Wolters Kluwer

Canadian Income Tax Act with Regulations, Annotated

108th Edition

2019 Autumn

R.S.C. 1985, c. 1 (5th Supp.), as amended

Consolidated to July 12, 2019

- Income Tax Application Rules, R.S.C. 1985, c. 2 (5th Supp.), as amended
- Multilateral Instrument in Respect of Tax Conventions Act
- Canada-U.S. Tax Convention as amended by Protocols
- Article-by-article commentary by Dentons LLP on the Canada-U.S. Tax Convention
- Technical Explanation of Canada-U.S. Tax Convention
- Technical Explanation to Third, Fourth and Fifth Protocols
- Canada–U.S. Enhanced Tax Information Exchange Agreement
- Canada-U.K. Tax Convention as amended by Protocols
- Income Tax Conventions Interpretation Act
- Interpretation Act
- Proposed Amendments, including Draft Legislation and Explanatory Notes
- Department of Finance Comfort Letters
- Editorial Notes
- History Notes
- References to Related Sections and Regulations
- References to Income Tax Folios, Interpretation Bulletins, Information Circulars, CRA Forms and Guides
- References to Canadian Tax Foundation Articles and Other Publications
- References to selected CRA Technical Interpretations and Rulings
- Selected Case Annotations
- Selected News Releases
- Selected Remission Orders
- Tax Rates and Other Reference Tables
- Topical Index

Published by Wolters Kluwer Canada Limited

Typeset by Wolters Kluwer Canada Limited.
Printed in Canada.

Editorial Board – As of July 2019

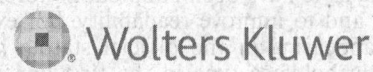

How to Use This Book

This Edition of the Wolters Kluwer *Canadian Income Tax Act with Regulations, Annotated* contains the consolidated text of the *Income Tax Act*, R.S.C. 1985, c. 1 (5th Supp.) (the "Act"), the transitional provisions known as the *Income Tax Application Rules*, R.S.C. 1985, c. 2 (5th Supp.), and the *Income Tax Regulations*. It consolidates all amendments made by legislation passed by Parliament and all regulations promulgated on or before the date of publication, July 12, 2019.

The "Fifth Supplement" version of the Act was proclaimed in force on March 1, 1994, replacing the former version of the Act (S.C. 70-71-72, c. 63). The former Act, which reflected the 1972 tax reform legislation, replaced the earlier *Income Tax Act*, R.S.C. 1952, c. 148, effective January 1, 1972. Information on the "Fifth Supplement" is included in this book at page lxxix.

Tax Charts

The following charts are included at the beginning of the book:

- the 2019 federal and provincial tax rates and personal tax credits
- prescribed interest rates
- automobile rates and limits
- annual average exchange rates for major currencies
- capital cost allowance rates
- tax calendar
- lists of deadlines, offences, and penalties under the Act
- rates of withholding tax on selected types of payments under the tax conventions signed by Canada.

Proposed Amendments

All proposed amendments to the Act issued on or before July 12, 2019 are reproduced in place. Each proposal appears in a greyed box immediately following the provision affected. All draft regulations outstanding at the time of publication are reproduced in place throughout the Regulations. Department of Finance Explanatory Notes to proposed amendments are included as well. Federal Budget proposals not yet enacted, government press releases outlining proposed changes to income tax provisions, and Department of Finance comfort letters describing possible future amendments are also reproduced in greyed boxes following the provisions to which they relate. See the list of proposed amendments for the Act at page lxxxv and for the Regulations at page lxxxvii.

In-depth historical notes outlining the evolution of the Act and Regulations have been added by Wolters Kluwer at the end of each section. These notes are essential to the interpretation of the Act and Regulations in both current and prior taxation years. The full text of each provision as it read prior to an amendment is included in the history notes. Due to space constraints, the notes in this print edition begin with amendments starting in 2009. Full history notes for 2008 and prior years are in Wolters Kluwer's *Income Tax Act and Regulations* online and on DVD.

Many useful cross-references have been incorporated at the end of sections of the Act and Regulations. These cross-references direct you to a regulation, section of the Act, definition, form, guide, Income Tax Folio, Interpretation Bulletin, Information Circular, Technical News, Registered Plans Directorate Newsletter, Transfer Pricing Memorandum, or to an article in *Tax Topics*, *Tax Profile*, *Canadian Tax Journal*, *Conference Report*, or the *Canadian Petroleum Tax Journal* that applies to the particular section. In situations where a reference applies to the section as a whole, it is noted following subsection (1) of the section, rather than for each subsection. If subsection (1) is a series of definitions, the general reference is noted in the charging subsection for that section. You will also find many case annotations throughout the book, which provide practical illustrations of how various provisions have been interpreted by the courts. Selected references to CRA technical interpretations and rulings have been added for certain provisions, and these are listed under the heading *Tax Window Files*. As well, with input from members of the Editorial Board for Wolters Kluwer's *Income Tax Act with Regulations, Annotated,* descriptive editorial notes have been added for certain provisions. The editorial notes highlight the most important issues relating to the subsection, each under a separate heading, with references to the most relevant cases, related sections, or government documents. These are generally located before the history notes.

The full texts of the Canada–U.S. and Canada–U.K. Tax Conventions consolidated with amending protocols and full-text history notes, and the Canada–U.S. Enhanced Tax Information Exchange Agreement and associated Annexes are reproduced in this book. Article-by-article commentary by Dentons LLP has also been included in the Canada–U.S. Tax Convention, as well as the "Technical Explanations" of the Canada–U.S. Tax Convention and the Third, Fourth, and Fifth Protocols issued by the U.S. Treasury Department and endorsed as authoritative by the Canadian Department of Finance. The *Multilateral Instrument in Respect of Tax Conventions Act*, S.C. 2019, c. 12 (formerly Bill C-82), which alters the current agreements, has also been reproduced.

Other features contained in this book include:

- a list of Department of Finance comfort letters that are reproduced throughout the Act and Regulations;
- a list of the tax conventions signed by Canada and those under negotiation;
- several relevant Remission Orders;
- a detailed sectional list of the *Income Tax Act*;
- a detailed sectional list of the *Income Tax Regulations*;
- the full texts of the *Income Tax Conventions Interpretation Act* and the *Interpretation Act*; and
- an easy-to-use, comprehensive topical index.

In the publication of this book, meticulous care has been exercised to set out an exact reproduction of the *Income Tax Act* and the *Income Tax Regulations* with all amendments incorporated in place. Some changes in printing style have been adopted, however, both for convenience and to improve readability. For example, marginal notes appearing in the official statute have been reproduced in boldface type in the first line of the section or subsection to which they apply, and in some places, where no marginal notes appear in the official statute, marginal notes have been inserted by Wolters Kluwer in square brackets. None of these changes affects the substance, punctuation, indentation, or wording of the statute.

July 12, 2019 — Wolters Kluwer Canada Ltd.

General Table of Contents

Current Tax Rates and Credits

Personal Income Tax Components — 2019 (Including Surtaxes)

(Prepared from information available as of June 14, 2019)

		Basic Tax Rates	Basic Tax Brackets	Surtax
Federal[1]		15.00%	$0	
		20.50%	$47,630	
		26.00%	$95,259	
		29.00%	$147,667	
		33.00%	$210,371	
Provincial or Territorial	Alberta	10.00%	$0	No surtax
		12.00%	$131,220	
		13.00%	$157,464	
		14.00%	$209,952	
		15.00%	$314,928	
	British Columbia[2]	5.06%	$0	
		7.70%	$40,707	
		10.50%	$81,416	
		12.29%	$93,476	
		14.70%	$113,506	
		16.80%	$153,900	
	Manitoba	10.80%	$0	
		12.75%	$32,670	
		17.40%	$70,610	
	New Brunswick	9.68%	$0	
		14.82%	$42,592	
		16.52%	$85,184	
		17.84%	$138,491	
		20.30%	$157,778	
	Newfoundland and Labrador[2]	8.70%	$0	
		14.50%	$37,591	
		15.80%	$75,181	
		17.30%	$134,224	
		18.30%	$187,913	
	Northwest Territories	5.90%	$0	
		8.60%	$43,137	
		12.20%	$86,277	
		14.05%	$140,267	
	Nova Scotia	8.79%	$0	
		14.95%	$29,590	
		16.67%	$59,180	
		17.50%	$93,000	
		21.00%	$150,000	
	Nunavut	4.00%	$0	
		7.00%	$45,414	
		9.00%	$90,829	
		11.50%	$147,667	
	Ontario[2]	5.05%	$0	20% of tax above $4,740 + 36% of tax above $6,067
		9.15%	$43,906	
		11.16%	$87,813	
		12.16%	$150,000	
		13.16%	$220,000	
	Prince Edward Island	9.80%	$0	10% of tax above $12,500
		13.80%	$31,984	
		16.70%	$63,969	
	Quebec[1, 2]	15.00%	$0	No surtax
		20.00%	$43,790	
		24.00%	$87,575	
		25.75%	$106,555	
	Saskatchewan	10.50%	$0	
		12.50%	$45,225	
		14.50%	$129,214	
	Yukon	6.40%	$0	
		9.00%	$47,630	
		10.90%	$95,259	
		12.80%	$147,667	
		15.00%	$500,000	
Non-residents[3]		7.20%	$0	No surtax
		9.84%	$47,630	
		12.48%	$95,259	
		13.92%	$147,667	
		15.84%	$210,371	

Notes:

1. In Quebec, federal tax is reduced by 16.5% for Quebec's abatement of basic federal tax.
2. Individuals may also be subject to provincial health levies or other personal tax levies. See **Provincial Health Care Premiums and Personal Tax Levies – 2019**.
3. Instead of provincial or territorial tax, non-residents pay an additional 48% of basic federal tax on income taxable in Canada that is not earned in a province or territory. Non-residents are subject to provincial or territorial rates (in this table) on employment income earned, and business income connected with a permanent establishment, in the respective province or territory. Different rates may apply to non-residents in other circumstances.

Non-Refundable Personal Tax Credits — 2019

(Prepared from information available as of June 14, 2019)

The two tables below contain information concerning select non-refundable personal tax credits. The first contains the federal and provincial/territorial rates used in the calculation of personal tax credits. The second shows the value of the credits. Provinces and territories use their own prescribed amounts to determine their personal tax credits.

		Federal	Alt.	B.C.	Man.	N.B.	Nfld. & Lab.	N.W.T.	N.S.	Nun.	Ont.	P.E.I.	Que.[1]	Sask.	Yukon
		Personal tax credit rates (See table below for some limitations)													
General factor[2]		15%[4]	10%	5.06%	10.8%	9.68%	8.7%	5.9%	8.79%	4%	5.05%	9.8%	15%[1]	10.5%	6.4%
Charitable donations	First $200												20%[1]		
	Amount over $200	29% or 33%[4]	21%	16.8%	17.4%	17.95%	18.3%	14.05%	21%	11.5%	11.16%	16.7%	24% or 25.75%[1]	14.5%	12.8%
Dividend tax credit[3] (on grossed-up amount)	Eligible	15.0198%	10%	12%	8%	14%	5.4%	11.5%	8.85%	5.51%	10%	10.5%	11.78%	11%	12.02%
	Non-eligible	9.0301%	2.18%	1.96%	0.7835%	2.75%	3.5%	6%	2.99%	2.61%	3.2863%	2.74%	5.55%	3.362%	2.3%

		Federal amounts	Federal[6]	Alt.	B.C.	Man.	N.B.	Nfld. & Lab.	N.W.T.	N.S.	Nun.	Ont.	P.E.I.	Que.[1]	Sask.	Yukon
			Maximum value (before surtaxes) of credits that are based on prescribed amounts													
Basic		$12,069	$1,810	$1,937	$541	$1,040	$994	$819	$874	$745[7]	$640	$534	$898	$2,290[1]	$1,687	$772
Spouse					$463	$986	$844	$669				$454	$762	N/A		
Equivalent to spouse																
Age 65		$7,494	$1,124	$540	$242	$403	$485	$523	$427	$364[7]	$409	$261	$369	$482[1]	$514[8]	$480
Disability	Basic	$8,416	$1,262	$1,494	$405	$667	$804	$553	$709	$645	$545	$432	$675	$509		$539
	Under 18 supplement	$4,909	$736							$303			$394			$314
Infirm dependant (18 or over)		$7,140[5]	$1,071[5]	$1,121	$237[5]	$389	$469	$260	$290	$246	$196	$252[5]	$240	N/A[1]	$994	$457[5]
Caregiver										$431						
Pension income		$2,000	$300	$149	$51	$108	$97	$87	$59	$103	$80	$74	$98	$428[1]	$105	$128
Adoption		$16,255	$2,438	$1,325	$823	$1,080	N/A	$1,105	N/A			$652	N/A	N/A[1]	N/A	$1,040
Canada Pension Plan (CPP)		$2,668[9]	$400	$267	$135	$288	$258	$232	$157	$235	$107	$135	$261	N/A	$280	$171
Quebec Pension Plan (QPP)		$2,911[1, 9]	$437	N/A										N/A[1]	N/A	
Employment Insurance (EI)	Not in Quebec	$860	$129	$86	$44	$93	$83	$75	$51	$76	$34	$43	$84	N/A	$90	$55
	In Quebec	$664[1]	$100	N/A										N/A[1]	N/A	
Canada Employment		$1,222	$183	N/A												$78
Education (per month)	Full-time	N/A	N/A	$75	N/A	$43	N/A	$17	$24	$18	$16	N/A	$39	$440[1]	N/A	N/A
	Part-time			$23		$13		$5	$7	$5	$5		$12	N/A		
Textbook (per month)	Full-time			N/A							$3	N/A				
	Part-time										$1					
												× 1.2 or × 1.56	*× 1.1*			

Factors at bottom of table increase value of credits to reflect surtaxes.[10]

Notes:

1. See below for Quebec's special credits and rules.
2. The general factor, multiplied by the federal (or provincial/territorial) amount, yields the value of the federal (or provincial/territorial) credit.
3. Eligible dividends are designated as such by the payor. They are grossed up by 38% and include dividends paid by:
   - public corporations or other corporations that are not Canadian-controlled private corporations (CCPCs), are resident in Canada and are subject to the federal general corporate income tax rate (i.e., 15% in 2019); or
   - CCPCs, to the extent that the CCPC's income is:
     - not investment income (other than eligible dividends from public corporations); and
     - subject to the federal general corporate income tax rate (i.e., the income is active business income not subject to the federal small business rate).

   Non-eligible dividends are grossed up by 15% and include dividends paid out of income eligible for the federal small business rate or a CCPC's investment income (other than eligible dividends received from public corporations).

Reference Material

Non-Refundable Personal Tax Credits — 2019 (continued)

4. For charitable donations exceeding $200, the tax credit rate is:
   - 33% for donations made after 2015, to the extent the individual has income that is subject to the federal 33% personal income tax rate; and
   - 29% for all other donations.
5. The Canada Caregiver Credit amount is:
   - $7,140 (value of $1,071; $457 in the Yukon) for infirm dependants (parents/grandparents, brothers/sisters, aunts/uncles, nieces/nephews, adult children); and
   - $2,230 (value of $335; $143 in the Yukon) for an infirm dependant:
     - spouse or common-law partner, if the spouse or common-law partner amount is claimed;
     - eligible dependant, if the eligible dependant (equivalent to spouse) amount is claimed; and
     - child under age 18 at the end of the year.

   British Columbia and Ontario also have a Caregiver Tax Credit. The Canada Caregiver Credit and the Ontario Caregiver Tax Credit do not apply to non-infirm seniors who reside with their adult children, while the British Columbia Caregiver Tax Credit does not require the dependant to live with the caregiver.
6. In Quebec, federal values are reduced by 16.5%.
7. For Nova Scotia, when taxable income is under $75,000, the basic/spouse/equivalent to spouse tax credit and the age tax credit will be as high as $1,009 and $493, respectively.
8. In Saskatchewan, an additional credit of $136 is available to individuals who are 65 or older, regardless of their income.
9. Starting 2019, employee contributions that relate to the enhanced portion of the CPP/QPP will be deductible. As a result:
   - the maximum CPP of $2,749 qualifies for a deduction of $81 and a non-refundable credit of 2,668; and
   - the maximum QPP of $2,991 qualifies for a deduction of $81 and a non-refundable tax credit of $2,911.
10. For taxpayers in Ontario or Prince Edward Island affected by provincial surtaxes, the value of the credits shown will be higher by the factors indicated. For example, for a taxpayer in Ontario's top bracket, the $534 shown for the basic Ontario credit would be worth $833 (i.e., $534 × 1.56).

Quebec's Special Credits and Rules — 2019

The following special rules apply to Quebec's non-refundable tax credits:

- the minimum basic personal credit, the Quebec Pension Plan (QPP), Employment Insurance (EI), Health Services Fund and Quebec Parental Insurance Plan (QPIP) credits are combined into a single basic personal credit of $15,269 (value of $2,290);
- employees, employers and the self-employed must contribute to the QPIP, from which maternity, adoption and parental leave benefits are paid. As a result, federal EI premiums are lower for Quebec employees than for other employees ($664 instead of $860). A federal credit is available to individuals for QPIP premiums;
- an adult student can transfer the unused portion of the basic personal credit to a parent, but if this transfer is made, the other dependant (18 or over) credit of $4,274 (value of $641) cannot be claimed for that student;
- most non-refundable credits, such as the basic personal credit and the age credit, can be transferred to a spouse, if not used by the taxpayer;
- the age, pension and living alone credits are reduced if net family income exceeds $34,610;
- the age to qualify for the age credit is 65;
- a person that lives alone, with a dependant, or with a grandchild or great-grandchild who is an eligible student, can claim a credit of $1,750 (value of $263);
- a person that qualifies for the living alone credit and lives with an eligible student is eligible for an additional $2,160 (value of $324) credit;
- the maximum education credit of $2,933 (value of $440) per term (maximum two terms per year) can be claimed by a supporting Quebec parent (but is not transferable) for a child under 18 who attends post-secondary school full-time (part-time for infirm dependants);
- a student can transfer the unused portion of the tuition and examination tax credits to a parent or grandparent;
- the medical expense credit is based on the amount by which qualifying expenses exceed 3% of net family income (see below for details on the refundable medical expense credit), and the factor is 20% for purposes of the medical expense tax credit;
- the factor is 20% for purposes of the tax credit on student loan interest; and
- the tax credit rate for charitable donations exceeding $200 is:
  - 25.75% for donations made after 2016, to the extent the individual has income that is subject to the 25.75% personal income tax rate; and
  - 24% for all other donations.

Select Quebec refundable tax credits are listed in the table below.

	Details
Adoption	50% of eligible adoption expenses (maximum credit of $10,000)
Child care	26% to 75% of qualifying child care expenses (limits apply[1])
Youth activities	Maximum credit is $100 for children age six to under 17; $200 for children with a disability, age six to under 19; available to families with incomes of $138,525 or less
Seniors' activities	Maximum credit is $40 for seniors age 70 or older with incomes of $42,215 or less
Caregivers[2]	Basic credit of $663 plus supplement of $542; the supplement is reduced if the dependant's income exceeds $24,105
Respite expenses for informal caregivers	30% of eligible respite expenses paid for the care of a person who resides with the caregiver and has a significant disability; maximum credit of $1,560 is reduced if family income exceeds $58,380
Informal caregivers	Maximum credit of $1,500 for each care recipient can be allocated to all volunteers who provide home respite to informal caregivers of the care recipient (maximum credit ranging from $250 to $750 can be allocated to each volunteer, depending on minimum volunteer hours)
Home support for seniors	35% of eligible expenses; maximum credit of $6,825 for independent seniors (reduced if family income exceeds $58,380) and $8,925 for dependent seniors, age 70 and over; expenses eligible for this credit will not qualify for the medical expense credit
Senior assistance	Maximum credit is $200 for seniors age 70 and older ($400 for an eligible senior couple); reduced if family income exceeds $22,500 (if no eligible spouse) and $36,600 (for an eligible senior couple)
Medical	25% of medical expenses eligible for the non-refundable credit and 25% of amount deducted for impairment support products and services; maximum credit of $1,205 is reduced if family income exceeds $23,300

Notes:

1. The child care expense limits follow, for a child:
   - under 7, $9,660;
   - that has a severe and prolonged impairment, $13,220; and
   - under 16, or who has an impairment, $5,085.
2. The caregivers credit has four components:
   i. caregivers who house, in the strict sense of the term, an eligible relative – see table for details of the credit;
   ii. caregivers who cohabit with an eligible relative unable to live alone – see table for details of the credit;
   iii. caregivers caring for an elderly spouse – these caregivers qualify only for a basic credit of $1,032; and
   iv. caregivers who do not cohabit with an eligible relative (provided the relative does not reside in a private seniors' residence or public network facility) qualify for the supplemental credit (i.e. up to $542 in 2019).

Credits: Federal Limitations and Other Information — 2019

This table presents additional information related to federal credits. Other restrictions may also apply. The provinces/territories may have comparable thresholds and rules.

	Limitations	To whom the credit may be transferred	Carry-forward
Tuition	Credit is available only if at least $100 is paid in fees to an institution	Spouse, parent or grandparent (Maximum credit transferable is $750)	Indefinite
Medical	Credit is based on amount by which qualifying medical expenses exceed the lesser of $2,352 and 3% of net income (generally, expenses for any twelve-month period ending in the year can be claimed)	Either spouse may claim	
CPP/QPP and EI	For employees, maximum credit is $529 (in Quebec, $448[1]) and a deduction is available for the enhanced portion of the CPP/QPP (maximum deduction of $80.85). Self-employed persons deduct 50% of base CPP/QPP premiums and 100% of the enhanced portion of CPP/QPP premiums paid for their own coverage (maximum deduction of $2,830; in Quebec $3,072), and claim a credit for the non-deductible portion of premiums paid (maximum credit $400; in Quebec $365[1]); self-employed persons are not required to pay EI premiums, but may opt to do so	N/A	
Canada Employment	Credit is based on employment income		
Student loan interest	Interest must be paid on qualifying student loans	N/A	5 years
Charitable donations	Eligible donations are limited to 75% of net income	Either spouse may claim	
Spousal and equivalent to spouse	Reduced by any net income of the spouse or qualifying dependant	N/A	
Canada Caregiver (includes infirm dependant and caregiver)	Reduced if infirm dependant/relative's income exceeds $16,766 (infirm dependant is not required to live with the caregiver)		
Age	Reduced if income exceeds $37,790	Spouse	
Pension	Credit is not available for CPP, QPP, Old Age Security or Guaranteed Income Supplement payments		
Adoption	Must be claimed in the year the adoption period ends	Either parent may claim	
Disability — Basic	For individuals with severe and prolonged impairment. Individuals must submit certification from a medical practitioner to obtain Canada Revenue Agency approval to claim the credit	Spouse, parent, grandparent, child, grandchild, sibling, aunt, uncle, niece or nephew	
Disability — Under 18 supplement	Reduced if child care expenses and attendant care expenses (claimed as a medical expense for child) exceed $2,875		

Notes:

1. In Quebec, federal values are reduced by 16.5%. The amounts shown reflect this reduction.

Provincial Health Care Premiums and Personal Tax Levies — 2019

(Prepared from information available as of June 14, 2019)

Only British Columbia, Newfoundland and Labrador, Ontario and Quebec have health care premiums or personal tax levies that are payable by individuals.

British Columbia Medical Services Plan Premiums

British Columbia monthly premium[1] 2019	
Single[1]	**Couples[1]**
$37.50	$75

1. In British Columbia:
   - low-income earners can get assistance;
   - Medical Services Plan (MSP) premiums do not apply to children under 19 and dependent post-secondary students enrolled in full-time studies; and
   - MSP premiums will be eliminated on January 1, 2020.

Newfoundland and Labrador Temporary Deficit Reduction Levies

Newfoundland and Labrador imposes a temporary deficit reduction levy on individuals who are residents of Newfoundland and Labrador on the last day of the taxation year, depending on taxable income, as shown in the table below.

		Newfoundland and Labrador annual levy per individual[1] 2019[2]	
		Fixed portion	+ 10% of taxable income >
Taxable income	Up to $51,000	$0	$50,000
	$51,000 to $56,000	$100	$55,000
	$56,000 to $61,000	$200	$60,000
	$61,000 to $66,000	$300	$65,000
	$66,000 to $71,000	$400	$70,000
	$71,000 to $76,000	$500	$75,000
	$76,000 to $81,000	$600	$80,000
	$81,000 to $101,000	$700	$100,000
	$101,000 to $126,000	$800	$125,000
	$126,000 to $176,000	$900	$175,000
	$176,000 to $251,000	$1,000	$250,000
	$251,000 to $301,000	$1,100	$300,000
	$301,000 to $351,000	$1,200	$350,000
	$351,000 to $401,000	$1,300	$400,000
	$401,000 to $451,000	$1,400	$450,000
	$451,000 to $501,000	$1,500	$500,000
	$501,000 to $551,000	$1,600	$550,000
	$551,000 to $601,000	$1,700	$600,000
	$601,000 and over	$1,800	n/a

1. Trusts are not liable for premiums.
2. The levy will be eliminated at the end of the 2019 taxation year.

Provincial Health Care Premiums and Personal Tax Levies — 2019 (continued)

Ontario Health Premiums

Ontario imposes a health care premium on individuals who are residents of Ontario on the last day of the taxation year, depending on taxable income, as shown in the table below.

		Ontario annual premium per individual[1] 2019
Taxable income	Up to $25,000	6% of income > $20,000
	$25,000 to $38,500	$300 + 6% of income > $36,000
	$38,500 to $48,600	$450 + 25% of income > $48,000
	$48,600 to $72,600	$600 + 25% of income > $72,000
	$72,600 to $200,600	$750 + 25% of income > $200,000
	$200,600 and over	$900

1. Trusts are not liable for premiums.

Quebec Health Services Fund Premiums

Individuals 18 years of age or older who are residents of Quebec on the last day of the taxation year and whose income from certain sources, excluding remuneration, exceeds a certain threshold ($14,915 for 2019) must contribute to the Health Services Fund, as shown in the table below.

		Health Services Fund annual contribution per individual[1] 2019
Income (subject to contribution)	Up to $29,915	1% of income > $14,915[2]
	$29,915 to $136,855	$150 + 1% of income > $51,855[2]
	$136,855 and over	$1,000

1. The Health Services Fund contribution gives rise to a tax credit.
2. Indexed income thresholds for 2019.

Federal and Provincial/Territorial Income Taxes Payable by Individuals at Various Levels of Taxable Income — 2019

(Prepared from information available as of June 14, 2019)

This table shows the combined federal and provincial (or territorial) income taxes payable, including surtaxes, assuming only the basic personal tax credit is claimed (except for non-residents — see footnote 2, below), and that all income is either interest or ordinary income (such as salary). When income includes at least $1,222 of salary, the Canada Employment Credit, described under **Non-Refundable Personal Tax Credits — 2019** (see table), will reduce the results shown by $183 ($153 in Quebec). The amounts do not take into account employee payroll taxes, provincial health levies or other personal tax levies (see **Provincial Health Care Premiums and Personal Tax Levies — 2019**). Depending on the types of income and deductions, the alternative minimum tax (AMT) may apply.

2019	Alberta	British Columbia[1]	Manitoba[1]	New Brunswick[1]	Newfoundland and Labrador[1]	Non-resident[2]	Northwest Territories	Nova Scotia[1,6]	Nunavut	Ontario[1]	Prince Edward Island[1]	Quebec[5]	Saskatchewan	Yukon
$1,000,000	$446,101	$463,950	$476,526	$500,146	$482,617	$457,758	$440,246	$507,878	$414,975	$497,482	$485,501	$504,403	$447,310	$439,860
$500,000	$206,101	$214,950	$224,526	$233,646	$226,117	$213,558	$204,996	$237,878	$192,475	$229,834	$228,651	$237,878	$209,810	$199,860
$400,000	$158,101	$165,150	$174,126	$180,346	$174,817	$164,718	$157,946	$183,878	$147,975	$176,305	$177,281	$184,573	$162,310	$154,060
$300,000	$110,250	$115,350	$123,726	$127,046	$123,517	$115,878	$110,896	$129,878	$103,475	$122,775	$125,911	$131,268	$114,810	$108,260
$250,000	$86,750	$90,450	$98,526	$100,396	$97,867	$91,458	$87,371	$102,878	$81,225	$96,010	$100,226	$104,616	$91,060	$85,360
$200,000	$63,765	$65,965	$73,741	$74,160	$72,632	$67,652	$64,261	$76,293	$59,390	$69,972	$74,955	$78,310	$67,725	$62,874
$150,000	$42,839	$43,147	$50,541	$49,702	$49,361	$46,192	$42,736	$51,293	$39,140	$45,988	$51,270	$53,327	$45,975	$41,974
$100,000	$24,394	$23,053	$28,771	$28,220	$28,154	$26,849	$23,386	$29,473	$21,512	$24,213	$29,015	$29,653	$26,239	$23,410
$90,000	$21,083	$19,575	$24,720	$24,257	$24,263	$23,429	$19,855	$25,437	$18,318	$20,205	$25,018	$25,324	$22,679	$20,109
$80,000	$18,033	$16,515	$20,930	$20,643	$20,633	$20,395	$16,811	$21,720	$15,568	$17,005	$21,298	$21,515	$19,379	$17,159
$70,000	$14,983	$13,695	$17,168	$17,111	$17,071	$17,361	$13,901	$17,977	$12,818	$13,990	$17,578	$17,803	$16,079	$14,209
$60,000	$11,933	$10,875	$13,843	$13,579	$13,571	$14,327	$10,991	$14,207	$10,068	$11,025	$13,973	$14,092	$12,779	$11,259
$50,000	$8,883	$8,055	$10,518	$10,047	$10,071	$11,293	$8,081	$10,595	$7,318	$8,060	$10,543	$10,380	$9,479	$8,309
$40,000	$6,253	$5,673	$7,613	$7,068	$6,990	$8,880	$5,676	$7,417	$5,150	$5,675	$7,533	$7,208	$6,703	$5,977
$30,000	$3,753	$3,667	$4,890	$4,600	$4,481	$6,660	$3,586	$4,369	$3,250	$3,670	$4,732	$4,456	$4,153	$3,837
$20,000	$1,253	$1,661	$2,310	$2,132	$2,111	$4,440	$1,496	$1,938	$1,350	$1,665	$2,252	$1,703	$1,603	$1,697
Top marginal rates:														
Canadian dividends														
(eligible)	31.71%	31.44%	37.78%	33.51%	42.61%	36.72%[3]	28.33%	41.58%	33.08%	39.34%	34.22%	40.00%	29.64%	28.93%
(non-eligible)	42.31%	44.63%	46.67%	47.75%	44.59%	40.80%[3]	36.82%	48.28%	37.79%	47.40%	45.22%	46.25%	40.37%	42.17%
Capital gains	24.00%	24.90%	25.20%	26.65%	25.65%	24.42%	23.53%	27.00%	22.25%	26.76%	25.69%	26.65%	23.75%	24.00%
Other income	48.00%	49.80%	50.40%	53.30%	51.30%	48.84%[3]	47.05%	54.00%	44.50%	53.53%	51.37%	53.31%	47.50%	48.00%
Maximum value:[4]														
Dividend tax credit:														
(eligible)	25.02%	27.02%	23.02%	29.02%	20.42%	22.23%	26.52%	23.87%	20.53%	25.02%	26.57%	24.32%	26.02%	27.04%
(non-eligible)	11.21%	10.99%	9.81%	11.78%	12.53%	13.36%	15.03%	12.02%	11.64%	12.32%	12.04%	13.09%	12.39%	11.33%
Other tax credits	25.00%	20.06%	25.80%	24.68%	23.70%	22.20%	20.90%	23.79%	19.00%	22.88%	25.78%	27.53%	25.50%	21.40%

1 These provinces have low-income tax reductions, which may decrease some amounts shown.

2 This table assumes the non-resident will not qualify for the federal basic personal tax credit of $12,069. Non-residents can claim this credit only if all or substantially all (i.e., 90% or more) of the non-resident's worldwide income is included in his or her taxable income earned in Canada for the year. The non-resident amounts apply to income taxable in Canada that is not earned in a province or territory.

3 Non-resident rates for interest and dividends apply only in limited circumstances. Generally, interest (other than most interest paid to arm's length non-residents) and dividends paid to non-residents are subject to Part XIII withholding tax.

4 When personal tax credits in addition to the basic personal tax credit are available, the results in this table are too high. The maximum value of the dividend tax credit is determined by multiplying the dividend tax credit rate by the amount of eligible dividends (grossed up by 38%) or of non-eligible dividends (grossed up by 15%). The maximum value of other personal tax credits is determined by multiplying the other tax credit rate by the amount of those other personal tax credits. The maximum values reflect the surtax rates levied by Ontario (except for dividend tax credit rates, which are calculated before surtaxes in Ontario) and Prince Edward Island. Charitable donations over $200 have a higher maximum value.

5 Taxable income may differ for federal and Quebec purposes, in which case the amounts shown in the table may require adjustment.

6 For Nova Scotia, the amounts reflect the increase in Nova Scotia's basic personal amount by up to $3,000 if taxable income is under $75,000.

Individual Marginal Tax Rates for 2019

(Prepared from information available as of June 14, 2019)

These tables show combined federal and provincial (or federal and territorial) marginal tax rates – the percentage of tax paid on the last dollar of income, or on additional income. These tables do not take into account provincial health levies or other personal tax levies (see **Provincial Health Care Premiums and Personal Tax Levies — 2019**).

	Taxable income $12,069 to $47,630					Taxable income $47,630 to $95,259				
	Brackets	Ordinary income & interest	Capital gains	Canadian dividends Eligible[2]	Canadian dividends Non-eligible[2]	Brackets	Ordinary income & interest	Capital gains	Canadian dividends Eligible[2]	Canadian dividends Non-eligible
Federal only	$12,069	15.00%	7.50%	(0.03%) to 0%	6.87%	$47,630	20.50%	10.25%	7.56%	13.19%
Alberta	$19,369	25.00%	12.50%	(0.03%) to 0%	15.86%	$47,630	30.50%	15.25%	7.56%	22.18%
	$12,069	15.00%	7.50%	(0.03%) to 0%	6.87%					
British Columbia[1]	$40,707	22.70%	11.35%	(5.96%) to 0%	13.47%	$93,476	32.79%	16.40%	7.96%	25.07%
	$12,069	20.06%	10.03%	(9.60%) to 0%	10.43%	$81,416	31.00%	15.50%	5.49% to 7.56%	23.01%
						$47,630	28.20%	14.10%	1.63% to 7.56%	19.79%
Manitoba[1]	$32,670	27.75%	13.88%	6.53% to 6.56%	20.63%	$70,610	37.90%	18.95%	20.53%	32.30%
	$12,069	25.80%	12.90%	3.84% to 3.86%	18.38%	$47,630	33.25%	16.63%	14.12%	26.95%
New Brunswick[1]	$42,592	29.82%	14.91%	1.10% to 1.13%	20.75%	$85,184	37.02%	18.51%	11.04%	29.03%
	$12,069	24.68%	12.34%	(5.99%) to 0%	14.83%	$47,630	35.32%	17.66%	8.69%	27.07%
Newfoundland and	$37,591	29.50%	14.75%	12.53% to 12.56%	19.52%	$75,181	36.30%	18.15%	21.91%	27.34%
Labrador[1]	$12,069	23.70%	11.85%	4.53% to 4.55%	12.85%	$47,630	35.00%	17.50%	20.12%	25.84%
Non-resident[3]	$12,069	22.20%	11.10%	(0.04%) to 0%	10.16%	$47,630	30.34%	15.17%	11.19%	19.52%
Northwest Territories	$43,137	23.60%	11.80%	(4.03%) to 0%	9.86%	$86,277	32.70%	16.35%	8.53%	20.32%
	$14,811	20.90%	10.45%	(7.76%) to 0%	6.75% to 6.87%	$47,630	29.10%	14.55%	3.56% to 7.56%	16.18%
	$12,069	15.00%	7.50%	(0.03%) to 0%	6.87%					
Nova Scotia[1]	$29,590	29.95%	14.98%	8.39% to 8.42%	20.62%	$93,000	38.00%	19.00%	19.50%	29.88%
	$12,069	23.79%	11.90%	(0.11%) to 0%	13.54%	$59,180	37.17%	18.59%	18.35%	28.92%
						$47,630	35.45%	17.73%	15.98%	26.94%
Nunavut	$45,414	22.00%	11.00%	2.03% to 2.06%	11.91%	$90,829	29.50%	14.75%	12.38%	20.54%
	$16,000	19.00%	9.50%	(2.11%) to 0%	8.46%	$47,630	27.50%	13.75%	9.62%	18.24%
	$12,069	15.00%	7.50%	(0.03%) to 0%	6.87%					
Ontario[1]	$43,906	24.15%	12.08%	(1.20%) to 0%	13.61%	$91,098[4]	37.91%	18.95%	17.79%	29.43%
	$12,069	20.05%	10.03%	(6.86%) to 0%	8.89%	$87,813	33.89%	16.95%	12.24%	24.81%
						$77,317[4]	31.48%	15.74%	8.92%	22.04%
						$47,630	29.65%	14.83%	6.39% to 7.56%	19.93%
Prince Edward Island[1]	$31,984	28.80%	14.40%	4.53% to 4.55%	19.58%	$63,969	37.20%	18.60%	16.12%	29.24%
	$12,069	24.80%	12.40%	(0.99%) to 0%	14.98%	$47,630	34.30%	17.15%	12.12%	25.91%
Quebec	$43,790	32.53%	16.26%	11.32% to 11.34%	22.35%	$87,575	41.12%	20.56%	23.18%	32.23%
	$15,269	27.53%	13.76%	4.42% to 4.44%	16.60%	$47,630	37.12%	18.56%	17.66%	27.63%
	$12,069	12.53%	6.26%	(0.02%) to 0%	5.73%					
Saskatchewan	$45,225	27.50%	13.75%	2.04% to 2.07%	17.37%	$47,630	33.00%	16.50%	9.63%	23.70%
	$16,065	25.50%	12.75%	(0.72%) to 0%	15.07%					
	$12,069	15.00%	7.50%	(0.03%) to 0%	6.87%					
Yukon	$12,069	21.40%	10.70%	(7.78%) to 0%	11.58%	$47,630	29.50%	14.75%	3.40% to 7.56%	20.90%

Individual Marginal Tax Rates for 2019 (continued)

	Taxable income $95,259 to $147,667					Taxable income $147,667 to $210,371				
	Brackets	Ordinary income & interest	Capital gains	Canadian dividends Eligible[2]	Canadian dividends Non-eligible	Brackets	Ordinary income & interest	Capital gains	Canadian dividends Eligible	Canadian dividends Non-eligible
Federal only	$95,259	26.00%	13.00%	15.15%	19.52%	$147,667	29.00%	14.50%	19.29%	22.97%
Alberta	$131,220	38.00%	19.00%	17.91%	30.81%	$209,952	43.00%	21.50%	24.81%	36.56%
	$95,259	36.00%	18.00%	15.15%	28.51%	$157,464	42.00%	21.00%	23.43%	35.41%
						$147,667	41.00%	20.50%	22.05%	34.26%
British Columbia	$113,506	40.70%	20.35%	18.88%	34.17%	$153,900	45.80%	22.90%	25.92%	40.03%
	$95,259	38.29%	19.15%	15.55%	31.39%	$147,667	43.70%	21.85%	23.02%	37.62%
Manitoba	$95,259	43.40%	21.70%	28.12%	38.62%	$147,667	46.40%	23.20%	32.26%	42.07%
New Brunswick	$138,491	43.84%	21.92%	20.45%	36.87%	$157,778	49.30%	24.65%	27.99%	43.15%
	$95,259	42.52%	21.26%	18.63%	35.35%	$147,667	46.84%	23.42%	24.59%	40.32%
Newfoundland and	$134,224	43.30%	21.65%	31.57%	35.39%	$187,913	47.30%	23.65%	37.09%	39.99%
Labrador	$95,259	41.80%	20.90%	29.50%	33.66%	$147,667	46.30%	23.15%	35.71%	38.84%
Non-resident[3]	$95,259	38.48%	19.24%	22.43%	28.88%	$147,667	42.92%	21.46%	28.55%	33.99%
Northwest Territories	$140,267	40.05%	20.03%	18.67%	28.77%	$147,667	43.05%	21.53%	22.81%	32.22%
	$95,259	38.20%	19.10%	16.12%	26.65%					
Nova Scotia	$95,259	43.50%	21.75%	27.09%	36.20%	$150,000	50.00%	25.00%	36.06%	43.68%
						$147,667	46.50%	23.25%	31.23%	39.65%
Nunavut	$95,259	35.00%	17.50%	19.97%	26.86%	$147,667	40.50%	20.25%	27.56%	33.19%
Ontario	$95,259	43.41%	21.70%	25.38%	35.76%	$150,000	47.97%	23.98%	31.67%	41.00%
						$147,667	46.41%	23.20%	29.52%	39.21%
Prince Edward Island	$98,995[4]	44.37%	22.19%	24.56%	37.17%	$147,667	47.37%	23.69%	28.70%	40.62%
	$95,259	42.70%	21.35%	23.71%	35.57%					
Quebec	$106,555	47.46%	23.73%	31.93%	39.53%	$147,667	49.97%	24.98%	35.39%	42.41%
	$95,259	45.71%	22.86%	29.52%	37.51%					
Saskatchewan	$129,214	40.50%	20.25%	19.98%	32.32%	$147,667	43.50%	21.75%	24.12%	35.77%
	$95,259	38.50%	19.25%	17.22%	30.02%					
Yukon	$95,259	36.90%	18.45%	13.61% to 15.15%	29.41%	$147,667	41.80%	20.90%	20.37%	35.04%

	Taxable income over $210,371				
	Brackets	Ordinary income & interest	Capital gains	Canadian dividends Eligible	Canadian dividends Non-eligible
Federal only	$210,371	33.00%	16.50%	24.81%	27.57%
Alberta	$314,928	48.00%	24.00%	31.71%	42.31%
	$210,371	47.00%	23.50%	30.33%	41.16%
British Columbia	$210,371	49.80%	24.90%	31.44%	44.63%
Manitoba	$210,371	50.40%	25.20%	37.78%	46.67%
New Brunswick	$210,371	53.30%	26.65%	33.51%	47.75%
Newfoundland and Labrador	$210,371	51.30%	25.65%	42.61%	44.59%
Non-resident[3]	$210,371	48.84%	24.42%	36.72%	40.80%
Northwest Territories	$210,371	47.05%	23.53%	28.33%	36.82%
Nova Scotia	$210,371	54.00%	27.00%	41.58%	48.28%
Nunavut	$210,371	44.50%	22.25%	33.08%	37.79%
Ontario	$220,000	53.53%	26.76%	39.34%	47.40%
	$210,371	51.97%	25.98%	37.19%	45.60%
Prince Edward Island	$210,371	51.37%	25.69%	34.22%	45.22%
Quebec	$210,371	53.31%	26.65%	40.00%	46.25%
Saskatchewan	$210,371	47.50%	23.75%	29.64%	40.37%
Yukon	$500,000	48.00%	24.00%	28.93%	42.17%
	$210,371	45.80%	22.90%	25.89%	39.64%

(1) The table does not take into account the low-income tax reductions federally or in British Columbia, New Brunswick, Newfoundland and Labrador, Nova Scotia, Ontario and Prince Edward Island, or the Manitoba Family Tax Benefit (for low-income taxpayers), which may affect the rates shown.

(2) When two dividend rates are indicated, the lower rate has a negative federal and/or provincial/territorial component. A negative federal component shelters other income from federal tax and a negative provincial/territorial component shelters other income from provincial/territorial tax. As a result, the combined federal and provincial/territorial rate that applies depends on the level of the taxpayer's other income, with the higher rate applying if the taxpayer has no other income.

(3) A non-resident can claim the personal basic credit only if all or substantially all (i.e., 90% or more) of the non-resident's worldwide income is included in his or her taxable income earned in Canada for the year.

Non-resident rates for interest and dividends apply only in limited circumstances. Generally, interest (other than most interest paid to arm's length non-residents) and dividends paid to non-residents are subject to Part XIII withholding tax.)

(4) The bracket relates to surtaxes levied by Ontario or Prince Edward Island, and assumes that only the basic personal credit is available.

Top Marginal Rates — A 17-Year History

(Prepared from information available as of June 14, 2019)

<table>
<tr><th></th><th></th><th>2003</th><th>2004</th><th>2005</th><th>2006</th><th>2007</th><th>2008</th><th>2009</th><th>2010</th><th>2011</th><th>2012</th><th>2013</th><th>2014</th><th>2015</th><th>2016</th><th>2017</th><th>2018</th><th>2019</th></tr>
<tr><td colspan="2">Federal rates</td><td colspan="13">29.00</td><td colspan="4">33.00</td></tr>
<tr><td rowspan="15">Combined rates (%) (including surtaxes)</td><td>Alberta</td><td colspan="12">39.00</td><td>40.25 [1]</td><td colspan="4">48.00 [1]</td></tr>
<tr><td>British Columbia</td><td colspan="11">43.70</td><td colspan="2">45.80</td><td colspan="2">47.70</td><td colspan="2">49.80</td></tr>
<tr><td>Manitoba</td><td colspan="13">46.40</td><td colspan="4">50.40</td></tr>
<tr><td>New Brunswick</td><td colspan="4">46.84</td><td colspan="2">46.95</td><td>46.00</td><td colspan="3">43.30</td><td>45.07</td><td>46.84</td><td>54.75 [2]</td><td colspan="4">53.30</td></tr>
<tr><td>Newfoundland and Labrador</td><td colspan="4">48.64</td><td>47.04</td><td>45.00</td><td colspan="2">43.40</td><td colspan="4">42.30</td><td>43.30</td><td>49.80</td><td colspan="3">51.30</td></tr>
<tr><td>Non-resident</td><td colspan="13">42.92</td><td colspan="4">48.84</td></tr>
<tr><td>Northwest Territories</td><td>42.05</td><td>42.55</td><td colspan="11">43.05</td><td colspan="4">47.05</td></tr>
<tr><td>Nova Scotia</td><td>47.34</td><td colspan="6">48.25</td><td colspan="6">50.00</td><td colspan="4">54.00</td></tr>
<tr><td>Nunavut</td><td colspan="13">40.50</td><td colspan="4">44.50</td></tr>
<tr><td>Ontario</td><td colspan="9">46.41</td><td>47.97 [3]</td><td colspan="3">49.53 [3]</td><td colspan="4">53.53 [3]</td></tr>
<tr><td>Prince Edward Island</td><td colspan="13">47.37</td><td colspan="4">51.37</td></tr>
<tr><td>Quebec</td><td colspan="10">48.22</td><td colspan="3">49.97</td><td colspan="4">53.31</td></tr>
<tr><td>Saskatchewan</td><td colspan="13">44.00</td><td>48.00</td><td>47.75</td><td colspan="2">47.50</td></tr>
<tr><td>Yukon</td><td colspan="12">42.40</td><td>44.00 [4]</td><td colspan="4">48.00 [4]</td></tr>
</table>

(1) For Alberta, the top combined federal/Alberta marginal rate applies to incomes over $300,000 in 2015 and 2016, $303,900 in 2017, $307,547 in 2018 and $314,928 in 2019. The rate is: (i) 40.00% in 2015 and 47.00% in 2016, if the individual's income is $300,000 or less, but over $200,000; (ii) 47.00% in 2017, 2018 and 2019, if the individual's income is $303,900 or less, but over $202,800 in 2017, $307,547 or less, but over $205,842 in 2018 and $314,928 or less, but over $210,371 in 2019.

(2) For New Brunswick, in 2015, the top combined federal/New Brunswick marginal rate applies to incomes over $250,000. The rate is 50.00%, if the individual's income is $250,000 or less, but over $150,000.

(3) For Ontario, the top combined federal/Ontario marginal rate applies to incomes over $500,000 in 2012, $509,000 in 2013 and $220,000 in 2014 to 2019. The rate is: (i) 46.41%, if the individual's income is $500,000 or less, but over $132,406 in 2012 or $509,000 or less, but over $135,054 in 2013; (ii) 47.97%, if the individual's income is $220,000 or less, but over $150,000 in 2014 and 2015; and (iii) 51.97%, if the individual's income is $220,000 or less, but over $200,000 in 2016, $202,800 in 2017, $205,842 in 2018, and $210,371 in 2019.

(4) For the Yukon, in 2015 to 2019, the top combined federal/Yukon marginal rate applies to incomes over $500,000. The rate is: (i) 41.80%, if the individual's income is $500,000 or less, but over $138,586 in 2015; and (ii) 45.80%, if the individual's income is $500,000 or less, but over $200,000 in 2016, $202,800 in 2017, $205,842 in 2018, and $210,371 in 2019.

Registered Plan Contributions Limits — 2015–2020

The deductible RRSP, TFSA, DPSP, and money RPP contribution limits for 2015 to 2020 are shown in the table below:

	2015	2016	2017	2018	2019	2020
Dollar limits:						
RRSP	$24,930	$25,370	$26,010	$26,230	$26,500	$27,230
TFSA	$10,000	$5,500	$5,500	$5,500	$6,000	Indexed*
DPSP	$12,685	$13,005	$13,115	$13,250	$13,615	Indexed*
Money Purchase RPP	$25,370	$26,010	$26,230	$26,500	$27,230	Indexed*

* Increased by increases in the Average Wage.

Federal Corporate Tax Rates — 2013–2019 (%)

(Prepared from information available as of June 10, 2019)

The rates shown are in effect for 12-month taxation years ended December 31. All rates that change must be pro-rated for taxation years that straddle the effective date.

			2013 – 2015	2016 – 2017	2018	2019
General and manufacturing & processing (M&P) income		Basic rate	38			
		Less: provincial abatement	10			
		General federal rate (before deductions)	28			
		Less: general rate reduction or M&P deduction[1]	13			
		General federal and M&P rate	**15**			
Canadian-controlled private corporations (CCPCs)	**Threshold**	Small business deduction threshold[2]	$500,000			
	Active business income up to threshold	General federal rate (before deductions)[1]	28			
		Less: small business deduction[2]	17	17.5	18	19
		CCPC small business rate	**11**	**10.5**	**10**	**9**
	Investment income	General federal rate (before deductions)[1]	28			
		Additional refundable tax[3]	6.67	10.67		
		CCPC investment income rate	**34.67**	**38.67**		

Notes:

1. The general rate reduction and M&P deduction do not apply to: income benefiting from the small business deduction; investment income of CCPCs; and income of certain corporations (e.g., mutual fund corporations, mortgage investment corporations and investment corporations). In addition, income from a personal services business is:
   - not eligible for the general rate reduction; and
   - subject to a federal corporate tax rate of 33% (up from 28%) for taxation years ending after December 31, 2015 (pro-rated for taxation years straddling this date).
2. The small business deduction applies to active business income earned in Canada of associated CCPCs, up to $500,000. As a result of a clawback, the small business deduction is reduced if taxable capital employed in Canada, on an associated basis, exceeded $10 million in the preceding year.

   For taxation years beginning after 2018, the small business deduction for a year of a CCPC that (together with associated CCPCs) earns more than $50,000 of passive investment income in the previous year, is reduced by $5 for every $1 of that investment income over $50,000 (it is eliminated at $150,000 of investment income). The CCPC's small business deduction will be reduced by the greater of this new reduction and the existing clawback (see above) that applies when associated taxable capital employed in Canada exceeds $10 million.

   Recent changes to the small business deduction are shown in the following table:

	Changes effective after December 31, 2014		
	From	**To**	**Effective**
Small business deduction	17%	17.5%	January 1, 2016
	17.5%	18%	January 1, 2018
	18%	19%	January 1, 2019

3. See "Refundable Investment Tax" in the table, **Other Federal Corporate Tax Rates for 2019**, and footnote 2 to that table for recent changes to the refundable investment tax.

Other Federal Corporate Tax Rates for 2019

(Prepared from information available as of June 10, 2019)

The rates shown in the table are in effect for a 12-month taxation year ended December 31, 2019. All rates that change must be pro-rated for taxation years that straddle the effective date, except as noted.

	Rate	Corporations affected	Description	Special rules
Income not earned in a province or territory	25%	All corporations	Income tax for 2019 is calculated as follows: Basic federal rate 38% Less: General rate reduction -13% General federal rate 25% Therefore, the federal rate is 25%, instead of 15%.	Corporate income not earned in a province or territory is neither: • eligible for the provincial abatement; nor • subject to provincial or territorial tax (exceptions apply).
Branch tax	25%	Non-resident corporations, except: • transportation, communications and iron-ore mining companies; and • insurers (other than in special circumstances).	Applies to after-tax profits that are not invested in qualifying property in Canada.	The 25% rate may be reduced by the relevant tax treaty (generally to the withholding tax rate on dividends, which is usually 5%, 10% or 15%). Some treaties prohibit the imposition of branch tax or provide that the tax is payable only on earnings exceeding a threshold.
Part III.1 Tax on Excess Eligible Dividend Designations	20% or 30%	Canadian-resident corporations	Applies if: • a CCPC has designated as eligible dividends during the year an amount that exceeds the corporation's general rate income pool (GRIP) at the end of the year; or • a non-CCPC pays an eligible dividend when it has a positive balance in its low rate income pool (LRIP).	A corporation subject to Part III.1 tax at the 20% rate (i.e., the excess designation was inadvertent) can elect, with shareholder concurrence, to treat all or part of the excess designation as a separate non-eligible dividend, in which case Part III.1 tax will not apply to the amount that is the subject of the election.
Refundable Part IV tax	38⅓%[1]	Private corporations and certain public corporations	Payable on taxable dividends received from certain Canadian corporations and foreign affiliates.	
Refundable Investment Tax	10⅔%[2]	Canadian-Controlled Private Corporations (CCPCs)	Increases the total federal rate that applies to investment income of a CCPC to 38.67% (34.67% for taxation years ending before 2016). Generally, 30⅔% (26⅔% for taxation years ending before 2016) of a CCPC's aggregate investment income is added to its non-eligible RDTOH (RDTOH for taxation years beginning before 2019).[3]	Refundable to the corporation through the refundable dividend tax on hand (RDTOH) mechanism, at a rate of 38⅓% (33⅓% for taxation years ending before 2016) of taxable dividends paid.[3]
Part VI Financial Institutions Capital Tax	1.25%	Banks Trust and loan corporations Life insurance companies	Applies if capital employed in Canada is over $1 billion. The threshold is shared by related corporations.	Reduced by the corporation's federal income tax liability. Any unused federal income tax liability can be applied to reduce Financial Institutions Capital Tax for the previous three years and the next seven.

Notes:

1. Recent changes to the refundable Part IV tax are shown in the following table:

	Changes effective after December 31, 2014		
	From	**To**	**Effective**
Refundable Part IV tax	33⅓%	38⅓%*	January 1, 2016*

* Applies to dividends received after 2015.

2. Recent changes to the refundable investment tax are shown in the following table:

	Changes effective after December 31, 2014		
	From	**To**	**Effective**
Refundable investment tax	6⅔%	10⅔%	January 1, 2016

3. For taxation years beginning after 2018:
   - eligible dividends paid by a CCPC will produce a refund (at the 38⅓% rate) only to the extent of its "eligible RDTOH account," that will include (subject to transitional rules) Part IV tax paid on eligible dividends from non-connected corporations and on taxable dividends from connected corporations to the extent the dividend generated a refund from the connected corporation's eligible RDTOH account; and
   - the refundable portion of the CCPC's other investment income, and the portion of Part IV tax on dividends from connected corporations that is not included in the eligible RDTOH account, is added to its "non-eligible RDTOH account," which is refunded to the extent of 38⅓% of non-eligible dividends paid by the CCPC (if this calculated amount exceeds the non-eligible RDTOH account, the excess can then recover any remaining eligible RDTOH account balance).

Corporate Income Tax Rates by Province — 2019 (%)

(Prepared from information available as of June 10, 2019)

All rates that change must be pro-rated for taxation years that straddle the effective date. Use the rate changes to determine rates for taxation years ending on December 31, 2015 or later.

Tax holidays may reduce or eliminate provincial tax.

In addition to income tax, financial institutions may also be subject to Part VI Financial Institution Capital Tax (see **Other Federal Corporate Tax Rates for 2019**) and provincial capital taxes (see **Financial Institutions Capital Tax Rates and Exemptions for 2019**).

General and M&P Corporate Income Tax Rates

(for December 31, 2019 year end) (%)

The percentages shown in the table below reflect the combined federal and provincial/territorial corporate rates (general, as well as manufacturing and processing (M&P)) for a 12-month taxation year ended December 31, 2019, on income allocated to provinces or territories. For Canadian-controlled private corporations (CCPCs), this table does not apply to:

- the first $500,000 ($600,000 in Saskatchewan) of active business income; and
- investment income.

For more CCPC rates, see the table, **Canadian-Controlled Private Corporation (CCPC) Income Tax Rates**.

		General and Manufacturing & Processing (M&P)	
Basic federal rate			**38**
Provincial abatement			(10)
Federal rate (before deductions)			**28**
General rate reduction or M&P deduction			(13)[1]
Federal rate			**15**[1] ↓
		Provincial/Territorial	**Combined**
Alberta[2]		11.5	**26.5**
British Columbia[3]		12	**27**
Manitoba		12	**27**
New Brunswick[4]		14	**29**
Newfoundland and Labrador[5]		15 **H**	**30**
Northwest Territories		11.5	**26.5**
Nova Scotia		16	**31**
Nunavut		12	**27**
Ontario[6]	General	11.5 **H**	**26.5**
	M&P	10 **H**	**25**
Prince Edward Island		16 **H**	**31**
Quebec[7]		11.6 **H**	**26.6**
Saskatchewan[8]	General	12	**27**
	M&P	10[9]	**25**
Yukon[10]	General	12	**27**
	M&P	2.5	**17.5**

H Tax holidays are available to certain corporations in the provinces indicated.

Notes:

1. Footnote 1 to the table, **Federal Corporate Tax Rates**, indicates when the general rate reduction and M&P deduction do not apply.
2. Recent and planned Alberta changes are shown in the following table:

	Alberta changes effective after December 31, 2014		
	From	**To**	**Effective**
General and M&P	10%	12%	July 1, 2015
	12%	11%	July 1, 2019
	11%	10%	January 1, 2020
	10%	9%	January 1, 2021
	9%	8%	January 1, 2022

3. Recent British Columbia changes are shown in the following table:

	British Columbia changes effective after December 31, 2014		
	From	**To**	**Effective**
General and M&P	11%	12%	January 1, 2018

Corporate Income Tax Rates by Province — 2019 (continued)

4. Recent New Brunswick changes are shown in the following table:

	New Brunswick changes effective after December 31, 2014		
	From	**To**	**Effective**
General and M&P	12%	14%	April 1, 2016

5. Recent Newfoundland and Labrador changes are shown in the following table:

	Newfoundland and Labrador changes effective after December 31, 2014		
	From	**To**	**Effective**
General	14%	15%	January 1, 2016
M&P	5%		

6. Corporations subject to Ontario income tax that, on an associated basis, have annual gross revenues of $100 million or more and total assets of $50 million or more may also be liable for a 2.7% corporate minimum tax (CMT) based on adjusted book income. The minimum tax is payable only to the extent that it exceeds the regular Ontario income tax liability.

7. Recent and planned Quebec changes are shown in the following table:

	Quebec changes effective after December 31, 2014		
	From	**To**	**Effective**
General and M&P	11.9%	11.8%	January 1, 2017
	11.8%	11.7%	January 1, 2018
	11.7%	11.6%	January 1, 2019
	11.6%	11.5%	January 1, 2020

8. Recent Saskatchewan changes are shown in the following table:

	Saskatchewan changes effective after December 31, 2014		
	From	**To**	**Effective**
General	12%	11.5%	July 1, 2017
	11.5%*	12%*	January 1, 2018
M&P**	10%	9.5%	July 1, 2017
	9.5%*	10%*	January 1, 2018

* Saskatchewan's October 25, 2017 throne speech:

- cancelled the general rate reduction from 11.5% to 11%, and the minimum M&P rate reduction from 9.5% to 9% that were to be effective on July 1, 2019; and
- restored on January 1, 2018, the rates that applied before July 1, 2017.

** See footnote 9 below.

9. The rate is the minimum rate that applies to M&P profits in Saskatchewan. The reduction from the general corporate rate is determined by multiplying the maximum rate reduction (2%) by the corporation's allocation of income to Saskatchewan.

10. Recent Yukon changes are shown in the following table:

	Yukon changes effective after December 31, 2014		
	From	**To**	**Effective**
General	15%	12%	July 1, 2017

Canadian-Controlled Private Corporation (CCPC) Income Tax Rates

(for December 31, 2019 year end) (%)

	Active business income of CCPCs up to $500,000[1]		Investment income[4]	
Federal rate (before deductions)		**28**		**28**
Small business deduction[2, 3]		(19)		n/a
Refundable investment tax		n/a		10.67
Federal rate		**9** ↓		**38.67** ↓
	Provincial/ Territorial	**Combined**	Provincial/ Territorial	**Combined**
Alberta[5]	2	**11**	11.5	**50.16***
British Columbia[6]	2	**11**	12	**50.67**
Manitoba[7]	Nil	**9**	12	**50.67**
New Brunswick[8]	2.5	**11.5**	14	**52.67**
Newfoundland and Labrador	3 **H**	**12**	15 **H**	**53.67**
Northwest Territories	4	**13**	11.5	**50.17**
Nova Scotia[9]	3 **H**	**12**	16	**54.67**
Nunavut[10]	3.5	**12.5**	12	**50.67**
Ontario[11, 12]	3.5 **H**	**12.5**	11.5 **H**	**50.17**
Prince Edward Island[13]	3.5 **H**	**12.5**	16 **H**	**54.67**
Quebec[14] M&P[15]	4 **H**	**13**	n/a	
Quebec[14] Regular[15]	6 **H**	**15**	11.6 **H**	**50.27**
Saskatchewan[16]	2[1]	**11**	12	**50.67**
Yukon[17] M&P	1.5	**10.5**	n/a	
Yukon[17] Non-M&P	2	**11**	12	**50.67**

H Tax holidays are available to certain corporations in the provinces indicated.

* Although 38.67% (federal) + 11.5% (Alberta) = 50.17%, the exact rate is 50.1626%.

Notes:

1. See the table, **General and M&P Corporate Income Tax Rates**, for the rates that apply to CCPCs on active business income above $500,000 ($600,000 for Saskatchewan).

   The $500,000 federal small business threshold also applies in all provinces and territories, except in Saskatchewan, where the CCPC threshold is $600,000; therefore, in Saskatchewan, the combined rate that applies to active business income from $500,000 to $600,000 is 17%.

2. See footnote 2 to the table, **Federal Corporate Tax Rates**, for a description of the federal small business deduction threshold and situations in which the small business deduction is reduced.

   These reductions also apply for the purposes of all provincial/territorial small business deductions, except that:

   - New Brunswick and Ontario will not parallel the federal measure that phases out the small business deduction for CCPCs that earn passive investment income exceeding $50,000 (on an associated basis) in a previous taxation year, for taxation years beginning after 2018; and
   - for Quebec, the $10 million threshold is based on paid-up capital (on an associated basis), instead of taxable capital.

3. For recent changes to the federal small business deduction, see footnote 2 to the table, **Federal Corporate Tax Rates**.

4. Rates on investment income are 23.67% higher than the general rates for 2019 (see the table, **General and M&P Corporate Income Tax Rates**), because:

   - CCPC investment income does not benefit from the 13% federal general rate reduction; and
   - the rates on investment income include a $10\frac{2}{3}$% tax that is refundable when the CCPC pays taxable dividends.

   See also "Refundable Investment Tax" in the table, **Other Federal Corporate Tax Rates for 2019**, and footnote 2 to that table for recent changes to the refundable investment tax.

5. Recent Alberta changes are shown in the following table:

	Alberta changes effective after December 31, 2014		
	From	**To**	**Effective**
CCPC rate	3%	2%	January 1, 2017

6. Recent British Columbia changes are shown in the following table:

	British Columbia changes effective after December 31, 2014		
	From	**To**	**Effective**
CCPC rate	2.5%	2%	April 1, 2017

7. Recent Manitoba changes are shown in the following table:

	Manitoba changes effective after December 31, 2014		
	From	**To**	**Effective**
Threshold up to which CCPC rate applies	$425,000	$450,000	January 1, 2016
	$450,000	$500,000	January 1, 2019

8. Recent New Brunswick changes are shown in the following table:

	New Brunswick changes effective after December 31, 2014		
	From	**To**	**Effective**
CCPC rate	4.5%	4%	January 1, 2015
	4%	3.5%	April 1, 2016
	3.5%	3%	April 1, 2017
	3%	2.5%	April 1, 2018

CCPC Income Tax Rates — 2019 (continued)

9. Recent Nova Scotia changes are shown in the following table:

	Nova Scotia changes effective after December 31, 2014		
	From	To	Effective
Threshold up to which CCPC rate applies	$350,000	$500,000	January 1, 2017

10. Planned Nunavut changes are shown in the following table:

	Nunavut changes effective after December 31, 2014		
	From	To	Effective
CCPC rate	4%	3%*	July 1, 2019

* Because Nunavut has a non-partisan government, it is uncertain whether draft legislation to decrease the rate to 3% will be enacted.

11. Recent Ontario changes are shown in the following table:

	Ontario changes effective after December 31, 2014		
	From	To	Effective
CCPC rate	4.5%	3.5%	January 1, 2018

12. Corporations subject to Ontario income tax may also be liable for corporate minimum tax (CMT) based on adjusted book income. The minimum tax is payable only to the extent that it exceeds the regular Ontario income tax liability. For the rate and thresholds, see the table, **General and M&P Corporate Income Tax Rates** (footnote 6).

13. Recent Prince Edward Island changes are shown in the following table:

	Prince Edward Island changes effective after December 31, 2014		
	From	To	Effective
CCPC rate	4.5%	4%	January 1, 2018
	4%	3.5%	January 1, 2019

14. Recent changes to Quebec's CCPC rates that apply for taxation years beginning after December 31, 2016:
   - require a CCPC to meet additional criteria (i.e., number of hours paid, percentage of activities in the M&P and primary sector) to be eligible for the province's regular CCPC rate;
   - increase the regular CCPC rate in certain cases;
   - extend the M&P CCPC rate to CCPCs in the primary sector (i.e., agriculture, forestry, fishing and hunting, mining, quarrying, and oil and gas extraction); and
   - determine the percentage of activities attributable to M&P and primary activities based only on labour costs (assets are no longer a factor).

15. Recent and planned Quebec changes are shown in the following table:

	Quebec changes effective after December 31, 2014		
	From	To	Effective
CCPC rate (M&P)	6%*	4%*, **	April 1, 2015
CCPC rate (Regular)	8%	7%	March 28, 2018
	7%	6%	January 1, 2019
	6%	5%	January 1, 2020
	5%	4%	January 1, 2021

* For taxation years beginning before January 1, 2017, the rates apply to all active business income up to $500,000 if 50% or more of the CCPC's activities are attributable to M&P (based on M&P assets and labour). If this percentage is under 50% and over 25%, the rates will increase proportionately (straight line) to 8% (i.e., the rate is 8% when the M&P percentage is 25% or less).

** For taxation years beginning after December 31, 2016, the 4% rate applies to all active business income up to $500,000 if 50% or more of the CCPC's activities are attributable to M&P and the primary sector (based on M&P and primary sector labour). If this percentage is under 50% and over 25%, the rates will increase proportionately (straight line) to the regular CCPC rate, or the general rate, depending on the circumstances (i.e., the rate is the regular CCPC rate [for 2019, 6%], or the general rate [for 2019, 11.6%], when the M&P and primary sector percentage is 25% or less).

16. Recent Saskatchewan changes are shown in the following table:

	Saskatchewan changes effective after December 31, 2014		
	From	To	Effective
Threshold up to which CCPC rate applies	$500,000	$600,000	January 1, 2018

17. Recent Yukon changes are shown in the following table:

	Yukon changes effective after December 31, 2014		
	From	To	Effective
CCPC rate (non-M&P)	3%	2%	July 1, 2017

Financial Institutions Capital Tax Rates and Exemptions for 2019

In addition to federal capital taxes on financial institutions, six provinces levy a capital tax on financial institutions, such as trust and loan corporations and banks. Alberta, British Columbia, Ontario, Quebec and the territories do not impose a financial institutions capital tax.

The calculation of the tax base may differ from province to province.

The table below sets out capital tax rates for financial institutions (other than insurance companies) for a twelve-month taxation year ending December 31, 2019.

All rates that change must be pro-rated for taxation years that straddle the effective date, except as noted. Use these changes to determine rates for taxation years ending on December 31, 2015 or later.

Financial Institutions

		Rate (for December 31, 2019 year-end)	Exemption[1] (for December 31, 2019 year-end)
Federal	Part VI Financial Institutions Capital Tax[2]	1.25%	$1 billion
Alberta		No capital tax	
British Columbia		No capital tax	
Manitoba[3]	If taxable paid-up capital < $4 billion		
	If taxable paid-up capital ≥ $4 billion	6%	Nil
New Brunswick[4]	Trust and loan corporations	4%	$10 million
	Banks	5%	$10 million
Newfoundland and Labrador[5]	If taxable capital ≤ $10 million	6%	$5 million
	If taxable capital > $10 million	6%	Nil
Nova Scotia[6]	Trust and loan corporations — Head office in N.S.	4%	$30 million
	Trust and loan corporations — Other	4%	$500,000
	Banks	4%	$500,000
Ontario		No capital tax	
Prince Edward Island		5%	$2 million
Quebec (compensation tax on payroll[7])		No capital tax	
Saskatchewan[8]	If taxable paid-up capital ≤ $1.5 billion	0.7%	Up to $20 million[9]
	If taxable paid-up capital > $1.5 billion — If taxable paid-up capital ≤ $1.5 billion in taxation year ending after October 31, 2008 and before November 1, 2009 — On first $1.5 billion of taxable paid-up capital	0.7%	Up to $20 million[9]
	If taxable paid-up capital > $1.5 billion — If taxable paid-up capital ≤ $1.5 billion in taxation year ending after October 31, 2008 and before November 1, 2009 — On taxable paid-up capital > $1.5 billion	4%	Up to $20 million[9]
	If taxable paid-up capital > $1.5 billion — Other	4%	Up to $20 million[9]

Notes:

1. Associated or related corporations may be required to share the exemption.
2. See the table, **Other Federal Corporate Tax Rates for 2019**.
3. Recent changes in Manitoba's capital tax rates and exemption are shown below:

	Manitoba changes effective after December 31, 2014 — From	To	Effective
Capital tax rates	5%	6%	Taxation years ending after April 30, 2015
Capital tax exemption	$10 million	Nil	Taxation years ending after April 30, 2017

Financial Institutions Capital Tax Rates and Exemptions for 2019 (continued)

4. Recent changes in New Brunswick's capital tax rates are shown below:

		New Brunswick changes effective after December 31, 2014		
		From	**To**	**Effective**
Capital tax rates	Banks*	4%	5%	April 1, 2016

* Effective April 1, 2016, a financial corporation that is a bank can reduce its capital tax payable by an "employment tax credit," which relates to certain salaries and wages incurred in New Brunswick.

5. Recent changes in Newfoundland and Labrador's capital tax rates are shown below:

	Newfoundland and Labrador changes effective after December 31, 2014		
	From	**To**	**Effective**
Capital tax rates	4%	5%	April 1, 2015
	5%	6%	January 1, 2016

6. In Nova Scotia, the maximum tax payable by financial institutions under the *Corporations Capital Tax Act* is $12 million annually, starting January 1, 2015.

7. Quebec imposes a compensation tax on payroll. Recent and planned changes to this tax are shown below:

		Quebec changes effective after December 31, 2014		
		From	**To**	**Effective**
Compensation tax on payroll*	Banks and loan, trust and security trading companies	4.48%	4.29%	April 1, 2018
		4.29%	4.22%	April 1, 2019
		4.22%	4.14%	April 1, 2020
		4.14%	2.8%	April 1, 2022
		2.8%	Nil	April 1, 2024
	Savings and credit unions	3.52%	3.39%	April 1, 2018
		3.39%	3.30%	April 1, 2019
		3.30%	3.26%	April 1, 2020
		3.26%	2.2%	April 1, 2022
		2.2%	Nil	April 1, 2024
	Other (excluding insurance companies)**	1.44%	1.37%	April 1, 2018
		1.37%	1.34%	April 1, 2019
		1.34%	1.32%	April 1, 2020
		1.32%	0.9%	April 1, 2022
		0.9%	Nil	April 1, 2024

* Starting April 1, 2018, the maximum payroll for a taxation year that is subject to the compensation tax is, for:

- banks and loan, trust and security trading companies – 1.1 billion;
- savings and credit unions – $550 million; and
- other (excluding insurance companies) – $275 million.

** Financial institutions in the "Other" category are exempt from the compensation tax on payroll, unless the financial institution made a joint election under section 150 of the *Excise Tax Act,* with a bank, a loan, trust or security trading company, a savings and credit union, or an insurance company (or with any person that made this election).

8. Recent changes in Saskatchewan's capital tax rates are shown below:

		Saskatchewan changes effective after December 31, 2014		
		From	**To**	**Effective**
Capital tax rates	If taxable paid-up capital > $1.5 billion	3.25%	4%	April 1, 2017

9. Saskatchewan's $20 million exemption includes a $10 million exemption, which is available to each corporation, and an additional $10 million exemption, which must be shared by the associated group. The extent to which the additional exemption is available to a corporation depends on the proportion of salaries and wages paid in Saskatchewan by that corporation in relation to the total salaries and wages paid by the associated group.

Payroll Tax Rates for 2019

Only those provinces and territories listed in the table below have payroll taxes (by various names).

		Rate	Payroll[1]	Payroll tax
British Columbia[2]	Employer Health Tax	1.95%	Over $1,500,000	Payroll × 1.95%
		2.925%	$500,000 to $1,500,000	(Payroll − $500,000) × 2.925%
		0%	$0 to $500,000	$0
Manitoba	Health and Post-Secondary Education Tax	2.15%	Over $2,500,000	Payroll × 2.15%
		4.3%	$1,250,000 to $2,500,000	(Payroll − $1,250,000) × 4.3%
		0%	$0 to $1,250,000	$0
Newfoundland and Labrador[3]		2%	Over $1,300,000	(Payroll − $1,300,000) × 2%
		0%	$0 to $1,300,000	$0
Northwest Territories[4]	Payroll Tax	2%	Over $0	Payroll × 2%
Nunavut[4]				
Ontario[5]	Employer Health Tax	1.95%	Over $5,000,000	Payroll × 1.95%
			$490,000 to $5,000,000	(Payroll − $490,000) × 1.95%
		0%	$0 to $490,000	$0
Quebec[6]	Health Services Fund	4.26%	Over $6,000,000	Payroll × rate
		Reduced rates	$1,000,000 to $6,000,000	
		1.25% or 1.7%	$0 to $1,000,000	

Notes:

1. Associated employers must aggregate their payroll costs to apply the thresholds.
2. British Columbia's Employer Health Tax became effective on January 1, 2019. Registered charities and non-profit organizations are eligible for higher exemption thresholds.
3. Recent changes to the exemption threshold for Newfoundland and Labrador's Health and Post-Secondary Education Tax follow:

	Newfoundland and Labrador changes effective after December 31, 2014		
	From	**To**	**Effective**
Exemption threshold	$1.2 million	$1.3 million	January 1, 2019

4. In the Northwest Territories and Nunavut, payroll tax is paid by employees. It is not levied on employers, but employers must deduct the tax from remuneration paid to employees.
5. Recent changes to the exemption for Ontario's Employer Health Tax follow:

	Ontario changes effective after December 31, 2014		
	From	**To**	**Effective**
Exemption threshold*	$450,000	$490,000	January 1, 2019

* The exemption is indexed every 5 years. Registered charities can claim the exemption regardless of their payroll.

6. Quebec's Health Services Fund rate is reduced for employers with annual payrolls between $1 million and $6 million (see below), using a formula that reflects both the calendar year and the employer's total payroll.

   Recent and planned changes to the minimum Health Services Fund rate for small- and medium-sized businesses follow:

		Quebec changes effective after December 31, 2014		
		From	**To**	**Effective**
Sector	Primary and manufacturing	2.7%	1.6%	January 1, 2015
		1.6%	1.55%	January 1, 2017
		1.55%	1.5%	January 1, 2018
		1.5%	1.45%	March 28, 2018
		1.45%	1.25%	August 16, 2018
	Other	2.7%	2.5%	January 1, 2017
		2.5%	2.3%	January 1, 2018
		2.3%	1.95%	March 28, 2018
		1.95%	1.75%	August 16, 2018
		1.75%	1.7%	January 1, 2019
		1.7%	1.65%	January 1, 2020

Payroll Tax Rates for 2019 (cont'd)

Recent and planned changes to the threshold above which the 4.26% rate applies follow:

	Quebec changes effective after December 31, 2014		
	From	**To**	**Effective**
Exemption threshold	$5 million	$5.5 million	January 1, 2018
	$5.5 million	$6 million	January 1, 2019
	$6 million	$6.5 million	January 1, 2021
	$6.5 million	$7 million*	January 1, 2022*

* The threshold is indexed after 2022.

Every Quebec employer with a payroll exceeding $2 million ($1 million before 2015) must:

- allot at least 1% of payroll to training; or
- contribute to a provincial fund the difference between that amount and the amount actually spent on training.

In certain cases, Health Services Fund contributions can be reduced or eliminated, and refunds may be made. Financial institutions (excluding insurers) may also be subject to a compensation tax on payroll (see footnote 7 to the table **Financial Institutions**).

Employees, employers and the self-employed must contribute to the Quebec Parental Insurance Plan (QPIP), from which maternity, adoption and parental leave benefits will be paid. Individuals may be required to contribute to the Quebec Health contribution (before January 1, 2017) and the Health Services Fund.

Integration Tables — 2019

(Prepared from information available as of June 14, 2019)

Table 1: Active Business Income (based on a December 31, 2019 year end and $10,000 of active business income)[1]

This table shows:

- the income tax deferral, if active business income is earned and retained in a corporation, as opposed to being paid out of the corporation as salary to the shareholder; and
- the tax saving (cost), if the after-tax corporate income is paid out as a dividend to the shareholder, instead of being paid out of the corporation as salary.

		Eligible for Small Business Deduction[3]		No Small Business Deduction[3]	
		Deferral	Saving (Cost)	Deferral	Saving (Cost)
Alberta[4]		3,700	(65)	2,150	(181)
British Columbia		3,976	4	2,376	81
Manitoba		4,244	(3)	2,444	(314)
New Brunswick[5]		4,180	(46)	2,430	51
Newfoundland and Labrador		4,025	101	2,225	(758)
Northwest Territories		3,605	401	2,255	173
Nova Scotia		4,200	(48)	2,300	(569)
Nunavut		3,400	93	1,950	(465)
Ontario[6, 7]	General	4,192	45	2,792	(100)
	M&P			2,942	(9)
Prince Edward Island		3,887	(70)	2,037	(324)
Quebec	General	4,022[8]	91[8]	2,862	(74)
	M&P	4,222[9]	199[9]		
Saskatchewan	General	3,650	57	2,050	(114)
	M&P			2,250	27
Yukon[10]	General	3,700	(53)	2,100	(12)
	M&P	3,750	(24)	3,050	664

Table 2: Investment Income (based on a December 31, 2019 year end and $10,000 of investment income)[2]

This table shows:

- the income tax deferral or prepayment, if investment income is earned and retained in a corporation, as opposed to being earned directly by an individual; and
- the tax saving (cost), if the after-tax corporate income is paid out as a dividend to the shareholder.

	Portfolio Dividends		Capital Gains		Interest	
	Deferral (Prepayment)	(Cost)	Deferral (Prepayment)	(Cost)	Deferral (Prepayment)	(Cost)
Alberta[4]	(662)	Nil	(108)	(278)	(216)	(555)
British Columbia	(689)	Nil	(43)	(295)	(87)	(591)
Manitoba	(55)	Nil	(13)	(347)	(27)	(694)
New Brunswick	(482)	Nil	32	(297)	63	(594)
Newfoundland and Labrador	428	Nil	(118)	(302)	(237)	(603)
Northwest Territories	(1,000)	Nil	(155)	(104)	(312)	(209)
Nova Scotia	325	Nil	(33)	(335)	(67)	(669)
Nunavut	(525)	Nil	(308)	(287)	(617)	(573)
Ontario[6]	101	Nil	168	(207)	336	(412)
Prince Edward Island	(411)	Nil	(164)	(350)	(330)	(700)
Quebec	167	Nil	152	(174)	304	(347)
Saskatchewan	(869)	Nil	(158)	(240)	(317)	(480)
Yukon[10]	(940)	Nil	(133)	(287)	(267)	(574)

Notes to Tables 1 and 2:

1. Table 1 assumes that the individual is taxed at the top marginal income tax rate (only federal and provincial/territorial income tax, the employer portion of provincial health tax and the employee portion of Northwest Territories and Nunavut payroll taxes are considered). Different results may arise in special circumstances (e.g., for credit unions).
2. Table 2 assumes that:
   - the individual is taxed at the top marginal income tax rate;
   - portfolio dividends received are designated as "eligible" dividends;
   - no capital gains deductions are available;
   - the non-taxable portion of the capital gain is distributed as a tax-free capital dividend; and

Integration Tables — 2019 (continued)

- the taxable dividend paid (eligible, for portfolio dividends; non-eligible, for capital gains and interest) generates a full refund of the refundable tax (i.e., $3,833 refund on $10,000 (dividend), $1,533 refund on $4,000 (capital gains), $3,067 refund on $8,000 (interest)). For 2019, the taxable dividend paid for:
  - o Alberta, Northwest Territories, Ontario and Quebec – is greater than $4,000 (capital gains) and $8,000 (interest) because excess funds are available.
  - o British Columbia, Manitoba, Nunavut, Saskatchewan and the Yukon – is $4,000 (capital gains) and $8,000 (interest) because there is not an excess or shortfall of funds.
  - o New Brunswick, Newfoundland and Labrador, Nova Scotia and Prince Edward Island – is $4,000 (capital gains) and $8,000 (interest); although there is a shortfall of funds from investment income, it is assumed that the corporation has other income from which it can pay the dividend (however, the figures in this table do not reflect the individual tax on the portion of the dividend paid from the other income).

3. The federal small business threshold of $500,000 applies in all provinces and territories, except for Saskatchewan, where the threshold is $600,000 (the figures in Table 1 do not apply to income between $500,000 and $600,000).
4. For Alberta, the figures in the table assume the individual is taxed at Alberta's personal income tax rate on incomes over $314,928. If the individual's income is $314,928 or less, but over $210,371, the figures are as follows:
   - Table 1:
     - o Eligible for small business deduction [deferral: $3,600, cost: ($63)]; and
     - o No small business deduction [deferral: $2,050, cost: ($179)].
   - Table 2:
     - o Portfolio dividends [prepayment: ($800), cost: nil];
     - o Capital gains [prepayment: ($158), cost: ($282)]; and
     - o Interest [prepayment: ($316), cost: ($563)].
5. For New Brunswick, the figures in Table 1 do not apply in situations in which a Canadian-controlled private corporation (CCPC) is not eligible for the federal small business deduction (SBD), but is eligible for the New Brunswick SBD. This situation occurs because New Brunswick will not parallel the federal For New Brunswick, the figures in Table 1 do not apply in situations in which a Canadian-controlled private corporation (CCPC) is not eligible for the federal small business deduction (SBD), but is eligible for the New Brunswick SBD. This situation occurs because New Brunswick will not parallel the federal rules that phase-out the $500,000 SBD for CCPCs that earn between $50,000 and $150,000 of passive investment income in a previous taxation year. This mismatch in the federal/New Brunswick SBD rules results in a lower integrated tax rate on ABI.
6. For Ontario, the figures in the table assume the individual is taxed at Ontario's personal income tax rate on incomes over $220,000. If the individual's income is $220,000 or less, but over $210,371, the figures are as follows:
   - Table 1:
     - o Eligible for small business deduction [deferral: $4,039, saving: $49]; and
     - o No small business deduction [General - deferral: $2,639, cost: ($95); M&P - deferral: $2,789, cost: nil].
   - Table 2:
     - o Portfolio dividends [prepayment: ($114), cost: nil];
     - o Capital gains [deferral: $90, cost: ($212)]; and
     - o Interest [deferral: $180, cost: ($424)].
7. For Ontario, the figures in Table 1 and in note 6 do not apply in situations in which a CCPC is not eligible for the federal SBD, but is eligible for the Ontario SBD. This situation occurs because Ontario will not parallel the federal rules that phase-out the $500,000 SBD for CCPCs that earn between $50,000 and $150,000 of passive investment income in a previous taxation year. This mismatch in the federal/Ontario SBD rules results in a lower integrated tax rate on ABI.
8. For Quebec, the figures in the table assume the corporation is eligible for Quebec's small business regular income tax rate (6% for 2019), which is the case if the corporation meets the requirements of the "activities" test or the "hours paid" test. If it does not, the regular small business tax rate will increase proportionately (straight line), in certain circumstances, to the general Quebec rate (11.6% for 2019).
9. For Quebec, the figures in the table assume the corporation is eligible for Quebec's small business M&P and primary sector rate of 4%, which is the case if 50% or more of the corporation's activities are attributable to M&P and the primary sector (based on M&P and primary sector labour costs). If the M&P and primary sector percentage is under 50% and more than 25%, the M&P and primary sector rate of 4% will increase proportionately (straight line) to Quebec's small business regular income tax rate (6% for 2019) or the general Quebec rate (11.6% for 2019), depending on the circumstances.
10. For the Yukon, the figures in the table assume the individual is taxed at Yukon's personal income tax rate on incomes over $500,000. If the individual's income is $500,000 or less, but over $210,371, the figures are as follows:
    - Table 1:
      - o Eligible for small business deduction [No M&P - deferral: $3,480, cost: ($48); M&P - deferral: $3,530, cost: ($18)]; and
      - o No small business deduction [General - deferral: $1,880, cost: ($10); M&P - deferral: $2,830, saving: $694].
    - Table 2:
      - o Portfolio dividends [prepayment: ($1,244), cost: nil];
      - o Capital gains [prepayment: ($243), cost: ($296)]; and
      - o Interest [prepayment: ($487), cost: ($591)].

Prescribed Quarterly Interest Rates

- (white) Deemed interest on employee and shareholder loans and effective July 1, 2010, rate also applies to overpaid taxes for corporate taxpayers
- (light grey) Rate for overpaid taxes for all taxpayers prior to July 1, 2010 and for non-corporate taxpayers after June 30, 2010
- (dark grey) Late or deficient income tax payments and unremitted withholdings

	Jan. 1 - Mar. 31			Apr. 1 - June 30			July 1 - Sept. 30			Oct. 1 - Dec. 31		
2000	5	7	9	6	8	10	6	8	10	6	8	10
2001	6	8	10	6	8	10	5	7	9	5	7	9
2002	3	5	7	2	4	6	3	5	7	3	5	7
2003	3	5	7	3	5	7	4	6	8	3	5	7
2004	3	5	7	3	5	7	2	4	6	3	5	7
2005	3	5	7	3	5	7	3	5	7	3	5	7
2006	3	5	7	4	6	8	4	6	8	5	7	9
2007	5	7	9	5	7	9	5	7	9	5	7	9
2008	4	6	8	4	6	8	3	5	7	3	5	7
2009	2	4	6	1	3	5	1	3	5	1	3	5
2010	1	3	5	1	3	5	1	3	5	1	3	5
2011	1	3	5	1	3	5	1	3	5	1	3	5
2012	1	3	5	1	3	5	1	3	5	1	3	5
2013	1	3	5	1	3	5	1	3	5	2	4	6
2014	1	3	5	1	3	5	1	3	5	1	3	5
2015	1	3	5	1	3	5	1	3	5	1	3	5
2016	1	3	5	1	3	5	1	3	5	1	3	5
2017	1	3	5	1	3	5	1	3	5	1	3	5
2018	1	3	5	2	4	6	2	4	6	2	4	6
2019	2	4	6	2	4	6	2	4	6			

Prescribed Interest Rates for Leasing Rules (%)

	2014	2015	2016	2017	2018	2019
January	4.01	3.36	3.17	3.06	3.16	3.39
February	4.09	3.22	3.04	3.24	3.15	3.12
March	3.80	2.75	2.90	3.34	3.35	3.11
April	3.80	2.76	2.78	3.29	3.35	3.10
May	3.82	2.79	2.86	3.14	3.22	2.76
June	3.76	3.01	2.94	3.01	3.45	2.90
July	3.60	3.08	2.87	2.87	3.28	2.75
August	3.72	3.29	2.67	2.99	3.15	
September	3.59	3.09	2.60	3.29	3.31	
October	3.44	3.08	2.53	3.19	3.33	
November	3.61	3.09	2.52	3.42	3.43	
December	3.46	3.13	2.68	3.32	3.52	

Automobile Rates and Limits

The following rates and limits are prescribed in sections 7305.1 to 7307 of the Income Tax Regulations. In recent years, the Department of Finance has been adjusting the amounts by News Release issued at the end of the calendar year.

See the definitions of "automobile", "passenger vehicle", and "zero-emission passenger vehicle" in subsection 248(1) of the Income Tax Act.

	Jan. 1/13-Dec. 31/13	Jan. 1/14-Dec. 31/14	Jan. 1/15-Dec. 31/15	Jan. 1/16-Dec. 31/16	Jan. 1/17-Dec. 31/17	Jan. 1/18-Dec. 31/18	Jan. 1/19-Dec. 31/19
Operating expense benefit - per kilometre [1]							
Employees	27¢	27¢	27¢	26¢	25¢	26¢	28¢
Employees employed principally in selling or leasing automobiles	24¢	24¢	24¢	23¢	22¢	23¢	25¢

	Jan. 1/13-Dec. 31/13	Jan. 1/14-Dec. 31/14	Jan. 1/15-Dec. 31/15	Jan. 1/16-Dec. 31/16	Jan. 1/17-Dec. 31/17	Jan. 1/18-Dec. 31/18	Jan. 1/19-Dec. 31/19
Reasonable allowance per kilometre [2]							
Deductible by employer where tax-free allowance paid to employee:							
All Provinces*	54¢/48¢	54¢/48¢	55¢/49¢	54¢/48¢	54¢/48¢	55¢/49¢	58¢/52¢
Nunavut, Yukon and Northwest Territories*	58¢/52¢	58¢/52¢	59¢/53¢	58¢/52¢	58¢/52¢	59¢/53¢	62¢/56¢

	Jan. 1/13-Dec. 31/13	Jan. 1/14-Dec. 31/14	Jan. 1/15-Dec. 31/15	Jan. 1/16-Dec. 31/16	Jan. 1/17-Dec. 31/17	Jan. 1/18-Dec. 31/18	Jan. 1/19-Dec. 31/19
Cost of passenger vehicle [3]	$30,000**	$30,000**	$30,000**	$30,000**	$30,000**	$30,000**	$30,000**
Cost of zero-emission passenger vehicle[4]							$55,000**
Prescribed monthly interest [5]	$300	$300	$300	$300	$300	$300	$300
Monthly lease amount [6]	$800**	$800**	$800**	$800**	$800**	$800**	$800**

* First number applies to the first 5,000 kilometres driven in the year. The second number applies to subsequent kilometres driven in the year.

** Applicable federal and provincial sales taxes are added to these figures to calculate the ceiling amount.

[1] Reg. 7305.1; prescribed for s. 6(1)(*k*).

[2] Reg. 7306; prescribed for s. 18(1)(*r*).

[3] Reg. 7307(1); prescribed for ss. 13(2), 13(7)(*g*), 13(7)(*h*)(iii), 20(4), 20(16.1), the description of B in s. 67.3(*d*), and s. 85(1)(*e*.4)(i).

[4] Reg. 7307(1.1); prescribed for ss. 13(7)(*i*). Effective March 19, 2019.

[5] Reg. 7307(2); prescribed for the description of A in s. 67.2.

[6] Reg. 7307(3); prescribed for the description of A in s. 67.3(*c*).

Mileage Rates and Meal Allowances

Certain amounts for travel are allowed in connection with northern residents' deductions (s. 110.7), moving expenses (s. 62), and transportation to obtain medical services (s. 118.2(2)). Generally speaking, travel expenses for these purposes may include any of the following amounts:

- air, train, and bus fares;
- vehicle expenses;
- meals;
- hotel and motel accommodations, and camping fees; and
- other incidental expenses, such as taxis and road or ferry tolls.

Where actual vehicle and meal expenses are claimed, they should be supported by receipts. The CRA does permit a simplified alternative calculation for these items; however, the CRA states that although taxpayers need not keep detailed receipts for actual expenses if they choose to use the simplified flat-rate methods, they may still ask the taxpayer to provide some documentation to support the claim.

Mileage

In limited situations, the CRA will permit mileage deductions to be calculated on an arbitrary cents per kilometre basis, rather than as a proration of actual annual expenditures prorated by mileage. This option is available in calculating northern residents' deductions (s. 110.7), moving expenses (s. 62), and transportation to obtain medical services (s. 118.2(2)). This option is not available for employees claiming deduction of auto expenses in the course of employment.

Where the option is permitted, the acceptable mileage rates are:

Province or Territory	*Cents per kilometre for taxation year*				
	2014	2015	2016	2017	2018
Alberta	45.5	44.5	43.5	45.0	48.5
British Columbia	49.5	48.5	47.5	50.0	53.0
Manitoba	48.5	47.0	47.0	47.0	50.5
New Brunswick	51.0	49.0	48.5	50.5	53.5
Newfoundland and Labrador	53.5	52.0	53.0	54.0	57.5
Northwest Territories	63.0	61.5	58.0	59.5	63.5
Nova Scotia	51.5	49.5	48.5	50.0	52.5
Nunavut	61.0	61.0	57.5	58.5	59.0
Ontario	57.5	57.5	54.0	55.5	58.5
Prince Edward Island	50.5	48.5	47.5	49.0	52.0
Quebec	52.0	50.5	49.5	50.5	53.0
Saskatchewan	47.5	46.5	45.5	46.0	50.0
Yukon	64.0	60.5	59.0	60.5	65.0

For travel from one province to another, or for travel from Canada to outside Canada, use the per kilometre rate for the province or territory where travel began. For travel from outside Canada into Canada, use the per kilometre rate for the province or territory of final destination. For travel between countries outside Canada, the actual expense method should be used.

Flat Rate Meal Allowances

Similarly, in calculating northern residents' deductions (s. 110.7), moving expenses (s. 62), and transportation to obtain medical services (s. 118.2(2)), the CRA will allow flat rate meal allowances for the travel period in lieu of actual "reasonable" expenses. The rates for 2014–2018 are $17 per meal to a maximum of $51 per day.

Actual expenses must be supported by receipts; the CRA states that although taxpayers need not keep detailed receipts for actual expenses if they choose to use the simplified flat-rate methods, they may still ask the taxpayer to provide some documentation to support the claim.

Yearly Average Conversion Rates for Major Currencies

Effective March 1, 2017, the Bank of Canada ceased providing average annual exchange rates for 32 currencies, but continued to report such rates with respect to the 26 most widely-traded currencies. Consequently, the list of average annual exchange rates for 2017 contains only rates for the remaining 26 currencies — much less than what was published in previous editions of *Canadian Income Tax Act with Regulations, Annotated*. The historical rates for the currencies that were removed have been retained for your reference, and are provided below remain in a separate table, entitled "Historical Rates".

For a complete list of monthly and annual conversion rate averages, see the "Exchange Rates" page on the Bank of Canada website at https://www.bankofcanada.ca/rates/exchange/.

Country	Monetary Unit	2017	2018
Australia	*dollar*	0.9951	0.9687
Brazil	*new real*	0.4071	0.3566
China	*renminbi*	0.1921	0.1961
Europe	*Euro*	1.4650	1.5302
Hong Kong	*dollar*	0.1667	0.1653
India	*rupee*	0.01995	0.01897
Indonesia	*rupiah*	0.000097	0.000091
Japan	*yen*	0.01158	0.01174
Malaysia	*ringgit*	0.3020	0.3213
Mexico	*peso*	0.06884	0.06744
New Zealand	*dollar*	0.9229	0.8973
Norway	*krone*	0.1570	0.1594
Peru	*nuevo sol*	0.3982	0.3943
Russia	*rouble*	0.02228	0.02071
Saudi Arabia	*riyal*	0.3463	0.3455
Singapore	*dollar*	0.9404	0.9607
South Africa	*rand*	0.09767	0.09844
South Korea	*won*	0.001149	0.001178
Sweden	*krona*	0.1520	0.1492
Switzerland	*franc*	1.3189	1.3246
Taiwan	*new Taiwan dollar*	0.04269	0.04299
Thailand	*baht*	0.03827	0.04011
Turkey	*lira*	0.3565	0.2759
United Kingdom	*pound*	1.6720	1.7299
United States	*dollar*	1.2986	1.2957
Vietnam	*dong*	0.000057	0.000056

The historical rates for the currencies that were removed have been provided below for your reference. Where you need to convert an amount that is denominated in a foreign currency that is no longer reported by the Bank of Canada, an alternative rate that is acceptable to the CRA must be used.

Historical Rates

Country	Monetary Unit	2015	2016
Argentina	*peso*	0.1388	0.08991
Bahamas	*dollar*	1.2787	1.3248
Burma (Myanmar)	*kyat*	0.00110	0.00107
Chile	*peso*	0.001956	0.001960
Colombia	*peso*	0.000469	0.000434
Communauté Financière Africaine	*franc*	0.002162	0.002235
Comptoirs Français du Pacifique	*franc*	0.01188	0.01229

Croatia	*kuna*	0.1863	0.1946
Czech Republic	*koruna*	0.05199	0.05423
Denmark	*krone*	0.1901	0.1969
East Caribbean	*dollar*	0.4755	0.4926
Fiji	*dollar*	0.6133	0.6345
Ghana	*cedi*	0.3393	0.3353
Guatemala	*quetzal*	0.1632	0.1697
Honduras	*lempira*	0.05929	0.05847
Hungary	*forint*	0.004576	0.004707
Iceland	*krona*	0.009701	0.01098
Israel	*new shekel*	0.3292	0.3450
Jamaica	*dollar*	0.01095	0.01059
Morocco	*dirham*	0.1311	0.1351
Neth. Antilles	*guilder*	0.7214	0.7422
Pakistan	*rupee*	0.01244	0.01265
Panama	*balboa*	1.2787	1.3248
Philippines	*peso*	0.02808	0.02791
Poland	*zloty*	0.3389	0.3360
Romania	*nouveau leu*	0.3191	0.3265
Serbia	*dinar*	0.01175	0.01191
Sri Lanka	*rupee*	0.009399	0.009066
Trinidad & Tobago	*dollar*	0.2012	0.1999
Tunisia	*dinar*	0.6514	0.6191
United Arab Emirates	*dirham*	0.3481	0.3607
Venezuela	*bolivar fuerte*	0.2030	0.1431

All Canadian tax returns (except for those of certain corporations which may operate primarily in a foreign currency and elect to use foreign currency reporting) must report income in Canadian dollars. Where you have a major transaction where you received proceeds (or acquired capital or depreciable property) in a foreign currency, you should use the currency value on the actual date of the transaction. This can be obtained from the Bank of Canada website (https://www.bankofcanada.ca/rates/exchange/). Where a sale is followed by a currency conversion, there may be a separate gain or loss on the conversion date. Where you receive periodic income in a foreign currency, or have a series of relatively small transactions, the CRA will normally accept the reporting of all transactions converted at (i.e., multiplied by) the average rate for the year. A table of average rates for several currencies is posted on the Bank of Canada website (https://www.bankofcanada.ca/rates/exchange/).

Where you receive income reported to you in foreign currency, multiply by the rate above to report in Canadian dollars. For example, if you received 2018 income reported to you as US$100 (100 US dollars), you must report Canadian income of $100 × 1.2957 = CDN$129.57 (129.57 Canadian dollars). If you were reporting Canadian dollar receipts to a foreign government, you would divide the Canadian dollars by the number shown. For example, if you have to report CDN$100 (100 Canadian dollars) on a US tax return, you would report CDN$100 / 1.2957 = US$77.18.

Alphabetical List of Assets — Capital Cost Allowance Classes and Rates

The following table sets out the capital cost allowance rates and classes for certain types of assets — listed alphabetically. This table is for use only as a quick reference guide. See Part XI and Schedules II, III, IV, V, and VI of the *Income Tax Regulations* for detailed rules relating to capital cost allowance.

Bill C-97 enacted the Accelerated Investment Incentive, which applies to nearly all types of depreciable property, provided that it is "accelerated investment incentive property". The half-year rule will not apply to qualifying depreciable property that is acquired after November 20, 2018 and is available for use before 2028. Also, property that is available for use before 2024 is eligible for an additional 50% first-year CCA deduction, so taxpayers can deduct three times what they can normally claim in the year that a depreciable asset is acquired.

Also, certain classes are eligible for a temporary first-year 100% write-off: Class 53 manufacturing and processing equipment, Class 43.1/43.2 clean energy and conservation equipment, and Class 54/55 zero emissions vehicles. Class 53 and 43.1/43.2 assets that are acquired after November 20, 2018 and are available for use before 2024 are eligible for the 100% write-off. Class 54/55 zero emissions vehicles acquired on or after March 19, 2019 and are available for use before 2024 are also eligible for a 100% write-off. The accelerate first-year CCA for Classes 43.1, 43.2, 53, 54, and 55 is phased out to 75% for 2024 and 2025, 55% for 2026 and 2027, and is not available for 2028 and onward.

Item	Rate	Class
Access roads and trails for the protection of standing timber	30%	10
Air conditioning equipment — same rate as building[1]		
Aircraft	25%	9
furniture and fittings	25%	9
hangars[1]	10%	6
Airplane runways	8%	17
Amusement park components (including fences, bridges, canals, stalls, tractors, etc.)	15%	37
land improvements[35]	15%	37
Apparel, used for earning rental income[1,26]	100%	12
Asphalt surface, storage yard	8%	17
Assets, tangible capital[1,2]	20%	8
used primarily in manufacturing or processing[10,15]		29, 39, 40, 43, 53
Automobiles[1]	30%	10
in excess of prescribed amount (Reg. 7307(1))[1,7]	30%	10.1
for lease or rental[22]	40%	16
Automotive equipment[1]	30%	10
designed for and used in amusement parks	15%	37
Bar code scanners — see Cash registers		
Billboards	20%	8
Boats — see Vessels		
Boilers		
heating use — same rate as building		
used primarily in manufacturing or processing[10,15]		29, 39, 43, 53
Books of lending libraries[26]	100%	12
Breakwaters		
wooden	10%	6
other	5%	3
Bridges[1]	4%	1
Buildings[1]		
addition or alteration — same class as buildings[13]		
amusement park stalls	15%	37
brick, stone, cement, etc., acquired before 1988	5%	3
brick, stone, cement, etc., acquired after 1987	4%	1
component parts — generally same class as building (see individual items)		
farm ensilage storage	20%	8
foundation excavation — same rate as building		
frame, log, stucco on frame, galvanized iron or corrugated metal[25]	10%	6
kiln, tank, vat used in manufacturing or processing	20%	8
liquefaction buildings acquired after Feb. 19, 2015, and before 2025.[5]	4%	1
manufacturing or processing[39]	4%	1
mining (except refineries and office buildings not at mine)	30%	10
multiple-unit residential[7,18]	4%	1
non-residential[39]	4%	1
portable camp	30%	10
rental property[7]		
storage of fresh fruits and vegetables	20%	8
Buses	30%	10
Cable TV converters and descramblers	40%	30
Cables — telephone, telegraph or data communication		
acquired after Feb. 22, 2005	12%	42
fibre optic	12%	42
Calculator	20%	8
Canals[1]	4%	1
Canoes	15%	7
Capital tangible assets[1,2]	20%	8
used primarily in manufacturing or processing[10,15]		29, 39, 40, 43, 53
Cash registers	20%	8

electronic, to record multiple sales taxes acquired after Aug. 8, 1989 and before 1993	100%	12
Catalyst	5%	26
Cattle	nil	—
Chinaware[26]	100%	12
Cold storage structures	20%	8
Computer hardware and systems software	55%	50
acquired after Jan. 27, 2009 and before Feb. 2011[40]	100%	52
Computer software[10,24]	100%	12
Concessions, for a limited period		14
Contractors' movable equipment, heavy	30%	10
Power-operated and designed for the purpose of excavating, moving, placing or compacting earth, rock, concrete or asphalt.	30%	38
Conversion cost — see Vessels		
Copyrights	5%	14.1
Costume and accessories for earning rental income[1,26]	100%	12
Culverts[1,10]	4%	1
Customer lists[21]	5%	14.1
Cutlery[26]	100%	12
Cutting part of a machine[1]	100%	12
Dams[1]	4%	1
Data communication equipment — wire and cable		
acquired after Feb. 22, 2005	12%	42
Data communication switching equipment[16]	8%	17
Dental instruments costing less than $500[1,26,28]	100%	12
Dies[1]	100%	12
Digital video disk — See DVD		
Display fixtures (window)	20%	8
Distribution equipment for heat, electrical energy, or water[4]	4%	1
for water or steam, acquired after Feb. 27, 2000	8%	17
for electrical energy, acquired after Feb. 22, 2005[32]	8%	47
Docks[1]	5%	3
Drone, aerial[41]	25%	9
Drive-in theatre property	30%	10
DVD, for rental[23,26]	100%	12
Electric vehicle charging stations	20%	8
greater than 10kw but less than 90kw	30%	43.1
at least 90kw, acquired before 2025	50%	43.2
Electrical advertising signs[10,16]	20%	8
Electrical energy storage equipment	30%	43.1
acquired before 2025	50%	43.2
Electrical generating and distributing equipment[6,10]		
acquired after 1987	4%	1
acquired after Feb. 27, 2000 for generation[10]	8%	17
acquired after Feb. 22, 2005 for transmission or distribution[32]	8%	47
combustion turbines acquired after Feb. 22, 2005[32]	15%	48
energy efficient generating equipment[19,32,33]	30%, 50%	43.1, 43.2
portable or maximum load 15 kw	20%	8
Electric wiring — same rate as building		
Electronic communications equipment including fax machines and telephone equipment[10]	20%	8
Electronic data processing equipment[1,15,16,40]		
used primarily in manufacturing or processing[15]		10, 29, 40
Electronic data processing equipment — data network infrastructure and systems software	30%	46
Electronic data processing equipment — general purpose and systems software	55%	50
acquired after Jan. 27, 2009 and before Feb. 2011[40]	100%	52
Elevators — same rate as building		
Equipment (see specific types)		
if not specifically mentioned[2]	20%	8
manufacturing or processing[10,15]		29, 39, 40, 43, 53
Escalators — same rate as building		
Fences[1]	10%	6
Fibre-optic cable	12%	42
Films, motion pictures	30%	10
Canadian production[7]	30%	10
certified production	100%	12
television commercials	100%	12
Franchises		
for a limited period		14
for an unlimited period	5%	14.1
Furniture (not otherwise listed)	20%	8
Gas manufacturing and distributing equipment, plants and pipelines acquired after 1987[8]	4%	1
distribution pipelines acquired after Mar. 18, 2007[31]	6%	51
liquefied natural gas equipment acquired after Mar. 18, 2007[32]	8%	47
liquefied natural gas equipment acquired after Feb. 19, 2015, and before 2025.[11]	8%	47
liquefaction buildings equipment acquired after Feb. 19, 2015, and before 2025.[16]	4%	1
transmission pipelines acquired after Feb. 22, 2005[10,31]	8%	49
Gas well equipment acquired after 1987	25%	41
Generating equipment and plant of producer or distributor of electrical energy[4,6]		
acquired after 1987	4%	1
acquired after Feb. 27, 2000	8%	17
energy efficient[32,33]	30%, 50%	43.1, 43.2
wave and tidal energy equipment[32,33]	30%, 50%	43.1, 43.2

Glass tableware[1, 26]	100%	12
Goodwill	5%	14.1
Government Rights	5%	14.1
Grain storage facilities — see buildings		
Greenhouses[1]	10%	6
rigid frame with plastic cover	20%	8
Hangars[1]	10%	6
Harness equipment[1]	30%	10
Heat production and recovery equipment[19, 32, 33]	50%, 30%, 50%	34, 43.1, 43.2
Heating equipment		
distribution plant, acquired after 1987	4%	1
general — same rate as building		
solar or energy efficient[19, 32, 33]	30%, 50%	43.1, 43.2
Herbs	nil	—
Horses	nil	—
Incorporation Expenses (exceeding $3,000)	5%	14.1
Instruments, dental or medical costing less than $500[1, 26, 28]	100%	12
Jetties	5%	3
wood	10%	6
Jigs[1]	100%	12
Kitchen utensils costing less than $500[1, 26, 28]	100%	12
Land	nil	—
deemed depreciable[7]	nil	36
Lasts[1]	100%	12
Leasehold interest		13
Lending library books[1, 26]	100%	12
Licences		
for a limited period		14
for an unlimited period	5%	14.1
Lighting fixture — same rate as building		
Linen[1, 26]	100%	12
Logging mechanical equipment[3]	30%	10
Machinery and equipment		
additional capital cost allowance on grain elevators	14%	8
not specifically listed	20%	8
used primarily in manufacturing or processing[10, 15]		29, 39, 40, 43, 53
Marine railways	15%	7
Medical instruments costing less than $500[1, 26, 28]	100%	12
Milk quota[42]	5%	14.1
Mining equipment	30%	10
Mining equipment, acquired for processing foreign ore in Canada	30%	43
Mining equipment, new or expanded mines[7, 14]		
mining property acquired after 1987	25%	41
oil sands property acquired after March 18, 2007	25%	41.1
mining property acquired after March 20, 2013, other than "eligible mine development property"	25%	41.2
Moles[1]	5%	3
Motion picture drive-in theatres	30%	10
Motion picture films — see Films		
Moulds[1]	100%	12
Multiple-unit residential buildings[7, 18]	5%, 10%	31, 32
Office equipment	20%	8
Offshore drilling platforms		
acquired after 1987	25%	41
Offshore drilling vessels[7, 17]		
acquired after 1987	25%	41
Oil pipelines		
acquired after 1987	4%	1
acquired after Feb. 22, 2005 — transmission[31]	8%	49
Oil sands — see Mining equipment, new or expanded mines		
Oil storage tanks[1, 15]	10%	6
used primarily in manufacturing or processing[15]		29, 39, 43, 53
Oil well equipment[1]		
acquired after 1987[14]	25%	41
Overburden removal cost, designated[1, 26]	100%	12
Parking area	8%	17
Passenger vehicles — see Automobiles		
Patents[20]		14
	25%	44
	5%, 7%	14.1
Patterns[1]	100%	12
Photocopy machines[10]	20%	8
Pinball machines — see Video games		
Pipelines		
acquired after 1987	4%	1
acquired after February 22, 2005 and used for transmission of oil and natural gas[31]	8%	49
acquired after March 18, 2007 for distribution of natural gas[31]	6%	51
acquired after Feb. 25, 2008 for transmission of carbon dioxide	8%	49
Plumbing — same rate as building		
Pollution control equipment[12]		
Portable construction camp buildings	30%	10
Portable electrical generating equipment	20%	8
Portable tool used for temporary rentals	30%	10
Power operated movable equipment[15]		

acquired after 1987	30%	38
Power plants — see Electrical power plants		
Producer gas generating equipment	30%	43.1
acquired after February 10, 2014	50%	43.2
Production equipment of distributor of heat (including structures)		
acquired after 1987	4%	1
acquired after Feb. 27, 2000	8%	17
Pumping and compression equipment		
Gas and oil acquired before Feb. 23, 2005	20%	8
Gas and oil acquired after Feb. 22, 2005[10,31]	15%	7
Carbon dioxide acquired after Feb. 25, 2008[31]	15%	7
Radar equipment	20%	8
Radio communication equipment (excluding satellites)	20%	8
Radium	nil	—
Railway car and rail suspension devices[1,7,29]		
acquired before Feb. 28, 2000[29]	7%	35
acquired after Feb. 27, 2000[29]	15%	7
Railway locomotive (excluding automotive railway car)		
acquired after Feb. 27, 2000[29]	15%	7
acquired after Feb. 25, 2008[29]	30%	10
Railway, marine	15%	7
Railway track or grading[1,7,29]	4%	1
Railway traffic control or signaling equipment[1,7,29]	4%	1
Rapid transit car[36]	20%	8
Refrigeration equipment	20%	8
Renewable energy generation equipment[6,19,32,33]		
acquired after Feb. 22, 2005 and before 2025[33]	50%	43.2
Rental property[7]		
Roads[1]	8%	17
acquired in relation to a mine	25%	41
forestry (may be depreciated with timber limit)[3]		
oil and gas mining temporary access[37]		
Roller rink floors	30%	10
Rowboats	15%	7
Satellites	30%	10
Scows	15%	7
Shaping part of a machine[1]	100%	12
Ships, including ships under construction[17]	15%	7
Shrubs	nil	—
Sidewalks	8%	17
Sleighs[1]	30%	10
Smart phone[43]	55%	50
Solar heating equipment acquired after Feb. 22, 2005 and before 2025[32,33]	50%	43.2
Solar panel[44]	30%	43.1
Spare parts for an aircraft	25%	9
Sprinkler systems — same rate as building		
Stable equipment[1]	30%	10
Storage area	8%	17
Storage tanks, oil or water[1]	10%	6
direct manufacturing use[15]		29, 39, 43, 53
Subway or tunnel[1]	4%	1
Systems software — general purpose electronic data processing equipment[1,40]		
acquired after Mar. 22, 2004 and before Mar. 19 2007[40]	45%	45
acquired after Mar. 18, 2007[40]	55%	50
acquired after Jan. 27, 2009 and before Feb. 2011[40]	100%	52
primary manufacturing purpose, acquired after March 18, 2007 and before January 28, 2009[15,40]		10, 29, 40
Tableware, glass[1,26]	100%	12
Tangible capital assets[1,2]	20%	8
Tank cars, railway[1,7]	7%	35
Tanks, oil and water storage[1]	10%	6
used primarily in manufacturing or processing[15]		29, 39, 43, 53
Taxicabs	40%	16
Telecommunication spacecraft	30%	10
Telegraph and telephone equipment, wires and cables		
acquired before Feb. 23, 2005[1]	5%	3
new and acquired after Feb. 22, 2005	12%	42
poles and masts[1]	5%	3
fibre-optic cable	12%	42
Telephone or telegraph communication non-electronic switching equipment	8%	17
Telephone system (purchased)	20%	8
Television aerial	20%	8
Television commercials	100%	12
Television set-top boxes	40%	30
Timber cutting and removing equipment[3]		10, 15
Timber limits — see Sched. VI of the *Income Tax Regulations*[3,7]		
Timber resource property[3]	15%	33
Tools costing less than $500[1,26,28]	100%	12
Tractors[1]	30%	10
for hauling freight[27]	40%	16
Trademarks	5%	14.1
Trailers[1,34]	30%	10
Tramways[4,9]	6%	4
Trees	nil	—
Trestles[1]	5%	3
Trolley bus	30%	10
Trolley bus system[4]	6%	4
Trucks, automotive[1]	30%	10

for hauling freight[27]	40%	16
Tunnel[1]	4%	1
Uniforms[1,26]	100%	12
Vessels[7,17]	15%	7
furniture, fittings and spare engines[17]	15%	7
offshore drilling after 1987[30]	25%	41
Video cassettes, video laser disks and DVDs[23,26]	100%	12
Video games (coin operated)	40%	16
Video tapes[1]	30%	10
television commercial	100%	12
Wagons[1]	30%	10
Water current energy equipment	30%	43.1
acquired after Feb. 10, 2014	50%	43.2
Water pipelines	4%	1
Water pollution control equipment — see Pollution control equipment		
Water storage tanks[1]	10%	6
primary manufacturing purpose[15]		
Water distribution plant and equipment	4%	1
Web page[45]	100%	12
Well equipment, oil or gas (for use above ground)		
acquired after 1987	25%	41
oil sands property acquired after Mar. 18, 2007	25%	41.1
certain mining property acquired after March 20, 2013[14]	25%	41.2
Wharves[1]	5%	3
wooden[1]	10%	6
Wind energy conversion system acquired after Feb. 22, 2005 and before 2025[32,33]	50%	43.2
Windmills[1,38]	5%	3
Wiring, electric — same rate as building		
Zero-emissions vehicle[46]		
otherwise included in Class 10 or 10.1	100%	54
otherwise included in Class 16	100%	55

Notes:

[1] Unless included in another class of assets subject to a different rate.

[2] Not applicable to land, animals, herbs, trees, shrubs or similar growing things, gas wells, mines, oil wells, radium, rights of way, timber limits, tramway track or certain vessels.

[3] See IT-481 and IT-501 regarding timber limits, timber resource property, and logging assets.

[4] Except property included in Class 10, 13, 14, 26 or 28. For distributors of gas, not including a property acquired to produce or distribute gas normally distributed in portable containers, to process natural gas before its delivery to a gas distribution system and to produce oxygen or nitrogen. See also under Gas manufacturing and distribution equipment, plants and pipelines; and Pipelines.

[5] Additional allowances are available for buildings in Class 1 acquired after February 19, 2015, and before 2025 that are considered eligible liquefaction buildings. The additional allowances are 6% for such buildings, and additions are required to be placed in a separate class in order to claim the additional allowance.

[6] Electrical generating equipment may be allocated to one of the following different classes: Class 1, if large and acquired by a producer; Class 8, if small; or Class 17, if new and acquired after February 27, 2000 (with certain exclusions). Energy-efficient equipment may be in Class 43.1; or Class 43.2, if acquired after February 22, 2005 and before 2025, and certain requirements are met (see note 35). Only a detailed reading of the classes can determine the appropriate one; see Schedule II of the *Income Tax Regulations*. If used in manufacturing or processing, see note 15.

[7] Separate classes may be required for each asset, including: certain rental properties costing $50,000 or more; automobiles in Class 10.1; certain vessels, including Canadian vessels and offshore drilling vessels; and Class 28, 41, 41.1, or 41.2 property relating to a particular mine or group of mines. See Regulation 1101 for the provisions regarding separate classes.

[8] Unless, in the case of a pipeline for oil or natural gas, the Minister is satisfied that the main source of supply for the business is likely to be exhausted within 15 years; such pipelines, not being specifically listed, fall under the general rate of 20% (Class 8).

[9] Tramway tracks: 100% on cessation of tramcar operation.

[10] Separate class elections may be available for certain assets or groups of assets, including: non-residential buildings in Class 1; certain electronic equipment in Class 8; transmission pipelines in Class 49; and equipment relating to transmission pipelines in Class 7. See Regulation 1101 for the provisions regarding separate classes.

[11] Additional allowances are available for equipment in Class 47 acquired after February 19, 2015, and before 2025 that are considered eligible liquefaction equipment. The additional allowance is 22% for such equipment, and additions are required to be placed in a separate class in order to claim the additional allowance.

[12] The equipment may be Class 8, 39 or 43 if used primarily in manufacturing, or Class 1, 3 or 6, depending on its nature.

[13] An addition or alteration to a building originally placed in Class 3, 6 or 20, but which would no longer be in that class under current rules, may be added to the old class within certain dollar and transitional rule limitations. See IT-79R3 and Regulation 1102(19).

[14] Qualifying assets are included in a special class for each mine. The full amount of UCC up to the amount of income from a mine may be claimed on property for new or expanded mines. This additional allowance is being phased out for oil sands property acquired after March 18, 2007 and for certain mining property acquired after March 20, 2013. See paragraphs 1100(1)(*w*) to (*ya.2*) of the *Income Tax Regulations*.

[15] Specified property used primarily in manufacturing or processing may be allocated to one of the following classes: Class 53, if acquired after 2015 and before 2026, Class 29 (25%/50%/25% straight line), if acquired after March 18, 2007 and before 2016. See note 44 for general-purpose electronic data processing equipment and system software used primarily in manufacturing or processing (Class 29 if acquired after March 18, 2007 and before January 28, 2009). The description of the specified property varies depending on the date it is acquired and the class. See the descriptions of the classes in Schedule II of the *Income Tax Regulations*.

[16] Additional allowances are available for buildings in Class 1 acquired after February 19, 2015, and before 2025 that are considered eligible liquefaction buildings. The additional allowances are 6% for such buildings, and additions are required to be placed in a separate class in order to claim the additional allowance.

[17] Accelerated capital cost allowances of 33¹⁄3% are provided on certain prescribed vessels and conversion costs (generally, Canadian vessels and furniture and fittings attached thereto). See Regulations 1100(1)(*va*) and 1101(2a).

[18] Multiple-unit residential buildings acquired after June 17, 1987 are Class 1 (4%).

[19] Such assets acquired after February 21, 1994 are eligible for CCA at 30% in Class 43.1. Certain Class 43.1 assets acquired after February 22, 2005 and before 2025 may be eligible for a CCA rate of 50% in Class 43.2. See Regulation 1102(16.1) that would allow a taxpayer to elect Class 29 treatment for property acquired after March 18, 2007 and before 2016 that would otherwise be in Class 43.1 or Class 43.2 and is used in manufacturing or processing.

20 Patents for a limited or unlimited period acquired after April 26, 1993 are in Class 44 (25%). Patents for a limited period acquired before April 27, 1993 are in Class 14, written off on a straight-line basis over the life of the patent, but a taxpayer can elect out of Class 44 into Class 14 for limited period patents acquired after April 26, 1993. A taxpayer can make the same election out of Class 44 with respect to unlimited life patents to include them in Class 14.1 (eligible capital property prior to 2017).

21 Effective January 1, 2017, property that was eligible capital property will be added to Class 14.1 and subject to a 7% CCA rate in years prior to 2027. Property acquired in 2017 and going forward that would have been considered ECP is also added to Class 14.1 and is subject to a 5% CCA rate. See ¶5649

22 Automobiles acquired for lease or rental other than to any one person for more than 30 days in a 12-month period.

23 Items must be acquired for the purpose of renting to any one person for no more than 7 days in any 30-day period.

24 Computer software in Class 12 is subject to the half-year rule. Systems software is in Class 10, 29, 45, 50, or 52, depending on the date acquired. See note 44.

25 Building must be used in farming or fishing business, or be unsupported below the ground, or have been acquired before 1979.

26 The half-year rule does not apply to this item. It may be written off in full in the first year claimed.

27 Trucks or tractors acquired after December 6, 1991 that have a gross vehicle weight rating in excess of 11,788 kg.

28 Tools, kitchen utensils, and medical and dental instruments costing more than the $500 limit are Class 8. Portable tools acquired to earn short-term rental income are Class 10 (30%).

29 Railway equipment may be subject to additional allowances over and above the class rate. Railway locomotives, railway cars and railway suspension devices acquired after February 27, 2000, (other than property included in paragraph (*y*) of Class 10) are eligible for Class 7 (15%) rather than a combined rate of 10% or 13% (7% + additional allowance of 3% or 6%) previously available for Class 35 assets. Leased assets are included in Class 7 (15%) only if the lessor elects specified leasing property treatment. Railway locomotives acquired after February 25, 2008 and not used previously by any taxpayer for any purpose are Class 10(*y*) (30%).

30 After November 7, 2001, Class 41 for offshore drilling vessels is not available if the Minister of Industry has agreed to a structured financing facility. In such a case, the maximum CCA rate applicable to the vessel and its attachments will be 15% under Class 7 (see Regulation 1101(2c)).

31 Class 49 applies to new transmission pipelines. Taxpayers may elect in the year the pipelines are acquired, to place them in a separate CCA class. The rate for new natural gas distribution pipelines acquired after March 18, 2007 changed from Class 1 (4%) to Class 51 (6%). Eligible assets will include control and monitoring devices, valves, metering and regulating equipment and other equipment ancillary to a distribution pipeline, but not buildings or other structures. See Class 7 for pumping and compression equipment used to move product along a transmission pipeline.

32 Specified energy property rules may apply. See Regulations 1100(24) to (29).

33 Class 43.2 (50%) applies to certain assets in Class 43.1 (30%) if they are acquired after February 22, 2005 and before 2025. Co-generation equipment described in paragraphs (*a*) to (*c*) of Class 43.1 will be eligible for Class 43.2 if the equipment has a heat rate attributable to fossil fuel not exceeding 4,750 BTU (Class 43.1 allows up to 6,000 BTU). Paragraph (*d*) of Class 43.1 sets out various other types of renewable energy assets that are eligible for Class 43.2, including active solar equipment, geothermal equipment, photovoltaic equipment, ground source heat pump systems, wind energy conversion systems, equipment used to collect, store, clean, or upgrade landfill gas and digester gas, equipment used to generate heat energy from eligible waste fuel, equipment used to generate electricity using waste heat, equipment used to produce and store biogas, and cleaning and upgrading equipment used to produce biomethane.

34 Includes trailers designed for use on both highways and railway tracks.

35 This item excludes landscaping costs deductible under paragraph 20(1)(*aa*) of the Act.

36 Used for public transportation within a metropolitan area and not part of a railway system.

37 Temporary access roads in the oil and gas mining sectors may qualify as Canadian exploration or development expenses.

38 Not to be confused with wind energy conversion systems included in Class 43.1 or 43.2.

39 Additional allowances are available for buildings in Class 1 acquired after May 18, 2007 (including new buildings which are under construction on March 19, 2007) that are used at least 90% (measured by square footage) for manufacturing or processing in Canada or for other non-residential purposes at the end of the year. The additional allowances are 6% for such a building used for manufacturing or processing and 2% for other non-residential buildings. In each case, the building is required to be placed in a separate class in order to claim the additional allowance.

40 Class 52 (100%) applies to certain general-purpose electronic data processing equipment and systems software for that equipment, acquired after January 27, 2009 and before February 2011 (i.e., situated in Canada and not previously used). Property that is general-purpose electronic data processing equipment and systems software for that equipment is included in Class 29 if acquired after March 18, 2007 and before January 28, 2009 and used primarily in manufacturing or processing. Property that is general-purpose electronic data processing equipment and systems software for that equipment acquired after March 18, 2007, that is not in Class 29 or Class 52, is Class 50 (55%).

41 See 2016-0633111E5.

42 See IT-143R3.

43 See 2009-0344551I7.

44 Question of fact, see 2009-0344551I7.

45 If capital in nature, see 2010-0380521E5.

46 Vehicle must meet the definition "zero emissions vehicle" under s. 248(1), and certain restrictions apply to a "zero emission passenger vehicle" which is also defined under s. 248(1). The capital cost with respect to zero-emissions passenger vehicles included in Class 54 is limited to $55,000 plus the equivalent sales taxes on that amount. The first-year CCA claim for zero emissions vehicles is phased out as follows: 75% in 2024 and 2025, 55% in 2026 and 2027, and the classes will be closed for new additions after 2027. Since CCA is computed using a declining balance method, where a zero emissions vehicle is acquired during the phase- out period, the CCA rates applicable after the enhanced first-year claim are 30% for Class 54 and 40% for Class 55.

Tax Calendar

Scope of Calendar

The following calendar shows the principal dates of the *Income Tax Act* and Regulations that govern the collection of federal income tax (including withholding, remittance, refund, assessment, and objection) and the filing of tax information (including information returns, tax returns, and common elections applicable to individuals). If one of the dates falls on a Sunday or other holiday, it is extended to the next business day by virtue of section 26 of the *Interpretation Act*. If one of the dates falls on a Saturday, it is also extended to the next business day by virtue of administrative policy.

Updated to June 2019

Monthly Requirements

10th — Date by which employers with an average monthly withholding of $25,000 or more but less than $100,000 (for the second calendar year preceding a particular calendar year) must remit the income tax withheld from the remuneration paid after the 15th of the previous month (ITR s. 108(1.1)(*a*)(ii))

15th — Date by which employers with an average monthly withholding of under $25,000 must remit the income tax withheld from the remuneration paid for the previous month (ITR s. 108(1))

25th — Date by which employers with an average monthly withholding of $25,000 or more but less than $100,000 (for the second calendar year preceding a particular calendar year) must remit the income tax withheld from the remuneration paid before the 16th of the current month (ITR s. 108(1.1)(*a*)(i))

Last day — Date by which corporations (including SIFT trusts) must make income tax instalments. No instalments are required if a corporation's first instalment base or total taxes payable under Parts I, VI, VI.1, and XIII.1 of the Act is $3,000 or less (ITA s. 157(1), 157(2), and 157(2.1))

Quarterly Requirements

15th — (March, June, September, December) — Dates by which income tax instalments must be made by individuals (excluding farmers, fishers, and SIFT trusts) whose expected taxability for the current year or each of the two preceding years exceeds their source deductions by $1,800 of federal income tax for a Quebec resident or $3,000 of combined federal and provincial income taxes for a non-Quebec resident. Graduated rate estates do not have to pay tax instalments but must pay their tax owing within 90 days after the end of their taxation year. (ITA s. 156(1), 156(3), 156(4), 156.1(1) "instalment threshold", 156.1(2), and ITR s. 5300)

15th — (April, July, October, January) — Dates by which employers who have an average monthly withholding of less than $3,000 for either the first or second preceding calendar year and no compliance irregularities for the preceding 12 months must remit the income tax withheld from the remuneration paid for the previous quarter. (ITR s. 108(1.12))

15th — (April, July, October, January) — Dates by which a "new employer" (with a monthly withholding under $1,000 for a particular month and no compliance irregularities for the last 12 months) must remit the income tax withheld from the remuneration paid for the previous quarter. (ITR s. 108(1.13), 108(1.4), and 108(1.41))

Last day of fiscal quarter Date by which a small Canadian-controlled private corporation may pay its tax instalments if: (1) it has a perfect income tax, sales tax, EI, and CPP compliance history; (2) it claimed the small business deduction in the current or previous year; and (3) it had a taxable capital employed in Canada of $10 million or less and a taxable income of $500,000 or less in the current or previous year where those two limits are calculated on an associated basis (ITA s. 157(1.1), 157(1.2), 157(1.3), and 157(1.4))

Annual Calendar

Feb. 14 — Date by which employees must reimburse their employer for all the operating costs incurred in the previous year for the personal use of an employer-provided automobile. Otherwise, an automobile operating cost benefit will be included in their income (ITA s. 6(1)(*k*))

Feb. 29 — Last day for individuals to make their RRSP contribution for a year preceding a leap year (ITA s. 146(5))

Feb. (last day) — Date by which a T4, T4A, or T4A-RCA information return is due to report an employee's remuneration and benefits (ITR s. 200 and 205(1))

Date by which a T4A-NR information return is due to report fees paid to non-residents for services rendered in Canada (ITA s. 153(1)(*g*); ITR s. 105)

Date by which a T4A information return is due to report patronage payments (ITA s. 135; ITR s. 205(1) and 218)

Date by which a T4RSP information return is due to report amounts included in a taxpayer's income under an RRSP, HBP, or LLP (ITA s. 146, 146.01, and 146.02; ITR s. 205(1), 214, and 214.1)

Date by which a T4RIF information return is due to report amounts included in a taxpayer's income under a RRIF (ITA s. 146.3; ITR s. 205(1) and 215)

Date by which a T5 information return is due to report interest, eligible or non-eligible dividends, capital gains dividends, or other investment income (ITR s. 201 and 205(1))

Date by which a T5003 information return is due to report the acquisition of an interest in a tax shelter. If the business in respect of which the form is required was discontinued, the form is due by the earlier of the last day of February or 30 days after the discontinuance of the business (ITA s. 237.1(7), (7.1), and (7.2))

Date by which a T5008 information return is due to report proceeds paid in respect of securities transactions (mostly dispositions) (ITR s. 205(1) and 230)

Date by which a TFSA issuer must report a TFSA individual record for each of its TFSA planholders and a TFSA return summary totaling those individual records. Those records include the TFSA contributions, withdrawals and other related amounts, and must only be sent to the CRA, not to the individual TFSA account holders (ITR s. 205(1) and 223)

Mar. 1 — Last day for individuals to make their RRSP contribution for a year preceding a non-leap year (ITA s. 146(5))

Mar. 31 — Date by which an NR4 information return is due to report interest, dividends, royalties, trust income, and other amounts paid to or received for the account of a non-resident in the preceding calendar year (ITA s. 212; ITR s. 202)

Date by which a T5013 information return is due when all partners (including end members of tiered partnerships) are individuals (including trusts) or investment clubs filing on a modified partnership basis throughout the fiscal period of the partnership (ITR s. 229(5)(*b*))

Apr. 30 — Date by which the balance of tax owed by any individual (including one having until June 15 to file his/her T1 income tax return) is due (ITA s. 156.1(4) and 248(1) "balance-due day")

Date by which individuals not carrying on a business in the year and whose cohabiting spouse or common-law partner is not carrying on such a business either must file their T1 income tax return (ITA s. 150(1)(*d*)(i))

June 15 — Date by which individuals carrying on a business in the year or whose cohabiting spouse or common-law partner is carrying on such a business must file their T1 income tax return (ITA s. 122.6 "cohabiting spouse or common-law partner" and 150(1)(*d*)(ii))

June 30 — Date by which the T2 income tax return of a corporation operating on a calendar-year basis is due (ITA s. 150(1)(*a*))

Date by which persons with a TFSA account must file Form RC243 (including Schedule A — Excess TFSA Amounts and Schedule B — Non-Resident Contributions to a Tax-Free Savings Account (TFSA) if applicable) and pay Part XI.01 Tax owed for the preceding year for any excess TFSA amount, non-resident contribution, non-qualified investment, prohibited investment, or advantage received by them or by a person related to them in respect of their TFSA account. If the account holder dies before June 30, the filing due date is the later of June 30 and six months after the date of death. (ITA s. 207.07(1))

Date by which Form RC312 is due to report reportable transactions (i.e., aggressive tax avoidance transactions). The form must be filed, in the year following the year in which the transaction became a reportable transaction, by any person entering into the transaction for him or herself or someone else, or by any promoter or adviser entitled to fees in respect of the transaction. (ITA s. 237.3(1) "advisor", 237.3(1) "avoidance transaction", 237.3(1) "fee", 237.3(1) "promoter", "reportable transaction"; 237.3(2); 237.3(5))

Dec. 31 — Date by which the income tax instalment payable by a farmer or fisherman for a particular year is due. The instalment is only required if the farmer's or fisherman's net tax owing for the particular year or either of the two preceding years exceeds $1,800 of federal income tax for a Quebec resident or $3,000 of combined federal and provincial income taxes for a non-Quebec resident (ITA s. 155(1), 156.1(1) "instalment threshold", and 156.1(2)(*a*))

Contingent Calendar

The principal tax requirements which do not fall upon fixed dates but are instead related to some other event or duty are listed below under two categories: tax collection and tax filing.

Tax Collection

- Employers with an average monthly withholding of $100,000 or more (for the second calendar year preceding a particular calendar year) must remit the income tax withheld from the remuneration paid in each of the following periods within three days (excluding Saturdays, Sundays, or holidays) from each period: (i) the first seven days of the month; (ii) the period after the 7th and before the 15th day; (iii) the period after the 14th but before the 22nd day; and (iv) the part of the month after the 21st day. The remittances must be made to the account of the Receiver General at a designated financial institution or directly to the Receiver General on the day before the normal due date. (ITA s. 153(1) and 153(1.4); ITR s. 108(1.1)(*b*) and 110)
- Employers required to remit their deductions twice a month by virtue of ITR s. 108(1.1)(*a*) or four times a month by virtue of ITR s. 108(1.1)(*b*) in respect of a given calendar year may elect to remit them only once a month or twice a month respectively if they qualified for this decelerated remittance in the immediately preceding calendar year (ITR s. 108(1.11))
- Employers ceasing to carry on their business on a given date have only seven days after that given date to remit their deductions (ITR s. 108(2))
- Taxpayers owing amounts of taxes, interest, or penalties may be informed, by a registered letter sent by the Minister to their last known address, that their goods, chattels, or movable properties will be seized and sold unless those amounts are paid within 30 days (ITA s. 225)
- Taxpayers owing amounts of taxes, interest, or penalties and leaving (or intending to leave) Canada may be asked, by a notice served personally or a registered letter sent by the Minister to their last known address, to pay those amounts immediately. If they fail to pay, their goods, chattels, or movable properties may be seized to pay the tax debt. (ITA s. 226)
- Taxpayers having filed a tax return within three years from the end of a taxation year may apply for a refund within three years from the earlier of (i) the date of sending of the original notice of assessment; or (ii) the date of notification that no tax was payable. The Minister is allowed by the Taxpayer Relief Provisions to grant a refund beyond the three-year period, provided the period does not exceed 10 years from the taxation year end. No refund is allowed unless all returns under the following legislation were timely filed: the *Income Tax Act*, the *Excise Act (2001)*, the *Excise Tax Act*, and the *Air Travellers Security Charge Act*. Non-residents having been withheld tax from fees or commissions paid for services rendered in Canada or amounts paid for the sale of certain properties would also qualify for the favourable 10-year refund rule, provided their Part I tax return was filed within two years from the date the withholding agent was reassessed. (ITA 152(3.1), 152(4), 152(4.2), 164(1)(*a*)(iii), 164(1)(*b*), 164(1.5), 164(2.01), 164(7), 227(10), and 227(10.1))
- Taxpayers holding amounts of unclaimed dividends, interest, or sales proceeds at the end of their taxation year for the account of unknown beneficial owners must withhold and remit a tax on those amounts within 60 days from the end of the taxation year (ITA s. 153(4))
- Taxpayers objecting to an assessment must generally serve their notice of objection within 90 days from the sending date of the notice of assessment. For individuals (other than trusts) and graduated rate estates, notices of objection from assessments concerning Part I and I.2 taxes must be served on or before the later of 90 days after the sending of the notice of assessment or one year after the taxpayer's filing-due date for the year. (ITA s. 165(1))
- Taxpayers appealing to the Tax Court of Canada must serve their notice of appeal within 90 days from the sending date of the reassessment or confirmed assessment, or after 90 days have elapsed from the service date of the notice of objection if the Minister never replied to that notice (ITA s. 169(1))
- Taxpayers receiving a notice of assessment showing an amount of tax assessed but remaining unpaid must pay the remainder immediately (ITA s. 158)
- Corporations with interest refunds and interest arrears have 90 days after the latest of the following dates to apply for an offset of the two amounts: (1) sending dates of original notices of assessment giving rise to the interests; (2) sending dates of Minister's notifications where notices of objection were filed; and (3) issue dates of court decisions if appeals were filed (ITA s. 161.1(2) and (3)(*c*))
- The Minister cannot normally reassess a taxpayer more than:
  - four years after sending the original notice of assessment (including a nil assessment) for a mutual fund trust or a corporation other than a Canadian-controlled private corporation (CCPC); and
  - three years after that time for an individual, CCPC, or any other person.

  However, the above time limits may be extended in the following circumstances:
  - taxpayer having made misrepresentations attributable to negligence, carelessness, or wilful default (no time limit);
  - taxpayer filing a waiver (no time limit);
  - taxpayer carrying back a loss (three years after the regular deadline);

- taxpayer claiming a loss, gift, credit, or deduction in a prior year (three years after the regular deadline);
- taxpayer disposing of a real or movable property in the year and not reporting the disposition on their income tax return for that year;
- corporate taxpayer receiving a provincial reassessment caused by reallocation of its taxable income earned in a province (one year after the later of: (1) the date the CRA was informed of the provincial reassessment; and (2) 90 days after the date of reassessment);
- tax shelter participant not filing the Statement of Tax Shelter Information (T5003) on time (three years after the date Form T5003 was filed); and
- taxpayer not reporting foreign property income on an annual tax return and: (1) not filing the Foreign Income Verification Statement (T1135) on time; or (2) incorrectly or not identifying the foreign property on the form (three years after the regular deadline).

(ITA s. 152(3.1), 152(4), 152(5), and 152(6))

- The Minister must wait 90 days after the sending of the notice of assessment to commence actions to collect a tax debt if a notice of objection was not filed by the taxpayer and 90 days after the sending of the notice confirming or varying the assessment if a notice of objection was filed by the taxpayer (ITA s. 225.1(1), (1.1), and (2))
- The Minister has 10 years from the day that is 90 days after the sending of the notice of assessment concerning a tax debt to commence an action to collect the tax debt, but this 10-year period can be restarted in certain circumstances (ITA s. 222(3), (4), and (5))
- The Minister has two years after an individual has ceased to be a director of a corporation to commence an action to recover amounts that were not deducted or remitted by the corporation (ITA s. 227.1(4))
- Corporations with a balance of tax due after having paid their instalments must pay that balance as follows: (1) Within three months after taxation year end for Canadian-controlled private corporations who claimed the small business deduction in the current year or preceding year and had a taxable income calculated on an associated basis not exceeding $500,000 in the preceding year; and (2) Within two months after year end for all other corporations (ITA s. 125(2), 157(1) to 157(4) and 248(1) "balance due-day")
- Trusts governed by a deferred profit sharing plan that acquire a non-qualified investment or use a trust property as a security for a loan must pay the Part X tax within 10 days from the day of its acquisition or use (ITA s. 198(2))

Tax Filing

- Registered charities must file a T3010 information return within six months from the end of their fiscal period (ITA s. 149.1(14))
- Registered journalism organizations must file an information return within six months from the end of their fiscal period, including the name of each donor whose total gifts to the organization in a taxation year exceed $5,000 and the total amount of donations from each such donor. (ITA s. 149.1(14.1))
- Persons earning more than 50% of their business income from construction activities and making annual payments of at least $500 to subcontractors for construction services must file a T5018 information return within six months from the end of their business period. If they cease their operations, they have 30 days to file that return (ITR s. 238(2) and 238(4))
- Corporations must file a T2 income tax return within six months from the end of their taxation year if they have Part I tax payable for the year or if, at any time in the year, they are resident in Canada, carry on business in Canada, have a taxable capital gain, or dispose of a taxable Canadian property (ITA s. 150(1)(*a*))
- The legal representative of a deceased taxpayer must file his/her T1 return (1) by the return's normal filing due date if the date of death is before November; (2) by the later of the normal filing due date and six months after the date of death if the date of death is after October but before the filing due date (ITA s. 150(1)(*b*))
- Taxpayers discontinuing a business must file the T3, T4, T5, T5008, NR4, and other information returns required under Part II of the *Income Tax Regulations* within 30 days from the date of discontinuance of the business (ITR s. 205(2))
- Trustees, estate administrators, or any other person controlling and receiving trust income (i.e., interest, dividends, capital gains, etc.) in a fiduciary capacity for trust beneficiaries must file a T3 information return within 90 days from the end of the trust's taxation year. Trusts that were assigned a trust account number (TAN) by the CRA must enter it in the space provided to that effect on the T3 information return. Those having to apply for a TAN may use either Form T3APP or T3RET for that purpose. However, this reporting obligation does not apply to the following trusts: deferred profit sharing plan trusts, employee profit sharing plan trusts, registered education savings plan trusts, eligible funeral arrangement trusts, cemetery care trusts, tax-free savings account trusts, registered disability savings plan trusts, and registered charity trusts. Public trusts must post prescribed financial information on the CDS Innovations Inc. website at the earlier of the following due dates:
  - 67 days from the end of the calendar year in which their fiscal period ends if they are public investment trusts; and
  - 60 days from the end of their fiscal period for other public trusts.

  (ITR s. 204 and 204.1)

- A T600 Ownership Certificate must be filed on or before the 15th day of the month following the month of payment or negotiation by: (1) a financial company paying accrued interest on transfers of bonds, debentures, or similar securities; (2) a debtor or encashing agent negotiating bearer coupons or warrants representing interest or dividend paid by any debtor or cheques representing interest or dividend paid by a non-resident debtor (ITA s. 234; ITR s. 207 and 211)
- Registered amateur athletic associations must file a T2052 information return within six months from the end of their fiscal period (ITA s. 149.1(14))
- Corporations and trusts wanting to certify for a taxation year that their shares, units, or interests are qualified investments for the purpose of an RRSP, RESP, RRIF, DPSP, RDSP, and TFSA must file a T3F information return within 90 days from the end of their taxation year (ITA s. 146(1) "qualified investment", 146.1(1) "qualified investment", 146.3(1) "qualified investment", 146.4(1) "qualified investment", 204 "qualified investment", and 207.01(1) "qualified investment"; ITR s. 221(2))
- Canadian partnerships, specified investment flow-through (SIFT) partnerships, and other partnerships carrying on business in Canada required to file a T5013 information return must file that form by the following due dates:
  - March 31 of the year following the calendar year in which their fiscal period ends if all partners or end members of a tiered partnership throughout the fiscal period are individuals (including trusts) or investment clubs filing on a modified partnership basis;
  - within five months after the end of their fiscal period if all partners or end members of a tiered partnership throughout the fiscal period are corporations; and
  - earlier of March 31 following the calendar year in which their fiscal period ends and five months after the end of the fiscal period, in all other situations, including if the partners and members of a tiered partnership are a combination of individuals, trusts, and corporations.

  Publicly traded partnerships must post prescribed financial information on the CDS Innovations Inc. website at the earlier of the following due dates:
  - 67 days from the end of the calendar year in which their fiscal period ends if they are public investment partnerships; and
  - the earlier of: (1) 60 days after the end of the calendar year in which their fiscal period ends; and (2) four months after the end of their fiscal period for other public partnerships.

  (ITR s. 229(5)(*a*), 229(5)(*b*), 229(5)(*c*), and 229.1)
- Partnerships discontinuing their business must file a T5013 partnership information return on or before the earlier of their normal filing due date and 90 days after the discontinuance of their activities (ITR s. 229(6))
- Corporations having renounced Canadian exploration or development expenses for the benefit of flow-through share investors must file a T101A information return in the month following the month the renunciation was made (ITA s. 66(12.7); ITR s. 228(2))
- The ultimate parent of a multinational enterprise (MNE) group if resident in Canada (or a non-parent Canadian resident entity of the group if certain conditions are met) must file the RC4649 Country-by-Country report by the following deadlines: (1) Within 30 days from the receipt of a systemic failure notification by the constituent entity if the entity receives such a notification; and (2) Within 12 months from the end of the reporting fiscal year of the group if no notification was received. The purpose of the report is to comply with standards developed by the OECD to enhance transparency to provide tax authorities with all required information to assess high-level transfer pricing, base erosion, and profit-shifting. (ITA s. 233.8(3), 233.8(6))
- Canadian taxpayers with controlled or non-controlled foreign affiliates must file a Form T1134 within 15 months from the end of their taxation year. For taxation years or fiscal periods that begin in 2020, the filing deadline is within 12 months from the end of the taxation year, and for taxation years or fiscal periods that begin after 2020, the filing deadline is within 10 months from the end of the taxation year. (ITA s. 233.4(4))

[illegible] (ITA s. 149.1(14)).

(ITR ss. 229(1), 229(5)(b), 229(6), and 229.1)

Deadlines and Limitation Periods: Returns, Assessments, Appeals, Payments, Refunds, and Collection

The following chart shows the principal deadlines and limitation periods under the *Income Tax Act*.

Updated to June 2019

Legislative Provisions	Obligations	Deadlines
116(3)	Non-resident persons disposing of taxable Canadian properties must send to the Minister a notice with the following information: name and address of the purchaser, description of the properties, proceeds of disposition, and adjusted cost base of the properties.	10 days after the disposition of the properties.
146(2)(*b*.4)	The Registered Retirement Savings Plan (RRSP) must mature (e.g., be converted to a Registered Retirement Income Fund (RRIF)) no later than a certain date.	End of the year in which the annuitant reaches the age of 71.
146(5)	Contributions to a Registered Retirement Savings Plan (RRSP) must be made within a certain number of days after the end of a calendar year to qualify for a deduction in that year.	Within 60 days after the end of that year.
146.1(2)(*h*)	The subscriber under a Registered Education Savings Plan (RESP) must stop making contributions to the plan after a certain number of years.	31 years after the plan is entered into for a regular plan and 35 years after the plan is entered into for a specified plan (i.e., for a disabled beneficiary).
146.1(2)(*i*)	The RESP must be terminated in a particular year.	35th year following the year the plan was opened for a regular plan and 40th year following the year the plan was opened for a specified plan (i.e., for a disabled beneficiary).
146.1(2)(*i*.1)	The RESP must be terminated if an accumulated income payment is made out of the plan.	Before March of the year after the year in which such first payment is made.
146.1(2)(*j*)	The subscriber under a family Registered Education Savings Plan must stop making contributions once the plan beneficiary reaches a certain age.	Once the beneficiary is 31 years of age.
146.2(5)	The issuer of a Tax-Free Savings Account in respect of a particular individual must file an election to register the arrangement with the Minister of National Revenue.	By the last day of February of the year following the calendar year in which the arrangement is entered into.
146.4(4)(*g*)	Contributions to a Registered Disability Savings Plan (RDSP) must stop after the beneficiary reaches a certain age.	After the calendar year during which the beneficiary turns 59.
146.4(4)(*k*)	Lifetime disability assistance payments must start once the RDSP beneficiary turns a certain age.	By the end of the calendar year during which the beneficiary turns 60.
149.1(14) 149.1(14.1)	Information return and public information return to be filed by a registered charity (Form T3010), registered Canadian amateur athletic association (Form T2052), or registered journalism organization.	Within six months after the end of the taxation year.
150(1)(*a*) 150(1.1)	Return of income to be filed by a corporation other than a registered charity (Form T2).	Within six months after the end of the taxation year.
150(1)(*b*)	Return of income to be filed by a deceased individual (Form T1).	• Death between January 1 and October 31, and individual and cohabiting spouse were not carrying on a business: by the filing due date of April 30. • Death between January 1 and October 31,

		and individual or cohabiting spouse was carrying on a business: by the filing due date of June 15. • Death between November 1 and April 30 of the following year, and individual and cohabiting spouse were not carrying on a business: by the later of the filing due date of April 30 and six months after the date of death. • Death between November 1 and June 15 of the following year, and individual or cohabiting spouse was carrying on a business: by the later of the filing due date of June 15 and six months after the date of death.
150(1)(*c*)	Return of income to be filed by a trust or estate (Form T3).	Within 90 days from the end of the year.
150(1)(*d*)(i) 150(5)	Return of income (Form T1) to be filed by an individual meeting any of the following conditions: • individual being subject to tax; • individual claiming the Canada Child Benefit or Goods and Services Tax Credit; • Canadian resident having a taxable capital gain or selling a capital property; • non-resident having a taxable capital gain or selling a taxable Canadian property not excluded under subsection 150(5); or • individual having a positive HBP or LLP balance as defined in subsection 146.01(1) or 146.02(1).	No later than April 30 of the following year.
150(1)(*d*)(ii)	Return of income to be filed by an individual carrying on a business (other than a tax shelter) during the year. The same deadline applies to his/her cohabiting spouse or common-law partner (Form T1).	No later than June 15 of the following year.
152(4) 152(3.1) 152(4.2) 152(6)	Minister's assessment or reassessment of tax, interest, and penalties under Part I of the Act.	• Regular deadline — Within four years from the sending of a notice of original assessment (or notification that no tax is payable for the year) for a mutual fund trust or a corporation other than a Canadian-controlled private corporation ("CCPC"). Within three years from such sending for a CCPC or an individual. • Extended deadline — The deadline is extended by three years for taxpayers claiming a deduction listed in subsection 152(6). • No deadline — The deadline does not apply to a taxpayer having filed a valid waiver with the Minister or having made misrepresentations attributable to neglect, carelessness, or willful default, and to a taxpayer having failed to report the disposition of a real or movable property (including a principal residence) on his/her income tax return. • Taxpayer Relief Provisions — The Minister is allowed under the Taxpayer Relief Provisions to reassess individuals or graduated rate estates and reduce or refund their taxes for the preceding 10 calendar years. • Provincial reassessment — The normal reassessment period of corporations having

received a provincial income tax reassessment caused by the reallocation of their taxable income earned in a province will be extended by one year from the later of: the date the Minister is advised of the reassessment; or 90 days after the sending of the provincial notice of reassessment.

- Tax shelter participants (T5003) — The normal reassessment period of a tax shelter participant is extended to three years after the date the Statement of Tax Shelter Information (T5003) is filed, regardless of the date the original notice of assessment was sent.
- Foreign property (T1135) — The normal reassessment period of a taxpayer is extended by three years if: (1) he/she did not report a foreign property income on his/her annual income tax return; and (2) he/she did not file the Foreign Income Verification Statement (T1135) on time or did not properly identify the specified foreign property on that form.
- Extended deadline — The deadline is extended an additional three years where the CRA reassesses a return because of a non-arm's length transaction with a non-resident person that affects a loss carryback.

153 Reg. 108	Employers having deducted income tax from their employees' remuneration must remit the tax to the Receiver General by certain dates varying with the size of their average monthly deductions and their new or old employer status.	For employers whose average monthly deductions: • Are less than $3,000 and who are not in default of payment of their remittances over the previous 12 months: no later than April 15 re January, February, and March payments; July 15 re April, May, and June payments; October 15 re July, August, and September payments; and January 15 re October, November, and December payments. Those quarterly deadlines will also apply to "new employers" having a monthly withholding under $1,000 and no compliance irregularities for the last 12 months. • Are less than $25,000: no later than the 15th day of the month following the month during which the source deductions were made. • Are between $25,000 and $99,999.99: no later than the 25th day of the same month for the remuneration paid in the first 15 days of the month and the 10th day of the following month for the remuneration paid from the 16th day of the month to the end of the month. • Are $100,000 or more: no later than the third working day after the end of the following periods: from the 1st to the 7th day of the month, from the 8th to the 14th day of the month, from the 15th to the 21st day of the month, and from the 22nd to the last day of the month. Employers ceasing to carry on their business on a particular date have seven days after that date to remit their deductions.
155 156.1(2)	Farmers and fishermen whose net tax owing for the current and two preceding years is not	The first instalment is equal to two-thirds of the lesser of (i) the estimated tax for the

	less than $1,800 for a Quebec resident and $3,000 for another Canadian resident must pay their income tax by instalments.	current year, and (ii) the instalment base for the immediately preceding year, and must be paid by December 31 of the current year. The second one is equal to the balance of tax due and must be paid by April 30 of the following year.
156 156.1(2)	Individuals (other than farmers, fishers, and SIFT trusts) whose net tax owing for the current and two preceding years is not less than $1,800 for a Quebec resident and $3,000 for another Canadian resident must pay their income tax by instalments.	Under the first method, one-quarter of the lesser of (i) the estimated tax payable for the current year, or (ii) the actual tax payable for the preceding year must be paid by March 15, June 15, September 15, and December 15. Under the second method, one-quarter of the actual tax payable for the second preceding year must be paid by March 15 and June 15, and one-half of the excess of the actual tax payable for the preceding year over one-half of the actual tax payable for the second preceding year must be paid by September 15 and December 15. Any balance of tax due by the individual for the year must be paid by April 30 of the following year.
157(1) 157(1.1) 157(1.2) 157(2) 157(2.1)	• Corporations (including SIFT trusts) whose total annual tax payable under Parts I, VI, VI.1, and XIII.1 of the Act exceeds $3,000 must normally make monthly income tax instalments. • Canadian-controlled private corporations (CCPCs) which meet the following conditions are small CCPCs entitled to make their instalments quarterly: (i) they have a perfect compliance history; (ii) they claimed the small business deduction in the current or preceding year; and (iii) they have a taxable capital employed in Canada of $10 million or less and a taxable income of $500,000 or less in the current or previous year where those two limits are calculated on an associated basis.	• Corporations required to make monthly instalments must pay them by the last day of each month and those eligible for quarterly instalments must pay them by the last day of each quarter of the calendar year. • Any balance of tax due must be paid: (1) Within three months after year end for a CCPC having claimed the small business deduction in the current or prior year, and having a taxable income calculated on an associated basis not exceeding $500,000 in that prior year; and (2) Within two months from year end in the case of any other corporation.
164(1)(*a*)	Automatic refund by the Minister.	Provided an income tax return was filed within three years from the end of a taxation year, the Minister will automatically refund any overpayment for the year, with no need for the taxpayer to file a refund application.
164(1)(*b*) 152(3.1) 152(4)(*b*) 152(6)	Refund application submitted in respect of a loss, gift, credit, or other eligible deduction carried back or claimed in a preceding taxation year under paragraph 152(4)(*b*) and subsection 152(6).	Within seven years from the sending of the original notice of assessment for a mutual fund trust or a corporation other than a Canadian-controlled private corporation, and six years for another taxpayer.
164(1)(*b*) 152(3.1)	Other refund application.	Within four years from the sending of the notice of original assessment for a mutual fund trust or a corporation other than a Canadian-controlled private corporation, and three years for another taxpayer.
164(1.5) 152(4.2) 227(10) 227(10.1)	Refund available under the Taxpayer Relief Provisions.	• Ten-year claim — The Minister is permitted under the Taxpayer Relief Provisions to reassess an individual or a graduated rate estate to refund or reduce their taxes if they file their return more than three years but not more than 10 years after the end of the taxation year in question. • Redetermination — This relief is also available to taxpayers having applied for a redetermination of their refund under subsection 152(4.2).

		• Non-resident tax — The relief is also applicable to non-resident tax withheld and remitted on fees and commissions paid for services rendered in Canada and to amounts paid for the sale of certain properties by non-residents, but only if they file their Part I tax return within two years from the date the person who withheld and remitted the tax was reassessed. • Waiver of penalties and interest — Penalties and interest waived under subsection 220(3.1) may also be refunded to a taxpayer at the Minister's discretion.
165(1)(*a*)	Objection to an assessment for an individual (other than a trust) or for a graduated rate estate.	No later than: • One year after the filing due date of the return of income; and • 90 days after the sending date of the notice of assessment.
165(1)(*b*)	Objection to an assessment for other taxpayers.	Within 90 days from the sending date of the notice of assessment.
166.1(1) 166.1(7)(*a*)	Application to the Minister for an extension of the time allowed to serve a notice of objection or make a request for adjustments under subsection 245(6).	Within one year from the deadline for serving the notice of objection or making the request.
166.2(1)	Application to the Tax Court of Canada for an extension of the time allowed to serve a notice of objection or make a request for adjustments under subsection 245(6) if the Minister refused the application or had not yet notified the taxpayer more than 90 days after the application was filed.	Within 90 days from the date the Minister's notification of his decision was sent to the taxpayer.
167(1) 167(5)(*a*)	Extension of time to appeal to the Tax Court of Canada.	Within one year from the expiration of the time limit to appeal to the Tax Court of Canada.
169(1)	Appeal to the Tax Court of Canada.	Within 90 days from the date the Minister sent a notice to the taxpayer to confirm, modify, or cancel the old assessment.
180 172(3)	Appeal to the Federal Court of Appeal from Minister's refusal or revocation of registration.	Within 30 days from the date of written notification of the Minister's decision.
185.1(2)	Any Canadian resident corporation that has made an excessive eligible dividend designation (as defined in subsection 89(1)) and become subject to a 20% Part III.1 tax on the designation can avoid having to pay the tax by electing by a particular date to treat the designation as an ordinary dividend instead of an eligible dividend.	Within 90 days from the date of sending the notice of assessment in respect of the Part III.1 tax otherwise payable.
198(2)	Requirement for the trustee of a trust governed by a deferred profit sharing plan having (i) acquired a non-qualified investment, or (ii) used a trust property as security for a loan, to remit Part X Tax to the Receiver General.	Within 10 days from the date the non-qualified investment was acquired by the trust or the trust property was used to secure the loan.
207.01(1) "excess TFSA amount" 207.01(1) "exempt contribution" 207.02 207.03	Following the death of a Tax-Free Savings Account planholder, the surviving spouse or common-law partner may transfer funds from the deceased's plan to his/her own plan without triggering the payment of Part XI.01 tax on an excess amount by making and designating that exempt contribution before the expiry of certain deadlines.	The exempt contribution must be made to the survivor's plan account no later than the end of the calendar year following the year of death and must be designated by filing a prescribed form in prescribed manner within 30 days after the date the exempt contribution was made.
207.07(1)	Individuals liable for Part XI.01 Tax on an excess TFSA amount, non-resident contribution,	By June 30 of the following calendar year.

	non-qualified investment, prohibited investment, or advantage received on their TFSA account for a calendar year must pay the tax and file a return in prescribed form (Form RC243, RC243-SCH-A, and RC243-SCH-B).	
220(3.1)	Application for the cancellation of interest and penalties otherwise payable by a taxpayer in respect of a taxation year. The Minister has the authority to do it under the Taxpayer Relief Provisions.	Within 10 calendar years from the end of the taxation year in respect of which the interest and penalties were assessed.
220(3.2)	Application for an extension of the time available to a taxpayer to make, amend, or revoke an election. The Minister has the authority under the Taxpayer Relief Provisions to grant such extension.	Within 10 calendar years from the end of the taxation year in respect of which the election was made.
220(3.201) 60.03(2)	Extension of the limitation period available to spouses or common-law partners to make, revoke, or amend the joint election to split their pension income.	Within three calendar years from the filing-due date for the taxation year to which the election applies.
222(4)	Beginning of initial 10-year limitation period to collect a tax debt.	90 days after the day on which the last regular or jeopardy notice of assessment was served or sent to the taxpayer.
222(5) 222(6)	Restarting of another 10-year limitation period to collect a tax debt.	On any day that one of the following conditions is met: • when the taxpayer acknowledges the debt in accordance with subsection 222(6); • when the Minister commences an action to collect the debt; or • when the Minister assesses a person in respect of the personal liability of the legal representative under subsection 159(3), of a debt concerning a transfer of properties between related persons under subsection 160(2), or of source deductions under paragraph 227(10)(*a*).
222(8) 222(4)(*a*) 225.1(1) 225.1(2) 225.1(3) 225.1(4) 225.1(5)	Extension of the limitation period for the collection of a tax debt: • when the Minister may not take any of the actions described in subsection 225.1(1) in respect of the debt; • when the Minister has accepted and holds security in lieu of payment of the debt; • for the period during which the tax debtor is non-resident; or • when an action that the Minister may otherwise exercise in respect of the debt is restricted or prohibited by the *Bankruptcy and Insolvency Act*, the *Companies' Creditors Arrangement Act*, or the *Farm Debt Mediation Act*.	Extension equivalent to the period during which: • the Minister could not act in respect of the debt because of subsection 225.1(1); • the Minister accepted and held security in lieu of payment of the debt; • the tax debtor was non-resident; or • the Minister was restricted or prohibited by the *Bankruptcy and Insolvency Act*, the *Companies' Creditors Arrangement Act*, or the *Farm Debt Mediation Act* to act in respect of the debt.
225.1(1.1)(*c*) 225.1(2)	Earlier date by which the Minister may normally start collecting a tax debt.	90 days after the sending of the taxpayer's notice of assessment when a notice of objection is not filed, and 90 days after the sending of the Minister's notice that the assessment is confirmed or varied when a notice of objection is filed.
227(6)	Refund application to recover non-resident withholding tax improperly deducted from payments to a non-resident person.	Within two years from the end of the calendar year in which the non-resident tax was paid to the Receiver General.
227.1(4)	Action to collect an amount payable by the director of a corporation.	Two years from the date the director last ceased to be a director of that corporation.

230(2)(*b*) 230(4)(*a*) 149.1(1) "qualified donee" Reg. 5800(1)(*f*)	Retention of duplicate receipts received by qualified donees.	Two years after the end of the calendar year to which the receipts relate.
230(4)(*b*)	Retention of books and records for tax purposes.	Six years after the end of the taxation year to which the books and records relate unless otherwise prescribed by regulation (for example, the retention period is two years for corporate records, including minutes of shareholders' and directors' meetings).
233.4(4)	Filing of Form T1134 by Canadian taxpayer for controlled or non-controlled foreign affiliates.	Within 15 months of the end of the taxation year. For taxation years or fiscal periods that begin in 2020, within 12 months of the end of the taxation year. For taxation years or fiscal periods that begin after 2020, within 10 months of the end of the taxation year.
233.8(6)	Filing of country-by-country report by the ultimate parent of an MNE group if resident in Canada (or by a non-parent Canadian resident entity of the group if certain conditions are met) to comply with standards developed by OECD to enhance transparency for the purpose of providing tax authorities with all required information to assess high-level transfer pricing, base erosion, and profit-shifting. See Form RC4649.	Within 30 days from receipt of a systemic failure notification by the constituent entity if the entity received such a notification. Otherwise, within 12 months from the end of the reporting fiscal year of the MNE group.
244(4)	An information or complaint under the *Criminal Code* may be made in respect of an offence under the *Income Tax Act*, but only within a certain period.	No later than eight years after the day on which the matter of the information or complaint arose.
261(3)(*b*)	Filing an election in prescribed form (T1296) and manner to be able to report Canadian tax results in a currency other than the Canadian dollar for a particular taxation year.	Within the first 61 days of the taxation year for which the election is filed.
261(4)	Filing a revocation of the above election (with the above prescribed form T1296) to be able to stop reporting Canadian tax results in a currency other than the Canadian dollar for a particular taxation year.	At least six months before the beginning of the particular taxation year, but the revocation cannot be filed in the taxpayer's first functional currency year.
278(1)	Any reporting financial institution that maintains a reportable account at any time during a calendar year must file an information return with the CRA.	By May 1 of the next calendar year.

Offences under the *Income Tax Act*

The following chart shows the principal offences under the *Income Tax Act*.

Updated to June 2019

Legislative Provisions	Offences	Punishment
238(1)	Failure to make a return as and when required by the Act or a regulation.	On summary conviction, a fine between $1,000 and $25,000, or both the fine and imprisonment for a term not exceeding 12 months. The fine is in addition to any penalty otherwise provided.
238(1) 116(1) 116(3) 116(5.2)	Failure by a non-resident person to send to the Minister the prescribed notice (Form T2062) required under subsection 116(3) in respect of the disposition of a taxable Canadian property (other than an excluded property or a property described in subsection 116(5.2)) no later than 10 days after the disposition. The notice is not required if another notice was filed under subsection 116(1).	On summary conviction, a fine between $1,000 and $25,000, or both the fine and imprisonment for a term not exceeding 12 months. The fine is in addition to any penalty otherwise provided.
238(1) 127(3) 127(3.1) 127(3.2)	Issuance of a tax receipt in respect of a political contribution contravening the *Income Tax Act*.	On summary conviction, a fine between $1,000 and $25,000, or both the fine and imprisonment for a term not exceeding 12 months. The fine is in addition to any penalty otherwise provided.
238(1) 147.1(7)	Failure by the administrator of a registered pension plan to comply with certain obligations.	On summary conviction, a fine between $1,000 and $25,000, or both the fine and imprisonment for a term not exceeding 12 months. The fine is in addition to any penalty otherwise provided.
238(1) 147.1(18)	Contravention of registered pension plan regulations made under subsection 147.1(18).	On summary conviction, a fine between $1,000 and $25,000, or both the fine and imprisonment for a term not exceeding 12 months. The fine is in addition to any penalty otherwise provided.
238(1) 153(1)	Failure to withhold, deduct, or remit certain tax amounts.	On summary conviction, a fine between $1,000 and $25,000, or both the fine and imprisonment for a term not exceeding 12 months. The fine is in addition to any penalty otherwise provided.
238(1) 230 to 232	Failure to comply with various obligations, including keeping records and books of account; providing additional information, including foreign-based information at the Minister's request; and cooperating with the Minister's representatives in the course of an inspection, inquiry, or seizure of documents under an authorized search warrant.	On summary conviction, a fine between $1,000 and $25,000, or both the fine and imprisonment for a term not exceeding 12 months. The fine is in addition to any penalty otherwise provided.
238(1) 238(2)	Contravention of a compliance order of the Court made under subsection 238(2).	On summary conviction, a fine between $1,000 and $25,000, or both the fine and imprisonment for a term not exceeding 12 months. The fine is in addition to any penalty otherwise provided.
238(1) 244.7	Failure to keep proper records in respect of electronic funds transfer reporting and comply with Part XV.1 of the Act.	On summary conviction, a fine between $1,000 and $25,000, or both the fine and imprisonment for a term not exceeding 12 months. The fine is in addition to any penalty otherwise provided.
238(1) 267	Failure by Canadian financial institutions to keep proper records for enhanced international information reporting and comply with Part XVIII of the Act.	On summary conviction, a fine between $1,000 and $25,000, or both the fine and imprisonment for a term not exceeding 12 months. The fine is in addition to any penalty otherwise provided.

239(1)(*a*)	Tax evasion: Make, or participate, assent, or acquiesce in the making of, false or deceptive statements in a return or any other document filed under the Act or a regulation.	On summary conviction, a fine between 50% and 200% of the evaded tax, or both the fine and imprisonment for a term not exceeding two years. The fine is in addition to any penalty otherwise provided.
239(1)(*b*)	Tax evasion: Destroy, alter, or otherwise dispose of a record or book of account.	On summary conviction, a fine between 50% and 200% of the evaded tax, or both the fine and imprisonment for a term not exceeding two years. The fine is in addition to any penalty otherwise provided.
239(1)(*c*)	Tax evasion: Make, assent, or acquiesce in the making of false/deceptive entries, or omit, assent, or acquiesce in the omission of material from a taxpayer's records or books of account.	On summary conviction, a fine between 50% and 200% of the evaded tax, or both the fine and imprisonment for a term not exceeding two years. The fine is in addition to any penalty otherwise provided.
239(1)(*d*)	Tax evasion: Wilfully evade or attempt to evade compliance with the Act or payment of taxes.	On summary conviction, a fine between 50% and 200% of the evaded tax, or both the fine and imprisonment for a term not exceeding two years. The fine is in addition to any penalty otherwise provided.
239(1)(*e*)	Tax evasion: Conspire with any person to commit an offence described in paragraphs 239(1)(*a*) to 239(1)(*d*).	On summary conviction, a fine between 50% and 200% of the evaded tax, or both the fine and imprisonment for a term not exceeding two years. The fine is in addition to any penalty otherwise provided.
239(1.1)(*a*) 239(1.1)(*b*) 239(1.1)(*c*) 239(1.1)(*d*) 239(1.1)(*e*) 239(1.1)(*f*)	Tax evasion: Undue full or partial refunds or credits.	On summary conviction, a fine between 50% and 200% of the undue refunds or credits, or both the fine and imprisonment for a term not exceeding two years. The fine is in addition to any penalty otherwise provided.
239(2)	Prosecution on indictment, at the election of the Attorney General of Canada, of any person charged with an offence described in subsections 239(1) or 239(1.1).	On indictment and conviction, a fine between 100% and 200% of the evaded tax, or undue refund or credit, and imprisonment for a term not exceeding five years. The fine is in addition to any penalty otherwise provided.
239(2.1)	Wilfully provide an incorrect tax shelter identification number.	On summary conviction, a fine between 100% and 200% of the cost to the other person of the person's share in the tax shelter and/or imprisonment for a term not exceeding two years. The fine is in addition to any penalty otherwise provided.
239(2.2) 241(1) 241(4.1)	Unauthorized wilful communication of taxpayer information or contravention of an order to prevent unauthorized use or disclosure of taxpayer information.	On summary conviction, a fine not exceeding $5,000, or imprisonment for a term not exceeding 12 months, or both the fine and imprisonment.
239(2.21) 241(4)	Unauthorized disclosure of confidential information on a taxpayer provided for a purpose authorized under subsection 241(4).	On summary conviction, a fine not exceeding $5,000, or imprisonment for a term not exceeding 12 months, or both the fine and imprisonment.
239(2.3)	Unauthorized communication of an identification number like: • the social insurance number of an individual; • the business number of an individual or a partnership; or • the trust account number of a trust.	On summary conviction, a fine not exceeding $5,000, or imprisonment for a term not exceeding 12 months, or both the fine and imprisonment.

239.1(2) 239.1(3)	Any person • using electronic suppression of sales (ESS) devices or software in respect of records required to be kept under section 230; • acquiring or possessing such devices or software; • designing, developing, manufacturing, possessing, or offering for sale, selling, or transferring such devices or software to another person; • supplying, installing, upgrading, or servicing such devices or software; or • participating or conspiring in the commission of any of the above offences.	• On summary conviction, a fine between $10,000 and $500,000. • In the case of prosecution on indictment, a fine between $50,000 and $1 million, an imprisonment term not exceeding five years, or both.
240(2) Reg. 807	Failure to comply with the regulatory provisions concerning the identification of interest coupons by the letters "A" for taxable obligations and "F" for non-taxable obligations.	On summary conviction, a maximum fine of $500.

Penalties Assessed under the *Income Tax Act*

The following chart shows the principal penalties under the *Income Tax Act.*

Updated to June 2019

Legislative Provisions	Default	Penalty
48.1(4)	Late filed election on Form T2101 by an individual to take advantage of the capital gains exemption and realize latent capital gains on the shares of a small business corporation becoming public.	The lesser of: • 0.25% of the excess of the deemed proceeds of disposition of the shares over their adjusted cost base, immediately before the corporation became public, times the number of months or parts of months between the due date and actual filing date of the election; and • $100 times that same number of months/parts of months comprised in the above period.
66(12.75) 66(12.68) 66(12.69) 66(12.691) 66(12.7) 66(12.701) 66(12.74) 66(12.741)	Late filed renunciation, prescribed form, or documents in respect of Canadian exploration or development expenses.	The lesser of $15,000 and the greater of the following amounts: • $100; and • 0.25% times (1) Maximum amount of Canadian exploration expenses or Canadian development expenses renounced or attributed, or to be renounced or attributed as set out in the document; (2) Assistance reported in the document; or (3) Amount of the renunciation.
66(14.5)	Late filed or amended designation in respect of Canadian exploration or development expenses.	The lesser of: • 0.25% times (1) The designated amount; or (2) The difference between the designated amounts, multiplied by the number of months/parts of months between the due date and actual filing date of the designation; and • An amount, not exceeding $8,000, equal to the product of $100 times the number of months/parts of months comprised in the above period.
83(4) 83(1) 83(2) 83(3)	Late filed election on Form T2054 for qualifying dividends described in subsection 83(1) or capital dividends described in subsection 83(2).	The lesser of: • One-twelfth of 1% of the dividend amount; and • $41.67 times the number of months/parts of months between the dividend payment date and the actual filing date of the election.
85(8) 85(7) 85(7.1)	Late filed or amended election on Form T2057 for the tax-free rollover transfer of a property by a shareholder to a corporation.	The lesser of: • 0.25% of the excess of the fair market value of the property subject to the election over the rollover amount agreed in the election, times the number of months or parts of months between the due date and actual filing date of the election; and • An amount, not exceeding $8,000, equal to the product of $100 times the number of months/parts of months comprised in the above period.
93(6) 93(5) 93(5.1)	Late filed or amended election on Form T2107 on the disposition of shares in a foreign affiliate.	The lesser of: • 0.25% of the amount designated in the election times the number of months/parts of months between the due date and actual filing date of the election; and • An amount, not exceeding $8,000, equal to the product of $100 times the number of months/parts of months comprised in the above period.
96(6) 96(5)	Late filed or amended election on Form T2059 for the tax-free rollover transfer of	The lesser of: • 0.25% of the excess of the fair market value of the

96(5.1) 97(2)	a property by a taxpayer to a Canadian partnership.	property being transferred over the amount agreed in the election, times the number of months/parts of months between the due date and actual filing date of the election; and • An amount, not exceeding $8,000, equal to the product of $100 times the number of months/parts of months comprised in the above period.
96(6) 96(5) 96(5.1) 98(3)	Late filed or amended election on Form T2060 for the tax-free rollover transfer of a property by a Canadian partnership to a partner where the partnership ceases to exist.	The lesser of: • 0.25% of the difference between (1) Total of all amounts of money and fair market value of other properties received by former members; and (2) Total of proceeds of disposition of the partnership interest of each former member, times the number of months/parts of months between the due date and actual filing date of the election; and • An amount, not exceeding $8,000, equal to the product of $100 times the number of months/parts of months comprised in the above period.
110.6(29) 110.6(19) 110.6(24) 110.6(26) 110.6(27)	Late filed or amended election for the deemed disposition of a property owned on February 22, 1994 to use the capital gains exemption.	One-third of 1% of the taxable capital gain resulting from the election times the number of months/parts of months between the day following the due date of the election and its actual filing date.
131(1.3) 131(1) 131(1.1)	Late filed election on Form T2055 for capital gains dividends paid by a mutual fund corporation.	The lesser of: • One-twelfth of 1% of the dividend amount; and • $41.67 times the number of months/parts of months between the dividend payment date and the actual filing date of the election.
149(7.1) 149(1)(*j*) 149(7)	Non-profit corporation for scientific research and experimental development not filing a prescribed form on time.	The greater of: • $500; and • 2% of the corporation's taxable income for the year times the number of months/parts of months (not exceeding 12) between the due date and actual filing date of the prescribed form.
162(1) 150(1)	Failure to file a return of income on time.	5% of the tax payable that was unpaid when the return was required to be filed, plus an additional 1% of that tax for each complete month (not exceeding 12) between the due date and the actual filing date of the return.
162(2) 150(1) 150(2)	Repeated failure (within a three-year period) to file a return of income on time after receiving a formal demand from the Minister.	10% of the tax payable that was unpaid when the return was required to be filed plus an additional 2% of that tax for each complete month (not exceeding 20) between the due date and the actual filing date of the return.
162(2.1) 150(1)(*a*) 150(2)	Failure or repeated failure by a non-resident corporation to file a return of income on time.	The greater of: • The amount of the penalty determined for a resident under subsection 162(1) or 162(2) as appropriate; and • The greater of $100 and $25 times the number of days (not exceeding 100) between the due date and the actual filing date of the return.
162(3) 150(3)	Failure by a trustee, liquidator, or any other person administering the property of a person to file a return of income on time.	$10 per day of default but not exceeding $50.
162(4) 234	Failure to prepare or deliver an ownership certificate required by section 234,	$50.

	or cashing a coupon or warrant for which no such certificate was prepared.	
162(5)	Failure to provide information on a prescribed form.	$100 for each failure unless (1) a reasonable effort was made by the person required to get the information from another person; or (2) the person required to provide a social insurance number on a return of income had already applied but not received that number.
162(5.1) 162(5.2) 162(5.3)	Provision of false or incomplete claim preparer information on Form T661, "Scientific Research and Experimental Development (SR&ED) Claim", required by subsection 37(11). This information includes the identity of the claim preparer and the terms of any agreement with him/her.	$1,000 for each failure. The claim preparer will be jointly liable with the taxpayer for the penalty unless he/she can prove that he/she exercised enough care to prevent the making of the false statement.
162(6)	Failure to provide on request a Social Insurance Number (SIN), a Business Number (BN), a Trust Account Number (TAN), or a US federal Taxpayer Identification Number (TIN) to a person required to make an information return requiring that number.	$100 for each failure unless an application to obtain a number is filed within 15 days and the number is provided within 15 days of its receipt.
162(7) Reg. 205 Reg. 205.1	Failure by a person (other than a registered charity) or partnership to file an information return or comply with a duty as and when required by the Act or the regulations.	The greater of $100 and $25 times the number of days (no more than 100) during which the failure continues; but this penalty does not apply to failures penalized under another provision of the Act. If the failure is for not filing electronically, the penalty applies only once to the summary form and not to each individual supplementary form (i.e., $100 per day of failure up to a maximum of $2,500).
162(7.01) Reg. 205(3)	Failure by a person (other than a registered charity) or partnership to file a prescribed information return when required by the Act or the regulations.	Regular legislated penalties for the following tax forms or information returns • T1204 • International Electronic Funds Transfer Report • International Exchange of Information on Financial Accounts Information Return (Part XVIII of the Act) • T215 • T10 • Pooled Registered Pension Plan (PRPP) Information Return • Registered Retirement Savings Plan (RRSP) Contribution Information Return • NR4 • T5007 • T4A(P) • T5018 • T4A-RCA • T4PS • T4E • AGR-1 • T4A-NR • T4RIF • T5 • T4A(OAS) • T4A • T4RSP

		• T4 • T5008 • T3 • TFSA Annual Information Return • Tuition and Enrolment Certificate • RC62 are calculated as follows: the greater of $100 and: • $10 per day of failure (max: $1,000) for less than 51 returns; • $15 per day of failure (max: $1,500) for 51 to 500 returns; • $25 per day of failure (max: $2,500) for 501 to 2,500 returns; • $50 per day of failure (max: $5,000) for 2,501 to 10,000 returns; and • $75 per day of failure (max $7,500) for more than 10,000 returns. As per administrative policy on the CRA website, reduced administrative penalties for the following tax forms or information returns • NR4 • T4 • T4A • T4E • T5 • T5018 are calculated as follows: the greater of $100 and: • $100 flat penalty for less than 6 returns; • $5 per day of failure (max: $500) for 6 to 10 returns; • $10 per day of failure (max: $1,000) for 11 to 50 returns; • $15 per day of failure (max: $1,500) for 51 to 500 returns; • $25 per day of failure (max: $2,500 for 501 to 2,500 returns; • $50 per day of failure (max: $5,000) for 2,501 to 10,000 returns; and • $75 per day of failure (max: $7,500) for more than 10,000 returns.
162(7.02) Reg. 205 Reg. 205.1	Failure by a person (other than a registered charity) or partnership to file a prescribed information return as required by regulation (electronically by Internet as opposed to manually) if more than 50 returns must be filed.	For the following forms and returns: • T1204 • International Electronic Funds Transfer Report • Part XVIII Information Return • PRPP Information Return • RRSP Contribution Information Return • RRSP and RRIF Non-qualified Investments • NR4 • T5007 • T4A(P)

		• T5018 • T4E • AGR-1 • T4A-NR • T4RIF • T5 • T4A(OAS) • T5013 • T4A • T4 • T4RSP • T5008 • T3 • TFSA Annual Information Return • Tuition and Enrolment Certificate • RC62 the penalty is calculated as follows: • nil for less than 51 returns; • $250 for 51 to 250 returns; • $500 for 251 to 500 returns; • $1,500 for 501 to 2,500 returns; and • $2,500 for more than 2,500 returns.
162(7.1)	Failure by a member of a partnership to file an information return as a member of the partnership.	The partnership is liable to a penalty equal to the greater of $100 and $25 times the number of days (not exceeding 100) during which the failure continues.
150.1(2.1) 162(7.2) Reg. 205.1(2)	Failure by a prescribed corporation (i.e., a corporation with a gross revenue exceeding $1 million but excluding insurance, non-resident, and tax-exempt corporations, and those reporting in functional currency) to file a return of income electronically.	$1,000.
162(7.3) 150.1(2.3)	Tax preparers failing to file a return electronically, as required under subsection 150.1(2.3). Tax preparers are persons accepting consideration to prepare more than 10 corporate or individual income returns during the year.	$25 per individual return and $100 per corporate return not filed electronically.
162(8) 162(7.1) 233	Repeated failure within a three-year period by a member of a partnership to file an information return after being served a formal demand by the Minister.	The partnership is liable to the total of the penalties imposed under subsection 162(7.1) and $100 for each partner and each month or part of month (not exceeding 24) during which the failure continues.
162(10) 233 233.1 233.2 233.3 233.4 233.8	Failure by a person or partnership, knowingly or under circumstances amounting to gross negligence, to file an information return (RC4649, T106, T1141, T1135, or T1134) required by formal demand under section 233 or provide the Minister with foreign-based information required under sections 233.1 to 233.4, and 233.8.	$500 per month of failure up to 24 months (or, if the person or partnership failed to comply with a formal demand served under section 233, $1,000 per month of failure up to 24 months) less the penalty provided under subsection 162(7).
162(10.1) 162(7) 162(10) 233.2	Delay of more than 24 months in the filing by a person or partnership of an information return in respect of a non-resident trust under section 233.2.	5% of the total of all amounts each of which is the fair market value, at the time it was made, of a contribution of the person or partnership made to the trust before the end of its last taxation year in respect of which the return is required, less the penalties provided under subsections 162(7) and 162(10).

162(10.1) 233.3	Delay of more than 24 months in the filing by a person or partnership of an information return in respect of specified foreign properties.	5% of the greatest of all amounts each of which is the total of the cost amounts to the person or partnership at any time in the year of the specified foreign properties, less the penalties provided under subsections 162(7) and 162(10).
162(10.1) 233.4	Delay of more than 24 months in the filing by a person or partnership of an information return in respect of a foreign affiliate.	5% of the greatest of all amounts each of which is the total of the cost amounts to the person or partnership at any time in the year of a share of the capital stock or indebtedness of the foreign affiliate, less the penalties provided under subsections 162(7) and 162(10).
163(1) 150(1) 163(2)	Failure to report an amount of at least $500 in a return of income for a taxation year after a similar failure had occurred for any of the three preceding taxation years.	Lesser of: (1) 10% of the unreported income; and (2) 50% of difference between the tax understatement on the unreported amount and income tax paid on the unreported amount (for details, see paragraphs 163(2)(*a*) to (*g*)). Penalty does not apply if a penalty is already applicable under 163(2).
163(2)	Make, participate, or acquiesce in the making, knowingly or in circumstances amounting to gross negligence, of a false statement or omission in a return, form, certificate, statement, or answer.	The greater of $100 and 50% of the avoided taxes or excess tax credits claimed.
163(2.2) 66(12.6) 66(12.601) 66(12.62) 66(12.66)	Make, participate, or acquiesce in the making, knowingly or in circumstances amounting to gross negligence, of a false statement or omission in respect of a flow-through share renunciation.	25% of the difference between the amount indicated in the renunciation and the one the corporation was entitled to renounce.
163(2.21) 163(2.22) 66(12.66) 66(12.73)	Make, participate, or acquiesce in the making, knowingly or in circumstances amounting to gross negligence, of a false statement or omission in respect of a renunciation purported to have been made for the so-called look-back rule.	25% of the difference (if any) between: • The excess of the actual amount renounced by the corporation over the amount the corporation was entitled to renounce, as outlined in subsection 66(12.73); and • The excess identified in the document to be filed under subsection 66(12.73) if paragraph 163(2.21)(*b*) is applicable and nil if it is not applicable.
163(2.3) 66(12.691) 66(12.701)	Make, participate, or acquiesce in the making, knowingly or in circumstances amounting to gross negligence, of a false statement or omission in a prescribed form concerning assistance re flow-through shares.	25% of the excess of the assistance that had to be reported on the prescribed form over the assistance that was actually reported on the form.
163(2.4) 233.1	Make, participate, or acquiesce in the making, knowingly or in circumstances amounting to gross negligence, of a false statement or omission in a return concerning reportable transactions with non-resident non-arm's length persons.	$24,000.
163(2.4) 233.2	Make, participate, or acquiesce in the making, knowingly or in circumstances amounting to gross negligence, of a false statement or omission in a return concerning a non-resident trust under section 233.2.	The greater of: • $24,000; and • 5% of the total of all amounts each of which is the fair market value, at the time it was made, of a contribution of the person or partnership made to the trust before the end of its last taxation year in respect of which the return is required.
163(2.4) 233.3	Make, participate, or acquiesce in the making, knowingly or in circumstances amounting to gross negligence, of a false statement or omission in a return concerning a specified foreign property.	The greater of: • $24,000; and • 5% of the greatest of all amounts each of which is the total of the cost amounts to the person or partnership at any time in the year of the speci-

		fied foreign property in respect of which the false statement or omission is made.
163(2.4) 233.4	Make, participate, or acquiesce in the making, knowingly or in circumstances amounting to gross negligence, of a false statement or omission in a return concerning a foreign affiliate.	The greater of: • $24,000; and • 5% of the greatest of all amounts each of which is the total of the cost amounts to the person or partnership at any time in the year of a share of the capital stock or indebtedness of the foreign affiliate in respect of which the return is filed.
163(2.4) 233.6	Person or partnership making, participating, or acquiescing in the making, knowingly or in circumstances amounting to gross negligence, of a false statement or an omission in a return made in respect of distributions from a non-resident trust.	The greater of: • $2,500; and • 5% of the total of the following amounts: (1) All amounts each of which is the fair market value of a property distributed to the person or partnership in the year by the trust and in respect of which the false statement or omission is made; and (2) All amounts each of which is the greatest unpaid principal amount of a debt owing to the trust by the person or partnership in the year and in respect of which the false statement or omission is made.
163.1 161	Late or deficient Part I tax instalments.	50% of the difference (if any) between: • Interest payable under section 161 on all instalments for the year; and • The greater of $1,000 and 25% of the interest that would have been payable under section 161 if no instalments had been made for the year.
163.2(2) 163.2(3) 163.2(6) 163.2(14)	Misrepresentation in tax planning arrangements (*tax planner penalty*). Make, furnish, or participate in the making of or cause another person to make or furnish, knowingly or through culpable conduct, a statement that the tax planner knows is false and could be used by another person for a purpose of the Act.	• If the statement is made in the course of a planning activity or a valuation activity: The greater of $1,000 and the planner's total gross entitlements (generally the professional fees received in respect of that activity); and • If the statement is not made in the course of such activity: $1,000. If both the subsection 163.2(2) tax planner penalty and the subsection 163.2(4) tax preparer penalty are applicable to the same false statement, the taxpayer will only be liable to the greater penalty.
163.2(4) 163.2(5) 163.2(6) 163.2(14)	Participation in a misrepresentation (*tax preparer penalty*). Make, participate, or acquiesce in the making, knowingly or through culpable conduct, of a statement that the tax preparer knows is false and could be used by another person for a purpose of the Act.	The greater of the following amounts: • $1,000; and • The lesser of: (1) The penalty to which the other person would be liable under subsection 163(2) if he/she had made the statement in a return filed for the purpose of the Act while knowing that it was false; and (2) The total of $100,000 and the tax preparer's gross compensation. If both the subsection 163.2(2) tax planner penalty and the subsection 163.2(4) tax preparer penalty are applicable to the same false statement, the taxpayer will only be liable to the greater penalty.
163.3(2) 163.3(3)	Acquiring, owning, using, or allowing Electronic Suppression of Sales (ESS) software or devices to falsify or hide electronic cash register records required to be kept under section 230. These penalties imposed under the *Income Tax Act* are in addition to any other penalties assessed under the *Excise Tax Act* (ETA).	• $5,000 for a first use or possession penalty assessment under the ITA or ETA; and • $50,000 for a second use or possession penalty assessment under the ITA or ETA.
163.3(4)	Designing, developing, manufacturing, selling, possessing for sale, or offering for sale Electronic Suppression of Sales (ESS) software or devices which are used	• $10,000 for a first manufacturing penalty assessment under the ITA or ETA; • $50,000 for a first manufacturing penalty assessment under the ITA or ETA if a use or possession

	to falsify or hide electronic cash register records required to be kept under section 230.	penalty was already imposed previously; and • $100,000 for a second manufacturing penalty assessment under the ITA or ETA.
179.1	Appeal to the Tax Court of Canada when the Court determines that there were no reasonable grounds for appeal.	10% of the amount in controversy.
180.01(4) 180.2(6) 181.7 183.2(2) 185(3) 185.2(2) 187(3) 187.6 189(8) 190.21 191.4(2) 193(8) 195(8) 196(4) 197(6) 202(3) 204.3(2) 204.7(3) 204.87 204.93 204.94(4) 207.07(3) 207.2(3) 207.4(2) 207.7(4) 207.8(5) 209(5) 210.2(7) 211.5(1) 211.6(5) 211.82(2) 211.91(3) 218.2(5) 218.3(10) 219(3) 247(11)	Failure to comply with the requirements of subsections 162 to 163.2 in respect of the following Parts of the Act: I.01, I.2, I.3, II.1, III, III.1, IV, IV.1, V, VI, VI.1, VII, VIII, IX, IX.1, X, X.1, X.2, X.3, X.4, X.5, XI.01, XI.1, XI.2, XI.3, XI.4, XII.1, XII.2, XII.3, XII.4, XII.5, XII.6, XIII.1, XIII.2, XIV, and XVI.1.	Same penalties as the ones described under subsections 162 to 163.2.
188.1(1) 149.1(1) "related business"	Charity — Private foundation carrying on any business, or registered charity or registered Canadian amateur athletic association carrying on a business that is not a related business.	5% of the gross revenue from the business carried on by the private foundation or business that is not a related business carried on by the registered charity or registered Canadian amateur athletic association.
188.1(2) 149.1(1) "related business"	Charity — Private foundation, registered charity, or registered Canadian amateur athletic association subject to a penalty under subsection 188.1(1) in the previous five years.	100% of the gross revenue for a subsequent taxation year from the business carried on by the private foundation or business that is not a related business carried on by the registered charity or registered Canadian amateur athletic association.
188.1(3)(*a*) 149.1(12)	Charity — Acquisition of control of a corporation by a charitable foundation.	5% of the dividends received from the corporation unless a penalty is already applicable under paragraph 188.1(3)(*b*).
188.1(3)(*b*) 149.1(12)	Charitable foundation subject to a penalty under paragraph 188.1(3)(*a*) in the previous five years.	100% of the dividends received by the foundation from the corporation at the particular time after the five-year period when the foundation still controlled the corporation.
188.1(3.1)	Charity — Private foundation having failed to reduce to 0%, by the end of its taxation year, its divestment obligation percentage in respect of a class of shares of the capital stock of a corporation.	5% of the fair market value of the shares represented by the outstanding portion of that divestment obligation percentage. The penalty is doubled to 10% if either: (1) The foundation was assessed a 5% penalty in respect of any class of shares of a corporation less than five years before; or (2) The foundation failed

		to disclose any of the following information on Form T3010: material transaction of the foundation in respect of the class of shares, material interest held by a relevant person in respect of the foundation, or its total corporate holdings percentage in respect of the class of shares at year end unless the foundation held at any time during the year only an insignificant interest in that class.
188.1(4)(*a*) 188.1(5)	Undue benefit conferred to a person by a registered charity or registered Canadian amateur athletic association.	105% of the benefit except if the registered charity or registered Canadian amateur athletic association is liable to the penalty under paragraph 188.1(4)(*b*).
188.1(4)(*b*) 188.1(5)	Registered charity or registered Canadian amateur athletic association that was subject to a penalty under paragraph 188.1(4)(*a*) in the previous five years.	110% of the undue benefit conferred by the registered charity or registered Canadian amateur athletic association.
188.1(6) 149.1(14) 149.1(14.1)	Failure by registered charity, registered Canadian amateur athletic association, or registered journalism organization to file information return and public information return required under subsection 149.1(14) or (14.1).	$500.
188.1(7)	Registered charity, registered Canadian amateur athletic association, or registered journalism organization reported incorrect information on a tax receipt.	5% of the amount reported on the tax receipt.
188.1(8)	Registered charity, registered Canadian amateur athletic association, or registered journalism organization was subject to a penalty under subsection 188.1(7) in the previous five years.	10% of the amount reported on the tax receipt.
188.1(9)	Registered charity, registered Canadian amateur athletic association, or registered journalism organization made, furnished, or participated in the making, or caused another person to make or furnish, a false statement on a receipt in circumstances amounting to culpable conduct.	125% of the amount reported on the receipt.
188.1(11)	Charity — Any transaction (including a gift by a registered charity to another registered charity) the purpose of which is to avoid or unduly delay the expenditure of amounts on charitable activities.	The registered charity is liable to a penalty equal to 110% of the expenditure amount avoided or delayed and, in the case of a gift between charities, both charities are jointly liable to the penalty.
188.1(12)	Charity — Amount transferred by way of a gift (other than a designated gift defined under s. 149.1(1)) between non-arm's length registered charities where the recipient charity failed to spend the whole amount by the end of the year following the year of gift. The amount should be spent in addition to the charity's disbursement quota on its own charitable activities or by way of gifts to arm's length qualified donees.	The recipient charity is liable to a penalty equal to 110% of the difference between the fair market value of the gift and the actual amount spent in addition to its disbursement quota.
192(9) 192(8)	Late filed designation for the purpose of Part VII, Refundable Tax on Corporations Issuing Qualifying Shares.	The lesser of $500 and 1% of the designated amount in respect of the shares.
194(8) 194(7)	Late filed designation for the purpose of Part VIII, Refundable Tax on Corporations in Respect of Scientific Research and Experimental Development Tax	The lesser of: (1) 1% of the designated amount in respect of the share or debt obligation issued, or right granted times the number of months or parts of months between the last day the designation

	Credit.	could be made and the actual day it was made; and (2) $500.
204.82(4) 204.82(3)	Labour-sponsored venture capital corporation not meeting certain investment requirements for 12 consecutive months.	An amount equal to the Part X.3 tax payable under subsection 204.82(3).
204.84 204.81(6)(*c*)	Labour-sponsored venture capital corporation issuing an information return concerning the issuance of a share when it is revoked or subscribing in respect of a share not issued within 180 days after issuing the return.	Amount of the consideration for which the share was issued or was to be issued.
220(3.5) 220(3.2) 220(3.201) Reg. 600	Late filed, amended, or revoked election (excluding pension income splitting election in subsection 220(3.201)) where the Minister has extended the time to make the election or granted permission to amend or revoke it. Elections under the following provisions are covered: *Income Tax Act* sections: 12(2.2)(*b*), 13(4), 13(7.4), 13(29), 20(24), 21, 44(1), 44(6), 45(2), 45(3), 50(1), 53(2.1), 56.4(13), 66.7(7)(*c*), 66.7(7)(*d*), 66.7(7)(*e*), 66.7(8)(*c*), 66.7(8)(*d*), 66.7(8)(*e*), 70(6.2), 70(9.01), 70(9.11), 70(9.21), 70(9.31), 72(2), 73(1), 80.01(4)(*c*), 80.1(1), 82(3), 83(2), 86.1(2)(*f*), 91(1.4), 104(14), 107(2.001), 128.1(4)(*d*), 128.1(6)(*a*), 128.1(6)(*c*), 128.1(7)(*d*), 128.1(7)(*g*), 128.1(8)(*c*), 143(2), 146.01(7), 146.02(7), 164(6), 164(6.1), 184(3), 251.2(6), 256(9); *Income Tax Regulations* sections: 1103(1), 1103(2), 1103(2d) and 5907(2.1).	The lesser of: • $8,000; and • $100 times the number of complete months between the due date of the election and the date the above application was filed with the Minister.
227(8) 153(1) 215	Failure to withhold a tax amount under subsection 153(1) or section 215. "Qualifying non-resident employers" may be exempt from the penalty under subsection 227(8.6) if, after reasonable inquiry, they had no reason to believe that the employee was not a qualifying non-resident employee not subject to withholding tax.	10% of the amount that should have been deducted. If the payer is already subject to this penalty in respect of another amount and the failure was made knowingly or in circumstances amounting to gross negligence, 20% of the amount required to be deducted.
227(9) 116(1) 215(4)	Failure to remit a tax amount deducted at source or to pay a tax amount under subsection 116(1) or a regulation made under subsection 215(4).	3% if the remittance is no more than three days late or made on time but not in the manner required (e.g., not paid to a designated financial institution by a large employer); 5% if four or five days late; 7% if six or seven days late; or 10% if more than seven days late. If the payer is already subject to the penalty for the same year and the failure was made knowingly or in circumstances amounting to gross negligence, 20% of the amount required to be paid or remitted.
227(9.1)	Failure to remit an amount before a prescribed date under subsection 153(1) of the *Income Tax Act*, subsection 21(1) of the *Canada Pension Plan*, or subsection 82(1) of the *Employment Insurance Act*.	The remittance failure penalty under s. 227(9) applies only to the excess of the remittance over $500 unless the remittance was delayed knowingly or in circumstances amounting to gross negligence.
235 150(1)(*a*) 190.2 225.1(8)	Failure by a large corporation (as defined in subsection 225.1(8)) to file a corporate return required under section 150 or 190.2.	The total of 0.0005% of the corporation's taxable capital employed in Canada at the end of its taxation year and 0.25% of the Part VI tax (if applicable) times the number of complete months (not exceeding 40) between the due date and actual filing date of the return.

237.1(7.4) 237.1(2)	Filing of false or misleading information in an application for the attribution of a tax shelter identification number, or selling, issuing, or accepting a contribution in respect of a tax shelter before the issuance of that number.	If the tax shelter is not a gifting arrangement, the penalty is the greater of: (1) $500; and (2) 25% of the total of all amounts each of which is the consideration received or receivable in respect of the tax shelter. If the tax shelter is a gifting arrangement, the penalty is the greater of: (1) the above penalty, and (2) 25% of the amount promised by the tax shelter promoter to be the value of the property that tax shelter participants can transfer to a qualified donee.
237.1(7.5)	Failing to file a tax shelter information return demanded by the Minister or report information required in the return.	If the tax shelter is not a gifting arrangement, the penalty is 25% of the total consideration received from tax shelter participants in respect of whom the information was demanded. If the tax shelter is a gifting arrangement, the penalty is the greater of: (1) the above penalty; and (2) 25% of the amount promised by the tax shelter promoter to be the value of the property that tax shelter participants can transfer to a qualified donee.
237.3(8)	Failure to report an aggressive tax avoidance transaction on Form RC312 by June 30 of the calendar year following the calendar year in which the transaction became reportable. The reporting is required for any person entering into a reportable transaction for him or herself or someone else, or any promoter or adviser entitled to fees in respect of the transaction.	The total of all fees that the promoter or adviser is entitled to receive for the reportable transaction. The penalty is applicable regardless of any agreement as to who is required to file Form RC312. The penalty imposed on the promoter or adviser cannot exceed the maximum fees that he or she may receive for the transaction.
247(3)	Transfer pricing adjustments.	10% of the excess (if any) of: • The taxpayer's transfer pricing capital and income adjustments or setoff adjustments less the portion of such adjustments related to either qualifying cost contribution arrangements or transfer prices resulting from a reasonable effort from the taxpayer to establish an arm's length price; over • The lesser of $5 million and 10% of the taxpayer's annual gross revenue. If there is no excess, then there is no penalty.
281(3) 270(1) "TIN"	Failure by a reportable person to provide a taxpayer identification number (TIN) to a person required to prepare an information return for the reportable person unless the reportable person applies for a TIN within 90 days of the request and provides it within 15 days from its receipt or the reportable person does not qualify for a TIN in its jurisdiction. For a Canadian, the TIN is the social insurance number (SIN), the business number (BN) or the trust account number (TAN). For a non-resident, the TIN is the TIN used in the foreign country of residence.	$500

International Tax Conventions

The following is a list of countries with which Canada has signed tax conventions. The date noted beside the country is the date that the most recent treaty was signed. If the treaty is not yet in force (as noted beside the date), the earlier treaty (if one exists) remains in force until the new treaty comes into force. Countries with which agreements are being negotiated or re-negotiated are also noted. The chart that follows shows the rates of withholding tax under the various treaties for selected types of payments.

Algeria	February 28, 1999
Argentina	April 29, 1993
Armenia	June 29, 2004
Australia	May 21, 1980 (Protocol January 23, 2002)
Austria	December 9, 1976 (Protocol June 15, 1999; Protocol March 9, 2012)
Azerbaijan	September 7, 2004
Bangladesh	February 15, 1982
Barbados	January 22, 1980 (Protocol November 8, 2011)
Belgium	May 23, 2002 (Protocol April 1, 2014 (not yet in force))
Brazil	June 4, 1984
Bulgaria	March 3, 1999
Cameroon	May 26, 1982
Chile	January 21, 1998
China, People's Republic of	May 12, 1986 (does not apply to Hong Kong)
Colombia	November 21, 2008
Croatia	December 9, 1997
Cyprus	May 2, 1984
Czech Republic	May 25, 2001
Denmark	September 17, 1997
Dominican Republic	August 6, 1976
Ecuador	June 28, 2001
Egypt	May 30, 1983
Estonia	June 2, 1995
Finland	July 20, 2006
France	May 2, 1975 (Protocol January 16, 1987; Protocol November 30, 1995; Protocol February 2, 2010)
Gabon	November 14, 2002
Germany	April 19, 2001
Greece	June 29, 2009
Guyana	October 15, 1985
Hong Kong	November 11, 2012
Hungary	April 15, 1992 (Protocol May 3, 1994)
Iceland	June 19, 1997
India	January 11, 1996
Indonesia	January 16, 1979 (Protocol April 1, 1998)
Ireland	October 8, 2003
Israel	September 21, 2016
Italy	June 3, 2002
Ivory Coast	June 16, 1983
Jamaica	March 30, 1978
Japan	May 7, 1986 (Protocol February 19, 1999)
Jordan	September 6, 1999
Kazakhstan	September 25, 1996
Kenya	April 27, 1983
Korea, Republic of	September 5, 2006
Kuwait	January 28, 2002
Kyrgyzstan	June 4, 1998
Latvia	April 26, 1995
Lebanon	December 29, 1998 (not yet in force)

Lithuania	August 29, 1996
Luxembourg	September 10, 1999 (Protocol May 8, 2012)
Madagascar	November 24, 2016 (not yet in force)
Malaysia	October 15, 1976
Malta	July 25, 1986
Mexico	September 12, 2006
Moldova	July 4, 2002
Mongolia	May 27, 2002
Morocco	December 22, 1975
Namibia	March 25, 2010 (not yet in force)
Netherlands	May 27, 1986 (Protocol March 4, 1993; Protocol August 25, 1997)
New Zealand	May 3, 2012 (Protocol September 12, 2014)
Nigeria	August 4, 1992
Norway	July 12, 2002
Oman	June 30, 2004
Pakistan	February 24, 1976
Papua New Guinea	October 16, 1987
Peru	July 20, 2001
Philippines	March 11, 1976
Poland	May 14, 2012
Portugal	June 14, 1999
Romania	April 8, 2004
Russia	October 5, 1995
Senegal	August 2, 2001
Serbia	April 27, 2012
Singapore	March 6, 1976 (Protocol November 29, 2011)
Slovak Republic	May 22, 2001
Slovenia	September 15, 2000
South Africa	November 27, 1995
Spain	November 23, 1976 (Protocol November 18, 2014)
Sri Lanka	June 23, 1982
Sweden	August 27, 1996
Switzerland	May 5, 1997 (Protocol October 22, 2010; Article 25 Interpretation Agreement June 28, 2012 / July 23, 2012)
Taiwan	January 15, 2016
Tanzania	December 15, 1995
Thailand	April 11, 1984
Trinidad and Tobago	September 11, 1995
Tunisia	February 10, 1982
Turkey	July 14, 2009
Ukraine	March 4, 1996
United Arab Emirates	June 9, 2002
United Kingdom	September 8, 1978 (Protocol April 15, 1980; Protocol October 16, 1985; Protocol May 7, 2003; Protocol July 21, 2014; Agreement July 25, 2015/August 11, 2015)
United States	September 26, 1980 (Protocol June 14, 1983; Protocol March 28, 1984; Protocol March 17, 1995; Protocol July 29, 1997; Protocol September 21, 2007; Agreement February 5, 2014)
Uzbekistan	June 17, 1999
Venezuela	July 10, 2001
Vietnam	November 14, 1997
Zambia	February 16, 1984
Zimbabwe	April 16, 1992

The Department of Finance has announced that agreements are being negotiated or re-negotiated with the following countries: Australia, Brazil, China (PRC), Germany, Malaysia, Netherlands, San Marino, and Switzerland.

Rates of Withholding Tax under Income Tax Agreements Signed by Canada

This chart is intended for use only as a quick reference guide for the rates of withholding tax for selected types of payments under the income tax agreements Canada has signed with various countries. The rates listed in the chart are the maximum rates that Canada and the other country may withhold for the type of payment noted. Many of the treaties have unique exceptions and qualifications on withholding tax which cannot be listed in a chart such as this. Therefore, the specific treaty should be consulted when determining whether or not there is a tax liability exigible on a payment.

Countries	*Date*	*Interest*	*Dividends — % of Ownership*	*Regular Dividends*	*Royalties*	*Pension and Annuity*	*From Estate or Trust*
Algeria	1999	15%[3]	15%	15%	15%, royalties for use of computer software and patents exempt.	15%[9,14,16]	—
Argentina	1993	12.5%[3]	10%[5]	15%	15% generally 3%, 5%, 10% for specific items	15%[9,14,16]	—
Armenia	2004	10%[3]	5%[5]for investment >US $100,000.	15%	10%	pen. 15%[9,14,16]	15%
Australia	1980[2,19]	10%	5%[4,6]	15%	10%	15%[10,17]	15% (Can)
Austria	1976[2]	10%[3]	5%[4,6]	15%	10%[8]	[9,11]	15% (Can)
Azerbaijan	2004	10%[3]	10%[4]	15%	5% on computer software, patents, industrial, commercial or scientific experience royalties; 10% on other royalties	—	15%
Bangladesh	1982	15%[3]	15%	15%	10%	15%[9]	—
Barbados	1980[2]	15%[3]	15%	15%	10%[7]	15%[9,14,16]	15% (Can)
Belgium	2002[1,2]	10%[3]	5%[4]	15%	10%[8]	[9,11] [13] for certain pensions	15%
Brazil	1984[19]	15%[3] 10% Brazil in certain circumstances	15%[4]	[11]	15% 25% on trademarks	[15,] [9] unless over $4,000	—
Bulgaria	1999	10%[3]	10%[4,6]	15%	10%[7]	pen. 15% ann. 10%[9]	15% (Can)
Cameroon	1982	15% (Can) 20% (Cam)	15% (Can) 20% (Cam)	15% (Can) 20% (Cam)	15% (Can) 20% (Cam)	[11]	—
Chile.........	1998	15%	10%[5]	15%	15%	pen. [13,] ann. 15%[9]	15% (Can)
China	1986[19]	10%[3]	10%[4]	15%	10%	[11]	—
Colombia	2008	10%[3]	5%[4]	15%	10%	15%[9,14,16]	15% (Can)
Croatia	1997	10%	5%[4,5,6]	15%	10%	pen. 15%[15,] ann. 10%[9]	15%
Cyprus	1984	15%[3]	15%	15%	10%[7]	15%[9] [13,] for certain pensions[15,16]	15%
Czech Republic	2001	10%[3]	5%[4]	15%	10%	15%[9]	15%
Denmark	1997	10%[3]	5%[5](if owned by a company) 10% if paid by Cdn. NRO invest. corp.	15%	10%[8]	[9,13]	15%
Dominican Republic	1976	18%[3]	18%	18%	18%[7]	18%[9,16]	18%
Ecuador	2001	10%[3]	5%[5]	15%	10% on use of industrial, commercial, or scientific equipment; 15% on other	pen. 15%[14,15,16,] ann. 15%[9]	15%

Egypt	1983	15%[3]	15%	15% (20% if paid to an individual resident in Canada)	15%	[11]	15%
Estonia	1995	10%[3]	5%[5,6]	15%	10%	15%[16], ann. 10%[9]	15%
Finland	2006	10%[3]	5%[4]	15%	10%[8]	pen. 20%[14], ann. 15%[9]	15%
France	1975[2]	10%[3]	5%[4] 10% if paid by Cdn. NRO invest. corp.	15%	10%[8]	pen.[13,14], ann.[9,11]	15%
Gabon........	2002	10%[3]	15%	15%	10%	pen.[11], ann.[11]	—
Germany......	2001[19]	10%[3]	5%[4]	15%	10%[8]	pen.[11], ann.[9,11]	—
Greece	2009	10%[3]	5%[5]	15%	10%[7]	15%[9,14,15,16]	15%
Guyana.......	1985	15% (Can)[3], 25% (Guy)[3]	15%	15%	10%	[9,11,14]	—
Hong Kong (PRC)	2012	10%[3]	5%[4]	15%	10%	pen.[11]	—
Hungary	1992[2]	10%[3]	5%[5] 10% if paid by Cdn. NRO invest. corp.	15%	10%[7]	pen. 15%[14,16], ann. 10%[9]	15%
Iceland	1997	10%[3]	5%[4,6]	15%	10%[8]	pen. 15%[14,16], ann. 15%[9]	15%
India	1996	15%[3]	15%[4]	25%	10% 15% 20%	[13]	15%
Indonesia	1979[2]	10%[3]	10%[5]	15%	10%	15%[9,14]	—
Ireland	2003	10%[3]	5%[4,6]	15%	10%[8]	pen. 15%[14,16] ann. 15%	15%
Israel.........	2016	10%[3]	5%[5]	15%	10%[7]	pen. 15%[14,16], ann. 15%[9]	15%
Italy..........	2002	10%[3]	5%[4,6]	15%	5%[7], on computer software, patents, industrial, commercial or scientific experience royalties, 10% on other royalties[7]	pen. 15%[14,15,16]	15%
Ivory Coast	1983	15%[3]	15% 18% on certain divs. from Ivory Coast	15% 18% on certain divs. from Ivory Coast	10%	15%	—
Jamaica.......	1978	15%[3]	15% 22.5% (Jam)[4]	15%	10%	pen.[11,14,16], ann. 15%[9]	15% (Can)
Japan	1986[2]	10%[3]	5%[5]	15%	10%	[11]	—
Jordan........	1999	10%[3]	10%[4,6]	15%	10%	[13]	—
Kazakhstan	1996	10%[3]	5%[4,6]	15%	10%	pen. 15%[9], [13] for certain pensions	—
Kenya	1983	15%[3]	15%[4]	25%	15%	15%	—
Korea	2006	10%[3]	5%[5]	15%	10%	pen. 15%[9,16] ann. 10%	—
Kuwait	2002	10%[3]	5%[4,5,6]	15%	10%	15%	—
Kyrgyzstan	1998	15%[3]	15%	15%	10%[8]	15%[9,14,16]	15%
Latvia	1995	10%[3]	5%[5,6]	15%	10%	pen. 15%[16], ann. 10%[9]	15%
Lebanon	1998[1]	10%[3]	5%[4,6]	15%	5% on cultural, computer software, industrial, commercial	pen. 15%[9,14]	—

					or scientific "know-how" royalties, 10% on other royalties		
Lithuania	1996	10%[3]	5%[5,6]	15%	10%	pen. 15%[16], ann. 10%[9]	15%
Luxembourg . . .	1999[2]	10%[3]	5%[4](if owned by a company) 10% if paid by Cdn. NRO invest. corp.	15%	10%[8]	[9,11,14], [13] for certain pensions	15%
Madagascar	2016[1]	10%[3]	5%[5]	15%	10% (5% on cultural, computer software, industrial, commercial or scientific experience royalties)	pen. 15%[9,14,16], ann. 15%[9]	15%
Malaysia	1976[19]	15%[3]	15%	15%	15% certain royalties excluded	15%[14,16]	15% (Can)
Malta	1986	15%[3]	15% (Can) not to exceed tax on profits (Malta)	15% (Can) not to exceed tax on profits (Malta)	10%[7]	15%[9,14,16]	15%
Mexico	2006	10%[3]	5%[4]	15%	10%[7]	pen. 15%[9,14,16] ann. 15%	15%
Moldova	2002	10%[3]	5%[5]	15%	10%	15%[14]	15%
Mongolia	2002	10%[3]	5%[4]	15%	5% on cultural, computer software, patent, industrial, commercial or scientific experience royalties, 10% on other royalties	pen. 15%[14,16], ann. 15%[9]	15%
Morocco	1975	15%[3]	15%	15%	10% 5% on cultural royalties	[11]	—
Namibia	2010[1]	10%[3]	5%[5]	15%	10%[7]	pen.[12]	15%
Netherlands . . .	1986[2,19]	10%[3]	5%[4,5](if owned by a company) 10% if paid by Cdn. NRO invest. corp.	15%	10%[8]	15%[9]	15% (Can)
New Zealand	2012	10%[3]	5%[4]	15%	5% on cultural, computer software, industrial, commercial or scientific info; 10% on other royalties	pen. 15%[14,16], ann. 15%[9]	15% (Can)
Nigeria	1992	12.5%[3]	12.5%[4]	15%	12.5%	[14,11]	—
Norway	2002	10%[3]	5%[4,6]	15%	10%[8]	15[9,14]	15%
Oman	2004	10%[3]	5%[4]	15%	10%[8]	pen. 15%[14,16], ann. 15%[9]	15%
Pakistan	1976	15% (Can)[3], 25% (Pak)[3]	15% (Can) 15% (Pak)[5]	15% (Can) 20% (Pak)	15% (Can)[7], 20% (Pak)[7]copyright, trademark equipment, films 15% (Pak) technical know-how	[13] Canada may withhold 15% on alimony	15% (Can)
Papua New Guinea	1987	10%[3]	15% (Can) 25% (PNG)	15% (Can) 25% (PNG)	10%	15%[10,14,16]	—
Peru	2001	15%	10%[4]	15%	15%	15%[9,14]	15%
Philippines	1976	15%[3]	15% (Can) 15% (Phil)[4]	15% (Can) 25% (Phil)	10% (Can) 25% (Phil)	[13]	—
Poland	2012	10%[3]	5%[4]	15%	5% on cultural, industrial, commercial, or scientific info; 10% on other royalties	pen. 15%[14,16], ann. 15%[9]	15%
Portugal	1999	10%[3]	10%[5,6]	15%	10%	15%[9,14,16]	15%
Romania	2004	10%[3]	5%[4]	15%	10% 5% on cultural, software, industrial, commercial, scientific info.	pen. 15%	—
Russia	1995	10%[3]	10%[4]	15%	10%[8]	[13]	—

Senegal	2001	15% (Can)[3], 20% (Sen)[3], 16% (Sen)[3]	15% (Can) 16% (Sen)	15% (Can) 16% (Sen)	15%	15%[9,14]	15%
Serbia	2012	10%[3]	5%[5]	15%	10%	pen. 15%	15%
Singapore	1976[2]	15%[3]	15% 0% (Sing) depending on domestic law	15% 0% (Sing) depending on domestic law	15%	[13] Canada may withhold 15% on alimony	15% (Can)
Slovak Republic	2001	10%[3]	5%[4]	15%	10%[7]	pen. 15%[14,16] ann. 15%	15%
Slovenia.......	2000	10%[3]	5% (Can)[4,6], 5% (Slo)[5]	15%	10%	pen. 15%[16], (Can) (Slo)[13], ann. 10%[9]	15%
South Africa	1995	10%[3]	5%[4,6]	15%	10% 6% on cultural, software, industrial, commercial, scientific info.	[11]	15%
Spain.........	1976[2]	10%[3]	5%[4]	15%	10%[7]	15%[9,14,16]	—
Sri Lanka	1982	15%[3]	15%	15%	10%[7]	15%[9,14,16]	15% (Can)
Sweden	1996	10%[3]	5%[5] 10% if paid by Cdn. NRO invest corp.	15%	10%[8]	[9,11,14]	15% (Can)
Switzerland....	1997[2,19]	10%[3]	5%[4]	15%	10%[8]	15%[9,14]	—
Taiwan	2016	10%[3]	10%[5]	15%	10%	pen. 15%[16], ann. 15%[9]	15%
Tanzania......	1995	15%[3]	20%[5]	25%	20%	15%[9,11,14,16] (Can)	—
Thailand	1984	15% (Can) 10% (Thai) if to fin. instit. 25% (Thai) otherwise[3]	15% (Can) 15% (Thai) in certain cases 20%[5] (Thai)	15% (Can) taxed under laws of Thailand	15% 5% on cultural	[13]	15% (Can)
Trinidad and Tobago	1995	10%[3]	5%[4,6]	15%	10%[7]	pen. 15%[9,14]	—
Tunisia	1982	15%[3]	15%	15%	20%[7] on patents, trademarks, films, videos, industrial, commercial, scientific or harbour equip.; 15% on other	[11]	15%
Turkey........	2009	15%[3]	15%[4]	20%	10%	15%[9,14,15,16]	—
Ukraine.......	1996	10%[3]	5%[5,6]	15%	10% computer software exempt	[13]	15%
United Arab Emirates	2002	10%[3]	5%[4] 10% if paid by Cdn. NRO invest. corp.	15%	10%[8]	[11]	15%
United Kingdom	1978[2]	10%[3]	5%[4]	15%	10%[8]	pen.[12], ann. 10%[9]	15% (Can)
U.S.A.	1980[2]	0%[3,18]	5%[4]	15%	10%[8]	15%[9,14]	15%
Uzbekistan	1999	10%[3]	5%[4]	15%	5% on cultural, computer software, industrial, commercial or scientific "know-how" royalties, 10% on other royalties	[13]	—
Venezuela	2001	10%[3]	10%[5]	15%	5% on cultural, computer software, industrial, commercial or scientific experience royalties, 10% on other royalties	[11,14]	—
Socialist Republic of Vietnam	1997	10%[3]	5% (if 70% controlled by corporate owner) 10% (if 25%–69% controlled by corporate owner)	15%	10%	pen. 15% ann.[9,11]	15%

Zambia	1984	15%[3]	15%	15%	15%	15%[14]	15% (Can)
Zimbabwe	1992	15%[3]	10%[5]	15% (Can) 20% (Zim)	10%	15%[9, 14, 16]	15% (Can)

Notes:

[1] Signed but not yet in force.

[2] Revised by subsequent Protocol.

[3] No withholding tax under the treaty on certain types of interest. After 2007, the Canadian *Income Tax Act* exempts interest payments to non-residents from withholding tax, except for certain interest paid or payable to a non-arms length person or participating debt interest. See paragraph 212(1)(*b*).

[4] If recipient company owns at least 10% of capital or voting stock or has 10% of voting power of stock on which dividends are paid (see specific treaty).

[5] If recipient company owns a specified percentage of capital or voting power of stock on which dividends are paid (see specific treaty for level of ownership specified).

[6] Does not apply to dividends from a non-resident-owned investment corporation resident in Canada.

[7] Cultural royalties are exempt from withholding tax. These include copyright royalties for production or reproduction of literary, dramatic, musical or artistic work. They usually do not include royalties on films or videotapes.

[8] Cultural royalties, computer software, industrial, commercial or scientific "know-how" royalties are exempt.

[9] Alimony and child support taxed only in the country of person receiving the payment.

[10] Alimony and child support taxed only in the paying country.

[11] May be taxed in source country — No treaty rate.

[12] Exempt from tax in source country.

[13] Taxed only in source country.

[14] Certain pensions exempt from tax in both countries.

[15] Tax withheld only if payment over a certain amount.

[16] For pensions, tax withheld is not to exceed the amount that would be payable if the recipient were resident in the source country.

[17] For pensions and annuities, tax withheld is not to exceed the amount that would be payable if the recipient were resident in the source country.

[18] Under the Canada–U.S. Treaty, the Fifth Protocol provides that withholding tax on interest will be completely eliminated for interest paid or credited after December 31, 2009. The maximum rate for withholding on interest paid or credited between January 1, 2008 and December 31, 2008 is 7%, and 4% on interest paid or credited between January 1, 2009 and December 31, 2009.

[19] Under negotiation/re-negotiation

The Fifth Supplement

The present version of the *Income Tax Act* has a complex history. Its origins are to be found in chapter 52 of the 1948 Statutes of Canada. That Act became chapter 148 of the 1952 Revised Statutes of Canada. A complete transformation of the tax legislation was introduced with S.C. 1970-71-72, c. 63, the legislation that implemented the 1972 tax reform. Section 1 of that Act was a sweeping amendment to the 1952 Act, which repealed and replaced nearly all its contents. That amending Act also introduced the *Income Tax Application Rules, 1971*.

Numerous amendments were made over the years to the 1972 Act — as well as to all other Acts of Parliament. Private publishers, such as CCH, issue consolidated versions of these Acts, for reasons of convenience. However, those are not official versions of the legislation. Legally, the official version of these texts is in the very form adopted by Parliament: an initial Act, and all the amendments subsequently made.

To alleviate the inevitable and ever-increasing complexity of the documentary mass resulting from this rule, Parliament periodically reissues all of the Acts in force at a given time. For instance, such revisions were made in 1952, in 1970, and in 1985. The revision process is a delicate one, which requires years of work by a Statute Revision Commission established for that purpose.

The mandate of the Commission, as it was for the most recent revision, permits it to: arrange, revise and consolidate the public general statutes of Canada; omit from the revision all Acts or parts thereof that have expired, have been repealed or suspended, or have had their effect; omit from the revisions all Acts or parts thereof that have reference only to a particular country, province, locality, place or body politic, or otherwise have no general application; include in the revision Acts or parts thereof that, although enacted as or in private Acts, or although deemed to be local Acts or enactments, are of such a character that they impose duties or obligations on, or limit the rights or privileges of, the public; alter the numbering and arrangement of the statutes and of the different Parts, sections and other divisions thereof; make such alterations in the language of the statutes as may be required to preserve a uniform mode of expression, without changing the substance of any enactment; make such minor improvements in the language of the statutes as may be required to bring out more clearly the intention of Parliament, or make the form of expression of the statute in one of the official languages more compatible with its expression in the other official language, without changing the substance of any enactment; make such changes in the statutes as are required to reconcile seemingly inconsistent enactments; and correct editing, grammatical or typographical errors in the statutes.

The Commission did prepare a revision of the public general statutes of Canada, which became law by virtue of the *Revised Statutes of Canada, 1985 Act*, R.S.C. 1985, c. 40 (3rd Supp.). However, the *Income Tax Act* was not part of the initial release of the Statutes. The Commission postponed the revision of that Act for a few years, and only recently added it to the *corpus* of the work. This procedure was allowed by section 12 of the *Revised Statutes of Canada, 1985 Act*.

Thus, the *Income Tax Act*, along with the *Income Tax Application Rules*, were introduced in their revised form in the Fifth Supplement of the Revised Statutes of Canada, 1985. The cut-off date for that supplement was November 30, 1991; in other words, the Fifth Supplement contained provisions equivalent to the 1970-71-72 Act, with all the amendments that had come into force before December 1, 1991. A schedule to the Supplement provided for the repeal of the former Act and Income Tax Application Rules, and all amendments to the Act and Rules that received Royal Assent before December 1, 1991.

The Fifth Supplement was proclaimed in force effective March 1, 1994. On that date, the 1972 Act, and all the amendments that had been made to it over the years, were repealed, and replaced by the Fifth Supplement. The *Income Tax Act* became chapter 1 of R.S.C. 1985 (5th Supp.), while the *Income Tax Application Rules* became chapter 2.

Amending legislation enacted after November 1991, however, still had some validity: it still embodied the rules that Parliament wanted to implement. As a result, it was necessary for Parliament to re-enact that legislation, but this time, with a view to amending the text of the new Act. This was done by Bill C-15, which contained amendments equivalent to those assented to between November 30, 1991, and July 1, 1993. When Bill C-15 received Royal Assent on May 12, 1994, the new Act was up-to-date as of the date of its proclamation. Extensive amendments have been made since that time, and are reflected in the text of this book.

Income Tax Act — Amending Acts
R.S.C. 1985 (5th Supp.), c. 1 as amended.

The current version of the Income Tax Act was proclaimed in force on March 1, 1994, replacing the former Act, S.C. 1970-71-72, c. 63. The current version of the Act has been amended by the following statutes.

Date last reviewed: June 2019

Year	Bill	Title	Chapter	Royal Assent
1994	C-15	*An Act to revise certain income tax law amendments in terms of the revised Income Tax Act and Income Tax Application Rules*	7	May 12, 1994
	C-9	*An Act to amend the Income Tax Act*	8	May 12, 1994
	C-2	*An Act to amend the Department of National Revenue Act and to amend certain other Acts in consequence thereof*	13	May 12, 1994
	C-27	*An Act to amend the Income Tax Application Rules, the Canada Pension Plan, the Canada Business Corporations Act, the Excise Tax Act, the Unemployment Insurance Act and certain related Acts*	21	June 15, 1994
	C-28	*Canada Student Financial Assistance Act*	28	June 23, 1994
	C-32	*An Act to amend the Excise Tax Act, the Excise Act and the Income Tax Act*	29	June 23, 1994
	C-49	*Department of Agriculture and Agri-Food Act*	38	November 24, 1994
	C-48	*Department of Natural Resources Act*	41	December 15, 1994
1995	C-46	*Department of Industry Act*	1	March 16, 1995
	C-59	*An Act to amend the Income Tax Act and the Income Tax Application Rules*	3	March 26, 1995
	C-53	*Department of Canadian Heritage Act*	11	June 15, 1995
	C-67	*Veterans Review and Appeal Board Act*	18	June 22, 1995
	C-70	*An Act to amend the Income Tax Act, the Income Tax Application Rules and related Acts*	21	June 22, 1995
	C-93	*An Act to amend the Cultural Property Export and Import Act, the Income Tax Act and the Tax Court of Canada Act*	38	December 5, 1995
	C-103	*An Act to amend the Excise Tax Act and Income Tax Act*	46	December 15, 1995
1996	C-11	*Department of Human Resources Development Act*	11	May 29, 1996
	C-36	*Income Tax Budget Amendment Act*	21	June 20, 1996
	C-12	*Employment Insurance Act*	23	June 20, 1996
1997	C-70	*An Act to amend the Excise Tax Act, the Federal–Provincial Fiscal Arrangements Act, the Income Tax Act, the Debt Servicing and Reduction Account Act and related Acts*	10	March 20, 1997
	C-5	*An Act to amend the Bankruptcy and Insolvency Act, the Companies' Creditors Arrangement Act and the Income Tax Act*	12	April 25, 1997
	C-92	*Income Tax Budget Amendments Act*	25	April 25, 1997
	C-93	*Budget Implementation Act, 1997*	26	April 25, 1997
1998	C-28	*Income Tax Amendments Act, 1997*	19	June 18, 1998
	C-36	*Budget Implementation Act, 1998*	21	June 18, 1998
	S-21	*Corruption of Foreign Public Officials Act*	34	December 10, 1998
1999	C-61	*An Act to amend the War Veterans Allowance Act, the Pension Act, the Merchant Navy Veteran and Civilian War-related Benefits Act, the Department of Veterans Affairs Act, the Veterans Review and Appeal Board Act and the Halifax Relief Commission Pension Continuation Act and to amend certain other Acts in consequence thereof*	10	March 25, 1999
	C-43	*Canada Customs and Revenue Agency Act*	17	April 29, 1999
	C-72	*Income Tax Amendments Act, 1998*	22	June 17, 1999

	C-71	*Budget Implementation Act, 1999*	26	June 17, 1999
	C-84	*Miscellaneous Statute Law Amendment Act, 1999*	31	June 17, 1999
2000	C-2	*Canada Elections Act*	9	May 31, 2000
	C-23	*Modernization of Benefits and Obligations Act*	12	June 29, 2000
	C-32	*Budget Implementation Act, 2000*	14	June 29, 2000
	C-25	*Income Tax Amendments Act, 1999*	19	June 29, 2000
	C-24	*Sales Tax and Excise Tax Amendments Act, 1999*	30	October 20, 2000
2001	C-26	*Tobacco Tax Amendments Act, 2001*	16	June 14, 2001
	C-22	*Income Tax Amendments Act, 2000*	17	June 14, 2001
	C-11	*Immigration and Refugee Protection Act*	27	November 1, 2001
	C-36	*Anti-terrorism Act*	41	December 18, 2001
2002	C-30	*Courts Administration Service Act*	8	March 27, 2002
	C-49	*Budget Implementation Act, 2001*	9	March 27, 2002
2003	C-28	*Budget Implementation Act, 2003*	15	June 19, 2003
	C-24	*An Act to amend the Canada Elections Act and the Income Tax Act (political financing)*	19	June 19, 2003
	C-48	*An Act to amend the Income Tax Act (natural resources)*	28	November 7, 2003
2004	C-8	*Library and Archives of Canada Act*	11	April 22, 2004
	C-30	*Budget Implementation Act, 2004*	22	May 14, 2004
	C-3	*An Act to amend the Canada Elections Act and the Income Tax Act*	24	May 14, 2004
	S-10	*Federal Law–Civil Law Harmonization Act, No. 2*	25	December 15, 2004
	C-5	*Canada Education Savings Act*	26	December 15, 2004
2005	C-33	*Budget Implementation Act, 2004, No. 2*	19	May 13, 2005
	C-45	*Canadian Forces Members and Veterans Re-establishment and Compensation Act*	21	May 13, 2005
	C-43	*Budget Implementation Act, 2005*	30	June 29, 2005
	C-38	*Civil Marriage Act*	33	July 20, 2005
	C-23	*Department of Human Resources and Skills Development Act*	34	July 20, 2005
	C-22	*Department of Social Development Act*	35	July 20, 2005
	C-26	*An Act to establish the Canada Border Services Agency*	38	November 3, 2005
	C-66	*Energy Costs Assistance Measures Act*	49	November 25, 2005
2006	C-4	*An Act to amend An Act to amend the Canada Elections Act and the Income Tax Act*	1	May 11, 2006
	C-13	*Budget Implementation Act, 2006*	4	June 22, 2006
	C-2	*Federal Accountability Act*	9	December 12, 2006
	C-25	*An Act to amend the Proceeds of Crime (Money Laundering) and Terrorist Financing Act and the Income Tax Act*	12	December 14, 2006
2007	C-28	*Budget Implementation Act, 2006, No. 2*	2	February 21, 2007
	C-294	*An Act to amend the Income Tax Act (sports and recreation programs)*	16	June 22, 2007
	C-52	*Budget Implementation Act, 2007*	29	June 22, 2007
	C-28	*Budget and Economic Statement Implementation Act, 2007*	35	December 14, 2007
	C-12	*An Act to amend the Bankruptcy and Insolvency Act, the Companies' Creditors Arrangement Act, the Wage Earner Protection Program Act and chapter 47 of the Statutes of Canada, 2005*	36	December 14, 2007
2008	C-50	*Budget Implementation Act, 2008*	28	June 18, 2008
2009	C-10	*Budget Implementation Act, 2009*	2	March 12, 2009
	C-51	*Economic Recovery Act (stimulus)*	31	December 15, 2009
2010	C-9	*Jobs and Economic Growth Act*	12	July 12, 2010
	C-47	*Sustaining Canada's Economic Recovery Act*	25	December 15, 2010

2011	C-3	*Supporting Vulnerable Seniors and Strengthening Canada's Economy Act*	15	June 26, 2011
	C-13	*Keeping Canada's Economy and Jobs Growing Act*	24	December 15, 2011
2012	C-38	*Jobs, Growth and Long-term Prosperity Act*	19	June 29, 2012
	C-44	*Helping Families in Need Act*	27	December 14, 2012
	C-45	*Jobs and Growth Act, 2012*	31	December 14, 2012
2013	C-48	*Technical Amendments Act, 2012*	34	June 26, 2013
	C-60	*Economic Action Plan Act, No. 1*	33	June 26, 2013
	C-4	*Economic Action Plan Act, No. 2*	40	December 12, 2013
2014	C-5	*Offshore Health and Safety Act*	13	June 19, 2014
	C-23	*Fair Elections Act*	12	June 19, 2014
	C-31	*Economic Action Plan 2014 Act, No. 1*	20	June 19, 2014
	C-43	*Economic Action Plan 2014 Act, No. 2*	39	December 16, 2014
2015	C-51	*Anti-terrorism Act, 2015*	20	June 18, 2015
	C-59	*An Act to Implement Certain Provisions of the Budget Tabled in Parliament on April 21, 2015 and Other Measures*	36	June 23, 2015
	C-377	*An Act to Amend the Income Tax Act (Requirements for Labour Organizations)*	41	June 30, 2015
2016	C-2	*An Act to amend the Income Tax Act*	11	December 15, 2016
	C-15	*Budget Implementation Act, 2016, No. 1*	7	June 22, 2016
	C-26	*An Act to amend the Canada Pension Plan, the Canada Pension Plan Investment Board Act and the Income Tax Act*	14	December 15, 2016
	C-29	*Budget Implementation Act, 2016, No. 2*	12	December 15, 2016
2017	C-4	*An Act to amend the Canada Labour Code, the Parliamentary Employment and Staff Relations Act, the Public Service Labour Relations Act and the Income Tax Act*	12	June 19, 2017
	C-44	*Budget Implementation Act, 2017, No. 1*	20	June 22, 2017
	C-63	*Budget Implementation Act, 2017, No. 2*	33	December 14, 2017
2018	C-51	*An Act to amend the Criminal Code and the Department of Justice Act and to make consequential amendments to another Act*	29	December 13, 2018
	C-74	*Budget Implementation Act, 2018, No. 1*	12	June 21, 2018
	C-86	*Budget Implementation Act, 2018, No. 2*	27	December 13, 2018
2019	C-59	*National Security Act, 2017*	13	June 21, 2019
	C-97	*Budget Implementation Act, 2019, No. 1*	29	June 21, 2019

Proposed Amendments
Income Tax Act

The following table lists proposed amendments that have been tabled as Bills or draft legislation, followed by Budget announcements and news releases, in reverse chronological order. Bills and draft legislation include the provisions of a government Bill that is tabled or a private member's Bill that has passed through the House of Commons, as well as draft legislation released by the Department of Finance. The proposed amendments listed below are reproduced in the *Income Tax Act* in a box immediately following the provision affected.

Bill or Release Name	Date	Description
Bills and Draft Legislation		
Notice of Ways and Means Motion to amend the *Income Tax Act* [Employee Stock Options]	June 17, 2019	Proposes to add a $200,000 annual maximum to the employee stock option deduction, modify the rules for the deduction for employers, and add reporting requirements for employers.
Legislative Proposals Relating to the *Income Tax Act*, Employee Life and Health Trusts	May 27, 2019	Will allow for the conversion of Health and Welfare Trusts into Employee Life and Health Trusts.
Legislative Proposals Relating to Income Tax and Other Legislation [Reporting Requirements for Trusts]	July 27, 2018	Proposes to enhance information and tax reporting requirements for trusts, and Budget 2019 expressed the government's commitment to enact these measures.
Bill C-74, Canada–Quebec Gulf of St. Lawrence Petroleum Resources Accord Implementation Act	June 18, 2015	Establishes a joint regulatory body between the Government of Canada and the Government of Quebec, which will oversee offshore petroleum activities in the Gulf of St. Lawrence. Note that Bill C-74 died when Parliament dissolved in 2015. It is unclear whether the new government plans on reintroducing this Bill.

Budget Announcements and Other Releases		
2019 Federal Budget (Special Report 119H)	March 19, 2019	Proposes to enact the numerous measures announced in the 2019 federal Budget. Many of these measures were enacted with Bill C-97, and others remain proposed.
2019 Indexation Factor	November 16, 2018	Canada Revenue Agency Fact Sheet sets out the 2019 indexation factor for personal amounts and income tax brackets, as well as other amounts. See s. 117.1(1).

Proposed Amendments
Income Tax Regulations

The following table lists proposed amendments that have been tabled in Bills, releases of draft regulations, Budget announcements or news releases, in reverse chronological order. The proposed amendments are reproduced in the *Income Tax Regulations* in a box immediately following the provision affected.

Bill, Draft Regulation, or Release Name	**Date**	**Regulations**	**Subject**
Bills and Draft Legislation			
Legislative Proposals Relating to Income Tax and Other Legislation [Reporting Requirements for Trusts]	July 27, 2018	204.2	Proposed amendments from Budget 2018 that are intended to add additional tax information reporting requirements for trusts.
Legislative Proposals Relating to the *Income Tax Act* and the *Income Tax Regulations* and to Related Legislation	September 16, 2016	6204(1)	Proposes to enact a proposed technical change with respect to the definition of a prescribed share for the purposes of 110(1)(*d*)(i).

Budget Announcements and Other Releases			
2019 Federal Budget (Special Report 119H)	March 19, 2019	Various provisions	Proposes to enact the various measures announced in the 2019 federal Budget. Many of these were enacted with Bill C-97, but others remain proposed.
Livestock Producers Receive Tax Relief for 2018	January 30, 2019	7305.01	Subsections 80.3(4) and (4.1) allow livestock farmers to defer a portion of their proceeds from selling livestock or bees until the following tax year where they are in a designated region affected by drought, flood, or excess moisture. These regions are designated by Agriculture and Agri-Food Canada.
Government Announces the 2019 Automobile Deduction Limits and Expense Benefit Rates for Business	December 27, 2018	7305.1, 7306, 7307	Increases the limit on tax exempt allowances paid to employees, and increases the prescribed rate that computes an employee's benefit from personal automobile use. All other amounts remain the same as their 2018 amounts.

Department of Finance Comfort Letters

The following list notes the Department of Finance comfort letters that are reproduced in Wolters Kluwer's *Income Tax Act with Regulations*. The issues described in these letters have not yet been addressed by proposed legislation or draft regulations but the letters provide some insight into possible future amendments. Where more than one letter has been released on the same issue, generally one representative letter has been reproduced.

Provision Where Letter is Reproduced	**Topic**	**Date**
Income Tax Act		
7(1.11)	Expansion of scope of subsection 7(1.11) — Non-arm's length relationship with trusts	December 4, 2006
60.03(1) "eligible pension income", 118(7) "pension income"	Ensuring that variable benefits paid from the Saskatchewan Pension Plan are eligible for the pension credit and pension income splitting	May 11, 2018
86.1(2)	Prescribed distribution for 86.1 foreign spinoff rules: Svenska Cellulosa Aktiebolaget's distribution of Essity Aktiebolag shares	April 30, 2018
90(6)–(15)	Adding deemed repayment provisions to the upstream loan rules	May 1, 2018
95(2)(*b*)	Removing income from FAPI where it arises from the payment of inter-company service fees of two FAs where certain conditions are met	December 23, 2016
95(2)(*b*)	Foreign accrual property income resulting from the application of paragraph 95(2)(*b*) of the *Income Tax Act* to inter-affiliate payments for services	June 12, 2017
142.2(1) "financial institution"	Exempting a particular financial institution from the mark-to-market rules	June 18, 2018
144.1(2)	Employee Life and Health Trust Making Loan To an Investment In a Participating Employer	December 19, 2012
Income Tax Regulations		
6802	Trust and partnership used to fund registered pension plan not considered Retirement Compensation Arrangements	June 19, 2017
8514	A person or partnership in which a Registered Pension Plan invests not a prohibited investment	June 12, 2017
9002.1	Shares held by financial institutions prescribed to be "excluded property" under subsection 142.2(1)	January 30, 2018

SECTIONAL LIST OF THE INCOME TAX ACT

[R.S.C. 1985 (5th Supp.), c. 1 as amended.]

New provisions added by any of the proposed amendments reproduced throughout the text of the Act are included in the list preceded by the prefix "Prop.".

Section	Subject
1	Short Title

PART I
INCOME TAX

DIVISION A LIABILITY FOR TAX

Section	Subject
2(1)	Tax payable by persons resident in Canada
2(2)	Taxable income
2(3)	Tax payable by non-resident persons

DIVISION B COMPUTATION OF INCOME

Section	Subject
3	Income for taxation year
4(1)	Income or loss from a source or from sources in a place
4(2)	Idem
4(3)	Deductions applicable
4(4)	Limitation respecting inclusions and deductions (Repealed.)

SUBDIVISION A
INCOME OR LOSS FROM AN OFFICE OR EMPLOYMENT

Section	Subject
5(1)	Income from office or employment
5(2)	Loss from office or employment
6(1)	Amounts to be included as income from office or employment
6(1)(*a*)	Value of benefits
6(1)(*b*)	Personal or living expenses
6(1)(*c*)	Director's or other fees
6(1)(*d*)	Allocations, etc., under profit sharing plan
6(1)(*e*)	Standby charge for automobile
6(1)(*e*.1)	Group sickness or accident insurance plans
6(1)(*f*)	Employment insurance benefits
6(1)(*f*.1)	Canadian Forces members and veterans amounts
6(1)(*g*)	Employee benefit plan benefits
6(1)(*h*)	Employee trust
6(1)(*i*)	Salary deferral arrangement payments
6(1)(*j*)	Reimbursements and awards
6(1)(*k*)	Automobile operating expense benefit
6(1)(*l*)	Where standby charge does not apply
6(1.1)	Parking cost
6(1.2)	Deeming rule — amount received
6(2)	Reasonable standby charge
6(2.1)	Automobile salesman
6(2.2)	Benefit re auto operation (Repealed.)
6(3)	Payments by employer to employee
6(3.1)	Amount receivable for covenant
6(4)	Group term life insurance
6(5)	Reference to policy year ending in taxation year (Repealed.)
6(6)	Employment at special work site or remote location
6(7)	Cost of property or service
6(8)	GST rebates re costs of property or service
6(9)	Amount in respect of interest on employee debt
6(10)	Contributions to an employee benefit plan
6(11)	Salary deferral arrangement
6(12)	Idem
6(13)	Application
6(14)	Part of plan or arrangement
6(15)	Forgiveness of employee debt
6(15.1)	Forgiven amount
6(16)	Disability-related employment benefits
6(17)	Definitions
	"disability policy"
	"employer"
	"top-up disability payment"
6(18)	Group disability benefits — insolvent insurer
6(19)	Benefit re housing loss
6(20)	Benefit re eligible housing loss
6(21)	Housing loss
6(22)	Eligible housing loss
6(23)	Employer-provided housing subsidies
7(1)	Agreement to issue securities to employees
7(1.1)	Employee stock options
7(1.11)	Non-arm's length relationship with trusts
7(1.2)	Idem (Repealed.)
7(1.3)	Order of disposition of securities
7(1.31)	Disposition of newly-acquired security
7(1.4)	Exchange of options
7(1.5)	Rules where securities exchanged
7(1.6)	Emigrant
7(1.7)	Rights ceasing to be exercisable
7(2)	Securities held by trustee
7(3)	Special provision
7(4)	Application of s. (1)
7(5)	Non-application of this section
7(6)	Sale to trustee for employees
7(7)	Definitions
	"qualifying person"
	"security"

Section	Subject
7(8)	Deferral in respect of non-CCPC employee options (Repealed.)
7(9)	Meaning of "qualifying acquisition" (Repealed.)
7(9.1)	Reorganization (Repealed.)
7(10)	Election for the purpose of subsection (8) (Repealed.)
7(11)	Meaning of "specified value" (Repealed.)
7(12)	Identical options — order of exercise (Repealed.)
7(13)	Revoked election (Repealed.)
7(14)	Deferral deemed valid (Repealed.)
7(15)	Withholding (Repealed.)
7(16)	Prescribed form for deferral
8(1)	Deductions allowed
8(1)(*a*)	Volunteers' deduction (Repealed.)
8(1)(*b*)	Legal expenses of employee
8(1)(*c*)	Clergy residence
8(1)(*d*)	Teachers' exchange fund contribution
8(1)(*e*)	Expenses of railway employees
8(1)(*f*)	Sales expenses
8(1)(*g*)	Transport employee's expenses
8(1)(*h*)	Travel expenses
8(1)(*h*.1)	Motor vehicle travel expenses
8(1)(*i*)	Dues and other expenses of performing duties
8(1)(*j*)	Motor vehicle and aircraft costs
8(1)(*k*)	Unemployment insurance premium (Repealed.)
8(1)(*l*)	Canada Pension Plan contribution (Repealed.)
8(1)(*l*.1)	C.P.P. contributions and U.I.A. [E.I.] premiums
8(1)(*l*.2)	Quebec parental insurance plan
8(1)(*m*)	Employee's registered pension plan contributions
8(1)(*m*.1)	Idem (Repealed.)
8(1)(*m*.2)	Employee RCA contributions
8(1)(*n*)	Salary reimbursement
8(1)(*n*.1)	Reimbursement of disability payments
8(1)(*o*)	Forfeited amounts
8(1)(*o*.1)	Idem
8(1)(*o*.2)	Excess EPSP amounts
8(1)(*p*)	Musical instrument costs
8(1)(*q*)	Artists' employment expenses
8(1)(*r*)	Apprentice mechanics' tool costs
8(1)(*s*)	Deduction — tradesperson's tools
8(2)	General limitation
8(3)	Limitation re employment expense deduction (Repealed.)
8(4)	Meals
8(5)	Dues not deductible
8(6)	Apprentice mechanics
8(6.1)	Eligible tool of tradesperson
8(7)	Cost of tool
8(8)	Employees' contributions to pension fund for arrears (Repealed.)
8(9)	Presumption
8(10)	Certificate of employer
8(11)	Goods and services tax
8(12)	Forfeiture of securities by employee
8(13)	Work space in home

SUBDIVISION B
INCOME OR LOSS FROM A BUSINESS OR PROPERTY

Section	Subject
9(1)	Income
9(2)	Loss
9(3)	Gains and losses not included
10(1)	Valuation of inventory
10(1.01)	Adventures in the nature of trade
10(1.1)	Certain expenses included in cost
10(2)	Continuation of valuation
10(2.1)	Methods of valuation to be the same
10(3)	Incorrect valuation
10(4)	Fair market value
10(5)	Inventory
10(6)	Artistic endeavour
10(7)	Value in later years
10(8)	Definition of "business that is an individual's artistic endeavour"
10(9)	Transition
10(10)	Loss restriction event
10(11)	Loss restriction event
10(12)	Removing property from inventory
10(13)	Adding property to inventory
10(14)	Work in progress
Pend. 10(14)	Work in progress (Repealed.)
10(14.1)	Work in progress — transitional
Pend. 10(14.1)	Work in progress — transitional (Repealed.)
10(15)	Derivatives
10.1(1)	Mark-to-market election
10.1(2)	Revocation
10.1(3)	Subsequent election
10.1(4)	Application
10.1(5)	Definition of *eligible derivative*
10.1(6)	Deemed disposition
10.1(7)	Election year — gains and losses
10.1(8)	Default realization method
10.1(9)	Interpretation
11(1)	Proprietor of business
11(2)	Reference to "taxation year"
12(1)	Income inclusions
12(1)(*a*)	Services, etc., to be rendered
12(1)(*b*)	Amounts receivable
12(1)(*c*)	Interest
12(1)(*d*)	Reserve for doubtful debts
12(1)(*d*.1)	Reserve for guarantees, etc.
12(1)(*e*)	Reserves for certain goods and services, etc.
12(1)(*e*.1)	Negative reserves
12(1)(*f*)	Insurance proceeds expended
12(1)(*g*)	Payments based on production or use
12(1)(*g*.1)	Proceeds of disposition of right to receive production
12(1)(*h*)	Previous reserve for quadrennial survey
12(1)(*i*)	Bad debts recovered
12(1)(*i*.1)	Bad debts recovered
12(1)(*j*)	Dividends from resident corporations
12(1)(*k*)	Foreign corporations, trusts and investment entities
12(1)(*l*)	Partnership income
12(1)(*l*.1)	Partnership — interest deduction add back
12(1)(*m*)	Benefits from trusts
12(1)(*n*)	Employees profit sharing plan
12(1)(*n*.1)	Employee benefit plan
12(1)(*n*.2)	Forfeited salary deferral amounts
12(1)(*n*.3)	Retirement compensation arrangement
12(1)(*o*)	Royalties, etc. (Repealed.)
12(1)(*o*.1)	Foreign oil and gas production taxes
12(1)(*p*)	Certain payments to farmers
12(1)(*q*)	Employment tax deduction
12(1)(*r*)	Inventory adjustment
12(1)(*s*)	Reinsurance commission (Repealed.)
12(1)(*t*)	Investment tax credit
12(1)(*u*)	Home insulation or energy conversion grants
12(1)(*v*)	Research and development deductions
12(1)(*w*)	S. 80.4(1) benefit

Section	Subject
12(1)(*x*)	Inducement, reimbursement, etc.
12(1)(*x*.1)	Fuel tax rebates
12(1)(*x*.2)	Crown charge rebates
12(1)(*y*)	Automobile provided to partner
12(1)(*z*)	Amateur athlete trust payments
12(1)(*z*.1)	Qualifying environmental trusts
12(1)(*z*.2)	Dispositions of interests in qualifying environmental trusts
12(1)(*z*.3)	Debt forgiveness
12(1)(*z*.4)	Eligible funeral arrangements
12(1)(*z*.5)	TFSA amounts
12(1)(*z*.6)	Refunds
12(1)(*z*.7)	Derivative forward agreement
12(2)	Interpretation
12(2.01)	No deferral of section 9 income under paragraph (1)(g)
12(2.02)	Source of income
12(2.1)	Receipt of inducement, reimbursement, etc
12(2.2)	Deemed outlay or expense
12(3)	Interest income
12(4)	Interest from investment contract
12(4.1)	Impaired debt obligations
12(5)–(8)	(Repealed.)
12(9)	Deemed accrual
12(9.1)	Exclusion of proceeds of disposition
12(10)	Application (Repealed.)
12(10.1)	Income from R.H.O.S.P
12(10.2)	NISA receipts
12(10.3)	Amount credited or added not included in income
12(10.4)	Acquisition of control — corporate NISA Fund No. 2
12(11)	Definitions
	"anniversary day"
	"investment contract"
12.1	Cash bonus on Canada Savings Bonds
12.2(1)	Amount to be included
12.2(2)	Interest not disposed of before 1985 (Repealed.)
12.2(3)	Amounts included in income (Repealed.)
12.2(4)	Election (Repealed.)
12.2(4.1)	Revocation of election (Repealed.)
12.2(5)	Idem
12.2(6)	Application (Repealed.)
12.2(7)	Idem (Repealed.)
12.2(8)	Deemed acquisition of interest in annuity
12.2(9)	Rules where premium paid (Repealed.)
12.2(10)	Riders
12.2(11)	Definitions
	"anniversary day"
	"exempt policy"
12.2(12)	Application of ss. 138(12) and 148(9)
12.2(13)	Application of s. 148(10)
12.3	Transition inclusion re unpaid claims reserve (Repealed.)
12.4	Bad debt inclusion
12.5(1)	Definitions
	"base year"
	"insurance business"
	"reserve transition amount"
	"transition year"
12.5(2)	Transition year income inclusion
12.5(3)	Transition year income deduction reversal
12.5(4)	Winding-up
12.5(5)	Amalgamations
12.5(6)	Application of subsection (7)
12.5(7)	Transfer of insurance business
12.5(8)	Ceasing to carry on business
12.5(9)	Ceasing to exist
12.6(1)	Definitions
12.6(2)	Where subsection (3) applies

Section	Subject
12.6(3)	Income inclusion
12.6(4)	Deemed excess
13(1)	Recaptured depreciation
13(1.1)	Idem (Repealed.)
13(2)	Idem
13(3)	"Taxation year", "year" and "income" of individual
13(4)	Exchanges of property
13(4.1)	Replacement for a former property
13(4.2)	Election — limited period franchise, concession or license
13(4.3)	Effect of election
13(5)	Reclassification of property
13(5.1)	Rules applicable
13(5.2)	Deemed cost and depreciation
13(5.3)	Deemed recapture
13(5.4)	Idem
13(5.5)	Lease cancellation payment
13(6)	Misclassified property
13(7)	Rules applicable
13(7.1)	Deemed capital cost of certain property
13(7.2)	Receipt of public assistance
13(7.3)	Control of corporations by one trustee
13(7.4)	Deemed capital cost
13(7.41)	Deemed capital cost
13(7.42)	Timing of deduction
13(7.5)	Deemed capital cost
13(8)	Disposition after ceasing business
13(9)	Meaning of "gaining or producing income"
13(10)	Deemed capital cost
13(11)	Deduction in respect of property used in performance of duties
13(12)	Application of para. 20(1)(cc)
13(13)	Deduction under Canadian Vessel Construction Assistance Act
13(14)	Conversion cost
13(15)	Where s. (1) and subdivision c do not apply
13(16)	Election concerning vessel
13(17)	Separate prescribed class concerning vessel
13(18)	Reassessments
13(18.1)	Ascertainment of certain property
13(19)	Disposition of deposit
13(20)	Idem
13(21)	Definitions
	"appropriate minister"
	"conversion"
	"conversion cost"
	"depreciable property"
	"disposition of property" (Repealed.)
	"proceeds of disposition"
	"timber resource property"
	"total depreciation"
	"undepreciated capital cost"
	"vessel"
13(21.1)	Disposition of building
13(21.2)	Loss on certain transfers
13(22)	Deduction for insurer (Repealed.)
13(23)	Deduction for life insurer (Repealed.)
13(23.1)	Application of s. 138(12) (Repealed.)
13(24)	Loss restriction event
13(25)	Affiliation — subsection (24)
13(26)	Restriction on deduction before available for use
13(27)	Interpretation — available for use
13(28)	Idem
13(29)	Idem
13(30)	Transfers of property
13(31)	Idem
13(32)	Leased property

Section	Subject
13(33)	Consideration given for depreciable property
13(34)	Goodwill
13(35)	Outlays not relating to property
13(36)	No addition to goodwill
13(37)	Receipts not relating to property
13(38)	Class 14.1 — transitional rules
13(39)	Class 14.1 — transitional rule
13(40)	Class 14.1 — transitional rule
13(41)	Class 14.1 — transitional rule
13(42)	Class 14.1 — transitional rules
14(1)	Eligible capital property — inclusion in income from business (Repealed.)
14(1.01)	Election re capital gain (Repealed.)
14(1.02)	Election re property acquired with pre-1972 outlays or expenditures (Repealed.)
14(1.03)	Non-application of subsections (1.01) and (1.02) (Repealed.)
14(1.1)	Deemed taxable capital gain (Repealed.)
14(1.2)	Deemed capital gain (Repealed.)
14(2)	Amount deemed payable (Repealed.)
14(3)	Acquisition of eligible capital property (Repealed.)
14(4)	References to "taxation year" or "year" (Repealed.)
14(5)	Definitions (Repealed.)
	"adjustment time" (Repealed.)
	"cumulative eligible capital" (Repealed.)
	"eligible capital expenditure" (Repealed.)
	"exempt gains balance" (Repealed.)
14(5.1)	Restrictive covenant amount (Repealed.)
14(6)	Exchange of property (Repealed.)
14(7)	Replacement property (Repealed.)
14(8)	Deemed residence in Canada (Repealed.)
14(9)	Effect of election under subsection 110.6(19) (Repealed.)
14(10)	Deemed eligible capital expenditure (Repealed.)
14(11)	Receipt of public assistance (Repealed.)
14(12)	Loss on certain transfers (Repealed.)
14(13)	Deemed identical property (Repealed.)
14(14)	Ceasing to use property in Canadian business (Repealed.)
14(15)	Beginning to use property in Canadian business (Repealed.)
15(1)	Benefit conferred on shareholder
15(1.1)	Conferring of benefit
15(1.2)	Forgiveness of shareholder debt
15(1.21)	Forgiven amount
15(1.3)	Cost of property or service
15(1.4)	Interpretation — subsection (1)
15(1.5)	Division of corporation under foreign laws
15(2)	Shareholder debt
15(2.1)	Meaning of connected
15(2.11)	Pertinent loan or indebtedness
15(2.12)	Late-filed elections
15(2.13)	Penalty for late-filed election
15(2.14)	Partnerships
15(2.15)	Mergers
15(2.16)	Back-to-back arrangement — application
15(2.17)	Back-to-back arrangement — consequences
15(2.18)	Back-to-back arrangement — conditions for deemed repayment
15(2.19)	Back-to-back arrangement — deemed repayment
15(2.191)	Negative amounts
15(2.192)	Back-to-back arrangement — definitions
	"funder"
	"funding arrangement"
	"specified right"
	"ultimate funder"
15(2.2)	When s. 15(2) not to apply — non-resident persons
15(2.3)	When s. 15(2) not to apply — ordinary lending business
15(2.4)	When s. 15(2) not to apply — certain employees
15(2.5)	When s. 15(2) not to apply — certain trusts
15(2.6)	When s. 15(2) not to apply — repayment within one year
15(2.7)	Employee of partnership
15(3)	Interest or dividend on income bond or debenture
15(4)	Idem, where corporation not resident
15(5)	Automobile benefit
15(6)	Application of ss. 6(2) (Repealed.)
15(7)	Application of ss. (1), (2) and (5)
15(8)	Where s. (2) does not apply (Repealed.)
15(9)	Deemed benefit to shareholder by corporation
15.1(1)	Interest on small business development bonds
15.1(2)	Rules for small business development bonds
15.1(3)	Definitions
	"eligible small business corporation"
	"joint election"
	"majority interest partner" (Repealed.)
	"property used for specified purposes" (Repealed.)
	"qualifying debt obligation"
	"small business development bond"
	"specified property" (Repealed.)
15.1(4)	Money borrowed
15.1(5)	False declaration
15.1(6)	Disqualification
15.1(7)	Exception
15.1(8)–(12)	[Small business development bonds] (Repealed.)
15.2(1)	Interest on small business bond
15.2(2)	Rules for small business bonds
15.2(3)	Definitions
	"eligible issuer"
	"joint election"
	"majority interest partner" (Repealed.)
	"qualifying debt obligation"
	"small business bond"
15.2(4)	Status of interest
15.2(5)	False declaration
15.2(6)	Partnerships
15.2(7)	Deemed eligible issuer
15.2(8)	Presumption (Repealed.)
15.2(9)	Penalty (Repealed.)
16(1)	Income and capital combined
16(2)	Obligation issued at discount
16(3)	Obligation issued at discount
16(4)	Where s. (1) does not apply
16(5)	Idem
16(6)	Indexed debt obligations
16(7)	Impaired indexed debt obligations
16.1(1)	Leasing properties
16.1(2)	Assignments and subleases
16.1(3)	Idem
16.1(4)	Amalgamations and windings-up
16.1(5)	Replacement property
16.1(6)	Additional property
16.1(7)	Renegotiation of lease
17(1)	Amount owing by non-resident
17(1.1)	Amount owing by non-resident
17(2)	Anti-avoidance rule — indirect loan
17(3)	Exception to anti-avoidance rule — indirect loan
17(4)	Anti-avoidance rule — loan through partnership
17(5)	Anti-avoidance rule — loan through trust
17(6)	Anti-avoidance rule — loan to partnership
17(7)	Exception
17(8)	Exception
17(8.1)	Borrowed money
17(8.2)	Deemed use
17(9)	Exception

Section	Subject
17(10)	Determination of whether related and controlled foreign affiliate status
17(11)	Determination of whether related
17(11.1)	Determination of whether persons related
17(11.2)	Back-to-back loans
17(11.3)	Determination of whether persons related
17(12)	Determination of controlled foreign affiliate status
17(13)	Extended definition of controlled foreign affiliate
17(14)	Anti-avoidance rule — where rights or shares issued, acquired or disposed of to avoid tax
17(15)	Definitions
	"controlled foreign affiliate"
	"exempt loan or transfer"
	"non-discretionary trust"
	"settlor"
17.1(1)	Deemed interest income — sections 15 and 212.3
17.1(2)	Acquisition of control
17.1(3)	Tax treaties
18(1)	General limitations
18(1)(*a*)	General limitation
18(1)(*b*)	Capital outlay or loss
18(1)(*c*)	Limitation re exempt income
18(1)(*d*)	Annual value of property
18(1)(*e*)	Reserves, etc.
18(1)(*e*.1)	Unpaid claims under insurance policies
18(1)(*f*)	Payments on discounted bonds
18(1)(*g*)	Payments on income bonds
18(1)(*h*)	Personal and living expenses
18(1)(*i*)	Limitation re employer's contribution under supplementary unemployment benefit plan
18(1)(*j*)	Limitation re employer's contribution under deferred profit sharing plan
18(1)(*k*)	Limitation re employer's contribution under profit sharing plan
18(1)(*l*)	Use of recreational facilities and club dues
18(1)(*l*.1)	Safety deposit box
18(1)(*m*)	Limitation re employee stock option expenses
18(1)(*n*)	Political contributions
18(1)(*o*)	Employee benefit plan contributions
18(1)(*o*.1)	Salary deferral arrangement
18(1)(*o*.2)	Retirement compensation arrangement
18(1)(*o*.3)	Employee life and health trust
18(1)(*p*)	Limitation re personal services business expenses
18(1)(*q*)	Limitation re cancellation of lease
18(1)(*r*)	Certain automobile expenses
18(1)(*s*)	Loans or lending assets
18(1)(*t*)	Payments under different acts
18(1)(*u*)	Fees — individual saving plans
18(1)(*v*)	Interest — authorized foreign bank
18(1)(*w*)	Underlying payments on qualified securities
18(1)(*x*)	Derivatives — lower of cost and market
18(1)(*y*)	Payment for shares
18(2)	Limit on certain interest and property tax
18(2.1)	Where taxpayer member of partnership
18(2.2)	Base level deduction
18(2.3)	Associated corporations
18(2.4)	Failure to file agreement
18(2.5)	Special rules for base level deduction
18(3)	Definitions
	"interest on debt relating to the acquisition of land"
	"land"
18(3.1)	Costs relating to construction of building or ownership of land
18(3.2)	Included costs
18(3.3)	Completion
18(3.4)	Where s. (3.1) does not apply
18(3.5)	Idem
18(3.6)	Undue delay

Section	Subject
18(3.7)	Commencement of footings
18(4)	Limitation on deduction of interest
18(5)	Definitions
	"beneficiary"
	"equity amount"
	"equity contribution"
	"outstanding debts to specified non-residents"
	"security interest"
	"specified beneficiary"
	"specified non-resident beneficiary"
	"specified non-resident shareholder"
	"specified proportion" (Repealed.)
	"specified right"
	"specified shareholder"
	"tax-paid earnings"
18(5.1)	Specified shareholder or specified beneficiary
18(5.2)	Specified shareholder or specified beneficiary
18(5.3)	Property used in business — cost attribution
18(5.4)	Rules — trust income
18(6)	Back-to-back loan arrangement
18(6.1)	Back-to-back loan arrangement
18(7)	Partnership debts and property
18(8)	Exception — foreign accrual property income
18(9)	Limitation respecting prepaid expenses
18(9.01)	Group term life insurance
18(9.02)	Application of subsection (9) to insurers
18(9.1)	Penalties, bonuses and rate-reduction payments
18(9.2)	Interest on debt obligations
18(9.3)	Interest on debt obligations
18(9.4)	Idem
18(9.5)	Idem
18(9.6)	Idem
18(9.7)	Idem
18(9.8)	Idem
18(10)	Employee benefit plan
18(11)	Limitation
18(12)	Work space in home
18(13)	When s. (15) applies to money lenders
18(14)	When s. (15) applies to adventurers in trade
18(15)	Loss on certain properties
18(16)	Deemed identical property
18(17)	Definitions
	"offsetting position"
	"position"
	"successor position"
	"unrecognized loss"
	"unrecognized profit"
18(18)	Application of subsection (19)
18(19)	Straddle losses
18(20)	Exceptions
18(21)	Application
18(22)	Different taxation years
18(23)	Different taxation years
18.1(1)	Definitions
	"matchable expenditure"
	"right to receive production"
	"tax benefit"
	"tax shelter"
	"taxpayer"
18.1(2)	Limitation on the deductibility of matchable expenditure
18.1(3)	Deduction of matchable expenditure
18.1(4)	Amount of deduction
18.1(5)	Special rules
18.1(6)	Proceeds of disposition considered income
18.1(7)	Arm's length disposition

Section	Subject
18.1(8)	Non-arm's length disposition
18.1(9)	Special case
18.1(10)	Amount of deduction if non-arm's length disposition
18.1(11)	Partnerships
18.1(12)	Identical property
18.1(13)	Application of section 143.2
18.1(14)	Debt obligations
18.1(15)	Non-application — risks ceded between insurers
18.1(16)	Non-application — no rights, tax benefits or shelters
18.1(17)	Revenue exception
18.2	[Double-dip financing] (Repealed.)
18.3(1)	Definitions
	"security"
	"stapled security"
	"subsidiary"
	"transition period"
18.3(2)	Property representing security
18.3(3)	Amounts not deductible
19(1)	Limitation re advertising expense — newspapers
19(2)	Idem (Repealed.)
19(3)	Where s. (1) does not apply
19(4)	Idem (Repealed.)
19(5)	Definitions
	"Canadian issue"
	"Canadian newspaper"
	"issue of a non-Canadian newspaper or periodical" (Repealed.)
	"substantially the same" (Repealed.)
	"United States"
19(5.1)	Interpretation
19(6)	Trust property
19(7)	Grace period
19(8)	Non-Canadian newspaper
19.01(1)	Definitions
	"advertisement directed at the Canadian market"
	"original editorial content"
	"periodical"
19.01(2)	Limitation re advertising expenses — periodicals
19.01(3)	100% deduction
19.01(4)	50% deduction
19.01(5)	Application
19.01(6)	Editions of issues
19.1(1)	Limitation re advertising expense on broadcasting undertaking
19.1(2)	Exception
19.1(3)	Limitation to exception in paragraph (2)(a) (Repealed.)
19.1(4)	Definitions
	"foreign broadcasting undertaking"
	"network"
20(1)	Deductions permitted in computing income from business or property
20(1)(*a*)	Capital cost of property
20(1)(*b*)	Incorporation expenses
20(1)(*c*)	Interest
20(1)(*d*)	Compound interest
20(1)(*e*)	Expenses re financing
20(1)(*e*.1)	Annual fees, etc.
20(1)(*e*.2)	Premiums on life insurance used as collateral
20(1)(*f*)	Discount on certain obligations
20(1)(*g*)	Share transfer and other fees
20(1)(*h*)	Certification fee paid to a bank (Repealed.)
20(1)(*i*)	Sale of bill (Repealed.)
20(1)(*j*)	Repayment of loan by shareholder
20(1)(*k*)	Combined income and capital (Repealed.)
20(1)(*l*)	Doubtful or impaired debts
20(1)(*l*.1)	Reserve for guarantees, etc.
20(1)(*m*)	Reserve in respect of certain goods and services
20(1)(*m*.1)	Manufacturer's warranty reserve
20(1)(*m*.2)	Repayment of amount previously included in income
20(1)(*m*.3)	[Reserve for bond premiums]
20(1)(*n*)	Reserve for unpaid amounts
20(1)(*o*)	Reserve for quadrennial survey
20(1)(*p*)	Bad debts
20(1)(*q*)	Employer's contributions to RPP or PRPP
20(1)(*r*)	Employer's contributions under retirement compensation arrangement
20(1)(*s*)	Employer's contributions under employee life and health trust
20(1)(*t*)	Scientific research and experimental development (Repealed.)
20(1)(*u*)	Patronage dividends
20(1)(*v*)	Mining taxes
20(1)(*v*.1)	Resource allowance (Repealed.)
20(1)(*w*)	Employer's contributions under profit sharing plan
20(1)(*x*)	Employer's contributions under registered supplementary unemployment benefit plan
20(1)(*y*)	Employer's contributions under deferred profit sharing plan
20(1)(*z*)	Cancellation of lease
20(1)(*z*.1)	Idem
20(1)(*aa*)	Landscaping of grounds
20(1)(*bb*)	Fees paid to investment counsel
20(1)(*cc*)	Expenses of representation
20(1)(*dd*)	Investigation of site
20(1)(*ee*)	Utilities service connection
20(1)(*ff*)	Payments by farmers
20(1)(*gg*)	Disability-related modifications to buildings (Repealed.)
20(1)(*hh*)	Repayments of inducements, etc.
20(1)(*hh*.1)	Repayment of obligation
20(1)(*ii*)	Inventory adjustment
20(1)(*jj*)	Reinsurance commission (Repealed.)
20(1)(*kk*)	Exploration and development grants
20(1)(*ll*)	Repayment of interest
20(1)(*mm*)	Cost of substances injected in reservoir
20(1)(*nn*)	Part XII.6 tax
20(1)(*nn*.1)	Recapture of investment tax credits — child care space amount status (Repealed.)
20(1)(*oo*)	Salary deferral arrangement
20(1)(*pp*)	Idem
20(1)(*qq*)	Disability-related modifications to buildings
20(1)(*rr*)	Disability-related equipment
20(1)(*ss*)	Qualifying environmental trusts
20(1)(*tt*)	Acquisition of interests in qualifying environmental trusts
20(1)(*uu*)	Debt forgiveness
20(1)(*vv*)	Countervailing or anti-dumping duty
20(1)(*ww*)	Split income
20(1)(*xx*)	Derivative forward agreement
20(1.1)	Application of s. 13(21)
20(1.2)	Application of s. 12.2(11)
20(2)	Borrowed money
20(2.01)	Limitation of expression "interest" — 10/8 policy
20(2.1)	Limitation of expression "interest"
20(2.2)	Limitation of expression "life insurance policy"
20(2.3)	Sectoral reserve
20(2.4)	Specified percentage
20(3)	Borrowed money
20(4)	Bad debts — dispositions of depreciable property
20(4.1)	Idem
20(4.11)	Bad debts — zero-emission passenger vehicles
20(4.2)	Former eligible capital property
20(4.3)	Deemed allowable capital loss (Repealed.)
20(5)	Sale of agreement for sale, mortgage or hypothecary claim included in proceeds of disposition

Section	Subject
20(5.1)	Sale of agreement for sale, mortgage or hypothecary claim included in proceeds of disposition
20(6)	Special reserves
20(7)	Where para. (1)(m) does not apply
20(8)	No deduction in respect of property in certain circumstances
20(9)	Application of para. (1)(cc)
20(10)	Convention expenses
20(11)	Foreign taxes on income from property exceeding 15%
20(12)	Foreign non-business income tax
20(12.1)	Foreign tax where no economic profit
20(13)	Deductions under subdivision i
20(14)	Accrued bond interest
20(14.1)	Interest on debt obligation
20(14.2)	Sales of linked notes
20(15)	Regulations (Repealed.)
20(16)	Terminal loss
20(16.1)	Non-application of subsection (16)
20(16.2)	Reference to "taxation year" and "year" of individual
20(16.3)	Disposition after ceasing business
20(17)	Reduction of inventory allowance deduction (Repealed.)
20(18)	Definitions (Repealed.)
20(19)	Annuity contract
20(20)	Life insurance policy
20(21)	Debt obligation
20(22)	Deduction for negative reserves
20(23)	"Member's portion" (Repealed.)
20(24)	Amounts paid for undertaking future obligations
20(25)	Manner of election
20(26)	Transition deduction re unpaid claims reserve (Repealed.)
20(27)	Loans, etc., acquired in ordinary course of business
20(27.1)	Application of ss. 13(21) and 138(12)
20(28)	Deduction before available for use
20(29)	Idem
20(30)	Specified reserve adjustment
20.01(1)	PHSP premiums
20.01(2)	Limit
20.01(3)	Equivalent coverage
20.1(1)	Borrowed money used to earn income from property
20.1(2)	Borrowed money used to earn income from business
20.1(3)	Deemed dispositions
20.1(4)	Amount payable for property
20.1(5)	Interest in partnership
20.1(6)	Refinancings
20.2(1)	Interest — authorized foreign bank — interpretation
	"branch advance"
	"branch financial statements"
	"calculation period"
20.2(2)	Formula elements
20.2(3)	Interest deduction
20.2(4)	Branch amounts
20.2(5)	Notional interest
20.3(1)	Weak currency debt — interpretation
	"exchange date"
	"hedge"
	"weak currency debt"
20.3(2)	Interest and gain
20.3(3)	Hedges
20.3(4)	Repayment of principal
20.4(1)	Definitions
20.4(2)	Transition year income deduction
20.4(3)	Transition year income inclusion reversal
20.4(4)	Ceasing to carry on business
21(1)	Cost of borrowed money
21(2)	Borrowed money used for exploration or development
21(3)	Borrowing for depreciable property

Section	Subject
21(4)	Borrowing for exploration, etc
21(5)	Reassessments
22(1)	Sale of accounts receivable
22(2)	Statement by vendor and purchaser
23(1)	Sale of inventory
23(2)	Agreement as to price by vendor and purchaser (Repealed.)
23(3)	Reference to property in inventory
24(1)	Ceasing to carry on business (Repealed.)
24(2)	Business carried on by spouse or common-law partner or controlled corporation
24(3)	Where partnership has ceased to exist (Repealed.)
24.1	Judges
25(1)	Fiscal period of business disposed of by individual
25(2)	Election
25(3)	Dispositions in extended fiscal period
26(1)	Banks — inclusions in income
26(2)	Banks — deductions from income
26(3)	Write-offs and recoveries
26(4)	Definition of "Minister's rules"
27(1)	Application of Part I to Crown corporation
27(2)	Presumption
27(3)	Transfers of land for disposition
27.1(1)	Emissions allowances
27.1(2)	Determination of cost of emissions allowances
27.1(3)	Expense restriction
27.1(4)	Income inclusion in following year
27.1(5)	Proceeds of disposition
27.1(6)	Loss restriction event
28(1)	Farming or fishing business
28(1.1)	Acquisition of inventory
28(1.2)	Valuation of inventory
28(1.3)	Short fiscal period
28(2)	Where joint farming or fishing business
28(3)	Concurrence of Minister
28(4)	Non-resident
28(4.1)	Idem (Repealed.)
28(5)	Accounts receivable
29(1)	Disposition of animal of basic herd class
29(2)	Reduction in basic herd
29(3)	Interpretation
30	Improving land for farming
31(1)	Restricted farm loss
31(1.1)	Restricted farm loss
31(2)	Farming and manufacturing or processing
32(1)	Insurance agents and brokers
32(2)	Reserve to be included
32(3)	Additional reserve
32.1(1)	Employee benefit plan deductions
32.1(2)	Allocation
32.1(3)	Income of employee benefit plan
33	[Lending of money on security]
33.1	[International Banking Centres]
34	Professional business
Pend. 34	Professional business (Repealed.)
34.1(1)	Additional business income
34.1(2)	Additional income election
34.1(3)	Deduction
34.1(4)	Deemed December 31, 1995 income (Repealed.)
34.1(5)	Deemed December 31, 1995 income (Repealed.)
34.1(6)	Deemed December 31, 1995 income (Repealed.)
34.1(7)	Maximum December 31, 1995 income (Repealed.)
34.1(8)	No additional income inclusion
34.1(9)	Death of partner or proprietor
34.2(1)	Definitions
	"adjusted stub period accrual"
	"eligible alignment income"

Section	Subject
	"multi-tier alignment"
	"qualified resource expense"
	"qualifying transitional income"
	"significant interest"
	"single-tier alignment"
	"specified percentage"
34.2(2)	Income inclusion — adjusted stub period accrual
34.2(3)	Income inclusion — new partner designation
34.2(4)	Treatment in following year
34.2(5)	Character of amounts
34.2(6)	Designation — qualified resource expense
34.2(7)	No additional income — bankrupt
34.2(8)	Foreign affiliates
34.2(9)	Special case — multi-tier alignment
34.2(10)	Designations
34.2(11)	Transitional reserve
34.2(12)	Inclusion of prior year reserve
34.2(13)	No reserve
34.2(14)	Deemed partner
34.2(15)	Computing qualifying transitional income — special rules
34.2(16)	Qualifying transition income adjustment — conditions for application
34.2(17)	Adjustment of qualifying transitional income
34.2(18)	Anti-avoidance
34.3(1)	Definitions
	"actual stub period accrual"
	"base year"
	"income shortfall adjustment"
	"qualifying partnership"
34.3(2)	Application of subsection (3)
34.3(3)	Income shortfall adjustment — inclusion
35(1)	Prospectors and grubstakers
35(2)	Definitions
	"mining property"
	"prospector"
36	Railway companies (Repealed.)
37(1)	Scientific research and experimental development
37(1.1)	Business of related corporations
37(1.2)	Deemed time of capital expenditure
37(1.3)	SR&ED in the exclusive economic zone
37(1.4)	Salary or wages for SR&ED outside Canada
37(1.5)	Salary or wages outside Canada — limit determined
37(2)	Research outside Canada
37(3)	Minister may obtain advice
37(4)	Where no deduction allowed under section
37(5)	Where no deduction allowed under ss. 110.1 and 118.1
37(6)	Expenditures of a capital nature
37(6.1)	Loss restriction event
37(7)	Definitions
	"approved"
	"scientific research and experimental development" (Repealed.)
37(8)	Interpretation
37(9)	Salary or wages
37(9.1)	Limitation re specified employees
37(9.2)	Associated corporations
37(9.3)	Agreement among associated corporations
37(9.4)	Filing
37(9.5)	Deemed corporation
37(10)	Time for election
37(11)	Filing requirement
37(11.1)	Failure to file
37(12)	Misclassified expenditures
37(13)	Non-arm's length contract — linked work
37(14)	Look-through rule
37(15)	Reporting of certain payments
37.1	Additional allowance for scientific research and experimental development (Repealed.)
37.2	Application of s. 37.1 (Repealed.)
37.3	Application of ss. 37.1(1) and (2) (Repealed.)

SUBDIVISION C
TAXABLE CAPITAL GAINS AND ALLOWABLE CAPITAL LOSSES

Section	Subject
38	Taxable capital gain and allowable capital loss
38.1	Tax-deferred transaction — Flow-through shares
38.2	Allocation of gain re certain gifts
39(1)	Meaning of capital gain and capital loss
39(1.1)	Foreign currency dispositions by an individual
39(2)	Foreign exchange capital gains and losses
39(2.01)	Deemed gain — parked obligation
39(2.02)	Parked obligation
39(2.03)	Interpretation
39(2.1)	Upstream loans — transitional set-off
39(2.2)	Definition of *qualifying entity*
39(2.3)	Upstream loan — transitional set-off election
39(3)	Gain in respect of purchase of bonds, etc., by issuer
39(4)	Election concerning disposition of Canadian securities
39(4.1)	Members of partnerships
39(5)	Exception
39(6)	Definition of "Canadian security"
39(7)	Unused share-purchase tax credit
39(8)	Unused scientific research and experimental development tax credit
39(9)	Deduction from business investment loss
39(10)	Idem, of a trust
39(11)	Recovery of bad debt
39(12)	Guarantees
39(13)	Repayment of assistance
39.1(1)	Definitions
	"exempt capital gains balance"
	"flow-through entity"
39.1(2)	Reduction of capital gain
39.1(3)	Reduction of taxable capital gain
39.1(4)	Reduction in share of partnership's taxable capital gains
39.1(5)	Reduction in share of partnership's income from a business (Repealed.)
39.1(6)	Reduction of capital gains
39.1(7)	Nil exempt capital gains balance
40(1)	General rules
40(1.01)	Gift of non-qualifying security
40(1.1)	Reserve — property disposed of to a child
40(2)	Limitations
40(3)	Deemed gain where amounts to be deducted from adjusted cost base exceed cost plus amounts to be added to adjusted cost base
40(3.1)	Deemed gain for certain partners
40(3.11)	Amount of gain
40(3.111)	Meaning of "professional partnership"
40(3.12)	Deemed loss for certain partners
40(3.13)	Artificial transactions
40(3.131)	Specified member of a partnership
40(3.14)	Limited partner
40(3.15)	Excluded interest
40(3.16)	Amounts considered not to be substantial
40(3.17)	Whether carrying on business before February 22, 1994
40(3.18)	Deemed partner

Section	Subject
40(3.19)	Non-application of subsection (3)
40(3.2)	Non-application of subsection (3.1)
40(3.21)	Deemed capital gain under section 180.01
40(3.3)	When subsection (3.4) applies
40(3.4)	Loss on certain properties
40(3.5)	Deemed identical property
40(3.6)	Loss on shares
40(3.61)	Exception — estate loss carried back
40(3.7)	Losses of non-resident
40(4)	Disposal of principal residence to spouse or trust for spouse
40(5)	Where principal residence is property of trust for spouse (Repealed.)
40(6)	Principal residence — property owned at end of 1981
40(6.1)	Principal residence — property owned at end of 2016
40(7)	Property in satisfaction of interest in trust
40(7.1)	Effect of election under subsection 110.6(19)
40(8)	Application of s. 70(10)
40(9)	Additions to taxable Canadian property
40(10)	Application of subsection (11)
40(11)	Gain or loss on foreign currency debt
40(12)	Donated flow-through shares
40(13)	Class 14.1 — transitional rules
40(14)	Class 14.1 — transitional rules
40(15)	Class 14.1 — transitional rules
40(16)	Class 14.1 — transitional rules
41(1)	Taxable net gain from disposition of listed personal property
41(2)	Determination of net gain
41(3)	Definition of "listed-personal-property loss"
42(1)	Dispositions subject to warranty
42(2)	Meaning of "specified date"
43(1)	General rule for part dispositions
43(2)	Ecological gifts
43(3)	Payments out of trust income, etc.
43.1(1)	Life estates in real property
43.1(2)	Idem
44(1)	Exchanges of property
44(1.1)	Reserve — property disposed of to a child
44(2)	Time of disposition and of receipt of proceeds
44(3)	Where s. 70(3) does not apply
44(4)	Deemed election
44(5)	Replacement property
44(6)	Deemed proceeds of disposition
44(7)	Where subpara. (1)(e)(iii) does not apply
44(8)	Application of s. 70(10)
44.1(1)	Definitions
	"ACB reduction"
	"active business corporation"
	"carrying value"
	"common share"
	"eligible pooling arrangement"
	"eligible small business corporation"
	"eligible small business corporation share"
	"permitted deferral"
	"qualifying cost" (Repealed.)
	"qualifying disposition"
	"qualifying portion of a capital gain" (Repealed.)
	"qualifying portion of the proceeds of disposition" (Repealed.)
	"replacement share"
44.1(2)	Capital gain deferral
44.1(3)	Special rule — re eligible pooling arrangements
44.1(4)	Special rule — re acquisitions on death
44.1(5)	Special rule — re breakdown of relationships
44.1(6)	Special rule — re eligible small business corporation share exchanges
44.1(7)	Special rule — re active business corporation share exchanges
44.1(8)	Special rule — re carrying on an active business
44.1(9)	Special rule — re qualifying disposition
44.1(10)	Special rule — re exceptions
44.1(11)	Determination rule
44.1(12)	Anti-avoidance rule
44.1(13)	Order of disposition of shares
45(1)	Property with more than one use
45(2)	Election where change of use
45(3)	Election concerning principal residence
45(4)	Where election cannot be made
46(1)	Personal-use property
46(2)	Where part only of property disposed of
46(3)	Properties ordinarily disposed of as a set
46(4)	Decrease in value of personal-use property of corporation, etc
46(5)	Excluded property
47(1)	Identical properties
47(2)	Where identical properties are bonds, etc
47(3)	Securities acquired by employee
47(4)	Meaning of "property" (Repealed.)
47.1(26.1)	Application of s. 47.1 of R.S.C., 1952, c. 148
47.1(27)	Capital losses in 1986
47.1(28)	Transition for 1986
48(1)	Deemed disposition of property where taxpayer has ceased to be resident in Canada (Repealed.)
48(1.1)	Gains and losses from indexed security investment plans where taxpayer has ceased to be resident in Canada (Repealed.)
48(2)	Property in respect of which election made deemed to be taxable Canadian property (Repealed.)
48(3)	Deemed acquisition of property on becoming a resident of Canada (Repealed.)
48(4)	Exception where taxpayer resident in Canada for short term only (Repealed.)
48(5)	Where corporation becomes resident in Canada (Repealed.)
48.1(1)	Gain when small business corporation becomes public
48.1(2)	Time for election
48.1(3)	Late filed election
48.1(4)	Penalty for late filed election
48.1(5)	Unpaid balance of penalty
49(1)	Granting of options
49(2)	Expired option — shares
49(2.1)	Expired option — trust units
49(3)	Where option to acquire exercised
49(3.01)	Option to acquire specified property exercised
49(3.1)	Where option to dispose exercised
49(3.2)	Option granted before February 23, 1994
49(4)	Reassessment where option exercised in subsequent year
49(5)	Idem
49.1	No disposition where obligation satisfied
50(1)	Debts established to be bad debts and shares of bankrupt corporation
50(1.1)	Idem
50(2)	Where debt a personal-use property
50(3)	Disposal of R.H.O.S.P. properties
51(1)	Convertible property
51(2)	Idem
51(3)	Computation of paid-up capital
51(4)	Application
51.1	Conversion of debt obligation
52(1)	Cost of certain property the value of which is included in income
52(1.1)	Idem, where owner non-resident (Repealed.)
52(2)	Cost of property received as dividend in kind
52(3)	Cost of stock dividend

Sectional List of the Income Tax Act

Section	Subject
52(4)	Cost of property acquired as prize
52(5)	Cost of property transferred by trustee under employees profit sharing plan (Repealed.)
52(6)	Cost of right to receive from trust (Repealed.)
52(7)	Cost of shares of subsidiary
52(8)	Cost of shares of immigrant corporation
53(1)	Adjustments to cost base
53(1)(*a*)	[Adjustments to cost base — Deemed gain resulting from negative ACB]
53(1)(*b*)	[Adjustments to cost base — Deemed dividend]
53(1)(*b*.1)	[Adjustments to cost base — Deemed dividend from immigrating corporation]
53(1)(*c*)	[Adjustments to cost base — Contributions of capital]
53(1)(*d*)	[Adjustments to cost base — Share of foreign affiliate]
53(1)(*d*.01)	[Adjustments to cost base — Share of demutualized insurer]
53(1)(*d*.1)	[Adjustments to cost base — Capital interest in a trust]
53(1)(*d*.2)	[Adjustments to cost base — Unit in a mutual fund trust]
53(1)(*d*.3)	[Adjustments to cost base — Denied deduction for interest or soft costs]
53(1)(*e*)	[Adjustments to cost base — Interest in a partnership]
53(1)(*f*)	[Adjustments to cost base — Substituted property]
53(1)(*f*.1)	[Adjustments to cost base — Previously denied capital loss]
53(1)(*f*.11)	[Adjustments to cost base — Previously denied capital loss]
53(1)(*f*.12)	[Adjustments to cost base — Commercial obligation]
53(1)(*f*.2)	[Adjustments to cost base — Denied loss on transfer of shares to corporation]
53(1)(*g*)	[Adjustments to cost base — Obligation issued at a discount]
53(1)(*g*.1)	[Adjustments to cost base — Indexed debt obligation]
53(1)(*h*)	[Adjustments to cost base — Land]
53(1)(*i*)	[Adjustments to cost base — Land used in farming]
53(1)(*j*)	[Adjustments to cost base — Share or fund unit taxed as stock option benefit]
53(1)(*k*)	[Adjustments to cost base — Expropriation asset]
53(1)(*l*)	[Adjustments to cost base — Interest in related segregated fund trust]
53(1)(*m*)	[Adjustments to cost base — Offshore investment fund property]
53(1)(*n*)	[Adjustments to cost base — Costs of surveying or valuing property]
53(1)(*o*)	[Adjustments to cost base — Remainder interests in land]
53(1)(*p*)	[Adjustments to cost base — Flow-through entity, after 2004]
53(1)(*q*)	[Adjustments to cost base — Debt forgiveness]
53(1)(*r*)	[Adjustments to cost base — Flow-through entity, before 2005]
53(1)(*s*)	[Adjustments to cost base — Derivative forward agreement]
53(1)(*t*)	[Adjustments to cost base — Derivative forward agreement]
53(1.1)	Deemed contribution of capital
53(1.2)	Flow-through entity before 2005
53(2)	Amounts to be deducted
53(2)(*a*)	[Amounts to be deducted — Share of the capital stock of a corporation]
53(2)(*b*)	[Amounts to be deducted — Share of non-resident corporation]
53(2)(*b*.1)	[Amounts to be deducted — Capital interest in a non-resident trust]
53(2)(*b*.2)	[Amounts to be deducted — Non-depreciable capital property of a corporation]
53(2)(*c*)	[Amounts to be deducted — Interest in a partnership]
53(2)(*d*)	[Amounts to be deducted — Part dispositions]
53(2)(*e*)	[Amounts to be deducted — Share, where shareholder incurred exploration and development expenses]
53(2)(*f*)	[Amounts to be deducted — Property received from joint exploration corporation]
53(2)(*f*.1)	[Amounts to be deducted — Share of the capital stock of joint exploration corporation]
53(2)(*f*.2)	[Amounts to be deducted — Resource expenses renounced by joint exploration corporation]
53(2)(*g*)	[Amounts to be deducted — Debt forgiveness]
53(2)(*g*.1)	[Amounts to be deducted — Debt forgiveness]
53(2)(*h*)	[Amounts to be deducted — Capital interest in a trust]
53(2)(*i*)	[Amounts to be deducted — Capital interest in a non-resident trust]
53(2)(*j*)	[Amounts to be deducted — Non-resident unit trust]
53(2)(*k*)	[Amounts to be deducted — Government assistance]
53(2)(*l*)	[Amounts to be deducted — Accrued interest on transferred debt obligation]
53(2)(*l*.1)	[Amounts to be deducted — Indexed debt obligation]
53(2)(*m*)	[Amounts to be deducted — Deductible cost of property]
53(2)(*n*)	[Amounts to be deducted — Expropriation asset]
53(2)(*o*)	[Amounts to be deducted — Right to receive partnership property]
53(2)(*p*)	[Amounts to be deducted — Debt owing by a corporation]
53(2)(*q*)	[Amounts to be deducted — Interest in related segregated fund trust]
53(2)(*r*)	(Repealed.)
53(2)(*s*)	[Amounts to be deducted — Inducement payments]
53(2)(*t*)	[Amounts to be deducted — Right to acquire shares or units]
53(2)(*u*)	[Amounts to be deducted — Non-qualifying real property]
53(2)(*v*)	[Amounts to be deducted — Capital gains election]
53(2)(*w*)	[Amounts to be deducted — Derivative forward agreement]
53(2)(*x*)	[Amounts to be deducted — Derivative forward agreement]
53(2.1)	Election
53(3)	Application of paragraphs (2)(i) and (j) (Repealed.)
53(4)	Recomputation of adjusted cost base on transfers and deemed dispositions
53(5)	Recomputation of adjusted cost base on other transfer
53(6)	Recomputation of adjusted cost base on amalgamation
54	Definitions
	"adjusted cost base"
	"capital property"
	"disposition" (Repealed.)
	"eligible capital property" (Repealed.)
	"exemption threshold"
	"flow-through share class of property"
	"fresh-start date"
	"listed personal property"
	"personal-use property"
	"principal residence"
	"proceeds of disposition"
	"specified property"
	"superficial loss"
54.1(1)	Exception to principal residence rules
54.1(2)	Definition of "property"
54.2	Certain shares deemed to be capital property
55(1)	Definitions
	"distribution"
	"permitted acquisition"
	"permitted exchange"
	"permitted redemption"
	"qualified person"
	"safe-income determination time"
	"specified class"
	"specified corporation"
	"specified wholly-owned corporation"
55(2)	Deemed proceeds or gain
55(2.1)	Application of subsection (2)
55(2.2)	Special rule — amount of the stock dividend
55(2.3)	Stock dividends and safe income

Section	Subject
55(2.4)	Application of subsection (2.3)
55(2.5)	Determination of reduction in fair market value
55(3)	Application
55(3.01)	Interpretation for par. (3)(a)
55(3.02)	Distribution by a specified corporation
55(3.1)	Where paragraph (3)(b) not applicable
55(3.2)	Interpretation of paragraph (3.1)(b)
55(3.3)	Interpretation of "specified shareholder" changed
55(3.4)	Specified shareholder exclusion
55(3.5)	Amalgamation of related corporations
55(4)	Avoidance of subsection (2)
55(5)	Applicable rules
55(6)	Unlisted shares deemed listed

SUBDIVISION D
OTHER SOURCES OF INCOME

Section	Subject
56(1)	Amounts to be included in income for year
56(1)(*a*)	Pension benefits, unemployment insurance benefits, etc.
56(1)(*a*.1)	Benefits under CPP/QPP
56(1)(*a*.2)	Pension income reallocation
56(1)(*a*.3)	Parents of victims of crime
56(1)(*b*)	Support
56(1)(*c*)	Maintenance (Repealed.)
56(1)(*c*.1)	Idem (Repealed.)
56(1)(*c*.2)	Reimbursement of support payments
56(1)(*d*)	Annuity payments
56(1)(*d*.1)	Idem (Repealed.)
56(1)(*d*.2)	Idem
56(1)(*e*)	Disposition of income-averaging annuity contract
56(1)(*f*)	Idem
56(1)(*g*)	Supplementary unemployment benefit plan
56(1)(*h*)	Registered retirement savings plan, etc.
56(1)(*h*.1)	Home buyers' plan
56(1)(*h*.2)	Lifelong learning plan
56(1)(*i*)	Deferred profit sharing plan
56(1)(*j*)	Life insurance policy proceeds
56(1)(*k*)	Certain tools of an employee, re proceeds
56(1)(*l*)	Legal expenses
56(1)(*l*.1)	Idem
56(1)(*m*)	Bad debt recovered
56(1)(*n*)	Scholarships, bursaries, etc.
56(1)(*n*.1)	Apprenticeship grants
56(1)(*o*)	Research grants
56(1)(*p*)	Refund of scholarships, bursaries and research grants
56(1)(*q*)	Education savings plan payments
56(1)(*q*.1)	Registered disability savings plan payments
56(1)(*r*)	Financial assistance
56(1)(*s*)	Grants under prescribed programs
56(1)(*t*)	Registered retirement income fund
56(1)(*u*)	Social assistance payments
56(1)(*v*)	Worker's compensation
56(1)(*w*)	Salary deferral arrangement
56(1)(*x*)	Retirement compensation arrangement
56(1)(*y*)	Idem
56(1)(*z*)	Idem
56(1)(*z*.1)	Value of benefits
56(1)(*z*.2)	Employee life and health trust
56(1)(*z*.3)	Pooled registered pension plan
56(1)(*z*.4)	Tax informant program
56(1.1)	Application of s. 12.2(11)
56(2)	Indirect payments
56(3)	Exemption for scholarships, fellowships, bursaries and prizes
56(3.1)	Limitations of scholarship exemption
56(4)	Transfer of rights to income
56(4.1)	Interest free or low interest loans
56(4.2)	Exception
56(4.3)	Repayment of existing indebtedness
56(5)	Exception for split income
56(6)	Child care benefit
56(6.1)	Designation
56(7)	Idem (Repealed.)
56(8)	CPP/QPP and UCCB amounts for previous years
56(9)	Meaning of "income for the year"
56(9.1)	Meaning of "income"
56(10)	Severability of retirement compensation arrangement
56(11)	Disposition of property by RCA trust
56(12)	Foreign retirement arrangement (Repealed.)
56.1(1)	Support
56.1(2)	Agreement
56.1(3)	Prior payments
56.1(4)	Definitions
	"child support amount"
	"commencement day"
	"support amount"
56.2	Reserve claimed for debt forgiveness
56.3	Reserve claimed for debt forgiveness
56.4(1)	Definitions
	"eligible corporation"
	"eligible individual"
	"eligible interest"
	"goodwill amount"
	"permanent establishment"
	"restrictive covenant"
	"taxpayer"
56.4(2)	Income — restrictive covenants
56.4(3)	Non-application of subsection (2)
56.4(4)	Treatment of purchaser
56.4(5)	Non-application of section 68
56.4(6)	Application of subsection (5) — if employee provides covenant
56.4(7)	Application of subsection (5) — realization of goodwill amount and disposition of property
56.4(8)	Application of subsection (7) and section 69 — special rules
56.4(9)	Anti-avoidance rule — non-application of paragraph (3)(c)
56.4(10)	Anti-avoidance — non-application of subsection (7)
56.4(11)	Clarification if subsection (2) applies — where another person receives the amount
56.4(12)	Clarification if subsection (5) applies
56.4(13)	Filing of prescribed form
56.4(14)	Non-application of section 42
57(1)	Certain superannuation or pension benefits
57(2)	Exception
57(3)	Limitation
57(4)	Certain payments from pension plan
57(5)	Payments to widow, etc., of contributor
58(1)	Government annuities and like annuities
58(2)	Annuities before 1940
58(3)	Limitation
58(4)	Capital element
58(5)	Spouses or common-law partners
58(6)	Pension benefits
58(7)	Enlargement of annuity
59(1)	Consideration for foreign resource property
59(1.1)	Partnerships
59(1.2)	Idem (Repealed.)
59(2)	Deduction under former s. 64 in preceding year

Section	Subject
59(2.1)	Idem (Repealed.)
59(3)	Disposition of resource property acquired before 1972 (Repealed.)
59(3.1)	Idem (Repealed.)
59(3.2)	Recovery of exploration and development expenses
59(3.3)	Amounts to be included in income
59(3.4)	Definitions
	"specified predecessor"
	"stated percentage"
	"successor corporation"
59(3.5)	Variation of stated percentage
59(4)	Determination of "relevant percentage" (Repealed.)
59(5)	Definition of "proceeds of disposition"
59(6)	Definitions in regulations under s. 65
59.1	Involuntary disposition of resource property

SUBDIVISION E
DEDUCTIONS IN COMPUTING INCOME

Section	Subject
60	Other deductions
60(*a*)	Capital element of annuity payments
60(*b*)	Support
60(*c*)	Pension income reallocation
60(*c*.1)	Idem (Repealed.)
60(*c*.2)	Repayment of support payments
60(*d*)	Interest on death duties
60(*e*)	CPP/QPP contributions on self-employed earnings
60(*e*.1)	Enhanced CPP contributions
60(*f*)	Restrictive covenant — bad debt
60(*g*)	Quebec parental insurance plan — self-employed premiums
60(*h*)	Canada Pension Plan contributions (Repealed.)
60(*i*)	Premium or payment under RRSP or RRIF
60(*j*)	Transfer of superannuation benefits
60(*j*.01)	Transfer of surplus
60(*j*.02)	Payment to registered pension plan
60(*j*.03)	Repayments of pre-1990 pension benefits
60(*j*.04)	Repayments of post-1989 pension benefits
60(*j*.1)	Transfer of retiring allowances
60(*j*.2)	Transfer to spousal RRSP
60(*k*)	Transfers to deferred profit sharing plans (Repealed.)
60(*l*)	Transfer of refund of premiums under RRSP
60(*m*)	[Payments to registered disability savings plans]
60(*m*.1)	Succession duties applicable to certain property
60(*n*)	Repayment of pension or benefits
60(*n*.1)	Repayment of pension benefits
60(*o*)	Legal expenses
60(*o*.1)	Idem
60(*p*)	Repayment of apprenticeship grants
60(*q*)	Refund of income payments
60(*r*)	Amounts included under s. 146.2(6)
60(*s*)	Repayment of policy loan
60(*t*)	RCA distributions
60(*u*)	RCA dispositions
60(*v*)	Repayment — parents of victims of crime
60(*v*.1)	UI and EI benefit repayment
60(*w*)	Tax under Part I.2
60(*x*)	Repayment under Canada Education Savings Act
60(*y*)	Repayment of UCCB
60(*z*)	Repayment under the Canada Disability Savings Act
60(*z*.1)	Tax informant program
60.001	Application of subpara. 60(c.1)(i) (Repealed.)
60.01	Eligible amount
60.011(1)	Meaning of "lifetime benefit trust"
60.011(2)	Meaning of "qualifying trust annuity"
60.011(3)	Application of paragraph 60(l) to "qualifying trust annuity"
60.02(1)	Definitions
	"eligible individual"
	"eligible proceeds"
	"specified RDSP payment"
	"transitional eligible proceeds"
60.02(2)	Rollover to RDSP on death
60.02(3)	Application of subsections (4) and (5)
60.02(4)	Transitional rule
60.02(5)	Transitional rule — deceased taxpayer
60.02(6)	Limitation
60.021(1)	Additions to clause 60(l)(v)(B.2) for 2008
60.021(2)	Meaning of eligible RRIF withdrawal amount
60.021(3)	Meaning of eligible variable benefit withdrawal amount
60.021(4)	Expressions used in this section
60.022(1)	Additions to clause 60(l)(v)(B.2) for 2015
60.022(2)	Eligible RRIF withdrawal amount
60.022(3)	Eligible variable benefit withdrawal amount
60.022(4)	Eligible PRPP withdrawal amount
60.022(5)	Expressions used in this section
60.03(1)	Definitions
	"eligible pension income"
	"joint election"
	"pension income"
	"pension transferee"
	"pensioner"
	"qualified pension income"
	"split-pension amount"
60.03(2)	Effect of pension income split
60.03(3)	Limitation
60.03(4)	False declaration
60.1(1)	Support
60.1(2)	Agreement
60.1(3)	Prior payments
60.1(4)	Definitions
60.11	Application of subpara. 60.1(1)(a)(ii) (Repealed.)
60.2(1)	Refund of undeducted past service AVCs
60.2(2)	Definition of "balance of the annuitized voluntary contributions"
61(1)	Payment made as consideration for income-averaging annuity
61(2)	Idem
61(3)	Where income-averaging annuity contract ceases to be such (Repealed.)
61(4)	Definitions
	"annual annuity amount"
	"income-averaging annuity contract"
	"qualifying payment"
61.1(1)	Where income-averaging annuity contract ceases to be such
61.1(2)	Where annuitant dies and payments continued
61.2	Reserve for debt forgiveness for resident individuals
61.3(1)	Deduction for insolvency with respect to resident corporations
61.3(2)	Reserve for insolvency with respect to non-resident corporations
61.3(3)	Anti-avoidance
61.4	Reserve for debt forgiveness for corporations and others
62(1)	Moving expenses
62(2)	Moving expenses of students
62(3)	Definition of "moving expenses"
63(1)	Child care expenses
63(2)	Income exceeding income of supporting person

Section	Subject
63(2.1)	Taxpayer and supporting person with equal incomes
63(2.2)	Expenses while at school
63(2.3)	Amount deductible
63(3)	Definitions
	"annual child care expense amount"
	"child care expense"
	"earned income"
	"eligible child"
	"periodic child care expense amount"
	"supporting person"
63(4)	Commuter's child care expense
63.1	Application to deemed residents (Repealed.)
64	Disability supports deduction
64.1	Individuals absent from Canada
65(1)	Allowance for oil or gas well, mine or timber limit
65(2)	Regulations
65(3)	Lessee's share of allowance
66(1)	Exploration and development expenses of principal-business corporations
66(2)	Expenses of special product corporations
66(3)	Expenses of other taxpayers
66(4)	Foreign exploration and development expenses
66(4.1)	Country-by-country FEDE allocations
66(4.2)	Method of allocation
66(4.3)	FEDE deductions where change of individual's residence
66(5)	Dealers
66(6)	Successor corporation's Canadian exploration and development expenses (Repealed.)
66(7)	Second successor corporation's Canadian exploration and development expenses (Repealed.)
66(8)	Successor corporation's foreign exploration and development expenses (Repealed.)
66(9)	Second successor corporation's foreign exploration and development expenses (Repealed.)
66(10)	Joint exploration corporation (Repealed.)
66(10.1)	Idem (Repealed.)
66(10.2)	Idem (Repealed.)
66(10.3)	Idem (Repealed.)
66(10.4)	Idem
66(11)	Acquisition of control
66(11.1)	Idem (Repealed.)
66(11.2)	Idem (Repealed.)
66(11.3)	Control
66(11.4)	Loss restriction event
66(11.5)	Affiliation — subsection (11.4)
66(11.6)	Trust loss restriction event — successor
66(12)	Computation of exploration and development expenses
66(12.1)	Limitations of Canadian exploration and development expenses
66(12.2)	Unitized oil or gas field in Canada
66(12.3)	Idem
66(12.4)	Limitation of FEDE
66(12.41)	Limitations of foreign resource expenses
66(12.42)	Partnerships
66(12.5)	Unitized oil or gas field in Canada
66(12.6)	Canadian exploration expenses to flow-through shareholder
66(12.601)	Flow-through share rules for first $1 million of Canadian development expenses
66(12.6011)	Taxable capital amount
66(12.6012)	Taxable capital employed in Canada
66(12.6013)	Amalgamations and mergers
66(12.602)	Idem
66(12.61)	Effect of renunciation
66(12.62)	Canadian development expenses to flow-through shareholder
66(12.63)	Effect of renunciation
66(12.64)	Canadian oil and gas property expenses to flow-through shareholder (Repealed.)

Section	Subject
66(12.65)	Effect of renunciation (Repealed.)
66(12.66)	Expenses in the first 60 days of year
66(12.67)	Restrictions on renunciation
66(12.671)	Prohibited relationship
66(12.68)	Filing selling instruments
66(12.69)	Filing re partners
66(12.6901)	Consequences of failure to file
66(12.691)	Filing re assistance
66(12.7)	Filing re renunciation
66(12.7001)	Consequences of failure to file
66(12.701)	Filing re assistance
66(12.702)	Consequences of failure to file
66(12.71)	Restriction on renunciation
66(12.72)	Application of sections 231 to 231.3 (Repealed.)
66(12.73)	Reductions in renunciations
66(12.74)	Late filed forms
66(12.741)	Late renunciation
66(12.75)	Penalty
66(13)	Limitation
66(13.1)	Short taxation year
66(14)	Amounts deemed deductible under this subdivision
66(14.1)	Designation respecting Canadian exploration expense
66(14.2)	Designation respecting cumulative Canadian development expense
66(14.3)	Definition of "adjusted cumulative Canadian development expense"
66(14.4)	Special cases
66(14.5)	Penalty for late designation
66(14.6)	Deduction of carved-out income
66(15)	Definitions
	"agreed portion"
	"assistance"
	"Canadian exploration and development expenses"
	"Canadian resource property"
	"drilling or exploration expense"
	"expense"
	"flow-through share"
	"foreign exploration and development expenses"
	"foreign resource property"
	"joint exploration corporation"
	"original owner"
	"outlay"
	"predecessor owner"
	"principal-business corporation"
	"production"
	"reserve amount"
	"selling instrument"
	"shareholder corporation"
	"specified foreign exploration and development expense"
66(15.1)	Other definitions
66(16)	Partnerships
66(17)	Non-arm's length partnerships
66(18)	Members of partnerships
66(19)	Renunciation by corporate partner, etc
66(20)	Specified amount
66.1(1)	Amount to be included in income
66.1(2)	Deduction for certain principal-business corporations
66.1(3)	Expenses of other taxpayer
66.1(4)	Successor corporation's Canadian exploration expense (Repealed.)
66.1(5)	Second successor corporation's Canadian exploration expenses (Repealed.)
66.1(6)	Definitions
	"bitumen mine development project"
	"bitumen upgrading development project"
	"Canadian exploration expense"
	"Canadian renewable and conservation expense"

Section	Subject
	"completion"
	"cumulative Canadian exploration expense"
	"designated asset"
	"eligible oil sands mine development expense"
	"oil sands mine development project"
	"preliminary work activity"
	"restricted expense"
	"specified oil sands mine development expense"
	"specified oil sands mine development project"
	"specified purpose"
66.1(6.1)	Application of ss. 66(15), 66.2(5) and 66.4(5)
66.1(6.2)	Deductible expense
66.1(7)	Share of partner
66.1(8)	Expenses in first 60 days of year (Repealed.)
66.1(9)	Canadian development expenses for preceding years
66.1(10)	Certificate ceasing to be valid
66.1(11)	Second successor (Repealed.)
66.2(1)	Amount to be included in income
66.2(2)	Deduction for cumulative Canadian development expenses
66.2(3)	Successor corporation's Canadian development expense (Repealed.)
66.2(4)	Second successor corporation's Canadian development expense (Repealed.)
66.2(5)	Definitions
	"accelerated Canadian development expense"
	"Canadian development expense"
	"cumulative Canadian development expense"
66.2(5.1)	Application of ss. 66(15), 66.1(6) and 66.4(5)
66.2(6)	Share of partner
66.2(7)	Exception
66.2(8)	Presumption
66.21(1)	Definitions
	"adjusted cumulative foreign resource expense"
	"cumulative foreign resource expense"
	"foreign resource expense"
	"foreign resource income"
	"foreign resource loss"
	"global foreign resource limit"
66.21(2)	Application of subsection 66(15)
66.21(3)	Amount to be included in income
66.21(4)	Deduction for cumulative foreign resource expense
66.21(5)	Individual changing residence
66.3(1)	Exploration and development shares
66.3(2)	Deductions from paid-up capital
66.3(3)	Cost of flow-through shares
66.3(4)	Paid-up capital
66.4(1)	Recovery of costs
66.4(2)	Deduction for cumulative Canadian oil and gas property expense
66.4(3)	Successor corporation's Canadian oil and gas property expense (Repealed.)
66.4(4)	Second successor corporation's Canadian oil and gas property expense (Repealed.)
66.4(5)	Definitions
	"accelerated Canadian oil and gas property expense"
	"Canadian oil and gas property expense"
	"cumulative Canadian oil and gas property expense"
	"proceeds of disposition"
66.4(5.1)	Application of ss. 66(15) and 66.1(6)
66.4(6)	Share of partner
66.4(7)	Exception
66.5(1)	Deduction from income
66.5(2)	Definition of "cumulative offset account"
66.5(3)	Change of control
66.6	Acquisition from tax-exempt
66.7(1)	Successor of Canadian exploration and development expenses
66.7(2)	Successor of foreign exploration and development expenses
66.7(2.1)	Country-by-country successor FEDE allocations
66.7(2.2)	Method of allocation
66.7(2.3)	Successor of foreign resource expenses
66.7(3)	Successor of Canadian exploration expense
66.7(4)	Successor of Canadian development expense
66.7(5)	Successor of Canadian oil and gas property expense
66.7(6)	Where s. 29(25) of ITAR and ss. (1) to (5) do not apply
66.7(7)	Application of s. 29(25) of ITAR and ss. (1), (3), (4) and (5)
66.7(8)	Application of subsections (2) and (2.3)
66.7(9)	Canadian development expense becoming Canadian exploration expense
66.7(10)	Change of control
66.7(10.1)	Amalgamation — partnership property
66.7(11)	Idem
66.7(12)	Reduction of Canadian resource expenses
66.7(12.1)	Specified amount
66.7(13)	Reduction of foreign resource expenses
66.7(13.1)	Reduction of foreign resource expenses
66.7(13.2)	Specified amount — foreign resource expenses
66.7(14)	Disposal of Canadian resource properties
66.7(15)	Disposal of foreign resource properties
66.7(15.1)	Disposal of foreign resource properties — subsection (2.3)
66.7(16)	Non-successor acquisitions
66.7(17)	Restriction on deductions
66.7(18)	Application of interpretation provisions
66.8(1)	Resource expenses of limited partner
66.8(2)	Expenses in following fiscal period
66.8(3)	Interpretation

SUBDIVISION F
RULES RELATING TO COMPUTATION OF INCOME

Section	Subject
67	General limitation re expenses
67.1(1)	Expenses for food, etc
67.1(1.1)	Meal expenses for long-haul truck drivers
67.1(2)	Exceptions
67.1(3)	Fees for convention, etc
67.1(4)	Interpretation
67.1(5)	Definitions
	"eligible travel period"
	"long-haul truck"
	"long-haul truck driver"
	"specified percentage"
	"specified place"
67.2	Interest on money borrowed for certain vehicle
67.3	Limitation re cost of leasing passenger vehicle
67.4	More than one owner
67.5(1)	Non-deductibility of illegal payments
67.5(2)	Reassessments
67.6	Non-deductibility of fines and penalties
68	Allocation of amounts in consideration for property, services or restrictive covenants
69(1)	Inadequate considerations
69(1.1)	Idem, where s. 70(3) applies
69(1.2)	Idem
69(2)	Unreasonable consideration (Repealed.)
69(3)	Idem (Repealed.)
69(4)	Shareholder appropriations
69(5)	Idem
69(6)	Disposition of petroleum, etc (Repealed.)

Section	Subject
	"person"
	"property"
	"specified amount"
79(2)	Surrender of property
79(3)	Proceeds of disposition for debtor
79(4)	Subsequent payment by debtor
79(5)	Subsequent application with respect to employee or shareholder debt
79(6)	Surrender of property not payment or repayment by debtor
79(7)	Foreign exchange
79.1(1)	Definitions
	"creditor"
	"debt"
	"person"
	"property"
	"specified amount"
	"specified cost"
79.1(2)	Seizure of property
79.1(2.1)	Exception
79.1(3)	Creditor's capital gains reserves
79.1(4)	Creditor's inventory reserves
79.1(5)	Adjustment where disposition and reacquisition of capital property in same year
79.1(6)	Cost of seized properties for creditor
79.1(7)	Treatment of debt
79.1(8)	Claims for debts
80(1)	Definitions
	"commercial debt obligation"
	"commercial obligation"
	"debtor"
	"directed person"
	"distress preferred share"
	"eligible Canadian partnership"
	"excluded obligation"
	"excluded property"
	"excluded security"
	"forgiven amount"
	"person"
	"relevant loss balance"
	"successor pool"
	"unrecognized loss"
80(2)	Application of debt forgiveness rules
80(3)	Reductions of non-capital losses
80(4)	Reductions of capital losses
80(5)	Reductions with respect to depreciable property
80(6)	Restriction with respect to depreciable property
80(7)	Reductions of cumulative eligible capital (Repealed.)
80(8)	Reductions of resource expenditures
80(9)	Reductions of adjusted cost bases of capital properties
80(10)	Reduction of adjusted cost bases of certain shares and debts
80(11)	Reduction of adjusted cost bases of certain shares, debts and partnership interests
80(12)	Capital gain where current year capital loss
80(13)	Income inclusion
80(14)	Residual balance
80(14.1)	Gross tax attributes
80(15)	Members of partnerships
80(16)	Designations by Minister
80(17)	Income inclusion where residual balance a positive amount (Repealed.)
80(18)	Partnership designations
80.01(1)	Definitions
	"commercial debt obligation"
	"commercial obligation"
	"debtor"
	"distress preferred share"

Section	Subject
	"forgiven amount"
	"person"
	"specified cost"
80.01(2)	Application
80.01(3)	Deemed settlement on amalgamation
80.01(4)	Deemed settlement on winding-up
80.01(5)	Deemed settlement on winding-up
80.01(5.1)	Deemed settlement on SIFT trust wind-up event
80.01(6)	Specified obligation in relation to debt parking
80.01(7)	Parked obligation
80.01(8)	Deemed settlement after debt parking
80.01(9)	Statute-barred debt
80.01(10)	Subsequent payments in satisfaction of debt
80.01(11)	Foreign currency gains and losses
80.02(1)	Definitions
80.02(2)	General rules for distress preferred shares
80.02(3)	Substitution of distress preferred share for debt
80.02(4)	Substitution of commercial debt obligation for distress preferred share
80.02(5)	Substitution of distress preferred share for other distress preferred share
80.02(6)	Substitution of non-commercial obligation for distress preferred share
80.02(7)	Deemed settlement on expiry of term
80.03(1)	Definitions
80.03(2)	Deferred recognition of debtor's gain on settlement of debt
80.03(3)	Surrender of capital property
80.03(4)	Dispositions by corporations (Repealed.)
80.03(5)	Specified period (Repealed.)
80.03(6)	When property acquired (Repealed.)
80.03(7)	Alternative treatment
80.03(8)	Lifetime capital gains exemption
80.04(1)	Definitions
80.04(2)	Eligible transferee
80.04(3)	Application
80.04(4)	Agreement respecting transfer of forgiven amount
80.04(5)	Consideration for agreement
80.04(5.1)	No benefit conferred
80.04(6)	Manner of filing agreement
80.04(7)	Filing by partnership
80.04(8)	Related corporations
80.04(9)	Assessment of taxpayers in respect of agreement
80.04(10)	Liability of debtor
80.04(11)	Joint and several, or solidary, liability
80.04(12)	Assessments in respect of liability
80.04(13)	Application of Division I
80.04(14)	Partnership members
80.1(1)	Expropriation assets acquired as compensation for, or as consideration for sale of, foreign property taken by or sold to foreign issuer
80.1(2)	Election re interest received or to be received on expropriation assets acquired by taxpayer
80.1(3)	Where interest amount and capital amount received at same time
80.1(4)	Assets acquired from foreign affiliate of taxpayer as dividend in kind or as benefit to shareholder
80.1(5)	Assets acquired from foreign affiliate of taxpayer as consideration for settlement, etc., of debt
80.1(6)	Assets acquired from foreign affiliate of taxpayer on winding-up, etc
80.1(7)	Definition of "adjusted principal amount"
80.1(8)	Currency in which adjusted principal amount to be computed or expressed
80.1(9)	Election in respect of two or more expropriation assets acquired by taxpayer
80.2(1)	Application
80.2(2)	Rules relating to time of payment
80.2(3)	Applying paragraph 18(1)(m)
80.2(4)	Exception for certain partnership reimbursements

Section	Subject
80.2(5)	Specified amount deemed to be paid at end of taxation year
80.2(6)	Inclusion in recipient's income
80.2(7)	Interpretation — portion of the original amount
80.2(8)	Inclusion in recipient's income
80.2(9)	Deduction by taxpayer
80.2(10)	Specified amount deemed not to be payable or receivable
80.2(11)	Eligible portion of a specified amount
80.2(12)	Taxpayer's share of original amount
80.2(13)	Reduction in original amount for Part XII of the regulations
80.3(1)	Definitions
	"breeding animals"
	"breeding bee stock"
	"breeding bees"
	"breeding herd"
80.3(2)	Income deferral from the destruction of livestock
80.3(3)	Inclusion of deferred amount
80.3(4)	Income deferral for regions of drought, flood or excessive moisture
80.3(4.1)	Income deferral
80.3(5)	Inclusion of deferred amount
80.3(6)	Subsections (2), (4) and (4.1) not applicable
80.3(7)	Measuring breeding bee stock
80.4(1)	Loans
80.4(1.1)	Interpretation
80.4(2)	Idem
80.4(3)	Where ss. (1) and (2) do not apply
80.4(4)	Interest on loans for home purchase or relocation
80.4(5)	Idem
80.4(6)	Deemed new home purchase loans
80.4(7)	Definitions
	"home purchase loan"
	"prescribed rate"
	"specified interest amount"
80.4(8)	Meaning of connected
80.5	Deemed interest
80.6(1)	Synthetic disposition
80.6(2)	Exception

SUBDIVISION G
AMOUNTS NOT INCLUDED IN COMPUTING INCOME

Section	Subject
81(1)	Amounts not included in income
81(1)(*a*)	Statutory exemptions
81(1)(*b*)	War Savings Certificate
81(1)(*c*)	Ship or aircraft of non-residents
81(1)(*d*)	Service pension, allowance or compensation
81(1)(*d*.1)	Canadian Forces members and veterans amounts
81(1)(*e*)	War pensions
81(1)(*f*)	Halifax disaster pensions, grants or allowances
81(1)(*g*)	Compensation by Federal Republic of Germany
81(1)(*g*.1)	Income from personal injury award property
81(1)(*g*.2)	Income from income exempt under para. (g.1)
81(1)(*g*.3)	Certain government funded trusts
81(1)(*g*.4)	Relief for increased heating expenses
81(1)(*g*.5)	Energy cost relief
81(1)(*g*.6)	Ontario Electricity Support Program
81(1)(*h*)	Social assistance
81(1)(*h*.1)	Social assistance for informal care programs
81(1)(*i*)	R.C.M.P. pension or compensation
81(1)(*j*)	Memorial grant
81(1)(*k*)	Employees profit sharing plan
81(1)(*l*)	Prospecting
81(1)(*m*)	Interest on certain obligations
81(1)(*n*)	Governor General
81(1)(*o*)	RESP refunds (Repealed.)
81(1)(*p*)	Educational assistance payments (Repealed.)
81(1)(*q*)	Provincial indemnities
81(1)(*r*)	Foreign retirement arrangements
81(1)(*s*)	Salary deferral leave plans
81(1.1)	Interpretation (Repealed.)
81(2)	M.L.A.'s expense allowance (Repealed.)
81(3)	Municipal officers' expense allowance (Repealed.)
81(3.1)	Travel expenses
81(4)	Payments for volunteer services
81(5)	Election

SUBDIVISION H
CORPORATIONS RESIDENT IN CANADA AND THEIR SHAREHOLDERS

Section	Subject
82(1)	Taxable dividends received
82(1.1)	Limitation as to paragraph (1)(c)
82(2)	Certain dividends received by taxpayer
82(3)	Dividends received by spouse or common-law partner
83(1)	Qualifying dividends
83(2)	Capital dividend
83(2.1)	Idem
83(2.2)	Where s. 83(2.1) does not apply
83(2.3)	Idem
83(2.4)	Idem
83(3)	Late filed elections
83(3.1)	Request for election
83(4)	Penalty for late filed election
83(5)	Unpaid balance of penalty
83(6)	Definition of "qualifying dividend"
83(7)	Amalgamation where there are tax-deferred preferred shares
84(1)	Deemed dividend
84(2)	Distribution on winding-up, etc
84(3)	Redemption, etc.
84(4)	Reduction of paid-up capital
84(4.1)	Deemed dividend on reduction of paid-up capital
84(4.2)	Deemed dividend on term preferred share
84(4.3)	Deemed dividend on guaranteed share
84(5)	Amount distributed or paid where a share
84(6)	Where s. (2) or (3) does not apply
84(7)	When dividend payable
84(8)	Where s. (3) does not apply
84(9)	Shares disposed of on redemptions, etc
84(10)	Reduction of contributed surplus
84(11)	Computation of contributed surplus
84.1(1)	Non-arm's length sale of shares
84.1(2)	Idem
84.1(2.01)	Rules for par. 84.1(2)(a.1)
84.1(2.1)	Idem
84.1(2.2)	Rules for par. 84.1(2)(b)
84.1(3)	Addition to paid-up capital
84.2(1)	Computation of paid-up capital in respect of particular class of shares
84.2(2)	Debt deficiency
84.2(3)	Idem
85(1)	Transfer of property to corporation by shareholders
85(1.1)	Definition of "eligible property"
85(1.11)	Exception

Section	Subject
85(1.12)	Eligible derivatives
85(1.2)	Application of subsection (1)
85(1.3)	Meaning of "wholly owned corporation"
85(1.4)	Definitions
85(2)	Transfer of property to corporation from partnership
85(2.1)	Computing paid-up capital
85(3)	Where partnership wound up
85(4)	Loss from disposition to controlled corporation (Repealed.)
85(5)	Rules on transfers of depreciable property
85(5.1)	Acquisition of certain tools — capital cost and deemed depreciation
85(6)	Time for election
85(7)	Late filed election
85(7.1)	Special cases
85(8)	Penalty for late filed election
85(9)	Unpaid balance of penalty
85.1(1)	Share for share exchange
85.1(2)	Where s. (1) does not apply
85.1(2.1)	Computation of paid-up capital
85.1(2.2)	Issuance deemed made to vendor
85.1(3)	Disposition of shares of foreign affiliate
85.1(4)	Exception
85.1(5)	Foreign share for foreign share exchange
85.1(6)	Where subsection (5) does not apply
85.1(6.1)	Issuance deemed made to vendor
85.1(7)	Application of subsection (8)
85.1(8)	Rollover on SIFT unit for share exchange
86(1)	Exchange of shares by a shareholder in course of reorganization of capital
86(2)	Idem
86(2.1)	Computation of paid-up capital
86(3)	Application
86(4)	Computation of adjusted cost base
86.1(1)	Eligible distribution not included in income
86.1(2)	Eligible distribution
86.1(3)	Cost adjustments
86.1(4)	Inventory
86.1(5)	Reassessments
87(1)	Amalgamations
87(1.1)	Shares deemed to have been received by virtue of merger
87(1.2)	New corporation continuation of a predecessor
87(1.3)	Shareholder corporation (Repealed.)
87(1.4)	Definition of "subsidiary wholly-owned corporation"
87(1.5)	Definitions
87(2)	Rules applicable
87(2)(*a*)	Taxation year
87(2)(*b*)	Inventory
87(2)(*c*)	Method adopted for computing income
87(2)(*d*)	Depreciable property
87(2)(*d*.1)	Depreciable property acquired from predecessor corporation
87(2)(*e*)	Capital property
87(2)(*e*.1)	Partnership interest
87(2)(*e*.2)	Security or debt obligation
87(2)(*e*.3)	Financial institutions — specified debt obligation
87(2)(*e*.4)	Financial institutions — mark-to-market property
87(2)(*e*.41)	[Eligible derivative — cost amount]
87(2)(*e*.42)	[Continuation of predecessor corporation — eligible derivative]
87(2)(*e*.5)	Financial institutions — mark-to-market property
87(2)(*f*)	Eligible capital property (Repealed.)
87(2)(*f*.1)	Idem (Repealed.)
87(2)(*g*)	Reserves
87(2)(*g*.1)	Continuation
87(2)(*g*.2)	Financial institution rules
87(2)(*g*.3)	Superficial losses
87(2)(*g*.4)	Superficial losses — capital property
87(2)(*g*.5)	Patronage dividends
87(2)(*h*)	Debts
87(2)(*h*.1)	Debts
87(2)(*i*)	Special reserve
87(2)(*j*)	Special reserves
87(2)(*j*.1)	Inventory adjustment
87(2)(*j*.2)	Prepaid expenses and matchable expenditures
87(2)(*j*.3)	Employee benefit plans etc.
87(2)(*j*.4)	Accrual rules
87(2)(*j*.5)	Cancellation of lease
87(2)(*j*.6)	Continuing corporation
87(2)(*j*.7)	Certain transfers and loans
87(2)(*j*.8)	International banking centre business (Repealed.)
87(2)(*j*.9)	Part I.3 tax
87(2)(*j*.91)	Part I.3 and Part VI tax
87(2)(*j*.92)	Subsections 125(5.1) and 157.1(1)
87(2)(*j*.93)	Mining reclamation trusts
87(2)(*j*.94)	Film or video productions
87(2)(*j*.95)	Non-resident entities
87(2)(*j*.96)	Journalism organizations
87(2)(*k*)	Certain payments to employees
87(2)(*l*)	Scientific research and experimental development
87(2)(*l*.1)	Idem
87(2)(*l*.2)	Definition of "predecessor corporation"
87(2)(*l*.21)	Forgiven amount
87(2)(*l*.3)	Replacement property
87(2)(*l*.4)	Subsection 13(4.2) election
87(2)(*l*.5)	Contingent amount — section 143.4
87(2)(*m*)	Reserves
87(2)(*m*.1)	Gift of non-qualifying security
87(2)(*m*.2)	Gift of predecessor's property
87(2)(*n*)	Outlays made pursuant to warranty
87(2)(*o*)	Expiration of options previously granted
87(2)(*p*)	Consideration for resource property disposition
87(2)(*q*)	Registered plans
87(2)(*r*)	Employees profit sharing plan
87(2)(*s*)	Tax deferred cooperative shares
87(2)(*s*.1)	Deemed SIFT wind-up corporation
87(2)(*t*)	Pre-1972 capital surplus on hand
87(2)(*u*)	Shares of foreign affiliate
87(2)(*v*)	Gifts
87(2)(*w*)	Losses (Repealed.)
87(2)(*x*)	Taxable dividends
87(2)(*y*)	Contributed surplus
87(2)(*y*.1)	Preferred-earnings amount (Repealed.)
87(2)(*z*)	Foreign tax carryover
87(2)(*z*.1)	Capital dividend account
87(2)(*z*.2)	Application of Parts III and III.1
87(2)(*aa*)	Refundable dividend tax on hand
87(2)(*bb*)	Mutual fund and investment corporations
87(2)(*bb*.1)	Flow-through entities
87(2)(*cc*)	Non-resident-owned investment corporation
87(2)(*dd*)	Tax in respect of ineligible investments (Repealed.)
87(2)(*ee*)	Preferred-rate amount (Repealed.)
87(2)(*ff*)	Application of Part VII (Repealed.)
87(2)(*gg*)	Designated surplus (Repealed.)
87(2)(*hh*)	1971 undistributed income on hand (Repealed.)
87(2)(*ii*)	Public corporation
87(2)(*jj*)	Interest on certain obligations
87(2)(*kk*)	Disposition of shares of controlled corporation
87(2)(*ll*)	Para. 20(1)(n) and subpara. 40(1)(a)(iii) amounts
87(2)(*mm*)	Idem (Repealed.)
87(2)(*nn*)	Refundable Part VII tax on hand
87(2)(*oo*)	Investment tax credit (Repealed.)
87(2)(*oo*.1)	Refundable investment tax credit and balance-due day
87(2)(*pp*)	Cumulative offset account computation
87(2)(*qq*)	Continuation of corporation
87(2)(*rr*)	Tax on taxable preferred shares
87(2)(*ss*)	Transferred liability for Part VI.1 tax

Section	Subject
87(2)(*tt*)	Livestock — inclusion of deferred amount
87(2)(*uu*)	Fuel tax rebates
87(2)(*vv*)	General rate income pool
87(2)(*ww*)	Low rate income pool
87(2.01)	Application of s. 37.1(5)
87(2.1)	Non-capital losses, etc., of predecessor corporations
87(2.11)	Vertical amalgamations
87(2.2)	Amalgamation of insurers
87(2.3)	Quebec credit unions
87(3)	Computation of paid-up capital
87(3.1)	Election for non-application of subsection (3)
87(4)	Shares of predecessor corporation
87(4.1)	Exchanged shares
87(4.2)	Idem
87(4.3)	Exchanged rights
87(4.4)	Flow-through shares
87(5)	Options to acquire shares of predecessor corporation
87(5.1)	Adjusted cost base of option
87(6)	Obligations of predecessor corporation
87(6.1)	Adjusted cost base
87(7)	Idem
87(8)	Foreign merger
87(8.1)	Definition of "foreign merger"
87(8.2)	Absorptive mergers
87(8.3)	Anti-avoidance
87(8.4)	Taxable Canadian property — conditions for rollover
87(8.5)	Foreign merger — taxable Canadian property rollover
87(9)	Rules applicable in respect of certain mergers
87(10)	Share deemed listed
87(11)	Vertical amalgamations
88(1)	Winding-up
88(1)(*a*)	[Winding-up — Proceeds of disposition of subsidiary's property]
88(1)(*a*.1)	[Winding-up — Pre-1972 capital surplus of subsidiary]
88(1)(*a*.2)	[Winding-up — Partnership interest of subsidiary]
88(1)(*a*.3)	[Winding-up — Specified debt obligations of financial institutions]
88(1)(*b*)	[Winding-up — Disposition of shares of subsidiary]
88(1)(*c*)	[Winding-up — Cost of property received by parent]
88(1)(*c*.1)	[Winding-up — Eligible capital property] (Repealed.)
88(1)(*c*.2)	[Winding-up — Specified person and specified shareholder]
88(1)(*c*.3)	[Winding-up — Substituted property]
88(1)(*c*.4)	[Winding-up — Specified property]
88(1)(*c*.5)	[Winding-up — Specified subsidiary corporation]
88(1)(*c*.6)	[Winding-up — Control acquired by way of articles of arrangement]
88(1)(*c*.7)	[Winding-up — Leasehold interests in and options for depreciable property]
88(1)(*c*.8)	[Winding-up — Specified class of capital stock]
88(1)(*c*.9)	[Winding-up — Right to acquire share]
88(1)(*d*)	[Winding-up — Addition to cost of property acquired by parent (the "bump")]
88(1)(*d*.1)	[Winding-up — Provisions not applicable]
88(1)(*d*.2)	[Winding-up — Timing of acquisition of control]
88(1)(*d*.3)	[Winding-up — Control acquired as consequence of death]
88(1)(*e*)	[Winding-up — Fair market value of interest in partnership]
88(1)(*e*.1)	[Winding-up — Reserves for subsidiary]
88(1)(*e*.2)	[Winding-up — Application of amalgamation provisions]
88(1)(*e*.3)	[Winding-up — Investment tax credit]
88(1)(*e*.4)	[Winding-up — Employment tax credit]
88(1)(*e*.5)	[Winding-up — Refundable dividend tax on hand] (Repealed.)
88(1)(*e*.6)	[Winding-up — Charitable gifts]
88(1)(*e*.61)	[Winding-up — Donation of non-qualifying securities]
88(1)(*e*.7)	[Winding-up — Unused foreign tax credits of subsidiary]
88(1)(*e*.8)	[Winding-up — Expenditure limit of parent or associated corporation] (Repealed.)

Section	Subject
88(1)(*e*.9)	[Winding-up — Business limit and balance-due day of parent]
88(1)(*f*)	[Winding-up — Depreciable property]
88(1)(*g*)	[Winding-up — Insurance corporations]
88(1)(*h*)	[Winding-up — Stop-loss rules and mark-to-market property]
88(1)(*i*)	[Winding-up — Mark-to-market property]
88(1)(*j*)	[Winding-up — Eligible derivative]
88(1.1)	Non-capital losses, etc., of subsidiary
88(1.2)	Net capital losses of subsidiary
88(1.3)	Computation of income and tax of parent
88(1.4)	Qualified expenditure of subsidiary
88(1.41)	Application of s. 37.1(5)
88(1.5)	Parent continuation of subsidiary
88(1.6)	Idem
88(1.7)	Interpretation
88(1.8)	Application of subsection (1.9)
88(1.9)	Amended designation
88(2)	Winding-up of Canadian corporation
88(2.1)	Definition of "pre-1972 capital surplus on hand"
88(2.2)	Determination of pre-1972 capital surplus on hand
88(2.3)	Actual cost of certain depreciable property
88(3)	Liquidation and dissolution of foreign affiliate
88(3.1)	Qualifying liquidation and dissolution
88(3.2)	Net distribution amount
88(3.3)	Suppression election
88(3.4)	Conditions for subsection (3.3) election
88(3.5)	Taxable Canadian property
88(4)	Amalgamation deemed not to be acquisition of control
88.1(1)	Application
88.1(2)	SIFT trust wind-up event
89(1)	Definitions
	"adjusted taxable income"
	"Canadian corporation"
	"capital dividend account"
	"designated property"
	"eligible dividend"
	"excessive eligible dividend designation"
	"general rate factor"
	"general rate income pool"
	"Life insurance capital dividend account" (Repealed.)
	"low rate income pool"
	"paid-up capital"
	"private corporation"
	"public corporation"
	"taxable Canadian corporation"
	"taxable dividend"
89(1.01)	Application of s. 138(12)
89(1.1)	Capital dividend account where control acquired
89(1.2)	Capital dividend account of tax-exempt corporation
89(2)	Where corporation is beneficiary
89(3)	Simultaneous dividends
89(4)	GRIP addition — becoming CCPC
89(5)	GRIP addition — post-amalgamation
89(6)	GRIP addition — post-winding-up
89(7)	GRIP addition for 2006
89(8)	LRIP addition — ceasing to be CCPC
89(9)	LRIP addition — amalgamation
89(10)	LRIP addition — winding-up
89(11)	Election: non-CCPC
89(12)	Revoking election
89(13)	Repeated elections — consent required
89(14)	Dividend designation
89(14.1)	Late designation
89(15)	Meaning of expression "deposit insurance corporation"
89.1	Paid-up capital (Repealed.)

Section	Subject
	SUBDIVISION I
	SHAREHOLDERS OF CORPORATIONS NOT RESIDENT IN CANADA
90(1)	Dividend from non-resident corporation
90(2)	Dividend from foreign affiliate
90(3)	Qualifying return of capital
90(4)	Connected person or partnership
90(5)	Exclusion
90(6)	Loan from foreign affiliate
90(6.1)	Upstream loan continuity — Reorganizations
90(6.11)	Upstream loan continuity — Reorganizations
90(7)	Back-to-back loans
90(8)	Exceptions to subsection (6)
90(8.1)	Upstream deposit — eligible bank affiliate
90(9)	Corporations: deduction for amounts included under subsection (6) or (12)
90(10)	Corporate partners: application of subsection (9)
90(11)	Downstream surplus
90(12)	Add-back for subsection (9) deduction
90(13)	No double deduction
90(14)	Repayment of loan
90(15)	Definitions
	"eligible bank affiliate"
	"eligible Canadian bank"
	"eligible Canadian indebtedness"
	"excess liquidity"
	"specified amount"
	"specified debtor"
	"upstream deposit"
91(1)	Amounts to be included in respect of share of foreign affiliate
91(1.1)	Conditions for application of subsection (1.2)
91(1.2)	Deemed year-end
91(1.3)	Definitions
	"aggregate participating percentage"
	"connected person"
	"connected partnership"
	"excluded acquisition or disposition"
	"triggering event"
91(1.4)	Election for application of subsection (1.2)
91(1.5)	Election for application of subsection (1.2) (Repealed.)
91(2)	Reserve where foreign exchange restriction
91(3)	Reserve for preceding year to be included
91(4)	Amounts deductible in respect of foreign taxes
91(4.1)	Denial of foreign accrual tax
91(4.2)	Specified owner
91(4.3)	Pertinent person or partnership
91(4.4)	Series of transactions
91(4.5)	Exception — hybrid entities
91(4.6)	Exceptions — partnerships
91(4.7)	Deemed ownership
91(5)	Amounts deductible in respect of dividends received
91(5.1)	Deduction of dividend by shareholder (Repealed.)
91(5.2)	Deduction of dividend by member of partnership (Repealed.)
91(5.3)	Deduction of capital gain by member of partnership (Repealed.)
91(6)	Idem
91(7)	Shares acquired from a partnership
92(1)	Adjusted cost base of share of foreign affiliate
92(1.1)	Adjustment for prescribed amount
92(1.2)	Adjustment re adjusted cost base
92(2)	Deduction in computing adjusted cost base
92(3)	Idem
92(4)	Disposition of a partnership interest
92(5)	Deemed gain from the disposition of a share
92(6)	Formula
93(1)	Election re disposition of share of foreign affiliate
93(1.1)	Application of subsection (1.11)
93(1.11)	Deemed election
93(1.2)	Disposition of shares of a foreign affiliate held by a partnership
93(1.3)	Deemed election
93(2)	Application of subsection (2.01)
93(2.01)	Loss limitation on disposition of share of foreign affiliate
93(2.02)	Specified gain
93(2.1)	Application of subsection (2.11)
93(2.11)	Loss limitation on disposition of foreign affiliate share by a partnership
93(2.12)	Specified gain
93(2.2)	Application of subsection (2.21)
93(2.21)	Loss limitation on disposition of partnership that has foreign affiliate shares
93(2.22)	Specified gain
93(2.3)	Application of subsection (2.31)
93(2.31)	Loss limitation on disposition by a partnership of an indirect interest in foreign affiliate shares
93(2.32)	Specified gain
93(3)	Exempt dividends
93(4)	Loss on disposition of shares of foreign affiliate
93(5)	Late filed elections
93(5.1)	Special cases
93(5.2)	Amended election
93(6)	Penalty for late filed election
93(7)	Unpaid balance of penalty
93.1(1)	Shares held by partnership
93.1(1.1)	Specified provisions for subsection (1)
93.1(2)	Where dividends received by a partnership
93.1(3)	Tiered partnerships
93.1(4)	Partnership deemed to be corporation
93.1(5)	Computing FAPI in respect of partnership
93.1(6)	Relevant provisions and assumptions
93.2(1)	Definitions
	"equity interest"
	"non-resident corporation without share capital"
93.2(2)	Non-resident corporation without share capital
93.2(3)	Non-resident corporation without share capital
93.3(1)	Definition of "Australian trust"
93.3(2)	Conditions for subsection (3)
93.3(3)	Australian trusts
93.3(4)	Specified purposes
93.3(5)	Mergers
94(1)	Definitions
	"arm's length transfer"
	"beneficiary"
	"closely held corporation"
	"connected contributor"
	"contribution"
	"contributor"
	"electing contributor"
	"electing trust"
	"exempt amount"
	"exempt foreign trust"
	"exempt person"
	"exempt service"
	"fixed interest"
	"joint contributor"
	"mutual fund"
	"non-resident portion"
	"non-resident time"
	"promoter"
	"qualifying services"
	"resident beneficiary"
	"resident contributor"

Section	Subject
	"resident portion"
	"restricted property"
	"specified party"
	"specified share"
	"specified time"
	"successor beneficiary"
	"transaction"
	"trust"
94(2)	Rules of application
94(3)	Liabilities of non-resident trusts and others
94(4)	Excluded provisions
94(5)	Deemed cessation of residence — loss of resident contributor or resident beneficiary
94(5.1)	Deemed cessation of residence — becoming an exempt foreign trust
94(5.2)	Administrative relief — changes in status
94(6)	Ceasing to be an exempt foreign trust
94(7)	Limit to amount recoverable
94(8)	Recovery limit
94(8.1)	Application of subsection (8.2)
94(8.2)	Deemed transfer of restricted property
94(9)	Determination of contribution amount — restricted property
94(10)	Contributor — resident in Canada within 60 months after contribution
94(11)	Application of subsections (12) and (13)
94(12)	Deemed resident contributor
94(13)	Deemed contributor
94(14)	Restricted property — exception
94(15)	Anti-avoidance
94(16)	Attribution to electing contributors
94(17)	Liability for joint contribution
94.1(1)	Offshore investment fund property
94.1(2)	Definitions
	"designated cost"
	"non-resident entity"
94.1(3)	Interpretation
94.2(1)	Investments in non-resident commercial trusts
94.2(2)	Deemed corporation
94.2(3)	Relief from double tax
94.2(4)	Request for information
95(1)	Definitions for this subdivision
	"active business"
	"antecedent corporation"
	"calculating currency"
	"controlled foreign affiliate"
	"designated acquired corporation"
	"designated liquidation and dissolution"
	"eligible trust"
	"entity"
	"excluded property"
	"exempt trust"
	"foreign accrual property income"
	"foreign accrual tax"
	"foreign affiliate"
	"foreign bank"
	"income from a non-qualifying business"
	"income from an active business"
	"income from property"
	"investment business"
	"investment property"
	"lease obligation"
	"lending of money"
	"licensing of property"
	"non-qualifying business"
	"non-qualifying country"
	"participating percentage"
	"permanent establishment"
	"relevant tax factor"
	"specified fixed interest"
	"specified person or partnership"
	"specified predecessor corporation"
	"specified purchaser"
	"surplus entitlement percentage"
	"taxable Canadian business"
	"taxation year"
	"trust company"
95(1.1)	British Virgin Islands
95(2)	Determination of certain components of foreign accrual property income
95(2)(*a*)	[Determination of FAPI — Property income deemed active business income]
95(2)(*a*.1)	[Determination of FAPI — Income from sale of property]
95(2)(*a*.2)	[Determination of FAPI — Income from insurance of Canadian risks]
95(2)(*a*.21)	[Determination of FAPI — Income from insurance of Canadian risks]
95(2)(*a*.22)	[Determination of FAPI — Income from insurance of Canadian risks]
95(2)(*a*.23)	[Determination of FAPI — Income from insurance of Canadian risks]
95(2)(*a*.24)	[Determination of FAPI — Deemed specified Canadian risk]
95(2)(*a*.3)	[Determination of FAPI — Income from indebtedness and lease obligations]
95(2)(*a*.4)	[Determination of FAPI — Income from indebtedness and lease obligations in respect of partnership business]
95(2)(*b*)	[Determination of FAPI — Provision of services]
95(2)(*c*)	[Determination of FAPI — Transfer of shares]
95(2)(*d*)	[Determination of FAPI — Foreign merger]
95(2)(*d*.1)	[Determination of FAPI — Foreign merger — surplus entitlement percentage of 90% or more]
95(2)(*e*)	[Determination of FAPI — Dissolution of foreign affiliate]
95(2)(*e*.1)	[Determination of FAPI — Dissolution of foreign affiliate — surplus entitlement percentage of 90% or more] (Repealed.)
95(2)(*f*)	[Determination of FAPI — Deemed residence in Canada]
95(2)(*f*.1)	[Determination of FAPI — Exclusion of amounts]
95(2)(*f*.11)	[Determination of FAPI — Application of other provisions]
95(2)(*f*.12)	[Determination of FAPI — Use of calculating currency]
95(2)(*f*.13)	[Determination of FAPI — Conversion to Canadian currency]
95(2)(*f*.14)	[Determination of FAPI — Use of Canadian currency]
95(2)(*f*.15)	[Determination of FAPI — Currency for s. 39(2)]
95(2)(*g*)	[Determination of FAPI — Foreign currency fluctuations]
95(2)(*g*.01)	[Determination of FAPI — Currency hedging agreements]
95(2)(*g*.02)	[Determination of FAPI — Application of s. 39(2)] (Repealed.)
95(2)(*g*.03)	[Determination of FAPI — Foreign currency fluctuations where member of partnership]
95(2)(*g*.04)	[Determination of FAPI — Upstream loans]
95(2)(*g*.1)	[Determination of FAPI — Debt forgiveness rules]
95(2)(*g*.2)	[Determination of FAPI — Elections for foreign spin-off rules]
95(2)(*h*)	[Gain or loss on currency fluctuations] (Repealed.)
95(2)(*i*)	[Determination of FAPI — Settlement of debt or currency hedging agreement]
95(2)(*j*)	[Determination of FAPI — ACB of partnership interest]
95(2)(*j*.1)	[Determination of FAPI — Insurance business]
95(2)(*j*.2)	[Determination of FAPI — life insurance business]
95(2)(*k*)	[Determination of FAPI — Fresh start rules]
95(2)(*k*.1)	[Determination of FAPI — Fresh start rules]
95(2)(*k*.2)	[Determination of FAPI — Deemed separate business]
95(2)(*l*)	[Determination of FAPI — Trading or dealing in indebtedness]
95(2)(*m*)	[Determination of FAPI — Qualifying interest in foreign affiliate]

Section	Subject
95(2)(n)	[Determination of FAPI — Foreign affiliate and qualifying interest]
95(2)(o)	[Determination of FAPI — Qualifying member of partnership]
95(2)(p)	[Determination of FAPI — Qualifying shareholder]
95(2)(q)	[Determination of FAPI — Look-through rules]
95(2)(r)	[Determination of FAPI — Deemed qualifying member of partnership]
95(2)(s)	[Determination of FAPI — Designated corporation]
95(2)(t)	[Determination of FAPI — Designated partnership]
95(2)(u)	[Determination of FAPI — Tiered partnerships] (Repealed.)
95(2)(v)	[Determination of FAPI — Look-through rule for s. 95(2)(p)]
95(2)(w)	[Determination of FAPI — Where business carried on]
95(2)(x)	[Determination of FAPI — Determination of losses]
95(2)(y)	[Determination of FAPI — Qualifying interest in foreign affiliate — property of partnership]
95(2)(z)	[Determination of FAPI — Member of partnership]
95(2.01)	Rules for the definition "controlled foreign affiliate"
95(2.02)	Rule against double-counting
95(2.1)	Rule for definition "investment business"
95(2.11)	Rule for "investment business" definition and paragraph (2)(l)
95(2.2)	Qualifying interest throughout year
95(2.201)	Controlled foreign affiliate throughout year
95(2.21)	Rule re subsection (2.2)
95(2.3)	Application of paragraph (2)(a.1)
95(2.31)	Application of paragraphs (2)(a.1) and (a.3)
95(2.32)	Definition of "specified property"
95(2.4)	Application of paragraph (2)(a.3)
95(2.41)	Application of paragraph (2)(a.3)
95(2.42)	Exception re paragraph (2)(a.3)
95(2.43)	Definitions — subsections (2.43) to (2.45)
	"Canadian indebtedness"
	"eligible bank affiliate"
	"eligible Canadian bank"
	"eligible Canadian indebtedness"
	"eligible currency hedge"
	"excess liquidity"
	"organic assets"
	"qualifying indebtedness"
	"relationship deposits"
	"total specified indebtedness"
	"upstream deposit"
95(2.44)	FAPI adjustment — eligible bank affiliate
95(2.45)	Investment business and excluded property
95(2.5)	Definitions for paragraph (2)(a.3)
	"excluded income" and "excluded revenue"
	"indebtedness"
	specified deposit
95(2.6)	Rule for the definition "specified person or partnership"
95(3)	Definition of "services"
95(3.01)	Application of paragraph (2)(b) — eligible Canadian bank
95(3.02)	Rules for clause (2)(b)(ii)(B)
95(3.1)	Designated property — subparagraph (2)(a.1)(i)
95(3.2)	Contract manufacturing
95(4)	Definitions
	"direct equity percentage"
	"eligible controlled foreign affiliate"
	"equity percentage"
	"relevant cost base"
95(4.1)	Application of s. 87(8.1)
95(5)	Income bonds or debentures issued by foreign affiliates
95(6)	Where rights or shares issued, acquired or disposed of to avoid tax
95(7)	Stock dividends from foreign affiliates
95(8)	Tracking interests — interpretation
95(9)	Tracking interests — "investment business" definition
95(10)	Conditions for subsection (11)
95(11)	Tracking class — separate corporation
95(12)	Tracking interests — controlled foreign affiliate

SUBDIVISION J
PARTNERSHIPS AND THEIR MEMBERS

Section	Subject
96(1)	General rules
96(1.01)	Income allocation to former member
96(1.1)	Allocation of share of income to retiring partner
96(1.11)	Deemed dividend of SIFT partnership
96(1.2)	Disposal of right to share in income, etc
96(1.3)	Deductions
96(1.4)	Right deemed not to be capital property
96(1.5)	Disposition by virtue of death of taxpayer
96(1.6)	Members deemed carrying on business
96(1.7)	Gains and losses
96(1.71)	Application
96(1.8)	Loan of property
96(2)	Construction
96(2.01)	Tiered partnerships
96(2.1)	Limited partnership losses
96(2.11)	Tiered partnerships — adjustments
96(2.2)	At-risk amount
96(2.3)	Idem
96(2.4)	Limited partner
96(2.5)	Exempt interest
96(2.6)	Artificial transactions
96(2.7)	Idem
96(3)	Agreement or election of partnership members
96(4)	Election
96(5)	Late filing
96(5.1)	Special cases
96(6)	Penalty for late-filed election
96(7)	Unpaid balance of penalty
96(8)	Foreign partnerships
96(9)	Application of foreign partnership rule
97(1)	Contribution of property to partnership
97(2)	Rules if election by partners
97(3)	Election not available — section 88
97(3.1)	Deemed majority interest partner (Repealed.)
97(4)	Where capital cost to partner exceeds proceeds of disposition
97(5)	Acquisition of certain tools — capital cost and deemed depreciation
98(1)	Disposition of partnership property
98(1.1)	Continuing partnership interest (Repealed.)
98(2)	Deemed proceeds
98(3)	Rules applicable if partnership ceases to exist
98(4)	Where s. (3) does not apply
98(5)	Where partnership business carried on as sole proprietorship
98(6)	Continuation of predecessor partnership by new partnership
98(7)	Depreciable property — leasehold interests and options
98.1(1)	Residual interest in partnership
98.1(2)	Continuation of original partnership
98.2	Transfer of interest on death
99(1)	Fiscal period of terminated partnership
99(2)	Fiscal period of terminated partnership for individual member
99(3)	Validity of election
99(4)	Idem
100(1)	Disposition of interest in partnership

Section	Subject
100(1.1)	Acquisition by certain persons or partnerships
100(1.2)	De minimis
100(1.3)	Exception — non-resident person
100(1.4)	Anti-avoidance — dilution
100(1.5)	Deemed gain — dilution
100(2)	Gain from disposition of interest in partnership
100(2.1)	Idem
100(3)	Transfer of interest on death
100(4)	Loss re interest in partnership
100(5)	Replacement of partnership capital
101	Disposition of farmland by partnership
102(1)	Definition of "Canadian partnership"
102(2)	Member of a partnership
103(1)	Agreement to share income, etc., so as to reduce or postpone tax otherwise payable
103(1.1)	Agreement to share income, etc., in unreasonable proportions
103(2)	Definition of "losses"

SUBDIVISION K
TRUSTS AND THEIR BENEFICIARIES

Section	Subject
104(1)	Reference to trust or estate
104(1.1)	Restricted meaning of "beneficiary"
104(2)	Taxed as individual
104(3)	Deduction not permitted (Repealed.)
104(4)	Deemed disposition by trust
104(5)	Depreciable property
104(5.1)	NISA Fund No. 2
104(5.2)	Resource property
104(5.3)	Election (Repealed.)
104(5.31)	Revocation of election (Repealed.)
104(5.4)	Exempt beneficiary (Repealed.)
104(5.5)	Beneficiary (Repealed.)
104(5.6)	Designated contributor (Repealed.)
104(5.7)	Idem (Repealed.)
104(5.8)	Trust transfers
104(6)	Deduction in computing income of trust
104(7)	Non-resident beneficiary
104(7.01)	Trusts deemed to be resident in Canada
104(7.02)	Limitation — amount claimed as gift
104(7.1)	Capital interest greater than income interest
104(7.2)	Avoidance of s. (7.1)
104(8)	Limitation on deduction (Repealed.)
104(9)	Idem (Repealed.)
104(10)	Where property owned for non-residents (Repealed.)
104(11)	Dividend received from non-resident-owned investment corporation (Repealed.)
104(12)	Deduction of amounts included in preferred beneficiaries' incomes
104(13)	Income of beneficiary
104(13.1)	Amounts deemed not paid
104(13.2)	Idem
104(13.3)	Invalid designation
104(13.4)	Death of beneficiary — spousal and similar trusts
104(14)	Election by trust and preferred beneficiary
104(14.01)	Late, amended or revoked election (Repealed.)
104(14.02)	Late, amended or revoked election (Repealed.)
104(14.1)	NISA election (Repealed.)
104(15)	Allocable amount for preferred beneficiary
104(16)	SIFT deemed dividend
104(17)	Depletion allowance (Repealed.)
104(17.1)	Determination, etc., ineffective (Repealed.)
104(17.2)	Idem (Repealed.)
104(18)	Trust for minor
104(19)	Designation in respect of taxable dividends
104(20)	Designation in respect of non-taxable dividends
104(21)	Designation in respect of taxable capital gains
104(21.01)	Late, amended or revoked designation
104(21.02)	Late, amended or revoked designation
104(21.03)	Late, amended or revoked designation
104(21.1)	Beneficiary's taxable capital gain (Repealed.)
104(21.2)	Beneficiaries' taxable capital gain
104(21.21)	Beneficiaries QFFP taxable capital gain
104(21.22)	Trusts to designate amounts
104(21.23)	Beneficiaries' taxable capital gain — QFFP taxable capital gain (Repealed.)
104(21.24)	Trusts to designate amounts (Repealed.)
104(21.3)	Net taxable capital gains of trust determined
104(21.4)	Deemed gains (Repealed.)
104(21.5)	Deemed gains (Repealed.)
104(21.6)	Deemed gains — subsection (21.4) applies (Repealed.)
104(21.7)	Deemed gains — subsection (21.4) does not apply (Repealed.)
104(22)	Designation in respect of foreign source income
104(22.1)	Foreign tax deemed paid by beneficiary
104(22.2)	Recalculation of trust's foreign source income
104(22.3)	Recalculation of trust's foreign tax
104(22.4)	Definitions
104(23)	Deceased beneficiary of graduated rate estate
104(24)	Amount payable
104(25)	Excess amount (Repealed.)
104(25.1)	Idem (Repealed.)
104(26)	Portion of interest deemed interest of beneficiary (Repealed.)
104(27)	Pension benefits
104(27.1)	DPSP benefits
104(28)	Death benefit
104(29)	Amounts deemed payable to beneficiaries (Repealed.)
104(30)	Tax under Part XII.2
104(31)	Idem
105(1)	Benefits under trust
105(2)	Upkeep, etc
106(1)	Income interest in trust
106(1.1)	Cost of income interest in a trust
106(2)	Disposition by taxpayer of income interest
106(3)	Proceeds of disposition of income interest
107(1)	Disposition by taxpayer of capital interest
107(1.1)	Cost of capital interest in a trust
107(1.2)	Deemed fair market value — non-capital property
107(2)	Distribution by personal trust
107(2.001)	No rollover on election by a trust
107(2.002)	No rollover on election by a beneficiary
107(2.01)	Distribution of principal residence
107(2.1)	Other distributions
107(2.11)	Gains not distributed to beneficiaries
107(2.12)	Election — Subsection (2.11)
107(2.2)	Flow-through entity
107(3)	Application of subsection (3.1)
107(3.1)	SIFT trust wind-up event
107(4)	Trusts in favour of spouse, common-law partner or self
107(4.1)	Where subsection 75(2) applicable to trust
107(4.2)	Distribution of property received on qualifying disposition
107(5)	Distribution to non-resident
107(5.1)	Instalment interest
107(6)	Loss reduction
107.1	Distribution by certain employment-related trusts
107.2	Distribution by a retirement compensation arrangement
107.3(1)	Treatment of beneficiaries under qualifying environmental trusts

Section	Subject
107.3(2)	Transfers to beneficiaries
107.3(3)	Ceasing to be qualifying environmental trust
107.3(4)	Application
107.4(1)	Qualifying disposition
107.4(2)	Application of paragraph (1)(a)
107.4(2.1)	Fractional interests
107.4(3)	Tax consequences of qualifying dispositions
107.4(4)	Fair market value of vested interest in trust
108(1)	Definitions
	"accumulating income"
	"beneficiary"
	"capital interest"
	"cost amount"
	"eligible offset"
	"eligible real property gain" (Repealed.)
	"eligible real property loss" (Repealed.)
	"eligible taxable capital gains"
	"excluded property"
	"exempt property"
	"income interest"
	"inter vivos trust"
	"non-qualifying real property" (Repealed.)
	"pre-1972 spousal trust"
	"preferred beneficiary"
	"qualified farm property" (Repealed.)
	"qualified fishing property" (Repealed.)
	"qualified small business corporation share" (Repealed.)
	"settlor"
	"testamentary trust"
	"trust"
108(1.1)	Testamentary trust not disqualified
108(2)	When trust is a unit trust
108(3)	Income of a trust in certain provisions
108(4)	Trust not disqualified
108(5)	Interpretation
108(6)	Variation of trusts
108(7)	Interests acquired for consideration

DIVISION C COMPUTATION OF TAXABLE INCOME

Section	Subject
109	Deductions permitted by individuals
Prop. 110(0.1)	Definitions
Prop.	"specified person"
Prop.	"vesting year"
110(1)	Deductions permitted
110(1)(*a*)	Charitable gifts (Repealed.)
110(1)(*b*)	Gifts to Her Majesty (Repealed.)
110(1)(*b*.1)	Gifts to institutions (Repealed.)
110(1)(*c*)	Medical expenses (Repealed.)
110(1)(*d*)	Employee options
110(1)(*d*.01)	Charitable donation of employee option securities
110(1)(*d*.1)	Idem
110(1)(*d*.2)	Prospector's and grubstaker's shares
110(1)(*d*.3)	Employer's shares
110(1)(*e*)	Mental or physical impairment (Repealed.)
Prop. 110(1)(*e*)	Employer deduction — non-qualified securities
110(1)(*e*.1)	Dependant having impairment (Repealed.)
110(1)(*e*.2)	Deduction transfer (Repealed.)
110(1)(*f*)	Deductions for payments
110(1)(*g*)	Financial assistance
110(1)(*h*)	[U.S. social security benefits]
110(1)(*i*)	Unemployment insurance benefit repayment (Repealed.)
110(1)(*j*)	Home relocation loan (Repealed.)
110(1)(*k*)	Part VI.1 tax
110(1.1)	Election by particular qualifying person
110(1.2)	Designated amount
110(1.3)	Designated mission (Repealed.)
Prop. 110(1.3)	Determination of non-qualified securities
Prop. 110(1.31)	Annual vesting limit
110(1.4)	Replacement of home relocation loan (Repealed.)
Prop. 110(1.4)	Non-qualified security designation
Prop. 110(1.41)	Ordering of acquisition of securities
110(1.5)	Determination of amounts relating to employee security options
110(1.6)	Meaning of "specified event"
110(1.7)	Reduction in exercise price
110(1.8)	Conditions for subsection (1.7) to apply
Prop. 110(1.9)	Notification — non-qualified security
110(2)	Charitable gifts
110(2.1)	Charitable donation — proceeds of disposition of employee option securities
110(2.2)–(9)	(Repealed.)
110.1(1)	Deduction for gifts
110.1(1)(*a*)	Charitable gifts
110.1(1)(*a*.1)	Gifts of medicine (Repealed.)
110.1(1)(*b*)	Gifts to Her Majesty
110.1(1)(*c*)	Gifts to institutions
Prop. 110.1(1)(*c*.1)	Gifts to food banks
110.1(1)(*d*)	Ecological gifts
110.1(1.1)	Limitation on deductibility
110.1(1.2)	Where control acquired
110.1(2)	Proof of gift
110.1(2.1)	Where subsection (3) applies
110.1(3)	Gifts of capital property
110.1(4)	Gifts made by partnership
Prop. 110.1(4.1)	Food product gifts
110.1(5)	Ecological gifts
110.1(6)	Non-qualifying securities
110.1(7)	Corporation ceasing to exist
110.1(8)	Eligible medical gift (Repealed.)
110.1(9)	Rules governing international medical charities (Repealed.)
110.1(10)	Options
110.1(11)	Application of subsection (12)
110.1(12)	Granting of an option
110.1(13)	Disposition of an option
110.1(14)	Returned property
110.1(15)	Returned property
110.1(16)	Information return
110.1(17)	Reassessment
110.2(1)	Definitions
	"eligible taxation year"
	"qualifying amount"
	"specified portion"
110.2(2)	Deduction for lump-sum payments
110.3	Transfer of unused deductions (Repealed.)
110.4	Forward averaging
110.5	Additions for foreign tax deductions
110.6(1)	Definitions
	"annual gains limit"
	"child"
	"cumulative gains limit"
	"cumulative net investment loss"
	"eligible real property gain" (Repealed.)
	"eligible real property loss" (Repealed.)
	"interest in a family farm or fishing partnership"
	"interest in a family farm partnership" (Repealed.)
	"interest in a family fishing partnership" (Repealed.)
	"investment expense"
	"investment income"
	"non-qualifying real property" (Repealed.)
	"qualified farm or fishing property"

Section	Subject
	"qualified farm property" (Repealed.)
	"qualified fishing property" (Repealed.)
	"qualified small business corporation share"
	"share of the capital stock of a family farm corporation" (Repealed.)
	"share of the capital stock of a family farm or fishing corporation"
	"share of the capital stock of a family fishing corporation" (Repealed.)
110.6(1.1)	Value of NISA
110.6(1.2)	Property used in a fishing business (Repealed.)
110.6(1.3)	Farming or fishing property — conditions
110.6(2)	Capital gains deduction — qualified farm or fishing property
110.6(2.1)	Capital gains deduction — qualified small business corporation shares
110.6(2.2)	Additional deduction — qualified farm or fishing property
110.6(2.3)	Additional deduction — ordering rule
110.6(3)	Capital gains deduction — other property (Repealed.)
110.6(4)	Maximum capital gains deduction
110.6(5)	Deemed resident in Canada
110.6(6)	Failure to report capital gain
110.6(7)	Deduction not permitted
110.6(8)	Deduction not permitted
110.6(9)	Average annual rate of return
110.6(10)	Gain from extension or renewal of option (Repealed.)
110.6(11)	Where deduction not permitted
110.6(12)	Trust deduction — death of spouse or common-law partner (Repealed.)
110.6(13)	Determination under paragraph 3(b)
110.6(14)	Related persons, etc
110.6(15)	Value of assets of corporations
110.6(16)	Personal trust
110.6(17)	Order of deduction
110.6(18)	Eligible real property gains and losses (Repealed.)
110.6(19)	Election for property owned on February 22, 1994
110.6(20)	Application of subsection (19)
110.6(21)	Effect of election on non-qualifying real property
110.6(22)	Adjusted cost base
110.6(23)	Disposition of partnership interest
110.6(24)	Time for election
110.6(25)	Revocation of election
110.6(26)	Late election
110.6(27)	Amended election
110.6(28)	Election that cannot be revoked or amended
110.6(29)	Amount of penalty
110.6(30)	Unpaid balance of penalty
110.6(31)	Reserve limit
110.6(32)	Deduction denied (Repealed.)
110.7(1)	Residing in prescribed zone
110.7(2)	Specified percentage
110.7(3)	Restriction
110.7(4)	Board and lodging allowances, etc
110.7(5)	Idem
111(1)	Losses deductible
111(1)(*a*)	Non-capital losses
111(1)(*b*)	Net capital losses
111(1)(*c*)	Restricted farm losses
111(1)(*d*)	Farm losses
111(1)(*e*)	Limited partnership losses
111(1.1)	Net capital losses
111(2)	Year of death
111(3)	Limitation on deductibility
111(4)	Loss restriction event — capital losses
111(5)	Loss restriction event — non-capital losses and farm losses
111(5.1)	Loss restriction event — UCC computation
111(5.2)	Loss restriction event — CEC computation (Repealed.)
111(5.3)	Loss restriction event — doubtful debts and bad debts
111(5.4)	Non-capital loss
111(5.5)	Loss restriction event — special rules
111(6)	Limitation
111(7)	Idem
111(7.1)	Effect of election by insurer under s. 138(9) in respect of 1975 taxation year (Repealed.)
111(7.11)	Application of s. 138(12) (Repealed.)
111(7.2)	Non-capital loss of life insurer (Repealed.)
111(7.3)	Non-capital losses of employee life and health trusts
111(7.4)	Non-capital losses of employee life and health trusts
111(7.5)	Non-capital losses of employee life and health trusts
111(8)	Definitions
	"exchange rate"
	"farm loss"
	"foreign currency debt"
	"net capital loss"
	"non-capital loss"
	"pre-1986 capital loss balance"
111(9)	Exception
111(10)	Fuel tax rebate loss abatement
111(11)	Fuel tax rebate — partnerships
111(12)	Foreign currency debt on loss restriction event
111.1	Order of applying provisions
112(1)	Deduction of taxable dividends received by corporation resident in Canada
112(2)	Dividends received from non-resident corporation
112(2.1)	No deduction permitted
112(2.2)	Guaranteed shares
112(2.21)	Exceptions
112(2.22)	Interpretation
112(2.3)	Where no deduction permitted
112(2.31)	Dividend rental arrangements — exception
112(2.32)	Representations
112(2.33)	End of particular period
112(2.34)	Interpretation
112(2.4)	Where no deduction permitted
112(2.5)	Application of s. (2.4)
112(2.6)	Definitions
	"exempt share"
	"investor"
	"issuer"
112(2.7)	Change in agreement or condition
112(2.8)	Loss sustained by investor
112(2.9)	Related corporations
112(3)	Loss on share that is capital property
112(3.01)	Loss on share that is capital property — excluded dividends
112(3.1)	Loss on share held by partnership
112(3.11)	Loss on share held by partnership — excluded dividends
112(3.12)	Loss on share held by partnership — excluded dividends
112(3.2)	Loss on share held by trust
112(3.3)	Loss on share held by trust — special cases
112(3.31)	Loss on share held by trust — excluded dividends
112(3.32)	Loss on share held by trust — excluded dividends
112(4)	Loss on share that is not capital property
112(4.01)	Loss on share that is not capital property — excluded dividends
112(4.1)	Fair market value of shares held as inventory
112(4.11)	Fair market value of shares held as inventory — excluded dividends
112(4.2)	Loss on share held by trust
112(4.21)	Loss on share held by trust — excluded dividends
112(4.22)	Loss on share held by trust — excluded dividends
112(4.3)	Loss on share that is not capital property of trust (Repealed.)
112(5)	Disposition of share by financial institution
112(5.1)	Share held for less than one year
112(5.2)	Adjustment re dividends

Section	Subject
112(5.21)	Subsection (5.2) — excluded dividends
112(5.3)	Adjustment not applicable
112(5.4)	Deemed dispositions
112(5.5)	Stop-loss rules not applicable
112(5.6)	Stop-loss rules restricted
112(6)	Meaning of certain expressions
112(6.1)	Interpretation — qualified dividend
112(7)	Rules where shares exchanged
112(8)	Synthetic disposition — holding period
112(9)	Exception
112(9.1)	Exception
112(10)	Synthetic equity arrangements — ordering
112(11)	Interest in a partnership — cost reduction
112(12)	Application
112(13)	Application
113(1)	Deduction in respect of dividend received from foreign affiliate
113(2)	Additional deduction
113(3)	Definitions
	"non-business-income tax"
	"relevant tax factor"
113(4)	Portion of dividend deemed paid out of exempt surplus
113(5)	Limitation on foreign accrual tax where treaty (Repealed.)
113(6)	Construction of other provisions (Repealed.)
113(7)	Meaning of "foreign accrual tax applicable" (Repealed.)
114	Individual resident in Canada for only part of year
114.1	Application of s. 115(2)
114.2	Deductions in separate returns

DIVISION D TAXABLE INCOME EARNED IN CANADA BY NON-RESIDENTS

Section	Subject
115(1)	Non-resident's taxable income in Canada
115(2)	Idem
115(2.1)	Non-resident actors
115(2.2)	Deferred payment by actor's corporation
115(2.3)	Non-resident persons — 2010 Olympic and Paralympic Winter Games
115(3)	Non-resident employed as aircraft pilot
115(4)	Non-resident's income from Canadian resource property
115(4.1)	Foreign resource pool expenses
115(5)	Interpretation of "partnership"
115(6)	Application of s. 138(12)
115.1(1)	Competent authority agreements
115.1(2)	Transfer of rights and obligations
115.2(1)	Definitions
	"Canadian investor"
	"Canadian service provider"
	"designated investment services"
	"promoter"
	"qualified investment"
	"qualified non-resident" (Repealed.)
115.2(2)	Not carrying on business in Canada
115.2(3)	Interpretation
115.2(4)	Transfer pricing
116(1)	Disposition by non-resident person of certain property
116(2)	Certificate in respect of proposed disposition
116(3)	Notice to Minister
116(4)	Certificate in respect of property disposed of
116(5)	Liability of purchaser
116(5.01)	Treaty-protected property
116(5.02)	Notice by purchaser in respect of an acquisition of property
116(5.1)	Gifts, etc
116(5.2)	Certificates for dispositions
116(5.3)	Liability of purchaser in certain cases
116(5.4)	Presumption
116(6)	Definition of "excluded property"
116(6.1)	Treaty-exempt property
116(7)	Application of s. 138(12)

DIVISION E COMPUTATION OF TAX

SUBDIVISION A RULES APPLICABLE TO INDIVIDUALS

Section	Subject
117(1)	Tax payable under this Part
117(2)	Rates for taxation years after 2015
117(2.1)	Tax payable — WITB advance payment
117(3)	Minimum thresholds for 2004
117(4)–(5.1)	(Repealed.)
117(5.2)	1982 and subsequent taxation years rates (Repealed.)
117(6)	Special table (Repealed.)
117(7)	Notch provision (Repealed.)
117.1(1)	Annual adjustment
117.1(1.1)	Adjustment of certain amounts (Repealed.)
117.1(2)	Idem (Repealed.)
117.1(3)	Rounding
117.1(4)	Consumer Price Index
117.1(5)	Idem (Repealed.)
117.1(6)	Rounding of amounts (Repealed.)
117.1(7)	Determination of "Consumer Price Index for a 12 month period" (Repealed.)
117.1(7.1)	Annual adjustment of amounts expressed in dollars (Repealed.)
117.1(8)	Limitation (Repealed.)
118(1)	Personal credits
118(1)(*a*)	Married or common-law partnership status
118(1)(*b*)	Wholly dependent person
118(1)(*b*.1)	Caregiver amount for infirm child
118(1)(*c*)	Single status
118(1)(*c*.1)	In-home care of relative (Repealed.)
118(1)(*d*)	Canada caregiver credit
118(1)(*e*)	Additional amount
118(2)	Age credit
118(3)	Pension credit
118(3.1)	Additions to personal credits — basic personal amount (Repealed.)
118(3.2)	Additions to personal credits — spouse or common-law partner or wholly dependent person (Repealed.)
118(3.3)	Additions to personal credits — net income threshold (Repealed.)
118(4)	Limitations re s. (1)
118(5)	Support
118(5.1)	Where subsection (5) does not apply
118(6)	Definition of "dependant"
118(7)	Definitions
	"eligible pension income"
	"pension income"
	"qualified pension income"
118(8)	Interpretation
118(8.1)	Bridging benefits
118(9)	Rounding (Repealed.)
118(9.1)	Child tax credit
118(10)	Canada Employment Credit
118.01(1)	Definitions

Section	Subject
	"adoption period"
	"eligible adoption expense"
	"eligible child"
118.01(2)	Adoption expense tax credit
118.01(3)	Apportionment of credit
118.02(1)	Definitions (Repealed.)
Pend. 118.02(1)	Definitions
Pend.	"digital news subscription"
Pend.	"qualifying subscription expense"
118.02(2)	Transit pass tax credit (Repealed.)
Pend. 118.02(2)	Digital news subscription tax credit
118.02(3)	Apportionment of credit (Repealed.)
Pend. 118.02(3)	Apportionment of credit
118.03(1)	Definitions (Repealed.)
118.03(2)	Child fitness tax credit (Repealed.)
118.03(2.1)	Child fitness tax credit — child with disability (Repealed.)
118.03(3)	Apportionment of credit (Repealed.)
118.031(1)	Definitions (Repealed.)
118.031(2)	Children's arts tax credit (Repealed.)
118.031(3)	Children's arts tax credit — child with disability (Repealed.)
118.031(4)	Apportionment of credit (Repealed.)
118.04(1)	Definitions
	"eligible dwelling"
	"eligible period"
	"individual"
	"qualifying expenditure"
	"qualifying relation"
	"qualifying renovation"
118.04(2)	Rules of application
118.04(3)	Home renovation tax credit
118.04(4)	Interaction with medical expense credit
118.04(5)	Apportionment of credit
118.041(1)	Definitions
	"eligible dwelling"
	"eligible individual"
	"individual"
	"qualifying expenditure"
	"qualifying individual"
	"qualifying renovation"
118.041(2)	Qualifying expenditure rules
118.041(3)	Home accessibility tax credit
118.041(4)	Interaction with medical expense credit
118.041(5)	Limits
118.041(6)	Effect of bankruptcy
118.041(7)	In the event of death and bankruptcy
118.05(1)	Definitions
	"qualifying home"
	"specified person"
118.05(2)	Rules of application
118.05(3)	First-time home buyers' tax credit
118.05(4)	Apportionment of credit
118.06(1)	Definition of "eligible volunteer firefighting services"
118.06(2)	Volunteer firefighter tax credit
118.06(3)	Certificate
118.07(1)	Definitions
	"eligible search and rescue organization"
	"eligible search and rescue volunteer services"
118.07(2)	Search and rescue volunteer tax credit
118.07(3)	Certificate
118.1(1)	Definitions
	"first-time donor" (Repealed.)
	"total charitable gifts"
	"total Crown gifts" (Repealed.)
	"total cultural gifts"
	"total ecological gifts"
	"total gifts"
118.1(2)	Proof of gift
118.1(2.1)	Ordering of gifts
118.1(3)	Deduction by individuals for gifts
118.1(3.1)	First-time donor credit (Repealed.)
118.1(3.2)	Apportionment of credit (Repealed.)
118.1(4)	Gifts — deaths before 2016
118.1(4.1)	Gifts — deaths after 2015
118.1(5)	Gifts — deaths after 2015
118.1(5.1)	Gifts by graduated rate estate
118.1(5.2)	Deemed gifts — eligible transfers
118.1(5.3)	Direct designation — RRSPs, RRIFs and TFSAs (Repealed.)
118.1(5.4)	Where subsection (6) applies
118.1(6)	Gifts of capital property
118.1(7)	Gift of art
118.1(7.1)	Gift of art
118.1(8)	Gifts made by partnership
118.1(9)	Commuter's charitable donations
118.1(10)	Determination of fair market value
118.1(10.1)	Determination of fair market value
118.1(10.2)	Request for determination by the Minister of the Environment
118.1(10.3)	Duty of Minister of the Environment
118.1(10.4)	Ecological gifts — redetermination
118.1(10.5)	Certificate of Fair Market Value
118.1(11)	Assessments
118.1(12)	Ecological gifts
118.1(13)	Non-qualifying securities
118.1(13.1)	Application of subsection (13.2)
118.1(13.2)	Non-qualifying securities — third-party accommodation
118.1(13.3)	Non-qualifying securities — anti-avoidance
118.1(14)	Exchanged security
118.1(14.1)	Exchange of beneficial interest in trust
118.1(15)	Death of donor
118.1(16)	Loanbacks
118.1(17)	Ordering rule
118.1(18)	Non-qualifying security defined
118.1(19)	Excepted gift
118.1(20)	Financial institution defined
118.1(21)	Options
118.1(22)	Application of subsection (23)
118.1(23)	Granting of an option
118.1(24)	Disposition of an option
118.1(25)	Returned property
118.1(26)	Returned property
118.1(27)	Information return
118.1(28)	Reassessment
118.2(1)	Medical expense credit
118.2(2)	Medical expenses
118.2(2.1)	Cosmetic purposes
118.2(2.2)	Fertility expenses
118.2(3)	Deemed medical expense
118.2(4)	Deemed payment of medical expenses
118.3(1)	Credit for mental or physical impairment
118.3(1.1)	Time spent on therapy
118.3(2)	Dependant having impairment
118.3(3)	Partial dependency
118.3(4)	Additional information
118.4(1)	Nature of impairment
118.4(2)	Reference to medical practitioners, etc.
118.5(1)	Tuition credit
118.5(1.1)	Minimum amount
118.5(1.2)	Canada training credit reduction
118.5(2)	Application to deemed residents
118.5(3)	Inclusion of ancillary fees and charges
118.5(4)	Ancillary fees and charges for examinations
118.6(1)	Definitions
	"designated educational institution"
	"qualifying educational program"
	"qualifying student"

Section	Subject
	"specified educational program"
118.6(2)	Education credit (Repealed.)
118.6(2.1)	Post-secondary textbook credit (Repealed.)
118.6(3)	Students eligible for disability tax credit
118.61(1)	Unused tuition, textbook and education tax credits
118.61(2)	Deduction of carryforward
118.61(3)	Unused tuition and education tax credits at the end of 2000 (Repealed.)
118.61(4)	Change of appropriate percentage
118.62	Credit for interest on student loan
118.7	Credit for EI and QPIP premiums and CPP contributions
118.8	Transfer of unused credits to spouse or common-law partner
118.81	Tuition tax credit transferred
118.9	Transfer to parent or grandparent
118.91	Part-year residents
118.92	Ordering of credits
118.93	Credits in separate returns
118.94	Tax payable by non-residents (credits restricted)
118.95	Credits in year of bankruptcy
119	Former resident — credit for tax paid
119.1(1)	Definitions (Repealed.)
119.1(2)	Family tax cut credit (Repealed.)
119.1(3)	Deduction not available (Repealed.)
119.1(4)	Taxation year deeming rules (Repealed.)
120(1)	Income not earned in a province
120(2)	Amount deemed paid in prescribed manner
120(2.1)	Idem (Repealed.)
120(2.2)	Amount deemed paid
120(3)	Definition of "the individual's income for the year"
120(3.1)	Additional deduction from tax (Repealed.)
120(4)	Definitions
	"income earned in the year in a province"
	"province" (Repealed.)
	"tax otherwise payable under this Part"
120.1	Forward averaging credit
120.2(1)	Minimum tax carry-over
120.2(2)	Death of individual (Repealed.)
120.2(3)	Additional tax determined
120.2(4)	Where subsection (1) does not apply
120.3	CPP/QPP disability benefits [and other CPP/QPP benefits] for previous years
120.31(1)	Definitions
120.31(2)	Addition to tax payable
120.31(3)	Notional tax payable
120.4(1)	Definitions
	"arm's length capital"
	"excluded amount"
	"excluded business"
	"excluded shares"
	"reasonable return"
	"related business"
	"safe harbour capital return"
	"source individual"
	"specified individual"
	"split income"
120.4(1.1)	Additional rules — specified individual
120.4(2)	Tax on split income
120.4(3)	Tax payable by a specified individual
120.4(4)	Taxable capital gain
120.4(5)	Taxable capital gain of trust
121	Deduction for taxable dividends
122(1)	Tax payable by trust
122(1.1)	Credits available to trusts
122(2)	Qualified disability trust — application of (1)(c)
122(3)	Definitions
	"beneficiary"

Section	Subject
	"electing beneficiary"
	"non-deductible distributions amount"
	"qualified disability trust"
	"taxable SIFT trust distributions"
122.1(1)	Definitions
	"eligible resale property"
	"entity"
	"equity"
	"equity value"
	"excluded subsidiary entity"
	"gross REIT revenue"
	"investment"
	"non-portfolio earnings"
	"non-portfolio property"
	"portfolio investment entity"
	"public market"
	"publicly-traded liability"
	"qualified REIT property"
	"real estate investment trust"
	"real or immovable property"
	"regulated innovative capital"
	"rent from real or immovable properties"
	"security"
	"SIFT trust"
	"subject entity"
	"unaffiliated publicly-traded liability"
122.1(1.1)	Application of subsection (1.2)
122.1(1.2)	Character preservation rule
122.1(1.3)	Character of revenue — hedging arrangements
122.1(2)	Application of definition "SIFT trust"
122.2(1)	Amount deemed paid in prescribed manner (Repealed.)
122.2(2)	Definitions (Repealed.)
	"eligible child" (Repealed.)
	"supporting person" (Repealed.)
122.3	Overseas employment tax credit
122.3(1.01)	Specified amount
122.3(1.02)	Specified percentage
122.3(1.1)	Excluded income
122.3(2)	Definitions
	"specified employer"
	"tax otherwise payable under this Part for the year"
122.4	[Sales tax credit] (Repealed.)
122.5(1)	Definitions
	"adjusted income"
	"cohabiting spouse or common-law partner"
	"eligible individual"
	"qualified dependant"
	"qualified relation"
	"return of income"
122.5(2)	Persons not eligible individuals, qualified relations or qualified dependants
122.5(3)	Deemed payment on account of tax
122.5(3.01)	Shared-custody parent
122.5(3.1)	When advance payment applies
122.5(3.2)	Advance payment
122.5(4)	Months specified
122.5(5)	Only one eligible individual
122.5(5.1)	Exception (Repealed.)
122.5(6)	Exception re qualified dependant
122.5(6.1)	Notification to Minister
122.5(6.2)	Non-residents and part-year residents
122.5(7)	Effect of bankruptcy
122.51(1)	Definitions
	"adjusted income"
	"eligible individual"
122.51(2)	Deemed payment on account of tax

SUBDIVISION A.1
CANADA CHILD BENEFIT

Section	Subject
122.6	Definitions
	"adjusted earned income" (Repealed.)
	"adjusted income"
	"base taxation year"
	"cohabiting spouse or common-law partner"
	"earned income" (Repealed.)
	"eligible individual"
	"qualified dependant"
	"return of income"
	"shared-custody parent"
122.61(1)	Deemed overpayment
122.61(1.1)	Shared-custody parent
122.61(2)	Exceptions
122.61(3)	Non-residents and part-year residents
122.61(3.1)	Effect of bankruptcy
122.61(4)	Amount not to be charged, etc
122.61(5)	Annual adjustment
122.61(5.1)	Annual adjustment (Repealed.)
122.61(6)	Additions to NCB supplement — July 2005 and 2006
122.61(6.1)	Agreement with a province
122.61(7)	Rounding
122.62(1)	Eligible individuals
122.62(2)	Extension for notices
122.62(3)	Exception
122.62(4)	Person ceasing to be an eligible individual
122.62(5)	Death of cohabiting spouse
122.62(6)	Separation from cohabiting spouse
122.62(7)	Person becoming a cohabiting spouse
122.62(8)	Ordering of events
122.62(9)	Advice of Department of Human Resources Development (Repealed.)
122.63(1)	Agreement
122.63(2)	Agreement
122.63(3)	Agreement
122.64(1)	Confidentiality of information (Repealed.)
122.64(2)	Communication of information (Repealed.)
122.64(3)	Taxpayer's address (Repealed.)
122.64(4)	Offence (Repealed.)
122.64(5)	"Official" and "authorized person" (Repealed.)

SUBDIVISION A.2
CANADA WORKERS BENEFIT

Section	Subject
122.7(1)	Definitions
	"adjusted net income"
	"cohabiting spouse or common-law partner"
	"designated educational institution"
	"eligible dependant"
	"eligible individual"
	"eligible spouse"
	"ineligible individual"
	"return of income"
	"working income"
122.7(1.1)	Optional amounts
122.7(1.2)	Receipt of social assistance
122.7(2)	Deemed payment on account of tax
122.7(3)	Deemed payment on account of tax — disability supplement
122.7(4)	Eligible spouse deemed not to be an eligible individual
122.7(5)	Only one eligible individual
122.7(6)	Application for advance payment
122.7(7)	Advance payment
122.7(8)	Limitation — advance payment
122.7(9)	Notification to Minister
122.7(10)	Special rule for eligible dependant
122.7(11)	Effect of bankruptcy
122.7(12)	Special rules in the event of death
122.71	Modification for purposes of provincial program

SUBDIVISION A.3
CLIMATE ACTION INCENTIVE

Section	Subject
122.8(1)	Definitions
	"cohabiting spouse or common-law partner"
	"eligible individual"
	"qualified dependant"
	"qualified relation"
	"return of income"
122.8(2)	Persons not eligible individuals, qualified relations or qualified dependants
122.8(3)	Residence
122.8(4)	Deemed overpayment
122.8(5)	Authority to specify amounts
122.8(6)	Deemed rebate in respect of fuel charges
122.8(7)	Only one eligible individual
122.8(8)	Exception — qualified dependant
122.8(9)	Effect of bankruptcy

SUBDIVISION A.4
SCHOOL SUPPLIES TAX CREDIT

Section	Subject
122.9(1)	Definitions
	"eligible educator"
	"eligible supplies expense"
	"return of income"
	"teaching supplies"
122.9(2)	Deemed overpayment
122.9(3)	Certificate
122.9(4)	Effect of bankruptcy
122.9(5)	Part-year residents
122.9(6)	Non-residents

SUBDIVISION A.5
CANADA TRAINING CREDIT

Section	Subject
122.91(1)	Claimed amount
122.91(2)	Definition of training amount limit
122.91(3)	Effect of bankruptcy
122.91(4)	Special rules in the event of death

SUBDIVISION B
RULES APPLICABLE TO CORPORATIONS

Section	Subject
123(1)	Rate for corporations
123(2)	Definitions — "Amount taxable earned by the corporation in the year in the Nova Scotia offshore area", "Nova Scotia offshore area" (Repealed.)
123.1	Corporation surtax
123.2(1)	Corporation surtax (Repealed.)
123.2(2)	Specified percentage (Repealed.)
123.2(3)	Taxable income (Repealed.)
123.3	Refundable tax on CCPC's investment income
123.4	Corporation tax reductions
123.4(1)	Definitions
	"CCPC rate reduction percentage" (Repealed.)
	"full rate taxable income"
	"general rate reduction percentage"
123.4(2)	General deduction from tax
123.4(3)	CCPC deduction (Repealed.)
123.5	Tax on personal services business income
124(1)	Deduction from corporation tax
124(2)	Idem (Repealed.)
124(2.1)	Idem (Repealed.)
124(2.2)	Calculation of percentage for particular taxation year (Repealed.)
124(3)	Crown agents
124(4)	Definitions
	"province"
	"taxable income earned in the year in a province"
124.1	"Taxable production profits from a mineral resource in Canada" defined
124.2	"Taxable production profits from oil or gas wells in Canada" defined (Repealed.)
125(1)	Small business deduction
125(1.1)	Small business deduction rate
125(2)	Business limit
125(3)	Associated corporations
125(3.1)	Reduction — business limit
125(3.2)	Assignment
125(4)	Failure to file agreement
125(5)	Special rules for business limit
125(5.1)	Business limit reduction
125(5.2)	Anti-avoidance
125(6)	Corporate partnerships
125(6.1)	Corporation deemed member of partnership
125(6.2)	Specified partnership income deemed nil
125(6.3)	Partnership deemed to be controlled
125(7)	Definitions
	"active asset"
	"active business carried on by a corporation"
	"adjusted aggregate investment income"
	"Canadian-controlled private corporation"
	"designated member"
	"income of the corporation for the year from an active business"
	"personal services business"
	"specified cooperative income" (Repealed.)
	"specified corporate income"
	"specified farming or fishing income"
	"specified investment business"
	"specified partnership business limit"
	"specified partnership income"
	"specified partnership loss"
125(8)	Assignment — specified partnership business limit
125(9)	Anti-avoidance
125(10)	Computational rule — specified corporate income
125(11)–(15)	(Repealed.)
125.1(1)	Manufacturing and processing profits deductions
125.1(2)	Electrical energy and steam
125.1(3)	Definitions
	"Canadian manufacturing and processing profits"
	"manufacturing or processing"
125.1(4)	Determination of gross revenue
125.1(5)	Interpretation
125.11(1)	Definitions (Repealed.)
	"resource rate reduction percentage" (Repealed.)
	"taxable resource income" (Repealed.)
125.11(2)	Resource deduction (Repealed.)
125.2(1)	Deduction of Part VI tax (Repealed.)
125.2(2)	Idem (Repealed.)
125.2(3)	Definition of "unused Part VI tax credit" (Repealed.)
125.21	Part XIII tax — eligible bank affiliate
125.3(1)	Deduction of Part I.3 tax
125.3(1.1)	Idem
125.3(2)	Special rules
125.3(3)	Acquisition of control
125.3(4)	Definitions
	"Canadian surtax payable"
	"unused Part I.3 tax credit"
125.4(1)	Definitions
	"assistance"
	"Canadian film or video production"
	"Canadian film or video production certificate"
	"investor" (Repealed.)
	"labour expenditure"
	"production commencement time"
	"qualified corporation"
	"qualified labour expenditure"
	"salary or wages"
	"script material"
125.4(2)	Rules governing labour expenditure of a corporation
125.4(3)	Tax credit
125.4(4)	Exception
125.4(5)	When assistance received
125.4(6)	Revocation of certificate
125.4(7)	Guidelines
125.5(1)	Definitions
	"accredited film or video production certificate"
	"accredited production"
	"assistance"
	"Canadian labour expenditure"
	"eligible production corporation"
	"qualified Canadian labour expenditure"
	"salary or wages"
125.5(2)	Rules governing Canadian labour expenditure of a corporation
125.5(3)	Tax credit

Section	Subject
125.5(4)	Canadian film or video production
125.5(5)	When assistance received
125.5(6)	Revocation of certificate
125.6(1)	Definitions
	"assistance"
	"eligible newsroom employee"
	"qualifying journalism organization"
	"qualifying labour expenditure"
125.6(2)	Tax credit
125.6(3)	When assistance received

SUBDIVISION C
RULES APPLICABLE TO ALL TAXPAYERS

Section	Subject
126(1)	Foreign tax deduction
126(1.1)	Authorized foreign bank
126(2)	Idem
126(2.1)	Amount determined for purposes of para. (2)(b)
126(2.2)	Non-resident's foreign tax deduction
126(2.21)	Former resident — deduction
126(2.22)	Former resident — trust beneficiary
126(2.23)	Where foreign credit available
126(2.3)	Rules relating to unused foreign tax credit
126(3)	Employees of international organizations
126(4)	Portion of foreign tax not included
126(4.1)	No economic profit
126(4.11)	Denial of foreign tax credit
126(4.12)	Exceptions
126(4.13)	Tiered partnerships
126(4.2)	Short-term securities acquisitions
126(4.3)	Exceptions
126(4.4)	Dispositions ignored
126(4.5)	Synthetic disposition — holding period
126(4.6)	Exception
126(5)	Foreign oil and gas levies
126(5.1)	Deductions for specified capital gains
126(6)	Rules of construction
126(7)	Definitions
	"business-income tax"
	"commercial obligation"
	"economic profit"
	"foreign oil and gas business"
	"Foreign-tax carryover" (Repealed.)
	"non-business-income tax"
	"production tax amount"
	"qualifying incomes"
	"qualifying losses"
	"related transactions"
	"tax for the year otherwise payable under this Part"
	"tax-exempt income"
	"taxing country"
	"unused foreign tax credit"
126(8)	Deemed dividend — partnership
126(9)	Computation of qualifying incomes and losses
126.1(1)	Definitions (Repealed.)
126.1(2)	Associated employers (Repealed.)
126.1(3)	Idem (Repealed.)
126.1(4)	Business carried on by another employer (Repealed.)
126.1(5)	Definition of "specified employer" (Repealed.)
126.1(6)	UI premium tax credit (Repealed.)
126.1(7)	Idem (Repealed.)
126.1(8)	Definition of "UI premium tax credit" (Repealed.)
126.1(9)	Allocation by associated employers (Repealed.)
126.1(10)	Allocation by the Minister (Repealed.)
126.1(11)	UI premium tax credit — associated employers (Repealed.)
126.1(12)	Prepayment of UI premium tax credit (Repealed.)
126.1(13)	Idem (Repealed.)
126.1(14)	Excess prepayment (Repealed.)
126.1(15)	Idem (Repealed.)
127(1)	Logging tax deduction
127(2)	Definitions
	"income for the year from logging operations in the province"
	"logging tax"
127(3)	Contributions to registered parties and candidates
127(3.1)	Issue of receipts
127(3.2)	Authorization required for receipts from registered associations
127(3.3)	Prohibition — issuance of receipts
127(4)	Definitions (Repealed.)
127(4.1)	Monetary contributions — form and content
127(4.2)	Allocation of amount contributed among partners (Repealed.)
127(5)	Investment tax credit
127(6)	Investment tax credit of cooperative corporation
127(7)	Investment tax credit of certain trusts
127(8)	Investment tax credit of partnership
127(8.1)	Investment tax credit of limited partner
127(8.2)	Expenditure base
127(8.3)	Investment tax credit — allocation of unallocated partnership ITCs
127(8.31)	Amount of unallocated partnership ITC
127(8.4)	Idem
127(8.5)	Definitions
127(9)	Idem
	"annual investment tax credit limit" (Repealed.)
	"apprenticeship expenditure"
	"approved project"
	"approved project property" (Repealed.)
	"Cape Breton"
	"certified property"
	"child care space amount" (Repealed.)
	"contract payment"
	"designated region" (Repealed.)
	"eligible apprentice"
	"eligible child care space expenditure" (Repealed.)
	"eligible salary and wages"
	"eligible taxpayer"
	"first term shared-use-equipment"
	"flow-through mining expenditure"
	"Gaspé Peninsula"
	"government assistance"
	"investment tax credit"
	"non-government assistance"
	"non-qualifying corporation"
	"phase"
	"pre-production mining expenditure"
	"qualified Canadian exploration expenditure" (Repealed.)
	"qualified construction equipment" (Repealed.)
	"qualified expenditure"
	"qualified property"
	"qualified resource property"
	"qualified small-business property" (Repealed.)
	"qualified transportation equipment" (Repealed.)
	"second term shared-use-equipment"
	"specified child care start-up expenditure" (Repealed.)
	"specified percentage"

Section	Subject
	"specified property" (Repealed.)
	"specified sampling"
	"SR&ED qualified expenditure pool"
	"super-allowance benefit amount"
	"taxable supplier"
127(9.01)	Transitional application of investment tax credit definition
127(9.02)	Transitional application of investment tax credit definition
127(9.1)	Loss restriction event before end of year
127(9.2)	Loss restriction event after end of year
127(10)	Ascertainment of certain property
127(10.1)	Additions to investment tax credit
127(10.2)	Expenditure limit
127(10.21)	Expenditure limits — associated CCPCs
127(10.22)	Deemed non-association of corporations
127(10.23)	Application of subsection (10.22)
127(10.3)	Associated corporations
127(10.4)	Failure to file agreement
127(10.5)	Failure to file agreement (Repealed.)
127(10.6)	Expenditure limit determination in certain cases
127(10.7)	Further additions to investment tax credit
127(10.8)	Further additions to investment tax credit
127(11)	Interpretation
127(11.1)	Investment tax credit
127(11.2)	Time of acquisition
127(11.3)	Decertification of approved project property
127(11.4)	Special rule for eligible salary and wages — apprentices
127(11.5)	Adjustments to qualified expenditures
127(11.6)	Non-arm's length costs
127(11.7)	Definitions
	"adjusted selling cost"
	"adjusted service cost"
127(11.8)	Interpretation for non-arm's length costs
127(12)	Interpretation
127(12.1)	Idem
127(12.2)	Idem
127(12.3)	Idem
127(13)	Agreement to transfer qualified expenditures
127(14)	Identification of amounts transferred
127(15)	Invalid agreements
127(16)	Non-arm's length parties
127(17)	Assessment
127(18)	Reduction of qualified expenditures
127(19)	Reduction of qualified expenditures
127(20)	Agreement to allocate
127(21)	Failure to allocate
127(22)	Invalid agreements
127(23)	Partnership's taxation year
127(24)	Exclusion from qualified expenditure
127(25)	Deemed contract payment
127(26)	Unpaid amounts
127(27)	Recapture of investment tax credit
127(27.1)	Recapture of investment tax credit — child care space amount (Repealed.)
127(27.11)	Disposition (Repealed.)
127(27.12)	Amount of recapture (Repealed.)
127(28)	Recapture of investment tax credit of partnership
127(28.1)	Recapture of partnership's investment tax credits — child care property (Repealed.)
127(29)	Recapture of investment tax credit of allocating taxpayer
127(30)	Addition to tax
127(31)	Tiered partnership
127(32)	Meaning of cost

Section	Subject
127(33)	Certain non-arm's length transfers
127(34)	Recapture of investment tax credit
127(35)	Recapture of investment tax credit
127(36)	Transitional application of investment tax credit recapture
127.1(1)	Refundable investment tax credit
127.1(2)	Definitions
	"excluded corporation"
	"qualifying corporation"
	"qualifying income limit"
	"refundable investment tax credit"
127.1(2.01)	Addition to refundable investment tax credit
127.1(2.1)	Application of s. 127(9)
127.1(2.2)	Refundable investment tax credit — associated CCPCs
127.1(2.3)	Application of subsection (2.2)
127.1(3)	Deemed deduction
127.1(4)	Qualifying income limit determined in certain cases
127.2(1)	Share-purchase tax credit
127.2(2)	Persons exempt from tax
127.2(3)	Trust
127.2(3.1)	Exclusion of certain trusts
127.2(4)	Partnership
127.2(5)	Cooperative corporation
127.2(6)	Definitions
	"share-purchase tax credit"
	"unused share-purchase tax credit"
127.2(7)	Definition of "tax otherwise payable"
127.2(8)	Deemed cost of acquisition
127.2(9)	Partnership
127.2(10)	Election re first holder
127.2(11)	Calculation of consideration
127.3(1)	Scientific research and experimental development tax credit
127.3(2)	Definitions
	"scientific research and experimental development tax credit"
	"unused scientific research and experimental development tax credit"
127.3(3)	Trust
127.3(3.1)	Exclusion of certain trusts
127.3(4)	Partnership
127.3(5)	Cooperative corporation
127.3(6)	Deduction from cost
127.3(7)	Partnership
127.3(8)	Definition of "tax otherwise payable"
127.3(9)	Election re first holder
127.3(10)	Calculation of consideration
127.4(1)	Definitions
	"approved share"
	"labour-sponsored funds tax credit" (Repealed.)
	"net cost"
	"original acquisition"
	"qualifying trust"
	"tax otherwise payable"
127.4(1.1)	Amalgamations or mergers
127.4(2)	Deduction of labour-sponsored funds tax credit
127.4(3)	3-year cooling-off period (Repealed.)
127.4(4)	Exceptions to cooling-off period (Repealed.)
127.4(5)	Labour-sponsored funds tax credit limit
127.4(5.1)	Deemed original acquisition
127.4(6)	Labour-sponsored funds tax credit
127.41(1)	Part XII.4 tax credit
127.41(2)	Reduction of Part I tax
127.41(3)	Deemed payment of Part I tax

DIVISION E.1 MINIMUM TAX

Section	Subject
127.5	Obligation to pay minimum tax
127.51	Minimum amount determined
127.52(1)	Adjusted taxable income determined
127.52(2)	Partnerships
127.52(2.1)	Specified member of a partnership
127.52(3)	Definitions
	"film property"
	"limited partner"
	"rental or leasing property"
	"residential property" (Repealed.)
127.53(1)	Basic exemption (Repealed.)
127.53(2)	Multiple trusts (Repealed.)
127.53(3)	Failure to file agreement (Repealed.)
127.531	Basic minimum tax credit determined
127.54(1)	Definitions
	"foreign income"
	"foreign taxes"
127.54(2)	Foreign tax credit
127.55	Application of s. 127.5

DIVISION F SPECIAL RULES APPLICABLE IN CERTAIN CIRCUMSTANCES

Section	Subject
128(1)	Where corporation bankrupt
128(2)	Where individual bankrupt
128(3)	Definitions of "bankrupt" and "estate of the bankrupt" (Repealed.)
128.1(1)	Immigration
128.1(1)*(a)*	Year-end, fiscal period
128.1(1)*(b)*	Deemed disposition
128.1(1)*(c)*	Deemed acquisition
128.1(1)*(c.1)*	Deemed dividend to immigrating corporation
128.1(1)*(c.2)*	Deemed dividend to shareholder of immigrating corporation
128.1(1)*(c.3)*	Foreign affiliate dumping — immigrating corporation
128.1(1)*(d)*	Foreign affiliate
128.1(1.1)	Trusts subject to subsection 94(3)
128.1(1.2)	Trusts and partnerships look-through rule
128.1(2)	Paid-up capital adjustment
128.1(3)	Paid-up capital adjustment
128.1(4)	Emigration
128.1(4)*(a)*	Year-end, fiscal period
128.1(4)*(a.1)*	Fiscal period
128.1(4)*(b)*	Deemed disposition
128.1(4)*(b.1)*	Employee life and health trust
128.1(4)*(c)*	Reacquisition
128.1(4)*(d)*	Individual — elective disposition
128.1(4)*(d.1)*	Employee CCPC stock option shares
128.1(4)*(e)*	Deemed property (Repealed.)
128.1(4)*(f)*	Losses on election (Repealed.)
128.1(5)	Instalment interest
128.1(6)	Returning former resident
128.1(6.1)	Deemed taxable Canadian property
128.1(7)	Returning trust beneficiary
128.1(8)	Post-emigration loss
128.1(9)	Information reporting
128.1(10)	Definitions
	"excluded right or interest"
	"reportable property"
128.2(1)	Cross-border mergers
128.2(2)	Idem
128.2(3)	Windings-up excluded
128.3	Former resident — replaced shares
129(1)	Dividend refund to private corporation
129(1.1)	Dividends paid to bankrupt controlling corporation
129(1.2)	Dividends deemed not to be taxable dividends
129(2)	Application to other liability
129(2.1)	Interest on dividend refund
129(2.2)	Excess interest on dividend refund
129(3)	Definition of "refundable dividend tax on hand" (Repealed.)
129(3.1)	Application
129(3.2)–(3.5)	(Repealed.)
129(4)	Definitions
	"aggregate investment income"
	"Canadian investment income" (Repealed.)
	"eligible portion"
	"eligible refundable dividend tax on hand"
	"foreign investment income"
	"income" or "loss"
	"non-eligible refundable dividend tax on hand"
129(4.1)	Conditions for subsection (4.2)
129(4.2)	Part IV tax — allocation of losses
129(4.3)	Definition of "designated property" (Repealed.)
129(5)	2019 transitional RDTOH
129(5.1)	2019 transitional RDTOH — amalgamations
129(6)	Investment income from associated corporation deemed to be active business income
129(7)	Meaning of "taxable dividend"
129(8)	Application of s. 125
130(1)	Deduction from tax
130(2)	Application of subsections 131(1) to (3.2), (4.1) and (6)
130(3)	Meaning of expressions "investment corporation" and "taxed capital gains"
130(4)	Wholly owned subsidiaries
130.1(1)	Deduction from tax
130.1(2)	Dividend equated to bond interest
130.1(3)	Application of s. (2)
130.1(4)	Election re capital gains dividend
130.1(4.1)	Application of ss. 131(1.1) to (1.4)
130.1(4.2)	Reporting (Repealed.)
130.1(4.3)	Allocation (Repealed.)
130.1(4.4)	Allocation (Repealed.)
130.1(4.5)	Allocation (Repealed.)
130.1(5)	Public corporation
130.1(6)	Meaning of "mortgage investment corporation"
130.1(7)	How shareholders counted
130.1(8)	First taxation year
130.1(9)	Definitions
	"liabilities"
	"non-qualifying real property" (Repealed.)
	"non-qualifying taxed capital gains" (Repealed.)
	"qualifying taxed capital gains" (Repealed.)
	"taxed capital gains"
131(1)	Election re capital gains dividend
131(1.1)	Deemed date of election
131(1.2)	Request to make election
131(1.3)	Penalty
131(1.4)	Assessment and payment of penalty
131(1.5)	Reporting (Repealed.)
131(1.6)	Allocation (Repealed.)
131(1.7)	Allocation (Repealed.)
131(1.8)	Allocation (Repealed.)
131(1.9)	Allocation (Repealed.)
131(2)	Capital gains refund to mutual fund corporation
131(3)	Application to other liability
131(3.1)	Interest on capital gains refund
131(3.2)	Excess interest on capital gains refund

Section	Subject
131(4)	Application of s. 84
131(4.1)	Sections not applicable
131(5)	Dividend refund to mutual fund corporation
131(5.1)	TCP gains distribution
131(5.2)	Application of subsection (5.1)
131(6)	Definitions
	“capital gains dividend account”
	“capital gains redemptions”
	“non-qualifying real property” (Repealed.)
	“non-qualifying real property capital gains dividend account” (Repealed.)
	“pro rata portion”
	“refundable capital gains tax on hand”
	“TCP gains balance”
	“TCP gains distribution”
131(7)	Definition of “taxed capital gains”
131(8)	Meaning of “mutual fund corporation”
131(8.01)	Election to be a mutual fund corporation
131(8.1)	Idem
131(9)	Reduction of refundable capital gains tax on hand
131(10)	Restricted financial institution
131(11)	Rules respecting prescribed labour-sponsored venture capital corporations
132(1)	Capital gains refund to mutual fund trust
132(2)	Application to other liability
132(2.1)	Interest on capital gains refund
132(2.2)	Excess interest on capital gains refund
132(3)	Application of s. 104(20)
132(4)	Definitions
	“capital gains redemptions”
	“pro rata portion”
	“refundable capital gains tax on hand”
	“TCP gains balance”
	“TCP gains distribution”
132(5)	Definition of “taxed capital gains”
132(5.1)	TCP gains distribution
132(5.2)	Application of subsection (5.1)
Prop. 132(5.3)	Allocation to redeemers
132(6)	Meaning of “mutual fund trust”
132(6.1)	Election to be mutual fund
132(6.2)	Retention of status as mutual fund trust
132(7)	Idem
132.1(1)	Amounts designated by mutual fund trust
132.1(2)	Adjusted cost base of unit where designation made
132.1(3)	Limitation on current year deduction
132.1(4)	Carryover of excess
132.1(5)	Where designation has no effect
132.11(1)	Taxation year of mutual fund trust
132.11(1.1)	Revocation of election
132.11(2)	Electing trust’s share of partnership income and losses
132.11(3)	Electing trust’s income from other trusts
132.11(4)	Amounts paid or payable to beneficiaries
132.11(5)	Special rules where change in status of beneficiary
132.11(6)	Additional income of electing trust
132.11(7)	Deduction
132.11(8)	Anti-avoidance
132.2(1)	Definitions re qualifying exchange of mutual funds
	“first post-exchange year”
	“qualifying exchange”
	“share”
132.2(2)	Timing
132.2(3)	General
132.2(4)	Qualifying exchange — non-depreciable property
132.2(5)	Depreciable property
132.2(6)	Due date
132.2(7)	Amendment or revocation of election
133(1)	Computation of income

Section	Subject
133(2)	Non-resident-owned investment corporations
133(3)	Special tax rate
133(4)	No deduction for foreign taxes
133(5)	1971 undistributed income and capital surplus on hand (Repealed.)
133(6)	Allowable refund to non-resident-owned investment corporations
133(7)	Application to other liability
133(7.01)	Interest on allowable refund
133(7.02)	Excess interest on allowable refund
133(7.1)	Election re capital gains dividend
133(7.2)	Simultaneous dividends
133(7.3)	Application of ss. 131(1.1) to (1.4)
133(7.4)	Request to make election (Repealed.)
133(7.5)	Penalty (Repealed.)
133(7.6)	Assessment and payment of penalty (Repealed.)
133(8)	Definitions
	“allowable refund”
	“Canadian property”
	“capital gains dividend account”
	“increase in capital”
	“non-resident-owned investment corporation”
	“taxable dividend”
133(9)	Definitions
	“allowable refundable tax on hand”
	“cumulative taxable income”
134	Non-resident-owned corporation not a Canadian corporation, etc.
134.1(1)	NRO — transition
134.1(2)	Application
134.2(1)	Revocation
134.2(2)	Consequences
135(1)	Deduction in computing income
135(1.1)	Limitation where non-arm’s length customer
135(2)	Limitation where non-member customer
135(2.1)	Deduction carried over
135(3)	Amount to be deducted or withheld from payment to customer
135(4)	Definitions
	“allocation in proportion to patronage”
	“consumer goods or services”
	“customer”
	“income of the taxpayer attributable to business done with members”
	“member”
	“non-member customer”
	“payment”
135(5)	Holding out prospect of allocations
135(6)	Amount of payment to customer
135(7)	Payment to customer to be included in income
135(8)	Patronage dividends
135.1(1)	Definitions
	“agricultural business”
	“agricultural cooperative corporation”
	“allowable disposition”
	“eligible member”
	“tax deferred cooperative share”
	“tax paid balance”
135.1(2)	Income inclusion
135.1(3)	Deductibility limit
135.1(4)	Deemed disposition
135.1(5)	Reacquisition
135.1(6)	Exclusion from withholding obligation
135.1(7)	Withholding on redemption
135.1(8)	Application of subsections 84(2) and (3)
135.1(9)	Application of subsection (10)
135.1(10)	Shares issued on corporate reorganizations

Section	Subject
135.2(1)	Definitions
	"application for continuance"
	"Canadian Wheat Board"
	"Canadian Wheat Board continuance"
	"eligible debt"
	"eligible share"
	"eligible trust"
	"eligible unit"
	"eligible wind-up distribution"
	"participating farmer"
	"person"
135.2(2)	Trust acquires an eligible debt
135.2(3)	Disposition of eligible debt
135.2(4)	Eligible trust
135.2(5)	Participating farmer — acquisition of eligible unit
135.2(6)	Eligible unit issued to estate
135.2(7)	Eligible unit — gain (loss)
135.2(8)	Death of a participating farmer
135.2(9)	Participating farmer — disposition of eligible unit
135.2(10)	Eligible wind-up distribution
135.2(11)	Ceasing to be an eligible trust
135.2(12)	Stock dividends — Canadian Wheat Board shares
135.2(13)	Reorganization of capital — Canadian Wheat Board
135.2(14)	Rollover of shares on reorganization
135.2(15)	Information filing requirement
135.2(16)	Failure to file prescribed form
136(1)	Cooperative not private corporation
136(2)	Definition of "cooperative corporation"
137(1)	Deductions in computing income (Repealed.)
137(2)	Payments pursuant to allocations in proportion to borrowing
137(3)	Additional deduction
137(4)	Amount deemed deductible under s. 125
137(4.1)	Payments in respect of shares
137(4.2)	Deemed interest not a dividend
137(4.3)	Determination of preferred-rate amount of a corporation
137(5)	Member's income
137(5.1)	Allocations of taxable dividends and capital gains
137(5.2)	Idem
137(6)	Definitions
	"allocation in proportion to borrowing"
	"bonus interest payment"
	"credit union"
	"maximum cumulative reserve"
	"member"
137(7)	Credit union not private corporation
137.1(1)	Amounts included in income of deposit insurance corporation
137.1(2)	Amounts not included in income
137.1(3)	Amounts deductible in computing income of deposit insurance corporation
137.1(4)	Limitation on deduction
137.1(5)	Definitions
	"amortized cost" (Repealed.)
	"deposit insurance corporation"
	"investment property"
	"member institution"
137.1(5.1)	Deeming provision
137.1(6)	Deemed not to be a private corporation
137.1(7)	Deposit insurance corporation deemed not a credit union
137.1(8)	Deemed compliance
137.1(9)	Special tax rate
137.1(10)	Amounts paid by a deposit insurance corporation
137.1(10.1)	Principal amount of an obligation to pay interest
137.1(11)	Deduction by member institutions
137.1(12)	Repayment excluded

Section	Subject
137.2	Computation of income for 1975 and subsequent years
138(1)	Insurance corporations
138(2)	Insurer's income or loss
138(2.1)	Income — designated foreign insurance business
138(2.2)	Insurance swaps
138(2.3)	Insurance swaps
138(2.4)	Insurance swaps
138(2.5)	Ceding of Canadian risks
138(2.6)	Anti-avoidance
138(3)	Deductions allowed in computing income
138(3.1)	Excess policy dividend deduction deemed deductible (Repealed.)
138(4)	Amounts included in computing income
138(4.01)	Life insurance policy
138(4.1)	Idem (Repealed.)
138(4.2)	Idem (Repealed.)
138(4.3)	Idem (Repealed.)
138(4.4)	Income inclusion
138(4.5)	Application
138(4.6)	Completion
138(5)	Deductions not allowed
138(5.1)	No deduction
138(5.2)	Idem (Repealed.)
138(6)	Deduction for dividends from taxable corporations
138(7)	Amounts paid to shareholders included in taxable income (Repealed.)
138(8)	No deduction for foreign tax
138(9)	Computation of income
138(9.1)	Gross investment revenue (Repealed.)
138(10)	Application of financial institution rules
138(11)	Profit or loss in respect of Canada security (Repealed.)
138(11.1)	Identical properties
138(11.2)	Computation of capital gain on pre-1969 depreciable property
138(11.3)	Deemed disposition
138(11.31)	Exclusion from deemed disposition
138(11.4)	Deduction of loss
138(11.41)	Inclusion of gain (Repealed.)
138(11.5)	Transfer of insurance business by non-resident insurer
138(11.6)	Time of election
138(11.7)	Computation of paid-up capital
138(11.8)	Rules on transfers of depreciable property
138(11.9)	Computation of contributed surplus
138(11.91)	Computation of income of non-resident insurer
138(11.92)	Computation of income where insurance business is transferred
138(11.93)	Property acquired on default in payment
138(11.94)	Transfer of insurance business by resident insurer
138(12)	Definitions
	"1975 branch accounting election deficiency" (Repealed.)
	"1975-76 excess additional group term reserve" (Repealed.)
	"1975-76 excess capital cost allowance" (Repealed.)
	"1975-76 excess investment reserve" (Repealed.)
	"1975-76 excess policy dividend deduction" (Repealed.)
	"1975-76 excess policy dividend reserve" (Repealed.)
	"1975-76 excess policy reserves" (Repealed.)
	"accumulated 1968 deficit" (Repealed.)
	"amortized cost" (Repealed.)
	"amount payable"
	"base year"
	"Canada security" (Repealed.)
	"cost" (Repealed.)
	"deposit accounting insurance policy"
	"designated foreign insurance business"
	"designated insurance property"
	"excluded policy"

Section	Subject
	"gross investment revenue"
	"insurance"
	"interest"
	"life insurance policy"
	"life insurance policy in Canada"
	"maximum tax actuarial reserve"
	"net Canadian life investment income" (Repealed.)
	"non-segregated property"
	"participating life insurance policy"
	"policy loan"
	"property used by it in the year in, or held by it in the year in the course of" (Repealed.)
	"qualified related corporation"
	"relevant authority" (Repealed.)
	"reserve transition amount"
	"segregated fund"
	"specified Canadian risk"
	"surplus funds derived from operations"
	"transition year"
138(13)	Variation in "tax basis" and "amortized cost"
138(14)	Meaning of certain expressions
138(15)	Definition not to apply
138(16)	Transition year income inclusion
138(17)	Transition year income deduction
138(17.1)	IFRS transition — reversals
138(18)	Transition year income inclusion reversal
138(19)	Transition year income deduction reversal
138(20)	Winding-up
138(21)	Amalgamations
138(22)	Application of subsection (23)
138(23)	Transfer of life insurance business
138(24)	Ceasing to carry on business
138(25)	Ceasing to exist
138(26)	Policy reserve transition — application rules
138.1(1)	Rules relating to segregated funds
138.1(2)	Rules relating to property in segregated funds at end of 1977 taxation year
138.1(2.1)	Transition — pre-2018 non-capital losses
138.1(3)	Capital gains and capital losses of related segregated fund trusts
138.1(3.1)	Deemed gains and losses (Repealed.)
138.1(3.2)	Deemed gains and losses — taxpayer (Repealed.)
138.1(4)	Election and allocation
138.1(5)	Adjusted cost base of property in related segregated fund trust
138.1(6)	Definition of "acquisition fee"
138.1(7)	Non-application of subsections (1) to (6)
138.2(1)	Qualifying transfer of funds
138.2(2)	General
138.2(3)	Transferor — capital gains and losses
138.2(4)	Transferee — capital gains and losses
138.2(5)	Loss limitation
138.2(6)	Due date
139	Conversion of insurance corporations into mutual corporations
139.1(1)	Definitions
	"conversion benefit"
	"deadline"
	"demutualization"
	"holding corporation"
	"initial deadline"
	"mutual holding corporation"
	"ownership rights"
	"person"
	"share"
	"specified insurance benefit"
	"stakeholder"
	"taxable conversion benefit"
139.1(2)	Rules of general application
139.1(3)	Special cases
139.1(4)	Consequences of demutualization
139.1(5)	Fair market value of ownership rights
139.1(6)	Paid-up capital — insurance corporation
139.1(7)	Paid-up capital — holding corporation
139.1(8)	Policy dividends
139.1(9)	Payment and receipt of premium
139.1(10)	Cost of taxable conversion benefit
139.1(11)	No shareholder benefit
139.1(12)	Exclusion of benefit from RRSP and other rules
139.1(13)	RRSP registration rules, etc
139.1(14)	Retirement benefit
139.1(15)	Employee-paid insurance
139.1(16)	Flow-through of conversion benefits to employees and others
139.1(17)	Flow-through of share benefits to employees and others
139.1(18)	Acquisition of control
139.2	Mutual holding corporations
140(1)	Deductions in computing income
140(2)	Inclusion in computing income
141(1)	Definitions
141(2)	Life insurance corporation deemed to be public corporation
141(3)	Holding corporation deemed to be public corporation
141(4)	Specified period
141(5)	Exclusion from taxable Canadian property
141.1	Deemed not to be a private corporation
142	Taxable capital gains etc. (Repealed.)
142.1	Application of s. 138(12) (Repealed.)
142.2(1)	Definitions
	"excluded property"
	"fair value property"
	"financial institution"
	"investment dealer"
	"mark-to-market property"
	"specified debt obligation"
	"tracking property"
142.2(2)	Significant interest
142.2(3)	Rules re significant interest
142.2(4)	Extension of meaning of "related"
142.2(5)	Significant interest — transition (Repealed.)
142.3(1)	Amounts to be included and deducted
142.3(2)	Failure to report accrued amounts
142.3(3)	Exception for certain obligations
142.3(4)	Impaired specified debt obligations
142.4(1)	Definitions
	"tax basis"
	"transition amount"
142.4(2)	Scope of section
142.4(3)	Rules applicable to disposition
142.4(4)	Inclusions and deductions re disposition
142.4(5)	Gain or loss not amortized
142.4(6)	Gain or loss from disposition of obligation
142.4(7)	Current amount
142.4(8)	Residual portion of gain or loss
142.4(9)	Disposition of part of obligation
142.4(10)	Penalties and bonuses
142.4(11)	Payments received on or after disposition
142.5(1)	Income treatment for profits and losses
142.5(2)	Mark-to-market requirement
142.5(3)	Mark-to-market debt obligation
142.5(4)	Proceeds — mark-to-market property
142.5(5)	Transition — inclusion re non-capital amounts (Repealed.)
142.5(6)	Transition — deduction re net capital gains (Repealed.)

Section	Subject
142.5(7)	Transition — inclusion re net capital gains (Repealed.)
142.5(8)	First deemed disposition of debt obligation
142.5(8.1)	Application of subsection (8.2)
142.5(8.2)	Rules applicable to first deemed disposition of debt obligation
142.5(9)	Transition — property acquired on rollover
142.51(1)	Definitions
	"base year"
	"transition amount"
	"transition property"
	"transition year"
142.51(2)	Transition year income inclusion
142.51(3)	Transition year income deduction
142.51(4)	Transition year income inclusion reversal
142.51(5)	Transition year income deduction reversal
142.51(6)	Winding-up
142.51(7)	Amalgamations
142.51(8)	Application of subsection (9)
142.51(9)	Transfer of a business
142.51(10)	Continuation of a partnership
142.51(11)	Ceasing to carry on a business
142.51(12)	Ceasing to exist
142.6(1)	Becoming or ceasing to be a financial institution
142.6(1.1)	Ceasing to use property in Canadian business
142.6(1.2)	Beginning to use property in a Canadian business
142.6(1.3)	Specified debt obligation marked to market
142.6(1.4)	Change in status — prescribed payment card corporation share
142.6(1.5)	Change in status — prescribed securities exchange investment
142.6(1.6)	Change in status — significant interest
142.6(2)	Deemed disposition not applicable
142.6(3)	Property not inventory
142.6(4)	Property that ceases to be inventory
142.6(5)	Debt obligations acquired in rollover transactions
142.6(6)	Definition of "rollover transaction"
142.6(7)	Superficial loss rule not applicable
142.6(8)	Accrued capital gains and losses election
142.6(9)	Accrued capital gains election limit
142.6(10)	Accrued capital losses election limit
142.7(1)	Definitions
	"Canadian affiliate"
	"eligible property"
	"entrant bank"
	"qualifying foreign merger"
142.7(2)	Qualifying foreign merger
142.7(3)	Branch-establishment rollover
142.7(4)	Deemed fair market value
142.7(5)	Specified debt obligations
142.7(6)	Mark-to-market property
142.7(7)	Reserves
142.7(8)	Assumption of debt obligation
142.7(9)	Branch-establishment dividend
142.7(10)	Treatment of dividend
142.7(11)	Elections
142.7(12)	Winding-up of Canadian affiliate: losses
142.7(13)	Winding-up of Canadian affiliate: stop loss
142.7(14)	Winding-up of Canadian affiliate: SDOs
143(1)	Communal organizations
143(2)	Election in respect of income
143(3)	Refusal to accept election
143(3.1)	Election in respect of gifts
143(4)	Definitions
	"adult"
	"business agency"
	"congregation"
	"family"
	"member of a congregation"
	"participating member"
	"religious organization"
	"total charitable gifts"
	"total Crown gifts" (Repealed.)
	"total cultural gifts"
	"total ecological gifts"
143(5)	Specification of family members
143.1(1)	Definitions
	"amateur athlete"
	"professional athlete"
	"qualifying performance income"
	"third party"
143.1(1.1)	Where subsection (1.2) applies
143.1(1.2)	Amateur athletes' reserve funds
143.1(2)	Amounts included in beneficiary's income
143.1(3)	Termination of amateur athlete trust
143.1(4)	Death of beneficiary
143.2(1)	Definitions
	"expenditure"
	"limited partner"
	"limited-recourse amount"
	"tax shelter investment"
	"taxpayer"
143.2(2)	At-risk adjustment
143.2(3)	Amount or benefit not included
143.2(4)	Amount or benefit
143.2(5)	Amount or benefit
143.2(6)	Amount of expenditure
143.2(6.1)	Limited-recourse debt in respect of a gift or monetary contribution
143.2(7)	Repayment of indebtedness
143.2(8)	Limited-recourse amount
143.2(9)	Timing
143.2(10)	Timing
143.2(11)	Short-term debt
143.2(12)	Series of loans or repayments
143.2(13)	Information located outside Canada
143.2(14)	Information located outside Canada
143.2(15)	Assessments
143.3(1)	Definitions
	"expenditure"
	"option"
	"taxpayer"
143.3(2)	Options — limitation
143.3(3)	Corporate shares — limitation
143.3(4)	Non-corporate interests — limitation
143.3(5)	Clarification
143.4(1)	Definitions
	"contingent amount"
	"expenditure"
	"right to reduce"
	"taxpayer"
143.4(2)	Limitation of amount of expenditure
143.4(3)	Payment of contingent amount
143.4(4)	Subsequent years
143.4(5)	Subsequent contingent amount
143.4(6)	Anti-avoidance
143.4(7)	Assessments

DIVISION G DEFERRED AND OTHER SPECIAL INCOME ARRANGEMENTS

Section	Subject
144(1)	Definitions
	"employees profit sharing plan"
	"unused portion of a beneficiary's exempt capital gains balance"
144(2)	No tax while trust governed by plan
144(3)	Allocation contingent or absolute taxable
144(4)	Allocated capital gains and losses
144(4.1)	Idem
144(4.2)	Idem
144(5)	Employer's contribution to trust deductible
144(6)	Beneficiary's receipts deductible
144(7)	Beneficiary's receipts that are not deductible
144(7.1)	Where property other than money received by beneficiary
144(8)	Allocation of credit for dividends
144(8.1)	Foreign tax deduction
144(8.2)	Allocation of interest income deduction (Repealed.)
144(9)	Deduction for forfeited amounts
144(10)	Payments out of profits
144(11)	Taxation year of trust
144.1(1)	Definitions
	"actuary"
	"class of beneficiaries"
	"designated employee benefit"
	"employee"
	"key employee"
144.1(2)	Employee life and health trust
144.1(3)	Breach of terms etc
144.1(4)	Deductibility of employer contributions
144.1(5)	Actuarial determination
144.1(6)	Multi-employer plans
Prop. 144.1(6)	Deductibility — collective agreement
144.1(7)	Maximum deductible
144.1(8)	Employer promissory note
144.1(9)	Trust status — subsequent times
144.1(10)	Employee contributions
144.1(11)	Income inclusion
144.1(12)	Deemed separate trusts
144.1(13)	Non-capital losses
Prop. 144.1(14)	Conditions — deemed employee life and health trust
Prop. 144.1(15)	Deemed employee life and health trust
Prop. 144.1(16)	Trust-to-trust transfer
Prop. 144.1(17)	Deductibility of transferred property
145(1)	Definitions
	"registered supplementary unemployment benefit plan"
	"supplementary unemployment benefit plan"
145(2)	No tax while trust governed by plan
145(3)	Amounts received taxable
145(4)	Amounts received on amendment or winding-up of plan
145(5)	Payments by employer deductible
146(1)	Definitions
	"annuitant"
	"benefit"
	"earned income"
	"issuer"
	"maturity"
	"net past service pension adjustment"
	"non-qualified investment"
	"premium"
	"qualified investment"
	"refund of premiums"
	"registered retirement savings plan"
	"retirement income"
	"retirement savings plan"
	"RRSP deduction limit"
	"RRSP dollar limit"
	"spousal or common-law partner plan"
	"spousal plan" (Repealed.)
	"tax-paid amount"
	"unused RRSP deduction room"
146(1.1)	Restriction — financially dependent
146(2)	Acceptance of plan for registration
146(3)	Idem
146(4)	No tax while trust governed by plan
146(5)	Amount of RRSP premiums deductible
146(5.1)	Amount of spousal RRSP premiums deductible
146(5.2)	RRSP premium
146(5.201)	Transitional rule
146(5.21)	Anti-avoidance
146(5.3)–(5.5)	(Repealed.)
146(6)	Disposition of non-qualified investment (Repealed.)
146(6.1)	Recontribution of certain withdrawals
146(7)	Recovery of property used as security
146(8)	Benefits taxable
146(8.01)	Subsequent re-calculation
146(8.1)	Deemed receipt of refund of premiums
146(8.2)	Amount deductible
146(8.21)	Premium deemed not paid
146(8.3)	Spousal or common-law partner payments
146(8.4)	Interpretation (Repealed.)
146(8.5)	Ordering
146(8.6)	Spouse's [or common-law partner's] income
146(8.7)	Where s. (8.3) does not apply
146(8.8)	Effect of death where person other than spouse becomes entitled
146(8.9)	Idem
146(8.91)	Amounts deemed receivable by spouse or common-law partner
146(8.92)	Deduction for post-death reduction in value
146(8.93)	Subsection (8.92) not applicable
146(9)	Where disposition of property by trust
146(10)	Property used as security for loan
146(10.1)	Where tax payable
146(11)	Life insurance policies (Repealed.)
146(11.1)	Exception (Repealed.)
146(12)	Change in plan after registration
146(13)	Idem
146(13.1)	RRSP advantages (Repealed.)
146(13.2)	Maturity after age 69 (Repealed.)
146(13.3)	Notice (Repealed.)
146(14)	Premiums paid in taxation year
146(15)	Plan not registered at end of year entered into
146(16)	Transfer of funds
146(17)	Interpretation (Repealed.)
146(18)	Where plan matures before annuitant attains age of 60 (Repealed.)
146(19)	Transitional (Repealed.)
146(20)	Credited or added amount deemed not received
146(21)	Specified pension plan
146(21.1)	Specified pension plan — contribution
146(21.2)	Specified pension plan — account
146(21.3)	Specified pension plan — payment
146(22)	Deemed payment of RRSP premiums
146.01(1)	Definitions
	"annuitant"
	"benefit"
	"completion date"
	"designated withdrawal"
	"eligible amount"
	"excluded premium"
	"excluded withdrawal"

Section	Subject
	"HBP balance"
	"issuer"
	"participation period"
	"premium"
	"qualifying home"
	"quarter" (Repealed.)
	"regular eligible amount"
	"replacement property"
	"specified disabled person"
	"supplemental eligible amount"
146.01(2)	Special Rules
Pend. 146.01(2.1)	Marriage or common-law partnership
146.01(3)	Repayment of eligible amount
146.01(4)	Portion of eligible amount not repaid
146.01(5)	Where individual becomes a non-resident
146.01(6)	Death of individual
146.01(7)	Exception
146.01(8)	Filing of prescribed form (Repealed.)
146.01(9)–(13)	(Repealed.)
146.02(1)	Definitions
	"annuitant"
	"benefit"
	"eligible amount"
	"excluded premium"
	"excluded withdrawal"
	"full-time student"
	"LLP balance"
	"participation period"
	"premium"
	"qualifying educational program"
	"repayment period"
146.02(2)	Rule of application
146.02(3)	Repayment of eligible amount
146.02(4)	If portion of eligible amount not repaid
146.02(5)	Ceasing residence in Canada
146.02(6)	Death of individual
146.02(7)	Exception
146.1(1)	Definitions
	"accumulated income payment"
	"beneficiary"
	"contribution"
	"designated provincial program"
	"education savings plan"
	"educational assistance payment"
	"post-secondary educational institution"
	"post-secondary school level"
	"pre-1972 income" (Repealed.)
	"promoter"
	"public primary caregiver"
	"qualified investment"
	"qualifying educational program"
	"refund of payments"
	"registered education savings plan" or "RESP"
	"RESP annual limit" (Repealed.)
	"specified educational program"
	"specified plan"
	"subscriber"
	"tax-paid income" (Repealed.)
	"trust"
146.1(1.1)	Election
146.1(1.2)	Effect of election
146.1(2)	Conditions for registration
146.1(2.1)	RESP is revocable
146.1(2.2)	Waiver of conditions for accumulated income payments
146.1(2.21)	Extension for making educational assistance payments
146.1(2.22)	Timing of payment
146.1(2.3)	Social Insurance Number not required
146.1(3)	Deemed registration
146.1(4)	Registration of plans without prospectus
146.1(4.1)	Obligation to file amendment
146.1(5)	Trust not taxable
146.1(6)	Subscriber not taxable
146.1(6.1)	Transfers between plans
146.1(7)	Educational assistance payments
146.1(7.1)	Other income inclusions
146.1(7.2)	Excluded amount
146.1(8)	Definition of "beneficiary's portion of the tax-paid income" (Repealed.)
146.1(9)	Limitation on allocation of tax-paid income (Repealed.)
146.1(10)	Allocation of tax-paid income (Repealed.)
146.1(11)	Trust deemed to be inter vivos trust (Repealed.)
146.1(12)	Deemed date of registration
146.1(12.1)	Notice of intent to revoke registration
146.1(12.2)	Notice of revocation
146.1(13)	Revocation of registration
146.1(13.1)	RESP information
146.1(14)	Former Act
146.1(15)	Regulations
146.2(1)	Definitions
	"distribution"
	"holder"
	"issuer"
	"qualifying arrangement"
	"survivor"
146.2(2)	Qualifying arrangement conditions
146.2(3)	Paragraphs (2)(a), (b) and (e) not applicable
146.2(4)	Using TFSA interest as security for a loan
146.2(5)	TFSA
146.2(6)	Trust not taxable
146.2(6.1)	Carrying on a business
146.2(7)	Amount credited to a deposit
146.2(8)	Trust ceasing to be a TFSA
146.2(9)	Trust ceasing to be a TFSA on death of holder
146.2(10)	Annuity contract ceasing to be a TFSA
146.2(11)	Deposit ceasing to be a TFSA
146.2(12)	Arrangement is TFSA only
146.2(13)	Regulations
146.3(1)	Definitions
	"annuitant"
	"carrier"
	"designated benefit"
	"minimum amount"
	"property held"
	"qualified investment"
	"registered retirement income fund"
	"retirement income fund"
146.3(1.1)	Adjusted minimum amount for 2008
146.3(1.2)	Exceptions
146.3(1.3)	Exceptions
146.3(2)	Acceptance of fund for registration
146.3(3)	No tax while trust governed by fund
146.3(3.1)	Exception
146.3(4)	Disposition or acquisition of property by trust
146.3(5)	Benefits taxable
146.3(5.1)	Amount included in income
146.3(5.2)	Interpretation (Repealed.)
146.3(5.3)	Ordering
146.3(5.4)	Spouse's [or common-law partner's] income
146.3(5.5)	Where s. (5.1) does not apply
146.3(6)	Where last annuitant dies
146.3(6.1)	Designated benefit deemed received
146.3(6.11)	Transfer of designated benefit
146.3(6.2)	Amount deductible
146.3(6.3)	Deduction for post-death reduction in value

Section	Subject
146.3(6.4)	Subsection (6.3) not applicable
146.3(7)	Property used as security for loan
146.3(8)	Disposition of non-qualified investment (Repealed.)
146.3(9)	Tax payable on income from non-qualified investment
146.3(10)	Recovery of property used as security
146.3(11)	Change in fund after registration
146.3(11.1)	Idem (Repealed.)
146.3(12)	Idem
146.3(13)	Idem (Repealed.)
146.3(14)	Transfer on breakdown of marriage or common-law partnership
146.3(14.1)	Transfer to PRPP or RPP
146.3(14.2)	Taxation of amount transferred
146.3(15)	Credited or added amount deemed not received
146.4(1)	Definitions
	"assistance holdback amount"
	"contribution"
	"designated provincial program"
	"disability assistance payment"
	"disability savings plan"
	"DTC-eligible individual"
	"holder"
	"issuer"
	"lifetime disability assistance payments"
	"plan trust"
	"qualified investment"
	"qualifying family member"
	"qualifying person"
	"registered disability savings plan" or "RDSP"
	"specified maximum amount"
	"specified Minister"
	"specified year"
146.4(1.1)	Specified disability savings plan
146.4(1.2)	Ceasing to be a specified disability savings plan
146.4(1.3)	Waiting period
146.4(1.4)	Waiver
146.4(1.5)	Beneficiary replacing holder
146.4(1.6)	Entity replacing holder
146.4(1.7)	Rules applicable in case of dispute
146.4(2)	Registered status
146.4(3)	Registered status nullified
146.4(4)	Plan conditions
146.4(4.1)	Election on cessation of DTC-eligibility
146.4(4.2)	Election
146.4(4.3)	Transitional rule
146.4(5)	Trust not taxable
146.4(6)	Taxation of disability assistance payments
146.4(7)	Non-taxable portion of disability assistance payment
146.4(8)	Transfer of funds
146.4(9)	No income inclusion on transfer
146.4(10)	Non-compliance — cessation of registered status
146.4(11)	Non-compliance
146.4(12)	Non-application of subsection (11)
146.4(13)	Obligations of issuer
146.4(14)	Issuer's liability
147(1)	Definitions
	"deferred profit sharing plan"
	"forfeited amount"
	"licensed annuities provider"
	"profit sharing plan"
147(1.1)	Participating employer
147(2)	Acceptance of plan for registration
147(2.1)	Terms limiting contributions
147(2.2)	Reallocation of forfeitures
147(3)	Acceptance of employees profit sharing plan for registration
147(4)	Capital gains determined
147(5)	Registration date
147(5.1)	Contribution limits
147(5.11)	Compensation (Repealed.)
147(6)	Deferred plan not employees profit sharing plan
147(7)	No tax while trust governed by plan
147(8)	Amount of employer's contribution deductible
147(9)	Limitation on deduction
147(9.1)	No deduction
147(10)	Amounts received taxable
147(10.1)	Single payment on retirement, etc
147(10.2)	Idem
147(10.3)	Amount contributed to or forfeited under a plan
147(10.4)	Income on disposal of shares
147(10.5)	Amended contract
147(10.6)	Commencement of annuity after age 69 (Repealed.)
147(11)	Portion of receipts deductible
147(12)	Idem
147(13)	Appropriation of trust property by employer
147(14)	Revocation of registration
147(14.1)	Idem
147(15)	Rules applicable to revoked plan
147(16)	Payments out of profits
147(17)	Interpretation of "other beneficiary"
147(18)	Inadequate consideration on purchase from or sale to trust
147(19)	Transfer to RPP, RRSP or DPSP
147(20)	Taxation of amount transferred
147(21)	Restriction re transfers
147(22)	Excess transfer
147.1(1)	Definitions
	"actuary"
	"administrator"
	"average wage"
	"compensation"
	"defined benefit provision"
	"former limit"
	"member"
	"money purchase limit"
	"money purchase provision"
	"multi-employer plan"
	"participating employer"
	"past service event"
	"single amount"
	"specified multi-employer plan"
	"spouse" (Repealed.)
	"wage measure"
147.1(2)	Registration of plan
147.1(3)	Deemed registration
147.1(4)	Acceptance of amendments
147.1(5)	Additional conditions
147.1(6)	Administrator
147.1(7)	Obligations of administrator
147.1(8)	Pension adjustment limits
147.1(9)	Idem — multi-employer plans
147.1(10)	Past service benefits
147.1(11)	Revocation of registration — notice of intention
147.1(12)	Notice of revocation
147.1(13)	Revocation of registration
147.1(14)	Anti-avoidance — multi-employer plans
147.1(15)	Plan as registered
147.1(16)	Separate liability for obligations
147.1(17)	Superintendent of Financial Institutions
147.1(18)	Regulations
147.1(19)	Reasonable error
147.2(1)	Pension contributions deductible — employer contributions
147.2(2)	Employer contributions — defined benefit provisions

Section	Subject
147.2(3)	Filing of actuarial report
147.2(4)	Amount of employee's pension contributions deductible
147.2(4)(*a*)	Service after 1989
147.2(4)(*b*)	Service before 1990 while not a contributor
147.2(4)(*c*)	Service before 1990 while a contributor
147.2(5)	Teachers
147.2(6)	Deductible contributions when taxpayer dies
147.2(7)	Letter of credit
147.2(8)	Former employee of predecessor employer
147.3(1)	Transfer — money purchase to money purchase, RRSP or RRIF
147.3(2)	Transfer — money purchase to defined benefit
147.3(3)	Transfer — defined benefit to defined benefit
147.3(4)	Transfer — defined benefit to money purchase, RRSP or RRIF
147.3(4.1)	Transfer of surplus — defined benefit to money purchase
147.3(5)	Transfer to RPP, RRSP or RRIF for spouse on marriage breakdown
147.3(6)	Transfer — pre-1991 contributions
147.3(7)	Transfer — lump sum benefits on death
147.3(7.1)	Transfer where money purchase plan replaces money purchase plan
147.3(8)	Transfer where money purchase plan replaces defined benefit plan
147.3(9)	Taxation of amount transferred
147.3(10)	Idem
147.3(11)	Division of transferred amount
147.3(12)	Restriction re transfers
147.3(13)	Excess transfer
147.3(13.1)	Withdrawal of excessive transfers to RRSPs and RRIFs
147.3(14)	Deemed transfer
147.3(14.1)	Transfer of property between provisions
147.3(15)	Annuity contract commencing after age 69 (Repealed.)
147.4(1)	RPP annuity contract
147.4(2)	Amended contract
147.4(3)	New contract
147.4(4)	RPP annuity contract beginning after age 69 (Repealed.)
147.5(1)	Definitions
	"administrator"
	"designated pooled pension plan"
	"exempt earned income"
	"exempt-income contribution amount"
	"member"
	"participating employer"
	"pooled pension plan"
	"pooled registered pension plan" or "PRPP"
	"qualifying annuity"
	"qualifying survivor"
	"restricted investment"
	"single amount"
	"successor member"
	"unused non-deductible PRPP room"
147.5(2)	Registration conditions
147.5(3)	Conditions applicable to PRPPs
147.5(4)	Non-payment of minimum amount
147.5(5)	Permissible benefits
147.5(6)	Additional conditions
147.5(7)	Acceptance of amendments
147.5(8)	Trust not taxable
147.5(9)	Obligations of administrator
147.5(10)	Employer contributions deductible
147.5(11)	Member contributions
147.5(12)	Member's account
147.5(13)	Taxable amounts
147.5(14)	Treatment on death — no successor member
147.5(15)	Treatment on death — successor member
147.5(16)	Qualifying survivor
147.5(17)	Deemed distribution to qualifying survivor
147.5(18)	Post-death increase in value
147.5(19)	Post-death decrease in value
147.5(20)	Subsection (19) not applicable
147.5(21)	Transfer of amounts
147.5(22)	Taxation of transfers
147.5(23)	Taxation of qualifying annuity
147.5(24)	Notice of intent
147.5(25)	Date of revocation
147.5(26)	Notice of revocation
147.5(27)	Revocation of registration
147.5(28)	Voluntary revocation
147.5(29)	Single employer
147.5(30)	Significant interest
147.5(31)	Contributions from exempt income
147.5(32)	Non-deductible contributions
147.5(32.1)	Contribution deemed not paid
147.5(33)	Exempt contributions not over-contributions
147.5(34)	Designation of exempt-income contribution amount
147.5(35)	Regulations — other
148	Life Insurance Policies
148(1)	Amounts included in computing policyholder's income
148(1.1)	Amount included in computing taxpayer's income
148(2)	Deemed proceeds of disposition
148(3)	Special rules for certain policies
148(4)	Partial surrender — ACB prorated
148(4.01)	Repayment of policy loan on partial surrender
148(4.1)	Interest deduction from tax (Repealed.)
148(5)	10/8 policy surrender
148(6)	Proceeds receivable as annuity
148(7)	Disposition at non-arm's length and similar cases
148(8)	Idem
148(8.1)	Inter vivos transfer to spouse
148(8.2)	Transfer to spouse at death
148(9)	Definitions
	"adjusted cost basis"
	"amount payable"
	"cash surrender value"
	"child"
	"disposition"
	"interest"
	"policy loan"
	"premium"
	"proceeds of the disposition"
	"relevant authority" (Repealed.)
	"tax anniversary date"
	"value"
148(9.1)	Application of s. 12.2(11)
148(10)	Life annuity contracts
148(11)	Loss of grandfathering
148.1(1)	Definitions
	"cemetery care trust"
	"cemetery services"
	"custodian"
	"eligible funeral arrangement"
	"funeral or cemetery services"
	"funeral services"
	"qualifying person"
	"relevant contribution"
148.1(2)	Exemption for eligible funeral arrangements
148.1(3)	Income inclusion on return of funds
148.1(4)	Deemed distribution on transfer
148.1(5)	Non-application of subsection (4)

DIVISION H EXEMPTIONS

Section	Subject
149(1)	Miscellaneous exemptions
149(1)(*a*)	Employees of a country other than Canada
149(1)(*b*)	Members of the family and servants of employees of a country other than Canada
149(1)(*c*)	Municipal authorities
149(1)(*d*)	Corporations owned by the Crown
149(1)(*d*.1)	Corporations 90% owned by the Crown
149(1)(*d*.2)	Wholly-owned corporations
149(1)(*d*.3)	90% owned corporations
149(1)(*d*.4)	Combined ownership
149(1)(*d*.5)	Income within boundaries of entities
149(1)(*d*.6)	Subsidiaries of municipal corporations
149(1)(*e*)	Certain organizations
149(1)(*f*)	Registered charities
149(1)(*g*)	Registered Canadian amateur athletic association
149(1)(*h*)	Charitable trusts (Repealed.)
Pend. 149(1)(*h*)	Registered journalism organizations
149(1)(*h*.1)	Association of Universities and Colleges of Canada
149(1)(*i*)	Certain housing corporations
149(1)(*j*)	Non-profit corporations for scientific research and experimental development
149(1)(*k*)	Labour organizations
149(1)(*l*)	Non-profit organizations
149(1)(*m*)	Mutual insurance corporations
149(1)(*n*)	Housing companies
149(1)(*o*)	Pension trusts
149(1)(*o*.1)	Pension corporations
149(1)(*o*.2)	Idem
149(1)(*o*.3)	Prescribed small business investment corporations
149(1)(*o*.4)	Master trusts
149(1)(*p*)	Trusts under profit sharing plan
149(1)(*q*)	Trusts under a registered supplementary unemployment benefit plan
149(1)(*q*.1)	RCA trusts
149(1)(*r*)	Trusts under registered retirement savings plan
149(1)(*s*)	Trusts under deferred profit sharing plan
149(1)(*s*.1)	Trust governed by eligible funeral arrangement
149(1)(*s*.2)	Cemetery care trust
149(1)(*t*)	Farmers' and fishermen's insurer (Repealed.)
149(1)(*u*)	Registered education savings plans
149(1)(*u*.1)	Trusts under registered disability savings plans
149(1)(*u*.2)	TFSA trust
149(1)(*u*.3)	Pooled registered pension plan
149(1)(*v*)	Amateur athlete trust
149(1)(*w*)	Trusts to provide compensation
149(1)(*x*)	Registered retirement income funds
149(1)(*y*)	Trusts to provide vacation pay
149(1)(*z*)	Qualifying environmental trust
149(1)(*z*.1)	Environmental Quality Acttrust
149(1)(*z*.2)	Nuclear Fuel Waste Acttrust
149(1.1)	Exception
149(1.11)	Election
149(1.12)	Deemed election
149(1.2)	Income test
149(1.3)	Votes or de facto control
149(2)	Determination of income
149(3)	Application of s. (1)
149(4)	Idem
149(4.1)	Income exempt under 149(1)(t) (Repealed.)
149(4.2)	Idem (Repealed.)
149(4.3)	Computation of taxable income of insurer (Repealed.)
149(5)	Exception — investment income of certain clubs
149(6)	Apportionment rule
149(7)	Time for filing
149(7.1)	Penalty for failure to file on time
149(8)	Interpretation of para. (1)(j)
149(9)	Rules for determining gross revenue
149(10)	Becoming or ceasing to be exempt
149(11)	Geographical boundaries — body performing government functions
149(12)	Information returns
149.01(1)	Definitions (Repealed.)
149.01(2)	Information return (Repealed.)
149.01(3)	Content of return (Repealed.)
149.01(4)	Communication of information (Repealed.)
149.01(5)	Disbursement (Repealed.)
149.01(6)	Subsection (2) does not apply (Repealed.)
149.01(7)	Reporting not required (Repealed.)
149.1(1)	Definitions
	"Canadian amateur athletic association"
	"capital gains pool" (Repealed.)
	"charitable activities"
	"charitable foundation"
	"charitable organization"
	"charitable purposes"
	"charity"
	"designated gift"
	"disbursement quota"
	"divestment obligation percentage"
	"enduring property" (Repealed.)
	"entrusted shares percentage" (Repealed.)
	"equity percentage"
	"excess corporate holdings percentage"
	"exempt shares"
	"exempt shares percentage"
	"ineligible individual"
	"material transaction"
	"non-qualified investment"
	"original corporate holdings percentage"
	"political activity" (Repealed.)
	"private foundation"
	"promoter"
	"public foundation"
	"qualified donee"
	"qualified investment" (Repealed.)
Pend.	"qualifying journalism organization"
	"related business"
	"relevant criminal offence"
	"relevant offence"
	"relevant person"
	"specified gift" (Repealed.)
	"substituted shares"
	"taxation year"
	"total corporate holdings percentage"
149.1(1.01)	Deeming rule — Safe Streets and Communities Act
149.1(1.1)	Exclusions
149.1(1.2)	Authority of Minister
149.1(2)	Revocation of registration of charitable organization
149.1(3)	Revocation of registration of public foundation
149.1(4)	Revocation of registration of private foundation
149.1(4.1)	Revocation of registration of registered charity
149.1(4.2)	Revocation of registration of Canadian amateur athletic association
149.1(4.3)	Revocation of a qualified donee
149.1(5)	Reduction
149.1(6)	Devoting resources to charitable activity
149.1(6.01)	Devoting resources to purpose and function
149.1(6.1)	Charitable purposes
149.1(6.2)	Charitable purposes
149.1(6.201)	Activities of Canadian amateur athletic associations
149.1(6.21)	Marriage for civil purposes

Section	Subject
149.1(6.3)	Designation as public foundation, etc
149.1(6.4)	National arts service organizations
149.1(6.5)	Revocation of designation
149.1(7)	Designation of associated charities
149.1(8)	Accumulation of property
149.1(9)	Idem (Repealed.)
149.1(10)	Deemed charitable activity
149.1(10.1)	Public policy activities
149.1(11)	Partnership look-through rule
149.1(12)	Rules
149.1(13)	Designation of private foundation as public
149.1(14)	Information returns
Pend. 149.1(14.1)	Information returns
149.1(15)	Information may be communicated
149.1(16)	Penalty tax (Repealed.)
149.1(17)	Idem (Repealed.)
149.1(18)	Rules relating to computation of income (Repealed.)
149.1(19)	Election in respect of first taxation year (Repealed.)
149.1(20)	Rule regarding disbursement excess
149.1(21)	Definition of "disbursement excess"
149.1(22)	Refusal to register
149.1(23)	Annulment of registration
149.1(24)	Receipts issued before annulment
149.1(25)	Refusal to register — ineligible individual
149.1(26)	Foreign charities
149.2(1)	Material and insignificant interests
149.2(2)	Material transaction — anti-avoidance
149.2(2.1)	Ownership
149.2(3)	Net increase in excess corporate holdings percentage
149.2(4)	Net decrease in excess corporate holdings percentage
149.2(5)	Allocation of net increase in excess corporate holdings percentage
149.2(6)	Minister's discretion
149.2(7)	Allocation of net decrease in excess corporate holdings percentage
149.2(8)	Transitional rule
149.2(9)	Where subsection (10) applies
149.2(10)	Shares held through a trust on March 18, 2007
149.2(11)	Discretionary trusts

DIVISION I RETURNS, ASSESSMENTS, PAYMENT AND APPEALS

150(1)	Filing returns of income — general rule
150(1)(*a*)	Corporations
150(1)(*b*)	Deceased individuals
150(1)(*c*)	Trusts or estates
150(1)(*d*)	Individuals
150(1)(*e*)	Designated persons
150(1.1)	Exception
Prop. 150(1.2)	Exception trusts
150(2)	Demands for returns
150(3)	Trustees, etc
150(4)	Death of partner or proprietor
150(5)	Excluded disposition
150.1(1)	Definition of "electronic filing"
150.1(2)	Filing of return by electronic transmission
150.1(2.1)	Mandatory filing of return by electronic transmission
150.1(2.2)	Definition of "tax preparer"
150.1(2.3)	Electronic filing — tax preparer
150.1(2.4)	Exceptions
150.1(3)	Deemed date of filing
150.1(4)	Declaration
150.1(5)	Application to other Parts
151	Estimate of tax
152(1)	Assessment
152(1.01)	Determination of disability tax credit eligibility
152(1.1)	Determination of losses
152(1.11)	Determination pursuant to s. 245(2)
152(1.111)	Application of s. 245(1)
152(1.12)	When determination not to be made
152(1.2)	Provisions applicable
152(1.3)	Determination binding
152(1.4)	Determination in respect of a partnership
152(1.5)	Notice of determination
152(1.6)	Absence of notification
152(1.7)	Binding effect of determination
152(1.8)	Time to assess
152(1.9)	Waiver of determination limitation period
152(2)	Notice of assessment
152(3)	Liability not dependent on assessment
152(3.1)	Definition of "normal reassessment period"
152(3.2)	Determination of deemed overpayment
152(3.3)	Notice of determination
152(3.4)	Determination of UI premium tax credit (Repealed.)
152(3.5)	Notice of determination (Repealed.)
152(4)	Assessment and reassessment
152(4.01)	Extended period of assessment
152(4.1)	If waiver revoked
152(4.2)	Reassessment with taxpayer's consent
152(4.3)	Consequential assessment
152(4.4)	Definition of "balance"
152(5)	Limitation on assessments
152(6)	Reassessment where certain deductions claimed
152(6.1)	Reassessment if amount under subsection 91(1) is reduced
152(6.2)	Extended reassessment period
152(6.3)	Reassessment for section 119 credit
152(7)	Assessment not dependent on return or information
152(8)	Assessment deemed valid and binding
152(9)	Alternative basis for assessment
152(10)	Tax deemed not assessed
153(1)	Withholding
153(1.01)	Withholding — stock option benefits
153(1.1)	Undue hardship
153(1.2)	Election to increase withholding
153(1.3)	Reduction not permitted
153(1.31)	Non-cash stock option benefit
153(1.4)	Exception — remittance to designated financial institution
153(2)	Deemed withholding
153(3)	Deemed effect of deduction
153(3.1)	Amounts paid in error
153(4)	Unclaimed dividends, interest and proceeds
153(5)	Deemed effect of remittance
153(6)	Definitions
	"designated financial institution"
	"qualifying non-resident employee"
	"qualifying non-resident employer"
153(7)	Certification by Minister
154(1)	Agreements providing for tax transfer payments
154(2)	Tax transfer payment
154(3)	Payment deemed received by individual
154(4)	Payment deemed received by Receiver General
154(5)	Amount not to include refund
155(1)	Farmers and fishermen
155(2)	Definition of "instalment base"
156(1)	Other individuals
156(2)	Payment by mutual fund trusts
156(3)	Definition of "instalment base"
156(4)	Payments by SIFT trusts

Section	Subject
156.1(1)	Definitions
	"instalment threshold"
	"net tax owing"
156.1(1.1)	Values of A and B in "net tax owing"
156.1(1.2)	Value of D in "net tax owing"
156.1(1.3)	Value of F in "net tax owing"
156.1(2)	No instalment required
156.1(3)	Idem
156.1(4)	Payment of remainder
157(1)	Payment by corporation
157(1.1)	Special case
157(1.2)	Small-CCPC
157(1.3)	Taxable income — small-CCPC
157(1.4)	Taxable capital — small-CCPC
157(1.5)	No longer a small-CCPC
157(2)	Application to SIFT trusts
157(2.1)	$3,000 threshold
157(3)	Reduced instalments
157(3.1)	Amount of payment — three-month period
157(4)	Definitions
157.1(1)	Instalment deferral for January, February and March 2002 — definitions
	"eligible corporation"
	"eligible instalment day"
157.1(2)	Deferred balance-due day
157.1(3)	Deferred instalment day
158	Payment of remainder
159(1)	Person acting for another
159(2)	Certificate before distribution
159(3)	Personal liability
159(3.1)	Appropriation of property
159(4)	Election on emigration (Repealed.)
159(4.1)	Idem (Repealed.)
159(5)	Election where certain provisions applicable
159(5.1)	Idem
159(6)	Idem
159(6.1)	Election where subsection 104(4) applicable
159(7)	Form and manner of election and interest
160(1)	Tax liability re property transferred not at arm's length
160(1.1)	Joint and several, or solidary, liability — subsection 69(11)
160(1.2)	Joint and several, or solidary, liability — tax on split income
160(1.3)	Joint liability — tax on split-pension income
160(1.4)	Joint liability — spousal and similar trusts
160(2)	Assessment
160(2.1)	Assessment
160(3)	Discharge of liability
160(3.1)	Fair market value of undivided interest or right
160(4)	Special rules re transfer of property to spouse or common-law partner
160.1(1)	Where excess refunded
160.1(1.1)	Liability for refund by reason of s. 122.5
160.1(2)	Liability under other provisions
160.1(2.1)	Liability for refunds by reason of section 122.61
160.1(2.2)	Liability for excess refunds under section 126.1 to partners
160.1(3)	Assessment
160.1(4)	Where amount applied to liability
160.2(1)	Joint and several liability in respect of amounts received out of or under RRSP
160.2(2)	Joint and several liability in respect of amounts received out of or under RRIF
160.2(2.1)	Joint and several liability in respect of a qualifying trust annuity
160.2(2.2)	No limitation on liability
160.2(3)	Assessment
160.2(4)	Rules applicable
160.2(5)	Rules applicable — qualifying trust annuity
160.21(1)	Joint and several liability — registered disability savings plan
160.21(2)	No limitation on liability
160.21(3)	Rules applicable — registered disability savings plans
160.21(4)	Assessment
160.3(1)	Liability in respect of amounts received out of or under RCA trust
160.3(2)	Assessment
160.3(3)	Rules applicable
160.4(1)	Liability in respect of transfers by insolvent corporations
160.4(2)	Indirect transfers
160.4(3)	Assessment
160.4(4)	Rules applicable
161(1)	General
161(2)	Interest on instalments
161(2.1)	Exception (Repealed.)
161(2.2)	Contra interest
161(3)	Special case (Repealed.)
161(4)	Limitation — farmers and fishermen
161(4.01)	Limitation — other individuals
161(4.1)	Limitation — corporations
161(5)	Participation certificates (Repealed.)
161(6)	Income of resident from a foreign country in blocked currency
161(6.1)	Foreign tax credit adjustment
161(6.2)	Flow-through share renunciations
161(7)	Effect of carryback of loss, etc
161(8)	Certain amounts deemed to be paid as instalments
161(9)	Definitions of "instalment base", etc
161(10)	When amount deemed paid
161(11)	Interest on penalties
161(12)	Partnership liable to interest (Repealed.)
161.1(1)	Definitions
	"accumulated overpayment amount"
	"accumulated underpayment amount"
	"arrears interest"
	"overpayment amount"
	"refund interest"
	"underpayment amount"
161.1(2)	Concurrent refund interest and arrears interest
161.1(3)	Contents of application
161.1(4)	Reallocation
161.1(5)	Repayment of refund
161.1(6)	Consequential reallocations
161.1(7)	Assessments
161.2	Period where interest not payable
161.3	Interest and penalty amounts of $25 or less
161.4(1)	Taxpayer
161.4(2)	Minister
162(1)	Failure to file return of income
162(2)	Repeated failure to file
162(2.1)	Failure to file — non-resident corporation
162(3)	Failure to file by trustee
162(4)	Ownership certificate
162(5)	Failure to provide information on form
162(5.1)	Failure to provide claim preparer information
162(5.2)	Due diligence
162(5.3)	Definitions
	"claim preparer"
	"claim preparer information"
	"SR&ED form"
162(6)	Failure to provide identification number
162(7)	Failure to comply
162(7.01)	Late filing penalty — prescribed information returns
162(7.02)	Failure to file in appropriate manner — prescribed information returns
162(7.1)	Failure to make partnership information return

Section	Subject
162(7.2)	Failure to file in appropriate manner — return of income
162(7.3)	Failure to file in appropriate manner — tax preparer
162(8)	Repeated failure to file
162(8.1)	Rules — partnership liable to a penalty
162(9)	Tax shelter identification number (Repealed.)
162(10)	Failure to furnish foreign-based information
162(10.1)	Additional penalty
162(10.11)	Application to trust contributions
162(10.2)	Shares or debt owned by controlled foreign affiliate
162(10.3)	Application to partnerships
162(10.4)	Application to non-resident trusts
162(11)	Effect of subsequent events
163(1)	Repeated failure to report income
163(1.1)	Amount of penalty
163(2)	False statements or omissions
163(2.1)	Interpretation
163(2.2)	False statement or omission
163(2.21)	False statement or omissions with respect to look-back rule
163(2.22)	Penalty
163(2.3)	Idem
163(2.4)	False statement or omission
163(2.41)	Application to trust contributions
163(2.5)	Shares or debt owned by controlled foreign affiliate
163(2.6)	Application to partnerships
163(2.7)	Application to partnerships
163(2.8)	Application to members of partnerships
163(2.9)	Partnership liable to penalty
163(2.91)	Application to non-resident trusts
163(3)	Burden of proof in respect of penalties
163(4)	Effect of carryback of losses etc
Prop. 163(5)	False statement or omission — trust return
Prop. 163(6)	False statement or omission — trust return
163.1	Penalty for late or deficient instalments
163.2(1)	Definitions
	"culpable conduct"
	"entity"
	"excluded activity"
	"false statement"
	"gross compensation"
	"gross entitlements"
	"participate"
	"person"
	"planning activity"
	"subordinate"
	"tax benefit"
	"valuation activity"
163.2(2)	Penalty for misrepresentations in tax planning arrangements
163.2(3)	Amount of penalty
163.2(4)	Penalty for participating in a misrepresentation
163.2(5)	Amount of penalty
163.2(6)	Reliance in good faith
163.2(7)	Non-application of subsection (6)
163.2(8)	False statements in respect of a particular arrangement
163.2(9)	Clerical services
163.2(10)	Valuations
163.2(11)	Exception
163.2(12)	Special rules
163.2(13)	Assessment void
163.2(14)	Maximum penalty
163.2(15)	Employees
163.3(1)	Definitions
	"electronic cash register"
	"electronic suppression of sales device"
	"service"

Section	Subject
163.3(2)	Penalty — use
163.3(3)	Penalty — possession
163.3(4)	Penalty — manufacturing or making available
163.3(5)	Assessment
163.3(6)	Limitation
163.3(7)	Certain defences not available
163.3(8)	Due diligence
163.3(9)	Assessment vacated
164(1)	Refunds
164(1.1)	Repayment on objections and appeals
164(1.2)	Collection in jeopardy
164(1.3)	Notice of application
164(1.31)	Application of ss. 225.2(4), (10), (12) and (13)
164(1.4)	Provincial refund
164(1.5)	Exception
164(1.51)	When subsection (1.52) applies
164(1.52)	Instalment refund
164(1.53)	Penalties, interest not affected
164(1.6)	Refund of UI premium tax credit (Repealed.)
164(1.7)	Limitation of repayment on objections and appeals
164(1.8)	Request to pay refund to province
164(2)	Application to other debts
164(2.01)	Withholding of refunds
164(2.1)	Application respecting refunds under s. 122.5
164(2.2)	Application respecting refunds re section 122.61
164(2.3)	Form deemed to be return of income
164(3)	Interest on refunds and repayments
164(3.1)	Idem
164(3.2)	Interest where amounts cancelled
164(4)	Interest on interest repaid
164(4.1)	Duty of Minister
164(5)	Effect of carryback of loss, etc
164(5.1)	Interest — disputed amounts
164(6)	Disposition by legal representative of deceased
164(6.1)	Realization of deceased employees' options
164(7)	Definition of "overpayment"
164.1	Prepayment of child tax credit
165(1)	Objections to assessment
165(1.1)	Limitation of right to object to assessments or determinations
165(1.11)	Objections by large corporations
165(1.12)	Late compliance
165(1.13)	Limitation on objections by large corporations
165(1.14)	Application of subsection (1.13)
165(1.15)	Partnership
165(1.2)	Limitation on objections
165(2)	Service
165(2.1)	Application
165(3)	Duties of Minister
165(3.1)	Decision by Minister of Human Resources Development (Repealed.)
165(3.2)	Reconsideration of determination (Repealed.)
165(4)	Effect of filing of notice of objection (Repealed.)
165(5)	Validity of reassessment
165(6)	Validity of notice of objection
165(7)	Notice of objection not required
166	Irregularities
166.1(1)	Extension of time by Minister
166.1(2)	Contents of application
166.1(3)	How application made
166.1(4)	Idem
166.1(5)	Duties of Minister
166.1(6)	Date of objection or request if application granted
166.1(7)	When order to be made
166.2(1)	Extension of time by Tax Court
166.2(2)	How application made

Section	Subject
166.2(3)	Copy to Commissioner of Revenue
166.2(4)	Powers of Court
166.2(5)	When application to be granted
167(1)	Extension of time to appeal
167(2)	Contents of application
167(3)	How application made
167(4)	Copy to Deputy Attorney General
167(5)	When order to be made
168(1)	Notice of intention to revoke registration
168(2)	Revocation of registration
168(3)	Charities Registration (Security Information) Act
168(4)	Objection to proposal or designation

DIVISION J APPEALS TO THE TAX COURT OF CANADA AND THE FEDERAL COURT OF APPEAL

Section	Subject
169(1)	Appeal
169(1.1)	Ecological gifts
169(2)	Limitation of right to appeal from assessments or determinations
169(2.1)	Limitation on appeals by large corporations
169(2.2)	Waived issues
169(3)	Disposition of appeal on consent
169(4)	Provisions applicable
170(1)	Notice to Commissioner
170(2)	Notice, etc., to be forwarded to Tax Court of Canada (Repealed.)
171(1)	Disposal of Appeal
171(1.1)	Ecological gifts
171(2)	Partial disposition of appeal
171(3)	Disposal of remaining issues
171(4)	Appeal to Federal Court of Appeal
172(1)	Appeal from refusal to register, revocation of registration, etc (Repealed.)
172(2)	Appeal to Federal Court of Canada (Repealed.)
172(3)	Appeal from refusal to register, revocation of registration, etc
172(3.1)	Exception — Charities Registration (Security Information) Act
172(4)	Deemed refusal to register
172(4.1)	Exception — Charities Registration (Security Information) Act
172(5)	Idem
172(6)	Application of s. 149.1(1)
173(1)	References to Tax Court of Canada
173(2)	Time during consideration not to count
174(1)	Common questions
174(2)	Application to Court
174(3)	Determination of question by Tax Court
174(4)	Determination final and conclusive
174(4.1)	Appeal
174(4.2)	Binding to appeal
174(5)	Time during consideration of question not counted
175	Institution of appeals
176(1)	Notice, etc., to be forwarded to Tax Court of Canada (Repealed.)
176(2)	Documents to be transferred to Federal Court of Appeal (Repealed.)
177	Disposal of appeal (Repealed.)
178(1)	Court may order payment of tax, etc. (Repealed.)
178(2)	Costs payable by Minister in certain cases (Repealed.)
179	Hearingsin camera
179.1	No reasonable grounds for appeal
180(1)	Appeals to Federal Court of Appeal
180(2)	No jurisdiction in a Tax Court of Canada or Federal Court
180(3)	Summary disposition of appeal

PART I.01
TAX IN RESPECT OF STOCK OPTION BENEFIT DEFERRAL

Section	Subject
180.01(1)	Election — special tax and relief for deferral of stock option benefits
180.01(2)	Effect of election
180.01(3)	Non-application for employment insurance purposes
180.01(4)	Provisions applicable to this Part

PART I.1
INDIVIDUAL SURTAX

Section	Subject
180.1	Individual surtax (Repealed.)

PART I.2
TAX ON OLD AGE SECURITY BENEFITS

Section	Subject
180.2(1)	Definitions
	"adjusted income"
	"base taxation year"
	"return of income"
180.2(2)	Tax payable
180.2(3)	Withholding
180.2(4)	Determination of amount to be withheld
180.2(5)	Return
180.2(6)	Provisions applicable to this Part

PART I.3
TAX ON LARGE CORPORATIONS

Section	Subject
181(1)	Definitions
	"financial institution"
	"long-term debt"
	"reserves"
181(2)	Prescribed expressions
181(3)	Determining values and amounts
181(4)	Limitations respecting inclusions and deductions
181.1(1)	Tax payable
181.1(1.1)	Specified percentage
181.1(1.2)	Exceptions
181.1(2)	Short taxation years
181.1(3)	Where tax not payable
181.1(4)	Deduction
181.1(5)	Idem

Section	Subject	Section	Subject
181.1(6)	Definitions "Canadian surtax payable" "unused surtax credit"	181.5(1)	Capital deduction
		181.5(1.1)	Exceptions
		181.5(2)	Related corporations
181.1(7)	Acquisition of control	181.5(3)	Allocation by Minister
181.2(1)	Taxable capital employed in Canada	181.5(4)	Idem
181.2(2)	Taxable capital	181.5(4.1)	Exceptions
181.2(3)	Capital	181.5(5)	Idem
181.2(4)	Investment allowance	181.5(6)	Idem
181.2(5)	Value of interest in partnership	181.5(7)	Related corporations that are not associated
181.2(6)	Loan	181.6	Return
181.3(1)	Taxable capital employed in Canada of financial institution	181.7(1)	Provisions applicable to Part
		181.7(2)	Instalment bases (Repealed.)
181.3(2)	Taxable capital of financial institution	181.71	Provisions applicable — Crown corporations
181.3(3)	Capital of financial institution	181.8	Interest (Repealed.)
181.3(4)	Investment allowance of financial institution	181.9	Provisions applicable to Part (Repealed.)
181.3(5)	Interpretation		
181.4	Taxable capital employed in Canada of non-resident		

PART II
TOBACCO MANUFACTURERS' SURTAX [REPEALED.]

Section	Subject	Section	Subject
182(1)	Surtax (Repealed.)	183(2)	Payment (Repealed.)
182(2)	Definitions (Repealed.)	183(3)	Provisions applicable (Repealed.)
183(1)	Return (Repealed.)		

PART II.1
TAX ON CORPORATE DISTRIBUTIONS

Section	Subject	Section	Subject
183.1(1)	Application of Part	183.1(6)	Where s. (2) does not apply
183.1(2)	Tax payable	183.1(7)	Where s. 110.6(8) does not apply
183.1(3)	Stock dividend	183.2(1)	Return
183.1(4)	Purchase of shares	183.2(2)	Provisions applicable to Part
183.1(5)	Indirect payment		

PART III
ADDITIONAL TAX ON EXCESSIVE ELECTIONS

Section	Subject	Section	Subject
184(1)	Tax on excess of dividend paid over portion payable out of tax-paid undistributed surplus or 1971 capital surplus (Repealed.)	184(5)	Exception for non-taxable shareholders
		185(1)	Assessment of tax
184(2)	Tax on excessive elections	185(2)	Payment of tax and interest
184(2.1)	Reduction of excess (Repealed.)	185(3)	Provisions applicable to Part
184(3)	Election to treat excess as separate dividend	185(4)	Joint and several, or solidary, liability from excessive elections
184(3.1)	Election to treat dividend as loan (Repealed.)	185(5)	Assessment
184(3.2)	Idem (Repealed.)	185(6)	Rules applicable
184(4)	Concurrence with election		

PART III.1
ADDITIONAL TAX ON EXCESSIVE ELIGIBLE DIVIDEND DESIGNATIONS

Section	Subject	Section	Subject
185.1(1)	Tax on excessive eligible dividend designations	185.2(2)	Provisions applicable to Part
185.1(2)	Election to treat excessive eligible dividend designation as an ordinary dividend	185.2(3)	Joint and several liability from excessive eligible dividend designations
185.1(3)	Concurrence with election	185.2(4)	Assessment
185.1(4)	Exception for non-taxable shareholders	185.2(5)	Rules applicable
185.2(1)	Return		

PART IV
TAX ON TAXABLE DIVIDENDS RECEIVED BY PRIVATE CORPORATIONS

Section	Subject	Section	Subject
186(1)	Tax on assessable dividends	186(6)	Partnerships
186(1.1)	Reduction where Part IV.1 tax payable	186(7)	Interpretation
186(2)	When corporation controlled	186.1	Exempt corporations
186(3)	Definitions "assessable dividend" "subject corporation"	186.2	Exempt dividends
		187(1)	Information return
		187(2)	Interest
186(4)	Corporations connected with particular corporation	187(3)	Provisions applicable to Part
186(5)	Deemed private corporation		

PART IV.1
TAXES ON DIVIDENDS ON CERTAIN PREFERRED SHARES RECEIVED BY CORPORATIONS

Section	Subject
187.1	Definition of "excepted dividend"
187.2	Tax on dividends on taxable preferred shares
187.3(1)	Tax on dividends on taxable RFI shares
187.3(2)	Time of acquisition of share
187.4	Partnerships
187.5	Information return
187.6	Provisions applicable to Part
187.61	Provisions applicable — Crown corporations

PART V
TAX AND PENALTIES IN RESPECT OF QUALIFIED DONEES

Section	Subject
187.7	Application of s. 149.1(1)
188(1)	Deemed year-end on notice of revocation
188(1.1)	Revocation tax
188(1.2)	Winding-up period
188(1.3)	Eligible donee
188(1.4)	Eligible donee
188(2)	Shared liability — revocation tax
188(2.1)	Non-application of revocation tax
188(3)	Transfer of property tax
188(3.1)	Non-application of subsection (3)
188(4)	Joint and several, or solidary, liability — tax transfer
188(5)	Definitions
	"net asset amount"
	"net value"
188.1(1)	Penalty — carrying on business
188.1(2)	Increased penalty for subsequent assessment
188.1(3)	Control of corporation by a charitable foundation
188.1(3.1)	Penalty for excess corporate holdings
188.1(3.2)	Avoidance of divestiture
188.1(3.3)	Where subsection (3.5) applies
188.1(3.4)	Rules applicable
188.1(3.5)	Avoidance of divestiture
188.1(4)	Undue benefits
188.1(5)	Meaning of undue benefits
188.1(6)	Failure to file information returns
188.1(7)	Incorrect information
188.1(8)	Increased penalty for subsequent assessment
188.1(9)	False information
188.1(10)	Maximum amount
188.1(11)	Delay of expenditure
188.1(12)	Gifts not at arm's length
188.2(1)	Notice of suspension with assessment
188.2(2)	Notice of suspension — general
188.2(2.1)	Suspension — failure to report
188.2(3)	Effect of suspension
188.2(4)	Application for postponement
188.2(5)	Grounds for postponement
189(1)	Tax regarding non-qualified investment
189(2)	Computation of interest on debt
189(3)	Share deemed to be debt
189(4)	Computation of interest with respect to a share
189(5)	Share substitution
189(6)	Taxpayer to file return and pay tax
189(6.1)	Revoked charity to file returns
189(6.2)	Reduction of revocation tax liability
189(6.3)	Reduction of liability for penalties
189(7)	Minister may assess
189(8)	Provisions applicable to Part
189(8.1)	Clarification re objections under subsection 168(4)
189(9)	Interest

PART VI
TAX ON CAPITAL OF FINANCIAL INSTITUTIONS

Section	Subject
190(1)	Definitions
	"financial institution"
	"long-term debt"
	"reserves"
190(1.1)	Prescribed meanings
190(2)	Application of ss. 181(3) and (4)
190.1(1)	Tax payable
190.1(1.1)	Additional tax payable by life insurance corporations (Repealed.)
190.1(1.2)	Additional tax payable by deposit-taking institutions (Repealed.)
190.1(2)	Short taxation years
190.1(3)	Deduction
190.1(4)	Idem
190.1(5)	Definitions
	"unused Part I tax credit"
	"unused surtax credit"
190.1(6)	Acquisition of control
190.11	Taxable capital employed in Canada
190.12	Taxable capital
190.13	Capital
190.14(1)	Investment in related institutions
190.14(2)	Interpretation
190.15(1)	Capital deduction
190.15(2)	Related financial institution
190.15(3)	Allocation by Minister
190.15(4)	Idem
190.15(5)	Idem
190.15(6)	Idem
190.16(1)	Application to taxation year including July 1, 2006 (Repealed.)
190.16(2)	Proportionate allocation (Repealed.)
190.16(3)	Capital deduction deemed (Repealed.)
190.16(4)	Idem (Repealed.)
190.16(5)	Provisions applicable to Part (Repealed.)
190.17	Enhanced capital deduction (Repealed.)
190.18	Special Rules (Repealed.)
190.19	Artificial reduction of capital tax (Repealed.)
190.2	Return
190.21	Provisions applicable to Part
190.211	Provisions applicable — Crown corporations
190.22	Instalment bases (Repealed.)
190.23	Interest (Repealed.)
190.24	Provisions applicable to Part (Repealed.)

PART VI.1
TAX ON CORPORATIONS PAYING DIVIDENDS ON TAXABLE PREFERRED SHARES

Section	Subject
191(1)	Definitions
	"excluded dividend"
	"financial intermediary corporation"
	"private holding corporation"
191(2)	Substantial interest
191(3)	Idem
191(4)	Deemed dividends
191(5)	Where subsection (4) does not apply
191(6)	Excluded dividend — partner
191.1(1)	Tax on taxable dividends
191.1(2)	Dividend allowance
191.1(3)	Associated corporations
191.1(4)	Total dividend allowance
191.1(5)	Failure to file agreement
191.1(6)	Dividend allowance in short years
191.2(1)	Election
191.2(2)	Time of election
191.2(3)	Assessment
191.3(1)	Agreement respecting liability for tax
191.3(1.1)	Consideration for agreement
191.3(2)	Manner of filing agreement
191.3(3)	Assessment
191.3(4)	Related corporations
191.3(5)	Assessment of transferor corporation
191.3(6)	Payment by transferor corporation
191.4(1)	Information return
191.4(2)	Provisions applicable to Part
191.4(3)	Provisions applicable — Crown corporations

PART VII
REFUNDABLE TAX ON CORPORATIONS ISSUING QUALIFYING SHARES

Section	Subject
192(1)	Corporation to pay tax
192(2)	Definition of "Part VII refund"
192(3)	Definition of "refundable Part VII tax on hand"
192(4)	Corporation may designate amount
192(4.1)	Computing paid-up capital after designation
192(5)	Presumption
192(6)	Definition of "qualifying share"
192(7)	Effect of obligation to acquire shares
192(8)	Late designation
192(9)	Penalty for late designation
192(10)	Deemed deduction
192(11)	Restriction
193(1)	Corporation to file return
193(2)	Corporation to make payment on account of tax
193(3)	Interest
193(4)	Idem
193(5)	Evasion of tax
193(6)	Undue deferral
193(7)	Avoidance of tax
193(7.1)	Tax on excess
193(8)	Provisions applicable to Part

PART VIII
REFUNDABLE TAX ON CORPORATIONS IN RESPECT OF SCIENTIFIC RESEARCH AND EXPERIMENTAL DEVELOPMENT TAX CREDIT

Section	Subject
194(1)	Corporation to pay tax
194(2)	Definition of "Part VIII refund"
194(3)	Definitions
	"debt obligation"
	"refundable Part VIII tax on hand"
194(4)	Corporation may designate amount
194(4.1)	Computing paid-up capital after designation
194(4.2)	Where amount may not be designated
194(5)	Presumption
194(6)	Definition of "scientific research and experimental development financing contract"
194(7)	Late designation
194(8)	Penalty for late designation
194(9)	Restriction
195(1)	Corporation to file return
195(2)	Corporation to make payment on account of tax
195(3)	Interest
195(4)	Idem
195(5)	Evasion of tax
195(6)	Undue deferral
195(7)	Avoidance of tax
195(7.1)	Tax on excess
195(8)	Provisions applicable to Part

PART IX
TAX ON DEDUCTION UNDER SECTION 66.5

Section	Subject
196(1)	Tax in respect of cumulative offset account
196(2)	Return
196(3)	Instalments
196(4)	Provisions applicable to Part

PART IX.1
TAX ON SIFT PARTNERSHIPS

Section	Subject
197(1)	Definitions
	"non-portfolio earnings"
	"SIFT partnership"
	"taxable non-portfolio earnings"
197(2)	Tax on partnership income
197(3)	Ordering
197(4)	Partnership to file return
197(5)	Authority to file return
197(6)	Provisions applicable to Part

Section	Subject
197(7)	Payment
197(8)	Application of definition "SIFT partnership"

PART X
TAXES ON DEFERRED PROFIT SHARING PLANS AND REVOKED PLANS

Section	Subject
198(1)	Tax on non-qualified investments and use of assets as security
198(2)	Payment of tax
198(3)	Trustee liable for tax
198(4)	Refund of tax on disposition of non-qualified investment
198(5)	Refund of tax on recovery of property given as security
198(6)	Special rules relating to life insurance policies
198(6.1)	Idem
198(7)	Idem
198(8)	Idem
199(1)	Tax on initial non-qualified investments not disposed of
199(2)	Refund
200	Distribution deemed disposition
201	Tax where inadequate consideration on purchase or sale
202(1)	Returns and payment of estimated tax
202(2)	Consideration of application for refund
202(3)	Provisions applicable to Part
202(4)	Provisions applicable to refunds
202(5)	Interest
202(6)	Deemed payment of tax
203	Application to other taxes
204	Definitions
	"debt obligation"
	"equity share"
	"excluded property"
	"excluded share"
	"initial base"
	"initial non-qualified investment"
	"non-participating share"
	"non-qualified investment"
	"paid-up capital value"
	"qualified investment"
	"revoked plan"

PART X.1
TAX IN RESPECT OF OVER-CONTRIBUTIONS TO DEFERRED INCOME PLANS

Section	Subject
204.1(1)	Tax payable by individuals
204.1(2)	Amount deemed repaid
204.1(2.1)	Tax payable by individuals — contributions after 1990
204.1(3)	Tax payable by deferred profit sharing plan
204.1(4)	Waiver of tax
204.2(1)	Definition of "excess amount for a year in respect of registered retirement savings plans"
204.2(1.1)	Cumulative excess amount in respect of RRSPs
204.2(1.2)	Undeducted RRSP premiums
204.2(1.3)	Group plan amount
204.2(1.31)	Qualifying group plan amount
204.2(1.32)	Qualifying arrangement
204.2(1.4)	Deemed receipt where RRSP or RRIF amended
204.2(1.5)	Transitional amount
204.2(2)	Where terminated plan deemed to continue to exist
204.2(3)	When retirement savings plan deemed to be a registered plan
204.2(4)	Definition of "excess amount" for a DPSP
204.2(5)	PRPP withdrawals
204.3(1)	Return and payment of tax
204.3(2)	Provisions applicable to Part

PART X.2
TAX IN RESPECT OF REGISTERED INVESTMENTS

Section	Subject
204.4(1)	Definition of "registered investment"
204.4(2)	Acceptance of applicant for registration
204.4(3)	Revocation of registration
204.4(4)	Suspension of revocation
204.4(5)	Cancellation of revocation
204.4(6)	Successor trust
204.4(7)	Deemed registration of registered investment
204.5	Publication of list in Canada Gazette
204.6(1)	Tax payable
204.6(2)	Tax payable
204.6(3)	Tax payable — real property or immovables
204.7(1)	Return and payment of tax
204.7(2)	Liability of trustee
204.7(3)	Provisions applicable to Part

PART X.3
LABOUR-SPONSORED VENTURE CAPITAL CORPORATIONS

Section	Subject
204.8(1)	Definitions
	"annuitant"
	"eligible business entity"
	"eligible investment"
	"eligible labour body"
	"labour-sponsored funds tax credit" (Repealed.)
	"national central labour body" (Repealed.)
	"original acquisition"
	"original purchaser" (Repealed.)
	"registered labour-sponsored venture capital corporation" (Repealed.)
	"reserve"
	"revoked corporation"
	"specified active business"
	"specified individual"
	"start-up period"
	"terminating corporation"
204.8(2)	When venture capital business discontinued
204.8(3)	Date of issue of Class A shares
204.81(1)	Conditions for registration
204.81(1.1)	Corporations incorporated before March 6, 1996
204.81(1.2)	Deemed provisions in articles
204.81(2)	Registration number

Section	Subject
204.81(3)	Successive registrations
204.81(4)	Determination of cost
204.81(5)	Registration date
204.81(6)	Revocation of registration
204.81(7)	Notice of intent to revoke registration
204.81(8)	Idem
204.81(8.1)	Voluntary de-registration
204.81(8.2)	Application of subsection 248(7)
204.81(8.3)	Transitional rules
204.81(8.4)	Discontinuance of provincial program
204.81(9)	Right of appeal
204.82(1)	Recovery of credit
204.82(2)	Liability for tax
204.82(2.1)	Determination of investment shortfall
204.82(2.2)	Investment shortfall
204.82(3)	Recovery of credit
204.82(4)	Penalty
204.82(5)	Provincially registered LSVCCs
204.82(6)	Further matching of amounts payable to a province
204.83(1)	Refunds for federally registered LSVCCs
204.83(2)	Refunds of amounts payable to provinces
204.84	Penalty
204.841	Penalty tax where venture capital business discontinued
204.85(1)	Dissolution of federally registered LSVCCs
204.85(2)	Dissolution of other LSVCCs
204.85(3)	Amalgamations and mergers
204.86(1)	Return and payment of tax for federally-registered LSVCCs
204.86(2)	Return and payment of tax for other LSVCCs
204.87	Provisions applicable to Part

PART X.4
TAX IN RESPECT OF OVERPAYMENT TO REGISTERED EDUCATION SAVINGS PLANS

Section	Subject
204.9(1)	Definitions
	"excess amount"
	"RESP lifetime limit"
	"subscriber's gross cumulative excess"
	"subscriber's share of the excess amount"
204.9(1.1)	Application of s. 146.1(1)
204.9(2)	Agreements before February 21, 1990
204.9(3)	Refunds from unregistered plans
204.9(4)	New beneficiary
204.9(5)	Transfers between plans
204.91(1)	Tax payable by subscribers
204.91(2)	Waiver of tax
204.91(3)	Marriage or common-law partnership breakdown
204.91(4)	Deceased subscribers
204.92	Return and payment of tax
204.93	Provisions applicable to Part
204.94(1)	Definitions
204.94(2)	Charging provision
204.94(3)	Return and payment of tax

PART X.5
PAYMENTS UNDER REGISTERED EDUCATION SAVINGS PLANS

Section	Subject
204.94(1)	Definitions
204.94(2)	Charging provision
204.94(3)	Return and payment of tax
204.94(4)	Administrative rules

PART XI
TAXES IN RESPECT OF REGISTERED DISABILITY SAVINGS PLANS [REPEALED]

Section	Subject
205(1)	Definitions (Repealed.)
205(2)	Definitions in subsection 146.4(1) (Repealed.)
206(1)	Tax payable where inadequate consideration (Repealed.)
206(2)	Amount of tax payable (Repealed.)
206(3)	Liability for tax (Repealed.)
206(4)	Payment of amount collected to RDSP (Repealed.)
206(5)	Deemed not to be a contribution (Repealed.)
206.1(1)	Tax payable on non-qualified investment (Repealed.)
206.1(2)	Amount of tax payable (Repealed.)
206.1(3)	Liability for tax (Repealed.)
206.1(4)	Refund of tax on disposition of non-qualified investment (Repealed.)
206.1(5)	Apportionment of refund (Repealed.)
206.1(6)	Deemed disposition and reacquisition (Repealed.)
206.2(1)	Tax payable where advantage extended (Repealed.)
206.2(2)	Amount of tax payable (Repealed.)
206.2(3)	Liability for tax (Repealed.)
206.3(1)	Tax payable on use of property as security (Repealed.)
206.3(2)	Amount of tax payable (Repealed.)
206.4	Waiver of liability (Repealed.)
207(1)	Return and payment of tax (Repealed.)
207(2)	Refund (Repealed.)
207(3)	Multiple holders (Repealed.)
207(4)	Provisions applicable to Part (Repealed.)

PART XI.01
TAXES IN RESPECT OF REGISTERED PLANS

Section	Subject
207.01(1)	Definitions
	"advantage"
	"allowable refund"
	"controlling individual"
	"deliberate over-contribution"
	"equity"
	"excess TFSA amount"
	"excluded property"
	"exempt contribution"
	"non-qualified investment"
	"prohibited investment"
	"qualified investment"
	"qualifying transfer"
	"registered plan"
	"registered plan strip"
	"restricted property" (Repealed.)

Section	Subject
	"RRSP strip" (Repealed.)
	"specified distribution"
	"specified non-qualified investment income"
	"swap transaction"
	"TFSA dollar limit"
	"transitional prohibited investment benefit"
	"transitional prohibited property"
	"unused TFSA contribution room"
207.01(2)	Exempt contribution to survivor TFSA (Repealed.)
207.01(3)	Survivor as successor holder
207.01(4)	Significant interest
207.01(5)	Obligation of issuer
207.01(6)	Deemed disposition and reacquisition of investments
207.01(7)	Adjusted cost base
207.01(8)	Prohibited investment status
207.01(9)	Prohibited investment status
207.01(10)	Breakdown of marriage or common-law partnership
207.01(11)	Breakdown of marriage or common-law partnership
207.01(12)	Exchange of property
207.01(13)	Exchange of property
207.02	Tax payable on excess TFSA amount
207.03	Tax payable on non-resident contributions
207.04(1)	Tax payable on prohibited or non-qualified investment
207.04(2)	Amount of tax payable
207.04(3)	Both prohibited and non-qualified investment
207.04(4)	Refund of tax on disposition of investment
207.04(5)	Apportionment of refund
207.04(6)	Liability for tax
207.04(7)	Amount of additional tax payable (Repealed.)
207.05(1)	Tax payable in respect of advantage
207.05(2)	Amount of tax payable
207.05(3)	Liability for tax
207.05(4)	Transitional rule
207.06(1)	Waiver of tax payable
207.06(2)	Waiver of tax payable
207.06(3)	Waiver of tax payable — advantage (Repealed.)
207.06(4)	Other powers of Minister
207.061	Income inclusion
207.062	Special limit on tax payable
207.07(1)	Return and payment of tax
207.07(1.1)	Multiple holders or subscribers
207.07(2)	Refund
207.07(3)	Provisions applicable to Part

PART XI.1
TAX IN RESPECT OF DEFERRED INCOME PLANS AND OTHER TAX EXEMPT PERSONS

Section	Subject
207.1(1)	Tax payable by trust under registered retirement savings plan (Repealed.)
207.1(2)	Tax payable by trust under deferred profit sharing plan
207.1(3)	Tax payable by trust under registered education savings plan (Repealed.)
207.1(4)	Tax payable by trust under registered retirement income fund (Repealed.)
207.1(5)	Tax payable in respect of agreement to acquire shares
207.2(1)	Return and payment of tax
207.2(2)	Liability of trustee
207.2(3)	Provisions applicable to Part

PART XI.2
TAX IN RESPECT OF DISPOSITIONS OF CERTAIN PROPERTIES

Section	Subject
207.3	Tax payable by institution or public authority
207.31(1)	Ecological gift — tax payable
207.31(2)	Ecological gift — amount of tax
207.4(1)	Return and payment of tax
207.4(2)	Provisions applicable to Part

PART XI.3
TAX IN RESPECT OF RETIREMENT COMPENSATION ARRANGEMENTS

Section	Subject
207.5(1)	Definitions
	"advantage"
	"prohibited investment"
	"RCA strip"
	"RCA trust"
	"refundable tax"
	"significant interest"
	"specified beneficiary"
	"subject property of a retirement compensation arrangement"
207.5(2)	Election
207.5(3)	Limitation on election
207.6(1)	Creation of trust
207.6(2)	Life insurance policies
207.6(3)	Incorporated employee
207.6(4)	Deemed contribution
207.6(5)	Residents' arrangement
207.6(5.1)	Resident's contribution
207.6(6)	Prescribed plan or arrangement
207.6(7)	Transfers
207.61(1)	Tax payable on prohibited investment
207.61(2)	Amount of tax payable
207.61(3)	Refund
207.61(4)	Deemed disposition and reacquisition
207.62(1)	Tax payable in respect of advantage
207.62(2)	Amount of tax payable
207.63	Joint liability
207.64	Waiver of tax payable
207.65	Deemed distribution
207.7(1)	Tax payable
207.7(2)	Refund
207.7(3)	Payment of tax
207.7(4)	Provisions applicable to Part

PART XI.4
TAX ON EXCESS EPSP AMOUNTS

Section	Subject
207.8(1)	Excess EPSP amount
207.8(2)	Tax payable
207.8(3)	Waiver or cancellation
207.8(4)	Return and payment of tax
207.8(5)	Provisions applicable to this Part

PART XI.5
TAX IN RESPECT OF EMPLOYEE LIFE AND HEALTH TRUST

Section	Subject
Prop. 207.9(1)	Definitions
Prop.	"participating employer"
Prop.	"prohibited investment"
Prop. 207.8(2)	Tax payable on prohibited investment
Prop. 207.8(3)	Amount of tax payable
Prop. 207.8(4)	Refund
Prop. 207.8(5)	Deemed disposition and reacquisition

PART XII
TAX IN RESPECT OF CERTAIN ROYALTIES, TAXES, LEASE RENTALS, ETC., PAID TO A GOVERNMENT BY A TAX EXEMPT PERSON [REPEALED]

Section	Subject
208(1)	Tax payable by exempt person (Repealed.)
208(1.1)	Definition of "specified stage" (Repealed.)
208(2)	Return and payment of tax (Repealed.)
208(3)	Liability of trustee (Repealed.)
208(4)	Provisions applicable to Part (Repealed.)

PART XII.1
TAX ON CARVED-OUT INCOME

Section	Subject
209(1)	Definitions
	"carved-out income"
	"carved-out property"
	"head lease"
	"term"
209(2)	Tax
209(3)	Return
209(4)	Payment of tax
209(5)	Provisions applicable to Part
209(6)	Partnerships
209(6)	Partnerships

PART XII.2
TAX ON DESIGNATED INCOME OF CERTAIN TRUSTS

Section	Subject
210(1)	Definitions
	"designated beneficiary"
	"designated income"
210(2)	Tax not payable
210.1	Application of Part (Repealed.)
210.2(1)	Tax on income of trust
210.2(1.1)	Amateur athlete trusts (Repealed.)
210.2(2)	Amateur athlete trusts
210.2(3)	Tax deemed paid by beneficiary
210.2(4)	Designations in respect of partnerships
210.2(5)	Returns
210.2(6)	Liability of trustee
210.2(7)	Provisions applicable to Part
210.3(1)	Where no designated beneficiaries
210.3(2)	Where beneficiary deemed not designated

PART XII.3
TAX ON INVESTMENT INCOME OF LIFE INSURERS

Section	Subject
211(1)	Definitions
	"existing guaranteed life insurance policy"
	"life insurance policy"
	"life insurance policy in Canada"
	"net interest rate"
	"non-participating life insurance policy"
	"participating life insurance policy"
	"policy loan"
	"registered life insurance policy"
	"reinsurance arrangement"
	"segregated fund"
	"specified transaction or event"
	"taxable life insurance policy"
211(2)	Riders and changes in terms
211.1(1)	Tax payable
211.1(2)	Taxable Canadian life investment income
211.1(3)	Canadian life investment income
211.1(4)	Short taxation year
211.2	Return
211.3(1)	Instalments
211.3(2)	Annualized tax payable
211.4	Payment of remainder of tax
211.5(1)	Provisions applicable to Part
211.5(2)	Interest on instalments

PART XII.4
TAX ON QUALIFYING ENVIRONMENTAL TRUSTS

Section	Subject
211.6(1)	Definitions
	"excluded trust"
	"prohibited investment"
	"QET income tax rate"
	"qualifying contract"
	"qualifying environmental trust"
	"qualifying law"
	"qualifying site"
211.6(2)	Charging provision
211.6(3)	Return
211.6(4)	Payment of tax
211.6(5)	Provisions applicable to Part

PART XII.5
RECOVERY OF LABOUR-SPONSORED FUNDS TAX CREDIT

Section	Subject
211.7(1)	Definitions
	"approved share"
	"labour-sponsored funds tax credit"
	"net cost"
	"original acquisition"
	"qualifying exchange"
	"qualifying trust"
	"revoked corporation"
211.7(2)	Amalgamations and mergers
211.7(3)	Exchangeable shares
211.8(1)	Disposition of approved share
211.8(1.1)	Rules of application
211.8(2)	Withholding and remittance of tax
211.8(3)	Liability for tax
211.81	Tax for failure to reacquire certain shares
211.82(1)	Return
211.82(2)	Provisions applicable to this Part
211.9	Refund (Repealed.)

PART XII.6
TAX ON FLOW-THROUGH SHARES

Section	Subject
211.91(1)	Tax imposed
211.91(2)	Return and payment of tax
211.91(3)	Provisions applicable to Part

PART XIII
TAX ON INCOME FROM CANADA OF NON-RESIDENT PERSONS

Section	Subject
212(1)	Tax
212(1)(*a*)	Management fee
212(1)(*b*)	Interest
212(1)(*c*)	Estate or trust income
212(1)(*d*)	Rents, royalties, etc.
212(1)(*e*)	Timber royalties
212(1)(*f*)	Alimony (Repealed.)
212(1)(*g*)	Patronage dividend
212(1)(*h*)	Pension benefits
212(1)(*i*)	Restrictive covenant amount
212(1)(*j*)	Benefits
212(1)(*j*.1)	Retiring allowances
212(1)(*k*)	Supplementary unemployment benefit plan payments
212(1)(*l*)	Registered retirement savings plan payments
212(1)(*m*)	Deferred profit sharing plan payments
212(1)(*n*)	Income-averaging annuity contract payments
212(1)(*o*)	Other annuity payments
212(1)(*p*)	Former TFSA
212(1)(*q*)	Registered retirement income fund payments
212(1)(*r*)	Registered education savings plan
212(1)(*r*.1)	Registered disability savings plan
212(1)(*s*)	Home insulation or energy conversion grants
212(1)(*t*)	NISA Fund No. 2 payments
212(1)(*u*)	Amateur athlete trust payments
212(1)(*v*)	Payments under an eligible funeral arrangement
212(1)(*w*)	[Employee life and health trust payments]
212(1)(*x*)	Tax informant program
212(2)	Tax on dividends
212(2.1)	Exempt dividends
212(3)	Interest — definitions
	"fully exempt interest"
	"participating debt interest"
212(3.1)	Back-to-back loan arrangement
212(3.2)	Back-to-back loan arrangement
212(3.21)	Back-to-back arrangement — election
212(3.22)	Back-to-back arrangement — election
212(3.3)	Excess funding
212(3.4)	Excess funding — deemed funding allocation
212(3.5)	Multiple funding arrangements
212(3.6)	Back-to-back loan arrangement — character substitution
212(3.7)	Back-to-back loan arrangement — character substitution
212(3.8)	Back-to-back loan arrangement — definitions
	"relevant funder"
	"relevant funding arrangement"
	"specified licensee"
	"specified licensor"
	"specified right"
	"specified royalty arrangement"
	"specified share"
	"ultimate funder"
212(3.81)	Specified shares
212(3.9)	Back-to-back arrangement — rents, royalties, similar payments
212(3.91)	Back-to-back arrangement — rents, royalties, similar payments
212(3.92)	Back-to-back arrangement — character substitution
212(3.93)	Back-to-back arrangement — character substitution
212(3.94)	Back-to-back arrangement — definitions
	"lease, licence or similar agreement"
	"relevant licensor"
	"relevant royalty arrangement"
	"rent, royalty or similar payment"
	"specified royalty arrangement"
	"ultimate licensor"
212(4)	Interpretation of "management or administration fee or charge"
212(5)	Motion picture films
212(5.1)	Acting services
212(5.2)	Relief from double taxation
212(5.3)	Reduction of withholding
212(6)	Interest on provincial bonds from wholly-owned subsidiaries
212(7)	Where s. (6) does not apply
212(8)	Bonds issued after December 20, 1960 in exchange for earlier bonds
212(9)	Exemptions
212(10)	Trust beneficiaries residing outside of Canada
212(11)	Payment to beneficiary as income of trust
212(11.1)	Idem (Repealed.)
212(11.2)	Idem (Repealed.)
212(12)	Deemed payments to spouse, etc
212(13)	Rent and other payments
212(13.1)	Application of Part XIII tax where payer or payee is a partnership
212(13.2)	Application of Part XIII tax — non-resident operates in Canada
212(13.3)	Application of Part XIII to authorized foreign bank
212(14)	Certificate of exemption (Repealed.)

Section	Subject
212(15)	Certain obligations
212(16)	Payments for temporary use of rolling stock
212(17)	Exception
212(17.1)	Payments to the International Olympic Committee and the International Paralympic Committee
212(18)	Undertaking
212(19)	Tax on registered securities dealers
212(20)	Designated SLA
212.1(1)	Non-arm's length sales of shares by non-residents
212.1(1.1)	Non-arm's length sales of shares by non-residents
212.1(1.2)	Deemed consideration
212.1(2)	Idem
212.1(3)	Idem
212.1(4)	Where section does not apply
212.1(5)	Tiered trusts and partnerships
212.1(6)	Trusts and partnerships look-through rule
212.1(7)	Avoidance of subsections (5) and (6)
212.2(1)	Application
212.2(2)	Deemed dividend
212.3(1)	Foreign affiliate dumping — conditions for application
212.3(2)	Foreign affiliate dumping — consequences
212.3(3)	Dividend substitution election
212.3(4)	Definitions "cross-border class" "dividend time" "qualifying substitute corporation"
212.3(5)	Modification of terms — paragraph (10)(e)
212.3(5.1)	Sequential investments — paragraph (10)(f)
212.3(6)	Anti-avoidance rule — cross-border class
212.3(7)	Reduction of deemed dividend
212.3(7.1)	Election to not reduce deemed dividend
212.3(8)	Paid-up capital adjustment
212.3(9)	Paid-up capital reinstatement
212.3(9.1)	Exchange of debt obligation for shares
212.3(9.2)	Continuity for paid-up capital reinstatement
212.3(10)	Investment in subject corporation
212.3(11)	Pertinent loan or indebtedness
212.3(12)	Late-filed elections
212.3(13)	Penalty for late-filed election
212.3(14)	Rules for paragraph (10)(f)
212.3(15)	Control
212.3(16)	Exception — more closely connected business activities
212.3(17)	Dual officers
212.3(18)	Exception — corporate reorganizations
212.3(18.1)	Exchange — pertinent loan or indebtedness
212.3(19)	Preferred shares
212.3(20)	Assumption of debt on liquidation or distribution
212.3(21)	Persons deemed not to be related
212.3(22)	Mergers
212.3(23)	Indirect investment
212.3(24)	Indirect funding
212.3(25)	Partnerships
213(1)	Tax non-payable by non-resident person
213(2)	Idem
213(3)	Corporation deemed to be foreign business corporation
214(1)	No deductions
214(2)	Income and capital combined
214(3)	Deemed payments
214(3.1)	Time of deemed payment
214(4)	Securities
214(5)	Interpretation
214(6)	Deemed interest
214(7)	Sale of obligation
214(7.1)	Idem
214(8)	Meaning of "excluded obligation"
214(9)	Deemed resident
214(10)	Reduction of tax
214(11)	Application of para. 212(1)(b) (Repealed.)
214(12)	Where s. (2) does not apply
214(13)	Regulations respecting residents
214(14)	Assignment of obligation
214(15)	Standby charges and guarantee fees
214(16)	Deemed dividends
214(17)	Deemed interest payments
215(1)	Withholding and remittance of tax
215(1.1)	Exception — corporate immigration
215(2)	Idem
215(3)	Idem
215(4)	Regulations creating exceptions
215(5)	Regulations reducing deduction or withholding
215(6)	Liability for tax
216(1)	Alternatives re rents and timber royalties
216(2)	Idem
216(3)	Idem
216(4)	Optional method of payment
216(4.1)	Optional method of payment
216(5)	Disposition by non-resident
216(6)	Saving provision
216(7)	Election (Repealed.)
216(8)	Restriction on deduction
216.1(1)	Alternative re: acting services
216.1(2)	Deemed Part I payment
216.1(3)	Deemed election and restriction
217(1)	Alternative re Canadian benefits
217(2)	Part I return
217(3)	Taxable income earned in Canada
217(4)	Tax credits — limitation
217(5)	Tax credits allowed
217(6)	Special credit
218(1)	Loan to wholly-owned subsidiary
218(2)	Idem
218(3)	Election
218(4)	Application of election
218.1	Application of s. 138.1

PART XIII.1
ADDITIONAL TAX ON AUTHORIZED FOREIGN BANKS

Section	Subject
218.2(1)	Branch interest tax
218.2(2)	Taxable interest expense
218.2(3)	Where tax not payable
218.2(4)	Rate limitation
218.2(5)	Provisions applicable to Part

PART XIII.2
NON-RESIDENT INVESTORS IN CANADIAN MUTUAL FUNDS

Section	Subject
218.3(1)	Definitions "assessable distribution" "Canadian property mutual fund investment" "Canadian property mutual fund loss" "non-resident investor" "unused Canadian property mutual fund loss"

Section	Subject
218.3(2)	Tax payable
218.3(3)	Use of losses
218.3(4)	Deemed tax paid
218.3(5)	Refund
218.3(6)	Excess loss — carryback
218.3(7)	Ordering
218.3(8)	Partnership filing-due date
218.3(9)	Partnership — member resident in Canada
218.3(10)	Provisions applicable

PART XIV
ADDITIONAL TAX ON NON-RESIDENT CORPORATIONS

Section	Subject
219(1)	Additional tax
219(1.1)	Excluded gains
219(2)	Exempt corporations
219(3)	Provisions applicable to Part
219(4)	Non-resident insurers
219(5)	Additional tax on insurer (Repealed.)
219(5.1)	Additional tax on insurer
219(5.2)	Election by non-resident insurer
219(5.3)	Deemed payment of dividend
219(6)	Where election under ss. 138(9) (Repealed.)
219(7)	Definitions
	"accumulated 1968 deficit"
	"attributed surplus"
	"Canadian investment fund"
	"maximum tax actuarial reserves"
	"surplus funds derived from operations"
	"tax deferred account"
219(8)	Meaning of "qualified related corporation"
219.1(1)	Corporate emigration
219.1(2)	Foreign affiliate dumping — emigrating corporation
219.1(3)	Application of subsection (4)
219.1(4)	Paid-up capital reinstatement
219.1(5)	Assigned meanings from section 212.3
219.2	Limitation on rate of branch tax
219.3	Effect of tax treaty

PART XV
ADMINISTRATION AND ENFORCEMENT

Section	Subject
220(1)	Minister's Duty
220(2)	Officers, clerks and employees
220(2.01)	Delegation
220(2.1)	Waiver of filing of documents
220(2.2)	Exception
220(3)	Extensions for returns
220(3.1)	Waiver of penalty or interest
220(3.2)	Late, amended or revoked elections
220(3.201)	Joint election — pension income split
220(3.21)	Designations and allocations
220(3.3)	Date of late election, amended election or revocation
220(3.4)	Assessments
220(3.5)	Penalty for late filed, amended or revoked elections
220(3.6)	Unpaid balance of penalty
220(3.7)	Idem
220(3.8)	Dishonoured instruments
220(4)	Security
220(4.1)	Idem
220(4.2)	Surrender of excess security
220(4.3)	Security furnished by a member institution of a deposit insurance corporation
220(4.4)	Additional security
220(4.5)	Security for departure tax
220(4.51)	Deemed security
220(4.52)	Limit
220(4.53)	Inadequate security
220(4.54)	Extension of time
220(4.6)	Security for tax on distributions of taxable Canadian property to non-resident beneficiaries
220(4.61)	Limit
220(4.62)	Inadequate security
220(4.63)	Extension of time
220(4.7)	Undue hardship
220(4.71)	Limit
220(5)	Administration of oaths
220(6)	Assignment by corporation
220(7)	Effect of assignment
221(1)	Regulations
221(2)	Effect
221(3)	Regulations binding Crown
221(4)	Incorporation by reference
221.01	Providing information returns in electronic format
221.1	Application of interest
221.2(1)	Re-appropriation of amounts
221.2(2)	Re-appropriation of amounts
222(1)	Definitions
	"action"
	"tax debt"
222(2)	Debts to Her Majesty
222(3)	No actions after limitation period
222(4)	Limitation period
222(5)	Limitation period restarted
222(6)	Acknowledgement of tax debts
222(7)	Agent or legal representative
222(8)	Extension of limitation period
222(9)	Bar to claims
222(10)	Orders after March 3, 2004 and before effect
222.1	Court costs
223(1)	Definition of "amount payable"
223(2)	Certificates
223(3)	Registration in court
223(4)	Costs
223(5)	Charge on property
223(6)	Creation of charge
223(7)	Proceedings in respect of memorial
223(8)	Presentation of documents
223(9)	Sale, etc
223(10)	Completion of notices, etc
223(11)	Application for an order
223(11.1)	Deemed security
223(12)	Details in certificates and memorials
223.1(1)	Application of ss. 223(1) to (8) and (12)
223.1(2)	Application of ss. 223(9) to (11)
224(1)	Garnishment
224(1.1)	Idem
224(1.2)	Garnishment
224(1.3)	Definitions
	"secured creditor"
	"security interest"
	"similar provision"
224(1.4)	Garnishment

Section	Subject
224(2)	Minister's receipt discharges original liability
224(3)	Idem
224(4)	Failure to comply with s. (1), (1.2) or (3) requirement
224(4.1)	Failure to comply with s. (1.1) requirement
224(5)	Service of garnishee
224(6)	Idem
224.1	Recovery by deduction or set-off
224.2	Acquisition of debtor's property
224.3(1)	Payment of moneys seized from tax debtor
224.3(2)	Receipt of Minister
225(1)	Seizure of goods, chattels or movable property
225(2)	Sale of seized property
225(3)	Notice of sale
225(4)	Surplus returned to owner
225(5)	Exemptions from seizure
225.1(1)	Collection restrictions
225.1(1.1)	Collection-commencement day
225.1(2)	No action by Minister
225.1(3)	Idem
225.1(4)	Idem
225.1(5)	Idem
225.1(6)	Where ss. (1) to (4) do not apply
225.1(7)	One-half collection
225.1(8)	Definition of "large corporation"
225.2(1)	Definition of "judge"
225.2(2)	Authorization to proceed forthwith
225.2(3)	Notice of assessment not sent
225.2(4)	Affidavits
225.2(5)	Service of authorization and of notice of assessment
225.2(6)	How service effected
225.2(7)	Application to judge for direction
225.2(8)	Review of authorization
225.2(9)	Limitation period for review application
225.2(10)	Hearingin camera
225.2(11)	Disposition of application
225.2(12)	Directions
225.2(13)	No appeal from review order
226(1)	Taxpayer leaving Canada
226(2)	Seizure in case of default of payment
227(1)	Withholding taxes
227(2)	Return filed with person withholding
227(3)	Failure to file return
227(4)	Trust for moneys deducted
227(4.1)	Extension of trust
227(4.2)	Meaning of security interest
227(4.3)	Application to Crown
227(5)	Payments by trustees, etc
227(5.1)	Definition of "specified person"
227(5.2)	"Person" includes partnership
227(6)	Excess withheld, returned or applied
227(6.1)	Repayment of non-resident shareholder loan
227(6.2)	Foreign affiliate dumping — late-filed form
227(7)	Application for assessment
227(7.1)	Application for determination
227(8)	Penalty
227(8.1)	Joint and several, or solidary, liability
227(8.2)	Retirement compensation arrangement deductions
227(8.3)	Interest on amounts not deducted or withheld
227(8.4)	Liability to pay amount not deducted or withheld
227(8.5)	No penalty — certain deemed payments
227(8.6)	No penalty — qualifying non-resident employers
227(9)	Penalty
227(9.1)	Penalty
227(9.2)	Interest on amounts deducted or withheld but not remitted
227(9.3)	Interest on certain tax not paid
227(9.4)	Liability to pay amount not remitted
227(9.5)	Payment from same establishment
227(10)	Assessment
227(10.01)	Part XII.5
227(10.1)	Idem
227(10.2)	Joint and several, or solidary, liability re contributions to RCA
227(10.3)–(10.9)	[Tax withholding and remittance] (Repealed.)
227(11)	Withholding tax
227(12)	Agreement not to deduct void
227(13)	Minister's receipt discharges debtor
227(14)	Application of other Parts
227(15)	Partnership included in "person"
227(16)	Municipal or provincial corporation excepted
227.1(1)	Liability of directors for failure to deduct
227.1(2)	Limitations on liability
227.1(3)	Idem
227.1(4)	Limitation period
227.1(5)	Amount recoverable
227.1(6)	Preference
227.1(7)	Contribution
228	Applying payments under collection agreements
229	Receipt of taxes by banks (Repealed.)
229.1(1)	Repeal of s. 229
229.1(2)	Coming into force
230(1)	Records and books
230(1.1)	Idem (Repealed.)
230(2)	Records and books
230(2.1)	Idem, lawyers
230(3)	Minister's requirement to keep records, etc
230(4)	Limitation period for keeping records, etc
230(4.1)	Electronic records
230(4.2)	Exemptions
230(5)	Exception where no return filed
230(6)	Exception where objection or appeal
230(7)	Exception where demand by Minister
230(8)	Permission for earlier disposal
230.1(1)	Records re monetary contributions — Canada Elections Act
230.1(2)	Information return
230.1(3)	Application of subsections 230(3) to (8)
230.1(4)	Reports to chief electoral officer (Repealed.)
230.1(5)	No report to enable identification of contributor (Repealed.)
230.1(6)	Definitions (Repealed.)
230.1(7)	Definition of "amount contributed" (Repealed.)
231	Definitions
	"authorized person"
	"document"
	"dwelling-house"
	"judge"
231.1(1)	Inspections
231.1(2)	Prior authorization
231.1(3)	Application
231.2(1)	Requirement to provide documents or information
Prop. 231.2(1.1)	Notice
231.2(2)	Unnamed persons
231.2(3)	Judicial authorization
231.2(4)	Service of authorization (Repealed.)
231.2(5)	Review of authorization (Repealed.)
231.2(6)	Powers on review (Repealed.)
231.2(7)	Additional remedy (Repealed.)
231.3(1)	Search warrant
231.3(2)	Evidence in support of application
231.3(3)	Evidence
231.3(4)	Contents of warrant
231.3(5)	Seizure of document
231.3(6)	Retention of things seized

Section	Subject
231.3(7)	Return of things seized
231.3(8)	Access and copies
231.4(1)	Inquiry
231.4(2)	Appointment of hearing officer
231.4(3)	Powers of hearing officer
231.4(4)	When powers to be exercised
231.4(5)	Rights of witness at inquiry
231.4(6)	Rights of person whose affairs are investigated
231.5(1)	Copies
231.5(2)	Compliance
231.6(1)	Definition of "foreign-based information or document"
231.6(2)	Requirement to provide foreign-based information
231.6(3)	Notice
Prop. 231.6(3.1)	Notice
231.6(4)	Review of foreign information requirement
231.6(5)	Powers on review
231.6(6)	Idem
231.6(7)	Time period not to count
231.6(8)	Consequence of failure
231.7(1)	Compliance order
231.7(2)	Notice required
231.7(3)	Judge may impose conditions
231.7(4)	Contempt of court
231.7(5)	Appeal
231.8	Time period not to count
232(1)	Definitions
	"custodian"
	"judge"
	"lawyer"
	"officer"
	"solicitor-client privilege"
232(2)	Solicitor-client privilege defence
232(3)	Seizure of certain documents where privilege claimed
232(3.1)	Examination of certain documents where privilege claimed
232(4)	Application to judge
232(5)	Disposition of application
232(6)	Order to deliver or make available
232(7)	Delivery by custodian
232(8)	Continuation by another judge
232(9)	Costs
232(10)	Directions
232(11)	Prohibition
232(12)	Idem
232(13)	Authority to make copies
232(14)	Waiver of claim of privilege
232(15)	Compliance
233(1)	Information return
233(2)	Partnerships
233(3)	Application to members of partnerships
233.1(1)	Definitions
	"reportable transaction"
	"reporting partnership"
	"reporting person"
	"transaction"
233.1(2)	Reporting person's information return
233.1(3)	Reporting partnership's information return
233.1(4)	De minimisexception
233.1(5)	Deemed member of partnership
233.2(1)	Definitions
	"exempt trust"
	"specified beneficiary" (Repealed.)
	"specified foreign trust" (Repealed.)
233.2(2)	Rule of application
233.2(3)	Partnerships (Repealed.)
233.2(4)	Filing information on foreign trusts
233.2(4.1)	Similar arrangements
233.2(5)	Joint filing
233.3(1)	Definitions
	"reporting entity"
	"specified Canadian entity"
	"specified foreign property"
233.3(2)	Application to members of partnerships
233.3(3)	Returns respecting foreign property
233.4(1)	Reporting entity
233.4(2)	Rules of application
233.4(3)	Application to members of partnerships
233.4(4)	Returns respecting foreign affiliates
233.5	Due diligence exception
233.6(1)	Returns respecting distributions from non-resident trusts
233.6(2)	Excluded trust defined
233.7	Exception for first-year residents
233.8(1)	Country-by-country report — definitions
	"business entity"
	"consolidated financial statements"
	"constituent entity"
	"excluded MNE group"
	"fiscal year"
	"multinational enterprise group"
	"permanent establishment"
	"qualifying competent authority agreement"
	"reporting fiscal year"
	"surrogate parent entity"
	"systemic failure"
	"ultimate parent entity"
233.8(2)	Determination of residence — ultimate parent entity
233.8(3)	Filing obligations
233.8(4)	Designation for multiple constituent entities
233.8(5)	Surrogate filing
233.8(6)	Time for filing
234(1)	Ownership certificates
234(2)	Idem
234(3)	Idem
234(4)	Idem (Repealed.)
234(5)	Withholding (Repealed.)
234(6)	Amount withheld deemed paid or credited (Repealed.)
234.1	Aviation turbine fuel
235	Penalty for failing to file corporate returns
236	Execution of documents by corporations
237(1)	Social Insurance Number
237(1.1)	Production of number
237(1.2)	Designated number
237(2)	Number required in information returns
237(3)	Authority to communicate number
237(4)	Authority to communicate number
237.1(1)	Definitions
	"gifting arrangement"
	"person"
	"promoter"
	"tax shelter"
237.1(2)	Application
237.1(3)	Identification
237.1(4)	Sales prohibited
237.1(5)	Providing tax shelter number
237.1(6)	Deductions and claims disallowed
237.1(6.1)	Deductions and claims disallowed
237.1(6.2)	Assessments
237.1(7)	Information return
237.1(7.1)	Time for filing return
237.1(7.2)	Time for filing — special case
237.1(7.3)	Copies to be provided
237.1(7.4)	Penalty
237.1(7.5)	Penalty

Section	Subject
237.1(8)	Application of ss. 231 to 231.3
237.2	Application of s. 237.1
237.3(1)	Definitions
	“advisor”
	“avoidance transaction”
	“confidential protection”
	“contractual protection”
	“fee”
	“person”
	“promoter”
	“reportable transaction”
	“solicitor-client privilege”
	“tax benefit”
	“transaction”
237.3(2)	Application
237.3(3)	Clarification of reporting transactions in series
237.3(4)	Application
237.3(5)	Time for filing return
237.3(6)	Tax benefits disallowed
237.3(7)	Assessments
237.3(8)	Penalty
237.3(9)	Joint and several liability
237.3(10)	Joint and several liability — special cases
237.3(11)	Due diligence
237.3(12)	Reporting not an admission
237.3(13)	Application of sections 231 to 231.3
237.3(14)	Tax shelters and flow-through shares
237.3(15)	Tax shelters and flow-through shares — penalty
237.3(16)	Anti-avoidance
237.3(17)	Solicitor-client privilege
238(1)	Offences and punishment
238(2)	Compliance orders
238(3)	Saving
239(1)	Other offences and punishment
239(1.1)	Offences re refunds and credits
239(2)	Prosecution on indictment
239(2.1)	Providing incorrect tax shelter identification number
239(2.2)	Offence with respect to confidential information
239(2.21)	Idem
239(2.22)	Definitions
239(2.3)	Offence with respect to an identification number
239(2.31)	Offence: section 149.01 (Repealed.)
239(3)	Penalty on conviction
239(4)	Stay of appeal
239(5)	Offence and punishment without reference to subsection 120(2.2)
239.1(1)	Definitions
239.1(2)	Offences
239.1(3)	Prosecution on indictment
239.1(4)	Penalty on conviction
239.1(5)	Stay of appeal
240(1)	Definition of “taxable obligation” and “non-taxable obligation”
240(2)	Interest coupon to be identified in prescribed manner — offence and punishment
241(1)	Provision of information
241(2)	Evidence relating to taxpayer information
241(3)	Communication where proceedings have been commenced
241(3.1)	Circumstances involving danger
241(3.2)	Registered charities and registered Canadian amateur athletic associations
Pend. 241(3.2)	Certain qualified donees

Section	Subject
241(3.3)	Information may be communicated
241(3.4)	Information may be communicated
241(4)	Where taxpayer information may be disclosed
241(4.1)	Measures to prevent unauthorized use or disclosure
241(5)	Disclosure to taxpayer or on consent
241(6)	Appeal from order or direction
241(7)	Disposition of appeal
241(8)	Stay of order or direction
241(9)	Threats to security
241(9.1)	Threats to security
241(9.2)	Restrictions on information sharing
241(9.3)	Public disclosure
241(9.4)	Public disclosure by representative of government entity
241(9.5)	Serious offences
241(10)	Definitions
	“aboriginal government”
	“authorized person”
	“business number” (Repealed.)
	“contact information”
	“corporate information”
	“court of appeal”
	“designated donor information”
	“designated person”
	“designated taxpayer information” (Repealed.)
	“excluded individual”
	“government entity”
	“official”
	“publicly accessible charity information”
	“registration information”
	“representative”
	“taxpayer information”
241(11)	References to “this Act”
242	Officers, etc., of corporations
243	Power to decrease punishment
244(1)	Information or complaint
244(2)	Two or more offences
244(3)	Venue
244(4)	Limitation period
244(5)	Proof of service by mail
244(6)	Proof of personal service
Prop. 244(6.1)	Proof of electronic delivery
244(7)	Proof of failure to comply
244(8)	Proof of time of compliance
244(9)	Proof of documents
244(10)	Proof of no appeal
244(11)	Presumption
244(12)	Judicial notice
244(13)	Proof of documents
244(13.1)	Revenue Canada, Taxation (Repealed.)
244(14)	Mailing or sending date
244(14.1)	Date when electronic notice sent
244(15)	Date when assessment made
244(16)	Forms prescribed or authorized
244(17)	Proof of return in prosecution for offence
244(18)	Idem, in proceedings under Division J of Part I
244(19)	Proof of statement of non-receipt
244(20)	Members of partnerships
244(21)	Proof of return filed
244(22)	Filing of information returns

PART XV.1
REPORTING OF ELECTRONIC FUNDS TRANSFER

Section	Subject
244.1	Definitions
	"cash"
	"casino"
	"client"
	"credit union central"
	"electronic funds transfer"
	"entity"
	"funds"
	"money services business"
	"reporting entity"
244.2(1)	Electronic funds transfer
244.2(2)	Transfer within Canada
244.2(3)	Intermediary
244.2(4)	Transfer conducted by agent
Pend. 244.2(5)	Entities outside Canada
244.3	Casino
244.4(1)	Single transaction
244.4(2)	Exception
244.5	Foreign currency
244.6	Filing of return
244.7(1)	Record keeping
244.7(2)	Form of records
244.7(3)	Retention of records

PART XVI
TAX AVOIDANCE

Section	Subject
245(1)	Definitions
	"tax benefit"
	"tax consequences"
	"transaction"
245(1.1)	Idem (Repealed.)
245(2)	General anti-avoidance provision
245(3)	Avoidance transaction
245(4)	Application of subsection (2)
245(5)	Determination of tax consequences
245(6)	Request for adjustments
245(7)	Exception
245(8)	Duties of Minister
246(1)	Benefit conferred on a person
246(2)	Arm's length

PART XVI.1
TRANSFER PRICING

Section	Subject
247(1)	Definitions
	"arm's length allocation"
	"arm's length transfer price"
	"documentation-due date"
	"qualifying cost contribution arrangement"
	"tax benefit"
	"transaction"
	"transfer price"
	"transfer pricing capital adjustment"
	"transfer pricing capital setoff adjustment"
	"transfer pricing income adjustment"
	"transfer pricing income setoff adjustment"
Prop. 247(1.1)	Order of applying provisions
247(2)	Transfer pricing adjustment
247(3)	Penalty
247(4)	Contemporaneous documentation
247(5)	Partner's gross revenue
247(6)	Deemed member of partnership
247(7)	Exclusion for loans to certain controlled foreign affiliates
247(7.1)	Exclusion — certain guarantees
247(8)	Provisions not applicable
Prop. 247(8)	Provisions not applicable (Repealed.)
247(9)	Anti-avoidance
247(10)	No adjustment unless appropriate
247(11)	Provisions applicable to Part
247(12)	Deemed dividends to non-residents
247(13)	Repatriation
247(14)	Repatriation — interest
247(15)	Non-application of provisions

PART XVII
INTERPRETATION

Section	Subject
248(1)	Definitions
	"10/8 policy"
	"1971 capital surplus on hand" (Repealed.)
	"1971 undistributed income on hand" (Repealed.)
	"active business"
	"additional voluntary contribution"
	"adjusted cost base"
	"adjustment time" (Repealed.)
	"aggregate investment income"
	"allowable business investment loss"
	"allowable capital loss"
	"alter ego trust"
	"amateur athlete trust"
	"amortized cost"
	"amount"
	"annuity"
	"appropriate percentage"
	"assessment"
	"authorized foreign bank"
	"automobile"
	"balance-due day"
	"bank"
	"bankrupt"
	"benefit under a deferred profit sharing plan"
	"bituminous sands"
	"borrowed money"
	"business"
	"business limit"
	"business number"
	"Canadian banking business"
	"Canadian corporation"
	"Canadian development expense"

Section	Subject
	"Canadian exploration and development expenses"
	"Canadian exploration expense"
	"Canadian field processing"
	"Canadian oil and gas property expense"
	"Canadian partnership"
	"Canadian real, immovable or resource property"
	"Canadian resident partnership"
	"Canadian resource property"
	"Canadian-controlled private corporation"
	"capital dividend"
	"capital gain"
	"capital interest"
	"capital loss"
	"capital property"
	"cash method"
	"cemetery care trust"
	"common share"
	"common-law partner"
	"common-law partnership"
	"controlled foreign affiliate"
	"corporation"
	"corporation incorporated in Canada"
	"cost amount"
	"credit union"
	"cumulative eligible capital" (Repealed.)
	"death benefit"
	"deferred amount"
	"deferred profit sharing plan"
	"depreciable property"
	"derivative forward agreement"
	"designated insurance property"
	"designated stock exchange"
	"designated surplus" (Repealed.)
	"disposition"
	"dividend"
	"dividend rental arrangement"
	"DRA share"
	"eligible capital amount" (Repealed.)
	"eligible capital expenditure" (Repealed.)
	"eligible capital property" (Repealed.)
	"eligible dividend"
	"eligible funeral arrangement"
	"eligible relocation"
	"emissions allowance"
	"emissions obligation"
	"employed"
	"employee"
	"employee benefit plan"
	"employee life and health trust"
	"employee trust"
	"employees profit sharing plan"
	"employer"
	"employment"
	"estate"
	"estate of the bankrupt"
	"excessive eligible dividend designation"
	"exempt income"
	"farm loss"
	"farming"
	"federal credit union"
	"filing-due date"
	"fiscal period" (Repealed.)
	"fishing"
	"flow-through share"
	"foreign accrual property income"
	"foreign affiliate"
	"foreign currency"
	"foreign currency debt"
	"foreign exploration and development expenses"
	"foreign resource expense"
	"foreign resource pool expenses"
	"foreign resource property"
	"foreign retirement arrangement"
	"former business property"
Prop.	"fully collateralized arrangement"
	"functional currency" (Repealed.)
	"general rate income pool"
	"goods and services tax"
	"graduated rate estate"
	"grandfathered share"
	"gross revenue"
	"group term life insurance policy"
	"highest individual percentage"
	"home relocation loan"
	"income bond" or "income debenture"
	"income interest"
	"income-averaging annuity contract"
	"indexed debt obligation"
	"indexed security" (Repealed.)
	"indexed security investment plan" (Repealed.)
	"individual"
	"insurance corporation"
	"insurance policy"
	"insurer"
	"inter vivos trust"
	"international shipping"
	"international traffic"
	"inventory"
	"investment corporation"
	"investment tax credit"
Prop.	"joint management area"
	"joint spousal or common-law partner trust"
	"lawyer"
	"legal representative"
	"lending asset"
	"LIA policy"
	"licensed annuities provider"
	"life insurance business"
	"life insurance capital dividend"
	"life insurance corporation"
	"life insurance policy"
	"life insurance policy in Canada"
	"life insurer"
	"limited partnership loss"
	"limited-recourse amount"
	"listed international agreement"
	"listed personal property"
	"low rate income pool"
	"majority-interest partner"
	"mineral"
	"mineral resource"
	"minerals" (Repealed.)
	"mining reclamation trust" (Repealed.)
	"Minister"
	"money purchase limit"
	"mortgage investment corporation"
	"motor vehicle"
	"mutual fund corporation"
	"mutual fund trust"
	"net capital loss"
	"net corporate income tax rate"
	"net income stabilization account"
	"Newfoundland offshore area"
	"NISA Fund No. 2"

Section	Subject
	"non-capital loss"
	"non-portfolio property"
	"non-resident"
	"non-resident-owned investment corporation"
	"Nova Scotia offshore area"
	"office"
	"oil or gas well"
	"OSFI risk-weighting guidelines"
	"overseas Canadian Forces school staff"
	"paid-up capital"
	"paid-up capital deficiency" (Repealed.)
	"Part VII refund"
	"Part VIII refund"
	"participant" (Repealed.)
	"passenger vehicle"
	"past service pension adjustment"
	"pension adjustment"
	"person"
	"personal or living expenses"
	"personal services business"
	"personal trust"
	"personal-use property"
	"pooled pension plan"
	"pooled registered pension plan" or "PRPP"
	"post-1971 spousal or common-law partner trust"
	"preferred share"
	"prescribed"
	"principal amount"
	"private corporation"
	"private foundation"
	"private health services plan"
	"professional corporation"
	"profit sharing plan"
	"property"
	"Province" (Repealed.)
	"provincial SIFT tax factor" (Repealed.)
	"provincial SIFT tax rate"
	"public corporation"
	"public foundation"
	"public market"
	"qualified Canadian journalism organization"
	"qualified donee"
	"qualifying environmental trust"
	"qualifying share"
	"qualifying trust annuity"
	"recognized derivatives exchange"
	"recognized stock exchange"
	"record"
	"refundable Part VII tax on hand"
	"refundable Part VIII tax on hand"
	"registered Canadian amateur athletic association"
	"registered charity"
	"registered disability savings plan" or "RDSP"
	"registered education savings plan" or "RESP"
	"registered home ownership savings plan" (Repealed.)
	"registered investment"
Pend.	"registered journalism organization"
	"registered labour-sponsored venture capital corporation"
	"registered national arts service organization"
	"registered pension fund or plan" (Repealed.)
	"registered pension plan"
	"registered retirement income fund" or "RRIF"
	"registered retirement savings plan" or "RRSP"
	"registered securities dealer"
	"registered supplementary unemployment benefit plan"
	"regulation"

Section	Subject
	"relevant factor"
	"restricted farm loss"
	"restricted financial institution"
	"retirement compensation arrangement"
	"retirement income fund"
	"retirement savings plan"
	"retiring allowance"
	"RRSP deduction limit"
	"RRSP dollar limit"
	"salary deferral arrangement"
	"salary or wages"
	"scientific research and experimental development"
	"scientific research and experimental development financing contract"
	"scientific research and experimental development tax credit"
	"securities lending arrangement"
	"self-contained domestic establishment"
	"separation agreement"
	"share"
	"shareholder"
	"share-purchase tax credit"
	"short-term preferred share"
	"SIFT partnership"
	"SIFT partnership balance-due day"
	"SIFT trust"
	"SIFT trust wind-up event"
	"SIFT wind-up corporation"
	"SIFT wind-up entity"
	"SIFT wind-up entity equity"
	"small business bond"
	"small business corporation"
	"small business development bond"
	"specified employee"
	"specified financial institution"
	"specified future tax consequence"
	"specified individual"
	"specified investment business"
	"specified member"
	"specified mutual fund trust"
	"specified pension plan"
	"specified proportion"
Prop.	"specified securities lending arrangement"
	"specified shareholder"
	"specified synthetic equity arrangement"
	"specified unitholder"
	"split income"
	"stock dividend"
	"subsidiary controlled corporation"
	"subsidiary wholly-owned corporation"
	"superannuation or pension benefit"
	"supplementary unemployment benefit plan"
	"synthetic disposition arrangement"
	"synthetic disposition period"
	"synthetic equity arrangement"
	"synthetic equity arrangement chain"
	"tar sands"
	"tax shelter"
	"tax treaty"
	"taxable Canadian corporation"
	"taxable Canadian property"
	"taxable capital gain"
	"taxable dividend"
	"taxable income"
	"taxable income earned in Canada"
	"taxable net gain"
	"taxable preferred share"

Section	Subject
	"taxable RFI share"
	"tax-indifferent investor"
	"tax-paid undistributed surplus on hand" (Repealed.)
	"taxpayer"
	"term preferred share"
	"termination payment" (Repealed.)
	"testamentary trust"
	"TFSA"
	"timber resource property"
	"total pension adjustment reversal"
	"Treasury Board"
	"treaty-protected business"
	"treaty-protected property"
	"trust"
	"trust account number"
	"undepreciated capital cost"
	"unit trust"
	"unused RRSP deduction room"
	"unused scientific research and experimental development tax credit"
	"unused share-purchase tax credit"
	"zero-emission passenger vehicle"
	"zero-emission vehicle"
248(1.1)	Non-disposition before December 24, 1998
248(2)	Tax payable
248(3)	Property subject to certain Quebec institutions and arrangements
248(3.1)	Gift of bare ownership of immovables
248(3.2)	Qualifying arrangement
248(4)	Interest in real property
248(4.1)	Real right in immovables
248(5)	Substituted property
248(6)	"Class" of shares issued in series
248(7)	Receipt of things mailed
248(8)	Occurrences as a consequence of death
248(9)	Definitions
	"disclaimer"
	"release or surrender"
248(9.1)	How trust created
248(9.2)	Vested indefeasibly
248(10)	Series of transactions
248(11)	Compound interest
248(12)	Identical properties
248(13)	Interests in trusts and partnerships
248(14)	Related corporations
248(15)	Goods and services tax — change of use
248(16)	Goods and services tax — input tax credit and rebate
248(16.1)	Quebec input tax refund and rebate
248(17)	Application of subsection (16) to certain vehicles and aircraft
248(17.1)	Application of subsection (16.1) to certain vehicles and aircraft
248(17.2)	Input tax credit on assessment
248(17.3)	Quebec input tax refund on assessment
248(18)	Goods and services tax — repayment of input tax credit
248(18.1)	Repayment of Quebec input tax refund
248(19)	When property available for use
248(20)	Partition of property
248(21)	Subdivision of property
248(22)	Matrimonial regimes
248(23)	Dissolution of a matrimonial regime
248(23.1)	Transfers after death
248(24)	Accounting methods
248(25)	Beneficially interested
248(25.1)	Trust-to-trust transfers
248(25.2)	Trusts to ensure obligations fulfilled
248(25.3)	Cost of trust interest
248(25.4)	Where acquisition by another of right to enforce

Section	Subject
248(26)	Debt obligations
248(27)	Parts of debt obligations
248(28)	Limitation respecting inclusions, deductions and tax credits
248(29)	Farming or fishing business
248(30)	Intention to give
248(31)	Eligible amount of gift or monetary contribution
248(32)	Amount of advantage
248(33)	Cost of property acquired by donor
248(34)	Repayment of limited-recourse debt
248(35)	Deemed fair market value
248(36)	Non-arm's length transaction
248(37)	Non-application of subsection (35)
248(38)	Artificial transactions
248(39)	Substantive gift
248(40)	Inter-charity gifts
248(41)	Information not provided
248(42)	Synthetic equity arrangements – disaggregation
249(1)	Definition of "taxation year"
249(1.1)	References to calendar year
249(2)	References to certain taxation years and fiscal periods
249(3)	Fiscal period exceeding 365 days
249(3.1)	Year end on status change
249(4)	Loss restriction event — year end
249(4.1)	Trust transition from graduated rate estate
249(5)	Graduated rate estate
249(6)	Loss of testamentary trust status (Repealed.)
249.1(1)	Definition of "fiscal period"
249.1(2)	Not a member of a partnership
249.1(3)	Subsequent fiscal periods
249.1(4)	Alternative method
249.1(5)	Alternative method not applicable to tax shelter investments
249.1(6)	Revocation of election
249.1(7)	Change of fiscal period
249.1(8)	Single-tier fiscal period alignment
249.1(9)	Multi-tier fiscal period alignment — one-time election
249.1(9.1)	When subsection (9) ceases to apply
249.1(10)	Conditions to align a partnership fiscal period
249.1(11)	Deemed multi-tier alignment election
250(1)	Person deemed resident
250(2)	Idem
250(3)	Ordinarily resident
250(4)	Corporation deemed resident
250(5)	Deemed non-resident
250(5.1)	Continued corporation
250(6)	Residence of international shipping corporation
250(6.01)	Partner's gross revenue
250(6.02)	Service providers
250(6.03)	Service providers
250(6.04)	Definitions
	"eligible entity"
	"eligible interest"
250(6.05)	Holdings in eligible entities
250(6.1)	Residence of inter vivos trusts
250(7)	Residence of a qualifying environmental trust (Repealed.)
250.1	Non-resident person's taxation year and income
251(1)	Arm's length
251(2)	Definition of "related persons"
251(3)	Corporations related through a third corporation
251(3.1)	Relation where amalgamation or merger
251(3.2)	Amalgamation of related corporations
251(4)	Definitions concerning groups
	"related group"
	"unrelated group"
251(5)	Control by related groups, options, etc

Section	Subject
251(6)	Blood relationship, etc
251.1(1)	Definition of "affiliated persons"
251.1(2)	Affiliation where amalgamation or merger
251.1(3)	Definitions
	"affiliated group of persons"
	"beneficiary"
	"contributor"
	"controlled"
	"majority-interest beneficiary"
	"majority-interest group of beneficiaries"
	"majority-interest group of partners"
251.1(4)	Interpretation
251.2(1)	Definitions
	"beneficiary"
	"equity"
	"equity value"
	"fixed interest"
	"investment fund"
	"majority-interest beneficiary"
	"majority-interest group of beneficiaries"
	"majority-interest group of partners"
	"person"
	"portfolio investment fund" (Repealed.)
	"specified right"
	"subsidiary"
251.2(2)	Loss restriction event
251.2(3)	Trusts — exceptions
251.2(4)	Trusts — additional cases
251.2(5)	Trusts — special rules of application
251.2(6)	Trusts — time of day
251.2(7)	Filing and other deadlines
252(1)	Extended meaning of "child"
252(2)	Relationships
252(3)	Extended meaning of "spouse" and "former spouse"
252(4)	Idem (Repealed.)
252.1	Union employer
253	Extended meaning of "carrying on business"
253.1(1)	Investments in limited partnerships
253.1(2)	Investments in limited partnerships
254	Contract under pension plan
255	"Canada"
256(1)	Associated corporations
256(1.1)	Definition of "specified class"
256(1.2)	Control, etc
256(1.3)	Parent deemed to own shares
256(1.4)	Options and rights
256(1.5)	Person related to himself, herself or itself
256(1.6)	Exception
256(2)	Corporations associated through a third corporation
256(2.1)	Anti-avoidance
256(3)	Saving provision
256(4)	Saving provision
256(5)	Idem
256(5.1)	Control in fact
256(5.11)	Factual control — Interpretation
256(6)	Idem
256(6.1)	Simultaneous control
256(6.2)	Application to control in fact
256(7)	Acquiring control
256(8)	Deemed exercise of right
256(8.1)	Corporations without share capital
256(9)	Date of acquisition of control
256.1(1)	Definitions
	"attribute trading restriction"
	"person"
	"specified provision"
256.1(2)	Application of subsection (3)

Section	Subject
256.1(3)	Deemed acquisition of control
256.1(4)	Special rules
256.1(5)	Deeming rules — if share value nil
256.1(6)	Deemed acquisition of control
257	Negative amounts
258(1)	Deemed dividend on term preferred share (Repealed.)
258(2)	Idem
258(3)	Deemed interest on preferred shares
258(4)	Exception
258(5)	Deemed interest on certain shares
258(6)	Exception
259(1)	Proportional holdings in trust property
259(2)	Proportional holdings in corporate property (Repealed.)
259(3)	Election
259(4)	Requirement to provide information
259(5)	Definitions
	"designated provisions"
	"qualified corporation" (Repealed.)
	"qualified trust"
	"specified taxpayer"
260(1)	Definitions
	"dealer compensation payment"
	"qualified security"
	"qualified trust unit"
	"securities lending arrangement"
	"security distribution"
	"SLA compensation payment"
	"specified securities lending arrangement"
	"underlying payment"
260(1.1)	Eligible dividend
Prop. 260(1.2)	References — borrower and lender
260(2)	Non-disposition
260(3)	Disposition of right
260(4)	Idem
260(5)	Where subsection (5.1) applies
260(5.1)	Deemed character of compensation payments
260(6)	Deductibility
260(6.1)	Deductible amount
260(7)	Dividend refund
260(8)	Non-resident withholding tax
260(8.1)	Deemed fee for borrowed security
260(8.2)	Effect for tax treaties
Prop. 260(8.2)	Effect for tax treaties — interest
Prop. 260(8.3)	Effect for tax treaties — dividend
Prop. 260(8.4)	Idem
260(9)	Restricted financial institution
260(9.1)	Non-arm's length compensation payment
260(10)	Partnerships
260(11)	Corporate members of partnerships
260(12)	Individual members of partnerships
261(1)	Definitions
	"Canadian currency year"
	"Canadian tax results"
	"consolidated financial statements" (Repealed.)
	"currency exchange rate" (Repealed.)
	"elected functional currency"
	"functional currency"
	"functional currency year"
	"generally accepted accounting principles" (Repealed.)
	"initial functional currency year" (Repealed.)
	"initial reversionary year" (Repealed.)
	"last Canadian currency year" (Repealed.)
	"last functional currency year" (Repealed.)
	"legal-entity financial statements" (Repealed.)
	"pre-reversion debt"
	"pre-transition debt"
	"qualifying currency"

Section	Subject
	"qualified credit card issuer"
	"related entity"
	"reportable account"
	"reportable jurisdiction"
	"reportable jurisdiction person"
	"reportable person"
	"reporting financial institution"
	"specified insurance company"
	"TIN"
	"USD"
270(2)	Interpretation
270(3)	Interpretation — investment entity
270(4)	Equity or debt interest — deeming rule
271(1)	General reporting requirements
271(2)	Currency
271(3)	TIN and date of birth
271(4)	Exceptions
272(1)	General due diligence rules
272(2)	Timing — determination of balance or value
272(3)	Determination — balance or value
272(4)	Service provider
272(5)	Optional due diligence procedures
272(6)	Documentation of due diligence procedures
273(1)	Due diligence for preexisting individual accounts
273(2)	Lower value accounts
273(3)	Enhanced review procedure — high value accounts
273(4)	Timing of review
273(5)	Reportable preexisting individual accounts
274(1)	Due diligence - new individual accounts
274(2)	Determination of reportable account
274(3)	Requirement to obtain new self-certification
275(1)	Due diligence — preexisting entity accounts
275(2)	Application of subsection (4)
275(3)	Determination of reportable accounts
275(4)	Review procedures — preexisting entity account
275(5)	Timing of review
275(6)	Change of circumstances
276	Due diligence for new entity accounts
277(1)	Special due diligence rules
277(2)	Exception — individual beneficiary receiving death benefit
277(3)	Aggregation rules
277(4)	Dealer accounts
277(5)	Dealer accounts
277(6)	Group insurance and annuities
278(1)	Reporting
278(2)	Electronic filing
279(1)	Record keeping
279(2)	Form of records
279(3)	Retention of records
280	Anti-avoidance
281(1)	Production of TIN
281(2)	Confidentiality of TIN
281(3)	Penalty for failure to provide TIN
281(4)	Assessment

SCHEDULE
LISTED CORPORATIONS

Section	Subject
Schedule	*(Subsection 181(1))*

Canadian Income Tax Act

R.S.C. 1985, Chapter 1 (5th Supp.), as amended

An Act respecting Income Taxes

Short Title

SECTION 1: Short Title

This Act may be cited as the *Income Tax Act*.

Editorial Note: The current Income Tax Act was proclaimed in force effective March 1, 1994. It replaced the former Act (c. 63, S.C. 1970-71-72) which was repealed by a schedule to the 5th Supplement of Revised Statutes of Canada, 1985.

The Income Tax Act was first enacted as chapter 52 of 1948, and later became chapter 148 of the Revised Statutes of Canada, 1952. At the time of the statute revision of 1970, the Income Tax Act was printed as chapter I-5, but its coming into force was prevented by the enactment of tax reform legislation. Section 1 of that legislation (c. 63, S.C. 1970-71-72) took the form of an amendment which repealed and replaced the Act almost in its entirety.

Part I
Income Tax

DIVISION A — Liability for Tax

SECTION 2: [Tax payable]

► 2(1) ◄

(1) Tax payable by persons resident in Canada. An income tax shall be paid, as required by this Act, on the taxable income for each taxation year of every person resident in Canada at any time in the year.

Editorial Note: The determination of whether a person is resident in Canada for the purposes of the Act is normally based on common law principles, although certain rules in s. 250 deem a person to be resident (or not). The determination of residency is also subject to the provisions of any applicable income tax treaty, and s. 250(5) generally ensures that a person cannot claim non-resident status under a treaty while simultaneously claiming resident status for the purposes of the Act.

Related Sections: S. 2(2) Taxable income; s. 3 Income for taxation year; s. 114 Individual resident in Canada for only part of year; s. 248(1), "person"; s. 249 Definition of "taxation year"; s. 250(1) Person deemed resident; s. 250(3) Ordinarily resident; s. 250(4) Corporation deemed resident.

Canadian Petroleum Tax Journal: Moving Forward With Mobile Income, Chris Roberge, CA, CPA, 2001, Vol. 14, No. 1.

Canadian Tax Foundation: Atlas, *A Review of the Residence Rules for Individuals, Trusts, and Corporations*, 2013 Ontario Tax Conference 11:1–26; Strawson and Jankovic, *Interprovincial Tax Planning: What's Trending?*, 2013 Ontario Tax Conference 7:1–19; Gartner, *Residence of Individuals*, 2013 Prairie Provinces Tax Conference 4B:1–23; Monaco et al., *New Approach to Compliance Activities (CRA Roundtable, Question 1)*, 2012 Ontario Tax Conference 14:1.

Tax Profile: January 2013 — Canadian Taxation of E-Commerce — An Overview; November 2012 — Canadian Residency Traps for Former Canadian Residents; May 2012 — Supreme Court Confirms Central Management and Control Test for Trust Residency; January 2011 — FCA Confirms Trust Residency to be Based on Central Management and Control; March 2011 — Canada 2010 — Year in Review; December 2010 — Problems for Canadians Using LLCs; December 2010 — Holding Companies Under Attack; December 2009 — *Lingle v. The Queen* — How Subjective Is the Habitual Abode Test?; October 2009 — Corporate Management and Control Extended to Trust Residency: A New and Novel Approach; July 2009 — Residency of Trusts — Under Attack?; December 2008 — Tax Planning for Emigration from Canada to the United States; April 2007 — Tax Planning for Emigration from Canada; June 2002 — Canadian Residency Update for Individuals.

Tax Topics: No. 2115, *Mark Higgins Rallying (a Firm) v. The Commissioners for Her Majesty's Revenue and Customs* — A Guide to Management and Control; No. 1980, *Garron v. The Queen:* Missing the Trees for the Forest?; No. 1969, Does the *Garron Family Trust* Decision Change Anything?; No. 1966, Case Comment — *Garron Family Trust*.

Guides: P151 Canadian Residents Going Down South; T4131 Canadian Residents Abroad.

Income Tax Folios: *Primary* — S5-F1-C1 Determining an Individual's Residence Status; S6-F1-C1 Residence of a Trust or Estate.

Income Tax Technical News: Issue No. 38, Canada-U.S. Treaty's Competent Authority Provision; Issue No. 33, Permanent Establishment — The Dudney Case Update; Issue No. 25, E-Commerce.

Interpretation Bulletins: *Secondary* — IT-106R3 Crown Corporation Employees Abroad.

Cases: There is no inconsistency between being a resident of Canada for the purposes of the Act and being a resident of the UK for purposes of the Canada-UK Tax Convention. The taxpayer was resident in Canada throughout 2002 for the purposes of the Act and was thus subject to tax on his worldwide income from employment, including employment outside Canada, unless the Convention otherwise determined, which it did not. *Black v. The Queen*, 2015 DTC 5024 (F.C.A.), affirming 2014 DTC 1046 (T.C.C.)

Interest income was "income from a business carried on in Canada", rather than income from property since the taxpayer's core activity was the operation of an investment holding business and earning interest income was its major business activity. *Inter-Leasing Inc. v. Ontario (Revenue)*, 2013 DTC 5124 (Ont. S.C.J.)

A central management and control test was applied to find a trust resident in Canada since its decisions were made by Canadian beneficiaries and not by the Barbados-resident trustee. *St. Michael Trust Corp. v. The Queen*, 2012 DTC 5063 (S.C.C.), affirming 2010 DTC 5189 (F.C.A.) and 2009 DTC 1287 (T.C.C.)

The taxpayer, a U.S. resident, worked as a consulting engineer for a Canadian company. Factors such as higher profit coupled with higher risk, mobility and independence, indicate that the taxpayer was an independent contractor. Since he had no fixed base in Canada, he could not be taxed in Canada under Article XIV of the Canada-U.S. Tax Convention. *Wolf v. The Queen*, 2002 DTC 6853 (F.C.A.), reversing 2000 DTC 2595 (T.C.C.)

Rental income derived by a non-resident from a single family dwelling in Canada was income from property and not income from a business. There was no merit in the taxpayer's argument that inconsistency existed between the Minister's assessments under s. 155 and Part XIII. The onus was on the taxpayer to demonstrate that these two assessments cover the same income and he failed to do so. *Gupta v. The Queen*, 2000 DTC 6326 (F.C.A.), affirming 99 DTC 224 (T.C.C.)

A U.S. resident performing services in Canada under contract was not subject to Canadian tax under Article XIV of the Convention because he did not have a "fixed base" in Canada. The expression "fixed base" is to be given a liberal interpretation. However, there is little difference in meaning between a "fixed base" and a "permanent establishment". *The Queen v. Dudney*, 2000 DTC 6169 (F.C.A.), affirming 99 DTC 147 (T.C.C.)

A taxpayer with permanent homes in both Canada and Germany was deemed for the purposes of the tax treaty with West Germany to be a resident of West Germany; he lived with his wife and children there, his coin business was located there, he was involved in the community there, his church ties were there and he had been appointed an honorary director of his local band there. *Hertel v. M.N.R.*, 93 DTC 721 (T.C.C.)

A non-resident partner in a business in which he did not actively participate carried on a business in Canada because he participated in the profits and was not merely investing. *Randall v. The Queen*, 85 DTC 5208 (F.C.T.D.)

The Minister argued that a certain trust was a resident of Bermuda and Canada because the Canadian trustee had sole power to appoint other trustees and that he took a very active role in investment programs of the trust. The Court held that the trust was a resident in Bermuda only because the majority of the trustees were resident in Bermuda and the trust document permitted a majority decision on all matters of trustee discretion. *Thibodeau Family Trust v. The Queen*, 78 DTC 6376 (F.C.T.D.)

Profits on the purchase and sale in Canada of speculative mining shares by a mining exploration company operating in Ireland were not taxable as the company was not resident in Canada. Notwithstanding the fact that the company had a "head office" in Toronto and the fact that it had other facilities and carried on certain activities in Canada, the central management and control of the company was in Ireland. *M.N.R. v. Tara Exploration and Development Co. Ltd.*, 72 DTC 6288 (S.C.C.), affirming 70 DTC 6370 (Ex. Ct.)

► 2(2) ◄

(2) Taxable income. The taxable income of a taxpayer for a taxation year is the taxpayer's income for the year plus the additions and minus the deductions permitted by Division C.

Related Sections: 2(1) Tax payable by persons resident in Canada; 2(3) Tax payable by non-resident persons; 110 Deductions permitted; 110.1 Deduction for gifts; 110.2 Lump-sum payments; 110.4 Forward averaging; 110.5 Additions for foreign tax deductions; 110.6 [Capital gains exemption]; 110.7 Residing in prescribed zone; 111 Losses deductible; 111.1 Order of applying provisions; 112 Deduction of taxable dividends received by corporation resident in Canada; 114 Individual resident in Canada for only part of year.

Canadian Petroleum Tax Journal: Moving Forward With Mobile Income, Chris Roberge, CA, CPA, 2001, Vol. 14, No. 1.

Forms: T1248 — Information About Your Residency Status.

► 2(3) ◄

(3) Tax payable by non-resident persons. Where a person who is not taxable under subsection (1) for a taxation year

(*a*) was employed in Canada,

(*b*) carried on a business in Canada, or

(*c*) disposed of a taxable Canadian property,

at any time in the year or a previous year, an income tax shall be paid, as required by this Act, on the person's taxable income earned in Canada for the year determined in accordance with Division D.

Editorial Note: A non-resident's Part I income is computed in accordance with the rules provided in Division D (ss. 115 through 116). However, most forms of passive investment income are subject to withholding tax under Part XIII. In either case, the non-resident's tax liability under the Act may be reduced or eliminated by an income tax treaty; see, for example, s. 110(1)(*f*)(i), which allows a deduction of treaty-exempt amounts in computing taxable income.

Related Sections: S. 2(2) Taxable income; s. 111(9) Exception; s. 114 Individual resident in Canada for only part of year; s. 115 Non-resident's taxable income in Canada; s. 212 Taxation of non-residents; s. 219 Branch tax; s. 248(1), "business", "employed", "non-resident", "taxable Canadian property", "taxable income earned in Canada"; s. 249 Definition of "taxation year"; s. 253 Extended meaning of "carrying on business"; s. 255 Canada.

Canadian Petroleum Tax Journal: Taxable Canadian Property, Tony Van Rooyen, 2000, Vol. 13, No. 1.

Canadian Tax Foundation: Nitikman, *More on Services PEs — What Is a Connected Project?*, 2014 Canadian Tax Journal 2:317–382; Ormrod and Bain, *Taxation Aspects of Cloud Computing*, 2012 Conference Report 18:1–25; Di Maio and Hutchinson, *Cross-Border Potpourri Issues for Small and Mid-Sized Businesses (Canada-U.S. Tax Treaty Update)*, 2012 Ontario Tax Conference 3:1–49.

Tax Profile: January 2013 — Canadian Taxation of E-Commerce — An Overview; May 2011 — Creating a Canada-U.S. Service Joint Venture; April 2011 — Canadian Tax Issues for Non-Resident Franchisors; October 2009 — New Rules under the Canada-U.S. Treaty and Canadian Withholding Taxes on Cross-Border Services; August 2008 — Fifth Protocol to the Canada–U.S. Tax Convention: A Canadian Perspective; June 2008 — International Tax Planning for the Owner-Manager; October 2007 — Important Changes Announced to the Canada — U.S. Income Tax Convention; December 2005 — Sales of Shares of Real Estate Companies by a Non-Resident of Canada — Canadian Tax Consequences; June 2005 — Are You Sure That You Don't Have a Permanent Establishment?.

Tax Topics: No. 2107, Interpretation of Article VII of the Canada-U.S. Tax Convention; No. 2075, 2011 Canadian Tax Foundation Roundtable; No. 1971-72, 2009 Canadian Tax Foundation Conference: Wizards, Tiny Taxes and "Evil" Kirk; No. 1965, Potential Double Taxation of Rental Income to Non-Residents?; No. 1963, The CRA Interprets the Fifth: An Update; No. 1859, The CRA Finally Asks for Water; No. 1834, OECD: Attribution of Profits to Permanent Establishments; No. 1737, Why Tax Lawyers Should Care that the Toronto Blue Jays Struck Out.

Forms: NR73 — Determination of Residency Status (leaving Canada); NR74 — Determination of Residency Status (Entering Canada); T2062 — Notice by a Non-Resident of Canada Concerning the Disposition or Proposed Disposition of Canadian Taxable Property.

Guides: T4058 Non-Residents and Income Tax.

Income Tax Technical News: Issue No. 44, Services Provided by a US Resident to a Canadian Subsidiary of a US Customer; Issue No. 44, Services Provided by a US Employee to a Canadian Subsidiary; Issue No. 44, Services Provided by a US Employee to a Customer of a Canadian Subsidiary; Issue No. 35, Treaty Residence — Resident of Convenience; Issue No. 34, Permanent Establishments; Issue No. 34, Treaty Interpretation and the Meaning of "Liable to Tax"; Issue No. 25, E-Commerce.

Interpretation Bulletins: *Secondary* — IT-168R3 Athletes and players employed by football, hockey and similar clubs; IT-176R2 Taxable Canadian Property — Interests in and Options on Real Property and Shares; IT-262R2 Losses of non-residents and part-year residents; IT-420R3 Non-residents — Income earned in Canada; IT-434R Rental of real property by individual.

Cases: For references to relevant cases on this provision, please see the case annotations following s. 2(1)

Division B — Computation of Income

Basic Rules

SECTION 3: Income for taxation year

The income of a taxpayer for a taxation year for the purposes of this Part is the taxpayer's income for the year determined by the following rules:

(*a*) determine the total of all amounts each of which is the taxpayer's income for the year (other than a taxable capital gain from the disposition of a property) from a source inside or outside Canada, including, without restricting the generality of the foregoing, the taxpayer's income for the year from each office, employment, business and property,

(*b*) determine the amount, if any, by which

(i) the total of

(A) all of the taxpayer's taxable capital gains for the year from dispositions of property other than listed personal property, and

(B) the taxpayer's taxable net gain for the year from dispositions of listed personal property,

exceeds

(ii) the amount, if any, by which the taxpayer's allowable capital losses for the year from dispositions of property other than listed personal property exceed the taxpayer's allowable business investment losses for the year,

(*c*) determine the amount, if any, by which the total determined under paragraph (*a*) plus the amount determined under paragraph (*b*) exceeds the total of the deductions permitted by subdivision e in computing the taxpayer's income for the year (except to the extent that those deductions, if any, have been taken into account in determining the total referred to in paragraph (*a*)), and

(*d*) determine the amount, if any, by which the amount determined under paragraph (*c*) exceeds the total of all amounts each of which is the taxpayer's loss for the year from an office, employment, business or property or the taxpayer's allowable business investment loss for the year,

and for the purposes of this Part,

(*e*) where an amount is determined under paragraph (*d*) for the year in respect of the taxpayer, the taxpayer's income for the year is the amount so determined, and

(*f*) in any other case, the taxpayer shall be deemed to have income for the year in an amount equal to zero.

Editorial Note: A taxpayer's income cannot be negative. To the extent that losses under s. 3(*d*) exceed the amount determined after the application of ss. 3(*a*) through (*c*), the excess will constitute a non-capital loss (or farm loss, etc.), which will be subject to carryover rules found in s. 111. Similarly, the excess, if any, of the amount determined under s. 3(*b*)(ii) over the amount determined under s. 3(*b*)(i) will constitute a net capital loss, also subject to carryover rules. Note that s. 3 also includes income from "unenumerated sources" — that is, from sources other than those expressly described in s. 3 or other provisions of the Act (see the Supreme Court of Canada's decision in *Schwartz*, (96 DTC 6103)).

Related Sections: S. 4(1) Income or loss from a source or from sources in a place; s. 5(1) Income from office or employment; s. 6(1) Amounts to be included as income from office or employment; s. 7(1) Agreement to issue securities to employees; s. 8(1) Deductions allowed; s. 9 Income; s. 12(1) Income inclusions; s. 18(1) General limitations; 31(1) Restricted farm loss; s. 38 Taxable capital gain and allowable capital loss; s. 39 Meaning of capital gain and capital loss; s. 41 Taxable net gain from disposition of listed personal property; s. 54, "listed personal property"; s. 56 Amounts to be included in income for year; s. 60 Other deductions; s. 104(2) Taxed as individual; s. 248(1), "amount", "business", "corporation", "employment", "office"; s. 249 Definition of "taxation year".

Canadian Tax Foundation: Alarie, *The Taxation of Winnings from Poker and Other Gambling Activities in Canada*, 2011 Canadian Tax Journal 4:731–763; Wentzell, *Taxation of Income from Unlisted Sources: An Analysis of Schwartz v. The Queen*, 1996 Conference Report 67:1–15.

Tax Profile: March 2012 — Ponzi Schemes — No Source of Income.

Tax Topics: No. 2123, Federal Court of Appeal Finds Payments from Ponzi Scheme are Taxable as Income; No. 1653, REOP Resurrected — This Year's Hallowe'en Trick; No. 1621, Non-Comp Non-Taxable.

Income Tax Folios: S4-F8-C1 Business Investment Losses; *Primary* — S3-F9-C1 Lottery Winnings, Miscellaneous Receipts, and Income (and Losses) from Crime; *Secondary* — S5-F2-C1 Foreign Tax Credit.

Income Tax Technical News: Issue No. 39, Settlement of a Shareholder Class Action Suit — Compensation by Way of Cash and Shares.

Interpretation Bulletins: *Primary* — IT-206R Separate businesses; IT-365R2 Damages, settlement, and similar receipts; IT-434R Rental of real property by individual; IT-490 Barter transactions. *Secondary* — IT-232R3 Losses — Their deductibility in the loss year or in other Years; IT-262R2 Losses of non-residents and part-year residents; IT-302R3 Losses of a corporation — The effect that acquisitions of control, amalgamations, and windings-up have on their deductibility.

Tax Window Files: Retirement Gift from Union, *Technical Interpretation, Business and Partnerships Division, March 15, 2005*, CRA Document No. 2005-0114061I7. Cash gift provided by union upon retirement of member in good standing not taxable; Per Diem Indemnities and Allowances Paid to Jurors and Witnesses, *Technical Interpretation, Business and Partnerships Division, October 5, 2004*, CRA Document No. 2004-0067741E5. Per diem indemnities received by jurors or witnesses are considered fees for services rendered and are taxable; allowances paid to cover expenses incurred by jurors or witnesses to render the services are not taxable.

Cases: As part of a wrongful dismissal settlement, the taxpayer received $3,080,000 to compensate him for the loss of an interest in his former employer's estate (which he had previously been promised). The settlement was not taxable because the estate interest it was intended to replace would not have been taxable, as granting it was not a term of the taxpayer's employment contract. *The Queen v. Au*, 2006 DTC 6074 (F.C.A.), affirming 2005 DTC 794 (T.C.C.)

The right to compete is not "property", and therefore payments under a non-competition agreement are non-taxable capital receipts. *Manrell v. The Queen*, 2003 DTC 5225 (F.C.A.), reversing 2002 DTC 1222 (T.C.C.)

The taxpayers received payments as consideration for signing non-competition agreements with Loblaws, after selling their shares of their own supermarket corporation to Loblaws. These payments were not income from a productive source under s. 3. *The Queen v. Fortino et al.*, 2000 DTC 6060 (F.C.A.), affirming 97 DTC 55 (T.C.C.)

The lump sum of $360,000 in damages that a taxpayer received when an employment offer was withdrawn was not a retiring allowance under s. 56(1)(*a*) since the key element of the definition of employment in s. 248(1) was missing and there was no factual basis to justify the allocation of such sum to losses of income relating to salary. *Schwartz v. The Queen*, 96 DTC 6103 (S.C.C.) reversing 94 DTC 6249 (F.C.A.) and affirming 93 DTC 555 (T.C.C.)

When the contracts signed by a taxpayer provided for his services in the writing of texts for a television series with payments to be made to his personal company, these payments were included in his income. *Giguère v. M.N.R.*, 93 DTC 488 (T.C.C.)

When considering fees paid to taxicab associations by members on certain conditions, the court decided that the fee was not income. The property in the money that was paid passed only in the event that the member left without providing a satisfactory successor. It was really a deposit. *Dominion Taxicab Ass'n v. M.N.R.*, 54 DTC 1020 (S.C.C.).

SECTION 4: Income or loss from a source or from sources in a place

► 4(1) ◄

(1) Income or loss from a source or from sources in a place. For the purposes of this Act,

(*a*) a taxpayer's income or loss for a taxation year from an office, employment, business, property or other source, or from sources in a particular place, is the taxpayer's income or loss, as the case may be, computed in accordance with this Act on the assumption that the taxpayer had during the taxation year no income or loss except from that source or no income or loss except from those sources, as the case may be, and was allowed no deductions in computing the taxpayer's income for the taxation year except such deductions as may reasonably be regarded as wholly applicable to that source or to those sources, as the case may be, and except such part of any other deductions as may reasonably be regarded as applicable thereto; and

(*b*) where the business carried on by a taxpayer or the duties of the office or employment performed by a taxpayer was carried on or were performed, as the case may be, partly in one place and partly in another place, the taxpayer's income or loss for the taxation year from the business carried on, or the duties performed, by the taxpayer in a particular place is the taxpayer's income or loss, as the case may be, computed in accordance with this Act on the assumption that the taxpayer had during the taxation year no income or loss except from the part of the business that was carried on in that particular place or no income or loss except from the part of those duties that were performed in that particular place, as the case may be, and was allowed no deductions in computing the taxpayer's income for the taxation year except such deductions as may reasonably be regarded as wholly applicable to that part of the business or to those duties, as the case may be, and except such part of any other deductions as may reasonably be regarded as applicable thereto.

Related Sections: S. 248(28) Limitation respecting inclusions, deductions and tax credits.

Canadian Tax Foundation: Arnold and Darmo, *Summary of the Proceedings of an Invitational Seminar on the Attribution of Profits to Permanent Establishments*, 2001 Canadian Tax Journal 3:525–549.

Income Tax Folios: *Secondary*— S3-F9-C1 Lottery Winnings, Miscellaneous Receipts, and Income (and Losses) from Crime.

Interpretation Bulletins: *Secondary* — IT-328R3 Losses on shares on which dividends have been received; IT-362R Patronage dividends.

Tax Window Files: Sourcing Income to the United States, *Technical Interpretation, International Tax and Trusts Division, October 16, 2007*, CRA Document No. 2007-0224221I7; Per Diem Indemnities and Allowances Paid to Jurors and Witnesses, *Technical Interpretation, Business and Partnerships Division, October 5, 2004*, CRA Document No. 2004-0067741E5.

Cases: The corporate resident taxpayer earned bond interest income arising in Brazil, and earned income from other sources that was taxable in Canada. Under the Act, interest income such as the bond interest in this case is taxed on a net basis after deducting the expenses incurred to earn that interest. The expenses relevant to income from a source in a particular place are found in subsection 4(1). *Société Générale Valeurs Mobilières Inc. v. The Queen*, 2017 DTC 5007 (FCA)

The explosives division sold by the taxpayer was not a separate business, therefore, the taxpayer was not subject to recapture of capital cost allowance or an increased s. 14(1) income inclusion. Indicators of integration included centralized financing and credit management, centralized purchasing, and common research facilities. *Du Pont Canada Inc. v. The Queen*, 2001 DTC 5269 (F.C.A.), reversing 99 DTC 1132 (T.C.C.)

The Supreme Court held that the interest expense deduction was to be allocated to the various sources of the taxpayer's income, with the result that the amount taken into account in computing the foreign tax credit was the foreign interest income reduced by the interest expense allocated to that source. *Interprovincial Pipeline Co. v. M.N.R.*, 68 DTC 5093 decision (S.C.C.)

► 4(2) ◄

(2) Idem. Subject to subsection (3), in applying subsection (1) for the purposes of this Part, no deductions permitted by sections 60 to 64 apply either wholly or in part to a particular source or to sources in a particular place.

► 4(3) ◄

(3) Deductions applicable. In applying subsection (1) for the purposes of subsections 104(22) and (22.1) and sections 115 and 126,

(*a*) subject to paragraph (*b*), all deductions permitted in computing a taxpayer's income for a taxation year for the purposes of this Part, except any deduction permitted by any of paragraphs 60(*b*) to (*o*), (*p*), (*r*) and (*v*) to (*z*), apply either wholly or in part to a particular source or to sources in a particular place; and

(*b*) any deduction permitted by subsection 104(6) or (12) shall not apply either wholly or in part to a source in a country other than Canada.

History: S. 4(3)(*a*) was replaced by S.C. 2013, c. 34, s. 169(1), applicable to the 2002 and subsequent taxation years, except that, for taxation years that end before 2007, paragraph 4(3)(*a*) is to be read as follows:

"(*a*) subject to paragraph (*b*), all deductions permitted in computing a taxpayer's income for a taxation year for the purposes of this Part, except any deduction permitted by any of paragraphs 60(*b*) to (*o*), (*p*), (*r*) and (*v*) to (*x*), apply either wholly or in part to a particular source or to sources in a particular place; and"

S. 4(3)(*a*) formerly read:

(*a*) subject to paragraph (*b*), all deductions permitted in computing a taxpayer's income for a taxation year for the purposes of this Part, except any deduction permitted by any of paragraphs 60(*b*) to (*o*), (*p*), (*r*) and (*v*) to (*z*), shall apply either wholly or in part to a particular source or to sources in a particular place; and

Income Tax Folios: *Secondary*— S5-F2-C1 Foreign tax credit.

Interpretation Bulletins: *Secondary* — IT-420R3 Non-residents — Income earned in Canada.

► 4(4) ◄

(4) Limitation respecting inclusions and deductions — (Repealed by S.C. 1996, c. 21, s. 2(1).)

Related Sections: S. 248(1), "amount", "business", "employment", "office", "property"; s. 249 Definition of "taxation year".

Subdivision a — Income or Loss from an Office or Employment

Basic Rules

SECTION 5: [Income or loss from office or employment]

▶ 5(1) ◀

(1) Income from office or employment. Subject to this Part, a taxpayer's income for a taxation year from an office or employment is the salary, wages and other remuneration, including gratuities, received by the taxpayer in the year.

Editorial Note: The often contentious issue of whether a person is an employee or an independent contractor relates largely to the fact that employees are only allowed those deductions specifically set out in s. 8, whereas independent contractors are allowed deductions in accordance with the (broader) rules regarding the computation of income from a business. Also, withholding is required in respect of remuneration paid to employees but not amounts paid for services rendered by independent contractors.

Related Sections: S. 3(*a*) Income for taxation year; s. 4(1)(*a*) Income or loss from a source or from sources in a place; s. 6 Amounts to be included as income from office or employment; s. 7 Agreement to issue securities to employees; s. 8(2) General limitation; s. 15(2.4) When s. 15(2) not to apply — certain employees; s. 81 Amounts not included in income; s. 115(1)(*a*)(i) Non-resident's taxable income in Canada; s. 149(1)(*a*) Employees of a country other than Canada; s. 149(1)(*b*) Members of the family and servants of employees of a country other than Canada; s. 153(1)(*a*) Withholding; s. 249(1) Definition of "taxation year".

Canadian Tax Foundation: Larre, *The Role of Intention in Distinguishing Employees from Independent Contractors*, 2014 Canadian Tax Journal 4:927–970; Doobay and MacPherson, *Intent in Service Contracts*, 2013 Canadian Tax Highlights 21(5):5–6; Donohoe, *Owner-Manager: Employee or Independent Contractor?*, 2013 Canadian Tax Highlights 21(1):1–2; Jung and McIntyre, *Current Issues: Owner-Managers: Employee or Independent Contractor*, 2013 Ontario Tax Conference 1:15–17; Navkar, *The Role of Intention in the Employee-Independent Contractor Determination*, 2013 Tax for the Owner-Manager 13(3):3–4; Peermohamed, *The Role of Intention in Characterizing a Worker*, 2013 Canadian Tax Focus 3(1):5–6; Clarke, *Tax Litigation Issues Relevant to Small and Medium-Sized Business*, 2012 British Columbia Tax Conference 7:1–17; Melville et al., *Personal Tax Planning: Tax Considerations for the Newly Self-Employed*, 2011 Canadian Tax Journal 4:843–868; Clarke, *The Employee/Independent Contractor Conundrum*, 2004 British Columbia Tax Conference 10:1–33; Friedlander, *What Has Tort Law Got to Do With It? Distinguishing Between Employees and Independent Contractors in the Federal Income Tax, Employment Insurance, and Canada Pension Plan Contexts*, 2003 Canadian Tax Journal 4:1467–1519; Gaucher, *A Worker's Status as Employee or Independent Contractor*, 1999 Conference Report 33:1–98.

Tax Topics: No. 2152, Just as Intended: *1392644 Ontario Inc. et al. v. The Queen*.

Forms: T4 — Statement of Remuneration Paid; T4 Sum. — Summary of Remuneration Paid; T4A — Statement of Pension, Retirement, Annuity, and Other Income; T4A Sum. — Summary of Pension, Retirement Annuity, and Other Income; T4A(P) Supp. — Statement of Canada Pension Plan Benefits; T4F Sum. — Summary of Fishing Income; T4F — Statement of Fishing Income.

Guides: RC4110 Employee or Self-employed?.

Income Tax Folios: S2-F3-C2 Benefits and Allowances Received from Employment.

Secondary — S1-F2-C3 Scholarships, Research Grants and Other Education Assistance; S2-F3-C1 Payments from Employer to Employee; S3-F9-C1 Lottery Winnings, Miscellaneous Receipts, and Income (and Losses) from Crime.

Interpretation Bulletins: *Primary* — IT-68R2 Exemption from income tax in Canada — Professors and teachers from other countries. *Secondary* — IT-113R4 Benefits to employees — Stock options; IT-168R3 Athletes and players employed by football, hockey and similar clubs; IT-202R2 Employees' or workers' compensation; IT-257R Canada Council grants; IT-292 Taxation of elected officers of incorporated municipalities, school boards, municipal commissions and similar bodies.

Tax Window Files: Settlement for Loss of Employment — Lost Vacation Pay, Expenses not Covered by Medical Plan and Human Rights Violation, *Technical Interpretation, Business and Partnerships Division, February 17, 2005*, CRA Document No. 2004-0104331E5. Indemnities for loss of annual vacation credits and reimbursement of psychotherapy and drug costs were taxable; indemnity for moral prejudice granted in accordance with Canadian Human Rights Act was not taxable; Retiring Allowance — Collective Agreement — Severance Pay, *Technical Interpretation, Financial Industries Division, January 16, 2004*, CRA Document No. 2003-0046491E5. Employee who had option under a collective agreement to collect "severance pay" immediately or upon retirement would be receiving employment income and not a retiring allowance; Timing of Income Recognition — Cheques Mailed to Taxpayer, *Technical Interpretation, Business and Partnerships Division, December 23, 2003*, CRA Document No. 2003-0049497. Lump-sum from employer in lieu of previous pay cheques that were not received was included in the year in which the lump sum was received; Employee Awards — Points Exchangeable for Goods, *Technical Interpretation, Business and Partnerships Division, November 12, 2003*, CRA Document No. 2003-0020275. Whether employer "points" program, under which points redeemable for goods, are cash or non-cash gifts under CRA employee gift policy.

Cases: A member of a regulatory body held an "office", since she was entitled to receive *per diem* payments when she worked that were fixed or ascertainable stipends. Even though she received nothing when there was no work, the entitlement requirement means nothing more than a position for pay. *M.N.R. v. Real Estate Council of Alberta*, 2012 DTC 5099 (F.C.A.), reversing 2011 UDTC 1 (T.C.C.)

Dancers at the Royal Winnipeg Ballet were independent contractors, not employees. Although the company exercised extensive control over their work, this was required to stage a season of performances. The understanding of the parties as to the nature of their legal relationship was relevant, although not conclusive. *The Royal Winnipeg Ballet v. M.N.R.*, 2006 DTC 6323 (F.C.A.), reversing (T.C.C.), unreported

As part of a wrongful dismissal settlement, the taxpayer received $3,080,000 to compensate him for the loss of an interest in his former employer's estate (which he had previously been promised). The settlement was not taxable because the estate interest it was intended to replace would not have been taxable, as granting it was not a term of the taxpayer's employment contract. *The Queen v. Au*, 2006 DTC 6074 (F.C.A.), affirming 2005 DTC 794 (T.C.C.)

The taxpayer, a U.S. resident, worked as a consulting engineer for a Canadian company. Factors such as higher profit coupled with higher risk, mobility and independence, indicate that the taxpayer was an independent contractor. Since he had no fixed base in Canada, he could not be taxed in Canada under Article XIV of the Canada-U.S. Tax Convention. *Wolf v. The Queen*, 2002 DTC 6853 (F.C.A.), reversing 2000 DTC 2595 (T.C.C.)

Considering that the tax equalization payment received by the taxpayer from the taxpayer's U.S. employer was made pursuant to an element of the overall ongoing compensation package and was designed to induce the taxpayer to serve outside the U.S., it constituted part of the taxpayer's remuneration for services within the meaning of s. 5(1). *Gernhart v. The Queen*, 98 DTC 6026 (F.C.A.), affirming 96 DTC 1672 (T.C.C.)

The Federal Court of Appeal, in determining whether a relationship is between an employer and employee or between two businesses, held that the test was whether the alleged employees were providing services in a business or employment capacity. *Wiebe Door Services Ltd. v. M.N.R.*, 87 DTC 5025 (F.C.A.).

▶ 5(2) ◀

(2) Loss from office or employment. A taxpayer's loss for a taxation year from an office or employment is the amount of the taxpayer's loss, if any, for the taxation year from that source computed by applying, with such modifications as the circumstances require, the provisions of this Act respecting the computation of income from that source.

Interpretation Bulletins: *Secondary* — IT-168R3 Athletes and players employed by football, hockey and similar clubs.

Inclusions

SECTION 6: Amounts to be included as income from office or employment

▶ 6(1) ◀

(1) Amounts to be included as income from office or employment. There shall be included in computing the income of a taxpayer for a taxation year as income from an office or employment such of the following amounts as are applicable:

Income Tax Folios: *Primary* — S2-F1-C1 Health and Welfare Trusts. *Secondary* — S2-F3-C1 Payments from Employer to Employee.

Interpretation Bulletins: *Primary* — IT-63R5 Benefits, including standby charge for an automobile, from the personal use of a motor vehicle supplied by an employer — After 1992; IT-168R3 Athletes and players employed by football, hockey and similar clubs; IT-529 Flexible employee benefit programs. *Secondary* — IT-227R Group term life insurance premiums; IT-339R3 Meaning of "private health services plan"; IT-357R2 Expenses of training; IT-365R2 Damages, settlement, and similar receipts; IT-421R2 Benefits to individuals, corporations and shareholders from loans or debt; IT-428 Wage loss replacement plans; IT-432R2 Benefits conferred on shareholders; IT-502 Employee benefit plans and employee trusts.

Other Publications: AD-18-01 Taxable benefit for the personal use of an aircraft.

► 6(1)(a) ◄

(a) **Value of benefits** — the value of board, lodging and other benefits of any kind whatever received or enjoyed by the taxpayer, or by a person who does not deal at arm's length with the taxpayer, in the year in respect of, in the course of, or by virtue of the taxpayer's office or employment, except any benefit

(i) derived from the contributions of the taxpayer's employer to or under a deferred profit sharing plan, an employee life and health trust, a group sickness or accident insurance plan, a group term life insurance policy, a pooled registered pension plan, a private health services plan, a registered pension plan or a supplementary unemployment benefit plan,

(ii) under a retirement compensation arrangement, an employee benefit plan or an employee trust,

(iii) that was a benefit in respect of the use of an automobile,

(iv) derived from counselling services in respect of

(A) the mental or physical health of the taxpayer or an individual related to the taxpayer, other than a benefit attributable to an outlay or expense to which paragraph 18(1)(*l*) applies, or

(B) the re-employment or retirement of the taxpayer,

(v) under a salary deferral arrangement, except to the extent that the benefit is included under this paragraph because of subsection (11), or

(vi) that is received or enjoyed by an individual other than the taxpayer under a program provided by the taxpayer's employer that is designed to assist individuals to further their education, if the taxpayer deals with the employer at arm's length and it is reasonable to conclude that the benefit is not a substitute for salary, wages or other remuneration of the taxpayer;

Editorial Note: Certain benefits excluded under s. 6(1)(*a*) are dealt with elsewhere in the Act, e.g., s. 6(4) for group term life insurance, s. 6(1)(*e*) for automobile standby charge, and s. 6(1)(*k*) and (l) for employer-paid automobile operating costs. The provision may not necessarily apply to an employee who is also a shareholder of a corporate employer and receives the benefit as a shareholder and not as an employee. If this is the case, the benefit is considered received under s. 15(1). The benefits are normally included in the employee's income even when they are enjoyed by his/her relatives and are calculated as the fair market value of the goods or services to the employee (including applicable sales taxes) less any amount paid or reimbursed to the employer.

History: S. 6(1)(*a*)(i) was replaced by S.C. 2013, c. 34, s. 426(2), in force June 26, 2013, and formerly read:

(i) derived from the contributions of the taxpayer's employer to or under a deferred profit sharing plan, an employee life and health trust, a group sickness or accident insurance plan, a group term life insurance policy, a private health services plan, a registered pension plan or a supplementary unemployment benefit plan,

S. 6(1)(*a*) was replaced by S.C. 2013, c. 34, s. 170(1), applicable in respect of benefits received or enjoyed on or after October 31, 2011. S. 6(1)(*a*) formerly read:

(*a*) *Value of benefits* — the value of board, lodging and other benefits of any kind whatever received or enjoyed by the taxpayer in the year in respect of, in the course of, or by virtue of an office or employment, except any benefit

(i) derived from the contributions of the taxpayer's employer to or under a deferred profit sharing plan, an employee life and health trust, a group sickness or accident insurance plan, a group term life insurance policy, a pooled registered pension plan, a private health services plan, a registered pension plan or a supplementary unemployment benefit plan,

(ii) under a retirement compensation arrangement, an employee benefit plan or an employee trust,

(iii) that was a benefit in respect of the use of an automobile,

(iv) derived from counselling services in respect of

(A) the mental or physical health of the taxpayer or an individual related to the taxpayer, other than a benefit attributable to an outlay or expense to which paragraph 18(1)(*l*) applies, or

(B) the re-employment or retirement of the taxpayer, or

(v) under a salary deferral arrangement, except to the extent that the benefit is included under this paragraph because of subsection (11);

S. 6(1)(*a*)(i) was replaced by S.C. 2012, c. 31, s. 2(1), in force December 14, 2012, and formerly read:

(i) derived from the contributions of the taxpayer's employer to or under a deferred profit sharing plan, an employee life and health trust, a group sickness or accident insurance plan, a group term life insurance policy, a private health services plan, a registered pension plan or a supplementary unemployment benefit plan,

S. 6(1)(*a*)(i) was replaced by S.C. 2010, c. 25, s. 2(1), applicable after 2009. S. 6(1)(*a*)(i) formerly read:

(i) derived from the contributions of the taxpayer's employer to or under a registered pension plan, group sickness or accident insurance plan, private health services plan, supplementary unemployment benefit plan, deferred profit sharing plan or group term life insurance policy,

Related Regulations: 200(3).

Related Sections: S. 5(1) Income from office or employment; s. 6(1.1) Parking cost; s. 6(2) Reasonable standby charge; s. 6(2.1) Automobile salesman; s. 6(4) Group term life insurance; s. 6(6) Employment at special work site or remote location; s. 6(7) Cost of property or service; s. 6(9) Amount in respect of interest on employee debt; s. 6(14) Part of plan or arrangement; s. 6(15) Forgiveness of employee debt; s. 6(16) Disability-related employment benefits; s. 6(18) Group disability benefits — insolvent insurer; s. 6(19) Benefit re housing loss; s. 6(20) Benefit re eligible housing loss; s. 6(23) Employer-provided housing subsidies; s. 7(1) Agreement to issue securities to employees; s. 8(11) Goods and services tax; s. 15(9) Deemed benefit to shareholder by corporation; s. 20.01(1) PHSP premiums; s. 56(1)(*a*) Pension benefits, unemployment insurance benefits, etc.; s. 56(1)(*g*) Supplementary unemployment benefit plan; s. 56(1)(*i*) Deferred profit sharing plan; s. 56(1)(*w*) Salary deferral arrangement; s. 56(1)(*x*) Retirement compensation arrangement — employee recipient; s. 56(1)(*y*) Retirement compensation arrangement — proceeds of disposition; s. 56(1)(*z*) Retirement compensation arrangement — non-employee recipient; s. 79(3) Proceeds of disposition for debtor; s. 79(5) Subsequent application with respect to employee or shareholder debt; s. 80(1), "forgiven amount"; s. 80(2)(*q*) Application of debt forgiveness rules; s. 80.01(1), "forgiven amount"; s. 81(3.1) Travel expenses; s. 145(1), "supplementary unemployment benefit plan"; s. 145(3) Amounts received taxable; s. 147(1), "deferred profit sharing plan"; s. 147(10) Amounts received taxable; s. 147.5 Pooled registered pension plans; s. 248(1), "benefit under a deferred profit sharing plan", "deferred amount", "employee benefit plan", "employee trust", "group term life insurance policy", "private health services plan", "registered pension plan", "retirement compensation arrangement", "retiring allowance", "salary deferral arrangement".

Canadian Petroleum Tax Journal: Attracting and Retaining Executives and Employees with Tax-Efficient Incentives, Julie Y. Lee, 2001, Vol. 14, No. 1; Current Trends in Executive Compensation Structures and Their Taxation, Rachel Colabella and Denise McMullen, 2000, Vol. 13, No. 1.

Canadian Tax Foundation: Truster, *Taxable Benefits: How Much Is Taxable?*, 2014 Tax for the Owner-Manager 14(2):2; Bassindale and Kreklewetz, *Employer's In-House Fitness Centre Taxable*, 2013 Tax for the Owner-Manager 13(1):4–6; Carenza, *Incentive Compensation for Small and Medium-Sized Private Companies*, 2012 Ontario Tax Conference 6:1–21; Bordeleau et al., *Taxable Benefit: Bring Your Own Device (Canada Revenue Agency and Revenu Québec Round Table, Question 12)*, 2011 Conference Report 4:8–9; Aiken, *Current Cases: Tax Court of Canada — "Non-Section 7 Options": When Does the Benefit from Employment Arise? (Henley v. The Queen, 2006 TCC 347)*,

2006 Canadian Tax Journal 4:930–936; Heddema and Lee, *Shareholder and Employee Benefits and Deductions: Selected Issues*, 2006 British Columbia Tax Conference 15:1–48; Ebel and Stewart, *Update on Employee Stock Options and Employee Benefits*, 2002 Conference Report 27:1–39; Van Cauwenberghe, *Taxation of Employee Stock Options — A Review and Update*, 2001 Prairie Provinces Tax Conference 2:1–53; Wong, *Current Cases: Federal Court of Appeal — Payment Made for the Cancellation of Stock Options: Taxable Benefit? (Bernier v. The Queen, 99 DTC 5656)*, 2000 Canadian Tax Journal 1:144–148; Woltersdorf, *Recent Challenges to Employee Benefits and Tax Consequences of Termination Benefits*, 1999 Prairie Provinces Tax Conference 5:2–49; Friedlander and Steele, *The Income Taxation of Flexible Benefit Plans in Canada*, 1998 Canadian Tax Journal 4:786–818; Arnold and Li, *The Appropriate Tax Treatment of the Reimbursement of Moving Expenses*, 1996 Canadian Tax Journal 1:1–37.

Tax Profile: July 2010 — Employee Compensation Planning: Stock-Based Incentive Compensation Plans; February 2010 — Employee Scholarship Programs.

Tax Topics: No. 2075, 2011 Canadian Tax Foundation Roundtable.

Guides: T4130 Employers Guide to Payroll Deductions — Taxable Benefits.

Income Tax Folios: S2-F3-C2 Benefits and Allowances Received from Employment.

Secondary — S1-F2-C3 Scholarships, Research Grants and Other Education Assistance; S2-F1-C1 Health and Welfare Trusts; S2-F3-C1 Payments from Employer to Employee.

Income Tax Technical News: Issue No. 25, Health and welfare trusts.

Interpretation Bulletins: *Primary* — IT-63R5 Benefits, including standby charge for an automobile, from the personal use of a motor vehicle supplied by an employer — After 1992; IT-529 Flexible employee benefit programs. *Secondary* — IT-227R Group term life insurance premiums; IT-339R3 Meaning of "private health services plan"; IT-357R2 Expenses of training; IT-421R2 Benefits to individuals, corporations and shareholders from loans or debt; IT-428 Wage loss replacement plans; IT-432R2 Benefits conferred on shareholders; IT-502 Employee benefit plans and employee trusts.

Tax Window Files: Employee insurance discounts, *March 26, 2019*, CRA Document No. 2017-0729441E5; Taxable benefits, *April 13, 2018*, CRA Document No. 2017-0682891E5; CPA Alberta 2017 Q17: Electric Vehicle Taxable Benefits, *September 14, 2017*, CRA Document No. 2017-0703881C6; Temporary living expenses and travel costs, *September 21, 2016*, CRA Document No. 2016-0639401E5; Taxable benefit – cell phones, *March 6, 2015*, CRA Document No. 2014-0553481I7; City uniforms - footwear, *February 2, 2015*, CRA Document No. 2014-0552421E5; Employee Recognition Program, *August 8, 2013*, CRA Document No. 2013-0479271E5; Wage Loss Replacement Plan — Employee-Shareholder Beneficiaries, *Technical Interpretation, Financial Sector and Exempt Entities Division, February 12, 2007*, CRA Document No. 2006-0214141E5; Private Health Services Plan for Shareholder-Employee, *Technical Interpretation, Business and Partnerships Division, October 19, 2006*, CRA Document No. 2006-0204951I7; Health and Welfare Trusts, *Technical Interpretation, Business and Partnerships Division, May 5, 2005*, CRA Document No. 2005-0121151E5. General comments regarding health and welfare trusts; Retirement Gift from Union, *Technical Interpretation, Business and Partnerships Division, March 15, 2005*, CRA Document No. 2005-0114061I7. Cash gift provided by union upon retirement of member in good standing not taxable; Taxable Benefit — Weight-Loss Program, *Technical Interpretation, Business and Partnerships Division, March 4, 2005*, CRA Document No. 2005-0109731E5. Weight loss program provided by employer results in taxable benefit for participating employees; Settlement for Loss of Employment — Lost Vacation Pay, Expenses not Covered by Medical Plan and Human Rights Violation, *Technical Interpretation, Business and Partnerships Division, February 17, 2005*, CRA Document No. 2004-0104331E5. Indemnities for loss of annual vacation credits and reimbursement of psychotherapy and drug costs were taxable; indemnity for moral prejudice granted in accordance with Canadian Human Rights Act was not taxable; Employee Parking, *Technical Interpretation, Business and Partnerships Division, November 26, 2004*, CRA Document No. 2004-0101151E5. No taxable benefit from free parking space for employee required to use vehicle for employment-related travel three or more days per week; Free Tuition for Employee's Dependant, *Technical Interpretation, Business and Partnerships Division, June 1, 2004*, CRA Document No. 2004-0069811E5. Tuition fees for employee's child were taxable benefit; Professional Membership Initiation or Admission Fees, *Technical Interpretation, Business and Partnerships Division, April 14, 2004*, CRA Document No. 2004-0058301E5. Employer-paid initiation fees for professional organization generally taxable benefits, but annual membership fees generally not taxable benefits; both deductible for employer; Employee Benefits — Reimbursement of Computer, Modem and Internet Costs — Computer Allowance, *Technical Interpretation, Business and Partnerships Division, March 4, 2004*, CRA Document No. 2003-0049831E5. Employer reimbursements for employees' costs of computers were taxable benefits; reimbursements of modem and internet costs were not taxable.

Cases: The taxpayer was the sole shareholder and director of his corporation and was reassessed for unreported income arising from alleged taxable benefits received from the company. The Court must "determine whether the person received the payment for his activities in the performance of his office or whether he received it simply as an individual". None of the items at issue were payments made to him for "activities in the performance of his office". Any benefits received were not compensation for services rendered. *Kootenay Management v. The Queen*, 2019 DTC 1068 (TCC)

The taxpayer received $140,000 from his former employer in appreciation for his years of service. This was included in his employment income, even though he was no longer employed by the payor. Benefits are included in employment income if they are received "in respect of ... or by virtue of ... employment". The provisions are very broad and only the smallest connection to employment is needed *Shaw v. The Queen*, 2013 DTC 1214 (T.C.C.)

Free parking provided by the taxpayers' employer was a taxable benefit equal to the fair market value of a parking spot near their workplace (rather than the cost to the employer). *Anthony v. The Queen*, 2012 DTC 5019 (F.C.A.), affirming 2010 DTC 1356 (T.C.C.)

The taxpayers' employer partially reimbursed their children's university tuition in recognition of the students' academic achievement. The scholarship cheques were issued directly to the students. These were not employment benefits because the taxpayers received no measurable economic advantage from them. *The Queen v. Bartley et al.*, 2009 DTC 5019 (F.C.A.), affirming 2008 DTC 3012 (T.C.C.) and 2008 DTC 3027 (T.C.C.)

The cost of the taxpayer's golf club membership was not included in his income since it was primarily for his employer's benefit. The value of a benefit to a particular taxpayer should be determined on an individual basis, taking into account actual use, as opposed to availability. *Rachfalowski v. The Queen*, 2008 DTC 3626 (T.C.C.)

The taxpayer's daughter qualified for a $1,200 award from the university where the taxpayer worked. It was paid to the taxpayer who, in turn, gave it to her daughter to put towards her tuition. It was not an employment benefit since the taxpayer received it on a resulting trust for her daughter and received no measurable economic advantage from it. *Okonski v. The Queen*, 2008 DTC 2992 (T.C.C.)

The taxpayers were given free parking passes by their employer. For most of them, this was a taxable benefit since it eliminated their need to pay for parking. However, one taxpayer had no taxable benefit since the parking pass reduced the employer's costs associated with his extensive use of his car for employer business. Another taxpayer had no taxable benefit since he never used the pass. *Adler et al. v. The Queen*, 2007 DTC 783 (T.C.C.)

Generally, an employer's reimbursement of tuition fees for an employee's children constitutes a benefit under s. 6(1)(*a*), unless the fees are required to be paid due to the nature of the employment. *Guay v. A.G. of Canada*, 2005 DTC 5217 (F.C.A.), affirming 2003 DTC 3957 (T.C.C.)

Free parking spaces provided to employees were not considered to be taxable benefits where the employer received an economic benefit by providing the space. *Chow et al. v. The Queen*, 2001 DTC 164 (T.C.C.)

The taxpayer sued her employer's group insurance carrier regarding denial of long-term disability benefits. The lump-sum settlement she received was taxable under s. 6(1)(*a*) as a benefit received by virtue of her employment. *Dumas v. The Queen*, 2000 DTC 2603 (T.C.C.)

A business trip which involved some travel by cruise ship and some sightseeing was not a taxable benefit. The test does not exclude pleasurable activities undertaken during the trip, so long as the business aspect predominates. The fact that it may help advance the taxpayer's career does not make it a taxable benefit. *Romeril v. The Queen*, 99 DTC 221 (T.C.C.)

Considering that the tax equalization payment received by the taxpayer from the taxpayer's U.S. employer was made pursuant to an element of the overall ongoing compensation package and was designed to induce the taxpayer to serve outside the U.S., it constituted part of the taxpayer's remuneration for services within the meaning of s. 5(1). *Gernhart v. The Queen*, 98 DTC 6026 (F.C.A.), affirming 96 DTC 1672 (T.C.C.)

Since s. 6(1)(*a*) includes "any kind" of economic advantage arising from a taxpayer's employment which renders his office of greater value to him, the benefit received by the taxpayer by virtue of his and his guests' attendance at a Christmas party and staying overnight at the hotel was taxable. *Dunlap v. The Queen*, 98 DTC 2053 (T.C.C.)

Having regard to the fact that the overwhelming portion of the time spent by the taxpayer and his spouse in New Orleans had been devoted to business activities, no part of the trip expenses were to be regarded as a personal benefit. *Lowe v. The Queen*, 96 DTC 6226 (F.C.A.)

Airline travel received by a taxpayer as a result of "frequent flyer" points acquired while travelling on the employer's business constituted a benefit from employment. The correct measure of the amount of the benefit was the price that the taxpayer would have had to pay to purchase a ticket to travel on the same flight, in the same class, and subject to the same restrictions. *Mommersteeg et al. v. The Queen*, 96 DTC 1011 (T.C.C.)

Although each of five taxpayers' houses in Toronto may have been a significantly more valuable asset than their previous houses in Calgary, their equity in both houses was the same, so that the subsidization payments their employer had paid, when they were relocated to Toronto were merely a reimbursement of an employment expense from which they received no economic advantage. *Attorney General of Canada v. Hoefele et al.*, 95 DTC 5602 (F.C.A.)

As part of a housing program termination package, the taxpayer received from his employer $7,240, which was included in his income considering that it arose out of an agreement entered into at the time of or before the period of his employment and it represented the money's worth of certain contractual rights which were of benefit to him. *The Queen v. Blanchard*, 95 DTC 5479 (F.C.A.), reversing 92 DTC 6585 (F.C.T.D.)

A police officer who received $500 per year from his employer to assist him in defraying the cost of clothing worn on the job was held not to have enjoyed any economic benefit. The taxpayer spent more on the clothing than he received, and the $500 was therefore nothing more than a reimbursement (as opposed to an "allowance"). *The Queen v. Huffman*, 90 DTC 6405 (F.C.A.)

Other Publications: AD-18-01 Taxable benefit for the personal use of an aircraft.

▶ 6(1)(b) ◀

(b) Personal or living expenses — all amounts received by the taxpayer in the year as an allowance for personal or living expenses or as an allowance for any other purpose, except

(i) travel, personal or living expense allowances

(A) expressly fixed in an Act of Parliament, or

(B) paid under the authority of the Treasury Board to a person who was appointed or whose services were engaged pursuant to the *Inquiries Act*, in respect of the discharge of the person's duties relating to the appointment or engagement,

(ii) travel and separation allowances received under service regulations as a member of the Canadian Forces,

(iii) representation or other special allowances received in respect of a period of absence from Canada as a person described in paragraph 250(1)(*b*), (*c*), (*d*) or (*d*.1),

(iv) representation or other special allowances received by a person who is an agent-general of a province in respect of a period while the person was in Ottawa as the agent-general of the province,

(v) reasonable allowances for travel expenses received by an employee from the employee's employer in respect of a period when the employee was employed in connection with the selling of property or negotiating of contracts for the employee's employer,

(v.1) allowances for board and lodging of the taxpayer, to a maximum total of $300 for each month of the year, if

(A) the taxpayer is, in that month, a registered participant with, or member of, a sports team or recreation program of the employer in respect of which membership or participation is restricted to persons under 21 years of age,

(B) the allowance is in respect of the taxpayer's participation or membership and is not attributable to services of the taxpayer as a coach, instructor trainer, referee, administrator or other similar occupation,

(C) the employer is a registered charity or a non-profit organization described in paragraph 149(1)(*l*), and

(D) the allowance is reasonably attributable to the cost to the taxpayer of living away from the place where the employee would, but for the employment, ordinarily reside,

(vi) reasonable allowances received by a minister or clergyman in charge of or ministering to a diocese, parish or congregation for expenses for transportation incident to the discharge of the duties of that office or employment,

(vii) reasonable allowances for travel expenses (other than allowances for the use of a motor vehicle) received by an employee (other than an employee employed in connection with the selling of property or the negotiating of contracts for the employer) from the employer for travelling away from

(A) the municipality where the employer's establishment at which the employee ordinarily worked or to which the employee ordinarily reported was located, and

(B) the metropolitan area, if there is one, where that establishment was located,

in the performance of the duties of the employee's office or employment,

(vii.1) reasonable allowances for the use of a motor vehicle received by an employee (other than an employee employed in connection with the selling of property or the negotiating of contracts for the employer) from the employer for travelling in the performance of the duties of the office or employment,

(viii) (Repealed by S.C. 1999, c. 22, S. 2(1).)

(ix) allowances (not in excess of reasonable amounts) received by an employee from the employee's employer in respect of any child of the employee living away from the employee's domestic establishment in the place where the employee is required by reason of the employee's employment to live and in full-time attendance at a school in which the language primarily used for instruction is the official language of Canada primarily used by the employee if

(A) a school suitable for that child primarily using that language of instruction is not available in the place where the employee is so required to live, and

(B) the school the child attends primarily uses that language for instruction and is not farther from that place than the community nearest to that place in which there is such a school having suitable boarding facilities,

and, for the purposes of subparagraphs (v), (vi) and (vii.1), an allowance received in a taxation year by a taxpayer for the use of a motor vehicle in connection with or in the course of the taxpayer's office or employment shall be deemed not to be a reasonable allowance

(x) where the measurement of the use of the vehicle for the purpose of the allowance is not based solely on the number of kilometres for which the vehicle is used in connection with or in the course of the office or employment, or

(xi) where the taxpayer both receives an allowance in respect of that use and is reimbursed in whole or in part for expenses in respect of that use (except where the reimbursement is in respect of supplementary business insurance or toll or ferry charges and the amount of the allowance was determined without reference to those reimbursed expenses);

CRA News Release

2.2% Indexation Factor for 2019

See the CRA Fact Sheet, dated November 16, 2018, that is reproduced following subsection117.1(1). This release announces a 2.2% indexation factor applicable for 2019 tax bracket thresholds, personal amounts and other amounts relating to non-refundable credits, as well as the refundable medical expense supplement, Old Age Security repayment threshold, certain board and lodging allowances, and the tradesperson's tools deduction. Increases to tax bracket thresholds, amounts relating to non-refundable credits, and most other amounts will take effect on January 1, 2019. However, increases in amounts for certain income-tested benefits (for example, the goods and services tax credit) will take effect on July 1, 2019.

Editorial Note: In contrast to s. 6(1)(*a*), which generally requires that an economic benefit be conferred upon an employee, s. 6(1)(*b*) includes any allowance in income regardless of whether an economic benefit is conferred, unless one of the listed exceptions applies. A specific reimbursement of an employee's expense is not an allowance, and will normally not be included in income if it reimburses an employment-related expense but will be included under s. 6(1)(*a*) if the expense was personal in nature. An allowance differs from a reimbursement in that the former is not a targeted repayment of an expense incurred, but rather an amount that is meant to more generally cover the employee's expenses without a specific accounting of the amount to an actual expense incurred.

Related Sections: S. 5(1) Income from office or employment; s. 6(6) Employment at special work site or remote location; s. 6(16) Disability-related employment benefits; s. 8(1)(*f*) Sales expenses; s. 8(1)(*g*) Transport employee's expenses; s. 8(1)(*h*) Travel expenses; s. 8(1)(*h*.1) Motor vehicle travel expenses; s. 8(1)(*j*) Motor vehicle and aircraft costs; s. 18(1)(*r*) Certain automobile expenses; s. 67.4 More than one owner or lessor; s. 81(3.1) Travel expenses; s. 248(1), "motor vehicle", "personal or living expenses".

Canadian Tax Foundation: Tang and Katz, *Automobile Taxable Benefits and Expenses: Part 2*, 1998 Canadian Tax Journal 1:125–146.

Guides: T4130 Employers Guide to Payroll Deductions — Taxable Benefits.

Income Tax Folios: S2-F3-C2 Benefits and Allowances Received from Employment.

Secondary — S1-F2-C2 Tuition Tax Credit.

Interpretation Bulletins: *Secondary* — IT-522R Vehicle, travel and sales expenses of employees.

Tax Window Files: Representation or other special allowances, *January 31, 2019*, CRA Document No. 2017-0695931E5; Motor vehicle allowances, *September 28, 2018*, CRA Document No. 2016-0673831E5; Payments received for work-related travel expenses, *February 25, 2016*, CRA Document No. 2015-0613001E5; Reasonable allowance for travel, *January 4, 2016*, CRA Document No. 2015-0608281E5; Employment at a Special Work Site, *April 10, 2015*, CRA Document No. 2014-055888117; Motor Vehicle Allowance, *April 7, 2005*, CRA Document No. 2005-0115061E5; Mv Benefits-Employer's Record Keeping Requirements., *March 14, 2005*, CRA Document No. 2005-0119451E5; Allocation Automobile, *June 29, 2004*, CRA Document No. 2004-0057181E5; Allocation Pour L'achat D'ordinateur, *March 4, 2004*, CRA Document No. 2003-0049831E5; Combined Employee Motor Vehicle Allow., *February 20, 2003*, CRA Document No. 2002-0176735.

Cases: The amount of $10,000 given by the CNR to assist a taxpayer with the purchase of a home in Winnipeg to replace the one he had sold in Moncton when he agreed to work at the CNR Winnipeg facility following the closing of the Moncton facility was taxable inasmuch as this sum increased the taxpayer's net worth by $10,000 and did not simply restore him to his previous financial state. *The Queen v. Phillips*, 94 DTC 6177 (F.C.A.), reversing 93 DTC 5247 (F.C.T.D.) and 90 DTC 1274 (T.C.C.)

As a result of changes in passenger services effected by Via Rail, the taxpayer was given the option of receiving either a $22,000 lump sum or certain relocation benefits. The lump sum he elected to receive had not been paid to reimburse him for specific expenses actually incurred by him. It was an allowance that had to be included in his income. *Vickery v. The Queen*, 93 DTC 993 (T.C.C.)

▶ 6(1)(c) ◀

(c) Director's or other fees — director's or other fees received by the taxpayer in the year in respect of, in the course of, or by virtue of an office or employment;

Editorial Note: An individual representing a corporation on another corporation's board of directors does not have to include the directors' fees in income if the fees are repaid or turned over to the individual's corporate employer.

Tax Window Files: Power of Attorney fees, *March 11, 2019*, CRA Document No. 2018-0749251E5.

▶ 6(1)(d) ◀

(d) Allocations, etc., under profit sharing plan — amounts allocated to the taxpayer in the year by a trustee under an employees profit sharing plan as provided by section 144 except subsection 144(4), and amounts required by subsection 144(7) to be included in computing the taxpayer's income for the year;

Related Regulations: 212.

Related Sections: S. 8(1)(*o*.1) Forfeited amounts re employee profit sharing plans; s. 8(1)(*o*.2) Excess EPSP amounts; s. 12(1)(*n*) Employees profit sharing plan; s. 128.1(10), "excluded right or interest", s. 144(1), "employees profit sharing plan"; s. 144(9) Deduction for forfeited amounts; s. 207.8 Excess EPSP amount; s. 248(1), "employee benefit plan".

Interpretation Bulletins: *Secondary* — IT-379R Employees Profit Sharing Plans — Allocations to Beneficiaries.

▶ 6(1)(e) ◀

(e) Standby charge for automobile — where the taxpayer's employer or a person related to the employer made an automobile available to the taxpayer, or to a person related to the taxpayer, in the year, the amount, if any, by which

(i) an amount that is a reasonable standby charge for the automobile for the total number of days in the year during which it was made so available

exceeds

(ii) the total of all amounts, each of which is an amount (other than an expense related to the operation of the automobile) paid in the year to the employer or the person related to the employer by the taxpayer or the person related to the taxpayer for the use of the automobile;

Editorial Note: The amount of the reasonable standby charge is computed under s. 6(2). The period during which the automobile is made available to the employee starts on the day the vehicle and the keys are made available to the employee and ends on the day they are returned to the employer or a person related to the employer. An automobile is available to the employee if it is used by the employee all day or for any part of the day or even if the automobile sits unused in the employee's garage, parking spot, or driveway. An employee required by his/her employer to use an automobile in the course of employment but not using it at all for personal driving does not receive a taxable benefit even if the automobile is available to him/her.

Related Regulations: 200(3).

Related Sections: S. 6(1)(*a*)(iii) Value of benefits; s. 6(1)(*k*) Automobile operating expense benefit — employer automobile; s. 6(1)(*l*) Automobile operating expense benefit — employee automobile; s. 6(1.1) Parking cost; 6(2) Reasonable standby charge; s. 6(2.1) Automobile salesman; s. 6(7) Cost of property or service; s. 8(1)(*f*) Sales expenses; s. 8(1)(*h*.1) Motor vehicle travel expenses; s. 8(1)(*j*) Motor vehicle and aircraft costs; s. 12(1)(*y*) Automobile provided to partner; s. 15(5) Automobile benefit; s. 248(1), "automobile".

Canadian Tax Foundation: Tollstam, *Personal Use of Logo-Emblazoned Company Car*, 2015 Canadian Tax Highlights 23(12):2; Tang and Katz, *Automobile Taxable Benefits and Expenses: Part 1*, 1997 Canadian Tax Journal 5:1150–1163.

Tax Topics: No. 2240, The Case of Szymczyk v. The Queen: The Limit of Administrative "One-Offs".

Forms: RC18 — Calculating Automobile Benefits.

Guides: T4130 Employers Guide to Payroll Deductions — Taxable Benefits.

Income Tax Folios: S2-F3-C2 Benefits and Allowances Received from Employment.

Interpretation Bulletins: *Primary* — IT-63R5 Benefits, including standby charge for an automobile, from the personal use of a motor vehicle supplied by an employer — After 1992.

Tax Window Files: Stand-by charge - employee required to use vehicle, *August 31, 2015*, CRA Document No. 2015-0582411E5.

Cases: An automobile salesperson was required to include a standby charge in income for the use of company vehicle even though the vehicle was subject to sale at any time and the taxpayer's use of the vehicle was restricted. *The Queen v. Adams*, 98 DTC 6266 (F.C.A.), reversing 97 DTC 228 (T.C.C.)

► 6(1)(e.1) ◄

(e.1) Group sickness or accident insurance plans — the total of all amounts contributed in the year in respect of the taxpayer by the taxpayer's employer to a group sickness or accident insurance plan, except to the extent that the contributions are attributable to benefits under the plan that, if received by the taxpayer, would be included in the taxpayer's income under paragraph (*f*) in the year the benefits are received if that paragraph were read without regard to its subparagraph (v);

History: S. 6(1)(*e*.1) was replaced by S.C. 2012, c. 31, s. 2(3), applicable to the 2014 and subsequent taxation years, and formerly read:

(*e*.1) *Group sickness or accident insurance plans* — the total of

(i) all amounts (or the portions of those amounts) contributed by the taxpayer's employer after March 28, 2012 and before 2013 that are attributable to the taxpayer's coverage after 2012 under a group sickness or accident insurance plan, except to the extent that the contributions (or portions of those contributions) are attributable to benefits under the plan that, if received by the taxpayer, would be included in the taxpayer's income under paragraph (*f*) in the year the benefits are received if that paragraph were read without regard to its subparagraph (v), and

(ii) all amounts contributed in 2013 in respect of the taxpayer by the taxpayer's employer to a group sickness or accident insurance plan, except to the extent that the contributions are attributable to benefits under the plan that, if received by the taxpayer, would be included in the taxpayer's income under paragraph (*f*) in the year the benefits are received if that paragraph were read without regard to its subparagraph (v);

S. 6(1)(*e*.1) was added by S.C. 2012, c. 31, s. 2(2), applicable to the 2013 taxation year.

Related Sections: S. 6(7) Cost of property or service.

Tax Topics: No. 2240, The Case of Szymczyk v. The Queen: The Limit of Administrative "One-Offs".

Income Tax Folios: S2-F3-C2 Benefits and Allowances Received from Employment.

► 6(1)(f) ◄

(f) Employment insurance benefits — the total of all amounts received by the taxpayer in the year that were payable to the taxpayer on a periodic basis in respect of the loss of all or any part of the taxpayer's income from an office or employment, pursuant to

(i) a sickness or accident insurance plan,

(ii) a disability insurance plan,

(iii) an income maintenance insurance plan, or

(iii.1) a plan described in any of subparagraphs (i) to (iii) that is administered or provided by an employee life and health trust,

to or under which the taxpayer's employer has made a contribution, not exceeding the amount, if any, by which

(iv) the total of all such amounts received by the taxpayer pursuant to the plan before the end of the year and

(A) where there was a preceding taxation year ending after 1971 in which any such amount was, by virtue of this paragraph, included in computing the taxpayer's income, after the last such year, and

(B) in any other case, after 1971,

exceeds

(v) the total of the contributions made by the taxpayer under the plan before the end of the year and

(A) where there was a preceding taxation year described in clause (iv)(A), after the last such year, and

(B) in any other case, after 1967;

Editorial Note: This provision does not apply to benefits from an employee-pay-all plan for which the premiums are paid only by the employee and not by the employer. If both the employer and the employee pay premiums to the plan, only the excess of the periodic benefits received by the employee over the premiums paid by the employee will be taxable to the employee.

History: S. 6(1)(*f*)(iii.1) was added by S.C. 2010, c. 25, s. 2(2), applicable after 2009.

Related Regulations: Part II.

Related Sections: S. 6(17) Definitions; s. 6(18) Group disability benefits — insolvent insurer; s. 8(1)(*n*.1)(iii) Reimbursement of disability payments; s. 110.2(1), "qualifying amount"; s. 122.51(1), "eligible individual"; s. 139.1(15) Employee-paid insurance. ITAR s. 19 Income maintenance payments.

Canadian Tax Foundation: O'Brien, *Surrogatum, Source, and Tsiaprailis: Is There a Principled Basis for the Tax Treatment of Replacement Payments?*, 2006 Canadian Tax Journal 4:862–906; Spiro et al., *Legislative, Administrative, and Judicial Developments: Current Cases — The Surrogatum Principle (Tsiaprailis)*, 2005 Conference Report 5:4–6; Friedlan, *Disability Payments: Lump Sum Partly Taxable*, 2005 Tax for the Owner-Manager 5(2):2–3; Prendergast, *Current Case Law: An Update on Recent Court Decisions of Interest to Tax Practitioners*, 2004 Prairie Provinces Tax Conference 1:1–53; Théroux and Millard, *Trends and Developments in Group Benefit Plans*, 2002 Conference Report 29:1–74.

Tax Topics: No. 2240, The Case of Szymczyk v. The Queen: The Limit of Administrative "One-Offs"; No. 1725, The Supreme Court's Take on the "Surrogatum Principle"; No. 1622, New Ways to Tax the Disabled on Disability Insurance Settlements.

Income Tax Folios: S2-F3-C2 Benefits and Allowances Received from Employment.

Secondary — S2-F1-C1 Health and Welfare Trusts.

Interpretation Bulletins: *Primary* — IT-428 Wage loss replacement plans. *Secondary* — IT-529 Flexible employee benefit programs.

Tax Window Files: Settlement amount for disability benefits, *August 11, 2015*, CRA Document No. 2015-0580521E5.

Cases: The taxpayer sued her employer's insurer after it discontinued long-term disability benefits. Since part of the lump-sum settlement she received was intended to replace accumulated arrears of disability payments, the *surrogatum* principle required that this portion be included in her income under s. 6(1)(*f*). *Tsiaprailis v. The Queen*, 2005 DTC 5119 (S.C.C.), affirming 2003 DTC 5246 (F.C.A.), reversing in part 2002 DTC 1563 (T.C.C.)

The taxpayer negotiated a lump-sum settlement with his employer's insurer after being denied disability payments. The portion of the settlement that was intended to replace past benefits was taxable under s. 6(1)(*f*). *Switzer v. The Queen*, 2005 DTC 431 (T.C.C.)

The taxpayer sued her insurer after it discontinued disability payments. A portion of her lump-sum settlement attributable to arrears is includable in income under s. 6(1)(*f*). Since no such allocation had been calculated, the matter was remitted to the Minister for reassessment in accordance with the *Tsiaprailis* decision. *The Queen v. Siftar*, 2003 DTC 5243 (F.C.A.), reversing in part 2001 DTC 938 (T.C.C.)

When the taxpayer was injured in an accident, her employer's group disability insurer denied her claim. But, following mediation, the taxpayer received a lump-sum settlement. Paragraph 6(1)(*f*) was inapplicable, since the settlement amount was not payable on a periodic basis. *Fry v. The Queen*, 2001 DTC 846 (T.C.C.)

The taxpayer was employed with a corporation having a group disability insurance policy. When the policy carrier refused to meet his disability claim, he sued the carrier, but later received a settlement of $138,000 in return for an absolute release. Paragraph 6(1)(*f*) was inapplicable, since the amount received by the taxpayer was not payable to him on a periodic basis. *Whitehouse v. The Queen*, 2000 DTC 1616 (T.C.C.)

A taxpayer was not required to include in her income a lump sum settlement of $25,000 she had received under her employer's group long-term disability policy since it did not represent the aggregate of a series of payments which the taxpayer might have received over her lifetime. *Landry v. The Queen*, 98 DTC 1416 (T.C.C.)

► 6(1)(f.1) ◄

(f.1) Canadian Forces members and veterans amounts — the total of all amounts received by the taxpayer in the year on account of

(i) an earnings loss benefit, an income replacement benefit (other than an amount determined under subsection 19.1(1), paragraph 23(1)(*b*) or subsection 26.1(1) of the *Veterans Well-being Act*, as modified, where applicable, under Part 5 of that Act), a supplementary retirement benefit or a career impact allowance payable to the taxpayer under Part 2 of the *Veterans Well-being Act*, or

(ii) an amount payable under any of subsections 99(6), 109(1) and 115(5) and sections 124 to 126 of the *Veterans Well-being Act*;

History: S. 6(1)(*f*.1) was replaced by S.C. 2018, c. 12, s. 2(1), in force April 1, 2019, and formerly read:

> (*f*.1) *Canadian Forces members and veterans income replacement benefits* — the total of all amounts received by the taxpayer in the year on account of an earnings loss benefit, a supplementary retirement benefit or a career impact allowance payable to the taxpayer under Part 2 of the *Veterans Well-being Act*;

S. 6(1)(*f*.1) was replaced by S.C. 2017, c. 20, s. 2(1), in force April 1, 2018, and formerly read:

> (*f*.1) *Canadian Forces members and veterans income replacement benefits* — the total of all amounts received by the taxpayer in the year on account of an earnings loss benefit, a supplementary retirement benefit or a career impact allowance payable to the taxpayer under Part 2 of the *Canadian Forces Members and Veterans Re-establishment and Compensation Act*;

S. 6(1)(*f*.1) was replaced by S.C. 2016, c. 7, s. 114, in force April 1, 2017, and formerly read:

> (*f*.1) *Canadian Forces members and veterans income replacement benefits* — the total of all amounts received by the taxpayer in the year on account of an earnings loss benefit, a supplementary retirement benefit or a permanent impairment allowance payable to the taxpayer under Part 2 of the *Canadian Forces Members and Veterans Re-establishment and Compensation Act*;

Related Sections: S. 110.2 Lump-sum Payments.

Tax Topics: No. 2240, The Case of Szymczyk v. The Queen: The Limit of Administrative "One-Offs".

► 6(1)(g) ◄

(g) Employee benefit plan benefits — the total of all amounts each of which is an amount received by the taxpayer in the year out of or under an employee benefit plan or from the disposition of any interest in any such plan, other than the portion thereof that is

(i) a death benefit or an amount that would, but for the deduction provided in the definition of that term in subsection 248(1), be a death benefit,

(ii) a return of amounts contributed to the plan by the taxpayer or a deceased employee of whom the taxpayer is an heir or legal representative, to the extent that the amounts were not deducted in computing the taxable income of the taxpayer or the deceased employee for any taxation year,

(iii) a superannuation or pension benefit attributable to services rendered by a person in a period throughout which the person was not resident in Canada, or

(iv) a designated employee benefit (as defined in subsection 144.1(1));

Editorial Note: Employee members of an Employee Benefit Plan (EBP) are not required to include any amount in their income when the employer makes a contribution to the EBP by virtue of s. 6(1)(*a*)(ii) but must include an amount in their income under s. 6(1)(*g*) when they receive an amount under the plan from the custodian. At the same time, the employer is prevented by s. 18(1)(*o*) to claim a deduction at the time the contribution is made but is allowed under s. 32.1 to claim such deduction within limits after the EBP made payments to the employee members.

History: S. 6(1)(*g*)(iv) was added by S.C. 2010, c. 25, s. 2(3), applicable after 2009.

S. 6(1)(*g*)(ii) was replaced by S.C. 2009, c. 2, s. 2(1), applicable to the 2009 and subsequent taxation years. S. 6(1)(*g*)(ii) formerly read:

> (ii) a return of amounts contributed to the plan by the taxpayer or a deceased employee of whom the taxpayer is an heir or legal representative, or

Related Sections: S. 6(1)(*a*)(ii) Value of benefits; s. 6(1.2) Deeming rule — amount received; s. 6(10) Contributions to an employee benefit plan; s. 12(1)(*n*) Employees profit sharing plan; s. 12(1)(*n*.1) Employee benefit plan; s. 18(1)(*o*) Employee benefit plan contributions; s. 32.1 Employee benefit plan contributions; s. 104(6)(*a*.1) Deduction in computing income of trust; s. 107.1 Distribution by certain employment-related trusts; s. 128.1(10), "excluded right or interest"; s. 212(17) Exception; s. 248(1), "death benefit", "employee benefit plan".

Canadian Petroleum Tax Journal: Current Trends in Executive Compensation Structures and Their Taxation, Rachel Colabella and Denise McMullen, 2000, Vol. 13, No. 1.

Canadian Tax Foundation: Horner, *Canadian Taxation and Cross-Border Pensions*, 2009 Canadian Tax Journal 4:905–930.

Tax Topics: No. 2240, The Case of Szymczyk v. The Queen: The Limit of Administrative "One-Offs".

Interpretation Bulletins: *Primary* — IT-502 Employee benefit plans and employee trusts. *Secondary* — IT-499R Superannuation or pension benefits; IT-529 Flexible employee benefit programs.

► 6(1)(h) ◄

(h) Employee trust — amounts allocated to the taxpayer for the year by a trustee under an employee trust;

Related Regulations: Part II.

Related Sections: S. 6(1)(*a*)(ii) Value of benefits; s. 12(1)(*n*) Employees profit sharing plan; s. 12(1)(*n*.1) Employee benefit plan; s. 32.1 Insurance agents and brokers; s. 104(6)(*a*) Deduction in computing income of trust; s. 104(13)

Income of beneficiary; s. 107.1 Distribution by certain employment-related trusts; s. 248(1), "employee trust".

Tax Topics: No. 2240, The Case of Szymczyk v. The Queen: The Limit of Administrative "One-Offs".

Interpretation Bulletins: *Primary* — IT-502 Employee benefit plans and employee trusts. *Secondary* — IT-499R Superannuation or pension benefits; IT-529 Flexible employee benefit programs.

► 6(1)(i) ◄

(i) Salary deferral arrangement payments — the amount, if any, by which the total of all amounts received by any person as benefits (other than amounts received by or from a trust governed by a salary deferral arrangement) in the year out of or under a salary deferral arrangement in respect of the taxpayer exceeds the amount, if any, by which

(i) the total of all deferred amounts under the arrangement that were included under paragraph (*a*) as benefits in computing the taxpayer's income for preceding taxation years

exceeds

(ii) the total of

(A) all deferred amounts received by any person in preceding taxation years out of or under the arrangement, and

(B) all deferred amounts under the arrangement that were deducted under paragraph 8(1)(*o*) in computing the taxpayer's income for the year or preceding taxation years;

Related Sections: S. 6(11) Salary deferral arrangement; s. 6(12) Salary deferral arrangement — accrued interest; s. 6(13) Application; s. 6(14) Part of plan or arrangement; s. 20(1)(*pp*) Salary deferral arrangement; s. 56(1)(*w*) Salary deferral arrangement; s. 128.1(10), "excluded right or interest"; s. 248(1), "deferred amount", "salary deferral arrangement".

Canadian Tax Foundation: Horner, *Canadian Taxation and Cross-Border Pensions,* 2009 Canadian Tax Journal 4:905–930.

Tax Topics: No. 2240, The Case of Szymczyk v. The Queen: The Limit of Administrative "One-Offs".

Interpretation Bulletins: *Primary* — IT-529 Flexible employee benefit programs.

► 6(1)(j) ◄

(j) Reimbursements and awards — amounts received by the taxpayer in the year as an award or reimbursement in respect of an amount that would, if the taxpayer were entitled to no reimbursements or awards, be deductible under subsection 8(1) in computing the income of the taxpayer, except to the extent that the amounts so received

(i) are otherwise included in computing the income of the taxpayer for the year, or

(ii) are taken into account in computing the amount that is claimed under subsection 8(1) by the taxpayer for the year or a preceding taxation year;

Tax Topics: No. 2240, The Case of Szymczyk v. The Queen: The Limit of Administrative "One-Offs".

► 6(1)(k) ◄

(k) Automobile operating expense benefit — where

(i) an amount is determined under subparagraph (*e*)(i) in respect of an automobile in computing the taxpayer's income for the year,

(ii) amounts related to the operation (otherwise than in connection with or in the course of the taxpayer's office or employment) of the automobile for the period or periods in the year during which the automobile was made available to the taxpayer or a person related to the taxpayer are paid or payable by the taxpayer's employer or a person related to the taxpayer's employer (each of whom is in this paragraph referred to as the "payor"), and

(iii) the total of the amounts so paid or payable is not paid in the year or within 45 days after the end of the year to the payor by the taxpayer or by the person related to the taxpayer,

the amount in respect of the operation of the automobile determined by the formula

$$A - B$$

where

A is

(iv) where the automobile is used primarily in the performance of the duties of the taxpayer's office or employment during the period or periods referred to in subparagraph (ii) and the taxpayer notifies the employer in writing before the end of the year of the taxpayer's intention to have this subparagraph apply, $\frac{1}{2}$ of the amount determined under subparagraph (*e*)(i) in respect of the automobile in computing the taxpayer's income for the year, and

(v) in any other case, the amount equal to the product obtained when the amount prescribed for the year is multiplied by the total number of kilometres that the automobile is driven (otherwise than in connection with or in the course of the taxpayer's office or employment) during the period or periods referred to in subparagraph (ii), and

B is the total of all amounts in respect of the operation of the automobile in the year paid in the year or within 45 days after the end of the year to the payor by the taxpayer or by the person related to the taxpayer; and

Editorial Note: Paragraph 6(1)(*k*) requires employees with an employer-provided automobile, and who are including a standby charge under s. 6(1)(*e*)(i) in their income, to include an operating cost benefit for any payment or reimbursement made by their employer for operating expenses connected with their personal use of the automobile.

Related Persons: The operating cost benefit must be included in their income even if the automobile is not used by them but by persons related to them (e.g., wife) and even if the automobile is not provided to them by their employer but by persons related to the employer (e.g., another corporation) (IT-63R5, *Benefits, Including Standby Charge for a Automobile, from the Personal Use of a Motor Vehicle Supplied by an Employer — after 1992*) (archived, as it doesn't meet current government web standards). To determine if two persons are related to each other, see s. 251(2). The CRA confirmed that it would be administratively acceptable to consider payments to third parties as amounts eligible in order to reduce operating expense benefit (see CRA Document No. 2008-0274071I7).

Personal Use: The personal use of an automobile includes any travel between the residence and the workplace of the employees. In Technical Interpretation No. 2012-0438001E5, the employees were required to include an operating expense benefit in their income if they used a motor vehicle leased by their employer and assigned to them for out-of-town travel to instead commute between their residence and place of work. The employer paid for all operating expenses of the automobile. Transportation benefits or allowances in respect of expenses incurred for travel between an employee's principal place of residence and a special work site or remote work location are excluded from employment income subject to s. 6(6) (see CRA Document No. 2005-0164991E5).

Reimbursement: Regardless of the method used to calculate the operating cost benefit, the benefit is reduced by any payments and reimbursements made by the employees (or persons related to them) to the employers (or persons related to them) within the year or before February 15 of the following year.

Rates: Employees may use an optional method to include 50% of their standby charge in their income if they use the automobile for employment purposes for more than 50% of the distance driven, and if they inform their employer in writing before year-end of their intention to use the optional method. If the conditions are not met, they must use the regular method to multiply the actual number of kilometres driven for personal purposes by a prescribed rate per kilometre. The rate is found in Regulation 7305.1(*a*) for employees spending more than 50% of their time selling or leasing automobiles, and Regulation 7305.1(*b*) for other employees. Note that the Department of Finance releases the rates for the following year at the end of December. For 2019, the rates are 25 cents/km for employees selling or leasing automobiles and 28 cents/km in other cases.

Related Regulations: S. 7305.1.

Related Sections: S. 6(1)(*a*)(iii) Value of benefits; s. 6(1)(*e*) Standby charge for automobile; s. 6(1)(*l*) Automobile operating expense benefit — employee automobile; s. 6(1.1) Parking cost; s. 6(2) Reasonable standby charge; s. 6(2.1) Automobile salesman; s. 6(7) Cost of property or service; s. 12(1)(*y*) Automobile provided to partner; s. 15(5) Automobile benefit; s. 15(9) Deemed benefit to shareholder by corporation; s. 80.5 Deemed interest; s. 248(1), "automobile"; s. 257 Negative amounts.

Canadian Tax Foundation: Tang and Katz, *Automobile Taxable Benefits and Expenses: Part 1*, 1997 Canadian Tax Journal 5:1150–1163.

Tax Topics: No. 2240, The Case of Szymczyk v. The Queen: The Limit of Administrative "One-Offs".

Forms: RC18 — Calculating Automobile Benefits.

Guides: T4130 Employers Guide to Payroll Deductions — Taxable Benefits.

Income Tax Folios: S2-F3-C2 Benefits and Allowances Received from Employment.

Tax Window Files: Stand-by charge - employee required to use vehicle, *August 31, 2015*, CRA Document No. 2015-0582411E5.

► 6(1)(l) ◄

(l) Where standby charge does not apply — the value of a benefit in respect of the operation of an automobile (other than a benefit to which paragraph (*k*) applies or would apply but for subparagraph (*k*)(iii)) received or enjoyed by the taxpayer, or by a person related to the taxpayer, in the year in respect of, in the course of or because of, the taxpayer's office or employment.

History: S. 6(1)(*l*) was replaced by S.C. 2013, c. 34, s. 170(2), applicable in respect of benefits received or enjoyed on or after October 31, 2011. S. 6(1)(*l*) formerly read:

(*l*) *Idem* — the value of a benefit in respect of the operation of an automobile (other than a benefit to which paragraph (*k*) applies or would apply but for subparagraph (*k*)(iii)) received or enjoyed by the taxpayer in the year in respect of, in the course of or because of, the taxpayer's office or employment.

Related Sections: S. 6(1)(*a*)(iii) Value of benefits; s. 6(1)(*e*) Standby charge for automobile; s. 6(1)(*k*) Automobile operating expense benefit — employer automobile.

Income Tax Folios: S2-F3-C2 Benefits and Allowances Received from Employment.

► 6(1.1) ◄

(1.1) Parking cost. For the purposes of this section, an amount or a benefit in respect of the use of a motor vehicle by a taxpayer does not include any amount or benefit related to the parking of the vehicle.

Related Sections: S. 6(1)(*a*)(iii) Value of benefits; s. 6(1)(*e*) Standby charge for automobile; s. 6(1)(*k*) Automobile operating expense benefit — employer automobile.

► 6(1.2) ◄

(1.2) Deeming rule — amount received. For the purposes of paragraph (1)(*g*), an amount received by an individual out of or under an employee benefit plan is deemed to have been received by a taxpayer and not by the individual if

(*a*) the individual does not deal at arm's length with the taxpayer;

(*b*) the amount is received in respect of an office or employment of the taxpayer; and

(*c*) the taxpayer is living at the time the amount is received by the individual.

History: S. 6(1.2) was added by S.C. 2013, c. 34, s. 170(3), applicable in respect of benefits received or enjoyed on or after October 31, 2011.

► 6(2) ◄

(2) Reasonable standby charge. For the purposes of paragraph (1)(*e*), a reasonable standby charge for an automobile for the total number of days (in this subsection referred to as the "total available days") in a taxation year during which the automobile is made available to a taxpayer or to a person related to the taxpayer by the employer of the taxpayer or by a person related to the employer (both of whom are in this subsection referred to as the "employer") shall be deemed to be the amount determined by the formula

$$A/B \times [2\% \times (C \times D) + 2/3 \times (E - F)]$$

where

A is

(*a*) the lesser of the total kilometres that the automobile is driven (otherwise than in connection with or in the course of the taxpayer's office or employment) during the total available days and the value determined for the description of B for the year in respect of the standby charge for the automobile during the total available days, if

(i) the taxpayer is required by the employer to use the automobile in connection with or in the course of the office or employment, and

(ii) the distance travelled by the automobile in the total available days is primarily in connection with or in the course of the office or employment, and

(*b*) the value determined for the description of B for the year in respect of the standby charge for the automobile during the total available days, in any other case;

B is the product obtained when 1,667 is multiplied by the quotient obtained by dividing the total available days by 30 and, if the quotient so obtained is not a whole number and exceeds one, by rounding it to the nearest whole number or, where that quotient is equidistant from two consecutive whole numbers, by rounding it to the lower of those two numbers;

C is the cost of the automobile to the employer where the employer owns the vehicle at any time in the year;

D is the number obtained by dividing such of the total available days as are days when the employer owns the automobile by 30 and, if the quotient so obtained is not a whole number and exceeds one, by rounding it to the nearest whole number or, where that quotient is equidistant from two consecutive whole numbers, by rounding it to the lower of those two numbers;

E is the total of all amounts that may reasonably be regarded as having been payable by the employer to a lessor for the purpose of leasing the automobile during such of the total available days as are days when the automobile is leased to the employer; and

F is the part of the amount determined for E that may reasonably be regarded as having been payable to the lessor in respect of all or part of the cost to the lessor of insuring against

(*a*) loss of, or damage to, the automobile, or

(*b*) liability resulting from the use or operation of the automobile.

Editorial Note: Generally speaking, the standby charge for employer-provided automobiles is reduced only if the employee is required by his/her employer to use the automobile in the course of employment, the distance travelled in the course of employment exceeds the distance of personal travel and the personal travel does not exceed 1,667 kilometres per month.

Related Sections: S. 6(2.1) Automobile salesman; s. 6(7) Cost of property or service; s. 12(1)(*y*) Automobile provided to partner; s. 15(5) Automobile benefit; s. 85(1)(*e*.4) Transfer of property to corporation by shareholders; s. 85(1)(*e*.5) Transfer of property to corporation by shareholders; s. 248(1), "automobile".

Canadian Tax Foundation: Tang and Katz, *Automobile Taxable Benefits and Expenses: Part 1*, 1997 Canadian Tax Journal 5:1150–1163.

Interpretation Bulletins: *Primary* — IT-63R5 Benefits, including standby charge for an automobile, from the personal use of a motor vehicle supplied by an employer — After 1992. *Secondary* — IT-291R3 Transfer of property to a corporation under subsection 85(1).

Tax Window Files: Use of Employer Provided Vehicle — Logbook, *Technical Interpretation, Business and Partnerships Division, March 14, 2005*, CRA Document No. 2005-0119451E5. Employer obligated to ensure that an employee maintains a logbook in respect of the personal use of an employer-provided motor vehicle; Stand-by charge - employee required to use vehicle, *August 31, 2015*, CRA Document No. 2015-0582411E5.

► 6(2.1) ◄

(2.1) Automobile salesman. Where in a taxation year

(*a*) a taxpayer was employed principally in selling or leasing automobiles,

(*b*) an automobile owned by the taxpayer's employer was made available by the employer to the taxpayer or to a person related to the taxpayer, and

(*c*) the employer has acquired one or more automobiles,

the amount that would otherwise be determined under subsection (2) as a reasonable standby charge shall, at the option of the employer, be computed as if

(*d*) the reference in the formula in subsection (2) to "2%" were read as a reference to "1½%", and

(*e*) the cost to the employer of the automobile were the greater of

(i) the quotient obtained by dividing

(A) the cost to the employer of all new automobiles acquired by the employer in the year for sale or lease in the course of the employer's business

by

(B) the number of automobiles described in clause (A), and

(ii) the quotient obtained by dividing

(A) the cost to the employer of all automobiles acquired by the employer in the year for sale or lease in the course of the employer's business

by

(B) the number of automobiles described in clause (A).

Interpretation Bulletins: *Primary* — IT-63R5 Benefits, including standby charge for an automobile, from the personal use of a motor vehicle supplied by an employer — After 1992.

► 6(2.2) ◄

(2.2) Benefit re auto operation — (Repealed by S.C. 1994, c. 21, s. 2(5).)

► 6(3) ◄

(3) Payments by employer to employee. An amount received by one person from another

(*a*) during a period while the payee was an officer of, or in the employment of, the payer, or

(*b*) on account, in lieu of payment or in satisfaction of an obligation arising out of an agreement made by the payer with the payee immediately prior to, during or immediately after a period that the payee was an officer of, or in the employment of, the payer,

shall be deemed, for the purposes of section 5, to be remuneration for the payee's services rendered as an officer or during the period of employment, unless it is established that, irrespective of when the agreement, if any, under which the amount was received was made or the form or legal effect thereof, it cannot reasonably be regarded as having been received

(*c*) as consideration or partial consideration for accepting the office or entering into the contract of employment,

(*d*) as remuneration or partial remuneration for services as an officer or under the contract of employment, or

(*e*) in consideration or partial consideration for a covenant with reference to what the officer or employee is, or is not, to do before or after the termination of the employment.

Editorial Note: In general terms, s. 6(3) ensures that inducement payments made to prospective employees and non-competition payments made to departing employees are considered remuneration and therefore are taxable under s. 5 upon receipt (see also s. 6(3.1)).

Related Sections: S. 87(2)(*k*) Certain payments to employees.

Income Tax Folios: S2-F3-C2 Benefits and Allowances Received from Employment.

Primary — S2-F1-C2 Retiring Allowances; S2-F3-C1 Payments from Employer to Employee.

Tax Window Files: Taxation of a lump-sum from a former employer, *January 27, 2016*, CRA Document No. 2015-0599581E5.

► 6(3.1) ◄

(3.1) Amount receivable for covenant. If an amount (other than an amount to which paragraph (1)(*a*) applies because of subsection (11)) is receivable at the end of a taxation year by a taxpayer in respect of a covenant, agreed to by the taxpayer more than 36 months before the end of that taxation year, with reference to what the taxpayer is, or is not, to do, and the amount would be included in the taxpayer's income for the year under this subdivision if it were received by the taxpayer in the year, the amount

(*a*) is deemed to be received by the taxpayer at the end of the taxation year for services rendered as an officer or during the period of employment; and

(*b*) is deemed not to be received at any other time.

History: S. 6(3.1) was added by S.C. 2013, c. 34, s. 170(4), applicable to amounts receivable in respect of a covenant agreed to after October 7, 2003.

Related Sections: S. 60(*f*) Restrictive covenant — bad debt.

► 6(4) ◄

(4) Group term life insurance. Where at any time in a taxation year a taxpayer's life is insured under a group term life insurance policy, there shall be included in computing the taxpayer's income for the year from an office or employment the amount, if any, prescribed for the year in respect of the insurance.

Related Regulations: 2700 to 2705.

Related Sections: S. 6(1)(*a*)(i) Value of benefits; s. 139.1(15) Employee-paid insurance; s. 146(1), "earned income"; s. 248(1), "group term life insurance policy".

Forms: T2030 — Direct Transfer Under Subparagraph 60(1)(v).

Guides: T4130 Employers Guide to Payroll Deductions — Taxable Benefits.

Income Tax Folios: S2-F3-C2 Benefits and Allowances Received from Employment.

Secondary — S2-F1-C1 Health and Welfare Trusts.

Interpretation Bulletins: *Primary* — IT-227R Group term life insurance premiums. *Secondary* — IT-529 Flexible employee benefit programs.

Cases: In 2011, former employees (and surviving spouses of former employees) of Nortel received distributions from a health and welfare trust established by Nortel in 1980. In some cases, the amounts distributed related to group term life insurance plans; others pertained to survivor transition benefits. While the provision of a group term life insurance benefit would have been taxable to the taxpayers during their employment, section 6 was not sufficiently broad to capture the distributions paid in 2011, and such distributions were not taxable. Distributions made in relation to survivor benefits were governed by section 56, which includes the phrase "any amount received... on account... of... a death benefit", and those distributions must be included in income. *Scott et al. v. The Queen*, 2017 DTC 1143 (TCC)

► 6(5) ◄

(5) Reference to policy year ending in taxation year — (Repealed by S.C. 1995, c. 3, s. 1(3).)

► 6(6) ◄

(6) Employment at special work site or remote location. Notwithstanding subsection (1), in computing the income of a taxpayer for a taxation year from an office or employment, there shall not be included any amount received or enjoyed by the taxpayer in respect of, in the course or by virtue of the office or employment that is the value of, or an allowance (not in excess of a reasonable amount) in respect of expenses the taxpayer has incurred for,

(*a*) the taxpayer's board and lodging for a period at

(i) a special work site, being a location at which the duties performed by the taxpayer were of a temporary nature, if the taxpayer maintained at another location a self-contained domestic establishment as the taxpayer's principal place of residence

(A) that was, throughout the period, available for the taxpayer's occupancy and not rented by the taxpayer to any other person, and

(B) to which, by reason of distance, the taxpayer could not reasonably be expected to have returned daily from the special work site, or

(ii) a location at which, by virtue of its remoteness from any established community, the taxpayer could not reasonably be expected to establish and maintain a self-contained domestic establishment,

if the period during which the taxpayer was required by the taxpayer's duties to be away from the taxpayer's principal place of residence, or to be at the special work site or location, was not less than 36 hours; or

(*b*) transportation between

(i) the principal place of residence and the special work site referred to in subparagraph (*a*)(i), or

(ii) the location referred to in subparagraph (*a*)(ii) and a location in Canada or a location in the country in which the taxpayer is employed,

in respect of a period described in paragraph (*a*) during which the taxpayer received board and lodging, or a reasonable allowance in respect of board and lodging, from the taxpayer's employer.

Related Sections: S. 67.1(2)(*e*.1)(ii) Exceptions; s. 110.7(4)(*a*) Board and lodging allowances, etc; s. 248(1), "self-contained domestic establishment".

Canadian Petroleum Tax Journal: Canada Customs and Revenue Agency 1999 Roundtable Questions and Answers, Question 19, 2000, Vol. 13, No. 1.

Canadian Tax Foundation: Winters and Novotny, *The "Special Work Site" and "Remote Location" Exemptions*, 2014 Prairie Provinces Tax Conference 10:1–34.

Forms: TD4 — Declaration of Exemption — Employment at Special Work Site; T2200 — Declaration of Conditions of Employment.

Income Tax Folios: S2-F3-C2 Benefits and Allowances Received from Employment.

Interpretation Bulletins: *Primary* — IT-91R4 Employment at special work sites or remote locations; IT-254R2 Fishermen-employees and seafarers — Value of rations and quarters. *Secondary* — IT-522R Vehicle, travel and sales expenses of employees.

Tax Window Files: Remote work location, *June 24, 2015*, CRA Document No. 2015-0570251E5; Employment at a Special Work Site, *April 10, 2015*, CRA Document No. 2014-0558881I7.

Cases: The term "maintain" in s. 6(6) means "preserve for use" or "keep available" and does not require payment. A shared home, where the taxpayer provided household chores in lieu of rent, was a self-contained domestic establishment and her principal place of residence. Accordingly, a living allowance from her employer, for a job site apartment, was not taxable. *Spannier v. The Queen*, 2013 DTC 1062 (T.C.C.)

► 6(7) ◄

(7) Cost of property or service. To the extent that the cost to a person of purchasing a property or service or an amount payable by a person for the purpose of leasing property is taken into account in determining an amount required under this section to be included in computing a taxpayer's income for a taxation year, that cost or amount payable, as the case may be, shall include any tax that was payable by the person in respect of the property or service or that would have been so payable if the person were not exempt from the payment of that tax because of the nature of the person or the use to which the property or service is to be put.

Related Sections: S. 6(1)(*a*) Value of benefits; s. 6(1)(*e*) Standby charge for automobile; s. 6(1)(*k*) Automobile operating expense benefit — employer automobile; s. 6(2) Reasonable standby charge; s. 8(11) Goods and services tax.

Canadian Tax Foundation: Winters and Novotny, *The "Special Work Site" and "Remote Location" Exemptions*, 2014 Prairie Provinces Tax Conference 10:1–34.

► 6(8) ◄

(8) GST rebates re costs of property or service. If

(*a*) an amount in respect of an outlay or expense is deducted under section 8 in computing the income of a taxpayer for a taxation year from an office or employment, or

(*b*) an amount is included in the capital cost to a taxpayer of a property described in subparagraph 8(1)(*j*)(ii) or 8(1)(*p*)(ii),

and a particular amount is paid to the taxpayer in a particular taxation year as a rebate under the *Excise Tax Act* in respect of any goods and services tax included in the amount of the outlay or expense, or the capital cost of the property, as the case may be, the particular amount

(*c*) to the extent that it relates to an outlay or expense referred to in paragraph (*a*), shall be included in computing the taxpayer's income from an office or employment for the particular taxation year, and

(*d*) to the extent that it relates to the capital cost of property referred to in paragraph (*b*), is deemed, for the purposes of subsection 13(7.1), to have been received by the taxpayer in the particular taxation year as assistance from a government for the acquisition of the property.

Editorial Note: An employee's deductible expenses for income tax purposes can include any GST or HST payable in respect of the expenses. The GST or HST is typically refunded to the employee by way of a rebate, which is either included in the employee's income (paragraph 6(8)(*a*)) or serves to reduce the capital cost of the property on which the GST or HST was payable (paragraph 6(8)(*b*)).

Related Sections: S. 8(11) Goods and services tax.

► 6(9) ◄

(9) Amount in respect of interest on employee debt. Where an amount in respect of a loan or debt is deemed by subsection 80.4(1) to be a benefit received in a taxation year by an individual, the amount of the benefit shall be included in computing the income of the individual for the year as income from an office or employment.

Editorial Note: If the employee loan or debt is for income-earning purposes, a deduction of part or all of the interest benefit may be allowed under s. 8(1)(*j*)(i) or s. 20(1)(*c*); see s. 80.5.

Related Regulations: Part II.

Related Sections: S. 6(23) Employer-provided housing subsidies; s. 15(9) Deemed benefit to shareholder by corporation; s. 80.5 Deemed interest.

Income Tax Folios: S2-F3-C2 Benefits and Allowances Received from Employment.

Interpretation Bulletins: *Secondary* — IT-421R2 Benefits to individuals, corporations and shareholders from loans or debt.

► 6(10) ◄

(10) Contributions to an employee benefit plan. For the purposes of subparagraph (1)(*g*)(ii),

(*a*) an amount included in the income of an individual in respect of an employee benefit plan for a taxation year preceding the year in which it was paid out of the plan shall be deemed to be an amount contributed to the plan by the individual; and

(*b*) where an amount is received in a taxation year by an individual from an employee benefit plan that was in a preceding year an employee trust, such portion of the amount so received by the individual as does not exceed the amount, if any, by which the lesser of

(i) the amount, if any, by which

(A) the total of all amounts allocated to the individual or a deceased person of whom the individual is an heir or legal representative by the trustee of the plan at a time when it was an employee trust

exceeds

(B) the total of all amounts previously paid out of the plan to or for the benefit of the individual or the deceased person at a time when the plan was an employee trust, and

(ii) the portion of the amount, if any, by which the cost amount to the plan of its property immediately before it ceased to be an employee trust exceeds its liabilities at that time that

(A) the amount determined under subparagraph (i) in respect of the individual

is of

(B) the total of amounts determined under subparagraph (i) in respect of all individuals who were beneficiaries under the plan immediately before it ceased to be an employee trust

exceeds

(iii) the total of all amounts previously received out of the plan by the individual or a deceased person of whom the individual is an heir or legal representative at a time when the plan was an employee benefit plan to the extent that the amounts were deemed by this paragraph to be a return of amounts contributed to the plan

shall be deemed to be the return of an amount contributed to the plan by the individual.

Related Sections: S. 248(1), "employee benefit plan", "employee trust".

Interpretation Bulletins: *Secondary* — IT-502 Employee benefit plans and employee trusts.

► 6(11) ◄

(11) Salary deferral arrangement. Where at the end of a taxation year any person has a right under a salary deferral arrangement in respect of a taxpayer to receive a deferred amount, an amount equal to the deferred amount shall be deemed, for the purposes only of paragraph (1)(*a*), to have been received by the taxpayer as a benefit in the year, to the extent that the amount was not otherwise included in computing the taxpayer's income for the year or any preceding taxation year.

Related Sections: S. 6(1)(*a*)(v) Value of benefits; s. 6(1)(*i*) Salary deferral arrangement payments; 6(12) Idem; 6(13) Application; 6(14) Part of plan or arrangement; s. 8(1)(*o*) Forfeited amounts re salary deferral arrangements; s. 12(1)(*n.2*) Forfeited salary deferral amounts; s. 20(1)(*oo*) Salary deferral arrangement; s. 56(1)(*w*) Salary deferral arrangement; s. 248(1), "deferred amount", "salary deferral arrangement".

Canadian Petroleum Tax Journal: Attracting and Retaining Executives and Employees with Tax-Efficient Incentives, Julie Y. Lee, 2001, Vol. 14, No. 1.

Tax Topics: No. 2108, Existing Retirement Compensation Arrangements Under Attack.

► 6(12) ◄

(12) Idem. Where at the end of a taxation year any person has a right under a salary deferral arrangement (other than a trust governed by a salary deferral arrangement) in respect of a taxpayer to receive a deferred amount, an amount equal to any interest or other additional amount that accrued to, or for the benefit of, that person to the end of the year in respect of the deferred amount shall be deemed at the end of the year, for the purposes only of subsection (11), to be a deferred amount that the person has a right to receive under the arrangement.

Related Sections: S. 6(13) Application; s. 6(14) Part of plan or arrangement.

Tax Topics: No. 2108, Existing Retirement Compensation Arrangements Under Attack.

▶ 6(13) ◀

(13) Application. Subsection (11) does not apply in respect of a deferred amount under a salary deferral arrangement in respect of a taxpayer that was established primarily for the benefit of one or more non-resident employees in respect of services to be rendered in a country other than Canada, to the extent that the deferred amount

(*a*) was in respect of services rendered by an employee who

(i) was not resident in Canada at the time the services were rendered, or

(ii) was resident in Canada for a period (in this subsection referred to as an "excluded period") of not more than 36 of the 72 months preceding the time the services were rendered and was an employee to whom the arrangement applied before the employee became resident in Canada; and

(*b*) cannot reasonably be regarded as being in respect of services rendered or to be rendered during a period (other than an excluded period) when the employee was resident in Canada.

Related Sections: S. 6(12) Salary deferral arrangement — accrued interest; s. 6(14) Part of plan or arrangement.

▶ 6(14) ◀

(14) Part of plan or arrangement. Where deferred amounts under a salary deferral arrangement in respect of a taxpayer (in this subsection referred to as "that arrangement") are required to be included as benefits under paragraph (1)(*a*) in computing the taxpayer's income and that arrangement is part of a plan or arrangement (in this subsection referred to as the "plan") under which amounts or benefits not related to the deferred amounts are payable or provided, for the purposes of this Act, other than this subsection,

(*a*) that arrangement shall be deemed to be a separate arrangement independent of other parts of the plan of which it is a part; and

(*b*) where any person has a right to a deferred amount under that arrangement, an amount received by the person as a benefit at any time out of or under the plan shall be deemed to have been received out of or under that arrangement except to the extent that it exceeds the amount, if any, by which

(i) the total of all deferred amounts under that arrangement that were included under paragraph (1)(*a*) as benefits in computing the taxpayer's income for taxation years ending before that time

exceeds

(ii) the total of

(A) all deferred amounts received by any person before that time out of or under the plan that were deemed by this paragraph to have been received out of or under that arrangement, and

(B) all deferred amounts under that arrangement that were deducted under paragraph 8(1)(*o*) in computing the taxpayer's income for the year or preceding taxation years.

Related Sections: S. 6(11) Salary deferral arrangement; s. 6(12) Salary deferral arrangement — accrued interest; s. 6(13) Application; s. 56(10) Severability of retirement compensation arrangement.

▶ 6(15) ◀

(15) Forgiveness of employee debt. For the purpose of paragraph (1)(*a*),

(*a*) a benefit shall be deemed to have been enjoyed by a taxpayer at any time an obligation issued by any debtor (including the taxpayer) is settled or extinguished; and

(*b*) the value of that benefit shall be deemed to be the forgiven amount at that time in respect of the obligation.

Related Sections: S. 79(3) Proceeds of disposition for debtor; s. 80(1), "forgiven amount".

Income Tax Folios: S2-F3-C2 Benefits and Allowances Received from Employment.

Tax Window Files: Employee loan extinguished or settled by employer, *March 8, 2017*, CRA Document No. 2016-0637781I7.

▶ 6(15.1) ◀

(15.1) Forgiven amount. For the purpose of subsection (15), the "forgiven amount" at any time in respect of an obligation issued by a debtor has the meaning that would be assigned by subsection 80(1) if

(*a*) the obligation were a commercial obligation (within the meaning assigned by subsection 80(1)) issued by the debtor;

(*b*) no amount included in computing income because of the obligation being settled or extinguished at that time were taken into account;

(*c*) the definition "forgiven amount" in subsection 80(1) were read without reference to paragraphs (*f*) and (*h*) of the description of B in that definition; and

(*d*) section 80 were read without reference to paragraphs (2)(*b*) and (*q*) of that section.

Related Sections: S. 79 Surrender of property by debtor; s. 80.01(1), "forgiven amount".

▶ 6(16) ◀

(16) Disability-related employment benefits. Notwithstanding subsection (1), in computing an individual's income for a taxation year from an office or employment, there shall not be included any amount received or enjoyed by the individual in respect of, in the course of or because of the individual's office or employment that is the value of a benefit relating to, or an allowance (not in excess of a reasonable amount) in respect of expenses incurred by the individual for,

(*a*) the transportation of the individual between the individual's ordinary place of residence and the individual's work location (including parking near that location) if the individual is blind or is a person in respect of whom an amount is deductible, or would but for paragraph 118.3(1)(*c*) be deductible, because of the individual's mobility impairment, under section 118.3 in computing a taxpayer's tax payable under this Part for the year; or

(*b*) an attendant to assist the individual in the performance of the individual's duties if the individual is a person in respect of whom an amount is deductible, or would but for paragraph 118.3(1)(*c*) be deductible, under section 118.3 in computing a taxpayer's tax payable under this Part for the year.

Related Sections: S. 6(1.1) Parking cost; s. 6(17) Definitions; s. 64 Disability supports deduction; s. 118.4(1) Nature of impairment.

Income Tax Folios: S2-F3-C2 Benefits and Allowances Received from Employment; S1-F1-C3 Disability Supports Deduction.

▶ 6(17) ◀

(17) Definitions. The definitions in this subsection apply in this subsection and subsection (18).

"disability policy" —"disability policy" means a group disability insurance policy that provides for periodic payments to individuals in respect of the loss of remuneration from an office or employment.

"employer" —"employer" of an individual includes a former employer of the individual.

"top-up disability payment" —"top-up disability payment" in respect of an individual means a payment made by an employer of the individual as a consequence of the insolvency of an insurer that was obligated to make payments to the individual under a disability policy where

(*a*) the payment is made to an insurer so that periodic payments made to the individual under the policy will not be reduced because of the insolvency, or will be reduced by a lesser amount, or

(*b*) the following conditions are satisfied:

(i) the payment is made to the individual to replace, in whole or in part, periodic payments that would have been made under the policy to the individual but for the insolvency, and

(ii) the payment is made under an arrangement by which the individual is required to reimburse the payment to the extent that the individual subsequently receives an amount from an insurer in respect of the portion of the periodic payments that the payment was intended to replace.

For the purposes of paragraphs (*a*) and (*b*), an insurance policy that replaces a disability policy is deemed to be the same policy as, and a continuation of, the disability policy that was replaced.

Related Sections: S. 8(1)(*n*) Salary reimbursement; s. 8(1)(*n*.1) Reimbursement of disability payments.

▶ 6(18) ◀

(18) Group disability benefits — insolvent insurer. Where an employer of an individual makes a top-up disability payment in respect of the individual,

(*a*) the payment is, for the purpose of paragraph (1)(*a*), deemed not to be a benefit received or enjoyed by the individual;

(*b*) the payment is, for the purpose of paragraph (1)(*f*), deemed not to be a contribution made by the employer to or under the disability insurance plan of which the disability policy in respect of which the payment is made is or was a part; and

(*c*) if the payment is made to the individual, it is, for the purpose of paragraph (1)(*f*), deemed to be an amount payable to the individual pursuant to the plan.

Related Sections: S. 6(17) Definitions; s. 8(1)(*n*.1) Reimbursement of disability payments.

▶ 6(19) ◀

(19) Benefit re housing loss. For the purpose of paragraph (1)(*a*), an amount paid at any time in respect of a housing loss (other than an eligible housing loss) to or on behalf of a taxpayer or a person who does not deal at arm's length with the taxpayer in respect of, in the course of or because of, an office or employment is deemed to be a benefit received by the taxpayer at that time because of the office or employment.

Editorial Note: See the editorial note for s. 6(20).

Related Sections: S. 6(21) Housing loss; s. 251(1) Arm's length.

Canadian Tax Foundation: Arnold and Li, *The Appropriate Tax Treatment of the Reimbursement of Moving Expenses*, 1996 Canadian Tax Journal 1:1–37.

Income Tax Folios: S2-F3-C2 Benefits and Allowances Received from Employment.

▶ 6(20) ◀

(20) Benefit re eligible housing loss. For the purpose of paragraph (1)(*a*), an amount paid at any time in a taxation year in respect of an eligible housing loss to or on behalf of a taxpayer or a person who does not deal at arm's length with the taxpayer in respect of, in the course of or because of, an office or employment is deemed to be a benefit received by the taxpayer at that time because of the office or employment to the extent of the amount, if any, by which

(*a*) one half of the amount, if any, by which the total of all amounts each of which is so paid in the year or in a preceding taxation year exceeds $15,000

exceeds

(*b*) the total of all amounts each of which is an amount included in computing the taxpayer's income because of this subsection for a preceding taxation year in respect of the loss.

Editorial Note: An "eligible housing loss" is defined in s. 6(22) and is generally a loss incurred on the disposition of a house in respect of an "eligible relocation". An eligible relocation is defined in s. 248(1) and generally means a relocation to enable the taxpayer to carry on employment or business at a new work location, where the taxpayer's new residence is at least 40 kilometres closer to the new work location than the taxpayer's former residence (the one that gave rise to the loss). One-half of a reimbursement of a taxpayer's eligible housing loss in excess of $15,000 is included in the taxpayer's income under s. 6(20). In contrast, if the loss is not an eligible housing loss, the reimbursement will be fully included in the taxpayer's income under s. 6(19).

Related Sections: S. 6(22) Eligible housing loss; s. 251(1) Arm's length.

Income Tax Folios: S2-F3-C2 Benefits and Allowances Received from Employment.

Tax Window Files: Eligible housing loss, *June 4, 2018*, CRA Document No. 2016-0669531E5.

► 6(21) ◄

(21) Housing loss. In this section, "housing loss" at any time in respect of a residence of a taxpayer means the amount, if any, by which the greater of

(*a*) the adjusted cost base of the residence at that time to the taxpayer or to another person who does not deal at arm's length with the taxpayer, and

(*b*) the highest fair market value of the residence within the six-month period that ends at that time

exceeds

(*c*) if the residence is disposed of by the taxpayer or the other person before the end of the first taxation year that begins after that time, the lesser of

(i) the proceeds of disposition of the residence, and

(ii) the fair market value of the residence at that time, and

(*d*) in any other case, the fair market value of the residence at that time.

Related Sections: S. 6(19) Benefit re housing loss.

Income Tax Folios: S2-F3-C2 Benefits and Allowances Received from Employment.

► 6(22) ◄

(22) Eligible housing loss. In this section, "eligible housing loss" in respect of a residence designated by a taxpayer means a housing loss in respect of an eligible relocation of the taxpayer or a person who does not deal at arm's length with the taxpayer and, for these purposes, no more than one residence may be so designated in respect of an eligible relocation.

Editorial Note: See the editorial note for s. 6(20).

Related Sections: S. 6(20) Benefit re eligible housing loss; s. 248(1), "eligible relocation".

Income Tax Folios: S2-F3-C2 Benefits and Allowances Received from Employment.

► 6(23) ◄

(23) Employer-provided housing subsidies. For greater certainty, an amount paid or the value of assistance provided by any person in respect of, in the course of or because of, an individual's office or employment in respect of the cost of, the financing of, the use of or the right to use, a residence is, for the purposes of this section, a benefit received by the individual because of the office or employment.

Related Sections: S. 6(9) Amount in respect of interest on employee debt; s. 80.4(1) Loans; s. 80.4(1.1) Loan or debt from office or employment; s. 110(1)(*j*) Home relocation loan; s. 248(1), "home relocation loan".

Income Tax Folios: S2-F3-C2 Benefits and Allowances Received from Employment.

SECTION 7: [Employee stock options]

► 7(1) ◄

(1) Agreement to issue securities to employees. Subject to subsection (1.1), where a particular qualifying person has agreed to sell or issue securities of the particular qualifying person (or of a qualifying person with which the particular qualifying person does not deal at arm's length) to an employee of the particular qualifying person (or of a qualifying person with which the particular qualifying person does not deal at arm's length),

(*a*) if the employee has acquired securities under the agreement, a benefit equal to the amount, if any, by which

(i) the value of the securities at the time the employee acquired them

exceeds the total of

(ii) the amount paid or to be paid to the particular qualifying person by the employee for the securities, and

(iii) the amount, if any, paid by the employee to acquire the right to acquire the securities

is deemed to have been received, in the taxation year in which the employee acquired the securities, by the employee because of the employee's employment;

(*b*) if the employee has transferred or otherwise disposed of rights under the agreement in respect of some or all of the securities to a person with whom the employee was dealing at arm's length, a benefit equal to the amount, if any, by which

(i) the value of the consideration for the disposition

exceeds

(ii) the amount, if any, paid by the employee to acquire those rights

shall be deemed to have been received, in the taxation year in which the employee made the disposition, by the employee because of the employee's employment;

(*b*.1) if the employee has transferred or otherwise disposed of rights under the agreement in respect of some or all of the securities to the particular qualifying person (or a qualifying person with which the particular qualifying person does not deal at arm's length) with whom the employee was not dealing at arm's length, a benefit equal to the amount, if any, by which

(i) the value of the consideration for the disposition

exceeds

(ii) the amount, if any, paid by the employee to acquire those rights

is deemed to have been received, in the taxation year in which the employee made the disposition, by the employee because of the employee's employment;

(*c*) if rights of the employee under the agreement have, by one or more transactions between persons not dealing at arm's length, become vested in a person who has acquired securities under the agreement, a benefit equal to the amount, if any, by which

(i) the value of the securities at the time the person acquired them

exceeds the total of

(ii) the amount paid or to be paid to the particular qualifying person by the person for the securities, and

(iii) the amount, if any, paid by the employee to acquire the right to acquire the securities,

is deemed to have been received, in the taxation year in which the person acquired the securities, by the employee because of the employee's employment, unless at the time the person acquired the securities the employee was deceased, in which case such a benefit is deemed to have been received by the person in that year as income from the duties of an employment performed by the person in that year in the country in which the employee primarily performed the duties of the employee's employment;

(*d*) if rights of the employee under the agreement have, by one or more transactions between persons not dealing at arm's length, become vested in a particular person who has transferred or otherwise disposed of rights under the agreement to another person with whom the particular person was dealing at arm's length, a benefit equal to the amount, if any, by which

(i) the value of the consideration for the disposition

exceeds

(ii) the amount, if any, paid by the employee to acquire those rights

shall be deemed to have been received, in the taxation year in which the particular person made the disposition, by the employee because of the employee's employment, unless at the time the other person acquired the rights the employee was deceased, in which case such a benefit shall be deemed to have been received by the particular person in that year as income from the duties of an employment performed by the particular person in that year in the country in which the employee primarily performed the duties of the employee's employment; and

(*d*.1) if rights of the employee under the agreement have, by one or more transactions between persons not dealing at arm's length, become vested in a particular person who has transferred or otherwise disposed of rights under the agreement to a particular qualifying person (or a qualifying person with which the particular qualifying person does not deal at arm's length) with whom the particular person was not dealing at arm's length, a benefit equal to the amount, if any, by which

(i) the value of the consideration for the disposition

exceeds

(ii) the amount, if any, paid by the employee to acquire those rights

is deemed to have been received, in the taxation year in which the particular person made the disposition, by the employee because of the employee's employment, unless at the time of the disposition the employee was deceased, in which case such a benefit is deemed to have been received by the particular person in that year as income from the duties of an employment performed by the particular person in that year in the country in which the employee primarily performed the duties of the employee's employment; and

(*e*) if the employee has died and immediately before death owned a right to acquire securities under the agreement, a benefit equal to the amount, if any, by which

(i) the value of the right immediately after the death

exceeds

(ii) the amount, if any, paid by the employee to acquire the right

shall be deemed to have been received, in the taxation year in which the employee died, by the employee because of the employee's employment, and paragraphs (*b*), (*c*) and (*d*) do not apply.

Editorial Note: Employee stock option benefits are generally included in income in the year of the exercise or disposition of the option. However, in the case of options granted by Canadian-controlled private corporations, the inclusion of the benefit is deferred to the year in which the securities are disposed of, by virtue of s. 7(1.1). One-half of the benefit is deductible in computing the employee's taxable income if the requirements of s. 110(1)(*d*) or (*d.1*) are fulfilled.

For the ability to claim the s. 110(1)(*d*) deduction where an option's exercise price is subsequently reduced after having been granted, see the editorial notes for s. 110(1.7)-(1.8).

History: S. 7(1), the portion before paragraph (*a*) was replaced by S.C. 2010, c. 25, s. 3(1), applicable in respect of rights exercised after 4:00 p.m. Eastern Standard Time, March 4, 2010. S. 7(1), the portion before paragraph (*a*) formerly read:

(1) *Agreement to issue securities to employees.* Subject to subsections (1.1) and (8), where a particular qualifying person has agreed to sell or issue securities of the particular qualifying person (or of a qualifying person with which it does not deal at arm's length) to an employee of the particular qualifying person (or of a qualifying person with which the particular qualifying person does not deal at arm's length),

S. 7(1)(*b.1*) was added by S.C. 2010, c. 25, s. 3(2), applicable to dispositions of rights occurring after 4:00 p.m. Eastern Standard Time, March 4, 2010.

S. 7(1)(*d.1*) was added by S.C. 2010, c. 25, s. 3(3), applicable to dispositions of rights occurring after 4:00 p.m. Eastern Standard Time, March 4, 2010.

Related Sections: S. 8(12) Forfeiture of securities by employee; s. 47(3) Securities acquired by employee; s. 49(3) Where option to acquire exercised; s. 52(1) Cost of certain property the value of which included in income; s. 53(1)(*j*) Share or fund unit taxed as stock option benefit; s. 53(2)(*t*) Amounts to be deducted — Right to acquire shares or units; s. 110(1)(*d*) Employee options; s. 110(1)(*d*.01) Charitable donation of employee option securities; s. 110(1)(*d*.1) Employee options for CCPC shares; s. 110(1.5) Determination of amounts relating to employee security options; s. 110(1.6) Meaning of "specified event"; s.110(1.7) Definitions in subsection 7(7); s. 110(2.1) Charitable donation — proceeds of disposition of employee option securities; s. 128.1(4)(*d*.1) Employee CCPC stock option shares; s. 128.1(10), "excluded right or interest"; s. 153(1.01) Withholding — stock option benefits; s. 153(1.31) Non-cash stock option benefit; s. 164(6.1) Realization of deceased employees' options; s. 180.01 Tax in Respect of Stock Option Benefit Deferral; s. 251 Arm's length.

Canadian Petroleum Tax Journal: Attracting and Retaining Executives and Employees with Tax-Efficient Incentives, Julie Y. Lee, 2001, Vol. 14, No. 1; Current Trends in Executive Compensation Structures and Their Taxation, Rachel Colabella and Denise McMullen, 2000, Vol. 13, No. 1.

Canadian Tax Foundation: Coburn, *Stock Options, With a Focus on Start-Ups*, 2017 British Columbia Tax Conference 13:1–23; Infanti, *Employee Stock Option Rules and Legally Binding Agreements*, 2017 Tax for the Owner Manager 17(2):1–2; Tollstam, *Unexercised Employee Stock Options on Death*, 2013 Canadian Tax Highlights 21(5):13–14; Yager, *Relief for Stock Option Buyout*, 2013 Canadian Tax Highlights 21(2):3–4; Lee, *Death of a Taxpayer: Employee Stock Option Benefits*, 2013 Tax for the Owner-Manager 13(2):6–7; Carenza, *Incentive Compensation for Small and Medium-Sized Private Companies*, 2012 Ontario Tax Conference 6:1–21; Hickey, *Stock Option Roundup*, 2011 Canadian Tax Highlights 19(2):2; Michalarias, *2010 Legislative Update: Including Administrative Announcements*, 2010 Ontario Tax Conference 1:1–34; Toaze and Pantry, *Current Issues Forum: Stock Options*, 2010 British Columbia Tax Conference 1:23–27; Yager, *Budget: Employee Stock Options*, 2010 Canadian Tax Highlights 18(4):7–8; Macnaughton and Mawami, *Addendum — CRA: Employee Stock Options and TFSAs*, 2009 Canadian Tax Highlights 17(5):10; Nijhawan and Sieker, *Topical Issues in Equity-Based Employee Compensation*, 2008 Conference Report 15:1–36; Macnaughton and Mawani, *Contributions of Employee Stock Options to RRSPs and TFSAs:*

Valuation Issues and Policy Anomalies, 2008 Canadian Tax Journal 4:893–922; Diksic and Desjardins, *Tax Treatment of Transaction Costs*, 2006 Conference Report 38:1–36; Aiken, *Current Cases: Tax Court of Canada — "Non-Section 7 Options": When Does the Benefit from Employment Arise? (Henley v. The Queen, 2006 TCC 347)*, 2006 Canadian Tax Journal 4:930–936; Tennant, *The Taxation of Derivatives: The Basic Rules*, 2005 Conference Report 41:1–15; Spadorcia and Montgomery, *Equity Compensation: Emerging Trends*, 2004 Conference Report 24:1–20; Kagan, *Update on Non-Cash Executive Compensation: ESOPs, DSPs, and SERPs*, 2004 Prairie Provinces Tax Conference 11:1–23; Mawani, *Tax Deductibility of Employee Stock Options*, 2003 Canadian Tax Journal 3:1230–1258; Sandler, *The Benchmark Income Tax Treatment of Employee Stock Options: A Basis for Comparison*, 2003 Canadian Tax Journal 3:1204–1229; Tunney, *Stock Options: The Solution or the Problem?*, 2002 Conference Report 28:1–39; Ebel and Stewart, *Update on Employee Stock Options and Employee Benefits*, 2002 Conference Report 27:1–39; Sandler, *The Tax Treatment of Employee Stock Options: Generous to a Fault*, 2001 Canadian Tax Journal 2:259–302; Van Cauwenberghe, *Taxation of Employee Stock Options — A Review and Update*, 2001 Prairie Provinces Tax Conference 2:1–53; Smith et al., *Taxation of Stock Options: Still Not Good Enough*, 2001 Tax for the Owner-Manager 1(1):2; Spadorcia and Diles, *Compensating the Cross-Border Executive: Stock Option Plans*, 2000 Conference Report 30:1–32; Addison and Korn, *Employee Stock Options: An Update*, 2000 Canadian Tax Journal 3:778–811; Wong, *Current Cases: Federal Court of Appeal — Payment Made for the Cancellation of Stock Options: Taxable Benefit? (Bernier v. The Queen, 99 DTC 5656)*, 2000 Canadian Tax Journal 1:144–148.

Tax Profile: July 2010 — Employee Compensation Planning: Stock-Based Incentive Compensation Plans; July 2007; March 2006 — Some Tax Considerations for Investing in Silicon Valley North.

Tax Topics: No. 1630, No Relief for Stock Options.

Information Circulars: IC 73-25R4 Business equity valuations; IC 89-3 Policy statement on business equity valuations.

Interpretation Bulletins: *Primary* — IT-113R4 Benefits to employees — Stock options.

Tax Window Files: Employee stock options - Bankruptcy, *May 28, 2018*, CRA Document No. 2017-0692931E5; RSU Plan-Cash Dividend Equivalents, *March 20, 2015*, CRA Document No. 2014-0526941E5; Employee Stock Options — Choice to Sell or Exercise Options, *August 15, 2007*, CRA Document No. 2006-0213941R3; Tax Treatment of Employee Stock Options, *June 7, 2007*, CRA Document No. 2006-0217731E5; Bad Debt for Amount Owing Under Employee Stock Option, *2006 APFF Conference Round Table on the Federal Taxation, Question 10, October 6, 2006*, CRA Document No. 2006-0196271C6; Employee Share Purchase Plan (ESPP), *Technical Interpretation, Financial Industries Division, April 25, 2005*, CRA Document No. 2005-0112901E5; Stock Option Benefit — Share Losing Value Between Acquisition and Disposal Date, *Technical Interpretation, Financing and Plans Division, November 29, 2004*, CRA Document No. 2004-0010513E5; Cashless Exercise of Employee Stock Options, *Technical Interpretation, Financial Industries Division, August 18, 2004*, CRA Document No. 2004-0070361E5. "Cashless exercise" of employee stock option generally results in acquisition date being the same as the settlement date of the sale, but depends on the circumstances; Employee Stock Option — Election To Receive/Pay Cash, *Technical Interpretation, Income Tax Rulings Directorate, December 23, 2003*, CRA Document No. 2003-0049927. Cash payment made to employee in lieu of the employee receiving shares under a stock option agreement; Recognition of Stock Option Benefit as a Result of Share Redemption, *Technical Interpretation, Financial Industries Division, March 26, 2003*, CRA Document No. 2002-0179145. Application of subsections 7(1) and 84(3) on employee stock option and subsequent redemption of shares.

Cases: In December 2001, the taxpayers were granted options to acquire shares of Cybectec, a CCPC. On January 26, 2007, Cooper Inc. acquired practically all Cybectec's assets and two days later the taxpayers took up their options to acquire Cybectec shares at the option price of 20 cents per share. They resold these the same day to Cybectec's parent corporation for $1.2583 per share, subsequently reporting as income for tax benefit purposes the difference between the option take up price and the proceeds of disposition of the shares. Regulation 6204(1) did not invalidate their claim, and the taxpayers were allowed a stock option deduction under paragraph 110(1)(*d*). *Montminy et al v. The Queen*, 2017 DTC 5091 (CAF)

In return for helping him to find employment, the taxpayer paid a consultant a portion of the stock option benefits that he received from his new employer. These payments were not deductible under s. 7(1)(*a*)(iii). *Morin v. The Queen*, 2006 DTC 6057 (F.C.A.), reversing 2005 DTC 813 (T.C.C.)

The taxpayer received a lump sum payment in consideration of his releasing a company from its obligations under various stock option agreements. This amount had to be included in the taxpayer's income since he clearly "transferred or disposed of" his rights under his stock option agreements. *Dundas v. The Queen*, 95 DTC 5116 (F.C.A.), affirming 93 DTC 5162 (F.C.T.D.), and 90 DTC 1529 (T.C.C.)

There was a potential conflict between s. 6(1)(*g*) and s. 7, when attempts were made to construe both groups of provisions as they applied to the taxpayer's employee stock ownership plan. However, the provisions of s. 7 prevailed since its language was more specific than the general language contained in s. 6(1)(*g*). *M.N.R. v. Chrysler Canada Ltd. et al.*, 92 DTC 6346 (F.C.T.D.)

An agreement executed in Quebec by an employee to purchase shares of a non-arm's length corporation was considered to be a stock option. *Gesser v. The Queen*, 92 DTC 6273 (F.C.A.), reversing 89 DTC 5274 (F.C.T.D.), and affirming 84 DTC 1570 (T.C.C.)

► 7(1.1) ◄

(1.1) Employee stock options. Where after March 31, 1977 a Canadian-controlled private corporation (in this subsection referred to as "the corporation") has agreed to sell or issue a share of the capital stock of the corporation or of a Canadian-controlled private corporation with which it does not deal at arm's length to an employee of the corporation or of a Canadian-controlled private corporation with which it does not deal at arm's length and at the time immediately after the agreement was made the employee was dealing at arm's length with

(*a*) the corporation,

(*b*) the Canadian-controlled private corporation, the share of the capital stock of which has been agreed to be sold by the corporation, and

(*c*) the Canadian-controlled private corporation that is the employer of the employee,

in applying paragraph (1)(*a*) in respect of the employee's acquisition of the share, the reference in that paragraph to "the taxation year in which the employee acquired the securities" shall be read as a reference to "the taxation year in which the employee disposed of or exchanged the securities".

Editorial Note: The deferral of the recognition of the stock option benefit under s. 7(1.1) continues to apply if the Canadian-controlled private corporation (CCPC) issuing or selling the shares subsequently ceases to be a CCPC. See also the editorial note under s. 7(1). The benefit can qualify for the one-half deduction in computing taxable income under either s. 110(1)(*d*) or (*d.1*). The benefit is not subject to the withholding requirement that otherwise applies to s. 7(1) benefits (s. 153(1.01)).

Related Sections: S. 47(3) Securities acquired by employee; s. 53(1)(*j*) Share or fund unit taxed as stock option benefit; s. 110(1)(*d.1*) Employee options for CCPC shares; s. 125(7), "Canadian-controlled private corporation"; s. 128.1(4)(*d.1*) Employee CCPC stock option shares; s. 251 Arm's length.

Canadian Tax Foundation: Coburn, *Stock Options, With a Focus on Start-Ups*, 2017 British Columbia Tax Conference 13:1–23; Infanti, *Employee Stock Option Rules and Legally Binding Agreements*, 2017 Tax for the Owner Manager 17(2):1–2.

Tax Profile: July 2010 — Employee Compensation Planning: Stock-Based Incentive Compensation Plans; March 2006 — Some Tax Considerations for Investing in Silicon Valley North.

Interpretation Bulletins: *Primary* — IT-113R4 Benefits to employees — Stock options.

Tax Window Files: ACB of CCPC Shares Acquired by Trust on Behalf of Employees, *August 18, 2005*, CRA Document No. 2005-0126131E5; Employee Stock Options — Substituted Property, *Technical Interpretation, Financial Industries Division, January 13, 2005*, CRA Document No. 2004-0101701E5 [Sale of shares that were received as stock dividend in respect of CCPC shares acquired under an employee stock option did not affect the timing of the subsection 7(1) inclusion].

Cases: In December 2001, the taxpayers were granted options to acquire shares of Cybectec, a CCPC. On January 26, 2007, Cooper Inc. acquired practically all Cybectec's assets and two days later the taxpayers took up their options to acquire Cybectec shares at the option price of 20 cents per share. They resold these the same day to Cybectec's parent corporation for $1.2583 per share, subsequently reporting as income for tax benefit purposes the difference between the option take up price and the proceeds of disposition of the shares. Regulation 6204(1) did not invalidate their claim, and the taxpayers were allowed a stock option deduction under paragraph 110(1)(*d*). *Montminy et al v. The Queen*, 2017 DTC 5091 (CAF)

▶ 7(1.11) ◀

(1.11) Non-arm's length relationship with trusts. For the purposes of this section, a mutual fund trust is deemed not to deal at arm's length with a corporation only if the trust controls the corporation.

Department of Finance Comfort Letters

(December 4, 2006) [Expansion of Scope of Subsection 7(1.11) — Non Arm's Length Relationship with Trusts]

Dear XXXX

I am writing in response to your letters and e-mails concerning subsection 7(1.11) of the *Income Tax Act* (the "Act"). I also acknowledge phone conversations that you and your colleague, XXXX have had with officials of this Branch.

Section 7 of the Act contains provisions dealing with agreements under which an employee of a corporation or mutual fund trust may acquire securities of the employer or of an entity that deals at non-arm's length with the employer. Subsection 7(1.11) deems a mutual fund trust to deal at non-arm's length with a corporation, for the purpose of section 7, only if the trust controls the corporation. Thus, in any other situation in which a corporation and a mutual fund trust deal at non-arm's length, the provisions of section 7 will not apply.

You have suggested that subsection 7(1.11) excludes certain other non-arm's length relationships between a mutual fund trust and a corporation that may not be offensive from a policy perspective, and have asked that the scope of subsection 7(1.11) be expanded accordingly.

We have considered this issue carefully and are prepared to recommend that the scope of subsection 7(1.11) be expanded to include a corporation and a mutual fund trust where the corporation owns securities that would give it more than 50% of the votes that could be cast under all circumstances at a meeting of unitholders of the trust. As discussed, the securities to which such voting rights are attached would not be limited to units of the trust and could thus include, for example, securities that are exchangeable into units of the trust.

We will recommend to the Minister of Finance that the proposed amendment apply to rights exercised or disposed of after 2004 under agreements to sell or issue securities made after 2002.

While I cannot offer any assurance that the Minister or Parliament will agree with our recommendation in this regard, I hope that this statement of our position is helpful to you.

Yours sincerely,

Brian Ernewein
General Director — Legislation
Tax Policy Branch

Related Sections: S. 104(1) Reference to trust or estate; s. 104(2) Taxed as individual; s. 132(6) Meaning of "mutual fund trust"; s. 251 Arm's length.

▶ 7(1.2) ◀

(1.2) Idem — (Repealed by 1986, c. 6, s. 2(2).)

▶ 7(1.3) ◀

(1.3) Order of disposition of securities. For the purposes of this subsection, subsection (1.1), subdivision c, paragraph 110(1)(*d.01*), subparagraph 110(1)(*d.1*)(ii) and subsections 110(2.1) and 147(10.4), and subject to subsection (1.31), a taxpayer is deemed to dispose of securities that are identical properties in the order in which the taxpayer acquired them and, for this purpose,

(*a*) if a taxpayer acquires a particular security (other than under circumstances to which subsection (1.1) or 147(10.1) applies) at a time when the taxpayer also acquires or holds one or more other securities that are identical to the particular security and are, or were, acquired under circumstances to which subsection (1.1) or 147(10.1) applied, the taxpayer is deemed to have acquired the particular security at the time immediately preceding the earliest of the times at which the taxpayer acquired those other securities; and

(*b*) if a taxpayer acquires, at the same time, two or more identical securities under circumstances to which subsection (1.1) applied, the taxpayer is deemed to have acquired the securities in the order in which the agreements under which the taxpayer acquired the rights to acquire the securities were made.

Editorial Note: S. 7(1.3) provides that identical securities are disposed of in the order in which they were acquired for the purposes of the deferral rules — that is, those cases where the benefit is included in the year of the disposition of the securities rather than the year of acquisition (see s. 7(1.1)). The ordering rule also applies for the purposes of determining the capital gain or loss on the disposition of the securities. Furthermore, if a taxpayer acquires securities that qualify for deferral and subsequently acquires identical securities that do not qualify for deferral, the latter are deemed to be acquired first, such that they will be deemed to have been disposed of prior to the deferral securities. Thus, a taxpayer holding both deferral securities and non-deferral securities that are identical will be deemed to dispose of the non-deferral securities first. The effect of the ordering rules is to defer, until all non-deferral securities have been disposed of, the benefit and capital gain or loss in respect of the identical deferral securities. The ordering rules in s. 7(1.3) are subject to the elective rule in s. 7(1.31) which can apply where a security is disposed of within 30 days of its acquisition. See also s. 47(3), which provides that the securities eligible for the deferral are not identical to other securities, such that the averaging cost rules of s. 47(1) do not apply.

History: S. 7(1.3) was replaced by S.C. 2010, c. 25, s. 3(4), applicable in respect of rights exercised after 4:00 p.m. Eastern Standard Time, March 4, 2010. S. 7(1.3) formerly read:

(1.3) *Order of disposition of securities.* For the purposes of this subsection, subsections (1.1) and (8), subdivision c, paragraph 110(1)(*d*.01), subparagraph 110(1)(*d*.1)(ii) and subsections 110(2.1) and 147(10.4), and subject to subsection (1.31) and paragraph (14)(*c*), a taxpayer is deemed to dispose of securities that are identical properties in the order in which the taxpayer acquired them and, for this purpose,

(*a*) where a taxpayer acquires a particular security (other than under circumstances to which subsection (1.1) or (8) or 147(10.1) applies) at a time when the taxpayer also acquires or holds one or more other securities that are identical to the particular security and are, or were, acquired under circumstances to which any of subsections (1.1), (8) or 147(10.1) applied, the taxpayer is deemed to have acquired the particular security at the time immediately preceding the earliest of the times at which the taxpayer acquired those other securities; and

(*b*) where a taxpayer acquires, at the same time, two or more identical securities under circumstances to which either subsection (1.1) or (8) applied, the taxpayer is deemed to have acquired the securities in the order in which the agreements under which the taxpayer acquired the rights to acquire the securities were made.

Related Sections: S. 7(1.31) Disposition of newly-acquired security; s. 47(3) Securities acquired by employee.

▶ 7(1.31) ◀

(1.31) Disposition of newly-acquired security. Where a taxpayer acquires, at a particular time, a particular security under an agreement referred to in subsection (1) and, on a day that is no later than 30 days after the day that includes the particular time, the taxpayer disposes of a security that is identical to the particular security, the particular security is deemed to be the security that is so disposed of if

(*a*) no other securities that are identical to the particular security are acquired, or disposed of, by the taxpayer after the particular time and before the disposition;

(*b*) the taxpayer identifies the particular security as the security so disposed of in the taxpayer's return of income under this Part for the year in which the disposition occurs; and

(*c*) the taxpayer has not so identified the particular security, in accordance with this subsection, in connection with the disposition of any other security.

Editorial Note: See the editorial note to s. 7(1.3).

Related Sections: S. 47(3) Securities acquired by employee.

Tax Window Files: Disposition of Securities — Designation by Estate, *Technical Interpretation, Financial Sector and Exempt Entities Division, July 26, 2005*, CRA Document No. 2005-0115091E5.

► 7(1.4) ◄

(1.4) Exchange of options. Where

(*a*) a taxpayer disposes of rights under an agreement referred to in subsection (1) to acquire securities of a particular qualifying person that made the agreement or of a qualifying person with which it does not deal at arm's length (which rights and securities are referred to in this subsection as the "exchanged option" and the "old securities", respectively),

(*b*) the taxpayer receives no consideration for the disposition of the exchanged option other than rights under an agreement with a person (in this subsection referred to as the "designated person") that is

(i) the particular person,

(ii) a qualifying person with which the particular person does not deal at arm's length immediately after the disposition,

(iii) a corporation formed on the amalgamation or merger of the particular person and one or more other corporations,

(iv) a mutual fund trust to which the particular person has transferred property in circumstances to which subsection 132.2(1) applied,

(v) a qualifying person with which the corporation referred to in subparagraph (iii) does not deal at arm's length immediately after the disposition, or

(vi) if the disposition is before 2013 and the old securities were equity in a SIFT wind-up entity that was at the time of the disposition a mutual fund trust, a SIFT wind-up corporation in respect of the SIFT wind-up entity

to acquire securities of the designated person or a qualifying person with which the designated person does not deal at arm's length (which rights and securities are referred to in this subsection as the "new option" and the "new securities", respectively), and

(*c*) the amount, if any, by which

(i) the total value of the new securities immediately after the disposition

exceeds

(ii) the total amount payable by the taxpayer to acquire the new securities under the new option

does not exceed the amount, if any, by which

(iii) the total value of the old securities immediately before the disposition

exceeds

(iv) the amount payable by the taxpayer to acquire the old securities under the exchanged option,

for the purposes of this section,

(*d*) the taxpayer is deemed (other than for the purposes of subparagraph (9)(*d*)(ii)) not to have disposed of the exchanged option and not to have acquired the new option,

(*e*) the new option is deemed to be the same option as, and a continuation of, the exchanged option, and

(*f*) if the designated person is not the particular person, the designated person is deemed to be the same person as, and a continuation of, the particular person.

Editorial Note: S. 7(1.4) provides a tax-free rollover and effective continuation of the option in the circumstances described therein. A key prerequisite is that the amount, if any, by which the new option is "in the money" (value of new securities in excess of exercise price) cannot exceed the amount by which the old option is in the money; see s. 7(1.4)(*c*).

History: S. 7(1.4)(*b*)(vi) was added by S.C. 2009, c. 2, s. 3(1), applicable after December 19, 2007.

Related Sections: S. 87(5) Options to acquire shares of predecessor corporation; s. 110(1)(*d*) Employee options; s. 110(1.5) Determination of amounts relating to employee security options; s. 251 Arm's length.

Canadian Petroleum Tax Journal: The Recent Take-Over Phenomenon, D. Alan Ross and Stanley R. Ebel, 2001, Vol. 14, No. 1.

Tax Window Files: Stock Options — Exchange, *December 1, 2004*, CRA Document No. 2004-0058171R3; Option Exercise Price Reduction, *Technical Interpretation, Financial Industries Division, October 29, 2004*, CRA Document No. 2004-0093241E5.

► 7(1.5) ◄

(1.5) Rules where securities exchanged. For the purposes of this section and paragraphs 110(1)(*d*) to (*d*.1), where

(*a*) a taxpayer disposes of or exchanges securities of a particular qualifying person that were acquired by the taxpayer under circumstances to which subsection (1.1) applied (in this subsection referred to as the "exchanged securities"),

(*b*) the taxpayer receives no consideration for the disposition or exchange of the exchanged securities other than securities (in this subsection referred to as the "new securities") of

(i) the particular qualifying person,

(ii) a qualifying person with which the particular qualifying person does not deal at arm's length immediately after the disposition or exchange,

(iii) a corporation formed on the amalgamation or merger of the particular qualifying person and one or more other corporations,

(iv) a mutual fund trust to which the particular qualifying person has transferred property in circumstances to which subsection 132.2(1) applied, or

(v) a qualifying person with which the corporation referred to in subparagraph (iii) does not deal at arm's length immediately after the disposition or exchange, and

(*c*) the total value of the new securities immediately after the disposition or exchange does not exceed the total value of the old securities immediately before the disposition or exchange,

the following rules apply:

(*d*) the taxpayer is deemed not to have disposed of or exchanged the exchanged securities and not to have acquired the new securities,

(*e*) the new securities are deemed to be the same securities as, and a continuation of, the exchanged securities, except for the purpose of determining if the new securities are identical to any other securities,

(*f*) the qualifying person that issued the new securities is deemed to be the same person as, and a continuation of, the qualifying person that issued the exchanged securities, and

(*g*) where the exchanged securities were issued under an agreement, the new securities are deemed to have been issued under that agreement.

Editorial Note: S. 7(1.5) effectively provides that the recognition of the benefit in respect of the option under s. 7(1), which would have been deferred under either s. 7(1.1) or (8), can continue to be deferred notwithstanding that the taxpayer has acquired the new securities in exchange for the old shares that were acquired under the option. The recognition of the benefit will be deferred until the disposition of the new securities.

History: S. 7(1.5)(*a*) was replaced by S.C. 2010, c. 25, s. 3(5), applicable in respect of rights exercised after 4:00 p.m. Eastern Standard Time, March 4, 2010. S. 7(1.5)(*a*) formerly read:

(*a*) a taxpayer disposes of or exchanges securities of a particular qualifying person that were acquired by the taxpayer under circumstances to which either subsection (1.1) or (8) applied (in this subsection referred to as the "exchanged securities"),

Related Sections: S. 47(3) Securities acquired by employee; s. 251 Arm's length.

► 7(1.6) ◄

(1.6) Emigrant. For the purposes of this section and paragraph 110(1)(*d*.1), a taxpayer is deemed not to have disposed of a share acquired under circumstances to which subsection (1.1) applied solely because of subsection 128.1(4).

Editorial Note: While subsection 128.1(4) emigration rules deem a taxpayer's property to be disposed of upon cessation of Canadian residency, subsection 7(1.6) defers taxation of the section 7 employee benefit on CCPC shares until the shares' actual disposition.

Tax Profile: April 2007 — Tax Planning for Emigration from Canada.

► 7(1.7) ◄

(1.7) Rights ceasing to be exercisable. For the purposes of subsections (1) and 110(1), if a taxpayer receives at a particular time one or more particular amounts in respect of rights of the taxpayer to acquire securities under an agreement referred to in subsection (1) ceasing to be exercisable in accordance with the terms of the agreement, and the cessation would not, if this Act were read without reference to this subsection, constitute a transfer or disposition of those rights by the taxpayer,

(*a*) the taxpayer is deemed to have disposed of those rights at the particular time to a person with whom the taxpayer was dealing at arm's length and to have received the particular amounts as consideration for the disposition; and

(*b*) for the purpose of determining the amount, if any, of the benefit that is deemed to have been received as a consequence of the disposition referred to in paragraph (*a*), the taxpayer is deemed to have paid an amount to acquire those rights equal to the amount, if any, by which

(i) the amount paid by the taxpayer to acquire those rights (determined without reference to this subsection)

exceeds

(ii) the total of all amounts each of which is an amount received by the taxpayer before the particular time in respect of the cessation.

Editorial Note: S. 7(1.7) overrides the effect of the decision in *Buccini v. The Queen*, 2000 DTC 6685 (F.C.A.).

History: S. 7(1.7) was replaced by S.C. 2010, c. 25, s. 3(6), applicable in respect of rights exercised after 4:00 p.m. Eastern Standard Time, March 4, 2010. S. 7(1.7) formerly read:

(1.7) *Rights ceasing to be exercisable.* For the purposes of paragraphs (1)(*b*) and 110(1)(*d*), where a taxpayer receives at a particular time one or more particular amounts in respect of rights of the taxpayer to acquire securities under an agreement referred to in subsection (1) ceasing to be exercisable in accordance with the terms of the agreement, and the cessation would not, if this Act were read without reference to this subsection, constitute a transfer or disposition of those rights by the taxpayer,

(*a*) the taxpayer is deemed to have disposed of those rights at the particular time to a person with whom the taxpayer was dealing at arm's length and to have received the particular amounts as consideration for the disposition; and

(*b*) for the purpose of determining the amount, if any, of the benefit that the taxpayer is deemed by paragraph (1)(*b*) to have received as a consequence of the disposition referred to in paragraph (*a*), the taxpayer is deemed to have paid an amount to acquire those rights equal to the amount, if any, by which

(i) the amount paid by the taxpayer to acquire those rights (determined without reference to this subsection)

exceeds

(ii) the total of all amounts each of which is an amount received by the taxpayer before the particular time in respect of the cessation.

Related Sections: S. 251 Arm's length.

Canadian Tax Foundation: Yager, *Relief for Stock Option Buyout*, 2013 Canadian Tax Highlights 21(2):3–4.

► 7(2) ◄

(2) Securities held by trustee. If a security is held by a trustee in trust or otherwise, whether absolutely, conditionally or contingently, for an employee, the employee is deemed, for the purposes of this section and paragraphs 110(1)(*d*) to (*d*.1),

(*a*) to have acquired the security at the time the trust began to so hold it; and

(*b*) to have exchanged or disposed of the security at the time the trust exchanged it or disposed of it to any person other than the employee.

Related Sections: S. 8(12) Forfeiture of securities by employee; s. 104(21.2) Beneficiaries' taxable capital gain; s. 110.6(16) Personal trust.

Tax Window Files: ACB of CCPC Shares Acquired by Trust on Behalf of Employees, *Technical Interpretation, Financial Sector and Exempt Entities Division, August 18, 2005*, CRA Document No. 2005-0126131E5.

► 7(3) ◄

(3) Special provision. If a particular qualifying person has agreed to sell or issue securities of the particular person, or of a qualifying person with which it does not deal at arm's length, to an employee of the particular person or of a qualifying person with which it does not deal at arm's length,

(*a*) except as provided by this section, the employee is deemed to have neither received nor enjoyed any benefit under or because of the agreement; and (*b*) the income for a taxation year of any person is deemed to be not less than its income for the year would have been if a benefit had not been conferred on the employee by the sale or issue of the securities.

Tax Window Files: Deduction on Share Based Deferred Compensation Plans, *April 12, 2017,* CRA Document No. 2015-0600941I7.

Editorial Note: S. 7(3)(*a*) ensures that the grant of the employee stock option does not itself generate a taxable benefit to the employee. S. 7(3)(*b*) prohibits a deduction by the qualifying person (e.g., the employer corporation) in respect of the issuance or sale of the securities to the employee.

Related Sections: S. 6(1)(*a*) Value of benefits; s. 7(7) Definitions; s. 251 Arm's length.

Canadian Petroleum Tax Journal: Attracting and Retaining Executives and Employees with Tax-Efficient Incentives, Julie Y. Lee, 2001, Vol. 14, No. 1.

Tax Profile: March 2006 — Some Tax Considerations for Investing in Silicon Valley North.

Tax Topics: No. 2093, Paying Employees — An Option That is Not a Stock Option.

Cases: No stock option benefit could be included as a "benefit" in the taxpayer's income under the general employee benefit provisions of s. 6(1)(*a*) because of the specific language in s. 7(3)(*a*), which makes s. 6(1)(*a*) inapplicable in this case. *Mathieu v. The Queen*, 2014 DTC 1165 (T.C.C.)

Payments to compensate employees for surrendering their stock options, as part of a corporate reorganization, were non-deductible capital outlays. *Imperial Tobacco Canada Limited v. The Queen*, 2012 DTC 5003 (F.C.A.), affirming 2011 DTC 1037 (T.C.C.).

► 7(4) ◄

(4) Application of s. (1). For greater certainty it is hereby declared that, where a person to whom any provision of subsection (1) would otherwise apply has ceased to be an employee before all things have happened that would make that provision applicable, subsection (1) shall continue to apply as though the person were still an employee and as though the employment were still in existence.

► 7(5) ◄

(5) Non-application of this section. This section does not apply if the benefit conferred by the agreement was not received in respect of, in the course of, or by virtue of, the employment.

Related Sections: S. 248(1), "employee", "employment".

► 7(6) ◄

(6) Sale to trustee for employees. If a particular qualifying person has entered into an arrangement under which securities of the particular person, or of a qualifying person with which it does not deal at arm's length, are sold or issued by either person to a trustee to be held by the trustee in trust for sale to an employee of the particular person or of a qualifying person with which it does not deal at arm's length,

(*a*) for the purposes of this section (other than subsection (2)) and paragraphs 110(1)(*d*) to (*d.1*),

(i) any particular rights of the employee under the arrangement in respect of those securities are deemed to be rights under a particular agreement with the particular person under which the particular person has agreed to sell or issue securities to the employee,

(ii) any securities acquired under the arrangement by the employee or by a person in whom the particular rights have become vested are deemed to be securities acquired under the particular agreement, and

(iii) any amounts paid or agreed to be paid to the trustee for any securities acquired under the arrangement by the employee or by a person in whom the particular rights have become vested are deemed to be amounts paid or agreed to be paid to the particular person for securities acquired under the particular agreement; and

(*b*) subsection (2) does not apply in respect of securities held by the trustee under the arrangement.

Related Sections: S. 104(1) Reference to trust or estate; s. 251 Arm's length.

Tax Window Files: Use of Trust To Acquire Employer Shares for Employees, *Technical Interpretation, Financial Industries Division, May 3, 2005,* CRA Document No. 2005-0124261E5.

Cases: To circumvent Stock Exchange rules, the taxpayer acquired shares under option agreements that he resold to a stock promoter at cost. It could not be said that these shares were impressed with a trust, nor that the taxpayer had acted as the promoter's agent. The stock option benefits were included in the taxpayer's income. *Stafford v. The Queen*, 93 DTC 438 (T.C.C.)

► 7(7) ◄

(7) Definitions. The following definitions apply in this section and in subsection 47(3), paragraphs 53(1)(*j*) and 110(1)(*d*) and (*d.01*) and subsections 110(1.1), (1.2), (1.5) to (1.8) and (2.1).

Proposed Amendment

Notice of Ways and Means Motion to amend the Income Tax Act (June 17, 2019)

The portion of subsection 7(7) of the *Income Tax Act* before the first definition is replaced by the following:

(7) Definitions. The following definitions apply in this section and in subsection 47(3), paragraph 53(1)(*j*), subsection 110(0.1), paragraphs 110(1)(*d*), (*d*.01) and (*e*) and subsections 110(1.1) to (1.9) and (2.1).

Applicable: On January 1, 2020.

History: S. 7(7), the portion before the definition "qualifying person" was replaced by S.C. 2013, c. 34, s. 171(1), deemed to have come into force on January 1, 1999. However,

(*a*) it does not apply to a right under an agreement to which subsection 7(7) does not (except for the purpose of applying paragraph 7(3)(*b*)) apply; and

(*b*) before 2000, the portion of subsection 7(7) before the definition "qualifying person" is to be read as follows:

"(7) The definitions in this subsection apply in this section and in paragraph 110(1)(*d*) and subsections 110(1.5) to (1.8)."

(*c*) in respect of rights (other than rights referred to in paragraph (*a*)) exercised after 2000 but on or before 4:00 p.m. Eastern Standard Time, March 4, 2010, the portion of subsection 7(7) before the definition "qualifying person" is to be read as follows:

"(7) The following definitions apply in this section and in subsection 47(3), paragraphs 53(1)(*j*) and 110(1)(*d*) and (*d.01*) and subsections 110(1.5) to (1.8) and (2.1)."

S. 7(7), the portion before the definition "qualifying person" formerly read:

(7) *Definitions.* The following definitions apply in this section and in subsection 47(3), paragraphs 53(1)(*j*) and 110(1)(*d*) and (*d.01*) and subsections 110(1.1), (1.2), (1.5), (1.6) and (2.1).

S. 7(7), the portion before the definition "qualifying person" was replaced by S.C. 2010, c. 25, s. 3(7), applicable in respect of rights exercised after 4:00 p.m. Eastern Standard Time, March 4, 2010. S. 7(7), the portion before the definition "qualifying person" formerly read:

(7) *Definitions.* The definitions in this subsection apply in this section and in subsection 47(3), paragraphs 53(1)(*j*), 110(1)(*d*) and (*d*.01) and subsections 110(1.5), (1.6) and (2.1).

"qualifying person" —"qualifying person" means a corporation or a mutual fund trust.

Related Sections: S. 132(6) Meaning of "mutual fund trust".

"security" —"security" of a qualifying person means

(*a*) if the person is a corporation, a share of the capital stock of the corporation; and

(*b*) if the person is a mutual fund trust, a unit of the trust.

Related Sections: S. 8(12) Forfeiture of securities by employee; s. 132(6) Meaning of "mutual fund trust".

▶ 7(8) ◀

(8) Deferral in respect of non-CCPC employee options — (Repealed by S.C. 2010, c. 25, s. 3(8).)

History: See the application provision under s. 110(1.7) in respect of an extended deadline for a deferral election.

S. 7(8) was repealed by S.C. 2010, c. 25, s. 3(8), applicable in respect of rights exercised after 4:00 p.m. Eastern Standard Time, March 4, 2010. S. 7(8) formerly read:

(8) *Deferral in respect of non-CCPC employee options.* Where a particular qualifying person (other than a Canadian-controlled private corporation) has agreed to sell or issue securities of the particular qualifying person (or of a qualifying person with which it does not deal at arm's length) to a taxpayer who is an employee of the particular qualifying person (or of a qualifying person with which the particular qualifying person does not deal at arm's length), in applying paragraph (1)(*a*) in respect of the taxpayer's acquisition of a security under the agreement, the reference in that paragraph to "the taxation year in which the employee acquired the securities" shall be read as a reference to "the taxation year in which the employee disposed of or exchanged the securities" if

(*a*) the acquisition is a qualifying acquisition; and

(*b*) the taxpayer elects, in accordance with subsection (10), to have this subsection apply in respect of the acquisition.

Canadian Tax Foundation: Smith and Churchill, *Update on Employee Compensation — A Changing Environment*, 2010 Atlantic Provinces Tax Conference 9:8–9.

▶ 7(9) ◀

(9) Meaning of "qualifying acquisition" — (Repealed by S.C. 2010, c. 25, s. 3(8).)

History: S. 7(9) was repealed by S.C. 2010, c. 25, s. 3(8), applicable in respect of rights exercised after 4:00 p.m. Eastern Standard Time, March 4, 2010. S. 7(9) formerly read:

(9) *Meaning of "qualifying acquisition".* For the purpose of subsection (8), a taxpayer's acquisition of a security under an agreement made by a particular qualifying person is a qualifying acquisition if

(*a*) the acquisition occurs after February 27, 2000;

(*b*) the taxpayer would, if this Act were read without reference to subsection (8), be entitled to deduct an amount under paragraph 110(1)(*d*) in respect of the acquisition in computing income for the taxation year in which the security is acquired;

(*c*) where the particular qualifying person is a corporation, the taxpayer was not, at the time immediately after the agreement was made, a person who would, if the references in the portion of the definition "specified shareholder" in subsection 248(1) before paragraph (*a*) to "in a taxation year" and "at any time in the year" were read as references to "at any time" and "at that time", respectively, be a specified shareholder of any of

(i) the particular qualifying person,

(ii) any qualifying person that, at that time, was an employer of the taxpayer and was not dealing at arm's length with the particular qualifying person, and

(iii) the qualifying person of which the taxpayer had, under the agreement, a right to acquire a security; and

(*d*) where the security is a share,

(i) it is of a class of shares that, at the time the acquisition occurs, is listed on a designated stock exchange, and

(ii) where rights under the agreement were acquired by the taxpayer as a result of one or more dispositions to which subsection (1.4) applied, none of the rights that were the subject of any of the dispositions included a right to acquire a share of a class of shares that, at the time the rights were disposed of, was not listed on any designated stock exchange.

▶ 7(9.1) ◀

(9.1) Reorganization — (Repealed by S.C. 2010, c. 25, s. 3(10).)

History: S. 7(9.1) was repealed by S.C. 2010, c. 25, s. 3(10), applicable in respect of rights exercised after 4:00 p.m. Eastern Standard Time, March 4, 2010. S. 7(9.1) formerly read:

(9.1) *Reorganization.* If, in the course of a reorganization that gives rise to a dividend that would, in the absence of paragraph 55(3)(*b*), be subject to subsection 55(2), rights to acquire securities listed on a designated stock exchange (referred to in this subsection as "public options") under an agreement to sell or issue securities referred to in subsection (1) are exchanged for rights to acquire securities that are not listed on a designated stock exchange (referred to in this subsection as "private options"), and the private options are subsequently exchanged for public options, the private options are deemed to be rights to acquire shares that are listed on a designated stock exchange for the purposes of subparagraph 7(9)(*d*)(ii).

S. 7(9.1) was added by S.C. 2010, c. 25, s. 3(9), applicable after 1999 and before 4:00 p.m. Eastern Standard Time, March 4, 2010, except that, for the period before December 14, 2007, the reference in subsection 7(9.1) to "designated stock exchange" shall be read as a reference to "prescribed stock exchange".

▶ 7(10) ◀

(10) Election for the purpose of subsection (8) — (Repealed by S.C. 2010, c. 25, s. 3(10).)

History: See the application provision under s. 110(1.7) in respect of an extended deadline for a deferral election.

S. 7(10) was repealed by S.C. 2010, c. 25, s. 3(10), applicable in respect of rights exercised after 4:00 p.m. Eastern Standard Time, March 4, 2010. S. 7(10) formerly read:

(10) *Election for the purpose of subsection (8).* For the purpose of subsection (8), a taxpayer's election to have that subsection apply in respect of the taxpayer's acquisition of a particular security under an agreement referred to in subsection (1) is in accordance with this subsection if

(*a*) the election is filed, in the prescribed form and manner at a particular time that is before January 16 of the year following the year in which the acquisition occurs, with a person who would be required to file an information return in respect of the acquisition if subsection (8) were read without reference to paragraph (8)(*b*);

(*b*) the taxpayer is resident in Canada at the time the acquisition occurs; and

(*c*) the specified value of the particular security does not exceed the amount by which

(i) $100,000

exceeds

(ii) the total of all amounts each of which is the specified value of another security acquired by the taxpayer at or before the particular time under an agreement referred to in subsection (1), where

(A) the taxpayer's right to acquire that other security first became exercisable in the year that the taxpayer's right to acquire the particular security first became exercisable, and

(B) at or before the particular time, the taxpayer has elected in accordance with this subsection to have subsection (8) apply in respect of the acquisition of that other security.

▶ 7(11) ◀

(11) Meaning of "specified value" — (Repealed by S.C. 2010, c. 25, s. 3(10).)

History: S. 7(11) was repealed by S.C. 2010, c. 25, s. 3(10), applicable in respect of rights exercised after 4:00 p.m. Eastern Standard Time, March 4, 2010. S. 7(11) formerly read:

(11) *Meaning of "specified value".* For the purpose of paragraph (10)(*c*), the specified value of a particular security acquired by a taxpayer under an agreement referred to in subsection (1) is the amount determined by the formula

$$A/B$$

where

A is the fair market value, determined at the time the agreement was made, of a security that was the subject of the agreement at the time the agreement was made; and

B is

(*a*) except where paragraph (*b*) applies, 1, and

(*b*) where the number or type of securities that are the subject of the agreement has been modified in any way after the time the agreement was made, the number of securities (including any fraction of a security) that it is reasonable to consider the taxpayer would, at the time the particular security was acquired, have a right to acquire under the agreement in lieu of one of the securities that was the subject of the agreement at the time the agreement was made.

▶ 7(12) ◀

(12) Identical options — order of exercise — (Repealed by S.C. 2010, c. 25, s. 3(10).)

History: S. 7(12) was repealed by S.C. 2010, c. 25, s. 3(10), applicable in respect of rights exercised after 4:00 p.m. Eastern Standard Time, March 4, 2010. S. 7(12) formerly read:

(12) *Identical options — order of exercise.* Unless the context otherwise requires, a taxpayer is deemed to exercise identical rights to acquire securities under agreements referred to in subsection (1)

(*a*) where the taxpayer has designated an order, in the order so designated; and

(*b*) in any other case, in the order in which those rights first became exercisable and, in the case of identical rights that first became exercisable at the same time, in the order in which the agreements under which those rights were acquired were made.

Related Sections: S. 7(1.3) Order of disposition of securities.

▶ 7(13) ◀

(13) Revoked election — (Repealed by S.C. 2010, c. 25, s. 3(10).)

History: S. 7(13) was repealed by S.C. 2010, c. 25, s. 3(10), applicable in respect of rights exercised after 4:00 p.m. Eastern Standard Time, March 4, 2010. S. 7(13) formerly read:

(13) *Revoked election.* For the purposes of this section (other than this subsection), an election filed by a taxpayer to have subsection (8) apply to the taxpayer's acquisition of a security is deemed never to have been filed if, before January 16 of the year following the year in which the acquisition occurs, the taxpayer files with the person with whom the election was filed a written revocation of the election.

▶ 7(14) ◀

(14) Deferral deemed valid — (Repealed by S.C. 2010, c. 25, s. 3(10).)

History: S. 7(14) was repealed by S.C. 2010, c. 25, s. 3(10), applicable in respect of rights exercised after 4:00 p.m. Eastern Standard Time, March 4, 2010. S. 7(14) formerly read:

(14) *Deferral deemed valid.* For the purposes of this section and paragraph 110(1)(*d*), where a taxpayer files an election to have subsection (8) apply in respect of the taxpayer's acquisition of a particular security and subsection (8) would not apply to the acquisition if this section were read without reference to this subsection, the following rules apply if the Minister so notifies the taxpayer in writing:

(*a*) the acquisition is deemed, for the purpose of subsection (8), to be a qualifying acquisition;

(*b*) the taxpayer is deemed to have elected, in accordance with subsection (10), at the time of the acquisition, to have subsection (8) apply in respect of the acquisition; and

(*c*) if, at the time the Minister sends the notice, the taxpayer has not disposed of the security, the taxpayer is deemed (other than for the purpose of subsection (1.5)) to have disposed of the security at that time and to have acquired the security immediately after that time other than under an agreement referred to in subsection (1).

▶ 7(15) ◀

(15) Withholding — (Repealed by S.C. 2010, c. 25, s. 3(10).)

History: S. 7(15) was repealed by S.C. 2010, c. 25, s. 3(10), applicable in respect of rights exercised after 4:00 p.m. Eastern Standard Time, March 4, 2010. S. 7(15) formerly read:

(15) *Withholding.* Where, because of subsection (8), a taxpayer is deemed by paragraph (1)(*a*) to have received a benefit from employment in a taxation year, the benefit is deemed to be nil for the purpose of subsection 153(1).

▶ 7(16) ◀

(16) Prescribed form for deferral. Where, at any time in a taxation year, a taxpayer holds a security that was acquired under circumstances to which subsection (8) applied, the taxpayer shall file with the Minister, with the taxpayer's return of income for the year, a prescribed form containing prescribed information relating to the taxpayer's acquisition and disposition of securities under agreements referred to in subsection (1).

Forms: T1212 — Statement of Deferred Security Option Benefits.

Deductions

SECTION 8: Deductions allowed

▶ 8(1) ◀

(1) Deductions allowed. In computing a taxpayer's income for a taxation year from an office or employment, there may be deducted such of the following amounts as are wholly applicable to that source or such part of the following amounts as may reasonably be regarded as applicable thereto:

Editorial Note: By virtue of subsection 8(2), these are the only permissible deductions for employees.

Related Sections: S. 4(1) Income or loss from a source or from sources in a place; s. 5(1) Income from office or employment; s. 5(2) Loss from office or employment; s. 6(1)(*j*) Reimbursements and awards; s. 6(8) GST rebates re costs of property or service; s. 8(2) General limitation.

Forms: T777 — Statement of Employment Expenses.

▶ 8(1)(a) ◀

(a) Volunteers' deduction — (Repealed by S.C. 2001, c. 17, s. 3(1).)

▶ 8(1)(b) ◀

(b) Legal expenses of employee — amounts paid by the taxpayer in the year as or on account of legal expenses incurred by the taxpayer to collect, or to establish a right to, an amount owed to the taxpayer that, if received by the taxpayer, would be required by this subdivision to be included in computing the taxpayer's income;

History: S. 8(1)(*b*) was replaced by S.C. 2013, c. 34, s. 172(1), applicable to amounts paid in the 2001 and subsequent taxation years. S. 8(1)(*b*) formerly read:

(*b*) *Legal expenses of employee* — amounts paid by the taxpayer in the year as or on account of legal expenses incurred by the taxpayer to collect or establish a right to salary or wages owed to the taxpayer by the employer or former employer of the taxpayer;

Related Sections: S. 6(1)(*j*) Reimbursements and awards; s. 6(8) GST rebates re costs of property or service; s. 56(1)(*a*)(ii) Pension benefits, unemployment insurance benefits, etc.; s. 60(*o*.1)(i)(B) Legal expenses for pension benefit or retiring allowance; s. 110.2(1), "qualifying amount".

Guides: T4044 Employment Expenses — Supplementary Income Tax Guide.

Interpretation Bulletins: *Secondary* — IT-99R5 (Consolid.) Legal and accounting fees.

Tax Window Files: Deduction of legal expense, *April 11, 2018*, CRA Document No. 2017-0699751E5; Legal Expenses of Employee, *Technical Interpretation, Business and Partnerships Division, June 1, 2005*, CRA Document No. 2005-0113991E5. Legal fees relating to inappropriate termination notice and negotiating a settlement not deductible under paragraph 8(1)(*b*) or paragraph 60(*o*.1).

Cases: Relief under paragraph 8(1)(*b*) is not available where the claim defended against extended beyond the employer-employee relationship into corporate claims based on allegations of unjust enrichment and breach of fiduciary duty. *Catlos et al v. The Queen*, 2018 DTC 1126 (TCC) [under appeal]

The expenditure of legal fees paid to defend against criminal charges in order to preserve a taxpayer's employment is not sufficient to fall within the terms of section 8. Unless legal fees are incurred to collect amounts owed from employment, they are not deductible. The protection or preservation of a future source of income is not enough. *Geick v. The Queen*, 2017 DTC 1067 (TCC)

The taxpayer unsuccessfully sued two of his children for control of a family-run insurance business. He claimed that their actions deprived him of his ability to continue earning employment income, but his legal expenses were not deductible under s. 8(1)(*b*) as expenditures to collect employment income or under s. 18(1)(*a*) as expenses laid out to earn income from business or property. *Hollinger Estate v. The Queen*, 2013 DTC 1210 (T.C.C.)

The damages claimed by a taxpayer as a result of a flawed competition for a job promotion did not relate to salary or wages "owed", but to an amount in lieu of the salary or wages that she would have earned, had the competition been fair. *Turner-Lienaux v. The Queen*, 97 DTC 5293 (F.C.A.), affirming 97 DTC 261 (T.C.C.)

A teacher's expenses of defending criminal charges were held not deductible since they could not be considered as expenses incurred for the purpose of collecting salary or wages. *Wilson v. The Queen*, 91 DTC 5407 (F.C.A.), affirming 90 DTC 6382 (F.C.T.D.) and (T.C.C.) unreported

▶ 8(1)(c) ◀

(c) Clergy residence — where, in the year, the taxpayer

(i) is a member of the clergy or of a religious order or a regular minister of a religious denomination, and

(ii) is

(A) in charge of a diocese, parish or congregation,

(B) ministering to a diocese, parish or congregation, or

(C) engaged exclusively in full-time administrative service by appointment of a religious order or religious denomination,

the amount, not exceeding the taxpayer's remuneration for the year from the office or employment, equal to

(iii) the total of all amounts including amounts in respect of utilities, included in computing the taxpayer's income for the year under section 6 in respect of the residence or other living accommodation occupied by the taxpayer in the course of, or because of, the taxpayer's office or employment as such a member or minister so in charge of or ministering to a diocese, parish or congregation, or so engaged in such administrative service, or

(iv) rent and utilities paid by the taxpayer for the taxpayer's principal place of residence (or other principal living accommodation), ordinarily occupied during the year by the taxpayer, or the fair rental value of such a residence (or other living accommodation), including utilities, owned by the taxpayer or the taxpayer's spouse or common-law partner, not exceeding the lesser of

(A) the greater of

(I) $1,000 multiplied by the number of months (to a maximum of ten) in the year, during which the taxpayer is a person described in subparagraphs (i) and (ii), and

(II) one-third of the taxpayer's remuneration for the year from the office or employment, and

(B) the amount, if any, by which

(I) the rent paid or the fair rental value of the residence or living accommodation, including utilities

exceeds

(II) the total of all amounts each of which is an amount deducted, in connection with the same accommodation or residence, in computing an individual's income for the year from an office or employment or from a business (other than an amount deducted under this paragraph by the taxpayer), to the extent that the amount can reasonably be considered to relate to the period, or a portion of the period, in respect of which an amount is claimed by the taxpayer under this paragraph;

Related Sections: S. 8(10) Certificate of employer; s. 146(1), "earned income".

Forms: T1223 — Clergy Residence Deduction.

Interpretation Bulletins: *Primary* — IT-141R (Consolid.) Clergy residence deduction.

Tax Window Files: Clergy Deduction - Aboriginal Spiritual Caregivers, *June 13, 2016*, CRA Document No. 2015-0620371E5; Clergy Residence Deduction, *July 22, 2015*, CRA Document No. 2015-0576461E5.

Cases: Although an interfaith chaplain was not an ordained member of the clergy, she was a "regular minister of a religious denomination" and was therefore entitled to the clergyman's residence deduction. *Noseworthy v. The Queen*, 99 DTC 541 (T.C.C.)

To be a member of the "clergy", one does not have to be "ordained", and the word "ordain" is not restricted to churches using that word. *Kraft et al. v. The Queen*, 99 DTC 693 (T.C.C.)

Missionaries were considered to be regular ministers of a religious order ministering to a congregation and therefore entitled to a deduction for clergyman's residence. *McGorman et al. v. The Queen*, 99 DTC 699 (T.C.C.)

Considering that in his capacity as the Manitoba Secretary of the Canadian Bible Society, the taxpayer, an ordained minister, participated in the worship services of the 200 Lutheran churches he visited every year, all the requirements of s. 8(1)(*c*) had been met by him. *Vibe v. The Queen*, 98 DTC 1684 (T.C.C.)

The president of the Ontario Bible College (OBC) was denied a clergyman's residence deduction on the ground that OBC was not a religious order and he was not "in charge of or ministering to a congregation". *McRae v. The Queen*, 97 DTC 5124 (F.C.A.), affirming 94 DTC 6687 (F.C.T.D.)

▶ 8(1)(d) ◀

(d) Teachers' exchange fund contribution — a single amount, in respect of all employments of the taxpayer as a teacher, not exceeding $250 paid by the taxpayer in the year to a fund established by the Canadian Education Association for the benefit of teachers from Commonwealth countries present in Canada under a teachers' exchange arrangement;

▶ 8(1)(e) ◀

(e) Expenses of railway employees — amounts disbursed by the taxpayer in the year for meals and lodging while employed by a railway company

(i) away from the taxpayer's ordinary place of residence as a relieving telegrapher or station agent or on maintenance and repair work, or

(ii) away from the municipality and the metropolitan area, if there is one, where the taxpayer's home terminal was located, and at a location from which, by reason of distance from the place where the taxpayer maintained a self-contained domestic establishment in which the taxpayer resided and actually supported a spouse or common-law partner or a person dependent on the taxpayer for support and connected with the taxpayer by blood relationship, marriage or common-law partnership or adoption, the taxpayer could not reasonably be expected to return daily to that place,

to the extent that the taxpayer has not been reimbursed and is not entitled to be reimbursed in respect thereof;

Related Sections: S. 6(6) Employment at special work site or remote location; s. 6(8) GST rebates re costs of property or service; s. 8(1)(*f*) Sales expenses; s 8(1)(*g*) Transport employee's expenses; s. 8(1)(*h*) Travel expenses;

s. 8(11) Goods and services tax; s. 67.1(1) Expenses for food, etc; s. 67.1(2) Exceptions; s. 248(1), "common-law partner", "self-contained domestic establishment"; s. 251(6) Blood relationship, etc.

Forms: TL2 — Claim for Board and Lodging Expenses.

Information Circulars: IC 73-21R9 Claims for Meals and Lodging Expenses of Transport Employees.

Interpretation Bulletins: *Secondary* — IT-522R Vehicle, travel and sales expenses of employees.

► 8(1)(f) ◄

(f) Sales expenses — where the taxpayer was employed in the year in connection with the selling of property or negotiating of contracts for the taxpayer's employer, and

(i) under the contract of employment was required to pay the taxpayer's own expenses,

(ii) was ordinarily required to carry on the duties of the employment away from the employer's place of business,

(iii) was remunerated in whole or part by commissions or other similar amounts fixed by reference to the volume of the sales made or the contracts negotiated, and

(iv) was not in receipt of an allowance for travel expenses in respect of the taxation year that was, by virtue of subparagraph 6(1)(*b*)(v), not included in computing the taxpayer's income,

amounts expended by the taxpayer in the year for the purpose of earning the income from the employment (not exceeding the commissions or other similar amounts referred to in subparagraph (iii) and received by the taxpayer in the year) to the extent that those amounts were not

(v) outlays, losses or replacements of capital or payments on account of capital, except as described in paragraph (*j*),

(vi) outlays or expenses that would, by virtue of paragraph 18(1)(*l*), not be deductible in computing the taxpayer's income for the year if the employment were a business carried on by the taxpayer, or

(vii) amounts the payment of which reduced the amount that would otherwise be included in computing the taxpayer's income for the year because of paragraph 6(1)(*e*);

Editorial Note: The deduction for a salesperson's expenses under s. 8(1)(*f*) is limited to the amount of commission or bonus income received in the year. Alternatively, a salesperson can deduct travel and automobile expenses under s. 8(1)(*h*) and (*h*.1) without the commission or bonus income limitation. However, the salesperson can claim a deduction under the latter provisions only if no deduction is made under s. 8(1)(*f*) in respect of any expenses. See the s. 8(4) limitation regarding meal expenses.

Related Regulations: 102(2)(*d*).

Related Sections: S. 6(8) GST rebates re costs of property or service; s. 6(9) Amount in respect of interest on employee debt; s. 8(1)(*h*) Travel expenses; s. 8(1)(*h*.1) Motor vehicle travel expenses; s. 8(1)(*j*) Motor vehicle and aircraft costs; s. 8(4) Meals; s. 8(9) Presumption; s. 8(10) Certificate of employer; s. 8(11) Goods and services tax; s. 8(13) Work space in home; s. 18(1)(*h*) Personal and living expenses; s. 18(1)(*l*) Use of recreational facilities and club dues; s. 18(1)(*r*) Certain automobile expenses; s. 67.1(1) Expenses for food, etc; s. 67.1(2) Exceptions; s. 67.3 Limitation re cost of leasing passenger vehicle.

Tax Profile: April 2004 — Interest is Almost Always a Capital Expense.

Tax Topics: No. 1673, Supreme Court's Decision on Interest Deductibility Defies Logic; No. 1517, Interest Not (Necessarily) a Capital Expense.

Forms: T777 — Statement of Employment Expenses; T2200 — Declaration of Conditions of Employment; TD1X — Statement of Commission Income and Expenses for Payroll Tax Deductions.

Guides: T4044 Employment Expenses — Supplementary Income Tax Guide.

Interpretation Bulletins: *Primary* — IT-522R Vehicle, travel and sales expenses of employees. *Secondary* — IT-352R2 Employee's expenses, including work space in home expenses.

Cases: The taxpayer was a salesman who worked largely on commission. He claimed a number of employment expenses, including salaries paid to his children, home office costs, motor vehicle expenses, meals and entertainment expenses, and the cost of supplies. He also declared a rental loss from a condominium of which he was a joint owner. In order to claim employment expenses, the taxpayer's terms of employment must require that he incur and pay such expenses. Filing Form T2200 prepared by the employer is a condition precedent to claiming certain employment expense deductions and provides evidence of the terms of employment. The taxpayer failed to meet his burden of proof for a deduction for salaries paid to his children. No record was kept of the number of hours worked, and the compensation paid was arbitrarily determined. The taxpayer had not met the conditions to claim home office expenses: he performed duties at home only 20% of the time and did not meet clients there. For motor vehicle expenses, meals and entertainment expenses, and the cost of supplies, in the absence of any supporting documentation, the amounts allowed by the Minister were reasonable. While the taxpayer claimed the source of the monthly deposits to his condominium bank account was transfers from his personal bank account, he failed to provide any supporting evidence to rebut the undeclared rental income assessed. *Brown v. The Queen*, 2017 DTC 1148 (TCC)

Salesperson expenses are only deductible to the extent that the contract of employment requires the employee to pay for them, and a prescribed form must be signed by the employer and filed. The taxpayer made false statements on his returns. Claiming amounts for clothing, not differentiating between personal and business use of cars, and failing to allocate expenses between personal and rental use showed the taxpayer was wilfully blind. Gross negligence penalties were properly assessed. *Kalryzian v. The Queen*, 2016 DTC 1161 (TCC)

The taxpayer was not remunerated by commissions related to sales volumes but by bonuses, which are not akin to commissions under s. 8. In addition, the taxpayer was not required by his employer to pay for business trip expenses, but was permitted by his employer to do so. The taxpayer failed to meet the deductibility criteria. *Tulman v. The Queen*, 2014 DTC 1144 (T.C.C.)

A stockbroker was successfully sued after resigning from his employment without notice. The judgment amount plus costs and legal fees were deductible as employment-related expenses since they were incurred as a consequence of leaving his former employer to earn more income with a larger firm. *Raphael v. The Queen*, 2008 DTC 3559 (T.C.C.)

The purchase of a client list and the related interest payments were both on account of capital and therefore not deductible under s. 8(1)(*f*). *Gifford v. The Queen et al.*, 2004 DTC 6120 (S.C.C.), affirming 2002 DTC 7197 (F.C.A.), reversing 2001 DTC 168 (T.C.C.)

A stockbroker incurred legal fees for representation before the Montreal Exchange's Disciplinary Committee and Governing Committee, before the Commission des valeurs mobilières du Québec, and in criminal proceedings. These expenses were deductible since they had been incurred for the purpose of earning income from the taxpayer's employment. *Mercille v. The Queen*, 2000 DTC 1915 (T.C.C.)

When a commissioned salesman had received from his employer a reimbursement of 25 cents per kilometre for his travelling expenses and had also been reimbursed for his meals and lodging expenses, this reasonable allowance was excluded from income so that the taxpayer could not claim sales expenses under s. 8(1)(*f*). *Lavigne v. The Queen*, 94 DTC 1571 (T.C.C.)

Occasional absences from the place of employment do not qualify the taxpayer as being "ordinarily required" to carry his duties away from his place of employment. *Stromberg v. M.N.R.*, 54 DTC 28 (T.A.B.) and 56 DTC 61. See also *Turnbull v. M.N.R.*, 60 DTC 634 (T.A.B.); *Neufeld v. M.N.R.*, 81 DTC 18 (T.R.B.); *Jalbert v. M.N.R.*, 86 DTC 1766 (T.C.C.)

► 8(1)(g) ◄

(g) Transport employee's expenses — where the taxpayer was an employee of a person whose principal business was passenger, goods, or passenger and goods transport and the duties of the employment required the taxpayer, regularly,

(i) to travel, away from the municipality where the employer's establishment to which the taxpayer reported for work was located and away from the metropolitan area, if there is one, where it was located, on vehicles used by the employer to transport the goods or passengers, and

(ii) while so away from that municipality and metropolitan area, to make disbursements for meals and lodging,

amounts so disbursed by the taxpayer in the year to the extent that the taxpayer has not been reimbursed and is not entitled to be reimbursed in respect thereof;

Related Sections: S. 6(1)(*b*)(vii) Amounts to be included as income from office or employment; s. 6(8) GST rebates re costs of property or service; s. 8(1)(*e*) Expenses of railway employees; s. 8(1)(*h*) Travel expenses; s. 8(11) Goods and services tax; s. 67.1(1) Expenses for food, etc; s. 67.1(2) Exceptions.

Forms: TL2 — Claim for Board and Lodging Expenses.

Information Circulars: IC 73-21R9 Claims for Meals and Lodging Expenses of Transport Employees.

Interpretation Bulletins: *Secondary* — IT-522R Vehicle, travel and sales expenses of employees.

▶ 8(1)(h) ◀

(h) Travel expenses — where the taxpayer, in the year,

(i) was ordinarily required to carry on the duties of the office or employment away from the employer's place of business or in different places, and

(ii) was required under the contract of employment to pay the travel expenses incurred by the taxpayer in the performance of the duties of the office or employment,

amounts expended by the taxpayer in the year (other than motor vehicle expenses) for travelling in the course of the office or employment, except where the taxpayer

(iii) received an allowance for travel expenses that was, because of subparagraph 6(1)(*b*)(v), (vi) or (vii), not included in computing the taxpayer's income for the year, or

(iv) claims a deduction for the year under paragraph (*e*), (*f*) or (*g*);

Editorial Note: Generally speaking, travel expenses include those incurred on meals, accommodation, and travel (other than automobile expenses) in the course of work-related travel. See the s. 8(4) limitation regarding meal expenses.

Related Regulations: 102(2)(*d*).

Related Sections: S. 6(8) GST rebates re costs of property or service; s. 6(9) Amount in respect of interest on employee debt; s. 8(1)(*h*.1) Motor vehicle travel expenses; s. 8(1)(*j*) Motor vehicle and aircraft costs; s. 8(1) Deductions allowed; s. 8(4) Meals; s. 8(9) Presumption; s. 8(10) Certificate of employer; s. 8(13) Work space in home; s. 81(3.1) Travel expenses; s. 248(1), "motor vehicle".

Forms: T777 — Statement of Employment Expenses; T2200 — Declaration of Conditions of Employment; TD1X — Statement of Commission Income and Expenses for Payroll Deductions.

Guides: T4044 Employment Expenses — Supplementary Income Tax Guide.

Information Circulars: IC 73-21R9 Claims for Meals and Lodging Expenses of Transport Employees.

Interpretation Bulletins: *Primary* — IT-522R Vehicle, travel and sales expenses of employees.

Tax Window Files: Employee travel - board and lodging, *April 12, 2017*, CRA Document No. 2016-0642571E5; Automobile Expenses, *Technical Interpretation, Business and Partnerships Division, July 15, 2004*, CRA Document No. 2004-0077791E5. If car expenses exceed the amount of the car allowance received, the expenses will be deductible if employee voluntarily includes the allowance in income.

Cases: While the motor vehicle expenses incurred by the taxpayer were work-related and not personal, his claim could not be allowed under paragraph 8(1)(*h*.1). The allowance was a "fixed allowance" and not a "reasonable allowance", which would have been computed by reference to the number of kilometres travelled, and the statutory requirements had not been met. A claim of 50% of cell phone expenses could be permitted under paragraph 8(1)(*h*). *Tilahun v. The Queen*, 2018 DTC 1093 (TCC)

Living expenses incurred by an R.C.M.P. officer while attending an English course in Montreal were deducible from his employment income on the ground that he had been required to carry on the duties of his office or employment away from his employer's place of business. *A.G. of Canada v. Tremblay*, 98 DTC 6008 (F.C.A.), affirming 96 DTC 3215 (T.C.C.)

As long as the requirement in their contract of employment to attend an annual Teacher's Convention took them away from the places where they usually worked, the taxpayers were entitled to deduct their convention expenses. *Imray et al. v. The Queen*, 98 DTC 6580 (F.C.T.D.)

Although provided with a free pass by the Montreal Urban Transit Authority to check the traffic flow, the taxpayer was entitled to deduct his travel expenses for the use of his own automobile in travelling to and from certain check points since it was the most practical way to perform his job as a "checker". *Stokes v. The Queen*, 93 DTC 201 (T.C.C.)

Where the terms of a taxpayer's employment as school principal did not require him ordinarily to be elsewhere than at his school, his travelling expenses for delivering reports and picking up materials could not be deducted. *Krause v. The Queen*, 93 DTC 594 (T.C.C.)

▶ 8(1)(h.1) ◀

(h.1) Motor vehicle travel expenses — where the taxpayer, in the year,

(i) was ordinarily required to carry on the duties of the office or employment away from the employer's place of business or in different places, and

(ii) was required under the contract of employment to pay motor vehicle expenses incurred in the performance of the duties of the office or employment,

amounts expended by the taxpayer in the year in respect of motor vehicle expenses incurred for travelling in the course of the office or employment, except where the taxpayer

(iii) received an allowance for motor vehicle expenses that was, because of paragraph 6(1)(*b*), not included in computing the taxpayer's income for the year, or

(iv) claims a deduction for the year under paragraph (*f*);

Related Regulations: 102(2)(*d*).

Related Sections: S. 6(8) GST rebates re costs of property or service; s. 8(1)(*j*) Motor vehicle and aircraft costs; s. 8(10) Certificate of employer; s. 18(1)(*r*) Certain automobile expenses; s. 67.3 Limitation re cost of leasing passenger vehicle; s. 81(3.1) Travel expenses; s. 248(1), "motor vehicle".

Canadian Tax Foundation: Tang and Katz, *Automobile Taxable Benefits and Expenses: Part 2*, 1998 Canadian Tax Journal 1:125–146.

Forms: T777 — Statement of Employment Expenses; T2200 — Declaration of Conditions of Employment.

Guides: T4044 Employment Expenses — Supplementary Income Tax Guide.

Cases: The taxpayer was a health care worker who used her own vehicle to travel to attend to patients in their homes. Her employer provided a per kilometre travel allowance. She included this in her income and also claimed a deduction for motor vehicle travel expenses under paragraph 8(1)(*h*.1). Although the taxpayer was not required to include the travel allowance in her income, she did so and paid tax on it. This was not caught by the statutory provision prohibiting employees who receive a motor vehicle allowance which they do not include in income from claiming a deduction for motor vehicle expenses. The qualifying travel expenses were deductible from employment income. *Kassa v. The Queen*, 2017 DTC 1139 (TCC)

Although the taxpayer received a reasonable allowance from her employer in respect of the use of her motor vehicle in the performance of her duties of employment, this did not bar her from claiming a deduction in relation to that portion of her motor vehicle travel expenses for which she was not reimbursed. *Evans v. The Queen*, 99 DTC 168 (T.C.C.)

▶ 8(1)(i) ◀

(i) Dues and other expenses of performing duties — an amount paid by the taxpayer in the year, or on behalf of the taxpayer in the year if the amount paid on behalf of the taxpayer is required to be included in the taxpayer's income for the year, as

(i) annual professional membership dues the payment of which was necessary to maintain a professional status recognized by statute,

(ii) office rent, or salary to an assistant or substitute, the payment of which by the officer or employee was required by the contract of employment,

(iii) the cost of supplies that were consumed directly in the performance of the duties of the office or employment and that the officer or employee was required by the contract of employment to supply and pay for,

(iv) annual dues to maintain membership in a trade union as defined

(A) by section 3 of the *Canada Labour Code*, or

(B) in any provincial statute providing for the investigation, conciliation or settlement of industrial disputes,

or to maintain membership in an association of public servants the primary object of which is to promote the improvement of the members' conditions of employment or work,

(v) annual dues that were, pursuant to the provisions of a collective agreement, retained by the taxpayer's employer from the taxpayer's remuneration and paid to a trade union or association designated in subparagraph (iv) of which the taxpayer was not a member,

(vi) dues to a parity or advisory committee or similar body, the payment of which was required under the laws of a province in respect of the employment for the year, and

(vii) dues to a professions board, the payment of which was required under the laws of a province, to the extent that the taxpayer has not been reimbursed, and is not entitled to be reimbursed in respect thereof;

Editorial Note: Certain expenses incurred to earn employment income are allowed to be deducted under certain circumstances. These items and the circumstances under which they are allowed to be deducted are listed below.

Professional Membership Dues: Professional dues are deductible if the fees are required to be paid to maintain a professional status recognized by statute (see *M.N.R. v. Montgomery*, 70 DTC 6080 (Ex. Ct.), reversing 69 DTC 161 (T.A.B.)). Examples of such dues would be fees payable by a lawyer to his provincial Law Society, or dues paid by a doctor, engineer or chartered accountant to his professional association. The membership dues must be payable on an annual basis (see *Daley v. M.N.R.*, 50 DTC 877 (Ex. Ct.), affirming 50 DTC 145 (T.A.B.)). A mining engineer could not deduct membership dues paid to the Canadian Institute of Mining and Metallurgy because such dues were not necessary to maintain his professional status. *Ad die v. M.N.R.*, 80 DTC 1556 (T.R.B.).

Office Rent or Assistant Salary: An employee, who is required to provide for the cost of an office under the terms of his or her employment as well as pay for an assistant or substitute, is entitled to a deduction for such costs. The employee must not be reimbursed or entitled for reimbursement, and the expenses must be reasonable. The employee must allocate qualifying home expenses on a reasonable and equitable basis. An expense deduction related to the salary of an assistant was denied in this case, since the taxpayer failed to provide the required details and documentation (see *Desouza v. The Queen*, 2005 DTC 1778 (T.C.C.)). The cost of home workspace expenses was denied because, as the owner of his corporate employer, he would not in fact have been subject by that employer to any disciplinary action for failing to pay those expenses (see *Adler v. The Queen*, 2010 DTC 1020 (T.C.C.)). In order for the taxpayer to deduct an assistant's salary under s. 8(1)(*i*)(ii), he did not have to show that his contract of employment required him to have an assistant. He only had to show that he was required to pay the salary of any assistant that he had decided to hire (see *Longtin v. The Queen*, 2006 DTC 3254 (T.C.C.)).

Cost of Supplies: An employee may deduct the cost of supplies consumed directly in the performance of the duties of his office or employment, if he is required by the contract of employment to pay for such supplies. The meaning of the word "supplies" in s. 8(1)(*i*)(iii) is limited to things or material used directly in the performance of employment duties. Therefore, the cost of a training course was not a deductible supply. *Auclair v. The Queen*, 2013 DTC 1199 (T.C.C.). A teacher was allowed a deduction for various supplies (pencils, pens, paper clips and charts) but not books, which were not "consumed" (see *Carson v. M.N.R.*, 66 DTC 424 (T.A.B.); *Krauss v. M.N.R.*, 71 DTC 577 (T.A.B.)).

Union Dues: Annual dues paid to maintain membership in a trade union, or paid as a member to an association of public servants which promotes the improvement of employee conditions, are deductible. A trade union is defined in s. 3 of the *Canada Labour Code* (or s. 26 of the present version of the *Canada Labour Code*, which supersedes clause 3 of the old version referenced in s. 8(1)(*i*)(iv)(A)).

Dues Pursuant to a Collective Agreement: Payments made to an employer pursuant to the provisions of a collective agreement, or retained by the employer from the remuneration of the employee, and paid by the employer to the trade union or association are deductible under s. 8(1)(*i*)(v). Payments of the kind contemplated in this subparagraph would ordinarily be made under the "Rand formula", a plan under which employees of the employer in question are not required to join a trade union, but are nevertheless required to pay union dues under a compulsory check-off.

Dues to a Professions Board: Dues paid by an employee to a professional board, as required under provincial or territorial law, are deductible. Such fees would not include initiation fees, licences, or special assessments for anything other than the organizations' normal operating costs. Membership fees for the Appraisal Institute of Canada are deductible (see *Montgomery et al. v. The Queen*, 99 DTC 5186 (F.C.A.), reversing 97 DTC 5510 (F.C.T.D.), reversing 96 DTC 3201 (T.C.C.)).

For home office expenses deducted under subparagraphs 8(1)(*i*)(ii) and 8(1)(*i*)(iii), see the requirements under subsection 8(13).

History: S. 8(1)(*i*), the portion before subparagraph (i) was replaced by S.C. 2013, c. 34, s. 172(2), in force June 26, 2013. S. 8(1)(*i*), the portion before subparagraph (i) formerly read:

(*i*) *Dues and other expenses of performing duties* — amounts paid by the taxpayer in the year as

Related Regulations: 102(2)(*d*); 100(3)(*b*).

Related Sections: S. 6(8) GST rebates re costs of property or service; s. 8(1)(*l*.1) C.P.P. contributions and E.I. premiums; s. 8(5) Dues not deductible; s. 8(10) Certificate of employer; s. 8(11) Goods and services tax; s. 8(13) Work space in home; s. 18(13) When s. (15) applies to money lenders.

Forms: T777 — Statement of Employment Expenses; T2200 — Declaration of Conditions of Employment; TD1X — Statement of Commission Income and Expenses for Payroll Deductions.

Guides: T4044 Employment Expenses — Supplementary Income Tax Guide.

Interpretation Bulletins: *Primary* — IT-103R Dues paid to a union or to a parity or advisory committee; IT-158R2 Employees' professional membership dues; IT-352R2 Employee's expenses, including work space in home expenses.

Tax Window Files: Deductibility of annual membership dues, *May 5, 2017*, CRA Document No. 2016-0681161E5; Employment expense-deductibility cell service plan, *July 19, 2016*, CRA Document No. 2015-0603631I7; Employment expense-deductibility cell service plan, *July 19, 2016*, CRA Document No. 2015-0603631I7; Professional membership dues, *March 5, 2015*, CRA Document No. 2014-0530691E5; Deduction — Dues Paid to Trade Union Outside Canada, *Technical Interpretation, Business and Partnerships Division, May 27, 2003*, CRA Document No. 2003-0015727. Annual dues paid to trade union located outside of Canada deductible.

Cases: The taxpayer claimed an employment expense deduction for salary paid to his wife for administrative work. There was no evidence of the taxpayer being required by his contract of employment to pay such expenses and the relevant form prepared by the taxpayer's employer indicated he was not required to pay for an assistant. There was not any evidence of a salary being paid to the wife, no T4 was issued, and no evidence of the work performed. The deduction was denied. *Blott v. The Queen*, 2018 DTC 1014 (TCC)

The meaning of the word "supplies" in s. 8(1)(*i*)(iii) is limited to things or material used directly in the performance of employment duties. Therefore, the cost of a training course was not a deductible supply. *Auclair v. The Queen*, 2013 DTC 1199 (T.C.C.)

Provincial court judges are not public servants within the meaning of s. 8(1)(*i*)(iv), and hence are not entitled to deduct membership dues in a provincial judges' association. *Crowe et al. v. The Queen*, 2002 DTC 1463 (T.C.C.)

Membership fees for the Appraisal Institute of Canada are deductible. *Montgomery et al. v. The Queen*, 99 DTC 5186 (F.C.A.), reversing 97 DTC 5510 (F.C.T.D.) which reversed 97 DTC 5510 (T.C.C.)

► 8(1)(j) ◄

(j) Motor vehicle and aircraft costs — where a deduction may be made under paragraph (*f*), (*h*) or (*h*.1) in computing the taxpayer's income from an office or employment for a taxation year,

(i) any interest paid by the taxpayer in the year on borrowed money used for the purpose of acquiring, or on an amount payable for the acquisition of, property that is

(A) a motor vehicle that is used, or

(B) an aircraft that is required for use

in the performance of the duties of the taxpayer's office or employment, and

(ii) such part, if any, of the capital cost to the taxpayer of

(A) a motor vehicle that is used, or

(B) an aircraft that is required for use

in the performance of the duties of the office or employment as is allowed by regulation;

Editorial Note: The capital cost allowance deduction allowed by this paragraph and paragraph 8(1)(*p*) (musical instruments) are the only tax depreciation deductions that are allowed for income tax purposes for employees.

Related Regulations: 102(2)(*d*); 1100(1)(*a*)(x), (x.1); Sch. II.

Related Sections: S. 6(8) GST rebates re costs of property or service; s. 8(1)(*q*) Artists' employment expenses; s. 8(9) Presumption; s. 13(7) Rules applicable; s. 13(11) Deduction in respect of property used in performance of duties; s. 67.2 Interest on money borrowed for passenger vehicle; s. 67.3 Limitation re cost of leasing passenger vehicle; s. 80(9) Reductions of adjusted cost bases of capital properties; s. 80.4 Loans; s. 80.5 Deemed interest; s. 248(1), "motor vehicle".

Forms: T777 — Statement of Employment Expenses; T2200 — Declaration of Conditions of Employment.

Guides: T4044 Employment Expenses — Supplementary Income Tax Guide.

Income Tax Folios: *Primary* — S3-F4-C1 General Discussion of Capital Cost Allowance.

Interpretation Bulletins: *Primary* — IT-522R Vehicle, travel and sales expenses of employees. *Secondary* — IT-525R (Consolid.) Performing artists.

Cases: Sections 8(1)(*j*) and 20(1)(*c*) do not provide a complete code dealing with interest deductibility. In circumstances where interest is not a payment on account of capital, it may be deducted as long as it meets the other requirements, such as those set out in s. 8(1)(*f*) or s. 18(1)(*a*), and is not precluded by some other section of the Act. *Gifford v. The Queen et al.*, 2004 DTC 6120 (S.C.C.), affirming 2002 DTC 7197 (F.C.A.), reversing 2001 DTC 168 (T.C.C.)

► 8(1)(k) ◄

(k) Unemployment insurance premium — (Repealed by 1988, c. 55, s. 2(1).)

► 8(1)(l) ◄

(l) Canada Pension Plan contribution — (Repealed by 1988, c. 55, s. 2(1).)

► 8(1)(l.1) ◄

(l.1) C.P.P. contributions and U.I.A. [E.I.] premiums — any amount payable by the taxpayer in the year

(i) as an employer's premium under the *Employment Insurance Act*, or

(ii) as an employer's contribution under the *Canada Pension Plan* or under a provincial pension plan as defined in section 3 of the *Canada Pension Plan*,

in respect of salary, wages or other remuneration, including gratuities, paid to an individual employed by the taxpayer as an assistant or substitute to perform the duties of the taxpayer's office or employment if an amount is deductible by the taxpayer for the year under subparagraph (*i*)(ii) in respect of that individual;

Related Sections: S. 60(*e*) CPP/QPP contributions on self-employed earnings; s. 118.7 Credit for EI premium and CPP contribution.

Interpretation Bulletins: *Secondary* — IT-352R2 Employee's expenses, including work space in home expenses.

► 8(1)(l.2) ◄

(l.2) Quebec parental insurance plan — an amount payable by the taxpayer in the year as an employer's premium under the *Act respecting parental insurance*, R.S.Q., c. A-29.011 in respect of salary, wages or other remuneration, including gratuities, paid to an individual employed by the taxpayer as an assistant or substitute to perform the duties of the taxpayer's office or employment if an amount is deductible by the taxpayer for the year under subparagraph (*i*)(ii) in respect of that individual;

History: S. 8(1)(*l*.2) was added by S.C. 2013, c. 34, s. 172(3), applicable to the 2006 and subsequent taxation years.

► 8(1)(m) ◄

(m) Employee's registered pension plan contributions — the amount in respect of contributions to registered pension plans that, by reason of subsection 147.2(4), is deductible in computing the taxpayer's income for the year;

Related Regulations: 100(3)(*a*).

Related Sections: S. 18(11) Borrowed money used for contribution; s. 20(1)(*q*) Employer's contributions to registered pension plan; s. 60(*j*) Transfer of superannuation benefits; s. 60(*j*.01) Transfer of surplus; s. 60(*j*.02) Payment to registered pension plan; s. 60(*j*.03) Repayments of pre-1990 pension benefits; s. 60(*j*.04) Repayments of post-1989 pension benefits; s. 60(*j*.1) Transfer of retiring allowances; s. 60.2 Refund of undeducted past service AVCs; s. 146(1), "earned income"; s. 147.1 Registered pension plans; s. 248(1), "additional voluntary contribution", "registered pension plan".

Tax Profile: October 2007 — Important Changes Announced to the Canada — U.S. Income Tax Convention.

Information Circulars: IC 72-13R8 Employees' pension plans.

Interpretation Bulletins: *Primary* — IT-167R6 Registered pension plans — Employee's contributions.

► 8(1)(m.1) ◄

(m.1) Idem — (Repealed by 1990, c. 35, s. 2(2).)

► 8(1)(m.2) ◄

(m.2) Employee RCA contributions — an amount contributed by the taxpayer in the year to a pension plan in respect of services rendered by the taxpayer where the plan is a prescribed plan established by an enactment of Canada or a province or where

(i) the plan is a retirement compensation arrangement,

(ii) the amount was paid to a custodian (within the meaning assigned by the definition "retirement compensation arrangement" in subsection 248(1)) of the arrangement who is resident in Canada, and

(iii) either

(A) the taxpayer was required, by the terms of the taxpayer's office or employment, to contribute the amount, and the total of the amounts contributed to the plan in the year by the taxpayer does not exceed the total of the amounts contributed to the plan in the year by any other person in respect of the taxpayer, or

(B) the plan is a pension plan the registration of which under this Act was revoked (other than a plan the registration of which was revoked as of the effective date of its registration) and the amount was contributed in accordance with the terms of the plan as last registered;

(C) (Repealed by S.C. 1994, c. 21, s. 4(2).)

Related Regulations: 100(3)(*b*.1); 6802; 6802.1(1); 6803.

Related Sections: S. 18(11)(*e*) Borrowed money used for contribution; s. 20(1)(*r*) Employer's contributions under retirement compensation arrangement; s. 56(1)(*x*) Retirement compensation arrangement — employee recipient; s. 56(1)(*y*) Retirement compensation arrangement — proceeds of disposition; s. 56(1)(*z*) Retirement compensation arrangement — non-employee recipient; s. 60(*t*)(ii) RCA distributions; s. 60(*u*)(ii) RCA dispositions; s. 146(1), "earned income"; s. 207.6(6) Prescribed plan or arrangement; s. 207.6(7) Transfers; s. 248(1), "prescribed".

Canadian Tax Foundation: Kahane et al., *A Fresh Look at Retirement Compensation Arrangements: A Flexible Vehicle for Retirement Planning*, 2013 Canadian Tax Journal 2:479–502.

► 8(1)(n) ◄

(n) Salary reimbursement — an amount paid by or on behalf of the taxpayer in the year pursuant to an arrangement (other than an arrangement described in subparagraph (*b*)(ii) of the definition "top-up disability payment" in subsection 6(17)) under which the taxpayer is required to reimburse any amount paid to the taxpayer for a period throughout which the taxpayer did not perform the duties of the office or employment, to the extent that

(i) the amount so paid to the taxpayer for the period was included in computing the taxpayer's income from an office or employment, and

(ii) the total of amounts so reimbursed does not exceed the total of amounts received by the taxpayer for the period throughout which the taxpayer did not perform the duties of the office or employment;

Related Sections: S. 5(1) Income from office or employment; s. 8(1)(*n*.1) Reimbursement of disability payments.

Interpretation Bulletins: *Secondary* — IT-202R2 Employees' or workers' compensation.

► 8(1)(n.1) ◄

(n.1) Reimbursement of disability payments — where,

(i) as a consequence of the receipt of a payment (in this paragraph referred to as the "deferred payment") from an insurer, a payment (in this paragraph referred to as the "reimbursement payment") is made by or on behalf of an individual to an employer or former employer of the individual pursuant to an arrangement described in subparagraph (*b*)(ii) of the definition "top-up disability payment" in subsection 6(17), and

(ii) the reimbursement payment is made

(A) in the year, other than within the first 60 days of the year if the deferred payment was received in the immediately preceding taxation year, or

(B) within 60 days after the end of the year, if the deferred payment was received in the year,

an amount equal to the lesser of

(iii) the amount included under paragraph 6(1)(*f*) in respect of the deferred payment in computing the individual's income for any taxation year, and

(iv) the amount of the reimbursement payment;

Related Sections: S. 6(18) Group disability benefits — insolvent insurer; s. 8(1)(*n*) Salary reimbursement.

► 8(1)(o) ◄

(o) Forfeited amounts — where at the end of the year the rights of any person to receive benefits under a salary deferral arrangement in respect of the taxpayer have been extinguished or no person has any further right to receive any amount under the arrangement, the amount, if any, by which the total of all deferred amounts under the arrangement included in computing the taxpayer's income for the year and preceding taxation years as benefits under paragraph 6(1)(*a*) exceeds the total of

(i) all such deferred amounts received by any person in that year or preceding taxation years out of or under the arrangement,

(ii) all such deferred amounts receivable by any person in subsequent taxation years out of or under the arrangement, and

(iii) all amounts deducted under this paragraph in computing the taxpayer's income for preceding taxation years in respect of deferred amounts under the arrangement;

Related Sections: S. 6(1)(*i*) Salary deferral arrangement payments; s. 6(14) Part of plan or arrangement; s. 12(1)(*n*.2) Forfeited salary deferral amounts; s. 248(1), "deferred amount", "salary deferral arrangement".

► 8(1)(o.1) ◄

(o.1) Idem — an amount that is deductible in computing the taxpayer's income for the year because of subsection 144(9);

Related Sections: S. 6(1)(*d*) Allocations, etc., under profit sharing plan.

Interpretation Bulletins: *Secondary* — IT-379R Employees profit sharing plans — Allocations to beneficiaries.

► 8(1)(o.2) ◄

(o.2) Excess EPSP amounts — an amount that is an excess EPSP amount (as defined in subsection 207.8(1)) of the taxpayer for the year, other than any portion of the excess EPSP amount for which the taxpayer's tax for the year under subsection 207.8(2) is waived or cancelled;

Editorial Note: To address concerns that employee profit sharing plans ("EPSPs") have been used by business owners to direct profits to members of their families to reduce or defer payment of income tax on these profits *and* reduce excessive employer contributions, Part XI.4 tax was introduced. The tax is payable by a specified employee (defined in subsection 248(1)). To prevent double taxation, the excess EPSP amount is deducted in computing the employee's income under paragraph 8(1)(o.2).

History: S. 8(1)(*o*.2) was added by S.C. 2012, c. 31, s. 3(1), applicable to the 2012 and subsequent taxation years.

Related Sections: S. 6(1)(*d*) Allocations, etc., under profit sharing plan.

▶ 8(1)(p) ◀

(p) Musical instrument costs — where the taxpayer was employed in the year as a musician and as a term of the employment was required to provide a musical instrument for a period in the year, an amount (not exceeding the taxpayer's income for the year from the employment, computed without reference to this paragraph) equal to the total of

(i) amounts expended by the taxpayer before the end of the year for the maintenance, rental or insurance of the instrument for that period, except to the extent that the amounts are otherwise deducted in computing the taxpayer's income for any taxation year, and

(ii) such part, if any, of the capital cost to the taxpayer of the instrument as is allowed by regulation;

Editorial Note: See the note to paragraph 8(1)(*j*).

Related Regulations: 1100(1)(*a*)(viii); Sch. II.

Related Sections: S. 6(8) GST rebates re costs of property or service; s. 8(1)(*q*) Artists' employment expenses; s. 13(7) Rules applicable; s. 13(11) Deduction in respect of property used in performance of duties; s. 80(9) Reductions of adjusted cost bases of capital properties.

Income Tax Folios: *Primary* — S3-F4-C1 General Discussion of Capital Cost Allowance.

Interpretation Bulletins: *Secondary* — IT-525R (Consolid.) Performing artists; IT-257R Canada Council grants.

▶ 8(1)(q) ◀

(q) Artists' employment expenses — where the taxpayer's income for the year from the office or employment includes income from an artistic activity

(i) that was the creation by the taxpayer of, but did not include the reproduction of, paintings, prints, etchings, drawings, sculptures or similar works of art,

(ii) that was the composition by the taxpayer of a dramatic, musical or literary work,

(iii) that was the performance by the taxpayer of a dramatic or musical work as an actor, dancer, singer or musician, or

(iv) in respect of which the taxpayer was a member of a professional artists' association that is certified by the Minister of Canadian Heritage,

amounts paid by the taxpayer before the end of the year in respect of expenses incurred for the purpose of earning the income from those activities to the extent that they were not deductible in computing the taxpayer's income for a preceding taxation year, but not exceeding a single amount in respect of all such offices and employments of the taxpayer equal to the amount, if any, by which

(v) the lesser of $1,000 and 20% of the total of all amounts each of which is the taxpayer's income from an office or employment for the year, before deducting any amount under this section, that was income from an artistic activity described in any of subparagraphs (i) to (iv),

exceeds

(vi) the total of all amounts deducted by the taxpayer for the year under paragraph (*j*) or (*p*) in respect of costs or expenses incurred for the purpose of earning the income from such an activity for the year;

Forms: T777 — Statement of Employment Expenses.

Interpretation Bulletins: *Primary* — IT-525R (Consolid.) Performing artists. *Secondary* — IT-257R Canada Council grants; 504R2 Visual artists and writers.

▶ 8(1)(r) ◀

(r) Apprentice mechanics' tool costs — if the taxpayer was an eligible apprentice mechanic at any time after 2001 and before the end of the taxation year, the amount claimed by the taxpayer for the taxation year under this paragraph not exceeding the lesser of

(i) the taxpayer's income for the taxation year computed without reference to this paragraph, and

(ii) the amount determined by the formula

$$(A - B) + C$$

where

A is the total of all amounts each of which is the cost to the taxpayer of an eligible tool acquired in the taxation year by the taxpayer or, if the taxpayer first becomes employed as an eligible apprentice mechanic in the taxation year, the cost to the taxpayer of an eligible tool acquired by the taxpayer in the last three months of the preceding taxation year,

B is the lesser of

(A) the value of A for the taxation year in respect of the taxpayer, and

(B) the greater of

(I) the amount that is the total of $500 and the amount determined for the taxation year for B in subsection 118(10), and

(II) 5% of the total of

1. the total of all amounts each of which is the taxpayer's income from employment for the taxation year as an eligible apprentice mechanic, computed without reference to this paragraph, and

2. the amount, if any, by which the amount required by paragraph 56(1)(*n*.1) to be included in computing the taxpayer's income for the taxation year exceeds the amount

required by paragraph 60(*p*) to be deducted in computing that income, and

C is the amount by which the amount determined under this subparagraph for the preceding taxation year in respect of the taxpayer exceeds the amount deducted under this paragraph for that preceding taxation year by the taxpayer; and

Related Sections: S. 6(8) GST rebates re costs of property or service; s. 8(1)(*s*) Deduction — tradesperson's tools; s. 8(6) Apprentice mechanics; s. 8(7) Cost of tool; s. 53(2)(*m*) Amounts to be deducted — Deductible cost of property; s. 56(1)(*k*) Certain tools of an employee, re proceeds; s. 85(5.1) Acquisition of certain tools — capital cost and deemed depreciation; s. 97(5) Acquisition of certain tools — capital cost and deemed depreciation.

Guides: T4044 Employment Expenses — Supplementary Income Tax Guide.

Interpretation Bulletins: *Secondary* — IT-291R3 Transfer of property to a corporation under subsection 85(1).

▶ 8(1)(s) ◀

(s) Deduction — tradesperson's tools — if the taxpayer is employed as a tradesperson at any time in the taxation year, the lesser of $500 and the amount determined by the formula

A - $1,000

where

A is the lesser of

(i) the total of all amounts each of which is the cost of an eligible tool acquired by the taxpayer in the year, and

(ii) the total of

(A) the amount that would, if this subsection were read without reference to this paragraph, be the taxpayer's income for the taxation year from employment as a tradesperson in the taxation year, and

(B) the amount, if any, by which the amount required by paragraph 56(1)(*n*.1) to be included in computing the taxpayer's income for the taxation year exceeds the amount required by paragraph 60(*p*) to be deducted in computing that income.

> **CRA News Release**
>
> **2.2% Indexation Factor for 2019**
>
> **See the CRA Fact Sheet, dated November 16, 2018, that is reproduced following subsection117.1(1). This release announces a 2.2% indexation factor applicable for 2019 tax bracket thresholds, personal amounts and other amounts relating to non-refundable credits, as well as the refundable medical expense supplement, Old Age Security repayment threshold, certain board and lodging allowances, and the tradesperson's tools deduction. Increases to tax bracket thresholds, amounts relating to non-refundable credits, and most other amounts will take effect on January 1, 2019. However, increases in amounts for certain income-tested benefits (for example, the goods and services tax credit) will take effect on July 1, 2019.**

Related Sections: S. 8(6.1) Eligible tool of tradesperson; s. 8(7) Cost of tool.

Guides: T4044 Employment Expenses — Supplementary Income Tax Guide.

▶ 8(2) ◀

(2) General limitation. Except as permitted by this section, no deductions shall be made in computing a taxpayer's income for a taxation year from an office or employment.

Income Tax Folios: *Secondary* — S3-F4-C1 General Discussion of Capital Cost Allowance.

Interpretation Bulletins: *Secondary* — IT-352R2 Employee's expenses, including work space in home expenses.

Tax Window Files: Reimbursement of Moving Expenses, *Technical Interpretation, Business and Partnerships Division, October 25, 2004,* CRA Document No. 2004-0080871E5. No deduction for individual required to repay reimbursed relocation expenses to his former employer.

▶ 8(3) ◀

(3) Limitation re employment expense deduction — (Repealed by 1988, c. 55, s. 2(3).)

▶ 8(4) ◀

(4) Meals. An amount expended in respect of a meal consumed by a taxpayer who is an officer or employee shall not be included in computing the amount of a deduction under paragraph (1)(*f*) or (*h*) unless the meal was consumed during a period while the taxpayer was required by the taxpayer's duties to be away, for a period of not less than twelve hours, from the municipality where the employer's establishment to which the taxpayer ordinarily reported for work was located and away from the metropolitan area, if there is one, where it was located.

Related Sections: S. 67.1(1) Expenses for food, etc.

Forms: T777 — Statement of Employment Expenses; TD1X — Statement of Commission Income and Expenses for Payroll Deductions.

Information Circulars: IC 73-21R9 Claims for Meals and Lodging Expenses of Transport Employees.

Interpretation Bulletins: *Secondary* — IT-522R Vehicle, travel and sales expenses of employees.

▶ 8(5) ◀

(5) Dues not deductible. Notwithstanding subparagraphs (1)(*i*)(i), (iv), (vi) and (vii), dues are not deductible under those subparagraphs in computing a taxpayer's income from an office or employment to the extent that they are, in effect, levied

(*a*) for or under a superannuation fund or plan;

(*b*) for or under a fund or plan for annuities, insurance (other than professional or malpractice liability insurance that is necessary to maintain a professional status recognized by statute) or similar benefits; or

(*c*) for any other purpose not directly related to the ordinary operating expenses of the committee or similar body, association, board or trade union, as the case may be.

Interpretation Bulletins: *Secondary* — IT-103R Dues paid to a union or to a parity or advisory committee; IT-158R2 Employees' professional membership dues.

▶ 8(6) ◀

(6) Apprentice mechanics. For the purpose of paragraph (1)(*r*),

(*a*) a taxpayer is an eligible apprentice mechanic in a taxation year if, at any time in the taxation year, the taxpayer

(i) is registered in a program established in accordance with the laws of Canada or of a province that leads to designation under those laws as a mechanic licensed to repair self-propelled motorized vehicles, and

(ii) is employed as an apprentice mechanic;

(*b*) an eligible tool is a tool (including ancillary equipment) that

(i) is acquired by a taxpayer for use in connection with the taxpayer's employment as an eligible apprentice mechanic,

(ii) has not been used for any purpose before it is acquired by the taxpayer,

(iii) is certified in prescribed form by the taxpayer's employer to be required to be provided by the taxpayer as a condition of, and for use in, the taxpayer's employment as an eligible apprentice mechanic, and

(iv) is, unless the device or equipment can be used only for the purpose of measuring, locating or calculating, not an electronic communication device or electronic data processing equipment; and

(*c*) a taxpayer who, for a taxation year, is not an eligible apprentice mechanic and has an excess amount determined under the description of C in subparagraph (1)(*r*)(ii) is, for the taxation year, entitled to claim a deduction under that paragraph as if that excess amount were wholly applicable to an employment of the taxpayer.

Forms: T2200 — Declaration of Conditions of Employment.

▶ 8(6.1) ◀

(6.1) Eligible tool of tradesperson. For the purposes of paragraph (1)(*s*), an eligible tool of a taxpayer is a tool (including ancillary equipment) that

(*a*) is acquired by the taxpayer on or after May 2, 2006 for use in connection with the taxpayer's employment as a tradesperson;

(*b*) has not been used for any purpose before it is acquired by the taxpayer;

(*c*) is certified in prescribed form by the taxpayer's employer to be required to be provided by the taxpayer as a condition of, and for use in, the taxpayer's employment as a tradesperson; and

(*d*) is, unless the device or equipment can be used only for the purpose of measuring, locating or calculating, not an electronic communication device or electronic data processing equipment.

Forms: T2200 — Declaration of Conditions of Employment.

Guides: T4044 Employment Expenses — Supplementary Income Tax Guide.

▶ 8(7) ◀

(7) Cost of tool. Except for the purposes of the description of A in subparagraph (1)(*r*)(ii) and the description of A in paragraph (1)(*s*), the cost to a taxpayer of an eligible tool the cost of which was included in determining the value of one or both of those descriptions in respect of the taxpayer for a taxation year is the amount determined by the formula

$$K - (K \times L/M)$$

where

K is the cost to the taxpayer of the tool determined without reference to this subsection;

L is

(*a*) if the tool is a tool to which only paragraph (1)(*r*) applies in the taxation year, the amount that would be determined under subparagraph (1)(*r*)(ii) in respect of the taxpayer for the taxation year if the value of C in that subparagraph were nil,

(*b*) if the tool is a tool to which only paragraph (1)(*s*) applies in the taxation year, the amount determined under that paragraph to be deductible by the taxpayer in the taxation year, or

(*c*) if the tool is a tool to which both paragraphs (1)(*r*) and (*s*) apply in the taxation year, the amount that is the total of

(i) the amount that would be determined under subparagraph (1)(*r*)(ii) in respect of the taxpayer for the taxation year if the value of C in that subparagraph were nil, and

(ii) the amount determined under paragraph (1)(*s*) to be deductible by the taxpayer in the taxation year; and

M is the amount that is

(*a*) if the tool is a tool to which only paragraph (1)(*r*) applies in the taxation year, the value of A determined under subparagraph (1)(*r*)(ii) in respect of the taxpayer for the taxation year,

(*b*) if the tool is a tool to which only paragraph (1)(*s*) applies in the taxation year, the amount determined under subparagraph (i) of the description of A in paragraph (1)(*s*) in respect of the taxpayer for the taxation year, and

(*c*) if the tool is a tool to which both paragraphs (1)(*r*) and (*s*) apply in the taxation year, the amount that is the greater of the value of A determined under subparagraph (1)(*r*)(ii) in respect of the taxpayer for the taxation year and the amount determined under subparagraph (i) of the description of A in paragraph (1)(*s*) in respect of the taxpayer for the taxation year.

Related Sections: S. 85(5.1) Acquisition of certain tools — capital cost and deemed depreciation; s. 97(5) Acquisition of certain tools — capital cost and deemed depreciation.

Interpretation Bulletins: *Secondary* — IT-291R3 Transfer of property to a corporation under subsection 85(1).

▶ 8(8) ◀

(8) Employees' contributions to pension fund for arrears — (Repealed by 1990, c. 35, s. 2(6).)

▶ 8(9) ◀

(9) Presumption. Notwithstanding any other provision of this Act, the total of all amounts that would otherwise be deductible by a taxpayer pursuant to paragraph (1)(*f*), (*h*) or (*j*) for travelling in the course of the taxpayer's employment in an aircraft that is owned or rented by the taxpayer, may not exceed an amount that is reasonable in the circumstances having regard to the relative cost and availability of other modes of transportation.

Related Sections: S. 67 General limitation re expenses.

Interpretation Bulletins: *Secondary* — IT-522R Vehicle, travel and sales expenses of employees.

▶ 8(10) ◀

(10) Certificate of employer. An amount otherwise deductible for a taxation year under paragraph (1)(*c*), (*f*), (*h*) or (*h*.1) or subparagraph (1)(*i*)(ii) or (iii) by a taxpayer shall not be deducted unless a prescribed form, signed by the taxpayer's employer certifying that the conditions set out in the applicable provision were met in the year in respect of the taxpayer, is filed with the taxpayer's return of income for the year.

Forms: T2200 — Declaration of Conditions of Employment.

Information Circulars: IC 73-21R9 Claims for meals and lodging expenses of transport employees.

Interpretation Bulletins: *Secondary* — IT-352R2 Employee's expenses, including work space in home expenses; IT-522R Vehicle, travel and sales expenses of employees.

Tax Window Files: Employment Expenses — Work Space In Home, *Technical Interpretation, Business and Partnerships Division, May 26, 2005,* CRA Document No. 2005-0124821E5. General guidelines as to when an employer should issue Form T2200 to an employee.

▶ 8(11) ◀

(11) Goods and services tax. For the purposes of this section and section 6, the amount of any rebate paid or payable to a taxpayer under the *Excise Tax Act* in respect of the goods and services tax shall be deemed not to be an amount that is reimbursed to the taxpayer or to which the taxpayer is entitled.

Related Sections: S. 6(7) Cost of property or service; s. 6(8) GST rebates re costs of property or service; s. 248(17) Application of s. (16) to passenger vehicles and aircraft; s. 248(18) Goods and services tax — repayment of input tax credit.

▶ 8(12) ◀

(12) Forfeiture of securities by employee. If, in a taxation year,

(*a*) an employee is deemed by subsection 7(2) to have disposed of a security (as defined in subsection 7(7)) held by a trust,

(*b*) the trust disposed of the security to the person that issued the security,

(*c*) the disposition occurred as a result of the employee not meeting the conditions necessary for title to the security to vest in the employee, and

(*d*) the amount paid by the person to acquire the security from the trust or to redeem or cancel the security did not exceed the amount paid to the person for the security,

the following rules apply:

(*e*) there may be deducted in computing the employee's income for the year from employment the amount, if any, by which

(i) the amount of the benefit deemed by subsection 7(1) to have been received by the employee in the year or a preceding taxation year in respect of the security

exceeds

(ii) any amount deducted under paragraph 110(1)(*d*) or (*d*.1) in computing the employee's taxable income for the year or a preceding taxation year in respect of that benefit, and

(*f*) notwithstanding any other provision of this Act, the employee's gain or loss from the disposition of the security is deemed to be nil and section 84 does not apply to deem a dividend to have been received in respect of the disposition.

Forms: T777 — Statement of Employment Expenses.

▶ 8(13) ◀

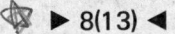

(13) Work space in home. Notwithstanding paragraphs (1)(*f*) and (*i*),

(*a*) no amount is deductible in computing an individual's income for a taxation year from an office or employment in respect of any part (in this subsection referred to as the "work space") of a self-contained domestic establishment in which the individual resides, except to the extent that the work space is either

(i) the place where the individual principally performs the duties of the office or employment, or

(ii) used exclusively during the period in respect of which the amount relates for the purpose of earning income from the office or employment and used on a regular and continuous basis for meeting customers or other persons in the ordinary course of performing the duties of the office or employment;

(*b*) where the conditions set out in subparagraph (*a*)(i) or (ii) are met, the amount in respect of the work space that is deductible in computing the individual's income for the year from the office or employment shall not exceed the individual's income for the year from the office or employment, computed without reference to any deduction in respect of the work space; and

(*c*) any amount in respect of a work space that was, solely because of paragraph (*b*), not deductible in computing the individual's income for the immediately preceding taxation year from the office or employment shall be deemed to be an amount in respect of a work space that is otherwise deductible in computing the individual's income for the year from that office or employment and that, subject to paragraph (*b*), may be deducted in computing the individual's income for the year from the office or employment.

Editorial Note: A deduction for home office expenses is limited to the taxpayer's employment income (before the expenses). Any excess expenses can be carried forward and deducted in the following year, subject to the same limitation. Non-commissioned and commissioned employees can deduct a portion of rent (s. 8(1)(*i*)(ii)), and heat and utilities (which are considered "supplies" under s. 8(1)(*i*)(iii)). Commissioned employees can deduct a portion of property taxes and house insurance (s. 8(1)(*f*)). Neither can deduct capital cost allowance in respect of the house or mortgage interest.

Related Sections: S. 248(1), "self-contained domestic establishment".

Canadian Tax Foundation: Gaucher, *A Worker's Status as Employee or Independent Contractor,* 1999 Conference Report 33:1–98; Roy, *Taxing the Virtual Office,* 1996 Conference Report 31:1–19.

Forms: T2200 — Declaration of Conditions of Employment.

Guides: T4044 Employment Expenses — Supplementary Income Tax Guide.

Interpretation Bulletins: *Secondary* — IT-352R2 Employee's expenses, including work space in home expenses.

Tax Window Files: Employment Expenses — Work Space In Home, *Technical Interpretation, Business and Partnerships Division, May 26, 2005,* CRA Document No. 2005-0124821E5. General guidelines as to when an employer should issue Form T2200 to an employee.

Subdivision b — Income or Loss from a Business or Property

Basic Rules

SECTION 9: Income

► 9(1) ◄

(1) Income. Subject to this Part, a taxpayer's income for a taxation year from a business or property is the taxpayer's profit from that business or property for the year.

Editorial Note: The computation of profit is subject to six "guiding principles" set out by the Supreme Court of Canada in the *Canderel* (98 DTC 6100 (S.C.C.), reversing 95 DTC 5101 (F.C.A.)) and *Toronto College Park* (98 DTC 6088 (S.C.C.), reversing 96 DTC 6407 (F.C.A.)) decisions (see "Cases" below). According to these principles, a taxpayer is "free to adopt any method which is not inconsistent with" the provisions of the Act, legal principles and well-accepted business principles, although the method must also provide an accurate picture of the taxpayer's income position. However, since well-accepted business principles are interpretive aids only, and not rules of law, it appears that a method of computing profit which is consistent with the provisions of the Act and the legal principles will suffice, assuming that it provides an accurate picture of income (see, for example, the *Urbandale Realty* (2000 DTC 6118 (F.C.A.), reversing 97 DTC 5353 (F.C.T.D.) and 93 DTC 154 (T.C.C.)) decision under "Cases" below).

Related Sections: S. 10 Valuation of inventory; s. 11 Proprietor of business; s. 12(1) Income inclusions; s. 12(2) Interpretation; s. 18(1)(a) General limitation; s. 18(1)(b) Capital outlay or loss; s. 20(1) Deductions permitted in computing income from business or property; s. 34 Professional business; s. 248(1), "business", "property"; s. 249 Definition of "taxation year".

Canadian Tax Foundation: Man et al., *Current Cases: Federal Court of Appeal — No Break on Break Fees (Morguard Corporation v. Canada, 2012 FCA 306)*, 2013 Canadian Tax Journal 2:435–440; Woltersdorf and Gislason, *Selected Topics: Purchase and Sale of a Business*, 2013 Prairie Provinces Tax Conference 5:1–49; Tollstam, *Crowdfunding Proceeds Are Business Income*, 2013 Canadian Tax Highlights 21(11):8; Gill, *CRA: Crowdfunding Receipts Are Taxable*, 2013 Canadian Tax Focus 3(4):6–7; Alarie, *The Taxation of Winnings from Poker and Other Gambling Activities in Canada*, 2011 Canadian Tax Journal 4:731–763; McDonnell, *REOP Revisited*, 2003 Tax for the Owner-Manager 3(3):8; Sibson, *Reasonable Expectation of Profit: A Return to Sanity?*, 2002 Conference Report 6:1–10; Laiken and Laiken, *Working With the Source Test: The Supreme Court's Replacement for the Reasonable Expectation of Profit Test*, 2002 Canadian Tax Journal 3:1147–1177; Walker, *Timing and Recognition of Income*, 2001 Conference Report 29:1–42; Arnold and Darmo, *Summary of the Proceedings of an Invitational Seminar on the Attribution of Profits to Permanent Establishments*, 2001 Canadian Tax Journal 3:525–549; Weinstein, *Damages, Fines, And Penalties: An Update*, 2000 Conference Report 7:1–29; Carr, *Current Receipts and Expenses After Canderel, Toronto College Park, and Ikea*, 1998 Canadian Tax Journal 5:953–991; Frankovic, *The Matching of "Current" Expense Under Canada's Income Tax Laws*, 1998 Canadian Tax Journal 1:1–28; Beam and Laiken, *"Adventure or Concern in the Nature of Trade": "Badges of Trade" as the Key Indicator of Taxpayer Intention*, 1996 Canadian Tax Journal 3:888–913.

Tax Profile: February 2005 — The Canadian Treatment of Derivatives.

Tax Topics: No. 2321, Mark-to-Market: Established Legal Principle?; No. 2261, Principles in the Computation of Profit: Unanswered Questions?; No. 2092, The "Business" of Earning Break Fees; No. 1971-72, 2009 Canadian Tax Foundation Conference: Wizards, Tiny Taxes and "Evil" Kirk; No. 1961, Impact of IFRS on the Canadian Tax Practitioner; No. 1928, Potential Conflict? Sections 9 and 10 of the *Income Tax Act*; No. 1872, Lease Cancellation Payment Received by Landlord; No. 1838, Conversion of Vacant Land from Capital Property to Inventory; No. 1805, The Matching Principle: RIP; No. 1791, Budget Proposals Regarding Functional Currency Tax Reporting; No. 1745, Characterizing Convertible Hedges: Round Holes Cannot Fit Into Square Pegs; No. 1578, After REOP, Where Do We GAAR From Here?; No. 1506, Supreme Court to Rule on the "reasonable expectation of profit" and Related Issues.

Forms: T776 — Statement of Real Estate Rentals; T2042 — Statement of Farming Activities; T2121 — Statement of Fishing Activities; T2125 — Statement of Business or Professional Activities.

Guides: RC4110 Employee or Self-employed?; P134 Using Your Home for Day Care; RC4015 Reconciliation of Business Income for Tax Purposes; T4002 Self-employed Business, Professional, Commission, Farming, and Fishing Income; T4004 Fishing Income.

Income Tax Folios: *Secondary* — S4-F11-C1 Meaning of Farming and Farming Business; S3-F6-C1 Interest Deductibility.

Income Tax Technical News: Issue No. 44, IFRS and Foreign GAAP; Issue No. 41, Conversion from Canadian GAAP to IFRS; Issue No. 38, Criteria for Determining Hedge Effectiveness for Tax Purposes; Issue No. 32, Reserve for Prepaid Amount: Impact of the Ellis Vision case; Issue No. 30, Prepaid Income — Whether Subsection 9(1) or Paragraph 12(1)(a) Applies?; Issue No. 25, Reasonable Expectation of Profit.

Interpretation Bulletins: *Primary* — IT-92R2 Income of contractors; IT-95R Foreign exchange gains and losses; IT-129R Lawyers' trust accounts and disbursements; IT-200 Surface rentals and farming operations; IT-218R Profit, capital gains and losses from the sale of real estate, including farmland and inherited land and conversion of real estate from capital property to inventory and vice versa; IT-261R Prepayments of rents; IT-346R Commodity futures and certain commodities; IT-359R2 Premiums and other amounts with respect to leases; IT-373R2 (Consolid.) Woodlots; IT-417R2 Prepaid expenses and deferred charges; IT-454 Business transactions prior to incorporation; IT-504R2 (Consolid.) Visual artists and writers. *Secondary* — IT-99R5 (Consolid.) Legal and accounting fees; IT-293R Debtor's gain on settlement of debt; IT-403R Options on real estate; IT-434R Rental of real property by individual; IT-444R Corporations — Involuntary dissolutions; IT-479R Transactions in securities; IT-490 Barter transactions.

Tax Window Files: Treatment of bond locks, *October 21, 2015*, CRA Document No. 2015-0592781I7; Crowdfunding, *April 1, 2015*, CRA Document No. 2015-0579031I7; Lottery Ticket Retailers, *July 5, 2013*, CRA Document No. 2013-0491991I7.

Cases: The taxpayer entered into a forward contract with respect to bank shares he owned in the expectation such shares would decline in value over the short term but would constitute a good long-term investment. The value did not decrease and the taxpayer made cash settlement payments under the contract of about $10 million in 2004-2006. The shares held by the taxpayer were capital property in his hands, so if the contract had the effect of hedging the risk linked to those shares any losses incurred by making cash settlements would be capital (not business) losses. The contract would be a hedging instrument if it neutralized or mitigated the risk to which the underlying asset was exposed. This was the effect of the contract, and it was a hedging instrument, and the losses were capital losses. *The Queen v. MacDonald*, 2018 DTC 5077 (FCA), reversing 2017 DTC 1104 [Under appeal]

The taxpayer and a predecessor corporation made payments to individuals who held options to acquire shares of the corporations. When the payments were made, the options were automatically extinguished at the moment of the transaction and were not acquired by the payor corporation. The payments were consideration for the termination of those options and were not the cost of the options. They were incurred by the corporations in respect of their businesses, on account of capital, for the purpose of gaining or producing income from those businesses, thus satisfying the definition of eligible capital expenditure, and were deductible. *Devon Canada Corporation v. The Queen*, 2018 DTC 1117 (TCC)

In determining whether a taxpayer's conduct constituted an adventure in the nature of trade, the critical factor is the intention of the taxpayer at the time the property in question is acquired, and such intention is to be ascertained from the taxpayer's whole course of conduct. The taxpayer, who was employed in the securities industry for several years, was found to be trading in securities personally as a business activity, or at least as part of an adventure in the nature of trade. *Andrew Foote v. The Queen*, 2017 DTC 1032 (TCC)

The taxpayer accepted $15.8 million from the government to dispose of all its right and interest in a property that had been rezoned. This amount was not income; it was a non-taxable capital receipt. *Henco Industries Limited v. The Queen*, 2014 DTC 1161 (T.C.C.)

The limited partnerships' yacht chartering business was a Ponzi-like fraudulent scheme that could not give rise to a source of income and could not be considered a business. The limited partnerships were not partnerships at law because they were not carrying on business in common with a view to profit. *Garber v. The Queen*, 2014 DTC 1045 (T.C.C.) [Under appeal]

Following an unsuccessful takeover bid, the taxpayer received a break fee from the target corporation. This was business income and not a capital gain since the taxpayer's business included acquiring controlling positions in public corporations and the break fee was received in the ordinary course of that business. *Morguard Corporation v. The Queen*, 2013 DTC 5009 (F.C.A.), affirming 2012 DTC 1099 (T.C.C.)

A lawyer could not deduct $121,991 in gambling losses since his "professional" poker playing did not constitute a business. *Cohen v. The Queen*, 2011 DTC 1195 (T.C.C.)

The taxpayers participated extensively in sports lotteries using a methodology that increased their potential payout and risk significantly. Although they lost 95% of the time, they had net winnings of $5,523,088. However, they were not professional gamblers who had a system to assess and minimize risks. The winnings were not business income but tax-exempt capital gains. *Leblanc et al. v. The Queen*, 2007 DTC 307 (T.C.C.)

A storage park operation carried on by a limited partnership constituted a source of income. Since it was commercial in nature, with no evidence of any personal element, the REOP test did not arise. Although the taxpayers were clearly motivated by tax considerations when purchasing their partnership interests, this does not detract from the commercial nature of the operation or its characterization as a source of income. *The Queen v. Walls et al.*, 2002 DTC 6960 (S.C.C.), affirming 2000 DTC 6025 (F.C.A.), reversing 96 DTC 6142 (F.C.T.D.)

A two-stage approach is required in determining whether a taxpayer's activities constitute a source of income. First, has the activity been undertaken in pursuit of profit, or is it a personal endeavour? Secondly, if not personal, is the source of income a business or property? If there is a personal element, it will only be considered as a source of income if undertaken in a sufficiently commercial manner. REOP is only one of several considerations to be taken into account at this stage. *Stewart v. The Queen*, 2002 DTC 6969 (S.C.C.), reversing 2000 DTC 6163 (F.C.A.) and 98 DTC 1600 (T.C.C.)

Considering that the required approval of the taxpayer's invoices for progress payments had been given by its subcontractor prior to June 30, 1991, the holdbacks were receivable in 1991 and, as such, had to be included in income for that year. *Supreme Steel Limited v. The Queen*, 2001 DTC 5121 (F.C.A.), affirming 96 DTC 1430 (T.C.C.)

A land developer was entitled to deduct a $2.9 million regional development charge in the year it was paid, even though none of the lands affected by the charge were sold by the taxpayer during that year. *Urbandale Realty Corporation Limited v. The Queen*, 2000 DTC 6118 (F.C.A.), reversing 97 DTC 5353 (F.C.T.D.) and 93 DTC 154 (T.C.C.)

An over-quota levy in relation to the excess production of eggs was deductible since it was incurred as part of the taxpayer's day-to-day operations and was incurred for the purposes of earning income. The characterization of the levy as a "fine or penalty" was of no consequence. *65302 British Columbia Limited v. The Queen*, 99 DTC 5814 (S.C.C.), reversing 98 DTC 6002 (F.C.A.), which reversed 96 DTC 2049 (T.C.C.)

The corporate taxpayer had a "participation clause" in its lease, entitling it to a percentage of the lessor's annual net profits. In 1989, the taxpayer accepted a payment from its lessor to "buy-out" and cancel the participation clause. The "buy-out" payment was a capital receipt rather than income. *The T. Eaton Company Limited v. The Queen*, 99 DTC 5178 (F.C.A.), reversing 96 DTC 1846 (T.C.C.)

The annual profit or loss of a business may be determined by any method that produces an accurate picture of the financial result of the operation of the business, and is consistent with the Act, established case law, and well accepted business principles. Well accepted business principles are not limited to GAAP and are not rules of law, but merely interpretive aids to be applied on a case-by-case basis. *Toronto College Park v. The Queen*, 98 DTC 6088 (S.C.C.), reversing 96 DTC 6407 (F.C.A.)

The measure of damages paid to the taxpayer had been determined by reference to the present value of the income lost as a result of the reduced management fees brought about by its solicitor's errors. Considering that the taxpayer did not lose its capital asset inasmuch as he continued to provide management services and its solicitor's errors did not cripple its profit-making structure, the amounts received as damages were income. *Prince Rupert Hotel (1957) Ltd v. The Queen*, 95 DTC 5227 (F.C.A.), affirming 93 DTC 5243 (F.C.T.D.)

In reporting his income from his trading in gold futures, the taxpayer had used the "lowest cost of market" method. Although this method had led to substantial deferrals of income, there was nothing "artificial" involved since the taxpayer had reported his losses when they were incurred and his gains when they were realized. The "market to market" method was inappropriate to describe income since it involved recognizing all unrealized losses and gains. *The Queen v. Friedberg*, 93 DTC 5507 (S.C.C.), affirming 92 DTC 6031 (F.C.A.), reversing in part 89 DTC 5115 (F.C.T.D.)

Amounts earned but not billed were included in the taxpayer's income where the taxpayer had a clear legal right to payment for any electricity delivered and in any amount reasonably estimated. *West Kootenay Power and Light Limited v. The Queen*, 92 DTC 6023 (F.C.A.), affirming 91 DTC 5214 (F.C.T.D.).

▶ 9(2) ◀

(2) Loss. Subject to section 31, a taxpayer's loss for a taxation year from a business or property is the amount of the taxpayer's loss, if any, for the taxation year from that source computed by applying the provisions of this Act respecting computation of income from that source with such modifications as the circumstances require.

Related Sections: See subsection 9(1).

Guides: RC4015 Reconciliation of Business Income for Tax Purposes; T4002 Business and Professional Income.

Cases: Mark to market methodology provided a picture of the taxpayer's income which was as accurate and as acceptable, from the CRA's perspective, as that which the principle of realization would provide. *Kruger Incorporated v. The Queen*, 2016 DTC 5079 (FCA)

▶ 9(3) ◀

(3) Gains and losses not included. In this Act, "income from a property" does not include any capital gain from the disposition of that property and "loss from a property" does not include any capital loss from the disposition of that property.

Related Sections: S. 39(1) Meaning of capital gain and capital loss.

SECTION 10: Valuation of inventory

▶ 10(1) ◀

(1) Valuation of inventory. For the purpose of computing a taxpayer's income for a taxation year from a business that is not an adventure or concern in the nature of trade, property described in an inventory shall be valued at the end of the year at the cost at which the taxpayer acquired the property or its fair market value at the end of the year, whichever is lower, or in a prescribed manner.

Editorial Note: Since the cost of inventory for purposes of s. 10(1) means its acquisition cost, under the lower of cost or fair market value method, any write-down in the value of inventory must be written "back up" if the value subsequently increases, but only to the acquisition cost. Regulation 1801 allows all inventories of a business to be valued at fair market value; see s. 1802 for rules regarding the valuation of animals.

Related Regulations: Part XVIII.

Related Sections: S. 18(2) Limit on certain interest and property tax; s. 23 Sale of inventory; s. 28(1.2) Valuation of inventory; s. 85(1)(*c*.1) Transfer of property to corporation by shareholders; s. 87(2)(*b*) Inventory; s. 107(1.2) Deemed fair market value — non-capital property; s. 112(4.1) Fair market value of shares held as inventory; s. 248(1), "business", "fiscal period", "inventory"; s. 249.1 Definition of "fiscal period".

Tax Profile: February 2005 — The Canadian Treatment of Derivatives.

Forms: T2034 — Election to Establish Inventory Unit Prices for Animals.

Income Tax Folios: *Secondary* — S4-F7-C1 Amalgamations of Canadian Corporations.

Interpretation Bulletins: *Primary* — IT-473R Inventory valuation. *Secondary* — IT-51R2 Supplies on hand at the end of a fiscal period; IT-142R3 Settlement of debts on the winding-up of a corporation; IT-153R3 Land developers — Subdivision and development costs and carrying charges on land; IT-165R Returnable containers; IT-189R2 Corporations used by practising members of professions; IT-482R Pipelines; IT-504R2 (Consolid.) Visual artists and writers.

Tax Window Files: Land Development Costs, *October 27, 2005*, CRA Document No. 2005-0152891E5.

Cases: The foreign exchange options purchased by the taxpayer were "property", but they were not "inventory" since they were not held for sale. The foreign exchange options written by the taxpayer, however, were neither property, capital property, nor inventory, since they only embodied the obligation to deliver funds in the future. *Kruger Incorporated v. The Queen*, 2016 DTC 5079 (FCA)

Consultants providing information technology services were entitled to value their work-in-progress inventory, for work performed but unbilled, using the lower of cost or market method under s. 10(1). The application of s. 10(1) is not confined to the professional practices enumerated under s. 34. *CGI Information Systems and Management Consultants Inc. et al. v. The Queen*, 2009 DTC 5030 (F.C.A.), reversing 2008 DTC 2812 (T.C.C.)

The taxpayer was entitled to deduct the decline in the fair market value of an unsold single piece of land as a business loss in the years immediately following its acquisition since the property involved was inventory to the extent that its cost or value was relevant to the computation of business income in the year of disposition and the valuation of stock-in trade at the lower of cost and fair market value under s. 10(1) applied to all inventory used in the computation of business income. *Friesen v. The Queen*, 95 DTC 5551 (S.C.C.), reversing 93 DTC 5313 (F.C.A.) and 92 DTC 6248 (F.C.T.D.)

A change in the method of valuing inventory during a tax exempt period was not in line with the consistency principle and therefore not permitted by statute. *The Queen v. Cyprus Anvil Corp.*, 90 DTC 6063 (F.C.A.), reversing 85 DTC 5306 (F.C.T.D.).

▶ 10(1.01) ◀

(1.01) Adventures in the nature of trade. For the purpose of computing a taxpayer's income from a business that is an adventure or concern in the nature of trade, property described in an inventory shall be valued at the cost at which the taxpayer acquired the property.

Editorial Note: S. 10(1.01) effectively overrides the Supreme Court of Canada's decision in the *Friesen* case (95 DTC 5551).

Related Sections: S. 18(14) When s. (15) applies to adventurers in trade; s. 18(15) Loss on certain properties; s. 18(16) Deemed identical property; s. 248(1), "business".

Tax Profile: February 2005 — The Canadian Treatment of Derivatives.

Cases: The taxpayers purchased residential condominium units from a developer, which they later resold. The transactions were adventures in the nature of trade because the taxpayers had a reasonable expectation of profit from resale. The properties themselves were inventory which is subject to the prohibition of writedowns in s. 10(1.01). However, the taxpayers were entitled to deduct the carrying costs relating to the units in the years in which they were incurred. *Stremler et al. v. The Queen*, 2000 DTC 1757 (T.C.C.).

► 10(1.1) ◄

(1.1) Certain expenses included in cost. For the purposes of subsections (1), (1.01) and (10), where land is described in an inventory of a business of a taxpayer, the cost at which the taxpayer acquired the land shall include each amount that is

(*a*) described in paragraph 18(2)(*a*) or (*b*) in respect of the land and for which no deduction is permitted to the taxpayer, or to another person or partnership that is

(i) a person or partnership with whom the taxpayer does not deal at arm's length,

(ii) if the taxpayer is a corporation, a person or partnership that is a specified shareholder of the taxpayer, or

(iii) if the taxpayer is a partnership, a person or partnership whose share of any income or loss of the taxpayer is 10% or more; and

(*b*) not included in or added to the cost to that other person or partnership of any property otherwise than because of paragraph 53(1)(*d*.3) or subparagraph 53(1)(*e*)(xi).

Editorial Note: S. 10(1.1) provides that interest expense and property taxes in respect of land inventory that are not deductible under s. 18(2) shall form part of the acquisition cost of the inventory, notwithstanding that a shareholder or partner of the taxpayer may add such amounts to the adjusted cost base of its share in the taxpayer under s. 53(1)(*d*.3) or its partnership interest in the taxpayer under s. 53(1)(*e*)(xi), as the case may be.

Related Sections: S. 18(3), "land", "interest on debt relating to the acquisition of land".

Tax Window Files: Interest Deductibility; Inventory, *Technical Interpretation, Financial Industries Division, April 21, 2004*, CRA Document No. 2004-0061651E5; Compound Interest, *Technical Interpretation, Financial Industries Division, April 10, 2003*, CRA Document No. 2002-0147295.

► 10(2) ◄

(2) Continuation of valuation. Notwithstanding subsection (1), for the purpose of computing income for a taxation year from a business, the inventory at the commencement of the year shall be valued at the same amount as the amount at which it was valued at the end of the preceding taxation year for the purpose of computing income for that preceding year.

► 10(2.1) ◄

(2.1) Methods of valuation to be the same. Where property described in an inventory of a taxpayer's business that is not an adventure or concern in the nature of trade is valued at the end of a taxation year in accordance with a method permitted under this section, that method shall, subject to subsection (6), be used in the valuation of property described in the inventory at the end of the following taxation year for the purpose of computing the taxpayer's income from the business unless the taxpayer, with the concurrence of the Minister and on any terms and conditions that are specified by the Minister, adopts another method permitted under this section.

► 10(3) ◄

(3) Incorrect valuation. Where the inventory of a business at the commencement of a taxation year has, according to the method adopted by the taxpayer for computing income from the business for that year, not been valued as required by subsection (1), the inventory at the commencement of that year shall, if the Minister so directs, be deemed to have been valued as required by that subsection.

► 10(4) ◄

(4) Fair market value. For the purpose of subsection (1), the fair market value of property (other than property that is obsolete, damaged or defective or that is held for sale or lease or for the purpose of being processed, fabricated, manufactured, incorporated into, attached to, or otherwise converted into property for sale or lease) that is

(*a*) work in progress at the end of a taxation year of a business that is a profession means the amount that can reasonably be expected to become receivable in respect thereof after the end of the year; and

(*b*) advertising or packaging material, parts, supplies or other property (other than work in progress of a business that is a profession) that is included in inventory means the replacement cost of the property.

Interpretation Bulletins: *Primary* — IT-51R2 Supplies on hand at the end of a fiscal period.

► 10(5) ◄

(5) Inventory. Without restricting the generality of this section,

(*a*) property (other than capital property) of a taxpayer that is advertising or packaging material, parts or supplies or work in progress of a business that is a profession is, for greater certainty, inventory of the taxpayer;

(*b*) anything used primarily for the purpose of advertising or packaging property that is included in the inventory of a taxpayer shall be deemed not to be property held for sale or lease or for any of the purposes referred to in subsection (4); and

(*c*) property of a taxpayer, the cost of which to the taxpayer was deductible by virtue of paragraph 20(1)(*mm*), is, for greater certainty, inventory of the taxpayer having a cost to the taxpayer, except for the purposes of that paragraph, of nil.

Editorial Note: See the election (being phased out, starting for taxation years that begin after March 21, 2017) in s. 34 to exclude work-in-progress, which applies to certain professional businesses.

Related Sections: S. 34 Professional business.

Tax Topics: No. 1928, Potential Conflict? Sections 9 and 10 of the *Income Tax Act*.

Interpretation Bulletins: *Primary* — IT-51R2 Supplies on hand at the end of a fiscal period. *Secondary* — IT-457R Election by professionals to exclude work in progress from income.

Cases: The transitional provisions of s. 10(6) required a professional trustee in bankruptcy to include in its income for 1983 one-half of its work in progress at the end of 1982. Since its work in progress for 1984 was deemed to be what it was at the end of 1983, the overall result was to include in its 1984 income any portion of its work in progress at the end of 1982 that was not included in its 1983 income. *170635 Canada Ltée v. M.N.R.*, 93 DTC 1129 (T.C.C.)

▶ 10(6) ◀

(6) Artistic endeavour. Notwithstanding subsection (1), for the purpose of computing the income of an individual other than a trust for a taxation year from a business that is the individual's artistic endeavour, the value of the inventory of the business for that year shall, if the individual so elects in the individual's return of income under this Part for the year, be deemed to be nil.

Interpretation Bulletins: *Secondary* — IT-212R3 Income of deceased persons — Rights or things; IT-504R2 (Consolid.) Visual artists and writers.

Tax Window Files: Inventory of a Deceased Artist, *Technical Interpretation, Business and Partnerships Division, April 7, 2005*, CRA Document No. 2004-0099191E5.

▶ 10(7) ◀

(7) Value in later years. Where an individual has made an election pursuant to subsection (6) for a taxation year, the value of the inventory of a business that is the individual's artistic endeavour shall, for each subsequent taxation year, be deemed to be nil unless the individual, with the concurrence of the Minister and on such terms and conditions as are specified by the Minister, revokes the election.

Interpretation Bulletins: *Secondary* — IT-504R2 (Consolid.) Visual artists and writers.

▶ 10(8) ◀

(8) Definition of "business that is an individual's artistic endeavour". For the purpose of this section, "business that is an individual's artistic endeavour" means the business of creating paintings, prints, etchings, drawings, sculptures or similar works of art, where such works of art are created by the individual, but does not include a business of reproducing works of art.

Interpretation Bulletins: *Secondary* — IT-504R2 (Consolid.) Visual artists and writers.

▶ 10(9) ◀

(9) Transition. Where, at the end of a taxpayer's last taxation year at the end of which property described in an inventory of a business that is an adventure or concern in the nature of trade was valued under subsection (1), the property was valued at an amount that is less than the cost at which the taxpayer acquired the property, after that time the cost to the taxpayer at which the property was acquired is, subject to subsection (10), deemed to be that amount.

▶ 10(10) ◀

(10) Loss restriction event. Notwithstanding subsection (1.01), property described in an inventory of a taxpayer's business that is an adventure or concern in the nature of trade at the end of the taxpayer's taxation year that ends immediately before the time at which the taxpayer is subject to a loss restriction event is to be valued at the cost at which the taxpayer acquired the property, or its fair market value at the end of the year, whichever is lower, and after that time the cost at which the taxpayer acquired the property is, subject to a subsequent application of this subsection, deemed to be that lower amount.

Editorial Note: Subsection 10(1.01) requires inventory in an adventure or concern in the nature of trade to be valued at the original cost of the property. Subsection 10(10) provides an exception. Upon a loss restriction event of a taxpayer, there is a deemed taxation year end immediately before that time, and such inventory is valued at the lower of the original cost and its fair market value at that time. As such, any accrued losses will be recognized, and the property's new cost will be deemed to be this lower amount.

A loss restriction event is, in the case of a corporation, an acquisition of control of the corporation. In the case of a trust, the event occurs when a person becomes a majority-interest beneficiary or a group becomes a majority-interest group of beneficiaries. See subsection 251.2(2).

History: S. 10(10) was replaced by S.C. 2013, c. 40, s. 2(1), deemed to have come into force on March 21, 2013, and formerly read:

(10) *Acquisition of control.* Notwithstanding subsection (1.01), property described in an inventory of a corporation's business that is an adventure or concern in the nature of trade at the end of the corporation's taxation year that ends immediately before the time at which control of the corporation is acquired by a person or group of persons shall be valued at the cost at which the corporation acquired the property, or its fair market value at the end of the year, whichever is lower, and, after that time, the cost at which the corporation acquired the property is, subject to a subsequent application of this subsection, deemed to be that lower amount.

Related Sections: S. 111(4) Loss restriction event — non-capital losses and farm losses; s. 111(5) Loss restriction event — capital losses; s. 251.2(2) Loss restriction event; s. 256(8) Deemed exercise of right; s. 256.1 [Corporate tax-attribute trading].

▶ 10(11) ◀

(11) Loss restriction event. For the purposes of subsections 88(1.1) and 111(5), a taxpayer's business that is at any time an adventure or concern in the nature of trade is deemed to be a business carried on at that time by the taxpayer.

History: S. 10(11) was replaced by S.C. 2013, c. 40, s. 2(1), deemed to have come into force on March 21, 2013, and formerly read:

(11) *Acquisition of control.* For the purposes of subsections 88(1.1) and 111(5), a corporation's business that is at any time an adventure or concern in the nature of trade is deemed to be a business carried on at that time by the corporation.

▶ 10(12) ◀

(12) Removing property from inventory. If at any time a non-resident taxpayer ceases to use, in connection with a business or part of a business carried on by the taxpayer in Canada immediately before that time, a property that was immediately before that time described in the inventory of the business or the part of the business, as the case may be, (other than a property that was disposed of by the taxpayer at that time), the taxpayer is deemed

(*a*) to have disposed of the property immediately before that time for proceeds of disposition equal to its fair market value at that time; and

(*b*) to have received those proceeds immediately before that time in the course of carrying on the business or the part of the business, as the case may be.

Related Sections: S. 14(14) References to "taxation year" or "year"; s. 45(1)(*d*) Property with more than one use; s. 126(4.4) Dispositions ignored; s. 248(1), "taxable Canadian property".

▶ 10(13) ◀

(13) Adding property to inventory. If at any time a property becomes included in the inventory of a business or part of a business that a non-resident taxpayer carries on in Canada after that time (other than a property that was, otherwise than because of this subsection, acquired by the taxpayer at that time), the taxpayer is deemed to have acquired the property at that time at a cost equal to its fair market value at that time.

Related Sections: S. 14(14) References to "taxation year" or "year"; s. 45(1)(*d*) Property with more than one use; s. 126(4.4) Dispositions ignored.

► 10(14) ◄

(14) Work in progress. For the purposes of subsections (12) and (13), property that is included in the inventory of a business includes property that would be so included if paragraph 34(*a*) did not apply.

> **Amendment not yet in force**
> **Budget Implementation Act, 2017, No. 2 [S.C. 2017, c. 33]**
> **S. 10(14) will be repealed by S.C. 2017, c. 33, s. 2(1).**
> **Applicable:** Comes into force on January 1, 2024.

Canadian Tax Foundation: Infanti, *WIP Election Applies to New Partners*, 2018 Tax for the Owner Manager 18(4):1–2; Infanti, *CRA Confirms Partner Time Not Part of Professional's WIP Cost*, 2018 Tax for the Owner Manager 18(3):1–3.

► 10(14.1) ◄

(14.1) Work in progress — transitional. If paragraph 34(*a*) applies in computing a taxpayer's income from a business for the last taxation year of the taxpayer that begins before March 22, 2017, then

(*a*) for the purpose of computing the income of the taxpayer from the business, at the end of the first taxation year that begins after March 21, 2017,

(i) the amount of the cost of the taxpayer's work in progress is deemed to be one-fifth of the amount of its cost determined without reference to this paragraph, and

(ii) the amount of the fair market value of the taxpayer's work in progress is deemed to be one-fifth of the amount of its fair market value determined without reference to this paragraph;

(*b*) for the purpose of computing the income of the taxpayer from the business, at the end of the second taxation year that begins after March 21, 2017,

(i) the amount of the cost of the taxpayer's work in progress is deemed to be two-fifths of the amount of its cost determined without reference to this paragraph, and

(ii) the amount of the fair market value of the taxpayer's work in progress is deemed to be two-fifths of the amount of its fair market value determined without reference to this paragraph;

(*c*) for the purpose of computing the income of the taxpayer from the business, at the end of the third taxation year that begins after March 21, 2017,

(i) the amount of the cost of the taxpayer's work in progress is deemed to be three-fifths of the amount of its cost determined without reference to this paragraph, and

(ii) the amount of the fair market value of the taxpayer's work in progress is deemed to be three-fifths of the amount of its fair market value determined without reference to this paragraph; and

(*d*) for the purpose of computing the income of the taxpayer from the business, at the end of the fourth taxation year that begins after March 21, 2017,

(i) the amount of the cost of the taxpayer's work in progress is deemed to be four-fifths of the amount of its cost determined without reference to this paragraph, and

(ii) the amount of the fair market value of the taxpayer's work in progress is deemed to be four-fifths of the amount of its fair market value determined without reference to this paragraph.

> **Amendment not yet in force**
> **Budget Implementation Act, 2017, No. 2 [S.C. 2017, c. 33]**
> **S. 10(14.1) will be repealed by S.C. 2017, c. 33, s. 2(3).**
> **Applicable:** Comes into force on January 1, 2024.

History: S. 10(14.1) was added by S.C. 2017, c. 33, s. 2(2), applicable to taxation years ending after March 21, 2017.

► 10(15) ◄

(15) Derivatives. For the purposes of this section, property of a taxpayer that is a swap agreement, a forward purchase or sale agreement, a forward rate agreement, a futures agreement, an option agreement, or any similar agreement is deemed not to be inventory of the taxpayer.

History: S. 10(15) was added by S.C. 2016, c. 12, s. 2(1), applicable to agreements entered into after March 21, 2016.

Related Sections: 10(1) Valuation of inventory; 18(1)(x) Derivatives — lower of cost and market; 18(1)(y) Payment for shares.

SECTION 10.1: [Mark-to-market election]

► 10.1(1) ◄

(1) Mark-to-market election. Subsection (4) applies to a taxpayer in respect of a taxation year and subsequent taxation years if the taxpayer elects to have subsection (4) apply to the taxpayer and has filed that election in prescribed form on or before its filing-due date for the taxation year.

History: S. 10.1(1) was added by S.C. 2017, c. 33, s. 3(1), applicable to taxation years that begin after March 21, 2017.

Related Sections: 18(1)(x) Derivatives — lower of cost and market; 142.2(1) financial institution; 142.2(1) mark-to-market property.

Canadian Tax Foundation: Robson, *Section 10.1*, 2018 Canadian Tax Highlights 26(1):2–3.

Tax Topics: No. 2366, Amendments to the Taxation of Derivatives.

Forms: T217 — Election, or Revocation of an Election, to use the Mark-to-Market method.

► 10.1(2) ◄

(2) Revocation. The Minister may, on application by the taxpayer in prescribed form, grant permission to the taxpayer to revoke its election under subsection (1). The revocation applies to each taxation year of the taxpayer that begins after the day on which the taxpayer is notified in writing that the Minister concurs with the revocation, on such terms and conditions as are specified by the Minister.

History: S. 10.1(2) was added by S.C. 2017, c. 33, s. 3(1), applicable to taxation years that begin after March 21, 2017.

▶ 10.1(3) ◀

(3) Subsequent election. Notwithstanding subsection (1), if a taxpayer has, under subsection (2), revoked an election, any subsequent election under subsection (1) shall result in subsection (4) applying to the taxpayer in respect of each taxation year that begins after the day on which the prescribed form in respect of the subsequent election is filed by the taxpayer.

History: S. 10.1(3) was added by S.C. 2017, c. 33, s. 3(1), applicable to taxation years that begin after March 21, 2017.

▶ 10.1(4) ◀

(4) Application. If this subsection applies to a taxpayer in respect of a taxation year,

(*a*) if the taxpayer is a *financial institution* (as defined in subsection 142.2(1)) in the taxation year, each eligible derivative held by the taxpayer at any time in the taxation year is, for the purpose of applying the provisions of this Act and with such modifications as the context requires, deemed to be *mark-to-market property* (as defined in subsection 142.2(1)) of the taxpayer for the taxation year; and

(*b*) in any other case, subsection (6) applies to the taxpayer in respect of each eligible derivative held by the taxpayer at the end of the taxation year.

History: S. 10.1(4) was added by S.C. 2017, c. 33, s. 3(1), applicable to taxation years that begin after March 21, 2017.

Related Sections: 142.2(1) excluded property; 142.2(1) tracking property.

▶ 10.1(5) ◀

(5) Definition of *eligible derivative*. For the purposes of this section, an *eligible derivative*, of a taxpayer for a taxation year, means a swap agreement, a forward purchase or sale agreement, a forward rate agreement, a futures agreement, an option agreement or a similar agreement, held at any time in the taxation year by the taxpayer, if

(*a*) the agreement is not a capital property, a Canadian resource property, a foreign resource property or an obligation on account of capital of the taxpayer;

(*b*) either

(i) the taxpayer has produced audited financial statements prepared in accordance with generally accepted accounting principles in respect of the taxation year, or

(ii) if the taxpayer has not produced audited financial statements described in subparagraph (i), the agreement has a readily ascertainable fair market value; and

(*c*) where the agreement is held by a *financial institution* (as defined in subsection 142.2(1)), the agreement is not a *tracking property* (as defined in subsection 142.2(1)), other than an *excluded property* (as defined in subsection 142.2(1)), of the financial institution.

History: S. 10.1(5) was added by S.C. 2017, c. 33, s. 3(1), applicable to taxation years that begin after March 21, 2017.

Related Sections: 85(1.12) Eligible derivatives; 85(2) Transfer of property to corporation from partnership.

▶ 10.1(6) ◀

(6) Deemed disposition. If this subsection applies to a taxpayer in respect of each eligible derivative held by the taxpayer at the end of a taxation year, for each eligible derivative held by the taxpayer at the end of the taxation year, the taxpayer is deemed

(*a*) to have disposed of the eligible derivative immediately before the end of the year and received proceeds or paid an amount, as the case may be, equal to its fair market value at the time of disposition; and

(*b*) to have reacquired, or reissued or renewed, the eligible derivative at the end of the year at an amount equal to the proceeds or the amount, as the case may be, determined under paragraph (*a*).

History: S. 10.1(6) was added by S.C. 2017, c. 33, s. 3(1), applicable to taxation years that begin after March 21, 2017.

Related Sections: 87(2)(e.41) [Eligible derivative — cost amount]; 87(2)(e.42) [Continuation of predecessor corporation — eligible derivative].

▶ 10.1(7) ◀

(7) Election year — gains and losses. If a taxpayer holds, at the beginning of its first taxation year in respect of which an election referred to in subsection (1) applies (in this subsection referred to as the "election year"), an eligible derivative and, in the taxation year immediately preceding the election year, the taxpayer did not compute its profit or loss in respect of that eligible derivative in accordance with a method of profit computation that produces a substantially similar effect to subsection (6), then

(*a*) the taxpayer is deemed

(i) to have disposed of the eligible derivative immediately before the beginning of the election year and received proceeds or paid an amount, as the case may be, equal to its fair market value at that time, and

(ii) to have reacquired, or reissued or renewed, the eligible derivative at the beginning of the election year at an amount equal to the proceeds or the amount, as the case may be, determined under subparagraph (i);

(*b*) the profit or loss that would arise (determined without reference to this paragraph) on the deemed disposition in subparagraph (*a*)(i)

(i) is deemed not to arise in the taxation year immediately preceding the election year, and

(ii) is deemed to arise in the taxation year in which the taxpayer disposes of the eligible derivative (otherwise than because of paragraphs (6)(*a*) or 142.5(2)(*a*)); and

(*c*) for the purpose of applying subsection 18(15) in respect of the disposition of the eligible derivative referred to in subparagraph (*b*)(ii), the profit or loss deemed to arise because of that subparagraph is included in determining the amount of the transferor's loss, if any, from the disposition.

History: S. 10.1(7) was added by S.C. 2017, c. 33, s. 3(1), applicable to taxation years that begin after March 21, 2017.

▶ 10.1(8) ◀

(8) Default realization method. If subsection (4) does not apply to a taxpayer referred to in paragraph (4)(*b*) in respect of a taxation year, a method of profit computation that produces a substantially similar effect to subsection (6) shall not be used for the purpose of computing the taxpayer's income from a business or property in respect of a swap agreement, a forward purchase or sale agreement, a forward rate agreement, a futures agreement, an option agreement or a similar agreement for the taxation year.

History: S. 10.1(8) was added by S.C. 2017, c. 33, s. 3(1), applicable to taxation years that begin after March 21, 2017.

▶ 10.1(9) ◀

(9) Interpretation. For the purposes of subsections (4) to (7), if an agreement that is an eligible derivative of a taxpayer is not a property of the taxpayer, the taxpayer is deemed

(*a*) to hold the eligible derivative at any time while the taxpayer is a party to the agreement; and

(*b*) to have disposed of the eligible derivative when it is settled or extinguished in respect of the taxpayer.

History: S. 10.1(9) was added by S.C. 2017, c. 33, s. 3(1), applicable to taxation years that begin after March 21, 2017.

SECTION 11: Proprietor of business

▶ 11(1) ◀

(1) Proprietor of business. Subject to section 34.1, if an individual is a proprietor of a business, the individual's income from the business for a taxation year is deemed to be the individual's income from the business for the fiscal periods of the business that end in the year.

Editorial Note: The end of the fiscal period of an individual's business must coincide with the calendar year end, unless the individual has elected under s. 249.1(4) to use the "alternative method" of computing business income under s. 34.1.

History: S. 11(1) was replaced by S.C. 2013, c. 40, s. 3(1), applicable to taxation years that end after March 22, 2011, and formerly read:

(1) *Proprietor of business.* Subject to sections 34.1 and 34.2, where an individual is a proprietor of a business, the individual's income from the business for a taxation year is deemed to be the individual's income from the business for the fiscal periods of the business that end in the year.

Related Sections: S. 248(1), "business"; s. 249 Definition of "taxation year"; s. 249.1 Definition of "fiscal period".

Cases: The fiscal period adopted by an individual in respect of a business applies only to income from the business itself. *Prefontaine v. M.N.R.*, 84 DTC 1688 (T.C.C.).

▶ 11(2) ◀

(2) Reference to "taxation year". Where an individual's income for a taxation year includes income from a business the fiscal period of which does not coincide with the calendar year, unless the context otherwise requires, a reference in this subdivision or section 80.3 to a "taxation year" or "year" shall, in respect of the business, be read as a reference to a fiscal period of the business ending in the year.

Related Regulations: S. 1104(1).

Related Sections: S. 25 Fiscal period for individual proprietor of business disposed of; s. 248(1), "business"; s. 249 Definition of "taxation year"; s. 249.1(1) Definition of "fiscal period".

Inclusions

SECTION 12: Income inclusions

▶ 12(1) ◀

(1) Income inclusions. There shall be included in computing the income of a taxpayer for a taxation year as income from a business or property such of the following amounts as are applicable:

▶ 12(1)(a) ◀

(a) Services, etc., to be rendered — any amount received by the taxpayer in the year in the course of a business

(i) that is on account of services not rendered or goods not delivered before the end of the year or that, for any other reason, may be regarded as not having been earned in the year or a previous year, or

(ii) under an arrangement or understanding that it is repayable in whole or in part on the return or resale to the taxpayer of articles in or by means of which goods were delivered to a customer;

Editorial Note: Prepaid (unearned) income included under s. 12(1)(*a*) is often eligible for the s. 20(1)(*m*) reserve. S. 12(1)(*a*) does not apply to unearned income from property, although such amounts would normally be included under s. 9 as a taxpayer's profit if they had attained the "quality of income". The CRA generally allows the recognition of prepaid income from property to be deferred to the year to which it relates, so that the net result is normally the same as that seen where the s. 20(1)(*m*) reserve applies; see CRA Document No. 2004-0105461R3, June 1, 2005.

Related Sections: S. 12(1)(*e*) Reserves for certain goods and services, etc.; s. 12(2) Interpretation; s. 20(1)(*m*) Reserve in respect of certain goods and services; s. 20(1)(*m.1*) Manufacturer's warranty reserve; s. 20(1)(*m.2*) Repayment of amount previously included in income; s. 20(6) Special reserves; s. 20(7) Where para. (1)(m) does not apply; s. 20(24) Amounts paid for undertaking future obligations; s. 87(2)(*j*) Special reserves.

Canadian Tax Foundation: Frankovic, *The Taxation of Prepaid Income*, 2002 Canadian Tax Journal 4:1239–1298; Walker, *Timing and Recognition of Income*, 2001 Conference Report 29:1–42; Allard, *The Retroactive Effect of Conditional Obligations in Tax Law*, 2001 Canadian Tax Journal 6:1729–1826; Stoddard, *Current Cases: Federal Court of Appeal — Meaning of "Receivable" in Paragraph 12(1)(b) (The Queen v. Huang and Danczkay Ltd., 2000 DTC 6549)*, 2001 Canadian Tax Journal 1:137–141; Du Pont and Cloutier, *Canderel Ltd. v. Canada, [1998] 1 SCR. 147*, 2000 Ontario Tax Conference 1A:1–20; Philp, *Is It Time To Place More Reliance on GAAP?*, 1991 Conference Report 25:1–55.

Tax Profile: November 2004 — Reserve for Pre-paid Amount — Impact of Ellis Vision; November 2003 — Revenue Canada Round Table.

Tax Topics: No. 1700, 2004 Canadian Tax Foundation Conference - CRA Round Table; No. 1598, Prepayments and the "Quality of Income".

Income Tax Technical News: Issue No. 32, Reserve for Prepaid Amount: Impact of the Ellis Vision case; Issue No. 30, Prepaid Income — Whether Subsection 9(1) or Paragraph 12(1)(a) Applies.

Interpretation Bulletins: *Primary* — IT-165R Returnable containers; IT-246 Funeral directors — Prepaid funeral costs. *Secondary* — IT-154R Special reserves; IT-457R Election by professionals to exclude work in progress from income.

Tax Window Files: Taxation of insurance contract commission income, *August 20, 2015*, CRA Document No. 2015-0588871E5; Services Invoiced in Advance, *Technical Interpretation, Business and Partnerships Division, February 4, 2005*, CRA Document No. 2004-0101781E5. Amounts invoiced but not paid in the current taxation year for services to be performed in the subsequent taxation year not included in income for the current taxation year under paragraph 12(1)(*a*) or (*b*); Site Reclamation Costs, *Technical Interpretation, Reorganizations and Resources Division, September 27, 2004*, CRA Document No. 2003-0048241E5. A reserve may be claimed where a taxpayer has received a specifically identifiable amount in respect of the future reclamation costs which it is obligated to incur and the amount is included in the taxpayer's income under paragraph 12(1)(*a*); Software Maintenance Agreements, *Technical Interpretation, Business and Partnerships Division, October 7, 2003*, CRA Document No. 2003-0037947. Fees in respect of software maintenance plan included in income under paragraph 12(1)(*a*); partly eligible for paragraph 20(1)(*m*) reserve; Refundable Membership Fees, *Technical Interpretation, Financial Industries Division, September 25, 2003*, CRA Document No. 2003-0022405. Returnable membership fee may be included under paragraph 12(1)(*a*) if it does not have the quality of income.

Cases: Licence fees received in advance for the future use of television productions were eligible for a s. 20(1)(*m*) reserve. The reference to "amounts described in paragraph 12(1)(*a*)" does not mean only amounts that were included in income *by virtue of* s. 12(1)(*a*). *Ellis Vision Incorporated v. The Queen*, 2004 DTC 2024 (T.C.C.)

Revenue from the sale of season passes to a recreational facility was included in income but the taxpayer could claim a reserve in respect of services to be rendered after the end of the year. Since the services would all be rendered after October 31, it was reasonable that the entire amount should be deductible as a reserve. *Blue Mountain Resorts Limited v. The Queen*, 2002 DTC 1886 (T.C.C.)

A waste disposal company was required to perform various tasks associated with reconstituting dump sites for thirty years following the closing thereof. A portion of the fees charged by the taxpayer was intended to meet those future costs. This amount was deductible as a reserve since it was not "earned" in the year it was received. *Deputy Minister of Revenue for Quebec v. La Compagnie Meloche Inc.*, 2002 DTC 7169 (Que. C.A.)

Progress payments received by the taxpayer for the construction of ships had the quality of income when received. Because these amounts were earned, the taxpayer was not entitled to claim a reserve on them. *Burrard Yarrows Corporation v. The Queen*, 88 DTC 6352 (F.C.A.), affirming 86 DTC 6459 (F.C.T.D.)

An agreement of purchase and sale was entered into one year with the attendant conditions precedent being fulfilled the next. It was held that sale took place, and tax was payable in the year the conditions were fulfilled, as the balance of purchase price was not payable until that time and entitlement to deposits was also contingent upon fulfillment. *The Queen v. Imperial General Properties Limited*, 85 DTC 5045 (F.C.A.), reversing 83 DTC 5059 (F.C.T.D.).

► 12(1)(b) ◄

(b) Amounts receivable — any amount receivable by the taxpayer in respect of property sold or services rendered in the course of a business in the year, notwithstanding that the amount or any part thereof is not due until a subsequent year, unless the method adopted by the taxpayer for computing income from the business and accepted for the purpose of this Part does not require the taxpayer to include any amount receivable in computing the taxpayer's income for a taxation year unless it has been received in the year, and for the purposes of this paragraph, an amount shall be deemed to have become receivable in respect of services rendered in the course of a business on the day that is the earlier of

(i) the day on which the account in respect of the services was rendered, and

(ii) the day on which the account in respect of those services would have been rendered had there been no undue delay in rendering the account in respect of the services;

Editorial Note: Amounts included under s. 12(1)(*b*) may be eligible for the s. 20(1)(*n*) reserve in respect of property sold in the course of a business. It is possible that amounts for services rendered may be receivable under general principles, notwithstanding that they are not deemed to be receivable under the deeming language of s. 12(1)(*b*).

Related Sections: S. 12(1)(*e*) Reserves for certain goods and services, etc.; s. 12(2) Interpretation; s. 20(1)(*n*) Reserve for unpaid amounts; s. 20(8) No deduction in respect of property in certain circumstances; s. 34 Professional business.

Interpretation Bulletins: *Primary* — IT-170R Sale of property — When included in income computation. *Secondary* — IT-129R Lawyers' trust accounts and disbursements; IT-457R Election by professionals to exclude work in progress from income.

Tax Window Files: Services Invoiced in Advance, *Technical Interpretation, Business and Partnerships Division, February 4, 2005*, CRA Document No. 2004-0101781E5. Amounts invoiced but not paid in the current taxation year for services to be performed in the subsequent taxation year not included in income for the current taxation year under paragraph 12(1)(*a*) or (*b*); Contingent Legal Fees, *Technical Interpretation, Business and Partnerships Division, June 20, 2003*, CRA Document No. 2003-0015775. Legal fees under a contingency fee agreement included in income at the earlier of the time the fees are billed or become billable.

Cases: Considering that the required approval of the taxpayer's invoices for progress payments had been given by its subcontractor prior to June 30, 1991, the holdbacks were receivable in 1991 and, as such, had to be included in income for that year. *Supreme Steel Limited v. The Queen*, 2001 DTC 5121 (F.C.A.), affirming 96 DTC 1430 (T.C.C.)

For an amount to be "receivable", there is no requirement that the right to payment be immediate. In addition, the taxpayer's right to receive the amounts of notes and mortgages became absolute when the obligations were made and signed. The existence of an express right of set off did not convert the absolute obligations to contingent ones. *The Queen v. Huang & Danczkay Ltd.*, 2000 DTC 6549 (F.C.A.), reversing 98 DTC 6393 (F.C.T.D.) and 93 DTC 1028 (T.C.C.)

The taxpayer reported income for tax purposes using the "billed method" so that income which was earned but not yet billed was not reported in the period. For general accounting purposes it continued to use the "earned method". The "earned method" produced a "truer picture" of the taxpayer's income and must therefore be used for tax purposes. *Maritime Telegraph and Telephone Company, Limited v. The Queen*, 92 DTC 6191 (F.C.A.), affirming 91 DTC 5038 (F.C.T.D.)

A taxpayer is not necessarily required to use the same method of calculating income for tax purposes as that used for calculating income for accounting purposes. *West Kootenay Power and Light Co. Ltd. v. The Queen*, 92 DTC 6023 (F.C.A.)

In the absence of a statutory definition, an amount is receivable when the so-called recipient has a clearly legal, though not necessarily immediate, right to receive it. Progress payments to a building contractor that were not to be made until an architect's certificate had been issued were held to be "receivable" only when the certificate had been issued. *M.N.R. v. John Colford Contracting Co. Ltd.*, 62 DTC 1338 (S.C.C.), affirming 60 DTC 1131 (Ex. Ct.) and 57 DTC 45 (T.A.B.).

► 12(1)(c) ◄

(c) Interest — subject to subsections (3) and (4.1), any amount received or receivable by the taxpayer in the year (depending on the method regularly followed by the taxpayer in computing the taxpayer's income) as, on account of, in lieu of payment of or in satisfaction of, interest to the extent that the interest was not included in computing the taxpayer's income for a preceding taxation year;

Editorial Note: Despite the receipt and receivable methods of reporting interest set out in s. 12(1)(*c*), corporations, partnerships and certain trusts must generally include interest on an accrual basis under s. 12(3), even if it is not received or has not become receivable in the year. An accrual rule also applies to individuals in s. 12(4), although it is based on an accrual of interest up to an "anniversary day" of an "investment contract" in the taxation year (both terms are defined in s. 12(11)).

Related Regulations: Part II; 7000.

Related Sections: S. 12(3) Interest income; s. 12(4) Interest from investment contract; s. 12(9) Deemed accrual; s. 12.1 Cash bonus on Canada Savings Bonds; s. 16 Income and capital combined; s. 17 Amount owing by non-resident; s. 20(14) Accrued bond interest; s. 20(21) Debt obligation; s. 81(1)(*m*) Interest on certain obligations.

Canadian Tax Foundation: Friedlan, *Not All Ponzi Proceeds Are Taxable*, 2014 Tax for the Owner-Manager 14(4); Fabbro, *Proving the Existence of a Spousal Partnership*, 2014 Canadian Tax Focus 4(2):8.

Tax Profile: November 2003 — Revenue Canada Round Table.

Forms: T5 Sum. — Return of Investment Income; T5 — Statement of Investment Income.

Income Tax Technical News: Issue No. 43, Taxation of Roth IRAs; Issue No. 30, Pre-judgment Interest.

Interpretation Bulletins: *Primary* — IT-396R Interest income.

Tax Window Files: Interest Income Renunciation, *Technical Interpretation, Financial Industries Division, June 11, 2004*, CRA Document No.

2004-0076291E5. Paragraph 12(1)(*c*) and subsection 12(3) not applicable when right to interest renounced by creditor; Indexed Debt Obligations — Various Issues, *Technical Interpretation, Financial Industries Division, December 22, 2003*, CRA Document No. 2003-0000125. Various comments regarding the inclusion of interest under indexed debt obligations.

Cases: The Quebec government was indebted to the judges of the Quebec Court (including the taxpayer) relating to their entitlement to compensation. The taxpayer was taxed on the salary adjustment plus the interest received. Although she argued a portion of the interest represented damages and not income, the amount in question qualified as "interest" on the government's indebtedness and was income. Even if the amount was damages, such damages were intended to compensate the taxpayer with respect to salary owing and must be given the same tax treatment as that salary. *Gaboury v. The Queen*, 2015 DTC 1199 (CCI)

The Minister reassessed the taxpayer to impute interest income of $156,000 stemming from his involvement in what was later discovered to be a Ponzi scheme. On appeal, it was decided the amount received was not interest income — the taxpayer was simply defrauded and given his money back (or that of other participants). *Roszko v. The Queen*, 2014 DTC 1083 (T.C.C.)

Pre-judgment interest was not "interest" for the purposes of s. 12(1)(*c*) since it related to damages arising in tort, and not in contract. Since the taxpayer did not have any right to a principal amount prior to judgment, there could be no interest until judgment. *Ahmad v. The Queen*, 2002 DTC 2065 (T.C.C.)

Since interest was paid to a taxpayer not as compensation for the expropriation of his land but as compensation for the expropriating authority's failure to pay promptly the balance of the value of the land taken, such interest had to be included in his income. *The Queen v. Shaw*, 93 DTC 5121 (F.C.A.), reversing 93 DTC 6145 (F.C.T.D.)

The sum of $3,090,900 in interest, which had accrued but not been paid on the debentures which the taxpayer had surrendered in return for shares of a joint venture corporation was not included in its income when the shares were not worth their par value because of the conditions attached thereto; the interest had in fact been received by the taxpayer. *Praxair Canada Inc. v. The Queen*, 93 DTC 5100 (F.C.T.D.).

► 12(1)(d) ◄

(d) Reserve for doubtful debts — any amount deducted under paragraph 20(1)(*l*) as a reserve in computing the taxpayer's income for the immediately preceding taxation year;

Editorial Note: The reserve may be claimed again if the debt remains doubtful. If the debt has become bad in the year, a final reserve may be deducted under paragraph 20(1)(*p*). See also paragraph 12(1)(*i*) regarding the recovery of bad debts.

Interpretation Bulletins: *Secondary* — IT-442R Bad debts and reserves for doubtful debts.

► 12(1)(d.1) ◄

(d.1) Reserve for guarantees, etc. — any amount deducted under paragraph 20(1)(*l*.1) as a reserve in computing the taxpayer's income for the immediately preceding taxation year;

► 12(1)(d.2) ◄

(d.2) [Reserve for bond premiums] — any amount deducted under paragraph 20(1)(*m*.3) as a reserve in computing the taxpayer's income for the immediately preceding taxation year;

History: S. 12(1)(*d*.2) was added by S.C. 2017, c. 33, s. 4(1), applicable in respect to bonds issued after 2000.

Related Sections: 20(1)(m.3) [Reserve for bond premiums]; 20(1)(xx) Derivative forward agreement.

► 12(1)(e) ◄

(e) Reserves for certain goods and services, etc. — any amount

(i) deducted under paragraph 20(1)(*m*) (including any amount substituted by virtue of subsection 20(6) for any amount deducted under that paragraph), paragraph 20(1)(*m*.1) or subsection 20(7), or

(ii) deducted under paragraph 20(1)(*n*),

in computing the taxpayer's income from a business for the immediately preceding year;

Editorial Note: The reserve deducted in the previous year is added back into income in the current year, and a further reserve may be claimed in the current year if the criteria of the reserve provision apply (e.g. paragraph 20(1)(*m*) if the income remains unearned in the year, or paragraph 20(1)(*n*) if the amount receivable is due after the year).

Related Sections: S. 12(1)(*a*) Services, etc., to be rendered; s. 12(1)(*b*) Amounts receivable; s. 20(1)(*m*) Reserve in respect of certain goods and services; s. 20(1)(*m*.1) Manufacturer's warranty reserve; s. 20(7) Where para. (1)(m) does not apply; s. 20(22) Deduction for negative reserves; s. 66.4(2) Deduction for cumulative Canadian oil and gas property expense.

Interpretation Bulletins: *Secondary* — IT-73R6 The small business deduction; IT-154R Special reserves.

Tax Window Files: Amounts Paid for Undertaking Future Obligations, *Technical Interpretation, Business and Partnerships Division, March 7, 2005*, CRA Document No. 2005-0114981E5. Subsection 20(24) deduction not limited to year of paragraph 12(1)(*a*) inclusion and therefore can be claimed in year of paragraph 12(1)(*e*) inclusion.

Cases: The taxpayer operated a club and charged its new members an initiation fee which was amortized over 10 years. There was no basis for the amortization since the initiation fees were earned in the year of receipt. The taxpayer had, in effect, deducted a reserve under s. 20(1)(*m*). However, it would be a gross distortion of the taxpayer's income picture if the entire balance of its "Deferred Initiation Fees" account were to be taxed in one year under s. 12(1)(*e*). *Argus Holdings Limited v. The Queen*, 2000 DTC 6681 (F.C.A.), reversing 99 DTC 597 (T.C.C.).

► 12(1)(e.1) ◄

(e.1) Negative reserves — where the taxpayer is an insurer, the amount prescribed in respect of the insurer for the year;

Related Regulations: 1400(2); 1400(3); 1400(4); 1402; 1402.1; 1408.

Related Sections: S. 20(22) Deduction for negative reserves.

► 12(1)(f) ◄

(f) Insurance proceeds expended — such part of any amount payable to the taxpayer as compensation for damage to, or under a policy of insurance in respect of damage to, property that is depreciable property of the taxpayer as has been expended by the taxpayer

(i) within the year, and

(ii) within a reasonable time after the damage,

on repairing the damage;

► 12(1)(g) ◄

(g) Payments based on production or use — any amount received by the taxpayer in the year that was dependent on the use of or production from property whether or not that amount was an instalment of the sale price of the property, except that an instalment of the sale price of agricultural land is not included by virtue of this paragraph;

Editorial Note: Although s. 12(1)(*g*) can apply to share sales that are subject to earn-out agreements, the CRA generally allows a cost recovery method of reporting capital gains or losses in such cases; see Interpretation Bulletin IT-426R, "Shares Sold Subject to an Earnout Agreement" (archived, as it doesn't meet current government web standards). .

Related Regulations: Part II.

Related Sections: S. 12(2.01) No deferral of section 9 income under paragraph (1)(*g*).

Canadian Petroleum Tax Journal: High Tech in the Oil Patch: Planning Considerations For Transferring Technology Offshore, Derek A. Kurrant, 2000, Vol. 13, No. 1.

Canadian Tax Foundation: Hanson and Yaskowich, *There is more to the Family Farm than Meets the Eye,* 2014 Prairie Provinces Tax Conference

5:1–28; Choudhury and Connell, *Select Issues in the Purchase and Sale of a Business*, 2012 Ontario Tax Conference 11:1–31.

Tax Profile: August 2012 — U.S. Purchases and Sales of Canadian Businesses: Tax and Corporate Issues; July 2012 — Intangibles; November 2009 — Purchase and Sale of a Canadian Business.

Tax Topics: No. 1713, Payments Based on Use or Production.

Income Tax Folios: *Secondary* — S4-F11-C1 Meaning of Farming and Farming Business.

Interpretation Bulletins: *Primary* — IT-462 Payments based on production or use. *Secondary* — IT-373R2 (Consolid.) Woodlots; IT-426R Shares sold subject to an earnout agreement.

Tax Window Files: Sale of Goodwill Subject to Earnout Agreement, *Technical Interpretation, Business and Partnerships Division, December 16, 2004*, CRA Document No. 2004-0098121E5. Consideration received for eligible capital property dependent upon the use or production from that property was taxable under paragraph 12(1)(*g*).

Cases: The entire proceeds of disposition must be included in income for tax purposes, even though the maximum purchase price stipulated in the agreement could be subject to subsequent reduction through the operation of price adjustment provisions. The production or use provisions of s. 12(1)(*g*) require the inclusion in income of all amounts attributable to the production or use of property. *Deragon v. The Queen*, 2016 DTC 1188 (TCC)

▶ 12(1)(g.1) ◀

(g.1) Proceeds of disposition of right to receive production — any proceeds of disposition to which subsection 18.1(6) applies;

▶ 12(1)(h) ◀

(h) Previous reserve for quadrennial survey — any amount deducted as a reserve under paragraph 20(1)(*o*) in computing the taxpayer's income for the immediately preceding year;

▶ 12(1)(i) ◀

(i) Bad debts recovered — any amount, other than an amount referred to in paragraph (*i*.1), received in the year on account of a debt or a loan or lending asset in respect of which a deduction for bad debts or uncollectable loans or lending assets was made in computing the taxpayer's income for a preceding taxation year;

Related Sections: S. 20(1)(*p*) Bad debts; s. 22(1) Sale of accounts receivable.

Income Tax Folios: *Primary* — S3-F4-C1 General Discussion of Capital Cost Allowance.

Interpretation Bulletins: *Secondary* — IT-442R Bad debts and reserves for doubtful debts.

▶ 12(1)(i.1) ◀

(i.1) Bad debts recovered — where an amount is received in the year on account of a debt in respect of which a deduction for bad debts was made under subsection 20(4.2) in computing the taxpayer's income for a preceding taxation year, the amount determined by the formula

$$A \times B/C$$

where

A is $^1/_2$ of the amount so received,

B is the amount that was deducted under subsection 20(4.2) in respect of the debt, and

C is the total of the amount that was so deducted under subsection 20(4.2) and the amount that was deemed by that subsection or subsection 20(4.3) to be an allowable capital loss in respect of the debt;

Related Sections: S. 39(11) Recovery of bad debt.

▶ 12(1)(j) ◀

(j) Dividends from resident corporations — any amount of a dividend in respect of a share of the capital stock of a corporation resident in Canada that is required by subdivision h to be included in computing the taxpayer's income for the year;

History: S. 12(1)(*j*) was replaced by S.C. 2013, c. 34, s. 173(1), deemed to have come into force on November 6, 2010, and formerly read:

(*j*) *Dividends from resident corporations* — any amount required by subdivision h to be included in computing the taxpayer's income for the year in respect of a dividend paid by a corporation resident in Canada on a share of its capital stock;

Related Regulations: Part II.

Related Sections: S. 82 Taxable dividends received.

Tax Profile: October 2004 — Taxation of Dividends: A Survey in the Context of Private Corporations and Their Shareholders.

Interpretation Bulletins: *Primary* — IT-67R3 Taxable dividends from corporations resident in Canada.

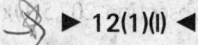

▶ 12(1)(k) ◀

(k) Foreign corporations, trusts and investment entities — any amount required by subdivision i to be included in computing the taxpayer's income for the year;

History: S. 12(1)(*k*) was replaced by S.C. 2013, c. 34, s. 2(1), applicable to taxation years that end after 2006, and formerly read:

(*k*) *Dividends from other corporations* — any amount required by subdivision i to be included in computing the taxpayer's income for the year in respect of a dividend paid by a corporation not resident in Canada on a share of its capital stock or in respect of a share owned by the taxpayer of the capital stock of a foreign affiliate of the taxpayer;

Related Regulations: Part II.

Related Sections: S. 90 Dividends received from non-resident corporation; s. 91 Amounts to be included in respect of share of foreign affiliate; s. 94 [Non-resident trusts]; s. 94.2 Investments in non-resident commercial trusts.

▶ 12(1)(l) ◀

(l) Partnership income — any amount that is, by virtue of subdivision j, income of the taxpayer for the year from a business or property;

Editorial Note: The character of the income as either business or property income flows through from the partnership to the partner; see generally s. 96(1).

Related Sections: S. 96 General rules.

Canadian Tax Foundation: Jamal, *Partnership Withdrawal Creates a Paragraph 12(1)(l.1) Anomaly*, 2015 Canadian Tax Focus 4(2):3–4.

Forms: T2032 — Statement of Professional Activities.

Interpretation Bulletins: *Secondary* — IT-278R2 Death of a partner or of a retired partner.

▶ 12(1)(l.1) ◀

(l.1) Partnership — interest deduction add back — the total of all amounts, each of which is the amount, if any, determined in respect of a partnership by the formula

$$A \times B/C - D$$

where

A is the total of all amounts each of which is an amount of interest that is

(i) deductible by the partnership, and

(ii) paid by the partnership in, or payable by the partnership in respect of, the taxation year of the taxpayer (depending on the method regularly followed by the taxpayer in computing the taxpayer's income) on a debt amount included in the taxpayer's outstanding debts to specified non-residents (as defined in subsection 18(5)),

B is the amount determined under paragraph 18(4)(*a*) in respect of the taxpayer for the year,

C is the amount determined under paragraph 18(4)(*b*) in respect of the taxpayer for the year, and

D is the total of all amounts each of which is an amount included under subsection 91(1) in computing the income of the taxpayer for the year or a subsequent taxation year, or of the partnership for a fiscal period, that may reasonably be considered to be in respect of interest described in A;

History: S. 12(1)(*l*.1) was added by S.C. 2012, c. 31, s. 4(1), applicable to taxation years that begin after March 28, 2012.

Related Sections: S. 12(2.02) Source of income.

Canadian Tax Foundation: Jamal, *Partnership Withdrawal Creates a Paragraph 12(1)(l.1) Anomaly,* 2015 Canadian Tax Focus 4(2):3–4.

► 12(1)(m) ◄

(m) Benefits from trusts — any amount required by subdivision k or subsection 132.1(1) to be included in computing the taxpayer's income for the year, except

(i) any amount deemed by that subdivision to be a taxable capital gain of the taxpayer, and

(ii) any amount paid or payable to the taxpayer out of or under an RCA trust (within the meaning assigned by subsection 207.5(1));

► 12(1)(n) ◄

(n) Employees profit sharing plan — any amount received by the taxpayer in the year out of or under

(i) an employees profit sharing plan, or

(ii) an employee trust

established for the benefit of employees of the taxpayer or of a person with whom the taxpayer does not deal at arm's length;

Related Regulations: 212.

Related Sections: S. 6(1)(*a*) Value of benefits; s. 6(1)(*d*) Allocations, etc., under profit sharing plan; s. 6(1)(*g*) Employee benefit plan benefits; s. 6(10) Contributions to an employee benefit plan; s. 32.1 Employee benefit plan contributions; s. 107.1 Distribution by certain employment-related trusts; s. 144(1), "employees profit sharing plan".

Interpretation Bulletins: *Secondary* — IT-502 Employee benefit plans and employee trusts.

► 12(1)(n.1) ◄

(n.1) Employee benefit plan — the amount, if any, by which the total of amounts received by the taxpayer in the year out of or under an employee benefit plan to which the taxpayer has contributed as an employer (other than amounts included in the income of the taxpayer by virtue of paragraph (*m*)) exceeds the amount, if any, by which the total of all amounts

(i) so contributed by the taxpayer to the plan, or

(ii) included in computing the taxpayer's income for any preceding taxation year by virtue of this paragraph

exceeds the total of all amounts

(iii) deducted by the taxpayer in respect of the taxpayer's contributions to the plan in computing the taxpayer's income for the year or any preceding taxation year, or

(iv) received by the taxpayer out of or under the plan in any preceding taxation year (other than an amount included in the taxpayer's income by virtue of paragraph (*m*));

Related Sections: S. 6(1)(*a*) Value of benefits; s. 6(1)(*g*) Employee benefit plan benefits; s. 6(10) Contributions to an employee benefit plan; s. 18(1)(*o*) Employee benefit plan contributions; s. 32.1 Employee benefit plan contributions; s. 107.1 Distribution by certain employment-related trusts; s. 248(1), "employee benefit plan".

Interpretation Bulletins: *Secondary* — IT-502 Employee benefit plans and employee trusts.

► 12(1)(n.2) ◄

(n.2) Forfeited salary deferral amounts — where deferred amounts under a salary deferral arrangement in respect of another person have been deducted under paragraph 20(1)(*oo*) in computing the taxpayer's income for preceding taxation years, any amount in respect of the deferred amounts that was deductible under paragraph 8(1)(*o*) in computing the income of the person for a taxation year ending in the year;

Related Sections: 6(11) Salary deferral arrangement; 6(12) Idem; 6(13) Application; s. 87(2)(*j*.3) Employee benefit plans, etc.

► 12(1)(n.3) ◄

(n.3) Retirement compensation arrangement — the total of all amounts received by the taxpayer in the year in the course of a business out of or under a retirement compensation arrangement to which the taxpayer, another person who carried on a business that was acquired by the taxpayer, or any person with whom the taxpayer or that other person does not deal at arm's length, has contributed an amount that was deductible under paragraph 20(1)(*r*) in computing the contributor's income for a taxation year;

Related Sections: S. 248(1), "retirement compensation arrangement".

Forms: T4A-RCA — Statement of Amounts Paid from a Retirement Compensation Arrangement (RCA).

Guides: T4041 Retirement Compensation Arrangements Guide.

► 12(1)(o) ◄

(o) Royalties, etc. — (Repealed by S.C. 2003, c. 28, s. 1(2).)

► 12(1)(o.1) ◄

(o.1) Foreign oil and gas production taxes — the total of all amounts, each of which is the taxpayer's production tax amount for a foreign oil and gas business of the taxpayer for the year, within the meaning assigned by subsection 126(7);

▶ 12(1)(p) ◀

(p) Certain payments to farmers — any amount received by the taxpayer in the year as a stabilization payment, or as a refund of a levy, under the *Western Grain Stabilization Act* or as a payment, or a refund of a premium, in respect of the gross revenue insurance program established under the *Farm Income Protection Act*;

Related Sections: S. 20(1)(*ff*) Payments by farmers; s. 248(1), "amount", "gross revenue".

▶ 12(1)(q) ◀

(q) Employment tax deduction — any amount deducted under subsection 127(13) or (14) of the *Income Tax Act*, chapter 148 of the Revised Statutes of Canada, 1952, by the taxpayer for the year;

▶ 12(1)(r) ◀

(r) Inventory adjustment — the total of all amounts each of which, in respect of a property described in the taxpayer's inventory at the end of the year and valued at its cost amount to the taxpayer for the purposes of computing the taxpayer's income for the year, is an allowance in respect of depreciation, obsolescence or depletion included in that cost amount;

Related Sections: S. 87(2)(*j*.1) Inventory adjustment.

▶ 12(1)(s) ◀

(s) Reinsurance commission — (Repealed by S.C. 2013, c. 34, s. 173(2).)

History: S. 12(1)(*s*) was repealed by S.C. 2013, c. 34, s. 173(2), applicable to reinsurance commissions paid after 1999, and formerly read:

> (s) *Reinsurance commission* — the total of all amounts each of which is the maximum amount that an insurer may claim in the year in respect of a reserve for a reinsurance commission for a policy as allowed by regulations made under paragraph 20(7)(*c*) in respect of a risk the reinsurance of which is assumed by the taxpayer;

▶ 12(1)(t) ◀

(t) Investment tax credit — the amount deducted under subsection 127(5) or (6) in respect of a property acquired or an expenditure made in a preceding taxation year in computing the taxpayer's tax payable for a preceding taxation year to the extent that it was not included in computing the taxpayer's income for a preceding taxation year under this paragraph or is not included in an amount determined under paragraph 13(7.1)(*e*) or 37(1)(*e*), subparagraph 53(2)(*c*)(vi) or (*h*)(ii) or for I in the definition "undepreciated capital cost" in subsection 13(21) or L in the definition "cumulative Canadian exploration expense" in subsection 66.1(6);

Information Circulars: IC 78-4R3 Investment tax credit rates.

Interpretation Bulletins: *Secondary* — IT-273R2 Government assistance — General comments.

▶ 12(1)(u) ◀

(u) Home insulation or energy conversion grants — the amount of any grant received by the taxpayer in the year under a prescribed program of the Government of Canada relating to home insulation or energy conversion in respect of a property used by the taxpayer principally for the purpose of gaining or producing income from a business or property;

Related Regulations: 224; 5500; 5501.

Related Sections: S. 13(7.1) Deemed capital cost of certain property; s. 53(1)(*k*) Adjustments to cost base — Expropriation asset; s. 56(1)(*s*) Grants under prescribed programs; s. 212(1)(*s*) Home insulation or energy conversion grants.

▶ 12(1)(v) ◀

(v) Research and development deductions — the amount, if any, by which the total of amounts determined at the end of the year in respect of the taxpayer under paragraphs 37(1)(*d*) to (*h*) exceeds the total of amounts determined at the end of the year in respect of the taxpayer under paragraphs 37(1)(*a*) to (*c*.1);

Forms: T661 — Claim for Scientific Research and Experimental Development Expenditures (SR&ED) Carried on in Canada.

SR&ED Publications: Pool of Deductible SR&ED Expenditures Policy.

▶ 12(1)(w) ◀

(w) S. 80.4(1) benefit — where the taxpayer is a corporation that carried on a personal services business at any time in the year or a preceding taxation year, the amount deemed by subsection 80.4(1) to be a benefit received by it in the year from carrying on a personal services business;

Canadian Tax Foundation: Fyfe, *The Taxation of Renewable Energy Investments in Canada*, 2011 Conference Report 42:1–42.

Interpretation Bulletins: *Secondary* — IT-421R2 Benefits to Individuals, Corporations and Shareholders from Loans or Debt.

▶ 12(1)(x) ◀

(x) Inducement, reimbursement, etc. — any particular amount (other than a prescribed amount) received by the taxpayer in the year, in the course of earning income from a business or property, from

(i) a person or partnership (in this paragraph referred to as the "payer") who pays the particular amount

(A) in the course of earning income from a business or property,

(B) in order to achieve a benefit or advantage for the payer or for persons with whom the payer does not deal at arm's length, or

(C) in circumstances where it is reasonable to conclude that the payer would not have paid the amount but for the receipt by the payer of amounts from a payer, government, municipality or public authority described in this subparagraph or in subparagraph (ii), or

(ii) a government, municipality or other public authority,

where the particular amount can reasonably be considered to have been received

(iii) as an inducement, whether as a grant, subsidy, forgivable loan, deduction from tax, allowance or any other form of inducement, or

(iv) as a refund, reimbursement, contribution or allowance or as assistance, whether as a grant, subsidy, forgivable loan, deduction from tax, allowance or any other form of assistance, in respect of

(A) an amount included in, or deducted as, the cost of property, or

(B) an outlay or expense,

to the extent that the particular amount

(v) was not otherwise included in computing the taxpayer's income, or deducted in computing, for the purposes of this Act, any balance of undeducted outlays, expenses or other amounts, for the year or a preceding taxation year,

(v.1) is not an amount received by the taxpayer in respect of a restrictive covenant, as defined by subsection 56.4(1), that was included, under subsection 56.4(2), in computing the income of a person related to the taxpayer,

(vi) except as provided by subsection 127(11.1), (11.5) or (11.6), does not reduce, for the purpose of an assessment made or that may be made under this Act, the cost or capital cost of the property or the amount of the outlay or expense, as the case may be,

(vii) does not reduce, under subsection (2.2) or 13(7.4) or paragraph 53(2)(*s*), the cost or capital cost of the property or the amount of the outlay or expense, as the case may be, and

(viii) may not reasonably be considered to be a payment made in respect of the acquisition by the payer or the public authority of an interest in the taxpayer, an interest in, or for civil law a right in, the taxpayer's business or an interest in, or for civil law a real right in, the taxpayer's property;

Editorial Note: Taxpayers can elect that an amount that would otherwise be included in income under s. 12(1)(*x*) in respect of the cost of a property or the amount of an outlay or expense can instead serve to reduce the cost of the property or the amount of the outlay or expense, as the case may be (see ss. 12(2.2), 13(7.4) and s. 53(2)(*s*)). However, the elections are not available if the amount is included in income other than under s. 12(1)(*x*) (for example, s. 9 profit).

History: S. 12(1)(*x*)(viii) was replaced by S.C. 2013, c. 34, s. 91(1), in force June 26, 2013, and formerly read:

(viii) may not reasonably be considered to be a payment made in respect of the acquisition by the payer or the public authority of an interest in the taxpayer or the taxpayer's business or property;

S. 12(1)(*x*)(v.1) was added by S.C. 2013, c. 34, s. 173(3), deemed to have come into force on October 8, 2003.

Related Regulations: 7300.

Related Sections: S. 12(2.1) Receipt of inducement, reimbursement, etc.; s. 12(2.2) Deemed outlay or expense; s. 13(7.4) Deemed capital cost; s. 20(1)(*hh*) Repayments of inducements, etc.; s. 53(2)(*s*) Amounts to be deducted — Inducement payments; s. 53(2.1) Election; s. 87(2)(*j*.6) Continuing corporation; s. 248(1), "assessment".

Canadian Tax Foundation: Lamarre, *Critical Issues in the Determination of Cost Under the Income Tax Act*, 2012 Conference Report 17:1–28; Fyfe, *The Taxation of Renewable Energy Investments in Canada*, 2011 Conference Report 42:1–42; Weinstein, *Damages, Fines, And Penalties: An Update*, 2000 Conference Report 7:1–29.

Tax Profile: March 2002 — Selected Tax Issues for Commercial Landlords and Tenants.

Tax Topics: No. 1677, Income Tax Implications of Lease Cancellation Payments.

Forms: T1273 — Statement A — Harmonized AgriStability and AgriInvest Program Information and Statement of Farming Activity for Individuals; T1274 — Statement B — Harmonized AgriStability and AgriInvest Program Information and Statement of Farming Activities for Additional Farming Operation; T1275 — AgriStability and AgriInvest Additional Information and Adjustment Request Form.

Guides: RC4408 Farming Income and the CAIS Program Harmonized Guide.

Income Tax Technical News: Issue No. 29, Application of paragraph 12(1)(x).

Interpretation Bulletins: *Primary* — IT-273R2 Government Assistance — General Comments.

SR&ED Publications: Assistance and Contract Payments Policy.

Tax Window Files: Cash back incentives on renewed mortgages, *May 31, 2017*, CRA Document No. 2016-0681271E5; Inducements — Mortgage Interest Rebate, *Technical Interpretation, Business and Partnerships Division, January 19, 2005*, CRA Document No. 2004-0091601E5. Mortgage interest rebate included in income; Inducements — Quebec Tax Deduction for Securities Acquired under a Cooperative Investment Plan, *Technical Interpretation, Financial Industries Division, April 28, 2004*, CRA Document No. 2004-0071331I7. Tax deduction under the Quebec *Taxation Act* was not a grant, subsidy or other assistance; Refund of Non-deductible Interest, *Technical Interpretation, Reorganizations and Resources Division, January 16, 2003*, CRA Document No. 2002-0164407. Refund of non-deductible interest included under subparagraph 12(1)(*x*)(iv) but taxpayer entitled to elect pursuant to subsection 12(2.2).

Cases: The taxpayer accepted $15.8 million from the government to dispose of all its right and interest in a property that had been rezoned. This amount was not income; it was a non-taxable capital receipt. An additional $650,000 paid to the taxpayer was a non-taxable windfall that did not fall under s. 12(1)(x). *Henco Industries Limited v. The Queen*, 2014 DTC 1161 (T.C.C.)

A break fee received following an unsuccessful takeover bid was held to be ordinary business income. Accordingly, the Tax Court did not rule on the s. 12(1)(*x*) arguments, but did comment that the evidence did not support a finding that the entire $7.7 million break fee was intended as a reimbursement of costs and expenses of mounting the bid. *Morguard Corporation v. The Queen*, 2012 DTC 1099 (T.C.C.), affirmed by 2013 DTC 5009 (F.C.A.)

The tenant inducement payment received by the taxpayer before the enactment of s. 12(1)(*x*) had to be included in income in the year received. *Ikea Limited v. The Queen*, 98 DTC 6092 (S.C.C.), affirming 96 DTC 6526 (F.C.A.)

The refund that the taxpayer received in 1994 of the federal sales tax paid and deducted by its predecessors between 1985 and 1989 had to be brought into its income for the years in which it was originally deducted rather than in its 1994 income. *Canada Safeway Ltd. v. The Queen*, 98 DTC 6060 (F.C.A.), affirming 97 DTC 187 (T.C.C.)

The lease inducement payment received by a taxpayer in the auto glass business upon leasing premises for use as a new head office was included in its income, considering that such payment could not be connected with any capital purpose and was directly and inextricably bound up with the economics of the taxpayer's operation. *The Queen v. TCG International Inc. (formerly Trans Canada Glass Ltd.)*, 96 DTC 6547 (F.C.T.D.) reversing 93 DTC 1260 (T.C.C.)

A tax credit received by the taxpayer under s. 1029.7 of the *Quebec Taxation Act* was an inducement payment for the purposes of s. 12(1)(*x*). *Tioxide Canada Inc. v. The Queen*, 96 DTC 6296 (F.C.A.), affirming 93 DTC 1499 (T.C.C.)

The amount paid to a partnership for entering into a lease could not be considered to be "a reimbursement, contribution, allowance or assistance ... in respect of the costs" of term deposits in which it had been obliged to invest the inducement payments until the commencement of the term of the lease, so that the taxpayer's share was included in his income. *Hill v. The Queen*, 95 DTC 5225 (F.C.A.), affirming 94 DTC 1078 (T.C.C.)

The $1 million inducement payment received by a taxpayer in consideration for an increased rent was income from his business considering that, from the moment he undertook to lease the premises, the taxpayer had signalled his intention of engaging in the business of subleasing. Had that arrangement been carried out, his profit from business would have been the difference between his rent and the rent charged to his sub-lessees. When the deal was changed so as to increase his own rent, his profit was expected to come from the lease inducement as well as from the rent differential. *The Queen v. Remington*, 94 DTC 6548 (F.C.A.), reversing 93 DTC 1020 (T.C.C.)

However, when a computer manufacturing taxpayer corporation received lease inducement payments from different landlords with respect to seven leases, such payments were included income. In this case, the primary consideration granted by the taxpayer was its acceptance of its obligations under the various leases to pay rent and these obligations were on revenue account. The inducement payments were just as much revenue payments as were the periodic rental payments to the landlords. *IBM Canada Ltd. v. M.N.R.*, 93 DTC 1266 (T.C.C.)

▶ 12(1)(x.1) ◀

(x.1) Fuel tax rebates — the total of all amounts each of which is

(i) a fuel tax rebate received in the year by the taxpayer under subsection 68.4(3) of the *Excise Tax Act*, or

(ii) the amount determined by the formula

$$10(A - B) - C$$

where

A is the total of all fuel tax rebates under subsections 68.4(2) and (3.1) of that Act received in the year by the taxpayer,

B is the total of all amounts, in respect of fuel tax rebates under section 68.4 of that Act received in the year by the taxpayer, repaid by the taxpayer under subsection 68.4(7) of that Act, and

C is the total of all amounts, in respect of fuel tax rebates under section 68.4 of that Act received in the year, deducted under subsection 111(10) in computing the taxpayer's non-capital losses for other taxation years;

► 12(1)(x.2) ◄

(x.2) Crown charge rebates — the total of all amounts each of which is an amount that

(i) was received by the taxpayer, including by way of a deduction from tax, in the year as a refund, reimbursement, contribution or allowance, in respect of an amount that was at any time receivable, directly or indirectly in any manner whatever, by Her Majesty in right of Canada or of a province in respect of

(A) the acquisition, development or ownership of a Canadian resource property, or

(B) the production in Canada from a mineral resource, a natural accumulation of petroleum or natural gas, or an oil or a gas well, and

(ii) was not otherwise included in computing the taxpayer's income for the year or a preceding taxation year;

Related Sections: S. 12(1)(*o*) Royalties, etc.; s. 18(1)(*m*) Limitation re employee stock option expenses; s. 66(15), "Canadian resource property"; s. 80.2 Reimbursement by taxpayer.

► 12(1)(y) ◄

(y) Automobile provided to partner — where the taxpayer is an individual who is a member of a partnership or an employee of a member of a partnership and the partnership makes an automobile available in the year to the taxpayer or to a person related to the taxpayer, the amounts that would be included by reason of paragraph 6(1)(*e*) in the income of the taxpayer for the year if the taxpayer were employed by the partnership;

Interpretation Bulletins: *Secondary* — IT-63R5 Benefits, including standby charge for an automobile, from the personal use of a motor vehicle supplied by an employer — After 1992.

► 12(1)(z) ◄

(z) Amateur athlete trust payments — any amount in respect of an amateur athlete trust required by section 143.1 to be included in computing the taxpayer's income for the year;

Related Sections: S. 143.1(1) Definitions; s. 248(1), "amateur athlete trust", "amount".

Forms: T1061 — Canadian Amateur Athletic Trust Group Information Return.

► 12(1)(z.1) ◄

(z.1) Qualifying environmental trusts — the total of all amounts received by the taxpayer in the year as a beneficiary under a qualifying environmental trust, whether or not the amounts are included because of subsection 107.3(1) in computing the taxpayer's income for any taxation year;

Editorial Note: The amounts received out of the trust are included in the taxpayer's income under s. 12(1)(z.1), and are subsequently deductible under general principles if they are spent on environmental reclamation incurred in the course of the taxpayer's business. See the Frankovic article cited below, at 35-6, and 41-53.

Related Sections: S. 20(1)(*ss*) Qualifying environmental trusts; s. 107.3(1) Treatment of beneficiaries under qualifying environmental trusts; s. 127.41 Part XII.4 tax credit.

Canadian Tax Foundation: Frankovic, *The Case for "Reverse Depreciation" of Reclamation Costs*, 2004 Canadian Tax Journal 1:1–58.

► 12(1)(z.2) ◄

(z.2) Dispositions of interests in qualifying environmental trusts — the total of all amounts each of which is the consideration received by the taxpayer in the year for the disposition to another person or partnership of all or part of the taxpayer's interest as a beneficiary under a qualifying environmental trust, other than consideration that is the assumption of a reclamation obligation in respect of the trust;

► 12(1)(z.3) ◄

(z.3) Debt forgiveness — any amount required because of subsection 80(13) or (17) to be included in computing the taxpayer's income for the year;

► 12(1)(z.4) ◄

(z.4) Eligible funeral arrangements — any amount required because of subsection 148.1(3) to be included in computing the taxpayer's income for the year;

► 12(1)(z.5) ◄

(z.5) TFSA amounts — any amount required by subsection 146.2(9) or section 207.061 to be included in computing the taxpayer's income for the year;

History: S. 12(1)(z.5) was replaced by S.C. 2010, c. 25, s. 4(1), applicable after October 16, 2009. S. 12(1)(z.5) formerly read:

(z.5) *Former TFSA* — any amount required because of subsection 146.2(9) to be included in computing the taxpayer's income for the year; and

S. 12(1)(z.5) was added by S.C. 2009, c. 2, s. 4(1), applicable to the 2009 and subsequent taxation years.

Related Regulations: 1100(1)(*w*)(i), 1100(1)(*x*)(i), 1100(1)(*y*)(i), 1100(1)(*ya*)(i); 1210.1; 5203(1), "adjusted business income".

Related Sections: S. 96(1)(*d*) General rules.

Forms: T81(IND) — British Columbia Royalty and Deemed Income Rebate (Individuals); T2 SCH 420 — British Columbia Royalty and Deemed Income Rebate Calculation and Application (Corporations).

► 12(1)(z.6) ◄

(z.6) Refunds — any amount received by the taxpayer in the year in respect of a refund of an amount that was deducted under paragraph 20(1)(*vv*) in computing income for any taxation year; and

Related Sections: S. 13(21), "undepreciated capital cost".

► 12(1)(z.7) ◄

(z.7) Derivative forward agreement — the total of all amounts each of which is

(i) if the taxpayer acquires a property under a derivative forward agreement in the year, the portion of the amount by which the fair market value of the property at the time it is acquired by the taxpayer exceeds the cost to the taxpayer of the property that is attributable to an underlying interest other than an underlying interest referred to in subparagraphs (*b*)(i) to (iii) of the definition *derivative forward agreement* in subsection 248(1), or

(ii) if the taxpayer disposes of a property under a derivative forward agreement in the year, the portion of the amount by which the *proceeds of disposition* (within the meaning assigned by subdivision c) of the property exceeds the fair market value of the property at the time the agreement is entered into by the taxpayer that is attributable to an underlying interest other than an underlying interest referred to in clauses (*c*)(i)(A) to (C) of the definition *derivative forward agreement* in subsection 248(1).

Editorial Note: Paragraph 12(1)(z.7) requires a taxpayer to include in income any profit derived from the acquisition or disposition of property under a derivative forward agreement. A "derivative forward agreement" is defined in s. 248(1) and in general terms includes an agreement made to buy or sell capital property, at a date more than 180 days in the future, with a total price which is linked to some unrelated underlying interest other than the value of the property and/or economic return on the property. This provision was introduced by the 2013 Budget to target "character conversion transactions" designed to convert ordinary income into capital gains through the use of derivative contracts. Where an amount is included in income under s. 12(1)(z.7), an adjustment is made to the cost base of property under s. 53(1)(*s*) or (*t*), to ensure the amount is not taxed again as a capital gain. Where the purchase or sale under a derivative forward agreement results in a loss, a corresponding deduction is available under 20(1)(*xx*).

History: S. 12(1)(z.7)(i) and (ii) were replaced by S.C. 2017, c. 33, s. 4(2), applicable to acquisitions and dispositions of property that occur after September 15, 2016, and formerly read:

(i) if the taxpayer acquires a property under a derivative forward agreement in the year, the amount by which the fair market value of the property at the time it is acquired by the taxpayer exceeds the cost to the taxpayer of the property, or

(ii) if the taxpayer disposes of a property under a derivative forward agreement in the year, the amount by which the proceeds of disposition (within the meaning assigned by subdivision c) of the property exceeds the fair market value of the property at the time the agreement is entered into by the taxpayer.

S. 12(1)(z.7) was added by S.C. 2013, c. 40, s. 4(1), applicable to acquisitions and dispositions of property by a taxpayer that occur

(*a*) under a derivative forward agreement entered into after March 20, 2013 unless

(i) the agreement is part of a series of agreements and the series

(A) includes a derivative forward agreement entered into after March 20, 2013 and before July 11, 2013, and

(B) has a term of 180 days or less (determined without reference to agreements entered into before March 21, 2013), or

(ii) the agreement is entered into after the final settlement of another derivative forward agreement (in this paragraph referred to as the "prior agreement") and

(A) having regard to the source of the funds used to purchase the property to be sold under the agreement, it is reasonable to conclude that the agreement is a continuation of the prior agreement,

(B) the terms of the agreement and the prior agreement are substantially similar,

(C) the final settlement date under the agreement is before 2015,

(D) paragraph 12(1)(z.7) would not apply to any acquisitions or dispositions under the prior agreement if this paragraph were read without reference to subparagraph (i), and

(E) the notional amount of the agreement is at all times less than or equal to the amount determined by the formula

$$(A + B + C + D + E) - (F + G)$$

where

A is the notional amount of the agreement when it is entered into,

B is the total of all amounts each of which is an increase in the notional amount of the agreement, at or before that time, that is attributable to the underlying interest,

C is the amount of the taxpayer's cash on hand immediately before March 21, 2013 that was committed, before March 21, 2013, to be invested under the agreement,

D is the total of all amounts each of which is an increase, at or before that time, in the notional amount of the agreement that is attributable to the final settlement of another derivative forward agreement (in this description referred to as the "terminated agreement") if subsection (1) would not apply to any acquisitions or dispositions under the terminated agreement if this subsection were read without reference to subparagraph (i),

E is the lesser of

(I) either

1. if the prior agreement was entered into before March 21, 2013, the amount, if any, by which the amount determined under clause (A) of the description of F in subparagraph (*b*)(ii) for the prior agreement immediately before it was finally settled exceeds the total determined under clause (B) of the description of F in subparagraph (*b*)(ii) for the prior agreement immediately before it was finally settled, or

2. in any other case, the amount, if any, by which the amount determined under this subclause for the prior agreement immediately before it was finally settled exceeds the total determined under subclause (II) for the prior agreement immediately before it was finally settled, and

(II) the total of all amounts each of which is an increase in the notional amount of the agreement before July 11, 2013 that is not otherwise described in this formula,

F is the total of all amounts each of which is a decrease in the notional amount of the agreement, at or before that time, that is attributable to the underlying interest, and

G is the total of all amounts each of which is the amount of a partial settlement of the agreement, at or before that time, to the extent that it is not reinvested in the agreement;

(*b*) after March 20, 2013 and before March 22, 2018 under a derivative forward agreement entered into before March 21, 2013, if

(i) after March 20, 2013, the term of the agreement is extended beyond 2014, or

(ii) at any time after March 20, 2013, the notional amount of the agreement exceeds the amount determined by the formula

$$(A + B + C + D + E + F) - (G + H)$$

where

A is the notional amount of the agreement immediately before March 21, 2013,

B is the total of all amounts each of which is an increase in the notional amount of the agreement, after March 20, 2013 and at or before that time, that is attributable to the underlying interest,

C is the amount of the taxpayer's cash on hand immediately before March 21, 2013 that was committed, before March 21, 2013, to be invested under the agreement,

D is the amount, if any, of an increase, after March 20, 2013 and at or before that time, in the notional amount of the agreement as a consequence of the exercise of an over-allotment option granted before March 21, 2013,

E is the total of all amounts each of which is an increase, after March 20, 2013 and at or before that time, in the notional amount of the agreement that is attributable to the final settlement of another derivative forward agreement (in this description referred to as the "terminated agreement") if

(A) the final settlement date under the agreement is

(I) before 2015, or

(II) on or before the date on which the terminated agreement, as it read immediately before March 21, 2013, was to be finally settled, and

(B) paragraph 12(1)(*z.7*) would not apply to any acquisitions or dispositions under the terminated agreement if this application were read without reference to subparagraph (*a*)(i),

F is the lesser of

(A) 5% of the notional amount of the agreement immediately before March 21, 2013, and

(B) the total of all amounts each of which is an increase in the notional amount of the agreement after March 20, 2013 and before July 11, 2013 that is not otherwise described in this formula,

G is the total of all amounts each of which is a decrease in the notional amount of the agreement, after March 20, 2013 and at or before that time, that is attributable to the underlying interest, and

H is the total of all amounts each of which is the amount of a partial settlement of the agreement, after March 20, 2013 and at or before that time, to the extent that it is not reinvested in the agreement; or

(*c*) after March 21, 2018.

For the purposes of the above application, the notional amount of a derivative forward agreement at any time is

(*a*) in the case of a purchase agreement, the fair market value at that time of the property that would be acquired under the agreement if the agreement were finally settled at that time; and

(*b*) in the case of a sale agreement, the sale price of the property that would be sold under the agreement if the agreement were finally settled at that time.

Related Sections: S. 13(21) "proceeds of disposition"; s. 20(1)(*xx*) Derivative forward agreement ITA; s. 53(1)(*s*) [Adjustments to cost base — Derivative forward agreement]; s. 53(1)(*t*) [Adjustments to cost base — Derivative forward agreement]; s. 54 "proceeds of disposition"; 248(1) derivative forward agreement.

Canadian Tax Foundation: Miller and Milet, *Derivative Forward Agreements and Synthetic Disposition Arrangements*, 2013 Conference Report 10:1–50.

Tax Profile: June 2013 — Supreme Court of Canada Clarifies that Assuming Obligations "Embedded" in a Property is not Consideration for the Property; June 2013 — Exchangeable Shares and UPREITS — At Risk in Canada; June 2013 — 2013 Federal Budget.

► 12(2) ◄

(2) Interpretation. Paragraphs (1)(*a*) and (*b*) are enacted for greater certainty and shall not be construed as implying that any amount not referred to in those paragraphs is not to be included in computing income from a business for a taxation year whether it is received or receivable in the year or not.

► 12(2.01) ◄

(2.01) No deferral of section 9 income under paragraph (1)(*g*). Paragraph (1)(*g*) does not defer the inclusion in income of any amount that would, if this section were read without reference to that paragraph, be included in computing the taxpayer's income in accordance with section 9.

History: S. 12(2.01) was added by S.C. 2013, c. 34, s. 173(5), in force June 26, 2013.

► 12(2.02) ◄

(2.02) Source of income. For the purposes of this Act, if an amount is included in computing the income of a taxpayer for a taxation year because of paragraph (1)(*l.1*) and the amount is in respect of interest that is deductible by a partnership in computing its income from a particular source or from sources in a particular place, the amount is deemed to be from the particular source or from sources in the particular place, as the case may be.

Editorial Note: Effective for taxation years that begin after 2013, the thin capitalization rules of subsection 18(4) can apply to non-resident trusts or corporations that are members of a partnership that earns Part I business or rental income. The interest deduction is not disallowed at the partnership level. Instead, the affected trust or corporate partner adds back the amount in its income under paragraph 12(1)(*l.1*). Subsection 12(2.02) provides that the amount included in under paragraph 12(1)(*l.1*) is deemed to have the same source as the income against which the relevant interest expense is deductible at the partnership level.

History: S. 12(2.02) was added by S.C. 2013, c. 40, s. 4(2), applicable to taxation years that begin after 2013.

Related Sections: S. 18(4) Limitation on deduction of interest; s. 18(5) Definitions.

► 12(2.1) ◄

(2.1) Receipt of inducement, reimbursement, etc. For the purposes of paragraph (1)(*x*), where at a particular time a taxpayer who is a beneficiary of a trust or a member of a partnership has received an amount as an inducement, whether as a grant, subsidy, forgivable loan, deduction from tax, allowance or any other form of inducement, in respect of the activities of the trust or partnership, or as a reimbursement, contribution, allowance or as assistance, whether as a grant, subsidy, forgivable loan, deduction from tax, allowance or any other form of assistance, in respect of the cost of property or in respect of an expense of the trust or partnership, the amount shall be deemed to have been received at that time by the trust or partnership, as the case may be, as such an inducement, reimbursement, contribution, allowance or assistance.

Interpretation Bulletins: *Secondary* — IT-273R2 Government assistance — General comments.

► 12(2.2) ◄

(2.2) Deemed outlay or expense. Where

(*a*) in a taxation year a taxpayer receives an amount that would, but for this subsection, be included under paragraph (1)(*x*) in computing the taxpayer's income for the year in respect of an outlay or expense (other than an outlay or expense in respect of the cost of property of the taxpayer) made or incurred by the taxpayer before the end of the following taxation year, and

(*b*) the taxpayer elects under this subsection on or before the day on or before which the taxpayer's return of income under this Part for the year is required to be filed, or would be required to be filed if tax under this Part were payable by the taxpayer for the year or, where the outlay or expense is made or incurred in the following taxation year, for that following year,

the amount of the outlay or expense shall be deemed for the purpose of computing the taxpayer's income, other than for the purposes of this subsection and paragraphs (1)(*x*) and 20(1)(*hh*), to have always been the amount, if any, by which

(*c*) the amount of the outlay or expense

exceeds

(*d*) the lesser of the amount elected by the taxpayer under this subsection and the amount so received by the taxpayer,

and, notwithstanding subsections 152(4) to (5), such assessment or reassessment of the taxpayer's tax, interest and penalties under this Act for any taxation year shall be made as is necessary to give effect to the election.

Editorial Note: See the editorial note under s. 12(1)(*x*).

Related Regulations: 600(*c*).

Related Sections: S. 13(7.4) Deemed capital cost; s. 53(2.1) Election; s. 220(3.2) Late, amended or revoked elections.

Interpretation Bulletins: *Secondary* — IT-273R2 Government assistance — General comments.

► 12(3) ◄

(3) Interest income. Subject to subsection (4.1), in computing the income for a taxation year of a corporation, partnership, unit trust or any trust of which a corporation or a partnership is a beneficiary, there shall be included any interest on a debt obligation (other than interest in respect of an income bond, an income debenture, a small business bond, a small business development bond, a net income stabilization account or an indexed debt obligation) that accrues to it to the end of the year, or becomes receivable or is received by it before the end of the year, to the extent that the interest was not included in computing its income for a preceding taxation year.

Editorial Note: See the editorial note under s. 12(1)(*c*).

Related Regulations: 201(4); 201(4.1); 201(4.2); 7000(2).

Related Sections: S. 12(1)(*c*) Interest; s. 12(1)(*p*) Certain payments to farmers; s. 12(4) Interest from investment contract; s. 12(5) Exception; s. 12(9) Deemed accrual; s. 15.2(3), "small business bond"; s. 16(6) Indexed debt obligations; s. 20(14) Accrued bond interest; s. 20(19) Annuity contract; s. 20(21) Debt obligation; s. 87(2)(*j*.4) Accrual rules; s. 248(1), "corporation", "income bond", "net income stabilization account", "small business bond", "small business development bond".

Interpretation Bulletins: *Secondary* — IT-142R3 Settlement of debts on the winding-up of a corporation; IT-265R3 Payments of income and capital combined; IT-396R Interest income.

Tax Window Files: Interest Income Renunciation, *Technical Interpretation, Financial Industries Division, June 11, 2004*, CRA Document No. 2004-0076291E5. Paragraph 12(1)(*c*) and subsection 12(3) not applicable when right to interest renounced by creditor.

► 12(4) ◄

(4) Interest from investment contract. Subject to subsection (4.1), if in a taxation year a taxpayer (other than a taxpayer to whom subsection (3) applies) holds an interest in, or for civil law a right in, an investment contract on any anniversary day of the contract, there shall be included in computing the taxpayer's income for the year the interest that accrued to the taxpayer to the end of that day with respect to the investment contract, to the extent that the interest was not otherwise included in computing the taxpayer's income for the year or any preceding taxation year.

Editorial Note: See the editorial note under s. 12(1)(*c*).

History: S. 12(4) was replaced by S.C. 2013, c. 34, s. 91(2), in force June 26, 2013, and formerly read:

(4) *Interest from investment contract.* Subject to subsection (4.1), where in a taxation year a taxpayer (other than a taxpayer to whom subsection (3) applies) holds an interest in an investment contract on any anniversary day of the contract, there shall be included in computing the taxpayer's income for the year the interest that accrued to the taxpayer to the end of that day with respect to the investment contract, to the extent that the interest was not otherwise included in computing the taxpayer's income for the year or any preceding taxation year.

Related Regulations: 201(4); 201(4.1); 201(4.2).

Related Sections: S. 12(9) Deemed accrual; s. 12(11) Definitions; s. 20(14) Accrued bond interest; s. 20(21) Debt obligation; s. 87(2)(*j*.4) Accrual rules.

Income Tax Technical News: Issue No. 43, Taxation of Roth IRAs.

Interpretation Bulletins: *Secondary* — IT-396R Interest income.

Tax Window Files: Investment Contract — Anniversary Day — Accrued Interest on Rate-Riser Investment, *Technical Interpretation, Financial Industries Division, May 31, 2005*, CRA Document No. 2005-0122641E5. Subsections 12(4) and (9) applied to "rate-riser" investment; Accrued Interest on Callable Step-up Bond, *Technical Interpretation, Financial Industries Division, September 9, 2003*, CRA Document No. 2003-0006645. Application of subsections 12(4) and (9) to "callable step-up bonds".

► 12(4.1) ◄

(4.1) Impaired debt obligations. Paragraph (1)(*c*) and subsections (3) and (4) do not apply to a taxpayer in respect of a debt obligation for the part of a taxation year throughout which the obligation is impaired where an amount in respect of the obligation is deductible because of subparagraph 20(1)(*l*)(ii) in computing the taxpayer's income for the year.

► 12(5)-(8) ◄

(5)-(8) — (Repealed by S.C. 1990, c. 39, s. 4(1).)

► 12(9) ◄

(9) Deemed accrual. For the purposes of subsections (3), (4) and (11) and 20(14) and (21), if a taxpayer acquires an interest in, or for civil law a right in, a prescribed debt obligation, an amount determined in prescribed manner is deemed to accrue to the taxpayer as interest on the obligation in each taxation year during which the taxpayer holds the interest or the right in the obligation.

Editorial Note: The prescribed debt obligations are prescribed under Regulation 7000(1), while the prescribed manner of accrual is prescribed under Regulation 7000(2).

History: S. 12(9) was replaced by S.C. 2013, c. 34, s. 91(3), in force June 26, 2013, and formerly read:

(9) *Deemed accrual.* For the purposes of subsections (3), (4) and (11) and 20(14) and (21), where a taxpayer acquires an interest in a prescribed debt obligation, an amount determined in prescribed manner shall be deemed to accrue to the taxpayer as interest on the obligation in each taxation year during which the taxpayer holds the interest in the obligation.

Related Regulations: 201(7); 7000.

Interpretation Bulletins: *Secondary* — IT-396R Interest income.

Tax Window Files: Investment Contract — Anniversary Day — Accrued Interest on Rate-Riser Investment, *Technical Interpretation, Financial Industries Division, May 31, 2005*, CRA Document No. 2005-0122641E5. Subsections 12(4) and (9) applied to "rate-riser" investment; Interest Calculation on Escalating Debt Obligation, *Technical Interpretation, Financing and Plans Division, March 30, 2005*, CRA Document No. 2004-0102421E5. Application of subsection 12(9) to escalating debt obligations; Interest Income Calculation — Coupon Bonds Issued at a Premium or Discount, *Technical Interpretation, Financial Industries Division, May 31, 2004*, CRA Document No. 2004-0074381E5. General comments regarding the accrual of interest on bonds issued at a premium or discount; Accrued Interest on Callable Step-up Bond, *Technical Interpretation, Financial Industries Division, September 9, 2003*, CRA Document No. 2003-0006645. Application of subsections 12(4) and (9) to "callable step-up bonds".

► 12(9.1) ◄

(9.1) Exclusion of proceeds of disposition. If a taxpayer disposes of an interest in, or for civil law a right in, a debt obligation that is a debt obligation in respect of which the proportion of the payments of principal to which the taxpayer is entitled is not equal to the proportion of the payments of interest to which the taxpayer is entitled, the portion of the proceeds of disposition received by the taxpayer that can reasonably be considered to represent a recovery of the cost to the taxpayer of the interest or the right in the debt obligation shall, notwithstanding any other provision of this Act, not be included in computing the taxpayer's income, and for the purpose of this subsection, a debt obligation includes, for greater certainty, all of the issuer's obligations to pay principal and interest under that obligation.

History: S. 12(9.1) was replaced by S.C. 2013, c. 34, s. 91(3), in force June 26, 2013, and formerly read:

(9.1) *Exclusion of proceeds of disposition.* Where a taxpayer disposes of an interest in a debt obligation that is a debt obligation in respect of which the proportion of the payments of principal to which the taxpayer is entitled is not equal to the proportion of the payments of interest to which the taxpayer is entitled, such portion of the proceeds of disposition received by the taxpayer as can reasonably be considered to represent a recovery of the cost to the taxpayer of the interest in the debt obligation shall, notwithstanding any other provision of this Act, not be included in computing the income of the taxpayer, and for the purpose of this subsection, a debt obligation includes, for greater certainty, all of the issuer's obligations to pay principal and interest under that obligation.

▶ 12(10) ◀

(10) Application — (Repealed by S.C. 1990, c. 39, s. 4(3).)

▶ 12(10.1) ◀

(10.1) Income from R.H.O.S.P. Notwithstanding any other provision of this Act, where an individual was at the end of 1985 a beneficiary under a registered home ownership savings plan (within the meanings assigned by paragraphs 146.2(1)(*a*) and (*h*) of the *Income Tax Act*, chapter 148 of the Revised Statutes of Canada, 1952, as they read in their application to the 1985 taxation year), that portion of the income that can reasonably be considered to have accrued under the plan before 1986 (other than the portion thereof that can reasonably be considered to be attributable to amounts contributed after May 22, 1985 to or under the plan) shall not be included in computing the income of the individual or of any other person.

Related Sections: S. 50(3) Disposal of R.H.O.S.P. properties; s. 146.2(22) Contributions to R.H.O.S.P. after May 22, 1985.

▶ 12(10.2) ◀

(10.2) NISA receipts. There shall be included in computing a taxpayer's income for a taxation year from a property the total of all amounts each of which is the amount determined by the formula

$$A - B$$

where

A is an amount paid at a particular time in the year out of the taxpayer's NISA Fund No. 2; and

B is the amount, if any, by which

(*a*) the total of all amounts each of which is

(i) deemed by subsection (10.4) or 104(5.1) or (14.1) (as it read for the taxpayer's 2015 taxation year) to have been paid out of the taxpayer's NISA Fund No. 2 before the particular time, or

(ii) deemed by subsection 70(5.4) or 73(5) to have been paid out of another person's NISA Fund No. 2 on being transferred to the taxpayer's NISA Fund No. 2 before the particular time,

exceeds

(*b*) the total of all amounts each of which is the amount by which an amount otherwise determined under this subsection in respect of a payment out of the taxpayer's NISA Fund No. 2 before the particular time was reduced because of this description.

History: S. 12(10.2), subparagraph (*a*)(i) of the description of B was replaced by S.C. 2014, c. 39, s. 2(1), applicable to the 2016 and subsequent taxation years, and formerly read:

(i) deemed by subsection (10.4) or 104(5.1) or (14.1) to have been paid out of the taxpayer's NISA Fund No. 2 before the particular time, or

Related Regulations: 202(2.1); 202(3).

Related Sections: S. 70(5.4) NISA on death; s. 73(5) Disposition of a NISA; s. 104(5.1) Interest in NISA Fund No. 2; s. 104(14.1) NISA election; s. 212(1)(*t*) NISA Fund No. 2 payments; s. 214(3)(*l*) Deemed payments; s. 248(1), "NISA Fund No. 2", "property"; s. 249(1) Definition of "taxation year".

Forms: T1163 — Statement A — AgriStability and AgriInvest Programs Account Information and Statement of Farming Activities for Individuals; T1175 — AgriStability and AgriInvest Programs/Farming - Calculation of Capital Cost Allowance (CCA) and Business-Use-of-Home Expenses.

Guides: RC4060 Farming Income and AgriStability and AgriInvest Programs — Joint Forms and Guide.

▶ 12(10.3) ◀

(10.3) Amount credited or added not included in income. Notwithstanding any other provision of this Act, an amount credited or added to a taxpayer's NISA Fund No. 2 shall not be included in computing the taxpayer's income solely because of that crediting or adding.

Related Sections: S. 70(5.4) NISA on death; s. 73(5) Disposition of a NISA; s. 104(5.1) Interest in NISA Fund No. 2; s. 104(14.1) NISA election; s. 248(1), "NISA Fund No. 2", "property"; s. 249(1) Definition of "taxation year".

▶ 12(10.4) ◀

(10.4) Acquisition of control — corporate NISA Fund No. 2. For the purpose of subsection (10.2), if at any time there is an acquisition of control of a corporation, the balance of the corporation's NISA Fund No. 2, if any, at that time is deemed to be paid out to the corporation immediately before that time.

▶ 12(11) ◀

(11) Definitions. In this section,

"anniversary day" — "anniversary day" of an investment contract means

(*a*) the day that is one year after the day immediately preceding the date of issue of the contract,

(*b*) the day that occurs at every successive one year interval from the day determined under paragraph (*a*), and

(*c*) the day on which the contract was disposed of;

"investment contract" — "investment contract", in relation to a taxpayer, means any debt obligation other than

(*a*) a salary deferral arrangement or a plan or arrangement that, but for any of paragraphs (*a*), (*b*) and (*d*) to (*l*) of the definition "salary deferral arrangement" in subsection 248(1), would be a salary deferral arrangement,

(*b*) a retirement compensation arrangement or a plan or arrangement that, but for any of paragraphs (*a*), (*b*), (*d*) and (*f*) to (*n*) of the definition "retirement compensation arrangement" in subsection 248(1), would be a retirement compensation arrangement,

(*c*) an employee benefit plan or a plan or arrangement that, but for any of paragraphs (*a*) to (*e*) of the definition "employee benefit plan" in subsection 248(1), would be an employee benefit plan,

(*d*) a foreign retirement arrangement,

(*d*.1) a TFSA,

(*e*) an income bond,

(*f*) an income debenture,

(*g*) a small business development bond,

(*h*) a small business bond,

(*i*) an obligation in respect of which the taxpayer has (otherwise than because of subsection (4)) at periodic intervals of not more than one year, included, in computing the taxpayer's income throughout the period in which the taxpayer held an interest in, or for civil law a right in, the obligation, the income accrued on it for those intervals, (*j*) an obligation in respect of a net income stabilization account,

(*k*) an indexed debt obligation, and

(*l*) a prescribed contract.

History: S. 12(11), paragraph (*i*) of the definition "investment contract", was replaced by S.C. 2013, c. 34, s. 91(4), in force June 26, 2013, and formerly read:

(*i*) an obligation in respect of which the taxpayer has (otherwise than because of subsection (4)) at periodic intervals of not more than one year, included, in computing the taxpayer's income throughout the period in which the taxpayer held an interest in the obligation, the income accrued thereon for such intervals,

S. 12(11), paragraph (*d.1*) of the definition "investment contract", was added by S.C. 2009, c. 2, s. 4(2), applicable to the 2009 and subsequent taxation years.

Related Regulations: 7000(6).

Related Sections: S. 12(1)(*c*) Interest; s. 12(4) Interest from investment contract; s. 16(6) Indexed debt obligations; s. 248(1), "foreign retirement arrangement", "net income stabilization account", "prescribed".

Interpretation Bulletins: *Secondary* — IT-396R Interest income.

SECTION 12.1: Cash bonus on Canada Savings Bonds

Notwithstanding any other provision of this Act, where in a taxation year a taxpayer receives an amount from the Government of Canada in respect of a Canada Savings Bond as a cash bonus that the Government of Canada has undertaken to pay (other than any amount of interest, bonus or principal agreed to be paid at the time of the issue of the bond under the terms of the bond), the taxpayer shall, in computing the taxpayer's income for the year, include as interest in respect of the Canada Savings Bond 1/2 of the cash bonus so received.

Related Regulations: Part II; 220.

Related Sections: S. 12(1)(*c*) Interest.

SECTION 12.2: [Life insurance policies and annuity contracts]

▶ 12.2(1) ◀

(1) Amount to be included. Where in a taxation year a taxpayer holds an interest, last acquired after 1989, in a life insurance policy that is not

(*a*) an exempt policy,

(*b*) a prescribed annuity contract, and

(*c*) a contract under which the policyholder has, under the terms and conditions of a life insurance policy that was not an annuity contract and that was last acquired before December 2, 1982, received the proceeds therefrom in the form of an annuity contract,

on any anniversary day of the policy, there shall be included in computing the taxpayer's income for the taxation year the amount, if any, by which the accumulating fund on that day in respect of the interest in the policy, as determined in prescribed manner, exceeds the adjusted cost basis to the taxpayer of the interest in the policy on that day.

Related Regulations: 201(5); 304; 307.

Related Sections: S. 148(9) Definitions.

Interpretation Bulletins: *Primary* — IT-87R2 Policyholders' income from life insurance policies. *Secondary* — IT-365R2 Damages, settlement, and similar receipts.

▶ 12.2(2) ◀

(2) Interest not disposed of before 1985 — (Repealed by S.C. 1990, c. 39, s. 5(1).)

▶ 12.2(3) ◀

(3) Amounts included in income — (Repealed by S.C. 1994, c. 7, Sched. II, s. 8(2).)

▶ 12.2(4) ◀

(4) Election — (Repealed by S.C. 1990, c. 39, s. 5(1).)

▶ 12.2(4.1) ◀

(4.1) Revocation of election — (Repealed by S.C. 1990, c. 39, s. 5(1).)

▶ 12.2(5) ◀

(5) Idem. Where in a taxation year subsection (1) applies with respect to a taxpayer's interest in an annuity contract (or would apply if the contract had an anniversary day in the year at a time when the taxpayer held the interest), there shall be included in computing the taxpayer's income for the year the amount, if any, by which

(*a*) the total of all amounts each of which is an amount determined at the end of the year, in respect of the interest, for any of H to L in the definition "adjusted cost basis" in subsection 148(9)

exceeds

(*b*) the total of all amounts each of which is an amount determined at the end of the year, in respect of the interest, for any of A to G in the definition referred to in paragraph (*a*).

Related Regulations: 201(5).

▶ 12.2(6) ◀

(6) Application — (Repealed by S.C. 1990, c. 39, s. 5(2).)

▶ 12.2(7) ◀

(7) Idem — (Repealed by S.C. 1990, c. 39, s. 5(2).)

▶ 12.2(8) ◀

(8) Deemed acquisition of interest in annuity. For the purposes of this section, the first premium that was not fixed before 1990 and that was paid after 1989 by or on behalf of a taxpayer under an annuity contract, other than a contract described in paragraph (1)(*d*) of this section, or paragraph 12.2(3)(*e*) of the *Income Tax Act*, chapter 148 of the Revised Statutes of Canada, 1952, or to which subsection (1) of this section or subsection 12.2(4) of the *Income Tax Act*, chapter 148 of the Revised Statutes of Canada, 1952, applies (as those paragraphs and subsections, the numbers of which are those in force immediately before December 17, 1991, read in their application to life insurance policies last acquired before 1990) or to which subsection 12(3) applies, last acquired by the taxpayer before 1990 (in this subsection referred to as the "original contract") shall be deemed to have been paid to acquire, at the time the premium was paid, an interest in a separate annuity contract issued at that time, to the extent that the amount of the premium was not fixed before 1990, and each subsequent premium paid under the original contract shall be deemed to have been paid under that separate contract to the extent that the amount of that subsequent premium was not fixed before 1990.

▶ 12.2(9) ◀

(9) Rules where premium paid — (Repealed by S.C. 1990, c. 39, s. 5(4).)

Editorial Note: This provision is still relevant for policies acquired before 1990.

Related Regulations: 309.

▶ 12.2(10) ◀

(10) Riders. For the purposes of this Act, a rider added at any time after 1989 to a life insurance policy last acquired before 1990 that provides additional life insurance is deemed to be a separate life insurance policy issued at that time unless

(*a*) the policy is an exempt policy last acquired after December 1, 1982 or an annuity contract; or

(*b*) the only additional life insurance provided by the rider is an accidental death benefit.

▶ 12.2(11) ◀

(11) Definitions. In this section and paragraph 56(1)(*d*.1) of the *Income Tax Act*, chapter 148 of the Revised Statutes of Canada, 1952,

Canadian Tax Foundation: Wark, *Review of Proposed Changes to the Exempt Test Legislation*, 2013 Ontario Tax Conference 13A:1–16.

"anniversary day" —"anniversary day" of a life insurance policy means

(*a*) the day that is one year after the day immediately preceding the day on which the policy was issued, and

(*b*) each day that occurs at each successive one-year interval after the day determined under paragraph (*a*).

"exempt policy" —"exempt policy" has the meaning prescribed by regulation.

Related Regulations: 306.

STEP Canada: Kevin Wark, "Practitioner's Update: Life Insurance," PowerPoint presentation to the 15th National Conference of STEP Canada, Toronto, June 10-11, 2013.

▶ 12.2(12) ◀

(12) Application of ss. 138(12) and 148(9). The definitions in subsections 138(12) and 148(9) apply to this section.

▶ 12.2(13) ◀

(13) Application of s. 148(10). Subsection 148(10) applies to this section.

SECTION 12.3: Transition inclusion re unpaid claims reserve

(Repealed by S.C. 2013, c. 34, s. 174(1).)

History: S. 12.3 was repealed by S.C. 2013, c. 34, s. 174(1), applicable to taxation years that begin after October 31, 2011, and formerly read:

S. 12.3 *Transition inclusion re unpaid claims reserve.* Where an amount has been deducted under subsection 20(26) in computing the income of an insurer for its taxation year that includes February 23, 1994, there shall be included in computing the insurer's income for that taxation year and each subsequent taxation year that begins before 2004, the prescribed portion for the year of the amount so deducted.

Related Regulations: 8101(2); 8101(3); 8101(4); 8101(5).

Related Sections: S. 87(2)(*g*.1) Continuation.

SECTION 12.4: Bad debt inclusion

Where, in a taxation year, a taxpayer disposes of a property that was a property described in an inventory of the taxpayer and in the year or a preceding taxation year an amount has been deducted under paragraph 20(1)(*p*) in computing the taxpayer's income in respect of the property, there shall be included in computing the taxpayer's income for the year from the business in which the property was used or held, the amount, if any, by which

(*a*) the total of all amounts deducted under paragraph 20(1)(*p*) by the taxpayer in respect of the property in computing the taxpayer's income for the year or a preceding taxation year

exceeds

(*b*) the total of all amounts included under paragraph 12(1)(*i*) by the taxpayer in respect of the property in computing the taxpayer's income for the year or a preceding taxation year.

Related Sections: S. 87(2)(*g*.1) Continuation.

SECTION 12.5: [Insurer's reserve inclusion]

▶ 12.5(1) ◀

(1) Definitions. The definitions in this section apply for the purposes of this section and section 20.4.

"base year" —"base year" of an insurer means the insurer's taxation year that immediately precedes its transition year.

History: S. 12.5(1), the definition "base year" was added by S.C. 2009, c. 2, s. 5(1), applicable to taxation years that begin after September 2006.

"insurance business" —"insurance business" of an insurer, is an insurance business carried on by the insurer, other than a life insurance business.

History: S. 12.5(1), the definition "insurance business" was added by S.C. 2009, c. 2, s. 5(1), applicable to taxation years that begin after September 2006.

"reserve transition amount" —"reserve transition amount" of an insurer, in respect of an insurance business carried on by it in Canada in its transition year, is the positive or negative amount determined by the formula

$$A - B$$

where

A is the maximum amount that the insurer would be permitted to claim under paragraph 20(7)(*c*) (and that would be prescribed by section 1400 of the Regulations for the purpose of paragraph 20(7)(*c*)) as a policy reserve for its base year in respect of its insurance policies if

(*a*) the generally accepted accounting principles that applied to the insurer in valuing its assets and liabilities for its transition year had applied to it for its base year, and (*b*) section 1400 of the Regulations were read in respect of the insurer's base year as it reads in respect of its transition year, and

B is the maximum amount that the insurer is permitted to claim under paragraph 20(7)(*c*) as a policy reserve for its base year.

History: S. 12.5(1), the definition "reserve transition amount" was added by S.C. 2009, c. 2, s. 5(1), applicable to taxation years that begin after September 2006.

"transition year" —"transition year" of an insurer means the insurer's first taxation year that begins after September 2006.

History: S. 12.5(1), the definition "transition year" was added by S.C. 2009, c. 2, s. 5(1), applicable to taxation years that begin after September 2006.

► 12.5(2) ◄

(2) Transition year income inclusion. There shall be included in computing an insurer's income for its transition year from an insurance business carried on by it in Canada in the transition year, the positive amount, if any, of the insurer's reserve transition amount in respect of that insurance business.

History: S. 12.5(2) was added by S.C. 2009, c. 2, s. 5(1), applicable to taxation years that begin after September 2006.

► 12.5(3) ◄

(3) Transition year income deduction reversal. If an amount has been deducted under subsection 20.4(2) in computing an insurer's income for its transition year from an insurance business carried on by it in Canada, there shall be included in computing the insurer's income, for each particular taxation year of the insurer that ends after the beginning of the transition year, from that insurance business, the amount determined by the formula

$$A \times B/1825$$

where

A is the amount deducted under subsection 20.4(2) in computing the insurer's income for the transition year from that insurance business; and

B is the number of days in the particular taxation year that are before the day that is 1825 days after the first day of the transition year.

History: S. 12.5(3) was added by S.C. 2009, c. 2, s. 5(1), applicable to taxation years that begin after September 2006.

► 12.5(4) ◄

(4) Winding-up. If an insurer has, in a winding-up to which subsection 88(1) has applied, been wound-up into another corporation (referred to in this subsection as the "parent"), and immediately after the winding-up the parent carries on an insurance business, in applying subsections (3) and 20.4(3) in computing the incomes of the insurer and of the parent for particular taxation years that end on or after the first day (referred to in this subsection as the "start day") on which assets of the insurer were distributed to the parent on the winding-up,

(*a*) the parent is, on and after the start day, deemed to be the same corporation as and a continuation of the insurer in respect of

(i) any amount included under subsection (2) or deducted under subsection 20.4(2) in computing the insurer's income from an insurance business for its transition year,

(ii) any amount included under subsection (3) or deducted under subsection 20.4(3) in computing the insurer's income from an insurance business for a taxation year of the insurer that begins before the start day, and

(iii) any amount that would — in the absence of this subsection and if the insurer existed and carried on an insurance business on each day that is the start day or a subsequent day and on which the parent carries on an insurance business — be required to be included or deducted, in respect of any of those days, under subsection (3) or 20.4(3) in computing the insurer's income from an insurance business; and

(*b*) the insurer is, in respect of each of its particular taxation years, to determine the value for B in the formulas in subsections (3) and 20.4(3) without reference to the start day and days after the start day.

History: S. 12.5(4) was added by S.C. 2009, c. 2, s. 5(1), applicable to taxation years that begin after September 2006.

► 12.5(5) ◄

(5) Amalgamations. If there is an amalgamation (within the meaning assigned by subsection 87(1)) of an insurer with one or more other corporations to form one corporation (referred to in this subsection as the "new corporation"), and immediately after the amalgamation the new corporation carries on an insurance business, in applying subsections (3) and 20.4(3) in computing the new corporation's income for particular taxation years that begin on or after the day on which the amalgamation occurred, the new corporation is, on and after that day, deemed to be the same corporation as and a continuation of the insurer in respect of

(*a*) any amount included under subsection (2) or deducted under subsection 20.4(2) in computing the insurer's income from an insurance business for its transition year,

(*b*) any amount included under subsection (3) or deducted under subsection 20.4(3) in computing the insurer's income from an insurance business for a taxation year of the insurer that begins before the day on which the amalgamation occurred; and

(*c*) any amount that would — in the absence of this subsection and if the insurer existed and carried on an insurance business on each day that is the day on which the amalgamation occurred or a subsequent day and on which the new corporation carries on an insurance business — be required to be included or deducted, in respect of any of those days, under subsection (3) or 20.4(3) in computing the insurer's income from an insurance business.

History: S. 12.5(5) was added by S.C. 2009, c. 2, s. 5(1), applicable to taxation years that begin after September 2006.

► 12.5(6) ◄

(6) Application of subsection (7). Subsection (7) applies if, at any time, an insurer (referred to in this subsection and subsection (7) as the "transferor") transfers, to a corporation (referred to in this subsection and subsection (7) as the "transferee") that is related to the transferor, property in respect of an insurance business carried on by the transferor in Canada (referred to in this subsection and subsection (7) as the "transferred business") and

(*a*) subsection 138(11.5) or (11.94) applies to the transfer; or

(*b*) subsection 85(1) applies to the transfer, the transfer includes all or substantially all of the property and liabilities of the transferred business and, immediately after the transfer, the transferee carries on an insurance business.

History: S. 12.5(6) was added by S.C. 2009, c. 2, s. 5(1), applicable to taxation years that begin after September 2006.

▶ 12.5(7) ◀

(7) Transfer of insurance business. If this subsection applies in respect of the transfer, at any time, of property

(*a*) the transferee is, at and after that time, deemed to be the same corporation as and a continuation of the transferor in respect of

(i) any amount included under subsection (2) or deducted under subsection 20.4(2) in computing the transferor's income for its transition year that can reasonably be attributed to the transferred business,

(ii) any amount included under subsection (3) or deducted under subsection 20.4(3) in computing the transferor's income for a taxation year of the transferor that begins before that time that can reasonably be attributed to the transferred business,

(iii) any amount that would — in the absence of this subsection and if the transferor existed and carried on an insurance business on each day that includes that time or is a subsequent day and on which the transferee carries on an insurance business — be required to be included or deducted, in respect of any of those days, under subsection (3) or 20.4(3) in computing the transferor's income that can reasonably be attributed to the transferred business; and

(*b*) in determining, in respect of the day that includes that time or any subsequent day, any amount that is required under subsection (3) or 20.4(3) to be included or deducted in computing the transferor's income for each particular taxation year from the transferred business, the description of A in the formulas in those subsections is deemed to be nil.

History: S. 12.5(7) was added by S.C. 2009, c. 2, s. 5(1), applicable to taxation years that begin after September 2006.

▶ 12.5(8) ◀

(8) Ceasing to carry on business. If at any time an insurer ceases to carry on all or substantially all of an insurance business (referred to in this subsection as the "discontinued business"), and none of subsections (4) to (6) apply, there shall be included in computing the insurer's income from the discontinued business for the insurer's taxation year that includes the time that is immediately before that time, the amount determined by the formula

$$A - B$$

where

A is the amount deducted under subsection 20.4(2) in computing the insurer's income from the discontinued business for its transition year; and

B is the total of all amounts each of which is an amount included under subsection (3) in computing the insurer's income from the discontinued business for a taxation year that began before that time.

History: S. 12.5(8) was added by S.C. 2009, c. 2, s. 5(1), applicable to taxation years that begin after September 2006.

▶ 12.5(9) ◀

(9) Ceasing to exist. If at any time an insurer that carried on an insurance business ceases to exist (otherwise than as a result of a winding-up or amalgamation described in subsection (4) or (5)), for the purposes of subsections (8) and 20.4(4), the insurer is deemed to have ceased to carry on the insurance business at the earlier of

(*a*) the time (determined without reference to this subsection) at which the insurer ceased to carry on the insurance business, and

(*b*) the time that is immediately before the end of the last taxation year of the insurer that ended at or before the time at which the insurer ceased to exist.

History: S. 12.5(9) was added by S.C. 2009, c. 2, s. 5(1), applicable to taxation years that begin after September 2006.

SECTION 12.6: [Stapled securities – anti-avoidance]

▶ 12.6(1) ◀

(1) Definitions. The definitions in section 18.3 apply in this section.

History: S. 12.6(1) was added by S.C. 2013, c. 40, s. 5(1), deemed to have come into force on July 20, 2011.

▶ 12.6(2) ◀

(2) Where subsection (3) applies. Subsection (3) applies for a taxation year of an entity in respect of a security of the entity if

(*a*) the security becomes, at a particular time in the year, a stapled security of the entity and, as a consequence, amounts described in paragraphs 18.3(3)(*a*) and (*b*) are not deductible because of subsection 18.3(3);

(*b*) the security (or any security for which the security was substituted) ceased, at an earlier time, to be a stapled security of any entity and, as a consequence, subsection 18.3(3) ceased to apply to deny the deductibility of amounts that would be described in paragraphs 18.3(3)(*a*) and (*b*) if the security were a stapled security; and

(*c*) throughout the period that began immediately after the most recent time referred to in paragraph (*b*) and that ends at the particular time, the security (or any security for which the security was substituted) was not a stapled security of any entity.

History: S. 12.6(2) was added by S.C. 2013, c. 40, s. 5(1), deemed to have come into force on July 20, 2011.

▶ 12.6(3) ◀

(3) Income inclusion. If this subsection applies for a taxation year of an entity in respect of a security of the entity, the entity shall include in computing its income for the year each amount that (*a*) was deducted by the entity (or by another entity that issued a security for which the security was substituted) in computing its income for a taxation year that includes any part of the period described in paragraph 2(*c*); and

(*b*) would not have been deductible if subsection 18.3(3) had applied in respect of the amount.

Editorial Note: Section 12.6 sets out anti-avoidance rules relating to the denial of certain deductions under section 18.3 involving stapled securities. In general terms, a stapled security is a publicly-traded security instrument that is bundled with one or more other securities such that each security is not independently transferable (see s. 18.3(1)). Section 18.3 denies the deduction of certain interest amounts and rent amounts in respect of REITs involving stapled securities. To avoid section 18.3, securities may be unstapled. However, where this unstapling may be temporary, section 12.6 disregards any separation that is not permanent or irrevocable. Subsection 12.6(3) requires a taxpayer to include in income any amounts deducted in the year that would not be deductible under section 18.3 during a period of temporary unstapling of otherwise stapled securities. Under subsection 12.6(2) this anti-avoidance rule applies to both unstapled and restapled securities and substituted securities. Under subsection 12.6(4), interest is applicable to each deducted amount subsequently included in income, from the end of the taxation year in which the deduction was taken.

History: S. 12.6(3) was added by S.C. 2013, c. 40, s. 5(1), deemed to have come into force on July 20, 2011.

▶ 12.6(4) ◀

(4) Deemed excess. For the purposes of subsection 161(1), if an amount described in paragraph (3)(*a*) is included in the income of an entity for a taxation year under subsection (3), the entity is deemed to have an excess immediately after the entity's balance-due day for the year computed as if

(*a*) the entity were resident in Canada throughout the year;

(*b*) the entity's tax payable for the year were equal to the tax payable by the entity on its taxable income for the year;

(*c*) the amount were the entity's only taxable income for the year;

(*d*) the entity claimed no deductions under Division E for the year;

(*e*) the entity had not paid any amounts on account of its tax payable for the year; and

(*f*) the tax payable determined under paragraph (*b*) had been outstanding throughout the period that begins immediately after the end of the taxation year for which the amount was deducted and that ends on the entity's balance-due day for the year.

History: S. 12.6(4) was added by S.C. 2013, c. 40, s. 5(1), deemed to have come into force on July 20, 2011.

SECTION 13: Recaptured depreciation

▶ 13(1) ◀

(1) Recaptured depreciation. If, at the end of a taxation year, the total of the amounts determined for E to K in the definition "undepreciated capital cost" in subsection (21) in respect of a taxpayer's depreciable property of a particular prescribed class exceeds the total of the amounts determined for A to D.1 in that definition in respect of that property, the excess shall be included in computing the taxpayer's income of the year.

Editorial Note: S. 13(1) includes in income the negative balance of the undepreciated capital cost (UCC) in respect of a class of depreciable property, if any, at the end of a taxation year. In general terms, the inclusion is normally meant to reflect previously deducted depreciation to the extent it is "recaptured" on a sale of depreciable property (for example, when the sole property in a class is sold for proceeds in excess of the UCC). The amount included under s. 13(1) is added to the UCC balance at the beginning of the next taxation year (see amount B in the UCC definition in s. 13(21)).

History: S. 13(1) was replaced by S.C. 2013, c. 34, s. 175(1), applicable to taxation years that end after February 23, 1998, and formerly read:

(1) *Recaptured depreciation.* Where, at the end of a taxation year, the total of the amounts determined for E to J in the definition "undepreciated capital cost" in subsection (21) in respect of a taxpayer's depreciable property of a particular prescribed class exceeds the total of the amounts determined for A to D in that definition in respect thereof, the excess shall be included in computing the taxpayer's income for the year.

Related Sections: S. 13(2) Recaptured depreciation for passenger vehicle; s. 13(3) "Taxation year", "year" and "income" of individual; s. 13(5.2) Lease-option agreement — exercise of option; s. 13(5.3) Lease-option agreement — disposition of option; s. 13(8) Disposition after ceasing business; s. 13(13) Deduction under Canadian Vessel Construction Assistance Act; s. 13(15) Where s. (1) and subdivision c do not apply; s. 13(21) Definitions; s. 28(1)(*d*) Farming or fishing business; s. 37(6) Expenditures of a capital nature; s. 45(2) Election where change of use; s. 70(5) Capital property of a deceased taxpayer; s. 73(2) Capital cost and amount deemed allowed to spouse, etc., or trust; s. 85(5) Rules on transfers of depreciable property; s. 87(2)(*d*) Depreciable property; s. 87(2)(*l.3*) Replacement property; s. 88(1) Winding-up; s. 97(4) Where capital cost to partner exceeds proceeds of disposition; s. 98(3) Rules applicable where partnership ceases to exist; s. 104(5), Depreciable property; s. 107(2) Distribution by personal trust; s. 110.1(3) Gifts of capital property; s. 110.6(1), "investment income"; s. 115(1)(*a*)(iii.2) Non-resident's taxable income in Canada; s. 118.1(6) Gift of capital property; s. 138(12) Definitions; s. 216(6) Saving provision; and ITAR s. 20(2) Recapture of capital cost allowances.

Income Tax Folios: *Primary* — S3-F4-C1 General Discussion of Capital Cost Allowance.

Interpretation Bulletins: *Secondary* — IT-206R Separate businesses; IT-267R2 Capital cost allowance — Vessels; IT-472 SR Capital cost allowance — Class 8 property; IT-481 (Consolid.) Timber resource property and timber limits.

Tax Window Files: Election to Transfer Property to CCA Class, *Technical Interpretation, Business Incentives & Capital Transactions Section, March 6, 2006*, CRA Document No. 2006-0171111E5; Allocation of Partnership Income Between Spouse Partners, *Technical Interpretation, Business and Partnerships Division, January 14, 2004*, CRA Document No. 2003-0029571E5; Estate — Transfer of Building to Income Beneficiary, *Technical Interpretation, International and Trusts Division, December 9, 2003*, CRA Document No. 2003-0032585; Dispositions — Transfer of Buildings from Nominee Corporation to Principal, *Tax Ruling, Business and Partnerships Division, January 7, 2003*, CRA Document No. 2003-0045613.

Cases: The explosives division sold by the taxpayer was not a separate business, therefore, the taxpayer was not subject to recapture of capital cost allowance or an increased s. 14(1) income inclusion. Indicators of integration included centralized financing and credit management, centralized purchasing, and common research facilities. *Du Pont Canada Inc. v. The Queen*, 2001 DTC 5269 (F.C.A.), reversing 99 DTC 1132 (T.C.C.)

A building was allocated a value greater than its undepreciated capital cost regardless of the fact that the purchaser was only interested in the land. *Stanley v. M.N.R.*, 72 DTC 6004 (S.C.C.).

▶ 13(1.1) ◀

(1.1) Idem — (Repealed by 1976-77, c. 4, s. 3(1).)

▶ 13(2) ◀

(2) Idem. Notwithstanding subsection (1), where an excess amount is determined under that subsection at the end of a taxation year in respect of a passenger vehicle having a cost to a taxpayer in excess of $20,000 or such other amount as may be prescribed, that excess amount shall not be included in computing the taxpayer's income for the year but shall be deemed, for the purposes of B in the definition "undepreciated capital cost" in subsection (21), to be an amount included in the taxpayer's income for the year by reason of this section.

Editorial Note: Subsection 13(2) provides that depreciation recapture will not be included in income in respect of a passenger vehicle with a cost exceeding a prescribed amount) which is set out under Regulation 7307(1) ($30,000 plus GST/HST and PST). However, the recapture is deemed for the purpose of B in the definition "undepreciated capital cost" in s. 13(21) to have been included in the taxpayer's income for the year, ensuring that the result of the computation of undepreciated capital cost of the particular class will be nil.

Related Regulations: 1100(2.5); 7307(1); Sched. II, Class 10.1.

Related Sections: s. 13(3) "Taxation year", "year" and "income" of individual; s. 13(4.2) Election — limited period franchise, concession or license; s. 13(4.3) Effect of election; s. 13(7)(*g*) Rules applicable; s. 20(16.1) Terminal loss for passenger vehicle; s. 67.2 Interest on money borrowed for passenger vehicle; s. 248(1), "passenger vehicle".

Income Tax Folios: *Primary* — S3-F4-C1 General Discussion of Capital Cost Allowance.

Interpretation Bulletins: *Secondary* — IT-521R Motor vehicle expenses claimed by self-employed individuals; IT-522R Vehicle, travel and sales expenses of employees.

► 13(3) ◄

(3) "Taxation year", "year" and "income" of individual. Where a taxpayer is an individual whose income for a taxation year includes income from a business the fiscal period of which does not coincide with the calendar year and depreciable property acquired for the purpose of gaining or producing income from the business has been disposed of,

(*a*) for greater certainty, each reference in subsections (1) and (2) to a "taxation year" and "year" shall be read as a reference to a "fiscal period"; and

(*b*) a reference in subsection (1) to "the income" shall be read as a reference to "the income from the business".

Related Sections: S. 13(8) Disposition after ceasing business; s. 20(16.2) Reference to "taxation year" and "year" of individual.

Income Tax Folios: *Primary* — S3-F4-C1 General Discussion of Capital Cost Allowance.

Interpretation Bulletins: *Secondary* — IT-172R Capital cost allowance — Taxation year of individual.

► 13(4) ◄

(4) Exchanges of property. Where an amount in respect of the disposition in a taxation year (in this subsection referred to as the "initial year") of depreciable property (in this section referred to as the "former property") of a prescribed class of a taxpayer would, but for this subsection, be the amount determined for F or G in the definition "undepreciated capital cost" in subsection (21) in respect of the disposition of the former property that is either

(*a*) property the proceeds of disposition of which were proceeds referred to in paragraph (*b*), (*c*) or (*d*) of the definition "proceeds of disposition" in subsection (21), or

(*b*) a property that was, immediately before the disposition, a former business property of the taxpayer,

and the taxpayer so elects under this subsection in the taxpayer's return of income for the taxation year in which the taxpayer acquires a depreciable property of a prescribed class of the taxpayer that is a replacement property for the taxpayer's former property,

(*c*) the amount otherwise determined for F or G in the definition "undepreciated capital cost" in subsection (21) in respect of the disposition of the former property shall be reduced by the lesser of

(i) the amount, if any, by which the amount otherwise determined for F or G in that definition exceeds the undepreciated capital cost to the taxpayer of property of the prescribed class to which the former property belonged at the time immediately before the time that the former property was disposed of, and

(ii) the amount that has been used by the taxpayer to acquire

(A) if the former property is described in paragraph (*a*), before the later of the end of the second taxation year following the initial year and 24 months after the end of the initial year, or

(B) in any other case, before the later of the end of the first taxation year following the initial year and 12 months after the end of the initial year,

a replacement property of a prescribed class that has not been disposed of by the taxpayer before the time at which the taxpayer disposed of the former property, and

(*d*) the amount of the reduction determined under paragraph (*c*) shall be deemed to be proceeds of disposition of a depreciable property of the taxpayer that had a capital cost equal to that amount and that was property of the same class as the replacement property, from a disposition made on the later of

(i) the time the replacement property was acquired by the taxpayer, and

(ii) the time the former property was disposed of by the taxpayer.

Editorial Note: Subsection 13(4) allows a taxpayer who is required under s. 13(1) to include in income recaptured depreciation from the disposition of certain depreciable property to elect to defer until the later of two periods any tax on the recapture, to the extent that the taxpayer reinvests the proceeds of disposition in a replacement property. In the case of certain involuntary dispositions (e.g., theft or expropriation), the proceeds must be reinvested before (a) the end of the taxpayer's second subsequent taxation year, or (b) within 24 months after the end of the taxpayer's taxation year in which the property was disposed of. In other situations, the proceeds must be reinvested before (a) the end of the first subsequent taxation year, or (b) within 12 months after the end of the taxpayer's taxation year in which the property was disposed of.

History: S. 13(4)(*c*)(ii) was replaced by S.C. 2013, c. 34, s. 175(2), applicable in respect of dispositions that occur in taxation years that end on or after December 20, 2000, except that for those dispositions that occur in taxation years that end before December 20, 2001, clause 13(4)(*c*)(ii)(B) is to be read as follows:

> "(B) in any other case, before the end of the first taxation year following the initial year,"

S. 13(4)(*c*)(ii) formerly read:

> (ii) the amount that has been used by the taxpayer to acquire
>
> (A) where the former property is referred to in paragraph (*a*), before the end of the second taxation year following the initial year, or
>
> (B) in any other case, before the end of the first taxation year following the initial year,
>
> a replacement property of a prescribed class that has not been disposed of by the taxpayer before the time at which the taxpayer disposed of the former property, and

Related Regulations: 600(b).

Related Sections: S. 13(4.1) Replacement for a former property; s. 13(4.2) Election — limited period franchise, concession or license; s. 13(4.3) Effect of election; s. 13(18) Reassessments; s. 13(21) Definitions; s. 14(6) Exchange of property; s. 44(1) Exchanges of property; s. 44(4) Deemed election; s. 44(6) Deemed proceeds of disposition; s. 87(2)(*l.3*) Replacement property; s. 96(3) Agreement or election of partnership members; s. 220(3.2) Late, amended or revoked elections; s. 248(1), "former business property".

Canadian Tax Foundation: Shapiro, *The Replacement Property Rules: A Bit More Than Before*, 2002 Canadian Tax Journal 6:2141–2165.

Tax Profile: July 2003 — The Replacement Property Rules.

Information Circulars: IC 07-1 Taxpayer relief provisions.

Interpretation Bulletins: *Primary* — IT-259R4 Exchange of property. *Secondary* — IT-267R2 Capital cost allowance — Vessels.

Tax Window Files: New Class 14.1 and replacement property rules, *November 4, 2016*, CRA Document No. 2016-0666901E5; Location of Former Business Property, *Technical Interpretation, Business and Partnerships Division, December 4, 2006*, CRA Document No. 2006-0213921E5; Replacement Property Rules, *Technical Interpretation, Business and Partnerships Division, July 31, 2006*, CRA Document No. 2005-0156171E5; Replacement Property — Partnership Interest, *Technical Interpretation, Business and Partnerships Division, February 17, 2005*, CRA Document No. 2004-0090411E5; Replacement Property Rules — Building on Leased Land, *Technical Interpretation, Business and Partnerships Division, January 24, 2003*, CRA Document No. 2002-0173815.

▶ 13(4.1) ◀

(4.1) Replacement for a former property. For the purposes of subsection (4), a particular depreciable property of a prescribed class of a taxpayer is a replacement for a former property of the taxpayer if

(*a*) it is reasonable to conclude that the property was acquired by the taxpayer to replace the former property;

(*a*.1) it was acquired by the taxpayer and used by the taxpayer or a person related to the taxpayer for a use that is the same as or similar to the use to which the taxpayer or a person related to the taxpayer put the former property;

(*b*) where the former property was used by the taxpayer or a person related to the taxpayer for the purpose of gaining or producing income from a business, the particular depreciable property was acquired for the purpose of gaining or producing income from that or a similar business or for use by a person related to the taxpayer for such a purpose;

(*c*) where the former property was a taxable Canadian property of the taxpayer, the particular depreciable property is a taxable Canadian property of the taxpayer; and

(*d*) where the former property was a taxable Canadian property (other than treaty-protected property) of the taxpayer, the particular depreciable property is a taxable Canadian property (other than treaty-protected property) of the taxpayer.

Editorial Note: S. 13(4.2) and (4.3) allow elections under s. 13(4) and 44(1) (to defer recapture of depreciation and capital gains, respectively) to be made in respect of a franchise, concession or limited period license if the transferor and transferee elect jointly. However, s. 20(16.1)(*b*) provides that a terminal loss will not be available to the transferee in respect of such property.

Related Sections: S. 44(5) Replacement property; s. 248(1), "treaty-protected property".

Interpretation Bulletins: *Primary* — IT-259R4 Exchange of property.

Tax Window Files: Location of Former Business Property, *Technical Interpretation, Business and Partnerships Division, December 4, 2006*, CRA Document No. 2006-0213921E5; Replacement Property Rules, *Technical Interpretation, Business and Partnerships Division, July 31, 2006*, CRA Document No. 2005-0156171E5; Acquisition of a Replacement Property from a Related Person, *Technical Interpretation, Business and Partnerships Division, October 15, 2004*, CRA Document No. 2004-0068421E5; Replacement Property Rules, *Technical Interpretation, Business and Partnerships Division, May 28, 2004*, CRA Document No. 2004-0066251E5; Replacement Property Rules — Same or Similar Use, *Technical Interpretation, Business and Partnerships Division, June 6, 2003*, CRA Document No. 2003-0012135.

▶ 13(4.2) ◀

(4.2) Election — limited period franchise, concession or license. Subsection (4.3) applies if

(*a*) a taxpayer (in this subsection and subsection (4.3) referred to as the "transferor") has, pursuant to a written agreement with a person or partnership (in this subsection and subsection (4.3) referred to as the "transferee"), at any time disposed of or terminated a former property that is a franchise, concession or licence for a limited period that is wholly attributable to the carrying on of a business at a fixed place;

(*b*) the transferee acquired the former property from the transferor or, on the termination, acquired a similar property in respect of the same fixed place from another person or partnership; and

(*c*) the transferor and the transferee jointly elect in their returns of income for their taxation years that include that time to have subsection (4.3) apply in respect of the acquisition and the disposition or termination.

History: S. 13(4.2) was added by S.C. 2013, c. 34, s. 175(3), applicable in respect of dispositions and terminations that occur after December 20, 2002.

▶ 13(4.3) ◀

(4.3) Effect of election. If this subsection applies in respect of an acquisition and a disposition or termination,

(*a*) if the transferee acquired a similar property referred to in paragraph (4.2)(*b*), the transferee is deemed to have also acquired the former property at the time that the former property was terminated and to own the former property until the transferee no longer owns the similar property;

(*b*) if the transferee acquired the former property referred to in paragraph (4.2)(*b*), the transferee is deemed to own the former property until such time as the transferee owns neither the former property nor a similar property in respect of the same fixed place to which the former property related;

(*c*) for the purpose of calculating the amount deductible under paragraph 20(1)(*a*) in respect of the former property in computing the transferee's income, the life of the former property remaining on its acquisition by the transferee is deemed to be equal to the period that was the life of the former property remaining on its acquisition by the transferor; and

(*d*) any amount that would, if this Act were read without reference to this subsection, be included in the cost of a property of the transferor included in Class 14.1 of Schedule II to the *Income Tax Regulations* (including a deemed acquisition under subsection (35)) or included in the proceeds of disposition of a property of the transferee included in that Class (including a deemed disposition under subsection (37)) in respect of the disposition or termination of the former property by the transferor is deemed to be

(i) neither included in the cost nor the proceeds of disposition of property included in that Class,

(ii) an amount required to be included in computing the capital cost to the transferee of the former property, and

(iii) an amount required to be included in computing the proceeds of disposition to the transferor in respect of a disposition of the former property.

History: S. 13(4.3)(*d*), the portion preceding subparagraph (ii) was replaced by S.C. 2016, c. 12, s. 3(1), applicable in respect of dispositions and terminations that occur after 2016, and formerly read:

(*d*) any amount that would, if this Act were read without reference to this subsection, be an eligible capital amount to the transferor or an eligible capital expenditure to the transferee in respect of the disposition or termination of the former property by the transferor is deemed to be

(i) neither an eligible capital amount nor an eligible capital expenditure,

S. 13(4.3) was added by S.C. 2013, c. 34, s. 175(3), applicable in respect of dispositions and terminations that occur after December 20, 2002.

Related Sections: S. 20(16.1) Non-application of subsection (16); s. 87(2)(*l.4*) Subsection 13(4.2) election.

▶ 13(5) ◀

(5) Reclassification of property. Where one or more depreciable properties of a taxpayer that were included in a prescribed class (in this subsection referred to as the "old class") become included at any time (in this subsection referred to as the "transfer time") in another prescribed class (in this subsection referred to as the "new class"), for the purpose of determining at any subsequent time the undepreciated capital cost to the taxpayer of depreciable property of the old class and the new class

(*a*) the value of A in the definition "undepreciated capital cost" in subsection (21) shall be determined as if each of those depreciable properties were

(i) properties of the new class acquired before the subsequent time, and

(ii) never included in the old class; and

(*b*) there shall be deducted in computing the total depreciation allowed to the taxpayer for property of the old class before the subsequent time, and added in computing the total depreciation allowed to the taxpayer for property of the new class before the subsequent time, the greater of

(i) the amount determined by the formula

$$A - B$$

where

A is the total of all amounts each of which is the capital cost to the taxpayer of each of those depreciable properties, and

B is the undepreciated capital cost to the taxpayer of depreciable property of the old class at the transfer time, and

(ii) the total of all amounts each of which is an amount that would have been deducted under paragraph 20(1)(*a*) in respect of a depreciable property that is one of those properties in computing the taxpayer's income for a taxation year that ended before the transfer time and at the end of which the property was included in the old class if

(A) the property had been the only property included in a separate prescribed class, and

(B) the rate allowed by the regulations made for the purpose of paragraph 20(1)(*a*) in respect of that separate class had been the effective rate that was used by the taxpayer to calculate a deduction under that paragraph in respect of the old class for the year.

Editorial Note: Subsections 13(5) and (5.1) provide the rules to be applied where depreciable property is transferred from one prescribed class to another; they also apply to determine the undepreciated capital cost of property. A transfer from one class to another class can occur when certain types of property are converted from a leasehold interest to a freehold interest, or when a new class is created from a class that already exists by an amendment to the Regulations.

Related Regulations: 1103; Sched. II.

Related Sections: S. 87(2)(*d*) Depreciable property.

Income Tax Folios: *Primary* — S3-F4-C1 General Discussion of Capital Cost Allowance.

Information Circulars: IC 84-1 Revision of capital cost allowance claims and other permissive deductions.

Interpretation Bulletins: *Secondary* — IT-521R Motor vehicle expenses claimed by self-employed individuals; IT-522R Vehicle, travel and sales expenses of employees.

Tax Window Files: Class 43.1 Generating Heat from Wood Pellets, *Technical Interpretation, Reorganizations and Resources Division, November 25, 2005*, CRA Document No. 2005-0151611E5; Definition of Automobile — Pick up Truck, *Technical Interpretation, Business and Partnerships Division, January 19, 2004*, CRA Document No. 2003-0045911I7.

▶ 13(5.1) ◀

(5.1) Rules applicable. Where at any time in a taxation year a taxpayer acquires a particular property in respect of which, immediately before that time, the taxpayer had a leasehold interest that was included in a prescribed class, for the purposes of this section, section 20 and any regulations made under paragraph 20(1)(*a*), the following rules apply:

(*a*) the leasehold interest shall be deemed to have been disposed of by the taxpayer at that time for proceeds of disposition equal to the amount, if any, by which

(i) the capital cost immediately before that time of the leasehold interest

exceeds

(ii) the total of all amounts claimed by the taxpayer in respect of the leasehold interest and deductible under paragraph 20(1)(*a*) in computing the taxpayer's income in previous taxation years;

(*b*) the particular property shall be deemed to be depreciable property of a prescribed class of the taxpayer acquired by the taxpayer at that time and there shall be added to the capital cost to the taxpayer of the property an amount equal to the capital cost referred to in subparagraph (*a*)(i); and

(*c*) the total referred to in subparagraph (*a*)(ii) shall be added to the total depreciation allowed to the taxpayer before that time in respect of the class to which the particular property belongs.

Income Tax Folios: *Primary* — S3-F4-C1 General Discussion of Capital Cost Allowance.

Interpretation Bulletins: *Primary* — IT-464R Capital cost allowance — Leasehold interests.

▶ 13(5.2) ◀

(5.2) Deemed cost and depreciation. If, at any time, a taxpayer has acquired a capital property that is depreciable property or real or immovable property in respect of which, before that time, the taxpayer or any person with whom the taxpayer was not dealing at arm's length was entitled to a deduction in computing income in respect of any amount paid or payable for the use of, or the right to use, the property and the cost or the capital cost (determined without reference to this subsection) at that time of the property to the taxpayer is less than the fair market value thereof at that time determined without reference to any option with respect to that property, for the purposes of this section, section 20 and any regulations made under paragraph 20(1)(*a*), the following rules apply:

(*a*) the property shall be deemed to have been acquired by the taxpayer at that time at a cost equal to the lesser of

(i) the fair market value of the property at that time determined without reference to any option with respect to that property, and

(ii) the total of the cost or the capital cost (determined without reference to this subsection) of the property to the taxpayer and all amounts (other than amounts paid or payable to a person with whom the taxpayer was not dealing at arm's length) each of which is an outlay or expense made or incurred by the taxpayer or by a person with whom the taxpayer was not dealing at arm's length at any time for the use of, or the right to use, the property,

and for the purposes of this paragraph and subsection (5.3), where a particular corporation has been incorporated or otherwise formed after the time any other corporation with which the particular corporation would not have been dealing at arm's length had the particular corporation been in existence before that time, the particular corporation shall be deemed to have been in existence from the time of the formation of the other corporation and to have been not dealing at arm's length with the other corporation;

(*b*) the amount by which the cost to the taxpayer of the property determined under paragraph (*a*) exceeds the cost or the capital cost thereof (determined without reference to this subsection) shall be added to the total depreciation allowed to the taxpayer before that time in respect of the prescribed class to which the property belongs; and

(*c*) where the property would, but for this paragraph, not be depreciable property of the taxpayer, it shall be deemed to be depreciable property of a separate prescribed class of the taxpayer.

Editorial Note: S. 13(5.2) applies when a taxpayer has paid rent for property (e.g., a building) and later acquires the property. Essentially, if the property is later sold for a profit, the rent paid is "recaptured" because it is treated as CCA claimed, which is recaptured under s. 13(1).

History: S. 13(5.2), the portion before paragraph (*a*) was replaced by S.C. 2013, c. 34, s. 92(1), in force June 26, 2013, and formerly read:

(5.2) *Idem.* Where, at any time, a taxpayer has acquired a capital property that is depreciable property or real property in respect of which, before that time, the taxpayer or any person with whom the taxpayer was not dealing at arm's length was entitled to a deduction in computing income in respect of any amount paid or payable for the use of, or the right to use, the depreciable property or real property and the cost or the capital cost (determined without reference to this subsection) at that time of the property to the taxpayer is less than the fair market value thereof at that time determined without reference to any option with respect to that property, for the purposes of this section, section 20 and any regulations made under paragraph 20(1)(*a*), the following rules apply:

Related Regulations: S. 1101(5g); Sched. II, Class 36.

Forms: T776 — Statement of Real Estate Rentals.

Interpretation Bulletins: *Primary* — IT-233R Lease option agreements.

▶ 13(5.3) ◀

(5.3) Deemed recapture. If, at any time in a taxation year, a taxpayer has disposed of a capital property that is an option with respect to depreciable property or real or immovable property in respect of which the taxpayer or any person with whom the taxpayer was not dealing at arm's length was entitled to a deduction in computing income in respect of any amount paid for the use of, or the right to use, the property, for the purposes of this section, the amount, if any, by which the proceeds of disposition to the taxpayer of the option exceed the taxpayer's cost in respect thereof is deemed to be an excess referred to in subsection (1) in respect of the taxpayer for the year.

History: S. 13(5.3) was replaced by S.C. 2013, c. 34, s. 92(2), in force June 26, 2013, and formerly read:

(5.3) *Idem.* Where, at any time in a taxation year, a taxpayer has disposed of a capital property that is an option with respect to depreciable property or real property in respect of which the taxpayer or any person with whom the taxpayer was not dealing at arm's length was entitled to a deduction in computing income in respect of any amount paid for the use of, or the right to use, the depreciable property or real property, for the purposes of this section, the amount, if any, by which the proceeds of disposition to the taxpayer of the option exceed the taxpayer's cost in respect thereof shall be deemed to be an excess referred to in subsection (1) in respect of the taxpayer for the year.

Related Sections: S. 13(5.2) Lease-option agreement — exercise of option; s. 49 Granting of options.

▶ 13(5.4) ◀

(5.4) Idem. Where, before the time of disposition of a capital property that was depreciable property of a taxpayer, the taxpayer, or any person with whom the taxpayer was not dealing at arm's length, was entitled to a deduction in computing income in respect of any outlay or expense made or incurred for the use of, or the right to use, during a period of time, that capital property (other than an outlay or expense made or incurred by the taxpayer or a person with whom the taxpayer was not dealing at arm's length before the acquisition of the property), except where the taxpayer disposed of the property to a person with whom the taxpayer was not dealing at arm's length and that person was subject to the provisions of subsection (5.2) with respect to the acquisition by that person of the property, the following rules apply:

(*a*) an amount equal to the lesser of

(i) the total of all amounts (other than amounts paid or payable to the taxpayer or a person with whom the taxpayer was not dealing at arm's length) each of which was a deductible outlay or expense made or incurred before the time of disposition by the taxpayer, or by a person with whom the taxpayer was not dealing at arm's length, for the use of, or the right to use, during the period of time, the property, and

(ii) the amount, if any, by which the fair market value of the property at the earlier of

(A) the expiration of the last period of time in respect of which the deductible outlay or expense referred to in subparagraph (i) was made or incurred, and

(B) the time of the disposition

exceeds the capital cost to the taxpayer of the property immediately before that time

shall, immediately before the time of the disposition, be added to the capital cost of the property to the person who owned the property at that time; and

(*b*) the amount added to the capital cost to the taxpayer of the property pursuant to paragraph (*a*) shall be added immediately before the time of the disposition to the total depreciation allowed to the taxpayer before that time in respect of the prescribed class to which the property belongs.

Editorial Note: Subsections 13(5.4) and (5.5) provide rules to be applied where a taxpayer, or a person with whom the taxpayer was not dealing at arm's length, disposes of a property for which a deduction in respect of an outlay or expense — usually rent — was made or incurred for the use of or right to use the property. Subsection 13(5.5) specifically provides that lease cancellation payments deductible under paragraphs (*z*) and 20(1)(*z*.1) are excluded from the amount which may be recaptured.

Related Sections: S. 13(5.5) Lease cancellation payment.

► 13(5.5) ◄

(5.5) Lease cancellation payment. For the purposes of subsection (5.4), an amount deductible by a taxpayer under paragraph 20(1)(*z*) or (*z*.1) in respect of a cancellation of a lease of property shall, for greater certainty, be deemed not to be an outlay or expense that was made or incurred by the taxpayer for the use of, or the right to use, the property.

Editorial Note: See the editorial note under 13(5.4).

► 13(6) ◄

(6) Misclassified property. Where, in calculating the amount of a deduction allowed to a taxpayer under subsection 20(16) or regulations made for the purposes of paragraph 20(1)(*a*) in respect of depreciable property of the taxpayer of a prescribed class (in this subsection referred to as the "particular class"), there has been added to the capital cost to the taxpayer of depreciable property of the particular class the capital cost of depreciable property (in this subsection referred to as "added property") of another prescribed class, for the purposes of this section, section 20 and any regulations made for the purposes of paragraph 20(1)(*a*), the added property shall, if the Minister so directs with respect to any taxation year for which, under subsection 152(4), the Minister may make any reassessment or additional assessment or assess tax, interest or penalties under this Part, be deemed to have been property of the particular class and not of the other class at all times before the beginning of the year and, except to the extent that the added property or any part thereof has been disposed of by the taxpayer before the beginning of the year, to have been transferred from the particular class to the other class at the beginning of the year.

Related Sections: S. 152(4) Assessment and reassessment.

Income Tax Folios: *Primary* — S3-F4-C1 General Discussion of Capital Cost Allowance.

Information Circulars: IC 84-1 Revision of capital cost allowance claims and other permissive deductions.

► 13(7) ◄

(7) Rules applicable. Subject to subsection 70(13), for the purposes of paragraphs 8(1)(*j*) and (*p*), this section, section 20 and any regulations made for the purpose of paragraph 20(1)(*a*),

(*a*) where a taxpayer, having acquired property for the purpose of gaining or producing income, has begun at a later time to use it for some other purpose, the taxpayer shall be deemed to have disposed of it at that later time for proceeds of disposition equal to its fair market value at that time and to have reacquired it immediately thereafter at a cost equal to that fair market value;

(*b*) where a taxpayer, having acquired property for some other purpose, has begun at a later time to use it for the purpose of gaining or producing income, the taxpayer shall be deemed to have acquired it at that later time at a capital cost to the taxpayer equal to the lesser of

(i) the fair market value of the property at that later time, and

(ii) the total of

(A) the cost to the taxpayer of the property at that later time determined without reference to this paragraph, paragraph (*a*) and subparagraph (*d*)(ii), and

(B) $1/2$ of the amount, if any, by which

(I) the fair market value of the property at that later time

exceeds the total of

(II) the cost to the taxpayer of the property as determined under clause (A), and

(III) twice the amount deducted by the taxpayer under section 110.6 in respect of the amount, if any, by which the fair market value of the property at that later time exceeds the cost to the taxpayer of the property as determined under clause (A);

(*c*) where property has, since it was acquired by a taxpayer, been regularly used in part for the purpose of gaining or producing income and in part for some other purpose, the taxpayer shall be deemed to have acquired, for the purpose of gaining or producing income, the proportion of the property that the use regularly made of the property for gaining or producing income is of the whole use regularly made of the property at a capital cost to the taxpayer equal to the same proportion of the capital cost to the taxpayer of the whole property and, if the property has, in such a case, been disposed of, the proceeds of disposition of the proportion of the property deemed to have been acquired for gaining or producing income shall be deemed to be the same proportion of the proceeds of disposition of the whole property;

(*d*) where, at any time after a taxpayer has acquired property, there has been a change in the relation between the use regularly made by the taxpayer of the property for gaining or producing income and the use regularly made of the property for other purposes,

(i) if the use regularly made by the taxpayer of the property for the purpose of gaining or producing income has increased, the taxpayer shall be deemed to have acquired at that time depreciable property of that class at a capital cost equal to the total of

(A) the proportion of the lesser of

(I) its fair market value at that time, and

(II) its cost to the taxpayer at that time determined without reference to this subparagraph, subparagraph (ii) and paragraph (*a*)

that the amount of the increase in the use regularly made by the taxpayer of the property for that purpose is of the whole of the use regularly made of the property, and

(B) 1/2 of the amount, if any, by which

(I) the amount deemed under subparagraph 45(1)(*c*)(ii) to be the taxpayer's proceeds of disposition of the property in respect of the change

exceeds the total of

(II) that proportion of the cost to the taxpayer of the property as determined under subclause (A)(II) that the amount of the increase in the use regularly made by the taxpayer of the property for that purpose is of the whole of the use regularly made of the property, and

(III) twice the amount deducted by the taxpayer under section 110.6 in respect of the amount, if any, by which the amount determined under subclause (I) exceeds the amount determined under subclause (II), and

(ii) if the use regularly made of the property for the purpose of gaining or producing income has decreased, the taxpayer shall be deemed to have disposed at that time of depreciable property of that class and the proceeds of disposition shall be deemed to be an amount equal to the proportion of the fair market value of the property as of that time that the amount of the decrease in the use regularly made by the taxpayer of the property for that purpose is of the whole use regularly made of the property;

(*e*) notwithstanding any other provision of this Act except subsection 70(13), where at a particular time a person or partnership (in this paragraph referred to as the "taxpayer") has, directly or indirectly, in any manner whatever, acquired (otherwise than as a consequence of the death of the transferor) a depreciable property (other than a timber resource property) of a prescribed class from a person or partnership with whom the taxpayer did not deal at arm's length (in this paragraph referred to as the "transferor") and, immediately before the transfer, the property was a capital property of the transferor,

(i) where the transferor was an individual resident in Canada or a partnership any member of which was either an individual resident in Canada or another partnership and the cost of the property to the taxpayer at the particular time determined without reference to this paragraph exceeds the cost, or where the property was depreciable property, the capital cost of the property to the transferor immediately before the transferor disposed of it, the capital cost of the property to the taxpayer at the particular time shall be deemed to be the amount that is equal to the total of

(A) the cost or capital cost, as the case may be, of the property to the transferor immediately before the particular time, and

(B) 1/2 of the amount, if any, by which

(I) the transferor's proceeds of disposition of the property

exceed the total of

(II) the cost or capital cost, as the case may be, to the transferor immediately before the particular time,

(III) twice the amount deducted by any person under section 110.6 in respect of the amount, if any, by which the amount determined under subclause (I) exceeds the amount determined under subclause (II), and

(IV) the amount, if any, required by subsection 110.6(21) to be deducted in computing the capital cost to the taxpayer of the property at that time

and, for the purposes of paragraph (*b*) and subparagraph (*d*)(i), the cost of the property to the taxpayer shall be deemed to be the same amount,

(ii) where the transferor was neither an individual resident in Canada nor a partnership any member of which was either an individual resident in Canada or another partnership and the cost of the property to the taxpayer at the particular time determined without reference to this paragraph exceeds the cost, or where the property was depreciable property, the capital cost of the property to the transferor immediately before the transferor disposed of it, the capital cost of the property to the taxpayer at that time shall be deemed to be the amount that is equal to the total of

(A) the cost or capital cost, as the case may be, of the property to the transferor immediately before the particular time, and

(B) 1/2 of the amount, if any, by which the transferor's proceeds of disposition of the property exceed the cost or capital cost, as the case may be, to the transferor immediately before the particular time

and, for the purposes of paragraph (*b*) and subparagraph (*d*)(i), the cost of the property to the taxpayer shall be deemed to be the same amount, and

(iii) where the cost or capital cost, as the case may be, of the property to the transferor immediately before the transferor disposed of it exceeds the capital cost of the property to the taxpayer at that time determined without reference to this paragraph, the capital cost of the property to the taxpayer at that time shall be deemed to be the amount that was the cost or capital cost, as the case may be, of the property to the transferor immediately before the transferor disposed of it and the excess shall be deemed to have been allowed to the taxpayer in respect of the property under regulations made under paragraph 20(1)(*a*) in computing the taxpayer's income for taxation years ending before the acquisition of the property by the taxpayer;

(*e*.1) where a taxpayer is deemed by paragraph 110.6(19)(*a*) to have disposed of and reacquired a property that immediately before the disposition was a depreciable property, the taxpayer shall be deemed to have acquired the property from himself, herself or itself and, in so having acquired the property, not to have been dealing with himself, herself or itself at arm's length;

(*f*) if a taxpayer is deemed under paragraph 111(4)(*e*) to have disposed of and reacquired depreciable property (other than a timber resource property), the capital cost to the taxpayer of the property at the time of the reacquisition is deemed to be equal to the total of

(i) the capital cost to the taxpayer of the property at the time of the disposition, and

(ii) 1/2 of the amount, if any, by which the taxpayer's proceeds of disposition of the property exceed the capital cost to the taxpayer of the property at the time of the disposition;

(*g*) where the cost to a taxpayer of a passenger vehicle exceeds $20,000 or such other amount as is prescribed, the capital cost to the taxpayer of the vehicle shall be deemed to be $20,000 or that other prescribed amount, as the case may be;

(*h*) notwithstanding paragraph (*g*), where a passenger vehicle is acquired by a taxpayer at any time from a person with whom the taxpayer does not deal at arm's length, the capital cost at that time to the taxpayer of the vehicle shall be deemed to be the least of

(i) the fair market value of the vehicle at that time,

(ii) the amount that immediately before that time was the cost amount to that person of the vehicle, and

(iii) $20,000 or such other amount as is prescribed; and

(*i*) if the cost to a taxpayer of a zero-emission passenger vehicle exceeds the prescribed amount,

(i) the capital cost to the taxpayer of the vehicle is deemed to be equal to the prescribed amount, and

(ii) for the purposes of paragraph (*a*) of the description of F in the definition "undepreciated capital cost" in subsection (21), the proceeds of disposition of the vehicle are deemed to be the amount determined by the formula

$$A \times B/C$$

where

A is the amount that would, in the absence of this subparagraph, be the proceeds of disposition of the vehicle,

B is

(A) if the vehicle is disposed of to a person or partnership with which the taxpayer deals at arm's length, the capital cost to the taxpayer of the vehicle, and

(B) in any other case, the cost to the taxpayer of the vehicle, and

C is the cost to the taxpayer of the vehicle.

History: S. 13(7)(*i*) was added by S.C. 2019, c. 29, s. 2(1), deemed to have come into force on March 19, 2019.

S. 13(7)(*f*) was replaced by S.C. 2013, c. 40, s. 6(1), deemed to have come into force on March 21, 2013, and formerly read:

(*f*) where a corporation is deemed under paragraph 111(4)(*e*) to have disposed of and reacquired depreciable property (other than a timber resource property), the capital cost to the corporation of the property at the time of the reacquisition is deemed to be the amount that is equal to the total of

(i) the capital cost to the corporation of the property at the time of the disposition, and

(ii) $^1/_2$ of the amount, if any, by which the corporation's proceeds of disposition of the property exceed the capital cost to the corporation of the property at the time of the disposition;

Related Regulations: 1100(2.5); 1101(1af); 1102(14); 7307(1); 7307(1.1); Sched. II, Class 10.1.

Related Sections: S. 13(2) Recaptured depreciation for passenger vehicle; s. 13(4) Exchanges of property; s. 13(7.3) Control of corporations by one trustee; s. 13(9) Meaning of "gaining or producing income"; s. 13(21) "undepreciated capital cost"; s. 13(21.2) Loss on certain transfers; s. 20(4) Bad debts — dispositions of depreciable property; s. 20(4.11) Bad debts — zero-emission passenger vehicles; s. 20(16.1) Terminal loss for passenger vehicle; s. 44(1) Exchanges of property; s. 45(1) Property with more than one use; s. 45(2) Election where change of use; s. 67.3 Limitation re cost of leasing passenger vehicle; s. 67.4 More than one owner or lessor; s. 67.41 More than one owner; s. 70(13) Capital cost of certain depreciable property; s. 85(1)(*e*.4) Transfer of property to corporation by shareholders; s. 85(1)(*e*.5) Transfer of property to corporation by shareholders; s. 85(5) Rules on transfers of depreciable property; s. 97(4) Where capital cost to partner exceeds proceeds of disposition; s. 248(1), "cost amount".

Canadian Tax Foundation: Irvine, *Current Cases: Federal Court of Appeal — Capital Gain Versus Income: Flying into Fog (CAE Inc. v. Canada, 2013 FCA 92)*, 2013 Canadian Tax Journal 3:729–739; Truster, *Inventory Versus Capital Property and the Change-in-Use Rules*, 2013 Tax for the Owner-Manager 13(4):6–7.

Tax Topics: No. 2182, A Revisit of the Change-in-Use Rules.

Income Tax Folios: *Primary* — S3-F4-C1 General Discussion of Capital Cost Allowance. *Secondary* — S1-F3-C2 Principal Residence.

Interpretation Bulletins: *Primary* — IT-102R2 Conversion of property, other than real property, from or to inventory. *Secondary* — IT-291R3 Transfer of property to a corporation under subsection 85(1); IT-302R3 Losses of a corporation — the effect that acquisitions of control, amalgamations and windings-up have on their deductibility — after January 15, 1987; IT-521R Motor vehicle expenses claimed by self-employed individuals.

Tax Window Files: Change in Use of a Duplex Given to a Grandson, *Technical Interpretation, International and Trust Division, January 26, 2007,*

CRA Document No. 2005-0157751E5; Automobile — Multiple Owners, *Technical Interpretation, Business and Partnerships Division, January 2, 2007*, CRA Document No. 2006-0217551I7; Resale of Depreciable Property Acquired from Related Person, *Technical Interpretation, Business and Partnerships Division, November 8, 2006*, CRA Document No. 2006-0176171E5; Election under Subsection 110.6(19) of the Act — Impact on Undepreciated Capital Cost of Non-Qualifying Real Property, *Technical Interpretation, Business and Partnerships Division, July 7, 2006*, CRA Document No. 2006-0185961I7; Definition of Automobile, *Technical Interpretation, Business and Partnerships Division, January 10, 2005*, CRA Document No. 2004-0091251I7; Shareholder's Use of Automobile in Corporate Activity, *APFF Conference 2004, Question 18, October 8, 2004*, CRA Document No. 2004-0086861C6; Deceased Taxpayer — Transfer of Depreciable Property to Spouse, *Technical Interpretation, Business and Partnerships Division, September 15, 2004*, CRA Document No. 2004-0075001I7; Capital Cost Allowance — Leasehold Interest, *Technical Interpretation, Financial Industries Division, June 14, 2004*, CRA Document No. 2004-0071821E5; Definition of Automobile — Pick up Truck, *Technical Interpretation, Business and Partnerships Division, January 19, 2004*, CRA Document No. 2003-0045911I7; Capital Cost Allowance — Acquisition of Computer Software from Related Non-Resident Company, *Technical Interpretation, Business and Publications Division, June 30, 2003*, CRA Document No. 2003-0014995.

Cases: When a taxpayer acquired new vehicles each year just before its year end, and traded in its old vehicles just after year-end, the vehicles were not disposed of at year-end merely because they were held for disposal and paragraph 13(7)(*a*) did not apply. *Hewlett Packard (Canada) Ltd. v. The Queen*, 2004 DTC 6498 (F.C.A.)

► 13(7.1) ◄

(7.1) Deemed capital cost of certain property. For the purposes of this Act, where section 80 applied to reduce the capital cost to a taxpayer of a depreciable property or a taxpayer deducted an amount under subsection 127(5) or (6) in respect of a depreciable property or received or is entitled to receive assistance from a government, municipality or other public authority in respect of, or for the acquisition of, depreciable property, whether as a grant, subsidy, forgivable loan, deduction from tax, investment allowance or as any other form of assistance other than

(*a*) an amount described in paragraph 37(1)(*d*),

(*b*) an amount deducted as an allowance under section 65, or

(*b*.1) an amount included in income by virtue of paragraph 12(1)(*u*) or 56(1)(*s*),

the capital cost of the property to the taxpayer at any particular time shall be deemed to be the amount, if any, by which the total of

(*c*) the capital cost of the property to the taxpayer, determined without reference to this subsection, subsection (7.4) and section 80, and

(*d*) such part, if any, of the assistance as has been repaid by the taxpayer, pursuant to an obligation to repay all or any part of that assistance, in respect of that property before the disposition thereof by the taxpayer and before the particular time

exceeds the total of

(*e*) where the property was acquired in a taxation year ending before the particular time, all amounts deducted under subsection 127(5) or (6) by the taxpayer for a taxation year ending before the particular time,

(*f*) the amount of assistance the taxpayer has received or is entitled, before the particular time, to receive, and

(*g*) all amounts by which the capital cost of the property to the taxpayer is required because of section 80 to be reduced at or before that time,

in respect of that property before the disposition thereof by the taxpayer.

Editorial Note: If a GST input tax credit or other government assistance cannot be applied to reduce the capital cost of depreciable property under s. 13(7.1) or the adjusted cost base of capital property under s. 53(2)(*k*), it is generally included in income under s. 12(1)(*t*) or (*x*).

Related Sections: S. 6(8) GST rebates re costs of property or service; s. 12(1)(*t*) Investment tax credit; s. 13(7.2) Receipt of public assistance; s. 13(7.4) Deemed capital cost; s. 13(7.41) Deemed capital cost; s. 13(7.42) Timing of deduction; s. 80(1), "excluded obligation"; s. 80(5) Reductions with respect to depreciable property; s. 80(9) Reductions of adjusted cost bases of capital properties; s. 87(2)(*j*.6) Continuing corporation; s. 127(11.5) Adjustments to qualified expenditures; s. 127(12) Deemed capital cost of depreciable property; s. 248(16) Goods and services tax — input tax credit and rebate; s. 248(16.1) Quebec input tax refund and rebate; s. 248(18) Goods and services tax — repayment of input tax credit; s. 248(18.1) Repayment of Quebec input tax refund.

Income Tax Folios: *Primary* — S3-F4-C1 General Discussion of Capital Cost Allowance.

Interpretation Bulletins: *Primary* — IT-273R2 Government assistance — General comments.

Tax Window Files: Quebec Capital Tax Credit, *Technical Interpretation, Business and Partnerships Division, January 22, 2007*, CRA Document No. 2006-0212641E5.

► 13(7.2) ◄

(7.2) Receipt of public assistance. For the purposes of subsection (7.1), where at any time a taxpayer who is a beneficiary of a trust or a member of a partnership has received or is entitled to receive assistance from a government, municipality or other public authority whether as a grant, subsidy, forgivable loan, deduction from tax, investment allowance or as any other form of assistance, the amount of the assistance that may reasonably be considered to be in respect of, or for the acquisition of, depreciable property of the trust or partnership shall be deemed to have been received at that time by the trust or partnership, as the case may be, as assistance from the government, municipality or other public authority for the acquisition of depreciable property.

Related Sections: S. 53(2)(*c*)(ix) Amounts to be deducted — Interest in a partnership; s. 53(2)(*h*)(v) Amounts to be deducted — Capital interest in a trust.

► 13(7.3) ◄

(7.3) Control of corporations by one trustee. For the purposes of paragraph (7)(*e*), where at a particular time one corporation would, but for this subsection, be related to another corporation by reason of both corporations being controlled by the same executor, liquidator of a succession or trustee and it is established that

(*a*) the executor, liquidator or trustee did not acquire control of the corporations as a result of one or more estates or trusts created by the same individual or by two or more individuals not dealing with each other at arm's length, and

(*b*) the estate or trust under which the executor, liquidator or trustee acquired control of each of the corporations arose only on the death of the individual creating the estate or trust, the two corporations are deemed not to be related to each other at the particular time.

Editorial Note: Subsection 13(7.3) is a "saving provision" for the purposes of paragraph 13(7)(*e*) and deals with non-arm's length purchases of depreciable property. It provides that under certain circumstances two corporations controlled by the same trustee or executor will not be treated as related and, therefore, will be regarded as dealing at arm's length.

Related Sections: S. 256(6) Saving provision — controlled corporations; s. 256(7) Acquiring control; s. 256(8) Deemed exercise of right; s. 256(9) Date of acquisition of control.

► 13(7.4) ◄

(7.4) Deemed capital cost. Notwithstanding subsection (7.1), where a taxpayer has in a taxation year received an amount that would, but for this subsection, be included in the taxpayer's income under paragraph 12(1)(*x*) in respect of the cost of a depreciable property acquired by the taxpayer in the year, in the three taxation years immediately preceding the year or in the taxation year immediately following the year and the taxpayer elects under this subsection on or before the day on or before which the taxpayer is required to file the taxpayer's return of income under this Part for the year, or, where the property is acquired in the taxation year immediately following the year, for that following year, the capital cost of the property to the taxpayer shall be deemed to be the amount by which the total of

(*a*) the capital cost of the property to the taxpayer otherwise determined, applying the provisions of subsection (7.1), where necessary, and

(*b*) such part, if any, of the amount received by the taxpayer as has been repaid by the taxpayer pursuant to a legal obligation to repay all or any part of that amount, in respect of that property and before the disposition thereof by the taxpayer, and as may reasonably be considered to be in respect of the amount elected under this subsection in respect of the property

exceeds the amount elected by the taxpayer under this subsection, but in no case shall the amount elected under this subsection exceed the least of

(*c*) the amount so received by the taxpayer,

(*d*) the capital cost of the property to the taxpayer otherwise determined, and

(*e*) where the taxpayer has disposed of the property before the year, nil.

Editorial Note: See the editorial note under s. 12(1)(*x*).

Related Regulations: 600(b).

Related Sections: S. 87(2)(*j*.6) Continuing corporation; s. 125.4(5) When assistance received; s. 125.5(5) When assistance received; s. 127(11.5) Adjustments to qualified expenditures; s. 220(3.2) Late, amended or revoked elections.

Tax Profile: March 2002 — Selected Tax Issues for Commercial Landlords and Tenants.

Income Tax Folios: *Primary* — S3-F4-C1 General Discussion of Capital Cost Allowance.

Information Circulars: IC 07-1 Taxpayer relief provisions.

Interpretation Bulletins: *Secondary* — IT-273R2 Government assistance — General comments.

► 13(7.41) ◄

(7.41) Deemed capital cost. Subsection (38) applies in respect of an amount repaid after 2016 as if that amount was repaid immediately before 2017, if

(*a*) the amount is repaid by the taxpayer under a legal obligation to repay all or part of an amount the taxpayer received or was entitled to receive that was assistance from a government, municipality or other public authority (whether as a grant, subsidy, forgivable loan, deduction from tax, investment allowance or as any other form of assistance) in respect of, or for the acquisition of, property the cost of which was an eligible capital expenditure of the taxpayer in respect of the business;

(*b*) the amount of an eligible capital expenditure of the taxpayer in respect of the business was reduced by paragraph 14(10)(*c*) because of the assistance referred to in paragraph (*a*); and

(*c*) paragraph 20(1)(*hh*.1) does not apply in respect of the amount repaid.

History: Subsection 13(7.41) was added by S.C. 2016, c. 12, s. 3(2), in force on January 1, 2017.

Related Sections: 13(7.1) Deemed capital cost of certain property.

► 13(7.42) ◄

(7.42) Timing of deduction. No amount may be deducted under paragraph 20(1)(*a*) in respect of an amount of repaid assistance referred to in subsection (7.41) for any taxation year prior to the taxation year in which the assistance is repaid.

History: Subsection 13(7.42) was added by S.C. 2016, c. 12, s. 3(2), in force on January 1, 2017.

Related Sections: 13(7.1) Deemed capital cost of certain property.

► 13(7.5) ◄

(7.5) Deemed capital cost. For the purposes of this Act,

(*a*) where a taxpayer, to acquire a property prescribed in respect of the taxpayer, is required under the terms of a contract made after March 6, 1996 to make a payment to Her Majesty in right of Canada or a province or to a Canadian municipality in respect of costs incurred or to be incurred by the recipient of the payment

(i) the taxpayer is deemed to have acquired the property at a capital cost equal to the portion of that payment made by the taxpayer that can reasonably be regarded as being in respect of those costs, and

(ii) the time of acquisition of the property by the taxpayer is deemed to be the later of the time the payment is made and the time at which those costs are incurred;

(*b*) where

(i) at any time after March 6, 1996 a taxpayer incurs a cost on account of capital for the building of, for the right to use or in respect of, a prescribed property, and

(ii) the amount of the cost would, if this paragraph did not apply, not be included in the capital cost to the taxpayer of depreciable property of a prescribed class, the taxpayer is deemed to have acquired the property at that time at a capital cost equal to the amount of the cost;

(*c*) if a taxpayer acquires an intangible property, or for civil law an incorporeal property, as a consequence of making a payment to which paragraph (*a*) applies or incurring a cost to which paragraph (*b*) applies,

(i) the property referred to in paragraph (*a*) or (*b*) is deemed to include the intangible or incorporeal property, and

(ii) the portion of the capital cost referred to in paragraph (*a*) or (*b*) that applies to the intangible or incorporeal property is deemed to be the amount determined by the formula

A x B/C

where

A is the lesser of the amount of the payment made or cost incurred and the amount determined for C,

B is the fair market value of the intangible or incorporeal property at the time the payment was made or the cost was incurred, and

C is the fair market value at the time the payment was made or the cost was incurred of all intangible or incorporeal properties acquired as a consequence of making the payment or incurring the cost; and

(*d*) any property deemed by paragraph (*a*) or (*b*) to have been acquired at any time by a taxpayer as a consequence of making a payment or incurring a cost

(i) is deemed to have been acquired for the purpose for which the payment was made or the cost was incurred, and

(ii) is deemed to be owned by the taxpayer at any subsequent time that the taxpayer benefits from the property.

Editorial Note: Subsection 13(7.5) deems certain costs incurred by a taxpayer that might not otherwise be depreciable property to be depreciable property. As well, payments for intangible assets relating to these costs will also be considered to be depreciable property. Deemed properties are also deemed to have been owned by the taxpayer at any future time in which the taxpayer benefits from the property.

History: S. 13(7.5)(*c*) was replaced by S.C. 2013, c. 34, s. 92(3), in force June 26, 2013, and formerly read:

(*c*) where a taxpayer acquires an intangible property as a consequence of making a payment to which paragraph (*a*) applies or incurring a cost to which paragraph (*b*) applies,

(i) the property referred to in paragraph (*a*) or (*b*) is deemed to include the intangible property, and

(ii) the portion of the capital cost referred to in paragraph (*a*) or (b) that applies to the intangible property is deemed to be the amount determined by the formula

A x B/C

where

A is the lesser of the amount of the payment made or cost incurred and the amount determined for C,

B is the fair market value of the intangible property at the time the payment was made or the cost was incurred, and

C is the fair market value at the time the payment was made or the cost was incurred of all intangible properties acquired as a consequence of making the payment or incurring the cost; and

Related Regulations: 1102(14.2); 1102(14.3).

Income Tax Folios: *Primary* — S3-F4-C1 General Discussion of Capital Cost Allowance.

Interpretation Bulletins: *Secondary* — IT-143R3 Meaning of eligible capital expenditure.

▶ 13(8) ◀

(8) Disposition after ceasing business. Notwithstanding subsections (3) and 11(2), where a taxpayer, after ceasing to carry on a business, has disposed of depreciable property of the taxpayer of a prescribed class that was acquired by the taxpayer for the purpose of gaining or producing income from the business and that was not subsequently used by the taxpayer for some other purpose, in applying subsection (1) or (2), each reference therein to a "taxation year" and "year" shall not be read as a reference to a "fiscal period".

Related Sections: S. 13(1) Recaptured depreciation; s. 13(3) "Taxation year", "year" and "income" of individual; s. 20(16.3) Disposition after ceasing business; s. 25(3) Dispositions in the extended fiscal period.

Income Tax Folios: *Primary* — S3-F4-C1 General Discussion of Capital Cost Allowance.

▶ 13(9) ◀

(9) Meaning of "gaining or producing income". In applying paragraphs (7)(*a*) to (*d*) in respect of a non-resident taxpayer, a reference to "gaining or producing income" in relation to a business shall be read as a reference to "gaining or producing income from a business wholly carried on in Canada or such part of a business as is wholly carried on in Canada".

Income Tax Folios: *Primary* — S3-F4-C1 General Discussion of Capital Cost Allowance.

▶ 13(10) ◀

(10) Deemed capital cost. For the purposes of this Act, where a taxpayer has, after December 3, 1970 and before April 1, 1972, acquired prescribed property

(*a*) for use in a prescribed manufacturing or processing business carried on by the taxpayer, and

(*b*) that was not used for any purpose whatever before it was acquired by the taxpayer,

the taxpayer shall be deemed to have acquired that property at a capital cost to the taxpayer equal to 115% of the amount that, but for this subsection and section 21, would have been the capital cost to the taxpayer of that property.

Related Regulations: 1102(15).

Interpretation Bulletins: *Secondary* — IT-273R2 Government assistance — General comments.

▶ 13(11) ◀

(11) Deduction in respect of property used in performance of duties. Any amount deducted under subparagraph 8(1)(*j*)(ii) or (*p*)(ii) of this Act or subsection 11(11) of *The Income Tax Act*, chapter 52 of the Statutes of Canada, 1948, shall be deemed, for the purposes of this section to have been deducted under regulations made under paragraph 20(1)(*a*).

Interpretation Bulletins: *Secondary* — IT-522R Vehicle, travel and sales expenses of employees.

Tax Window Files: Earned Income — Recaptured CCA, *Technical Interpretation, Business and Partnerships Division, January 27, 2004*, CRA Document No. 2004-0055367.

▶ 13(12) ◀

(12) Application of para. 20(1)(cc). Where, in computing the income of a taxpayer for a taxation year, an amount has been deducted under paragraph 20(1)(*cc*) or the taxpayer has elected under subsection 20(9) to make a deduction in respect of an amount that would otherwise have been deductible under that paragraph, the amount shall, if it was a payment on account of the capital cost of depreciable property, be deemed to have been allowed to the taxpayer in respect of the property under regulations made under paragraph 20(1)(*a*) in computing the income of the taxpayer

(*a*) for the year, or

(*b*) for the year in which the property was acquired,

whichever is the later.

Interpretation Bulletins: *Primary* — IT-99R5 Legal and accounting fees.

► 13(13) ◄

(13) Deduction under Canadian Vessel Construction Assistance Act. Where a deduction has been made under the *Canadian Vessel Construction Assistance Act* for any taxation year, subsection (1) is applicable in respect of the prescribed class created by that Act or any other prescribed class to which the vessel may have been transferred.

► 13(14) ◄

(14) Conversion cost. For the purposes of this section, section 20 and any regulations made under paragraph 20(1)(*a*), a vessel in respect of which any conversion cost is incurred after March 23, 1967 shall, to the extent of the conversion cost, be deemed to be included in a separate prescribed class.

Related Regulations: S. 1100(1)(v); s. 1101(2a).

Related Sections: S. 13(17) Separate prescribed class concerning vessel.

Interpretation Bulletins: *Secondary* — IT-267R2 Capital cost allowance — Vessels.

► 13(15) ◄

(15) Where s. (1) and subdivision c do not apply. Where a vessel owned by a taxpayer on January 1, 1966 or constructed pursuant to a construction contract entered into by the taxpayer prior to 1966 and not completed by that date was disposed of by the taxpayer before 1974,

(*a*) subsection (1) and subdivision c do not apply to the proceeds of disposition

(i) if an amount at least equal to the proceeds of disposition was used by the taxpayer, before May, 1974 and during the taxation year of the taxpayer in which the vessel was disposed of or within 4 months after the end of that taxation year, under conditions satisfactory to the appropriate minister, either for replacement or to incur any conversion cost with respect to a vessel owned by the taxpayer, or

(ii) if the appropriate minister certified that the taxpayer had, on satisfactory terms, deposited

(A) on or before the day on which the taxpayer was required to file a return of the taxpayer's income for the taxation year in which the vessel was disposed of, or

(B) on or before such day subsequent to the day referred to in clause (A) as the appropriate minister specified in respect of the taxpayer,

an amount at least equal to the tax that would, but for this subsection, have been payable by the taxpayer under this Part in respect of the proceeds of disposition, or satisfactory security therefor, as a guarantee that the proceeds of disposition would be used before 1975 for replacement; and

(*b*) if within the time specified for the filing of a return of the taxpayer's income for the taxation year in which the vessel was disposed of

(i) the taxpayer elected to have the vessel constituted a prescribed class, or

(ii) where any conversion cost in respect of the vessel was included in a separate prescribed class, the taxpayer elected to have the vessel transferred to that class,

the vessel shall be deemed to have been so transferred immediately before the disposition thereof, but this paragraph does not apply unless the proceeds of disposition of the vessel exceed the amount that would be the undepreciated capital cost of property of the class to which it would be so transferred.

Related Sections: S. 13(16) Election concerning vessel; s. 13(17) Separate prescribed class concerning vessel; s. 13(18) Reassessments; s. 13(18.1) Ascertainment of certain property; s. 13(19) Reassessments; s. 13(20) Refund of deposit; s. 13(21), "appropriate minister".

► 13(16) ◄

(16) Election concerning vessel. Where a vessel owned by a taxpayer is disposed of by the taxpayer, the taxpayer may, if subsection (15) does not apply to the proceeds of disposition or if the taxpayer did not make an election under paragraph (15)(*b*) in respect of the vessel, within the time specified for the filing of a return of the taxpayer's income for the taxation year in which the vessel was disposed of, elect to have the proceeds that would be included in computing the taxpayer's income for the year under this Part treated as proceeds of disposition of property of another prescribed class that includes a vessel owned by the taxpayer.

Related Sections: S. 13(17) Separate prescribed class concerning vessel; s. 96(3) Agreement or election of partnership members.

Interpretation Bulletins: *Secondary* — IT-267R2 Capital cost allowance — Vessels.

Tax Window Files: Disposition of Vessel — Election to Treat Recapture as Proceeds of Property of Another Prescribed Class, *Technical Interpretation, Business and Partnerships Division, March 9, 2004*, CRA Document No. 2004-0059661E5.

► 13(17) ◄

(17) Separate prescribed class concerning vessel. Where a separate prescribed class has been constituted either under this Act or the *Canadian Vessel Construction Assistance Act* by reason of the conversion of a vessel owned by a taxpayer and the vessel is disposed of by the taxpayer, if no election in respect of the vessel was made under paragraph (15)(*b*), the separate prescribed class constituted by reason of the conversion shall be deemed to have been transferred to the class in which the vessel was included immediately before the disposition thereof.

Interpretation Bulletins: *Secondary* — IT-267R2 Capital cost allowance — Vessels.

► 13(18) ◄

(18) Reassessments. Notwithstanding any other provision of this Act, where a taxpayer has

(a) used an amount as described in paragraph (4)(c), or

(b) made an election under paragraph (15)(b) in respect of a vessel and the proceeds of disposition of the vessel were used before 1975 for replacement under conditions satisfactory to the appropriate minister,

such reassessments of tax, interest or penalties shall be made as are necessary to give effect to subsections (4) and (15).

▶ 13(18.1) ◀

(18.1) Ascertainment of certain property. For the purpose of determining whether property meets the criteria set out in the *Income Tax Regulations* in respect of prescribed energy conservation property, the *Technical Guide to Class 43.1 and 43.2*, as amended from time to time and published by the Department of Natural Resources, shall apply conclusively with respect to engineering and scientific matters.

History: S. 13(18.1) was replaced by S.C. 2013, c. 40, s. 6(2), deemed to have come into force on the day on which the *Technical Guide to Class 43.1 and 43.2* is first published by the Department of Natural Resources, and formerly read:

(18.1) *Ascertainment of certain property.* For the purpose of determining whether property meets the criteria set out in the Regulations in respect of prescribed energy conservation property, the Technical Guide to Class 43.1, as amended from time to time and published by the Department of Natural Resources, shall apply conclusively with respect to engineering and scientific matters.

Related Regulations: 8200.1.

Related Sections: S. 241(4)(*d*)(vi.1) Where taxpayer information may be disclosed.

Tax Window Files: Request for description of property encompassed by paragraph (d) of Class 43.1 and Class 43.2, *Reorganizations and Resources Division Income Tax Rulings Directorate, March 9, 2007*, CRA Document No. 2007-0225661E5.

▶ 13(19) ◀

(19) Disposition of deposit. All or any part of a deposit made under subparagraph (15)(a)(ii) or under the *Canadian Vessel Construction Assistance Act* may be paid out to or on behalf of any person who, under conditions satisfactory to the appropriate minister and as a replacement for the vessel disposed of, acquires a vessel before 1975

(a) that was constructed in Canada and is registered in Canada or is registered under conditions satisfactory to the appropriate minister in any country or territory to which the British Commonwealth Merchant Shipping Agreement, signed at London on December 10, 1931, applies, and

(b) in respect of the capital cost of which no allowance has been made to any other taxpayer under this Act or the *Canadian Vessel Construction Assistance Act*,

or incurs any conversion cost with respect to a vessel owned by that person that is registered in Canada or is registered under conditions satisfactory to the appropriate minister in any country or territory to which the agreement referred to in paragraph (a) applies, but the ratio of the amount paid out to the amount of the deposit shall not exceed the ratio of the capital cost to that person of the vessel or the conversion cost to that person of the vessel, as the case may be, to the proceeds of disposition of the vessel disposed of, and any deposit or part of a deposit not so paid out before July 1, 1975 or not paid out pursuant to subsection (20) shall be paid to the Receiver General and form part of the Consolidated Revenue Fund.

Related Sections: S. 13(21), "appropriate minister".

▶ 13(20) ◀

(20) Idem. Notwithstanding any other provision of this section, where a taxpayer made a deposit under subparagraph (15)(a)(ii) and the proceeds of disposition in respect of which the deposit was made were not used by any person before 1975 under conditions satisfactory to the appropriate minister as a replacement for the vessel disposed of,

(a) to acquire a vessel described in paragraphs (19)(a) and (b), or

(b) to incur any conversion cost with respect to a vessel owned by that person that is registered in Canada or is registered under conditions satisfactory to the appropriate minister in any country or territory to which the agreement referred to in paragraph (19)(a) applies,

the appropriate minister may refund to the taxpayer the deposit, or the part thereof not paid out to the taxpayer under subsection (19), as the case may be, in which case there shall be added, in computing the income of the taxpayer for the taxation year of the taxpayer in which the vessel was disposed of, that proportion of the amount that would have been included in computing the income for the year under this Part had the deposit not been made under subparagraph (15)(a)(ii) that the portion of the proceeds of disposition not so used before 1975 as such a replacement is of the proceeds of disposition, and, notwithstanding any other provision of this Act, such reassessments of tax, interest or penalties shall be made as are necessary to give effect to this subsection.

▶ 13(21) ◀

(21) Definitions. In this section,

Related Sections: S. 20(1.1) Application of s. 13(21); s. 20(27.1) Application of ss. 13(21) and 138(12).

Tax Topics: No. 2120, Tax Treatment of Contingent Liabilities in an Asset Sale: Canada's *Daishowa v. The Queen*; No. 2105, Supreme Court to Hear *Daishowa* Appeal — Back to Basics on Basis and Proceeds.

Interpretation Bulletins: *Secondary* — IT-273R2 Government assistance — General comments.

Tax Window Files: *Catégorie d'amortissement - bateau, November 25, 2010*, CRA Document No. 2010-0377841E5; *Catégorie d'amortissement-maison flottante, March 12, 2012*, CRA Document No. 2011-0431631I7; British Columbia Forestry Revitalization Act and Forest (Revitalization) Amendment Act, *Technical Interpretation, Reorganizations and Resources Division, December 1, 2003*, CRA Document No. 2003-0020445.

"appropriate minister" —"appropriate minister" means the Canadian Maritime Commission, the Minister of Industry, Trade and Commerce, the Minister of Regional Industrial Expansion, the Minister of Industry, Science and Technology or the Minister of Industry or any other minister or body that was or is legally authorized to perform the act referred to in the provision in which this expression occurs at the time the act was or is performed;

"conversion" —"conversion", in respect of a vessel, means a conversion or major alteration in Canada by a taxpayer;

Interpretation Bulletins: *Secondary* — IT-267R2 Capital cost allowance — Vessels.

"conversion cost" —"conversion cost", in respect of a vessel, means the cost of a conversion;

Related Sections: S. 13(1) Recaptured depreciation; 13(13) Deduction under Canadian Vessel Construction Assistance Act; 13(14) Conversion cost; 13(15) Where s. (1) and subdivision c do not apply; 13(16) Election concerning vessel; 13(17) Separate prescribed class concerning vessel; 13(18) Reassessments; 13(18.1) Ascertainment of certain property; 13(19) Disposition of deposit; 13(20) Idem.

Interpretation Bulletins: *Secondary* — IT-267R2 Capital cost allowance — Vessels.

"depreciable property" —"depreciable property" of a taxpayer as of any time in a taxation year means property acquired by the taxpayer in respect of which the taxpayer has been allowed, or would, if the taxpayer owned the property at the end of the year and this Act were read without reference to subsection (26), be entitled to, a deduction under paragraph 20(1)(*a*) in computing income for that year or a preceding taxation year;

Related Regulations: Part XI.

Related Sections: S. 13(1) Recaptured depreciation; s. 13(5.2)(*c*) Lease-option agreement — exercise of option; s. 13(33) Consideration given for depreciable property; s. 20(1)(*a*) Capital cost of property; s. 54, "capital property"; s. 88(1)(*c.7*) Winding-up; s. 107.4(3)(*d*) Tax consequences of qualifying dispositions; s. 248(1), "depreciable property".

Income Tax Folios: *Primary* — S3-F4-C1 General Discussion of Capital Cost Allowance.

Interpretation Bulletins: *Primary* — IT-102R2 Conversion of property, other than real property, from or to inventory.

Tax Window Files: Depreciable Property, *Technical Interpretation, Business and Partnerships Division, January 27, 2003*, CRA Document No. 2002-0177677.

"disposition of property" — (Repealed by S.C. 2001, c. 17, s. 6(5).)

"proceeds of disposition" —"proceeds of disposition" of property includes

(*a*) the sale price of property that has been sold,

(*b*) compensation for property unlawfully taken,

(*c*) compensation for property destroyed and any amount payable under a policy of insurance in respect of loss or destruction of property,

(*d*) compensation for property taken under statutory authority or the sale price of property sold to a person by whom notice of an intention to take it under statutory authority was given,

(*e*) compensation for property injuriously affected, whether lawfully or unlawfully or under statutory authority or otherwise,

(*f*) compensation for property damaged and any amount payable under a policy of insurance in respect of damage to property, except to the extent that the compensation or amount, as the case may be, has within a reasonable time after the damage been expended on repairing the damage,

(*g*) an amount by which the liability of a taxpayer to a mortgagee or hypothecary creditor is reduced as a result of the sale of mortgaged or hypothecated property under a provision of the mortgage or hypothec, plus any amount received by the taxpayer out of the proceeds of the sale, and

(*h*) any amount included because of section 79 in computing a taxpayer's proceeds of disposition of the property;

Editorial Note: Any event or transaction giving rise to proceeds of disposition is considered a disposition; see 248(1) "disposition".

Related Sections: S. 12(1)(*f*) Insurance proceeds expended; s. 13(4) Exchanges of property; s. 13(21), "undepreciated capital cost"; s. 13(21.1) Disposition of building; s. 44 Exchanges of property; s. 54, "proceeds of disposition"; s. 79(3) Proceeds of disposition for debtor; S. 248(39) Substantive gift.

Canadian Tax Foundation: Morris, *Current Cases: Supreme Court of Canada — Supreme Court Weighs In on Age-Old Question: If a Tree Falls in the Forest ... (Daishowa-Marubeni International Ltd. v. Canada, 2013 SCC 29)*, 2013 Canadian Tax Journal 3:723–729; Blackler and Nitikman, *Case Comment: Daishowa-Marubeni International Ltd. v. The Queen, 2013 DTC 5085*, 2013 British Columbia Tax Conference 2:1–5.

Tax Profile: Supreme Court of Canada Clarifies that Assuming Obligations "Embedded" in a Property is not Consideration for the Property.

Income Tax Folios: *Primary* — S3-F4-C1 General Discussion of Capital Cost Allowance.

Interpretation Bulletins: *Secondary* — IT-170R Sale of property — When included in income computation; IT-259R4 Exchange of property; IT-460 Dispositions — Absence of consideration.

Cases: Alberta required the purchasers of forest tenures to assume reforestation obligations. The cost of these obligations was not included in the vendor's proceeds of disposition since the purchasers were not assuming an existing liability. The reforestation costs could not be severed from the tenures and were simply a future cost that would decrease the purchase price. *Morguard Corporation v. The Queen*, 2013 DTC 5009 (F.C.A.), affirming 2012 DTC 1099 (T.C.C.)

When, following the taxpayers' mortgage default, their mortgagee was allowed to purchase their condominium property for a stipulated sum and granted judgment for the balance of the amount owing, the taxpayers could report as "proceeds of disposition" their shares of the stipulated sum rather than their shares of the full principal amount still outstanding on the mortgage. *Brill et al. v. The Queen*, 96 DTC 6572 (F.C.A.), reversing in part 95 DTC 5435 (F.C.T.D.)

Since paragraph (*h*) of the definition "proceeds of disposition" in s. 13(21) specifically refers to any amount included in a taxpayer's proceeds of disposition by virtue of s. 79(*c*), the taxpayers' principal indebtedness to the mortgagees at the time they acquired the beneficial ownership of various condominiums in consequence of the failure to pay the mortgage amount owing was included in their proceeds of disposition. *Farn et al. v. The Queen*, 95 DTC 5426 (F.C.T.D.).

"timber resource property" —"timber resource property" of a taxpayer means

(*a*) a right or licence to cut or remove timber from a limit or area in Canada (in this definition referred to as an "original right") if

(i) that original right was acquired by the taxpayer (other than in the manner referred to in paragraph (*b*)) after May 6, 1974, and

(ii) at the time of the acquisition of the original right

(A) the taxpayer may reasonably be regarded as having acquired, directly or indirectly, the right to extend or renew that original right or to acquire another such right or licence in substitution therefor, or

(B) in the ordinary course of events, the taxpayer may reasonably expect to be able to extend or renew that original right or to acquire another such right or licence in substitution therefor, or

(*b*) any right or licence owned by the taxpayer to cut or remove timber from a limit or area in Canada if that right or licence may reasonably be regarded

(i) as an extension or renewal of or as one of a series of extensions or renewals of an original right of the taxpayer, or

(ii) as having been acquired in substitution for or as one of a series of substitutions for an original right of the taxpayer or any renewal or extension thereof;

Related Regulations: Sch. II, Class 33.

Related Sections: S. 13(21), "Undepreciated capital cost"; s. 128.1(4)(*b*)(i) Emigration; s. 248(1) Definition applies to entire Act.

Income Tax Folios: *Secondary* — S4-F11-C1 Meaning of Farming and Farming Business.

Interpretation Bulletins: *Primary* — IT-481 (Consolid.) Timber resource property and timber limits. *Secondary* — IT-373R2 (Consolid.) Woodlots; IT-393R2 Election re tax on rents and timber royalties — non-residents.

Cases: The proceeds from the transfer of cutting licences were income from the disposition of "timber resource properties" because original rights become timber resource properties when initially obtained, renewed, extended or substituted for earlier rights after May 6, 1974 and it is irrelevant whether the licenses were extensions, renewals or substitutions for original rights initially acquired before or after May 6, 1974. *The Queen v. Kettle River Sawmills Ltd. et al.*, 94 DTC 6086 (F.C.A.), reversing 92 DTC 6525 (F.C.T.D.)

"total depreciation"—"total depreciation" allowed to a taxpayer before any time for property of a prescribed class means the total of all amounts each of which is an amount deducted by the taxpayer under paragraph 20(1)(*a*) in respect of property of that class or an amount deducted under subsection 20(16), or that would have been so deducted but for subsection 20(16.1), in computing the taxpayer's income for taxation years ending before that time;

Related Regulations: Part XI.

Income Tax Folios: *Primary* — S3-F4-C1 General Discussion of Capital Cost Allowance.

Interpretation Bulletins: *Secondary* — IT-522R Vehicle, travel and sales expenses of employees.

"undepreciated capital cost"—"undepreciated capital cost" to a taxpayer of depreciable property of a prescribed class as of any time means the amount determined by the formula

$$(A+B+C+D+D.1)-(E+E.1+F+G+H+I+J+K)$$

where

A is the total of all amounts each of which is the capital cost to the taxpayer of a depreciable property of the class acquired before that time,

B is the total of all amounts included in the taxpayer's income under this section for a taxation year ending before that time, to the extent that those amounts relate to depreciable property of the class,

C is the total of all amounts each of which is such part of any assistance as has been repaid by the taxpayer, pursuant to an obligation to repay all or any part of that assistance, in respect of a depreciable property of the class subsequent to the disposition thereof by the taxpayer that would have been included in an amount determined under paragraph (7.1)(*d*) had the repayment been made before the disposition,

D is the total of all amounts each of which is an amount repaid in respect of a property of the class subsequent to the disposition thereof by the taxpayer that would have been an amount described in paragraph (7.4)(*b*) had the repayment been made before the disposition,

D.1 is the total of all amounts each of which is an amount paid by the taxpayer before that time as or on account of an existing or proposed countervailing or anti-dumping duty in respect of depreciable property of the class,

E is the total depreciation allowed to the taxpayer for property of the class before that time, including, if the taxpayer is an insurer, depreciation deemed to have been allowed before that time under subsection (22) or (23) as they read in their application to the taxpayer's last taxation year that began before November 2011,

E.1 is the total of all amounts each of which is an amount by which the undepreciated capital cost to the taxpayer of depreciable property of that class is required (otherwise than because of a reduction in the capital cost to the taxpayer of depreciable property) to be reduced at or before that time because of subsection 80(5),

F is the total of all amounts each of which is an amount in respect of a disposition before that time of property (other than a timber resource property) of the taxpayer of the class, and is the lesser of

(*a*) the proceeds of disposition of the property minus any outlays and expenses to the extent that they were made or incurred by the taxpayer for the purpose of making the disposition, and

(*b*) the capital cost to the taxpayer of the property,

G is the total of all amounts each of which is the proceeds of disposition before that time of a timber resource property of the taxpayer of the class minus any outlays and expenses to the extent that they were made or incurred by the taxpayer for the purpose of making the disposition,

H is, where the property of the class was acquired by the taxpayer for the purpose of gaining or producing income from a mine and the taxpayer so elects in prescribed manner and within a prescribed time in respect of that property, the amount equal to that portion of the income derived from the operation of the mine that is, by virtue of the provisions of the *Income Tax Application Rules* relating to income from the operation of new mines, not included in computing income of the taxpayer or any other person,

I is the total of all amounts deducted under subsection 127(5) or (6), in respect of a depreciable property of the class of the taxpayer, in computing the taxpayers' tax payable for a taxation year ending before that time and subsequent to the disposition of that property by the taxpayer,

J is the total of all amounts of assistance that the taxpayer received or was entitled to receive before that time, in respect of or for the acquisition of a depreciable property of the class of the taxpayer subsequent to the disposition of that property by the taxpayer, that would have been included in an amount determined under paragraph (7.1)(*f*) had the assistance been received before the disposition, and

K is the total of all amounts each of which is an amount received by the taxpayer before that time in respect of a refund of an amount added to the undepreciated capital cost of depreciable property of the class because of the description of D.1;

History: S. 13(21), the description of E in the definition "undepreciated capital cost" was replaced by S.C. 2013, c. 34, s. 175(4), applicable to taxation years that begin after October 31, 2011. S. 13(21), the description of E in the definition "undepreciated capital cost" formerly read:

E is the total depreciation allowed to the taxpayer for property of the class before that time,

Related Regulations: 1100(2); 1100(2.1) Property Acquired in the Year; 1100(2.2) Property Acquired in the Year; 1100(2.21) Property Acquired in the Year; 1100(2.3); 1100(2.4) Property Acquired in the Year.

Related Sections: S. 12(1)(*f*) Insurance proceeds expended; S. 12(1)(*t*) Investment tax credit; s. 12(1)(*z*6) Refunds; s. 13(1) Recaptured depreciation; s. 13(2) Recaptured depreciation for passenger vehicle; s. 13(4) Exchanges of property; s. 13(5) Reclassification of property; s. 13(5.2) Lease-option agreement — exercise of option; s. 13(7) Rules applicable; s. 13(21), "proceeds of disposition"; s. 13(22) Deduction for insurer; s. 13(23) Deduction for life insurer; s. 13(24) Loss restriction event; s. 13(26) Restriction on deduction before available for use; s. 20(1)(*vv*) Countervailing or anti-dumping duty; s. 20(16) Terminal loss; s. 70(13) Capital cost of certain depreciable property; s. 87(2)(*j*.6) Continuing corporation; s. 138(11.31)(*b*) Exclusion from deemed disposition; s. 248(1), "undepreciated capital cost" s. 257 Negative amounts; ITAR 18 General depreciation provisions.

Income Tax Folios: *Primary* — S3-F4-C1 General Discussion of Capital Cost Allowance.

Interpretation Bulletins: *Secondary* — IT-481 (Consolid.) Timber resource property and timber limits.

Tax Window Files: Resale of Depreciable Property Acquired from Related Person, *Technical Interpretation, Business and Partnerships Division, November 8, 2006*, CRA Document No. 2006-0176171E5; Purchase of Vehicle Using GM Points, *Technical Interpretation, Business and Partnerships Division, September 8, 2006*, CRA Document No. 2006-0175841E5.

"vessel" —"vessel" means a vessel as defined in the *Canada Shipping Act*.

Canadian Petroleum Tax Journal: Offshore Oil & Gas Interests: A Perspective on Exploration & Development of Offshore Petroleum and Natural Gas Resources in Eastern Canada, Michael R. Smith, CA and B. David Nielsen, CA, 2000, Vol. 13, No. 1.

Interpretation Bulletins: *Primary* — IT-267R2 Capital cost allowance — Vessels.

▶ 13(21.1) ◀

(21.1) Disposition of building. Notwithstanding subsection (7) and the definition "proceeds of disposition" in section 54, where at any particular time in a taxation year a taxpayer disposes of a building of a prescribed class and the proceeds of disposition of the building determined without reference to this subsection and subsection (21.2) are less than the lesser of the cost amount and the capital cost to the taxpayer of the building immediately before the disposition, for the purposes of paragraph (*a*) of the description of F in the definition "undepreciated capital cost" in subsection (21) and subdivision c,

(*a*) where in the year the taxpayer or a person with whom the taxpayer does not deal at arm's length disposes of land subjacent to, or immediately contiguous to and necessary for the use of, the building, the proceeds of disposition of the building are deemed to be the lesser of

(i) the amount, if any, by which

(A) the total of the fair market value of the building at the particular time and the fair market value of the land immediately before its disposition

exceeds

(B) the lesser of the fair market value of the land immediately before its disposition and the amount, if any, by which the cost amount to the vendor of the land (determined without reference to this subsection) exceeds the total of the capital gains (determined without reference to subparagraphs 40(1)(*a*)(ii) and (iii)) in respect of dispositions of the land within 3 years before the particular time by the taxpayer or by a person with whom the taxpayer was not dealing at arm's length to the taxpayer or to another person with whom the taxpayer was not dealing at arm's length, and

(ii) the greater of

(A) the fair market value of the building at the particular time, and

(B) the lesser of the cost amount and the capital cost to the taxpayer of the building immediately before its disposition,

and, notwithstanding any other provision of this Act, the proceeds of disposition of the land are deemed to be the amount, if any, by which

(iii) the total of the proceeds of disposition of the building and of the land determined without reference to this subsection and subsection (21.2)

exceeds

(iv) the proceeds of disposition of the building as determined under this paragraph,

and the cost to the purchaser of the land shall be determined without reference to this subsection; and

(*b*) where paragraph (*a*) does not apply with respect to the disposition and, at any time before the disposition, the taxpayer or a person with whom the taxpayer did not deal at arm's length owned the land subjacent to, or immediately contiguous to and necessary for the use of, the building, the proceeds of disposition of the building are deemed to be an amount equal to the total of

(i) the proceeds of disposition of the building determined without reference to this subsection and subsection (21.2), and

(ii) 1/2 of the amount by which the greater of

(A) the cost amount to the taxpayer of the building, and

(B) the fair market value of the building immediately before its disposition exceeds the proceeds of disposition referred to in subparagraph (i).

Editorial Note: Subsection 13(21.1) allocates the proceeds of disposition between a building and its contiguous land. Subsection 13(21.1) applies before s. 13(21.2), but does not prevent s. 13(21.2) from applying. If both apply, s. 13(21.2) may defer the recognition of a terminal loss arising after the application of s. 13(21.1).

Related Regulations: 1103(1).

Related Sections: S. 70(5)(*c*) Capital property of a deceased taxpayer; s. 70(5)(*d*) Capital property of a deceased taxpayer.

Tax Topics: No. 2014, Terminal Loss of Building Reduced — Land Not Disposed Of; No. 1846, Demolition of Buildings; No. 1676, Demolition of Buildings.

Income Tax Folios: *Primary* — S3-F4-C1 General Discussion of Capital Cost Allowance.

Interpretation Bulletins: *Primary* — IT-349R3 Intergenerational transfers of farm property on death.

Tax Window Files: Allocation of Proceeds of Disposition to Building, *Technical Interpretation, Business and Partnerships Division, November 8, 2006*, CRA Document No. 2006-0203301I7; Election under Regulation 1103(1) to reduce the affect of S. 13(21), *Technical Interpretation, Income Tax Rulings Directorate, September 20, 2004*, CRA Document No. 2004-0072411E5.

Cases: The taxpayer leased its shopping plaza for 25 years on August 31, 1961, granting the lessee an option to purchase it no later than 60 days prior to the end of the term. On January 20, 1986, an assignee of the lessee exercised such option and on August 29, 1986, the plaza was sold. Since the taxpayer was bound to give effect to the option granted by it to its original lessor in 1961 and the written agreement was in effect on May 9, 1985, s. 13(21.1) permitted the taxpayer to allocate the entire proceeds of sale to the land and to claim a terminal loss on the building. *The Queen v. Trade Investments Shopping Centre Ltd*, 93 DTC 486 (F.C.T.D.)

► 13(21.2) ◄

(21.2) Loss on certain transfers. Where

(*a*) a person or partnership (in this subsection referred to as the "transferor") disposes at a particular time (otherwise than in a disposition described in any of paragraphs (*c*) to (*g*) of the definition "superficial loss" in section 54) of a depreciable property — other than, for the purposes of computing the exempt surplus or exempt deficit and taxable surplus or taxable deficit of a foreign affiliate of a taxpayer, in respect of the taxpayer, where the transferor is the affiliate or is a partnership of which the affiliate is a member, depreciable property that is, or would be, if the transferor were a foreign affiliate of the taxpayer, excluded property (within the meaning assigned by subsection 95(1)) of the transferor — of a particular prescribed class of the transferor,

(*b*) the lesser of

(i) the capital cost to the transferor of the transferred property, and

(ii) the proportion of the undepreciated capital cost to the transferor of all property of the particular class immediately before that time that

(A) the fair market value of the transferred property at that time

is of

(B) the fair market value of all property of the particular class immediately before that time

exceeds the amount that would otherwise be the transferor's proceeds of disposition of the transferred property at the particular time, and

(*c*) on the 30th day after the particular time, a person or partnership (in this subsection referred to as the "subsequent owner") who is the transferor or a person affiliated with the transferor owns or has a right to acquire the transferred property (other than a right, as security only, derived from a mortgage, hypothec, agreement for sale or similar obligation),

the following rules apply:

(*d*) sections 85 and 97 do not apply to the disposition,

(*e*) for the purposes of applying this section and section 20 and any regulations made for the purpose of paragraph 20(1)(*a*) to the transferor for taxation years that end after the particular time,

(i) the transferor is deemed to have disposed of the transferred property for proceeds equal to the lesser of the amounts determined under subparagraphs (*b*)(i) and (ii) with respect to the transferred property,

(ii) where two or more properties of a prescribed class of the transferor are disposed of at the same time, subparagraph (i) applies as if each property so disposed of had been separately disposed of in the order designated by the transferor or, if the transferor does not designate an order, in the order designated by the Minister,

(iii) the transferor is deemed to own a property that was acquired before the beginning of the taxation year that includes the particular time at a capital cost equal to the amount of the excess described in paragraph (*b*), and that is property of the particular class, until the time that is immediately before the first time, after the particular time,

(A) at which a 30-day period begins throughout which neither the transferor nor a person affiliated with the transferor owns or has a right to acquire the transferred property (other than a right, as security only, derived from a mortgage, hypothec, agreement for sale or similar obligation),

(B) at which the transferred property is not used by the transferor or a person affiliated with the transferor for the purpose of earning income and is used for another purpose,

(C) at which the transferred property would, if it were owned by the transferor, be deemed by section 128.1 or subsection 149(10) to have been disposed of by the transferor,

(D) that is immediately before the transferor is subject to a loss restriction event, or

(E) if the transferor is a corporation,

(I) for the purposes of computing the transferor's foreign accrual property income, exempt surplus or exempt deficit, and taxable surplus or taxable deficit, in respect of a taxpayer for a taxation year of the transferor where the transferor is a foreign affiliate of the taxpayer, at which the liquidation and dissolution of the transferor begins, unless the liquidation and dissolution is

1. a qualifying liquidation and dissolution (within the meaning assigned by subsection 88(3.1)) of the transferor, or

2. a designated liquidation and dissolution (within the meaning assigned by subsection 95(1)) of the transferor, and

(II) for any other purposes, at which the winding-up (other than a winding-up to which subsection 88(1) applies) of the transferor begins, and

(iv) the property described in subparagraph (iii) is considered to have become available for use by the transferor at the time at which the transferred property is considered to have become available for use by the subsequent owner,

(*f*) for the purposes of subparagraphs (*e*)(iii) and (iv), where a partnership otherwise ceases to exist at any time after the particular time, the partnership is deemed not to have ceased to exist, and each person who was a member of the partnership immediately before the partnership would, but for this paragraph, have ceased to exist is deemed to remain a member of the partnership, until the time that is immediately after the first time described in clauses (*e*)(iii)(A) to (E), and

(*g*) for the purposes of applying this section and section 20 and any regulations made for the purpose of paragraph 20(1)(*a*) to the subsequent owner,

(i) the subsequent owner's capital cost of the transferred property is deemed to be the amount that was the transferor's capital cost of the transferred property, and

(ii) the amount by which the transferor's capital cost of the transferred property exceeds its fair market value at the particular time is deemed to have been deducted under paragraph 20(1)(*a*) by the subsequent owner in respect of property of that class in computing income for taxation years that ended before the particular time.

Editorial Note: Subsection 13(21.2) denies the deduction of a terminal loss on the disposition of certain depreciable property, where either the transferor or a person or partnership affiliated with the transferor owns the property or a right to acquire the property 30 days after the disposition. Similar stop-loss rules are found in s. 14(12) for dispositions of eligible capital property (prior to 2017), in s. 18(15) for property held in an adventure or concern in the nature of trade, and in s. 40(3.4) for non-depreciable capital property.

History: S. 13(21.2)(*e*)(iii)(D) was replaced by S.C. 2013, c. 40, s. 6(3), deemed to have come into force on March 21, 2013, and formerly read:

(D) that is immediately before control of the transferor is acquired by a person or group of persons, where the transferor is a corporation, or

S. 13(21.2)(*a*) was replaced by S.C. 2013, c. 34, s. 54(1), applicable to dispositions that occur after August 19, 2011.

Any assessment of a taxpayer's tax, interest and penalties payable under the Act for any taxation year that ends before June 26, 2013 that would, in the absence of this section, be precluded because of subsections 152(4) to (5) of the Act shall be made to the extent necessary to take into account the amendments by S.C. 2013, c. 34, s. 54 to 89.

S. 13(21.2)(*a*) formerly read:

(*a*) a person or partnership (in this subsection referred to as the "transferor") disposes at a particular time (otherwise than in a disposition described in any of paragraphs (*c*) to (*g*) of the definition "superficial loss" in section 54) of a depreciable property of a particular prescribed class of the transferor,

S. 13(21.2)(*e*)(iii)(E) was replaced by S.C. 2013, c. 34, s. 54(2), applicable to windings-up and liquidations and dissolutions that begin after August 19, 2011.

See the application provision above for the extension of assessment periods to take into account the amendments by S.C. 2013, c. 34, s. 54 to 89

S. 13(21.2)(*e*)(iii)(E) formerly read:

(E) at which the winding-up of the transferor begins (other than a winding-up to which subsection 88(1) applies), where the transferor is a corporation, and

Related Sections: S. 14(12) Loss on certain transfers; 18(13) When s. (15) applies to money lenders; 18(14) When s. (15) applies to adventurers in trade; 18(15) Loss on certain properties; 18(16) Deemed identical property; s. 40(3.3) When subsection (3.4) applies; s. 40(3.4) Loss on certain properties; s. 69(5)(*d*) Winding-up of corporation; s. 87(2)(*g*.3) Superficial losses; s. 88(1)(*d*.1) Winding-up; s. 139.1(18) Acquisition of control; s. 251.1 Definition of "affiliated persons"; s. 251.2(2) Loss restriction event.

Canadian Tax Foundation: Courage, *Utilization of Tax Losses and Debt Restructuring,* 2006 Ontario Tax Conference 9:1–86.

Tax Profile: May 2004 — The Stop-Loss Rules.

Interpretation Bulletins: *Secondary* — IT-291R3 Transfer of property to a corporation under subsection 85(1).

Tax Window Files: Depreciable Property Transferred from Trust to Majority Interest Beneficiary, *Technical Interpretation, International and Trusts Division, March 21, 2007,* CRA Document No. 2004-0091061E5; Suspended Loss With Respect to Depreciable Property, *Technical Interpretation, Reorganizations and Resources Division, July 25, 2005,* CRA Document No. 2005-0125501E5; Capital Cost Allowance — Leasehold Interest, *Technical Interpretation, Financial Industries Division, June 14, 2004,* CRA Document No. 2004-0071821E5.

► 13(22) ◄

(22) Deduction for insurer — (Repealed by S.C. 2013, c. 34, s. 175(5).)

History: S. 13(22) was repealed by S.C. 2013, c. 34, s. 175(5), applicable to taxation years that begin after October 31, 2011, and formerly read:

(22) *Deduction for insurer.* For the purposes of E in the definition "undepreciated capital cost" in subsection (21), an insurer shall be deemed to have been allowed a deduction for depreciation for property of a prescribed class under paragraph 20(1)(*a*) in computing income for taxation years before its 1977 taxation year equal to the total of

(*a*) the amount determined, immediately after the end of its 1976 taxation year, for E in that definition, with respect to property of the particular prescribed class of the insurer (determined without reference to this subsection),

(*b*) the lesser of

(i) the amount of its 1975-76 excess capital cost allowance with respect to property of the particular prescribed class of the insurer, and

(ii) that proportion of the amount, if any, by which its 1975 branch accounting election deficiency exceeds the amount determined under subparagraph 138(4.1)(*d*)(ii) that

(A) the amount of its 1975-76 excess capital cost allowance with respect to property of the particular prescribed class of the insurer

is of

(B) the total of all its 1975-76 excess capital cost allowances with respect to properties of a prescribed class of the insurer, and

(*c*) the lesser of

(i) the amount, if any, by which

(A) the undepreciated capital cost of property of the particular prescribed class of the insurer immediately after the end of its 1976 taxation year (determined without reference to this subsection),

exceeds

(B) the amount determined under paragraph (*b*) in respect of property of the particular prescribed class of the insurer, and

(ii) that proportion of the amount, if any, by which its 1975 branch accounting election deficiency exceeds the total of

(A) the amount determined under subparagraph 138(4.1)(*d*)(ii),

(B) the total of all amounts determined under paragraph (*b*) with respect to property of a prescribed class of the insurer,

(C) the total described in subclause 138(4.1)(*a*)(ii)(B)(IV),

(D) the amount determined under subparagraph 138(4.1)(*b*)(ii), and

(E) the amount determined under subparagraph 138(4.1)(*a*)(ii)

that

(F) the undepreciated capital cost of property of the particular prescribed class of the insurer immediately after the end of its 1976 taxation year (determined without reference to this subsection),

is of

(G) the total of all amounts each of which is the undepreciated capital cost of property of a prescribed class of the insurer immediately after the end of its 1976 taxation year (determined without reference to this subsection).

► 13(23) ◄

(23) Deduction for life insurer — (Repealed by S.C. 2013, c. 34, s. 175(5).)

History: S. 13(23) was repealed by S.C. 2013, c. 34, s. 175(5), applicable to taxation years that begin after October 31, 2011, and formerly read:

(23) *Deduction for life insurer.* For the purposes of E in the definition "undepreciated capital cost" in subsection (21), a life insurer shall be deemed to have been allowed a deduction for depreciation for property of a pre-

scribed class under paragraph 20(1)(*a*) in computing income for taxation years before its 1978 taxation year equal to the total of

(*a*) the amount determined immediately after the end of its 1977 taxation year for E in that definition, with respect to property of the particular prescribed class of the insurer (determined without reference to this subsection), and

(*b*) the amount, if any, by which

(i) the total of all maximum amounts the insurer was entitled to claim with respect to property of the particular prescribed class of the insurer in taxation years ending before 1978 and after 1968

exceeds

(ii) the amount determined under paragraph (*a*).

► 13(23.1) ◄

(23.1) Application of s. 138(12) — (Repealed by S.C. 2013, c. 34, s. 175(5).)

History: S. 13(23.1) was repealed by S.C. 2013, c. 34, s. 175(5), applicable to taxation years that begin after October 31, 2011, and formerly read:

(23.1) *Application of s. 138(12).* The definitions in subsection 138(12) apply to this section.

► 13(24) ◄

(24) Loss restriction event. If at any time a taxpayer is subject to a loss restriction event and, within the 12-month period that ended immediately before that time, the taxpayer, a partnership of which the taxpayer was a majority-interest partner or a trust of which the taxpayer was a majority-interest beneficiary (as defined in subsection 251.1(3)) acquired depreciable property (other than property that was held, by the taxpayer, partnership or trust or by a person that would be affiliated with the taxpayer if section 251.1 were read without reference to the definition "controlled" in subsection 251.1(3), throughout the period that began immediately before the 12-month period began and ended at the time the property was acquired by the taxpayer, partnership or trust) that was not used, or acquired for use, by the taxpayer, partnership or trust in a business that was carried on by it immediately before the 12-month period began

(*a*) subject to paragraph (*b*), for the purposes of the description of A in the definition "undepreciated capital cost" in subsection (21) and of sections 127 and 127.1, the property is deemed

(i) not to have been acquired by the taxpayer, partnership or trust, as the case may be, before that time, and

(ii) to have been acquired by it immediately after that time; and

(*b*) if the property was disposed of by the taxpayer, partnership or trust, as the case may be, before that time and was not reacquired by it before that time, for the purposes of the description of A in that definition, the property is deemed to have been acquired by it immediately before the property was disposed of.

History: S. 13(24) was replaced by S.C. 2013, c. 40, s. 6(4), deemed to have come into force on March 21, 2013, except that subsection 13(24) is to be read as follows before September 13, 2013:

"(24) If at any time a taxpayer is subject to a loss restriction event and, within the 12-month period that ended immediately before that time, the taxpayer or a partnership of which the taxpayer was a majority-interest partner acquired depreciable property (other than property that was held, by the taxpayer or partnership or by a person that would be affiliated with the taxpayer if section 251.1 were read without reference to the definition "controlled" in subsection 251.1(3), throughout the period that began immediately before the 12-month period began and ended at the time the property was acquired by the taxpayer or partnership) that was not used, or acquired for use, by the taxpayer or partnership in a business that was carried on by it immediately before the 12-month period began

(*a*) subject to paragraph (*b*), for the purposes of the description of A in the definition "undepreciated capital cost" in subsection (21) and of sections 127 and 127.1, the property is deemed

(i) not to have been acquired by the taxpayer or partnership, as the case may be, before that time, and

(ii) to have been acquired by it immediately after that time; and

(*b*) if the property was disposed of by the taxpayer or partnership, as the case may be, before that time and was not reacquired by it before that time, for the purposes of the description of A in that definition, the property is deemed to have been acquired by it immediately before the property was disposed of."

S. 13(24) formerly read:

(24) *Acquisition of control.* Where control of a corporation has been acquired at any time by a person or group of persons and, within the 12-month period that ended immediately before that time, the corporation or a partnership of which it was a majority interest partner acquired depreciable property (other than property that was owned by the corporation or partnership or by a person that would, if section 251.1 were read without reference to the definition "controlled" in subsection 251.1(2) [(*sic*) 251.1(3) — CCH], be affiliated with the corporation throughout the period that began immediately before the 12-month period began and ended at the time the property was acquired by the corporation or partnership) that was not used, or acquired for use, by the corporation or partnership in a business that was carried on by it immediately before the 12-month period began,

(*a*) for the purposes of the description of A in the definition "undepreciated capital cost" in subsection (21) and of sections 127 and 127.1, the property is, subject to paragraph (*b*), deemed not to have been acquired by the corporation or partnership before that time and to have been acquired by it immediately after that time; and

(*a*) where the property was disposed of by it before that time and was not reacquired by it before that time, for the purpose of the description of A in that definition, the property is deemed to have been acquired by the corporation or partnership immediately before the property was disposed of.

Related Sections: S. 13(25) Affiliation – subsection (24); s. 87(2)(*j*.6) Continuing corporation; s. 139.1(18) Acquisition of control; s. 251.2(2) Loss restriction event; 256(6) Idem; 256(6.1) Simultaneous control; 256(6.2) Application to control in fact; 256(7) Acquiring control; 256(8) Deemed exercise of right; 256(8.1) Corporations without share capital; 256(9) Date of acquisition of control; s. 256.1 [Corporate tax-attribute trading].

Interpretation Bulletins: *Primary* — IT-302R3 Losses of a corporation — the effect that acquisitions of control, amalgamations and windings-up have on their deductibility — after January 15, 1987.

► 13(25) ◄

(25) Affiliation — subsection (24). For the purposes of subsection (24), if the taxpayer referred to in that subsection was formed or created in the 12-month period referred to in that subsection, the taxpayer is deemed to have been, throughout the period that began immediately before the 12-month period and ended immediately after it was formed or created,

(*a*) in existence; and

(*b*) affiliated with every person with whom it was affiliated (otherwise than because of a right referred to in paragraph 251(5)(*b*)) throughout the period that began when it was formed or created and that ended immediately before the time at which the taxpayer was subject to the loss restriction event referred to in that subsection.

History: S. 13(25) was replaced by S.C. 2013, c. 40, s. 6(4), deemed to have come into force on March 21, 2013, and formerly read:

(25) *Early change of control.* For the purpose of subsection (24), where a corporation referred to in that subsection was incorporated or otherwise formed in the 12-month period referred to in that subsection, the corporation is deemed to have been, throughout the period that began immediately before the 12-month period and ended immediately after it was incorporated or otherwise formed,

(*a*) in existence; and

(*b*) affiliated with every person with whom it was affiliated (otherwise than because of a right referred to in paragraph 251(5)(*b*)) throughout the period that began when it was incorporated or otherwise formed and ended immediately before its control is acquired.

► 13(26) ◄

(26) Restriction on deduction before available for use. In applying the definition "undepreciated capital cost" in subsection (21) for the purpose of paragraph 20(1)(*a*) and any regulations made for the purpose of that paragraph, in computing a taxpayer's income for a taxation year from a business or property, no amount shall be included in calculating the undepreciated capital cost to the taxpayer of depreciable property of a prescribed class in respect of the capital cost to the taxpayer of a property of that class (other than property that is a certified production, as defined by regulations made for the purpose of paragraph 20(1)(*a*)) before the time the property is considered to have become available for use by the taxpayer.

Editorial Note: S. 13(26) essentially provides that if depreciable property is not "available for use", as defined in s. 13(27) and (28), no CCA can be claimed for the year the property is acquired or the following year. However, this limitation is effectively restricted by the "two-year rolling start" rule in s. 13(27)(*b*) and 13(28)(*c*). When a CCA claim has been delayed under s. 13(26), the full (not half) claim will be available once s. 13(26) ceases to apply. This is because the "half-year rule" in Regulation 1100(2)(*a*)(i) applies only to property "acquired in the year." Also, see Regulation 1100(2)(*a*)(vii).

Related Regulations: 1100(2)(*a*)(i); 1100(2)(*a*)(vii); 1103(2g).

Related Sections: 13(27) Interpretation — available for use; 13(28) Idem; 13(29) Idem; 13(30) Transfers of property; 13(31) Idem; 13(32) Leased property; s. 20(1)(*a*) Capital cost of property; s. 20(28) Exception to available-for-use rule; s. 20(29) Exception to soft costs capitalization rule; s. 37(1.2) Deemed time of capital expenditure; s. 127(11.2) Time of expenditure and acquisition; s. 248(19) When property available for use.

Canadian Petroleum Tax Journal: Offshore Oil & Gas Interests: A Perspective on Exploration & Development of Offshore Petroleum and Natural Gas Resources in Eastern Canada, Michael R. Smith, CA and B. David Nielsen, CA, 2000, Vol. 13, No. 1.

Income Tax Folios: *Primary* — S3-F4-C1 General Discussion of Capital Cost Allowance.

► 13(27) ◄

(27) Interpretation — available for use. For the purposes of subsection (26) and subject to subsection (29), property (other than a building or part thereof) acquired by a taxpayer shall be considered to have become available for use by the taxpayer at the earliest of

(*a*) the time the property is first used by the taxpayer for the purpose of earning income,

(*b*) the time that is immediately after the beginning of the first taxation year of the taxpayer that begins more than 357 days after the end of the taxation year of the taxpayer in which the property was acquired by the taxpayer,

(*c*) the time that is immediately before the disposition of the property by the taxpayer,

(*d*) the time the property

(i) is delivered to the taxpayer, or to a person or partnership (in this paragraph referred to as the "other person") that will use the property for the benefit of the taxpayer, or, where the property is not of a type that is deliverable, is made available to the taxpayer or the other person, and

(ii) is capable, either alone or in combination with other property in the possession at that time of the taxpayer or the other person, of being used by or for the benefit of the taxpayer or the other person to produce a commercially saleable product or to perform a commercially saleable service, including an intermediate product or service that is used or consumed, or to be used or consumed, by or for the benefit of the taxpayer or the other person in producing or performing any such product or service,

(*e*) in the case of property acquired by the taxpayer for the prevention, reduction or elimination of air or water pollution created by operations carried on by the taxpayer or that would be created by such operations if the property had not been acquired, the time at which the property is installed and capable of performing the function for which it was acquired,

(*f*) in the case of property acquired by

(i) a corporation a class of shares of the capital stock of which is listed on a designated stock exchange,

(ii) a corporation that is a public corporation because of an election made under subparagraph (*b*)(i) of the definition "public corporation" in subsection 89(1) or a designation made by the Minister in a notice to the corporation under subparagraph (*b*)(ii) of that definition, or

(iii) a subsidiary wholly-owned corporation of a corporation described in subparagraph (i) or (ii),

the end of the taxation year for which depreciation in respect of the property is first deducted in computing the earnings of the corporation in accordance with generally accepted accounting principles and for the purpose of the financial statements of the corporation for the year presented to its shareholders,

(*g*) in the case of property acquired by the taxpayer in the course of carrying on a business of farming or fishing, the time at which the property has been delivered to the taxpayer and is capable of performing the function for which it was acquired,

(*h*) in the case of property of a taxpayer that is a motor vehicle, trailer, trolley bus, aircraft or vessel for which one or more permits, certificates or licences evidencing that the property may be operated by the taxpayer in accordance with any laws regulating the use of such property are required to be obtained, the time all those permits, certificates or licences have been obtained,

(*i*) in the case of property that is a spare part intended to replace a part of another property of the taxpayer if required due to a breakdown of that other property, the time the other property became available for use by the taxpayer,

(*j*) in the case of a concrete gravity base structure and topside modules intended to be used at an oil production facility in a commercial discovery area (within the meaning assigned by section 2 of the *Canada Petroleum Resources Act*) on which the drilling of the first well that indicated the discovery began before March 5, 1982, in an offshore region prescribed for the purposes of subsection 127(9), the time the gravity base structure deballasts and lifts the assembled topside modules, and

(*k*) where the property is (within the meaning assigned by subsection (4.1)) a replacement for a former property described in paragraph (4)(*a*) that was acquired before 1990 or that became available for use at or before the time the replacement property is acquired, the time the replacement property is acquired,

and, for the purposes of paragraph (*f*), where depreciation is calculated by reference to a portion of the cost of the property, only that portion of the property shall be considered to have become available for use at the end of the taxation year referred to in that paragraph.

Related Regulations: 1100(2)(*a*)(vii).

Related Sections: S. 13(21.2)(*e*)(iv) Loss on certain transfers; s. 13(26) Restriction on deduction before available for use; 13(28) Idem; 13(29) Idem; 13(30) Transfers of property; 13(31) Idem; 13(32) Leased property; s. 20(1)(*a*) Capital cost of property; s. 20(28) Exception to available-for-use rule; s. 20(29) Exception to soft costs capitalization rule; s. 37(1.2) Deemed time of capital expenditure; s. 87(2)(*j*.6) Continuing corporation; s. 139.1(18) Acquisition of control; s. 127(11.2) Time of expenditure and acquisition; s. 248(19) When property available for use; s. 262(1) Authority to designate stock exchange.

Canadian Petroleum Tax Journal: Offshore Oil & Gas Interests: A Perspective on Exploration & Development of Offshore Petroleum and Natural Gas Resources in Eastern Canada, Michael R. Smith, CA and B. David Nielsen, CA, 2000, Vol. 13, No. 1.

Income Tax Folios: *Primary* — S3-F4-C1 General Discussion of Capital Cost Allowance.

▶ 13(28) ◀

(28) Idem. For the purposes of subsection (26) and subject to subsection (29), property that is a building or part thereof of a taxpayer shall be considered to have become available for use by the taxpayer at the earliest of

(*a*) the time all or substantially all of the building is first used by the taxpayer for the purpose for which it was acquired,

(*b*) the time the construction of the building is complete,

(*c*) the time that is immediately after the beginning of the taxpayer's first taxation year that begins more than 357 days after the end of the taxpayer's taxation year in which the property was acquired by the taxpayer,

(*d*) the time that is immediately before the disposition of the property by the taxpayer, and

(*e*) where the property is (within the meaning assigned by subsection (4.1)) a replacement for a former property described in paragraph (4)(*a*) that was acquired before 1990 or that became available for use at or before the time the replacement property is acquired, the time the replacement property is acquired,

and, for the purpose of this subsection, a renovation, alteration or addition to a particular building shall be considered to be a building separate from the particular building.

Related Regulations: 1100(2)(*a*)(vii).

Related Sections: S.13(21.2)(*e*)(iv) Loss on certain transfers; s. 13(30) Transfers of property; s. 13(31) Transfers of property — continuity of ownership; s. 87(2)(*j*.6) Continuing corporation.

Income Tax Folios: *Primary* — S3-F4-C1 General Discussion of Capital Cost Allowance.

Tax Window Files: Available for Use Rules, *Technical Interpretation, Business and Partnerships Division, December 19, 2003,* CRA Document No. 2003-0035347.

▶ 13(29) ◀

(29) Idem. For the purposes of subsection (26), where a taxpayer acquires property (other than a building that is used or is to be used by the taxpayer principally for the purpose of gaining or producing gross revenue that is rent) in the taxpayer's first taxation year (in this subsection referred to as the "particular year") that begins more than 357 days after the end of the taxpayer's taxation year in which the taxpayer first acquired property after 1989, that is part of a project of the taxpayer, or in a taxation year subsequent to the particular year, and at the end of any taxation year (in this subsection referred to as the "inclusion year") of the taxpayer

(*a*) the property can reasonably be considered to be part of the project, and

(*b*) the property has not otherwise become available for use,

if the taxpayer so elects in prescribed form filed with the taxpayer's return of income under this Part for the particular year, that particular portion of the property the capital cost of which does not exceed the amount, if any, by which

(*c*) the total of all amounts each of which is the capital cost to the taxpayer of a depreciable property (other than a building that is used or is to be used by the taxpayer principally for the purpose of gaining or producing gross revenue that is rent) that is part of the project, that was acquired by the taxpayer after 1989 and before the end of the taxpayer's last taxation year that ends more than 357 days before the beginning of the inclusion year and that has not become available for use at or before the end of the inclusion year (except where the property has first become available for use before the end of the inclusion year because of this subsection or paragraph (27)(*b*) or (28)(*c*))

exceeds

(*d*) the total of all amounts each of which is the capital cost to the taxpayer of a depreciable property, other than the particular portion of the property, that is part of the project to the extent that the property is considered, because of this subsection, to have become available for use before the end of the inclusion year

shall be considered to have become available for use immediately before the end of the inclusion year.

Related Regulations: 600(*b*); 4609.

Related Sections: S. 220(3.2) Late, amended or revoked elections.

Canadian Petroleum Tax Journal: Offshore Oil & Gas Interests: A Perspective on Exploration & Development of Offshore Petroleum and Natural Gas Resources in Eastern Canada, Michael R. Smith, CA and B. David Nielsen, CA, 2000, Vol. 13, No. 1.

Forms: T1031 — Subsection 13(29) Election in Respect of Certain Depreciable Properties, Acquired for Use in a Long Term Project.

Income Tax Folios: *Primary* — S3-F4-C1 General Discussion of Capital Cost Allowance.

▶ 13(30) ◀

(30) Transfers of property. Notwithstanding subsections (27) to (29), for the purpose of subsection (26), property of a taxpayer shall be deemed to have become available for use by the taxpayer at the earlier of the time the property was acquired by the taxpayer and, if applicable, a prescribed time, where

(*a*) the property was acquired

(i) from a person with whom the taxpayer was not dealing at arm's length (otherwise than because of a right referred to in paragraph 251(5)(*b*)) at the time the property was acquired by the taxpayer, or

(ii) in the course of a reorganization in respect of which, if a dividend were received by a corporation in the course of the reorganization, subsection 55(2) would not apply to the dividend because of paragraph 55(3)(*b*); and

(*b*) before the property was acquired by the taxpayer, it became available for use (determined without reference to paragraphs (27)(*c*) and (28)(*d*)) by the person from whom it was acquired.

Related Regulations: 1100(2.2)(*j*).

▶ 13(31) ◀

(31) Idem. For the purposes of paragraphs (27)(*b*) and (28)(*c*) and subsection (29), where a property of a taxpayer was acquired from a person (in this subsection referred to as "the transferor")

(*a*) with whom the taxpayer was, at the time the taxpayer acquired the property, not dealing at arm's length (otherwise than because of a right referred to in paragraph 251(5)(*b*)), or

(*b*) in the course of a reorganization in respect of which, if a dividend were received by a corporation in the course of the reorganization, subsection 55(2) would not apply to the dividend because of the application of paragraph 55(3)(*b*),

the taxpayer shall be deemed to have acquired the property at the time it was acquired by the transferor.

▶ 13(32) ◀

(32) Leased property. Where a taxpayer has leased property that is depreciable property of a person with whom the taxpayer does not deal at arm's length, the amount, if any, by which

(*a*) the total of all amounts paid or payable by the taxpayer for the use of, or the right to use, the property in a particular taxation year and before the time the property would have been considered to have become available for use by the taxpayer if the taxpayer had acquired the property, and that, but for this subsection, would be deductible in computing the taxpayer's income for any taxation year

exceeds

(*b*) the total of all amounts received or receivable by the taxpayer for the use of, or the right to use, the property in the particular taxation year and before that time and that are included in the income of the taxpayer for any taxation year

shall be deemed to be a cost to the taxpayer of a property included in Class 13 in Schedule II to the *Income Tax Regulations* and not to be an amount paid or payable for the use of, or the right to use, the property.

Related Sections: 13(26) Restriction on deduction before available for use; 13(27) Interpretation — available for use; 13(28) Idem; 13(29) Idem; 13(30) Transfers of property; 13(31) Idem; s. 20(1)(*a*) Capital cost of property; s. 20(28) Exception to available-for-use rule; s. 20(29) Exception to soft costs capitalization rule; s. 37(1.2) Deemed time of capital expenditure; s. 127(11.2) Time of expenditure and acquisition; s. 248(19) When property available for use.

▶ 13(33) ◀

(33) Consideration given for depreciable property. For greater certainty, where a person acquires a depreciable property for consideration that can reasonably be considered to include a transfer of property, the portion of the cost to the person of the depreciable property attributable to the transfer shall not exceed the fair market value of the transferred property.

Related Sections: S. 13(21) Definitions; s. 13(30) Transfers of property; s. 68 Allocation of amounts in consideration for disposition of property; s. 69(1) Inadequate considerations.

Income Tax Folios: *Primary* — S3-F4-C1 General Discussion of Capital Cost Allowance.

▶ 13(34) ◀

(34) Goodwill. Where a taxpayer carries on a particular business,

(*a*) there is deemed to be a single goodwill property in respect of the particular business;

(*b*) if at any time the taxpayer acquires goodwill as part of an acquisition of all or a part of another business that is carried on, after the acquisition, as part of the particular business — or is deemed by subsection (35) to acquire goodwill in respect of the particular business — the cost of the goodwill is added at that time to the cost of the goodwill property in respect of the particular business;

(*c*) if at any time the taxpayer disposes of goodwill as part of the disposition of part of the particular business, receives proceeds of disposition a portion of which is attributable to goodwill and continues to carry on the particular business or is deemed by subsection (37) to dispose of goodwill in respect of the particular business,

(i) the taxpayer is deemed to dispose at that time of a portion of the goodwill property in respect of the particular business having a cost equal to the lesser of the cost of the goodwill property in respect of the particular business otherwise determined and the portion of the proceeds attributable to goodwill, and

(ii) the cost of the goodwill property in respect of the particular business is reduced at that time by the amount determined under subparagraph (i); and

(*d*) if paragraph (*c*) applies to more than one disposition of goodwill at the same time, that paragraph and subsection (39) apply as if each disposition had occurred separately in the order designated by the taxpayer or, if the taxpayer does not designate an order, in the order designated by the Minister.

Editorial Note: The eligible capital property rules in former section 14 were repealed on January 1, 2017 and effective that date, property that was eligible capital property is now treated as depreciable property and included in CCA Class 14.1. Simultaneously, rules that provide specific tax treatment of goodwill were introduced effective January 1, 2017. These "goodwill rules" are discussed below;

Single Goodwill Property for Each Business: Subsection 13(34) provides that each particular business of a taxpayer is deemed to have a single goodwill property that is included in Class 14.1. Where a taxpayer acquires goodwill by acquiring another business that becomes a part of the existing business, the cost of that acquired goodwill is added to the cost of the single goodwill property of that business.

Paragraph 13(34)(*c*) provides two separate computations where a portion of goodwill is disposed of but the business continues to operate. Subparagraph (i) computes the cost of the goodwill portion that is disposed of. Subparagraph (ii) reduces the cost of the single goodwill property of the business by the amount of the deemed cost of the portion disposed of. If multiple goodwill dispositions occur simultaneously, the taxpayer can choose the order in which the computation occurs.

History: S. 13(34) was replaced by S.C. 2016, c. 12, s. 3(3), in force January 1, 2017, and formerly read:

(34) *Deductible expenses.* Notwithstanding paragraph 1102(1)(*a*) of the Regulations, for taxation years that end after 1987 and before December 6, 1996, the classes of property prescribed for the purpose of paragraph 20(1)(*a*) are deemed to include property of a taxpayer that, if the Act were read without reference to sections 66 to 66.4, would be included in one of the classes.

Related Regulations: Schedule II Class 14.1.

Canadian Tax Foundation: Paproski, *Effectively Dealing with Eligible Capital Property Under the New Regime*, 2017 Prairie Provinces Tax Conference 9B:1–25.

Tax Topics: No. 2345, February 16, 2017, CRA Interpretations of the New Class 14.1 Rules.

▶ 13(35) ◀

(35) Outlays not relating to property. If at any time a taxpayer makes or incurs an outlay or expense on account of capital for the purpose of gaining or producing income from a business carried on by the taxpayer, the taxpayer is deemed to acquire at that time goodwill in respect of the business with a cost equal to the amount of the outlay or expense if no portion of the amount is

(*a*) the cost, or any part of the cost, of a property;

(*b*) deductible in computing the taxpayer's income from the business (determined without reference to this subsection);

(*c*) not deductible in computing the taxpayer's income from the business because of any provision of this Act (other than paragraph 18(1)(*b*)) or the *Income Tax Regulations*;

(*d*) paid or payable to a creditor of the taxpayer as, on account of or in lieu of payment of, any debt, or on account of the redemption, cancellation or purchase of any bond or debenture; or

(*e*) where the taxpayer is a corporation, partnership or trust, paid or payable to a person as a shareholder, partner or beneficiary, as the case may be, of the taxpayer.

Editorial Note: *Deemed Acquisition of Goodwill:* Essentially, where a taxpayer incurs an outlay or expense that does not relate to property, subsection 13(35) deems them to have acquired goodwill. The eligible capital property rules (prior to 2017) provided nearly identical tax treatment of such amounts.

Effective January 1, 2017, where a taxpayer incurs an amount on account of capital for the purpose of producing income from a business, the taxpayer is deemed to acquire goodwill with a cost equal to that amount, provided that the amount does not fall under paragraphs (*a*) to (*e*). As a result, capital costs incurred that do not relate to property are deemed to be a goodwill acquisition. Subsection 13(36) further clarifies that consideration paid to acquire shares cannot be allocated to goodwill.

History: Subsection 13(35) was added by S.C. 2016, c. 12, s. 3(3), in force on January 1, 2017.

Related Regulations: Schedule II Class 14.1.

Tax Window Files: 2018 CTF - Q15 - Class 14.1, *November 27, 2018*, CRA Document No. 2018-0780011C6.

▶ 13(36) ◀

(36) No addition to goodwill. For greater certainty, no amount paid or payable may be included in Class 14.1 of Schedule II to the *Income Tax Regulations*, if the amount is

(*a*) in consideration for the purchase of shares; or

(*b*) in consideration for the cancellation or assignment of an obligation to pay consideration referred to in paragraph (*a*).

Editorial Note: See editorial note to s. 13(35).

History: Subsection 13(36) was added by S.C. 2016, c. 12, s. 3(3), in force on January 1, 2017.

Related Regulations: Schedule II Class 14.1.

▶ 13(37) ◀

(37) Receipts not relating to property. If at any time in a taxation year a taxpayer has or may become entitled to receive an amount (in this subsection referred to as the receipt) on account of capital in respect of a business that is or was carried on by the taxpayer, the taxpayer is deemed to dispose, at that time, of goodwill in respect of the business for proceeds of disposition equal to the amount by which the receipt exceeds the total of all outlays or expenses that were made or incurred by the taxpayer for the purpose of obtaining the receipt and that were not otherwise deductible in computing the taxpayer's income, if the following conditions are satisfied (determined without reference to this subsection):

(*a*) the receipt is not included in computing the taxpayer's income, or deducted in computing, for the purposes of this Act, any balance of undeducted outlays, expenses or other amounts for the taxation year or a preceding taxation year;

(*b*) the receipt does not reduce the cost or capital cost of a property or the amount of an outlay or expense; and

(*c*) the receipt is not included in computing any gain or loss of the taxpayer from a disposition of a capital property.

Editorial Note: *Deemed Disposition of Goodwill:* Where a taxpayer sells property that is goodwill, the taxpayer is selling Class 14.1 property, and the disposition is treated the same as any other disposition of depreciable property, subject to the single goodwill property computations, as discussed in the editorial note at s. 13(34). Furthermore, effective January 1, 2017, subsection 13(37) deems taxpayers to have disposed of goodwill where they receive proceeds that basically relate to "nothing."

Where a taxpayer becomes entitled to receive an amount in respect of a business, that amount is deemed to be proceeds of disposition of goodwill, provided that the amount: is not included in income (or deducted therefrom), does not reduce the cost of property, or is not otherwise included in computing a gain or loss from a disposition of a capital property. Therefore, receipts that do not relate to property are deemed to be proceeds of goodwill.

History: Subsection 13(37) was added by S.C. 2016, c. 12, s. 3(3), in force on January 1, 2017.

Related Regulations: Schedule II Class 14.1.

Tax Window Files: ECP Rules NAL Disposition, *June 7, 2016*, CRA Document No. 2016-0641851E5; partial disposition of farm quota, *September 27, 2016*, CRA Document No. 2016-0660861E5.

► 13(38) ◄

(38) Class 14.1 — transitional rules. If a taxpayer has incurred an eligible capital expenditure in respect of a business before January 1, 2017,

(*a*) at the beginning of that day, the total capital cost of all property of the taxpayer included in Class 14.1 of Schedule II to the *Income Tax Regulations* in respect of the business, each of which was an eligible capital property of the taxpayer immediately before that day or is the goodwill property in respect of the business, is deemed to be the amount determined by the formula

$$4/3 \times (A + B - C)$$

where

A is the amount that is the cumulative eligible capital in respect of the business at the beginning of that day,

B is the amount determined for F in the definition "cumulative eligible capital" in subsection 14(5) (as that subsection applied immediately before that day) in respect of the business at the beginning of that day, and

C is the amount by which the total of all amounts determined, in respect of the business, for E or F in the definition "cumulative eligible capital" in subsection 14(5) (as that subsection applied immediately before that day), exceeds the total of all amounts determined for A to D.1 in that definition in respect of the business at the beginning of that day, including any adjustment required by subparagraph (*d*)(i);

(*b*) at the beginning of that day, the capital cost of each property of the taxpayer included in the class in respect of the business, each of which was an eligible capital property of the taxpayer immediately before that day or is the goodwill property in respect of the business, is to be determined as follows:

(i) the taxpayer shall designate the order in which the capital cost of each property that is not the goodwill property is determined and, if the taxpayer does not designate an order, the Minister may designate the order,

(ii) the capital cost of a particular property that is not the goodwill property in respect of the business is deemed to be the lesser of the eligible capital expenditure of the taxpayer in respect of the particular property and the amount by which the total capital cost of the class determined under paragraph (*a*) exceeds the total of all amounts each of which is an amount deemed by this subparagraph to be the capital cost of a property that is determined in advance of the determination of the capital cost of the particular property, and

(iii) the capital cost of the goodwill property is deemed to be the amount by which the total capital cost of the class exceeds the total of all amounts each of which is an amount deemed by subparagraph (ii) to be the capital cost of a property;

(*c*) an amount is deemed to have been allowed to the taxpayer in respect of property of the class under regulations made under paragraph 20(1)(*a*) in computing the taxpayer's income for taxation years ending before that day equal to the amount by which

(i) the total of the total capital cost of the class and the amount determined for C in paragraph (*a*)

exceeds

(ii) the amount determined for A in paragraph (*a*); and

(*d*) if no taxation year of the taxpayer ends immediately before that day and the taxpayer would have had a particular amount included, because of paragraph 14(1)(*b*) (as that paragraph applied immediately before that day), in computing the taxpayer's income from the business for the particular taxation year that includes that day if the particular year had ended immediately before that day,

(i) for the purposes of the formula in paragraph (*a*), 3/2 of the particular amount is to be included in computing the amount for B of the definition "cumulative eligible capital" in subsection 14(5) (as that subsection applied immediately before that day),

(ii) the taxpayer is deemed to dispose of a capital property in respect of the business immediately before that day for proceeds of disposition equal to twice the particular amount,

(iii) if the taxpayer elects in writing to have this subparagraph apply and files that election with the Minister on or before the filing-due date for the particular year, subparagraph (ii) does not apply and an amount equal to the particular amount is to be included in computing the taxpayer's income from the business for the particular year,

(iv) if, on or after that day and in the particular year, the taxpayer acquires a property included in the class in respect of the business, or is deemed by subsection (35) to acquire goodwill in respect of the business, and the taxpayer elects in writing to have this subparagraph apply and files that election with the Minister on or before the filing-due date for the particular year

(A) for the purposes of subparagraphs (ii) and (iii), the particular amount is to be reduced by the lesser of the particular amount otherwise determined and 1/2 of the capital cost of the property or goodwill acquired (determined without reference to clause (B)), and

(B) the capital cost of the property or goodwill acquired, as the case may be, is to be reduced by twice the amount by which the particular amount is reduced under clause (A), and

(v) if, in the particular year and before that day, the taxpayer disposed of a "qualified farm or fishing property" (as defined in subsection 110.6(1)) that was an eligible capital property of the taxpayer, the capital property disposed of under subparagraph (ii), if any, is deemed to be a qualified farm or fishing property to the extent of the lesser of

(A) the proceeds of disposition of the capital property, and

(B) the amount by which the proceeds of disposition of the qualified farm or fishing property exceed its cost.

Editorial Note: The eligible capital rules in former section 14 were repealed on January 1, 2017 and effective that date, property that was eligible capital property is now treated as depreciable property and included in CCA Class 14.1. There are a number of transitional rules that apply in respect of expenditures incurred prior to 2017. Basically, the end result of the transitional provisions is to place taxpayers in a position similar to what they would have been in if the eligible capital property rules never existed and Class 14.1 existed all along.

Determining Capital Cost: Subsection 13(38) contains several rules for computing the capital cost of Class 14.1 property acquired before 2017. Paragraph 13(38)*(a)* provides that on January 1, 2017, the total capital cost of all property included in Class 14.1 is 4/3 of the CEC balance immediately before that time, plus 4/3 of previously-claimed unrecaptured deductions (under the old rules), less 4/3 of any negative CEC balance immediately before that time. Paragraph 13(38)*(b)* allocates the total capital cost between all the properties (including goodwill) that are included in Class 14.1.

Subparagraph 13(38)*(b)*(i) provides that the taxpayer must designate the order in which the capital cost of each property that is not goodwill is determined, failing which the Minister can designate. The maximum amount that can be allocated to a particular non-goodwill property is limited to its eligible capital expenditure amount (basically its cost) and the excess capital cost, if any, is deemed to be the capital cost of goodwill.

Paragraph 13(38)*(c)* effectively ensures that the undepreciated capital cost of Class 14.1 on January 1, 2017 is equal to what would have been the CEC pool at the time, while also taking into account any negative CEC balance. Subparagraph 13(38)*(d)* provides the transitional rules for taxation years that straddle January 1, 2017, including an election to treat pre-2017 receipts as income from a business.

History: Subsection 13(38) was added by S.C. 2016, c. 12, s. 3(3), in force on January 1, 2017.

Related Regulations: 1100(1)*(c.1)*; Schedule II Class 14.1.

Canadian Tax Foundation: Paproski, *Effectively Dealing with Eligible Capital Property Under the New Regime*, 2017 Prairie Provinces Tax Conference 9B:1–25; Adkin and Gimpel, *Eligible Capital Expenditure Changes*, 2016 British Columbia Tax Conference 14:1–30.

Tax Topics: No. 2345, February 16, 2017, CRA Interpretations of the New Class 14.1 Rules.

Tax Window Files: Transitional Rules for Eligible Capital Expenditures, *May 10, 2017*, CRA Document No. 2016-0680141E5.

► 13(39) ◄

(39) Class 14.1 — transitional rule. If at any time a taxpayer disposes of a particular property included in Class 14.1 of Schedule II to the *Income Tax Regulations* in respect of a business and none of subsections 24(2), 70(5.1), 73(3.1), 85(1), 88(1), 98(3) and (5), 107(2) and 107.4(3) apply to the disposition, then for the purpose of determining the undepreciated capital cost of the class, the taxpayer is deemed to have acquired a property of the class immediately before that time with a capital cost equal to the least of 1/4 of the proceeds of disposition of the particular property, 1/4 of the capital cost of the particular property and

(*a*) if the particular property is not goodwill and is acquired before January 1, 2017 by the taxpayer, 1/4 of the capital cost of the particular property;

(*b*) if the particular property is not goodwill, is acquired on or after that day by the taxpayer and subsection (40) deems an amount to have been allowed under paragraph 20(1)(*a*) in respect of the taxpayer's acquisition of the particular property, that amount;

(*c*) if the particular property (other than a property to which paragraph (*b*) applies) is not goodwill and is acquired on or after that day by the taxpayer — in circumstances under which any of subsections 24(2), 70(5.1), 73(3.1), 85(1), 88(1), 98(3) and (5), 107(2) and 107.4(3) apply — from a person or partnership that would have been deemed under this subsection to have acquired a property if none of those subsections had applied, the capital cost of the property that would have been deemed under this subsection to have been acquired by the person or partnership;

(*d*) if the particular property is goodwill, the amount by which

(i) the total of all amounts each of which is

(A) 1/4 of the amount determined under subparagraph (38)(*b*)(iii) in respect of the business,

(B) if goodwill is acquired on or after that day by the taxpayer and subsection (40) deems an amount to have been allowed under paragraph 20(1)(*a*) in respect of the taxpayer's acquisition of the goodwill, that amount, or

(C) if goodwill is acquired (other than an acquisition in respect of which clause (B) applies) on or after that day by the taxpayer — in circumstances under which any of subsections 24(2), 70(5.1), 73(3.1), 85(1), 88(1), 98(3) and (5), 107(2) and 107.4(3) apply — from a person or partnership that would have been deemed under this subsection to have acquired a property if none of those subsections had applied, the capital cost of the property that would have been deemed under this subsection to have been acquired by the person or partnership

exceeds

(ii) the total of all amounts each of which is the capital cost of a property deemed by this subsection to have been acquired by the taxpayer at or before that time in respect of another disposition of goodwill in respect of the business; and

(*e*) in any other case, nil.

Editorial Note: *Dispositions of Former Eligible Capital Property:* Subsection 13(39) is a provision that reduces the rate at which proceeds of disposition reduce the undepreciated capital cost balance of Class 14.1 property from 100% to 75%, if a related eligible capital expenditure was incurred prior to January 1, 2017. Subsection 13(39) provides that, where property that was eligible capital property prior to 2017 is disposed of on or after January 1, 2017, the undepreciated capital cost of Class 14.1 is increased to the extent necessary to prevent excess recapture of CCA. The rule ensures that a receipt from the disposition of property the cost of which was included in the CEC pool (and the undepreciated capital cost as a result) at a 75% rate does not reduce the undepreciated capital cost at a 100% rate. To this end, a taxpayer is deemed to have acquired a Class 14.1 property with a cost equal to the least of: 1/4 of the proceeds, 1/4 of the capital cost, and an amount determined pursuant to paragraphs 13(39)*(a)* to *(e)*.

History: Subsection 13(39) was added by S.C. 2016, c. 12, s. 3(3), in force on January 1, 2017.

Related Regulations: Schedule II Class 14.1.

► 13(40) ◄

(40) Class 14.1 — transitional rule. If at any time a taxpayer acquires a particular property included in Class 14.1 of Schedule II to the *Income Tax Regulations* in respect of a business, the acquisition of the particular property is part of a transaction or series of transactions or events that includes a disposition (in this subsection referred to as the "prior disposition") at or before that time of the particular property, or a similar property, by the taxpayer or a person or partnership that does not deal at arm's length with the taxpayer and subsection (39) applies in respect of the prior disposition, then for the purpose of determining the undepreciated capital cost of the class, an amount is deemed to have been allowed under paragraph 20(1)(*a*) to the taxpayer in respect of the particular property in computing the taxpayer's income for taxation years ending before the acquisition equal to the lesser of the capital cost of the property deemed by subsection (39) to be acquired in respect of the prior disposition and $^1/_4$ of the capital cost of the particular property.

Editorial Note: ***Non-Arm's Length Transfers:*** In order to prevent the use of subsection 13(39) to increase the depreciable base of Class 14.1 by means of non-arm's length transfers of eligible capital property acquired before January 1, 2017, subsection 13(40) decreases the undepreciated capital cost of the property to the acquirer in certain circumstances. Essentially, where a taxpayer acquires property from a non-arm's length person and subsection 13(39) (see note at that subsection) applied to the transfer of that property, the taxpayer is deemed to have made a prior CCA claim of 1/4 of the capital cost of the property, which thus reduces the undepreciated capital cost. Note that paragraph 13(39)(*b*) will bump the taxpayer's undepreciated capital cost back up to prevent excess recapture when the property is eventually disposed of.

History: Subsection 13(40) was added by S.C. 2016, c. 12, s. 3(3), in force on January 1, 2017.

Related Regulations: Schedule II Class 14.1.

► 13(41) ◄

(41) Class 14.1 — transitional rule. For the purposes of subsections (38) to (40) and (42), paragraph 20(1)(*hh.1*), subsections 40(13) to (16) and paragraph 79(4)(*b*), "cumulative eligible capital", "eligible capital expenditure", "eligible capital property" and "exempt gains balance" have the meanings that would be assigned to those expressions if the Act read as it did immediately before 2017.

History: Subsection 13(41) was added by S.C. 2016, c. 12, s. 3(3), in force on January 1, 2017.

Related Regulations: Schedule II Class 14.1.

► 13(42) ◄

(42) Class 14.1 — transitional rules. If a taxpayer owns property included in Class 14.1 of Schedule II to the *Income Tax Regulations* in respect of a business at the beginning of 2017, that was an eligible capital property in respect of the business immediately before 2017,

(*a*) for the purposes of the Act and its regulations (other than this section, section 20 and any regulations made for the purposes of paragraph 20(1)(*a*)), if the amount determined for A in the definition "cumulative eligible capital" in subsection 14(5) would have been increased immediately before 2017 if the property had been disposed of immediately before that time, the capital cost of the property is deemed to be increased by $^4/_3$ of the amount of that increase;

(*b*) for purposes of this section, section 20 and any regulations made for the purposes of paragraph 20(1)(*a*), if the taxpayer was deemed by subsection 14(12) to continue to own eligible capital property in respect of the business and not to have ceased to carry on the business until a time that is after 2016, the taxpayer is deemed to continue to own the property and to continue to carry on the business until the time that is immediately before the first time one of the events that would be described in any of paragraphs 14(12)(*c*) to (*g*) (as they read immediately before 2017, if the reference to "eligible capital property" in paragraph 14(12)(*d*) were read as "eligible capital property or capital property") occurs;

(*c*) for the purposes of the descriptions of D.1 and K in the definition "undepreciated capital cost" in subsection (21), the taxpayer is deemed not to have paid or received any amounts before 2017 as or on account of an existing or proposed countervailing or anti-dumping duty in respect of depreciable property of the class; and

(*d*) subsection (7.1) does not apply to assistance that a taxpayer received or is entitled to receive before 2017 in respect of a property that was an eligible capital property immediately before 2017.

Editorial Note: Prior to 2017, where eligible capital property was transferred at non-arm's length, the transferee's CEC pool was reduced by the non-taxable portion of the transferor's capital gain — this reduction prohibited the taxpayer from depreciating the non-taxable portion of the gain realized by the non-arm's length transferor. Where such a prior reduction to the CEC pool applied to a Class 14.1 property, paragraph 13(42)(*a*) increases a taxpayer's capital cost (on January 1, 2017) of that property by 4/3 of the amount of the previous reduction. Moreover, the CRA has taken the position (2016-0664451E5) that paragraph 13(42)(*a*) also bumps a taxpayer's capital cost by the amount of a prior reduction pursuant to former subsection 14(3), which reduced a transferee's eligible capital expenditure by the amount of the capital gains exemption claimed by a non-arm's length transferor.

History: Subsection 13(42) was added by S.C. 2016, c. 12, s. 3(3), in force on January 1, 2017.

Related Regulations: Schedule II Class 14.1.

SECTION 14: [Eligible capital property]

(Repealed.)

► 14(1) ◄

(1) Eligible capital property — inclusion in income from business — (Repealed by S.C. 2016, c. 12, s. 4(1).)

History: S. 14(1) was repealed by S.C. 2016, c. 12, s. 4(1), in force January 1, 2017, and formerly read:

(1) *Eligible capital property — inclusion in income from business.* Where, at the end of a taxation year, the total of all amounts each of which is an amount determined, in respect of a business of a taxpayer, for E in the definition "cumulative eligible capital" in subsection (5) (in this section referred to as an "eligible capital amount") or for F in that definition exceeds the total of all amounts determined for A to D in that definition in respect of the business (which excess is in this subsection referred to as "the excess"), there shall be included in computing the taxpayer's income from the business for the year the total of

(*a*) the amount, if any, that is the lesser of

(i) the excess, and

(ii) the amount determined for F in the definition "cumulative eligible capital" in subsection (5) at the end of the year in respect of the business, and

(*b*) the amount, if any, determined by the formula

$$2/3 \times (A - B - C - D)$$

where

A is the excess,

B is the amount determined for F in the definition "cumulative eligible capital" in subsection (5) at the end of the year in respect of the business,

C is $^1/_2$ of the amount determined for Q in the definition "cumulative eligible capital" in subsection (5) at the end of the year in respect of the business, and

D is the amount claimed by the taxpayer, not exceeding the taxpayer's exempt gains balance for the year in respect of the business.

Canadian Tax Foundation: Kerr, *Eligible Capital Property: Update on the Rules,* 2006 British Columbia Tax Conference 17:1–29; Thivierge, *Planning for the Purchase or Sale of a Business,* 2005 Conference Report 10:1–30;

Branham, *Update on Non-Taxable Payments and Eligible Capital Property*, 2003 British Columbia Tax Conference 14:1–39; Severin, *Eligible Capital Property Update*, 2003 Prairie Provinces Tax Conference 4:1–35; Dalsin, *Corporate Tax Planning: Post October 18, 2000 Mini-Budget*, 2001 Prairie Provinces Tax Conference 1:1–57.

▶ 14(1.01) ◀

(1.01) Election re capital gain — (Repealed by S.C. 2016, c. 12, s. 4(1).)

History: S. 14(1.01) was repealed by S.C. 2016, c. 12, s. 4(1), in force January 1, 2017, and formerly read:

(1.01) *Election re capital gain.* A taxpayer may, in the taxpayer's return of income for a taxation year, or with an election under subsection 83(2) filed on or before the taxpayer's filing-due date for the taxation year, elect that the following rules apply to a disposition made at any time in the year of an eligible capital property in respect of a business, if the taxpayer's actual proceeds of the disposition exceed the taxpayer's eligible capital expenditure in respect of the acquisition of the property, that eligible capital expenditure can be determined and, for taxpayers who are individuals, the taxpayer's exempt gains balance in respect of the business for the taxation year is nil:

(*a*) for the purpose of subsection (5) other than the description of A in the definition "cumulative eligible capital", the proceeds of disposition of the property are deemed to be equal to the amount of that eligible capital expenditure;

(*b*) the taxpayer is deemed to have disposed at that time of a capital property that had, immediately before that time, an adjusted cost base to the taxpayer equal to the amount of that eligible capital expenditure, for proceeds of disposition equal to the actual proceeds; and

(*c*) if the eligible capital property is a qualified farm or fishing property (within the meaning assigned by subsection 110.6(1)) of the taxpayer at that time, the capital property deemed by paragraph (*b*) to have been disposed of by the taxpayer is deemed to be a qualified farm or fishing property of the taxpayer at that time.

S. 14(1.01)(*c*) was replaced by S.C. 2014, c. 39, s. 3(1), applicable to dispositions and transfers that occur in the 2014 and subsequent taxation years, and formerly read:

(*c*) if the eligible capital property is

(i) a qualified farm property (within the meaning assigned by subsection 110.6(1)) of the taxpayer at that time, the capital property deemed by paragraph (*b*) to have been disposed of by the taxpayer is deemed to be a qualified farm property of the taxpayer at that time, and

(ii) a qualified fishing property (within the meaning assigned by subsection 110.6(1)) of the taxpayer at that time, the capital property deemed by paragraph (*b*) to have been disposed of by the taxpayer is deemed to be a qualified fishing property of the taxpayer at that time.

▶ 14(1.02) ◀

(1.02) Election re property acquired with pre-1972 outlays or expenditures — (Repealed by S.C. 2016, c. 12, s. 4(1).)

History: S. 14(1.02) was repealed by S.C. 2016, c. 12, s. 4(1), in force January 1, 2017, and formerly read:

(1.02) *Election re property acquired with pre-1972 outlays or expenditures.* If at any time in a taxation year a taxpayer has disposed of an eligible capital property in respect of which an outlay or expenditure to acquire the property was made before 1972 (which outlay or expenditure would have been an eligible capital expenditure if it had been made or incurred as a result of a transaction that occurred after 1971), the taxpayer's actual proceeds of the disposition exceed the total of those outlays or expenditures, that total can be determined, subsection 21(1) of the *Income Tax Application Rules* applies in respect of the disposition and, for taxpayers who are individuals, the taxpayer's exempt gains balance in respect of the business for the taxation year is nil, the taxpayer may, in the taxpayer's return of income for the taxation year, or with an election under subsection 83(2) filed on or before the taxpayer's filing-due date for the taxation year, elect that the following rules apply:

(*a*) for the purpose of subsection (5) other than the description of A in the definition "cumulative eligible capital", the proceeds of disposition of the property are deemed to be nil;

(*b*) the taxpayer is deemed to have disposed at that time of a capital property that had, immediately before that time, an adjusted cost base to the taxpayer equal to nil, for proceeds of disposition equal to the amount determined, in respect of the disposition, under subsection 21(1) of the *Income Tax Application Rules*; and

(*c*) if the eligible capital property is a qualified farm or fishing property (within the meaning assigned by subsection 110.6(1)) of the taxpayer at that time, the capital property deemed by paragraph (*b*) to have been disposed of by the taxpayer is deemed to be a qualified farm or fishing property of the taxpayer at that time.

S. 14(1.02)(*c*) was replaced by S.C. 2014, c. 39, s. 3(2), applicable to dispositions and transfers that occur in the 2014 and subsequent taxation years, and formerly read:

(*c*) if the eligible capital property is

(i) a qualified farm property (within the meaning assigned by subsection 110.6(1)) of the taxpayer at that time, the capital property deemed by paragraph (*b*) to have been disposed of by the taxpayer is deemed to be a qualified farm property of the taxpayer at that time, and

(ii) a qualified fishing property (within the meaning assigned by subsection 110.6(1)) of the taxpayer at that time, the capital property deemed by paragraph (*b*) to have been disposed of by the taxpayer is deemed to be a qualified fishing property of the taxpayer at that time.

▶ 14(1.03) ◀

(1.03) Non-application of subsections (1.01) and (1.02) — (Repealed by S.C. 2016, c. 12, s. 4(1).)

History: S. 14(1.03) was repealed by S.C. 2016, c. 12, s. 4(1), in force January 1, 2017, and formerly read:

(1.03) *Non-application of subsections (1.01) and (1.02).* Subsections (1.01) and (1.02) do not apply to a disposition by a taxpayer of a property

(*a*) that is goodwill; or

(*b*) that was acquired by the taxpayer

(i) in circumstances where an election was made under subsection 85(1) or (2) and the amount agreed on in that election in respect of the property was less than the fair market value of the property at the time it was so acquired, and

(ii) from a person or partnership with whom the taxpayer did not deal at arm's length and for whom the eligible capital expenditure in respect of the acquisition of the property cannot be determined.

▶ 14(1.1) ◀

(1.1) Deemed taxable capital gain — (Repealed by S.C. 2016, c. 12, s. 4(1).)

History: S. 14(1.1) was repealed by S.C. 2016, c. 12, s. 4(1), in force January 1, 2017, and formerly read:

(1.1) *Deemed taxable capital gain.* For the purposes of section 110.6 and paragraph 3(*b*) as it applies for the purposes of that section, an amount included under paragraph (1)(*b*) in computing a taxpayer's income for a particular taxation year from a business is deemed to be a taxable capital gain of the taxpayer for the year from the disposition in the year of qualified farm or fishing property to the extent of the lesser of

(*a*) the amount included under paragraph (1)(*b*) in computing the taxpayer's income for the particular year from the business, and

(*b*) the amount determined by the formula

$$A - B$$

where

A is the amount by which the total of

(i) 3/4 of the total of all amounts each of which is the taxpayer's proceeds from a disposition in a preceding taxation year that began after 1987 and ended before February 28, 2000 of eligible capital property in respect of the business that, at the time of the disposition, was a qualified farm property (within the meaning assigned by subsection 110.6(1)) of the taxpayer,

(ii) 2/3 of the total of all amounts each of which is the taxpayer's proceeds from a disposition in the particular year or a preceding taxation year that ended after February 27, 2000 and before October 18, 2000 of eligible capital property in respect of the business that, at the time of the disposition, was a qualified farm property (within the meaning assigned by subsection 110.6(1)) of the taxpayer, and

(iii) 1/2 of the total of all amounts each of which is the taxpayer's proceeds from a disposition in the particular year or a preceding taxation year that ended after October 17, 2000 of eligible capital property in respect of the business that, at the time of the disposition, was a qualified farm property, a qualified fishing property or a qualified farm or fishing property (within the meaning assigned by subsection 110.6(1)) of the taxpayer

exceeds the total of

(iv) 3/4 of the total of all amounts each of which is

(A) an eligible capital expenditure of the taxpayer in respect of the business that was made or incurred in respect of a property that was, at the time of disposition, a qualified farm property disposed of by the taxpayer in a preceding taxation year that began after 1987 and ended before February 28, 2000, or

(B) an outlay or expense of the taxpayer that was not deductible in computing the taxpayer's income and that was made or incurred for the purpose of making a disposition referred to in clause (A),

(v) 2/3 of the total of all amounts each of which is

(A) an eligible capital expenditure of the taxpayer in respect of the business that was made or incurred in respect of a property that was, at the time of disposition, a qualified farm property disposed of by the taxpayer in the particular year or a preceding taxation year that ended after February 27, 2000 and before October 18, 2000, or

(B) an outlay or expense of the taxpayer that was not deductible in computing the taxpayer's income and that was made or incurred for the purpose of making a disposition referred to in clause (A), and

(vi) 1/2 of the total of all amounts each of which is

(A) an eligible capital expenditure of the taxpayer in respect of the business that was made or incurred in respect of a property that was, at the time of disposition, a qualified farm property, a qualified fishing property or a qualified farm or fishing property disposed of by the taxpayer in the particular year or a preceding taxation year that ended after October 17, 2000, or

(B) an outlay or expense of the taxpayer that was not deductible in computing the taxpayer's income and that was made or incurred for the purpose of making a disposition referred to in clause (A), and

B is the total of all amounts each of which is

(i) that portion of an amount deemed by subparagraph (1)(*a*)(v) (as it applied in respect of the business to fiscal periods that began after 1987 and ended before February 23, 1994) to be a taxable capital gain of the taxpayer that can reasonably be attributed to a disposition of a property that was, at the time of disposition, a qualified farm property of the taxpayer, or

(ii) an amount deemed by this section to be a taxable capital gain of the taxpayer for a taxation year preceding the particular year from the disposition of a property that was, at the time of disposition, a qualified farm property, a qualified fishing property or a qualified farm or fishing property of the taxpayer.

S. 14(1.1), the portion before paragraph (*a*) was replaced by S.C. 2014, c. 39, s. 3(3), applicable to dispositions and transfers that occur in the 2014 and subsequent taxation years, and formerly read:

(1.1) *Deemed taxable capital gain.* For the purposes of section 110.6 and paragraph 3(*b*) as it applies for the purposes of that section, an amount included under paragraph (1)(*b*) in computing a taxpayer's income for a particular taxation year from a business is deemed to be a taxable capital gain of the taxpayer for the year from the disposition in the year of qualified farm property to the extent of the lesser of

S. 14(1.1)(*b*), the descriptions of A and B were replaced by S.C. 2014, c. 39, s. 3(4), applicable to dispositions and transfers that occur in the 2014 and subsequent taxation years, and formerly read:

A is the amount by which the total of

(i) $^3/_4$ of the total of all amounts each of which is the taxpayer's proceeds from a disposition in a preceding taxation year that began after 1987 and ended before February 28, 2000 of eligible capital property in respect of the business that, at the time of the disposition, was a qualified farm property (within the meaning assigned by subsection 110.6(1)) of the taxpayer,

(ii) $^2/_3$ of the total of all amounts each of which is the taxpayer's proceeds from a disposition in the particular year or a preceding taxation year that ended after February 27, 2000 and before October 18, 2000 of eligible capital property in respect of the business that, at the time of the disposition, was a qualified farm property (within the meaning assigned by subsection 110.6(1)) of the taxpayer, and

(iii) $^1/_2$ of the total of all amounts each of which is the taxpayer's proceeds from a disposition in the particular year or a preceding taxation year that ended after October 17, 2000 of eligible capital property in respect of the business that, at the time of the disposition, was a qualified farm property (within the meaning assigned by subsection 110.6(1)) of the taxpayer

exceeds the total of

(iv) $^3/_4$ of the total of all amounts each of which is

(A) an eligible capital expenditure of the taxpayer in respect of the business that was made or incurred in respect of a qualified farm property disposed of by the taxpayer in a preceding taxation year that began after 1987 and ended before February 28, 2000, or

(B) an outlay or expense of the taxpayer that was not deductible in computing the taxpayer's income and that was made or incurred for the purpose of making a disposition referred to in clause (A),

(v) $^2/_3$ of the total of all amounts each of which is

(A) an eligible capital expenditure of the taxpayer in respect of the business that was made or incurred in respect of a qualified farm property disposed of by the taxpayer in the particular year or a preceding taxation year that ended after February 27, 2000 and before October 18, 2000, or

(B) an outlay or expense of the taxpayer that was not deductible in computing the taxpayer's income and that was made or incurred for the purpose of making a disposition referred to in clause (A), and

(vi) $^1/_2$ of the total of all amounts each of which is

(A) an eligible capital expenditure of the taxpayer in respect of the business that was made or incurred in respect of a qualified farm property disposed of by the taxpayer in the particular year or a preceding taxation year that ended after October 17, 2000, or

(B) an outlay or expense of the taxpayer that was not deductible in computing the taxpayer's income and that was made or incurred for the purpose of making a disposition referred to in clause (A), and

B is the total of all amounts each of which is

(i) that portion of an amount deemed by subparagraph (1)(*a*)(v) (as it applied in respect of the business to fiscal periods that began after 1987 and ended before February 23, 1994) to be a taxable capital gain of the taxpayer that can reasonably be attributed to a disposition of a qualified farm property of the taxpayer, or

(ii) an amount deemed by this section to be a taxable capital gain of the taxpayer for a taxation year preceding the particular year from the disposition of qualified farm property of the taxpayer.

► 14(1.2) ◄

(1.2) Deemed capital gain — (Repealed by S.C. 2014, c. 39, s. 3(5).)

History: S. 14(1.2) was repealed by S.C. 2014, c. 39, s. 3(5), applicable to dispositions and transfers that occur in the 2014 and subsequent taxation years, and formerly read:

(1.2) *Deemed capital gain.* For the purposes of section 110.6 and paragraph 3(*b*) as it applies for the purposes of that section, an amount included under paragraph (1)(*b*) in computing a taxpayer's income for a particular taxation year from a fishing business is deemed to be a taxable capital gain of the taxpayer for the year from the disposition in the year of qualified fishing property to the extent of the lesser of

(*a*) the amount included under paragraph (1)(*b*) in computing the taxpayer's income for the particular year from the fishing business, and

(*b*) the amount determined by the formula

$$A - B$$

where

A is the amount by which

(i) $^1/_2$ of the total of all amounts each of which is the taxpayer's proceeds from a disposition on or after May 2, 2006 and in the particular taxation year or a preceding taxation year of eligible capital property (referred to in this subsection as a "disposed property") that was at the time of the disposition a qualified fishing property (within the meaning assigned by subsection 110.6(1)) of the taxpayer exceeds the total of

(ii) $^1/_2$ of the total of all amounts each of which is

(A) an eligible capital expenditure of the taxpayer in respect of the fishing business that was made or incurred in respect of a disposed property, or

(B) an outlay or expense of the taxpayer that was not deductible in computing the taxpayer's income and that was made or incurred for the purpose of making a disposition of a disposed property, and

B is the total of all amounts each of which is an amount deemed by this section to be a taxable capital gain of the taxpayer for a taxation year preceding the particular year from the disposition of qualified fishing property of the taxpayer.

► 14(2) ◄

(2) Amount deemed payable — (Repealed by S.C. 2016, c. 12, s. 4(1).)

History: S. 14(2) was repealed by S.C. 2016, c. 12, s. 4(1), in force January 1, 2017, and formerly read:

(2) *Amount deemed payable.* Where any amount is, by any provision of this Act, deemed to be a taxpayer's proceeds of disposition of any property disposed of by the taxpayer at any time, for the purposes of this section, that amount shall be deemed to have become payable to the taxpayer at that time.

► 14(3) ◄

(3) Acquisition of eligible capital property — (Repealed by S.C. 2016, c. 12, s. 4(1).)

History: S. 14(3) was repealed by S.C. 2016, c. 12, s. 4(1), in force January 1, 2017, and formerly read:

(3) *Acquisition of eligible capital property.* Notwithstanding any other provision of this Act, where at any particular time a person or partnership (in this subsection referred to as the "taxpayer") has, directly or indirectly, in any manner whatever, acquired an eligible capital property in respect of a business from a person or partnership with which the taxpayer did not deal at arm's length (in this subsection referred to as the "transferor") and the property was an eligible capital property of the transferor (other than property acquired by the taxpayer as a consequence of the death of the transferor), the eligible capital expenditure of the taxpayer in respect of the business is, in respect of that acquisition, deemed to be equal to $^4/_3$ of the amount, if any, by which

(*a*) the amount determined for E in the definition "cumulative eligible capital" in subsection (5) in respect of the disposition of the property by the transferor or, if the property is the subject of an election under subsection (1.01) or (1.02) by the transferor, $^3/_4$ of the actual proceeds referred to in that subsection,

exceeds the total of

(*b*) the total of all amounts that can reasonably be considered to have been claimed as deductions under section 110.6 for taxation years that ended before February 28, 2000 by any person with whom the taxpayer was not dealing at arm's length in respect of the disposition of the property by the transferor, or any other disposition of the property before the particular time,

(*b*.1) $^9/_8$ of the total of all amounts that can reasonably be considered to have been claimed as deductions under section 110.6 for taxation years that ended after February 27, 2000 and before October 18, 2000 by any person with whom the taxpayer was not dealing at arm's length in respect of the disposition of the property by the transferor, or any other disposition of the property before the particular time, and

(*b*.2) $^3/_2$ of the total of all amounts that can reasonably be considered to have been claimed as deductions under section 110.6 for taxation years that end after October 17, 2000 by any person with whom the taxpayer was not dealing at arm's length in respect of the disposition of the property by the transferor, or any other disposition of the property before the particular time,

except that, where the taxpayer disposes of the property after the particular time, the amount of the eligible capital expenditure deemed by this subsection to be made by the taxpayer in respect of the property shall be determined at any time after the disposition as if the total of the amounts determined under paragraphs (*b*), (*b*.1) and (*b*.2) in respect of the disposition were the lesser of

(*c*) the amount otherwise so determined, and

(*d*) the amount, if any, by which

(i) the amount determined under paragraph (*a*) in respect of the disposition of the property by the transferor

exceeds

(ii) the amount determined for E in the definition "cumulative eligible capital" in subsection (5) in respect of the disposition of the property by the taxpayer.

S. 14(3)(*a*) was replaced by S.C. 2013, c. 34, s. 176(1), applicable to taxation years that end after February 27, 2000, except that the reference to "subsection (1.01) or (1.02)" in paragraph 14(3)(*a*) is to be read as a reference to "subsection (1.01)" for taxation years that end after February 27, 2000 and before December 20, 2002.

S. 14(3)(*a*) formerly read:

(*a*) the amount determined for E in the definition "cumulative eligible capital" in subsection (5) in respect of the disposition of the property by the transferor

▶ 14(4) ◀

(4) References to "taxation year" or "year" — (Repealed by S.C. 2016, c. 12, s. 4(1).)

History: S. 14(4) was repealed by S.C. 2016, c. 12, s. 4(1), in force January 1, 2017, and formerly read:

(4) *References to "taxation year" or "year".* Where a taxpayer is an individual and the taxpayer's income for a taxation year includes income from a business the fiscal period of which does not coincide with the calendar year, for greater certainty a reference in this section to a "taxation year" or "year" shall be read as a reference to a "fiscal period" or "period".

▶ 14(5) ◀

(5) Definitions. (Repealed.)

"adjustment time" — (Repealed by S.C. 2016, c. 12, s. 4(1).)

History: S. 14(5), the definition "adjustment time" was repealed by S.C. 2016, c. 12, s. 4(1), in force January 1, 2017, and formerly read:

"adjustment time"—"adjustment time", of a taxpayer in respect of a business, means

(*a*) for a corporation, the time immediately after the commencement of its first taxation year commencing after June 1988, and

(*b*) for any other taxpayer, the time immediately after the commencement of the taxpayer's first fiscal period commencing after 1987 in respect of the business;

S. 14(5), the definition "adjustment time" was replaced by S.C. 2013, c. 34, s. 176(2), deemed to have come into force on November 1, 2011, and formerly read:

"adjustment time"—"adjustment time" of a taxpayer in respect of a business is

(*a*) in the case of a corporation formed as a result of an amalgamation occurring after June 30, 1988, the time immediately before the amalgamation,

(*b*) in the case of any other corporation, the time immediately after the commencement of its first taxation year commencing after June 30, 1988, and

(*c*) for any other taxpayer, the time immediately after the commencement of the taxpayer's first fiscal period commencing after 1987 in respect of the business;

"cumulative eligible capital" — (Repealed by S.C. 2016, c. 12, s. 4(1).)

History: S. 14(5), the definition "cumulative eligible capital" was repealed by S.C. 2016, c. 12, s. 4(1), in force January 1, 2017, and formerly read:

"cumulative eligible capital"—"cumulative eligible capital" of a taxpayer at any time in respect of a business of the taxpayer means the amount determined by the formula

$$(A + B + C + D + D.1) - (E + F)$$

where

A is the amount, if any, by which $^3/_4$ of the total of all eligible capital expenditures in respect of the business made or incurred by the taxpayer after the taxpayer's adjustment time and before that time exceeds the total of all amounts each of which is determined by the formula

$$1/2 \times (A.1 - A.2) \times (A.3/A.4)$$

where

A.1 is the amount required, because of paragraph (1)(*b*) or 38(*a*), to be included in the income of a person or partnership (in this definition referred to as the "transferor") not dealing at arm's length with the taxpayer in respect of the disposition after December 20, 2002 of a property that was an eligible capital property acquired by the taxpayer directly or indirectly, in any manner whatever, from the transferor and not disposed of by the taxpayer before that time,

A.2 is the total of all amounts that can reasonably be considered to have been claimed as deductions under section 110.6 by the transferor in respect of that disposition,

A.3 is the transferor's proceeds from that disposition, and

A.4 is the transferor's total proceeds of disposition of eligible capital property in the taxation year of the transferor in which the property described in A.1 was disposed of,

B is the total of

(*a*) $^3/_2$ of all amounts included under paragraph (1)(*b*) in computing the taxpayer's income from the business for taxation years that ended before that time and after October 17, 2000,

(*b*) $^9/_8$ of all amounts included under paragraph (1)(*b*) in computing the taxpayer's income from the business for taxation years that ended

(i) before that time, and

(ii) after February 27, 2000 and before October 18, 2000,

(*c*) all amounts included under paragraph (1)(*b*) in computing the taxpayer's income from the business for taxation years that ended

(i) before the earlier of that time and February 28, 2000, and

(ii) after the taxpayer's adjustment time,

(*d*) all amounts each of which is the amount that would have been included under subparagraph (1)(*a*)(v) (as that subparagraph applied for taxation years that ended before February 28, 2000) in computing the taxpayer's income from the business, if the amount determined for D in that subparagraph for the year were nil, for taxation years that ended

(i) before the earlier of that time and February 28, 2000, and

(ii) after February 22, 1994, and

(*e*) all taxable capital gains included, because of the application of subparagraph (1)(*a*)(v) (as that subparagraph applied for taxation years that ended before February 28, 2000) to the taxpayer in respect of the business, in computing the taxpayer's income for taxation years that began before February 23, 1994,

C is $^3/_2$ of the amount, if any, of the taxpayer's cumulative eligible capital in respect of the business at the taxpayer's adjustment time,

D is the amount, if any, by which

(*a*) the total of all amounts deducted under paragraph 20(1)(*b*) in computing the taxpayer's income from the business for taxation years ending before the taxpayer's adjustment time

exceeds

(*b*) the total of all amounts included under subsection (1) in computing the taxpayer's income from the business for taxation years ending before the taxpayer's adjustment time,

D.1 is, where the amount determined by B exceeds zero, $^1/_2$ of the amount determined for Q in respect of the business

E is the total of all amounts each of which is $^3/_4$ of the amount, if any, by which

(*a*) an amount that the taxpayer has or may become entitled to receive, after the taxpayer's adjustment time and before that time, on account of capital in respect of the business carried on or formerly carried on by the taxpayer, other than an amount that

(i) is included in computing the taxpayer's income, or deducted in computing, for the purposes of this Act, any balance of undeducted outlays, expenses or other amounts for the year or a preceding taxation year,

(ii) reduces the cost or capital cost of a property or the amount of an outlay or expense, or

(iii) is included in computing any gain or loss of the taxpayer from a disposition of a capital property

exceeds

(*b*) all outlays and expenses that were not otherwise deductible in computing the taxpayer's income and were made or incurred by the taxpayer for the purpose of obtaining the amount described by paragraph (*a*), and

F is the amount determined by the formula

$$(P + P.1 + Q) - R$$

where

P is the total of all amounts deducted under paragraph 20(1)(*b*) in computing the taxpayer's income from the business for taxation years ending before that time and after the taxpayer's adjustment time,

P.1 is the total of all amounts each of which is an amount by which the cumulative eligible capital of the taxpayer in respect of the business is required to be reduced at or before that time because of subsection 80(7);

Q is the amount, if any, by which

(*a*) the total of all amounts deducted under paragraph 20(1)(*b*) in computing the taxpayer's income from the business for taxation years ending before the taxpayer's adjustment time

exceeds

(*b*) the total of all amounts included under subsection (1) in computing the taxpayer's income for taxation years ending before the taxpayer's adjustment time, and

R is the total of all amounts each of which is an amount included, in computing the taxpayer's income from the business for a taxation year that ended before that time and after the taxpayer's adjustment time

(*a*) in the case of a taxation year that ends after February 27, 2000, under paragraph (1)(*a*), or

(*b*) in the case of a taxation year that ended before February 28, 2000,

(i) under subparagraph (1)(*a*)(iv), as that subparagraph applied in respect of that taxation year, or

(ii) under paragraph (1)(*b*), as that paragraph applied in respect of that taxation year, to the extent that the amount so included is in respect of an amount included in the amount determined for P;

S. 14(5), the description of A in the definition "cumulative eligible capital" was replaced by S.C. 2013, c. 34, s. 176(3), applicable to taxation years that end after February 27, 2000, except that the reference to "disposition after December 20, 2002 of a property that was an eligible capital property" in the description of A.1 in the definition "cumulative eligible capital" in subsection 14(5) is to be read as a reference to "disposition after 2003 of a property that was an eligible capital property" if

(i) the taxpayer referred to in that description of A.1 acquired the property referred to in that description from the transferor referred to in that description,

(ii) the property was so acquired under an agreement in writing made before December 21, 2002 between the transferor, or a particular person that controlled the transferor, and another person who dealt at arm's length with the transferor and the particular person, and

(iii) no clause in the agreement or any other arrangement allows an obligation of any party to the agreement to be changed, reduced or waived in the event of a change to, or an adverse assessment under, the Act.

S. 14(5), the description of A in the definition "cumulative eligible capital" formerly read:

A is $^3/_4$ of the total of all eligible capital expenditures in respect of the business made or incurred by the taxpayer before that time and after the taxpayer's adjustment time,

S. 14(5), the description of R in the definition "cumulative eligible capital" was replaced by S.C. 2013, c. 34, s. 176(4), applicable to taxation years that end after February 27, 2000, and formerly read:

R is the total of all amounts included, in computing the taxpayer's income from the business for taxation years that ended before that time and after the taxpayer's adjustment time, under subparagraph (1)(*a*)(iv) in respect of taxation years that ended before February 28, 2000 and under paragraph (1)(*a*) in respect of taxation years that end after February 27, 2000;

Tax Window Files: ECP Rules NAL Disposition, *June 7, 2016*, CRA Document No. 2016-0641851E5.

"eligible capital expenditure" — (Repealed by S.C. 2016, c. 12, s. 4(1).)

History: S. 14(5), the definition "eligible capital expenditure" was repealed by S.C. 2016, c. 12, s. 4(1), in force January 1, 2017, and formerly read:

"eligible capital expenditure"—"eligible capital expenditure" of a taxpayer in respect of a business means the portion of any outlay or expense made or incurred by the taxpayer, as a result of a transaction occurring after 1971, on account of capital for the purpose of gaining or producing income from the business, other than any such outlay or expense

(*a*) in respect of which any amount is or would be, but for any provision of this Act limiting the quantum of any deduction, deductible (otherwise than under paragraph 20(1)(*b*)) in computing the taxpayer's income from the business, or in respect of which any amount is, by virtue of any provision of this Act other than paragraph 18(1)(*b*), not deductible in computing that income,

(*b*) made or incurred for the purpose of gaining or producing income that is exempt income, or

(*c*) that is the cost of, or any part of the cost of,

(i) tangible property, or for civil law corporeal property, of the taxpayer,

(ii) intangible property, or for civil law incorporeal property, that is depreciable property of the taxpayer,

(iii) property in respect of which any deduction (otherwise than under paragraph 20(1)(*b*)) is permitted in computing the taxpayer's income from the business or would be so permitted if the taxpayer's income from the business were sufficient for the purpose, or

(iv) an interest in, or for civil law a right in, or a right to acquire any property described in any of subparagraphs (i) to (iii)

but, for greater certainty and without restricting the generality of the foregoing, does not include any portion of

(*d*) any amount paid or payable to any creditor of the taxpayer as, on account or in lieu of payment of any debt or as or on account of the redemption, cancellation or purchase of any bond or debenture,

(*e*) where the taxpayer is a corporation, any amount paid or payable to a person as a shareholder of the corporation, or

(*f*) any amount that is the cost of, or any part of the cost of,

(i) an interest in a trust,

(ii) an interest in a partnership,

(iii) a share, bond, debenture, mortgage, hypothecary claim, note, bill or other similar property, or

(iv) an interest in, or for civil law a right in, or a right to acquire any property described in any of subparagraphs (i) to (iii).

S. 14(5), paragraph (*c*) of the definition "eligible capital expenditure" was replaced by S.C. 2013, c. 34, s. 93(1), in force June 26, 2013, and formerly read:

(*c*) that is the cost of, or any part of the cost of,

(i) tangible property of the taxpayer,

(ii) intangible property that is depreciable property of the taxpayer,

(iii) property in respect of which any deduction (otherwise than under paragraph 20(1)(*b*)) is permitted in computing the taxpayer's income from the business or would be so permitted if the taxpayer's income from the business were sufficient for the purpose, or

(iv) an interest in, or right to acquire, any property described in any of subparagraphs (i) to (iii)

S. 14(5), paragraph (f)(iv) of the definition "eligible capital expenditure" was replaced by S.C. 2013, c. 34, s. 93(2), in force June 26, 2013, and formerly read:

(iv) an interest in, or right to acquire, any property described in any of subparagraphs (i) to (iii);

"exempt gains balance" — (Repealed by S.C. 2016, c. 12, s. 4(1).)

History: S. 14(5), the definition "exempt gains balance" was repealed by S.C. 2016, c. 12, s. 4(1), in force January 1, 2017, and formerly read:

"exempt gains balance"—"exempt gains balance" of an individual in respect of a business of the individual for a taxation year means the amount determined by the formula

A - B

where

A is the lesser of

(a) the amount by which

(i) the amount that would have been the individual's taxable capital gain determined under paragraph 110.6(19)(b) in respect of the business if

(A) the amount designated in an election under subsection 110.6(19) in respect of the business were equal to the fair market value at the end of February 22, 1994 of all the eligible capital property owned by the elector at that time in respect of the business, and

(B) this Act were read without reference to subsection 110.6(20)

exceeds

(ii) the amount determined by the formula

0.75(C - 1.1D)

where

C is the amount designated in the election that was made under subsection 110.6(19) in respect of the business, and

D is the fair market value at the end of February 22, 1994 of the property referred to in clause (i)(A), and

(b) the individual's taxable capital gain determined under paragraph 110.6(19)(b) in respect of the business, and

B is the total of all amounts each of which is the amount determined for D in subparagraph (1)(a)(v) in respect of the business for a preceding taxation year that ended before February 28, 2000 or the amount determined for D in paragraph (1)(b) for a preceding taxation year that ended after February 27, 2000.

▶ 14(5.1) ◀

(5.1) Restrictive covenant amount — (Repealed by S.C. 2016, c. 12, s. 4(1).)

History: S. 14(5.1) was repealed by S.C. 2016, c. 12, s. 4(1), in force January 1, 2017, and formerly read:

(5.1) *Restrictive covenant amount.* The description of E in the definition "cumulative eligible capital" in subsection (5) does not apply to an amount that is received or receivable by a taxpayer in a taxation year if that amount is required to be included in the taxpayer's income because of subsection 56.4(2).

S. 14(5.1) was added by S.C. 2013, c. 34, s. 176(5), deemed to have come into force on October 8, 2003.

▶ 14(6) ◀

(6) Exchange of property — (Repealed by S.C. 2016, c. 12, s. 4(1).)

History: S. 14(6) was repealed by S.C. 2016, c. 12, s. 4(1), in force January 1, 2017, and formerly read:

(6) *Exchange of property.* If in a taxation year (in this subsection referred to as the "initial year") a taxpayer disposes of an eligible capital property (in this section referred to as the taxpayer's "former property") and the taxpayer so elects under this subsection in the taxpayer's return of income for the year in which the taxpayer acquires an eligible capital property that is a replacement property for the taxpayer's former property, the amount, not exceeding the amount that would otherwise be included in the amount determined for E in the definition "cumulative eligible capital" in subsection (5) (if the description of E in that definition were read without reference to "$^3/_4$ of") in respect of a business, that has been used by the taxpayer to acquire the replacement property before the later of the end of the first taxation year after the initial year and 12 months after the end of the initial year

(a) shall, subject to paragraph (b), not be included in the amount determined for E in that definition for the purpose of determining the cumulative eligible capital of the taxpayer in respect of the business; and

(b) shall, to the extent of $^3/_4$ thereof, be included in the amount determined for E in that definition for the purpose of determining the cumulative eligible capital of the taxpayer in respect of the business at a time that is the later of

(i) the time the replacement property was acquired by the taxpayer, and

(ii) the time the former property was disposed of by the taxpayer.

S. 14(6), the portion before paragraph (a) was replaced by S.C. 2013, c. 34, s. 176(6), applicable in respect of dispositions that occur in taxation years that end on or after December 20, 2001. S. 14(6), the portion before paragraph (a) formerly read:

(6) *Exchange of property.* Where in a taxation year (in this subsection referred to as the "initial year") a taxpayer disposes of an eligible capital property (in this section referred to as the taxpayer's "former property") and the taxpayer so elects under this subsection in the taxpayer's return of income for the year in which the taxpayer acquires an eligible capital property that is a replacement property for the taxpayer's former property, such amount, not exceeding the amount that would otherwise be included in the amount determined for E in the definition "cumulative eligible capital" in subsection (5) (if the description of E in that definition were read without reference to "$^3/_4$ of") in respect of a business, as has been used by the taxpayer before the end of the first taxation year after the initial year to acquire the replacement property

▶ 14(7) ◀

(7) Replacement property — (Repealed by S.C. 2016, c. 12, s. 4(1).)

History: S. 14(7) was repealed by S.C. 2016, c. 12, s. 4(1), in force January 1, 2017, and formerly read:

(7) *Replacement property.* For the purposes of subsection (6), a particular eligible capital property of a taxpayer is a replacement property for a former property of the taxpayer if

(a) it is reasonable to conclude that the property was acquired by the taxpayer to replace the former property;

(a.1) it was acquired by the taxpayer for a use that is the same as or similar to the use to which the taxpayer put the former property;

(b) it was acquired for the purpose of gaining or producing income from the same or a similar business as that in which the former property was used; and

(c) where the former property was used by the taxpayer in a business carried on in Canada, the particular property was acquired for use by the taxpayer in a business carried on by the taxpayer in Canada.

▶ 14(8) ◀

(8) Deemed residence in Canada — (Repealed by S.C. 2016, c. 12, s. 4(1).)

History: S. 14(8) was repealed by S.C. 2016, c. 12, s. 4(1), in force January 1, 2017, and formerly read:

(8) *Deemed residence in Canada.* Where an individual was resident in Canada at any time in a particular taxation year and throughout

(a) the preceding taxation year, or

(b) the following taxation year,

for the purpose of paragraph (1)(a), the individual shall be deemed to have been resident in Canada throughout the particular year.

▶ 14(9) ◀

(9) Effect of election under subsection 110.6(19) — (Repealed by S.C. 2016, c. 12, s. 4(1).)

History: S. 14(9) was repealed by S.C. 2016, c. 12, s. 4(1), in force January 1, 2017, and formerly read:

(9) *Effect of election under subsection 110.6(19).* Where an individual elects under subsection 110.6(19) in respect of a business, the individual shall be deemed to have received proceeds of a disposition on February 23, 1994 of eligible capital property in respect of the business equal to the amount determined by the formula

(A - B)4/3

where

A is the amount determined in respect of the business under subparagraph (a)(ii) of the description of A in the definition "exempt gains balance" in subsection (5), and

B is the amount determined in respect of the business under subparagraph (a)(i) of the description of A in the definition "exempt gains balance" in subsection (5).

▶ 14(10) ◀

(10) Deemed eligible capital expenditure — (Repealed by S.C. 2016, c. 12, s. 4(1).)

History: S. 14(10) was repealed by S.C. 2016, c. 12, s. 4(1), in force January 1, 2017, and formerly read:

(10) *Deemed eligible capital expenditure.* For the purposes of this Act, where a taxpayer received or is entitled to receive assistance from a government, municipality or other public authority in respect of, or for the acquisition of, property the cost of which is an eligible capital expenditure of the taxpayer in respect of a business, whether as a grant, subsidy, forgivable loan, deduction from tax, investment allowance or as any other form of assistance, that eligible capital expenditure shall at any time be deemed to be the amount, if any, by which the total of

(*a*) that eligible capital expenditure, determined without reference to this subsection, and

(*b*) such part, if any, of the assistance as the taxpayer repaid before

(i) the taxpayer ceased to carry on the business, and

(ii) that time

under a legal obligation to pay all or any part of the assistance

exceeds

(*c*) the amount of the assistance the taxpayer received or is entitled to receive before the earlier of that time and the time the taxpayer ceases to carry on the business.

▶ 14(11) ◀

(11) Receipt of public assistance — (Repealed by S.C. 2016, c. 12, s. 4(1).)

History: S. 14(11) was repealed by S.C. 2016, c. 12, s. 4(1), in force January 1, 2017, and formerly read:

(11) *Receipt of public assistance.* For the purpose of subsection (10), where at any time a taxpayer who is a beneficiary under a trust or a member of a partnership received or is entitled to receive assistance from a government, municipality or other public authority, whether as a grant, subsidy, forgivable loan, deduction from tax, investment allowance or as any other form of assistance, the amount of the assistance that can reasonably be considered to be in respect of, or for the acquisition of, property the cost of which was an eligible capital expenditure of the trust or partnership shall be deemed to have been received at that time by the trust or partnership, as the case may be, as assistance from the government, municipality or other public authority for the acquisition of such property.

▶ 14(12) ◀

(12) Loss on certain transfers — (Repealed by S.C. 2016, c. 12, s. 4(1).)

History: S. 14(12) was repealed by S.C. 2016, c. 12, s. 4(1), in force January 1, 2017, and formerly read:

(12) *Loss on certain transfers.* Where

(*a*) a corporation, trust or partnership (in this subsection referred to as the "transferor") disposes at any time in a taxation year of a particular eligible capital property — other than, for the purposes of computing the exempt surplus or exempt deficit and taxable surplus or taxable deficit of a foreign affiliate of a taxpayer, in respect of the taxpayer, where the transferor is the affiliate or is a partnership of which the affiliate is a member, eligible capital property that is, or would be, if the transferor were a foreign affiliate of the taxpayer, excluded property (within the meaning assigned by subsection 95(1)) of the transferor — in respect of a business of the transferor in respect of which it would, but for this subsection, be permitted a deduction under paragraph 24(1)(*a*) as a consequence of the disposition, and

(*b*) during the period that begins 30 days before and ends 30 days after the disposition, the transferor or a person affiliated with the transferor acquires a property (in this subsection referred to as the "substituted property") that is, or is identical to, the particular property and, at the end of that period, a person or partnership that is either the transferor or a person or partnership affiliated with the transferor owns the substituted property,

the transferor is deemed, for the purposes of this section and sections 20 and 24, to continue to own eligible capital property in respect of the business, and not to have ceased to carry on the business, until the time that is immediately before the first time, after the disposition,

(*c*) at which a 30-day period begins throughout which neither the transferor nor a person affiliated with the transferor owns

(i) the substituted property, or

(ii) a property that is identical to the substituted property and that was acquired after the day that is 31 days before the period begins,

(*d*) at which the substituted property is not eligible capital property in respect of a business carried on by the transferor or a person affiliated with the transferor,

(*e*) at which the substituted property would, if it were owned by the transferor, be deemed by section 128.1 or subsection 149(10) to have been disposed of by the transferor,

(*f*) that is immediately before the transferor is subject to a loss restriction event, or

(*g*) if the transferor is a corporation,

(i) for the purposes of computing the transferor's foreign accrual property income, exempt surplus or exempt deficit, and taxable surplus or taxable deficit, in respect of a taxpayer for a taxation year of the transferor where the transferor is a foreign affiliate of the taxpayer, at which the liquidation and dissolution of the transferor begins, unless the liquidation and dissolution is

(A) a qualifying liquidation and dissolution (within the meaning assigned by subsection 88(3.1)) of the transferor, or

(B) a designated liquidation and dissolution (within the meaning assigned by subsection 95(1)) of the transferor, and

(ii) for any other purposes, at which the winding-up (other than a winding-up to which subsection 88(1) applies) of the transferor begins.

S. 14(12)(*f*) was replaced by S.C. 2013, c. 40, s. 7(1), deemed to have come into force on March 21, 2013, and formerly read:

(*f*) that is immediately before control of the transferor is acquired by a person or group of persons, where the transferor is a corporation, or

S. 14(12)(*a*) was replaced by S.C. 2013, c. 34, s. 55(1), applicable to dispositions that occur after August 19, 2011.

Any assessment of a taxpayer's tax, interest and penalties payable under the Act for any taxation year that ends before June 26, 2013 that would, in the absence of this section, be precluded because of subsections 152(4) to (5) of the Act shall be made to the extent necessary to take into account the amendments by S.C. 2013, c. 34, s. 54 to 89.

S. 14(12)(*a*) formerly read:

(*a*) a corporation, trust or partnership (in this subsection referred to as the "transferor") disposes at any time in a taxation year of a particular eligible capital property in respect of a business of the transferor in respect of which it would, but for this subsection, be permitted a deduction under paragraph 24(1)(*a*) as a consequence of the disposition, and

S. 14(12)(*g*) was replaced by S.C. 2013, c. 34, s. 55(2), applicable to windings-up and liquidations and dissolutions that begin after August 19, 2011.

See the application provision above for the extension of assessment periods to take into account the amendments by S.C. 2013, c. 34, s. 54 to 89.

S. 14(12)(*g*) formerly read:

(*g*) at which the winding-up of the transferor begins (other than a winding-up to which subsection 88(1) applies), where the transferor is a corporation.

▶ 14(13) ◀

(13) Deemed identical property — (Repealed by S.C. 2016, c. 12, s. 4(1).)

History: S. 14(13) was repealed by S.C. 2016, c. 12, s. 4(1), in force January 1, 2017, and formerly read:

(13) *Deemed identical property.* For the purpose of subsection (12),

(*a*) a right to acquire a property (other than a right, as security only, derived from a mortgage, hypothec, agreement for sale or similar obligation) is deemed to be a property that is identical to the property; and

(*b*) where a partnership otherwise ceases to exist at any time after the disposition, the partnership is deemed not to have ceased to exist and each person who, immediately before the partnership would, but for this paragraph, have ceased to exist, was a member of the partnership is deemed to remain a member of the partnership, until the time that is immediately after the first time described in paragraphs (12)(*c*) to (*g*).

▶ 14(14) ◀

(14) Ceasing to use property in Canadian business — (Repealed by S.C. 2016, c. 12, s. 4(1).)

History: S. 14(14) was repealed by S.C. 2016, c. 12, s. 4(1), in force January 1, 2017, and formerly read:

(14) *Ceasing to use property in Canadian business.* If at a particular time a non-resident taxpayer ceases to use, in connection with a business or part of a business carried on by the taxpayer in Canada immediately before the particular time, a property that was immediately before the particular time eligible capital property of the taxpayer (other than a property that was disposed of by the taxpayer at the particular time), the taxpayer is deemed to have disposed of the property immediately before the particular time for proceeds of disposition equal to the amount determined by the formula

$$A - B$$

where

A is the fair market value of the property immediately before the particular time, and

B is

(*a*) where at a previous time before the particular time the taxpayer ceased to use the property in connection with a business or part of a business carried on by the taxpayer outside Canada and began to use it in connection with a business or part of a business carried on by the taxpayer in Canada, the amount, if any, by which the fair market value of the property at the previous time exceeded its cost to the taxpayer at the previous time, and

(*b*) in any other case, nil.

▶ 14(15) ◀

(15) Beginning to use property in Canadian business — (Repealed by S.C. 2016, c. 12, s. 4(1).)

History: S. 14(14) was repealed by S.C. 2016, c. 12, s. 4(1), in force January 1, 2017, and formerly read:

(15) *Beginning to use property in Canadian business.* If at a particular time a non-resident taxpayer ceases to use, in connection with a business or part of a business carried on by the taxpayer outside Canada immediately before the particular time, and begins to use, in connection with a business or part of a business carried on by the taxpayer in Canada, a property that is an eligible capital property of the taxpayer, the taxpayer is deemed to have disposed of the property immediately before the particular time and to have reacquired the property at the particular time for consideration equal to the lesser of the cost to the taxpayer of the property immediately before the particular time and its fair market value immediately before the particular time.

SECTION 15: Benefit conferred on shareholder

▶ 15(1) ◀

(1) Benefit conferred on shareholder. If, at any time, a benefit is conferred by a corporation on a shareholder of the corporation, on a member of a partnership that is a shareholder of the corporation or on a contemplated shareholder of the corporation, then the amount or value of the benefit is to be included in computing the income of the shareholder, member or contemplated shareholder, as the case may be, for its taxation year that includes the time, except to the extent that the amount or value of the benefit is deemed by section 84 to be a dividend or that the benefit is conferred on the shareholder

(*a*) where the corporation is resident in Canada at the time,

(i) by the reduction of the paid-up capital of the corporation,

(ii) by the redemption, acquisition or cancellation by the corporation of shares of its capital stock,

(iii) on the winding-up, discontinuance or reorganization of the corporation's business, or

(iv) by way of a transaction to which subsection 88(1) or (2) applies;

(*a*.1) where the corporation is not resident in Canada at the time,

(i) by way of a distribution to which subsection 86.1(1) applies,

(ii) by a reduction of the paid-up capital of the corporation to which subclause 53(2)(*b*)(i)(B)(II) or subparagraph 53(2)(*b*)(ii) applies,

(iii) by the redemption, acquisition or cancellation by the corporation of shares of its capital stock, or

(iv) on the winding-up, or liquidation and dissolution, of the corporation;

(*b*) by the payment of a dividend or a stock dividend;

(*c*) by conferring, on all owners of common shares of the capital stock of the corporation at that time, a right in respect of each common share, that is identical to every other right conferred at that time in respect of each other such share, to acquire additional shares of the capital stock of the corporation, and, for the purposes of this paragraph,

(i) the shares of a particular class of common shares of the capital stock of the corporation are deemed to be property that is identical to the shares of another class of common shares of the capital stock of the corporation if

(A) the voting rights attached to the particular class differ from the voting rights attached to the other class, and

(B) there are no other differences between the terms and conditions of the classes of shares that could cause the fair market value of a share of the particular class to differ materially from the fair market value of a share of the other class, and

(ii) rights are not considered identical if the cost of acquiring the rights differs; or

(*d*) by an action to which paragraph 84(1)(*c.1*), (*c.2*) or (*c.3*) applies.

Editorial Note: Subsection 15(1) prevents shareholders from extracting or enjoying benefits from a corporation on a tax-free basis. The provision applies where a benefit is conferred by a corporation on a shareholder, a member of a partnership that is a shareholder, or a "contemplated shareholder" (defined in s. 15(1.4)(*a*)). The amount or value of the benefit is included in income of the recipient, and is treated as ordinary income and not as a dividend, such that the dividend tax credit (individual shareholder) and the intercorporate deduction (corporate shareholder) are not applicable. The corporation will not normally be allowed a deduction on account of the benefit. There are some exceptions to the application of s. 15(1), which are noted below.

A benefit conferred on an individual who does not deal at arm's length with, or is affiliated with, a shareholder, member of a partnership, or contemplated shareholder, as the case may be, is included in the income of the shareholder, member or contemplated shareholder rather than the individual (unless it is otherwise included in the income of the individual); see s. 15(1.4)(*c*).

Amount or value of benefit: The Federal Court of Appeal has held that the amount or value of the benefit is the amount that "the shareholder would have had to pay for the same benefit in the same circumstances had he not been a shareholder of the company" (*Youngman*, 90 DTC 6322). In that case, the shareholder's corporation built a luxury home for him and his wife. After he moved in, he paid the corporation monthly rent, which was apparently well below fair market value ("FMV") rent. It was appropriate to measure the amount of the benefit using the corporation's required rate of return on its investment (i.e., the house it built).

Generally, in the case of a single purpose corporation holding property for the benefit of a shareholder, the CRA's view is that the amount or value of a benefit is based on the FMV rent for the property minus any consideration paid to the corporation by the shareholder for the use of the property. If FMV rent cannot be determined or does not exist, the amount or value of a benefit would then usually be determined by multiplying a normal rate of return times the greater of the cost or FMV of the property and adding the operating costs related to the property. This would be the "imputed rent" for the property. Any consideration paid to the corporation by the shareholder for the use of the property would then be subtracted from the imputed rent (CRA Document No. 2010-0360001E5).

For a general discussion on how much is to be included as a benefit under s. 15(1), see Truster, Taxable Benefits: How Much Is Taxable?, *Tax for the Owner-Manager*, (2014) vol. 14 no. 2. See also Interpretation Bulletin IT-432R2 (archived, as it doesn't meet current government web standards).

If the benefit is a forgiven debt, the amount included is the "forgiven amount" of the debt (s. 15(1.21) and s. 80(1)).

In case of an automobile provided by a corporation to a shareholder, the benefit is computed using the standby charge formula (see s. 6(1)(*e*) and s. 6(2)).

Exceptions: An amount that is a deemed dividend under s. 84 is excluded from s. 15(1), but it will of course be taxed as a dividend. Similarly, a benefit conferred by the reduction of the paid-up capital of the corporation, by the redemption, acquisition, or cancellation by the corporation of any of its shares or on the winding-up, discontinuance, or reorganization of the corporation's business is not subject to s. 15(1), but may be a deemed dividend under s. 84(2)–(4).

When a corporation grants all holders of common shares an identical right to purchase additional shares, there will be no income inclusion under s. 15(1) for the value of that right. Shares are deemed to be identical for the s. 15(1)(*c*) exemption where the only difference between two or more classes of common shares is the voting rights attached to the shares. The meaning of "identical right" is considered in CRA Document No. 2004-0093731E5.

Non-resident shareholder: The benefit is deemed to be a dividend received, and is subject to withholding tax under Part XIII (see s. 214(3)(*a*)).

History: S. 15(1) was replaced by S.C. 2013, c. 34, s. 177(1), applicable in respect of benefits conferred on or after October 31, 2011, and formerly read:

(1) *Benefit conferred on shareholder.* Where at any time in a taxation year a benefit is conferred on a shareholder, or on a person in contemplation of the person becoming a shareholder, by a corporation otherwise than by

(*a*) the reduction of the paid-up capital, the redemption, cancellation or acquisition by the corporation of shares of its capital stock or on the winding-up, discontinuance or reorganization of its business, or otherwise by way of a transaction to which section 88 applies,

(*b*) the payment of a dividend or a stock dividend,

(*c*) conferring, on all owners of common shares of the capital stock of the corporation at that time, a right in respect of each common share, that is identical to every other right conferred at that time in respect of each other such share, to acquire additional shares of the capital stock of the corporation, and, for the purpose of this paragraph,

(i) where

(A) the voting rights attached to a particular class of common shares of the capital stock of a corporation differ from the voting rights attached to another class of common shares of the capital stock of the corporation, and

(B) there are no other differences between the terms and conditions of the classes of shares that could cause the fair market value of a share of the particular class to differ materially from the fair market value of a share of the other class,

the shares of the particular class shall be deemed to be property that is identical to the shares of the other class, and

(ii) rights are not considered identical if the cost of acquiring the rights differs, or

(*d*) an action described in paragraph 84(1)(*c*.1), (*c*.2) or (*c*.3),

the amount or value thereof shall, except to the extent that it is deemed by section 84 to be a dividend, be included in computing the income of the shareholder for the year.

Related Sections: S. 7(3) Special provision; s. 51(1) Convertible property; s. 52(1) Cost of certain property the value of which included in income; s. 69(4) Shareholder appropriations; s. 69(5) Winding-up of corporation; s. 79(3) Proceeds of disposition for debtor; s. 79(5) Subsequent application with respect to employee or shareholder debt; s. 80(1), "forgiven amount"; s. 80(2) Application of debt forgiveness rules; s. 80.4(2) Loan or debt by virtue of shareholding; 84(1) Deemed dividend; 84(2) Distribution on winding-up, etc; 84(3) Redemption, etc.; 84(4) Reduction of paid-up capital; 84(4.1) Deemed dividend on reduction of paid-up capital; 84(4.2) Deemed dividend on term preferred share; 84(4.3) Deemed dividend on guaranteed share; 84(5) Amount distributed or paid where a share; s. 85(1) Transfer of property to corporation by shareholders; s. 86(1) Exchange of shares by a shareholder in course of reorganization of capital; s. 120.4 Tax on split income; s. 139.1(11) No shareholder benefit; s. 214(3) Deemed payments; s. 246(1) Benefit conferred on a person; s. 248(1), "share", "shareholder"; s. 249(1) Definition of "taxation year".

Canadian Tax Foundation: Hennessey, *Another Reason To Avoid Shareholder Benefits*, 2016 Canadian Tax Focus 6(1):3–4; Truster, *Taxable Benefits: How Much Is Taxable?*, 2014 Tax for the Owner-Manager 14(2):2; Junkin, *Section 15 — Shareholder Benefits Update*, 2009 British Columbia Tax Conference 12:1–18; Diksic and Desjardins, *Tax Treatment of Transaction Costs*, 2006 Conference Report 38:1–36; Heddema and Lee, *Shareholder and Employee Benefits and Deductions: Selected Issues*, 2006 British Columbia Tax Conference 15:1–48; Goldberg, *Single-Purpose and Professional Corporations: Recent Developments and CRA Administrative Policies*, 2005 Conference Report 11:1–33; Heddema, *Section 15 Shareholder Benefits: A Review and Update*, 2004 British Columbia Tax Conference 12:1–32; Tunney, *SPC Benefit Eliminated*, 2004 Canadian Tax Highlights 12(7):1; Lerman, *Hot Issues in Tax Compliance: Section 15 — Shareholder Benefits and Shareholder Debt*, 2002 Ontario Tax Conference 16:50–61; Chowscano, *No Benefit, No Doubt*, 2002 Canadian Tax Highlights 10(3):22; Belley and Bienvenue, *Taxable Shareholder Benefits: Sailing Close to the Wind under Section 15*, 2001 Tax for the Owner-Manager 1(1):2–3; Beam and Laiken, *Benefits Under Subsection 15(1)*, 1994 Canadian Tax Journal 2:479–511.

Tax Profile: November 2010 — Canadian Acquisition of U.S. Real Estate; November 2004 — New Administrative Policy on Single-Purpose Corporations; May 2004 — Ownership of U.S. Residential Property by Canadian Residents.

Tax Topics: No. 2455, Court Finds Corporation's Cost of Space Trip Resulted in Substantial Benefit to Shareholder; No. 2040, CRA Roundtable at Association de planification fiscale et financière (APFF) 2010 Conference; No. 1971-72, 2009 Canadian Tax Foundation Conference: Wizards, Tiny Taxes and "Evil" Kirk; No. 1700, 2004 Canadian Tax Foundation Conference — CRA Round Table.

Forms: T2 SCH 11 — Transactions with Shareholders, Officers, or Employees.

Income Tax Folios: S2-F3-C2 Benefits and Allowances Received from Employment; *Primary* — S4-F3-C1 Price Adjustment Clauses; *Secondary* — S3-F9-C1 Lottery Winnings, Miscellaneous Receipts, and Income (and Losses) from Crime.

Income Tax Technical News: Issue No. 44, Corporate-Held Life Insurance; Issue No. 32, New Administrative Policy on Single-Purpose Corporations; Issue No. 31R2, Single-Purpose Corporations; Issue No. 25, Dividend Reinvestment Plans.

Information Circulars: IC 76-19R3 Transfer of property to a corporation under section 85; IC 87-2R International Transfer Pricing.

Interpretation Bulletins: *Primary* — IT-116R3 Right to buy additional shares; IT-432R2 Benefits conferred on shareholders. *Secondary* — IT-63R5 Benefits, including standby charge for an automobile, from the personal use of a motor vehicle supplied by an employer — After 1992; IT-96R6 Options granted by corporations to acquire shares, bonds or debentures; IT-291R3 Transfer of property to a corporation under subsection 85(1); IT-335R2 Indirect payments; IT-357R2 Expenses of training.

Tax Window Files: CPA Alberta 2017 Q17: Electric Vehicle Taxable Benefits, *September 14, 2017*, CRA Document No. 2017-0703881C6; PHSP for relatives of shareholder-employee, *March 8, 2017*, CRA Document No. 2016-0635351E5; Disposition of Property, *Income Tax Rulings Directorate, Legislative Policy and Regulatory Affairs Branch, November 14, 2008*, CRA Document No. 2008-0295871E5; Wage Loss Replacement Plan — Employee-Shareholder Beneficiaries, *Technical Interpretation, Financial Sector and Exempt Entities Division, February 12, 2007*, CRA Document No. 2006-0214141E5; Automobile Used by Shareholder's Spouse, *Technical Interpretation, Business and Partnerships Division, January 4, 2007*, CRA Document No. 2006-0187051E5; Shareholders' Benefits — Critical Illness Insurance, *Technical Interpretation, Financial Sector and Exempt Entities Division, November 3, 2006*, CRA Document No. 2006-0178561E5; Private Health Services Plan for Shareholder-Employee, *Technical Interpretation, Business and Partnerships Division, October 19, 2006*, CRA Document No. 2006-0204951I7; Single Purpose Corporations, *Technical Interpretation, Reorganizations and Resources Division, June 22, 2005*, CRA Document No. 2005-0136421E5; Transfer of Life Insurance Policy for No Consideration, *Technical Interpretation, Financial Industries Division, April 4, 2005*, CRA Document No. 2005-0110941E5; Shareholders' Benefits — Life Insurance Policy, *Technical Interpretation, Reorganizations and Resources Division, June 29, 2004*, CRA Document No. 2004-0081901I7. For corporate-owned insurance policy on the life of a shareholder where the shareholder's spouse was the beneficiary, the shareholder benefit was based on the insurance premiums paid by the corporation and not the death benefit paid under the policy. However, if the corporation is the beneficiary, there is no shareholder benefit — see Document number 2004-0072971I7; Shareholder Loans — Loan to Shareholder's Adult Child, *Technical Interpretation, Business and Partnerships Division, March 23, 2004*, CRA Document No. 2003-0049031E5; Repayment of Contributed Surplus, *Technical Interpretation, Reorganizations and Resources Division, August 25, 2003*, CRA Document No. 2003-0031585; Changes in Terms of Debt Obligation, *Technical Interpretation, Financial Industries Division, March 26, 2003*, CRA Document No. 2001-0105315. Conversion of interest-bearing inter-corporate loan (from one subsidiary to another subsidiary) to a non-interest bearing loan does not generally result in a taxable benefit for the parent corporation; Benefit Resulting from Issue of Shares, *Technical Interpretation, Reorganizations and Resources Division, January 3, 2003*, CRA Document No. 2002-0143965. Taxable benefit conferred when a corporation's first share is issued for a nominal price after the corporation has carried on business and has accumulated value.

Cases: The taxpayer's trip to the ISS was a personal trip with some significant business aspects, but the overarching reasons were personal. The business-related portion was in the 10% range at most, and 90% of the cost was the the shareholder's benefit to be included in his income. *Laliberté v. The Queen*, 2018 DTC 1132 (TCC)

Despite the payment not being recorded in the corporation's books, the taxpayer's testimony clearly showed the $94,000 was not a shareholder's benefit but the repayment of a loan. *Latham v. The Queen*, 2015 DTC 1104 (T.C.C.)

The employer, B&N, did not intend to confer a benefit to the taxpayer. The value of the transfer to the taxpayer was incorrect due to the error of B&N's accounting firm. The amount was a loan receivable by the taxpayer and the

Minister was ordered to remove $79,779 from the taxpayer's income and increase his shareholder loan account. *Charania v. The Queen*, 2015 DTC 1103 (T.C.C.)

The taxpayer and two corporations he owned each invested in a third party. He later received a payment representing return of the investments and deposited it in his own bank account. The part belonging to the corporations was a shareholder's benefit and penalties were imposed since the corporations conferred a benefit on him, representing virtually all of their assets, allowing him to wind them up without paying tax on distributions. *Carrier v. The Queen*, 2013 DTC 1164 (T.C.C.)

A release of claims under a guarantee did not constitute a shareholder's benefit since there were no quantifiable claims at the time the release was granted and all obligations under the guarantee were satisfied. *Axa Canada Inc. v. The Queen*, 2006 DTC 2198 (T.C.C.)

There was no shareholder's benefit where payments owed to a corporation were paid directly to a shareholder who then used the funds to acquire assets for the company. Although the transactions were not properly recorded in the corporation's financial statements, the taxpayer himself received no benefit. *The Queen v. Franklin*, 2002 DTC 6803 (F.C.A.), affirming 2000 DTC 2456 (T.C.C.)

Although certain expenses claimed by a family corporation were disallowed, they were not to be included in a shareholder's income since there was no evidence of an intent to confer a benefit, or that any benefit was actually conferred. Even if they could be construed as benefits, they should be allocated among all of the company's shareholders. *Robson et al. v. The Queen*, 2001 DTC 1039 (T.C.C.)

When a taxpayer did not know of the bookkeeping error resulting in the overstated credit balance in his shareholder loan account and did not attempt to use it for his own benefit or advantage, the amount was not to be included in his income since, in order for the value of a benefit to be included in a shareholder's income, it must be conferred with his knowledge or consent. *The Queen v. Chopp*, 98 DTC 6014 (F.C.A.), affirming 95 DTC 527 (T.C.C.)

The taxpayer's corporation purchased a condominium which was occupied by the taxpayer and his wife during part of the year. This gave rise to a shareholder's benefit, calculated on the assumption that the condominium had been acquired for personal use. The calculation was based on what the corporation could have earned on the money committed to the acquisition and renovation, not just on the fair rental value for the periods of personal use. It was calculated on the basis of what the taxpayer would have had to pay to get the same benefit from a company of which he was not a shareholder. *The Queen v. Fingold*, 97 DTC 5449 (F.C.A.), reversing 96 DTC 1305 (T.C.C.)

Payments made by a corporation to a taxpayer's divorced spouse constituted a shareholder benefit to the taxpayer. *Osadchuk v. The Queen*, 96 DTC 6083 (F.C.A.), affirming 95 DTC 98 (T.C.C.)

A house built by the taxpayer's corporation on land which was to be subdivided was not built for business purposes and was a shareholder benefit. The calculation should be based on the company's rate of return, expressed as a percentage of its equity in the house, as opposed to free-market rental. *Youngman v. The Queen*, 90 DTC 6322 (F.C.A.), reversing 86 DTC 6584 (F.C.T.D.) and unreported (T.R.B.)

The word "benefit" refers to the monetary amounts received from a corporation and not the shareholder's overall financial or physical well-being. Therefore amounts received by a shareholder from one corporation used to meet losses of another corporation were shareholder benefits and properly included in income. *Vine Estate v. The Queen*, 89 DTC 5528 (F.C.T.D.)

Other Publications: AD-18-01 Taxable benefit for the personal use of an aircraft.

► 15(1.1) ◄

(1.1) Conferring of benefit. Notwithstanding subsection (1), if in a taxation year a corporation has paid a stock dividend to a person and it may reasonably be considered that one of the purposes of that payment was to significantly alter the value of the interest of any specified shareholder of the corporation, the fair market value of the stock dividend shall, except to the extent that it is otherwise included in computing that person's income under any of paragraphs 82(1)(*a*), (*a*.1) and (*c*) to (*e*), be included in computing the income of that person for the year.

Related Sections: S. 248(1), "stock dividend".

Interpretation Bulletins: *Secondary* — IT-432R2 Benefits conferred on shareholders.

Cases: A corporation declared stock dividends to the controlling shareholder and his wife and children (who owned non-voting shares). Although the effect of issuing the stock dividends was to significantly alter the controlling shareholder's interest in the corporation, this was not the purpose of the payment. Subsection 15(1.1) was inapplicable. *Wong et al. v. The Queen*, 99 DTC 458 (T.C.C.)

► 15(1.2) ◄

(1.2) Forgiveness of shareholder debt. For the purpose of subsection (1), the value of the benefit where an obligation issued by a debtor is settled or extinguished at any time shall be deemed to be the forgiven amount at that time in respect of the obligation.

Editorial Note: See s. 15(1.21), below, regarding the computation of the forgiven amount.

Interpretation Bulletins: *Secondary* — IT-432R2 Benefits conferred on shareholders.

Tax Window Files: Benefit from Settlement of Debt on Dissolution of Foreign Affiliate, *Technical Interpretation, International and Trusts Division, August 30, 2004*, CRA Document No. 2003-0001351E5.

► 15(1.21) ◄

(1.21) Forgiven amount. For the purpose of subsection (1.2), the "forgiven amount" at any time in respect of an obligation issued by a debtor has the meaning that would be assigned by subsection 80(1) if

(*a*) the obligation were a commercial obligation (within the meaning assigned by subsection 80(1)) issued by the debtor;

(*b*) no amount included in computing income (otherwise than because of paragraph 6(1)(*a*)) because of the obligation being settled or extinguished were taken into account;

(*c*) the definition "forgiven amount" in subsection 80(1) were read without reference to paragraphs (*f*) and (*h*) of the description B in that definition; and

(*d*) section 80 were read without reference to paragraphs (2)(*b*) and (*q*) of that section.

Interpretation Bulletins: *Secondary* — IT-432R2 Benefits conferred on shareholders.

► 15(1.3) ◄

(1.3) Cost of property or service. To the extent that the cost to a person of purchasing a property or service or an amount payable by a person for the purpose of leasing property is taken into account in determining an amount required under this section to be included in computing a taxpayer's income for a taxation year, that cost or amount payable, as the case may be, shall include any tax that was payable by the person in respect of the property or service or that would have been so payable if the person were not exempt from the payment of that tax because of the nature of the person or the use to which the property or service is to be put.

Interpretation Bulletins: *Secondary* — IT-432R2 Benefits conferred on shareholders.

► 15(1.4) ◄

(1.4) Interpretation — subsection (1). For the purposes of this subsection and subsection (1),

(*a*) a contemplated shareholder of a corporation is

(i) a person or partnership on whom a benefit is conferred by the corporation in contemplation of the person or partnership becoming a shareholder of the corporation, or

(ii) a member of a partnership on whom a benefit is conferred by the corporation in contemplation of the partnership becoming a shareholder of the corporation;

(*b*) a person or partnership that is (or is deemed by this paragraph to be) a member of a particular partnership that is a member of another partnership is deemed to be a member of the other partnership;

(*c*) a benefit conferred by a corporation on an individual is a benefit conferred on a shareholder of the corporation, a member of a partnership that is a shareholder of the corporation or a contemplated shareholder of the corporation — except to the extent that the amount or value of the benefit is included in computing the income of the individual or any other person — if the individual is an individual, other than an excluded trust in respect of the corporation, who does not deal at arm's length with, or is affiliated with, the shareholder, member of the partnership or contemplated shareholder, as the case may be; and

(*d*) for the purposes of paragraph (*c*), an excluded trust in respect of a corporation is a trust in which no individual (other than an excluded trust in respect of the corporation) who does not deal at arm's length with, or is affiliated with, a shareholder of the corporation, a member of a partnership that is a shareholder of the corporation or a contemplated shareholder of the corporation, is beneficially interested.

(*e*) (Repealed by S.C. 2018, c. 27, s. 2(1).)

History: S. 15(1.4)(*e*) was repealed by S.C. 2018, c. 27, s. 2(1), deemed in force October 24, 2012, and formerly read:

(*e*) if a non-resident corporation (in this paragraph referred to as the "original corporation") governed by the laws of a foreign jurisdiction is divided under those laws into two or more non-resident corporations and, as a consequence of the division, a shareholder of the original corporation acquires at any time one or more shares of another corporation (in this paragraph referred to as the "new corporation"), the original corporation is deemed at that time to have conferred a benefit on the shareholder equal to the value at that time of the shares of the new corporation acquired by the shareholder except to the extent that any of subparagraphs (1)(*a.1*)(i) to (iii) and paragraph (1)(*b*) applies to the acquisition of the shares.

S. 15(1.4) was added by S.C. 2013, c. 34, s. 177(3), applicable in respect of benefits conferred on or after October 31, 2011.

S. 15(1.4)(*e*) was added by S.C. 2013, c. 34, s. 177(4), applicable in respect of divisions of non-resident corporations that occur on or after October 24, 2012.

Interpretation Bulletins: *Secondary* — IT-432R2 Benefits conferred on shareholders.

▶ 15(1.5) ◀

(1.5) Division of corporation under foreign laws. If a non-resident corporation (in this subsection referred to as the "original corporation") governed by the laws of a foreign jurisdiction undergoes a division under those laws that results in all or part of its property and liabilities becoming the property and liabilities of one or more other non-resident corporations (each of which is referred to in this subsection as a "new corporation") and, as a consequence of the division, a shareholder of the original corporation acquires one or more shares (referred to in this subsection as "new shares") of the capital stock of a new corporation at a particular time, the following rules apply:

(*a*) except to the extent that any of subparagraphs (1)(*a*.1)(i) to (iii) and paragraph (1)(*b*) applies (determined without reference to this subsection) to the acquisition of the new shares

(i) in the case where, for each class of shares of the capital stock of the original corporation of which shares are held by the shareholder immediately before the division, new shares are received at the particular time by shareholders of that class on a pro rata basis in respect of all the shares (referred to in this subsection as the "original shares") of that class

(A) at the particular time, the original corporation is deemed to have distributed, and the shareholder is deemed to have received, as a dividend in kind in respect of the original shares, the new shares acquired by the shareholder at the particular time, and

(B) the amount of the dividend in kind received by the shareholder in respect of an original share is deemed to be equal to the fair market value, immediately after the particular time, of the new shares acquired by the shareholder at the particular time in respect of the original share, and

(ii) in any case where subparagraph (i) does not apply, the original corporation is deemed, at the particular time, to have conferred a benefit on the shareholder equal to the total fair market value, at that time, of the new shares acquired by the shareholder as a consequence of the division;

(*b*) any gain or loss of the original corporation from a distribution of the new shares as a consequence of the division is deemed to be nil; and

(*c*) each property of the original corporation that becomes at any time (referred to in this paragraph as the "disposition time") property of the new corporation as a consequence of the division is deemed to be

(i) disposed of by the original corporation immediately before the disposition time for proceeds of disposition equal to the property's fair market value, and

(ii) acquired by the new corporation at the disposition time at a cost equal to the amount determined under subparagraph (i) to be the original corporation's proceeds of disposition.

History: S. 15(1.5) was added by S.C. 2018, c. 27, s. 2(2), applicable in respect of divisions that occur after October 23, 2012.

Related Regulations: 5907(1), "designated person or partnership"; 5907(2.011).

▶ 15(2) ◀

(2) Shareholder debt. Where a person (other than a corporation resident in Canada) or a partnership (other than a partnership each member of which is a corporation resident in Canada) is

(*a*) a shareholder of a particular corporation,

(*b*) connected with a shareholder of a particular corporation, or (*c*) a member of a partnership, or a beneficiary of a trust, that is a shareholder of a particular corporation

and the person or partnership has in a taxation year received a loan from or become indebted to (otherwise than by way of a pertinent loan or indebtedness) the particular corporation, any other corporation related to the particular corporation or a partnership of which the particular corporation or a corporation related to the particular corporation is a member, the amount of the loan or indebtedness is included in computing the income for the year of the person or partnership.

Editorial Note: Subsection 15(2) is designed to prevent the effective distribution of funds of a corporation to or for the benefit of its shareholders free of tax through the use of loans or other transactions where the shareholder becomes indebted to a corporation. The provision can also apply to a loan or debt of a "connected shareholder" (see s. 15(2.1)). It can also apply to a loan received or debt incurred by a member of a partnership or a beneficiary of a trust, that is a shareholder of the corporation.

Where the provision applies, the principal amount of the loan or debt is included in income. In such case, the imputed interest benefit provisions of s. 80.4(2) do not apply.

Exceptions: The provision does not apply to a loan received or debt incurred by a corporation resident in Canada or a partnership, each member of which is a corporation resident in Canada. The provision also does not apply to indebtedness between non-resident persons.

Furthermore, there are several explicit exceptions (see s. 15(2.3)–(2.6)).

The employee exception in s. 15(2.4) applies to a "specified employee" only if the loan is used for one of the purposes set out in paragraphs (*b*) through (*d*) therein. A "specified employee" means an employee of the creditor who is a specified shareholder of the creditor, or an employee who does not deal at arm's length with the creditor. A "specified shareholder" of the creditor generally means a taxpayer who owns 10% or more of the issued shares of any class of the capital stock of the creditor or any other corporation that is related to the creditor. For these purposes, a taxpayer is deemed to own each share owned by a person with whom the taxpayer does not deal at arm's length, and there are "look-through" rules for beneficiaries of trusts and members of partnerships.

The repayment exception in s. 15(2.6) does not apply if the repayment was made as part of a series of loans or other transactions and repayments. For these purposes, *bona fide* repayments of shareholder loans that result from the payment of dividends, salaries, or bonuses, are not part of a series of loans or other transactions and repayments (see *Uphill Holdings Ltd., et al v. M.N.R.,* 93 DTC 148 (T.C.C.), and paragraph 29 of Interpretation Bulletin IT-119R4 (archived, as it doesn't meet current government web standards); see also MacPherson, Shareholder Loans: Meaning of "Series of Loans and Repayments", *Tax for the Owner Manager,* (2013) vol. 13, no. 1 , 6-7).

For the Canada Revenue Agency's ("CRA") views on the "ordinary money lending business" exception in s. 15(2.3), see CRA Document No. 2003-0047891E5, January 23, 2004.

If one of the exceptions to s. 15(2) applies, a low- or no-interest shareholder loan may be subject to the imputed interest provisions of s. 80.4(2).

Non-residents: Subsection 15(2) can apply if the corporate lender is non-resident if the debtor is resident in Canada (other than a Canadian resident corporation or partnership, each member of which is Canadian resident). It can also apply to a non-resident shareholder of a Canadian resident corporation, in which case the debt is treated as a dividend for Part XIII withholding tax purposes (s. 214(3)(*a*)).

Repayment: In the year that part or all of the loan is repaid, a deduction is allowed for the amount of the repayment under s. 20(1)(*j*). The deduction is not allowed if the repayment was made as part of a series of loans or other transactions and repayments. For these purposes, *bona fide* repayments of shareholder loans that result from the payment of dividends, salaries, or bonuses are not part of a series of loans or other transactions and repayments (see the discussion above on s. 15(2.6)).

The CRA will generally accept that a loan or indebtedness has been repaid by set-off if the intention to do so is evidenced in the relevant books and records, including any contracts or agreements between the parties and the accounting records of the parties (CRA Document No. 2013-0508141C6).

If a shareholder debt owed to a creditor corporation is assigned by that corporation as payment of another debt that it owes to another related corporation, the assignment does not constitute repayment of the first debt (CRA Document No. 2013-0482991E5).

History: S. 15(2), the portion after paragraph (*c*) was replaced by S.C. 2012, c. 31, s. 5(2), applicable to loans received and indebtedness incurred after March 28, 2012. S. 15(2), the portion after paragraph (*c*) formerly read:

and the person or partnership has in a taxation year received a loan from or has become indebted to the particular corporation, any other corporation related to the particular corporation or a partnership of which the particular corporation or a corporation related to the particular corporation is a member, the amount of the loan or indebtedness is included in computing the income for the year of the person or partnership.

Related Sections: S. 17(1) Amount owing by non-resident; s. 17(7) Exception; s. 20(1)(*j*) Repayment of loan by shareholder; s. 80.4(2) Loan or debt by virtue of shareholding; s. 80.4(3) Where ss. (1) and (2) do not apply; s. 214(3)(*a*) Deemed payments; s. 227(6.1) Repayment of non-resident shareholder loan; s. 248(10) Series of transactions; s. 251(2) Definition of "related persons".

Canadian Tax Foundation: Bonanno and Vercillo, *Related Party Loan Arrangements,* 2018 Ontario Tax Conference 11:1–21; Hennessey, *Another Reason To Avoid Shareholder Benefits,* 2016 Canadian Tax Focus 6(1):3–4; Gill, *Fixing Mistakes: Rectification & Rescission,* 2014 British Columbia Tax Conference 9:1–11; Morphy, *The Modern Approach to Statutory Interpretation, Applied to the Section 15 Anomaly in Foreign Affiliate Financing,* 2013 Canadian Tax Journal 2:367–385; MacPherson, *Shareholder Loans: Meaning of "Series of Loans and Repayments",* 2013 Tax for the Owner-Manager 13(1):6–7; Tremblay and Wilkie, *The Canadian Triangle: Tax Policy Reflections on the Uneasy Interaction of 15(2), 17 and 95(2),* 2002 Conference Report 18:1–16; Smith, *15(2) Anomaly Exposed,* 2002 Canadian Tax Highlights 10(5):36; Robinson and Folkins, *Shareholder Loans to Employees,* 2002 Tax for the Owner-Manager 2(3):18–19; Truster, *Secrets of Subsection 15(2),* 2001 Tax for the Owner-Manager 1(3):15–16; Belley and Bienvenue, *Taxable Shareholder Benefits: Sailing Close to the Wind under Section 15,* 2001 Tax for the Owner-Manager 1(1):2–3; Teltscher, *Loans to Shareholder-Employees: Salary Versus Dividends,* 1996 Conference Report 53:1–74.

Tax Topics: No. 2073, Upstream Loan Rules — Why Now?.

Forms: T2 SCH 11 — Transactions with Shareholders, Officers, or Employees.

Interpretation Bulletins: *Primary* — IT-119R4 Debts of shareholders and certain persons connected with shareholders.

Tax Window Files: Transitioning from 15(2) to a PLOI, *October 2, 2014,* CRA Document No. 2013-0506551E5; Reduction of PUC, *Technical Interpretation, International and Trusts Division, February 28, 2008,* CRA Document No. 2008-0266181I7; Non-Shareholder Employee at the Time of a Loan, *Technical Interpretation, Business and Partnerships Division, September 7, 2006,* CRA Document No. 2006-0172841E5; Shareholder Loan to Acquire Home, *Technical Interpretation, Business and Partnerships Division, February 20, 2006,* CRA Document No. 2005-0159061E5; Loans to Related Foreign Corporations, *Technical Interpretation, International and Trusts Division, February 8, 2006,* CRA Document No. 2004-0064811E5; Assignment of Shareholder Loan, *Technical Interpretation, Business and Partnerships Division, June 21, 2005,* CRA Document No. 2005-0129551E5. Assignment of loan did not affect paragraph 15(2.4)(*b*) exception to shareholder loan rules; Home Purchase Loan by Company to Shareholder-Employee, *Technical Interpretation, Business and Partnerships Division, October 27, 2004,* CRA Document No. 2004-0088581E5. Home purchase loan made to sole employee who was also president and sole shareholder; whether paragraph 15(2.4)(*b*) exception could apply; Loan by a Corporation to a Partnership, *Financial Services Round Table of the 2004 Conference of the Fiscal and Financial Planning Association, Question 4, October 8, 2004,* CRA Document No. 2004-0088411C6; Novation of Debt — Shareholder Loan, *Technical Interpretation, Business and Partnerships Division, June 1, 2004,* CRA Document No. 2004-0077171I7. Issuance of a new promissory note, which replaces an existing promissory note, results in a new loan subject to subsection 15(2); Shareholder Loans — Loan to Shareholder's Adult Child, *Technical Interpretation, Business and Partnerships Division, March 23, 2004,* CRA Document No. 2003-0049031E5; Loan to Shareholder — Assignment of Debt, *Technical Interpretation, International and Trusts Division, March 22, 2004,* CRA Document No. 2004-0062761E5. Subsection 15(2) applies where a shareholder of a corporation initially owes a debt to someone other than the corporation and the debt is later assigned to the corporation; Housing Loan by a Corporation to its Sole Shareholder, *Technical Interpretation, Business and Partnerships Division, February 26, 2004,* CRA Document No. 2003-0045471E5. Housing loan made to sole shareholder included under subsection 15(2) and not eligible for paragraph 15(2)(*b*) exception; Lending Money in the Ordinary Course of Business, *Technical Interpretation, Financial Industries Division, January 23, 2004,* CRA Document No. 2003-0047891E5. General comments regarding the subsection 15(2.3) exception, and in particular, whether the corporation made a loan in the ordinary course of its ordinary business of lending money.

Cases: The taxpayers were seeking rectification of articles of incorporation that failed to give the directors sufficient authority to determine the redemption amounts for shares the corporation had issued either as dividends or consideration. That error resulted in the taxpayer being reassessed under the shareholder benefit provisions to have over $17 million included in his income. It was clear there was a drafting error and the articles did not reflect the intent of the parties. The application for rectification was granted. *Lau v. Canada (Attorney General)*, 2015 DTC 5020 (B.C.S.C.)

The taxpayers were unable to avoid the unpaid shareholder loan income inclusion provisions of s. 15(2). Their application for rectification of their restructuring arrangements was merely an attempt at retroactive tax planning and could not be approved. *Graymar Equipment (2008) Inc. v. Canada (AG)*, 2014 DTC 5051 (Alta.Q.B.)

The Act does not require a provision for repayment of a shareholder's loan on a certain date. All that is required is simply an arrangement for payment within a reasonable time. In addition, any *bona fide* repayment arrangement does not have to be in writing, but certainly does have to be contractually binding. *Davidson v. The Queen*, 99 DTC 933 (T.C.C.)

When the five-year promissory note dated January 10, 1986 on the strength of which a corporation's shareholder borrowed $100,000 to purchase a house provided for annual capital repayments of $20,000 and no capital payments were made until 1992, it still could be said that *at the time of the loan* there were *bona fide* arrangements made for its repayments within a reasonable time. *Kalousdian v. The Queen*, 94 DTC 1722 (T.C.C.)

JK, who was related to the taxpayers, sold them shares in exchange of demand promissory notes which he assigned to a corporation controlled by him. The amounts of their respective indebtedness to the company were included in their income under s. 15(2) which should not be confined to situations where the indebtedness to the corporation has arisen directly rather than by way of the assignment to it of debt from a third party. *Kwong et al. v. The Queen*, 93 DTC 588 (T.C.C.)

When a corporation caused its Canadian subsidiary, of which the taxpayer was an employee and shareholder, to advance $55,000 to him to be repayable in full if he were to quit or sell his property, this amount was included in his income as a shareholder loan since, pursuant to the arrangement, the loan was not to be reimbursed within a reasonable time. *The Queen v. Silden*, 93 DTC 5362 (F.C.A.), reversing 90 DTC 6576

▶ 15(2.1) ◀

(2.1) Meaning of connected. For the purposes of subsection (2), a person or partnership is connected with a shareholder of a particular corporation if that person or partnership does not deal at arm's length with, or is affiliated with, the shareholder, unless, in the case of a person, that person is

(*a*) a foreign affiliate of the particular corporation; or

(*b*) a foreign affiliate of a person resident in Canada with which the particular corporation does not deal at arm's length.

History: S. 15(2.1), the portion before paragraph (*a*) was replaced by S.C. 2013, c. 34, s. 177(5), applicable in respect of loans made and indebtedness arising after October 31, 2011, and formerly read:

(2.1) *Persons connected with a shareholder.* For the purposes of subsection (2), a person is connected with a shareholder of a particular corporation if that person does not deal at arm's length with the shareholder and if that person is a person other than

Related Sections: S. 15(7) Application of ss. (1), (2) and (5); s. 95(1), "foreign affiliate", s. 251(1) Arm's length.

Tax Window Files: Loans to Related Foreign Corporations, *Technical Interpretation, International and Trusts Division, February 8, 2006*, CRA Document No. 2004-0064811E5; Loan by a Corporation to a Partnership, *Financial Services Round Table of the 2004 Conference of the Fiscal and Financial Planning Association, Question 4, October 8, 2004*, CRA Document No. 2004-0088411C6.

▶ 15(2.11) ◀

(2.11) Pertinent loan or indebtedness. For the purposes of subsection (2) and subject to subsection 17.1(3), "pertinent loan or indebtedness" means a loan received, or an indebtedness incurred, at any time, by a non-resident corporation (in this subsection referred to as the "subject corporation"), or by a partnership of which the subject corporation is, at that time, a member, that is an amount owing to a corporation resident in Canada (in this subsection and subsections (2.12) and (2.14) referred to as the "CRIC") or to a qualifying Canadian partnership in respect of the CRIC and in respect of which amount owing all of the following apply:

(*a*) subsection (2) would, in the absence of this subsection, apply to the amount owing;

(*b*) the amount becomes owing after March 28, 2012;

(*c*) at that time, the CRIC is controlled by a non-resident corporation that

(i) is the subject corporation, or

(ii) does not deal at arm's length with the subject corporation; and

(*d*) either

(i) in the case of an amount owing to the CRIC, the CRIC and a non-resident corporation that controls the CRIC jointly elect in writing under this subparagraph in respect of the amount owing and file the election with the Minister on or before the filing-due date of the CRIC for the taxation year that includes that time, or

(ii) in the case of an amount owing to the qualifying Canadian partnership, all the members of the qualifying Canadian partnership and a non-resident corporation that controls the CRIC jointly elect in writing under this subparagraph in respect of the amount owing and file the election with the Minister on or before the filing-due date of the CRIC for its taxation year in which ends the fiscal period of the qualifying Canadian partnership that includes that time.

Editorial Note: A loan or indebtedness that is a "pertinent loan or indebtedness" ("PLOI") for purposes of s. 15(2.11) is excluded from the application of s. 15(2) and is instead governed by s. 17.1. See the editorial note to s. 17.1. To qualify as a PLOI for purposes of s. 15(2), the requirements of s. 15(2.11) must be met: (i) the amount must be a loan received or an indebtedness incurred, at any time, by a non-resident corporation (the "subject corporation" or a partnership of which a subject corporation is a member) that is owing to a corporation resident in Canada (a "CRIC") or to a qualifying Canadian partnership (as defined in s. 15(2.14)) in respect of the CRIC; (ii) s. 15(2) would ordinarily apply to the amount, absent the application of s. 15(2.11); (iii) the amount became owing after March 28, 2012; (iv) at that time, the CRIC must be controlled by a non-resident corporation that is either the subject corporation or a corporation that does not deal at arm's length with the subject corporation; (v) the CRIC and a non-resident that controls the CRIC jointly elect in writing with the Minister of National Revenue in respect of the amount on or before the CRIC's filing-due date for the year that includes the time that the loan was received or the indebtedness arose.

History: S. 15(2.11) was added by S.C. 2012, c. 31, s. 5(3), applicable to loans received and indebtedness incurred after March 28, 2012. However, any election referred to in paragraph 15(2.11)(*d*) that would otherwise be required to be filed with the Minister of National Revenue on or before the day that is 120 days after December 14, 2012 is deemed to have been filed with the Minister on a timely basis if it is filed with the Minister on or before the day that is 365 days after December 14, 2012.

▶ 15(2.12) ◀

(2.12) Late-filed elections. Where an election referred to in paragraph (2.11)(*d*) was not made on or before the day on or before which the election was required by that paragraph to be made, the election is deemed to have been made on that day if the election is made on or before the day that is three years after that day and the penalty in respect of the election is paid by the CRIC when the election is made.

Editorial Note: Under s. 15(2.12) and (2.13) a late filed election made within three years of the date the election was required to be filed is deemed to have been timely filed provided that the appropriate penalty is paid. The penalty is $100 for each month all or part or which falls in the period between when the election was required to be made and when the election is actually made.

History: S. 15(2.12) was added by S.C. 2012, c. 31, s. 5(3), applicable to loans received and indebtedness incurred after March 28, 2012.

► 15(2.13) ◄

(2.13) Penalty for late-filed election. For the purposes of subsection (2.12), the penalty in respect of an election referred to in that subsection is the amount equal to the product obtained by multiplying $100 by the number of months each of which is a month all or part of which is during the period commencing with the day on or before which the election is required by paragraph (2.11)(*d*) to be made and ending on the day the election is made.

History: S. 15(2.13) was added by S.C. 2012, c. 31, s. 5(3), applicable to loans received and indebtedness incurred after March 28, 2012.

► 15(2.14) ◄

(2.14) Partnerships. For purposes of this subsection, subsection (2.11), section 17.1 and subsection 18(5),

(*a*) a "qualifying Canadian partnership", at any time in respect of a CRIC, means a partnership each member of which is, at that time, the CRIC or another corporation resident in Canada to which the CRIC is, at that time, related; and

(*b*) a person or partnership that is (or is deemed by this paragraph to be) a member of a particular partnership that is a member of another partnership is deemed to be a member of the other partnership.

Editorial Note: S. 15(2.14) defines a "qualifying Canadian partnership" for purposes of the PLOI rules in s. 15(2.11) and s. 17.1. A qualifying Canadian partnership in respect of a CRIC is one in which each member of the partnership is the CRIC or another corporation resident in Canada to which the CRIC is related. A partnership "look through" rule in paragraph 15(2.14)(*b*) provides that a member of a partnership that is itself a member of another partnership is considered to be a member of the other partnership. For example, if "Aco" is a member of "B partnership" and B partnership is a member of "C partnership", Aco will be considered to be a member of C partnership for purposes of determining if C partnership is a qualifying Canadian partnership. The rule provides that any number of partnerships can be looked through to determine whether a particular partnership qualifies.

History: S. 15(2.14), the portion before paragraph (*a*) was replaced by S.C. 2014, c. 39, s. 4(1), applicable to taxation years that end after March 28, 2012, except that, if an election is made by a taxpayer under subsection 49(3) of the *Jobs and Growth Act, 2012* [S.C. 2012, c. 31], this amendment does not apply to taxation years of the taxpayer that end before August 14, 2012. The portion of s. 15(2.14) before paragraph (*a*) formerly read:

(2.14) *Partnerships.* For the purposes of this subsection, subsection (2.11) and section 17.1,

S. 15(2.14) was added by S.C. 2012, c. 31, s. 5(3), applicable to loans received and indebtedness incurred after March 28, 2012.

► 15(2.15) ◄

(2.15) Mergers. For the purposes of subsections (2.11) and (2.14),

(*a*) if there has been an amalgamation to which subsection 87(1) applies, the new corporation referred to in that subsection is deemed to be the same corporation as, and a continuation of, each predecessor corporation referred to in that subsection; and

(*b*) if there has been a winding-up to which subsection 88(1) applies, the parent referred to in that subsection is deemed to be the same corporation as, and a continuation of, the subsidiary referred to in that subsection.

Editorial Note: S. 15(2.15) provides certain continuity rules in the event of certain corporate reorganizations. Generally, s. 15(2.15)(*a*) provides that where there has been a qualifying amalgamation for purposes of s. 87(1) of the Act, the new corporation formed on amalgamation is deemed to be the same as each predecessor corporation for purposes of the PLOI rules. Paragraph 15(2.15)(*b*) provides a parallel rule in the case of a s. 88(1) windup. This rule applies to amalgamations that occur, and windings up that begin, after March 28, 2012.

History: S. 15(2.15) was added by S.C. 2012, c. 31, s. 5(3), applicable to amalgamations that occur, and windings-up that begin, after March 28, 2012.

► 15(2.16) ◄

(2.16) Back-to-back arrangement — application. Subsection (2.17) applies at any time if

(*a*) at that time, a person or partnership (referred to in this subsection and subsections (2.17) to (2.192) as the "intended borrower") has an amount outstanding as or on account of a debt or other obligation to pay an amount (in this subsection and subsections (2.17) to (2.192) referred to as the "shareholder debt") to a person or partnership (in this subsection and subsections (2.17) to (2.192) referred to as the "immediate funder");

(*b*) subsection (2) would not, in the absence of this subsection and subsection (2.17), apply to the shareholder debt;

(*c*) at that time, a funder, in respect of a particular funding arrangement,

(i) has an amount outstanding as or on account of a debt or other obligation to pay an amount (other than a debt or other obligation to pay an amount to which subsection (2) applies or would apply if it were not a "pertinent loan or indebtedness", as defined in subsection (2.11)) to a person or partnership that meets either of the following conditions:

(A) recourse in respect of the debt or other obligation is limited in whole or in part, either immediately or in the future and either absolutely or contingently, to a funding arrangement, or

(B) it can reasonably be concluded that all or a portion of the particular funding arrangement was entered into or was permitted to remain outstanding because

(I) all or a portion of the debt or other obligation was entered into or was permitted to remain outstanding, or

(II) the funder anticipated that all or a portion of the debt or other obligation would become owing or remain outstanding, or

(ii) has a specified right in respect of a particular property that was granted directly or indirectly by a person or partnership and

(A) the existence of the specified right is required under the terms and conditions of the particular funding arrangement, or

(B) it can reasonably be concluded that all or a portion of the particular funding arrangement was entered into, or was permitted to remain in effect, because

(I) the specified right was granted, or

(II) the funder anticipated that the specified right would be granted; and

(*d*) at that time, one or more funders is an ultimate funder.

History: Subsection 15(2.16) was added by S.C. 2016, c. 12, s. 5(1), applicable in respect of

(a) if the immediate funder in respect of a shareholder debt is a debtor, or holder of a specified right, under a funding arrangement under which an ultimate funder is the creditor or the grantor of the specified right,

(i) loans received and indebtedness incurred in respect of the shareholder debt after March 21, 2016, and

(ii) any portion of a particular loan received or indebtedness incurred in respect of the shareholder debt before March 22, 2016 that remains outstanding on that day, as if that portion were a separate loan or indebtedness that was received or incurred, as the case may be, on March 22, 2016 in the same manner and on the same terms as the particular loan or indebtedness; and

(b) in any other case,

(i) loans received and indebtedness incurred after 2016, and

(ii) any portion of a particular loan received or indebtedness incurred before January 1, 2017 that remains outstanding on that day, as if that portion were a separate loan or indebtedness that was received or incurred, as the case may be, on January 1, 2017 in the same manner and on the same terms as the particular loan or indebtedness.

▶ 15(2.17) ◀

(2.17) Back-to-back arrangement — consequences. If this subsection applies at a particular time, then for the purposes of this section and section 80.4, the intended borrower is deemed to receive a loan from each particular ultimate funder at the particular time, the amount of which is equal to the amount determined by the formula

$$A \times B/C - (D - E)$$

where

A is the lesser of

(*a*) the amount outstanding as or on account of the shareholder debt at the particular time, and

(*b*) the total of all amounts, each of which is, at the particular time,

(i) an amount outstanding as or on account of a debt or other obligation that is owed by a funder (other than an ultimate funder) to an ultimate funder under a funding arrangement in respect of the shareholder debt, or

(ii) the fair market value of a particular property in respect of which an ultimate funder has granted a specified right to a funder (other than an ultimate funder) under a funding arrangement in respect of the shareholder debt;

B is the total of all amounts, each of which is, at the particular time,

(*a*) an amount outstanding as or on account of a debt or other obligation that is owed by a funder (other than an ultimate funder) to the particular ultimate funder under a funding arrangement in respect of the shareholder debt, or

(*b*) the fair market value of a particular property in respect of which the particular ultimate funder has granted a specified right to a funder (other than an ultimate funder) under a funding arrangement in respect of the shareholder debt;

C is the total amount determined under paragraph (*b*) of the description of A;

D is the total of all amounts, each of which is, in respect of the shareholder debt, an amount that the intended borrower has been deemed by this subsection to have received from the particular ultimate funder as a loan at any time before the particular time; and

E is the total amount of any repayments deemed by subsections (2.19) and (2.191) to have occurred before the particular time, in respect of any deemed loans from the particular ultimate funder that are referred to in the description of D.

History: Subsection 15(2.17) was added by S.C. 2016, c. 12, s. 5(1), applicable in respect of

(a) if the immediate funder in respect of a shareholder debt is a debtor, or holder of a specified right, under a funding arrangement under which an ultimate funder is the creditor or the grantor of the specified right,

(i) loans received and indebtedness incurred in respect of the shareholder debt after March 21, 2016, and

(ii) any portion of a particular loan received or indebtedness incurred in respect of the shareholder debt before March 22, 2016 that remains outstanding on that day, as if that portion were a separate loan or indebtedness that was received or incurred, as the case may be, on March 22, 2016 in the same manner and on the same terms as the particular loan or indebtedness; and

(b) in any other case,

(i) loans received and indebtedness incurred after 2016, and

(ii) any portion of a particular loan received or indebtedness incurred before January 1, 2017 that remains outstanding on that day, as if that portion were a separate loan or indebtedness that was received or incurred, as the case may be, on January 1, 2017 in the same manner and on the same terms as the particular loan or indebtedness.

▶ 15(2.18) ◀

(2.18) Back-to-back arrangement — conditions for deemed repayment. Subsection (2.19) applies in respect of an intended borrower and a particular ultimate funder at a particular time if

(*a*) prior to the particular time, subsection (2.17) has applied in respect of a shareholder debt to deem one or more loans to have been received by the intended borrower from the particular ultimate funder; and

(*b*) at the particular time,

(i) an amount owing in respect of the shareholder debt is repaid in whole or in part,

(ii) an amount owing in respect of a debt or other obligation owing to the particular ultimate funder by a funder (other than an ultimate funder) under a funding arrangement in respect of the shareholder debt is repaid in whole or in part, or

(iii) either

(A) there is a decrease in the fair market value of a property in respect of which a specified right was granted by the particular ultimate funder to a funder (other than an ultimate funder) under a funding arrangement in respect of the shareholder debt, or

(B) a right described in clause (A) is extinguished.

History: Subsection 15(2.18) was added by S.C. 2016, c. 12, s. 5(1), applicable in respect of

(a) if the immediate funder in respect of a shareholder debt is a debtor, or holder of a specified right, under a funding arrangement under which an ultimate funder is the creditor or the grantor of the specified right,

(i) loans received and indebtedness incurred in respect of the shareholder debt after March 21, 2016, and

(ii) any portion of a particular loan received or indebtedness incurred in respect of the shareholder debt before March 22, 2016 that remains outstanding on that day, as if that portion were a separate loan or indebtedness that was received or incurred, as the case may be, on March 22, 2016 in the same manner and on the same terms as the particular loan or indebtedness; and

(b) in any other case,

(i) loans received and indebtedness incurred after 2016, and

(ii) any portion of a particular loan received or indebtedness incurred before January 1, 2017 that remains outstanding on that day, as if that portion were a separate loan or indebtedness that was received or incurred, as the case may be, on January 1, 2017 in the same manner and on the same terms as the particular loan or indebtedness.

▶ 15(2.19) ◀

(2.19) Back-to-back arrangement — deemed repayment. If this subsection applies in respect of an intended borrower and a particular ultimate funder at a particular time,

(*a*) the intended borrower is deemed, for the purposes of this section, paragraph 20(1)(*j*), section 80.4 and subsection 227(6.1), to repay, in whole or in part, one or more of the deemed loans referred to in paragraph (2.18)(*a*) at the particular time; and

(*b*) the total amount of the deemed repayments referred to in paragraph (*a*) is to be determined by the following formula:

$$A - B - C$$

where

A is the total of all amounts, each of which is the amount of a loan deemed by subsection (2.17) to have been received, at any time before the particular time, by the intended borrower from the particular ultimate funder in respect of the shareholder debt,

B is the total of all amounts deemed by this subsection to have been repaid, at any time before the particular time, by the intended borrower in respect of any loans referred to in the description of A, and

C is the amount determined by the formula

$$D \times E/F$$

where

D is the lesser of

(i) the amount outstanding as or on account of the shareholder debt, immediately after the particular time, and

(ii) the total of all amounts, each of which is, immediately after the particular time,

(A) an amount outstanding as or on account of a debt or other obligation that is owed by a funder (other than an ultimate funder) to an ultimate funder under a funding arrangement in respect of the shareholder debt, or

(B) the fair market value of a particular property in respect of which an ultimate funder has granted a specified right to a funder (other than an ultimate funder) under a funding arrangement in respect of the shareholder debt,

E is the total of all amounts, each of which is, immediately after the particular time

(i) an amount outstanding as or on account of a debt or other obligation that is owed by a funder (other than an ultimate funder) to the particular ultimate funder under a funding arrangement in respect of the shareholder debt, or

(ii) the fair market value of a particular property in respect of which the particular ultimate funder has granted a specified right to a funder (other than an ultimate funder) under a funding arrangement in respect of the shareholder debt, and

F is the amount determined under subparagraph (ii) in the description of D.

History: Subsection 15(2.19) was added by S.C. 2016, c. 12, s. 5(1), applicable in respect of

(a) if the immediate funder in respect of a shareholder debt is a debtor, or holder of a specified right, under a funding arrangement under which an ultimate funder is the creditor or the grantor of the specified right,

(i) loans received and indebtedness incurred in respect of the shareholder debt after March 21, 2016, and

(ii) any portion of a particular loan received or indebtedness incurred in respect of the shareholder debt before March 22, 2016 that remains outstanding on that day, as if that portion were a separate loan or indebtedness that was received or incurred, as the case may be, on March 22, 2016 in the same manner and on the same terms as the particular loan or indebtedness; and

(b) in any other case,

(i) loans received and indebtedness incurred after 2016, and

(ii) any portion of a particular loan received or indebtedness incurred before January 1, 2017 that remains outstanding on that day, as if that portion were a separate loan or indebtedness that was received or incurred, as the case may be, on January 1, 2017 in the same manner and on the same terms as the particular loan or indebtedness.

▶ 15(2.191) ◀

(2.191) Negative amounts. If, in the absence of section 257, the formula in subsection (2.17) would result in a negative amount at a particular time,

(*a*) the intended borrower is deemed, for the purposes of this section, paragraph 20(1)(*j*), section 80.4 and subsection 227(6.1), to repay, in whole or in part, one or more of the loans deemed by subsection (2.17) to have been received by the intended borrower from the particular ultimate funder before the particular time; and

(*b*) the total amount of the deemed repayments referred to in paragraph (*a*) is equal to the absolute value of that negative amount.

History: Subsection 15(2.191) was added by S.C. 2016, c. 12, s. 5(1), applicable in respect of

(a) if the immediate funder in respect of a shareholder debt is a debtor, or holder of a specified right, under a funding arrangement under which an ultimate funder is the creditor or the grantor of the specified right,

(i) loans received and indebtedness incurred in respect of the shareholder debt after March 21, 2016, and

(ii) any portion of a particular loan received or indebtedness incurred in respect of the shareholder debt before March 22, 2016 that remains outstanding on that day, as if that portion were a separate loan or indebtedness that was received or incurred, as the case may be, on March 22, 2016 in the same manner and on the same terms as the particular loan or indebtedness; and

(b) in any other case,

(i) loans received and indebtedness incurred after 2016, and

(ii) any portion of a particular loan received or indebtedness incurred before January 1, 2017 that remains outstanding on that day, as if that portion were a separate loan or indebtedness that was received or incurred, as the case may be, on January 1, 2017 in the same manner and on the same terms as the particular loan or indebtedness.

▶ 15(2.192) ◀

(2.192) Back-to-back arrangement — definitions. The following definitions apply in this subsection and subsections (2.16) to (2.191).

"funder" —"funder", in respect of a funding arrangement, means

(*a*) if the funding arrangement is described in paragraph (*a*) of the definition "funding arrangement", the immediate funder;

(*b*) if the funding arrangement is described in paragraph (*b*) of the definition "funding arrangement", the creditor in respect of the debt or other obligation or the grantor of the specified right, as the case may be; and

(*c*) a person or partnership that does not deal at arm's length with a person or partnership referred to in paragraph (*a*) or (*b*).

"funding arrangement" —"funding arrangement" means

(*a*) the shareholder debt; and

(*b*) each debt or other obligation or specified right, owing by or granted to a funder, in respect of a particular funding arrangement, if the debt or other obligation or specified right meets the conditions in subparagraph (2.16)(*c*)(i) or (ii) in respect of a funding arrangement.

"specified right" —"specified right" has the same meaning as in subsection 18(5).

"ultimate funder" —"ultimate funder" means a funder, if subsection (2) would apply to the shareholder debt if the creditor under the shareholder debt were the funder instead of the immediate funder.

History: Subsection 15(2.192) was added by S.C. 2016, c. 12, s. 5(1), applicable in respect of

(a) if the immediate funder in respect of a shareholder debt is a debtor, or holder of a specified right, under a funding arrangement under which an ultimate funder is the creditor or the grantor of the specified right,

(i) loans received and indebtedness incurred in respect of the shareholder debt after March 21, 2016, and

(ii) any portion of a particular loan received or indebtedness incurred in respect of the shareholder debt before March 22, 2016 that remains outstanding on that day, as if that portion were a separate loan or indebtedness that was received or incurred, as the case may be, on March 22, 2016 in the same manner and on the same terms as the particular loan or indebtedness; and

(b) in any other case,

(i) loans received and indebtedness incurred after 2016, and

(ii) any portion of a particular loan received or indebtedness incurred before January 1, 2017 that remains outstanding on that day, as if that portion were a separate loan or indebtedness that was received or incurred, as the case may be, on January 1, 2017 in the same manner and on the same terms as the particular loan or indebtedness.

▶ 15(2.2) ◀

(2.2) When s. 15(2) not to apply — non-resident persons. Subsection (2) does not apply to indebtedness between non-resident persons.

▶ 15(2.3) ◀

(2.3) When s. 15(2) not to apply — ordinary lending business. Subsection (2) does not apply to a debt that arose in the ordinary course of the creditor's business or a loan made in the ordinary course of the lender's ordinary business of lending money where, at the time the indebtedness arose or the loan was made, *bona fide* arrangements were made for repayment of the debt or loan within a reasonable time.

Tax Window Files: Loans to Related Foreign Corporations, *Technical Interpretation, International and Trusts Division, February 8, 2006*, CRA Document No. 2004-0064811E5; Application of Subsection 15(2.3), *Technical Interpretation, Financial Industries Division, January 23, 2004*, CRA Document No. 2003-0047891E5.

▶ 15(2.4) ◀

(2.4) When s. 15(2) not to apply — certain employees. Subsection (2) does not apply to a loan made or a debt that arose

(*a*) in respect of an individual who is an employee of the lender or creditor but not a specified employee of the lender or creditor,

(*b*) in respect of an individual who is an employee of the lender or creditor or who is the spouse or common-law partner of an employee of the lender or creditor to enable or assist the individual to acquire a dwelling or a share of the capital stock of a cooperative housing corporation acquired for the sole purpose of acquiring the right to inhabit a dwelling owned by the corporation, where the dwelling is for the individual's habitation,

(*c*) where the lender or creditor is a particular corporation, in respect of an employee of the particular corporation or of another corporation that is related to the particular corporation, to enable or assist the employee to acquire from the particular corporation, or from another corporation related to the particular corporation, previously unissued fully paid shares of the capital stock of the particular corporation or the related corporation, as the case may be, to be held by the employee for the employee's own benefit, or

(*d*) in respect of an employee of the lender or creditor to enable or assist the employee to acquire a motor vehicle to be used by the employee in the performance of the duties of the employee's office or employment,

where

(*e*) it is reasonable to conclude that the employee or the employee's spouse or common-law partner received the loan, or became indebted, because of the employee's employment and not because of any person's share-holdings, and

(*f*) at the time the loan was made or the debt was incurred, *bona fide* arrangements were made for repayment of the loan or debt within a reasonable time.

Editorial Note: The exception in paragraph (*a*) applies only to employees who are not specified employees while the exceptions in paragraphs (*b*) through (*d*) can apply to any employee. "Specified employee" is defined in s. 248(1) and generally means an employee who owns at least 10% of the shares of a class of the capital stock of the employer corporation or any related corporation (see also the deeming rules in the definition of "specified shareholder") or who is non-arm's length with the corporation. See s. 15(2.7) regarding employees of a partnership.

Related Sections: S. 248(1), "specified employee"; s. 251(2) Definition of "related persons".

Canadian Petroleum Tax Journal: Attracting and Retaining Executives and Employees with Tax-Efficient Incentives, Julie Y. Lee, 2001, Vol. 14, No. 1.

Tax Window Files: Shareholder Loan to Acquire Home, *Technical Interpretation, Business and Partnerships Division, February 20, 2006*, CRA Document No. 2005-0159061E5; Assignment of Shareholder Loan, *Technical Interpretation, Business and Partnerships Division, June 21, 2005*, CRA Document No. 2005-0129551E5. Assignment of loan did not affect paragraph 15(2.4)(*b*) exception to shareholder loan rules; Home Purchase Loan by Company to Shareholder-Employee, *Technical Interpretation, Business and Partnerships Division, October 27, 2004*, CRA Document No. 2004-0088581E5. Home purchase loan made to sole employee who was also president and sole shareholder; whether paragraph 15(2.4)(*b*) exception could apply.

Cases: The loan was consistent with one being made to a shareholder and it would be unreasonable to conclude that it was an employee loan under s. 15(2.4). *Mast v. The Queen*, 2014 DTC 1001 (T.C.C.)

▶ 15(2.5) ◀

(2.5) When s. 15(2) not to apply — certain trusts. Subsection (2) does not apply to a loan made or a debt that arose in respect of a trust where

(*a*) the lender or creditor is a private corporation;

(*b*) the corporation is the settlor and sole beneficiary of the trust;

(*c*) the sole purpose of the trust is to facilitate the purchase and sale of the shares of the corporation, or of another corporation related to the corporation, for an amount equal to their fair market value at the time of the purchase or sale, as the case may be, from or to the employees of the corporation or of the related corporation (other than employees who are specified employees of the corporation or of another corporation related to the corporation), as the case may be; and

(*d*) at the time the loan was made or the debt incurred, *bona fide* arrangements were made for repayment of the loan or debt within a reasonable time.

▶ 15(2.6) ◀

(2.6) When s. 15(2) not to apply — repayment within one year. Subsection (2) does not apply to a loan or an indebtedness repaid within one year after the end of the taxation year of the lender or creditor in which the loan was made or the indebtedness arose, where it is established, by subsequent events or otherwise, that the repayment was not part of a series of loans or other transactions and repayments.

Editorial Note: *Bona fide* repayments of shareholder loans that result from the payment of dividends, salaries, or bonuses, are not part of a series of loans or other transactions and repayments for these purposes; see paragraph 29 of IT-119R4 (archived, as it doesn't meet current government web standards).

▶ 15(2.7) ◀

(2.7) Employee of partnership. For the purpose of this section, an individual who is an employee of a partnership is deemed to be a specified employee of the partnership where the individual is a specified shareholder of one or more corporations that, in total, are entitled, directly or indirectly, to a share of any income or loss of the partnership, which share is not less than 10% of the income or loss.

Related Sections: S. 248(1), "specified shareholder".

▶ 15(3) ◀

(3) Interest or dividend on income bond or debenture. An amount paid as interest or a dividend by a corporation resident in Canada to a taxpayer in respect of an income bond or income debenture shall be deemed to have been paid by the corporation and received by the taxpayer as a dividend on a share of the capital stock of the corporation, unless the corporation is entitled to deduct the amount so paid in computing its income.

Related Sections: S. 15.1 Interest on small business development bonds; s. 18(1)(*g*) Payments on income bonds; s. 112(2.1) Where no deduction permitted; s. 248(1), "income bond"; s. 258 Deemed dividend.

▶ 15(4) ◀

(4) Idem, where corporation not resident. An amount paid as interest or a dividend by a corporation not resident in Canada to a taxpayer in respect of an income bond or income debenture shall be deemed to have been received by the taxpayer as a dividend on a share of the capital stock of the corporation unless the amount so paid was, under the laws of the country in which the corporation was resident, deductible in computing the amount for the year on which the corporation was liable to pay income or profits tax imposed by the government of that country.

Related Sections: S. 15.1 Interest on small business development bonds; s. 18(1)(*g*) Payments on income bonds; s. 112(2.2) Guaranteed shares; s. 248(1), "income bond"; s. 258 Deemed dividend.

▶ 15(5) ◀

(5) Automobile benefit. For the purposes of subsection (1), the value of the benefit to be included in computing a shareholder's income for a taxation year with respect to an automobile made available to the shareholder, or a person related to the shareholder, by a corporation shall (except where an amount is determined under subparagraph 6(1)(*e*)(i) in respect of the automobile in computing the shareholder's income for the year) be computed on the assumption that subsections 6(1), (1.1), (2) and (7) apply, with such modifications as the circumstances require, and as though the references therein to "the employer of the taxpayer", "the taxpayer's employer" and "the employer" were read as "the corporation".

Editorial Note: The amount of the shareholder automobile benefit is computed by reference to the "standby charge" otherwise applicable to employee automobile benefits; see especially s. 6(1)(*e*) and s. 6(2).

Related Regulations: 200(4).

Interpretation Bulletins: *Secondary* — IT-63R5 Benefits, including standby charge for an automobile, from the personal use of a motor vehicle supplied by an employer — After 1992.

Tax Window Files: Automobile Used by Shareholder's Spouse, *Technical Interpretation, Business and Partnerships Division, January 4, 2007*, CRA Document No. 2006-0187051E5; Shareholder's Use of Automobile in Corporate Activity, *APFF Conference 2004, Question 18, October 8, 2004*, CRA Document No. 2004-0086861C6.

▶ 15(6) ◀

(6) Application of ss. 6(2) — (Repealed by S.C. 1980-81-82-83, c. 140, s. 7(4).)

▶ 15(7) ◀

(7) Application of ss. (1), (2) and (5). For greater certainty, subsections (1), (2) and (5) are applicable in computing, for the purposes of this Part, the income of a shareholder or of a person or partnership whether or not the corporation, or the lender or creditor, as the case may be, was resident or carried on business in Canada.

Interpretation Bulletins: *Secondary* — IT-119R4 Debts of shareholders, certain persons connected with shareholders, etc; IT-432R2 Benefits conferred on shareholders.

▶ 15(8) ◀

(8) Where s. (2) does not apply — (Repealed by S.C. 1998, c. 19, s. 75(4).)

▶ 15(9) ◀

(9) Deemed benefit to shareholder by corporation. Where an amount in respect of a loan or debt is deemed by section 80.4 to be a benefit received by a person or partnership in a taxation year, the amount is deemed for the purpose of subsection (1) to be a benefit conferred in the year on a shareholder, unless subsection 6(9) or paragraph 12(1)(*w*) applies to the amount.

Editorial Note: The benefit under s. 80.4 is based on the prescribed rates of interest (Regulation 4301) in effect during the period of the loan or debt. The deemed amount is deductible by virtue of s. 80.5 to the extent that the loan is used for income-earning purposes.

Related Regulations: Part II.

Related Sections: S. 80.5 Deemed interest.

Interpretation Bulletins: *Secondary* — IT-421R2 Benefits to Individuals, Corporations and Shareholders from Loans or Debt.

SECTION 15.1: Interest on small business development bonds

▶ 15.1(1) ◀

(1) Interest on small business development bonds. Any amount received by a taxpayer as or on account of interest on a small business development bond shall, except for the purposes of Part IV, be deemed to have been received as a taxable dividend.

Related Sections: S. 15(3) Interest or dividend on income bond or debenture; s. 15(4) Idem, where corporation not resident; s. 18(1)(*g*) Payments on income bonds; s. 89(1) Capital dividend account; s. 248(1), "income bond", "taxable dividend".

▶ 15.1(2) ◀

(2) Rules for small business development bonds. Where a corporation (in this section referred to as the "issuer") has issued an obligation that is at any time a small business development bond, notwithstanding any other provision of this Act,

(*a*) in computing the issuer's income for a taxation year, no deduction shall be made in respect of any amount paid or payable (depending on the method regularly followed in computing the issuer's income) as or on account of interest on the obligation in respect of a period that includes that time;

(*b*) except for the purpose of subsection 129(1), to the extent that any amount paid by the issuer as or on account of interest on the obligation is not allowed as a deduction because of paragraph (*a*), it shall, when paid, be deemed to have been paid as a taxable dividend; and

(*c*) except for the purposes of paragraph 125(1)(*b*), the issuer's taxable income for any taxation year that includes a period throughout which the obligation was a small business development bond but

(i) the issuer was not an eligible small business corporation, or

(ii) all or substantially all of the proceeds from the issue of the obligation cannot reasonably be regarded as having been used by the issuer or a corporation with which it was not dealing at arm's length in the financing of an active business carried on in Canada immediately before the obligation was issued

shall be deemed to be an amount equal to the total of

(iii) the amount paid or payable (depending on the method regularly followed in computing the issuer's income) as or on account of interest on the obligation in respect of that period, and

(iv) the issuer's taxable income otherwise determined for the year.

Related Sections: S. 15.1(3), "small business development bond"; s. 15.1(4) Money borrowed; s. 15.1(6) Disqualification; s. 125(1) Small business deduction; s. 125(7), "active business carried on by a corporation"; s. 129(1) Dividend refund to private corporation; s. 143(1)(*m*) Communal organizations; s. 248(1), "active business", "taxable income", "taxable dividend"; s. 249(1) Definition of "taxation year"; s. 255 Canada.

▶ 15.1(3) ◀

(3) Definitions. In this section,

"eligible small business corporation" —"eligible small business corporation" at any time means a taxable Canadian corporation that at that time is

(*a*) a small business corporation, or

(*b*) a cooperative corporation (within the meaning assigned by subsection 136(2)) all or substantially all of the assets of which are used in an active business carried on by it in Canada;

Related Sections: S. 89(1), "taxable Canadian corporation"; s. 136(2) Definition of "cooperative corporation"; s. 248(1), "active business", "small business corporation", "taxable Canadian corporation".

"joint election" —"joint election" means an election that is made in prescribed form, containing prescribed information, jointly by the issuer of an obligation and the person who is the holder of the obligation at the time of the election, that is filed with the Minister by the holder, and in which the holder and the issuer elect that this section apply to the obligation;

Related Sections: S. 248(1), "prescribed".

"majority interest partner" — (Repealed by S.C. 1998, c. 19, s. 76(1).)

"property used for specified purposes" — (Repealed by S.C. 1994, c. 7, Sched. VIII, s. 6(1).)

"qualifying debt obligation" —"qualifying debt obligation" of a corporation at a particular time means an obligation that is a bond, debenture, bill, note, mortgage, hypothecary claim or similar obligation issued after February 25, 1992 and before 1995,

(*a*) the principal amount of which is not less than $10,000 or more than $500,000,

(*b*) that is issued for a term of not more than 5 years and, except in the event of a failure or default under the terms or conditions of the obligation, not less than one year, and

(*c*) that was issued not more than 5 years before the particular time,

if the obligation is issued by the corporation

(*d*) as part of a proposal to, or an arrangement with, its creditors that has been approved by a court under the *Bankruptcy and Insolvency Act*, (*e*) at a time when all or substantially all of its assets are under the control of a receiver, receiver-manager, sequestrator or trustee in bankruptcy, or

(*f*) at a time when, because of financial difficulty, the corporation is in default, or could reasonably be expected to default, on a debt held by a person with whom the corporation was dealing at arm's length and the obligation is issued, in whole or in part, directly or indirectly in exchange or substitution for that debt;

Related Sections: S. 248(1), "corporation", "principal amount".

"small business development bond" —"small business development bond" at any time means

(*a*) an obligation that is at that time a qualifying debt obligation issued after 1981 and before 1988 by a Canadian-controlled private corporation in respect of which a joint election was made within 90 days after the later of its issue date and March 30, 1983,

(*b*) an obligation that is at that time a qualifying debt obligation issued after February 25, 1992 by a Canadian-controlled private corporation in respect of which a joint election was made within 90 days after its issue date, or

(*c*) an obligation that is at that time a qualifying debt obligation issued by a Canadian-controlled private corporation if

(i) it is reasonable to consider that the corporation and the holder of the obligation intended that this section apply to the obligation, having regard to such factors as may be relevant, including the rate of interest stipulated under the terms of the obligation and the manner in which the corporation and the holder have treated the obligation for the purposes of this Act, and

(ii) the holder files with the Minister a joint election in respect of the obligation within 90 days after the date of notification by the Minister that a joint election in respect of the obligation has not been filed.

Related Sections: S. 125(7), "Canadian-controlled private corporation"; s. 248(1), "corporation".

"specified property" — (Repealed by S.C. 1994, c. 7, Sched. VIII, s. 6(1).)

► 15.1(4) ◄

(4) Money borrowed. Notwithstanding any other provision of this Act, an amount paid or payable by a taxpayer pursuant to a legal obligation to pay interest on borrowed money used for the purpose of acquiring a small business development bond shall be deemed to be an amount paid or payable, as the case may be, on borrowed money used for the purpose of earning income from a business or property.

Related Sections: S. 248(1), "borrowed money", "business", "property".

► 15.1(5) ◄

(5) False declaration. Where the Minister establishes that an issuer has knowingly or under circumstances amounting to gross negligence made a false declaration in a joint election in respect of an obligation, the reference in subparagraph (2)(*c*)(iii) to "the amount paid or payable" shall in respect of the obligation be read as a reference to "3 times the amount paid or payable".

Related Sections: S. 15.1(3), "small business development bond"; s. 248(1), "amount".

► 15.1(6) ◄

(6) Disqualification. Where at a particular time an issuer makes a joint election in respect of an obligation and

(*a*) the issuer or any other corporation associated at the time the obligation was issued with the issuer,

(*b*) an individual who controls or is a member of a related group that controls the issuer, or

(*c*) a partnership any member of which, who is a majority interest partner of the partnership, controls, or is a member of a related group that controls, the issuer

had at or before the particular time made a joint election in respect of any small business development bond or small business bond, as the case may be, for the purposes of this section, the issuer shall be deemed not to be an eligible small business corporation in respect of the obligation.

Related Sections: S. 15.1(3), "majority interest partner"; s. 248(1), "corporation", "individual"; s. 251(4) Definitions concerning groups; s. 256(1) Associated corporations.

► 15.1(7) ◄

(7) Exception. Subsection (6) does not apply in respect of an obligation issued at any time where the issue price of the obligation does not exceed the amount, if any, by which

(*a*) $500,000

exceeds

(*b*) the total of all amounts each of which is the principal amount outstanding immediately after that time in respect of

(i) another obligation that is a small business development bond issued by

(A) the issuer, or

(B) a corporation associated with the issuer, or

(ii) a small business bond issued by

(A) an individual who controls, or is a member of a related group that controls, the issuer, or

(B) a partnership any member of which, who is a majority interest partner of the partnership, controls, or is a member of a related group that controls, the issuer.

Related Sections: S. 15.1(3), "majority interest partner"; s. 248(1), "amount", "corporation", "individual", "principal amount"; s. 251(4) Definitions concerning groups; s. 256(1) Associated corporations.

► 15.1(8)-(12) ◄

(8)-(12) [Small business development bonds] — (Repealed by S.C. 1994, c. 7, Sched. VIII, s. 6(1).)

SECTION 15.2: Interest on small business bond

► 15.2(1) ◄

(1) Interest on small business bond. Any amount received by a taxpayer as or on account of interest on a small business bond shall, except for the purposes of Part IV, be deemed to have been received as a taxable dividend from a taxable Canadian corporation.

Related Sections: S. 89(1) Capital dividend account; s. 248(1), "taxable Canadian corporation", "taxable dividend".

▶ 15.2(2) ◀

(2) Rules for small business bonds. Where an individual or a partnership (in this section referred to as the "issuer") has issued an obligation that is at any time a small business bond, notwithstanding any other provision of this Act,

(*a*) in computing the issuer's income for a taxation year, no deduction shall be made in respect of any amount paid or payable (depending on the method regularly followed in computing the issuer's income) as or on account of interest on the bond in respect of a period that includes that time; and

(*b*) for any taxation year that includes a period throughout which the obligation was a small business bond but

(i) the issuer was not an eligible issuer, or

(ii) all or substantially all of the proceeds from the issue of the obligation were not used by the issuer in the financing of an active business carried on by the issuer in Canada immediately before the time of the issue of the obligation,

there shall be added to the tax otherwise payable under this Part by the issuer for that taxation year an amount equal to 29% of the amount of interest paid or payable (depending on the method regularly followed in computing the issuer's income) in respect of the bond for that period.

Related Sections: S. 15.2(5) False declaration; s. 15.2(6) Partnerships; s. 248(1), "active business", "individual"; s. 255 Canada.

▶ 15.2(3) ◀

(3) Definitions. In this section,

"eligible issuer" —"eligible issuer" at any time means

(*a*) an individual (other than a trust) who is resident in Canada and who

(i) has not made a joint election before that time in respect of a small business bond,

(ii) is not a majority interest partner of a partnership that has made a joint election before that time in respect of a small business bond, and

(iii) neither controls nor is a member of a related group that controls

(A) a corporation that has made a joint election before that time in respect of a small business development bond, or

(B) a corporation that is associated with a corporation referred to in clause (A), or

(*b*) a partnership

(i) each member of which is an individual (other than a trust) who is resident in Canada,

(ii) each majority interest partner, if any, of which is an eligible issuer, and

(iii) that has not made a joint election before that time in respect of a small business bond;

Related Sections: S. 15.2(3), "majority interest partner"; s. 104(1) Reference to trust or estate; s. 248(1), "corporation", "individual", "trust"; s. 250(1) Person deemed resident; s. 251(4) Definitions concerning groups; s. 251(5) Control by related groups, options, etc; s. 255 Canada; s. 256(1) Associated corporations.

"joint election" —"joint election" means an election that is made in prescribed form, containing prescribed information, jointly by the issuer of an obligation and the person who is the holder of the obligation at the time of the election, that is filed with the Minister by the holder and in which the holder and the issuer elect that the provisions of this section apply to that obligation;

Related Sections: S. 248(1), "prescribed".

"majority interest partner" — (Repealed by S.C. 1998, c. 19, s. 77(1).)

"qualifying debt obligation" —"qualifying debt obligation" of an issuer at a particular time means an obligation that is a bill, note, mortgage, hypothecary claim or similar obligation issued after February 25, 1992 and before 1995,

(*a*) the principal amount of which is not less than $10,000 or more than $500,000,

(*b*) that is issued for a term of not more than 5 years and, except in the event of a failure or default under the terms or conditions of the obligation, not less than one year, and

(*c*) that was issued not more than 5 years before the particular time,

if the obligation is issued

(*d*) as part of a proposal to, or an arrangement with, the issuer's creditors that has been approved by a court under the *Bankruptcy and Insolvency Act*,

(*e*) at a time when all or substantially all of the issuer's assets are under the control of a receiver, receiver-manager, sequestrator or trustee in bankruptcy, or

(*f*) at a time when, because of financial difficulty, the issuer is in default, or could reasonably be expected to default, on a debt incurred in the course of the issuer's business and held by a person with whom the issuer was dealing at arm's length or, where the issuer is a partnership, by a person with whom each member of the partnership was dealing at arm's length, and it is issued, in whole or in part, directly or indirectly in exchange or substitution for that debt,

and the funds from the issue of the obligation are used in Canada in a business of the issuer carried on immediately before the time of issue;

Related Sections: S. 248(1), "business", "principal amount".

"small business bond" —"small business bond" at any time means

(*a*) an obligation that is at that time a qualifying debt obligation, issued by an individual or a partnership, in respect of which a joint election was made within 90 days after its issue date, or

(*b*) an obligation that is at that time a qualifying debt obligation issued by an individual or a partnership if

(i) it is reasonable to consider that the issuer and the holder of the obligation intended that this section apply to the obligation, having regard to such factors as may be relevant, including the rate of interest stipulated under the terms of the obligation and the manner in which the issuer and the holder have treated the obligation for the purposes of this Act, and

(ii) the holder files with the Minister a joint election in respect of the obligation within 90 days after the date of notification by the Minister that a joint election in respect of the obligation has not been filed under paragraph (*a*).

Related Sections: S. 248(1), "individual", "prescribed".

▶ 15.2(4) ◀

(4) Status of interest. Notwithstanding any other provision of this Act, an amount paid or payable by a taxpayer pursuant to a legal obligation to pay interest on borrowed money used for the purpose of acquiring a small business bond shall be deemed to be an amount paid or payable, as the case may be, on borrowed money used for the purpose of earning income from a business or property.

Related Sections: S. 15.2(3), "small business bond"; s. 248(1), "amount", "borrowed money", "business", "property".

▶ 15.2(5) ◀

(5) False declaration. Where the Minister establishes that an issuer has knowingly or under circumstances amounting to gross negligence made a false declaration in a joint election in respect of an obligation, the reference in paragraph (2)(*b*) to "29%" shall, in respect of the obligation, be read as a reference to "87%".

Related Sections: S. 15.2(2) Rules for small business bonds; s. 15.2(3), "small business bond"; s. 248(1), "small business bond".

▶ 15.2(6) ◀

(6) Partnerships. For the purpose of paragraph (2)(*b*), in the case of an issuer that is a partnership, the expression "tax otherwise payable under this Part by the issuer" shall be read as a reference to the "tax otherwise payable under this Part by each member of the partnership" and each member shall add to that member's tax otherwise payable under this Part for the taxation year that includes the period described in paragraph (2)(*b*) the amount that can reasonably be regarded as that member's share of the amount determined under that paragraph with respect to the partnership.

Related Sections: S. 15.2(2) Rules for small business bonds; s. 248(1), "amount"; s. 249(1) Definition of "taxation year".

▶ 15.2(7) ◀

(7) Deemed eligible issuer. Where, but for subparagraphs (*a*)(i), (ii) and (iii) and (*b*)(ii) of the definition "eligible issuer" in subsection (3), an individual or a partnership would be an "eligible issuer", the individual or partnership shall be deemed to be an eligible issuer in respect of a small business bond at any time where the issue price of the bond does not exceed the amount, if any, by which

(*a*) $500,000

exceeds

(*b*) where the issuer is an individual, the total of all amounts each of which is the principal amount outstanding immediately after that time in respect of

(i) another obligation that is a small business bond issued by

(A) the individual, or

(B) a partnership of which the individual is a majority interest partner, or

(ii) a small business development bond issued by

(A) a corporation that is controlled by the individual or by a related group of which the individual is a member, or

(B) a corporation that is associated with a corporation referred to in clause (A), or

(*c*) where the issuer is a partnership, the total of all amounts each of which is the principal amount outstanding immediately after that time in respect of

(i) another obligation that is a small business bond issued by

(A) the partnership,

(B) an individual who is a majority interest partner of the partnership, or

(C) a partnership of which the individual referred to in clause (B) is a majority interest partner, or

(ii) a small business development bond issued by

(A) a corporation that is controlled by the individual referred to in clause (i)(B) or by a related group of which the individual is a member, or

(B) a corporation that is associated with a corporation referred to in clause (A).

Related Sections: S. 15.2(3), "majority interest partner", "small business bond"; s. 248(1), "corporation", "individual", "principal amount"; s. 251(4) Definitions concerning groups; s. 256(1) Associated corporations.

▶ 15.2(8) ◀

(8) Presumption — (Repealed by S.C. 1994, c. 7, Sched. VIII, s. 6(1).)

▶ 15.2(9) ◀

(9) Penalty — (Repealed by S.C. 1994, c. 7, Sched. VIII, s. 6(1).)

SECTION 16: Income and capital combined

▶ 16(1) ◀

(1) Income and capital combined. Where, under a contract or other arrangement, an amount can reasonably be regarded as being in part interest or other amount of an income nature and in part an amount of a capital nature, the following rules apply:

(*a*) the part of the amount that can reasonably be regarded as interest shall, irrespective of when the contract or arrangement was made or the form or legal effect thereof, be deemed to be interest on a debt obligation held by the person to whom the amount is paid or payable; and

(*b*) the part of the amount that can reasonably be regarded as an amount of an income nature, other than interest, shall, irrespective of when the contract or arrangement was made or the form or legal effect thereof, be included in the income of the taxpayer to whom the amount is paid or payable for the taxation year in which the amount was received or became due to the extent it has not otherwise been included in the taxpayer's income.

Editorial Note: The courts have applied s. 16(1)(*a*) to deferred payment transactions where the deferred purchase price of property can reasonably be considered to contain an interest element. Generally speaking, where property is disposed of and the payment of the purchase price is deferred, the extent to which the purchase price (not including stipulated interest thereon) exceeds the fair market value of the property at the time of the disposition may be considered interest. See the cases cited below ("Cases").

Related Regulations: 201(1)(*d*).

Related Sections: S. 12(3) Interest income; s. 12(4) Interest from investment contract; s. 16(4) Where s. (1) does not apply; s. 16(5) Where s. 1 does not apply; s. 20(1)(*c*) Interest; s. 214(2) Income and capital combined; s. 214(12) Where s. (2) does not apply.

Forms: T5 Sum. — Return of Investment Income; T5 — Statement of Investment Income.

Income Tax Folios: *Secondary* — S3-F6-C1 Interest Deductibility.

Interpretation Bulletins: *Secondary* — IT-365R2 Damages, settlement, and similar receipts; IT-396R Interest income.

Cases: The agreements under which Amoco assumed liability for the $225 million loan were entered into on account of capital. Subsection 16(1) is an anti-avoidance provision intended to apply where an agreement does not explicitly identify an amount as being interest and that amount can reasonably be regarded to be interest for both parties. It is impossible under paragraph 16(1)(*a*) for an amount to be classified as deemed interest for the debtor and capital for the creditor. *Plains Midstream v. The Queen*, 2017 DTC 1125 (TCC), affirmed 2019 DTC 5040 (FCA)

Where an interest-free loan was equivalent to the fair market value of the property furnished as security payments to a non-resident in liquidation, the loan could not be regarded as including an interest element on which withholding tax was payable. *Rodmon Construction Inc. v. The Queen*, 75 DTC 5038 (F.C.T.D.), reversing T.R.B. (unreported)

The sale price for timber limits was paid in instalments without interest. No part of the instalments should be regarded as interest since the sale price was not in excess of fair market value and there was no evidence that interest affected the price or that it was the taxpayer's invariable practice to charge interest. *Vanwest Logging Co. v. MNR*, 71 DTC 5120 (Ex. Ct.)

The taxpayer sold his farm through instalment payments without interest. Part of each instalment could reasonably be regarded as interest since the property was sold for more than fair market value and the taxpayer, who must have appreciated the benefits of capitalization, proposed the non-payment of interest despite common business practice. *Groulx v. MNR*, 67 DTC 5284 (S.C.C.), affirming 66 DTC 5126 (Ex. Ct.), reversing 64 DTC 739 (T.A.B.)

► 16(2) ◄

(2) Obligation issued at discount. Where, in the case of a bond, debenture, bill, note, mortgage or similar obligation issued after December 20, 1960 and before June 19, 1971 by a person exempt from tax under section 149, a non-resident person not carrying on business in Canada, or a government, municipality or municipal or other public body performing a function of government,

(*a*) the obligation was issued for an amount that is less than the principal amount of the obligation,

(*b*) the interest stipulated to be payable on the obligation, expressed in terms of an annual rate on

(i) the principal amount thereof, if no amount is payable on account of the principal amount before the maturity of the obligation, or

(ii) the amount outstanding from time to time as or on account of the principal amount thereof, in any other case,

is less than 5%, and

(*c*) the yield from the obligation, expressed in terms of an annual rate on the amount for which the obligation was issued (which annual rate shall, if the terms of the obligation or any agreement relating thereto conferred on the holder thereof a right to demand payment of the principal amount of the obligation or the amount outstanding as or on account of the principal amount, as the case may be, before the maturity of the obligation, be calculated on the basis of the yield that produces the highest annual rate obtainable either on the maturity of the obligation or conditional on the exercise of any such right) exceeds the annual rate determined under paragraph (*b*) by more than 1/3 thereof,

the amount by which the principal amount of the obligation exceeds the amount for which the obligation was issued shall be included in computing the income of the first owner of the obligation who is a resident of Canada and is not a person exempt from tax under section 149 or a government, for the taxation year of that owner of the obligation in which he, she or it became the owner thereof.

Related Sections: S. 16(5) Where s. 1 does not apply; s. 53 Adjustments to cost base — Obligation issued at a discount.

► 16(3) ◄

(3) Obligation issued at discount. Where, in the case of a bond, debenture, bill, note, mortgage, hypothecary claim or similar obligation (other than an obligation that is a prescribed debt obligation for the purpose of subsection 12(9)) issued after June 18, 1971 by a person exempt, because of section 149, from Part I tax on part or on all of the person's income, a non-resident person not carrying on business in Canada or a government, municipality or municipal or other public body performing a function of government,

(*a*) the obligation was issued for an amount that is less than the principal amount of the obligation, and

(*b*) the yield from the obligation, expressed in terms of an annual rate on the amount for which the obligation was issued (which annual rate shall, if the terms of the obligation or any agreement relating thereto conferred on the holder thereof a right to demand payment of the principal amount of the obligation or the amount outstanding as or on account of the principal amount, as the case may be, before the maturity of the obligation, be calculated on the basis of the yield that produces the highest annual rate obtainable either on the maturity of the obligation or conditional on the exercise of any such right) exceeds 4/3 of the interest stipulated to be payable on the obligation, expressed in terms of an annual rate on

(i) the principal amount of the obligation, if no amount is payable on account of the principal amount before the maturity of the obligation, or

(ii) the amount outstanding from time to time as or on account of the principal amount thereof, in any other case,

the amount by which the principal amount of the obligation exceeds the amount for which the obligation was issued shall be included in computing the income of the first owner of the obligation

(*c*) who is resident in Canada,

(*d*) who is not a government nor a person exempt, because of section 149, from tax under this Part on all or part of the person's taxable income, and

(*e*) of whom the obligation is a capital property,

for the taxation year in which the owner acquired the obligation.

Editorial Note: The amount included under s. 16(3) is added to the taxpayer's adjusted cost base of the debt obligation under s. 53(1)(*g*).

Related Sections: S. 53(1)(*g*) Adjustments to cost base — Obligation issued at a discount; s. 142.4(1), "tax basis"; s. 214(7) Sale of obligation; s. 214(7.1) Obligation transfer between a resident and a non-resident; s. 253 Extended meaning of "carrying on business".

▶ 16(4) ◀

(4) Where s. (1) does not apply. Subsection (1) does not apply to any amount received by a taxpayer in a taxation year

(*a*) as an annuity payment; or

(*b*) in satisfaction of the taxpayer's rights under an annuity contract.

Related Regulations: Part III.

Related Sections: S. 12.2(1) Amount to be included; s. 56(1)(*d*) Annuity payments; s. 248(1), "annuity".

▶ 16(5) ◀

(5) Idem. Subsection (1) does not apply in any case where subsection (2) or (3) applies.

▶ 16(6) ◀

(6) Indexed debt obligations. Subject to subsection (7) and for the purposes of this Act, where at any time in a taxpayer's taxation year

(*a*) an interest in an indexed debt obligation is held by the taxpayer,

(i) an amount determined in prescribed manner shall be deemed to be received and receivable by the taxpayer in the year as interest in respect of the obligation, and

(ii) an amount determined in prescribed manner shall be deemed to be paid and payable in respect of the year by the taxpayer as interest under a legal obligation of the taxpayer to pay interest on borrowed money used for the purpose of earning income from a business or property;

(*b*) an indexed debt obligation is an obligation of the taxpayer,

(i) an amount determined in prescribed manner shall be deemed to be payable in respect of the year by the taxpayer as interest in respect of the obligation, and

(ii) an amount determined in prescribed manner shall be deemed to be received and receivable by the taxpayer in the year as interest in respect of the obligation; and

(*c*) the taxpayer pays or credits an amount in respect of an amount determined under subparagraph (*b*)(i) in respect of an indexed debt obligation, the payment or crediting shall be deemed to be a payment or crediting of interest on the obligation.

Related Regulations: 7001.

Related Sections: S. 12(1)(*c*) Interest; s. 20(1)(*c*) Interest; s. 53(1)(*g*.1) Adjustments to cost base — Indexed debt obligation; s. 53(2)(*l*.1) Amounts to be deducted — Indexed debt obligation; s. 212(1)(*b*) Interest; s. 248(1), "amount", "borrowed money", "business", "indexed debt obligation".

Tax Window Files: Excluded Amount with Respect to Indexed Debt Obligation, *Technical Interpretation, Financial Sector and Exempt Entities Division, December 21, 2005,* CRA Document No. 2005-0154191E5; Indexed Debt Obligations — Various Issues, *Technical Interpretation, Financial Industries Division, December 22, 2003,* CRA Document No. 2003-0000125.

▶ 16(7) ◀

(7) Impaired indexed debt obligations. Paragraph (6)(*a*) does not apply to a taxpayer in respect of an indexed debt obligation for the part of a taxation year throughout which the obligation is impaired where an amount in respect of the obligation is deductible because of subparagraph 20(1)(*l*)(ii) in computing the taxpayer's income for the year.

SECTION 16.1: Leasing properties

▶ 16.1(1) ◀

(1) Leasing properties. Where a taxpayer (in this section referred to as the "lessee") leases tangible property, or for civil law corporeal property, that is not prescribed property and that would, if the lessee acquired the property, be depreciable property of the lessee, from a person resident in Canada other than a person whose taxable income is exempt from tax under this Part, or from a non-resident person who holds the lease in the course of carrying on a business through a permanent establishment in Canada, as defined by regulation, any income from which is subject to tax under this Part, who owns the property and with whom the lessee was dealing at arm's length (in this section referred to as the "lessor") for a term of more than one year, if the lessee and the lessor jointly elect in prescribed form filed with their returns of income for their respective taxation years that include the particular time when the lease began, the following rules apply for the purpose of computing the income of the lessee for the taxation year that includes the particular time and for all subsequent taxation years:

(*a*) in respect of amounts paid or payable for the use of, or for the right to use, the property, the lease shall be deemed not to be a lease;

(*b*) the lessee shall be deemed to have acquired the property from the lessor at the particular time at a cost equal to its fair market value at that time;

(*c*) the lessee shall be deemed to have borrowed money from the lessor at the particular time, for the purpose of acquiring the property, in a principal amount equal to the fair market value of the property at that time;

(*d*) interest shall be deemed to accrue on the principal amount of the borrowed money outstanding from time to time, compounded semi-annually, not in advance, at the prescribed rate in effect

(i) at the earlier of

(A) the time, if any, before the particular time, at which the lessee last entered into an agreement to lease the property, and

(B) the particular time, or

(ii) where the lease provides that the amount payable by the lessee for the use of, or the right to use, the property varies according to prevailing interest rates in effect from time to time, and the lessee so elects, in respect of all of the property that is subject to the lease, in the lessee's return of income under this Part for the taxation year of the lessee in which the lease began, at the beginning of the period for which the interest is being calculated;

(*e*) all amounts paid or payable by or on behalf of the lessee for the use of, or the right to use, the property in the year shall be deemed to be blended payments, paid or payable by the lessee, of principal and interest on the borrowed money outstanding from time to time, calculated in accordance with paragraph (*d*), applied firstly on account of interest on principal, secondly on account of interest on unpaid interest and thirdly on account of unpaid principal, if any, and the amount, if any, by which any such payment exceeds the total of those amounts shall be deemed to be paid or payable on account of interest, and any amount deemed by reason of this paragraph to be a payment of interest shall be deemed to have been an amount paid or payable, as the case may be, pursuant to a legal obligation to pay interest in respect of the year on the borrowed money;

(*f*) at the time of the expiration or cancellation of the lease, the assignment of the lease or the sublease of the property by the lessee, the lessee shall (except where subsection (4) applies) be deemed to have disposed of the property at that time for proceeds of disposition equal to the amount, if any, by which

(i) the total of

(A) the amount referred to in paragraph (*c*), and

(B) all amounts received or receivable by the lessee in respect of the cancellation or assignment of the lease or the sublease of the property

exceeds

(ii) the total of

(A) all amounts deemed under paragraph (*e*) to have been paid or payable, as the case may be, by the lessee on account of the principal amount of the borrowed money, and

(B) all amounts paid or payable by or on behalf of the lessee in respect of the cancellation or assignment of the lease or the sublease of the property;

(*g*) for the purposes of subsections 13(5.2) and (5.3), each amount paid or payable by or on behalf of the lessee that would, but for this subsection, have been an amount paid or payable for the use of, or the right to use, the property shall be deemed to have been deducted in computing the lessee's income as an amount paid or payable by the lessee for the use of, or the right to use, the property after the particular time;

(*h*) any amount paid or payable by or on behalf of the lessee in respect of the granting or assignment of the lease or the sublease of the property that would, but for this paragraph, be the capital cost to the lessee of a leasehold interest in the property shall be deemed to be an amount paid or payable, as the case may be, by the lessee for the use of, or the right to use, the property for the remaining term of the lease; and

(*i*) where the lessee elects under this subsection in respect of a property and, at any time after the lease was entered into, the owner of the property is a non-resident person who does not hold the lease in the course of carrying on a business through a permanent establishment in Canada, as defined by regulation, any income from which is subject to tax under this Part, for the purposes of this subsection the lease shall be deemed to have been cancelled at that time.

History: S. 16.1(1), the portion before paragraph (*a*) was replaced by S.C. 2013, c. 34, s. 94, in force June 26, 2013, and formerly read:

(1) *Leasing properties.* Where a taxpayer (in this section referred to as the "lessee") leases tangible property (other than prescribed property) that would, if the lessee acquired the property, be depreciable property of the lessee, from a person resident in Canada other than a person whose taxable income is exempt from tax under this Part, or from a non-resident person who holds the lease in the course of carrying on a business through a permanent establishment in Canada, as defined by regulation, any income from which is subject to tax under this Part, who owns the property and with whom the lessee was dealing at arm's length (in this section referred to as the "lessor") for a term of more than one year, if the lessee and the lessor jointly elect in prescribed form filed with their returns of income for their respective taxation years that include the particular time when the lease began, the following rules apply for the purpose of computing the income of the lessee for the taxation year that includes the particular time and for all subsequent taxation years:

(*a*) in respect of amounts paid or payable for the use of, or for the right to use, the property, the lease shall be deemed not to be a lease;

(*b*) the lessee shall be deemed to have acquired the property from the lessor at the particular time at a cost equal to its fair market value at that time;

(*c*) the lessee shall be deemed to have borrowed money from the lessor at the particular time, for the purpose of acquiring the property, in a principal amount equal to the fair market value of the property at that time;

(*d*) interest shall be deemed to accrue on the principal amount of the borrowed money outstanding from time to time, compounded semi-annually, not in advance, at the prescribed rate in effect

(i) at the earlier of

(A) the time, if any, before the particular time, at which the lessee last entered into an agreement to lease the property, and

(B) the particular time, or

(ii) where the lease provides that the amount payable by the lessee for the use of, or the right to use, the property varies according to prevailing interest rates in effect from time to time, and the lessee so elects, in respect of all of the property that is subject to the lease, in the lessee's return of income under this Part for the taxation year of the lessee in which the lease began, at the beginning of the period for which the interest is being calculated;

(*e*) all amounts paid or payable by or on behalf of the lessee for the use of, or the right to use, the property in the year shall be deemed to be blended payments, paid or payable by the lessee, of principal and interest on the borrowed money outstanding from time to time, calculated in accordance with paragraph (*d*), applied firstly on account of interest on principal, secondly on account of interest on unpaid interest and thirdly on account of unpaid principal, if any, and the amount, if any, by which any such payment exceeds the total of those amounts shall be deemed to be paid or payable on account of interest, and any amount deemed by reason of this paragraph to be a payment of interest shall be deemed to have been an amount paid or payable, as the case may be, pursuant to a legal obligation to pay interest in respect of the year on the borrowed money;

(*f*) at the time of the expiration or cancellation of the lease, the assignment of the lease or the sublease of the property by the lessee, the lessee shall (except where subsection (4) applies) be deemed to have disposed of the property at that time for proceeds of disposition equal to the amount, if any, by which

(i) the total of

(A) the amount referred to in paragraph (*c*), and

(B) all amounts received or receivable by the lessee in respect of the cancellation or assignment of the lease or the sublease of the property

exceeds

(ii) the total of

(A) all amounts deemed under paragraph (*e*) to have been paid or payable, as the case may be, by the lessee on account of the principal amount of the borrowed money, and

(B) all amounts paid or payable by or on behalf of the lessee in respect of the cancellation or assignment of the lease or the sublease of the property;

(*g*) for the purposes of subsections 13(5.2) and (5.3), each amount paid or payable by or on behalf of the lessee that would, but for this subsection, have been an amount paid or payable for the use of, or the right to use, the property shall be deemed to have been deducted in computing the lessee's income as an amount paid or payable by the lessee for the use of, or the right to use, the property after the particular time;

(*h*) any amount paid or payable by or on behalf of the lessee in respect of the granting or assignment of the lease or the sublease of the property that would, but for this paragraph, be the capital cost to the lessee of a leasehold interest in the property shall be deemed to be an amount paid or payable, as the case may be, by the lessee for the use of, or the right to use, the property for the remaining term of the lease; and

(*i*) where the lessee elects under this subsection in respect of a property and, at any time after the lease was entered into, the owner of the property is a non-resident person who does not hold the lease in the course of carrying on a business through a permanent establishment in Canada, as defined by regulation, any income from which is subject to tax under this Part, for the purposes of this subsection the lease shall be deemed to have been cancelled at that time.

Related Regulations: 1100(1.13)(a); 4302; 8200; 8201.

Canadian Tax Foundation: Ashton, *Leasing: Recent Developments*, 1997 Corporate Management Tax Conference 11:1–46.

Forms: T2145 — Election in Respect of the Leasing of Property.

Income Tax Folios: *Secondary* — S3-F4-C1 General Discussion of Capital Cost Allowance.

Tax Window Files: Whether s. 16.1 applies to a transport truck, *April 28, 2015*, CRA Document No. 2015-0566011E5.

▶ 16.1(2) ◀

(2) Assignments and subleases. Subject to subsections (3) and (4), where at any particular time a lessee who has made an election under subsection (1) in respect of a leased property assigns the lease or subleases the property to another person (in this section referred to as the "assignee"),

(*a*) subsection (1) shall not apply in computing the income of the lessee in respect of the lease for any period after the particular time; and

(*b*) if the lessee and the assignee jointly elect in prescribed form filed with their returns of income under this Part for their respective taxation years that include the particular time, subsection (1) shall apply to the assignee as if

(i) the assignee leased the property at the particular time from the owner of the property for a term of more than one year, and

(ii) the assignee and the owner of the property jointly elected under subsection (1) in respect of the property with their returns of income under this Part for their respective taxation years that include the particular time.

Forms: T2146 — Election in Respect of Assigned Leases or Subleased Property.

▶ 16.1(3) ◀

(3) Idem. Subject to subsection (4), where at any particular time a lessee who has made an election under subsection (1) in respect of a leased property assigns the lease or subleases the property to another person with whom the lessee is not dealing at arm's length, the other person shall, for the purposes of subsection (1) and for the purposes of computing that person's income in respect of the lease for any period after the particular time, be deemed to be the same person as, and a continuation of, the lessee, except that, notwithstanding paragraph (1)(*b*), that other person shall be deemed to have acquired the property from the lessee at the time that it was acquired by the lessee at a cost equal to the amount that would be the lessee's proceeds of disposition of the property determined under paragraph (1)(*f*) if that amount were determined without reference to clauses (1)(*f*)(i)(B) and (ii)(B).

▶ 16.1(4) ◀

(4) Amalgamations and windings-up. Notwithstanding subsection (2), where at any time a particular corporation that has made an election under subsection (1) in respect of a lease assigns the lease

(*a*) by reason of an amalgamation (within the meaning assigned by subsection 87(1)), or

(*b*) in the course of the winding-up of a Canadian corporation in respect of which subsection 88(1) applies,

to another corporation with which it does not deal at arm's length, the other corporation shall, for the purposes of subsection (1) and for the purposes of computing its income in respect of the lease after that time, be deemed to be the same person as, and a continuation of, the particular corporation.

▶ 16.1(5) ◀

(5) Replacement property. For the purposes of subsection (1), where at any time a property (in this subsection referred to as a "replacement property") is provided by a lessor to a lessee as a replacement for a similar property of the lessor (in this subsection referred to as the "original property") that was leased by the lessor to the lessee, and the amount payable by the lessee for the use of, or the right to use, the replacement property is the same as the amount that was so payable in respect of the original property, the replacement property shall be deemed to be the same property as the original property.

▶ 16.1(6) ◀

(6) Additional property. For the purposes of subsection (1), where at any particular time

(*a*) an addition or alteration (in this subsection referred to as "additional property") is made by a lessor to a property (in this subsection referred to as the "original property") of the lessor that is the subject of a lease,

(*b*) the lessor and the lessee of the original property have jointly elected under subsection (1) in respect of the original property, and

(*c*) as a consequence of the addition or alteration, the total amount payable by the lessee for the use of, or the right to use, the original property and the additional property exceeds the amount so payable in respect of the original property,

the following rules apply:

(*d*) the lessee shall be deemed to have leased the additional property from the lessor at the particular time,

(*e*) the term of the lease of the additional property shall be deemed to be greater than one year, (*f*) the lessor and the lessee shall be deemed to have jointly elected under subsection (1) in respect of the additional property,

(*g*) the prescribed rate in effect at the particular time in respect of the additional property shall be deemed to be equal to the prescribed rate in effect in respect of the original property at the particular time,

(*h*) the additional property shall be deemed not to be prescribed property, and

(*i*) the excess referred to in paragraph (*c*) shall be deemed to be an amount payable by the lessee for the use of, or the right to use, the additional property.

Related Regulations: 4302.

► 16.1(7) ◄

(7) Renegotiation of lease. For the purposes of subsection (1), where at any time

(*a*) a lease (in this subsection referred to as the "original lease") of property is renegotiated in the course of a *bona fide* renegotiation, and

(*b*) as a result of the renegotiation, the amount payable by the lessee of the property for the use of, or the right to use, the property is altered in respect of a period after that time (otherwise than because of an addition or alteration to which subsection (6) applies),

the original lease shall be deemed to have expired and the renegotiated lease shall be deemed to be a new lease of the property entered into at that time.

SECTION 17: Amount owing by non-resident

► 17(1) ◄

(1) Amount owing by non-resident. If this subsection applies to a corporation resident in Canada in respect of an amount owing to the corporation (in this subsection referred to as the "debt"), the corporation shall include in computing its income for a taxation year the amount determined by the formula

$$A - B$$

where

A is the amount of interest that would be included in computing the corporation's income for the year in respect of the debt if interest on the debt were computed at the prescribed rate for the period in the year during which the debt was outstanding; and

B is the total of all amounts each of which is

(*a*) an amount included in computing the corporation's income for the year as, on account of, in lieu of or in satisfaction of, interest in respect of the debt,

(*b*) an amount received or receivable by the corporation from a trust that is included in computing the corporation's income for the year or a subsequent taxation year and that can reasonably be attributed to interest on the debt for the period in the year during which the debt was outstanding, or

(*c*) an amount included in computing the corporation's income for the year or a subsequent taxation year under subsection 91(1) that can reasonably be attributed to interest on an amount owing (in this paragraph referred to as the "original debt") — or if the amount of the original debt exceeds the amount of the debt, a portion of the original debt that is equal to the amount of the debt — for the period in the year during which the debt was outstanding if

(i) without the existence of the original debt, subsection (2) would not have deemed the debt to be owed by the non-resident person referred to in paragraph (1.1)(*a*),

(ii) the original debt was owed by a non-resident person or a partnership each member of which is a non-resident person, and

(iii) where subsection (11.2) applies to the original debt,

(A) an amount determined under paragraph (11.2)(*a*) or (*b*) in respect of the original debt is an amount referred to in paragraph (2)(*a*), and because of the amount referred to in paragraph (2)(*a*), the debt is deemed to be owed by the non-resident person referred to in paragraph (1.1)(*a*), and

(B) the original debt was owing by an intermediate lender to an initial lender or by an intended borrower to an intermediate lender (within the meanings of those terms assigned by subsection (11.2)).

Editorial Note: S. 17(1) was enacted to prevent corporations resident in Canada from avoiding Canadian tax by providing loans or other amounts at low interest or no interest to non-residents. For the provision to apply, (a) a corporation resident in Canada must be owed funds by a non-resident person (the creditor must be a Canadian-resident corporation but the debtor can be any person who is a non-resident), (b) the amount owed to the Canadian-resident corporation must have been outstanding for more than a year, and (c) interest amounts calculated for the Canadian-resident corporation's income per Variable B of subsection 17(1) in respect of the outstanding amount must be less than interest computed at a reasonable rate for the period in the year during which the amount was owing. If these conditions are satisfied, the difference between the amount of such interest received (if any) and interest calculated at the prescribed interest rate under Regulation 4301 is included in the Canadian-resident corporation's income for the year. It should be noted that s. 17 contains many anti-avoidance rules which may cause a loan or transfer to be "caught" and that exceptions to the application of s. 17(1) are found in ss. (7), (8) and (9). The term "interest computed at a reasonable rate" is not defined in the Act but the CRA has published numerous technical interpretations setting out its views on the meaning of this term. It should also be noted that if a non-resident owes an amount to a Canadian resident and such amount is not subject to s. 17(1) because of an exception to s. 17 or because the amount is not owed to a Canadian-resident corporation, s. 247, which deals with transfer pricing may apply. For taxation years ending after March 28, 2012, s. 17 does not apply to an amount owed to a corporation resident in Canada (or a qualifying Canadian partnership) that is a "pertinent loan or indebtedness" for purposes of s. 15(2.11) or 212.3(11). These loans are subject to a special regime under s. 17.1.

History: S. 17(1) was replaced by S.C. 2014, c. 39, s. 5(1), applicable to taxation years that begin after February 23, 1998. In addition, any assessment of a taxpayer's tax, interest and penalties payable under the Act for any taxation year that ends before the day on which this amendment receives royal assent [December 16, 2014] that would, in the absence of this section, be precluded because of the time references in subsection 152(4) of the Act is to be made to the extent necessary to take into account this amendment.

S. 17(1) formerly read:

(1) *Amount owing by non-resident.* Where, at any time in a taxation year of a corporation resident in Canada, a non-resident person owes an amount to the corporation, that amount has been or remains outstanding for more than a year and the total determined under paragraph (*b*) for the year is less than the amount of interest that would be included in computing the corporation's income for the year in respect of the amount owing if that interest were computed at a reasonable rate for the period in the year during which the amount was owing, the corporation shall include an amount in computing its income for the year equal to the amount, if any, by which

(*a*) the amount of interest that would be included in computing the corporation's income for the year in respect of the amount owing if that interest were computed at the prescribed rate for the period in the year during which the amount was owing

exceeds

(*b*) the total of all amounts each of which is

(i) an amount included in computing the corporation's income for the year as, on account of, in lieu of or in satisfaction of, interest in respect of the amount owing,

(ii) an amount received or receivable by the corporation from a trust that is included in computing the corporation's income for the year or a subsequent year and that can reasonably be attributed to interest on the amount owing for the period in the year during which the amount was owing, or

(iii) an amount that is included in computing the corporation's income for the year or a subsequent year under subsection 91(1) and that can reasonably be attributed to interest on the amount owing for the period in the year during which the amount was owing.

Related Regulations: 4301.

Canadian Tax Foundation: Bonanno and Vercillo, *Related Party Loan Arrangements*, 2018 Ontario Tax Conference 11:1–21; Grosman and Buttenham, *Foreign Affiliate Taxation: An Update For Owner-Managers and Their Advisors*, 2005 Ontario Tax Conference 2:1–38; McDowell, *Section 17: Practical Issues Arising From the Indirect Indebtedness Rule*, 2004 Conference Report 19:1–22; Tremblay and Wilkie, *The Canadian Triangle: Tax Policy Reflections on the Uneasy Interaction of 15(2), 17 and 95(2)*, 2002 Conference Report 18:1–16; Holms and Charpentier, *Financing Foreign Affiliates: Some Things Old and Some Things New*, 2001 British Columbia Tax Conference 12:1–32; Moskowitz, *Financing of Non-Residents and the Recent Amendments to Section 17*, 1999 Conference Report 43:1–61; Woolford-Marshall, *Amendments to Section 17: Imputed Income to Canadian Resident Corporations on Certain Loans to Non-Residents*, 1999 Canadian Tax Journal 3:640–662.

Tax Profile: February 2013 — The Purchase of US Businesses by Canadians; September 2011 — Acquisition of Canadian Business by Non-Residents.

Tax Topics: No. 2062, CRA Seeks to Clarify Application of Section 17; No. 1631, Tinkering with Section 17.

Tax Window Files: Loan to Non-Resident — Doubtful Debt, *Technical Interpretation, International and Trusts Division, March 29, 2006*, CRA Document No. 2004-0093541E5; Reasonable Rate of Interest, *Technical Interpretation, International and Trusts Division, March 6, 2003*, CRA Document No. 2002-0178357.

Cases: The amendment to subsection 17(1), substituting "prescribed rates" for the previously stipulated 5 per cent per annum rate, did not have the effect of creating new obligations on the taxpayer with respect to loan transactions entered into prior to January 1, 1979. *Upper Lakes Shipping Limited v. M.N.R.*, 92 DTC 2381 (T.C.C.)

▶ 17(1.1) ◀

(1.1) Amount owing by non-resident. Subsection (1) applies to a corporation resident in Canada in respect of an amount owing to the corporation if, at any time in a taxation year of the corporation,

(*a*) a non-resident person owes the amount to the corporation;

(*b*) the amount has been or remains outstanding for more than a year; and

(*c*) the amount that would be determined for B in subsection (1), if that subsection applied, for the year in respect of the amount owing is less than the amount of interest that would be included in computing the corporation's income for the year in respect of the amount owing if that interest were computed at a reasonable rate for the period in the year during which the amount was outstanding.

History: S. 17(1.1) was added by S.C. 2014, c. 39, s. 5(1), applicable to taxation years that begin after February 23, 1998. In addition, any assessment of a taxpayer's tax, interest and penalties payable under the Act for any taxation year that ends before the day on which this amendment receives royal assent [December 16, 2014] that would, in the absence of this section, be precluded because of the time references in subsection 152(4) of the Act is to be made to the extent necessary to take into account this amendment.

▶ 17(2) ◀

(2) Anti-avoidance rule — indirect loan. For the purpose of this section and subject to subsection (3), where

(*a*) a non-resident person owes an amount at any time to a particular person or partnership (other than a corporation resident in Canada), and

(*b*) it is reasonable to conclude that the amount or a portion of the amount became owing, or was permitted to remain owing, to the particular person or partnership because

(i) a corporation resident in Canada made a loan or transfer of property, or

(ii) the particular person or partnership anticipated that a corporation resident in Canada would make a loan or transfer of property,

either directly or indirectly, in any manner whatever, to or for the benefit of any person or partnership (other than an exempt loan or transfer),

the non-resident person is deemed at that time to owe to the corporation an amount equal to the amount, or the portion of the amount, as the case may be, owing to the particular person or partnership.

Editorial Note: S. 17(2) is an anti-avoidance provision which deals with indirect loans. For the subsection to apply, the following tests must be met: (a) a non-resident person owes an amount at any time to a person or partnership other than a Canadian resident corporation; (b) a Canadian resident corporation made a loan or transfer of property, either directly or indirectly in any manner whatsoever to or for the benefit of any person or partnership; and (c) it is reasonable to conclude that the particular person or partnership entered into the transaction under (a) above, because of the loan or transfer under (b) above. If these conditions are met, the non-resident person is deemed to owe money to the Canadian resident corporation in an amount equal to the amount or portion of the amount owing to the particular person or partnership. It should be noted that because the test is a subjective "reasonable to conclude" test, it is often difficult to ascertain when this anti-avoidance provision applies. It should also be noted that the provision does not apply if it involves an "exempt loan or transfer" which is defined in s. 17(15) to generally include (a) loan made by a Canadian resident corporation at arm's length interest; (b) a transfer of property or payment at arm's length types of terms and conditions (other than a transfer of property made for the purpose of acquiring shares of a foreign affiliate of a corporation or a corporation with whom the corporation does not deal at arm's length); (c) a dividend paid by a Canadian resident corporation; and (d) payment made by a Canadian resident corporation on a reduction of paid-up capital, or if the exceptions provided in subsection (3) apply.

S. 17(2) is extended by further anti-avoidance rules dealing with partnerships, trusts and multi-tiered entities found in subsections (4), (5) and (6) and an anti-avoidance rule relating to back-to-back loans found in subsection (11.2).

History: S. 17(2)(*b*), the portion before subparagraph (i) was replaced by S.C. 2014, c. 39, s. 5(2), applicable to taxation years that begin after July 12, 2013. In addition, any assessment of a taxpayer's tax, interest and penalties payable under the Act for any taxation year that ends before the day on which this amendment receives royal assent [December 16, 2014] that would, in the absence of this section, be precluded because of the time references in subsection 152(4) of the Act is to be made to the extent necessary to take into account this amendment.

The portion of s. 17(2)(*b*) before subparagraph (i) formerly read:

(*b*) it is reasonable to conclude that the particular person or partnership entered into the transaction under which the amount became owing or the particular person or partnership permitted the amount owing to remain outstanding because

S. 17(2), the portion after paragraph (*b*) was replaced by S.C. 2014, c. 39, s. 5(3), applicable to taxation years that begin after July 12, 2013. In addition, any assessment of a taxpayer's tax, interest and penalties payable under the Act for any taxation year that ends before the day on which this amendment receives royal assent [December 16, 2014] that would, in the absence of this section, be precluded because of the time references in subsection 152(4) of the Act is to be made to the extent necessary to take into account this amendment.

The portion of s. 17(2) after paragraph (*b*) formerly read:

the non-resident person is deemed at that time to owe to the corporation an amount equal to the amount owing to the particular person or partnership.

Related Sections: S. 245(2) General anti-avoidance provision.

Canadian Petroleum Tax Journal: Recent Developments in Corporate Reorganizations and International Transactions, Doug Richardson and Edward Rowe, 2000, Vol. 13, No. 1.

Canadian Tax Foundation: McDowell, *Section 17: Practical Issues Arising From the Indirect Indebtedness Rule*, 2004 Conference Report 19:1–22.

Tax Topics: No. 1631, Tinkering with Section 17.

Tax Window Files: Related Foreign Entity Financing, *Advance Income Tax Ruling, International Division, 2012*, CRA Document No. 2011-0418711R3; Transfer of Property, *Technical Interpretation, International & Trusts Division, May 19, 2005*, CRA Document No. 2004-0072331E5.

► 17(3) ◄

(3) Exception to anti-avoidance rule — indirect loan. Subsection (2) does not apply to an amount owing at any time by a non-resident person to a particular person or partnership where

(*a*) at that time, the non-resident person and the particular person or each member of the particular partnership, as the case may be, are controlled foreign affiliates of the corporation resident in Canada; or

(*b*) at that time,

(i) the non-resident person and the particular person are not related or the non-resident person and each member of the particular partnership are not related, as the case may be,

(ii) the terms or conditions made or imposed in respect of the amount owing, determined without reference to any loan or transfer of property by a corporation resident in Canada described in paragraph (2)(*b*) in respect of the amount owing, are such that persons dealing at arm's length would have been willing to enter into them at the time that they were entered into, and

(iii) if there were an amount of interest payable on the amount owing at that time that would be required to be included in computing the income of a foreign affiliate of the corporation resident in Canada for a taxation year, that amount of interest would not be required to be included in computing the foreign accrual property income of the affiliate for that year.

Editorial Note: One exception to the anti-avoidance rule in s. 17(2) is found in subsection (3) which provides that subsection (2) does not apply to an amount owing at any time by a non-resident person to a particular person or a partnership if (a) the non-resident person and the particular person or each member of the particular partnership as the case may be, are controlled foreign affiliates of the corporation resident in Canada; or (b) the non-resident person and the particular person are not related, the terms in respect of the amount owing are such that persons dealing at arm's length would have been willing to enter into them, and, if there were an amount of interest payable on the amount owing at the time that would be required to be included in computing the income of a foreign affiliate of the corporation resident in Canada, that amount of interest would not be required to be included in computing the FAPI of the affiliate for the year.

The second exception deals with debts owed to unrelated third parties on arm's length terms. An example would be a Canadian resident corporation lending funds at a preferential rate to an unrelated third party in order to induce the third party to make a loan to one of its non-resident suppliers and the loan from the third party to the non-resident is on arm's length terms and any interest payable is not FAPI to the Canadian resident corporation.

It should be noted that for purposes of s. 17, the definition of "controlled foreign affiliate" which is defined in s. 95(1) (subject to the interpretational rules in ss. 95(2.01) and (2.02)) is modified by ss. 17(10), (12), (13) and (15). These modifications are generally designed to ensure that, in determining whether an income inclusion under s. 17 is warranted, it is the level of Canadian ownership of the foreign entity that is ultimately determinative. For example, a foreign entity will not be considered a "controlled foreign affiliate" of a corporation resident in Canada (and therefore no exemption from the income inclusion rules in s. 17 will be available) if the entity is considered a "controlled foreign affiliate" of the corporation resident in Canada solely because of the attribution of shareholdings in the foreign entity by another foreign entity that is related to the corporation resident in Canada (i.e., a foreign parent or sister company).

It should also be noted that for purposes of determining whether parties are related, reference should be made to s. 251 as modified by ss. 17(10), (11), (11.1) and (11.3).

Related Sections: S. 17(10) Determination of whether related and controlled foreign affiliate status; s. 17(11) Determination of whether related; s. 17(11.1) Determination of whether persons related; s. 17(12) Determination of controlled foreign affiliate status; s. 17(13) Extended definition of controlled foreign affiliate; s. 17(15) Definitions; s. 95(1), "foreign affiliate", "controlled foreign affiliate", " foreign accrual property income"; s. 248(1), "corporation", "non-resident"; s. 251 Arm's length.

► 17(4) ◄

(4) Anti-avoidance rule — loan through partnership. For the purpose of this section, where a non-resident person owes an amount at any time to a partnership and subsection (2) does not deem the non-resident person to owe an amount equal to that amount to a corporation resident in Canada, the non-resident person is deemed at that time to owe to each member of the partnership, on the same terms as those that apply in respect of the amount owing to the partnership, that proportion of the amount owing to the partnership at that time that

(*a*) the fair market value of the member's interest in the partnership at that time

is of

(*b*) the fair market value of all interests in the partnership at that time.

Editorial Note: S. 17(4) is an anti-avoidance rule which deals with situations where a non-resident person owes an amount to a partnership and subsection (2) does not deem a like amount to be owing to a Canadian resident corporation. In such case, the non-resident person is deemed to owe each member of the partnership a portion of the amount owing at the particular time. A similar anti-avoidance rule applies to amounts owed to a trust under s. 17(5). In such case, if the trust is a non-discretionary trust, the non-resident person is deemed to owe an amount to each beneficiary of the trust based on the beneficiary's interest in the trust. For purposes of this provision, "non-discretionary trust" is defined in s. 17(15). In the case of any other trust, the non-resident person is deemed to owe each settlor an amount equal to the entire amount owing to the trust. Therefore, if there is more than one settlor, the same amount owing may give rise to more than one income inclusion. The definition of "settlor" is also found in s. 17(15). S. 17(6) provides a similar anti-avoidance rule for tiered entities. It applies where a partnership owes an amount to any person or any other partnership. In such event, each member of the partnership owing the amount is deemed to owe a share of the amount owing. The apportionment of the amount owing is based on the fair market value of the interest of each member of the partnership owing the amount.

► 17(5) ◄

(5) Anti-avoidance rule — loan through trust. For the purpose of this section, where a non-resident person owes an amount at any time to a trust and subsection (2) does not deem the non-resident person to owe an amount equal to that amount to a corporation resident in Canada,

(*a*) where the trust is a non-discretionary trust at that time, the non-resident person is deemed at that time to owe to each beneficiary of the trust, on the same terms as those that apply in respect of the amount owing to the trust, that proportion of the amount owing to the trust that

(i) the fair market value of the beneficiary's interest in the trust at that time

is of

(ii) the fair market value of all the beneficial interests in the trust at that time; and

(*b*) in any other case, the non-resident person is deemed at that time to owe to each settlor in respect of the trust, on the same terms as those that apply in respect of the amount owing to the trust, an amount equal to the amount owing to the trust.

Editorial Note: See the Editorial Note following s. 17(4).

▶ 17(6) ◀

(6) Anti-avoidance rule — loan to partnership. For the purpose of this section, where a particular partnership owes an amount at any time to any person or any other partnership (in this subsection referred to as the "lender"), each member of the particular partnership is deemed to owe at that time to the lender, on the same terms as those that apply in respect of the amount owing by the particular partnership to the lender, that proportion of the amount owing to the lender that

(*a*) the fair market value of the member's interest in the particular partnership at that time

is of

(*b*) the fair market value of all interests in the particular partnership at that time.

Editorial Note: See the Editorial Note following s. 17(4).

▶ 17(7) ◀

(7) Exception. Subsection (1) does not apply in respect of an amount owing to a corporation resident in Canada by a non-resident person if a tax has been paid under Part XIII on the amount owing, except that, for the purpose of this subsection, tax under Part XIII is deemed not to have been paid on that portion of the amount owing in respect of which an amount was repaid or applied under subsection 227(6.1).

Editorial Note: S. 17(7) provides another exception to the inclusion rule in subsection (1). Specifically, if there is an amount owing to a Canadian resident corporation by a non-resident person, s. 17(1) does not apply if withholding tax has been paid under Part XIII of the Act on the amount owing. However, if withholding tax was refunded under s. 227(6.1) in respect of a repayment of a non-resident shareholder loan, Part XIII non-resident withholding tax is deemed not to have been paid for the purpose of s. 17(7).

Related Sections: S. 15(2) Shareholder debt; s. 214(3)(*a*) Deemed payments; s. 227(6.1) Repayment of non-resident shareholder loan.

▶ 17(8) ◀

(8) Exception. Subsection (1) does not apply to a corporation resident in Canada for a taxation year of the corporation in respect of an amount owing to the corporation by a non-resident person if the non-resident person is a controlled foreign affiliate of the corporation throughout the period in the year during which the amount is owing to the extent that it is established that the amount owing

(*a*) arose as a loan or advance of money to the affiliate that the affiliate has used, throughout the period that began when the loan or advance was made and that ended at the earlier of the end of the year and the time at which the amount was repaid,

(i) for the purpose of earning

(A) income from an active business, as defined in subsection 95(1), of the affiliate, or

(B) income that was included in computing the income from an active business of the affiliate under subsection 95(2), or

(ii) for the purpose of making a loan or advance to another controlled foreign affiliate of the corporation where, if interest became payable on the loan or advance at any time in the period and the affiliate was required to include the interest in computing its income for a taxation year, that interest would not be required to be included in computing the affiliate's foreign accrual property income for that year; or

(*b*) arose in the course of an active business, as defined in subsection 95(1), carried on by the affiliate throughout the period that began when the amount owing arose and that ended at the earlier of the end of the year and the time at which the amount was repaid.

Editorial Note: S. 17(8) is another exception to subsection (1) and limits, in certain circumstances, the income inclusion to a Canadian resident under s. (1) if the non-resident person owing the amount is a controlled foreign affiliate of the Canadian resident corporation throughout the period during which the amount is owed. The definition of "controlled foreign affiliate" is found in s. 95(1) (subject to the interpretational rules in ss. 95(2.01) and (2.02), as modified for purposes of s. 17 (see the editorial note for s. 17(3))).

S. 17(8)(*a*)(i) provides that there is no income inclusion to the extent that a loan or advance of money was made and that loan or advance was used by the controlled foreign affiliate either to earn income from an active business or to earn income that was included in the affiliate's income from an active business pursuant to s. 95(2). It should be noted that this use must occur throughout the period that began when the loan or advance was made and that ended at the earlier of the end of the year and the time at which the amount was repaid.

S. 17(8)(*a*)(ii) provides that there is no income inclusion to the extent that a loan or advance was made and that loan or advance was used by the controlled foreign affiliate to make a loan or advance to another controlled foreign affiliate of the Canadian resident corporation and interest, if payable and included in the first affiliate's income, will not be required to be included in computing the first affiliate's FAPI for the year.

S. 17(8)(*a*) limits the income inclusion under s. 17(1) only in circumstances where a controlled foreign affiliate owes an amount to a corporation resident in Canada as a loan or advance of money. S. 17(8)(*b*) limits the income inclusion in circumstances where a controlled foreign affiliate owes other amounts to the Canadian-resident corporation to the extent the amounts arose in the course of an active business carried on by the controlled foreign affiliate. The active business must be carried on by the affiliate throughout the period that began when the amount owing arose and that ended at the earlier of the end of the year and the time at which the amount was repaid. If the Canadian-resident corporation is controlled by a non-resident corporation, a loan made (or extended) on or after March 28, 2012, to a foreign affiliate may trigger a deemed dividend and paid-up capital reduction under the "foreign affiliate dumping" rules in s. 212.3.

Related Sections: S. 95(1) Foreign affiliate; s. 95(2) Determination of certain components of foreign accrual property income.

Tax Topics: No. 1631, Tinkering with Section 17.

Tax Window Files: Transfer Pricing Adjustment — Loan to Non-resident Corporation, *Technical Interpretation, International and Trusts Division, February 6, 2004*, CRA Document No. 2003-0033891E5; Return of capital by controlled foreign affiliate, *May 31, 2017*, CRA Document No. 2016-0676701E5.

▶ 17(8.1) ◀

(8.1) Borrowed money. Subsection (8.2) applies in respect of money (referred to in this subsection and in subsection (8.2) as "new borrowings") that a controlled foreign affiliate of a particular corporation resident in Canada has borrowed from the particular corporation to the extent that the affiliate has used the new borrowings (*a*) to repay money (referred to in this subsection and in subsection (8.2) as "previous borrowings") previously borrowed from any person or partnership, if

(i) the previous borrowings became owing after the last time at which the affiliate became a controlled foreign affiliate of the particular corporation, and

(ii) the previous borrowings were, at all times after they became owing, used for a purpose described in subparagraph (8)(*a*)(i) or (ii); or

(*b*) to pay an amount owing (referred to in this subsection and in subsection (8.2) as the "unpaid purchase price") by the affiliate for property previously acquired from any person or partnership, if

(i) the property was acquired, and the unpaid purchase price became owing, by the affiliate after the last time at which it became a controlled foreign affiliate of the particular corporation,

(ii) the unpaid purchase price is in respect of the property, and

(iii) throughout the period that began when the unpaid purchase price became owing by the affiliate and ended when the unpaid purchase price was so paid, the property had been used principally to earn income described in clause (8)(*a*)(i)(A) or (B).

► 17(8.2) ◄

(8.2) Deemed use. To the extent that this subsection applies in respect of new borrowings, the new borrowings are, for the purpose of subsection (8), deemed to have been used for the purpose for which the proceeds from the previous borrowings were used or were deemed by this subsection to have been used, or to acquire the property in respect of which the unpaid purchase price was payable, as the case may be.

► 17(9) ◄

(9) Exception. Subsection (1) does not apply to a corporation resident in Canada for a taxation year of the corporation in respect of an amount owing to the corporation by a non-resident person if

(*a*) the corporation is not related to the non-resident person throughout the period in the year during which the amount owing is outstanding;

(*b*) the amount owing arose in respect of goods sold or services provided to the non-resident person by the corporation in the ordinary course of the business carried on by the corporation; and

(*c*) the terms and conditions in respect of the amount owing are such that persons dealing at arm's length would have been willing to enter into them at the time that they were entered into.

Editorial Note: S. 17(9) provides a further exception to the income inclusion under subsection (1). To qualify for this exception, the following test must be met: (a) the corporation is not related to the non-resident person while the amount owed is outstanding ("related" is defined in s. 251 as modified for purposes of s. 17 by s. 17(10), (11) and (11.1)); (b) the amount owing is for goods or services sold to the non-resident person by the Canadian-resident corporation in the ordinary course of its business; and (c) the terms and conditions for the amount owing are those that parties at arm's length would have been willing to enter into. Essentially, this provision ensures that trade receivables incurred in the ordinary course of a Canadian corporation's business are not caught by the rule in s. 17.

Related Sections: S. 251(1) Arm's length.

Tax Window Files: Reasonable Rate of Interest, *Technical Interpretation, International and Trusts Division, March 6, 2003,* CRA Document No. 2002-0178357.

► 17(10) ◄

(10) Determination of whether related and controlled foreign affiliate status. For the purpose of this section, in determining whether persons are related to each other and whether a non-resident corporation is a controlled foreign affiliate of a corporation resident in Canada at any time,

(*a*) each member of a partnership is deemed to own that proportion of the number of shares of a class of the capital stock of a corporation owned by the partnership at that time that

(i) the fair market value of the member's interest in the partnership at that time

is of

(ii) the fair market value of all interests in the partnership at that time; and

(*b*) each beneficiary of a non-discretionary trust is deemed to own that proportion of the number of shares of a class of the capital stock of a corporation owned by the trust at that time that

(i) the fair market value of the beneficiary's interest in the trust at that time

is of

(ii) the fair market value of all the beneficial interests in the trust at that time.

► 17(11) ◄

(11) Determination of whether related. For the purpose of this section, in determining whether persons are related to each other at any time, each settlor in respect of a trust, other than a non-discretionary trust, is deemed to own the shares of a class of the capital stock of a corporation owned by the trust at that time.

Related Sections: S. 251(2) Definition of "related persons"; s. 251(3) Corporations related through a third corporation; s. 251(3.1) Relation where amalgamation or merger; s. 251(3.2) Amalgamation of related corporations; s. 251(4) Definitions concerning groups; s. 251(5) Control by related groups, options, etc; s. 251(6) Blood relationship, etc.

► 17(11.1) ◄

(11.1) Determination of whether persons related. For the purposes of this section, in determining whether persons are related to each other at any time, any rights referred to in subparagraph 251(5)(*b*)(i) that exist at that time are deemed not to exist at that time to the extent that the exercise of those rights is prohibited at that time under a law of the country under the law of which the corporation was formed or last continued and is governed, that restricts the foreign ownership or control of the corporation.

► 17(11.2) ◄

(11.2) Back-to-back loans. For the purposes of subsection (2) and paragraph (3)(*b*), where a non-resident person, or a partnership each member of which is non-resident, (in this subsection referred to as the "intermediate lender") makes a loan to a non-resident person, or a partnership each member of which is non-resident, (in this subsection referred to as the "intended borrower") because the intermediate lender received a loan from another non-resident person, or a partnership each member of which is non-resident, (in this subsection referred to as the "initial lender")

(*a*) the loan made by the intermediate lender to the intended borrower is deemed to have been made by the initial lender to the intended borrower (to the extent of the lesser of the amount of the loan made by the initial lender to the intermediate lender and the amount of the loan made by the intermediate lender to the intended borrower) under the same terms and conditions and at the same time as it was made by the intermediate lender; and

(*b*) the loan made by the initial lender to the intermediate lender and the loan made by the intermediate lender to the intended borrower are deemed not to have been made to the extent of the amount of the loan deemed to have been made under paragraph (*a*).

Editorial Note: S. 17(11.2) prevents the use of back-to-back loans to avoid the application of subsection (2). If a non-resident person loans an amount to a non-resident person because the lender received a loan from another non-resident person, s. 17(11.2) will apply to deem the initial lender to have made the loan directly to the intended borrower for purposes of subsection (2).

Tax Topics: No. 1631, Tinkering with Section 17.

► 17(11.3) ◄

(11.3) Determination of whether persons related. For the purpose of applying paragraph (3)(*b*) in respect of a corporation resident in Canada described in paragraph (2)(*b*), in determining whether persons described in subparagraph (3)(*b*)(i) are related to each other at any time, any rights referred to in paragraph 251(5)(*b*) that otherwise exist at that time are deemed not to exist at that time where, if the rights were exercised immediately before that time,

(*a*) all of those persons would at that time be controlled foreign affiliates of the corporation resident in Canada; and

(*b*) because of subsection (8), subsection (1) would not apply to the corporation resident in Canada in respect of the amount that would, but for this subsection, have been deemed to have been owing at that time to the corporation resident in Canada by the non-resident person described in subparagraph (3)(*b*)(i).

► 17(12) ◄

(12) Determination of controlled foreign affiliate status. For the purpose of this section, in determining whether a non-resident person is a controlled foreign affiliate of a corporation resident in Canada at any time, each settlor in respect of a trust, other than a non-discretionary trust, is deemed to own that proportion of the number of shares of a class of the capital stock of a corporation owned by the trust at that time that one is of the number of settlors in respect of the trust at that time.

► 17(13) ◄

(13) Extended definition of controlled foreign affiliate. For the purpose of this section, where, at any time, two corporations resident in Canada are related (otherwise than because of a right referred to in paragraph 251(5)(*b*)), any corporation that is a controlled foreign affiliate of one of the corporations at that time is deemed to be a controlled foreign affiliate of the other corporation at that time.

► 17(14) ◄

(14) Anti-avoidance rule — where rights or shares issued, acquired or disposed of to avoid tax. For the purpose of this section,

(*a*) where any person or partnership has a right under a contract, in equity or otherwise, either immediately or in the future and either absolutely or contingently, to, or to acquire, shares of the capital stock of a corporation and it can reasonably be considered that the principal purpose for the existence of the right is to avoid or reduce the amount of income that subsection (1) would otherwise require any corporation to include in computing its income for any taxation year, those shares are deemed to be owned by that person or partnership; and

(*b*) where any person or partnership acquires or disposes of shares of the capital stock of a corporation, either directly or indirectly, and it can reasonably be considered that the principal purpose for the acquisition or disposition of the shares is to avoid or reduce the amount of income that subsection (1) would otherwise require any corporation to include in computing its income for any taxation year, those shares are deemed not to have been acquired or disposed of, as the case may be, and where the shares were unissued by the corporation immediately before the acquisition, those shares are deemed not to have been issued.

► 17(15) ◄

(15) Definitions. The definitions in this subsection apply in this section.

"controlled foreign affiliate" — "controlled foreign affiliate", at any time, of a taxpayer resident in Canada, means a corporation that would, at that time, be a controlled foreign affiliate of the taxpayer within the meaning assigned by the definition "controlled foreign affiliate" in subsection 95(1) if the word "or" were added at the end of paragraph (*a*) of that definition and

(*a*) subparagraph (*b*)(ii) of that definition were read as "all of the shares of the capital stock of the foreign affiliate that are owned at that time by persons resident in Canada who do not deal at arm's length with the taxpayer,"; and

(*b*) subparagraph (*b*)(iv) of that definition were read as "all of the shares of the capital stock of the foreign affiliate that are owned at that time by persons resident in Canada who do not deal at arm's length with any relevant Canadian shareholder;".

"exempt loan or transfer" — "exempt loan or transfer" means

(*a*) a loan made by a corporation resident in Canada where the interest rate charged on the loan is not less than the interest rate that a lender and a borrower would have been willing to agree to if they were dealing at arm's length with each other at the time the loan was made;

(*b*) a transfer of property (other than a transfer of property made for the purpose of acquiring shares of the capital stock of a foreign affiliate of a corporation or a foreign affiliate of a person resident in Canada with whom the corporation was not dealing at arm's length) or payment of an amount owing by a corporation resident in Canada pursuant to an agreement made on terms and conditions that persons who were dealing at arm's length at the time the agreement was entered into would have been willing to agree to;

(*c*) a dividend paid by a corporation resident in Canada on shares of a class of its capital stock; and

(*d*) a payment made by a corporation resident in Canada on a reduction of the paid-up capital in respect of shares of a class of its capital stock (not exceeding the total amount of the reduction).

"non-discretionary trust" —"non-discretionary trust", at any time, means a trust in which all interests were vested indefeasibly at the beginning of the trust's taxation year that includes that time.

"settlor" —"settlor" in respect of a trust at any time means any person or partnership that has made a loan or transfer of property, either directly or indirectly, in any manner whatever, to or for the benefit of the trust at or before that time, other than, where the person or partnership deals at arm's length with the trust at that time,

(*a*) a loan made by the person or partnership to the trust at a reasonable rate of interest; or

(*b*) a transfer made by the person or partnership to the trust for fair market value consideration.

SECTION 17.1: Deemed interest income — sections 15 and 212.3

► 17.1(1) ◄

(1) Deemed interest income — sections 15 and 212.3. Subject to subsection (2), if — at any time in a taxation year of a corporation resident in Canada (in this section referred to as the "CRIC") or in a fiscal period of a qualifying Canadian partnership in respect of the CRIC — a non-resident corporation, or a partnership of which the non-resident corporation is a member, owes an amount to the CRIC or the qualifying Canadian partnership and the amount owing is a pertinent loan or indebtedness (as defined in subsection 15(2.11) or 212.3(11)),

(*a*) section 17 does not apply in respect of the amount owing; and

(*b*) the amount, if any, determined by the following formula is to be included in computing the income of the CRIC for the year or of the qualifying Canadian partnership for the fiscal period, as the case may be:

$$A - B$$

where

A is the amount that is the greater of

(i) the amount of interest that would be included in computing the income of the CRIC for the year or of the qualifying Canadian partnership for the fiscal period, as the case may be, in respect of the amount owing for the particular period in the year, or the fiscal period, during which the amount owing was a pertinent loan or indebtedness if that interest were computed at the prescribed rate for the particular period, and

(ii) the total of all amounts of interest payable in respect of the period in the year, or the fiscal period, during which the amount owing was a pertinent loan or indebtedness, by the CRIC, the qualifying Canadian partnership, a person resident in Canada with which the CRIC did not, at the time the amount owing arose, deal at arm's length or a partnership of which the CRIC or the person is a member, in respect of a debt obligation — entered into as part of a series of transactions or events that includes the transaction by which the amount owing arose — to the extent that the proceeds of the debt obligation can reasonably be considered to have directly or indirectly funded, in whole or in part, the amount owing, and

B is an amount included in computing the income of the CRIC for the year or of the qualifying Canadian partnership for the fiscal period, as the case may be, as, on account of, in lieu of or in satisfaction of, interest in respect of the amount owing for the period in the year, or the fiscal period, during which the amount owing was a pertinent loan or indebtedness.

Editorial Note: S. 17.1 of the Act applies to an amount that is a "pertinent loan or indebtedness" ("PLOI") for purposes of either s. 15(2.11) or 212.3(11). Very generally, a PLOI is an amount owing by a non-resident corporation to a corporation resident in Canada (a "CRIC") where certain conditions are met. See the editorial note to s. 15(2.11) and the editorial note to s. 212.3(11) for commentary on when a loan or indebtedness qualifies as a PLOI. Generally, the loan must have been made (or, in certain cases, the maturity date of the loan extended) after March 28, 2012, in order to qualify.

S. 17.1 requires the CRIC to include an amount in income in each year the PLOI is outstanding. The amount of income to be included is the amount prescribed under Regulation 4301(b.1), less any actual interest on the PLOI included in income. Generally, the prescribed interest rate under Regulation 4301(b.1) is 4% plus the amount that would be determined under Regulation 4301(a) if that amount were not rounded up to the nearest whole integer but were instead rounded to two decimal points.

History: S. 17.1(1) was added by S.C. 2012, c. 31, s. 6(1), applicable to taxation years and fiscal periods that end after March 28, 2012.

Tax Window Files: S. 17.1 and debt denominated in foreign currency, *June 4, 2014*, CRA Document No. 2014-0517151E5.

► 17.1(2) ◄

(2) Acquisition of control. If at any time a parent referred to in section 212.3 acquires control of a CRIC and the CRIC was not controlled by a non-resident corporation immediately before that time, no amount is to be included under subsection (1) in computing the income of the CRIC in respect of a pertinent loan or indebtedness (as defined in subsection 212.3(11)) for the period that begins at that time and ends on the day that is 180 days after that time.

> **Proposed Amendment**
> **2019 Federal Budget Resolutions**
> **Subsection 17.1(2) of the Act is replaced by the following:**
>
> **(2) Acquisition of control.** If at any time a parent or group of parents referred to in section 212.3 acquires control of a CRIC and the CRIC was not controlled by a non-resident person, or a group of non-resident persons not dealing with each other at arm's length, immediately before that time, no amount is to be included under subsection (1) in computing the income of the CRIC in respect of a *pertinent loan or indebtedness* (as defined in subsection 212.3(11)) for the period that begins at that time and ends on the day that is 180 days after that time.
>
> **Applicable:** In respect of transactions or events that occur on or after March 19, 2019.

Editorial Note: Subsection 17.1(2) is a transitional relieving rule for a CRIC that first becomes controlled by a single non-resident corporation. For the first 180 days following the acquisition of control of the CRIC, no amount of deemed interest is required to be included under s. 17.1(1) in respect of a PLOI.

History: S. 17.1(2) was added by S.C. 2012, c. 31, s. 6(1), applicable to taxation years and fiscal periods that end after March 28, 2012. However, in respect of acquisitions of control of a corporation resident in Canada that occur before October 15, 2012, subsection 17.1(2) is to be read as follows:

"(2) If at any time a parent referred to in section 212.3 acquires control of a CRIC and the CRIC was not controlled by a non-resident corporation immediately before that time, no amount is to be included under subsection (1) in computing the income of the CRIC in respect of a pertinent loan or indebtedness (as defined in subsection 212.3(11)) for the period that begins on March 29, 2012 and ends on the day that is 180 days after the day on which the ways and means motion to implement this subsection is tabled in the House of Commons."

▶ 17.1(3) ◀

(3) Tax treaties. A particular loan or indebtedness that would, in the absence of this subsection, be a pertinent loan or indebtedness is deemed not to be a pertinent loan or indebtedness if, because of a provision of a tax treaty, the amount included in computing the income of the CRIC for any taxation year or of the qualifying Canadian partnership for any fiscal period, as the case may be, in respect of the particular loan or indebtedness is less than it would be if no tax treaty applied.

Editorial Note: S. 17.1(3) is an anti-avoidance provision that deems a particular loan or indebtedness that would otherwise be a PLOI not to be a PLOI where, because of a tax treaty, the income of the CRIC in respect of the particular loan or indebtedness is lower than it would be absent the treaty. The provision is intended to prevent taxpayers from obtaining competent authority relief in respect of the PLOI interest inclusion; however, because it is worded broadly, it may catch other situations that were likely not intended.

History: S. 17.1(3) was added by S.C. 2012, c. 31, s. 6(1), applicable to taxation years and fiscal periods that end after March 28, 2012.

Deductions

SECTION 18: General limitations

▶ 18(1) ◀

(1) General limitations. In computing the income of a taxpayer from a business or property no deduction shall be made in respect of

Editorial Note: S. 18(1) expressly disallows the deduction of certain amounts that might otherwise be deductible under general principles. The rest of s. 18 similarly sets out restrictions on the deductibility of amounts that might otherwise be deductible.

Related Sections: S. 9(1) Income; s. 9(2) Loss; s. 20(1) Deductions permitted in computing income from business or property; s. 248(1), "business", "property"; s. 249 Definition of "taxation year".

Interpretation Bulletins: *Primary* — IT-357R2 Expenses of training.

Cases: Child care expenses are not business expenses and as such are not deductible under s. 18(1). Furthermore such expenses are dealt with specifically under section 63 of the Act. *Symes v. The Queen et al.*, 94 DTC 6001 (S.C.C.)

▶ 18(1)(a) ◀

(a) General limitation — an outlay or expense except to the extent that it was made or incurred by the taxpayer for the purpose of gaining or producing income from the business or property;

Editorial Note: A taxpayer's income from a business or property is the profit therefrom for the year, subject to Part I (subsection 9(1)). By prohibiting a deduction "except to the extent" the outlay or expense was made or incurred for the purpose of gaining or producing income from a business or property, paragraph 18(1)(*a*) (in conjunction with subsection 9(1)) effectively permits the deduction of expenses incurred for those purposes. Unlike previous versions of paragraph 18(1)(*a*), it is not necessary that the expense be made "wholly, exclusively, and necessarily" for the purpose of earning income.

Expenses incurred, and not just expenses laid out or paid, can be deducted. Personal or living expenses cannot be deducted (see paragraph 18(1)(*h*)). Before an expense will be allowed, it must be "reasonable in the circumstances" (see section 67). The onus of proving that an expense was laid out to produce the income is on the taxpayer (*Gilbert v. M.N.R.*, 50 DTC 393 (T.A.B.)). See also IT-487 — General limitation on deduction of outlays or expenses (archived, as it doesn't meet current government web standards).

When Incurred: An expense is incurred when the taxpayer has a clearly legal, though not necessarily immediate, obligation to pay the amount (see in *J.L. Guay Ltée*, 71 DTC 5423 (F.C.T.D.) (affirmed in 73 DTC 5373 (F.C.A.) and 75 DTC 5094 (S.C.C.))). It is not enough that the liability to pay is relatively certain to arise in the future (*Winter et al. v. Inland Revenue Commissioners*, [1963] A.C. 235 (H.L.)).

"Purpose of Gaining or Producing Income": To determine whether a taxpayer incurred an expense for the purpose of gaining or producing income from a business or property, apply the "but for" test to the need which the expense meets. Would the need for the expense exist apart from — or "but for" — the existence of the business or property? If the answer is no, then the expense will generally be considered deductible. Courts look for objective manifestations of purpose, and purpose is ultimately a question of fact to be decided with regard for all of the circumstances. See *Symes v. The Queen*, 94 DTC 6001 (S.C.C.).

Types of Expenses or Outlays: Once it has been determined that an expense is deductible in computing income from a business or property, it is necessary to determine the classification of the expense for income tax purposes: capital expense; current expense (sometimes called expenses on income account); or cost of inventory. A current expense is normally deductible in the year in which it is incurred, although there are exceptions. The deduction of capital expenses is restricted except as expressly provided (see paragraph 18(1)(*b*)). If an expense forms part of the cost of inventory, it is normally deducted when the inventory is sold or decreases in value (see also section 10).

Mixed Purpose or Use: Where expenses are incurred partly for the purpose of earning income from a business or property and partly for another purpose (e.g., a personal purpose), only the amount expended in respect of the income from the business or property is deductible (see, for example, *Harvey v. The Queen*, 2013 DTC 1236 (T.C.C.)).

Repairs and Maintenance: Amounts expended on repairs and maintenance of capital property used for the purpose of earning income from a business or property are often deductible as current expenses. However, where major alterations of a capital property are made, the costs of making the alterations may be on capital account and therefore non-deductible (see paragraph 18(1)(*b*)). The general rule is that an expenditure is on capital account if it is made with a view to bringing into existence an asset or advantage for the enduring benefit of a trade (see *Minister of National Revenue v. Haddon Hall Realty Inc.*, 62 DTC 1001 (S.C.C.) and Income Tax Folio S3-F4-C1, *General Discussion of Capital Cost Allowance*.

Fines and Penalties: The deduction of fines or penalties imposed under the law of a country, including a state, province, or territory, are specifically prohibited, except for penalties imposed under paragraph 110(1)(*a*) of the *Excise Tax Act* (see section 67.6 and regulation 7309). No deduction is allowed for interest, penalties, or fines imposed under the Act (see paragraph 18(1)(*t*)), and the deduction of interest payable under the GST/HST provisions of Part XI of the *Excise Tax Act* is prohibited (paragraph 18(1)(*t*)). See also Income Tax Folio S4-F2-C1, *Deductibility of Fines and Penalties*.

Related Sections: S. 9(1) Income; s. 9(2) Loss; s. 18(1)(*h*) Personal and living expenses; s. 20(1) Deductions permitted in computing income from business or property; s. 20(16) Terminal loss; s. 21(1) Cost of borrowed money; s. 26(2) Banks — deductions from income; s. 30 Improving land for farming.

Canadian Petroleum Tax Journal: Tax Treatment and Classification of Costs in the Energy Sector, Chan and Van Dyke, 2008, Vol. 139, No. 1; Recent Cases of Interest — Deduction of Fines, Penalties, and Damage Awards, Gerald Grenon, 2000, Vol. 13, No. 1.

Canadian Tax Foundation: Morrison and Strawson, *Professional Fees Incurred for Voluntary Disclosure*, 2015 Canadian Tax Highlights 23(10):2–3; Gosselin, *Quebec Finds Big Cavity in Dentist's Management Services Company*, 2014 Tax for the Owner-Manager 14(4):1; Gervais and Power, *Can I Deduct That?*, 2013 Ontario Tax Conference 10:1–15; Neilson, *Deductibility of Expenses*, 2013 Prairie Provinces Tax Conference 14:1–21; Hally, *Taxpayer Misconduct and the Deductibility of Damages*, 2013 Canadian Tax Focus 3(4):10–11; Woon, *Current Cases: Canada v. Doiron, 2012 FCA 71 — The Business Purpose Test in s. 18(1)(a) of the Income Tax Act Is Not the "But For" Test*, 2012 Atlantic Provinces Tax Conference 1C:12–14; Rachert, *Proving Business Expenses: Checklists and Commentary*, 2012 British Columbia Tax Conference 11:1–21; Palmer and Walker, *Current Cases: The Deductibility of Advisory Fees Incurred to Reduce Withholding Taxes on Inbound Payments (Potash Corporation of Saskatchewan Inc. v. The Queen, 2011 TCC 213)*, 2011 Canadian Tax Journal 3:554–561; Tamaki and Richards, *The Significance of Commercial and Accounting Principles in Canadian Tax Cases*, 2010 Canadian Tax Journal SS:101–109; Blanchet, *Purchase and Sale of Assets: The Treatment to the Vendor of Contingent Liabilities Assumed*, 2009 Conference Report 11:1–22; Diksic and Desjardins, *Tax Treatment of Transaction Costs*, 2006 Conference Report 38:1–36; Ebel, *Transaction Costs*, 2005 Conference Report 35:1–27; Aiken, *Current Cases: A Reasonable Victim (Tax Court of Canada, Hammill v. The Queen, 2004 DTC 3271)*, 2005 Canadian Tax Journal 1:206–209; Sibson, *Reasonable Expectation of Profit: A Return to Sanity?*, 2002 Conference Report 6:1–10; Laiken and Laiken, *Working With the Source Test: The Supreme Court's Replacement for the Reasonable Expectation of Profit Test*, 2002 Canadian Tax Journal 3:1147–1177; Weinstein, *Damages, Fines, And Penalties: An Update*, 2000 Conference Report 7:1–29; Frankovic, *The Income Tax Treatment of Prepaid Expenses and Similar Costs: A Time Value Analysis*, 2000 Canadian Tax Journal 5:1371–1443; Lobsinger, *Current Cases: Federal Court of Appeal — Section 18(1)(a) Versus GAAP: Deduction for Amortized Rent Denied (Buck Consultants Limited v. The Queen, 2000 DTC 6015)*, 2000 Canadian Tax Journal 1:142–144; Carr, *Current Receipts and Expenses After Canderel, Toronto College Park, and Ikea*, 1998 Canadian Tax Journal 5:953–991; Frankovic, *The Matching of "Current" Expense Under Canada's Income Tax Laws*, 1998 Canadian Tax Journal 1:1–28; Harris, *Deductibility of Takeover Bid Costs*, 1996 Conference Report 23:1–29; Magee, *Real Estate Rental Losses and the Application of the Reasonable Expectation of Profit Test After the Tonn Decision*, 1996 Canadian Tax Journal 4:1150–1176; Owen, *The Reasonable Expectation of Profit Test: Is There a Better Approach?*, 1996 Canadian Tax Journal 4:979–1015; Fien, *To Profit or Not To Profit: A Historical Review and Critical Analysis of the "Reasonable Expectation of Profit" Test*, 1995 Canadian Tax Journal 5:1287–1315.

Tax Topics: No. 2292, *Grenon v. The Queen*: Deduction for Legal Fees in Determining Support Obligations; No. 2158, *Drouin v. The Queen*: Business, Sham, and Reasonableness; No. 1999, *Opacic et al. v. The Queen*, 2010 DTC 1079 (T.C.C.); No. 1897, Unmasking "Management Fees" — What's in a Name?; No. 1862, The Deduction of Professional Fees — *Bolen v. The Queen*; No. 1805, The Matching Principle: RIP; No. 1667, *BJ Services:* The Porosity of Paragraph 18(1)(*a*); No. 1526, Contingent expenses.

Guides: T4036 Rental Income.

Income Tax Folios: *Primary* — S3-F9-C1 Lottery Winnings, Miscellaneous Receipts, and Income (and Losses) from Crime.

Income Tax Technical News: Issue No. 24, Legal Costs to Obtain Support Amounts.

Information Circulars: IC 77-11 Sales tax reassessments — Deductibility in computing income; IC 88-2 para. 18 — General anti-avoidance rule — Section 245 of the Income Tax Act.

Interpretation Bulletins: *Primary* — IT-99R5 (Consolid.) Legal and accounting fees; IT-211R Membership dues — Associations and societies; IT-261R Prepayments of rents; IT-357R2 Expenses of training; IT-364 Commencement of business operations; IT-467R2 Damages, settlements and similar payments; IT-475 Expenditures on research and for business expansion; IT-487 General limitation on deduction of outlays or expenses; IT-521 Motor vehicle expenses claimed by self-employed individuals. *Secondary* — IT-153R3 Land developers — Subdivision and development costs and carrying charges on land; IT-341R4 Expenses of issuing or selling shares, units in a trust, interests in a partnership or syndicate and expenses of borrowing money.

Tax Window Files: Damages Received for Cancellation of a Service Contract, *Technical Interpretation, Business and Partnerships Division, December 6, 2006*, CRA Document No. 2005-0163291E5; Legal Fees Incurred with Respect to Shareholder Oppression Remedy Suit, *Technical Interpretation, Business and Partnerships Division, October 3, 2006*, CRA Document No. 2006-0181191I7; Contractors Payments to Subcontractors — Deduction for Reasonable Expenses, *Technical Interpretation, Business and Partnerships Division, May 31, 2006*, CRA Document No. 2006-0181651I7; Deductibility of Professional Liability Insurance, *Technical Interpretation, Business and Partnerships Division, December 21, 2004*, CRA Document No. 2004-0091011E5. Liability insurance premiums paid after a professional closed his business but in respect of acts performed in the course of the previous business practice remained deductible; Deduction of Various Expenses Connected with an Illegal Business, *Technical Interpretation, Business and Partnerships Division, June 8, 2004*, CRA Document No. 2004-0067401I7. Expenses incurred for purpose of earning income from illegal business deductible, but expenses incurred by taxpayer to defend against personal criminal accusations not deductible; Professional Membership Initiation or Admission Fees, *Technical Interpretation, Business and Partnerships Division, April 14, 2004*, CRA Document No. 2004-0058301E5. Employer-paid initiation fees and annual membership fees for employees of professional organization deductible for employer; Deductibility of Unrealized Losses on FX Contracts, *Technical Interpretation, International and Trusts Division, January 28, 2004*, CRA Document No. 2003-0028891E5. Accrued losses at year end from foreign exchange contracts deductible if incurred for purposes of paragraph 18(1)(*a*) and not contingent for purposes of paragraph 18(1)(*e*).

Cases: The amounts in question were not deductible charitable gifts because: (a) the taxpayer received consideration for them in the form of a percentage of the proceeds of the ultimate sale of the company's factory; (b) the taxpayer was obligated to make them; and (c) the taxpayer had no donative intent when paying them. The amounts were not deductible as business expenses since they were not paid with a view to repairing or enhancing the taxpayer's reputation, as claimed, but were paid for other reasons not directly related to the earning of income. *Fonds de Solidarité des Travailleurs du Québec v. The Queen*, 2018 DTC 1028 (TCC), affirmed 2019 DTC 5024 (FCA)

Legal expenses are deductible if incurred for the purpose of gaining or producing income from a business or property. The right to support is "property", and income which flows from the exercise of that right is associated with it. Expenses incurred by the payer of support cannot be considered to have been incurred for the purpose of producing income from property. *Grenon v. The Queen*, 2016 DTC 5009 (FCA)

Legal expenses incurred by a taxpayer making support payments, including expenses to terminate those payments, are not deductible as expenses incurred to earn income. *Landry v. The Queen*, 2014 DTC 1198 (T.C.C.)

Legal expenses were incurred to obtain an increased entitlement to a portion of the taxpayer's father's estate. This did not constitute a legal expense incurred to earn income and was not deductible. *Deschenes v. The Queen*, 2016 DTC 5026 (F.C.A.), application for leave to appeal to S.C.C. dismissed.

Despite certain information being excluded by virtue of solicitor-client privilege, some fees related to legal invoices were allowable deductions. *Richard A. Kanan Corporation v. The Queen*, 2014 DTC 1121 (T.C.C.)

Neither the Minister nor the Court is obliged to determine a factual dispute in a taxpayer's favour simply because that taxpayer refuses to waive a claim of solicitor-client privilege with respect to the admission of evidence that could resolve the dispute. *Dr. Mike Orth Inc. v. The Queen*, 2014 DTC 5032 (F.C.A.)

The taxpayer claimed deductions for legal expenses to defend against charges brought by the O.S.C. and a class action lawsuit. The connection between the legal expenses and the taxpayer's consulting activities was too remote to be deductible, and the deduction of legal fees incurred to preserve the taxpayer's reputation and capacity to earn income was prohibited by s. 18(1)(*b*). *Gouveia v. The Queen*, 2014 DTC 1035 (TCC), affirmed 2019 DTC 5022 (FCA).

The taxpayer failed to establish the requisite connection between the legal and professional expenses and his income in order for the expenses to be deductible. *Ironside v. The Queen*, 2014 DTC 1002 (T.C.C.)

The taxpayer unsuccessfully sued two of his children for control of a family-run insurance business. He claimed that their actions deprived him of his ability to continue earning employment income, but his legal expenses were not deductible under s. 8(1)(*b*) as expenditures to collect employment income or under s. 18(1)(*a*) as expenses laid out to earn income from business or property. *Hollinger Estate v. The Queen*, 2013 DTC 1210 (T.C.C.)

On the advice of a financial planner, the taxpayer acquired a software development franchise from a Barbados corporation which operated the franchise as his agent. Although tax considerations were important, he acquired the franchise to earn income and his investment was not a sham. He was carrying on business and could deduct expenses. *Drouin v. The Queen*, 2013 DTC 1146 (T.C.C.)

The taxpayer purchased term deposits to post as security for potential liabilities to US trade authorities. The cost was not deductible under s. 18(1)(*a*) since it was not an expense that was "once and for all, without recourse", as the taxpayer retained an interest in the funds. It was also a non-deductible reserve under s. 18(1)(*e*) in respect of a contingent liability. *Industries Perron Inc. v. The Queen*, 2013 DTC 5131 (F.C.A.), affirming 2012 DTC 1072 (T.C.C.)

A lawyer could not deduct $121,991 in gambling losses since his "professional" poker playing did not constitute a business. *Cohen v. The Queen*, 2011 DTC 1195 (T.C.C.)

Under a collective agreement, the taxpayer contributed to a contingency fund for employee programs. After previous court decisions held that these obligations were contingent, the documentation was amended specifically to create an absolute liability. Despite the amendment, the unexpended portion of the fund remained a contingent liability that was not deductible by virtue of s. 18(1)(*e*). *The Queen v. General Motors of Canada Limited*, 2008 DTC 6381 (F.C.A.), reversing 2007 DTC 272 (T.C.C.)

The taxpayer's parent company paid the taxpayer's employees to surrender options to purchase shares of the parent. The taxpayer reimbursed its parent for these payments and was entitled to deduct the amount reimbursed. The reimbursement payments could not be recharacterized as capital expenditures just because they were made in the context of the parent's corporate reorganization. *Shoppers Drug Mart Limited v. The Queen*, 2008 DTC 2043 (T.C.C.)

Professional fees incurred to reorganize capital structure and to update shareholder agreements were deductible as a current expense since they were incurred to earn income. *Truckbase Corporation et al. v. The Queen*, 2006 DTC 2930 (T.C.C.)

A lawyer could not deduct legal fees paid to defend himself on criminal charges. Although he argued that he would have lost his license to practice law if convicted, the legal fees were not a business expense, but a non-deductible personal expenditure. *Leduc v. The Queen*, 2005 DTC 250 (T.C.C.)

Financial and legal expenses incurred in defending against a hostile take-over bid were deductible. The expenses were a cost of doing business, and were so integral to conducting the target corporation's business that they could not be divorced from the corporate activities of gaining and producing income. *BJ Services Company Canada v. The Queen*, 2004 DTC 2032 (T.C.C.)

The taxpayer hired a firm of financial advisors which recommended a share for share exchange arrangement under which taxpayer's shareholders would become shareholders of a third party. The $1.2 million fee paid to the financial advisors was deductible as a current expense. *International Colin Energy Corporation v. The Queen*, 2002 DTC 2185 (T.C.C.)

Partnership losses with respect to a storage park operation were deductible since it constituted a source of income. Since it was commercial in nature, with no evidence of any personal element, the REOP test did not arise. Although the taxpayers were clearly motivated by tax considerations when purchasing their partnership interests, this does not detract from the commercial nature of the operation or its characterization as a source of income. *The Queen v. Walls et al.*, 2002 DTC 6960 (S.C.C.), affirming 2000 DTC 6025 (F.C.A.), reversing 96 DTC 6142 (F.C.T.D.)

The taxpayer, who purchased condominium units for rental purposes, was able to deduct related losses since the rental activity lacked any personal element and was clearly a commercial activity. REOP was not the appropriate test. The taxpayer's hope of realizing an eventual capital gain with the expectation of deducting interest expenses, did not detract from the commercial nature of his rental operation, or its characterization as a source of income. *Stewart v. The Queen*, 2002 DTC 6969 (S.C.C.), reversing 2000 DTC 6163 (F.C.A.) and 98 DTC 1600 (T.C.C.)

Employer contributions in respect of vacation pay were deductible in the year the contributions were made even though the vacations were not actually taken until a subsequent year. It is not a non-deductible reserve because the employer's obligation to pay such contributions is "incurred" as soon as the employee's entitlement to the vacation pay has been earned. *Fédération des Caisses Populaires Desjardins de Montréal et al. v. The Queen*, 2001 DTC 5173 (F.C.A.)

The taxpayers held back a portion of their payments to independent contractors until they received workers' compensation clearance certificates. The taxpayers were entitled to claim a deduction for the holdbacks since the contract price was not a contingent liability. It became an absolute obligation when the contractors had completed their work. *Wawang Forest Products Limited et al. v. The Queen*, 2001 DTC 5212 (F.C.A.), reversing 99 DTC 759 (T.C.C.)

The taxpayer was entitled to deduct legal fees in connection with divorce proceedings since the fees were incurred to obtain maintenance payments to which she was entitled under the *Divorce Act*. *Gallien v. The Queen*, 2000 DTC 2514 (T.C.C.)

The taxpayer sought to deduct notional (but unpaid) rent during a rent-free period provided in its lease. This was calculated in accordance with an amortization formula said to reflect GAAP. It was not deductible for tax purposes because s. 18(1)(*a*) requires that the "outlay or expense" be "made or incurred" to earn income. *Buck Consultants Limited v. The Queen*, 2000 DTC 6015 (F.C.A.), affirming 96 DTC 1464 (T.C.C.)

A land developer was entitled to deduct a $2.9 million regional development charge in the year it was paid, even though none of the lands affected by the charge were sold by the taxpayer during that year. *Urbandale Realty Corporation Limited v. The Queen*, 2000 DTC 6118 (F.C.A.), reversing 97 DTC 5353 (F.C.T.D.) and 93 DTC 154 (T.C.C.)

An over-quota levy in relation to the excess production of eggs was deductible since it was incurred as part of the taxpayer's day-to-day operations and was incurred for the purposes of earning income. The characterization of the levy as a "fine or penalty" was of no consequence. *65302 British Columbia Limited v. The Queen*, 99 DTC 5799 (S.C.C.), reversing 98 DTC 6002 (F.C.A.), which reversed 96 DTC 2049. (T.C.C.)

The deduction by a "foot and transit" courier of the cost of extra food and water was allowed as a business expense because he was using them as a replacement for automobile fuel. *Scott v. The Queen*, 98 DTC 6530 (F.C.A.)

The estimated costs of a taxpayer's silviculture obligations under its provincial timber harvesting licence were not deductible since the obligation to pay them had not come into existence in the taxation years in issue. *Northwood Pulp and Timber Ltd. v. The Queen*, 98 DTC 6640 (F.C.A.), affirming 96 DTC 1104 (T.C.C.)

Tenant inducement payments paid by the taxpayer were not required to be amortized over the course of the lease, and were deductible in the year incurred. *Toronto College Park v. The Queen*, 98 DTC 6088 (S.C.C.), reversing 96 DTC 6407 (F.C.A.). *Canderel Limited v. The Queen*, 98 DTC 6100 (S.C.C.), reversing 95 DTC 5101 (F.C.A.)

Although the circulars sent by a taxpayer to outline its position on take-over bids were not financial reports, they were required by securities legislation and their costs were deductible. *The Queen v. Boulangerie St-Augustin Inc.*, 97 DTC 5012 (F.C.A.), affirming 95 DTC 164 (T.C.C.)

The taxpayers' rental losses could not be disallowed, under the reasonable expectation of profit test, without giving their enterprise a reasonable length of time beyond the three start-up years to prove itself capable of yielding profits. *Tonn et al. v. The Queen*, 96 DTC 6001 (F.C.A.)

► 18(1)(b) ◄

(b) Capital outlay or loss — an outlay, loss or replacement of capital, a payment on account of capital or an allowance in respect of depreciation, obsolescence or depletion except as expressly permitted by this Part;

Editorial Note: The deduction (depreciation) of the cost of depreciable property is provided under the capital cost allowance provisions of s. 20(1)(*a*) and the regulations thereunder. The costs of certain intangible capital expenses are deductible under specific provisions (for example, financing costs and similar amounts under ss. 20(1)(*c*) through (*f*)). Most other intangible capital expenses fall into the "catch-all" category of eligible capital expenditure and are deducted (amortized) under s. 20(1)(*b*).

Certain other intangible expenses that are capital in nature (e.g. financing expenses) are deductible under other provisions of subsection 20(1).

Related Sections: S. 14(5), "Eligible capital expenditure"; s. 20(1) Deductions permitted in computing income from business or property; s. 20(1)(*a*) Capital cost of property; s. 20(1)(*b*) Cumulative eligible capital amount; s. 20(10) Convention expenses; s. 20(16) Terminal loss; s. 24(1) Ceasing to carry on business; s. 26(2) Banks — deductions from income; s. 30 Improving land for farming; s. 39(1)(*b*) and (*c*) Meaning of capital gain and capital loss.

Canadian Petroleum Tax Journal: Tax Treatment and Classification of Costs in the Energy Sector, Chan and Van Dyke, 2008, Vol. 139, No. 1; Pot Pourri of Income Tax Issues, John Chan, 2001, Vol. 14, No. 1.

Canadian Tax Foundation: Morris and Templeton, *Current Cases: Federal Court of Appeal — Deductibility of Stock Option Cashouts Denied (Imperial Tobacco Canada Limited v. Canada, 2011 FCA 308)*, 2012 Canadian Tax Journal 1:143–148; Ebel, *Transaction Costs*, 2005 Conference Report 35:1–27; Flatters, *The Distinction Between Income and Capital in the Income Tax Act*, 2005 Prairie Provinces Tax Conference 16:1–15; Frankovic, *Why Interest Should Be Considered a Current Expense*, 2001 Canadian Tax Journal 4:859–872; Durnford, *The Deductibility of Building Repair and Renovation Costs*, 1997 Canadian Tax Journal 3:395–416.

Tax Profile: April 2004 — Interest is Almost Always a Capital Expense.

Tax Topics: No. 2027, On Account of Income or Capital?; No. 1882, Stock Market Losses: Might They Be Fully Deductible?; No. 1740, Lease Negotiation and Finder Fees; No. 1673, Supreme Court's Decision on Interest Deductibility Defies Logic.

Income Tax Folios: *Primary* — S3-F4-C1 General Discussion of Capital Cost Allowance. *Secondary* — S4-F2-C1 Deductibility of Fines and Penalties.

Interpretation Bulletins: *Primary* — IT-187 Customer lists and ledger accounts; IT-467R2 Damages, settlements and similar payments; IT-475 Expenditures on research and for business expansion. *Secondary* — IT-99R5 (Consolid.) Legal and accounting fees; IT-143R3 Meaning of eligible capital expenditure; IT-261R Prepayments of rents; IT-341R4 Expenses of issuing or selling shares, units in a trust, interests in a partnership or syndicate and expenses of borrowing money; IT-364 Commencement of business operations.

Tax Window Files: Clothing Expenses of a Personal Style Consultant, *Technical Interpretation, Business and Partnerships Division, January 16, 2007*, CRA Document No. 2006-0217641E5; Damages Received for Cancellation of a Service Contract, *Technical Interpretation, Business and Partnerships Division, December 6, 2006*, CRA Document No. 2005-0163291E5; Discount on Sales of Accounts Receivable, *Technical Interpretation, Financial Sector and Exempt Entities Division, October 30, 2006*, CRA Document No. 2006-0199721I7; Contract Termination Payment, *Technical Interpretation, Business and Partnerships Division, November 5, 2003*, CRA Document No. 2003-0043297. Contract termination payment normally on income account if contract settled in the course of an ongoing business, but on capital account if made as a consequence of the termination of the business.

Cases: The taxpayer claimed deductions for legal expenses to defend against charges brought by the O.S.C. and a class action lawsuit. The connection between the legal expenses and the taxpayer's consulting activities was too remote to be deductible, and the deduction of legal fees incurred to preserve the taxpayer's reputation and capacity to earn income was prohibited by s. 18(1)(*b*). *Gouveia v. The Queen*, 2014 DTC 1035 (TCC), affirmed 2019 DTC 5022 (FCA)

The taxpayer and a predecessor corporation made payments to individuals who held options to acquire shares of the corporations. When the payments were made, the options were automatically extinguished at the moment of the transaction and were not acquired by the payor corporation. The payments were consideration for the termination of those options and were not the cost of the options. They were incurred by the corporations in respect of their businesses, on account of capital, for the purpose of gaining or producing income from those businesses, thus satisfying the definition of eligible capital expenditure, and were deductible. *Devon Canada Corporation v. The Queen*, 2018 DTC 1117 (TCC)

Oversight expenses were currently deductible on the basis they were frequent and recurring for the taxpayer and part of its annual costs of business. The costs were incurred by the company's board of directors in the discharge of its oversight responsibilities with respect to the management of the company's income-earning process, as evaluation of corporate opportunities was an ongoing quest for the directors and intrinsically linked to the income-earning process. Expenses for advertising and reporting fees were capital expenses and not currently deductible. *The Queen v. Rio Tinto Alcan Inc.*, 2018 DTC 5075 (FCA)

The taxpayer purchased two rental properties and carried out major renovations (kitchens, bathrooms, floors, windows, etc.) prior to renting them. In evaluating a series of repairs, the collective approach is required, rather than an analysis of each individual repair. The costs were on capital account since they were incurred to ready the properties for rental and were part of the acquisition cost. *Hare v. The Queen*, 2013 DTC 5066 (F.C.A.), affirming 2011 DTC 1215 (T.C.C.)

Payments to compensate employees for surrendering their stock options, as part of a corporate reorganization, were non-deductible capital outlays. *Imperial Tobacco Canada Limited v. The Queen*, 2012 DTC 5003 (F.C.A.), affirming 2011 DTC 1037 (T.C.C.)

Professional fees incurred to reorganize capital structure and to update shareholder agreements were not subject to the s. 18(1)(*b*) restrictions on the deductibility of capital expenses. *Truckbase Corporation et al. v. The Queen*, 2006 DTC 2930 (T.C.C.)

Fees paid to an agent to find new store locations and to negotiate leases and renewals were deductible expenses, not capital outlays. *Pantorama Industries Inc. v. The Queen*, 2005 DTC 5230 (F.C.A.), reversing 2004 DTC 2536 (T.C.C.)

Considering that the only asset that a taxpayer was trying to maintain and preserve in a libel suit was a capital asset (his professional reputation), his legal expenses were not deductible. *Upenieks v. The Queen et al.*, 94 DTC 6656 (F.C.A.)

When properties had been purchased for less than their normal capital value at that time, the expenditures needed (due to their condition) to restore them to their normal value was capital in nature. *Fiore v. The Queen*, 93 DTC 5215 (F.C.A.)

The taxpayer was in the business of open pit asbestos mining. As the size of the pit expanded, the taxpayer was required to purchase adjoining land from time to time in order to maintain the stability of the pit walls. The cost of the land purchases was found to be a deductible business expense rather than a capital expenditure. *Johns-Manville Canada Inc. v. The Queen*, 85 DTC 5373 (S.C.C.), reversing 82 DTC 6054 (F.C.A.), which reversed 79 DTC 5270 (F.C.T.D.)

Cost of a geological survey undertaken by a railway company to place the resulting information with interested members of the public in the hope that it would lead to development of the area and attract business was not a capital expenditure. The result of the survey was not an acquisition of an advantage of an enduring benefit but merely the procurement of some information. *Algoma Central Railway v. M.N.R.*, 68 DTC 5096 (S.C.C.), affirming 67 DTC 5091 (Ex. Ct.)

► 18(1)(c) ◄

(c) Limitation re exempt income — an outlay or expense to the extent that it may reasonably be regarded as having been made or incurred for the purpose of gaining or producing exempt income or in connection with property the income from which would be exempt;

Income Tax Folios: *Secondary* — S4-F2-C1 Deductibility of Fines and Penalties.

Interpretation Bulletins: *Primary* — IT-467R2 Damages, settlements and similar payments. *Secondary* — IT-341R4 Expenses of issuing or selling shares, units in a trust, interests in a partnership or syndicate and expenses of borrowing money.

► 18(1)(d) ◄

(d) Annual value of property — the annual value of property except rent for property leased by the taxpayer for use in the taxpayer's business;

► 18(1)(e) ◄

(e) Reserves, etc. — an amount as, or on account of, a reserve, a contingent liability or amount or a sinking fund except as expressly permitted by this Part;

Editorial Note: The restriction in the predecessor to s. 18(1)(*e*) was apparently construed by reference to accounting principles; see the Supreme Court of Canada decision in the *Time Motors* case (69 DTC 5149). Whether the restriction in current s. 18(1)(*e*) is construed by reference to accounting principles or legal principles is explored in the Frankovic article cited below (see "Canadian Tax Foundation", below, at 41-50 of the article). The author concludes that legal principles should apply for the purpose of determining whether an amount is contingent.

Related Sections: S. 20(1)(*l*) Doubtful or impaired debts; s. 20(1)(*l*.1) Reserve for guarantees, etc.; s. 20(1)(*m*) Reserve in respect of certain goods and services; s. 20(1)(*m*.1) Manufacturer's warranty reserve; s. 20(1)(*n*) Reserve for unpaid amounts; s. 20(1)(*o*) Reserve for quadrennial survey; s. 20(1)(*p*) Bad debts.

Canadian Tax Foundation: Frankovic, *The Case for "Reverse Depreciation" of Reclamation Costs*, 2004 Canadian Tax Journal 1:1–58; Templeton, *Current Cases: Ontario Court of Appeal — Contingency: Accounting or Legal Concept? (Canadian Pacific Limited v. The Minister of Revenue (Ontario), 99 DTC 5286)*, 1999 Canadian Tax Journal 4:968–974.

Tax Profile: February 2005 — The Canadian Treatment of Derivatives.

Tax Topics: No. 1793, Contingent Liabilities: The Gathering Storm; No. 1526, Contingent Expenses.

Interpretation Bulletins: *Primary* — IT-467R2 Damages, settlements and similar payments. *Secondary* — IT-109R2 Unpaid amounts.

Tax Window Files: Site Reclamation Costs, *Technical Interpretation, Reorganizations and Resources Division, September 27, 2004*, CRA Document No. 2003-0048241E5. Comments regarding the deduction of reclamation costs; Contingent Liability — Payment on Death of Member, *Technical Interpretation, Financial Industries Division, March 25, 2004*, CRA Document No. 2003-0043431E5. Refundable fees payable in the event of death were contingent; Deductibility of Unrealized Losses on FX Contracts, *Technical Interpretation, International and Trusts Division, January 28, 2004*, CRA Document No. 2003-0028891E5. Accrued losses at year end from foreign exchange contracts deductible only if incurred as a legal matter for purposes of paragraph 18(1)(*a*) and if not contingent for purposes of paragraph 18(1)(*e*).

Cases: The taxpayer purchased term deposits to post as security for potential liabilities to US trade authorities. The cost was not deductible under s. 18(1)(*a*) since it was not an expense that was "once and for all, without recourse", as the taxpayer retained an interest in the funds. It was also a non-deductible reserve under s. 18(1)(*e*) in respect of a contingent liability. *Industries Perron Inc. v. The Queen*, 2013 DTC 5131 (F.C.A.), affirming 2012 DTC 1072 (T.C.C.)

Under a collective agreement, the taxpayer contributed to a contingency fund for employee programs. After previous court decisions held that these obligations were contingent, the documentation was amended specifically to create an absolute liability. Despite the amendment, the unexpended portion of the fund remained a contingent liability that was not deductible by virtue of s. 18(1)(*e*). *The Queen v. General Motors of Canada Limited*, 2008 DTC 6381 (F.C.A.), reversing 2007 DTC 272 (T.C.C.)

The taxpayer acquired an interest in seismic data for a cash payment and a promissory note. He agreed to pay $85,000 plus 8% interest under the terms of the note and, accordingly, his liability was absolute. The fact that it was a limited-recourse debt and might not be repaid in full did not render the liability contingent. *The Queen v. McLarty*, 2008 DTC 6354 (S.C.C.), affirming in part 2006 DTC 6340 (F.C.A.), affirming in part 2005 DTC 217 (T.C.C.)

When the taxpayer purchased a property, it assumed whatever liability the vendor might have had for environmental clean up. The taxpayer could not add the "cost" of this assumed liability to the purchase price of the buildings and equipment for CCA purposes since no amount had actually been spent on clean-up and there was no evidence that the vendor actually had any legally enforceable liability. *A & D Holdings Inc. v. The Queen*, 2006 DTC 2219 (T.C.C.)

Under a collective agreement, the taxpayer established a contingency fund, from which payments were made to certain benefit plans when prescribed thresholds in those plans were reached. Payments were also made to an employee child care program upon acceptance of union requests. Annual allocations to the fund were not deductible since any obligation to make payments out of the fund was contingent. *General Motors of Canada Limited v. The Queen*, 2004 DTC 6716 (F.C.A.), affirming 2003 DTC 1533 (T.C.C.)

Employer contributions in respect of vacation pay were deductible in the year the contributions were made even though the vacations were not actually taken until a subsequent year. It is not a non-deductible reserve because the employer's obligation to pay such contributions is "incurred" as soon as the employee's entitlement to the vacation pay has been earned. *Fédération des Caisses Populaires Desjardins de Montréal et al. v. The Queen*, 2001 DTC 5173 (F.C.A.), reversing 99 DTC 1275 (T.C.C.)

The taxpayer's Deferred Liability-Workmen's Compensation account was not a contingent account within the meaning of s.18(1)*(e)*. *Canadian Pacific Limited v. The Minister of Revenue (Ontario)*, 99 DTC 5286 (Ont. C.A.)

The estimated costs of a taxpayer's silviculture obligations under its provincial timber harvesting licence were not deductible since the obligation to pay them had not come into existence in the taxation years in issue. *Northwood Pulp and Timber Ltd. v. The Queen*, 98 DTC 6640 (F.C.A.), affirming 96 DTC 1104 (T.C.C.)

► 18(1)(e.1) ◄

(e.1) Unpaid claims under insurance policies — an amount in respect of claims that were received by an insurer before the end of the year under insurance policies and that are unpaid at the end of the year, except as expressly permitted by this Part;

Related Regulations: Part XIV.

Related Sections: S. 138(3)*(a)* Deductions allowed in computing income.

► 18(1)(f) ◄

(f) Payments on discounted bonds — an amount paid or payable as or on account of the principal amount of any obligation described in paragraph 20(1)*(f)* except as expressly permitted by that paragraph;

Editorial Note: Since the restriction in s. 18(1)*(f)* relates to a discount that is part of the principal amount of a debt obligation, it does not apply to a discount that is considered interest.

Related Sections: S. 248(1), "principal amount".

Interpretation Bulletins: *Secondary* — IT-341R4 Expenses of issuing or selling shares, units in a trust, interests in a partnership or syndicate and expenses of borrowing money.

► 18(1)(g) ◄

(g) Payments on income bonds — an amount paid by a corporation as interest or otherwise to holders of its income bonds or income debentures unless the bonds or debentures have been issued or the income provisions thereof have been adopted since 1930

(i) to afford relief to the debtor from financial difficulties, and

(ii) in place of or as an amendment to bonds or debentures that at the end of 1930 provided unconditionally for a fixed rate of interest;

Related Sections: S. 15(3) Interest or dividend on income bond or debenture; s. 15(4) Idem, where corporation not resident; s. 15.1 Interest on small business development bonds; s. 248(1), "income bond".

► 18(1)(h) ◄

(h) Personal and living expenses — personal or living expenses of the taxpayer, other than travel expenses incurred by the taxpayer while away from home in the course of carrying on the taxpayer's business;

Related Sections: S. 20(1) Deductions permitted in computing income from business or property; s. 20(16) Terminal loss; s. 248(1), "personal or living expenses".

Canadian Tax Foundation: Gervais and Power, *Can I Deduct That?*, 2013 Ontario Tax Conference 10:1–15.

Income Tax Folios: *Secondary* — S4-F11-C1 Meaning of Farming and Farming Business; S4-F2-C1 Deductibility of Fines and Penalties.

Interpretation Bulletins: *Secondary* — IT-322R Farm losses; IT-521R Motor vehicle expenses claimed by self-employed individuals.

Cases: A lawyer could not deduct legal fees paid to defend himself on criminal charges. Although he argued that he would have lost his license to practice law if convicted, the legal fees were not a business expense, but a non-deductible personal expenditure. *Leduc v. The Queen*, 2005 DTC 250 (T.C.C.)

The deduction by a "foot and transit" courier of the cost of extra food and water was allowed as a business expense because he was using them as a replacement for automobile fuel. *Scott v. The Queen*, 98 DTC 6530 (F.C.A.)

A deduction in respect of a nanny's salary is limited to the amount deductible under s. 63 as child care expenses. Such salary is a personal rather than a business expense. *Symes v. The Queen*, 94 DTC 6001 (S.C.C.), affirming 91 DTC 5397 (F.C.A.), reversing 89 DTC 5243 (F.C.T.D.)

► 18(1)(i) ◄

(i) Limitation re employer's contribution under supplementary unemployment benefit plan — an amount paid by an employer to a trustee under a supplementary unemployment benefit plan except as permitted by section 145;

► 18(1)(j) ◄

(j) Limitation re employer's contribution under deferred profit sharing plan — an amount paid by an employer to a trustee under a deferred profit sharing plan except as expressly permitted by section 147;

► 18(1)(k) ◄

(k) Limitation re employer's contribution under profit sharing plan — an amount paid by an employer to a trustee under a profit sharing plan that is not

(i) an employees profit sharing plan,

(ii) a deferred profit sharing plan, or

(iii) a pooled registered pension plan or registered pension plan;

History: S. 18(1)*(k)*(iii) was replaced by S.C. 2012, c. 31, s. 7(1), in force December 14, 2012, and formerly read:

(iii) a registered pension plan;

Related Sections: S. 144 Definitions; s. 147 Deferred profit sharing plans.

Interpretation Bulletins: *Secondary* — IT-502 Employee benefit plans and employee trusts.

► 18(1)(l) ◄

(l) Use of recreational facilities and club dues — an outlay or expense made or incurred by the taxpayer after 1971,

(i) for the use or maintenance of property that is a yacht, a camp, a lodge or a golf course or facility, unless the taxpayer made or incurred the outlay or expense in the ordinary course of the taxpayer's business of providing the property for hire or reward, or

(ii) as membership fees or dues (whether initiation fees or otherwise) in any club the main purpose of which is to provide dining, recreational or sporting facilities for its members;

Related Sections: S. 6(1)(*a*)(iv)(A) Value of benefits; s. 8(1)(*f*) Sales expenses.

Income Tax Folios: S2-F3-C2 Benefits and Allowances Received from Employment.

Interpretation Bulletins: *Secondary* — IT-211R Membership dues — Associations and societies.

Cases: The word "lodge" in s. 18(1)(*l*) does not include large resort hotels with modern amenities. *Hewlett-Packard (Canada) Co. v. The Queen*, 2005 DTC 976 (T.C.C.)

▶ 18(1)(l.1) ◀

(l.1) Safety deposit box — an amount paid or payable in respect of the use of a safety deposit box of a financial institution;

History: S. 18(1)(*l.1*) was added by S.C. 2013, c. 33, s. 2(1), applicable to taxation years that begin after March 20, 2013.

▶ 18(1)(m) ◀

(m) Limitation re employee stock option expenses — an amount in respect of which an election was made by or on behalf of the taxpayer under subsection 110(1.1);

History: S. 18(1)(*m*) was added by S.C. 2010, c. 25, s. 5(1), applicable in respect of transfers or dispositions of rights occurring after 4:00 p.m. Eastern Standard Time, March 4, 2010.

▶ 18(1)(n) ◀

(n) Political contributions — a political contribution;

Related Sections: S. 127(3) Monetary contributions — Canada Elections Act.

▶ 18(1)(o) ◀

(o) Employee benefit plan contributions — an amount paid or payable as a contribution to an employee benefit plan;

Related Sections: S. 6(1)(*a*) Value of benefits; s. 6(1)(*g*) Employee benefit plan benefits; s. 12(1)(*n.*1) Employee benefit plan; s. 18(10) Employee benefit plan; s. 32.1 Additional allowance for scientific research and experimental development; s. 107.1 Distribution by certain employment-related trusts.

Interpretation Bulletins: *Secondary* — IT-502 Employee benefit plans and employee trusts.

▶ 18(1)(o.1) ◀

(o.1) Salary deferral arrangement — except as expressly permitted by paragraphs 20(1)(*oo*) and (*pp*), an outlay or expense made or incurred under a salary deferral arrangement in respect of another person, other than such an arrangement established primarily for the benefit of one or more non-resident employees in respect of services to be rendered outside Canada;

▶ 18(1)(o.2) ◀

(o.2) Retirement compensation arrangement — except as expressly permitted by paragraph 20(1)(*r*), contributions made under a retirement compensation arrangement;

▶ 18(1)(o.3) ◀

(o.3) Employee life and health trust — except as expressly permitted by paragraph 20(1)(*s*), contributions to an employee life and health trust;

History: S. 18(1)(*o.3*) was added by S.C. 2010, c. 25, s. 5(2), applicable after 2009.

▶ 18(1)(p) ◀

(p) Limitation re personal services business expenses — an outlay or expense to the extent that it was made or incurred by a corporation in a taxation year for the purpose of gaining or producing income from a personal services business, other than

(i) the salary, wages or other remuneration paid in the year to an incorporated employee of the corporation,

(ii) the cost to the corporation of any benefit or allowance provided to an incorporated employee in the year,

(iii) any amount expended by the corporation in connection with the selling of property or the negotiating of contracts by the corporation if the amount would have been deductible in computing the income of an incorporated employee for a taxation year from an office or employment if the amount had been expended by the incorporated employee under a contract of employment that required the employee to pay the amount, and

(iv) any amount paid by the corporation in the year as or on account of legal expenses incurred by it in collecting amounts owing to it on account of services rendered

that would, if the income of the corporation were from a business other than a personal services business, be deductible in computing its income;

Editorial Note: S. 18(1)(*p*) severely limits the expenses that can be claimed by a personal services business (essentially an "incorporated employee"). All deductions are disallowed except (i) remuneration paid (not payable) to an incorporated employee including benefits or allowances; (ii) selling expenses and similar expenses that would have been deductible in computing the individual's employment income if he or she had expended them; and (iii) legal expenses incurred in collecting amounts owing for services rendered.

Related Sections: s. 125(7), "personal services business".

Tax Profile: August 2009 — Structuring a Services Business.

Interpretation Bulletins: *Secondary* — IT-73R6 The small business deduction; IT-168R3 Athletes and players employed by football, hockey and similar clubs.

▶ 18(1)(q) ◀

(q) Limitation re cancellation of lease — an amount paid or payable by the taxpayer for the cancellation of a lease of property of the taxpayer leased by the taxpayer to another person, except to the extent permitted by paragraph 20(1)(*z*) or (*z*.1);

Tax Topics: No. 1677, Income Tax Implications of Lease Cancellation Payments.

Interpretation Bulletins: *Secondary* — IT-359R2 Premiums and other amounts with respect to leases.

▶ 18(1)(r) ◀

(r) Certain automobile expenses — an amount paid or payable by the taxpayer as an allowance for the use by an individual of an automobile to the extent that the amount exceeds an amount determined in accordance with prescribed rules, except where the amount so paid or payable is required to be included in computing the individual's income;

Related Regulations: 7306.

Related Sections: S. 6(1)(*b*) Personal or living expenses; s. 67.2 Interest on money borrowed for passenger vehicle; s. 67.3 Limitation re cost of leasing passenger vehicle; s. 67.4 More than one owner or lessor.

► 18(1)(s) ◄

(s) Loans or lending assets — any loss, depreciation or reduction in a taxation year in the value or amortized cost of a loan or lending asset of a taxpayer made or acquired by the taxpayer in the ordinary course of the taxpayer's business of insurance or the lending of money and not disposed of by the taxpayer in the year, except as expressly permitted by this Part;

► 18(1)(t) ◄

(t) Payments under different acts — any amount paid or payable

(i) under this Act (other than tax paid or payable under Part XII.2 or Part XII.6),

(ii) as interest under Part IX of the *Excise Tax Act*, or

(iii) as interest under the *Air Travellers Security Charge Act*;

Income Tax Folios: *Secondary* — S4-F2-C1 Deductibility of Fines and Penalties.

Income Tax Technical News: Issue No. 38, Income Tax Treatment of GST.

Information Circulars: IC 77-11 Sales tax reassessments — Deductibility in computing income.

Cases: An unrecovered withholding tax could not be considered as an expense laid out to produce income and so it was not deductible. *Harrowston Corporation v. The Queen*, 96 DTC 6544 (F.C.A.), affirming 93 DTC 995 (T.C.C.)

► 18(1)(u) ◄

(u) Fees — individual saving plans — any amount paid or payable by the taxpayer for services in respect of a retirement savings plan, retirement income fund or TFSA under or of which the taxpayer is the annuitant or holder;

Related Sections: S. 147.5(12) Member's account.

► 18(1)(v) ◄

(v) Interest — authorized foreign bank — where the taxpayer is an authorized foreign bank, an amount in respect of interest that would otherwise be deductible in computing the taxpayer's income from a business carried on in Canada, except as provided in section 20.2;

Related Sections: S. 248(1), "authorized foreign bank".

► 18(1)(w) ◄

(w) Underlying payments on qualified securities — except as expressly permitted, an amount that is deemed by subsection 260(5.1) to have been received by another person as an amount described in any of paragraphs 260(5.1)(*a*) to (*c*);

History: S. 18(1)(*w*) was added by S.C. 2013, c. 34, s. 178(1), deemed to have come into force on January 1, 2002.

► 18(1)(x) ◄

(x) Derivatives — lower of cost and market — any reduction in a taxation year in the value of a property if

(i) the method used by the taxpayer to value the property at the end of the year for purposes of computing the taxpayer's profit from a business or property is the cost at which the taxpayer acquired it or its fair market value at the end of the year, whichever is lower,

(ii) the property is described in subsection 10(15), and

(iii) the property is not disposed of by the taxpayer in the year; and

History: S. 18(1)(*x*) was added by S.C. 2016, c. 12, s. 6(1), applicable to agreements entered into after March 21, 2016.

Related Sections: 10(15) Derivatives; 10.1(1) Mark-to-market election.

► 18(1)(y) ◄

(y) Payment for shares — an amount referred to in subsection 13(36).

History: S. 18(1)(*y*) was added by S.C. 2016, c. 12, s. 6(1), in force January 1, 2017.

Related Sections: 10(15) Derivatives.

► 18(2) ◄

(2) Limit on certain interest and property tax. Notwithstanding paragraph 20(1)(*c*), in computing the taxpayer's income for a particular taxation year from a business or property, no amount shall be deductible in respect of any expense incurred by the taxpayer in the year as, on account or in lieu of payment of, or in satisfaction of,

(*a*) interest on debt relating to the acquisition of land, or

(*b*) property taxes (not including income or profits taxes or taxes computed by reference to the transfer of property) paid or payable by the taxpayer in respect of land to a province or to a Canadian municipality,

unless, having regard to all the circumstances (including the cost to the taxpayer of the land in relation to the taxpayer's gross revenue, if any, from the land for the particular year or any preceding taxation year), the land can reasonably be considered to have been, in the year,

(*c*) used in the course of a business carried on in the particular year by the taxpayer, other than a business in the ordinary course of which land is held primarily for the purpose of resale or development, or

(*d*) held primarily for the purpose of gaining or producing income of the taxpayer from the land for the particular year,

except to the extent of the total of

(*e*) the amount, if any, by which the taxpayer's gross revenue, if any, from the land for the particular year exceeds the total of all amounts deducted in computing the taxpayer's income from the land for the year, and (*f*) in the case of a corporation whose principal business is the leasing, rental or sale, or the development for lease, rental or sale, or any combination thereof, of real or immovable property owned by it, to or for a person with whom the corporation is dealing at arm's length, the corporation's base level deduction for the particular year.

Editorial Note: The exceptions in ss. 18(2)(*c*) and (*d*) are independent of the thresholds in paragraphs (*e*) and (*f*); in other words, if a taxpayer falls within one of the exceptions in paragraphs (*c*) and (*d*), there is no limitation to the deduction of interest or property taxes under s. 18(2).

History: S. 18(2)(*f*) was replaced by S.C. 2013, c. 34, s. 95(1), in force June 26, 2013, and formerly read:

(*f*) in the case of a corporation whose principal business is the leasing, rental or sale, or the development for lease, rental or sale, or any combination thereof, of real property owned by it, to or for a person with whom the corporation is dealing at arm's length, the corporation's base level deduction for the particular year.

Related Sections: S. 18(2.1) Where taxpayer member of partnership; s. 18(3), "interest on debt relating to the acquisition of land"; s. 53(1)(*d.3*) Adjustments to cost base — Denied deduction for interest or soft costs; s. 53(1)(*h*) Adjustments to cost base — Land; s. 212(1)(*b*)(iii)(E) Interest.

Canadian Tax Foundation: MacLean, *Subsection 18(2): Easily Overlooked*, 2001 Tax for the Owner-Manager 1(2):6–7.

Tax Profile: March 2013 — Non-Resident Investment in Canadian Real Estate.

Interpretation Bulletins: *Primary* — IT-153R3 Land developers — Subdivision and development costs and carrying charges on land. *Secondary* — IT-142R3 Settlement of debts on the winding-up of a corporation; IT-373R2 (Consolid.) Woodlots.

Tax Window Files: Carrying Charges — Inventory of Land Developers, *Technical Interpretation, Financial Industries Division, April 21, 2004*, CRA Document No. 2004-0061651E5. Land developer allowed to add interest expense to cost of land inventory instead of deducting on a current basis; Compound Interest — Incurred with Respect to Vacant Land and Construction of Building, *Technical Interpretation, Financial Industries Division, April 10, 2003*, CRA Document No. 2002-0147295. Subsections 18(2) and (3.1) can apply to compound interest only when paid.

► 18(2.1) ◄

(2.1) Where taxpayer member of partnership. Where a taxpayer who is a member of a partnership was obligated to pay any amount as, on account or in lieu of payment of, or in satisfaction of, interest (in this subsection referred to as an "interest amount") on money that was borrowed by the taxpayer before April 1, 1977 and that was used to acquire land owned by the partnership before that day or on an obligation entered into by the taxpayer before April 1, 1977 to pay for land owned by the partnership before that day, and, in a taxation year of the taxpayer, either,

(*a*) the partnership has disposed of all or any portion of the land, or

(*b*) the taxpayer has disposed of all or any portion of the taxpayer's interest in the partnership

to a person other than a person with whom the taxpayer does not deal at arm's length, in computing the taxpayer's income for the year or any subsequent year, there may be deducted such portion of the taxpayer's interest amount

(*c*) that was, by virtue of subsection (2), not deductible in computing the income of the taxpayer for any previous taxation year,

(*d*) that was not deductible in computing the income of any other taxpayer for any taxation year,

(*e*) that was not included in computing the adjusted cost base to the taxpayer of any property, and

(*f*) that was not deductible under this subsection in computing the income of the taxpayer for any previous taxation year

as is reasonable having regard to the portion of the land or interest in the partnership, as the case may be, so disposed of.

Related Regulations: Part XLIII.

► 18(2.2) ◄

(2.2) Base level deduction. For the purposes of this section, a corporation's base level deduction for a taxation year is the amount that would be the amount of interest, computed at the prescribed rate, for the year in respect of a loan of $1,000,000 outstanding throughout the year, unless the corporation is associated in the year with one or more other corporations in which case, except as otherwise provided in this section, its base level deduction for the year is nil.

Related Regulations: 4301.

Related Sections: S. 256(1) Associated corporations.

► 18(2.3) ◄

(2.3) Associated corporations. Notwithstanding subsection (2.2), if all of the corporations that are associated with each other in a taxation year have filed with the Minister in prescribed form an agreement whereby, for the purposes of this section, they allocate an amount to one or more of them for the taxation year and the amount so allocated or the total of the amounts so allocated, as the case may be, does not exceed $1,000,000, the base level deduction for the year for each of the corporations is the base level deduction that would be computed under subsection (2.2) in respect of the corporation if the reference in that subsection to $1,000,000 were read as a reference to the amount so allocated to it.

Forms: T2005 — Agreement Among Associated Corporations to Allocate an Amount to Calculate Their Base Level Deduction.

► 18(2.4) ◄

(2.4) Failure to file agreement. If any of the corporations that are associated with each other in a taxation year has failed to file with the Minister an agreement as contemplated by subsection (2.3) within 30 days after notice in writing by the Minister has been forwarded to any of them that such an agreement is required for the purpose of any assessment of tax under this Part, the Minister shall, for the purpose of this section, allocate an amount to one or more of them for the taxation year, which amount or the total of which amounts, as the case may be, shall equal $1,000,000 and in any such case, the amount so allocated to any corporation shall be deemed to be an amount allocated to the corporation pursuant to subsection (2.3).

► 18(2.5) ◄

(2.5) Special rules for base level deduction. Notwithstanding any other provision of this section,

(*a*) where a corporation, in this paragraph referred to as the "first corporation", has more than one taxation year ending in the same calendar year and is associated in two or more of those taxation years with another corporation that has a taxation year ending in that calendar year, the base level deduction of the first corporation for each taxation year in which it is associated with the other corporation ending in that calendar year is, subject to the application of paragraph (*b*), an amount equal to its base level deduction for the first such taxation year determined without reference to paragraph (*b*); and

(*b*) where a corporation has a taxation year that is less than 51 weeks, its base level deduction for the year is that proportion of its base level deduction for the year determined without reference to this paragraph that the number of days in the year is of 365.

Forms: T2005 — Agreement Among Associated Corporations to Allocate an Amount to Calculate Their Base Level Deduction.

▶ 18(3) ◀

(3) Definitions. In subsection (2),

Related Sections: S. 20(1)(*c*) Interest.

Interpretation Bulletins: *Primary* — IT-153R3 Land developers — Subdivision and development costs and carrying charges on land.

"interest on debt relating to the acquisition of land" — "interest on debt relating to the acquisition of land" includes

(*a*) interest paid or payable in a year in respect of borrowed money that cannot be identified with particular land but that may nonetheless reasonably be considered (having regard to all the circumstances) as interest on borrowed money used in respect of or for the acquisition of land, and

(*b*) interest paid or payable in the year by a taxpayer in respect of borrowed money that may reasonably be considered (having regard to all the circumstances) to have been used to assist, directly or indirectly,

(i) another person with whom the taxpayer does not deal at arm's length,

(ii) a corporation of which the taxpayer is a specified shareholder, or

(iii) a partnership of which the taxpayer's share of any income or loss is 10% or more,

to acquire land to be used or held by that person, corporation or partnership otherwise than as described in paragraph (2)(*c*) or (*d*), except where the assistance is in the form of a loan to that person, corporation or partnership and a reasonable rate of interest on the loan is charged by the taxpayer;

"land" — "land" does not, except to the extent that it is used for the provision of parking facilities for a fee or charge, include

(*a*) any property that is a building or other structure affixed to land,

(*b*) the land subjacent to any property described in paragraph (*a*), or

(*c*) such land immediately contiguous to the land described in paragraph (*b*) that is a parking area, driveway, yard, garden or similar land as is necessary for the use of any property described in paragraph (*a*).

▶ 18(3.1) ◀

(3.1) Costs relating to construction of building or ownership of land. Notwithstanding any other provision of this Act, in computing a taxpayer's income for a taxation year,

(*a*) no deduction shall be made in respect of any outlay or expense made or incurred by the taxpayer (other than an amount deductible under paragraph 20(1)(*a*), (*aa*) or (*qq*) or subsection 20(29)) that can reasonably be regarded as a cost attributable to the period of the construction, renovation or alteration of a building by or on behalf of the taxpayer, a person with whom the taxpayer does not deal at arm's length, a corporation of which the taxpayer is a specified shareholder or a partnership of which the taxpayer's share of any income or loss is 10% or more and relating to the construction, renovation or alteration, or a cost attributable to that period and relating to the ownership during that period of land

(i) that is subjacent to the building, or

(ii) that

(A) is immediately contiguous to the land subjacent to the building,

(B) is used, or is intended to be used, for a parking area, driveway, yard, garden or any other similar use, and

(C) is necessary for the use or intended use of the building; and

(*b*) the amount of such an outlay or expense shall, to the extent that it would otherwise be deductible in computing the taxpayer's income for the year, be included in computing the cost or capital cost, as the case may be, of the building to the taxpayer, to the person with whom the taxpayer does not deal at arm's length, to the corporation of which the taxpayer is a specified shareholder or to the partnership of which the taxpayer's share of any income or loss is 10% or more, as the case may be.

Editorial Note: The construction-period expenses referred to in s. 18(3.1) that are required to be capitalized are often referred to as "soft costs", and include the costs listed in s. 18(3.3). S. 20(29) provides an exception to the capitalization of soft costs under s. 18(3.1), and allows a taxpayer to deduct such costs incurred in a year to the extent of the taxpayer's rental income from the building computed before taking into account any capital cost allowance under s. 20(28).

Related Sections: S. 18(3.2) Included costs; s. 18(3.3) Completion; s. 18(3.4) Where s. (3.1) does not apply; s. 18(3.5) Transitional rules; s. 20(1)(*gg*) Disability-related modifications to buildings; s. 20(29) Exception to soft costs capitalization rule; s. 53(1)(*d*.3) Adjustments to cost base — Denied deduction for interest or soft costs.

Tax Profile: March 2013 — Non-Resident Investment in Canadian Real Estate.

Income Tax Folios: *Primary* — S3-F4-C1 General Discussion of Capital Cost Allowance.

Interpretation Bulletins: *Secondary* — IT-142R3 Settlement of debts on the winding-up of a corporation.

Cases: Construction interest capitalized under s. 18(3.1) lost its character as "interest" and was therefore not subject to Part XIII tax when paid out to a non-resident lender*Eastern Success Co. Ltd. v. The Queen*, 2004 DTC 3521 (T.C.C.)

▶ 18(3.2) ◀

(3.2) Included costs. For the purposes of subsection (3.1), costs relating to the construction, renovation or alteration of a building or to the ownership of land include

(*a*) interest paid or payable by a taxpayer in respect of borrowed money that cannot be identified with a particular building or particular land, but that can reasonably be considered (having regard to all the circumstances) as interest on borrowed money used by the taxpayer in respect of the construction, renovation or alteration of a building or the ownership of land; and

(*b*) interest paid or payable by a taxpayer in respect of borrowed money that may reasonably be considered (having regard to all the circumstances) to have been used to assist, directly or indirectly,

(i) another person with whom the taxpayer does not deal at arm's length,

(ii) a corporation of which the taxpayer is a specified shareholder, or

(iii) a partnership of which the taxpayer's share of any income or loss is 10% or more,

to construct, renovate or alter a building or to purchase land, except where the assistance is in the form of a loan to that other person, corporation or partnership and a reasonable rate of interest on the loan is charged by the taxpayer.

Income Tax Folios: *Primary* — S3-F4-C1 General Discussion of Capital Cost Allowance.

▶ 18(3.3) ◀

(3.3) Completion. For the purposes of subsection (3.1), the construction, renovation or alteration of a building is completed at the earlier of the day on which the construction, renovation or alteration is actually completed and the day on which all or substantially all of the building is used for the purpose for which it was constructed, renovated or altered.

Income Tax Folios: *Primary* — S3-F4-C1 General Discussion of Capital Cost Allowance.

▶ 18(3.4) ◀

(3.4) Where s. (3.1) does not apply. Subsection (3.1) does not apply to prohibit a deduction in a taxation year of the specified percentage of any outlay or expense described in that subsection made or incurred before 1992 by

(*a*) a corporation whose principal business is throughout the year the leasing, rental or sale, or the development for lease, rental or sale, or any combination thereof, of real or immovable property owned by it, to or for a person with whom the corporation is dealing at arm's length, or

(*b*) a partnership

(i) each member of which is a corporation described in paragraph (*a*), and

(ii) the principal business of which is throughout the year the leasing, rental or sale, or the development for lease, rental or sale, or any combination thereof, of real or immovable property held by it, to or for a person with whom each member of the partnership is dealing at arm's length,

and for the purposes of this subsection, "specified percentage" means, in respect of an outlay or expense made or incurred in 1988, 80%, in 1989, 60%, in 1990, 40%, and in 1991, 20%.

History: S. 18(3.4)(*a*) and (*b*) were replaced by S.C. 2013, c. 34, s. 95(2), in force June 26, 2013, and formerly read:

(*a*) a corporation whose principal business is throughout the year the leasing, rental or sale, or the development for lease, rental or sale, or any combination thereof, of real property owned by it to or for a person with whom the corporation is dealing at arm's length, or

(*b*) a partnership

(i) each member of which is a corporation described in paragraph (*a*), and

(ii) the principal business of which is throughout the year the leasing, rental or sale, or the development for lease, rental or sale, or any combination thereof, of real property held by it, to or for a person with whom each member of the partnership is dealing at arm's length,

Income Tax Folios: *Primary* — S3-F4-C1 General Discussion of Capital Cost Allowance.

▶ 18(3.5) ◀

(3.5) Idem. Subsection (3.1) does not apply in respect of an outlay or expense in respect of a building or the land described in subparagraph (3.1)(*a*)(i) or (ii) in respect of the building,

(*a*) where the construction, renovation or alteration of the building was in progress on November 12, 1981,

(*b*) where the installation of the footings or other base support of the building commenced after November 12, 1981 and before 1982,

(*c*) if, in the case of a new building being constructed in Canada or an existing building being renovated or altered in Canada, arrangements, evidenced in writing, for the construction, renovation or alteration were substantially advanced before November 13, 1981 and the installation of footings or other base support for the new building or the renovation or alteration of the existing building, as the case may be, commenced before June 1, 1982, or

(*d*) if, in the case of a new building being constructed in Canada, the taxpayer was obligated to construct the building under the terms of an agreement in writing entered into before November 13, 1981 and arrangements, evidenced in writing, respecting the construction of the building were substantially advanced before June 1, 1982 and the installation of footings or other base support for the building commenced before 1983,

and the construction, renovation or alteration, as the case may be, of the building proceeds after 1982 without undue delay (having regard to acts of God, labour disputes, fire, accidents or unusual delay by common carriers or suppliers of materials or equipment).

Income Tax Folios: *Primary* — S3-F4-C1 General Discussion of Capital Cost Allowance.

▶ 18(3.6) ◀

(3.6) Undue delay. For the purposes of subsection (3.5), where more than one building is being constructed under any of the circumstances described in that subsection on one site or on immediately contiguous sites, no undue delay shall be regarded as occurring in the construction of any such building if construction of at least one such building proceeds after 1982 without undue delay and continuous construction of all other such buildings proceeds after 1983 without undue delay.

Income Tax Folios: *Primary* — S3-F4-C1 General Discussion of Capital Cost Allowance.

► 18(3.7) ◄

(3.7) Commencement of footings. For the purposes of this section, the installation of footings or other base support for a building shall be deemed to commence on the first placement of concrete, pilings or other material that is to provide permanent support for the building.

Income Tax Folios: *Primary* — S3-F4-C1 General Discussion of Capital Cost Allowance.

► 18(4) ◄

(4) Limitation on deduction of interest. Notwithstanding any other provision of this Act (other than subsection (8)), in computing the income for a taxation year of a corporation or a trust from a business (other than the Canadian banking business of an authorized foreign bank) or property, no deduction shall be made in respect of that proportion of any amount otherwise deductible in computing its income for the year in respect of interest paid or payable by it on outstanding debts to specified non-residents that

(*a*) the amount, if any, by which

(i) the average of all amounts each of which is, in respect of a calendar month that ends in the year, the greatest total amount at any time in the month of the outstanding debts to specified non-residents of the corporation or trust,

exceeds

(ii) 1.5 times the equity amount of the corporation or trust for the year,

is of

(*b*) the amount determined under subparagraph (*a*)(i) in respect of the corporation or trust for the year.

Editorial Note: The thin capitalization rules of subsection 18(4) limit the deduction of interest expense where the payer corporation's debt-equity ratio exceeds 1.5. Historically, the rules applied only to payers who were Canadian resident corporations. Effective for taxation years that begin after 2013, the rules also apply to Canadian resident trusts, and to non-resident corporations and trusts that earn business income in Canada. The rules can also apply where the corporation or trust is a member of a partnership; see subsection 18(7).

The 2014 Budget introduced anti-avoidance measures which provide that interest payments in certain back-to-back loan arrangements will be subject to the thin capitalization rules, effective for taxation years that begin after 2014. Basically, the new measures ensure that the thin capitalization rules cannot be avoided through the imposition of an arm's length intermediary between a resident payor of interest and a specified non-resident shareholder or beneficiary payor (subsections 18(6) and (6.1)).

History: S. 18(4) was replaced by S.C. 2013, c. 40, s. 8(1), applicable to taxation years that begin after 2013.

S. 18(4) formerly read:

(4) *Limitation — deduction of interest by certain corporations.* Notwithstanding any other provision of this Act (other than subsection (8)), in computing the income for a taxation year of a corporation resident in Canada from a business or property, no deduction shall be made in respect of that proportion of any amount otherwise deductible in computing its income for the year in respect of interest paid or payable by it on outstanding debts to specified non-residents that

(*a*) the amount, if any, by which

(i) the average of all amounts each of which is, in respect of a calendar month that ends in the year, the greatest total amount at any time in the month of the corporation's outstanding debts to specified non-residents,

exceeds

(ii) 1.5 times the total of

(A) the retained earnings of the corporation at the beginning of the year, except to the extent that those earnings include retained earnings of any other corporation,

(B) the average of all amounts each of which is the corporation's contributed surplus (other than any portion of that contributed surplus that arose in connection with an investment, as defined in subsection 212.3(10), to which subsection 212.3(2) applies) at the beginning of a calendar month that ends in the year, to the extent that it was contributed by a specified non-resident shareholder of the corporation, and

(C) the average of all amounts each of which is the corporation's paid-up capital at the beginning of a calendar month that ends in the year, excluding the paid-up capital in respect of shares of any class of the capital stock of the corporation owned by a person other than a specified non-resident shareholder of the corporation,

is of

(*b*) the amount determined under subparagraph (*a*)(i) in respect of the corporation for the year.

S. 18(4), the portion before paragraph (*a*) was replaced by S.C. 2012, c. 31, s. 7(2), applicable to taxation years that end after March 28, 2012. S. 18(4), the portion before paragraph (*a*) formerly read:

(4) *Limitation re deduction of interest by certain corporations.* Notwithstanding any other provision of this Act, in computing the income for a taxation year of a corporation resident in Canada from a business or property, no deduction shall be made in respect of that proportion of any amount otherwise deductible in computing its income for the year in respect of interest paid or payable by it on outstanding debts to specified non-residents that

S. 18(4)(*a*)(ii), the portion before clause (A) was replaced by S.C. 2012, c. 31, s. 7(3), applicable to taxation years that begin after 2012. S. 18(4)(*a*)(ii), the portion before clause (A) formerly read:

(ii) two times the total of

S. 18(4)(*a*)(ii)(B) was replaced by S.C. 2012, c. 31, s. 7(4), deemed to have come into force on March 29, 2012. S. 18(4)(*a*)(ii)(B) formerly read:

(ii) two times the total of

Related Sections: S. 12(1)(*l.1*) Partnership — interest deduction add back; s. 12(2.02) Source of income; s. 18(5) Definitions; s. 18(6) Loans made on condition; s. 18(8) Where s. (4) does not apply; s. 20(1)(*c*) Interest; s. 89 (1) "paid-up capital"; s. 212(3.1) Back-to-back loan arrangement; s. 214(16) Deemed dividends; s. 214(17) Deemed interest payments; s. 251(2) Definition of "related persons".

Canadian Tax Foundation: Sherman and Smit, *Thin Cap Gains Weight*, 2012 Conference Report 25:1–17; Choudhury and Connell, *Select Issues in the Purchase and Sale of a Business*, 2012 Ontario Tax Conference 11:1–31; Edgar et al., *Foreign Direct Investment, Thin Capitalization, and the Interest Expense Deduction: A Policy Analysis*, 2008 Canadian Tax Journal 4:803–869; Monaghan and Juneja, *Selected Issues in Cross-Border Debt Financing*, 2006 Conference Report 16:1–58; Lanthier, *Thin Capitalization: Cross-Border Issues and Strategies*, 2003 Conference Report 25:1–23; Fontaine and Kong, *The March 16, 2001 Draft Legislation: Thin Capitalization, Non-Resident-Owned Investment Corporations and Foreign Spinoff Relief*, 2001 Canadian Tax Journal 2:383–401.

Tax Profile: June 2013 — 2013 Federal Budget; March 2013 — Non-Resident Investment in Canadian Real Estate; August 2012 — U.S. Purchases and Sales of Canadian Businesses: Tax and Corporate Issues; June 2012 — Use of Canadian Partnerships by Non-Residents; September 2011 — Acquisition of Canadian Business by Non-Residents; January 2009 — Enhancing Canada's International Tax Advantage.

Tax Topics: No. 2114, Thin Capitalization Amendments — Denied Interest May Be Subject to Withholding Tax; No. 2106, More on Rectification in Quebec; No. 2095, Thin Capitalization; No. 1930, Budget 2009 Provides Initial Response to Final Report Issued by the Advisory Panel on Canada's System of International Taxation; No. 1867-68, 2007 Canadian Tax Foundation Annual Conference CRA Round Table; No. 1814, 2006 Canadian Tax Foundation Annual Conference CRA Round Table.

Income Tax Technical News: Issue No. 38, Thin Capitalization.

Information Circulars: IC 87-2R International Transfer Pricing.

Interpretation Bulletins: *Primary* — IT-59R3 Interest on debts owing to specified non-residents (thin capitalization).

Tax Window Files: 2015 CTF Q.10 Thin cap - foreign currency debt, *November 24, 2015*, CRA Document No. 2015-0610601C6.

Cases: Since the mortgage loan of the taxpayer and a corporation it had entered into a partnership agreement with was their debt and not that of the partnership, the thin capitalization rules applied. *Wildenburg Holdings Limited v. Minister of Revenue (Ont.)*, 2001 DTC 5145 (Ont. C.A.)

The thin capitalization rules were used to restrict the corporate taxpayer's deduction of interest which it had paid on funds borrowed from two related U.S. corporations. The Canada–U.S. Tax Treaty does not operate to limit the application of the thin capitalization rules to the taxpayer's situation. *Specialty Manufacturing Limited v. The Queen*, 99 DTC 5222 (F.C.A.), affirming 97 DTC 1511 (T.C.C.)

Since the mortgage loan the taxpayer and a corporation it had entered into a partnership agreement with was their debt and not that of the partnership, the taxpayer could not use the deeming provisions of s. 96(1) to prevent the application of the thin capitalization rules. *Wildenburg Holdings Ltd. v. M.N.R.*, 98 DTC 6462 (Ont. (Gen. Div.))

▶ 18(5) ◀

(5) Definitions. Notwithstanding any other provision of this Act (other than subsection (5.1)), in this subsection and subsections (4) and (5.1) to (6.1),

History: S. 18(5), the portion before the definitions was replaced by S.C. 2014, c. 39, s. 6(1), applicable to taxation years that begin after 2014, and formerly read:

Definitions Notwithstanding any other provision of this Act (other than subsection (5.1)), in this subsection and subsections (4) to (6),

S. 18(5), the portion before the definition "outstanding debts to specified non-residents" was replaced by S.C. 2013, c. 34, s. 427(*a*), applicable on the first day on which both the *Jobs and Growth Act, 2012* [2012, c. 31] and *Technical Amendments Act, 2012* [S.C. 2013, c. 34] receive royal assent [June 26, 2013], and formerly read:

(5) *Definitions.* Notwithstanding any other provision of this Act (other than subsection (5.1)), in this subsection and subsections (4) to (7),

S 18(5), the portion before the definition "outstanding debts to specified non-residents" was replaced by S.C. 2012, c. 31, s. 7(5), applicable to taxation years that begin after March 28, 2012. That part formerly read:

(5) *Definitions.* Notwithstanding any other provision of this Act (other than subsection (5.1)), in this subsection and subsections (4) to (6),

Related Regulations: 8201.

Related Sections: S. 248(1), "corporation", "individual", "insurance corporation", "non-resident", "property", "shareholder"; s. 249(1) Definition of "taxation year".

Interpretation Bulletins: *Secondary* — IT-59R3 Interest on debts owing to specified non-residents (thin capitalization).

Tax Window Files: 2015 TEI Liaison Meeting Q.6 - Specified Right, *November 17, 2015*, CRA Document No. 2015-0614241C6; Canadian Branch of Authorized Foreign Bank, *March 12, 2010*, CRA Document No. 2009-0355691I7.

"beneficiary" — "beneficiary" has the same meaning as in subsection 108(1);

History: S. 18(5), the definition "beneficiary" was added by S.C. 2013, c. 40, s. 8(3), applicable to taxation years that begin after 2013.

"equity amount" — "equity amount", of a corporation or trust for a taxation year, means

(*a*) in the case of a corporation resident in Canada, the total of

(i) the retained earnings of the corporation at the beginning of the year, except to the extent that those earnings include retained earnings of any other corporation,

(ii) the average of all amounts each of which is the corporation's contributed surplus (other than any portion of that contributed surplus that arose at a time when the corporation was non-resident, or that arose in connection with a disposition to which subsection 212.1(1.1) applies or an "investment", as defined in subsection 212.3(10), to which subsection 212.3(2) applies) at the beginning of a calendar month that ends in the year, to the extent that it was contributed by a specified non-resident shareholder of the corporation, and

(iii) the average of all amounts each of which is the corporation's paid-up capital at the beginning of a calendar month that ends in the year, excluding the paid-up capital in respect of shares of any class of the capital stock of the corporation owned by a person other than a specified non-resident shareholder of the corporation,

(*b*) in the case of a trust resident in Canada, the amount, if any, by which

(i) the total of

(A) the average of all amounts each of which is the total amount of all equity contributions to the trust made before a calendar month that ends in the year, to the extent that the contributions were made by a specified non-resident beneficiary of the trust, and

(B) the tax-paid earnings of the trust for the year,

exceeds

(ii) the average of all amounts each of which is the total of all amounts that were paid or became payable by the trust to a beneficiary of the trust in respect of the beneficiary's interest under the trust before a calendar month that ends in the year except to the extent that the amount is

(A) included in the beneficiary's income for a taxation year because of subsection 104(13),

(B) an amount from which tax was deducted under Part XIII because of paragraph 212(1)(*c*), or

(C) paid or payable to a person other than a specified non-resident beneficiary of the trust, and

(*c*) in the case of a corporation or trust that is not resident in Canada, including a corporation or trust that files a return under this Part in accordance with subsection 216(1) in respect of the year, 40% of the amount, if any, by which

(i) the average of all amounts each of which is the cost of a property, other than an interest as a member of a partnership, owned by the corporation or trust at the beginning of a calendar month that ends in the year

(A) that is used by the corporation or trust in the year in, or held by it in the year in the course of, carrying on business in Canada, or

(B) that is an interest in real property, or a real right in immovables, in Canada, or an interest in, or for civil law a right in, timber resource properties and timber limits, in Canada, and in respect of which the corporation or trust files a return under this Part in accordance with subsection 216(1) in respect of the year,

exceeds

(ii) the average of all amounts each of which is the total of all amounts outstanding, at the beginning of a calendar month that ends in the year, as or on account of a debt or other obligation to pay an amount that was payable by the corporation or trust that may reasonably be regarded as relating to a business carried on by it in Canada or to an interest or right described in clause (i)(B), other than a debt or obligation that is included in the outstanding debts to specified non-residents of the corporation or trust;

History: S. 18(5), subparagraph (*a*)(ii) of the definition "equity amount" was replaced by S.C. 2018, c. 27, s. 3(1), applicable in respect of transactions or events that occur after February 26, 2018, and formerly read:

(ii) the average of all amounts each of which is the corporation's contributed surplus (other than any portion of that contributed surplus that arose in connection with an investment, as defined in subsection 212.3(10), to which subsection 212.3(2) applies) at the beginning of a calendar month that ends in the year, to the extent that it was contributed by a specified non-resident shareholder of the corporation, and

S. 18(5), the definition "equity amount" was added by S.C. 2013, c. 40, s. 8(3), applicable to taxation years that begin after 2013, except that if a trust that is resident in Canada on March 21, 2013 elects in writing and files the election with the Minister of National Revenue on or before the trust's filing-due date for its first taxation year that begins after 2013,

(*a*) for the purpose of determining the trust's equity amount, as defined in subsection 18(5), the trust is deemed

(i) to not have received any equity contributions, as defined in subsection 18(5), before March 21, 2013,

(ii) to not have paid or made payable any amount to a beneficiary of the trust before March 21, 2013, and

(iii) to have tax-paid earnings, as defined in subsection 18(5), of nil for each taxation year that ends before March 21, 2013, and

(*b*) each beneficiary of the trust at the beginning of March 21, 2013 is deemed to have made an equity contribution at that time to the trust equal to the amount determined by the formula

$$A/B \times (C - D)$$

where

A is the fair market value of the beneficiary's interest as a beneficiary under the trust at that time,

B is the fair market value of all the beneficial interests under the trust at that time,

C is the total fair market value of all the properties of the trust at that time, and

D is the total amount of the trust's liabilities at that time.

Tax Window Files: Thin Cap.-Retained Earnings-Other Income (Loss), *January 19, 2018*, CRA Document No. 2017-0721641I7; Thin cap rules and trusts, *August 19, 2016*, CRA Document No. 2015-0585471E5.

"equity contribution"—"equity contribution", to a trust, means a transfer of property to the trust that is made

(*a*) in exchange for an interest as a beneficiary under the trust,

(*b*) in exchange for a right to acquire an interest as a beneficiary under the trust, or

(*c*) for no consideration by a person beneficially interested in the trust;

History: S. 18(5), the definition "equity contribution" was added by S.C. 2013, c. 40, s. 8(3), applicable to taxation years that begin after 2013.

"outstanding debts to specified non-residents"—"outstanding debts to specified non-residents", of a corporation or trust at any particular time in a taxation year, means

(*a*) the total of all amounts each of which is an amount outstanding at that time as or on account of a debt or other obligation to pay an amount

(i) that was payable by the corporation or trust to a person who was, at any time in the year,

(A) a specified non-resident shareholder of the corporation or a specified non-resident beneficiary of the trust, or

(B) a non-resident person who was not dealing at arm's length with a specified shareholder of the corporation or a specified beneficiary of the trust, as the case may be, and

(ii) on which any amount in respect of interest paid or payable by the corporation or trust is or would be, but for subsection (4), deductible in computing the income of the corporation or trust for the year,

but does not include

(*b*) an amount outstanding at the particular time as or on account of a debt or other obligation

(i) to pay an amount to

(A) a non-resident insurance corporation to the extent that the obligation was, for the non-resident insurance corporation's taxation year that included the particular time, designated insurance property in respect of an insurance business carried on in Canada through a permanent establishment as defined by regulation, or

(B) an authorized foreign bank, if the bank uses or holds the obligation at the particular time in its Canadian banking business, or

(ii) that is a debt obligation described in subparagraph (ii) of the description of A in paragraph 17.1(1)(*b*) to the extent that the proceeds of the debt obligation can reasonably be considered to directly or indirectly fund at the particular time, in whole or in part, a pertinent loan or indebtedness (as defined in subsection 212.3(11)) owing to the corporation or another corporation resident in Canada that does not, at the particular time, deal at arm's length with the corporation;

History: S. 18(5), paragraph (*b*) of the definition "outstanding debts to specified non-residents" was amended by S.C. 2014, c. 39, s. 6(2), applicable to taxation years that end after March 28, 2012, except that, if an election is made by a taxpayer under subsection 49(3) of the *Jobs and Growth Act, 2012* [S.C. 2012, c. 31], this amendment does not apply to taxation years of the taxpayer that end before August 14, 2012.

Paragraph (*b*) of the definition "outstanding debts to specified non-residents" formerly read:

(*b*) an amount outstanding at the particular time as or on account of a debt or other obligation to pay an amount to

(i) a non-resident insurance corporation to the extent that the obligation was, for the non-resident insurance corporation's taxation year that included the particular time, designated insurance property in respect of an insurance business carried on in Canada through a permanent establishment as defined by regulation, or

(ii) an authorized foreign bank, if the bank uses or holds the obligation at the particular time in its Canadian banking business;

S. 18(5), the portion before paragraph (*b*) of the definition "outstanding debts to specified non-residents" was replaced by S.C. 2013, c. 40, s. 8(2), applicable to taxation years that begin after 2013.

S. 18(5), the portion before paragraph (*b*) of the definition "outstanding debts to specified non-residents" formerly read:

"outstanding debts to specified non-residents"—"outstanding debts to specified non-residents" of a corporation at any particular time in a taxation year means

(*a*) the total of all amounts each of which is an amount outstanding at that time as or on account of a debt or other obligation to pay an amount

(i) that was payable by the corporation to a person who was, at any time in the year,

(A) a specified non-resident shareholder of the corporation, or

(B) a non-resident person, or a non-resident-owned investment corporation, who was not dealing at arm's length with a specified shareholder of the corporation, and

(ii) on which any amount in respect of interest paid or payable by the corporation is or would be, but for subsection (4), deductible in computing the corporation's income for the year,

but does not include

Related Regulations: 8201.

Related Sections: S. 248(1), "corporation", "individual", "insurance corporation", "non-resident", "property", "shareholder"; s. 249(1) Definition of "taxation year".

Interpretation Bulletins: *Secondary* — IT-59R3 Interest on debts owing to specified non-residents (thin capitalization).

"security interest" —"security interest" in respect of a property, means an interest in, or for civil law a right in, the property that secures payment of an obligation;

History: S. 18(5), the definition "security interest" was added by S.C. 2014, c. 39, s. 6(3), applicable to taxation years that begin after 2014.

"specified beneficiary" —"specified beneficiary", of a trust at any time, means a person who at that time, either alone or together with persons with whom that person does not deal at arm's length, has an interest as a beneficiary under the trust with a fair market value that is not less than 25% of the fair market value of all interests as a beneficiary under the trust and for the purpose of determining whether a particular person is a specified beneficiary of a trust,

(*a*) if the particular person, or a person with whom the particular person does not deal at arm's length, has at that time a right under a contract, in equity or otherwise, either immediately or in the future and either absolutely or contingently, to, or to acquire, an interest as a beneficiary under a trust, the particular person or the person with whom the particular person does not deal at arm's length, as the case may be, is deemed at that time to own the interest,

(*b*) if the particular person, or a person with whom the particular person does not deal at arm's length, has at that time a right under a contract, in equity or otherwise, either immediately or in the future and either absolutely or contingently to cause a trust to redeem, acquire or terminate any interest in it as a beneficiary (other than an interest held by the particular person or a person with whom the particular person does not deal at arm's length), the trust is deemed at that time to have redeemed, acquired or terminated the interest, unless the right is not exercisable at that time because the exercise of the right is contingent on the death, bankruptcy or permanent disability of an individual, and

(*c*) if the amount of income or capital of the trust that the particular person, or a person with whom the particular person does not deal at arm's length, may receive as a beneficiary of the trust depends on the exercise by any person of, or the failure by any person to exercise, a discretionary power, that person is deemed to have fully exercised, or to have failed to exercise, the power, as the case may be;

History: S. 18(5), the definition "specified beneficiary" was added by S.C. 2013, c. 40, s. 8(3), applicable to taxation years that begin after 2013.

"specified non-resident beneficiary" —"specified non-resident beneficiary", of a trust at any time, means a specified beneficiary of the trust who at that time is a non-resident person;

History: S. 18(5), the definition "specified non-resident beneficiary" was added by S.C. 2013, c. 40, s. 8(3), applicable to taxation years that begin after 2013.

"specified non-resident shareholder" —"specified non-resident shareholder" of a corporation at any time means a specified shareholder of the corporation who was at that time a non-resident person or a non-resident-owned investment corporation;

"specified proportion" — (Repealed by S.C. 2013, c. 34, s. 427(2)(*b*).)

History: S. 18(5), the definition "specified proportion" was repealed by S.C. 2013, c. 34, s. 427(2)(*b*), applicable on the first day on which both the *Jobs and Growth Act, 2012* [2012, c. 31] and *Technical Amendments Act, 2012* [S.C. 2013, c. 34] receive royal assent [June 26, 2013], and formerly read:

"specified proportion" —"specified proportion", of a member of a partnership for a fiscal period of the partnership, means the proportion that the member's share of the total income or loss of the partnership for the partnership's fiscal period is of the partnership's total income or loss for that period and, for the purposes of this definition, where that income or loss for a period is nil, that proportion shall be computed as if the partnership had income for that period in the amount of $1,000,000;

S. 18(5), the definition "specified proportion" was added by S.C. 2012, c. 31, s. 7(6), applicable to taxation years that begin after March 28, 2012.

Related Sections: S. 248(1), "specified proportion".

"specified right" —"specified right", at any time in respect of a property, means a right to, at that time, mortgage, hypothecate, assign, pledge or in any way encumber the property to secure payment of an obligation — other than the particular debt or other obligation described in paragraph (6)(*a*) or a debt or other obligation described in subparagraph (6)(*d*)(ii) — or to use, invest, sell or otherwise dispose of, or in any way alienate, the property unless it is established by the taxpayer that all of the proceeds (net of costs, if any) received, or that would be received, from exercising the right must first be applied to reduce an amount described in subparagraph (6)(*d*)(i) or (ii);

History: S. 18(5), the definition "specified right" was added by S.C. 2014, c. 39, s. 6(3), applicable to taxation years that begin after 2014.

Canadian Tax Foundation: Spiro and Bazarkewich, *Specified Right: Back-to-Back Shareholder Loans*, 2018 Canadian Tax Highlights 26(1):8–9.

Tax Window Files: CPA Alberta 2017 Q11: Shareholder loans, *September 14, 2017*, CRA Document No. 2017-0703901C6.

"specified shareholder" —"specified shareholder" of a corporation at any time means a person who at that time, either alone or together with persons with whom that person is not dealing at arm's length, owns

(*a*) shares of the capital stock of the corporation that give the holders thereof 25% or more of the votes that could be cast at an annual meeting of the shareholders of the corporation, or

(*b*) shares of the capital stock of the corporation having a fair market value of 25% or more of the fair market value of all of the issued and outstanding shares of the capital stock of the corporation,

and, for the purpose of determining whether a particular person is a specified shareholder of a corporation at any time, where the particular person or a person with whom the particular person is not dealing at arm's length has at that time a right under a contract, in equity or otherwise, either immediately or in the future and either absolutely or contingently

(*c*) to, or to acquire, shares in a corporation or to control the voting rights of shares in a corporation, or

(*d*) to cause a corporation to redeem, acquire or cancel any of its shares (other than shares held by the particular person or a person with whom the particular person is not dealing at arm's length), the particular person or the person with whom the particular person is not dealing at arm's length, as the case may be, shall be deemed at that time to own the shares referred to in paragraph (*c*) and the corporation referred to in paragraph (*d*) shall be deemed at that time to have redeemed, acquired or cancelled the shares referred to in paragraph (*d*), unless the right is not exercisable at that time because the exercise thereof is contingent on the death, bankruptcy or permanent disability of an individual;

Related Sections: S. 248(1), "corporation", "individual", "insurance corporation", "non-resident", "property", "shareholder"; s. 249(1) Definition of "taxation year"; s. 251 Arm's length.

Interpretation Bulletins: *Secondary* — IT-59R3 Interest on debts owing to specified non-residents (thin capitalization).

"tax-paid earnings" —"tax-paid earnings", of a trust resident in Canada for a taxation year, means the total of all amounts each of which is the amount in respect of a particular taxation year of the trust that ended before the year determined by the formula

$$A - B$$

where

A is the taxable income of the trust under this Part for the particular year, and

B is the total of tax payable under this Part by the trust, and all income taxes payable by the trust under the laws of a province, for the particular year.

History: S. 18(5), the definition "tax-paid earnings" was added by S.C. 2013, c. 40, s. 8(3), applicable to taxation years that begin after 2013.

► 18(5.1) ◄

(5.1) Specified shareholder or specified beneficiary. For the purposes of subsections (4) to (6), if

(*a*) a particular person would, but for this subsection, be a specified shareholder of a corporation or a specified beneficiary of a trust at any time,

(*b*) there was in effect at that time an agreement or arrangement under which, on the satisfaction of a condition or the occurrence of an event that it is reasonable to expect will be satisfied or will occur, the particular person will cease to be a specified shareholder of the corporation or a specified beneficiary of the trust, and

(*c*) the purpose for which the particular person became a specified shareholder or specified beneficiary was the safeguarding of rights or interests of the particular person or a person with whom the particular person is not dealing at arm's length in respect of any indebtedness owing at any time to the particular person or a person with whom the particular person is not dealing at arm's length,

the particular person is deemed not to be a specified shareholder of the corporation or a specified beneficiary of the trust, as the case may be, at that time.

History: S. 18(5.1) was replaced by S.C. 2013, c. 40, s. 8(4), applicable to taxation years that begin after 2013.

S. 18(5.1) formerly read:

(5.1) *Person deemed not to be specified shareholder.* For the purposes of subsections (4) to (6), where

(*a*) a particular person would, but for this subsection, be a specified shareholder of a corporation at any time,

(*b*) there was in effect at that time an agreement or arrangement under which, on the satisfaction of a condition or the occurrence of an event that it is reasonable to expect will be satisfied or will occur, the particular person will cease to be a specified shareholder, and

(*c*) the purpose for which the particular person became a specified shareholder was the safeguarding of rights or interests of the particular person or a person with whom the particular person is not dealing at arm's length in respect of any indebtedness owing at any time to the particular person or a person with whom the particular person is not dealing at arm's length,

the particular person shall be deemed not to be a specified shareholder of the corporation at that time.

Related Sections: S. 248(1), "corporation", "specified shareholder"; s. 251 Arm's length.

► 18(5.2) ◄

(5.2) Specified shareholder or specified beneficiary. For the purposes of subsections (4) to (6), a non-resident corporation is deemed to be a specified shareholder of itself and a non-resident trust is deemed to be a specified beneficiary of itself.

History: S. 18(5.2) was added by S.C. 2013, c. 40, s. 8(4), applicable to taxation years that begin after 2013.

► 18(5.3) ◄

(5.3) Property used in business — cost attribution. For the purposes of subparagraph (*c*)(i) of the definition "equity amount" in subsection (5),

(*a*) if a property is partly used or held by a taxpayer in a taxation year in the course of carrying on business in Canada, the cost of the property to the taxpayer is deemed for the year to be equal to the same proportion of the cost to the taxpayer of the property (determined without reference to this subsection) that the proportion of the use or holding made of the property in the course of carrying on business in Canada in the year is of the whole use or holding made of the property in the year; and

(*b*) if a corporation or trust is deemed to own a portion of a property of a partnership because of subsection (7) at any time,

(i) the property is deemed to have, at that time, a cost to the corporation or trust equal to the same proportion of the cost of the property to the partnership as the proportion of the debts and other obligations to pay an amount of the partnership allocated to it under subsection (7) is of the total amount of all debts and other obligations to pay an amount of the partnership, and

(ii) in the case of a partnership that carries on business in Canada, the corporation or trust is deemed to use or hold the property in the course of carrying on business in Canada to the extent the partnership uses or holds the property in the course of carrying on business in Canada for the fiscal period of the partnership that includes that time.

History: S. 18(5.3) was added by S.C. 2013, c. 40, s. 8(4), applicable to taxation years that begin after 2013.

► 18(5.4) ◄

(5.4) Rules — trust income. For the purposes of this Act, a trust resident in Canada may designate in its return of income under this Part for a taxation year that all or any portion of an amount paid or credited as interest by the trust, or by a partnership, in the year to a non-resident person is deemed to be income of the trust that has been paid to the non-resident person as a beneficiary of the trust, and not to have been paid or credited by the trust or the partnership as interest, to the extent that an amount in respect of the interest

(*a*) is included in computing the income of the trust for the year under paragraph 12(1)(*l.1*); or

(*b*) is not deductible in computing the income of the trust for the year because of subsection (4).

History: S. 18(5.4) was added by S.C. 2013, c. 40, s. 8(4), applicable to taxation years that begin after 2013.

▶ 18(6) ◀

(6) Back-to-back loan arrangement. Subsection (6.1) applies at any time in respect of a taxpayer if at that time

(*a*) the taxpayer has a particular amount outstanding as or on account of a particular debt or other obligation to pay an amount to a person (in this subsection and subsection (6.1) referred to as the "intermediary");

(*b*) the intermediary is neither

(i) a person resident in Canada with whom the taxpayer does not deal at arm's length, nor

(ii) a person that is, in respect of the taxpayer, described in subparagraph (*a*)(i) of the definition "outstanding debts to specified non-residents" in subsection (5);

(*c*) the intermediary or a person that does not deal at arm's length with the intermediary

(i) has an amount outstanding as or on account of a debt or other obligation to pay an amount to a particular non-resident person that is, in respect of the taxpayer, described in subparagraph (*a*)(i) of the definition "outstanding debts to specified non-residents" in subsection (5) that meets any of the following conditions (in this subsection and subsection (6.1) referred to as the "intermediary debt"):

(A) recourse in respect of the debt or other obligation is limited in whole or in part, either immediately or in the future and either absolutely or contingently, to the particular debt or other obligation, or

(B) it can reasonably be concluded that all or a portion of the particular amount became owing, or was permitted to remain owing, because

(I) all or a portion of the debt or other obligation was entered into or was permitted to remain outstanding, or

(II) the intermediary anticipated that all or a portion of the debt or other obligation would become owing or remain outstanding, or

(ii) has a specified right in respect of a particular property that was granted directly or indirectly by a person that is, in respect of the taxpayer, a particular non-resident person described in subparagraph (*a*)(i) of the definition "outstanding debts to specified non-residents" in subsection (5) and

(A) the existence of the specified right is required under the terms and conditions of the particular debt or other obligation, or

(B) it can reasonably be concluded that all or a portion of the particular amount became owing, or was permitted to remain owing, because

(I) the specified right was granted, or

(II) the intermediary anticipated that the specified right would be granted; and

(*d*) the total of all amounts — each of which is, in respect of the particular debt or other obligation, an amount outstanding as or on account of an intermediary debt or the fair market value of a particular property described in subparagraph (*c*)(ii) — is equal to at least 25% of the total of

(i) the particular amount, and

(ii) the total of all amounts each of which is an amount (other than the particular amount) that the taxpayer, or a person that does not deal at arm's length with the taxpayer, has outstanding as or on account of a debt or other obligation to pay an amount to the intermediary under the agreement, or an agreement that is connected to the agreement, under which the particular debt or other obligation was entered into if

(A) the intermediary is granted a security interest in respect of a property that is the intermediary debt or the particular property, as the case may be, and the security interest secures the payment of two or more debts or other obligations that include the debt or other obligation and the particular debt or other obligation, and

(B) each security interest that secures the payment of a debt or other obligation referred to in clause (A) secures the payment of every debt or other obligation referred to in that clause.

Editorial Note: This provision was enacted as a result of a 2014 Budget measure to combat certain back-to-back loan arrangements that previously avoided the thin capitalization rules. The provision ensures that the thin capitalization rules cannot be avoided through the imposition of an arm's length intermediary between a resident payor of interest and a specified non-resident (see the conditions in paragraph 18(6)(*c*)). Similar rules were enacted to ensure that back-to-back loan arrangements cannot be utilized to avoid the non-resident withholding tax rules (subsection 212(3.1)).

History: S. 18(6) was replaced by S.C. 2014, c. 39, s. 6(4), applicable to taxation years that begin after 2014, and formerly read:

(6) *Loans made on condition.* If any loan (in this subsection referred to as the "first loan") has been made

(*a*) by a specified non-resident shareholder of a corporation or a specified non-resident beneficiary of a trust, or

(*b*) by a non-resident person who was not dealing at arm's length with a specified shareholder of a corporation or a specified non-resident beneficiary of a trust,

to another person on condition that a loan (in this subsection referred to as the "second loan") be made by any person to a particular corporation or trust, for the purposes of subsections (4) and (5), the lesser of

(*c*) the amount of the first loan, and

(*d*) the amount of the second loan

is deemed to be a debt incurred by the particular corporation or trust to the person who made the first loan.

S. 18(6) was replaced by S.C. 2013, c. 40, s. 8(4), applicable to taxation years that begin after 2013.

S. 18(6) formerly read:

(6) *Loans made on condition.* Where any loan (in this subsection referred to as the "first loan") has been made

(*a*) by a specified non-resident shareholder of a corporation, or

(*b*) by a non-resident person, or a non-resident-owned investment corporation, who was not dealing at arm's length with a specified shareholder of a corporation,

to another person on condition that a loan (in this subsection referred to as the "second loan") be made by any person to a particular corporation resident in Canada, for the purposes of subsections (4) and (5), the lesser of

(*c*) the amount of the first loan, and

(*d*) the amount of the second loan

shall be deemed to be a debt incurred by the particular corporation to the person who made the first loan.

Related Sections: 212(3.1) Back-to-back loan arrangement; 214(6) Deemed interest; 214(7) Sale of obligation.

Canadian Tax Foundation: Spiro and Bazarkewich, *Specified Right: Back-to-Back Shareholder Loans*, 2018 Canadian Tax Highlights 26(1):8–9.

Tax Topics: No. 1715, Thin Capitalization Rules — "Back-to-Back" Loans.

Interpretation Bulletins: *Secondary* — IT-59R3 Interest on debts owing to specified non-residents (thin capitalization).

Tax Window Files: 2015 TEI Liaison Meeting Q.6 - Specified Right, *November 17, 2015*, CRA Document No. 2015-0614241C6.

▶ 18(6.1) ◀

(6.1) Back-to-back loan arrangement. If this subsection applies at any time in respect of a taxpayer,

(*a*) then for the purpose of applying subsections (4) and (5),

(i) the portion of the particular amount, at that time, referred to in paragraph (6)(*a*) that is equal to the lesser of the following amounts is deemed to be an amount outstanding as or on account of a debt or other obligation to pay an amount to the particular non-resident person referred to in subparagraph (6)(*c*)(i) or (ii), as the case may be, and not to the intermediary:

(A) the amount outstanding as or on account of the intermediary debt or the fair market value of the particular property referred to in subparagraph (6)(*c*)(ii), as the case may be, and

(B) the proportion of the particular amount that the amount outstanding or the fair market value, as the case may be, is of the total of all amounts each of which is

(I) an amount outstanding as or on account of an intermediary debt in respect of the particular debt or other obligation, owed to the particular non-resident or any other non-resident person that is, in respect of the taxpayer, described in the definition "outstanding debts to specified non-residents" in subsection (5), or

(II) the fair market value of a particular property referred to in subparagraph (6)(*c*)(ii) in respect of the particular debt or other obligation, and

(ii) the portion of the interest paid or payable by the taxpayer, in respect of a period throughout which subparagraph (*a*)(i) applies, on the particular debt or other obligation referred to in paragraph (6)(*a*) that is equal to the amount determined by the following formula is deemed to be paid or payable by the taxpayer to the particular non-resident, and not to the intermediary, as interest for the period on the amount deemed by subparagraph (*a*)(i) to be outstanding to the particular non-resident:

$$A \times B/C$$

where

A is the interest paid or payable,

B is the average of all amounts each of which is an amount that is deemed by subparagraph (*a*)(i) to be outstanding to the particular non-resident at a time during the period, and

C is the average of all amounts each of which is the particular amount outstanding at a time during the period; and

(*b*) for the purposes of Part XIII and subject to subsections 214(16) and (17), interest deemed under subparagraph (*a*)(ii) to be paid or payable to the particular non-resident in respect of a period is, to the extent that the interest is not deductible in computing the income of the taxpayer for the year because of subsection 18(4), deemed to be paid or payable by the taxpayer to the particular non-resident, and not to the intermediary, in respect of the period.

History: S. 18(6.1) was added by S.C. 2014, c. 39, s. 6(4), applicable to taxation years that begin after 2014.

▶ 18(7) ◀

(7) Partnership debts and property. For the purposes of this subsection, paragraph (4)(*a*), subsections (5) to (6.1) and paragraph 12(1)(*l.1*), each member of a partnership at any time is deemed at that time

(*a*) to owe the portion (in this subsection and paragraph 12(1)(*l.1*) referred to as the "debt amount") of each debt or other obligation to pay an amount of the partnership and to own the portion of each property of the partnership that is equal to

(i) the member's specified proportion for the last fiscal period, if any, of the partnership ending

(A) at or before the end of the taxation year referred to in subsection (4), and

(B) at a time when the member is a member of the partnership, and

(ii) if the member does not have a specified proportion described in subparagraph (i), the proportion that

(A) the fair market value of the member's interest in the partnership at that time

is of

(B) the fair market value of all interests in the partnership at that time;

(*b*) to owe the debt amount to the person to whom the partnership owes the debt or other obligation to pay an amount; and

(*c*) to have paid interest on the debt amount that is deductible in computing the member's income to the extent that an amount in respect of interest paid or payable on the debt amount by the partnership is deductible in computing the partnership's income.

History: S. 18(7), the portion before paragraph (*a*) was replaced by S.C. 2014, c. 39, s. 6(5), applicable to taxation years that begin after 2014, and formerly read:

(7) *Partnership debts.* For the purposes of this subsection, paragraph (4)(*a*), subsections (5) to (6) and paragraph 12(1)(*l.1*), each member of a partnership at any time is deemed at that time

S. 18(7)(*a*), the portion before subparagraph (i) was replaced by S.C. 2013, c. 40, s. 8(5), applicable to taxation years that begin after 2013.

S. 18(7)(*a*), the portion before subparagraph (i) formerly read:

(*a*) to owe the portion (in this subsection and paragraph 12(1)(*l.1*) referred to as the "debt amount") of each debt or other obligation to pay an amount of the partnership that is equal to

S. 18(7) was added by S.C. 2012, c. 31, s.7(7), applicable to taxation years that begin after March 28, 2012.

► 18(8) ◄

(8) Exception — foreign accrual property income. An amount in respect of interest paid or payable to a controlled foreign affiliate of a corporation resident in Canada that would otherwise not be deductible by the corporation for a taxation year because of subsection (4) may be deducted to the extent that an amount included under subsection 91(1) in computing the corporation's income for the year or a subsequent year can reasonably be considered to be in respect of the interest.

History: S. 18(8) was added by S.C. 2012, c. 31, s.7(7), applicable to taxation years that end after 2004.

Related Sections: S. 18(1)(*c*) Limitation re exempt income.

Interpretation Bulletins: *Secondary* — IT-59R3 Interest on debts owing to specified non-residents (thin capitalization).

► 18(9) ◄

(9) Limitation respecting prepaid expenses. Notwithstanding any other provision of this Act,

(*a*) in computing a taxpayer's income for a taxation year from a business or property (other than income from a business computed in accordance with the method authorized by subsection 28(1)), no deduction shall be made in respect of an outlay or expense to the extent that it can reasonably be regarded as having been made or incurred

(i) as consideration for services to be rendered after the end of the year,

(ii) as, on account of, in lieu of payment of or in satisfaction of, interest, taxes (other than taxes imposed on an insurer in respect of insurance premiums of a non-cancellable or guaranteed renewable accident and sickness insurance policy, or a life insurance policy other than a group term life insurance policy that provides coverage for a period of 12 months or less), rent or royalties in respect of a period that is after the end of the year,

(iii) as consideration for insurance in respect of a period after the end of the year, other than

(A) where the taxpayer is an insurer, consideration for reinsurance, and

(B) consideration for insurance on the life of an individual under a group term life insurance policy where all or part of the consideration is for insurance that is (or would be if the individual survived) in respect of a period that ends more than 13 months after the consideration is paid, or

(iv) subject to clause (iii)(B) and subsections 144.1(4) to (7), as consideration for a "designated employee benefit" (as defined in subsection 144.1(1)) to be provided after the end of the year (other than consideration payable in the year, to a corporation that is licensed to provide insurance, for insurance coverage in respect of the year);

(*b*) such portion of each outlay or expense (other than an outlay or expense of a corporation, partnership or trust as, on account of, in lieu of payment of or in satisfaction of, interest) made or incurred as would, but for paragraph (*a*), be deductible in computing a taxpayer's income for a taxation year shall be deductible in computing the taxpayer's income for the subsequent year to which it can reasonably be considered to relate;

(*c*) for the purposes of section 37.1, such portion of each qualified expenditure (within the meaning assigned by subsection 37.1(5)) as was made by a taxpayer in a taxation year and as would, but for paragraph (*a*), have been deductible in computing the taxpayer's income for the year shall be deemed

(i) not to be a qualified expenditure made by the taxpayer in the year, and

(ii) to be a qualified expenditure made by the taxpayer in the subsequent year to which the expenditure can reasonably be considered to relate;

(*d*) for the purpose of paragraph (*a*), an outlay or expense of a taxpayer is deemed not to include any payment referred to in subparagraph 37(1)(*a*)(ii) or (iii) that

(i) is made by the taxpayer to a person or partnership with which the taxpayer deals at arm's length, and

(ii) is not an expenditure described in subparagraph 37(1)(*a*)(i); and

(*e*) for the purposes of section 37 and the definition "qualified expenditure" in subsection 127(9), the portion of an expenditure that is made or incurred by a taxpayer in a taxation year and that would, but for paragraph (*a*), have been deductible under section 37 in computing the taxpayer's income for the year, is deemed

(i) not to be made or incurred by the taxpayer in the year, and

(ii) to be made or incurred by the taxpayer in the subsequent taxation year to which the expenditure can reasonably be considered to relate.

(*f*) (Repealed by S.C. 2017, c. 20, s. 3(1).)

Editorial Note: See also s. 18(9.2) regarding prepaid interest incurred by corporations, trusts and partnerships, and s. 18(9.1) regarding early repayment penalties, bonuses, and interest-rate reduction payments. The CRA historically applied the matching principle of accounting to amortize or defer the deduction of expenses such as deferred charges that were similar in nature to prepaid expenses but not specifically covered by s. 18(9). However, the CRA position was cast into doubt as a result of the Supreme Court decisions in *Canderel* and *Toronto College Park* cited below; in this regard, see also the lead article in Tax Topics No. 1805, October 12, 2006.

History: S. 18(9)(*f*) was repealed by S.C. 2017, c. 20, s. 3(1), applicable in respect of expenditures incurred after March 21, 2017, except that this amendment does not apply in respect of expenditures incurred before 2020 under a written agreement entered into before March 22, 2017. S. 18(9)(*f*) formerly read:

(*f*) for the purpose of the definition "eligible child care space expenditure" in subsection 127(9), the portion of an expenditure (other than for the acquisition of depreciable property) that is made or incurred by a taxpayer in a taxation year and that would, but for paragraph (*a*), have been deductible under this Act in computing the taxpayer's income for the year, is deemed

(i) not to be made or incurred by the taxpayer in the year, and

(ii) to be made or incurred by the taxpayer in the subsequent taxation year to which the expenditure can reasonably be considered to relate.

S. 18(9)(*a*)(iv) was added by S.C. 2010, c. 25, s. 5(3), applicable after 2009.

Related Sections: S. 18(1)(*a*) General limitation; s. 18(1)(*b*) Capital outlay or loss; s. 18(9.2) Interest on debt obligations — notional principal; s. 18.1 Definitions; s. 18.1(4) Amount of deduction; s. 87(2)(*j*.2) Prepaid expenses and matchable expenditures.

Canadian Tax Foundation: Frankovic, *The Income Tax Treatment of Prepaid Expenses and Similar Costs: A Time Value Analysis*, 2000 Canadian Tax Journal 5:1371–1443; Frankovic, *The Matching of "Current" Expense Under Canada's Income Tax Laws*, 1998 Canadian Tax Journal 1:1–28.

Income Tax Technical News: Issue No. 25, Health and Welfare Trusts.

Interpretation Bulletins: *Primary* — IT-417R2 Prepaid expenses and deferred charges. *Secondary* — IT-109R2 Unpaid amounts; IT-211R Membership dues — Associations and societies.

Tax Window Files: Straight-Line Amortization or Averaging of Rent, *May 26, 2008*, CRA Document No. 2008-027277117; Prepaid Lease Payments, *Technical Interpretation, Financial Industries Division, February 22, 2005*, CRA Document No. 2004-0109381E5. Application of subsection 18(9) when section 16.1 election is made; Lump-Sum Rent Payment, *Technical Interpretation, Business and Partnerships Division, December 15, 2004*, CRA Document No. 2004-0093841E5. Treatment of lump sum additional rent payment required at beginning of fourth year of twenty-year lease; Lump-Sum Prepayment of Automobile Lease, *Technical Interpretation, Financial Industries Division, June 3, 2003*, CRA Document No. 2003-0015675. Subsection 18(9) applies to amortize prepayment under car lease over the period of the lease; section 67.3 then applies to limit the amount otherwise deductible in each year; Amortization of Product Liability Insurance Premiums, *Technical Interpretation, Business and Partnerships Division, January 30, 2003*, CRA Document No. 2002-0169785. Product liability insurance purchased by manufacturer subject to amortization under subsection 18(9); amortization can be based on expected claims against the manufacturer over the life of the manufactured goods, and if not feasible, straight-line amortization acceptable over life of goods.

Cases: Tenant inducement payments paid by the taxpayer were not required to be amortized over the course of the lease, and were deductible in the year incurred. *Toronto College Park v. The Queen*, 98 DTC 6088 (S.C.C.), reversing 96 DTC 6407 (F.C.A.). *Canderel Limited v. The Queen*, 98 DTC 6100 (S.C.C.), reversing 95 DTC 5101 (F.C.A.)

▶ 18(9.01) ◀

(9.01) Group term life insurance. Where

(*a*) a taxpayer pays a premium after February 1994 and before 1997 under a group term life insurance policy for insurance on the life of an individual,

(*b*) the insurance is for the remainder of the individual's lifetime, and

(*c*) no further premiums will be payable for the insurance,

no amount may be deducted in computing the taxpayer's income for a taxation year from a business or property in respect of the premium except that there may be so deducted,

(*d*) where the year is the taxation year in which the premium was paid or a subsequent taxation year and the individual is alive at the end of the year, the lesser of

(i) the amount determined by the formula

$$A - B$$

and

(ii) $1/3$ of the amount determined by the formula

$$(A \times C)/365$$

where

A is the amount that would, if this Act were read without reference to this subsection, be deductible in respect of the premium in computing the taxpayer's income,

B is the total amount deductible in respect of the premium in computing the taxpayer's income for preceding taxation years, and

C is the number of days in the year, and

(*e*) where the individual died in the year, the amount determined under subparagraph (*d*)(i).

▶ 18(9.02) ◀

(9.02) Application of subsection (9) to insurers. For the purpose of subsection (9), an outlay or expense made or incurred by an insurer on account of the acquisition of an insurance policy (other than a non-cancellable or guaranteed renewable accident and sickness insurance policy or a life insurance policy other than a group term life insurance policy that provides coverage for a period of 12 months or less) is deemed to be an expense incurred as consideration for services rendered consistently throughout the period of coverage of the policy.

▶ 18(9.1) ◀

(9.1) Penalties, bonuses and rate-reduction payments. Subject to subsection 142.4(10), where at any time a payment, other than a payment that

(*a*) can reasonably be considered to have been made in respect of the extension of the term of a debt obligation or in respect of the substitution or conversion of a debt obligation to another debt obligation or share, or

(*b*) is contingent or dependent on the use of or production from property or is computed by reference to revenue, profit, cash flow, commodity price or any other similar criterion or by reference to dividends paid or payable to shareholders of any class of shares of the capital stock of a corporation,

is made to a person or partnership by a taxpayer in the course of carrying on a business or earning income from property in respect of borrowed money or on an amount payable for property acquired by the taxpayer (in this subsection referred to as a "debt obligation")

(*c*) as consideration for a reduction in the rate of interest payable by the taxpayer on the debt obligation, or

(*d*) as a penalty or bonus payable by the taxpayer because of the repayment by the taxpayer of all or part of the principal amount of the debt obligation before its maturity,

the payment shall, to the extent that it can reasonably be considered to relate to, and does not exceed the value at that time of, an amount that, but for the reduction described in paragraph (*c*) or the repayment described in paragraph (*d*), would have been paid or payable by the taxpayer as interest on the debt obligation for a taxation year of the taxpayer ending after that time, be deemed,

(*e*) for the purposes of this Act, to have been paid by the taxpayer and received by the person or partnership at that time as interest on the debt obligation, and

(*f*) for the purpose of computing the taxpayer's income in respect of the business or property for the year, to have been paid or payable by the taxpayer in that year as interest pursuant to a legal obligation to pay interest,

(i) in the case of a reduction described in paragraph (*c*), on the debt obligation, and

(ii) in the case of a repayment described in paragraph (*d*),

(A) where the repayment was in respect of all or part of the principal amount of the debt obligation that was borrowed money, except to the extent that the borrowed money was used by the taxpayer to acquire property, on borrowed money used in the year for the purpose for which the borrowed money that was repaid was used, and

(B) where the repayment was in respect of all or part of the principal amount of the debt obligation that was either borrowed money used to acquire property or an amount payable for property acquired by the taxpayer, on the debt obligation to the extent that the property or property substituted therefor is used by the taxpayer in the year for the purpose of gaining or producing income therefrom or for the purpose of gaining or producing income from a business.

Related Sections: S. 18(9) Limitation respecting prepaid expenses; s. 18(9.2) Interest on debt obligations — notional principal; s. 20(1)(*c*) Interest; s. 20(1)(*e*) Expenses re financing; s. 248(1), "principal amount".

Canadian Tax Foundation: Diksic and Desjardins, *Tax Treatment of Transaction Costs*, 2006 Conference Report 38:1–36; Frankovic, *The Income Tax Treatment of Prepaid Expenses and Similar Costs: A Time Value Analysis*, 2000 Canadian Tax Journal 5:1371–1443.

Income Tax Folios: *Secondary* — S4-F2-C1 Deductibility of Fines and Penalties.

Tax Window Files: Deduction of Interest Penalty After Disposition of Property, *Round Table on Federal Taxation — 2003 APFF Conference, Question 8, October 10, 2003*, CRA Document No. 2003-0030055. Subsection 18(9.1) not applicable to interest rate penalty on mortgage after the mortgaged property was sold; Determining the Penalty Amount, *Technical Interpretation, Financial Industries Division, September 30, 2003*, CRA Document No. 2003-0023137. Possible bifurcation between penalty or bonus component and restructuring fee component of payment; former could be subject to subsection 18(9.1).

► 18(9.2) ◄

(9.2) Interest on debt obligations. For the purposes of this Part, the amount of interest payable on borrowed money or on an amount payable for property (in this subsection and subsections (9.3) to (9.8) referred to as the "debt obligation") by a corporation, partnership or trust (in this subsection and subsections (9.3) to (9.7) referred to as the "borrower") in respect of a taxation year shall, notwithstanding subparagraph (9.1)(*f*)(i), be deemed to be an amount equal to the lesser of

(*a*) the amount of interest, not in excess of a reasonable amount, that would be payable on the debt obligation by the borrower in respect of the year if no amount had been paid before the end of the year in satisfaction of the obligation to pay interest on the debt obligation in respect of the year and if the amount outstanding at each particular time in the year that is after 1991 on account of the principal amount of the debt obligation were the amount, if any, by which

(i) the amount outstanding at the particular time on account of the principal amount of the debt obligation

exceeds the total of

(ii) all amounts each of which is an amount paid before the particular time in satisfaction, in whole or in part, of the obligation to pay interest on the debt obligation in respect of a period or part thereof that is after 1991, after the beginning of the year, and after the time the amount was so paid (other than a period or part thereof that is in the year where no such amount was paid before the particular time in respect of a period, or part of a period, that is after the end of the year), and

(iii) the amount, if any, by which

(A) the total of all amounts of interest payable on the debt obligation (determined without reference to this subsection) by the borrower in respect of taxation years ending after 1991 and before the year (to the extent that the interest does not exceed a reasonable amount)

exceeds

(B) the total of all amounts of interest deemed by this subsection to have been payable on the debt obligation by the borrower in respect of taxation years ending before the year, and

(*b*) the amount, if any, by which

(i) the total of all amounts of interest payable on the debt obligation (determined without reference to this subsection) by the borrower in respect of the year or taxation years ending after 1991 and before the year (to the extent that the interest does not exceed a reasonable amount)

exceeds

(ii) the total of all amounts of interest deemed by this subsection to have been payable on the debt obligation by the borrower in respect of taxation years ending before the year.

Related Sections: S. 18(9) Limitation respecting prepaid expenses; s. 20(1)(*c*) Interest; s. 20(1)(*e*) Expenses re financing; s. 104(1) Reference to trust or estate; s. 248(1), "borrowed money", "principal amount".

Canadian Tax Foundation: Frankovic, *The Income Tax Treatment of Prepaid Expenses and Similar Costs: A Time Value Analysis*, 2000 Canadian Tax Journal 5:1371–1443.

► 18(9.3) ◄

(9.3) Interest on debt obligations. Where at any time in a taxation year of a borrower a debt obligation of the borrower is settled or extinguished or the holder of the obligation acquires or reacquires property of the borrower in circumstances in which section 79 applies in respect of the debt obligation and the total of

(*a*) all amounts each of which is an amount paid at or before that time in satisfaction, in whole or in part, of the obligation to pay interest on the debt obligation in respect of a period or part of a period that is after that time, and (*b*) all amounts of interest payable on the debt obligation (determined without reference to subsection (9.2)) by the borrower in respect of taxation years ending after 1991 and before that time, or in respect of periods, or parts of periods, that are in such years and before that time (to the extent that the interest does not exceed a reasonable amount),

exceeds the total of

(*c*) all amounts of interest deemed by subsection (9.2) to have been payable on the debt obligation by the borrower in respect of taxation years ending before that time, and

(*d*) the amount of interest that would be deemed by subsection (9.2) to have been payable on the debt obligation by the borrower in respect of the year if the year had ended immediately before that time,

(which excess is in this subsection referred to as the "excess amount"), the following rules apply:

(*e*) for the purpose of applying section 79 in respect of the borrower, the principal amount at that time of the debt obligation shall be deemed to be equal to the amount, if any, by which

(i) the principal amount at that time of the debt obligation

exceeds

(ii) the excess amount, and

(*f*) the excess amount shall be deducted at that time in computing the forgiven amount in respect of the obligation (within the meaning assigned by subsection 80(1)).

Related Sections: S. 18(9.2) Interest on debt obligations — notional principal; s. 18(9.3) Interest on debt obligations — extinguished obligations; s. 80(1) Definitions; s. 248(1), "amount", "principal amount"; s. 249(1) Definition of "taxation year".

► 18(9.4) ◄

(9.4) Idem. Where an amount is paid at any time by a person or partnership in respect of a debt obligation of a borrower

(*a*) as, on account of, in lieu of payment of or in satisfaction of, interest on the debt obligation in respect of a period or part thereof that is after 1991 and after that time, or

(*b*) as consideration for a reduction in the rate of interest payable on the debt obligation (excluding, for greater certainty, a payment described in paragraph (9.1)(*a*) or (*b*)) in respect of a period or part thereof that is after 1991 and after that time,

that amount shall be deemed, for the purposes of subsection (9.5) and, subject to that subsection, for the purposes of clause (9.2)(*a*)(iii)(A), subparagraph (9.2)(*b*)(i), paragraph (9.3)(*b*) and subsection (9.6), to be an amount of interest payable on the debt obligation by the borrower in respect of that period or part thereof and shall be deemed, for the purposes of subparagraph (9.2)(*a*)(ii) and paragraph (9.3)(*a*), to be an amount paid at that time in satisfaction of the obligation to pay interest on the debt obligation in respect of that period or part thereof.

Related Sections: S. 18(9.1) Penalties, bonuses and rate-reduction payments; s. 18(9.2) Interest on debt obligations — notional principal; s. 248(1), "amount".

► 18(9.5) ◄

(9.5) Idem. Where the amount of interest payable on a debt obligation (determined without reference to subsection (9.2)) by a borrower in respect of a particular period or part thereof that is after 1991 can reasonably be regarded as an amount payable as consideration for

(*a*) a reduction in the amount of interest that would otherwise be payable on the debt obligation in respect of a subsequent period, or

(*b*) a reduction in the amount that was or may be paid before the beginning of a subsequent period in satisfaction of the obligation to pay interest on the debt obligation in respect of that subsequent period

(determined without reference to the existence of, or the amount of any interest paid or payable on, any other debt obligation), that amount shall, for the purposes of clause (9.2)(*a*)(iii)(A), subparagraph (9.2)(*b*)(i), paragraph (9.3)(*b*) and subsection (9.6), be deemed to be an amount of interest payable on the debt obligation by the borrower in respect of the subsequent period and not to be an amount of interest payable on the debt obligation by the borrower in respect of the particular period and shall, when paid, be deemed for the purposes of subparagraph (9.2)(*a*)(ii) and paragraph (9.3)(*a*) to be an amount paid in satisfaction of the obligation to pay interest on the debt obligation in respect of the subsequent period.

Related Sections: S. 18(9.2) Interest on debt obligations — notional principal; s. 248(1), "amount".

► 18(9.6) ◄

(9.6) Idem. Where the liability in respect of a debt obligation of a person or partnership is assumed by a borrower at any time,

(*a*) the amount of interest payable on the debt obligation (determined without reference to subsection (9.2)) by any person or partnership in respect of a period shall, to the extent that that period is included in a taxation year of the borrower ending after 1991, be deemed, for the purposes of clause (9.2)(*a*)(iii)(A), subparagraph (9.2)(*b*)(i) and paragraph (9.3)(*b*), to be an amount of interest payable on the debt obligation by the borrower in respect of that year, and

(*b*) the application of subsections (9.2) and (9.3) to the borrower in respect of the debt obligation after that time shall be determined on the assumption that subsection (9.2) applied to the borrower in respect of the debt obligation before that time,

and, for the purposes of this subsection, where the borrower came into existence at a particular time that is after the beginning of the particular period beginning at the beginning of the first period in respect of which interest was payable on the debt obligation by any person or partnership and ending at the particular time, the borrower shall be deemed

(*c*) to have been in existence throughout the particular period, and

(*d*) to have had, throughout the particular period, taxation years ending on the day of the year on which its first taxation year ended.

Related Sections: S. 18(9.2) Interest on debt obligations — notional principal; s. 249(1) Definition of "taxation year".

▶ 18(9.7) ◀

(9.7) Idem. Where the amount paid by a borrower at any particular time, in satisfaction of the obligation to pay a particular amount of interest on a debt obligation in respect of a subsequent period or part thereof, exceeds the particular amount of that interest, discounted

(*a*) for the particular period beginning at the particular time and ending at the end of the subsequent period or part thereof, and

(*b*) at the rate or rates of interest applying under the debt obligation during the particular period (or, where the rate of interest of any part of the particular period is not fixed at the particular time, at the prescribed rate of interest in effect at the particular time),

that excess shall

(*c*) for the purposes of applying subsections (9.2) to (9.6) and (9.8), be deemed to be neither an amount of interest payable on the debt obligation nor an amount paid in satisfaction of the obligation to pay interest on the debt obligation, and

(*d*) be deemed to be a payment described in paragraph (9.1)(*d*) in respect of the debt obligation.

Related Regulations: 4301.

Related Sections: S. 18(9.2) Interest on debt obligations — notional principal; s. 248(1), "amount", "prescribed".

▶ 18(9.8) ◀

(9.8) Idem. Nothing in any of subsections (9.2) to (9.7) shall be construed as providing that

(*a*) the total of all amounts each of which is the amount of interest payable on a debt obligation by an individual (other than a trust), or deemed by subsection (9.2) to be payable on the debt obligation by a corporation, partnership or trust, in respect of a taxation year ending after 1991 and before any particular time,

may exceed

(*b*) the total of all amounts each of which is the amount of interest payable on the debt obligation (determined without reference to subsection (9.2)) by a person or partnership in respect of a taxation year ending after 1991 and before that particular time.

Related Sections: S. 18(9.2) Interest on debt obligations — notional principal; s. 104(1) Reference to trust or estate; s. 248(1), "amount", "corporation", "trust"; s. 249(1) Definition of "taxation year".

▶ 18(10) ◀

(10) Employee benefit plan. Paragraph (1)(*o*) does not apply in respect of a contribution to an employee benefit plan

(*a*) to the extent that the contribution

(i) is made in respect of services performed by an employee who is not resident in Canada and is regularly employed in a country other than Canada, and

(ii) cannot reasonably be regarded as having been made in respect of services performed or to be performed during a period when the employee is resident in Canada;

(*b*) the custodian of which is non-resident, to the extent that the contribution

(i) is in respect of an employee who is non-resident at the time the contribution is made, and

(ii) cannot reasonably be regarded as having been made in respect of services performed or to be performed during a period when the employee is resident in Canada; or

(*c*) the custodian of which is non-resident, to the extent that the contribution can reasonably be regarded as having been made in respect of services performed by an employee in a particular calendar month where

(i) the employee was resident in Canada throughout no more than 60 of the 72 calendar months ending with the particular month, and

(ii) the employee became a member of the plan before the end of the month following the month in which the employee became resident in Canada,

and, for the purpose of this paragraph, where benefits provided to an employee under a particular employee benefit plan are replaced by benefits provided under another employee benefit plan, the other plan shall be deemed, in respect of the employee, to be the same plan as the particular plan.

Interpretation Bulletins: *Secondary* — IT-502 Employee benefit plans and employee trusts.

▶ 18(11) ◀

(11) Limitation. Notwithstanding any other provision of this Act, in computing the income of a taxpayer for a taxation year, no amount is deductible under paragraph 20(1)(*c*), (*d*), (*e*), (*e*.1) or (*f*) in respect of borrowed money (or other property acquired by the taxpayer) in respect of any period after which the money (or other property) is used by the taxpayer for the purpose of

(*a*) making a payment after November 12, 1981 as consideration for an income-averaging annuity contract, unless the contract was acquired pursuant to an agreement in writing entered into before November 13, 1981;

(*b*) paying a premium (within the meaning assigned by subsection 146(1) read without reference to the portion of the definition "premium" in that subsection following paragraph (*b*) of that definition) under a registered retirement savings plan after November 12, 1981;

(*c*) making a contribution to a deferred profit sharing plan, a pooled registered pension plan or a registered pension plan, other than

(i) a contribution described in subparagraph 8(1)(*m*)(ii) or (iii) (as they read in their application to the 1990 taxation year) that was required to be made pursuant to an obligation entered into before November 13, 1981, or

(ii) a contribution deductible under paragraph 20(1)(*q*) or (*y*) in computing the taxpayer's income;

(*d*) making a payment as consideration for an annuity the payment for which was deductible in computing the taxpayer's income by virtue of paragraph 60(*l*);

(*e*) making a contribution to a retirement compensation arrangement where the contribution was deductible under paragraph 8(1)(*m*.2) in computing the taxpayer's income;

(*f*) making a contribution to a net income stabilization account;

(*g*) (Repealed.)

(*h*) making a contribution into a registered education savings plan;

(*i*) making a contribution to a registered disability savings plan; or

(*j*) making a contribution under a TFSA,

and, for the purposes of this subsection, to the extent that an indebtedness is incurred by a taxpayer in respect of a property and at any time that property or a property substituted therefor is used for any of the purposes referred to in this subsection, the indebtedness shall be deemed to be incurred at that time for that purpose.

History: S. 18(11)(*c*), the portion before subparagraph (i) was replaced by S.C. 2012, c. 31, s. 7(8), in force December 14, 2012. S. 18(11)(*c*), the portion before subparagraph (i) formerly read:

(*c*) making a contribution to a registered pension plan or a deferred profit sharing plan after November 12, 1981, other than

S. 18(11)(*g*) was repealed by S.C. 2011, c. 24, s. 2(1), applicable after 2009. S. 18(11)(*g*) formerly read:

(*g*) making a contribution to any account under a provincial pension plan prescribed for the purpose of paragraph 60(*v*),

Related Sections: S. 146(1), "premium", "registered retirement savings plan"; s. 248(1), "net income stabilization account", "property".

Interpretation Bulletins: *Secondary* — IT-124R6 Contributions to registered retirement savings plans; IT-307R4 Spousal or common-law partner registered retirement savings plans.

▶ 18(12) ◀

(12) Work space in home. Notwithstanding any other provision of this Act, in computing an individual's income from a business for a taxation year,

(*a*) no amount shall be deducted in respect of an otherwise deductible amount for any part (in this subsection referred to as the "work space") of a self-contained domestic establishment in which the individual resides, except to the extent that the work space is either

(i) the individual's principal place of business, or

(ii) used exclusively for the purpose of earning income from business and used on a regular and continuous basis for meeting clients, customers or patients of the individual in respect of the business;

(*b*) if the conditions set out in subparagraph (*a*)(i) or (ii) are met, the amount for the work space that is deductible in computing the individual's income for the year from the business shall not exceed the individual's income for the year from the business, computed without reference to the amount and section 34.1; and

(*c*) any amount not deductible by reason only of paragraph (*b*) in computing the individual's income from the business for the immediately preceding taxation year shall be deemed to be an amount otherwise deductible that, subject to paragraphs (*a*) and (*b*), may be deducted for the year for the work space in respect of the business.

Editorial Note: A deduction for home office business expenses is limited to the individual's income from the business (before the expenses). Any excess expenses can be carried forward and deducted in the following year, subject to the same limitation.

History: S. 18(12)(*b*) was replaced by S.C. 2017, c. 33, s. 5(1), applicable to the 2011 and subsequent taxation years, and formerly read:

(*b*) where the conditions set out in subparagraph (*a*)(i) or (ii) are met, the amount for the work space that is deductible in computing the individual's income for the year from the business shall not exceed the individual's income for the year from the business, computed without reference to the amount and sections 34.1 and 34.2; and

Canadian Tax Foundation: Caron-Morin, *Work Space in Home and Elsewhere*, 2013 Canadian Tax Focus 3(3):7–8; Roy, *Taxing the Virtual Office*, 1996 Conference Report 31:1–19.

Income Tax Folios: *Primary* — S4-F2-C1 Deductibility of Fines and Penalties.

Interpretation Bulletins: *Secondary* — IT-504R2 (Consolid.) Visual artists and writers.

Cases: Although the taxpayer's studio had its own separate entrance and created a sense of a separate entity, it was physically connected to her residence and was "part of the self-contained domestic establishment" comprising her residence. *Ellis v. The Queen*, 94 DTC 1731 (T.C.C.)

▶ 18(13) ◀

(13) When s. (15) applies to money lenders. Subsection (15) applies, subject to subsection 142.6(7), when

(*a*) a taxpayer (in this subsection and subsection (15) referred to as the "transferor") disposes of a particular property (other than, for the purposes of computing the exempt surplus or exempt deficit and taxable surplus or taxable deficit of a foreign affiliate of a taxpayer, in respect of the taxpayer, where the transferor is the affiliate or is a partnership of which the affiliate is a member, property that is, or would be, if the transferor were a foreign affiliate of the taxpayer, excluded property (within the meaning assigned by subsection 95(1)) of the transferor);

(*b*) the disposition is not described in any of paragraphs (*c*) to (*g*) of the definition "superficial loss" in section 54;

(*c*) the transferor is not an insurer;

(*d*) the ordinary business of the transferor includes the lending of money and the particular property was used or held in the ordinary course of that business;

(*e*) the particular property is a share, or a loan, bond, debenture, mortgage, hypothecary claim, note, agreement for sale or any other indebtedness;

(*f*) the particular property was, immediately before the disposition, not a capital property of the transferor;

(*g*) during the period that begins 30 days before and ends 30 days after the disposition, the transferor or a person affiliated with the transferor acquires a property (in this subsection and subsection (15) referred to as the "substituted property") that is, or is identical to, the particular property; and (*h*) at the end of the period, the transferor or a person affiliated with the transferor owns the substituted property.

History: S. 18(13)(*a*) was replaced by S.C. 2013, c. 34, s. 56(1), applicable to dispositions that occur after August 19, 2011.

Any assessment of a taxpayer's tax, interest and penalties payable under the Act for any taxation year that ends before June 26, 2013 that would, in the absence of this section, be precluded because of subsections 152(4) to (5) of the Act shall be made to the extent necessary to take into account the amendments by S.C. 2013, c. 34, s. 54 to 89.

S. 18(13)(*a*) formerly read:

(*a*) a taxpayer (in this subsection and subsection (15) referred to as the "transferor") disposes of a particular property;

Related Sections: S. 248(12) Identical properties.

Tax Profile: May 2004 — The Stop-Loss Rules.

▶ 18(14) ◀

(14) When s. (15) applies to adventurers in trade. Subsection (15) applies where

(*a*) a person (in this subsection and subsection (15) referred to as the "transferor") disposes of a particular property;

(*b*) the particular property is described in an inventory of a business that is an adventure or concern in the nature of trade;

(*c*) the disposition is not a disposition that is deemed to have occurred by subsection 10.1 (6) or (7), section 70, subsection 104(4), section 128.1, paragraph 132.2(3)(*a*) or (*c*) or subsection 138(11.3), 138.2(4) or 149(10);

(*d*) during the period that begins 30 days before and ends 30 days after the disposition, the transferor or a person affiliated with the transferor acquires property (in this subsection and subsection (15) referred to as the "substituted property") that is, or is identical to, the particular property; and

(*e*) at the end of the period, the transferor or a person affiliated with the transferor owns the substituted property.

History: S. 18(14)(*c*) was replaced by S.C. 2017, c. 33, s. 5(3), applicable to taxation years that begin after 2017, and formerly read:

(*c*) the disposition is not a disposition that is deemed to have occurred by subsection 10.1(6) or (7), section 70, subsection 104(4), section 128.1, paragraph 132.2(3)(*a*) or (*c*) or subsection 138(11.3) or 149(10);

S. 18(14)(*c*) was replaced by S.C. 2017, c. 33, s. 5(2), applicable to taxation years that begin after March 21, 2017, and formerly read:

(*c*) the disposition is not a disposition that is deemed to have occurred by section 70, subsection 104(4), section 128.1, paragraph 132.2(3)(*a*) or (*c*) or subsection 138(11.3) or 149(10);

S. 18(14)(*c*) was replaced by S.C. 2013, c. 34, s. 178(2), applicable to dispositions that occur after 1998, and formerly read:

(*c*) the disposition is not a disposition that is deemed to have occurred by section 70, subsection 104(4), section 128.1, paragraph 132.2(1)(*f*) or subsection 138(11.3) or 149(10);

Tax Profile: May 2004 — The Stop-Loss Rules.

▶ 18(15) ◀

(15) Loss on certain properties. If this subsection applies because of subsection (13) or (14) to a disposition of a particular property,

(*a*) the transferor's loss, if any, from the disposition is deemed to be nil, and

(*b*) the amount of the transferor's loss, if any, from the disposition (determined without reference to this subsection) is deemed to be a loss of the transferor from a disposition of the particular property at the first time, after the disposition,

(i) at which a 30-day period begins throughout which neither the transferor nor a person affiliated with the transferor owns

(A) the substituted property, or

(B) a property that is identical to the substituted property and that was acquired after the day that is 31 days before the period begins,

(ii) at which the substituted property would, if it were owned by the transferor, be deemed by section 128.1 or subsection 149(10) to have been disposed of by the transferor,

(iii) that is immediately before the transferor is subject to a loss restriction event, or

(iv) if the transferor is a corporation,

(A) for the purposes of computing the transferor's foreign accrual property income, exempt surplus or exempt deficit, and taxable surplus or taxable deficit, in respect of a taxpayer for a taxation year of the transferor where the transferor is a foreign affiliate of the taxpayer, at which the liquidation and dissolution of the transferor begins, unless the liquidation and dissolution is

(I) a qualifying liquidation and dissolution (within the meaning assigned by subsection 88(3.1)) of the transferor, or

(II) a designated liquidation and dissolution (within the meaning assigned by subsection 95(1)) of the transferor, and

(B) for any other purposes, at which the winding-up (other than a winding-up to which subsection 88(1) applies) of the transferor begins, and

and for the purpose of paragraph (*b*), where a partnership otherwise ceases to exist at any time after the disposition, the partnership is deemed not to have ceased to exist, and each person who was a member of the partnership immediately before the partnership would, but for this subsection, have ceased to exist is deemed to remain a member of the partnership, until the time that is immediately after the first time described in subparagraphs (*b*)(i) to (iv).

Editorial Note: Similar stop-loss rules are found in s. 13(21.2) for dispositions of depreciable capital property, s. 14(12) for eligible capital property (prior to 2017), and s. 40(3.4) for non-depreciable capital property.

History: S. 18(15)(*b*)(iii) was replaced by S.C. 2013, c. 40, s. 8(6), deemed to have come into force on March 21, 2013, and formerly read:

(iii) that is immediately before control of the transferor is acquired by a person or group of persons, where the transferor is a corporation, or

S. 18(15)(*b*)(iv) was replaced by S.C. 2013, c. 34, s. 56(2), applicable to windings-up and liquidations and dissolutions that begin after August 19, 2011.

See the application for s. 18(13)(*a*) for the extension of assessment periods to take into account the amendments by S.C. 2013, c. 34, s. 54 to 89.

S. 18(15)(*b*)(iv) formerly read:

(iv) at which the winding-up of the transferor begins (other than a winding-up to which subsection 88(1) applies), where the transferor is a corporation,

Related Sections: S. 13(21.2) Loss on certain transfers; s. 14(12) Loss on certain transfers; s. 18(16) Deemed identical property; s. 251.2(2) Loss restriction event.

▶ 18(16) ◀

(16) Deemed identical property. For the purposes of subsections (13), (14) and (15), a right to acquire a property (other than a right, as security only, derived from a mortgage, hypothec, agreement for sale or similar obligation) is deemed to be a property that is identical to the property.

▶ 18(17) ◀

(17) Definitions. The following definitions apply in this subsection and subsections (18) to (23).

offsetting position, in respect of a particular position of a person or partnership (in this definition referred to as the "holder"), means one or more positions that

(*a*) are held by

(i) the holder,

(ii) a person or partnership that does not deal at arm's length with, or is affiliated with, the holder (in this subsection and subsections (20), (22) and (23) referred to as the "connected person"), or

(iii) for greater certainty, by any combination of the holder and one or more connected persons;

(*b*) have the effect, or would have the effect if each of the positions held by a connected person were held by the holder, of eliminating all or substantially all of the holder's risk of loss and opportunity for gain or profit in respect of the particular position; and

(*c*) if held by a connected person, can reasonably be considered to have been held with the purpose of obtaining the effect described in paragraph (*b*).

position, of a person or partnership, means one or more properties, obligations or liabilities of the person or partnership, if

(*a*) each property, obligation or liability is

(i) a share in the capital stock of a corporation,

(ii) an interest in a partnership,

(iii) an interest in a trust,

(iv) a commodity,

(v) foreign currency,

(vi) a swap agreement, a forward purchase or sale agreement, a forward rate agreement, a futures agreement, an option agreement or a similar agreement,

(vii) a debt owed to or owing by the person or partnership that, at any time,

(A) is denominated in a foreign currency,

(B) would be described in paragraph 7000(1)(*d*) of the *Income Tax Regulations* if that paragraph were read without reference to the words "other than one described in paragraph (*a*), (*b*) or (*c*)", or

(C) is convertible into or exchangeable for an interest, or for civil law a right, in any property that is described in any of subparagraphs (i) to (iv),

(viii) an obligation to transfer or return to another person or partnership a property identical to a particular property described in any of subparagraphs (i) to (vii) that was previously transferred or lent to the person or partnership by that other person or partnership, or

(ix) an interest, or for civil law a right, in any property that is described in any of subparagraphs (i) to (vii); and

(*b*) it is reasonable to conclude that, if there is more than one property, obligation or liability, each of them is held in connection with each other.

successor position, in respect of a position (in this definition referred to as the "initial position"), means a particular position if

(*a*) the particular position is an offsetting position in respect of a second position;

(*b*) the second position was an offsetting position in respect of the initial position that was disposed of at a particular time; and

(*c*) the particular position was entered into during the period that begins 30 days before, and ends 30 days after, the particular time.

unrecognized loss, in respect of a position of a person or partnership at a particular time in a taxation year, means the loss, if any, that would be deductible in computing the income of the person or partnership for the year with respect to the position if it were disposed of immediately before the particular time at its fair market value at the time of disposition.

unrecognized profit, in respect of a position of a person or partnership at a particular time in a taxation year, means the profit, if any, that would be included in computing the income of the person or partnership for the year with respect to the position if it were disposed of immediately before the particular time at its fair market value at the time of disposition.

History: S. 18(17) was added by S.C. 2017, c. 33, s. 5(4), applicable in respect of a "position" (as defined in subsection 18(17)), of a person or partnership if

(a) the position is acquired, entered into, renewed or extended, or becomes owing, by the person or partnership after March 21, 2017; or

(b) an offsetting position (as defined in subsection 18(17)) in respect of the position is acquired, entered into, renewed or extended, or becomes owing, by the person or partnership or a "connected person" (within the meaning of subsection 18(17)) after March 21, 2017.

▶ 18(18) ◀

(18) Application of subsection (19). Subject to subsection (20), subsection (19) applies in respect of a disposition of a particular position by a person or partnership (in this subsection and subsections (19), (20) and (22) referred to as the "transferor"), if

(*a*) the disposition is not a disposition that is deemed to have occurred by section 70, subsection 104(4), section 128.1 or subsection 138(11.3) or 149(10);

(*b*) the transferor is not a *financial institution* (as defined in subsection 142.2(1)), a mutual fund corporation or a mutual fund trust; and

(*c*) the particular position was, immediately before the disposition, not a capital property, or an obligation or liability on account of capital, of the transferor.

Editorial Note: As paragraphs 18(18)(*a*) through (*c*) are framed in the negative, they effectively provide for exceptions to the application of the stop-loss rule in subsection 18(19). For example, losses upon death (subsection 70(5)) and losses on capital account are not subject to the stop-loss rule.

History: S. 18(18) was added by S.C. 2017, c. 33, s. 5(4), applicable in respect of a "position" (as defined in subsection 18(17)), of a person or partnership if

(a) the position is acquired, entered into, renewed or extended, or becomes owing, by the person or partnership after March 21, 2017; or

(b) an offsetting position (as defined in subsection 18(17)) in respect of the position is acquired, entered into, renewed or extended, or becomes owing, by the person or partnership or a "connected person" (within the meaning of subsection 18(17)) after March 21, 2017.

► 18(19) ◄

(19) Straddle losses. If this subsection applies in respect of a disposition of a particular position by a transferor, the portion of the transferor's loss, if any, from the disposition of the particular position that is deductible in computing the transferor's income for a particular taxation year is the amount determined by the formula

$$A + B - C$$

where

A is

(*a*) if the particular taxation year is the taxation year in which the disposition occurs, the amount of the loss determined without reference to this subsection (which is, for greater certainty, subject to subsection (15)), and

(*b*) in any other taxation year, nil;

B is

(*a*) if the disposition occurred in a preceding taxation year, the amount determined for C in respect of the disposition for the immediately preceding taxation year, and

(*b*) in any other case, nil; and

C is the lesser of

(*a*) the amount determined for A for the taxation year in which the disposition occurs, and

(*b*) the amount determined by the formula

$$D - (E + F)$$

where

D is the total of all amounts each of which is the amount of unrecognized profit at the end of the particular taxation year in respect of

(i) the particular position,

(ii) positions that are offsetting positions in respect of the particular position (or would be, to the extent that there is no successor position in respect of the particular position, if the particular position continued to be held by the transferor),

(iii) successor positions in respect of the particular position (for this purpose, a successor position in respect of a position includes a successor position that is in respect of a successor position in respect of the position), and

(iv) positions that are offsetting positions in respect of any successor position referred to in subparagraph (iii) (or would be, if any such successor position continued to be held by the holder),

E is the total of all amounts each of which is the amount of unrecognized loss at the end of the particular taxation year in respect of positions referred to in subparagraphs (i) to (iv) of the description of D, and

F is the total of all amounts each of which is an amount determined by the formula

$$G - H$$

where

G is the amount determined for A for the taxation year in which the disposition occurs in respect of any position that was disposed of prior to the disposition of the particular position, if

(i) the particular position was a successor position in respect of that position (for this purpose, a successor position in respect of a position includes a successor position that is in respect of a successor position in respect of the position), and

(ii) that position was

(A) an offsetting position in respect of the particular position,

(B) an offsetting position in respect of a position in respect of which the particular position was a successor position (for this purpose, a successor position in respect of a position includes a successor position that is in respect of a successor position in respect of the position), or

(C) the particular position, and

H is the total of all amounts each of which is, in respect of a position described in G, an amount determined under the first formula in this subsection for the particular taxation year or a preceding taxation year.

Editorial Note: Sections 18(17) through (23) were introduced in the 2017 Federal Budget to deal with the selective recognition of losses in so-called straddle transactions. Under previous rules, under a typical straddle a taxpayer could settle or otherwise realize a loss position in respect of a derivative (or other agreement or property or obligation) in one taxation year while deferring the recognition of an offsetting gain position to a later taxation year. The actual stop-loss rule is found in subsection 18(19). Basically, it applies to reduce the loss on a disposition by a person or partnership (the "transferor") of a particular position in a taxation year by the total of the "unrecognized profit" in respect of each "offsetting position" in respect of the particular position at the end of the year (amount D in the formula). The unrecognized profit means the profit that would be realized if the position were disposed of immediately before the end of the taxation year for proceeds equal to its fair market value (subsection 18(17)). (If there is an unrecognized loss in respect of an offsetting position, that amount will serve to decrease the reduction in the loss of the particular position (amount E in the formula).)

The amount of the denied loss of the initial position is regenerated in the next taxation year (amount B in the formula), where it may be recognized if there is no unrecognized profit in respect of any offsetting positions at the end of that year, or may be reduced again to the extent of any unrecognized profit in respect of offsetting positions at the end of that year.

The stop-loss rule also takes into account unrecognized profits (net of unrecognized losses) in respect of "successor positions" in respect of the particular position and offsetting positions in respect of successor positions (amount D).

If there is more than one loss position disposed of in a taxation year, the reduction of the loss on the second or subsequent disposition(s) takes into account the amount of the loss denied for the previous disposition(s) (amount F).

History: S. 18(19) was added by S.C. 2017, c. 33, s. 5(4), applicable in respect of a "position" (as defined in subsection 18(17)), of a person or partnership if

(a) the position is acquired, entered into, renewed or extended, or becomes owing, by the person or partnership after March 21, 2017; or

(b) an offsetting position (as defined in subsection 18(17)) in respect of the position is acquired, entered into, renewed or extended, or becomes owing, by the person or partnership or a "connected person" (within the meaning of subsection 18(17)) after March 21, 2017.

▶ 18(20) ◀

(20) Exceptions. Subsection (19) does not apply in respect of a particular position of a transferor if

(*a*) it is the case that

(i) either the particular position, or the offsetting position in respect of the particular position, consists of

(A) commodities that the holder of the position manufactures, produces, grows, extracts or processes, or

(B) debt that the holder of the position incurs in the course of a business that consists of one or any combination of the activities described in clause (A), and

(ii) it can reasonably be considered that the position not described in subparagraph (i) — the particular position if the offsetting position is described in subparagraph (i) or the offsetting position if the particular position is described in that subparagraph — is held to reduce the risk, with respect to the position described in subparagraph (i), from

(A) in the case of a position described in clause (i)(A), price changes or fluctuations in the value of currency with respect to the goods described in clause (i)(A), or

(B) in the case of a position described in clause (i)(B), fluctuations in interest rates or in the value of currency with respect to the debt described in clause (i)(B);

(*b*) the transferor or a connected person (in this paragraph referred to as the "holder") continues to hold a position — that would be an offsetting position in respect of the particular position if the particular position continued to be held by the transferor — throughout a 30-day period beginning on the date of disposition of the particular position, and at no time during the period

(i) is the holder's risk of loss or opportunity for gain or profit with respect to the position reduced in any material respect by another position entered into or disposed of by the holder, or

(ii) would the holder's risk of loss or opportunity for gain or profit with respect to the position be reduced in any material respect by another position entered into or disposed of by a connected person, if the other position were entered into or disposed of by the holder; or

(*c*) it can reasonably be considered that none of the main purposes of the series of transactions or events, or any of the transactions or events in the series, of which the holding of both the particular position and offsetting position are part, is to avoid, reduce or defer tax that would otherwise be payable under this Act.

History: S. 18(20) was added by S.C. 2017, c. 33, s. 5(4), applicable in respect of a "position" (as defined in subsection 18(17)), of a person or partnership if

(a) the position is acquired, entered into, renewed or extended, or becomes owing, by the person or partnership after March 21, 2017; or

(b) an offsetting position (as defined in subsection 18(17)) in respect of the position is acquired, entered into, renewed or extended, or becomes owing, by the person or partnership or a "connected person" (within the meaning of subsection 18(17)) after March 21, 2017.

▶ 18(21) ◀

(21) Application. For the purposes of subsections (17) to (23),

(*a*) if a position of a person or partnership is not a property of the person or partnership, the person or partnership is deemed

(i) to hold the position at any time while it is a position of the person or partnership, and

(ii) to have disposed of the position when the position is settled or extinguished in respect of the person or partnership;

(*b*) a disposition of a position is deemed to include a disposition of a portion of the position;

(*c*) a position held by one or more persons or partnerships referred to in paragraph (*a*) of the definition *offsetting position* in subsection (17) is deemed to be an offsetting position in respect of a particular position of a person or partnership if

(i) there is a high degree of negative correlation between changes in value of the position and the particular position, and

(ii) it can reasonably be considered that the principal purpose of the series of transactions or events, or any of the transactions in the series, of which the holding of both the position and the particular position are part, is to avoid, reduce or defer tax that would otherwise be payable under this Act; and

(*d*) one or more positions held by one or more persons or partnerships referred to in paragraph (*a*) of the definition *offsetting position* in subsection (17) are deemed to be a successor position in respect of a particular position of a person or partnership if

(i) a portion of the particular position was disposed of at a particular time,

(ii) the position is, or the positions include, as the case may be, a position that consists of the portion of the particular position that was not disposed of (in this paragraph referred to as the "remaining portion of the particular position"),

(iii) where there is more than one position, the position or positions that do not consist of the remaining portion of the particular position were entered into during the period that begins 30 days before, and ends 30 days after, the particular time,

(iv) the position is, or the positions taken together would be, as the case may be, an offsetting position in respect of a second position (within the meaning of the definition *successor position* in subsection (17)),

(v) the second position was an offsetting position in respect of the particular position, and

(vi) it can reasonably be considered that the principal purpose of the series of transactions or events, or any of the transactions in the series, of which the disposition of a portion of the particular position and the holding of one or more positions are part, is to avoid, reduce or defer tax that would otherwise be payable under this Act.

History: S. 18(21) was added by S.C. 2017, c. 33, s. 5(4), applicable in respect of a "position" (as defined in subsection 18(17)), of a person or partnership if

(a) the position is acquired, entered into, renewed or extended, or becomes owing, by the person or partnership after March 21, 2017; or

(b) an offsetting position (as defined in subsection 18(17)) in respect of the position is acquired, entered into, renewed or extended, or becomes owing, by the person or partnership or a "connected person" (within the meaning of subsection 18(17)) after March 21, 2017.

▶ 18(22) ◀

(22) Different taxation years. Subsection (23) applies if

(*a*) at any time in a particular taxation year of a transferor, a position referred to in any of subparagraphs (ii) to (iv) of the description of D in subsection (19) (in this subsection and subsection (23) referred to as the "gain position") is held by a connected person;

(*b*) the connected person disposes of the gain position in the particular taxation year; and

(*c*) the taxation year of the connected person in which the disposition referred to in paragraph (*b*) occurs ends after the end of the particular taxation year.

History: S. 18(22) was added by S.C. 2017, c. 33, s. 5(4), applicable in respect of a "position" (as defined in subsection 18(17)), of a person or partnership if

(a) the position is acquired, entered into, renewed or extended, or becomes owing, by the person or partnership after March 21, 2017; or

(b) an offsetting position (as defined in subsection 18(17)) in respect of the position is acquired, entered into, renewed or extended, or becomes owing, by the person or partnership or a "connected person" (within the meaning of subsection 18(17)) after March 21, 2017.

▶ 18(23) ◀

(23) Different taxation years. If this subsection applies, for the purposes of the definition *unrecognized profit* in subsection (17) and subsection (19), the portion of the profit, if any, realized from the disposition of the gain position referred to in paragraph (22)(*b*) that is determined by the following formula is deemed to be unrecognized profit in respect of the gain position until the end of the taxation year of the connected person in which the disposition occurs:

$$A \times B/C$$

where

A is the amount of the profit otherwise determined;

B is the number of days in the taxation year of the connected person in which the disposition referred to in paragraph (22)(*b*) occurs that are after the end of the particular taxation year; and

C is the total number of days in the taxation year of the connected person in which the disposition referred to in paragraph (22)(*b*) occurs.

Editorial Note: Subsection 18(23) is an anti-avoidance rule, generally meant to ensure that the stop-loss rule in subsection 18(19) is not avoided when a taxation year of a "connected person" does not coincide with the transferor's taxation year.

History: S. 18(23) was added by S.C. 2017, c. 33, s. 5(4), applicable in respect of a "position" (as defined in subsection 18(17)), of a person or partnership if

(a) the position is acquired, entered into, renewed or extended, or becomes owing, by the person or partnership after March 21, 2017; or

(b) an offsetting position (as defined in subsection 18(17)) in respect of the position is acquired, entered into, renewed or extended, or becomes owing, by the person or partnership or a "connected person" (within the meaning of subsection 18(17)) after March 21, 2017.

SECTION 18.1: [Matchable expenditures]

▶ 18.1(1) ◀

(1) Definitions. The definitions in this subsection apply in this section.

"matchable expenditure" —"matchable expenditure" of a taxpayer means the amount of an expenditure that is made by the taxpayer to

(*a*) acquire a right to receive production,

(*b*) fulfil a covenant or obligation arising in circumstances in which it is reasonable to conclude that a relationship exists between the covenant or obligation and a right to receive production, or

(*c*) preserve or protect a right to receive production,

but does not include an amount for which a deduction is provided under section 20 in computing the taxpayer's income.

"right to receive production" —"right to receive production" means a right under which a taxpayer is entitled, either immediately or in the future and either absolutely or contingently, to receive an amount all or a portion of which is computed by reference to use of property, production, revenue, profit, cash flow, commodity price, cost or value of property or any other similar criterion or by reference to dividends paid or payable to shareholders of any class of shares where the amount is in respect of another taxpayer's activity, property or business but such a right does not include an income interest in a trust, a Canadian resource property or a foreign resource property.

"tax benefit" —"tax benefit" means a reduction, avoidance or deferral of tax or other amount payable under this Act or an increase in a refund of tax or other amount under this Act.

"tax shelter" —"tax shelter" means a property that would be a tax shelter (as defined in subsection 237.1(1)) if

(*a*) the cost of a right to receive production were the total of all amounts each of which is a matchable expenditure to which the right relates; and

(*b*) subsections (2) to (13) did not apply for the purpose of computing an amount, or in the case of a partnership a loss, represented to be deductible.

"taxpayer"—"taxpayer" includes a partnership.

▶ 18.1(2) ◀

(2) Limitation on the deductibility of matchable expenditure. In computing a taxpayer's income from a business or property for a taxation year, no amount of a matchable expenditure may be deducted except as provided by subsection (3).

Tax Profile: March 2004 — Loss Utilization By Individuals.

▶ 18.1(3) ◀

(3) Deduction of matchable expenditure. If a taxpayer's matchable expenditure would, but for subsection (2) and this subsection, be deductible in computing the taxpayer's income, there may be deducted in respect of the matchable expenditure in computing the taxpayer's income for a taxation year the amount that is determined under subsection (4) for the year in respect of the expenditure.

▶ 18.1(4) ◀

(4) Amount of deduction. For the purpose of subsection (3), the amount determined under this subsection for a taxation year in respect of a taxpayer's matchable expenditure is the amount, if any, that is the least of

(*a*) the total of

(i) the lesser of

(A) $^1/_5$ of the matchable expenditure, and

(B) the amount determined by the formula

$$(A/B) \times C$$

where

A is the number of months that are in the year and after the day on which the right to receive production to which the matchable expenditure relates is acquired,

B is the lesser of 240 and the number of months that are in the period that begins on the day on which the right to receive production to which the matchable expenditure relates is acquired and that ends on the day the right is to terminate, and

C is the amount of the matchable expenditure, and

(ii) the amount, if any, by which the amount determined under this paragraph for the preceding taxation year in respect of the matchable expenditure exceeds the amount of the matchable expenditure deductible in computing the taxpayer's income for that preceding year,

(*b*) the total of

(i) all amounts each of which is included in computing the taxpayer's income for the year (other than any portion of such amount that is the subject of a reserve claimed by the taxpayer for the year under this Act) in respect of the right to receive production to which the matchable expenditure relates, and

(ii) the amount by which the amount determined under this paragraph for the preceding taxation year in respect of the matchable expenditure exceeds the amount of the matchable expenditure deductible in computing the taxpayer's income for that preceding year, and

(*c*) the amount, if any, by which

(i) the total of all amounts each of which is an amount of the matchable expenditure that would, but for this section, have been deductible in computing the taxpayer's income for the year or a preceding taxation year

exceeds

(ii) the total of all amounts each of which is an amount of the matchable expenditure deductible under subsection (3) in computing the taxpayer's income for a preceding taxation year.

▶ 18.1(5) ◀

(5) Special rules. For the purpose of this section,

(*a*) where a taxpayer's matchable expenditure is made before the day on which the related right to receive production is acquired by the taxpayer, the expenditure is deemed to have been made on that day;

(*b*) where a taxpayer has one or more rights to renew a particular right to receive production to which a matchable expenditure relates for one or more additional terms, after the term that includes the time at which the particular right was acquired, the particular right is deemed to terminate on the latest day on which the latest possible such term could terminate if all rights to renew the particular right were exercised;

(*c*) where a taxpayer has 2 or more rights to receive production that can reasonably be considered to be related to each other, the rights are deemed to be one right; and

(*d*) where the term of a taxpayer's right to receive production is for an indeterminate period, the right is deemed to terminate 240 months after it is acquired.

▶ 18.1(6) ◀

(6) Proceeds of disposition considered income. Where in a taxation year a taxpayer disposes of all or part of a right to receive production to which a matchable expenditure relates, the proceeds of the disposition shall be included in computing the taxpayer's income for the year.

▶ 18.1(7) ◀

(7) Arm's length disposition. Subject to subsections (8) to (10), where in a taxation year a taxpayer disposes (otherwise than in a disposition to which subsection 87(1) or 88(1) applies) of all of the taxpayer's right to receive production to which a matchable expenditure (other than an expenditure no portion of which would, if this section were read without reference to this subsection, be deductible under subsection (3) in computing the taxpayer's income) relates, or the taxpayer's right expires, the amount deductible in respect of the expenditure under subsection (3) in computing the taxpayer's income for the year is deemed to be the amount, if any, determined under paragraph (4)(*c*) for the year in respect of the expenditure.

► 18.1(8) ◄

(8) Non-arm's length disposition. Subsection (10) applies where

(*a*) a taxpayer's particular right to receive production to which a matchable expenditure (other than an expenditure no portion of which would, if this section were read without reference to subsections (7) and (10), be deductible under subsection (3) in computing the taxpayer's income) relates has expired or the taxpayer has disposed of all of the right (otherwise than in a disposition to which subsection 87(1) or 88(1) applies);

(*b*) during the period that begins 30 days before and ends 30 days after the disposition or expiry, the taxpayer or a person affiliated, or who does not deal at arm's length, with the taxpayer acquires a right to receive production (in this subsection and subsection (10) referred to as the "substituted property") that is, or is identical to, the particular right; and

(*c*) at the end of the period, the taxpayer or a person affiliated, or who does not deal at arm's length, with the taxpayer owns the substituted property.

► 18.1(9) ◄

(9) Special case. Subsection (10) applies where

(*a*) a taxpayer's particular right to receive production to which a matchable expenditure (other than an expenditure no portion of which would, if this section were read without reference to subsections (7) and (10), be deductible under subsection (3) in computing the taxpayer's income) relates has expired or the taxpayer has disposed of all of the right (otherwise than in a disposition to which subsection 87(1) or 88(1) applies); and

(*b*) during the period that begins at the time of the disposition or expiry and ends 30 days after that time, a taxpayer that had an interest, directly or indirectly, in the right has another interest, directly or indirectly, in another right to receive production, which other interest is a tax shelter or a tax shelter investment (as defined by section 143.2).

► 18.1(10) ◄

(10) Amount of deduction if non-arm's length disposition. Where this subsection applies because of subsection (8) or (9) to a disposition or expiry in a taxation year or a preceding taxation year of a taxpayer's right to receive production to which a matchable expenditure relates,

(*a*) the amount deductible under subsection (3) in respect of the expenditure in computing the taxpayer's income for a taxation year that ends at or after the disposition or expiry of the right is the least of the amounts determined under subsection (4) for the year in respect of the expenditure; and

(*b*) the least of the amounts determined under subsection (4) in respect of the expenditure for a taxation year is deemed to be the amount, if any, determined under paragraph (4)(*c*) in respect of the expenditure for the year where the year includes the time that is immediately before the first time, after the disposition or expiry,

(i) at which the right would, if it were owned by the taxpayer, be deemed by section 128.1 or subsection 149(10) to have been disposed of by the taxpayer,

(ii) that is immediately before the taxpayer is subject to a loss restriction event,

(iii) at which winding-up of the taxpayer begins (other than a winding-up to which subsection 88(1) applies), if the taxpayer is a corporation,

(iv) if subsection (8) applies, at which a 30-day period begins throughout which neither the taxpayer nor a person affiliated, or who does not deal at arm's length, with the taxpayer owns

(A) the substituted property, or

(B) a property that is identical to the substituted property and that was acquired after the day that is 31 days before the period began, or

(v) if subsection (9) applies, at which a 30-day period begins throughout which no taxpayer who had an interest, directly or indirectly, in the right has an interest, directly or indirectly, in another right to receive production if one or more of those direct or indirect interests in the other right is a tax shelter or tax shelter investment (as defined by section 143.2).

History: S. 18.1(10)(*b*)(ii) was replaced by S.C. 2013, c. 40, s. 9(1), deemed to have come into force on March 21, 2013, and formerly read:

(ii) that is immediately before control of the taxpayer is acquired by a person or group of persons, if the taxpayer is a corporation,

► 18.1(11) ◄

(11) Partnerships. For the purpose of paragraph (10)(*b*), where a partnership otherwise ceases to exist at any time after a disposition or expiry referred to in subsection (10), the partnership is deemed not to have ceased to exist, and each taxpayer who was a member of the partnership immediately before the partnership would, but for this subsection, have ceased to exist is deemed to remain a member of the partnership until the time that is immediately after the first of the times described in subparagraphs (10)(*b*)(i) to (v).

► 18.1(12) ◄

(12) Identical property. For the purposes of subsections (8) and (10), a right to acquire a particular right to receive production (other than a right, as security only, derived from a mortgage, hypothec, agreement of sale or similar obligation) is deemed to be a right to receive production that is identical to the particular right.

► 18.1(13) ◄

(13) Application of section 143.2. For the purpose of applying section 143.2 to an amount that would, if this section were read without reference to this subsection, be a matchable expenditure any portion of the cost of which is deductible under subsection (3), the expenditure is deemed to be a tax shelter investment and that section shall be read without reference to subparagraph 143.2(6)(*b*)(ii).

▶ 18.1(14) ◀

(14) Debt obligations. Where the rate of return on a taxpayer's right to receive production to which a matchable expenditure (other than an expenditure no portion of which would, if this section were read without reference to this subsection, be deductible under subsection (3) in computing the taxpayer's income) relates is reasonably certain at the time the taxpayer acquires the right,

(*a*) the right is, for the purposes of subsection 12(9) and Part LXX of the *Income Tax Regulations*, deemed to be a debt obligation in respect of which no interest is stipulated to be payable in respect of its principal amount and the obligation is deemed to be satisfied at the time the right terminates for an amount equal to the total of the return on the obligation and the amount that would otherwise be the matchable expenditure that is related to the right; and

(*b*) notwithstanding subsection (3), no amount may be deducted in computing the taxpayer's income in respect of any matchable expenditure that relates to the right.

▶ 18.1(15) ◀

(15) Non-application — risks ceded between insurers. Subsections (2) to (13) do not apply to a taxpayer's matchable expenditure in respect of a right to receive production if

(*a*) the expenditure is in respect of commissions, or other expenses, related to the issuance of an insurance policy for which all or a portion of a risk has been ceded to the taxpayer, and

(*b*) the taxpayer and the person to whom the expenditure is made, or is to be made, are both insurers who are subject to the supervision of

(i) the Superintendent of Financial Institutions, if the taxpayer or that person, as the case may be, is an insurer who is required by law to report to the Superintendent of Financial Institutions, or

(ii) the Superintendent of Insurance, or other similar officer or authority, of the province under whose laws the insurer is incorporated, in any other case.

History: S. 18.1(15) was replaced by S.C. 2013, c. 34, s. 179(1), applicable, subject to subsection (3) [below], in respect of expenditures made by a taxpayer on or after September 18, 2001 in respect of a right to receive production, except if

(*a*) the expenditure was

(i) required to be made under a written agreement made by the taxpayer before September 18, 2001,

(ii) made under, or described in, the terms of a prospectus, preliminary prospectus or registration statement that was, before September 18, 2001, filed with a public authority in Canada in accordance with the securities legislation of Canada or of a province and, if required by law, accepted for filing by the public authority before September 18, 2001, or

(iii) made under, or described in, the terms of an offering memorandum distributed as part of an offering of securities if

(A) the memorandum contains a complete, or substantially complete, description of the securities contemplated in the offering as well as the terms and conditions of the offering,

(B) the memorandum was distributed before September 18, 2001,

(C) solicitations in respect of a sale of the securities contemplated in the offering were made before September 18, 2001, and

(D) the sale of the securities contemplated in the offering was substantially in accordance with the memorandum;

(*b*) the expenditure was made before 2002;

(*c*) the expenditure was made in consideration for services that were rendered in Canada before 2002 in respect of an activity, or a business, all or substantially all of which was carried on in Canada;

(*d*) there is no agreement or other arrangement under which the obligation of any taxpayer in respect of the expenditure can, on or after September 18, 2001, be changed, reduced or waived if there is a change to, or an adverse assessment under, the Act;

(*e*) if the right to receive production is, or is related to, a tax shelter investment, a tax shelter identification number in respect of the tax shelter was obtained before September 18, 2001; and

(*f*) if the expenditure was made under, or described in, the terms of a document that is a prospectus, a preliminary prospectus, a registration statement or an offering memorandum (and regardless of whether the expenditure was also made under a written agreement)

(i) all of the funds raised pursuant to the document that may reasonably be used to make a matchable expenditure were received by the taxpayer before 2002,

(ii) all or substantially all of the securities distributed pursuant to the document for the purpose of raising the funds described in subparagraph (i) were acquired before 2002 by a person who is not

(A) a promoter, or an agent of a promoter, of the securities, other than an agent of the promoter who acquired the security as principal and not for resale,

(B) a vendor of the right to receive production,

(C) a broker or dealer in securities, other than a person who acquired the security as principal and not for resale, or

(D) a person who does not deal at arm's length with a person to whom clause (A) or (B) applies, and

(iii) all or substantially all of the funds raised pursuant to the document before 2002 were used to make expenditures that were required to be made pursuant to agreements in writing made before September 18, 2001.

(3) [The amendment] does not apply to an expenditure made by a taxpayer in respect of a right to receive production in respect of a particular film or video production if

(*a*) expenditures in respect of the particular film or video production

(i) were made before September 18, 2001 (as determined, for the purpose of this paragraph, without reference to subsection 143.2(10) of the Act, except if a repaid amount for the purposes of that subsection is paid after 2002), or

(ii) were required to be made by the taxpayer under a written agreement made before September 18, 2001 by the taxpayer;

(*b*) principal photography of the particular film or video production

(i) began before 2002,

(ii) was primarily completed before April 2002, and

(iii) was conducted primarily in Canada;

(*c*) the expenditure

(i) was made before April 2002 in the course of the taxpayer's business of providing film production services in respect of the particular film or video production (as determined for the purpose of this subparagraph without reference to subsection 143.2(10) of the Act, except to the extent that a repaid amount for the purposes of that subsection is paid after 2002),

(ii) was made under, or described in, the terms of

(A) a prospectus, preliminary prospectus or registration statement that was, before September 18, 2001, filed with a public authority in Canada in accordance with the securities legislation of Canada or of a province and, if required by law, accepted for filing by the public authority before September 18, 2001, or

(B) an offering memorandum distributed as part of an offering of securities if

(I) the memorandum contains a complete, or substantially complete, description of the securities contemplated in the offering as well as the terms and conditions of the offering,

(II) the memorandum was distributed before September 18, 2001,

(III) solicitations in respect of a sale of the securities contemplated in the offering have been made before September 18, 2001, and

(IV) the sale of the securities contemplated in the offering was substantially in accordance with the memorandum, and

(iii) was not an amount in respect of advertising, marketing, promotion or market research;

(*d*) except where the particular film or video production is a designated production of the taxpayer, at least 75% of the total of all expenditures, each of which is an expenditure made by the taxpayer in the course of the business referred to in subparagraph (*c*)(i), is an expenditure described for the purpose of that subparagraph made in consideration for the supply of goods or services that are supplied or rendered in Canada before April 2002 by persons that are subject to tax on the expenditure under Part I or XIII of the Act;

(*e*) there is no agreement or other arrangement under which the obligation of any taxpayer to acquire a security distributed pursuant to the prospectus, preliminary prospectus, registration statement or offering memorandum can, after September 18, 2001, be changed, reduced or waived if there is a change to, or an adverse assessment under, the Act;

(*f*) if the right to receive production is, or is related to, a tax shelter investment, a tax shelter identification number in respect of the tax shelter was obtained before September 18, 2001;

(*g*) all of the funds raised pursuant to the prospectus, preliminary prospectus, registration statement or offering memorandum that may reasonably be used to make a matchable expenditure before April 2002 in respect of the particular film or video production are received by the taxpayer before 2003;

(*h*) all of the securities distributed pursuant to the prospectus, preliminary prospectus, registration statement or offering memorandum for the purpose of raising the funds described in paragraph (*g*) [above] were acquired before 2002;

(*i*) all or substantially all of the securities distributed pursuant to the prospectus, preliminary prospectus, registration statement or offering memorandum for the purpose of raising the funds described in paragraph (*g*) were acquired by a person who is not

(i) a promoter, or an agent of a promoter, of the securities, other than an agent of the promoter who acquired the security as principal and not for resale,

(ii) a vendor of the right to receive production,

(iii) a broker or dealer in securities, other than a person who acquired the security as principal and not for resale, or

(iv) a person who does not deal at arm's length with a person referred to in subparagraph (i) or (ii); and

(*j*) except where the particular film or video production is a designated production of the taxpayer, all or substantially all of the matchable expenditures made by the taxpayer that are wholly attributable to the principal photography of the particular film or video production are wholly attributable to principal photography conducted in Canada.

(4) For the purpose of paragraphs (3)(*d*) and (*j*) [above], a designated production of a taxpayer is

(*a*) a film or video production in respect of which

(i) all of the expenditures made by the taxpayer in respect of the particular film or video production were required to be made under a written agreement made by the taxpayer before September 18, 2001,

(ii) if the taxpayer is a partnership,

(A) the taxpayer's expenditures in respect of the particular film or video production were funded, in whole or in part, with funds raised from the initial contribution of capital of members of the taxpayer, pursuant to subscriptions in writing for the issue of units in the taxpayer,

(B) all or substantially all of those written subscriptions were received by the taxpayer on or before September 18, 2001,

(C) at least one member of the taxpayer referred to in subparagraph (i) is a partnership (in this subsection referred to as a "master partnership"),

(D) the subscriptions in writing of all master partnerships for units in the taxpayer were funded, in whole or in part, with funds raised from the initial contribution of capital of members of the master partnerships, pursuant to subscriptions in writing for the issue of units in the master partnerships, and

(E) all or substantially all of the subscriptions in writing referred to in clause (D) were received by the master partnership on or before September 18, 2001,

(iii) if a member of a particular master partnership is a partnership (in this subsection referred to as an "original master partnership"),

(A) the subscriptions in writing of all original master partnerships for units in the particular master partnership were funded, in whole or in part, with funds raised from the initial contribution of capital of members of the original master partnerships, pursuant to subscriptions in writing for the issue of units in the original master partnerships, and

(B) all or substantially all of those written subscriptions were received by the original master partnership on or before September 18, 2001, and

(iv) no member of an original master partnership is a partnership, an interest in which is a tax shelter; or

(*b*) a film or video production in respect of which

(i) principal photography was all or substantially all complete before September 18, 2001, and

(ii) all or substantially all of the taxpayer's expenditures were made on or before September 18, 2001 (as determined, for the purpose of this paragraph, without reference to subsection 143.2(10) of the Act, except if a repaid amount for the purposes of that subsection is paid after 2002).

S. 18.1(15) formerly read:

(15) *Non-applicability of section 18.1.* Subject to subsections (1) and (14), this section does not apply to a taxpayer's matchable expenditure in respect of a right to receive production if

(*a*) no portion of the expenditure can reasonably be considered to have been paid to another taxpayer, or to a person with whom the other taxpayer does not deal at arm's length, to acquire the right from the other taxpayer and

(i) the taxpayer's expenditure cannot reasonably be considered to relate to a tax shelter or tax shelter investment (within the meaning assigned by subsection 143.2(1)) and none of the main purposes for making the expenditure is that the taxpayer, or a person with whom the taxpayer does not deal at arm's length, obtain a tax benefit, or

(ii) before the end of the taxation year in which the expenditure is made, the total of all amounts each of which is included in computing the taxpayer's income for the year (other than any portion of such an amount that is the subject of a reserve claimed by the taxpayer for the year under this Act) in respect of the right to receive production to which the matchable expenditure relates exceeds 80% of the expenditure; or

(*b*) the expenditure is in respect of commissions or other expenses related to the issuance of an insurance policy for which all or a portion of a risk has been ceded to the taxpayer (in this paragraph referred to as the "reinsurer") and both the reinsurer and the person to whom the expenditure is made or is to be made are insurers subject to the supervision of

(i) the Superintendent of Financial Institutions, in the case of an insurer that is required by law to report to the Superintendent of Financial Institutions, or

(ii) in any other case, the Superintendent of Insurance or other similar officer or authority of the province under whose laws the insurer is incorporated.

► 18.1(16) ◄

(16) Non-application — no rights, tax benefits or shelters. Subsections (2) to (13) do not apply to a taxpayer's matchable expenditure in respect of a right to receive production if

(*a*) no portion of the matchable expenditure can reasonably be considered to have been paid to another taxpayer, or to a person or partnership with whom the other taxpayer does not deal at arm's length, to acquire the right from the other taxpayer;

(*b*) no portion of the matchable expenditure can reasonably be considered to relate to a tax shelter or a tax shelter investment (within the meaning assigned by subsection 143.2(1)); and

(*c*) none of the main purposes for making the matchable expenditure can reasonably be considered to have been to obtain a tax benefit for the taxpayer, a person or partnership with whom the taxpayer does not deal at arm's length, or a person or partnership that holds, directly or indirectly, an interest in the taxpayer.

History: S. 18.1(16) was added by S.C. 2013, c. 34, s. 179(1). See the history note for the amendment to s. 18.1(15) for the application of s. 18.1(16).

► 18.1(17) ◄

(17) Revenue exception. Paragraph (4)(*a*) does not apply in determining the amount for a taxation year that may be deducted in respect of a taxpayer's matchable expenditure in respect of a right to receive production if

(*a*) before the end of the taxation year in which the matchable expenditure is made, the total of all amounts each of which is included in computing the taxpayer's income for the year (other than any portion of any of those amounts that is the subject of a reserve claimed by the taxpayer for the year under this Act) in respect of the right to receive production that relates to the matchable expenditure exceeds 80% of the matchable expenditure; and

(*b*) no portion of the matchable expenditure can reasonably be considered to have been paid to another taxpayer, or to a person or partnership with whom the other taxpayer does not deal at arm's length, to acquire the right from the other taxpayer.

History: S. 18.1(17) was added by S.C. 2013, c. 34, s. 179(1). See the history note for the amendment to s. 18.1(15) for the application of s. 18.1(17)

SECTION 18.2: [Double-dip financing]

(Repealed by S.C. 2009, c. 2, s. 6(1).)

History: S. 18.2 was repealed by S.C. 2009, c. 2, s. 6(1), applicable in respect of interest and other borrowing costs paid or payable in respect of a period or periods that begin after 2011. S. 18.2(1) was previously added by S.C. 2007, c. 35, s. 12(1), applicable in respect of interest and other borrowing costs paid or payable in respect of the same period.

S. 18.2 formerly read:

(1) *Definitions.* The following definitions apply in this section.

"aggregate double-dip income"—"aggregate double-dip income", of a particular corporation for a taxation year in respect of an inter-affiliate loan, means the total of the double-dip exempt earnings amount and the double-dip taxable earnings amount of the particular corporation for the taxation year in respect of the inter-affiliate loan.

"double-dip exempt earnings amount"—"double-dip exempt earnings amount", of a particular corporation for a taxation year in respect of an inter-affiliate loan owing to a foreign affiliate (referred to in this definition as the "earning foreign affiliate") of the particular corporation or of a corporation that does not deal at arm's length with the particular corporation, means the total of all amounts each of which is the amount, in respect of a share (referred to in this definition as the "specified share") of the capital stock of a particular foreign affiliate of the particular corporation or of a corporation that does not deal at arm's length with the particular corporation, determined by the formula

$$A \times [B - (C \times D)]$$

where

A is the participating percentage of the specified share in respect of the earning foreign affiliate at the end of a taxation year of the earning foreign affiliate that ends in the taxation year of the particular corporation;

B is the amount of the re-characterized exempt earnings income of the earning foreign affiliate in respect of the inter-affiliate loan for the taxation year of the earning foreign affiliate;

C is the foreign accrual tax applicable to the amount determined under the description of B; and

D is the relevant tax factor of the particular corporation for the taxation year of the particular corporation.

"double-dip taxable earnings amount"—"double-dip taxable earnings amount" of a particular corporation for a taxation year in respect of an inter-affiliate loan owing to a foreign affiliate (referred to in this definition as the "earning foreign affiliate"), of the particular corporation or of a corporation that does not deal at arm's length with the particular corporation, means the total of all amounts each of which is the amount, in respect of a share (referred to in this definition as the "specified share") of the capital stock of a particular foreign affiliate of the particular corporation or of a corporation that does not deal at arm's length with the particular corporation, determined by the formula

$$A \times [B - (C \times D)]$$

where

A is the participating percentage of the specified share in respect of the earning foreign affiliate at the end of a taxation year of the earning foreign affiliate that ends in the taxation year of the particular corporation;

B is the amount of the re-characterized taxable earnings income of the earning foreign affiliate in respect of the inter-affiliate loan for the taxation year of the earning foreign affiliate;

C is the foreign accrual tax applicable to the amount determined under the description of B; and

D is the relevant tax factor of the particular corporation for the taxation year of the particular corporation.

"foreign accrual tax"—"foreign accrual tax" applicable to an amount of re-characterized income of a foreign affiliate (referred to in this definition as the "earning foreign affiliate"), of a particular corporation or of a corporation that does not deal at arm's length with the particular corporation, for a taxation year in respect of an inter-affiliate loan owing to the earning foreign affiliate means the total of

(*a*) the amount equal to that portion of any foreign income or profit taxes that was paid by the earning foreign affiliate or any other foreign affiliate, of the particular corporation or of a corporation that does not deal at arm's length with the particular corporation, that can reasonably be regarded as applicable to the re-characterized income, and

(*b*) the amount that would, if the re-characterized income were an amount included in computing the particular corporation's income under subsection 91(1) in respect of the earning foreign affiliate, be prescribed in respect of the earning foreign affiliate to be foreign accrual tax that is applicable to the re-characterized income for the purpose of the definition "foreign accrual tax" in subsection 95(1).

"inter-affiliate loan"—"inter-affiliate loan" in respect of a particular corporation for a taxation year means a debt that is owing to a foreign affiliate of the particular corporation or of a corporation that does not deal at arm's length with the particular corporation or to a partnership of which such a foreign affiliate is a member, if the income that the foreign affiliate derives in a taxation year from the interest paid or payable in respect of the debt is re-characterized income of the foreign affiliate for the taxation year.

"participating percentage"—"participating percentage" of a share (referred to in this definition as the "specified share") of the capital stock of a particular foreign affiliate of a particular corporation or of a corporation that does not deal at arm's length with the particular corporation, held by the particular corporation at the end of a particular taxation year of a non-resident corporation (referred to in this definition as the "earning foreign affiliate") that ends in the particular corporation's taxation year, which earning foreign affiliate was, at the end of the particular taxation year, a foreign affiliate of the particular corporation or of a corporation that does not deal at arm's length with the particular corporation, means the percentage that would, if the earning foreign affiliate were a controlled foreign affiliate of the particular corporation, be determined under subparagraph (*b*)(i) or (ii) of the definition "participating percentage" in subsection 95(1) in respect of the specified share in respect of the earning foreign affiliate at the end of the particular taxation year.

"re-characterized income"—"re-characterized income" of a foreign affiliate of a corporation for a taxation year in respect of a debt owing to the foreign affiliate means the total of the re-characterized exempt earnings income and the re-characterized taxable earnings income of the foreign affiliate for the taxation year from the debt.

"re-characterized exempt earnings income"—"re-characterized exempt earnings income" of a foreign affiliate of a corporation for a taxation year in respect of a debt owing to the foreign affiliate means that portion of the income of the foreign affiliate for the taxation year from the debt that is included

(*a*) under subparagraph 95(2)(*a*)(ii) in computing the income from an active business of the foreign affiliate for the taxation year, or that would be so included if the income were income from property; and

(*b*) in computing the amount prescribed to be the exempt earnings of the foreign affiliate for the taxation year.

"re-characterized taxable earnings income"—"re-characterized taxable earnings income" of a foreign affiliate of a corporation for a taxation year in respect of a debt owing to the foreign affiliate means that portion of the income of the foreign affiliate for the taxation year from the debt that is included

(*a*) under subparagraph 95(2)(*a*)(ii) in computing the income from an active business of the foreign affiliate for the taxation year, or that would be so included if the income were income from property; and

(*b*) in computing the amount prescribed to be the taxable earnings of the foreign affiliate for the taxation year.

"re-characterized taxable earnings income"—"re-characterized taxable earnings income" of a foreign affiliate of a corporation for a taxation year in respect of a debt owing to the foreign affiliate means that portion of the income of the foreign affiliate for the taxation year from the debt that is included

(*a*) under subparagraph 95(2)(*a*)(ii) in computing the income from an active business of the foreign affiliate for the taxation year, or that would be so included if the income were income from property; and (*b*) in computing the amount prescribed to be the taxable earnings of the foreign affiliate for the taxation year.

"taxable earnings base adjustment"—"taxable earnings base adjustment" of a particular corporation for a taxation year in respect of a share (referred to in this definition as the "specified share") of a particular foreign affiliate of the particular corporation or of a corporation that does not deal at arm's length with the particular corporation and in respect of an inter-affiliate loan owing to a foreign affiliate of the particular corporation or of a corporation that does not deal at arm's length with the particular corporation, means the amount determined by the formula

$$A \times B/C$$

where

A is the amount of interest deduction denied under subsection (2) in respect of the particular corporation in respect of interest relating to the inter-affiliate loan for the taxation year;

B is the amount determined to be the double-dip taxable earnings amount of the particular corporation in respect of the inter-affiliate loan that can be attributed to the specified share for the taxation year; and

C is the aggregate double-dip income of the particular corporation in respect of the inter-affiliate loan for the taxation year.

(2) *Double-dip interest not deductible.* Notwithstanding any other provision of this Act, in computing the income of a corporation for a taxation year, no amount may be deducted in respect of the corporation's specified financing expense in respect of an inter-affiliate loan for the taxation year, except to the extent that that specified financing expense exceeds the corporation's aggregate double-dip income for the taxation year in respect of that inter-affiliate loan.

(3) *Specified financing expense.* A particular corporation's specified financing expense in respect of an inter-affiliate loan for a taxation year, is the amount, if any, by which

(*a*) the total of all amounts of interest paid or payable in the taxation year by the particular corporation on, and other costs referred to in paragraph 20(1)(*e*) deductible in computing the particular corporation's income for the taxation year in respect of,

(i) borrowed money, to the extent that it is reasonable to consider that the borrowed money is used, in that taxation year, directly or indirectly, for the purpose of funding, in whole or in part, the inter-affiliate loan, and

(ii) an amount payable for property where it is reasonable to consider that the property, or property substituted for it (or, where the property or property substituted for it is a share of the capital stock of a corporation, property of the corporation or of a person related to the corporation, or property substituted for such property) is used, directly or indirectly, for the purpose of funding, in whole or in part, the inter-affiliate loan,

exceeds

(*b*) if the particular corporation has subsequently loaned the property referred to in paragraph (*a*), the total of all amounts that are, in respect of that subsequent loan, included in computing the income of the particular corporation for the taxation year and that relate to the period or periods of use referred to in that paragraph.

(4) *Aggregate double-dip income — related parties.* Subsection (5) applies to a corporation (referred to in this subsection and subsections (5) to (7) as the "debtor corporation") and another corporation in respect of a particular taxation year of the debtor corporation and an inter-affiliate loan if

(*a*) the debtor corporation's specified financing expense for the particular taxation year in respect of the inter-affiliate loan exceeds the debtor corporation's aggregate double-dip income for the particular taxation year in respect of the inter-affiliate loan;

(*b*) the other corporation's aggregate double-dip income for a taxation year in respect of the inter-affiliate loan exceeds the other corporation's specified financing expense for that taxation year in respect of the inter-affiliate loan;

(*c*) the other corporation's taxation year referred to in paragraph (*b*) ends in the particular taxation year; and

(*d*) at the end of the particular taxation year, the other corporation and the debtor corporation are related.

(5) *Deemed effects.* If this subsection applies to a debtor corporation and another corporation in respect of a particular taxation year of the debtor corporation and an inter-affiliate loan,

(*a*) the lesser of the excess determined under paragraph (4)(*b*) in respect of the other corporation and the excess determined under paragraph (4)(*a*) in respect of the debtor corporation is deemed to be included in the aggregate double-dip income of the debtor corporation in respect of the inter-affiliate loan and not to be included in the aggregate double-dip income of the other corporation;

(*b*) this subsection shall not apply to any other corporation in respect of the amount determined under paragraph (*a*); and

(*c*) for the purpose of determining the taxable earnings base adjustment of the other corporation, the amount determined under paragraph (*a*) is deemed to be

(i) an amount of interest deduction denied to it under subsection (2) in respect of interest relating to the inter-affiliate loan for its taxation year referred to in paragraph 4(*b*), and

(ii) an amount that is included in the aggregate double-dip income in respect of the inter-affiliate loan for its taxation year referred to in paragraph 4(*b*).

(6) *Allocation by debtor corporation.* If subsections (4) and (5) apply to more than one other corporation in respect of a debtor corporation and an inter-affiliate loan, the debtor corporation may allocate the excess double-dip incomes of the other corporations against the specified financing expense of the debtor corporation.

(7) *Allocation by Minister.* If a debtor corporation is entitled to make an allocation under subsection (6) but fails to do so, or does so in a manner that allows an excess to remain under subparagraph (4)(*a*) in respect of the debtor corporation and an excess to remain under subparagraph (4)(*b*) in respect of one or more other corporations, the Minister may allocate the excess double-dip incomes of the other corporations against the specified financing expense of the debtor corporation.

(8) *Inter-affiliate loans — exceptions.* A debt that would, at any time, otherwise be an inter-affiliate loan in respect of a corporation for a taxation year of a particular foreign affiliate is not an inter-affiliate loan at that time, if

(*a*) it is the case that

(i) another foreign affiliate, of the corporation or a corporation that does not deal at arm's length with the corporation, owes the debt,

(ii) the particular foreign affiliate and the other foreign affiliate are, at the end of their taxation years that include that time, resident in the same country, and

(iii) the particular foreign affiliate and the other foreign affiliate determine their income, for income tax purposes under the income tax laws of that country, on a consolidated or combined basis; or

(*b*) it is the case that

(i) the corporation is a taxpayer described in paragraph 95(2)(*l*)(iv),

(ii) the particular foreign affiliate holds the debt, and the other foreign affiliate owes the debt, in the ordinary course of businesses that are described in subparagraph (*a*)(i) of the definition "investment business" in subsection 95(1) and conducted principally with persons with which those affiliates deal at arm's length, and

(iii) the terms and conditions of the debt are substantially the same as the terms and conditions of similar debt entered into between persons dealing at arm's length.

(9) *Partnership rules.* If a partnership that holds, directly or indirectly, a share of the capital stock of a specified corporation in respect of the partnership has borrowed money or become liable for an amount payable (in this subsection referred to as the "partnership indebtedness") the interest in respect of which is deductible under paragraph 20(1)(*c*),

(*a*) there shall be added to the income of each corporation or partnership that is a member of the partnership, an amount equal to the member's specified proportion of the interest and other borrowing costs referred to in paragraph 20(1)(*e*) that are deductible in computing the partnership's income in respect of that member's specified proportion of the partnership indebtedness;

(*b*) for the purpose of this section and paragraphs 20(1)(*c*) and (*e*), an amount equal to the amount added to the member's income by paragraph (*a*) shall be deemed to be an amount of interest or other borrowing cost, as the case may be, that is deductible by the member; and

(*c*) the member shall be deemed to have incurred its specified proportion of the partnership indebtedness and to use the proceeds or property acquired in respect of that indebtedness in the same manner as the partnership.

(10) *Interpretation.* For the purpose of subsection (9),

(*a*) a specified corporation in respect of a partnership means a corporation that is, for the purpose of section 95,

(i) a foreign affiliate of a member of the partnership,

(ii) a foreign affiliate of a person with whom the partnership does not deal at arm's length, or

(iii) a foreign affiliate of a person that does not deal at arm's length with a member of the partnership; and

(*b*) the specified proportion of a member of a partnership for a fiscal period of the partnership means the proportion that the member's share of the total income or loss of the partnership for the partnership's fiscal period is of the partnership's total income or loss for that period and, for the purpose of this definition, where that income or loss for a period is nil, that proportion shall be computed as if the partnership had income for that period in the amount of $1,000,000.

SECTION 18.3: [Stapled securities]

► 18.3(1) ◄

(1) Definitions. The following definitions apply in this section.

History: S. 18.3(1) was added by S.C. 2013, c. 40, s. 10(1), deemed to have come into force on July 20, 2011.

"entity"—"entity" has the same meaning as in subsection 122.1(1).

"equity value"—"equity value" has the same meaning as in subsection 122.1(1).

"real estate investment trust"—"real estate investment trust" has the same meaning as in subsection 122.1(1).

"security"—"security", of an entity, means

(*a*) a liability of the entity;

(*b*) if the entity is a corporation,

(i) a share of the capital stock of the corporation, and

(ii) a right to control in any manner whatever the voting rights of a share of the capital stock of the corporation if it can reasonably be concluded that one of the reasons that a person or partnership holds the right to control is to avoid the application of subsection (3) or 12.6(3);

(*c*) if the entity is a trust, an income or a capital interest in the trust; and

(*d*) if the entity is a partnership, an interest as a member of the partnership.

"stapled security"—"stapled security", of a particular entity at any time, means a particular security of the particular entity if at that time

(*a*) another security (referred to in this section as the "reference security")

(i) is or may be required to be transferred together or concurrently with the particular security as a term or condition of the particular security, the reference security, or an agreement or arrangement to which the particular entity (or if the reference security is a security of another entity, the other entity) is a party, or

(ii) is listed or traded with the particular security on a stock exchange or other public market under a single trading symbol;

(*b*) the particular security or the reference security is listed or traded on a stock exchange or other public market; and

(*c*) any of the following applies:

(i) the reference security and the particular security are securities of the particular entity and the particular entity is a corporation, SIFT partnership or SIFT trust,

(ii) the reference security is a security of another entity, one of the particular entity or the other entity is a subsidiary of the other, and the particular entity or the other entity is a corporation, SIFT partnership or SIFT trust, or

(iii) the reference security is a security of another entity and the particular entity or the other entity is a real estate investment trust or a subsidiary of a real estate investment trust.

"subsidiary"—"subsidiary", of a particular entity at any time, means

(*a*) an entity in which the particular entity holds at that time securities that have a total fair market value greater than 10% of the equity value of the entity; and

(*b*) an entity that at that time is a subsidiary of an entity that is a subsidiary of the particular entity.

"transition period"—"transition period", of an entity, means

(*a*) if one or more securities of the entity would have been stapled securities of the entity on October 31, 2006 and July 19, 2011 had the definition "stapled security" in this subsection come into force on October 31, 2006, the period that begins on July 20, 2011 and ends on the earliest of

(i) January 1, 2016,

(ii) the first day after July 20, 2011 on which any of those securities is materially altered, and

(iii) the first day after July 20, 2011 on which any security of the entity becomes a stapled security other than by way of

(A) a transaction

(I) that is completed under the terms of an agreement in writing entered into before July 20, 2011 if no party to the agreement may be excused from completing the transaction as a result of amendments to this Act, and

(II) that is not the issuance of a security in satisfaction of a right to enforce payment of an amount by the entity, or

(B) the issuance of the security in satisfaction of a right to enforce payment of an amount that became payable by the entity on another security of the entity before July 20, 2011, if the other security was a stapled security on July 20, 2011 and the issuance was made under a term or condition of the other security in effect on July 20, 2011;

(*b*) if paragraph (*a*) does not apply to the entity and one or more securities of the entity would have been stapled securities of the entity on July 19, 2011 had the definition "stapled security" in this subsection come into force on July 19, 2011, the period that begins on July 20, 2011 and ends on the earliest of

(i) July 20, 2012,

(ii) the first day after July 20, 2011 on which any of those securities is materially altered, and

(iii) the first day after July 20, 2011 on which any security of the entity becomes a stapled security other than by way of

(A) a transaction

(I) that is completed under the terms of an agreement in writing entered into before July 20, 2011 if no party to the agreement may be excused from completing the transaction as a result of amendments to this Act, and

(II) that is not the issuance of a security in satisfaction of a right to enforce payment of an amount by the entity, or

(B) the issuance of the security in satisfaction of a right to enforce payment of an amount that became payable by the entity on another security of the entity before July 20, 2011, if the other security was a stapled security on July 20, 2011 and the issuance was made under a term or condition of the other security in effect on July 20, 2011; and

(*c*) in any other case, if the entity is a subsidiary of another entity on July 20, 2011 and the other entity has a transition period, the period that begins on July 20, 2011 and ends on the earliest of

(i) the day on which the other entity's transition period ends,

(ii) the first day after July 20, 2011 on which the entity ceases to be a subsidiary of the other entity, and

(iii) the first day after July 20, 2011 on which any security of the entity becomes a stapled security other than by way of

(A) a transaction

(I) that is completed under the terms of an agreement in writing entered into before July 20, 2011 if no party to the agreement may be excused from completing the transaction as a result of amendments to this Act, and

(II) that is not the issuance of a security in satisfaction of a right to enforce payment of an amount by the entity, or

(B) the issuance of the security in satisfaction of a right to enforce payment of an amount that became payable by the entity on another security of the entity before July 20, 2011, if the other security was a stapled security on July 20, 2011 and the issuance was made under a term or condition of the other security in effect on July 20, 2011.

► 18.3(2) ◄

(2) Property representing security. For the purpose of determining whether a particular security of an entity is a stapled security, if a receipt or similar property (referred to in this subsection as the "receipt") represents all or a portion of the particular security and the receipt would be described in paragraphs (*a*) and (*b*) of the definition "stapled security" in subsection (1) if it were a security of the entity, then

(*a*) the particular security is deemed to be described in those paragraphs; and

(*b*) a security that would be a reference security in respect of the receipt is deemed to be a reference security in respect of the particular security.

History: S. 18.3(2) was added by S.C. 2013, c. 40, s. 10(1), deemed to have come into force on July 20, 2011.

► 18.3(3) ◄

(3) Amounts not deductible. Notwithstanding any other provision of this Act, in computing the income of a particular entity for a taxation year from a business or property, no deduction may be made in respect of an amount

(*a*) that is paid or payable after July 19, 2011, unless the amount is paid or payable in respect of the entity's transition period; and

(*b*) that is

(i) interest paid or payable on a liability of the particular entity that is a stapled security, unless each reference security in respect of the stapled security is a liability, or

(ii) if a security of the particular entity, a subsidiary of the particular entity or an entity of which the particular entity is a subsidiary is a reference security in respect of a stapled security of a real estate investment trust or a subsidiary of a real estate investment trust, an amount paid or payable to

(A) the real estate investment trust,

(B) a subsidiary of the real estate investment trust, or

(C) any person or partnership on condition that any person or partnership pays or makes payable an amount to the real estate investment trust or a subsidiary of the real estate investment trust.

Editorial Note: Section 18.3 denies the deduction of certain interest amounts on debt and rent amounts in respect of REITs under stapled securities arrangements. In general terms, a "stapled security" is a publicly-traded security instrument that is bundled with one or more other securities such that each security is not independently transferrable as a matter of common commercial practice. Paragraph 18.3(3)(*b*) denies the deduction of interest on a liability that is part of a stapled security, unless the other security is another liability. Where debt is stapled to a share, for example, an interest deduction is denied. Also denied are amounts paid or payable to a REIT, where the REIT is part of a stapled security arrangement. Section 18.3 was introduced with the purpose of denying certain deductions relating to arrangements that frustrate policy objectives with respect to the taxation of REITs and SIFT trusts.

To avoid the application of section 18.3, securities may be unstapled. However, where that unstapling is temporary so that separation is not permanent and irrevocable, section 12.6 sets out an anti-avoidance rule requiring deducted amounts to be included in income that would otherwise be nondeductible under section 18.3.

History: S. 18.3(3) was added by S.C. 2013, c. 40, s. 10(1), deemed to have come into force on July 20, 2011.

Related Sections: S. 12.6 [Stapled securities–anti-avoidance].

SECTION 19: Limitation re advertising expense — newspapers

► 19(1) ◄

(1) Limitation re advertising expense — newspapers. In computing income, no deduction shall be made in respect of an otherwise deductible outlay or expense of a taxpayer for advertising space in an issue of a newspaper for an advertisement directed primarily to a market in Canada unless

(*a*) the issue is a Canadian issue of a Canadian newspaper; or

(*b*) the issue is an issue of a newspaper that would be a Canadian issue of a Canadian newspaper except that

(i) its type has been wholly set in the United States or has been partly set in the United States with the remainder having been set in Canada, or

(ii) it has been wholly printed in the United States or has been partly printed in the United States with the remainder having been printed in Canada.

Related Sections: S. 19(3) Where s. (1) does not apply; s. 19(5) Definitions.

Tax Window Files: Deductibility of foreign online advertising, *June 14, 2017*, CRA Document No. 2017-0691521M4.

▶ 19(2) ◀

(2) Idem — (Repealed by 1974-75-76, c. 106, s. 1.)

▶ 19(3) ◀

(3) Where s. (1) does not apply. Subsection (1) does not apply with respect to an advertisement in a special issue or edition of a newspaper that is edited in whole or in part and printed and published outside Canada if that special issue or edition is devoted to features or news related primarily to Canada and the publishers thereof publish such an issue or edition not more frequently than twice a year.

▶ 19(4) ◀

(4) Idem — (Repealed by 1974-75-76, c. 106, s. 2.)

▶ 19(5) ◀

(5) Definitions. In this section,

"Canadian issue" — "Canadian issue" of a newspaper means an issue, including a special issue,

(*a*) the type of which, other than the type for advertisements or features, is set in Canada,

(*b*) all of which, exclusive of any comics supplement, is printed in Canada,

(*c*) that is edited in Canada by individuals resident in Canada, and

(*d*) that is published in Canada;

"Canadian newspaper" — "Canadian newspaper" means a newspaper the exclusive right to produce and publish issues of which is held by one or more of the following:

(*a*) a Canadian citizen,

(*b*) a partnership

(i) in which interests representing in value at least 3/4 of the total value of the partnership property are beneficially owned by, and

(ii) at least 3/4 of each income or loss of which from any source is included in the determination of the income of,

corporations described in paragraph (*e*) or Canadian citizens or any combination thereof,

(*c*) an association or society of which at least 3/4 of the members are Canadian citizens,

(*d*) Her Majesty in right of Canada or a province, or a municipality in Canada, or

(*e*) a corporation

(i) that is incorporated under the laws of Canada or a province,

(ii) of which the chairperson or other presiding officer and at least 3/4 of the directors or other similar officers are Canadian citizens, and

(iii) that, if it is a corporation having share capital, is

(A) a public corporation a class or classes of shares of the capital stock of which are listed on a designated stock exchange in Canada, other than a corporation controlled by citizens or subjects of a country other than Canada, or

(B) a corporation of which at least 3/4 of the shares having full voting rights under all circumstances, and shares having a fair market value in total of at least 3/4 of the fair market value of all of the issued shares of the corporation, are beneficially owned by Canadian citizens or by public corporations a class or classes of shares of the capital stock of which are listed on a designated stock exchange in Canada, other than a public corporation controlled by citizens or subjects of a country other than Canada,

and, for the purposes of clause (B), where shares of a class of the capital stock of a corporation are owned, or deemed by this definition to be owned, at any time by another corporation (in this definition referred to as the "holding corporation"), other than a public corporation a class or classes of shares of the capital stock of which are listed on a designated stock exchange in Canada, each shareholder of the holding corporation shall be deemed to own at that time that proportion of the number of such shares of that class that

(C) the fair market value of the shares of the capital stock of the holding corporation owned at that time by the shareholder

is of

(D) the fair market value of all the issued shares of the capital stock of the holding corporation outstanding at that time,

and, where at any time shares of a class of the capital stock of a corporation are owned, or are deemed by this definition to be owned, by a partnership, each member of the partnership shall be deemed to own at that time the least proportion of the number of such shares of that class that

(E) the member's share of the income or loss of the partnership from any source for its fiscal period that includes that time

is of

(F) the income or loss of the partnership from that source for its fiscal period that includes that time,

and for this purpose, where the income and loss of a partnership from any source for a fiscal period are nil, the partnership shall be deemed to have had income from that source for that period in the amount of $1,000,000;

"issue of a non-Canadian newspaper or periodical" — (Repealed by 1988, c. 65, s. 133(2).)

"substantially the same" — (Repealed by S.C. 2001, c. 17, s. 11(2).)

"United States" —"United States" means

(*a*) the United States of America, but does not include Puerto Rico, the Virgin Islands, Guam or any other United States possession or territory, and

(*b*) any areas beyond the territorial sea of the United States within which, in accordance with international law and its domestic laws, the United States may exercise rights with respect to the seabed and subsoil and the natural resources of those areas.

► 19(5.1) ◄

(5.1) Interpretation. In this section, each of the following is deemed to be a Canadian citizen:

(*a*) a trust or corporation described in paragraph 149(1)(*o*) or (*o*.1) formed in connection with a pension plan that exists for the benefit of individuals a majority of whom are Canadian citizens;

(*b*) a trust described in paragraph 149(1)(*r*) or (*x*), the annuitant in respect of which is a Canadian citizen;

(*c*) a mutual fund trust, within the meaning assigned by subsection 132(6), other than a mutual fund trust the majority of the units of which are held by citizens or subjects of a country other than Canada;

(*d*) a trust, each beneficiary of which is a person, partnership, association or society described in any of paragraphs (*a*) to (*e*) of the definition "Canadian newspaper" in subsection (5); and

(*e*) a person, association or society described in paragraph (*c*) or (*d*) of the definition "Canadian newspaper" in subsection (5).

► 19(6) ◄

(6) Trust property. Where the right that is held by any person, partnership, association or society described in the definition "Canadian newspaper" in subsection (5) to produce and publish issues of a newspaper is held as property of a trust or estate, the newspaper is not a Canadian newspaper unless each beneficiary under the trust or estate is a person, partnership, association or society described in that definition.

► 19(7) ◄

(7) Grace period. A Canadian newspaper that would, but for this subsection, cease to be a Canadian newspaper, is deemed to continue to be a Canadian newspaper until the end of the 12th month that follows the month in which it would, but for this subsection, have ceased to be a Canadian newspaper.

Related Sections: S. 89(1), s. 181(2), "paid-up capital"; s. 104(1) Reference to trust or estate; s. 248(1), "business", "corporation", "property"; s. 255 Canada.

► 19(8) ◄

(8) Non-Canadian newspaper. Where at any time one or more persons or partnerships that are not described in any of paragraphs (*a*) to (*e*) of the definition "Canadian newspaper" in subsection (5) have any direct or indirect influence that, if exercised, would result in control in fact of a person or partnership that holds a right to produce or publish issues of a newspaper, the newspaper is deemed not to be a Canadian newspaper at that time.

SECTION 19.01: [Limitation re advertising expenses — periodicals]

► 19.01(1) ◄

(1) Definitions. The definitions in this subsection apply in this section.

"advertisement directed at the Canadian market" — "advertisement directed at the Canadian market" has the same meaning as the expression "directed at the Canadian market" in section 2 of the *Foreign Publishers Advertising Services Act* and includes a reference to that expression made by or under that Act.

"original editorial content" —"original editorial content" in respect of an issue of a periodical means non-advertising content

(*a*) the author of which is a Canadian citizen or a permanent resident of Canada within the meaning assigned by the *Immigration Act* and, for this purpose, "author" includes a writer, a journalist, an illustrator and a photographer; or

(*b*) that is created for the Canadian market and has not been published in any other edition of that issue of the periodical published outside Canada.

"periodical" —"periodical" has the meaning assigned by section 2 of the *Foreign Publishers Advertising Services Act*.

► 19.01(2) ◄

(2) Limitation re advertising expenses — periodicals. Subject to subsections (3) and (4), in computing income, no deduction shall be made by a taxpayer in respect of an otherwise deductible outlay or expense for advertising space in an issue of a periodical for an advertisement directed at the Canadian market.

Tax Window Files: Deductibility of foreign online advertising, *June 14, 2017*, CRA Document No. 2017-0691521M4.

► 19.01(3) ◄

(3) 100% deduction. A taxpayer may deduct in computing income an outlay or expense of the taxpayer for advertising space in an issue of a periodical for an advertisement directed at the Canadian market if

(*a*) the original editorial content in the issue is 80% or more of the total non-advertising content in the issue; and

(*b*) the outlay or expense would, but for subsection (2), be deductible in computing the taxpayer's income.

► 19.01(4) ◄

(4) 50% deduction. A taxpayer may deduct in computing income 50% of an outlay or expense of the taxpayer for advertising space in an issue of a periodical for an advertisement directed at the Canadian market if

(*a*) the original editorial content in the issue is less than 80% of the total non-advertising content in the issue; and (*b*) the outlay or expense would, but for subsection (2), be deductible in computing the taxpayer's income.

► 19.01(5) ◄

(5) Application. For the purposes of subsections (3) and (4),

(*a*) the percentage that original editorial content is of total non-advertising content is the percentage that the total space occupied by original editorial content in the issue is of the total space occupied by non-advertising content in the issue; and

(*b*) the Minister may obtain the advice of the Department of Canadian Heritage for the purpose of

(i) determining the result obtained under paragraph (*a*), and

(ii) interpreting any expression defined in this section that is defined in the *Foreign Publishers Advertising Services Act*.

► 19.01(6) ◄

(6) Editions of issues. For the purposes of this section,

(*a*) where an issue of a periodical is published in several versions, each version is an edition of that issue; and

(*b*) where an issue of a periodical is published in only one version, that version is an edition of that issue.

SECTION 19.1: Limitation re advertising expense on broadcasting undertaking

► 19.1(1) ◄

(1) Limitation re advertising expense on broadcasting undertaking. Subject to subsection (2), in computing income, no deduction shall be made in respect of an otherwise deductible outlay or expense of a taxpayer made or incurred after September 21, 1976 for an advertisement directed primarily to a market in Canada and broadcast by a foreign broadcasting undertaking.

Tax Window Files: Section 19.1, *May 25, 2017*, CRA Document No. 2017-0684351E5; Deductibility of foreign online advertising, *June 14, 2017*, CRA Document No. 2017-0691521M4.

► 19.1(2) ◄

(2) Exception. In computing income, a deduction may be made in respect of an outlay or expense made or incurred before September 22, 1977 for an advertisement directed primarily to a market in Canada and broadcast by a foreign broadcasting undertaking pursuant to

(*a*) a written agreement entered into on or before January 23, 1975; or

(*b*) a written agreement entered into after January 23, 1975 and before September 22, 1976 if the agreement is for a term of one year or less and by its express terms is not capable of being extended or renewed.

► 19.1(3) ◄

(3) Limitation to exception in paragraph (2)(a) — (Repealed by 1977-78, c. 1, s. 13(2).)

► 19.1(4) ◄

(4) Definitions. In this section,

"foreign broadcasting undertaking" — "foreign broadcasting undertaking" means a network operation or a broadcasting transmitting undertaking located outside Canada or on a ship or aircraft not registered in Canada;

"network" — "network" includes any operation involving two or more broadcasting undertakings whereby control over all or any part of the programs or program schedules of any of the broadcasting undertakings involved in the operation is delegated to a network operator.

SECTION 20: Deductions permitted in computing income from business or property

► 20(1) ◄

(1) Deductions permitted in computing income from business or property. Notwithstanding paragraphs 18(1)(*a*), (*b*) and (*h*), in computing a taxpayer's income for a taxation year from a business or property, there may be deducted such of the following amounts as are wholly applicable to that source or such part of the following amounts as may reasonably be regarded as applicable thereto:

Editorial Note: S. 20(1) allows the deduction of certain amounts that might not otherwise be deductible under general principles or owing to the restrictions in s. 18(1)(*a*) (expense not deductible unless incurred for the purpose of earning income from business or property), 18(1)(*b*) (capital expenses not deductible except as expressly permitted), or 18(1)(*h*) (personal and living expenses not deductible).

Related Sections: S. 13(21), "depreciable property"; s. 14(5), "cumulative eligible capital"; s. 108(2) When trust is a unit trust; s. 248(1), "amount", "business", "property", s. 249 Definition of "taxation year"; s. 255 Canada; ITAR s. 20(3) Depreciable property of partnership of prescribed class.

Income Tax Folios: *Primary* — S3-F4-C1 General Discussion of Capital Cost Allowance.

► 20(1)(a) ◄

(a) Capital cost of property — such part of the capital cost to the taxpayer of property, or such amount in respect of the capital cost to the taxpayer of property, if any, as is allowed by regulation;

Editorial Note: The rate of capital cost allowance applicable to each class of property is set out in Regulation 1100 and its related schedules. Most classes are (or have been) subject to the half-year rule in the year of acquisition of property; see regulation 1100(2).

However, as a result of the November 20, 2018 Fall Economic Statement and the 2019 Federal Budget, the half-year rule does not apply to accelerated investment incentive property ("AIIP") or property in Classes 54 or 55. AIIP includes depreciable property that is acquired after November 20, 2018, becomes available for use before 2028, and meets other conditions of regulation 1104(4). Classes 54 and 55 include zero-emission vehicles.

Instead of being subject to the half-year rule in the year of acquisition, AIIP qualifies for an enhanced CCA rate in the year of acquisition. The enhanced rate is generally 50% more than the normal applicable CCA for acquisitions before 2024 (meaning it is 3 times the former half-year rate). The half-year rule is scheduled to be reinstated beginning in 2028. For class 54 and 55 property, a 100% CCA rate is allowed for acquisitions before 2024, with declining rates thereafter. See generally regulations 1102(2) and 1104(4).

Related Regulations: Part XI; Part XVII; Schedules II to VI.

Related Sections: S. 13(5) Reclassification of property; s. 13(6) Misclassified property; s. 13(7) Rules applicable; s. 13(11) Deduction in respect of property used in performance of duties; s. 13(12) Application of para. 20(1)(cc); s. 13(14) Conversion cost; s. 13(21) Definitions; s. 13(34) Deductible expenses; s. 21 Cost of borrowed money; s. 28(1) Farming or fishing business; s. 37(6) Expenditures of a capital nature; s. 85(5) Rules on transfers of depreciable property; s. 87(2)(*d*) Depreciable property; s. 87(2)(*d*.1) Depreciable property acquired from predecessor corporation; s. 88 Winding-up; s. 97(4) Where capital cost to partner exceeds proceeds of disposition; s. 98(3) Rules applicable where partnership ceases to exist; s. 98(5) Where partnership business carried on as sole proprietorship; s. 104(5) Depreciable property; s. 107(2) Distribution by personal trust; s. 164(6) Where disposition of property by legal representative of deceased taxpayer; s. 216(5) Disposition by non-resident of interest in real property, timber resource property or timber limit; and ITAR s. 18(2) Depreciable property acquired before 1949; s. 20(1) Depreciable property, (2) Recapture of capital cost allowances, (3) Depreciable property of partnership of prescribed class.

Canadian Tax Foundation: Robson, *Late UCC Additions*, 2013 Canadian Tax Highlights 21(12):6–7; Fitzgerald and Albert, *Mining Update*, 2011 Conference Report 16:1–25.

Tax Topics: No. 2439, Accelerated CCA and Other Measures From the 2018 Fall Economic Statement; No. 1961, Impact of IFRS on the Canadian Tax Practitioner.

Forms: T2 SCH 8 — Capital Cost Allowance (CCA).

Income Tax Folios: S4-F15-C1 Manufacturing and Processing.

Primary — S3-F4-C1 General Discussion of Capital Cost Allowance.

Information Circulars: IC 84-1 Revision of capital cost allowance claims and other permissive deductions.

Interpretation Bulletins: *Primary* — IT-79R3 Capital cost allowance — Buildings or other structures; IT-172R Capital cost allowance — Taxation year of individual; IT-291R3 Transfer of property to a corporation under subsection 85(1); IT-267R2 Capital cost allowance — Vessels; IT-304R2 Condominiums; IT-306R2 Capital cost allowance — Contractor's movable equipment; IT-422 Definition of tools; IT-464R Capital cost allowance — Leasehold interests; IT-469R Capital cost allowance — Earth-moving equipment; IT-472 Capital cost allowance — Class 8 property; IT-477 (Consolid.) Capital cost allowance — Patents, franchises, concessions and licences; IT-485 Cost of clearing or levelling land; IT-492 Capital cost allowance — Industrial mineral mines; IT-501 Capital cost allowance — Logging assets. *Secondary* — IT-121R3 Election to capitalize cost of borrowed money; IT-187 Customer lists and ledger accounts; IT-371 Rental property — Meaning of "principal business"; IT-481 (Consolid.) Timber resource property and timber limits.

Tax Window Files: Class 43.2 - Solar Thermal System, *March 31, 2015*, CRA Document No. 2015-0568271E5; Paragraph 1102(5)(a) of the Regulations, *15XXXX*, CRA Document No. 2014-0552291R3.

Cases: When the taxpayer purchased a property, it assumed whatever liability the vendor might have had for environmental clean up. The taxpayer could not add the "cost" of this assumed liability to the purchase price of the buildings and equipment for CCA purposes since no amount had actually been spent on clean-up and there was no evidence that the vendor actually had any legally enforceable liability. *A & D Holdings Inc. v. The Queen*, 2006 DTC 2219 (T.C.C.)

The taxpayer purchased equipment and circuitously leased it back to the vendor, while using prepayment arrangements and bonds to minimize financial risk. The Court rejected the Minister's argument that, without real financial risk or economic cost, GAAR should be used to deny CCA claims. There is nothing in GAAR or the object of the CCA provisions that permits "cost" to be interpreted as "amount economically at risk". *The Queen v. Canada Trustco Mortgage Company*, 2005 DTC 5523 (S.C.C.), affirming 2004 DTC 6119 (F.C.A.), affirming 2003 DTC 587 (T.C.C.)

When during the five-day period between the wind-up of its subsidiaries and their sale to a related corporation, the depreciable assets acquired by the taxpayer had been used to produce some business income, they were eligible for CCA treatment in its hands. *Hickman Motors Ltd. v. The Queen*, 97 DTC 5363 (S.C.C.), reversing 95 DTC 5575 (F.C.A.) and 93 DTC 5040 (F.C.T.D.).

► 20(1)(b) ◄

(b) Incorporation expenses — the lesser of

(i) the portion of the amount (that is not otherwise deductible in computing the income of the taxpayer) that is an expense incurred in the year for the incorporation of a corporation, and

(ii) $3,000 less the total of all amounts each of which is an amount deducted by another taxpayer in respect of the incorporation of the corporation;

History: S. 20(1)(*b*) was replaced by S.C. 2016, c. 12, s. 7(1), applicable in respect of expenses incurred after 2016, and formerly read:

(*b*) *Cumulative eligible capital amount* — such amount as the taxpayer claims in respect of a business, not exceeding 7% of the taxpayer's cumulative eligible capital in respect of the business at the end of the year except that, where the year is less than 12 months, the amount allowed as a deduction under this paragraph shall not exceed that proportion of the maximum amount otherwise allowable that the number of days in the taxation year is of 365;

Related Sections: S. 14(1) Eligible capital property — inclusion in income from business; s. 14(5), "cumulative eligible capital", "eligible capital expenditure"; s. 20(4.2) Bad debts re eligible capital property; s. 24(1) Ceasing to carry on business; s. 28(1) Farming or fishing business; s. 70(5.1) Eligible capital property of deceased; s. 70(9.8) Leased farm and fishing property; s. 87(2)(*f*) Eligible capital property; s. 111(5.2) Computation of cumulative eligible capital.

Tax Profile: July 2012 — Intangibles; July 2012 — Asset Sale — Price Allocation.

Tax Topics: No. 1718, Eligible Capital — Some Big Changes Part I.

Forms: T2 SCH 10 — Cumulative Eligible Capital Deduction.

Interpretation Bulletins: *Secondary* — IT-123R6 Transactions involving eligible capital property; IT-143R3 Meaning of eligible capital expenditure; IT-291R3 Transfer of property to a corporation under subsection 85(1); IT-302R3 Losses of a corporation — The effect on their deductibility of changes in control, amalgamation and winding-up; IT-313R2 Eligible capital property — Rules where a taxpayer has ceased carrying on a business or has died; IT-341R4 Expenses of issuing or selling shares, units in a trust, interests in a partnership or syndicate and expenses of borrowing money.

► 20(1)(c) ◄

(c) Interest — an amount paid in the year or payable in respect of the year (depending on the method regularly followed by the taxpayer in computing the taxpayer's income), pursuant to a legal obligation to pay interest on

(i) borrowed money used for the purpose of earning income from a business or property (other than borrowed money used to acquire property the income from which would be exempt or to acquire a life insurance policy),

(ii) an amount payable for property acquired for the purpose of gaining or producing income from the property or for the purpose of gaining or producing income from a business (other than property the income from which would be exempt or property that is an interest in a life insurance policy),

(iii) an amount paid to the taxpayer under

(A) an appropriation Act and on terms and conditions approved by the Treasury Board for the purpose of advancing or sustaining the technological capability of Canadian manufacturing or other industry, or

(B) the *Northern Mineral Exploration Assistance Regulations* made under an appropriation Act that provides for payments in respect of the Northern Mineral Grants Program, or

(iv) borrowed money used to acquire an interest in an annuity contract in respect of which section 12.2 applies (or would apply if the contract had an anniversary day in the year at a time when the taxpayer held the interest) except that, where annuity payments have begun under the contract in a preceding taxation year, the amount of interest paid or payable in the year shall not be deducted to the extent that it exceeds the amount included under section 12.2 in computing the taxpayer's income for the year in respect of the taxpayer's interest in the contract,

or a reasonable amount in respect thereof, whichever is the lesser;

Editorial Note: A specific provision is required to permit the deduction of interest as the Canadian courts have generally held that interest expense is on capital account and therefore not deductible under general principles. (see *Canada Safeway Ltd.*, 57 DTC 1239 (S.C.C.) and *Bronfman Trust*, 87 DTC 5059 (S.C.C.)) However, for financial institutions and other taxpayers in the business of lending money, interest expense is apparently not on account of capital, so that it may be deducted under general principles in the computation of profit (see *Gifford*, 2004 DTC 6120 (S.C.C.)).

Income-Earning Requirement: In *Ludco*, (2001 DTC 5505), the Supreme Court held that a "reasonable expectation of profit" test is not an appropriate source test for income tax purposes, and that the term "income" in s. 20(1)(*c*) refers to gross income rather than net income. Taxpayers arranging their affairs in order to fit within the direct use requirement of paragraph 20(1)(*c*) will be entitled to an interest deduction, provided that the current and direct use of the borrowed money is for the purpose of earning income from a business or property (see *Singleton*, 2001 DTC 5533 (S.C.C.) and CRA document No. 2001-0084055).

Loan to Purchase Shares: Interest expense incurred on borrowed money used to redeem shares is deductible under paragraph 20(1)(*c*) to the extent that the money originally received on the issuance of the shares was used for the purpose of earning income. (See Income Tax Folio S3-F6-C1, ¶1.48 *et seq.*) There must be a reasonable expectation that the shares will generate income if interest paid on a related loan is deductible (see *Swirsky*, 2014 DTC 5037 (F.C.A.)).

Loss Utilization Arrangements: A common method for effectively transferring losses within a Canadian resident corporate group is to have a profitable corporation in the group borrow money and use the money to invest in preferred shares in a company with losses. So long as the transactions are legally effective, the CRA does not find them offensive. See Income Tax Folio S3-F6-C1, ¶1.71, and "Interest Deductibility: Where From, Where To, Where Now?", Report of Proceedings of Fifty-Fourth Tax Conference, 2002 Tax Conference (Toronto: Canadian Tax Foundation, 2003), 11:1–18, at 11:10–11).

Related Sections: S. 18(2) Limit on certain interest and property tax; s. 18(3.1) Costs relating to construction of building or ownership of land; s. 18(4) Limitation re deduction of interest by certain corporations; s. 18(9.1) Penalties, bonuses and rate-reduction payments; s. 18(9.2) Interest on debt obligations — notional principal; s. 20(1)(*d*) Compound interest; s. 20(1)(*e*) Expenses re financing; s. 20(2) Borrowed money; s. 20(2.01) Limitation of expression "interest"; s. 20(3) Borrowed money; s. 20(14) Accrued bond interest; s. 21 Cost of borrowed money.

Canadian Petroleum Tax Journal: Recent Trends In Interest Expense Deductibility, J. Scott Bodie and Jehad Haymour, 2002, Vol. 15, No. 1; Café Annie's Tasty Inbound Financing, Jim McKee, 2002, Vol. 15, No. 1; Selected Current Issues Regarding Interest Deductibility, Sandra E. Jack, 2002, Vol. 15, No. 1.

Canadian Tax Foundation: McClure, *TDL Interest Deduction Allowed*, 2016 Canadian Tax Highlights 24(4):2–3; Bernstein, *Purpose of Borrowing*, 2015 Canadian Tax Highlights 23(4):2–3; Cepparo, *Folio Updates Interest Deductibility Policies*, 2015 Canadian Tax Highlights 23(4):1–2; Friedlan and Friedlan, *TDL Group: Interest Deductibility and the "Purpose" Test*, 2015 Tax for the Owner-Manager 15(3):6–7; Jones, *The Interest Deductibility Interpretation in TDL: Some Wider Implications*, 2015 Canadian Tax Focus 5(2):2; Klyguine, *Interest Deductibility Denied on Intra-Group Loan for Novel Reasons*, 2015 Canadian Tax Focus 5(2):1–2; Morrison, *Interest on Money Borrowed To Acquire Common Shares of Private Corporation Not Deductible*, 2014 Tax for the Owner-Manager 14(2):4–5; Blackler and Nitikman, *Case Comment: Swirsky v. The Queen*, 2013 British Columbia Tax Conference 2:15–18; Hudson, *Deductibility of Interest Paid to Earn Interest Income*, 2013 Tax for the Owner-Manager 13(2):8–9; MacKnight, *Swirsky v. The Queen: Of Interest to Dr. Jekyll and Mr. Hyde?*, 2013 Tax for the Owner-Manager 13(2):2; Doobay and MacPherson, *Interest Deduction Denied: Swirsky*, 2013 Canadian Tax Highlights 21(4):5–6; Fréchette and Rabinovitch, *Recent Issues Relating to Interest Deductability and Non-Traditional Forms of Indebtedness*, 2011 Conference Report 27:1–36; Hickey, *Collins: Interest Payable*, 2010 Canadian Tax Highlights 18(3):8–9; McClure, *Planning for Interest Deductibility*, 2010 Tax for the Owner-Manager 10(4):9–10; Maclagan, *Interest Deductibility — An Update*, 2009 British Columbia Tax Conference 10:1–20; Thomson and Quinn, *Financing Alternatives for Small and Medium-Sized Businesses*, 2007 Conference Report 33:1–23; McDonnell, *Current Cases: The Federal Court of Appeal — The Relevance of "Overall Purpose" in a GAAR Analysis (Lipson et al. v. The Queen, 2007 DTC 5172)*, 2007 Canadian Tax Journal 3:720–730; McDonnell, *Current Cases: Tax Court of Canada — GAAR Applied To Reverse Attribution Plan (Lipson et al. v. The Queen, 2006 DTC 148)*, 2006 Canadian Tax Journal 3:711–719; Jack et al., *Income Trusts and Interest Deductibility (Canada Revenue Agency Round Table)*, 2005 Conference Report 6A:1–2; Friedlander, *What Does Gifford Mean?*, 2005 Canadian Tax Journal 4:897–940; Weekes, *Recent Developments Regarding Interest Deductibility*, 2005 Prairie Provinces Tax Conference 3:1–17; Johnson and Tamaki, *Deductibility of Interest and Other Expenses — Proposed Section 3.1*, 2004 Ontario Tax Conference 6:1–21; Tamaki, *Interest Deductibility*, 2003 Conference Report 1:1–19; Carr, *Interest Deductibility*, 2003 Canadian Tax Journal 3:1422–1449; Belley, *Deductibility of Interest and Repayment of Principal*, 2003 Tax for the Owner-Manager 3(1):5; Kakkar, *Compound Interest Deductibility: The Meaning of "Paid"*, 2003 Tax for the Owner-Manager 3(1):4–5; Jack et al., *Interest Deductibility: Where From, Where To, Where Now?*, 2002 Conference Report 11:1–18; Wertschek, *Interest Deductibility — Current CCRA Policy*, 2002 British Columbia Tax Conference 3:1–5; Martin, *The Fundamentals of the Interest Expense Deduction*, 2002 Prairie Provinces Tax Conference 3:1–30; Jack, *Interest Deductibility Update*, 2002 Canadian Tax Highlights 10(10):73–74; McDonnell, *Interest Deductibility: New CCRA Policy?*, 2002 Tax for the Owner-Manager 2(1):8; Du Pont and Jodoin, *Interest Deductibility: An Update*, 2001 Conference Report 40:1–22; Wong, *Current Cases: Supreme Court of Canada — Goodbye "Economic Realities", Hello "Legal Substance" (The Queen v. Singleton, 2001 SCC 61)*, 2001 Canadian Tax Journal 6:1571–1575; Taylor, *Current Cases: Supreme Court of Canada — LUDCO Enterprises Ltd.: New Solutions for Old Problems (Ludco Enterprises et al. v. The Queen, 2001 SCC 62)*, 2001 Canadian Tax Journal 6:1563–1571; Frankovic, *Why Interest Should Be Considered a Current Expense*, 2001 Canadian Tax Journal 4:859–872; Templeton, *Current Cases: The Earth is Not Flat (Gifford v. The Queen, 2001 DTC 168)*, 2001 Canadian Tax Journal 3:720–726; Owen, *Subparagraph 20(1)(c)(i): What Is Its Purpose?*, 2000 Canadian Tax Journal 2:231–273; Nitikman, *Current Cases: Supreme Court of Canada — Is Interest a Current Expense? (Shell Canada Limited v. The Queen et al., 99 DTC 5669)*, 2000 Canadian Tax Journal 1:133–142; Edgar, *Some Lessons From the Saga of Weak-Currency Borrowings*, 2000 Canadian Tax Journal 1:1–34; Lewin, *Interest Deductibility: The Ongoing Saga*, 1999 Conference Report 23:1–30; Richardson et al., *Fundamentals of Canadian Taxation of Financial Instruments*, 1999 Conference Report 5:1–57; Wong, *Current Cases: Federal Court of Appeal — Deductibility of Interest: The Singleton "Two-Step" (Singleton v. R., 99 DTC 5362)*, 1999 Canadian Tax Journal 4:952–957; Hanly, *Current Cases: Federal Court of Appeal — Interest on Money Borrowed to Buy Common Shares — What is your Real Purpose? Dividends or Capital Gains? (Les Entreprises Ludco Ltée et al. v. The Queen, 99 DTC 5153)*, 1999 Canadian Tax Journal 3:624–629; Barette, *Interest: Where Are We Now?*, 1997 Corporate Management Tax Conference 8:1–34; Edgar, *The Concept of Interest Under the Income Tax Act*, 1996 Canadian Tax Journal 2:277–346; Arnold and Edgar, *Deductibility of Interest Expense*, 1995 Canadian Tax Journal 5:1216–1244; Arnold, *Is Interest a Capital Expense?*, 1992 Canadian Tax Journal 3:533.

STEP Canada: Jamie Golombek, "Taxation of Investments: So, you thought you knew everything?," PowerPoint presentation to the 15th National Conference of STEP Canada, Toronto, June 10-11, 2013.

Tax Profile: February 2013 — The Purchase of US Businesses by Canadians; December 2012 — Taxpayer's Equity Characterization of Hybrid Instruments — Canadian Implications; July 2012 — Asset Sale — Price Allocation; April 2011 — Proposed Changes to Canada's Tax Laws — The Canadian Government Reacts To Close Perceived Abuses; November 2010 — Canadian Acquisition of U.S. Real Estate; February 2009 — SCC on the GAAR — Taxpayer Loses in Lipson; May 2007 — Impact of 2007 Federal Budget on Cross-Border Transactions; April 2004 — Interest is Almost Always a Capital Expense; February 2004 — Interest and Other Financing Costs; December 2003 — Proposed Amendments to the Income Tax Act (Canada) Related to the Deductibility of Interest and Other Expenses: the Reintroduction of Reasonable Expectation of Profit; November 2003 — Revenue Canada Round Table; July 2003 — One Foot in the Present and One Foot in the Past: Interest Deductibility and Anti-Avoidance.

Tax Topics: No. 2414, Crossing Provincial Lines: Alberta Courts Tackle 20(1)(*c*); No. 2411, Interest Deductibility and Changing Uses of Borrowed Money; No. 2253, The Purpose Test — Where Does It End?; No. 2199, Interest Deductibility — Has the Bar Been Raised for Share Purchases?; No. 2023-24, 2010 Canadian Tax Foundation CRA Roundtable: Pipelines, Privilege and Working Papers (Again!); No. 1981, Which Amount of Interest Is Deductible? — *Collins et al. v. The Queen*; No. 1924, Lipson (SCC) — A Unanimously Divided Supreme Court; No. 1919-20, 2008 Canadian Tax Foundation Annual Conference — Department of Finance Presentation and CRA Round Table; No. 1883, Supreme Court To Consider GAAR in *Lipson Appeal*; No. 1843, Finance's May 14, 2007 Revised Interest Deductibility Proposals — An "Anti-Double-Dip Initiative"; No. 1829, The Federal Budget's Interest Restrictions — Clear and Present Danger?; No. 1782, Walk the Line — *Lipson v. The Queen*; No. 1774, Deduction of Interest: Cash or Accrual Basis?; No. 1675, Canadian Tax Foundation's Interest Deductibility Symposium; No. 1673, Supreme Court's Decision on Interest Deductibility Defies Logic; No. 1653, REOP Resurrected - This Year's Hallowe'en Trick; No. 1651, Supreme Court of Canada to Rule on the Characterization of Interest Expense; No. 1591, Federal Court of Appeal Rules on the Nature of Interest Expense; No. 1580, Refinancing a Partnership Interest — More on the "Singleton Shuffle"; No. 1506, Supreme Court to rule on the "Reasonable Expectation of Profit" and related issues.

Income Tax Folios: *Primary* — S3-F6-C1 Interest Deductibility. *Secondary* — S4-F2-C1 Deductibility of Fines and Penalties.

Income Tax Technical News: Issue No. 41, Deductibility of Interest on Money Borrowed to Acquire Common Shares; Issue No. 34, Income Trusts and Interest Deductibility.

Information Circulars: IC 88-2 General anti-avoidance rule — Section 245 of the Income Tax Act (paras. 19 and 20, Supp. 1 para. 5).

Interpretation Bulletins: *Secondary* — IT-341R4 Expenses of issuing or selling shares, units in a trust, interests in a partnership or syndicate, and expenses of borrowing money; IT-362R Patronage dividends.

Tax Window Files: Interest deductibility and share repurchases, *January 29, 2016*, CRA Document No. 2015-0621401I7; Loss consolidation arrangements, *August 19, 2015*, CRA Document No. 2015-0589611E5; loss consolidation, *14XXXX*, CRA Document No. 2014-0543911R3; Reorganization, *14XXXX*, CRA Document No. 2013-0516071R3; Monetization of Securities - 2010 CTF Conference, *October 8, 2010*, CRA Document No. 2013-0507191C6; Interest deductibility, *August 27, 2010*, CRA Document No. 2009-0335101E5. Tracing rule where property transferred; Tax Considerations in an International Insolvency, *Income Tax Rulings Directorate, Business and Partnerships Division, October 15, 2009*, CRA Document No. 2009-0314641I7; Backdating of Completed Transaction, *Income Tax Rulings Directorate, Financial Industries Division, October 8, 2009*, CRA Document No. 2009-0338861E5; Interest Deduction — Issuance of a New Promissory Note, *Technical Interpretation, Financial Sector and Exempt Entities Division, July 21, 2009*, CRA Document No. 2009-0322591I7; Interest Deductibility, *Technical Interpretation, Financial Industries Division, July 16, 2009*, CRA Document No. 2009-0329171E5; Interest Deductibility — Borrowing to Redeem Shares, *Technical Interpretation, Financial Sector and Exempt Entities Division, May 27, 2009*, CRA Document No. 2008-0296731E5; Forgiveness of Debt — Commercial Obligation and Commercial Debt Obligation, *Technical Interpretation, Financial Sector and Exempt Entities Division, January 12, 2009*, CRA Document No. 2008-0293901E5; Interest Deductibility — Borrowing to Make Interest-Free Loan, *Technical Interpretation, Financial Sector and Exempt Entities Division, November 25, 2008*, CRA Document No. 2008-0297631E5; Interest Deductibility — Investment in Mutual Fund Trusts, *Technical Interpretation, Financial Sector and Exempt Entities Division, September 24, 2008*, CRA Document No. 2008-0268511E5; Money Borrowed to Pay a Dividend, *Technical Interpretation, Financial Sector and Exempt Entities Division, September 12, 2008*, CRA Document No. 2007-0228931E5; Interest Deductibility — Disposition of Mutual Fund Units, *Technical Interpretation, Financial Sector and Exempt Entities Division, June 5, 2008*, CRA Document No. 2007-0252211E5; Interest Deductibility, *April 24, 2008*, CRA Document No. 2008-0275171E5. Discussion on net or gross income concept and pending draft legislation; Interest Deductibility — Capitalization of Interest, *Technical Interpretation, Financial Sector and Exempt Entities Division, April 21, 2008*, CRA Document No. 2007-0251761I7; Interest Deduction, *March 10, 2008*, CRA Document No. 2008-0267961E5. Current use of funds relevant; Interest Deductibility — Borrowing to Replace Retained Earnings and Pay Dividends, *Technical Interpretation, Financial Sector and Exempt Entities Division, March 18, 2008*, CRA Document No. 2007-0249601E5; Interest Deductibility — Cash Damming, *Technical Interpretation, Financial Sector and Exempt Entities Division, January 14, 2008*, CRA Document No. 2007-0263241E5; Deduction of Interest, *Round Table on Federal Taxation 2007 APFF Conference, Question 25, October 5, 2007*, CRA Document No. 2007-0243181C6; Shareholders — Loans to Corporations, *Round Table on Federal Taxation 2007 APFF Conference, Question 14, October 5, 2007*, CRA Document No. 2007-0243361C6; Deductible Interest — Commingled Funds, *Technical Interpretation, Financial Sector and Exempt Entities Division, September 7, 2007*, CRA Document No. 2006-0218381E5; Interest Deductibility, *Technical Interpretation, Financial Sector and Exempt Entities Division, September 6, 2007*, CRA Document No. 2007-0244231I7; Redemption of Shares Acquired with Borrowed Money, *Technical Interpretations, Financial Sector and Exempt Entities Division, August 16, 2007, August 21, 2007, and August 23, 2007*, CRA Document No. 2007-0236351E5; Cash Damming, *Technical Interpretation, Financial Sector and Exempt Entities Division, August 14, 2007*, CRA Document No. 2006-0218241E5; Interest Deductibility — Return of Capital, *Technical Interpretation, Financial Sector and Exempt Entities Division, May 11, 2007*, CRA Document No. 2005-0156891E5; Interest Deductibility — Return of Capital, *Technical Interpretation, Financial Sector and Exempt Entities Division, May 11, 2007*, CRA Document No. 2006-0191681E5; Deduction for Financing Expenses — Indirect Use of Funds, *Technical Interpretation, Financial Sector and Exempt Entities Division, March 14, 2007*, CRA Document No. 2005-0161661E5; Deductibility of Accrued Interest — Period of Stay Ordered under the Companies' Creditors Arrangement Act, *Technical Interpretation, Financial Sector and Exempt Entities Division, March 14, 2007*, CRA Document No. 2006-0214681I7; Interest Deductibility, *Technical Interpretation, Financial Sector and Exempt Entities Section, March 6, 2007*, CRA Document No. 2007-0219791E5; Interest Deductibility — Borrowing for Loan Repayment, *Technical Interpretation, Financial Sector and Exempt Entities Division, October 31, 2006*, CRA Document No. 2006-0173731E5; Interest Deductibility — Leveraged Buyout, *Technical Interpretation, 2006 APFF Conference Round Table on the Federal Taxation Question 7, October 6, 2006*, CRA Document No. 2006-0202091E5; Interest Deduction — Corporation Borrowing from Shareholders to Pay Their Dividends, *Technical Interpretation, Financial Sector and Exempt Entities Division, May 18, 2006*, CRA Document No. 2006-0182321I7; Interest Deductibility — Dividends Paid with Promissory Notes Issued to Shareholders, *Technical Interpretation, Financial Sector and Exempt Entities Division, March 3, 2006*, CRA Document No. 2005-0151871I7; Financing Fees Paid by Parent Company on Behalf of Subsidiary, *Technical Interpretation, Financial Sector and Exempt Entities Division, October 19, 2005*, CRA Document No. 2005-0151211I7; Deductibility of Legal Fees and Interest, *Technical Interpretation, Business and Partnerships Division, June 9, 2005*, CRA Document No. 2004-0105421I7; Interest Deductibility — Co-Borrowers, *Technical Interpretation, Financing and Plans Division, June 7, 2005*, CRA Document No. 2005-0121551E5; Interest Expense — Insurer, *CLHIA Conference, Question 8, May 26, 2005*, CRA Document No. 2005-0126051C6; Interest Deductibility, *Income Tax Rulings Directorate, May 14, 2005*, CRA Document No. 2008-0304841I7; Interest on Loan To Pay Interest, *2005 Conference for Advance Life Underwriting (2005), May 3, 2005*, CRA Document No. 2005-0116661C6. Interest on second loan used to pay interest on original loan deductible since original loan used to earn income from business; Life Insurance as Collateral for Loan, *2005 Conference for Advance Life Underwriting, Question 4, May 3, 2005*, CRA Document No. 2005-0116651C6; Participating Loan, *February 8, 2005*, CRA Document No. 2004-0103941E5; Interest Expense — Borrowing to Pay for Current Expenditures, *Technical Interpretation, Financing and Plans Division, February 3, 2005*, CRA Document No. 2005-0111871E5. Interest on loan used to pay current expenses remained deductible after the year in which current expenses were incurred; Interest Expense — Return of Capital, *Technical Interpretation, Financial Industries Division, January 21, 2005*, CRA Document No. 2004-0103721E5; Interest Deductibility — Notion of Capital, *Technical Interpretation, Financial Industries Division, May 31, 2004*, CRA Document No. 2003-0051971E5. Interest deductible on borrowed money used to redeem shares — Trans-Prairie rationale applies and generally based on legal stated capital of shares rather than tax paid-up capital (see also paragraph 23 of Interpretation Bulletin IT-533); Interest Expense — Double Dip Deduction and Thin Capitalization, *Technical Interpretation, Financial Industries Division, May 18, 2004*, CRA Document No. 2004-0063351I7. Structure of cross-border "double-dip" loan does not, in itself, preclude an interest deduction under paragraph 20(1)(*c*), although GAAR may apply; Deductibility of Penalties and Interest Under the CPP Act and Ei Act, *Technical Interpretation, Business and Partnerships Division, January 28, 2004*, CRA Document No. 2004-0054881I7. Interest paid pursuant to the *CPP Act* or *EI Act* in respect of un-remitted source deductions is interest paid on borrowed money; Interest Free Loans to Related Company, *Technical Interpretation, Financial Industries Division, April 9, 2003*, CRA Document No. 2003-0181655. Interest on borrowed money used to make interest-free loan generally not deductible, unless loan made to wholly-owned corporation or under "exceptional circumstances"; Loss Consolidation Interest Deductibility, *Tax Ruling, February 11, 2003*, CRA Document No. 2003-0044293. Interest deduction allowed in "in-house" corporate loss utilization transaction.

Cases: Any determination of whether interest paid was reasonable required consideration of the underlying legislative scheme, the purpose of which was to level the playing field between utilities companies exempt from tax and those that were not. Not only was the interest rate required to be objectively reasonable, but the structure of each loan was required to be objectively reasonable to the extent it affected the amount of interest paid. Given the purpose and object of the balancing pool payments regime, the arm's length market rate interest rate, properly determined and in the absence of exceptional circumstances, was determinative of reasonableness. *Alberta v. ENMAX Energy Corporation*, 2018 DTC 5054 (ABCA)

Almost two-thirds of the original amount invested in the mutual fund was returned to the taxpayer and more than one-half of that money was used for personal purposes. The requirement to trace the borrowed money to a current eligible use applies whether or not there has been a disposition, in whole or in part, of the original investment. There was no longer any link between the borrowed funds and the investment in the mutual fund and the taxpayer was not entitled to deduct the interest on the portion used for personal purposes. *Van Steenis v. The Queen*, 2018 DTC 1063 (TCC), affirmed 2019 DTC 5056 (FCA)

The agreements under which Amoco assumed liability for the $225 million loan were entered into on account of capital. It is impossible under section 16(1)(*a*) for an amount to be classified as deemed interest for the debtor and capital for the creditor. As a result, the amounts claimed by the taxpayer were not deductible interest under paragraph 20(1)(*c*). *Plains Midstream v. The Queen*, 2017 DTC 1125 (TCC), affirmed 2019 DTC 5040 (FCA)

The taxpayer's purpose when using borrowed monies was to be assessed at the time the monies were used. Consequently, the taxpayer's purpose at the time it subscribed for shares in its US subsidiary must be examined and not the series of transactions that resulted in a loan to the parent company. *TDL v. The Queen*, 2016 DTC 5075 (FCA)

Interest payable by the taxpayer was not deductible. The taxpayer obtained loans to purchase and cancel its own shares and the shares of a subsidiary. This transaction was not for the purpose of gaining, producing or protecting income from a business, and there were no exceptional circumstances to justify a deduction. *A.P. Toldo Holding Corporation v. The Queen*, 2014 DTC 1042 (T.C.C.)

The taxpayer's wife obtained a bank loan to purchase shares of a family corporation from him. He used the proceeds to buy a new house. They then took out a mortgage on the house and used it to pay off the bank loan. The mortgage interest was deducted from her dividend income and the resulting loss was attributed to him under s. 74.1(1). This was not an abuse of s. 20(1)(*c*) or 20(3). However, it was an abuse of the attribution rules and GAAR was used to disallow deduction of the mortgage interest. *Lipson et al. v. The Queen*, 2009 DTC 5015 (S.C.C.), affirming 2007 DTC 5172 (F.C.A.), affirming 2006 DTC 2687 (T.C.C.)

Days before emigrating from Canada, the taxpayers executed a departure trade designed to create a $1.7 million interest deduction. The deduction was disallowed under s. 114(*c*) since the phrase, "any other deduction permitted for the purpose of computing taxable income" is restricted to Division C deductions, which excludes a s. 20(1)(*c*) interest deduction. *Grant et al. v. The Queen*, 2007 DTC 5351 (F.C.A.), affirming 2006 DTC 3071 (T.C.C.)

Paragraph 20(1)(*c*) does not require compliance with GAAP. The only requirement to be taken from the plain meaning of the provision is that interest be accounted for on a consistent basis: either cash or accrual. *Crown Forest Industries Ltd. v. The Queen*, 2006 DTC 2321 (T.C.C.)

Sections 8(1)(*j*) and 20(1)(*c*) do not provide a complete code dealing with interest deductibility. In circumstances where interest is not a payment on account of capital, it may be deducted as long as it meets the other requirements, such as those set out in s. 8(1)(*f*) or s. 18(1)(*a*), and is not precluded by some other section of the Act. *Gifford v. The Queen et al.*, 2004 DTC 6120 (S.C.C.), affirming 2002 DTC 7197 (F.C.A.), reversing 2001 DTC 168 (T.C.C.)

The taxpayer entered into a series of transactions designed to create an interest deduction. The direct use of the borrowed funds was to purchase shares in a company to earn dividend income. While this met the requirements of s. 20(1)(*c*), the deduction was denied because it artificially reduced the taxpayer's income, contrary to the 1987 version of s. 245(1). *Novopharm Limited v. The Queen*, 2003 DTC 5195 (F.C.A.), affirming 2002 DTC 1307 (T.C.C.)

The taxpayer and others purchased land which they immediately sold and leased back. They borrowed funds from the purchaser to construct an office building on the land. Cash flow above a certain amount was paid to the owner as either interest or rent based on a formula. Such "excess interest" payments were deductible. *Hill v. The Queen*, 2002 DTC 1749 (T.C.C.)

Interest relating to a highly leveraged condominium purchase fell within the scope of s. 20(1)(*c*). The rental activity lacked any personal element and was clearly a commercial activity. REOP was not the appropriate test. S. 20(1)(*c*) is not a tax avoidance mechanism and the taxpayer's hope of realizing an eventual capital gain with the expectation of deducting interest expenses, did not detract from the commercial nature of his rental operation, or its characterization as a source of income. *Stewart v. The Queen*, 2002 DTC 6969 (S.C.C.), reversing 2000 DTC 6163 (F.C.A.) and 98 DTC 1600 (T.C.C.)

The taxpayer borrowed funds which it loaned on an interest-free basis to a holding corporation, to enable the latter's parent to purchase V corporation. The interest was deductible because of "exceptional circumstances", namely that the taxpayer expected to earn business income from management fees and the take-over of some of V's operations. *The Queen v. Canadian Helicopters Limited*, 2002 DTC 6805 (F.C.A.), affirming 2001 DTC 339 (T.C.C.)

The taxpayers borrowed money to acquire the shares of two Panamanian corporations. Although the dividends they received were significantly less than the interest on the borrowed money, the bulk of the return being in capital gains, the interest was deductible since one of the purposes of the borrowed funds was to earn (dividend) income. It was not necessary to establish a prime or dominant purpose, and "income" means gross, not net income. *Ludco Enterprises Ltd. et al. v. The Queen*, 2001 DTC 5505 (S.C.C.), reversing 99 DTC 5153 (F.C.A.), 98 DTC 6045 (F.C.T.D.) and 93 DTC 1351 (T.C.C.)

The taxpayer withdrew funds from his law firm capital account and used this amount to assist in the purchase of a house. Later on the same day, he borrowed funds from a bank which he used to refinance his capital account. Interest on the loan was deductible because the transactions were viewed independently and the proceeds from the loan were used to earn income. *The Queen v. Singleton*, 2001 DTC 5533 (S.C.C.), affirming 99 DTC 5362 (F.C.A.) which reversed 96 DTC 1850 (T.C.C.)

The taxpayer invested in units of a limited partnership carrying on the business of renting apartments. Almost all of the purchase price was financed by arm's length borrowings. The Minister had argued that the taxpayer had no reasonable expectation of profit because his interest payments exceeded his income from the partnership. However, the partnership was a viable business with a reasonable expectation of profit and therefore the interest was deductible. *The Queen v. Milewski*, 2000 DTC 6559 (F.C.A.), affirming 99 DTC 968 (T.C.C.)

Interest was not deductible where the corporate taxpayer borrowed funds from a bank for the purpose of financing the purchase by a third party of the corporations which owned the taxpayer's issued and outstanding shares. *C.R.B. Logging Co. Ltd. v. The Queen*, 2000 DTC 6547 (F.C.A.), affirming 99 DTC 840 (T.C.C.)

A bank advanced $36 million to its subsidiary which then paid the bank a $45 million dividend. The subsidiary was denied a deduction for interest paid on the advanced funds because the direct use of the funds was to pay a dividend, which was an ineligible use. *The Chase Manhattan Bank of Canada v. The Queen*, 2000 DTC 6018 (F.C.A.), affirming 97 DTC 349 (T.C.C.)

Rather than borrowing in Canadian funds, the taxpayer borrowed foreign funds, converted these to Canadian funds, and entered into foreign exchange swap agreements to meet foreign currency interest and principal payments. Based on the S.C.C. decision in *The Queen v. Shell Canada Limited*, the interest paid on the foreign currency loans was deductible. *Canadian Pacific Limited v. The Queen*, 2000 DTC 6174 (F.C.A.), reversing 99 DTC 5132 (F.C.A.) and 98 DTC 2021 (T.C.C.)

Rather than borrowing in U.S. dollars at 9.1%, the taxpayer borrowed in New Zealand dollars at 15.4%, converted the funds into U.S. dollars (which it required for operations) and concurrently entered into a forward foreign exchange contract to hedge its N.Z. dollar obligations. The 15.4% interest was deductible because, between Shell and the lenders, the payments were consideration for the use of the N.Z. dollars that Shell had borrowed. The 15.4% rate was the N.Z. market rate between arm's length parties and therefore a reasonable rate. *Shell Canada Limited v. The Queen*, 99 DTC 5669 (S.C.C.), reversing 98 DTC 6177 (F.C.A.) which reversed in part 97 DTC 395 (T.C.C.)

Construction period interest may be treated as an expense, deductible under s. 20(1)(c), or may be capitalized under s. 21(1), but not otherwise. Capitalized interest is not part of the capital cost for ITC purposes. *Alberta Wheat Pool et al. v. The Queen*, 99 DTC 5198 (F.C.A.), affirming 96 DTC 1795 (T.C.C.)

The corporate taxpayer purchased its own debentures in the open market at a discounted purchase price which included accrued interest. The taxpayer was entitled to interest deductions in respect of the accrued interest. *Hudson Bay Mining and Smelting Co., Limited v. The Queen*, 99 DTC 5269 (F.C.A.), reversing 96 DTC 1246 (T.C.C.)

When the agreement reached during the course of a trial made no reference to a debenture held by the taxpayer's bank against all of its assets, the deduction by the taxpayer of interest on the debenture was disallowed on the ground that it had been "settled". *Central City Financial Services Ltd. v. The Queen*, 98 DTC 6645 (F.C.A.), affirming 98 DTC 1021 (T.C.C.)

In keeping with the new commercial realities, participating interest paid on the taxpayer's long-term bonds was deductible both as interest under s. 20(1)(*c* and as an expense incurred in the course of borrowing money under s. 20(1)(*e*). *The Queen v. Sherway Centre Limited*, 98 DTC 6121 (F.C.A.), affirming 96 DTC 1640 (T.C.C.)

Where property is exchanged for property acquired with a loan, the deduction under s. 20(1)(*c*) is based not on the value of the replacement property, but on the amount of the original loan. Accordingly, where a taxpayer acquired property worth $1,000 in exchange for a rollover of property purchased with a $1 million loan, he was entitled to continue to claim an interest deduction on the basis of the amount of that loan. *Tennant v. The Queen*, 96 DTC 6121 (S.C.C.), reversing 94 DTC 6505 (F.C.A.) and 93 DTC 5067 (F.C.T.D.)

A trust wanted to make capital allocations to the beneficiary but it did not want to liquidate any assets in order to do so. Instead, the trust borrowed the money and claimed a deduction for the interest paid on the borrowed money. The S.C.C. held that the interest was not deductible. Despite the fact that the borrowing could be characterized as indirectly preserving income, the trust in fact borrowed money for an ineligible direct purpose (i.e., making capital allocations to the beneficiary) and the deduction was therefore prohibited. *The Queen v. Bronfman Trust*, 87 DTC 5059 (S.C.C.), reversing 83 DTC 5243 (F.C.A.) and 79 DTC 5438 (F.C.T.D.), which reversed 78 DTC 1752 (T.R.B.).

► 20(1)(d) ◄

(d) Compound interest — an amount paid in the year pursuant to a legal obligation to pay interest on an amount that would be deductible under paragraph (*c*) if it were paid in the year or payable in respect of the year;

Editorial Note: Compound interest is deductible only in the year in which it is paid, in contrast to simple interest which is effectively deductible on an accrual basis under s. 20(1)(*c*).

Related Sections: S. 20(2.01) Limitation of expression "interest"; s. 20(2.1) Limitation of expression "interest"; s. 20(2.2) Limitation of expression "life insurance policy"; s. 21 Cost of borrowed money.

Income Tax Folios: *Secondary* — S3-F6-C1 Interest Deductibility; S4-F2-C1 Deductibility of Fines and Penalties.

Interpretation Bulletins: *Secondary* — IT-362R Patronage dividends.

Tax Window Files: Compound Interest — Incurred with Respect to Vacant Land and Construction of Building, *Technical Interpretation, Financial Industries Division, April 10, 2003*, CRA Document No. 2002-0147295. The restrictions in subsections 18(2) and (3.1) can apply to compound interest in the year it is paid and otherwise deductible under paragraph 20(1)(*d*).

▶ 20(1)(e) ◀

(e) Expenses re financing — such part of an amount (other than an excluded amount) that is not otherwise deductible in computing the income of the taxpayer and that is an expense incurred in the year or a preceding taxation year

(i) in the course of an issuance or sale of units of the taxpayer where the taxpayer is a unit trust, of interests in a partnership or syndicate by the partnership or syndicate, as the case may be, or of shares of the capital stock of the taxpayer,

(ii) in the course of a borrowing of money used by the taxpayer for the purpose of earning income from a business or property (other than money used by the taxpayer for the purpose of acquiring property the income from which would be exempt),

(ii.1) in the course of incurring indebtedness that is an amount payable for property acquired for the purpose of gaining or producing income therefrom or for the purpose of gaining or producing income from a business (other than property the income from which would be exempt or property that is an interest in a life insurance policy), or

(ii.2) in the course of a rescheduling or restructuring of a debt obligation of the taxpayer or an assumption of a debt obligation by the taxpayer, where the debt obligation is

(A) in respect of a borrowing described in subparagraph (ii), or

(B) in respect of an amount payable described in subparagraph (ii.1),

and, in the case of a rescheduling or restructuring, the rescheduling or restructuring, as the case may be, provides for the modification of the terms or conditions of the debt obligation or the conversion or substitution of the debt obligation to or with a share or another debt obligation,

(including a commission, fee, or other amount paid or payable for or on account of services rendered by a person as a salesperson, agent or dealer in securities in the course of the issuance, sale or borrowing) that is the lesser of

(iii) that proportion of 20% of the expense that the number of days in the year is of 365 and

(iv) the amount, if any, by which the expense exceeds the total of all amounts deductible by the taxpayer in respect of the expense in computing the taxpayer's income for a preceding taxation year,

and, for the purposes of this paragraph,

(iv.1) "excluded amount" means

(A) an amount paid or payable as or on account of the principal amount of a debt obligation or interest in respect of a debt obligation,

(B) an amount that is contingent or dependent on the use of, or production from, property, or

(C) an amount that is computed by reference to revenue, profit, cash flow, commodity price or any other similar criterion or by reference to dividends paid or payable to shareholders of any class of shares of the capital stock of a corporation,

(v) where in a taxation year all debt obligations in respect of a borrowing described in subparagraph (ii) or in respect of indebtedness described in subparagraph (ii.1) are settled or extinguished (otherwise than in a transaction made as part of a series of borrowings or other transactions and repayments), by the taxpayer for consideration that does not include any unit, interest, share or debt obligation of the taxpayer or any person with whom the taxpayer does not deal at arm's length or any partnership or trust of which the taxpayer or any person with whom the taxpayer does not deal at arm's length is a member or beneficiary, this paragraph shall be read without reference to the words "the lesser of" and to subparagraph (iii), and

(vi) where a partnership has ceased to exist at any particular time in a fiscal period of the partnership,

(A) no amount may be deducted by the partnership under this paragraph in computing its income for the period, and

(B) there may be deducted for a taxation year ending at or after that time by any person or partnership that was a member of the partnership immediately before that time, that proportion of the amount that would, but for this subparagraph, have been deductible under this paragraph by the partnership in the fiscal period ending in the year had it continued to exist and had the partnership interest not been redeemed, acquired or cancelled, that the fair market value of the member's interest in the partnership immediately before that time is of the fair market value of all the interests in the partnership immediately before that time;

Editorial Note: Effective generally after November 1999, participation payments and similar "excluded amounts" are not deductible under s. 20(1)(*e*); the provision was amended in this regard in response to the decision in *Sherway Centre Limited* (see "Cases", below).

Related Sections: S. 18(9.1) Penalties, bonuses and rate-reduction payments; s. 20(1)(*e*.1) Annual fees, etc.; s. 20(3) Borrowed money; s. 21 Cost of borrowed money; s. 53(2)(*c*) Amounts to be deducted — Interest in a partnership; s. 248(10) Series of transactions.

Canadian Petroleum Tax Journal: Canada Customs and Revenue Agency 1999 Roundtable Questions and Answers, Question 10, Vol. 13, No. 1 2000.

Canadian Tax Foundation: Ebel, *Transaction Costs*, 2005 Conference Report 35:1–27; Richardson et al., *Fundamentals of Canadian Taxation of Financial Instruments*, 1999 Conference Report 5:1–57.

Tax Profile: November 2003 — Current Cases.

Tax Topics: No. 1636, Investment Banking and Other Fees Incurred in Connection with Purchase and Sales of Shares.

Interpretation Bulletins: *Primary* — IT-341R4 Expenses of issuing or selling shares, units in a trust, interests in a partnership or syndicate and expenses of borrowing money.

Tax Window Files: Expense of Borrowing Money, *Round Table — 2004 APFF Conferences, Question 34, October 8, 2004*, CRA Document No. 2004-0087021C6. Member of a corporate group borrowed on behalf of the group and incurred costs in the course of the borrowing; a reimbursement of those costs by another member of the group deductible under subparagraph 20(1)(e)(ii); Financing Costs Incurred During Construction of Building, *Technical Interpretation, Financial Industries Division, February 24, 2004*, CRA Document No. 2004-0056861E5. Interaction of subsection 18(3.1) and paragraph 20(1)(e); Demutualization Expenses, *Technical Interpretation, Financial Industries Division, October 24, 2003*, CRA Document No. 2003-0183447; Guarantee Fee, *Technical Interpretation, Financial Industries Division, May 13, 2003*, CRA Document No. 2003-0013655. Payment made in the course of borrowing money, as consideration for a lender agreeing to charge a borrower a lower interest rate than the borrower could otherwise negotiate with another lender, could be deductible under paragraph 20(1)(e); Deductibility of Break-Up Fee, *Technical Interpretations, Financial Industries Division and Reorganizations and Resources Division, March 5, 2003*, CRA Document No. 2002-0151425; Investment Banker Fees, *Technical Interpretation, Financial Industries Division, March 4, 2003*, CRA Document No. 2002-0151485.

Cases: Financial and legal expenses incurred in defending against a hostile takeover bid were deductible under s. 20(1)(e) as expenses incurred during the eventual sale of the target corporation's shares. *BJ Services Company Canada v. The Queen*, 2004 DTC 2032 (T.C.C.)

The taxpayer entered into a series of transactions designed to create an interest deduction. Because the interest deduction artificially reduced the taxpayer's income, the interest deduction, along with the deduction of a related loan arrangement fee, were denied on the basis of the 1987 version of s. 245(1). *Novopharm Limited v. The Queen*, 2003 DTC 5195 (F.C.A.), affirming 2002 DTC 1307 (T.C.C.)

The taxpayer hired a firm of financial advisors which recommended a share for share exchange arrangement under which taxpayer's shareholders would become shareholders of a third party. The fee paid to the financial advisors was deductible under s. 18(1)(a) but there were also "respectable arguments" that it may have been deductible under s. 20(1)(e), even though it was a sale by shareholders and not by the corporation itself. *International Colin Energy Corporation v. The Queen*, 2002 DTC 2185 (T.C.C.)

In keeping with the new commercial realities, participating interest paid on the taxpayer's long-term bonds was deductible both as interest under s. 20(1)(c) and as an expense incurred in the course of borrowing money under s. 20(1)(e). *The Queen v. Sherway Centre Limited*, 98 DTC 6121 (F.C.A.), affirming 96 DTC 1640 (T.C.C.)

A company which was required under a loan agreement to pay 1% of its gross rental income from its new office building for 25 years to the company that had helped to finance the project was entitled to deduct these payments from its income. *M.N.R. v. Yonge-Eglinton Building Ltd.*, 74 DTC 6180 (F.C.A.), affirming 72 DTC 6465 (F.C.T.D.).

► 20(1)(e.1) ◄

(e.1) Annual fees, etc. — an amount payable by the taxpayer (other than a payment that is contingent or dependent on the use of, or production from, property or is computed by reference to revenue, profit, cash flow, commodity price or any other similar criterion or by reference to dividends paid or payable to shareholders of any class of shares of the capital stock of a corporation) as a standby charge, guarantee fee, registrar fee, transfer agent fee, filing fee, service fee or any similar fee, that can reasonably be considered to relate solely to the year and that is incurred by the taxpayer

(i) for the purpose of borrowing money to be used by the taxpayer for the purpose of earning income from a business or property (other than borrowed money used by the taxpayer for the purpose of acquiring property the income from which would be exempt income),

(ii) in the course of incurring indebtedness that is an amount payable for property acquired for the purpose of gaining or producing income therefrom or for the purpose of gaining or producing income from a business (other than property the income from which would be exempt income or property that is an interest in a life insurance policy), or

(iii) for the purpose of rescheduling or restructuring a debt obligation of the taxpayer or an assumption of a debt obligation by the taxpayer, where the debt obligation is

(A) in respect of a borrowing described in subparagraph (i), or

(B) in respect of an amount payable described in subparagraph (ii),

and, in the case of a rescheduling or restructuring, the rescheduling or restructuring, as the case may be, provides for the modification of the terms or conditions of the debt obligation or the conversion or substitution of the debt obligation to or with a share or another debt obligation.

Related Sections: S. 20(3) Borrowed money.

Interpretation Bulletins: *Primary* — IT-341R4 Expenses of issuing or selling shares, units in a trust, interests in a partnership or syndicate, and expenses of borrowing money.

► 20(1)(e.2) ◄

(e.2) Premiums on life insurance used as collateral — the least of the following amounts in respect of a life insurance policy (other than an annuity contract or LIA policy):

(i) the premiums payable by the taxpayer under the policy in respect of the year, if

(A) an interest in the policy is assigned to a restricted financial institution in the course of a borrowing from the institution,

(B) the interest payable in respect of the borrowing is or would, but for subsections 18(2) and (3.1) and sections 21 and 28, be deductible in computing the taxpayer's income for the year, and

(C) the assignment referred to in clause (A) is required by the institution as collateral for the borrowing,

(ii) the net cost of pure insurance in respect of the year (other than in respect of a period after 2013 during which the policy is a 10/8 policy), as determined in accordance with the regulations, in respect of the interest in the policy referred to in clause (i)(A), and

(iii) the portion, of the lesser of the amounts determined under subparagraphs (i) and (ii) in respect of the policy, that can reasonably be considered to relate to the amount owing from time to time during the year by the taxpayer to the institution under the borrowing;

Editorial Note: Paragraph 20(1)(e.2) permits the deduction of life insurance premiums paid under a life insurance policy which has been assigned as collateral for a loan. It is not necessary that the person claiming the deduction under s. 20(1)(e.2) be the person whose life is insured under the policy. Thus, for example, a corporation with a life insurance policy on the life of one of its executives may claim the deduction.

History: S. 20(1)(e.2), the portion before clause (i)(A) was replaced by S.C. 2013, c. 40, s. 11(1), applicable to taxation years that end after March 20, 2013, and formerly read:

(e.2) *Premiums on life insurance — collateral* — such portion of the lesser of

(i) the premiums payable by the taxpayer under a life insurance policy (other than an annuity contract) in respect of the year, where

S. 20(1)(e.2), the portion after clause (i)(C) was replaced by S.C. 2013, c. 40, s. 11(2), applicable to taxation years that end after March 20, 2013, and formerly read:

(ii) the net cost of pure insurance in respect of the year, as determined in accordance with the regulations, in respect of the interest in the policy referred to in clause (i)(A),

as can reasonably be considered to relate to the amount owing from time to time during the year by the taxpayer to the institution under the borrowing;

Related Regulations: 308(1), 308(1.1).

Tax Profile: January 2010 — Shareholders' Agreements — A Survey of Income Tax Issues; September 2004 — Review of Tax Implications of Corporate-Owned Life Insurance Buy-Sell Arrangements.

Tax Topics: No. 1681, Life Insurance: Exploring the Corporate Edge — Part I.

Interpretation Bulletins: *Primary* — IT-309R2 Premiums on life insurance used as collateral. *Secondary* — IT-341R4 Expenses of issuing or selling shares, units in a trust, interests in a partnership or syndicate, and expenses of borrowing money.

Tax Window Files: Deductibility of Life Insurance and Disability Insurance Premiums — Loan Collateral, *Technical Interpretation, Business and Partnerships Division, March 31, 2005*, CRA Document No. 2004-0093651E5.

Cases: Life insurance premiums may be deducted where an interest in a life insurance policy is assigned to a lending institution in the context of a borrowing transaction, the assignment is required by the lending institution as collateral, and interest on the loan is otherwise deductible to the borrower. A deduction is allowed for the lesser of the premiums actually paid and the "net cost of pure insurance". *Emjo Holdings Ltd. v. The Queen*, 2018 DTC 1076 (TCC)

► 20(1)(f) ◄

(f) Discount on certain obligations — an amount paid in the year in satisfaction of the principal amount of any bond, debenture, bill, note, mortgage, hypothecary claim or similar obligation issued by the taxpayer after June 18, 1971 on which interest was stipulated to be payable, to the extent that the amount so paid does not exceed,

(i) in any case where the obligation was issued for an amount not less than 97% of its principal amount, and the yield from the obligation, expressed in terms of an annual rate on the amount for which the obligation was issued (which annual rate shall, if the terms of the obligation or any agreement relating thereto conferred on its holder a right to demand payment of the principal amount of the obligation or the amount outstanding as or on account of its principal amount, as the case may be, before the maturity of the obligation, be calculated on the basis of the yield that produces the highest annual rate obtainable either on the maturity of the obligation or conditional on the exercise of any such right) does not exceed $4/3$ of the interest stipulated to be payable on the obligation, expressed in terms of an annual rate on

(A) the principal amount of the obligation, if no amount is payable on account of the principal amount before the maturity of the obligation, or

(B) the amount outstanding from time to time as or on account of the principal amount of the obligation, in any other case,

the amount by which the lesser of the principal amount of the obligation and all amounts paid in the year or in any preceding year in satisfaction of its principal amount exceeds the amount for which the obligation was issued, and

(ii) in any other case, $1/2$ of the lesser of the amount so paid and the amount by which the lesser of the principal amount of the obligation and all amounts paid in the year or in any preceding taxation year in satisfaction of its principal amount exceeds the amount for which the obligation was issued;

Editorial Note: S. 20(1)(*f*) only applies if the discount is part of the principal amount of the debt obligation, so that it does not apply, for example, to a discount that is considered interest. At the 2009 Canadian Tax Foundation's Annual Conference, the CRA announced that it was reversing its long-standing position that previously allowed a deduction under s. 20(1)(*f*) upon the issuance or transfer of shares by a corporate taxpayer on the conversion or exchange of a convertible or exchangeable debenture issued by the taxpayer (i.e., where the fair market value of the shares exceeded the amount for which the debenture was issued). Effective for debentures issued on or after January 1, 2010, the CRA will not allow a deduction under s. 20(1)(*f*) in such circumstances. See also *Tembec Inc. et al. v. The Queen*, 2008 DTC 3232 (T.C.C.), affirmed 2009 DTC 5089 (F.C.A.).

Related Sections: S. 18(1)(*f*) Payments on discounted bonds; s. 18(11) Borrowed money used for contribution; s. 110.6(1) Definitions — fair market value of NISA; s. 127.52(1) Adjusted taxable income determined.

Canadian Tax Foundation: McBean, *Current Cases: Foreign Exchange Losses: No win for Imperial Oil and Inco at the Supreme Court of Canada*, 2006 Canadian Tax Journal 4:922–928; Spiro et al., *Legislative, Administrative, and Judicial Developments: Current Cases — Foreign Exchange Losses (Imperial Oil and Inco)*, 2005 Conference Report 5:6–9; Weekes, *Recent Developments Regarding Interest Deductibility*, 2005 Prairie Provinces Tax Conference 3:1–17; Mitchell, *Current Cases: You Can't Get There From Here (Imperial Oil Limited v. The Queen, 2004 TCC 207)*, 2004 Canadian Tax Journal 2:570–573; Quo Vadis, *Recent Cases of Significance*, 2004 British Columbia Tax Conference 5:1–21; Kopstein and Pantry, *Foreign Exchange Issues*, 2003 Conference Report 27:1–54; Kopstein and Pantry, *Foreign Exchange Issues*, 2003 British Columbia Tax Conference 3:1–88.

Tax Topics: No. 1971-72, 2009 Canadian Tax Foundation Conference: Wizards, Tiny Taxes and "Evil" Kirk; No. 1826, Recognition of FX Gains and Losses in Doubt After Supreme Court Decision; No. 1814, 2006 Canadian Tax Foundation Annual Conference CRA Round Table; No. 1808, Supreme Court Rules FX Losses Not Deductible as "Discounts"; No. 1683, *Imperial Oil Limited v. The Queen*.

Income Tax Folios: *Secondary* — S3-F6-C1 Interest Deductibility.

Income Tax Technical News: Issue No. 44, Exchangeable Debentures: Paragraph 20(1)(f); Issue No. 44, Convertible Debentures: Paragraph 20(1)(f); Issue No. 41, Exchangeable Debentures — Paragraph 20(1)(f); Issue No. 25, Foreign Exchange Losses.

Interpretation Bulletins: *Secondary* — IT-341R4 Expenses of issuing or selling shares, units in a trust, interests in a partnership or syndicate, and expenses of borrowing money.

Cases: The taxpayer issued convertible debentures with a conversion rate of $10/share. They were not issued at a discount. Most of the debentures were later converted into shares with a market value of $13 to $14. The taxpayer could not claim a s. 20(1)(*f*) deduction for the difference between the market value of the shares issued on the conversion date and the amount received for the debentures on the issuance date. *Provigo Inc. et al. v. The Queen*, 2008 DTC 6601 (F.C.A.), affirming 2008 DTC 3232 (T.C.C.)

The taxpayers redeemed U.S. dollar debentures which had been issued at a discount. Foreign exchange losses incurred on the redemption were not deductible under s. 20(1)(*f*) and could only be claimed as a capital loss under s. 39. *The Queen v. Imperial Oil Limited and Inco Limited*, 2006 DTC 6639 (S.C.C.), reversing 2004 DTC 6702 (F.C.A.) and affirming 2004 DTC 2377 (T.C.C.) re *Imperial Oil*, and reversing 2005 DTC 5109 (F.C.A.) and affirming 2004 DTC 3586 (T.C.C.) re *Inco*.

► 20(1)(g) ◄

(g) Share transfer and other fees — where the taxpayer is a corporation,

(i) an amount payable in the year as a fee for services rendered by a person as a registrar of or agent for the transfer of shares of the capital stock of the taxpayer or as an agent for the remittance to shareholders of the taxpayer of dividends declared by it,

(ii) an amount payable in the year as a fee to a stock exchange for the listing of shares of the capital stock of the taxpayer, and

(iii) an expense incurred in the year in the course of printing and issuing a financial report to shareholders of the taxpayer or to any other person entitled by law to receive the report;

► 20(1)(h) ◄

(h) Certification fee paid to a bank — (Repealed by 1984, c. 45, s. 10(1).)

► 20(1)(i) ◄

(i) Sale of bill — (Repealed by 1984, c. 45, s. 10(1).)

► 20(1)(j) ◄

(j) Repayment of loan by shareholder — such part of any loan or indebtedness repaid by the taxpayer in the year as was by virtue of subsection 15(2) included in computing the taxpayer's income for a preceding taxation year (except to the extent that the amount of the loan or indebtedness was deductible from the taxpayer's income for the purpose of computing the taxpayer's taxable income for that preceding taxation year), if it is established by subsequent events or otherwise that the repayment was not made as part of a series of loans or other transactions and repayments;

Editorial Note: *Bona fide* repayments of shareholder loans that result from the payment of dividends, salaries, or bonuses are not considered part of a series of loans or other transactions and repayments; see paragraphs 29 and 31 of Interpretation Bulletin IT-119R4 (archived, as it doesn't meet current government web standards).

Related Sections: S. 248(10) Series of transactions.

Interpretation Bulletins: *Secondary* — IT-119R4 Debts of shareholders and certain persons connected with shareholders.

► 20(1)(k) ◄

(k) Combined income and capital — (Repealed by 1988, c. 55, s. 12(4).)

► 20(1)(l) ◄

(l) Doubtful or impaired debts — a reserve determined as the total of

(i) a reasonable amount in respect of doubtful debts (other than a debt to which subparagraph (ii) applies) that have been included in computing the taxpayer's income for the year or a preceding taxation year, and

(ii) where the taxpayer is a financial institution (as defined in subsection 142.2(1)) in the year or a taxpayer whose ordinary business includes the lending of money, an amount in respect of properties (other than mark-to-market properties, as defined in that subsection) that are

(A) impaired loans or lending assets that are specified debt obligations (as defined in that subsection) of the taxpayer, or

(B) impaired loans or lending assets that were made or acquired by the taxpayer in the ordinary course of the taxpayer's business of insurance or the lending of money

equal to the total of

(C) the percentage (not exceeding 100%) that the taxpayer claims of the prescribed reserve amount for the taxpayer for the year, and

(D) in respect of loans, lending assets or specified debt obligations that are impaired and for which an amount is not deductible for the year because of clause (C) (each of which in this clause is referred to as a "loan"), the taxpayer's specified percentage for the year of the lesser of

(I) the total of all amounts each of which is a reasonable amount as a reserve (other than any portion of which is in respect of a sectoral reserve) for a loan in respect of the amortized cost of the loan to the taxpayer at the end of the year, and

(II) the amount determined by the formula

$$0.9M - N$$

where

M is the amount that is the taxpayer's reserve or allowance for impairment (other than any portion of the amount that is in respect of a sectoral reserve) for all loans that is determined for the year in accordance with generally accepted accounting principles, and

N is the total of all amounts each of which is the specified reserve adjustment for a loan (other than an income bond, an income debenture, a small business bond or small business development bond) for the year or a preceding taxation year;

Editorial Note: The amount claimed as a doubtful or impaired debt reserve is included in income in the following taxation year under s. 12(1)(*d*), and a reserve may be claimed in that following year if the debt remains doubtful or impaired. If a doubtful debt becomes a bad debt, a final deduction is allowed under s. 20(1)(*p*), subject to any subsequent recovery and inclusion of the debt under s. 12(1)(*i*).

Related Regulations: 8000; 8002; 8003; 8005; 8006.

Related Sections: S. 12(1)(*d*) Reserve for doubtful debts; s. 20(27) Loans, etc., acquired in ordinary course of business; s. 22(1) Sale of accounts receivable; s. 79 Surrender of property by debtor; s. 87(2)(*h*) Debts; s. 138(5) Deductions not allowed; and ITAR s. 23(5) Definitions.

Forms: T2 SCH 13 — Continuity of Reserves.

Interpretation Bulletins: *Primary* — IT-442R Bad debts and reserves for doubtful debts. *Secondary* — IT-291R3 Transfer of property to a corporation under subsection 85(1).

Cases: The taxpayer sold a building and claimed a reserve for doubtful accounts based on the assumption that the security he held for payment of the purchase price had deteriorated in value. The reserve could not be deducted because the taxpayer had not included amounts payable under the contract of sale in his income. Also, there had been no objective basis supporting the taxpayer's calculation of the reserve amount. *Langdon v. The Queen*, 2000 DTC 6203 (F.C.A.), affirming 98 DTC 1690 (T.C.C.)

A taxpayer claimed a reserve of $3,084,000 for doubtful debts, using the same generally accepted accounting principles it used for calculating doubtful accounts for financial statements. This method was accepted but the reserve was reduced to $2,921,000. *The Queen v. Coppley Noyes & Randall Ltd.*, 93 DTC 5196 (F.C.A.), reversing 91 DTC 5291 (F.C.T.D.).

► 20(1)(l.1) ◄

(l.1) Reserve for guarantees, etc. — a reserve in respect of credit risks under guarantees, indemnities, letters of credit or other credit facilities, bankers' acceptances, interest rate or currency swaps, foreign exchange or other future or option contracts, interest rate protection agreements, risk participations and other similar instruments or commitments issued, made or assumed by a taxpayer who was an insurer or whose ordinary business included the lending of money in favour of persons with whom the taxpayer deals at arm's length in the ordinary course of the taxpayer's business of insurance or the lending of money, equal to the lesser of

(i) a reasonable amount as a reserve for credit risk losses of the taxpayer expected to arise after the end of the year under or in respect of those instruments or commitments, and

(ii) 90% of the reserve for credit risk losses of the taxpayer expected to arise after the end of the year under or in respect of those instruments or commitments determined for the year in accordance with generally accepted accounting principles,

or such lesser amount as the taxpayer may claim;

Related Sections: S. 12(1)(*d.1*) Reserve for guarantees, etc.; s. 20(27) Loans, etc., acquired in ordinary course of business; s. 87(2)(*h*) Debts.

Forms: T2 SCH 13 — Continuity of Reserves.

Cases: The taxpayer sold a building and claimed a reserve for doubtful accounts based on the assumption that the security he held for payment of the purchase price had deteriorated in value. The reserve could not be deducted because the taxpayer had not included amounts payable under the contract of sale in his income. Also, there had been no objective basis supporting the taxpayer's calculation of the reserve amount. *Langdon v. The Queen*, 2000 DTC 6203 (F.C.A.), affirming 98 DTC 1690 (T.C.C.).

► 20(1)(m) ◄

(m) Reserve in respect of certain goods and services — subject to subsection (6), where amounts described in paragraph 12(1)(*a*) have been included in computing the taxpayer's income from a business for the year or a previous year, a reasonable amount as a reserve in respect of

(i) goods that it is reasonably anticipated will have to be delivered after the end of the year,

(ii) services that it is reasonably anticipated will have to be rendered after the end of the year,

(iii) periods for which rent or other amounts for the possession or use of land or of chattels or movables have been paid in advance, or

(iv) repayments under arrangements or understandings of the class described in subparagraph 12(1)(*a*)(ii) that it is reasonably anticipated will have to be made after the end of the year on the return or resale to the taxpayer of articles other than bottles;

Editorial Note: The s. 20(1)(*m*) reserve does not apply to receipts of prepaid rent that is (or will be) income from property, nor does it apply to receipts of prepaid interest or prepayments for the sale of land (land is apparently not a "good"). However, in the past, the CRA has indicated that the inclusion of prepaid rent that is income from property can be deferred to the year to which it relates, in accordance with financial accounting principles; see Interpretation Bulletin IT-261R (archived, as it doesn't meet current government web standards). The *Ellis Vision* decision (2004 DTC 2024 (T.C.C.)) (see "Cases", below) indicates that the reserve can apply to amounts included under s. 9 profit, as long as they are amounts described in s. 12(1)(*a*); see also the *Doteasy Technology* case (2009 DTC 1187).

History: S. 20(1)(*m*)(iii) was replaced by S.C. 2013, c. 34, s. 97(1), in force June 26, 2013, and formerly read:

(iii) periods for which rent or other amounts for the possession or use of land or chattels have been paid in advance, or

Related Sections: S. 12(1)(*e*) Reserves for certain goods and services, etc.; s. 20(7) Where para. (1)(m) does not apply; s. 20(24) Amounts paid for undertaking future obligations; s. 32(1) Insurance agents and brokers; s. 34 Professional business; s. 87(2)(*j*) Special reserves.

Canadian Tax Foundation: Frankovic, *The Taxation of Prepaid Income*, 2002 Canadian Tax Journal 4:1239–1298.

Tax Profile: November 2004 — New Restrictions Repeal Patronage Deduction for Canadian Corporations; November 2003 — Revenue Canada Round Table.

Tax Topics: No. 1700, 2004 Canadian Tax Foundation Conference - CRA Round Table; No. 1598, Prepayments and the "Quality of Income".

Forms: T2 SCH 13 — Continuity of Reserves.

Income Tax Technical News: Issue No. 32, Reserve for Prepaid Amount: Impact of the Ellis Vision Case.

Interpretation Bulletins: *Primary* — IT-154R Special reserves. *Secondary* — IT-92R2 Income of contractors; IT-261R Prepayments of rents.

Tax Window Files: Taxation of insurance contract commission income, *August 20, 2015*, CRA Document No. 2015-0588871E5; Site Reclamation Costs, *Technical Interpretation, Reorganizations and Resources Division, September 27, 2004*, CRA Document No. 2003-0048241E5. A reserve may be claimed where a taxpayer has received a specifically identifiable amount in respect of the future reclamation costs which it is obligated to incur and the amount is included in the taxpayer's income under paragraph 12(1)(*a*); Software Maintenance Agreements, *Technical Interpretation, Business and Partnerships Division, October 7, 2003*, CRA Document No. 2003-0037947. Reserve allowed for portion of payments made under computer software maintenance agreement, based on elements of maintenance plan not in the nature of an indemnity.

Cases: Licence fees received in advance for the future use of television productions were eligible for a s. 20(1)(*m*) reserve. The reference to "amounts described in paragraph 12(1)(*a*)" does not mean only amounts that were included in income *by virtue of* s. 12(1)(*a*). *Ellis Vision Incorporated v. The Queen*, 2004 DTC 2024 (T.C.C.)

Revenue from the sale of season passes to a recreational facility was included in income but the taxpayer could claim a reserve in respect of services to be rendered after the end of the year. Since the services would all be rendered after October 31, it was reasonable that the entire amount should be deductible as a reserve. *Blue Mountain Resorts Limited v. The Queen*, 2002 DTC 1886 (T.C.C.)

A waste disposal company was required to perform various tasks associated with reconstituting dump sites for thirty years following the closing thereof. A portion of the fees charged by the taxpayer was intended to meet those future costs. This amount was deductible as a reserve since it was not "earned" in the year it was received. *Deputy Minister of Revenue for Quebec v. La Compagnie Meloche Inc.*, 2002 DTC 7169 (Que. C.A.)

The taxpayer operated a club and charged its new members an initiation fee which was amortized over 10 years. There was no basis for the amortization since the initiation fees were earned in the year of receipt. The taxpayer had, in effect, deducted a reserve under s. 20(1)(*m*). However, it would be a gross distortion of the taxpayer's income picture if the entire balance of its "Deferred Initiation Fees" account were to be taxed in one year under s. 12(1)(*e*). *Argus Holdings Limited v. The Queen*, 2000 DTC 6681 (F.C.A.), reversing 99 DTC 597 (T.C.C.)

Progress payments received by the taxpayer for the construction of ships had the quality of income when received. Because these amounts were earned, the taxpayer was not entitled to claim a reserve on them. *Burrard Yarrows Corporation v. The Queen*, 88 DTC 6352 (F.C.A.), affirming (F.C.T.D.) 86 DTC 6459.

► 20(1)(m.1) ◄

(m.1) Manufacturer's warranty reserve — where an amount described in paragraph 12(1)(*a*) has been included in computing the taxpayer's income from a business for the year or a preceding taxation year, a reasonable amount as a reserve in respect of goods or services that it is reasonably anticipated will have to be delivered or rendered after the end of the year pursuant to an agreement for an extended warranty

(i) entered into by the taxpayer with a person with whom the taxpayer was dealing at arm's length, and

(ii) under which the only obligation of the taxpayer is to provide those goods or services with respect to property manufactured by the taxpayer or by a corporation related to the taxpayer,

not exceeding that portion of the amount paid or payable by the taxpayer to an insurer that carries on an insurance business in Canada to insure the taxpayer's liability under the agreement in respect of an outlay or expense made or incurred after December 11, 1979 and in respect of the period after the end of the year;

Editorial Note: Any reserve taken under s. 20(1)(*m*), (*m*.1), or (*n*) in one year must be added to income in the next year under s. 12(1)(*e*), subject to the taxpayer's right to claim a further reserve if permissible.

Forms: T2 SCH 13 — Continuity of Reserves.

Interpretation Bulletins: *Primary* — IT-154R Special reserves.

► 20(1)(m.2) ◄

(m.2) Repayment of amount previously included in income — a repayment in the year by the taxpayer of an amount required by paragraph 12(1)(*a*) to be included in computing the taxpayer's income from a business for the year or a preceding taxation year;

Editorial Note: Paragraph 20(1)(*m*.2) provides a deduction (as opposed to a reserve, which is brought back into income later) when a taxpayer repays an amount that was brought into income under s. 12(1)(*a*).

Interpretation Bulletins: *Primary* — IT-154R Special reserves.

► 20(1)(m.3) ◄

(m.3) [Reserve for bond premiums] — the unamortized amount at the end of the year in respect of the amount that was received in excess of the principal amount of a bond (in this paragraph referred to as the "premium") received by the issuer in the year, or a previous year, for issuing the bond (in this paragraph referred to as the "new bond") if

(i) the terms of the new bond are identical to the terms of bonds previously issued by the taxpayer (in this paragraph referred to as the "old bonds"), except for the date of issuance and total principal amount of the bonds,

(ii) the old bonds were part of an issuance (in this paragraph referred to as the "original issuance") of bonds by the taxpayer,

(iii) the interest rate on the old bonds was reasonable at the time of the original issuance,

(iv) the new bond is issued on the re-opening of the original issuance,

(v) the amount of the premium at the time of issuance of the new bond is reasonable, and

(vi) the amount of the premium has been included in the taxpayer's income for the year or a previous taxation year;

Editorial Note: Paragraph 20(1)(*m*.3) is relevant when a corporation or other taxpayer issues a "new bond" on the re-opening of a previous issuance of an "old bond". Typically, the interest rate on the new bond will not reflect the relevant market rate at the re-opening. Rather, the rate on the new bond will typically be the same as the rate under the old bond. If the new bond rate is higher than the relevant market interest rate at the time of the re-opening, the issuing taxpayer will typically receive a premium. Under general principles, it appears that the premium is included in the taxpayer's income. Paragraph 20(1)(*m*.3) allows a deduction in a taxation year in respect of the premium received in these circumstances. The deduction is equal to the unamortized amount of the premium at the end of the year. More particularly, the provision refers to the unamortized amount at the end of the year in respect of the amount received by the taxpayer on the issuance of the new bond in the year or a previous year in excess of its principal amount of the new bond (such amount referred to as the "premium").

The amount deducted in one year is added back into income in the following year under subsection 12(1)(*d*.2). An additional deduction is allowed in the following year if there is a remaining unamortized amount in respect of the premium.

History: S. 20(1)(*m*.3) was added by S.C. 2017, c. 33, s. 6(1), applicable in respect of bonds issued after 2000.

Related Sections: 12(1)(d.2) [Reserve for bond premiums].

12(1)(d.2) [Reserve for bond premiums].

► 20(1)(n) ◄

(n) Reserve for unpaid amounts — if an amount included in computing the taxpayer's income from the business for the year or for a preceding taxation year in respect of property sold in the course of the business is payable to the taxpayer after the end of the year and, except where the property is real or immovable property, all or part of the amount was, at the time of the sale, not due until at least two years after that time, a reasonable amount as a reserve in respect of any part of the amount that can reasonably be regarded as a portion of the profit from the sale;

Editorial Note: By virtue of s. 20(8), the reserve under s. 20(1)(*n*) is generally not available after the second taxation year following the year of sale (more particularly, it is not allowed in a year if the sale occurred more than 36 months before the end of the year).

History: S. 20(1)(*n*) was replaced by S.C. 2013, c. 34, s. 97(2), in force June 26, 2013, and formerly read:

> (*n*) *Reserve for unpaid amounts* — where an amount included in computing the taxpayer's income from the business for the year or for a preceding taxation year in respect of property sold in the course of the business is payable to the taxpayer after the end of the year and, except where the property is real property, all or part of the amount was, at the time of the sale, not due until at least 2 years after that time, a reasonable amount as a reserve in respect of such part of the amount as can reasonably be regarded as a portion of the profit from the sale;

Related Sections: S. 12(1)(*e*) Reserves for certain goods and services, etc.; s. 20(8) No deduction in respect of property in certain circumstances; s. 66.2(2) Deduction for cumulative Canadian development expenses; s. 66.4(2) Deduction for cumulative Canadian oil and gas property expense; s. 72 Reserves, etc., for year of death; s. 79 Surrender of property by debtor; s. 87(2)(*i*) Special reserve.

Tax Profile: August 2012 — U.S. Purchases and Sales of Canadian Businesses: Tax and Corporate Issues.

Forms: T2 SCH 13 — Continuity of Reserves; T2069 — Election in Respect of Amounts Not Deductible as Reserves for the Year of Death.

Information Circulars: IC 88-2 General anti-avoidance rule — Section 245 of the Income Tax Act.

Interpretation Bulletins: *Primary* — IT-152R3 Special reserves — Sale of land; IT-154R Special reserves; IT-436R Reserves — Where promissory notes are included in disposal proceeds.

Tax Window Files: Continuity of Reserves on Dissolution of Partnership, *Technical Interpretation, Business and Partnerships Division, November 20, 2003*, CRA Document No. 2003-0033545. Where partnership dissolves, reserves formerly claimed under 20(1)(*m*) and (*n*) can continue to be claimed by sole proprietor to whom subsection 98(5) applies.

► 20(1)(o) ◄

(o) Reserve for quadrennial survey — such amount as may be prescribed as a reserve for expenses to be incurred by the taxpayer by reason of quadrennial or other special surveys required under the *Canada Shipping Act*, or the regulations under that Act, or under the rules of any society or association for the classification and registry of shipping approved by the Minister of Transport for the purposes of the *Canada Shipping Act*;

Related Regulations: 3600.

Related Sections: S. 12(1)(*h*) Previous reserve for quadrennial survey.

Forms: T2 SCH 13 — Continuity of Reserves.

► 20(1)(p) ◄

(p) Bad debts — the total of

(i) all debts owing to the taxpayer that are established by the taxpayer to have become bad debts in the year and that have been included in computing the taxpayer's income for the year or a preceding taxation year, and

(ii) all amounts each of which is that part of the amortized cost to the taxpayer at the end of the year of a loan or lending asset (other than a mark-to-market property, as defined in subsection 142.2(1)) that is established in the year by the taxpayer to have become uncollectible and that,

(A) where the taxpayer is an insurer or a taxpayer whose ordinary business includes the lending of money, was made or acquired in the ordinary course of the taxpayer's business of insurance or the lending of money, or

(B) where the taxpayer is a financial institution (as defined in subsection 142.2(1)) in the year, is a specified debt obligation (as defined in that subsection) of the taxpayer;

Editorial Note: Bad debts that are subsequently recovered are included in income under s. 12(1)(*i*).

Related Sections: S. 12(1)(*i*) Bad debts recovered; s. 20(27) Loans, etc., acquired in ordinary course of business; s. 22(1) Sale of accounts receivable; s. 79 Surrender of property by debtor; s. 87(2)(*g*) Reserves; s. 87(2)(*h*) Debts.

Canadian Tax Foundation: Cepparo, *No ABIL for Loans to Canco*, 2015 Canadian Tax Highlights 23(2):3.

Interpretation Bulletins: *Primary* — IT-442R Bad debts and reserves for doubtful debts. *Secondary* — IT-123R6 Transactions involving eligible capital property; IT-159R3 Capital debts established to be bad debts; IT-291R3 Transfer of property to a corporation under subsection 85(1).

Cases: The taxpayers failed to make an honest and reasonable assessment that the debts had become bad; past and present circumstances as well as future prospects were all major considerations. *Coveley v. The Queen*, 2015 DTC 5014 (F.C.A.), affirming 2014 DTC 1041 (T.C.C.)

The amount owing on a promissory note had previously been included in the taxpayer's income as a deemed dividend. Therefore, since it was deemed to have been paid and received, it was not deductible as a bad debt. *Mills Estate v. The Queen*, 2011 DTC 5124 (F.C.A.), affirming 2010 DTC 1301 (T.C.C.)

Loans made by the taxpayer were made in the ordinary course of a moneylending business and associated bad debts were deductible. The taxpayer typically lent money for terms of two to three years and he kept track of interest payment due dates and outstanding balances, so that there was a "continuity or system" in his lending activities. He had even purchased certain bonds in the course of the carrying on of that business. *Langhammer v. The Queen*, 2001 DTC 45 (T.C.C.)

The taxpayer advanced funds to a related corporation and the loan later became uncollectible. Although the advance was clearly a loan, the taxpayer was not entitled to bad debt deductions because the taxpayer was not in the money-lending business and the loan was not made as part of the taxpayer's ordinary business. *Loman Warehousing Ltd. v. The Queen*, 2000 DTC 6610 (F.C.A.), affirming 99 DTC 1113 (T.C.C.)

The taxpayer supplied the labour of its own employees to a related corporation but recorded the accounts receivable as a reduction of its own expenses, rather than as revenue from the supply of services. The related company later became insolvent and the taxpayer treated the amounts owing as bad debts. Although the taxpayer's accounting records did not show that the amounts had been included in the taxpayer's income prior to the deduction, they were no less revenue just because they were improperly recorded. Therefore the bad debts deduction was allowed. *Williams Gold Refining Co. of Canada Limited v. The Queen*, 2000 DTC 1829 (T.C.C.).

► 20(1)(q) ◄

(q) Employer's contributions to RPP or PRPP — such amount in respect of employer contributions to registered pension plans or pooled registered pension plans as is permitted under subsection 147.2(1) or 147.5(10);

Editorial Note: Paragraph 20(1)(*q*), in conjunction with subsection 147.5(10), also allows an employer to deduct its contributions to a pooled registered pension plan (PRPP). The employer's contributions to the PRPP in respect of an employee in a taxation year reduce the employee's RRSP deduction room for that year under paragraph 146(5)(*b*).

History: S. 20(1)(*q*) was replaced by S.C. 2012, c. 31, s. 8(1), in force December 14, 2012. S. 20(1)(*q*) formerly read:

> (*q*) *Employer's contributions to registered pension plan* — such amount in respect of employer contributions to registered pension plans as is permitted by subsection 147.2(1);

Related Regulations: Part XXVII.

Related Sections: S. 146(5) Amount of RRSP premiums deductible; s. 147(8) Amount of employer's contribution deductible.

Forms: T2 SCH 15 — Deferred Income Plans.

Information Circulars: IC 72-13R8 Employees' pension plans.

► 20(1)(r) ◄

(r) Employer's contributions under retirement compensation arrangement — amounts paid by the taxpayer in the year as contributions under a retirement compensation arrangement in respect of services rendered by an employee or former employee of the taxpayer, other than where it is established, by subsequent events or otherwise, that the amounts were paid as part of a series of payments and refunds of contributions under the arrangement;

Related Sections: S. 248(1), "retirement compensation arrangement".

Canadian Tax Foundation: Kahane et al., *A Fresh Look at Retirement Compensation Arrangements: A Flexible Vehicle for Retirement Planning*, 2013 Canadian Tax Journal 2:479–502.

Tax Profile: May 2012 — Retirement Compensation Arrangements; December 2010 — RCAs Under Attack; September 2010 — RCAs Under Attack.

Forms: T737-RCA — Statement of Contributions Paid to a Custodian of a Retirement Compensation Arrangement (RCA).

Guides: T4041 Retirement Compensation Arrangements Guide.

► 20(1)(s) ◄

(s) Employer's contributions under employee life and health trust — such amount in respect of employer contributions paid to a trustee under an employee life and health trust as is permitted by subsections 144.1(4) to (7);

History: S. 20(1)(*s*) was added by S.C. 2010, c. 25, s. 6(1), applicable after 2009.

► 20(1)(t) ◄

(t) Scientific research and experimental development — (Repealed by 1988, c. 55, s. 12(7).)

► 20(1)(u) ◄

(u) Patronage dividends — such amounts in respect of payments made by the taxpayer pursuant to allocations in proportion to patronage as are permitted by section 135;

Related Regulations: 219.

▶ 20(1)(v) ◀

(v) Mining taxes — such amount as is allowed by regulation in respect of taxes on income for the year from mining operations;

Related Regulations: 3900.

▶ 20(1)(v.1) ◀

(v.1) Resource allowance — (Repealed by S.C. 2003, c. 28, s. 3(1).)

▶ 20(1)(w) ◀

(w) Employer's contributions under profit sharing plan — an amount paid by the taxpayer to a trustee in trust for employees of the taxpayer or of a corporation with whom the taxpayer does not deal at arm's length, under an employees profit sharing plan as permitted by section 144;

Forms: T2 SCH 15 — Deferred Income Plans.

▶ 20(1)(x) ◀

(x) Employer's contributions under registered supplementary unemployment benefit plan — an amount paid by the taxpayer to a trustee under a registered supplementary unemployment benefit plan as permitted by section 145;

Forms: T2 SCH 15 — Deferred Income Plans.

▶ 20(1)(y) ◀

(y) Employer's contributions under deferred profit sharing plan — an amount paid by the taxpayer to a trustee under a deferred profit sharing plan as permitted by subsection 147(8);

Forms: T2 SCH 15 — Deferred Income Plans.

▶ 20(1)(z) ◀

(z) Cancellation of lease — the proportion of an amount not otherwise deductible that was paid or that became payable by the taxpayer before the end of the year to a person for the cancellation of a lease of property of the taxpayer leased by the taxpayer to that person that

(i) the number of days that remained in the term of the lease (including all renewal periods of the lease), not exceeding 40 years, immediately before its cancellation and that were in the year

is of

(ii) the number of days that remained in the term of the lease (including all renewal periods of the lease), not exceeding 40 years, immediately before its cancellation,

in any case where the property was owned at the end of the year by the taxpayer or by a person with whom the taxpayer was not dealing at arm's length and no part of the amount was deductible by the taxpayer under paragraph (z.1) in computing the taxpayer's income for a preceding taxation year;

Editorial Note: By virtue of s. 18(1)(*q*), no deduction is allowed for a lease cancellation payment made by a lessor except as provided under s. 20(1)(*z*) or (z.1).

Tax Profile: March 2002 — Selected Tax Issues for Commercial Landlords and Tenants.

Tax Topics: No. 1677, Income Tax Implications of Lease Cancellation Payments.

Interpretation Bulletins: *Secondary* — IT-359R2 Premiums and other amounts with respect to leases; IT-467R2 Damages, settlements and similar payments.

▶ 20(1)(z.1) ◀

(z.1) Idem — an amount not otherwise deductible that was paid or that became payable by the taxpayer before the end of the year to a person for the cancellation of a lease of property of the taxpayer leased by the taxpayer to that person, in any case where

(i) the property was not owned at the end of the year by the taxpayer or by a person with whom the taxpayer was not dealing at arm's length, and

(ii) no part of the amount was deductible by the taxpayer under this paragraph in computing the taxpayer's income for any preceding taxation year,

to the extent of the amount thereof (or in the case of capital property, 1/2 of the amount thereof) that was not deductible by the taxpayer under paragraph (z) in computing the taxpayer's income for any preceding taxation year;

Editorial Note: By virtue of s. 18(1)(*q*), no deduction is allowed for a lease cancellation payment made by a lessor except as provided under s. 20(1)(*z*) or (z.1).

Related Sections: S. 13(5.5) Lease cancellation payment; s. 18(1)(*q*) Limitation re cancellation of lease; s. 20(1)(*z*) Cancellation of lease — before sale of leased property; s. 87(2)(*j*.5) Cancellation of lease.

Tax Profile: March 2002 — Selected Tax Issues for Commercial Landlords and Tenants.

Tax Topics: No. 1677, Income Tax Implications of Lease Cancellation Payments.

Interpretation Bulletins: *Secondary* — IT-359R2 Premiums and other amounts with respect to leases; IT-467R2 Damages, settlements and similar payments.

▶ 20(1)(aa) ◀

(aa) Landscaping of grounds — an amount paid by the taxpayer in the year for the landscaping of grounds around a building or other structure of the taxpayer that is used by the taxpayer primarily for the purpose of gaining or producing income therefrom or from a business;

Related Sections: S. 18(3.1) Costs relating to construction of building or ownership of land.

Interpretation Bulletins: *Primary* — IT-485 Cost of clearing or levelling land. *Secondary* — IT-304R2 Condominiums.

▶ 20(1)(bb) ◀

(bb) Fees paid to investment counsel — an amount, other than a commission, that

(i) is paid by the taxpayer in the year to a person or partnership the principal business of which

(A) is advising others as to the advisability of purchasing or selling specific shares or securities, or

(B) includes the provision of services in respect of the administration or management of shares or securities, and

(ii) is paid for

(A) advice as to the advisability of purchasing or selling a specific share or security of the taxpayer, or

(B) services in respect of the administration or management of shares or securities of the taxpayer;

History: S. 20(1)(*bb*) was replaced by S.C. 2013, c. 34, s. 180(1), applicable to amounts paid after June 2005, and formerly read:

(*bb*) *Fees paid to investment counsel* — an amount other than a commission paid by the taxpayer in the year to a person

(i) for advice as to the advisability of purchasing or selling a specific share or security of the taxpayer, or

(ii) for services in respect of the administration or management of shares or securities of the taxpayer,

if that person's principal business

(iii) is advising others as to the advisability of purchasing or selling specific shares or securities, or

(iv) includes the provision of services in respect of the administration or management of shares or securities.

Interpretation Bulletins: *Primary* — IT-238R2 Fees paid to investment counsel. *Secondary* — IT-124R6 Contributions to registered retirement savings plans.

Tax Window Files: Paragraph 20(1)(bb) - segregated funds, *August 24, 2016*, CRA Document No. 2014-0542581E5.

Cases: Oversight expenses were currently deductible, on the basis they were frequent and recurring for the taxpayer and part of its annual costs of business. The costs were incurred by the company's board of directors in the discharge of its oversight responsibilities with respect to the management of the company's income-earning process, as evaluation of corporate opportunities was an ongoing quest for the directors and intrinsically linked to the income-earning process. Expenses for advertising and reporting fees were capital expenses and not currently deductible. *The Queen v. Rio Tinto Alcan Inc.*, 2018 DTC 5075 (FCA)

The fees paid to S. by the taxpayer's estate were not personal but to earn income from property and were deductible. *Wickham Estate v. The Queen*, 2015 DTC 1025 (T.C.C.)

▶ 20(1)(cc) ◀

(cc) Expenses of representation — an amount paid by the taxpayer in the year as or on account of expenses incurred by the taxpayer in making any representation relating to a business carried on by the taxpayer,

(i) to the government of a country, province or state or to a municipal or public body performing a function of government in Canada, or

(ii) to an agency of a government or of a municipal or public body referred to in subparagraph (i) that had authority to make rules, regulations or by-laws relating to the business carried on by the taxpayer,

including any representation for the purpose of obtaining a licence, permit, franchise or trade-mark relating to the business carried on by the taxpayer;

Related Sections: S. 13(12) Application of para. 20(1)(cc); s. 20(9) Application of para. (1)(cc).

Interpretation Bulletins: *Secondary* — IT-99R5 (Consolid.) Legal and accounting fees.

▶ 20(1)(dd) ◀

(dd) Investigation of site — an amount paid by the taxpayer in the year for investigating the suitability of a site for a building or other structure planned by the taxpayer for use in connection with a business carried on by the taxpayer;

Interpretation Bulletins: *Primary* — IT-350R Investigation of site.

▶ 20(1)(ee) ◀

(ee) Utilities service connection — an amount paid by the taxpayer in the year to a person (other than a person with whom the taxpayer was not dealing at arm's length) for the purpose of making a service connection to the taxpayer's place of business for the supply, by means of wires, pipes or conduits, of electricity, gas, telephone service, water or sewers supplied by that person, to the extent that the amount so paid was not paid

(i) to acquire property of the taxpayer, or

(ii) as consideration for the goods or services for the supply of which the service connection was undertaken or made;

Interpretation Bulletins: *Secondary* — IT-482R Pipelines.

▶ 20(1)(ff) ◀

(ff) Payments by farmers — an amount paid by the taxpayer in the year as a levy under the *Western Grain Stabilization Act*, as a premium in respect of the gross revenue insurance program established under the *Farm Income Protection Act* or as an administration fee in respect of a net income stabilization account;

Related Sections: S. 12(1)(*p*) Certain payments to farmers; s. 248(1), "amount", "gross revenue", "net income stabilization account".

▶ 20(1)(gg) ◀

(gg) Disability-related modifications to buildings — (Repealed by S.C. 1994, c. 7, Sched. VIII, s. 157(1).)

▶ 20(1)(hh) ◀

(hh) Repayments of inducements, etc. — an amount repaid by the taxpayer in the year pursuant to a legal obligation to repay all or part of a particular amount

(i) included under paragraph 12(1)(*x*) in computing the taxpayer's income for the year or a preceding taxation year, or

(ii) that is, by reason of subparagraph 12(1)(*x*)(vi) or subsection 12(2.2), not included under paragraph 12(1)(*x*) in computing the taxpayer's income for the year or a preceding taxation year,

where the particular amount relates to an outlay or expense (other than an outlay or expense that is in respect of the cost of property of the taxpayer or that is or would be, if amounts deductible by the taxpayer were not limited by reason of paragraph 66(4)(*b*), subsection 66.1(2), subparagraph 66.2(2)(*a*)(ii), the words "30% of" in clause 66.21(4)(*a*)(ii)(B), clause 66.21(4)(*a*)(ii)(C) or (D) or subparagraph 66.4(2)(*a*)(ii), deductible under section 66, 66.1, 66.2, 66.21 or 66.4) that would, if the particular amount had not been received, have been deductible in computing the taxpayer's income for the year or a preceding taxation year;

Related Sections: S. 12(2.2) Deemed outlay or expense; s. 87(2)(*j*.6) Continuing corporation.

Interpretation Bulletins: *Secondary* — IT-273R2 Government assistance — General comments.

Tax Window Files: Repayment of cash back incentives on renewed mortgages, May 31, 2017, CRA Document No. 2016-0681271E5.

▶ 20(1)(hh.1) ◀

(hh.1) Repayment of obligation — ¾ of any amount repaid by the taxpayer in the year (on or after the time the taxpayer ceases to carry on a business) under a legal obligation to repay all or part of an amount the taxpayer received or was entitled to receive that was assistance from a government, municipality or other public authority (whether as a grant, subsidy, forgivable loan, deduction from tax, investment allowance or as any other form of assistance) in respect of, or for the acquisition of, property the cost of which was an eligible capital expenditure of the taxpayer in respect of the business if the amount of the eligible capital expenditure of the taxpayer in respect of the business was reduced by paragraph 14(10)(*c*) because of the amount of the assistance the taxpayer received or was entitled to receive;

History: S. 20(1)(*hh.1*) was replaced by S.C. 2016, c. 12, s. 7(2), in force January 1, 2017, and formerly read:

(*hh.*1) *Repayment of obligation* — ¾ of any amount (other than an amount to which paragraph 14(10)(*b*) applies in respect of the taxpayer) repaid by the taxpayer in the year under a legal obligation to repay all or part of an amount to which paragraph 14(10)(*c*) applies in respect of the taxpayer;

Interpretation Bulletins: *Secondary* — IT-273R2 Government assistance — General comments.

▶ 20(1)(ii) ◀

(ii) Inventory adjustment — the amount required by paragraph 12(1)(*r*) to be included in computing the taxpayer's income for the immediately preceding taxation year;

Related Sections: S. 12(1)(*r*) Inventory adjustment; s. 87(2)(*j.*1) Inventory adjustment.

▶ 20(1)(jj) ◀

(jj) Reinsurance commission — (Repealed by S.C. 2013, c. 34, s. 180(2).)

History: S. 20(1)(*jj*) was repealed by S.C. 2013, c. 34, s. 180(2), applicable to reinsurance commissions paid after 1999, and formerly read:

(*jj*) *Reinsurance commission* — the amount required by paragraph 12(1)(*s*) to be included in computing the taxpayer's income for the immediately preceding taxation year;

Related Sections: S. 12(1)(*s*) Reinsurance commission.

▶ 20(1)(kk) ◀

(kk) Exploration and development grants — the amount of any assistance or benefit received by the taxpayer in the year as a deduction from or reimbursement of an expense that is a tax (other than the goods and services tax) or royalty to the extent that

(i) the tax or royalty is, by reason of the receipt of the amount by the taxpayer, not deductible in computing the taxpayer's income for a taxation year, and

(ii) the deduction or reimbursement was included by the taxpayer in the amount determined for J in the definition "cumulative Canadian exploration expense" in subsection 66.1(6), for M in the definition "cumulative Canadian development expense" in subsection 66.2(5) or for I in the definition "cumulative Canadian oil and gas property expense" in subsection 66.4(5);

▶ 20(1)(ll) ◀

(ll) Repayment of interest — such part of any amount payable by the taxpayer because of a provision of this Act, or of an Act of a province that imposes a tax similar to the tax imposed under this Act, as was paid in the year and as can reasonably be considered to be a repayment of interest that was included in computing the taxpayer's income for the year or a preceding taxation year;

Editorial Note: Paragraph 20(1)(*ll*) permits a deduction from income for the repayment of interest (but not the interest thereon) in the year the repayment is made, if it can reasonably be regarded as a repayment of interest which was previously included in the taxpayer's income by virtue of a legal Act.

▶ 20(1)(mm) ◀

(mm) Cost of substances injected in reservoir — the portion claimed by the taxpayer of an amount that is an outlay or expense made or incurred by the taxpayer before the end of the year that is a cost to the taxpayer of any substance injected before that time into a natural reservoir to assist in the recovery of petroleum, natural gas or related hydrocarbons to the extent that that portion was not

(i) otherwise deducted in computing the taxpayer's income for the year, or

(ii) deducted in computing the taxpayer's income for any preceding taxation year,

except that where the year is less than 51 weeks, the amount that may be claimed under this paragraph by the taxpayer for the year shall not exceed the greater of

(iii) that proportion of the maximum amount that may otherwise be claimed under this paragraph by the taxpayer for the year that the number of days in the year is of 365, and

(iv) the amount of such outlay or expense that was made or incurred by the taxpayer in the year and not otherwise deducted in computing the taxpayer's income for the year;

▶ 20(1)(nn) ◀

(nn) Part XII.6 tax — the tax, if any, under Part XII.6 paid in the year or payable in respect of the year by the taxpayer (depending on the method regularly followed by the taxpayer in computing the taxpayer's income);

Canadian Petroleum Tax Journal: Flow-Through Shares: An Update, Angelo F. Toselli, 1997, Vol. 10, No. 1.

▶ 20(1)(nn.1) ◀

(nn.1) Recapture of investment tax credits — child care space amount — (Repealed by S.C. 2017, c. 20, s. 4(1).)

History: S. 20(1)(*nn.*1) was repealed by S.C. 2017, c. 20, s. 4(1), applicable in respect of expenditures incurred after March 21, 2017, except that this amendment does not apply in respect of expenditures incurred before 2020 under a written agreement entered into before March 22, 2017. S. 20(1)(*nn.*1) formerly read:

(*nn.*1) *Recapture of investment tax credits — child care space amount* — total of all amounts (other than an amount in respect of a disposition of a depreciable property) added because of subsection 127(27.1) or (28.1) to the taxpayer's tax otherwise payable under this Part for any preceding taxation year;

► 20(1)(oo) ◄

(oo) Salary deferral arrangement — any deferred amount under a salary deferral arrangement in respect of another person to the extent that it was

(i) included under paragraph 6(1)(*a*) as a benefit in computing the income of the other person for the taxation year of the other person that ends in the taxpayer's taxation year, and

(ii) in respect of services rendered to the taxpayer;

Related Sections: S. 87(2)(*j*.3) Employee benefit plans, etc.

► 20(1)(pp) ◄

(pp) Idem — any amount under a salary deferral arrangement in respect of another person (other than an arrangement established primarily for the benefit of one or more non-resident employees in respect of services to be rendered outside Canada) to the extent that it was

(i) included under paragraph 6(1)(*i*) in computing the income of the other person for the taxation year of the other person that ends in the taxpayer's taxation year, and

(ii) in respect of services rendered to the taxpayer;

► 20(1)(qq) ◄

(qq) Disability-related modifications to buildings — an amount paid by the taxpayer in the year for prescribed renovations or alterations to a building used by the taxpayer primarily for the purpose of gaining or producing income from the building or from a business that are made to enable individuals who have a mobility impairment to gain access to the building or to be mobile within it;

Related Regulations: 8800.

Related Sections: S. 18(3.1) Costs relating to construction of building or ownership of land; s. 248(1), "amount", "business", "individual", "prescribed".

► 20(1)(rr) ◄

(rr) Disability-related equipment — an amount paid by the taxpayer in the year for any prescribed disability-specific device or equipment;

Related Regulations: 8801.

Related Sections: S. 248(1), "prescribed".

► 20(1)(ss) ◄

(ss) Qualifying environmental trusts — a contribution made in the year by the taxpayer to a qualifying environmental trust under which the taxpayer is a beneficiary;

Editorial Note: Although the contributions to the trust are deductible, the income earned on the contributions while inside the trust is taxed under s. 211.6. Each beneficiary of the trust will also include its share of the income earned by the trust under s. 107.3(1), but the beneficiary will be eligible for the refundable credit under s. 127.41 in respect of the tax paid by the trust in respect of that income under s. 211.6.

Related Sections: S. 12(1)(*z*.1) Qualifying environmental trusts; s. 107.3(1) Treatment of beneficiaries under qualifying environmental trusts; s. 127.41 Part XII.4 tax credit.

Canadian Tax Foundation: Frankovic, *The Case for "Reverse Depreciation" of Reclamation Costs,* 2004 Canadian Tax Journal 1:1–58.

Tax Window Files: Site Reclamation Costs, *Technical Interpretation, Reorganizations and Resources Division, September 27, 2004,* CRA Document No. 2003-0048241E5.

► 20(1)(tt) ◄

(tt) Acquisition of interests in qualifying environmental trusts — the consideration paid by the taxpayer in the year for the acquisition from another person or partnership of all or part of the taxpayer's interest as a beneficiary under a qualifying environmental trust, other than consideration that is the assumption of a reclamation obligation in respect of the trust;

► 20(1)(uu) ◄

(uu) Debt forgiveness — any amount deducted in computing the taxpayer's income for the year because of paragraph 80(15)(*a*) or subsection 80.01(10);

► 20(1)(vv) ◄

(vv) Countervailing or anti-dumping duty — an amount paid in the year by the taxpayer as or on account of an existing or proposed countervailing or anti-dumping duty in respect of property (other than depreciable property);

Related Sections: S. 12(1)(*z*6) Refunds; s. 13(21), "undepreciated capital cost".

► 20(1)(ww) ◄

(ww) Split income — where the taxpayer is a specified individual in relation to the year, the individual's split income for the year; and

Related Sections: S. 120.4(1), "specified individual", "split income"; s. 160(1.2) Joint liability — tax on split income.

► 20(1)(xx) ◄

(xx) Derivative forward agreement — in respect of a derivative forward agreement of a taxpayer, the amount determined by the formula

$$A - B$$

where

A is the lesser of

(i) the total of all amounts each of which is

(A) if the taxpayer acquires a property under the agreement in the year or a preceding taxation year, the portion of the amount by which the cost to the taxpayer of the property exceeds the fair market value of the property at the time it is acquired by the taxpayer that is attributable to an underlying interest other than an underlying interest referred to in subparagraphs (*b*)(i) to (iii) of the definition *derivative forward agreement* in subsection 248(1), or

(B) if the taxpayer disposes of a property under the agreement in the year or a preceding taxation year, the portion of the amount by which the fair market value of the property at the time the agreement is entered into by the taxpayer exceeds the *proceeds of disposition* (within the meaning assigned by subdivision c) of the property that is attributable to an underlying interest other than an underlying interest referred to in clauses (*c*)(i)(A) to (C) of the definition *derivative forward agreement* in subsection 248(1), and

(ii) the amount that is,

(A) if final settlement of the agreement occurs in the year and it cannot reasonably be considered that one of the main reasons for entering into the agreement is to obtain a deduction under this paragraph, the amount determined under subparagraph (i), or

(B) in any other case, the total of all amounts included under paragraph 12(1)(*z*.7) in computing the taxpayer's income in respect of the agreement for the year or a preceding taxation year, and

B is the total of all amounts deducted under this paragraph in respect of the agreement for a preceding taxation year.

Editorial Note: Paragraph 20(1)(*xx*) allows an income deduction to be made for losses derived from derivative forward agreements. A "derivative forward agreement" is defined in s. 248(1) and in general terms includes an agreement made to buy or sell capital property, at a date more than 180 days in the future, with a total price linked to an unrelated underlying interest other than the value of the property. This provision was introduced by the 2013 Budget as a means to address "character conversion transactions" designed to convert ordinary income into capital gains through the use of derivative contracts. Where an amount is deducted under 20(1)(*xx*), a corresponding decrease in the adjusted cost base of the capital property is available under paragraph 53(1)(*w*) or (*x*), to ensure the amount is not deductible again as a capital loss. For profits from derivative forward agreements, see paragraph 12(1)(*z*.7).

History: S. 20(1)(*xx*), clauses (A) and (B) of the description of A were replaced by S.C. 2017, c. 33, s. 6(2), applicable in respect of acquisitions and dispositions of property that occur after September 15, 2016, and formerly read:

(A) if the taxpayer acquires a property under the agreement in the year or a preceding taxation year, the amount by which the cost to the taxpayer of the property exceeds the fair market value of the property at the time it is acquired by the taxpayer, or

(B) if the taxpayer disposes of a property under the agreement in the year or a preceding taxation year, the amount by which the fair market value of the property at the time the agreement is entered into by the taxpayer exceeds the proceeds of disposition (within the meaning assigned by subdivision c) of the property, and

History: S. 20(1)(*xx*) was added by S.C. 2013, c. 40, s. 11(3), applicable to acquisitions and dispositions of property to which new paragraph 12(1)(*z*.7) applies.

Related Sections: 12(1)(d.2) [Reserve for bond premiums]; S. 53(2)(*w*) [Amounts to be deducted — Derivative forward agreement]; s. 53(2)(*x*) [Amounts to be deducted — Derivative forward agreement].

Canadian Tax Foundation: Miller and Milet, *Derivative Forward Agreements and Synthetic Disposition Arrangements*, 2013 Conference Report 10:1–50.

► 20(1.1) ◄

(1.1) Application of s. 13(21). The definitions in subsection 13(21) apply to any regulations made under paragraph (1)(*a*).

► 20(1.2) ◄

(1.2) Application of s. 12.2(11). The definitions in subsection 12.2(11) apply to paragraph (1)(*c*).

► 20(2) ◄

(2) Borrowed money. For the purposes of paragraph (1)(*c*), where a person has borrowed money in consideration of a promise by the person to pay a larger amount and to pay interest on the larger amount,

(*a*) the larger amount shall be deemed to be the amount borrowed; and

(*b*) where the amount actually borrowed has been used in whole or in part for the purpose of earning income from a business or property, the proportion of the larger amount that the amount actually so used is of the amount actually borrowed shall be deemed to be the amount so used.

Editorial Note: The CRA takes the position that a discount on a debt obligation that pays stipulated interest cannot be considered interest, because s. 20(2)(*a*) provides that the discount is deemed to be part of the amount borrowed for the purposes of s. 20(1)(*c*). However, s. 20(1)(*f*) allows for a full or partial deduction of the discount when the debt is repaid, depending on how "deep" the discount is (see paragraph 1.94 of Income Tax Folio S3-F6-C1).

Income Tax Folios: *Secondary* — S3-F6-C1 Interest Deductibility.

► 20(2.01) ◄

(2.01) Limitation of expression "interest" — 10/8 policy. For the purposes of paragraphs (1)(*c*) and (*d*), interest does not include an amount if

(*a*) the amount

(i) is paid, after March 20, 2013 in respect of a period after 2013, in respect of a life insurance policy that is, at the time of the payment, a 10/8 policy, and

(ii) is described in paragraph (*a*) of the definition "10/8 policy" in subsection 248(1); or

(*b*) the amount

(i) is payable, in respect of a life insurance policy, after March 20, 2013 in respect of a period after 2013 during which the policy is a 10/8 policy, and

(ii) is described in paragraph (*a*) of the definition "10/8 policy" in subsection 248(1).

History: S. 20(2.01) was added by S.C. 2013, c. 40, s. 11(4), applicable to taxation years that end after March 20, 2013.

Canadian Tax Foundation: Everett, *Life Insurance Planning After the 2013 Budget*, 2013 Conference Report 32:1–23.

► 20(2.1) ◄

(2.1) Limitation of expression "interest". For the purposes of paragraphs (1)(*c*) and (*d*), "interest" does not include an amount that is paid after the taxpayer's 1977 taxation year or payable in respect of a period after the taxpayer's 1977 taxation year, depending on the method regularly followed by the taxpayer in computing the taxpayer's income, in respect of interest on a policy loan made by an insurer except to the extent that the amount of that interest is verified by the insurer in prescribed form and within the prescribed time to be

(*a*) interest paid in the year on that loan; and

(*b*) interest (other than interest that would, but for paragraph (2.2)(*b*), be interest on money borrowed before 1978 to acquire a life insurance policy or on an amount payable for property acquired before 1978 that is an interest in a life insurance policy) that is not added to the adjusted cost basis (within the meaning given that expression in subsection 148(9)) to the taxpayer of the taxpayer's interest in the policy.

Related Regulations: 4001.

Forms: T2210 — Verification of Policy Loan Interest by the Insurer.

► 20(2.2) ◄

(2.2) Limitation of expression "life insurance policy". For the purposes of paragraphs (1)(*c*) and (*d*), a "life insurance policy" does not include a policy

(*a*) that is or is issued pursuant to a pooled registered pension plan, a registered pension plan, a registered retirement savings plan, an income-averaging annuity contract or a deferred profit sharing plan;

(*b*) that was an annuity contract issued before 1978 that provided for annuity payments to commence not later than the day on which the policyholder attains 75 years of age; or

(*c*) that is an annuity contract all of the insurer's reserves for which vary in amount depending on the fair market value of a specified group of properties.

History: S. 20(2.2)(*a*) was replaced by S.C. 2012, c. 31, s. 8(2), in force December 14, 2012 and formerly read:

(*a*) that is or is issued pursuant to a registered pension plan, a registered retirement savings plan, an income-averaging annuity contract or a deferred profit sharing plan;

Income Tax Folios: *Primary* — S3-F6-C1 Interest Deductibility.

► 20(2.3) ◄

(2.3) Sectoral reserve. For the purpose of clause (1)(*l*)(ii)(D), a sectoral reserve is a reserve or an allowance for impairment for a loan that is determined on a sector-by-sector basis (including a geographic sector, an industrial sector or a sector of any other nature) and not on a property-by-property basis.

► 20(2.4) ◄

(2.4) Specified percentage. For the purpose of clause (1)(*l*)(ii)(D), a taxpayer's specified percentage for a taxation year is

(*a*) where the taxpayer has a prescribed reserve amount for the year, the percentage that is the percentage of the prescribed reserve amount of the taxpayer for the year claimed by the taxpayer under clause (1)(*l*)(ii)(C) for the year, and

(*b*) in any other case, 100%.

► 20(3) ◄

(3) Borrowed money. For greater certainty, if a taxpayer uses borrowed money to repay money previously borrowed, or to pay an amount payable for property described in subparagraph (1)(*c*)(ii) previously acquired (which previously borrowed money or amount payable in respect of previously acquired property is, in this subsection, referred to as the "previous indebtedness"), subject to subsection 20.1(6), for the purposes of paragraphs (1)(*c*), (*e*) and (*e.1*), subsections 20.1(1) and (2), section 21 and subparagraph 95(2)(*a*)(ii), and for the purpose of paragraph 20(1)(*k*) of the *Income Tax Act*, Chapter 148 of the Revised Statutes of Canada, 1952, the borrowed money is deemed to be used for the purpose for which the previous indebtedness was used or incurred, or was deemed by this subsection to have been used or incurred.

History: S. 20(3) was replaced by S.C. 2009, c. 2, s. 7(1), applicable in respect of interest paid or payable in respect of a period or periods that begin after January 27, 2009. S. 20(3) was replaced by S.C. 2007, c. 35, s. 14(2), applicable in respect of interest paid or payable in respect of a period or periods that begin after 2011, to read as above except for a reference to s. 18.2 included. However, as a result of the repeal of s. 18.2, the reference to s. 18.2 was deleted in the amendment to s. 20(3) by S.C. 2009, c. 2, for interest paid or payable in respect of a period or periods that begin after January 27, 2009. S. 20(3) formerly read:

(3) *Borrowed money.* For greater certainty, it is hereby declared that where a taxpayer has used borrowed money

(*a*) to repay money previously borrowed, or

(*b*) to pay an amount payable for property described in subparagraph (1)(*c*)(ii) previously acquired,

subject to subsection 20.1(6), the borrowed money shall, for the purposes of paragraphs (1)(*c*), (*e*) and (*e.1*), subsections 20.1(1) and (2), section 21 and subparagraph 95(2)(*a*)(ii) and for the purpose of paragraph 20(1)(*k*) of the *Income Tax Act*, Chapter 148 of the Revised Statutes of Canada, 1952, be deemed to have been used for the purpose for which the money previously borrowed was used or was deemed by this subsection to have been used, or to acquire the property in respect of which the amount was payable, as the case may be.

Related Sections: S. 20.1 Borrowed money used to earn income from property.

Income Tax Folios: *Secondary* — S3-F6-C1 Interest Deductibility.

Interpretation Bulletins: *Secondary* — IT-533 Interest deductibility and related issues.

► 20(4) ◄

(4) Bad debts — dispositions of depreciable property. If an amount that is owing to a taxpayer as or on account of the proceeds of disposition of depreciable property (other than a timber resource property, a passenger vehicle to which paragraph 13(7)(*g*) applies or a zero-emission passenger vehicle to which paragraph 13(7)(*i*) applies) of the taxpayer of a prescribed class is established by the taxpayer to have become a bad debt in a taxation year, there may be deducted in computing the taxpayer's income for the year the lesser of

(*a*) the amount so owing to the taxpayer, and

(*b*) the amount, if any, by which the capital cost to the taxpayer of that property exceeds the total of the amounts, if any, realized by the taxpayer on account of the proceeds of disposition.

Editorial Note: Subsection 20(4) allows a deduction if an amount owing to a taxpayer on account of proceeds of disposition of depreciable property (other than timber resource property or Class 10.1 property) becomes a bad debt in the taxation year. The deduction equals the lesser of the amount of the bad debt, and the amount by which the capital cost of the property disposed of exceeds the amount realized on the disposition. As to what constitutes a bad debt, see the caselaw summarized under paragraph 20(1)(*p*).

History: S. 20(4), the portion before paragraph (*a*) was amended by S.C. 2019, c. 29, s. 3(1), deemed to have come into force on March 19, 2019. S. 20(4) formerly read:

Bad debts from dispositions of depreciable property Where an amount that is owing to a taxpayer as or on account of the proceeds of disposition of depreciable property (other than a timber resource property or a passenger vehicle having a cost to the taxpayer in excess of $20,000 or such other amount as may be prescribed) of the taxpayer of a prescribed class is established by the taxpayer to have become a bad debt in a taxation year, there may be deducted in computing the taxpayer's income for the year the lesser of

Related Regulations: 7307(1).

Related Sections: S. 13(7)(*g*), (*i*) Rules applicable; s. 13(21) Definitions; s. 20(1)(*a*) Capital cost of property.

Income Tax Folios: *Primary* — S3-F4-C1 General Discussion of Capital Cost Allowance.

Interpretation Bulletins: *Secondary* — IT-159R3 Capital debts established to be bad debts.

► 20(4.1) ◄

(4.1) Idem. Where an amount that is owing to a taxpayer as or on account of the proceeds of disposition of a timber resource property of the taxpayer is established by the taxpayer to have become a bad debt in a taxation year, the amount so owing to the taxpayer may be deducted in computing the taxpayer's income for the year.

Related Sections: S. 13(2) Recaptured depreciation for passenger vehicle; s. 20(1)(*a*) Capital cost of property.

Income Tax Folios: *Primary* — S3-F4-C1 General Discussion of Capital Cost Allowance.

► 20(4.11) ◄

(4.11) Bad debts — zero-emission passenger vehicles. If an amount that is owing to a taxpayer as or on account of the proceeds of disposition of a zero-emission passenger vehicle of the taxpayer to which paragraph 13(7)(*i*) applies is established by the taxpayer to have become a bad debt in a taxation year, there may be deducted in computing the taxpayer's income for the year the lesser of

(*a*) the amount that would be determined by the formula in subparagraph 13(7)(*i*)(ii) in respect of the disposition if the amount determined for A in the formula were the amount owing to the taxpayer, and

(*b*) the amount determined by the formula

$$A - B$$

where

A is the capital cost to the taxpayer of the vehicle, and

B is the amount that would be determined by the formula in subparagraph 13(7)(*i*)(ii) in respect of the disposition if the amount determined for A in the formula were the total amount, if any, realized by the taxpayer on account of the proceeds of disposition.

Editorial Note: Subsection 20(4.11) allows a deduction where a taxpayer's proceeds of disposition of a "zero-emission passenger vehicle" (subsection 248(1)) are owing to the taxpayer but have become a bad debt, equal to the lesser of:

(1) the amount of the bad debt; for this purpose, if the vehicle was disposed of to an arm's length person or partnership, the amount of the bad debt is the bad debt otherwise determined multiplied by a fraction equalling the capital cost of the vehicle divided by the cost of the vehicle to the taxpayer (fraction B/C in subparagraph 13(7)(*i*)(ii)), and

(2) the amount by which the capital cost to the taxpayer of the vehicle exceeds the amount, if any, realized on the disposition; for this purpose, the amount realized is the amount otherwise determined multiplied by a fraction equalling the capital cost of the vehicle divided by the cost of the vehicle to the taxpayer (fraction B/C in subparagraph 13(7)(*i*)(ii)).

History: S. 20(4.11) was added by S.C. 2019, c. 29, s. 3(2), deemed to have come into force on March 19, 2019.

Related Sections: S. 13(7)(*i*) Rules applicable.

► 20(4.2) ◄

(4.2) Former eligible capital property. If an amount is deductible under subsection (4) in respect of the disposition of a depreciable property and subsection 13(39) applied to the disposition of the depreciable property, the amount deductible under subsection (4) is equal to ¾ of the amount that would be deductible without reference to this subsection.

History: S. 20(4.2) was replaced by S.C. 2016, c. 12, s. 7(3), applicable to dispositions that occur after 2016, and formerly read:

(4.2) *Bad debts re eligible capital property.* Where, in respect of one or more dispositions of eligible capital property by a taxpayer, an amount that is described in paragraph (*a*) of the description of E in the definition "cumulative eligible capital" in subsection 14(5) in respect of the taxpayer is established by the taxpayer to have become a bad debt in a taxation year, there shall be deducted in computing the taxpayer's income for the year the amount determined by the formula

$$(A + B) - (C + D + E + F + G + H)$$

where

A is the lesser of

(*a*) ½ of the total of all amounts each of which is such an amount that was so established to have become a bad debt in the year or a preceding taxation year, and

(*b*) the amount that is

(i) where the year ended after February 27, 2000, the amount, if any, that would be the total of all amounts determined by the formula in paragraph 14(1)(*b*) (if that formula were read without reference to the description of D) for the year, or for a preceding taxation year that ended after February 27, 2000, and

(ii) where the year ended before February 28, 2000, nil;

B is the amount, if any, by which

(*a*) ¾ of the total of all amounts each of which is such an amount that was so established to be a bad debt in the year or a preceding taxation year

exceeds the total of

(*b*) $^3/_2$ of the amount by which

(i) the value of A exceeds

(ii) the amount included in the value of A because of subparagraph (*b*)(i) of the description of A in respect of taxation years that ended after February 27, 2000 and before October 18, 2000, and

(*c*) $^9/_8$ of the amount included in the value of A because of subparagraph (*b*)(i) of the description of A in respect of taxation years that ended after February 27, 2000 and before October 18, 2000;

C is the total of all amounts each of which is an amount determined under subsection 14(1) or (1.1) for the year, or a preceding taxation year, that ends after October 17, 2000 and in respect of which a deduction can reasonably be considered to have been claimed under section 110.6 by the taxpayer;

D is the total of all amounts each of which is an amount determined under subsection 14(1) or (1.1) for the year, or a preceding taxation year, that ended after February 27, 2000 and before October 18, 2000 and in respect of which a deduction can reasonably be considered to have been claimed under section 110.6 by the taxpayer;

E is the total of all amounts each of which is an amount determined under subsection 14(1) or (1.1) for a preceding taxation year that ended before February 28, 2000 and in respect of which a deduction can reasonably be considered to have been claimed under section 110.6 by the taxpayer;

F is the total of

(*a*) $^2/_3$ of the total of all amounts each of which is the value determined in respect of the taxpayer for D in the formula in paragraph 14(1)(*b*) for the year, or a preceding taxation year, that ends after October 17, 2000, and

(*b*) $^8/_9$ of the total of all amounts each of which is the value determined in respect of the taxpayer for D in the formula in paragraph 14(1)(*b*) for the year, or a preceding taxation year, that ended after February 27, 2000 and before October 18, 2000;

G is the total of all amounts each of which is the value determined in respect of the taxpayer for D in the formula in subparagraph 14(1)(*a*)(v) (as that subparagraph applied for taxation years that ended before February 28, 2000) for a preceding taxation year; and

H is the total of all amounts deducted by the taxpayer under this subsection for preceding taxation years.

Related Sections: S. 12(1)(*i*.1) Bad debts recovered; s. 20(4.3) Deemed allowable capital loss; s. 39(11) Recovery of bad debt; s. 50(1)(*a*) Debts established to be bad debts and shares of bankrupt corporation; s. 79.1(7) Treatment of debt; s. 79.1(8) Claims for debts; s. 89(1), "capital dividend account".

Interpretation Bulletins: *Primary* — IT-442R Bad debts and reserves for doubtful debts. *Secondary* — IT-123R6 Transactions involving eligible capital property.

► 20(4.3) ◄

(4.3) Deemed allowable capital loss — (Repealed by S.C. 2016, c. 12, s. 7(3).)

History: S. 20(4.3) was repealed by S.C. 2016, c. 12, s. 7(3), applicable to dispositions that occur after 2016, and formerly read:

(4.3) *Deemed allowable capital loss.* Where, in respect of one or more dispositions of eligible capital property by a taxpayer, an amount that is described in paragraph (*a*) of the description of E in the definition "cumulative eligible capital" in subsection 14(5) in respect of the taxpayer is established by the taxpayer to have become a bad debt in a taxation year, the taxpayer is deemed to have an allowable capital loss from a disposition of capital property in the year equal to the lesser of

(*a*) the total of the value determined for A and 2/3 of the value determined for B in the formula in subsection (4.2) in respect of the taxpayer for the year; and

(*b*) the total of all amounts each of which is

(i) the value determined for C or paragraph (*a*) of the description of F in the formula in subsection (4.2) in respect of the taxpayer for the year,

(ii) 3/4 of the value determined for D or paragraph (*b*) of the description of F in the formula in subsection (4.2) in respect of the taxpayer for the year, or

(iii) 2/3 of the value determined for E or G in the formula in subsection (4.2) in respect of the taxpayer for the year.

Related Sections: S. 20(4.2) Bad debts re eligible capital property.

► 20(5) ◄

(5) Sale of agreement for sale, mortgage or hypothecary claim included in proceeds of disposition. Where depreciable property, other than a timber resource property, of a taxpayer has, in a taxation year, been disposed of to a person with whom the taxpayer was dealing at arm's length, and the proceeds of disposition include an agreement for the sale of, or a mortgage or hypothecary claim on, land that the taxpayer has, in a subsequent taxation year, sold to a person with whom the taxpayer was dealing at arm's length, there may be deducted in computing the income of the taxpayer for the subsequent year an amount equal to the lesser of

(*a*) the amount, if any, by which the principal amount of the agreement for sale, mortgage or hypothecary claim outstanding at the time of the sale exceeds the consideration paid by the purchaser to the taxpayer for the agreement for sale, mortgage or hypothecary claim, and

(*b*) the amount determined under paragraph (*a*) less the amount, if any, by which the proceeds of disposition of the depreciable property exceed the capital cost to the taxpayer of that property.

Related Sections: S. 13(2) Recaptured depreciation for passenger vehicle; s. 13(3) "Taxation year", "year" and "income" of individual; s. 13(21) Definitions.

► 20(5.1) ◄

(5.1) Sale of agreement for sale, mortgage or hypothecary claim included in proceeds of disposition. Where a timber resource property of a taxpayer has, in a taxation year, been disposed of to a person with whom the taxpayer was dealing at arm's length, and the proceeds of disposition include an agreement for sale of, or a mortgage or hypothecary claim on, land that the taxpayer has, in a subsequent taxation year, sold to a person with whom the taxpayer was dealing at arm's length, there may be deducted in computing the income of the taxpayer for the subsequent year the amount, if any, by which the principal amount of the agreement for sale, mortgage or hypothecary claim outstanding at the time of the sale exceeds the consideration paid by the purchaser to the taxpayer for the agreement for sale, mortgage or hypothecary claim.

Related Sections: S. 13(2) Recaptured depreciation for passenger vehicle; s. 13(3) "Taxation year", "year" and "income" of individual; s. 13(21), "proceeds of disposition", "timber resource property".

► 20(6) ◄

(6) Special reserves. Where an amount is deductible in computing income for a taxation year under paragraph (1)(*m*) as a reserve in respect of

(*a*) articles of food or drink that it is reasonably anticipated will have to be delivered after the end of the year, or

(*b*) transportation that it is reasonably anticipated will have to be provided after the end of the year,

there shall be substituted for the amount determined under that paragraph an amount not exceeding the total of amounts included in computing the taxpayer's income from the business for the year that were received or receivable (depending on the method regularly followed by the taxpayer in computing the taxpayer's profit) in the year in respect of

(*c*) articles of food or drink not delivered before the end of the year, or

(*d*) transportation not provided before the end of the year,

as the case may be.

Related Sections: S. 12(1)(*e*) Reserves for certain goods and services, etc.

Interpretation Bulletins: *Secondary* — IT-154R Special reserves.

► 20(7) ◄

(7) Where para. (1)(m) does not apply. Paragraph (1)(*m*) does not apply to allow a deduction

(*a*) as a reserve in respect of guarantees, indemnities or warranties;

(*b*) in computing the income of a taxpayer for a taxation year from a business in any case where the taxpayer's income for the year from that business is computed in accordance with the method authorized by subsection 28(1);

(*c*) as a reserve in respect of insurance, except that in computing an insurer's income for a taxation year from an insurance business, other than a life insurance business, carried on by it, there may be deducted as a policy reserve any amount that the insurer claims not exceeding the amount prescribed in respect of the insurer for the year; or

(*d*) as a reserve in respect of a reclamation obligation.

History: S. 20(7)(*d*) was added by S.C. 2013, c. 33, s. 3(1), applicable in respect of amounts received after March 20, 2013. However, this amendment does not apply in respect of an amount received that is directly attributable to a reclamation obligation, that was authorized by a government or regulatory authority before March 21, 2013 and that is received

(*a*) under a written agreement between the taxpayer and another party (other than a government or regulatory authority) that was entered into before March 21, 2013 and not extended or renewed on or after that day; or

(*b*) before 2018.

Related Regulations: 1400(1), 1400(3),1400(4), 1400(5); 1402; 1402.1; 1408.

Related Sections: S. 12(1)(*e*) Reserves for certain goods and services, etc.; s. 12(1)(*e*.1) Negative reserves; s. 139.1(8) Policy dividends.

Canadian Tax Foundation: Frankovic, *The Taxation of Prepaid Income*, 2002 Canadian Tax Journal 4:1239–1298.

Interpretation Bulletins: *Secondary* — IT-154R Special reserves.

Tax Window Files: Deductibility of a Reserve in Respect of a Class Action, *Technical Interpretation, Financial Sector and Exempt Entities Division, April 11, 2006*, CRA Document No. 2006-0169571I7; Continuity of Reserves on Dissolution of Partnership, *Technical Interpretation, Business and Partnerships Division, November 20, 2003*, CRA Document No.

2003-0033545; Software Maintenance Agreements, *Technical Interpretation, Business and Partnerships Division, October 7, 2003*, CRA Document No. 2003-0037947. Reserve allowed for portion of payments made under computer software maintenance agreement, based on elements of maintenance plan not in the nature of an indemnity.

▶ 20(8) ◀

(8) No deduction in respect of property in certain circumstances. Paragraph (1)(*n*) does not apply to allow a deduction in computing the income of a taxpayer for a taxation year from a business in respect of a property sold in the course of the business if

(*a*) the taxpayer, at the end of the year or at any time in the immediately following taxation year,

(i) was exempt from tax under any provision of this Part, or

(ii) was not resident in Canada and did not carry on the business in Canada;

(*b*) the sale occurred more than 36 months before the end of the year;

(*c*) the purchaser of the property sold was a corporation that, immediately after the sale,

(i) was controlled, directly or indirectly, in any manner whatever, by the taxpayer,

(ii) was controlled, directly or indirectly, in any manner whatever, by a person or group of persons that controlled the taxpayer, directly or indirectly, in any manner whatever, or

(iii) controlled the taxpayer, directly or indirectly, in any manner whatever; or

(*d*) the purchaser of the property sold was a partnership in which the taxpayer was, immediately after the sale, a majority-interest partner.

History: S. 20(8)(*d*) was replaced by S.C. 2013, c. 40, s. 11(5), in force December 12, 2013, and formerly read:

(*d*) the purchaser of the property sold was a partnership in which the taxpayer was, immediately after the sale, a majority interest partner.

S. 20(8)(*c*) and (*d*) were added by S.C. 2013, c. 34, s. 180(3), applicable in respect of property sold by a taxpayer after December 20, 2002. However, if a property so sold pursuant to an agreement in writing made before December 21, 2002 is transferred to the purchaser before 2004

(*a*) subsection 20(8), as it read immediately before the amendment by S.C. 2013, c. 34, s. 180(3), applies in respect of the property; and

(*b*) for the purpose of applying paragraph 20(1)(*n*) to the taxpayer for a taxation year in respect of the property, a reasonable amount as a reserve in respect of an amount not due in respect of the sale may not exceed the amount that would be reasonable if the proceeds from any subsequent disposition of the property that the purchaser receives before the end of the taxation year were received by the taxpayer.

Related Sections: S. 12(1)(*b*) Amounts receivable; s. 20(1)(*n*) Reserve for unpaid amounts; s. 149 Miscellaneous exemptions; s. 212 Taxation of non-residents.

Interpretation Bulletins: *Primary* — IT-152R3 Special reserves — Sale of land. *Secondary* — IT-154R Special reserves.

▶ 20(9) ◀

(9) Application of para. (1)(cc). In lieu of making any deduction of an amount permitted by paragraph (1)(*cc*) in computing a taxpayer's income for a taxation year from a business, the taxpayer may, if the taxpayer so elects in prescribed manner, make a deduction of 1/10 of that amount in computing the taxpayer's income for that taxation year and a like deduction in computing the taxpayer's income for each of the 9 immediately following taxation years.

Related Regulations: 4100.

Related Sections: S. 13(12) Application of para. 20(1)(cc); s. 249(1) Definition of "taxation year".

▶ 20(10) ◀

(10) Convention expenses. Notwithstanding paragraph 18(1)(*b*), there may be deducted in computing a taxpayer's income for a taxation year from a business an amount paid by the taxpayer in the year as or on account of expenses incurred by the taxpayer in attending, in connection with the business, not more than two conventions held during the year by a business or professional organization at a location that may reasonably be regarded as consistent with the territorial scope of that organization.

Editorial Note: Subsection 20(10) is permissive in nature in respect of convention expenses that are on capital account. If a convention expense is a current expense, it may be deductible under general principles.

Related Sections: S. 67 General limitation re expenses; s. 67.1(3) Fees for convention, etc.

Interpretation Bulletins: *Secondary* — IT-357R2 Expenses of training.

▶ 20(11) ◀

(11) Foreign taxes on income from property exceeding 15%. In computing the income of an individual from a property other than real or immovable property for a taxation year after 1975 that is income from a source outside Canada, there may be deducted the amount, if any, by which,

(*a*) such part of any income or profits tax paid by the taxpayer to the government of a country other than Canada for the year as may reasonably be regarded as having been paid in respect of an amount that has been included in computing the taxpayer's income for the year from the property,

exceeds

(*b*) 15% of the amount referred to in paragraph (*a*).

Editorial Note: The first 15% of such foreign tax (the amount described in s. 20(11)(*b*)) is generally eligible for the non-business income tax credit under s. 126(1).

History: S. 20(11), the portion before paragraph (*a*) was amended by S.C. 2013, c. 34, s. 97(3), in force June 26, 2013, and formerly read:

(11) *Foreign taxes on income from property exceeding 15%.* In computing the income of an individual from a property other than real property for a taxation year after 1975 that is income from a source outside Canada, there may be deducted the amount, if any, by which,

Related Sections: S. 20(12) Foreign non-business income tax; s. 95(1), "foreign affiliate"; s. 104(22) Designation of foreign source income by trust; s. 104(22.1) Foreign tax deemed paid by beneficiary; s. 126(7) Definitions; s. 144(8.1) Foreign tax deduction; s. 248(1), "corporation", "share"; s. 249(1) Definition of "taxation year"; s. 255 Canada.

Tax Profile: February 2007 — U.S. Limited Liability Companies — The Good, the Bad and the Ugly; January 2006 — Foreign Source Income: Outbound Structures and Foreign Tax Credit Planning — Part I.

Income Tax Folios: *Secondary* — S5-F2-C1 Foreign Tax Credit.

Interpretation Bulletins: *Primary* — IT-506 Foreign income taxes as a deduction from income. *Secondary* — IT-201R2 Foreign tax credit — Trust and beneficiaries.

Tax Window Files: Foreign tax deduction, *March 7, 2016*, CRA Document No. 2015-0572461I7; U.S. tax paid in respect of an LLC's income, *February 3, 2016*, CRA Document No. 2014-0548111E5.

▶ 20(12) ◀

(12) Foreign non-business income tax. In computing the income of a taxpayer who is resident in Canada at any time in a taxation year from a business or property for the year, there may be deducted any amount that the taxpayer claims that does not exceed the non-business income tax paid by the taxpayer for the year to the government of a country other than Canada (within the meaning assigned by subsection 126(7) read without reference to paragraphs (*c*) and (*e*) of the definition "non-business income tax" in that subsection) in respect of that income, other than any of those taxes paid that can, in whole or in part, reasonably be regarded as having been paid by a corporation in respect of income from a share of the capital stock of a foreign affiliate of the corporation.

Editorial Note: An amount deducted under s. 20(12) does not qualify for the foreign tax credit under s. 126(1). The deduction may be desirable if the foreign tax paid exceeds the amount of the credit available under s. 126(1).

The deduction is available in the year for which the non-business income tax was paid, regardless of whether it relates to that year or another year.

History: S. 20(12) was replaced by S.C. 2013, c. 34, s. 180(4), applicable after December 20, 2002 in respect of taxes paid at any time. S. 20(12) formerly read:

(12) *Foreign non-business income tax.* In computing a taxpayer's income for a taxation year from a business or property, there may be deducted such amount as the taxpayer claims not exceeding the non-business income tax paid by the taxpayer for the year to the government of a country other than Canada (within the meaning assigned by subsection 126(7) read without reference to paragraphs (*c*) and (*e*) of the definition "non-business-income tax" in that subsection) in respect of that income, other than any such tax, or part thereof, that can reasonably be regarded as having been paid by a corporation in respect of income from a share of the capital stock of a foreign affiliate of the corporation.

Related Sections: S. 20(11) Foreign taxes on income from property exceeding 15%; s. 95(1), "foreign affiliate"; s. 104(22.1) Foreign tax deemed paid by beneficiary; s. 104(22) Designation of foreign source income by trust; s. 126(7), "business-income tax", "non-business-income tax"; s. 138(5.1) No deduction; s. 248(1), "corporation", "share", "foreign affiliate".

Canadian Tax Foundation: Stirling, *Current Cases: Tax Court of Canada — Foreign Tax Deduction Denied for Tower Structure (FLSmidth Ltd. v. The Queen, 2012 TCC 3)*, 2012 Canadian Tax Journal 2:404–415.

Tax Profile: February 2013 — The Purchase of US Businesses by Canadians; February 2007 — U.S. Limited Liability Companies — The Good, the Bad and the Ugly; January 2006 — Foreign Source Income: Outbound Structures and Foreign Tax Credit Planning — Part I.

Tax Topics: No. 2089, FLSmidth: The Tax Court of Canada Causes a Tower Structure To Lean (if Ever so Slightly).

Income Tax Folios: *Secondary* — S5-F2-C1 Foreign Tax Credit.

Interpretation Bulletins: *Primary* — IT-506 Foreign income taxes as a deduction from income. *Secondary* — IT-201R2 Foreign tax credit — Trust and beneficiaries.

Tax Window Files: Foreign tax deduction, *March 7, 2016*, CRA Document No. 2015-0572461I7; Subsection 20(12) deduction, *December 15, 2015*, CRA Document No. 2014-0560371I7; U.S. tax paid in respect of an LLC's income, *February 3, 2016*, CRA Document No. 2014-0548111E5; Subsection 20(12) deduction, *December 15, 2015*, CRA Document No. 2014-0560371I7.

Cases: A US partnership owned a NSULC which owned shares in a US LLC. Since the NSULC and LLC were disregarded for US tax purposes, the partnership paid US tax on interest earned by the LLC. A Canadian corporate partner could not deduct any of this tax since it was paid "in respect of" income from foreign affiliate shares. *FLSmidth LTD. v. The Queen*, 2013 DTC 5118 (F.C.A.), affirming 2012 DTC 1052 (T.C.C.)

► 20(12.1) ◄

(12.1) Foreign tax where no economic profit. In computing a taxpayer's income for a taxation year from a business, there may be deducted the amount that the taxpayer claims not exceeding the lesser of

(*a*) the amount of foreign tax (within the meaning assigned by subsection 126(4.1)) that

(i) is in respect of a property used in the business for a period of ownership by the taxpayer or in respect of a related transaction (as defined in subsection 126(7)),

(ii) is paid by the taxpayer for the year,

(iii) is, because of subsection 126(4.1), not included in computing the taxpayer's business-income tax or non-business-income tax, and

(iv) where the taxpayer is a corporation, is not an amount that can reasonably be regarded as having been paid in respect of income from a share of the capital stock of a foreign affiliate of the taxpayer, and

(*b*) the portion of the taxpayer's income for the year from the business that is attributable to the property for the period or to a related transaction (as defined in subsection 126(7)).

Related Sections: S. 248(28) Limitation respecting inclusions, deductions and tax credits.

► 20(13) ◄

(13) Deductions under subdivision i. In computing the income for a taxation year of a taxpayer resident in Canada, there may be deducted such amounts as are provided by subdivision i.

History: S. 20(13) was replaced by S.C. 2013, c. 34, s. 57(1), applicable to taxation years that end after 1994.

Any assessment of a taxpayer's tax, interest and penalties payable under the Act for any taxation year that ends before June 26, 2013 that would, in the absence of this section, be precluded because of subsections 152(4) to (5) of the Act shall be made to the extent necessary to take into account the amendments by S.C. 2013, c. 34, s. 54 to 89.

S. 20(13) formerly read:

(13) *Dividend on share from foreign affiliate of taxpayer.* In computing the income for a taxation year of a taxpayer resident in Canada, there may be deducted such amount in respect of a dividend received by the taxpayer in the year on a share owned by the taxpayer of the capital stock of a foreign affiliate of the taxpayer as is provided by subdivision i.

Related Sections: S. 91(5) Amounts deductible in respect of dividends received.

► 20(14) ◄

(14) Accrued bond interest. Where, by virtue of an assignment or other transfer of a debt obligation, other than an income bond, an income debenture, a small business development bond or a small business bond, the transferee has become entitled to an amount of interest that accrued on the debt obligation for a period commencing before the time of transfer and ending at that time that is not payable until after that time, that amount

(*a*) shall be included as interest in computing the transferor's income for the transferor's taxation year in which the transfer occurred, except to the extent that it was otherwise included in computing the transferor's income for the year or a preceding taxation year; and

(*b*) may be deducted in computing the transferee's income for a taxation year to the extent that the amount was included as interest in computing the transferee's income for the year.

Editorial Note: Generally speaking, pre-transfer accrued interest is included in the transferor's income and excluded from the transferee's income.

Related Regulations: 211.

Related Sections: S. 12(9) Deemed accrual; s. 20(14.1) Interest on debt obligation; s. 20(21) Debt obligation; s. 53(2)(*l*) Amounts to be deducted — Accrued interest on transferred debt obligation; s. 214(6) Deemed interest; s. 214(7) Sale of obligation; s. 214(7.1) Obligation transfer between a resident and a non-resident; s. 214(9) Deemed resident.

Interpretation Bulletins: *Secondary* — IT-396R Interest income.

Tax Window Files: 2018 CTF Q. 14 - Foreign exchange, *November 27, 2018*, CRA Document No. 2018-0779911C6; Interest Income Calculation — Coupon Bonds Issued at a Premium or Discount, *May 31, 2004*, CRA Document No. 2004-0074381E5.

► 20(14.1) ◄

(14.1) Interest on debt obligation. Where a person who has issued a debt obligation, other than an income bond, an income debenture, a small business development bond or a small business bond, is obligated to pay an amount that is stipulated to be interest on that debt obligation in respect of a period before its issue (in this subsection referred to as the "unearned interest amount") and it is reasonable to consider that the person to whom the debt obligation was issued paid to the issuer consideration for the debt obligation that included an amount in respect of the unearned interest amount,

(*a*) for the purposes of subsection (14) and section 12, the issue of the debt obligation shall be deemed to be an assignment of the debt obligation from the issuer, as transferor, to the person to whom the obligation was issued, as transferee, and an amount equal to the unearned interest amount shall be deemed to be interest that accrued on the obligation for a period commencing before the issue and ending at the time of issue; and

(*b*) notwithstanding paragraph (*a*) or any other provision of this Act, no amount that can reasonably be considered to be an amount in respect of the unearned interest amount shall be deducted or included in computing the income of the issuer.

▶ 20(14.2) ◀

(14.2) Sales of linked notes. For the purposes of subsection (14), the amount determined by the following formula is deemed to be interest that accrued on an assigned or otherwise transferred debt obligation — that is, at any time, described in paragraph 7000(1)(*d*) of the *Income Tax Regulations* — to which the transferee has become entitled to for a period commencing before the time of the transfer and ending at that particular time that is not payable until after that particular time:

$$A - B$$

where

A is the price for which the debt obligation was assigned or otherwise transferred at the particular time; and

B is the amount by which the price (converted to Canadian currency using the exchange rate prevailing at the particular time, if the debt obligation is denominated in a foreign currency) for which the debt obligation was issued exceeds the portion, if any, of the principal amount of the debt obligation (converted to Canadian currency using the exchange rate prevailing at the particular time, if the debt obligation is denominated in a foreign currency) that was repaid by the issuer on or before the particular time.

History: S. 20(14.2) was added by S.C. 2016, c. 12, s. 7(4), applicable to transfers occurring after 2016.

▶ 20(15) ◀

(15) Regulations — (Repealed by S.C. 2003, c. 28, s. 3(2).)

Related Sections: S. 20(1)(*v*.1) Resource allowance.

▶ 20(16) ◀

(16) Terminal loss. Notwithstanding paragraphs 18(1)(*a*), (*b*) and (*h*), where at the end of a taxation year,

(*a*) the total of all amounts used to determine A to D.1 in the definition "undepreciated capital cost" in subsection 13(21) in respect of a taxpayer's depreciable property of a particular class exceeds the total of all amounts used to determine E to K in that definition in respect of that property, and

(*b*) the taxpayer no longer owns any property of that class,

in computing the taxpayer's income for the year

(*c*) there shall be deducted the amount of the excess determined under paragraph (*a*), and

(*d*) no amount shall be deducted for the year under paragraph (1)(*a*) in respect of property of that class.

Editorial Note: In general terms, a terminal loss occurs when there is no property left in a class of depreciable property and the undepreciated capital cost (UCC) balance of the class is positive at the end of a taxation year. The loss is fully deductible in computing income in the year. Despite the positive UCC balance, capital cost allowance is not deductible in the year under s. 20(1)(*a*). Unlike capital cost allowance, which is a permissive deduction, a terminal loss must be deducted in the year it occurs.

History: S. 20(16)(*a*) was replaced by S.C. 2013, c. 34, s. 180(5), applicable to taxation years that end after February 23, 1998, and formerly read:

(*a*) the total of all amounts used to determine A to D in the definition "undepreciated capital cost" in subsection 13(21) in respect of a taxpayer's depreciable property of a particular class exceeds the total of all amounts used to determine E to J in that definition in respect of that property, and

Related Sections: S. 13(1) Recaptured depreciation; s. 13(21) Definitions; s. 20(16.1) Terminal loss for passenger vehicle. s. 20(16.2) Reference to "taxation year" and "year" of individual; s. 20(16.3) Disposition after ceasing business.

Canadian Petroleum Tax Journal: Canada Customs and Revenue Agency 1999 Roundtable Questions and Answers, Question 14, Vol. 13, No. 1, 2000.

Income Tax Folios: *Primary* — S3-F4-C1 General Discussion of Capital Cost Allowance.

Interpretation Bulletins: *Primary* — IT-464R Capital cost allowance — Leasehold interests. *Secondary* — IT-172R Capital cost allowance — Taxation year of individual; IT-288R2 Gifts of capital properties to a charity and others; IT-465R Non-resident beneficiaries of trusts.

▶ 20(16.1) ◀

(16.1) Non-application of subsection (16). Subsection (16) does not apply

(*a*) in respect of a passenger vehicle of a taxpayer that has a cost to the taxpayer in excess of $20,000 or any other amount that is prescribed;

(*b*) in respect of a taxation year in respect of a property that was a former property deemed by paragraph 13(4.3)(*a*) or (*b*) to be owned by the taxpayer, if

(i) within 24 months after the taxpayer last owned the former property, the taxpayer or a person not dealing at arm's length with the taxpayer acquires a similar property in respect of the same fixed place to which the former property applied, and

(ii) at the end of the taxation year, the taxpayer or the person owns the similar property or another similar property in respect of the same fixed place to which the former property applied; and

(*c*) in respect of a taxation year in respect of property included in Class 14.1 of Schedule II to the *Income Tax Regulations* unless the taxpayer has ceased to carry on the business to which the class relates.

History: S. 20(16.1)(*c*) was added by S.C. 2016, c. 12, s. 7(5), in force January 1, 2017.

S. 20(16.1) was replaced by S.C. 2013, c. 34, s. 180(6), applicable in respect of taxation years that end after December 20, 2002, and formerly read:

(16.1) *Idem.* Subsection (16) does not apply in respect of a passenger vehicle of a taxpayer that has a cost to the taxpayer in excess of $20,000 or such other amount as is prescribed.

Related Regulations: 1100(2.5); 7307(1); Sched. II, Class 10.1.

Related Sections: S. 13(2) Recaptured depreciation for passenger vehicle; s. 248(1), "passenger vehicle", "prescribed".

Income Tax Folios: *Primary* — S3-F4-C1 General Discussion of Capital Cost Allowance.

Interpretation Bulletins: *Secondary* — IT-521R Motor vehicle expenses claimed by self-employed individuals; IT-522R Vehicle, Travel and Sales Expenses of Employees.

▶ 20(16.2) ◀

(16.2) Reference to "taxation year" and "year" of individual. Where a taxpayer is an individual and the taxpayer's income for a taxation year includes income from a business the fiscal period of which does not coincide with the calendar year, if depreciable property acquired for the purpose of gaining or producing income from the business has been disposed of, each reference in subsections (16) and (16.1) to a "taxation year" and "year" shall, for greater certainty, be read as a reference to a "fiscal period".

Income Tax Folios: *Primary* — S3-F4-C1 General Discussion of Capital Cost Allowance.

▶ 20(16.3) ◀

(16.3) Disposition after ceasing business. Where a taxpayer, after ceasing to carry on a business, has disposed of depreciable property of the taxpayer of a prescribed class that was acquired by the taxpayer for the purpose of gaining or producing income from the business and that was not subsequently used by the taxpayer for some other purpose, in applying subsection (16) or (16.1), each reference in that subsection to a "taxation year" and "year" shall, notwithstanding anything in subsection (16.2), not be read as a reference to a "fiscal period".

Income Tax Folios: *Primary* — S3-F4-C1 General Discussion of Capital Cost Allowance.

▶ 20(17) ◀

(17) Reduction of inventory allowance deduction — (Repealed by S.C. 2013, c. 34, s. 180(7).)

History: S. 20(17) was repealed by S.C. 2013, c. 34, s. 180(7), in force June 26, 2013, and formerly read:

(17) *Reduction of inventory allowance deduction.* Notwithstanding paragraph 20(1)(*gg*) of the *Income Tax Act*, chapter 148 of the Revised Statutes of Canada, 1952, the deduction allowed under that paragraph to a taxpayer for a taxation year shall be reduced by 3% of that proportion of the lesser of

(*a*) the cost amount to the taxpayer of the taxpayer's qualifying inventory that was disposed of during the year by the taxpayer in a specified transaction to a person with whom the taxpayer was not dealing at arm's length, and

(*b*) the cost amount to the taxpayer of the taxpayer's qualifying inventory at the beginning of the year,; that the number of days in the year and after the date of disposition is of 365.

▶ 20(18) ◀

(18) Definitions — (Repealed by S.C. 2013, c. 34, s. 180(7).)

History: S. 20(18) was repealed by S.C. 2013, c. 34, s. 180(7), in force June 26, 2013, and formerly read:

(18) *Definitions.* For the purposes of this subsection and subsection (17),

"qualifying inventory" — "qualifying inventory" means tangible property described in subparagraphs 20(1)(*gg*)(i) and (ii) of the *Income Tax Act*, chapter 148 of the Revised Statutes of Canada, 1952, other than real property or an interest therein or property of a taxpayer that becomes property of a new corporation by virtue of an amalgamation or merger;

"specified transaction" — "specified transaction" means

(*a*) a distribution by a corporation of qualifying inventory on or in the course of its winding-up,

(*b*) a disposition by a taxpayer of all or a substantial part of the taxpayer's qualifying inventory, or

(*c*) a disposition at a particular time of qualifying inventory by a taxpayer one of the principal purposes of which was to permit a person with whom the taxpayer does not deal at arm's length to obtain a deduction in respect thereof under paragraph 20(1)(*gg*) of the *Income Tax Act*, chapter 148 of the Revised Statutes of Canada, 1952, for that person's first taxation year commencing after the particular time,

but does not include any such distribution or disposition by a taxpayer to another person during a taxation year of that other person that ends at least 11 months after the commencement of the taxation year of the taxpayer during which the distribution or disposition occurs.

▶ 20(19) ◀

(19) Annuity contract. Where a taxpayer has in a particular taxation year received a payment under an annuity contract in respect of which an amount was by virtue of subsection 12(3) included in computing the taxpayer's income for a taxation year commencing before 1983, there may be deducted in computing the taxpayer's income for the particular year such amount, if any, as is allowed by regulation.

Related Regulations: 303.

Related Sections: S. 87(2)(*j*.4) Accrual rules.

▶ 20(20) ◀

(20) Life insurance policy. Where in a taxation year a taxpayer disposes of an interest in a life insurance policy that is not an annuity contract (otherwise than as a consequence of a death) or of an interest in an annuity contract (other than a prescribed annuity contract), there may be deducted in computing the taxpayer's income for the year an amount equal to the lesser of

(*a*) the total of all amounts in respect of the interest in the policy that were included under section 12.2 of this Act or paragraph 56(1)(*d*.1) of the *Income Tax Act*, chapter 148 of the Revised Statutes of Canada, 1952, in computing the taxpayer's income for the year or a preceding taxation year, and

(*b*) the amount, if any, by which the adjusted cost basis (within the meaning assigned by section 148) to the taxpayer of that interest immediately before the disposition exceeds the proceeds of the disposition (within the meaning assigned by section 148) of the interest that the policyholder, a beneficiary or an assignee became entitled to receive.

Related Regulations: 304.

Related Sections: S. 148(2) Deemed proceeds of disposition.

▶ 20(21) ◀

(21) Debt obligation. If a taxpayer has in a particular taxation year disposed of a property that is an interest in, or for civil law a right in, a debt obligation for consideration equal to its fair market value at the time of disposition, there may be deducted in computing the taxpayer's income for the particular year the amount, if any, by which

(*a*) the total of all amounts each of which is an amount that was included in computing the taxpayer's income for the particular year or a preceding taxation year as interest in respect of that property

exceeds the total of all amounts each of which is

(*b*) the portion of an amount that was received or became receivable by the taxpayer in the particular year or a preceding taxation year that can reasonably be considered to be in respect of an amount described in paragraph (*a*) and that was not repaid by the taxpayer to the issuer of the debt obligation because of an adjustment in respect of interest received before the time of disposition by the taxpayer, or

(*c*) an amount in respect of that property that was deductible by the taxpayer by virtue of paragraph (14)(*b*) in computing the taxpayer's income for the particular year or a preceding taxation year.

History: S. 20(21), the portion before paragraph (*a*) was replaced by S.C. 2013, c. 34, s. 97(4), in force June 26, 2013, and formerly read:

(21) *Debt obligation.* Where a taxpayer has in a particular taxation year disposed of a property that is an interest in a debt obligation for consideration equal to its fair market value at the time of disposition, there may be deducted in computing the taxpayer's income for the particular year the amount, if any, by which

Related Sections: S. 12(3) Interest income; s. 12(4) Interest from investment contract; s. 12(9) Deemed accrual; s. 20(14) Accrued bond interest; s. 248(1), "amount"; s. 249(1) Definition of "taxation year".

Interpretation Bulletins: *Secondary* — IT-396R Interest income.

Tax Window Files: Interest Income Calculation — Coupon Bonds Issued at a Premium or Discount, *Technical Interpretation, Financial Industries Division, May 31, 2004*, CRA Document No. 2004-0074381E5.

► 20(22) ◄

(22) Deduction for negative reserves. In computing an insurer's income for a taxation year, there may be deducted the amount included under paragraph 12(1)(*e.1*) in computing the insurer's income for the preceding taxation year.

Related Sections: S. 12(1)(*e*.1) Negative reserves.

► 20(23) ◄

(23) "Member's portion" — (Repealed by 1990, c. 35, s. 4(3).)

► 20(24) ◄

(24) Amounts paid for undertaking future obligations. Where an amount is included under paragraph 12(1)(*a*) in computing a taxpayer's income for a taxation year in respect of an undertaking to which that paragraph applies and the taxpayer paid a reasonable amount in a particular taxation year to another person as consideration for the assumption by that other person of the taxpayer's obligations in respect of the undertaking, if the taxpayer and the other person jointly so elect,

(*a*) the payment may be deducted in computing the taxpayer's income for the particular year and no amount is deductible under paragraph (1)(*m*) or (*m*.1) in computing the taxpayer's income for that or any subsequent taxation year in respect of the undertaking; and

(*b*) where the amount was received by the other person in the course of business, it shall be deemed to be an amount described in paragraph 12(1)(*a*).

Editorial Note: S. 20(24) applies where a taxpayer receives prepaid (unearned) income in respect of goods to be delivered or services to be provided after the year of receipt, and subsequently the obligation to deliver or provide is assumed by another person. A reasonable amount paid to the other person as consideration for the assumption is deducted in computing the taxpayer's income, meaning that the taxpayer will effectively report net income (loss) equal to the amount by which the original prepayment exceeds (is less than) the amount paid to the other person. The provision is subject to a joint election by the taxpayer and the other person; see also s. 20(25) below.

Related Regulations: 600(*b*).

Related Sections: S. 12(1)(*a*) Services, etc., to be rendered; s. 20(1)(*m*) Reserve in respect of certain goods and services; s. 20(1)(*m*.1) Manufacturer's warranty reserve; s. 20(25) Manner of election; s. 220(3.2) Late, amended or revoked elections; s. 248(1), "amount", "business"; s. 249(1) Definition of "taxation year".

Tax Profile: January 2014–ITA Subsection 20(24)–A Critical Look.

Interpretation Bulletins: *Secondary* — IT-154R Special reserves.

Tax Window Files: Amounts Paid for Undertaking Future Obligations, *Technical Interpretation, Business and Partnerships Division, March 7, 2005*, CRA Document No. 2005-0114981E5. Subsection 20(24) deduction not limited to year of paragraph 12(1)(*a*) inclusion and therefore can be claimed in year of paragraph 12(1)(*e*) inclusion.

► 20(25) ◄

(25) Manner of election. An election under subsection (24) shall be made by notifying the Minister in writing on or before the earlier of the days on or before which either the payer or the recipient is required to file a return of income pursuant to section 150 for the taxation year in which the payment to which the election relates was made.

Interpretation Bulletins: *Secondary* — IT-154R Special reserves.

► 20(26) ◄

(26) Transition deduction re unpaid claims reserve — (Repealed by S.C. 2013, c. 34, s. 180(8).)

History: S. 20(26) was repealed by S.C. 2013, c. 34, s. 180(8), applicable to taxation years that begin after October 31, 2011, and formerly read:

(26) *Transition deduction re unpaid claims reserve.* An insurer may deduct, in computing its income for its taxation year that includes February 23, 1994, such amount as the insurer claims not exceeding the amount prescribed to be the insurer's unpaid claims reserve adjustment.

Related Regulations: 8100.

Related Sections: S. 12.3 Transition inclusion re unpaid claims reserve.

► 20(27) ◄

(27) Loans, etc., acquired in ordinary course of business. For the purposes of computing a deduction under paragraph (1)(*l*), (*l*.1) or (*p*) from the income for a taxation year of a taxpayer who was an insurer or whose ordinary business included the lending of money, a loan or lending asset or an instrument or commitment described in paragraph (1)(*l*.1) acquired from a person with whom the taxpayer did not deal at arm's length for an amount equal to its fair market value shall be deemed to have been acquired by the taxpayer in the ordinary course of the taxpayer's business of insurance or the lending of money where

(*a*) the person from whom the loan or lending asset or instrument or commitment was acquired carried on the business of insurance or the lending of money; and

(*b*) the loan or lending asset was made or acquired or the instrument or commitment was issued, made or assumed by the person in the ordinary course of the person's business of insurance or the lending of money.

► 20(27.1) ◄

(27.1) Application of ss. 13(21) and 138(12). The definitions in subsections 13(21) and 138(12) apply to this section.

► 20(28) ◄

(28) Deduction before available for use. In computing a taxpayer's income from a business or property for a taxation year ending before the time a building or a part thereof acquired after 1989 by the taxpayer becomes available for use by the taxpayer, there may be deducted an amount not exceeding the amount by which the lesser of (*a*) the amount that would be deductible under paragraph (1)(*a*) for the year in respect of the building if subsection 13(26) did not apply, and

(*b*) the taxpayer's income for the year from renting the building, computed without reference to this subsection and before deducting any amount in respect of the building under paragraph (1)(*a*)

exceeds

(*c*) the amount deductible under paragraph (1)(*a*) for the year in respect of the building, computed without reference to this subsection,

and any amount so deducted shall be deemed to be an amount deducted by the taxpayer under paragraph (1)(*a*) in computing the taxpayer's income for the year.

Editorial Note: The income limitation in s. 20(28)(*b*) is net of any deduction claimed under s. 20(29).

Related Sections: 13(26) Restriction on deduction before available for use; 13(27) Interpretation — available for use; 13(28) Idem; 13(29) Idem; 13(30) Transfers of property; 13(31) Idem; 13(32) Leased property; s. 20(1)(*a*) Capital cost of property; s. 20(29) Exception to soft costs capitalization rule.

► 20(29) ◄

(29) Idem. Where, because of subsection 18(3.1), a deduction would, but for this subsection, not be allowed to a taxpayer in respect of an outlay or expense in respect of a building, or part thereof, and the outlay or expense would, but for that subsection and without reference to this subsection, be deductible in computing the taxpayer's income for a taxation year, there may be deducted in respect of such outlays and expenses in computing the taxpayer's income for the year an amount equal to the lesser of

(*a*) the total of all such outlays or expenses, and

(*b*) the taxpayer's income for the year from renting the building or the part thereof computed without reference to subsection (28) and this subsection.

Editorial Note: S. 20(29) provides an exception to the capitalization of soft costs under s. 18(3.1), and allows a taxpayer to deduct such costs incurred in a year to the extent of the taxpayer's rental income from the building computed before taking into account any capital cost allowance under s. 20(28).

Related Sections: 13(26) Restriction on deduction before available for use; 13(27) Interpretation — available for use; 13(28) Idem; 13(29) Idem; 13(30) Transfers of property; 13(31) Idem; 13(32) Leased property; s. 18(3.1) Costs relating to construction of building or ownership of land; s. 20(1)(*gg*) Disability-related modifications to buildings.

► 20(30) ◄

(30) Specified reserve adjustment. For the purpose of the description of N in subclause (1)(*l*)(ii)(D)(II), the specified reserve adjustment for a loan of a taxpayer for a taxation year is the amount determined by the formula

$$0.1(A \times B \times C/365)$$

where

A is the carrying amount of the impaired loan that is used or would be used in determining the interest income on the loan for the year in accordance with generally accepted accounting principles;

B is the effective interest rate on the loan for the year determined in accordance with generally accepted accounting principles; and

C is the number of days in the year on which the loan is impaired.

SECTION 20.01: PHSP premiums

► 20.01(1) ◄

(1) PHSP premiums. Notwithstanding paragraphs 18(1)(*a*) and (*h*) and subject to subsection (2), there may be deducted in computing an individual's income for a taxation year from a business carried on by the individual and in which the individual is actively engaged on a regular and continuous basis, directly or as a member of a partnership, an amount payable by the individual or partnership in respect of the year as a premium, contribution or other consideration under a private health services plan in respect of the individual, the individual's spouse or common-law partner or any person who is a member of the individual's household if

(*a*) in the year or in the preceding taxation year

(i) the total of all amounts each of which is the individual's income from such a business for a fiscal period that ends in the year exceeds 50% of the individual's income for the year, or

(ii) the individual's income for the year does not exceed the total of $10,000 and the total referred to in subparagraph (i) in respect of the individual for the year,

on the assumption that the individual's income from each business is computed without reference to this subsection and the individual's income is computed without reference to this subsection and subdivision e; and

(*b*) the amount is payable under a contract between the individual or partnership and

(i) a person licensed or otherwise authorized under the laws of Canada or a province to carry on in Canada an insurance business or the business of offering to the public its services as trustee,

(ii) a person or partnership engaged in the business of offering to the public its services as an administrator of private health services plans, or

(iii) a person the taxable income of which is exempt under section 149 and that is a business or professional organization of which the individual is a member or a trade union of which the individual or a majority of the individual's employees are members.

Related Sections: S. 6(1)(*a*) Value of benefits; s. 18(1)(*a*) General limitation; s. 118.2(2)(*q*) Medical expenses; s. 248(1), "disposition", "private health services plan".

► 20.01(2) ◄

(2) Limit. For the purpose of calculating the amount deductible under subsection (1) in computing an individual's income for a taxation year from a particular business,

(*a*) no amount may be deducted to the extent that

(i) it is deducted under this section in computing another individual's income for any taxation year, or

(ii) it is included in calculating a deduction under section 118.2 in computing an individual's tax payable under this Part for any taxation year;

(*b*) where an amount payable under a private health services plan relates to a period in the year throughout which

(i) each of one or more persons

(A) is employed on a full-time basis (other than on a temporary or seasonal basis) in the particular business or in another business carried on by

(I) the individual (otherwise than as a member of a partnership),

(II) a partnership of which the individual is a majority-interest partner, or

(III) a corporation affiliated with the individual, and

(B) has accumulated not less than three months of service in that employment since the person last became so employed, and

(ii) the total number of persons employed in a business described in clause (i)(A), with whom the individual deals at arm's length and to whom coverage is extended under the plan, is not less than 50% of the total number of persons each of whom is a person

(A) who carries on the particular business or is employed in a business described in clause (i)(A), and

(B) to whom coverage is extended under the plan,

the amount so deductible in relation to the period shall not exceed the individual's cost of equivalent coverage under the plan in respect of each employed person who deals at arm's length with the individual and who is described in subparagraph (i) in relation to the period;

(*c*) subject to paragraph (*d*), where an amount payable under a private health services plan relates to a particular period in the year, other than a period described in paragraph (*b*), the amount so deductible in relation to the particular period shall not exceed the amount determined by the formula

$$(A/365) \times (B + C)$$

where

A is the number of days in the year that are included in the particular period,

B is the product obtained when $1,500 is multiplied by the number of persons each of whom is covered under the plan, and

(i) is the individual or the individual's spouse or common-law partner, or

(ii) is a member of the individual's household and has attained the age of 18 years before the beginning of the particular period, and

C is the product obtained when $750 is multiplied by the number of members of the individual's household who, but for the fact that they have not attained the age of 18 years before the particular period began, would be included in computing the product under the description of B; and

(*d*) where an amount payable under a private health services plan relates to a particular period in the year (other than a period described in paragraph (*b*)) and one or more persons with whom the individual deals at arm's length are described in subparagraph (*b*)(i) in relation to the particular period, the amount so deductible in relation to the particular period shall not exceed the lesser of the amount determined under the formula set out in paragraph (*c*) and the individual's cost of equivalent coverage in respect of any such person in relation to the particular period.

History: S. 20.01(2)(*b*)(i)(A)(II) was replaced by S.C. 2013, c. 40, s. 12, in force December 12, 2013, and formerly read:

(II) a partnership of which the individual is a majority interest partner, or

► 20.01(3) ◄

(3) Equivalent coverage. For the purpose of subsection (2), an amount payable in respect of an individual under a private health services plan in relation to a period does not exceed the individual's cost of equivalent coverage under the plan in respect of another person in relation to the period to the extent that, in relation to the period, the amount does not exceed the product obtained when

(*a*) the amount that would be the individual's cost of coverage under the plan if the benefits and coverage in respect of the individual, the individual's spouse or common-law partner and the members of the individual's household were identical to the benefits and coverage made available in respect of the other person, the other person's spouse or common-law partner and the members of the other person's household

is multiplied by

(*b*) the percentage of the cost of coverage under the plan in respect of the other person that is payable by the individual or a partnership of which the individual is a member.

SECTION 20.1: [Borrowed money used to earn income from business or property]

► 20.1(1) ◄

(1) Borrowed money used to earn income from property. Where

(*a*) at any time after 1993 borrowed money ceases to be used by a taxpayer for the purpose of earning income from a capital property (other than real or immovable property or depreciable property), and

(*b*) the amount of the borrowed money that was so used by the taxpayer immediately before that time exceeds the total of

(i) where the taxpayer disposed of the property at that time for an amount of consideration that is not less than the fair market value of the property at that time, the amount of the borrowed money used to acquire the consideration,

(ii) where the taxpayer disposed of the property at that time and subparagraph (i) does not apply, the amount of the borrowed money that, if the taxpayer had received as consideration an amount of money equal to the amount by which the fair market value of the property at that time exceeds the amount included in the total by reason of subparagraph (iii), would be considered to be used to acquire the consideration,

(iii) where the taxpayer disposed of the property at that time for consideration that includes a reduction in the amount of the borrowed money, the amount of the reduction, and

(iv) where the taxpayer did not dispose of the property at that time, the amount of the borrowed money that, if the taxpayer had disposed of the property at that time and received as consideration an amount of money equal to the fair market value of the property at that time, would be considered to be used to acquire the consideration,

an amount of the borrowed money equal to the excess shall, to the extent that the amount is outstanding after that time, be deemed to be used by the taxpayer for the purpose of earning income from the property.

Editorial Note: S. 20.1 effectively overrules the decision in *Emerson v. The Queen*, 86 DTC 6184 (F.C.A.), which held that interest on borrowed money ceased to be deductible under s. 20(1)(*c*) when the source of income to which the interest related no longer existed, unless the borrowed money could be traced to another income-producing use.

History: S. 20.1(1)(*a*) was replaced by S.C. 2013, c. 34, s. 98(2), in force June 26, 2013, and formerly read:

(*a*) at any time after 1993 borrowed money ceases to be used by a taxpayer for the purpose of earning income from a capital property (other than real property or depreciable property), and

Related Sections: S. 20(1)(*c*) Interest; s. 20(3) Borrowed money.

Income Tax Folios: *Secondary* — S3-F6-C1 Interest Deductibility.

► 20.1(2) ◄

(2) Borrowed money used to earn income from business. Where at any particular time after 1993 a taxpayer ceases to carry on a business and, as a consequence, borrowed money ceases to be used by the taxpayer for the purpose of earning income from the business, the following rules apply:

(*a*) where, at any time (in this paragraph referred to as the "time of disposition") at or after the particular time, the taxpayer disposes of property that was last used by the taxpayer in the business, an amount of the borrowed money equal to the lesser of

(i) the fair market value of the property at the time of disposition, and

(ii) the amount of the borrowed money outstanding at the time of disposition that is not deemed by this paragraph to have been used before the time of disposition to acquire any other property

shall be deemed to have been used by the taxpayer immediately before the time of disposition to acquire the property;

(*b*) subject to paragraph (*a*), the borrowed money shall, after the particular time, be deemed not to have been used to acquire property that was used by the taxpayer in the business;

(*c*) the portion of the borrowed money outstanding at any time after the particular time that is not deemed by paragraph (*a*) to have been used before that subsequent time to acquire property shall be deemed to be used by the taxpayer at that subsequent time for the purpose of earning income from the business; and

(*d*) the business shall be deemed to have fiscal periods after the particular time that coincide with the taxation years of the taxpayer, except that the first such fiscal period shall be deemed to begin at the end of the business's last fiscal period that began before the particular time.

Related Sections: S. 20(1)(*c*) Interest; s. 20(3) Borrowed money.

Cases: The unpaid balance of borrowed money for use in a taxpayer's business which is outstanding after the business has ceased to exist is deemed to have been used by the taxpayer to earn income from that business. The deduction by the taxpayer of the interest expense for 2013–2014 was justified. *Moras v. The Queen*, 2019 DTC 1071 (TCC)

The taxpayer ceased to operate a business and later disposed of property used in that business. Interest on funds borrowed to acquire such property was deductible under s. 20.1(2). *Ciebien v. The Queen*, 2002 DTC 1589 (T.C.C.)

► 20.1(3) ◄

(3) Deemed dispositions. For the purpose of paragraph (2)(*a*),

(*a*) where a property was used by a taxpayer in a business that the taxpayer has ceased to carry on, the taxpayer shall be deemed to dispose of the property at the time at which the taxpayer begins to use the property in another business or for any other purpose;

(*b*) where a taxpayer, who has at any time ceased to carry on a business, regularly used a property in part in the business and in part for some other purpose,

(i) the taxpayer shall be deemed to have disposed of the property at that time, and

(ii) the fair market value of the property at that time shall be deemed to equal the proportion of the fair market value of the property at that time that the use regularly made of the property in the business was of the whole use regularly made of the property; and

(*c*) where the taxpayer is a trust, subsections 104(4) to (5.2) do not apply.

Related Sections: S. 20(3) Borrowed money.

► 20.1(4) ◄

(4) Amount payable for property. Where an amount is payable by a taxpayer for property, the amount shall be deemed, for the purposes of this section and, where subsection (2) applies with respect to the amount, for the purposes of this Act, to be payable in respect of borrowed money used by the taxpayer to acquire the property.

Related Sections: S. 20(3) Borrowed money.

Income Tax Folios: *Secondary* — S3-F6-C1 Interest Deductibility.

► 20.1(5) ◄

(5) Interest in partnership. For the purposes of this section, where borrowed money that has been used to acquire an interest in a partnership is, as a consequence, considered to be used at any time for the purpose of earning income from a business or property of the partnership, the borrowed money shall be deemed to be used at that time for the purpose of earning income from property that is the interest in the partnership and not to be used for the purpose of earning income from the business or property of the partnership.

Related Sections: S. 20(3) Borrowed money.

▶ 20.1(6) ◀

(6) Refinancings. Where at any time a taxpayer uses borrowed money to repay money previously borrowed that was deemed by paragraph (2)(*c*) immediately before that time to be used for the purpose of earning income from a business,

(*a*) paragraphs (2)(*a*) to (*c*) apply with respect to the borrowed money; and

(*b*) subsection 20(3) does not apply with respect to the borrowed money.

Related Sections: S. 20(3) Borrowed money.

SECTION 20.2: [Interest — authorized foreign bank]

▶ 20.2(1) ◀

(1) Interest — authorized foreign bank — interpretation. The following definitions apply in this section.

"branch advance" —"branch advance" of an authorized foreign bank means an amount allocated or provided by, or on behalf of, the bank to, or for the benefit of, its Canadian banking business under terms that were documented, before the amount was so allocated or provided, to the same extent as, and in a form similar to the form in which, the bank would ordinarily document a loan by it to a person with whom it deals at arm's length.

"branch financial statements" —"branch financial statements" of an authorized foreign bank for a taxation year means the unconsolidated statements of assets and liabilities and of income and expenses for the year, in respect of its Canadian banking business,

(*a*) that form part of the bank's annual report for the year filed with the Superintendent of Financial Institutions as required under section 601 of the *Bank Act*, and accepted by the Superintendent, and

(*b*) if no filing is so required for the taxation year, that are prepared in a manner consistent with the statements in the annual report or reports so filed and accepted for the period or periods in which the taxation year falls,

except if the Minister demonstrates that the statements are not prepared in accordance with generally-accepted accounting principles in Canada as modified by any specifications applicable to the bank made by the Superintendent of Financial Institutions under subsection 308(4) of the *Bank Act* (in this definition referred to as "modified GAAP"), in which case it means the statements subject to such modifications as are required to make them comply with modified GAAP.

"calculation period" —"calculation period" of an authorized foreign bank for a taxation year means any one of a series of regular periods into which the year is divided in a designation by the bank in its return of income for the year or, in the absence of such a designation, by the Minister,

(*a*) none of which is longer than 31 days;

(*b*) the first of which commences at the beginning of the year and the last of which ends at the end of the year; and

(*c*) that are, unless the Minister otherwise agrees in writing, consistent with the calculation periods designated for the bank's preceding taxation year.

▶ 20.2(2) ◀

(2) Formula elements. The following descriptions apply for the purposes of the formulae in subsection (3) for any calculation period in a taxation year of an authorized foreign bank:

A is the amount of the bank's assets at the end of the period;

BA is the amount of the bank's branch advances at the end of the period;

IBA is the total of all amounts each of which is a reasonable amount on account of notional interest for the period, in respect of a branch advance, that would be deductible in computing the bank's income for the year if it were interest payable by, and the advance were indebtedness of, the bank to another person and if this Act were read without reference to paragraph 18(1)(*v*) and this section;

IL is the total of all amounts each of which is an amount on account of interest for the period in respect of a liability of the bank to another person or partnership that would be deductible in computing the bank's income for the year if this Act were read without reference to paragraph 18(1)(*v*) and this section; and

L is the amount of the bank's liabilities to other persons and partnerships at the end of the period.

▶ 20.2(3) ◀

(3) Interest deduction. In computing the income of an authorized foreign bank from its Canadian banking business for a taxation year, there may be deducted on account of interest for each calculation period of the bank for the year,

(*a*) where the total amount at the end of the period of its liabilities to other persons and partnerships and branch advances is 95% or more of the amount of its assets at that time, an amount not exceeding

(i) if the amount of liabilities to other persons and partnerships at that time is less than 95% of the amount of its assets at that time, the amount determined by the formula

$$IL + IBA \times (0.95 \times A - L)/BA$$

and

(ii) if the amount of those liabilities at that time is greater than or equal to 95% of the amount of its assets at that time, the amount determined by the formula

$$IL \times (0.95 \times A)/L$$

and

(*b*) in any other case, the total of

(i) the amount determined by the formula

IL + IBA

and

(ii) the product of

(A) the amount claimed by the bank, in its return of income for the year, not exceeding the amount determined by the formula

(0.95 × A) - (L + BA)

and

(B) the average, based on daily observations, of the Bank of Canada bank rate for the period.

► 20.2(4) ◄

(4) Branch amounts. Only amounts that are in respect of an authorized foreign bank's Canadian banking business, and that are recorded in the books of account of the business in a manner consistent with the manner in which they are required to be treated for the purposes of the branch financial statements, shall be used to determine

(*a*) the amounts in subsection (2); and

(*b*) the amounts in subsection (3) of an authorized foreign bank's assets, liabilities to other persons and partnerships, and branch advances.

► 20.2(5) ◄

(5) Notional interest. For the purposes of the description of IBA in subsection (2), a reasonable amount on account of notional interest for a calculation period in respect of a branch advance is the amount that would be payable on account of interest for the period by a notional borrower, having regard to the duration of the advance, the currency in which repayment is required and all other terms, as adjusted by paragraph (*c*), of the advance, if

(*a*) the borrower were a person that dealt at arm's length with the bank, that carried on the bank's Canadian banking business and that had the same credit-worthiness and borrowing capacity as the bank;

(*b*) the advance were a loan by the bank to the borrower; and

(*c*) any of the terms of the advance (excluding the rate of interest, but including the structure of the interest calculation, such as whether the rate is fixed or floating and the choice of any reference rate referred to) that are not terms that would be made between the bank as lender and the borrower, having regard to all the circumstances, including the nature of the Canadian banking business, the use of the advanced funds in the business and normal risk management practices for banks, were instead terms that would be agreed to by the bank and the borrower.

Related Sections: S. 18(1)(*v*) Interest — authorized foreign bank; s. 212(13.3) Application of Part XIII to authorized foreign bank; s. 218.2(2) Taxable interest expense; s. 248(1), "authorized foreign bank", "Canadian banking business".

SECTION 20.3: [Weak currency debt]

► 20.3(1) ◄

(1) Weak currency debt — interpretation. The definitions in this subsection apply in this section.

"exchange date" — "exchange date" in respect of a debt of a taxpayer that is at any time a weak currency debt means, if the debt is incurred or assumed by the taxpayer

(*a*) in respect of borrowed money that is denominated in the final currency, the day that the debt is incurred or assumed by the taxpayer; and

(*b*) in respect of borrowed money that is not denominated in the final currency, or in respect of the acquisition of property, the day on which the taxpayer uses the borrowed money or the acquired property, directly or indirectly, to acquire funds that are, or to settle an obligation that is, denominated in the final currency.

"hedge" — "hedge" in respect of a debt of a taxpayer that is at any time a weak currency debt means any agreement made by the taxpayer

(*a*) that can reasonably be regarded as having been made by the taxpayer primarily to reduce the taxpayer's risk, with respect to payments of principal or interest in respect of the debt, of fluctuations in the value of the weak currency; and

(*b*) that is identified by the taxpayer as a hedge in respect of the debt in a designation in prescribed form filed with the Minister on or before the 30th day after the day the taxpayer enters into the agreement.

"weak currency debt" — "weak currency debt" of a taxpayer at a particular time means a particular debt in a foreign currency (in this section referred to as the "weak currency"), incurred or assumed by the taxpayer at a time (in this section referred to as the "commitment time") after February 27, 2000, in respect of a borrowing of money or an acquisition of property, where

(*a*) any of the following applies, namely,

(i) the borrowed money is denominated in a currency (in this section referred to as the "final currency") other than the weak currency, is used for the purpose of earning income from a business or property and is not used to acquire funds in a currency other than the final currency,

(ii) the borrowed money or the acquired property is used, directly or indirectly, to acquire funds that are denominated in a currency (in this section referred to as the "final currency") other than the weak currency, that are used for the purpose of earning income from a business or property and that are not used to acquire funds in a currency other than the final currency,

(iii) the borrowed money or the acquired property is used, directly or indirectly, to settle an obligation that is denominated in a currency (in this section referred to as the "final currency") other than the weak currency, that is incurred or assumed for the purpose of earning income from a business or property and that is not incurred or assumed to acquire funds in a currency other than the final currency, or

(iv) the borrowed money or the acquired property is used, directly or indirectly, to settle another debt of the taxpayer that is at any time a weak currency debt in respect of which the final currency (which is deemed to be the final currency in respect of the particular debt) is a currency other than the currency of the particular debt;

(*b*) the amount of the particular debt (together with any other debt that would, but for this paragraph, be at any time a weak currency debt, and that can reasonably be regarded as having been incurred or assumed by the taxpayer as part of a series of transactions that includes the incurring or assumption of the particular debt) exceeds $500,000; and

(*c*) either of the following applies, namely,

(i) if the rate at which interest is payable at the particular time in the weak currency in respect of the particular debt is determined under a formula based on the value from time to time of a reference rate (other than a reference rate the value of which is established or materially influenced by the taxpayer), the interest rate at the commitment time, as determined under the formula as though interest were then payable, exceeds by more than two percentage points the rate at which interest would have been payable at the commitment time in the final currency if

(A) the taxpayer had, at the commitment time, instead incurred or assumed an equivalent amount of debt in the final currency on the same terms as the particular debt (excluding the rate of interest but including the structure of the interest calculation, such as whether the rate is fixed or floating) with those modifications that the difference in currency requires, and

(B) interest on the equivalent amount of debt referred to in clause (A) was payable at the commitment time, or

(ii) in any other case, the rate at which interest is payable at the particular time in the weak currency in respect of the particular debt exceeds by more than two percentage points the rate at which interest would have been payable at the particular time in the final currency if at the commitment time the taxpayer had instead incurred or assumed an equivalent amount of debt in the final currency on the same terms as the particular debt (excluding the rate of interest but including the structure of the interest calculation, such as whether the rate is fixed or floating), with those modifications that the difference in currency requires.

► 20.3(2) ◄

(2) Interest and gain. Notwithstanding any other provision of this Act, the following rules apply in respect of a particular debt of a taxpayer (other than a corporation described in one or more of paragraphs (*a*), (*b*), (*c*) and (*e*) of the definition "specified financial institution" in subsection 248(1)) that is at any time a weak currency debt:

(*a*) no deduction on account of interest that accrues on the debt for any period that begins after the day that is the later of June 30, 2000 and the exchange date during which it is a weak currency debt shall exceed the amount of interest that would, if at the commitment time the taxpayer had instead incurred or assumed an equivalent amount of debt, the principal and interest in respect of which were denominated in the final currency, on the same terms as the particular debt (excluding the rate of interest but including the structure of the interest calculation, such as whether the rate is fixed or floating) have accrued on the equivalent debt during that period, with those modifications that the difference in currency requires;

(*b*) the amount, if any, of the taxpayer's gain or loss (in this section referred to as a "foreign exchange gain or loss") for a taxation year on the settlement or extinguishment of the debt that arises because of the fluctuation in the value of any currency shall be included or deducted, as the case may be, in computing the taxpayer's income for the year from the business or the property to which the debt relates; and

(*c*) the amount of any interest on the debt that was, because of this subsection, not deductible is deemed, for the purpose of computing the taxpayer's foreign exchange gain or loss on the settlement or extinguishment of the debt, to be an amount paid by the taxpayer to settle or extinguish the debt.

Related Sections: S. 20(1)(*c*) Interest.

Canadian Petroleum Tax Journal: Café Annie's Tasty Inbound Financing, Jim McKee, 2002, Vol. 15, No. 1.

Canadian Tax Foundation: Chapman and Marcovitz, *Weak-Currency Borrowing Transactions*, 2001 Canadian Tax Journal 4:961–983.

► 20.3(3) ◄

(3) Hedges. In applying subsection (2) in circumstances where a taxpayer has entered into a hedge in respect of a debt of the taxpayer that is at any time a weak currency debt, the amount paid or payable in the weak currency for a taxation year on account of interest on the debt, or paid in the weak currency in the year on account of the debt's principal, shall be decreased by the amount of any foreign exchange gain, or increased by the amount of any foreign exchange loss, on the hedge in respect of the amount so paid or payable.

► 20.3(4) ◄

(4) Repayment of principal. If the amount (expressed in the weak currency) outstanding on account of principal in respect of a debt of the taxpayer that is at any time a weak currency debt is reduced before maturity (whether by repayment or otherwise), the amount (expressed in the weak currency) of the reduction is deemed, except for the purposes of determining the rate of interest that would have been charged on an equivalent loan in the final currency and applying paragraph (*b*) of the definition "weak currency debt" in subsection (1), to have been a separate debt from the commitment time.

SECTION 20.4: [Insurer's reserve deduction]

▶ 20.4(1) ◀

(1) Definitions. The definitions in section 12.5 apply for the purposes of this section.

History: S. 20.4(1) was added by S.C. 2009, c. 2, s. 8(1), applicable to taxation years that begin after September 2006.

▶ 20.4(2) ◀

(2) Transition year income deduction. There shall be deducted in computing an insurer's income for its transition year from an insurance business carried on by it in Canada in the transition year the absolute value of the negative amount, if any, of the insurer's reserve transition amount in respect of that insurance business.

History: S. 20.4(2) was added by S.C. 2009, c. 2, s. 8(1), applicable to taxation years that begin after September 2006.

▶ 20.4(3) ◀

(3) Transition year income inclusion reversal. If an amount has been included under subsection 12.5(2) in computing an insurer's income for its transition year from an insurance business carried on by it in Canada, there shall be deducted in computing the insurer's income, for each particular taxation year of the insurer that ends after the beginning of the transition year, from that insurance business, the amount determined by the formula

$$A \times B/1825$$

where

A is the amount included under subsection 12.5(2) in computing the insurer's income for the transition year from that insurance business; and

B is the number of days in the particular taxation year that are before the day that is 1825 days after the first day of the transition year.

History: S. 20.4(3) was added by S.C. 2009, c. 2, s. 8(1), applicable to taxation years that begin after September 2006.

▶ 20.4(4) ◀

(4) Ceasing to carry on business. If at any time an insurer ceases to carry on all or substantially all of an insurance business (referred to in this subsection as the "discontinued business"), and none of subsections 12.5(4) to (6) apply, there shall be deducted in computing the insurer's income from the discontinued business for the insurer's taxation year that includes the time that is immediately before that time, the amount determined by the formula

$$A - B$$

where

A is any amount included under subsection 12.5(2) in computing the insurer's income from the discontinued business for its transition year; and

B is the total of all amounts each of which is an amount deducted under subsection (3) in computing the insurer's income from the discontinued business for a taxation year that began before that time.

History: S. 20.4(4) was added by S.C. 2009, c. 2, s. 8(1), applicable to taxation years that begin after September 2006.

SECTION 21: Cost of borrowed money

▶ 21(1) ◀

(1) Cost of borrowed money. Where in a taxation year a taxpayer has acquired depreciable property, if the taxpayer elects under this subsection in the taxpayer's return of income under this Part for the year,

(*a*) in computing the taxpayer's income for the year and for such of the 3 immediately preceding taxation years as the taxpayer had, paragraphs 20(1)(*c*), (*d*), (*e*) and (*e*.1) do not apply to the amount or to the part of the amount specified in the taxpayer's election that, but for an election under this subsection in respect thereof, would be deductible in computing the taxpayer's income (other than exempt income) for any such year in respect of borrowed money used to acquire the depreciable property or the amount payable for the depreciable property; and

(*b*) the amount or the part of the amount, as the case may be, described in paragraph (*a*) shall be added to the capital cost to the taxpayer of the depreciable property so acquired by the taxpayer.

Related Regulations: 600(*a*).

Related Sections: S. 20(3) Borrowed money; s. 21(5) Reassessments; s. 212(1)(*b*)(iii)(E) Interest; s. 220(3.2) Late, amended or revoked elections.

Tax Profile: March 2013 — Non-Resident Investment in Canadian Real Estate.

Tax Topics: No. 2023-24, 2010 Canadian Tax Foundation CRA Roundtable: Pipelines, Privilege and Working Papers (Again!).

Information Circulars: IC 07-1 Taxpayer relief provisions.

Interpretation Bulletins: *Primary* — IT-121R3 Election to capitalize cost of borrowed money. *Secondary* — IT-142R3 Settlement of debts on the winding-up of a corporation; IT-341R4 Expenses of issuing or selling shares, units in a trust, interests in a partnership or syndicate and expenses of borrowing money.

Cases: Construction period interest may be treated as an expense, deductible under s. 20(1)(c), or may be capitalized under s. 21(1), but not otherwise. Capitalized interest is not part of the capital cost for ITC purposes. *Alberta Wheat Pool et al. v. The Queen*, 99 DTC 5198 (F.C.A.), affirming 96 DTC 1795 (T.C.C.).

▶ 21(2) ◀

(2) Borrowed money used for exploration or development. Where in a taxation year a taxpayer has used borrowed money for the purpose of exploration, development or the acquisition of property and the expenses incurred by the taxpayer in respect of those activities are Canadian exploration and development expenses, Canadian exploration expenses, Canadian development expenses, Canadian oil and gas property expenses, foreign resource expenses in respect of a country, or foreign exploration and development expenses, as the case may be, if the taxpayer so elects under this subsection in the taxpayer's return of income for the year,

(*a*) in computing the taxpayer's income for the year and for such of the three immediately preceding taxation years as the taxpayer had, paragraphs 20(1)(*c*), (*d*), (*e*) and (*e*.1) do not apply to the amount or to the part of the amount specified in the taxpayer's election that, but for that election, would be deductible in computing the taxpayer's income (other than exempt income or income that is exempt from tax under this Part) for any such year in respect of the borrowed money used for the exploration, development or acquisition of property, as the case may be; and

(*b*) the amount or the part of the amount, as the case may be, described in paragraph (*a*) is deemed to be Canadian exploration and development expenses, Canadian exploration expenses, Canadian development expenses, Canadian oil and gas property expenses, foreign resource expenses in respect of a country, or foreign exploration and development expenses, as the case may be, incurred by the taxpayer in the year.

Related Regulations: 600(*a*).

Related Sections: S. 21(5) Reassessments; s. 66 Exploration and development expenses of principal-business corporations s. 220(3.2) Late, amended or revoked elections.

Information Circulars: IC 07-1 Taxpayer relief provisions.

Interpretation Bulletins: *Primary* — IT-121R3 Election to capitalize cost of borrowed money. *Secondary* — IT-142R3 Settlement of debts on the winding-up of a corporation; IT-341R4 Expenses of issuing or selling shares, units in a trust, interests in a partnership or syndicate and expenses of borrowing money.

▶ 21(3) ◀

(3) Borrowing for depreciable property. In computing the income of a taxpayer for a particular taxation year, where the taxpayer

(*a*) in any preceding taxation year

(i) made an election under subsection (1) in respect of borrowed money used to acquire depreciable property or an amount payable for depreciable property acquired by the taxpayer, or

(ii) was, by virtue of subsection 18(3.1), required to include an amount in respect of the construction of a depreciable property in computing the capital cost to the taxpayer of the depreciable property, and

(*b*) in each taxation year, if any, after that preceding taxation year and before the particular year, made an election under this subsection covering the total amount that, but for an election under this subsection in respect thereof, would have been deductible in computing the taxpayer's income (other than exempt income) for each such year in respect of the borrowed money used to acquire the depreciable property or the amount payable for the depreciable property acquired by the taxpayer,

if an election under this subsection is made in the taxpayer's return of income under this Part for the particular year, paragraphs 20(1)(*c*), (*d*), (*e*) and (*e*.1) do not apply to the amount or to the part of the amount specified in the election that, but for an election under this subsection in respect thereof, would be deductible in computing the taxpayer's income (other than exempt income) for the particular year in respect of the borrowed money used to acquire the depreciable property or the amount payable for the depreciable property acquired by the taxpayer, and the amount or part of the amount, as the case may be, shall be added to the capital cost to the taxpayer of the depreciable property.

Related Regulations: 600(*a*).

Related Sections: S. 220(3.2) Late, amended or revoked elections.

Interpretation Bulletins: *Primary* — IT-121R3 Election to capitalize cost of borrowed money. *Secondary* — IT-142R3 Settlement of debts on the winding-up of a corporation; IT-341R4 Expenses of issuing or selling shares, units in a trust, interests in a partnership or syndicate and expenses of borrowing money.

▶ 21(4) ◀

(4) Borrowing for exploration, etc. In computing the income of a taxpayer for a particular taxation year, where the taxpayer

(*a*) in any preceding taxation year made an election under subsection (2) in respect of borrowed money used for the purpose of exploration, development or acquisition of property,

(*b*) in each taxation year, if any, after that preceding taxation year and before the particular year, made an election under this subsection covering the total amount that, but for that election, would have been deductible in computing the taxpayer's income (other than exempt income or income that is exempt from tax under this Part) for each such year in respect of the borrowed money used for the exploration, development or acquisition of property, as the case may be, and

(*c*) so elects in the taxpayer's return of income for the particular year,

the following rules apply:

(*d*) paragraphs 20(1)(*c*), (*d*), (*e*) and (*e*.1) do not apply to the amount or to the part of the amount specified in the election that, but for the election, would be deductible in computing the taxpayer's income (other than exempt income or income that is exempt from tax under this Part) for the particular year in respect of the borrowed money used for the exploration, development or acquisition of property, and

(*e*) the amount or part of the amount, as the case may be, is deemed to be Canadian exploration and development expenses, Canadian exploration expenses, Canadian development expenses, Canadian oil and gas property expenses, foreign resource expenses in respect of a country, or foreign exploration and development expenses, as the case may be, incurred by the taxpayer in the particular year.

Related Regulations: 600(*a*).

Related Sections: S. 220(3.2) Late, amended or revoked elections.

Interpretation Bulletins: *Primary* — IT-121R3 Election to capitalize cost of borrowed money. *Secondary* — IT-142R3 Settlement of debts on the winding-up of a corporation; IT-341R4 Expenses of issuing or selling shares, units in a trust, interests in a partnership or syndicate and expenses of borrowing money.

▶ 21(5) ◀

(5) Reassessments. Notwithstanding any other provision of this Act, where a taxpayer has made an election in accordance with the provisions of subsection (1) or (2), such reassessments of tax, interest or penalties shall be made as are necessary to give effect thereto.

Related Regulations: 600(*a*).

Related Sections: S. 13(10) Deemed capital cost; s. 13(21), "depreciable property"; s. 20(3) Borrowed money; s. 248(1), "amount", "assessment", "exempt income", "prescribed", "regulation".

Interpretation Bulletins: *Primary* — IT-121R3 Election to capitalize cost of borrowed money. *Secondary* — IT-142R3 Settlement of debts on the winding-up of a corporation; IT-341R4 Expenses of issuing or selling shares, units in a trust, interests in a partnership or syndicate and expenses of borrowing money.

Ceasing to carry on business

SECTION 22: Sale of accounts receivable

► 22(1) ◄

(1) Sale of accounts receivable. Where a person who has been carrying on a business has, in a taxation year, sold all or substantially all the property used in carrying on the business, including the debts that have been or will be included in computing the person's income for that year or a previous year and that are still outstanding, and including the debts arising from loans made in the ordinary course of the person's business if part of the person's ordinary business was the lending of money and that are still outstanding, to a purchaser who proposes to continue the business which the vendor has been carrying on, if the vendor and the purchaser have executed jointly an election in prescribed form to have this section apply, the following rules are applicable:

(*a*) there may be deducted in computing the vendor's income for the taxation year an amount equal to the difference between the face value of the debts so sold (other than debts in respect of which the vendor has made deductions under paragraph 20(1)(*p*)), and the consideration paid by the purchaser to the vendor for the debts so sold;

(*b*) an amount equal to the difference described in paragraph (*a*) shall be included in computing the purchaser's income for the taxation year;

(*c*) the debts so sold shall be deemed, for the purposes of paragraphs 20(1)(*l*) and (*p*), to have been included in computing the purchaser's income for the taxation year or a previous year but no deduction may be made by the purchaser under paragraph 20(1)(*p*) in respect of a debt in respect of which the vendor has previously made a deduction; and

(*d*) each amount deducted by the vendor in computing income for a previous year under paragraph 20(1)(*p*) in respect of any of the debts so sold shall be deemed, for the purpose of paragraph 12(1)(*i*), to have been so deducted by the purchaser.

Editorial Note: In the absence of the s. 22 election, a loss incurred by the vendor on the sale of the accounts receivable would likely be on capital account. S. 22 does not specify the time period for filing the election, although the CRA indicates that the election should be filed with the tax return of either party for the year of sale (see Form T2022).

Related Sections: S. 22(2) Statement by vendor and purchaser.

Tax Profile: August 2012 — U.S. Purchases and Sales of Canadian Businesses: Tax and Corporate Issues; July 2012 — Asset Sale — Price Allocation.

Tax Topics: No. 2075, 2011 Canadian Tax Foundation Roundtable.

Forms: T2022 — Election in Respect of the Sale of Debts Receivable.

Interpretation Bulletins: *Primary* — IT-188R Sale of accounts receivable. *Secondary* — IT-291R3 Transfer of property to a corporation under subsection 85(1); IT-442R Bad debts and reserves for doubtful debts.

► 22(2) ◄

(2) Statement by vendor and purchaser. An election executed for the purposes of subsection (1) shall contain a statement by the vendor and the purchaser jointly as to the consideration paid for the debts sold by the vendor to the purchaser and that statement shall, subject to subsection 69(1), as against the Minister, be binding on the vendor and the purchaser in so far as it may be relevant in respect of any matter arising under this Act.

Related Sections: S. 248(1), "amount", "business", "prescribed", "property".

SECTION 23: Sale of inventory

► 23(1) ◄

(1) Sale of inventory. Where, on or after disposing of or ceasing to carry on a business or a part of a business, a taxpayer has sold all or any part of the property that was included in the inventory of the business, the property so sold shall, for the purposes of this Part, be deemed to have been sold by the taxpayer in the course of carrying on the business.

Related Sections: S. 10(1) Valuation of inventory.

Interpretation Bulletins: *Primary* — IT-287R2 Sale of inventory. *Secondary* — IT-427R Livestock of Farmers; IT-457R Election by professionals to exclude work in progress from income.

► 23(2) ◄

(2) Agreement as to price by vendor and purchaser — (Repealed by 1974-75-76, c. 26, s. 11(1).)

► 23(3) ◄

(3) Reference to property in inventory. A reference in this section to property that was included in the inventory of a business shall be deemed to include a reference to property that would have been so included if the income from the business had not been computed in accordance with the method authorized by subsection 28(1) or paragraph 34(*a*).

Related Sections: S. 61(2) Income-averaging annuity — eligible income; s. 248(1), "business", "inventory", "property".

Interpretation Bulletins: *Primary* — IT-287R2 Sale of inventory. *Secondary* — IT-427R Livestock of Farmers; IT-457R Election by professionals to exclude work in progress from income.

SECTION 24: Ceasing to carry on business

► 24(1) ◄

(1) Ceasing to carry on business — (Repealed by S.C. 2016, c. 12, s. 8(1).)

Editorial Note: S. 70(5.1), rather than s. 24(1), applies upon an individual's death where the eligible capital property in respect of the individual's business is acquired by a beneficiary as a consequence of the individual's death. S. 24(2) generally applies if the eligible capital property in respect of an individual's business is acquired by the individual's spouse or common-law partner or a corporation controlled by the individual that carries on the business. In either case, the individual is not allowed the terminal allowance deduction under s. 24(1)(*a*); rather, the eligible capital property is effectively rolled over to the person who acquires the property. See also the stop-loss rule in s. 14(12) (repealed January 1, 2017), which can apply if the taxpayer is a corporation, trust or partnership and an affiliated person acquires the eligible capital property.

As of January 1, 2017, subsection 24(1) is repealed as a result of the repeal of the eligible capital property rules. Beginning in 2017, such property is considered depreciable capital property described in Class 14.1. A similar deduction is now allowed under the terminal loss rules of subsection 20(16).

History: S. 24(1) was repealed by S.C. 2016, c. 12, s. 8(1), in force January 1, 2017, and formerly read:

(1) *Ceasing to carry on business.* Notwithstanding paragraph 18(1)(*b*), where at any time after a taxpayer ceases to carry on a business the taxpayer no longer owns any property that was eligible capital property in respect of the business and that has value, in computing the taxpayer's income for taxation years ending after that time,

(*a*) there shall be deducted, for the first such taxation year, the amount of the taxpayer's cumulative eligible capital in respect of the business at that time;

(*b*) no amount may be deducted under paragraph 20(1)(*b*) in respect of the business;

(*c*) for the purposes of determining the value of P in the definition "cumulative eligible capital" in subsection 14(5), the amount deducted by the taxpayer under paragraph (*a*) shall be deemed to be an amount deducted under paragraph 20(1)(*b*) in computing the taxpayer's income from the business for the taxation year that included that time; and

(*d*) for the purposes of subsection 14(1), section 14 shall be read without reference to subsection 14(4).

Related Sections: S. 14(12) Loss on certain transfers; s. 54(1), "eligible capital property"; s. 70(5.1) Eligible capital property of deceased.

Interpretation Bulletins: *Primary* — IT-313R2 Eligible capital property — Rules where a taxpayer has ceased carrying on a business or has died. *Secondary* — IT-123R6 Transactions involving eligible capital property; IT-291R3 Transfer of property to a corporation under subsection 85(1).

► 24(2) ◄

(2) Business carried on by spouse or common-law partner or controlled corporation. If, at any time, an individual ceases to carry on a business and the individual's spouse or common-law partner, or a corporation controlled directly or indirectly in any manner whatever by the individual, carries on the business and acquires all of the property included in Class 14.1 of Schedule II to the *Income Tax Regulations* in respect of the business owned by the individual immediately before that time and that had value at that time, the following rules apply:

(*a*) the individual is deemed to have, immediately before that time, disposed of the property and received proceeds of disposition equal to the lesser of the capital cost and the cost amount to the individual of the property immediately before the disposition;

(*b*) the spouse, common-law partner or corporation, as the case may be, is deemed to have acquired the property at a cost equal to those proceeds; and

(*c*) if the amount that was the capital cost to the individual of the property exceeds the amount determined under paragraph 70(5)(*b*) to be the cost to the person that acquired the property, for the purposes of sections 13 and 20 and any regulations made for the purpose of paragraph 20(1)(*a*),

(i) the capital cost to the person of the property is deemed to be the amount that was the capital cost to the individual of the property, and

(ii) the excess is deemed to have been allowed to the person in respect of the property under regulations made for the purposes of paragraph 20(1)(*a*) in computing income for taxation years that ended before the person acquired the property.

Editorial Note: The rollover under s. 24(2) effectively results in the acquiring spouse or common-law partner or controlled corporation assuming the individual's former eligible capital property pool. The individual is not allowed the terminal allowance deduction under s. 24(1)(*a*). Note that s. 24(2) takes precedence over the rollover under s. 70(5.1) upon an individual's death.

Subsection 24(2) was amended, effective as of January 1, 2017, as a result of the repeal of the eligible capital property rules. Beginning in 2017, such property is considered depreciable capital property described in Class 14.1. Therefore, the rollover in subsection 24(2) is now allowed in respect of property described in Class 14.1.

History: S. 24(2) was replaced by S.C. 2016, c. 12, s. 8(2), in force January 1, 2017, and formerly read:

(2) *Business carried on by spouse or common-law partner or controlled corporation.* Notwithstanding subsection (1), where at any time an individual ceases to carry on a business and thereafter the individual's spouse or common-law partner, or a corporation controlled directly or indirectly in any manner whatever by the individual, carries on the business and acquires all of the property that was eligible capital property in respect of the business owned by the individual before that time and that had value at that time,

(*a*) in computing the individual's income for the individual's first taxation year ending after that time, subsection (1) shall be read without reference to paragraph (1)(*a*) and the reference in paragraph (1)(*c*) to "the amount deducted by the taxpayer under paragraph (*a*)" shall be read as a reference to "an amount equal to the taxpayer's cumulative eligible capital in respect of the business immediately before that time";

(*b*) in computing the cumulative eligible capital of the spouse or common-law partner or the corporation, as the case may be, in respect of the business, the spouse or common-law partner or corporation shall be deemed to have acquired an eligible capital property and to have made an eligible capital expenditure at that time at a cost equal to $4/3$ of the total of

(i) the cumulative eligible capital of the taxpayer in respect of the business immediately before that time, and

(ii) the amount, if any, determined for F in the definition "cumulative eligible capital" in subsection 14(5) in respect of the business of the individual at that time;

(*c*) for the purposes of determining the cumulative eligible capital in respect of the business of the spouse or common-law partner or corporation after that time, an amount equal to the amount determined under subparagraph (*b*)(ii) shall be added to the amount otherwise determined in respect thereof for P in the definition "cumulative eligible capital" in subsection 14(5); and

(*d*) for the purpose of determining after that time the amount required to be included under paragraph 14(1)(*b*) in computing the income of the spouse, the common-law partner or the corporation in respect of any subsequent disposition of property of the business, there shall be added to the amount otherwise determined for Q in the definition "cumulative eligible capital" in subsection 14(5) the amount, if any, determined for Q in that definition in respect of the business of the individual immediately before the individual ceased to carry on business.

Related Sections: S. 14(5), "cumulative eligible capital"; s. 70(5.1) Eligible capital property of deceased; s. 256(5.1) Control in fact.

► 24(3) ◄

(3) Where partnership has ceased to exist — (Repealed by S.C. 2016, c. 12, s. 8(3).)

History: S. 24(3) was repealed by S.C. 2016, c. 12, s. 8(3), in force January 1, 2017, and formerly read:

(3) *Where partnership has ceased to exist.* Notwithstanding subsection (1), where at any time a partnership ceases to exist in circumstances to which neither subsection 98(3) nor subsection 98(5) applies, there may be deducted, in computing the income for the first taxation year beginning after that time of a taxpayer who was a member of the partnership immediately before that time, an amount determined by the formula

$$A \times B/C$$

where

A is the amount that would, had the partnership continued to exist, have been deductible under subsection (1) in computing its income;

B is the fair market value of the taxpayer's interest in the partnership immediately before that time; and

C is the fair market value of all interests in the partnership immediately before that time.

SECTION 24.1: Judges

(Repealed by S.C. 1996, c. 21, s. 6(1).)

SECTION 25: Fiscal period of business disposed of by individual

► 25(1) ◄

(1) Fiscal period of business disposed of by individual. Where an individual was the proprietor of a business and disposed of it during a fiscal period of the business, the fiscal period may, if the individual so elects and subsection 249.1(4) does not apply in respect of the business, be deemed to have ended at the time it would have ended if the individual had not disposed of the business during the fiscal period.

Related Sections: S. 25(2) Election; s. 249.1(4) Alternative method.

Information Circulars: IC 76-19R3 Transfer of property to a corporation under section 85.

Interpretation Bulletins: *Secondary* — IT-287R2 Sale of inventory; IT-313R2 Eligible capital property — Rules where a taxpayer has ceased carrying on a business or has died.

► 25(2) ◄

(2) Election. An election under subsection (1) is not valid unless the individual, at the time when the fiscal period of the business would, if the election were valid, be deemed to have ended, is resident in Canada.

Related Sections: S. 248(1), "business", "fiscal period", "individual"; s. 255 Canada.

► 25(3) ◄

(3) Dispositions in extended fiscal period. If subsection (1) applies in respect of a fiscal period of a business of an individual, for the purpose of computing the individual's income for the fiscal period, section 13 is to be read without reference to its subsection (8).

History: S. 25(3) was replaced by S.C. 2016, c. 12, s. 9(1), in force January 1, 2017, and formerly read:

(3) *Dispositions in the extended fiscal period.* Where subsection (1) applies in respect of a fiscal period of a business of an individual, for the purpose of computing the individual's income for the fiscal period,

(*a*) section 13 shall be read without reference to subsection 13(8); and

(*b*) section 24 shall be read without reference to paragraph 24(1)(*d*).

Income Tax Folios: *Secondary* — S3-F4-C1 General Discussion of Capital Cost Allowance.

Special Cases

SECTION 26: [Banks]

► 26(1) ◄

(1) Banks — inclusions in income. There shall be included in computing the income of a bank for its first taxation year that commences after June 17, 1987 and ends after 1987 the total of

(*a*) the total of the specific provisions of the bank, as determined, or as would be determined if such a determination were required, under the Minister's rules, as at the end of its immediately preceding taxation year,

(*b*) the total of the general provisions of the bank, as determined, or as would be determined if such a determination were required, under the Minister's rules, as at the end of its immediately preceding taxation year,

(*c*) the amount, if any, by which

(i) the amount of the special provision for losses on trans-border claims of the bank, as determined, or as would be determined if such a determination were required, under the Minister's rules, that was deductible by the bank under subsection (2) in computing its income for its immediately preceding taxation year

exceeds

(ii) that part of the amount determined under subparagraph (i) that was a realized loss of the bank for that immediately preceding taxation year, and

(*d*) the amount, if any, of the tax allowable appropriations account of the bank, as determined, or as would be determined if such a determination were required, under the Minister's rules, at the end of its immediately preceding taxation year.

Related Sections: S. 248(1), "amount".

► 26(2) ◄

(2) Banks — deductions from income. In computing the income for a taxation year of a bank, there may be deducted an amount not exceeding the total of

(*a*) that part of the total of the amounts of the five-year average loan loss experiences of the bank, as determined, or as would be determined if such a determination were required, under the Minister's rules, for all taxation years before its first taxation year that commences after June 17, 1987 and ends after 1987 that is specified by the bank for the year and was not deducted by the bank in computing its income for any preceding taxation year,

(*b*) that part of the total of the amounts transferred by the bank to its tax allowable appropriations account, as permitted under the Minister's rules, for all taxation years before its first taxation year that commences after June 17, 1987 and ends after 1987 that is specified by the bank for the year and was not deducted by the bank in computing its income for any preceding taxation year,

(*c*) that part of the amount, if any, by which

(i) the amount of the special provision for losses on trans-border claims, as determined, or as would be determined if such a determination were required, under the Minister's rules, that was deductible by the bank under this subsection in computing its income for its last taxation year before its first taxation year that commences after June 17, 1987 and ends after 1987

exceeds

(ii) that part of the amount determined under subparagraph (i) that was a realized loss of the bank for that last taxation year

that is specified by the bank for the year and was not deducted by the bank in computing its income for any preceding taxation year,

(*d*) where the tax allowable appropriations account of the bank at the end of its last taxation year before its first taxation year that commences after June 17, 1987 and ends after 1987, as determined, or as would be determined if such a determination were required, under the Minister's rules, is a negative amount, that part of such amount expressed as a positive number that is specified by the bank for the year and was not deducted by the bank in computing its income for any preceding taxation year, and

(*e*) that part of the total of the amounts calculated in respect of the bank for the purposes of the Minister's rules, or that would be calculated for the purposes of those rules if such a calculation were required, under Procedure 8 of the Procedures for the Determination of the Provision for Loan Losses as set out in Appendix 1 of those rules, for all taxation years before its first taxation year that commences after June 17, 1987 and ends after 1987 that is specified by the bank for the year and was not deducted by the bank in computing its income for any preceding taxation year.

► 26(3) ◄

(3) Write-offs and recoveries. In computing the income of a bank, the following rules apply:

(*a*) any amount that was recorded by the bank as a realized loss or a write-off of an asset that was included by the bank in the calculation of an amount deductible under the Minister's rules, or would have been included in the calculation of such an amount if such a calculation had been required, for any taxation year before its first taxation year that commences after June 17, 1987 and ends after 1987, shall, for the purposes of paragraph 12(1)(*i*) and section 12.4, be deemed to have been deducted by the bank under paragraph 20(1)(*p*) in computing its income for the year for which it was so recorded; and

(*b*) any amount that was recorded by the bank as a recovery of a realized loss or a write-off of an asset that was included by the bank in the calculation of an amount deductible under the Minister's rules, or would have been included in the calculation of such an amount if such a calculation had been required, for any taxation year before its first taxation year that commences after June 17, 1987 and ends after 1987 shall, for the purposes of section 12.4, be deemed to have been included by the bank under paragraph 12(1)(*i*) in computing its income for the year for which it was so recorded.

► 26(4) ◄

(4) Definition of "Minister's rules". For the purposes of this section, "Minister's rules" means the *Rules for the Determination of the Appropriations for Contingencies of a Bank* issued under the authority of the Minister of Finance pursuant to section 308 of the *Bank Act* for the purposes of subsections (1) and (2) of this section.

SECTION 27: Application of Part I to Crown corporation

► 27(1) ◄

(1) Application of Part I to Crown corporation. This Part applies to a federal Crown corporation as if

(*a*) any income or loss from a business carried on by the corporation as agent of Her Majesty, or from a property of Her Majesty administered by the corporation, were an income or loss of the corporation from the business or the property, as the case may be; and

(*b*) any property, obligation or debt of any kind whatever held, administered, entered into or incurred by the corporation as agent of Her Majesty were a property, obligation or debt, as the case may be, of the corporation.

Tax Topics: No. 1625, Provincial Crown Corporation Not Bound by the *Income Tax Act*.

► 27(2) ◄

(2) Presumption. Notwithstanding any other provision of this Act, a prescribed federal Crown corporation and any corporation controlled by such a corporation are each deemed not to be a private corporation and paragraphs 149(1)(*d*) to (*d*.4) do not apply to those corporations.

Related Regulations: 7100.

► 27(3) ◄

(3) Transfers of land for disposition. Where land of Her Majesty has been transferred to a prescribed federal Crown corporation for purposes of disposition, the acquisition of the property by the corporation and any disposition thereof shall be deemed not to have been in the course of the business carried on by the corporation.

Related Regulations: 7100.

Related Sections: S. 89(1), "private corporation"; s. 248(1), "business", "corporation", "property".

SECTION 27.1: Emissions allowances

► 27.1(1) ◄

(1) Emissions allowances. Notwithstanding section 10, for the purpose of computing a taxpayer's income from a business, an emissions allowance shall be valued at the cost at which the taxpayer acquired it.

History: S. 27.1(1) was added by S.C. 2016, c. 12, s. 10(1), applicable in respect of emissions allowances acquired in taxation years that begin after 2016. However, if a taxpayer elects in their return of income for their 2016 or 2017 taxation year, s. 27.1(1) applies in respect of emissions allowances acquired by the taxpayer in taxation years that end after 2012.

► 27.1(2) ◄

(2) Determination of cost of emissions allowances. If at any particular time a taxpayer that owns one emissions allowance, or two or more identical emissions allowances (for the purposes of this subsection two or more emissions allowances will be considered identical if they could be used to settle the same emissions obligations), acquires one or more other emissions allowances (in this subsection referred to as "newly acquired emissions allowances"), each of which is identical to each of the previously-acquired emissions allowances, for the purposes of computing, at any subsequent time, the cost of the taxpayer of each of the identical emissions allowances,

(*a*) the taxpayer is deemed to have disposed of each of the previously-acquired emissions allowances immediately before the particular time for proceeds equal to its cost to the taxpayer immediately before the particular time; and

(*b*) the taxpayer is deemed to have acquired each of the identical emissions allowances at the particular time at a cost equal to the amount determined by the formula

$$(A + B)/C$$

where

A is the total cost to the taxpayer immediately before the particular time of the previously-acquired emissions allowances,

B is the total cost to the taxpayer (determined without reference to this section) of the newly-acquired emissions allowances, and

C is the number of the identical emissions allowances owned by the taxpayer immediately after the particular time.

History: S. 27.1(2) was added by S.C. 2016, c. 12, s. 10(1), applicable in respect of emissions allowances acquired in taxation years that begin after 2016. However, if a taxpayer elects in their return of income for their 2016 or 2017 taxation year, s. 27.1(2) applies in respect of emissions allowances acquired by the taxpayer in taxation years that end after 2012.

Related Regulations: 7300.

Related Sections: S. 248(1) "emissions allowance", "emissions obligation".

▶ 27.1(3) ◀

(3) Expense restriction. Notwithstanding any other provision of this Act, in computing a taxpayer's income from a business for a taxation year, the total amount deductible in respect of a particular emissions obligation for a taxation year shall not exceed the amount determined by the formula

$$A + B \times C$$

where

A is the total cost of emissions allowances either

(*a*) used by the taxpayer to settle the particular emissions obligation in the year, or

(*b*) held by the taxpayer at the end of the taxation year that can be used to satisfy the particular emissions obligation in respect of the year;

B is the amount determined by the formula

$$D - (E + F)$$

where

D is the number of emissions allowances required to satisfy the particular emissions obligation in respect of the taxation year,

E is the number of emissions allowances used by the taxpayer to settle the particular emissions obligation in the year, and

F is the number of emissions allowances held by the taxpayer at the end of the taxation year that can be used to satisfy the particular emissions obligation in respect of the year; and

C is the fair market value of an emissions allowance at the end of the taxation year that could be used to satisfy the particular emissions obligation in respect of the year.

History: S. 27.1(3) was added by S.C. 2016, c. 12, s. 10(1), applicable in respect of emissions allowances acquired in taxation years that begin after 2016. However, if a taxpayer elects in their return of income for their 2016 or 2017 taxation year, s. 27.1(3) applies in respect of emissions allowances acquired by the taxpayer in taxation years that end after 2012.

Related Regulations: 7300.

Related Sections: S. 248(1) "emissions allowance", "emissions obligation".

▶ 27.1(4) ◀

(4) Income inclusion in following year. There shall be included in computing the income of a taxpayer for a taxation year as income from a business the amount deducted in respect of an emissions obligation referred to in subsection (3) for the immediately preceding taxation year to the extent that the emissions obligation was not settled in the immediately preceding taxation year.

History: S. 27.1(4) was added by S.C. 2016, c. 12, s. 10(1), applicable in respect of emissions allowances acquired in taxation years that begin after 2016. However, if a taxpayer elects in their return of income for their 2016 or 2017 taxation year, s. 27.1(4) applies in respect of emissions allowances acquired by the taxpayer in taxation years that end after 2012.

▶ 27.1(5) ◀

(5) Proceeds of disposition. If a taxpayer surrenders an emissions allowance to settle an emissions obligation, the taxpayer's proceeds from the disposition of the emissions allowance are deemed to be equal to the taxpayer's cost of the emissions allowance.

History: S. 27.1(5) was added by S.C. 2016, c. 12, s. 10(1), applicable in respect of emissions allowances acquired in taxation years that begin after 2016. However, if a taxpayer elects in their return of income for their 2016 or 2017 taxation year, s. 27.1(5) applies in respect of emissions allowances acquired by the taxpayer in taxation years that end after 2012.

▶ 27.1(6) ◀

(6) Loss restriction event. Notwithstanding subsection (1), each emissions allowance held at the end of the taxpayer's taxation year that ends immediately before the time at which the taxpayer is subject to a loss restriction event is to be valued at the cost at which the taxpayer acquired the property, or its fair market value at the end of the year, whichever is lower, and after that time the cost at which the taxpayer acquired the property is, subject to a subsequent application of this subsection and subsection (2), deemed to be that lower amount.

History: S. 27.1(6) was added by S.C. 2016, c. 12, s. 10(1), applicable in respect of emissions allowances acquired in taxation years that begin after 2016. However, if a taxpayer elects in their return of income for their 2016 or 2017 taxation year, s. 27.1(6) applies in respect of emissions allowances acquired by the taxpayer in taxation years that end after 2012.

SECTION 28: Farming or fishing business

▶ 28(1) ◀

(1) Farming or fishing business. For the purpose of computing the income of a taxpayer for a taxation year from a farming or fishing business, the income from the business for that year may, if the taxpayer so elects, be computed in accordance with a method (in this section referred to as the "cash method") whereby the income therefrom for that year shall be deemed to be an amount equal to the total of

(*a*) all amounts that

(i) were received in the year, or are deemed by this Act to have been received in the year, in the course of carrying on the business, and

(ii) were in payment of or on account of an amount that would, if the income from the business were not computed in accordance with the cash method, be included in computing income from the business for that or any other year,

(*b*) with respect to a farming business, such amount, if any, as is specified by the taxpayer in respect of the business in the taxpayer's return of income under this Part for the year, not exceeding the amount, if any, by which

(i) the fair market value at the end of the year of inventory owned by the taxpayer in connection with the business at that time

exceeds

(ii) the amount determined under paragraph (*c*) for the year,

(*c*) with respect to a farming business, the amount, if any, that is the lesser of

(i) the taxpayer's loss from the business for the year computed without reference to this paragraph and to paragraph (*b*), and

(ii) the value of inventory purchased by the taxpayer that was owned by the taxpayer in connection with the business at the end of the year, and

(*d*) the total of all amounts each of which is an amount included in computing the taxpayer's income for the year from the business because of subsection 13(1), 80(13) or 80.3(3) or (5),

minus the total of

(*e*) all amounts, other than amounts described in section 30, that

(i) were paid in the year, or are deemed by this Act to have been paid in the year, in the course of carrying on the business,

(ii) in the case of amounts paid, or deemed by this Act to have been paid, for inventory, were in payment of or on account of an amount that would be deductible in computing the income from the business for the year or any other taxation year if that income were not computed in accordance with the cash method, and

(iii) in any other case, were in payment of or on account of an amount that would be deductible in computing the income from the business for a preceding taxation year, the year or the following taxation year if that income were not computed in accordance with the cash method,

(*e*.1) all amounts, other than amounts described in section 30, that

(i) would be deductible in computing the income from the business for the year if that income were not computed in accordance with the cash method,

(ii) are not deductible in computing the income from the business for any other taxation year, and

(iii) were paid in a preceding taxation year in the course of carrying on the business,

(*f*) the total of all amounts each of which is the amount, if any, included under paragraph (*b*) or (*c*) in computing the taxpayer's income from the business for the immediately preceding taxation year, and

(*g*) the total of all amounts each of which is an amount deducted for the year under paragraph 20(1)(*a*) or (*uu*), subsection 20(16), section 30 or subsection 80.3(2) or (4) in respect of the business,

except that paragraphs (*b*) and (*c*) do not apply in computing the income of the taxpayer for the taxation year in which the taxpayer dies.

History: S. 28(1)(*d*) was replaced by S.C. 2016, c. 12, s. 11(1), in force January 1, 2017, and formerly read:

(*d*) the total of all amounts each of which is an amount included in computing the taxpayer's income for the year from the business because of subsection 13(1), 14(1), 80(13) or 80.3(3) or (5),

S. 28(1)(*g*) was replaced by S.C. 2016, c. 12, s. 11(2), in force January 1, 2017, and formerly read:

(*g*) the total of all amounts each of which is an amount deducted for the year under paragraph 20(1)(*a*), (*b*) or (*uu*), subsection 20(16) or 24(1), section 30 or subsection 80.3(2), (4) or (4.1) in respect of the business,

S. 28(1)(*g*) was replaced by S.C. 2014, c. 39, s. 7(1), applicable to the 2014 and subsequent taxation years, and formerly read:

(*g*) the total of all amounts each of which is an amount deducted for the year under paragraph 20(1)(*a*), (*b*) or (*uu*), subsection 20(16) or 24(1), section 30 or subsection 80.3(2) or (4) in respect of the business,

S. 28(1)(*a*)(ii) was replaced by S.C. 2013, c. 40, s. 13, in force December 12, 2013, and formerly read"

(ii) were in payment of or on account of an amount that would, if the income from the business were not computed in accordance with the cash method, be included in computing income therefrom for that or any other year, and

Related Sections: S. 20(7) Where para. (1)(m) does not apply; s. 23(3) Reference to property in inventory; 28(1.1) Acquisition of inventory; 28(1.2) Valuation of inventory; 28(1.3) Short fiscal period; 28(2) Where joint farming or fishing business; 28(3) Concurrence of Minister; 28(4) Non-resident; s. 87(2)(*b*) Inventory.

Forms: T1273 — Statement A — Harmonized AgriStability and AgriInvest Program Information and Statement of Farming Activity for Individuals; T1274 — Statement B — Harmonized AgriStability and AgriInvest Program Information and Statement of Farming Activities for Additional Farming Operation; T1275 — AgriStability and AgriInvest Additional Information and Adjustment Request Form for 2005; T2042 — Statement of Farming Activities; T2121 — Statement of Fishing Activities.

Guides: RC4408 Farming Income and the AgriStability and AgriInvest Program Harmonized Guide; T4002 Self-employed Business, Professional, Commission, Farming, and Fishing Income; T4004 Fishing Income.

Income Tax Folios: *Primary* — S4-F11-C1 Meaning of Farming and Farming Business.

Interpretation Bulletins: *Primary* — IT-427R Livestock of farmers; IT-433R Farming or fishing — Use of cash method. *Secondary* — IT-154R Special reserves; IT-184R Deferred cash purchase tickets issued for grain; IT-291R3 Transfer of property to a corporation under subsection 85(1); IT-373R2 (Consolid.) Woodlots.

Cases: The election to use the cash method of accounting can only be made with the filing of the return. Once the taxpayer filed his return on the accrual basis, the cash option no longer existed for that taxation year. *Hadler Turkey Farms Inc. v. The Queen*, 86 DTC 6013 (F.C.T.D.)

► 28(1.1) ◄

(1.1) Acquisition of inventory. Where at any time, and in circumstances where paragraph 69(1)(*a*) or (*c*) applies, a taxpayer acquires inventory that is owned by the taxpayer in connection with a farming business the income from which is computed in accordance with the cash method, for the purposes of this section an amount equal to the cost to the taxpayer of the inventory shall be deemed

(*a*) to have been paid by the taxpayer at that time and in the course of carrying on that business, and

(*b*) to be the only amount so paid for the inventory by the taxpayer,

and the taxpayer shall be deemed to have purchased the inventory at the time it was so acquired.

Forms: T2034 — Election to Establish Inventory Unit Prices for Animals.

Income Tax Folios: *Primary* — S4-F11-C1 Meaning of Farming and Farming Business.

Interpretation Bulletins: *Primary* — IT-427R Livestock of farmers; IT-433R Farming or fishing — Use of cash method.

► 28(1.2) ◄

(1.2) Valuation of inventory. For the purpose of paragraph (1)(*c*) and notwithstanding section 10, inventory of a taxpayer shall be valued at any time at the lesser of the total amount paid by the taxpayer at or before that time to acquire it (in this section referred to as its "cash cost") and its fair market value, except that an animal (in this section referred to as a "specified animal") that is a horse or, where the taxpayer has so elected in respect thereof for the taxation year that includes that time or for any preceding taxation year, is a bovine animal registered under the *Animal Pedigree Act*, shall be valued

(*a*) at any time in the taxation year in which it is acquired, at such amount as is designated by the taxpayer not exceeding its cash cost to the taxpayer and not less than 70% of its cash cost to the taxpayer; and

(*b*) at any time in a subsequent taxation year, at such amount as is designated by the taxpayer not exceeding its cash cost to the taxpayer and not less than 70% of the total of

(i) its value determined under this subsection at the end of the preceding taxation year, and

(ii) the total amount paid on account of the purchase price of the animal during the year.

Forms: T2034 — Election to Establish Inventory Unit Prices for Animals.

Income Tax Folios: *Primary* — S4-F11-C1 Meaning of Farming and Farming Business.

Interpretation Bulletins: *Primary* — IT-427R Livestock of farmers; IT-433R Farming or fishing — Use of cash method. *Secondary* — IT-291R3 Transfer of property to a corporation under subsection 85(1).

► 28(1.3) ◄

(1.3) Short fiscal period. For each taxation year that is less than 51 weeks, the reference in subsection (1.2) to "70" shall be read as a reference to the number determined by the formula

$$100 - (30 \times A/365)$$

where

A is the number of days in the taxation year.

Income Tax Folios: *Primary* — S4-F11-C1 Meaning of Farming and Farming Business.

Interpretation Bulletins: *Primary* — IT-427R Livestock of farmers; IT-433R Farming or fishing — Use of cash method.

► 28(2) ◄

(2) Where joint farming or fishing business. Subsection (1) does not apply for the purpose of computing the income of a taxpayer for a taxation year from a farming or fishing business carried on by the taxpayer jointly with one or more other persons, unless each of the other persons by whom the business is jointly carried on has elected to have his or her income from the business for that year computed in accordance with the cash method.

Income Tax Folios: *Primary* — S4-F11-C1 Meaning of Farming and Farming Business.

Interpretation Bulletins: *Primary* — IT-427R Livestock of farmers; IT-433R Farming or fishing — Use of cash method. *Secondary* — IT-373R2 (Consolid.) Woodlots.

► 28(3) ◄

(3) Concurrence of Minister. Where a taxpayer has filed a return of income under this Part for a taxation year wherein the taxpayer's income for that year from a farming or fishing business has been computed in accordance with the cash method, income from the business for each subsequent taxation year shall, subject to the other provisions of this Part, be computed in accordance with that method unless the taxpayer, with the concurrence of the Minister and on such terms and conditions as are specified by the Minister, adopts some other method.

Interpretation Bulletins: *Primary* — IT-427R Livestock of farmers; IT-433R Farming or fishing — Use of cash method. *Secondary* — IT-373R2 (Consolid.) Woodlots.

► 28(4) ◄

(4) Non-resident. Notwithstanding subsections (1) and (5), where at the end of a taxation year a taxpayer who carried on a business the income from which was computed in accordance with the cash method is non-resident and does not carry on that business in Canada, an amount equal to the total of all amounts each of which is the fair market value of an amount outstanding during the year as or on account of a debt owing to the taxpayer that arose in the course of carrying on the business and that would have been included in computing the taxpayer's income for the year if the amount had been received by the taxpayer in the year, shall (to the extent that the amount was not otherwise included in computing the taxpayer's income for the year or a preceding taxation year) be included in computing the taxpayer's income from the business

(*a*) for the year, if the taxpayer was non-resident throughout the year; and

(*b*) for the part of the year throughout which the taxpayer was resident in Canada, if the taxpayer was resident in Canada at any time in the year.

Related Sections: S. 61(2) Income-averaging annuity — eligible income.

Interpretation Bulletins: *Primary* — IT-427R Livestock of farmers; IT-433R Farming or fishing — Use of cash method.

► 28(4.1) ◄

(4.1) Idem — (Repealed by S.C. 2001, c. 17, s. 18(2).)

► 28(5) ◄

(5) Accounts receivable. There shall be included in computing the income of a taxpayer for a taxation year such part of an amount received by the taxpayer in the year, on or after disposing of or ceasing to carry on a business or a part of a business, for, on account or in lieu of payment of, or in satisfaction of debts owing to the taxpayer that arose in the course of carrying on the business as would have been included in computing the income of the taxpayer for the year had the amount so received been received by the taxpayer in the course of carrying on the business.

Related Sections: S. 248(1), "amount", "business", "farming", "fishing".

Interpretation Bulletins: *Primary* — IT-427R Livestock of farmers; IT-433R Farming or fishing — Use of cash method.

SECTION 29: Disposition of animal of basic herd class

► 29(1) ◄

(1) Disposition of animal of basic herd class. Where a taxpayer has a basic herd of a class of animals and disposes of an animal of that class in the course of carrying on a farmingbusiness in a taxation year, if the taxpayer so elects in the taxpayer's return of income under this Part for the year the following rules apply:

(*a*) there shall be deducted in computing the taxpayer's basic herd of that class at the end of the year such number as is designated by the taxpayer in the taxpayer's election, not exceeding the least of

(i) the number of animals of that class so disposed of by the taxpayer in that year,

(ii) $^{1}/_{10}$ of the taxpayer's basic herd of that class on December 31, 1971, and

(iii) the taxpayer's basic herd of that class of animal at the end of the immediately preceding taxation year; and

(*b*) there shall be deducted in computing the taxpayer's income from the farming business for the taxation year the product obtained when

(i) the number determined under paragraph (*a*) in respect of the taxpayer's basic herd of that class for the year

is multiplied by

(ii) the quotient obtained when the fair market value on December 31, 1971 of the taxpayer's animals of that class on that day is divided by the number of the taxpayer's animals of that class on that day.

Related Sections: S. 29(2) Reduction in basic herd; s. 61(2) Income-averaging annuity — eligible income.

Forms: T2034 — Election to Establish Inventory Unit Prices for Animals.

Cases: Where a dairy herd has not been treated as a capital asset in the past, proceeds from the sale of the herd will be treated as income and not as a capital gain. *Syrico Corp. v. M.N.R.*, 88 DTC 1001 (T.C.C.)

▶ 29(2) ◀

(2) Reduction in basic herd. Where a taxpayer carries on a farming business in a taxation year and the taxpayer's basic herd of any class at the end of the immediately preceding year, minus the deduction, if any, required by paragraph (1)(*a*) to be made in computing the taxpayer's basic herd of that class at the end of the year, exceeds the number of animals of that class owned by the taxpayer at the end of the year,

(*a*) there shall be deducted in computing the taxpayer's basic herd of that class at the end of the year the number of animals comprising the excess; and

(*b*) there shall be deducted in computing the taxpayer's income from the farming business for the taxation year the product obtained when

(i) the number of animals comprising the excess is multiplied by

(ii) the quotient obtained when the fair market value on December 31, 1971 of the taxpayer's animals of that class on that day is divided by the number of the taxpayer's animals of that class on that day.

▶ 29(3) ◀

(3) Interpretation. For the purposes of this section,

(*a*) a taxpayer's "basic herd" of any class of animals at a particular time means such number of the animals of that class that the taxpayer had on hand at the end of his 1971 taxation year as were, for the purpose of assessing the taxpayer's tax under this Part for that year, accepted by the Minister, as a consequence of an application made by the taxpayer, to be capital properties and not to be stock-in-trade, minus the numbers, if any, required by virtue of this section to be deducted in computing the taxpayer's basic herd of that class at the end of taxation years of the taxpayer ending before the particular time;

(*b*) "class of animals" means animals of a particular species, namely, cattle, horses, sheep or swine, that are

(i) purebred animals of that species for which a certificate of registration has been issued by a person recognized by breeders in Canada of purebred animals of that species to be the registrar of the breed to which such animals belong, or issued by the Canadian Livestock Records Corporation, or

(ii) animals of that species other than purebred animals described in subparagraph (i),

each of which descriptions in subparagraphs (i) and (ii) shall be deemed to be of separate classes, except that where the number of the taxpayer's animals described in subparagraph (i) or (ii), as the case may be, of a particular species is not greater than 10% of the total number of the taxpayer's animals of that species that would otherwise be of two separate classes by virtue of this paragraph, the taxpayer's animals described in subparagraphs (i) and (ii) of that species shall be deemed to be of a single class; and

(*c*) in determining the number of animals of any class on hand at any time, an animal shall not be included if it was acquired for a feeder operation, and an animal shall be included only if its actual age is not less than,

(i) in the case of cattle, 2 years,

(ii) in the case of horses, 3 years, and

(iii) in the case of sheep or swine, one year,

except that 2 animals of a class under the age specified in subparagraph (i), (ii) or (iii), as the case may be, shall be counted as one animal of the age so specified.

Related Sections: S. 54, "capital property"; s. 248(1), "business", "farming".

SECTION 30: Improving land for farming

Notwithstanding paragraphs 18(1)(*a*) and (*b*), there may be deducted in computing a taxpayer's income for a taxation year from a farming business any amount paid by the taxpayer before the end of the year for clearing land, levelling land or installing a land drainage system for the purposes of the business, to the extent that the amount has not been deducted in a preceding taxation year.

Related Sections: S. 248(1), "amount", "business", "farming".

Interpretation Bulletins: *Primary* — IT-485 Cost of clearing or levelling land.

SECTION 31: [Loss from farming where chief source of income not farming]

▶ 31(1) ◀

(1) Restricted farm loss. If a taxpayer's chief source of income for a taxation year is neither farming nor a combination of farming and some other source of income that is a subordinate source of income for the taxpayer, then for the purposes of sections 3 and 111 the taxpayer's loss, if any, for the year from all farming businesses carried on by the taxpayer is deemed to be the total of

(*a*) the lesser of

(i) the amount by which the total of the taxpayer's losses for the year, determined without reference to this section and before making any deduction under section 37, from all farming businesses carried on by the taxpayer exceeds the total of the taxpayer's incomes for the year, so determined from all such businesses, and

(ii) $2,500 plus the lesser of

(A) $1/2$ of the amount by which the amount determined under subparagraph (i) exceeds $2,500, and

(B) $15,000, and

(*b*) the amount, if any, by which

(i) the amount that would be determined under subparagraph (*a*)(i) if it were read without reference to "and before making any deduction under section 37",

exceeds

(ii) the amount determined under subparagraph (*a*)(i).

History: S. 31(1), the portion before paragraph (*a*) was replaced by S.C. 2013, c. 40, s. 14(1), applicable to taxation years that end after March 20, 2013, and formerly read:

(1) *Loss from farming where chief source of income not farming.* Where a taxpayer's chief source of income for a taxation year is neither farming nor a combination of farming and some other source of income, for the purposes of sections 3 and 111 the taxpayer's loss, if any, for the year from all farming businesses carried on by the taxpayer shall be deemed to be the total of

S. 31(1)(*a*)(i) was replaced by S.C. 2013, c. 40, s. 14(2), applicable to taxation years that end after March 20, 2013, and formerly read:

(i) the amount by which the total of the taxpayer's losses for the year, determined without reference to this section and before making any deduction under section 37 or 37.1, from all farming businesses carried on by the taxpayer exceeds the total of the taxpayer's incomes for the year, so determined from all such businesses, and

S. 31(1)(*a*)(ii)(B) was replaced by S.C. 2013, c. 40, s. 14(3), applicable to taxation years that end after March 20, 2013, and formerly read:

(B) $6,250, and

S. 31(1)(*b*)(i) was replaced by S.C. 2013, c. 40, s. 14(4), applicable to taxation years that end after March 20, 2013, and formerly read:

(i) the amount that would be determined under subparagraph (*a*)(i) if it were read as though the words "and before making any deduction under section 37 or 37.1" were deleted,

Related Sections: S. 9(2) Loss; s. 53(1) Adjustments to cost base; s. 101 Disposition of farmland by partnership.

Canadian Tax Foundation: Hanson and Yaskowich, *There is more to the Family Farm than Meets the Eye,* 2014 Prairie Provinces Tax Conference 5:1–28; Swanson, *The Difference a Farm Makes,* 2004 Prairie Provinces Tax Conference 12:1–35; Little and Colborne, *Current Cases: Federal Court of Appeal — Will a "Gentleman" Farmer Who Suffers Farm Losses Ever Be Successful Before the Federal Court of Appeal? (The Queen v. Donnelly, 97 DTC 5499),* 1998 Canadian Tax Journal 1:87–90.

Tax Profile: November 2003 — Revenue Canada Round Table.

Tax Topics: No. 2156, Tax Policy Bewilderment — *Moldowan* Is Reincarnated in Budget 2013; No. 2041, Restricted Farm Losses (Section 31 of the *Income Tax Act*) — A Judicial Revolution is Upon Us.

Income Tax Folios: *Primary* — S4-F11-C1 Meaning of Farming and Farming Business.

Income Tax Technical News: Issue No. 30, Restricted Farm Losses.

Interpretation Bulletins: *Primary* — IT-322R Farm losses. *Secondary* — IT-232R3 Non-capital losses, net capital losses, restricted farm losses, farm losses and limited partnership losses — Their composition and deductibility in computing taxable income; IT-262R2 Losses of non-residents and part-year residents; IT-302R3 Losses of a corporation — The effect on their deductibility of changes in control, amalgamation and winding-up; IT-373R2 (Consolid.) Woodlots.

Cases: The taxpayer earned most of his income as a lawyer, but also invested significant time and capital to raising race horses. His farm losses were not restricted since farming, in combination with his law practice, was a chief source of income. The *Moldowan* approach, which effectively read out the combination test in s. 31(1), was incorrect. *The Queen v. Craig,* 2012 DTC 5115 (S.C.C.), affirming 2011 DTC 5047 (F.C.A.) and 2010 DTC 1032 (T.C.C.)

The taxpayer's deductible farming losses were not restricted since her chief source of income was farming and her medical practice combined. Although she dedicated four days a week to her medical practice, she still spent part of those days, and the remaining days of the week, on her farm. All of her excess income was invested in the farm, and it was potentially profitable. *Stackhouse v. The Queen,* 2007 DTC 620 (T.C.C.)

A lawyer's farming losses were not restricted to the s. 31(1) amounts since his chief source of income was a combination of farming and law. The farm did have profit potential and there was a synergy between it and the law practice. The combination question does not require that farming be the predominant element in the combination or that there be a connection between farming and the second source. *Gunn v. The Queen,* 2006 DTC 6544 (F.C.A.), reversing 2005 DTC 1074 (T.C.C.)

Where the owner of a racing horse showed insufficient command of the facts involved in his horse racing enterprise to indicate that he seriously regarded it as a business proposition, it was found that his expenses were not put out with a reasonable expectation of profit and were not deductible. *Moldowan v. The Queen,* 77 DTC 5213 (S.C.C.), affirming 75 DTC 5216 (F.C.A.), affirming 74 DTC 6496 (F.C.T.D.), affirming 73 DTC 228 (T.R.B.)

► 31(1.1) ◄

(1.1) Restricted farm loss. For the purposes of this Act, a taxpayer's "restricted farm loss" for a taxation year is the amount, if any, by which

(*a*) the amount determined under subparagraph (1)(*a*)(i) in respect of the taxpayer for the year

exceeds

(*b*) the total of the amount determined under subparagraph (1)(*a*)(ii) in respect of the taxpayer for the year and all amounts each of which is an amount by which the taxpayer's restricted farm loss for the year is required to be reduced because of section 80.

► 31(2) ◄

(2) Farming and manufacturing or processing. Subsection (1) does not apply to a taxpayer for a taxation year if the taxpayer's chief source of income for the year is a combination of farming and manufacturing or processing in Canada of goods for sale and all or substantially all output from all farming businesses carried on by the taxpayer is used in the manufacturing or processing.

History: S. 31(2) was replaced by S.C. 2013, c. 40, s. 14(5), applicable to taxation years that end after March 20, 2013, and formerly read:

(2) *Determination by Minister.* For the purpose of this section, the Minister may determine that a taxpayer's chief source of income for a taxation year is neither farming nor a combination of farming and some other source of income.

Related Sections: S. 9(2) Loss; s. 31(1) Loss from farming where chief source of income not farming; s. 248(1), "amount", "business", "farming".

Cases: When a taxpayer had purchased a cattle farm with the specific purpose of supplying its supermarket chain, its farming and retail food sales operations became so intimately connected as to make its chief source of income a combination of farming and another source and the taxpayer's farm losses could be deducted. *Gestion S.A.P. Inc. v. M.N.R.,* 94 DTC 1349 (T.C.C.)

A taxpayer's chief source of income was a combination of farming and dentistry where his dental practice had contributed such a substantial amount of income to his farming operation that farming became the central focus of his life rather than a sideline business. *Hover v. M.N.R.,* 93 DTC 98 (T.C.C.).

SECTION 32: Insurance agents and brokers

► 32(1) ◄

(1) Insurance agents and brokers. In computing a taxpayer's income for a taxation year from the taxpayer's business as an insurance agent or broker, no amount may be deducted under paragraph 20(1)(*m*) for the year in respect of unearned commissions from the business, but in computing the taxpayer's income for the year from the business there may be deducted, as a reserve in respect of such commissions, an amount equal to the lesser of

(*a*) the total of all amounts each of which is that proportion of an amount that has been included in computing the taxpayer's income for the year or a preceding taxation year as a commission in respect of an insurance contract (other than a life insurance contract) that

(i) the number of days in the period provided for in the insurance contract that are after the end of the taxation year

is of

(ii) the number of days in that period, and

(*b*) the total of all amounts each of which is the amount that would, but for this subsection, be deductible under paragraph 20(1)(*m*) for the year in respect of a commission referred to in paragraph (*a*).

Related Sections: S. 32(2) Reserve to be included; s. 72 Reserves, etc., for year of death.

Tax Window Files: Taxation of insurance contract commission income, *August 20, 2015,* CRA Document No. 2015-0588871E5.

Cases: The use of the phrase "unearned commissions" is merely an arbitrary label. Consequently, the reserve allowed against income received by an insurance agent or broker does not involve any subjective assessment of whether commissions are earned or unearned. *J. W. Baker Agency (1976) Ltd. v. The Queen,* 89 DTC 5078 (F.C.A.), affirming 88 DTC 6030 (F.C.T.D.)

► 32(2) ◄

(2) Reserve to be included. There shall be included as income of a taxpayer for a taxation year from a business as an insurance agent or broker, the amount deducted under subsection (1) in computing the taxpayer's income therefrom for the immediately preceding year.

Related Sections: S. 101 Disposition of farmland by partnership; s. 248(1), "amount", "business".

► 32(3) ◄

(3) Additional reserve. In computing a taxpayer's income for a taxation year ending after 1990 from a business carried on by the taxpayer throughout the year as an insurance agent or broker, there may be deducted as an additional reserve an amount not exceeding

(*a*) where the year ends in 1991, 90%,

(*b*) where the year ends in 1992, 80%,

(*c*) where the year ends in 1993, 70%,

(*d*) where the year ends in 1994, 60%,

(*e*) where the year ends in 1995, 50%,

(*f*) where the year ends in 1996, 40%,

(*g*) where the year ends in 1997, 30%,

(*h*) where the year ends in 1998, 20%,

(*i*) where the year ends in 1999, 10%, and

(*j*) where the year ends after 1999, 0%

of the amount, if any, by which

(*k*) the reserve that was deducted by the taxpayer under subsection (1) for the taxpayer's last taxation year ending before 1991

exceeds

(*l*) the amount deductible by the taxpayer under subsection (1) for the taxpayer's first taxation year ending after 1990,

and any amount so deducted by the taxpayer for a taxation year shall be deemed for the purposes of subsection (2) to have been deducted for that year under subsection (1).

SECTION 32.1: [Employee benefit plan]

► 32.1(1) ◄

(1) Employee benefit plan deductions. Where a taxpayer has made contributions to an employee benefit plan in respect of the taxpayer's employees or former employees, the taxpayer may deduct in computing the taxpayer's income for a taxation year

(*a*) such portion of an amount allocated to the taxpayer for the year under subsection (2) by the custodian of the plan as does not exceed the amount, if any, by which

(i) the total of all amounts each of which is a contribution by the taxpayer to the plan for the year or a preceding year

exceeds the total of all amounts each of which is

(ii) an amount in respect of the plan deducted by the taxpayer in computing the taxpayer's income for a preceding year, or

(iii) an amount received by the taxpayer in the year or a preceding year that was a return of amounts contributed by the taxpayer to the plan; and

(*b*) where at the end of the year all of the obligations of the plan to the taxpayer's employees and former employees have been satisfied and no property of the plan will thereafter be paid to or otherwise be available for the benefit of the taxpayer, the amount, if any, by which

(i) the total of all amounts each of which is a contribution by the taxpayer to the plan for the year or a preceding year

exceeds the total of all amounts each of which is

(ii) an amount in respect of the plan deducted by the taxpayer in computing the taxpayer's income for a preceding year, or, by virtue of paragraph (*a*), for the year, or

(iii) an amount received by the taxpayer in the year or a preceding year that was a return of amounts contributed by the taxpayer to the plan.

Related Sections: S. 6(1)(*a*) Value of benefits; s. 6(1)(*g*) Employee benefit plan benefits; s. 12(1)(*n*) Employees profit sharing plan; s. 12(1)(*n*.1) Employee benefit plan; s. 18(1)(*o*) Employee benefit plan contributions; s. 87(2)(*j*.3) Employee benefit plans, etc.; s. 107.1 Distribution by certain employment-related trusts.

Interpretation Bulletins: *Secondary* — IT-502 Employee benefit plans and employee trusts.

► 32.1(2) ◄

(2) Allocation. Every custodian of an employee benefit plan shall each year allocate to persons who have made contributions to the plan in respect of their employees or former employees the amount, if any, by which the total of

(*a*) all payments made in the year out of or under the plan to or for the benefit of their employees or former employees (other than the portion thereof that, by virtue of subparagraph 6(1)(*g*)(ii), is not required to be included in computing the income of a taxpayer), and

(*b*) all payments made in the year out of or under the plan to the heirs or the legal representatives of their employees or former employees

exceeds the income of the plan for the year.

Interpretation Bulletins: *Secondary* — IT-502 Employee benefit plans and employee trusts.

► 32.1(3) ◄

(3) Income of employee benefit plan. For the purposes of subsection (2), the income of an employee benefit plan for a year

(*a*) in the case of a plan that is a trust, is the amount that would be its income for the year if section 104 were read without reference to subsections 104(4) to (24); and

(*b*) in any other case, is the total of all amounts each of which is the amount, if any, by which a payment under the plan by the custodian thereof in the year exceeds

(i) in the case of an annuity, that part of the payment determined in prescribed manner to have been a return of capital, and

(ii) in any other case, that part of the payment that could, but for paragraph 6(1)(*g*), reasonably be regarded as being a payment of a capital nature.

Related Regulations: 300.

Interpretation Bulletins: *Secondary* — IT-502 Employee benefit plans and employee trusts.

SECTION 33: [Lending of money on security]

(1) (Repealed by 1988, c. 55, s. 17(1).)

► 33(2) ◄

(2) [Reserve to be included]. (Repealed by 1988, c. 55, s. 17(1).)

► 33(3) ◄

(3) [Amortized cost of an obligation]. (Repealed by 1988, c. 55, s. 17(1).)

SECTION 33.1: [International Banking Centres]

► 33.1(1) ◄

(1) International banking centres — definitions. (Repealed by S.C. 2013, c. 33, s. 4(1).)

History: S. 33.1(1) was repealed by S.C. 2013, c. 33, s. 4(1), applicable to taxation years that begin after March 20, 2013, and formerly read:

S. 33.1 *[International Banking Centres].*

(1) *International banking centres — definitions.* In this section,

"eligible deposit"—"eligible deposit", at any particular time, means a debt owing at the particular time by a taxpayer that is a prescribed financial institution as or on account of an amount deposited with the taxpayer by

(*a*) a non-resident person with whom the taxpayer is dealing at arm's length at the particular time, where

(i) at the particular time, the deposit is recorded in the books of account of an international banking centre business of the taxpayer,

(ii) at the particular time, the taxpayer is not obligated, either immediately or in the future and either absolutely or contingently, to repay any portion of the debt to a person other than a non-resident person, and

(iii) before the deposit was recorded in the books of account of the international banking centre business, the taxpayer made reasonable inquiries and had no reasonable cause to believe that any portion of the amount was deposited on behalf of, for the benefit of or as a condition of any transaction with, a person (other than a non-resident person with whom the taxpayer was dealing at arm's length), or

(*b*) another prescribed financial institution with whom the taxpayer is dealing at arm's length at the particular time, where

(i) at or before the time at which the deposit was made, the prescribed financial institution provided written notice to the taxpayer that the deposit was being made from deposits recorded in the books of account of an international banking centre business of that prescribed financial institution, and

(ii) a reasonable rate of interest is paid or payable by the taxpayer in respect of the deposit;

"eligible loan"—"eligible loan", at any particular time, means

(*a*) a loan or deposit (in this paragraph referred to as a "loan") made by a taxpayer that is a prescribed financial institution to a non-resident person (in this paragraph referred to as the "borrower") with whom the taxpayer is dealing at arm's length at the particular time, where

(i) at the particular time, neither a person other than a non-resident person nor a person with whom the taxpayer is not dealing at arm's length is obligated to the taxpayer, either immediately or in the future and either absolutely or contingently, to pay to the taxpayer any amount in respect of the loan,

(ii) the loan was recorded in the books of account of an international banking centre business of the taxpayer throughout the period commencing with the later of

(A) the time at which the loan was made, and

(B) the earliest of

(I) the time at which the loan was first recorded in the books of account of a branch or office of the taxpayer located in Canada,

(II) the end of the first taxation year in respect of which the taxpayer has made any designation under subsection (3), and

(III) the end of 1992

and ending at the particular time,

(iii) in the case of a loan made before the end of the first taxation year in respect of which the taxpayer has made any designation under subsection (3) (other than a loan recorded in the books of account of an international banking centre business of the taxpayer at the time at which the loan was made) or a loan made to a foreign bank, the taxpayer made reasonable inquiries before the loan was recorded in the books of account of the international banking centre business and had no reasonable cause to believe that the borrower had used or would use any proceeds of the loan, directly or indirectly, for the purpose of

(A) earning income in Canada, or

(B) making a loan to a person other than a non-resident person, and

(iv) in the case of any other loan, the taxpayer, before the loan was recorded in the books of account of the international banking centre business,

(A) obtained a statement signed by or on behalf of the borrower that the borrower would not use any proceeds of the loan, directly or indirectly, for a purpose described in subparagraph (iii), and

(B) had no reasonable cause to believe that the borrower would use any proceeds of the loan, directly or indirectly, for a purpose described in subparagraph (iii),

(*b*) a loan acquired by a taxpayer that is a prescribed financial institution from a foreign bank with which the taxpayer is not dealing at arm's length at the time the loan was acquired, where the conditions described in subparagraphs (*a*)(i) to (iii) are met at the particular time, or

(*c*) a deposit made by a taxpayer that is a prescribed financial institution with another prescribed financial institution with whom the taxpayer is dealing at arm's length at the particular time where, at or before the time at which the deposit was made, the taxpayer provided written notice to the prescribed financial institution that the deposit was being made from deposits recorded in the books of account of an international banking centre business of the taxpayer;

"foreign bank"—"foreign bank" has the meaning assigned by the definition "foreign bank" in section 2 of the *Bank Act* (read without reference to paragraph (*g*)), except that an authorized foreign bank is not considered to be a foreign bank in respect of its Canadian banking business;

"non-resident person"—"non-resident person" at any time, with respect to a taxpayer, includes a person that the taxpayer, based on reasonable inquiries, believes at that time to be a person not resident in Canada.

► 33.1(2) ◄

(2) Interpretation. (Repealed by S.C. 2013, c. 33, s. 4(1).)

History: S. 33.1(2) was repealed by S.C. 2013, c. 33, s. 4(1), applicable to taxation years that begin after March 20, 2013, and formerly read:

(2) *Interpretation.* For the purposes of this section,

(*a*) a partnership shall be deemed to be a person;

(*b*) where a member of a partnership and a person do not deal with each other at arm's length, the partnership and the person shall be deemed not to deal with each other at arm's length;

(*c*) a partnership is a non-resident person only where all of its members are non-resident persons; and

(*d*) a deposit made by or to a non-resident person or a loan made to a non-resident person does not include a deposit made by or to, or a loan made to, as the case may be, a fixed place of business in Canada of the non-resident person.

► 33.1(3) ◄

(3) Designation and exemption. (Repealed by S.C. 2013, c. 33, s. 4(1).)

History: S. 33.1(3) was repealed by S.C. 2013, c. 33, s. 4(1), applicable to taxation years that begin after March 20, 2013, and formerly read:

(3) *Designation and exemption.* Where a taxpayer that was, throughout a taxation year, a prescribed financial institution has designated in respect of the year, by filing a prescribed form with the Minister on or before the day that is 90 days after the commencement of the year, a branch or office of the taxpayer in the metropolitan area of Montreal in the Province of Quebec or in the metropolitan area of Vancouver in the Province of British Columbia as a branch or office in which an international banking centre business of the taxpayer is to be carried on and has not revoked that designation by filing a prescribed form with the Minister on or before that day, in computing the income of the taxpayer for the year no amount shall be added or deducted in respect of the taxpayer's income or loss, as the case may be, for the year from the international banking centre business.

► 33.1(4) ◄

(4) Income or loss from an international banking centre business. (Repealed by S.C. 2013, c. 33, s. 4(1).)

History: S. 33.1(4) was repealed by S.C. 2013, c. 33, s. 4(1), applicable to taxation years that begin after March 20, 2013, and formerly read:

(4) *Income or loss from an international banking centre business.* Subject to subsection (5), the amount of a taxpayer's income or loss, as the case may be, for a taxation year from an international banking centre business shall be determined on the assumption that

(*a*) the international banking centre business was a separate business carried on by the taxpayer the only income or loss of which was derived from eligible loans for the period in the year during which they were recorded in the books of account of the business; and

(*b*) the only amount payable for the year by the taxpayer in respect of interest on money borrowed for the purpose of earning income from the business was equal to the total of

(i) the total of all amounts each of which is the interest payable by the taxpayer in respect of an eligible deposit for the period in the year during which it was recorded in the books of account of the business, and

(ii) the amount equal to that proportion of

(A) the total of all amounts each of which is the amount determined in respect of a day in the year equal to the amount, if any, by which

(I) 96% of the total of all amounts each of which is the amount outstanding on account of the principal amount of an eligible loan recorded in the books of account of the business at the end of the day

exceeds

(II) the total of all amounts each of which is the amount outstanding on account of the principal amount of an eligible deposit recorded in the books of account of the business at the end of the day

that

(B) the total determined under subparagraph (i)

is of

(C) the total of all amounts each of which is the amount outstanding on account of the principal amount of an eligible deposit recorded in the books of account of the business at the end of a day in the year.

▶ 33.1(5) ◀

(5) Restriction. (Repealed by S.C. 2013, c. 33, s. 4(1).)

History: S. 33.1(5) was repealed by S.C. 2013, c. 33, s. 4(1), applicable to taxation years that begin after March 20, 2013, and formerly read:

(5) *Restriction.* A taxpayer's income for a taxation year from an international banking centre business shall not exceed that proportion of that income determined in accordance with subsection (4) that

(*a*) the total of all amounts each of which is an amount determined in respect of a day in the year equal to the lesser of

(i) 96% of the total of all amounts each of which is the amount outstanding on account of the principal amount of an eligible loan recorded in the books of account of the business at the end of the day, and

(ii) the total of all amounts each of which is the amount outstanding on account of the principal amount of an eligible deposit recorded in the books of account of the business at the end of the day

is of

(*b*) 96% of the total of all amounts each of which is the amount outstanding on account of the principal amount of an eligible loan recorded in the books of account of the business at the end of a day in the year.

▶ 33.1(6) ◀

(6) Election. (Repealed by S.C. 2013, c. 33, s. 4(1).)

History: S. 33.1(6) was repealed by S.C. 2013, c. 33, s. 4(1), applicable to taxation years that begin after March 20, 2013, and formerly read:

(6) *Election.* For the purposes of subsections (4) and (5), where a taxpayer so elects in the taxpayer's return of income for a taxation year or in a prescribed form filed with the Minister within 90 days after the day of sending of a notice of assessment for the year or a notification that no tax is payable for the year, an eligible deposit recorded in the books of account of an international banking centre business of the taxpayer at the end of a day in the year is deemed not to have been recorded at any time in the day in the books of account of that business and is deemed to have been recorded throughout that day in the books of account of another international banking centre business of the taxpayer designated by the taxpayer in the election.

S. 33.1(6) was replaced by S.C. 2010, c. 25, s. 7, in force on Royal Assent, December 15, 2010. S. 33.1(6) formerly read:

(6) *Election.* For the purposes of subsections (4) and (5), where a taxpayer so elects in the taxpayer's return of income for a taxation year or in a prescribed form filed with the Minister within 90 days after the day of mailing of a notice of assessment for the year or a notification that no tax is payable for the year, an eligible deposit recorded in the books of account of an international banking centre business of the taxpayer at the end of a day in the year shall be deemed not to have been recorded at any time in the day in the books of account of that business and shall be deemed to have been recorded throughout that day in the books of account of another international banking centre business of the taxpayer designated by the taxpayer in the election.

▶ 33.1(7) ◀

(7) Election restriction. (Repealed by S.C. 2013, c. 33, s. 4(1).)

History: S. 33.1(7) was repealed by S.C. 2013, c. 33, s. 4(1), applicable to taxation years that begin after March 20, 2013, and formerly read:

(7) *Election restriction.* A taxpayer may elect, as provided in subsection (6), only in respect of eligible deposits recorded in the books of account of an international banking centre business at the end of a day to the extent that the total of those deposits exceeds 96% of the total of all amounts outstanding on account of the principal amounts of eligible loans recorded in the books of account of the business at the end of the day.

▶ 33.1(8) ◀

(8) Limitation. (Repealed by S.C. 2013, c. 33, s. 4(1).)

History: S. 33.1(8) was repealed by S.C. 2013, c. 33, s. 4(1), applicable to taxation years that begin after March 20, 2013, and formerly read:

(8) *Limitation.* In computing the income of a taxpayer for a taxation year, an amount paid or payable by the taxpayer on a deposit for the period in the year during which it was an eligible deposit shall, notwithstanding any other provision of this Act, be deductible only in computing the income or loss of the taxpayer from an international banking centre business.

▶ 33.1(9) ◀

(9) Exception. (Repealed by S.C. 2013, c. 33, s. 4(1).)

History: S. 33.1(9) was repealed by S.C. 2013, c. 33, s. 4(1), applicable to taxation years that begin after March 20, 2013, and formerly read:

(9) *Exception.* Where less than 90% of the revenue of a taxpayer for a taxation year from loans or deposits for the period in the year during which they were recorded in the books of account of an international banking centre business was derived from eligible loans in respect of which employees of the taxpayer actively participated in the solicitation, negotiation, analysis or management thereof while employed at a branch or office designated under subsection (3) as a branch or office in which an international banking centre business of the taxpayer is to be carried on, the amount, if any, of the taxpayer's income for the year from the international banking centre business shall, notwithstanding subsection (3), be included in computing the taxpayer's income for the year.

▶ 33.1(10) ◀

(10) No deduction permitted. (Repealed by S.C. 2013, c. 33, s. 4(1).)

History: S. 33.1(10) was repealed by S.C. 2013, c. 33, s. 4(1), applicable to taxation years that begin after March 20, 2013, and formerly read:

(10) *No deduction permitted.* Notwithstanding any other provision of this Act, in computing the income of a taxpayer no deduction shall be made in respect of any amount paid or payable in respect of indebtedness of the taxpayer to any person where, under an arrangement of which the taxpayer was aware or ought to have been aware at the time the indebtedness was incurred by the taxpayer, any portion of the indebtedness may reasonably be regarded as having been provided directly or indirectly from proceeds of a loan recorded in the books of account of an international banking centre business of a prescribed financial institution and any person has, in respect of that loan, signed a statement described in subparagraph (*a*)(iv) of the definition "eligible loan" in subsection (1).

▶ 33.1(11) ◀

(11) Application. (Repealed by S.C. 2013, c. 33, s. 4(1).)

History: S. 33.1(11) was repealed by S.C. 2013, c. 33, s. 4(1), applicable to taxation years that begin after March 20, 2013, and formerly read:

(11) *Application.* For greater certainty,

(*a*) where at any time a loan or deposit of a taxpayer ceases to be an eligible loan otherwise than by virtue of its disposition to another person, the taxpayer shall be deemed to have disposed of the loan or deposit in the course of carrying on an international banking centre business and to have received proceeds of disposition therefor equal to the fair market value of the loan or deposit at that time and to have reacquired the loan or deposit immediately after that time at a cost equal to its fair market value at that time;

(*b*) a taxpayer's loss for a taxation year from an international banking centre business shall not be included in determining the taxpayer's non-capital loss for the year; and

(*c*) the amount, if any, by which

(i) the amount that would be a taxpayer's income for a taxation year from an international banking centre business if this section were read without reference to subsection (5)

exceeds

(ii) the taxpayer's income for the year from the international banking centre business

shall be added in computing the income of the taxpayer for the year.

▶ 33.1(12) ◀

(12) Return. (Repealed by S.C. 2013, c. 33, s. 4(1).)

History: S. 33.1(12) was repealed by S.C. 2013, c. 33, s. 4(1), applicable to taxation years that begin after March 20, 2013, and formerly read:

(12) *Return.* Every taxpayer that has, in respect of a taxation year, designated a branch or office under subsection (3) as a branch or office in which an international banking centre business of the taxpayer is to be carried on

shall, within six months after the end of the year, file with the Minister a return in prescribed form containing prescribed information.

Related Regulations: 7900.

Related Sections: S. 248(1), "amount", "principal amount"; s. 255 Canada; S. 248(1), "authorized foreign bank", "Canadian banking business".

Forms: T781 — Designation as an International Banking Centre; T781-C — Revocation of designation as an international banking centre; T781-B — Election re: Deemed Transfers or Eligible Deposits Between International Banking Centres; T781-A — International Banking Centre Information Return.

SECTION 34: Professional business

In computing the income of a taxpayer for a taxation year from a business that is the professional practice of an accountant, dentist, lawyer, medical doctor, veterinarian or chiropractor, the following rules apply:

(*a*) if the taxpayer so elects in the taxpayer's return of income under this Part for the year and the year begins before March 22, 2017, there shall not be included any amount in respect of work in progress at the end of the year; and

(*b*) where the taxpayer has made an election under this section, paragraph (*a*) shall apply in computing the taxpayer's income from the business for all subsequent taxation years unless the taxpayer, with the concurrence of the Minister and on such terms and conditions as are specified by the Minister, revokes the election to have that paragraph apply.

Amendment not yet in force
Budget Implementation Act, 2017, No. 2 [S.C. 2017, c. 33]

S. 34 will be repealed by S.C. 2017, c. 33, s. 7(2).

Applicable: Comes into force on January 1, 2024.

History: S. 34(*a*) was replaced by S.C. 2017, c. 33, s. 7(1), applicable to taxation years ending after March 21, 2017, and formerly read:

(*a*) where the taxpayer so elects in the taxpayer's return of income under this Part for the year, there shall not be included any amount in respect of work in progress at the end of the year; and

Related Sections: S. 23(3) Reference to property in inventory.

Tax Topics: No. 1928, Potential Conflict? Sections 9 and 10 of the *Income Tax Act*.

Forms: T2125 — Statement of Business and Professional Activities.

Interpretation Bulletins: *Primary* — IT-457R Election by professionals to exclude work in progress from income. *Secondary* — IT-189R2 Corporations used by practising members of professions; IT-212R3 Income of deceased persons — Rights or things; IT-278R2 Death of a partner or of a retired partner.

SECTION 34.1: Additional business income

▶ 34.1(1) ◀

(1) Additional business income. Where

(*a*) an individual (other than a graduated rate estate) carries on a business in a taxation year,

(*b*) a fiscal period of the business begins in the year and ends after the end of the year (in this subsection referred to as the "particular period"), and

(*c*) the individual has elected under subsection 249.1(4) in respect of the business and the election has not been revoked,

there shall be included in computing the individual's income for the year from the business, the amount determined by the formula

$$(A - B) \times C/D$$

where

A is the total of the individual's income from the business for the fiscal periods of the business that end in the year,

B is the lesser of

(i) the total of all amounts each of which is an amount included in the value of A in respect of the business and that is deemed to be a taxable capital gain for the purpose of section 110.6, and

(ii) the total of all amounts deducted under section 110.6 in computing the individual's taxable income for the year,

C is the number of days on which the individual carries on the business that are both in the year and in the particular period, and

D is the number of days on which the individual carries on the business that are in fiscal periods of the business that end in the year.

Editorial Note: An individual carrying on a business must normally have a calendar year fiscal period (see s. 249.1(1)(*b*)). However, if the individual chooses to use the "alternative method" of computing business income, he or she may choose a fiscal period for his or her business other than the calendar year. if the individual chooses the alternative method, the individual must make the additional computations under s. 34.1 to account for income occurring in the period between the end of the fiscal period and the taxation year (i.e. the "stub period"), if any.

History: S. 34.1(1)(*a*) was replaced by S.C. 2014, c. 39, s. 8(1), applicable to the 2016 and subsequent taxation years, and formerly read:

(*a*) an individual (other than a testamentary trust) carries on a business in a taxation year,

Related Sections: 248(1) "testamentary trust"; 248(1) "graduated rate estate"; 249(2) References to certain taxation years and fiscal periods; 249.1 Definition of "fiscal period".

▶ 34.1(2) ◀

(2) Additional income election. Where

(*a*) an individual (other than a graduated rate estate) begins carrying on a business in a taxation year and not earlier than the beginning of the first fiscal period of the business that begins in the year and ends after the end of the year (in this subsection referred to as the "particular period"), and

(*b*) the individual has elected under subsection 249.1(4) in respect of the business and the election has not been revoked,

there shall be included in computing the individual's income for the year from the business the lesser of

(*c*) the amount designated in the individual's return of income for the year, and

(*d*) the amount determined by the formula

$$(A - B) \times C/D$$

where

A is the individual's income from the business for the particular period,

B is the lesser of

(i) the total of all amounts each of which is an amount included in the value of A in respect of the business and that is deemed to be a taxable capital gain for the purpose of section 110.6, and

(ii) the total of all amounts deducted under section 110.6 in computing the individual's taxable income for the taxation year that includes the end of the particular period,

C is the number of days on which the individual carries on the business that are both in the year and in the particular period, and

D is the number of days on which the individual carries on the business that are in the particular period.

History: S. 34.1(2)(*a*) was replaced by S.C. 2014, c. 39, s. 8(2), applicable to the 2016 and subsequent years, and formerly read:

(*a*) an individual (other than a testamentary trust) begins carrying on a business in a taxation year and not earlier than the beginning of the first fiscal period of the business that begins in the year and ends after the end of the year (in this subsection referred to as the "particular period"), and

▶ 34.1(3) ◀

(3) Deduction. There shall be deducted in computing an individual's income for a taxation year from a business the amount, if any, included under subsection (1) or (2) in computing the individual's income for the preceding taxation year from the business.

Related Sections: S. 249.1 Definition of "fiscal period".

▶ 34.1(4) ◀

(4) Deemed December 31, 1995 income — (Repealed by S.C. 2013, c. 40, s. 15.)

History: S. 34.1(4) was repealed by S.C. 2013, c. 40, s. 15, in force December 12, 2013, and formerly read:

(4) *Deemed December 31, 1995 income.* For the purpose of section 34.2, where

(*a*) at the end of 1994 an individual carried on a particular business no fiscal period of which ended at that time, and

(*b*) an amount is included under subsection (1) in computing the individual's income for the 1995 taxation year in respect of

(i) the particular business, or

(ii) another business that would, if subsection 34.2(3) applied for the purpose of this subparagraph, be included in the particular business,

subject to subsection (7), the December 31, 1995 income of the individual in respect of the particular business or the other business, as the case may be, is deemed to be the amount that would have been so included if the descriptions of A and B in subsection (1) were read as follows:

"A is the total of the individual's income from the business for the fiscal periods of the business that end in the year (determined as if paragraphs 34.2(2)(*a*) to (*d*) applied in computing that income),

B is the lesser of

(i) the total of all amounts each of which is an amount included in the value of A in respect of the business and that is deemed to be a taxable capital gain for the purpose of section 110.6, and

(ii) the total of the maximum amounts deductible under section 110.6 in computing the individual's taxable income for the year,".

▶ 34.1(5) ◀

(5) Deemed December 31, 1995 income — (Repealed by S.C. 2013, c. 40, s. 15.)

History: S. 34.1(5) was repealed by S.C. 2013, c. 40, s. 15, in force December 12, 2013, and formerly read:

(5) *Deemed December 31, 1995 income.* For the purpose of section 34.2, where

(*a*) at the end of 1994 an individual carried on a particular business no fiscal period of which ended at that time, and

(*b*) an amount is included under subsection (2) in computing the individual's income for the 1995 taxation year in respect of another business that would, if subsection 34.2(3) applied for the purpose of this paragraph, be included in the particular business,

the December 31, 1995 income of the individual in respect of the other business is deemed to be the amount that would have been so included if the descriptions of A and B in paragraph (2)(*d*) were read as follows:

"A is the individual's income from the business for the particular period (determined as if paragraphs 34.2(2)(*a*) to (*d*) applied in computing that income),

B is the lesser of

(i) the total of all amounts each of which is an amount included in the value of A in respect of the business and that is deemed to be a taxable capital gain for the purpose of section 110.6, and

(ii) the total of the maximum amounts deductible under section 110.6 in computing the individual's taxable income for the taxation year that includes the end of the particular period,".

▶ 34.1(6) ◀

(6) Deemed December 31, 1995 income — (Repealed by S.C. 2013, c. 40, s. 15.)

History: S. 34.1(6) was repealed by S.C. 2013, c. 40, s. 15, in force December 12, 2013, and formerly read:

(6) *Deemed December 31, 1995 income.* For the purpose of section 34.2, where

(*a*) at the end of 1995 an individual carries on a business as a member of a partnership no fiscal period of which ended at the end of 1994,

(*b*) the business was carried on by a professional corporation as a member of the partnership at the end of 1994,

(*c*) the professional corporation transferred its interest in the partnership to the individual before the end of 1995,

(*d*) the individual is a practising member of the professional body under the authority of which the professional corporation practised the profession,

(*e*) the individual was a specified shareholder of the professional corporation immediately before the transfer,

(*f*) the professional corporation does not have a share of the income or loss of the partnership for the first fiscal period of the partnership that ends after the end of 1995, and

(*g*) an amount is included under subsection (2) in computing the individual's income for the 1995 taxation year in respect of the business,

the December 31, 1995 income of the individual in respect of the business is deemed to be the amount that would have been so included if the descriptions of A and B in paragraph (2)(*d*) were read as follows:

"A is the individual's income from the business for the particular period (determined as if paragraphs 34.2(2)(*a*) to (*d*) applied in computing that income),

B is the lesser of

(i) the total of all amounts each of which is an amount included in the value of A in respect of the business and that is deemed to be a taxable capital gain for the purpose of section 110.6, and

(ii) the total of the maximum amounts deductible under section 110.6 in computing the individual's taxable income for the taxation year that includes the end of the particular period,"

and, for the purpose of computing the values of C and D in paragraph (2)(*d*), the individual is deemed to carry on the business on the days on which the corporation carried on the business.

▶ 34.1(7) ◀

(7) Maximum December 31, 1995 income — (Repealed by S.C. 2013, c. 40, s. 15.)

History: S. 34.1(7) was repealed by S.C. 2013, c. 40, s. 15, in force December 12, 2013, and formerly read:

(7) *Maximum December 31, 1995 income.* Where an amount was included under subsection (1) in computing an individual's income for the 1995 taxation year from a business and

(*a*) the individual's December 31, 1995 income otherwise determined under subsection (4) in respect of the business for the purpose of section 34.2

exceeds

(*b*) the amount that would be described under paragraph (*a*) if the descriptions of A, B and D in subsection (1) were read as follows:

"A is the individual's income from the business for the particular period (determined as if paragraphs 34.2(2)(*a*) to (*d*) applied in computing that income),

B is the lesser of

(i) the total of all amounts each of which is an amount included in the value of A in respect of the business and that is deemed to be a taxable capital gain for the purpose of section 110.6, and

(ii) the total of the maximum amounts deductible under section 110.6 in computing the individual's taxable income for the taxation year that includes the end of the particular period,

D is the number of days on which the individual carries on the business that are in the particular period.",

for the purpose of applying subsection 34.2(4) to the 1996 and subsequent taxation years, the December 31, 1995 income of the individual in respect of the business is deemed to be the amount determined under paragraph (*b*).

▶ 34.1(8) ◀

(8) No additional income inclusion. Subsections (1) and (2) do not apply in computing an individual's income for a taxation year from a business where (*a*) the individual dies or otherwise ceases to carry on the business in the year; or

(*b*) the individual becomes a bankrupt in the calendar year in which the taxation year ends.

▶ 34.1(9) ◀

(9) Death of partner or proprietor. Where

(*a*) an individual carries on a business in a taxation year,

(*b*) the individual dies in the year and after the end of a fiscal period of the business that ends in the year,

(*c*) another fiscal period of the business ends because of the individual's death (in this subsection referred to as the "short period"), and

(*d*) the individual's legal representative

(i) elects that this subsection apply in computing the individual's income for the year, or

(ii) files a separate return of income under subsection 150(4) in respect of the individual's business,

notwithstanding subsection (8), there shall be included in computing the individual's income for the year from the business, the amount determined by the formula

$$(A - B) \times C/D$$

where

A is the total of the individual's income from the business for fiscal periods (other than the short period) of the business that end in the year,

B is the lesser of

(i) the total of all amounts, each of which is an amount included in the value of A in respect of the business that is deemed to be a taxable capital gain for the purpose of section 110.6, and

(*ii*) the total of all amounts deducted under section 110.6 in computing the individual's taxable income for the year,

C is the number of days in the short period, and

D is the total number of days in fiscal periods of the business (other than the short period) that end in the year.

SECTION 34.2: [Corporate partners — income adjustment]

▶ 34.2(1) ◀

(1) Definitions. The definitions in this subsection apply in this section.

Editorial Note: See the editorial note under s. 249.1(1).

History: S. 34.2(1) was replaced by S.C. 2011, c. 24, s. 3(1), applicable to taxation years ending after March 22, 2011. See the history note following s. 34.2(18) for the former reading of s. 34.2.

"adjusted stub period accrual" — "adjusted stub period accrual" of a corporation in respect of a partnership — in which the corporation has a significant interest at the end of the last fiscal period of the partnership that ends in the corporation's taxation year in circumstances where another fiscal period (in this definition referred to as the "particular period") of the partnership begins in the year and ends after the year — means

(*a*) if paragraph (*b*) does not apply, the amount determined by the formula

$$[(A - B) \times C/D] - (E + F)$$

where

A is the total of all amounts each of which is the corporation's share of an income or taxable capital gain of the partnership for a fiscal period of the partnership that ends in the year (other than any amount for which a deduction is available under section 112 or 113),

B is the total of all amounts each of which is the corporation's share of a loss or allowable capital loss — to the extent that the total of all allowable capital losses does not exceed the total of all taxable capital gains included in the description of A — of the partnership for a fiscal period of the partnership that ends in the year,

C is the number of days that are in both the year and the particular period,

D is the number of days in fiscal periods of the partnership that end in the year,

E is the amount of the qualified resource expense in respect of the particular period of the partnership that is designated by the corporation for the year under subsection (6) in its return of income for the year filed with the Minister on or before its filing-due date for the year, and

F is an amount designated by the corporation in its return of income for the year (other than an amount included in the description of E) and filed with the Minister on or before its filing-due date for the year; and

(*b*) if a fiscal period of the partnership ends in the corporation's taxation year and the year is the first taxation year in which the fiscal period of the partnership is aligned with the fiscal period of one or more other partnerships under a multi-tier alignment (in this paragraph referred to as the "eligible fiscal period"),

(i) where a fiscal period of the partnership ends in the year and before the eligible fiscal period, the amount determined by the formula

$$[(A - B) \times C/D] - (E + F)$$

where

A is the total of all amounts each of which is the corporation's share of an income or taxable capital gain of the partnership for the first fiscal period of the partnership that ends in the year (other than any amount for which a deduction is available under section 112 or 113),

B is the total of all amounts each of which is the corporation's share of a loss or allowable capital loss — to the extent that the total of all allowable capital losses does not exceed the total of all taxable capital gains included in the description of A — of the partnership for the first fiscal period of the partnership that ends in the year,

C is the number of days that are in both the year and the particular period,

D is the number of days in the first fiscal period of the partnership that ends in the year,

E is the amount of the qualified resource expense in respect of the particular period of the partnership that is designated by the corporation for the year under subsection (6) in its return of income for the year filed with the Minister on or before its filing-due date for the year, and

F is an amount designated by the corporation in its return of income for the year (other than an amount included in the description of E) and filed with the Minister on or before its filing-due date for the year, and

(ii) where the eligible fiscal period of the partnership is the first fiscal period of the partnership that ends in the corporation's taxation year, the amount determined by the formula

$$(A - B - C) \times D/E - (F + G)$$

where

A is the total of all amounts each of which is the corporation's share of an income or taxable capital gain of the partnership for the eligible fiscal period (other than any amount for which a deduction is available under section 112 or 113),

B is the total of all amounts each of which is the corporation's share of a loss or allowable capital loss — to the extent that the total of all allowable capital losses does not exceed the total of all taxable capital gains included in the description of A — of the partnership for the eligible fiscal period,

C is the corporation's eligible alignment income for the eligible fiscal period,

D is the number of days that are in both the year and the particular period,

E is the number of days that are in the eligible fiscal period that ends in the year,

F is the amount of the qualified resource expense in respect of the particular period of the partnership that is designated by the corporation for the year under subsection (6) in its return of income for the year filed with the Minister on or before its filing-due date for the year, and

G is an amount designated by the corporation in its return of income for the year (other than an amount included in the description of F) and filed with the Minister on or before its filing-due date for the year.

Editorial Note: If a corporation has a significant interest at the end of the last fiscal period of the partnership that ends in the corporation's taxation year in circumstances where another fiscal period (the "particular period") of the partnership begins in the year and ends after the year, then the adjusted stub period accrual ("ASPA") for such corporation is its share of the income of the partnership for a fiscal period of the partnership that ends in the year multiplied by the fraction in which the numerator is the number of days that are in both the taxation year of the corporation and the particular period and in which the denominator is the number of days in fiscal periods of the partnership that end in the year. ASPA may be reduced by the aggregate of the amount of qualified resource expense in respect of the particular period of the partnership that is designated by the corporation and an amount designated by the corporation (the "F designation"). (The term "F designation" was used in a presentation of Mitchell Sherman and Marisa Wyse to the Taxation Section Ontario Bar Association on February 23, 2012.) Each of the designations must be made by the corporation in its return of income for the year filed with the Minister on or before its filing-due date for the year.

ASPA is determined on a partnership-by-partnership basis and in accordance with s. 257, cannot be negative. A corporation cannot therefore reduce the ASPA in respect of a partnership, if it has realized losses from another partnership. It may be possible, however, to make an F designation in respect of a profitable partnership.

If a fiscal period of the partnership ends in the corporation's taxation year and the taxation year of the corporation is the first taxation year in which the fiscal period of the partnership is aligned with the fiscal period of one or more other partnerships under a multi-tier alignment (the "eligible fiscal period") where a fiscal period of the partnership ends in the year and before the eligible fiscal period, then the ASPA is calculated in the same manner as set out above and the first fiscal period of the partnership that ends in the corporation's taxation year is used in the calculations. Where the eligible fiscal period of the partnership is the first fiscal period of the partnership that ends in the corporation's taxation year, then the ASPA is calculated using the eligible fiscal period of the partnership.

Related Sections: S. 34.2(2) Inclusion in income; s. 34.2(6) Designation by corporation to reduce ASPA for qualifying resource expense; s. 34.2(10) E and F designations cannot be amended or revoked; s. 34.2(16), (17) Determining a corporation's qualifying transitional income; s. 257 Formula cannot yield negative result.

"eligible alignment income" — "eligible alignment income", of a corporation, means

(*a*) if a partnership is subject to a single-tier alignment, the first aligned fiscal period of the partnership ends in the first taxation year of the corporation ending after March 22, 2011 (in this paragraph referred to as the "eligible fiscal period") and the corporation is a member of the partnership at the end of the eligible fiscal period,

(i) where the eligible fiscal period is preceded by another fiscal period of the partnership that ends in the corporation's first taxation year that ends after March 22, 2011 and the corporation is a member of the partnership at the end of that preceding fiscal period, the amount determined by the formula

$$A - B - C$$

where

A is the total of all amounts each of which is the corporation's share of an income or taxable capital gain of the partnership for the eligible fiscal period (other than any amount for which a deduction is available under section 112 or 113),

B is the total of all amounts each of which is the corporation's share of a loss or allowable capital loss — to the extent that the total of all allowable capital losses does not exceed the total of all taxable capital gains included in the description of A — of the partnership for the eligible fiscal period, and

C is, where an outlay or expense of the partnership is deemed by subsection 66(18) to be made or incurred by the corporation at the end of the eligible fiscal period, the total of all amounts each of which is an amount that would be deductible by the corporation for the taxation year under any of sections 66.1, 66.2, 66.21 and 66.4 determined as if each such outlay or expense were the only amount relevant in determining the amount deductible, or

(ii) where the eligible fiscal period is the first fiscal period of the partnership that ends in the corporation's first taxation year ending after March 22, 2011, nil; and (*b*) if a partnership is subject to a multi-tier alignment, the first aligned fiscal period of the partnership ends in the taxation year of the corporation (in this paragraph referred to as the "eligible fiscal period") and the corporation is a member of the partnership at the end of the eligible fiscal period, the amount determined by the formula

$$A - B - C$$

where

A is the total of all amounts each of which is the corporation's share of an income or taxable capital gain of the partnership for the eligible fiscal period, other than any amount

(i) for which a deduction is available under section 112 or 113, or

(ii) that would be included in computing the income of the corporation for the year if there were no multi-tier alignment,

B is the total of all amounts each of which is the corporation's share of a loss or allowable capital loss — to the extent that the total of all allowable capital losses does not exceed the total of all taxable capital gains included in the description of A — of a partnership for the eligible fiscal period, and

C is, where an outlay or expense of the partnership is deemed by subsection 66(18) to be made or incurred by the corporation at the end of the eligible fiscal period, the total of all amounts each of which is an amount that would be deductible by the corporation for the taxation year under any of sections 66.1, 66.2, 66.21 and 66.4 determined as if each such outlay or expense were the only amount relevant in determining the amount deductible.

"multi-tier alignment" —"multi-tier alignment", in respect of a partnership, means the alignment under subsection 249.1(9) or (11) of the fiscal period of the partnership and the fiscal period of one or more other partnerships.

Related Sections: S. 249.1(9) Election to end fiscal period; s. 249.1(11) Deemed multi-tier election to end fiscal period on December 31, 2011.

"qualified resource expense" —"qualified resource expense", of a corporation for a taxation year in respect of a fiscal period of a partnership that begins in the year and ends after the year, means an expense incurred by the partnership in the portion of the fiscal period that is in the year and that is described in any of the following definitions:

(*a*) "Canadian exploration expense" in subsection 66.1(6);

(*b*) "Canadian development expense" in subsection 66.2(5);

(*c*) "foreign resource expense" in subsection 66.21(1); and

(*d*) "Canadian oil and gas property expense" in subsection 66.4(5).

Related Sections: S. 34.2(6) Designation to reduce ASPA.

"qualifying transitional income" —"qualifying transitional income", of a corporation that is a member of a partnership on March 22, 2011, means the amount that is the total of the following amounts, computed in accordance with subsection (15),

(*a*) the corporation's eligible alignment income in respect of the partnership, and

(*b*) the corporation's adjusted stub period accrual in respect of the partnership for

(i) if there is a multi-tier alignment in respect of the partnership, the corporation's taxation year during which ends the fiscal period of the partnership that is aligned with the fiscal period of one or more other partnerships under the multi-tier alignment, or

(ii) in any other case, the corporation's first taxation year that ends after March 22, 2011.

"significant interest" —"significant interest", of a corporation in a partnership at any time, means a membership interest of the corporation in the partnership if the corporation, or the corporation together with one or more persons or partnerships related to or affiliated with the corporation, is entitled at that time to more than 10% of

(*a*) the income or loss of the partnership; or

(*b*) the assets (net of liabilities) of the partnership if it were to cease to exist.

Related Sections: S. 34.2(2) Inclusions in income for corporations.

"single-tier alignment" —"single-tier alignment", in respect of a partnership, means the ending of a fiscal period of the partnership under subsection 249.1(8).

"specified percentage" —"specified percentage", of a corporation for a particular taxation year in respect of a partnership, means

(*a*) if the first taxation year for which the corporation has qualifying transitional income ends in 2011 and the particular year ends in

(i) 2011, 100%,

(ii) 2012, 85%,

(iii) 2013, 65%,

(iv) 2014, 45%,

(v) 2015, 25%, and

(vi) 2016, 0%;

(*b*) if the first taxation year for which the corporation has qualifying transitional income ends in 2012 and the particular year ends in

(i) 2012, 100%,

(ii) 2013, 85%,

(iii) 2014, 65%,

(iv) 2015, 45%,

(v) 2016, 25%, and

(vi) 2017, 0%; and

(*c*) if the first taxation year for which the corporation has qualifying transitional income ends in 2013 and the particular year ends in

(i) 2013, 85%,

(ii) 2014, 65%,

(iii) 2015, 45%,

(iv) 2016, 25%, and

(v) 2017, 0%.

Related Sections: S. 34.2(11) Transitional reserve to avoid large inclusion in income in first year.

► 34.2(2) ◄

(2) Income inclusion — adjusted stub period accrual. Subject to subsections (5) and (9), a corporation (other than a professional corporation) shall include in computing its income for a taxation year its adjusted stub period accrual in respect of a partnership if

(*a*) the corporation has a significant interest in the partnership at the end of the last fiscal period of the partnership that ends in the year;

(*b*) another fiscal period of the partnership begins in the year and ends after the year; and

(*c*) at the end of the year, the corporation is entitled to a share of an income, loss, taxable capital gain or allowable capital loss of the partnership for the fiscal period referred to in paragraph (*b*).

History: S. 34.2(2) was replaced by S.C. 2011, c. 24, s. 3(1), applicable to taxation years ending after March 22, 2011. See the history note following s. 34.2(18) for the former reading of s. 34.2.

Related Sections: S. 34.2(3) New partner has option in first year of including ASPA; s. 34.2(4) Deduction in following year; s. 34.2(5)(*a*) Components of ASPA retain their character; s. 34.2(5)(*b*) Allowable capital loss can reduce taxable capital gain; s. 34.2(7) Non application of 34.2(2) if corporation is bankrupt; s. 34.2(8) FAPI rules are not applicable in determining ASPA; s. 34.2(9) Limited inclusion in income where there is multi-tier alignment; s. 34.3(1), (2), (3) Increase in income if ASPA is reduced.

Canadian Tax Foundation: Oldewening et al., *An Update on Amendments Affecting Partnerships*, 2013 Ontario Tax Conference 3:1–23; Lindsey and Pashkowich, *Anti-Deferral Rules for Partnership Income: Update and Selected Issues*, 2012 Conference Report 15:1–22; Oldewening and Carr, *Limitation on Deferral of Partnership Income by a Corporation*, 2012 Canadian Tax Journal 1:219–256; Calvert and Young, *New Anti-Deferral Rules for Partnership Income*, 2011 Conference Report 40:1–28.

Forms: T2 Sch 73 Income Inclusion Summary for Corporations that are Members of Partnerships; T2 Sch 71 Income Inclusion for Corporations that are Members of Single Tier Partnerships.

► 34.2(3) ◄

(3) Income inclusion — new partner designation. Subject to subsection (5), if a corporation (other than a professional corporation) becomes a member of a partnership during a fiscal period of the partnership (in this subsection referred to as the "particular period") that begins in the corporation's taxation year and ends after the taxation year but on or before the filing-due date for the taxation year and the corporation has a significant interest in the partnership at the end of the particular period, the corporation may include in computing its income for the taxation year the lesser of

(*a*) the amount, if any, designated by the corporation in its return of income for the taxation year, and

(*b*) the amount determined by the formula

$$A \times B/C$$

where

A is the corporation's income from the partnership for the particular period (other than any amount for which a deduction is available under section 112 or 113),

B is the number of days that are both in the corporation's taxation year and the particular period, and

C is the number of days in the particular period.

Editorial Note: Subsection 34.2(3) applies to corporations that become members of a partnership in a taxation year during a fiscal period of the partnership (the "particular period") that begins in the corporation's taxation year and ends after the taxation year, but on or before the filing-due date of the corporation for that taxation year. If the corporation has a significant interest in the partnership at the end of the fiscal period of the partnership, then the corporation may include in its income for the taxation year the lesser of the amount designated by it, and the amount of the corporation's income for the partnership for the particular period multiplied by the fraction of the numerator of which is the number of days that are both in the corporation's taxation year and the particular period of the partnership and the denominator of which is the number of days in the particular period of the partnership. As stated in the Explanatory Notes, in this type of situation, the corporation may apportion its income from the partnership for a particular period between two taxation years — the taxation year in which the fiscal period of the partnership began and the taxation year in which it ends.

History: S. 34.2(3) was replaced by S.C. 2011, c. 24, s. 3(1), applicable to taxation years ending after March 22, 2011. See the history note following s. 34.2(18) for the former reading of s. 34.2.

Related Sections: S. 34.2(4) Deduction in following year; s. 34.2(5) Components of ASPA retain their character; s. 34.2(7) Non application of 34.2(3) when corporation is bankrupt; s. 34.2(8) FAPI not applicable in determining ASPA.

Forms: T2 Sch 73 Income Inclusion Summary for Corporations that are Members of Partnerships; T2 Sch 71 Income Inclusion for Corporations that are Members of Single Tier Partnerships.

► 34.2(4) ◄

(4) Treatment in following year. If an amount was included in computing the income of a corporation in respect of a partnership for the immediately preceding taxation year under subsection (2) or (3),

(*a*) the portion of the amount that, because of subparagraph (5)(*a*)(i) or (ii), was income for that preceding year is deductible in computing the income of the corporation for the current taxation year; and

(*b*) the portion of the amount that, because of subparagraph (5)(*a*)(i) or (ii), was taxable capital gains for that preceding year is deemed to be an allowable capital loss of the corporation for the current taxation year from the disposition of property.

History: S. 34.2(4) was replaced by S.C. 2013 c. 40, s. 16(1), applicable to taxation years that end after March 22, 2011, and formerly read:

(4) *Deduction in following year.* A corporation may deduct in computing its income for a taxation year each amount that was included in computing its income in respect of a partnership for the immediately preceding taxation year under subsection (2) or (3).

S. 34.2(4) was replaced by S.C. 2011, c. 24, s. 3(1), applicable to taxation years ending after March 22, 2011. See the history note following s. 34.2(18) for the former reading of s. 34.2.

Related Sections: S. 34.2(2) and 34.2(3) Inclusion in previous year; s. 34.2(5) Deduction retaining same character as inclusion in preceding year.

► 34.2(5) ◄

(5) Character of amounts. For the purposes of this Act, the following rules apply:

(*a*) in computing the income of a corporation for a taxation year,

(i) an adjusted stub period accrual included under subsection (2) in respect of a partnership for the year is deemed to be income, and taxable capital gains from the disposition of property, having the same character and to be in the same proportions as any income and taxable capital gains that were allocated by the partnership to the corporation for all fiscal periods of the partnership ending in the year,

(ii) an amount included under subsection (3) in respect of a partnership for the year is deemed to be income, and taxable capital gains from the disposition of property, having the same character and to be in the same proportions as any income and taxable capital gains that were allocated by the partnership to the corporation for the particular period referred to in that subsection,

(iii) an amount, a portion of which is deductible or is an allowable capital loss under subsection (4) in respect of a partnership for the year, is deemed to have the same character and to be in the same proportions as the income and taxable capital gains included in the corporation's income for the immediately preceding taxation year under subsection (2) or (3) in respect of the partnership,

(iv) an amount claimed as a reserve under subsection (11) in respect of a partnership for the year is deemed to have the same character and to be in the same proportions as the qualifying transitional income in respect of the partnership for the year, and

(v) an amount, a portion of which is included in income under paragraph (12)(*a*), or is deemed to be a taxable capital gain under paragraph (12)(*b*), in respect of a partnership for the year, is deemed to have the same character and to be in the same proportions as the amount claimed as a reserve under subsection (11) in respect of the partnership for the immediately preceding taxation year;

(*b*) a corporation's capital dividend account, as defined in subsection 89(1), is to be determined without reference to this section; and

(*c*) the reference in subparagraph 53(2)(*c*)(i.4) to an amount deducted under subsection (11) by a taxpayer includes an amount deemed to be an allowable capital loss under subparagraph (11)(*b*)(ii).

Editorial Note: Paragraph 34.2(5)(*b*) prevents corporations that are subject to the s. 34.2 adjustments from including those adjustments in the s. 89(1) calculation of their capital dividend accounts. Because certain s. 34.2 adjustments — such as the addition of taxable capital gains arising from the adjusted stub period accrual ("ASPA") — are deemed to be "from property", the explicitness of this preventative provision is necessary to prevent an inappropriate increase in the capital dividend account of the corporation. In the case of a corporation with an ASPA deemed allowable capital loss, s. 34.2(5)(*b*) similarly prevents that loss from reducing the corporation's capital dividend account.

History: S. 34.2(5)(*a*)(i) to (v) were replaced by S.C. 2013 c. 40, s. 16(2), applicable to taxation years that end after March 22, 2011, and formerly read:

(i) an adjusted stub period accrual included under subsection (2) in respect of a partnership for the year is deemed to be income and taxable capital gains having the same character and to be in the same proportions as any income and taxable capital gains that were allocated by the partnership to the corporation for all fiscal periods of the partnership ending in the year,

(ii) an amount included under subsection (3) in respect of a partnership for the year is deemed to be income and taxable capital gains having the same character and to be in the same proportions as any income and taxable capital gains that were allocated by the partnership to the corporation for the particular period referred to in that subsection,

(iii) an amount deductible under subsection (4) in respect of a partnership for the year is deemed to have the same character and to be in the same proportions as the income and taxable capital gains included in the corporation's income for the immediately preceding taxation year under subsection (2) or (3) in respect of the partnership,

(iv) an amount deductible as a reserve under subsection (11) in respect of a partnership for the year is deemed to have the same character and to be in the same proportions as the qualifying transitional income in respect of the partnership for the year, and

(v) an amount included in income under subsection (12) in respect of the partnership for the year is deemed to have the same character and to be in the same proportions as the amount deducted under subsection (11) for the immediately preceding taxation year; and

S. 34.2(5)(*b*) was replaced by S.C. 2013 c. 40, s. 16(3), applicable to taxation years that end after March 22, 2011, and formerly read:

(*b*) a corporation is deemed to have realized at the end of a taxation year an allowable capital loss equal to the amount determined by the formula

$$A - (B - C)$$

where

A is the amount deductible by the corporation under subsection (4) for the year in respect of taxable capital gains of a partnership,

B is the amount that is the total of

(i) all taxable capital gains allocated by the partnership to the corporation for the year,

(ii) the amount included in the corporation's income under subsection (2) for the year in respect of taxable capital gains of the partnership, and

(iii) the amount included in the corporation's income under subsection (12) for the year in respect of taxable capital gains of the partnership, and

C is the amount, if any, that is the lesser of

(i) the amount that is the total of all allowable capital losses allocated by the partnership to the corporation for the year, and

(ii) the amount determined under subparagraph (i) of the description of B.

S. 34.2(5)(*c*) was added by S.C. 2013 c. 40, s. 16(3), applicable to taxation years that end after March 22, 2011.

S. 34.2(5) was replaced by S.C. 2011, c. 24, s. 3(1), applicable to taxation years ending after March 22, 2011. See the history note following s. 34.2(18) for the former reading of s. 34.2.

▶ 34.2(6) ◀

(6) Designation — qualified resource expense. A corporation may designate an amount for a taxation year in respect of a qualified resource expense under the definition "adjusted stub period accrual" in subsection (1) subject to the following rules:

(*a*) the corporation cannot designate an amount for the year in respect of a qualified resource expense in respect of a partnership except to the extent the corporation obtains from the partnership, before the corporation's filing-due date for the year, information in writing identifying the corporation's qualified resource expenses described

(i) in paragraph (*h*) of the definition "Canadian exploration expense" in subsection 66.1(6), determined as if those expenses had been incurred by the partnership in its last fiscal period that ended in the year,

(ii) in paragraph (*f*) of the definition "Canadian development expense" in subsection 66.2(5), determined as if those expenses had been incurred by the partnership in its last fiscal period that ended in the year,

(iii) in paragraph (*e*) of the definition "foreign resource expense" in subsection 66.21(1), determined as if those expenses had been incurred by the partnership in its last fiscal period that ended in the year, and

(iv) in paragraph (*b*) of the definition "Canadian oil and gas property expense" in subsection 66.4(5), determined as if those expenses had been incurred by the partnership in its last fiscal period that ended in the year; and

(*b*) the amount designated for the year by the corporation is not to exceed the maximum amount that would be deductible by the corporation under any of sections 66.1, 66.2, 66.21 and 66.4 in computing its income for the year if

(i) the amounts referred to in paragraph (*a*) in respect of the partnership were the only amounts relevant in determining the maximum amount, and

(ii) the fiscal period of the partnership that begins in the year and ends after the year had ended at the end of the year and each qualified resource expense were deemed under subsection 66(18) to be incurred by the corporation at the end of the year.

History: S. 34.2(6) was replaced by S.C. 2011, c. 24, s. 3(1), applicable to taxation years ending after March 22, 2011. See the history note following s. 34.2(18) for the former reading of s. 34.2.

Related Sections: S. 34.2(1) Adjusted stub period accrual can be reduced; s. 34.2(10) Designation cannot be amended nor revoked; s. 34.2(17) Qualifying transitional income can be reduced.

▶ 34.2(7) ◀

(7) No additional income — bankrupt. Subsections (2) and (3) do not apply in computing a corporation's income for a taxation year in respect of a partnership if the corporation becomes a bankrupt in the year.

History: S. 34.2(7) was replaced by S.C. 2011, c. 24, s. 3(1), applicable to taxation years ending after March 22, 2011. See the history note following s. 34.2(18) for the former reading of s. 34.2.

▶ 34.2(8) ◀

(8) Foreign affiliates. This section does not apply for the purposes of computing, for a taxation year of a foreign affiliate of a corporation resident in Canada,

(*a*) the foreign accrual property income of the affiliate in respect of the corporation; and

(*b*) except to the extent that the context otherwise requires, the exempt surplus or exempt deficit, the hybrid surplus or hybrid deficit, and the taxable surplus or taxable deficit (as those terms are defined in subsection 5907(1) of the *Income Tax Regulations*) of the affiliate in respect of the corporation.

History: S. 34.2(8)(*b*) was replaced by S.C. 2013, c. 34, s. 58(1), applicable to taxation years that end after August 19, 2011.

Any assessment of a taxpayer's tax, interest and penalties payable under the Act for any taxation year that ends before June 26, 2013 that would, in the absence of this section, be precluded because of subsections 152(4) to (5) of the Act shall be made to the extent necessary to take into account the amendments by S.C. 2013, c. 34, s. 54 to 89.

S. 34.2(8)(*b*) formerly read:

(*b*) except to the extent that the context otherwise requires, the exempt surplus or exempt deficit and the taxable surplus or taxable deficit (as those terms are defined in subsection 5907(1) of the *Income Tax Regulations*) of the affiliate in respect of the corporation.

S. 34.2(8) was replaced by S.C. 2011, c. 24, s. 3(1), applicable to taxation years ending after March 22, 2011. See the history note following s. 34.2(18) for the former reading of s. 34.2.

▶ 34.2(9) ◀

(9) Special case — multi-tier alignment. If a corporation is a member of a partnership subject to a multi-tier alignment, subsection (2) does not apply to the corporation in respect of the partnership for taxation years preceding the taxation year that includes the end of the first aligned fiscal period of the partnership under the multi-tier alignment.

History: S. 34.2(9) was added by S.C. 2011, c. 24, s. 3(1), applicable to taxation years ending after March 22, 2011.

▶ 34.2(10) ◀

(10) Designations. Once a corporation makes a designation in calculating its adjusted stub period accrual in respect of a partnership for a taxation year under any of the description of E or F of paragraph (*a*), the description of E or F of subparagraph (*b*)(i) and the description of F or G of subparagraph (*b*)(ii) of the definition "adjusted stub period accrual" in subsection (1), the designation cannot be amended or revoked.

History: S. 34.2(10) was added by S.C. 2011, c. 24, s. 3(1), applicable to taxation years ending after March 22, 2011.

▶ 34.2(11) ◀

(11) Transitional reserve. If a corporation has qualifying transitional income in respect of a partnership for a particular taxation year,

(*a*) the corporation may, in computing its income for the particular year, claim an amount, as a reserve, not exceeding the least of

(i) the specified percentage for the particular year of the corporation's qualifying transitional income in respect of the partnership,

(ii) if, for the immediately preceding taxation year, an amount was claimed under this subsection in computing the corporation's income in respect of the partnership, the amount that is the total of

(A) the amount included under subsection (12) in computing the corporation's income for the particular year in respect of the partnership, and

(B) the amount by which the corporation's qualifying transitional income in respect of the partnership is increased in the particular year because of the application of subsections (16) and (17), and

(iii) the amount determined by the formula

$$A - B$$

where

A is the corporation's income for the particular year computed before deducting or claiming any amount under this subsection in respect of the partnership or under section 61.3 and 61.4, and

B is the total of all amounts each of which is an amount deductible by the corporation for the year under section 112 or 113 in respect of a dividend received by the corporation after December 20, 2012; and

(*b*) the portion of the amount claimed under paragraph (*a*) for the particular year that, because of subparagraph (5)(*a*)(iv), has

(i) a character other than capital is deductible in computing the income of the corporation for the particular year, and

(ii) the character of capital is deemed to be an allowable capital loss of the corporation for the particular year from the disposition of property.

History: S. 34.2(11) was replaced by S.C. 2013, c. 40, s. 16(4), applicable to taxation years ending after March 22, 2011, and formerly read:

(11) *Transitional reserve.* A corporation that has qualifying transitional income in respect of a partnership for a particular taxation year may deduct in computing its income, as a reserve, for the particular year such amount as the corporation claims not exceeding the least of

(*a*) the specified percentage for the particular year of the corporation's qualifying transitional income in respect of the partnership,

(*b*) if, for the immediately preceding taxation year, an amount was deductible under this subsection in computing the corporation's income in respect of the partnership, the amount that is the total of

(i) the amount included under subsection (12) in computing the corporation's income for the particular year in respect of the partnership, and

(ii) the amount by which the corporation's qualifying transitional income in respect of the partnership is increased in the particular year because of the application of subsections (16) and (17), and

(c) the corporation's income for the particular year computed before deducting any amount under this subsection in respect of the partnership or under sections 61.3 and 61.4.

S. 34.2(11) was added by S.C. 2011, c. 24, s. 3(1), applicable to taxation years ending after March 22, 2011.

Related Sections: S. 34.2(12) Reserve included in income in following year; s. 34.2(13) When reserve is denied; s. 34.2(16) and 34.2(17) Adjustment of qualifying transitional income; s. 53(2)(c)(i.4) Increase in ACB of partnership interest.

▶ 34.2(12) ◀

(12) Inclusion of prior year reserve. Subject to subsection (5), if a reserve was claimed by a corporation under subsection (11) in respect of a partnership for the immediately preceding taxation year,

(a) the portion of the reserve that was deducted under subparagraph (11)(b)(i) for that preceding year is to be included in computing the income of the corporation for the current taxation year; and

(b) the portion of the reserve that was deemed by subparagraph (11)(b)(ii) to be an allowable capital loss of the corporation for that preceding year is deemed to be a taxable capital gain of the corporation for the current taxation year from the disposition of property.

History: S. 34.2(12) was replaced by S.C. 2013, c. 40, s. 16(5), applicable to taxation years ending after March 22, 2011, and formerly read:

(12) *Inclusion of prior year reserve.* A corporation shall include in computing its income in respect of a partnership for a taxation year the amount, if any, deducted by it under subsection (11) in respect of the partnership for its immediately preceding taxation year.

S. 34.2(12) was added by S.C. 2011, c. 24, s. 3(1), applicable to taxation years ending after March 22, 2011.

Related Sections: S. 34.2(5)(a)(v) Amounts included retain same character; s. 34.2(11) Amount of reserve may be limited by reserve claimed in previous year.

▶ 34.2(13) ◀

(13) No reserve. No claim shall be made under subsection (11) in computing a corporation's income for a taxation year in respect of a partnership

(a) unless,

(i) in the case of a corporation that is a member of a partnership in respect of which there is a multi-tier alignment, the corporation has been a member of the partnership continuously since before March 22, 2011 to the end of the year,

(ii) in the case of a corporation that is a member of a partnership in respect of which there is no multi-tier alignment, the corporation is a member of the partnership

(A) at the end of the partnership's fiscal period that begins before March 22, 2011 and ends in the year of the corporation that includes March 22, 2011,

(B) at the end of the partnership's fiscal period commencing immediately after the fiscal period referred to in clause (A) and continues to be a member until after the end of the year of the corporation that includes March 22, 2011, and

(C) continuously since before March 22, 2011 until the end of the year;

(b) if at the end of the year or at any time in the following taxation year,

(i) the corporation's income is exempt from tax under this Part, or

(ii) the corporation is non-resident and the partnership does not carry on business through a permanent establishment (as defined for the purpose of subsection 16.1(1)) in Canada; or

(c) if the year ends immediately before another taxation year

(i) at the beginning of which the partnership no longer principally carries on the activities to which the reserve relates,

(ii) in which the corporation becomes a bankrupt, or

(iii) in which the corporation is dissolved or wound up (other than in circumstances to which subsection 88(1) applies).

Editorial Note: There are a number of problems relating to situations where a corporation may be prevented from claiming a reserve. If a corporation has a short year and the partnership does not have a fiscal period ending in the corporation's first year ending after March 22, 2011, then the corporation will not have an ASPA. The reserve may also be lost in the transitional period if the corporation has little or no income in a subsequent year.

The reserve may be denied if the partnership no longer principally carries on the activities to which the reserve relates. The submission of the Joint Committee on Taxation of the Canadian Bar Association and the Canadian Institute of Chartered Accountants poses questions as to whether the partnership principally carries on the activities to which the reserve relates. Problems may arise if a partnership had realized a large taxable capital gain (and does not during the reserve period realize a capital gain) or the business of the partnership changes naturally due to market conditions, or if the partnership disposes of some properties and acquires properties that provide similar sources of income.

History: S. 34.2(13), the portion before paragraph (a) was replaced by S.C. 2013, c. 40, s. 16(6), applicable to taxation years ending after March 22, 2011, and formerly read:

(13) *No reserve.* No deduction shall be made under subsection (11) in computing a corporation's income for a taxation year in respect of a partnership

S. 34.2(13) was added by S.C. 2011, c. 24, s. 3(1), applicable to taxation years ending after March 22, 2011.

Related Sections: S. 34.2(14) When former partner is deemed to be a partner; s. 34.2(18) Anti-avoidance rule to deny recognition as a partner.

▶ 34.2(14) ◀

(14) Deemed partner. A corporation that cannot claim an amount under subsection (11) for a taxation year in respect of a partnership solely because it has disposed of its interest in the partnership is deemed for the purposes of paragraph (13)(a) to be a member of a partnership continuously until the end of the taxation year if

(a) the corporation disposed of its interest to another corporation related to, or affiliated with, the corporation at the time of the disposition; and

(b) a corporation related to, or affiliated with, the corporation has the partnership interest referred to in paragraph (a) at the end of the taxation year.

History: S. 34.2(14), the portion before paragraph (a) was replaced by S.C. 2013, c. 40, s. 16(7), applicable to taxation years ending after March 22, 2011, and formerly read:

(14) *Deemed partner.* A corporation that cannot deduct an amount under subsection (11) for a taxation year in respect of a partnership solely because it has disposed of its interest in the partnership is deemed for the purposes of paragraph (13)(a) to be a member of the partnership continuously until the end of the taxation year if

S. 34.2(14) was added by S.C. 2011, c. 24, s. 3(1), applicable to taxation years ending after March 22, 2011.

▶ 34.2(15) ◀

(15) Computing qualifying transitional income — special rules. For the purposes of determining a corporation's qualifying transitional income, the income or loss, as the case may be, of a partnership for a fiscal period shall be computed as if (*a*) the partnership had deducted for the period the maximum amount deductible in respect of any expense, reserve, allowance or other amount;

(*b*) this Act were read without reference to paragraph 28(1)(*b*); and

(*c*) the partnership had made an election under paragraph 34(*a*).

History: S. 34.2(15) was added by S.C. 2011, c. 24, s. 3(1), applicable to taxation years ending after March 22, 2011.

▶ 34.2(16) ◀

(16) Qualifying transition income adjustment — conditions for application. Subsection (17) applies for a particular taxation year of a corporation and for each subsequent taxation year for which the corporation may claim an amount under subsection (11) in respect of a partnership if the particular year is the first taxation year

(*a*) that is after the taxation year in which the corporation has, or would have if the partnership had income, an adjusted stub period accrual that is included in the corporation's qualifying transitional income in respect of the partnership by reason of paragraph (*b*) of the definition "qualifying transitional income" in subsection (1); and

(*b*) in which ends the fiscal period of the partnership that began in the taxation year referred to in paragraph (*a*).

History: S. 34.2(16), the portion before paragraph (*a*) was replaced by S.C. 2013, c. 40, s. 16(8), applicable to taxation years ending after March 22, 2011, and formerly read:

(16) *Qualifying transition income adjustment — conditions for application.* Subsection (17) applies for a particular taxation year of a corporation and for each subsequent taxation year for which the corporation may deduct an amount under subsection (11) in respect of a partnership if the particular year is the first taxation year

S. 34.2(16) was added by S.C. 2011, c. 24, s. 3(1), applicable to taxation years ending after March 22, 2011.

Related Sections: S. 34.2(11)(*b*)(ii) Increase in QTI may increase reserve.

▶ 34.2(17) ◀

(17) Adjustment of qualifying transitional income. If this subsection applies in respect of a partnership for a taxation year of a corporation, the adjusted stub period accrual included in the corporation's qualifying transitional income in respect of the partnership for the year is computed as if

(*a*) the descriptions in paragraph (*a*) and subparagraph (*b*)(i) of the definition "adjusted stub period accrual" in subsection (1) read as follows:

A is the total of all amounts each of which is the corporation's share of an income or taxable capital gain of the partnership for the particular period (other than any amount for which a deduction is available under section 112 or 113),

B is the total of all amounts each of which is the corporation's share of a loss or allowable capital loss — to the extent that the total of all allowable losses does not exceed the total of all taxable capital gains included in the description of A — of the partnership for the particular period,

C is the number of days that are in both the year and the particular period,

D is the number of days in the particular period,

E is the amount of the qualified resource expense in respect of the particular period of the partnership that is designated by the corporation for the year under subsection (6) in its return of income for the year filed with the Minister on or before its filing-due date for the year, and

F is nil; and

(*b*) the descriptions in subparagraph (*b*)(ii) of the definition "adjusted stub period accrual" in subsection (1) read as follows:

A is the total of all amounts each of which is the corporation's share of an income or taxable capital gain of the partnership for the particular period (other than any amount for which a deduction is available under section 112 or 113),

B the total of all amounts each of which is the corporation's share of a loss or allowable capital loss — to the extent that the total of all allowable capital losses does not exceed the total of all taxable capital gains included in the description of A — of the partnership for the particular period,

C is nil,

D is the number of days that are in both the year and the particular period,

E is the number of days in the particular period,

F is the amount of the qualified resource expense in respect of the particular period of the partnership that is designated by the corporation for the year under subsection (6) in its return of income for the year filed with the Minister on or before its filing-due date for the year, and

G is nil.

History: S. 34.2(17)(*b*), the description of C was replaced by S.C. 2013, c. 40, s. 16(9), applicable to taxation years ending after March 22, 2011, and formerly read:

C is the corporation's eligible alignment income for the eligible fiscal period,

S. 34.2(17) was added by S.C. 2011, c. 24, s. 3(1), applicable to taxation years ending after March 22, 2011.

Related Sections: S. 34.2(11)(*b*)(ii) May increase amount of reserve; s. 34.2(16) When adjustment is made.

▶ 34.2(18) ◀

(18) Anti-avoidance. If it is reasonable to conclude that one of the main reasons a corporation is a member of a partnership in a taxation year is to avoid the application of subsection (13), the corporation is deemed not to be a member of the partnership for the purposes of that subsection.

History: S. 34.2(18) was added by S.C. 2011, c. 24, s. 3(1), applicable to taxation years ending after March 22, 2011.

S. 34.2 was replaced by S.C. 2011, c. 24, s. 3(1). S. 34.2 formerly read:

S. 34.2 *[Reserve for December 31, 1995 income].*

(1) *Definitions.* The definitions in this subsection apply in this section.

"December 31, 1995 income" — "December 31, 1995 income" in respect of a business carried on by a taxpayer means the amount determined by the formula

$$(A - B - C + D) \times E$$

where

A is the total of all amounts each of which is the taxpayer's income from the business for a qualifying fiscal period,

B is the total of all amounts each of which is the taxpayer's loss from the business for a qualifying fiscal period,

C is the lesser of

(*a*) the total of all amounts each of which is an amount included in computing the taxpayer's income or loss from the business for a qualifying fiscal period and that is deemed to be a taxable capital gain for the purpose of section 110.6, and

(*b*) the total of the maximum amounts deductible under section 110.6 in computing the taxpayer's taxable income for the taxation year in which the qualifying fiscal periods end,

D is

(*a*) where the taxpayer is a professional corporation, the total salary or wages deductible in computing the value of A or B in respect of the business that is payable by the corporation to an individual

(i) who is a practising member of the professional body under the authority of which the corporation practised the profession, and

(ii) who is a specified shareholder of the corporation, and

(*b*) in any other case, nil, and

E is

(*a*) where the taxpayer is a professional corporation a taxation year of which ended at the end of 1995 because of the application of paragraph 249.1(1)(*b*), the amount determined by the formula

(F-G)/F

where

F is the number of days in all qualifying fiscal periods of the business, and

G is the number of days in the year, and

(*b*) in any other case, 1.

"qualifying fiscal period"—"qualifying fiscal period" of a business of a taxpayer means

(*a*) where at the end of 1994 the taxpayer carried on the business and no fiscal period of the business ended at that time, a fiscal period of the business that

(i) begins after the beginning of the taxpayer's taxation year that includes the end of 1995, and

(ii) ends

(A) at the end of 1995 because of the application of paragraph 249.1(1)(*b*) or because of the application of section 25 and paragraph 249.1(1)(*b*), or

(B) immediately before the end of 1995 because of the application of subsection 99(2) and paragraph 249.1(1)(*b*),

(*b*) a fiscal period of the business that ends at the end of 1995 because of the application of paragraph 249.1(1)(*b*) where

(i) the taxpayer is an individual who carries on the business as a member of a partnership at the end of 1995,

(ii) the individual acquired the individual's interest in the partnership in 1995 from a professional corporation,

(iii) the professional corporation carried on the business at the end of 1994 as a member of the partnership and does not have a share of the income or loss of the partnership for the fiscal period,

(iv) the individual is a practising member of the professional body under the authority of which the professional corporation practised the profession, and

(v) the individual was a specified shareholder of the professional corporation immediately before acquiring the interest, and

(*c*) where

(i) the taxpayer is a professional corporation that has a taxation year that ends at the end of 1995 because of the application of paragraph 249.1(1)(*b*), and

(ii) at the end of 1994 the business was carried on by the professional corporation as a member of a partnership, or by an individual

(A) who transferred an interest in the partnership to the professional corporation before the end of 1995,

(B) who is a practising member of the professional body under the authority of which the professional corporation practises the profession,

(C) who was a specified shareholder of the professional corporation immediately after the transfer, and

(D) who does not have a share of the income or loss of the partnership for the first fiscal period of the partnership that ends in 1995,

a fiscal period of the business that ends in that taxation year.

"specified percentage"—"specified percentage" of a taxpayer for a particular taxation year in respect of a business means

(*a*) where the first taxation year in which a qualifying fiscal period of the business ends is 1995, or subsection 34.1(4), (5) or (6) applies in respect of the business, and the particular year ends in

(i) 1995, 95%,

(ii) 1996, 85%,

(iii) 1997, 75%,

(iv) 1998, 65%,

(v) 1999, 55%,

(vi) 2000, 45%,

(vii) 2001, 35%,

(viii) 2002, 25%,

(ix) 2003, 15%, and

(x) any other year, 0%, and

(*b*) where the first taxation year in which a qualifying fiscal period of a business of the taxpayer ends is 1996 and the particular year ends in

(i) 1996, 95%,

(ii) 1997, 85%,

(iii) 1998, 75%,

(iv) 1999, 65%,

(v) 2000, 55%,

(vi) 2001, 45%,

(vii) 2002, 35%,

(viii) 2003, 25%,

(ix) 2004, 15%, and

(x) any other year, 0%.

(2) *Computation of December 31, 1995 income.* For the purpose of the definition "December 31, 1995 income" in subsection (1), a taxpayer's income or loss from a business for a qualifying fiscal period shall be computed as if

(*a*) this Act were read without reference to paragraph 28(1)(*b*);

(*b*) the taxpayer had made the election referred to in paragraph 34(*a*) in respect of the business for the period;

(*c*) the maximum amount deductible in respect of any reserve, allowance or other amount were deducted; and

(*d*) the taxpayer had not received any taxable dividend.

(3) *Business defined.* For the purposes of the definition "qualifying fiscal period" in subsection (1) and subparagraphs (6)(*b*)(i) and (*c*)(i), a reference to a particular business of a taxpayer includes another business substituted therefor, or for which the particular business was substituted, by the taxpayer where

(*a*) all or substantially all of the gross revenue of the particular business is derived from the sale, leasing, rental or development of properties or the rendering of services; and

(*b*) all or substantially all of the gross revenue of the other business is derived from the sale, leasing, rental or development, as the case may be, of similar properties or the rendering of similar services.

(4) *Reserve.* Subject to subsection (6), where a taxpayer carries on a business in a taxation year, there may be deducted in computing the taxpayer's income for the year from the business, as a reserve in respect of December 31, 1995 income, such amount as the taxpayer claims not exceeding the least of

(*a*) the specified percentage for the year of the taxpayer's December 31, 1995 income in respect of the business;

(*b*) where an amount was deductible under this subsection in computing the taxpayer's income for a preceding taxation year from the business, the amount included under subsection (5) in computing the taxpayer's income for the particular year from the business; and

(*c*) the taxpayer's income for the particular year computed before deducting any amount under this subsection in respect of the business or under any of paragraph 60(*w*), sections 61.2 to 61.4 and subsection 80(17).

(5) *Reserve included in income.* There shall be included in computing a taxpayer's income for a taxation year from a business the amount deducted under subsection (4) in computing the taxpayer's income therefrom for the preceding taxation year.

(6) *No reserve.* No deduction shall be made under subsection (4) in computing a taxpayer's income for a taxation year from a business where

(*a*) at the end of the year or at any time in the following taxation year,

(i) the taxpayer's income from the business is exempt from tax under this Part, or

(ii) the taxpayer is non-resident and does not carry on the business through a permanent establishment (as defined by regulation) in Canada;

(*b*) the taxpayer is a corporation and the year ends immediately before another taxation year

(i) at the beginning of which the business is not carried on principally by the corporation nor by members of a partnership of which the corporation is a member,

(ii) in which the corporation becomes a bankrupt, or

(iii) in which the corporation is dissolved or wound up (other than in circumstances to which subsection 88(1) applies); or

(*c*) the taxpayer is an individual, and

(i) at the beginning of the year, the business is not carried on principally by the individual nor by members of a partnership of which the individual is a member,

(ii) the individual dies or becomes a bankrupt in the calendar year in which the taxation year ends, or

(iii) the individual is a trust that ceases to exist in the year.

(7) *Anti-avoidance rule.* Where it is reasonable to conclude that one of the main reasons a person carries on a business or is a member of a partnership is to avoid the application of subparagraph (6)(*b*)(i) or (*c*)(i), the person is deemed not to carry on the business, and not to be a member of the partnership, for the purposes of those subparagraphs.

(8) *Death of partner or proprietor.* Where

(*a*) an individual carries on a business in a taxation year,

(*b*) the individual dies in the year,

(*c*) an amount is included under subsection (5) in computing the individual's income for the year from the business, and

(*d*) the individual's legal representative

(i) elects that this subsection apply in computing the individual's income for the year, or

(ii) files a separate return of income under subsection 150(4) in respect of the individual's business,

there shall be deducted in computing the individual's income for the year from the business the lesser of

(*e*) the greatest amount that would have been deductible under subsection (4) in computing the individual's income for the year from the business if the individual had not died, and

(*f*) any amount that the representative claims.

SECTION 34.3: [Corporate partners — income shortfall adjustment]

► 34.3(1) ◄

(1) Definitions. The definitions in this subsection and in subsection 34.2(1) apply in this section.

"actual stub period accrual" —"actual stub period accrual", of a corporation in respect of a qualifying partnership for a taxation year, means the positive or negative amount determined by the formula

$$(A - B) \times C/D - E$$

where

A is the total of all amounts each of which is the corporation's share of an income or taxable capital gain of the qualifying partnership for the last fiscal period of the partnership that began in the base year (other than any amount for which a deduction was available under section 112 or 113);

B is the total of all amounts each of which is the corporation's share of a loss or allowable capital loss of the qualifying partnership for the last fiscal period of the partnership that began in the base year (to the extent that the total of all allowable capital losses included under this description in respect of all qualifying partnerships for the taxation year does not exceed the corporation's share of all taxable capital gains of all qualifying partnerships for the taxation year);

C is the number of days that are in both the base year and the fiscal period;

D is the number of days in the fiscal period; and

E is the amount of the qualified resource expense in respect of the qualifying partnership that was designated by the corporation for the base year under subsection 34.2(6) in its return of income for the base year filed with the Minister on or before its filing-due date for the base year.

"base year" —"base year", of a corporation in respect of a qualifying partnership for a taxation year, means the preceding taxation year of the corporation in which began a fiscal period of the partnership that ends in the corporation's taxation year.

"income shortfall adjustment" —"income shortfall adjustment", of a corporation in respect of a qualifying partnership for a taxation year, means the positive or negative amount determined by the formula

$$(A - B) \times C \times D$$

where

A is the amount that is the lesser of

(*a*) the actual stub period accrual in respect of the qualifying partnership, and

(*b*) the amount that would be the corporation's adjusted stub period accrual for the base year in respect of the qualifying partnership if the value of F in paragraph (*a*) of the definition "adjusted stub period accrual" in subsection 34.2(1) were nil;

B is the amount included under subsection 34.2(2) in computing the corporation's income for the base year in respect of the qualifying partnership;

C is the number of days in the period that

(*a*) begins on the day after the day on which the base year ends, and

(*b*) ends on the day on which the taxation year ends; and

D is the average daily rate of interest determined by reference to the rate of interest prescribed under paragraph 4301(*a*) of the *Income Tax Regulations* for the period referred to in the description of C.

Related Sections: S. 34.2(1), "adjusted stub period accrual".

"qualifying partnership" —"qualifying partnership", in respect of a corporation for a particular taxation year, means a partnership

(*a*) a fiscal period of which began in a preceding taxation year and ends in the particular taxation year; and

(*b*) in respect of which the corporation was required to calculate an adjusted stub period accrual for the preceding taxation year.

History: S. 34.3(1) was added by S.C. 2011, c. 24, s. 3(1), applicable to taxation years ending after March 22, 2011.

► 34.3(2) ◄

(2) Application of subsection (3). Subsection (3) applies to a corporation for a taxation year if

(*a*) the corporation has designated an amount for the purpose of the description of F in paragraph (*a*) of the definition "adjusted stub period accrual" in subsection 34.2(1) in calculating its adjusted stub period accrual for the base year in respect of a qualifying partnership for the taxation year; and

(*b*) where the corporation has qualifying transitional income, the taxation year is after the first taxation year of the corporation to which subsection 34.2(17) applies.

History: S. 34.3(2) was added by S.C. 2011, c. 24, s. 3(1), applicable to taxation years ending after March 22, 2011.

Related Sections: S. 34.2(1), "qualifying transitional income".

► 34.3(3) ◄

(3) Income shortfall adjustment — inclusion. If this subsection applies to a corporation for a taxation year, the corporation shall include in computing its income for the taxation year the amount determined by the formula

$$A + 0.50 \times (A - B)$$

where

A is the amount that is the total of all amounts each of which is the corporation's income shortfall adjustment in respect of a qualifying partnership for the year; and

B is the amount that is the lesser of A and the total of all amounts each of which is 25% of the positive amount, if any, that would be the income shortfall adjustment in respect of a qualifying partnership for the year if the value of the description of B in the definition "income shortfall adjustment" in subsection (1) were nil.

Editorial Note: The income shortfall adjustments of a corporation in respect of a qualifying partnership can be either a positive or negative amount and is described in the Explanatory Notes as the accrued interest on the underreported ASPA. If a corporation has made an F designation, with the result that the ASPA is less than both the amount determined under the formulaic approach and the actual stub period accrual, then the income shortfall adjustment is the amount by which the lesser of the actual stub period accrual and the amount that would be the corporation's ASPA (without the F designation) exceeds the corporation's ASPA that was included in the corporation's income multiplied by the average daily rate of prescribed interest for the period between the end of the corporation's base year and the end of the corporation's taxation year. (The base year is the preceding taxation year of the corporation in which began a fiscal period of the partnership that ends in the corporation's taxation year).

If the shortfall exceeds 25% of the amount (the "threshold amount") that is the lesser of the aggregate of all amounts that are income shortfall adjustments and the aggregate of amounts determined under the formulaic approach, subsection 34.3(3) provides that there will be an additional income inclusion of 50% of the aggregate shortfall income adjustments in excess of the threshold amount.

Although some may take the view that this inclusion is tantamount to a penalty or interest, it appears that an inclusion income is neither a penalty nor interest, and the taxpayer relief provisions in subsection 220(3.1) should not be available to a corporate taxpayer.

History: S. 34.3(3) was added by S.C. 2011, c. 24, s. 3(1), applicable to taxation years ending after March 22, 2011.

Related Sections: S. 34.3(2) When 34.3(3) applies.

SECTION 35: Prospectors and grubstakers

► 35(1) ◄

(1) Prospectors and grubstakers. Where a share of the capital stock of a corporation

(*a*) is received in a taxation year by an individual as consideration for the disposition by the individual to the corporation of a mining property or an interest, or for civil law a right, therein acquired by the individual as a result of the individual's efforts as a prospector, either alone or with others, or

(*b*) is received in a taxation year

(i) by a person who has, either under an arrangement with a prospector made before the prospecting, exploration or development work or as an employer of a prospector, advanced money for, or paid part or all of, the expenses of prospecting or exploring for minerals or of developing a property for minerals, and

(ii) as consideration for the disposition by the person referred to in subparagraph (i) to the corporation of a mining property or an interest, or for civil law a right, therein acquired under the arrangement under which that person made the advance or paid the expenses, or if the prospector's employee, acquired by the person through the employee's efforts,

the following rules apply:

(*c*) notwithstanding any other provision of this Act, no amount in respect of the receipt of the share shall be included

(i) in computing the income for the year of the individual or person, as the case may be, except as provided in paragraph (*d*), or

(ii) in computing at any time the amount to be determined for F in the definition "cumulative Canadian development expense" in subsection 66.2(5) in respect of the individual or person, as the case may be,

(*d*) in the case of an individual or partnership (other than a partnership each member of which is a taxable Canadian corporation), an amount in respect of the receipt of the share equal to the lesser of its fair market value at the time of acquisition and its fair market value at the time of disposition or exchange of the share shall be included in computing the income of the individual or partnership, as the case may be, for the year in which the share is disposed of or exchanged,

(*e*) notwithstanding subdivision c, in computing the cost to the individual, person or partnership, as the case may be, of the share, no amount shall be included in respect of the disposition of the mining property or the interest, or for civil law the right, therein, as the case may be,

(*f*) notwithstanding sections 66 and 66.2, in computing the cost to the corporation of the mining property or the interest, or for civil law the right, therein, as the case may be, no amount shall be included in respect of the share, and

(*g*) for the purpose of paragraph (*d*), an individual or partnership shall be deemed to have disposed of or exchanged shares that are identical properties in the order in which they were acquired.

History: S. 35(1)(*a*) was replaced by S.C. 2013, c. 34, s. 99(1), in force June 26, 2013, and formerly read:

(*a*) is received in a taxation year by an individual as consideration for the disposition by the individual to the corporation of a mining property or interest therein acquired by the individual as a result of the individual's efforts as a prospector, either alone or with others, or

S. 35(1)(*b*)(ii) was replaced by S.C. 2013, c. 34, s. 99(2), in force June 26, 2013, and formerly read:

(ii) as consideration for the disposition by the person referred to in subparagraph (i) to the corporation of a mining property or interest therein acquired under the arrangement under which that person made the advance or paid the expenses, or if the prospector was the person's employee, acquired by the person through the employee's efforts,

S. 35(1)(*e*) was replaced by S.C. 2013, c. 34, s. 99(3), in force June 26, 2013, and formerly read:

(*e*) notwithstanding subdivision c, in computing the cost to the individual, person or partnership, as the case may be, of the share, no amount shall be included in respect of the disposition of the mining property or the interest therein, as the case may be,

S. 35(1)(*f*) was replaced by S.C. 2013, c. 34, s. 99(3), in force June 26, 2013, and formerly read:

(*f*) notwithstanding sections 66 and 66.2, in computing the cost to the corporation of the mining property or the interest therein, as the case may be, no amount shall be included in respect of the share, and

Related Sections: S. 81(1) Amounts not included in income; s. 110(1)(*d.2*) Prospector's and grubstaker's shares.

Canadian Tax Foundation: Koubrak, *Tax Deferral for Mining Prospectors and Grubstakers,* 2013 Canadian Tax Focus 3(3):12–13.

Tax Window Files: Income Inclusion for Prospectors, *June 11, 2018,* CRA Document No. 2017-0733221E5.

Cases: For the purposes of section 35 a prospector must be an individual. In *Kay v. M.N.R.,* 71 DTC 5085 (Ex. Ct.) the major portion of what might have been regarded as prospecting work was performed by a company and the grubstaker exemption was held not to apply. See also *Keevil Consultants Ltd. v. M.N.R.,* 73 DTC 5409 (F.C.T.D.); and *Geophysical Engineering Ltd. v. M.N.R.,* 76 DTC 6390 (S.C.C.), affirming 74 DTC 6650 (F.C.A.)

► 35(2) ◄

(2) Definitions. In this section,

"mining property" —"mining property" means

(*a*) a right, licence or privilege to prospect, explore, drill or mine for minerals in a mineral resource in Canada, or

(*b*) real property or an immovable in Canada (other than depreciable property) the principal value of which depends on its mineral resource content;

History: S. 35(2), paragraph (*b*) of the definition "mining property" was replaced by S.C. 2013, c. 34, s. 100, in force June 26, 2013, and formerly read:

(*b*) real property in Canada (other than depreciable property) the principal value of which depends on its mineral resource content;

Related Sections: S. 81(1) Amounts not included in income; s. 248(1), "corporation", "employee", "individual", "minerals", "property", "share".

"prospector" —"prospector" means an individual who prospects or explores for minerals or develops a property for minerals on behalf of the individual, on behalf of the individual and others or as an employee.

SECTION 36: Railway companies

(Repealed by S.C. 2013, c. 40, s. 17(1).)

History: S. 36 was repealed by S.C. 2013, c. 40, s. 17(1), applicable in respect of expenditures incurred in taxation years that begin after December 21, 2012, and formerly read:

S. 36. *Railway companies.* Where any amount in respect of an expenditure incurred by a taxpayer on or in respect of the repair, replacement, alteration or renovation of depreciable property of the taxpayer of a prescribed class is, under a uniform classification and system of accounts and returns prescribed by the National Transportation Agency pursuant to the *Railway Act*, required to be entered in the books of the taxpayer otherwise than as an expense,

(*a*) no deduction may be made in respect of that expenditure in computing the income of the taxpayer for a taxation year; and

(*b*) for the purposes of section 13 and regulations made under paragraph 20(1)(*a*), the taxpayer shall be deemed to have acquired, at the time the expenditure was incurred, depreciable property of a class prescribed by regulation at a capital cost equal to that amount.

Related Regulations: 1102(10).

Related Sections: S. 13(21), "depreciable property"; s. 248(1), "prescribed", "regulation".

SECTION 37: Scientific research and experimental development

► 37(1) ◄

(1) Scientific research and experimental development. Where a taxpayer carried on a business in Canada in a taxation year, there may be deducted in computing the taxpayer's income from the business for the year such amount as the taxpayer claims not exceeding the amount, if any, by which the total of

(*a*) the total of all amounts each of which is an expenditure of a current nature made by the taxpayer in the year or in a preceding taxation year ending after 1973

(i) on scientific research and experimental development related to a business of the taxpayer, carried on in Canada and directly undertaken by the taxpayer,

(i.01) on scientific research and experimental development related to a business of the taxpayer, carried on in Canada and directly undertaken on behalf of the taxpayer,

(i.1) by payments to a corporation resident in Canada to be used for scientific research and experimental development carried on in Canada that is related to a business of the taxpayer, but only where the taxpayer is entitled to exploit the results of that scientific research and experimental development,

(ii) by payments to

(A) an approved association that undertakes scientific research and experimental development,

(B) an approved university, college, research institute or other similar institution,

(C) a corporation resident in Canada and exempt from tax under paragraph 149(1)(*j*), or

(D) (Repealed.)

(E) an approved organization that makes payments to an association, institution or corporation described in any of clauses (A) to (C)

to be used for scientific research and experimental development carried on in Canada that is related to a business of the taxpayer, but only where the taxpayer is entitled to exploit the results of that scientific research and experimental development, or

(iii) where the taxpayer is a corporation, by payments to a corporation resident in Canada and exempt from tax because of paragraph 149(1)(*j*), for scientific research and experimental development that is basic research or applied research carried on in Canada

(A) the primary purpose of which is the use of results therefrom by the taxpayer in conjunction with other scientific research and experimental development activities undertaken or to be undertaken by or on behalf of the taxpayer that relate to a business of the taxpayer, and

(B) that has the technological potential for application to other businesses of a type unrelated to that carried on by the taxpayer,

(*b*) (Repealed.)

(*c*) the total of all amounts each of which is an expenditure made by the taxpayer in the year or in a preceding taxation year ending after 1973 by way of repayment of amounts described in paragraph (*d*),

(*c*.1) all amounts included by virtue of paragraph 12(1)(*v*), in computing the taxpayer's income for any previous taxation year,

(*c*.2) all amounts added because of subsection 127(27), (29) or (34) to the taxpayer's tax otherwise payable under this Part for any preceding taxation year, and

(*c*.3) in the case of a partnership, all amounts each of which is an excess referred to in subsection 127(30) in respect of the partnership for any preceding fiscal period,

exceeds the total of

(*d*) the total of all amounts each of which is the amount of any government assistance or non-government assistance (as defined in subsection 127(9)) in respect of an expenditure described in paragraph (*a*) or (*b*), as paragraph (*a*) or (*b*), as the case may be, read in its application in respect of the expenditure, that at the taxpayer's filing-due date for the year the taxpayer has received, is entitled to receive or can reasonably be expected to receive,

(*d*.1) the total of all amounts each of which is the super-allowance benefit amount (within the meaning assigned by subsection 127(9)) for the year or for a preceding taxation year in respect of the taxpayer in respect of a province,

(*e*) that part of the total of all amounts each of which is an amount deducted under subsection 127(5) in computing the tax payable under this Part by the taxpayer for a preceding taxation year where the amount can reasonably be attributed to

(i) a prescribed proxy amount for a preceding taxation year,

(ii) an expenditure of a current nature incurred in a preceding taxation year that was a qualified expenditure incurred in that preceding year in respect of scientific research and experimental development for the purposes of section 127, or

(iii) an amount included because of paragraph 127(13)(*e*) in the taxpayer's SR&ED qualified expenditure pool at the end of a preceding taxation year within the meaning assigned by subsection 127(9),

(*f*) the total of all amounts each of which is an amount deducted under this subsection in computing the taxpayer's income for a preceding taxation year, except amounts described in subsection (6),

(*f*.1) the total of all amounts each of which is the lesser of

(i) the amount deducted under section 61.3 in computing the taxpayer's income for a preceding taxation year, and

(ii) the amount, if any, by which the amount that was deductible under this subsection in computing the taxpayer's income for that preceding year exceeds the amount claimed under this subsection in computing the taxpayer's income for that preceding year,

(*g*) the total of all amounts each of which is an amount equal to twice the amount claimed under subparagraph 194(2)(*a*)(ii) by the taxpayer for the year or any preceding taxation year, and

(*h*) if the taxpayer was subject to a loss restriction event before the end of the year, the amount determined for the year under subsection (6.1) with respect to the taxpayer.

Editorial Note: Capital expenditures made after 2013 no longer qualify for the SR&ED deduction or investment tax credit. Furthermore, SR&ED treatment no longer applies to expenditures made to another party (those described in subparagraphs (1)(*a*)(i.01) to (iii)) to the extent that the other party's related expenditures are capital (see subsection 37(14)).

S. 37(1) generally allows a full deduction for SR&ED expenditures carried on in Canada, even if the expenditure was not incurred to produce income and would otherwise be disallowed by s. 18(1)(*a*), or is on account of capital and would otherwise be disallowed by s. 18(1)(*b*). Expenditures that are deductible under s. 37(1) (except in the case of used equipment and non-arm's length contract payments) are also "qualified expenditures" under s. 127(9) and give rise to investment tax credits of 15% (20% for taxation years ending before 2013) or 35%. SR&ED expenditures carried on outside Canada qualify for a deduction under s. 37(2) and will not qualify for investment tax credits.

History: S. 37(1)(*h*) was replaced by S.C. 2013, c. 40, s. 18(1), deemed to have come into force on March 21, 2013, and formerly read:

(*h*) where the taxpayer is a corporation control of which has been acquired by a person or group of persons before the end of the year, the amount determined for the year under subsection (6.1) with respect to the corporation.

S. 37(1)(*a*)(i) was replaced by S.C. 2012, c. 31, s. 9(1), applicable in respect of expenditures made after 2012. S. 37(1)(*a*)(i) formerly read:

(i) on scientific research and experimental development carried on in Canada, directly undertaken by or on behalf of the taxpayer, and related to a business of the taxpayer,

S. 37(1)(*a*)(i.01) was added by S.C. 2012, c. 31, s. 9(1), applicable in respect of expenditures made after 2012.

S. 37(1)(*b*) was repealed by S.C. 2012, c. 31, s. 9(2), applicable in respect of expenditures made after 2013 and expenditures that subsection 37(1.2) deems not to have been made before 2014. S. 37(1)(*b*) formerly read:

(*b*) the lesser of

(i) the total of all amounts each of which is an expenditure of a capital nature made by the taxpayer (in respect of property acquired that would be depreciable property of the taxpayer if this section were not applicable in respect of the property, other than land or a leasehold interest in land) in the year or in a preceding taxation year ending after 1958 on scientific research and experimental development carried on in Canada, directly undertaken by or on behalf of the taxpayer, and related to a business of the taxpayer, and

(ii) the undepreciated capital cost to the taxpayer of the property so acquired as of the end of the taxation year (before making any deduction under this paragraph in computing the income of the taxpayer for the taxation year),

S. 37(1)(*d*) was replaced by S.C. 2012, c. 31, s. 9(3), and comes into force on January 1, 2014. S. 37(1)(*d*) formerly read:

(*d*) the total of all amounts each of which is the amount of any government assistance or non-government assistance (within the meanings assigned to those expressions by subsection 127(9)) in respect of an expenditure described in paragraph (*a*) or (*b*) that, at the taxpayer's filing-due date for the year, the taxpayer has received, is entitled to receive or can reasonably be expected to receive,

Related Regulations: 1102(1)(*d*).

Related Sections: S. 12(1)(*t*) Investment tax credit; s. 12(1)(*v*) Research and development deductions; s. 18(9)(*d*), (*e*) Limitation respecting prepaid expenses; s. 37(1.1) Business of related corporations; s. 37(1.2) Research outside Canada; s. 37(1.3) SR&ED in the exclusive economic zone; s. 37(2) Research outside Canada; s. 37(4) Where no deduction allowed under section; s. 37(6) Expenditures of a capital nature; s. 37(6.1) Loss restriction event; s. 37(7), "approved"; s. 37(8) Interpretation; s. 37(11) Filing requirement; s. 53(2)(*k*) Amounts to be deducted — Government assistance; s. 87(2)(*l*) Scientific research and experimental development; s. 96(1)(*e*.1) General rules; s. 125.4(2)(*c*) Rules governing labour expenditure of a corporation; s. 127(9), "contract payment", "investment tax credit", "qualified expenditure"; s. 127(10.1) Additions to investment tax credit; s. 127(10.8) Further additions to investment tax credit; s. 127(11.2) Time of expenditure and acquisition; s. 127(12.1) Scientific research and experimental development; s. 149(1)(*j*) Non-profit corporations for scientific research and experimental development; s. 248(1), "scientific research and experimental development"; s. 251.2(2) Loss restriction event; s. 256(8) Deemed exercise of right; s. 256.1 [Corporate tax-attribute trading].

Canadian Petroleum Tax Journal: Recent Cases of Interest — Capital Vs. Current Expense (Plus a Little SR&ED) — Pipeline Replacement and Repair, Gerald Grenon, 2000, Vol. 13, No. 1; High Tech in the Oil Patch: Planning Considerations For Transferring Technology Offshore, Derek A. Kurrant, 2000, Vol. 13, No. 1; Offshore Oil & Gas Interests: A Perspective on Exploration & Development of Offshore Petroleum and Natural Gas Resources in Eastern Canada, Michael R. Smith, CA and B. David Nielsen, CA, 2000, Vol. 13, No. 1; Recent Cases of Interest — SR&ED, Gerald Grenon, 2000, Vol. 13, No. 1.

Canadian Tax Foundation: Regan and Cepparo, *CRA Loses*, 2015 Canadian Tax Highlights 23(5):6–7; Hearn, *Abeilles on SR & ED Eligibility*, 2015 Canadian Tax Highlights 23(1):9–10; Doobay, *Government Assistance or Loan?*, 2013 Canadian Tax Highlights 21(8):7–9; Jung and McIntyre, *Current Issues: Scientific Research & Experimental Development (SR&ED) Update*, 2013 Ontario Tax Conference 1:10; De Luca et al., *The New SR & ED Regime: Evolution Rather Than Revolution*, 2012 Conference Report 16:1–25; Hearn, *Are Tax Adviser Fees an Eligible SR&ED Expenditure?*, 2008 Tax for the Owner-Manager 8(2):8–9; Feely and Pringle, *Resolving SR&ED Disputes with the CRA*, 2007 Tax for the Owner-Manager 7(2):5–6; Feely and Pringle, *The CRA's SR&ED Claim-Processing Procedures*, 2007 Tax for the Owner-Manager 7(1):7–8; Aronshtam and Hutson, *Recent Developments in R&D*, 2006 Conference Report 28:1–20; Murray and De Luca, *SR & ED and Outsourcing*, 2006 Canadian Tax Highlights 14(4):6; MacDonald and Robinson, *Supporting SR & ED Claims*, 2006 Tax for the Owner-Manager 6(4):8–9; Robinson and Pringle, *SR&ED: All You Need Is an "Infinitesimal Advancement"*, 2006 Tax for the Owner-Manager 6(3):7–8; Robinson, *Shop Floor SR & ED: Are You Missing Out?*, 2006 Tax for the Owner-Manager 6(2):6; Hausch, *SR&ED in the Owner Managed Company*, 2005 British Columbia Tax Conference 15:1–31; Chikhani, *SR&ED Program: Perspective from the field*, 2003 Conference Report 46:1–13; Katiya, *Scientific Research and Experimental Development (SR&ED): Roundup of Recent Developments*, 2003 Conference Report 37:1–12; Braithwaite, *Software Development Work as SR&ED*, 2000 Ontario Tax Conference 9:2–55; Blumenthal, *SR&ED — Recent Developments*, 2000 Prairie Provinces Tax Conference 10:1–30; Braithwaite, *Setting Up Research Facilities and Contracts*, 1999 Corporate Management Tax Conference 13:1–32; Côté and Katiya, *Due Diligence and Structural Issues in Acquiring and Financing Corporations Performing Scientific Research and Experimental Development*, 1999 Corporate Management Tax Conference 12:1–18; DeSousa et al., *Administration and Compliance Issues: Application of the Scientific Research and Experimental Development Program to the Pharmaceutical Industry*, 1999 Corporate Management Tax Conference 7:1–11; Gibney and Wensley, *A Review of Recent Scientific Research and Experimental Development Cases*, 1999 Corporate Management Tax Conference 6:1–23; Fyfe and Viner, *An Introduction to the Scientific Research and Experimental Development Program*, 1999 Corporate Management Tax Conference 2:1–17; Heselton, *Seizing the Opportunities: The New and Improved SR&ED Program/Pour Saisir l'Occasion: Le Programme de la RS & DE Nouveau et Ameliore*, 1999 Corporate Management Tax Conference 1:1–15; Millen, *Building Partnerships with Industry: New Directions for the Scientific Research and Experimental Development (SR&ED) Program*, 1998 Conference Report 28:1–13; Murray, *Scientific Research and Experimental Development: A New Beginning?*, 1998 Conference Report 27:1–15; Murray, *The Mintz Committee and R&D Incentives*, 1998 Corporate Management Tax Conference 16:1–15; Hausch, *SR&ED Building Partnerships*, 1998 British Columbia Tax Conference 17:1–28; Murray, *SR&ED Draft Surprise*, 1998 Canadian Tax Highlights 6(11):84–85.

Tax Profile: April 2006 — The SR&ED Deduction and Investment Tax Credits; March 2006 — Some Tax Considerations for Investing in Silicon Valley North.

Tax Topics: No. 1844, SR&ED Investment Tax Credit Claims: Making the CRA's Revised Procedures Work; No. 1830, The CRA's Revised Position on SR&ED Contracts; No. 1792, An Axe Instead of a Scalpel: Finance Canada's Response to the Alcatel Decision; No. 1767, Draft Legislation Overrides Alcatel — Affects SR&ED ITCs and More; No. 1564, Software and Life Sciences SR&ED Guidelines; No. 1561, Documentation for Scientific Research and Experimental Development Claims.

Forms: T2 SCH 31 — Investment Tax Credit — Corporations; T2 SCH 301 — Newfoundland Research and Development Tax Credit; T2 SCH 340 — Nova Scotia Research and Development Tax Credit; T2 SCH 360 — New Brunswick Research and Development Tax Credit; T2 SCH 380 — Manitoba Research and Development Tax Credit; T2 SCH 403 — Saskatchewan Research and Development Tax Credit; T2 SCH 442 — Yukon Research and Development Tax Credit; T661 — Claim for Scientific Research and Experimental Development Expenditures (SR&ED) Carried out in Canada; T666 — British Columbia Scientific Research and Experimental Development Tax Credit; T1129 — Newfoundland and Labrador Research and Development Tax Credit (Individuals); T1232 — Yukon Research and Development Tax Credit (Individuals); T1263 — Schedule A — Additional — Third-party payment for SR&ED.

Guides: T4088 Claiming Scientific Research and Experimental Development Expenditures — Guide to Form T661.

SR&ED Publications: Assistance and Contract Payments Policy; Claiming SR&ED tax incentives; Contract Expenditures for SR&ED Performed on Behalf of a Claimant Policy; Pool of Deductible SR&ED Expenditures Policy; Prescribed Proxy Amount Policy; Recapture of SR&ED Investment Tax Credit Policy; SR&ED Capital Expenditures Policy; SR&ED Claims for Partnerships Policy; SR&ED During Production Runs Policy; SR&ED Filing Requirements Policy; SR&ED Lease Expenditures Policy; SR&ED Overhead and Other Expenditures Policy; SR&ED Salary or Wages Policy; Third-Party Payments Policy; Total Qualified SR&ED Expenditures for Investment Tax Credit Purposes Policy; Traditional and Proxy Methods Policy; 96-03R, Claimants' entitlements and responsibilities; 95-04R, Conflict of Interest.

Tax Window Files: SR&ED Government Assistance, *May 3, 2007*, CRA Document No. 2007-0224191E5; SR&ED Used Equipment, *January 30, 2007*, CRA Document No. 2006-0211041E5; Politique d'application RS & DE 1996-02, *January 17, 2007*, CRA Document No. 2005-0152601E5; Approved Organization, *June 9, 2006*, CRA Document No. 2006-0168111E5; Soutien Administratif à Une Filiale, *July 30, 2004*, CRA Document No. 2004-0063811E5; SR&ED Approved University, *March 26, 2003*, CRA Document No. 2003-0004967.

Cases: The corporate taxpayer expended amounts on two projects involving the removal of linings from large metal pipes used to transport bitumen. The taxpayer did not meet the last of the five criteria set out in *Northwest Hydraulic Consultants Ltd. v. The Queen* — the need to keep detailed records of hypotheses, tests, and results of the SR&ED work done. The handwritten notes did not contain any hypotheses and could not be used to replicate or confirm any of the results obtained from the taxpayer's SR&ED work. *Mac & Mac v. The Queen*, 2018 DTC 1008 (TCC)

Bonuses paid to employees were not SR&ED expenditures since they were not related to SR&ED activities and did not meet the SR&ED-related criteria for bonuses set out by the Tax Court. Instead, they were paid to allow employees to share the financial success resulting from the sale of the company and to encourage them to remain with the new organization. *CalAmp Wireless Networks Inc. v. The Queen*, 2013 DTC 1172 (T.C.C.)

Two partnerships carried out SR&ED through a research corporation, which they paid with Brazilian currency promissory notes. Due to a devaluation of the Brazilian currency and rampant inflation in Brazil, the partnerships sustained significant unhedged losses. In the absence of relevant Canadian accounting principles, the Tax Court was justified in using American accounting principles to significantly discount the SR&ED expenses and promissory notes. *Romar et al. v. The Queen*, 2009 DTC 5057 (F.C.A.), affirming in part 2008 DTC 2647 (T.C.C.)

Stock option benefits provided by the taxpayer to its employees, who were engaged in SR&ED, were an "expenditure of a current nature...on scientific research and experimental development" within the meaning of s. 37(1)(*a*)(i). *Alcatel Canada Inc. v. The Queen*, 2005 DTC 387 (T.C.C.)

The communication charges incurred by the taxpayer for a telephone line to pass instructions and data between its employees in Ottawa an a corporation testing its software in Alabama qualified as SR&ED since the telephone line had formed a necessary part of the taxpayer's SR&ED activities. *Data Kinetics Ltd. v. The Queen*, 98 DTC 1877 (T.C.C.)

The expenditures on a computer-aided learning research project did not constitute SR&ED expenditures since "scientific research" connotes systematic investigation involving the existence of controlled experiment and of highly accurate measurements entailing the testing of one's theories against empirical evidence and would not include activities of research in social sciences or the routine collection of data. *ETA Performance Systems Corporation v. M.N.R.*, 93 DTC 451 (T.C.C.)

► 37(1.1) ◄

(1.1) Business of related corporations. Notwithstanding paragraph (8)(*c*), for the purposes of subsection (1), where a taxpayer is a corporation, scientific research and experimental development, related to a business carried on by another corporation to which the taxpayer is related (otherwise than by reason of a right referred to in paragraph 251(5)(*b*)) and in which that other corporation is actively engaged, at the time at which an expenditure or payment in respect of the scientific research and experimental development is made by the taxpayer, shall be considered to be related to a business of the taxpayer at that time.

► 37(1.2) ◄

(1.2) Deemed time of capital expenditure. For the purposes of paragraph (1)(*b*), an expenditure made by a taxpayer in respect of property shall be deemed not to have been made before the property is considered to have become available for use by the taxpayer.

Related Sections: S. 13(26) Restriction on deduction before available for use; s. 127(11.2) Time of expenditure and acquisition; s. 248(19) When property available for use.

SR&ED Publications: SR&ED Capital Expenditures Policy; 2003-01, Capital Property Intended to be Used All or Substantially All for SR&ED.

► 37(1.3) ◄

(1.3) SR&ED in the exclusive economic zone. For the purposes of this section and section 127 of this Act and Part XXIX of the Income Tax Regulations, an expenditure is deemed to have been made by a taxpayer in Canada if the expenditure is

(*a*) made by the taxpayer in the course of a business carried on by the taxpayer in Canada; and

(*b*) made for the prosecution of scientific research and experimental development in the exclusive economic zone of Canada, within the meaning of the *Oceans Act*, or in the airspace above that zone or the seabed or subsoil below that zone.

Editorial Note: The definition of "exclusive economic zone" in s. 37(1.3) is broader than the one in s. 35(1) of the *Interpretation Act* because it includes airspace.

► 37(1.4) ◄

(1.4) Salary or wages for SR&ED outside Canada. For the purposes of this section, section 127 and Part XXIX of the *Income Tax Regulations*, the amount of a taxpayer's expenditure for a taxation year determined under subsection (1.5) is deemed to be made in the taxation year in respect of scientific research and experimental development carried on in Canada by the taxpayer.

History: S. 37(1.4) was added by 2008, c. 28, s. 3(1), applicable in respect of taxation years that end on or after February 26, 2008.

▶ 37(1.5) ◀

(1.5) Salary or wages outside Canada — limit determined. The amount of a taxpayer's expenditure for a taxation year determined under this subsection is the lesser of

(*a*) the amount that is the total of all expenditures each of which is an expenditure made by the taxpayer, in the taxation year and after February 25, 2008, in respect of an expense incurred in the taxation year for salary or wages paid to the taxpayer's employee who was resident in Canada at the time the expense was incurred in respect of scientific research and experimental development,

(i) that was carried on outside Canada,

(ii) that was directly undertaken by the taxpayer,

(iii) that related to a business of the taxpayer, and

(iv) that was solely in support of scientific research and experimental development carried on in Canada by the taxpayer, and

(*b*) the amount that is 10 per cent of the total of all expenditures, made by the taxpayer in the year, each of which would, if this Act were read without reference to subsection (1.4), be an expenditure made in respect of an expense incurred in the year for salary or wages paid to an employee in respect of scientific research and experimental development that was carried on in Canada, that was directly undertaken by the taxpayer and that related to a business of the taxpayer.

History: S. 37(1.5) was added by 2008, c. 28, s. 3(1), applicable in respect of taxation years that end on or after February 26, 2008, except that in respect of taxation years that include February 26, 2008, the reference in paragraph 37(1.5)(*b*) to "10 per cent" shall be read as a reference to the percentage determined by the formula

$$10\% \times A/B$$

where

A is the number of days in the taxation year that are after February 25, 2008; and

B is the number of days in the taxation year.

▶ 37(2) ◀

(2) Research outside Canada. In computing the income of a taxpayer for a taxation year from a business of the taxpayer, there may be deducted expenditures of a current nature made by the taxpayer in the year

(*a*) on scientific research and experimental development carried on outside Canada, directly undertaken by or on behalf of the taxpayer, and related to the business (except to the extent that subsection (1.4) deems the expenditures to have been made in Canada); or

(*b*) by payments to an approved association, university, college, research institute or other similar institution to be used for scientific research and experimental development carried on outside Canada related to the business provided that the taxpayer is entitled to exploit the results of that scientific research and experimental development.

Editorial Note: S. 37(2) allows a full deduction for current R&D expenditures carried on outside Canada, even if the expenditure was not incurred to produce income and would be otherwise disallowed by s. 18(1)(*a*). Expenditures that are deductible under s. 37(2) are not "qualified expenditures" under s. 127(9) and therefore do not give rise to investment tax credits. (See s. 37(1) for R&D expenditures carried on in Canada.)

Related Sections: S. 241(4)(*a*) Where taxpayer information may be disclosed.

SR&ED Publications: Contract Expenditures for SR&ED Performed on Behalf of a Claimant Policy; SR&ED Capital Expenditures Policy.

Tax Window Files: Politique d'application RS & DE 1996-02, *January 17, 2007*, CRA Document No. 2005-0152601E5.

▶ 37(3) ◀

(3) Minister may obtain advice. The Minister may obtain the advice of the Department of Industry, the National Research Council of Canada, the Defence Research Board or any other agency or department of the Government of Canada carrying on activities in the field of scientific research as to whether any particular activity constitutes scientific research and experimental development.

Cases: A taxpayer's rights under s. 15 of the Charter are not infringed where the Minister fails to seek advice before proposing to reassess him because the taxpayer can challenge the basis and validity of the assessment once it is issued. *Stromotich v. The Queen*, 88 DTC 6172 (F.C.T.D.)

▶ 37(4) ◀

(4) Where no deduction allowed under section. No deduction may be made under this section in respect of an expenditure made to acquire rights in, or arising out of, scientific research and experimental development.

SR&ED Publications: Pool of Deductible SR&ED Expenditures Policy.

Tax Window Files: SR&ED — Acquiring Rights, *April 24, 2003*, CRA Document No. 2002-0169537.

▶ 37(5) ◀

(5) Where no deduction allowed under ss. 110.1 and 118.1. Where, in respect of an expenditure on scientific research and experimental development made by a taxpayer in a taxation year, an amount is otherwise deductible under this section and under section 110.1 or 118.1, no deduction may be made in respect of the expenditure under section 110.1 or 118.1 in computing the taxable income of, or the tax payable by, the taxpayer for any taxation year.

▶ 37(6) ◀

(6) Expenditures of a capital nature. For the purposes of section 13, an amount claimed under subsection (1) that may reasonably be considered to be in respect of a property described in paragraph (1)(*b*), as that paragraph read in its application in respect of the property, is deemed to be an amount allowed to the taxpayer in respect of the property under regulations made under paragraph 20(1)(*a*), and for that purpose the property is deemed to be of a separate prescribed class.

Editorial Note: S. 37(6) provides that the recapture provisions of the capital cost allowance system (see s. 13(1)) will apply in respect of capital property that is later sold. For this purpose, the property will be deemed to be in a separate prescribed class.

History: S. 37(6) was replaced by S.C. 2012, c. 31, s. 9(4), and comes into force on January 1, 2014. S. 37(6) formerly read:

> (6) *Expenditures of a capital nature.* An amount claimed under subsection (1) that may reasonably be considered to be in respect of a property described in paragraph (1)(*b*) shall, for the purpose of section 13, be deemed to be an amount allowed to the taxpayer in respect of the property under regulations made under paragraph 20(1)(*a*), and for that purpose the property shall be deemed to be of a separate prescribed class.

Related Regulations: Part XI.

Related Sections: S. 87(2)(*d*)(ii)(D) Depreciable property.

▶ 37(6.1) ◀

(6.1) Loss restriction event. If a taxpayer was, at any time (in this subsection referred to as "that time") before the end of a taxation year of the taxpayer, last subject to a loss restriction event, the amount determined for the purposes of paragraph (1)(*h*) for the year with respect to the taxpayer in respect of a business is the amount, if any, by which

(*a*) the amount, if any, by which

(i) the total of all amounts each of which is

(A) an expenditure described in paragraph (1)(*a*) or (*c*) that was made by the taxpayer before that time,

(B) the lesser of the amounts determined immediately before that time in respect of the taxpayer under subparagraphs (1)(*b*)(i) and (ii), as those paragraphs read on March 29, 2012, in respect of expenditures made, and property acquired, by the taxpayer before 2014, or

(C) an amount determined in respect of the taxpayer under paragraph (1)(*c.1*) for its taxation year that ended immediately before that time

exceeds the total of all amounts each of which is

(ii) the total of all amounts determined in respect of the taxpayer under paragraphs (1)(*d*) to (*g*) for its taxation year that ended immediately before that time, or

(iii) the amount deducted under subsection (1) in computing the taxpayer's income for its taxation year that ended immediately before that time

exceeds

(*b*) the total of

(i) if the business to which the amounts described in any of clauses (*a*)(i)(A) to (C) can reasonably be considered to have been related was carried on by the taxpayer for profit or with a reasonable expectation of profit throughout the year, the total of

(A) the taxpayer's income for the year from the business before making any deduction under subsection (1), and

(B) if properties were sold, leased, rented or developed, or services were rendered, in the course of carrying on the business before that time, the taxpayer's income for the year, before making any deduction under subsection (1), from any other business substantially all the income of which was derived from the sale, leasing, rental or development, as the case may be, of similar properties or the rendering of similar services, and

(ii) the total of all amounts each of which is an amount determined in respect of a preceding taxation year of the taxpayer that ended after that time equal to the lesser of

(A) the amount determined under subparagraph (i) with respect to the taxpayer in respect of the business for that preceding year, and

(B) the amount in respect of the business deducted under subsection (1) in computing the taxpayer's income for that preceding year.

Editorial Note: Subsection 37(6.1) provides a limit to the deduction of SR&ED deduction after an acquisition of control of a taxpayer corporation. Generally, such expenses will be deductible after an acquisition of control only if the business continues to be carried on for profit or with a reasonable expectation of profit and only to the extent of income earned from that business or a similar business. Effective March 21, 2013, the limitation similarly applies to trusts after a "loss restriction event", which occurs when a person has become a majority-interest beneficiary, or a group of persons has become a majority-interest group of beneficiaries, of the trust.

History: S. 37(6.1), the portion before paragraph (*a*) was replaced by S.C. 2013, c. 40, s. 18(2), deemed to have come into force on March 21, 2013, and formerly read:

(6.1) *Amount referred to in para. (1)(h).* Where a taxpayer is a corporation control of which was last acquired by a person or group of persons at any time (in this subsection referred to as "that time") before the end of a taxation year of the corporation, the amount determined for the purposes of paragraph (1)(*h*) for the year with respect to the corporation in respect of a business is the amount, if any, by which

S. 37(6.1)(*a*)(i)(A) to (C) were replaced by S.C. 2013, c. 40, s. 18(3), deemed to have come into force on March 21, 2013, except that, before January 1, 2014, clause 37(6.1)(*a*)(i)(B) is to be read as follows:

"(B) the lesser of the amounts determined immediately before that time in respect of the taxpayer under subparagraphs (1)(*b*)(i) and (ii), as those paragraphs read on March 29, 2012, in respect of expenditures made, and property acquired, by the taxpayer before that time, or"

S. 37(6.1)(*a*)(i)(A) to (C) formerly read:

(A) an expenditure described in paragraph (1)(*a*) or (*c*) that was made by the corporation before that time,

(B) the lesser of the amounts determined in respect of the corporation under subparagraphs (1)(*b*)(i) and (ii) immediately before that time, or

(C) an amount determined in respect of the corporation under paragraph (1)(*c*.1) for its taxation year ending immediately before that time

S. 37(6.1)(*a*)(ii) and (iii) were replaced by S.C. 2013, c. 40, s. 18(4), deemed to have come into force on March 21, 2013, and formerly read:

(ii) the total of all amounts determined in respect of the corporation under paragraphs (1)(*d*) to (*g*) for its taxation year ending immediately before that time, or

(iii) the amount deducted by virtue of subsection (1) in computing the corporation's income for its taxation year ending immediately before that time

S. 37(6.1)(*b*)(i) and (ii) were replaced by S.C. 2013, c. 40, s. 18(5), deemed to have come into force on March 21, 2013, and formerly read:

(i) where the business to which the amounts described in clause (*a*)(i)(A), (B) or (C) may reasonably be considered to have been related was carried on by the corporation for profit or with a reasonable expectation of profit throughout the year, the total of

(A) the corporation's income for the year from the business before making any deduction under subsection (1), and

(B) where properties were sold, leased, rented or developed, or services were rendered, in the course of carrying on the business before that time, the corporation's income for the year, before making any deduction under subsection (1), from any other business substantially all the income of which was derived from the sale, leasing, rental or development, as the case may be, of similar properties or the rendering of similar services, and

(ii) the total of all amounts each of which is an amount determined in respect of a preceding taxation year of the corporation that ended after that time equal to the lesser of

(A) the amount determined under subparagraph (i) with respect to the corporation in respect of the business for that preceding year, and

(B) the amount in respect of the business deducted by virtue of subsection (1) in computing the corporation's income for that preceding year.

Related Sections: S. 127(9.1) Loss restriction event before end of year; s. 127(9.2) Loss restriction event after end of year; s. 251.2(2) Loss restriction event.

SR&ED Publications: Pool of Deductible SR&ED Expenditures Policy.

▶ 37(7) ◀

(7) Definitions. In this section,

"approved" — "approved" means approved by the Minister after the Minister has, if the Minister considers it necessary, obtained the advice of the Department of Industry or the National Research Council of Canada.

Income Tax Technical News: Issue No. 23, List of "Approved" Entities for the Purpose of Scientific Research and Experimental Development.

Tax Window Files: Approved Organization, *June 9, 2006,* CRA Document No. 2006-0168111E5; Sr&Ed Approved Status, *December 2, 2004,* CRA Document No. 2004-0096811E5; SR&ED Approved University, *March 26, 2003,* CRA Document No. 2003-0004967.

"scientific research and experimental development" — (Repealed by S.C. 1996, c. 21, s. 9(8).)

Related Regulations: 2900(1).

▶ 37(8) ◀

(8) Interpretation. In this section,

(*a*) references to expenditures on or in respect of scientific research and experimental development

(i) where the references occur in subsection (2), include only

(A) expenditures each of which was an expenditure incurred for and all or substantially all of which was attributable to the prosecution of scientific research and experimental development, and

(B) expenditures of a current nature that were directly attributable, as determined by regulation, to the prosecution of scientific research and experimental development, and

(ii) where the references occur other than in subsection (2), include only

(A) expenditures incurred by a taxpayer in a taxation year (other than a taxation year for which the taxpayer has elected under clause (B)), each of which is

(I) an expenditure of a current nature all or substantially all of which was attributable to the prosecution, or to the provision of premises, facilities or equipment for the prosecution, of scientific research and experimental development in Canada, or

(II) an expenditure of a current nature directly attributable, as determined by regulation, to the prosecution, or to the provision of premises, facilities or equipment for the prosecution, of scientific research and experimental development in Canada, and

(III) (Repealed.)

(B) where a taxpayer has elected in prescribed form and in accordance with subsection (10) for a taxation year, expenditures incurred by the taxpayer in the year each of which is

(I) (Repealed.)

(II) an expenditure of a current nature for the prosecution of scientific research and experimental development in Canada directly undertaken on behalf of the taxpayer,

(III) (Repealed.)

(IV) that portion of an expenditure made in respect of an expense incurred in the year for salary or wages of an employee who is directly engaged in scientific research and experimental development in Canada that can reasonably be considered to relate to such work having regard to the time spent by the employee thereon, and, for this purpose, where that portion is all or substantially all of the expenditure, that portion shall be deemed to be the amount of the expenditure, or

(V) the cost of materials consumed or transformed in the prosecution of scientific research and experimental development in Canada, or

(VI) (Repealed.)

(*b*) for greater certainty, references to scientific research and experimental development related to a business include any scientific research and experimental development that may lead to or facilitate an extension of that business;

(*c*) except in the case of a taxpayer who derives all or substantially all of the taxpayer's revenue from the prosecution of scientific research and experimental development (including the sale of rights arising out of scientific research and experimental development carried on by the taxpayer), the prosecution of scientific research and experimental development shall not be considered to be a business of the taxpayer to which scientific research and experimental development is related; and

(*d*) references to expenditures of a current nature include any expenditure made by a taxpayer other than an expenditure made by the taxpayer for

(i) the acquisition from a person or partnership of a property that is a capital property of the taxpayer, or

(ii) the use of, or the right to use, property that would be capital property of the taxpayer if it were owned by the taxpayer.

History: S. 37(8)(*a*)(ii)(B)(II) was replaced by S.C. 2017, c. 33, s. 8(1), applicable in respect of expenditures incurred after September 16, 2016, and formerly read:

(II) an expenditure of a current nature in respect of the prosecution of scientific research and experimental development in Canada directly undertaken on behalf of the taxpayer,

S. 37(8)(*a*)(ii)(B)(V) was replaced by S.C. 2013, c. 34, s. 181(1), applicable to costs incurred after February 23, 1998, and formerly read:

(V) the cost of materials consumed in the prosecution of scientific research and experimental development in Canada;

S. 37(8)(*a*)(ii)(A)(III) was repealed by S.C. 2012, c. 31, s. 9(6), applicable in respect of expenditures made after 2013 and expenditures that subsection 37(1.2) deems not to have been made before 2014. S. 37(8)(*a*)(ii)(A)(III) formerly read:

(III) an expenditure of a capital nature that at the time it was incurred was for the provision of premises, facilities or equipment, where at that time it was intended

1. that it would be used during all or substantially all of its operating time in its expected useful life for, or

2. that all or substantially all of its value would be consumed in,

the prosecution of scientific research and experimental development in Canada, and

S. 37(8)(*a*)(ii)(B)(I) was repealed by S.C. 2012, c. 31, s. 9(7), applicable in respect of expenditures made after 2013 and expenditures that subsection 37(1.2) deems not to have been made before 2014. S. 37(8)(*a*)(ii)(B)(I) formerly read:

(I) an expenditure of a current nature for, and all or substantially all of which was attributable to, the lease of premises, facilities or equipment for the prosecution of scientific research and experimental development in Canada, other than an expenditure in respect of general purpose office equipment or furniture,

S. 37(8)(*a*)(ii)(B)(II) was replaced by S.C. 2012, c. 31, s. 9(8), applicable in respect of expenditures made after 2013 and expenditures that subsection 37(1.2) deems not to have been made before 2014. S. 37(8)(*a*)(ii)(B)(II) formerly read:

(II) an expenditure in respect of the prosecution of scientific research and experimental development in Canada directly undertaken on behalf of the taxpayer,

S. 37(8)(*a*)(ii)(B)(III) was repealed by S.C. 2012, c. 31, s. 9(9), applicable in respect of expenditures made after 2013 and expenditures that subsection 37(1.2) deems not to have been made before 2014. S. 37(8)(*a*)(ii)(B)(III) formerly read:

(III) an expenditure described in subclause (A)(III), other than an expenditure in respect of general purpose office equipment or furniture,

S. 37(8)(*a*)(ii)(B)(VI) was repealed by S.C. 2012, c. 31, s. 9(10), applicable in respect of expenditures made after 2013 and expenditures that subsection 37(1.2) deems not to have been made before 2014. S. 37(8)(*a*)(ii)(B)(VI) formerly read:

(VI) 1/2 of any other expenditure of a current nature in respect of the lease of premises, facilities or equipment used primarily for the prosecution of scientific research and experimental development in Canada, other than an expenditure in respect of general purpose office equipment or furniture;

S. 37(8)(*d*) was replaced by S.C. 2012, c. 31, s. 9(11), applicable in respect of expenditures made after 2013 and expenditures that subsection 37(1.2) deems not to have been made before 2014. S. 37(8)(*d*) formerly read:

(*d*) notwithstanding paragraph (*a*), references to expenditures on or in respect of scientific research and experimental development shall not include

(i) any capital expenditure made in respect of the acquisition of a building, other than a prescribed special-purpose building, including a leasehold interest therein,

(ii) any outlay or expense made or incurred for the use of, or the right to use, a building other than a prescribed special-purpose building, and

(iii) payments made by a taxpayer to

(A) a corporation resident in Canada and exempt from tax under paragraph 149(1)(*j*), an approved research institute or an approved association, with which the taxpayer does not deal at arm's length,

(B) a corporation other than a corporation referred to in clause (A), or

(C) an approved university, college or organization

to be used for scientific research and experimental development

(D) in the case of such a payment to a person described in clause (A) or (B), to the extent that the amount of the payment may reasonably be considered to have been made to enable the recipient to acquire a building or a leasehold interest in a building or to pay an amount in respect of the rental expense in respect of a building, and

(E) in the case of a payment to a person described in clause (C), to the extent that the amount of the payment may reasonably be considered to have been made to enable the recipient to acquire a building, or a leasehold interest in a building, in which the taxpayer has, or may reasonably be expected to acquire, an interest.

Related Regulations: 2900(2) [Expenditures directly attributable to SR&ED]; 2900(3) [Expenditures directly attributable to premises, facilities and equipment]; 2900(4) [Calculation of prescribed proxy amount]; 2902; 2903.

Related Sections: S. 37(1.1) Business of related corporations; s. 37(9) Salary or wages; 37(9.1) Limitation re specified employees; 37(9.2) Associated corporations; 37(9.3) Agreement among associated corporations; 37(9.4) Filing; 37(9.5) Deemed corporation; s. 37(10) Time for election; s. 96(3) Agreement or election of partnership members; s. 127(9), "qualified expenditure"; S. 143.3 Expenditure — Limitations; s. 149(1)(*j*)(ii)(A) Miscellaneous exemptions.

Tax Topics: No. 1767, Draft Legislation Overrides Alcatel — Affects SR&ED ITCs and More.

Forms: T661 — Scientific Research and Experimental Development (SR&ED) Expenditures Claim.

SR&ED Publications: Traditional and Proxy Methods Policy; Materials for SR&ED Policy; Contract Expenditures for SR&ED Performed on Behalf of a Claimant Policy; SR&ED Lease Expenditures Policy; SR&ED Overhead and Other Expenditures Policy; SR&ED Capital Expenditures Policy.

Tax Window Files: Lease of used equipment & non-arm's length party, *February 15, 2007*, CRA Document No. 2006-0206761I7; R&D Credits and Subcontracting, *October 7, 2005*, CRA Document No. 2005-0140991C6; Soutien Administratif à Une Filiale, *July 30, 2004*, CRA Document No. 2004-0063811E5.

Cases: Stock option benefits provided by the taxpayer to its employees, who were engaged in SR&ED, were "expenditures made in respect of...salary or wages" within the meaning of s. 37(8)(*a*)(ii)(B)(IV). *Alcatel Canada Inc. v. The Queen*, 2005 DTC 387 (T.C.C.)

► 37(9) ◄

(9) Salary or wages. An expenditure of a taxpayer

(*a*) does not include, for the purposes of clauses (8)(*a*)(ii)(A) and (B), remuneration based on profits or a bonus, where the remuneration or bonus, as the case may be, is in respect of a specified employee of the taxpayer, and

(*b*) includes, for the purpose of paragraph (1.5)(*a*), an amount paid in respect of an expense incurred for salary or wages paid to an employee only if the taxpayer reasonably believes that the salary or wages is not subject to an income or profits tax imposed, because of the employee's presence or activity in a country other than Canada, by a government of that other country.

Editorial Note: Paragraph 37(9)(*a*) explains that any remuneration paid to a specified employee that is based on profits, or is a bonus paid to that employee, does not qualify as an expenditure for scientific research and experimental development ("SR&ED"). For more information on what a specified employee is, see the definition in s. 248(1).

Paragraph 37(9)(*b*) provides that an expense for salary or wages paid to a Canadian-resident employee working outside the country is treated as having been incurred in Canada by a taxpayer for the purpose of s. 37(1.5)(*a*) only if the taxpayer reasonably believes that the salary or wages is not subject to an income or profits tax imposed by a foreign government. If the taxpayer knows or has reason to believe that the amount is being taxed in the foreign country where its employees are carrying out the SR&ED, then salary or wages paid to the employee would not be included in the amount determined under s. 37(1.5)(*a*) for the purposes of determining the amount of SR&ED expenditures considered to have been made in Canada.

Related Sections: S. 248(1), "specified employee".

► 37(9.1) ◄

(9.1) Limitation re specified employees. For the purposes of clauses (8)(*a*)(ii)(A) and (B), expenditures incurred by a taxpayer in a taxation year do not include expenses incurred in the year in respect of salary or wages of a specified employee of the taxpayer to the extent that those expenses exceed the amount determined by the formula

$$A \times B/365$$

where

A is 5 times the Year's Maximum Pensionable Earnings (as determined under section 18 of the *Canada Pension Plan*) for the calendar year in which the taxation year ends; and

B is the number of days in the taxation year on which the employee is a specified employee of the taxpayer.

Editorial Note: Subsection 37(9.1) limits the amount of salary and wages paid to a specified employee in respect of scientific research and experimental development expenses, to an amount equal to five times the maximum pensionable earnings for the year as determined for the Canada Pension Plan. The limit is prorated for the number of days that the employee is a specified employee during the year. For further information on what constitutes a specified employee, see the definition in s. 248(1).

► 37(9.2) ◄

(9.2) Associated corporations. Where

(*a*) in a taxation year of a corporation that ends in a calendar year, the corporation employs an individual who is a specified employee of the corporation,

(*b*) the corporation is associated with another corporation (in this subsection and subsection (9.3) referred to as the "associated corporation") in a taxation year of the associated corporation that ends in the calendar year, and

(*c*) the individual is a specified employee of the associated corporation in the taxation year of the associated corporation that ends in the calendar year,

for the purposes of clauses (8)(*a*)(ii)(A) and (B), the expenditures incurred by the corporation in its taxation year or years that end in the calendar year and by each associated corporation in its taxation year or years that end in the calendar year do not include expenses incurred in those taxation years in respect of salary or wages of the specified employee unless the corporation and all of the associated corporations have filed with the Minister an agreement referred to in subsection (9.3) in respect of those years.

Editorial Note: Associated corporations employing the same specified employee in their taxation years ending in a particular calendar year must agree to allocate the maximum amount (five times the year's maximum pensionable earnings as defined for the Canada Pension Plan) in respect of that employee's wages and salary amongst themselves; otherwise, none of the wages and salary qualify as scientific research and experimental development expenses.

Related Sections: S. 37(9.5) Deemed corporation.

▶ 37(9.3) ◀

(9.3) Agreement among associated corporations. Where all of the members of a group of associated corporations of which an individual is a specified employee file, in respect of their taxation years that end in a particular calendar year, an agreement with the Minister in which they allocate an amount in respect of the individual to one or more of them for those years and the amount so allocated or the total of the amounts so allocated, as the case may be, does not exceed the amount determined by the formula

$$A \times B/365$$

where

A is 5 times the Year's Maximum Pensionable Earnings (as determined under section 18 of the *Canada Pension Plan*) for the particular calendar year, and

B is the lesser of 365 and the number of days in those taxation years on which the individual was a specified employee of one or more of the corporations,

the maximum amount that may be claimed in respect of salary or wages of the individual for the purposes of clauses (8)(*a*)(ii)(A) and (B) by each of the corporations for each of those years is the amount so allocated to it for each of those years.

Editorial Note: Where an agreement is filed by associated groups in respect of wages paid to a specified employee, the amount of maximum wages that may be split as scientific research and experimental development expenses for an individual is the lesser of the wages so paid or an amount that is limited to five times the maximum pensionable earnings for the year as defined for the Canada Pension Plan.

Related Sections: S. 37(9.5) Deemed corporation.

Forms: T1174 — Agreement Among Associated Corporations to Allocate Salaries or Wages of Specified Employees for Scientific Research and Experimental Development (SR&ED) Expenditures.

SR&ED Publications: SR&ED Filing Requirements Policy.

▶ 37(9.4) ◀

(9.4) Filing. An agreement referred to in subsection (9.3) is deemed not to have been filed by a taxpayer unless

(*a*) it is in prescribed form; and

(*b*) where the taxpayer is a corporation, it is accompanied by

(i) where its directors are legally entitled to administer its affairs, a certified copy of their resolution authorizing the agreement to be made, and

(ii) where its directors are not legally entitled to administer its affairs, a certified copy of the document by which the person legally entitled to administer its affairs authorized the agreement to be made.

▶ 37(9.5) ◀

(9.5) Deemed corporation. For the purposes of subsections (9.2) and (9.3) and this subsection, each

(*a*) individual related to a particular corporation,

(*b*) partnership of which a majority-interest partner is

(i) an individual related to a particular corporation, or

(ii) a corporation associated with a particular corporation, and

(*c*) limited partnership of which a member whose liability as a member is not limited is

(i) an individual related to a particular corporation, or

(ii) a corporation associated with a particular corporation,

is deemed to be a corporation associated with the particular corporation.

History: S. 37(9.5)(*b*), the portion before subparagraph (i) was replaced by S.C. 2013, c. 40, s. 18(6), in force December 12, 2013, and formerly read:

(*b*) partnership of which a majority interest partner is

▶ 37(10) ◀

(10) Time for election. Any election made under clause (8)(*a*)(ii)(B) for a taxation year by a taxpayer shall be filed by the taxpayer on the day on which the taxpayer first files a prescribed form referred to in subsection (11) for the year.

▶ 37(11) ◀

(11) Filing requirement. A prescribed form must be filed by a taxpayer with the Minister in respect of any expenditure, that would be incurred by the taxpayer in a taxation year that begins after 1995 if this Act were read without reference to subsection 78(4), that is claimed by the taxpayer for the year as a deduction under this section, on or before the day that is 12 months after the taxpayer's filing due-date for the taxation year, containing

(*a*) prescribed information in respect of the expenditure; and

(*b*) *claim preparer information*, as defined in subsection 162(5.3).

Editorial Note: The prescribed form in respect of the SR&ED is T661. If the form is not filed on a timely basis, subsection 37(12) deems the expenditure not to be an SR&ED expenditure. In this case, the expenditure will be subject to the ordinary rules for the deduction of business expenditures. Similarly, if the prescribed information in respect of an expenditure is not contained in the form, subsection 37(11.1) provides that no amount of the expenditure can be claimed as a deduction under subsection 37(1).

History: S. 37(11) was replaced by S.C. 2017, c. 33, s. 8(2), in force December 14, 2017, and formerly read:

(11) *Filing requirement.* Subject to subsection (12), no amount in respect of an expenditure that would be incurred by a taxpayer in a taxation year that begins after 1995 if this Act were read without reference to subsection 78(4) may be deducted under subsection (1) unless the taxpayer files with the Minister a prescribed form containing prescribed information in respect of the expenditure on or before the day that is 12 months after the taxpayer's filing-due date for the year.

Related Sections: S. 127(9), "investment tax credit"; s. 162(5.1) Failure to provide claim preparer information; s. 220(2) Officers, clerks and employees; s. 220(2.2) Exception.

Tax Topics: No. 1844, SR&ED Investment Tax Credit Claims: Making the CRA's Revised Procedures Work; No. 1824, Stamping of Hand-Delivered Mail at CRA Local Offices — SR&ED Implications.

Forms: T661 — Claim for Scientific Research and Experimental Development Expenditures (SR&ED) Carried out in Canada.

Guides: T4088 Claiming Scientific Research and Experimental Development Expenditures — Guide to Form T661.

SR&ED Publications: SR&ED Filing Requirements Policy; 2000-02R, Guidelines for Resolving Claimants' SR&ED Concerns.

▶ 37(11.1) ◀

(11.1) Failure to file. Subject to subsection (12), if the prescribed information in respect of an expenditure referred to in paragraph (11)(*a*) is not contained in the form referred to in subsection (11), no amount in respect of the expenditure may be deducted under subsection (1).

Editorial Note: The prescribed form in respect of the SR&ED is T661. If the form is not filed on a timely basis, subsection 37(12) deems the expenditure not to be an SR&ED expenditure. In this case, the expenditure will be subject to the ordinary rules for the deduction of business expenditures. Similarly, if the prescribed information in respect of an expenditure is not contained in the form, subsection 37(11.1) provides that no amount of the expenditure can be claimed as a deduction under subsection 37(1).

History: S. 37(11.1) was added by S.C. 2017, c. 33, s. 8(2), in force December 14, 2017.

▶ 37(12) ◀

(12) Misclassified expenditures. If a taxpayer has not filed a prescribed form in respect of an expenditure in accordance with subsection (11), for the purposes of this Act, the expenditure is deemed not to be an expenditure on or in respect of scientific research and experimental development.

Editorial Note: If the filing deadline in s. 37(11) has not been met in respect of an expenditure, s. 37(12) deems the expenditure not to be an SR&ED expenditure. In this case, the expenditure will be subject to the ordinary rules for capital or current expenditures.

▶ 37(13) ◀

(13) Non-arm's length contract — linked work. For the purposes of this section and sections 127 and 127.1, where

(*a*) work is performed by a taxpayer for a person or partnership at a time when the person or partnership does not deal at arm's length with the taxpayer, and

(*b*) the work would be scientific research and experimental development if it were performed by the person or partnership,

the work is deemed to be scientific research and experimental development.

Editorial Note: Work performed by a taxpayer who does not deal at arm's length with a person or partnership qualifies as scientific research and experimental development ("SR&ED") work. This subsection deems certain work that would not otherwise be SR&ED work to be SR&ED work for the purposes of s. 37, 127, and 127.1.

Related Sections: S. 248(1), "scientific research and experimental development".

Tax Window Files: Soutien Administratif à Une Filiale, *July 30, 2004*, CRA Document No. 2004-0063811E5.

▶ 37(14) ◀

(14) Look-through rule. For the purposes of subparagraphs (1)(*a*)(i.01) to (iii), the amount of a particular expenditure made by a taxpayer shall be reduced by the amount of any related expenditure of the person or partnership to whom the particular expenditure is made that is not an expenditure of a current nature of the person or partnership.

Editorial Note: Capital expenditures made after 2013 do not qualify for the SR&ED deduction (paragraph 37(1)(*b*) was repealed). As a consequence of that measure, subsection 37(14) similarly provides that a taxpayer's expenditure made to another party to be used in SR&ED (described in subparagraphs (1)(*a*)(i.01) to (iii)) is reduced to the extent that the other party's related expenditures are not current, i.e., they are capital.

History: S. 37(14) was added by S.C. 2012, c. 31, s. 9(12), applicable in respect of expenditures made after 2013 and expenditures that subsection 37(1.2) deems not to have been made before 2014.

Related Sections: S. 127(9), "contract payment".

▶ 37(15) ◀

(15) Reporting of certain payments. If an expenditure is required to be reduced because of subsection (14), the person or the partnership referred to in that subsection is required to inform the taxpayer in writing of the amount of the reduction without delay if requested by the taxpayer and in any other case no later than 90 days after the end of the calendar year in which the expenditure was made.

History: S. 37(15) was added by S.C. 2012, c. 31, s. 9(12), applicable in respect of expenditures made after 2013 and expenditures that subsection 37(1.2) deems not to have been made before 2014.

SECTION 37.1: Additional allowance for scientific research and experimental development

(Repealed by S.C. 1998, c. 19, s. 87(1).)

SECTION 37.2: Application of s. 37.1

(Repealed by S.C. 1998, c. 19, s. 87(1).)

SECTION 37.3: Application of ss. 37.1(1) and (2)

(Repealed by S.C. 1998, c. 19, s. 87(1).)

Subdivision c — Taxable Capital Gains and Allowable Capital Losses

SECTION 38: Taxable capital gain and allowable capital loss

For the purposes of this Act,

(*a*) subject to paragraphs (*a.1*) to (*a.3*), a taxpayer's taxable capital gain for a taxation year from the disposition of any property is 1/2 of the taxpayer's capital gain for the year from the disposition of the property;

(*a*.1) a taxpayer's taxable capital gain for a taxation year from the disposition of a property is equal to zero if

(i) the disposition is the making of a gift to a qualified donee of a share, debt obligation or right listed on a designated stock exchange, a share of the capital stock of a mutual fund corporation, a unit of a mutual fund trust, an interest in a related segregated fund trust (within the meaning assigned by paragraph 138.1(1)(*a*)) or a prescribed debt obligation,

(ii) the disposition is deemed by section 70 to have occurred and the property is

(A) a security described in subparagraph (i), and

(B) the subject of a gift to which subsection 118.1(5.1) applies and that is made by the taxpayer's estate to a qualified donee, or

(iii) the disposition is the exchange, for a security described in subparagraph (i), of a share of the capital stock of a corporation, which share included, at the time it was issued and at the time of the disposition, a condition allowing the holder to exchange it for the security, and the taxpayer

(A) receives no consideration on the exchange other than the security, and

(B) makes a gift of the security to a qualified donee not more than 30 days after the exchange;

Tax Window Files: Donation to private foundation, *May 31, 2017*, CRA Document No. 2016-0642621E5.

(*a*.2) a taxpayer's taxable capital gain for a taxation year from the disposition of a property is equal to zero if

(i) the disposition is the making of a gift to a qualified donee (other than a private foundation) of a property described, in respect of the taxpayer, in paragraph 110.1(1)(*d*) or in the definition "total ecological gifts" in subsection 118.1(1), or

(ii) the disposition is deemed by section 70 to have occurred and the property is

(A) described in subparagraph (i), and

(B) the subject of a gift to which subsection 118.1(5.1) applies and that is made by the taxpayer's estate to a qualified donee (other than a private foundation);

(*a*.3) a taxpayer's taxable capital gain for a taxation year, from the disposition of an interest in a partnership (other than a prescribed interest in a partnership) that would be an exchange described in subparagraph (*a.1*)(iii) if the interest were a share in the capital stock of a corporation, is equal to the lesser of

(i) that taxable capital gain determined without reference to this paragraph, and

(ii) 1/2 of the amount, if any, by which

(A) the total of

(I) the cost to the taxpayer of the partnership interest, and

(II) each amount required by subparagraph 53(1)(*e*)(iv) or (x) to be added in determining the taxpayer's adjusted cost base of the partnership interest,

exceeds

(B) the adjusted cost base to the taxpayer of the partnership interest (determined without reference to subparagraphs 53(2)(*c*)(iv) and (v));

(*b*) a taxpayer's allowable capital loss for a taxation year from the disposition of any property is 1/2 of the taxpayer's capital loss for the year from the disposition of that property; and

(*c*) a taxpayer's allowable business investment loss for a taxation year from the disposition of any property is 1/2 of the taxpayer's business investment loss for the year from the disposition of that property.

Editorial Note: Allowable capital losses are only deductible against taxable capital gains; see s. 3(*c*) (an exception is made in the year of death and the preceding year pursuant to s. 111(2)). Excess allowable capital losses in a year become net capital losses, which can be carried forward indefinitely or back three years.

However, allowable business investment losses are deductible against all forms of income; see s. 3(*d*).

The capital gains inclusion rate is zero for charitable gifts of publicly listed securities (s. 38(*a*.1)) and certified ecologically sensitive lands (s. 38(*a*.2)) to qualified donees. Where a taxpayer dies holding such property and is subject to a capital gain as a result of the deemed disposition rules of s. 70, if the property is subsequently donated to a qualified donee by the taxpayer's "graduated rate estate" (defined in s. 248(1)), the taxpayer's taxable capital gain upon death is also nil. The same rule applies if the donation is made by the taxpayer's estate within 60 months after death if it would qualify as a graduated rate estate but for the fact that more than 36 months have passed since the death; 36 months is the maximum duration of a graduated rate estate.

Prior to 2016, if a deceased taxpayer made donation of such property under the taxpayer's will, the deemed disposition under s. 70 would similarly give rise to a nil taxable capital gain.

History: S. 38(*a.1*)(ii)(B) was replaced by S.C. 2016, c. 12, s. 12(1), applicable to the 2016 and subsequent taxation years, and formerly read:

> (B) the subject of a gift to which subsection 118.1(5.1) applies and that is made by the taxpayer's graduated rate estate to a qualified donee, or

S. 38(*a.2*)(ii)(B) was replaced by S.C. 2016, c. 12, s. 12(2), applicable to the 2016 and subsequent taxation years, and formerly read:

> (B) the subject of a gift to which subsection 118.1(5.1) applies and that is made by the taxpayer's graduated rate estate to a qualified donee (other than a private foundation);

S. 38(*a.1*)(ii) was replaced by S.C. 2014, c. 39, s. 9(1), applicable to the 2016 and subsequent taxation years, and formerly read:

> (ii) the disposition is deemed by section 70 to have occurred and the taxpayer is deemed by subsection 118.1(5) to have made a gift described in subparagraph (i) of the property, or

S. 38(*a.2*)(ii) was replaced by S.C. 2014, c. 39, s. 9(2), applicable to the 2016 and subsequent taxation years, and formerly read:

> (ii) the disposition is deemed by section 70 to have occurred and the taxpayer is deemed by subsection 118.1(5) to have made a gift described in subparagraph (i) of the property;

Related Regulations: 6210.

Related Sections: S. 38.2 Allocation of gain re certain gifts; s. 39(1) Meaning of capital gain and capital loss; s. 53 Adjustments to cost base; s. 70(5) Capital property of a deceased taxpayer; s. 100 Disposition of an interest in a partnership; s. 118.1(5.1) Gifts by graduated rate estate; s. 248(1), "disposition", "graduated rate estate", "property"; s. 262 Designated stock exchanges.

Tax Profile: January 2009 — Market Meltdown — Capital Loss Utilization.

Tax Topics: No. 1523, No ABIL Please!.

Forms: T1 SCH 3 — Capital Gains (or Losses); T2 SCH 6 — Summary of Dispositions of Capital Property; T3 SCH 1 — Dispositions of Capital Property.

Guides: RC4169 Tax Treatment of Mutual Funds for Individuals.

Income Tax Folios: S4-F8-C1 Business Investment Losses.

Information Circulars: IC 89-3 Policy statement on business equity valuations.

Interpretation Bulletins: *Secondary* — IT-381R3 Trusts — Capital Gains and Losses and the Flow-Through of Taxable Capital Gains to Beneficiaries.

Cases: The donation was a *bona fide* gift, and the nature of a gift does not change because there were favourable tax consequences. Even if there had been a secondary intention to develop the land, nothing was carried out and there was no adventure in the nature of trade. The gift yielded a capital gain, the taxable half of which was deemed to be zero as the land was certified as ecologically sensitive. *Staltari v. The Queen*, 2015 DTC 1130 (T.C.C.)

SECTION 38.1: Tax-deferred transaction — Flow-through shares

If a taxpayer acquires a property (in this section referred to as the "acquired property") that is included in a flow-through share class of property in the course of a transaction or series of transactions to which any of section 51, subsections 73(1), 85(1) and (2) and 85.1(1), sections 86 and 87 and subsections 88(1) and 98(3) apply

(*a*) if the transfer of the acquired property is part of a gifting arrangement (within the meaning assigned by section 237.1) or of a transaction or series of transactions to which subsection 98(3) applies, or the transferor is a person with whom the taxpayer was, at the time of the acquisition, not dealing at arm's length, there shall be added, at the time of the transfer, to the taxpayer's exemption threshold in respect of the flow-through share class of property, and deducted from the transferor's exemption threshold in respect of the flow-through share class of property, the amount determined by the formula

$$A \times B$$

where

A is the amount by which the transferor's exemption threshold in respect of the flow-through share class of property immediately before that time exceeds the capital gain, if any, of the transferor as a result of the transfer, and

B is the proportion that the fair market value of the acquired property immediately before the transfer is of the fair market value of all property of the transferor immediately before the transfer that is included in the flow-through share class of property; and

(*b*) if the transferor receives particular shares of the capital stock of the taxpayer as consideration for the acquired property and those particular shares are listed on a designated stock exchange or are shares of a mutual fund corporation, then for the purposes of this section and subsection 40(12)

(i) the particular shares are deemed to be flow-through shares of the transferor, and

(ii) there shall be added to the transferor's exemption threshold in respect of the flow-through share class of property that includes the particular shares the amount that is determined under paragraph (*a*) or that would be so determined if paragraph (*a*) applied to the taxpayer.

History: S. 38.1 was added by S.C. 2011, c. 24, s. 4(1), deemed to have come into force on March 22, 2011.

Related Sections: S. 40(12) Donated flow-through shares; s. 54, "exemption threshold", "flow-through share class of property".

SECTION 38.2: Allocation of gain re certain gifts

If a taxpayer is entitled to an amount of an advantage in respect of a gift of property described in paragraph 38(*a.1*) or (*a.2*),

(*a*) those paragraphs apply only to that proportion of the taxpayer's capital gain in respect of the gift that the eligible amount of the gift is of the taxpayer's proceeds of disposition in respect of the gift; and

(*b*) paragraph 38(*a*) applies to the extent that the taxpayer's capital gain in respect of the gift exceeds the amount of the capital gain to which paragraph 38(*a.1*) or (*a.2*) applies.

Editorial Note: Section 38.2 applies to limit the amount of the special inclusion rate as set out in s. 38(*a.1*) and (*a.2*) on gifts donated to qualified donees to an amount that excludes any advantage or benefit that the taxpayer may have obtained or may be entitled to as a result of the gift. The amount that will be allowed the special inclusion rate will be the amount of the eligible amount of the gift as defined in s. 248(31). For additional details regarding eligible amounts of gifts and the amount of the advantage, see the editorial notes for s. 248(31) and (32).

History: S. 38.2 was added by S.C. 2013, c. 34, s. 182(1), applicable to gifts made after December 20, 2002.

Related Sections: s. 248(31) Eligible amount of gift or monetary contribution; s. 248(32) Amount of advantage.

SECTION 39: Meaning of capital gain and capital loss

▶ 39(1) ◀

(1) Meaning of capital gain and capital loss. For the purposes of this Act,

(*a*) a taxpayer's capital gain for a taxation year from the disposition of any property is the taxpayer's gain for the year determined under this subdivision (to the extent of the amount thereof that would not, if section 3 were read without reference to the expression "other than a taxable capital gain from the disposition of a property" in paragraph 3(*a*) and without reference to paragraph 3(*b*), be included in computing the taxpayer's income for the year or any other taxation year) from the disposition of any property of the taxpayer other than

(i) (Repealed by S.C. 2016, c. 12, s. 13(1).)

(i.1) an object that the Canadian Cultural Property Export Review Board has determined meets the criterion set out in paragraph 29(3)(*b*) of the *Cultural Property Export and Import Act* if

(A) the disposition is to an institution or a public authority in Canada that was, at the time of the disposition, designated under subsection 32(2) of that Act either generally or for a specified purpose related to that object, or

(B) the disposition is deemed by section 70 to have occurred and the object is the subject of a gift to which subsection 118.1(5.1) applies and that is made by the taxpayer's estate to an institution that would be described in clause (A) if the disposition were made at the time the estate makes the gift,

(ii) a Canadian resource property,

(ii.1) a foreign resource property,

(ii.2) a property if the disposition is a disposition to which subsection 142.4(4) or (5) or 142.5(1) applies,

(iii) an insurance policy, including a life insurance policy, except for that part of a life insurance policy in respect of which a policyholder is deemed by paragraph 138.1(1)(*e*) to have an interest in a related segregated fund trust,

(iv) a timber resource property; or

(v) an interest of a beneficiary under a qualifying environmental trust;

(*b*) a taxpayer's capital loss for a taxation year from the disposition of any property is the taxpayer's loss for the year determined under this subdivision (to the extent of the amount thereof that would not, if section 3 were read in the manner described in paragraph (*a*) of this subsection and without reference to the expression "or the taxpayer's allowable business investment loss for the year" in paragraph 3(*d*), be deductible in computing the taxpayer's income for the year or any other taxation year) from the disposition of any property of the taxpayer other than

(i) depreciable property, or

(ii) property described in any of subparagraphs 39(1)(*a*)(ii) to (iii) and (v); and

(*c*) a taxpayer's business investment loss for a taxation year from the disposition of any property is the amount, if any, by which the taxpayer's capital loss for the year from a disposition after 1977

(i) to which subsection 50(1) applies, or

(ii) to a person with whom the taxpayer was dealing at arm's length

of any property that is

(iii) a share of the capital stock of a small business corporation, or

(iv) a debt owing to the taxpayer by a Canadian-controlled private corporation (other than, where the taxpayer is a corporation, a debt owing to it by a corporation with which it does not deal at arm's length) that is

(A) a small business corporation,

(B) a bankrupt that was a small business corporation at the time it last became a bankrupt, or

(C) a corporation referred to in section 6 of the *Winding-up Act* that was insolvent (within the meaning of that Act) and was a small business corporation at the time a winding-up order under that Act was made in respect of the corporation,

exceeds the total of

(v) in the case of a share referred to in subparagraph (iii), the amount, if any, of the increase after 1977 by virtue of the application of subsection 85(4) in the adjusted cost base to the taxpayer of the share or of any share (in this subparagraph referred to as a "replaced share") for which the share or a replaced share was substituted or exchanged,

(vi) in the case of a share referred to in subparagraph (iii) that was issued before 1972 or a share (in this subparagraph and subparagraph (vii) referred to as a "substituted share") that was substituted or exchanged for such a share or for a substituted share, the total of all amounts each of which is an amount received after 1971 and before or on the disposition of the share or an amount receivable at the time of such a disposition by

(A) the taxpayer,

(B) where the taxpayer is an individual, the taxpayer's spouse or common-law partner, or

(C) a trust of which the taxpayer or the taxpayer's spouse or common-law partner was a beneficiary

as a taxable dividend on the share or on any other share in respect of which it is a substituted share, except that this subparagraph shall not apply in respect of a share or substituted share that was acquired after 1971 from a person with whom the taxpayer was dealing at arm's length,

(vii) in the case of a share to which subparagraph (vi) applies and where the taxpayer is a trust for which a day is to be, or has been, determined under paragraph 104(4)(*a*), or (*a.4*) by reference to a death or later death, as the case may be, the total of all amounts each of which is an amount received after 1971 or receivable at the time of the disposition, as a taxable dividend on the share or on any other share in respect of which it is a substituted share, by an individual whose death is that death or later death, as the case may be, or a spouse or common-law partner of the individual, and

(viii) the amount determined in respect of the taxpayer under subsection (9) or (10), as the case may be.

Editorial Note: Paragraphs 39(1)(*a*), (*b*), and (*c*) define "capital gain", "capital loss", and "business investment loss" respectively. Neither the definition of capital gain nor that of capital loss spells out the distinction between a gain or loss that constitutes a capital gain or loss and one that constitutes ordinary business income. It is therefore necessary to refer to court decisions which provide guidelines for distinguishing between business income and capital receipts. Section 39 also excludes gains from dispositions of certain types of property in the definition of capital gain.

Capital Gain: A gain is considered a capital gain only to the extent that it would not otherwise be included in income under the Act. Since there are no provisions which clearly differentiate between a capital gain and a gain from an adventure in the nature of trade, the latter of which is taxed as business income, taxpayers will still have to refer to the numerous Canadian and foreign court decisions that provide the rules for distinguishing between ordinary income and capital receipts. Presently one-half of capital gains are included as taxable capital gains.

In one instance, proceeds from a sale of land were treated as income, rather than a capital gain, since the taxpayer had expressed an intention to sell the land for commercial development, had created a partnership for that purpose, and had made marketing efforts. The fact that the land remained in farm use until its sale did not take away from the intent to sell the property. *Bodine v. The Queen*, 2011 DTC 5084 (F.C.A.), affirming 2010 DTC 1296 (T.C.C.). In another case, the taxpayer's gain on the sale of the land was on capital account. There was nothing to indicate any intention other than that the land had been purchased for the business of a logging operation, and that it was later sold as a residue of a timber limit. *Twin Islands Estates Ltd. v. The Queen*, 2004 DTC 2515 (T.C.C.).

Capital Loss: A capital loss is generally defined by s. 39(1)(*b*) as a loss which is not deductible in computing income, and does not include an allowable business investment loss, which are accounted for separately under s. 39(1). Presently, one-half of capital losses are treated as allowable capital losses. Generally, aggregate taxable capital gains are offset by aggregate allowable capital losses, but special rules apply under s. 40 for gains and losses from personal-use assets. A loss sustained by a shareholder for a guarantee of corporate debt is usually capital in nature, unless he has provided the guarantee in the ordinary course of business, or holds the shares as a trading asset. *DeCicco v. The Queen*, 2007 DTC 388 (T.C.C.).

Allowable Business Investment Loss (ABIL): A business investment loss is defined to be a capital loss realized in certain circumstances on the disposition of shares or debt of a "small business corporation" (s. 248(1)). The disposition must either be to an arm's length person, or one to which the bad debt/share provisions of s. 50(1) apply. By virtue of s. 39(1)(*c*)(iv), a capital loss realized by a corporation on a disposition of a debt owing to it by another corporation with which it does not deal at arm's length will not be a business investment loss. Allowable business investment losses as defined in s. 38 are applied against all forms of income and not just taxable capital gains under s. 3.

"Active business" (relevant for purposes of the term "small business corporation") simply means "any business carried on by the taxpayer". A corporation pursuing oil and gas ventures was carrying on an active business and was therefore a small business corporation, allowing the taxpayer to claim an ABIL deduction for money he loaned to it. *Ollenberger v. The Queen*, 2013 DTC 5064 (F.C.A.), reversing 2012 DTC 1094 (T.C.C.). It is not necessary for a creditor to exhaust all possible recourses of collection before declaring a debt to be unrecoverable. The taxpayer made an honest and reasonable determination that the loans had become non-collectable, and was entitled to ABIL deductions. *Netolitzky v. The Queen*, 2006 DTC 2953 (T.C.C.).

Definition of "Property": Subsection 248(1) provides that "property" means property of any kind whatever, whether real or personal, or corporeal or incorporeal, and includes, but is not limited to: (i) a right of any kind whatever, a share or a chose in action; (ii) money, unless a contrary intention is evident; (iii) a timber resource property; and (iv) the work in progress of a business that is a profession. The statutory definition of "property" thus appears to be extremely broad, particularly since it means "property of any kind whatever" and includes "a right of any kind whatever". The Federal Court of Appeal applied the broad definition in the *Kieboom* decision (92 DTC 6382), where it held that a taxpayer's "ownership equity" in a corporation constituted "property" for the purposes of the Act.

Definition of "Capital Property": "Capital property" is defined in s. 54 as meaning depreciable property and any other property in respect of which any gain or loss on its disposition would be a capital gain or loss.

A capital gain does not arise on the disposition of the following types of property:

(1) Property, the sale of which would be taken into account in computing ordinary income. This would include inventory of a business or property acquired as part of an adventure in the nature of trade.

(2) Prior to 2017, eligible capital property was defined in s. 54, which must be read with former s. 14. It includes goodwill and other non-deductible intangibles acquired in connection with a business. Beginning in 2017, this type of property is now depreciable property (Class 14.1), and capital gains from dispositions of depreciable property are included in the amount determined under paragraph 39(1)(*a*).

(3) Cultural property disposed of to an institution or public authority in Canada designated under the *Canadian Cultural Property Export and Import Act*. If the deemed disposition occurs upon a taxpayer's death as a result of the deemed disposition rules of section 70, if the property is subsequently donated to a qualified donee by the taxpayer's "graduated rate estate" (defined in s. 248(1)), the deemed disposition gives rise to no capital gain. The same rule applies if the donation is made by the taxpayer's estate within 60 months after death if it would qualify as a graduated rate estate but for the fact that more than 36 months have passed since the death; 36 months is the maximum duration of a graduated rate estate.

(4) Canadian and foreign resource properties.

(5) An insurance policy including a life insurance policy other than a segregated fund policy.

(6) "Specified debt obligations" to which s. 142.4(4) or 142.4(5) apply, or "mark-to-market properties" to which s. 142.5(1) applies.

(7) Property that is a timber resource property. This is defined in s. 13(21) to mean a renewable right or license to cut or remove timber acquired after May 6, 1974.

(8) A beneficiary's interest in a mining reclamation trust. A mining reclamation trust is defined in s. 248(1).

Foreign Exchange (FX) Gains and Losses: FX gains and losses from the disposition of property are determined under subsection 39(1), generally by converting the cost and the proceeds of disposition to Canadian dollars. However, for individuals other than trusts, FX gains and losses from the disposition of currency is determined under subsection 39(1.1). For FX gains and losses realized on the repayment of foreign debt or similar obligations, subsection 39(2) applies.

History: S. 39(1)(*a*)(i.1), the portion before clause (A) was replaced by S.C. 2019, c. 29, s. 4(1), deemed to have come into force on March 19, 2019, and formerly read:

(i.1) an object that the Canadian Cultural Property Export Review Board has determined meets the criteria set out in paragraphs 29(3)(*b*) and (*c*) of the *Cultural Property Export and Import Act* if

S. 39(1)(*c*)(iv)(B) was replaced by S.C. 2017, c. 33, s. 9(1), applicable in respect of bankruptcies that occur after April 26, 1995, and formerly read:

(B) a bankrupt (within the meaning assigned by subsection 128(3)) that was a small business corporation at the time it last became a bankrupt, or

S. 39(1)(*a*)(i) was repealed by S.C. 2016, c. 12, s. 13(1), in force January 1, 2017, and formerly read:

(i) eligible capital property,

S. 39(1)(*a*)(i.1)(B) was replaced by S.C. 2016, c. 12, s. 13(2), applicable to the 2016 and subsequent taxation years, and formerly read:

(B) the disposition is deemed by section 70 to have occurred and the object is the subject of a gift to which subsection 118.1(5.1) applies and that is made by the taxpayer's graduated rate estate to an institution that would be described in clause (A) if the disposition were made at the time the estate makes the gift,

S. 39(1)(*b*)(ii) was replaced by S.C. 2016, c. 12, s. 13(3), in force January 1, 2017, and formerly read:

(ii) property described in any of subparagraphs (*a*)(i), (ii) to (iii) and (v); and

S. 39(1)*a*)(i.1) was replaced by S.C. 2014, c. 39, s. 10(1), applicable to the 2016 and subsequent taxation years, and formerly read:

(i.1) an object that the Canadian Cultural Property Export Review Board has determined meets the criteria set out in paragraphs 29(3)(*b*) and (*c*) of the *Cultural Property Export and Import Act* and that has been disposed of,

(A) in the case of a gift to which subsection 118.1(5) applies, within the period ending 36 months after the death of the taxpayer or, where written application therefor has been made to the Minister by the taxpayer's legal representative within that period, within such longer period as the Minister considers reasonable in the circumstances, and

(B) in any other case, at any time,

to an institution or a public authority in Canada that was, at the time of the disposition, designated under subsection 32(2) of that Act either generally or for a specified purpose related to that object,

S. 39(1)*c*)(vii) was replaced by S.C. 2014, c. 39, s. 10(3), applicable to the 2016 and subsequent taxation years, and formerly read:

(vii) in the case of a share to which subparagraph (vi) applies and where the taxpayer is a trust referred to in paragraph 104(4)(*a*) or (*a.4*), the total of all amounts each of which is an amount received after 1971 or receivable at the time of the disposition by the settlor (within the meaning assigned by subsection 108(1)) or by the settlor's spouse as a taxable dividend on the share or on any other share in respect of which it is a substituted share, and

S. 39(1)(*c*)(vii) was replaced by S.C. 2014, c. 39, s. 10(2), applicable to the 2014 and 2015 taxation years, and formerly read:

(vii) in the case of a share to which subparagraph (vi) applies and where the taxpayer is a trust referred to in paragraph 104(4)(*a*), the total of all amounts each of which is an amount received after 1971 or receivable at the time of the disposition by the settlor (within the meaning assigned by subsection 108(1)) or by the settlor's spouse or common-law partner as a taxable dividend on the share or on any other share in respect of which it is a substituted share, and

S. 39(1)(*a*)(ii.2) was replaced by S.C. 2009, c. 2, s. 9(1), applicable to taxation years that begin after September 2006. S. 39(1)(*a*)(ii.2) formerly read:

(ii.2) a property to the disposition of which subsection 142.4(4) or (5) or 142.5(1) applies,

Related Sections: S. 13(21), "depreciable property"; s. 38 Taxable capital gain and allowable capital loss; s. 39(2) Capital gains and losses in respect of foreign currencies; s. 39(3) Gain in respect of purchase of bonds, etc., by issuer; s. 39(9) Deduction from business investment loss; s. 39(10) Idem, of a trust; s. 40(1) General rules; s. 40(2) Limitations; s. 41(2) Determination of net gain; s. 41(3) Definition of "listed-personal-property loss"; s. 54, "capital property", "eligible capital property"; s. 70(5) Capital property of a deceased taxpayer; s. 118.1(5.1) Gifts by graduated rate estate; s. 248(1), "disposition", "graduated rate estate", "property", "share", "taxable dividend".

Canadian Tax Foundation: Jung, *Effect of BIA Proposal on ABIL Claim*, 2015 Tax for the Owner-Manager 15(3):5–6; Morrison, *Belcourt Properties: Developers Real Estate Properties on Capital Account*, 2015 Tax for the Owner-Manager 15(1):5–6; Desilets, *Currency Swaps: CRA's Linkage Principle Overturned*, 2015 Canadian Tax Focus 5(2):2–3; Hickey, *Hybrid Capital/Inventory*, 2013 Canadian Tax Highlights 21(5):6–7; Beswick and Young, *The Use of Holding Companies in the Private Business Context*, 2012 Canadian Tax Journal 1:169–191; Kakkar and Yan, *Practical Considerations in Claiming an ABIL or the Capital Gains Exemption*, 2012 Ontario Tax Conference 5:1–28.

Tax Profile: January 2009 — Market Meltdown — Capital Loss Utilization; February 2005 — The Canadian Treatment of Derivatives; March 2004 — Loss Utilization By Individuals.

Tax Topics: No. 2027, On Account of Income or Capital?; No. 1882, Stock Market Losses: Might They Be Fully Deductible?; No. 1838, Conversion of Vacant Land from Capital Property to Inventory; No. 1766, Two Recent Real Estate Decisions; No. 1649, Restricting the Tax Advantage of Restrictive Covenants; No. 1621, Non-Comp Non-Taxable; No. 1523, No ABIL Please!.

Guides: T4037 Capital Gains.

Income Tax Folios: S4-F8-C1 Business Investment Losses.

Secondary — S3-F4-C1 General Discussion of Capital Cost Allowance.

Secondary — S3-F9-C1 Lottery Winnings, Miscellaneous Receipts, and Income (and Losses) from Crime.

Income Tax Technical News: Issue No. 39, Settlement of a Shareholder Class Action Suit — Compensation by Way of Cash and Shares.

Interpretation Bulletins: *Primary* — IT-407R4 (Consolid.) Dispositions of cultural property to designated Canadian institutions; IT-426R Shares sold subject to an earnout agreement; IT-479R Transactions in securities. *Secondary* — IT-125R4 Disposition of resource properties; IT-159R3 Capital debts established to be bad debts; IT-262R2 Losses of non-residents and part-year residents; IT-297R2 Gifts in kind to charity and others; IT-346R Commodity futures and certain commodities; IT-359R2 Premiums and other amounts with respect to leases; IT-444R Corporations — Involuntary dissolutions; IT-481 (Consolid.) Timber resource property and timber limits.

Tax Window Files: Loss on solar panels, *March 26, 2015*, CRA Document No. 2015-0572221E5; Sale of Land — Subsection 110.6(2), *November 9, 2010*, CRA Document No. 2010-0381361E5; Income/capital treatment — commodity transactions, *October 26, 2010*, CRA Document No. 2010-0381521E5; Sale of Foreign Patent, *April 22, 2010*, CRA Document No. 2010-0353301E5.

Cases: The tax treatment of any gain or loss from a hedging instrument is determined by the character of the asset being hedged. The shares held were capital property in the taxpayer's hands. The contract entered into by the taxpayer would be a hedging instrument if it neutralized or mitigated the risk to the underlying asset. This was the effect of the contract, meaning it was a hedging instrument and the losses arising under that contract were capital losses. *The Queen v. MacDonald*, 2018 DTC 5077 (FCA)

A former employee's client list was not a property of the employee such that a "disposition" of that list upon the employee's termination did not give rise to a capital loss. Furthermore, expenses incurred for the purpose of making the disposition, if any, could not include the employee's estimated value of foregone revenues caused by the loss of the clients. *Louis-Fred Martin v. The Queen*, 2017 DTC 5058 (FCA)

There is a presumption that the sale of shares of a corporation carrying on business gives rise to a capital gain. The taxpayer's disposition of the shares she purchased from her husband gave rise to a capital gain. The taxpayer's disposition of the shares given to her by him also gave rise to a capital gain. *Gervais v. The Queen* and *The Queen v. Gendron*, 2016 DTC 5008 (CAF)

The donation was a bona fide gift, and the nature of a gift does not change because there were favourable tax consequences. Even if there had been a secondary intention to develop the land, nothing was carried out and there was no adventure in the nature of trade. The gift yielded a capital gain, the taxable half of which was deemed to be zero as the land was certified as ecologically sensitive. *Staltari v. The Queen*, 2015 DTC 1130 (T.C.C.)

The proceeds from the termination of cross-currency basis swap contracts were capital. There was no intent on the part of the taxpayer to make a profit from the swaps, and there was no speculation involved. The sole purpose was to protect the value of its US operations from currency fluctuations. *George Weston Limited v. The Queen*, 2015 DTC 1079 (T.C.C.)

The transactions in issue were all similar, in that the taxpayer incorporated a new corporation, received its common shares at fair market value, received a preferred share stock dividend (on the common shares) with a high redemptive value and a low PUC, and then disposed of the common shares at a loss. These transactions constitute an abuse of s. 39(1)(*b*) (and others) contrary to the GAAR. *Barrasso v. The Queen*, 2014 DTC 1130 (T.C.C.)

Alberta required the purchasers of forest tenures to assume reforestation obligations. The cost of these obligations was not included in the vendor's proceeds of disposition since the purchasers were not assuming an existing liability. The reforestation costs could not be severed from the tenures and were simply a future cost that would decrease the purchase price. *Daishowa-Marubeni International Ltd. v. The Queen*, 2013 DTC 5085 (S.C.C.), reversing 2011 DTC 5157 (F.C.A.)

"Active business" simply means "any business carried on by the taxpayer". A corporation pursuing oil and gas ventures was carrying on an active business and was therefore a small business corporation, allowing the taxpayer to claim an ABIL deduction for money he loaned to it. *Ollenberger v. The Queen*, 2013 DTC 5064 (F.C.A.), reversing 2012 DTC 1094 (T.C.C.)

Under a government program, a commercial fisherman received $2,583,465 for transferring his fishing licences to an aboriginal organization. Since the licences were not "property", the payment was not included in his income as a capital gain. *Haché v. The Queen*, 2010 DTC 1088 (T.C.C.)

The taxpayer was awarded damages for wrongful cancellation of a dealer agreement. The damage award constituted proceeds from the disposition of capital property, consisting of the taxpayer's rights under the agreement, and was therefore a taxable capital gain. *Valley Equipment Limited v. The Queen*, 2008 DTC 6200 (F.C.A.), affirming 2006 DTC 3593 (T.C.C.)

The right to compete is not "property", and therefore payments under a non-competition agreement are not proceeds of disposition giving rise to a taxable capital gain. *Manrell v. The Queen*, 2003 DTC 5225 (F.C.A.), reversing 2002 DTC 1222 (T.C.C.)

The taxpayer loaned funds to a partnership. When the loan became unrecoverable, the taxpayer was entitled to an ABIL deduction because the partnership's debt was a debt of the partners (who were CCPCs and small business corporations). *Klein v. The Queen*, 2001 DTC 443 (T.C.C.)

The corporate taxpayer had a "participation clause" in its lease, entitling it to a percentage of the lessor's annual net profits. In 1989, the taxpayer accepted a payment from its lessor to "buy-out" and cancel the participation clause. The "buy-out" payment was a capital receipt rather than income. *The T. Eaton Company Limited v. The Queen*, 99 DTC 5178 (F.C.A.), reversing 96 DTC 1846 (T.C.C.)

When a real estate agent purchased a residential property in December 1987, listed it for sale in January 1988 and sold it a profit in May 1988, the profit was characterized as income on the ground that the transaction was related to her occupational activities as a real estate agent. *Gratl v. The Queen*, 94 DTC 6255 (F.C.A.)

When a mining engineer with a 30-year background in natural resources disposed of shares of resource companies, most of which he had acquired through the exercise of employee stock options, their sale fell within the purview of an adventure in the nature of trade and yielded income. *Pollock v. The Queen*, 94 DTC 6050 (F.C.A.), affirming 90 DTC 6142 (F.C.T.D.)

A taxpayer's background and experience as a former licensed stockbroker were consistent with that of a security trader. His share purchases were highly leveraged and involved those of resource companies not paying dividends. The high volume of transactions, the relatively quick turnover and the considerable outlay of the taxpayer's time lead to conclude that the profits from the transactions were business income. *McGroarty v. The Queen*, 94 DTC 6276 (F.C.T.D.), affirming 89 DTC 185 (T.C.C.)

A developer sold land, reported the profit as income and took back a mortgage which it later sold at a discount. The discount was treated as a loss on income account, rather than as a capital loss as it had been acquired in the course of the taxpayer's normal trading activities. *Millford Development Limited v. The Queen*, 93 DTC 5052 (F.C.T.D.), reversing 85 DTC 248 (T.C.C.)

Where an SRTC debenture was redeemed by a taxpayer six months after buying it as a tax shelter, the resulting gain was treated as business income from an adventure in the nature of trade. *The Queen v. Loewen*, 93 DTC 5109 (F.C.T.D.), reversing 90 DTC 1009 (T.C.C.) . See also *Morello v. M.N.R.*, 93 DTC 1072 (T.C.C.)

The frequency of the real estate transactions in which a taxpayer had engaged, the short length of the period of ownership, the lack of perseverance in the face of problems inherent in property rentals and the lack of interest shown in analyzing the return on the rentals were all factors indicating purchases of a speculative nature. *Dauphinais v. M.N.R.*, 93 DTC 631 (T.C.C.)

The sale of commercial properties yielded capital where the taxpayers' whole course of conduct confirmed their stated intention to purchase them as investments. They investigated the rental market, converting existing structures to provide greater rental accommodation, they complied with municipal requirements, they advertised for desirable tenants, they made cash-flow projections and they arranged permanent financing for two of the properties. *600166 Ontario Ltd. et al. v. M.N.R.*, 93 DTC 910 (T.C.C.)

A taxpayer could not be heard to argue that the method of calculating capital gains in Canadian dollars does not reflect the true economic selling price or cost of the asset because of the fluctuating purchasing power of the Canadian dollar. *Macdonald v. The Queen*, 93 DTC 5318 (F.C.A.)

The loss from an investment in shares of a construction company was characterized as a business investment loss. *H.Y. Louie Co. Ltd. v. The Queen*, 86 DTC 6228 (F.C.T.D.).

► 39(1.1) ◄

(1.1) Foreign currency dispositions by an individual. If, because of any fluctuation after 1971 in the value of one or more currencies other than Canadian currency relative to Canadian currency, an individual (other than a trust) has made one or more particular gains or sustained one or more particular losses in a taxation year from dispositions of currency other than Canadian currency and the particular gains or losses would, in the absence of this subsection, be capital gains or losses described under subsection (1)

(*a*) subsection (1) does not apply to any of the particular gains or losses;

(*b*) the amount determined by the following formula is deemed to be a capital gain of the individual for the year from the disposition of currency other than Canadian currency:

$$A - (B + C)$$

where

A is the total of all the particular gains made by the individual in the year,

B is the total of all the particular losses sustained by the individual in the year, and

C is $200; and

(*c*) the amount determined by the following formula is deemed to be a capital loss of the individual for the year from the disposition of currency other than Canadian currency:

$$D - (E + F)$$

where

D is the total of all the particular losses sustained by the individual in the year,

E is the total of all the particular gains made by the individual in the year, and

F is $200.

Editorial Note: Subsection 39(1.1) applies in respect of foreign exchange gains or losses realized by an individual (other than a trust) from dispositions of foreign currency itself. For dispositions of property other than the currency (e.g., property purchased and sold in foreign currency), foreign exchange gains or losses will be determined under the regular rule in subsection 39(1). For foreign exchange gains or losses from the repayment of foreign current debt or other amounts, see subsection 39(2).

History: S. 39(1.1) was added by S.C. 2013, c. 34, s. 59(1), applicable

(*a*) in determining the capital gain or capital loss of a foreign affiliate of a taxpayer, in respect of taxation years of the foreign affiliate that end after August 19, 2011, except that, if the taxpayer has elected under the election described in the application for s. 95(2)(*f.11*), subsection 39(1.1) applies in respect of taxation years of all foreign affiliates of the taxpayer that end after June 2011; and

(*b*) in any other case, in respect of gains made and losses sustained in taxation years that begin after August 19, 2011.

See the application for the amendment to s. 39(2) for the extension of assessment periods to take into account the amendments by S.C. 2013, c. 34, s. 54 to 89.

► 39(2) ◄

(2) Foreign exchange capital gains and losses. If, because of any fluctuation after 1971 in the value of a currency other than Canadian currency relative to Canadian currency, a taxpayer has made a gain or sustained a loss in a taxation year (other than a gain or loss that would, in the absence of this subsection, be a capital gain or capital loss to which subsection (1) or (1.1) applies, or a gain or loss in respect of a transaction or event in respect of shares of the capital stock of the taxpayer)

(*a*) the amount of the gain (to the extent of the amount of that gain that would not, if section 3 were read in the manner described in paragraph (1)(*a*), be included in computing the taxpayer's income for the year or any other taxation year), if any, is deemed to be a capital gain of the taxpayer for the year from the disposition of currency other than Canadian currency; and

(*b*) the amount of the loss (to the extent of the amount of that loss that would not, if section 3 were read in the manner described in paragraph (1)(*a*), be deductible in computing the taxpayer's income for the year or any other taxation year), if any, is deemed to be a capital loss of the taxpayer for the year from the disposition of currency other than Canadian currency.

Editorial Note: Since subsection 39(2) carves out from its application gains or losses that would otherwise be determined under subsections 39(1) and (1.1), it normally applies when a debt or other obligation in foreign currency is repaid such that a foreign currency exchange gain or loss is realized. Foreign currency exchange gains or losses from dispositions of currency itself or other property will be subject to the provisions of subsection 39(1) and (1.1).

History: S. 39(2) was replaced by S.C. 2013, c. 34, s. 59(1), applicable

(*a*) in determining the capital gain or capital loss of a foreign affiliate of a taxpayer, in respect of taxation years of the foreign affiliate that end after August 19, 2011, except that, if the taxpayer has elected under the election described in the application for s. 95(2)(*f.11*), subsection 39(2) applies in respect of taxation years of all foreign affiliates of the taxpayer that end after June 2011; and

(*b*) in any other case, in respect of gains made and losses sustained in taxation years that begin after August 19, 2011.

Any assessment of a taxpayer's tax, interest and penalties payable under the Act for any taxation year that ends before June 26, 2013 that would, in the absence of this section, be precluded because of subsections 152(4) to (5) of the Act shall be made to the extent necessary to take into account the amendments by S.C. 2013, c. 34, s. 54 to 89.

S. 39(2) formerly read:

(2) *Capital gains and losses in respect of foreign currencies.* Notwithstanding subsection (1), where, by virtue of any fluctuation after 1971 in the value of the currency or currencies of one or more countries other than Canada relative to Canadian currency, a taxpayer has made a gain or sustained a loss in a taxation year, the following rules apply:

(*a*) the amount, if any, by which

(i) the total of all such gains made by the taxpayer in the year (to the extent of the amounts thereof that would not, if section 3 were read in the manner described in paragraph (1)(*a*) of this section, be included in computing the taxpayer's income for the year or any other taxation year)

exceeds

(ii) the total of all such losses sustained by the taxpayer in the year (to the extent of the amounts thereof that would not, if section 3 were read in the manner described in paragraph (1)(*a*) of this section, be deductible in computing the taxpayer's income for the year or any other taxation year), and

(iii) if the taxpayer is an individual, $200,

shall be deemed to be a capital gain of the taxpayer for the year from the disposition of currency of a country other than Canada, the amount of which capital gain is the amount determined under this paragraph; and

(*b*) the amount, if any, by which

(i) the total determined under subparagraph (*a*)(ii),

exceeds

(ii) the total determined under subparagraph (*a*)(i), and

(iii) if the taxpayer is an individual, $200,

shall be deemed to be a capital loss of the taxpayer for the year from the disposition of currency of a country other than Canada, the amount of which capital loss is the amount determined under this paragraph.

Related Sections: S. 20(1)(*f*) Discount on certain obligations; s. 40(10) Application; s. 40(11) Gain or loss on foreign currency debt; s. 111(12) Foreign currency debt on acquisition of control; s. 248(1), "principal amount".

Canadian Tax Foundation: Sandler and Korkh, *No Forex Gain on US-Dollar Debenture Conversion*, 2016 Canadian Tax Highlights 24(7):1–2; Korkh and Nikolakakis, *Taxation of Derivatives*, 2015 Canadian Tax Highlights 23(5):5–6; Korkh, *No Forex Gain on Conversion of USD-Denominated Debentures*, 2015 Canadian Tax Focus 1(1):7–8; Guimont, *Denial of Capital Losses from Foreign Currency Fluctuations*, 2013 Canadian Tax Focus 13(2):4–5; Maikawa and Martin, *Foreign Exchange and Foreign Affiliates: Continuing Problems and Possible Solutions*, 2006 Canadian Tax Journal 1:241–261.

Tax Topics: No. 2149, Foreign Exchange Revisited; No. 1826, Recognition of FX Gains and Losses in Doubt After Supreme Court Decision; No. 1814, 2006 Canadian Tax Foundation Annual Conference CRA Round Table; No. 1808, Supreme Court Rules FX Losses Not Deductible as "Discounts"; No. 1683, *Imperial Oil Limited v. The Queen*.

Income Tax Folios: *Secondary* — S5-F2-C1 Foreign Tax Credit.

Income Tax Technical News: Issue No. 44, Foreign Exchange Gains and Losses; Issue No. 38, Imperial Oil and the Treatment of Foreign Currency Loans.

Interpretation Bulletins: *Secondary* — IT-95R Foreign exchange gains and losses.

Tax Window Files: IFA 2018 - Question 7, *May 16, 2018*, CRA Document No. 2018-0750261C6.

Cases: The indebtedness of the taxpayer (evidenced by the convertible debentures that were converted) was repaid by the issuance of the stipulated number of common shares. The results of such conversion and issuance was to be determined using Canadian dollars and any foreign currency amount was required to be converted to Canadian dollars using a stipulated rate of exchange on the date the foreign currency amount first "arose". The issue was whether, in Canadian dollars, the taxpayer paid less on the repayment of its indebtedness than it received on the issuance of the convertible debentures in 2002. The foreign currency amount that related to each repayment by the taxpayer arose on the date of that repayment. The sale price of the common shares was to be determined by reference to their trading price on the conversion date. The repayment amount in respect of each convertible debenture was effectively the amount determined when the sale price of a common share on each conversion date was multiplied by the number of shares issued. A separate calculation would therefore be required with respect to each conversion. *Agnico-Eagle Mines Limited v. The Queen*, 2016 DTC 5056 (F.C.A.).

The taxpayer borrowed U.S. dollars to build a plant. When the U.S. dollar appreciated, the taxpayer used hedge accounting to effectively net its increased profit from U.S. revenues against the foreign currency losses realized on its debt repayments. The Court rejected its argument that a loss on a foreign currency hedge takes its character from the item being hedged. The losses took their character from the nature of the loan and were therefore capital losses. Also, hedge accounting is not appropriate for tax purposes. *Saskferco Products ULC v. The Queen*, 2008 DTC 6698 (F.C.A.), affirming 2007 DTC 1183 (T.C.C.)

The taxpayers redeemed U.S. dollar debentures which had been issued at a discount. Foreign exchange losses incurred on the redemption were not deductible under s. 20(1)(*f*) and could only be claimed as a capital loss under s. 39. *The Queen v. Imperial Oil Limited and Inco Limited*, 2006 DTC 6639 (S.C.C.), reversing 2004 DTC 6702 (F.C.A.) and affirming 2004 DTC 2377 (T.C.C.) re Imperial Oil, and reversing 2005 DTC 5109 (F.C.A.) and affirming 2004 DTC 3586 (T.C.C.) re Inco.

► 39(2.01) ◄

(2.01) Deemed gain — parked obligation. For the purposes of subsection (2), if a debt obligation owing by a taxpayer (referred to in this subsection and subsections (2.02) and (2.03) as the debtor) is denominated in a foreign currency and the debt obligation has become a parked obligation at a particular time, the debtor is deemed at that time to have made the gain, if any, that the debtor otherwise would have made if it had paid an amount at the particular time in satisfaction of the debt obligation equal to

(*a*) if the debt obligation has become a parked obligation at the particular time as a result of its acquisition by the holder of the debt obligation, the amount paid by the holder to acquire the debt obligation; and

(*b*) in any other case, the fair market value of the debt obligation at the particular time.

Editorial Note: In the 2016 federal Budget, the government introduced a new rule to combat "debt parking", under which some taxpayers attempt to avoid realizing a foreign exchange gain that would occur if a foreign debt obligation were repaid. Instead of repaying the obligation, the taxpayer (debtor) would arrange for a non-arm's length party to acquire the debt from the creditor or other holder of the obligation. The non-arm's length party would continue to hold the "parked" debt, such that no foreign currency gain was realized until ultimate repayment, if at all.

Subsection 39(2.01) provides that when a foreign currency debt becomes a "parked obligation" (defined in subsection 39(2.02)), the debtor is deemed to have a gain equal to the amount that the debtor would have realized if it had made a payment in satisfaction of the obligation. Where the debt became a parked obligation as a result of its acquisition by the holder of the debt, the amount of the notional payment equals the amount paid by the holder to acquire the debt. In any other case, the amount of the notional payment equals the fair market value of the debt.

History: S. 39(2.01) was added by S.C. 2016, c. 12, s. 13(4), deemed to have come into force on March 22, 2016. However, this subsection does not apply to a debtor in respect of a debt obligation owing by that debtor at the time that the obligation meets the conditions to become a parked obligation under subsection 39(2.02) because of a written agreement entered into before March 22, 2016, if that time is before 2017.

Related Sections: S. 39(2), Foreign exchange capital gains and losses; 80(2)(*j*); 80.01(2)(*b*).

► 39(2.02) ◄

(2.02) Parked obligation. For the purposes of subsection (2.01), a debt obligation owing by a debtor is a parked obligation at a particular time if

(*a*) both

(i) at that time, the holder of the debt obligation does not deal at arm's length with the debtor or, if the debtor is a corporation, has a significant interest in the debtor, and

(ii) at any previous time, a person who held the debt obligation dealt at arm's length with the debtor and, where the debtor is a corporation, did not have a significant interest in the debtor; and

(*b*) it can reasonably be considered that one of the main purposes of the transaction or event or series of transactions or events that resulted in the debt obligation meeting the condition in subparagraph (*a*)(i) is to avoid the application of subsection (2).

Editorial Note: A debt becomes a parked obligation at a particular time if the holder at that time does not deal at arm's length with the debtor, or has a significant interest in the debtor (where the debtor is a corporation), and at a previous time, a person who held the obligation was dealing at arm's length with the debtor, and did not have a significant interest in the debtor. However, the debt does not become a parked obligation unless it can reasonably be considered that one of the main purposes of the transaction or event that resulted in the non-arm's length holder (or significant interest holder) owning the debt at the particular time was to avoid the recognition of a capital gain under the foreign exchange rules.

Generally, a holder has a significant interest in a corporate debtor if it owns shares in the corporation with a value equal to 25% or more of the value of all of the shares in the corporation or that carry 25% or more of the shareholder votes (see paragraph 80.01(2)(*b*), which applies for these purposes).

History: S. 39(2.02) was added by S.C. 2016, c. 12, s. 13(4), deemed to have come into force on March 22, 2016.

► 39(2.03) ◄

(2.03) Interpretation. For the purposes of subsections (2.01) and (2.02),

(*a*) paragraph 80(2)(*j*) applies for the purpose of determining whether two persons are related to each other or whether any person is controlled by any other person; and

(*b*) paragraph 80.01(2)(*b*) applies for the purpose of determining whether a person has a significant interest in a corporation.

History: S. 39(2.03) was added by S.C. 2016, c. 12, s. 13(4), deemed to have come into force on March 22, 2016.

▶ 39(2.1) ◀

(2.1) Upstream loan — transitional set-off. If at any time a corporation resident in Canada or a partnership of which such a corporation is a member (such corporation or partnership referred to in this subsection and subsections (2.2) and (2.3) as the "borrowing party") has received a loan from, or become indebted to, a creditor that is a foreign affiliate (referred to in this subsection and subsections (2.2) and (2.3) as a "creditor affiliate") of a qualifying entity, or that is a partnership (referred to in this subsection and subsection (2.3) as a "creditor partnership") of which such an affiliate is a member, and the loan or indebtedness is at a later time repaid, in whole or in part, then the amount of the borrowing party's capital gain or capital loss determined, in the absence of this subsection, under subsection (2) in respect of the repayment, is to be reduced

(*a*) in the case of a capital gain

(i) if the creditor is a creditor affiliate, by an amount, not exceeding that capital gain, that is equal to twice the amount that would — in the absence of subparagraph 40(2)(*g*)(ii) and paragraph 95(2)(*g*.04) and on the assumption that the creditor affiliate's capital loss in respect of the repayment of the loan or indebtedness were a capital gain of the creditor affiliate, the creditor affiliate had no other income, loss, capital gain or capital loss for any taxation year, and no other foreign affiliate of a qualifying entity had any income, loss, capital gain or capital loss for any taxation year — be the total of all amounts each of which is an amount that would be included in computing a qualifying entity's income under subsection 91(1) for its taxation year that includes the last day of the taxation year of the creditor affiliate that includes the later time, or

(ii) if the creditor is a creditor partnership, by an amount, not exceeding that capital gain, that is equal to twice the amount that is the total of each amount, determined in respect of a particular member of the creditor partnership that is a foreign affiliate of a qualifying entity, that would — in the absence of subparagraph 40(2)(*g*)(ii) and paragraph 95(2)(*g*.04) and on the assumption that the creditor partnership's capital loss in respect of the repayment of the loan or indebtedness were a capital gain of the creditor partnership, the particular member had no other income, loss, capital gain or capital loss for any taxation year, and no other foreign affiliate of a qualifying entity had any income, loss, capital gain or capital loss for any taxation year — be the total of all amounts each of which is an amount that would be included in computing a qualifying entity's income under subsection 91(1) for its taxation year that includes the last day of the taxation year of the particular member that includes the last day of the creditor partnership's fiscal period that includes that later time; and

(*b*) in the case of a capital loss

(i) if the creditor is a creditor affiliate, by an amount, not exceeding that capital loss, that is equal to twice the amount, in respect of the creditor affiliate's capital gain in respect of the repayment of the loan or indebtedness, that would — in the absence of paragraph 95(2)(*g*.04) and on the assumption that the creditor affiliate had no other income, loss, capital gain or capital loss for any taxation year, and no other foreign affiliate of a qualifying entity had any income, loss, capital gain or capital loss for any taxation year — be the total of all amounts each of which is an amount that would be included in computing a qualifying entity's income under subsection 91 (1) for its taxation year that includes the last day of the taxation year of the creditor affiliate that includes the later time, or

(ii) if the creditor is a creditor partnership, by an amount, not exceeding that capital loss, that is equal to twice the amount, in respect of the creditor partnership's capital gain in respect of the repayment of the loan or indebtedness, that is the total of each amount, determined in respect of a particular member of the creditor partnership that is a foreign affiliate of a qualifying entity, that would — in the absence of paragraph 95(2)(*g*.04) and on the assumption that the particular member had no other income, loss, capital gain or capital loss for any taxation year, and no other foreign affiliate of a qualifying entity had any income, loss, capital gain or capital loss for any taxation year — be the total of all amounts each of which is an amount that would be included in computing a qualifying entity's income under subsection 91 (1) for its taxation year that includes the last day of the taxation year of the particular member that includes the last day of the creditor partnership's fiscal period that includes the later time.

Editorial Note: Subsection 39(2.1) provides transitional relief to a Canadian resident corporation, or a partnership with a member that is a Canadian resident corporation ("borrowing party"), that is required to repay an upstream loan to a foreign affiliate of a "qualifying entity" (defined in subsection 39(2.2)). The relief is intended to apply where the borrowing party repays the loan in order to reduce or avoid the income inclusion and deduction rules of subsection 90(6) in conjunction with 90(14). Subsection 39(2.1) serves to reduce the borrowing party's foreign exchange capital gain or loss on the partial or whole repayment of the loan, if any, but generally only to the extent of the affiliate's related capital gain or loss that would result from the repayment.

History: S. 39(2.1) was replaced by S.C. 2017, c. 33, s. 9(2), applicable in respect of portions of loans received and indebtedness incurred before August 20, 2011 that remain outstanding on August 19, 2011 and that are repaid, in whole or in part, before August 20, 2016, and formerly read:

(2.1) *Upstream loans — transitional set-off.* If at any time a corporation resident in Canada or a partnership of which such a corporation is a member (such corporation or partnership referred to in this subsection as the "borrowing party") has received a loan from, or become indebted to, a creditor that is a foreign affiliate (referred to in this subsection as a "creditor affiliate") of the borrowing party or that is a partnership (referred to in this subsection as a "creditor partnership") of which such an affiliate is a member, the loan or indebtedness is at a later time repaid, in whole or in part, and the amount of the borrowing party's capital gain or capital loss determined, in the absence of this subsection, under subsection (2) in respect of the repayment is equal to the amount of the creditor affiliate's or creditor partnership's capital loss or capital gain, as the case may be, determined, in the absence of paragraph 95(2)(*g.04*), in respect of the repayment, then the borrowing party's capital gain or capital loss so determined is to be reduced

(*a*) in the case of a capital gain

(i) if the creditor is a creditor affiliate, by an amount, not exceeding that capital gain, that is equal to twice the amount that would — in the absence of paragraph 95(2)(*g.04*) and on the assumption that the creditor affiliate's capital loss in respect of the repayment of the loan or indebtedness were a capital gain of the creditor affiliate, the creditor affiliate had no other income, loss, capital gain or capital loss for any taxation year, and no other foreign affiliate of the borrowing party had any income, loss, capital gain or capital loss for any taxation year — be included in computing the borrowing party's income under subsection 91(1) for its taxation year that includes the last day of the taxation year of the creditor affiliate that includes the later time, or

(ii) if the creditor is a creditor partnership, by an amount, not exceeding that capital gain, that is equal to twice the amount that is the total of each amount, determined in respect of a particular member of the creditor partnership that is a foreign affiliate of the borrowing party, that would — in the absence of paragraph 95(2)(*g.04*) and on the assumption that the creditor partnership's capital loss in respect of the repayment of the loan or indebtedness were a capital gain of the creditor partnership, the particular member had no other income, loss, capital gain or capital loss for any taxation year, and no other foreign affiliate of the borrowing party had any income, loss, capital gain or capital loss for any taxation year — be included in computing the borrowing party's income under subsection 91(1) for its taxation year that includes the last day of the taxation year of the particular member that includes the last day of the creditor partnership's fiscal period that includes the later time, and

(*b*) in the case of a capital loss

(i) if the creditor is a creditor affiliate, by an amount, not exceeding that capital loss, that is equal to twice the amount, in respect of the creditor affiliate's capital gain in respect of the repayment of the loan or indebtedness, that would — in the absence of paragraph 95(2)(*g.04*) and on the assumption that the creditor affiliate had no other income, loss, capital gain or capital loss for any taxation year, and no other foreign affiliate of the borrowing party had any income, loss, capital gain or capital loss for any taxation year — be included in computing the borrowing party's income under subsection 91(1) for its taxation year that includes the last day of the taxation year of the creditor affiliate that includes the later time, or

(ii) if the creditor is a creditor partnership, by an amount, not exceeding that capital loss, that is equal to twice the amount, in respect of the creditor partnership's capital gain in respect of the repayment of the loan or indebtedness, that is the total of each amount, determined in respect of a particular member of the creditor partnership that is a foreign affiliate of the borrowing party, that would — in the absence of paragraph 95(2)(*g.04*) and on the assumption that the particular member had no other income, loss, capital gain or capital loss for any taxation year, and no other foreign affiliate of the borrowing party had any income, loss, capital gain or capital loss for any taxation year — be included in computing the borrowing party's income under subsection 91(1) for its taxation year that includes the last day of the taxation year of the particular member that includes the last day of the creditor partnership's fiscal period that includes the later time.

S. 39(2.1) was added by S.C. 2013, c. 34, s. 59(1), applicable in respect of the portions of loans received and indebtedness incurred on or before August 19, 2011 that remain outstanding on that date and that are repaid, in whole or in part, on or before August 19, 2016.

See the application for the amendment to s. 39(2) for the extension of assessment periods to take into account the amendments by S.C. 2013, c. 34, s. 54 to 89.

Related Sections: 90(6) Loan from foreign affiliate.

► 39(2.2) ◄

(2.2) Definition of *qualifying entity*. For purposes of subsections (2.1) and (2.3), *qualifying entity* means

(*a*) in the case of a borrowing party that is a corporation,

(i) the borrowing party,

(ii) a corporation resident in Canada of which

(A) the borrowing party is a subsidiary wholly-owned corporation, or

(B) a corporation described in this paragraph is a subsidiary wholly-owned corporation,

(iii) a corporation resident in Canada

(A) each share of the capital stock of which is owned by

(I) the borrowing party, or

(II) a corporation that is described in this subparagraph or subparagraph (ii), or

(B) all or substantially all of the capital stock of which is owned by one or more corporations resident in Canada that are borrowing parties in respect of the creditor affiliate because of subsection 90(7), or

(iv) a partnership each member of which is

(A) a corporation described in any of subparagraphs (i) to (iii), or

(B) another partnership described in this subparagraph; and

(*b*) in the case of a borrowing party that is a partnership,

(i) the borrowing party,

(ii) if each member — determined as if each member of a partnership that is a member of another partnership is a member of that other partnership — of the borrowing party is either a particular corporation resident in Canada (in this paragraph referred to as the "parent") or a corporation resident in Canada that is a *subsidiary wholly-owned corporation*, as defined in subsection 87(1.4), of the parent,

(A) the parent, or

(B) a corporation resident in Canada that is a *subsidiary wholly-owned corporation*, as defined in subsection 87(1.4), of the parent, or

(iii) a partnership each member of which is any of

(A) the borrowing party,

(B) a corporation described in subparagraph (ii), and

(C) another partnership described in this subparagraph.

History: S. 39(2.2) was added by S.C. 2017, c. 33, s. 9(2), applicable in respect of portions of loans received and indebtedness incurred before August 20, 2011 that remain outstanding on August 19, 2011 and that are repaid, in whole or in part, before August 20, 2016.

► 39(2.3) ◄

(2.3) Upstream loan — transitional set-off election. Subsection (2.1) and paragraph 95(2)(*g.04*) do not apply in respect of a repayment, in whole or in part, of a loan or indebtedness if an election has been filed with the Minister before 2019 jointly by

(*a*) the borrowing party;

(*b*) if the creditor is a creditor affiliate, each qualifying entity of which the creditor affiliate is a foreign affiliate; and

(*c*) if the creditor is a creditor partnership, each qualifying entity of which a member of the creditor partnership is a foreign affiliate.

History: S. 39(2.3) was added by S.C. 2017, c. 33, s. 9(2), applicable in respect of portions of loans received and indebtedness incurred before August 20, 2011 that remain outstanding on August 19, 2011 and that are repaid, in whole or in part, before August 20, 2016.

▶ 39(3) ◀

(3) Gain in respect of purchase of bonds, etc., by issuer. Where a taxpayer has issued any bond, debenture or similar obligation and has at any subsequent time in a taxation year and after 1971 purchased the obligation in the open market, in the manner in which any such obligation would normally be purchased in the open market by any member of the public,

(*a*) the amount, if any, by which the amount for which the obligation was issued by the taxpayer exceeds the purchase price paid or agreed to be paid by the taxpayer for the obligation shall be deemed to be a capital gain of the taxpayer for the taxation year from the disposition of a capital property, and

(*b*) the amount, if any, by which the purchase price paid or agreed to be paid by the taxpayer for the obligation exceeds the greater of the principal amount of the obligation and the amount for which it was issued by the taxpayer shall be deemed to be a capital loss of the taxpayer for the taxation year from the disposition of a capital property,

to the extent that the amount determined under paragraph (*a*) or (*b*) would not, if section 3 were read in the manner described in paragraph (1)(*a*) and this Act were read without reference to subsections 80(12) and (13), be included or be deductible, as the case may be, in computing the taxpayer's income for the year or any other taxation year.

Related Sections: ITAR s. 26(1.1) Principal amount of certain obligations.

▶ 39(4) ◀

(4) Election concerning disposition of Canadian securities. Except as provided in subsection (5), where a Canadian security has been disposed of by a taxpayer in a taxation year and the taxpayer so elects in prescribed form in the taxpayer's return of income under this Part for that year,

(*a*) every Canadian security owned by the taxpayer in that year or any subsequent taxation year shall be deemed to have been a capital property owned by the taxpayer in those years; and

(*b*) every disposition by the taxpayer of any such Canadian security shall be deemed to be a disposition by the taxpayer of a capital property.

Editorial Note: See the editorial note under s. 39(5).

Tax Profile: October 2011 — Hedge Funds and Private Equity Funds in Canada; January 2009 — Market Meltdown — Capital Loss Utilization; June 2007 — Selected Tax Issues For Hedge Funds; November 2006 — Structuring and Taxation of Canadian Hedge Funds; February 2005 — The Canadian Treatment of Derivatives; August 2004 — Canadian Tax Treatment of Index Participation Units and Exchange-Traded Index Derivatives; March 2004 — Loss Utilization By Individuals.

Forms: T123 — Election on Disposition of Canadian Securities.

▶ 39(4.1) ◀

(4.1) Members of partnerships. For the purpose of determining the income of a taxpayer who is a member of a partnership, subsections (4) and (5) apply as if

(*a*) every Canadian security owned by the partnership were owned by the taxpayer; and

(*b*) every Canadian security disposed of by the partnership in a fiscal period of the partnership were disposed of by the taxpayer at the end of that fiscal period.

Tax Window Files: 39(4) Election — Tiered Partnerships, *Technical Interpretation, Business and Partnerships Division, February 12, 2003*, CRA Document No. 2002-0141425. Subsection 39(4.1) not applicable to securities owned by lower-tier partnership where member of higher-tier partnership makes subsection 39(4) election.

▶ 39(5) ◀

(5) Exception. An election under subsection (4) does not apply to a disposition of a Canadian security by a taxpayer (other than a mutual fund corporation or a mutual fund trust) who at the time of the disposition is

(*a*) a trader or dealer in securities,

(*b*) a financial institution (as defined in subsection 142.2(1)),

(*c*) (Repealed by 1995, c. 21, s. 49(3).)

(*d*) (Repealed by 1995, c. 21, s. 49(3).)

(*e*) (Repealed by 1995, c. 21, s. 49(3).)

(*f*) a corporation whose principal business is the lending of money or the purchasing of debt obligations or a combination thereof, or

(*g*) a non-resident,

or any combination thereof.

Editorial Note: Since the s. 39(4) election does not apply to dispositions made by traders or dealers in securities, which apparently include all persons found to be in the business of buying and selling securities (see the *Vancouver Art Metal Works* decision (93 DTC 5116 (F.C.A.), reversing 91 DTC 5643 (F.C.T.D.)) in "Cases", below), the election essentially only covers dispositions that would otherwise be adventures or concerns in the nature of trade.

Cases: Considering that the words "trader or dealer" should be given their ordinary meaning, a person loses the benefit of the capital gain election when he professionally engages in dealing in securities or when his dealings amount to carrying on a business and can no longer be characterized as investor's transactions, or mere adventures in the nature of trade. *The Queen v. Vancouver Art Metal Works Ltd.*, 93 DTC 5116 (F.C.A.), reversing 91 DTC 5643 (F.C.T.D.).

▶ 39(6) ◀

(6) Definition of "Canadian security". For the purposes of this section, "Canadian security" means a security (other than a prescribed security) that is a share of the capital stock of a corporation resident in Canada, a unit of a mutual fund trust or a bond, debenture, bill, note, mortgage, hypothecary claim or similar obligation issued by a person resident in Canada.

Related Regulations: 6200.

Tax Profile: February 2005 — The Canadian Treatment of Derivatives; August 2004 — Canadian Tax Treatment of Index Participation Units and Exchange-Traded Index Derivatives.

▶ 39(7) ◀

(7) Unused share-purchase tax credit. The amount of any unused share-purchase tax credit of a taxpayer for a particular taxation year, to the extent that it was not deducted from the taxpayer's tax otherwise payable under this Part for the immediately preceding taxation year, shall be deemed to be a capital loss of the taxpayer from a disposition of property for the year immediately following the particular taxation year.

▶ 39(8) ◀

(8) Unused scientific research and experimental development tax credit. The amount of any unused scientific research and experimental development tax credit of a taxpayer for a particular taxation year, to the extent that it was not deducted from the taxpayer's tax otherwise payable under this Part for the immediately preceding taxation year, shall be deemed to be a capital loss of the taxpayer from a disposition of property for the year immediately following the particular taxation year, except that where the taxpayer is an individual the capital loss shall be deemed to be 147% of that amount.

Related Sections: S. 127.3(1) Scientific research and experimental development tax credit; s. 127.3(2), "unused scientific research and experimental development tax credit".

► 39(9) ◄

(9) Deduction from business investment loss. In computing the business investment loss of a taxpayer who is an individual (other than a trust) for a taxation year from the disposition of a particular property, there shall be deducted an amount equal to the lesser of

(*a*) the amount that would be the taxpayer's business investment loss for the year from the disposition of that particular property if paragraph (1)(*c*) were read without reference to subparagraph (1)(*c*)(viii), and

(*b*) the amount, if any, by which the total of

(i) the total of all amounts each of which is twice the amount deducted by the taxpayer under section 110.6 in computing the taxpayer's taxable income for a preceding taxation year that

(A) ended before 1988, or

(B) begins after October 17, 2000,

(i.1) the total of all amounts each of which is

(A) $^3/_2$ of the amount deducted under section 110.6 in computing the taxpayer's taxable income for a preceding taxation year that

(I) ended after 1987 and before 1990, or

(II) began after February 27, 2000 and ended before October 18, 2000, or

(B) the amount determined by multiplying the reciprocal of the fraction in paragraph 38(*a*) that applies to the taxpayer for each of the taxpayer's taxation years that includes February 28, 2000 or October 18, 2000 by the amount deducted under section 110.6 in computing the taxpayer's taxable income for that year, and

(i.2) the total of all amounts each of which is $^4/_3$ of the amount deducted under section 110.6 in computing the taxpayer's taxable income for a preceding taxation year that ended after 1989 and before February 28, 2000

exceeds

(ii) the total of all amounts each of which is an amount deducted by the taxpayer under paragraph (1)(*c*) by virtue of subparagraph (1)(*c*)(viii) in computing the taxpayer's business investment loss

(A) from the disposition of property in taxation years preceding the year, or

(B) from the disposition of property other than the particular property in the year,

except that, where a particular amount was included under subparagraph 14(1)(*a*)(v) in the taxpayer's income for a taxation year that ended after 1987 and before 1990, the reference in subparagraph (i.1) to "$^3/_2$" shall, in respect of that portion of any amount deducted under section 110.6 in respect of the particular amount, be read as "$^4/_3$".

Income Tax Folios: S4-F8-C1 Business Investment Losses.

► 39(10) ◄

(10) Idem, of a trust. In computing the business investment loss of a trust for a taxation year from the disposition of a particular property, there shall be deducted an amount equal to the lesser of

(*a*) the amount that would be the trust's business investment loss for the year from the disposition of that particular property if paragraph (1)(*c*) were read without reference to subparagraph (1)(*c*)(viii), and

(*b*) the amount, if any, by which the total of

(i) the total of all amounts each of which is twice the amount designated by the trust under subsection 104(21.2) in respect of a beneficiary in its return of income for a preceding taxation year that

(A) ended before 1988, or

(B) begins after October 17, 2000,

(i.1) the total of all amounts each of which is

(A) $^3/_2$ of the amount designated by the trust under subsection 104(21.2) in respect of a beneficiary in its return of income for a preceding taxation year that

(I) ended after 1987 and before 1990, or

(II) began after February 27, 2000 and ended before October 18, 2000, or

(B) the amount determined by multiplying the reciprocal of the fraction in paragraph 38(*a*) that applies to the trust for each of the trust's taxation years that includes February 28, 2000 or October 18, 2000 by the amount designated by the trust under subsection 104(21.2) in respect of a beneficiary in its return of income for that year, and

(i.2) the total of all amounts each of which is $^4/_3$ of the amount designated by the trust under subsection 104(21.2) in respect of a beneficiary in its return of income for a preceding taxation year that ended after 1989 and before February 28, 2000

exceeds

(ii) the total of all amounts each of which is an amount deducted by the trust under paragraph (1)(*c*) by virtue of subparagraph (1)(*c*)(viii) in computing its business investment loss

(A) from the disposition of property in taxation years preceding the year, or

(B) from the disposition of property other than the particular property in the year except that, where a particular amount was included under subparagraph 14(1)(*a*)(v) in the trust's income for a taxation year that ended after 1987 and before 1990, the reference in subparagraph (i.1) to "3/2" shall, in respect of that portion of any amount deducted under section 110.6 in respect of the particular amount, be read as "4/3".

Income Tax Folios: S4-F8-C1 Business Investment Losses.

▶ 39(11) ◀

(11) Recovery of bad debt. Where an amount is received in a taxation year on account of a debt (in this subsection referred to as the "recovered amount") in respect of which a deduction for bad debts had been made under subsection 20(4.2) in computing a taxpayer's income for a preceding taxation year, the amount, if any, by which 1/2 of the recovered amount exceeds the amount determined under paragraph 12(1)(*i*.1) in respect of the recovered amount is deemed to be a taxable capital gain of the taxpayer from a disposition of capital property in the year.

▶ 39(12) ◀

(12) Guarantees. For the purpose of paragraph (1)(*c*), where

(*a*) an amount was paid by a taxpayer in respect of a debt of a corporation under an arrangement under which the taxpayer guaranteed the debt,

(*b*) the amount was paid to a person with whom the taxpayer was dealing at arm's length, and

(*c*) the corporation was a small business corporation

(i) at the time the debt was incurred, and

(ii) at any time in the 12 months before the time an amount first became payable by the taxpayer under the arrangement in respect of a debt of the corporation,

that part of the amount that is owing to the taxpayer by the corporation shall be deemed to be a debt owing to the taxpayer by a small business corporation.

▶ 39(13) ◀

(13) Repayment of assistance. The total of all amounts paid by a taxpayer in a taxation year each of which is

(*a*) such part of any assistance described in subparagraph 53(2)(*k*)(i) in respect of, or for the acquisition of, a capital property (other than depreciable property) by the taxpayer that was repaid by the taxpayer in the year where the repayment is made after the disposition of the property by the taxpayer and under an obligation to repay all or any part of that assistance, or

(*b*) an amount repaid by the taxpayer in the year in respect of a capital property (other than depreciable property) acquired by the taxpayer that is repaid after the disposition thereof by the taxpayer and that would have been an amount described in subparagraph 53(2)(*s*)(ii) had the repayment been made before the disposition of the property,

shall be deemed to be a capital loss of the taxpayer for the year from the disposition of property by the taxpayer in the year and, for the purpose of section 110.6, that property shall be deemed to have been disposed of by the taxpayer in the year.

Related Sections: S. 13(21), "disposition of property"; s. 39(1)(*b*) Meaning of capital gain and capital loss; s. 54, "capital property", "disposition"; s. 248(1), "amount", "capital loss", "property".

SECTION 39.1: [Exempt capital gains balance in respect of flow-through entity]

▶ 39.1(1) ◀

(1) Definitions. In this section,

"exempt capital gains balance" — "exempt capital gains balance" of an individual for a taxation year that ends before 2005 in respect of a flow-through entity means the amount determined by the formula

$$A - B - C - F$$

where

A is

(*a*) if the entity is a trust referred to in any of paragraphs (*f*) to (*j*) of the definition "flow-through entity" in this subsection, the amount determined under paragraph 110.6(19)(*c*) in respect of the individual's interest or interests therein, and

(*b*) in any other case, the lesser of

(i) 4/3 of the total of the taxable capital gains that resulted from elections made under subsection 110.6(19) in respect of the individual's interests in or shares of the capital stock of the entity, and

(ii) the amount that would be determined under subparagraph (i) if

(A) the amount designated in the election in respect of each interest or share were equal to the amount determined by the formula

$$D - E$$

where

D is the fair market value of the interest or share at the end of February 22, 1994, and

E is the amount, if any, by which the amount designated in the election that was made in respect of the interest or share exceeds 11/10 of its fair market value at the end of February 22, 1994, and

(B) this Act were read without reference to subsection 110.6(20),

B is the total of all amounts each of which is the amount by which the individual's capital gain for a preceding taxation year, determined without reference to subsection (2), from the disposition of an interest in or a share of the capital stock of the entity was reduced under that subsection,

C is

(*a*) if the entity is a trust described in any of paragraphs (*d*) and (*h*) to (*j*) of the definition "flow-through entity" in this subsection, the total of

(i) 3/2 of the total of all amounts each of which is the amount by which the individual's taxable capital gain (determined without reference to this section), for a preceding taxation year that began after February 27, 2000 and ended before October 18, 2000 that resulted from a designation made under subsection 104(21) by the trust, was reduced under subsection (3),

(ii) 4/3 of the total of all amounts each of which is the amount by which the individual's taxable capital gain (determined without reference to this section), for a preceding taxation year that ended before February 28, 2000 and that resulted from a designation made under subsection 104(21) by the trust, was reduced under subsection (3),

(iii) the amount claimed by the individual under subparagraph 104(21.4)(*a*)(ii) or (21.7)(*b*)(ii) for a preceding taxation year, and

(iv) twice the total of all amounts each of which is the amount by which the individual's taxable capital gain (determined without reference to this section) for a preceding taxation year that began after October 17, 2000 and that resulted from a designation made under subsection 104(21) by the trust, was reduced under subsection (3),

(*b*) if the entity is a partnership, the total of

(i) 3/2 of the total of

(A) the total of all amounts each of which is the amount by which the individual's share of the partnership's taxable capital gains (determined without reference to this section), for its fiscal period that began after February 27, 2000 and ended before October 18, 2000, was reduced under subsection (4), and

(B) the total of all amounts each of which is the amount by which the individual's share of the partnership's income from a business (determined without reference to this section), for its fiscal period that began after February 27, 2000 and ended before October 18, 2000, was reduced under subsection (5),

(ii) 4/3 of the total of

(A) the total of all amounts each of which is the amount by which the individual's share of the partnership's taxable capital gains (determined without reference to this section), for its fiscal period that ended before February 28, 2000 and in a preceding taxation year was reduced under subsection (4), and

(B) the total of all amounts each of which is the amount by which the individual's share of the partnership's income from a business (determined without reference to this section), for its fiscal period that ended before February 28, 2000 and in a preceding taxation year, was reduced under subsection (5),

(iii) the product obtained when the reciprocal of the fraction in paragraph 38(*a*) that applies to the partnership for its fiscal period that includes February 28, 2000 or October 17, 2000 is multiplied by the total of

(A) the total of all amounts each of which is the amount by which the individual's share of the partnership's taxable capital gains (determined without reference to this section), for its fiscal period that includes February 28, 2000 or October 17, 2000 and ended in a preceding taxation year, was reduced under subsection (4), and

(B) the total of all amounts each of which is the amount by which the individual's share of the partnership's income from a business (determined without reference to this section), for its fiscal period that includes February 28, 2000 or October 17, 2000 and ended in a preceding taxation year was reduced under subsection (5), and

(iv) twice the total of

(A) the total of all amounts each of which is the amount by which the individual's share of the partnership's taxable capital gains (determined without reference to this section), for its fiscal period that began after October 17, 2000 and ended in a preceding taxation year, was reduced under subsection (4), and

(B) the total of all amounts each of which is the amount by which the individual's share of the partnership's income from a business (determined without reference to this section), for its fiscal period that began after October 17, 2000 and ended in a preceding taxation year, was reduced under subsection (5), and

(*c*) in any other case, the total of all amounts each of which is the amount by which the total of the individual's capital gains otherwise determined under subsection 130.1(4) or 131(1), subsections 138.1(3) and (4) or subsection 144(4), as the case may be, for a preceding taxation year in respect of the entity was reduced under subsection (6); and

F is

(*a*) if the entity is a trust described in any of paragraphs (*g*) to (*j*) of the definition "flow-through entity" in this subsection, the total of all amounts each of which is an amount included before the year in the cost to the individual of a property under subsection 107(2.2) or paragraph 144(7.1)(*c*) because of the individual's exempt capital gains balance in respect of the entity, and (*b*) in any other case, nil;

"flow-through entity" —"flow-through entity" means

(*a*) an investment corporation,

(*b*) a mortgage investment corporation,

(*c*) a mutual fund corporation,

(*d*) a mutual fund trust,

(*e*) a partnership,

(*f*) a related segregated fund trust for the purpose of section 138.1,

(*g*) a trust governed by an employees profit sharing plan,

(*h*) a trust maintained primarily for the benefit of employees of a corporation or two or more corporations that do not deal at arm's length with each other, where one of the main purposes of the trust is to hold interests in, or for civil law rights in, shares of the capital stock of the corporation or corporations, as the case may be, or any corporation not dealing at arm's length therewith,

(*i*) a trust established exclusively for the benefit of one or more persons each of whom was, at the time the trust was created, either a person from whom the trust received property or a creditor of that person, where one of the main purposes of the trust is to secure the payments required to be made by or on behalf of that person to such creditor, and

(*j*) a trust all or substantially all of the properties of which consist of shares of the capital stock of a corporation, where the trust was established pursuant to an agreement between 2 or more shareholders of the corporation and one of the main purposes of the trust is to provide for the exercise of voting rights in respect of those shares pursuant to that agreement.

History: S. 39.1(1), paragraph (*h*) of the definition "flow-through entity" was replaced by S.C. 2013, c. 34, s. 101, in force June 26, 2013, and formerly read:

(*h*) a trust maintained primarily for the benefit of employees of a corporation or 2 or more corporations that do not deal at arm's length with each other, where one of the main purposes of the trust is to hold interests in shares of the capital stock of the corporation or corporations, as the case may be, or any corporation not dealing at arm's length therewith,

▶ 39.1(2) ◀

(2) Reduction of capital gain. Where at any time after February 22, 1994 an individual disposes of an interest in or a share of the capital stock of a flow-through entity, the individual's capital gain, if any, otherwise determined for a taxation year from the disposition shall be reduced by such amount as the individual claims, not exceeding the amount determined by the formula

$$A - B - C$$

where

A is the exempt capital gains balance of the individual for the year in respect of the entity,

B is

(*a*) if the entity made a designation under subsection 104(21) in respect of the individual for the year, twice the amount, if any, claimed under subsection (3) by the individual for the year in respect of the entity,

(*b*) if the entity is a partnership, twice the amount, if any, claimed under subsection (4) by the individual for the year in respect of the entity, and

(*c*) in any other case, the amount, if any, claimed under subsection (6) by the individual for the year in respect of the entity, and

C is the total of all reductions under this subsection in the individual's capital gains otherwise determined for the year from the disposition of other interests in or shares of the capital stock of the entity.

History: S. 39.1(2), paragraph (*b*) of the description of B was replaced by S.C. 2016, c. 12, s. 14(1), applicable in respect of taxation years that begin after 2016, and formerly read:

(*b*) if the entity is a partnership, twice the total of

(i) the amount, if any, claimed under subsection (4) by the individual for the year in respect of the entity, and

(ii) the amount, if any, claimed under subsection (5) by the individual for the year in respect of the entity, and

▶ 39.1(3) ◀

(3) Reduction of taxable capital gain. The taxable capital gain otherwise determined under subsection 104(21) of an individual for a taxation year as a result of a designation made under that subsection by a flow-through entity shall be reduced by such amount as the individual claims, not exceeding $\frac{1}{2}$ of the individual's exempt capital gains balance for the year in respect of the entity.

▶ 39.1(4) ◀

(4) Reduction in share of partnership's taxable capital gains. An individual's share otherwise determined for a taxation year of a taxable capital gain of a partnership from the disposition of a property (other than property acquired by the partnership after February 22, 1994 in a transfer to which subsection 97(2) applied) for its fiscal period that ends after February 22, 1994 and in the year shall be reduced by such amount as the individual claims, not exceeding the amount determined by the formula

$$A - B$$

where

A is $\frac{1}{2}$ of the individual's exempt capital gains balance for the year in respect of the partnership, and

B is the total of amounts claimed by the individual under this subsection in respect of other taxable capital gains of the partnership for that fiscal period.

▶ 39.1(5) ◀

(5) Reduction in share of partnership's income from a business — (Repealed by S.C. 2016, c. 12, s. 14(2).)

History: S. 39.1(5) was repealed by S.C. 2016, c. 12, s. 14(2), applicable in respect of taxation years that begin after 2016, and formerly read:

(5) *Reduction in share of partnership's income from a business.* An individual's share otherwise determined for a taxation year of the income of a partnership from a business for the partnership's fiscal period that ends in the year and the individual's share of the partnership's taxable capital gain, if any, arising under paragraph 14(1)(*b*) shall be reduced by such amount as the individual claims, not exceeding the lesser of

(*a*) the amount, if any, by which $\frac{1}{2}$ of the individual's exempt capital gains balance for the year in respect of the partnership exceeds the total of

(i) the amount, if any, claimed under subsection (4) by the individual for the year in respect of the partnership, and

(ii) all amounts, if any, claimed under this subsection by the individual for the year in respect of other businesses of the partnership, and (*b*) the amount determined by the formula

$$A \times (B/C)$$

where

A is the amount included under paragraph 14(1)(*b*) in computing the income of the partnership from the business for the fiscal period,

B is the amount that would otherwise be the individual's share of the partnership's income from the business for the fiscal period, and

C is the partnership's income from the business for the fiscal period.

► 39.1(6) ◄

(6) Reduction of capital gains. The total capital gains otherwise determined under subsection 130.1(4) or 131(1), subsections 138.1(3) and (4) or subsection 144(4), as the case may be, of an individual for a taxation year as a result of one or more elections, allocations or designations made after February 22, 1994 by a flow-through entity shall be reduced by such amount as the individual claims, not exceeding the individual's exempt capital gains balance for the year in respect of the entity.

► 39.1(7) ◄

(7) Nil exempt capital gains balance. Notwithstanding subsection (1), where at any time an individual ceases to be a member or shareholder of, or a beneficiary under, a flow-through entity, the exempt capital gains balance of the individual in respect of the entity for each taxation year that begins after that time is deemed to be nil.

SECTION 40: [Calculation of gain, loss or reserve]

► 40(1) ◄

(1) General rules. Except as otherwise expressly provided in this Part

(*a*) a taxpayer's gain for a taxation year from the disposition of any property is the amount, if any, by which

(i) if the property was disposed of in the year, the amount, if any, by which the taxpayer's proceeds of disposition exceed the total of the adjusted cost base to the taxpayer of the property immediately before the disposition and any outlays and expenses to the extent that they were made or incurred by the taxpayer for the purpose of making the disposition, or

(ii) if the property was disposed of before the year, the amount, if any, claimed by the taxpayer under subparagraph (iii) in computing the taxpayer's gain for the immediately preceding year from the disposition of the property,

exceeds

(iii) subject to subsection (1.1), such amount as the taxpayer may claim

(A) in the case of an individual (other than a trust) in prescribed form filed with the taxpayer's return of income under this Part for the year, and

(B) in any other case, in the taxpayer's return of income under this Part for the year,

as a deduction, not exceeding the lesser of

(C) a reasonable amount as a reserve in respect of such of the proceeds of disposition of the property that are payable to the taxpayer after the end of the year as can reasonably be regarded as a portion of the amount determined under subparagraph (i) in respect of the property, and

(D) an amount equal to the product obtained when 1/5 of the amount determined under subparagraph (i) in respect of the property is multiplied by the amount, if any, by which 4 exceeds the number of preceding taxation years of the taxpayer ending after the disposition of the property; and

(*b*) a taxpayer's loss for a taxation year from the disposition of any property is,

(i) if the property was disposed of in the year, the amount, if any, by which the total of the adjusted cost base to the taxpayer of the property immediately before the disposition and any outlays and expenses to the extent that they were made or incurred by the taxpayer for the purpose of making the disposition, exceeds the taxpayer's proceeds of disposition of the property, and

(ii) in any other case, nil.

Income Tax Folios: *Primary* — S3-F4-C1 General Discussion of Capital Cost Allowance.

Editorial Note: Whether the gain or loss under s. 40(1) is a capital gain or capital loss (or business investment loss) is determined under the provisions of s. 39(1). Generally speaking, the rest of s. 40 either qualifies, expands, or imposes limitations on the recognition of gains or losses. The capital gain reserve (see clauses *a*)(iii)(C) and (D)) is the lesser of 1) the gain otherwise determined multiplied by proceeds due after year / total proceeds (the reasonable portion in (C)), and 2) 4/5 of the gain for the year of disposition (year 1), 3/5 of the gain for year 2, 2/5 of the gain for year 3, 1/5 of the gain for year 4, and nil afterwards.

Related Sections: S. 40(2) Limitations; s. 44 Exchanges of property; s. 45(1) Property with more than one use; s. 46(1) Personal-use property; s. 53(1) Adjustments to cost base; s. 53(2) Amounts to be deducted; s. 54, "adjusted cost base", "capital property", "listed personal property", "principal residence", "proceeds of disposition"; s. 69(1) Inadequate considerations; s. 72 Reserves, etc., for year of death; s. 79 Surrender of property by debtor; s. 87(2)(*m*) Reserves; s. 100(2) Gain from disposition of interest in partnership; s. 104(1) Reference to trust or estate; s. 248(1), "amount", "business", "corporation", "disposition", "exempt income", "farming", "individual", "property"; s. 255 Canada.

Forms: T3 SCH 2 — Reserves on Dispositions of Capital Property; T2017 — Summary of Reserves on Dispositions of Capital Property; T2091(IND) — Designation of a Property as a Principal Residence by an Individual (Other than a Personal Trust).

Guides: T4037 Capital Gains.

Income Tax Folios: *Primary* — S3-F2-C1 Capital Dividends. *Secondary* — S3-F9-C1 Lottery Winnings, Miscellaneous Receipts, and Income (and Losses) from Crime; S4-F2-C1 Deductibility of Fines and Penalties.

Information Circulars: IC 88-2 General anti-avoidance rule — Section 245 of the Income Tax Act.

Interpretation Bulletins: *Secondary* — IT-95R Foreign exchange gains and losses; IT-259R4 Exchange of property; IT-268R4 Inter vivos transfer of farm property to child; IT-426R Shares sold subject to an earnout agreement; IT-467R2 Damages, settlements and similar payments.

Tax Window Files: Beneficial Ownership, *June 14, 2016*, CRA Document No. 2016-0647461E5; Transfer of Silver Bullion, *March 30, 2007*, CRA Document No. 2006-0196641E5.

Cases: A former employee's client list was not a property of the employee such that a "disposition" of that list upon the employee's termination did not give rise to a capital loss. Furthermore, expenses incurred for the purpose of making the disposition, if any, could not include the employee's estimated value of foregone revenues caused by the loss of the clients. *Louis-Fred Martin v. The Queen*, 2017 DTC 5058 (FCA)

No reserve may be claimed for a promissory note of which the taxpayer is entitled to enforce payment but does not do so. *The Queen v. Derbecker*, 84 DTC 6549 (F.C.A.), reversing 84 DTC 6136 (F.C.T.D.). See also: *Pineo v. The Queen*, 86 DTC 6322 (F.C.T.D.).

► 40(1.01) ◄

(1.01) Gift of non-qualifying security. A taxpayer's gain for a particular taxation year from a disposition of a non-qualifying security of the taxpayer (as defined in subsection 118.1(18)) that is the making of a gift (other than an excepted gift, within the meaning assigned by subsection 118.1(19)) to a qualified donee (as defined in subsection 149.1(1)) is the amount, if any, by which

(*a*) where the disposition occurred in the particular year, the amount, if any, by which the taxpayer's proceeds of disposition exceed the total of the adjusted cost base to the taxpayer of the security immediately before the disposition and any outlays and expenses to the extent they were made or incurred by the taxpayer for the purpose of making the disposition, and

(*b*) where the disposition occurred in the 60-month period that ends at the beginning of the particular year, the amount, if any, deducted under paragraph (*c*) in computing the taxpayer's gain for the preceding taxation year from the disposition of the security

exceeds

(*c*) the amount that the taxpayer claims in prescribed form filed with the taxpayer's return of income for the particular year, not exceeding the eligible amount of the gift, where the taxpayer is not deemed by subsection 118.1(13) to have made a gift of property before the end of the particular year as a consequence of a disposition of the security by the donee or as a consequence of the security ceasing to be a non-qualifying security of the taxpayer before the end of the particular year.

History: S. 40(1.01)(*c*) was replaced by S.C. 2013, c. 34, s. 183(1), applicable to gifts made after December 20, 2002, and formerly read:

(*c*) the amount that the taxpayer claims in prescribed form filed with the taxpayer's return of income for the particular year, where the taxpayer is not deemed by subsection 118.1(13) to have made a gift of property before the end of the particular year as a consequence of a disposition of the security by the donee or as a consequence of the security ceasing to be a non-qualifying security of the taxpayer before the end of the particular year.

Related Sections: s. 248(31) Eligible amount of gift or monetary contribution.

▶ 40(1.1) ◀

(1.1) Reserve — property disposed of to a child. In computing the amount that a taxpayer may claim under subparagraph (1)(*a*)(iii) in computing the taxpayer's gain from the disposition of a property, that subparagraph shall be read as if the references in that subparagraph to "1/5" and "4" were references to "1/10" and "9" respectively, if,

(*a*) the property was disposed of by the taxpayer to the taxpayer's child,

(*b*) that child was resident in Canada immediately before the disposition, and

(*c*) the property was immediately before the disposition,

(i) any land in Canada or depreciable property in Canada of a prescribed class that was used by the taxpayer, the spouse or common-law partner of the taxpayer, a child or a parent of the taxpayer in a farming or fishing business carried on in Canada,

(ii) a share of the capital stock of a family farm or fishing corporation of the taxpayer or an interest in a family farm or fishing partnership of the taxpayer (such a share or an interest having the meaning assigned by subsection 70(10)), or

(iii) a qualified small business corporation share of the taxpayer (within the meaning assigned by subsection 110.6(1)).

(iv) (Repealed by S.C. 2014, c. 39, s. 11(2).)

History: S. 40(1.1)(*c*)(ii) was replaced by S.C. 2014, c. 39, s. 11(1), applicable to dispositions and transfers that occur in the 2014 and subsequent taxation years, and formerly read:

(ii) a share of the capital stock of a family farm corporation of the taxpayer or an interest in a family farm partnership of the taxpayer (such a share or an interest having the meaning assigned by subsection 70(10)),

S. 40(1.1)(*c*)(iv) was repealed by S.C. 2014, c. 39, s. 11(2), applicable to dispositions and transfers that occur in the 2014 and subsequent taxation years, and formerly read:

(iv) a share of the capital stock of a family fishing corporation of the taxpayer or an interest in a family fishing partnership (such a share or an interest having the meaning assigned by subsection 70(10)).

Related Sections: 248(29) Farming or fishing business.

Interpretation Bulletins: *Secondary* — IT-268R4 Inter vivos transfer of farm property to child.

▶ 40(2) ◀

(2) Limitations. Notwithstanding subsection (1),

(*a*) subparagraph (1)(*a*)(iii) does not apply to permit a taxpayer to claim any amount under that subparagraph in computing a gain for a taxation year if

(i) the taxpayer, at the end of the year or at any time in the immediately following year, was not resident in Canada or was exempt from tax under any provision of this Part,

(ii) the purchaser of the property sold is a corporation that, immediately after the sale,

(A) was controlled, directly or indirectly, in any manner whatever, by the taxpayer,

(B) was controlled, directly or indirectly, in any manner whatever, by a person or group of persons by whom the taxpayer was controlled, directly or indirectly, in any manner whatever, or

(C) controlled the taxpayer, directly or indirectly, in any manner whatever, where the taxpayer is a corporation, or

(iii) the purchaser of the property sold is a partnership in which the taxpayer was, immediately after the sale, a majority-interest partner;

(*b*) where the taxpayer is an individual, the taxpayer's gain for a taxation year from the disposition of a property that was the taxpayer's principal residence at any time after the date (in this section referred to as the "acquisition date") that is the later of December 31, 1971 and the day on which the taxpayer last acquired or reacquired it, as the case may be, is the amount determined by the formula

$$A - (A \times B/C) - D$$

where

A is the amount that would, if this Act were read without reference to this paragraph and subsections 110.6(19) and (21), be the taxpayer's gain therefrom for the year,

B is

(i) if the taxpayer was resident in Canada during the year that includes the acquisition date, one plus the number of taxation years that end after the acquisition date for which the property is the taxpayer's principal residence and during which the taxpayer was resident in Canada, or

(ii) if it is not the case that the taxpayer was resident in Canada during the year that includes the acquisition date, the number of taxation years that end after the acquisition date for which the property was the taxpayer's principal residence and during which the taxpayer was resident in Canada,

C is the number of taxation years that end after the acquisition date during which the taxpayer owned the property whether jointly with another person or otherwise, and

D is

(i) if the acquisition date is before February 23, 1994 and the taxpayer or the taxpayer's spouse or common-law partner elected under subsection 110.6(19) in respect of the property or an interest, or for civil law a right, therein that was owned, immediately before the disposition, by the taxpayer, $4/3$ of the lesser of

(A) the total of all amounts each of which is the taxable capital gain of the taxpayer or of their spouse or common-law partner that would have resulted from an election by the taxpayer or spouse or common-law partner under subsection 110.6(19) in respect of the property or the interest or right if

(I) this Act were read without reference to subsection 110.6(20), and

(II) the amount designated in the election were equal to the amount, if any, by which the fair market value of the property or the interest or right at the end of February 22, 1994 exceeds the amount determined by the formula

$$E - 1.1F$$

where

E is the amount designated in the election that was made in respect of the property or the interest or right, and

F is the fair market value of the property or the interest or right at the end of February 22, 1994, and

(B) the total of all amounts each of which is the taxable capital gain of the taxpayer or of their spouse or common-law partner that would have resulted from an election that was made under subsection 110.6(19) in respect of the property or the interest or right if the property were the principal residence of neither the taxpayer nor the spouse or common-law partner for each particular taxation year unless the property was designated, in a return of income for the taxation year that includes February 22, 1994 or for a preceding taxation year, to be the principal residence of either of them for the particular taxation year, and

(ii) in any other case, zero;

Canadian Tax Foundation: Wang and Bernier, *Principal and Cottage Residence Planning: A Review of Selected Issues — Part 2,* 2013 Ontario Tax Conference 8B:1–20; Friedlan and Friedlan, *Principal and Cottage Residence Planning: A Review of Selected Issues — Part 1,* 2013 Ontario Tax Conference 8A:1–23; Freedman and Nakonechny, *The Tax Principles of Family Law,* 2012 Ontario Tax Conference 4:1–52.

(*c*) where the taxpayer is an individual, the taxpayer's gain for a taxation year from the disposition of land used in a farming business carried on by the taxpayer that includes property that was at any time the taxpayer's principal residence is

(i) the taxpayer's gain for the year, otherwise determined, from the disposition of the portion of the land that does not include the property that was the taxpayer's principal residence, plus the taxpayer's gain for the year, if any, determined under paragraph (*b*) from the disposition of the property that was the taxpayer's principal residence, or

(ii) if the taxpayer so elects in prescribed manner in respect of the land, the taxpayer's gain for the year from the disposition of the land including the property that was the taxpayer's principal residence, determined without regard to paragraph (*b*) or subparagraph (i) of this paragraph, less the total of

(A) $1,000, and

(B) $1,000 for each taxation year ending after the acquisition date for which the property was the taxpayer's principal residence and during which the taxpayer was resident in Canada;

(*d*) where the taxpayer is a corporation, its loss for a taxation year from the disposition of a bond or debenture is its loss therefrom for the year otherwise determined, less the total of such amounts received by it as, on account or in lieu of payment of, or in satisfaction of interest thereon as were, by virtue of paragraph 81(1)(*m*), not included in computing its income;

(*e*) (Repealed.)

(*e*.1) a particular taxpayer's loss, if any, from the disposition at any time to a particular person or partnership of an obligation — other than, for the purposes of computing the exempt surplus or exempt deficit and taxable surplus or taxable deficit of the particular taxpayer in respect of another taxpayer, where the particular taxpayer or, if the particular taxpayer is a partnership, a member of the particular taxpayer is a foreign affiliate of the other taxpayer, an obligation that is, or would be, if the particular taxpayer were a foreign affiliate of the other taxpayer, excluded property (within the meaning assigned by subsection 95(1)) of the particular taxpayer — that was, immediately after that time, payable by another person or partnership to the particular person or partnership is nil if the particular taxpayer, the particular person or partnership and the other person or partnership are related to each other at that time or would be related to each other at that time if paragraph 80(2)(*j*) applied for the purpose of this paragraph;

(*e*.2) subject to paragraph (*e*.3), a taxpayer's loss on the settlement or extinguishment of a particular commercial obligation (in this paragraph having the meaning assigned by subsection 80(1)) issued by a person or partnership and payable to the taxpayer is deemed to be the amount determined by the following formula if any part of the consideration given by the person or partnership for the settlement or extinguishment of the particular obligation consists of one or more other commercial obligations issued by the person or partnership to the taxpayer:

$$A \times (B - C)/B$$

where

A is the amount, if any, that would be the taxpayer's loss from the disposition of the particular obligation if this Act were read without reference to this paragraph,

B is the total fair market value of all the consideration given by the person or partnership for the settlement or extinguishment of the particular obligation, and

C is the total fair market value of the other obligations;

(*e*.3) paragraph (*e*.2) does not apply, for the purposes of computing the exempt surplus or exempt deficit and taxable surplus or taxable deficit of the taxpayer in respect of another taxpayer, where the taxpayer or, if the taxpayer is a partnership, a member of the taxpayer is a foreign affiliate of the other taxpayer, to the particular commercial obligation if the particular commercial obligation is, or would be, if the taxpayer were a foreign affiliate of the other taxpayer, excluded property (within the meaning assigned by subsection 95(1)) of the taxpayer;

(*f*) a taxpayer's gain or loss from the disposition of

(i) a chance to win a prize or bet, or

(ii) a right to receive an amount as a prize or as winnings on a bet,

in connection with a lottery scheme or a pool system of betting referred to in section 205 of the *Criminal Code* is nil;

(*g*) a taxpayer's loss, if any, from the disposition of a property (other than, for the purposes of computing the exempt surplus or exempt deficit, hybrid surplus or hybrid deficit, and taxable surplus or taxable deficit of the taxpayer in respect of another taxpayer, where the taxpayer or, if the taxpayer is a partnership, a member of the taxpayer is a foreign affiliate of the other taxpayer, a property that is, or would be, if the taxpayer were a foreign affiliate of the other taxpayer, excluded property (within the meaning assigned by subsection 95(1)) of the taxpayer), to the extent that it is

(i) a superficial loss,

(ii) a loss from the disposition of a debt or other right to receive an amount, unless the debt or right, as the case may be, was acquired by the taxpayer for the purpose of gaining or producing income from a business or property (other than exempt income) or as consideration for the disposition of capital property to a person with whom the taxpayer was dealing at arm's length,

(iii) a loss from the disposition of any personal-use property of the taxpayer (other than listed personal property or a debt referred to in subsection 50(2)), or

(iv) a loss from the disposition of property to

(A) a trust governed by a deferred profit sharing plan, an employees profit sharing plan, a registered disability savings plan, a registered retirement income fund or a TFSA under which the taxpayer is a beneficiary or immediately after the disposition becomes a beneficiary, or

(B) a trust governed by a registered retirement savings plan under which the taxpayer or the taxpayer's spouse or common-law partner is an annuitant or becomes, within 60 days after the end of the taxation year, an annuitant,

is nil;

Canadian Tax Foundation: Magee, *Tax Writeoffs for Investment Losses: Lessons from Cases Involving Victims of Investment Fraud*, 2014 Canadian Tax Journal 1:221–244; Ouelette and Warner, *Estate Planning: US-Resident Beneficiaries of a Canadian Estate — Part 1*, 2014 Canadian Tax Journal 1:197–219; Samuel, *Stopping The Losses: The Application Of Stop-Loss Rules To Transactions Involving Foreign Affiliates*, 2010 Canadian Tax Journal 4:897–925; Katz and Haber, *The Principal Residence Exemption*, 2001 Canadian Tax Journal 4:990–1020; Wong, *Current Cases: Federal Court of Appeal — Allowable Capital Losses on the Disposition of Debt: Loans Versus Guarantees (The Queen v. Byram, 99 DTC 5117 and Cadillac Fairview Corp. v. R., 99 DTC 5121)*, 1999 Canadian Tax Journal 4:945–952.

(*h*) where the taxpayer is a corporation, its loss otherwise determined from the disposition at any time in a taxation year of shares of the capital stock of a corporation (in this paragraph referred to as the "controlled corporation") that was controlled, directly or indirectly in any manner whatever, by it at any time in the year, is its loss therefrom otherwise determined less the amount, if any, by which

(i) all amounts added under paragraph 53(1)(*f*.1) to the cost to a corporation, other than the controlled corporation, of property disposed of to that corporation by the controlled corporation that were added to the cost of the property during the period while the controlled corporation was controlled by the taxpayer and that can reasonably be attributed to losses on the property that accrued during the period while the controlled corporation was controlled by the taxpayer,

exceeds

(ii) all amounts by which losses have been reduced by virtue of this paragraph in respect of dispositions before that time of shares of the capital stock of the controlled corporation; and

(*i*) where at a particular time a taxpayer has disposed of a share of the capital stock of a corporation that was at any time a prescribed venture capital corporation or a prescribed labour-sponsored venture capital corporation or a share of the capital stock of a taxable Canadian corporation that was held in a prescribed stock savings plan or of a property substituted for such a share, the taxpayer's loss from the disposition thereof shall be deemed to be the amount, if any, by which

(i) the loss otherwise determined

exceeds

(ii) the amount, if any, by which

(A) the amount of prescribed assistance that the taxpayer (or a person with whom the taxpayer was not dealing at arm's length) received or is entitled to receive in respect of the share

exceeds

(B) the total of all amounts determined under subparagraph (i) in respect of any disposition of the share or of the property substituted for the share before the particular time by the taxpayer or by a person with whom the taxpayer was not dealing at arm's length.

(*j*) (Repealed by 1986, c. 6, s. 18(3).)

Editorial Note: S. 40(2) sets out a number of provisions which override the general rules in s. 40(1) for the computation of a capital gain or loss, or a reserve for proceeds not due. Each of these overrides is described below by reference to the paragraph in which it appears.

(a) No Reserve: A taxpayer cannot claim a reserve under s. 40(1)(*a*)(iii) if: i) the taxpayer is either not resident in Canada at the end of the year or is exempt from tax; ii) the property was sold to a corporation which was controlled, directly or indirectly, by the taxpayer, or which controls the taxpayer; or iii) the property was sold to a partnership in which the taxpayer is a majority interest partner. Despite the fact that two public corporations collectively owned 50% and a private corporation owned the other 50%, a corporation was found to be indirectly controlled by the public corporations as they had the right to appoint four of five directors (see *International Mercantile Factors Ltd.*, 94 DTC 6365 (F.C.A.)). A taxpayer need not be a partner in a partnership to be a majority interest partner as the definition in s. 248(1) includes all partnership interests owned by affiliated persons.

(b) Principal Residence: The portion of a gain that is taxable is reduced where the taxpayer designates the property sold as a principal residence. S. 54 contains the definition of "principal residence". The definition normally limits the area of the subjacent land to 1/2 hectare, but there is a long line of case law that modifies this limit where zoning does not permit smaller lots. The zoning test is applied annually (see *Cassidy*, 2011 DTC 5160 (F.C.A.)). It is possible for a personal trust to claim the principal residence exemption on the disposition of a property (see Income Tax Folio S1-F3-C2 for the CRA's interpretation of s. 40(2)).

(c) Principal Residence on Farmland: Rather than use the general principal residence exemption, a taxpayer can elect to treat the sum of $1,000 plus $1,000 for each year of ownership as the exempt portion of the gain on the disposition of a principal residence of farmland. Making the election eliminates the otherwise subjective requirement to allocate a portion of the farmland to the principal residence.

(d) Certain Debt Losses: S. 81(1)(*m*) exempts from tax certain interest received on debt taken back on pre-1972 business sales. If a corporate taxpayer realizes a loss on the disposition of such a debt, the loss is reduced by the interest that was not taken into income.

(e.1) Related Party Debt: A loss on the disposition of a debt is deemed to be nil where the vendor, purchaser, and creditor are related. The loss denied is added to the purchaser's adjusted cost base of the property under s. 53(1)(*f*.1). In applying this test, the expanded definition of relationship in s. 80(2)(*j*) applies to look through partnerships and trusts to their partners and beneficiaries.

(e.2)(e.3) Commercial Debt Obligation: A taxpayer's loss on a commercial debt obligation is reduced where part of the consideration received is another commercial debt obligation. Paragraph 40(2)(*e*.3) may modify this rule where the loss arises on a commercial debt obligation issued by a foreign affiliate. "Commercial debt obligation" is defined in s. 80(1) as one on which interest is deductible or would be deductible if the obligation bore interest.

(g) Superficial Losses: A superficial loss and a loss on a debt that was not acquired for the purposes of earning income are deemed to be nil. S. 54 defines "superficial loss" which applies only to individuals. A superficial loss increases the adjusted cost base of the property to the purchaser under s. 53(1)(*f*). A loss was allowed on the disposition of non-interest bearing debt where the creditor was an indirect shareholder in the debtor, as there was a connection between the loan and the potential for receiving dividends (see *Byram*, 99 DTC 5117 (F.C.A.)). A loss on honouring a guarantee of a loan made to a corporation owned by the taxpayer's son was allowed, as one of the purposes of the guarantee was to permit the corporation to pay amounts it owed to a corporation owned by the guarantor (see *Neil MacCallum*, 2011 DTC 1225 (T.C.C.)). A related party loan of $115,000 was found to be made for the purposes of earning income where the lender was entitled only to a fee of $6,000 at the end of the loan's term (see *Russell Scott*, 2010 DTC 1273 (T.C.C.)).

(h) Loss on Shares: A corporation's loss on the disposition of shares of a controlled corporation is reduced to the extent that the controlled corporation, during the period it was controlled, transferred property to another corporation (the transferee), and a stop-loss rule applied to deny that loss and add it to the adjusted cost base of the property to the transferee. As a decline in the value of property owned by a corporation is reflected both in the property itself and in the value of the shares of the corporation, this rule ensures the stop-loss rule in s. 40(2)(*e*.1) cannot be avoided by transferring shares of the company owning the property rather than the property itself.

(i) Venture Capital and Other Shares: An investment in certain securities may qualify for government assistance which is prescribed as not reducing the adjusted cost base of the property. A loss realized on such property is reduced to the extent that the taxpayer received such prescribed assistance.

History: S. 40(2)(*b*), the description of B was replaced by S.C. 2017, c. 33, s. 10(1), applicable in respect of dispositions that occur after October 2, 2016, and formerly read:

B is one plus the number of taxation years that end after the acquisition date for which the property was the taxpayer's principal residence and during which the taxpayer was resident in Canada,

S. 40(2)(*a*)(iii) was replaced by S.C. 2013, c. 40, s. 19(1), in force December 12, 2013, and formerly read:

(iii) the purchaser of the property sold is a partnership in which the taxpayer was, immediately after the sale, a majority interest partner;

S. 40(2)(*e.1*) was replaced by S.C. 2013, c. 34, s. 60(1), applicable in respect of dispositions that occur after August 19, 2011.

Any assessment of a taxpayer's tax, interest and penalties payable under the Act for any taxation year that ends before June 26, 2013 that would, in the absence of this section, be precluded because of subsections 152(4) to (5) of the Act shall be made to the extent necessary to take into account the amendments by S.C. 2013, c. 34, s. 54 to 89.

S. 40(2)(*e.1*) formerly read:

(*e*.1) a taxpayer's loss, if any, from the disposition at any time to a particular person or partnership of an obligation that was, immediately after that time, payable by another person or partnership to the particular person or partnership is nil where the taxpayer, the particular person or partnership and the other person or partnership are related to each other at that time or would be related to each other at that time if paragraph 80(2)(*j*) applied for the purpose of this paragraph;

S. 40(2)(*e.2*), the portion before the formula was replaced by S.C. 2013, c. 34, s. 60(2), applicable in respect of settlements and extinguishments that occur after August 19, 2011.

See the application provision above for the extension of assessment periods to take into account the amendments by S.C. 2013, c. 34, s. 54 to 89.

S. 40(2)(*e.2*), the portion before the formula formerly read:

(*e*.2) a taxpayer's loss on the settlement or extinguishment of a particular commercial obligation (in this paragraph having the meaning assigned by subsection 80(1)) issued by a person or partnership and payable to the taxpayer shall, where any part of the consideration given by the person or partnership for the settlement or extinguishment of the particular obligation consists of one or more other commercial obligations issued by the person or partnership to the taxpayer, be deemed to be the amount determined by the formula

S. 40(2)(*e.3*) was added by S.C. 2013, c. 34, s. 60(3), applicable in respect of settlements and extinguishments that occur after August 19, 2011.

See the application provision above for the extension of assessment periods to take into account the amendments by S.C. 2013, c. 34, s. 54 to 89.

S. 40(2)(*g*), the portion before subparagraph (i) was replaced by S.C. 2013, c. 34, s. 60(4), applicable in respect of dispositions that occur after August 19, 2011.

See the application provision above for the extension of assessment periods to take into account the amendments by S.C. 2013, c. 34, s. 54 to 89.

S. 40(2)(*g*), the portion before subparagraph (i) formerly read:

(*g*) a taxpayer's loss, if any, from the disposition of a property, to the extent that it is

S. 40(2)(*b*), subparagraph (i) of the description of D was replaced by S.C. 2013, c. 34, s. 102, in force June 26, 2013, and formerly read:

(i) where the acquisition date is before February 23, 1994 and the taxpayer or a spouse or common-law partner of the taxpayer elected under subsection 110.6(19) in respect of the property or an interest therein that was owned, immediately before the disposition, by the taxpayer, 4/3 of the lesser of

(A) the total of all amounts each of which is the taxable capital gain of the taxpayer or of a spouse or common-law partner of the taxpayer that would have resulted from an election by the taxpayer or spouse or common-law partner under subsection 110.6(19) in respect of the property or interest if

(I) this Act were read without reference to subsection 110.6(20), and

(II) the amount designated in the election were equal to the amount, if any, by which the fair market value of the property or interest at the end of February 22, 1994 exceeds the amount determined by the formula

$$E - 1.1F$$

where

E is the amount designated in the election that was made in respect of the property or interest, and

F is the fair market value of the property or interest at the end of February 22, 1994, and

(B) the total of all amounts each of which is the taxable capital gain of the taxpayer or of a spouse or common-law partner of the taxpayer that would have resulted from an election that was made under subsection 110.6(19) in respect of the property or interest if the property were the principal residence of neither the taxpayer nor the spouse or common-law partner for each particular taxation year unless the property was designated, in a return of income for the taxation year that includes February 22, 1994 or for a preceding taxation year, to be the principal residence of either of them for the particular taxation year, and

S. 40(2)(*a*)(iii) was added by S.C. 2013, c. 34, s. 183(2), applicable to sales that occur after December 20, 2002.

Related Regulations: 6700; 6700.1; 6700.2; 6701; 6702; 6705.

Related Sections: S. 40(1) General rules; s. 40(4) Disposal of principal residence to spouse or trust for spouse; 40(6.1) Principal residence — property owned at end of 2016; s. 53(2) Amounts to be deducted; s. 54, "principal residence", "superficial loss"; s. 69(5) Winding-up of corporation; s. 85(4) Loss from disposition to controlled corporation; s. 87(2)(*kk*) Disposition of shares of controlled corporation; s. 248(1), "disposition"; s. 256(5.1) Control in fact.

Canadian Tax Foundation: Woolley, *Principal Residences - Selected Issues: An Update*, 2017 British Columbia Tax Conference 7A:1–41; Bernstein and Santia, *Principal-Residence Exemption: Trusts and Non-Residents*, 2017 Canadian Tax Highlights 25(1):6–7.

Tax Profile: January 2012 — The Top 10 Cases of 2011; July 2011 — Personal Trusts and Cottage Properties Residence — Pitfalls and Planning; January 2009 — Market Meltdown — Capital Loss Utilization; July 2007 — Canadian Tax Traps; May 2004 — The Stop-Loss Rules; March 2004 — Loss Utilization By Individuals.

Tax Topics: No. 2332, November 17, 2016, A Primer on the New Principal Residence Rules; No. 2148, Principal Residence Exemption And Zoning Requirements: The Half-Hectare Rule Made Twice As Clear; No. 2082, Principal Residence Exemption — Excess Lands.

Income Tax Folios: S4-F8-C1 Business Investment Losses.

Primary — S1-F3-C2 Principal Residence; S3-F9-C1 Lottery Winnings, Miscellaneous Receipts, and Income (and Losses) from Crime.

Interpretation Bulletins: *Primary* — IT-291R3 Transfer of property to a corporation under subsection 85(1). *Secondary* — IT-95R Foreign exchange gains and losses; IT-124R6 Contributions to registered retirement savings plans; IT-159R3 Capital debts established to be bad debts; IT-218R Profit, capital gains and losses from the sale of real estate, including farmland and inherited land and conversion of real estate from capital property to inventory and vice versa; IT-268R4 Inter vivos transfer of farm property to child; IT-273R2 Government assistance — General comments; IT-373R2 (Consolid.) Woodlots.

Tax Window Files: Principal residence, land, *July 13, 2017*, CRA Document No. 2017-0702001E5.

Cases: The taxpayer sold his home with 2.43 hectares of land. The CRA denied a principal residence exemption beyond a half hectare since, just prior to the sale, the land was rezoned allowing it to be subdivided. However, exemption eligibility is determined annually and the recent rezoning did not affect his eligibility for previous years. *Cassidy v. The Queen*, 2011 DTC 5160 (F.C.A.), reversing 2010 DTC 1336 (T.C.C.)

The taxpayers participated extensively in sports lotteries using a methodology that increased their potential payout and risk significantly. Although they lost 95% of the time, they had net winnings of $5,523,088. However, they were not professional gamblers who had a system to assess and minimize risks. The winnings were not business income but tax-exempt capital gains. *Leblanc et al. v. The Queen*, 2007 DTC 307 (T.C.C.)

The taxpayer was allowed to claim a capital loss on the disposition of non-interest bearing loans made to a corporation even though the taxpayer was a shareholder of the corporation for only part of the relevant time and a shareholder of its parent corporation for the rest of the time. There was still a connection to the dividend income generating stream. *The Queen v. Byram*, 99 DTC 5117 (F.C.A.), affirming 95 DTC 5069 (F.C.T.D.)

The taxpayer was not allowed to claim a capital loss on amounts paid to extricate several of its subsidiaries from U.S. partnerships and itself from guarantees in respect of the partnerships, because no property was disposed of. *The Cadillac Fairview Corporation Limited v. The Queen*, 99 DTC 5121 (F.C.A.), affirming 97 DTC 405 (T.C.C.)

The taxpayer met the objective test that her entire 32.75-acre parcel of land qualified for principal residence treatment. *Carlile v. The Queen*, 95 DTC 5483 (F.C.A.), reversing 93 DTC 5336 (F.C.T.D.)

The application date of the income earning test under s. 40(2)(*g*) was the date when a collateral was furnished by a taxpayer to a corporation to enable it to become successful again and pay dividends. The taxpayer could therefore deduct the capital loss arising from the insolvency of that corporation. *National Developments Ltd. v. The Queen*, 94 DTC 1061 (T.C.C.)

When the only reason for the taxpayer to have guaranteed the bank loan of a corporation incorporated for the benefit of his children was to facilitate the highly leveraged transfer of his business assets to his children, the taxpayer could not deduct a capital loss. *W. F. Botkin Construction Ltd. v. The Queen*, 93 DTC 448 (T.C.C.)

A taxpayer could claim the principal residence exemption on the sale of 8.9 acres of land which at the time of purchase in 1966 a zoning by-law had compelled him to buy in its entirety. He was not allowed at any time to retain the minimum lot size of 3 acres prevailing in 1966 and sell the remaining acres. *Augart v. The Queen*, 93 DTC 5205 (F.C.A.), reversing 92 DTC 6610 (F.C.T.D.).

► 40(3) ◄

(3) Deemed gain where amounts to be deducted from adjusted cost base exceed cost plus amounts to be added to adjusted cost base. Where

(*a*) the total of all amounts required by subsection 53(2) (except paragraph 53(2)(*c*)) to be deducted in computing the adjusted cost base to a taxpayer of any property at any time in a taxation year

exceeds

(*b*) the total of

(i) the cost to the taxpayer of the property determined for the purpose of computing the adjusted cost base to the taxpayer of that property at that time, and

(ii) all amounts required by subsection 53(1) to be added to the cost to the taxpayer of the property in computing the adjusted cost base to the taxpayer of that property at that time,

the following rules apply:

(*c*) subject to paragraph 93(1)(*b*), the amount of the excess is deemed to be a gain of the taxpayer for the year from a disposition at that time of the property,

(*d*) for the purposes of section 93 and subsections 116(6) and (6.1), the property is deemed to have been disposed of by the taxpayer at that time, and

(*e*) for the purposes of subsection 2(3) and sections 110.6 and 150, the property is deemed to have been disposed of by the taxpayer in the year.

Editorial Note: Subsections 53(1) and (2) provide additions and deductions, respectively, in the computation of the adjusted cost base of a capital property. Under s. 40(3), if the deductions exceed the adjusted cost base (otherwise determined) and the additions, the difference is deemed to be a gain of the taxpayer from a notional disposition of the property. The rule under s. 40(3) does not apply to deductions in computing the adjusted cost base of a partnership interest under s. 53(2)(*c*). However, a similar rule applies under s. 40(3.1) to the interests of limited partners and specified members of a partnership, and s. 40(3.11) calculates the value of the gain.

History: S. 40(3)(*d*) and (*e*) were replaced by S.C. 2017, c. 33, s. 10(2), applicable in respect of gains from dispositions that occur after September 15, 2016, and formerly read:

(*d*) for the purposes of section 93, the property is deemed to have been disposed of by the taxpayer at that time, and

(*e*) for the purposes of section 110.6, the property is deemed to have been disposed of by the taxpayer in the year.

S. 40(3)(*c*) to (*e*) were replaced by S.C. 2013, c. 34, s. 60(5), deemed to have come into force on August 20, 2011.

See the application provision following s. 40(2) for the extension of assessment periods to take into account the amendments by S.C. 2013, c. 34, s. 54 to 89.

S. 40(3)(*c*) to (*e*) formerly read:

(*c*) subject to paragraph 93(1)(*b*), the amount of the excess shall be deemed to be a gain of the taxpayer for the year from a disposition at that time of the property, (*d*) for the purposes of section 93, the definition "foreign accrual property income" in subsection 95(1) and section 110.6, the property shall be deemed to have been disposed of by the taxpayer in the year, and

(*e*) for the purposes of section 93, the amount of the excess shall be deemed to be proceeds of disposition of the property to the taxpayer.

Related Sections: S. 53 Adjustments to cost base — Deemed gain resulting from negative ACB; 116(6) Definition of "excluded property"; 116(6.1) Treaty-exempt property.

Interpretation Bulletins: *Secondary* — IT-278R2 Death of a partner or of a retired partner.

Cases: The taxpayer received a cash payment for reducing his interest in a partnership. At the same time, one of the other partners increased its investment in the partnership by contributing capital so that the total capital of the partnership prior to and after these transactions was the same. The cash received by the taxpayer was not a distribution of capital but proceeds of disposition of an interest in the partnership. *Stursberg v. The Queen*, 93 DTC 5271 (F.C.A.), affirming 91 DTC 5607 (F.C.T.D.), and 90 DTC 1159 (T.C.C.).

► 40(3.1) ◄

(3.1) Deemed gain for certain partners. Where, at the end of a fiscal period of a partnership, a member of the partnership is a limited partner of the partnership, or is a member of the partnership who was a specified member of the partnership at all times since becoming a member, except where the member's partnership interest was held by the member on February 22, 1994 and is an excluded interest at the end of the fiscal period,

(*a*) the amount determined under subsection (3.11) is deemed to be a gain from the disposition, at the end of the fiscal period, of the member's interest in the partnership; and

(*b*) for the purposes of subsection 2(3), section 110.6, subsections 116(6) and (6.1) and section 150, the interest is deemed to have been disposed of by the member at that time.

Editorial Note: A member of a partnership (including a professional partnership) has a deemed gain equal to the negative ACB of its interest (as calculated in s. 40(3.11)) if, at the end of the partnership's fiscal period, the member is either (a) a limited partner (unless, of course, one takes part in the control of the business and thereby loses limited liability protection; see, for example, *Foley*, 2003 DTC 1320 (TCC)), including pursuant to special rules in s. 40(3.14) (special arrangements, other than LLPs, designed to limit liability or losses); or (b) was at *all times since becoming a partner* a "specified member" of the partnership (basically inactive — see the definition of "specified member" in s. 248(1)). Anti-avoidance rules (s. 40(3.131)) may deem specified-partner-at-all-times status where such status is avoided to escape this subsection. The deemed gain is added to partnership ACB, *per* s. 53(1)(*e*)(vi), in the subsequent fiscal period. Subsection 40(3.12) may provide some relief where a positive partnership ACB subsequently arises. Grandfathering may apply for interests held by the member on February 22, 1994, if they are "excluded interests", *per* s. 40(3.15), at the end of the fiscal period. If a former partner or an heir of a deceased partner repays all or part of the deficit and the payment would have been a capital contribution if the former partner was still a partnership member, then s. 100(5) deems the taxpayer to have a capital loss.

See also the editorial notes for s. 40(3) and (3.11).

History: S. 40(3.1)(*b*) was replaced by S.C. 2017, c. 33, s. 10(3), applicable in respect of gains from dispositions that occur after September 15, 2016, and formerly read:

(*b*) for the purpose of section 110.6, the interest is deemed to have been disposed of by the member at that time.

Related Sections: S. 40(3) Deemed gain where amounts to be deducted from adjusted cost base exceed cost plus amounts to be added to adjusted cost base; s. 40(3.11) Amount of gain; s. 40(3.14) Limited partner; s. 40(3.15) Excluded interest; 116(6) Definition of "excluded property"; 116(6.1) Treaty-exempt property; s. 248(1), "specified member".

Canadian Tax Foundation: Ewens, *Tax Issues Affecting Partnerships*, 1997 Conference Report 8:1–85.

Tax Topics: No. 1921, Ontario Limited Liability Partnerships — A Hidden Danger for Many.

► 40(3.11) ◄

(3.11) Amount of gain. For the purpose of subsection (3.1), the amount determined at any time under this subsection in respect of a member's interest in a partnership is the amount determined by the formula

A - B

where

A is the total of

(*a*) all amounts required by subsection 53(2) to be deducted in computing the adjusted cost base to the member of the interest in the partnership at that time, and

(*b*) if the member is a member of a professional partnership, and that time is the end of the fiscal period of the partnership, the amount referred to in subparagraph 53(2)(*c*)(i) in respect of the taxpayer for that fiscal period; and

B is the total of

(*a*) the cost to the member of the interest determined for the purpose of computing the adjusted cost base to the member of the interest at that time,

(*b*) all amounts required by subsection 53(1) to be added to the cost to the member of the interest in computing the adjusted cost base to the member of the interest at that time, and

(*c*) if the member is a member of a professional partnership, and that time is the end of the fiscal period of the partnership, the amount referred to in subparagraph 53(1)(*e*)(i) in respect of the taxpayer for that fiscal period.

Editorial Note: Subsection 40(3.11) provides the calculation of negative ACB for the purpose of s. 40(3.1). Since the gain is calculated at the end of the fiscal period of the partnership, the addition/reduction for current year income/loss is ignored, since these adjustments relate to income or loss "before that time" (see s. 53(1)(*e*)(i) and 53(2)(*c*)(i)). The lag relating to income may result in negative cost base, e.g., due to distributions during the year; thus, consideration should be given to loans rather than distributions.

Amendments applicable to fiscal taxation years ending after November 2001 partially remedy this deficiency by adding variables A(b) and B(c) to the formula in this subsection, picking up current-year loss/income. These provisions apply to members of "professional partnerships" (*per* s. 40(3.111). Professional partnerships are partnerships where one or more persons carry on the practice of a profession governed or regulated under provincial or federal law. However, since partial-shield partnerships are carved out of limited partner status, *per* s. 40(3.14)(*a*), the amendments have significance to "full-shield" professional partnerships.

History: S. 40(3.11), the descriptions of A and B were replaced by S.C. 2013, c. 34, s. 183(3), applicable to fiscal periods that end after November 2001, and formerly read:

A is the total of all amounts required by subsection 53(2) to be deducted in computing the adjusted cost base to the member of the interest in the partnership at that time, and

B is the total of

(*a*) the cost to the member of the interest determined for the purpose of computing the adjusted cost base to the member of the interest at that time, and

(*b*) all amounts required by subsection 53(1) to be added to the cost to the member of the interest in computing the adjusted cost base to the member of the interest at that time.

Related Sections: S. 40(3) Deemed gain where amounts to be deducted from adjusted cost base exceed cost plus amounts to be added to adjusted cost base.

► 40(3.111) ◄

(3.111) Meaning of "professional partnership". In this section, "professional partnership" means a partnership through which one or more persons carry on the practice of a profession that is governed or regulated under a law of Canada or a province.

History: S. 40(3.111) was added by S.C. 2013, c. 34, s. 183(4), applicable to fiscal periods that end after November 2001.

▶ 40(3.12) ◀

(3.12) Deemed loss for certain partners. If a corporation, an individual (other than a trust) or a graduated rate estate (each of which is referred to in this subsection as the "taxpayer") is a member of a partnership at the end of a fiscal period of the partnership, the taxpayer is deemed to have a loss from the disposition at that time of the member's interest in the partnership equal to the amount that the taxpayer elects in the taxpayer's return of income under this Part for the taxation year that includes that time, not exceeding the lesser of

(*a*) the amount, if any, by which

(i) the total of all amounts each of which was an amount deemed by subsection (3.1) to be a gain of the taxpayer from a disposition of the interest before that time

exceeds

(ii) the total of all amounts each of which was an amount deemed by this subsection to be a loss of the taxpayer from a disposition of the interest before that time, and

(*b*) the adjusted cost base to the taxpayer of the interest at that time.

Editorial Note: S. 40(3.12) provides limited relief from s. 40(3.1): a corporation, individual or a testamentary trust (taxation years before 2016) or a graduated rate estate (post-2015 taxation years) which is a member of a partnership at the end of a fiscal period of the partnership may be able to elect to treat a positive adjusted cost base ("ACB") as a capital loss from the disposition of the partnership interest at that time. See subsection 248(1) for a definition of a graduated rate estate. (The CRA has stated that the election is not open to a partnership that is a member of a partnership; see CRA Document No. 2012-0449701E5.) The loss may not exceed previous gains required to be reported under s. 40(3.1) (in excess of previous losses claimed under s. 40(3.12)). The loss (which reduces partnership ACB, per s. 53(2)(*c*)(i.1)) may then be carried back pursuant to the normal rules. S. 40(3.13) provides rules against the artificial creation of cost base, e.g., where a loan is made by the partnership as part of a series of contributions to the partnership.

History: S. 40(3.12), the portion before paragraph (*a*) was replaced by S.C. 2014, c. 39, s. 11(3), applicable to the 2016 and subsequent taxation years, and formerly read:

(3.12) *Deemed loss for certain partners.* Where a corporation, an individual (other than a trust) or a testamentary trust (each of which is referred to in this subsection as the "taxpayer") is a member of a partnership at the end of a fiscal period of the partnership, the taxpayer shall be deemed to have a loss from the disposition at that time of the member's interest in the partnership equal to the amount that the taxpayer elects in the taxpayer's return of income under this Part for the taxation year that includes that time, not exceeding the lesser of

Related Sections: S. 40(3) Deemed gain where amounts to be deducted from adjusted cost base exceed cost plus amounts to be added to adjusted cost base.

▶ 40(3.13) ◀

(3.13) Artificial transactions. For the purpose of applying section 53 at any time to a member of a partnership who would be a member described in subsection (3.1) of the partnership if the fiscal period of the partnership that includes that time ended at that time, where at any time after February 21, 1994 the member of the partnership makes a contribution of capital to the partnership and

(*a*) the partnership or a person or partnership with whom the partnership does not deal at arm's length

(i) makes a loan to the member or to a person with whom the member does not deal at arm's length, or

(ii) pays an amount as, on account of, in lieu of payment of or in satisfaction of, a distribution of the member's share of the partnership profits or partnership capital, or

(*b*) the member or a person with whom the member does not deal at arm's length becomes indebted to the partnership or a person or partnership with whom the partnership does not deal at arm's length,

and it is established, by subsequent events or otherwise, that the loan, payment or indebtedness, as the case may be, was made or arose as part of a series of contributions and such loans, payments or other transactions, the contribution of capital shall be deemed not to have been made.

▶ 40(3.131) ◀

(3.131) Specified member of a partnership. Where it can reasonably be considered that one of the main reasons that a member of a partnership was not a specified member of the partnership at all times since becoming a member of the partnership is to avoid the application of subsection (3.1) to the member's interest in the partnership, the member is deemed for the purpose of that subsection to have been a specified member of the partnership at all times since becoming a member of the partnership.

▶ 40(3.14) ◀

(3.14) Limited partner. For the purpose of subsection (3.1), a member of a partnership at a particular time is a limited partner of the partnership at that time if, at that time or within 3 years after that time,

(*a*) by operation of any law governing the partnership arrangement, the liability of the member as a member of the partnership is limited (except by operation of a provision of a statute of Canada or a province that limits the member's liability only for debts, obligations and liabilities of the partnership, or any member of the partnership, arising from negligent acts or omissions, from misconduct or from fault of another member of the partnership or an employee, an agent or a representative of the partnership in the course of the partnership business while the partnership is a limited liability partnership);

(*b*) the member or a person not dealing at arm's length with the member is entitled, either immediately or in the future and either absolutely or contingently, to receive an amount or to obtain a benefit that would be described in paragraph 96(2.2)(*d*) if that paragraph were read without reference to subparagraphs (ii) and (vi);

(*c*) one of the reasons for the existence of the member who owns the interest

(i) can reasonably be considered to be to limit the liability of any person with respect to that interest, and

(ii) cannot reasonably be considered to be to permit any person who has an interest in the member to carry on the person's business (other than an investment business) in the most effective manner; or

(*d*) there is an agreement or other arrangement for the disposition of an interest in the partnership and one of the main reasons for the agreement or arrangement can reasonably be considered to be to attempt to avoid the application of this subsection to the member.

History: S. 40(3.14)(*a*) was replaced by S.C. 2013, c. 34, s. 183(5), deemed to have come into force on June 21, 2001, and formerly read:

(*a*) by operation of any law governing the partnership arrangement, the liability of the member as a member of the partnership is limited (except by operation of a provision of a statute of Canada or a province that limits the member's liability only for debts, obligations and liabilities of the partnership, or any member of the partnership, arising from negligent acts or omissions or misconduct that another member of the partnership or an employee, agent or representative of the partnership commits in the course of the partnership business while the partnership is a limited liability partnership);

Tax Topics: No. 1921, Ontario Limited Liability Partnerships — A Hidden Danger for Many.

▶ 40(3.15) ◀

(3.15) Excluded interest. For the purpose of subsection (3.1), an excluded interest in a partnership at any time means an interest in a partnership that actively carries on a business that was carried on by it throughout the period beginning February 22, 1994 and ending at that time, or that earns income from a property that was owned by it throughout that period, unless in that period there was a substantial contribution of capital to the partnership or a substantial increase in the indebtedness of the partnership.

Editorial Note: This subsection may provide grandfathering relief from s. 40(3.1) in respect of an "excluded interest". In addition to the requirements in s. (3.15) itself, the partnership interest must be held by the member on February 22, 1994. Grandfathered status may be lost if the partnership interest is transferred, as there are only limited provisions for successor members (see s. 40(3.18)). Substantial contribution of capital or increases of partnership indebtedness may also adversely affect grandfathered status, although s. (3.16) details circumstances pursuant to which amounts will not be considered to be substantial. These largely relate to agreements or offering documents entered into or filed before February 22, 1994; however, s. 40(3.16)(*d*) stipulates that an amount will not be considered to be substantial where it was used for an activity that was carried on by the partnership on February 22, 1994 other than a "significant expansion" of the activity.

Related Sections: S. 40(3) Deemed gain where amounts to be deducted from adjusted cost base exceed cost plus amounts to be added to adjusted cost base.

▶ 40(3.16) ◀

(3.16) Amounts considered not to be substantial. For the purpose of subsection (3.15), an amount will be considered not to be substantial where

(*a*) the amount

(i) was raised pursuant to the terms of a written agreement entered into by a partnership before February 22, 1994 to issue an interest in the partnership and was expended on expenditures contemplated by the agreement before 1995 (or before March 2, 1995 in the case of amounts expended to acquire a film production prescribed for the purpose of subparagraph 96(2.2)(*d*)(ii) the principal photography of which or, in the case of such a production that is a television series, one episode of the series, commences before 1995 and the production is completed before March 2, 1995, or an interest in one or more partnerships all or substantially all of the property of which is such a film production),

(ii) was raised pursuant to the terms of a written agreement (other than an agreement referred to in subparagraph (i)) entered into by a partnership before February 22, 1994 and was expended on expenditures contemplated by the agreement before 1995 (or before March 2, 1995 in the case of amounts expended to acquire a film production prescribed for the purpose of subparagraph 96(2.2)(*d*)(ii) the principal photography of which or, in the case of such a production that is a television series, one episode of the series, commences before 1995 and the production is completed before March 2, 1995, or an interest in one or more partnerships all or substantially all of the property of which is such a film production),

(iii) was used by the partnership before 1995 (or before March 2, 1995 in the case of amounts expended to acquire a film production prescribed for the purpose of subparagraph 96(2.2)(*d*)(ii) the principal photography of which or, in the case of such a production that is a television series, one episode of the series, commences before 1995 and the production is completed before March 2, 1995, or an interest in one or more partnerships all or substantially all of the property of which is such a film production) to make an expenditure required to be made pursuant to the terms of a written agreement entered into by the partnership before February 22, 1994, or

(iv) was used to repay a loan, debt or contribution of capital that had been received or incurred in respect of any such expenditure;

(*b*) the amount was raised before 1995 pursuant to the terms of a prospectus, preliminary prospectus, offering memorandum or registration statement filed before February 22, 1994 with a public authority in Canada pursuant to and in accordance with the securities legislation of Canada or of a province and, where required by law, accepted for filing by the public authority, and expended before 1995 (or before March 2, 1995 in the case of amounts expended to acquire a film production prescribed for the purpose of subparagraph 96(2.2)(*d*)(ii), or an interest in one or more partnerships all or substantially all of the property of which is such a film production) on expenditures contemplated by the document that was filed before February 22, 1994;

(*c*) the amount was raised before 1995 pursuant to the terms of an offering memorandum distributed as part of an offering of securities where

(i) the memorandum contained a complete or substantially complete description of the securities contemplated in the offering as well as the terms and conditions of the offering,

(ii) the memorandum was distributed before February 22, 1994,

(iii) solicitations in respect of the sale of the securities contemplated by the memorandum were made before February 22, 1994,

(iv) the sale of the securities was substantially in accordance with the memorandum, and

(v) the funds are expended in accordance with the memorandum before 1995 (except that the funds may be expended before March 2, 1995 in the case of a partnership all or substantially all of the property of which is a film production prescribed for the purpose of subparagraph 96(2.2)(*d*)(ii) the principal photography of which or, in the case of such a production that is a television series, one episode of the series, commences before 1995 and the production is completed before March 2, 1995, or an interest in one or more partnerships all or substantially all of the property of which is such a film production); or

(*d*) the amount was used for an activity that was carried on by the partnership on February 22, 1994 but not for a significant expansion of the activity nor for the acquisition or production of a film production.

Editorial Note: See the editorial note to s. 40(3.15).

▶ 40(3.17) ◀

(3.17) Whether carrying on business before February 22, 1994. For the purpose of subsection (3.15), a partnership in respect of which paragraph (3.16)(*a*), (*b*) or (*c*) applies shall be considered to have actively carried on the business, or earned income from the property, contemplated in the document referred to in that paragraph throughout the period beginning February 22, 1994 and ending on the earlier of the closing date, if any, stipulated in the document and January 1, 1995.

▶ 40(3.18) ◀

(3.18) Deemed partner. For the purpose of subsection (3.1), a member of a partnership who acquired an interest in the partnership after February 22, 1994 shall be deemed to have held the interest on February 22, 1994 where the member acquired the interest

(*a*) in circumstances in which

(i) paragraph 70(6)(*d*.1) applied,

(ii) where the member is an individual, the member's spouse or common-law partner held the partnership interest on February 22, 1994,

(iii) where the member is a trust, the taxpayer by whose will the trust was created held the partnership interest on February 22, 1994, and

(iv) the partnership interest was, immediately before the death of the spouse or common-law partner or the taxpayer, as the case may be, an excluded interest;

(*b*) in circumstances in which

(i) paragraph 70(9.2)(*c*) applied,

(ii) the member's parent held the partnership interest on February 22, 1994, and

(iii) the partnership interest was, immediately before the parent's death, an excluded interest;

(*c*) in circumstances in which

(i) paragraph 70(9.3)(*e*) applied,

(ii) the trust referred to in subsection 70(9.3) or the taxpayer by whose will the trust was created held the partnership interest on February 22, 1994, and

(iii) the partnership interest was, immediately before the death of the spouse or common-law partner referred to in subsection 70(9.3), an excluded interest; or

(*d*) before 1995 pursuant to a document referred to in subparagraph (3.16)(*a*)(i) or paragraph (3.16)(*b*) or (*c*).

▶ 40(3.19) ◀

(3.19) Non-application of subsection (3). Subsection (3) does not apply in any case where subsection (3.1) applies.

▶ 40(3.2) ◀

(3.2) Non-application of subsection (3.1). Subsection (3.1) does not apply in any case where paragraph 98(1)(*c*) or 98.1(1)(*c*) applies.

▶ 40(3.21) ◀

(3.21) Deemed capital gain under section 180.01. If, in respect of a taxation year, a taxpayer has made an election under subsection 180.01(1), the amount deemed to be a capital gain under paragraph 180.01(2)(*b*) is deemed to be a gain from the disposition of property for the taxation year.

History: S. 40(3.21) was added by S.C. 2010, c. 25, s. 8(1), deemed to have come into force on March 4, 2010.

▶ 40(3.3) ◀

(3.3) When subsection (3.4) applies. Subsection (3.4) applies when

(*a*) a corporation, trust or partnership (in this subsection and subsection (3.4) referred to as the "transferor") disposes of a particular capital property — other than depreciable property of a prescribed class and other than, for the purposes of computing the exempt surplus or exempt deficit, hybrid surplus or hybrid deficit, and taxable surplus or taxable deficit of a foreign affiliate of a taxpayer, in respect of the taxpayer, where the transferor is the affiliate or is a partnership of which the affiliate is a member, property that is, or would be, if the transferor were a foreign affiliate of the taxpayer, excluded property (within the meaning assigned by subsection 95(1)) of the transferor — otherwise than in a disposition described in any of paragraphs (*c*) to (*g*) of the definition "superficial loss" in section 54;

(*b*) during the period that begins 30 days before and ends 30 days after the disposition, the transferor or a person affiliated with the transferor acquires a property (in this subsection and subsection (3.4) referred to as the "substituted property") that is, or is identical to, the particular property; and

(*c*) at the end of the period, the transferor or a person affiliated with the transferor owns the substituted property.

Editorial Note: Similar stop-loss rules are found in s. 13(21.2) for dispositions of depreciable capital property, s. 14(12) for dispositions of eligible capital property (prior to 2017), and s. 18(15) for property held in an adventure or concern in the nature of trade.

History: S. 40(3.3)(*a*) was replaced by S.C. 2013, c. 34, s. 60(6), applicable in respect of dispositions that occur after August 19, 2011.

See the application for s. 40(2)(*e.1*) for the extension of assessment periods to take into account the amendments by S.C. 2013, c. 34, s. 54 to 89.

S. 40(3.3)(*a*) formerly read:

(*a*) a corporation, trust or partnership (in this subsection and subsection (3.4) referred to as the "transferor") disposes of a particular capital property (other than depreciable property of a prescribed class) otherwise than in a disposition described in any of paragraphs (*c*) to (*g*) of the definition "superficial loss" in section 54;

Canadian Tax Foundation: Man and Tse, *Tax in Troubled Times — Opportunities and Techniques for Loss Utilization*, 2009 British Columbia Tax Conference 5:1–40; Goodman and Cuperfain, *Life Insurance Planning*, 2001 Prairie Provinces Tax Conference 12:1–40.

Tax Profile: January 2009 — Market Meltdown — Capital Loss Utilization; May 2004 — The Stop-Loss Rules.

Tax Window Files: FX Loss on Disposition of Cash, *International & Trusts Division, Income Tax Rulings Division, January 6, 2009*, CRA Document No. 2008-0280111I7; Loss Denial Rules, *Technical Interpretation, Reorganizations and Resources Division, August 13, 2008*, CRA Document No.

2008-0274451E5; Stop loss rules for depreciable property, *Technical Interpretation, International & Trusts Division, March 21, 2007*, CRA Document No. 2004-0091061E5.

▶ 40(3.4) ◀

(3.4) Loss on certain properties. If this subsection applies because of subsection (3.3) to a disposition of a particular property,

(*a*) the transferor's loss, if any, from the disposition is deemed to be nil, and

(*b*) the amount of the transferor's loss, if any, from the disposition (determined without reference to paragraph (2)(*g*) and this subsection) is deemed to be a loss of the transferor from a disposition of the particular property at the time that is immediately before the first time, after the disposition,

(i) at which a 30-day period begins throughout which neither the transferor nor a person affiliated with the transferor owns

(A) the substituted property, or

(B) a property that is identical to the substituted property and that was acquired after the day that is 31 days before the period begins,

(ii) at which the property would, if it were owned by the transferor, be deemed by section 128.1 or subsection 149(10) to have been disposed of by the transferor,

(iii) that is immediately before the transferor is subject to a loss restriction event,

(iv) at which the transferor or a person affiliated with the transferor is deemed by section 50 to have disposed of the property, where the substituted property is a debt or a share of the capital stock of a corporation, or

(v) if the transferor is a corporation,

(A) for the purposes of computing the transferor's foreign accrual property income, exempt surplus or exempt deficit, hybrid surplus or hybrid deficit, and taxable surplus or taxable deficit, in respect of a taxpayer for a taxation year of the transferor where the transferor is a foreign affiliate of the taxpayer, at which the liquidation and dissolution of the transferor begins, unless the liquidation and dissolution is

(I) a qualifying liquidation and dissolution (within the meaning assigned by subsection 88(3.1)) of the transferor, or

(II) a designated liquidation and dissolution (within the meaning assigned by subsection 95(1)) of the transferor, and

(B) for any other purposes, at which the winding-up (other than a winding-up to which subsection 88(1) applies) of the transferor begins,

and, for the purpose of paragraph (*b*), where a partnership otherwise ceases to exist at any time after the disposition, the partnership is deemed not to have ceased to exist, and each person who was a member of the partnership immediately before the partnership would, but for this subsection, have ceased to exist is deemed to remain a member of the partnership, until the time that is immediately after the first time described in subparagraphs (*b*)(i) to (v).

Editorial Note: Subsection 40(3.4) applies, generally, where a trust, corporation or partnership disposes of non-depreciable capital property and the transferor or an affiliated person acquires the property or an identical property within 30 days before or 30 days after the disposition, and either the transferor or affiliated person owns such property on the day that is 30 days after the disposition. Where s. 40(3.4) applies, any loss arising from the disposition is denied, but may be realized where one of the events in s. 40(3.4)(*b*) occur.

History: S. 40(3.4)(*b*)(iii) was replaced by S.C. 2013, c. 40, s. 19(2), deemed to have come into force March 21, 2013, and formerly read:

(iii) that is immediately before control of the transferor is acquired by a person or group of persons, where the transferor is a corporation,

S. 40(3.4)(*b*)(v) was replaced by S.C. 2013, c. 34, s. 60(7), applicable in respect of windings-up and liquidations and dissolutions that begin after August 19, 2011.

See the application for s. 40(2)(*e.1*) for the extension of assessment periods to take into account the amendments by S.C. 2013, c. 34, s. 54 to 89.

S. 40(3.4)(*b*)(v) formerly read:

(v) at which the winding-up of the transferor begins (other than a winding-up to which subsection 88(1) applies), where the transferor is a corporation,

Related Sections: S. 13(21.2) Loss on certain transfers; s. 14(12) Loss on certain transfers; s. 18(15) Loss on certain properties; s. 40(3.5) Deemed identical property; s. 251.2(2) Loss restriction event.

Canadian Tax Foundation: Samuel, *Stopping The Losses: The Application Of Stop-Loss Rules To Transactions Involving Foreign Affiliates*, 2010 Canadian Tax Journal 4:897–925.

Tax Profile: January 2009 — Market Meltdown — Capital Loss Utilization; May 2004 — The Stop-Loss Rules.

Tax Topics: No. 2065, Exchangeable Shares: Not Just Rights to Foreign Shares.

Interpretation Bulletins: *Secondary* — IT-291R3 Transfer of property to a corporation under subsection 85(1).

Tax Window Files: Interaction of subsections 100(4) and 40(3.4), *November 12, 2009*, CRA Document No. 2009-0315431I7; FX Loss on Disposition of Cash, *International & Trusts Division, Income Tax Rulings Division, January 6, 2009*, CRA Document No. 2008-0280111I7.

▶ 40(3.5) ◀

(3.5) Deemed identical property. For the purposes of subsections (3.3) and (3.4),

(*a*) a right to acquire a property (other than a right, as security only, derived from a mortgage, hypothec, agreement for sale or similar obligation) is deemed to be a property that is identical to the property;

(*b*) a share of the capital stock of a corporation that is acquired in exchange for another share in a transaction is deemed to be a property that is identical to the other share if

(i) section 51, 86 or 87 applies to the transaction, or

(ii) the following conditions are met, namely,

(A) section 85.1 applies to the transaction,

(B) subsection (3.4) applied to a prior disposition of the other share, and

(C) none of the times described in any of subparagraphs (3.4)(*b*)(i) to (v) has occurred in respect of the prior disposition;

(*b.1*) a share of the capital stock of a SIFT wind-up corporation in respect of a SIFT wind-up entity is, if the share was acquired before 2013, deemed to be a property that is identical to equity in the SIFT wind-up entity;

(*c*) if subsections (3.3) and (3.4) apply to the disposition by a transferor of a share of the capital stock of a particular corporation and after the disposition

(i) the particular corporation is merged or combined with one or more other corporations, otherwise than in a transaction in respect of which paragraph (*b*) applies to the share, then the corporation formed on the merger or combination is deemed to own the share while the corporation so formed is affiliated with the transferor,

(ii) the particular corporation is wound up in a winding-up to which subsection 88(1) applies, then the parent (within the meaning assigned by subsection 88(1)) is deemed to own the share while the parent is affiliated with the transferor, or

(iii) the particular corporation is liquidated and dissolved, the liquidation and dissolution is a qualifying liquidation and dissolution (within the meaning assigned by subsection 88(3.1)) of the corporation or a designated liquidation and dissolution (within the meaning assigned by subsection 95(1)) of the corporation, and the transferor is a foreign affiliate of a taxpayer, then for the purposes of computing the transferor's foreign accrual property income, exempt surplus or exempt deficit, hybrid surplus or hybrid deficit, and taxable surplus or taxable deficit, in respect of the taxpayer for a taxation year of the transferor, the taxpayer referred to in subsection 88(3.1) or the particular shareholder referred to in the definition "designated liquidation and dissolution" in subsection 95(1), as the case may be, is deemed to own the share while the taxpayer or particular shareholder is affiliated with the transferor; and

(*d*) where subsections (3.3) and (3.4) apply to the disposition by a transferor of a share of the capital stock of a corporation, and after the disposition the share is redeemed, acquired or cancelled by the corporation, otherwise than in a transaction in respect of which paragraph (*b*) or (*c*) applies to the share, the transferor is deemed to own the share while the corporation is affiliated with the transferor.

History: S. 40(3.5)(*c*) was replaced by S.C. 2013, c. 34, s. 60(8), applicable in respect of mergers or combinations that occur, and windings-up and liquidations and dissolutions that begin, after August 19, 2011.

See the application for s. 40(2)(*e.1*) for the extension of assessment periods to take into account the amendments by S.C. 2013, c. 34, s. 54 to 89.

S. 40(3.5)(*c*) formerly read;

(*c*) where subsections (3.3) and (3.4) apply to the disposition by a transferor of a share of the capital stock of a corporation, and after the disposition the corporation is merged with one or more other corporations, otherwise than in a transaction in respect of which paragraph (*b*) applies to the share, or is wound up in a winding-up to which subsection 88(1) applies, the corporation formed on the merger or the parent (within the meaning assigned by subsection 88(1)), as the case may be, is deemed to own the share while it is affiliated with the transferor; and

S. 40(3.5)(*b*) was replaced by S.C. 2013, c. 34, s. 183(6), applicable to dispositions of property that occur after April 26, 1995, except that it does not apply to any of those dispositions by a person or partnership that occurred before 1996 and that is described in subsection 247(1) of the *Income Tax Amendments Act, 1997* unless the person or partnership, as the case may be, made an election under subsection 247(2) of that Act.

S. 40(3.5)(*b*) formerly read:

(*b*) a share of the capital stock of a corporation that is acquired in exchange for another share in a transaction to which section 51, 85.1, 86 or 87 applies is deemed to be a property that is identical to the other share;

S. 40(3.5)(*b.1*) was added by S.C. 2009, c. 2, s. 10(1), applicable to dispositions that occur on or after November 28, 2008.

Tax Topics: No. 2065, Exchangeable Shares: Not Just Rights to Foreign Shares.

Cases: Subsection 40(3.4) applied to deny a capital loss where the taxpayer sold shares to an affiliated corporation. Although, as a result of a merger, the shares no longer existed 30 days after the disposition, the requirement in s. 40(3.3)(*c*) was met due to the application of the deeming provision in s. 40(3.5)(*c*). *The Queen v. Cascades Inc.*, 2009 DTC 5139 (F.C.A.), reversing 2008 DTC 2387 (T.C.C.)

▶ 40(3.6) ◀

(3.6) Loss on shares. If at any time a taxpayer disposes, to a corporation that is affiliated with the taxpayer immediately after the disposition, of a share of a class of the capital stock of the corporation (other than a share that is a distress preferred share (within the meaning assigned by subsection 80(1)) and other than, for the purposes of computing the exempt surplus or exempt deficit, hybrid surplus or hybrid deficit, and taxable surplus or taxable deficit of the taxpayer in respect of another taxpayer, where the taxpayer or, if the taxpayer is a partnership, a member of the taxpayer is a foreign affiliate of the other taxpayer, a property that is, or would be, if the taxpayer were a foreign affiliate of the other taxpayer, excluded property (within the meaning assigned by subsection 95(1)) of the taxpayer),

(*a*) the taxpayer's loss, if any, from the disposition is deemed to be nil; and

(*b*) in computing the adjusted cost base to the taxpayer after that time of a share of a class of the capital stock of the corporation owned by the taxpayer immediately after the disposition, there shall be added the proportion of the amount of the taxpayer's loss from the disposition (determined without reference to paragraph (2)(*g*) and this subsection) that

(i) the fair market value, immediately after the disposition, of the share

is of

(ii) the fair market value, immediately after the disposition, of all shares of the capital stock of the corporation owned by the taxpayer.

History: S. 40(3.6), the portion before paragraph (*a*) was replaced by S.C. 2013, c. 34, s. 60(9), applicable in respect of dispositions that occur after August 19, 2011.

See the application for s. 40(2)(*e.1*) for the extension of assessment periods to take into account the amendments by S.C. 2013, c. 34, s. 54 to 89.

S. 40(3.6), the portion before paragraph (*a*) formerly read

(3.6) *Loss on shares.* Where at any time a taxpayer disposes, to a corporation that is affiliated with the taxpayer immediately after the disposition, of a share of a class of the capital stock of the corporation (other than a share that is a distress preferred share as defined in subsection 80(1)),

Canadian Tax Foundation: Cepparo, *Foreign Exchange Losses on CFA Windup*, 2015 Canadian Tax Highlights 23(3):10; Kopstein and Pantry, *Subparagraph 212(1)(b)(vii) Withholding Tax Exemption*, 2005 Conference Report 15:1–44; Everett and Ireland, *Impact of the Proposed New Stop-Loss Rules*, 1997 Conference Report 17:1–26.

Tax Profile: February 2012 — Post-Mortem Planning — Double Taxation on Death; May 2004 — The Stop-Loss Rules.

Tax Topics: No. 1582, Estate Planning in the 21st Century.

Tax Window Files: FX losses on CFA wind-up, *January 12, 2015*, CRA Document No. 2014-0560421I7.

▶ 40(3.61) ◀

(3.61) Exception — estate loss carried back. If, in the course of administering the estate of a deceased taxpayer, the taxpayer's legal representative elects in accordance with subsection 164(6) to treat all or any portion of the estate's capital loss (determined without reference to subsections (3.4) and (3.6)) from the disposition of a share of the capital stock of a corporation as a capital loss of the deceased taxpayer from the disposition of the share, subsections (3.4) and (3.6) apply to the estate in respect of the loss only to the extent that the amount of the loss exceeds the portion of the loss to which the election applies.

Tax Window Files: STEP CRA Roundtable Question 5, *June 12, 2012*, CRA Document No. 2012-0449801C6; Attribution Rules and Suspended Loss Rules, *January 9, 2012*, CRA Document No. 2011-0427461E5; Capital

Losses, *April 23, 2012,* CRA Document No. 2012-0436921I7; 2012 BC CTF Q8 - Subsection 40(3.61), September 25, 2012, CRA Document No. 2012-0457541C6.

▶ 40(3.7) ◀

(3.7) Losses of non-resident. If an individual disposes of a property at any time after having ceased to be resident in Canada, for the purposes of applying subsections 100(4), 107(1) and 112(3) to (3.32) and (7) in computing the individual's loss from the disposition,

(*a*) the individual is deemed to be a corporation in respect of dividends received by the individual, or deemed under Part XIII to have been paid to the individual, at a particular time that is after the time at which the individual last acquired the property and at which the individual was non-resident; and

(*b*) an amount on account of

(i) each taxable dividend received by the individual at a particular time described in paragraph (*a*), and

(ii) each amount deemed under Part XIII to have been paid to the individual at a particular time described in paragraph (*a*), as a dividend from a corporation resident in Canada, to the extent that the amount can reasonably be considered to relate to the property,

is deemed to be a taxable dividend that was received by the individual and that was deductible under section 112 in computing the individual's taxable income or taxable income earned in Canada for the taxation year that includes that particular time.

Related Sections: S. 212(2) Tax on dividends.

Tax Profile: December 2008 — Tax Planning for Emigration from Canada to the United States.

▶ 40(4) ◀

(4) Disposal of principal residence to spouse or trust for spouse. Where a taxpayer has, after 1971, disposed of property to an individual in circumstances to which subsection 70(6) or 73(1) applied, for the purposes of computing the individual's gain from the disposition of the property under paragraph (2)(*b*) or (*c*), as the case may be,

(*a*) the individual shall be deemed to have owned the property throughout the period during which the taxpayer owned it;

(*b*) the property shall be deemed to have been the individual's principal residence

(i) in any case where subsection 70(6) is applicable, for any taxation year for which it would, if the taxpayer had designated it in prescribed manner to have been the taxpayer's principal residence for that year, have been the taxpayer's principal residence, and

(ii) in any case where subsection 73(1) is applicable, for any taxation year for which it was the taxpayer's principal residence; and

(*c*) where the individual is a trust, the trust shall be deemed to have been resident in Canada during each taxation year during which the taxpayer was resident in Canada.

Editorial Note: The general effect of s. 40(4) is that, for the purposes of the principal residence exemption, the transferee spouse or trust inherits the transferor's years of ownership of the residence and the years of qualifying principal residence status.

Forms: T1255 — Designation of a Property as a Principal Residence by the Legal Representative of a Deceased Individual.

Income Tax Folios: *Secondary* — S1-F3-C2 Principal Residence.

▶ 40(5) ◀

(5) Where principal residence is property of trust for spouse — (Repealed by S.C. 1994, c. 7, Sched. VIII, s. 12(1).)

▶ 40(6) ◀

(6) Principal residence — property owned at end of 1981. Subject to subsection (6.1), if a property was owned by a taxpayer, whether jointly with another person or otherwise, at the end of 1981 and continuously from the beginning of 1982 until disposed of by the taxpayer, the amount of the gain determined under paragraph (2)(*b*) in respect of the disposition shall not exceed the amount, if any, by which the total of

(*a*) the taxpayer's gain calculated in accordance with paragraph (2)(*b*) on the assumption that the taxpayer had disposed of the property on December 31, 1981 for proceeds of disposition equal to its fair market value on that date, and

(*b*) the taxpayer's gain calculated in accordance with paragraph (2)(*b*) on the assumption that that paragraph applies and that

(i) the taxpayer acquired the property on January 1, 1982 at a cost equal to its proceeds of disposition as determined under paragraph (*a*), and

(ii) the description of B in paragraph (2)(*b*) is read without reference to "one plus"

exceeds

(*c*) the amount, if any, by which the fair market value of the property on December 31, 1981 exceeds the proceeds of disposition of the property determined without reference to this subsection.

History: S. 40(6), the portion before paragraph (*a*) was replaced by S.C. 2017, c. 33, s. 10(4), in force December 14, 2017, and formerly read:

(6) *Special rule concerning principal residence.* Where a property was owned by a taxpayer, whether jointly with another person or otherwise, at the end of 1981 and continuously thereafter until disposed of by the taxpayer, the amount of the gain determined under paragraph (2)(*b*) in respect of the disposition shall not exceed the amount, if any, by which the total of

Income Tax Folios: *Secondary* — S1-F3-C2 Principal Residence.

▶ 40(6.1) ◀

(6.1) Principal residence — property owned at end of 2016. If a trust owns property at the end of 2016, the trust is not in its first taxation year that begins after 2016 a trust described in subparagraph (*c*.1)(iii.1) of the definition *principal residence* in section 54, the trust disposes of the property after 2016, the disposition is the trust's first disposition of the property after 2016 and the trust owns the property, whether jointly with another person or otherwise, continuously from the beginning of 2017 until the disposition,

(*a*) subsection (6) does not apply to the disposition; and

(*b*) the trust's gain determined under paragraph (2)(*b*) in respect of the disposition is the amount, if any, determined by the formula

$$A + B - C$$

where

A is the trust's gain calculated in accordance with paragraph (2)(*b*) on the assumption that
(i) the trust disposed of the property on December 31, 2016 for proceeds of disposition equal to its fair market value on that date, and
(ii) paragraph (*a*) did not apply in respect of the disposition described in subparagraph (i),

B is the trust's gain in respect of the disposition calculated in accordance with paragraph (2)(*b*) on the assumption that
(i) the description of B in that paragraph is read without reference to "one plus", and
(ii) the trust acquired the property on January 1, 2017 at a cost equal to its fair market value on December 31, 2016, and

C is the amount, if any, by which the fair market value of the property on December 31, 2016 exceeds the proceeds of disposition of the property determined without reference to this subsection.

History: S. 40(6.1) was added by S.C. 2017, c. 33, s. 10(5), in force December 14, 2017.

Related Sections: 40(2) Limitations; 54 principal residence.

▶ 40(7) ◀

(7) Property in satisfaction of interest in trust. Where property has been acquired by a taxpayer in satisfaction of all or any part of the taxpayer's capital interest in a trust, in circumstances to which subsection 107(2) applies and subsection 107(4) does not apply, for the purposes of paragraph (2)(*b*) and the definition "principal residence" in section 54 the taxpayer shall be deemed to have owned the property continuously since the trust last acquired it.

Editorial Note: If the trust makes the election under s. 107(2.01), which provides a deemed disposition and reacquisition by the trust of the property at its fair market value immediately before the s. 107(2) rollover, the deeming rule in s. 40(7) is of no practical consequence (since it only extends back to the time that the trust last acquired the property, namely, the time that is immediately before the s. 107(2) rollover).

Related Sections: S. 108(1), "capital interest".

Tax Profile: July 2011 — Personal Trusts and Cottage Properties Residence — Pitfalls and Planning.

Income Tax Folios: *Secondary* — S1-F3-C2 Principal Residence.

▶ 40(7.1) ◀

(7.1) Effect of election under subsection 110.6(19). Where an election was made under subsection 110.6(19) in respect of a property of a taxpayer that was the taxpayer's principal residence for the 1994 taxation year or that, in the taxpayer's return of income for the taxation year in which the taxpayer disposes of the property or grants an option to acquire the property, is designated as the taxpayer's principal residence, in determining, for the purposes of paragraph (2)(*b*) and subsections (4) to (7), the day on which the property was last acquired or reacquired by the taxpayer and the period throughout which the property was owned by the taxpayer this Act shall be read without reference to subsection 110.6(19).

Income Tax Folios: *Secondary* — S1-F3-C2 Principal Residence.

▶ 40(8) ◀

(8) Application of s. 70(10). The definitions in subsection 70(10) apply to this section.

▶ 40(9) ◀

(9) Additions to taxable Canadian property. If a non-resident person disposes of a taxable Canadian property

(*a*) that the person last acquired before April 27, 1995,

(*b*) that would not be a taxable Canadian property immediately before the disposition if section 115 were read as it applied to dispositions that occurred on April 26, 1995, and

(*c*) that would be a taxable Canadian property immediately before the disposition if section 115 were read as it applied to dispositions that occurred on January 1, 1996,

the person's gain or loss from the disposition is deemed to be the amount determined by the formula

$$A \times B/C$$

where

A is the amount of the gain or loss determined without reference to this subsection;

B is the number of calendar months in the period that begins with May 1995 and ends with the calendar month that includes the time of the disposition; and

C is the number of calendar months in the period that begins with the calendar month in which the person last acquired the property and ends with the calendar month that includes the time of the disposition.

▶ 40(10) ◀

(10) Application of subsection (11). Subsection (11) applies in computing at any particular time a taxpayer's gain or loss (in this subsection and subsection (11) referred to as the "new gain" or "new loss", as the case may be), in respect of any part (which in this subsection and subsection (11) is referred to as the "relevant part" and which may for greater certainty be the whole) of a foreign currency debt of the taxpayer, arising from a fluctuation in the value of the currency of the foreign currency debt (other than, for greater certainty, a gain or a capital loss that arises because of the application of subsection 111(12)), if at any time before the particular time the taxpayer realized a capital loss or gain in respect of the foreign currency debt because of subsection 111(12).

Editorial Note: See the Editorial Note following s. 40(11).

History: S. 40(10) was replaced by S.C. 2013, c. 40, s. 19(3), deemed to have come into force March 21, 2013, and formerly read:

(10) *Application.* Subsection (11) applies in computing at any particular time a corporation's gain or loss (in this subsection and subsection (11) referred to as the "new gain" or "new loss", as the case may be), in respect of any part (which in this subsection and subsection (11) is referred to as the "relevant part" and which may for greater certainty be the whole) of a foreign currency debt of the corporation, arising from a fluctuation in the value of the currency of the foreign currency debt (other than, for greater certainty, a gain or a capital loss that arises because of the application of subsection 111(12)), if at any time before the particular time the corporation realized a capital loss or gain in respect of the foreign currency debt because of subsection 111(12).

S. 40(10) was added by S.C. 2009, c. 2, s. 10(2), applicable after 2005.

Related Sections: S. 39(2) Capital gains and losses in respect of foreign currencies; s. 111(4) Acquisition of control; s. 111(8), "exchange rate", "foreign currency debt"; s. 111(12) Foreign currency debt on acquisition of control.

▶ 40(11) ◀

(11) Gain or loss on foreign currency debt. If this subsection applies, the new gain is the positive amount, or the new loss is the negative amount, as the case may be, determined by the formula

$$A + B - C$$

where

A is

(*a*) if the taxpayer would, but for any application of subsection 111(12), recognize a new gain, the amount of the new gain, determined without reference to this subsection, or

(*b*) if the taxpayer would, but for any application of subsection 111(12), recognize a new loss, the amount of the new loss, determined without reference to this subsection, multiplied by (-1);

B is the total of all amounts each of which is that portion of the amount of a capital loss realized by the taxpayer at any time before the particular time, in respect of the foreign currency debt and because of subsection 111(12), that is reasonably attributable to

(*a*) the relevant part of the foreign currency debt at the particular time, or

(*b*) the forgiven amount, if any, (as defined in subsection 80(1)) in respect of the foreign currency debt at the particular time; and

C is the total of all amounts each of which is that portion of the amount of a gain realized by the taxpayer at any time before the particular time, in respect of the foreign currency debt and because of subsection 111(12), that is reasonably attributable to

(*a*) the relevant part of the foreign currency debt at the particular time, or

(*b*) the forgiven amount, if any, (as defined in subsection 80(1)) in respect of the foreign currency debt at the particular time.

Editorial Note: Where a corporation or trust incurs a loss restriction event (i.e., an acquisition of control of a corporation or a person becomes a majority-interest beneficiary of a trust), s. 111(12) effectively requires the write-down and realization of accrued foreign exchange losses in respect of foreign currency debts owed by the corporation or trust, and allows the corporation or trust to trigger any accrued gains in respect of foreign currency debt owed to the corporation (which can then be offset by the losses). In general terms, s. 40(11) ensures that the loss or gain in respect of the foreign currency debt that was realized upon the loss restriction event is taken into account in computing a subsequent gain or loss, if any, upon the actual repayment or settlement of the debt.

History: S. 40(11) was replaced by S.C. 2013, c. 40, s. 19(3), deemed to have come into force March 21, 2013, and formerly read:

(11) *Gain or loss on foreign currency debt.* If this subsection applies, the new gain is the positive amount, or the new loss is the negative amount, as the case may be, determined by the formula

$$A + B - C$$

where

A is

(*a*) if the corporation would, but for any application of subsection 111(12), recognize a new gain, the amount of the new gain, determined without reference to this subsection, or

(*b*) if the corporation would, but for any application of subsection 111(12), recognize a new loss, the amount of the new loss, determined without reference to this subsection, multiplied by (-1);

B is the total of all amounts each of which is that portion of the amount of a capital loss realized by the corporation at any time before the particular time, in respect of the foreign currency debt and because of subsection 111(12), that is reasonably attributable to

(*a*) the relevant part of the foreign currency debt at the particular time, or

(*b*) the forgiven amount, if any, (within the meaning assigned by subsection 80(1)) in respect of the foreign currency debt at the particular time; and

C is the total of all amounts each of which is that portion of the amount of a gain realized by the corporation at any time before the particular time, in respect of the foreign currency debt and because of subsection 111(12), that is reasonably attributable to

(*a*) the relevant part of the foreign currency debt at the particular time, or

(*b*) the forgiven amount, if any, (within the meaning assigned by subsection 80(1)) in respect of the foreign currency debt at the particular time.

S. 40(11) was added by S.C. 2009, c. 2, s. 10(2), applicable after 2005.

Related Sections: S. 39(2) Capital gains and losses in respect of foreign currencies; s. 111(4) Acquisition of control; s. 111(8), "exchange rate", "foreign currency debt"; s. 111(12) Foreign currency debt on acquisition of control.

► 40(12) ◄

(12) Donated flow-through shares. If at any time a taxpayer disposes of one or more capital properties that are included in a flow-through share class of property and subparagraph 38(*a.1*)(i) or (iii) applies to the disposition (in this subsection referred to as the "actual disposition"), then the taxpayer is deemed to have a capital gain from a disposition at that time of another capital property equal to the lesser of

(*a*) the taxpayer's exemption threshold at that time in respect of the flow-through share class of property, and

(*b*) the total of all amounts each of which is a capital gain from the actual disposition (for greater certainty, calculated without reference to this subsection).

Editorial Note: Flow-through shares (FTS) that are disposed of in respect of donations to qualified donees are eligible for the zero taxable capital gain inclusion rate under paragraph 38(*a.1*)(i) or 38(*a.1*)(iii). The Department of Finance apparently felt that this treatment was unwarranted, owing to the fact that in many cases the FTS will have previously generated significant flow-through deductions or credits to the holder of the FTS.

As a result, subsection 40(12) was enacted to effectively provide that the zero inclusion rate for such a capital gain applies only to the amount by which the capital gain exceeds the actual amount paid for the FTS. More particularly, under new subsection 40(12), the donor will be deemed to have a capital gain from a disposition of another capital property equal to the lesser of (a) the taxpayer's "exemption threshold" at that time in respect of the flow-through share class of property; and (b) the capital gain from the actual disposition at that time by the taxpayer. The exemption threshold generally equals the original amount paid by the investor for all of the FTS of the class of shares in excess of capital gains previously realized on the disposition of an FTS of the same class. Since the other capital property will not be the shares described in paragraph 38(*a.1*)(i) or 38(*a.1*)(iii), the resulting taxable capital gain will be subject to the regular 1/2 inclusion rate.

History: S. 40(12) was added by S.C. 2011, c. 24, s. 5(1), applicable to dispositions made on or after March 22, 2011.

Related Sections: S. 38.1 Tax-deferred transaction — Flow-through shares; s. 54, "exemption threshold", "flow-through share class of property".

► 40(13) ◄

(13) Class 14.1 — transitional rules. Subsection (14) applies in respect of a disposition by a taxpayer of a property that is included in Class 14.1 of Schedule II to the *Income Tax Regulations* in respect of a business of the taxpayer if

(*a*) the property was an eligible capital property of the taxpayer immediately before January 1, 2017;

(*b*) the amount determined for Q in the definition "cumulative eligible capital" in subsection 14(5) in respect of the business immediately before January 1, 2017 is greater than nil;

(*c*) the amount determined for B in that definition in respect of the business immediately before January 1, 2017 is nil; and

(*d*) no amount is included in the taxpayer's income for a taxation year because of paragraph 13(38)(*d*).

History: S. 40(13) was added by S.C. 2016, c. 12, s. 15(1), in force January 1, 2017.

► 40(14) ◄

(14) Class 14.1 — transitional rules. If this subsection applies in respect of a disposition at any time by a taxpayer of a property, the taxpayer's capital gain from the disposition is to be reduced by such amount as the taxpayer claims, not exceeding the amount by which

(*a*) 2/3 of the amount determined for Q in the definition "cumulative eligible capital" in subsection 14(5) in respect of the business immediately before 2017

exceeds

(*b*) the total of all amounts each of which is an amount claimed under this subsection in respect of another disposition at or before that time.

History: S. 40(14) was added by S.C. 2016, c. 12, s. 15(1), in force January 1, 2017.

► 40(15) ◄

(15) Class 14.1 — transitional rules. Subsection (16) applies in respect of a disposition by an individual of a property that is included in Class 14.1 of Schedule II to the *Income Tax Regulations* in respect of a business of the individual if

(*a*) the property was an eligible capital property of the individual immediately before January 1, 2017; and

(*b*) the individual's exempt gains balance in respect of the business is greater than nil for the taxation year that includes January 1, 2017.

History: S. 40(15) was added by S.C. 2016, c. 12, s. 15(1), in force January 1, 2017.

► 40(16) ◄

(16) Class 14.1 — transitional rules. If this subsection applies in respect of a disposition at any time by an individual of a property, the individual's capital gain from the disposition is to be reduced by such amount as the individual claims, not exceeding the amount by which

(*a*) twice the amount of the individual's exempt gains balance in respect of the business for the taxation year that includes January 1, 2017

exceeds

(*b*) the total of

(i) if paragraph 13(38)(*d*) applies in respect of the business for the individual's taxation year that includes January 1, 2017, the amount determined for D in paragraph 14(1)(*b*) for the purposes of paragraph 13(38)(*d*), and

(ii) the total of all amounts each of which is an amount claimed under this subsection in respect of another disposition at or before that time.

History: S. 40(16) was added by S.C. 2016, c. 12, s. 15(1), in force January 1, 2017.

SECTION 41: Taxable net gain from disposition of listed personal property

► 41(1) ◄

(1) Taxable net gain from disposition of listed personal property. For the purposes of this Part, a taxpayer's taxable net gain for a taxation year from dispositions of listed personal property is 1/2 of the amount determined under subsection (2) to be the taxpayer's net gain for the year from dispositions of such property.

Editorial Note: Losses in a taxation year from dispositions of listed personal property can be deducted from gains from dispositions of listed personal property in the year, if any. If there are excess losses in the year from listed personal property, the excess can be carried back three years or forward seven years and deducted from gains from listed personal property in any of those other years. If there is a net gain in a year from listed personal properties, one-half of the net gain is included in income by virtue of s. 41(1) and s. 3(*b*)(i)(B).

Related Sections: S. 3(*b*) Income for taxation year; s. 53(1) Adjustments to cost base; s. 54, "listed personal property"; s. 127.5 Obligation to pay minimum tax; s. 127.52(1)(*d*)(i) Adjusted taxable income determined.

Forms: T1A — Request for Loss Carryback.

► 41(2) ◄

(2) Determination of net gain. A taxpayer's net gain for a taxation year from dispositions of listed personal property is an amount determined as follows:

(*a*) determine the amount, if any, by which the total of the taxpayer's gains for the year from the disposition of listed personal property, other than property described in subparagraph 39(1)(*a*)(i.1), exceeds the total of the taxpayer's losses for the year from dispositions of listed personal property, and

(*b*) deduct from the amount determined under paragraph (*a*) such portion as the taxpayer may claim of the taxpayer's listed-personal-property losses for the 7 taxation years immediately preceding and the 3 taxation years immediately following the taxation year, except that for the purposes of this paragraph

(i) an amount in respect of a listed-personal-property loss is deductible for a taxation year only to the extent that it exceeds the total of amounts deducted under this paragraph in respect of that loss for preceding taxation years,

(ii) no amount is deductible in respect of the listed-personal-property loss of any year until the deductible listed-personal-property losses for previous years have been deducted, and

(iii) no amount is deductible in respect of listed-personal-property losses from the amount determined under paragraph (*a*) for a taxation year except to the extent of the amount so determined for the year,

and the remainder determined under paragraph (*b*) is the taxpayer's net gain for the year from dispositions of listed personal property.

Editorial Note: See the editorial note following s. 41(1).

Forms: T1A — Request for Loss Carryback.

Interpretation Bulletins: *Secondary* — IT-262R2 Losses of non-residents and part-year residents; IT-407R4 (Consolid.) Dispositions of cultural property to designated Canadian institutions.

► 41(3) ◄

(3) Definition of "listed-personal-property loss". In this section, "listed-personal-property loss" of a taxpayer for a taxation year means the amount, if any, by which the total of the taxpayer's losses for the year from dispositions of listed personal property exceeds the total of the taxpayer's gains for the year from dispositions of listed personal property, other than property described in subparagraph 39(1)(*a*)(i.1).

Related Sections: S. 41(1) Taxable net gain from disposition of listed personal property; s. 54, "listed personal property"; s. 248(1), "amount", "property".

Interpretation Bulletins: *Secondary* — IT-159R3 Capital debts established to be bad debts; IT-232R3 Losses — Their Deductibility in the Loss Year or in Other Years; IT-262R2 Losses of non-residents and part-year residents.

SECTION 42: Dispositions subject to warranty

▶ 42(1) ◀

(1) Dispositions subject to warranty. For the purposes of this subdivision,

(*a*) an amount received or receivable by a person or partnership (referred to in this subsection as the "vendor"), as the case may be, as consideration for a warranty, covenant or other conditional or contingent obligation given or incurred by the vendor in respect of a property (referred to in this section as the "subject property") disposed of by the vendor,

(i) if it is received or receivable on or before the specified date, is deemed to be received as consideration for the disposition by the vendor of the subject property (and not to be an amount received or receivable by the vendor as consideration for the obligation) and is to be included in computing the vendor's proceeds of disposition of the subject property for the taxation year or fiscal period in which the disposition occurred, and

(ii) in any other case, is deemed to be a capital gain of the vendor from the disposition of a property by the vendor that occurs at the earlier of the time when the amount is received or becomes receivable; and

(*b*) an outlay or expense paid or payable by the vendor under a warranty, covenant or other conditional or contingent obligation given or incurred by the vendor in respect of the subject property disposed of by the vendor,

(i) if it is paid or payable on or before the specified date, is deemed to reduce the consideration for the disposition by the vendor of the subject property (and not to be an outlay or expense paid or payable by the vendor under the obligation) and is to be deducted in computing the vendor's proceeds of disposition of the subject property for the taxation year or fiscal period in which the disposition occurred, and

(ii) in any other case, is deemed to be a capital loss of the vendor from the disposition of a property by the vendor that occurs at the earlier of the time when the outlay or expense is paid or becomes payable.

History: S. 42 was replaced and renumbered as s. 42(1) by S.C. 2013, c. 34, s. 184(1), applicable to taxation years and fiscal periods that end after February 27, 2004 except that, in its application to taxation years and fiscal periods that end before November 5, 2010, section 42 is to be read as follows:

S. 42. "For the purposes of this subdivision,

(*a*) an amount received or receivable by a taxpayer in a taxation year as consideration for a warranty, a covenant or another conditional or contingent obligation given or incurred by the taxpayer in respect of a property disposed of, at any time, by the taxpayer

(i) is, if the amount is received or becomes receivable on or before the taxpayer's filing-due date for the taxpayer's taxation year in which the taxpayer disposed of the property, to be included in computing the taxpayer's proceeds of disposition of the property, and

(ii) is, if the amount is received or becomes receivable after that filing-due date, deemed to be a capital gain of the taxpayer from the disposition, by the taxpayer of the property, that occurs at the time when the amount is received or becomes receivable; and

(*b*) an outlay or expense paid or payable by the taxpayer in a taxation year under a warranty, covenant or another conditional or contingent obligation given or incurred by the taxpayer in respect of property disposed of, at any time, by the taxpayer

(i) is, if the amount is paid or becomes payable on or before the taxpayer's filing-due date for the taxpayer's taxation year in which the taxpayer disposed of the property, to be deducted in computing the taxpayer's proceeds of disposition of the property, and

(ii) is, if the amount is paid or becomes payable after that filing-due date, deemed to be a capital loss of the taxpayer from the disposition, by the taxpayer of the property, that occurs at the time when the amount is paid or becomes payable."

S. 42 formerly read:

S. 42. *Dispositions subject to warranty.* In computing a taxpayer's proceeds of disposition of any property for the purposes of this subdivision, there shall be included all amounts received or receivable by the taxpayer as consideration for warranties, covenants or other conditional or contingent obligations given or incurred by the taxpayer in respect of the disposition, and in computing the taxpayer's income for the taxation year in which the property was disposed of and for each subsequent taxation year, any outlay or expense made or incurred by the taxpayer in any such year pursuant to or by reason of any such obligation shall be deemed to be a loss of the taxpayer for that year from a disposition of a capital property and for the purposes of section 110.6, that capital property shall be deemed to have been disposed of by the taxpayer in that year.

Related Sections: S. 54, "capital property", "proceeds of disposition"; s. 56.4(14) Non-application of section 42; s. 87(2)(*n*) Outlays made pursuant to warranty.

Tax Topics: No. 2176, Escrow Arrangements in Acquisition Agreements: What Are You Creating?; No. 1699, Principal Residence Exemption — Filing Requirements.

Tax Window Files: Disposition of a Principal Residence — Damages Paid Under a Warranty for Hidden Defects, *Technical Interpretation, Business and Partnerships Division, October 30, 2008*, CRA Document No. 2006-0198381E5.

▶ 42(2) ◀

(2) Meaning of "specified date". In subsection (1), "specified date" means,

(*a*) if the vendor is a partnership, the last day of the vendor's fiscal period in which the vendor disposed of the subject property; and

(*b*) in any other case, the vendor's filing-due date for the vendor's taxation year in which the vendor disposed of the subject property.

History: S. 42(2) was added by S.C. 2013, c. 34, s. 184(1), generally applicable to taxation years and fiscal periods that end after February 27, 2004. However, see the history note for s. 42(1) for the alternate reading of s. 42 for taxation years and fiscal periods that end before November 5, 2010.

SECTION 43: General rule for part dispositions

▶ 43(1) ◀

(1) General rule for part dispositions. For the purpose of computing a taxpayer's gain or loss for a taxation year from the disposition of part of a property, the adjusted cost base to the taxpayer, immediately before the disposition, of that part is the portion of the adjusted cost base to the taxpayer at that time of the whole property that can reasonably be regarded as attributable to that part.

Editorial Note: When only part of a capital property is sold or disposed of, the adjusted cost base of that part is a portion of the adjusted cost base of the whole property that may be attributed in a reasonable manner. See also s. 46(2), which deals with the part disposition of personal-use property.

Related Sections: S. 40(1) General rules; s. 53(2) Amounts to be deducted; s. 54, "adjusted cost base"; "proceeds of disposition"; s. 248(1), "disposition", "property".

Tax Topics: No. 1967, Conversion of Partnership Interests into Income and Capital Components.

Income Tax Folios: *Secondary* — S3-F4-C1 General Discussion of Capital Cost Allowance.

Interpretation Bulletins: *Primary* — IT-264R Part dispositions. *Secondary* — IT-200 Surface rentals and farming operations; IT-226R Gift to a charity of a residual interest in real property or an equitable interest in a trust; IT-278R2 Death of a partner or of a retired partner; IT-359R2 Premiums and other amounts with respect to leases; IT-373R2 (Consolid.) Woodlots.

▶ 43(2) ◀

(2) Ecological gifts. For the purposes of subsection (1) and section 53, if at any time a taxpayer disposes of a covenant or an easement to which land is subject or, in the case of land in the Province of Quebec, a real or personal servitude, in circumstances where subsection 110.1(5) or 118.1(12) applies,

(*a*) the portion of the adjusted cost base to the taxpayer of the land immediately before the disposition that can reasonably be regarded as attributable to the covenant, easement or servitude, as the case may be, is deemed to be equal to the amount determined by the formula

$$A \times B/C$$

where

A is the adjusted cost base to the taxpayer of the land immediately before the disposition,

B is the amount determined under subsection 110.1(5) or 118.1(12) in respect of the disposition, and

C is the fair market value of the land immediately before the disposition; and

(*b*) for greater certainty, the cost to the taxpayer of the land shall be reduced at the time of the disposition by the amount determined under paragraph (*a*).

Editorial Note: When a covenant or easement (or a servitude, under the laws of Quebec) is donated as an ecological gift, then the adjusted cost base of that portion of the property is calculated based on the proportionate decrease in the value of the property that results from that donation.

History: S. 43(2), the portion before the formula in paragraph (*a*) was replaced by S.C. 2017, c. 33, s. 11(1), applicable in respect of gifts made after March 21, 2017, and formerly read:

(2) *Ecological gifts.* For the purposes of subsection (1) and section 53, if at any time a taxpayer disposes of a covenant or an easement to which land is subject or, in the case of land in the Province of Quebec, a real servitude, in circumstances where subsection 110.1(5) or 118.1(12) applies,

(*a*) the portion of the adjusted cost base to the taxpayer of the land immediately before the disposition that can reasonably be regarded as attributable to the covenant, easement or real servitude, as the case may be, is deemed to be equal to the amount determined by the formula

S. 43(2), the portion before the formula in paragraph (*a*) was replaced by S.C. 2013, c. 34, s. 185(1), applicable to gifts made after December 20, 2002, and formerly read:

(2) *Ecological gifts.* For the purposes of subsection (1) and section 53, where at any time a taxpayer disposes of a servitude, covenant or easement to which land is subject in circumstances where subsection 110.1(5) or 118.1(12) applies,

(*a*) the portion of the adjusted cost base to the taxpayer of the land immediately before the disposition that can reasonably be regarded as attributable to the servitude, covenant or easement, as the case may be, is deemed to be equal to the amount determined by the formula

▶ 43(3) ◀

(3) Payments out of trust income, etc. Notwithstanding subsection (1), where part of a capital interest of a taxpayer in a trust would, but for paragraph (*h*) or (*i*) of the definition "disposition" in subsection 248(1), be disposed of solely because of the satisfaction of a right to enforce payment of an amount by the trust, no part of the adjusted cost base to the taxpayer of the taxpayer's capital interest in the trust shall be allocated to that part of the capital interest.

Editorial Note: Where a payment is made from a trust to a beneficiary which is excluded from the definition of a "disposition" under s. 248(1)(*h*) and (*i*), then no part of the adjusted cost base will be allocated to that part of the capital interest in respect of which the payment is made. In other words, there can be no disposition of a "part" when there is no disposition of the "whole".

Paragraphs (h) and (i) of the definition of "disposition" in s. 248(1) provide that no disposition of a capital interest occurs where:

- the capital interest is described by reference to units issued by the trust and the number of units owned by the beneficiary is not reduced because of the payment;
- the payment is out of the income or capital gains of the trust for the same year in which the payment was made; or
- the payment is in respect of a non-taxable dividend designated by the trust in respect of the beneficiary under s. 104(20).

SECTION 43.1: Life estates in real property

▶ 43.1(1) ◀

(1) Life estates in real property. Notwithstanding any other provision of this Act, if at any time a taxpayer disposes of a remainder interest in real property (except as a result of a transaction to which subsection 73(3) would otherwise apply or by way of a gift to a qualified donee) to a person or partnership and retains a life estate or an estate*pur autre vie* (in this section referred to as the "life estate") in the property, the taxpayer is deemed

(*a*) to have disposed at that time of the life estate in the property for proceeds of disposition equal to its fair market value at that time; and

(*b*) to have reacquired the life estate immediately after that time at a cost equal to the proceeds of disposition referred to in paragraph (*a*).

Editorial Note: S. 43.1 effectively results in a "freeze" upon the disposition of a remainder interest in real property. Although the taxpayer may realize a gain on the (actual) disposition of the remainder interest and the deemed disposition of the life interest under s. 43.1(1), the life interest is subject to a rollover upon the taxpayer's death under s. (2). Thus, any further accrued gain on the property can be deferred until the holder of the remainder interest disposes of the property. Note that s. 43.1(1) does not apply to charitable donations of remainder interests.

History: S. 43.1(1), the portion before paragraph (*a*) was replaced by S.C. 2011, c. 24, s. 6(2), in force January 1, 2012. S. 43.1(1), the portion before paragraph (*a*) formerly read:

S. 43.1

(1) *Life estates in real property.* Notwithstanding any other provision of this Act, if at any time a taxpayer disposes of a remainder interest in real property (except as a result of a transaction to which subsection 73(3) would otherwise apply or by way of a gift to a donee described in the definition "total charitable gifts", "total Crown gifts" or "total ecological gifts" in subsection 118.1(1)) to a person or partnership and retains a life estate or an estate *pur autre vie* (in this section referred to as the "life estate") in the property, the taxpayer is deemed

S. 43.1(1), the portion before paragraph (*a*) was replaced by S.C. 2011, c. 24, s. 6(1), applicable to dispositions that occur after February 27, 1995. S. 43.1(1), the portion before paragraph (*a*) formerly read:

S. 43.1

(1) *Life estates in real property.* Notwithstanding any other provision of this Act, where at any time a taxpayer disposes of a remainder interest in real property (except as a result of a transaction to which subsection 73(3) would otherwise apply or by way of a gift to a donee described in the definition "total charitable gifts" or "total Crown gifts" in subsection 118.1(1)) to a person or partnership and retains a life estate or an estate *pur autre vie* (in this section called the "life estate") in the property, the taxpayer shall be deemed

Related Sections: S. 13(21), "proceeds of disposition"; s. 54, "proceeds of disposition"; s. 248(1), "disposition", "property"; s. 248(4) Interest in real property.

Canadian Tax Foundation: Lam, *Charitable Remainder Trusts*, 2005 Canadian Tax Journal 2:506–538.

Tax Window Files: Rooftop Solar Electricity Generation Projects, *November 25, 2009*, CRA Document No. 2009-0343881E5.

▶ 43.1(2) ◀

(2) Idem. Where, as a result of an individual's death, a life estate to which subsection (1) applied is terminated,

(*a*) the holder of the life estate immediately before the death shall be deemed to have disposed of the life estate immediately before the death for proceeds of disposition equal to the adjusted cost base to that person of the life estate immediately before the death; and

(*b*) where a person who is the holder of the remainder interest in the real property immediately before the death was not dealing at arm's length with the holder of the life estate, there shall, after the death, be added in computing the adjusted cost base to that person of the real property an amount equal to the lesser of

(i) the adjusted cost base of the life estate in the property immediately before the death, and

(ii) the amount, if any, by which the fair market value of the real property immediately after the death exceeds the adjusted cost base to that person of the remainder interest immediately before the death.

Editorial Note: See the editorial note under s. 43.1(1).

Related Sections: S. 53(1)(*o*) Adjustments to cost base — Remainder interests in land; s. 54, "adjusted cost base"; s. 248(1), "adjusted cost base", "individual", "property"; s. 251 Arm's length.

Tax Topics: No. 1769, Unpleasant Tax Surprise for Donees of Remainder Interest.

SECTION 44: Exchanges of property

▶ 44(1) ◀

(1) Exchanges of property. Where at any time in a taxation year (in this subsection referred to as the "initial year") an amount has become receivable by a taxpayer as proceeds of disposition of a capital property that is not a share of the capital stock of a corporation (which capital property is in this section referred to as the taxpayer's "former property") that is either

(*a*) property the proceeds of disposition of which are described in paragraph (*b*), (*c*) or (*d*) of the definition "proceeds of disposition" in subsection 13(21) or paragraph (*b*), (*c*) or (*d*) of the definition "proceeds of disposition" in section 54, or

(*b*) a property that was, immediately before the disposition, a former business property of the taxpayer,

and the taxpayer has

(*c*) if the former property is described in paragraph (*a*), before the later of the end of the second taxation year following the initial year and 24 months after the end of the initial year, and

(*d*) in any other case, before the later of the end of the first taxation year following the initial year and 12 months after the end of the initial year,

acquired a capital property that is a replacement property for the taxpayer's former property and the replacement property has not been disposed of by the taxpayer before the time the taxpayer disposed of the taxpayer's former property, notwithstanding subsection 40(1), if the taxpayer so elects under this subsection in the taxpayer's return of income for the year in which the taxpayer acquired the replacement property,

(*e*) the gain for a particular taxation year from the disposition of the taxpayer's former property shall be deemed to be the amount, if any, by which

(i) where the particular year is the initial year, the lesser of

(A) the amount, if any, by which the proceeds of disposition of the former property exceed

(I) in the case of depreciable property, the lesser of the proceeds of disposition of the former property computed without reference to subsection (6) and the total of its adjusted cost base to the taxpayer immediately before the disposition and any outlays and expenses to the extent that they were made or incurred by the taxpayer for the purpose of making the disposition, and

(II) in any other case, the total of its adjusted cost base to the taxpayer immediately before the disposition and any outlays and expenses to the extent that they were made or incurred by the taxpayer for the purpose of making the disposition, and

(B) the amount, if any, by which the proceeds of disposition of the former property exceed the total of the cost to the taxpayer, or in the case of depreciable property, the capital cost to the taxpayer, determined without reference to paragraph (*f*), of the taxpayer's replacement property and any outlays and expenses to the extent that they were made or incurred by the taxpayer for the purpose of making the disposition, or

(ii) where the particular year is subsequent to the initial year, the amount, if any, claimed by the taxpayer under subparagraph (iii) in computing the taxpayer's gain for the immediately preceding year from the disposition of the former property,

exceeds

(iii) subject to subsection (1.1), such amount as the taxpayer claims,

(A) in the case of an individual (other than a trust), in prescribed form filed with the taxpayer's return of income under this Part for the particular year, and

(B) in any other case, in the taxpayer's return of income under this Part for the particular year,

as a deduction, not exceeding the lesser of

(C) a reasonable amount as a reserve in respect of such of the proceeds of disposition of the former property that are payable to the taxpayer after the end of the particular year as can reasonably be regarded as a portion of the amount determined under subparagraph (i) in respect of the property, and

(D) an amount equal to the product obtained when $1/5$ of the amount determined under subparagraph (i) in respect of the property is multiplied by the amount, if any, by which 4 exceeds the number of preceding taxation years of the taxpayer ending after the disposition of the property, and

(*f*) the cost to the taxpayer or, in the case of depreciable property, the capital cost to the taxpayer, of the taxpayer's replacement property at any time after the time the taxpayer disposed of the taxpayer's former property, shall be deemed to be

(i) the cost to the taxpayer or, in the case of depreciable property, the capital cost to the taxpayer of the taxpayer's replacement property otherwise determined,

minus

(ii) the amount, if any, by which the amount determined under clause (*e*)(i)(A) exceeds the amount determined under clause (*e*)(i)(B).

Editorial Note: Subsection 44(1) allows a taxpayer to defer the recognition of a capital gain when capital property is disposed of and a replacement property is acquired. In the case of voluntary dispositions, the replacement property must be acquired before the later of the end of the first taxation year following the disposition year and 12 months after the end of the disposition year. In the case of involuntary dispositions (e.g. destruction, expropriation), the replacement property must be acquired before the later of the end of the second taxation year following the disposition year and 24 months after the end of the disposition year. A similar election is available under subsection 13(4) in respect of any recapture of capital cost allowance arising from the same disposition.

History: S. 44(1)(*c*) was replaced by S.C. 2013, c. 34, s. 186(1), applicable in respect of dispositions that occur in taxation years that end on or after December 20, 2000, and formerly read:

(*c*) where the former property is described in paragraph (*a*), before the end of the second taxation year following the initial year, and

S. 44(1)(*d*) was replaced by S.C. 2013, c. 34, s. 186(1), applicable in respect of dispositions that occur in taxation years that end on or after December 20, 2001, and formerly read:

(*d*) in any other case, before the end of the first taxation year following the initial year,

Related Regulations: 600(b).

Related Sections: S. 13(4) Exchanges of property; s. 44(6) Deemed proceeds of disposition; s. 44(7) Where subpara. (1)(*e*)(iii) does not apply; s. 54, "capital property", "proceeds of disposition"; s. 87(2)(*l*.3) Replacement property; s. 96(3) Agreement or election of partnership members; s. 220(3.2) Late, amended or revoked elections; s. 248(1), "amount", "former business property", "property".

Canadian Tax Foundation: Shapiro, *The Replacement Property Rules: A Bit More Than Before*, 2002 Canadian Tax Journal 6:2141–2165.

Forms: T1030 — Election to Allow Individuals (Other Than Trusts) to Defer the Recognition of a Capital Gain in Respect of Dispositions of Capital Property.

Income Tax Technical News: Issue No. 25, Replacement Property Rules and Business Expansions.

Information Circulars: IC 07-1 Taxpayer Relief Provisions.

Interpretation Bulletins: *Primary* — IT-259R4 Exchanges of Property; IT-491 Former business property.

Tax Window Files: New Class 14.1 and replacement property rules, *November 4, 2016*, CRA Document No. 2016-0666901E5.

Cases: A rental building is not a former business property because it is used for producing income from property, not from a business. *Buonincontri v. The Queen*, 85 DTC 5277 (F.C.T.D.)

▶ 44(1.1) ◀

(1.1) Reserve — property disposed of to a child. In computing the amount that a taxpayer may claim under subparagraph (1)(*e*)(iii) in computing the taxpayer's gain from the disposition of a former property of the taxpayer, that subparagraph shall be read as if the references in that subparagraph to "1/5" and "4" were references to "1/10" and "9" respectively if that former property is real or immovable property in respect of the disposition of which, because of subsection 73(3), the rules in subsection 73(3.1) applied to the taxpayer and a child of the taxpayer.

▶ 44(2) ◀

(2) Time of disposition and of receipt of proceeds. For the purposes of this Act, the time at which a taxpayer has disposed of a property for which there are proceeds of disposition as described in paragraph (*b*), (*c*) or (*d*) of the definition "proceeds of disposition" in subsection 13(21) or paragraph (*b*), (*c*) or (*d*) of the definition "proceeds of disposition" in section 54, and the time at which an amount, in respect of those proceeds of disposition has become receivable by the taxpayer shall be deemed to be the earliest of

(*a*) the day the taxpayer has agreed to an amount as full compensation to the taxpayer for the property lost, destroyed, taken or sold,

(*b*) where a claim, suit, appeal or other proceeding has been taken before one or more tribunals or courts of competent jurisdiction, the day on which the taxpayer's compensation for the property is finally determined by those tribunals or courts,

(*c*) where a claim, suit, appeal or other proceeding referred to in paragraph (*b*) has not been taken before a tribunal or court of competent jurisdiction within two years of the loss, destruction or taking of the property, the day that is two years following the day of the loss, destruction or taking,

(*d*) the time at which the taxpayer is deemed by section 70 or paragraph 128.1(4)(*b*) to have disposed of the property, and

(*e*) where the taxpayer is a corporation other than a subsidiary corporation referred to in subsection 88(1), the time immediately before the winding-up of the corporation,

and the taxpayer shall be deemed to have owned the property continuously until the time so determined.

Related Sections: S. 59.1 Involuntary disposition of resource property.

Income Tax Folios: *Secondary* — S3-F9-C1 Lottery Winnings, Miscellaneous Receipts, and Income (and Losses) from Crime.

Interpretation Bulletins: *Secondary* — IT-125R4 Disposition of resource properties.

▶ 44(3) ◀

(3) Where s. 70(3) does not apply. Subsection 70(3) does not apply to compensation referred to in paragraph (*b*), (*c*) or (*d*) of the definition "proceeds of disposition" in subsection 13(21) or paragraph (*b*), (*c*) or (*d*) of the definition "proceeds of disposition" in section 54 that has been transferred or distributed to beneficiaries or other persons beneficially interested in an estate or trust.

Related Sections: S. 70(3) Rights or things transferred to beneficiaries.

▶ 44(4) ◀

(4) Deemed election. Where a former property of a taxpayer was a depreciable property of the taxpayer

(*a*) if the taxpayer has elected in respect of that property under subsection (1), the taxpayer shall be deemed to have elected in respect thereof under subsection 13(4); and

(*b*) if the taxpayer has elected in respect of that property under subsection 13(4), the taxpayer shall be deemed to have elected in respect thereof under subsection (1).

▶ 44(5) ◀

(5) Replacement property. For the purposes of this section, a particular capital property of a taxpayer is a replacement property for a former property of the taxpayer, if

(*a*) it is reasonable to conclude that the property was acquired by the taxpayer to replace the former property;

(*a*.1) it was acquired by the taxpayer and used by the taxpayer or a person related to the taxpayer for a use that is the same as or similar to the use to which the taxpayer or a person related to the taxpayer put the former property;

(*b*) where the former property was used by the taxpayer or a person related to the taxpayer for the purpose of gaining or producing income from a business, the particular capital property was acquired for the purpose of gaining or producing income from that or a similar business or for use by a person related to the taxpayer for such a purpose;

(*c*) where the former property was a taxable Canadian property of the taxpayer, the particular capital property is a taxable Canadian property of the taxpayer; and

(*d*) where the former property was a taxable Canadian property (other than treaty-protected property) of the taxpayer, the particular capital property is a taxable Canadian property (other than treaty-protected property) of the taxpayer.

Related Sections: S. 13(4) Exchanges of property; s. 13(4.1) Replacement for a former property; s. 13(6) Misclassified property; s. 13(7) Rules applicable; s. 248(1), "treaty-protected property".

Tax Window Files: Replacement property, *June 7, 2016*, CRA Document No. 2016-0648971E5.

▶ 44(6) ◀

(6) Deemed proceeds of disposition. If a taxpayer has disposed of property that was a former business property and was in part a building and in part the land (or an interest, or for civil law a right, therein) subjacent to, or immediately contiguous to and necessary for the use of, the building, for the purposes of this subdivision, the amount if any, by which

(*a*) the proceeds of disposition of one such part determined without regard to this subsection

exceed

(*b*) the adjusted cost base to the taxpayer of that part

shall, to the extent that the taxpayer so elects in the taxpayer's return of income under this Part for the year in which the taxpayer acquired a replacement property for the former business property, be deemed not to be proceeds of disposition of that part and to be proceeds of disposition of the other part.

History: S. 44(6), the portion before paragraph (*a*) was replaced by S.C. 2013, c. 34, s. 104, in force June 26, 2013, and formerly read:

(6) *Deemed proceeds of disposition.* Where a taxpayer has disposed of property that was a former business property and was in part a building and in part the land (or an interest therein) subjacent to, or immediately contiguous to and necessary for the use of, the building, for the purposes of this subdivision, the amount if any, by which

Related Regulations: 600(b).

Related Sections: S. 220(3.2) Late, amended or revoked elections.

Information Circulars: IC 07-1 Taxpayer Relief Provisions.

▶ 44(7) ◀

(7) Where subpara. (1)(e)(iii) does not apply. Subparagraph (1)(*e*)(iii) does not apply to permit a taxpayer to claim any amount under that subparagraph in computing a gain for a taxation year where

(*a*) the taxpayer, at the end of the year or at any time in the immediately following year, was not resident in Canada or was exempt from tax under any provision of this Part;

(*b*) the person to whom the former property of the taxpayer was disposed of was a corporation that, immediately after the disposition,

(i) was controlled, directly or indirectly in any manner whatever, by the taxpayer,

(ii) was controlled, directly or indirectly in any manner whatever, by a person or group of persons by whom the taxpayer was controlled, directly or indirectly in any manner whatever, or

(iii) controlled the taxpayer, directly or indirectly in any manner whatever, where the taxpayer is a corporation; or

(*c*) the former property of the taxpayer was disposed of to a partnership in which the taxpayer was, immediately after the disposition, a majority-interest partner.

History: S. 44(7)(*c*) was replaced by S.C. 2013, c. 40, s. 20, in force December 12, 2013, and formerly read:

(*c*) the former property of the taxpayer was disposed of to a partnership in which the taxpayer was, immediately after the disposition, a majority interest partner.

S. 44(7)(*c*) was added by S.C. 2013, c. 34, s. 186(2), applicable to dispositions of property by a taxpayer that occur after December 20, 2002. However, if a property so disposed of pursuant to an agreement in writing made before December 21, 2002 is transferred to the purchaser before 2004

(*a*) subsection 44(7), as it read immediately before the enactment of subsection (2), applies in respect of the disposition of property; and

(*b*) for the purpose of applying subparagraph 44(1)(*e*)(iii) to the taxpayer for a taxation year in respect of the property, a reasonable amount as a reserve in respect of the proceeds of disposition may not exceed the amount that would be reasonable if the proceeds from any subsequent disposition of the property that the purchaser receives before the end of the taxation year were received by the taxpayer.

Related Sections: S. 256(5.1) Control in fact.

▶ 44(8) ◀

(8) Application of s. 70(10). The definitions in subsection 70(10) apply to this section.

SECTION 44.1: [Capital gain deferral re small business investments]

▶ 44.1(1) ◀

(1) Definitions. The definitions in this subsection apply in this section.

Editorial Note: S. 44.1 offers a deferral of capital gains tax with respect to a gain from the disposition of the shares of certain active business corporations by an individual (other than a trust) where such individual reinvests the proceeds of disposition into eligible small business investments. Similar to the exchange of property provisions, this policy measure only provides a deferral which is reflected in a reduction of the cost base of the new investment. (See also the editorial notes re the definition of "eligible small business corporation share" and s. 44.1(2).)

Where a trust owns shares of such a corporation and an individual (other than such trust) could otherwise take advantage of section 44.1, consideration should be given to distributing such shares to the trust's beneficiaries — if such distribution may take place on a tax-deferred basis — prior to the disposition of the shares.

Canadian Tax Foundation: Wilkenfeld, *Rollover For Eligible SBC Shares*, 2001 Tax for the Owner-Manager 1(2):9–10.

"ACB reduction" — "ACB reduction" of an individual in respect of a replacement share of the individual in respect of a qualifying disposition of the individual means the amount determined by the formula

$$D \times (E/F)$$

where

D is the permitted deferral of the individual in respect of the qualifying disposition;

E is the cost to the individual of the replacement share; and

F is the cost to the individual of all the replacement shares of the individual in respect of the qualifying disposition.

"active business corporation" — "active business corporation" at any time means, subject to subsection (10), a corporation that is, at that time, a taxable Canadian corporation all or substantially all of the fair market value of the assets of which at that time is attributable to assets of the corporation that are

(*a*) assets used principally in an active business carried on by the corporation or by an active business corporation that is related to the corporation;

(*b*) shares issued by or debt owing by other active business corporations that are related to the corporation; or

(*c*) a combination of assets described in paragraphs (*a*) and (*b*).

Editorial Note: See the Editorial Note to the definition of "eligible small business corporation".

Related Sections: S. 44.1(8) Special rule — re carrying on an active business; s. 44.1(10) Special rule — re exceptions; s. 89(1), "taxable Canadian corporation".

"carrying value" —"carrying value" of the assets of a corporation at any time means the amount at which the assets of the corporation would be valued for the purpose of the corporation's balance sheet as of that time if that balance sheet were prepared in accordance with generally accepted accounting principles used in Canada at that time, except that an asset of a corporation that is a share or debt issued by a related corporation is deemed to have a carrying value of nil.

Related Sections: s. 248(24) Accounting methods.

"common share" —"common share" means a share prescribed for the purpose of paragraph 110(1)(*d*).

Related Regulations: 6204.

"eligible pooling arrangement" —"eligible pooling arrangement" in respect of an individual means an agreement in writing made between the individual and another person or partnership (which other person or partnership is referred to in this definition and subsection (3) as the "investment manager") where the agreement provides for

(*a*) the transfer of funds or other property by the individual to the investment manager for the purpose of making investments on behalf of the individual;

(*b*) the purchase of eligible small business corporation shares with those funds, or the proceeds of a disposition of the other property, within 60 days after receipt of those funds or the other property by the investment manager; and

(*c*) the provision of a statement of account to the individual by the investment manager at the end of each month that ends after the transfer disclosing the details of the investment portfolio held by the investment manager on behalf of the individual at the end of that month and the details of the transactions made by the investment manager on behalf of the individual during the month.

"eligible small business corporation" —"eligible small business corporation" at any time means, subject to subsection (10), a corporation that, at that time, is a Canadian-controlled private corporation all or substantially all of the fair market value of the assets of which at that time is attributable to assets of the corporation that are

(*a*) assets used principally in an active business carried on primarily in Canada by the corporation or by an eligible small business corporation that is related to the corporation;

(*b*) shares issued by or debt owing by other eligible small business corporations that are related to the corporation; or

(*c*) a combination of assets described in paragraphs (*a*) and (*b*).

Editorial Note: An "eligible small business corporation" is generally a Canadian-controlled private corporation, as defined under s. 125(7) (in contrast, an active business corporation need not be a Canadian-controlled private corporation). It is defined (subject to s. 44.1(10)) as a taxable Canadian corporation, all or substantially all of the fair market value of the assets of which is attributable to assets used principally in an active business carried on primarily in Canada by the corporation or a related corporation that is also an eligible small business corporation, and shares or debt of other eligible small business corporations that are related to the corporation. While the definition is similar to "small business corporation" in s. 248(1), there are a number of differences. (See also the Editorial Note to s. 44.1(2).)

Related Sections: S. 44.1(8) Special rule — re carrying on an active business; s. 44.1(10) Special rule — re exceptions; s. 125(7), "Canadian-controlled private corporation".

Tax Window Files: Paragraphe 44.1 — actions de remplacement, *May 11, 2010*, CRA Document No. 2009-0339151E5.

"eligible small business corporation share" —"eligible small business corporation share" of an individual means a common share issued by a corporation to the individual if

(*a*) at the time the share was issued, the corporation was an eligible small business corporation; and

(*b*) immediately before and after the share was issued, the total carrying value of the assets of the corporation and corporations related to it did not exceed $50,000,000.

Editorial Note: An "eligible small business corporation share" of an individual is a common share issued by an "eligible small business corporation", the total carrying value of the assets of which (together with related corporations) did not exceed $50,000,000 immediately before and after the issuance of the share. Because the shares must be from treasury, shares acquired by an individual from the initial investor will not be eligible for the deferral. The meaning of "common share" is prescribed under Regulation 6204. The "carrying value" of the assets is the amount determined for such property in accordance with Canadian GAAP except that shares or debt of a related corporation are deemed to have a carrying value of nil.

A share must be a share of an "active business corporation" but not necessarily a share of an "eligible small business corporation" throughout an individual's ownership period. The latter status is necessary only at the time the share was issued to the individual, thus allowing an individual to claim a deferral with respect to a share of a corporation that was not a Canadian-controlled private corporation throughout the period of ownership. The CRA takes the position that a corporation must have started its business before it can be considered an "eligible small business corporation". For a business to be seen as having started, a significant activity (i.e., a regular part of an income-earning process), must have been undertaken. (See also the Editorial Note to s. 44.1(2).)

"permitted deferral" —"permitted deferral" of an individual in respect of a qualifying disposition of the individual means the amount determined by the formula

$$(G/H) \times I$$

where

G is the lesser of the individual's proceeds of disposition from the qualifying disposition and the total of all amounts each of which is the cost to the individual of a replacement share in respect of the qualifying disposition;

H is the individual's proceeds of disposition from the qualifying disposition; and

I is the individual's capital gain from the qualifying disposition.

Editorial Note: Effective February 18, 2003, there is no limit on the amount of capital gains eligible for the deferral. (See also the Editorial Note to s. 44.1(2).)

Related Sections: S. 44.1(12) Anti-avoidance rule.

"qualifying cost" — (Repealed by S.C. 2003, c. 15, s. 70(1).)

"qualifying disposition" — "qualifying disposition" of an individual (other than a trust) means, subject to subsection (9), a disposition of shares of the capital stock of a corporation where each such share disposed of was

(*a*) an eligible small business corporation share of the individual;

(*b*) throughout the period during which the individual owned the share, a common share of an active business corporation; and

(*c*) throughout the 185-day period that ended immediately before the disposition of the share, owned by the individual.

Editorial Note: A "qualifying disposition" of a common share of an active business corporation by an individual requires that the active business of the corporation was carried on primarily in Canada by the corporation or a related active business corporation since the time at which the individual last acquired the share or a period of 730 days, whichever is less. (See also the Editorial Note to ss. 44.1(2) and 44.1(9).)

Related Sections: S. 44.1(9) Special rule — re qualifying disposition.

Tax Window Files: Actions de remplacement, *February 10, 2012*, CRA Document No. 2010-0385861E5.

"qualifying portion of a capital gain" — (Repealed by S.C. 2003, c. 15, s. 70(1).)

Related Sections: S. 39(1)(*a*) Meaning of capital gain and capital loss; s. 54, "adjusted cost base".

"qualifying portion of the proceeds of disposition" — (Repealed by S.C. 2003, c. 15, s. 70(1).)

"replacement share" — "replacement share" of an individual in respect of a qualifying disposition of the individual in a taxation year means an eligible small business corporation share of the individual that is

(*a*) acquired by the individual in the year or within 120 days after the end of the year; and

(*b*) designated by the individual in the individual's return of income for the year to be a replacement share in respect of the qualifying disposition.

Editorial Note: A "replacement share" is an eligible small business corporation share that is acquired by the individual in the year or within 120 days after the end of the year and is designated by the individual in his/her tax return for the year to be a replacement share in respect of the qualifying disposition. However, the late filing of, or the failure to make a designation, could prevent an individual from claiming the deferral, even though the shares would otherwise qualify as replacement shares. The designation is also not eligible for relief under s. 220(3.2). This highlights the importance of making a designation in respect of the replacement shares on a timely basis. (See also the Editorial Note to s. 44.1(2).)

Tax Window Files: Actions de remplacement, *February 10, 2012*, CRA Document No. 2010-0385861E5.

▶ 44.1(2) ◀

(2) Capital gain deferral. Where an individual has made a qualifying disposition in a taxation year,

(*a*) the individual's capital gain for the year from the qualifying disposition is deemed to be the amount by which the individual's capital gain for the year from the qualifying disposition, determined without reference to this section, exceeds the individual's permitted deferral in respect of the qualifying disposition;

(*b*) in computing the adjusted cost base to the individual of a replacement share of the individual in respect of the qualifying disposition at any time after its acquisition, there shall be deducted the amount of the ACB reduction of the individual in respect of the replacement share; and

(*c*) where the qualifying disposition was a disposition of a share that was taxable Canadian property of the individual, the replacement share of the individual in respect of the qualifying disposition is deemed to be, at any time that is within 60 months after the disposition, taxable Canadian property of the individual.

Editorial Note: The small business investment deferral allows an individual to defer the amount of his or her capital gain from a "qualifying disposition" as follows: (a) the individual's capital gain from the qualifying disposition is reduced by the amount of the individual's "permitted deferral" in respect of the disposition; (b) the adjusted cost base of the individual's "replacement shares" is reduced by the amount of the individual's ACB reduction in respect of such shares (the ACB reduction is the amount of the permitted deferral prorated over the number of replacement shares); and (c) the replacement shares of the individual in respect of the qualifying disposition are deemed to be, at any time that is within 60 months after the disposition, taxable Canadian property where the qualifying disposition was a disposition of shares that were taxable Canadian property.

An individual's permitted deferral is proportional to the percentage of the proceeds from a qualifying disposition that is reinvested in replacement shares.

History: S. 44.1(2)(*c*) was replaced by S.C. 2010, c. 12, s. 2(1), applicable in determining after March 4, 2010 whether a property is taxable Canadian property of a taxpayer. S. 44.1(2)(*c*) formerly read:

(*c*) where the qualifying disposition was a disposition of a share that was a taxable Canadian property of the individual, the replacement share of the individual in respect of the qualifying disposition is deemed to be taxable Canadian property of the individual.

Related Sections: S. 39(1)(*a*) Meaning of capital gain and capital loss; s. 53(2)(*a*)(v) Amounts to be deducted — Share of the capital stock of a corporation; s. 54, "adjusted cost base"; s. 107.4(3)(*f*) Tax consequences of qualifying dispositions; s. 248(1), "taxable Canadian property".

Canadian Tax Foundation: Shapiro, *The Replacement Property Rules: A Bit More Than Before*, 2002 Canadian Tax Journal 6:2141–2165.

Tax Window Files: Section 44.1, *July 19, 2007*, CRA Document No. 2006-0194571I7.

▶ 44.1(3) ◀

(3) Special rule — re eligible pooling arrangements. Except for the purpose of the definition "eligible pooling arrangement" in subsection (1), any transaction entered into by an investment manager under an eligible pooling arrangement on behalf of an individual is deemed to be a transaction of the individual and not a transaction of the investment manager.

Editorial Note: Any transaction entered into by an investment manager under an eligible pooling arrangement on behalf of an individual is deemed to be that of the individual.

▶ 44.1(4) ◀

(4) Special rule — re acquisitions on death. For the purpose of this section, a share of the capital stock of a corporation, acquired by an individual as a consequence of the death of a person who is the individual's spouse, common-law partner or parent, is deemed to be a share that was acquired by the individual at the time it was acquired by that person and owned by the individual throughout the period that it was owned by that person, if

(*a*) where the person was the spouse or common-law partner of the individual, the share was an eligible small business share of the person and subsection 70(6) applied to the individual in respect of the share; or

(*b*) where the person was the individual's parent, the share was an eligible small business share of the parent and subsection 70(9.2) applied to the individual in respect of the share.

Editorial Note: Where an individual acquires the shares of a corporation as a consequence of the death of his/her spouse, common-law partner or parent, the individual is deemed to have acquired the shares at the same time as the deceased individual and to have owned the shares throughout the period that they were owned by the deceased individual.

▶ 44.1(5) ◀

(5) Special rule — re breakdown of relationships. For the purpose of this section, a share of the capital stock of a corporation, acquired by an individual from a person who was the individual's former spouse or common-law partner as a consequence of the settlement of rights arising out of their marriage or common-law partnership, is deemed to be a share that was acquired by the individual at the time it was acquired by that person and owned by the individual throughout the period that it was owned by that person if the share was an eligible small business share of the person and subsection 73(1) applied to the individual in respect of the share.

Editorial Note: Where an individual acquires shares of a corporation from the individual's former spouse or common-law partner as a result of a settlement agreement with such former spouse or common-law partner, the individual is deemed to have acquired such shares at the time that the transferor acquired the shares and to have owned such shares throughout the period that the transferor owned the shares.

▶ 44.1(6) ◀

(6) Special rule — re eligible small business corporation share exchanges. For the purpose of this section, where an individual receives shares of the capital stock of a particular corporation that are eligible small business corporation shares of the individual (in this subsection referred to as the "new shares") as the sole consideration for the disposition by the individual of shares issued by the particular corporation or by another corporation that were eligible small business corporation shares of the individual (in this subsection referred to as the "exchanged shares"), the new shares are deemed to have been owned by the individual throughout the period that the exchanged shares were owned by the individual if

(*a*) section 51, paragraph 85(1)(*h*), subsection 85.1(1), section 86 or subsection 87(4) applied to the individual in respect of the new shares; and

(*b*) the individual's total proceeds of disposition of the exchanged shares was equal to the total of all amounts each of which was the individual's adjusted cost base of an exchanged share immediately before the disposition.

History: S. 44.1(6), the portion before paragraph (*b*) was replaced by S.C. 2013, c. 34, s. 187(1), applicable to dispositions that occur after February 27, 2000, and formerly read:

(6) *Special rule — re eligible small business corporation share exchanges.* For the purpose of this section, where an individual receives shares of the capital stock of a corporation that are eligible small business corporation shares of the individual (in this subsection referred to as the "new shares") as the sole consideration for the disposition of shares issued by another corporation that were eligible small business corporation shares of the individual (in this subsection referred to as the "exchanged shares"), the new shares are deemed to have been owned by the individual throughout the period that the exchanged shares were owned by the individual if

(*a*) paragraph 85(1)(*h*) or subsection 85.1(3) or 87(4) applied to the individual in respect of the new shares; and

▶ 44.1(7) ◀

(7) Special rule — re active business corporation share exchanges. For the purpose of this section, where an individual receives common shares of the capital stock of a particular corporation (in this subsection referred to as the "new shares") as the sole consideration for the disposition by the individual of common shares of the particular corporation or of another corporation (in this subsection referred to as the "exchanged shares"), the new shares are deemed to be eligible small business corporation shares of the individual and shares of the capital stock of an active business corporation that were owned by the individual throughout the period that the exchanged shares were owned by the individual, if

(*a*) section 51, paragraph 85(1)(*h*), subsection 85.1(1), section 86 or subsection 87(4) applied to the individual in respect of the new shares;

(*b*) the total of the individual's proceeds of disposition in respect of the disposition of the exchanged shares was equal to the total of the individual's adjusted cost bases immediately before the disposition of such shares; and

(*c*) the disposition of the exchanged shares was a qualifying disposition of the individual.

Editorial Note: The provisions of s. 44.1(6) and (7) allow certain share exchanges and rollovers to occur without jeopardizing the qualification of the shares as shares of an active business corporation held throughout the 185-day holding period. The individual who had rolled or exchanged shares for new shares of an eligible small business corporation is deemed to have owned the new shares throughout the period that he or she owned the exchanged or rolled shares.

History: S. 44.1(7), the portion before paragraph (*b*) was replaced by S.C. 2013, c. 34, s. 187(2), applicable to dispositions that occur after February 27, 2000, and formerly read:

(7) *Special rule — re active business corporation share exchanges.* For the purpose of this section, where an individual receives common shares of the capital stock of a corporation (in this subsection referred to as the "new shares") as the sole consideration for the disposition of common shares of another corporation (in this subsection referred to as the "exchanged shares"), the new shares are deemed to be eligible small business corporation shares of the individual and shares of the capital stock of an active business corporation that were owned by the individual throughout the period that the exchanged shares were owned by the individual, if

(*a*) paragraph 85(1)(*h*) or subsection 85.1(3) or 87(4) applied to the individual in respect of the new shares;

▶ 44.1(8) ◀

(8) Special rule — re carrying on an active business. For the purpose of the definitions in subsection (1), a property held at any particular time by a corporation that would, if this Act were read without reference to this subsection, be considered to carry on an active business at that time, is deemed to be used or held by the corporation in the course of carrying on that active business if the property (or other property for which the property is substituted property) was acquired by the corporation, at any time in the 36-month period ending at the particular time, because the corporation

(*a*) issued a debt or a share of a class of its capital stock in order to acquire money for the purpose of acquiring property to be used in or held in the course of, or making expenditures for the purpose of, earning income from an active business carried on by it;

(*b*) disposed of property used or held by it in the course of carrying on an active business in order to acquire money for the purpose of acquiring property to be used in or held in the course of, or making expenditures for the purpose of, earning income from an active business carried on by it; or

(*c*) accumulated income derived from an active business carried on by it in order to acquire property to be used in or held in the course of, or to make expenditures for the purpose of, earning income from an active business carried on by it.

Editorial Note: Cash will be deemed to be an active business asset during a 36-month period that begins after the corporation received the funds from certain transactions relating to its active business. This subsection, in effect, provides a 36-month grace period for a corporation to convert its cash into active business assets.

A similar grace period does not apply to the definition of a "small business corporation share" in s. 248(1) and a "qualifying small business corporation share" in s. 110.6.

An essential condition to the application of s. 44.1(8) is that the corporation be considered as carrying on an active business at any time for the purpose of determining if a particular property is used in the course of carrying on an active business. The CRA has indicated that this condition will not be met if the business had not started at the time the treasury shares were acquired by the individual (Doc. No. 2004-0083791I7).

Related Sections: S. 248(5) Substituted property.

▶ 44.1(9) ◀

(9) Special rule — re qualifying disposition. A disposition of a common share of an active business corporation (in this subsection referred to as the "subject share") by an individual that, but for this subsection, would be a qualifying disposition of the individual is deemed not to be a qualifying disposition of the individual unless the active business of the corporation referred to in paragraph (*a*) of the definition "active business corporation" in subsection (1) was carried on primarily in Canada

(*a*) at all times in the period that began at the time the individual last acquired the subject share and ended at the time of disposition, if that period is less than 730 days; or

(*b*) in any other case, for at least 730 days in the period referred to in paragraph (*a*).

Editorial Note: A disposition of a common share of an active business corporation by an individual is deemed not to be a qualifying disposition unless the active business of the corporation was carried on primarily in Canada by the corporation or a related active business corporation since the time at which the individual last acquired the share or for a period of 730 days, whichever is less.

▶ 44.1(10) ◀

(10) Special rule — re exceptions. For the purpose of this section, an eligible small business corporation and an active business corporation at any time do not include a corporation that is, at that time,

(*a*) a professional corporation;

(*b*) a specified financial institution;

(*c*) a corporation the principal business of which is the leasing, rental, development or sale, or any combination of those activities, of real or immovable property owned by it; or

(*d*) a corporation more than 50% of the fair market value of the property of which (net of debts incurred to acquire the property) is attributable to real or immovable property.

Editorial Note: An eligible small business corporation and an active business corporation do not include a "professional corporation" (as defined in s. 248(1)); a "specified financial institution" (as defined in s. 248(1)); a corporation, the principal business of which is the leasing, rental, development or sale, or any combination of those activities, of real or immovable property owned by it; and a corporation more than 50% of the fair market value of the property of which (net of debts incurred to acquire the property) is attributable to real or immovable property.

History: S. 44.1(10)(*c*) and (*d*) were replaced by S.C. 2013, c. 34, s. 105, in force June 26, 2013, and formerly read:

(*c*) a corporation the principal business of which is the leasing, rental, development or sale, or any combination of those activities, of real property owned by it; or

(*d*) a corporation more than 50 per cent of the fair market value of the property of which (net of debts incurred to acquire the property) is attributable to real property.

Related Sections: S. 248(1), "professional corporation", "specified financial institution".

▶ 44.1(11) ◀

(11) Determination rule. In determining whether a share owned by an individual is an eligible small business corporation share of the individual, this Act shall be read without reference to section 48.1.

Editorial Note: The Act is to be read without reference to s. 48.1 in determining whether a share owned by an individual is an eligible small business corporation share of the individual. S. 48.1 deems a share to be reacquired and therefore would be offside the definition of an eligible small business corporation share as the share would not be "issued".

▶ 44.1(12) ◀

(12) Anti-avoidance rule. The permitted deferral of an individual in respect of a qualifying disposition of shares issued by a corporation (in this subsection referred to as "new shares") is deemed to be nil where

(*a*) the new shares (or shares for which the new shares are substituted property) were issued to the individual or a person related to the individual as part of a series of transactions or events in which

(i) shares of the capital stock of a corporation (in this subsection referred to as the "old shares") were disposed of by the individual or a person related to the individual, or

(ii) the paid-up capital of old shares or the adjusted cost base to the individual or to a person related to the individual of the old shares was reduced;

(*b*) the new shares (or shares for which the new shares are substituted property) were

(i) issued by the corporation that issued the old shares,

(ii) issued by a corporation that, at or immediately after the time of issue of the new shares, was a corporation that was not dealing at arm's length with

(A) the corporation that issued the old shares, or

(B) the individual, or

(iii) issued, by a corporation that acquired the old shares (or by another corporation related to that corporation), as part of the transaction or event or series of transactions or events that included that acquisition of the old shares; and

(*c*) it is reasonable to conclude that one of the main reasons for the series of transactions or events or a transaction in the series was to permit the individual, persons related to the individual, or the individual and persons related to the individual to become eligible to deduct under subsection (2)permitted deferrals in respect of qualifying dispositions of new shares (or shares substituted for the new shares) the total of which would exceed the total that those persons would have been eligible to deduct under subsection (2) in respect of permitted deferrals in respect of qualifying dispositions of old shares.

Editorial Note: This anti-avoidance rule will deem the permitted deferral to be nil where an individual (or a related person) disposes of shares of a particular corporation and acquires new shares of the particular corporation (or of a corporation not at arm's length with the particular corporation) with the purpose of increasing the total amount of permitted deferrals with respect to qualifying dispositions of the individual (and/or related persons).

The provision is broadly worded to potentially encompass any internal reorganization, the purpose of which is to increase the permitted deferral of a related group of companies.

History: S. 44.1(12)(*b*) was replaced by S.C. 2013, c. 34, s. 187(3), applicable in respect of dispositions that occur after February 27, 2004, and formerly read:

(*b*) the new shares (or shares for which the new shares are substituted property) were issued by the corporation that issued the old shares or were issued by a corporation that, at or immediately after the time of issue of those shares, was a corporation that was not dealing at arm's length with the corporation that issued the old shares; and

Related Sections: S. 54, "adjusted cost base"; s. 248(1), "taxable Canadian property"; s. 248(5) Substituted property; s. 251(1) Arm's length; s. 251(6) Blood relationship, etc.

▶ 44.1(13) ◀

(13) Order of disposition of shares. For the purpose of this section, an individual is deemed to dispose of shares that are identical properties in the order in which the individual acquired them.

History: S. 44.1(13) was added by S.C. 2013, c. 34, s. 187(4), applicable in respect of dispositions that occur after December 20, 2002. However, if an individual so elects in writing and files the election with the Minister of National Revenue on or before the individual's filing-due date for the individual's taxation year which includes June 26, 2013, subsection 44.1(13) applies, in respect of the individual, to dispositions that occur after February 27, 2000.

SECTION 45: Property with more than one use

▶ 45(1) ◀

(1) Property with more than one use. For the purposes of this subdivision the following rules apply:

(*a*) where a taxpayer,

(i) having acquired property for some other purpose, has commenced at a later time to use it for the purpose of gaining or producing income, or

(ii) having acquired property for the purpose of gaining or producing income, has commenced at a later time to use it for some other purpose,

the taxpayer shall be deemed to have

(iii) disposed of it at that later time for proceeds equal to its fair market value at that later time, and

(iv) immediately thereafter reacquired it at a cost equal to that fair market value;

(*b*) where property has, since it was acquired by a taxpayer, been regularly used in part for the purpose of gaining or producing income and in part for some other purpose, the taxpayer shall be deemed to have acquired, for that other purpose, the proportion of the property that the use regularly made of the property for that other purpose is of the whole use regularly made of the property at a cost to the taxpayer equal to the same proportion of the cost to the taxpayer of the whole property, and, if the property has, in such a case, been disposed of, the proceeds of disposition of the proportion of the property deemed to have been acquired for that other purpose shall be deemed to be the same proportion of the proceeds of disposition of the whole property;

(*c*) where, at any time after a taxpayer has acquired property, there has been a change in the relation between the use regularly made by the taxpayer of the property for gaining or producing income and the use regularly made of the property for other purposes,

(i) if the use regularly made of the property for those other purposes has increased, the taxpayer shall be deemed to have

(A) disposed of the property at that time for proceeds equal to the proportion of the fair market value of the property at that time that the amount of the increase in the use regularly made by the taxpayer of the property for those other purposes is of the whole use regularly made of the property, and

(B) immediately thereafter reacquired the property so disposed of at a cost equal to the proceeds referred to in clause (A), and

(ii) if the use regularly made of the property for those other purposes has decreased, the taxpayer shall be deemed to have

(A) disposed of the property at that time for proceeds equal to the proportion of the fair market value of the property at that time that the amount of the decrease in use regularly made by the taxpayer of the property for those other purposes is of the whole use regularly made of the property, and

(B) immediately thereafter reacquired the property so disposed of at a cost equal to the proceeds referred to in clause (A); and

Tax Window Files: Change-in-use rules for principal residence exemption, *April 26, 2017*, CRA Document No. 2016-0673231E5; Paragraphe 7(1.5) - contrepartie reçue, *February 9, 2010*, CRA Document No. 2016-0673231E5.

(*d*) in applying this subsection in respect of a non-resident taxpayer, a reference to "gaining or producing income" shall be read as a reference to "gaining or producing income from a source in Canada".

Editorial Note: S. 45(1) does not appear to apply to conversions of inventory to income-producing capital property, or vice versa, since both types of property are used for income-producing purposes. For the CRA's views of the income tax consequences of such conversions, see IT-102R2 and IT-218R, noted below ("Interpretation Bulletins"), both of which have been archived as they don't meet current government web standards. If personal-use property is converted into an income-producing property, any loss under s. 45(1) will be denied (s. 40(2)(*g*)(iii)) unless the property is a listed personal-use property.

Related Sections: S. 13(7) Rules applicable; s. 40(1) General rules; s. 40(2)(*g*) Limitations; s. 45(2) Election where change of use; s. 45(3) Election concerning principal residence; s. 54, "principal residence", "proceeds of disposition".

Canadian Tax Foundation: Irvine, *Current Cases: Federal Court of Appeal — Capital Gain Versus Income: Flying into Fog (CAE Inc. v. Canada, 2013 FCA 92)*, 2013 Canadian Tax Journal 3:729–739; Truster, *Inventory Versus Capital Property and the Change-in-Use Rules*, 2013 Tax for the Owner-Manager 13(4):6–7.

Tax Topics: No. 1838, Conversion of Vacant Land from Capital Property to Inventory; No. 2182, A Revisit of the Change-in-Use Rules.

Income Tax Folios: *Secondary* — S1-F3-C2 Principal Residence.

Interpretation Bulletins: *Secondary* — IT-102R2 Conversion of property, other than real property, from or to inventory; IT-218R Profit, capital gains and losses from the sale of real estate, including farmland and inherited land and conversion of real estate from capital property to inventory and vice versa.

Tax Window Files: Conversion from inventory to capital, *September 25, 2015*, CRA Document No. 2015-0596921E5; Change in Use of a Duplex Given to a Grandson, *Technical Interpretation, International and Trust Division, January 26, 2007*, CRA Document No. 2005-0157751E5; Cottage — Intention of Purchaser, *Technical Interpretation, Business and Partnerships Division, December 18, 2006*, CRA Document No. 2006-0208681E5; Change in Use of Property Prior to Acquisition, *Technical Interpretation, Business and Partnerships Division, October 26, 2005*, CRA Document No. 2005-0125831E5; Principal Residence Exemption — Use of Residence for Rental and Business Purposes, *Technical Interpretation, Business and Partnerships Division, January 7, 2004*, CRA Document No. 2003-0038217; Principal Residence Exemption — Rental of Home Outside Canada, *Technical Interpretation, Business and Partnerships Division, May 14, 2003*, CRA Document No. 2003-0014907.

Cases: Where there has been a deemed disposition, the proceeds are deemed to have been received at the time the property was deemed to have been disposed of. *Derlago v. The Queen*, 88 DTC 6290 (F.C.T.D.), affirming 86 DTC 1503 (T.C.C.)

▶ 45(2) ◀

(2) Election where change of use. For the purposes of this subdivision and section 13, where subparagraph (1)(*a*)(i) or paragraph 13(7)(*b*) would otherwise apply to any property of a taxpayer for a taxation year and the taxpayer so elects in respect of the property in the taxpayer's return of income for the year under this Part, the taxpayer shall be deemed not to have begun to use the property for the purpose of gaining or producing income except that, if in the taxpayer's return of income under this Part for a subsequent taxation year the taxpayer rescinds the election in respect of the property, the taxpayer shall be deemed to have begun so to use the property on the first day of that subsequent year.

> **Proposed Amendment**
> **2019 Federal Budget Resolutions**
> **Subsection 45(2) of the Act is replaced by the following:**
>
> **(2) Election where change of use.** For the purposes of this subdivision and section 13, if a taxpayer elects in respect of any property of the taxpayer in the taxpayer's return of income for a taxation year under this Part,
>
> (*a*) if subparagraph (1)(*a*)(i) or paragraph 13(7)(*b*) would otherwise apply to the property for the taxation year, the taxpayer is deemed not to have begun to use the property for the purpose of gaining or producing income;
>
> (*b*) if subparagraph (1)(*c*)(ii) or 13(7)(*d*)(i) would otherwise apply to the property for the taxation year, the taxpayer is deemed not to have increased the use regularly made of the property for the purpose of gaining or producing income relative to the use regularly made of the property for other purposes; and
>
> (*c*) if the taxpayer rescinds the election in respect of the property in the taxpayer's return of income under this Part for a subsequent taxation year,
>
> (i) if paragraph (*a*) applied to the taxpayer in the taxation year, the taxpayer is deemed to have begun to use the property for the purpose of gaining or producing income on the first day of the subsequent taxation year, and
>
> (ii) if paragraph (*b*) applied to the taxpayer in the taxation year, the taxpayer is deemed to have increased the use regularly made of the property for the purpose of gaining or producing income on the first day of the subsequent taxation year by the amount that would have been the increase in the taxation year if the election had not been made.
>
> **Applicable:** In respect of changes in the use of property that occur on or after March 19, 2019.

Editorial Note: In the case of a change of use in a residential property, an election under s. 45(2) or (3) to preserve principal residence status (e.g., where the taxpayer moves out of the residence and subsequently rents it out, or vice versa) is normally applicable for up to four years; see paragraph (*d*) of the definition "principal residence" in s. 54. However, principal residence status can be extended beyond four years for taxpayers who are required to live away from their principal residence for longer periods of time by virtue of their employment; see s. 54.1.

Related Regulations: 600(b).

Related Sections: S. 13(7) Rules applicable; s. 54, "principal residence"; s. 54.1(1) Exception to principal residence rules; s. 220(3.2) Late, amended or revoked elections; s. 248(1), "business", "property".

Tax Profile: April 2007 — Tax Planning for Emigration from Canada.

Tax Topics: No. 1699, Draft Legislation Governing Non-Competition Payments.

Information Circulars: IC 07-1 Taxpayer relief provisions.

Tax Window Files: Principal Residence Exemption — Two Houses on Property, *Technical Interpretation, Business and Partnerships Division, April 28, 2006*, CRA Document No. 2005-0157441I7; Change in Use of Property Prior to Acquisition, *Technical Interpretation, Business and Partnerships Division, October 26, 2005*, CRA Document No. 2005-0125831E5; Principal Residence Exemption, *Technical Interpretation, Business and Partnerships Division, June 3, 2004*, CRA Document No. 2004-0056851E5; Principal Residence Exemption — Rental of Home Outside Canada, *Technical Interpretation, Business and Partnerships Division, May 14, 2003*, CRA Document No. 2003-0014907.

▶ 45(3) ◀

(3) Election concerning principal residence. Where at any time a property that was acquired by a taxpayer for the purpose of gaining or producing income ceases to be used for that purpose and becomes the principal residence of the taxpayer, subsection (1) shall not apply to deem the taxpayer to have disposed of the property at that time and to have reacquired it immediately thereafter if the taxpayer so elects by notifying the Minister in writing on or before the earlier of

> **Proposed Amendment**
> **2019 Federal Budget Resolutions**
> **The portion of subsection 45(3) of the Act before paragraph (*a*) is replaced by the following:**
>
> **(3) Election concerning principal residence.** If at any time a property that was acquired by a taxpayer for the purpose of gaining or producing income, or that was acquired in part for that purpose, ceases in whole or in part to be used for that purpose and becomes, or becomes part of, the principal residence of the taxpayer, paragraphs (1)(*a*) and (*c*) shall not apply to deem the taxpayer to have disposed of the property at that time and to have reacquired it immediately thereafter if the taxpayer so elects by notifying the Minister in writing on or before the earlier of
>
> **Applicable:** In respect of changes in the use of property that occur on or after March 19, 2019.

(*a*) the day that is 90 days after a demand by the Minister for an election under this subsection is sent to the taxpayer, and

(*b*) the taxpayer's filing-due date for the taxation year in which the property is actually disposed of by the taxpayer.

Editorial Note: See the editorial note under s. 45(2). The s. 45(3) election cannot be made if capital cost allowance has been claimed in respect of the property for a taxation year ending after 1984; see s. 45(4).

Related Regulations: 600(b).

Related Sections: S. 45(4) Where election cannot be made; s. 54, "principal residence"; s. 54.1(1) Exception to principal residence rules; s. 220(3.2) Late, amended or revoked elections; s. 248(1), "filing-due date".

Income Tax Folios: *Secondary* — S1-F3-C2 Principal Residence.

Information Circulars: IC 07-1 Taxpayer relief provisions.

▶ 45(4) ◀

(4) Where election cannot be made. Notwithstanding subsection (3), an election described in that subsection shall be deemed not to have been made in respect of a change in use of property if any deduction in respect of the property has been allowed for any taxation year ending after 1984 and on or before the change in use under regulations made under paragraph 20(1)(*a*) to the taxpayer, the taxpayer's spouse or common-law partner or a trust under which the taxpayer or the taxpayer's spouse or common-law partner is a beneficiary.

SECTION 46: Personal-use property

► 46(1) ◄

(1) Personal-use property. Where a taxpayer has disposed of a personal-use property (other than an excluded property disposed of in circumstances to which subsection 110.1(1), or the definition "total charitable gifts", "total cultural gifts" or "total ecological gifts" in subsection 118.1(1), applies) of the taxpayer, for the purposes of this subdivision

(*a*) the adjusted cost base to the taxpayer of the property immediately before the disposition shall be deemed to be the greater of $1,000 and the amount otherwise determined to be its adjusted cost base to the taxpayer at that time; and

(*b*) the taxpayer's proceeds of disposition of the property shall be deemed to be the greater of $1,000 and the taxpayer's proceeds of disposition of the property otherwise determined.

Editorial Note: The effect of the deeming rules in s. 46(1) with respect to personal-use property can be summarized as follows. If a taxpayer's actual adjusted cost base of the property is less than $1,000, the taxpayer cannot have a loss from the property and can only have a gain from the property to the extent that the actual proceeds of disposition exceed $1,000. If the taxpayer's actual proceeds of disposition are less than $1,000, the taxpayer cannot have a gain from the property and can only have a loss to the extent that the actual adjusted cost base of the property exceeds $1,000. (Note also that losses are recognized only in respect of listed personal property and arm's length personal-use property debts — see s. 40(2)(*g*)(iii)).

Related Sections: S. 40(2)(*g*) Limitations; s. 41(1) Taxable net gain from disposition of listed personal property; s. 41(2) Determination of net gain; s. 50(2) Where debt a personal-use property; s. 54, "personal-use property", "proceeds of disposition"; s. 248(1), "disposition".

Interpretation Bulletins: *Secondary* — IT-373R2 (Consolid.) Woodlots.

Tax Window Files: Personal-Use Property — Disposition of a Collection, *Technical Interpretation, Business and Partnerships Division, November 10, 2004,* CRA Document No. 2004-0077831E5.

► 46(2) ◄

(2) Where part only of property disposed of. Where a taxpayer has disposed of part of a personal-use property (other than a part of an excluded property disposed of in circumstances to which subsection 110.1(1), or the definition "total charitable gifts", "total cultural gifts" or "total ecological gifts" in subsection 118.1(1), applies) owned by the taxpayer and has retained another part of the property, for the purposes of this subdivision

(*a*) the adjusted cost base to the taxpayer, immediately before the disposition, of the part so disposed of shall be deemed to be the greater of

(i) the adjusted cost base to the taxpayer at that time of that part otherwise determined, and

(ii) that proportion of $1,000 that the amount determined under subparagraph (i) is of the adjusted cost base to the taxpayer at that time of the whole property; and

(*b*) the proceeds of disposition of the part so disposed of shall be deemed to be the greater of

(i) the proceeds of disposition of that part otherwise determined, and

(ii) the amount determined under subparagraph (*a*)(ii).

Editorial Note: The adjusted cost base of the part of the property "otherwise determined" (s. 46(2)(*a*)(i)) is presumably that in accordance with the rules in s. 43(1).

Related Sections: S. 43(1) General rule for part dispositions; s. 54, "adjusted cost base", "proceeds of disposition".

► 46(3) ◄

(3) Properties ordinarily disposed of as a set. For the purposes of this subdivision, where a number of personal-use properties of a taxpayer that would, if the properties were disposed of, ordinarily be disposed of in one disposition as a set,

(*a*) have been disposed of by more than one disposition so that all of the properties have been acquired by one person or by a group of persons not dealing with each other at arm's length, and

(*b*) had, immediately before the first disposition referred to in paragraph (*a*), a total fair market value greater than $1,000,

the properties shall be deemed to be a single personal-use property and each such disposition shall be deemed to be a disposition of a part of that property.

Editorial Note: Since s. 46(3) deems each disposition of a property in the set to be a disposition of part of a single personal-use property, the part-disposition rules in s. 46(2) apply.

Related Sections: S. 46(2) Where part only of property disposed of.

Tax Window Files: 2013 STEP Canada Roundtable, Question 8, *June 12, 2013,* CRA Document No. 2013-0481001C6; Personal-Use Property — Disposition of a Collection, *Technical Interpretation, Business and Partnerships Division, November 10, 2004,* CRA Document No. 2004-0077831E5.

► 46(4) ◄

(4) Decrease in value of personal-use property of corporation, etc. Where it may reasonably be regarded that, by reason of a decrease in the fair market value of any personal-use property of a corporation, partnership or trust,

(*a*) a taxpayer's gain, if any, from the disposition of a share of the capital stock of a corporation, an interest in a trust or an interest in a partnership has become a loss, or is less than it would have been if the decrease had not occurred, or

(*b*) a taxpayer's loss, if any, from the disposition of a share or interest described in paragraph (*a*) is greater than it would have been if the decrease had not occurred,

the amount of the gain or loss, as the case may be, shall be deemed to be the amount that it would have been but for the decrease.

Editorial Note: S. 46(4) ensures that an accrued personal-use property loss cannot be claimed indirectly by holding a personal-use property in a corporation, trust or partnership. For example, in the absence of the provision, one could claim a loss on the disposition of a share in a corporation attributable to an accrued loss in respect of personal-use property owned by the corporation.

► 46(5) ◄

(5) Excluded property. For the purpose of this section, "excluded property" of a taxpayer means property acquired by the taxpayer, or by a person with whom the taxpayer does not deal at arm's length, in circumstances in which it is reasonable to conclude that the acquisition of the property relates to an arrangement, plan or scheme that is promoted by another person or partnership and under which it is reasonable to conclude that the property will be the subject of a gift to which subsection 110.1(1), or the definition "total charitable gifts", "total cultural gifts" or "total ecological gifts" in subsection 118.1(1), applies.

Editorial Note: S. 46(5) was enacted in response to certain tax shelter gifting arrangements under which property was acquired and immediately donated to a charity at a purported fair market value that was in excess of the donor's cost but not more than $1,000. The practical effect of the provision has been diluted somewhat owing to the new gifting rules, particularly s. 248(35).

Related Sections: S. 251(1) Arm's length.

Tax Profile: May 2002 — Update on Charitable Giving.

SECTION 47: Identical properties

▶ 47(1) ◀

(1) Identical properties. Where at any particular time after 1971 a taxpayer who owns one property that was or two or more identical properties each of which was, as the case may be, acquired by the taxpayer after 1971, acquires one or more other properties (in this subsection referred to as "newly-acquired properties") each of which is identical to each such previously-acquired property, for the purposes of computing, at any subsequent time, the adjusted cost base of the taxpayer of each such identical property,

(*a*) the taxpayer shall be deemed to have disposed of each such previously-acquired property immediately before the particular time for proceeds equal to its adjusted cost base to the taxpayer immediately before the particular time;

(*b*) the taxpayer shall be deemed to have acquired the identical property at the particular time at a cost equal to the quotient obtained when

(i) the total of the adjusted cost bases to the taxpayer immediately before the particular time of the previously-acquired properties, and the cost to the taxpayer (determined without reference to this section) of the newly-acquired properties

is divided by

(ii) the number of the identical properties owned by the taxpayer immediately after the particular time;

(*c*) there shall be deducted, after the particular time, in computing the adjusted cost base to the taxpayer of each such identical property, the amount determined by the formula

$$A/B$$

where

A is the total of all amounts deducted under paragraph 53(2)(*g*.1) in computing immediately before the particular time the adjusted cost base to the taxpayer of the previously-acquired properties, and

B is the number of such identical properties owned by the taxpayer immediately after the particular time or, where subsection (2) applies, the quotient determined under that subsection in respect of the acquisition; and

(*d*) there shall be added, after the particular time, in computing the adjusted cost base to the taxpayer of each such identical property the amount determined under paragraph (*c*) in respect of the identical property.

Editorial Note: The deemed dispositions and acquisitions in ss. 47(1)(*a*) and (*b*) effectively provide for the averaging of the adjusted cost bases of a taxpayer's identical properties. Paragraphs (*c*) and (*d*) may be relevant, if at all, to the application of the debt forgiveness rules in s. 80.03.

Related Sections: S. 7(1.3) Order of disposition of securities; s. 7(1.31) Disposition of newly-acquired security; s. 54, "adjusted cost base"; s. 138(11.1) Identical properties; s. 248(12) Identical properties.

Canadian Tax Foundation: Gosselin, *TCC Shuts Down Strategy To Multiply Lifetime Capital Gains Exemption*, 2014 Tax for the Owner-Manager 14(3):4–5.

Interpretation Bulletins: *Secondary* — IT-88R2 Stock dividends; IT-115R2 Fractional interests in shares; IT-146R4 Shares entitling shareholders to choose taxable or capital dividends.

Tax Window Files: Identical Properties — Shares Acquired By Estate, *Technical Interpretation, International & Trusts Division, September 17, 2004*, CRA Document No. 2004-0083161E5.

▶ 47(2) ◀

(2) Where identical properties are bonds, etc. For the purposes of subsection (1), where a group of identical properties referred to in that subsection is a group of identical bonds, debentures, bills, notes or similar obligations issued by a debtor, subparagraph (1)(*b*)(ii) shall be read as follows:

"(ii) the quotient obtained when the total of the principal amounts of all such identical properties owned by the taxpayer immediately after the particular time is divided by the principal amount of the identical property."

Related Sections: S. 248(12) Identical properties.

▶ 47(3) ◀

(3) Securities acquired by employee. For the purpose of subsection (1), a security (within the meaning assigned by subsection 7(7)) acquired by a taxpayer after February 27, 2000 is deemed not to be identical to any other security acquired by the taxpayer if

(*a*) the security is acquired in circumstances to which any of subsections 7(1.1), (1.5) or (8) or 147(10.1) applies; or

(*b*) the security is a security to which subsection 7(1.31) applies.

Editorial Note: S. 47(3) provides that a security described therein is not subject to the cost averaging rules in s. 47(1), effectively meaning that the adjusted cost base of the security is determined without reference to other securities that might otherwise be identical properties.

Related Sections: S. 7(1.3) Order of disposition of securities; s. 7(1.31) Disposition of newly-acquired security.

Tax Window Files: Adjusted Cost Base of Stock Option Shares following Amalgamation, *Technical Interpretation, Financial Industries Division, August 14, 2003*, CRA Document No. 2002-0167465.

▶ 47(4) ◀

(4) Meaning of "property" — (Repealed by 1986, c. 6, s. 19(1).)

SECTION 47.1: Indexed Security Investment Plans

[Subsections 47.1(1) to (26) were repealed by S.C. 1986, c. 6, s. 20.]

▶ 47.1(26.1) ◀

(26.1) Application of s. 47.1 of R.S.C., 1952, c. 148. Words and expressions used in subsections (27) and (28) have the meanings assigned to them by subsections 47.1(1) to (26) of the *Income Tax Act*, chapter 148 of the Revised Statutes of Canada, 1952, as the latter subsections read on July 1, 1986 and in so far as they are not inconsistent with subsections (27) and (28).

▶ 47.1(27) ◀

(27) Capital losses in 1986. Notwithstanding any other provision of this Act, where paragraph 47.1(10)(*f*) of the *Income Tax Act*, chapter 148 of the Revised Statutes of Canada, 1952, as that paragraph read on January 1, 1986, applied in respect of the termination before 1986 of an indexed security investment plan under which a taxpayer was a participant, any amount that would have been deemed under that paragraph to be a capital loss of the taxpayer from the Plan for the 1986 or a subsequent taxation year shall be deemed to be a capital loss of the taxpayer for the 1986 taxation year from the disposition of property in 1986.

▶ 47.1(28) ◀

(28) Transition for 1986. Where a taxpayer was a participant under a Plan on January 1, 1986, the following rules apply:

(*a*) each indexed security owned under the Plan by the taxpayer on that date shall be deemed to have been disposed of under the Plan on that date for proceeds of disposition determined by the formula

$$A \times B/C$$

where

A is the indexing base of the Plan on that date determined as if subparagraph 47.1(3)(*a*)(i) of the *Income Tax Act*, chapter 148 of the Revised Statutes of Canada, 1952, were read as "the fair market value of all indexed securities owned by the taxpayer under the Plan at the end of the preceding taxation year",

B is the fair market value of the security on that date, and

C is the fair market value of all indexed securities owned under the Plan by the taxpayer on that date;

(*b*) each indexed security deemed under paragraph (*a*) to have been disposed of under the Plan shall be deemed to have been reacquired outside the Plan by the taxpayer immediately after that date at a cost equal to the amount deemed under paragraph (*a*) to be the proceeds of the disposition of that security;

(*c*) each put or call option referred to in clause 47.1(4)(*a*)(iv)(B) or (C) of the *Income Tax Act*, chapter 148 of the Revised Statutes of Canada, 1952, as that clause read on January 1, 1986, outstanding under the Plan on that date shall be deemed to have been closed out under the Plan on that date at a cost equal to the amount that the taxpayer would have had to pay on that date if the taxpayer had actually closed out the option on a prescribed stock exchange in Canada on that date;

(*d*) each put or call option deemed under paragraph (*c*) to have been closed out shall be deemed to be written outside the Plan immediately after that date for proceeds equal to the amount deemed under paragraph (*c*) to be the cost at which the option was closed out; and

(*e*) for greater certainty, the taxpayer's indexed gain or loss, as the case may be, for the 1986 taxation year from the Plan and unindexed gain or loss, as the case may be, for that year from the Plan shall be nil.

SECTION 48: [Ceasing to be or becoming a resident of Canada]

▶ 48(1) ◀

(1) Deemed disposition of property where taxpayer has ceased to be resident in Canada — (Repealed by S.C. 1994, c. 21, s. 19(1).)

▶ 48(1.1) ◀

(1.1) Gains and losses from indexed security investment plans where taxpayer has ceased to be resident in Canada — (Repealed by 1986, c. 6, s. 21(3).)

▶ 48(2) ◀

(2) Property in respect of which election made deemed to be taxable Canadian property — (Repealed by S.C. 1994, c. 21, s. 19(1).)

▶ 48(3) ◀

(3) Deemed acquisition of property on becoming a resident of Canada — (Repealed by S.C. 1994, c. 21, s. 19(1).)

▶ 48(4) ◀

(4) Exception where taxpayer resident in Canada for short term only — (Repealed by S.C. 1994, c. 21, s. 19(1).)

▶ 48(5) ◀

(5) Where corporation becomes resident in Canada — (Repealed by S.C. 1994, c. 21, s. 19(1).)

SECTION 48.1: Gain when small business corporation becomes public

▶ 48.1(1) ◀

(1) Gain when small business corporation becomes public. Where

(*a*) at any time in a taxation year an individual owns capital property that is a share of a class of the capital stock of a corporation that,

(i) at that time, is a small business corporation, and

(ii) immediately after that time, ceases to be a small business corporation because a class of its or another corporation's shares is listed on a designated stock exchange, and

(*b*) the individual elects in prescribed form to have this section apply,

the individual is deemed, except for the purposes of sections 7 and 35, paragraph 110(1)(*d.1*) and subsections 120.4(4) and (5),

(*c*) to have disposed of the share at that time for proceeds of disposition equal to the greater of

(i) the adjusted cost base to the individual of the share at that time, and

(ii) the lesser of the fair market value of the share at that time and such amount as is designated in the prescribed form by the individual in respect of the share, and

(*d*) to have reacquired the share immediately after that time at a cost equal to those proceeds of disposition.

History: S. 48.1(1), the portion after paragraph (*b*) and before paragraph (*c*) was replaced by S.C. 2011, c. 24, s. 7(1), applicable to dispositions that occur on or after March 22, 2011. S. 48.1(1), the portion after paragraph (*b*) and before paragraph (*c*) formerly read:

> the individual shall be deemed, except for the purposes of sections 7 and 35 and paragraph 110(1)(*d*.1),

Related Sections: S. 110.6(2.1) Capital gains deduction — qualified small business corporation shares s. 262 Designated stock exchanges.

Forms: T2101 — Election in Respect of Gains on Shares of a Corporation Becoming Public.

Tax Window Files: 2016 STEP - Q12 - Phantom Income, *June 10, 2016*, CRA Document No. 2016-0634921C6.

▶ 48.1(2) ◀

(2) Time for election. An election made under subsection (1) by an individual for a taxation year shall be made on or before the individual's filing-due date for the year.

Related Sections: S. 248(1), "filing-due date".

Forms: T2101 — Election in Respect of Gains on Shares of a Corporation Becoming Public.

▶ 48.1(3) ◀

(3) Late filed election. Where the election referred to in subsection (2) was not made on or before the day referred to therein, the election shall be deemed for the purposes of subsections (1) and (2) to have been made on that day if, on or before the day that is 2 years after that day,

(*a*) the election is made in prescribed form; and

(*b*) an estimate of the penalty in respect of that election is paid by the individual when the election is made.

Forms: T2101 — Election in Respect of Gains on Shares of a Corporation Becoming Public.

▶ 48.1(4) ◀

(4) Penalty for late filed election. For the purposes of this section, the penalty in respect of an election referred to in paragraph (3)(*a*) is an amount equal to the lesser of

(*a*) 1/4 of 1% of the amount, if any, by which

(i) the proceeds of disposition determined under subsection (1)

exceed

(ii) the amount referred to in subparagraph (1)(*c*)(i)

for each month or part of a month during the period commencing on the day referred to in subsection (2) and ending on the day the election is made, and

(*b*) an amount equal to the product obtained by multiplying $100 by the number of months each of which is a month all or part of which is during the period referred to in paragraph (*a*).

Forms: T2101 — Election in Respect of Gains on Shares of a Corporation Becoming Public.

▶ 48.1(5) ◀

(5) Unpaid balance of penalty. The Minister shall, with all due dispatch, examine each election referred to in paragraph (3)(*a*), assess the penalty payable and send a notice of assessment to the individual, who shall pay forthwith to the Receiver General the amount, if any, by which the penalty so assessed exceeds the total of all amounts previously paid on account of that penalty.

Forms: T2101 — Election in Respect of Gains on Shares of a Corporation Becoming Public.

SECTION 49: [Options]

▶ 49(1) ◀

(1) Granting of options. Subject to subsections (3) and (3.1), for the purposes of this subdivision, the granting of an option, other than

(*a*) an option to acquire or to dispose of a principal residence,

(*b*) an option granted by a corporation to acquire shares of its capital stock or bonds or debentures to be issued by it, or

(*c*) an option granted by a trust to acquire units of the trust to be issued by the trust,

is a disposition of a property the adjusted cost base of which to the grantor immediately before the grant is nil.

Editorial Note: Since the adjusted cost base of the granted option is deemed to be nil, the option premium received as consideration for the option (if any) will constitute a capital gain to the grantor of the option (unless the exceptions in ss. (*a*) through (*c*) apply). If the option is subsequently exercised, the capital gain can be effectively nullified and will instead serve to adjust the grantor's proceeds of disposition or cost of the optioned property, as the case may be. See ss. (3), (3.1) and (4).

If the option premium is on income account for the grantor of the option, s. 49(1) is not relevant. The CRA takes the position that a premium on income account is recognized by the grantor in the year in which the option is exercised or expires; see paragraphs 29 and 32 of IT-479R (archived, as it doesn't meet current government web standards).

Related Sections: S. 7(1) Agreement to issue securities to employees; s. 7(3) Special provision; s. 39(1) Meaning of capital gain and capital loss; s. 51(1) Convertible property.

Tax Profile: February 2005 — The Canadian Treatment of Derivatives; August 2004 — Canadian Tax Treatment of Index Participation Units and Exchange-Traded Index Derivatives.

Interpretation Bulletins: *Primary* — IT-96R6 Options granted by corporations to acquire shares, bonds or debentures and by trusts to acquire trust units; IT-403R Options on real estate. *Secondary* — IT-479R Transactions in securities.

Tax Window Files: Principal Residence Exemption — Capital Gains Exemption — Extension/Exercise of Purchase Option re Farm Property, *Technical Interpretation, International and Trust Division, December 21, 2006*, CRA Document No. 2006-0170851E5; Transfer of Leasing Agreement between Related Corporations, *Technical Interpretation, Business and Partnerships Division, April 4, 2005*, CRA Document No. 2004-0099411E5; Lease Option-Sale, *July 12, 2004*, CRA Document No. 2004-0076531E5; Lease-Bargain Purchase Option, *February 4, 2003*, CRA Document No. 2003-0028033.

▶ 49(2) ◀

(2) Expired option — shares. If at any time an option described in paragraph (1)(*b*) expires, the corporation that granted the option is deemed to have disposed of capital property at that time for proceeds equal to the proceeds received by it for the granting of the option, and the adjusted cost base to the corporation of that capital property immediately before that time is deemed to be nil, unless

(*a*) the option is held, at that time, by a person who deals at arm's length with the corporation and the option was granted by the corporation to a person who was dealing at arm's length with the corporation at the time that the option was granted, or

(*b*) the option is an option to acquire shares of the capital stock of the corporation in consideration for the incurring, pursuant to an agreement described in paragraph (*e*) of the definition "Canadian exploration and development expenses" in subsection 66(15), paragraph (*i*) of the definition "Canadian exploration expense" in subsection 66.1(6), paragraph (*g*) of the definition "Canadian development expense" in subsection 66.2(5) or paragraph (*c*) of the definition "Canadian oil and gas property expense" in subsection 66.4(5), of any expense described in whichever of those paragraphs is applicable.

Editorial Note: Where the option granted by the corporation expires, the holder is also deemed to have disposed of the option, which will normally result in a capital loss; see subparagraph (*b*)(iv) of the definition of "disposition" in s. 248(1). The CRA takes the position that a conversion right with respect to a security that is not severable from the security and cannot be separately traded is not subject to s. 49, such that the expiry of the conversion right will not be subject to s. 49(2) (paragraph 9, IT-96R6) (archived, as it doesn't meet current government web standards).

History: S. 49(2) was replaced by S.C. 2013, c. 34, s. 188(1), applicable to options issued after October 24, 2012, and formerly read:

(2) *Where option expires.* Where at any time an option described in paragraph (1)(*b*) (other than an option to acquire shares of the capital stock of a corporation in consideration for the incurring, pursuant to an agreement described in paragraph (*e*) of the definition "Canadian exploration and development expenses" in subsection 66(15), paragraph (*i*) of the definition "Canadian exploration expense" in subsection 66.1(6), paragraph (*g*) of the definition "Canadian development expense" in subsection 66.2(5) or paragraph (*c*) of the definition "Canadian oil and gas property expense" in subsection 66.4(5), of any expense described in whichever of those paragraphs is applicable) that has been granted by a corporation after 1971 expires,

(*a*) the corporation shall be deemed to have disposed of capital property at that time for proceeds equal to the proceeds received by it for the granting of the option; and

(*b*) the adjusted cost base to the corporation of that capital property immediately before that time shall be deemed to be nil.

Related Sections: S. 39(1) Meaning of capital gain and capital loss; s. 51(1) Convertible property; s. 54, "capital property"; s. 87(2)(*o*) Expiration of options previously granted; s. 248(1), "disposition".

Interpretation Bulletins: *Secondary* — IT-96R6 Options granted by corporations to acquire shares, bonds or debentures.

▶ 49(2.1) ◀

(2.1) Expired option — trust units. If, at a particular time, an option referred to in paragraph (1)(*c*) expires, and the option is held at that time by a person who does not deal at arm's length with the trust or was granted to a person who did not deal at arm's length with the trust at the time that the option was granted,

(*a*) the trust is deemed to have disposed of capital property at the particular time for proceeds equal to the proceeds received by it for the granting of the option; and

(*b*) the adjusted cost base to the trust of that capital property immediately before the particular time is deemed to be nil.

Editorial Note: Where the option granted by the trust expires, the holder is also deemed to have disposed of the option, which will normally result in a capital loss; see s. (*b*)(iv) of the definition of "disposition" in s. 248(1).

History: S. 49(2.1) was replaced by S.C. 2013, c. 34, s. 188(1), applicable to options issued after October 24, 2012, and formerly read:

(2.1) *Idem.* Where at any time an option referred to in paragraph (1)(*c*) expires,

(*a*) the trust shall be deemed to have disposed of capital property at that time for proceeds equal to the proceeds received by it for the granting of the option; and

(*b*) the adjusted cost base to the trust of that capital property immediately before that time shall be deemed to be nil.

Related Sections: S. 39(1) Meaning of capital gain and capital loss; s. 108(2)(*b*) When trust is a unit trust; s. 248(1), "disposition".

▶ 49(3) ◀

(3) Where option to acquire exercised. Where an option to acquire property is exercised so that property is disposed of by a taxpayer (in this subsection referred to as the "vendor") or so that property is acquired by another taxpayer (in this subsection referred to as the "purchaser"), for the purpose of computing the income of each such taxpayer the granting and the exercise of the option shall be deemed not to be dispositions of property and there shall be included

(*a*) in computing the vendor's proceeds of disposition of the property, the consideration received by the vendor for the option; and

(*b*) in computing the cost to the purchaser of the property,

(i) where paragraph 53(1)(*j*) applied to the acquisition of the property by the purchaser because a person who did not deal at arm's length with the purchaser was deemed because of the acquisition to have received a benefit under section 7, the adjusted cost base to that person of the option immediately before that person last disposed of the option, and

(ii) in any other case, the adjusted cost base to the purchaser of the option.

Editorial Note: In general terms, if a call option (to purchase capital property) is exercised, the option premium paid by the option holder/purchaser is included in the vendor's proceeds of disposition of the property and is added to the purchaser's adjusted cost base of the property. Under s. 49(4), the vendor may file an amended return for the year in which the option was granted to nullify the previous inclusion of the option premium (effectively, under s. 49(1)). If the option expires, the option holder realizes a capital loss, generally equal to the option premium (see subparagraph (*b*)(iv) of the definition of "disposition" in s. 248(1)).

Related Sections: S. 161(7) Effect of carryback of loss, etc.

Tax Profile: February 2005 — The Canadian Treatment of Derivatives; August 2004 — Canadian Tax Treatment of Index Participation Units and Exchange-Traded Index Derivatives.

Interpretation Bulletins: *Secondary* — IT-96R6 Options Granted by Corporations to Acquire Shares, Bonds, or Debentures and by Trusts to Acquire Trust Units.

Tax Window Files: Option to Buy an Automobile at a Favourable Price, *Technical Interpretation, Business and Partnerships Division, April 25, 2005*, CRA Document No. 2004-010830117; Lease Option-Sale, *July 12, 2004*, CRA Document No. 2004-0076531E5.

▶ 49(3.01) ◀

(3.01) Option to acquire specified property exercised. Where at any time a taxpayer exercises an option to acquire a specified property,

(*a*) there shall be deducted after that time in computing the adjusted cost base to the taxpayer of the specified property the total of all amounts deducted under paragraph 53(2)(*g*.1) in computing, immediately before that time, the adjusted cost base to the taxpayer of the option; and

(*b*) the amount determined under paragraph (*a*) in respect of that acquisition shall be added after that time in computing the adjusted cost base to the taxpayer of the specified property.

Editorial Note: Where the adjusted cost base of an option to acquire "specified property" has been subject to a deduction in computing its adjusted cost base under s. 53(2)(*g.1*), the adjusted cost base of the specified property acquired on the exercise of the option will also be reduced under that paragraph. A corresponding increase in the adjusted cost base is also provided, so that there is no net effect on the amount of the adjusted cost base of the specified property. For this purpose, "specified property" is defined in s. 54 as a capital property of a taxpayer that is a share, a capital interest in a trust, a partnership interest, or an option to acquire such property.

Related Sections: S. 53(1)(*q*) Adjustments to cost base — Debt forgiveness.

▶ 49(3.1) ◀

(3.1) Where option to dispose exercised. Where an option to dispose of property is exercised so that property is disposed of by a taxpayer (in this subsection referred to as the "vendor") or so that property is acquired by another taxpayer (in this subsection referred to as the "purchaser"), for the purpose of computing the income of each such taxpayer the granting and the exercise of the option shall be deemed not to be dispositions of property and there shall be deducted

(*a*) in computing the vendor's proceeds of disposition of the property, the adjusted cost base to the vendor of the option; and

(*b*) in computing the cost to the purchaser of the property, the consideration received by the purchaser for the option.

Editorial Note: In general terms, if a put option (to sell capital property) is exercised, the option premium paid by the option holder/vendor is deducted from the vendor's proceeds of disposition of the property and is deducted from the purchaser's cost of the property. Under s. 49(4), the purchaser may file an amended return for the year in which the option was granted to nullify the previous inclusion of the option premium (effectively, under s. 49(1)). If the option expires, the option holder realizes a capital loss, generally equal to the option premium (see subparagraph (*b*)(iv) of the definition of "disposition" in s. 248(1)).

Related Sections: S. 161(7) Effect of carryback of loss, etc.

Interpretation Bulletins: *Secondary* — IT-96R6 Options Granted by Corporations to Acquire Shares, Bonds, or Debentures and by Trusts to Acquire Trust Units.

▶ 49(3.2) ◀

(3.2) Option granted before February 23, 1994. Where an individual (other than a trust) who disposes of property pursuant to the exercise of an option that was granted by the individual before February 23, 1994 so elects in the individual's return of income for the taxation year in which the disposition occurs, subsection (3) does not apply in respect of the disposition in computing the income of the individual.

▶ 49(4) ◀

(4) Reassessment where option exercised in subsequent year. Where

(*a*) an option granted by a taxpayer in a taxation year (in this subsection referred to as the "initial year") is exercised in a subsequent taxation year (in this subsection referred to as the "subsequent year"),

(*b*) the taxpayer has filed a return of the taxpayer's income for the initial year as required by section 150, and

(*c*) on or before the day on or before which the taxpayer was required by section 150 to file a return of the taxpayer's income for the subsequent year, the taxpayer has filed an amended return for the initial year excluding from the taxpayer's income the proceeds received by the taxpayer for the granting of the option,

such reassessment of the taxpayer's tax, interest or penalties for the year shall be made as is necessary to give effect to the exclusion.

Editorial Note: See the notes under ss. 49(3) and (3.1).

Related Sections: S. 161(7) Effect of carryback of loss, etc; s. 163(4) Effect of carryback of losses etc; s. 164(5) Effect of carryback of loss, etc.

Interpretation Bulletins: *Primary* — IT-384R Reassessment where option exercised in subsequent year. *Secondary* — IT-96R6 Options granted by corporations to acquire shares, bonds or debentures.

▶ 49(5) ◀

(5) Idem. Where a taxpayer has granted an option (in this subsection referred to as the "original option") to which subsection (1), (2) or (2.1) applies, and grants one or more extensions or renewals of that original option,

(*a*) for the purposes of subsections (1), (2) and (2.1), the granting of each extension or renewal shall be deemed to be the granting of an option at the time the extension or renewal is granted;

(*b*) for the purposes of subsections (2) to (4) and subparagraph (*b*)(iv) of the definition "disposition" in subsection 248(1), the original option and each extension or renewal of it is deemed to be the same option; and

(*c*) subsection (4) shall be read as if the year in which the original option was granted and each year in which any extension or renewal thereof was granted were all initial years.

Interpretation Bulletins: *Secondary* — IT-96R6 Options granted by corporations to acquire shares, bonds or debentures and by trusts to acquire trust units.

SECTION 49.1: No disposition where obligation satisfied

For greater certainty, where a taxpayer acquires a particular property in satisfaction of an absolute or contingent obligation of a person or partnership to provide the particular property pursuant to a contract or other arrangement one of the main objectives of which was to establish a right, whether absolute or contingent, to the particular property and that right was not under the terms of a trust, partnership agreement, share or debt obligation, the satisfaction of the obligation is not a disposition of that right.

Related Sections: S. 139.1 Demutualization of insurance corporations; s. 248(1), "disposition".

SECTION 50: [Bad debts and shares of bankrupt corporation]

▶ 50(1) ◀

(1) Debts established to be bad debts and shares of bankrupt corporation. For the purposes of this subdivision, where

(*a*) a debt owing to a taxpayer at the end of a taxation year (other than a debt owing to the taxpayer in respect of the disposition of personal-use property) is established by the taxpayer to have become a bad debt in the year, or

(*b*) a share (other than a share received by a taxpayer as consideration in respect of the disposition of personal-use property) of the capital stock of a corporation is owned by the taxpayer at the end of a taxation year and

(i) the corporation has during the year become a bankrupt,

(ii) the corporation is a corporation referred to in section 6 of the *Winding-up Act* that is insolvent (within the meaning of that Act) and in respect of which a winding-up order under that Act has been made in the year, or

(iii) at the end of the year,

(A) the corporation is insolvent,

(B) neither the corporation nor a corporation controlled by it carries on business,

(C) the fair market value of the share is nil, and

(D) it is reasonable to expect that the corporation will be dissolved or wound up and will not commence to carry on business

and the taxpayer elects in the taxpayer's return of income for the year to have this subsection apply in respect of the debt or the share, as the case may be, the taxpayer shall be deemed to have disposed of the debt or the share, as the case may be, at the end of the year for proceeds equal to nil and to have reacquired it immediately after the end of the year at a cost equal to nil.

Editorial Note: The loss resulting from the deemed disposition in s. 50(1) may qualify as a business investment loss; see s. 39(1)(*c*). S. 50(2) provides for the treatment of bad debts that are personal-use property owed by arm's length persons.

History: S. 50(1)(*b*)(i) was replaced by S.C. 2013, c. 40, s. 21(1), deemed to have come into force December 21, 2012, and formerly read:

> (i) the corporation has during the year become a bankrupt (within the meaning of subsection 128(3)),

Related Regulations: 600(b).

Related Sections: S. 39(1) Meaning of capital gain and capital loss; s. 80.01(6) Specified obligation in relation to debt parking; s. 96(3) Agreement or election of partnership members; s. 220(3.2) Late, amended or revoked elections; s. 248(1), "small business corporation".

Canadian Tax Foundation: Magee, *Tax Writeoffs for Investment Losses: Lessons from Cases Involving Victims of Investment Fraud,* 2014 Canadian Tax Journal 1:221–244; Kakkar and Yan, *Practical Considerations in Claiming an ABIL or the Capital Gains Exemption,* 2012 Ontario Tax Conference 5:1–28; Friedlan, *Subsection 50(1) Election and an E-Filed Return,* 2012 Tax for the Owner-Manager 12(3):3; Donnelly and Young, *Substantiating an ABIL Deduction: An Analysis of the Key Elements,* 2010 Canadian Tax Journal 2:229–276; Schusheim and Hurst, *Allowable Business Investment Losses— An Update,* 2009 Ontario Tax Conference 6:1–25; Weder and MacDonald, *Allowable Business Investment Losses: What To Do When the CRA Calls,* 2009 British Columbia Tax Conference 7:1–21; Bauer, *Restructuring Debt Obligations,* 2008 Conference Report 37:1–30; Posthumus, *Tax Loss Planning for the Owner Manager— An Update on Claiming Allowable Business Investment Losses,* 2008 Prairie Provinces Tax Conference 12:1–24.

Tax Profile: October 2008 — Tax Consequences of Debt Restructuring and Workouts in Canada.

Income Tax Folios: S4-F8-C1 Business Investment Losses.

Secondary — S3-F4-C1 General Discussion of Capital Cost Allowance.

Information Circulars: IC 07-1 Taxpayer relief provisions.

Interpretation Bulletins: *Primary* — IT-159R3 Capital debts established to be bad debts.

Tax Window Files: Employee stock options - Bankruptcy, *May 28, 2018,* CRA Document No. 2017-0692931E5; Bad Debt for Amount Owing Under Employee Stock Option, *October 6, 2006,* CRA Document No. 2006-0196271C6; Capital Loss — Cease Trading Order, *Technical Interpretation, Business and Partnerships Division, April 28, 2006,* CRA Document No. 2006-0175701M4; Business Investment Loss — Bad Debt — Non-Profit Organization, *Technical Interpretation, Financing and Plans Division, June 9, 2005,* CRA Document No. 2005-0122511I7; Disposition of Capital Property — Treatment of Loss on Debt and Legal Costs, *Technical Interpretation, Business and Partnerships Division, November 13, 2003,* CRA Document No. 2003-0039637.

Cases: The taxpayer could not claim a capital loss for bad debts since the loans had not become uncollectible by the end of the year, as ongoing litigation was still in progress at that time. *Fisher v. The Queen,* 2013 DTC 1182 (T.C.C.); affirmed 2015 DTC 5135 (F.C.A.).

The taxpayer was not allowed to claim a capital loss on amounts paid to extricate several of its subsidiaries from U.S. partnerships and itself from guarantees in respect of the partnerships, because no property was disposed of. *The Cadillac Fairview Corporation Limited v. The Queen,* 99 DTC 5121 (F.C.A.), affirming 97 DTC 405 (T.C.C.)

In determining whether amounts in question became "bad debts", a taxpayer must act in a "pragmatic businesslike manner". A taxpayer is not required to attempt to collect the amounts in question if such attempt would result in the debtor's bankruptcy. *Granby Construction & Equipment Ltd. v. M.N.R.,* 89 DTC 456 (T.C.C.).

► 50(1.1) ◄

(1.1) Idem. Where

(*a*) a taxpayer is deemed because of subparagraph (1)(*b*)(iii) to have disposed of a share of the capital stock of a corporation at the end of a taxation year, and

(*b*) the taxpayer or a person with whom the taxpayer is not dealing at arm's length owns the share at the earliest time, during the 24-month period immediately following the disposition, that the corporation or a corporation controlled by it carries on business,

the taxpayer or the person, as the case may be, shall be deemed to have disposed of the share at that earliest time for proceeds of disposition equal to its adjusted cost base to the taxpayer determined immediately before the time of the disposition referred to in paragraph (*a*) and to have reacquired it immediately after that earliest time at a cost equal to those proceeds.

Editorial Note: S. 50(1.1) applies if a share of a corporation was subject to the deemed disposition for nil proceeds rule under s. 50(1)(*b*)(iii) (corporation insolvent, not carrying on business, fair market value of share is nil) and the corporation subsequently begins to carry on business within 24 months of the disposition. If the original shareholder or a non-arm's length person owns the share at that subsequent time, there is a deemed disposition of the share for proceeds equal to the original adjusted cost base, such that resulting gain effectively offsets the previous loss under s. 50(1).

► 50(2) ◄

(2) Where debt a personal-use property. Where at the end of a taxation year a debt that is a personal-use property of a taxpayer is owing to the taxpayer by a person with whom the taxpayer deals at arm's length and is established by the taxpayer to have become a bad debt in the year,

(*a*) the taxpayer shall be deemed to have disposed of it at the end of the year for proceeds equal to the amount, if any, by which

(i) its adjusted cost base to the taxpayer immediately before the end of the year

exceeds

(ii) the amount of the taxpayer's gain, if any, from the disposition of the personal-use property the proceeds of disposition of which included the debt; and

(*b*) the taxpayer shall be deemed to have reacquired the debt immediately after the end of the year at a cost equal to the amount of the proceeds determined under paragraph (*a*).

Editorial Note: The loss resulting from the deemed disposition of the debt is limited to the amount of the gain realized on the previous disposition of the personal-use property.

Related Sections: S. 40(2)(*g*) Limitations; s. 46 Personal-use property; s. 54, "adjusted cost base", "personal-use property"; s. 248(1), "amount".

Interpretation Bulletins: *Primary* — IT-159R3 Capital debts established to be bad debts.

► 50(3) ◄

(3) Disposal of R.H.O.S.P. properties. Each trust that was at the end of 1985 governed by a registered home ownership savings plan (within the meaning assigned by paragraph 146.2(1)(*h*) of the *Income Tax Act*, chapter 148 of the Revised Statutes of Canada, 1952, as it read in its application to the 1985 taxation year) shall be deemed to have disposed, immediately before 1986, of each property it holds at that time for proceeds of disposition equal to the fair market value of the property at that time and to have reacquired it immediately after 1985 at a cost equal to that fair market value.

Related Sections: S. 12(10.1) Income from R.H.O.S.P.

SECTION 51: Convertible property

► 51(1) ◄

(1) Convertible property. Where a share of the capital stock of a corporation is acquired by a taxpayer from the corporation in exchange for

(*a*) a capital property of the taxpayer that is another share of the corporation (in this section referred to as a "convertible property"), or

(*b*) a capital property of the taxpayer that is a bond, debenture or note of the corporation the terms of which confer on the holder the right to make the exchange (in this section referred to as a "convertible property")

and no consideration other than the share is received by the taxpayer for the convertible property,

(*c*) except for the purposes of subsections 20(21) and 44.1(6) and (7) and paragraph 94(2)(*m*), the exchange is deemed not to be a disposition of the convertible property,

(*d*) the cost to the taxpayer of all the shares of a particular class acquired by the taxpayer on the exchange shall be deemed to be the amount determined by the formula

$$A \times B/C$$

where

A is the adjusted cost base to the taxpayer of the convertible property immediately before the exchange,

B is the fair market value, immediately after the exchange, of all the shares of the particular class acquired by the taxpayer on the exchange, and

C is the fair market value, immediately after the exchange, of all the shares acquired by the taxpayer on the exchange,

(*d*.1) there shall be deducted, after the exchange, in computing the adjusted cost base to the taxpayer of a share acquired by the taxpayer on the exchange, the amount determined by the formula

$$A \times B/C$$

where

A is the total of all amounts deducted under paragraph 53(2)(*g*.1) in computing, immediately before the exchange, the adjusted cost base to the taxpayer of the convertible property,

B is the fair market value, immediately after the exchange, of that share, and

C is the fair market value, immediately after the exchange, of all the shares acquired by the taxpayer on the exchange,

(*d*.2) the amount determined under paragraph (*d*.1) in respect of a share shall be added, after the exchange, in computing the adjusted cost base to the taxpayer of the share,

(*e*) for the purposes of sections 74.4 and 74.5, the exchange shall be deemed to be a transfer of the convertible property by the taxpayer to the corporation, and

(*f*) where the convertible property is taxable Canadian property of the taxpayer, the share acquired by the taxpayer on the exchange is deemed to be, at any time that is within 60 months after the exchange, taxable Canadian property of the taxpayer.

Editorial Note: S. 51(1) provides a tax-free rollover upon the exchange of the share or debt of the corporation into another share of the corporation. The CRA takes the position that, where a conversion feature described in s. 51(1)(*b*) is not severable from the underlying security and cannot be separately traded, s. 51 applies to the exclusion of s. 49. However, if the conversion feature is severable and can be separately traded, it may be considered an option subject to s. 49. See paragraph 9 of IT-96R6 (archived, as it doesn't meet current government web standards). S. 51(1) does not apply if the exchange or conversion is otherwise subject to s. 85(1) or (2) or s. 86 (s. 51(4)).

History: S. 51(1)(*c*) was replaced by S.C. 2013, c. 34, s. 3(2), applicable to taxation years of a taxpayer that begin after 1999, except that, for any taxation year of the taxpayer that ends before 2007 in respect of which subsection 94(1) does not apply to the taxpayer, paragraph 51(1)(*c*) is to be read without reference to "and paragraph 94(2)(*m*)".

S. 51(1)(*c*) formerly read:

(*c*) except for the purpose of subsection 20(21), the exchange shall be deemed not to be a disposition of the convertible property,

S. 51(1)(*f*) was replaced by S.C. 2010, c. 12, s. 3(1), applicable in determining after March 4, 2010 whether a property is taxable Canadian property of a taxpayer. S. 51(1)(*f*) formerly read:

(*f*) where the convertible property is taxable Canadian property of the taxpayer, the share acquired by the taxpayer on the exchange shall be deemed to be taxable Canadian property of the taxpayer.

Related Sections: S. 40(3.5) Deemed identical property; s. 53(1)(*q*) Adjustments to cost base — Debt forgiveness; s. 53(2)(*g*.1) Amounts to be deducted — Debt forgiveness; s. 55(1), "permitted exchange"; s. 55(3)(*b*) Application; s. 84 Deemed dividend; s. 85 Transfer of property to corporation by shareholders; s. 86(1) Exchange of shares by a shareholder in course of reorganization of capital; s. 86(3) Application; s. 112(7) Rules where shares exchanged; s. 116(5) Liability of purchaser; ITAR 26(24).

Canadian Tax Foundation: Bernstein, *Valuation and Related Tax Issues, Part 1*, 2011 Conference Report 17:1–31; Ireland et al., *Disarming the Succession Time Bomb: The Role of Trusts, Insurance, and Shareholders' Agreements in the Transition of Family Businesses*, 2011 Conference Report 15:1–53; Tabuchi, *Share Capital Reorganizations for Private Corporations*, 2003 Canadian Tax Journal 3:1340–1378; Moch and Ebel, *Basics of Corporate Reorganizations: Sections 51, 85, 85.1, and 86*, 2002 Prairie Provinces Tax Conference 10:1–32; Moch and Ebel, *Share Reorganizations and Corporate Takeover Transactions: Using Tax Rollover Provisions*, 2000 Conference Report 8:1–20.

Tax Profile: October 2008 — Tax Consequences of Debt Restructuring and Workouts in Canada.

Interpretation Bulletins: *Primary* — IT-115R2 Fractional interests in shares. *Secondary* — IT-96R6 Options granted by corporations to acquire shares, bonds or debentures; IT-146R4 Shares entitling shareholders to choose taxable or capital dividends.

Tax Window Files: CÉLI — Notion d'avantage, *December 12, 2010*, CRA Document No. 2009-0351931R3; 2008 TEI — Section 51 Convertible Property, *Tax Executive Institute, December 9, 2008*, CRA Document No. 2008-0300391C6; Capital loss reduction under 112(3.2) for estate, *Technical Interpretation, International and Trusts Division, May 30, 2007*, CRA Document No. 2007-0224371I7; Grandfathering of Stop Loss Provision, *Technical Interpretation, Financial Sector and Exempt Entities Division, January 18, 2006*, CRA Document No. 2005-0145111E5; Application of Rollover Provisions to a Partnership, *Technical Interpretation, Reorganizations and Resources Division, December 16, 2005*, CRA Document No. 2005-0150411E5; Price Adjustment Clauses, *Technical Interpretation, Reorganizations and Resources Division, July 6, 2004*, CRA Document No. 2004-0081631E5; Disposition of Capital Property — Treatment of Loss on Debt and Legal Costs, *November 13, 2003*, CRA Document No. 2003-0039637.

Cases: A convertible debenture purchased at fair market value by an employee and later converted to shares gave rise to a taxable benefit under s. 7, regardless of whether s. 51 established a cost for the shares. *Mansfield v. The Queen*, 84 DTC 6535 (F.C.A.), affirming 83 DTC 5136 (F.C.T.D.)

► 51(2) ◄

(2) Idem. Notwithstanding subsection (1), where

(*a*) shares of the capital stock of a corporation have been acquired by a taxpayer in exchange for a convertible property in circumstances such that, but for this subsection, subsection (1) would have applied,

(*b*) the fair market value of the convertible property immediately before the exchange exceeds the fair market value of the shares immediately after the exchange, and

(*c*) it is reasonable to regard any portion of the excess (in this subsection referred to as the "gift portion") as a benefit that the taxpayer desired to have conferred on a person related to the taxpayer,

the following rules apply:

(*d*) the taxpayer shall be deemed to have disposed of the convertible property for proceeds of disposition equal to the lesser of

(i) the total of its adjusted cost base to the taxpayer immediately before the exchange and the gift portion, and

(ii) the fair market value of the convertible property immediately before the exchange, (*e*) the taxpayer's capital loss from the disposition of the convertible property shall be deemed to be nil, and

(*f*) the cost to the taxpayer of all the shares of a particular class acquired in exchange for the convertible property shall be deemed to be that proportion of the lesser of

(i) the adjusted cost base to the taxpayer of the convertible property immediately before the exchange, and

(ii) the total of the fair market value immediately after the exchange of all the shares acquired by the taxpayer in exchange for the convertible property and the amount that, but for paragraph (*e*), would have been the taxpayer's capital loss on the disposition of the convertible property,

that

(iii) the fair market value, immediately after the exchange, of all the shares of the particular class acquired by the taxpayer on the exchange

is of

(iv) the fair market value, immediately after the exchange, of all the shares acquired by the taxpayer on the exchange.

Income Tax Folios: *Secondary* — S4-F3-C1 Price Adjustment Clauses.

Interpretation Bulletins: *Primary* — IT-115R2 Fractional interests in shares. *Secondary* — IT-146R4 Shares entitling shareholders to choose taxable or capital dividends.

Tax Window Files: Price Adjustment Clause — Estate Freeze, *Technical Interpretation, Reorganizations and Resources Division, April 11, 2005*, CRA Document No. 2005-0112321E5.

▶ 51(3) ◀

(3) Computation of paid-up capital. Where subsection (1) applies to the exchange of convertible property described in paragraph (1)(*a*) (referred to in this subsection as the "old shares"), in computing the paid-up capital in respect of a particular class of shares of the capital stock of the corporation at any particular time that is the time of, or any time after, the exchange

(*a*) there shall be deducted the amount determined by the formula

$$(A - B) \times C/A$$

where

A is the total of all amounts each of which is the amount of the increase, if any, as a result of the exchange, in the paid-up capital in respect of a class of shares of the capital stock of the corporation, computed without reference to this subsection as it applies to the exchange,

B is the paid-up capital immediately before the exchange in respect of the old shares, and

C is the increase, if any, as a result of the exchange, in the paid-up capital in respect of the particular class of shares, computed without reference to this subsection as it applies to the exchange; and

(*b*) there shall be added an amount equal to the lesser of

(i) the amount, if any, by which

(A) the total of all amounts deemed by subsection 84(3), (4) or (4.1) to be a dividend on shares of that class paid by the corporation before the particular time

exceeds

(B) the total that would be determined under clause (A) if this Act were read without reference to paragraph (*a*), and

(ii) the total of all amounts required by paragraph (*a*) to be deducted in respect of that particular class of shares before the particular time.

Related Sections: S. 84(5) Amount distributed or paid where a share; s. 89(1), "paid-up capital".

▶ 51(4) ◀

(4) Application. Subsections (1) and (2) do not apply to any exchange to which subsection 85(1) or (2) or section 86 applies.

Interpretation Bulletins: *Secondary* — IT-115R2 Fractional interests in shares.

SECTION 51.1: Conversion of debt obligation

Where

(*a*) a taxpayer acquires a bond, debenture or note of a debtor (in this section referred to as the "new obligation") in exchange for a capital property of the taxpayer that is another bond, debenture or note of the same debtor (in this section referred to as the "convertible obligation"),

(*b*) the terms of the convertible obligation conferred on the holder the right to make the exchange, and

(*c*) the principal amount of the new obligation is equal to the principal amount of the convertible obligation,

the cost to the taxpayer of the new obligation and the proceeds of disposition of the convertible obligation shall be deemed to be equal to the adjusted cost base to the taxpayer of the convertible obligation immediately before the exchange.

Related Sections: S. 248(1), "principal amount".

Tax Profile: October 2008 — Tax Consequences of Debt Restructuring and Workouts in Canada.

SECTION 52: [Cost of certain property]

▶ 52(1) ◀

(1) Cost of certain property the value of which is included in income. In applying this subdivision, an amount equal to the particular amount described by paragraph (*d*) shall be added in computing the cost at any time to a taxpayer of a property if

(*a*) the taxpayer acquired the property after 1971;

(*b*) the amount was not at or before that time otherwise added to the cost, or included in computing the adjusted cost base, to the taxpayer of the property;

(*c*) the property is not an annuity contract, a right as a beneficiary under a trust to enforce payment of an amount by the trust to the taxpayer, property acquired in circumstances to which subsection (2) or (3) applies, or property acquired from a trust in satisfaction of all or part of the taxpayer's capital interest in the trust; and

(*d*) a particular amount in respect of the property's value was

(i) included, otherwise than under section 7, in computing

(A) the taxpayer's taxable income or taxable income earned in Canada, as the case may be, for a taxation year during which the taxpayer was non-resident, or

(B) the taxpayer's income for a taxation year throughout which the taxpayer was resident in Canada, or

(ii) for the purpose of computing the tax payable under Part XIII by the taxpayer, included in an amount that was paid or credited to the taxpayer.

Editorial Note: This subsection provides that, where an amount in respect of the value of a property has been included in computing a taxpayer's income, that amount is added in determining the cost to the taxpayer of the property for the purposes of determining capital gains and losses in respect of the property. It applies where a taxpayer acquired property, and an amount in respect of its value was included in computing the taxpayer's income for a taxation year throughout which the taxpayer was resident in Canada (or in computing a non-resident taxpayer's taxable income earned in Canada under s. 115, taxable income under s. 114, or an amount from which tax is withheld under Part XIII).

Although s. 52(1) does not apply to s. 7 employee stock option benefits included in income (see s. 52(1)(*b*)(i)), such amounts are added to the cost of the acquired securities under s. 53(1)(*j*).

History: S. 52(1) was replaced by S.C. 2013, c. 34, s. 189(1), applicable to taxation years that begin after 2006, and formerly read:

(1) *Cost of certain property the value of which included in income.* Where

(*a*) a taxpayer acquired property after 1971 (other than an annuity contract, a right as a beneficiary under a trust to enforce payment of an amount by the trust to the taxpayer, property acquired in circumstances to which subsection (2) or (3) applies or property acquired from a trust in satisfaction of all or part of the taxpayer's capital interest in the trust), and

(*b*) an amount in respect of its value was

(i) included, otherwise than under section 7, in computing

(A) the taxpayer's taxable income or taxable income earned in Canada, as the case may be, for a taxation year during which the taxpayer was non-resident, or

(B) the taxpayer's income for a taxation year throughout which the taxpayer was resident in Canada, or

(ii) for the purpose of computing the tax payable under Part XIII by the taxpayer, included in an amount that was paid or credited to the taxpayer,

for the purposes of this subdivision, the amount so included shall be added in computing the cost to the taxpayer of the property, except to the extent that the amount was otherwise added to the cost or included in computing the adjusted cost base to the taxpayer of the property.

Related Sections: S. 12(9) Deemed accrual; s. 15(1) Benefit conferred on shareholder; s. 53(1)(*b*) Adjustments to cost base — Deemed dividend; s. 54, "adjusted cost base"; s. 69(5) Winding-up of corporation; s. 107(2.1) Other distributions; s. 147(10.4) Income on disposal of shares.

Interpretation Bulletins: *Secondary* — IT-96R6 Options granted by corporations to acquire shares, bonds or debentures and by trusts to acquire trust units; IT-432R2 Benefits conferred on shareholders.

▶ 52(1.1) ◀

(1.1) Idem, where owner non-resident — (Repealed by S.C. 2001, c. 17, s. 35(1).)

▶ 52(2) ◀

(2) Cost of property received as dividend in kind. Where any property has, after 1971, been received by a shareholder of a corporation at any time as, on account or in lieu of payment of, or in satisfaction of, a dividend payable in kind (other than a stock dividend) in respect of a share owned by the shareholder of the capital stock of the corporation, the shareholder shall be deemed to have acquired the property at a cost to the shareholder equal to its fair market value at that time, and the corporation shall be deemed to have disposed of the property at that time for proceeds equal to that fair market value.

Editorial Note: The fair market value of the dividend will also be the amount of the dividend included in the shareholder's income. S. 52(3), rather than s. 52(2), applies to a stock dividend.

Related Sections: S. 69(5) Winding-up of corporation; s. 82(1) Taxable dividends received; s. 86.1(1) Eligible distribution not included in income; s. 142.7(4) Deemed fair market value.

▶ 52(3) ◀

(3) Cost of stock dividend. Where a shareholder of a corporation has, after 1971, received a stock dividend in respect of a share owned by the shareholder of the capital stock of the corporation, the shareholder shall be deemed to have acquired the share or shares received by the shareholder as a stock dividend at a cost to the shareholder equal to the total of

(*a*) where the stock dividend is a dividend,

(i) in the case of a shareholder that is an individual, the amount of the stock dividend, and

(ii) in any other case, the total of all amounts each of which is

(A) the amount, if any, by which

(I) the amount that is the lesser of the amount of the stock dividend and its fair market value

exceeds

(II) the amount of the dividend that the shareholder may deduct under subsection 112(1) in computing the shareholder's taxable income, except any portion of the dividend that, if paid as a separate dividend, would not be subject to subsection 55(2) because the amount of the separate dividend would not exceed the amount of the income earned or realized by any corporation — after 1971 and before the safe-income determination time for the transaction, event or series of transactions or events as part of which the dividend is received — that could reasonably be considered to contribute to the capital gain that could be realized on a disposition at fair market value, immediately before the dividend, of the share on which the dividend is received, and

(B) the amount determined by the formula

$$A + B$$

where

A is the amount of the deemed gain under paragraph 55(2)(*c*) in respect of that stock dividend, and

B is the amount, if any, by which the amount of the reduction under paragraph 55(2.3)(*b*) in respect of that stock dividend to which paragraph 55(2)(*a*) would otherwise apply exceeds the amount determined for clause (A) in respect of that dividend;

(*a*.1) where the stock dividend is not a dividend, nil, and

(*b*) where an amount is included in the shareholder's income in respect of the stock dividend under subsection 15(1.1), the amount so included.

Editorial Note: When a stock dividend is received by an individual the "amount" of the stock dividend (as per s. 248(1)) is generally the amount by which the corporation's paid-up capital has increased by reason of the payment of the dividend.

In all other cases (i.e., stock dividends received by corporations), the "amount" of the stock dividend (as per s. 55(2.2)) is generally equal to the greater of:

(1) the amount by which the corporation's paid-up capital has increased by reason of the payment of the dividend; or

(2) the fair market value of the shares that are issued as a stock dividend.

If subsection 15(1.1) applies to the stock dividend, the fair market value of the stock dividend in excess of the amount of the stock dividend is also added to the cost of the share.

History: S. 52(3)(*a*) was replaced by S.C. 2016, c. 7, s. 2(1), applicable to stock dividends received after April 20, 2015, except that, in respect of stock dividends that are declared after April 20, 2015 and before July 31, 2015, and that are received before September 30, 2015,

(*a*) clause 52(3)(*a*)(ii)(A) is to be read as follows:

(A) the lesser of the amount of the stock dividend and its fair market value, and

(*b*) the description of B in clause 52(3)(*a*)(ii)(B) is to be read without reference to the words "to which paragraph 55(2)(*a*) would otherwise apply".

S. 52(3)(*a*) formerly read:

(*a*) where the stock dividend is a dividend, the amount, if any, by which

(i) the amount of the stock dividend

exceeds

(ii) the amount of the dividend that the shareholder may deduct under subsection 112(1) in computing the shareholder's taxable income, except any portion of the dividend that, if paid as a separate dividend, would not be subject to subsection 55(2) because the capital gain referred to in that subsection could reasonably be considered not to be attributable to anything other than income earned or realized by any corporation after 1971 and before the safe-income determination time for the transaction or event or series of transactions or events as part of which the dividend was received,

S. 52(3)(*a*) was replaced by S.C. 2013, c. 34, s. 189(2), applicable in respect of amounts received on or after November 9, 2006, and formerly read:

(*a*) where the stock dividend is a dividend, the amount of the stock dividend,

Related Sections: S. 82(1) Taxable dividends received; s. 95(7) Stock dividends from foreign affiliates; s. 248(1), "amount".

Tax Topics: No. 2012, Accessing Safe Income through PUC Increases and Stock Dividends; No. 1820, Beware of Pitfalls in November 9, 2006 Technical Amendments When Crystallizing "Safe Income"!.

Interpretation Bulletins: *Secondary* — IT-88R2 Stock dividends.

► 52(4) ◄

(4) Cost of property acquired as prize. Where any property has been acquired by a taxpayer at any time after 1971 as a prize in connection with a lottery scheme, the taxpayer shall be deemed to have acquired the property at a cost to the taxpayer equal to its fair market value at that time.

Editorial Note: The receipt of the prize should not be included in income because lottery winnings are generally tax-free windfalls.

Income Tax Folios: *Secondary* — S3-F9-C1 Lottery Winnings, Miscellaneous Receipts, and Income (and Losses) from Crime.

► 52(5) ◄

(5) Cost of property transferred by trustee under employees profit sharing plan — (Repealed by 1973-74, c. 14, s. 12(2).)

► 52(6) ◄

(6) Cost of right to receive from trust — (Repealed by S.C. 2001, c. 17, s. 35(2).)

► 52(7) ◄

(7) Cost of shares of subsidiary. Notwithstanding any other provision of this Act, where a corporation disposes of property to another corporation in a transaction to which paragraph 219(1)(*l*) applies, the cost to it of any share of a particular class of the capital stock of the other corporation received by it as consideration for the property is deemed to be the lesser of the cost of the share to the corporation otherwise determined immediately after the disposition and the amount by which the paid-up capital in respect of that class increases because of the issuance of the share.

Interpretation Bulletins: *Secondary* — IT-137R3 Additional tax on certain corporations carrying on business in Canada.

► 52(8) ◄

(8) Cost of shares of immigrant corporation. Notwithstanding any other provision of this Act, where at any time a corporation becomes resident in Canada, the cost to any shareholder who is not at that time resident in Canada of any share of the corporation's capital stock, other than a share that was taxable Canadian property immediately before that time, is deemed to be equal to the fair market value of the share at that time.

Related Sections: S. 128.1(2) Paid-up capital adjustment.

SECTION 53: Adjustments to cost base

► 53(1) ◄

(1) Adjustments to cost base. In computing the adjusted cost base to a taxpayer of property at any time, there shall be added to the cost to the taxpayer of the property such of the following amounts in respect of the property as are applicable:

Related Sections: S. 54, "adjusted cost base".

► 53(1)(a) ◄

(a) [Adjustments to cost base — Deemed gain resulting from negative ACB] — any amount deemed by subsection 40(3) to be a gain of the taxpayer for a taxation year from a disposition before that time of the property;

Related Sections: ITAR s. 26(3) Cost of acquisition of capital property owned on Dec. 31, 1971.

► 53(1)(b) ◄

(b) [Adjustments to cost base — Deemed dividend] — where the property is a share of the capital stock of a corporation resident in Canada, the amount, if any, by which

(i) the total of all amounts each of which is the amount of a dividend on the share deemed by subsection 84(1) to have been received by the taxpayer before that time

exceeds

(ii) the portion of the total determined under subparagraph (i) that relates to dividends in respect of which the taxpayer was permitted a deduction under subsection 112(1) in computing the taxpayer's taxable income, except any portion of the dividend that, if paid as a separate dividend, would not be subject to subsection 55(2) because the amount of the separate dividend would not exceed the amount of the income earned or realized by any corporation — after 1971 and before the safe-income determination time for the transaction, event or series of transactions or events as part of which the dividend is received — that could reasonably be considered to contribute to the capital gain that could be realized on a disposition at fair market value, immediately before the dividend, of the share on which the dividend is received;

History: S. 53(1)(*b*)(ii) was replaced by S.C. 2016, c. 7, s. 3(1), applicable to dividends received after April 20, 2015, and formerly read:

(ii) the portion of the total determined under subparagraph (i) that relates to dividends in respect of which the taxpayer was permitted a deduction under subsection 112(1) in computing the taxpayer's taxable income, except any portion of the dividend that, if paid as a separate dividend, would not be subject to subsection 55(2) because the capital gain referred to in that subsection could reasonably be considered not to be attributable to anything other than income earned or realized by any corporation after 1971 and before the safe-income determination time for the transaction or event or series of transactions or events as part of which the dividend was received;

S. 53(1)(*b*) was replaced by S.C. 2013, c. 34, s. 190(1), applicable in respect of a dividend received by a taxpayer on or after November 9, 2006. However, if the taxpayer elects, no later than 180 days after June 26, 2013, by filing with the Minister of National Revenue an election in writing, in respect of the dividend received by the taxpayer before July 16, 2010, paragraph 53(1)(*b*) is to be read as follows:

"(*b*) where the property is a share of the capital stock of a corporation resident in Canada, the amount, if any, by which

(i) the total of all amounts each of which is the amount of a dividend on the share deemed by subsection 84(1) to have been received by the taxpayer before that time

exceeds

(ii) the portion of the total determined under subparagraph (i) that relates to dividends

(A) in respect of which the taxpayer was permitted a deduction under subsection 112(1) in computing the taxpayer's taxable income, and

(B) that arose directly or indirectly as a result of a conversion of contributed surplus into paid-up capital;"

S. 53(1)(*b*) formerly read:

(*b*) *[Adjustments to cost base — Deemed dividend]* — where the property is a share of the capital stock of a corporation resident in Canada, the amount of any dividend on the share deemed by subsection 84(1) to have been received by the taxpayer before that time;

Related Sections: ITAR s. 26(3) Cost of acquisition of capital property owned on Dec. 31, 1971.

Tax Topics: No. 2012, Accessing Safe Income through PUC Increases and Stock Dividends; No. 1820, Beware of Pitfalls in November 9, 2006 Technical Amendments When Crystallizing "Safe Income"!.

▶ 53(1)(b.1) ◀

(b.1) [Adjustments to cost base — Deemed dividend from immigrating corporation] — where the property is a share of the capital stock of a corporation, the amount of any dividend deemed by paragraph 128.1(1)(*c.2*) to have been received in respect of the share by the taxpayer before that time and while the taxpayer was resident in Canada;

Related Sections: ITAR s. 26(3) Cost of acquisition of capital property owned on Dec. 31, 1971.

▶ 53(1)(c) ◀

(c) [Adjustments to cost base — Contributions of capital] — where the property is a share of the capital stock of a corporation and the taxpayer has, after 1971, made a contribution of capital to the corporation otherwise than by way of a loan, by way of a disposition of shares of a foreign affiliate of the taxpayer to which subsection 85.1(3) or paragraph 95(2)(*c*) applies or, subject to subsection (1.1), a disposition of property in respect of which the taxpayer and the corporation have made an election under section 85, that proportion of such part of the amount of the contribution as cannot reasonably be regarded as a benefit conferred by the taxpayer on a person (other than the corporation) who was related to the taxpayer that

(i) the amount that may reasonably be regarded as the increase in the fair market value, as a result of the contribution, of the share

is of

(ii) the amount that may reasonably be regarded as the increase in the fair market value, as a result of the contribution, of all shares of the capital stock of the corporation owned by the taxpayer immediately after the contribution;

Related Sections: ITAR s. 26(3) Cost of acquisition of capital property owned on Dec. 31, 1971.

Interpretation Bulletins: *Primary* — IT-456R Capital property — Some adjustments to cost base. *Secondary* — IT-291R3 Transfer of property to a corporation under subsection 85(1).

Tax Window Files: Subsection 247(2), surplus, and FAPI, *October 27, 2017*, CRA Document No. 2017-0694231I7; Payments under a German profit transfer agreement "PTA", *16XXXX*, CRA Document No. 2015-0617351R3.

▶ 53(1)(d) ◀

(d) [Adjustments to cost base — Share of foreign affiliate] — if the property is a share of the capital stock of a foreign affiliate of the taxpayer, any amount required by section 92 to be added in computing the adjusted cost base to the taxpayer of the share;

History: S. 53(1)(*d*) was replaced by S.C. 2013, c. 34, s. 29(1), deemed to have come into force on December 21, 2002.

However, any assessment of a taxpayer's tax, interest and penalties payable under the Act for any taxation year that ends before June 26, 2013 that would otherwise be precluded because of subsections 152(4) to (5) of the Act, shall be made to the extent necessary to take into account this amendment, if the taxpayer

(i) elects in writing in respect of all of its foreign affiliates that this section apply in respect of that provision, and

(ii) files that election with the Minister of National Revenue on or before December 26, 2013 [the day that is six months after royal assent].

S. 53(1)(*d*) formerly read:

(*d*) *[Adjustments to cost base — Share of foreign affiliate]* — where the property is a share of the capital stock of a foreign affiliate of the taxpayer, any amount required by paragraph 92(1)(*a*) to be added in computing the adjusted cost base to the taxpayer of the share;

Related Sections: ITAR s. 26(3) Cost of acquisition of capital property owned on Dec. 31, 1971.

▶ 53(1)(d.01) ◀

(d.01) [Adjustments to cost base — Share of demutualized insurer] — where the property is a share of the capital stock of a corporation, any amount required by paragraph 139.1(16)(*l*) to be added in computing the adjusted cost base to the taxpayer of the share;

Related Sections: S. 53(1.1) Deemed contribution of capital; ITAR s. 26(3) Cost of acquisition of capital property owned on Dec. 31, 1971.

▶ 53(1)(d.1) ◀

(d.1) [Adjustments to cost base — Capital interest in a trust] — if the property is a capital interest in a trust, any amount included under subsection 91(1) or (3) in computing the taxpayer's income for a taxation year that ends at or before that time (or that would have been required to have been included under those subsections but for subsection 56(4.1) and sections 74.1 to 75 of this Act and section 74 of the *Income Tax Act*, chapter 148 of the Revised Statutes of Canada, 1952) in respect of that interest;

History: S. 53(1)(*d.1*) was replaced by S.C. 2013, c. 34, s. 4(1), applicable to taxation years that end after 2006. This amendment also applies in computing the adjusted cost base to a taxpayer of a capital interest in a trust for an earlier taxation year if subsection 94(1) applies to the trust for a taxation year that ends in that earlier taxation year of the taxpayer.

In computing the adjusted cost base of a capital interest in a trust disposed of on or before August 27, 2010, paragraph 53(1)(*d.1*) is to be read as follows:

"(*d*.1) where the property is a capital interest in a trust, any amount required to be included under subsection 91(1) or (3) in computing the taxpayer's income for a taxation year that ends before that time (or that would have been required to have been included under those subsections but for subsection 56(4.1) and sections 74.1 to 75 of this Act and section 74 of the *Income Tax Act*, chapter 148 of the Revised Statutes of Canada, 1952) in respect of that interest;"

S. 53(1)(*d.1*) formerly read:

(*d*.1) *[Adjustments to cost base — Capital interest in a trust]* — where the property is a capital interest of the taxpayer in a trust to which paragraph 94(1)(*d*) applies, any amount required by paragraph 94(5)(*a*) to be added in computing the adjusted cost base to the taxpayer of the interest;

Related Sections: ITAR s. 26(3) Cost of acquisition of capital property owned on Dec. 31, 1971.

▶ 53(1)(d.2) ◀

(d.2) [Adjustments to cost base — Unit in a mutual fund trust] — where the property is a unit in a mutual fund trust, any amount required by subsection 132.1(2) to be added in computing the adjusted cost base to the taxpayer of the unit;

Related Sections: ITAR s. 26(3) Cost of acquisition of capital property owned on Dec. 31, 1971.

▶ 53(1)(d.3) ◀

(d.3) [Adjustments to cost base — Denied deduction for interest or soft costs] — where the property is a share of the capital stock of a corporation of which the taxpayer was, at any time, a specified shareholder, any expense incurred by the taxpayer in respect of land or a building of the corporation that was by reason of subsection 18(2) or (3.1) not deductible by the taxpayer in computing the taxpayer's income for any taxation year commencing before that time;

Related Sections: ITAR s. 26(3) Cost of acquisition of capital property owned on Dec. 31, 1971.

▶ 53(1)(e) ◀

(e) [Adjustments to cost base — Interest in a partnership] — where the property is an interest in a partnership,

(i) an amount in respect of each fiscal period of the partnership ending after 1971 and before that time, equal to the total of all amounts each of which is the taxpayer's share (other than a share under an agreement referred to in subsection 96(1.1)) of the income of the partnership from any source for that fiscal period, computed as if this Act were read without reference to

(A) paragraphs 38(*a.1*) to (*a.3*) and the fractions set out in the formula in paragraph 14(1)(*b*) and in subsection 14(5), paragraph 38(*a*) and subsection 41(1),

(A.1) subparagraph 39(1)(*a*)(i.1) in respect of an object referred to in that subparagraph that is not the subject of a gifting arrangement, as defined in subsection 237.1(1), nor a property that is a tax shelter,

(A.2) the description of C in the formula in paragraph 14(1)(*b*), and

(B) paragraph (i), paragraphs 12(1)(*o*) and (*z*.5), 18(1)(*m*), 20(1)(*v*.1) and 29(1)(*b*) and (2)(*b*), section 55, subsections 69(6) and (7) and paragraph 82(1)(*b*) of this Act and paragraphs 20(1)(*gg*) and 81(1)(*r*) and (*s*) of the *Income Tax Act*, chapter 148 of the Revised Statutes of Canada, 1952, and the provisions of the *Income Tax Application Rules* relating to income from the operation of new mines,

(ii) the taxpayer's share of any capital dividends and any life insurance capital dividends received by the partnership before that time on shares of the capital stock of a corporation that were partnership property,

(iii) the taxpayer's share of the amount, if any, by which

(A) any proceeds of a life insurance policy received by the partnership after 1971 and before that time in consequence of the death of any person whose life was insured under the policy,

exceeds the total of all amounts each of which is

(B) the "adjusted cost basis" (in this subparagraph as defined in subsection 148(9)), immediately before the death, of

(I) if the death occurs before March 22, 2016, the policy to the partnership, and

(II) if the death occurs after March 21, 2016, a policyholder's interest in the policy,

(C) the amount by which the fair market value of consideration given in respect of a disposition of an interest in the policy exceeds the greater of the amount determined under subparagraph 148(7)(*a*)(i) in respect of the disposition and the adjusted cost basis to the policyholder of the interest immediately before the disposition, if

(I) the death occurs after March 21, 2016, and

(II) the disposition was by a policyholder (other than a taxable Canadian corporation) after 1999 and before March 22, 2016, or

(D) if the death occurs after March 21, 2016, an interest in the policy was disposed of by a policyholder (other than a taxable Canadian corporation) after 1999 and before March 22, 2016 and subsection 148(7) applied to the disposition, the amount, if any, determined by the formula

$$A - B$$

where

A is the amount, if any, by which the lesser of the adjusted cost basis to the policyholder of the interest immediately before the disposition and the fair market value of consideration given in respect of the disposition exceeds the amount determined under subparagraph 148(7)(*a*)(i) in respect of the disposition, and

B is the absolute value of the negative amount, if any, that would be, in the absence of section 257, the adjusted cost basis, immediately before the death, of the interest in the policy,

(iv) where the taxpayer has, after 1971, made a contribution of capital to the partnership otherwise than by way of loan, such part of the amount of the contribution as cannot reasonably be regarded as a benefit conferred on any other member of the partnership who was related to the taxpayer,

(iv.1) each amount that is in respect of a specified amount described in subsection 80.2(1) and that is paid by the taxpayer to the partnership, to the extent that the amount paid is not deductible in computing the income of the taxpayer,

(v) where the time is immediately before the taxpayer's death and the taxpayer was at that time a member of a partnership, the value, at the time of the taxpayer's death, of the rights or things referred to in subsection 70(2) in respect of a partnership interest held by the taxpayer immediately before the taxpayer's death, other than an interest referred to in subsection 96(1.5),

(vi) any amount deemed by subsection 40(3.1) to be a gain of the taxpayer for a taxation year from a disposition before that time of the property,

(vii) any amount deemed by paragraph 98(1)(*c*) or 98.1(1)(*c*) to be a gain of the taxpayer for a taxation year from a disposition before that time of the property,

(vii.1) a share of the taxpayer's Canadian development expense or Canadian oil and gas property expense that was deducted at or before that time in computing the adjusted cost base to the taxpayer of the interest because of subparagraph (2)(*c*)(ii) and in respect of which the taxpayer elected under paragraph (*f*) of the definition "Canadian development expense" in subsection 66.2(5) or paragraph (*b*) of the definition "Canadian oil and gas property expense" in subsection 66.4(5), as the case may be,

(viii) an amount deemed, before that time, by subsection 66.1(7), 66.2(6) or 66.4(6) to be an amount referred to in the description of G in the definition "cumulative Canadian exploration expense" in subsection 66.1(6), paragraph (*a*) of the description of F in the definition "cumulative Canadian development expense" in subsection 66.2(5) or the description of G in that definition, or paragraph (*a*) of the description of F in the definition "cumulative Canadian oil and gas property expense" in subsection 66.4(5) or the description of G in that definition in respect of the taxpayer,

(viii.1) an amount deemed, before that time, by subsection 59(1.1) to be proceeds of disposition receivable by the taxpayer in respect of the disposition of a foreign resource property,

(ix) the amount, if any, by which

(A) the taxpayer's share of the amount of any assistance or benefit that the partnership received or became entitled to receive after 1971 and before that time from a government, municipality or other public authority, whether as a grant, subsidy, forgivable loan, deduction from royalty or tax, investment allowance or any other form of assistance or benefit, in respect of or related to a Canadian resource property or an exploration or development expense incurred in Canada

exceeds

(B) the part, if any, of the amount included in clause (A) in respect of the interest that was repaid before that time by the taxpayer under a legal obligation to repay all or any part of the amount,

(x) any amount required by section 97 to be added before that time in computing the adjusted cost base to the taxpayer of the interest,

(xi) of which the taxpayer's share of any income or loss of the partnership was, at any time, 10% or more, any expense incurred by the taxpayer in respect of land or a building of the partnership that was by reason of subsection 18(2) or (3.1) not deductible by the taxpayer in computing the taxpayer's income for any taxation year commencing before that time,

(xii) any amount required by paragraph 110.6(23)(*a*) to be added at that time in computing the adjusted cost base to the taxpayer of the interest, and

(xiii) any amount required by subsection 127(30) to be added to the taxpayer's tax otherwise payable under this Part for a taxation year that ended before that time;

History: S. 53(1)(*e*)(iii) was replaced by S.C. 2016, c. 12, s. 16, in force December 15, 2016, and formerly read:

(iii) the taxpayer's share of the amount, if any, by which

(A) any proceeds of a life insurance policy received by the partnership after 1971 and before that time in consequence of the death of any person whose life was insured under the policy,

exceeds

(B) the adjusted cost basis (within the meaning assigned by subsection 148(9)) of the policy to the partnership immediately before that person's death,

S. 53(1)(*e*)(i)(A) was replaced by S.C. 2013, c. 40, s. 22(1), applicable in respect of gifts made after February 25, 2008, and formerly read:

(A) paragraphs 38(*a*.1) and (*a*.2) and the fractions set out in the formula in paragraph 14(1)(*b*) and in subsection 14(5), paragraph 38(*a*) and subsection 41(1),

S. 53(1)(*e*)(i)(A.1) was added by S.C. 2013, c. 34, s. 190(3), applicable in respect of the disposition of an object made after 2003.

S. 53(1)(*e*)(i)(A.1) was repealed by S.C. 2013, c. 34, s. 190(2), applicable in respect of amounts that became payable after December 20, 2002, and formerly read:

(A.1) paragraph 18(1)(*l*.1),

S. 53(1)(*e*)(iv.1) was added by S.C. 2013, c. 34, s. 190(4), applicable to payments made in taxation years that end after 2002.

S. 53(1)(*e*)(viii.1) was added by S.C. 2013, c. 34, s. 190(5), applicable for fiscal periods of a partnership that begin after 2000.

Related Sections: S. 53(2)(*c*) Amounts to be deducted — Interest in a partnership; s. 96(1) General rules; s. 100(2) Gain from disposition of interest in partnership; ITAR s. 26(3) Cost of acquisition of capital property owned on Dec. 31, 1971, s. 26(9) Cost of interest in partnership, s. 26(9.1) Determination of amounts for purpose of s. (9), s. 26(9.4) Application of s. 53 of amended Act in respect of interest in partnership.

Canadian Tax Foundation: Cormack and Pantry, *Negative Partnership Interest ACB*, 2016 Canadian Tax Highlights 24(8):1–2; Lille and Johnson, *Partnerships: An Update*, 2010 Conference Report 36:1–62; Goldlist, *Implications of Recent Tax Changes on Business Purchases and Sales*, 2007 Ontario Tax Conference 11:1–24; Hsu and Nixon, *Current Issues Forum: Recent Developments of Interest to Tax Advisors of Owner-Managed Businesses*, 2007 Ontario Tax Conference 1:1–19; Taylor and Gifford, *Bill C-33 — Part 2, Technical Amendments*, 2007 Prairie Provinces Tax Conference 15:1–31; Stephan, *Sale or Succession of the Owner Managed Business — Selected Topics*, 2007 Prairie Provinces Tax Conference 7:1–39; Kakkar, *Contributed Surplus ACB Trap*, 2007 Tax for the Owner-Manager 7(3):1–2.

Tax Profile: December 2011 — Partnership Taxation.

Forms: T2065 — Determination of Adjusted Cost Base of a Partnership Interest.

Interpretation Bulletins: *Primary* — IT-430R3 (Consolid.) — Life insurance proceeds received by a private corporation or a partnership as a consequence of death. *Secondary* — IT-153R3 Land developers — Subdivision and development costs and carrying charges on land; IT-242R Retired partners; IT-278R2 Death of a partner or of a retired partner; IT-471R Merger of partnerships.

▶ 53(1)(f) ◀

(f) [Adjustments to cost base — Substituted property] — where the property is substituted property (within the meaning assigned by paragraph (*a*) of the definition "superficial loss" in section 54) of the taxpayer, the amount, if any, by which

(i) the amount of the loss that was, because of the acquisition by the taxpayer of the property, a superficial loss of any taxpayer from a disposition of a property

exceeds

(ii) where the property disposed of was a share of the capital stock of a corporation, the amount that would, but for paragraph 40(2)(*g*), be deducted under subsection 112(3), (3.1) or (3.2) in computing the loss of any taxpayer in respect of the disposition of the share;

Related Sections: ITAR s. 26(3) Cost of acquisition of capital property owned on Dec. 31, 1971.

Tax Profile: January 2009 — Market Meltdown — Capital Loss Utilization; May 2004 — The Stop-Loss Rules.

Interpretation Bulletins: *Primary* — IT-456R Capital property — Some adjustments to cost base. *Secondary* — IT-291R3 Transfer of property to a corporation under subsection 85(1).

▶ 53(1)(f.1) ◀

(f.1) [Adjustments to cost base — Previously denied capital loss] — where the taxpayer is a taxable Canadian corporation and the property was disposed of by another taxable Canadian corporation to the taxpayer in circumstances such that

(i) paragraph (*f*.2) does not apply to increase the adjusted cost base to the other corporation of shares of the capital stock of the taxpayer, and

(ii) the capital loss from the disposition was deemed by paragraph 40(2)(*e*.1) (or, where the property was acquired by the taxpayer before 1996, by paragraph 40(2)(*e*) or 85(4)(*a*) as those paragraphs read in their application to property acquired before April 26, 1995) to be nil,

the amount that would otherwise have been the capital loss from the disposition;

Related Sections: ITAR s. 26(3) Cost of acquisition of capital property owned on Dec. 31, 1971.

Tax Profile: January 2009 — Market Meltdown — Capital Loss Utilization.

▶ 53(1)(f.11) ◀

(f.11) [Adjustments to cost base — Previously denied capital loss] — where the property was disposed of by a person (other than a non-resident person or a person exempt from tax under this Part on the person's taxable income) or by an eligible Canadian partnership (as defined in subsection 80(1)) to the taxpayer in circumstances such that

(i) paragraph (*f*.1) does not apply to increase the adjusted cost base to the taxpayer of the property,

(ii) paragraph (*f*.2) does not apply to increase the adjusted cost base to that person of shares of the capital stock of the taxpayer, and

(iii) the capital loss from the disposition was deemed by paragraph 40(2)(*e*.1) (or, where the property was acquired by the taxpayer before 1996, by paragraph 85(4)(*a*) as it read in its application to property acquired before April 26, 1995) to be nil,

the amount that would otherwise be the capital loss from the disposition;

Related Sections: ITAR s. 26(3) Cost of acquisition of capital property owned on Dec. 31, 1971.

Tax Profile: January 2009 — Market Meltdown — Capital Loss Utilization.

▶ 53(1)(f.12) ◀

(f.12) [Adjustments to cost base — Commercial obligation] — where the property is a particular commercial obligation (in this paragraph having the meaning assigned by subsection 80(1)) payable to the taxpayer as consideration for the settlement or extinguishment of another commercial obligation payable to the taxpayer and the taxpayer's loss from the disposition of the other obligation was reduced because of paragraph 40(2)(*e*.2), the proportion of the reduction that the principal amount of the particular obligation is of the total of all amounts each of which is the principal amount of a commercial obligation payable to the taxpayer as consideration for the settlement or extinguishment of that other obligation;

Related Sections: ITAR s. 26(3) Cost of acquisition of capital property owned on Dec. 31, 1971.

▶ 53(1)(f.2) ◀

(f.2) [Adjustments to cost base — Denied loss on transfer of shares to corporation] — where the property is a share, any amount required by paragraph 40(3.6)(*b*) (or, where the property was acquired by the taxpayer before 1996, by paragraph 85(4)(*b*) as it read in its application to property disposed of before April 26, 1995) to be added in computing the adjusted cost base to the taxpayer of the share;

Related Sections: ITAR s. 26(3) Cost of acquisition of capital property owned on Dec. 31, 1971.

Interpretation Bulletins: *Primary* — IT-456R Capital property — Some adjustments to cost base.

▶ 53(1)(g) ◀

(g) [Adjustments to cost base — Obligation issued at a discount] — where the property is a bond, debenture, bill, note, mortgage, hypothecary claim or similar obligation, the amount, if any, by which the principal amount of the obligation exceeds the amount for which the obligation was issued, if the excess was required by subsection 16(2) or (3) to be included in computing the income of the taxpayer for a taxation year commencing before that time;

Related Sections: ITAR s. 26(3) Cost of acquisition of capital property owned on Dec. 31, 1971.

▶ 53(1)(g.1) ◀

(g.1) **[Adjustments to cost base — Indexed debt obligation]** — where the property is an indexed debt obligation, any amount determined under subparagraph 16(6)(*a*)(i) in respect of the obligation and required to be included in computing the taxpayer's income for a taxation year beginning before that time;

Related Sections: S. 248(1), "indexed debt obligation"; ITAR s. 26(3) Cost of acquisition of capital property owned on Dec. 31, 1971.

▶ 53(1)(h) ◀

(h) **[Adjustments to cost base — Land]** — where the property is land of the taxpayer, any amount paid by the taxpayer or by another taxpayer in respect of whom the taxpayer was a person, corporation or partnership described in subparagraph (*b*)(i), (ii) or (iii) of the definition "interest on debt relating to the acquisition of land" in subsection 18(3), after 1971 and before that time pursuant to a legal obligation to pay

(i) interest on debt relating to the acquisition of land (within the meaning assigned by subsection 18(3)), or

(ii) property taxes (not including income or profits taxes or taxes imposed by reference to the transfer of property) paid by the taxpayer in respect of the property to a province or to a Canadian municipality

to the extent that the amount was, because of subsection 18(2),

(iii) not deductible in computing the taxpayer's income from the land or from a business for any taxation year beginning before that time, or

(iv) not deductible in computing the income of the other taxpayer and was not included in or added to the cost to the other taxpayer of any property otherwise than because of subparagraph (*d*.3) or subparagraph (*e*)(xi);

Related Sections: ITAR s. 26(3) Cost of acquisition of capital property owned on Dec. 31, 1971.

Interpretation Bulletins: *Primary* — IT-456R Capital property — Some adjustments to cost base.

▶ 53(1)(i) ◀

(i) **[Adjustments to cost base — Land used in farming]** — where the property is land used in a farming business carried on by the taxpayer, an amount in respect of each taxation year ending after 1971 and commencing before that time, equal to the taxpayer's loss, if any, for that year from the farming business, to the extent that the loss

(i) was not, by virtue of section 31, deductible in computing the taxpayer's income for that year,

(ii) was not deducted in computing the taxpayer's taxable income for the taxation year in which the taxpayer disposed of the property or any preceding taxation year,

(iii) did not exceed the total of

(A) taxes (other than income or profits taxes or taxes imposed by reference to the transfer of the property) paid by the taxpayer in that year or payable by the taxpayer in respect of that year to a province or a Canadian municipality in respect of the property, and

(B) interest, paid by the taxpayer in that year or payable by the taxpayer in respect of that year, pursuant to a legal obligation to pay interest on borrowed money used to acquire the property or on any amount as consideration payable for the property,

to the extent that those taxes and interest were included in computing the loss, and

(iv) did not exceed the remainder obtained when

(A) the total of each of the taxpayer's losses from the farming business for taxation years preceding that year (to the extent that they are required by this paragraph to be added in computing the taxpayer's adjusted cost base of the property),

is deducted from

(B) the amount, if any, by which the taxpayer's proceeds of disposition of the property exceed the adjusted cost base to the taxpayer of the property immediately before that time, determined without reference to this paragraph;

Related Sections: S. 111(6) Limitation; ITAR s. 26(3) Cost of acquisition of capital property owned on Dec. 31, 1971.

▶ 53(1)(j) ◀

(j) **[Adjustments to cost base — Share or fund unit taxed as stock option benefit]** — if the property is a security (within the meaning assigned by subsection 7(7)) and, in respect of its acquisition by the taxpayer, a benefit was deemed by section 7 to have been received in any taxation year that ends after 1971 and begins before that time by the taxpayer or by a person that did not deal at arm's length with the taxpayer or, if the security was acquired after February 27, 2000, would have been so deemed if section 7 were read without reference to subsections 7(1.1) and (8), the amount of the benefit that was, or would have been, so deemed to have been received;

Related Sections: ITAR s. 26(3) Cost of acquisition of capital property owned on Dec. 31, 1971.

Interpretation Bulletins: *Secondary* — IT-113R4 Benefits to employees — Stock options.

▶ 53(1)(k) ◀

(k) **[Adjustments to cost base — Expropriation asset]** — where the property is an expropriation asset of the taxpayer (within the meaning assigned by section 80.1) or an asset of the taxpayer assumed for the purposes of that section to be an expropriation asset thereof, any amount required by paragraph 80.1(2)(*b*) to be added in computing the adjusted cost base to the taxpayer of the asset;

Related Sections: ITAR s. 26(3) Cost of acquisition of capital property owned on Dec. 31, 1971.

▶ 53(1)(l) ◀

(l) **[Adjustments to cost base — Interest in related segregated fund trust]** — where the property is an interest in a related segregated fund trust referred to in section 138.1,

(i) each amount deemed by paragraph 138.1(1)(*f*) to be an amount payable to the taxpayer before that time in respect of that interest,

(ii) each amount required by subparagraph 138.1(1)(*g*)(ii) to be added before that time in respect of that interest,

(iii) each amount in respect of that interest that is a capital gain deemed to have been allocated under subsection 138.1(4) to the taxpayer before that time, and

(iv) each amount in respect of that interest that before that time was deemed by subsection 138.1(3) to be a capital gain of the taxpayer;

Related Sections: ITAR s. 26(3) Cost of acquisition of capital property owned on Dec. 31, 1971.

► 53(1)(m) ◄

(m) [Adjustments to cost base — Offshore investment fund property] — where the property is an offshore investment fund property (within the meaning assigned by subsection 94.1(1)),

(i) any amount included in respect of the property by virtue of subsection 94.1(1) in computing the taxpayer's income for a taxation year commencing before that time, or

(ii) where the taxpayer is a controlled foreign affiliate (within the meaning of subsection 95(1)), of a person resident in Canada, any amount included in respect of the property in computing the foreign accrual property income of the controlled foreign affiliate by reason of the description of C in the definition "foreign accrual property income" in subsection 95(1) for a taxation year commencing before that time;

Related Sections: ITAR s. 26(3) Cost of acquisition of capital property owned on Dec. 31, 1971.

► 53(1)(n) ◄

(n) [Adjustments to cost base — Costs of surveying or valuing property] — the reasonable costs incurred by the taxpayer, before that time, of surveying or valuing the property for the purpose of its acquisition or disposition (to the extent that those costs are not deducted by the taxpayer in computing the taxpayer's income for any taxation year or attributable to any other property);

Related Sections: ITAR s. 26(3) Cost of acquisition of capital property owned on Dec. 31, 1971.

Interpretation Bulletins: *Secondary* — IT-407R4 (Consolid.) Dispositions of cultural property to designated Canadian institutions.

► 53(1)(o) ◄

(o) [Adjustments to cost base — Remainder interests in land] — where the property is real property of the taxpayer, any amount required by paragraph 43.1(2)(*b*) to be added in computing the adjusted cost base to the taxpayer of the property;

Related Sections: ITAR s. 26(3) Cost of acquisition of capital property owned on Dec. 31, 1971.

► 53(1)(p) ◄

(p) [Adjustments to cost base — Flow-through entity, after 2004] — where the time is after 2004 and the property is an interest in or a share of the capital stock of a flow-through entity (within the meaning assigned by subsection 39.1(1)), the amount determined by the formula

$$A \times B/C$$

where

A is the amount, if any, that would, if the definition "exempt capital gains balance" in subsection 39.1(1) were read without reference to "that ends before 2005", be the taxpayer's exempt capital gains balance in respect of the entity for the taxpayer's 2005 taxation year,

B is the fair market value at that time of the property, and

C is the fair market value at that time of all the taxpayer's interests in or shares of the capital stock of the entity;

Related Sections: S. 107(2.2) Flow-through entity; ITAR s. 26(3) Cost of acquisition of capital property owned on Dec. 31, 1971.

► 53(1)(q) ◄

(q) [Adjustments to cost base — Debt forgiveness] — any amount required under paragraph (4)(*b*), (5)(*b*), (6)(*b*), 47(1)(*d*), 49(3.01)(*b*), 51(1)(*d.2*), 86(4)(*b*) or 87(5.1)(*b*) or (6.1)(*b*) to be added in computing the adjusted cost base to the taxpayer of the property;

Related Sections: ITAR s. 26(3) Cost of acquisition of capital property owned on Dec. 31, 1971.

► 53(1)(r) ◄

(r) [Adjustments to cost base — Flow-through entity, before 2005] — if the time is before 2005, the property is an interest in, or a share of the capital stock of, a flow-through entity described in any of paragraphs (*a*) to (*f*) and (*h*) of the definition "flow-through entity" in subsection 39.1(1) and immediately after that time the taxpayer disposed of all their interests in, and shares of the capital stock of, the entity, the amount determined by the formula

$$A \times B/C$$

where

A is the amount, if any, by which the taxpayer's exempt capital gains balance (as defined in subsection 39.1(1)) in respect of the entity for the taxpayer's taxation year that includes that time exceeds the total of all amounts each of which is

(i) the amount by which a capital gain is reduced under section 39.1 for the year because of the taxpayer's exempt capital gains balance in respect of the entity, or

(ii) twice an amount by which a taxable capital gain, or the income from a business, is reduced under section 39.1 for the year because of the taxpayer's exempt capital gains balance in respect of the entity,

B is the fair market value at that time of the property, and

C is the fair market value at that time of all the taxpayer's interests in, and shares of the capital stock of, the entity;

History: S. 53(1)(*r*), the portion before the formula, was replaced by S.C. 2013, c. 40, s. 22(2), applicable to dispositions that occur after 2001, and formerly read:

(r) where the time is before 2005, the property is an interest in, or a share of the capital stock of, a flow-through entity described in any of paragraphs (a) to (f) of the definition "flow-through entity" in subsection 39.1(1) and immediately after that time the taxpayer disposed of all of the taxpayer's interests in, and shares of the capital stock of, the entity, the amount determined by the formula

Related Sections: S. 53(1.2) Flow-through entity before 2005; s. 54, "adjusted cost base"; and ITAR s. 26(3) Cost of acquisition of capital property owned on Dec. 31, 1971.

▶ 53(1)(s) ◀

(s) [Adjustments to cost base — Derivative forward agreement] — if the property was acquired under a derivative forward agreement, any amount required to be included in respect of the property under subparagraph 12(1)(z.7)(i) in computing the income of the taxpayer for a taxation year; and

History: S. 53(1)(s) was added by S.C. 2013, c. 40, s. 22(3), deemed to have come into force on March 21, 2013.

▶ 53(1)(t) ◀

(t) [Adjustments to cost base — Derivative forward agreement] — if the property is disposed of under a derivative forward agreement, any amount required to be included in respect of the property under subparagraph 12(1)(z.7)(ii) in computing the income of the taxpayer for the taxation year that includes that time.

History: S. 53(1)(t) was added by S.C. 2013, c. 40, s. 22(3), deemed to have come into force on March 21, 2013.

▶ 53(1.1) ◀

(1.1) Deemed contribution of capital. For the purposes of paragraph (1)(c), where there has been a disposition of property before May 7, 1974 and

(a) the taxpayer and the corporation referred to in that paragraph have made an election under section 85 in respect of that property, and

(b) the consideration received by the taxpayer for the property did not include shares of the capital stock of the corporation,

the disposition of property shall be deemed to be a contribution of capital equal to the amount, if any, by which

(c) the amount that the taxpayer and the corporation have agreed on in the election

exceeds

(d) the fair market value at the time of the disposition of any consideration received by the taxpayer for the property so disposed of.

Related Sections: S. 53(1) Adjustments to cost base.

▶ 53(1.2) ◀

(1.2) Flow-through entity before 2005. For the purposes of paragraph (1)(r), if the fair market value of all of a taxpayer's interests in, and shares of the capital stock of, a flow-through entity is nil when the taxpayer disposes of those interests and shares, the fair market value of each such interest or share at that time is deemed to be $1.

History: S. 53(1.2) was added by S.C. 2013, c. 40, s. 22(4), applicable to dispositions that occur after 2001.

▶ 53(2) ◀

(2) Amounts to be deducted. In computing the adjusted cost base to a taxpayer of property at any time, there shall be deducted such of the following amounts in respect of the property as are applicable:

Related Sections: 112(4) Loss on share that is not capital property; 112(5.2) Adjustment re dividends.

▶ 53(2)(a) ◀

(a) [Amounts to be deducted — Share of the capital stock of a corporation] — where the property is a share of the capital stock of a corporation resident in Canada,

(i) any amount received by the taxpayer after 1971 and before that time as, on account or in lieu of payment of, or in satisfaction of, a dividend on the share (other than a taxable dividend or a dividend in respect of which the corporation paying the dividend has elected in accordance with subsection 83(2) or (2.1) in respect of the full amount thereof),

(ii) any amount received by the taxpayer after 1971 and before that time on a reduction of the paid-up capital of the corporation in respect of the share, except to the extent that the amount is deemed by subsection 84(4) or (4.1) to be a dividend received by the taxpayer,

(iii) any amount required to be deducted before that time under section 84.1 of the *Income Tax Act*, chapter 148 of the Revised Statutes of Canada, 1952, as it applied before May 23, 1985 in computing the adjusted cost base to the taxpayer of the share,

(iv) any amount, to the extent that such amount is not proceeds of disposition of a share, received by the taxpayer before that time that would, but for subsection 84(8), be deemed by subsection 84(2) to be a dividend received by the taxpayer, and

(v) any amount required by paragraph 44.1(2)(b) to be deducted in computing the adjusted cost base to the taxpayer of the share;

Related Sections: S. 40(3) Deemed gain where amounts to be deducted from adjusted cost base exceed cost plus amounts to be added to adjusted cost base; s. 83(1) Qualifying dividends; ITAR s. 26(3) Cost of acquisition of capital property owned on Dec. 31, 1971.

Income Tax Folios: *Primary* — S3-F2-C1 Capital Dividends.

Interpretation Bulletins: *Primary* — IT-456R Capital property — Some adjustments to cost base.

▶ 53(2)(b) ◀

(b) [Amounts to be deducted — Share of non-resident corporation] — where the property is a share of the capital stock of a non-resident corporation,

(i) if the corporation is a foreign affiliate of the taxpayer,

(A) any amount required under paragraph 80.1(4)(d) or section 92 to be deducted in computing the adjusted cost base to the taxpayer of the share, and

(B) any amount received by the taxpayer before that time, on a reduction of the paid-up capital of the corporation in respect of the share, that is so received

(I) after 1971 and on or before August 19, 2011, or

(II) after August 19, 2011, where the reduction is a qualifying return of capital (within the meaning assigned by subsection 90(3)) in respect of the share, or

(ii) in any other case, any amount received by the taxpayer after 1971 and before that time on a reduction of the paid-up capital of the corporation in respect of the share;

History: S. 53(2)(*b*) was replaced by S.C. 2013, c. 34, s. 61(1), deemed to have come into force on August 20, 2011.

Any assessment of a taxpayer's tax, interest and penalties payable under the Act for any taxation year that ends before June 26, 2013 that would, in the absence of this section, be precluded because of subsections 152(4) to (5) of the Act shall be made to the extent necessary to take into account the amendments by S.C. 2013, c. 34, s. 54 to 89.

S. 53(2)(*b*) formerly read:

(*b*) *[Amounts to be deducted — Share of non-resident corporation]* — where the property is a share of the capital stock of a corporation not resident in Canada,

(i) any amount required by paragraph 80.1(4)(*d*) or section 92 to be deducted in computing the adjusted cost base to the taxpayer of the share, and

(ii) any amount received by the taxpayer after 1971 and before that time on a reduction of the paid-up capital of the corporation in respect of the share;

Related Sections: 40(3) Deemed gain where amounts to be deducted from adjusted cost base exceed cost plus amounts to be added to adjusted cost base; 90(3) qualifying return of capital; ITAR s. 26(3) Cost of acquisition of capital property owned on Dec. 31, 1971.

Tax Window Files: Paid-up capital reduction of a foreign affiliate, *January 22, 2015*, CRA Document No. 2014-0560571I7.

▶ 53(2)(b.1) ◀

(b.1) [Amounts to be deducted — Capital interest in a non-resident trust] — if the property is a capital interest in a trust, any amount deducted by the taxpayer by reason of subsection 91(2) or (4) in computing the taxpayer's income for a taxation year that ends at or before that time (or that would have been so deductible by the taxpayer but for subsection 56(4.1) and sections 74.1 to 75 of this Act and section 74 of the *Income Tax Act*, chapter 148 of the Revised Statutes of Canada, 1952) in respect of that interest;

History: S. 53(2)(*b.1*) was replaced by S.C. 2013, c. 34, s. 4(2), applicable to taxation years that end after 2006. This amendment also applies in computing the adjusted cost base to a taxpayer of a capital interest in a trust for an earlier taxation year if subsection 94(1) applies to the trust for a taxation year that ends in that earlier taxation year of the taxpayer.

S. 53(2)(*b.1*) formerly read:

(*b.1*) *[Amounts to be deducted — Capital interest in a non-resident trust]* — where the property is a capital interest of the taxpayer in a trust to which paragraph 94(1)(*d*) applies, any amount required by paragraph 94(5)(*b*) to be deducted in computing the adjusted cost base to the taxpayer of the interest;

Related Sections: S. 40(3) Deemed gain where amounts to be deducted from adjusted cost base exceed cost plus amounts to be added to adjusted cost base; ITAR s. 26(3) Cost of acquisition of capital property owned on Dec. 31, 1971.

▶ 53(2)(b.2) ◀

(b.2) [Amounts to be deducted — Non-depreciable capital property of a corporation] — if the property is property of a taxpayer that was subject to a loss restriction event at or before that time, any amount required by paragraph 111(4)(*c*) to be deducted in computing the adjusted cost base of the property;

History: S. 53(2)(*b.2*) was replaced by S.C. 2013, c. 40, s. 22(5), deemed to have come into force on March 21, 2013, and formerly read:

(*b.2*) where the property is property of a corporation control of which was acquired by a person or group of persons at or before that time, any amount required by paragraph 111(4)(*c*) to be deducted in computing the adjusted cost base of the property;

Related Sections: S. 40(3) Deemed gain where amounts to be deducted from adjusted cost base exceed cost plus amounts to be added to adjusted cost base; s. 251.2(2) Loss restriction event; ITAR s. 26(3) Cost of acquisition of capital property owned on Dec. 31, 1971.

▶ 53(2)(c) ◀

(c) [Amounts to be deducted — Interest in a partnership] — where the property is an interest in a partnership,

(i) an amount in respect of each fiscal period of the partnership ending after 1971 and before that time, equal to the total of amounts each of which is the taxpayer's share (other than a share under an agreement referred to in subsection 96(1.1)) of any loss of the partnership from any source for that fiscal period, computed as if this Act were read without reference to

(A) the fractions set out in subsection 14(5), paragraph 38(*b*) and in the formula in paragraph 14(1)(*b*),

(A.1) (Repealed by S.C. 2013, c. 34, s. 190(6).)

(A.2) the description of C in the formula in paragraph 14(1)(*b*),

(B) paragraphs 12(1)(*o*) and (*z.5*), 18(1)(*m*) and 20(1)(*v.1*), section 31, subsection 40(2), section 55 and subsections 69(6) and (7) of this Act and paragraphs 20(1)(*gg*) and 81(1)(*r*) and (*s*) of the *Income Tax Act*, chapter 148 of the Revised Statutes of Canada, 1952, and

(C) subsections 100(4), 112(3.1), (4), (4.2) as it read in its application to dispositions of property that occurred before April 27, 1995 and (5.2),

except to the extent that all or a portion of such a loss may reasonably be considered to have been included in the taxpayer's limited partnership loss in respect of the partnership for the taxpayer's taxation year in which that fiscal period ended,

(i.1) an amount in respect of each fiscal period of the partnership ending before that time that is the taxpayer's limited partnership loss in respect of the partnership for the taxation year in which that fiscal period ends to the extent that such loss was deducted by the taxpayer in computing the taxpayer's taxable income for any taxation year that commenced before that time,

(i.2) any amount deemed by subsection 40(3.12) to be a loss of the taxpayer for a taxation year from a disposition before that time of the property,

(i.3) if at that time the property is not a tax shelter investment as defined by section 143.2 and the taxpayer would be a member, described in subsection 40(3.1), of the partnership if the fiscal period of the partnership that includes that time ended at that time, the unpaid principal amount of any indebtedness of the taxpayer for which recourse is limited, either immediately or in the future and either absolutely or contingently, and that can reasonably be considered to have been used to acquire the property,

(i.4) unless that time is immediately before a disposition of the interest, if the taxpayer is a member of the partnership and the taxpayer has been a specified member of the partnership at all times since becoming a member of the partnership, or the taxpayer is at that time a limited partner of the partnership for the purposes of subsection 40(3.1),

(A) where that time is in the taxpayer's first taxation year for which the taxpayer is eligible to deduct an amount in respect of the partnership under subsection 34.2(11), the portion of the amount deducted in computing the taxpayer's income for the taxation year under subsection 34.2(11) in respect of the partnership that would have been deductible if the definition "qualifying transitional income" in subsection 34.2(1) were read without reference to paragraph (*b*), and

(B) where that time is in any other taxation year, the portion of the amount deducted in computing the taxpayer's income for the taxation year immediately preceding that other year under subsection 34.2(11) in respect of the partnership that would have been deductible if the definition "qualifying transitional income" in subsection 34.2(1) were read without reference to paragraph (*b*),

(ii) an amount in respect of each fiscal period of the partnership ending after 1971 and before that time, other than a fiscal period after the fiscal period in which the taxpayer ceased to be a member of the partnership, equal to the taxpayer's share of the total of

(A) amounts that, but for paragraph 96(1)(*d*), would be deductible in computing the income of the partnership for the fiscal period by virtue of the provisions of the *Income Tax Application Rules* relating to the exploration and development expenses,

(B) the Canadian exploration and development expenses and foreign resource pool expenses, if any, incurred by the partnership in the fiscal period,

(C) the Canadian exploration expense, if any, incurred by the partnership in the fiscal period,

(D) the Canadian development expense, if any, incurred by the partnership in the fiscal period, and

(E) the Canadian oil and gas property expense, if any, incurred by the partnership in the fiscal period,

(iii) any amount deemed by subsection 110.1(4) or 118.1(8) to have been the eligible amount of a gift made by the taxpayer by reason of the taxpayer's membership in the partnership at the end of a fiscal period of the partnership ending before that time,

(iv) any amount required by section 97 to be deducted before that time in computing the adjusted cost base to the taxpayer of the interest,

(v) any amount received by the taxpayer after 1971 and before that time as, on account or in lieu of payment of, or in satisfaction of, a distribution of the taxpayer's share (other than a share under an agreement referred to in subsection 96(1.1)) of the partnership profits or partnership capital,

(vi) an amount equal to that portion of all amounts deducted under subsection 127(5) in computing the tax otherwise payable by the taxpayer under this Part for the taxpayer's taxation years ending before that time that may reasonably be attributed to amounts added in computing the investment tax credit of the taxpayer by virtue of subsection 127(8),

(vii) any amount added pursuant to subsection 127.2(4) in computing the taxpayer's share-purchase tax credit for a taxation year ending before or after that time,

(viii) an amount equal to 50% of the amount deemed to be designated pursuant to subsection 127.3(4) before that time in respect of each share, debt obligation or right acquired by the partnership and deemed to have been acquired by the taxpayer under that subsection,

(ix) the amount of all assistance received by the taxpayer before that time that has resulted in a reduction of the capital cost of a depreciable property to the partnership by virtue of subsection 13(7.2),

(x) any amount deductible by the taxpayer under subparagraph 20(1)(*e*)(vi) in respect of the partnership for a taxation year of the taxpayer ending at or after that time,

(xi) any amount required by paragraph 110.6(23)(*b*) to be deducted at that time in computing the adjusted cost base to the taxpayer of the interest,

(xii) any amount payable by the partnership, to the extent that the amount is deductible under subsection 20.01(1) in computing the taxpayer's income for a taxation year that began before that time, and

(xiii) the amount of any reduction (within the meaning of paragraph 247(13)(*a*)) of the amount of a dividend deemed to have been received by the taxpayer in respect of a transaction (as defined in subsection 247(1)) or series of transactions in which the partnership was a participant;

History: S. 53(2)(*c*)(i)(C) was replaced by S.C. 2017, c. 33, s. 12(1), deemed to have come into force on September 16, 2016, and formerly read:

> (C) subsections 100(4) and 112(3.1), and subsection 112(4.2) as it read in its application to dispositions of property that occurred before April 27, 1995,

S. 53(2)(*c*)(i)(A.1) was repealed by S.C. 2013, c. 34, s. 190(6), applicable in respect of amounts that became payable after December 20, 2002, and formerly read:

> (A.1) paragraph 18(1)(*l*.1),

S. 53(2)(*c*)(iii) was replaced by S.C. 2013, c. 34, s. 190(7), applicable in respect of gifts and contributions made after December 20, 2002, except that in its application before 2007, subparagraph 53(2)(*c*)(iii), is to be read as follows:

> "(iii) any amount deemed by subsection 110.1(4) or 118.1(8) to have been the eligible amount of a gift made, or by subsection 127(4.2) to have been an amount contributed, by the taxpayer by reason of the taxpayer's membership in the partnership at the end of a fiscal period of the partnership ending before that time,"

S. 53(2)(*c*)(iii) formerly read:

> (iii) any amount deemed by subsection 110.1(4) or 118.1(8) to have been a gift made, or by subsection 127(4.2) to have been an amount contributed, by the taxpayer by reason of the taxpayer's membership in the partnership at the end of a fiscal period of the partnership ending before that time,

S. 53(2)(*c*)(xiii) was added by S.C. 2012, c. 31, s. 10(1), deemed to have come into force on March 29, 2012.

S. 53(2)(*c*)(i.4) was replaced by S.C. 2011, c. 24, s. 8(1), applicable to the 2011 and subsequent taxation years. S. 53(2)(*c*)(i.4) formerly read:

(i.4) if the taxpayer is a member of the partnership who was a specified member of the partnership at all times since becoming a member of the partnership or the taxpayer is at that time a limited partner of the partnership for the purposes of subsection 40(3.1), the amount

(A) deducted under subsection 34.2(4) in computing the taxpayer's income for the taxation year in respect of the interest, where that time is in the taxpayer's first taxation year in which a qualifying fiscal period (within the meaning assigned by subsection 34.2(1)) of the business carried on by the taxpayer as a member of the partnership ends and is after the end of that period, and

(B) where that time is in any other taxation year, deducted under subsection 34.2(4) in respect of the interest in computing the taxpayer's income for the taxation year preceding that other year

unless

(C) that time is immediately before a disposition of the interest and no amount is deductible under subsection 34.2(4) in respect of the interest in computing the taxpayer's income for the taxation year following the taxation year that includes that time,

(D) the taxpayer has December 31, 1995 income in respect of the business because of section 34.1, or

(E) the taxpayer's partnership interest was held by the taxpayer on February 22, 1994 and is an excluded interest (within the meaning assigned by subsection 40(3.15)) at the end of the fiscal period of the partnership that includes that time,

Related Sections: S. 87(2)(*j*.6) Continuing corporation; s. 96(1) General rules; s. 98.1 Residual interest in partnership; s. 98.2 Transfer of interest on death; s. 100(2) Gain from disposition of interest in partnership; s. 127(12.2) Adjusted cost base deductions re partnership interest, trust capital interest and government assistance; ITAR s. 26(3) Cost of acquisition of capital property owned on Dec. 31, 1971; s. 26(9.3) Amounts deemed to be required to be deducted in respect of interest in partnership; s. 26(9.4) Application of s. 53 of amended Act in respect of interest in partnership.

Canadian Tax Foundation: Cormack and Pantry, *Negative Partnership Interest ACB*, 2016 Canadian Tax Highlights 24(8):1–2; Lille and Johnson, *Partnerships: An Update*, 2010 Conference Report 36:1–62.

Tax Profile: December 2011 — Partnership Taxation.

Tax Topics: No. 1921, Ontario Limited Liability Partnerships — A Hidden Danger for Many.

Forms: T2065 — Determination of Adjusted Cost Base of a Partnership Interest.

Interpretation Bulletins: *Secondary* — IT-278R2 Death of a partner or of a retired partner; IT-341R4 Expenses of issuing or selling shares, units in a trust, interests in a partnership or syndicate and expenses of borrowing money.

▶ 53(2)(d) ◀

(d) [Amounts to be deducted — Part dispositions] — where the property is such that the taxpayer has, after 1971 and before that time, disposed of a part of it while retaining another part of it, the amount determined under section 43 to be the adjusted cost base to the taxpayer of the part so disposed of;

Related Sections: S. 40(3) Deemed gain where amounts to be deducted from adjusted cost base exceed cost plus amounts to be added to adjusted cost base; ITAR s. 26(3) Cost of acquisition of capital property owned on Dec. 31, 1971.

Interpretation Bulletins: *Secondary* — IT-200 Surface rentals and farming operations.

▶ 53(2)(e) ◀

(e) [Amounts to be deducted — Share, where shareholder incurred exploration and development expenses] — if the property is a share, or an interest in or a right to — or, for civil law, a right in or to — a share, of the capital stock of a corporation acquired before August 1976, an amount equal to any expense incurred by the taxpayer in consideration therefor, to the extent that the expense was, by virtue of

(i) paragraph (*e*) of the definition "Canadian exploration and development expenses" in subsection 66(15), a Canadian exploration and development expense,

(ii) paragraph (*i*) of the definition "Canadian exploration expense" in subsection 66.1(6), a Canadian exploration expense,

(iii) paragraph (*g*) of the definition "Canadian development expense" in subsection 66.2(5), a Canadian development expense, or

(iv) paragraph (*c*) of the definition "Canadian oil and gas property expense" in subsection 66.4(5), a Canadian oil and gas property expense

incurred by the taxpayer;

History: S. 53(2)(*e*), the portion before subparagraph (i) was replaced by S.C. 2013, c. 34, s. 106(2), in force June 26, 2013, and formerly read:

(*e*) *[Amounts to be deducted — Share, where shareholder incurred exploration and development expenses]* — where the property is a share, or an interest in or a right to a share, of the capital stock of a corporation acquired before August, 1976, an amount equal to any expense incurred by the taxpayer in consideration therefor, to the extent that the expense was, by virtue of

Related Sections: S. 40(3) Deemed gain where amounts to be deducted from adjusted cost base exceed cost plus amounts to be added to adjusted cost base; ITAR s. 26(3) Cost of acquisition of capital property owned on Dec. 31, 1971.

▶ 53(2)(f) ◀

(f) [Amounts to be deducted — Property received from joint exploration corporation] — where the property was received by the taxpayer as consideration for any payment or loan

(i) made before April 20, 1983 by the taxpayer as a shareholder corporation (within the meaning assigned by subsection 66(15)) to a joint exploration corporation of the shareholder, and

(ii) described in paragraph (*a*) of the definition "agreed portion" in subsection 66(15),

or the property was substituted for such a property, such portion of the payment or loan as may reasonably be considered to be related to an agreed portion (within the meaning assigned by subsection 66(15)) of the joint exploration corporation's

(iii) Canadian exploration and development expenses,

(iv) Canadian exploration expense,

(v) Canadian development expense, or

(vi) Canadian oil and gas property expense,

as the case may be;

Related Sections: S. 40(3) Deemed gain where amounts to be deducted from adjusted cost base exceed cost plus amounts to be added to adjusted cost base; ITAR s. 26(3) Cost of acquisition of capital property owned on Dec. 31, 1971.

▶ 53(2)(f.1) ◀

(f.1) [Amounts to be deducted — Share of the capital stock of joint exploration corporation] — where the property is a share of the capital stock of a joint exploration corporation resident in Canada and the taxpayer has, after 1971, made a contribution of capital to the corporation otherwise than by way of a loan, which contribution was included in computing the adjusted cost base of the property by virtue of paragraph (1)(*c*), such portion of the contribution as may reasonably be considered to be part of an agreed portion (within the meaning assigned by subsection 66(15)) of the corporation's

(i) Canadian exploration and development expenses,

(ii) Canadian exploration expense,

(iii) Canadian development expense, or

(iv) Canadian oil and gas property expense,

as the case may be;

Related Sections: S. 40(3) Deemed gain where amounts to be deducted from adjusted cost base exceed cost plus amounts to be added to adjusted cost base; ITAR s. 26(3) Cost of acquisition of capital property owned on Dec. 31, 1971.

► 53(2)(f.2) ◄

(f.2) [Amounts to be deducted — Resource expenses renounced by joint exploration corporation] — any amount required by paragraph 66(10.4)(*a*) to be deducted before that time in computing the adjusted cost base to the taxpayer of the property;

Related Sections: S. 40(3) Deemed gain where amounts to be deducted from adjusted cost base exceed cost plus amounts to be added to adjusted cost base; ITAR s. 26(3) Cost of acquisition of capital property owned on Dec. 31, 1971.

► 53(2)(g) ◄

(g) [Amounts to be deducted — Debt forgiveness] — where section 80 is applicable in respect of the taxpayer, the amount, if any, by which the adjusted cost base to the taxpayer of the property is required in prescribed manner to be reduced before that time;

Related Sections: S. 40(3) Deemed gain where amounts to be deducted from adjusted cost base exceed cost plus amounts to be added to adjusted cost base; ITAR s. 26(3) Cost of acquisition of capital property owned on Dec. 31, 1971.

► 53(2)(g.1) ◄

(g.1) [Amounts to be deducted — Debt forgiveness] — any amount required under paragraph (4)(*a*), (5)(*a*), (6)(*a*), 47(1)(*c*), 49(3.01)(*a*), 51(1)(*d*.1), 86(4)(*a*) or 87(5.1)(*a*) or (6.1)(*a*) to be deducted in computing the adjusted cost base to the taxpayer of the property or any amount by which that adjusted cost base is required to be reduced because of subsection 80(9), (10) or (11);

Related Sections: S. 40(3) Deemed gain where amounts to be deducted from adjusted cost base exceed cost plus amounts to be added to adjusted cost base; ITAR s. 26(3) Cost of acquisition of capital property owned on Dec. 31, 1971.

► 53(2)(h) ◄

(h) [Amounts to be deducted — Capital interest in a trust] — where the property is a capital interest of the taxpayer in a trust (other than an interest in a personal trust that has never been acquired for consideration or an interest of a taxpayer in a trust described in any of paragraphs (*a*) to (*e*.1) of the definition "trust" in subsection 108(1)),

(i) any amount paid to the taxpayer by the trust after 1971 and before that time as a distribution or payment of capital by the trust (otherwise than as proceeds of disposition of the interest or part thereof), to the extent that the amount became payable before 1988,

(i.1) any amount that has become payable to the taxpayer by the trust after 1987 and before that time in respect of the interest (otherwise than as proceeds of disposition of the interest or part thereof), except to the extent of the portion thereof

(A) that was included in the taxpayer's income by reason of subsection 104(13) or from which an amount of tax was deducted under Part XIII by reason of paragraph 212(1)(*c*),

(A.1) that was deemed by subsection 104(16) to be a dividend received by the taxpayer, or

(B) where the trust was resident in Canada throughout its taxation year in which the amount became payable

(I) that is equal to the amount designated by the trust under subsection 104(21) in respect of the taxpayer,

(II) that was designated by the trust under subsection 104(20) in respect of the taxpayer, or

(III) that is an assessable distribution (as defined in subsection 218.3(1)) to the taxpayer,

(ii) an amount equal to that portion of all amounts deducted under subsection 127(5) in computing the tax otherwise payable by the taxpayer under this Part for the taxpayer's taxation years ending before that time that may reasonably be attributed to amounts added in computing the investment tax credit of the taxpayer by virtue of subsection 127(7),

(iii) any amount added pursuant to subsection 127.2(3) in computing the taxpayer's share-purchase tax credit for a taxation year ending before or after that time,

(iv) an amount equal to 50% of the amount deemed to be designated pursuant to subsection 127.3(3) before that time in respect of each share, debt obligation or right acquired by the trust and deemed to have been acquired by the taxpayer under that subsection, and

(v) an amount equal to the amount of all assistance received by the taxpayer before that time that has resulted in a reduction of the capital cost of a depreciable property to the trust by virtue of subsection 13(7.2);

Related Sections: S. 40(3) Deemed gain where amounts to be deducted from adjusted cost base exceed cost plus amounts to be added to adjusted cost base; s. 87(2)(*j*.6) Continuing corporation; s. 127(12.2) Adjusted cost base deductions re partnership interest, trust capital interest and government assistance; ITAR s. 26(3) Cost of acquisition of capital property owned on Dec. 31, 1971.

Interpretation Bulletins: *Primary* — IT-456R Capital property — Some adjustments to cost base. *Secondary* — IT-342R Trusts — Income payable to beneficiaries; IT-381R3 Trusts — Capital gains and losses and the flow-through of taxable capital gains to beneficiaries.

► 53(2)(i) ◄

(i) [Amounts to be deducted — Capital interest in a non-resident trust] — where the property is a capital interest in a trust (other than a unit trust) not resident in Canada that was purchased after 1971 and before that time by the taxpayer from a non-resident person at a time (in this paragraph referred to as the "purchase time") when the property was not taxable Canadian property and the fair market value of such of the trust property as was

(i) a Canadian resource property,

(ii) (Repealed.)

(iii) an income interest in a trust resident in Canada,

(iv) taxable Canadian property, or

(v) a timber resource property

was not less than 50% of the fair market value of all the trust property, that proportion of the amount, if any, by which

(vi) the fair market value at the purchase time of such of the trust properties as were properties described in any of subparagraphs (i) to (v)

exceeds

(vii) the total of the cost amounts to the trust at the purchase time of such of the trust properties as were properties described in any of subparagraphs (i) to (v),

that the fair market value at the purchase time of the interest is of the fair market value at the purchase time of all capital interests in the trust;

Related Sections: S. 40(3) Deemed gain where amounts to be deducted from adjusted cost base exceed cost plus amounts to be added to adjusted cost base; s. 53(3) Application of paragraphs (2)(i) and (j); ITAR s. 26(3) Cost of acquisition of capital property owned on Dec. 31, 1971.

► 53(2)(j) ◄

(j) [Amounts to be deducted — Non-resident unit trust] — where the property is a unit of a unit trust not resident in Canada that was purchased after 1971 and before that time by the taxpayer from a non-resident person at a time (in this paragraph referred to as the "purchase time") when the property was not taxable Canadian property and the fair market value of such of the trust property as was

(i) a Canadian resource property,

(ii) (Repealed.)

(iii) an income interest in a trust resident in Canada,

(iv) taxable Canadian property, or

(v) a timber resource property

was not less than 50% of the fair market value of all the trust property, that proportion of the amount, if any, by which

(vi) the fair market value at the purchase time of such of the trust properties as were properties described in any of subparagraphs (i) to (v)

exceeds

(vii) the total of the cost amounts to the trust at the purchase time of such of the trust properties as were properties described in any of subparagraphs (i) to (v),

that the fair market value at the purchase time of the unit is of the fair market value at the purchase time of all the issued units of the trust;

Related Sections: S. 40(3) Deemed gain where amounts to be deducted from adjusted cost base exceed cost plus amounts to be added to adjusted cost base; s. 53(3) Application of paragraphs (2)(i) and (j); ITAR s. 26(3) Cost of acquisition of capital property owned on Dec. 31, 1971.

► 53(2)(k) ◄

(k) [Amounts to be deducted — Government assistance] — where the property was acquired by the taxpayer after 1971, the amount, if any, by which the total of

(i) the amount of any assistance which the taxpayer has received or is entitled to receive before that time from a government, municipality or other public authority, in respect of, or for the acquisition of, the property, whether as a grant, subsidy, forgivable loan, deduction from tax not otherwise provided for under this paragraph, investment allowance or as any other form of assistance other than

(A) an amount described in paragraph 37(1)(*d*),

(B) an amount deducted as an allowance under section 65,

(C) the amount of prescribed assistance that the taxpayer has received or is entitled to receive in respect of, or for the acquisition of, shares of the capital stock of a prescribed venture capital corporation or a prescribed labour-sponsored venture capital corporation or shares of the capital stock of a taxable Canadian corporation that are held in a prescribed stock savings plan, or

(D) an amount included in income by virtue of paragraph 12(1)(*u*) or 56(1)(*s*), and

(ii) all amounts deducted under subsection 127(5) or (6) in respect of the property before that time,

exceeds such part, if any, of the assistance referred to in subparagraph (i) as has been repaid before that time by the taxpayer pursuant to an obligation to repay all or any part of that assistance;

Related Regulations: 6700; 6700.1; 6700.2; 6701; 6702; 6705.

Related Sections: S. 40(3) Deemed gain where amounts to be deducted from adjusted cost base exceed cost plus amounts to be added to adjusted cost base; s. 127(12.2) Adjusted cost base deductions re partnership interest, trust capital interest and government assistance; ITAR s. 26(3) Cost of acquisition of capital property owned on Dec. 31, 1971.

Interpretation Bulletins: *Primary* — IT-273R2 Government assistance — General comments.

► 53(2)(l) ◄

(l) [Amounts to be deducted — Accrued interest on transferred debt obligation] — where the property is a debt obligation, any amount that was deductible by virtue of subsection 20(14) in computing the taxpayer's income for any taxation year commencing before that time in respect of interest on that debt obligation;

Related Sections: S. 40(3) Deemed gain where amounts to be deducted from adjusted cost base exceed cost plus amounts to be added to adjusted cost base; ITAR s. 26(3) Cost of acquisition of capital property owned on Dec. 31, 1971.

► 53(2)(l.1) ◄

(l.1) [Amounts to be deducted — Indexed debt obligation] — where the property is an indexed debt obligation,

(i) any amount determined under subparagraph 16(6)(*a*)(ii) in respect of the obligation and deductible in computing the income of the taxpayer for a taxation year beginning before that time, and

(ii) the amount of any payment that was received or that became receivable by the taxpayer at or before that time in respect of an amount that was added under paragraph (1)(g.1) to the cost to the taxpayer of the obligation;

Related Sections: S. 40(3) Deemed gain where amounts to be deducted from adjusted cost base exceed cost plus amounts to be added to adjusted cost base; s. 248(1), "indexed debt obligation"; ITAR s. 26(3) Cost of acquisition of capital property owned on Dec. 31, 1971.

▶ 53(2)(m) ◀

(m) **[Amounts to be deducted — Deductible cost of property]** — any part of the cost to the taxpayer of the property that was deductible (otherwise than because of this subdivision or paragraph 8(1)(*r*)) in computing the taxpayer's income for any taxation year commencing before that time and ending after 1971;

Related Sections: S. 40(3) Deemed gain where amounts to be deducted from adjusted cost base exceed cost plus amounts to be added to adjusted cost base; ITAR s. 26(3) Cost of acquisition of capital property owned on Dec. 31, 1971.

Interpretation Bulletins: *Secondary* — IT-350R Investigation of site.

▶ 53(2)(n) ◀

(n) **[Amounts to be deducted — Expropriation asset]** — where the property is an expropriation asset of the taxpayer (within the meaning assigned by section 80.1) or an asset of the taxpayer assumed for the purposes of that section to be an expropriation asset thereof, any amount required by paragraph 80.1(2)(*b*) to be deducted in computing the adjusted cost base to the taxpayer of the asset;

Related Sections: S. 40(3) Deemed gain where amounts to be deducted from adjusted cost base exceed cost plus amounts to be added to adjusted cost base; ITAR s. 26(3) Cost of acquisition of capital property owned on Dec. 31, 1971.

▶ 53(2)(o) ◀

(o) **[Amounts to be deducted — Right to receive partnership property]** — where the property is a right to receive partnership property within the meaning assigned by paragraph 98.2(*a*) or 100(3)(*a*), any amount received by the taxpayer in full or partial satisfaction of that right;

Related Sections: S. 40(3) Deemed gain where amounts to be deducted from adjusted cost base exceed cost plus amounts to be added to adjusted cost base; ITAR s. 26(3) Cost of acquisition of capital property owned on Dec. 31, 1971.

▶ 53(2)(p) ◀

(p) **[Amounts to be deducted — Debt owing by a corporation]** — where the property is a debt owing to the taxpayer by a corporation, any amount required to be deducted before that time under section 84.1 of the *Income Tax Act*, chapter 148 of the Revised Statutes of Canada, 1952, as it applied before May 23, 1985 or subsection 84.2(2) in computing the adjusted cost base to the taxpayer of the debt;

Related Sections: S. 40(3) Deemed gain where amounts to be deducted from adjusted cost base exceed cost plus amounts to be added to adjusted cost base; ITAR s. 26(3) Cost of acquisition of capital property owned on Dec. 31, 1971.

▶ 53(2)(q) ◀

(q) **[Amounts to be deducted — Interest in related segregated fund trust]** — where the property is an interest in a related segregated fund trust referred to in section 138.1,

(i) each amount in respect of that interest that is a capital loss deemed to have been allocated under subsection 138.1(4) to the taxpayer before that time, and

(ii) each amount in respect of that interest that before that time was deemed by subsection 138.1(3) to be a capital loss of the taxpayer;

Related Sections: S. 40(3) Deemed gain where amounts to be deducted from adjusted cost base exceed cost plus amounts to be added to adjusted cost base; ITAR s. 26(3) Cost of acquisition of capital property owned on Dec. 31, 1971.

▶ 53(2)(r) ◀

(r) — (Repealed by 1986, c. 6, s. 26(4).)

▶ 53(2)(s) ◀

(s) **[Amounts to be deducted — Inducement payments]** — the amount, if any, by which

(i) the amount elected by the taxpayer before that time under subsection (2.1)

exceeds

(ii) any repayment before that time by the taxpayer of an amount received by the taxpayer as described in subsection (2.1) that may reasonably be considered to relate to the amount elected where the repayment is made pursuant to a legal obligation to repay all or any part of the amount so received;

Related Sections: S. 40(3) Deemed gain where amounts to be deducted from adjusted cost base exceed cost plus amounts to be added to adjusted cost base; s. 53(2.1) Election; s. 87(2)(*j*.6) Continuing corporation; ITAR s. 26(3) Cost of acquisition of capital property owned on Dec. 31, 1971.

Interpretation Bulletins: *Primary* — IT-456R Capital property — Some adjustments to cost base.

▶ 53(2)(t) ◀

(t) **[Amounts to be deducted — Right to acquire shares or units]** — if the property is a right to acquire shares or units under an agreement, any amount required by paragraph 164(6.1)(*b*) to be deducted in computing the adjusted cost base to the taxpayer of the right;

Related Sections: S. 40(3) Deemed gain where amounts to be deducted from adjusted cost base exceed cost plus amounts to be added to adjusted cost base; ITAR s. 26(3) Cost of acquisition of capital property owned on Dec. 31, 1971.

▶ 53(2)(u) ◀

(u) **[Amounts to be deducted — Non-qualifying real property]** — where the property was at the end of February 22, 1994 a non-qualifying real property (within the meaning assigned by subsection 110.6(1) as that subsection applies to the 1994 taxation year) of a taxpayer, any amount required by paragraph 110.6(21)(*b*) to be deducted in computing the adjusted cost base to the taxpayer of the property;

Related Sections: S. 40(3) Deemed gain where amounts to be deducted from adjusted cost base exceed cost plus amounts to be added to adjusted cost base; ITAR s. 26(3) Cost of acquisition of capital property owned on Dec. 31, 1971.

▶ 53(2)(v) ◀

(v) **[Amounts to be deducted — Capital gains election]** — where the taxpayer elected under subsection 110.6(19) in respect of the property, any amount required by subsection 110.6(22) to be deducted in computing the adjusted cost base to the taxpayer of the property at that time;

Related Sections: S. 40(3) Deemed gain where amounts to be deducted from adjusted cost base exceed cost plus amounts to be added to adjusted cost base; ITAR s. 26(3) Cost of acquisition of capital property owned on Dec. 31, 1971.

▶ 53(2)(w) ◀

(w) **[Amounts to be deducted — Derivative forward agreement]** — if the property was acquired under a derivative forward agreement, any amount deductible in respect of the property under paragraph 20(1)(*xx*) in computing the income of the taxpayer for a taxation year; and

History: S. 53(2)(*w*) was added by S.C. 2013, c. 40, s. 22(6), deemed to have come into force on March 21, 2013.

▶ 53(2)(x) ◀

(x) **[Amounts to be deducted — Derivative forward agreement]** — if the property is disposed of under a derivative forward agreement, any amount deductible in respect of the property under paragraph 20(1)(*xx*) in computing the income of the taxpayer for the taxation year that includes that time.

History: S. 53(2)(*x*) was added by S.C. 2013, c. 40, s. 22(6), deemed to have come into force on March 21, 2013.

▶ 53(2.1) ◀

(2.1) Election. For the purpose of paragraph (2)(*s*), where in a taxation year a taxpayer receives an amount that would, but for this subsection, be included in the taxpayer's income under paragraph 12(1)(*x*) in respect of the cost of a property (other than depreciable property) acquired by the taxpayer in the year, in the 3 taxation years preceding the year or in the taxation year following the year, the taxpayer may elect under this subsection on or before the date on or before which the taxpayer's return of income under this Part for the year is required to be filed or, where the property is acquired in the following year, for that following year, to reduce the cost of the property by such amount as the taxpayer specifies, not exceeding the least of

(*a*) the adjusted cost base, determined without reference to paragraph (2)(*s*), at the time the property was acquired,

(*b*) the amount so received by the taxpayer, and

(*c*) where the taxpayer has disposed of the property before the year, nil.

Editorial Note: See the editorial note under s. 12(1)(*x*).

Related Regulations: 600(b).

Related Sections: S. 13(21), "depreciable property"; s. 87(2)(*j*.6) Continuing corporation; s. 220(3.2) Late, amended or revoked elections; s. 248(1), "amount", "property".

Information Circulars: IC 07-1 Taxpayer relief provisions.

Interpretation Bulletins: *Secondary* — IT-273R2 Government assistance — General comments.

▶ 53(3) ◀

(3) Application of paragraphs (2)(i) and (j) — (Repealed by S.C. 2001, c. 17, s. 36(13).)

▶ 53(4) ◀

(4) Recomputation of adjusted cost base on transfers and deemed dispositions. If at any time in a taxation year a person or partnership (in this subsection referred to as the "vendor") disposes of a specified property and the proceeds of disposition of the property are determined under paragraph 48.1(1)(*c*), section 70 or 73, subsection 85(1), paragraph 87(4)(*a*) or (*c*) or 88(1)(a), subsection 97(2) or 98(2), paragraph 98(3)(*f*) or (5)(*f*), subsection 104(4), paragraph 107(2)(*a*) or (2.1)(*a*), 107.4(3)(*a*) or 111(4)(*e*) or section 128.1,

(*a*) there shall be deducted after that time in computing the adjusted cost base to the person or partnership (in this subsection referred to as the "transferee") who acquires or reacquires the property at or immediately after that time the amount, if any, by which

(i) the total of all amounts deducted under paragraph (2)(*g*.1) in computing, immediately before that time, the adjusted cost base to the vendor of the property,

exceeds

(ii) the amount that would be the vendor's capital gain for the year from that disposition if this Act were read without reference to subparagraph 40(1)(*a*)(iii) and subsection 100(2); and

(*b*) the amount determined under paragraph (*a*) in respect of that disposition shall be added after that time in computing the adjusted cost base to the transferee of the property.

History: S. 53(4), the portion before paragraph (*a*) was replaced by S.C. 2013, c. 34, s. 190(8), deemed to have come into force on February 28, 2004, and formerly read:

(4) *Recomputation of adjusted cost base on transfers and deemed dispositions.* Where at any time in a taxation year a person or partnership (in this subsection referred to as the "vendor") disposes of a specified property and the proceeds of disposition of the property are determined under paragraph 48.1(1)(*c*), section 70 or 73, subsection 85(1), paragraph 87(4)(*a*) or (*c*) or 88(1)(*a*), subsection 97(2) or 98(2), paragraph 98(3)(*f*) or (5)(*f*), subsection 104(4), paragraph 107(2)(*a*), (2.1)(*a*), (4)(*d*) or (5)(*a*), 107.4(3)(*a*) or 111(4)(*e*) or section 128.1,

▶ 53(5) ◀

(5) Recomputation of adjusted cost base on other transfer. Where

(*a*) at any time in a taxation year a person or partnership (in this subsection referred to as the "vendor") disposes of a specified property to another person or partnership (in this subsection referred to as the "transferee"),

(*b*) immediately before that time, the vendor and the transferee do not deal with each other at arm's length or would not deal with each other at arm's length if paragraph 80(2)(*j*) applied for the purpose of this subsection,

(*c*) paragraph (*b*) would apply in respect of the disposition if each right referred to in paragraph 251(5)(*b*) that is a right of the transferee to acquire the specified property from the vendor or a right of the transferee to acquire other property as part of a transaction or event or series of transactions or events that includes the disposition were not taken into account, and

(*d*) the proceeds of the disposition are not determined under any of the provisions referred to in subsection (4),

the following rules apply:

(*e*) there shall be deducted after that time in computing the adjusted cost base to the transferee of the property the amount, if any, by which

(i) the total of all amounts deducted under paragraph (2)(*g*.1) in computing the adjusted cost base to the vendor of the property immediately before that time

exceeds

(ii) the amount that would be the vendor's capital gain for the year from that disposition if this Act were read without reference to subparagraph 40(1)(*a*)(iii) and subsection 100(2), and

(*f*) the amount determined under paragraph (*e*) in respect of that disposition shall be added after that time in computing the adjusted cost base to the transferee of the property.

▶ 53(6) ◀

(6) Recomputation of adjusted cost base on amalgamation. Where a capital property that is a specified property is acquired by a new corporate entity at any time as a result of the amalgamation or merger of 2 or more predecessor corporations,

(*a*) there shall be deducted after that time in computing the adjusted cost base to the new entity of the property the total of all amounts deducted under paragraph (2)(*g*.1) in computing, immediately before that time, the adjusted cost base to a predecessor corporation of the property, unless those amounts are otherwise deducted under that paragraph in computing the adjusted cost base to the new entity of the property; and

(*b*) the amount deducted under paragraph (*a*) in respect of the acquisition shall be added after that time in computing the adjusted cost base to the new entity of the property.

SECTION 54: Definitions

In this subdivision,

"adjusted cost base" —"adjusted cost base" to a taxpayer of any property at any time means, except as otherwise provided,

(*a*) where the property is depreciable property of the taxpayer, the capital cost to the taxpayer of the property as of that time, and

(*b*) in any other case, the cost to the taxpayer of the property adjusted, as of that time, in accordance with section 53,

except that

(*c*) for greater certainty, where any property (other than an interest in or a share of the capital stock of a flow-through entity within the meaning assigned by subsection 39.1(1) that was last reacquired by the taxpayer as a result of an election under subsection 110.6(19)) of the taxpayer is property that was reacquired by the taxpayer after having been previously disposed of by the taxpayer, no adjustment to the cost to the taxpayer of the property that was required to be made under section 53 before its reacquisition by the taxpayer shall be made under that section to the cost to the taxpayer of the property as reacquired property of the taxpayer, and

(*d*) in no case shall the adjusted cost base to a taxpayer of any property at any time be less than nil;

Related Sections: S. 13(21), "depreciable property"; s. 40(1) General rules; s. 54, "capital property".

Canadian Tax Foundation: Fuller and Muise, *Recent Court Decisions: 2. Brosamler v. R, 2012 TCC 204*, 2013 Prairie Provinces Tax Conference 1:6–8; Lewin, *Tax Attributes: Cost or Capital Cost and Paid-Up Capital*, 1998 Conference Report 8:1–40.

Income Tax Folios: *Secondary* — S3-F4-C1 General Discussion of Capital Cost Allowance.

Interpretation Bulletins: *Secondary* — IT-102R2 Conversion of property, other than real property, from or to inventory; IT-218R Profit, capital gains and losses from the sale of real estate, including farmland and inherited land and conversion of real estate from capital property to inventory and vice versa; IT-373R2 (Consolid.) Woodlots.

Cases: In computing the ACB of their inherited shares, the taxpayers could not consider as additional cost of acquisition the monies they had paid to the estate by way of a loan or remittance to facilitate their sale to a third party. *Barabash et al. v. M.N.R.*, 93 DTC 1436 (T.C.C.)

Damage awards were properly excluded from the computation of the deceased's adjusted cost base of his shares since the awards could not be regarded as part of the price which he "had to give up in order to get the shares", which was the test laid down in *The Queen v. Stirling*, (85 DTC 5199). *Bodrug Estate v. The Queen*, 91 DTC 5621 (F.C.A.), affirming 90 DTC 6521 (F.C.T.D.).

"capital property" —"capital property" of a taxpayer means

(*a*) any depreciable property of the taxpayer, and

(*b*) any property (other than depreciable property), any gain or loss from the disposition of which would, if the property were disposed of, be a capital gain or a capital loss, as the case may be, of the taxpayer;

Related Sections: S. 39(1) Meaning of capital gain and capital loss; s. 40(1) General rules.

Canadian Petroleum Tax Journal: Canada Customs and Revenue Agency 1999 Roundtable Questions and Answers, Question 5, 2000, Vol. 13, No. 1.

Interpretation Bulletins: *Secondary* — IT-102R2 Conversion of property, other than real property, from or to inventory; IT-113R4 Benefits to employees — Stock options; IT-143R3 Meaning of eligible capital expenditure.

"disposition" — (Repealed by S.C. 2001, c. 17, s. 37(1).)

Editorial Note: The definition of "disposition" is found in s. 248(1).

"eligible capital property" — (Repealed by S.C. 2016, c. 12, s. 17(1).)

History: S. 54, the definition of "eligible capital property" was repealed by S.C. 2016, c. 12, s. 17(1), in force January 1, 2017, and formerly read:

"eligible capital property" —"eligible capital property" of a taxpayer means any property, a part of the consideration for the disposition of which would, if the taxpayer disposed of the property, be an eligible capital amount in respect of a business;

Related Sections: S. 14 Eligible capital property and expenditures.

Tax Topics: No. 1718, Eligible Capital — Some Big Changes Part I.

Interpretation Bulletins: *Secondary* — IT-123R6 Transactions involving eligible capital property; IT-143R3 Meaning of eligible capital expenditure.

"exemption threshold" —"exemption threshold", of a taxpayer at a particular time in respect of a flow-through share class of property, means the amount determined by the formula

$$A - B$$

where

A is the total of

(*a*) the total of all amounts, each of which is an amount that would be the cost to the taxpayer, computed without reference to subsection 66.3(3), of a flow-through share that was included at any time before the particular time in the flow-through share class of property and that was issued by a corporation to the taxpayer on or after the taxpayer's fresh-start date in respect of the flow-through share class of property at that time, other than a flow-through share that the taxpayer was obligated, before March 22, 2011, to acquire pursuant to the terms of a flow-through share agreement entered into between the corporation and the taxpayer, and

(*b*) the total of all amounts, each of which is an amount that would be the adjusted cost base to the taxpayer of an interest in a partnership —

computed as if subparagraph 53(1)(*e*)(vii.1) and clauses 53(2)(*c*)(ii)(C) and (D) did not apply to any amount incurred by the partnership in respect of a flow-through share held by the partnership, either directly or indirectly through another partnership — that was included at any time before the particular time in the flow-through share class of property, if

(i) the taxpayer

(A) acquired the interest on or after the taxpayer's fresh-start date in respect of the flow-through share class of property at the particular time (other than an interest that the taxpayer was obligated, before August 16, 2011, to acquire pursuant to the terms of an agreement in writing entered into by the taxpayer), or

(B) made a contribution of capital to the partnership on or after August 16, 2011,

(ii) at any time after the taxpayer acquired the interest or made the contribution of capital, the taxpayer is deemed by subsection 66(18) to have made or incurred an outlay or expense in respect of a flow-through share held by the partnership, either directly or indirectly through another partnership, and

(iii) at any time between the time that the taxpayer acquired the interest or made the contribution of capital and the particular time, more than 50% of the fair market value of the assets of the partnership is attributable to property included in a flow-through share class of property, and

B is the total, if any, of all amounts, each of which is the lesser of

(*a*) the total of all amounts, each of which is a capital gain from a disposition of a property included in the flow-through share class of property, other than a capital gain referred to in paragraph 38.1(*a*), at an earlier time that is

(i) before the particular time, and

(ii) after the first time that the taxpayer acquired a flow-through share referred to in paragraph (*a*) of the description of A or acquired a partnership interest referred to in paragraph (*b*) of the description of A, and

(*b*) the exemption threshold of the taxpayer in respect of the flow-th[r]ough share class of property immediately before that earlier time;

Editorial Note: See the note following subsection 40(12).

History: S. 54, the definition "exemption threshold" was added by S.C. 2011, c. 24, s. 9(1), deemed to have come into force on March 22, 2011.

"flow-through share class of property" —"flow-through share class of property" means a group of properties,

(*a*) in respect of a class of shares of the capital stock of a corporation, each of which is

(i) a share of the class, if any share of the class or any right described in subparagraph (ii) is, at any time, a flow-through share to any person,

(ii) a right to acquire a share of the class, if any share of that class or any right described in this subparagraph is, at any time, a flow-through share to any person, or

(iii) a property that is an identical property of a property described in subparagraph (i) or (ii), or

(*b*) each of which is an interest in a partnership, if at any time more than 50% of the fair market value of the partnership's assets is attributable to property included in a flow-through share class of property;

History: S. 54, the definition "flow-through share class of property" was added by S.C. 2011, c. 24, s. 9(1), deemed to have come into force on March 22, 2011.

"fresh-start date" —"fresh-start date", of a taxpayer at a particular time in respect of a flow-through share class of property, means

(*a*) in the case of a partnership interest that is included in the flow-through share class of property, the day that is the later of

(i) August 16, 2011, and

(ii) the last day, if any, before the particular time, on which the taxpayer held an interest in the partnership, and

(*b*) in the case of any other property that is included in the flow-th[r]ough share class of property, the day that is the later of

(i) March 22, 2011, and

(ii) the last day, if any, before the particular time, on which the taxpayer disposed of all property included in the flow-through share class of property;

History: S. 54, the definition "fresh-start date" was added by S.C. 2011, c. 24, s. 9(1), deemed to have come into force on March 22, 2011.

"listed personal property" —"listed personal property" of a taxpayer means the taxpayer's personal-use property that is all or any portion of, or any interest in or right to — or, for civil law, any right in or to — any

(*a*) print, etching, drawing, painting, sculpture, or other similar work of art,

(*b*) jewellery,

(*c*) rare folio, rare manuscript, or rare book,

(*d*) stamp, or

(*e*) coin;

History: S. 54, the portion before paragraph (*a*) of the definition "listed personal property" was replaced by S.C. 2013, c. 34, s. 107, in force June 26, 2013, and formerly read:

"listed personal property"—"listed personal property" of a taxpayer means the taxpayer's personal-use property that is all or any portion of, or any interest in or right to, any

Related Sections: S. 3(*b*) Income for taxation year; s. 41 Taxable net gain from disposition of listed personal property.

Interpretation Bulletins: *Secondary* — IT-159R3 Capital debts established to be bad debts.

"personal-use property" —"personal-use property" of a taxpayer includes

(*a*) property owned by the taxpayer that is used primarily for the personal use or enjoyment of the taxpayer or for the personal use or enjoyment of one or more individuals each of whom is

(i) the taxpayer,

(ii) a person related to the taxpayer, or

(iii) where the taxpayer is a trust, a beneficiary under the trust or any person related to the beneficiary, (*b*) any debt owing to the taxpayer in respect of the disposition of property that was the taxpayer's personal-use property, and

(*c*) any property of the taxpayer that is an option to acquire property that would, if the taxpayer acquired it, be personal-use property of the taxpayer,

and "personal-use property" of a partnership includes any partnership property that is used primarily for the personal use or enjoyment of any member of the partnership or for the personal use or enjoyment of one or more individuals each of whom is a member of the partnership or a person related to such a member;

Related Sections: S. 40(2)(*g*) Limitations; s. 46 Personal-use property; s. 50(2) Where debt a personal-use property.

Interpretation Bulletins: *Secondary* — IT-159R3 Capital debts established to be bad debts; IT-218R Profit, capital gains and losses from the sale of real estate, including farmland and inherited land and conversion of real estate from capital property to inventory and vice versa.

Cases: The taxpayers each purchased a group of limited edition prints and donated them to charities. The personal-use property provisions were inapplicable since the cost of acquisition and FMV of each *group* of prints exceeded $1,000, even though the value of the individual prints may have been less. *A.G. of Canada v. Nash et al.*, 2005 DTC 5696 (F.C.A.), reversing 2004 DTC 3391 (T.C.C.), 2004 DTC 3328 (T.C.C.) and 2004 DTC 3360 (T.C.C.)

"principal residence" —"principal residence" of a taxpayer for a taxation year means a particular property that is a housing unit, a leasehold interest in a housing unit or a share of the capital stock of a co-operative housing corporation acquired for the sole purpose of acquiring the right to inhabit a housing unit owned by the corporation and that is owned, whether jointly with another person or otherwise, in the year by the taxpayer, if

(*a*) where the taxpayer is an individual other than a personal trust, the housing unit was ordinarily inhabited in the year by the taxpayer, by the taxpayer's spouse or common-law partner or former spouse or common-law partner or by a child of the taxpayer,

(*a*.1) where the taxpayer is a personal trust, the housing unit was ordinarily inhabited in the calendar year ending in the year by a specified beneficiary of the trust for the year, by the spouse or common-law partner or former spouse or common-law partner of such a beneficiary or by a child of such a beneficiary, or

(*b*) where the taxpayer is a personal trust or an individual other than a trust, the taxpayer

(i) elected under subsection 45(2) that relates to the change in use of the particular property in the year or a preceding taxation year, other than an election rescinded under subsection 45(2) in the taxpayer's return of income for the year or a preceding taxation year, or

(ii) elected under subsection 45(3) that relates to a change in use of the particular property in a subsequent taxation year,

except that, subject to section 54.1, a particular property shall be considered not to be a taxpayer's principal residence for a taxation year

(*c*) where the taxpayer is an individual other than a personal trust, unless the particular property was designated by the taxpayer in prescribed form and manner to be the taxpayer's principal residence for the year and no other property has been designated for the purposes of this definition for the year

(i) where the year is before 1982, by the taxpayer, or

(ii) where the year is after 1981,

(A) by the taxpayer,

(B) by a person who was throughout the year the taxpayer's spouse or common-law partner (other than a spouse or common-law partner who was throughout the year living apart from, and was separated under a judicial separation or written separation agreement from, the taxpayer),

(C) by a person who was the taxpayer's child (other than a child who was at any time in the year a married person, a person who is in a common-law partnership or 18 years of age or older), or

(D) where the taxpayer was not at any time in the year a married person, a person who is in a common-law partnership or 18 years of age or older, by a person who was the taxpayer's

(I) mother or father, or

(II) brother or sister, where that brother or sister was not at any time in the year a married person, a person who is in a common-law partnership or 18 years of age or older,

(*c*.1) where the taxpayer is a personal trust, unless

(i) the particular property was designated by the trust in prescribed form and manner to be the taxpayer's principal residence for the year,

(ii) the trust specifies in the designation each individual (in this definition referred to as a "specified beneficiary" of the trust for the year) who, in the calendar year ending in the year,

(A) is beneficially interested in the trust, and

(B) except where the trust is entitled to designate it for the year solely because of paragraph (*b*), ordinarily inhabited the housing unit or has a spouse or common-law partner, former spouse or common-law partner or child who ordinarily inhabited the housing unit,

(iii) no corporation (other than a registered charity) or partnership is beneficially interested in the trust at any time in the year,

(iii.1) if the year begins after 2016, the trust is, in the year,

(A) a trust

(I) for which a day is to be determined under paragraph 104(4)(*a*), (*a*.1) or (*a*.4) by reference to the death or later death, as the case may be, that has not occurred before the beginning of the year, of an individual who is resident in Canada during the year, and

(II) a specified beneficiary of which for the year is the individual referred to in subclause (I),

(B) a trust

(I) that is a *qualified disability trust* (as defined in subsection 122(3)) for the year, and

(II) an *electing beneficiary* (in this clause, as defined in subsection 122(3)) of which for the year is

1 resident in Canada during the year,

2 a specified beneficiary of the trust for the year, and

3 a spouse, common-law partner, former spouse or common-law partner or child of the *settlor* (in this subparagraph, as defined in subsection 108(1)) of the trust, or

(C) a trust

(I) a specified beneficiary of which for the year is an individual

1 who is resident in Canada during the year,

2 who has not attained 18 years of age before the end of the year, and

3 a mother or father of whom is a settlor of the trust, and

(II) in respect of which either of the following conditions is met:

1 no mother or father of the individual referred to in subclause (I) is alive at the beginning of the year, or

2 the trust arose before the beginning of the year on and as a consequence of the death of a mother or father of the individual referred to in subclause (I), and

(iv) no other property has been designated for the purpose of this definition for the calendar year ending in the year by any specified beneficiary of the trust for the year, by a person who was throughout that calendar year such a beneficiary's spouse or common-law partner (other than a spouse or common-law partner who was throughout that calendar year living apart from, and was separated pursuant to a judicial separation or written separation agreement from, the beneficiary), by a person who was such a beneficiary's child (other than a child who was during that calendar year a married person or a person who is in a common-law partnership or a person 18 years or over) or, where such a beneficiary was not during that calendar year a married person or a person who is in a common-law partnership or a person 18 years or over, by a person who was such a beneficiary's

(A) mother or father, or

(B) brother or sister, where that brother or sister was not during that calendar year a married person or a person who is in a common-law partnership or a person 18 years or over, or

(*d*) because of paragraph (*b*), if solely because of that paragraph the property would, but for this paragraph, have been a principal residence of the taxpayer for 4 or more preceding taxation years,

and, for the purpose of this definition,

(*e*) the principal residence of a taxpayer for a taxation year shall be deemed to include, except where the particular property consists of a share of the capital stock of a co-operative housing corporation, the land subjacent to the housing unit and such portion of any immediately contiguous land as can reasonably be regarded as contributing to the use and enjoyment of the housing unit as a residence, except that where the total area of the subjacent land and of that portion exceeds $1/2$ hectare, the excess shall be deemed not to have contributed to the use and enjoyment of the housing unit as a residence unless the taxpayer establishes that it was necessary to such use and enjoyment, and

(*f*) a particular property designated under paragraph (*c*.1) by a trust for a year shall be deemed to be property designated for the purposes of this definition by each specified beneficiary of the trust for the calendar year ending in the year;

Editorial Note: Paragraph 40(2)(*b*) provides an exemption for an individual for a portion of a gain realized on the disposition of a principal residence. Subject to other criteria, a principal residence is a housing unit, leasehold interest in a housing unit, or a share of capital stock of a co-operative corporation. The housing unit must have been owned (individually or jointly), ordinarily inhabited, and designated as such in a prescribed form in the year of its disposition. For dispositions from October 3, 2016 onwards, the "one plus" rule in the formula only applies if the individual is resident in Canada in the year of acquisition. The disposition and relevant information must be reported on Form T2091, except for deceased taxpayers and trusts, where the disposition is reported on T1255 and T1079, respectively.

The definition of "principal residence" also applies to property owned by a personal trust with a "specified beneficiary". For tax years beginning after 2016, the types of trusts that qualify for the exemption are restricted. The types of trusts that currently qualify are spousal or common-law partner trust, joint spousal or common-law partner trust, an *alter ego* trust, and a self-benefit trust; a qualified disability trust; and certain trusts where the specified beneficiary is under the age of 18 and the parents of the beneficiary are deceased or the trust arose as a consequence of the death of one of the beneficiaries.

Ordinarily Inhabited: The housing unit must have been ordinarily inhabited by the taxpayer, his or her spouse or common-law partner (CLP), his or her former spouse or CLP, or his or her child in any year that it is designated as a principal residence. Where a housing unit is ordinarily inhabited only for a short length of time in the year, it will still qualify as a principal residence (see Folio S1-F3-C2, ¶2.11). Therefore, provided it was ordinarily inhabited at some time during the year, a seasonal residence such as a cottage can qualify as a principal residence (see CRA Document No. 2014-0528241E5). The CRA's position is that where a taxpayer moves permanently to a nursing home, his or her vacant housing unit ceases to be ordinarily inhabited (see CRA Document No. 9612345).

A housing unit that is owned by a personal trust may also qualify as a principal residence if the housing unit is ordinarily inhabited by a specified beneficiary, his or her spouse or CLP, his or her former spouse or CLP, or child. Each specified beneficiary must be identified on form T1079 and the beneficiary must have a beneficial interest in the trust. No specified beneficiary can claim the principal residence exemption on any property he or she owns for a year that the trust designates for its principal residence.

Designating a Property: In the case of a principal residence being designated by an individual or a personal trust, only one principal residence can be designated with respect to the individual/specified beneficiary, his or her spouse or CLP (except where the spouses or CLPs are living apart and separated due to judicial separation or a separation agreement), or the individual's child who was under 18. Only one principal residence can be designated by an individual taxpayer per year per married or common-law couple.

Land Area Restriction: A principal residence includes the land subjacent to the housing unit that is reasonably necessary for its use. When the total area exceeds half a hectare, the excess is not considered a part of the principal residence unless the taxpayer can establish that the excess is necessary for the use and enjoyment of the property. Land may be considered "subjacent" to a housing unit, and therefore qualifies as a principal residence, if a vehicle is parked on that land and that vehicle provides the amenities that a house would otherwise provide (see *Flanagan*, 89 DTC 615, TCC).

Zoning by-laws requiring a minimum lot size or restricting a lot from being subdivided are exceptions to the half-hectare limit (see Folio S1-F3-C2, ¶2.33 - ¶2.35). A taxpayer was eligible for the principal residence exemption on a home with a 2.43 hectare parcel of land, as zoning by-laws would not let him subdivide the property during the years in question (see *Cassidy*, 2011 DTC 5160, FCA).

Housing Unit: A housing unit generally encompasses a house, apartment or unit in a duplex, apartment building, condominium, cottage, mobile home, trailer, or houseboat. A share in the capital stock of a co-operative housing corporation will qualify as a principal residence provided that the sole purpose of acquiring the share was to obtain the right to inhabit a housing unit that is owned by the corporation (see Folio S1-F3-C2, ¶2.7, ¶2.88, ¶2.91). A housing unit outside Canada can qualify as a principal residence (see CRA Document 2010-0369351E5).

Change in Use: The various elections which defer the deemed disposition resulting from a change in use will also affect the property's status as a principal residence. Paragraphs 13(7)(*a*), 13(7)(*b*), and 45(1)(*a*) deem a taxpayer to have disposed of property where the use of the property changes from producing income to another purpose, or from another purpose to producing income. It is the CRA's position that a deemed disposition will not occur with respect to a partial change in use from a principal residence to an income-producing property if: the income-producing purpose is ancillary to the property's primary function as a principal residence, no structural changes to the property are made, and no CCA is claimed (see Folio S1-F3-C2, ¶2.59).

Subsections 45(2) and 45(3) allow a taxpayer to elect out of the deemed disposition on a change in use. Where a taxpayer so elects, the property qualifies as a principal residence even though the property is not ordinarily inhabited for up to four years.

Section 54.1 provides that the four-year limitation does not apply if the place of employment of the taxpayer (or CLP) has changed and the housing unit is being rented out. The distance between the old residence and new work location must be at least 40 kilometers greater than the distance between the new place of residence and the new work location. Moreover, the s. 54.1 exception will only apply if the housing unit is ordinarily inhabited again in the future (see CRA Document No. 2004-0056851E5).

History: S. 54, subparagraph (*c*.1)(iii.1) of the definition "principal residence" was added by S.C. 2017, c. 33, s. 13(1), in force December 14, 2017.

Related Regulations: 2301.

Related Sections: S. 40(2)(*b*) Gain from disposition of principal residence; s. 40(2)(*c*) Principal residence on farm property; s. 40(4) Disposal of principal residence to spouse or trust for spouse; s. 40(6) Special rule concerning principal residence; 40(6.1) Principal residence — property owned at end of 2016; s. 54.1 Exception to principal residence rules; s. 107(2.01) Distribution of principal residence; s. 248(1), "common-law partner", "corporation", "disposition", "individual", "share"; s. 252(1) Extended meaning of "child".

Canadian Tax Foundation: Sinclair and Paisley, *Planning for Principal Residences*, 2017 Ontario Tax Conference 15:1–20; Woolley, *Principal Residences - Selected Issues: An Update*, 2017 British Columbia Tax Conference 7A:1–41; Bernstein and Santia, *Principal-Residence Exemption: Trusts and Non-Residents*, 2017 Canadian Tax Highlights 25(1):6–7; Wang and Bernier, *Principal and Cottage Residence Planning: A Review of Selected Issues — Part 2*, 2013 Ontario Tax Conference 8B:1–20; Friedlan and Friedlan, *Principal and Cottage Residence Planning: A Review of Selected Issues — Part 1*, 2013 Ontario Tax Conference 8A:1–23; Katz and Haber, *The Principal Residence Exemption*, 2001 Canadian Tax Journal 4:990–1020.

Tax Profile: January 2012 — The Top 10 Cases of 2011; July 2011 — Personal Trusts and Cottage Properties Residence — Pitfalls and Planning; February 2009 — Residence Trust: Tips and Traps; April 2007 — Tax Planning for Emigration from Canada.

Tax Topics: No. 2332, November 17, 2016, A Primer on the New Principal Residence Rules; No. 2148, Principal Residence Exemption And Zoning Requirements: The Half-Hectare Rule Made Twice As Clear; No. 2082, Principal Residence Exemption — Excess Lands; No. 2040, Relevant Time for Determining When Excess Land is Necessary for Use and Enjoyment of Principal Residence; No. 1702, Income Tax Issues To Be Considered in Negotiating Marriage Contracts; No. 1699, Draft Legislation Governing Non-Competition Payments.

Forms: T1079 — Designation of a Property as a Principal Residence by a Personal Trust; T1255 — Designation of a Property as a Principal Residence by the Legal Representative of a Deceased Individual; T2091(IND) — Designation of a Property as a Principal Residence by an Individual (Other than a Personal Trust); T2091 (IND) - WS — Principal Residence Worksheet.

Income Tax Folios: *Primary* — S1-F3-C2 Principal Residence.

Interpretation Bulletins: *Secondary* — IT-218R Profit, capital gains and losses from the sale of real estate, including farmland and inherited land and conversion of real estate from capital property to inventory and vice versa; IT-268R4 Inter vivos transfer of farm property to child.

Tax Window Files: Principal Residence Exemption, *March 7, 2016*, CRA Document No. 2016-0629951I7.

Cases: A principal residence exemption was denied where the taxpayers built a house with the intent to sell at a profit. They lived in it for a few weeks in an attempt to establish it as a principal residence, but it was never furnished and was for sale the entire time. *Sangha v. The Queen*, 2013 DTC 1074 (T.C.C.)

The taxpayer sold his home with 2.43 hectares of land. The CRA denied a principal residence exemption beyond a half hectare since, just prior to the sale, the land was rezoned allowing it to be subdivided. However, exemption eligibility is determined annually and the recent rezoning did not affect his eligibility for previous years. *Cassidy v. The Queen*, 2011 DTC 5160 (F.C.A.), reversing 2010 DTC 1336 (T.C.C.)

An entire ten-acre parcel of land constituted the taxpayers' principal residence since the property could not legally be subdivided. *Brohman et al. v. The Queen*, 2001 DTC 71 (T.C.C.)

The taxpayer's entire 32.75-acre parcel of land qualified for principal residence treatment. The taxpayer had met the objective test because a zoning by-law set a 25-acre minimum allotment size for her property, and the local authority would not have authorized a partition of her lot between 25 acres and the remainder. *Carlile v. The Queen*, 95 DTC 5483 (F.C.A.), reversing 93 DTC 5336 (F.C.T.D.)

A taxpayer could claim the principal residence exemption on the sale of 8.9 acres of land which, at the time of purchase in 1966, a zoning by-law had compelled him to buy in its entirety. He was not allowed at any time to retain the minimum lot size of 3 acres prevailing in 1966 and sell the remaining acres. *Augurt v. The Queen*, 93 DTC 5205 (F.C.A.), reversing 92 DTC 6610 (F.C.T.D.).

"proceeds of disposition" — "proceeds of disposition" of property includes,

(*a*) the sale price of property that has been sold,

(*b*) compensation for property unlawfully taken,

(*c*) compensation for property destroyed, and any amount payable under a policy of insurance in respect of loss or destruction of property,

(*d*) compensation for property taken under statutory authority or the sale price of property sold to a person by whom notice of an intention to take it under statutory authority was given,

(*e*) compensation for property injuriously affected, whether lawfully or unlawfully or under statutory authority or otherwise,

(*f*) compensation for property damaged and any amount payable under a policy of insurance in respect of damage to property, except to the extent that such compensation or amount, as the case may be, has within a reasonable time after the damage been expended on repairing the damage,

(*g*) an amount by which the liability of a taxpayer to a mortgagee or hypothecary creditor is reduced as a result of the sale of mortgaged or hypothecated property under a provision of the mortgage or hypothec, plus any amount received by the taxpayer out of the proceeds of the sale,

(*h*) any amount included in computing a taxpayer's proceeds of disposition of the property because of section 79, and

(*i*) in the case of a share, an amount deemed by subparagraph 88(2)(*b*)(ii) not to be a dividend on that share,

but notwithstanding any other provision of this Part, does not include

(*j*) any amount that would otherwise be proceeds of disposition of a share to the extent that the amount is deemed by subsection 84(2) or (3) to be a dividend received except to the extent the dividend is deemed

(i) by paragraph 55(2)(*b*) to be proceeds of disposition of the share, or

(ii) by subparagraph 88(2)(*b*)(ii) not to be a dividend, or

(*k*) any amount that would otherwise be proceeds of disposition of property of a taxpayer to the extent that the amount is deemed by subsection 84.1(1), 212.1(1.1) or 212.2(2) to be a dividend paid to the taxpayer or, if the taxpayer is a partnership, to a member of the taxpayer;

Editorial Note: Any transaction or event that entitles a taxpayer to "proceeds of disposition" is deemed to be a disposition of property (s. 248(1), "disposition"), ensuring that the capital gain or loss provisions will apply (since they do not apply unless there is a disposition of property). The exceptions in paragraphs (*j*) and (*k*) of the definition ensure that dispositions of shares that result in deemed dividend treatment are not subject to double taxation (i.e., they do not generate capital gains in addition to the deemed dividends).

History: S. 54, paragraph (*k*) of the definition "proceeds of disposition" was replaced by S.C. 2018, c. 27, s. 4(1), applicable in respect of dispositions that occur after February 26, 2018, and formerly read:

(*k*) any amount that would otherwise be proceeds of disposition of property of a taxpayer to the extent that the amount is deemed by subsection 84.1(1), 212.1(1.1) or 212.2(2) to be a dividend paid to the taxpayer;

S. 54, paragraph (*k*) of the definition "proceeds of disposition" was replaced by S.C. 2016, c. 12, s. 17(2), applicable in respect of dispositions that occur after March 21, 2016, and formerly read:

(*k*) any amount that would otherwise be proceeds of disposition of property of a taxpayer to the extent that the amount is deemed by subsection 84.1(1), 212.1(1) or 212.2(2) to be a dividend paid to the taxpayer;

S. 54, paragraph (*j*) of the definition "proceeds of disposition" was replaced by S.C. 2016, c. 7, s. 4(1), applicable to dividends received after April 20, 2015, and formerly read:

(*j*) any amount that would otherwise be proceeds of disposition of a share to the extent that the amount is deemed by subsection 84(2) or (3) to be a dividend received and is not deemed by paragraph 55(2)(*a*) or subparagraph 88(2)(*b*)(ii) not to be a dividend, or

Related Sections: S. 13(21) Definitions; s. 40(1) General rules; s. 44 Exchanges of property; s. 59(5) Definition of "proceeds of disposition"; s. 248(1), "disposition".

Canadian Tax Foundation: Morris, *Current Cases: Supreme Court of Canada — Supreme Court Weighs In on Age-Old Question: If a Tree Falls in the Forest ... (Daishowa-Marubeni International Ltd. v. Canada, 2013 SCC 29)*, 2013 Canadian Tax Journal 3:723–729; Blackler and Nitikman, *Case Comment: Daishowa-Marubeni International Ltd. v. The Queen, 2013 DTC 5085*, 2013 British Columbia Tax Conference 2:1–5; Boidman et al, *Daishowa: Still No Tax Patrimony?*, 2013 Canadian Tax Highlights 21(6):6–7.

Tax Profile: Supreme Court of Canada Clarifies that Assuming Obligations "Embedded" in a Property is not Consideration for the Property.

Tax Topics: No. 1884, Amounts Received by Shareholders from Foreign Corporations in the Course of Winding Up.

Income Tax Folios: *Secondary* — S3-F9-C1 Lottery Winnings, Miscellaneous Receipts, and Income (and Losses) from Crime.

Interpretation Bulletins: *Secondary* — IT-125R4 Disposition of resource properties; IT-170R Sale of property — When included in income computation; IT-200 Surface rentals and farming operations; IT-259R4 Exchange of property; IT-460 Dispositions — Absence of consideration.

Cases: The entire proceeds of disposition must be included in income for tax purposes, even though the maximum purchase price stipulated in the agreement could be subject to subsequent reduction through the operation of price adjustment provisions. The production or use provisions of s. 12(1)(g) require the inclusion in income of all amounts attributable to the production or use of property. *Deragon v. The Queen, 2016 DTC*, 2016 DTC 1188 (TCC)

Alberta required the purchasers of forest tenures to assume reforestation obligations. The cost of these obligations was not included in the vendor's proceeds of disposition since the purchasers were not assuming an existing liability. The reforestation costs could not be severed from the tenures and were simply a future cost that would decrease the purchase price. *Daishowa-Marubeni International Ltd. v. The Queen*, 2013 DTC 5085 (S.C.C.), reversing 2011 DTC 5157 (F.C.A.)

When, following the taxpayers' mortgage default, their mortgagor was allowed to purchase their condominium property for a stipulated sum and granted judgment for the balance of the amount owing, the taxpayers could report as "proceeds of disposition" their shares of the stipulated sum rather than their shares of the full principal amount still outstanding on the mortgage. *Brill et al. v. The Queen*, 96 DTC 6572 (F.C.A.), reversing in part 95 DTC 5435 (F.C.T.D.)

The taxpayer received $350,000 as compensation for the expropriation of his property which included $286,534 for loss of business opportunity. This latter amount was included in the expression "compensation for property taken under statutory authority". *Sani Sport Inc. v. The Queen*, 90 DTC 6230 (F.C.A.), affirming 87 DTC 5253 (F.C.T.D.)

"specified property" — "specified property" of a taxpayer is capital property of the taxpayer that is

(*a*) a share,

(*b*) a capital interest in a trust,

(*c*) an interest in a partnership, or

(*d*) an option to acquire specified property of the taxpayer;

Related Sections: S. 49(3.01) Option to acquire specified property exercised; s. 53(4) Recomputation of adjusted cost base on transfers and deemed dispositions; s. 53(5) Recomputation of adjusted cost base on other transfer; s. 53(6) Recomputation of adjusted cost base on amalgamation.

"superficial loss" — "superficial loss" of a taxpayer means the taxpayer's loss from the disposition of a particular property where

(*a*) during the period that begins 30 days before and ends 30 days after the disposition, the taxpayer or a person affiliated with the taxpayer acquires a property (in this definition referred to as the "substituted property") that is, or is identical to, the particular property, and

(*b*) at the end of that period, the taxpayer or a person affiliated with the taxpayer owns or had a right to acquire the substituted property,

except where the disposition was

(*c*) a disposition deemed to have been made by subsection 45(1), section 48 as it read in its application before 1993, section 50 or 70, subsection 104(4), section 128.1, paragraph 132.2(3)(*a*) or (*c*), subsection 138(11.3), 138.2(4) or 142.5(2), section 142.6 or any of subsections 144(4.1) and (4.2) and 149(10),

(*d*) the expiry of an option,

(*e*) a disposition to which paragraph 40(2)(*e.1*) applies,

(*f*) a disposition by a taxpayer that was subject to a loss restriction event within 30 days after the disposition,

(*g*) a disposition by a person that, within 30 days after the disposition, became or ceased to be exempt from tax under this Part on its taxable income, or

(*h*) a disposition to which subsection 40(3.4) or 69(5) applies,

and, for the purpose of this definition,

(*i*) a right to acquire a property (other than a right, as security only, derived from a mortgage, hypothec, agreement for sale or similar obligation) is deemed to be a property that is identical to the property, and

(*j*) a share of the capital stock of a SIFT wind-up corporation in respect of a SIFT wind-up entity is, if the share was acquired before 2013, deemed to be a property that is identical to equity in the SIFT wind-up entity.

Editorial Note: A superficial loss applies only to individuals other than trusts. For trusts, partnerships, and corporations, the stop-loss rule in s. 40(3.4) may apply.

History: S. 54, paragraph (*c*) of the definition "superficial loss" was replaced by S.C. 2017, c. 33, s. 13(2), applicable to taxation years that begin after 2017, and formerly read:

(*c*) a disposition deemed to have been made by subsection 45(1), section 48 as it read in its application before 1993, section 50 or 70, subsection 104(4), section 128.1, paragraph 132.2(3)(*a*) or (*c*), subsection 138(11.3) or 142.5(2), section 142.6 or any of subsections 144(4.1) and (4.2) and 149(10),

S. 54, paragraph (*c*) of the definition "superficial loss" was replaced by S.C. 2013, c. 40, s. 23(1), applicable to taxation years that begin after March 20, 2013, and formerly read:

(*c*) a disposition deemed to have been made by paragraph 33.1(11)(*a*), subsection 45(1), section 48 as it read in its application before 1993, section 50 or 70, subsection 104(4), section 128.1, paragraph 132.2(3)(*a*) or (*c*), subsection 138(11.3) or 142.5(2), section 142.6 or any of subsections 144(4.1) and (4.2) and 149(10),

S. 54, paragraph (*f*) of the definition "superficial loss" was replaced by S.C. 2013, c. 40, s. 23(2), deemed to have come into force on March 21, 2013, and formerly read:

(*f*) a disposition by a corporation the control of which was acquired by a person or group of persons within 30 days after the disposition,

S. 54, paragraph (*c*) of the definition "superficial loss" was replaced by S.C. 2013, c. 34, s. 191(1), applicable to dispositions that occur after 1998, except that, in its application to taxation years that begin before October 2006, paragraph (*c*) of the definition "superficial loss" in section 54 is to be read as follows:

"(*c*) a disposition deemed by paragraph 33.1(11)(*a*), subsection 45(1), section 48 as it read in its application before 1993, section 50 or 70, subsection 104(4), section 128.1, paragraph 132.2(3)(*a*) or (*c*), subsection 138(11.3) or 142.5(2), paragraph 142.6(1)(*b*) or subsection 144(4.1) or (4.2) or 149(10) to have been made."

S. 54, paragraph (*c*) of the definition "superficial loss" formerly read:

(*c*) a disposition deemed to have been made by paragraph 33.1(11)(*a*), subsection 45(1), section 48 as it read in its application before 1993, section 50 or 70, subsection 104(4), section 128.1, paragraph 132.2(1)(*f*), subsection 138(11.3) or 142.5(2), section 142.6, or any of subsections 144(4.1) and (4.2) and 149(10),

S. 54, paragraph (*c*) of the definition "superficial loss" was replaced by S.C. 2009, c. 2, s. 12(1), applicable to taxation years that begin after September 2006. S. 54, paragraph (*c*) of the definition "superficial loss" formerly read:

(*c*) a disposition deemed by paragraph 33.1(11)(*a*), subsection 45(1), section 48 as it read in its application before 1993, section 50 or 70, subsection 104(4), section 128.1, paragraph 132.2(1)(*f*), subsection 138(11.3) or 142.5(2), paragraph 142.6(1)(*b*) or subsection 144(4.1) or (4.2) or 149(10) to have been made,

S. 54, the portion of the definition "superficial loss" after paragraph (*h*) was replaced, and paragraphs (*i*) and (*j*) were added, by S.C. 2009, c. 2, s. 12(2), applicable to dispositions that occur after February 2, 2009. S. 54, the portion of the definition "superficial loss" after paragraph (*h*) formerly read:

and, for the purpose of this definition, a right to acquire a property (other than a right, as security only, derived from a mortgage, hypothec, agreement for sale or similar obligation) is deemed to be a property that is identical to the property.

Related Sections: S. 13(21), "depreciable property"; s. 39(1) Meaning of capital gain and capital loss; s. 40(2)(*g*) Limitation on loss; s. 53 Adjustments to cost base; s. 54, "disposition", "proceeds of disposition"; s. 104(1) Reference to trust or estate; s. 248(1), "business", "disposition", "individual", "prescribed", "property", "share"; s. 250(5.1) Continued corporation; s. 251.1 Definition of "affiliated persons"; s. 251.2(2) Loss restriction event.

Canadian Tax Foundation: Man and Tse, *Tax in Troubled Times — Opportunities and Techniques for Loss Utilization*, 2009 British Columbia Tax Conference 5:1–40.

Tax Profile: *May 2004 — Superficial Losses — Capital Property.*

Interpretation Bulletins: *Secondary* — IT-159R3 Capital debts established to be bad debts; IT-291R3 Transfer of property to a corporation under subsection 85(1); IT-387R2 (Consolid.) Meaning of "identical properties".

Tax Window Files: Superficial Loss, *January 22, 2009*, CRA Document No. 2008-0299661E5; FX Loss on Disposition of Cash, *January 6, 2009*, CRA Document No. 2008-0280111I7; Stock Options/Superficial Loss, *October 10, 2008*, CRA Document No. 2008-0284441C6; Loss Denial Rules, *Technical Interpretation, Reorganizations and Resources Division, August 13, 2008*, CRA Document No. 2008-0274451E5; Superficial Loss on Security Transactions, *Technical Interpretation, Financial Sector and Exempt Entities Division, November 30, 2005*, CRA Document No. 2005-0150811E5.

SECTION 54.1: Exception to principal residence rules

► 54.1(1) ◄

(1) Exception to principal residence rules. A taxation year in which a taxpayer does not ordinarily inhabit the taxpayer's property as a consequence of the relocation of the place of employment of the taxpayer or the taxpayer's spouse or common-law partner while the taxpayer or the taxpayer's spouse or common-law partner, as the case may be, is employed by an employer who is not a person to whom the taxpayer or the taxpayer's spouse or common-law partner is related is deemed not to be a previous taxation year referred to in paragraph (*d*) of the definition "principal residence" in section 54 if

(*a*) the property subsequently becomes ordinarily inhabited by the taxpayer during the term of the taxpayer's or the taxpayer's spouse's or common-law partner's employment by that employer or before the end of the taxation year immediately following the taxation year in which the taxpayer's or the spouse's or common-law partner's employment by that employer terminates; or

(*b*) the taxpayer dies during the term of the taxpayer's or the spouse's or common-law partner's employment by that employer.

History: S. 54.1(1), the portion before paragraph (*a*) was replaced by S.C. 2013, c. 34, s. 192(1), applicable to the 2001 and subsequent taxation years, except that, if a taxpayer and a person have jointly elected under s. 144 of the *Modernization of Benefits and Obligations Act*, in respect of the 1998, 1999 or 2000 taxation years, s. 54.1(1), the portion before paragraph (*a*), applies to the taxpayer and the person in respect of the applicable taxation year and subsequent taxation years.

S. 54.1(1), the portion before paragraph (*a*) formerly read:

(1) *Exception to principal residence rules.* A taxation year in which a taxpayer does not ordinarily inhabit the taxpayer's property as a consequence of the relocation of the taxpayer's or the taxpayer's spouse's or common-law partner's place of employment while the taxpayer, spouse or common-law partner, as the case may be, is employed by an employer who is not a person to whom the taxpayer or the spouse is related is deemed not to be a previous taxation year referred to in paragraph (*d*) of the definition "principal residence" in section 54 if

Related Sections: S. 40(2)(*b*) Limitations.

Income Tax Folios: *Secondary* — S1-F3-C2 Principal Residence.

► 54.1(2) ◄

(2) Definition of "property". In this section, "property", in relation to a taxpayer, means a housing unit

(*a*) owned by the taxpayer,

(*b*) in respect of which the taxpayer has a leasehold interest, or

(*c*) in respect of which the taxpayer owned a share of the capital stock of a co-operative housing corporation if the share was acquired for the sole purpose of acquiring the right to inhabit a housing unit owned by the corporation

whether jointly with another person or otherwise in the year and that at all times was at least 40 kilometres farther from the taxpayer's or the taxpayer's spouse's or common-law partner's new place of employment than was the taxpayer's subsequent place or places of residence.

Related Sections: S. 54, "principal residence"; s. 251(2) Definition of "related persons".

SECTION 54.2: Certain shares deemed to be capital property

Where any person has disposed of property that consisted of all or substantially all of the assets used in an active business carried on by that person to a corporation for consideration that included shares of the corporation, the shares shall be deemed to be capital property of the person.

Editorial Note: S. 54.2 effectively provides that where a person incorporates a business, a subsequent sale of the shares in the corporation will be on capital account.

Related Sections: S. 39(1) Meaning of capital gain and capital loss; s. 40(1) General rules; s. 54, "capital property"; s. 248(1), "active business", "business", "corporation", "share".

Information Circulars: IC 88-2 General anti-avoidance rule — Section 245 of the Income Tax Act.

Cases: Section 54.2 does not contain an explicit reference to value, nor does it focus on the recipient receiving all the assets necessary to carry on the business. Based on fair market value, the percentage of the assets of the division transferred to the new company was around 68%. The judge also considered two alternative tests: whether the taxpayer transferred the "heart of the business" and the contribution of the transferred property to the division's profit. In this case, the fair market value was the most reliable method, and all or substantially all means more than just over two-thirds. *Atlantic Packaging Products Ltd. v. The Queen*, 2018 DTC 1133 (TCC) [under appeal]

SECTION 55: [Deemed proceeds or capital gain]

► 55(1) ◄

(1) Definitions. In this section,

"distribution" — "distribution" means a direct or indirect transfer of property of a corporation (referred to in this section as the "distributing corporation") to one or more corporations (each of which is referred to in this section as a "transferee corporation") where, in respect of each type of property owned by the distributing corporation immediately before the transfer, each transferee corporation receives property of that type the fair market value of which is equal to or approximates the amount determined by the formula

$$A \times B/C$$

where

A is the fair market value, immediately before the transfer, of all property of that type owned at that time by the distributing corporation,

B is the fair market value, immediately before the transfer, of all the shares of the capital stock of the distributing corporation owned at that time by the transferee corporation, and

C is the fair market value, immediately before the transfer, of all the issued shares of the capital stock of the distributing corporation;

"permitted acquisition" —"permitted acquisition", in relation to a distribution by a distributing corporation, means an acquisition of property by a person or partnership on, or as part of,

(*a*) a distribution, or

(*b*) a permitted exchange or permitted redemption in relation to a distribution by another distributing corporation;

"permitted exchange" —"permitted exchange", in relation to a distribution by a distributing corporation, means

(*a*) an exchange of shares for shares of the capital stock of the distributing corporation to which subsection 51(1) or 86(1) applies or would, if the shares were capital property to the holder thereof, apply, other than an exchange that resulted in an acquisition of control of the distributing corporation by any person or group of persons, and

(*b*) an exchange of shares of the capital stock of the distributing corporation by one or more shareholders of the distributing corporation (each of whom is referred to in this paragraph as a "participant") for shares of the capital stock of another corporation (referred to in this paragraph as the "acquiror") in contemplation of the distribution where

(i) no share of the capital stock of the acquiror outstanding immediately after the exchange (other than directors' qualifying shares) is owned at that time by any person or partnership other than a participant,

and either

(ii) the acquiror owns, immediately before the distribution, all the shares each of which is a share of the capital stock of the distributing corporation that was owned immediately before the exchange by a participant, or

(iii) the fair market value, immediately before the distribution, of each participant's shares of the capital stock of the acquiror is equal to or approximates the amount determined by the formula

$$(A \times B/C) + D$$

where

A is the fair market value, immediately before the distribution, of all the shares of the capital stock of the acquiror then outstanding (other than shares issued to participants in consideration for shares of a specified class all the shares of which were acquired by the acquiror on the exchange),

B is the fair market value, immediately before the exchange, of all the shares of the capital stock of the distributing corporation (other than shares of a specified class none or all of the shares of which were acquired by the acquiror on the exchange) owned at that time by the participant,

C is the fair market value, immediately before the exchange, of all the shares (other than shares of a specified class none or all of the shares of which were acquired by the acquiror on the exchange and shares to be redeemed, acquired or cancelled by the distributing corporation pursuant to the exercise of a statutory right of dissent by the holder of the share) of the capital stock of the distributing corporation outstanding immediately before the exchange, and

D is the fair market value, immediately before the distribution, of all the shares issued to the participant by the acquiror in consideration for shares of a specified class all of the shares of which were acquired by the acquiror on the exchange;

"permitted redemption" —"permitted redemption", in relation to a distribution by a distributing corporation, means

(*a*) a redemption or purchase for cancellation by the distributing corporation, as part of the reorganization in which the distribution was made, of all the shares of its capital stock that were owned, immediately before the distribution, by a transferee corporation in relation to the distributing corporation,

(*b*) a redemption or purchase for cancellation by a transferee corporation in relation to the distributing corporation, or by a corporation that, immediately after the redemption or purchase, was a subsidiary wholly-owned corporation of the transferee corporation, as part of the reorganization in which the distribution was made, of all of the shares of the capital stock of the transferee corporation or the subsidiary wholly-owned corporation that were acquired by the distributing corporation in consideration for the transfer of property received by the transferee corporation on the distribution, and

(*c*) a redemption or purchase for cancellation by the distributing corporation, in contemplation of the distribution, of all the shares of its capital stock each of which is

(i) a share of a specified class the cost of which, at the time of its issuance, to its original owner was equal to the fair market value at that time of the consideration for which it was issued, or

(ii) a share that was issued, in contemplation of the distribution, by the distributing corporation in exchange for a share described in subparagraph (i);

"qualified person" —"qualified person", in relation to a distribution, means a person or partnership with whom the distributing corporation deals at arm's length at all times during the course of the series of transactions or events that includes the distribution if

(*a*) at any time before the distribution,

(i) all of the shares of each class of the capital stock of the distributing corporation that includes shares that cause that person or partnership to be a specified shareholder of the distributing corporation (in this definition all of those shares in all of those classes are referred to as the "exchanged shares") are, in the circumstances described in paragraph (*a*) of the definition "permitted exchange", exchanged for consideration that consists solely of shares of a specified class of the capital stock of the distributing corporation (in this definition referred to as the "new shares"), or

(ii) the terms or conditions of all of the exchanged shares are amended (which shares are in this definition referred to after the amendment as the "amended shares") and the amended shares are shares of a specified class of the capital stock of the distributing corporation,

(*b*) immediately before the exchange or amendment, the exchanged shares are listed on a designated stock exchange,

(*c*) immediately after the exchange or amendment, the new shares or the amended shares, as the case may be, are listed on a designated stock exchange,

(*d*) the exchanged shares would be shares of a specified class if they were not convertible into, or exchangeable for, other shares,

(*e*) the new shares or the amended shares, as the case may be, and the exchanged shares are non-voting in respect of the election of the board of directors of the distributing corporation except in the event of a failure or default under the terms or conditions of the shares, and

(*f*) no holder of the new shares or the amended shares, as the case may be, is entitled to receive on the redemption, cancellation or acquisition of the new shares or the amended shares, as the case may be, by the distributing corporation or by any person with whom the distributing corporation does not deal at arm's length an amount (other than a premium for early redemption) that is greater than the total of the fair market value of the consideration for which the exchanged shares were issued and the amount of any unpaid dividends on the new shares or on the amended shares, as the case may be;

History: S. 55(1), the definition "qualified person" was added by S.C. 2013, c. 34, s. 193(2), applicable in respect of dividends received after 1999, except that for the period before December 14, 2007, the references to "designated stock exchange" in the definition "qualified person" in subsection 55(1) are to be read as references to "prescribed stock exchange".

"safe-income determination time" —"safe-income determination time" for a transaction or event or a series of transactions or events means the time that is the earlier of

(*a*) the time that is immediately after the earliest disposition or increase in interest described in any of subparagraphs (3)(*a*)(i) to (v) that resulted from the transaction, event or series, and

(*b*) the time that is immediately before the earliest time that a dividend is paid as part of the transaction, event or series;

Related Sections: S. 55(2) Deemed proceeds or capital gain; s. 55(5) Applicable rules.

"specified class" —"specified class" means a class of shares of the capital stock of a distributing corporation where

(*a*) the paid-up capital in respect of the class immediately before the beginning of the series of transactions or events that includes a distribution by the distributing corporation was not less than the fair market value of the consideration for which the shares of that class then outstanding were issued,

(*b*) under neither the terms and conditions of the shares nor any agreement in respect of the shares are the shares convertible into or exchangeable for shares other than shares of a specified class or shares of the capital stock of a transferee corporation in relation to the distributing corporation,

(*c*) no holder of the shares is entitled to receive on the redemption, cancellation or acquisition of the shares by the corporation or by any person with whom the corporation does not deal at arm's length an amount (other than a premium for early redemption) that is greater than the total of the fair market value of the consideration for which the shares were issued and the amount of any unpaid dividends on the shares, and

(*d*) the shares are non-voting in respect of the election of the board of directors except in the event of a failure or default under the terms or conditions of the shares;

History: S. 55(1), paragraph (*c*) of the definition "specified class" was replaced by S.C. 2013, c. 34, s. 193(1), applicable in respect of shares issued after December 20, 2002, and formerly read:

(c) under neither the terms and conditions of the shares nor any agreement in respect of the shares is any holder of the shares entitled to receive on the redemption, cancellation or acquisition of the shares by the corporation or by any person with whom the corporation does not deal at arm's length (excluding any premium for early redemption) an amount greater than the total of the fair market value of the consideration for which the shares were issued and the amount of any unpaid dividends thereon;

S. 55(1), paragraph (*d*) of the definition "specified class" was added by S.C. 2013, c. 34, s. 193(1), applicable in respect of shares issued after December 20, 2002.

"specified corporation" —"specified corporation" in relation to a distribution means a distributing corporation

(*a*) that is a public corporation or a specified wholly-owned corporation of a public corporation,

(*b*) shares of the capital stock of which are exchanged for shares of the capital stock of another corporation (referred to in this definition and subsection (3.02) as an "acquiror") in an exchange to which the definition "permitted exchange" in this subsection would apply if that definition were read without reference to paragraph (*a*) and subparagraph (*b*)(ii) of that definition,

(*c*) that does not make a distribution, to a corporation that is not an acquiror, after 1998 and before the day that is three years after the day on which the shares of the capital stock of the distributing corporation are exchanged in a transaction described in paragraph (*b*), and (*d*) no acquiror in relation to which makes a distribution after 1998 and before the day that is three years after the day on which the shares of the capital stock of the distributing corporation are exchanged in a transaction described in paragraph (*b*),

and, for the purposes of paragraphs (*c*) and (*d*),

(*e*) a corporation that is formed by an amalgamation of two or more other corporations is deemed to be the same corporation as, and a continuation of, each of the other corporations, and

(*f*) where there has been a winding-up of a corporation to which subsection 88(1) applies, the parent is deemed to be the same corporation as, and a continuation of, the subsidiary;

"specified wholly-owned corporation" —"specified wholly-owned corporation" of a public corporation means a corporation all of the outstanding shares of the capital stock of which (other than directors' qualifying shares and shares of a specified class) are held by

(*a*) the public corporation,

(*b*) a specified wholly-owned corporation of the public corporation, or

(*c*) any combination of corporations described in paragraph (*a*) or (*b*).

▶ 55(2) ◀

(2) Deemed proceeds or gain. If this subsection applies to a taxable dividend received by a dividend recipient, notwithstanding any other provision of this Act, the amount of the dividend (other than the portion of it, if any, subject to tax under Part IV that is not refunded as a consequence of the payment of a dividend by a corporation where the payment is part of the series referred to in subsection (2.1)) is deemed

(*a*) not to be a dividend received by the dividend recipient;

(*b*) if the dividend is received on a redemption, acquisition or cancellation of a share, by the corporation that issued the share, to which subsection 84(2) or (3) applies, to be proceeds of disposition of the share that is redeemed, acquired or cancelled except to the extent that the dividend is otherwise included in computing those proceeds; and

(*c*) if paragraph (*b*) does not apply to the dividend, to be a gain of the dividend recipient, for the year in which the dividend was received, from the disposition of a capital property.

Editorial Note: Section 55 contains rules under which intercorporate dividends that are not otherwise subject to tax may be treated as proceeds of disposition of shares or as a capital gain. The purpose of the provision is to prevent the avoidance of tax by strategies that convert accrued capital gains, FMV reductions, or ACB increases into tax-free intercorporate dividends.

The main provisions are found in s. 55(2) to 55(2.5). Dividends subject to Part IV tax are exempt from s. 55(2) provided the Part IV tax is not refunded as a result of the payment of a further dividend to any shareholder, including individuals.

Subsection 55(2) applies if the dividend was received as part of a transaction or event or a series of transactions or events and if all three of the conditions in s. 55(2.1) are met. The term "series of transactions or events" is defined in s. 248(10) to include any related transactions or events completed in contemplation of the series and has been the subject of much jurisprudence, including Supreme Court of Canada decisions in the context of the general anti-avoidance rule (*Canada Trustco*, 2005 DTC 5523, and *Copthorne Holdings*, 2012 DTC 5007).

The condition in paragraph 55(2.1)(*a*) will be met if the dividend recipient is entitled to a deduction under s. 138(6) (applicable to life insurers) or under s. 112(1) or (2) (applicable to corporations generally). Subsection 55(2) does not apply to a dividend paid to an individual or to a non-resident.

The condition in Paragraph 55(2.1)(b), which is often referred to as the purposes test, will be met if one of the purposes of the dividend is to effect:

(1) a significant reduction in the portion of the capital gain that, but for the dividend, would have been realized on the disposition of any share at fair market value;

(2) a significant reduction in the fair market value of any share if the dividend (other than a deemed dividend received to which subsection 84(2) or 84(3) applies) is received on a share that is capital property to the shareholder; or

(3) a significant increase in the cost of property of the dividend recipient immediately after the dividend, if the dividend (other than a deemed dividend received to which subsection 84(2) or 84(3) applies) is received on a share that is capital property to the shareholder.

Lastly, the condition in paragraph 55(2.1)(*c*) will be met if the dividend exceeds the amount of income earned or realized by any corporation after 1971 (commonly referred to as "safe income") and before the safe income determination time (defined in s. 55(1)) that could reasonably be considered to contribute to the capital gain that could be realized on a disposition at fair market value of the share on which the dividend is received. In general terms, safe income is the after-tax retained earnings of the corporation and intercorporate dividends should not exceed the corporation's safe income on hand at the time the dividend is paid. Subsection 55(5) contains rules for determining the safe income of a corporation. The CRA's administrative position as to the calculation of safe income has been the subject of numerous publications by the CRA and numerous judicial decisions (see *Brelco*, 99 DTC 5253 (FCA); *Kruco Inc.*, 2003 DTC 5506 (FCA); *Trico Industries*, 94 DTC 1740 (TCC); and *Deuce Holdings*, 97 DTC 921 (TCC)).

History: S. 55(2) was replaced by S.C. 2016, c. 7, s. 5(1), applicable to dividends received after April 20, 2015, and formerly read:

(2) *Deemed proceeds or capital gain.* Where a corporation resident in Canada has received a taxable dividend in respect of which it is entitled to a deduction under subsection 112(1) or (2) or 138(6) as part of a transaction or event or a series of transactions or events, one of the purposes of which (or, in the case of a dividend under subsection 84(3), one of the results of which) was to effect a significant reduction in the portion of the capital gain that, but for the dividend, would have been realized on a disposition at fair market value of any share of capital stock immediately before the dividend and that could reasonably be considered to be attributable to anything other than income earned or realized by any corporation after 1971 and before the safe-income determination time for the transaction, event or series, notwithstanding any other section of this Act, the amount of the dividend (other than the portion of it, if any, subject to tax under Part IV that is not refunded as a consequence of the payment of a dividend to a corporation where the payment is part of the series)

(*a*) shall be deemed not to be a dividend received by the corporation;

(*b*) where a corporation has disposed of the share, shall be deemed to be proceeds of disposition of the share except to the extent that it is otherwise included in computing such proceeds; and

(*c*) where a corporation has not disposed of the share, shall be deemed to be a gain of the corporation for the year in which the dividend was received from the disposition of a capital property.

Related Sections: S. 55(1), "safe-income determination time"; s. 55(3) Application; s. 55(4) Avoidance of subsection (2); s. 256(7) Acquiring control; s. 256(8) Deemed exercise of right.

Canadian Petroleum Tax Journal: A Comparative Study of Canadian and US Rules Regarding the Taxation of Corporate Reorganizations, Firoz Talakshi and Christy Palmer, 2000, Vol. 13, No. 1; Recent Developments in Corporate Reorganizations and International Transactions, Doug Richardson and Edward Rowe, 2000, Vol. 13, No. 1.

Canadian Tax Foundation: Carenza and Jacinto, *New 55(2): A Purposeful Review of the Results to Date*, 2017 Ontario Tax Conference 8:1–36; Keung, *Selected Safe Income Issues: Relevant Period, Global Computation and Allocation*, 2017 Prairie Provinces Tax Conference 8A:1–20; Cormack, *A Practical Approach to Calculating Safe Income – Case Study*, 2017 British Columbia Tax Conference 2:1–32; Talbot and Conrad, *Subsection 55(2): a Practical Perspective*, 2017 Atlantic Provinces Tax Conference 9:1–23; Keung, *Capital Gains Taxed Twice*, 2017 Tax for the Owner Manager 17(2):2–3; Welters, *Results Test in Subsection 55(2)*, 2017 Canadian Tax Highlights 25(3):6–7; Truster, *Cash Dividends and Amended Subsection 55(2)*, 2016 Tax for the Owner-Manager 16(2):6–7; Kakkar and Halil, *Subsection 55(2): The CRA's Recent Positions*, 2016 Tax for the Owner-Manager 16(1):1; Abdulla, *New Subsection 55(2) Issues*, 2016 Canadian Tax Highlights 24(1):2–3; Kakkar and Halil, *Corporate Beneficiary Can Add to Its Safe Income on Hand*, 2015 Tax for the Owner-Manager 15(3):7; Diep and Kopstein, *Current Cases: Tax Court of Canada--Statutory Interpretation: Subsection 55(2) and Double-Counting of Safe Income (D & D Livestock Ltd. v. The Queen, 2013 TCC 318)*, 2014 Canadian Tax Journal 1:192–196; Hudson and McCamis, *Refresher on Specific Anti-Avoidance Provisions*, 2014 Prairie Provinces Tax Conference 12:1–41; Gosselin, *CRA Confirms GRIP Trap When Dividend Not Paid Out of Safe Income*, 2014 Tax for the Owner-Manager 14(3):1–2; ZoBell, *A Subsection 55(2) Anomaly: Using Safe Income Twice*, 2014 Canadian Tax Focus 4(1):1; Chong, *Fight Against Surplus Stripping Continues*, 2013 Canadian Tax Highlights 21(8):9–10; Brender, *Subsection 55(2): Then and Now*, 2011 Conference Report 12:1–35; Pantry and Maclagan, *Issues and Updates — Safe Income*, 2008 British Columbia Tax Conference 4:1–35; McDonnell, *Current*

Cases: Federal Court of Appeal — Profit Trading as an Acceptable Tax-Minimization Technique, 2005 Canadian Tax Journal 3:754–761; Anderson, *Subsection 55(2): Phantom Income is Safe,* 2003 Tax for the Owner-Manager 3(4):7–8; Rogers, *Splitting Up and Reorganizing the Family Business — Some Tips and Traps,* 2001 British Columbia Tax Conference 8:1–30; James et al, *Butterflies and Rollovers Application to the Agricultural Industry,* 2000 Prairie Provinces Tax Conference 6:1–12; Ton-That and Sider, *Butterfly Revisited,* 1999 Conference Report 24:1–33; Ton-That and Bilodeau, *Breaking Up is Hard To Do,* 1996 Conference Report 11:1–70.

Tax Profile: August 2012 — U.S. Purchases and Sales of Canadian Businesses: Tax and Corporate Issues; November 2009 — Purchase and Sale of a Canadian Business; October 2003 — Split-Up of Corporate Business Partnerships.

Tax Topics: No. 2257, Proposed Amendments to Section 55 Contain Unwanted Surprise; No. 2196, D&D Livestock Ltd. V. The Queen: Is Double Counting Permitted under Subsection 55(2)?; No. 2194, Subsection 55(2) Anti-Avoidance Rule – Share Redemption; No. 2102, Eligible Dividends and Subsection 55(2); No. 2023-24, 2010 Canadian Tax Foundation CRA Roundtable: Pipelines, Privilege and Working Papers (Again!); No. 1876, Income Tax Technical News No. 37: Safe Income Calculation — Treatment of Non-Deductible Expenses; No. 1851, Subsection 55(2): No Recharacterization Based On What Could Have Been Done; No. 1814, 2006 Canadian Tax Foundation Annual Conference CRA Round Table; No. 1775, Series of Transactions After Canada *Trustco*: When Does Paragraph 55(3)(a) Apply?.

Income Tax Technical News: Issue No. 37, Safe Income Calculation — Treatment of Non-Deductible Expenses; Issue No. 34, Safe Income Calculation — the Kruco Case; Issue No. 33, Income Earned or Realized — The Kruco Case.

Information Circulars: IC 88-2 General anti-avoidance rule — Section 245 of the Income Tax Act (paras. 7, 13 and 15).

Tax Window Files: 2018 CTF - Q2 - Impact of 55(2) deeming rules, *November 27, 2018,* CRA Document No. 2018-0780071C6; 2018 CTF - Q1 - Allocation of safe income, *November 27, 2018,* CRA Document No. 2018-0780061C6; 2017 CTF - Q6 - Circular calculations Part IV tax, *November 21, 2017,* CRA Document No. 2017-0724071C6; 2017 CTF - Q4 - Timing of deemed gain under 55(2), *November 21, 2017,* CRA Document No. 2017-0724051C6; 2017 STEP – Q7 - 55(2) and pipeline planning, *June 13, 2017,* CRA Document No. 2017-0693421C6; 2016 CTF – Q4 – 55(2) and Part IV Tax, *November 29, 2016,* CRA Document No. 2016-0671491C6; Subsection 55(2) and Part IV tax, *October 11, 2016,* CRA Document No. 2016-0653451E5; Application of subsection 55(2) - holding period, *October 7, 2016,* CRA Document No. 2016-0652991C6; Computation of safe income - stub period, *April 20, 2016,* CRA Document No. 2016-0633961E5; 2015 CTF Q.6(e), Creditor Proofing, *November 24, 2015,* CRA Document No. 2015-0623551C6; 2015 CTF Q.6(c), Safe Income, *November 24, 2015,* CRA Document No. 2015-0610661C6; 2015 CTF Q. 4, Surplus Stripping and GAAR, *November 24, 2015,* CRA Document No. 2015-0610701C6; Cross-Border Butterfly, *14XXXX,* CRA Document No. 2014-0530961R3.

Cases: S. 55(2) does not apply to the stock dividend received by the taxpayer. While the taxpayer's actions defeated the purpose of s. 55(2), the Court could not rewrite the section to give effect to that purpose. *D & D Livestock Ltd. v. The Queen,* 2013 DTC 1251 (T.C.C.)

The taxpayer treated proceeds of redemption of shares as s. 55(2) capital gains. The Minister characterized them as deemed dividends. Instead of paying Part IV tax and applying for a dividend refund within the required time frames, the taxpayer chose to set off non-capital losses against the Part IV tax. Hence, s. 55(2) was inapplicable. *Ottawa Air Cargo Centre Ltd. v. The Queen,* 2008 DTC 6177 (F.C.A.), affirming 2007 DTC 661 (T.C.C.)

The taxpayers received s. 84(3) deemed dividends that were subject to Part IV tax, but this liability was offset by normal course dividends paid by the taxpayers. Subsection 55(2) applied since the dividends were held to be part of the series of transactions that gave rise to the deemed dividends. However, the Act does not require a *pro rata* allocation of Part IV refunds between dividends paid to corporations and those paid to individuals. The taxpayers can allocate the dividends in the manner most beneficial to them. *The Queen v. Canadian Utilities Limited et al.,* 2004 DTC 6475 (F.C.A.), reversing in part 2003 DTC 1029 (T.C.C.)

Safe income adjustments with respect to investment tax credits were not justified because it would result in double taxation and strayed from the very basis of the calculation set out in s. 55(5)(*c*). An adjustment was allowed with respect to the cost of a debt acquired by the company which gave rise to an SRED tax credit. *The Queen v. Kruco Inc.,* 2003 DTC 5506 (F.C.A.), affirming 2001 DTC 668 (T.C.C.)

The corporate taxpayer was deemed by s. 84(3) to have received a dividend upon the redemption of shares of G corporation. The same shareholders owned all of the shares of both the taxpayer and G. They subsequently sold their shares of G at arm's length. The redemption by G of its shares, and the sale by the shareholders of their G shares were part of a series of transactions coming within s. 55(2). *Granite Bay Charters Ltd. v. The Queen,* 2001 DTC 615 (T.C.C.)

Treatment of PUC and "safe income" in the calculation of deemed "proceeds of disposition" under s. 55(2). *943963 Ontario Inc. v. The Queen,* 99 DTC 802 (T.C.C.)

In the calculation of the taxpayer's "safe income", the surpluses of the taxpayer's foreign affiliates were netted against the deficits of the taxpayer's other foreign affiliates. *The Queen v. Brelco Drilling Ltd.,* 99 DTC 5253 (F.C.A.), reversing 98 DTC 1422 (T.C.C.)

Where the Minister would have allowed the corporate taxpayer the benefit of tax-free intercorporate dividends if its accountant had not failed to make a safe income designation, the taxpayer could not be said to have attempted to circumvent s. 55(2). *Nassau Walnut Investments Inc. v. The Queen,* 97 DTC 5051 (F.C.A.), affirming 95 DTC 367 (T.C.C.)

Cognizance by the taxpayer of the fact that the capital gain otherwise realizable on the sale of its shares could be significantly reduced, to the extent that it had been attributable to intercorporate dividends designated as safe income, could not be equated with a tax-avoidance purpose on the taxpayer's part. *The Queen v. Placer Dome Inc.,* 96 DTC 6562 (F.C.A.)

When the evidence adduced by two corporations claiming the deduction of intercorporate dividends failed to establish a reasonable nexus between the events leading up to the declaration of the dividends and any previous event or transaction, the Minister could rely on the avoidance provision of s. 55(2)(*b*) to treat the dividends as proceeds of disposition of their shares. *454538 Ontario Limited et al. v. M.N.R.,* 93 DTC 427 (T.C.C.).

► 55(2.1) ◄

(2.1) Application of subsection (2). Subsection (2) applies to a taxable dividend received by a corporation resident in Canada (in subsections (2) to (2.2) and (2.4) referred to as the *dividend recipient*) as part of a transaction or event or a series of transactions or events if

(*a*) the dividend recipient is entitled to a deduction in respect of the dividend under subsection 112(1) or (2) or 138(6);

(*b*) it is the case that

(i) one of the purposes of the payment or receipt of the dividend (or, in the case of a dividend under subsection 84(3), one of the results of which) is to effect a significant reduction in the portion of the capital gain that, but for the dividend, would have been realized on a disposition at fair market value of any share of capital stock immediately before the dividend, or

(ii) the dividend (other than a dividend that is received on a redemption, acquisition or cancellation of a share, by the corporation that issued the share, to which subsection 84(2) or (3) applies) is received on a share that is held as capital property by the dividend recipient and one of the purposes of the payment or receipt of the dividend is to effect

(A) a significant reduction in the fair market value of any share, or

(B) a significant increase in the cost of property, such that the amount that is the total of the cost amounts of all properties of the dividend recipient immediately after the dividend is significantly greater than the amount that is the total of the cost amounts of all properties of the dividend recipient immediately before the dividend; and

(*c*) the amount of the dividend exceeds the amount of the income earned or realized by any corporation — after 1971 and before the safe-income determination time for the transaction, event or series — that could reasonably be considered to contribute to the capital gain that could be realized on a disposition at fair market value, immediately before the dividend, of the share on which the dividend is received.

History: S. 55(2.1) was added by S.C. 2016, c. 7, s. 5(1), applicable to dividends received after April 20, 2015.

Canadian Tax Foundation: Wahidie and Templeton, *Current Cases — Safe Income — The Dangerous Impact of Future Taxes*, 2018 Canadian Tax Journal 66(3):611–617; Frydberg and Malik, *Subsection 55(2) and Safe Income*, 2018 Prairie Provinces Tax Conference 9:0; Shew, *Safe Income May Vary Within Shares of the Same Class*, 2018 Canadian Tax Focus 8(3):3–3; Kiefer and Taylor, *Lumpy Creditor-Protection Dividends and Subsection 55(2)*, 2016 Tax for the Owner-Manager 16(3):4–5.

Tax Topics: No. 2465, An Overview of Section 55 and Safe Income Part I — 55(2) Deemed Dividend.

Tax Window Files: 2017 CTF - Q5 - 55(5)(f) and 55(2.3) with 55(2.1), *November 21, 2017*, CRA Document No. 2017-0726381C6; 2017 CTF - Q3 - Meaning of purpose, *November 21, 2017*, CRA Document No. 2017-0724021C6; Purpose tests of a dividend or repurchase of share, *May 12, 2017*, CRA Document No. 2017-0683511E5; Purpose tests and Allocation of safe income, *April 6, 2017*, CRA Document No. 2016-0658841E5; 2016 CTF–Computation of safe income, *November 29, 2016*, CRA Document No. 2016-0669651C6; 2016 CTF–Q8–55(2) clause 55(2.1)(b)(ii)(B), *November 29, 2016*, CRA Document No. 2016-0671501C6; Guidance on determination of safe income, *November 15, 2016*, CRA Document No. 2016-0672321C6; Allocation of the safe income on hand, *October 7, 2016*, CRA Document No. 2016-0652981C6; Safe income and freeze preferred shares, *October 7, 2016*, CRA Document No. 2016-0653001C6; Safe income on hand - Preferred shares, *October 7, 2016*, CRA Document No. 2016-0655921C6; Application of proposed amendments to section 55, *June 23, 2016*, CRA Document No. 2016-0627571E5; Attribution of safe income, *April 27, 2016*, CRA Document No. 2016-0633101E5; Allocation of the safe income on hand, *December 3, 2015*, CRA Document No. 2015-0593941E5; 2015 CTF Q.6(b) Loss Consolidation and Section 55, *November 24, 2015*, CRA Document No. 2015-0610671C6; 2015 CTF Q.6(c), Safe Income, *November 24, 2015*, CRA Document No. 2015-0610661C6; 2015 CTF Q.6(a), Purpose Test, *November 24, 2015*, CRA Document No. 2015-0610651C6.

▶ 55(2.2) ◀

(2.2) Special rule — amount of the stock dividend. For the purpose of applying subsections (2), (2.1), (2.3) and (2.4), the amount of a stock dividend and the dividend recipient's entitlement to a deduction under subsection 112(1) or (2) or 138(6) in respect of the amount of that dividend are to be determined as if paragraph (*b*) of the definition *amount* in subsection 248(1) read as follows:

(*b*) in the case of a stock dividend paid by a corporation, the greater of

(i) the amount by which the paid-up capital of the corporation that paid the dividend is increased by reason of the payment of the dividend, and

(ii) the fair market value of the share or shares issued as a stock dividend at the time of payment,

History: S. 55(2.2) was added by S.C. 2016, c. 7, s. 5(1), applicable to dividends received after April 20, 2015.

▶ 55(2.3) ◀

(2.3) Stock dividends and safe income. If this subsection applies in respect of a stock dividend

(*a*) the amount of the stock dividend is deemed for the purpose of subsection (2) to be a separate taxable dividend to the extent of the portion of the amount that does not exceed the amount of the income earned or realized by any corporation — after 1971 and before the safe-income determination time for the transaction, event or series — that could reasonably be considered to contribute to the capital gain that could be realized on a disposition at fair market value, immediately before the dividend, of the share on which the dividend is received; and

(*b*) the amount of the separate taxable dividend referred to in paragraph (*a*) is deemed to reduce the amount of the income earned or realized by any corporation — after 1971 and before the safe-income determination time for the transaction, event or series — that could reasonably be considered to contribute to the capital gain that could be realized on a disposition at fair market value, immediately before the dividend, of the share on which the dividend is received.

History: S. 55(2.3) was added by S.C. 2016, c. 7, s. 5(1), applicable to dividends received after April 20, 2015.

Tax Window Files: Stock dividends and safe income, *June 6, 2017*, CRA Document No. 2016-0658351E5; Stock dividend, *December 12, 2016*, CRA Document No. 2016-0668341E5.

▶ 55(2.4) ◀

(2.4) Application of subsection (2.3). Subsection (2.3) applies in respect of a stock dividend if

(*a*) a dividend recipient holds a share upon which it receives the stock dividend;

(*b*) the fair market value of the share or shares issued as a stock dividend exceeds the amount by which the paid-up capital of the corporation that paid the stock dividend is increased because of the dividend; and

(*c*) subsection (2) would apply to the dividend if subsection (2.1) were read without reference to its paragraph (*c*).

History: S. 55(2.4) was added by S.C. 2016, c. 7, s. 5(1), applicable to dividends received after April 20, 2015.

▶ 55(2.5) ◀

(2.5) Determination of reduction in fair market value. For the purpose of applying clause (2.1)(*b*)(ii)(A), whether a dividend causes a significant reduction in the fair market value of any share is to be determined as if the fair market value of the share, immediately before the dividend, was increased by an amount equal to the amount, if any, by which the fair market value of the dividend received on the share exceeds the fair market value of the share.

History: S. 55(2.5) was added by S.C. 2016, c. 7, s. 5(1), applicable to dividends received after April 20, 2015.

▶ 55(3) ◀

(3) Application. Subsection (2) does not apply to any dividend received by a corporation (in this subsection and subsection (3.01) referred to as the "dividend recipient")

(*a*) in the case of a dividend that is received on a redemption, acquisition or cancellation of a share, by the corporation that issued the share, to which subsection 84(2) or (3) applies, if, as part of a transaction or event or a series of transactions or events as a part of which the dividend is received, there was not at any particular time

(i) a disposition of property, other than

(A) money disposed of on the payment of a dividend or on a reduction of the paid-up capital of a share, and

(B) property disposed of for proceeds that are not less than its fair market value,

to a person or partnership that was an unrelated person immediately before the particular time,

(ii) a significant increase (other than as a consequence of a disposition of shares of the capital stock of a corporation for proceeds of disposition that are not less than their fair market value) in the total direct interest in any corporation of one or more persons or partnerships that were unrelated persons immediately before the particular time,

(iii) a disposition, to a person or partnership who was an unrelated person immediately before the particular time, of

(A) shares of the capital stock of the corporation that paid the dividend (referred to in this paragraph and subsection (3.01) as the "dividend payer"), or

(B) property (other than shares of the capital stock of the dividend recipient) more than 10% of the fair market value of which was, at any time during the series, derived from any combination of shares of the capital stock and debt of the dividend payer,

(iv) after the time the dividend was received, a disposition, to a person or partnership that was an unrelated person immediately before the particular time, of

(A) shares of the capital stock of the dividend recipient, or

(B) property more than 10% of the fair market value of which was, at any time during the series, derived from any combination of shares of the capital stock and debt of the dividend recipient, and

(v) a significant increase in the total of all direct interests in the dividend payer of one or more persons or partnerships who were unrelated persons immediately before the particular time; or

(*b*) if the dividend was received

(i) in the course of a reorganization in which

(A) a distributing corporation made a distribution to one or more transferee corporations, and

(B) the distributing corporation was wound up or all of the shares of its capital stock owned by each transferee corporation immediately before the distribution were redeemed or cancelled otherwise than on an exchange to which subsection 51(1), 85(1) or 86(1) applies, and

(ii) on a permitted redemption in relation to the distribution or on the winding-up of the distributing corporation.

Editorial Note: Paragraph 55(3)(*a*) exempts a dividend that is received on a redemption, acquisition, or cancellation of a share, to which subsection 84(2) or 84(3) applies, from the application of s. 55(2) if none of the transactions or events in s. 55(3)(*a*)(i) to 55(3)(*a*)(v) occur as part of the transaction, event, or series of transactions or events as a part of which the dividend was received. The transactions and events prohibited by s. 55(3)(*a*)(i) to 55(3)(*a*)(v) involve either: (i) a disposition to an unrelated person; or (ii) a significant increase in an unrelated person's interest in a corporation. Therefore, s. 55(2) will generally have no application to subsection 84(2) or 84(3) dividends that are paid to related persons (ordinary dividends paid to related parties are subject to the s. 55(2) application rules). Subsection 55(4) deems persons not to be related if it is reasonable to consider that one of the main purposes of one or more transactions or events was to cause the persons to be related so that s. 55(2) would not apply. Further, s. 55(5)(*e*) provides that for the purposes of s. 55, brothers and sisters are deemed to deal at arm's length and to not be related. Similarly, persons who are related solely under s. 251(5)(*b*) (rights to acquire shares) or under s. 251(3) (corporations related to each other because each corporation is related to a third corporation) are deemed not to be related for the purposes of s. 55. Note that s. 55(3.01) also contains various rules regarding the interpretation of s. 55(3)(*a*).

Paragraph 55(3)(*b*) provides another exception to the application of s. 55(2). Specifically, s. 55(2) does not apply to a dividend received in the course of a reorganization, the objective of which is to separate the interests of shareholders and, in effect, "demerge" the corporation, provided the technical requirements of s. 55(3)(*b*) are met. For example, a corporation owned by two shareholders who are not related, such as two siblings each owning 50% of the shares of an operating company, may want to separate their interests. If properly structured, the transaction can take place free of tax and the deemed dividends which would be part of the transaction would not be caught by s. 55(2). This type of divisive reorganization is commonly referred to as a "butterfly" transaction. In order for s. 55(3)(*b*) to apply to such a transaction, each transferee corporation must obtain a *pro rata* share of the distributing corporation's assets in exchange (directly or indirectly) for its shares. This *pro rata* determination generally applies to each of the following types of property: (i) cash or near-cash; (ii) business assets; and (iii) investments. The rules for a s. 55(3)(*b*) butterfly reorganization are very complex and, in most cases, such a reorganization is only undertaken if an advance income tax ruling is obtained.

History: S. 55(3)(*a*), the portion before subparagraph (i) was replaced by S.C. 2016, c. 7, s. 5(2), applicable to dividends received after April 20, 2015, and formerly read:

(*a*) if, as part of a transaction or event or a series of transactions or events as a part of which the dividend was received, there was not at any particular time

S. 55(3)(*a*)(iii)(B) was replaced by S.C. 2013, c. 40, s. 24(1), applicable in respect of dividends received after December 20, 2012, and formerly read:

(B) property (other than shares of the capital stock of the dividend recipient) more than 10% of the fair market value of which was, at any time during the course of the series, derived from shares of the capital stock of the dividend payer,

S. 55(3)(*a*)(iv)(B) was replaced by S.C. 2013, c. 40, s. 24(2), applicable in respect of dividends received after December 20, 2012, and formerly read:

(B) property more than 10% of the fair market value of which was, at any time during the course of the series, derived from shares of the capital stock of the dividend recipient, and

S. 55(3)(*a*)(iii)(B) was replaced by S.C. 2013, c. 34, s. 193(3), applicable to dividends received after February 21, 1994, and formerly read:

(B) property more than 10% of the fair market value of which was, at any time during the course of the series, derived from shares of the capital stock of the dividend payer,

Related Sections: S. 55(3.01) Interpretation for par. (3)(a); s. 55(3.1) Where paragraph (3)(b) not applicable; 251(2) Definition of "related persons"; 251(3) Corporations related through a third corporation; 251(3.1) Relation where amalgamation or merger; 251(3.2) Amalgamation of related corporations; 251(4) Definitions concerning groups; 251(5) Control by related groups, options, etc.

Canadian Tax Foundation: Truster, *The Challenges of Creditor Proofing*, 2014 Tax for the Owner-Manager 14(3):7; Haughey, *Spinoff Butterflies in Trouble?*, 2013 Canadian Tax Focus 3(15): 3–4; Citrome, *An Introduction to Paragraph 55(3)(a)*, 2006 Conference Report 36:1–31; Truster, *Divisive Reorganizations: Breaking up the Family Business*, 2005 Conference Report 12:1–30; Wortsman, *The Public Company Spinoff Rule*, 2000 Conference Report 24:1–38.

STEP Canada: Mark Brender and Greg Boehmer, "Butterfly Case Study: Breaking Up is (Sometimes) Hard to Do," PowerPoint presentation to the 15th National Conference of STEP Canada, Toronto, June 10-11, 2013.

Tax Topics: No. 1775, Series of Transactions After Canada Trustco: When Does Paragraph 55(3)(a) Apply?.

Information Circulars: IC 88-2 General anti-avoidance rule — Section 245 of the Income Tax Act (para. 7).

Tax Window Files: 2017 STEP – Q6 - GAAR on share redemption-55(3)(a), *June 13, 2017*, CRA Document No. 2017-0693411C6; 2015 CTF Q.6(d), Use of 84(3) Dividend, *November 24, 2015*, CRA Document No. 2015-0610681C6; Internal Reorganization, *15XXXX*, CRA Document No. 2015-0604051R3; ACB increase in paragraph 55(3)(a) reorganization, *January 13, 2016*, CRA Document No. 2015-0604521E5.

► 55(3.01) ◄

(3.01) Interpretation for par. (3)(a). For the purposes of paragraph (3)(*a*),

(*a*) an unrelated person means a person (other than the dividend recipient) to whom the dividend recipient is not related or a partnership any member of which (other than the dividend recipient) is not related to the dividend recipient;

(*b*) a corporation that is formed by an amalgamation of 2 or more other corporations is deemed to be the same corporation as, and a continuation of, each of the other corporations;

(*c*) where there has been a winding-up of a corporation to which subsection 88(1) applies, the parent is deemed to be the same corporation as, and a continuation of, the subsidiary;

(*d*) proceeds of disposition are to be determined without reference to

(i) subparagraph (*j*)(i) of the definition *proceeds of disposition* in section 54, and

(ii) section 93;

(*e*) notwithstanding any other provision of this Act, where a non-resident person disposes of a property in a taxation year and the gain or loss from the disposition is not included in computing the person's taxable income earned in Canada for the year, the person is deemed to have disposed of the property for proceeds of disposition that are less than its fair market value unless, under the income tax laws of the country in which the person is resident, the gain or loss is computed as if the property were disposed of for proceeds of disposition that are not less than its fair market value and the gain or loss so computed is recognized for the purposes of those laws;

(*f*) a significant increase in the total direct interest in a corporation that would, but for this paragraph, be described in subparagraph (3)(*a*)(ii) is deemed not to be described in that subparagraph if the increase was the result of the issuance of shares of the capital stock of the corporation solely for money and the shares were redeemed, acquired or cancelled by the corporation before the dividend was received;

(*g*) a disposition of property that would, but for this paragraph, be described in subparagraph (3)(*a*)(i), or a significant increase in the total direct interest in a corporation that would, but for this paragraph, be described in subparagraph (3)(*a*)(ii), is deemed not to be described in those subparagraphs if

(i) the dividend payer was related to the dividend recipient immediately before the dividend was received,

(ii) the dividend payer did not, as part of the series of transactions or events that includes the receipt of the dividend, cease to be related to the dividend recipient,

(iii) the disposition or increase occurred before the dividend was received,

(iv) the disposition or increase was the result of the disposition of shares to, or the acquisition of shares of, a particular corporation, and

(v) at the time the dividend was received, all the shares of the capital stock of the dividend recipient and the dividend payer were owned by the particular corporation, a corporation that controlled the particular corporation, a corporation controlled by the particular corporation or any combination of those corporations; and

(*h*) a winding-up of a subsidiary wholly-owned corporation to which subsection 88(1) applies, or an amalgamation to which subsection 87(11) applies of a corporation with one or more subsidiary wholly-owned corporations, is deemed not to result in a significant increase in the total direct interest, or in the total of all direct interests, in the subsidiary or subsidiaries, as the case may be.

History: S. 52(3.01)(*d*)(i) was replaced by S.C. 2016, c. 7, s. 5(3), applicable to dividends received after April 20, 2015, and formerly read:

(i) the expression "paragraph 55(2)(*a*) or" in paragraph (*j*) of the definition "proceeds of disposition" in section 54, and

S. 55(3.01)(*f*) to (*h*) were added by S.C. 2013, c. 40, s. 24(3), applicable in respect of dividends received after 2003.

S. 55(3.01)(*d*) was replaced by S.C. 2013, c. 34, s. 193(4), applicable to dividends received after February 21, 1994, and formerly read:

(*d*) proceeds of disposition shall be determined without reference to "paragraph 55(2)(*a*) or" in paragraph (*j*) of the definition "proceeds of disposition" in section 54; and

► 55(3.02) ◄

(3.02) Distribution by a specified corporation. For the purposes of the definition "distribution" in subsection (1), where the transfer referred to in that definition is by a specified corporation to an acquiror described in the definition "specified corporation" in subsection (1), the references in the definition "distribution" to

(*a*) "each type of property" shall be read as "property"; and

(*b*) "property of that type" shall be read as "property".

► 55(3.1) ◄

(3.1) Where paragraph (3)(b) not applicable. Notwithstanding subsection (3), a dividend to which subsection (2) would, but for paragraph (3)(*b*), apply is not excluded from the application of subsection (2) where

(*a*) in contemplation of and before a distribution (other than a distribution by a specified corporation) made in the course of the reorganization in which the dividend was received, property became property of the distributing corporation, a corporation controlled by it or a predecessor corporation of any such corporation otherwise than as a result of

(i) an amalgamation of corporations each of which was related to the distributing corporation,

(ii) an amalgamation of a predecessor corporation of the distributing corporation and one or more corporations controlled by that predecessor corporation,

(iii) a reorganization in which a dividend was received to which subsection (2) would, but for paragraph (3)(*b*), apply, or

(iv) a disposition of property by

(A) the distributing corporation, a corporation controlled by it or a predecessor corporation of any such corporation to a corporation controlled by the distributing corporation or a predecessor corporation of the distributing corporation,

(B) a corporation controlled by the distributing corporation or by a predecessor corporation of the distributing corporation to the distributing corporation or predecessor corporation, as the case may be, or

(C) the distributing corporation, a corporation controlled by it or a predecessor corporation of any such corporation for consideration that consists only of money or indebtedness that is not convertible into other property, or of any combination thereof,

(*b*) the dividend was received as part of a series of transactions or events in which

(i) a person or partnership (referred to in this subparagraph as the "vendor") disposed of property and

(A) the property is

(I) a share of the capital stock of a distributing corporation that made a distribution as part of the series or of a transferee corporation in relation to the distributing corporation, or

(II) property 10% or more of the fair market value of which was, at any time during the course of the series, derived from one or more shares described in subclause (I),

(B) the vendor (other than a qualified person in relation to the distribution) was, at any time during the course of the series, a specified shareholder of the distributing corporation or of the transferee corporation, and

(C) the property or any other property (other than property received by the transferee corporation on the distribution) acquired by any person or partnership in substitution therefor was acquired (otherwise than on a permitted acquisition, permitted exchange or permitted redemption in relation to the distribution) by a person (other than the vendor) who was not related to the vendor or, as part of the series, ceased to be related to the vendor or by a partnership,

(ii) control of a distributing corporation that made a distribution as part of the series or of a transferee corporation in relation to the distributing corporation was acquired (otherwise than as a result of a permitted acquisition, permitted exchange or permitted redemption in relation to the distribution) by any person or group of persons, or

(iii) in contemplation of a distribution by a distributing corporation, a share of the capital stock of the distributing corporation was acquired (otherwise than on a permitted acquisition or permitted exchange in relation to the distribution or on an amalgamation of 2 or more predecessor corporations of the distributing corporation) by

(A) a transferee corporation in relation to the distributing corporation or by a person or partnership with whom the transferee corporation did not deal at arm's length from a person to whom the acquiror was not related or from a partnership,

(B) a person or any member of a group of persons who acquired control of the distributing corporation as part of the series,

(C) a particular partnership any interest in which is held, directly or indirectly through one or more partnerships, by a person referred to in clause (B), or

(D) a person or partnership with whom a person referred to in clause (B) or a particular partnership referred to in clause (C) did not deal at arm's length,

(*c*) the dividend was received by a transferee corporation from a distributing corporation that, immediately after the reorganization in the course of which a distribution was made and the dividend was received, was not related to the transferee corporation and the total of all amounts each of which is the fair market value, at the time of acquisition, of a property that

(i) was acquired, as part of the series of transactions or events that includes the receipt of the dividend, by a person (other than the transferee corporation) who was not related to the transferee corporation or, as part of the series, ceased to be related to the transferee corporation or by a partnership, otherwise than

(A) as a result of a disposition

(I) in the ordinary course of business, or

(II) before the distribution for consideration that consists solely of money or indebtedness that is not convertible into other property, or of any combination of the two,

(B) on a permitted acquisition in relation to a distribution, or

(C) as a result of an amalgamation of 2 or more corporations that were related to each other immediately before the amalgamation, and

(ii) is a property (other than money, indebtedness that is not convertible into other property, a share of the capital stock of the transferee corporation and property more than 10% of the fair market value of which is attributable to one or more such shares)

(A) that was received by the transferee corporation on the distribution,

(B) more than 10% of the fair market value of which was, at any time after the distribution and before the end of the series, attributable to property (other than money and indebtedness that is not convertible into other property) described in clause (A) or (C), or

(C) to which, at any time during the course of the series, the fair market value of property described in clause (A) was wholly or partly attributable

is greater than 10% of the fair market value, at the time of the distribution, of all the property (other than money and indebtedness that is not convertible into other property) received by the transferee corporation on the distribution, or

(*d*) the dividend was received by a distributing corporation that, immediately after the reorganization in the course of which a distribution was made and the dividend was received, was not related to the transferee corporation that paid the dividend and the total of all amounts each of which is the fair market value, at the time of acquisition, of a property that

(i) was acquired, as part of the series of transactions or events that includes the receipt of the dividend, by a person (other than the distributing corporation) who was not related to the distributing corporation or, as part of the series, ceased to be related to the distributing corporation or by a partnership, otherwise than

(A) as a result of a disposition

(I) in the ordinary course of business, or

(II) before the distribution for consideration that consists solely of money or indebtedness that is not convertible into other property, or of any combination of the two,

(B) on a permitted acquisition in relation to a distribution, or

(C) as a result of an amalgamation of 2 or more corporations that were related to each other immediately before the amalgamation, and

(ii) is a property (other than money, indebtedness that is not convertible into other property, a share of the capital stock of the distributing corporation and property more than 10% of the fair market value of which is attributable to one or more such shares)

(A) that was owned by the distributing corporation immediately before the distribution and not disposed of by it on the distribution,

(B) more than 10% of the fair market value of which was, at any time after the distribution and before the end of the series, attributable to property (other than money and indebtedness that is not convertible into other property) described in clause (A) or (C), or

(C) to which, at any time during the course of the series, the fair market value of property described in clause (A) was wholly or partly attributable

is greater than 10% of the fair market value at the time of the distribution, of all the property (other than money and indebtedness that is not convertible into other property) owned immediately before that time by the distributing corporation and not disposed of by it on the distribution.

Editorial Note: Subsection 55(3.1) provides certain situations in which the butterfly exception set out in s. 55(3)(*b*) does not apply even if the rules in s. 55(3)(*b*) are met. Paragraph 55(3.1)(*a*) provides that the butterfly exception will not apply if the distributing corporation, a corporation controlled by it, or a predecessor corporation of any such corporation acquired property in contemplation of the butterfly distribution, unless any of the circumstances in s. 55(3.1)(*a*)(i) to (iv) apply. This paragraph does not apply if the distribution is made by a "specified corporation". The term "property" is given a wide meaning in s. 248(1) and includes cash. The purpose of this rule is to stop a distributing corporation from "manoeuvring" to benefit from the butterfly.

Subparagraph 55(3.1)(*b*)(i) applies where a person or partnership (the "vendor") who was a "specified shareholder" of the distributing corporation or a transferee corporation at any time during the series of transactions or events as a part of which the dividend was received disposes of certain property, and the property or substituted property is acquired by a person who is not related, or as part of the series ceases to be related, to the vendor or by a partnership. This subparagraph does not apply where the vendor is a "qualified person" (defined in s. 55(1)). A "specified shareholder" is defined in s. 248(1) generally to mean any person who owns directly or indirectly 10% or more of the issued shares of any class of the corporation or a related corporation. Subparagraph 55(3.1)(*b*)(ii) disallows a butterfly reorganization in which there is an acquisition of control of the distributing corporation or a transferee corporation. Subparagraph 55(3.1)(*b*)(iii) applies, generally, where a share of the distributing corporation is acquired by a transferee corporation or certain other persons in contemplation of the distribution. It should be noted that there are exceptions to s. 55(3.1)(*b*) for certain permitted acquisitions, permitted exchanges, and permitted redemptions, as defined in s. 55(1).

Paragraphs 55(3.1)(*c*) and (*d*) prohibit most post-butterfly transfers of assets which were butterflied to a transferee corporation or left behind in a distributing corporation to a person not related to the transferee corporation or distributing corporation, as applicable, or to a partnership. This prohibition only applies when the distributing corporation and transferee corporation are not related immediately after the butterfly reorganization. Additionally, transfers to unrelated parties of 10% or less of the fair market value of the assets butterflied to the transferee corporation or 10% or less of the assets which were left behind in the distributing corporation are generally permitted. Other exceptions include dispositions of property in the ordinary course of business, dispositions before the distribution for consideration that consists solely of money or indebtedness that is not convertible into other property, and permitted acquisitions.

History: S. 55(3.1)(*a*), the portion before subparagraph (i) was replaced by S.C. 2013, c. 40, s. 24(4), applicable in respect of dividends received after 2003, and formerly read:

(*a*) in contemplation of and before a distribution made in the course of the reorganization in which the dividend was received, property became property of the distributing corporation, a corporation controlled by it or a predecessor corporation of any such corporation otherwise than as a result of

S. 55(3.1)(*c*)(i)(A) was replaced by S.C. 2013, c. 40, s. 24(5), applicable in respect of dividends received after 2003, and formerly read:

(A) as a result of a disposition in the ordinary course of business,

S. 55(3.1)(*d*)(i)(A) was replaced by S.C. 2013, c. 40, s. 24(6), applicable in respect of dividends received after 2003, and formerly read:

(A) as a result of a disposition in the ordinary course of business,

S. 55(3.1)(*b*)(i)(B) was replaced by S.C. 2013, c. 34, s. 193(5), applicable in respect of dividends received after 1999, and formerly read:

(B) the vendor was, at any time during the course of the series, a specified shareholder of the distributing corporation or of the transferee corporation, and

▶ 55(3.2) ◀

(3.2) Interpretation of paragraph (3.1)(b). For the purpose of paragraph (3.1)(*b*),

(*a*) in determining whether the vendor referred to in subparagraph (3.1)(*b*)(i) is at any time a specified shareholder of a transferee corporation or of a distributing corporation, the references in the definition "specified shareholder" in subsection 248(1) to "taxpayer" shall be read as "person or partnership";

(*b*) a corporation that is formed by the amalgamation of 2 or more corporations (each of which is referred to in this paragraph as a "predecessor corporation") shall be deemed to be the same corporation as, and a continuation of, each of the predecessor corporations;

(*c*) subject to paragraph (*d*), each particular person who acquired a share of the capital stock of a distributing corporation in contemplation of a distribution by the distributing corporation shall be deemed, in respect of that acquisition, not to be related to the person from whom the particular person acquired the share unless

(i) the particular person acquired all the shares of the capital stock of the distributing corporation that were owned, at any time during the course of the series of transactions or events that included the distribution and before the acquisition, by the other person, or

(ii) immediately after the reorganization in the course of which the distribution was made, the particular person was related to the distributing corporation;

(*d*) where a share is acquired by an individual from a personal trust in satisfaction of all or a part of the individual's capital interest in the trust, the individual shall be deemed, in respect of that acquisition, to be related to the trust;

(*e*) subject to paragraph (*f*), where at any time a share of the capital stock of a corporation is redeemed or cancelled (otherwise than on an amalgamation where the only consideration received or receivable for the share by the shareholder on the amalgamation is a share of the capital stock of the corporation formed by the amalgamation), the corporation shall be deemed to have acquired the share at that time;

(*f*) where a share of the capital stock of a corporation is redeemed, acquired or cancelled by the corporation pursuant to the exercise of a statutory right of dissent by the holder of the share, the corporation shall be deemed not to have acquired the share;

(*g*) control of a corporation shall be deemed not to have been acquired by a person or group of persons where it is so acquired solely because of

(i) the incorporation of the corporation, or

(ii) the acquisition by an individual of one or more shares for the sole purpose of qualifying as a director of the corporation; and

(*h*) in relation to a distribution each corporation (other than a qualified person in relation to the distribution) that is a shareholder and a specified shareholder of the distributing corporation at any time during the course of a series of transactions or events, a part of which includes the distribution made by the distributing corporation, is deemed to be a transferee corporation in relation to the distributing corporation.

History: S. 55(3.2)(*h*) was replaced by S.C. 2013, c. 34, s. 193(6), applicable in respect of dividends received after 1999, and formerly read:

(*h*) each corporation that is a shareholder and specified shareholder of a distributing corporation at any time during the course of a series of transactions or events, a part of which includes a distribution made by the distributing corporation, is deemed to be a transferee corporation in relation to the distributing corporation.

▶ 55(3.3) ◀

(3.3) Interpretation of "specified shareholder" changed. In determining whether a person is a specified shareholder of a corporation for the purposes of subparagraph (3.1)(*b*)(i) and paragraph (3.2)(*h*), the reference in the definition "specified shareholder" in subsection 248(1) to "or of any other corporation that is related to the corporation" shall be read as "or of any other corporation that is related to the corporation and that has a significant direct or indirect interest in any issued shares of the capital stock of the corporation".

▶ 55(3.4) ◀

(3.4) Specified shareholder exclusion. In determining whether a person is a specified shareholder of a corporation for the purposes of the definition "qualified person" in subsection (1), subparagraph (3.1)(*b*)(i) and paragraph (3.2)(*h*) as it applies for the purpose of subparagraph (3.1)(*b*)(iii), the reference to "not less than 10% of the issued shares of any class of the capital stock of the corporation" in the definition "specified shareholder" in subsection 248(1) is to be read as "not less than 10% of the issued shares of any class of the capital stock of the corporation, other than shares of a specified class (within the meaning of subsection 55(1))".

History: S. 55(3.4) was added by S.C. 2013, c. 34, s. 193(7), applicable in respect of dividends received after 1999.

▶ 55(3.5) ◀

(3.5) Amalgamation of related corporations. For the purposes of paragraphs (3.1)(*c*) and (*d*), a corporation formed by an amalgamation of two or more corporations (each of which is referred to in this subsection as a "predecessor corporation") that were related to each other immediately before the amalgamation, is deemed to be the same corporation as, and a continuation of, each of the predecessor corporations.

History: S. 55(3.5) was added by S.C. 2013, c. 34, s. 193(7), applicable in respect of dividends received after April 26, 1995.

▶ 55(4) ◀

(4) Avoidance of subsection (2). For the purposes of this section, where it can reasonably be considered that one of the main purposes of one or more transactions or events was to cause 2 or more persons to be related to each other or to cause a corporation to control another corporation, so that subsection (2) would, but for this subsection, not apply to a dividend, those persons shall be deemed not to be related to each other or the corporation shall be deemed not to control the other corporation, as the case may be.

Related Sections: 251(2) Definition of "related persons"; 251(3) Corporations related through a third corporation; 251(3.1) Relation where amalgamation or merger; 251(3.2) Amalgamation of related corporations; 251(4) Definitions concerning groups; 251(5) Control by related groups, options, etc.

▶ 55(5) ◀

(5) Applicable rules. For the purposes of this section,

(*a*) where a dividend referred to in subsection (2) was received by a corporation as part of a transaction or event or a series of transactions or events, the portion of a capital gain attributable to any income expected to be earned or realized by a corporation after the safe-income determination time for the transaction, event or series is deemed to be a portion of a capital gain attributable to anything other than income;

(*b*) the income earned or realized by a corporation for a period throughout which it was resident in Canada and not a private corporation shall be deemed to be the total of

(i) its income for the period otherwise determined on the assumption that no amounts were deductible by the corporation by reason of section 37.1 of this Act or paragraph 20(1)(*gg*) of the *Income Tax Act*, chapter 148 of the Revised Statutes of Canada, 1952,

(ii) the amount, if any, by which

(A) the amount, if any, by which the total of the capital gains of the corporation for the period exceeds the total of the taxable capital gains of the corporation for the period

exceeds

(B) the amount, if any, by which the total of the capital losses of the corporation for the period exceeds the total of the allowable capital losses of the corporation for the period,

(iii) the total of all amounts each of which is an amount required to have been included under this subparagraph as it read in its application to a taxation year that ended before February 28, 2000,

(iv) the amount, if any, by which

(A) 1/2 of the total of all amounts each of which is an amount required by paragraph 14(1)(*b*) to be included in computing the corporation's income in respect of a business carried on by the corporation for a taxation year that is included in the period and that ended after February 27, 2000 and before October 18, 2000,

exceeds

(B) where the corporation has deducted an amount under subsection 20(4.2) in respect of a debt established by it to have become a bad debt in a taxation year that is included in the period and that ended after February 27, 2000 and before October 18, 2000, or has an allowable capital loss for such a year because of the application of subsection 20(4.3), the amount determined by the formula

$$V + W$$

where

V is 1/2 of the value determined for A under subsection 20(4.2) in respect of the corporation for the last such taxation year that ended in the period, and

W is 1/3 of the value determined for B under subsection 20(4.2) in respect of the corporation for the last such taxation year that ended in the period, and

(C) in any other case, nil, and

(v) the amount, if any, by which

(A) the total of all amounts each of which is an amount required by paragraph 14(1)(*b*) to be included in computing the corporation's income in respect of a business carried on by the corporation for a taxation year that is included in the period and that ends after October 17, 2000,

exceeds

(B) where the corporation has deducted an amount under subsection 20(4.2) in respect of a debt established by it to have become a bad debt in a taxation year that is included in the period and that ends after October 17, 2000, or has an allowable capital loss for such a year because of the application of subsection 20(4.3), the amount determined by the formula

$$X + Y$$

where

X is the value determined for A under subsection 20(4.2) in respect of the corporation for the last such taxation year that ended in the period, and

Y is 1/3 of the value determined for B under subsection 20(4.2) in respect of the corporation for the last such taxation year that ended in the period, and

(C) in any other case, nil;

(*c*) the income earned or realized by a corporation for a period throughout which it was a private corporation is deemed to be its income for the period otherwise determined on the assumption that no amounts were deductible by the corporation under section 37.1 of this Act, as that section applies for taxation years that ended before 1995, or paragraph 20(1)(*gg*) of the *Income Tax Act*, chapter 148 of the Revised Statutes of Canada, 1952;

(*d*) the income earned or realized by a corporation (referred to in this paragraph as the "affiliate") for a period ending at a time when the affiliate was a foreign affiliate of another corporation is deemed to be the lesser of

(i) the amount that would, if the *Income Tax Regulations* were read without reference to their subsection 5905(5.6), be the tax-free surplus balance (within the meaning of their subsection 5905(5.5)) of the affiliate in respect of the other corporation at that time, and

(ii) the fair market value at that time of all the issued and outstanding shares of the capital stock of the affiliate;

(*e*) in determining whether 2 or more persons are related to each other, in determining whether a person is at any time a specified shareholder of a corporation and in determining whether control of a corporation has been acquired by a person or group of persons,

(i) a person shall be deemed to be dealing with another person at arm's length and not to be related to the other person if the person is the brother or sister of the other person,

(ii) where at any time a person is related to each beneficiary (other than a registered charity) under a trust who is or may (otherwise than by reason of the death of another beneficiary under the trust) be entitled to share in the income or capital of the trust, the person and the trust shall be deemed to be related at that time to each other and, for this purpose, a person shall be deemed to be related to himself, herself or itself,

(iii) a trust and a person shall be deemed not to be related to each other unless they are deemed by paragraph (3.2)(*d*) or subparagraph (ii) to be related to each other or the person is a corporation that is controlled by the trust, and

(iv) this Act shall be read without reference to subsection 251(3) and paragraph 251(5)(*b*); and

(*f*) unless subsection (2.3) applies, if a corporation has received a dividend any portion of which is a taxable dividend (such a portion referred to as the "taxable part" in this paragraph), as part of a transaction or event or series of transactions or events

(i) a portion of the dividend is deemed to be a separate taxable dividend equal to the lesser of

(A) the taxable part, and

(B) the amount of the income earned or realized by any corporation — after 1971 and before the safe-income determination time for the transaction, event or series — that could reasonably be considered to contribute to the capital gain that could be realized on a disposition at fair market value, immediately before the dividend, of the share on which the dividend is received, and

(ii) the amount, if any, by which the taxable part exceeds the portion referred to in subparagraph (i) is deemed to be a separate taxable dividend.

Editorial Note: Paragraph 55(5)(*f*) provides that where a corporation receives a taxable dividend, an automatic designation separates the amount of the taxable dividend into two separate taxable dividends, one of which is subject to subsection 55(2) and the other of which is not.

The portion of the dividend that is deemed to be a separate taxable dividend that is not subject to the provisions of s. 55(2) is equal to the lesser of the taxable part and the amount of safe income that could reasonably be considered to contribute to a capital gain that could be realized on an FMV disposition of the share on which the dividend is received. The amount, if any, by which the taxable part of the dividend exceeds the corporations safe income on hand is deemed to be a separate taxable dividend, which will be subject to the provisions of s. 55(2).

Paragraph 55(5)(*f*) no longer applies to stock dividends as these type of dividends are now subject to the rules in subsection 55(2.3).

History: S. 55(5)(*f*) was replaced by S.C. 2016, c. 7, s. 5(4), applicable to dividends received after April 20, 2015 except that, for dividends received after April 20, 2015 and before April 18, 2016, paragraph 55(5)(*f*) is to be read as follows:

(*f*) unless subsection (2.3) applies, if a corporation has received a dividend any portion of which is a taxable dividend

(i) the corporation may designate in its return of income under this Part for the taxation year during which the dividend was received any portion of the taxable dividend to be a separate taxable dividend, and

(ii) the amount, if any, by which the portion of the dividend that is a taxable dividend exceeds the portion designated under subparagraph (i) shall be deemed to be a separate dividend.

S. 55(5)(*f*) formerly read:

(*f*) where a corporation has received a dividend any portion of which is a taxable dividend,

(i) the corporation may designate in its return of income under this Part for the taxation year during which the dividend was received any portion of the taxable dividend to be a separate taxable dividend, and

(ii) the amount, if any, by which the portion of the dividend that is a taxable dividend exceeds the portion designated under subparagraph (i) shall be deemed to be a separate taxable dividend.

S. 55(5)(*d*) was replaced by S.C. 2013, c. 34, s. 62(1), applicable in respect of a dividend received after August 19, 2011 by a corporation resident in Canada, except where the dividend is received as part of a series of transactions or events that includes a disposition of the shares in respect of which the dividend is received that

(*a*) is made to a person or partnership that, at the time of the disposition, deals at arm's length with the corporation; and

(*b*) occurs under an agreement in writing entered into before August 19, 2011.

Any assessment of a taxpayer's tax, interest and penalties payable under the Act for any taxation year that ends before June 26, 2013 that would, in the absence of this section, be precluded because of subsections 152(4) to (5) of the Act shall be made to the extent necessary to take into account the amendments by S.C. 2013, c. 34, s. 54 to 89.

S. 55(5)(*d*) formerly read:

(*d*) the income earned or realized by a corporation for a period ending at a time when it was a foreign affiliate of another corporation shall be deemed to be the total of the amount, if any, that would have been deductible by that other corporation at that time by virtue of paragraph 113(1)(*a*) and the amount, if any, that would have been deductible by that other corporation at that time by virtue of paragraph 113(1)(*b*) if that other corporation

(i) owned all of the shares of the capital stock of the foreign affiliate immediately before that time,

(ii) had disposed at that time of all of the shares referred to in subparagraph (i) for proceeds of disposition equal to their fair market value at that time, and

(iii) had made an election under subsection 93(1) in respect of the full amount of the proceeds of disposition referred to in subparagraph (ii);

Related Sections: S. 53 Adjustments to cost base; s. 55(1), "safe-income determination time"; s. 104(1) Reference to trust or estate; s. 248(1), "amount", "corporation", "dividend", "private corporation", "property", "share".

Canadian Petroleum Tax Journal: Recent Cases of Interest — Safe Income, Gerald Grenon, 2000, Vol. 13, No. 1.

Canadian Tax Foundation: Drori, *CRA's (Re)interpretation of Paragraph 55(5)(f)*, 2015 Canadian Tax Focus 2(3):7; Thomas, *Current Cases: It's What Parliament Said That Counts, Not What it Meant to Say*, 2000 Canadian Tax Journal 4:1260–1264.

Tax Profile: October 2003 — Split-Up of Corporate Business Partnerships.

Tax Topics: No. 1876, Income Tax Technical News No. 37: Safe Income Calculation — Treatment of Non-Deductible Expenses; No. 1820, Beware of Pitfalls in November 9, 2006 Technical Amendments When Crystallizing "Safe Income"!.

Income Tax Technical News: Issue No. 37, Safe Income Calculation — Treatment of Non-Deductible Expenses; Issue No. 33, Income Earned or Realized — The Kruco Case.

Cases: Safe income adjustments with respect to investment tax credits were not justified because it would result in double taxation and strayed from the very basis of the calculation set out in paragraph 55(5)(*c*). An adjustment was allowed with respect to the cost of a debt acquired by the company which gave rise to an SRED tax credit. *Kruco Inc. v. The Queen*, 2003 DTC 5506 (F.C.A.), affirming 2001 DTC 668 (T.C.C.)

The words "any corporation" in subsection 55(2) are not limited to those corporations listed in paragraphs 55(5)(*b*), (*c*), and (*d*) and therefore could include a foreign non-affiliate. *Lamont Management Limited v. The Queen*, 2000 DTC 6256 (F.C.A.), reversing 99 DTC 871 (T.C.C.)

In the calculation of the taxpayer's "safe income", the surpluses of the taxpayer's foreign affiliates were netted against the deficits of the taxpayer's other foreign affiliates. *The Queen v. Brelco Drilling Ltd.*, 99 DTC 5253 (F.C.A.), reversing 98 DTC 1422 (T.C.C.).

► 55(6) ◄

(6) Unlisted shares deemed listed. A share (in this subsection referred to as the "reorganization share") is deemed, for the purposes of subsection 116(6) and the definition "taxable Canadian property" in subsection 248(1), to be listed on a designated stock exchange if

(*a*) a dividend, to which subsection (2) does not apply because of paragraph (3)(*b*), is received in the course of a reorganization;

(*b*) in contemplation of the reorganization

(i) the reorganization share is issued to a taxpayer by a public corporation in exchange for another share of that corporation (in this subsection referred to as the "old share") owned by the taxpayer, and

(ii) the reorganization share is exchanged by the taxpayer for a share of another public corporation (in this subsection referred to as the "new share") in an exchange that would be a permitted exchange if the definition "permitted exchange" were read without reference to paragraph (*a*) and subparagraph (*b*)(ii) of that definition;

(*c*) immediately before the exchange, the old share

(i) is listed on a designated stock exchange, and

(ii) is not taxable Canadian property of the taxpayer; and

(*d*) the new share is listed on a designated stock exchange.

History: S. 55(6) was added by S.C. 2013, c. 34, s. 193(8), applicable to shares that are issued after April 26, 1995, except that for the period before December 14, 2007, the references to "designated stock exchange" in subsection 55(6) are to be read as references to "prescribed stock exchange".

Subdivision d — Other Sources of Income

SECTION 56: Amounts to be included in income for year

► 56(1) ◄

(1) Amounts to be included in income for year. Without restricting the generality of section 3, there shall be included in computing the income of a taxpayer for a taxation year,

Editorial Note: The amounts described in s. 56 are included in a taxpayer's Part 1 income, notwithstanding that they might not be considered income from one of the sources listed in s. 3(*a*) (namely, income from office, employment, business or property).

► 56(1)(a) ◄

(a) Pension benefits, unemployment insurance benefits, etc. — any amount received by the taxpayer in the year as, on account or in lieu of payment of, or in satisfaction of,

(i) a superannuation or pension benefit including, without limiting the generality of the foregoing,

(A) the amount of any pension, supplement or spouse's or common-law partner's allowance under the *Old Age Security Act* and the amount of any similar payment under a law of a province,

(B) the amount of any benefit under the *Canada Pension Plan* or a provincial pension plan as defined in section 3 of that Act,

(C) the amount of any payment out of or under a specified pension plan, and

(C.1) the amount of any payment out of or under a foreign retirement arrangement established under the laws of a country, except to the extent that the amount would not, if the taxpayer were resident in the country, be subject to income taxation in the country,

but not including

(D) the portion of a benefit received out of or under an employee benefit plan that is required by paragraph 6(1)(*g*) to be included in computing the taxpayer's income for the year, or would be required to be so included if that paragraph were read without reference to subparagraph 6(1)(*g*)(ii),

(E) the portion of an amount received out of or under a retirement compensation arrangement that is required by paragraph (*x*) or (*z*) to be included in computing the taxpayer's income for the year,

(F) a benefit received under section 71 of the *Canada Pension Plan* or under a similar provision of a provincial pension plan as defined in section 3 of that Act, and

(G) an amount received out of or under a registered pension plan as a return of all or a portion of a contribution to the plan to the extent that the amount

(I) is a payment made to the taxpayer under subsection 147.1(19) or subparagraph 8502(*d*)(iii) of the *Income Tax Regulations*, and

(II) is not deducted in computing the taxpayer's income for the year or a preceding taxation year,

(ii) a retiring allowance, other than an amount received out of or under an employee benefit plan, a retirement compensation arrangement or a salary deferral arrangement,

(iii) a death benefit,

(iv) a benefit under the *Unemployment Insurance Act*, other than a payment relating to a course or program designed to facilitate the re-entry into the labour force of a claimant under that Act, or a benefit under Part I, VII.1, VIII or VIII.1 of the *Employment Insurance Act*,

(v) a benefit under regulations made under an appropriation Act providing for a scheme of transitional assistance benefits to persons employed in the production of products to which the Canada-United States Agreement on Automotive Products, signed on January 16, 1965 applies,

(vi) except to the extent otherwise required to be included in computing the taxpayer's income, a prescribed benefit under a government assistance program,

(vii) a benefit under the *Act respecting parental insurance*, R.S.Q., c. A-29.011, or

(viii) an income replacement benefit payable to the taxpayer under Part 2 of the *Veterans Well-being Act*, if the amount is determined under subsection 19.1(1), paragraph 23(1)(*b*) or subsection 26.1(1) of that Act (as modified, where applicable, under Part 5 of that Act);

History: S. 56(1)(*a*)(viii) was added by S.C. 2018, c. 12, s. 3(1), in force April 1, 2019.

S. 56(1)(*a*)(i)(G) was added by S.C. 2013, c. 40, s. 25(1), applicable to contributions made on or after January 1, 2014.

S. 56(1)(*a*)(iv) was replaced by S.C. 2013, c. 34, s. 194(1), applicable to the 2011 and subsequent taxation years, and formerly read:

> (iv) a benefit under the *Unemployment Insurance Act*, other than a payment relating to a course or program designed to facilitate the re-entry into the labour force of a claimant under that Act, or a benefit under Part I, VIII or VIII.1 of the *Employment Insurance Act*,

S. 56(1)(*a*)(vii) was added by S.C. 2013, c. 34, s. 194(2), applicable to the 2006 and subsequent taxation years.

S. 56(1)(*a*)(i)(C) was replaced by S.C. 2011, c. 24, s. 10(1), applicable to payments made after 2009. S. 56(1)(*a*)(i)(C) formerly read:

> (C) the amount of any payment out of or under a prescribed provincial pension plan, and

Related Regulations: 202(2), (3); 5502; 7800(1).

Related Sections: S. 6(1)(*a*)(i) Value of benefits; s. 56(1)(*l*) Legal expenses; s. 57 Certain superannuation or pension benefits; s. 60(*j*.02) Payment to registered pension plan; s. 60(*j*.03) Repayments of pre-1990 pension benefits; s. 60(*j*.04) Repayments of post-1989 pension benefits; s. 60(*l*) Transfer of refund of premiums under RRSP; s. 60(*n*) Repayment of pension or benefits; s. 60(*o*) Legal expenses; s. 60(*v*) Contribution to a provincial pension plan; s. 60(*v*.1) UI and EI benefit repayment; s. 110(1)(*f*) Deductions for payments; s. 110.2 Lump-sum Payments; s. 145(1), "supplementary unemployment benefit plan"; s. 146(1), "registered retirement savings plan"; s. 147(1), "deferred profit sharing plan"; s. 147(21) Restriction re transfers; s. 147(22) Excess transfer; 147.3(13.1) Withdrawal of excessive transfers to RRSPs and RRIFs; s. 153(1) Withholding; s. 212(1)(*h*) Pension benefits; s. 212(1)(*j*) Benefits; s. 212(1)(*j*.1) Retiring allowances; s. 248(1), "amount", "annuity", "assessment", "death benefit", "insurer", "property", "retirement compensation arrangement", "salary deferral arrangement", "superannuation or pension benefit"; s. 252(1) Extended meaning of "child".

Canadian Tax Foundation: Horner, *Canadian Taxation and Cross-Border Pensions*, 2009 Canadian Tax Journal 4:905–930; Carey and Levene, *Tools* *for Retirement Planning for Owner-Managers*, 2004 Prairie Provinces Tax Conference 6:1–26; Ball and Dietrich, *Canadian Taxation of Foreign Pensions*, 2000 Canadian Tax Journal 6:1908–1932.

Tax Topics: No. 1706, Retiring Allowances and E.I. Reimbursements: How Many Times Do You Have To Withhold?.

Forms: T4A(P) Supp. — Statement of Canada Pension Plan Benefits; T4E — Statement of Employment Insurance Benefits; T4A(OAS) Supp. — Statement of Old Age Security.

Income Tax Folios: *Primary* — S2-F1-C2 Retiring Allowances. *Secondary* — S1-F2-C3 Scholarships, Research Grants and Other Education Assistance.

Interpretation Bulletins: *Primary* — IT-499R Superannuation or pension benefits; IT-508R Death benefits. *Secondary* — IT-307R4 Spousal or common-law partner registered retirement savings plans; IT-365R2 Damages, settlement, and similar receipts; IT-397R Amounts excluded from income — Statutory exemptions and certain service or RCMP pensions, allowances and compensation; IT-499R Superannuation or pension benefits; IT-528 Transfers of funds between registered plans; IT-529 Flexible employee benefit programs.

Tax Window Files: Widowed Parent's Allowance, *March 21, 2016*, CRA Document No. 2015-0588521E5; Settlement amount for disability benefits, *August 11, 2015*, CRA Document No. 2015-0580521E5; Foreign Tax Credit on Transfer of 401(k) to RRSP, *15XXXX*, CRA Document No. 2015-0572541R3; General Info re IPPs, *July 23, 2015*, CRA Document No. 2014-0553991E5.

Cases: The taxpayer was the beneficiary of his father's U.S. individual retirement account ("IRA"). Following his father's death, the taxpayer's share of that IRA was rolled over to an IRA in his name. Funds from that IRA were distributed to him and amounts withheld for U.S. income taxes. While amounts distributed from an estate do not trigger tax, the taxpayer received the amount from an IRA and not from his father's estate. A payment out of a "foreign retirement arrangement" is included in computing the income of a taxpayer, and the payment from the IRA to the taxpayer was clearly a payment out of a foreign retirement arrangement and must be included in income. *Owen v. The Queen*, 2019 DTC 2071 (TCC)

Article 17(1) of the applicable Income Tax Convention entitled a taxpayer's state of residence to tax pension income arising in another state, even where such pension was on account of government service. The taxpayer, who was a resident of Canada, received pension payments from the government of Colombia. Canada, as the taxpayer's country of residence, was entitled to tax those benefits. *Reyes v. The Queen*, 2019 DTC 5008 (FCA), affirming TCC file no. 2016-4744(IT)I (unreported)

The issue was the date the taxpayer resumed Canadian residency, as any amounts received after would constitute income for Canadian tax purposes. At the time, the taxpayer was a resident of both the US and Canada. The taxpayer's habitual abode was in the US on the date he received the 401(k) proceeds and he was taxed in the US as a resident. As a dual treaty resident he was a resident of the US and not Canada by virtue of the tie-breaker rule in section 2(b) of Article IV of the *Canada-U.S. Income Tax Convention* and the income from the 401(k) was not taxable in Canada. *Davis v. The Queen*, 2018 DTC 1085 (TCC)

The payment from a US individual retirement account ("IRA") was clearly a payment out of a foreign retirement arrangement and must be included in income. *Owen v. The Queen*, 2018 DTC 1072 (TCC)

The taxpayer was discharged from his employment and instituted oppression proceedings and an action for damages against his employer. The taxpayer settled for a confidential amount arbitrarily arrived upon. It was not determinative that the taxpayer characterized the entire settlement in his tax return as a "retiring allowance". Not all awards of damages received by a taxpayer fall within the purview of a "retiring allowance" in 248(1), but only those damages related to the loss of employment. The oppression proceedings were concerned with damages arising from the oppressive conduct of the employer. The settlement would never have been paid had those oppression proceedings not been commenced. A portion of the settlement represented an award of damages not subject to tax, and the balance constituted an indemnity in lieu of notice subject to tax. *Abenaim v. The Queen*, 2017 DTC 1142 (CCI)

In 2011, former employees (and surviving spouses of former employees) of Nortel received distributions from a health and welfare trust established by Nortel in 1980. In some cases, the amounts distributed related to group term life insurance plans; others pertained to survivor transition benefits. While the provision of a group term life insurance benefit would have been taxable to the taxpayers during their employment, section 6 was not sufficiently broad to capture the distributions paid in 2011, and such distributions were not taxable. Distributions made in relation to survivor benefits were governed by section 56, which includes the phrase "any amount received... on account... of... a death benefit", and those distributions must be included in income. *Scott et al. v. The Queen*, 2017 DTC 1143 (TCC)

The taxpayer was demoted by his employer due to the interference of the employer's major customer. When the taxpayer sued the customer, the damage award he received was not a "retiring allowance" since it was not related to loss of employment. *Ahmad v. The Queen*, 2002 DTC 2065 (T.C.C.)

S. 56(1)(*a*) does not provide for the taxation of settlements for loss of intended employment. Accordingly, where a taxpayer's proposed employment was terminated before it had commenced, the amount of the settlement was not taxable. Further, it could not be characterized as a "retirement allowance". *Schwartz v. The Queen*, 96 DTC 6103 (S.C.C.), reversing 94 DTC 6249 (F.C.A.), and affirming 93 DTC 555 (T.C.C.)

The amount of $603,753 received by a taxpayer from his employer's "Incentive Performance Plan" was in respect of long service, so that it could reasonably be considered as a "retiring allowance" rather than as "remuneration" for services rendered during employment. The employees were encouraged to stay by virtue of the plan vesting provisions and they were not allowed to receive amounts before retirement. *The Queen v. Albino*, 94 DTC 6071 (F.C.T.D.)

The $100,000 lump-sum payment made to the taxpayer allegedly to terminate after eight years "his business relationship" with F was nothing more than a taxable retiring allowance paid to the taxpayer in respect of his loss of office or employment when there was simply an employee-employer relationship between the taxpayer and F. *Lyness v. The Queen*, 94 DTC 1242 (T.C.C.)

Within one year of his appointment to the National Parole Board, the taxpayer was forced to resign and executed a release in return for which he received a "termination allowance" of $90,000. This sum constituted a "retiring allowance" to be included in his income. *Blaker v. The Queen*, 93 DTC 1025 (T.C.C.)

The lump-sum payment received by a Canadian resident from the U.K. Civil Service Pension Scheme was a superannuation or pension benefit to be included in his income. *Merritt v. The Queen*, 93 DTC 978 (T.C.C.).

► 56(1)(a.1) ◄

(a.1) Benefits under CPP/QPP — where the taxpayer is an estate that arose on or as a consequence of the death of an individual, each benefit received under section 71 of the *Canada Pension Plan*, or under a similar provision of a provincial pension plan as defined in section 3 of that Act, after July 1997 and in the year in respect of the death of the individual;

► 56(1)(a.2) ◄

(a.2) Pension income reallocation — where the taxpayer is a pension transferee (as defined in subsection 60.03(1)), any amount that is a split-pension amount (as defined in that subsection) in respect of the pension transferee for the taxation year;

► 56(1)(a.3) ◄

(a.3) Parents of victims of crime — amounts received by the taxpayer in the year under a program established under the authority of the *Department of Employment and Social Development Act* in respect of children who are deceased or missing as a result of an offence, or a probable offence, under the *Criminal Code*;

History: S. 56(1)(*a.3*) was amended by S.C. 2013, c. 40, s. 236(1)(*e*)(i), by replacing "*Department of Human Resources and Skills Development Act*" with "*Department of Employment and Social Development Act*", in force December 12, 2013.

S. 56(1)(*a.3*) was replaced by S.C. 2012, c. 27, s. 36(2), in force March 1, 2013, and formerly read:

(*a.3*) *Parents of victims of crime* — amounts received by the taxpayer in the year under a program established under the authority of the *Department of Social Development Act* in respect of children who are deceased or missing as a result of an offence, or a probable offence, under the *Criminal Code*;

S. 56(1)(*a.3*) was added by S.C. 2012, c. 27, s. 26(1), in force January 1, 2013.

► 56(1)(b) ◄

(b) Support — the total of all amounts each of which is an amount determined by the formula

$$A - (B + C)$$

where

A is the total of all amounts each of which is a support amount received after 1996 and before the end of the year by the taxpayer from a particular person where the taxpayer and the particular person were living separate and apart at the time the amount was received,

B is the total of all amounts each of which is a child support amount that became receivable by the taxpayer from the particular person under an agreement or order on or after its commencement day and before the end of the year in respect of a period that began on or after its commencement day, and

C is the total of all amounts each of which is a support amount received after 1996 by the taxpayer from the particular person and included in the taxpayer's income for a preceding taxation year;

Editorial Note: Generally speaking, for orders and agreements made or amended after April 1997, child support amounts are neither deductible for the payer nor included in the income of the recipient; see also the definitions in s. 56.1(4).

Related Sections: S. 56(12) Definition of "allowance"; s. 56.1 Support; s. 60(*b*) Support; s. 60(*c*) Pension income reallocation; s. 60(*c*.2) Repayment of support payments; s. 60.1 Support; s. 109 Deductions permitted by individuals; s. 110.2 Lump-sum Payments; s. 146(1), "earned income"; s. 252(1) Extended meaning of "child"; s. 252(3) Extended meaning of "spouse" and "former spouse".

Canadian Tax Foundation: Freedman and Nakonechny, *The Tax Principles of Family Law*, 2012 Ontario Tax Conference 4:1–52; Corbin and Freedman, *Tax and Estate Planning and Family Law Considerations*, 2001 Conference Report 24:1–47; Prendergast, *Social Policy and the Income Tax Act — Tax Planning in Light of the New Definition of "Spouse"*, 2001 Prairie Provinces Tax Conference 10:1–B5.

Forms: T1157 — Election for Child Support Payments; T1158 — Registration of Family Support Payments.

Guides: P102 Support Payments.

Income Tax Folios: *Secondary* — S1-F3-C3 Support Payments.

Income Tax Technical News: Issue No. 24, Legal Costs to Obtain Support Amounts.

► 56(1)(c) ◄

(c) Maintenance — (Repealed by S.C. 1997, c. 25, s. 8(1).)

► 56(1)(c.1) ◄

(c.1) Idem — (Repealed by S.C. 1994, c. 7, Sched. VIII, s. 17(2).)

► 56(1)(c.2) ◄

(c.2) Reimbursement of support payments — an amount received by the taxpayer in the year under a decree, order or judgment of a competent tribunal as a reimbursement of an amount deducted under paragraph 60(*b*) or (*c*), or under paragraph 60(*c*.1) as it applies, in computing the taxpayer's income for the year or a preceding taxation year to decrees, orders and judgments made before 1993;

Related Sections: S. 248(1), "amount".

Income Tax Folios: *Secondary* — S1-F3-C3 Support Payments.

► 56(1)(d) ◄

(d) Annuity payments — any amount received by the taxpayer in the year as an annuity payment other than an amount

(i) otherwise required to be included in computing the taxpayer's income for the year,

(ii) with respect to an interest in an annuity contract to which subsection 12.2(1) applies (or would apply if the contract had an anniversary day in the year at a time when the taxpayer held the interest), or

(iii) received out of or under an annuity contract issued or effected as a TFSA;

(iv) (Repealed by 1990, c. 39. S. 11(1).)

History: S. 56(1)(*d*)(iii) was added by S.C. 2009, c. 2, s. 13(1), applicable to the 2009 and subsequent taxation years.

Related Sections: S. 58 Government annuities and like annuities; s. 60(*a*) Capital element of annuity payments; s. 81(1)(*g*) Compensation by Federal Republic of Germany.

Income Tax Folios: *Secondary* — S2-F1-C1 Health and Welfare Trusts.

Interpretation Bulletins: *Secondary* — IT-500R Registered retirement savings plans — Death of annuitant.

Tax Window Files: Structured Settlement, *15XXXX*, CRA Document No. 2015-0621341R3.

► 56(1)(d.1) ◄

(d.1) Idem — (Repealed by S.C. 1990, c. 39, s. 11(2).)

► 56(1)(d.2) ◄

(d.2) Idem — any amount received out of or under, or as proceeds of disposition of, an annuity the payment for which was

(i) deductible in computing the taxpayer's income because of paragraph 60(*l*) or because of subsection 146(5.5) of the *Income Tax Act*, chapter 148 of the Revised Statutes of Canada, 1952,

(ii) made in circumstances to which subsection 146(21) applied, or

(iii) made pursuant to or under a deferred profit sharing plan by a trustee under the plan to purchase the annuity for a beneficiary under the plan;

Related Sections: S. 147(10.6) Commencement of annuity after age 69.

► 56(1)(e) ◄

(e) Disposition of income-averaging annuity contract — any amount received by the taxpayer in the year as, on account or in lieu of payment of, or in satisfaction of, proceeds of the surrender, cancellation, redemption, sale or other disposition of an income-averaging annuity contract;

Related Regulations: Part II.

Related Sections: S. 61.1 Where income-averaging annuity contract ceases to be such.

► 56(1)(f) ◄

(f) Idem — any amount deemed by subsection 61.1(1) to have been received by the taxpayer in the year as proceeds of the disposition of an income-averaging annuity contract;

Related Regulations: Part II.

Related Sections: S. 214(3) Deemed payments.

► 56(1)(g) ◄

(g) Supplementary unemployment benefit plan — amounts received by the taxpayer in the year from a trustee under a supplementary unemployment benefit plan as provided by section 145;

Related Regulations: 202(2), (3).

► 56(1)(h) ◄

(h) Registered retirement savings plan, etc. — amounts required by section 146 in respect of a registered retirement savings plan or a registered retirement income fund to be included in computing the taxpayer's income for the year;

Related Regulations: 202(2), (3).

Related Sections: S. 146(8) Benefits taxable.

► 56(1)(h.1) ◄

(h.1) Home buyers' plan — amounts required by section 146.01 to be included in computing the taxpayer's income for the year;

Related Sections: S. 146.01(4) Portion of eligible amount not repaid; s. 146.01(5) Where individual becomes a non-resident; s. 146.01(6) Death of individual.

► 56(1)(h.2) ◄

(h.2) Lifelong learning plan — amounts required by section 146.02 to be included in computing the taxpayer's income for the year;

Related Sections: S. 146.02(4) If portion of eligible amount not repaid; s. 146.02(5) Ceasing residence in Canada; s. 146.02(6) Death of individual.

► 56(1)(i) ◄

(i) Deferred profit sharing plan — amounts received by the taxpayer in the year under a deferred profit sharing plan as provided by section 147;

► 56(1)(j) ◄

(j) Life insurance policy proceeds — any amount required by subsection 148(1) or (1.1) to be included in computing the taxpayer's income for the year;

Related Regulations: 217.

Tax Topics: No. 1858, Viatical Settlements ... What?.

Forms: T5 Sum. — Return of Investment Income; T5 — Statement of Investment Income.

Interpretation Bulletins: *Secondary* — IT-87R2 Policyholders' income from life insurance policies; IT-430R3 (Consolid.) — Life insurance proceeds received by a private corporation or a partnership as a consequence of death.

► 56(1)(k) ◄

(k) Certain tools of an employee, re proceeds — all amounts received in the year by a person or partnership (in this paragraph referred to as the "vendor") as consideration for the disposition by the vendor of a property the cost of which was included in computing an amount under paragraph 8(1)(*r*) or (*s*) in respect of the vendor or in respect of a person with whom the vendor does not deal at arm's length, to the extent that the total of those amounts received in respect of the disposition in the year and in preceding taxation years exceeds the total of the cost to the vendor of the property immediately before the disposition and all amounts included in respect of the disposition under this paragraph in computing the vendor's income for a preceding taxation year, unless the property was acquired by the vendor in circumstances to which subsection 85(5.1) or subsection 97(5) applied;

► 56(1)(l) ◄

(l) Legal expenses — amounts received by the taxpayer in the year as

(i) legal costs awarded to the taxpayer by a court on an appeal in relation to an assessment of any tax, interest or penalties referred to in paragraph 60(*o*),

(ii) reimbursement of costs incurred in relation to a decision of the Canada Employment Insurance Commission under the *Employment Insurance Act* or to an appeal of such a decision to the Social Security Tribunal,

(iii) reimbursement of costs incurred in relation to an assessment or a decision under the *Canada Pension Plan* or a provincial pension plan as defined in section 3 of that Act,

if with respect to that assessment or decision, as the case may be, an amount has been deducted or may be deductible under paragraph 60(*o*) in computing the taxpayer's income;

History: S. 56(1)(*l*)(ii) was replaced by S.C. 2012, c. 19, s. 277(1), applicable in respect of

(a) appeals to the Social Security Tribunal filed, and decisions made by the Canada Employment Insurance Commission, after March 2013; and

(b) appeals for which leave has deemed to have been granted by the Appeal Division of the Social Security Tribunal on April 1, 2013 or on April 1, 2014 for appeals fiiled before April 1, 2013.

S. 56(1)(*l*)(ii) formerly read:

(ii) reimbursement of costs incurred in relation to a decision of the Canada Employment and Immigration Commission, the Canada Employment and Insurance Commission, a board of referees or an umpire under the *Unemployment Insurance Act* or the *Employment Insurance Act*, or

Related Sections: S. 56(1)(*a*) Pension benefits, unemployment insurance benefits, etc.; s. 60(*n*) Repayment of pension or benefits; s. 60(*o*) Legal expenses; s. 60(*v*.1) UI and EI benefit repayment; s. 152(1.2) Provisions applicable.

► 56(1)(l.1) ◄

(l.1) Idem — amounts received by the taxpayer in the year as an award or a reimbursement in respect of legal expenses (other than those relating to a division or settlement of property arising out of, or on a breakdown of, a marriage or common-law partnership) paid to collect or establish a right to a retiring allowance or a benefit under a pension fund or plan (other than a benefit under the *Canada Pension Plan* or a provincial pension plan as defined in section 3 of that Act) in respect of employment;

Related Sections: S. 60(*o*.1) Legal expenses for pension benefit or retiring allowance; s. 248(1), "employment", "retiring allowance".

Income Tax Folios: *Primary* — S2-F1-C2 Retiring Allowances.

► 56(1)(m) ◄

(m) Bad debt recovered — any amount received by the taxpayer, or by a person who does not deal at arm's length with the taxpayer, in the year on account of a debt in respect of which a deduction was made under paragraph 60(*f*) in computing the taxpayer's income for a preceding taxation year;

History: S. 56(1)(*m*) was added by S.C. 2013, c. 34, s. 194(3), deemed to have come into force on October 8, 2003.

Related Regulations: Part II.

Related Sections: S. 63(3), "earned income".

► 56(1)(n) ◄

(n) Scholarships, bursaries, etc. — the amount, if any, by which

(i) the total of all amounts (other than amounts described in paragraph (*q*), amounts received in the course of business, and amounts received in respect of, in the course of or by virtue of an office or employment) received by the taxpayer in the year, each of which is an amount received by the taxpayer as or on account of a scholarship, fellowship or bursary, or a prize for achievement in a field of endeavour ordinarily carried on by the taxpayer, other than a prescribed prize,

exceeds

(ii) the taxpayer's scholarship exemption for the year computed under subsection (3);

Editorial Note: A scholarship, fellowship, bursary, or similar prize (but excluding a prescribed prize) that exceeds the scholarship exemption described in s. 56(3) must be included in the recipient's income in the year of receipt. A prescribed prize (see Regulation 7700) is one that is recognized by the general public and that is awarded for meritorious achievements in the fields of arts, sciences, or public service (e.g., Nobel Prize).

Related Regulations: 200(2); 7700.

Related Sections: S. 56(3) Exemption for scholarships, fellowships, bursaries and prizes; s. 56(3.1) Limitations of scholarship exemption; s. 60(*q*) Refund of income payments; s. 62(1) Moving expenses; s. 63(3), "earned income"; s. 115(2) Non-resident's taxable income in Canada; s. 248(1), "employment", "office", "prescribed".

Canadian Tax Foundation: Magee, *Tax Planning for Post-Secondary Education*, 2010 Canadian Tax Journal 2:393–416.

Tax Profile: February 2010 — Employee Scholarship Programs; September 2008 — Scholarships: The Enhanced Employee Incentive.

Guides: P105 Students and Income Tax; RC192 Information for Students — Educational Institutions Outside Canada; RC4054 Ceiling Amounts for Housing Benefits Paid in Prescribed Zones.

Income Tax Folios: *Primary* — S1-F2-C3 Scholarships, Research Grants and Other Education Assistance; *Secondary* — S1-F2-C2 Tuition Tax Credit; S1-F2-C1 Education and Textbook Tax Credits; S1-F1-C3 Disability Supports Deduction.

Secondary — S1-F3-C4 Moving Expenses.

Interpretation Bulletins: *Primary* — IT-257R Canada Council grants.

Tax Window Files: Educational Assistance, *July 17, 2018*, CRA Document No. 2017-0735391E5; Prescribed prizes won by Olympic athletes, *March 1, 2017*, CRA Document No. 2016-0664861M4; Polanyi Prizes - Prescribed prize, *November 20, 2015*, CRA Document No. 2015-0595091E5; Prescribed Prize, *February 8, 2016*, CRA Document No. 2015-0610461I7.

Cases: The taxpayer's daughter qualified for a $1,200 award from the university where the taxpayer worked. It was paid to the taxpayer who, in turn, gave it to her daughter to put towards her tuition. The award was scholarship income in the daughter's hands since she had to maintain an annual academic average of at least 70% to receive and retain it. *Okonski v. The Queen*, 2008 DTC 2992 (T.C.C.)

An employee received $300 from her insurance company employer for her success in a series of insurance examinations. The $300 was found not to be taxable. *The Queen v. Savage*, 83 DTC 5409 (S.C.C.), affirming 81 DTC 5258 (F.C.A.), reversing 80 DTC 6066 (F.C.T.D.), affirming 79 DTC 388 (T.R.B.)

► 56(1)(n.1) ◄

(n.1) Apprenticeship grants — the total of all amounts, each of which is an amount received by the taxpayer in the year under the Apprenticeship Incentive Grant program or the Apprenticeship Completion Grant program administered by the Department of Employment and Social Development;

History: S. 56(1)(*n.1*) was replaced by S.C. 2013, c. 34, s. 194(4), applicable for the 2007 and subsequent taxation years except that, for the 2007 and 2008 taxation years, paragraph 56(1)(*n.1*) is to be read as follows:

"(*n*.1) the total of all amounts, each of which is an amount received by the taxpayer in the year under the Apprenticeship Incentive Grant program administered by the Department of Human Resources and Skills Development;"

S. 56(1)(*n.1*) formerly read:

(*n*.1) *Apprenticeship incentive grant* — amounts received by the taxpayer in the year under the Apprenticeship Incentive Grant program administered by the Department of Human Resources and Social Development;

► 56(1)(o) ◄

(o) Research grants — the amount, if any, by which any grant received by the taxpayer in the year to enable the taxpayer to carry on research or any similar work exceeds the total of expenses incurred by the taxpayer in the year for the purpose of carrying on the work, other than

(i) personal or living expenses of the taxpayer except travel expenses (including the entire amount expended for meals and lodging) incurred by the taxpayer while away from home in the course of carrying on the work,

(ii) expenses in respect of which the taxpayer has been reimbursed, or

(iii) expenses that are otherwise deductible in computing the taxpayer's income for the year;

Editorial Note: Research grants do not qualify for the "scholarship exemption" that applies to amounts described in s. 56(1)(*n*).

Related Regulations: Part II.

Related Sections: S. 60(*q*) Refund of income payments; s. 62(1) Moving expenses; s. 63(3), "earned income"; s. 115(2) Non-resident's taxable income in Canada.

Income Tax Folios: *Primary* — S1-F2-C3 Scholarships, Research Grants and Other Education Assistance. *Secondary* — S1-F3-C4 Moving Expenses; S1-F1-C3 Disability Supports Deduction.

Interpretation Bulletins: *Secondary* — IT-257R Canada Council grants.

► 56(1)(p) ◄

(p) Refund of scholarships, bursaries and research grants — amounts as described in paragraph 60(*q*) received by the taxpayer in the year from an individual;

Related Sections: S. 56(1)(*n*) Scholarships, bursaries, etc; s. 60(*q*) Refund of income payments.

► 56(1)(q) ◄

(q) Education savings plan payments — amounts in respect of a registered education savings plan required by section 146.1 to be included in computing the taxpayer's income for the year;

Related Sections: S. 56(1)(*n*) Scholarships, bursaries, etc; s. 146.1(1) Definitions; s. 146.1(7) Educational assistance payments s. 146.1(7.1) Other income inclusions; s. 212(1)(*r*) Registered education savings plan.

Income Tax Folios: *Secondary* — S1-F2-C3 Scholarships, Research Grants and Other Education Assistance.

► 56(1)(q.1) ◄

(q.1) Registered disability savings plan payments — amounts in respect of a registered disability savings plan required by section 146.4 to be included in computing the taxpayer's income for the year;

► 56(1)(r) ◄

(r) Financial assistance — amounts received in the year by the taxpayer as

(i) earnings supplements provided under a project sponsored by a government or government agency in Canada to encourage individuals to obtain or keep employment,

(ii) financial assistance under a program established by the Canada Employment Insurance Commission under Part II of the *Employment Insurance Act*,

(iii) financial assistance under a program that is

(A) established by a government or government agency in Canada or by an organization,

(B) similar to a program established under Part II of that Act, and

(C) the subject of an agreement between the government, government agency or organization and the Canada Employment Insurance Commission because of section 63 of that Act,

(iv) financial assistance provided under a program established by a government, or government agency, in Canada that provides income replacement benefits similar to income replacement benefits provided under a program established under the *Employment Insurance Act*, or

(v) amounts received by the taxpayer in the year under the *Wage Earner Protection Program Act* in respect of wages (within the meaning of that Act);

History: S. 56(1)(*r*)(iv) and (v) were added by S.C. 2009, c. 2, s. 13(2), applicable to the 2003 and subsequent taxation years except that, in its application to the 2003 to 2007 taxation years, paragraph 56(1)(*r*) is to be read without reference to its subparagraph (v).

Related Regulations: 202(2).

Related Sections: S. 56(1)(*u*) Social assistance payments; s. 63(3), "earned income"; s. 110(1)(*g*) Financial assistance; s. 153(1)(*s*) Withholding.

Income Tax Folios: *Primary* — S1-F2-C3 Scholarships, Research Grants and Other Education Assistance; *Secondary* — S1-F1-C3 Disability Supports Deduction.

Tax Window Files: Assistance for laid off XXXXXXXXXX workers, *July 11, 2018*, CRA Document No. 2017-0735991E5; T4A reporting for services provided, *December 23, 2015*, CRA Document No. 2015-0601671E5.

► 56(1)(s) ◄

(s) Grants under prescribed programs — the amount of any grant received in the year under a prescribed program of the Government of Canada relating to home insulation or energy conversion by

(i) the taxpayer, other than a married taxpayer or a taxpayer who is in a common-law partnership who resided with the taxpayer's spouse or common-law partner at the time the grant was received and whose income for the year is less than the taxpayer's spouse's or common-law partner's income for the year, or

(ii) the spouse or common-law partner of the taxpayer with whom the taxpayer resided at the time the grant was received, if the spouse's or common-law partner's income for the year is less than the taxpayer's income for the year

to the extent that the amount is not required by paragraph 12(1)(*u*) to be included in computing the taxpayer's or the taxpayer's spouse's or common-law partner's income for the year or a subsequent year;

Related Regulations: 224; 5500; 5501.

Related Sections: S. 56(9) Meaning of "income for the year"; s. 212(1)(*s*) Home insulation or energy conversion grants.

Interpretation Bulletins: *Secondary* — IT-273R2 Government assistance — General comments.

► 56(1)(t) ◄

(t) Registered retirement income fund — amounts in respect of a registered retirement income fund required by section 146.3 to be included in computing the taxpayer's income for the year;

Related Sections: S. 146.3(5) Benefits taxable; s. 146.3(5.1) Amount included in income; s. 146.3(7) Acquisition of non-qualified investment by trust; s. 146.3(11) Change in fund after registration.

Forms: T2205 — Calculating Amounts from a Spousal RRSP or RRIF to Include in Income for ----.

► 56(1)(u) ◄

(u) Social assistance payments — a social assistance payment made on the basis of a means, needs or income test and received in the year by

(i) the taxpayer, other than a married taxpayer or a taxpayer who is in a common-law partnership who resided with the taxpayer's spouse or common-law partner at the time the payment was received and whose income for the year is less than the spouse's or common-law partner's income for the year, or

(ii) the taxpayer's spouse or common-law partner, if the taxpayer resided with the spouse or common-law partner at the time the payment was received and if the spouse's or common-law partner's income for the year is less than the taxpayer's income for the year,

except to the extent that the payment is otherwise required to be included in computing the income for a taxation year of the taxpayer or the taxpayer's spouse or common-law partner;

Editorial Note: Although the social assistance payment is included in computing income, a corresponding deduction is allowed in computing taxable income under s. 110(1)(*f*).

Related Regulations: 233.

Related Sections: S. 56(1)(*r*) Financial assistance; s. 81(1)(*h*) Social assistance; s. 110(1)(*f*) Deductions for payments.

Forms: T5007 — Statement of Benefits.

Guides: T4115 — T5007 Guide — Return of Benefits.

Tax Window Files: Training assistance for ABE, *August 9, 2016*, CRA Document No. 2016-0644171E5.

► 56(1)(v) ◄

(v) Workers' compensation — compensation received under an employees' or workers' compensation law of Canada or a province in respect of an injury, a disability or death;

Editorial Note: Although the workers' compensation payments are included in computing income, a corresponding deduction is allowed in computing taxable income under s. 110(1)(*f*).

Related Sections: S. 110(1)(*f*) Deductions for payments.

Interpretation Bulletins: *Primary* — IT-202R2 Employees' or workers' compensation.

Cases: Compensation received from the WCB is included in the calculation of income if it is received "in respect of an injury". "In respect of" is to be interpreted broadly and includes pain suffered as a result of an injury. If there had been no injury there would have been no award, and as such the award was to be included in income. *Butler v. The Queen*, 2016 DTC 5034 (F.C.A.)

When the taxpayer was injured at work, she was compensated by her employer (under a collective agreement) rather than from the Workers' Compensation Board (WCB). The portion of this compensation that would otherwise have been received from the WCB was taxable. *Whitney v. The Queen*, 2002 DTC 7145 (F.C.A.), reversing 2001 DTC 423 (T.C.C.).

► 56(1)(w) ◄

(w) Salary deferral arrangement — the total of all amounts each of which is an amount received by the taxpayer as a benefit (other than an amount received by or from a trust governed by a salary deferral arrangement) in the year out of or under a salary deferral arrangement in respect of a person other than the taxpayer except to the extent that the amount, or another amount that may reasonably be considered to relate thereto, has been included in computing the income of that other person for the year or for any preceding taxation year;

► 56(1)(x) ◄

(x) Retirement compensation arrangement — any amount, including a return of contributions, received in the year by the taxpayer or another person, other than an amount required to be included in that other person's income for a taxation year under paragraph 12(1)(*n*.3), out of or under a retirement compensation arrangement that can reasonably be considered to have been received in respect of an office or employment of the taxpayer;

Related Sections: S. 212(1)(*j*) Benefits.

Canadian Tax Foundation: Horner, *Canadian Taxation and Cross-Border Pensions*, 2009 Canadian Tax Journal 4:905–930.

Forms: T4A-RCA — Statement of Amounts Paid from a Retirement Compensation Arrangement (RCA).

Guides: T4041 Retirement Compensation Arrangements Guide.

▶ 56(1)(y) ◀

(y) Idem — any amount received or that became receivable in the year by the taxpayer as proceeds from the disposition of an interest in a retirement compensation arrangement;

Related Sections: S. 214(3) Deemed payments.

▶ 56(1)(z) ◀

(z) Idem — the total of all amounts, including a return of contributions, each of which is an amount received in the year by the taxpayer out of or under a retirement compensation arrangement that can reasonably be considered to have been received in respect of an office or employment of a person other than the taxpayer, except to the extent that the amount was required

(i) under paragraph 12(1)(*n*.3) to be included in computing the taxpayer's income for a taxation year, or

(ii) under paragraph (*x*) or subsection 70(2) to be included in computing the income for the year of a person resident in Canada other than the taxpayer;

Related Sections: S. 212(1)(*j*) Benefits.

▶ 56(1)(z.1) ◀

(z.1) Value of benefits — the value of benefits received or enjoyed by any person in the year in respect of workshops, seminars, training programs and similar development programs because of the taxpayer's membership in a registered national arts service organization;

History: S. 56(1)(*aa*) was renumbered as paragraph (*z.1*) by S.C. 2010, c. 25, s. 9(1), applicable after 2009.

Related Sections: S. 248(1), "registered national arts service organization".

Income Tax Folios: *Primary*— S1-F2-C3 Scholarships, Research Grants and Other Education Assistance.

▶ 56(1)(z.2) ◀

(z.2) Employee life and health trust — the total of all amounts, each of which is an amount received in the year by the taxpayer that is required to be included in income under subsection 144.1(11) except to the extent that the amount was required under subsection 70(2) to be included in computing the income for the year by the taxpayer or other person resident in Canada;

Editorial Note: Amounts received from an Employee Life and Health trust are to be included in the income of the recipient unless they were previously included as rights or things of a deceased taxpayer or their beneficiary. The recipient will receive a deduction for previous employee contributions to the trust.

History: S. 56(1)(*z.2*) was added by S.C. 2010, c. 25, s. 9(1), applicable after 2009.

▶ 56(1)(z.3) ◀

(z.3) Pooled registered pension plan — any amount required by section 147.5 to be included in computing the taxpayer's income for the year other than an amount distributed under a PRPP as a return of all or a portion of a contribution to the plan to the extent that the amount

(i) is a payment described under clause 147.5(3)(*d*)(ii)(A) or (B), and

(ii) is not deducted in computing the taxpayer's income for the year or a preceding taxation year; and

History: S. 56(1)(z3) was replaced by S.C. 2017, c. 33, s. 14(1), deemed to have come into force on December 14, 2012, and formerly read:

(z3) *Pooled registered pension plan* — any amount required by section 147.5 to be included in computing the taxpayer's income for the year; and

S. 56(1)(*z.3*) was added by S.C. 2012, c. 31, s. 11(1), in force December 14, 2012.

Related Sections: 147.3(13.1) Withdrawal of excessive transfers to RRSPs and RRIFs; 147.5(3) Conditions applicable to PRPPs.

▶ 56(1)(z.4) ◀

(z.4) Tax informant program — any amount received in the year by the taxpayer under a contract, to provide information to the Canada Revenue Agency, entered into by the taxpayer under a program administered by the Canada Revenue Agency to obtain information relating to tax non-compliance.

Editorial Note: Paragraph 56(1)(*z.4*) requires a taxpayer to include in income amounts received under contract with the CRA for the provision of information relating to tax non-compliance. This provision was added in conjunction with the launch of the CRA's Offshore Tax Informant Program ("OTIP"), under which the CRA may pay financial rewards to individuals who provide information regarding significant cases of international tax evasion that result in tax assessments of $100,000 or more. Withholding tax may be applied to such payments under s. 153(1)(*s*) or 212(1). A deduction is permitted under s. 60(*z.1*) for any reward amounts subsequently subject to repayment.

History: S. 56(1)(*z.4*) was added by S.C. 2014, c. 20, s. 2, in force June 19, 2014.

Related Regulations: 103(9).

Related Sections: S. 60(*z.1*) Tax informant program; s. 153(1) Withholding; s. 212(1) Tax.

▶ 56(1.1) ◀

(1.1) Application of s. 12.2(11). The definitions in subsection 12.2(11) apply to paragraph (1)(*d*).

History: S. 56(1.1) was not part of the former Act.

▶ 56(2) ◀

(2) Indirect payments. A payment or transfer of property made pursuant to the direction of, or with the concurrence of, a taxpayer to another person for the benefit of the taxpayer or as a benefit that the taxpayer desired to have conferred on the other person (other than by an assignment of any portion of a retirement pension under section 65.1 of the *Canada Pension Plan* or a comparable provision of a provincial pension plan as defined in section 3 of that Act) shall be included in computing the taxpayer's income to the extent that it would be if the payment or transfer had been made to the taxpayer.

Editorial Note: If s. 56(2) applies to include an amount in a taxpayer's income in respect of the transfer or payment of property, the CRA will reduce the transferee's income accordingly, in order to prevent double taxation; see paragraph 13 of IT-335R2 (archived, as it doesn't meet current government web standards). The Supreme Court of Canada has held that, as a general rule, s. 56(2) does not apply to dividends; see the *Neuman* and *McClurg* cases cited below (see "Cases").

History: S. 56(2) was replaced by S.C. 2011, c. 24, s. 10(2), applicable to payments and transfers made after 2010. S. 56(2) formerly read:

(2) *Indirect payments.* A payment or transfer of property made pursuant to the direction of, or with the concurrence of, a taxpayer to some other person for the benefit of the taxpayer or as a benefit that the taxpayer desired to have conferred on the other person (other than by an assignment of any portion of a retirement pension pursuant to section 65.1 of the *Canada Pension Plan* or a comparable provision of a provincial pension plan as defined in section 3 of that Act or of a prescribed provincial pension plan)

shall be included in computing the taxpayer's income to the extent that it would be if the payment or transfer had been made to the taxpayer.

Related Regulations: 7800(1).

Related Sections: S. 56(4) Transfer of rights to income; s. 56(5) Exception for split income; s. 135(4), "payment"; s. 214(3) Deemed payments; s. 246(1) Benefit conferred on a person.

Canadian Tax Foundation: Doobay, *Subsection 56(2) and a Discretionary Trust*, 2013 Canadian Tax Highlights 21(10):8–9; Hoffstein and Lee, *Revisiting the Attribution Rules*, 2012 Ontario Tax Conference 9:1–40; Brown and Wiener, *A Practical Look at the Attribution Rules: Tips and Traps*, 2011 Conference Report 38:1–49; MacNight, *Corporate Guarantee Payment Not a Subsection 56(2) Benefit*, 2005 Tax for the Owner-Manager 5(2):3–4; Rochwerg, *Using Trusts as an Income-Splitting Tool*, 2003 Conference Report 18:1–28; Théroux and Millard, *Trends and Developments in Group Benefit Plans*, 2002 Conference Report 29:1–74; Donnelly et al., *Income Splitting and the New Kiddie Tax: Major Changes for Minor Children*, 2000 Canadian Tax Journal 4:979–1018; Duff, *Interpreting the Income Tax Act — Part 1: Interpretive Doctrines*, 1999 Canadian Tax Journal 3:464–533; Bleiwas, *Income Splitting and the September 10, 1999 Draft Legislation*, 1999 Ontario Tax Conference 14:1–32; Cherniawsky and Toy, *Income Splitting*, 1996 Conference Report 52:1–70.

Tax Profile: April 2012 — Price Adjustment Clauses; February 2010 — Planning With Trusts; August 2009 — Structuring a Services Business; February 2008 — Income Splitting A–Z; May 2006 — Professional Corporations for Physicians and Dentists in Ontario.

Income Tax Folios: *Secondary* — S6-F2-C1 Disposition of an Income Interest in a Trust.

Interpretation Bulletins: *Primary* — IT-335R2 Indirect payments. *Secondary* — IT-362R Patronage dividends; IT-432R2 Benefits conferred on shareholders.

Tax Window Files: Non-cash long-service award and cash donation, *March 5, 2013*, CRA Document No. 2012-0440821E5; Application of 56(2) to discretionary trust, *October 30, 2012*, CRA Document No. 2012-0462891C6.

Cases: The taxpayer orchestrated share transfers under s. 85(1), as part of a legitimate succession plan, to leave shares to his children. The Court rejected the Minister's contention that, based on the FMV of the shares, the taxpayer had arranged the indirect transfer of the shares to his son's corporation for inadequate consideration. He did not confer a taxable benefit to his son's corporation within the meaning of s. 56(2). *Laflamme v. The Queen*, 2008 DTC 4829 (T.C.C.)

An insurance agent deposited his commission cheques in the bank account of a corporation and then drew a salary from the corporation. The commission income was held to be income of the company, and not of the agent, even though this arrangement was in violation of the agent's contract with the insurer. *Wallsten et al. v. The Queen*, 2001 DTC 215 (T.C.C.)

The taxpayer was the controlling shareholder of a corporation which paid dividends to the taxpayer's wife who held non-voting shares. Based on *Neuman v. M.N.R.*, no s. 56(2) dividend reallocations were to be included in the taxpayer's income. *Rao v. M.N.R.*, 99 DTC 413 (T.C.C.)

Management fees paid by a family holding company to the family trust and allocated to the taxpayer's minor children under preferred beneficiary elections were taxable in the hands of the children not the taxpayer. *The Queen v. Ferrel*, 99 DTC 5111 (F.C.A.), affirming 97 DTC 1565 (T.C.C.)

Since the dividends on share capital paid to the taxpayer's spouse by a closely held family corporation would otherwise have remained it its retained earnings and would not otherwise have been obtained by the taxpayer, the indirect payment provisions of ss. 56(2) did not apply. *Neuman v. The Queen*, 98 DTC 6297 (S.C.C.), reversing 96 DTC 6464 (F.C.A.) and affirming 94 DTC 6094 (F.C.T.D.) and 92 DTC 1652 (T.C.C.)

When a company, of which the taxpayer was the sole shareholder, bought a property at the request of the taxpayer's father and sold it to him three years later below its fair market value, the taxpayer's approach in determining the value of the property was not enough to infer a "desire" by him to confer a benefit on his father. *Jones. v. The Queen*, 96 DTC 6015 (F.C.A.)

A taxpayer and his partner owned all voting shares of a company, and their wives each held a number of non-voting common shares. Dividends paid to the taxpayer's wife did not constitute a "benefit" conferred upon her. Her efforts in establishing and operating the company justified the payment. *McClurg v. The Queen*, 91 DTC 5001 (S.C.C.), affirming 88 DTC 6047 (F.C.A.) and 86 DTC 6128 (F.C.T.D.), which reversed 84 DTC 1379 (T.C.C.). See also *Cliche v. M.N.R.*, 86 DTC 1571 (T.C.C.).

▶ 56(3) ◀

(3) Exemption for scholarships, fellowships, bursaries and prizes. For the purpose of subparagraph (1)(*n*)(ii), a taxpayer's scholarship exemption for a taxation year is the total of

(*a*) the total of all amounts each of which is the amount included under subparagraph (1)(*n*)(i) in computing the taxpayer's income for the taxation year in respect of a scholarship, fellowship or bursary received in connection with the taxpayer's enrolment

(i) in an educational program in respect of which the taxpayer is a *qualifying student* (as defined in subsection 118.6(1)) in the taxation year, in the immediately preceding taxation year or in the following taxation year, or

(ii) in an elementary or secondary school educational program,

(*b*) the total of all amounts each of which is the lesser of

(i) the amount included under subparagraph (1)(*n*)(i) in computing the taxpayer's income for the taxation year in respect of a scholarship, fellowship, bursary or prize that is to be used by the taxpayer in the production of a literary, dramatic, musical or artistic work, and

(ii) the total of all amounts each of which is an expense incurred by the taxpayer in the taxation year for the purpose of fulfilling the conditions under which the amount described in subparagraph (i) was received, other than

(A) personal or living expenses of the taxpayer (except expenses in respect of travel, meals and lodging incurred by the taxpayer in the course of fulfilling those conditions and while absent from the taxpayer's usual place of residence for the period to which the scholarship, fellowship, bursary or prize, as the case may be, relates),

(B) expenses for which the taxpayer is entitled to be reimbursed, and

(C) expenses that are otherwise deductible in computing the taxpayer's income, and

(*c*) the lesser of $500 and the amount by which the total described in subparagraph (1)(*n*)(i) for the taxation year exceeds the total of the amounts determined under paragraphs (*a*) and (*b*).

Editorial Note: The scholarship exemption is the total of the three amounts described below but will not reduce the taxpayer's scholarship income below zero or create a loss to use against the taxpayer's other sources of income.

(a) The full amount of a scholarship, fellowship, or bursary received by a taxpayer if, on or after January 1, 2017, it was received by a student (i) in connection with the student's enrolment at a designated educational institution in an educational program in respect of which the taxpayer is a "qualifying student" (as defined in subsection 118.6(1)) (for the taxation years from 2007 to 2016, prior to the repeal of the education tax credit, enrolment must be in a program which entitles the student to claim the education tax credit under subsection 118.6(2)) in the taxation year, in the immediately preceding taxation year, or in the following taxation year, or (ii) in connection with enrolment at an elementary or secondary school.

(b) The lesser of (i) the total amount of scholarships, fellowships, bursaries, and prizes received by a taxpayer for producing any literary, dramatic, musical, or artistic work, and (ii) the total expenses incurred by the taxpayer to fulfill the conditions of the scholarships, fellowships, bursaries, or prizes except for personal or living expenses and reimbursed or deductible expenses. Note that travel, meal, and lodging expenses incurred by an artist meeting those conditions and being away from his/her normal residence would qualify for the exemption.

(c) The lesser of (i) $500, and (ii) the total amount of scholarships, fellowships, bursaries, and prizes included in the taxpayer's income that are not eligible for an exemption under (a) or (b) above. In other words, scholarships, fellowships, bursaries, and prizes qualify for an exemption up to $500 even if they do not qualify for the other two more generous exemptions.

History: S. 56(3)(*a*)(i) was replaced by S.C. 2016, c. 7, s. 6(1), applicable to the 2017 and subsequent taxation years and

(*a*) for the 2016 taxation year, a taxpayer is considered to be entitled to deduct an amount under subsection 118.6(2) in respect of an educational program for the immediately following taxation year if the taxpayer is a "qualifying student" (as defined in subsection 118.6(1)) in respect of the educational program in that year; and (*b*) for the 2017 taxation year, a taxpayer is considered to be a qualifying student in respect of an educational program in the immediately preceding taxation year if the taxpayer was entitled to deduct an amount under subsection 118.6(2) in respect of the educational program for that year.

S. 56(3)(*a*)(i) formerly read:

(i) in an educational program in respect of which an amount may be deducted under subsection 118.6(2) in computing the taxpayer's tax payable under this Part for the taxation year, for the immediately preceding taxation year or for the following taxation year, or

Related Sections: S. 56(1)(*b*) Support; s. 56(3.1) Limitations of scholarship exemption; s. 56.1(4) Definitions; s. 67.1 Expenses for food, etc; s. 118.6(1), "qualifying educational program"; s. 248(1), "personal or living expenses".

Canadian Tax Foundation: Dumalski and Sarabalos, *Are Payments to Research Assistants Tax-Free?*, 2013 Canadian Tax Focus 13(2):11–12; Magee, *Tax Planning for Post-Secondary Education*, 2010 Canadian Tax Journal 2:393–416.

Tax Profile: February 2010 — Employee Scholarship Programs; September 2008 — Scholarships: The Enhanced Employee Incentive.

Guides: P105 Students and Income Tax; RC192 Information for Students — Educational Institutions Outside Canada.

Income Tax Folios: *Primary* — S1-F2-C3 Scholarships, Research Grants and Other Education Assistance. *Secondary* — S1-F2-C2 Tuition Tax Credit; S1-F2-C1 Education and Textbook Tax Credits.

Tax Window Files: Educational Assistance, *July 17, 2018*, CRA Document No. 2017-0735391E5; Scholarship Exemption — Post-Doctoral Fellowship Outside Canada, *Technical Interpretation, Financial Sector and Exempt Entities Division, May 1, 2007*, CRA Document No. 2007-0228871E5; Tuition Assistance Offered to Students, *Technical Interpretation, Financial Sector and Exempt Entities Division, July 18, 2005*, CRA Document No. 2005-0122271E5.

▶ 56(3.1) ◀

(3.1) Limitations of scholarship exemption. For the purpose of determining the total in paragraph (3)(*a*) for a taxation year,

(*a*) a scholarship, fellowship or bursary (in this subsection referred to as an "award") is not considered to be received in connection with the taxpayer's enrolment in an educational program described in subparagraph (3)(*a*)(i) except to the extent that it is reasonable to conclude that the award is intended to support the taxpayer's enrolment in the program, having regard to all the circumstances, including the terms and conditions that apply in respect of the award, the duration of the program and the period for which support is intended to be provided; and

(*b*) if an award is received in connection with an educational program in respect of which the taxpayer is a qualifying student because of subparagraph (*a*)(ii) of the definition *qualifying student* in subsection 118.6(1) in the taxation year, in the immediately preceding taxation year or in the following taxation year (in this paragraph referred to as the *claim year*), the amount included under subparagraph (1)(*n*)(i) in computing the taxpayer's income for the taxation year in respect of the award may not exceed the amount that is the total of amounts, each of which is the cost of materials related to the program or a fee paid to a *designated educational institution* in respect of the program, as defined in subsection 118.6(1), in respect of the claim year.

History: S. 56(3.1)(*b*) was replaced by S.C. 2016, c. 7, s. 6(2), applicable to the 2017 and subsequent taxation years and

(*a*) for the 2016 taxation year, a taxpayer is considered to be entitled to deduct an amount by reason of paragraph (*b*) of the description of B in subsection 118.6(2) in respect of an educational program for the immediately following taxation year if the taxpayer is a qualifying student in respect of the educational program because of subparagraph (*a*)(ii) of the definition "qualifying student" in subsection 118.6(1) for that year; and

(*b*) for the 2017 taxation year, a taxpayer is considered to be a qualifying student in respect of an educational program because of subparagraph (*a*)(ii) of the definition *qualifying student* in subsection 118.6(1) in the immediately preceding taxation year if the taxpayer was entitled to deduct an amount by reason of paragraph (*b*) of the description of B in subsection 118.6(2) in respect of the educational program for that year.

S. 56(3.1)(*b*) formerly read:

(*b*) if an award is received in connection with an educational program in respect of which the taxpayer may deduct an amount by reason of paragraph (*b*) of the description of B in subsection 118.6(2) for the taxation year, for the immediately preceding taxation year or for the following taxation year (in this paragraph referred to as the "claim year"), the amount included under subparagraph (1)(*n*)(i) in computing the taxpayer's income for the taxation year in respect of the award may not exceed the amount that is the total of amounts, each of which is the cost of materials related to the program or a fee paid to a designated educational institution in respect of the program, as defined in subsection 118.6(1), in respect of the claim year.

S. 56(3.1) was added by S.C. 2011, c. 24, s. 10(3), applicable to the 2010 and subsequent taxation years.

Income Tax Folios: *Primary* — S1-F2-C3 Scholarships, Research Grants and Other Education Assistance.

▶ 56(4) ◀

(4) Transfer of rights to income. Where a taxpayer has, at any time before the end of a taxation year, transferred or assigned to a person with whom the taxpayer was not dealing at arm's length the right to an amount (other than any portion of a retirement pension assigned by the taxpayer under section 65.1 of the *Canada Pension Plan* or a comparable provision of a provincial pension plan as defined in section 3 of that Act) that would, if the right had not been so transferred or assigned, be included in computing the taxpayer's income for the taxation year, the part of the amount that relates to the period in the year throughout which the taxpayer is resident in Canada shall be included in computing the taxpayer's income for the year unless the income is from property and the taxpayer has also transferred or assigned the property.

Editorial Note: The closing words of s. 56(4) indicate that the provision does not apply if the property is itself transferred, although in such case the attribution rules of s. 74.1 or 74.2 may apply if the transferee is a spouse, common-law partner or minor child.

Related Sections: S. 56(2) Indirect payments; s. 56(5) Exception for split income; 74.1 [Transfers and loans to spouse or common-law partner or minor]; 74.2 Gain or loss deemed that of lender or transferor; 74.3 Transfers or loans to a trust; 74.4 [Transfers and loans to corporations]; 74.5 Transfers for fair market consideration; s. 82(2) Certain dividends received by taxpayer; s. 212(12) Deemed payments to spouse, etc; s. 251 Arm's length and related persons.

Canadian Tax Foundation: Brown and Wiener, *A Practical Look at the Attribution Rules: Tips and Traps*, 2011 Conference Report 38:1–49.

Interpretation Bulletins: *Primary* — IT-440R2 Transfer of rights to income.

Cases: A financial planner earned trailer fees from mutual fund managers but transferred the right to receive the fees to a corporation. The fees then flowed through a family trust and back to the taxpayer. The fees were included in his income under s. 56(4). Although the corporation had already paid tax on them, there is nothing in the Act to prevent double taxation in these circumstances. *Boutilier v. The Queen*, 2007 DTC 479 (T.C.C.)

Where a doctor incorporated a company to operate a private hospital and paid all fees for medical services to the company and in return received a fixed salary, the income from the professional services was income of the hospital company. The arrangement was genuine, the doctor in effect limited his earnings from the provision of medical services in order to leave the hospital with sufficient working capital. *Campbell v. The Queen*, 80 DTC 6239 (S.C.C.), affirming 79 DTC 5202 (F.C.A.), reversing 76 DTC 6278 (F.C.T74 DTC 6598 (T.R.B.)

▶ 56(4.1) ◀

(4.1) Interest free or low interest loans. Where

(*a*) a particular individual (other than a trust) or a trust in which the particular individual is beneficially interested has, directly or indirectly by means of a trust or by any means whatever, received a loan from or become indebted to

(i) another individual (in this subsection referred to as the "creditor") who

(A) does not deal at arm's length with the particular individual, and

(B) is not a trust, or

(ii) a trust (in this subsection referred to as the "creditor trust") to which another individual (in this subsection referred to as the "original transferor") who

(A) does not deal at arm's length with the particular individual,

(B) was resident in Canada at any time in the period during which the loan or indebtedness is outstanding, and

(C) is not a trust,

has, directly or indirectly by means of a trust or by any means whatever, transferred property, and

(*b*) it can reasonably be considered that one of the main reasons for making the loan or incurring the indebtedness was to reduce or avoid tax by causing income from

(i) the loaned property,

(ii) property that the loan or indebtedness enabled or assisted the particular individual, or the trust in which the particular individual is beneficially interested, to acquire, or

(iii) property substituted for property referred to in subparagraph (i) or (ii)

to be included in the income of the particular individual,

the following rules apply:

(*c*) any income of the particular individual for a taxation year from the property referred to in paragraph (*b*) that relates to the period or periods in the year throughout which the creditor or the creditor trust, as the case may be, was resident in Canada and the particular individual was not dealing at arm's length with the creditor or the original transferor, as the case may be, shall be deemed,

(i) where subparagraph (*a*)(i) applies, to be income of the creditor for that year and not of the particular individual except to the extent that

(A) section 74.1 applies or would, but for subsection 74.5(3), apply, or

(B) subsection 75(2) applies

to that income, and

(ii) where subparagraph (*a*)(ii) applies, to be income of the creditor trust for that year and not of the particular individual except to the extent that

(A) subparagraph (i) applies,

(B) section 74.1 applies or would, but for subsection 74.5(3), apply, or

(C) subsection 75(2) applies (otherwise than because of paragraph (*d*))

to that income; and

(*d*) where subsection 75(2) applies to any of the property referred to in paragraph (*b*) and subparagraph (*c*)(ii) applies to income from the property, subsection 75(2) applies after subparagraph (*c*)(ii) is applied.

Editorial Note: Unlike the attribution rules in s. 74.1 and 74.2, which can apply to low or no-interest loans made to spouses, common-law partners or minor children, s. 56(4.1) can apply to low or no-interest loans made to any non-arm's length persons (e.g., adult children, parents).

Related Sections: S. 56(5) Exception for split income; 74.1 [Transfers and loans to spouse or common-law partner or minor]; 74.2 Gain or loss deemed that of lender or transferor; 74.3 Transfers or loans to a trust; 74.4 [Transfers and loans to corporations]; 74.5 Transfers for fair market consideration; s. 82(2) Certain dividends received by taxpayer; s. 104(1) Reference to trust or estate; s. 212(12) Deemed payments to spouse, etc; s. 248(1), "individual", "trust".

Canadian Tax Foundation: Hoffstein and Lee, *Revisiting the Attribution Rules*, 2012 Ontario Tax Conference 9:1–40; Brown and Wiener, *A Practical Look at the Attribution Rules: Tips and Traps*, 2011 Conference Report 38:1–49.

Tax Profile: February 2010 — Planning With Trusts; February 2008 — Income Splitting A–Z.

Interpretation Bulletins: *Secondary* — IT-394R2 Preferred beneficiary election.

▶ 56(4.2) ◀

(4.2) Exception. Notwithstanding any other provision of this Act, subsection (4.1) does not apply to any income derived in a particular taxation year where

(*a*) interest was charged on the loan or indebtedness at a rate equal to or greater than the lesser of

(i) the prescribed rate of interest in effect at the time the loan was made or the indebtedness arose, and

(ii) the rate that would, having regard to all the circumstances, have been agreed on, at the time the loan was made or the indebtedness arose, between parties dealing with each other at arm's length;

(*b*) the amount of interest that was payable in respect of the particular year in respect of the loan or indebtedness was paid not later than 30 days after the end of the particular year; and

(*c*) the amount of interest that was payable in respect of each taxation year preceding the particular year in respect of the loan or indebtedness was paid not later than 30 days after the end of each of those preceding taxation years.

Related Regulations: 4301.

▶ 56(4.3) ◀

(4.3) Repayment of existing indebtedness. For the purposes of subsection (4.1), where at any time a particular property is used to repay, in whole or in part, a loan or indebtedness that enabled or assisted an individual to acquire another property, there shall be included in computing the income from the particular property that proportion of the income or loss, as the case may be, derived after that time from the other property or from property substituted therefor that the amount so repaid is of the cost to the individual of the other property, but for greater certainty nothing in this subsection shall affect the application of subsection (4.1) to any income or loss derived from the other property or from property substituted therefor.

▶ 56(5) ◀

(5) Exception for split income. Subsections (2), (4) and (4.1) do not apply to any amount that is included in computing a specified individual's split income for a taxation year.

Related Sections: S. 60(*p*) Repayment of apprenticeship incentive grant; s. 120.4(1), "specified individual", "split income".

▶ 56(6) ◀

(6) Child care benefit. There shall be included in computing the income of a taxpayer for a taxation year the total of all amounts each of which is a benefit paid under section 4 of the *Universal Child Care Benefit Act* that is received in the taxation year by

(*a*) the taxpayer, if

(i) the taxpayer does not have a "cohabiting spouse or common-law partner" (within the meaning assigned by section 122.6) at the end of the year and the taxpayer does not make a designation under subsection (6.1) for the taxation year, or

(ii) the income, for the taxation year, of the person who is the taxpayer's cohabiting spouse or common-law partner at the end of the taxation year is equal to or greater than the income of the taxpayer for the taxation year;

(*b*) the taxpayer's cohabiting spouse or common-law partner at the end of the taxation year, if the income of the cohabiting spouse or common-law partner for the taxation year is greater than the taxpayer's income for the taxation year; or

(*c*) an individual who makes a designation under subsection (6.1) in respect of the taxpayer for the taxation year.

History: S. 56(6) was replaced by S.C. 2010, c. 12, s. 4(1), applicable to 2010 and subsequent years. S. 56(6) formerly read:

(6) *Child care benefit.* There shall be included in computing the income of a taxpayer for a taxation year the total of all amounts each of which is a benefit paid under section 4 of the *Universal Child Care Benefit Act* that is received in the taxation year by

(*a*) the taxpayer, if

(i) the taxpayer does not have a spouse or common-law partner at the end of the year, or

(ii) the income, for the taxation year, of the person who is the taxpayer's spouse or common-law partner at the end of the taxation year is equal to or greater than the income of the taxpayer for the taxation year; or

(*b*) the taxpayer's spouse or common-law partner at the end of the taxation year, if the income of the spouse or common-law partner for the taxation year is greater than the taxpayer's income for the taxation year.

Related Sections: S. 60(*y*) Repayment of UCCB; s. 122.5(1), "adjusted income"; s. 122.6, "adjusted income"; s. 180.2(1), "adjusted income".

► 56(6.1) ◄

(6.1) Designation. If, at the end of the taxation year, a taxpayer does not have a "cohabiting spouse or common-law partner" (within the meaning assigned by section 122.6), the taxpayer may designate, in the taxpayer's return of income for the taxation year, the total of all amounts, each of which is a benefit received in the taxation year by the taxpayer under section 4 of the *Universal Child Care Benefit Act*, to be income of

(*a*) if the taxpayer deducts an amount for the taxation year under subsection 118(1) because of paragraph (*b*) of the description of B in that subsection in respect of an individual, the individual; or

(*b*) in any other case, a child who is a "qualified dependant" (as defined in section 2 of the *Universal Child Care Benefit Act*) of the taxpayer.

History: S. 56(6.1) was added by S.C. 2010, c. 12, s. 4(1), applicable to 2010 and subsequent years.

► 56(7) ◄

(7) Idem — (Repealed by S.C. 1994, c. 7, Sched. VII, s. 1(1).)

History: S. 56(1)(*z.3*) was replaced by S.C. 2017, c. 33, s. 14(1), deemed to have come into force on December 14, 2012, and formerly read:

(z3) *Pooled registered pension plan* — any amount required by section 147.5 to be included in computing the taxpayer's income for the year; and

► 56(8) ◄

(8) CPP/QPP and UCCB amounts for previous years. Notwithstanding subsections (1) and (6), if

(*a*) one or more amounts

(i) are received by an individual (other than a trust) in a taxation year as, on account of, in lieu of payment of or in satisfaction of, any benefit under the *Canada Pension Plan* or a provincial pension plan as defined in section 3 of that Act, or

(ii) would be, but for this subsection, included in computing the income of an individual for a taxation year under subsection (6), and

(*b*) a portion, not less than $300, of the total of those amounts relates to one or more preceding taxation years,

that portion shall, at the option of the individual, not be included in the individual's income.

History: S. 56(8)(*a*) was replaced by S.C. 2013, c. 40, s. 25(3), applicable to the 2006 and subsequent taxation years, and formerly read:

(*a*) one or more amounts are received by an individual (other than a trust) in a taxation year as, on account of, in lieu of payment of or in satisfaction of, any benefit under the *Universal Child Care Benefit Act*, the *Canada Pension Plan* or a provincial pension plan as defined in section 3 of the *Canada Pension Plan*, and

Related Sections: S. 120.3 CPP/QPP disability benefits and other CPP/QPP benefits for previous years.

► 56(9) ◄

(9) Meaning of "income for the year". For the purposes of paragraphs (1)(*s*) and (*u*), "income for the year" of a person means the amount that would, but for those paragraphs, paragraphs 60(*v*.1) and (*w*) and section 63, be the income of that person for the year.

Related Sections: S. 248(1), "amount".

► 56(9.1) ◄

(9.1) Meaning of "income". For the purposes of subsection (6), "income" of a person for a taxation year means the amount that would, in the absence of that subsection, paragraphs (1)(*s*) and (*u*) and 60(*v.1*), (*w*) and (*y*) and section 63, be the income of the person for the taxation year.

History: S. 56(9.1) was added by S.C. 2013, c. 34, s. 194(5), applicable to the 2006 and subsequent taxation years.

► 56(10) ◄

(10) Severability of retirement compensation arrangement. Where a retirement compensation arrangement is part of a plan or arrangement (in this subsection referred to as the "plan") under which amounts not related to the retirement compensation arrangement are payable or provided, for the purposes of this Act, other than this subsection,

(*a*) the retirement compensation arrangement shall be deemed to be a separate arrangement independent of other parts of the plan of which it is a part; and

(*b*) subject to subsection 6(14), amounts paid out of or under the plan shall be deemed to have first been paid out of the retirement compensation arrangement unless a provision in the plan otherwise provides.

► 56(11) ◄

(11) Disposition of property by RCA trust. For the purposes of paragraphs (1)(*x*) and (*z*), where, at any time in a year, a trust governed by a retirement compensation arrangement

(*a*) disposes of property to a person for consideration less than the fair market value of the property at the time of the disposition, or for no consideration, (*b*) acquires property from a person for consideration greater than the fair market value of the property at the time of the acquisition, or

(*c*) permits a person to use or enjoy property of the trust for no consideration or for consideration less than the fair market value of such use or enjoyment,

the amount, if any, by which the fair market value differs from the consideration or, if there is no consideration, the amount of the fair market value shall be deemed to be an amount received at that time by the person out of or under the arrangement that can reasonably be considered to have been received in respect of an office or employment of a taxpayer.

► 56(12) ◄

(12) Foreign retirement arrangement. If an amount in respect of a foreign retirement arrangement is, as a result of a transaction, an event or a circumstance, considered to be distributed to an individual under the income tax laws of the country in which the arrangement is established, the amount is, for the purpose of paragraph (1)(*a*), deemed to be received by the individual as a payment out of the arrangement in the taxation year that includes the time of the transaction, event or circumstance.

History: S. 56(12) was added by S.C. 2013, c. 34, s. 194(6), applicable to the 1998 and subsequent taxation years except that, for taxation years that end before 2002, subsection 56(12) is to be read as follows:

"(12) For the purpose of paragraph (1)(*a*),

(*a*) if an amount in respect of a foreign retirement arrangement is considered, under section 408A(*d*)(3)(C) of the *Internal Revenue Code of 1986* of the United States (in this subsection referred to as the "Code"), to be distributed to an individual as a result of a conversion of the arrangement after 1998 and before 2002, the amount is deemed to be received by the individual as a payment out of the arrangement in the taxation year that includes the time of the conversion; and

(*b*) if an individual received an amount as a payment out of or under a foreign retirement arrangement in 1998, or an amount is considered under section 408A(*d*)(3)(C) of the Code to be distributed to the individual as a result of a conversion of the arrangement in 1998, the individual was resident in Canada at the time of the receipt or conversion and the amount is an amount to which section 408A(*d*)(3)(A)(iii) of the Code applies,

(i) the amount is deemed not to have been received by the individual, and

(ii) an amount equal to the amount that is included under section 408A(*d*)(3)(A)(iii) or 408A(*d*)(3)(E) of the Code in the individual's gross income for a particular taxable year is deemed to be an amount received by the individual, in the taxation year that includes the day on which the particular taxable year begins, as a payment out of the arrangement, where the expressions "gross income" and "taxable year" in this subparagraph have the meanings assigned to those expressions by the Code."

SECTION 56.1: Support

► 56.1(1) ◄

(1) Support. For the purposes of paragraph 56(1)(*b*) and subsection 118(5), where an order or agreement, or any variation thereof, provides for the payment of an amount to a taxpayer or for the benefit of the taxpayer, children in the taxpayer's custody or both the taxpayer and those children, the amount or any part thereof

(*a*) when payable, is deemed to be payable to and receivable by the taxpayer; and

(*b*) when paid, is deemed to have been paid to and received by the taxpayer.

Related Sections: S. 56.1(4) Definitions; s. 60.1 Support; s. 118(5) Support; s. 248(1), "amount"; s. 252(3) Extended meaning of "spouse" and "former spouse".

Canadian Tax Foundation: Bateman, *Personal Tax Planning: Marriage Breakdown: A Practical Review of Income Tax Considerations*, 2014 Canadian Tax Journal 4:1109–1131.

Income Tax Folios: *Secondary* — S1-F3-C3 Support Payments.

► 56.1(2) ◄

(2) Agreement. For the purposes of section 56, this section and subsection 118(5), the amount determined by the formula

$$A - B$$

where

A is the total of all amounts each of which is an amount (other than an amount that is otherwise a support amount) that became payable by a person in a taxation year, under an order of a competent tribunal or under a written agreement, in respect of an expense (other than an expenditure in respect of a self-contained domestic establishment in which the person resides or an expenditure for the acquisition of tangible property, or for civil law corporeal property, that is not an expenditure on account of a medical or education expense or in respect of the acquisition, improvement or maintenance of a self-contained domestic establishment in which the taxpayer described in paragraph (*a*) or (*b*) resides) incurred in the year or the preceding taxation year for the maintenance of a taxpayer, children in the taxpayer's custody or both the taxpayer and those children, if the taxpayer is

(*a*) the person's spouse or common-law partner or former spouse or common-law partner, or

(*b*) where the amount became payable under an order made by a competent tribunal in accordance with the laws of a province, an individual who is the parent of a child of whom the person is a legal parent,

and

B is the amount, if any, by which

(*a*) the total of all amounts each of which is an amount included in the total determined for A in respect of the acquisition or improvement of a self-contained domestic establishment in which the taxpayer resides, including any payment of principal or interest in respect of a loan made or indebtedness incurred to finance, in any manner whatever, such acquisition or improvement

exceeds

(*b*) the total of all amounts each of which is an amount equal to 1/5 of the original principal amount of a loan or indebtedness described in paragraph (*a*),

is, where the order or written agreement, as the case may be, provides that this subsection and subsection 60.1(2) shall apply to any amount paid or payable thereunder, deemed to be an amount payable to and receivable by the taxpayer as an allowance on a periodic basis, and the taxpayer is deemed to have discretion as to the use of that amount.

Editorial Note: Although s. 56.1(2) indicates that the court order or written agreement must provide that this subsection and s. 60.1(2) apply, the courts and the CRA have stated that the inclusion of a clause in the order or agreement stating the parties understand that the third-party payments will be taxable to the recipient and deductible to the payer is sufficient in this regard; see, for example, paragraph 3.58 of Income Tax Folio S1-F3-C3.

History: S. 56.1(2), the portion of the description of A before paragraph (*a*) was replaced by S.C. 2013, c. 34, s. 108, in force June 26, 2013, and formerly read:

A is the total of all amounts each of which is an amount (other than an amount that is otherwise a support amount) that became payable by a person in a taxation year, under an order of a competent tribunal or under a written agreement, in respect of an expense (other than an expenditure in respect of a self-contained domestic establishment in which the person resides or an expenditure for the acquisition of tangible property that is not an expenditure on account of a medical or education expense or in respect of the acquisition, improvement or maintenance of a self-contained domestic establishment in which the taxpayer described in paragraph (*a*) or (*b*) resides) incurred in the year or the preceding taxation year for the maintenance of a taxpayer, children in the taxpayer's custody or both the taxpayer and those children, where the taxpayer is

Related Regulations: 6502; Part LXV.

Related Sections: S. 56.1(4) Definitions; s. 60.1(2) Agreement; s. 118(5) Support; s. 248(1), "amount", "individual", "property", "self-contained domestic establishment"; s. 252(1) Extended meaning of "child"; s. 252(3) Extended meaning of "spouse" and "former spouse".

Income Tax Folios: *Primary*— S1-F3-C3 Support Payments.

▶ 56.1(3) ◀

(3) Prior payments. For the purposes of this section and section 56, where a written agreement or order of a competent tribunal made at any time in a taxation year provides that an amount received before that time and in the year or the preceding taxation year is to be considered to have been paid and received thereunder,

(*a*) the amount is deemed to have been received thereunder; and

(*b*) the agreement or order is deemed, except for the purpose of this subsection, to have been made on the day on which the first such amount was received, except that, where the agreement or order is made after April 1997 and varies a child support amount payable to the recipient from the last such amount received by the recipient before May 1997, each varied amount of child support received under the agreement or order is deemed to have been receivable under an agreement or order the commencement day of which is the day on which the first payment of the varied amount is required to be made.

Related Sections: S. 56(1)(*b*) Support; s. 56.1(4) Definitions; s. 60(*b*) Support; s. 60.1(3) Prior payments.

▶ 56.1(4) ◀

(4) Definitions. The definitions in this subsection apply in this section and section 56.

Tax Window Files: Spousal Support payments, *March 28, 2012*, CRA Document No. 2011-0415191E5; Tax Implications on Spousal Support, *March 2, 2012*, CRA Document No. 2011-0405131E5; Support Payments, *February 7, 2012*, CRA Document No. 2011-0426211E5; Retroactive spousal support, *March 18, 2011*, CRA Document No. 2010-0376821E5; Support Amount and Equalization of Family Assets, *Technical Interpretation, Business and Partnerships Division, October 6, 2008*, CRA Document No. 2008-0291251I7; Taxation of Compensatory Payments from France, *Technical Interpretation, Business and Partnerships Division, March 15, 2006*, CRA Document No. 2005-0124911E5; Arrears of Child Support Payments, *Technical Interpretation, Business and Partnerships Division, September 28, 2004*, CRA Document No. 2004-0079801I7; Child Support Payments — Commencement Day, *Technical Interpretation, Business and Partnerships Division, July 13, 2004*, CRA Document No. 2004-0068521I7; Wholly Dependent Person Credit — Divorced Taxpayer Amending Support Amount Retroactively, *Technical Interpretation, Business and Partnerships Division, March 2, 2004*, CRA Document No. 2003-0045921I7.

"child support amount" —"child support amount" means any support amount that is not identified in the agreement or order under which it is receivable as being solely for the support of a recipient who is a spouse or common-law partner or former spouse or common-law partner of the payer or who is a parent of a child of whom the payer is a legal parent.

Editorial Note: The definition effectively means that spousal support amounts must be specifically identified as such in the court order or written agreement; otherwise, they will be considered child support and normally not deductible for the payer or included for the recipient.

Related Sections: S. 56(1)(*b*) Support; s. 60(*b*) Support.

Income Tax Folios: *Primary*— S1-F3-C3 Support Payments.

"commencement day" —"commencement day" at any time of an agreement or order means

(*a*) where the agreement or order is made after April 1997, the day it is made; and

(*b*) where the agreement or order is made before May 1997, the day, if any, that is after April 1997 and is the earliest of

(i) the day specified as the commencement day of the agreement or order by the payer and recipient under the agreement or order in a joint election filed with the Minister in prescribed form and manner,

(ii) where the agreement or order is varied after April 1997 to change the child support amounts payable to the recipient, the day on which the first payment of the varied amount is required to be made,

(iii) where a subsequent agreement or order is made after April 1997, the effect of which is to change the total child support amounts payable to the recipient by the payer, the commencement day of the first such subsequent agreement or order, and

(iv) the day specified in the agreement or order, or any variation thereof, as the commencement day of the agreement or order for the purposes of this Act.

Tax Topics: No. 1702, Income Tax Issues To Be Considered in Negotiating Marriage Contracts.

Forms: T1157 — Election for Child Support Payments.

"support amount" —"support amount" means an amount payable or receivable as an allowance on a periodic basis for the maintenance of the recipient, children of the recipient or both the recipient and children of the recipient, if the recipient has discretion as to the use of the amount, and

(*a*) the recipient is the spouse or common-law partner or former spouse or common-law partner of the payer, the recipient and payer are living separate and apart because of the breakdown of their marriage or common-law partnership and the amount is receivable under an order of a competent tribunal or under a written agreement; or

(*b*) the payer is a legal parent of a child of the recipient and the amount is receivable under an order made by a competent tribunal in accordance with the laws of a province.

Editorial Note: Where s. 56.1(2) or 60.1(2) applies, the "periodic basis" and "discretion as to the use" requirements are deemed to be met.

Related Regulations: 6502.

Related Sections: S. 56(1)(*b*) Support; s. 56.1(2) Agreement; s. 60(*b*) Support; s. 60.1(2) Agreement.

Canadian Tax Foundation: Freedman and Nakonechny, *The Tax Principles of Family Law*, 2012 Ontario Tax Conference 4:1–52.

Tax Topics: No. 1702, Income Tax Issues To Be Considered in Negotiating Marriage Contracts.

Forms: T1157 — Election for Child Support Payments; T1158 — Registration of Family Support Payments.

Income Tax Folios: *Primary*— S1-F3-C3 Support Payments.

Tax Window Files: Lump-Sum Payment for Retroactive Spousal Support, *May 24, 2017*, CRA Document No. 2016-0669271E5.

Cases: Amounts are deductible as support payments if they are an allowance paid on a periodic basis for the maintenance of a former spouse. Payments made at intervals of greater than a year are generally not for maintenance. The payments here were made annually for 5 years, no interest was payable, and the payments could not be prepaid or accelerated. The obligation to pay did not survive the taxpayer's death. The fact the Minutes of Agreement stated the payments were made in full satisfaction of support claims could support the argument they were capital, but that one factor alone should not disqualify the deduction. The payments met the criteria for deductibility. *Blue v. The Queen*, 2016 DTC 1014 (TCC)

The language in the minutes of settlement and the court order left no doubt the payments were support payments. They met all of the indicia of support payments set out in the definition in s. 56.1(4), including that they be periodic and the taxpayer be free to use them as she saw fit. It was irrelevant that the payments were erroneously described as "non-taxable" in the minutes and court order. *McBride v. The Queen*, 2015 DTC 1091 (T.C.C.)

The support payments were specifically for the taxpayer's own personal benefit, the obligation to pay was unconditional, the taxpayer had complete discretion to increase or eliminate some expenses, and she was not required to account for the way she used the payments. The taxpayer had "discretion as to the use" and the full amount of the support payments must be included in her income. *Lemieux v. The Queen*, 2013 DTC 1246 (T.C.C.)

The taxpayer's former spouse agreed to pay her $1,000/week for four years, as consideration for her share of the value of his companies. This was a property settlement between the parties, not support payments, and the amounts did not have to be included in her income. *Maheu v. The Queen*, 2013 DTC 1261 (T.C.C.)

A court ordered the taxpayer to pay increased monthly spousal support retroactive to 2005. Although he paid the retroactive portion in a lump-sum, it was deductible as it reflected a periodic payment obligation. *James v. The Queen*, 2013 DTC 1135 (T.C.C.)

An amount paid under a separation agreement directly to the taxpayer's adult daughter was not a "support amount" since the taxpayer's wife was not the recipient thereof, and had no discretion as to its use. Accordingly, the payments were not deductible. *Larabie*, 2000 DTC 2336 (T.C.C.)

When, instead of making maintenance payments of $700 per month for his wife and three children, the taxpayer provided his wife with monthly cheques of $690 made payable to her landlord, these amounts were deductible since they were limited and predetermined and they represented a certain type of expense which the taxpayer's wife was thereby enabled to discharge. *The Queen v. Arsenault*, 96 DTC 6131 (F.C.A.)

The requirement to include in income the child support payments received by the taxpayer from her former spouse was held not to offend the rights of single custodial parents under the Charter. *The Queen v. Thibaudeau*, 95 DTC 5273 (S.C.C.), reversing 94 DTC 6230 (F.C.A.) and affirming 92 DTC 2098 (T.C.C.)

Under the terms of an agreement, the taxpayer undertook to pay to his former spouse five "maintenance payments" of $10,000 each over a five-year period, with interest to accrue on the remaining portion of the original $50,000 outstanding at the date of each payment. These payments were not deductible as alimony since they were predetermined by the clauses of an agreement whereas alimony payments are spread over an undetermined period. *Champagne v. M.N.R.*, 93 DTC 479 (T.C.C.)

A taxpayer was entitled to deduct monthly payments made to his former wife, even though his obligation to pay was contingent on her using the money to make mortgage and tax payments. She was entitled to dispose of the amounts completely, and derived an economic benefit from them. The restrictions placed on their use did not affect the benefit. *Gagnon v. The Queen*, 86 DTC 6179 (S.C.C.), reversing 82 DTC 6318 (F.C.A.), which reversed 80 DTC 6256 (F.C.T.D.).

SECTION 56.2: Reserve claimed for debt forgiveness

There shall be included in computing an individual's income for a taxation year during which the individual was not a bankrupt the amount, if any, deducted under section 61.2 in computing the individual's income for the preceding taxation year.

Related Sections: S. 80(13) Income inclusion.

SECTION 56.3: Reserve claimed for debt forgiveness

There shall be included in computing a taxpayer's income for a taxation year during which the taxpayer was not a bankrupt the amount, if any, deducted under section 61.4 in computing the taxpayer's income for the preceding taxation year.

Related Sections: S. 80(13) Income inclusion.

SECTION 56.4: Restrictive Covenants

► 56.4(1) ◄

(1) Definitions. The following definitions apply in this section.

"eligible corporation" —"eligible corporation", of a taxpayer, means a taxable Canadian corporation of which the taxpayer holds, directly or indirectly, shares of the capital stock.

History: S. 56.4(1), the definition "eligible corporation" was added by S.C. 2013, c. 34, s. 195(1), applicable to

(*a*) amounts received or receivable by a taxpayer after October 7, 2003 other than to amounts received by the taxpayer before 2005 under a grant of a restrictive covenant made in writing on or before October 7, 2003 between the taxpayer and a purchaser with whom the taxpayer deals at arm's length; and

(*b*) amounts paid or payable by a purchaser after October 7, 2003 other than to amounts paid or payable by the purchaser before 2005 under a grant of a restrictive covenant made in writing on or before October 7, 2003 between the purchaser and a taxpayer with whom the purchaser deals at arm's length.

"eligible individual" —"eligible individual", in respect of a vendor, at any time means an individual (other than a trust) who is related to the vendor and who has attained the age of 18 years at or before that time.

History: S. 56.4(1), the definition "eligible individual" was added by S.C. 2013, c. 34, s. 195(1).

See the application for amounts received or receivable by a taxpayer after October 7, 2003 and for amounts paid or payable by a purchaser after October 7, 2003 in the history note following s. 56.4(1), the definition "eligible corporation".

"eligible interest" —"eligible interest", of a taxpayer, means capital property of the taxpayer that is

(*a*) a partnership interest in a partnership that carries on a business;

(*b*) a share of the capital stock of a corporation that carries on a business; or

(*c*) a share of the capital stock of a corporation 90% or more of the fair market value of which is attributable to eligible interests in one other corporation.

History: S. 56.4(1), the definition "eligible interest" was added by S.C. 2013, c. 34, s. 195(1).

See the application for amounts received or receivable by a taxpayer after October 7, 2003 and for amounts paid or payable by a purchaser after October 7, 2003 in the history note following s. 56.4(1), the definition "eligible corporation".

"goodwill amount" —"goodwill amount", of a taxpayer, is an amount the taxpayer has or may become entitled to receive that would, if this Act were read without reference to this section, be required to be included in the proceeds of disposition of a property included in Class 14.1 of Schedule II to the *Income Tax Regulations*, or is an amount to which subsection 13(38) applies, in respect of a business carried on by the taxpayer through a permanent establishment located in Canada.

History: S. 56.4(1), the definition "goodwill amount" was replaced by S.C. 2016, c. 12, s. 18(1), in force January 1, 2017, and formerly read:

"goodwill amount"—"goodwill amount", of a taxpayer, is an amount the taxpayer has or may become entitled to receive that is required by the description of E in the definition "cumulative eligible capital" in subsection 14(5) to be included in computing the cumulative eligible capital of a business carried on by the taxpayer through a permanent establishment located in Canada.

S. 56.4(1), the definition "goodwill amount" was added by S.C. 2013, c. 34, s. 195(1).

See the application for amounts received or receivable by a taxpayer after October 7, 2003 and for amounts paid or payable by a purchaser after October 7, 2003 in the history note following s. 56.4(1), the definition "eligible corporation".

"permanent establishment" —"permanent establishment" means a permanent establishment as defined for the purpose of subsection 16.1(1).

History: S. 56.4(1), the definition "permanent establishment" was added by S.C. 2013, c. 34, s. 195(1).

See the application for amounts received or receivable by a taxpayer after October 7, 2003 and for amounts paid or payable by a purchaser after October 7, 2003 in the history note following s. 56.4(1), the definition "eligible corporation".

Related Regulations: 8201 Permanent Establishments.

"restrictive covenant" —"restrictive covenant", of a taxpayer, means an agreement entered into, an undertaking made, or a waiver of an advantage or right by the taxpayer, whether legally enforceable or not, that affects, or is intended to affect, in any way whatever, the acquisition or provision of property or services by the taxpayer or by another taxpayer that does not deal at arm's length with the taxpayer, other than an agreement or undertaking

(*a*) that disposes of the taxpayer's property; or

(*b*) that is in satisfaction of an obligation described in section 49.1 that is not a disposition except where the obligation being satisfied is in respect of a right to property or services that the taxpayer acquired for less than its fair market value.

History: S. 56.4(1), the definition "restrictive covenant" was added by S.C. 2013, c. 34, s. 195(1), applicable, subject to the application of section 56.4 to a restrictive covenant granted by a taxpayer before November 9, 2006 (described below) to

(*a*) amounts received or receivable by a taxpayer after October 7, 2003 other than to amounts received by the taxpayer before 2005 under a grant of a restrictive covenant made in writing on or before October 7, 2003 between the taxpayer and a purchaser with whom the taxpayer deals at arm's length; and

(*b*) amounts paid or payable by a purchaser after October 7, 2003 other than to amounts paid or payable by the purchaser before 2005 under a grant of a restrictive covenant made in writing on or before October 7, 2003 between the purchaser and a taxpayer with whom the purchaser deals at arm's length.

For the purpose of a restrictive covenant granted by a taxpayer before November 9, 2006, paragraph (*b*) of the definition "restrictive covenant" in subsection 56.4(1) is to be read as follows:

"(*b*) that is in satisfaction of an obligation described in section 49.1 that is not a disposition."

Canadian Tax Foundation: McDonnell, *Restrictive Covenants: The CRA Clarifies Its Position on Consideration*, 2015 Tax for the Owner-Manager 15(1):8.

"taxpayer" —"taxpayer" includes a partnership.

History: S. 56.4(1), the definition "taxpayer" was added by S.C. 2013, c. 34, s. 195(1).

See the application for amounts received or receivable by a taxpayer after October 7, 2003 and for amounts paid or payable by a purchaser after October 7, 2003 in the history note following s. 56.4(1), the definition "eligible corporation".

▶ 56.4(2) ◀

(2) Income — restrictive covenants. There is to be included in computing a taxpayer's income for a taxation year the total of all amounts each of which is an amount in respect of a restrictive covenant of the taxpayer that is received or receivable in the taxation year by the taxpayer or by a taxpayer with whom the taxpayer does not deal at arm's length (other than an amount that has been included in computing the taxpayer's income because of this subsection for a preceding taxation year or in the taxpayer's eligible corporation's income because of this subsection for the taxation year or a preceding taxation year).

Editorial Note: The income inclusion for amounts received in respect of restrictive covenants effectively overrides the Federal Court of Appeal decisions in *Manrell* (2003 DTC 5225) and *Fortino* (97 DTC 55, affirmed 2000 DTC 6060), which had held that such amounts were not taxable. See "Non-Comp Non-Taxable", in CCH *Tax Topics* No. 1621, April 3, 2003.

Subsection 56.4(2) applies to both amounts received and receivable. If a receivable amount is included under s. 56.4(2), but is subsequently not collected and becomes a bad debt, s. 60(*f*) allows a deduction.

History: S. 56.4(2) was added by S.C. 2013, c. 34, s. 195(1).

See the application for amounts received or receivable by a taxpayer after October 7, 2003 and for amounts paid or payable by a purchaser after October 7, 2003 in the history note following s. 56.4(1), the definition "eligible corporation".

Related Sections: S. 60(*f*) Restrictive covenant; s. 212(1)(*i*) Restrictive covenant amount.

Canadian Tax Foundation: Wen, *Restrictive Covenants and Withholding Tax*, 2018 Tax for the Owner Manager 18(3):10–11; Miazga, *Structuring a CCPC Shareholder's Exit with a Non-Compete*, 2017 Canadian Tax Focus 7(3):9–10; Arkin, *Restrictive Covenants — Selected Issues*, 2013 Atlantic Provinces Tax Conference 7B:1–17; Peters and Al-Shikarchy, *Restrictive Covenants and the Assumption of Liabilities in Purchase and Sale Transactions*, 2013 Ontario Tax Conference 6:1–A9; Woltersdorf and Gislason, *Selected Topics: Purchase and Sale of a Business*, 2013 Prairie Provinces Tax Conference 5:1–49; Kakkar, *Section 56.4 Restricted Covenant Trap*, 2013 Tax for the Owner-Manager 13(4):4–5; Butler, *Restrictive Covenants: A Summary of the Newly Enacted Rules*, 2013 Canadian Tax Focus 3(4):9; Bernstein, *Valuation and Related Tax Issues, Part 1*, 2011 Conference Report 17:1–31.

Tax Topics: No. 2135, Restrictive Covenants — The Final Chapter (For Now) — Part II; No. 2132, Restrictive Covenants — The Final Chapter (For Now) — Part I.

Tax Window Files: Q3 - Restrictive Covenants, *December 2, 2014*, CRA Document No. 2014-0547251C6.

▶ 56.4(3) ◀

(3) Non-application of subsection (2). Subsection (2) does not apply to an amount received or receivable by a particular taxpayer in a taxation year in respect of a restrictive covenant granted by the particular taxpayer to another taxpayer (referred to in this subsection and subsection (4) as the "purchaser") with whom the particular taxpayer deals at arm's length (determined without reference to paragraph 251(5)(*b*)), if

(*a*) section 5 or 6 applied to include the amount in computing the particular taxpayer's income for the taxation year or would have so applied if the amount had been received in the taxation year;

(*b*) the amount would, if this Act were read without reference to this section, be required to be included in the proceeds of disposition of a property included in Class 14.1 of Schedule II to the *Income Tax Regulations*, or is an amount to which subsection 13(38) applies, in respect of the business to which the restrictive covenant relates, and the particular taxpayer elects (or if the amount is payable by the purchaser in respect of a business carried on in Canada by the purchaser, the particular taxpayer and the purchaser jointly elect) in prescribed form to apply this paragraph in respect of the amount; or

(*c*) subject to subsection (9), the amount directly relates to the particular taxpayer's disposition of property that is, at the time of the disposition, an eligible interest in the partnership or corporation that carries on the business to which the restrictive covenant relates, or that is at that time an eligible interest by virtue of paragraph (*c*) of the definition "eligible interest" in subsection (1) where the other corporation referred to in that paragraph carries on the business to which the restrictive covenant relates, and

(i) the disposition is to the purchaser (or to a person related to the purchaser),

(ii) the amount is consideration for an undertaking by the particular taxpayer not to provide, directly or indirectly, property or services in competition with the property or services provided or to be provided by the purchaser (or by a person related to the purchaser),

(iii) the restrictive covenant may reasonably be considered to have been granted to maintain or preserve the value of the eligible interest disposed of to the purchaser;

(iv) if the restrictive covenant is granted on or after July 18, 2005, subsection 84(3) does not apply to the disposition,

(v) the amount is added to the particular taxpayer's proceeds of disposition, as defined by section 54, for the purpose of applying this Act to the disposition of the particular taxpayer's eligible interest, and

(vi) the particular taxpayer and the purchaser elect in prescribed form to apply this paragraph in respect of the amount.

Editorial Note: The exceptions to the s. 56.4(2) inclusion are found in s. 56.4(3). Under s. 56.4(3)(*a*), the amount must have otherwise been included in the recipient's employment income under s. 5 or 6 (see also s. 6(3.1), which can apply to include amounts receivable). The exception in paragraph (*b*), applies where the covenant relates to the recipient's business which is being sold, the receipt is considered proceeds of disposition from CCA Class 14.1 property and a joint election is filed. Under the exception in paragraph (*c*), the receipt is proceeds of disposition of the eligible interest, which may result in a capital gain or loss for the recipient.

History: S. 56.4(3)(*b*) was replaced by S.C. 2016, c. 12, s. 18(2), in force January 1, 2017, and formerly read:

(*b*) the amount would, if this Act were read without reference to this section, be required by the description of E in the definition "cumulative eligible capital" in subsection 14(5) to be included in computing the particular taxpayer's cumulative eligible capital in respect of the business to which the restrictive covenant relates, and the particular taxpayer elects (or if the amount is payable by the purchaser in respect of a business carried on in Canada by the purchaser, the particular taxpayer and the purchaser jointly elect) in prescribed form to apply this paragraph in respect of the amount; or

S. 56.4(3) was added by S.C. 2013, c. 34, s. 195(1), applicable, subject to the election below, to:

(*a*) amounts received or receivable by a taxpayer after October 7, 2003 other than to amounts received by the taxpayer before 2005 under a grant of a restrictive covenant made in writing on or before October 7, 2003 between the taxpayer and a purchaser with whom the taxpayer deals at arm's length; and

(*b*) amounts paid or payable by a purchaser after October 7, 2003 other than to amounts paid or payable by the purchaser before 2005 under a grant of a restrictive covenant made in writing on or before October 7, 2003 between the purchaser and a taxpayer with whom the purchaser deals at arm's length.

For the purpose of a restrictive covenant granted by a taxpayer before November 9, 2006, paragraph 56.4(3)(*c*) applies unless the taxpayer elects, no later than December 23, 2013 [180 days after royal assent], by filing with the Minister of National Revenue an election in writing, in which case paragraph 56.4(3)(*c*) is to be read in respect of the restrictive covenant as follows:

"(*c*) the amount directly relates to the particular taxpayer's disposition of property that is, at the time of the disposition, an eligible interest in the partnership or corporation that carries on the business to which the restrictive covenant relates, or that is at that time an eligible interest by virtue of paragraph (*c*) of the definition "eligible interest" in subsection (1) where the other corporation referred to in that paragraph carries on the business to which the restrictive covenant relates, and

(i) the disposition is to the purchaser (or to a person related to the purchaser),

(ii) the amount is consideration for an undertaking by the particular taxpayer not to provide, directly or indirectly, property or services in competition with the property or services provided or to be provided by the purchaser (or by a person related to the purchaser),

(iii) the amount does not exceed the amount determined by the formula

$$A - B$$

where

A is the amount that would be the fair market value of the particular taxpayer's eligible interest that is disposed of if all restrictive covenants that may reasonably be considered to relate to a disposition of an interest, or for civil law purposes a right, in the business by any taxpayer were provided for no consideration, and

B is the amount that would be the fair market value of the particular taxpayer's eligible interest that is disposed of if no covenant were granted by any taxpayer that held an interest, or for civil law purposes a right, in the business,

(iv) if the restrictive covenant is granted on or after July 18, 2005, subsection 84(3) does not apply to the disposition,

(v) the amount is added to the particular taxpayer's proceeds of disposition, as defined by section 54, for the purpose of applying this Act to the disposition of the particular taxpayer's eligible interest, and

(vi) the particular taxpayer and the purchaser elect in prescribed form to apply this paragraph in respect of the amount."

Related Sections: S. 6(3.1) Amount receivable for covenant.

► 56.4(4) ◄

(4) Treatment of purchaser. An amount paid or payable by a purchaser for a restrictive covenant is

(*a*) if the amount is required because of section 5 or 6 to be included in computing the income of an employee of the purchaser, to be considered to be wages paid or payable by the purchaser to the employee;

(*b*) if an election has been made under paragraph (3)(*b*) in respect of the amount, to be considered to be incurred by the purchaser on account of capital for the purpose of determining the cost of the property or for the purposes of subsection 13(35), as the case may be, and not to be an amount paid or payable for all other purposes of the Act; and

(*c*) if an election has been made under paragraph (3)(*c*), in respect of the amount and the amount relates to the purchaser's acquisition of property that is, immediately after the acquisition, an eligible interest of the purchaser, to be included in computing the cost to the purchaser of that eligible interest and considered not to be an amount paid or payable for all other purposes of the Act.

History: S. 56.4(4)(*b*) was replaced by S.C. 2016, c. 12, s. 18(3), in force January 1, 2017, and formerly read:

(*b*) if an election has been made under paragraph (3)(*b*) in respect of the amount, to be considered to be incurred by the purchaser on account of capital for the purpose of applying the definition "eligible capital expenditure" in subsection 14(5) and not to be an amount paid or payable for all other purposes of the Act; and

S. 56.4(4) was added by S.C. 2013, c. 34, s. 195(1).

See the application for amounts received or receivable by a taxpayer after October 7, 2003 and for amounts paid or payable by a purchaser after October 7, 2003 in the history note following s. 56.4(1), the definition "eligible corporation".

Related Sections: s. 6(3.1) Amount receivable for covenant.

► 56.4(5) ◄

(5) Non-application of section 68. If this subsection applies to a restrictive covenant granted by a taxpayer, section 68 does not apply to deem consideration to be received or receivable by the taxpayer for the restrictive covenant.

History: S. 56.4(5) was added by S.C. 2013, c. 34, s. 195(1).

See the application for amounts received or receivable by a taxpayer after October 7, 2003 and for amounts paid or payable by a purchaser after October 7, 2003 in the history note following s. 56.4(1), the definition "eligible corporation".

► 56.4(6) ◄

(6) Application of subsection (5) — if employee provides covenant. Subsection (5) applies to a restrictive covenant if

(*a*) the restrictive covenant is granted by an individual to another taxpayer with whom the individual deals at arm's length (referred to in this subsection as the "purchaser");

(*b*) the restrictive covenant directly relates to the acquisition from one or more other persons (in this subsection and subsection (12) referred to as the "vendors") by the purchaser of an interest, or for civil law purposes a right, in the individual's employer, in a corporation related to that employer or in a business carried on by that employer;

(*c*) the individual deals at arm's length with the employer and with the vendors;

(*d*) the restrictive covenant is an undertaking by the individual not to provide, directly or indirectly, property or services in competition with property or services provided or to be provided by the purchaser (or by a person related to the purchaser) in the course of carrying on the business to which the restrictive covenant relates;

(*e*) no proceeds are received or receivable by the individual for granting the restrictive covenant; and

(*f*) the amount that can reasonably be regarded to be consideration for the restrictive covenant is received or receivable only by the vendors.

Editorial Note: Effectively, s. 56.4(6) ensures that no amount will be included in an individual's (employee's) income when the individual's employer is sold and the individual provides a restrictive covenant not to compete — provided no consideration is received or receivable by the individual.

History: S. 56.4(6) was added by S.C. 2013, c. 34, s. 195(1).

See the application for amounts received or receivable by a taxpayer after October 7, 2003 and for amounts paid or payable by a purchaser after October 7, 2003 in the history note following s. 56.4(1), the definition "eligible corporation".

Canadian Tax Foundation: Kakkar, *More Problems with Restrictive Covenants*, 2014 Tax for the Owner-Manager 14(4):8.

▶ 56.4(7) ◀

(7) Application of subsection (5) — realization of goodwill amount and disposition of property. Subject to subsection (10), subsection (5) applies to a restrictive covenant granted by a taxpayer if

(*a*) the restrictive covenant is granted by the taxpayer (in this subsection and subsection (8) referred to as the "vendor") to

(i) another taxpayer (in this subsection referred to as the "purchaser") with whom the vendor deals at arm's length (determined without reference to paragraph 251(5)(*b*)) at the time of the grant of the restrictive covenant, or

(ii) another person who is an eligible individual in respect of the vendor at the time of the grant of the restrictive covenant;

(*b*) where subparagraph (*a*)(i) applies, the restrictive covenant is an undertaking of the vendor not to provide, directly or indirectly, property or services in competition with the property or services provided or to be provided by the purchaser (or by a person related to the purchaser) in the course of carrying on the business to which the restrictive covenant relates, and

(i) the amount that can reasonably be regarded as being consideration for the restrictive covenant is

(A) included by the vendor in computing a goodwill amount of the vendor, or

(B) received or receivable by a corporation that was an eligible corporation of the vendor when the restrictive covenant was granted and included by the eligible corporation in computing a goodwill amount of the eligible corporation in respect of the business to which the restrictive covenant relates, or

(ii) it is reasonable to conclude that the restrictive covenant is integral to an agreement in writing,

(A) under which the vendor or the vendor's eligible corporation disposes of property (other than property described in clause (B) or subparagraph (i)) to the purchaser, or the purchaser's eligible corporation, for consideration that is received or receivable by the vendor, or the vendor's eligible corporation, as the case may be, or

(B) under which shares of the capital stock of a corporation (in this subsection and subsection (12) referred to as the "target corporation") are disposed of to the purchaser or to another person that is related to the purchaser and with whom the vendor deals at arm's length (determined without reference to paragraph 251(5)(*b*)),

(*c*) where subparagraph (*a*)(ii) applies, the restrictive covenant is an undertaking of the vendor not to provide, directly or indirectly, property or services in competition with the property or services provided or to be provided by the eligible individual (or by an eligible corporation of the eligible individual) in the course of carrying on the business to which the restrictive covenant relates, and

(i) either

(A) the amount that can reasonably be regarded as being consideration for the restrictive covenant is

(I) included by the vendor in computing a goodwill amount of the vendor, or

(II) received or receivable by a corporation that was an eligible corporation of the vendor when the restrictive covenant was granted and included by the eligible corporation in computing a goodwill amount of the eligible corporation in respect of the business to which the restrictive covenant relates, or

(B) it is reasonable to conclude that the restrictive covenant is integral to an agreement in writing

(I) under which the vendor or the vendor's eligible corporation disposes of property (other than property described in subclause (II) or clause (A)) to the eligible individual, or the eligible individual's corporation, for consideration that is received or receivable by the vendor, or the vendor's eligible corporation, as the case may be, or

(II) under which shares of the capital stock of the vendor's eligible corporation (in this subsection and subsection (12) referred to as the "family corporation") are disposed of to the eligible individual or the eligible individual's eligible corporation,

(ii) the vendor is resident in Canada at the time of the grant of the restrictive covenant and the disposition referred to in clause (i)(B), and

(iii) the vendor does not, at any time after the grant of the restrictive covenant and whether directly or indirectly in any manner whatever, have an interest, or for civil law a right, in the family corporation or in the eligible corporation of the eligible individual, as the case may be;

(*d*) no proceeds are received or receivable by the vendor for granting the restrictive covenant;

(*e*) subsection 84(3) does not apply in respect of the disposition of a share of the target corporation or family corporation, as the case may be;

(*f*) the restrictive covenant can reasonably be regarded to have been granted to maintain or preserve the fair market value of any of

(i) the benefit of the expenditure derived from the goodwill amount referred to in subparagraph (*b*)(i) or clause (*c*)(i)(A) and for which a joint election referred to in paragraph (*g*) was made,

(ii) the property referred to in clause (*b*)(ii)(A) or subclause (*c*)(i)(B)(I), or

(iii) the shares referred to in clause (*b*)(ii)(B) or subclause (*c*)(i)(B)(II); and

(*g*) a joint election in prescribed form to apply subsection (5) to the amount referred to in subparagraph (*b*)(i) or clause (*c*)(i)(A), if otherwise applicable, is made by

(i) in the case of subparagraph (*b*)(i), the vendor, or the vendor's eligible corporation, if it is required to include the goodwill amount in computing its income, and the purchaser, or the purchaser's eligible corporation, if it incurs the expenditure that is the goodwill amount to the vendor or the vendor's eligible corporation, as the case may be, or

(ii) in the case of clause (*c*)(i)(A), the vendor, or the vendor's eligible corporation, if it is required to include the goodwill amount in computing its income, and the eligible individual, or the eligible individual's eligible corporation, if it incurs the expenditure that is the goodwill amount to the vendor or the vendor's eligible corporation, as the case may be.

Editorial Note: Subsection 56.4(7) provides a set of conditions that, if met, result in subsection 56.4(5) applying to a restrictive covenant granted by a taxpayer. Where subsection 56.4(5) applies, section 68 does not apply to deem consideration to have been received or receivable by the taxpayer for granting the restrictive covenant.

Subsection 56.4(7) covers two basic situations. First, it applies where a restrictive covenant is granted by a "vendor" to an arm's length "purchaser" to not provide property or services in competition with the purchaser or a person related to the purchaser in the course of carrying on the business to which the restrictive covenant relates. Generally speaking, the grant of the covenant must relate to the realization of a goodwill amount for the vendor (subparagraph (*b*)(i)) or the disposition of property by the vendor (subparagraph (*b*)(ii)).

The second situation to which s. 56.4(7) applies occurs where the restrictive covenant is granted in connection with a vendor's sale of property or shares in a corporation to an "eligible individual" in respect of the vendor — meaning a person who is related to the vendor and is at least 18 years of age. Generally, the grant of the covenant must relate to the realization of a goodwill amount for the vendor (subparagraph (*c*)(i)) or the disposition of property by the vendor (subparagraph (*c*)(ii)).

The joint election described in s. 56.4(7)(*g*) must be made within the time limits in s. 56.4(13). The due date for the filing if the vendor is resident in Canada is the vendor's filing-due date for the taxation year that includes the day on which the covenant was granted. If the vendor is not resident, the due date is six months after the day the covenant was granted (see s. 56.4(13)). However, the election is deemed to be filed on a timely basis if it is filed by the later of the above date (whichever applicable) and 180 days after the provision received Royal Assent (it received Royal Assent on June 26, 2013). Furthermore, this joint election is not required in respect of a restrictive covenant granted on or before October 24, 2012.

History: S. 56.4(7)(*g*)(i) and (ii) were replaced by S.C. 2017, c. 33, s. 15(3), applicable in respect of restrictive covenants granted after September 15, 2016, and formerly read:

(i) in the case of subparagraph (*b*)(i), the vendor, or the vendor's eligible corporation if it is required to include the goodwill amount in computing its income, and the purchaser, or the purchaser's eligible corporation if it incurs the expenditure that is the goodwill amount to the vendor or the vendor's eligible corporation, as the case may be, or

(ii) in the case of clause (*c*)(i)(A), the vendor, or the vendor's eligible corporation if it is required to include the goodwill amount in computing its income, and the eligible individual, or the eligible individual's eligible corporation if it incurs the expenditure that is the goodwill amount to the vendor or the vendor's eligible corporation, as the case may be.

S. 56.4(7)(*c*)(i)(B)(I) was replaced by S.C. 2017, c. 33, s. 15(2), applicable in respect of restrictive covenants granted after September 15, 2016, and formerly read:

(I) under which the vendor or the vendor's eligible corporation disposes of property (other than property described in subclause (II)) to the eligible individual, or eligible individual's eligible corporation, for consideration that is received or receivable by the vendor, or the vendor's eligible corporation, as the case may be, or

S. 56.4(7)(*b*)(ii)(A) was replaced by S.C. 2017, c. 33, s. 15(1), applicable in respect of restrictive covenants granted after September 15, 2016, and formerly read:

(A) under which the vendor or the vendor's eligible corporation disposes of property (other than property described in clause (B)) to the purchaser, or the purchaser's eligible corporation, for consideration that is received or receivable by the vendor, or the vendor's eligible corporation, as the case may be, or

S. 56.4(7) was added by S.C. 2013, c. 34, s. 195(1), applicable, subject to the applications below, to

(*a*) amounts received or receivable by a taxpayer after October 7, 2003 other than to amounts received by the taxpayer before 2005 under a grant of a restrictive covenant made in writing on or before October 7, 2003 between the taxpayer and a purchaser with whom the taxpayer deals at arm's length; and

(*b*) amounts paid or payable by a purchaser after October 7, 2003 other than to amounts paid or payable by the purchaser before 2005 under a grant of a restrictive covenant made in writing on or before October 7, 2003 between the purchaser and a taxpayer with whom the purchaser deals at arm's length.

For the purpose of applying a restrictive covenant granted by a taxpayer on or before July 16, 2010, paragraph 56.4(7)(*d*) is to be read as follows:

"(*d*) for the purpose of applying subparagraph (7)(*b*)(i) and paragraph (7)(*c*), no proceeds are received or receivable by the vendor for granting the restrictive covenant; and"

For the purpose of applying a restrictive covenant granted by a taxpayer on or before October 24, 2012,

(*a*) subparagraph 56.4(7)(*f*)(i) is to be read as follows:

"(i) the benefit of the expenditure made by the taxpayer derived from the goodwill amount referred to in subparagraph (*b*)(i) or clause (*c*)(i)(A),"

(*b*) subsection 56.4(7) is to be read without reference to paragraph (*g*).

Canadian Tax Foundation: Kakkar, *More Problems with Restrictive Covenants*, 2014 Tax for the Owner-Manager 14(4):8.

► 56.4(8) ◄

(8) Application of subsection (7) and section 69 — special rules. For the purpose

(*a*) of applying subsection (7), clause (7)(*b*)(ii)(A) and subclause (7)(*c*)(i)(B)(I) apply to a grant of a restrictive covenant only if

(i) the consideration that can reasonably be regarded as being in part the consideration for the restrictive covenant is received or receivable by the vendor or the vendor's eligible corporation, as the case may be, as consideration for the disposition of the property, and

(ii) if all or a part of the consideration can reasonably be regarded as being for a goodwill amount, subsection (2), paragraph (3)(*b*), subparagraph (7)(*b*)(i) or clause (7)(*c*)(i)(A) applies to that consideration; and

(*b*) of determining if the conditions described in paragraph (7)(*c*) have been met, and for the purpose of applying section 69, in respect of a restrictive covenant granted by a vendor, the fair market value of a property is the amount that can reasonably be regarded as being the fair market value of the property if the restrictive covenant were part of the property.

History: S. 56.4(8) was added by S.C. 2013, c. 34, s. 195(1), applicable, subject to the application below, to

(*a*) amounts received or receivable by a taxpayer after October 7, 2003 other than to amounts received by the taxpayer before 2005 under a grant of a restrictive covenant made in writing on or before October 7, 2003 between the taxpayer and a purchaser with whom the taxpayer deals at arm's length; and

(*b*) amounts paid or payable by a purchaser after October 7, 2003 other than to amounts paid or payable by the purchaser before 2005 under a grant of a restrictive covenant made in writing on or before October 7, 2003 between the purchaser and a taxpayer with whom the purchaser deals at arm's length.

For the purpose of applying a restrictive covenant granted by a taxpayer on or before July 16, 2010, paragraph 56.4(8)(*a*) is to be read as follows:

"(*a*) of applying subsection (7), clause (7)(*b*)(ii)(A) and subclause (7)(*c*)(i)(B)(I) do not apply to a grant of a restrictive covenant unless the consideration, that can reasonably be regarded as being in part the consideration for the restrictive covenant, is received or receivable by the vendor or the vendor's eligible corporation, as the case may be, as consideration for the disposition of the property;"

▶ 56.4(9) ◀

(9) Anti-avoidance rule — non-application of paragraph (3)(*c*). Paragraph (3)(*c*) does not apply to an amount that would, if this Act were read without reference to subsections (2) to (14), be included in computing a taxpayer's income from a source that is an office or employment or a business or property under paragraph 3(*a*).

History: S. 56.4(9) was added by S.C. 2013, c. 34, s. 195(1), applicable, subject to the application below, to

(*a*) amounts received or receivable by a taxpayer after October 7, 2003 other than to amounts received by the taxpayer before 2005 under a grant of a restrictive covenant made in writing on or before October 7, 2003 between the taxpayer and a purchaser with whom the taxpayer deals at arm's length; and

(*b*) amounts paid or payable by a purchaser after October 7, 2003 other than to amounts paid or payable by the purchaser before 2005 under a grant of a restrictive covenant made in writing on or before October 7, 2003 between the purchaser and a taxpayer with whom the purchaser deals at arm's length.

For the purpose of applying a restrictive covenant by a taxpayer before November 9, 2006, section 56.4 is to be read without reference to subsection (9).

▶ 56.4(10) ◀

(10) Anti-avoidance — non-application of subsection (7). Subsection (7) does not apply in respect of a taxpayer's grant of a restrictive covenant if one of the results of not applying section 68 to the consideration received or receivable in respect of the taxpayer's grant of the restrictive covenant would be that paragraph 3(*a*) would not apply to consideration that would, if this Act were read without reference to subsections (2) to (14), be included in computing a taxpayer's income from a source that is an office or employment or a business or property.

History: S. 56.4(10) was added by S.C. 2013, c. 34, s. 195(1), applicable, subject to the application below, to

(*a*) amounts received or receivable by a taxpayer after October 7, 2003 other than to amounts received by the taxpayer before 2005 under a grant of a restrictive covenant made in writing on or before October 7, 2003 between the taxpayer and a purchaser with whom the taxpayer deals at arm's length; and

(*b*) amounts paid or payable by a purchaser after October 7, 2003 other than to amounts paid or payable by the purchaser before 2005 under a grant of a restrictive covenant made in writing on or before October 7, 2003 between the purchaser and a taxpayer with whom the purchaser deals at arm's length.

For the purpose of applying a restrictive covenant by a taxpayer before November 9, 2006, section 56.4 is to be read without reference to subsection (10).

▶ 56.4(11) ◀

(11) Clarification if subsection (2) applies — where another person receives the amount. For greater certainty, if subsection (2) applies to include in computing a taxpayer's income an amount received or receivable by another taxpayer, that amount is not to be included in computing the income of that other taxpayer.

History: S. 56.4(11) was added by S.C. 2013, c. 34, s. 195(1).

See the application for amounts received or receivable by a taxpayer after October 7, 2003 and for amounts paid or payable by a purchaser after October 7, 2003 in the history note following s. 56.4(1), the definition "eligible corporation".

▶ 56.4(12) ◀

(12) Clarification if subsection (5) applies. For greater certainty, if subsection (5) applies in respect of a restrictive covenant,

(*a*) the amount referred to in paragraph (6)(*f*) is to be added in computing the amount received or receivable by the vendors as consideration for the disposition of the interest or right referred to in paragraph (6)(*b*); and

(*b*) the amount that can reasonably be regarded as being in part consideration received or receivable for a restrictive covenant to which clause (7)(*b*)(ii)(B) or subclause (7)(*c*)(i)(B)(II) applies is to be added in computing the consideration that is received or receivable by each taxpayer who disposes of shares of the target corporation, or shares of the family corporation, as the case may be, to the extent of the portion of the consideration that is received or receivable by that taxpayer.

History: S. 56.4(12) was added by S.C. 2013, c. 34, s. 195(1).

See the application for amounts received or receivable by a taxpayer after October 7, 2003 and for amounts paid or payable by a purchaser after October 7, 2003 in the history note following s. 56.4(1), the definition "eligible corporation".

▶ 56.4(13) ◀

(13) Filing of prescribed form. For the purpose of paragraphs (3)(*b*) and (*c*) and subsection (7), an election in prescribed form filed under any of those provisions is to include a copy of the restrictive covenant and be filed

(*a*) if the person who granted the restrictive covenant was a person resident in Canada when the restrictive covenant was granted, by the person with the Minister on or before the person's filing-due date for the taxation year that includes the day on which the restrictive covenant was granted; and

(*b*) in any other case, with the Minister on or before the day that is six months after the day on which the restrictive covenant is granted.

History: S. 56.4(13) was added by S.C. 2013, c. 34, s. 195(1), applicable, subject to the election below, to

(*a*) amounts received or receivable by a taxpayer after October 7, 2003 other than to amounts received by the taxpayer before 2005 under a grant of a restrictive covenant made in writing on or before October 7, 2003 between the taxpayer and a purchaser with whom the taxpayer deals at arm's length; and

(*b*) amounts paid or payable by a purchaser after October 7, 2003 other than to amounts paid or payable by the purchaser before 2005 under a grant of a restrictive covenant made in writing on or before October 7, 2003 between the purchaser and a taxpayer with whom the purchaser deals at arm's length.

For the purpose of applying a restrictive covenant, an election referred to in subsection 56.4(13) is deemed to be filed on a timely basis if it is filed on or before the later of the day that it is otherwise required to be filed and December 23, 2013 [180 days after royal assent].

Related Regulations: 600(*b*).

▶ 56.4(14) ◀

(14) Non-application of section 42. Section 42 does not apply to an amount received or receivable as consideration for a restrictive covenant.

History: S. 56.4(14) was added by S.C. 2013, c. 34, s. 195(1).

See the application for amounts received or receivable by a taxpayer after October 7, 2003 and for amounts paid or payable by a purchaser after October 7, 2003 in the history note following s. 56.4(1), the definition "eligible corporation".

SECTION 57: Certain superannuation or pension benefits

▶ 57(1) ◀

(1) Certain superannuation or pension benefits. Notwithstanding subparagraph 56(1)(*a*)(i), there shall be included in computing the income of a taxpayer in respect of a payment received by the taxpayer out of or under a superannuation or pension fund or plan the investment income of which has at some time been exempt from taxation under the *Income War Tax Act* by reason of an election for that exemption by the trustees or corporation administering the fund or plan, only that part of the payment that remains after deducting the proportion thereof

(*a*) that the total of the amounts paid by the taxpayer into or under the fund or plan during the period when its income was exempt by reason of that election is of the total of all amounts paid by the taxpayer into or under the fund or plan, or

(*b*) that the total of the amounts paid by the taxpayer into or under the fund or plan during the period when its income was exempt by reason of that election together with simple interest on each amount so paid from the end of the year of payment thereof to the commencement of the superannuation allowance or pension at 3% per annum is of the total of all amounts paid by the taxpayer into or under the fund or plan together with simple interest, computed in the same manner, on each amount so paid,

whichever is the greater.

Related Sections: S. 57(3) Limitation; s. 57(5) Payments to widow, etc., of contributor; s. 212(1)(*h*) Pension benefits.

▶ 57(2) ◀

(2) Exception. This section does not apply in respect of a payment received by a taxpayer out of or under a superannuation or pension fund or plan if the taxpayer made no payment into or under the fund or plan.

▶ 57(3) ◀

(3) Limitation. Where a payment, to which subsection (1) would otherwise be applicable, is received by a taxpayer out of or under a superannuation or pension fund or plan in respect of a period of service for part only of which the taxpayer made payments into or under the fund or plan, subsection (1) is applicable only to that part of the payment which may reasonably be regarded as having been received in respect of the period for which the taxpayer made payments into or under the fund or plan and any part of the payment which may reasonably be regarded as having been received in respect of a period for which the taxpayer made no payments into or under the fund or plan shall be included in computing the taxpayer's income for the year without any deduction whatever.

▶ 57(4) ◀

(4) Certain payments from pension plan. Where a taxpayer, during the period from August 15, 1944 to December 31, 1945, made a contribution in excess of $300 to or under a registered pension plan in respect of services rendered by the taxpayer before the taxpayer became a contributor, there shall be included in computing the taxpayer's income in respect of a payment received by the taxpayer out of or under the plan only that part of the payment that remains after deducting the proportion thereof that the contribution so made minus $300 is of the total of the amounts paid by the taxpayer to or under the plan.

Related Sections: S. 57(5) Payments to widow, etc., of contributor.

▶ 57(5) ◀

(5) Payments to widow, etc., of contributor. Where, in respect of the death of a taxpayer who was a contributor to or under a superannuation or pension fund or plan described in subsection (1) or (4), a payment is received by a person in a taxation year out of or under the fund or plan, there shall be included in computing the income of that person for the year in respect thereof only that part of the payment that would, if the payment had been received by the taxpayer in the year out of or under the fund or plan, have been included by virtue of this section in computing the income of the taxpayer for the year.

Related Sections: S. 212(1)(*h*) Pension benefits; s. 248(1), "amount", "corporation", "registered pension plan", "superannuation or pension benefit".

SECTION 58: Government annuities and like annuities

▶ 58(1) ◀

(1) Government annuities and like annuities. In determining the amount that shall be included in computing the income of a taxpayer in respect of payments received by the taxpayer in a taxation year under contracts entered into before May 26, 1932 with the Government of Canada or annuity contracts like those issued under the *Government Annuities Act* entered into before that day with the government of a province or a corporation incorporated or licensed to carry on an annuities business in Canada, there may be deducted from the total of the payments received the lesser of

(*a*) the total of the amounts that would have been so received if the contracts had continued in force as they were immediately before June 25, 1940, without the exercise of any option or contractual right to enlarge the annuity by the payment of additional sums or premiums unless those additional sums or premiums had been paid before that day, and

(*b*) $5,000.

Related Sections: S. 58(3) Limitation; s. 58(4) Capital element.

▶ 58(2) ◀

(2) Annuities before 1940. In determining the amount that shall be included in computing the income of a taxpayer in respect of payments received by the taxpayer in a taxation year under annuity contracts entered into after May 25, 1932, and before June 25, 1940, with the Government of Canada or annuity contracts like those issued under the *Government Annuities Act* entered into during that period with the government of a province or a corporation incorporated or licensed to carry on an annuities business in Canada, there may be deducted from the total of the payments received the lesser of

(*a*) the total of the amounts that would have been received under the contracts if they had continued in force as they were immediately before June 25, 1940, without the exercise of any option or contractual right to enlarge the annuity by the payment of additional sums or premiums unless such additional sums or premiums had been paid before that day, and

(*b*) $1,200.

Related Sections: S. 58(3) Limitation; s. 58(4) Capital element.

▶ 58(3) ◀

(3) Limitation. Where a taxpayer has received annuity payments in respect of which the taxpayer would otherwise be entitled to make deductions under both subsection (1) and subsection (2),

(*a*) if the amount deductible under subsection (1) is $1,200 or more, he may not make a deduction under subsection (2); and

(*b*) if the amount deductible under subsection (1) is less than $1,200, the taxpayer may make one deduction computed as though subsection (2) applied to all contracts entered into before June 25, 1940.

Related Sections: S. 58(4) Capital element.

▶ 58(4) ◀

(4) Capital element. The amount remaining after deducting from the total of the annuity payments to which this section applies received in a taxation year the deductions permitted by subsection (1), (2) or (3) shall be deemed to be the annuity payment in respect of which the capital element is deductible under paragraph 60(*a*).

▶ 58(5) ◀

(5) Spouses or common-law partners. Where a taxpayer and the taxpayer's spouse or common-law partner each received annuity payments in respect of which they may deduct amounts under this section, the amount deductible shall be computed as if their annuities belonged to one person and may be deducted by either of them or be apportioned between them in such manner as is agreed to by them or, in case of disagreement, as the Minister determines.

Related Sections: S. 248(1), "annuity", "common-law partner".

▶ 58(6) ◀

(6) Pension benefits. This section does not apply to superannuation or pension benefits received out of or under a registered pension plan.

▶ 58(7) ◀

(7) Enlargement of annuity. For the purpose of this section, an annuity shall be deemed to have been enlarged on or after June 25, 1940, if what is payable under the contract has, at any such time, been increased whether by increasing the amount of each periodic payment, by increasing the number of payments or otherwise.

Related Sections: S. 60(*a*) Capital element of annuity payments; s. 248(1), "annuity", "business", "corporation", "registered pension plan", "superannuation or pension benefit".

SECTION 59: Consideration for foreign resource property

▶ 59(1) ◀

(1) Consideration for foreign resource property. Where a taxpayer has disposed of a foreign resource property, there shall be included in computing the taxpayer's income for a taxation year the amount, if any, by which

(*a*) the portion of the taxpayer's proceeds of disposition from the disposition of the property that becomes receivable in the year

exceeds

(*b*) the total of

(i) all amounts each of which is an outlay or expense made or incurred by the taxpayer for the purpose of making the disposition that was not otherwise deductible for the purposes of this Part, and

(ii) where the property is a foreign resource property in respect of a country, the amount designated under this subparagraph in prescribed form filed with the taxpayer's return of income for the year in respect of the disposition.

Related Sections: S. 54, "proceeds of disposition"; s. 66(15), "foreign resource property"; s. 70(5.2) Resource properties and land inventories of a deceased taxpayer; s. 104(5.2) Resource property.

Canadian Petroleum Tax Journal: Foreign Exploration and Development Expenditures — The New Rules, Roch J. Martin, 2001, Vol. 14, No. 1.

Interpretation Bulletins: *Primary* — IT-125R4 Dispositions of resource properties.

▶ 59(1.1) ◀

(1.1) Partnerships. Where a taxpayer is a member of a partnership in a fiscal period of the partnership, the taxpayer's share of the amount that would be included under subsection (1) in respect of a disposition of a foreign resource property in computing the partnership's income for a taxation year if the partnership were a person, the fiscal period were a taxation year, subsection (1) were read without reference to subparagraph (1)(*b*)(ii) and section 96 were read without reference to paragraph 96(1)(*d*) is deemed to be proceeds of disposition that become receivable by the taxpayer at the end of the fiscal period in respect of a disposition of the property by the taxpayer.

▶ 59(1.2) ◀

(1.2) Idem — (Repealed by 1985, c. 45, s. 24(1).)

▶ 59(2) ◀

(2) Deduction under former s. 64 in preceding year. There shall be included in computing a taxpayer's income for a taxation year any amount that has been deducted as a reserve under subsection 64(1), (1.1) or (1.2) of the *Income Tax Act*, chapter 148 of the Revised Statutes of Canada, 1952, in computing the taxpayer's income for the immediately preceding taxation year.

Related Sections: S. 39(1) Meaning of capital gain and capital loss; s. 87(2)(*p*) Consideration for resource property disposition; s. 115(4) Non-resident's income from Canadian resource property.

▶ 59(2.1) ◀

(2.1) Idem — (Repealed by 1985, c. 45, s. 24(2).)

▶ 59(3) ◀

(3) Disposition of resource property acquired before 1972 — (Repealed by 1985, c. 45, s. 24(3).)

▶ 59(3.1) ◀

(3.1) Idem — (Repealed by 1985, c. 45, s. 24(3).)

▶ 59(3.2) ◀

(3.2) Recovery of exploration and development expenses. There shall be included in computing a taxpayer's income for a taxation year

(*a*) any amount referred to in paragraph 66(12.4)(*b*);

(*b*) any amount referred to in subsection 66.1(1);

(*c*) any amount referred to in subsection 66.2(1);

(*c*.1) any amount referred to in subsection 66.21(3);

(*d*) any amount referred to in subparagraph 66(10.4)(*b*)(ii); and

(*e*) any amount referred to in paragraph 66(10.4)(*c*).

Related Sections: S. 104(5.2) Resource property.

Interpretation Bulletins: *Primary* — IT-125R4 Disposition of resource properties.

Tax Window Files: Attribution of Royalty Income From Oil and Gas Property Acquired by Discretionary Trust, *Technical Interpretation, International and Trusts Division, February 7, 2003,* CRA Document No. 2002-012676.

▶ 59(3.3) ◀

(3.3) Amounts to be included in income. There shall be included in computing a taxpayer's income for a taxation year

(*a*) 33⅓% of the total of all amounts, each of which is the stated percentage of

(i) an amount that became receivable by the taxpayer after December 31, 1983 and in the year (other than an amount that would have been a Canadian oil and gas exploration expense if it had been an expense incurred by the taxpayer at the time it became receivable),

(ii) an amount that became receivable by the taxpayer after December 31, 1983 and in the year that would have been a Canadian oil and gas exploration expense described in paragraph (*c*) or (*d*) of the definition "Canadian exploration expense" in subsection 66.1(6) in respect of a qualified tertiary oil recovery project if it had been an expense incurred by the taxpayer at the time it became receivable, or

(iii) 30% of an amount that became receivable by the taxpayer in the year and in 1984 that would have been a Canadian oil and gas exploration expense (other than an expense described in paragraph (*c*) of the definition "Canadian exploration expense" in subsection 66.1(6) in respect of a qualified tertiary oil recovery project) incurred in respect of non-conventional lands if it had been an expense incurred by the taxpayer at the time it became receivable

and in respect of which the consideration given by the taxpayer was a property (other than a share, depreciable property of a prescribed class or a Canadian resource property) or services the cost of which may reasonably be regarded as having been an expenditure that was added in computing the earned depletion base of the taxpayer or in computing the earned depletion base of a predecessor where the taxpayer is a successor corporation to the predecessor;

(*b*) 33⅓% of the total of all amounts, each of which is the stated percentage of an amount in respect of a disposition of depreciable property of a prescribed class (other than a disposition of such property that had been used by the taxpayer to any person with whom the taxpayer was not dealing at arm's length) of the taxpayer after December 11, 1979 and in the year, the capital cost of which was added in computing the earned depletion base of the taxpayer or of a person with whom the taxpayer was not dealing at arm's length or in computing the earned depletion base of a predecessor where the taxpayer is a successor corporation to the predecessor, that is equal to the lesser of

(i) the proceeds of disposition of the property, and

(ii) the capital cost of the property to the taxpayer, the person with whom the taxpayer was not dealing at arm's length or the predecessor, as the case may be, computed as if no amount had been added thereto by virtue of paragraph 21(1)(*b*) or subsection 21(3);

(*c*) 33⅓% of the total of all amounts, each of which is an amount in respect of a disposition of depreciable property of a prescribed class that is bituminous sands equipment (other than a disposition of such property that had been used by the taxpayer to any person with whom the taxpayer was not dealing at arm's length) of the taxpayer after December 11, 1979 and before 1990 and in the year, the capital cost of which was added in computing the supplementary depletion base of the taxpayer or of a person with whom the taxpayer was not dealing at arm's length or in computing the supplementary depletion base of a predecessor where the taxpayer is a successor corporation to the predecessor, that is equal to the lesser of

(i) the proceeds of disposition of the property, and

(ii) the capital cost of the property to the taxpayer, the person with whom the taxpayer was not dealing at arm's length or the predecessor, as the case may be, computed as if no amount had been added thereto by virtue of paragraph 21(1)(*b*) or subsection 21(3);

(*d*) 50% of the total of all amounts, each of which is an amount in respect of a disposition of depreciable property of a prescribed class that is enhanced recovery equipment (other than a disposition of such property that had been used by the taxpayer to any person with whom the taxpayer was not dealing at arm's length) of the taxpayer after December 11, 1979 and before 1990 and in the year, the capital cost of which was added in computing the supplementary depletion base of the taxpayer or of a person with whom the taxpayer was not dealing at arm's length or in computing the supplementary depletion base of a predecessor where the taxpayer is a successor corporation to the predecessor, that is equal to the lesser of

(i) the proceeds of disposition of the property, and

(ii) the capital cost of the property to the taxpayer, the person with whom the taxpayer was not dealing at arms' length or the predecessor, as the case may be, computed as if no amount had been added thereto by virtue of paragraph 21(1)(*b*) or subsection 21(3);

(*e*) 66²/₃% of the total of all amounts, each of which is an amount that became receivable by the taxpayer after December 11, 1979 and before 1990 and in the year and in respect of which the consideration given by the taxpayer was a property (other than a share or a Canadian resource property) or services the cost of which may reasonably be regarded as having been an expenditure in connection with an oil or gas well in respect of which an amount was included in computing the taxpayer's frontier exploration base or in computing the frontier exploration base of a predecessor where the taxpayer is a successor corporation to the predecessor; and

(*f*) 33¹/₃% of the total of all amounts, each of which is the stated percentage of an amount that became receivable by the taxpayer after April 19, 1983 and in the year and in respect of which the consideration given by the taxpayer was a property (other than a share, depreciable property of a prescribed class or a Canadian resource property) or services the cost of which may reasonably be regarded as having been an expenditure that was included in computing the mining exploration depletion base of the taxpayer or in computing the mining exploration depletion base of a specified predecessor of the taxpayer.

Related Regulations: Part XI; Part XII.

Related Sections: 59(3.4) Definitions; 59(3.5) Variation of stated percentage; 59(5) Definition of "proceeds of disposition"; 59(6) Definitions in regulations under s. 65; s. 66.1(2) Deduction for certain principal-business corporations; s. 87(1.2) New corporation continuation of a predecessor; s. 88(1.5) Parent continuation of subsidiary.

► 59(3.4) ◄

(3.4) Definitions. For the purposes of this subsection and subsection (3.3),

"specified predecessor" —"specified predecessor" of a taxpayer means a person who is a predecessor of

(*a*) the taxpayer, or

(*b*) a person who is a specified predecessor of the taxpayer;

"stated percentage" —"stated percentage" means

(*a*) in respect of an amount described in paragraph (3.3)(*a*) or (*f*) that became receivable by a taxpayer,

(i) 100% where the amount became receivable before July, 1988,

(ii) 50% where the amount became receivable after June, 1988 and before 1990, and

(iii) 0% where the amount became receivable after 1989, and

(*b*) in respect of the disposition described in paragraph (3.3)(*b*) of a depreciable property of a taxpayer,

(i) 100% where the property was disposed of before July, 1988,

(ii) 50% where the property was disposed of after June, 1988 and before 1990, and

(iii) 0% where the property was disposed of after 1989;

Related Sections: S. 59(3.5) Variation of stated percentage.

"successor corporation" —"successor corporation" means a corporation that has at any time after November 7, 1969 acquired, by purchase, amalgamation, merger, winding-up or otherwise (other than pursuant to an amalgamation that is described in subsection 87(1.2) or a winding-up to which the rules in subsection 88(1) apply), from another person (in this subsection and subsection (3.3) referred to as the "predecessor") all or substantially all of the Canadian resource properties of the predecessor in circumstances in which any of subsection 29(25) of the *Income Tax Application Rules* and subsections 66.7(1) and (3) to (5) apply to the corporation.

► 59(3.5) ◄

(3.5) Variation of stated percentage. Notwithstanding the definition "stated percentage" in subsection (3.4), where

(*a*) an amount became receivable by a taxpayer within 60 days after the end of 1989 in respect of a disposition of property or services, and

(*b*) the person to whom the disposition was made is a corporation that, before the end of 1989, had issued, or had undertaken to issue, a flow-through share and the corporation renounces under subsection 66(12.66), effective on December 31, 1989, an amount in respect of Canadian exploration expenses that includes an expenditure in respect of the amount referred to in paragraph (*a*),

the stated percentage in respect of the amount described in paragraph (*a*) shall be 50%.

► 59(4) ◄

(4) Determination of "relevant percentage" — (Repealed by 1985, c. 45, s. 24(7).)

► 59(5) ◄

(5) Definition of "proceeds of disposition". In this section, "proceeds of disposition" has the meaning assigned by section 54.

Interpretation Bulletins: *Secondary* — IT-125R4 Disposition of resource properties.

Cases: The taxpayers sold certain coal licences in 1968 and received part payment in 1969. They received the balance in 1977 as a result of a further transfer of the licences. This constituted a disposition of a Canadian resource property in 1977 subject to tax. *De Luca v. The Queen*, 91 DTC 5540 (F.C.A.), affirming 87 DTC 5202 (F.C.T.D.) and 84 DTC 1796 (T.C.C)

► 59(6) ◄

(6) Definitions in regulations under s. 65. In this section, "bituminous sands equipment", "Canadian oil and gas exploration expense", "earned depletion base", "enhanced recovery equipment", "frontier exploration base", "mining exploration depletion base", "non-conventional lands", "qualified tertiary oil recovery project" and "supplementary depletion base" have the meanings assigned by regulations made for the purposes of section 65.

Related Regulations: 1200.

Related Sections: S. 54, "disposition", "proceeds of disposition"; s. 248(1), "amount", "disposition", "property"; s. 255 Canada.

SECTION 59.1: Involuntary disposition of resource property

Where in a particular taxation year an amount is deemed by subsection 44(2) to have become receivable by a taxpayer as proceeds of disposition described in paragraph (*d*) of the definition "proceeds of disposition" in section 54 of any Canadian resource property and the taxpayer elects, in the taxpayer's return of income under this Part for the year, to have this section apply to those proceeds of disposition,

(*a*) there shall be deducted in computing the taxpayer's income for the particular year such amount as the taxpayer may claim, not exceeding the least of,

(i) the total of all those proceeds so becoming receivable in the particular year by the taxpayer to the extent that they have been included in the amount referred to in paragraph (*a*) of the description of F in the definition "cumulative Canadian development expense" in subsection 66.2(5) or in paragraph (*a*) of the description of F in the definition "cumulative Canadian oil and gas property expense" in subsection 66.4(5) in respect of the taxpayer,

(ii) the amount required to be included in computing the taxpayer's income for the particular year by virtue of paragraph 59(3.2)(*c*), and

(iii) the taxpayer's income for the particular year determined without reference to this section;

(*b*) the amount, if any, by which

(i) the amount deducted under paragraph (*a*)

exceeds

(ii) the total of such of the Canadian exploration expenses, Canadian development expenses and Canadian oil and gas property expenses made or incurred by the taxpayer in the taxpayer's ten taxation years immediately following the particular year as were designated by the taxpayer in the taxpayer's return of income for the year in which the expense was made or incurred,

shall be included in computing the taxpayer's income for the particular year and, notwithstanding subsections 152(4) and (5), such reassessment of the taxpayer's tax, interest or penalties for any year shall be made as is necessary to give effect to the inclusion; and

(*c*) any Canadian exploration expense, Canadian development expense or Canadian oil and gas property expense made or incurred by the taxpayer and designated in the taxpayer's return of income in accordance with subparagraph (*b*)(ii) shall (except for the purposes of subsections 66(12.1), (12.2), (12.3) and (12.5) and for the purpose of computing the taxpayer's earned depletion base within the meaning assigned by regulations made for the purposes of section 65) be deemed not to be a Canadian exploration expense, a Canadian development expense or a Canadian oil and gas property expense, as the case may be, of the taxpayer.

Related Sections: S. 66(18) Members of partnerships.

Interpretation Bulletins: *Primary* — IT-125R4 Dispositions of resource properties.

Subdivision e — Deductions in Computing Income

SECTION 60: Other deductions

There may be deducted in computing a taxpayer's income for a taxation year such of the following amounts as are applicable:

Related Sections: S. 61(4), "income-averaging annuity contract"; s. 104(1) Reference to trust or estate; s. 248(1), "amount", "annuity", "assessment", "benefit under a deferred profit sharing plan", "death benefit", "property", "retirement compensation arrangement", "retiring allowance", "superannuation or pension benefit"; s. 249 Definition of "taxation year"; s. 255 Canada.

▶ 60(a) ◀

(a) Capital element of annuity payments — the capital element of each annuity payment included by virtue of paragraph 56(1)(*d*) in computing the taxpayer's income for the year, that is to say,

(i) if the annuity was paid under a contract, an amount equal to that part of the payment determined in prescribed manner to have been a return of capital, and

(ii) if the annuity was paid under a will or trust, such part of the payment as can be established by the recipient not to have been paid out of the income of the estate or trust;

Editorial Note: The deductions in s. 60 serve to reduce a taxpayer's Part 1 income (see also s. 3(*c*)), notwithstanding that the amounts described therein may not relate to a particular source of income.

Related Regulations: 300.

Related Sections: S. 4(2) Deductions not attributable to a source; s. 56(1)(*d*) Annuity payments; s. 58 Government annuities and like annuities.

Income Tax Folios: *Secondary* — S2-F1-C1 Health and Welfare Trusts.

Interpretation Bulletins: *Secondary* — IT-500R Registered retirement savings plans — Death of an annuitant.

▶ 60(b) ◀

(b) Support — the total of all amounts each of which is an amount determined by the formula

$$A - (B + C)$$

where

A is the total of all amounts each of which is a support amount paid after 1996 and before the end of the year by the taxpayer to a particular person, where the taxpayer and the particular person were living separate and apart at the time the amount was paid,

B is the total of all amounts each of which is a child support amount that became payable by the taxpayer to the particular person under an agreement or order on or after its commencement day and before the end of the year in respect of a period that began on or after its commencement day, and

C is the total of all amounts each of which is a support amount paid by the taxpayer to the particular person after 1996 and deductible in computing the taxpayer's income for a preceding taxation year;

Editorial Note: Generally speaking, for orders and agreements made or amended after April 1997, child support amounts are neither deductible for the payer nor included in the income of the recipient; see also the definitions in s. 56.1(4).

Related Regulations: 100(3)(d).

Related Sections: S. 4(1) Income or loss from a source or from sources in a place; s. 4(3) Deductions applicable; s. 56(1)(*b*) Support; s. 56(1)(*c*) Maintenance; s. 56(1)(*c.2*) Reimbursement of support payments; s. 56(12) Definition of "allowance"; s. 56.1 Support; s. 56.1(4) Definitions; s. 60.1 Support; s. 252(1) Extended meaning of "child"; s. 252(3) Extended meaning of "spouse" and "former spouse".

Canadian Tax Foundation: Freedman and Nakonechny, *The Tax Principles of Family Law*, 2012 Ontario Tax Conference 4:1–52.

Forms: T1157 — Election for Child Support Payments; T1158 — Registration of Family Support Payments.

Guides: P102 Support Payments.

Income Tax Folios: *Primary* — S1-F3-C3 Support Payments.

Income Tax Technical News: Issue No. 24, Legal Costs to Obtain Support Amounts.

Cases: Legal expenses are deductible if incurred for the purpose of gaining or producing income from a business or property. The right to support is "property", and income which flows from the exercise of that right is associated with it. Expenses incurred by the payer of support cannot be considered to have been incurred for the purpose of producing income from property. *Grenon v. The Queen*, 2016 DTC 5009 (FCA)

A separation agreement required the taxpayer to pay his former wife, as "lump sum child and spousal support", half of any bonus payments received from his employer. The payments were not deductible as they were not "periodic" or made entirely for his spouse's benefit. *Berty v. The Queen*, 2013 DTC 1171 (T.C.C.)

A separation agreement stating that payments to third parties were to be "taxable as income" in the recipient's hands and "deducted as support" by the taxpayer was sufficient in order for s. 60.1(2) to apply. The separation agreement does not have to specify subsection numbers. *Ferron v. The Queen*, 2001 DTC 450 (T.C.C.)

An amount paid under a separation agreement directly to the taxpayer's adult daughter was not a "support amount" since the taxpayer's wife was not the recipient thereof, and had no discretion as to its use. Accordingly, the payments were not deductible. *Larabie*, 2000 DTC 2336 (T.C.C.)

When, instead of making maintenance payments of $700 per month for his wife and three children, the taxpayer provided his wife with monthly cheques of $690 made payable to her landlord, these amounts were deductible since they were limited and predetermined and they represented a certain type of expense which the taxpayer's wife was thereby enabled to discharge. *The Queen v. Arsenault*, 96 DTC 6131 (F.C.A.)

Pursuant to a judgment of divorce, the taxpayer was required to pay his former wife a $100 weekly alimony but agreed under a subsequent document to pay her $10,000 as "lump-sum alimony" in return for a discharge of his obligations. This lump sum was not deductible as alimony. *Dubreuil v. M.N.R.*, 93 DTC 542 (T.C.C.)

A taxpayer was entitled to deduct monthly payments made to his former wife, even though his obligation to pay was contingent on her using the money to make mortgage and tax payments. She was entitled to dispose of the amounts completely, and derived an economic benefit from them. The restrictions placed on their use did not affect the benefit. *Gagnon v. The Queen*, 86 DTC 6179 (S.C.C.), reversing 82 DTC 6318 (F.C.A.), which reversed 80 DTC 6256 (F.C.T.D.)

▶ 60(c) ◀

(c) Pension income reallocation — where the taxpayer is a pensioner (as defined in subsection 60.03(1)), any amount that is a split-pension amount (as defined in that subsection) in respect of the pensioner for the taxation year;

▶ 60(c.1) ◀

(c.1) Idem — (Repealed by S.C. 1994, c. 7, Sched. VIII, s. 20(2).)

▶ 60(c.2) ◀

(c.2) Repayment of support payments — an amount paid by the taxpayer in the year or one of the 2 preceding taxation years under a decree, order or judgment of a competent tribunal as a repayment of an amount included under paragraph 56(1)(*b*) or (*c*), or under paragraph 56(1)(*c*.1) (as it applies, in computing the taxpayer's income for the year or a preceding taxation year, to decrees, orders and judgments made before 1993) to the extent that it was not so deducted for a preceding taxation year;

Related Sections: S. 56(1)(*c*.2) Reimbursement of support payments.

Income Tax Folios: *Secondary* — S1-F3-C3 Support Payments.

► 60(d) ◄

(d) Interest on death duties — an amount equal to annual interest accruing within the taxation year in respect of succession duties, inheritance taxes or estate taxes;

Related Sections: S. 4(1) Income or loss from a source or from sources in a place; s. 4(3) Deductions applicable.

Income Tax Folios: *Secondary* — S3-F6-C1 Interest Deductibility.

► 60(e) ◄

(e) CPP/QPP contributions on self-employed earnings — the total of

(i) 1/2 of the lesser of

(A) the total of all amounts each of which is an amount payable by the taxpayer in respect of self-employed earnings for the year as a contribution under subsection 10(1) of the *Canada Pension Plan* or as a like contribution under a "provincial pension plan", as defined in section 3 of that Act, and

(B) the maximum amount of such contributions payable by the taxpayer for the year under the plan, and

(ii) the lesser of

(A) the total of all amounts each of which is an amount payable by the taxpayer in respect of self-employed earnings for the year as a contribution under subsection 10(1.1) or (1.2) of the *Canada Pension Plan* or as a like contribution under a "provincial pension plan", as defined in section 3 of that Act, and

(B) the maximum amount of such contributions payable by the taxpayer for the year under the plan;

Editorial Note: One-half of the CPP or QPP amount is deductible for self-employed persons, while the other half is generally eligible for the credit under s. 118.7. Subparagraph 60(*e*)(ii) is amended, effective as of 2019, to allow a deduction for the increased CPP premiums payable under the "CPP enhancement", which begins in that year.

History: S. 60(*e*) was replaced by S.C. 2016, c. 14, s. 66(1), in force January 1, 2019. [Note: Clause 60(*e*)(ii)(A), as enacted by S.C. 2016, c. 14, s. 66(1), was further amended by S.C. 2018, c. 27, s. 34(*a*) before the amendment to s. 60(*e*) entered into force.] S. 60 *e*) formerly read:

(*e*) *CPP/QPP contributions on self-employed earnings* — 1/2 of the lesser of

(i) the total of all amounts each of which is an amount payable by the taxpayer in respect of self-employed earnings for the year as a contribution under the *Canada Pension Plan* or under a provincial pension plan within the meaning assigned by section 3 of that Act, and

(ii) the maximum amount of such contributions payable by the taxpayer for the year under the plan;

► 60(e.1) ◄

(e.1) Enhanced CPP contributions — the lesser of

(i) the total of all amounts each of which is an amount payable by the taxpayer for the year as an employee's contribution under subsection 8(1.1) or (1.2) of the *Canada Pension Plan* or as a like contribution under a "provincial pension plan", as defined in section 3 of that Act, and

(ii) the maximum amount of such contributions payable by the taxpayer for the year under the plan;

Editorial Note: Beginning in 2019, the CPP is being enhanced and funded with increased CPP contributions. Paragraph 60(*e*.1) provides that employee contributions to the enhanced portion of the CPP will be deductible.

History: S. 60(*e*.1) was added by S.C. 2016, c. 14, s. 66(1), in force January 1, 2019. [Note: Clause 60(*e*.1)(i), as enacted by S.C. 2016, c. 14, s. 66(1), was further amended by S.C. 2018, c. 27, s. 34(*b*) before new paragraph 60(*e*.1) entered into force.]

► 60(f) ◄

(f) Restrictive covenant — bad debt — all debts owing to a taxpayer that are established by the taxpayer to have become bad debts in the taxation year and that are in respect of an amount included because of the operation of subsection 6(3.1) or 56.4(2) in computing the taxpayer's income in a preceding taxation year;

Related Sections: S. 56(1)(*m*) Bad debt recovered.

► 60(g) ◄

(g) Quebec parental insurance plan — self-employed premiums — the amount determined by the formula

$$A - B$$

where

A is the total of all amounts each of which is an amount payable by the taxpayer in respect of self-employed earnings for the taxation year as a premium under the *Act respecting parental insurance*, R.S.Q., c. A-29.011, and

B is the total of all amounts each of which is an amount that would be payable by the taxpayer as an employee's premium under the *Act respecting parental insurance*, R.S.Q., c. A-29.011, if those earnings were employment income of the taxpayer for the taxation year;

History: S. 60(*g*) was added by S.C. 2013, c. 34, s. 196(1), applicable to the 2006 and subsequent taxation years.

► 60(h) ◄

(h) Canada Pension Plan contributions — (Repealed by 1988, c. 55, s. 37(2).)

► 60(i) ◄

(i) Premium or payment under RRSP or RRIF — any amount that is deductible under section 146 or 146.3 or subsection 147.3(13.1) in computing the income of the taxpayer for the year;

History: S. 60(*l*) was replaced by S.C. 2009, c. 2, s. 14(1), applicable in respect of a registered retirement income fund in respect of which the last payment out of the fund is made after 2008. S. 60(*l*) formerly read:

(*l*) *Premium or payment under RRSP or RRIF* — any amount that is deductible under section 146 or subsection 147.3(13.1) in computing the income of the taxpayer for the year;

Related Sections: S. 4(1) Income or loss from a source or from sources in a place; s. 4(3) Deductions applicable; s. 146 Registered retirement savings plans.

Interpretation Bulletins: *Secondary* — IT-124R6 Contributions to registered retirement savings plans.

► 60(j) ◄

(j) Transfer of superannuation benefits — such part of the total of all amounts each of which is

(i) a superannuation or pension benefit (other than any amount in respect of the benefit that is deducted in computing the taxable income of the taxpayer for a taxation year because of subparagraph 110(1)(*f*)(i) or a benefit that is part of a series of periodic payments) payable out of or under a pension plan that is not a registered pension plan, attributable to services rendered by the taxpayer or a spouse or common-law partner or former spouse or common-law partner of the taxpayer in a period throughout which that person was not resident in Canada, and included in computing the income of the taxpayer for the year because of subparagraph 56(1)(*a*)(i), or

(ii) an eligible amount in respect of the taxpayer for the year under section 60.01, subsection 104(27) or (27.1) or paragraph 147(10.2)(*d*),

as

(iii) is designated by the taxpayer in the taxpayer's return of income under this Part for the year, and

(iv) does not exceed the total of all amounts each of which is an amount paid by the taxpayer in the year or within 60 days after the end of the year

(A) as a contribution to or under a registered pension plan for the taxpayer's benefit, other than the portion thereof deductible under paragraph 8(1)(*m*) in computing the taxpayer's income for the year, or

(B) as a premium (within the meaning assigned by subsection 146(1)) under a registered retirement savings plan under which the taxpayer is the annuitant (within the meaning assigned by subsection 146(1)), other than the portion thereof designated for a taxation year for the purposes of paragraph (*l*),

to the extent that the amount was not deducted in computing the taxpayer's income for a preceding taxation year;

Related Sections: S. 8(1)(*m*) Employee's registered pension plan contributions; s. 8(8) Employees' contributions to pension fund for arrears; s. 56(1)(*a*) Pension benefits, unemployment insurance benefits, etc.; s. 60(*k*) Transfers to deferred profit sharing plans; s. 60.01 Eligible amount; s. 61 Payment made as consideration for income-averaging annuity; s. 104(27) Pension benefits; s. 146(5) Amount of RRSP premiums deductible; s. 146(22) Deemed payment of RRSP premiums and provincial pension plan contributions; s. 146.01(1), "excluded premium"; s. 146.02(1), "excluded premium"; s. 147(10) Amounts received taxable; s. 147.3(3) Transfer — defined benefit to defined benefit; s. 147.3(8) Transfer where money purchase plan replaces defined benefit plan; s. 147.5(11) Member contributions; s. 212(1)(*h*) Pension benefits; s. 248(1), "common-law partner"; s. 252(3) Extended meaning of "spouse" and "former spouse"; ITAR, s. 40(3) Determination of amount of payment.

Canadian Tax Foundation: Tollstam, *Foreign Tax Credit on 401(k) Transfer to RRSP*, 2016 Canadian Tax Highlights 24(1):6-7.

Interpretation Bulletins: *Primary* — IT-528 Transfers of funds between registered plans. *Secondary* — IT-124R6 Contributions to registered retirement savings plans; IT-167R6 Registered pension plans — Employee's contributions.

Tax Window Files: Transfer from an IRA to a RRSP, *October 29, 2018*, CRA Document No. 2018-0750411E5; Foreign Tax Credit on Transfer of 401(k) to RRSP, *15XXXX*, CRA Document No. 2015-0572541R3.

► 60(j.01) ◄

(j.01) Transfer of surplus — such part of the total of all amounts each of which is an amount received by the taxpayer before March 28, 1988 that can reasonably be considered to be a payment in respect of the actuarial surplus under a defined benefit provision (within the meaning assigned by subsection 147.1(1)) of a registered pension plan and that is included in computing the income of the taxpayer for the year by virtue of subparagraph 56(1)(*a*)(i) (other than any portion thereof deducted by the taxpayer under subsection 60.2(1) in computing the taxpayer's income for the year) as

(i) is designated by the taxpayer in the taxpayer's return of income under this Part for the year, and

(ii) does not exceed the total of all amounts each of which as an amount paid by the taxpayer in the year or within 60 days after the end of the year

(A) as a contribution to or under a registered pension plan for the taxpayer's benefit, other than the portion thereof deductible under paragraph (*j*) or (*j*.1) or 8(1)(*m*) of this Act or paragraph 8(1)(*m*.1) of the *Income Tax Act*, chapter 148 of the Revised Statutes of Canada, 1952, in computing the taxpayer's income for the year, or

(B) as a premium (within the meaning assigned by subsection 146(1)) under a registered retirement savings plan under which the taxpayer is the annuitant (within the meaning assigned by subsection 146(1)), other than the portion thereof that has been designated for the purposes of paragraph (*j*), (*j*.1) or (*l*),

to the extent that it was not deducted in computing the taxpayer's income for a preceding taxation year;

► 60(j.02) ◄

(j.02) Payment to registered pension plan — an amount equal to the lesser of

(i) the total of

(A) all contributions made in the year by the taxpayer to registered pension plans in respect of eligible service of the taxpayer before 1990 under the plans, where the taxpayer was obliged under the terms of an agreement in writing entered into before March 28, 1988 to make the contributions, and

(B) all amounts each of which is an amount paid in the year by the taxpayer to a registered pension plan as

(I) a repayment under a prescribed statutory provision of an amount received from the plan that was included under subsection 56(1) in computing the taxpayer's income for a taxation year ending before 1990, where the taxpayer was obliged as a consequence of a written election made before March 28, 1988 to make the repayment, or

(II) interest in respect of a repayment referred to in subclause (I),

other than the portion of that total that is deductible under paragraph 8(1)(*m*) or paragraph (*j*.03) in computing the taxpayer's income for the year, and

(ii) the total of all amounts each of which is an amount paid out of or under a registered pension plan as part of a series of periodic payments and included under subsection 56(1) in computing the taxpayer's income for the year, other than the portion of that total that can reasonably be considered to have been designated by the taxpayer for the purpose of paragraph (*j*.2);

Related Regulations: S. 6503.

Related Sections: S. 56(1)(*a*) Pension benefits, unemployment insurance benefits, etc.; s. 248(1), "amount", "registered pension plan".

► 60(j.03) ◄

(j.03) Repayments of pre-1990 pension benefits — an amount equal to the lesser of

(i) the total of all amounts each of which is an amount paid in the year or a preceding taxation year by the taxpayer to a registered pension plan that was not deductible in computing the taxpayer's income for a preceding taxation year and that was paid as

(A) a repayment under a prescribed statutory provision of an amount received from the plan that was included under subsection 56(1) in computing the taxpayer's income for a taxation year ending before 1990, or

(B) interest in respect of a repayment referred to in clause (A), and

(ii) the amount, if any, by which $3,500 exceeds the amount deducted under paragraph 8(1)(*m*) in computing the taxpayer's income for the year;

Related Regulations: S. 6503.

Related Sections: S. 56(1)(*a*) Pension benefits, unemployment insurance benefits, etc.; s. 248(1), "amount", "registered pension plan".

► 60(j.04) ◄

(j.04) Repayments of post-1989 pension benefits — the total of all amounts each of which is an amount paid in the year by the taxpayer to a registered pension plan as

(i) a repayment under a prescribed statutory provision of an amount received from the plan that

(A) was included under subsection 56(1) in computing the taxpayer's income for a taxation year ending after 1989, and

(B) can reasonably be considered not to have been designated by the taxpayer for the purpose of paragraph (*j*.2), or

(ii) interest in respect of a repayment referred to in subparagraph (i),

except to the extent that the total was deductible under paragraph 8(1)(*m*) in computing the taxpayer's income for the year;

Related Regulations: S. 6503.

Related Sections: S. 56(1)(*a*) Pension benefits, unemployment insurance benefits, etc.; s. 248(1), "amount", "registered pension plan".

► 60(j.1) ◄

(j.1) Transfer of retiring allowances — such part of the total of all amounts each of which is an amount paid to the taxpayer by an employer, or under a retirement compensation arrangement to which the employer has contributed, as a retiring allowance and included in computing the taxpayer's income for the year by virtue of subparagraph 56(1)(*a*)(ii) or paragraph 56(1)(*x*) as

(i) is designated by the taxpayer in the taxpayer's return of income under this Part for the year,

(ii) does not exceed the amount, if any, by which the total of

(A) $2,000 multiplied by the number of years before 1996 during which the employee or former employee in respect of whom the payment was made (in this paragraph referred to as the "retiree") was employed by the employer or a person related to the employer, and

(B) $1,500 multiplied by the number by which the number of years before 1989 described in clause (A) exceeds the number that can reasonably be regarded as the equivalent number of years before 1989 in respect of which employer contributions under either a pension plan or a deferred profit sharing plan of the employer or a person related to the employer had vested in the retiree at the time of the payment

exceeds the total of

(C) all amounts deducted under this paragraph in respect of amounts paid before the year in respect of the retiree

(I) by the employer or a person related to the employer, or

(II) under a retirement compensation arrangement to which the employer or a person related to the employer has contributed,

(C.1) all other amounts deducted under this paragraph for the year in respect of amounts paid in the year in respect of the retiree

(I) by a person related to the employer, or

(II) under a retirement compensation arrangement to which a person related to the employer has contributed, and

(D) all amounts deducted under paragraph (*t*) in computing the retiree's income for the year in respect of a retirement compensation arrangement to which the employer or a person related to the employer has contributed, and

(iii) does not exceed the total of all amounts each of which is an amount paid by the taxpayer in the year or within 60 days after the end of the year in respect of the amount so designated

(A) as a contribution to or under a registered pension plan, other than the portion thereof deductible under paragraph (*j*) or 8(1)(*m*) in computing the taxpayer's income for the year, or

(B) as a premium (within the meaning assigned by section 146) under a registered retirement savings plan under which the taxpayer is the annuitant (within the meaning assigned by section 146), other than the portion thereof that has been designated for the purposes of paragraph (*j*) or (*l*),

to the extent that it was not deducted in computing the taxpayer's income for a preceding taxation year

and for the purposes of this paragraph, "person related to the employer" includes

(iv) any person whose business was acquired or continued by the employer, and

(v) a previous employer of the retiree whose service therewith is recognized in determining the retiree's pension benefits;

Editorial Note: The deduction for retiring allowances transferred to a registered pension plan or RRSP does not apply in respect of years of employment after 1995.

Related Regulations: 100(3)(c).

Related Sections: S. 146(22) Deemed payment of RRSP premiums and provincial pension plan contributions; s. 146.01(1), "excluded premium"; s. 146.02(1), "excluded premium"; s. 147.5(11) Member contributions; s. 212(1)(*j*.1) Retiring allowances; s. 248(1), "retiring allowance".

Canadian Tax Foundation: Belley, *Owner-Manager Compensation 4: Retiring Allowances*, 2002 Tax for the Owner-Manager 2(2):13–14.

Tax Profile: November 2009 — Purchase and Sale of a Canadian Business.

Income Tax Folios: *Primary* — S2-F1-C2 Retiring Allowances.

Interpretation Bulletins: *Secondary* — IT-124R6 Contributions to registered retirement savings plans; IT-167R6 Registered pension plans — Employee's contributions.

Cases: Where a taxpayer engineered a corporate reorganization and then continued to do exactly the same work as before, he could not deduct a "retiring allowance". *Lorenzen v. The Queen*, 81 DTC 5251 (F.C.T.D.).

► 60(j.2) ◄

(j.2) Transfer to spousal RRSP — for taxation years ending after 1988 and before 1995, such part of the total of all amounts (other than amounts paid out of or under a registered retirement savings plan or a registered retirement income fund that by reason of section 254 are considered to be amounts paid out of or under a registered pension plan) paid on a periodic basis out of or under a registered pension plan or a deferred profit sharing plan and included, by reason of subsection 56(1), in computing the taxpayer's income for the year as

(i) is designated by the taxpayer in the taxpayer's return of income under this Part for the year, and

(ii) does not exceed the least of

(A) $6,000,

(B) the amount, if any, by which that total exceeds the part of that total designated for the year for the purposes of paragraph (*j*) of this Act or deducted under paragraph 60(*k*) of the *Income Tax Act*, chapter 148 of the Revised Statutes of Canada, 1952, in computing the taxpayer's income for the year, and

(C) the total of all amounts each of which is paid by the taxpayer in the year or within 60 days after the end of the year as a premium (within the meaning assigned by subsection 146(1)) under a registered retirement savings plan under which the taxpayer's spouse or common-law partner (or, where the taxpayer died in the year or within 60 days after the end of the year, an individual who was the taxpayer's spouse or common-law partner immediately before the death) is the annuitant (within the meaning assigned by subsection 146(1)), to the extent that the amount was not deducted in computing the taxpayer's income for a preceding taxation year;

Related Sections: S. 146.01(1), "excluded premium"; s. 212(1)(*h*) Pension benefits; s. 212(1)(*m*) Deferred profit sharing plan payments.

Interpretation Bulletins: *Secondary* — IT-307R4 Spousal or common-law partner registered retirement savings plans.

► 60(k) ◄

(k) Transfers to deferred profit sharing plans — (Repealed by 1990, c. 35, s. 5(5).)

► 60(l) ◄

(l) Transfer of refund of premiums under RRSP — the total of all amounts each of which is an amount paid by or on behalf of the taxpayer in the year or within 60 days after the end of the year (or within such longer period after the end of the year as is acceptable to the Minister)

(i) as a premium under a registered retirement savings plan under which the taxpayer is the annuitant,

(ii) to acquire, from a person licensed or otherwise authorized under the laws of Canada or a province to carry on in Canada an annuities business, an annuity

(A) under which the taxpayer is the annuitant

(I) for the taxpayer's life, or for the lives jointly of the taxpayer and the taxpayer's spouse or common-law partner either without a guaranteed period, or with a guaranteed period that is not greater than 90 years minus the lesser of the age in whole years of the taxpayer and the age in whole years of the taxpayer's spouse or common-law partner at the time the annuity was acquired, or

(II) for a term equal to 90 years minus the age in whole years of the taxpayer or the age in whole years of the taxpayer's spouse or common-law partner, at the time the annuity was acquired, or

(B) under which the taxpayer is the annuitant for a term not exceeding 18 years minus the age in whole years of the taxpayer at the time the annuity was acquired

that does not provide for any payment thereunder except

(C) the single payment by or on behalf of the taxpayer,

(D) annual or more frequent periodic payments

(I) beginning not later than one year after the date of the payment referred to in clause (C), and

(II) each of which is equal to all other such payments or not equal to all other such payments solely because of an adjustment that would, if the annuity were an annuity under a retirement savings plan, be in accordance with subparagraphs 146(3)(*b*)(iii) to (v), and

(E) payments in full or partial commutation of the annuity and, where the commutation is partial,

(I) equal annual or more frequent periodic payments thereafter, or

(II) annual or more frequent periodic payments thereafter that are not equal solely because of an adjustment that would, if the annuity were an annuity under a retirement savings plan, be in accordance with subparagraphs 146(3)(*b*)(iii) to (v);

or

(iii) to a carrier as consideration for a registered retirement income fund under which the taxpayer is the annuitant

where that total

(iv) is designated by the taxpayer in the taxpayer's return of income under this Part for the year,

(v) does not exceed the total of

(A) the amount included in computing the taxpayer's income for the year as a refund of premiums out of or under a registered retirement savings plan under which the taxpayer's spouse or common-law partner was the annuitant,

(A.1) the amount included in computing the taxpayer's income for the year as a payment (other than a payment that is part of a series of periodic payments) received by the taxpayer out of or under a pooled registered pension plan as a consequence of the death of an individual who was, immediately before the death, a spouse or common-law partner of the taxpayer,

(B) the amount included in computing the taxpayer's income for the year as a refund of premiums out of or under a registered retirement savings plan where the taxpayer was dependent by reason of physical or mental infirmity on the annuitant under the plan,

(B.01) the amount included in computing the taxpayer's income for the year as a payment (other than a payment that is part of a series of periodic payments or that relates to an actuarial surplus) received by the taxpayer out of or under a pooled registered pension plan, a registered pension plan or a specified pension plan as a consequence of the death of an individual of whom the taxpayer was a child or grandchild, if the taxpayer was, immediately before the death, financially dependent on the individual for support because of mental or physical infirmity,

(B.1) the least of

(I) the amount paid by or on behalf of the taxpayer to acquire an annuity that would be described in subparagraph (ii) if that subparagraph were read without reference to clause (A) thereof,

(II) the amount (other than any portion of it that is included in the amount determined under clause (B), (B.01) or (B.2)) that is included in computing the taxpayer's income for the year as

1. a payment (other than a payment that is part of a series of periodic payments or that relates to an actuarial surplus) received by the taxpayer out of or under a pooled registered pension plan, a registered pension plan or a specified pension plan,
2. a refund of premiums out of or under a registered retirement savings plan, or
3. a designated benefit in respect of a registered retirement income fund (in this clause having the meaning assigned by subsection 146.3(1))

as a consequence of the death of an individual of whom the taxpayer is a child or grandchild, and

(III) the amount, if any, by which the amount determined for the year under subclause (II) in respect of the taxpayer exceeds the amount, if any, by which

1. the total of all designated benefits of the taxpayer for the year in respect of registered retirement income funds

exceeds

2. the total of all amounts that would be eligible amounts of the taxpayer for the year in respect of those funds (within the meaning that would be assigned by subsection 146.3(6.11) if the taxpayer were described in paragraph (*b*) thereof), and

(B.2) all eligible amounts of the taxpayer for the year in respect of registered retirement income funds (within the meaning assigned by subsection 146.3(6.11)),

and, where the amount is paid by a direct transfer from the issuer of a registered retirement savings plan or a carrier of a registered retirement income fund,

(C) the amount included in computing the taxpayer's income for the year as a consequence of a payment described in subparagraph 146(2)(*b*)(ii), and

(D) the amount, if any, by which

(I) the amount received by the taxpayer out of or under a registered retirement income fund under which the taxpayer is the annuitant and included because of subsection 146.3(5) in computing the taxpayer's income for the year

exceeds

(II) the amount, if any, by which the minimum amount (within the meaning assigned by subsection 146.3(1)) under the fund for the year exceeds the total of all amounts received out of or under the fund in the year by an individual who was an annuitant under the fund before the taxpayer became the annuitant under the fund and that were included because of subsection 146.3(5) in computing that individual's income for the year, and

(vi) was not deducted in computing the taxpayer's income for a preceding taxation year;

History: S. 60(*l*)(ii)(B) was replaced by S.C. 2013, c. 34, s. 196(2), deemed to have come into force on January 1, 1989, and formerly read:

(B) under which the taxpayer, or a trust under which the taxpayer is the sole person beneficially interested in amounts payable under the annuity, is the annuitant for a term not exceeding 18 years minus the age in whole years of the taxpayer at the time the annuity was acquired

S. 60(*l*)(v)(A.1) was added by S.C. 2012, c. 31, s. 12(1), in force December 14, 2012.

S. 60(*l*)(v)(B.01) was replaced by S.C. 2012, c. 31, s. 12(2), in force December 14, 2012. S. 60(*l*)(v)(B.01) formerly read:

(B.01) the amount included in computing the taxpayer's income for the year as a payment (other than a payment that is part of a series of periodic payments or that relates to an actuarial surplus) received by the taxpayer out of or under a registered pension plan or a specified pension plan as a consequence of the death of an individual of whom the taxpayer was a child or grandchild, if the taxpayer was, immediately before the death, financially dependent on the individual for support because of mental or physical infirmity,

S. 60(*l*)(v)(B.1)(II)1. was replaced by S.C. 2012, c. 31, s. 12(3), in force December 14, 2012. S. 60(*l*)(v))(v)(B.1)(II)1 formerly read:

1. a payment (other than a payment that is part of a series of periodic payments or that relates to an actuarial surplus) received by the taxpayer out of or under a registered pension plan or a specified pension plan,

S. 60(*l*)(v)(B.01) was replaced by S.C. 2011, c. 24, s. 11(1), applicable to taxation years that begin after 2009. S. 60(*l*)(v)(B.01) formerly read:

(B.01) the amount included in computing the taxpayer's income for the year as a payment (other than a payment that is part of a series of periodic payments or that relates to an actuarial surplus) received by the taxpayer out of or under a registered pension plan as a consequence of the death of an individual of whom the taxpayer was a child or grandchild, if the taxpayer was, immediately before the death, financially dependent on the individual for support because of mental or physical infirmity,

S. 60(*l*)(v)(B.1)(II)1. was replaced by S.C. 2011, c. 24, s. 11(2), applicable to taxation years that begin after 2009. S. 60(*l*)(v)(B.1)(II)1. formerly read:

1. a payment (other than a payment that is part of a series of periodic payments or that relates to an actuarial surplus) received by the taxpayer out of or under a registered pension plan,

Related Sections: S. 56(1)(*a*) Pension benefits, unemployment insurance benefits, etc.; s. 60(*j*) Transfer of superannuation benefits; s. 60(*v*) Contribution to a provincial pension plan; s. 60.011 [Meaning of "qualifying trust annuity"]; s. 61 Payment made as consideration for income-averaging annuity; s. 75.2 Rules applicable with respect to "qualifying trust annuity"; s. 146(1), "refund of premiums"; s. 146(1.1) Restriction — financially dependent; s. 146(5) Amount of RRSP premiums deductible; s. 146(21) Prescribed provincial pension plans; s. 146(22) Deemed payment of RRSP premiums and provincial pension plan contributions; s. 146.02(1), "excluded premium"; s. 146.3 Registered retirement income funds; s. 146.3(5.5) Where s. (5.1) does not apply; s. 146.3(6.11) Transfer of designated benefit; s. 147.3(13.1) Withdrawal of excessive transfers to RRSPs and RRIFs; s. 147.5(11) Member contributions; s. 147.5(13) Taxable amounts; s. 212(1)(*l*) Registered retirement savings plan payments; s. 212(1)(*q*) Registered retirement income fund payments; s. 248(1), "annuity", "retirement savings plan".

Canadian Tax Foundation: Doobay, *Consent Order Not Rectification*, 2015 Canadian Tax Highlights 23(2):6–8.

Tax Topics: No. 1643, Leaving RRSP Funds to an Infirm Child or Grandchild.

Forms: T2030 — Direct Transfer Under Subparagraph 60(1)(v).

Information Circulars: IC 78-18R6 Registered retirement income funds.

Interpretation Bulletins: *Primary* — IT-528 Transfers of funds between registered plans. *Secondary* — IT-124R6 Contributions to registered retirement savings plans; IT-307R4 Spousal or common-law partner registered retirement savings plans; IT-500R Registered retirement savings plans — Death of an annuitant.

▶ 60(m) ◀

(m) [Payments to registered disability savings plans] — such amount in respect of payments to a registered disability savings plan as is permitted under section 60.02;

History: S. 60(*m*) was replaced by S.C. 2010, c. 25, s. 10(1), applicable after March 3, 2010. S. 60(*m*) formerly read:

(*m*) *Estate tax applicable to certain property* — that proportion of any superannuation or pension benefit, death benefit, benefit under a registered retirement savings plan or benefit under a deferred profit sharing plan, received by the taxpayer in the year, on or after the death of a predecessor, in payment of or on account of property to which the taxpayer is the successor, that

(i) such part of any tax payable under the *Estate Tax Act*, chapter E-9 of the Revised Statutes of Canada, 1970, in respect of the death of the predecessor as is determined under that Act to be the part thereof applicable to the property in payment of or on account of which the benefit was so received,

is of

(ii) the value of the property in payment of or on account of which the benefit was so received, computed as provided for the purpose of subsection 62(4) of the *Estate Tax Act*, chapter E-9 of the Revised Statutes of Canada, 1970;

Related Sections: S. 146(1), "earned income"; ITAR, s. 40(3) Determination of amount of payment; s. 40(4) Death benefit.

Tax Window Files: RDSP Rollover - 60.02, *September 29, 2016*, CRA Document No. 2016-0625061E5.

► 60(m.1) ◄

(m.1) Succession duties applicable to certain property — that proportion of any superannuation or pension benefit, death benefit, benefit under a registered retirement savings plan, benefit under a deferred profit sharing plan or benefit that is a payment under an income-averaging annuity contract, received by the taxpayer in the year, on or after the death of a predecessor, in payment of or on account of property to which the taxpayer is the successor, that

(i) such part of any succession duties payable under a law of a province in respect of the death of the predecessor as may reasonably be regarded as attributable to the property in payment of or on account of which the benefit was so received,

is of

(ii) the value of the property in payment of or on account of which the benefit was so received, as computed for the purposes of the law referred to in subparagraph (i);

► 60(n) ◄

(n) Repayment of pension or benefits — any amount paid by the taxpayer in the year as a repayment (otherwise than because of Part VII of the *Unemployment Insurance Act*, chapter U-1 of the Revised Statutes of Canada, 1985, or of Part VII of the *Employment Insurance Act*) of any of the following amounts to the extent that the amount was included in computing the taxpayer's income, and not deducted in computing the taxpayer's taxable income, for the year or for a preceding taxation year, namely,

(i) a pension described in clause 56(1)(*a*)(i)(A),

(ii) a benefit described in clause 56(1)(*a*)(i)(B),

(iii) an amount described in subparagraph 56(1)(*a*)(ii),

(iv) a benefit described in subparagraph 56(1)(*a*)(iv),

(v) a benefit described in subparagraph 56(1)(*a*)(vi),

(v.1) a benefit described in subparagraph 56(1)(*a*)(vii), and

(vi) an amount described in paragraph 56(1)(*r*);

History: S. 60(*n*)(v.1) was added by S.C. 2013, c. 34, s. 196(3), applicable to the 2006 and subsequent taxation years.

Related Sections: S. 60(v.1) UI and EI benefit repayment; s. 227(9.1) Penalty.

Income Tax Folios: *Secondary* — S1-F2-C3 Scholarships, Research Grants and Other Education Assistance.

► 60(n.1) ◄

(n.1) Repayment of pension benefits — an amount paid by the taxpayer in the year to a pooled registered pension plan or registered pension plan if

(i) the taxpayer is an individual,

(ii) the amount is paid as

(A) a repayment of an amount received from the plan that was included in computing the taxpayer's income for the year or a preceding year, if

(I) it is reasonable to consider that the amount was paid under the plan as a consequence of an error and not as an entitlement to benefits, or

(II) it was subsequently determined that, as a consequence of a settlement of a dispute in respect of the taxpayer's employment, the taxpayer was not entitled to the amount, or

(B) interest in respect of a repayment described in clause (A), and

(iii) no portion of the amount is deductible under any of paragraph 8(1)(*m*) and subsections 146(5) to (5.2) in computing the taxpayer's income for the year;

History: S. 60(*n.1*), the portion before subparagraph (i) was replaced by S.C. 2013, c. 34, s. 426(4)(*a*), applicable to the 2009 and subsequent taxation years, except that, before December 14, 2012 (the day the *Pooled Registered Pension Plans Act* came into force), the portion of paragraph 60(*n.1*) before subparagraph (i) is to be read without reference to "pooled registered pension plan or".

S. 60(*n.1*), the portion before subparagraph (i) formerly read:

(*n*.1) *Repayment of pension benefits* — an amount paid by the taxpayer in the year to a registered pension plan if

S. 60(*n.1*)(iii) was replaced by S.C. 2013, c. 34, s. 426(4)(*b*), applicable to the 2009 and subsequent taxation years, except that, before December 14, 2012 (the day the *Pooled Registered Pension Plans Act* came into force), subparagraph. 60(*n.1*)(iii) is to be read as follows:

(iii) "no portion of the amount is deductible under paragraph 8(1)(*m*) in computing the taxpayer's income for the year;"

S. 60(*n.1*)(iii) formerly read:

(iii) no portion of the amount is deductible under paragraph 8(1)(*m*) in computing the taxpayer's income for the year;

S. 60(*n.1*) was added by S.C. 2013, c. 34, s. 196(4), applicable to the 2009 and subsequent taxation years.

► 60(o) ◄

(o) Legal expenses — amounts paid by the taxpayer in the year in respect of fees or expenses incurred in preparing, instituting or prosecuting an objection to, or an appeal in relation to,

(i) an assessment of tax, interest or penalties under this Act or an Act of a province that imposes a tax similar to the tax imposed under this Act,

(ii) a decision of the Canada Employment Insurance Commission under the *Employment Insurance Act* or to an appeal of such a decision to the Social Security Tribunal,

(iii) an assessment of any income tax deductible by the taxpayer under section 126 or any interest or penalty with respect thereto, or

(iv) an assessment or a decision made under the *Canada Pension Plan* or a provincial pension plan as defined in section 3 of that Act;

History: S. 60(*o*)(ii) was replaced by S.C. 2012, c. 19, s. 278(1), applicable in respect of

(a) appeals to the Social Security Tribunal filed, and decisions made by the Canada Employment Insurance Commission, after March 2013; and

(b) appeals for which leave has deemed to have been granted by the Appeal Division of the Social Security Tribunal on April 1, 2013 or on April 1, 2014 for appeals fiiled before April 1, 2013.

S. 60(*o*)(ii) formerly read:

(ii) a decision of the Canada Employment and Immigration Commission, the Canada Employment and Insurance Commission, a board of referees or an umpire under the *Unemployment Insurance Act* or the *Employment Insurance Act*.

Related Sections: S. 56(1)(*l*) Legal expenses; s. 152(1.2) Provisions applicable.

Interpretation Bulletins: *Secondary* — IT-99R5 (Consolid.) Legal and accounting fees.

Tax Window Files: Cost of Making Voluntary Disclosure, *May 22, 2014*, CRA Document No. 2014-0528451C6.

► 60(o.1) ◄

(o.1) Idem — the amount, if any, by which the lesser of

(i) the total of all legal expenses (other than those relating to a division or settlement of property arising out of, or on a breakdown of, a marriage or common-law partnership) paid by the taxpayer in the year or in any of the 7 preceding taxation years to collect or establish a right to an amount of

(A) a benefit under a pension fund or plan (other than a benefit under the *Canada Pension Plan* or a provincial pension plan as defined in section 3 of that Act) in respect of the employment of the taxpayer or a deceased individual of whom the taxpayer was a dependant, relation or legal representative, or

(B) a retiring allowance of the taxpayer or a deceased individual of whom the taxpayer was a dependant, relation or legal representative, and

(ii) the amount, if any, by which the total of all amounts each of which is

(A) an amount described in clause (i)(A) or (B)

(I) that is received after 1985,

(II) in respect of which legal expenses described in subparagraph (i) were paid, and

(III) that is included in computing the income of the taxpayer for the year or a preceding taxation year, or

(B) an amount included in computing the income of the taxpayer under paragraph 56(1)(*l*.1) for the year or a preceding taxation year,

exceeds the total of all amounts each of which is an amount deducted under paragraph (*j*), (*j*.01), (*j*.1) or (*j*.2) in computing the income of the taxpayer for the year or a preceding taxation year, to the extent that the amount may reasonably be considered to have been deductible as a consequence of the receipt of an amount referred to in clause (A),

exceeds

(iii) the portion of the total described in subparagraph (i) in respect of the taxpayer that may reasonably be considered to have been deductible under this paragraph in computing the income of the taxpayer for a preceding taxation year;

Income Tax Folios: *Primary* — S2-F1-C2 Retiring Allowances.

Tax Window Files: Legal Expenses of Employee, *Technical Interpretation, Business and Partnerships Division, June 1, 2005*, CRA Document No. 2005-0113991E5. Legal fees relating to inappropriate termination notice and negotiating a settlement not deductible under paragraph 8(1)(*b*) or paragraph 60(*o*.1).

► 60(p) ◄

(p) Repayment of apprenticeship grants — the total of all amounts each of which is an amount paid in the taxation year as a repayment under the Apprenticeship Incentive Grant program or the Apprenticeship Completion Grant program of an amount that was included under paragraph 56(1)(*n.1*) in computing the taxpayer's income for the taxation year or a preceding taxation year;

History: S. 60(*p*) was replaced by S.C. 2013, c. 34, s. 196(5), applicable to the 2009 and subsequent years, and formerly read:

(*p*) *Repayment of apprenticeship incentive grant* — the total of all amounts each of which is an amount paid in the taxation year as a repayment under the Apprenticeship Incentive Grant program of an amount that was included because of paragraph 56(1)(*n*.1) in computing the taxpayer's income for the taxation year or a preceding taxation year;

► 60(q) ◄

(q) Refund of income payments — where the taxpayer is an individual, an amount paid by the taxpayer in the year to a person with whom the taxpayer was dealing at arm's length (in this paragraph referred to as the "payer") if

(i) the amount has been included in computing the income of the taxpayer for the year or a preceding taxation year as an amount described in subparagraph 56(1)(*n*)(i) or paragraph 56(1)(*o*) paid to the taxpayer by the payer,

(ii) at the time the amount was paid by the payer to the taxpayer a condition was stipulated for the taxpayer to fulfil,

(iii) as a result of the failure of the taxpayer to fulfil the condition referred to in subparagraph (ii) the taxpayer was required to repay the amount to the payer,

(iv) during the period for which the amount referred to in subparagraph (i) was paid the taxpayer did not provide other than occasional services to the payer as an officer or under a contract of employment, and

(v) the amount was paid to the taxpayer for the purpose of enabling the taxpayer to further the taxpayer's education;

History: S. 60(*q*)(i) was replaced by S.C. 2013, c. 40, s. 26(1), deemed to have come into force on March 1, 1994, and formerly read:

(i) the amount has been included in computing the income of the taxpayer in a preceding taxation year as an amount described in subparagraph 56(1)(*n*)(i) or paragraph 56(1)(*o*) paid to the taxpayer by the payer,

Related Sections: S. 56(1)(*n*) Scholarships, bursaries, etc; s. 56(1)(*o*) Research grants.

Income Tax Folios: *Secondary* — S1-F2-C3 Scholarships, Research Grants and Other Education Assistance.

▶ 60(r) ◀

(r) Amounts included under s. 146.2(6) — where an amount has been included in computing the income of the taxpayer by virtue of subsection 146.2(6) of the *Income Tax Act*, chapter 148 of the Revised Statutes of Canada, 1952 (as it read in its application to the 1985 taxation year) for any of the taxpayer's three immediately preceding taxation years, the taxpayer may deduct the lesser of

(i) the amount that had been so included in computing the taxpayer's income, and

(ii) the total of all amounts used by the taxpayer to acquire in the year the taxpayer's owner-occupied home (within the meaning assigned by paragraph 146.2(1)(*f*) of the *Income Tax Act*, chapter 148 of the Revised Statutes of Canada, 1952, as it read in its application to the 1985 taxation year),

except that no amount may be deducted by the taxpayer for the year under this paragraph if an amount has been deducted

(iii) under subsection 146.2(6.1) of the *Income Tax Act*, chapter 148 of the Revised Statutes of Canada, 1952 (as it read in its application to taxation years before 1986) in computing the taxpayer's income for any taxation year ending before 1986, or

(iv) under this paragraph for any preceding taxation year ending after 1985;

▶ 60(s) ◀

(s) Repayment of policy loan — the total of all repayments made by the taxpayer in the year in respect of a policy loan (within the meaning assigned by subsection 148(9)) made under a life insurance policy, not exceeding the amount, if any, by which

(i) the total of all amounts required by subsection 148(1) to be included in computing the taxpayer's income for the year or a preceding taxation year from a disposition described in paragraph (*b*) of the definition "disposition" in subsection 148(9) in respect of that policy

exceeds

(ii) the total of all repayments made by the taxpayer in respect of the policy loan that were deductible in computing the taxpayer's income for a preceding taxation year;

Related Sections: S. 148(9), "policy loan".

▶ 60(t) ◀

(t) RCA distributions — where an amount in respect of a particular retirement compensation arrangement is required by paragraph 56(1)(*x*) or (*z*) or subsection 70(2) to be included in computing the taxpayer's income for the year, an amount equal to the lesser of

(i) the total of all amounts in respect of the particular arrangement so required to be included in computing the taxpayer's income for the year, and

(ii) the amount, if any, by which the total of all amounts each of which is

(A) an amount (other than an amount deductible under paragraph 8(1)(*m*.2) or transferred to the particular arrangement under circumstances in which subsection 207.6(7) applies) contributed under the particular arrangement by the taxpayer while it was a retirement compensation arrangement and before the end of the year,

(A.1) an amount transferred in respect of the taxpayer before the end of the year to the particular arrangement from another retirement compensation arrangement under circumstances in which subsection 207.6(7) applies, to the extent that the amount would have been deductible under this paragraph in respect of the other arrangement in computing the taxpayer's income if it had been received by the taxpayer out of the other arrangement,

(B) an amount paid by the taxpayer before the end of the year and at a time when the taxpayer was resident in Canada to acquire an interest in the particular arrangement, or

(C) an amount that was received or became receivable by the taxpayer before the end of the year and at a time when the taxpayer was resident in Canada as proceeds from the disposition of an interest in the particular arrangement,

exceeds the total of all amounts each of which is

(D) an amount deducted under this paragraph or paragraph (*u*) in respect of the particular arrangement in computing the taxpayer's income for a preceding taxation year, or

(E) an amount transferred in respect of the taxpayer before the end of the year from the particular arrangement to another retirement compensation arrangement under circumstances in which subsection 207.6(7) applies, to the extent that the amount would have been deductible under this paragraph in respect of the particular arrangement in computing the taxpayer's income if it had been received by the taxpayer out of the particular arrangement;

▶ 60(u) ◀

(u) RCA dispositions — where an amount in respect of a particular retirement compensation arrangement is required by paragraph 56(1)(*y*) to be included in computing the taxpayer's income for the year, an amount equal to the lesser of

(i) the total of all amounts in respect of the particular arrangement so required to be included in computing the taxpayer's income for the year, and

(ii) the amount, if any, by which the total of all amounts each of which is

(A) an amount (other than an amount deductible under paragraph 8(1)(*m.2*) or transferred to the particular arrangement under circumstances in which subsection 207.6(7) applies) contributed under the particular arrangement by the taxpayer while it was a retirement compensation arrangement and before the end of the year,

(A.1) an amount transferred in respect of the taxpayer before the end of the year to the particular arrangement from another retirement compensation arrangement under circumstances in which subsection 207.6(7) applies, to the extent that the amount would have been deductible under paragraph (*t*) in respect of the other arrangement in computing the taxpayer's income if it had been received by the taxpayer out of the other arrangement, or

(B) an amount paid by the taxpayer before the end of the year and at a time when the taxpayer was resident in Canada to acquire an interest in the particular arrangement

exceeds the total of all amounts each of which is

(C) an amount deducted under paragraph (*t*) in respect of the particular arrangement in computing the taxpayer's income for the year or a preceding taxation year,

(D) an amount deducted under this paragraph in respect of the particular arrangement in computing the taxpayer's income for a preceding taxation year, or

(E) an amount transferred in respect of the taxpayer before the end of the year from the particular arrangement to another retirement compensation arrangement under circumstances in which subsection 207.6(7) applies, to the extent that the amount would have been deductible under paragraph (*t*) in respect of the particular arrangement in computing the taxpayer's income if it had been received by the taxpayer out of the particular arrangement;

► 60(v) ◄

(v) Repayment — parents of victims of crime — the total of all amounts each of which is an amount paid in the year as a repayment of a benefit that was included because of paragraph 56(1)(*a.3*) in computing the taxpayer's income for the year or a preceding taxation year;

History: S. 60(*v*) was added by S.C. 2012, C. 27, s. 27(1), in force January 1, 2013.

S. 60(*v*) was repealed by S.C. 2011, c. 24, s. 11(3), applicable to taxation years that begin after 2009. S. 60(*v*) formerly read:

(*v*) *Contribution to a provincial pension plan* — the least of

(i) the amount, if any, by which

(A) the total of all amounts each of which is a contribution made in the year, or within 60 days after the end of the year, by the taxpayer to the account of the taxpayer, or of the taxpayer's spouse or common-law partner, under a prescribed provincial pension plan

exceeds

(B) the portion of the total described in clause (A) that was deducted in computing the taxpayer's income for the preceding taxation year,

(ii) the prescribed amount for the year in respect of the plan, and

(iii) the amount by which the taxpayer's RRSP deduction limit for the year exceeds the total of the amounts deducted under subsections 146(5) and (5.1) in computing the taxpayer's income for the year;

Related Regulations: 7800(1); 7800(2).

Related Sections: S. 18(11) Borrowed money used for contribution; s. 56(1)(*a*) Pension benefits, unemployment insurance benefits, etc.; s. 60(*l*) Transfer of refund of premiums under RRSP; s. 60.02 Application of subpara. 60(v)(iii); s. 146(21) Prescribed provincial pension plans; s. 146(22) Deemed payment of RRSP premiums and provincial pension plan contributions; s. 146.01(1), "excluded premium"; s. 146.02(1), "excluded premium".

Interpretation Bulletins: *Secondary* — IT-124R6 Contributions to registered retirement savings plans.

► 60(v.1) ◄

(v.1) UI and EI benefit repayment — any benefit repayment payable by the taxpayer under Part VII of the *Unemployment Insurance Act* or Part VII of the *Employment Insurance Act* on or before April 30 of the following year, to the extent that the amount was not deductible in computing the taxpayer's income for any preceding taxation year;

Related Sections: S. 56(1)(*a*) Pension benefits, unemployment insurance benefits, etc.; s. 60(*n*) Repayment of pension or benefits; s. 153(1)(*d.1*) Withholding; s. 227(9.1) Penalty; s. 241(1) Provision of information; s. 241(3) Communication where proceedings have been commenced; s. 241(4) Where taxpayer information may be disclosed; s. 241(10) Definitions.

► 60(w) ◄

(w) Tax under Part I.2 — the amount of the taxpayer's tax payable under Part I.2 for the year;

Related Sections: S. 180.2 Tax on Old Age Security Benefits.

► 60(x) ◄

(x) Repayment under *Canada Education Savings Act* — the total of all amounts each of which is an amount paid by the taxpayer in the year as a repayment, under the *Canada Education Savings Act* or under a designated provincial program (as defined in subsection 146.1(1)), of an amount that was included because of subsection 146.1(7) in computing the taxpayer's income for the year or a preceding taxation year;

Related Sections: S. 146.1(14) Former Act.

► 60(y) ◄

(y) Repayment of UCCB — the total of all amounts each of which is an amount paid in the taxation year as a repayment, under the *Universal Child Care Benefit Act*, of a benefit that was included because of subsection 56(6) in computing the taxpayer's income for the taxation year or a preceding taxation year;

Related Sections: S. 122.5(1), "adjusted income"; s. 122.6, "adjusted income"; s. 180.2(1), "adjusted income".

► 60(z) ◄

(z) Repayment under the *Canada Disability Savings Act* — the total of all amounts each of which is an amount paid in the taxation year as a repayment, under or because of the *Canada Disability Savings Act* or a designated provincial program as defined in subsection 146.4(1), of an amount that was included because of section 146.4 in computing the taxpayer's income for the taxation year or a preceding taxation year; and

History: S. 60(*z*) was replaced by S.C. 2010, c. 12, s. 5(1), applicable to the 2009 and subsequent taxation years. S. 60(*z*) formerly read:

(*z*) *Repayment under the Canada Disability Savings Act* — the total of all amounts each of which is an amount paid in the taxation year as a repayment, under the *Canada Disability Savings Act*, of an amount that was included because of section 146.4 in computing the taxpayer's income for the taxation year or a preceding taxation year.

► 60(z.1) ◄

(z.1) Tax informant program — the total of all amounts each of which is an amount paid in the year as a repayment of an amount that was included, because of paragraph 56(1)(*z.4*), in computing the taxpayer's income for the year or a preceding taxation year.

Editorial Note: See the editorial note under s. 56(1)(*z.4*).

History: S. 60(*z.1*) was added by S.C. 2014, c. 20, s. 3, in force June 19, 2014.

SECTION 60.001: Application of subpara. 60(c.1)(i)

(Repealed by S.C. 2013, c. 40, s. 27(1).)

History: S. 60.001 was repealed by S.C. 2013, c. 40, s. 27(1), applicable to orders made after December 12, 2013, and formerly read:

S. 60.001 *Application of subpara. 60(c.1)(i).* In the application of subparagraph 60(*c.1*)(i) in respect of amounts received pursuant to orders made after December 11, 1979 under the laws of Ontario, the references in that subparagraph to "February 10, 1988" and "February 11, 1988" shall be read as references to "December 11, 1979" and "December 12, 1979", respectively.

SECTION 60.01: Eligible amount

For the purpose of paragraph 60(*j*), the amount, if any, by which

(*a*) the amount of any payment received by a taxpayer in a taxation year out of or under a foreign retirement arrangement and included in computing the taxpayer's income because of clause 56(1)(*a*)(i)(C.1) (other than any portion thereof that is included in respect of the taxpayer for the year under subparagraph 60(*j*)(i) or that is part of a series of periodic payments)

exceeds

(*b*) the portion, if any, of the payment included under paragraph (*a*) that can reasonably be considered to derive from contributions to the foreign retirement arrangement made by a person other than the taxpayer or the taxpayer's spouse or common-law partner or former spouse or common-law partner,

is an eligible amount in respect of the taxpayer for the year.

Related Sections: S. 60(*j*) Transfer of superannuation benefits; s. 248(1), "foreign retirement arrangement", "common-law partner".

Interpretation Bulletins: *Secondary* — IT-124R6 Contributions to registered retirement savings plans; IT-528 Transfers of funds between registered plans.

SECTION 60.011: [Qualifying trust annuity]

► 60.011(1) ◄

(1) Meaning of "lifetime benefit trust". For the purpose of subsection (2), a trust is at any particular time a lifetime benefit trust with respect to a taxpayer and the estate of a deceased individual if

(*a*) immediately before the death of the deceased individual, the taxpayer

(i) was both a spouse or common-law partner of the deceased individual and mentally infirm, or

(ii) was both a child or grandchild of the deceased individual and dependent on the deceased individual for support because of mental infirmity; and

(*b*) the trust is, at the particular time, a personal trust under which

(i) no person other than the taxpayer may receive or otherwise obtain the use of, during the taxpayer's lifetime, any of the income or capital of the trust, and

(ii) the trustees

(A) are empowered to pay amounts from the trust to the taxpayer, and

(B) are required — in determining whether to pay, or not to pay, an amount to the taxpayer — to consider the needs of the taxpayer including, without limiting the generality of the foregoing, the comfort, care and maintenance of the taxpayer.

History: S. 60.011(1) was added by S.C. 2013, c. 34, s. 197(1), deemed to have come into force on January 1, 1989.

Related Sections: S. 108(3) Income of a trust in certain provisions.

► 60.011(2) ◄

(2) Meaning of "qualifying trust annuity". Each of the following is a qualifying trust annuity with respect to a taxpayer:

(*a*) an annuity that meets the following conditions:

(i) it is acquired after 2005,

(ii) the annuitant under it is a trust that is, at the time the annuity is acquired, a lifetime benefit trust with respect to the taxpayer and the estate of a deceased individual,

(iii) it is for the life of the taxpayer (with or without a guaranteed period), or for a fixed term equal to 90 years minus the age in whole years of the taxpayer at the time it is acquired, and

(iv) if it is with a guaranteed period or for a fixed term, it requires that, in the event of the death of the taxpayer during the guaranteed period or fixed term, any amounts that would otherwise be payable after the death of the taxpayer be commuted into a single payment;

(*b*) an annuity that meets the following conditions:

(i) it is acquired after 1988,

(ii) the annuitant under it is a trust under which the taxpayer is the sole person beneficially interested (determined without regard to any right of a person to receive an amount from the trust only on or after the death of the taxpayer) in amounts payable under the annuity,

(iii) it is for a fixed term not exceeding 18 years minus the age in whole years of the taxpayer at the time it is acquired, and

(iv) if it is acquired after 2005, it requires that, in the event of the death of the taxpayer during the fixed term, any amounts that would otherwise be payable after the death of the taxpayer be commuted into a single payment; and

(*c*) an annuity that meets the following conditions:

(i) it is acquired

(A) after 2000 and before 2005 at a time at which the taxpayer was mentally or physically infirm, or

(B) in 2005 at a time at which the taxpayer was mentally infirm,

(ii) the annuitant under it is a trust under which the taxpayer is the sole person beneficially interested (determined without regard to any right of a person to receive an amount from the trust only on or after the death of the taxpayer) in amounts payable under the annuity, and

(iii) it is for the life of the taxpayer (with or without a guaranteed period), or for a fixed term equal to 90 years minus the age in whole years of the taxpayer at the time it is acquired.

History: S. 60.011(2) was added by S.C. 2013, c. 34, s. 197(1), deemed to have come into force on January 1, 1989.

▶ 60.011(3) ◀

(3) Application of paragraph 60(*l*) to "qualifying trust annuity". For the purpose of paragraph 60(*l*),

(*a*) in determining if a qualifying trust annuity with respect to a taxpayer is an annuity described in subparagraph 60(*l*)(ii), clauses 60(*l*)(ii)(A) and (B) are to be read without regard to their requirement that the taxpayer be the annuitant under the annuity; and

(*b*) if an amount paid to acquire a qualifying trust annuity with respect to a taxpayer would, if this Act were read without reference to this subsection, not be considered to have been paid by or on behalf of the taxpayer, the amount is deemed to have been paid on behalf of the taxpayer where

(i) it is paid

(A) by the estate of a deceased individual who was, immediately before death,

(I) a spouse or common-law partner of the taxpayer, or

(II) a parent or grandparent of the taxpayer on whom the taxpayer was dependent for support, or

(B) by the trust that is the annuitant under the qualifying trust annuity, and

(ii) it would, if it had been paid by the taxpayer, be deductible under paragraph 60(*l*) in computing the taxpayer's income for a taxation year and the taxpayer elects, in the taxpayer's return of income under this Part for that taxation year, to have this paragraph apply to the amount.

History: S. 60.011(3) was added by S.C. 2013, c. 34, s. 197(1), deemed to have come into force on January 1, 1989 and, for the purpose of applying subparagraph 60.011(3)(*b*)(ii) to a taxation year that ends before 2005, a taxpayer is deemed to have made the election referred to in that subparagraph in respect of an amount paid to acquire a qualifying trust annuity if the taxpayer claimed, in their return of income for that taxation year, an amount as a deduction under paragraph 60(*l*) in respect of the amount paid to acquire the qualifying trust annuity.

SECTION 60.02: [Rollover to RDSP on death]

▶ 60.02(1) ◀

(1) Definitions. The definitions in this subsection apply in this section and section 146.4.

History: S. 60.02(1) was added by S.C. 2010, c. 25, s. 11(1), applicable after March 3, 2010.

"eligible individual" — "eligible individual" means a child or grandchild of a deceased annuitant under a registered retirement savings plan or a registered retirement income fund, or of a deceased member of a pooled registered pension plan, a registered pension plan or a specified pension plan, who was financially dependent on the deceased for support, at the time of the deceased's death, by reason of mental or physical infirmity.

History: S. 60.02(1), the definition "eligible individual" was replaced by S.C. 2012, c. 31, s. 13(1), in force December 14, 2012. S. 60.02(1), the definition "eligible individual" formerly read:

"eligible individual"—"eligible individual" means a child or grandchild of a deceased annuitant under a registered retirement savings plan or registered retirement income fund, or of a deceased member of a registered pension plan or a specified pension plan, who was financially dependent on the deceased for support, at the time of the deceased's death, by reason of mental or physical infirmity.

S. 60.02(1), the definition "eligible individual" was replaced by S.C. 2011, c. 24, s. 12(1), deemed to have come into force on March 4, 2010. S. 60.02(1), the definition "eligible individual" formerly read:

"eligible individual"—"eligible individual" means a child or grandchild of a deceased annuitant under a registered retirement savings plan or a registered retirement income fund, or of a deceased member of a registered pension plan, who was financially dependent on the deceased for support, at the time of the deceased's death, by reason of mental or physical infirmity.

S. 60.02(1), the definition "eligible individual" was added by S.C. 2010, c. 25, s. 11(1), applicable after March 3, 2010.

"eligible proceeds" — "eligible proceeds" means an amount (other than an amount that was deducted under paragraph 60(*l*) in computing the eligible individual's income) received by an eligible individual as a consequence of the death after March 3, 2010 of a parent or grandparent of the eligible individual that is

(*a*) a refund of premiums (as defined in subsection 146(1));

(*b*) an eligible amount under subsection 146.3(6.11); or

(*c*) a payment (other than a payment that is part of a series of periodic payments or that relates to an actuarial surplus) out of or under a pooled registered pension plan, a registered pension plan or a specified pension plan.

History: S. 60.02(1), paragraph (*c*) of the definition "eligible proceeds" was replaced by S.C. 2012, c. 31, s. 13(2), in force December 14, 2012. S. 60.02(1), paragraph (*c*) of the definition "eligible proceeds" formerly read:

(c) a payment (other than a payment that is part of a series of periodic payments or that relates to an actuarial surplus) out of or under a registered pension plan or a specified pension plan.

S. 60.02(1), paragraph (*c*) of the definition "eligible proceeds" was replaced by S.C. 2011, c. 24, s. 12(2), deemed to have come into force on March 4, 2010. S. 60.02(1), paragraph (*c*) of the definition "eligible proceeds" formerly read:

(c) a payment (other than a payment that is part of a series of periodic payments or that relates to an actuarial surplus) out of or under a registered pension plan.

S. 60.02(1), the definition "eligible proceeds" was added by S.C. 2010, c. 25, s. 11(1), applicable after March 3, 2010.

"specified RDSP payment" —"specified RDSP payment" in respect of an eligible individual means a payment that

(*a*) is made to a registered disability savings plan under which the eligible individual is the beneficiary;

(*b*) complies with the conditions set out in paragraphs 146.4(4)(*f*) to (*h*);

(*c*) is made after June 2011; and

(*d*) has been designated in prescribed form for a taxation year by the holder of the plan and the eligible individual at the time that the payment is made.

History: S. 60.02(1), the definition "specified RDSP payment" was added by S.C. 2010, c. 25, s. 11(1), applicable after March 3, 2010.

"transitional eligible proceeds" —"transitional eligible proceeds" of a taxpayer means

(*a*) any amount (other than an amount that is eligible proceeds or an amount that was deducted under paragraph 60(*l*) in computing the taxpayer's income) that is received by the taxpayer as a consequence of the death of an individual after 2007 and before 2011 out of or under

(i) a registered retirement savings plan or registered retirement income fund, or

(ii) a registered pension plan (other than an amount that is received as part of a series of periodic payments or that relates to an actuarial surplus); or

(*b*) an amount withdrawn from the taxpayer's registered retirement savings plan or a registered retirement income fund (in this subsection referred to as the "RRSP withdrawal") if

(i) the taxpayer previously deducted an amount under paragraph 60(*l*) in respect of an amount that would be described by paragraph (*a*) if it were read without reference to "other than an amount that is eligible proceeds or an amount that was deducted under paragraph 60(*l*) in computing the taxpayer's income",

(ii) the RRSP withdrawal is included in computing the taxpayer's income for the year of the withdrawal, and

(iii) the RRSP withdrawal does not exceed the amount deducted under subparagraph (i).

History: S. 60.02(1), the definition "transitional eligible proceeds" was added by S.C. 2010, c. 25, s. 11(1), applicable after March 3, 2010.

▶ 60.02(2) ◀

(2) Rollover to RDSP on death. There may be deducted in computing the income for a taxation year of a taxpayer who is an eligible individual an amount that

(*a*) does not exceed the lesser of

(i) the total specified RDSP payments made in the year or within 60 days after the end of the year (or within any longer period after the end of the year that is acceptable to the Minister) in respect of the taxpayer; and

(ii) the total amount of eligible proceeds that is included in computing the taxpayer's income in the year; and

(*b*) was not deducted in computing the taxpayer's income for a preceding taxation year.

Editorial Note: If the eligible individual received transitional eligible proceeds instead of eligible proceeds (e.g. if the proceeds were received as a consequence of the death of a parent or grandparent before March 4, 2010), a deduction is allowed for RDSP contributions under s. 60.02(4) if made before 2012. S. 60.02(4) also allows other individuals to make such deductible contributions if the criteria of s. 60.02(3) are met.

History: S. 60.02(2) was added by S.C. 2010, c. 25, s. 11(1), applicable after March 3, 2010.

Related Sections: 60(m) [Payments to registered disability savings plans]; S. 60(*l*) Transfer of refund of premiums under RRSP; s. 146(1), "refund of premiums"; s. 146.3(6.11) Transfer of designated benefit.

Forms: RC4625 — Rollover to a Registered Disability Savings Plan (RDSP) Under Paragraph 60(m).

Tax Window Files: RDSP Rollover - 60.02, *September 29, 2016*, CRA Document No. 2016-0625061E5.

▶ 60.02(3) ◀

(3) Application of subsections (4) and (5). Subsections (4) and (5) do not apply unless

(*a*) a taxpayer who was the annuitant under a registered retirement savings plan or a registered retirement income fund or was a member of a registered pension plan died after 2007 and before 2011;

(*b*) the taxpayer was, immediately before the taxpayer's death, the parent or grandparent of an eligible individual;

(*c*) transitional eligible proceeds were received from the plan or fund by

(i) an eligible individual in respect of the taxpayer,

(ii) a person who was the spouse or common-law partner of the taxpayer immediately before the taxpayer's death, or

(iii) a person who is a beneficiary of the taxpayer's estate or who directly received transitional eligible proceeds as a consequence of the death of the taxpayer; and

(*d*) the transitional eligible proceeds were included in computing the income of a person for a taxation year.

History: S. 60.02(3) was added by S.C. 2010, c. 25, s. 11(1), applicable after March 3, 2010.

▶ 60.02(4) ◀

(4) Transitional rule. There may be deducted in computing the income of a taxpayer described in paragraph (3)(*c*) for a taxation year an amount approved by the Minister that does not exceed the lesser of

(*a*) the total specified RDSP payments made by the taxpayer before 2012, and

(*b*) the amount of transitional eligible proceeds included in computing the taxpayer's income for the year.

History: S. 60.02(4) was added by S.C. 2010, c. 25, s. 11(1), applicable after March 3, 2010.

▶ 60.02(5) ◀

(5) Transitional rule — deceased taxpayer. There may be deducted in computing the income of a taxpayer for the taxation year in which the taxpayer died an amount approved by the Minister that does not exceed the lesser of

(*a*) the total specified RDSP payments made before 2012 by an individual described in subparagraph (3)(*c*)(iii), and

(*b*) the amount by which the total of all amounts that were included in computing the taxpayer's income for the year under subsection 146(8.8) or 146.3(6) exceeds the total of all amounts, if any, that were deducted in computing the taxpayer's income for the year under subsection 146(8.92) or 146.3(6.3).

History: S. 60.02(5) was added by S.C. 2010, c. 25, s. 11(1), applicable after March 3, 2010.

▶ 60.02(6) ◀

(6) Limitation. The total amounts that may be deducted under subsections (4) and (5) in respect of transitional eligible proceeds received in respect of the death of a taxpayer shall not exceed the total transitional eligible proceeds received in respect of the deceased taxpayer.

History: S. 60.02(6) was added by S.C. 2010, c. 25, s. 11(1), applicable after March 3, 2010.

S. 60.02 was replaced by S.C. 2010, c. 25, s. 11(1), applicable after March 3, 2010. S. 60.02 formerly read:

S. 60.02 *Application of subpara. 60(v)(iii).* Subparagraph 60(*v*)(iii) is applicable to the 1991 and subsequent taxation years.

SECTION 60.021: [RRIF and variable benefit minimum amount rules — recontributions]

▶ 60.021(1) ◀

(1) Additions to clause 60(*l*)(v)(B.2) for 2008. In determining the amount that may be deducted because of paragraph 60(*l*) in computing a taxpayer's income for the 2008 taxation year, clause 60(*l*)(v)(B.2) shall be read as follows:

(B.2) the total of all amounts each of which is

(I) the taxpayer's eligible amount (within the meaning assigned by subsection 146.3(6.11)) for the year in respect of a registered retirement income fund,

(II) the taxpayer's eligible RRIF withdrawal amount (within the meaning assigned by subsection 60.021(2)) for the year in respect of a registered retirement income fund, or

(III) the taxpayer's eligible variable benefit withdrawal amount (within the meaning assigned by subsection 60.021(3)) for the year in respect of an account of the taxpayer under a money purchase provision of a registered pension plan,

History: S. 60.021(1) was added by S.C. 2009, c. 2, s. 15(1), in force on Royal Assent, March 12, 2009.

Amounts paid by a taxpayer, to a registered retirement savings plan or registered retirement income fund under which the taxpayer is the annuitant, during the period that begins on March 2, 2009 and that ends on the day that is 30 days after March 12, 2009, are deemed for the purpose of paragraph 60(*l*) to have been made on March 1, 2009, and not when they were actually made, except that the amounts so deemed shall not exceed the total of all amounts each of which is

(a) the taxpayer's eligible RRIF withdrawal amount for 2008 in respect of a registered retirement income fund, or

(b) the taxpayer's eligible variable benefit withdrawal amount for 2008 in respect of an account of the taxpayer under a money purchase provision of a registered pension plan.

[S.C. 2009, c. 2 was assented to on March 12, 2009. Due to statutory holidays within this 30-day period after Royal Assent, the period ends on April 14, 2009.]

▶ 60.021(2) ◀

(2) Meaning of eligible RRIF withdrawal amount. A taxpayer's eligible RRIF withdrawal amount for a taxation year in respect of a registered retirement income fund under which the taxpayer is the annuitant at the beginning of the taxation year is

(*a*) except where paragraph (*b*) applies, the amount determined by the formula

$$A - B$$

where

A is the lesser of

(i) the total of all amounts included, because of subsection 146.3(5), in computing the income of the taxpayer for the taxation year in respect of amounts received out of or under the fund (other than an amount paid by direct transfer from the fund to another fund or to a registered retirement savings plan), and

(ii) the amount that would, in the absence of subsection 146.3(1.1), be the minimum amount under the fund for the taxation year, and

B is the minimum amount under the fund for the taxation year; and

(*b*) if the taxpayer attained 70 years of age in 2007, nil.

History: S. 60.021(2) was added by S.C. 2009, c. 2, s. 15(1), in force on Royal Assent, March 12, 2009.

▶ 60.021(3) ◀

(3) Meaning of eligible variable benefit withdrawal amount. A taxpayer's eligible variable benefit withdrawal amount for a taxation year in respect of an account of the taxpayer under a money purchase provision of a registered pension plan is the amount determined by the formula

$$A - B - C$$

where

A is the lesser of

(*a*) the total of all amounts each of which is the amount of a retirement benefit (other than a retirement benefit permissible under any of paragraphs 8506(1)(*a*) to (*e*) of the Regulations) paid from the plan in the taxation year in respect of the account and included, because of paragraph 56(1)(*a*), in computing the taxpayer's income for the taxation year, and

(*b*) the amount that would, in the absence of paragraph 8506(7)(*b*) of the Regulations, be the minimum amount for the account for the taxation year;

B is the minimum amount for the account for the taxation year; and

C is the total of all contributions made by the taxpayer under the provision and designated for the purposes of subsection 8506(10) of the Regulations.

History: S. 60.021(3) was added by S.C. 2009, c. 2, s. 15(1), in force on Royal Assent, March 12, 2009.

▶ 60.021(4) ◀

(4) Expressions used in this section. For the purposes of this section,

(*a*) the term "money purchase provision" has the meaning assigned by subsection 147.1(1);

(*b*) the term "retirement benefit" has the meaning assigned by subsection 8500(1) of the Regulations; and

(*c*) the minimum amount for an account of a taxpayer under a money purchase provision of a registered pension plan is the amount determined in accordance with subsection 8506(5) of the Regulations.

History: S. 60.021(4) was added by S.C. 2009, c. 2, s. 15(1), in force on Royal Assent, March 12, 2009.

SECTION 60.022: [Transfer of Refund of premiums for 2015]

▶ 60.022(1) ◀

(1) Additions to clause 60(*l*)(v)(B.2) for 2015. In determining the amount that may be deducted because of paragraph 60(*l*) in computing a taxpayer's income for the 2015 taxation year, clause 60(*l*)(v)(B.2) is to be read as follows:

(B.2) the total of all amounts each of which is

(I) the taxpayer's eligible amount (within the meaning of subsection 146.3(6.11)) for the year in respect of a registered retirement income fund,

(II) the taxpayer's eligible RRIF withdrawal amount (within the meaning of subsection 60.022(2)) for the year in respect of a RRIF,

(III) the taxpayer's eligible variable benefit withdrawal amount (within the meaning of subsection 60.022(3)) for the year in respect of an account of the taxpayer under a money purchase provision of a registered pension plan, or

(IV) the taxpayer's eligible PRPP withdrawal amount (within the meaning of subsection 60.022(4)) for the year in respect of an account of the taxpayer under a PRPP,

History: S. 60.022(1) was added by S.C. 2015, c. 36, s. 2, in force on Royal Assent, June 23, 2015.

Related Sections: 60(l)(v).

▶ 60.022(2) ◀

(2) Eligible RRIF withdrawal amount. A taxpayer's eligible RRIF withdrawal amount for the taxation year in respect of a RRIF under which the taxpayer is the annuitant at the beginning of the taxation year is the amount determined by the formula

$$A - B$$

where

A is the lesser of

(*a*) the total of all amounts included, because of subsection 146.3(5), in computing the taxpayer's income for the taxation year in respect of amounts received out of or under the fund (other than an amount paid by direct transfer from the fund to another fund or to a registered retirement savings plan), and

(*b*) the amount that would be the minimum amount under the fund for the 2015 taxation year if it were determined using the prescribed factors under subsection 7308(3) or (4), as the case may be, of the *Income Tax Regulations* as they read on December 31, 2014; and

B is the minimum amount under the fund for the taxation year.

History: S. 60.022(2) was added by S.C. 2015, c. 36, s. 2, in force on Royal Assent, June 23, 2015.

▶ 60.022(3) ◀

(3) Eligible variable benefit withdrawal amount. A taxpayer's eligible variable benefit withdrawal amount for a taxation year in respect of an account of the taxpayer under a money purchase provision of a registered pension plan is the amount determined by the formula

$$A - B - C$$

where

A is the lesser of

(*a*) the total of all amounts each of which is the amount of a retirement benefit (other than a retirement benefit permissible under any of paragraphs 8506(1)(*a*) to (*e*) of the *Income Tax Regulations*) paid from the plan in the taxation year in respect of the account and included, because of paragraph 56(1)(*a*), in computing the taxpayer's income for the taxation year, and

(*b*) the amount that would be the minimum amount for the account for the 2015 taxation year if it were determined using the factor designated under subsection 7308(4) of the *Income Tax Regulations* as they read on December 31, 2014;

B is the minimum amount for the account for the taxation year; and

C is the total of all contributions made by the taxpayer under the provision and designated for the purposes of subsection 8506(12) of the *Income Tax Regulations*.

History: S. 60.022(3) was added by S.C. 2015, c. 36, s. 2, in force on Royal Assent, June 23, 2015.

▶ 60.022(4) ◀

(4) Eligible PRPP withdrawal amount. A taxpayer's eligible PRPP withdrawal amount for a taxation year in respect of an account of the taxpayer under a PRPP is the amount determined by the formula

$$A - B$$

where

A is the lesser of

(*a*) the total of all amounts each of which is the amount of a distribution made from the account in the taxation year and included, because of subsection 147.5(13), in computing the taxpayer's income for the taxation year, and

(*b*) the amount that would be the minimum amount for the account for the 2015 taxation year if it were determined using the factor designated under subsection 7308(4) of the *Income Tax Regulations* as they read on December 31, 2014, and

B is the minimum amount for the account for the taxation year.

History: S. 60.022(4) was added by S.C. 2015, c. 36, s. 2, in force on Royal Assent, June 23, 2015.

► 60.022(5) ◄

(5) Expressions used in this section. For the purposes of this section,

(*a*) "money purchase provision" has the same meaning as in subsection 147.1(1);

(*b*) "retirement benefits" has the same meaning as in subsection 8500(1) of the *Income Tax Regulations;*

(*c*) the minimum amount for an account of a taxpayer under a money purchase provision of a registered pension plan is the amount determined under subsection 8506(5) of the *Income Tax Regulations;* and

(*d*) the minimum amount for an account of a taxpayer under a PRPP is the amount that would be the minimum amount for the calendar year under subsection 8506(5) of the *Income Tax Regulations* if the taxpayer's account were an account under a money purchase provision of a registered pension plan.

History: S. 60.022(5) was added by S.C. 2015, c. 36, s. 2, in force on Royal Assent, June 23, 2015.

SECTION 60.03: [Pension income splitting]

► 60.03(1) ◄

(1) Definitions. The following definitions apply in this section.

"eligible pension income" —"eligible pension income" , of an individual for a taxation year, means the total of

(*a*) the eligible pension income (as defined in subsection 118(7)) of the individual for the year,

(*b*) if the individual has attained the age of 65 years before the end of the year, the lesser of

(i) the total of all amounts each of which is a payment made in the year to the individual

(A) out of or under a retirement compensation arrangement that provides benefits that supplement the benefits provided under a registered pension plan (other than an individual pension plan for the purposes of Part LXXXIII of the *Income Tax Regulations*), and

(B) in respect of a life annuity that is attributable to periods of employment for which benefits are also provided to the individual under the registered pension plan, and

(ii) the amount, if any, by which the defined benefit limit (as defined in subsection 8500(1) of the *Income Tax Regulations*) for the year multiplied by 35 exceeds the amount determined under paragraph (*a*), and

(*c*) the lesser of

(i) the total of all amounts received by the individual in the year on account of

(A) a retirement income security benefit payable to the individual under Part 2 of the *Veterans Well-being Act*, or

(B) an income replacement benefit payable to the individual under Part 2 of the *Veterans Well-being Act,* if the amount is determined under subsection 19.1(1), paragraph 23(1)(*b*) or subsection 26.1(1) of that Act (as modified, where applicable, under Part 5 of that Act), and

(ii) the amount, if any, by which the *defined benefit limit* (as defined in subsection 8500(1) of the *Income Tax Regulations)* for the year multiplied by 35 exceeds the total of the amounts determined under paragraphs (*a*) and (*b*). *(revenu de pension déterminé)*

Department of Finance Comfort Letters

(May 11, 2018) [Saskatchewan Pension Plan – Tax Treatment of Variable Benefit Option]

Dear XXXX:

I am writing in response to your letter of December 21, 2017 in which you request amendments to the *Income Tax Act* (the Act) to ensure that variable benefits paid from the Saskatchewan Pension Plan will be eligible for the pension income credit and for pension income splitting.

Officials from Finance Canada have had ongoing discussions with Saskatchewan Finance officials regarding the use of the existing tax framework for registered pension variable benefits as a model for tax accommodation of variable benefits paid out of the Saskatchewan Pension Plan. In conjunction with these discussions, we note that *The Saskatchewan Pension Plan Amendment Regulations, 2018* introduced variable benefits options for members and surviving spouses. We understand that the variable benefit option will become available under the Saskatchewan Pension Plan beginning in 2019.

These changes included references to pertinent sections of the *Income Tax Regulations* in order to ensure that variable benefits paid out of the Saskatchewan Pension Plan will satisfy the tax rules (including "minimum amount" withdrawals) that apply to variable benefits paid out of money purchase registered pension plans. However, as the Saskatchewan Pension Plan is not a registered plan *per se*, but rather is prescribed as a "specified pension plan", the Act would need to be amended to deem the tax provisions applicable to money purchase variable benefits to also apply to the Saskatchewan Pension Plan's variable benefits.

Given those recent changes to your regulations and the fact that the Act currently permits registered pension plans to offer variable benefits to members, we believe that your request is supported to income tax policy terms. We do note, however, that any amendments to the Act would need to include conditions with respect to variable benefits that are consistent with the conditions applicable to benefits paid out of these registered plans.

Consequently, we are prepared to recommend to the Minister of Finance that the Act be amended such that variable benefits paid out of a specified pension plan to a taxpayer:

i. would qualify for the pension income credit and pension income splitting after the taxpayer attains age 65; and

> ii. would be subject to the rules in section 8506 of the *Income Tax Regulations* that apply to variable benefits paid out of money purchase registered pension plans.
>
> If our recommendations are accepted, we would also recommend that these proposed amendments apply in respect of any variable benefit payments made from a specified pension plan after 2018. While I cannot offer any assurance that our recommendations with respect to this matter will be accepted, I hope this statement of our intention is helpful to you.
>
> Thank you for writing to us on this matter.
>
> Yours sincerely,
>
> Brian Ernewein
>
> General Director — Legislation
>
> Tax Policy Branch

History: S. 60.03(1), subparagraph (*c*)(i) of the definition "eligible pension income" was replaced by S.C. 2018, c. 12, s. 4(1), in force April 1, 2019, and formerly read:

(i) the total of all amounts received by the individual in the year on account of a retirement income security benefit payable to the individual under Part 2 of the *Canadian Forces Members and Veterans Re-establishment and Compensation Act*, and

S. 60.03(1), paragraph (*c*) of the definition "eligible pension income" was added by S.C. 2017, c. 33, s. 16(1), applicable to the 2015 and subsequent taxation years.

S. 60.03(1), the definition "eligible pension income" was replaced by S.C. 2012, c. 31, s. 14(1), applicable to the 2013 and subsequent taxation years. S. 60.03(1), the definition "eligible pension income" formerly read:

"eligible pension income"—"eligible pension income" has the same meaning as in subsection 118(7).

Related Regulations: 8500(1) defined benefit limit.

"joint election"—"joint election" in respect of a pensioner and a pension transferee for a taxation year means an election made jointly in prescribed form by the pensioner and the pension transferee and filed with the Minister with both the pensioner's and the pension transferee's returns of income for the taxation year in respect of which the election is made, on or before their respective filing-due dates for the taxation year.

Related Sections: S. 153(1.3) Split-pension amount; s. 220(3.201) Joint election — pension income split.

Forms: T1032 — Joint Election to Split Pension Income.

"pensioner"—"pensioner" for a taxation year means an individual who

(*a*) receives eligible pension income in the taxation year; and

(*b*) is resident in Canada,

(i) if the individual dies in the taxation year, at the time that is immediately before the individual's death, or

(ii) in any other case, at the end of the calendar year in which the taxation year ends.

Related Sections: S. 60(*c*) Other deductions; s. 153(2) Deemed withholding; s. 160(1.3) Joint liability — tax on split-pension income.

"pension income"—"pension income" has the meaning assigned by section 118.

Editorial Note: The amounts that may be split include annuity payments from superannuation or pension funds or, for pensioners over age 65, payments under a RRIF, RRSP, PRPP, or DPSP.

Related Sections: S. 118(7), "pension income".

"pension transferee"—"pension transferee" for a taxation year means an individual who

(*a*) is resident in Canada,

(i) if the individual dies in the taxation year, at the time that is immediately before the individual's death, or

(ii) in any other case, at the end of the calendar year in which the taxation year ends; and

(*b*) at any time in the taxation year is married to, or in a common-law partnership with, a pensioner and is not, by reason of the breakdown of their marriage or common-law partnership, living separate and apart from the pensioner at the end of the taxation year and for a period of at least 90 days commencing in the taxation year.

Related Sections: S. 56(1)(*a.2*) Amounts to be included in income for year; s. 153(2) Deemed withholding; s. 160(1.3) Joint liability — tax on split-pension income.

"qualified pension income"—"qualified pension income" has the meaning assigned by section 118.

Related Sections: S. 118(7) Definitions.

"split-pension amount"—"split-pension amount" for a taxation year is the amount elected by a pensioner and a pension transferee in a joint election for the taxation year not exceeding the amount determined by the formula

$$0.5A \times B/C$$

where

A is the eligible pension income of the pensioner for the taxation year;

B is the number of months in the pensioner's taxation year at any time during which the pensioner was married to, or was in a common-law partnership with, the pension transferee; and

C is the number of months in the pensioner's taxation year.

Related Sections: S. 56(1)(*a.2*) Amounts to be included in income for year; s. 60(*c*) Other deductions; s. 153(2) Deemed withholding; s. 160(1.3) Joint liability — tax on split-pension income.

► 60.03(2) ◄

(2) Effect of pension income split. For the purpose of subsection 118(3), if a pensioner and a pension transferee have made a joint election in a taxation year,

(*a*) the pensioner is deemed not to have received the portion of the pensioner's pension income or qualified pension income, as the case may be, for the taxation year that is equal to the amount of the pensioner's split-pension amount for that taxation year; and

(*b*) the pension transferee is deemed to have received the split-pension amount

(i) as pension income, to the extent that the split-pension amount was pension income to the pensioner, and

(ii) as qualified pension income, to the extent that the split-pension amount was qualified pension income to the pensioner.

Editorial Note: The main benefit of the election (to be made annually) will derive from a difference in the marginal tax brackets of the two parties; it will be most beneficial where the transferor has a large income and the transferee does not. The age and circumstance of the transferee may contribute further to the value of making the transfer. If the transferee qualifies for the pension credit, but otherwise has no other pension income to use it, the transferred-in income will qualify. A third bonus might include reduced OAS clawback burden for the transferor. Note that a change in income levels resulting from pension splitting may also affect access to the spouse/common-law partner credit and the age credit. These and other factors have to be carefully weighed to determine the optimal amount to be transferred. There will be no reduction of tax withheld based on the election to income split. Instalments may be paid based on split income. *Canada Pension Plan* income is not covered by s. 60.03. Rather, the CPP legislation allows spouses and common-law partners to split their CPP retirement pensions.

Related Sections: S. 118(3) Pension credit; s. 118(7) Definitions; s. 153(2) Deemed withholding; s. 160(1.3) Joint liability — tax on split-pension income; s. 220(3.201) Joint election — pension income split.

Tax Profile: February 2008 — Income Splitting A–Z.

Tax Topics: No. 1873, Understanding the New Pension Income Splitting Options.

Forms: T1032 — Joint Election to Split Pension Income.

Tax Window Files: Pension Income Splitting, *December 4, 2007*, CRA Document No. 2006-0214951M4; Pension Income Splitting, *September 27, 2006*, CRA Document No. 2006-0204981M4. Prior to the enactment of s. 60.03, there was no provision of the ITA that permitted the splitting of pension income between spouses.

► 60.03(3) ◄

(3) Limitation. A pensioner may file only one joint election for a particular taxation year.

► 60.03(4) ◄

(4) False declaration. A joint election is invalid if the Minister establishes that a pensioner or a pension transferee has knowingly or under circumstances amounting to gross negligence made a false declaration in the joint election.

SECTION 60.1: Support

► 60.1(1) ◄

(1) Support. For the purposes of paragraph 60(*b*) and subsection 118(5), where an order or agreement, or any variation thereof, provides for the payment of an amount by a taxpayer to a person or for the benefit of the person, children in the person's custody or both the person and those children, the amount or any part thereof

(*a*) when payable, is deemed to be payable to and receivable by that person; and

(*b*) when paid, is deemed to have been paid to and received by that person.

Related Sections: S. 56(1)(*b*) Support; s. 56(1)(*c*) Maintenance; s. 56(1)(*c.1*) Idem; s. 56.1 Support; s. 56.1(4) Definitions; s. 60(*b*) Support; s. 60(*c*) Pension income reallocation; s. 248(1), "amount", "individual", "self-contained domestic establishment"; s. 252(1) Extended meaning of "child"; s. 252(3) Extended meaning of "spouse" and "former spouse".

Income Tax Folios: *Secondary* — S1-F3-C3 Support Payments.

► 60.1(2) ◄

(2) Agreement. For the purposes of section 60, this section and subsection 118(5), the amount determined by the formula

$$A - B$$

where

A is the total of all amounts each of which is an amount (other than an amount that is otherwise a support amount) that became payable by a taxpayer in a taxation year, under an order of a competent tribunal or under a written agreement, in respect of an expense (other than an expenditure in respect of a self-contained domestic establishment in which the taxpayer resides or an expenditure for the acquisition of tangible property, or for civil law corporeal property, that is not an expenditure on account of a medical or education expense or in respect of the acquisition, improvement or maintenance of a self-contained domestic establishment in which the person described in paragraph (*a*) or (*b*) resides) incurred in the year or the preceding taxation year for the maintenance of a person, children in the person's custody or both the person and those children, if the person is

(*a*) the taxpayer's spouse or common-law partner or former spouse or common-law partner, or

(*b*) where the amount became payable under an order made by a competent tribunal in accordance with the laws of a province, an individual who is a parent of a child of whom the taxpayer is a legal parent,

and

B is the amount, if any, by which

(*a*) the total of all amounts each of which is an amount included in the total determined for A in respect of the acquisition or improvement of a self-contained domestic establishment in which that person resides, including any payment of principal or interest in respect of a loan made or indebtedness incurred to finance, in any manner whatever, such acquisition or improvement

exceeds

(*b*) the total of all amounts each of which is an amount equal to 1/5 of the original principal amount of a loan or indebtedness described in paragraph (*a*),

is, where the order or written agreement, as the case may be, provides that this subsection and subsection 56.1(2) shall apply to any amount paid or payable thereunder, deemed to be an amount payable by the taxpayer to that person and receivable by that person as an allowance on a periodic basis, and that person is deemed to have discretion as to the use of that amount.

Editorial Note: Although s. 60.1(2) indicates that the court order or written agreement must provide that this subsection and s. 56.1(2) apply, the courts and the CRA have stated that the inclusion of a clause in the order or agreement stating the parties understand that the third-party payments will be taxable to the recipient and deductible to the payer is sufficient in this regard; see, for example, paragraphs 3.56 to 3.61 of Income Tax Folio S1-F3-C3.

History: S. 60.1(2), the portion of the description of A before paragraph (*a*) was replaced by S.C. 2013, c. 34, s. 109, in force June 26, 2013, and formerly read:

A is the total of all amounts each of which is an amount (other than an amount that is otherwise a support amount) that became payable by a taxpayer in a taxation year, under an order of a competent tribunal or under a written agreement, in respect of an expense (other than an expenditure in respect of a self-contained domestic establishment in which the taxpayer resides or an expenditure for the acquisition of tangible property that is not an expenditure on account of a medical or education expense or in respect of the acquisition, improvement or maintenance of a self-contained domestic establishment in which the person described in paragraph (*a*) or (*b*) resides) incurred in the year or the preceding taxation year for the maintenance of a person, children in the person's custody or both the person and those children, where the person is

Related Regulations: 6502; Part LXV.

Related Sections: S. 56(12) Definition of "allowance"; s. 56.1(2) Agreement; s. 56.1(4) Definitions; s. 248(1), "amount", "property", "self-contained domestic establishment"; s. 252(1) Extended meaning of "child"; s. 252(3) Extended meaning of "spouse" and "former spouse".

Income Tax Folios: *Secondary*— S1-F3-C3 Support Payments.

Cases: A separation agreement stating that payments to third parties were to be "taxable as income" in the recipient's hands and "deducted as support" by the taxpayer was sufficient in order for s. 60.1(2) to apply. The separation agreement does not have to specify subsection numbers. *Ferron v. The Queen*, 2001 DTC 450 (T.C.C.)

When, instead of making maintenance payments of $700 per month for his wife and three children, the taxpayer provided his wife with monthly cheques of $690 made payable to her landlord, these amounts were deductible since they were limited and predetermined and they represented a certain type of expense which the taxpayer's wife was thereby enabled to discharge. *The Queen v. Arsenault*, 96 DTC 6131 (F.C.A.)

▶ 60.1(3) ◀

(3) Prior payments. For the purposes of this section and section 60, where a written agreement or order of a competent tribunal made at any time in a taxation year provides that an amount paid before that time and in the year or the preceding taxation year is to be considered to have been paid and received thereunder,

(*a*) the amount is deemed to have been paid thereunder; and

(*b*) the agreement or order is deemed, except for the purpose of this subsection, to have been made on the day on which the first such amount was paid, except that, where the agreement or order is made after April 1997 and varies a child support amount payable to the recipient from the last such amount paid to the recipient before May 1997, each varied amount of child support paid under the agreement or order is deemed to have been payable under an agreement or order the commencement day of which is the day on which the first payment of the varied amount is required to be made.

Related Sections: S. 56.1(3) Prior payments; s. 56.1(4) Definitions.

Cases: When the Minutes of Settlement signed by the taxpayer and his former spouse failed to provide that the taxpayer's prior payments of maintenance were to be considered as having been paid and received pursuant to them, their deduction was disallowed. *Chabros v. The Queen*, 95 DTC 5247 (F.C.A.).

▶ 60.1(4) ◀

(4) Definitions. The definitions in subsection 56.1(4) apply in this section and section 60.

SECTION 60.11: Application of subpara. 60.1(1)(a)(ii)

(Repealed by 2013, c. 40, s. 29.)

History: S. 60.11 was repealed by S.C. 2013, c. 40, s. 29, in force December 12, 2013, and formerly read:

S. 60.11 *Application of subpara. 60.1(1)(a)(ii).* In the application of subparagraph 60.1(1)(*a*)(ii) in respect of amounts paid pursuant to orders made after May 6, 1974 under the laws of Ontario, the reference in that subparagraph to "February 10, 1988" shall be read as a reference to "May 6, 1974".

SECTION 60.2: Refund of undeducted past service AVCs

▶ 60.2(1) ◀

(1) Refund of undeducted past service AVCs. There may be deducted in computing a taxpayer's income for a taxation year an amount equal to the total of

(*a*) where the taxation year ends before 1991, the total of all amounts each of which is that portion of an amount paid to the taxpayer before 1991 and included by reason of subparagraph 56(1)(*a*)(i) or paragraph 56(1)(*h*) or (*t*) in computing the taxpayer's income for the year or a preceding taxation year that can reasonably be considered to be a refund of additional voluntary contributions made by the taxpayer before October 9, 1986 to a registered pension plan for the taxpayer's benefit in respect of services rendered by the taxpayer before the year in which the contributions were made, to the extent that the contributions were not deducted in computing the taxpayer's income for any taxation year; and

(*b*) the least of

(i) $3,500,

(ii) the total of all amounts each of which is an amount included after 1986 by reason of subparagraph 56(1)(*a*)(i) or paragraph 56(1)(*d.2*), (*h*) or (*t*) in computing the taxpayer's income for the year, and

(iii) the balance of the annuitized voluntary contributions of the taxpayer at the end of the year.

Related Sections: S. 8(1)(*m*) Employee's registered pension plan contributions.

▶ 60.2(2) ◀

(2) Definition of "balance of the annuitized voluntary contributions". For the purposes of subsection (1), "balance of the annuitized voluntary contributions" of a taxpayer at the end of a taxation year means the amount, if any, by which

(*a*) such part of the total of all amounts each of which is an additional voluntary contribution made by the taxpayer to a registered pension plan before October 9, 1986 in respect of services rendered by the taxpayer before the year in which the contribution was made, to the extent that the contribution was not deducted in computing the taxpayer's income for any taxation year, as may reasonably be considered as having been

(i) used before October 9, 1986 to acquire or provide an annuity for the taxpayer's benefit under a registered pension plan or registered retirement savings plan, or

(ii) transferred before October 9, 1986 to a registered retirement income fund under which the taxpayer was the annuitant (within the meaning assigned by subsection 146.3(1)) at the time of the transfer

exceeds

(*b*) the total of all amounts each of which is

(i) an amount deducted under paragraph (1)(*b*) in computing the taxpayer's income for a preceding taxation year, or

(ii) an amount deducted under paragraph (1)(*a*) in computing the taxpayer's income for the year or a preceding taxation year, to the extent that the amount can reasonably be considered to be in respect of a refund of additional voluntary contributions included in determining the total under paragraph (*a*).

SECTION 61: Payment made as consideration for income-averaging annuity

▶ 61(1) ◀

(1) Payment made as consideration for income-averaging annuity. In computing the income for a taxation year of an individual resident in Canada, there may be deducted an amount equal to the lesser of

(*a*) such amount as the individual may claim, not exceeding the total of amounts each of which is a single payment

(i) made by the individual in the year or within 60 days after the end of the year as consideration for an income-averaging annuity contract of the individual, and

(ii) in respect of which no amount has been deducted in computing the individual's income for the immediately preceding taxation year, and

(*b*) the amount, if any, by which the total of

(i) the remainder obtained when the total of the amounts deductible in computing the individual's income for the year by reason of paragraphs 60(*j*) and (*l*) of this Act and paragraph 60(*k*) of the *Income Tax Act*, chapter 148 of the Revised Statutes of Canada, 1952, is deducted from the total of amounts described in subsection (2) in respect of the individual for the year,

(ii) the amount, if any, by which the amount determined under paragraph 3(*b*) in respect of the individual for the year exceeds the total of amounts each of which is an allowable business investment loss of the individual for the year,

(iii) the individual's income for the year from the production of a literary, dramatic, musical or artistic work,

(iv) the individual's income for the year from the individual's activities as an athlete, a musician or a public entertainer such as a theatre, motion picture, radio or television artist, and

(iv.1) the amount, if any, by which the amount included in computing the income of the individual for the year by virtue of section 59 exceeds the total of amounts deducted in computing the individual's income for the year under sections 64, 66, 66.1, 66.2 and 66.4 and under section 29 of the *Income Tax Application Rules*,

exceeds

(v) the total of amounts each of which is the annual annuity amount of the individual in respect of an income-averaging annuity contract in respect of the consideration for which any amount has been deducted under this subsection in computing the individual's income for the year.

Related Regulations: Part II.

Related Sections: S. 61(2) Income-averaging annuity — eligible income.

Interpretation Bulletins: *Secondary* — IT-500R Registered retirement savings plans — Death of an annuitant.

▶ 61(2) ◀

(2) Idem. For the purposes of subsection (1), an amount described in this subsection in respect of an individual for a taxation year is any following amount:

(*a*) any single payment received by the individual in the year

(i) out of or under a superannuation or pension fund or plan

(A) on the death, withdrawal or retirement from employment of an employee or former employee,

(B) on the winding-up of the fund or plan in full satisfaction of all rights of the payee in or under the fund or plan, or

(C) to which the payee is entitled by virtue of an amendment to the plan although the payee continues to be an employee to whom the plan is applicable,

(ii) on retirement as an employee in recognition of long service and not made out of or under a superannuation fund or plan,

(iii) pursuant to an employees profit sharing plan in full satisfaction of all the individual's rights in or under the plan, to the extent that the amount thereof is required to be included in computing the individual's income for the year in which the payment was received, or

(iv) pursuant to a deferred profit sharing plan on the death, withdrawal or retirement from employment of an employee or former employee, to the extent that the amount thereof is required to be included in computing the individual's income for the year;

(*b*) a payment or payments made by an employer to the individual as an employee or former employee on or after retirement in respect of loss of office or employment, if made in the year of retirement or within one year after that year;

(*c*) a payment or payments paid to the individual as a death benefit, if paid in the year of death or within one year after that year;

(*d*) any amount included in computing the individual's income for the year by virtue of subsection 146(8), to the extent that the amount is a refund of premiums, as defined by section 146, under a registered retirement savings plan received by the individual under the plan on or after the death of the person who was, immediately before the person's death, the annuitant thereunder;

(*e*) any amount included in computing the individual's income for the year by virtue of section 13, 14 or 23, subsection 28(4) or (5) or paragraph 106(2)(*a*) of this Act or subparagraph 56(1)(*a*)(viii) of the *Income Tax Act*, chapter 148 of the Revised Statutes of Canada, 1952;

(*f*) any amount deemed by section 7 to be a benefit received by the individual in the year by virtue of the individual's employment;

(*g*) the amount, if any, by which any amount received by the individual in the year as or on account of a prize for achievement in a field of endeavour ordinarily carried on by the individual exceeds $500;

(*h*) any amount included in computing the individual's income for the year by virtue of subsection 146.2(6) of the *Income Tax Act*, chapter 148 of the Revised Statutes of Canada, 1952;

(*i*) a payment made in the year to an individual by virtue of paragraph 51(2)(*b*) of the *Judges Act*;

(*j*) except where the individual claimed a deduction under paragraph 23(3)(*a*) of the *Income Tax Application Rules* in computing the individual's income for the year, any amount included in computing that income by virtue of paragraph 23(3)(*c*) of that Act; and

(*k*) where the individual ceased to be a member of a partnership in the year or the preceding year and paragraph 34(*a*) applied in computing the individual's income therefrom in the preceding year, the amount included in the individual's income for the year by virtue of paragraph 3(*a*) to the extent that, having regard to all the circumstances including the proportion in which the members of the partnership have agreed to share the profits of the partnership, it can reasonably be considered to be in respect of the individual's share of the work in progress of the partnership at the time the individual ceased to be a member thereof, if, during the remainder of the year in which the individual ceased to be a member and in the following year, the individual did not

(i) become employed in the business that had been carried on by the partnership,

(ii) carry on a business that is a profession, or

(iii) become a member of a partnership that carries on a business that is a profession.

► 61(3) ◄

(3) Where income-averaging annuity contract ceases to be such — (Repealed by 1976-77, c. 4, s. 18(2).)

► 61(4) ◄

(4) Definitions. In this section,

"annual annuity amount" —"annual annuity amount" of an individual in respect of an income-averaging annuity contract means the total of the equal payments described in paragraph (*c*) of the definition "income-averaging annuity contract" in this subsection that, under the contract, are receivable by the individual in the twelve month period commencing on the day that the first such payment under the contract becomes receivable by the individual;

"income-averaging annuity contract" —"income-averaging annuity contract" of an individual means a contract between the individual and a person licensed or otherwise authorized under the laws of Canada or a province to carry on in Canada an annuities business or a corporation licensed or otherwise authorized under the laws of Canada or a province to carry on in Canada the business of offering to the public its services as trustee, under which

(*a*) in consideration of a qualifying payment as consideration under the contract, that person agrees to pay to the individual, commencing at a time not later than 10 months after the individual has made the qualifying payment,

(i) an annuity to the individual for the individual's life, with or without a guaranteed term not exceeding the number of years that is the lesser of

(A) 15, and

(B) 85 minus the age of the individual at the time the annuity payments commence, or

(ii) an annuity to the individual for a guaranteed term described in subparagraph (i), or

(*b*) in consideration of a single payment in respect of the individual's 1981 taxation year, other than a qualifying payment, made by the individual as consideration under the contract, that person makes all payments provided for under the contract to the individual before 1983

and under which no payments are provided except the single payment by the individual and,

(*c*) in respect of a contract referred to in paragraph (*a*), equal annuity payments that are to be made annually or at more frequent periodic intervals, or

(*d*) in respect of a contract referred to in paragraph (*b*), payments described therein to the individual;

Related Regulations: 208.

Related Sections: S. 4(2) Deductions not attributable to a source; s. 56(1)(*e*) Disposition of income-averaging annuity contract; s. 144(1), "employees profit sharing plan"; s. 248(1), "amount", "annuity", "death benefit", "deferred profit sharing plan", "employee", "employment", "individual", "office"; s. 255 Canada.

"qualifying payment" —"qualifying payment" means a single payment made before November 13, 1981 (or made on or after November 13, 1981 pursuant to an agreement in writing entered into before that date to make such a payment in respect of the individual's 1981 taxation year, or pursuant to an arrangement in writing made before that date to have funds withheld before 1982 from any of the individual's remuneration described in paragraph (1)(*b*) earned or received before November 13, 1981 and paid by or on behalf of the individual).

SECTION 61.1: Where income-averaging annuity contract ceases to be such

▶ 61.1(1) ◀

(1) Where income-averaging annuity contract ceases to be such. Where a contract that was at any time an income-averaging annuity contract of an individual has, at a subsequent time, ceased to be an income-averaging annuity contract otherwise than by virtue of the surrender, cancellation, redemption, sale or the disposition thereof, the individual shall be deemed to have received at that subsequent time as proceeds of the disposition of an income-averaging annuity contract an amount equal to the fair market value of the contract at that subsequent time and to have acquired the contract, as another contract not being an income-averaging annuity contract, immediately thereafter at a cost to the individual equal to that fair market value.

Related Regulations: 202(2), (3).

Related Sections: S. 56(1)(*l*) Deemed disposition of income-averaging annuity contract; s. 61 Payment made as consideration for income-averaging annuity; s. 212(1)(*n*) Income-averaging annuity contract payments.

▶ 61.1(2) ◀

(2) Where annuitant dies and payments continued. Where an individual who was an annuitant under an income-averaging annuity contract has died and payments are subsequently made under that contract, the payments shall be deemed to be payments under an income-averaging annuity contract.

Interpretation Bulletins: *Secondary* — IT-212R3 Income of deceased persons — Rights or things.

SECTION 61.2: Reserve for debt forgiveness for resident individuals

There may be deducted in computing the income for a taxation year of an individual (other than a trust) resident in Canada throughout the year such amount as the individual claims not exceeding the amount determined by the formula

$$A + B - 0.2(C - \$40{,}000)$$

where

A is the amount, if any, by which

(*a*) the total of all amounts each of which is an amount that, because of the application of section 80 to an obligation payable by the individual (or a partnership of which the individual was a member) was included under subsection 80(13) in computing the income of the individual for the year or the income of the partnership for a fiscal period that ends in the year (to the extent that, where the amount was included in computing income of a partnership, it relates to the individual's share of that income)

exceeds

(*b*) the total of all amounts deducted because of paragraph 80(15)(*a*) in computing the individual's income for the year,

B is the amount, if any, included under section 56.2 in computing the individual's income for the year, and

C is the greater of $40,000 and the individual's income for the year, determined without reference to this section, paragraph 20(1)(*ww*), section 56.2, paragraph 60(*w*), subsection 80(13) and paragraph 80(15)(*a*).

Editorial Note: The amount that may be included in the income of an individual (other than a trust) resident in Canada under the debt forgiveness rules in a year is limited to 20% of the individual's other income for the year in excess of $40,000. This is achieved by a deduction under s. 61.2. The amount of the deduction is included in the individual's income in the following year under s. 56.2, and the reserve calculation is made again. This reserve does not eliminate tax on an income hit, but defers tax until the individual has sufficient income. Claiming a reserve allows the CRA to reduce the individual's tax attributes under s. 80(5) to (11) to the maximum extent possible, if the taxpayer has not already done so, thereby reducing the deduction available under s. 61.2 (s. 80(16)). Reserves for other taxpayers are governed by s. 61.3 and 61.4.

Related Sections: S. 34.2(4) Reserve; s. 56.2 Reserve claimed for debt forgiveness; s. 61.2 Reserve for debt forgiveness for resident individuals; s. 61.4 Reserve for debt forgiveness for corporations and others; s. 80(13) Income inclusion; s. 80(15) Members of partnerships; s. 80(16) Designations by Minister; s. 257 Negative amounts.

Canadian Tax Foundation: Ehinger, *Relief from Debt-Forgiveness Inclusions: The Basics*, 2013 Canadian Tax Focus 3(3):6–7.

SECTION 61.3: Deduction for insolvency with respect to resident corporations

▶ 61.3(1) ◀

(1) Deduction for insolvency with respect to resident corporations. There shall be deducted in computing the income for a taxation year of a corporation resident in Canada throughout the year that is not exempt from tax under this Part on its taxable income, the lesser of

(*a*) the amount, if any, by which

(i) the total of all amounts each of which is an amount that, because of the application of section 80 to a commercial obligation (in this section having the meaning assigned by subsection 80(1)) issued by the corporation (or a partnership of which the corporation was a member) was included under subsection 80(13) in computing the income of the corporation for the year or the income of the partnership for a fiscal period that ends in the year (to the extent that the amount, where it was included in computing income of a partnership, relates to the corporation's share of that income)

exceeds

(ii) the total of all amounts deducted because of paragraph 80(15)(*a*) in computing the corporation's income for the year, and

(*b*) the amount determined by the formula

$$A - 2(B - C - D - E)$$

where

A is the amount determined under paragraph (*a*) in respect of the corporation for the year,

B is the total of

(i) the fair market value of the assets of the corporation at the end of the year,

(ii) the amounts paid before the end of the year on account of the corporation's tax payable under this Part or any of Parts I.3, II, VI and XIV for the year or on account of a similar tax payable for the year under an Act of a province, and

(iii) all amounts paid by the corporation in the 12-month period preceding the end of the year to a person with whom the corporation does not deal at arm's length

(A) as a dividend (other than a stock dividend),

(B) on a reduction of paid-up capital in respect of any class of shares of its capital stock,

(C) on a redemption, acquisition or cancellation of its shares, or

(D) as a distribution or appropriation in any manner whatever to or for the benefit of the shareholders of any class of its capital stock, to the extent that the distribution or appropriation cannot reasonably be considered to have resulted in a reduction in the amount otherwise determined for C in respect of the corporation for the year,

C is the total liabilities of the corporation at the end of the year (determined without reference to the corporation's liabilities for tax payable under this Part or any of Parts I.3, II, VI and XIV for the year or for a similar tax payable for the year under an Act of a province) and, for this purpose,

(i) the equity and consolidation methods of accounting shall not be used, and

(ii) subject to subparagraph (i) and except as otherwise provided in this description, the total liabilities of the corporation shall

(A) where the corporation is not an insurance corporation, a federal credit union or a bank to which clause (B) or (C) applies and the balance sheet as of the end of the year was presented to the shareholders of the corporation and was prepared in accordance with generally accepted accounting principles, be considered to be the total liabilities shown on the balance sheet,

(B) where the corporation is a bank, a federal credit union or an insurance corporation that is required to report to the Superintendent of Financial Institutions and the balance sheet as of the end of the year was accepted by the Superintendent, be considered to be the total liabilities shown on that balance sheet,

(C) where the corporation is an insurance corporation that is required to report to the superintendent of insurance or other similar officer or authority of the province under whose laws the corporation is incorporated and the balance sheet as of the end of the year was accepted by that officer or authority, be considered to be the total liabilities shown on that balance sheet, and

(D) in any other case, be considered to be the amount that would be shown as total liabilities of the corporation at the end of the year on a balance sheet prepared in accordance with generally accepted accounting principles,

D is the total of all amounts each of which is the principal amount at the end of the year of a distress preferred share (within the meaning assigned by subsection 80(1)) issued by the corporation, and

E is 50% of the amount, if any, by which

(i) the amount that would be the corporation's income for the year if that amount were determined without reference to this section and section 61.4

exceeds

(ii) the amount determined under paragraph (*a*) in respect of the corporation for the year.

Editorial Note: This provision allows a debtor corporation resident in Canada throughout the year to claim a permanent offset deduction (i.e., not a reserve) of an "income inclusion hit" under the debt forgiveness rules (per paragraph (*a*)). The amount of offset is limited to an amount that is twice that corporation's "net tax assets" (paragraph (*b*)), so that in the absence of such assets a complete offset is available, even if there is only a small "tax deficit". (The provision's rationale is that an income inclusion should not "financially aggravate" an insolvent corporation). Net tax assets are based on the total of year-end assets at fair market value (subparagraph (i) of the description of B), most income taxes paid by year end (subparagraph (ii) of the description of B), and non-arm's length distributions/appropriations within 12 months of year-end (subparagraph (iii) of the description of B); less year-end liabilities/distress preferred shares (the descriptions of C and D) and 50% of income (ignoring the income inclusion and related provisions) (the description of E). A s. 61.3 deduction reduces undeducted SR&ED expenditures (s. 37(1)(*f.1*)) and allows the CRA to redesignate ss. 80(5) to (11) reductions to the maximum allowed, if not already done (s. 80(16)). A similar offset is available for non-resident corporations, per s. 61.3(2), both provisions being subject to an anti-avoidance rule in s. 61.3(3) (see editorial note).

History: S. 61.3(1)(*b*), clauses (ii)(A) and (B) of the description of C were replaced by S.C. 2010, c. 12, s. 2108, in force December 19, 2012 (P.C. 2012-1623, SI/2012-99). S. 61.3(1)(*b*), clauses (ii)(A) and (B) of the description of C formerly read:

(A) where the corporation is not an insurance corporation or a bank to which clause (B) or (C) applies and the balance sheet as of the end of the year was presented to the shareholders of the corporation and was prepared in accordance with generally accepted accounting principles, be considered to be the total liabilities shown on that balance sheet,

(B) where the corporation is a bank or an insurance corporation that is required to report to the Superintendent of Financial Institutions and the balance sheet as of the end of the year was accepted by the Superintendent, be considered to be the total liabilities shown on that balance sheet,

Related Sections: S. 37(1)(*f.1*) Scientific research and experimental development; s. 56.3 Reserve claimed for debt forgiveness; s. 61.3(2) Reserve for insolvency with respect to non-resident corporations; s. 61.3(3) Anti-avoidance; s. 61.4 Reserve for debt forgiveness for corporations and others; s. 80(13) Income inclusion; s. 80(15) Members of partnerships; s. 80(16) Designations by Minister; s. 80.01(10) Subsequent payments in satisfaction of debt; s. 80.04(4) Agreement respecting transfer of forgiven amount; s. 87(2)(*l.21*) Forgiven amount; s. 160.4(1) Liability in respect of transfers by insolvent corporations; s. 257 Negative amounts.

Canadian Tax Foundation: Ehinger, *Relief from Debt-Forgiveness Inclusions: The Basics*, 2013 Canadian Tax Focus 3(3):6–7; Vantil, *Corporate Debt Settlement and Forgiveness: The Technical Rules*, 2009 British Columbia Tax Conference 6:2–38; Hegedus, *Fond Memories of Section 80 and Distressed Preferred Share Rules*, 2009 Prairie Provinces Tax Conference 9:1–40; Bauer, *Restructuring Debt Obligations*, 2008 Conference Report 37:1–30.

► 61.3(2) ◄

(2) Reserve for insolvency with respect to non-resident corporations. There shall be deducted in computing the income for a taxation year of a corporation that is non-resident at any time in the year, the lesser of

(*a*) the amount, if any, by which

(i) the total of all amounts each of which is an amount that, because of the application of section 80 to a commercial obligation issued by the corporation (or a partnership of which the corporation was a member) was included under subsection 80(13) in computing the corporation's taxable income or taxable income earned in Canada for the year or the income of the partnership for a fiscal period that ends in the year (to the extent that, where the amount was included in computing income of a partnership, it relates to the corporation's share of the partnership's income added in computing the corporation's taxable income or taxable income earned in Canada for the year)

exceeds

(ii) the total of all amounts deducted because of paragraph 80(15)(*a*) in computing the corporation's taxable income or taxable income earned in Canada for the year, and

(*b*) the amount determined by the formula

$$A - 2(B - C - D - E)$$

where

A is the amount determined under paragraph (*a*) in respect of the corporation for the year,

B is the total of

(i) the fair market value of the assets of the corporation at the end of the year,

(ii) the amounts paid before the end of the year on account of the corporation's tax payable under this Part or any of Parts I.3, II, VI and XIV for the year or on account of a similar tax payable for the year under an Act of a province, and

(iii) all amounts paid in the 12-month period preceding the end of the year by the corporation to a person with whom the corporation does not deal at arm's length

(A) as a dividend (other than a stock dividend),

(B) on a reduction of paid-up capital in respect of any class of shares of its capital stock,

(C) on a redemption, acquisition or cancellation of its shares, or

(D) as a distribution or appropriation in any manner whatever to or for the benefit of the shareholders of any class of its capital stock, to the extent that the distribution or appropriation cannot reasonably be considered to have resulted in a reduction of the amount otherwise determined for C in respect of the corporation for the year,

C is the total liabilities of the corporation at the end of the year (determined without reference to the corporation's liabilities for tax payable under this Part or any of Parts I.3, II, VI and XIV for the year or for a similar tax payable for the year under an Act of a province), determined in the manner described in the description of C in paragraph (1)(*b*),

D is the total of all amounts each of which is the principal amount at the end of the year of a distress preferred share (within the meaning assigned by subsection 80(1)) issued by the corporation, and

E is 50% of the amount, if any, by which

(i) the amount that would be the corporation's taxable income or taxable income earned in Canada for the year if that amount were determined without reference to this section and section 61.4

exceeds

(ii) the amount determined under paragraph (*a*) in respect of the corporation for the year.

Editorial Note: See the Editorial Note to s. 61.3(1).

Related Sections: S. 37(1)(*f.1*) Scientific research and experimental development; s. 56.3 Reserve claimed for debt forgiveness; s. 61.3(2) Reserve for insolvency with respect to non-resident corporations; s. 61.3(3) Anti-avoidance; s. 61.4 Reserve for debt forgiveness for corporations and others; s. 80(13) Income inclusion; s. 80(15) Members of partnerships; s. 80(16) Designations by Minister; s. 80.01(10) Subsequent payments in satisfaction of debt; s. 80.04(4) Agreement respecting transfer of forgiven amount; s. 87(2)(*l.21*) Forgiven amount; s. 160.4(1) Liability in respect of transfers by insolvent corporations; s. 257 Negative amounts.

► 61.3(3) ◄

(3) Anti-avoidance. Subsections (1) and (2) do not apply to a corporation for a taxation year where property was transferred in the 12-month period preceding the end of the year or the corporation became indebted in that period and it can reasonably be considered that one of the reasons for the transfer or the indebtedness was to increase the amount that the corporation would, but for this subsection, be entitled to deduct under subsection (1) or (2).

Editorial Note: This provision nullifies the ss. 61.3(1) and (2) offsets (in their entirety), where property was transferred or the corporation became indebted within 12 months preceding year-end, if one of the main reasons for the foregoing is to increase the offsets.

SECTION 61.4: Reserve for debt forgiveness for corporations and others

There may be deducted as a reserve in computing the income for a taxation year of a taxpayer that is a corporation or trust resident in Canada throughout the year or a non-resident person who carried on business through a fixed place of business in Canada at the end of the year such amount as the taxpayer claims not exceeding the least of

(*a*) the amount determined by the formula

$$A - B$$

where

A is the amount, if any, by which

(i) the total of all amounts each of which is an amount that, because of the application of section 80 to a commercial obligation (within the meaning assigned by subsection 80(1)) issued by the taxpayer (or a partnership of which the taxpayer was a member) was included under subsection 80(13) in computing the income of the taxpayer for the year or a preceding taxation year or of the partnership for a fiscal period that ends in that year or preceding year (to the extent that, where the amount was included in computing income of a partnership, it relates to the taxpayer's share of that income)

exceeds the total of

(ii) all amounts each of which is an amount deducted under paragraph 80(15)(*a*) in computing the taxpayer's income for the year or a preceding taxation year, and

(iii) all amounts deducted under section 61.3 in computing the taxpayer's income for the year or a preceding taxation year, and

B is the amount, if any, by which the amount determined for A in respect of the taxpayer for the year exceeds the total of

(i) the amount that would be determined for A in respect of the taxpayer for the year if that value did not take into account amounts included or deducted in computing the taxpayer's income for any preceding taxation year, and

(ii) the amount, if any, included under section 56.3 in computing the taxpayer's income for the year,

(*b*) the total of

(i) 4/5 of the amount that would be determined for A in paragraph (*a*) in respect of the taxpayer for the year if that value did not take into account amounts included or deducted in computing the taxpayer's income for any preceding taxation year,

(ii) 3/5 of the amount that would be determined for A in paragraph (*a*) in respect of the taxpayer for the year if that value did not take into account amounts included or deducted in computing the taxpayer's income for the year or any preceding taxation year (other than the last preceding taxation year),

(iii) 2/5 of the amount that would be determined for A in paragraph (*a*) in respect of the taxpayer for the year if that value did not take into account amounts included or deducted in computing the taxpayer's income for the year or any preceding taxation year (other than the second last preceding taxation year), and

(iv) 1/5 of the amount that would be determined for A in paragraph (*a*) in respect of the taxpayer for the year if that value did not take into account amounts included or deducted in computing the taxpayer's income for the year or any preceding taxation year (other than the third last preceding taxation year), and

(*c*) where the taxpayer is a corporation that commences to wind up in the year (otherwise than in circumstances to which the rules in subsection 88(1) apply), nil.

Editorial Note: This provision (as well as s. 56.3) allows a qualifying person to spread an "income hit" under the debt forgiveness rules over 5 years, so that at least 20% of the amount is included each year. It applies to a corporation or trust resident in Canada throughout the year, or a non-resident person who carried on business through a fixed place of business in Canada at the end of the year, but does not apply where a corporation has commenced a wind-up other than on a rollover basis (see paragraph (*c*)).

Related Sections: S. 34.2(4) Reserve; s. 56.3 Reserve claimed for debt forgiveness; s. 61.2 Reserve for debt forgiveness for resident individuals; s. 61.3 Deduction for insolvency with respect to resident corporations; s. 80(13) Income inclusion; s. 80(15) Members of partnerships; s. 80.04(4) Agreement respecting transfer of forgiven amount; s. 87(2)(*h.1*) Debts; s. 257 Negative amounts.

Canadian Tax Foundation: Ehinger, *Relief from Debt-Forgiveness Inclusions: The Basics*, 2013 Canadian Tax Focus 3(3):6–7.

SECTION 62: Moving expenses

► 62(1) ◄

(1) Moving expenses. There may be deducted in computing a taxpayer's income for a taxation year amounts paid by the taxpayer as or on account of moving expenses incurred in respect of an eligible relocation, to the extent that

(*a*) they were not paid on the taxpayer's behalf in respect of, in the course of or because of, the taxpayer's office or employment;

(*b*) they were not deductible because of this section in computing the taxpayer's income for the preceding taxation year;

(*c*) the total of those amounts does not exceed

(i) in any case described in subparagraph (*a*)(i) of the definition "eligible relocation" in subsection 248(1), the total of all amounts, each of which is an amount included in computing the taxpayer's income for the taxation year from the taxpayer's employment at a new work location or from carrying on the business at the new work location, or because of subparagraph 56(1)(*r*)(v) in respect of the taxpayer's employment at the new work location, and

(ii) in any case described in subparagraph (*a*)(ii) of the definition "eligible relocation" in subsection 248(1), the total of amounts included in computing the taxpayer's income for the year because of paragraphs 56(1)(*n*) and (*o*); and

(*d*) all reimbursements and allowances received by the taxpayer in respect of those expenses are included in computing the taxpayer's income.

Editorial Note: If the taxpayer is resident in Canada for income tax purposes, the relocation can be inside or outside of Canada; see the postamble to the definition of "eligible relocation" in s. 248(1). For employees or self-employed persons, the deduction is limited to the income from the employment or business at the new work location for the relevant year, and any excess expenses can be carried forward and deducted in the next year, subject to the same income limitation. For students, the deduction is limited to the included amount of scholarship or bursary income (but for most students, these amounts are not included) and research grants.

History: S. 62(1)(*c*)(i) was replaced by S.C. 2009, c. 2, s. 16(1), applicable to the 2008 and subsequent taxation years. S. 62(1)(*c*)(i) formerly read:

(i) in any case described in subparagraph (*a*)(i) of the definition "eligible relocation" in subsection 248(1), the taxpayer's income for the year from the taxpayer's employment at a new work location or from carrying on the business at the new work location, as the case may be, and

Related Sections: S. 6(19) Benefit re housing loss; s. 6(20) Benefit re eligible housing loss; s. 6(21) Housing loss; s. 62(2) Moving expenses of students; s. 63.1 Application to deemed residents; s. 64.1 Individuals absent from Canada; s. 80.4(1.1) Loan or debt from office or employment; s. 110(1)(*j*) Home relocation loan; s. 115(2)(*f*) Non-resident's taxable income in Canada; s. 248(1), "eligible relocation"; s. 248(28) Limitation respecting inclusions, deductions and tax credits.

Canadian Tax Foundation: Arnold and Li, *The Appropriate Tax Treatment of the Reimbursement of Moving Expenses*, 1996 Canadian Tax Journal 1:1–37.

Forms: T1-M — Claim for Moving Expenses.

Income Tax Folios: *Primary* — S1-F3-C4 Moving Expenses.

Interpretation Bulletins: *Secondary* — IT-518R Food, beverages and entertainment expenses.

Tax Window Files: Provincial residency, Moving expenses, *January 26, 2015*, CRA Document No. 2014-0547981E5.

Cases: The taxpayer sold his home and moved to a smaller one for personal reasons. He failed to establish that he moved in order to continue working. It was not sufficient to state that he moved to get closer to work and continue working when there were no changes in his employment. *Dueck v. The Queen*, 2014 DTC 1183 (T.C.C.)

The taxpayer's employer relocated from Nanaimo, B.C. to Courtenay, B.C. in 1996. After commuting to work for seven years, the taxpayer moved to Courtenay in 2003. His moving expenses were deductible since there are no time restrictions in s. 62. *Beaudoin v. The Queen*, 2005 DTC 282 (T.C.C.)

The 40-kilometre distance referred to in s. 62(1) must be measured using the "shortest normal route". *Giannakopoulos v. M.N.R.*, 95 DTC 5447 (F.C.A.)

On moving from Ottawa to Vancouver, the taxpayer acquired a new home which was inferior to his former home but cost more. He attempted to include a deduction for the mortgage interest attributable to the difference in selling prices of the home as a moving expense, together with the cost of land registration, installation of a dishwasher and new locks. These expenses were extra costs incurred in replacing an asset, the old residence, not moving expenses. *Storrow v. The Queen*, 78 DTC 6551 (F.C.T.D.)

► 62(2) ◄

(2) Moving expenses of students. There may be deducted in computing a taxpayer's income for a taxation year the amount, if any, that the taxpayer would be entitled to deduct under subsection (1) if the definition *eligible relocation* in subsection 248(1) were read without reference to subparagraph (*a*)(i) of that definition and if the word "both" in paragraph (*c*) of that definition were read as "either or both".

History: S. 62(2) was replaced by S.C. 2017, c. 33, s. 17(1), applicable to taxation years that end after October 2011, and formerly read:

(2) *Moving expenses of students.* There may be deducted in computing a taxpayer's income for a taxation year the amount, if any, that the taxpayer would be entitled to deduct under subsection (1) if the definition "eligible relocation" in subsection 248(1) were read without reference to subparagraph (*a*)(i) of that definition and if the word "both" in paragraph (*b*) of that definition were read as "either or both".

Income Tax Folios: *Primary* — S1-F3-C4 Moving Expenses.

► 62(3) ◄

(3) Definition of "moving expenses". In subsection (1), "moving expenses" includes any expense incurred as or on account of

(*a*) travel costs (including a reasonable amount expended for meals and lodging), in the course of moving the taxpayer and members of the taxpayer's household from the old residence to the new residence,

(*b*) the cost to the taxpayer of transporting or storing household effects in the course of moving from the old residence to the new residence,

(*c*) the cost to the taxpayer of meals and lodging near the old residence or the new residence for the taxpayer and members of the taxpayer's household for a period not exceeding 15 days,

(*d*) the cost to the taxpayer of cancelling the lease by virtue of which the taxpayer was the lessee of the old residence,

(*e*) the taxpayer's selling costs in respect of the sale of the old residence,

(*f*) where the old residence is sold by the taxpayer or the taxpayer's spouse or common-law partner as a result of the move, the cost to the taxpayer of legal services in respect of the purchase of the new residence and of any tax, fee or duty (other than any goods and services tax or value-added tax) imposed on the transfer or registration of title to the new residence,

(*g*) interest, property taxes, insurance premiums and the cost of heating and utilities in respect of the old residence, to the extent of the lesser of $5,000 and the total of such expenses of the taxpayer for the period

(i) throughout which the old residence is neither ordinarily occupied by the taxpayer or by any other person who ordinarily resided with the taxpayer at the old residence immediately before the move nor rented by the taxpayer to any other person, and

(ii) in which reasonable efforts are made to sell the old residence, and

(*h*) the cost of revising legal documents to reflect the address of the taxpayer's new residence, of replacing drivers' licenses and non-commercial vehicle permits (excluding any cost for vehicle insurance) and of connecting or disconnecting utilities,

but, for greater certainty, does not include costs (other than costs referred to in paragraph (*f*)) incurred by the taxpayer in respect of the acquisition of the new residence.

Editorial Note: The CRA allows a "simplified method" of determining meal and vehicle expenses incurred in the course of moving, for which supporting receipts are not required. Under this method, a flat rate applies per qualifying meal and per kilometre driven in the course of moving. The current flat rates can be found on the CRA website at http://www.cra-arc.gc.ca/tx/ndvdls/tpcs/ncm-tx/rtrn/cmpltng/ddctns/lns248-260/255/rts-eng.html. The meal expenses are not subject to the 50% limitation in s. 67.1.

Related Sections: S. 56(1)(*n*) Scholarships, bursaries, etc; s. 56(1)(*o*) Research grants; s. 115(2) Non-resident's taxable income in Canada; s. 248(1), "amount", "business", "eligible location", "employed", "employer", "employment"; s. 255 Canada.

Income Tax Folios: *Primary* — S1-F3-C4 Moving Expenses.

Cases: Although they constituted an expense connected with moving, mortgage interest payments pending the sale of the taxpayer's old residence were not specifically included in the definition of "moving expenses" and, hence, were not deductible. *A. G. of Canada v. Séguin*, 97 DTC 5457 (F.C.A.), reversing 97 DTC 3255 (T.C.C.).

SECTION 63: Child care expenses

► 63(1) ◄

(1) Child care expenses. Subject to subsection (2), where a prescribed form containing prescribed information is filed with a taxpayer's return of income (other than a return filed under subsection 70(2) or 104(23), paragraph 128(2)(*e*) or subsection 150(4)) under this Part for a taxation year, there may be deducted in computing the taxpayer's income for the year such amount as the taxpayer claims not exceeding the total of all amounts each of which is an amount paid, as or on account of child care expenses incurred for services rendered in the year in respect of an eligible child of the taxpayer,

(*a*) by the taxpayer, where the taxpayer is described in subsection (2) and the supporting person of the child for the year is a person described in clause (i)(D) of the description of C in the formula in that subsection, or

(*b*) by the taxpayer or a supporting person of the child for the year, in any other case,

to the extent that

(*c*) the amount is not included in computing the amount deductible under this subsection by an individual (other than the taxpayer), and

(*d*) the amount is not an amount (other than an amount that is included in computing a taxpayer's income and that is not deductible in computing the taxpayer's taxable income) in respect of which any taxpayer is or was entitled to a reimbursement or any other form of assistance,

and the payment of which is proven by filing with the Minister one or more receipts each of which was issued by the payee and contains, where the payee is an individual, that individual's Social Insurance Number, but not exceeding the amount, if any, by which

(*e*) the lesser of

(i) $2/3$ of the taxpayer's earned income for the year, and

(ii) the total of all amounts each of which is the annual child care expense amount in respect of an eligible child of the taxpayer for the year

exceeds

(*f*) the total of all amounts each of which is an amount that is deducted, in respect of the taxpayer's eligible children for the year, under this section in computing the income for the year of an individual (other than the taxpayer) to whom subsection (2) applies for the year.

Editorial Note: Generally, in the case of two parents or spouses or common-law partners residing together, the deduction must be claimed by the lower-income-earning person. There are exceptions in s. 63(2) which allow the higher-income-earning person to claim the deduction under certain circumstances (for example, where the other person is attending school, or is incapable of caring for the children because of infirmity). The general limits on the deduction are $11,000 per year per disabled child, $8,000 per year per child under 7 years old, and $5,000 per year for any other child under 16 years old during the year. There are additional limitations on weekly expenses incurred for boarding school or camp (deductions limited to 1/40th of the above amounts per week).

Related Sections: S. 63(2.2) Expenses while at school; s. 63(3) Definitions; s. 64.1 Individuals absent from Canada; s. 118.4 Reference to medical practitioners, etc.; s. 248(1), "amount", "individual"; s. 252 Extended meaning of "child".

Canadian Tax Foundation: Gordon, *Child-Care Expense Deduction*, 1999 Canadian Tax Journal 6:1588–1626.

Forms: T778 — Child Care Expenses Deduction.

Income Tax Folios: *Primary* — S1-F3-C1 Child Care Expense Deduction; *Secondary* — S1-F1-C1 Medical Expense Tax Credit; S1-F1-C2 Disability Tax Credit.

Information Circulars: IC 82-2R2 Social insurance number legislation that relates to the preparation of information slips.

Interpretation Bulletins: *Secondary* — IT-518R Food, beverages and entertainment expenses.

Cases: Since baby-sitting expenses incurred during periods of orientation while a taxpayer may not actually be physically present at the work place are within the "object and spirit" of s. 63, the taxpayer could deduct the cost of a baby-sitter for the seven-day period immediately preceding her return to work. *McCluskie v. The Queen*, 94 DTC 1735 (T.C.C.)

A nanny's salary was not deductible as a business expense but was only deductible as a parental expense within the meaning of s. 63. *Symes v. The Queen et al.*, 94 DTC 6001 (S.C.C.)

► 63(2) ◄

(2) Income exceeding income of supporting person. Where the income for a taxation year of a taxpayer who has an eligible child for the year exceeds the income for that year of a supporting person of that child (on the assumption that both incomes are computed without reference to this section and paragraphs 60(*v*.1) and (*w*)), the amount that may be deducted by the taxpayer under subsection (1) for the year as or on account of child care expenses shall not exceed the lesser of

(*a*) the amount that would, but for this subsection, be deductible by the taxpayer for the year under subsection (1), and

(*b*) the amount determined by the formula

$$A \times C$$

where

A is the total of all amounts each of which is the periodic child care expense amount in respect of an eligible child of the taxpayer for the year, and

C is the total of

(i) the number of weeks in the year during which the child care expenses were incurred and throughout which the supporting person was

(A) a student in attendance at a designated educational institution or a secondary school and enrolled in a program of the institution or school of not less than 3 consecutive weeks duration that provides that each student in the program spend not less than 10 hours per week on courses or work in the program,

(B) a person certified in writing by a medical doctor or a nurse practitioner to be a person who

(I) was incapable of caring for children because of the person's mental or physical infirmity and confinement throughout a period of not less than 2 weeks in the year to bed, to a wheelchair or as a patient in a hospital, an asylum or other similar institution, or

(II) was in the year, and is likely to be for a long, continuous and indefinite period, incapable of caring for children, because of the person's mental or physical infirmity,

(C) a person confined to a prison or similar institution throughout a period of not less than 2 weeks in the year, or

(D) a person who, because of a breakdown of the person's marriage or common-law partnership, was living separate and apart from the taxpayer at the end of the year and for a period of at least 90 days that began in the year, and

(ii) the number of months in the year (other than a month that includes all or part of a week included in the number of weeks referred to in subparagraph (i)), each of which is a month during which the child care expenses were incurred and the supporting person was a student in attendance at a designated educational institution or a secondary school and enrolled in a program of the institution or school that is not less than 3 consecutive weeks duration and that provides that each student in the program spend not less than 12 hours in the month on courses in the program.

Editorial Note: S. 63(2) allows a limited deduction for the higher income-earner of a married or common-law couple. The amount so deducted reduces the amount deductible for the other spouse or common-law partner under s. 63(1).

History: S. 63(2)(*b*), the portion of clause (i)(B) of the description of C before subclause (I) was replaced by S.C. 2017, c. 33, s. 18(1), applicable in respect of certifications made after September 7, 2017, and formerly read:

> (B) a person certified in writing by a medical doctor to be a person who

S. 63(2)(*b*), the portion of clause (i)(B) before subclause (I) of the description of C was replaced by S.C. 2013, c. 34, s. 198(1), applicable to certifications made after December 20, 2002, and formerly read:

> (B) a person certified by a medical doctor to be a person who

Related Sections: S. 63(2.2) Expenses while at school; s. 63(3), "periodic child care expense amount".

▶ 63(2.1) ◀

(2.1) Taxpayer and supporting person with equal incomes. For the purposes of this section, where in any taxation year the income of a taxpayer who has an eligible child for the year and the income of a supporting person of the child are equal (on the assumption that both incomes are computed without reference to this section and paragraphs 60(*v*.1) and (*w*)), no deduction shall be allowed under this section to the taxpayer and the supporting person in respect of the child unless they jointly elect to treat the income of one of them as exceeding the income of the other for the year.

▶ 63(2.2) ◀

(2.2) Expenses while at school. There may be deducted in computing a taxpayer's income for a taxation year such part of the amount determined under subsection (2.3) as the taxpayer claims, where

(*a*) the taxpayer is, at any time in the year, a student in attendance at a designated educational institution or a secondary school and enrolled in a program of the institution or school of not less than 3 consecutive weeks duration that provides that each student in the program spend not less than

(i) 10 hours per week on courses or work in the program, or

(ii) 12 hours per month on courses in the program;

(*b*) there is no supporting person of an eligible child of the taxpayer for the year or the income of the taxpayer for the year exceeds the income for the year of a supporting person of the child (on the assumption that both incomes are computed without reference to this section and paragraphs 60(*v*.1) and (*w*)); and

(*c*) a prescribed form containing prescribed information is filed with the taxpayer's return of income (other than a return filed under subsection 70(2) or 104(23), paragraph 128(2)(*e*) or subsection 150(4)) for the year.

Related Sections: S. 60(*v*.1) UI and EI benefit repayment; s. 63(1) Child care expenses; s. 63(2)(*b*) Income exceeding income of supporting person.

▶ 63(2.3) ◀

(2.3) Amount deductible. For the purpose of subsection (2.2), the amount determined in respect of a taxpayer for a taxation year is the least of

(*a*) the amount by which the total of all amounts, each of which is an amount paid as or on account of child care expenses incurred for services rendered in the year in respect of an eligible child of the taxpayer, exceeds the amount that is deductible under subsection (1) in computing the taxpayer's income for the year,

(*b*) $2/3$ of the taxpayer's income for the year computed without reference to this section and paragraphs 60(*v*.1) and (*w*),

(*c*) the amount determined by the formula

$$A \times C$$

where

A is the total of all amounts each of which is the periodic child care expense amount in respect of an eligible child of the taxpayer for the year, and

C is

(i) if there is a supporting person of an eligible child of the taxpayer for the year,

(A) the number of weeks, in the year, in which both the taxpayer and the supporting person were students who would be described in paragraph (2.2)(*a*) if that paragraph were read without reference to subparagraph (ii), and

(B) the number of months in the year (other than a month that includes all or part of a week included in the number of weeks referred to in clause (A)), in which both the taxpayer and the supporting person were students described in paragraph (2.2)(*a*), and

(ii) in any other case,

(A) the number of weeks, in the year, in which the taxpayer was a student who would be described in paragraph (2.2)(*a*) if that paragraph were read without reference to subparagraph (ii), and

(B) the number of months in the year (other than a month that includes all or part of a week included in the number of weeks referred to in clause (A)), in which the taxpayer was a student described in paragraph (2.2)(*a*),

(*d*) the amount by which the total calculated under subparagraph (1)(*e*)(ii) in respect of eligible children of the taxpayer for the year exceeds the amount that is deductible under subsection (1) in computing the taxpayer's income for the year, and

(*e*) where there is a supporting person of an eligible child of the taxpayer for the year, the amount by which the amount calculated under paragraph (2)(*b*) for the year in respect of the taxpayer exceeds ⅔ of the taxpayer's earned income for the year.

Editorial Note: S. 63(2.2) and (2.3) may allow an additional deduction (that is, in addition to any amount deducted under s. 63(1)) for a single parent, or a married or common-law parent whose income exceeds that of the other parent, where the individual attends secondary school or a designated educational institution (defined in s. 118.6(1)).

Related Sections: S. 60(*v*.1) UI and EI benefit repayment; s. 63(1) Child care expenses; s. 63(2)(*b*) Income exceeding income of supporting person; s. 63(3) Definitions.

▶ 63(3) ◀

(3) Definitions. In this section,

"annual child care expense amount" —"annual child care expense amount", in respect of an eligible child of a taxpayer for a taxation year, means

(*a*) $11,000, if the child is a person in respect of whom an amount may be deducted under section 118.3 in computing a taxpayer's tax payable under this Part for the year, and

(*b*) if the child is not a person referred to in paragraph (*a*),

(i) $8,000, if the child is under 7 years of age at the end of the year, and

(ii) $5,000, in any other case;

History: S. 63(3), paragraphs (*a*) and (*b*) of the definition "annual child care expense amount" were replaced by S.C. 2015, c. 36, s. 29(1), applicable to the 2015 and subsequent taxation years, and formerly read:

(*a*) $10,000, where the child is a person in respect of whom an amount may be deducted under section 118.3 in computing a taxpayer's tax payable under this Part for the year, and

(*b*) where the child is not a person referred to in paragraph (*a*),

(i) $7,000, where the child is under 7 years of age at the end of the year, and

(ii) $4,000, in any other case;

"child care expense" —"child care expense" means an expense incurred in a taxation year for the purpose of providing in Canada, for an eligible child of a taxpayer, child care services including baby sitting services, day nursery services or services provided at a boarding school or camp if the services were provided

(*a*) to enable the taxpayer, or the supporting person of the child for the year, who resided with the child at the time the expense was incurred,

(i) to perform the duties of an office or employment,

(ii) to carry on a business either alone or as a partner actively engaged in the business,

(iii) (Repealed.)

(iv) to carry on research or any similar work in respect of which the taxpayer or supporting person received a grant, or

(v) to attend a designated educational institution or a secondary school, where the taxpayer is enrolled in a program of the institution or school of not less than three consecutive weeks duration that provides that each student in the program spend not less than

(A) 10 hours per week on courses or work in the program, or

(B) 12 hours per month on courses in the program, and

(*b*) by a resident of Canada other than a person

(i) who is the father or the mother of the child,

(ii) who is a supporting person of the child or is under 18 years of age and related to the taxpayer, or

(iii) in respect of whom an amount is deducted under section 118 in computing the tax payable under this Part for the year by the taxpayer or by a supporting person of the child,

except that

(*c*) any such expenses paid in the year for a child's attendance at a boarding school or camp to the extent that the total of those expenses exceeds the product obtained when the periodic child care expense amount in respect of the child for the year is multiplied by the number of weeks in the year during which the child attended the school or camp, and

(*d*) for greater certainty, any expenses described in subsection 118.2(2) and any other expenses that are paid for medical or hospital care, clothing, transportation or education or for board and lodging, except as otherwise expressly provided in this definition,

are not child care expenses;

Editorial Note: The child care provider must be resident in Canada in order for the expense to qualify. Note also the limitation for child's attendance at boarding school or camp; instead of the actual costs, the periodic child care expense amount applies per week of attendance.

Related Sections: S. 64.1 Individuals absent from Canada.

Cases: The payments made by a taxpayer to his wife to provide child care services for their children were excluded by s. 63(3)(*a*)(ii) as an allowable child care expense and such exclusion did not constitute discrimination on the basis of family status under s. 15 of the Charter, since a group based on marital status does not form a "distinct and insular minority", even though that group may be in a minority. *Boland v. M.N.R.,* 93 DTC 1558 (T.C.C.)

"earned income" —"earned income" of a taxpayer means the total of

(*a*) all salaries, wages and other remuneration, including gratuities, received by the taxpayer in respect of in the course of, or because of, offices and employments,

(*b*) all amounts that are included, or that would, but for paragraph 81(1)(*a*) or subsection 81(4), be included, because of section 6 or 7 or paragraph 56(1) (*n*), (*n.1*), (*o*) or (*r*), in computing the taxpayer's income,

(*c*) all the taxpayer's incomes or the amounts that would, but for paragraph 81(1)(*a*), be the taxpayer's incomes from all businesses carried on either alone or as a partner actively engaged in the business, and

(*d*) all amounts received by the taxpayer as, on account of, in lieu of payment of or in satisfaction of, a disability pension under the *Canada Pension Plan* or a provincial pension plan as defined in section 3 of that Act;

Interpretation Bulletins: *Secondary* — IT-434R Rental of real property by individual.

"eligible child" —"eligible child" of a taxpayer for a taxation year means

(*a*) a child of the taxpayer or of the taxpayer's spouse or common-law partner, or

(*b*) a child dependent on the taxpayer or the taxpayer's spouse or common-law partner for support and whose income for the year does not exceed the amount used under paragraph (*c*) of the description of B in subsection 118(1) for the year

if, at any time during the year, the child

(*c*) is under 16 years of age, or

(*d*) is dependent on the taxpayer or on the taxpayer's spouse or common-law partner and has a mental or physical infirmity;

"periodic child care expense amount" —"periodic child care expense amount", in respect of an eligible child of a taxpayer for a taxation year, means 1/40 of the annual child care expense amount in respect of the child for the year;

"supporting person" —"supporting person" of an eligible child of a taxpayer for a taxation year means a person, other than the taxpayer, who is

(*a*) a parent of the child,

(*b*) the taxpayer's spouse or common-law partner, or

(*c*) an individual who deducted an amount under section 118 for the year in respect of the child

if the parent, spouse or common-law partner or individual, as the case may be, resided with the taxpayer at any time during the year and at any time within 60 days after the end of the year.

Cases: The Minister was justified by s. 3(*f*) to deny the taxpayer her child care expense deduction when the income of her spouse was nil rather than some positive amount. *Fromstein v. The Queen,* 93 DTC 726 (T.C.C.)

► 63(4) ◄

(4) Commuter's child care expense. Where in a taxation year a person resides in Canada near the boundary between Canada and the United States and while so resident incurs expenses for child care services that would be child care expenses if

(*a*) the definition "child care expense" in subsection (3) were read without reference to the words "in Canada", and

(*b*) the reference in paragraph (*b*) of the definition "child care expense" in subsection (3) to "resident of Canada" were read as "person",

those expenses (other than expenses paid for a child's attendance at a boarding school or camp outside Canada) shall be deemed to be child care expenses for the purpose of this section if the child care services are provided at a place that is closer to the person's principal place of residence by a reasonably accessible route, having regard to the circumstances, than any place in Canada where such child care services are available and, in respect of those expenses, subsection (1) shall be read without reference to the words "and contains, where the payee is an individual, that individual's Social Insurance Number".

SECTION 63.1: Application to deemed residents

(Repealed by 1990, c. 39, s. 14(1).)

SECTION 64: Disability supports deduction

If a taxpayer files with the taxpayer's return of income (other than a return of income filed under subsection 70(2), paragraph 104(23)(*d*) or 128(2)(*e*) or subsection 150(4)) for the taxation year a prescribed form containing prescribed information, there may be deducted in computing the taxpayer's income for the year the lesser of

(*a*) the amount determined by the formula

$$A - B$$

where

A is the total of all amounts each of which is an amount paid by the taxpayer in the year and that

(i) was paid to enable the taxpayer

(A) to perform the duties of an office or employment,

(B) to carry on a business either alone or as a partner actively engaged in the business,

(C) to attend a designated educational institution or a secondary school at which the taxpayer is enrolled in an educational program, or

(D) to carry on research or any similar work in respect of which the taxpayer received a grant,

(ii) was paid

(A) where the taxpayer has a speech or hearing impairment, for the cost of sign-language interpretation services or real time captioning services and to a person engaged in the business of providing such services,

(B) where the taxpayer is deaf or mute, for the cost of a teletypewriter or similar device, including a telephone ringing indicator, prescribed by a medical practitioner, to enable the taxpayer to make and receive telephone calls,

(C) where the taxpayer is blind, for the cost of a device or equipment, including synthetic speech systems, Braille printers, and large-print on-screen devices, prescribed by a medical practitioner, and designed to be used by blind individuals in the operation of a computer,

(D) where the taxpayer is blind, for the cost of an optical scanner or similar device, prescribed by a medical practitioner, and designed to be used by blind individuals to enable them to read print,

(E) where the taxpayer is mute, for the cost of an electronic speech synthesizer, prescribed by a medical practitioner, and designed to be used by mute individuals to enable them to communicate by use of a portable keyboard,

(F) where the taxpayer has an impairment in physical or mental functions, for the cost of note-taking services and to a person engaged in the business of providing such services, if the taxpayer has been certified in writing by a medical practitioner to be a person who, because of that impairment, requires such services,

(G) where the taxpayer has an impairment in physical functions, for the cost of voice recognition software, if the taxpayer has been certified in writing by a medical practitioner to be a person who, because of that impairment, requires that software,

(H) where the taxpayer has a learning disability or an impairment in mental functions, for the cost of tutoring services that are rendered to, and supplementary to the primary education of, the taxpayer and to a person ordinarily engaged in the business of providing such services to individuals who are not related to the person, if the taxpayer has been certified in writing by a medical practitioner to be a person who, because of that disability or impairment, requires those services,

(I) where the taxpayer has a perceptual disability, for the cost of talking textbooks used by the taxpayer in connection with the taxpayer's enrolment at a secondary school in Canada or at a designated educational institution, if the taxpayer has been certified in writing by a medical practitioner to be a person who, because of that disability, requires those textbooks,

(J) where the taxpayer has an impairment in physical or mental functions, for the cost of attendant care services provided in Canada and to a person who is neither the taxpayer's spouse or common-law partner nor under 18 years of age, if the taxpayer is a taxpayer in respect of whom an amount may be deducted because of section 118.3, or if the taxpayer has been certified in writing by a medical practitioner to be a person who, because of that impairment is, and is likely to be indefinitely, dependent on others for their personal needs and care and who as a result requires a full-time attendant,

(K) where the taxpayer has a severe and prolonged impairment in physical or mental functions, for the cost of job coaching services (not including job placement or career counselling services) and to a person engaged in the business of providing such services if the taxpayer has been certified in writing by a medical practitioner to be a person who, because of that impairment, requires such services,

(L) where the taxpayer is blind or has a severe learning disability, for the cost of reading services and to a person engaged in the business of providing such services, if the taxpayer has been certified in writing by a medical practitioner to be a person who, because of that impairment or disability, requires those services,

(M) where the taxpayer is blind and profoundly deaf, for the cost of deaf-blind intervening services and to a person engaged in the business of providing such services,

(N) where the taxpayer has a speech impairment, for the cost of a device that is a Bliss symbol board, or a similar device, that is prescribed by a medical practitioner to help the taxpayer communicate by selecting the symbols or spelling out words,

(O) where the taxpayer is blind, for the cost of a device that is a Braille note-taker, prescribed by a medical practitioner, to allow the taxpayer to take notes (that can, by the device, be read back to them or printed or displayed in Braille) with the help of a keyboard,

(P) where the taxpayer has a severe and prolonged impairment in physical functions that markedly restricts their ability to use their arms or hands, for the cost of a device that is a page turner prescribed by a medical practitioner to help the taxpayer to turn the pages of a book or other bound document, and

(Q) where the taxpayer is blind, or has a severe learning disability, for the cost of a device or software that is prescribed by a medical practitioner and designed to enable the taxpayer to read print,

(iii) is evidenced by one or more receipts filed with the Minister each of which was issued by the payee and contains, where the payee is an individual who is a person referred to in clause (ii)(J), that individual's Social Insurance Number, and

(iv) is not included in computing a deduction under section 118.2 for any taxpayer for any taxation year, and

B is the total of all amounts each of which is the amount of a reimbursement or any other form of assistance (other than prescribed assistance or an amount that is included in computing a taxpayer's income and that is not deductible in computing the taxpayer's taxable income) that any taxpayer is or was entitled to receive in respect of an amount included in computing the value of A, and

(*b*) the total of

(i) the total of all amounts each of which is

(A) an amount included under section 5, 6 or 7 or paragraph 56(1)(*n*), (*o*) or (*r*) in computing the taxpayer's income for the year, or

(B) the taxpayer's income for the year from a business carried on either alone or as a partner actively engaged in the business, and

(ii) where the taxpayer is in attendance at a designated educational institution or a secondary school at which the taxpayer is enrolled in an educational program, the least of

(A) $15,000,

(B) $375 times the number of weeks in the year during which the taxpayer is in attendance at the institution or school, and

(C) the amount, if any, by which the amount that would, if this Act were read without reference to this section, be the taxpayer's income for the year exceeds the total determined under subparagraph (i) in respect of the taxpayer for the year.

Tax Topics: No. 1746, The Disability Supports Deduction; No. 1714, Committee Report Concerning Tax Credits for Disabled Individuals.

Forms: T929 — Attendant Care Expenses.

Guides: RC4064 Information Concerning People with Disabilities.

Income Tax Folios: *Primary*— S1-F1-C3 Disability Supports Deduction; *Secondary*— S1-F1-C1 Medical Expense Tax Credit; S1-F1-C2 Disability Tax Credit.

Information Circulars: IC 82-2R2 Social insurance number legislation that relates to the preparation of information slips.

SECTION 64.1: Individuals absent from Canada

In applying sections 63 and 64 in respect of a taxpayer who is, throughout all or part of a taxation year, absent from but resident in Canada, the following rules apply for the year or that part of the year, as the case may be:

(*a*) the definition "child care expense" in subsection 63(3), and section 64, shall be read without reference to the words "in Canada";

(*b*) subsection 63(1) and section 64 shall be read without reference to the words "and contains, where the payee is an individual, that individual's Social Insurance Number", if the payment referred to in that subsection or section, as the case may be, is made to a person who is not resident in Canada; and

(*c*) paragraph (*b*) of the definition "child care expense" in subsection 63(3) shall be read as if the word "person" were substituted for the words "resident of Canada" where they appear therein.

Income Tax Folios: *Secondary* — S1-F3-C4 Moving Expenses; S1-F3-C1 Child Care Expense Deduction; S1-F1-C3 Disability Supports Deduction.

SECTION 65: Allowance for oil or gas well, mine or timber limit

► 65(1) ◄

(1) Allowance for oil or gas well, mine or timber limit. There may be deducted in computing a taxpayer's income for a taxation year such amount as an allowance, if any, in respect of

(*a*) a natural accumulation of petroleum or natural gas, oil or gas well, mineral resource or timber limit,

(*b*) the processing of ore (other than iron ore or tar sands) from a mineral resource to any stage that is not beyond the prime metal stage or its equivalent,

(*c*) the processing of iron ore from a mineral resource to any stage that is not beyond the pellet stage or its equivalent, or

(*d*) the processing of tar sands from a mineral resource to any stage that is not beyond the crude oil stage or its equivalent

as is allowed to the taxpayer by regulation.

Editorial Note: S. 65 provides the legislative authority for the passage of regulations for the depletion allowances, earned depletion, frontier exploration allowance, supplementary depletion and mining exploration depletion. This section is largely of historical interest only. Taxpayers have not been able to add to any such allowances after 1989 although taxpayers can continue to claim any undeducted allowances.

Related Regulations: 1200 [Deductions allowed]; 1201 Earned Depletion Allowances; 1202 Earned Depletion Allowances; 1203 Mining Exploration Depletion; 1204 Resource Profits; 1205 Earned Depletion Base; 1206 Interpretation; 1207 Frontier Exploration Allowances; 1208 Additional Allowances in Respect of Certain Oil or Gas Wells; 1209 Additional Allowances in Respect of Certain Mines; 1212.

Related Sections: S. 53(2) Amounts to be deducted; s. 65(2) Regulations; s. 65(3) Lessee's share of allowance; s. 96(1) General rules; s. 127.5 Obligation to pay minimum tax; s. 133(1) Computation of income.

Cases: The formula for calculating the frontier exploration allowance for a company in the oil and gas business uses the phrase "threshold amount . . . minus". The word "minus" is used in its technical or mathematical sense and the calculation can therefore result in a negative amount. This interpretation had the effect of increasing the taxpayer's allowance. *Canterra Energy Ltd. v. The Queen*, 87 DTC 5019 (F.C.A.), reversing 85 DTC 5245 (F.C.T.D.)

▶ 65(2) ◀

(2) Regulations. For greater certainty it is hereby declared that, in the case of a regulation made under subsection (1) allowing to a taxpayer an amount in respect of a natural accumulation of petroleum or natural gas, an oil or gas well or a mineral resource or in respect of the processing of ore,

(*a*) there may be allowed to the taxpayer by that regulation an amount in respect of any or all

(i) natural accumulations of petroleum or natural gas, oil or gas wells or mineral resources in which the taxpayer has any interest or, for civil law, right, or

(ii) processing operations described in any of paragraphs (1)(*b*), (*c*) and (*d*) that are carried on by the taxpayer; and

(*b*) notwithstanding any other provision contained in this Act, the Governor in Council may prescribe the formula by which the amount that may be allowed to the taxpayer by that regulation shall be determined.

History: S. 65(2)(*a*)(i) was replaced by S.C. 2013, c. 34, s. 110, in force June 26, 2013, and formerly read:

(i) natural accumulations of petroleum or natural gas, oil or gas wells or mineral resources in which the taxpayer has any interest, or

▶ 65(3) ◀

(3) Lessee's share of allowance. Where a deduction is allowed under subsection (1) in respect of a coal mine operated by a lessee, the lessor and lessee may agree as to what portion of the allowance each may deduct and, in the event that they cannot agree, the Minister may fix the portions.

Related Sections: S. 66(1) Exploration and development expenses of principal-business corporations; s. 66(3) Expenses of other taxpayers; s. 87(6) Obligations of predecessor corporation — position of debtholder; s. 248(1), "amount", "mineral resource", "regulation"; ITAR s. 29 Deduction from income of petroleum or natural gas corporation.

SECTION 66: [Exploration and development expenses]

▶ 66(1) ◀

(1) Exploration and development expenses of principal-business corporations. A principal-business corporation may deduct, in computing its income for a taxation year, the lesser of

(*a*) the total of such of its Canadian exploration and development expenses as were incurred by it before the end of the taxation year, to the extent that they were not deductible in computing income for a previous taxation year, and

(*b*) of that total, an amount equal to its income for the taxation year if no deduction were allowed under this subsection, section 65 or subsection 66.1(2), minus the deductions allowed for the year by sections 112 and 113.

Related Sections: S. 13(21), "depreciable property"; s. 21(2) Borrowed money used for exploration or development; s. 35(1) Prospectors and grubstakers; s. 66(10) Joint exploration corporation; s. 66(15), "principal-business corporation"; s. 66.1(6), "Canadian exploration expense"; s. 66.4(5) Definitions; s. 87(6) Obligations of predecessor corporation — position of debtholder; s. 87(7) Obligations of predecessor corporation — position of amalgamated corporation; s. 96(1) General rules; s. 115(1) Non-resident's taxable income in Canada; s. 127.5 Obligation to pay minimum tax; s. 248(1), "amount", "corporation", "fiscal period", "individual", "mineral resource", "minerals", "property", "shareholder"; s. 255 Canada; ITAR s. 29 Deduction from income of petroleum or natural gas corporation.

Forms: T2 SCH12 — Resource-Related Deductions; T1229 — Statement of Exploration and Development Expenses; T2 SCH 421 — British Columbia Mining Exploration Tax Credit; T88 — BC Mining Exploration Tax Credit (Individuals); T2 SCH 441 — Yukon Mineral Exploration Tax Credit; T1199 — Yukon Mineral Exploration Tax Credit; T1221 — Ontario Focused Flow-Through Share Tax Credit.

Income Tax Folios: *Primary* — S3-F8-C2 Tax Incentives for Clean Energy Equipment. *Secondary* — S3-F8-C1 Principal-business Corporations in the Resource Industries.

Interpretation Bulletins: *Secondary* — IT-143R3 Meaning of eligible capital expenditure; IT-273R2 Government assistance — General comments.

Cases: A wholly-owned Canadian subsidiary of an American company, supplying natural gas to the parent in California as well as to other customers, was held to be a principal-business corporation and there was no artificial reduction of income. *The Queen v. Alberta and Southern Gas Co. Ltd.*, 78 DTC 6566 (S.C.C.), affirming 77 DTC 5244 (F.C.A.) and 76 DTC 6362 (F.C.T.D.)

▶ 66(2) ◀

(2) Expenses of special product corporations. A corporation (other than a principal-business corporation the principal business of which is described in paragraph (*a*) or (*b*) of the definition "principal-business corporation" in subsection (15)), whose principal business is the production or marketing of sodium chloride or potash or whose business includes manufacturing products the manufacturing of which involves processing sodium chloride or potash, may deduct, in computing its income for a taxation year, the drilling and exploration expenses incurred by it in the year and before May 7, 1974 on or in respect of exploring or drilling for halite or sylvite.

Related Sections: S. 66(1) Exploration and development expenses of principal-business corporations; s. 66(6) Successor corporation's Canadian exploration and development expenses.

Income Tax Folios: *Primary* — S3-F8-C2 Tax Incentives for Clean Energy Equipment.

▶ 66(3) ◀

(3) Expenses of other taxpayers. A taxpayer other than a principal-business corporation may deduct, in computing the taxpayer's income for a taxation year, the total of the taxpayer's Canadian exploration and development expenses to the extent that they were not deducted in computing the taxpayer's income for a preceding taxation year.

Related Sections: S. 53(2)(*e*) Amounts to be deducted — Share, where shareholder incurred exploration and development expenses; s. 66(5) Dealers; s. 66(10) Joint exploration corporation.

▶ 66(4) ◀

(4) Foreign exploration and development expenses. A taxpayer who is resident throughout a taxation year in Canada may deduct, in computing the taxpayer's income for that taxation year, the lesser of

(*a*) the amount, if any, by which

(i) the total of the foreign exploration and development expenses incurred by the taxpayer

(A) before the end of the year,

(B) at a time at which the taxpayer was resident in Canada, and

(C) where the taxpayer became resident in Canada before the end of the year, after the last time (before the end of the year) that the taxpayer became resident in Canada,

exceeds the total of

(ii) such of the expenses described in subparagraph (i) as were deductible in computing the taxpayer's income for a preceding taxation year, and

(iii) all amounts by which the amount described in this paragraph in respect of the taxpayer is required because of subsection 80(8) to be reduced at or before the end of the year, and

(*b*) of that total, the greater of

(i) the amount, if any, claimed by the taxpayer not exceeding 10% of the amount determined under paragraph (*a*) in respect of the taxpayer for the year, and

(ii) the total of

(A) the part of the taxpayer's income for the year, determined without reference to this subsection and subsection 66.21(4), that can reasonably be regarded as attributable to

(I) the production of petroleum or natural gas from natural accumulations outside Canada or from oil or gas wells outside Canada, or

(II) the production of minerals from mines outside Canada,

(B) the taxpayer's income for the year from royalties in respect of a natural accumulation of petroleum or natural gas outside Canada, an oil or gas well outside Canada or a mine outside Canada, determined without reference to this subsection and subsection 66.21(4), and

(C) all amounts each of which is an amount, in respect of a foreign resource property that has been disposed of by the taxpayer, equal to the amount, if any, by which

(I) the amount included in computing the taxpayer's income for the year by reason of subsection 59(1) in respect of the disposition

exceeds

(II) the total of all amounts each of which is that portion of an amount deducted under subsection 66.7(2) in computing the taxpayer's income for the year that

1. can reasonably be considered to be in respect of the foreign resource property, and

2. cannot reasonably be considered to have reduced the amount otherwise determined under clause (A) or (B) in respect of the taxpayer for the year.

Editorial Note: Subsection 66(4) provides for the deduction by a taxpayer of the taxpayer's foreign exploration development expenses ("FEDE"). FEDE cannot be incurred by a taxpayer for taxation years commencing after 2000. Expenses that would otherwise be FEDE will be foreign resource expenses ("FRE") if they are incurred after that time. Only taxpayers who are resident in Canada throughout a taxation year may deduct FEDE. The taxpayer is entitled to claim a discretionary deduction equal to the greater of 10% of its FEDE at the end of the year and its income attributable to foreign oil and gas and mining activities, including income from the disposition of foreign resource properties.

See the editorial note following s. 66.21(4) for a summary of the definition of FRE.

Related Sections: S. 66(5) Dealers; s. 87(7) Obligations of predecessor corporation — position of amalgamated corporation; s. 104(5.2) Resource property; S. 115(4.1) Foreign resource pool expenses.

▶ 66(4.1) ◀

(4.1) Country-by-country FEDE allocations. For greater certainty, the portion of an amount deducted under subsection (4) in computing a taxpayer's income for a taxation year that can reasonably be considered to be in respect of specified foreign exploration and development expenses of the taxpayer in respect of a country is considered to apply to a source in that country.

Editorial Note: Subsection 66(4.1) is relevant to the calculation by the taxpayer of its foreign tax credit in respect of the taxpayer's production tax amount for a country. The amount of the credit is based on the taxpayer's income allocable to the country. The income relevant for purposes of computing the credit is reduced by any specified foreign exploration and development expenses deducted.

Subsection 66(4.2) provides that the allocation must be reasonable in the circumstances and applied consistently.

Related Sections: S. 66(4) Foreign exploration and development expenses; s. 66(4.2) Method of allocation; s. 66(15) Definitions; s. 66.7(2) Successor of foreign exploration and development expenses; s. 66.7(2.1) Country-by-country successor FEDE allocations; s. 248(1), "foreign exploration and development expenses".

Canadian Petroleum Tax Journal: Foreign Exploration and Development Expenditures — The New Rules, Roch J. Martin, 2001, Vol. 14, No. 1.

▶ 66(4.2) ◀

(4.2) Method of allocation. For the purpose of subsection (4.1), where a taxpayer has incurred specified foreign exploration and development expenses in respect of two or more countries, an allocation to each of those countries for a taxation year shall be determined in a manner that is

(*a*) reasonable having regard to all the circumstances, including the level and timing of

(i) the taxpayer's specified foreign exploration and development expenses in respect of the country, and

(ii) the profits or gains to which those expenses relate; and

(*b*) not inconsistent with the allocation made under subsection (4.1) for the preceding taxation year.

Related Sections: S. 66(4) Foreign exploration and development expenses; s. 66(4.1) Country-by-country FEDE allocations; s. 66(15) Definitions; s. 66.7(2.1) Country-by-country successor FEDE allocations; s. 66.7(2.2) Method of allocation; s. 248(1), "foreign exploration and development expenses".

Canadian Petroleum Tax Journal: Foreign Exploration and Development Expenditures — The New Rules, Roch J. Martin, 2001, Vol. 14, No. 1.

▶ 66(4.3) ◀

(4.3) FEDE deductions where change of individual's residence. Where at any time in a taxation year an individual becomes or ceases to be resident in Canada,

(*a*) subsection (4) applies to the individual as if the year were the period or periods in the year throughout which the individual was resident in Canada; and

(*b*) for the purpose of applying subsection (4), subsection (13.1) does not apply to the individual for the year.

Related Sections: S. 66(4) Foreign exploration and development expenses; s. 66(4.1) Country-by-country FEDE allocations; s. 66(4.2) Method of allocation; s. 66(13.1) Short taxation year; s. 66.21(5) Individual changing residence; s. 128.1 Change in residence.

▶ 66(5) ◀

(5) Dealers. Subsections (3) and (4) and sections 59, 64, 66.1, 66.2, 66.21, 66.4 and 66.7 do not apply in computing the income for a taxation year of a taxpayer (other than a principal-business corporation) whose business includes trading or dealing in rights, licences or privileges to explore for, drill for or take minerals, petroleum, natural gas or other related hydrocarbons.

Editorial Note: A taxpayer who is in the business of trading or dealing in rights, licences or privileges to explore for or drill minerals or petroleum is not subject to a number of provisions. The determination of whether a taxpayer is "trading or dealing" is a question of fact. See the editorial notes and cases under section 39(5) for the meaning of "trader or dealer".

Income Tax Folios: *Secondary* — S3-F8-C1 Principal-business Corporations in the Resource Industries.

Interpretation Bulletins: *Secondary* — IT-291R3 Transfer of property to a corporation under subsection 85(1).

▶ 66(6) ◀

(6) Successor corporation's Canadian exploration and development expenses — (Repealed by 1987, c. 46, s. 18(1).)

▶ 66(7) ◀

(7) Second successor corporation's Canadian exploration and development expenses — (Repealed by 1987, c. 46, s. 18(1).)

▶ 66(8) ◀

(8) Successor corporation's foreign exploration and development expenses — (Repealed by 1987, c. 46, s. 18(1).)

▶ 66(9) ◀

(9) Second successor corporation's foreign exploration and development expenses — (Repealed by 1987, c. 46, s. 18(1).)

▶ 66(10) ◀

(10) Joint exploration corporation — (Repealed by S.C. 1997, c. 25, s. 13(1).)

▶ 66(10.1) ◀

(10.1) Idem — (Repealed by S.C. 1997, c. 25, s. 13(1).)

▶ 66(10.2) ◀

(10.2) Idem — (Repealed by S.C. 1997, c. 25, s. 13(1).)

▶ 66(10.3) ◀

(10.3) Idem — (Repealed by S.C. 1997, c. 25, s. 13(1).)

▶ 66(10.4) ◀

(10.4) Idem. Where a taxpayer has, after April 19, 1983, made a payment or loan described in paragraph (*a*) of the definition "agreed portion" in subsection (15) to a joint exploration corporation in respect of which the corporation has at any time renounced in favour of the taxpayer any Canadian exploration expenses, Canadian development expenses or Canadian oil and gas property expenses (in this subsection referred to as "resource expenses") under subsection (10.1), (10.2) or (10.3), the following rules apply:

(*a*) where the taxpayer receives as consideration for the payment or loan property that is capital property to the taxpayer,

(i) there shall be deducted in computing the adjusted cost base to the taxpayer of the property at any time the amount of any resource expenses renounced by the corporation in the taxpayer's favour in respect of the loan or payment at or before that time,

(ii) there shall be deducted in computing the adjusted cost base to the taxpayer at any time of any property for which the property, or any property substituted therefor, was exchanged the amount of any resource expenses renounced by the corporation in the taxpayer's favour in respect of the loan or payment at or before that time (except to the extent such amount has been deducted under subparagraph (i)), and

(iii) the amount of any resource expenses renounced by the corporation in favour of the taxpayer in respect of the loan or payment at any time, except to the extent that the renunciation of those expenses results in a deduction under subparagraph (i) or (ii), shall, for the purposes of this Act, be deemed to be a capital gain of the taxpayer from the disposition by the taxpayer of property at that time;

(*b*) where the taxpayer receives as consideration for the payment or loan property that is not capital property to the taxpayer,

(i) there shall be deducted in computing the cost to the taxpayer of the property at any time the amount of any resource expenses renounced by the corporation in the taxpayer's favour in respect of the loan or payment at or before that time, and

(ii) there shall be included in computing the amount referred to in paragraph 59(3.2)(*d*) for a taxation year the amount of any resource expenses renounced by the corporation in the taxpayer's favour in respect of the loan or payment at any time in the year, except to the extent that the amount has been deducted under subparagraph (i); and

(*c*) where the taxpayer does not receive any property as consideration for the payment, there shall be included in computing the amount referred to in paragraph 59(3.2)(*e*) for a taxation year the amount of any resource expenses renounced by the corporation in the taxpayer's favour in respect of the payment in the year, except to the extent that the amount has been deducted from the adjusted cost base to the taxpayer of shares of the corporation under paragraph 53(2)(*f*.1) in respect of the payment.

▶ 66(11) ◀

(11) Acquisition of control. Where after March 31, 1977 and before November 13, 1981 control of a corporation has been acquired by a person or persons who did not control the corporation at the time when it last ceased to carry on active business,

(*a*) the amount by which the Canadian exploration and development expenses incurred by the corporation before it last ceased to carry on active business exceeds the total of all amounts otherwise deductible by the corporation in respect of Canadian exploration and development expenses in computing its income for taxation years ending before control was so acquired, shall be deemed to have been deductible under this section by the corporation in computing its income for taxation years ending before control was so acquired;

(*b*) the amount by which the cumulative Canadian exploration expense of the corporation at the time it last ceased to carry on active business exceeds the total of amounts otherwise deducted under section 66.1 in computing its income for taxation years ending after that time and before control was so acquired, shall be deemed to have been deducted under that section by the corporation in computing its income for taxation years ending before control was so acquired;

(*c*) the amount by which the cumulative Canadian development expense of the corporation at the time it last ceased to carry on active business exceeds the total of amounts otherwise deducted under section 66.2 in computing its income for taxation years ending after that time and before control was so acquired, shall be deemed to have been deducted under that section by the corporation in computing its income for taxation years ending before control was so acquired;

(*d*) the amount by which the cumulative Canadian oil and gas property expense of the corporation at the time it last ceased to carry on active business exceeds the total of amounts otherwise deducted under section 66.4 in computing its income for taxation years ending after that time and before control was so acquired, shall be deemed to have been deducted under that section by the corporation in computing its income for taxation years ending before control was so acquired; and

(*e*) the amount by which the foreign exploration and development expenses incurred by the corporation before it last ceased to carry on active business exceeds the total of all amounts otherwise deductible by the corporation in respect of foreign exploration and development expenses in computing its income for taxation years ending before control was so acquired, shall be deemed to have been deductible under this section by the corporation in computing its income for taxation years ending before control was so acquired.

Related Regulations: 1202(1).

Related Sections: S. 66(11.3) Control; s. 66(15) Definitions; s. 256(7) Acquiring control; s. 256(8) Deemed exercise of right.

► 66(11.1) ◄

(11.1) Idem — (Repealed by 1987, c. 46, s. 18(2).)

► 66(11.2) ◄

(11.2) Idem — (Repealed by 1987, c. 46, s. 18(2).)

► 66(11.3) ◄

(11.3) Control. For the purposes of subsections (11) and 66.7(10), where a corporation acquired control of another corporation after November 12, 1981 and before 1983 by reason of the acquisition of shares of the other corporation pursuant to an agreement in writing concluded on or before November 12, 1981, it shall be deemed to have acquired that control on or before November 12, 1981.

► 66(11.4) ◄

(11.4) Loss restriction event. If

(*a*) at any time a taxpayer is subject to a loss restriction event,

(*b*) within the 12-month period that ended immediately before that time, the taxpayer, a partnership of which the taxpayer was a majority-interest partner or a trust of which the taxpayer was a majority-interest beneficiary (as defined in subsection 251.1(3)) acquired a Canadian resource property or a foreign resource property (other than a property that was held, by the taxpayer, partnership or trust or by a person that would be affiliated with the taxpayer if section 251.1 were read without reference to the definition "controlled" in subsection 251.1(3), throughout the period that began immediately before the 12-month period began and ended at the time the property was acquired by the taxpayer, partnership or trust), and

(*c*) immediately before the 12-month period began the taxpayer, partnership or trust was not, or would not be if it were a corporation, a principal-business corporation,

for the purposes of subsection (4) and sections 66.2, 66.21 and 66.4, except as those provisions apply for the purposes of section 66.7, the property is deemed not to have been acquired by the taxpayer, partnership or trust, as the case may be, before that time, except that if the property has been disposed of by it before that time and not reacquired by it before that time, the property is deemed to have been acquired by the taxpayer, partnership or trust, as the case may be, immediately before it disposed of the property.

Editorial Note: S. 66(11.4) applies in certain circumstances in which a corporation or trust, or a partnership of which the taxpayer was a majority-interest partner or trust in which the taxpayer was a majority-interest beneficiary, acquires a Canadian or foreign resource property within 12 months of a loss restriction event (i.e, an acquisition of control of the corporation or a person becoming a majority-interest partner of a trust). Where s. 66(11.4) applies, the corporation or partnership is deemed not to have acquired the property except for the purposes of the successor corporation rules. As a result, the corporation cannot deduct any of the expenses related to the acquisition of such property, except pursuant to the successor corporation rules.

History: S. 66(11.4) was replaced by S.C. 2013, c. 40, s. 30(1), deemed to have come into force on March 21, 2013, except that subsection 66(11.4) is to be read as follows before September 13, 2013:

"(11.4) If

(*a*) at any time a taxpayer is subject to a loss restriction event,

(*b*) within the 12-month period that ended immediately before that time, the taxpayer or a partnership of which the taxpayer was a majority-interest partner acquired a Canadian resource property or a foreign resource property (other than a property that was held, by the taxpayer or partnership or by a person that would be affiliated with the taxpayer if section 251.1 were read without reference to the definition "controlled" in subsection 251.1(3), throughout the period that began immediately before the 12-month period began and ended at the time the property was acquired by the taxpayer or partnership), and

(*c*) immediately before the 12-month period began the taxpayer or partnership was not, or would not be if it were a corporation, a principal-business corporation,

for the purposes of subsection (4) and sections 66.2, 66.21 and 66.4, except as those provisions apply for the purposes of section 66.7, the property is deemed not to have been acquired by the taxpayer or partnership, as the case may be, before that time, except that if the property has been disposed of by it before that time and not reacquired by it before that time, the property is deemed to have been acquired by the taxpayer or partnership, as the case may be, immediately before it disposed of the property."

S. 66(11.4) formerly read:

(11.4) *Change of control.* Where,

(*a*) at any time, control of a corporation has been acquired by a person or group of persons,

(*b*) within the 12-month period that ended immediately before that time, the corporation or a partnership of which it was a majority interest partner acquired a Canadian resource property or a foreign resource property (other than a property that was owned by the corporation or partnership or a person that would, if section 251.1 were read without reference to the definition "controlled" in subsection 251.1(3), be affiliated with the corporation throughout the period that began immediately before the 12-month period began and ended at the time the property was acquired by the corporation or partnership), and

(*c*) immediately before the twelve month period commenced, the corporation was not a principal-business corporation and the partnership, if it were a corporation, would not be a principal-business corporation,

for the purposes of subsection (4) and sections 66.2, 66.21 and 66.4, except as those provisions apply for the purposes of section 66.7, the property is deemed not to have been acquired by the corporation or partnership before that time and is deemed to have been acquired by it at that time, except that, where the property has been disposed of by it before that time and not reacquired by it before that time, the property is deemed to have been acquired by the corporation or partnership immediately before it disposed of the property.

Related Sections: S. 66(11.5) Affiliation – subsection (24); s. 66(15), "Canadian resource property", "foreign resource property"; s. 251.2(2) Loss restriction event; s. 256(8) Deemed exercise of right; s. 256.1 [Corporate tax-attribute trading].

▶ 66(11.5) ◀

(11.5) Affiliation — subsection (11.4). For the purposes of subsection (11.4), if the taxpayer referred to in that subsection was formed or created in the 12-month period referred to in that subsection, the taxpayer is deemed to have been, throughout the period that began immediately before the 12-month period and ended immediately after it was formed or created,

(*a*) in existence; and

(*b*) affiliated with every person with whom it was affiliated (otherwise than because of a right referred to in paragraph 251(5)(*b*)) throughout the period that began when it was formed or created and that ended immediately before the time at which the taxpayer was subject to the loss restriction event referred to in that subsection.

History: S. 66(11.5) was replaced by S.C. 2013, c. 40, s. 30(1), deemed to have come into force on March 21, 2013, and formerly read:

(11.5) *Early change of control.* For the purpose of subsection (11.4), where the corporation referred to in that subsection was incorporated or otherwise formed in the 12-month period referred to in that subsection, the corporation is deemed to have been, throughout the period that began immediately before the 12-month period and ended immediately after it was incorporated or otherwise formed,

(*a*) in existence; and

(*b*) affiliated with every person with whom it was affiliated (otherwise than because of a right referred to in paragraph 251(5)(*b*)) throughout the period that began when it was incorporated or otherwise formed and ended immediately before its control was acquired.

Related Sections: S. 256(7) Acquiring control; s. 256(8) Deemed exercise of right.

▶ 66(11.6) ◀

(11.6) Trust loss restriction event — successor. If at any time a trust is subject to a loss restriction event,

(*a*) for the purposes of the provisions of this Act relating to deductions in respect of drilling and exploration expenses, prospecting, exploration and development expenses, Canadian exploration and development expenses, foreign resource pool expenses, Canadian exploration expenses, Canadian development expenses and Canadian oil and gas property expenses (in this subsection referred to as "resource expenses") incurred by the trust before that time, the following rules apply:

(i) the trust is (other than for purposes of this subsection and subsections (11.4), (11.5) and 66.7(10) to (11)) deemed to be a corporation that

(A) after that time is a successor (within the meaning assigned by any of subsections 66.7(1), (2) and (2.3) to (5)), and

(B) at that time, acquired all the properties held by the trust immediately before that time from an original owner of those properties,

(ii) if the trust did not hold a foreign resource property immediately before that time, the trust is deemed to have owned a foreign resource property immediately before that time,

(iii) a joint election is deemed to have been filed in accordance with subsections 66.7(7) and (8) in respect of the acquisition described in clause (i)(B),

(iv) the resource expenses incurred by the trust before that time are deemed to have been incurred by an original owner of the properties and not by the trust,

(v) the original owner is deemed to have been resident in Canada at every time before that time at which the trust was resident in Canada,

(vi) if at that time the trust is a member of a partnership and the property of the partnership includes a Canadian resource property or a foreign resource property,

(A) for the purposes of clause (i)(B), the trust is deemed to have held immediately before that time that portion of the partnership's property at that time that is equal to the trust's percentage share of the total of amounts that would be paid to all members of the partnership if it were wound up at that time, and

(B) for the purposes of clauses 66.7(1)(*b*)(i)(C) and (2)(*b*)(i)(B), subparagraph 66.7(2.3)(*b*)(i) and clauses 66.7(3)(*b*)(i)(C), (4)(*b*)(i)(B) and (5)(*b*)(i)(B) for a taxation year that ends after that time, the lesser of the following amounts is deemed to be income of the trust for the year that can reasonably be regarded as attributable to production from the property:

(I) the trust's share of the part of the income of the partnership for the fiscal period of the partnership that ends in the year that can reasonably be regarded as attributable to the production from the property, and

(II) an amount that would be determined under subclause (I) for the year if the trust's share of the income of the partnership for the fiscal period of the partnership that ends in the year were determined on the basis of the percentage share referred to in clause (A), and

(vii) if after that time the trust disposes of property that was at that time held by the trust to another person, subsections 66.7(1) to (5) do not apply in respect of the acquisition by the other person of the property; and

(*b*) if before that time, the trust or a partnership of which the trust was a member acquired a property that is a Canadian resource property, a foreign resource property or an interest in a partnership and it can reasonably be considered that one of the main purposes of the acquisition is to avoid any limitation provided in any of subsections 66.7(1) to (5) on the deduction in respect of any expenses incurred by the trust, then the trust or the partnership, as the case may be, is deemed, for the purposes of applying those subsections to or in respect of the trust, not to have acquired the property.

History: S. 66(11.6) was added by S.C. 2013, c. 40, s. 30(1), deemed to have come into force on March 21, 2013.

Related Sections: s. 251.2(2) Loss restriction event.

► 66(12) ◄

(12) Computation of exploration and development expenses. In computing a taxpayer's Canadian exploration and development expenses,

(*a*) there shall be deducted any amount paid to the taxpayer before May 7, 1974

(i) and after 1971 under the *Northern Mineral Exploration Assistance Regulations* made under an appropriation Act that provides for payments in respect of the Northern Mineral Grants Program, or

(ii) pursuant to any agreement entered into between the taxpayer and Her Majesty in right of Canada under the Northern Mineral Grants Program or the Development Program of the Department of Indian Affairs and Northern Development, to the extent that the amount has been expended by the taxpayer as or on account of Canadian exploration and development expenses incurred by the taxpayer; and

(*b*) there shall be included any amount, except an amount in respect of interest, paid by the taxpayer after 1971 and before May 7, 1974 under the Regulations referred to in subparagraph (*a*)(i) to Her Majesty in right of Canada.

Related Sections: S. 66(15) Definitions.

► 66(12.1) ◄

(12.1) Limitations of Canadian exploration and development expenses. Except as expressly otherwise provided in this Act,

(*a*) if as a result of a transaction occurring after May 6, 1974 an amount has become receivable by a taxpayer at a particular time in a taxation year and the consideration given by the taxpayer therefor was property (other than a share or a Canadian resource property, or an interest in or a right to — or, for civil law, a right in or to — the share or the property) or services, the original cost of which to the taxpayer may reasonably be regarded as having been primarily Canadian exploration and development expenses of the taxpayer (or would have been so regarded if they had been incurred by the taxpayer after 1971 and before May 7, 1974) or a Canadian exploration expense, there shall at that time be included in the amount determined for G in the definition "cumulative Canadian exploration expense" in subsection 66.1(6) in respect of the taxpayer the amount that became receivable by the taxpayer at that time; and

(*b*) if as a result of a transaction occurring after May 6, 1974 an amount has become receivable by a taxpayer at a particular time in a taxation year and the consideration given by the taxpayer therefor was property (other than a share or a Canadian resource property, or an interest in or a right to — or, for civil law, a right in or to — the share or the property) or services, the original cost of which to the taxpayer may reasonably be regarded as having been primarily a Canadian development expense, there shall at that time be included in the amount determined for G in the definition "cumulative Canadian development expense" in subsection 66.2(5) in respect of the taxpayer the amount that became receivable by the taxpayer at that time.

Editorial Note: When a taxpayer incurs CEE and CDE and sells the property resulting from such expenses, s. 66(12.1)(*a*) and (*b*) require the taxpayer to reduce its cumulative Canadian exploration expenses or cumulative Canadian development expenses, respectively, by the proceeds of disposition. Property does not include a share or a Canadian resource property.

History: S. 66(12.1)(*a*) and (*b*) were replaced by S.C. 2013, c. 34, s. 111, in force June 26, 2013, and formerly read:

(*a*) where as a result of a transaction occurring after May 6, 1974 an amount has become receivable by a taxpayer at a particular time in a taxation year and the consideration given by the taxpayer therefor was property (other than a share or a Canadian resource property, or an interest therein or a right thereto) or services, the original cost of which to the taxpayer may reasonably be regarded as having been primarily Canadian exploration and development expenses of the taxpayer (or would have been so regarded if they had been incurred by the taxpayer after 1971 and before May 7, 1974) or a Canadian exploration expense, there shall at that time be included in the amount determined for G in the definition "cumulative Canadian exploration expense" in subsection 66.1(6) in respect of the taxpayer the amount that became receivable by the taxpayer at that time; and

(*b*) where as a result of a transaction occurring after May 6, 1974 an amount has become receivable by a taxpayer at a particular time in a taxation year and the consideration given by the taxpayer therefor was property (other than a share or a Canadian resource property, or an interest therein or a right thereto) or services, the original cost of which to the taxpayer may reasonably be regarded as having been primarily a Canadian development expense, there shall at that time be included in the amount determined for G in the definition "cumulative Canadian development expense" in subsection 66.2(5) in respect of the taxpayer the amount that became receivable by the taxpayer at that time.

Related Sections: S. 66(15) Definitions; s. 66.2(5) Definitions; s. 66.2(6) Share of partner.

Canadian Petroleum Tax Journal: A Practical Guide to the Flow-Through Share Rules, Greg Johnson, CA, 2002, Vol. 15, No. 1.

Income Tax Folios: *Primary* — S3-F8-C2 Tax Incentives for Clean Energy Equipment.

Interpretation Bulletins: *Secondary* — IT-125R4 Disposition of resource properties.

► 66(12.2) ◄

(12.2) Unitized oil or gas field in Canada. Where, pursuant to an agreement between a taxpayer and another person to unitize an oil or gas field in Canada, an amount has become receivable by the taxpayer at a particular time after May 6, 1974 from that other person in respect of Canadian exploration expense incurred by the taxpayer or Canadian exploration and development expenses incurred by the taxpayer (or expenses that would have been Canadian exploration and development expenses if they had been incurred by the taxpayer after 1971 and before May 7, 1974) in respect of that field or any part thereof, the following rules apply:

(*a*) there shall, at that time, be included by the taxpayer in the amount determined for G in the definition "cumulative Canadian exploration expense" in subsection 66.1(6) the amount that became receivable by the taxpayer; and

(*b*) there shall, at that time, be included by the other person in the amount referred to in paragraph (*c*) of the definition "Canadian exploration expense" in subsection 66.1(6) the amount that became payable by that person.

Related Sections: S. 66(15) Definitions.

Interpretation Bulletins: *Secondary* — IT-125R4 Disposition of resource properties.

► 66(12.3) ◄

(12.3) Idem. Where, pursuant to an agreement between a taxpayer and another person to unitize an oil or gas field in Canada, an amount has become receivable by the taxpayer at a particular time after May 6, 1974 from that other person in respect of Canadian development expense incurred by the taxpayer in respect of that field or any part thereof, the following rules apply:

(*a*) there shall, at that time, be included by the taxpayer in the amount determined for G in the definition "cumulative Canadian development expense" in subsection 66.2(5) the amount that became receivable by the taxpayer; and

(*b*) there shall, at that time, be included by the other person in the amount referred to in paragraph (*a*) of the definition "Canadian development expense" in subsection 66.2(5) the amount that became payable by that person.

Related Sections: S. 66.1(6), "restricted expense"; s. 66.1(9) Canadian development expenses for preceding years; s. 66.2(5) Definitions.

Interpretation Bulletins: *Secondary* — IT-125R4 Disposition of resource properties.

► 66(12.4) ◄

(12.4) Limitation of FEDE. Where, as a result of a transaction that occurs after May 6, 1974, an amount becomes receivable by a taxpayer at a particular time in a taxation year and the consideration given by the taxpayer for the amount receivable is property (other than a foreign resource property) or services, the original cost of which to the taxpayer can reasonably be regarded as having been primarily foreign exploration and development expenses of the taxpayer (or would have been so regarded if they had been incurred by the taxpayer after 1971 and the definition "foreign exploration and development expenses" in subsection (15) were read without reference to paragraph (*k*) of that definition), the following rules apply:

(*a*) in computing the taxpayer's foreign exploration and development expenses at that time, there shall be deducted the amount receivable by the taxpayer;

(*b*) where the amount receivable exceeds the total of the taxpayer's foreign exploration and development expenses incurred before that time to the extent that those expenses were not deducted or deductible, as the case may be, in computing the taxpayer's income for a preceding taxation year, there shall be included in the amount referred to in paragraph 59(3.2)(*a*) the amount, if any, by which the amount receivable exceeds the total of

(i) the taxpayer's foreign exploration and development expenses incurred before that time to the extent that those expenses were not deducted or deductible, as the case may be, in computing the taxpayer's income for a preceding taxation year, and

(ii) the amount, designated by the taxpayer in prescribed form filed with the taxpayer's return of income for the year, not exceeding the portion of the amount receivable for which the consideration given by the taxpayer was property (other than a foreign resource property) or services, the original cost of which to the taxpayer can reasonably be regarded as having been primarily

(A) specified foreign exploration and development expenses in respect of a country, or

(B) foreign resource expenses in respect of a country; and

(*c*) where an amount is included in the amount referred to in paragraph 59(3.2)(*a*) by virtue of paragraph (*b*), the total of the taxpayer's foreign exploration and development expenses at that time shall be deemed to be nil.

Editorial Note: Subsections 66(12.4) and (12.41) apply to foreign exploration and development expenses and foreign resource expenses in a country in the same manner as s. 66(12.1) applies to CEE and CDE.

Related Sections: S. 59(3.2) Recovery of exploration and development expenses; s. 95(1), "foreign affiliate".

Canadian Petroleum Tax Journal: Foreign Exploration and Development Expenditures — The New Rules, Roch J. Martin, 2001, Vol. 14, No. 1.

► 66(12.41) ◄

(12.41) Limitations of foreign resource expenses. Where a particular amount described in subsection (12.4) becomes receivable by a taxpayer at a particular time, there shall at that time be included in the value determined for G in the definition "cumulative foreign resource expense" in subsection 66.21(1) in respect of the taxpayer and a country the amount designated under subparagraph (12.4)(b)(ii) by the taxpayer in respect of the particular amount and the country.

Canadian Petroleum Tax Journal: Foreign Exploration and Development Expenditures — The New Rules, Roch J. Martin, 2001, Vol. 14, No. 1.

► 66(12.42) ◄

(12.42) Partnerships. For the purposes of subsections (12.4) and (12.41), where a person or partnership is a member of a particular partnership and a particular amount described in subsection (12.4) becomes receivable by the particular partnership in a fiscal period of the particular partnership,

(a) the member's share of the particular amount is deemed to be an amount that became receivable by the member at the end of the fiscal period; and

(b) the amount deemed by paragraph (a) to be an amount receivable by the member is deemed to be an amount

(i) that is described in subsection (12.4) in respect of the member, and

(ii) that has the same attributes for the member as it did for the particular partnership.

► 66(12.5) ◄

(12.5) Unitized oil or gas field in Canada. Where, pursuant to an agreement between a taxpayer and another person to unitize an oil or gas field in Canada, an amount has become receivable by the taxpayer at a particular time from that other person in respect of Canadian oil and gas property expense incurred by the taxpayer in respect of that field or any part thereof, the following rules apply:

(a) there shall, at that time, be included by the taxpayer in the amount determined for G in the definition "cumulative Canadian oil and gas property expense" in subsection 66.4(5) the amount that became receivable by the taxpayer; and

(b) there shall, at that time, be included by the other person in the amount referred to in paragraph (a) of the definition "Canadian oil and gas property expense" in subsection 66.4(5) the amount that became payable by that person.

Interpretation Bulletins: *Secondary* — IT-125R4 Disposition of resource properties.

► 66(12.6) ◄

(12.6) Canadian exploration expenses to flow-through shareholder. If a person gave consideration under an agreement to a corporation for the issue of a flow-through share of the corporation and, in the period that begins on the day on which the agreement was made and ends 24 months after the end of the month that includes that day, the corporation incurred Canadian exploration expenses (other than an expense deemed by subsection 66.1(9) to be a Canadian exploration expense of the corporation), the corporation may, after it complies with subsection (12.68) in respect of the share and before March of the first calendar year that begins after the period, renounce, effective on the day on which the renunciation is made or on an earlier day set out in the form prescribed for the purpose of subsection (12.7), to the person in respect of the share the amount, if any, by which the portion of those expenses that was incurred on or before the effective date of the renunciation (which portion is in this subsection referred to as the "specified expenses") exceeds the total of

(a) the assistance that the corporation has received, is entitled to receive or can reasonably be expected to receive at any time, and that can reasonably be related to the specified expenses or to Canadian exploration activities to which the specified expenses relate (other than assistance that can reasonably be related to expenses referred to in paragraph (b) or (b.1)),

(b) all specified expenses that are prescribed Canadian exploration and development overhead expenses of the corporation,

(b.1) all specified expenses each of which is a cost of, or for the use of, seismic data

(i) that had been acquired (otherwise than as a consequence of performing work that resulted in the creation of the data) by any other person before the cost was incurred,

(ii) in respect of which a right to use had been acquired by any other person before the cost was incurred, or

(iii) all or substantially all of which resulted from work performed more than one year before the cost was incurred, and

(c) the total of amounts that are renounced on or before the date on which the renunciation is made by any other renunciation under this subsection in respect of those expenses,

but not in any case

(d) exceeding the amount, if any, by which the consideration for the share exceeds the total of other amounts renounced under this subsection or subsection (12.601) or (12.62) in respect of the share on or before the day on which the renunciation is made, or

(e) exceeding the amount, if any, by which the cumulative Canadian exploration expense of the corporation on the effective date of the renunciation computed before taking into account any amounts renounced under this subsection on the date on which the renunciation is made, exceeds the total of all amounts renounced under this subsection in respect of any other share

(i) on the date on which the renunciation is made, and

(ii) effective on or before the effective date of the renunciation.

Editorial Note: Subsections 66(12.6) to (12.75) set out the rules relating to the flow-through share regime. These rules permit a corporation to renounce CEE and CDE incurred by the principal-business corporation to a person who enters into an agreement with the corporation to acquire flow-through shares.

Subsection 66(12.6) sets out the rules pursuant to which the corporation may renounce CEE, s. 66(12.601) sets out the rules pursuant to which a corporation may renounce certain CDE incurred in oil and gas activities as CEE, and s. 66(12.62) sets out the rules pursuant to which a corporation may renounce CDE.

Subsections 66(12.61) and (12.63) provide that the CEE and CDE so renounced are deemed to be incurred by the person who entered into the agreement and not by the corporation.

In order for a principal business corporation to make a renunciation under s. 66(12.6), it must comply with s. 66(12.68). Subsection 66.1(9) provides for the reclassification of certain CDE as CEE. This reclassified CDE is deemed to be incurred at the time of the reclassification and not at the time the reclassified CDE was actually incurred. To ensure that only expenses incurred after a flow-through share has been entered into can be renounced, for renunciations made after December 20, 2002, the preamble in s. 66(12.6) excludes reclassified CDE from CEE that may be renounced by a principal business corporation to its shareholders.

History: S. 66(12.6), the portion before paragraph (a) was replaced by S.C. 2013, c. 34, s. 199(1), applicable to renunciations made after December 20, 2002, and formerly read:

(12.6) *Canadian exploration expenses to flow-through shareholder.* Where a person gave consideration under an agreement to a corporation for the issue of a flow-through share of the corporation and, in the period that begins on the day the agreement was made and ends 24 months after the end of the month that includes that day, the corporation incurred Canadian exploration expenses, the corporation may, after it complies with subsection (12.68) in respect of the share and before March of the first calendar year that begins after the period, renounce, effective on the day on which the renunciation is made or on an earlier day set out in the form prescribed for the purposes of subsection (12.7), to the person in respect of the share the amount, if any, by which the part of those expenses that was incurred on or before the effective date of the renunciation (which part is in this subsection referred to as the "specified expenses") exceeds the total of

Related Regulations: 228; 1206(4.2), (4.3).

Related Sections: S. 66(12.7) Filing re renunciation; s. 66(12.73) Reductions in renunciations; s. 66(15), "assistance", "flow-through share"; s. 66(16) Partnerships; s. 66(19) Renunciation by corporate partner, etc; s. 66.1(6) Definitions; s. 163(2.2) False statement or omission.

Canadian Petroleum Tax Journal: Renewable Energy — Tax Developments and Opportunities, Leanne Sereda, 2000, Vol. 13, No. 1; Flow-Through Shares: An Update, Angelo F. Toselli, 1997, Vol. 10, No. 1.

Canadian Tax Foundation: Jog et al., *Flow-Through Shares: Premium-Sharing and Cost-Effectiveness*, 1996 Canadian Tax Journal 4:1016–1051.

Forms: T101 — Statement of Resource Expenses; T101A — Claim for Renouncing Canadian Exploration Expenditures (CEEs) and Canadian Development Expenditures (CDEs).

Income Tax Folios: *Primary* — S3-F8-C2 Tax Incentives for Clean Energy Equipment.

► 66(12.601) ◄

(12.601) Flow-through share rules for first $1 million of Canadian development expenses. Where

(*a*) a person gave consideration under an agreement to a corporation for the issue of a flow-through share of the corporation,

(*a*.1) the corporation's taxable capital amount at the time the consideration was given was not more than $15,000,000, and

(*b*) during the period beginning on the particular day the agreement was entered into and ending on the earlier of December 31, 2018 and the day that is 24 months after the end of the month that included that particular day, the corporation incurred Canadian development expenses (excluding expenses that are deemed by subsection (12.66) to have been incurred on December 31, 2018) described in paragraph (*a*) or (*b*) of the definition *Canadian development expense* in subsection 66.2(5) or that would be described in paragraph (*f*) of that definition if the words "paragraphs (*a*) to (*e*)" in that paragraph were read as "paragraphs (*a*) and (*b*)",

the corporation may, after it complies with subsection (12.68) in respect of the share and before March of the first calendar year that begins after that period, renounce, effective on the day on which the renunciation is made or on an earlier day set out in the form prescribed for the purposes of subsection (12.7), to the person in respect of the share the amount, if any, by which the part of those expenses that was incurred on or before the effective date of the renunciation (which part is in this subsection referred to as the "specified expenses") exceeds the total of

(*c*) the assistance that the corporation has received, is entitled to receive, or can reasonably be expected to receive at any time, and that can reasonably be related to the specified expenses or Canadian development activities to which the specified expenses relate (other than assistance that can reasonably be related to expenses referred to in paragraph (*d*)),

(*d*) all specified expenses that are prescribed Canadian exploration and development overhead expenses of the corporation, and

(*e*) all amounts that are renounced on or before the day on which the renunciation is made by any other renunciation under this subsection or subsection (12.62) in respect of those expenses.

History: S. 66(12.601)(*b*) was replaced by S.C. 2017, c. 33, s. 19(1), in force on December 14, 2017 except that, in its application in respect of agreements entered into after 2016 and before March 22, 2017, paragraph 66(12.601)(*b*) is to be read without reference to the phrase "the earlier of December 31, 2018 and". S. 66(12.601)(*b*) formerly read:

> (*b*) during the period beginning on the later of December 3, 1992 and the particular day the agreement was entered into and ending on the day that is 24 months after the end of the month that included that particular day, the corporation incurred Canadian development expenses described in paragraph (*a*) or (*b*) of the definition "Canadian development expense" in subsection 66.2(5) or that would be described in paragraph (*f*) of that definition if the words "paragraphs (*a*) to (*e*)" in that paragraph were read as "paragraphs (*a*) and (*b*)",

Related Regulations: 1206(4.2), (4.3).

Related Sections: S. 66(12.6) Canadian exploration expenses to flow-through shareholder; s. 66(12.61) Effect of renunciation; 66(12.7) Filing re renunciation; 66(12.7001) Consequences of failure to file; 66(12.701) Filing re assistance; 66(12.702) Consequences of failure to file; 66(12.71) Restriction on renunciation; 66(12.73) Reductions in renunciations; s. 66(15) Definitions; s. 66(19) Renunciation by corporate partner, etc; s. 66.1(6) Definitions; s. 66.2(5) Definitions; s. 161(6.2) Flow-through share renunciations; s. 163(2.2) False statement or omission; s. 181.2(1) Taxable capital employed in Canada; s. 181.2(4) Investment allowance.

Canadian Petroleum Tax Journal: A Practical Guide to the Flow-Through Share Rules, Greg Johnson, CA, 2002, Vol. 15, No. 1.

► 66(12.6011) ◄

(12.6011) Taxable capital amount. For the purpose of subsection (12.601), a particular corporation's taxable capital amount at any time is the total of

(*a*) its taxable capital employed in Canada for its last taxation year that ended more than 30 days before that time, and

(*b*) the total of all amounts each of which is the taxable capital employed in Canada of another corporation associated at that time with the particular corporation for the other corporation's last taxation year that ended more than 30 days before that time.

► 66(12.6012) ◄

(12.6012) Taxable capital employed in Canada. For the purpose of determining a corporation's taxable capital amount at a particular time under subsection (12.6011) and for the purpose of subsection (12.6013), a particular corporation's taxable capital employed in Canada for a taxation year is the amount that would be its taxable capital employed in Canada for the year, determined in accordance with subsection 181.2(1) and without reference to the portion of its investment allowance (as determined under subsection 181.2(4)) that is attributable to shares of the capital stock of, dividends payable by, or indebtedness of, another corporation that

(*a*) was not associated with the particular corporation at the particular time; and

(*b*) was associated with the particular corporation at the end of the particular corporation's last taxation year that ended more than 30 days before that time.

► 66(12.6013) ◄

(12.6013) Amalgamations and mergers. For the purpose of determining the taxable capital amount at a particular time under subsection (12.6011) of any corporation and for the purpose of this subsection, a particular corporation that was created as a consequence of an amalgamation or merger of other corporations (each of which is in this subsection referred to as a "predecessor corporation"), and that does not have a taxation year that ended more than 30 days before the particular time, is deemed to have taxable capital employed in Canada for a taxation year that ended more than 30 days before the particular time equal to the total of all amounts each of which is the taxable capital employed in Canada of a predecessor corporation for its last taxation year that ended more than 30 days before the particular time.

▶ 66(12.602) ◀

(12.602) Idem. A corporation shall be deemed not to have renounced any particular amount under subsection (12.601) in respect of a share where

(*a*) the particular amount exceeds the amount, if any, by which the consideration for the share exceeds the total of other amounts renounced in respect of the share under subsection (12.6), (12.601) or (12.62) on or before the day on which the renunciation is made;

(*b*) the particular amount exceeds the amount, if any, by which

(i) the cumulative Canadian development expense of the corporation on the effective date of the renunciation, computed before taking into account any amounts renounced under subsection (12.601) on the day on which the renunciation is made,

exceeds

(ii) the total of all amounts renounced under subsection (12.601) by the corporation in respect of any other share

(A) on the day on which the renunciation is made, and

(B) effective on or before the effective date of the renunciation; or

(*c*) the particular amount relates to Canadian development expenses incurred by the corporation in a calendar year and the total amounts renounced, on or before the day on which the renunciation is made, under subsection (12.601) in respect of

(i) Canadian development expenses incurred by the corporation in that calendar year, or

(ii) Canadian development expenses incurred in that calendar year by another corporation associated with the corporation at the time the other corporation incurred such expenses

exceeds $1,000,000.

Canadian Petroleum Tax Journal: A Practical Guide to the Flow-Through Share Rules, Greg Johnson, CA, 2002, Vol. 15, No. 1.

▶ 66(12.61) ◀

(12.61) Effect of renunciation. Subject to subsections (12.69) to (12.702), where under subsection (12.6) or (12.601) a corporation renounces an amount to a person,

(*a*) the Canadian exploration expenses or Canadian development expenses to which the amount relates shall be deemed to be Canadian exploration expenses incurred in that amount by the person on the effective date of the renunciation; and

(*b*) the Canadian exploration expenses or Canadian development expenses to which the amount relates shall, except for the purposes of that renunciation, be deemed on and after the effective date of the renunciation never to have been Canadian exploration expenses or Canadian development expenses incurred by the corporation.

Related Sections: 66(12.69) Filing re partners; 66(12.6901) Consequences of failure to file; 66(12.691) Filing re assistance; 66(12.7) Filing re renunciation; 66(12.7001) Consequences of failure to file; 66(12.701) Filing re assistance; 66(12.702) Consequences of failure to file.

Income Tax Folios: *Primary* — S3-F8-C2 Tax Incentives for Clean Energy Equipment.

▶ 66(12.62) ◀

(12.62) Canadian development expenses to flow-through shareholder. Where a person gave consideration under an agreement to a corporation for the issue of a flow-through share of the corporation and, in the period that begins on the day the agreement was made and ends 24 months after the end of the month that includes that day, the corporation incurred Canadian development expenses, the corporation may, after it complies with subsection (12.68) in respect of the share and before March of the first calendar year that begins after the period, renounce, effective on the day on which the renunciation is made or on an earlier day set out in the form prescribed for the purposes of subsection (12.7), to the person in respect of the share the amount, if any, by which the part of those expenses that was incurred on or before the effective date of the renunciation (which part is in this subsection referred to as the "specified expenses") exceeds the total of

(*a*) the assistance that the corporation has received, is entitled to receive, or can reasonably be expected to receive at any time, and that can reasonably be related to the specified expenses or to Canadian development activities to which the specified expenses relate (other than assistance that can reasonably be related to expenses referred to in paragraph (*b*) or (*b*.1)),

(*b*) all specified expenses that are prescribed Canadian exploration and development overhead expenses of the corporation,

(*b*.1) all specified expenses that are described in paragraph (*e*) of the definition "Canadian development expense" in subsection 66.2(5) or that are described in paragraph (*f*) of that definition because of the reference in the latter paragraph to paragraph (*e*), and

(*c*) the total of amounts that are renounced on or before the day on which the renunciation is made by any other renunciation under this subsection or subsection (12.601) in respect of those expenses,

but not in any case

(*d*) exceeding the amount, if any, by which the consideration for the share exceeds the total of other amounts renounced in respect of the share under this subsection or subsection (12.6) or (12.601) on or before the day on which the renunciation is made, or

(*e*) exceeding the amount, if any, by which the cumulative Canadian development expense of the corporation on the effective date of the renunciation computed before taking into account any amounts renounced under this subsection on the date on which the renunciation is made, exceeds the total of all amounts renounced under this subsection in respect of any other share

(i) on the date on which the renunciation is made, and

(ii) effective on or before the effective date of the renunciation.

Related Regulations: 1206(4.2), (4.3).

Related Sections: S. 66(12.6) Canadian exploration expenses to flow-through shareholder; s. 66(12.601) Flow-through share rules for first $1 million of Canadian development expenses; 66(12.7) Filing re renunciation; 66(12.7001) Consequences of failure to file; 66(12.701) Filing re assistance; 66(12.702) Consequences of failure to file; 66(12.71) Restriction on renunciation; 66(12.73) Reductions in renunciations; s. 66(15), "flow-through share"; s. 66(19) Renunciation by corporate partner, etc; s. 66.1(6), "restricted expense"; s. 66.2(5) Definitions; s. 163(2.2) False statement or omission.

Forms: T100A — Application for a Selling Instrument T100 Identification Number (SITIN); T101 — Statement of Resource Expenses; T101A — Claim for Renouncing Canadian Exploration Expenditures (CEEs) and Canadian Development Expenditures (CDEs); T101D — Summary of Assistance.

▶ 66(12.63) ◀

(12.63) Effect of renunciation. Subject to subsections (12.69) to (12.702), if under subsection (12.62) a corporation renounces an amount to a person,

(*a*) the Canadian development expenses to which the amount relates shall be deemed to be Canadian development expenses incurred in that amount by the person on the effective date of the renunciation; and

(*b*) the Canadian development expenses to which the amount relates shall, except for the purposes of that renunciation, be deemed on and after the effective date of the renunciation never to have been Canadian development expenses incurred by the corporation.

History: S. 66(12.63), the portion before paragraph (*a*) was replaced by S.C. 2013, c. 34, s. 199(2), applicable to renunciations made after December 20, 2002, and formerly read:

(12.63) *Effect of renunciation.* Subject to subsections (12.691) to (12.702), where under subsection (12.62) a corporation renounces an amount to a person,

Related Sections: 66(12.69) Filing re partners; 66(12.6901) Consequences of failure to file; 66(12.691) Filing re assistance; 66(12.7) Filing re renunciation; 66(12.7001) Consequences of failure to file; 66(12.701) Filing re assistance; 66(12.702) Consequences of failure to file; 66.1(9) Canadian development expenses for preceding years.

▶ 66(12.64) ◀

(12.64) Canadian oil and gas property expenses to flow-through shareholder — (Repealed by S.C. 1997, c. 25, s. 13(15).)

▶ 66(12.65) ◀

(12.65) Effect of renunciation — (Repealed by S.C. 1997, c. 25, s. 13(15).)

▶ 66(12.66) ◀

(12.66) Expenses in the first 60 days of year. Where

(*a*) a corporation that issues a flow-through share to a person under an agreement incurs, in a particular calendar year, Canadian exploration expenses or Canadian development expenses,

(*a*.1) the agreement was made in the preceding calendar year,

(*b*) the expenses

(i) are described in paragraph (*a*), (*d*), (*f*) or (*g*.1) of the definition "Canadian exploration expense" in subsection 66.1(6) or paragraph (*a*) or (*b*) of the definition "Canadian development expense" in subsection 66.2(5),

(ii) would be described in paragraph (*h*) of the definition "Canadian exploration expense" in subsection 66.1(6) if the reference to "paragraphs (*a*) to (*d*) and (*f*) to (*g.4*)" in that paragraph were read as "paragraphs (*a*), (*d*), (*f*) and (*g.1*)", or

(iii) would be described in paragraph (*f*) of the definition "Canadian development expense" in subsection 66.2(5) if the words "any of paragraphs (*a*) to (*e*)" were read as "paragraph (*a*) or (*b*)",

(*c*) before the end of that preceding year the person paid the consideration in money for the share to be issued,

(*d*) the corporation and the person deal with each other at arm's length throughout the particular year, and

(*e*) in January, February or March of the particular year, the corporation renounces an amount in respect of the expenses to the person in respect of the share in accordance with subsection (12.6) or (12.601) and the effective date of the renunciation is the last day of that preceding year,

the corporation is, for the purpose of subsection (12.6), or of subsection (12.601) and paragraph (12.602)(*b*), as the case may be, deemed to have incurred the expenses on the last day of that preceding year.

Editorial Note: A corporation may renounce, effective as of December 31 of a preceding calendar year ("Year 1"), the expenses referred to in s. 66(12.66) which it has incurred or will incur in a particular calendar year ("Year 2"). The corporation must make the renunciation in the first three months of Year 2. S. 66(12.66) is known as the "one-year look-back rule". Additionally, the corporation must enter into a flow-through share agreement with an investor, the investor must pay the subscription price in money for the shares in Year 1, and the corporation and the investor must deal with each other at arm's length throughout Year 2. If the conditions in s. 66(12.66) are satisfied, the corporation is deemed to have incurred the expenses on December 31 of Year 1.

History: S. 12.66(*b*)(ii) was replaced by S.C. 2013, c. 40, s. 30(2), deemed to have come into force on March 22, 2011, except that before March 21, 2013 subparagraph 66(12.66)(*b*)(ii) is to be read as follows:

"(ii) would be described in paragraph (h) of the definition 'Canadian exploration expense' in subsection 66.1(6) if the reference to 'paragraphs (*a*) to (*d*) and (*f*) to (*g.2*)' in that paragraph were 'paragraphs (*a*), (*d*), (*f*) and (*g.1*)', or"

S. 12.66(*b*)(ii) formerly read:

(ii) would be described in paragraph (*h*) of the definition "Canadian exploration expense" in subsection 66.1(6) if the words "paragraphs (*a*) to (*d*) and (*f*) to (*g*.1)" were read as "paragraphs (*a*), (*d*), (*f*) and (*g*.1)", or

S. 66(12.66), the portion after paragraph (*e*) was replaced by S.C. 2013, c. 34, s. 199(5), in force June 26, 2013, and formerly read:

the corporation is for the purpose of subsection (12.6) or for the purposes of subsection (12.601) and paragraph (12.602)(*b*), as the case may be, deemed to have incurred the expenses on the last day of the year.

Related Sections: S. 59(3.5)(*b*) Variation of stated percentage; s. 66(12.6) Canadian exploration expenses to flow-through shareholder; s. 66(12.601) Flow-through share rules for first $1 million of Canadian development expenses; s. 66(12.602)(*b*) Deemed non-renunciation of Canadian development expenses; s. 66(15), "flow-through share"; s. 66(16) Partnerships; s. 66(17) Non-arm's length partnerships; s. 66.1(6) "Canadian exploration expense"; s. 87(4.4) Flow-through shares; s. 127(9), "flow-through mining expenditure", "investment tax credit"; s. 161(6.2) Flow-through share renunciations; s. 163(2.2) False statement or omission; s. 163(2.21) False statement or omissions with respect to look-back rule; s. 211.91(1) Tax imposed; s. 248(1), "specified future tax consequence; s. 251(1) Arm's length.

Canadian Petroleum Tax Journal: A Practical Guide to the Flow-Through Share Rules, Greg Johnson, CA, 2002, Vol. 15, No. 1.

Income Tax Folios: *Primary* — S3-F8-C2 Tax Incentives for Clean Energy Equipment

▶ 66(12.67) ◀

(12.67) Restrictions on renunciation. A corporation shall be deemed

(*a*) not to have renounced under any of subsections (12.6), (12.601) and (12.62) any expenses that are deemed to have been incurred by it because of a renunciation under this section by another corporation that is not related to it;

(*b*) not to have renounced under subsection (12.601) to a trust, corporation or partnership any Canadian development expenses (other than expenses renounced to another corporation that renounces under subsection (12.6) any Canadian exploration expense deemed to have been incurred by it because of the renunciation under subsection (12.601)) if, in respect of the renunciation under subsection (12.601), it has a prohibited relationship with the trust, corporation or partnership;

(*c*) not to have renounced under subsection (12.601) any Canadian development expenses deemed to have been incurred by it because of a renunciation under subsection (12.62); and

(*d*) not to have renounced under subsection (12.6) to a particular trust, corporation or partnership any Canadian exploration expenses (other than expenses ultimately renounced by another corporation under subsection (12.6) to an individual (other than a trust) or to a trust, corporation or partnership with which that other corporation does not have, in respect of that ultimate renunciation, a prohibited relationship) deemed to be incurred by it because of a renunciation under subsection (12.601) if, in respect of the renunciation under subsection (12.6), it has a prohibited relationship with the particular trust, corporation or partnership.

Editorial Note: There are a number of restrictions imposed on the ability of a corporation to renounce expenses. A corporation may not renounce any expenses that have been renounced to it by a person that is not related to it. A corporation may not renounce Canadian development expenses as Canadian exploration expenses pursuant to s. 66(12.601) and therefore have no application to the renunciation of expenses which are Canadian exploration expenses without the deeming provisions of s. 66(12.601).

Related Sections: S. 66(12.6) Canadian exploration expenses to flow-through shareholder; s. 66(12.61) Effect of renunciation; s. 66(12.62) Canadian development expenses to flow-through shareholder; s. 66(12.63) Effect of renunciation; s. 66(12.64) Canadian oil and gas property expenses to flow-through shareholder; s. 66(12.65) Effect of renunciation; s. 66(12.671) Prohibited relationship.

▶ 66(12.671) ◀

(12.671) Prohibited relationship. For the purposes of subsection (12.67), where a trust, corporation (in paragraph (*b*) referred to as the "shareholder corporation") or partnership, as the case may be, gave consideration under a particular agreement for the issue of a flow-through share of a particular corporation, the particular corporation has, in respect of a renunciation under subsection (12.6) or (12.601) in respect of the share, a prohibited relationship

(*a*) with the trust if, at any time after the particular agreement was entered into and before the share is issued to the trust, the particular corporation or any corporation related to the particular corporation is beneficially interested in the trust;

(*b*) with the shareholder corporation if, immediately before the particular agreement was entered into, the shareholder corporation was related to the particular corporation; or

(*c*) with the partnership if any part of the amount renounced would, but for subsection (12.7001), be included, because of paragraph (*h*) of the definition "Canadian exploration expense" in subsection 66.1(6), in the Canadian exploration expense of

(i) the particular corporation, or

(ii) any other corporation that, at any time

(A) after the particular agreement was entered into, and

(B) before that part of the amount renounced would, but for this paragraph, be incurred,

would, if flow-through shares issued by the particular corporation under agreements entered into at the same time as or after the time the particular agreement was entered into were disregarded, be related to the particular corporation.

Related Sections: S. 248(25) Beneficially interested.

▶ 66(12.68) ◀

(12.68) Filing selling instruments. A corporation that agrees to issue or prepares a selling instrument in respect of flow-through shares shall file with the Minister a prescribed form together with a copy of the selling instrument or agreement to issue the shares on or before the last day of the month following the earlier of

(*a*) the month in which the agreement to issue the shares is entered into, and

(*b*) the month in which the selling instrument is first delivered to a potential investor,

and the Minister shall thereupon assign an identification number to the form and notify the corporation of the number.

Related Sections: S. 66(12.7) Filing re renunciation; s. 66(12.75) Penalty; s. 66(15), "selling instrument"; s. 163.2 Amount of penalty.

Forms: T100A — Application for a Selling Instrument T100 Identification Number (SITIN); T100B — Details of the Flow-Through Shares (FTSs) and Flow-Through Warrants (FTWs) Subscribed; T100C — Application for a T100 Identification Number (TIN) on the Exercise of Flow-Through Warrants (FTWs) and Details of the FTWs Exercised.

▶ 66(12.69) ◀

(12.69) Filing re partners. Where, in a fiscal period of a partnership, an expense is incurred by the partnership as a consequence of a renunciation of an amount under subsection (12.6), (12.601) or (12.62), the partnership shall, before the end of the third month that begins after the end of the period, file with the Minister a prescribed form identifying the share of the expense attributable to each member of the partnership at the end of the period.

Related Sections: S. 66(12.74) Late filed forms; s. 66(12.75) Penalty.

Forms: T5013SCH52 Summary Information for Partnership that Allocated Renounced Resource Expenses to their Members.

▶ 66(12.6901) ◀

(12.6901) Consequences of failure to file. Where a partnership fails to file a prescribed form as required under subsection (12.69) in respect of an expense, except for the purpose of subsection (12.69) the partnership is deemed not to have incurred the expense.

▶ 66(12.691) ◀

(12.691) Filing re assistance. Where a partnership receives or becomes entitled to receive assistance as an agent for its members or former members at a particular time in respect of any Canadian exploration expense or Canadian development expense that is or, but for paragraph (12.61)(*b*) or (12.63)(*b*), would be incurred by a corporation, the following rules apply:

(*a*) where the entitlement of any such member or former member to any part of the assistance is known by the partnership as of the end of the partnership's first fiscal period ending after the particular time and that part of the assistance was not required to be reported under paragraph (*b*) in respect of a calendar year ending before the end of that fiscal period, the partnership shall, on or before the last day of the third month following the end of that fiscal period, file with the Minister a prescribed form indicating the share of that part of the assistance paid to each of those members or former members before the end of that fiscal period or to which each of those members or former members is entitled at the end of that fiscal period;

(*b*) where the entitlement of any of those members or former members to any part of the assistance is known by the partnership as of the end of a calendar year that ends after the particular time and that part of the assistance was not required to be reported under paragraph (*a*) in respect of a fiscal period ending at or before the end of that calendar year, or under this paragraph in respect of a preceding calendar year, the partnership shall, on or before the last day of the third month following the end of that calendar year, file with the Minister a prescribed form indicating the share of that part of the assistance paid to each of those members or former members before the end of that fiscal period or to which each of those members or former members is entitled at the end of that calendar year; and

(*c*) where a prescribed form required to be filed under paragraph (*a*) or (*b*) is not so filed, the part of that expense relating to the assistance required to be reported in the prescribed form shall be deemed not to have been incurred by the partnership.

▶ 66(12.7) ◀

(12.7) Filing re renunciation. Where a corporation renounces an amount in respect of Canadian exploration expenses or Canadian development expenses under subsection (12.6), (12.601) or (12.62), the corporation shall file a prescribed form in respect of the renunciation with the Minister before the end of the first month after the month in which the renunciation is made.

Related Sections: S. 66(12.74) Late filed forms; s. 66(12.75) Penalty.

Forms: T101 — Statement of Resource Expenses; T101A — Claim for Renouncing Canadian Exploration Expenditures (CEEs) and Canadian Development Expenditures (CDEs).

▶ 66(12.7001) ◀

(12.7001) Consequences of failure to file. Where a corporation fails to file a prescribed form as required under subsection (12.7) in respect of a renunciation of an amount, subsections (12.61) and (12.63) do not apply in respect of the amount.

▶ 66(12.701) ◀

(12.701) Filing re assistance. Where a corporation receives or becomes entitled to receive assistance as an agent in respect of any Canadian exploration expense or Canadian development expense that is or, but for paragraph (12.61)(*b*) or (12.63)(*b*), would be incurred by the corporation, the corporation shall, before the end of the first month after the particular month in which it first becomes known to the corporation that a person that holds a flow-through share of the corporation is entitled to a share of any part of the assistance, file with the Minister a prescribed form identifying the share of the assistance to which each of those persons is entitled at the end of the particular month.

Forms: T101D — Summary of Assistance.

▶ 66(12.702) ◀

(12.702) Consequences of failure to file. Where a corporation fails to file a prescribed form as required under subsection (12.701) in respect of assistance, except for the purpose of subsection (12.701) the Canadian exploration expense or Canadian development expense to which the assistance relates is deemed not to have been incurred by the corporation.

▶ 66(12.71) ◀

(12.71) Restriction on renunciation. A corporation may renounce an amount under subsection (12.6), (12.601) or (12.62) in respect of Canadian exploration expenses or Canadian development expenses incurred by it only to the extent that, but for the renunciation, it would be entitled to a deduction in respect of the expenses in computing its income.

Tax Window Files: Flow through shares - farm-out agreement, *16XXXX*, CRA Document No. 2015-0614081R3.

▶ 66(12.72) ◀

(12.72) Application of sections 231 to 231.3 — (Repealed by S.C. 1997, c. 25, s. 13(23).)

▶ 66(12.73) ◀

(12.73) Reductions in renunciations. Where an amount that a corporation purports to renounce to a person under subsection (12.6), (12.601) or (12.62) exceeds the amount that it can renounce to the person under that subsection,

(*a*) the corporation shall file a statement with the Minister in prescribed form where

(i) the Minister sends a notice in writing to the corporation demanding the statement, or

(ii) the excess arose as a consequence of a renunciation purported to be made in a calendar year under subsection (12.6) or (12.601) because of the application of subsection (12.66) and, at the end of the year, the corporation knew or ought to have known of all or part of the excess;

(*b*) where subparagraph (*a*)(i) applies, the statement shall be filed not later than 30 days after the Minister sends a notice in writing to the corporation demanding the statement;

(*c*) where subparagraph (*a*)(ii) applies, the statement shall be filed before March of the calendar year following the calendar year in which the purported renunciation was made;

(*d*) except for the purpose of Part XII.6, any amount that is purported to have been so renounced to any person is deemed, after the statement is filed with the Minister, to have always been reduced by the portion of the excess identified in the statement in respect of that purported renunciation; and

(*e*) where a corporation fails in the statement to apply the excess fully to reduce one or more purported renunciations, the Minister may at any time reduce the total amount purported to be renounced by the corporation to one or more persons by the amount of the unapplied excess in which case, except for the purpose of Part XII.6, the amount purported to have been so renounced to a person is deemed, after that time, always to have been reduced by the portion of the unapplied excess allocated by the Minister in respect of that person.

Editorial Note: Subsection 66(12.73) applies where a corporation purports to renounce expenses in excess of the amount that it can renounce. The subsection contemplates two situations, one in which the Minister sends a notice to the corporation and the second in which the corporation knew it should have known of the excess. The subsection requires the corporation to file a statement reducing the renounced expenses. Where the corporation has not filed such a statement, the Minister may reduce the expenses. In *Forsberg v. The Queen*, 2005 DTC 1315 (TCC), the Court held that a taxpayer has a right to challenge the Minister's determination.

Related Sections: S. 161(6.2) Flow-through share renunciations.

Forms: T101B — Claims for Adjustments to Canadian Exploration Expenditures (CEEs) and Canadian Development Expenditures (CDEs) Previously Renounced.

► 66(12.74) ◄

(12.74) Late filed forms. A corporation or partnership may file with the Minister a document referred to in subsection (12.68), (12.69), (12.691), (12.7) or (12.701) after the particular day on or before which the document is required to be filed under the applicable subsection and the document shall, except for the purposes of this subsection and subsection (12.75), be deemed to have been filed on the day on or before which it was required to be filed if

(*a*) it is filed

(i) on or before the day that is 90 days after the particular day, or

(ii) after the day that is 90 days after the particular day where, in the opinion of the Minister, the circumstances are such that it would be just and equitable to permit the document to be filed; and

(*b*) the corporation or partnership, as the case may be, pays to the Receiver General at the time of filing a penalty in respect of the late filing.

Related Sections: S. 66(12.75) Penalty.

Forms: T100 — Flow-Through Share Information; T100A — Application for a Selling Instrument T100 Identification Number (SITIN); T101 — Statement of Resource Expenses; T101C Part XII.6 Tax Return; T101A — Claim for Renouncing Canadian Exploration Expenditures (CEEs) and Canadian Development Expenditures (CDEs); T101D — Summary of Assistance; T5013SCH52 Summary Information for Partnership that Allocated Renounced Resource Expenses to their Members.

► 66(12.741) ◄

(12.741) Late renunciation. Where a corporation purports to renounce an amount under subsection (12.6), (12.601) or (12.62) after the period in which the corporation was entitled to renounce the amount, the amount is deemed, except for the purposes of this subsection and subsections (12.7) and (12.75), to have been renounced at the end of the period if

(*a*) the corporation purports to renounce the amount

(i) on or before the day that is 90 days after the end of that period, or

(ii) after the day that is 90 days after the end of that period where, in the opinion of the Minister, the circumstances are such that it would be just and equitable that the amount be renounced; and

(*b*) the corporation pays to the Receiver General a penalty in respect of the renunciation not more than 90 days after the renunciation.

Related Sections: S. 66(12.75) Penalty.

Forms: T101A — Claim for Renouncing Canadian Exploration Expenditures (CEEs) and Canadian Development Expenditures (CDEs).

► 66(12.75) ◄

(12.75) Penalty. For the purposes of subsections (12.74) and (12.741), the penalty in respect of the late filing of a document referred to in subsection (12.68), (12.69), (12.691), (12.7) or (12.701) or in respect of a renunciation referred to in subsection (12.741) is the lesser of $15,000 and

(*a*) where the penalty is in respect of the late filing of a document referred to in subsection (12.68), (12.69) or (12.7), the greater of

(i) $100, and

(ii) 1/4 of 1% of the maximum amount in respect of the Canadian exploration expenses and Canadian development expenses renounced or attributed or to be renounced or attributed as set out in the document;

(*b*) where the penalty is in respect of the late filing of a document referred to in subsection (12.691) or (12.701), the greater of

(i) $100, and

(ii) 1/4 of 1% of the assistance reported in the document; and

(*c*) where the penalty is in respect of a renunciation referred to in subsection (12.741), the greater of

(i) $100, and

(ii) 1/4 of 1% of the amount of the renunciation.

Forms: T100 — Flow-Through Share Information; T100A — Application for a Selling Instrument T100 Identification Number (SITIN); T101 — Statement of Resource Expenses; T101C Part XII.6 Tax Return; T101A — Claim for Renouncing Canadian Exploration Expenditures (CEEs) and Canadian Development Expenditures (CDEs); T101D — Summary of Assistance; T5013SCH52 Summary Information for Partnership that Allocated Renounced Resource Expenses to their Members.

▶ 66(13) ◀

(13) Limitation. Where a taxpayer has incurred an outlay or expense in respect of which a deduction from income is authorized under more than one provision of this section or section 66.1, 66.2 or 66.4, the taxpayer is not entitled to make the deduction under more than one provision but is entitled to select the provision under which to make the deduction.

▶ 66(13.1) ◀

(13.1) Short taxation year. Where a taxpayer has a taxation year that is less than 51 weeks, the amount determined in respect of the year under each of subparagraph (4)(*b*)(i), paragraph 66.2(2)(*c*), subparagraph (*b*)(i) of the definition "global foreign resource limit" in subsection 66.21(1), subparagraph 66.21(4)(*a*)(i), clause 66.21(4)(*a*)(ii)(B) and paragraphs 66.4(2)(*b*) and 66.7(2.3)(*a*), (4)(*a*) and (5)(*a*) shall not exceed that proportion of the amount otherwise determined that the number of days in the year is of 365.

▶ 66(14) ◀

(14) Amounts deemed deductible under this subdivision. For the purposes of section 3, any amount deductible under the *Income Tax Application Rules* in respect of this subsection shall be deemed to be deductible under this subdivision.

Related Sections: ITAR s. 30(3) Reference to this Act in amended Act.

▶ 66(14.1) ◀

(14.1) Designation respecting Canadian exploration expense. A corporation may designate for a taxation year, by filing a designation in prescribed form with the Minister on or before the day on or before which it is required to file a return of its income for the year under section 150, a particular amount not exceeding the lesser of

(*a*) its prescribed Canadian exploration expense for the year, and

(*b*) its cumulative Canadian exploration expense at the end of the year,

and the particular amount shall be added in computing its cumulative offset account immediately before the end of the year and deducted in computing its cumulative Canadian exploration expense at any time after the end of the year.

Related Regulations: 1217.

Related Sections: S. 66(14.4) Special cases; s. 66.1(2) Deduction for certain principal-business corporations; s. 66.1(3) Expenses of other taxpayer; s. 66.1(6), "cumulative Canadian exploration expense"; s. 66.5 Deduction from income.

▶ 66(14.2) ◀

(14.2) Designation respecting cumulative Canadian development expense. A corporation may designate for a taxation year, by filing a designation in prescribed form with the Minister on or before the day on or before which it is required to file a return of its income for the year under section 150, a particular amount not exceeding

(*a*) where a deduction has been made under subsection 66.2(2) in computing its income for the year, the lesser of

(i) 30% of its prescribed Canadian development expense for the year, and

(ii) the amount, if any, by which 30% of its cumulative Canadian development expense at the end of the year exceeds the amount, if any, deducted for the year under subsection 66.2(2) in computing its income for the year, or

(*b*) where a deduction has not been made under subsection 66.2(2) in computing its income for the year, the lesser of

(i) 30% of its prescribed Canadian development expense for the year, and

(ii) 30% of the amount, if any, of its adjusted cumulative Canadian development expense at the end of the year,

and the particular amount shall be added in computing its cumulative offset account immediately before the end of the year and deducted in computing its cumulative Canadian development expense at any time after the end of the year.

Related Regulations: 1218.

Related Sections: S. 66(14.3) Definition of "adjusted cumulative Canadian development expense"; s. 66(14.4) Special cases; s. 66.5 Deduction from income.

▶ 66(14.3) ◀

(14.3) Definition of "adjusted cumulative Canadian development expense". For the purposes of paragraph (14.2)(*b*), "adjusted cumulative Canadian development expense" of a corporation at the end of a taxation year means the amount, if any, that would be its cumulative Canadian development expense at the end of the year, if no Canadian resource property were disposed of by it in the year.

▶ 66(14.4) ◀

(14.4) Special cases. Where, in the opinion of the Minister, the circumstances of a case are such that it would be just and equitable

(*a*) to permit a designation under subsection (14.1) or (14.2) to be filed after the day on or before which it is required by that subsection to be filed, or

(*b*) to permit a designation filed under subsection (14.1) or (14.2) to be amended,

the Minister may permit the designation to be filed or amended, as the case may be, after that day, and where the designation or amendment is filed pursuant to that permission, it shall be deemed to have been filed on the day on or before which it was required to be filed if

(*c*) it is filed with the Minister in prescribed form, and

(*d*) the corporation filing it pays to the Receiver General at the time of filing the penalty in respect of it,

and where a designation is amended under this subsection, the designation to which the amendment is made shall be deemed not to have been effective.

Related Sections: S. 66(14.5) Penalty for late designation.

▶ 66(14.5) ◀

(14.5) Penalty for late designation. For the purposes of this section, the penalty in respect of a designation or amended designation referred to in paragraph (14.4)(*a*) or (*b*) is the lesser of

(*a*) an amount determined by the formula

$$0.0025 \times A \times B$$

where

A is

(i) in the case of a late-filed designation, the amount designated therein, and

(ii) in the case of an amended designation, the amount, if any, by which the amount designated in the designation being amended differs from the amount designated in the amended designation, and

B is the number of months each of which is included in whole or in part in the period commencing on the day on or before which the designation was required to be filed under subsection (14.1) or (14.2), as the case may be, and ending on the day the late-filed designation or amended designation, as the case may be, is filed, and

(*b*) an amount, not exceeding $8,000, equal to the product obtained by multiplying $100 by the number of months each of which is included in whole or in part in the period referred to in the description of B in paragraph (*a*).

▶ 66(14.6) ◀

(14.6) Deduction of carved-out income. A taxpayer may deduct in computing the taxpayer's income under this Part for a taxation year, an amount equal to the total of the taxpayer's carved-out incomes for the year within the meaning assigned by subsection 209(1).

▶ 66(15) ◀

(15) Definitions. In this section,

"agreed portion" —"agreed portion" in respect of a corporation that was a shareholder corporation of a joint exploration corporation means such amount as may be agreed on between the joint exploration corporation and the shareholder corporation not exceeding

(*a*) the total of all amounts each of which is a payment or loan referred to in paragraph (*b*) of the definition "shareholder corporation" in this subsection (except to the extent that the payment or loan was made by a shareholder corporation that was not a Canadian corporation and was used by the joint exploration corporation to acquire a Canadian resource property after December 11, 1979 from a shareholder corporation that was not a Canadian corporation) made by the shareholder corporation to the joint exploration corporation during the period it was a shareholder corporation of the joint exploration corporation,

minus

(*b*) the total of the amounts, if any, previously renounced by the joint exploration corporation under any of subsections (10) to (10.3) in favour of the shareholder corporation;

Related Sections: S. 53(2) Amounts to be deducted; s. 66(10) Joint exploration corporation; s. 66(15), "joint exploration corporation".

"assistance" —"assistance" means any amount, other than a prescribed amount, received or receivable at any time from a person or government, municipality or other public authority whether the amount is by way of a grant, subsidy, rebate, forgivable loan, deduction from royalty or tax, rebate of royalty or tax, investment allowance or any other form of assistance or benefit;

"Canadian exploration and development expenses" — "Canadian exploration and development expenses" incurred by a taxpayer means any expense incurred before May 7, 1974 that is

(*a*) any drilling or exploration expense, including any general geological or geophysical expense, incurred by the taxpayer after 1971 on or in respect of exploring or drilling for petroleum or natural gas in Canada,

(*b*) any prospecting, exploration or development expense incurred by the taxpayer after 1971 in searching for minerals in Canada,

(*c*) the cost to the taxpayer of any Canadian resource property acquired by the taxpayer after 1971,

(*d*) the taxpayer's share of the Canadian exploration and development expenses incurred after 1971 by any association, partnership or syndicate in a fiscal period thereof, if at the end of that fiscal period the taxpayer was a member or partner thereof,

(*e*) any expense incurred by the taxpayer after 1971 pursuant to an agreement with a corporation under which the taxpayer incurred the expense solely in consideration for shares of the capital stock of the corporation issued to the taxpayer by the corporation or any interest in such shares or right thereto, to the extent that the expense was incurred as or on account of the cost of

(i) drilling or exploration activities, including any general geological or geophysical activities, in or in respect of exploring or drilling for petroleum or natural gas in Canada,

(ii) prospecting, exploration or development activities in searching for minerals in Canada, or

(iii) acquiring a Canadian resource property, and

(*f*) any annual payment made by the taxpayer for the preservation of a Canadian resource property,

but, for greater certainty, does not include

(*g*) any consideration given by the taxpayer for any share or any interest therein or right thereto, except as provided by paragraph (*e*), or

(*h*) any expense described in paragraph (*e*) incurred by another taxpayer to the extent that the expense was, by virtue of that paragraph, a Canadian exploration and development expense of that other taxpayer;

Editorial Note: See the editorial notes under s. 66(1).

Related Sections: S. 49(2) Where option granted by a corporation expires; s. 53(2) Amounts to be deducted.

"Canadian resource property" —"Canadian resource property" of a taxpayer means any property of the taxpayer that is

(*a*) any right, licence or privilege to explore for, drill for or take petroleum, natural gas or related hydrocarbons in Canada,

(*b*) any right, licence or privilege to

(i) store underground petroleum, natural gas or related hydrocarbons in Canada, or

(ii) prospect, explore, drill or mine for minerals in a mineral resource in Canada other than a bituminous sands deposit or an oil shale deposit,

(*c*) any oil or gas well in Canada or any real property or immovable in Canada the principal value of which depends on its petroleum, natural gas or related hydrocarbon content (not including any depreciable property),

(*d*) any right to a rental or royalty computed by reference to the amount or value of production from an oil or a gas well in Canada, or from a natural accumulation of petroleum, natural gas or a related hydrocarbon in Canada, if the payer of the rental or royalty has an interest in, or for civil law a right in, the well or accumulation, as the case may be, and 90% or more of the rental or royalty is payable out of, or from the proceeds of, the production from the well or accumulation,

(*e*) any right to a rental or royalty computed by reference to the amount or value of production from a mineral resource in Canada, other than a bituminous sands deposit or an oil shale deposit, if the payer of the rental or royalty has an interest in, or for civil law a right in, the mineral resource and 90% or more of the rental or royalty is payable out of, or from the proceeds of, the production from the mineral resource,

(*f*) any real property or immovable in Canada (not including any depreciable property) the principal value of which depends on its mineral resource content other than where the mineral resource is a bituminous sands deposit or an oil shale deposit,

(*g*) any right to or interest in — or, for civil law, any right to or in — any property described in any of paragraphs (*a*) to (*e*), other than a right or an interest that the taxpayer has because the taxpayer is a beneficiary under a trust or a member of a partnership, or

(*h*) an interest in real property described in paragraph (*f*) or a real right in an immovable described in that paragraph, other than an interest or a right that the taxpayer has because the taxpayer is a beneficiary under a trust or a member of a partnership;

Editorial Note: The definition of "Canadian resource property" generally classifies Canadian resource properties into Canadian oil and gas properties and Canadian mineral resource properties. The definition does not require the taxpayer to have an ownership interest in the lands producing the oil and gas or minerals. A Canadian resource property also includes a right, licence or privilege of the taxpayer to explore for or take hydrocarbons, or to explore for or mine for minerals other than a bituminous sands deposit or oil shale deposit by virtue of paragraphs (*a*) and (*b*). Additionally, a right to a rental or royalty acquired after December 20, 2002, generally computed by reference to the value of production from an oil or gas well in Canada, from a natural accumulation of petroleum, natural gas or other similar hydrocarbon in Canada or from a mineral resource in Canada, also constitutes a Canadian resource property by virtue of paragraphs (*d*) and (*e*), as long as the payer of the royalty has an interest in the well, accumulation or mineral resource and 90% or more of the rental or royalty is paid from the proceeds of the production from the well, accumulation or mineral resource. The definition expressly provides that a Canadian resource property does not include the cost of any depreciable property by virtue of paragraphs (*c*) and (*f*).

History: S. 66(15), subparagraph (*b*)(ii) of the definition "Canadian resource property" was replaced by S.C. 2011, c. 24, s. 13(1), applicable in respect of properties and rights acquired after March 21, 2011 except that, in respect of a property or right acquired by a person or partnership before 2012 if the person or partnership was obligated to acquire the property or right pursuant to an agreement in writing entered into by the person or partnership before March 22, 2011, subparagraph (*b*)(ii) of the definition "Canadian resource property" in subsection 66(15) is to be read without reference to "other than a bituminous sands deposit or an oil shale deposit".

S. 66(15), subparagraph (*b*)(ii) of the definition "Canadian resource property" formerly read:

(ii) prospect, explore, drill or mine for minerals in a mineral resource in Canada,

S. 66(15), paragraph (*c*) of the definition "Canadian resource property" was replaced by S.C. 2011, c. 24, s. 13(2), applicable in respect of properties and rights acquired after March 21, 2011 except that, in respect of a property or right acquired by a person or partnership before 2012 if the person or partnership was obligated to acquire the property or right pursuant to an agreement in writing entered into by the person or partnership before March 22, 2011, the reference to "petroleum, natural gas or related hydrocarbon content" in paragraph (*c*) of the definition "Canadian resource property" in subsection 66(15) is to be read as a reference to "petroleum or natural gas content".

S. 66(15), paragraph (*c*) of the definition "Canadian resource property" formerly read:

(*c*) any oil or gas well in Canada or any real property in Canada the principal value of which depends on its petroleum or natural gas content (but not including any depreciable property),

S. 66(15), paragraphs (*d*) and (*e*) of the definition "Canadian resource property" were replaced by S.C. 2011, c. 24, s. 13(3), applicable in respect of rights acquired after December 20, 2002 except that, in respect of a right acquired before March 22, 2011 or in respect of a right that is acquired by a person or partnership after March 21, 2011 and before 2012 and that the person or partnership is obligated to acquire pursuant to an agreement in writing entered into by the person or partnership before March 22, 2011,

(a) the reference to "petroleum, natural gas or related hydrocarbon" in paragraph (*d*) of the definition "Canadian resource property" in subsection 66(15) is to be read as a reference to "petroleum or natural gas"; and

(b) paragraph (*e*) of the definition "Canadian resource property" in subsection 66(15) is to be read without reference to ", other than a bituminous sands deposit or an oil shale deposit,".

S. 66(15), paragraphs (*d*) and (*e*) of the definition "Canadian resource property" formerly read:

(*d*) any rental or royalty computed by reference to the amount or value of production from an oil or gas well in Canada or from a natural accumulation of petroleum or natural gas in Canada,

(*e*) any rental or royalty computed by reference to the amount or value of production from a mineral resource in Canada,

S. 66(15), paragraphs (*f*) and (*g*) of the definition "Canadian resource property" were replaced, and paragraph (*h*) was added, by S.C. 2011, c. 24, s. 13(4), applicable in respect of properties and rights acquired after March 21, 2011 except that, in respect of a property or right acquired by a person or partnership before 2012 if the person or partnership was obligated to acquire the property or right pursuant to an agreement in writing entered into by the person or partnership before March 22, 2011, paragraph (*f*) of the definition "Canadian resource property" in subsection 66(15) is to be read without reference to "other than where the mineral resource is a bituminous sands deposit or an oil shale deposit".

S. 66(15), paragraphs (*f*) and (*g*) of the definition "Canadian resource property" formerly read:

(*f*) any real property in Canada the principal value of which depends on its mineral resource content (but not including any depreciable property), or

(*g*) any right to or interest in any property described in any of paragraphs (*a*) to (*f*), other than a right or an interest that the taxpayer has because the taxpayer is a beneficiary under a trust or a member of a partnership;

Related Regulations: 808(2), 808(5); 1204(1); 1206(4); 6200(*a*)(ii).

Related Sections: S. 12(1)(*o*) Royalties, etc.; s. 12(1)(x.2) Crown charge rebates; s. 18(1)(*m*) Limitation re employee stock option expenses; s. 18.1(1), "right to receive production"; s. 39(1)(a)(ii) Meaning of capital gain and capital loss; s. 53(1)(e)(ix) Adjustments to cost base — Interest in a partnership; s. 53(2)(h)(i) Amounts to be deducted — Capital interest in a non-resident trust; s. 53(2)(h)(i) Amounts to be deducted — Non-resident unit trust; s. 59(1) Consideration for foreign resource property; s. 66(5) Dealers; s. 66(11.4) Loss restriction event; s. 66(12.1) Limitations of Canadian exploration and development expenses; s. 66.1(6), "Canadian exploration expense"; s. 66.2(5), "Canadian development expense"; s. 66.2(7) Exception; s. 66.4(5), "Canadian oil and gas property expense"; s. 66.4(7) Exception; s. 66.7 Successor of Canadian exploration and development expenses; s. 69(13) Amalgamation or merger; s. 88(1)(a)(i) Winding-up; s. 104(5.2) Resource property; s. 115(4) Non-resident's income from Canadian resource property; s. 208(1.1) Definition of "specified stage"; s. 248(1), "Canadian resource property", "taxable Canadian property".

Canadian Petroleum Tax Journal: Offshore Oil & Gas Interests: A Perspective on Exploration & Development of Offshore Petroleum and Natural Gas Resources in Eastern Canada, Michael R. Smith, CA and B. David Nielsen, CA, 2000, Vol. 13, No. 1.

Income Tax Folios: *Primary* — S3-F8-C2 Tax Incentives for Clean Energy Equipment.

Interpretation Bulletins: *Secondary* — IT-125R4 Disposition of resource properties; IT-291R3 Transfer of property to a corporation under subsection 85(1).

"drilling or exploration expense" — "drilling or exploration expense" incurred on or in respect of exploring or drilling for petroleum or natural gas includes any expense incurred on or in respect of

(*a*) drilling or converting a well for the disposal of waste liquids from a petroleum or natural gas well,

(*b*) drilling for water or gas for injection into a petroleum or natural gas formation, or

(*c*) drilling or converting a well for the injection of water or gas to assist in the recovery of petroleum or natural gas from another well;

"expense" — "expense", incurred before a particular time by a taxpayer,

(*a*) includes an amount designated by the taxpayer at that time under paragraph 98(3)(*d*) or (5)(*d*) of the *Income Tax Act*, chapter 148 of the Revised Statutes of Canada, 1952, as a cost in respect of property that is a Canadian resource property or a foreign resource property,

but

(*b*) for greater certainty, does not include any amount paid or payable

(i) as consideration for services to be rendered after that time, or

(ii) as, on account or in lieu of payment of, or in satisfaction of, rent in respect of a period after that time;

"flow-through share" — "flow-through share" means a share (other than a prescribed share) of the capital stock of a principal-business corporation, or a right (other than a prescribed right) to acquire a share of the capital stock of a principal-business corporation, issued to a person under an agreement in writing made between the person and the corporation under which the corporation, for consideration that does not include property to be exchanged or transferred by the person under the agreement in circumstances to which any of sections 51, 85, 85.1, 86 and 87 applies, agrees

(*a*) to incur, in the period that begins on the day on which the agreement was made and ends 24 months after the month that includes that day, Canadian exploration expenses or Canadian development expenses in an amount not less than the consideration for which the share or right is to be issued, and

(*b*) to renounce, in prescribed form and before March of the first calendar year that begins after that period, to the person in respect of the share or right, an amount in respect of the Canadian exploration expenses or Canadian development expenses so incurred by it not exceeding the consideration received by the corporation for the share or right;

Editorial Note: See the editorial notes under s. 66(12.6). The flow-through share rules are an exception to the general rule in the Act that only the taxpayer that incurs an expense may deduct the expense from its income. The concept of a flow-through share is a uniquely Canadian tax concept and not a corporate concept. In order to be a flow-through share, it must be a share or a right to acquire a share of a principal-business corporation. A flow-through share cannot be a "prescribed share"; accordingly, a flow-through share must generally have the same characteristics as a simple common share; however, such shares can be non-voting common shares. The share must be issued to an investor pursuant to an agreement in writing under which the principal-business corporation agrees to incur qualifying CEE or CDE and to renounce such expenses to the investor. In *Jes Investments Ltd. v. The Queen*, 2006 DTC 3608 (TCC), affirmed 2007 DTC 5608 (FCA), the Federal Court of Appeal confirmed that the determination of whether a share qualifies as a "flow-through share" is made at the time the share is issued. A share will be a flow-through share only to the person who enters into the flow-through share agreement and not to a subsequent purchaser or assignee. The amount of CEE or CDE renounced to the investor under the terms of a flow-through share agreement is limited to the subscription price paid for the shares by the investor.

History: S. 66(15), the definition "flow-through share" was replaced by S.C. 2013, c. 34, s. 199(6), applicable to agreements made after December 20, 2002, and formerly read:

"flow-through share" — "flow-through share" means a share (other than a prescribed share) of the capital stock of a principal-business corporation that is issued to a person under an agreement in writing entered into between the person and the corporation after February 1986, under which the corporation agrees for consideration that does not include property to be exchanged or transferred by the person under the agreement in circumstances in which section 51, 85, 85.1, 86 or 87 applies

(*a*) to incur, in the period that begins on the day the agreement was made and ends 24 months after the end of the month that includes that day, Canadian exploration expenses or Canadian development expenses in an amount not less than the consideration for which the share is to be issued, and

(*b*) to renounce, before March of the first calendar year that begins after that period, in prescribed form to the person in respect of the share, an amount in respect of the Canadian exploration expenses or Canadian development expenses so incurred by it not exceeding the consideration received by the corporation for the share,

and includes a right of a person to have such a share issued to that person and any interest acquired in such a share by a person pursuant to such an agreement;

Related Regulations: 6202; 6202.1.

Related Sections: S. 66(12.6) Canadian exploration expenses to flow-through shareholder; s. 66(12.601) Flow-through share rules for first $1 million of Canadian development expenses; s. 66(12.62) Canadian development expenses to flow-through shareholder; s. 66(12.64) Canadian oil and gas property expenses to flow-through shareholder; s. 66(12.66) Expenses in the first 60 days of year; s. 66(12.68) Filing selling instruments; s. 66(15), "principal-business corporation", "selling instrument"; s. 66.3(3) Cost of flow-through shares; s. 66.3(4) Paid-up capital.

Canadian Petroleum Tax Journal: A Practical Guide to the Flow-Through Share Rules, Greg Johnson, CA, 2002, Vol. 15, No. 1; Renewable Energy — Tax Developments and Opportunities, Leanne Sereda, 2000, Vol. 13, No. 1.

Income Tax Folios: *Primary* — S3-F8-C2 Tax Incentives for Clean Energy Equipment. *Secondary* — S3-F8-C1 Principal-business Corporations in the Resource Industries.

Tax Window Files: RRSP or RRIF payments to a resident of New Zealand, *October 3, 2014*, CRA Document No. 2013-0509751E5.

"foreign exploration and development expenses" — "foreign exploration and development expenses" incurred by a taxpayer means

(*a*) any drilling or exploration expense, including any general geological or geophysical expense, incurred by the taxpayer after 1971 on or in respect of exploring or drilling for petroleum or natural gas outside Canada,

(*b*) any expense incurred by the taxpayer for the purpose of determining the existence, location, extent or quality of a mineral resource outside Canada, including any expense incurred in the course of

(i) prospecting,

(ii) carrying out geological, geophysical or geochemical surveys,

(iii) drilling by rotary, diamond, percussion or other method, or

(iv) trenching, digging test pits and preliminary sampling,

(*c*) the cost to the taxpayer of any foreign resource property acquired by him,

(*d*) subject to section 66.8, the taxpayer's share of the foreign exploration and development expenses incurred after 1971 by a partnership in a fiscal period thereof, if at the end of that period the taxpayer was a member of the partnership, and

(*e*) any annual payment made by the taxpayer for the preservation of a foreign resource property;

but does not include

(*f*) any amount included at any time in the capital cost to the taxpayer of any depreciable property of a prescribed class,

(*g*) an expenditure incurred at any time after the commencement of production from a foreign resource property of the taxpayer in order to evaluate the feasibility of a method of recovery of petroleum, natural gas or related hydrocarbons from the portion of a natural reservoir to which the foreign resource property relates,

(*h*) an expenditure (other than a drilling expense) incurred at any time after the commencement of production from a foreign resource property of the taxpayer in order to assist in the recovery of petroleum, natural gas or related hydrocarbons from the portion of a natural reservoir to which the foreign resource property relates,

(*i*) an expenditure incurred at any time relating to the injection of any substance to assist in the recovery of petroleum, natural gas or related hydrocarbons from a natural reservoir,

(*j*) an expenditure that is the cost, or any part of the cost, to the taxpayer of any depreciable property of a prescribed class that was acquired after December 21, 2000,

(*k*) foreign resource expenses in respect of a country, or

(*l*) an expenditure made after February 27, 2000 by the taxpayer unless the expenditure was made

(i) pursuant to an agreement in writing made by the taxpayer before February 28, 2000,

(ii) for the acquisition of foreign resource property by the taxpayer, or

(iii) for the purpose of

(A) enhancing the value of foreign resource property that the taxpayer owned at the time the expenditure was incurred or that the taxpayer had a reasonable expectation of owning after that time, or

(B) assisting in evaluating whether a foreign resource property is to be acquired by the taxpayer;

Related Sections: S. 66(15), "drilling or exploration expense", "foreign resource property".

Canadian Petroleum Tax Journal: Foreign Exploration and Development Expenditures — The New Rules, Roch J. Martin, 2001, Vol. 14, No. 1; Canada Customs and Revenue Agency 1999 Roundtable Questions and Answers, Question 8, 2000, Vol. 13, No. 1.

"foreign resource property" —"foreign resource property" of a taxpayer means any property that would be a Canadian resource property of the taxpayer if the definition "Canadian resource property" in this subsection were read as if the references therein to "in Canada" were references to "outside Canada";

Interpretation Bulletins: *Secondary* — IT-125R4 Disposition of resource properties.

"joint exploration corporation" —"joint exploration corporation" means a principal-business corporation that has not at any time since its incorporation had more than 10 shareholders, not including any individual holding a share for the sole purpose of qualifying as a director;

Related Sections: S. 66(10) Joint exploration corporation; s. 66(15), "agreed portion", "principal-business corporation".

Interpretation Bulletins: *Secondary* — IT-400 Exploration and development expenses — Meaning of principal-business corporation.

"original owner" —"original owner" of a Canadian resource property or a foreign resource property means a person

(*a*) who owned the property and disposed of it to a corporation that acquired it in circumstances in which subsection 29(25) of the *Income Tax Application Rules* or subsection 66.7(1), (2), (2.3), (3), (4) or (5) applies, or would apply if the corporation had continued to own the property, to the corporation in respect of the property, and

(*b*) who would, but for subsection 66.7(12), (13), (13.1) or (17), as the case may be, be entitled in computing that person's income for a taxation year that ends after that person disposed of the property to a deduction under section 29 of the *Income Tax Application Rules* or subsection (2), (3) or (4), 66.1(2) or (3), 66.2(2), 66.21(4) or 66.4(2) of this Act in respect of expenses described in subparagraph 29(25)(*c*)(i) or (ii) of that Act, Canadian exploration and development expenses, foreign resource pool expenses, Canadian exploration expenses, Canadian development expenses or Canadian oil and gas property expenses incurred by the person before the person disposed of the property;

"outlay" —"outlay", made before a particular time by a taxpayer, has the meaning assigned to the expression "expense" by this subsection;

"predecessor owner" —"predecessor owner" of a Canadian resource property or a foreign resource property means a corporation

(*a*) that acquired the property in circumstances in which subsection 29(25) of the *Income Tax Application Rules* or subsection 66.7(1), (2), (2.3), (3), (4) or (5) applies, or would apply if the corporation had continued to own the property, to the corporation in respect of the property,

(*b*) that disposed of the property to another corporation that acquired it in circumstances in which subsection 29(25) of the *Income Tax Application Rules* or subsection 66.7(1), (2), (2.3), (3), (4) or (5) applies, or would apply if the other corporation had continued to own the property, to the other corporation in respect of the property, and

(*c*) that would, but for subsection 66.7(14), (15), (15.1) or (17), as the case may be, be entitled in computing its income for a taxation year ending after it disposed of the property to a deduction under subsection 29(25) of the *Income Tax Application Rules* or subsection 66.7(1), (2), (2.3), (3), (4) or (5) in respect of expenses incurred by an original owner of the property;

"principal-business corporation" —"principal-business corporation" means a corporation the principal business of which is any of, or a combination of,

(*a*) the production, refining or marketing of petroleum, petroleum products or natural gas,

(*a*.1) exploring or drilling for petroleum or natural gas,

(*b*) mining or exploring for minerals,

(*c*) the processing of mineral ores for the purpose of recovering metals or minerals from the ores,

(*d*) the processing or marketing of metals or minerals that were recovered from mineral ores and that include metals or minerals recovered from mineral ores processed by the corporation,

(*e*) the fabrication of metals,

(*f*) the operation of a pipeline for the transmission of oil or gas,

(*f*.1) the production or marketing of calcium chloride, gypsum, kaolin, sodium chloride or potash,

(*g*) the manufacturing of products, where the manufacturing involves the processing of calcium chloride, gypsum, kaolin, sodium chloride or potash,

(*h*) the generation or distribution of energy, or the production of fuel, using property described in Class 43.1 or 43.2 of Schedule II to the *Income Tax Regulations*, and

(*i*) the development of projects for which it is reasonable to expect that at least 50% of the capital cost of the depreciable property to be used in each project would be the capital cost of property described in Class 43.1 or 43.2 of Schedule II to the *Income Tax Regulations*,

or a corporation all or substantially all of the assets of which are shares of the capital stock or indebtedness of one or more principal-business corporations that are related to the corporation (otherwise than because of a right referred to in paragraph 251(5)(*b*));

Editorial Note: There is no requirement in the definition of "principal-business corporation" that the corporation be a resident of Canada for purposes of the Act. It is the nature and scope of the business activities that are undertaken by the corporation which determine the status of the corporation rather than the tax residency of the corporation.

History: S. 66(15), paragraphs (*h*) and (*i*) of the definition "principal-business corporation" were replaced by S.C. 2010, c. 25, s. 12(1), applicable to 2004 and subsequent taxation years. S. 66(15), paragraphs (*h*) and (*i*) of the definition "principal-business corporation" formerly read:

(*h*) the generation of energy using property described in Class 43.1 or 43.2 of Schedule II to the regulations, or any combination thereof, and

(*i*) the development of projects for which it is reasonable to expect that at least 50% of the capital cost of the depreciable property to be used in each project would be the capital cost of property described in Class 43.1 or 43.2 of Schedule II to the regulations or any combination thereof,

Canadian Petroleum Tax Journal: A Practical Guide to the Flow-Through Share Rules, Greg Johnson, CA, 2002, Vol. 15, No. 1.

Income Tax Folios: *Primary* — S3-F8-C2 Tax Incentives for Clean Energy Equipment.

Interpretation Bulletins: *Primary* — IT-400 Exploration and development expenses — Meaning of principal-business corporation.

"production" —"production" from a Canadian resource property or a foreign resource property means

(*a*) petroleum, natural gas and related hydrocarbons produced from the property,

(*b*) heavy crude oil produced from the property processed to any stage that is not beyond the crude oil stage or its equivalent,

(*c*) ore (other than iron ore or tar sands) produced from the property processed to any stage that is not beyond the prime metal stage or its equivalent,

(*d*) iron ore produced from the property processed to any stage that is not beyond the pellet stage or its equivalent,

(*e*) tar sands produced from the property processed to any stage that is not beyond the crude oil stage or its equivalent, and

(*f*) any rental or royalty from the property computed by reference to the amount or value of the production of petroleum, natural gas or related hydrocarbons or ore;

"reserve amount" —"reserve amount" of a corporation for a taxation year in respect of an original owner or predecessor owner of a Canadian resource property means the amount determined by the formula

$$A - B$$

where

A is the total of all amounts that are

(*a*) required by subsection 59(2) to be included in computing the corporation's income for the year, and

(*b*) in respect of a reserve, deducted in computing the income of the original owner or predecessor owner and deemed by paragraph 87(2)(*g*) or by virtue of that paragraph and paragraph 88(1)(*e*.2) to have been deducted by the corporation as a reserve in computing its income for a preceding taxation year, and

B is the total of amounts deducted in computing the corporation's income for the year by virtue of subsection 64(1), (1.1) or (1.2) in respect of dispositions by the original owner or predecessor owner, as the case may be;

"selling instrument" —"selling instrument" in respect of flow-through shares means a prospectus, registration statement, offering memorandum, term sheet or other similar document that describes the terms of the offer (including the price and number of shares) pursuant to which a corporation offers to issue flow-through shares;

Related Sections: S. 66(12.68) Filing selling instruments; s. 66(15), "flow-through share".

"shareholder corporation" —"shareholder corporation" of a joint exploration corporation means a corporation that for the period in respect of which the expression is being applied

(*a*) was a shareholder of the joint exploration corporation, and

(*b*) made a payment or loan to the joint exploration corporation in respect of Canadian exploration and development expenses, a Canadian exploration expense, a Canadian development expense or a Canadian oil and gas property expense incurred or to be incurred by the joint exploration corporation;

"specified foreign exploration and development expense" —"specified foreign exploration and development expense" of a taxpayer in respect of a country (other than Canada) means an amount that is included in the taxpayer's foreign exploration and development expenses and that is

(*a*) a drilling or exploration expense, including any general geological or geophysical expense, incurred by the taxpayer on or in respect of exploring or drilling for petroleum or natural gas in that country,

(*a*.1) an expense incurred by the taxpayer after December 21, 2000 (otherwise than pursuant to an agreement in writing made before December 22, 2000) for the purpose of determining the existence, location, extent or quality of a mineral resource in that country, including any expense incurred in the course of

(i) prospecting,

(ii) carrying out geological, geophysical or geochemical surveys,

(iii) drilling by rotary, diamond, percussion or other methods, or

(iv) trenching, digging test pits and preliminary sampling,

(*b*) a prospecting, exploration or development expense incurred by the taxpayer before December 22, 2000 (or after December 21, 2000 pursuant to an agreement in writing made before December 22, 2000) in searching for minerals in that country,

(*c*) the cost to the taxpayer of the taxpayer's foreign resource property in respect of that country,

(*d*) an annual payment made by the taxpayer in a taxation year of the taxpayer for the preservation of a foreign resource property in respect of that country,

(*e*) an amount deemed by subsection 21(2) or (4) to be a foreign exploration and development expense incurred by the taxpayer, to the extent that it can reasonably be considered to relate to an amount that, without reference to this paragraph and paragraph (*f*), would be a specified foreign exploration and development expense in respect of that country, or

(*f*) subject to section 66.8, the taxpayer's share of the specified foreign exploration and development expenses of a partnership incurred in respect of that country in a fiscal period of the partnership if, at the end of that period, the taxpayer was a member of the partnership.

► 66(15.1) ◄

(15.1) Other definitions. The definitions in subsections 66.1(6), 66.2(5), 66.21(1), 66.4(5) and 66.5(2) apply in this section.

► 66(16) ◄

(16) Partnerships. For the purposes of subsections (12.6) to (12.73), the definitions "assistance" and "flow-through share" in subsection (15) and subsections (18), (19) and 66.3(3) and (4), a partnership is deemed to be a person and its taxation year is deemed to be its fiscal period.

Related Sections: 66(12.6) Canadian exploration expenses to flow-through shareholder; 66(12.601) Flow-through share rules for first $1 million of Canadian development expenses; 66(12.6011) Taxable capital amount; 66(12.6012) Taxable capital employed in Canada; 66(12.6013) Amalgamations and mergers; 66(12.602) Idem; 66(12.61) Effect of renunciation; 66(12.62) Canadian development expenses to flow-through shareholder; 66(12.63) Effect of renunciation; 66(12.66) Expenses in the first 60 days of year; 66(12.67) Restrictions on renunciation; 66(12.671) Prohibited relationship; 66(12.68) Filing selling instruments; 66(12.69) Filing re partners; 66(12.6901) Consequences of failure to file; 66(12.691; 66(12.7) Filing re renunciation; 66(12.7001) Consequences of failure to file; 66(12.701) Filing re assistance; 66(12.702) Consequences of failure to file; 66(12.71) Restriction on renunciation; 66(12.73) Reductions in renunciations.

► 66(17) ◄

(17) Non-arm's length partnerships. For the purpose of paragraph (12.66)(*d*), a partnership and a corporation are, at all times in a calendar year,

(*a*) deemed not to deal with each other at arm's length, if

(i) an expense is deemed by subsection (12.61) to be incurred by the partnership,

(ii) the expense would, if this Act were read without reference to paragraph (12.61)(*b*), be incurred in the calendar year by the corporation, and

(iii) a share of the expense is included, because of paragraph (*h*) of the definition "Canadian exploration expense" in subsection 66.1(6), in the Canadian exploration expense of the corporation or of a member of the partnership with whom the corporation, at any time in that calendar year, does not deal at arm's length; and

(*b*) deemed to deal with each other at arm's length, in any other case.

Related Sections: S. 66(12.61) Effect of renunciation; s. 66(12.66)(*a*) Expenses in the first 60 days of year; s. 66(16) Partnerships; s. 66.1(6) "Canadian exploration expense"; s. 127(9), "flow-through mining expenditure", "investment tax credit"; s. 163(2.2) False statement or omission; s. 211.91(1) Tax imposed; s. 251(1) Arm's length.

▶ 66(18) ◀

(18) Members of partnerships. For the purposes of this section, subsection 21(2), sections 59.1 and 66.1 to 66.7, paragraph (*d*) of the definition "investment expense" in subsection 110.6(1), the definition "pre-production mining expenditure" in subsection 127(9) and the descriptions of C and D in subsection 211.91(1), where a person's share of an outlay or expense made or incurred by a partnership in a fiscal period of the partnership is included in respect of the person under paragraph (*d*) of the definition "foreign exploration and development expenses" in subsection (15), paragraph (*h*) of the definition "Canadian exploration expense" in subsection 66.1(6), paragraph (*f*) of the definition "Canadian development expense" in subsection 66.2(5), paragraph (*e*) of the definition "foreign resource expense" in subsection 66.21(1) or paragraph (*b*) of the definition "Canadian oil and gas property expense" in subsection 66.4(5), the portion of the outlay or expense so included is deemed, except for the purposes of applying the definitions "foreign exploration and development expenses", "Canadian exploration expense", "Canadian development expense", "foreign resource expense" and "Canadian oil and gas property expense" in respect of the person, to be made or incurred by the person at the end of that fiscal period.

History: S. 66(18) was replaced by S.C. 2013, c. 34, s. 199(7), applicable to expenses incurred in fiscal periods that begin after 2001, and formerly read:

(18) *Members of partnerships.* For the purposes of this section, subsection 21(2), sections 59.1 and 66.1 to 66.7, paragraph (*d*) of the definition "investment expense" in subsection 110.6(1) and the descriptions of C and D in subsection 211.91(1), where a person's share of an outlay or expense made or incurred by a partnership in a fiscal period of the partnership is included in respect of the person under paragraph (*d*) of the definition "foreign exploration and development expenses" in subsection (15), paragraph (*h*) of the definition "Canadian exploration expense" in subsection 66.1(6), paragraph (*f*) of the definition "Canadian development expense" in subsection 66.2(5), paragraph (*e*) of the definition "foreign resource expense" in subsection 66.21(1) or paragraph (*b*) of the definition "Canadian oil and gas property expense" in subsection 66.4(5), the portion of the outlay or expense so included is deemed, except for the purposes of applying the definitions "foreign exploration and development expenses", "Canadian exploration expense", "Canadian development expense", "foreign resource expense" and "Canadian oil and gas property expense" in respect of the person, to be made or incurred by the person at the end of that fiscal period.

Related Sections: 66 [Exploration and development expenses]; 66.1 [Canadian exploration expenses]; 66.2 [Canadian development expenses]; 66.2.1; 66.3 Exploration and development shares; 66.4 Recovery of costs; 66.5 [Cumulative offset account]; 66.6 Acquisition from tax-exempt; 66.7 [Successor corporation rules].

▶ 66(19) ◀

(19) Renunciation by corporate partner, etc. A corporation is not entitled to renounce under subsection (12.6), (12.601) or (12.62) to a person a specified amount in respect of the corporation where the corporation would not be entitled to so renounce the specified amount if

(*a*) the expression "end of that fiscal period" in subsection (18) were read as "time the outlay or expense was made or incurred by the partnership"; and

(*b*) the expression "on the effective date of the renunciation" in each of paragraphs (12.61)(*a*) and (12.63)(*a*) were read as "at the earliest time that any part of such expense was incurred by the corporation".

▶ 66(20) ◀

(20) Specified amount. For the purpose of subsection (19), a specified amount in respect of a corporation is an amount that represents

(*a*) all or part of the corporation's share of an outlay or expense made or incurred by a partnership of which the corporation is a member or former member; or

(*b*) all or part of an amount renounced to the corporation under subsection (12.6), (12.601) or (12.62).

SECTION 66.1: [Canadian exploration expenses]

▶ 66.1(1) ◀

(1) Amount to be included in income. There shall be included in computing the amount referred to in paragraph 59(3.2)(*b*) in respect of a taxpayer for a taxation year the amount, if any, by which

(*a*) the total of all amounts referred to in the descriptions of F to M in the definition "cumulative Canadian exploration expense" in subsection (6) that are deducted in computing the taxpayer's cumulative Canadian exploration expense at the end of the year

exceeds the total of

(*b*) all amounts referred to in the descriptions of A to E.1 in the definition "cumulative Canadian exploration expense" in subsection (6) that are included in computing the taxpayer's cumulative Canadian exploration expense at the end of the year, and

(*c*) the total determined under subparagraph 66.7(12.1)(*a*)(i) in respect of the taxpayer for the year.

Editorial Note: Section 66.1 provides for the deduction by a taxpayer of its Canadian exploration expenses ("CEE"). CEE include certain oil and gas and drilling expenses and expenses in finding a mineral resource and bringing it into production. The taxpayer adds its CEE to its cumulative Canadian exploration expenses ("CCEE"). A taxpayer may claim a deduction in respect of its CCEE. A principal-business corporation is limited in the deduction it may claim to its income for the year as defined in s. 66.1(2)(*b*); accordingly, a principal-business corporation cannot create a loss by claiming a CCEE deduction in excess of its income for a particular year. A principal-business corporation may claim an additional amount that is relevant only if the corporation transfers in the year all of its Canadian resource properties to another corporation in accordance with the successor corporation rules. A taxpayer other than a principal-business corporation may claim an optional deduction up to the full amount of its CCEE at the end of the year by virtue of s. 66.1(3). Such a taxpayer may claim an additional amount if it transfers in the year all of its Canadian resource properties in accordance with the successor corporation rules. A taxpayer must include in income any amount by which its CCEE is negative at the end of the year less any amount that the taxpayer may deduct by virtue of disposing in the year of its Canadian resource properties in accordance with the successor corporation rules.

Related Sections: S. 59(3.2) Recovery of exploration and development expenses; s. 66(6) Successor corporation's Canadian exploration and development expenses; s. 66.1(6) Definitions; s. 66.4(5) Definitions; s. 127.5 Obligation to pay minimum tax.

Interpretation Bulletins: *Secondary* — IT-273R2 Government assistance — General comments.

▶ 66.1(2) ◀

(2) Deduction for certain principal-business corporations. In computing the income for a taxation year of a principal-business corporation (other than a corporation that would not be a principal-business corporation if the definition "principal-business corporation" in subsection 66(15) were read without reference to paragraphs (*h*) and (*i*) of that definition), there may be deducted any amount that the corporation claims not exceeding the lesser of

(*a*) the total of

(i) the amount, if any, by which its cumulative Canadian exploration expense at the end of the year exceeds the amount, if any, designated by it for the year under subsection 66(14.1), and

(ii) the amount, if any, by which

(A) the total determined under subparagraph 66.7(12.1)(*a*)(i) in respect of the corporation for the year

exceeds

(B) the amount that would be determined under subsection (1) in respect of the corporation for the year, if that subsection were read without reference to paragraph (*c*) thereof, and

(*b*) the amount, if any, by which

(i) the amount that would be its income for the year if no deduction (other than a prescribed deduction) were allowed under this subsection or section 65

exceeds

(ii) the total of all amounts each of which is an amount deducted by the corporation under section 112 or 113 in computing its taxable income for the year.

Related Regulations: 1202(2); 1213.

Related Sections: S. 59(3.3) Amounts to be included in income; s. 66.1(6), "cumulative Canadian exploration expense".

Income Tax Folios: *Secondary* — S3-F8-C1 Principal-business Corporations in the Resource Industries.

▶ 66.1(3) ◀

(3) Expenses of other taxpayer. In computing the income for a taxation year of a taxpayer that is not a principal-business corporation, or that is a corporation that would not be a principal-business corporation if the definition "principal-business corporation" in subsection 66(15) were read without reference to paragraphs (*h*) and (*i*) of that definition, there may be deducted such amount as the taxpayer claims not exceeding the total of

(*a*) the amount, if any, by which the taxpayer's cumulative Canadian exploration expense at the end of the year exceeds the amount, if any, designated by the taxpayer for the year under subsection 66(14.1), and

(*b*) the amount, if any, by which

(i) the total determined under subparagraph 66.7(12.1)(*a*)(i) in respect of the taxpayer for the year

exceeds

(ii) the amount that would, but for paragraph (1)(*c*), be the amount determined under subsection (1) in respect of the taxpayer for the year.

Related Sections: S. 66(15), "Canadian exploration and development expenses", "principal-business corporation"; s. 66.1(6), "cumulative Canadian exploration expense"; s. 127.5 Obligation to pay minimum tax.

▶ 66.1(4) ◀

(4) Successor corporation's Canadian exploration expense — (Repealed by 1987, c. 46, s. 19(2).)

▶ 66.1(5) ◀

(5) Second successor corporation's Canadian exploration expenses — (Repealed by 1987, c. 46, s. 19(2).)

▶ 66.1(6) ◀

(6) Definitions. In this section,

Related Sections: S. 13(7.5) Deemed capital cost.

"bitumen mine development project" — "bitumen mine development project", of a taxpayer, means an undertaking for the sole purpose of developing a new mine to extract and process tar sands from a mineral resource of the taxpayer to produce bitumen or a similar product;

History: S. 66.1(6), the definition "bitumen mine development project" was added by S.C. 2011, c. 24, s. 14(5), deemed to have come into force on March 22, 2011.

"bitumen upgrading development project" — "bitumen upgrading development project", of a taxpayer, means an undertaking for the sole purpose of constructing an upgrading facility to process bitumen or a similar feedstock (all or substantially all of which is from a mineral resource of the taxpayer) from a new mine to the crude oil stage or its equivalent;

History: S. 66.1(6), the definition "bitumen upgrading development project" was added by S.C. 2011, c. 24, s. 14(5), deemed to have come into force on March 22, 2011.

"Canadian exploration expense" — "Canadian exploration expense" of a taxpayer means any expense incurred after May 6, 1974 that is

(*a*) any expense incurred by the taxpayer (other than an expense incurred in drilling or completing an oil or gas well or in building a temporary access road to, or preparing a site in respect of, any such well) for the purpose of determining the existence, location, extent or quality of an accumulation of petroleum or natural gas (other than a mineral resource) in Canada, including such an expense that is

(i) a geological, geophysical or geochemical expense, or

(ii) an expense for environmental studies or community consultations (including studies or consultations that are undertaken to obtain a right, licence or privilege for the purpose of determining the existence, location, extent or quality of an accumulation of petroleum or natural gas),

(*b*) any expense (other than an expense incurred in drilling or completing an oil or gas well or in building a temporary access road to, or preparing a site in respect of, any such well) incurred by the taxpayer after March, 1985 for the purpose of bringing a natural accumulation of petroleum or natural gas (other than a mineral resource) in

Canada into production and incurred prior to the commencement of the production (other than the production from an oil or gas well) in reasonable commercial quantities from such accumulation, including

(i) clearing, removing overburden and stripping, and

(ii) sinking a shaft or constructing an adit or other underground entry,

(*c*) any expense incurred before April, 1987 in drilling or completing an oil or gas well in Canada or in building a temporary access road to, or preparing a site in respect of, any such well,

(i) incurred by the taxpayer in the year, or

(ii) incurred by the taxpayer in any previous year and included by the taxpayer in computing the taxpayer's Canadian development expense for a previous taxation year,

if, within six months after the end of the year, the drilling of the well is completed and

(iii) it is determined that the well is the first well capable of production in commercial quantities from an accumulation of petroleum or natural gas (other than a mineral resource) not previously known to exist, or

(iv) it is reasonable to expect that the well will not come into production in commercial quantities within twelve months of its completion,

(*d*) any expense incurred by the taxpayer after March, 1987 and in a taxation year of the taxpayer in drilling or completing an oil or gas well in Canada or in building a temporary access road to, or preparing a site in respect of, any such well if

(i) the drilling or completing of the well resulted in the discovery that a natural underground reservoir contains petroleum or natural gas, where

(A) before the time of the discovery, no person or partnership had discovered that the reservoir contained either petroleum or natural gas,

(B) the discovery occurred at any time before six months after the end of the year, and

(C) the expense is incurred

(I) before 2021 (excluding an expense that is deemed by subsection 66(12.66) to have been incurred on December 31, 2020), if the expense is incurred in connection with an obligation that was committed to in writing (including a commitment to a government under the terms of a license or permit) by the taxpayer before March 22, 2017, or

(II) before 2019 (excluding an expense that is deemed by subsection 66(12.66) to have been incurred on December 31, 2018), in any other case,

(ii) the well is abandoned in the year or within six months after the end of the year without ever having produced otherwise than for specified purposes,

(iii) the period of 24 months commencing on the day of completion of the drilling of the well ends in the year, the expense was incurred within that period and in the year and the well has not within that period produced otherwise than for specified purposes, or

(iv) there has been filed with the Minister, on or before the day that is 6 months after the end of the taxation year of the taxpayer in which the drilling of the well was commenced, a certificate issued by the Minister of Natural Resources certifying that, on the basis of evidence submitted to that Minister, that Minister is satisfied that

(A) the total of expenses incurred and to be incurred in drilling and completing the well, in building a temporary access road to the well and in preparing the site in respect of the well will exceed $5,000,000, and

(B) the well will not produce, otherwise than for a specified purpose, within the period of 24 months commencing on the day on which the drilling of the well is completed,

(*e*) any expense deemed by subsection (9) to be a Canadian exploration expense incurred by the taxpayer,

(*f*) any expense incurred by the taxpayer (other than an expense incurred in drilling or completing an oil or gas well or in building a temporary access road to, or preparing a site in respect of, any such well) for the purpose of determining the existence, location, extent or quality of a mineral resource in Canada including such an expense for environmental studies or community consultations (including, notwithstanding subparagraph (v), studies or consultations that are undertaken to obtain a right, licence or privilege for the purpose of determining the existence, location, extent or quality of a mineral resource in Canada) and any expense incurred in the course of

(i) prospecting,

(ii) carrying out geological, geophysical or geochemical surveys,

(iii) drilling by rotary, diamond, percussion or other methods, or

(iv) trenching, digging test pits and preliminary sampling,

but not including

(v) any Canadian development expense,

(v.1) any expense described in subparagraph (i), (iii) or (iv) in respect of the mineral resource, incurred before a new mine in the mineral resource comes into production in reasonable commercial quantities, that results in revenue or can reasonably be expected to result in revenue earned before the new mine comes into production in reasonable commercial quantities, except to the extent that the total of all such expenses exceeds the total of those revenues, or

(vi) any expense that may reasonably be considered to be related to a mine in the mineral resource that has come into production in reasonable commercial quantities or to be related to a potential or actual extension of the mine,

(*g*) any expense incurred by the taxpayer after November 16, 1978 and before March 21, 2013 for the purpose of bringing a new mine in a mineral resource in Canada, other than a bituminous sands deposit or an oil shale deposit, into production in reasonable commercial quantities and incurred before the new mine comes into production in such quantities, including an expense for clearing, removing overburden, stripping, sinking a mine shaft or constructing an adit or other underground entry, but not including any expense that results in revenue or can reasonably be expected to result in revenue earned before the new mine comes into production in reasonable commercial quantities, except to the extent that the total of all such expenses exceeds the total of those revenues,

(*g*.1) any Canadian renewable and conservation expense incurred by the taxpayer,

(*g*.2) any expense incurred by the taxpayer after March 21, 2011, that is

(i) a specified oil sands mine development expense, or

(ii) an eligible oil sands mine development expense,

(*g*.3) any expense incurred by the taxpayer that would be described in paragraph (*g*) if the reference to "March 21, 2013" in that paragraph were "2017" and that is incurred

(i) under an agreement in writing entered into by the taxpayer before March 21, 2013, or

(ii) as part of the development of a new mine, if

(A) the construction of the new mine was started by, or on behalf of, the taxpayer before March 21, 2013 (and for this purpose construction does not include obtaining permits or regulatory approvals, conducting environmental assessments, community consultations or impact benefit studies, and similar activities), or

(B) the engineering and design work for the construction of the new mine, as evidenced in writing, was started by, or on behalf of, the taxpayer before March 21, 2013 (and for this purpose engineering and design work does not include obtaining permits or regulatory approvals, conducting environmental assessments, community consultations or impact benefit studies, and similar activities),

(*g*.4) any expense incurred by the taxpayer, the amount of which is determined by the formula

$$A \times B$$

where

A is an expense that would be described in paragraph (*g*) if the reference to "March 21, 2013" in that paragraph were "2018" and that is not described in paragraph (*g.3*), and

B is

(i) 100% if the expense is incurred before 2015,

(ii) 80% if the expense is incurred in 2015,

(iii) 60% if the expense is incurred in 2016, and

(iv) 30% if the expense is incurred in 2017,

(*h*) subject to section 66.8, the taxpayer's share of any expense referred to in any of paragraphs (*a*) to (*d*) and (*f*) to (*g.4*) incurred by a partnership in a fiscal period of the partnership, if at the end of the period the taxpayer is a member of the partnership, or

(*i*) any expense referred to in any of paragraphs (*a*) to (*g*) incurred by the taxpayer pursuant to an agreement in writing with a corporation, entered into before 1987, under which the taxpayer incurred the expense solely as consideration for shares, other than prescribed shares, of the capital stock of the corporation issued to the taxpayer or any interest in or right to — or, for civil law, any right in or to — such shares,

but, for greater certainty, shall not include

(*j*) any consideration given by the taxpayer for any share or any interest in or right to — or, for civil law, any right in or to — a share, except as provided by paragraph (*i*),

(*k*) any expense described in paragraph (*i*) incurred by any other taxpayer to the extent that the expense was,

(i) by virtue of that paragraph, a Canadian exploration expense of that other taxpayer,

(ii) by virtue of paragraph (*g*) of the definition "Canadian development expense" in subsection 66.2(5), a Canadian development expense of that other taxpayer, or

(iii) by virtue of paragraph (*c*) of the definition "Canadian oil and gas property expense" in subsection 66.4(5), a Canadian oil and gas property expense of that other taxpayer,

(*k*.1) an expense that is the cost, or any part of the cost, to the taxpayer of any depreciable property of a prescribed class that was acquired after 1987,

(*k*.2) (Repealed.)

(*l*) any amount (other than a Canadian renewable and conservation expense) included at any time in the capital cost to the taxpayer of any depreciable property of a prescribed class,

(*m*) an expenditure incurred at any time after the commencement of production from a Canadian resource property of the taxpayer in order to evaluate the feasibility of a method of recovery of, or to assist in the recovery of, petroleum, natural gas or related hydrocarbons from the portion of a natural reservoir to which the Canadian resource property relates,

(*n*) an expenditure incurred at any time relating to the injection of any substance to assist in the recovery of petroleum, natural gas or related hydrocarbons from a natural reservoir, or

(*o*) the taxpayer's share of any consideration, expense, cost or expenditure referred to in any of paragraphs (*j*) to (*n*) given or incurred by a partnership,

but any assistance that a taxpayer has received or is entitled to receive after May 25, 1976 in respect of or related to the taxpayer's Canadian exploration expense shall not reduce the amount of any of the expenses described in any of paragraphs (*a*) to (*i*);

Editorial Note: The definition of "Canadian exploration expense" ("CEE") in s. 66.1(6) sets out a number of expenses incurred in connection with exploring for and developing oil and gas properties and mineral resource properties. The definition also specifically excludes a number of expenses, such as the cost of acquiring depreciable property. There is no requirement that a person own an interest in a particular Canadian resource property to be able to incur CEE on a particular property. This is accomplished by way of a simple "farm-out" arrangement, as described in CRA Document No. 2005-0119731E5 and IT-125R4, para. 14 (archived, as it doesn't meet current government web standards). Any revenue earned as a result of incurring exploration expenses will reduce the amount of CEE that can be claimed by virtue of subparagraph (*f*)(v.1) and paragraph (*g*) of the definition of CEE. Taxpayers may deduct CEE at the rate of 100% in any year subject to s. 66.1(2) and (3) and may carry forward any undeducted CEE indefinitely. Most CEE may be renounced pursuant to the flow-through share rules. The expenses in paragraph (*f*) of the definition of CEE are commonly referred to as "grassroots" exploration expenses that can be renounced by a principal-business corporation to investors pursuant to a flow-through share agreement and are eligible for the one-year look-back rule in s. 66(12.66).

Many amendments to the definition of CEE have been introduced over the years to better align the deductions available for expenses in the mining sector with those available in the oil and gas sector. The 2013 Budget made changes to the treatment of pre-production mine development expenses described in paragraph (*g*) of the definition of CEE, which are reclassified as "Canadian development expenses" ("CDE") (see s. 66.2) for expenses incurred after March 21, 2013, and the 2016 Budget included expenses for environmental studies and community consultations in the definition. In the case of pre-production oil sands development, CEE treatment is maintained for qualifying expenses incurred before 2015, subject to certain conditions. In the case of pre-production mine development expenses, CEE treatment is maintained for expenses incurred before 2017, subject to certain conditions. The 2017 Federal Budget provided that expenses related to the drilling or completion of a discovery well, or building a temporary access road to such a well, or preparing a site for such a well, incurred after 2018 (including expenses incurred in 2019 that are deemed to have been incurred in 2018 under the look-back rule) no longer qualify as CEE, subject to grandfathering.

History: S. 66.1(6), clause (*d*)(i)(C) of the definition "Canadian exploration expense" was added by S.C. 2017, c. 33, s. 20(1), in force on December 14, 2017.

S. 66.1(6), paragraph (*a*) of the definition "Canadian exploration expense" was replaced by S.C. 2016, c. 7, s. 7(1), applicable in respect of expenses incurred after February 2015, and formerly read:

(*a*) any expense including a geological, geophysical or geochemical expense incurred by the taxpayer (other than an expense incurred in drilling or completing an oil or gas well or in building a temporary access road to, or preparing a site in respect of, any such well) for the purpose of determining the existence, location, extent or quality of an accumulation of petroleum or natural gas (other than a mineral resource) in Canada,

S. 66.1(6), the portion of paragraph (*f*) of the definition "Canadian exploration expense" before subparagraph (i) was replaced by S.C. 2016, c. 7, s. 7(2), applicable in respect of expenses incurred after February 2015, and formerly read:

(*f*) any expense incurred by the taxpayer (other than an expense incurred in drilling or completing an oil or gas well or in building a temporary access road to, or preparing a site in respect of, any such well) for the purpose of determining the existence, location, extent or quality of a mineral resource in Canada including any expense incurred in the course of

S. 66.1(6), paragraph (*g*) of the definition "Canadian exploration expense" was replaced by S.C. 2013, c. 40, s. 31(2), deemed to have come into force on March 21, 2013, and formerly read:

(*g*) any expense incurred by the taxpayer after November 16, 1978 for the purpose of bringing a new mine in a mineral resource in Canada, other than a bituminous sands deposit or an oil shale deposit, into production, in reasonable commercial quantities and incurred before the new mine comes into production in such quantities, including an expense for clearing, removing overburden, stripping, sinking a mine shaft or constructing an adit or other underground entry, but not including any expense that results in revenue or can reasonably be expected to result in revenue earned before the new mine comes into production in reasonable commercial quantities, except to the extent that the total of all such expenses exceeds the total of those revenues,

S. 66.1(6), paragraphs (*g.3*) and (*g.4*) of the definition "Canadian exploration expense" were added by S.C. 2013, c. 40, s. 31(3), deemed to have come into force on March 21, 2013.

S. 66.1(6), paragraph (*h*) of the definition "Canadian exploration expense" was replaced by S.C. 2013, c. 40, s. 31(4), deemed to have come into force on March 21, 2013, except that before March 21, 2013 paragraph (*h*) of the definition "Canadian exploration expense" in subsection 66.1(6) is to be read as follows:

"(*h*) subject to section 66.8, the taxpayer's share of any expense referred to in any of paragraphs (*a*) to (*d*) and (*f*) to (*g.2*) incurred by a partnership in a fiscal period of the partnership, if at the end of the period the taxpayer is a member of the partnership, or"

S. 66.1(6), paragraph (*h*) of the definition "Canadian exploration expense" formerly read:

(*h*) subject to section 66.8, the taxpayer's share of any expense referred to in any of paragraphs (*a*) to (*d*) and (*f*) to (*g*.1) incurred by a partnership in a fiscal period thereof, if at the end of the period the taxpayer is a member of the partnership, or

S. 66.1(6), paragraph (*i*) of the definition "Canadian exploration expense" was replaced by S.C. 2013, c. 34, s. 112(1), in force June 26, 2013, and formerly read:

(*i*) any expense referred to in any of paragraphs (*a*) to (*g*) incurred by the taxpayer pursuant to an agreement in writing with a corporation, entered into before 1987, under which the taxpayer incurred the expense solely as consideration for shares, other than prescribed shares, of the capital stock of the corporation issued to the taxpayer or any interest in such shares or right thereto,

S. 66.1(6), paragraph (*j*) of the definition "Canadian exploration expense" was replaced by S.C. 2013, c. 34, s. 112(2), in force June 26, 2013, and formerly read:

(*j*) any consideration given by the taxpayer for any share or any interest therein or right thereto, except as provided by paragraph (*i*),

S. 66.1(6), subparagraph (*f*)(v.1) of the definition "Canadian exploration expense" was added, and subparagraph (vi) was replaced, by S.C. 2011, c. 24, s. 14(1), applicable to expenses incurred after November 5, 2010. S. 66.1(6), subparagraph (*f*)(vi) of the definition "Canadian exploration expense" formerly read:

(vi) any expense that may reasonably be considered to be related to a mine that has come into production in reasonable commercial quantities or to be related to a potential or actual extension thereof,

S. 66.1(6), paragraph (*g*) of the definition "Canadian exploration expense" was replaced by S.C. 2011, c. 24, s. 14(2), applicable to expenses incurred after November 5, 2010 except that in respect of expenses incurred before March 22, 2011 paragraph (*g*) of the definition "Canadian exploration expense" in subsection 66.1(6) is to be be read without reference to ", other than a bituminous sands deposit or an oil shale deposit,".

S. 66.1(6), paragraph (*g*) of the definition "Canadian exploration expense" formerly read:

(*g*) any expense incurred by the taxpayer after November 16, 1978 for the purpose of bringing a new mine in a mineral resource in Canada into production in reasonable commercial quantities and incurred before the new mine comes into production in such quantities, including an expense for clearing, removing overburden, stripping, sinking a mine shaft or constructing an adit or other underground entry,

S. 66.1(6), paragraph (*g.2*) of the definition "Canadian exploration expense" was added by S.C. 2011, c. 24, s. 14(3), applicable to expenses incurred after March 21, 2011.

S. 66.1(6), paragraph (*k.2*) of the definition "Canadian exploration expense" was repealed by S.C. 2011, c. 24, s. 14(4), applicable to expenses incurred after November 5, 2010. S. 66.1(6), paragraph (*k.2*) of the definition "Canadian exploration expense" formerly read:

(*k*.2) any portion of any expense that may reasonably be considered to have resulted in revenue earned by a taxpayer if

(i) the expense is otherwise described by subparagraph (*f*)(i), (iii) or (iv) and the revenue is earned before a new mine of the taxpayer in the mineral resource referred to in paragraph (*f*) comes into production in reasonable commercial quantities, or

(ii) the expense is otherwise described by paragraph (*g*) and the revenue is earned before the new mine referred to in that paragraph comes into production in reasonable commercial quantities,

Related Regulations: 1203(2); 1205(1); 1206; 1207; 1217; 4608; 6202(1).

Related Sections: S. 12(1)(*t*) Investment tax credit; s. 13(7.5) Deemed capital cost; s. 13(21), "depreciable property"; s. 53(2)(*c*) Amounts to be deducted — Interest in a partnership; s. 53(2)(*e*) Amounts to be deducted — Share, where shareholder incurred exploration and development expenses;

s. 53(2)(*f*) Amounts to be deducted — Property received from joint exploration corporation; s. 53(2)(*f*.1) Amounts to be deducted — Share of the capital stock of joint exploration corporation; s. 59(3.3) Amounts to be included in income; s. 66(10.1) Idem; s. 66(12.1)(*a*) Limitations of Canadian exploration and development expenses; s. 66(12.2) Unitized oil or gas field in Canada — Canadian exploration expenses; s. 66(12.6) Canadian exploration expenses to flow-through shareholder; s. 66(12.66) Expenses in the first 60 days of year; s. 66(12.67) Restrictions on renunciation; s. 66(14.1) Designation respecting Canadian exploration expense; s. 66(15), "assistance", "flow-through share"; s. 66.1(6), "Canadian renewable and conservation expense"; s. 66.1(7) Share of partner; s. 66.1(9) Canadian development expenses for preceding years; s. 66.2(2) Deduction for cumulative Canadian development expenses; s. 66.2(5), "Canadian development expense"; s. 66.3 Exploration and development shares; s. 66.4(5) "Canadian oil and gas property expense"; s. 66.7 Successor of Canadian exploration and development expenses; s. 66.8 Resource expenses of limited partner; s. 127(9) "flow-through mining expenditure", "pre-production mining expenditure"; s. 219(1)(*c*) Branch tax; s. 248(1), "Canadian exploration expense".

Canadian Petroleum Tax Journal: Legislation Dealing with CEE, CDE and COGPE & Proposed Policy on CEDOE, Ladak, 2003, Vol. 16, No. 1; Recent Cases of Interest — Canadian Exploration Expense ("CEE"), Gerald Grenon, 2000, Vol. 13, No. 1; Canada Customs and Revenue Agency 1999 Roundtable Questions and Answers, Question 15, , 2000, Vol. 13, No. 1; Renewable Energy — Tax Developments and Opportunities, Leanne Sereda, 2000, Vol. 13, No. 1; Flow-Through Shares: An Update, Angelo F. Toselli, 1997, Vol. 10, No. 1.

Canadian Tax Foundation: Colborne and Paton, *2013 Mining Update*, 2013 Conference Report 9:1–19.

Income Tax Folios: *Primary* — S3-F8-C2 Tax Incentives for Clean Energy Equipment.

Interpretation Bulletins: *Primary* — IT-476R Capital cost allowance — Equipment used in petroleum and natural gas activities.

Tax Window Files: Mining Expenditure Review Table, *February 21, 2019*, CRA Document No. 2019-0796791I7.

Cases: Canadian exploration expense ("CEE") must be incurred for the "purpose" of bringing a mine into production. These criteria must be applied objectively, without second-guessing the company's business decisions. In addition, the taxpayer, who had acquired flow-through shares, could not deduct the amounts in issue (that were not CEE) as expenses incurred to generate business income under s. 9. *Mickleborough v. The Queen*, 99 DTC 47 (T.C.C.)

Seismic data purchased for the purpose of resale or licensing does not qualify as CEE. *Global Communications Limited v. The Queen*, 99 DTC 5377 (F.C.A.), reversing 97 DTC 1293 (T.C.C.)

The costs incurred by the taxpayer for exploration, drilling and tunnelling in the development of its underground coal deposit were held to be "Canadian exploration expenses" since the expenses were related to a mine (i.e. the underground mine) separate and apart from the taxpayer's surface operations and had been incurred prior to the production from that mine in "reasonable commercial quantities". *Oro Del Norte S.A. v. The Queen*, 93 DTC 5217 (F.C.T.D.)

"Canadian renewable and conservation expense" —"Canadian renewable and conservation expense" has the meaning assigned by regulation, and for the purpose of determining whether an outlay or expense in respect of a prescribed energy conservation property is a Canadian renewable and conservation expense, the *Technical Guide to Canadian Renewable and Conservation Expenses (CRCE)*, as amended from time to time and published by the Department of Natural Resources, shall apply conclusively with respect to engineering and scientific matters;

History: S. 66.1(6), the definition "Canadian renewable and conservation expense" was replaced by S.C. 2013, c. 40, s. 31(1), deemed to have come into force on December 21, 2012, and formerly read:

"Canadian renewable and conservation expense" —"Canadian renewable and conservation expense" has the meaning assigned by regulation, and for the purpose of determining whether an outlay or expense meets the criteria set out in the Regulations in respect of Canadian renewable and conservation expenses, the *Technical Guide to Canadian Renewable and Conservation Expenses*, as amended from time to time and published by the Department of Natural Resources, shall apply conclusively with respect to engineering and scientific matters;

Related Regulations: 1219.

Canadian Petroleum Tax Journal: Renewable Energy — Tax Developments and Opportunities, Leanne Sereda, 2000, Vol. 13, No. 1; Flow-Through Shares: An Update, Angelo F. Toselli, 1997, Vol. 10, No. 1.

Tax Profile: August 2011 — Structuring Solar Projects in Canada.

"completion" —"completion", of a specified oil sands mine development project, means the first attainment of a level of average output, measured over a 60-day period, equal to at least 60% of the planned level of average daily output (as determined in paragraph (*b*) of the definition "specified oil sands mine development project") for the specified oil sands mine development project;

History: S. 66.1(6), the definition "completion" was added by S.C. 2011, c. 24, s. 14(5), deemed to have come into force on March 22, 2011.

"cumulative Canadian exploration expense" —"cumulative Canadian exploration expense" of a taxpayer at any time in a taxation year means the amount determined by the formula

$$(A + B + C + D + E + E.1) - (F + G + H + I + J + J.1 + K + L + M)$$

where

A is the total of all Canadian exploration expenses made or incurred by the taxpayer before that time,

B is the total of all amounts that were, because of subsection (1), included in computing the amount referred to in paragraph 59(3.2)(*b*) for the taxpayer's taxation years ending before that time,

C is the total of all amounts, except amounts in respect of interest, paid by the taxpayer after May 6, 1974 and before that time to Her Majesty in right of Canada in respect of amounts paid to the taxpayer before May 25, 1976 under the regulations referred to in paragraph (*a*) of the description of H,

D is the total of all amounts referred to in the description of G that are established by the taxpayer to have become bad debts before that time,

E is such part, if any, of the amount determined for J as has been repaid before that time by the taxpayer pursuant to a legal obligation to repay all or any part of that amount,

E.1 is the total of all specified amounts determined under paragraph 66.7(12.1)(*a*) in respect of the taxpayer for taxation years ending before that time,

F is the total of all amounts deducted or required to be deducted in computing the taxpayer's income for a taxation year ending before that time in respect of the taxpayer's cumulative Canadian exploration expense,

G is the total of all amounts that became receivable by the taxpayer before that time that are to be included in the amount determined under this description by virtue of paragraph 66(12.1)(*a*) or (12.2)(*a*),

H is the total of all amounts paid to the taxpayer after May 6, 1974 and before May 25, 1976

(*a*) under the *Northern Mineral Exploration Assistance Regulations* made under an appropriation Act that provides for payments in respect of the Northern Mineral Grants Program, or

(*b*) pursuant to any agreement entered into between the taxpayer and Her Majesty in right of Canada under the Northern Mineral Grants Program or the Development Program of the Department of Indian Affairs and Northern Development,

to the extent that the amounts have been expended by the taxpayer as or on account of Canadian exploration and development expenses or Canadian exploration expense incurred by the taxpayer,

I is the total of all amounts each of which is an amount received before that time on account of any amount referred to in the description of D,

J is the total amount of assistance that the taxpayer has received or is entitled to receive in respect of any Canadian exploration expense incurred after 1980 or that can reasonably be related to Canadian exploration activities after 1980, to the extent that the assistance has not reduced the taxpayer's Canadian exploration expense by virtue of paragraph (9)(*g*),

J.1 is the total of all amounts by which the cumulative Canadian exploration expense of the taxpayer is required because of subsection 80(8) to be reduced at or before that time,

K is the total of all amounts that are required to be deducted before that time under subsection 66(14.1) in computing the taxpayer's cumulative Canadian exploration expense,

L is that portion of the total of all amounts each of which was deducted by the taxpayer under subsection 127(5) or (6) for a taxation year that ended before that time and that can reasonably be attributed to a qualified Canadian exploration expenditure, a pre-production mining expenditure or a flow-through mining expenditure (each expenditure within the meaning assigned by subsection 127(9)) made in a preceding taxation year, and

M is the total of all amounts that are required to be deducted before that time under paragraph 66.7(12)(*b*) in computing the taxpayer's cumulative Canadian exploration expense;

History: S. 66.1(6), the description of B in the definition "cumulative Canadian exploration expense" was replaced by S.C. 2013, c. 34, s. 200(1), applicable to taxation years that end after November 5, 2010, and formerly read:

B is the total of all amounts required by subsection (1) to be included in computing the amount referred to in paragraph 59(3.2)(*b*) for the taxpayer's taxation years ending before that time,

Related Sections: S. 12(1)(*t*) Investment tax credit; s. 20(1)(*kk*) Exploration and development grants; s. 53(1)(*e*)(viii) Adjustments to cost base — Interest in a partnership; s. 59(3.2)(*b*) Recovery of exploration and development expenses; s. 66(11) Acquisition of control; s. 66(12.1)(*a*) Limitations of Canadian exploration and development expenses; s. 66(12.2) Unitized oil or gas field in Canada — Canadian exploration expenses; s. 66(12.3)(*a*) Unitized oil or gas field in Canada — Canadian development expenses; s. 66(12.6)(*e*) Canadian exploration expenses to flow-through shareholder; s. 66(14.1) Designation respecting Canadian exploration expense; s. 66(15), "assistance"; s. 66.1(6), "Canadian exploration expense"; s. 66.1(7) Share of partner; s. 66.1(9) Canadian development expenses for preceding years; s. 66.7(3) Successor of Canadian exploration expense; s. 66.7(9) Canadian development expense becoming Canadian exploration expense; s. 66.7(12) Reduction of Canadian resource expenses; s. 66.7(12.1)(*a*) Specified amount; s. 79(4)(*c*) Subsequent payment by debtor; s. 80(8) Reductions of resource expenditures; s. 127(5) Investment tax credit; s. 127(6) Investment tax credit of cooperative corporation; s. 127(9), "flow-through mining expenditure", "pre-production mining expenditure"; s. 127(12.3) Cumulative Canadian exploration expense.

"designated asset" — "designated asset", in respect of an oil sands mine development project of a taxpayer, means a property that is a building, a structure, machinery or equipment and is, or is an integral and substantial part of,

(*a*) in the case of a bitumen mine development project,

(i) a crusher,

(ii) a froth treatment plant,

(iii) a primary separation unit,

(iv) a steam generation plant,

(v) a cogeneration plant, or

(vi) a water treatment plant, or

(*b*) in the case of a bitumen upgrading development project,

(i) a gasifier unit,

(ii) a vacuum distillation unit,

(iii) a hydrocracker unit,

(iv) a hydrotreater unit,

(v) a hydroprocessor unit, or

(vi) a coker;

History: S. 66.1(6), the definition "designated asset" was added by S.C. 2011, c. 24, s. 14(5), deemed to have come into force on March 22, 2011.

"eligible oil sands mine development expense" — "eligible oil sands mine development expense", of a taxpayer, means an expense incurred by the taxpayer after March 21, 2011 and before 2016, the amount of which is determined by the formula

$$A \times B$$

where

A is an expense that would be a Canadian exploration expense of the taxpayer described in paragraph (*g*) of the definition "Canadian exploration expense" if that paragraph were read without reference to "and before March 21, 2013" and "other than a bituminous sands deposit or an oil shale deposit", but does not include an expense that is a specified oil sands mine development expense, and

B is

(*a*) 100% if the expense is incurred before 2013,

(*b*) 80% if the expense is incurred in 2013,

(*c*) 60% if the expense is incurred in 2014, and

(*d*) 30% if the expense is incurred in 2015;

History: S. 66.1(6), the description of A in the definition "eligible oil sands mine development expense" was replaced by S.C. 2013, c. 40, s. 31(5), deemed to have come into force on March 21, 2013, and formerly read:

A is an expense that would be a Canadian exploration expense of the taxpayer described in paragraph (*g*) of the definition "Canadian exploration expense" if that paragraph were read without reference to "other than a bituminous sands deposit or an oil shale deposit", but does not include an expense that is a specified oil sands mine development expense, and

S. 66.1(6), the definition "eligible oil sands mine development expense" was added by S.C. 2011, c. 24, s. 14(5), deemed to have come into force on March 22, 2011.

"oil sands mine development project" —"oil sands mine development project", of a taxpayer, means a bitumen mine development project or a bitumen upgrading development project of the taxpayer;

History: S. 66.1(6), the definition "oil sands mine development project" was added by S.C. 2011, c. 24, s. 14(5), deemed to have come into force on March 22, 2011.

"preliminary work activity" —"preliminary work activity", in respect of an oil sands mine development project, means activity that is preliminary to the acquisition, construction, fabrication or installation by or on behalf of a taxpayer of designated assets in respect of the taxpayer's oil sands mine development project including, without limiting the generality of the foregoing, the following activities:

(*a*) obtaining permits or regulatory approvals,

(*b*) performing design or engineering work,

(*c*) conducting feasibility studies,

(*d*) conducting environmental assessments, and

(*e*) entering into contracts;

History: S. 66.1(6), the definition "preliminary work activity" was added by S.C. 2011, c. 24, s. 14(5), deemed to have come into force on March 22, 2011.

"restricted expense" —"restricted expense" of a taxpayer means an expense

(*a*) incurred by the taxpayer before April, 1987,

(*b*) that is deemed by paragraph 66(10.2)(*c*) to have been incurred by the taxpayer, or included by the taxpayer in the amount referred to in paragraph (*a*) of the definition "Canadian development expense" in subsection 66.2(5) by virtue of paragraph 66(12.3)(*b*), to the extent that the expense was originally incurred before April, 1987,

(*c*) that was renounced by the taxpayer under subsection 66(10.2), (12.601) or (12.62),

(*d*) in respect of which an amount referred to in subsection 66(12.3) becomes receivable by the taxpayer,

(*e*) deemed to be a Canadian exploration expense of the taxpayer or any other taxpayer by virtue of subsection (9), or

(*f*) where the taxpayer is a corporation, that was incurred by the corporation before the time control of the corporation was last acquired by a person or persons;

Related Sections: S. 66.1(9) Canadian development expenses for preceding years.

"specified oil sands mine development expense" —"specified oil sands mine development expense", of a taxpayer, means an expense that

(*a*) would be a Canadian exploration expense described in paragraph (*g*) of the definition "Canadian exploration expense" if that paragraph were read without reference to "and before March 21, 2013" and "other than a bituminous sands deposit or an oil shale deposit",

(*b*) is incurred by the taxpayer after March 21, 2011 and before 2015, and

(*c*) is incurred by the taxpayer to achieve completion of a specified oil sands mine development project of the taxpayer;

History: S. 66.1(6), paragraph (*a*) of the definition "specified oil sands mine development expense" was replaced by S.C. 2013, c. 40, s. 31(6), deemed to have come into force on March 21, 2013, and formerly read:

(*a*) would be a Canadian exploration expense described in paragraph (*g*) of the definition "Canadian exploration expense" if that paragraph were read without reference to "other than a bituminous sands deposit or an oil shale deposit",

S. 66.1(6), the definition "specified oil sands mine development expense" was added by S.C. 2011, c. 24, s. 14(5), deemed to have come into force on March 22, 2011.

"specified oil sands mine development project" —"specified oil sands mine development project", of a taxpayer, means an oil sands mine development project (not including any preliminary work activity) in respect of which

(*a*) one or more designated assets was, before March 22, 2011,

(i) acquired by the taxpayer, or

(ii) in the process of being constructed, fabricated or installed, by or on behalf of the taxpayer, and

(*b*) the planned level of average daily output (where that output is bitumen or a similar product in the case of a bitumen mine development project, or synthetic crude oil or a similar product in the case of a bitumen upgrading development project) that can reasonably be expected, is the lesser of

(i) the level that was the demonstrated intention of the taxpayer as of March 21, 2011 to produce from the oil sands mine development project, and

(ii) the maximum level of output associated with the design capacity, as of March 21, 2011, of the designated asset referred to in paragraph (*a*);

History: S. 66.1(6), the definition "specified oil sands mine development project" was added by S.C. 2011, c. 24, s. 14(5), deemed to have come into force on March 22, 2011.

"specified purpose" —"specified purpose" means

(*a*) the operation of an oil or gas well for the sole purpose of testing the well or the well head and related equipment, in accordance with generally accepted engineering practices,

(*b*) the burning of natural gas and related hydrocarbons to protect the environment, and

(*c*) prescribed purposes.

Related Sections: S. 66.1(9) Canadian development expenses for preceding years.

► 66.1(6.1) ◄

(6.1) Application of ss. 66(15), 66.2(5) and 66.4(5). The definitions in subsections 66(15), 66.2(5) and 66.4(5) apply to this section.

► 66.1(6.2) ◄

(6.2) Deductible expense. An expense of a taxpayer that is not included in paragraph (*f*) or (*g*) of the definition "Canadian exploration expense" in subsection (6) because the taxpayer earned revenue from a mine in a mineral resource is deemed, for the purposes of this Part, not to be an outlay or payment described in paragraph 18(1)(*b*).

History: S. 66.1(6.2) was added by S.C. 2013, c. 34, s. 200(2), applicable in respect of expenses incurred after November 5, 2010.

► 66.1(7) ◄

(7) Share of partner. Where a taxpayer is a member of a partnership, the taxpayer's share of any amount that would be an amount referred to in the description of E, G or J in the definition "cumulative Canadian exploration expense" in subsection (6) in respect of the partnership for a taxation year of the partnership if section 96 were read without reference to paragraph 96(1)(*d*) shall, for the purposes of this Act, be deemed to be an amount referred to in the description of E, G or J, as the case may be, in that definition in respect of the taxpayer for the taxation year of the taxpayer in which the partnership's taxation year ends.

► 66.1(8) ◄

(8) Expenses in first 60 days of year — (Repealed by S.C. 1997, c. 25, s. 14(6).)

► 66.1(9) ◄

(9) Canadian development expenses for preceding years. Where at any time in a taxpayer's taxation year

(*a*) the drilling or completing of an oil or gas well resulted in the discovery that a natural underground reservoir contains petroleum or natural gas and, before the time of the discovery, no person or partnership had discovered that the reservoir contained either petroleum or natural gas,

(*b*) the period of 24 months commencing on the day of completion of the drilling of an oil or gas well ends and the well has not, within that period, produced otherwise than for specified purposes, or

(*c*) an oil or gas well that has never produced, otherwise than for specified purposes, is abandoned,

the amount, if any, by which the total of

(*d*) all Canadian development expenses (other than restricted expenses) described in subparagraph (*a*)(ii) of the definition "Canadian development expense" in subsection 66.2(5) in respect of the well that are deemed by subsection 66(10.2) or (12.63) to have been incurred by the taxpayer in the year or a preceding taxation year,

(*e*) all Canadian development expenses (other than restricted expenses) described in subparagraph (*a*)(ii) of the definition "Canadian development expense" in subsection 66.2(5) in respect of the well that are required by paragraph 66(12.3)(*b*) to be included by the taxpayer in the amount referred to in paragraph (*a*) of that definition for the year or a preceding taxation year, and

(*f*) all Canadian development expenses (other than expenses referred to in paragraph (*d*) or (*e*) and restricted expenses) described in subparagraph (*a*)(ii) of the definition "Canadian development expense" in subsection 66.2(5) incurred by the taxpayer in respect of the well in a taxation year preceding the year,

exceeds

(*g*) any assistance that the taxpayer or a partnership of which the taxpayer is a member has received or is entitled to receive in respect of the expenses referred to in any of paragraphs (*d*) to (*f*),

shall, for the purposes of this Act, be deemed to be a Canadian exploration expense referred to in paragraph (*e*) of the definition "Canadian exploration expense" in subsection (6) incurred by the taxpayer at that time.

Editorial Note: Many expenses which are incurred in drilling and completing an oil or gas well in Canada do not initially satisfy the tests in paragraph (*d*) of the definition of "Canadian exploration expense" and therefore are initially categorized as Canadian development expenses. Subsection 66.1(9) allows the taxpayer to subsequently classify the expenses as Canadian exploration expenses, other than expenses which are restricted expenses.

Related Sections: S. 66(15), "assistance"; s. 66.1(6) Definitions.

► 66.1(10) ◄

(10) Certificate ceasing to be valid. A certificate in respect of an oil or gas well issued by the Minister of Natural Resources for the purposes of subparagraph (*d*)(iv) of the definition "Canadian exploration expense" in subsection (6) shall be deemed never to have been issued and never to have been filed with the Minister where

(*a*) the well produces, otherwise than for a specified purpose, within the period of 24 months commencing on the day on which the drilling of the well was completed; or

(*b*) in applying for the certificate, the applicant, in any material respect, provided any incorrect information or failed to provide information.

Related Sections: S. 66.1(6), "specified purpose".

► 66.1(11) ◄

(11) Second successor — (Repealed by 1987, c. 46, s. 19(4).)

SECTION 66.2: [Canadian development expenses]

► 66.2(1) ◄

(1) Amount to be included in income. There shall be included in computing the amount referred to in paragraph 59(3.2)(*c*) in respect of a taxpayer for a taxation year the amount, if any, by which the total of

(*a*) all amounts referred to in the descriptions of E to O in the definition "cumulative Canadian development expense" in subsection (5) that are deducted in computing the taxpayer's cumulative Canadian development expense at the end of the year, and

(*b*) the amount that is designated by the taxpayer for the year under subsection 66(14.2)

exceeds the total of

(*c*) all amounts referred to in the descriptions of A to D.1 in the definition "cumulative Canadian development expense" in subsection (5) that are included in computing the taxpayer's cumulative Canadian development expense at the end of the year, and

(*d*) the total determined under subparagraph 66.7(12.1)(*b*)(i) in respect of the taxpayer for the year.

Editorial Note: Section 66.2 provides for the deduction by a taxpayer of its Canadian development expenses ("CDE"). CDE include expenses incurred in drilling oil and gas wells which are not CEE and expenses incurred in mining which include the cost of mineral resource properties and certain underground expenses incurred after a mine comes into production. A taxpayer (whether or not it is a principal-business corporation) does not claim a deduction directly in respect of any CDE that it has incurred. Instead, the CDE is added to the taxpayer's cumulative Canadian development expense ("CCDE") account. A taxpayer may claim an optional deduction of 30% of its CCDE at the end of the year. A taxpayer may claim an additional deduction if it disposed of its Canadian resource properties in the year in accordance with the successor corporation rules. The proceeds of disposition of a Canadian mineral resource property and any amount by which a taxpayer's cumulative Canadian oil and gas property expenses is negative at the end of the year are deducted from a taxpayer's CCDE. The taxpayer must include in income for the year the amount by which its CCDE is negative at the end of the year, less any amount that the taxpayer may deduct by virtue of disposing in the year of its Canadian resource properties pursuant to the successor corporation rules.

In addition to the 30% deduction rate, accelerated rates apply to "accelerated Canadian development expense" incurred after November 20, 2018 and before 2028. The accelerated rates equal the existing 30% plus an additional percentage depending on the taxation year (see paragraph 66.2(2)(d)). The additional percentage is 15% for taxation years that end before 2024 (for a total of 45%) and 7.5% for taxation years that begin after 2023 (for a total of 37.5%). For a taxation year that straddles December 31, 2023, the rate is 7.5% plus a portion of the 15% rate based on the expenditures incurred before 2024 relative to the total incurred in the taxation year.

Related Sections: S. 66(18) Members of partnerships; s. 66.2(5) Definitions; s. 104(5.2) Resource property; s. 127.5 Obligation to pay minimum tax.

Interpretation Bulletins: *Secondary* — IT-125R4 Dispositions of resource properties; IT-273R2 Government assistance — General comments.

► 66.2(2) ◄

(2) Deduction for cumulative Canadian development expenses. A taxpayer may deduct, in computing the taxpayer's income for a taxation year, such amount as the taxpayer may claim not exceeding the total of

(*a*) the lesser of

(i) the total of

(A) the taxpayer's cumulative Canadian development expense at the end of the year, and

(B) the amount, if any, by which

(I) the total determined under subparagraph 66.7(12.1)(*b*)(i) in respect of the taxpayer for the year

exceeds

(II) the amount that would, but for paragraph (1)(*d*), be determined under subsection (1) in respect of the taxpayer for the year, and

(ii) the amount, if any, by which the amount determined under subparagraph 66.4(2)(*a*)(ii) exceeds the amount determined under subparagraph 66.4(2)(*a*)(i),

(*b*) the lesser of

(i) the amount, if any, by which the amount determined under subparagraph (*a*)(i) exceeds the amount determined under subparagraph (*a*)(ii), and

(ii) the amount, if any, by which the total of all amounts each of which is

(A) an amount included in the taxpayer's income for the year by virtue of a disposition in the year of inventory described in section 66.3 that was a share or any interest in or right to — or, for civil law, any right in or to — a share, acquired by the taxpayer under circumstances described in paragraph (*g*) of the definition "Canadian development expense" in subsection (5) or paragraph (*i*) of the definition "Canadian exploration expense" in subsection 66.1(6), or

(B) an amount included by virtue of paragraph 12(1)(*e*) in computing the taxpayer's income for the year to the extent that it relates to inventory described in clause (A)

exceeds

(C) the total of all amounts deducted as a reserve by virtue of paragraph 20(1)(*n*) in computing the taxpayer's income for the year to the extent that the reserve relates to inventory described in clause (A),

(*c*) 30% of the amount, if any, by which the amount determined under subparagraph (*b*)(i) exceeds the amount determined under subparagraph (*b*)(ii), and

(*d*) the amount determined by the formula

$$A(B - C)$$

where

A is

(i) for taxation years that end before 2024, 15%,

(ii) for taxation years that begin before 2024 and end after 2023, the amount determined by the formula

$$0.15(I/J) + 0.075(K/J)$$

where

I is the total of all accelerated Canadian development expenses incurred by the taxpayer before 2024 and in the taxation year,

J is the total of all accelerated Canadian development expenses incurred by the taxpayer in the taxation year, and

K is the total of all accelerated Canadian development expenses incurred by the taxpayer after 2023 and in the taxation year, and

(iii) for taxation years that begin after 2023, 7.5%,

B is the total of all accelerated Canadian development expenses incurred by the taxpayer in the taxation year, and

C is the amount determined by the formula

$$(D - E) - (F - G - H)$$

where

D is the total of the amounts determined for E to O in the definition "cumulative Canadian development expense" in subsection (5) at the end of the taxation year,

E is the total of the amounts determined for E to O in the definition "cumulative Canadian development expense" in subsection (5) at the beginning of the taxation year,

F is the total of the amounts determined for A to D.1 in the definition "cumulative

Canadian development expense" in subsection (5) at the end of the taxation year,

G is the total of the amounts determined for A to D.1 in the definition "cumulative Canadian development expense" in subsection (5) at the end of the preceding taxation year, and

H is the amount determined for B.

Editorial Note: See the editorial note following subsection 66.2(1) regarding the deduction of Canadian development expenses, including the accelerated deduction.

History: S. 66.2(2)(*d*) was added by S.C. 2019, c. 29, s. 5(1), effective June 21, 2019.

S. 66.2(2)(*b*)(ii)(A) was replaced by S.C. 2013, c. 34, s. 113(1), in force June 26, 2013, and formerly read:

(A) an amount included in the taxpayer's income for the year by virtue of a disposition in the year of inventory described in section 66.3 that was a share, any interest therein or right thereto, acquired by the taxpayer under circumstances described in paragraph (*g*) of the definition "Canadian development expense" in subsection (5) or paragraph (*i*) of the definition "Canadian exploration expense" in subsection 66.1(6), or

Related Sections: S. 66(14.2) Designation respecting cumulative Canadian development expense; s. 66.2(5), "Canadian development expense".

Interpretation Bulletins: *Secondary* — IT-438R2 Crown charges — Resource properties in Canada.

Cases: Lease payments to the province for subsurface rights did not constitute "Canadian exploration expenses" because their purpose was not exclusively or even primarily exploration, but rather the accumulation of an acreage inventory which might or might not be used to serve exploration, development and production in the future. *The Queen v. Gulf Canada Limited*, 92 DTC 6123 (F.C.A.), affirming 90 DTC 6622 (F.C.T.D.)

▶ 66.2(3) ◀

(3) Successor corporation's Canadian development expense — (Repealed by 1987, c. 46, s. 20(2).)

▶ 66.2(4) ◀

(4) Second successor corporation's Canadian development expense — (Repealed by 1987, c. 46, s. 20(2).)

▶ 66.2(5) ◀

(5) Definitions. In this section,

accelerated Canadian development expense — "accelerated Canadian development expense", of a taxpayer, means any cost or expense incurred by the taxpayer during a taxation year if the cost or expense

(*a*) qualifies as a Canadian development expense at the time it is incurred, other than

(i) an expense in respect of which the taxpayer is a successor, within the meaning of subsection 66.7(4), and

(ii) a cost in respect of a Canadian resource property acquired by the taxpayer, or a partnership in which the taxpayer is a member, from a person or partnership with which the taxpayer does not deal at arm's length,

(*b*) is incurred after November 20, 2018 and before 2028, other than expenses deemed to have been incurred on December 31, 2027 because of subsection 66(12.66), and

(*c*) if the Canadian development expense is deemed to be a Canadian development expense incurred by the taxpayer because of paragraph 66(12.63)(*a*), is an amount renounced under an agreement entered into after November 20, 2018;

History: S. 66.2(5), the definition of "accelerated Canadian development expense" was added by S.C. 2019, c. 29, s. 5(2), effective June 21, 2019.

"Canadian development expense" — "Canadian development expense" of a taxpayer means any cost or expense incurred after May 6, 1974 that is

(*a*) any expense incurred by the taxpayer in

(i) drilling or converting a well in Canada for the disposal of waste liquids from an oil or gas well,

(ii) drilling or completing an oil or gas well in Canada, building a temporary access road to the well or preparing a site in respect of the well, to the extent that the expense was not a Canadian exploration expense of the taxpayer in the taxation year in which it was incurred,

(iii) drilling or converting a well in Canada for the injection of water, gas or any other substance to assist in the recovery of petroleum or natural gas from another well,

(iv) drilling for water or gas in Canada for injection into a petroleum or natural gas formation, or

(v) drilling or converting a well in Canada for the purposes of monitoring fluid levels, pressure changes or other phenomena in an accumulation of petroleum or natural gas,

(*b*) any expense incurred by the taxpayer in drilling or recompleting an oil or gas well in Canada after the commencement of production from the well,

(*c*) any expense incurred by the taxpayer before November 17, 1978 for the purpose of bringing a mineral resource in Canada into production and incurred prior to the commencement of production from the resource in reasonable commercial quantities, including

(i) clearing, removing overburden and stripping, and

(ii) sinking a mine shaft, constructing an adit or other underground entry,

(*c*.1) any expense, or portion of any expense, that is not a Canadian exploration expense, incurred by the taxpayer for the purpose of bringing a new mine in a mineral resource in Canada that is a bituminous sands deposit or an oil shale deposit into production and incurred before the new mine comes into production in reasonable commercial quantities, including an expense for clearing the land, removing overburden and stripping, or building an entry ramp,

(*c*.2) any expense, or portion of any expense, that is not a Canadian exploration expense, incurred by the taxpayer after March 20, 2013 for the purpose of bringing a new mine in a mineral resource in Canada, other than a bituminous sands deposit or an oil shale deposit, into production in reasonable commercial quantities and incurred before the new mine comes into production in such quantities, including an expense for clearing, removing overburden, stripping, sinking a mine shaft or constructing an adit or other underground entry,

(*d*) any expense (other than an amount included in the capital cost of depreciable property) incurred by the taxpayer after 1987

(i) in sinking or excavating a mine shaft, main haulage way or similar underground work designed for continuing use, for a mine in a mineral resource in Canada built or excavated after the mine came into production, or

(ii) in extending any such shaft, haulage way or work,

(*e*) the cost to the taxpayer of, including any payment for the preservation of a taxpayer's rights in respect of, any property described in paragraph (*b*), (*e*) or (*f*) of the definition "Canadian resource property" in subsection 66(15), or any right to or interest in — or for civil law, any right in or to — the property (other than a right or an interest that the taxpayer has by reason of being a beneficiary under a trust or a member of a partnership),

(*f*) subject to section 66.8, the taxpayer's share of any expense referred to in any of paragraphs (*a*) to (*e*) incurred by a partnership in a fiscal period thereof at the end of which the taxpayer was a member of the partnership, unless the taxpayer elects in respect of the share in prescribed form and manner on or before the day that is 6 months after the taxpayer's taxation year in which that period ends, or

(*g*) any cost or expense referred to in any of paragraphs (*a*) to (*e*) incurred by the taxpayer pursuant to an agreement in writing with a corporation, entered into before 1987, under which the taxpayer incurred the cost or expense solely as consideration for shares, other than prescribed shares, of the capital stock of the corporation issued to the taxpayer or any interest in or right to — or, for civil law, any right in or to — such shares,

but, for greater certainty, shall not include

(*h*) any consideration given by the taxpayer for any share or any interest in or right to — or, for civil law, any right in or to — a share, except as provided by paragraph (*g*),

(*i*) any expense described in paragraph (*g*) incurred by any other taxpayer to the extent that the expense was,

(i) by virtue of that paragraph, a Canadian development expense of that other taxpayer,

(ii) by virtue of paragraph (*i*) of the definition "Canadian exploration expense" in subsection 66.1(6), a Canadian exploration expense of that other taxpayer, or

(iii) by virtue of paragraph (*c*) of the definition "Canadian oil and gas property expense" in subsection 66.4(5), a Canadian oil and gas property expense of that other taxpayer,

(*i*.1) an expense that is the cost, or any part of the cost, to the taxpayer of any depreciable property of a prescribed class that was acquired after 1987,

(*j*) any amount included at any time in the capital cost to the taxpayer of any depreciable property of a prescribed class, or

(*k*) the taxpayer's share of any consideration, expense, cost or expenditure referred to in any of paragraphs (*h*) to (*j*) given or incurred by a partnership,

but any assistance that a taxpayer has received or is entitled to receive after May 25, 1976 in respect of or related to the taxpayer's Canadian development expense shall not reduce the amount of any of the expenses described in any of paragraphs (*a*) to (*g*);

Editorial Note: There is no requirement that a person have an interest in a particular Canadian resource property to be entitled to incur Canadian development expenses ("CDE") on a particular property. This is accomplished through a "farm-out" arrangement as described in CRA Document No. 2005-0119731E5 and IT-125R4, para. 14 (archived, as it doesn't meet current government web standards). Amendments to the definition of CDE have been introduced in recent years to better align the deductions available for expenses in the mining sector with those available in the oil and gas sector. The 2013 Budget made changes to the treatment of pre-production mine development expenses which are reclassified as CDE for expenses incurred after March 21, 2013, subject to certain transitional rules.

History: S. 66.2(5), paragraph (*c.2*) of the definition "Canadian development expense" was added by S.C. 2013, c. 40, s. 32(1) deemed to have come into force on March 21, 2013.

S. 66.2(5), paragraph (*e*) of the definition "Canadian development expense" was replaced by S.C. 2013, c. 34, s. 201(1), applicable to taxation years that begin after 2006, except that in its application to taxation years that begin in 2007, paragraph (*e*) of the definition "Canadian development expense" in subsection 66.2(5) is to be read as follows:

"(*e*) notwithstanding paragraph 18(1)(*m*), the cost to the taxpayer of, including any payment for the preservation of a taxpayer's rights in respect of, any property described in paragraph (*b*), (*e*) or (*f*) of the definition "Canadian resource property" in subsection 66(15), or any right to or interest in — or for civil law, any right in or to — the property (other than a right or an interest that the taxpayer has by reason of being a beneficiary under a trust or a member of a partnership), but not including any payment made to any of the persons referred to in subparagraph 18(1)(*m*)(i) for the preservation of a taxpayer's right in respect of a Canadian resource property, nor a payment to which paragraph 18(1)(*m*) applied because of clause 18(1)(*m*)(ii)(B),"

S. 66.2(5), paragraph (*e*) of the definition "Canadian development expense" formerly read:

(*e*) the cost to the taxpayer of, including any payment for the preservation of a taxpayer's rights in respect of, any property described in paragraph (*b*), (*e*) or (*f*) of the definition "Canadian resource property" in subsection 66(15), or any right to or interest in such property (other than a right or an interest that the taxpayer has by reason of being a beneficiary under a trust or a member of a partnership),

S. 66.2(5), paragraph (*g*) of the definition "Canadian development expense" was replaced by S.C. 2013, c. 34, s. 113(2), in force June 26, 2013, and formerly read:

(*g*) any cost or expense referred to in any of paragraphs (*a*) to (*e*) incurred by the taxpayer pursuant to an agreement in writing with a corporation, entered into before 1987, under which the taxpayer incurred the cost or expense solely as consideration for shares, other than prescribed shares, of the capital stock of the corporation issued to the taxpayer or any interest in such shares or right thereto,

S. 66.2(5), paragraph (*h*) of the definition "Canadian development expense" was replaced by S.C. 2013, c. 34, s. 113(3), in force June 26, 2013, and formerly read:

(*h*) any consideration given by the taxpayer for any share or any interest therein or right thereto, except as provided by paragraph (*g*),

S. 66.2(5), paragraph (*c.1*) of the definition "Canadian development expense" was added by S.C. 2011, c. 24, s. 15(1), applicable to expenses incurred after March 21, 2011.

Related Regulations: 6202(1).

Related Sections: S. 13(7.5) Deemed capital cost; s. 13(21), "depreciable property"; s. 18(1)(*m*) Limitation re employee stock option expenses; s. 53(1)(*e*)(vii.1) Adjustments to cost base — Interest in a partnership; s. 53(1)(*e*)(viii) Adjustments to cost base — Interest in a partnership; s. 53(2)(*c*) Amounts to be deducted — Interest in a partnership; s. 53(2)(*e*) Amounts to be deducted — Share, where shareholder incurred exploration and development expenses; s. 53(2)(*f*) Amounts to be deducted — Property received from joint exploration corporation; s. 53(2)(*f*.1) Amounts to be deducted — Share of the capital stock of joint exploration corporation; s. 66(10.2) Idem;

s. 66(12.1)(*b*) Limitations of Canadian exploration and development expenses; s. 66(12.601) Flow-through share rules for first $1 million of Canadian development expenses; s. 66(12.63) Effect of renunciation; s. 66(12.66) Expenses in the first 60 days of year; s. 66(15), "assistance", "Canadian resource property"; s. 66(18) Members of partnerships; s. 66.1(6), "Canadian exploration expense"; s. 66.2(2) Deduction for cumulative Canadian development expenses; s. 66.2(8) Presumption; s. 66.3 Exploration and development shares; s. 66.4(5), "Canadian oil and gas property expense"; s. 66.7(4) Successor of Canadian development expense; s. 66.8 Resource expenses of limited partner; s. 149(1)(*o*.2)(ii.1) Pension corporations.

Canadian Petroleum Tax Journal: Canada Customs and Revenue Agency 1999 Roundtable Questions and Answers, Question 15, , 2000, Vol. 13, No. 1; Flow-Through Shares: An Update, Angelo F. Toselli, 1997, Vol. 10, No. 1.

Canadian Tax Foundation: Colborne and Paton, *2013 Mining Update*, 2013 Conference Report 9:1–19.

Forms: T1086 — Election by a Partner Waiving Canadian Development Expenses or Oil and Gas Property Expenses.

Interpretation Bulletins: *Secondary* — IT-438R2 Crown charges — Resource properties in Canada; IT-476R Capital cost allowance — Equipment used in petroleum and natural gas activities.

"cumulative Canadian development expense" —"cumulative Canadian development expense" of a taxpayer at any time in a taxation year means the amount determined by the formula

$$(A + B + C + D + D.1) - (E + F + G + H + I + J + K + L + M + M.1 + N + O)$$

where

A is the total of all Canadian development expenses made or incurred by the taxpayer before that time,

B is the total of all amounts that were, because of subsection (1), included in computing the amount referred to in paragraph 59(3.2)(*c*) for taxation years ending before that time,

C is the total of all amounts referred to in the description of F or G that are established by the taxpayer to have become bad debts before that time,

D is such part, if any, of the amount determined for M as has been repaid before that time by the taxpayer pursuant to a legal obligation to repay all or any part of that amount,

D.1 is the total of all specified amounts, determined under paragraph 66.7(12.1)(*b*) in respect of the taxpayer for taxation years ending before that time,

E is the total of all amounts deducted in computing the taxpayer's income for a taxation year ending before that time in respect of the taxpayer's cumulative Canadian development expense,

F is the total of all amounts each of which is an amount in respect of property described in paragraph (*b*), (*e*) or (*f*) of the definition "Canadian resource property" in subsection 66(15) or property disposed of after March 21, 2011 which was described in any of those paragraphs and the cost of which when acquired by the taxpayer was included in the Canadian development expense of the taxpayer, or any right to or interest in — or, for civil law, any right in or to — such a property, other than such a right or an interest that the taxpayer has by reason of being a beneficiary under a trust or a member of a partnership, (in this description referred to as "the particular property") disposed of by the taxpayer before that time equal to the amount, if any, by which

(*a*) the amount, if any, by which the proceeds of disposition in respect of the particular property that became receivable by the taxpayer after May 6, 1974 and before that time exceed any outlays or expenses that were made or incurred by the taxpayer after May 6, 1974 and before that time for the purpose of making the disposition and that were not otherwise deductible for the purposes of this Part

exceeds

(*b*) the amount, if any, by which

(i) the total of all amounts that would be determined under paragraph 66.7(4)(*a*), immediately before the time (in this paragraph referred to as the "relevant time") when such proceeds of disposition became receivable, in respect of the taxpayer and an original owner of the particular property (or of any other property acquired by the taxpayer with the particular property in circumstances in which subsection 66.7(4) applied and in respect of which the proceeds of disposition became receivable by the taxpayer at the relevant time) if

(A) amounts that became receivable at or after the relevant time were not taken into account,

(B) each designation made under subparagraph 66.7(4)(*a*)(iii) in respect of an amount that became receivable before the relevant time were made before the relevant time,

(C) paragraph 66.7(4)(*a*) were read without reference to "30% of", and

(D) no reduction under subsection 80(8) at or after the relevant time were taken into account

exceeds the total of

(ii) all amounts that would be determined under paragraph 66.7(4)(*a*) at the relevant time in respect of the taxpayer and an original owner of the particular property (or of that other property) if

(A) amounts that became receivable after the relevant time were not taken into account,

(B) each designation made under subparagraph 66.7(4)(*a*)(iii) in respect of an amount that became receivable at or before the relevant time were made before the relevant time,

(C) paragraph 66.7(4)(*a*) were read without reference to "30% of",

(D) amounts described in subparagraph 66.7(4)(*a*)(iii) that became receivable at the relevant time were not taken into account, and

(E) no reduction under subsection 80(8) at or after the relevant time were taken into account, and

(iii) such portion of the amount otherwise determined under this paragraph as was otherwise applied to reduce the amount otherwise determined under this description,

G is the total of all amounts that became receivable by the taxpayer before that time that are to be included in the amount determined under this description by virtue of paragraph 66(12.1)(*b*) or (12.3)(*a*),

H is the total of all amounts each of which is an amount included by the taxpayer as an expense under paragraph (*a*) of the definition "Canadian development expense" in this subsection in computing the taxpayer's Canadian development expense for a previous taxation year that has become a Canadian exploration expense of the taxpayer by virtue of subparagraph (*c*)(ii) of the definition "Canadian exploration expense" in subsection 66.1(6),

I is the total of all amounts each of which is an amount that before that time has become a Canadian exploration expense of the taxpayer by virtue of subsection 66.1(9),

J is the total of all amounts each of which is an amount received before that time on account of any amount referred to in the description of C

K is the total of all amounts paid to the taxpayer after May 6, 1974 and before May 25, 1976

(*a*) under the *Northern Mineral Exploration Assistance Regulations* made under an appropriation Act that provides for payments in respect of the Northern Mineral Grants Program, or

(*b*) pursuant to any agreement, entered into between the taxpayer and Her Majesty in right of Canada under the Northern Mineral Grants Program or the Development Program of the Department of Indian Affairs and Northern Development,

to the extent that the amounts have been expended by the taxpayer as or on account of Canadian development expense incurred by the taxpayer,

L is the amount by which the total of all amounts determined under subsection 66.4(1) in respect of a taxation year of the taxpayer ending at or before that time exceeds the total of all amounts each of which is the least of

(*a*) the amount that would be determined under paragraph 66.7(4)(*a*), at a time (hereafter in this description referred to only as the "particular time") that is the end of the latest taxation year of the taxpayer ending at or before that time, in respect of the taxpayer as successor in respect of a disposition (in this description referred to as the "original disposition") of Canadian resource property by a person who is an original owner of the property because of the original disposition, if

(i) that paragraph were read without reference to "30% of",

(ii) where the taxpayer has disposed of all or part of the property in circumstances in which subsection 66.7(4) applied, that subsection continued to apply to the taxpayer in respect of the original disposition as if subsequent successors were the same person as the taxpayer, and

(iii) each designation made under subparagraph 66.7(4)(*a*)(iii) in respect of an amount that became receivable before the particular time were made before the particular time,

(*b*) the amount, if any, by which the total of all amounts each of which became receivable at or before the particular time and before 1993 by the taxpayer and is included in computing the amount determined under subparagraph 66.7(5)(*a*)(ii) in respect of the original disposition exceeds the amount, if any, by which

(i) where the taxpayer disposed of all or part of the property before the particular time in circumstances in which subsection 66.7(5) applied, the amount that would be determined at the particular time under subparagraph 66.7(5)(*a*)(i) in respect of the original disposition if that subparagraph continued to apply to the taxpayer in respect of the original disposition as if subsequent successors were the same person as the taxpayer, and

(ii) in any other case, the amount determined at the particular time under subparagraph 66.7(5)(*a*)(i) in respect of the original disposition

exceeds

(iii) the amount that would be determined at the particular time under subparagraph 66.7(5)(*a*)(ii) in respect of the original disposition if that subparagraph were read without reference to the words "or the successor", wherever they appear therein, and if amounts that became receivable after 1992 were not taken into account, and

(*c*) where

(i) after the original disposition and at or before the particular time, the taxpayer disposed of all or part of the property in circumstances in which subsection 66.7(4) applied, otherwise than by way of an amalgamation or merger or solely because of the application of paragraph 66.7(10)(*c*), and

(ii) the winding-up of the taxpayer began at or before that time or the taxpayer's disposition referred to in subparagraph (i) (other than a disposition under an agreement in writing entered into before December 22, 1992) occurred after December 21, 1992,

nil,

M is the total amount of assistance that the taxpayer has received or is entitled to receive in respect of any Canadian development expense (including an expense that has become a Canadian exploration expense of the taxpayer by virtue of subsection 66.1(9)) incurred after 1980 or that can reasonably be related to Canadian development activities after 1980,

M.1 is the total of all amounts by which the cumulative Canadian development expense of the taxpayer is required because of subsection 80(8) to be reduced at or before that time,

N is the total of all amounts that are required to be deducted before that time under subsection 66(14.2) in computing the taxpayer's cumulative Canadian development expense, and

O is the total of all amounts that are required to be deducted before that time under paragraph 66.7(12)(*c*) in computing the taxpayer's cumulative Canadian development expense.

History: S. 66.2(5), the description of B in the definition "cumulative Canadian development expense" was replaced by S.C. 2013, c. 34, s. 201(2), applicable to taxation years that end after November 5, 2010, and formerly read:

B is the total of all amounts required by virtue of subsection (1) to be included in computing the amount referred to in paragraph 59(3.2)(*c*) for taxation years ending before that time,

S. 66.2(5), the portion of the description of F before paragraph (*a*) in the definition "cumulative Canadian development expense" was replaced by S.C. 2011, c. 24, s. 15(2), deemed to have come into force on March 22, 2011. S. 66.2(5), the portion of the description of F before paragraph (*a*) in the definition "cumulative Canadian development expense" formerly read:

F is the total of all amounts each of which is an amount in respect of property described in paragraph (*b*), (*e*) or (*f*) of the definition "Canadian resource property" in subsection 66(15) or any right to or interest in such a property, other than such a right or an interest that the taxpayer has by reason of being a beneficiary under a trust or a member of a partnership, (in this description referred to as "the particular property") disposed of by the taxpayer before that time equal to the amount, if any, by which

Related Sections: S. 20(1)(*kk*) Exploration and development grants; s. 53(1)(*e*)(viii) Adjustments to cost base — Interest in a partnership; s. 59(3.2)(*c*) Recovery of exploration and development expenses; s. 66(11)(*c*) Acquisition of control; s. 66(12.1) Limitations of Canadian exploration and development expenses; s. 66(12.3) Unitized oil or gas field in Canada — Canadian development expenses; s. 66(12.62) Canadian development expenses to flow-through shareholder; s. 66(14.2) Designation respecting cumulative Canadian development expense; s. 66(15), "Canadian resource property"; s. 66.1(6) "Canadian exploration expense"; s. 66.1(9) Canadian development expenses for preceding years; s. 66.2(1) Amount to be included in income; s. 66.2(5), "Canadian development expense"; s. 66.2(6) Share of partner; s. 66.2(7) Exception; s. 66.2(8) Presumption; s. 66.4(1) Recovery of costs; s. 66.7(4) Successor of Canadian development expense; s. 66.7(5) Successor of Canadian oil and gas property expense; s. 66.7(9) Canadian development expense becoming Canadian exploration expense; s. 66.7(10) Change of control; s. 66.7(12) Reduction of Canadian resource expenses; s. 66.7(12.1)(*b*) Specified amount; s. 70(5.2) Resource properties and land inventories of a deceased taxpayer; s. 80(8) Reductions of resource expenditures; s. 104(5.2) Resource property.

Interpretation Bulletins: *Secondary* — IT-125R4 Disposition of resource properties.

▶ 66.2(5.1) ◀

(5.1) Application of ss. 66(15), 66.1(6) and 66.4(5). The definitions in subsections 66(15), 66.1(6) and 66.4(5) apply to this section.

▶ 66.2(6) ◀

(6) Share of partner. Except as provided in subsection (7), where a taxpayer is a member of a partnership, the taxpayer's share of any amount that would be an amount referred to in the description of D in the definition "cumulative Canadian development expense" in subsection (5), in paragraph (*a*) of the description of F in that definition or in the description of G or M in that definition in respect of the partnership for a taxation year of the partnership if section 96 were read without reference to paragraph 96(1)(*d*) shall, for the purposes of this Act, be deemed to be an amount referred to in the description of D in the definition "cumulative Canadian development expense" in subsection (5), in paragraph (*a*) of the description of F in that definition or in the description of G or M in that definition, whichever is applicable, in respect of the taxpayer for the taxation year of the taxpayer in which the partnership's taxation year ends.

Interpretation Bulletins: *Primary* — IT-125R4 Disposition of resource properties.

▶ 66.2(7) ◀

(7) Exception. Where a non-resident person is a member of a partnership that is deemed under paragraph 115(4)(*b*) to have disposed of any Canadian resource property, the person's share of any amount that would be an amount referred to in the description of D in the definition "cumulative Canadian development expense" in subsection (5), in paragraph (*a*) of the description of F in that definition or in the description of G or M in that definition in respect of the partnership for a taxation year of the partnership if section 96 were read without reference to paragraph 96(1)(*d*) shall, for the purposes of this Act, be deemed to be an amount referred to in the description of D in the definition "cumulative Canadian development expense" in subsection (5), in paragraph (*a*) of the description of F in that definition or in the description of G or M in that definition, whichever is applicable, in respect of the person for the taxation year of the person that is deemed under paragraph 115(4)(*a*) to have ended.

Interpretation Bulletins: *Secondary* — IT-125R4 Disposition of resource properties.

▶ 66.2(8) ◀

(8) Presumption. Where pursuant to the terms of an arrangement in writing entered into before December 12, 1979 a taxpayer acquired a property described in paragraph (*a*) of the definition "Canadian oil and gas property expense" in subsection 66.4(5), for the purposes of this Act, the cost of acquisition shall be deemed to be a Canadian development expense incurred at the time the taxpayer acquired the property.

SECTION 66.21: [Foreign resource expenses]

▶ 66.21(1) ◀

(1) Definitions. The definitions in this subsection apply in this section.

"adjusted cumulative foreign resource expense" — "adjusted cumulative foreign resource expense" of a taxpayer, in respect of a country, at the end of a taxation year means the total of (*a*) the cumulative foreign resource expense of the taxpayer, in respect of that country, at the end of the year; and

(*b*) the amount, if any, by which

(i) the total determined under paragraph 66.7(13.2)(*a*) in respect of that country and the taxpayer for the year

exceeds

(ii) the amount that would, but for paragraph (3)(*c*), be determined under subsection (3) in respect of that country and the taxpayer for the year.

Related Sections: S. 66.21(3) Amount to be included in income; s. 66.21(4) Deduction for cumulative foreign resource expense; s. 66.7(13.1) Reduction of foreign resource expenses; s. 66.7(13.2) Specified amount — foreign resource expenses.

"cumulative foreign resource expense" — "cumulative foreign resource expense" of a taxpayer, in respect of a country other than Canada at a particular time, means the amount determined by the formula

$$(A + A.1 + B + C + D) - (E + F + G + H + I + J)$$

where

A is the total of all foreign resource expenses, in respect of that country, made or incurred by the taxpayer

(*a*) before the particular time, and

(*b*) at a time (in this definition referred to as a "resident time")

(i) at which the taxpayer was resident in Canada, and

(ii) where the taxpayer became resident in Canada before the particular time, that is after the last time (before the particular time) that the taxpayer became resident in Canada;

A.1 is the total of all foreign resource expenses, in respect of that country, that is the cost to the taxpayer of any of the taxpayer's foreign resource property in respect of that country that is deemed to have been acquired by the taxpayer under paragraph 128.1(1)(*c*) at the last time (before the particular time) that the taxpayer became resident in Canada;

B is the total of all amounts included in computing the amount referred to in paragraph 59(3.2)(*c.1*) in respect of that country, for taxation years that ended before the particular time and at a resident time;

C is the total of all amounts referred to in the description of F or G that are established by the taxpayer to have become a bad debt before the particular time and at a resident time;

D is the total of all specified amounts determined under subsection 66.7(13.2), in respect of the taxpayer and that country, for taxation years that ended before the particular time and at a resident time;

E is the total of all amounts deducted, in computing the taxpayer's income for a taxation year that ended before the particular time and at a resident time, in respect of the taxpayer's cumulative foreign resource expense in respect of that country;

F is the total of all amounts each of which is an amount in respect of a foreign resource property, in respect of that country, (in this description referred to as the "particular property") disposed of by the taxpayer equal to the amount, if any, by which

(*a*) the amount designated under subparagraph 59(1)(*b*)(ii) by the taxpayer in respect of the portion of the proceeds of that disposition that became receivable before the particular time and at a resident time

exceeds

(*b*) the amount, if any, by which

(i) the total of all amounts that would be determined under paragraph 66.7(2.3)(*a*), immediately before the time (in this paragraph referred to as the "relevant time") when such proceeds of disposition became receivable, in respect of the taxpayer, that country and an original owner of the particular property (or of any other property acquired by the taxpayer with the particular property in circumstances to which subsection 66.7(2.3) applied and in respect of which the proceeds of disposition became receivable by the taxpayer at the relevant time) if

(A) amounts that became receivable at or after the relevant time were not taken into account,

(B) paragraph 66.7(2.3)(*a*) were read without reference to "30% of", and

(C) no reduction under subsection 80(8) at or after the relevant time were taken into account

exceeds the total of

(ii) all amounts that would be determined under paragraph 66.7(2.3)(*a*) at the relevant time in respect of the taxpayer, that country and an original owner of the particular property (or of that other property) if

(A) amounts that became receivable after the relevant time were not taken into account,

(B) paragraph 66.7(2.3)(*a*) were read without reference to "30% of", and

(C) no reduction under subsection 80(8) at or after the relevant time were taken into account, and

(iii) the portion of the amount otherwise determined under this paragraph that was otherwise applied to reduce the amount otherwise determined under this description;

G is the total of all amounts, in respect of that country, each of which is an amount included in the amount determined under this description by reason of subsection 66(12.41) that became receivable by the taxpayer before the particular time and at a resident time;

H is the total of all amounts each of which is an amount received before the particular time and at a resident time on account of any amount referred to in the description of C;

I is the total of all amounts each of which is an amount by which the cumulative foreign resource expense of the taxpayer, in respect of that country, is required, by reason of subsection 80(8), to be reduced at or before the particular time and at a resident time; and

J is the total of all amounts each of which is an amount that is required to be deducted, before the particular time and at a resident time, under paragraph 66.7(13.1)(*a*) in computing the taxpayer's cumulative foreign resource expense.

History: S. 66.21(1), the formula in the definition "cumulative foreign resource expense" was replaced by S.C. 2013, c. 34, s. 202(1), deemed to have come into force on January 1, 2005, and formerly read:

(A + B + C + D) - (E + F + G + H + I + J)

S. 66.21(1), the description of A.1 in the definition "cumulative foreign resource expense" was added by S.C. 2013, c. 34, s. 202(2), deemed to have come into force on January 1, 2005.

S. 66.21(1), the description of B in the definition "cumulative foreign resource expense" was replaced by S.C. 2013, c. 34, s. 202(3), applicable to taxation years that end after November 5, 2010, and formerly read:

B is the total of all amounts required to be included in computing the amount referred to in paragraph 59(3.2)(c.1), in respect of that country, for taxation years that ended before the particular time and at a resident time;

Related Sections: S. 59(1) Consideration for foreign resource property; s. 59(3.2) Recovery of exploration and development expenses; s. 66(5) Dealers; s. 66(11.4) Loss restriction event; s. 66(12.41) Limitations of foreign resource expenses; s. 66(12.42) Partnerships; s. 66.21(4) Deduction for cumulative foreign resource expense; s. 66.7(2.3) Successor of foreign resource expenses; s. 66.7(13.1) Reduction of foreign resource expenses; s. 66.7(13.2) Specified amount — foreign resource expenses; s. 80(8) Reductions of resource expenditures; s. 87(1.2) New corporation continuation of a predecessor; s. 88(1.5) Parent continuation of subsidiary; s. 104(5.2) Resource property; s. 110.6(1) Definitions — fair market value of NISA; s. 115(4.1) Foreign resource pool expenses; s. 248(1), "foreign resource property".

Canadian Petroleum Tax Journal: Selected Income Tax Considerations When Structuring Foreign Resource Ventures, William A. Brebber, 2002, Vol. 15, No. 1; Foreign Exploration and Development Expenditures — The New Rules, Roch J. Martin, 2001, Vol. 14, No. 1.

"foreign resource expense" — "foreign resource expense" of a taxpayer, in respect of a country other than Canada, means

(*a*) any drilling or exploration expense, including any general geological or geophysical expense, incurred by the taxpayer on or in respect of exploring or drilling for petroleum or natural gas in that country,

(*b*) any expense incurred by the taxpayer for the purpose of determining the existence, location, extent or quality of a mineral resource in that country, including any expense incurred in the course of

(i) prospecting,

(ii) carrying out geological, geophysical or geochemical surveys,

(iii) drilling by rotary, diamond, percussion or other methods, or

(iv) trenching, digging test pits and preliminary sampling,

(*c*) the cost to the taxpayer of any of the taxpayer's foreign resource property in respect of that country,

(*d*) any annual payment made by the taxpayer for the preservation of a foreign resource property in respect of that country, and

(*e*) subject to section 66.8, the taxpayer's share of an expense, cost or payment referred to in any of paragraphs (*a*) to (*d*) that is made or incurred by a partnership in a fiscal period of the partnership that begins after 2000 if, at the end of that period, the taxpayer was a member of the partnership

but does not include

(*f*) an expenditure that is the cost, or any part of the cost, to the taxpayer of any depreciable property of a prescribed class,

(*g*) an expenditure incurred at any time after the commencement of production from a foreign resource property of the taxpayer in order to evaluate the feasibility of a method of recovery of petroleum, natural gas or related hydrocarbons from the portion of a natural reservoir to which the foreign resource property relates,

(*h*) an expenditure (other than a drilling expense) incurred at any time after the commencement of production from a foreign resource property of the taxpayer in order to assist in the recovery of petroleum, natural gas or related hydrocarbons from the portion of a natural reservoir to which the foreign resource property relates,

(*i*) an expenditure, incurred at any time, that relates to the injection of any substance to assist in the recovery of petroleum, natural gas or related hydrocarbons from a natural reservoir,

(*j*) an expenditure incurred by the taxpayer, unless the expenditure was made

(i) for the acquisition of foreign resource property by the taxpayer, or

(ii) for the purpose of

(A) enhancing the value of foreign resource property that the taxpayer owned at the time the expenditure was incurred or that the taxpayer had a reasonable expectation of owning after that time, or

(B) assisting in evaluating whether a foreign resource property is to be acquired by the taxpayer, or

(*k*) the taxpayer's share of any cost or expenditure referred to in any of paragraphs (*f*) to (*j*) that is incurred by a partnership.

Editorial Note: Foreign resource expenses ("FRE") generally include expenses in respect of drilling, prospecting, exploration and acquisition costs relating to a foreign resource property. They do not include expenses incurred to acquire depreciable property. The category of expenses as set out in the definition of FRE is very similar to the expenses set out in the definition of FEDE, and the definition of FEDE contains similar but not identical aspects of the definitions of CEE, CDE and COGPE.

Related Sections: S. 66(18) Members of partnerships; s. 66.7(2.3) Successor of foreign resource expenses; s. 66.8 Resource expenses of limited partner; s. 248(1), "foreign resource property".

Canadian Petroleum Tax Journal: Selected Income Tax Considerations When Structuring Foreign Resource Ventures, William A. Brebber, 2002, Vol. 15, No. 1; Foreign Exploration and Development Expenditures — The New Rules, Roch J. Martin, 2001, Vol. 14, No. 1.

"foreign resource income" —"foreign resource income" of a taxpayer for a taxation year, in respect of a country other than Canada, means the total of

(*a*) that part of the taxpayer's income for the year, determined without reference to subsections (4) and 66(4), that is reasonably attributable to

(i) the production of petroleum or natural gas from natural accumulations of petroleum or natural gas in that country or from oil or gas wells in that country, or

(ii) the production of minerals from mines in that country;

(*b*) the taxpayer's income for the year from royalties in respect of a natural accumulation of petroleum or natural gas in that country, an oil or gas well in that country or a mine in that country, determined without reference to subsections (4) and 66(4); and

(*c*) all amounts each of which is an amount, in respect of a foreign resource property in respect of that country that has been disposed of by the taxpayer, equal to the amount, if any, by which

(i) the amount included in computing the taxpayer's income for the year by reason of subsection 59(1) in respect of that disposition

exceeds

(ii) the total of all amounts each of which is that portion of an amount deducted under subsection 66.7(2) in computing the taxpayer's income for the year that

(A) can reasonably be considered to be in respect of the foreign resource property, and

(B) cannot reasonably be considered to have reduced the amount otherwise determined under paragraph (*a*) or (*b*) in respect of the taxpayer for the year.

Related Sections: S. 59(1) Consideration for foreign resource property; s. 66(4) Foreign exploration and development expenses; s. 66.21(4) Deduction for cumulative foreign resource expense; s. 66.7(2) Successor of foreign exploration and development expenses; s. 66.7(2.3) Successor of foreign resource expenses; s. 248(1), "foreign resource property".

"foreign resource loss" —"foreign resource loss" of a taxpayer for a taxation year in respect of a country other than Canada means the taxpayer's loss for the year in respect of the country determined in accordance with the definition "foreign resource income" with such modifications as the circumstances require.

Related Sections: S. 66.21(4)(*a*)(ii) Deduction for cumulative foreign resource expense.

"global foreign resource limit" —"global foreign resource limit" of a taxpayer for a taxation year means the amount that is the lesser of

(*a*) the amount, if any, by which

(i) the amount determined under subparagraph 66(4)(*b*)(ii) in respect of the taxpayer for the year

exceeds the total of

(ii) the total of all amounts each of which is the maximum amount that the taxpayer would be permitted to deduct, in respect of a country, under subsection (4) in computing the taxpayer's income for the year if, in its application to the year, subsection (4) were read without reference to paragraph (4)(*b*), and

(iii) the amount deducted for the year under subsection 66(4) in computing the taxpayer's income for the year; and

(*b*) the amount, if any, by which

(i) 30% of the total of all amounts each of which is, at the end of the year, the taxpayer's adjusted cumulative foreign resource expense in respect of a country

exceeds

(ii) the total described in subparagraph (*a*)(ii).

Related Sections: S. 66(4) Foreign exploration and development expenses; s. 66(13.1) Short taxation year; s. 66.21(4) Deduction for cumulative foreign resource expense.

► 66.21(2) ◄

(2) Application of subsection 66(15). The definitions in subsection 66(15) apply in this section.

Related Sections: S. 66(15) Definitions.

► 66.21(3) ◄

(3) Amount to be included in income. For the purpose of paragraph 59(3.2)(*c*.1), the amount referred to in this subsection in respect of a taxpayer for a taxation year is the amount, if any, by which

(*a*) the total of all amounts referred to in the descriptions of E to J in the definition "cumulative foreign resource expense" in subsection (1) that are deducted in computing the taxpayer's cumulative foreign resource expense at the end of the year in respect of a country

exceeds the total of

(*b*) the total of all amounts referred to in the descriptions of A to D in the definition "cumulative foreign resource expense" in subsection (1) that are included in computing the taxpayer's cumulative foreign resource expense at the end of the year in respect of the country, and

(*c*) the total determined under paragraph 66.7(13.2)(*a*) for the year in respect of the taxpayer and the country.

Related Sections: S. 59(3.2) Recovery of exploration and development expenses; s. 66(5) Dealers; s. 66(11.4) Loss restriction event; s. 66.8 Resource expenses of limited partner; s. 70(5.2)(*a*) Resource properties and land inventories of a deceased taxpayer; s. 88(1.5) Parent continuation of subsidiary.

► 66.21(4) ◄

(4) Deduction for cumulative foreign resource expense. In computing a taxpayer's income for a taxation year throughout which the taxpayer is resident in Canada, the taxpayer may deduct the amount claimed by the taxpayer, in respect of a country other than Canada, not exceeding the total of

(*a*) the greater of

(i) 10% of a particular amount equal to the taxpayer's adjusted cumulative foreign resource expense in respect of the country at the end of the year, and

(ii) the least of

(A) if the taxpayer ceased to be resident in Canada immediately after the end of the year, the particular amount,

(B) if clause (A) does not apply, 30% of the particular amount,

(C) the amount, if any, by which the taxpayer's foreign resource income for the year in respect of the country exceeds the portion of the amount, deducted under subsection 66(4) in computing the taxpayer's income for the year, that applies to a source in the country, and

(D) the amount, if any, by which

(I) the total of all amounts each of which is the taxpayer's foreign resource income for the year in respect of a country

exceeds the total of

(II) all amounts each of which is the taxpayer's foreign resource loss for the year in respect of a country, and

(III) the amount deducted under subsection 66(4) in computing the taxpayer's income for the year, and

(*b*) the lesser of

(i) the amount, if any, by which the particular amount exceeds the amount determined for the year under paragraph (*a*) in respect of the taxpayer, and

(ii) that portion of the taxpayer's global foreign resource limit for the year that is designated for the year by the taxpayer, in respect of that country and no other country, in prescribed form filed with the Minister with the taxpayer's return of income for the year.

Editorial Note: Section 66.21 provides for the deduction of foreign resource expenses incurred in a country by a taxpayer. For taxation years commencing prior to 2001, all expenses incurred outside Canada in connection with oil and gas and mining activities were classified as FEDE. Starting with taxation years commencing after 2000, such expenses are categorized as foreign resource expenses ("FRE") in respect of a country. Such expenses are added to a taxpayer's cumulative foreign resource expense ("CFRE") in respect of the country. A taxpayer may claim a deduction in respect of each country based on its income incurred in that country. A taxpayer may claim a deduction equal to the greater of 10% of the taxpayer's adjusted CFRE and 30% of the taxpayer's income earned in the country in the year. The taxpayer is also entitled to an additional deduction in respect of its global foreign resource limit. A taxpayer may claim an additional deduction if it disposed of its foreign resource expenses in the year in accordance with the successor corporation rules. The taxpayer must include in income any amount by which its CFRE is negative at the end of the year less any amount which the taxpayer may claim by virtue of disposing in the year of its foreign resource properties in accordance with the successor corporation rules.

Related Sections: S. 20(1)(*hh*) Repayments of inducements, etc.; s. 66(5) Dealers; s. 66(8) Successor corporation's foreign exploration and development expenses; s. 66(11.4) Loss restriction event; s. 66(13.1) Short taxation year; s. 66.21(5) Individual changing residence; s. 70(5.2) Resource properties and land inventories of a deceased taxpayer; s. 87(1.2) New corporation continuation of a predecessor; s. 88(1.5) Parent continuation of subsidiary; s. 115(4.1) Foreign resource pool expenses; s. 127.52(1) Adjusted taxable income determined.

Canadian Petroleum Tax Journal: Selected Income Tax Considerations When Structuring Foreign Resource Ventures, William A. Brebber, 2002, Vol. 15, No. 1; Foreign Exploration and Development Expenditures — The New Rules, Roch J. Martin, 2001, Vol. 14, No. 1.

▶ 66.21(5) ◀

(5) Individual changing residence. Where at any time in a taxation year an individual becomes or ceases to be resident in Canada,

(*a*) subsection (4) applies to the individual as if the year were the period or periods in the year throughout which the individual was resident in Canada; and

(*b*) for the purpose of applying this section, subsection 66(13.1) does not apply to the individual for the year.

Related Sections: S. 66(4.3) FEDE deductions where change of individual's residence; s. 66(13.1) Short taxation year; s. 114 Individual resident in Canada for only part of year; s. 128.1 Immigration.

SECTION 66.3: Exploration and development shares

▶ 66.3(1) ◀

(1) Exploration and development shares. Any shares of the capital stock of a corporation or any interest in any such shares or right thereto acquired by a taxpayer under circumstances described in paragraph (*i*) of the definition "Canadian exploration expense" in subsection 66.1(6), paragraph (*g*) of the definition "Canadian development expense" in subsection 66.2(5) or paragraph (*c*) of the definition "Canadian oil and gas property expense" in subsection 66.4(5)

(*a*) shall, if acquired before November 13, 1981, be deemed

(i) not to be a capital property of the taxpayer,

(ii) subject to subsection 142.6(3), to be inventory of the taxpayer, and

(iii) to have been acquired by the taxpayer at a cost to the taxpayer of nil; and

(*b*) shall, if acquired after November 12, 1981, be deemed to have been acquired by the taxpayer at a cost to the taxpayer of nil.

Related Regulations: 5101 [Small business investment corporation]; 5102 [Small business investment limited partnership]; 5103 [Small business investment trust].

Related Sections: S. 66(18) Members of partnerships; s. 66.4(2) Deduction for cumulative Canadian oil and gas property expense.

▶ 66.3(2) ◀

(2) Deductions from paid-up capital. If, at any time after May 23, 1985, a corporation has issued a share of its capital stock under circumstances described in paragraph (*i*) of the definition "Canadian exploration expense" in subsection 66.1(6), paragraph (*g*) of the definition "Canadian development expense" in subsection 66.2(5) or paragraph (*c*) of the definition "Canadian oil and gas property expense" in subsection 66.4(5) or has issued a share of its capital stock on the exercise of an interest in or right to — or, for civil law, a right in or to — such a share granted under circumstances described in any of those paragraphs, in computing, at any particular time after that time, the paid-up capital in respect of the class of shares of the capital stock of the corporation that included that share

(*a*) there shall be deducted the amount, if any, by which

(i) the increase as a result of the issue of the share in the paid-up capital, determined without reference to this subsection as it applies to the share, in respect of all of the shares of that class

exceeds

(ii) the amount, if any, by which

(A) the total amount of consideration received by the corporation in respect of the share, including any consideration for the interest or right in respect of the share

exceeds

(B) 50% of the amount of the expense referred to in paragraph (*i*) of the definition "Canadian exploration expense" in subsection 66.1(6), paragraph (*g*) of the definition "Canadian development expense" in subsection 66.2(5) or paragraph (*c*) of the definition "Canadian oil and gas property expense" in subsection 66.4(5) that was incurred by a taxpayer who acquired the share or the interest or right on the exercise of which the share was issued, as the case may be, pursuant to an agreement with the corporation under which the taxpayer incurred the expense solely as consideration for the share, interest or right, as the case may be; and

(*b*) there shall be added an amount equal to the lesser of

(i) the amount, if any, by which

(A) the total of all amounts each of which is an amount deemed by subsection 84(3), (4) or (4.1) to be a dividend on shares of that class paid by the corporation after May 23, 1985 and before the particular time

exceeds

(B) the total that would be determined under clause (A) if this Act were read without reference to paragraph (*a*), and

(ii) the total of all amounts each of which is an amount required by paragraph (*a*) to be deducted in computing the paid-up capital in respect of that class of shares after May 22, 1985 and before the particular time.

History: S. 66.3(2), the portion before paragraph (*a*) was replaced by S.C. 2013, c. 34, s. 114, in force June 26, 2013, and formerly read:

(2) *Deductions from paid-up capital.* Where, at any time after May 23, 1985, a corporation has issued a share of its capital stock under circumstances described in paragraph (*i*) of the definition "Canadian exploration expense" in subsection 66.1(6), paragraph (*g*) of the definition "Canadian development expense" in subsection 66.2(5) or paragraph (*c*) of the definition "Canadian oil and gas property expense" in subsection 66.4(5) or has issued a share of its capital stock on the exercise of an interest in or right to such a share granted under circumstances described in any of those paragraphs, in computing, at any particular time after that time, the paid-up capital in respect of the class of shares of the capital stock of the corporation that included that share

Related Sections: S. 66.3(4) Paid-up capital.

► 66.3(3) ◄

(3) Cost of flow-through shares. Any flow-through share (within the meaning assigned by subsection 66(15)) of a corporation acquired by a person who was a party to the agreement pursuant to which it was issued shall be deemed to have been acquired by the person at a cost to the person of nil.

Editorial Note: In light of the preferential tax treatment given to subscribers of flow-through shares, this subsection confirms that the adjusted cost base of a flow-through share acquired by a taxpayer pursuant to a flow-through share agreement is nil. Generally speaking, flow-through shares are considered capital property to the investor; accordingly, the investor will realize a capital gain on the disposition of a flow-through share equal to the full proceeds received by the investor for the share.

Related Sections: 66(12.6) Canadian exploration expenses to flow-through shareholder; 66(12.601) Flow-through share rules for first $1 million of Canadian development expenses; 66(12.6011) Taxable capital amount; 66(12.6012) Taxable capital employed in Canada; 66(12.6013) Amalgamations and mergers; 66(12.602) Idem; 66(12.61) Effect of renunciation; 66(12.62) Canadian development expenses to flow-through shareholder; 66(12.63) Effect of renunciation; 66(12.66) Expenses in the first 60 days of year; 66(12.67) Restrictions on renunciation; 66(12.671) Prohibited relationship; 66(12.68) Filing selling instruments; 66(12.69) Filing re partners; 66(12.6901) Consequences of failure to file; 66(12.691) Filing re assistance; 66(12.7) Filing re renunciation; 66(12.7001) Consequences of failure to file; 66(12.701) Filing re assistance; 66(12.702) Consequences of failure to file; 66(12.71) Restriction on renunciation; 66(12.73) Reductions in renunciations.

► 66.3(4) ◄

(4) Paid-up capital. Where, at any time after February, 1986, a corporation has issued a flow-through share (within the meaning assigned by subsection 66(15)), in computing, at any particular time after that time, the paid-up capital in respect of the class of shares of the capital stock of the corporation that included that share

(*a*) there shall be deducted the amount, if any, by which

(i) the increase as a result of the issue of the share in the paid-up capital, determined without reference to this subsection as it applies to the share, in respect of all of the shares of that class

exceeds

(ii) the amount, if any, by which

(A) the total amount of consideration received by the corporation in respect of the share

exceeds

(B) 50% of the total of the expenses that were renounced by the corporation under subsection 66(12.6), (12.601), (12.62) or (12.64) in respect of the share; and

(*b*) there shall be added an amount equal to the lesser of

(i) the amount, if any, by which

(A) the total of all amounts each of which is an amount deemed by subsection 84(3), (4) or (4.1) to be a dividend on shares of that class paid by the corporation after February, 1986 and before the particular time

exceeds

(B) the total that would be determined under clause (A) if this Act were read without reference to paragraph (*a*), and

(ii) the total of all amounts each of which is an amount required by paragraph (*a*) to be deducted in computing the paid-up capital in respect of that class of shares after February, 1986 and before the particular time.

SECTION 66.4: Recovery of costs

▶ 66.4(1) ◀

(1) Recovery of costs. For the purposes of the description of B in the definition "cumulative Canadian oil and gas property expense" in subsection (5) and the description of L in the definition "cumulative Canadian development expense" in subsection 66.2(5) and for the purpose of subparagraph 64(1.2)(*a*)(ii) of the *Income Tax Act*, chapter 148 of the Revised Statutes of Canada, 1952, as it applies to dispositions occurring before November 13, 1981, the amount determined under this subsection in respect of a taxpayer for a taxation year is the amount, if any, by which

(*a*) the total of all amounts referred to in the descriptions of E to J in the definition "cumulative Canadian oil and gas property expense" in subsection (5) that are deducted in computing the taxpayer's cumulative Canadian oil and gas property expense at the end of the year

exceeds the total of

(*b*) all amounts referred to in the descriptions of A to D.1 in the definition "cumulative Canadian oil and gas property expense" in subsection (5) that are included in computing the taxpayer's cumulative Canadian oil and gas property expense at the end of the year, and

(*c*) the total determined under subparagraph 66.7(12.1)(*c*)(i) in respect of the taxpayer for the year.

Editorial Note: Section 66.4 provides for the deduction by a taxpayer of its Canadian oil and gas property expenses ("COGPE"). COGPE include the cost of purchasing oil and gas properties, including the cost of land, exploration rights, licences, permits and leases, and a royalty interest in an oil and gas property in Canada. The taxpayer adds its COGPE to its cumulative Canadian oil and gas property expense ("CCOGPE"). A taxpayer may claim an optional deduction of 10% of its CCOGPE at the end of the year. In addition, a taxpayer may also claim an additional deduction if it disposes in the year of its Canadian resource properties in accordance with the successor corporation rules. The proceeds of disposition of Canadian oil and gas properties are deducted from the taxpayer's CCOGPE in the year of disposition. If the CCOGPE account is negative at the end of the year, the taxpayer must deduct the negative amount from its CCDE account. A taxpayer may carry forward indefinitely any undeducted balance in its CCOGPE account and claim such amount in subsequent years.

In addition to the 10% deduction, accelerated rates apply to "accelerated Canadian oil and gas property expense" incurred after November 20, 2018 and before 2028. The accelerated rates equal the existing 10% plus an additional percentage depending on the taxation year (see paragraph 66.2(4)(c)). The additional percentage is 5% for taxation years that end before 2024 (for a total of 15%) and 2.5% for taxation years that begin after 2023 (for a total of 12.5%). For a taxation year that straddles December 31, 2023, the additional rate equals a portion of 5% plus a portion of 2.5% based on the expenditures incurred before and after 2024, respectively, relative to the total incurred in the taxation year.

Related Sections: S. 66(5) Dealers; s. 66(11) Acquisition of control; s. 66(13) Limitation; s. 66(15) Definitions; s. 66(18) Members of partnerships; s. 66.1(6) Definitions; s. 66.2(5) Definitions; s. 104(5.2) Resource property; s. 127.5 Obligation to pay minimum tax.

Interpretation Bulletins: *Secondary* — IT-273R2 Government assistance — General comments.

▶ 66.4(2) ◀

(2) Deduction for cumulative Canadian oil and gas property expense. A taxpayer may deduct, in computing the taxpayer's income for a taxation year, such amount as the taxpayer may claim not exceeding the total of

(*a*) the lesser of

(i) the total of

(A) the taxpayer's cumulative Canadian oil and gas property expense at the end of the year, and

(B) the amount, if any, by which

(I) the total determined under subparagraph 66.7(12.1)(*c*)(i) in respect of the taxpayer for the year

exceeds

(II) the amount that would, but for paragraph (1)(*c*), be determined under subsection (1) in respect of the taxpayer for the year, and

(ii) the amount, if any, by which the total of all amounts each of which is

(A) an amount included in the taxpayer's income for the year by virtue of a disposition in the year of inventory described in section 66.3 that was a share or any interest in or right to — or, for civil law, any right in or to — a share acquired by the taxpayer under circumstances described in paragraph (*c*) of the definition "Canadian oil and gas property expense" in subsection (5), or

(B) an amount included by virtue of paragraph 12(1)(*e*) in computing the taxpayer's income for the year to the extent that it relates to inventory described in clause (A)

exceeds

(C) the total of all amounts deducted as a reserve by virtue of paragraph 20(1)(*n*) in computing the taxpayer's income for the year to the extent that the reserve relates to inventory described in clause (A);

(*b*) 10% of the amount, if any, by which the amount determined under subparagraph (*a*)(i) exceeds the amount determined under subparagraph (*a*)(ii); and

(*c*) the amount determined by the formula

$$A(B - C)$$

where

A is

(i) for taxation years that end before 2024, 5%,

(ii) for taxation years that begin before 2024 and end after 2023, the amount determined by the formula

$$0.05(I/J) + 0.025(K/J)$$

where

I is the total of all accelerated Canadian oil and gas property expenses incurred by the taxpayer before 2024 and in the taxation year,

J is the total of all accelerated Canadian oil and gas property expenses incurred by the taxpayer in the taxation year, and

K is the total of all accelerated Canadian oil and gas property expenses incurred by the taxpayer after 2023 and in the taxation year, and

(iii) for taxation years that begin after 2023, 2.5%,

B is the total of all accelerated Canadian oil and gas property expenses incurred by the taxpayer in the taxation year, and

C is the amount determined by the formula

$$(D - E) - (F - G - H)$$

where

D is the total of the amounts determined for E to J in the definition "cumulative Canadian oil and gas property expense" in subsection (5) at the end of the taxation year,

E is the total of the amounts determined for E to J in the definition "cumulative Canadian oil and gas property expense" in subsection (5) at the beginning of the taxation year,

F is the total of the amounts determined for A to D.1 in the definition "cumulative Canadian oil and gas property expense" in subsection (5) at the end of the taxation year,

G is the total of the amounts determined for A to D.1 in the definition "cumulative Canadian oil and gas property expense" in subsection (5) at the end of the preceding taxation year, and

H is the amount determined for B.

Editorial Note: See the editorial note following subsection 66.4(1) regarding the deduction of Canadian oil and gas property expenses, including the accelerated deduction.

History: S. 66.4(2)(*c*) was added by S.C. 2019, c. 29, s. 6(1), effective June 21, 2019.

S. 66.4(2)(*a*)(ii)(A) was replaced by S.C. 2013, c. 34, s. 115(1), in force June 26, 2013, and formerly read:

(A) an amount included in the taxpayer's income for the year by virtue of a disposition in the year of inventory described in section 66.3 that was a share, any interest therein or right thereto acquired by the taxpayer under circumstances described in paragraph (*c*) of the definition "Canadian oil and gas property expense" in subsection (5), or

Related Sections: S. 66.2(2) Deduction for cumulative Canadian development expenses; s. 66.4(5) "cumulative Canadian oil and gas property expense"; s. 209 Tax on carved-out income.

Interpretation Bulletins: *Secondary* — IT-438R2 Crown charges — Resource properties in Canada.

► 66.4(3) ◄

(3) Successor corporation's Canadian oil and gas property expense — (Repealed by 1987, c. 46, s. 21(1).)

► 66.4(4) ◄

(4) Second successor corporation's Canadian oil and gas property expense — (Repealed by 1987, c. 46, s. 21(2).)

► 66.4(5) ◄

(5) Definitions. In this section,

accelerated Canadian oil and gas property expense — "accelerated Canadian oil and gas property expense", of a taxpayer, means any cost or expense incurred by the taxpayer during a taxation year, if the cost or expense

(*a*) qualifies as a Canadian oil and gas property expense at the time it is incurred, other than

(i) an expense in respect of which the taxpayer is a successor, within the meaning of subsection 66.7(5), and

(ii) a cost in respect of a Canadian resource property acquired by the taxpayer, or a partnership in which the taxpayer is a member, from a person or partnership with which the taxpayer does not deal at arm's length, and

(*b*) is incurred after November 20, 2018 and before 2028;

History: S. 66.4(5), the definition of "accelerated Canadian oil and gas property expense", was added by S.C. 2019, c. 29, s. 6(2), effective June 21, 2019.

"Canadian oil and gas property expense" — "Canadian oil and gas property expense" of a taxpayer means any cost or expense incurred after December 11, 1979 that is

(*a*) the cost to the taxpayer of, including any payment for the preservation of a taxpayer's rights in respect of, any property described in paragraph (*a*), (*c*) or (*d*) of the definition "Canadian resource property" in subsection 66(15) or any right to or interest in — or, for civil law, any right in or to — the property (other than a right or an interest that the taxpayer has by reason of being a beneficiary under a trust or a member of a partnership), or an amount paid to Her Majesty in right of the Province of Saskatchewan as a net royalty payment pursuant to a net royalty petroleum and natural gas lease that was in effect on March 31, 1977 to the extent that it can reasonably be regarded as a cost of acquiring the lease,

(*b*) subject to section 66.8, the taxpayer's share of any expense referred to in paragraph (*a*) incurred by a partnership in a fiscal period thereof at the end of which the taxpayer was a member of the partnership, unless the taxpayer elects in respect of the share in prescribed form and manner on or before the day that is 6 months after the taxpayer's taxation year in which that period ends, or

(*c*) any cost or expense referred to in paragraph (*a*) incurred by the taxpayer pursuant to an agreement in writing with a corporation, entered into before 1987, under which the taxpayer incurred the cost or expense solely as consideration for shares, other than prescribed shares, of the capital stock of the corporation issued to the taxpayer or any interest in or right to — or, for civil law, any right in or to — such shares,

but, for greater certainty, shall not include

(*d*) any consideration given by the taxpayer for any share or any interest therein or right thereto, except as provided by paragraph (*c*), or

(*e*) any expense described in paragraph (*c*) incurred by any other taxpayer to the extent that the expense was,

(i) by virtue of that paragraph, a Canadian oil and gas property expense of that other taxpayer,

(ii) by virtue of paragraph (*i*) of the definition "Canadian exploration expense" in subsection 66.1(6), a Canadian exploration expense of that other taxpayer, or

(iii) by virtue of paragraph (*g*) of the definition "Canadian development expense" in subsection 66.2(5), a Canadian development expense of that other taxpayer,

but any amount of assistance that a taxpayer has received or is entitled to receive in respect of or related to the taxpayer's Canadian oil and gas property expense shall not reduce the amount of any of the expenses described in any of paragraphs (*a*) to (*c*);

History: S. 66.4(5), paragraph (*a*) of the definition "Canadian oil and gas property expense" was replaced by S.C. 2013, c. 34, s. 203(1), applicable to taxation years that begin after 2006, except that in its application to the taxation years that begin in 2007, paragraph (*a*) of the definition "Canadian oil and gas property expense" in subsection 66.4(5) is to be read as follows:

"(*a*) notwithstanding paragraph 18(1)(*m*), the cost to the taxpayer of, including any payment for the preservation of a taxpayer's rights in respect of, any property described in paragraph (*a*), (*c*) or (*d*) of the definition "Canadian resource property" in subsection 66(15) or any right to or interest in — or, for civil law, any right in or to — the property (other than a right or an interest that the taxpayer has by reason of being a beneficiary under a trust or a member of a partnership), or an amount paid or payable to Her Majesty in right of the Province of Saskatchewan as a net royalty payment pursuant to a net royalty petroleum and natural gas lease that was in effect on March 31, 1977 to the extent that it can reasonably be regarded as a cost of acquiring the lease, but not including any payment made to any of the persons referred to in subparagraph 18(1)(*m*)(i) for the preservation of a taxpayer's right in respect of a Canadian resource property, nor a payment (other than a net royalty payment referred to in this paragraph) to which paragraph 18(1)(*m*) applied because of clause 18(1)(*m*)(ii)(B),"

S. 66.4(5), paragraph (*a*) of the definition "Canadian oil and gas property expense" formerly read:

(*a*) the cost to the taxpayer of, including any payment for the preservation of a taxpayer's rights in respect of, any property described in paragraph (*a*), (*c*) or (*d*) of the definition "Canadian resource property" in subsection 66(15), or any right to or interest in such property (other than a right or an interest that the taxpayer has by reason of being a beneficiary under a trust or a member of a partnership), or an amount paid to Her Majesty in right of the Province of Saskatchewan as a net royalty payment pursuant to a net royalty petroleum and natural gas lease that was in effect on March 31, 1977 to the extent that it can reasonably be regarded as a cost of acquiring the lease,

S. 66.4(5), paragraph (*c*) of the definition "Canadian oil and gas property expense" was replaced by S.C. 2013, c. 34, s. 115(2), in force June 26, 2013, and formerly read:

(*c*) any cost or expense referred to in paragraph (*a*) incurred by the taxpayer pursuant to an agreement in writing with a corporation, entered into before 1987, under which the taxpayer incurred the cost or expense solely as consideration for shares, other than prescribed shares, of the capital stock of the corporation issued to the taxpayer or any interest in such shares or right thereto,

Related Regulations: 6202(1).

Related Sections: S. 18(1)(*m*) Limitation re employee stock option expenses; s. 49(2) Where option granted by a corporation expires; s. 53(1)(*e*)(vii.1) Adjustments to cost base — Interest in a partnership; s. 53(2)(*c*) Amounts to be deducted — Interest in a partnership; s. 53(2)(*e*) Amounts to be deducted — Share, where shareholder incurred exploration and development expenses; s. 53(2)(*f*) Amounts to be deducted — Property received from joint exploration corporation; s. 53(2)(*f*.1) Amounts to be deducted — Share of the capital stock of joint exploration corporation; s. 66(12.5) Unitized oil or gas field in Canada; s. 66(15), "assistance", "Canadian resource property"; s. 66.1(6), "Canadian exploration expense"; s. 66.2(5), "Canadian development expense"; s. 66.2(8) Presumption; s. 66.3 Exploration and development shares; s. 66.4(6) Share of partner; s. 66.4(7) Exception; s. 66.8 Resource expenses of limited partner; s. 80(8) Reductions of resource expenditures.

Canadian Petroleum Tax Journal: Offshore Oil & Gas Interests: A Perspective on Exploration & Development of Offshore Petroleum and Natural Gas Resources in Eastern Canada, Michael R. Smith, CA and B. David Nielsen, CA, 2000, Vol. 13, No. 1.

Forms: T1086 — Election by a Partner Waiving Canadian Development Expenses or Oil and Gas Property Expenses.

Interpretation Bulletins: *Secondary* — IT-125R4 Disposition of resource properties; IT-438R2 Crown charges — Resource properties in Canada.

"cumulative Canadian oil and gas property expense" — "cumulative Canadian oil and gas property expense" of a taxpayer at any time in a taxation year means the amount determined by the formula

$$(A + B + C + D + D.1) - (E + F + G + H + I + I.1 + J)$$

where

A is the total of all Canadian oil and gas property expenses made or incurred by the taxpayer before that time,

B is the total of all amounts determined under subsection (1) in respect of the taxpayer for taxation years ending before that time,

C is the total of all amounts referred to in the description of F or G that are established by the taxpayer to have become bad debts before that time,

D is such part, if any, of the amount determined for I as has been repaid before that time by the taxpayer pursuant to a legal obligation to repay all or any part of that amount,

D.1 is the total of all specified amounts, determined under paragraph 66.7(12.1)(*c*) in respect of the taxpayer for taxation years ending before that time,

E is the total of all amounts deducted in computing the taxpayer's income for a taxation year ending before that time in respect of the taxpayer's cumulative Canadian oil and gas property expense,

F is the total of all amounts each of which is an amount in respect of property described in paragraph (*a*), (*c*) or (*d*) of the definition "Canadian resource property" in subsection 66(15) or any right to or interest in — or, for civil law, any right in or to — such a property, other than such a right or interest that the taxpayer has by reason of being a beneficiary under a trust or a member of a partnership, (in this description referred to as "the particular property") disposed of by the taxpayer before that time equal to the amount, if any, by which

(*a*) the amount, if any, by which the proceeds of disposition in respect of the particular property that became receivable by the taxpayer before that time exceed any outlays or expenses made or incurred by the taxpayer before that time for the purpose of making the disposition and that were not otherwise deductible for the purposes of this Part

exceeds the total of

(*b*) the amount, if any, by which

(i) the total of all amounts that would be determined under paragraph 66.7(5)(*a*), immediately before the time (in this paragraph and paragraph (*c*) referred to as the "relevant time") when such proceeds of disposition became receivable, in respect of the taxpayer and an original owner of the particular property (or of any other property acquired by the taxpayer with the particular property in circumstances in which subsection 66.7(5) applied and in respect of which the proceeds of disposition became receivable by the taxpayer at the relevant time) if

(A) amounts that became receivable at or after the relevant time were not taken into account,

(B) each designation made under subparagraph 66.7(4)(*a*)(iii) in respect of an amount that became receivable before the relevant time were made before the relevant time,

(C) paragraph 66.7(5)(*a*) were read without reference to "10% of", and

(D) no reduction under subsection 80(8) at or after the relevant time were taken into account

exceeds the total of

(ii) all amounts that would be determined under paragraph 66.7(5)(*a*) at the relevant time in respect of the taxpayer and an original owner of the particular property (or of that other property described in subparagraph (i)) if

(A) amounts that became receivable after the relevant time were not taken into account,

(B) each designation made under subparagraph 66.7(4)(*a*)(iii) in respect of an amount that became receivable at or before the relevant time were made before the relevant time,

(C) paragraph 66.7(5)(*a*) were read without reference to "10% of", and

(D) no reduction under subsection 80(8) at or after the relevant time were taken into account, and

(iii) such portion of the amount determined under this paragraph as was otherwise applied to reduce the amount otherwise determined under this description, and

(*c*) the amount, if any, by which

(i) the total of all amounts that would be determined under paragraph 66.7(4)(*a*), immediately before the relevant time, in respect of the taxpayer and an original owner of the particular property (or of any other property acquired by the taxpayer with the particular property in circumstances in which subsection 66.7(4) applied and in respect of which the proceeds of disposition became receivable by the taxpayer at the relevant time) if

(A) amounts that became receivable at or after the relevant time were not taken into account,

(B) each designation made under subparagraph 66.7(4)(*a*)(iii) in respect of an amount that became receivable before the relevant time were made before the relevant time,

(C) paragraph 66.7(4)(*a*) were read without reference to "30% of", and

(D) no reduction under subsection 80(8) at or after the relevant time were taken into account

exceeds the total of

(ii) all amounts that would be determined under paragraph 66.7(4)(*a*) at the relevant time in respect of the taxpayer and an original owner of the particular property (or of that other property described in subparagraph (i)) if

(A) amounts that became receivable after the relevant time were not taken into account,

(B) each designation made under subparagraph 66.7(4)(*a*)(iii) in respect of an amount that became receivable at or before the relevant time were made before the relevant time,

(C) paragraph 66.7(4)(*a*) were read without reference to "30% of",

(D) amounts described in subparagraph 66.7(4)(*a*)(ii) that became receivable at the relevant time were not taken into account, and

(E) no reduction under subsection 80(8) at or after the relevant time were taken into account, and

(iii) such portion of the amount otherwise determined under this paragraph as was otherwise applied to reduce the amount otherwise determined under this description,

G is the total of all amounts that became receivable by the taxpayer before that time that are to be included in the amount determined under this description by virtue of paragraph 66(12.5)(*a*),

H is the total of all amounts each of which is an amount received before that time on account of any amount referred to in the description of C,

I is the total amount of assistance that the taxpayer has received or is entitled to receive in respect of any Canadian oil and gas property expense incurred after 1980 or that can reasonably be related to any such expense after 1980,

I.1 is the total of all amounts by which the cumulative Canadian oil and gas property expense of the taxpayer is required because of subsection 80(8) to be reduced at or before that time, and

J is the total of all amounts that are required to be deducted before that time under paragraph 66.7(12)(*d*) in computing the taxpayer's cumulative Canadian oil and gas property expense;

History: S. 66.4(5), the portion of the description of F before paragraph (*a*) in the definition "cumulative Canadian oil and gas property expense" was replaced by S.C. 2013, c. 34, s. 115(3), in force June 26, 2013, and formerly read:

F is the total of all amounts each of which is an amount in respect of property described in paragraph (*a*), (*c*) or (*d*) of the definition "Canadian resource property" in subsection 66(15) or any right to or interest in such a property, other than such a right or an interest that the taxpayer has by reason of being a beneficiary under a trust or a member of a partnership, (in this description referred to as "the particular property") disposed of by the taxpayer before that time equal to the amount, if any, by which

Related Sections: S. 20(1)(*kk*) Exploration and development grants; s. 53(1)(*e*)(viii) Adjustments to cost base—Interest in a partnership; s. 66(11)(*d*) Acquisition of control; s. 66(12.5)(*a*) Unitized oil or gas field in Canada; s. 66(15), "Canadian resource property"; s. 66.4(1) Recovery of costs; s. 66.4(2) Deduction for cumulative Canadian oil and gas property expense; s. 66.4(5), "Canadian oil and gas property expense"; s. 66.4(6) Share of partner; s. 66.4(7) Exception; s. 66.7(4) Successor of Canadian development expense; s. 66.7(5) Successor of Canadian oil and gas property expense; s. 66.7(12) Reduction of Canadian resource expenses; s. 66.7(12.1)(*c*) Specified amount; s. 66.7(14)(*a*) Disposal of Canadian resource properties; s. 70(5.2) Resource properties and land inventories of a deceased taxpayer; s. 79(4)(*c*) Subsequent payment by debtor; s. 80(8) Reductions of resource expenditures; s. 96(2.2)(*d*) At-risk amount; s. 104(5.2) Resource property.

Interpretation Bulletins: *Secondary* — IT-125R4 Disposition of resource properties.

"proceeds of disposition" —"proceeds of disposition" has the meaning assigned by section 54.

▶ 66.4(5.1) ◀

(5.1) Application of ss. 66(15) and 66.1(6). The definitions in subsections 66(15) and 66.1(6) apply to this section.

▶ 66.4(6) ◀

(6) Share of partner. Except as provided in subsection (7), where a taxpayer is a member of a partnership, the taxpayer's share of any amount that would be an amount referred to in the description of D in the definition "cumulative Canadian oil and gas property expense" in subsection (5), in paragraph (*a*) of the description of F in that definition or in the description of G or I in that definition in respect of the partnership for a taxation year of the partnership if section 96 were read without reference to paragraph 96(1)(*d*) shall, for the purposes of this Act, be deemed to be an amount referred to in the description of D in the definition "cumulative Canadian oil and gas property expense" in subsection (5), in paragraph (*a*) of the description of F in that definition or in the description of G or I in that definition, whichever is applicable, in respect of the taxpayer for the taxation year of the taxpayer in which the partnership's taxation year ends.

Related Sections: S. 66.4(7) Exception.

Interpretation Bulletins: *Primary* — IT-125R4 Disposition of resource properties.

▶ 66.4(7) ◀

(7) Exception. Where a non-resident person is a member of a partnership that is deemed under paragraph 115(4)(*b*) to have disposed of any Canadian resource property, the person's share of any amount that would be an amount referred to in the description of D in the definition "cumulative Canadian oil and gas property expense" in subsection (5), in paragraph (*a*) of the description of F in that definition or in the description of G or I in that definition in respect of the partnership for a taxation year of the partnership if section 96 were read without reference to paragraph 96(1)(*d*) shall, for the purposes of this Act, be deemed to be an amount referred to in the description of D in the definition "cumulative Canadian oil and gas property expense" in subsection (5), in paragraph (*a*) of the description of F in that definition or in the description of G or I in that definition, whichever is applicable, in respect of the person for the taxation year of the person that is deemed under paragraph 115(4)(*a*) to have ended.

Interpretation Bulletins: *Secondary* — IT-125R4 Disposition of resource properties.

SECTION 66.5: [Cumulative offset account]

▶ 66.5(1) ◀

(1) Deduction from income. In computing its income for a taxation year that ends before 1995, a corporation that has not made a designation for the year under subsection 66(14.1) or (14.2) may deduct such amount as it may claim not exceeding its cumulative offset account at the end of the year.

Related Sections: S. 66(18) Members of partnerships; s. 196 Tax in respect of cumulative offset account.

▶ 66.5(2) ◀

(2) Definition of "cumulative offset account". In this section, "cumulative offset account" of a corporation at any time means the amount, if any, by which

(*a*) the total of all amounts required to be added under subsections 66(14.1) and (14.2) in computing its cumulative offset account before that time,

exceeds

(*b*) the total of all amounts deducted under subsection (1) in computing its income for taxation years ending before that time.

Related Sections: S. 87(2)(*pp*) Cumulative offset account computation; s. 88(1)(*e.2*) Winding-up.

▶ 66.5(3) ◀

(3) Change of control. Where at any time after June 5, 1987 control of a corporation has been acquired by a person or group of persons, the amount deductible under subsection (1) by the corporation in computing its income for a taxation year ending after that time shall not exceed the amount, if any, by which

(*a*) the part of its income for the year that may reasonably be regarded as attributable to production from Canadian resource properties owned by it immediately before that time

exceeds

(*b*) the total of all amounts deducted under subsection 29(25) of the *Income Tax Application Rules* and subsections 66.7(1), (3), (4) and (5) by it in respect of its income for the year in computing its income for the year.

Related Sections: S. 256(7) Acquiring control; s. 256(8) Deemed exercise of right.

SECTION 66.6: Acquisition from tax-exempt

Where a corporation acquires, by purchase, amalgamation, merger, winding-up or otherwise, all or substantially all of the Canadian resource properties or foreign resource properties of a person whose taxable income is exempt from tax under this Part, subsection 29(25) of the *Income Tax Application Rules* and subsections 66.7(1) to (5) do not apply to the corporation in respect of the acquisition of the properties.

Related Sections: S. 66(18) Members of partnerships.

Interpretation Bulletins: *Secondary* — IT-126R2 Meaning of "winding-up".

SECTION 66.7: [Successor corporation rules]

► 66.7(1) ◄

(1) Successor of Canadian exploration and development expenses. Subject to subsections (6) and (7), where after 1971 a corporation (in this subsection referred to as the "successor") acquired a particular Canadian resource property (whether by way of a purchase, amalgamation, merger, winding-up or otherwise), there may be deducted by the successor in computing its income for a taxation year an amount not exceeding the total of all amounts each of which is an amount determined in respect of an original owner of the particular property that is the lesser of

(*a*) the Canadian exploration and development expenses incurred by the original owner before the original owner disposed of the particular property to the extent that those expenses were not otherwise deducted in computing the income of the successor for the year, were not deducted in computing the income of the successor for a preceding taxation year and were not deductible under subsection 66(1) or deducted under subsection 66(2) or (3) by the original owner, or deducted by any predecessor owner of the particular property, in computing income for any taxation year, and

(*b*) the amount, if any, by which

(i) the part of the successor's income for the year that may reasonably be regarded as attributable to

(A) the amount included in computing its income for the year under paragraph 59(3.2)(*c*) that may reasonably be regarded as attributable to the disposition by it in the year or a preceding taxation year of any interest in or right to — or, for civil law, any right in or to — the particular property to the extent that the proceeds of the disposition have not been included in determining an amount under clause 29(25)(*d*)(i)(A) of the *Income Tax Application Rules*, this clause, clause (3)(*b*)(i)(A) or paragraph (10)(*g*) for a preceding taxation year,

(B) its reserve amount for the year in respect of the original owner and each predecessor owner, if any, of the particular property, or

(C) production from the particular property,

computed as if no deduction were allowed under section 29 of the *Income Tax Application Rules*, this section or any of sections 65 to 66.5,

exceeds the total of

(ii) all other amounts deducted under subsection 29(25) of the *Income Tax Application Rules*, this subsection and subsections (3), (4) and (5) for the year that can reasonably be regarded as attributable to the part of its income for the year described in subparagraph (i) in respect of the particular property, and

(iii) all amounts added because of subsection 80(13) in computing the amount determined under subparagraph (i).

Editorial Note: S. 66.7 sets out what are known as the successor corporation rules. These rules contemplate that an infinite number of people in succession may have owned a particular Canadian or foreign resource property before the successor acquired it. A person who incurred resource expenses while it owned a property (regardless of whether it is on that particular property) is an original owner of the property. A person who acquires a Canadian or foreign resource property in accordance with the rules may deduct the expenses of the original owner against income from and proceeds of disposition of the properties.

A corporation that owned the property before the successor and acquired it and disposed of it in a transaction that satisfied the rules is a "predecessor owner". A corporation can be both an original owner and a predecessor owner of a property.

History: S. 66.7(1)(*b*)(i)(A) was replaced by S.C. 2013, c. 34, s. 116(1), in force June 26, 2013, and formerly read:

> (A) the amount included in computing its income for the year under paragraph 59(3.2)(*c*) that may reasonably be regarded as attributable to the disposition by it in the year or a preceding taxation year of any interest in or right to the particular property to the extent that the proceeds of the disposition have not been included in determining an amount under clause 29(25)(*d*)(i)(A) of the *Income Tax Application Rules*, this clause, clause (3)(*b*)(i)(A) or paragraph (10)(*g*) for a preceding taxation year,

Related Sections: S. 59(3.4), "successor corporation"; s. 66(15), "Canadian exploration and development expenses", "original owner", "predecessor owner", "production", "reserve amount"; s. 66(18) Members of partnerships; s. 66.5(3) Change of control; s. 66.6 Acquisition from tax-exempt; s. 66.8(1) Resource expenses of limited partner.

Canadian Petroleum Tax Journal: Canada Customs and Revenue Agency 1999 Roundtable Questions and Answers, Question 16, 2000, Vol. 13, No. 1.

Canadian Tax Foundation: Haughey, *Tiered Partnerships: Successor Rules*, 2014 Canadian Tax Highlights 22(2):13–15.

Forms: T1046 — Designation of Resource Amount by an Original Owner; T2010 — Election to Deduct Resource Expenses Upon Acquisition of Resource Property by a Corporation.

Interpretation Bulletins: *Secondary* — IT-126R2 Meaning of "winding-up".

Cases: There is no specific requirement that a partnership continue to directly own the property at the time the successored resource expenses are deducted. The proportionate share of income earned from the resource property and allocated to the predecessor partnership may have reasonably been regarded as having been attributable to production for the purposes of s. 66.7(1)–(5). *Devon Canada Corporation v. The Queen*, 2014 DTC 1043 (T.C.C.)

► 66.7(2) ◄

(2) Successor of foreign exploration and development expenses. Subject to subsections (6) and (8), where after 1971 a corporation (in this subsection referred to as the "successor") acquired a particular foreign resource property (whether by way of a purchase, amalgamation, merger, winding-up or otherwise), there may be deducted by the successor in computing its income for a taxation year an amount not exceeding the total of all amounts each of which is an amount determined in respect of an original owner of the particular property that is the lesser of

(*a*) the amount, if any, by which

(i) the foreign exploration and development expenses incurred by the original owner before the original owner disposed of the particular property to the extent that those expenses were incurred when the original owner was resident in Canada, were not otherwise deducted in computing the successor's income for the year, were not deducted in computing the successor's income for a preceding taxation year and were not deductible by the original owner, nor deducted by any predecessor owner of the particular property, in computing income for any taxation year

exceeds

(ii) the total of all amounts each of which is an amount by which the amount described in this paragraph is required because of subsection 80(8) to be reduced at or before the end of the year, and

(*b*) the amount, if any, by which the total of

(i) the part of the successor's income for the year that can reasonably be regarded as attributable to

(A) the amount included under subsection 59(1) in computing its income for the year that can reasonably be regarded as attributable to the disposition by it of any interest in or right to — or, for civil law, any right in or to — the particular property, or

(B) production from the particular property,

computed as if no deduction were allowed under sections 65 to 66.5 and this section, and

(ii) the lesser of

(A) the total of all amounts each of which is the amount designated by the successor for the year in respect of a Canadian resource property owned by the original owner immediately before being acquired with the particular property by the successor or a predecessor owner of the particular property, not exceeding the amount included in the successor's income for the year, computed as if no deduction were allowed under section 29 of the *Income Tax Application Rules*, this section or any of sections 65 to 66.5, that can reasonably be regarded as being attributable to the production after 1988 from the Canadian resource property, and

(B) the amount, if any, by which 10% of the amount described in paragraph (*a*) for the year in respect of the original owner exceeds the total of all amounts each of which would, but for this subparagraph, clause (iii)(B) and subparagraph (10)(*h*)(vi), be determined under this paragraph for the year in respect of the particular property or other foreign resource property owned by the original owner immediately before being acquired with the particular property by the successor or a predecessor owner of the particular property

exceeds the total of

(iii) all other amounts deducted under this subsection for the year that can reasonably be regarded as attributable to

(A) the part of its income for the year described in subparagraph (i) in respect of the particular property, or

(B) a part of its income for the year described in clause (ii)(A) in respect of which an amount is designated by the successor under clause (ii)(A), and

(iv) all amounts added because of subsection 80(13) in computing the amount determined under subparagraph (i),

and income in respect of which an amount is designated under clause (*b*)(ii)(A) shall, for the purposes of clause 29(25)(*d*)(i)(B) of the *Income Tax Application Rules*, clauses (1)(*b*)(i)(C), (3)(*b*)(i)(C), (4)(*b*)(i)(B) and (5)(*b*)(i)(B) and subparagraph (10)(*g*)(iii), be deemed not to be attributable to production from a Canadian resource property.

History: S. 66.7(2)(*b*)(i)(A) was replaced by S.C. 2013, c. 34, s. 116(2), in force June 26, 2013, and formerly read:

(A) the amount included under subsection 59(1) in computing its income for the year that can reasonably be regarded as attributable to the disposition by it of any interest in or right to the particular property, or

Related Sections: S. 66(4) Foreign exploration and development expenses; s. 66.7(8) Application of subsections (2) and (2.3).

Canadian Petroleum Tax Journal: Canada Customs and Revenue Agency 1999 Roundtable Questions and Answers, Question 12, 2000, Vol. 13, No. 1.

► 66.7(2.1) ◄

(2.1) Country-by-country successor FEDE allocations. For greater certainty, the portion of an amount deducted under subsection (2) in computing a taxpayer's income for a taxation year that can reasonably be considered to be in respect of specified foreign exploration and development expenses of the taxpayer in respect of a country is considered to apply to a source in that country.

Related Sections: S. 66(4.1) Country-by-country FEDE allocations; s. 66.7(2.2) Method of allocation.

Canadian Petroleum Tax Journal: Foreign Exploration and Development Expenditures — The New Rules, Roch J. Martin, 2001, Vol. 14, No. 1.

► 66.7(2.2) ◄

(2.2) Method of allocation. For the purpose of subsection (2.1), where a taxpayer has incurred specified foreign exploration and development expenses in respect of two or more countries, an allocation to each of those countries for a taxation year shall be determined in a manner that is

(*a*) reasonable having regard to all the circumstances, including the level and timing of

(i) the taxpayer's specified foreign exploration and development expenses in respect of the country, and

(ii) the profits or gains to which those expenses relate; and

(*b*) not inconsistent with the allocation made under subsection (2.1) for the preceding taxation year.

Related Sections: S. 66(4.2) Method of allocation; s. 66.7(2.1) Country-by-country successor FEDE allocations.

Canadian Petroleum Tax Journal: Foreign Exploration and Development Expenditures — The New Rules, Roch J. Martin, 2001, Vol. 14, No. 1.

► 66.7(2.3) ◄

(2.3) Successor of foreign resource expenses. Subject to subsections (6) and (8), where a corporation (in this subsection referred to as the "successor") acquired a particular foreign resource property in respect of a country (whether by way of a purchase, amalgamation, merger, winding-up or otherwise), there may be deducted by the successor in computing its income for a taxation year an amount not exceeding the total of all amounts each of which is an amount determined in respect of an original owner of the particular property that is the lesser of

(*a*) 30% of the amount, if any, by which

(i) the cumulative foreign resource expense, in respect of the country, of the original owner determined immediately after the disposition of the particular property by the original owner to the extent that it has not been

(A) deducted by the original owner or any predecessor owner of the particular property in computing income for any taxation year,

(B) otherwise deducted in computing the income of the successor for the year, or

(C) deducted by the successor in computing its income for any preceding taxation year

exceeds the total of

(ii) all amounts each of which is an amount (other than any portion of the amount that can reasonably be considered to result in a reduction of the amount otherwise determined under this paragraph in respect of another original owner of a relevant resource property who is not a predecessor owner of a relevant resource property or who became a predecessor owner of a relevant resource property before the original owner became a predecessor owner of a relevant resource property) that became receivable by a predecessor owner of the particular property, or by the successor in the year or a preceding taxation year, and that

(A) was included by the predecessor owner or the successor in computing an amount determined under paragraph (*a*) of the description of F in the definition "cumulative foreign resource expense" in subsection 66.21(1) at the end of the year, and

(B) can reasonably be regarded as attributable to the disposition of a property (in this subparagraph referred to as a "relevant resource property") that is

(I) the particular property, or

(II) another foreign resource property in respect of the country that was acquired from the original owner with the particular property by the successor or a predecessor owner of the particular property, and

(iii) all amounts each of which is an amount by which the amount described in this paragraph is required by reason of subsection 80(8) to be reduced at or before the end of the year, and

(*b*) the amount, if any, by which the total of

(i) the part of the successor's income for the year that can reasonably be regarded as attributable to production from the particular property, computed as if no deduction were permitted under section 29 of the *Income Tax Application Rules*, this section or any of sections 65 to 66.5, except that, where the successor acquired the particular property from the original owner at any time in the year (otherwise than by way of an amalgamation or merger or solely by reason of the application of paragraph (10)(*c*)) and did not deal with the original owner at arm's length at that time, the amount determined under this subparagraph is deemed to be nil, and

(ii) unless the amount determined under subparagraph (i) is nil by reason of the exception provided under that subparagraph, the lesser of

(A) the total of all amounts each of which is the amount designated by the successor for the year in respect of a Canadian resource property owned by the original owner immediately before being acquired with the particular property by the successor or a predecessor owner of the particular property, not exceeding the amount included in the successor's income for the year, computed as if no deduction were permitted under section 29 of the *Income Tax Application Rules*, this section or any of sections 65 to 66.5, that can reasonably be regarded as being attributable to the production from the Canadian resource property, and

(B) the amount, if any, by which 10% of the amount described in paragraph (*a*) for the year, in respect of the original owner, exceeds the total of all amounts each of which would, but for this subparagraph, clause (2)(*b*)(iii)(B) and subparagraph (10)(*h*)(vi), be determined under this paragraph for the year in respect of the particular property or other foreign resource property, in respect of the country, owned by the original owner immediately before being acquired with the particular property by the successor or by a predecessor owner of the particular property

exceeds the total of

(iii) all other amounts each of which is an amount deducted for the year under this subsection or subsection (2) that can reasonably be regarded as attributable to

(A) the part of its income for the year described in subparagraph (i) in respect of the particular property, or

(B) a part of its income for the year described in clause (ii)(A) in respect of which an amount is designated by the successor under clause (ii)(A), and

(iv) all amounts added by reason of subsection 80(13) in computing the amount determined under subparagraph (i), and income in respect of which an amount is designated under clause (*b*)(ii)(A) is, for the purposes of clause 29(25)(*d*)(i)(B) of the *Income Tax Application Rules*, clauses (1)(*b*)(i)(C), (3)(*b*)(i)(C), (4)(*b*)(i)(B) and (5)(*b*)(i)(B) and subparagraph (10)(*g*)(iii), deemed not to be attributable to production from a Canadian resource property.

Related Sections: S. 66(13.1) Short taxation year; s. 66.21 Application of subsection 66(15); s. 66.7(8) Application of subsections (2) and (2.3); s. 66.7(10)(*h*) Change of control; s. 66.7(13.1) Reduction of foreign resource expenses; s. 66.7(15.1) Disposal of foreign resource properties — subsection (2.3); s. 80(8) Reductions of resource expenditures; s. 248(1), "foreign resource expense", "foreign resource property".

Canadian Petroleum Tax Journal: Foreign Exploration and Development Expenditures — The New Rules, Roch J. Martin, 2001, Vol. 14, No. 1.

▶ 66.7(3) ◀

(3) Successor of Canadian exploration expense. Subject to subsections (6) and (7), where after May 6, 1974 a corporation (in this subsection referred to as the "successor") acquired a particular Canadian resource property (whether by way of a purchase, amalgamation, merger, winding-up or otherwise), there may be deducted by the successor in computing its income for a taxation year an amount not exceeding the total of all amounts each of which is an amount determined in respect of an original owner of the particular property that is the lesser of

(*a*) the amount, if any, by which

(i) the total of

(A) the cumulative Canadian exploration expense of the original owner determined immediately after the disposition of the particular property by the original owner, and

(B) all amounts required to be added under paragraph (9)(*f*) to the cumulative Canadian exploration expense of the original owner in respect of a predecessor owner of the particular property, or the successor, as the case may be, at any time after the disposition of the particular property by the original owner and before the end of the year,

to the extent that an amount in respect of that total was not

(C) deducted or required to be deducted under subsection 66.1(2) or (3) by the original owner or deducted by any predecessor owner of the particular property in computing income for any taxation year,

(D) otherwise deducted in computing the successor's income for the year,

(E) deducted in computing the successor's income for a preceding taxation year, or

(F) designated by the original owner pursuant to subsection 66(14.1) for any taxation year,

exceeds

(ii) the total of all amounts each of which is an amount by which the amount described in this paragraph is required because of subsection 80(8) to be reduced at or before the end of the year, and

(*b*) the amount, if any, by which

(i) the part of the successor's income for the year that may reasonably be regarded as attributable to

(A) the amount included in computing its income for the year under paragraph 59(3.2)(*c*) that may reasonably be regarded as being attributable to the disposition by it in the year or a preceding taxation year of any interest in or right to — or, for civil law, any right in or to — the particular property to the extent that the proceeds have not been included in determining an amount under clause 29(25)(*d*)(i)(A) of the *Income Tax Application Rules*, this clause, clause (1)(*b*)(i)(A) or paragraph (10)(*g*) for a preceding taxation year,

(B) its reserve amount for the year in respect of the original owner and each predecessor owner, if any, of the particular property, or

(C) production from the particular property,

computed as if no deduction were allowed under section 29 of the *Income Tax Application Rules*, this section or any of sections 65 to 66.5,

exceeds the total of

(ii) all other amounts deducted under subsection 29(25) of the *Income Tax Application Rules*, this subsection and subsections (1), (4) and (5) for the year that can reasonably be regarded as attributable to the part of its income for the year described in subparagraph (i) in respect of the particular property, and

(iii) all amounts added because of subsection 80(13) in computing the amount determined under subparagraph (i).

History: S. 66.7(3)(*b*)(i)(A) was replaced by S.C. 2013, c. 34, s. 116(3), in force June 26, 2013, and formerly read:

> (A) the amount included in computing its income for the year under paragraph 59(3.2)(*c*) that may reasonably be regarded as being attributable to the disposition by it in the year or a preceding taxation year of any interest in or right to the particular property to the extent that the proceeds have not been included in determining an amount under clause 29(25)(*d*)(i)(A) of the *Income Tax Application Rules*, this clause, clause (1)(*b*)(i)(A) or paragraph (10)(*g*) for a preceding taxation year,

Related Sections: S. 66.1(6), "Canadian exploration expense", "cumulative Canadian exploration expense".

Canadian Petroleum Tax Journal: Pot Pourri of Income Tax Issues, John Chan, 2001, Vol. 14, No. 1.

▶ 66.7(4) ◀

(4) Successor of Canadian development expense. Subject to subsections (6) and (7), where after May 6, 1974 a corporation (in this subsection referred to as the "successor") acquired a particular Canadian resource property (whether by way of a purchase, amalgamation, merger, winding-up or otherwise), there may be deducted by the successor in computing its income for a taxation year an amount not exceeding the total of all amounts each of which is an amount determined in respect of an original owner of the particular property that is the lesser of

(*a*) 30% of the amount, if any, by which

(i) the amount, if any, by which

(A) the cumulative Canadian development expense of the original owner determined immediately after the disposition of the particular property by the original owner to the extent that it has not been

(I) deducted by the original owner or any predecessor owner of the particular property in computing income for any taxation year,

(I.1) otherwise deducted in computing the income of the successor for the year,

(II) deducted by the successor in computing its income for any preceding taxation year, or

(III) designated by the original owner pursuant to subsection 66(14.2) for any taxation year,

exceeds

(B) any amount required to be deducted under paragraph (9)(*e*) from the cumulative Canadian development expense of the original owner in respect of a predecessor owner of the particular property or the successor, as the case may be, at any time after the disposition of the particular property by the original owner and before the end of the year,

exceeds the total of

(ii) all amounts each of which is an amount (other than any portion thereof that can reasonably be considered to result in a reduction of the amount otherwise determined under this paragraph in respect of another original owner of a relevant mining property who is not a predecessor owner of a relevant mining property or who became a predecessor owner of a relevant mining property before the original owner became a predecessor owner of a relevant mining property) that became receivable by a predecessor owner of the particular property or the successor in the year or a preceding taxation year and that

(A) was included by the predecessor owner or the successor in computing an amount determined under paragraph (*a*) of the description of F in the definition "cumulative Canadian development expense" in subsection 66.2(5) at the end of the year, and

(B) can reasonably be regarded as attributable to the disposition of a property (in this subparagraph referred to as a "relevant mining property") that is the particular property or another Canadian resource property that was acquired from the original owner with the particular property by the successor or a predecessor owner of the particular property,

(iii) all amounts each of which is an amount (other than any portion thereof that can reasonably be considered to result in a reduction of the amount otherwise determined under paragraph (5)(*a*) in respect of the original owner or under this paragraph or paragraph (5)(*a*) in respect of another original owner of a relevant oil and gas property who is not a predecessor owner of a relevant oil and gas property or who became a predecessor owner of a relevant oil and gas property before the original owner became a predecessor owner of a relevant oil and gas property) that became receivable by a predecessor owner of the particular property or the successor after 1992 and in the year or a preceding taxation year and that

(A) is designated in respect of the original owner by the predecessor owner or the successor, as the case may be, in prescribed form filed with the Minister within 6 months after the end of the taxation year in which the amount became receivable,

(B) was included by the predecessor owner or the successor in computing an amount determined under paragraph (*a*) of the description of F in the definition "cumulative Canadian oil and gas property expense" in subsection 66.4(5) at the end of the year, and

(C) can reasonably be regarded as attributable to the disposition of a property (in this subparagraph referred to as a "relevant oil and gas property") that is the particular property or another Canadian resource property that was acquired from the original owner with the particular property by the successor or a predecessor owner of the particular property, and

(iv) all amounts each of which is an amount by which the amount described in this paragraph is required because of subsection 80(8) to be reduced at or before the end of the year, and

(*b*) the amount, if any, by which

(i) the part of the successor's income for the year that can reasonably be regarded as attributable to

(A) its reserve amount for the year in respect of the original owner and each predecessor owner of the particular property, or

(B) production from the particular property,

computed as if no deduction were allowed under section 29 of the *Income Tax Application Rules*, this section or any of sections 65 to 66.5, except that, where the successor acquired the particular property from the original owner at any time in the year (otherwise than by way of an amalgamation or merger or solely because of the application of paragraph (10)(*c*)) and did not deal with the original owner at arm's length at that time, the amount determined under this subparagraph shall be deemed to be nil,

exceeds the total of

(ii) all other amounts deducted under subsection 29(25) of the *Income Tax Application Rules*, this subsection and subsections (1), (3) and (5) for the year that can reasonably be regarded as attributable to the part of its income for the year described in subparagraph (i) in respect of the particular property, and

(iii) all amounts added because of subsection 80(13) in computing the amount determined under subparagraph (i).

► 66.7(5) ◄

(5) Successor of Canadian oil and gas property expense. Subject to subsections (6) and (7), where after December 11, 1979 a corporation (in this subsection referred to as the "successor") acquired a particular Canadian resource property (whether by way of a purchase, amalgamation, merger, winding-up or otherwise), there may be deducted by the successor in computing its income for a taxation year an amount not exceeding the total of all amounts each of which is an amount determined in respect of an original owner of the particular property that is the lesser of

(*a*) 10% of the amount, if any, by which

(i) the cumulative Canadian oil and gas property expense of the original owner determined immediately after the disposition of the particular property by the original owner to the extent it has not been

(A) deducted by the original owner or any predecessor owner of the particular property in computing income for any taxation year,

(A.1) otherwise deducted in computing the income of the successor for the year, or

(B) deducted by the successor in computing its income for any preceding taxation year

exceeds the total of

(ii) the total of all amounts each of which is an amount (other than any portion thereof that can reasonably be considered to result in a reduction of the amount otherwise determined under this paragraph or paragraph (4)(*a*) in respect of another original owner of a relevant oil and gas property who is not a predecessor owner of a relevant oil and gas property or who became a predecessor owner of a relevant oil and gas property before the original owner became a predecessor owner of a relevant oil and gas property) that became receivable by a predecessor owner of the particular property or the successor in the year or a preceding taxation year and that

(A) was included by the predecessor owner or the successor in computing an amount determined under paragraph (*a*) of the description of F in the definition "cumulative Canadian oil and gas property expense" in subsection 66.4(5) at the end of the year, and

(B) can reasonably be regarded as attributable to the disposition of a property (in this subparagraph referred to as a "relevant oil and gas property") that is the particular property or another Canadian resource property that was acquired from the original owner with the particular property by the successor or a predecessor owner of the particular property, and

(iii) the total of all amounts each of which is an amount by which the amount described in this paragraph is required because of subsection 80(8) to be reduced at or before the end of the year, and

(*b*) the amount, if any, by which

(i) the part of the successor's income for the year that can reasonably be regarded as attributable to

(A) its reserve amount for the year in respect of the original owner and each predecessor owner of the particular property, or

(B) production from the particular property,

computed as if no deduction were allowed under section 29 of the *Income Tax Application Rules*, this section or any of sections 65 to 66.5, except that, where the successor acquired the particular property from the original owner at any time in the year (otherwise than by way of an amalgamation or merger or solely because of the application of paragraph (10)(*c*)) and did not deal with the original owner at arm's length at that time, the amount determined under this subparagraph shall be deemed to be nil,

exceeds the total of

(ii) all other amounts deducted under subsection 29(25) of the *Income Tax Application Rules*, this subsection and subsections (1), (3) and (4) for the year that can reasonably be regarded as attributable to the part of its income for the year described in subparagraph (i) in respect of the particular property, and

(iii) all amounts added because of subsection 80(13) in computing the amount determined under subparagraph (i).

► 66.7(6) ◄

(6) Where s. 29(25) of ITAR and ss. (1) to (5) do not apply. Subsection 29(25) of the *Income Tax Application Rules* and subsections (1) to (5) do not apply

(*a*) in respect of a Canadian resource property or a foreign resource property acquired by way of an amalgamation to which subsection 87(1.2) applies or a winding-up to which subsection 88(1.5) applies; or

(*b*) to permit, in respect of the acquisition by a corporation before February 18, 1987 of a Canadian resource property or a foreign resource property, a deduction by the corporation of an amount that the corporation would not have been entitled to deduct under section 29 of the *Income Tax Application Rules* or section 66, 66.1, 66.2 or 66.4 if those sections, as they read in their application to taxation years ending before February 18, 1987, applied to taxation years ending after February 17, 1987.

▶ 66.7(7) ◀

(7) Application of s. 29(25) of ITAR and ss. (1), (3), (4) and (5). Subsection 29(25) of the *Income Tax Application Rules* and subsections (1), (3), (4) and (5) apply only to a corporation that has acquired a particular Canadian resource property

(*a*) where it acquired the particular property in a taxation year commencing before 1985 and, at the time it acquired the particular property, the corporation acquired all or substantially all of the property used by the person from whom it acquired the particular property in carrying on in Canada such of the businesses described in paragraphs (*a*) to (*g*) of the definition "principal-business corporation" in subsection 66(15) as were carried on by the person;

(*b*) where it acquired the particular property in a taxation year commencing after 1984 and, at the time it acquired the particular property, the corporation acquired all or substantially all of the Canadian resource properties of the person from whom it acquired the particular property;

(*c*) where it acquired the particular property after June 5, 1987 by way of an amalgamation or winding-up and it has filed an election in prescribed form with the Minister on or before the day on or before which the corporation is required to file a return of income pursuant to section 150 for its taxation year in which it acquired the particular property;

(*d*) where it acquired the particular property after November 16, 1978 and in a taxation year ending before February 18, 1987 by any means other than by way of an amalgamation or winding-up and it and the person from whom it acquired the particular property, have filed with the Minister a joint election under and in accordance with any of subsection 29(25) of the *Income Tax Application Rules*, subsection 29(29) of the *Income Tax Application Rules, 1971*, Part III of chapter 63 of the Statutes of Canada, 1970-71-72, and subsections 66(6) and (7), 66.1(4) and (5), 66.2(3) and (4) and 66.4(3) and (4) of the *Income Tax Act*, chapter 148 of the Revised Statutes of Canada, 1952, as all of those subsections read in their application to that year; and

(*e*) where it acquired the particular property in a taxation year ending after February 17, 1987 by any means other than by way of an amalgamation or winding-up and it and the person from whom it acquired the particular property have filed a joint election in prescribed form with the Minister on or before the earlier of the days on or before which either of them is required to file a return of income pursuant to section 150 for its or the person's taxation year in which the corporation acquired the particular property.

Related Regulations: 600(*c*).

Related Sections: S. 220(3.2) Late, amended or revoked elections.

Forms: T2010 — Election to Deduct Resource Expenses Upon Acquisition of Resource Property by a Corporation.

Information Circulars: IC 07-1 Taxpayer Relief Provisions.

▶ 66.7(8) ◀

(8) Application of subsections (2) and (2.3). Subsections (2) and (2.3) apply only to a corporation that has acquired a particular foreign resource property

(*a*) where it acquired the particular property in a taxation year commencing before 1985 and, at the time it acquired the particular property, the corporation acquired all or substantially all of the property used by the person from whom it acquired the particular property in carrying on outside Canada such of the businesses described in paragraphs (*a*) to (*g*) of the definition "principal-business corporation" in subsection 66(15) as were carried on by that person;

(*b*) where it acquired the particular property in a taxation year commencing after 1984 and, at the time it acquired the particular property, the corporation acquired all or substantially all of the foreign resource properties of the person from whom it acquired the particular property;

(*c*) where it acquired the particular property after June 5, 1987 by way of an amalgamation or winding-up and it has filed an election in prescribed form with the Minister on or before the day on or before which the corporation is required to file a return of income pursuant to section 150 for its taxation year in which it acquired the particular property;

(*d*) where it acquired the particular property after November 16, 1978 and in a taxation year ending before February 18, 1987 by any means other than by way of an amalgamation or winding-up and it and the person from whom it acquired the particular property, have filed with the Minister a joint election under and in accordance with subsection 66(6) or (7) (as modified by subsections 66(8) and (9), respectively) of the *Income Tax Act*, chapter 148 of the Revised Statutes of Canada, 1952, as those subsections read in their application to that year; and

(*e*) where it acquired the particular property in a taxation year ending after February 17, 1987 by any means other than by way of an amalgamation or winding-up and it and the person from whom it acquired the particular property have filed a joint election in prescribed form with the Minister on or before the earlier of the days on or before which either of them is required to file a return of income pursuant to section 150 for its or the person's taxation year in which the corporation acquired the particular property.

Related Regulations: 600(*c*).

Related Sections: S. 220(3.2) Late, amended or revoked elections.

Forms: T2010 — Election to Deduct Resource Expenses Upon Acquisition of Resource Property by a Corporation.

Information Circulars: IC 07-1 Taxpayer relief provisions.

▶ 66.7(9) ◀

(9) Canadian development expense becoming Canadian exploration expense. Where

(*a*) a corporation acquires a Canadian resource property,

(*b*) subsection (4) applies in respect of the acquisition, and

(*c*) the cumulative Canadian development expense of an original owner of the property determined under clause (4)(*a*)(i)(A) in respect of the corporation includes a Canadian development expense incurred by the original owner in respect of an oil or gas well that would, but for this subsection, be deemed by subsection 66.1(9) to be a Canadian exploration expense incurred in respect of the well by the original owner at any particular time after the acquisition by the corporation and before it disposed of the property,

the following rules apply:

(*d*) subsection 66.1(9) does not apply in respect of the Canadian development expense incurred in respect of the well by the original owner,

(*e*) an amount equal to the lesser of

(i) the amount that would be deemed by subsection 66.1(9) to be a Canadian exploration expense incurred in respect of the well by the original owner at the particular time if that subsection applied in respect of the expense, and

(ii) the cumulative Canadian development expense of the original owner as determined under clause (4)(*a*)(i)(A) in respect of the corporation immediately before the particular time

shall be deducted at the particular time from the cumulative Canadian development expense of the original owner in respect of the corporation for the purposes of subparagraph (4)(*a*)(i), and

(*f*) the amount required by paragraph (*e*) to be deducted shall be added at the particular time to the cumulative Canadian exploration expense of the original owner in respect of the corporation for the purpose of paragraph (3)(*a*).

▶ 66.7(10) ◀

(10) Change of control. Where at any time after November 12, 1981

(*a*) control of a corporation has been acquired by a person or group of persons, or

(*b*) a corporation ceased on or before April 26, 1995 to be exempt from tax under this Part on its taxable income,

for the purposes of the provisions of the *Income Tax Application Rules* and this Act (other than subsections 66(12.6), (12.601), (12.602), (12.62) and (12.71)) relating to deductions in respect of drilling and exploration expenses, prospecting, exploration and development expenses, Canadian exploration and development expenses, foreign resource pool expenses, Canadian exploration expenses, Canadian development expenses and Canadian oil and gas property expenses (in this subsection referred to as "resource expenses") incurred by the corporation before that time, the following rules apply:

(*c*) the corporation shall be deemed after that time to be a successor (within the meaning assigned by subsection 29(25) of the *Income Tax Application Rules* or any of subsections (1) to (5)) that had, at that time, acquired all the properties owned by the corporation immediately before that time from an original owner thereof,

(*c*.1) where the corporation did not own a foreign resource property immediately before that time, the corporation is deemed to have owned a foreign resource property immediately before that time,

(*d*) a joint election shall be deemed to have been filed in accordance with subsections (7) and (8) in respect of the acquisition,

(*e*) the resource expenses incurred by the corporation before that time shall be deemed to have been incurred by an original owner of the properties and not by the corporation,

(*f*) the original owner is deemed to have been resident in Canada before that time while the corporation was resident in Canada,

(*g*) where the corporation (in this paragraph referred to as the "transferee") was, immediately before and at that time,

(i) a parent corporation (within the meaning assigned by subsection 87(1.4)), or

(ii) a subsidiary wholly-owned corporation (within the meaning assigned by subsection 87(1.4))

of a particular corporation (in this paragraph referred to as the "transferor"), if both corporations agree to have this paragraph apply to them in respect of a taxation year of the transferor ending after that time and notify the Minister in writing of the agreement in the return of income under this Part of the transferor for that year, the transferor may, if throughout that year the transferee was such a parent corporation or subsidiary wholly-owned corporation of the transferor, designate in favour of the transferee, in respect of that year, for the purpose of making a deduction under subsection 29(25) of the *Income Tax Application Rules* or this section in respect of resource expenses incurred by the transferee before that time and when it was such a parent corporation or subsidiary wholly-owned corporation of the transferor, an amount not exceeding such portion of the amount that would be its income for the year, if no deductions were allowed under any of section 29 of the *Income Tax Application Rules*, this section and sections 65 to 66.5, that may reasonably be regarded as being attributable to

(iii) the production from Canadian resource properties owned by the transferor immediately before that time, and

(iv) the disposition in the year of any Canadian resource properties owned by the transferor immediately before that time,

to the extent that the portion of the amount so designated is not designated under this paragraph in favour of any other taxpayer, and the amount so designated shall be deemed, for the purposes of determining the amount under paragraph 29(25)(*d*) of the *Income Tax Application Rules* and paragraphs (1)(*b*), (3)(*b*), (4)(*b*) and (5)(*b*),

(v) to be income from the sources described in subparagraph (iii) or (iv), as the case may be, of the transferee for its taxation year in which that taxation year of the transferor ends, and

(vi) not to be income from the sources described in subparagraph (iii) or (iv), as the case may be, of the transferor for that year,

(*h*) where the corporation (in this paragraph referred to as the "transferee") was, immediately before and at that time,

(i) a parent corporation (within the meaning assigned by subsection 87(1.4)), or

(ii) a subsidiary wholly-owned corporation (within the meaning assigned by subsection 87(1.4))

of a particular corporation (in this paragraph referred to as the "transferor"), if both corporations agree to have this paragraph apply to them in respect of a taxation year of the transferor ending after that time and notify the Minister in writing of the agreement in the return of income under this Part of the transferor for that year, the transferor may, if throughout that year the transferee was such a parent corporation or subsidiary wholly-owned corporation of the transferor, designate in favour of the transferee, in respect of that year, for the purpose of making a deduction under this section in respect of resource expenses incurred by the transferee before that time and when it was such a parent corporation or subsidiary wholly-owned corporation of the transferor, an amount not exceeding such portion of the amount that would be its income for the year, if no deductions were allowed under this section and sections 65 to 66.5, that may reasonably be regarded as being attributable to

(iii) the production from foreign resource properties owned by the transferor immediately before that time, and

(iv) the disposition of any foreign resource properties owned by the transferor immediately before that time,

to the extent that the portion of the amount so designated is not designated under this paragraph in favour of any other taxpayer, and the amount so designated shall be deemed,

(v) for the purposes of determining the amounts under paragraphs (2)(*b*) and (2.3)(*b*), to be income from the sources described in subparagraph (iii) or (iv), as the case may be, of the transferee for its taxation year in which that taxation year of the transferor ends, and

(vi) for the purposes of determining the amounts under paragraphs (2)(*b*) and (2.3)(*b*), not to be income from the sources described in subparagraph (iii) or (iv), as the case may be, of the transferor for that year,

(*i*) where, immediately before and at that time, the corporation (in this paragraph referred to as the "transferee") and another corporation (in this paragraph referred to as the "transferor") were both subsidiary wholly-owned corporations (within the meaning assigned by subsection 87(1.4)) of a particular parent corporation (within the meaning assigned by subsection 87(1.4)), if the transferee and the transferor agree to have this paragraph apply to them in respect of a taxation year of the transferor ending after that time and notify the Minister in writing of the agreement in the return of income under this Part of the transferor for that year, paragraph (*g*) or (*h*), or both, as the agreement provides, shall apply for that year to the transferee and transferor as though one were the parent corporation (within the meaning of subsection 87(1.4)) of the other, and

(*j*) where that time is after January 15, 1987 and at that time the corporation was a member of a partnership that owned a Canadian resource property or a foreign resource property at that time

(i) for the purpose of paragraph (*c*), the corporation shall be deemed to have owned immediately before that time that portion of the property owned by the partnership at that time that is equal to its percentage share of the total of amounts that would be paid to all members of the partnership if it were wound up at that time, and

(ii) for the purposes of clause 29(25)(*d*)(i)(B) of the *Income Tax Application Rules*, clauses (1)(*b*)(i)(C) and (2)(*b*)(i)(B), subparagraph (2.3)(*b*)(i) and clauses (3)(*b*)(i)(C), (4)(*b*)(i)(B) and (5)(*b*)(i)(B) for a taxation year ending after that time, the lesser of

(A) its share of the part of the income of the partnership for the fiscal period of the partnership ending in the year that may reasonably be regarded as being attributable to the production from the property, and

(B) an amount that would be determined under clause (A) for the year if its share of the income of the partnership for the fiscal period of the partnership ending in the year were determined on the basis of the percentage share referred to in subparagraph (i),

shall be deemed to be income of the corporation for the year that may reasonably be attributable to production from the property.

Editorial Note: Where there has been an acquisition of control of a corporation by a person or group of persons, the corporation is considered to be a successor to itself. The corporation in such circumstances may deduct its undeducted resource expenses only in accordance with the successor corporation rules. S. 66.7(10) permits corporations in a group to deduct successor expenses of another corporation in a group.

S. 66.7(10)(*j*) permits the corporation to deduct its successored expenses against income from and proceeds of disposition of property realized by a partnership of which it was a partner at the time of the acquisition of control.

S. 66(11.6) extends these successor rules to trusts subject to a loss restriction event.

Related Sections: 66(11.3) Control; 66(11.6) Trust loss restriction event — successor; 87(2.1)(*b*) Non-capital losses, etc., of predecessor corporations; 149(10)(*b*) Exempt corporations; 256(7) Acquiring control; 256(8) Deemed exercise of right; 256.1 [Corporate tax-attribute trading].

Canadian Petroleum Tax Journal: Pot Pourri of Income Tax Issues, John Chan, 2001, Vol. 14, No. 1; Recent Developments in Corporate Reorganizations and International Transactions, Doug Richardson and Edward Rowe, 2000, Vol. 13, No. 1.

Canadian Tax Foundation: Haughey, *Tiered Partnerships: Successor Rules*, 2014 Canadian Tax Highlights 22(2):13–15.

▶ 66.7(10.1) ◀

(10.1) Amalgamation — partnership property. For the purposes of subsections (1) to (5) and the definition "original owner" in subsection 66(15), if at any particular time there has been an amalgamation within the meaning assigned by subsection 87(1), other than an amalgamation to which subsection 87(1.2) applies, of two or more corporations (each of which is referred to in this subsection as a "predecessor corporation") to form one corporate entity (referred to in this subsection as the "new corporation") and immediately before the particular time a predecessor corporation was a member of a partnership that owned a Canadian resource property or a foreign resource property,

(*a*) the predecessor corporation is deemed

(i) to have owned, immediately before the particular time, that portion of each Canadian resource property and of each foreign resource property owned by the partnership at the particular time that is equal to the predecessor corporation's percentage share of the total of the amounts that would be paid to all members of the partnership if the partnership were wound up immediately before the particular time, and

(ii) to have disposed of those portions to the new corporation at the particular time;

(*b*) the new corporation is deemed to have, by way of the amalgamation, acquired those portions at the particular time; and

(*c*) the income of the new corporation for a taxation year that ends after the particular time that can reasonably be attributable to production from those properties is deemed to be the lesser of

(i) the new corporation's share of the part of the income of the partnership for fiscal periods of the partnership that end in the year that can reasonably be regarded as being attributable to production from those properties, and

(ii) the amount that would be determined under subparagraph (i) for the year if the new corporation's share of the income of the partnership for the fiscal periods of the partnership that end in the year were determined on the basis of the percentage share referred to in paragraph (*a*).

History: S. 66.7(10.1) was added by S.C. 2013, c. 34, s. 204(1), applicable to amalgamations that occur after 1996.

▶ 66.7(11) ◀

(11) Idem. Where, at any time,

(*a*) control of a taxpayer that is a corporation has been acquired by a person or group of persons, or

(*b*) a taxpayer has disposed of all or substantially all of the taxpayer's Canadian resource properties or foreign resource properties,

and, before that time, the taxpayer or a partnership of which the taxpayer was a member acquired a property that is a Canadian resource property, a foreign resource property or an interest in a partnership and it may reasonably be considered that one of the main purposes of the acquisition was to avoid any limitation provided in subsection 29(25) of the *Income Tax Application Rules* or any of subsections (1) to (5) on the deduction in respect of any expenses incurred by the taxpayer or a corporation referred to as a transferee in paragraph (10)(*g*) or (*h*), the taxpayer or the partnership, as the case may be, shall be deemed, for the purposes of applying those subsections to or in respect of the taxpayer, not to have acquired the property.

Editorial Note: S. 66.7(11) is an anti-avoidance rule. Its purpose is to prevent a person from using artificially its resource expenses by buying a Canadian resource property or foreign resource property prior to an acquisition of control or disposition of all of its Canadian or foreign resource properties. But for this rule, a corporation could acquire such assets to produce income and proceeds of disposition against which the expenses of the person could be deducted in accordance with the successor corporation rules.

Related Sections: S. 87(2)(*j*.6) Continuing corporation; s. 256(7) Acquiring control; s. 256(8) Deemed exercise of right.

▶ 66.7(12) ◀

(12) Reduction of Canadian resource expenses. Where in a taxation year an original owner of Canadian resource properties disposes of all or substantially all of the original owner's Canadian resource properties to a particular corporation in circumstances in which subsection 29(25) of the *Income Tax Application Rules* or subsection (1), (3), (4) or (5) applies,

(*a*) the Canadian exploration and development expenses incurred by the original owner before that owner so disposed of the properties shall, for the purposes of this subdivision, be deemed after the disposition not to have been incurred by the original owner except for the purposes of making a deduction under subsection 66(1) or (2) for the year and of determining the amount that may be deducted under subsection (1) by the particular corporation or by any other corporation that subsequently acquires any of the properties;

(*b*) in determining the cumulative Canadian exploration expense of the original owner at any time after the time referred to in subparagraph (3)(*a*)(i), there shall be deducted the amount thereof determined immediately after the disposition;

(*b*.1) for the purposes of paragraph (3)(*a*), the cumulative Canadian exploration expenses of the original owner determined immediately after the disposition that was deducted or required to be deducted under subsection 66.1(2) or (3) in computing the original owner's income for the year shall be deemed to be equal to the lesser of

(i) the amount deducted under paragraph (*b*) in respect of the disposition, and

(ii) the amount, if any, by which

(A) the specified amount determined under paragraph (12.1)(*a*) in respect of the original owner for the year

exceeds

(B) the total of all amounts each of which is an amount determined under this paragraph in respect of any disposition made by the original owner before the disposition and in the year;

(*b*.2) for greater certainty, any amount (other than the amount determined under paragraph (*b*.1)) that was deducted or required to be deducted under subsection 66.1(2) or (3) by the original owner for the year or a subsequent taxation year shall, for the purposes of paragraph (3)(*a*), be deemed not to be in respect of the cumulative Canadian exploration expense of the original owner determined immediately after the disposition;

(*c*) in determining the cumulative Canadian development expense of the original owner at any time after the time referred to in clause (4)(*a*)(i)(A), there shall be deducted the amount thereof determined immediately after the disposition;

(*c*.1) for the purpose of paragraph (4)(*a*), the cumulative Canadian development expense of the original owner determined immediately after the disposition that was deducted under subsection 66.2(2) in computing the original owner's income for the year shall be deemed to be equal to the lesser of

(i) the amount deducted under paragraph (*c*) in respect of the disposition, and

(ii) the amount, if any, by which

(A) the specified amount determined under paragraph (12.1)(*b*) in respect of the original owner for the year

exceeds

(B) the total of all amounts determined under this paragraph in respect of any dispositions made by the original owner before the disposition and in the year;

(*c*.2) for greater certainty, any amount (other than the amount determined under paragraph (*c*.1)) that was deducted under subsection 66.2(2) by the original owner for the year or a subsequent taxation year shall, for the purpose of paragraph (4)(*a*), be deemed not to be in respect of the cumulative Canadian development expense of the original owner determined immediately after the disposition;

(*d*) in determining the cumulative Canadian oil and gas property expense of the original owner at any time after the time referred to in subparagraph (5)(*a*)(i), there shall be deducted the amount thereof determined immediately after the disposition;

(*d*.1) for the purpose of paragraph (5)(*a*), the cumulative Canadian oil and gas property expense of the original owner determined immediately after the disposition that was deducted under subsection 66.4(2) in computing the original owner's income for the year shall be deemed to be equal to the lesser of

(i) the amount deducted under paragraph (*d*) in respect of the disposition, and

(ii) the amount, if any, by which

(A) the specified amount determined under paragraph (12.1)(*c*) in respect of the original owner for the year

exceeds

(B) the total of all amounts determined under this paragraph in respect of any dispositions made by the original owner before the disposition and in the year;

(*d*.2) for greater certainty, any amount (other than the amount determined under paragraph (*d*.1)) that was deducted under subsection 66.4(2) by the original owner for the year or a subsequent taxation year shall, for the purpose of paragraph (5)(*a*), be deemed not to be in respect of the cumulative Canadian oil and gas property expense of the original owner determined immediately after the disposition; and

(*e*) the drilling and exploration expenses, including all general geological and geophysical expenses, incurred by the original owner before 1972 on or in respect of exploring or drilling for petroleum or natural gas in Canada and the prospecting, exploration and development expenses incurred by the original owner before 1972 in searching for minerals in Canada shall, for the purposes of section 29 of the *Income Tax Application Rules*, be deemed after the disposition not to have been incurred by the original owner except for the purposes of making a deduction under that section for the year and of determining the amount that may be deducted under subsection 29(25) of that Act by the particular corporation or any other corporation that subsequently acquires any of the properties.

Editorial Note: Where an original owner transfers all or substantially all of its Canadian resource properties in accordance with the successor corporation rules, its cumulative Canadian exploration expense ("CCEE"), cumulative Canadian development expense ("CCDE") and cumulative Canadian oil and gas property expense ("CCOGPE") are reduced to zero immediately after the disposition. Since the taxpayer claims a deduction in respect of its CCEE, CCDE and CCOGPE at the end of the year, the taxpayer would not be able to claim a deduction in respect of such CCEE, CCDE and CCOGPE, notwithstanding it might have income in the year from the Canadian resource properties disposed of. The rules in ss. 66.7(12) and (12.1) permit an original owner to claim a deduction in respect of its CCEE, CCDE and CCOGPE existing immediately after the disposition of all of its Canadian resource properties in computing its income for the year.

▶ 66.7(12.1) ◀

(12.1) Specified amount. Where in a taxation year an original owner of Canadian resource properties disposes of all or substantially all of the original owner's Canadian resource properties in circumstances in which subsection (3), (4) or (5) applies,

(*a*) the lesser of

(i) the total of all amounts each of which is the amount, if any, by which

(A) an amount deducted under paragraph (12)(*b*) in respect of a disposition in the year by the original owner

exceeds

(B) the amount, if any, designated by the original owner in prescribed form filed with the Minister within 6 months after the end of the year in respect of an amount determined under clause (A), and

(ii) the total of

(A) the amount claimed under subsection 66.1(2) or (3) by the original owner for the year, and

(B) the amount that would, but for paragraph 66.1(1)(*c*), be determined under subsection 66.1(1) in respect of the original owner for the year

is the specified amount in respect of the original owner for the year for the purposes of clause (12)(*b*.1)(ii)(A) and of determining the value of E.1 in the definition "cumulative Canadian exploration expense" in subsection 66.1(6);

(*b*) the lesser of

(i) the total of all amounts each of which is the amount, if any, by which

(A) an amount deducted under paragraph (12)(*c*) in respect of a disposition in the year by the original owner

exceeds

(B) the amount, if any, designated by the original owner in prescribed form filed with the Minister within 6 months after the end of the year in respect of an amount determined under clause (A), and

(ii) the total of

(A) the amount claimed under subsection 66.2(2) by the original owner for the year, and

(B) the amount that would, but for paragraph 66.2(1)(*d*), be determined under subsection 66.2(1) in respect of the original owner for the year

is the specified amount in respect of the original owner for the year for the purposes of clause (12)(*c*.1)(ii)(A) and of determining the value of D.1 in the definition "cumulative Canadian development expense" in subsection 66.2(5); and

(*c*) the lesser of

(i) the total of all amounts each of which is the amount, if any, by which

(A) an amount deducted under paragraph (12)(*d*) in respect of a disposition in the year by the original owner

exceeds

(B) the amount, if any, designated by the original owner in prescribed form filed with the Minister within 6 months after the end of the year in respect of an amount determined under clause (A), and

(ii) the total of

(A) the amount claimed under subsection 66.4(2) by the original owner for the year, and

(B) the amount that would, but for paragraph 66.4(1)(*c*), be determined under subsection 66.4(1) in respect of the original owner for the year

is the specified amount in respect of the original owner for the year for the purposes of clause (12)(*d*.1)(ii)(A) and of determining the value of D.1 in the definition "cumulative Canadian oil and gas property expense" in subsection 66.4(5).

► 66.7(13) ◄

(13) Reduction of foreign resource expenses. Where after June 5, 1987 an original owner of foreign resource properties disposes of all or substantially all of the original owner's foreign resource properties to a particular corporation in circumstances in which subsection (2) applies, the foreign exploration and development expenses incurred by the original owner before that owner so disposed of the properties shall be deemed after the disposition not to have been incurred by the original owner except for the purposes of determining the amounts that may be deducted under that subsection by the particular corporation or any other corporation that subsequently acquires any of the properties.

Editorial Note: The provisions of ss. 66.7(13) and (13.1) provide rules in respect of foreign resource expenses incurred in a country that are similar to the rules described in ss. 66.7(12) and (12.1) with respect to Canadian exploration expenses, Canadian development expenses and Canadian oil and gas property expenses incurred by an original owner.

► 66.7(13.1) ◄

(13.1) Reduction of foreign resource expenses. Where in a taxation year an original owner of foreign resource properties in respect of a country disposes of all or substantially all of the original owner's foreign resource properties in circumstances to which subsection (2.3) applies,

(*a*) in determining the cumulative foreign resource expense of the original owner in respect of the country at any time after the time referred to in subparagraph (2.3)(*a*)(i), there shall be deducted the amount of that cumulative foreign resource expense determined immediately after the disposition; and

(*b*) for the purpose of paragraph (2.3)(*a*), the cumulative foreign resource expense of the original owner in respect of the country determined immediately after the disposition that was deducted under subsection 66.21(4) in computing the original owner's income for the year is deemed to be equal to the lesser of

(i) the amount deducted under paragraph (*a*) in respect of the disposition, and

(ii) the amount, if any, by which

(A) the specified amount determined under subsection (13.2) in respect of the original owner and the country for the year

exceeds

(B) the total of all amounts determined under this paragraph in respect of another disposition of foreign resource property in respect of the country made by the original owner before the disposition and in the year.

Related Sections: S. 66.21(1), "cumulative foreign resource expense", "foreign resource expense"; s. 66.7(13.2) Specified amount — foreign resource expenses; s. 66.7(15.1) Disposal of foreign resource properties — subsection (2.3); s. 248(1), "foreign resource expense", "foreign resource property".

► 66.7(13.2) ◄

(13.2) Specified amount — foreign resource expenses. Where in a taxation year an original owner of foreign resource properties in respect of a country disposes of all or substantially all of the original owner's foreign resource properties in circumstances to which subsection (2.3) applies, the specified amount in respect of the country and the original owner for the year for the purposes of clause (13.1)(*b*)(ii)(A) and of determining the value of D in the definition "cumulative foreign resource expense" in subsection 66.21(1) is the lesser of

(*a*) the total of all amounts each of which is the amount, if any, by which

(i) an amount deducted under paragraph (13.1)(*a*) in respect of a disposition in the year by the original owner of foreign resource property in respect of the country

exceeds

(ii) the amount, if any, designated by the original owner in the prescribed form filed with the Minister within six months after the end of the year in respect of an amount described under subparagraph (i); and

(*b*) the total of

(i) the amount claimed under subsection 66.21(4) by the original owner in respect of the country for the year, and

(ii) the amount that would, but for paragraph 66.21(3)(*c*), be determined under subsection 66.21(3) in respect of the country and the original owner for the year.

Related Sections: S. 66.21(1) Definitions; s. 66.21(3) Amount to be included in income; s. 66.21(4) Deduction for cumulative foreign resource expense; s. 66.7(2.3) Successor of foreign resource expenses; s. 66.7(13.1) Reduction of foreign resource expenses.

► 66.7(14) ◄

(14) Disposal of Canadian resource properties. Where in a taxation year a predecessor owner of Canadian resource properties disposes of Canadian resource properties to a corporation in circumstances in which subsection 29(25) of the *Income Tax Application Rules* or subsection (1), (3), (4) or (5) applies,

(*a*) for the purposes of applying any of those subsections to the predecessor owner in respect of its acquisition of any Canadian resource property owned by it immediately before the disposition, it shall be deemed, after the disposition, never to have acquired any such properties except for the purposes of

(i) determining an amount deductible under subsection (1) or (3) for the year,

(ii) where the predecessor owner and the corporation dealt with each other at arm's length at the time of the disposition or the disposition was by way of an amalgamation or merger, determining an amount deductible under subsection (4) or (5) for the year, and

(iii) determining the amount for F in the definition "cumulative Canadian development expense" in subsection 66.2(5), the amounts for paragraphs (*a*) and (*b*) in the description of L in that definition and the amount for F in the definition "cumulative Canadian oil and gas property expense" in subsection 66.4(5); and

(*b*) where the corporation or another corporation acquires any of the properties on or after the disposition in circumstances in which subsection (4) or (5) applies, amounts that become receivable by the predecessor owner after the disposition in respect of Canadian resource properties retained by it at the time of the disposition shall, for the purposes of applying subsection (4) or (5) to the corporation or the other corporation in respect of the acquisition, be deemed not to have become receivable by the predecessor owner.

► 66.7(15) ◄

(15) Disposal of foreign resource properties. Where after June 5, 1987 a predecessor owner of foreign resource properties disposes of all or substantially all of its foreign resource properties to a corporation in circumstances in which subsection (2) applies, for the purpose of applying that subsection to the predecessor owner in respect of its acquisition of any of those properties (or other foreign resource properties retained by it at the time of the disposition which were acquired by it in circumstances in which subsection (2) applied), it shall be deemed, after the disposition, never to have acquired the properties.

► 66.7(15.1) ◄

(15.1) Disposal of foreign resource properties — subsection (2.3). Where in a taxation year a predecessor owner of foreign resource properties disposes of foreign resource properties to a corporation in circumstances to which subsection (2.3) applies,

(*a*) for the purpose of applying that subsection to the predecessor owner in respect of its acquisition of any foreign resource properties owned by it immediately before the disposition, it is deemed, after the disposition, never to have acquired any such properties except for the purposes of

(i) where the predecessor owner and the corporation dealt with each other at arm's length at the time of the disposition or the disposition was by way of an amalgamation or merger, determining an amount deductible under subsection (2.3) for the year, and

(ii) determining the value of F in the definition "cumulative foreign resource expense" in subsection 66.21(1); and

(*b*) where the corporation or another corporation acquires any of the properties on or after the disposition in circumstances to which subsection (2.3) applies, amounts that become receivable by the predecessor owner after the disposition in respect of foreign resource properties retained by it at the time of the disposition are, for the purposes of applying subsection (2.3) to the corporation or the other corporation in respect of the acquisition, deemed not to have become receivable by the predecessor owner.

Related Sections: S. 66.7(2.3) Successor of foreign resource expenses; s. 66.7(13.1) Reduction of foreign resource expenses.

► 66.7(16) ◄

(16) Non-successor acquisitions. If at any time a Canadian resource property or a foreign resource property is acquired by a person in circumstances in which none of subsections (1) to (5), nor subsection 29(25) of the *Income Tax Application Rules*, apply, every person who was an original owner or predecessor owner of the property before that time is, for the purpose of applying those subsections to or in respect of the person or any other person who after that time acquires the property, deemed after that time not to be an original owner or predecessor owner of the property before that time.

History: S. 66.7(16) was replaced by S.C. 2013, c. 34, s. 204(2), applicable to property acquired after November 5, 2010, and formerly read:

(16) *Non-successor acquisitions.* Where at any time a Canadian resource property or a foreign resource property is acquired by a person in circumstances in which none of subsection 29(25) of the *Income Tax Application Rules* and subsections (1) to (5) apply, every person who was an original owner or predecessor owner of the property by reason of having disposed of the property before that time shall, for the purpose of applying those subsections to or in respect of the person or any other person who after that time acquires the property, be deemed after that time not to be an original owner or predecessor owner of the property by reason of having disposed of the property before that time.

Canadian Tax Foundation: Haughey, *Tiered Partnerships: Successor Rules*, 2014 Canadian Tax Highlights 22(2):13–15.

► 66.7(17) ◄

(17) Restriction on deductions. Where in a particular taxation year and before June 6, 1987 a person disposed of a Canadian resource property or a foreign resource property in circumstances in which any of subsection 29(25) of the *Income Tax Application Rules* and subsections (1) to (5) applies, no deduction in respect of an expense incurred before the property was disposed of may be made under this section or section 66, 66.1, 66.2 or 66.4 by the person in computing the person's income for a taxation year subsequent to the particular taxation year.

► 66.7(18) ◄

(18) Application of interpretation provisions. The definitions in subsection 66(15) and sections 66.1 to 66.4 apply in this section.

SECTION 66.8: Resource expenses of limited partner

► 66.8(1) ◄

(1) Resource expenses of limited partner. Where a taxpayer is a limited partner of a partnership at the end of a fiscal period of the partnership, the following rules apply:

(*a*) determine the amount, if any, by which

(i) the total of all amounts each of which is the taxpayer's share of

(A) the Canadian oil and gas property expenses (in this subsection referred to as "property expenses"),

(B) the Canadian development expenses (in this subsection referred to as "development expenses"),

(C) the Canadian exploration expenses (in this subsection referred to as "exploration expenses"),

(D) the foreign resource expenses in respect of a country (in this subsection referred to as "country-specific foreign expenses"), or

(E) the foreign exploration and development expenses (in this subsection referred to as "global foreign expenses"),

incurred by the partnership in the fiscal period determined without reference to this subsection

exceeds

(ii) the amount, if any, by which

(A) the taxpayer's at-risk amount at the end of the fiscal period in respect of the partnership

exceeds

(B) the total of

(I) the amount required by subsection 127(8) in respect of the partnership to be added in computing the investment tax credit of the taxpayer in respect of the fiscal period, and

(II) the taxpayer's share of any losses of the partnership for the fiscal period from a farming business;

(*b*) the amount determined under paragraph (*a*) shall be applied

(i) first to reduce the taxpayer's share of property expenses,

(ii) if any remains unapplied, then to reduce the taxpayer's share of development expenses,

(iii) if any remains unapplied, then to reduce the taxpayer's share of exploration expenses,

(iv) if any remains unapplied, then to reduce (in the order specified by the taxpayer in writing filed with the Minister on or before the taxpayer's filing-due date for the taxpayer's taxation year in which the fiscal period ends or, where no such specification is made, in the order determined by the Minister) the taxpayer's share of country-specific foreign expenses, and

(v) if any remains unapplied, then to reduce the taxpayer's share of global foreign expenses; and

incurred by the partnership in the fiscal period; and

(*c*) for the purposes of subparagraph 53(2)(*c*)(ii), sections 66 to 66.7, subsection 96(2.1) and section 111, the taxpayer's share of each class of expenses described in subparagraph (*a*)(i) incurred by the partnership in the fiscal period shall be deemed to be the amount by which the taxpayer's share of that class of expenses as determined under subparagraph (*a*)(i) exceeds the amount, if any, that was applied under paragraph (*b*) to reduce the taxpayer's share of that class of expenses.

Editorial Note: S. 66.8 limits the deduction by a limited partner of resource expenses allocated to the limited partner in excess of the limited partner's "at-risk amount". Where the resource expenses allocated to a limited partner exceed the limited partner's at-risk amount, the limited partner's share of resource expenses incurred by the partnership in the fiscal period are reduced in the following order: Canadian oil and gas property expenses, Canadian development expenses, Canadian exploration expenses, foreign resource expenses incurred in a country and foreign exploration and development expenses.

Where such a reduction occurs in a year, the amount of the reduction may be carried forward and added to the limited partner's share of the class of resource expenses incurred by the partnership in the immediately following fiscal period of the partnership. Such expenses may be carried forward indefinitely and deducted in future years when the limited partner has a sufficient at-risk amount.

Related Sections: S. 66(15), "foreign exploration and development expenses"; s. 66.1(6), "Canadian exploration expense"; s. 66.2(5), "Canadian development expense"; s. 66.4(5), "Canadian oil and gas property expense"; s. 66.8(2) Expenses in following fiscal period; s. 66.8(3) Interpretation.

▶ 66.8(2) ◀

(2) Expenses in following fiscal period. For the purposes of subparagraph (1)(*a*)(i), the amount by which a taxpayer's share of a class of expenses incurred by a partnership is reduced under paragraph (1)(*b*) in respect of a fiscal period of the partnership shall be added to the taxpayer's share, otherwise determined, of that class of expenses incurred by the partnership in the immediately following fiscal period of the partnership.

▶ 66.8(3) ◀

(3) Interpretation. In this section,

(*a*) the expression "limited partner" of a partnership has the meaning that would be assigned by subsection 96(2.4), if in subsection 96(2.5) each reference to

(i) "February 25, 1986" were a reference to "June 17, 1987",

(ii) "February 26, 1986" were a reference to "June 18, 1987",

(iii) "January 1, 1987" were a reference to "January 1, 1988",

(iv) "June 12, 1986" were a reference to "June 18, 1987", and

(v) "prospectus, preliminary prospectus or registration statement" were a reference to "prospectus, preliminary prospectus, registration statement, offering memorandum or notice that is required to be filed before any distribution of securities may commence";

(*a*.1) the expression "at-risk amount" of a taxpayer in respect of a partnership has the meaning that would be assigned by subsection 96(2.2) if paragraph 96(2.2)(*c*) read as follows:

(*c*) all amounts each of which is an amount owing at that time to the partnership, or to a person or partnership not dealing at arm's length with the partnership, by the taxpayer or by a person or partnership not dealing at arm's length with the taxpayer, other than any amount deducted under subparagraph 53(2)(*c*)(i.3) in computing the adjusted cost base, or under section 143.2 in computing the cost, to the taxpayer of the taxpayer's partnership interest at that time, or any amount owing by the taxpayer to a person in respect of which the taxpayer is a subsidiary wholly-owned corporation or where the taxpayer is a trust, to a person that is the sole beneficiary of the taxpayer, and;

(*b*) a reference to a taxpayer who is a member of a particular partnership shall include a reference to another partnership that is a member if the particular partnership; and

(*c*) a taxpayer's share of Canadian development expenses or Canadian oil and gas property expenses incurred by a partnership in a fiscal period in respect of which the taxpayer has elected in respect of the share under paragraph (*f*) of the definition "Canadian development expense" in subsection 66.2(5) or paragraph (*b*) of the definition "Canadian oil and gas property expense" in subsection 66.4(5), as the case may be, shall be deemed to be nil.

History: S. 66.8(3)(*a*) was replaced by S.C. 2013, c. 34, s. 205(1), applicable to fiscal periods that end after 2003, and formerly read:

(*a*) the expressions "at-risk amount" of a taxpayer in respect of a partnership and "limited partner" of a partnership have the meanings assigned by subsections 96(2.2) and (2.4), respectively, except that, with respect to the definition "limited partner", the definition "exempt interest" in subsection 96(2.5) shall be read as though the reference therein to

(i) "February 25, 1986" were a reference to "June 17, 1987",

(ii) "February 26, 1986" were a reference to "June 18, 1987",

(iii) "January 1, 1987" were a reference to "January 1, 1988",

(iv) "June 12, 1986" were a reference to "June 18, 1987", and

(v) "prospectus, preliminary prospectus or registration statement" were read as "prospectus, preliminary prospectus, registration statement, offering memorandum or notice that is required to be filed before any distribution of securities may commence";

S. 66.8(3)(*a.1*) was added by S.C. 2013, c. 34, s. 205(1), applicable to fiscal periods that end after 2003.

Related Sections: S. 66.2(5), "Canadian development expense"; s. 66.4(5), "Canadian oil and gas property expense".

Subdivision f — Rules Relating to Computation of Income

SECTION 67: General limitation re expenses

In computing income, no deduction shall be made in respect of an outlay or expense in respect of which any amount is otherwise deductible under this Act, except to the extent that the outlay or expense was reasonable in the circumstances.

Related Sections: S. 8(9) Presumption; s. 18(1)(*a*) General limitation; s. 18(1)(*h*) Personal and living expenses. s. 248(1), "amount"; ITAR s. 31 Application of s. 67 of amended Act.

Canadian Tax Foundation: Moody, *Owner Manager Remuneration — Current Trends, Strategies, and Challenges*, 2013 Prairie Provinces Tax Conference 7:1–49; Rachert, *Proving Business Expenses: Checklists and Commentary*, 2012 British Columbia Tax Conference 11:1–21; Clarke, *Tax Litigation Issues Relevant to Small and Medium-Sized Business*, 2012 British Columbia Tax Conference 7:1–17; Kirby and Strawson, *More Planning for Professionals*, 2007 Conference Report 36:1–40; Clark, *Recent Development in Small Business Corporate Taxation*, 2006 Prairie Provinces Tax Conference 7:1–22; Gill, *Bonusing Down*, 2002 Canadian Tax Highlights 10(11):81–82.

Tax Profile: May 2012 — Retirement Compensation Arrangements; January 2012 — Highlights from the 2011 Ontario Tax Conference: Q&A with the Tax Administration Panel; June 2005 — Paying a Bonus After a Sale of Assets: Where Are We Now?; June 2004 — Owner-Manager Remuneration: Bonuses Out of Non-Active Business Income.

Tax Topics: No. 2107, Taxpayer Denied Deduction for "unreasonably" being the Victim of Fraud; No. 1814, 2006 Canadian Tax Foundation Annual Conference CRA Round Table; No. 1716, Adding Insult to Injury; No. 1686, Owner-Manager Remuneration: Bonuses Out of Non-Active Business Income.

Income Tax Folios: *Secondary* — S1-F2-C3 Scholarships, Research Grants and Other Education Assistance.

Secondary — S1-F3-C4 Moving Expenses.

Income Tax Technical News: Issue No. 30, Reasonableness of Shareholder/Manager Remuneration.

Information Circulars: IC 87-2R International transfer pricing.

Interpretation Bulletins: *Secondary* — IT-357R2 Expenses of training; IT-373R2 (Consolid.) Woodlots; IT-467R2 Damages, settlements and similar payments; IT-468R Management or administration fees paid to non-residents; IT-521R Motor vehicle expenses claimed by self-employed individuals; IT-525R (Consolid.) Performing artists.

Tax Window Files: Contractors Payments to Subcontractors — Deduction for Reasonable Expenses, *Technical Interpretation, Business and Partnerships Division, May 31, 2006*, CRA Document No. 2006-0181651I7.

Cases: A family construction company deducted $20,000 in 1962 and $30,000 in 1963 in respect of remuneration for the company president's young brother. It was held that the deductions were reasonable having regard to the services rendered by the brother and to his contemplated status as a key man in the company. *Gabco Ltd. v. M.N.R.*, 68 DTC 5210 (Ex. Ct.)

SECTION 67.1: Expenses for food, etc

► 67.1(1) ◄

(1) Expenses for food, etc. Subject to subsection (1.1), for the purposes of this Act, other than sections 62, 63, 118.01 and 118.2, an amount paid or payable in respect of the human consumption of food or beverages or the enjoyment of entertainment is deemed to be 50 per cent of the lesser of

(*a*) the amount actually paid or payable in respect thereof, and

(*b*) an amount in respect thereof that would be reasonable in the circumstances.

Editorial Note: Section 67.1 effectively reduces by 50% the deduction claimed by a taxpayer for food, beverages, and entertainment expenses incurred for the purpose of earning employment, business, or property income. If the actual amount paid for the expenses is unreasonable, the limited deduction is only calculated on a reasonable amount. The limit does not apply to moving, adoption, medical, or child care expenses or in the circumstances described in s. 67.1(2), but it is applicable to amounts that are capitalized or included in the cost of inventory. The limit is 80% for food and beverage expenses incurred by a long-haul truck driver meeting the conditions in subsections 67.1(1.1) and (5) regarding the type of travel and vehicle involved.

Canadian Tax Foundation: Gervais and Power, *Can I Deduct That?*, 2013 Ontario Tax Conference 10:1–15; Kakkar, *Some Not So Obvious Exceptions to the 50 Percent Meals and Entertainment Rules*, 2013 Tax for the Owner-Manager 13(1):3–4.

Forms: T2125 — Statement of Business or Professional Activities.

Guides: T4002 Business and Professional Income.

Income Tax Folios: *Secondary* — S3-F6-C1 Interest Deductibility.

Information Circulars: IC 73-21R9 Claims for meals and lodging expenses of transport employees.

Interpretation Bulletins: *Primary* — IT-518R Food, beverages and entertainment expenses; IT-525R (Consolid.) Performing artists. *Secondary* — IT-504R2 (Consolid.) Visual artists and writers; IT-522R Vehicle, travel and sales expenses of employees.

Tax Window Files: Coffee and Water Provided to Clients and Staff, *Technical Interpretation, Business and Partnerships Division, February 16, 2004*, CRA Document No. 2004-0057101E5.

Cases: The cost of food and entertainment vouchers that a real estate agent gave to his clients was subject to the 50% deductibility rule. *The Queen v. Stapley*, 2006 DTC 6075 (F.C.A.), reversing 2005 DTC 1095 (T.C.C.).

► 67.1(1.1) ◄

(1.1) Meal expenses for long-haul truck drivers. An amount paid or payable in respect of the consumption of food or beverages by a long-haul truck driver during an eligible travel period of the driver is deemed to be the amount determined by multiplying the specified percentage in respect of the amount so paid or payable by the lesser of

(*a*) the amount so paid or payable, and

(*b*) a reasonable amount in the circumstances.

Editorial Note: Subsection 67.1(1.1) allows long haul truck drivers incurring food and beverage expenses during an eligible travel period to deduct 80% of those expenses from their income. The same percentage may be used for allowances paid under the CRA's daily flat rate meal policy and by the employers of those long haul truck drivers reimbursing them for their expenses.

History: S. 67.1(1.1), the portion before paragraph (*a*) was replaced by S.C. 2013, c. 34, s. 206(1), applicable to amounts that are paid, or become payable, after March 18, 2007, and formerly read:

(1.1) *Expenses for food and beverages of long-haul truck drivers.* An amount paid or payable by a long-haul truck driver in respect of the consumption of food or beverages by the driver during an eligible travel period of the driver is deemed to be the amount determined by multiplying the specified percentage in respect of the amount so paid or payable by the lesser of

► 67.1(2) ◄

(2) Exceptions. Subsection (1) does not apply to an amount paid or payable by a person in respect of the consumption of food or beverages or the enjoyment of entertainment where the amount

(*a*) is paid or payable for food, beverages or entertainment provided for, or in expectation of, compensation in the ordinary course of a business carried on by that person of providing the food, beverages or entertainment for compensation;

(*b*) relates to a fund-raising event the primary purpose of which is to benefit a registered charity;

(*c*) is an amount for which the person is compensated and the amount of the compensation is reasonable and specifically identified in writing to the person paying the compensation;

(*d*) is required to be included in computing any taxpayer's income because of the application of section 6 in respect of food or beverages consumed or entertainment enjoyed by the taxpayer or a person with whom the taxpayer does not deal at arm's length, or would be so required but for subparagraph 6(6)(*a*)(ii);

(*e*) is an amount that

(i) is not paid or payable in respect of a conference, convention, seminar or similar event,

(ii) would, but for subparagraph 6(6)(*a*)(i), be required to be included in computing any taxpayer's income for a taxation year because of the application of section 6 in respect of food or beverages consumed or entertainment enjoyed by the taxpayer or a person with whom the taxpayer does not deal at arm's length, and

(iii) is paid or payable in respect of the taxpayer's duties performed at a work site in Canada that is

(A) outside any population centre, as defined by the last Census Dictionary published by Statistics Canada before the year, that has a population of at least 40,000 individuals as determined in the last census published by Statistics Canada before the year, and

(B) at least 30 kilometres from the nearest point on the boundary of the nearest such population centre;

(*e*.1) is an amount that

(i) is not paid or payable in respect of entertainment or of a conference, convention, seminar or similar event,

(ii) would, if this Act were read without reference to subparagraph 6(6)(*a*)(i), be required to be included in computing a taxpayer's income for a taxation year because of the application of section 6 in respect of food or beverages consumed by the taxpayer or by a person with whom the taxpayer does not deal at arm's length,

(iii) is paid or payable in respect of the taxpayer's duties performed at a site in Canada at which the person carries on a construction activity or at a construction work camp referred to in subparagraph (iv) in respect of the site, and

(iv) is paid or payable for food or beverages provided at a construction work camp, at which the taxpayer is lodged, that was constructed or installed at or near the site to provide board and lodging to employees while they are engaged in construction services at the site; or

(*f*) is in respect of one of six or fewer special events held in a calendar year at which the food, beverages or entertainment is generally available to all individuals employed by the person at a particular place of business of the person and consumed or enjoyed by those individuals.

History: S. 67.1(2)(*e*)(iii) was replaced by S.C. 2013, c. 40, s. 33(1), applicable to the 2013 and subsequent taxation years, and formerly read:

(iii) is paid or payable in respect of the taxpayer's duties performed at a work site in Canada that is

(A) outside any urban area, as defined by the last Census Dictionary published by Statistics Canada before the year, that has a population of at least 40,000 individuals as determined in the last census published by Statistics Canada before the year, and

(B) at least 30 kilometres from the nearest point on the boundary of the nearest such urban area;

▶ 67.1(3) ◀

(3) Fees for convention, etc. For the purposes of this section, where a fee paid or payable for a conference, convention, seminar or similar event entitles the participant to food, beverages or entertainment (other than incidental beverages and refreshments made available during the course of meetings or receptions at the event) and a reasonable part of the fee, determined on the basis of the cost of providing the food, beverages and entertainment, is not identified in the account for the fee as compensation for the food, beverages and entertainment, $50 or such other amount as may be prescribed shall be deemed to be the actual amount paid or payable in respect of food, beverages and entertainment for each day of the event on which food, beverages or entertainment is provided and, for the purposes of this Act, the fee for the event shall be deemed to be the actual amount of the fee minus the amount deemed by this subsection to be the actual amount paid or payable for the food, beverages and entertainment.

Editorial Note: The deductible expense for a convention, seminar or similar event is reduced by a reasonable amount for meals and entertainment provided. Where this amount is not specified a daily amount of $50 may be prescribed.

▶ 67.1(4) ◀

(4) Interpretation. For the purposes of this section,

(*a*) no amount paid or payable for travel on an airplane, train or bus shall be considered to be in respect of food, beverages or entertainment consumed or enjoyed while travelling thereon; and

(*b*) "entertainment" includes amusement and recreation.

▶ 67.1(5) ◀

(5) Definitions. The following definitions apply for the purpose of this section.

"eligible travel period" —"eligible travel period" in respect of a long-haul truck driver is a period during which the driver is away from the municipality or metropolitan area where the specified place in respect of the driver is located for a period of at least 24 continuous hours for the purpose of driving a long-haul truck that transports goods to, or from, a location that is beyond a radius of 160 kilometres from the specified place.

"long-haul truck" —"long-haul truck" means a truck or a tractor that is designed for hauling freight and that has a gross vehicle weight rating (as that term is defined in subsection 2(1) of the *Motor Vehicle Safety Regulations*) that exceeds 11 788 kilograms.

"long-haul truck driver" —"long-haul truck driver" means an individual whose principal business or principal duty of employment is driving a long-haul truck that transports goods.

"specified percentage" —"specified percentage" in respect of an amount paid or payable is

(*a*) 60 per cent, if the amount is paid or becomes payable on or after March 19, 2007 and before 2008;

(*b*) 65 per cent, if the amount is paid or becomes payable in 2008;

(*c*) 70 per cent, if the amount is paid or becomes payable in 2009;

(*d*) 75 per cent, if the amount is paid or becomes payable in 2010; and

(*e*) 80 per cent, if the amount is paid or becomes payable after 2010.

"specified place" —"specified place" means, in the case of an employee, the employer's establishment to which the employee ordinarily reports to work is located and, in the case of an individual whose principal business is to drive a long-haul truck to transport goods, the place where the individual resides.

SECTION 67.2: Interest on money borrowed for certain vehicles

For the purposes of this Act, if an amount is paid or payable for a period by a person in respect of interest on borrowed money used to acquire a passenger vehicle or zero-emission passenger vehicle, or on an amount paid or payable for the acquisition of such a vehicle, then in computing the person's income for a taxation year the amount of interest so paid or payable is deemed to be the lesser of the actual amount paid or payable and the amount determined by the formula

$$A/30 \times B$$

where

A is $250 or such other amount as may be prescribed; and

B is the number of days in the period in respect of which the interest was paid or payable, as the case may be.

Editorial Note: The prescribed limit has been $300 per 30-day period since 2001; see also Regulation 7307(2).

History: S. 67.2, the portion before the formula was replaced by S.C. 2019, c. 29, s. 7(1), deemed to have come into force on March 19, 2019. S. 67.2 formerly read:

S. 67.2 *Interest on money borrowed for passenger vehicle.* For the purposes of this Act, where an amount is paid or payable for a period by a person in respect of interest on borrowed money used to acquire a passenger vehicle or on an amount paid or payable for the acquisition of such a vehicle, in computing the person's income for a taxation year, the amount of interest so paid or payable shall be deemed to be the lesser of the actual amount paid or payable and the amount determined by the formula

Related Regulations: 7307(2).

Related Sections: S. 8(1)(*j*) Motor vehicle and aircraft costs; s. 18(1)(*r*) Certain automobile expenses; s. 20(1)(*c*) Interest; s. 67.4 More than one owner or lessor; s. 67.41 More than one owner; s. 248(1), "passenger vehicle".

Interpretation Bulletins: *Secondary* — IT-521 Motor vehicle expenses claimed by self-employed individuals; IT-522R Vehicle, travel and sales expenses of employees; IT-525R (Consolid.) Performing artists.

SECTION 67.3: Limitation re cost of leasing passenger vehicle

Notwithstanding any other section of this Act, where

(*a*) in a taxation year all or part of the actual lease charges in respect of a passenger vehicle are paid or payable, directly or indirectly, by a taxpayer, and

(*b*) in computing the taxpayer's income for the year an amount may be deducted in respect of those charges,

in determining the amount that may be so deducted, the total of those charges shall be deemed not to exceed the lesser of

(*c*) the amount determined by the formula

$$(A \times B)/30 - C - D - E$$

where

A is $600 or such other amount as is prescribed,

B is the number of days in the period commencing at the beginning of the term of the lease and ending at the earlier of the end of the year and the end of the lease,

C is the total of all amounts deducted in computing the taxpayer's income for preceding taxation years in respect of the actual lease charges in respect of the vehicle,

D is the amount of interest that would be earned on the part of the total of all refundable amounts in respect of the lease that exceeds $1,000 if interest were

(i) payable on the refundable amounts at the prescribed rate, and

(ii) computed for the period before the end of the year during which the refundable amounts were outstanding, and

E is the total of all reimbursements that became receivable before the end of the year by the taxpayer in respect of the lease, and

(*d*) the amount determined by the formula

$$(A \times B)/0.85C - D - E$$

where

A is the total of the actual lease charges in respect of the lease incurred in respect of the year or the total of the actual lease charges in respect of the lease paid in the year (depending on the method regularly followed by the taxpayer in computing income),

B is $20,000 or such other amount as is prescribed,

C is the greater of $23,529 (or such other amount as is prescribed) and the manufacturer's list price for the vehicle,

D is the amount of interest that would be earned on that part of the total of all refundable amounts paid in respect of the lease that exceeds $1,000 if interest were

(i) payable on the refundable amounts at the prescribed rate, and

(ii) computed for the period in the year during which the refundable amounts are outstanding, and

E is the total of all reimbursements that became receivable during the year by the taxpayer in respect of the lease.

Editorial Note: The general prescribed limit (amount A in the formula) has been $800 plus federal and provincial sales taxes per 30-day period since 2001; see also Regulation 7307(3).

Related Regulations: 4301; 7307(1), (3), (4).

Related Sections: S. 8(1)(*f*) Sales expenses; s. 8(1)(*h.1*) Travel expenses; s. 18(1)(*a*) General limitation; S. 67.4 More than one owner or lessor; s. 248(1), "passenger vehicle".

Interpretation Bulletins: *Secondary* — IT-521 Motor vehicle expenses claimed by self-employed individuals; IT-522R Vehicle, travel and sales expenses of employees; IT-525R (Consolid.) Performing artists.

SECTION 67.4: More than one owner or lessor

Where a person owns or leases a motor vehicle jointly with one or more other persons, the reference in paragraph 13(7)(*g*) to the amount of $20,000, in section 67.2 to the amount of $250 and in section 67.3 to the amounts of $600, $20,000 and $23,529 shall be read as a reference to that proportion of each of those amounts or such other amounts as may be prescribed for the purposes thereof that the fair market value of the first-mentioned person's interest in the vehicle is of the fair market value of the interests in the vehicle of all those persons.

Related Regulations: 7307(1), (2), (3).

Interpretation Bulletins: *Secondary* — IT-521 Motor vehicle expenses claimed by self-employed individuals; IT-522R Vehicle, travel and sales expenses of employees.

SECTION 67.41: More than one owner

If a person owns a zero-emission passenger vehicle jointly with one or more other persons, any reference in paragraph 13(7)(*i*) to the prescribed amount and in section 67.2 to the amount of $250 or such other amount as may be prescribed is to be read as a reference to that proportion of each of those amounts that the fair market value of the first-mentioned person's interest in the vehicle is of the fair market value of the interests in the vehicle of all those persons.

History: S. 67.41 was added by S.C. 2019, c. 29, s. 8(1), deemed to have come into force on March 19, 2019.

Related Sections: 13(7)(i) Rules applicable; 67.2 Interest on money borrowed for certain vehicles.

SECTION 67.5: Non-deductibility of illegal payments

► 67.5(1) ◄

(1) Non-deductibility of illegal payments. In computing income, no deduction shall be made in respect of an outlay made or expense incurred for the purpose of doing anything that is an offence under section 3 of the *Corruption of Foreign Public Officials Act* or under any of sections 119 to 121, 123 to 125, 393 and 426 of the *Criminal Code*, or an offence under section 465 of the *Criminal Code* as it relates to an offence described in any of those sections.

Related Sections: S. 18(1)(*a*) General limitation; s. 67.6 Non-deductibility of fines and penalties.

Canadian Petroleum Tax Journal: Recent Cases of Interest — Deduction of Fines, Penalties, and Damage Awards, Gerald Grenon, 2000, Vol. 13, No. 1.

Income Tax Folios: *Secondary* — S3-F6-C1 Interest Deductibility.

► 67.5(2) ◄

(2) Reassessments. Notwithstanding subsections 152(4) to (5), the Minister may make such assessments, reassessments and additional assessments of tax, interest and penalties and such determinations and redeterminations as are necessary to give effect to subsection (1) for any taxation year.

SECTION 67.6: Non-deductibility of fines and penalties

In computing income, no deduction shall be made in respect of any amount that is a fine or penalty (other than a prescribed fine or penalty) imposed under a law of a country or of a political subdivision of a country (including a state, province or territory) by any person or public body that has authority to impose the fine or penalty.

Editorial Note: S. 67.6 does not apply to fines and penalties imposed under private contracts.

Related Regulations: 7309.

Related Sections: S. 18(1)(*a*) General limitation; s. 18(1)(*t*) Payments under Act; s. 67.5 Non-deductibility of illegal payments.

Income Tax Folios: *Primary* — S4-F2-C1 Deductibility of Fines and Penalties.

Income Tax Technical News: Issue No. 38, Income Tax Treatment of GST.

SECTION 68: Allocation of amounts in consideration for property, services or restrictive covenants

If an amount received or receivable from a person can reasonably be regarded as being in part the consideration for the disposition of a particular property of a taxpayer, for the provision of particular services by a taxpayer or for a restrictive covenant as defined by subsection 56.4(1) granted by a taxpayer,

(*a*) the part of the amount that can reasonably be regarded as being the consideration for the disposition shall be deemed to be proceeds of disposition of the particular property irrespective of the form or legal effect of the contract or agreement, and the person to whom the property was disposed of shall be deemed to have acquired it for an amount equal to that part;

(*b*) the part of the amount that can reasonably be regarded as being consideration for the provision of particular services shall be deemed to be an amount received or receivable by the taxpayer in respect of those services irrespective of the form or legal effect of the contract or agreement, and that part shall be deemed to be an amount paid or payable to the taxpayer by the person to whom the services were rendered in respect of those services; and

(*c*) the part of the amount that can reasonably be regarded as being consideration for the restrictive covenant is deemed to be an amount received or receivable by the taxpayer in respect of the restrictive covenant irrespective of the form or legal effect of the contract or agreement, and that part is deemed to be an amount paid or payable to the taxpayer by the person to whom the restrictive covenant was granted.

Editorial Note: Basically, s. 68 applies where an amount is received as consideration for a property or service plus "something else" (i.e., another property or service). Generally speaking, the allocation of the consideration to the property or service must be made on a reasonable basis.

The provision was recently amended to apply where part of an amount received or receivable from a person can reasonably be regarded as consideration for a restrictive covenant granted by a taxpayer. This part of the consideration is considered to be an amount that is received or receivable by the taxpayer in respect of the restrictive covenant, and that part is also considered to be paid or payable to the taxpayer by the person to whom the restrictive covenant was granted. As such, the consideration may be included in the taxpayer's income under s. 56.4(2), unless one of the exceptions to that provision applies. Furthermore, s. 56.4(5) explicitly provides that s. 68 does not apply in certain circumstances.

History: S. 68, the portion before paragraph (*a*) was replaced by S.C. 2013, c. 34, s. 207(1), deemed to have come into force on February 27, 2004, except that section 68, the portion before paragraph (*a*) does not apply to a taxpayer's grant of a restrictive covenant made in writing by the taxpayer before February 27, 2004 between the taxpayer and a person with whom the taxpayer deals at arm's length.

S. 68, the portion before paragraph (*a*) formerly read:

S. 68. *Allocation of amounts in consideration for disposition of property.* Where an amount received or receivable from a person can reasonably be regarded as being in part the consideration for the disposition of a particular property of a taxpayer or as being in part consideration for the provision of particular services by a taxpayer,

S. 68(*c*) was added by S.C. 2013, c. 34, s. 207(2), deemed to have come into force on February 27, 2004, except that paragraph 68(*c*) does not apply to a taxpayer's grant of a restrictive covenant made in writing by the taxpayer before February 27, 2004 between the taxpayer and a person with whom the taxpayer deals at arm's length.

Related Sections: S. 40(1) General rules; 54, "proceeds of disposition"; 56.4(5) Non-application of section 68; 56.4(7) Application of subsection (5) — realization of goodwill amount and disposition of property; 67 General limitation re expenses; 248(1), "amount", "disposition", "property".

Canadian Tax Foundation: McCue, *The Section 68 Reasonableness Standard After TransAlta*, 2014 Canadian Tax Journal 1:43–67; Kakkar, *More Problems with Restrictive Covenants*, 2014 Tax for the Owner-Manager 14(4):8; Lamarre, *Critical Issues in the Determination of Cost Under the Income Tax Act*, 2012 Conference Report 17:1–28; Choudhury and Connell, *Select Issues in the Purchase and Sale of a Business*, 2012 Ontario Tax Conference 11:1–31; Lang and Taylor, *Tax Issues in Purchase and Sale Agreements*, 2011 Conference Report 14:1–52.

Tax Profile: August 2012 — U.S. Purchases and Sales of Canadian Businesses: Tax and Corporate Issues; July 2012 — Non-Competition Payments; July 2012 — Asset Sale — Price Allocation.

Tax Topics: No. 2135, Restrictive Covenants — The Final Chapter (For Now) — Part II; No. 2132, Restrictive Covenants — The Final Chapter (For Now) — Part I; No. 1875, Restrictive Covenants; No. 1638, Valuing a Non-Compete Agreement.

Interpretation Bulletins: *Secondary* — IT-96R6 Options granted by corporations to acquire shares, bonds or debentures; IT-143R3 Meaning of eligible capital expenditure.

Cases: Where an amount is received which is partly payment for the disposition of property and partly payment for "something else", the taxpayer must establish that the allocation of the amount between property and "something else" is reasonable. In this context, the expression "something else" is not limited to non-property, but includes different items and classes of property. Thus, where a transaction involved the sale of land and buildings, the buildings were "something else" and the taxpayer had the onus of showing that the allocation of the sale price was reasonable. *The Queen v. Golden*, 86 DTC 6138 (S.C.C.), affirming 83 DTC 5138 (F.C.A.), which reversed 80 DTC 6378 (F.C.T.D.)

SECTION 69: Inadequate considerations

► 69(1) ◄

(1) Inadequate considerations. Except as expressly otherwise provided in this Act,

(*a*) where a taxpayer has acquired anything from a person with whom the taxpayer was not dealing at arm's length at an amount in excess of the fair market value thereof at the time the taxpayer so acquired it, the taxpayer shall be deemed to have acquired it at that fair market value;

(*b*) where a taxpayer has disposed of anything

(i) to a person with whom the taxpayer was not dealing at arm's length for no proceeds or for proceeds less than the fair market value thereof at the time the taxpayer so disposed of it,

(ii) to any person by way of gift, or

(iii) to a trust because of a disposition of a property that does not result in a change in the beneficial ownership of the property;

the taxpayer shall be deemed to have received proceeds of disposition therefor equal to that fair market value; and

(*c*) where a taxpayer acquires a property by way of gift, bequest or inheritance or because of a disposition that does not result in a change in the beneficial ownership of the property, the taxpayer is deemed to acquire the property at its fair market value.

Editorial Note: The deeming rules in s. 69(1)(*a*) and (*b*) are one-sided, in that they only apply to the taxpayer and not the person disposing of the property (paragraph (*a*)) or the person acquiring the property (paragraph (*b*)), as the case may be. However, in the case of a gift or inheritance, the person acquiring the property is subject to the deemed acquisition at fair market value rule in s. 69(1)(*c*). Note that the deeming rules are subject to the express provisions of the Act that provide otherwise.

History: S. 69(1)(*b*)(ii) was replaced by S.C. 2014, c. 39, s. 12(1), applicable to the 2016 and subsequent taxation years, and formerly read:

(ii) to any person by way of gift *inter vivos*, or

S. 69(1)(*b*) was amended by S.C. 2013, c. 34, s. 208(1), by striking out "and" at the end of subparagraph (iii), applicable to dispositions that occur after December 23, 1998.

Related Sections: S. 15(1) Benefit conferred on shareholder; s. 51(1) Convertible property; s. 52(1.1) Idem, where owner non-resident; s. 52(2) Cost of property received as dividend in kind; s. 54, "proceeds of disposition"; s. 69(4) Shareholder appropriations; s. 69(5) Winding-up of corporation; s. 70(6) Where transfer or distribution to spouse or spouse trust; s. 70(9.11) Transfer of farming and fishing property from trust to settlor's children; s. 70(9.21) Transfer of family farm and fishing corporations and partnerships; s. 70(9.31) Transfer of family farm or fishing corporation or family farm or fishing partnership from trust to children of settlor; s. 73(1) Inter vivos transfers by individuals; s. 73(3.1) Inter vivos transfer of farm or fishing property to child; s. 73(4.1) Inter vivos transfer of family farm or fishing corporations and partnerships; s. 74.1(1) Transfers and loans to spouse; s. 74.2(1) Gain or loss deemed that of lender or transferor; s. 85(1) Transfer of property to corporation by shareholders; s. 86(1) Exchange of shares by a shareholder in course of reorganization of capital; s. 88(1) Winding-up; s. 97(2) Rules where election by partners; s. 107(2) Distribution by personal trust; s. 248(1), "amount", "disposition", "property"; s. 248(35) Deemed fair market value.

Canadian Tax Foundation: Kakkar, *Business Migrations: Is a Transfer for No Consideration a Gift?*, 2015 Tax for the Owner-Manager 15(2):8–9.

Tax Profile: April 2012 — Price Adjustment Clauses; July 2007 — Canadian Tax Traps.

Tax Topics: No. 2361, Tax Treatment of Non-Arm's Length Transfer for $1: Sale or Gift?; No. 1971-72, 2009 Canadian Tax Foundation Conference: Wizards, Tiny Taxes and "Evil" Kirk; No. 1854, The Effectiveness of Price Adjustment Clauses; No. 1814, 2006 Canadian Tax Foundation Annual Conference CRA Round Table.

Income Tax Folios: *Primary* — S4-F3-C1 Price Adjustment Clauses; *Secondary* — S3-F9-C1 Lottery Winnings, Miscellaneous Receipts, and Income (and Losses) from Crime.

Information Circulars: IC 72-25R4 Business equity valuations; IC 87-2R International Transfer Pricing; IC 89-3 Policy statement on business equity valuations.

Interpretation Bulletins: *Primary* — IT-209R Inter-vivos gifts of capital property to individuals directly or through trusts. *Secondary* — IT-125R4 Disposition of resource properties; IT-140R3 Buy-sell agreements; IT-143R3 Meaning of eligible capital expenditure; IT-212R3 Income of deceased persons — Rights or things; IT-226R Gift to a charity of a residual interest in real property or an equitable interest in a trust; IT-268R4 Inter vivos transfer of farm property to a child; IT-288R2 Gifts of capital properties to a charity and others; IT-297R2 Gifts in kind to charity and others; IT-335R2 Indirect payments; IT-427R Livestock of farmers; IT-432R2 Benefits conferred on shareholders; IT-433R Farming or fishing — Use of cash method; IT-490 Barter transactions; IT-504R2 (Consolid.) Visual artists and writers.

Tax Window Files: Paragraph 69(1)(c) and Nominal Consideration, *January 24, 2019*, CRA Document No. 2018-0773301E5.

Cases: The parties involved in a sale of seismic data were dealing at arm's length even though the vendor also acted as the purchaser's agent. *The Queen v. McLarty*, 2008 DTC 6354 (S.C.C.), reversing in part 2006 DTC 6340 (F.C.A.), reversing in part 2005 DTC 217 (T.C.C.)

The taxpayers each purchased a group of limited edition prints, donated them to charities and received donation receipts for approximately three times the purchase price. Since the prints were acquired and donated in groups, FMV should be determined on a group basis and was equal to the highest price that the art vendor charged for each group of prints. *A.G. of Canada v. Nash et al.*, 2005 DTC 5696 (F.C.A.), reversing 2004 DTC 3391 (T.C.C.), 2004 DTC 3328 and 2004 DTC 3360

A limited partner was denied partnership losses which resulted from CCA taken at the partnership level relating to the purchase of certain processing equipment. The purchase of the equipment was not at arm's length, and hence was deemed to have taken place at fair market value. *Deptuck v. The Queen*, 2003 DTC 5272 (F.C.A.), affirming 2002 DTC 1835 (T.C.C.)

A limited partnership, ITOLP, acquired equipment from a corporation, IRRI, of which G was the controlling shareholder. At that time, ITOLP's only partners were G and ITML, a corporation of which G was the sole shareholder and director. Paragraph 69(1)(a) was invoked to deem the purchase price to be the fair market value of the equipment. The taxpayers could not be heard to argue that the non-arm's length deeming rules of s. 69(1) were applicable only to "persons" and not to partnerships as separate entities. *Chutka et al. v. The Queen*, 2001 DTC 5093 (F.C.A.), affirming 98 DTC 1668 (T.C.C.)

The taxpayer was diluting his own shareholdings in a company and increasing those of his wife and children. Those dispositions by the taxpayer of his economic interest in the company gave rise to gifts, bringing into operation the "deemed proceeds" provisions of s. 69(1)(*b*)(ii) and justifying the inclusion in the taxpayer's income of his one-half share of such deemed proceeds. *The Queen v. Kieboom*, 92 DTC 6382 (F.C.A.), affirming 91 DTC 5478 (F.C.T.D.)

▶ 69(1.1) ◀

(1.1) Idem, where s. 70(3) applies. Where a taxpayer has acquired property that is a right or thing to which subsection 70(3) applies, the following rules apply:

(*a*) paragraph (1)(*c*) is not applicable to that property; and

(*b*) the taxpayer shall be deemed to have acquired the property at a cost equal to the total of

(i) such part, if any, of the cost thereof to the taxpayer who has died as had not been deducted by the taxpayer in computing the taxpayer's income for any year, and

(ii) any expenditures made or incurred by the taxpayer to acquire the property.

Related Sections: S. 70(3) Rights or things transferred to beneficiaries.

Interpretation Bulletins: *Secondary* — IT-212R3 Income of deceased persons — Rights or things; IT-427R Livestock of farmers.

▶ 69(1.2) ◀

(1.2) Idem. Where, at any time,

(*a*) a taxpayer disposed of property for proceeds of disposition (determined without reference to this subsection) equal to or greater than the fair market value at that time of the property, and

(*b*) there existed at that time an agreement under which a person with whom the taxpayer was not dealing at arm's length agreed to pay as rent, royalty or other payment for the use of or the right to use the property an amount less than the amount that would have been reasonable in the circumstances if the taxpayer and the person had been dealing at arm's length at the time the agreement was entered into,

the taxpayer's proceeds of disposition of the property shall be deemed to be the greater of

(*c*) those proceeds determined without reference to this subsection, and

(*d*) the fair market value of the property at the time of the disposition, determined without reference to the existence of the agreement.

Related Sections: S. 13(21), "proceeds of disposition"; s. 54, "proceeds of disposition"; s. 248(1), "property".

▶ 69(2) ◀

(2) Unreasonable consideration — (Repealed by S.C. 1998, c. 19, s. 107(1).)

▶ 69(3) ◀

(3) Idem — (Repealed by S.C. 1998, c. 19, s. 107(1).)

▶ 69(4) ◀

(4) Shareholder appropriations. Where at any time property of a corporation has been appropriated in any manner whatever to or for the benefit of a shareholder of the corporation for no consideration or for consideration that is less than the property's fair market value and a sale of the property at its fair market value would have increased the corporation's income or reduced a loss of the corporation, the corporation shall be deemed to have disposed of the property, and to have received proceeds of disposition therefor equal to its fair market value, at that time.

Related Sections: S. 15(1) Benefit conferred on shareholder; s. 88(1) Winding-up; s. 88(2) Winding-up of Canadian corporation.

▶ 69(5) ◀

(5) Idem. Where in a taxation year of a corporation property of the corporation has been appropriated in any manner whatever to, or for the benefit of, a shareholder, on the winding-up of the corporation, the following rules apply:

(*a*) the corporation is deemed, for the purpose of computing its income for the year, to have disposed of the property immediately before the winding-up for proceeds equal to its fair market value at that time;

(*b*) the shareholder shall be deemed to have acquired the property at a cost equal to its fair market value immediately before the winding-up;

(*c*) subsections 52(1) and (2) do not apply for the purposes of determining the cost to the shareholder of the property; and

(*d*) subsections 13(21.2), 18(15) and 40(3.4) and (3.6) do not apply in respect of any property disposed of on the winding-up.

History: S. 69(5)(*d*) was replaced by S.C. 2016, c. 12, s. 19(1), in force January 1, 2017, and formerly read:

(*d*) subsections 13(21.2), 14(12), 18(15) and 40(3.4) and (3.6) do not apply in respect of any property disposed of on the winding-up.

Related Sections: S. 15(1) Benefit conferred on shareholder; s. 88(1) Winding-up; s. 88(2) Winding-up of Canadian corporation.

▶ 69(6) ◀

(6) Disposition of petroleum, etc — (Repealed by S.C. 2003, c. 28, s. 8(2).)

▶ 69(7) ◀

(7) Idem — (Repealed by S.C. 2003, c. 28, s. 8(2).)

▶ 69(7.1) ◀

(7.1) Aviation turbine fuel — (Repealed by 1983-84, c. 1, s. 31(1).)

▶ 69(8) ◀

(8) Fair market value of resource output disposed of to Crown — (Repealed by S.C. 2003, c. 28, s. 8(2).)

▶ 69(9) ◀

(9) Fair market value of resource output acquired from Crown — (Repealed by S.C. 2003, c. 28, s. 8(2).)

▶ 69(10) ◀

(10) Certain persons deemed to be same person — (Repealed by S.C. 2003, c. 28, s. 8(2).)

▶ 69(11) ◀

(11) Deemed proceeds of disposition. Where, at any particular time as part of a series of transactions or events, a taxpayer disposes of property for proceeds of disposition that are less than its fair market value and it can reasonably be considered that one of the main purposes of the series is (*a*) to obtain the benefit of

(i) any deduction (other than a deduction under subsection 110.6(2.1) in respect of a capital gain from a disposition of a share acquired by the taxpayer in an acquisition to which subsection 85(3) or 98(3) applied) in computing income, taxable income, taxable income earned in Canada or tax payable under this Act, or

(ii) any balance of undeducted outlays, expenses or other amounts

available to a person (other than a person that would be affiliated with the taxpayer immediately before the series began, if section 251.1 were read without reference to the definition "controlled" in subsection 251.1(3)) in respect of a subsequent disposition of the property or property substituted for the property, or

(*b*) to obtain the benefit of an exemption available to any person from tax payable under this Act on any income arising on a subsequent disposition of the property or property substituted for the property,

notwithstanding any other provision of this Act, where the subsequent disposition occurs, or arrangements for the subsequent disposition are made, before the day that is 3 years after the particular time, the taxpayer is deemed to have disposed of the property at the particular time for proceeds of disposition equal to its fair market value at the particular time.

Editorial Note: S. 69(11) is an anti-avoidance provision which can have severe consequences. It prevents a taxpayer from disposing of property for less than fair market value, if the disposition is part of a series of transactions or events, where it may reasonably be considered that one of the main purposes thereof is to obtain the benefit of any tax deduction or other balance (including any balance of undeducted outlays, expenses or other amounts) available to a "non-affiliated" person in respect of a subsequent disposition of the property or a substituted property. (Where the benefit is tax-exempt status, the non-affiliated requirement does not apply.) Where the subsequent disposition or arrangements for the disposition are made within three years of the original disposition, the taxpayer is deemed to have disposed of the property at fair market value.

As a disposition for less than fair market value may arise from the elected proceeds of disposition pursuant to a rollover, the application of s. 69(11) would "knock out" the rollover. Note also that the benefit of the balances sought must be in respect of a subsequent disposition of the particular property (i.e., which was disposed of for less than fair market value) or a substituted property.

Very generally, one corporation will be "affiliated" with another corporation or individual only if that other corporation is controlled by the same person(s) and/or the spouse(s) of the person(s) who controls the other corporation. For more details regarding affiliated persons, see s. 251.1.

A simple example of the application of s. 69(11) would be where there is an attempted section 85 rollover into a non-affiliated corporation with tax losses, followed by a sale of the asset — i.e., sheltered by the losses. This could include a situation where the "lossco" is controlled by a sibling or parent, since they would not be affiliated persons.

Per s. 69(12), the Minister may assess or reassess as necessary to give effect to s. 69(11) without regard to assessment limitation periods; s. 69(13) provides special rules for the purpose of determining whether s. 69(11) is applicable in respect of amalgamations and mergers; s. 69(14) treats a taxpayer that comes into existence during a series of transactions or events as having existed immediately before the series, and as having been affiliated with every person with whom it is affiliated when it comes into existence.

S. 160(1.1) of the Act provides that where s. 69(11) of the Act applies to deem a disposition of property to have occurred at fair market value, both the person disposing of the property and the person to whom the benefit described in that subsection is available in respect of the subsequent disposition are jointly and severally liable for the payment of each other's liabilities arising under the Act as a result of that disposition. The Minister of National Revenue may assess the person for such a liability under s. 160(2) of the Act with interest applying to such assessment.

S. 248(5) provides a broad definition of the term "substituted property". Where a person has disposed of or exchanged a particular property and acquired substituted property and subsequently, by one or more further transactions, acquires further substitutions, any property acquired by any such transaction is deemed to have been substituted for the particular property. Also, any share received in payment of a stock dividend on a particular share is property substituted for the particular share.

Related Sections: S. 73(3) When subsection (3.1) applies; s. 73(4) When subsection (4.1) applies; s. 85(1) Transfer of property to corporation by shareholders; s. 85(2) Transfer of property to corporation from partnership; s. 87 Amalgamations; s. 88(1) Winding-up; s. 97(2) Rules where election by partners; s. 98(3) Rules applicable where partnership ceases to exist; s. 98(5) Where partnership business carried on as sole proprietorship; s. 112(2.4) Where no deduction permitted; s. 160(1.1) Joint liability where s. 69(11) applies; s. 160(2) Assessment; s. 160(3) Discharge of liability; s. 256.1 [Corporate tax-attribute trading].

Canadian Tax Foundation: Truster, *Loss Trading and Subsection 69(11): The Sequel*, 2017 Tax for the Owner Manager 17(3):3–4; Hudson and McCamis, *Refresher on Specific Anti-Avoidance Provisions*, 2014 Prairie Provinces Tax Conference 12:1–41; Man and Tse, *Tax in Troubled Times — Opportunities and Techniques for Loss Utilization*, 2009 British Columbia Tax Conference 5:1–40; De Angelis, *Stop-Loss Rules: Pitfalls and Opportunities*, 2003 Conference Report 50:1–16.

Tax Profile: January 2009 — Market Meltdown — Capital Loss Utilization; February 2008 — Income Splitting A–Z; July 2007 — Canadian Tax Traps; May 2004 — The Stop-Loss Rules.

Income Tax Folios: *Secondary* — S4-F7-C1 Amalgamations of Canadian Corporations.

Information Circulars: IC 88-2 General anti-avoidance rule — Section 245 of the Income Tax Act.

Interpretation Bulletins: *Secondary* — IT-291R3 Transfer of property to a corporation under subsection 85(1).

► 69(12) ◄

(12) Reassessments. Notwithstanding subsections 152(4) to (5), the Minister may at any time make any assessments or reassessments of the tax, interest and penalties payable by the taxpayer that are necessary to give effect to subsection (11).

Editorial Note: See editorial note to s. 69(11).

► 69(12.1) ◄

(12.1) Application of ss. (11) and (12) — (Repealed by S.C. 1998, c. 19, s. 107(4).)

► 69(12.2) ◄

(12.2) Obligation to acquire property, etc — (Repealed by S.C. 1998, c. 19, s. 107(4).)

► 69(13) ◄

(13) Amalgamation or merger. Where there is an amalgamation or merger of a corporation with one or more other corporations to form one corporate entity (in this subsection referred to as the "new corporation"), each property of the corporation that becomes property of the new corporation as a result of the amalgamation or merger is deemed, for the purpose of determining whether subsection (11) applies to the amalgamation or merger, to have been disposed of by the corporation immediately before the amalgamation or merger for proceeds equal to

(*a*) in the case of a Canadian resource property or a foreign resource property, nil; and

(*b*) in the case of any other property, the cost amount to the corporation of the property immediately before the amalgamation or merger.

Editorial Note: See editorial note to s. 69(11).

► 69(14) ◄

(14) New taxpayer. For the purpose of subsection (11), where a taxpayer is incorporated or otherwise comes into existence at a particular time during a series of transactions or events, the taxpayer is deemed

(*a*) to have existed at the time that was immediately before the series began; and

(*b*) to have been affiliated at that time with every person with whom the taxpayer is affiliated (otherwise than because of a right referred to in paragraph 251(5)(*b*)) at the particular time.

Editorial Note: See editorial note to s. 69(11).

Related Sections: S. 251.1 Definition of "affiliated persons".

SECTION 70: Death of a taxpayer

► 70(1) ◄

(1) Death of a taxpayer. In computing the income of a taxpayer for the taxation year in which the taxpayer died,

(*a*) an amount of interest, rent, royalty, annuity (other than an amount with respect to an interest in an annuity contract to which paragraph 148(2)(*b*) applies), remuneration from an office or employment, or other amount payable periodically, that was not paid before the taxpayer's death, shall be deemed to have accrued in equal daily amounts in the period for or in respect of which the amount was payable, and the value of the portion thereof so deemed to have accrued to the day of death shall be included in computing the taxpayer's income for the year in which the taxpayer died; and

(*b*) paragraph 12(1)(*t*) shall be read as follows:

"(*t*) the amount deducted under subsection 127(5) or (6) in computing the taxpayer's tax payable for the year or a preceding taxation year to the extent that it was not included in computing the taxpayer's income for a preceding taxation year under this paragraph or is not included in an amount determined under paragraph 13(7.1)(*e*) or 37(1)(*e*) or subparagraph 53(2)(*c*)(vi) or (*h*)(ii) or for I in the definition "undepreciated capital cost" in subsection 13(21) or L in the definition "cumulative Canadian exploration expense" in subsection 66.1(6);"

Editorial Note: Subsection 70(1) of the Act provides certain rules for calculating the income of a taxpayer in his or her year of death. It states that periodic payments that were earned prior to the time of the taxpayer's death but were not paid shall be accrued up to the time of death and reported in his or her tax return for the year of death.

As well, where a taxpayer claims an investment tax credit under s. 127(5) or (6) in a taxation year, the resulting reduction in the cost of the property to which it relates or the resulting income inclusion under s. 12(1)(*t*) will not occur until the following taxation year. However, this rule is not appropriate where the credit is claimed in the year in which the taxpayer died. Accordingly, in the year of the taxpayer's death, the amount of the investment tax credit claimed which would otherwise impact his or her following taxation year shall be taken into account.

The CRA allows the deduction of accrued expenses relating to the amount included in income under s. 70(1)(*a*) provided that the expenses would have been deductible had they been paid (e.g., interest expense and property taxes). Where there is "genuine doubt" about whether the nature of income arising before a taxpayer's death is a periodic payment (s. 70(1)) or a right or thing (s. 70(2)), the CRA generally allows the legal representative of the taxpayer to report the income as either amount. The right or thing treatment under s. 70(2) is normally advantageous because the income can be reported on a separate return. See para. 4 and 5 of Interpretation Bulletin IT-210R2 (archived, as it doesn't meet current government web standards).

Related Sections: S. 5(1) Income from office or employment; s. 12(1)(*c*) Interest; s. 12(4) Interest from investment contract; s. 12.2(1) Amount to be included; s. 56(1)(*d*) Annuity payments; s. 70(2) Amounts receivable.

Canadian Tax Foundation: Cohen and Bozzelli, *Death of a Taxpayer: Will & Estate Planning in Light of the 2014 Budget Changes*, 2014 Ontario Tax Conference 5A:1–24; Christian, *Post-Mortem Tax Planning*, 2007 Conference Report 37:1–27; Riggin, *Death of a Taxpayer*, 2005 Ontario Tax Conference 9:1–34; Stephan and van der Wissel, *Advising the Personal Representative of a Deceased Taxpayer: Selected Post Mortem Issues*, 2004 Conference Report 36:1–45.

Guides: T4011 Preparing Returns for Deceased Persons.

Interpretation Bulletins: *Primary* — IT-210R2 Income of deceased persons — Periodic payments. *Secondary* — IT-212R3 Income of deceased persons — Rights or things; IT-226R Gift to a charity of a residual interest in real property or an equitable interest in a trust; IT-234 Income of deceased persons — Farm crops; IT-259R4 Exchange of property; IT-396R Interest income; IT-427R Livestock of farmers.

Tax Window Files: Damages — Pay Equity Settlement Received by an Estate, *Technical Interpretation, International and Trust Division, January 19, 2007*, CRA Document No. 2006-0208561E5; Deceased Shareholder's Bonus, *Technical Interpretation, Business and Partnerships Division, May 31, 2006*, CRA Document No. 2006-0168181E5.

Cases: Because of their periodic nature, the payments received by the deceased taxpayer on the actual date of his death fell within the purview of s. 70(1) and could not be considered "rights or things" within the meaning of s. 70(2). *Estate of R. Fontaine v. The Queen*, 95 DTC 5580 (F.C.A.), affirming unreported (T.C.C.).

► 70(2) ◄

(2) Amounts receivable. If a taxpayer who has died had at the time of death rights or things (other than any capital property or any amount included in computing the taxpayer's income by virtue of subsection (1)), the amount of which when realized or disposed of would have been included in computing the taxpayer's income, the value of the rights or things at the time of death shall be included in computing the taxpayer's income for the taxation year in which the taxpayer died, unless the taxpayer's legal representative has, not later than the later of the day that is one year after the date of death of the taxpayer and the day that is 90 days after the sending of any notice of assessment in respect of the tax of the taxpayer for the year of death, elected otherwise, in which case the legal representative shall file a separate return of income for the year under this Part and pay the tax for the year under this Part as if

(*a*) the taxpayer were another person;

(*b*) that other person's only income for the year were the value of the rights or things; and

(*c*) subject to sections 114.2 and 118.93, that other person were entitled to the deductions to which the taxpayer was entitled under sections 110, 118 to 118.7 and 118.9 for the year in computing the taxpayer's taxable income or tax payable under this Part, as the case may be, for the year.

Editorial Note: Subsection 70(2) of the Act provides for an election by the deceased taxpayer's legal representative to file a separate return with respect to "rights or things" receivable at the date of death, to be made by the taxpayer's representative not later than the day that is the later of (i) one year after the date of death of the taxpayer, and (ii) the day that is 90 days after the sending of any notice of assessment in respect of the tax of the taxpayer for the year of death.

If the election is made to report rights and things in a separate return, all rights and things must be reported in that separate return, other than those transferred to beneficiaries pursuant to s. 70(3). In other words, rights and things cannot be "split" between the regular terminal return and the elective separate return.

The personal tax credits under s. 118(1) and (2) can be claimed on both the regular return and the separate return. Section 118.93 precludes the doubling-up of other personal credits, such that the total amount of these credits claimed on the returns cannot exceed the amount that could otherwise be claimed on the regular return only.

History: S. 70(2), the portion before paragraph (*a*) was replaced by S.C. 2010, c. 25, s. 13, in force on Royal Assent, December 15, 2010. S. 70(2), the portion before paragraph (*a*) formerly read:

(2) *Amounts receivable.* Where a taxpayer who has died had at the time of death rights or things (other than any capital property or any amount included in computing the taxpayer's income by virtue of subsection (1)), the amount of which when realized or disposed of would have been included in computing the taxpayer's income, the value thereof at the time of death shall be included in computing the taxpayer's income for the taxation year in which the taxpayer died, unless the taxpayer's legal representative has, not later than the day that is one year after the date of death of the taxpayer or the day that is 90 days after the mailing of any notice of assessment in respect of the tax of the taxpayer for the year of death, whichever is the later day, elected otherwise, in which case the legal representative shall file a separate return of income for the year under this Part and pay the tax for the year under this Part as if

Related Sections: S. 10(6) Artistic endeavour; s. 12(1)(*b*) Amounts receivable; s. 34(*a*) Professional business; s. 53(1)(*e*)(v) Adjustments to cost base — Interest in a partnership; s. 56(1)(*z*) Amounts to be included in income for year; s. 60(*t*) RCA distributions; s. 69(1)(*c*) Inadequate considerations; s. 96(1.5) Disposition by virtue of death of taxpayer; s. 118.93 Credits in separate returns; s. 127.55 Application of s. 127.5; s. 159(5) Election where certain provisions applicable. s. 159(6) Death of taxpayer — tax payable.

Income Tax Folios: *Primary* — S2-F1-C2 Retiring Allowances.

Interpretation Bulletins: *Primary* — IT-212R3 Income of deceased persons — Rights or things; IT-234 Income of deceased persons — Farm crops. *Secondary* — IT-210R2 Income of deceased persons — Periodic payments; IT-278R2 Death of a partner or of a retired partner; IT-326R3 Returns of deceased persons as "another person"; IT-457R Election by professionals to exclude work in progress from income; IT-502 Employee benefit plans and employee trusts.

Tax Window Files: Receipt of Retroactive CPP Lump Sum after death, *June 28, 2017*, CRA Document No. 2017-0709461E5; Damages — Pay Equity Settlement Received by an Estate, *Technical Interpretation, International and Trust Division, January 19, 2007*, CRA Document No. 2006-0208561E5; Lump sum retroactive pension payment, *November 3, 2006*, CRA Document No. 2006-0192051I7; Deceased Shareholder's Bonus, *May 31, 2006*, CRA Document No. 2006-0168181E5; Inventory of a Deceased Artist, *Technical Interpretation, Business and Partnerships Division, April 7, 2005*, CRA Document No. 2004-0099191E5; Taxation of IRA Upon Death, *April 16, 2004*, CRA Document No. 2003-0046111E5.

Cases: Because of their periodic nature, the payments received by the deceased taxpayer on the actual date of his death fell within the purview of s. 70(1) and could not be considered "rights or things" within the meaning of s. 70(2). *Estate of R. Fontaine v. The Queen*, 95 DTC 5580 (F.C.A.), affirming unreported (T.C.C.).

▶ 70(3) ◀

(3) Rights or things transferred to beneficiaries. Where before the time for making an election under subsection (2) has expired, a right or thing to which that subsection would otherwise apply has been transferred or distributed to beneficiaries or other persons beneficially interested in the estate or trust,

(*a*) subsection (2) is not applicable to that right or thing; and

(*b*) an amount received by one of the beneficiaries or persons on the realization or disposition of the right or thing shall be included in computing the income of the beneficiary or person for the taxation year in which the beneficiary or person received it.

Editorial Note: Under s. 70(2) of the Act, the value of certain "rights or things" owned by a taxpayer at death is required to be included in the taxpayer's income for the year of death. Subsection 70(3) provides that s. 70(2) does not apply in connection with rights or things transferred to beneficiaries of the deceased before the later of one year after the date of death of the deceased and 90 days after the sending of any notice of assessment for the year of death.

See s. 69(1.1) regarding the beneficiary's cost of the right or thing.

Related Sections: S. 44(3) Where s. 70(3) does not apply; s. 69(1.1) Inadequate considerations — where s. 70(3) applies; 118.1(5.2) Deemed gifts — eligible transfers; 118.1(7) Gift of art; s. 118.1(7.1) Gifts of cultural property.

Interpretation Bulletins: *Secondary* — IT-210R2 Income of deceased persons — Periodic payments; IT-212R3 Income of deceased persons — Rights or things; IT-278R2 Death of a partner or of a retired partner.

Tax Window Files: Inventory of a Deceased Artist, *Technical Interpretation, Business and Partnerships Division, April 7, 2005*, CRA Document No. 2004-0099191E5.

Cases: If the deceased was reporting the income of his business on the cash basis, amounts receivable would also be rights or things. Accounts receivable of the deceased from his law practice had not been transferred or distributed to his beneficiary within the meaning of what is now subsection 70(3) where the deceased's daughter had agreed to pay the estate for them. *Tory Estate v. M.N.R.*, 76 DTC 6312 (S.C.C.), affirming 73 DTC 5354 (F.C.A.) and 71 DTC 5271 (F.C.T.D.)

▶ 70(3.1) ◀

(3.1) Exception. For the purposes of this section, "rights or things" do not include an interest in a life insurance policy (other than an annuity contract of a taxpayer where the payment therefor was deductible in computing the taxpayer's income because of paragraph 60(*l*) or was made in circumstances in which subsection 146(21) applied), land included in the inventory of a business, a Canadian resource property or a foreign resource property.

History: S. 70(3.1) was replaced by S.C. 2016, c. 12, s. 20(1), in force January 1, 2017, and formerly read:

(3.1) *Exception.* For the purposes of this section, "rights or things" do not include an interest in a life insurance policy (other than an annuity contract of a taxpayer where the payment therefor was deductible in computing the taxpayer's income because of paragraph 60(*l*) or was made in circumstances in which subsection 146(21) applied), eligible capital property, land included in the inventory of a business, a Canadian resource property or a foreign resource property.

Related Sections: S. 54, "eligible capital property"; s. 66(15), "Canadian resource property", "foreign resource property"; s. 70(2) Amounts receivable; s. 70(3) Rights or things transferred to beneficiaries.

Interpretation Bulletins: *Secondary* — IT-212R3 Income of deceased persons — Rights or things; IT-313R2 Eligible capital property — Rules where a taxpayer has ceased carrying on a business or has died.

▶ 70(4) ◀

(4) Revocation of election. An election made under subsection (2) may be revoked by a notice of revocation signed by the legal representative of the taxpayer and filed with the Minister within the time that an election under that subsection may be made.

Interpretation Bulletins: *Secondary* — IT-212R3 Income of deceased persons — Rights or things.

▶ 70(5) ◀

(5) Capital property of a deceased taxpayer. Where in a taxation year a taxpayer dies,

(*a*) the taxpayer shall be deemed to have, immediately before the taxpayer's death, disposed of each capital property of the taxpayer and received proceeds of disposition therefor equal to the fair market value of the property immediately before the death;

(*b*) any person who as a consequence of the taxpayer's death acquires any property that is deemed by paragraph (*a*) to have been disposed of by the taxpayer shall be deemed to have acquired it at the time of the death at a cost equal to its fair market value immediately before the death;

(*c*) where any depreciable property of the taxpayer of a prescribed class that is deemed by paragraph (*a*) to have been disposed of is acquired by any person as a consequence of the taxpayer's death (other than where the taxpayer's proceeds of disposition of the property under paragraph (*a*) are redetermined under subsection 13(21.1)) and the amount that was the capital cost to the taxpayer of the property exceeds the amount determined under paragraph (*b*) to be the cost to the person thereof, for the purposes of sections 13 and 20 and any regulations made for the purpose of paragraph 20(1)(*a*),

(i) the capital cost to the person of the property shall be deemed to be the amount that was the capital cost to the taxpayer of the property, and

(ii) the excess shall be deemed to have been allowed to the person in respect of the property under regulations made for the purpose of paragraph 20(1)(*a*) in computing income for taxation years that ended before the person acquired the property; and

(*d*) where a property of the taxpayer that was deemed by paragraph (*a*) to have been disposed of is acquired by any person as a consequence of the taxpayer's death and the taxpayer's proceeds of disposition of the property under paragraph (*a*) are redetermined under subsection 13(21.1), notwithstanding paragraph (*b*),

(i) where the property was depreciable property of a prescribed class and the amount that was the capital cost to the taxpayer of the property exceeds the amount so redetermined under subsection 13(21.1), for the purposes of sections 13 and 20 and any regulations made for the purpose of paragraph 20(1)(*a*),

(A) its capital cost to the person shall be deemed to be the amount that was its capital cost to the taxpayer, and

(B) the excess shall be deemed to have been allowed to the person in respect of the property under regulations made for the purpose of paragraph 20(1)(*a*) in computing income for taxation years that ended before the person acquired the property, and

(ii) where the property is land (other than land to which subparagraph (i) applies), its cost to the person shall be deemed to be the amount that was the taxpayer's proceeds of disposition of the land as redetermined under subsection 13(21.1).

Editorial Note: Subsection 70(5) of the Act sets out the rules for the deemed realization of capital property owned by a taxpayer immediately before the death of the taxpayer.

A rollover is provided under s. 70(6) for capital property transferred or distributed to the deceased's spouse or common-law partner, or to a qualifying spousal or common-law partner trust. Rollovers are also available for transfers of farming and fishing property to a child of the deceased under ss. 70(9.01) and (9.21) (see the extended definition of "child" in s. 70(10)). See also ss. 70(5.1) and (5.2) for deemed disposition rules with respect to a deceased's eligible capital property, resource properties, and land inventory.

See also s. 248(8) and (23.1)(*a*) regarding the acquisition of property "as a consequence of" a taxpayer's death.

Related Sections: S. 13(21), "depreciable property", "proceeds of disposition"; s. 54, "capital property"; s. 98.2 Transfer of interest on death; s. 100(3) Transfer of interest on death; s. 111(1.1) Net capital losses; s. 111(2) Year of death; s. 118.1(10.1) Determination of fair market value; s. 118.1(12) Ecological gifts; s. 159(5) Election where certain provisions applicable; s. 248(8) Occurrences as a consequence of death; s. 248(9) Definitions; s. 248(23.1) Transfers after death.

Canadian Tax Foundation: Donahue and Crummey, *Tax Issues in Will Planning: Part 1*, 2000 Canadian Tax Journal 4:1299–1320.

STEP Canada: Mark Chartrand and Bryan McNulty, "Shareholders' Agreements: The Hard Stuff," PowerPoint presentation to the 15th National Conference of STEP Canada, Toronto, June 10-11, 2013.

Tax Profile: February 2012 — Post-Mortem Planning — Double Taxation on Death; January 2012 — Highlights from the 2011 Ontario Tax Conference: Q&A with the Tax Administration Panel; January 2010 — Shareholders' Agreements — A Survey of Income Tax Issues; February 2009 — Voting Shares — Premium for Control on Estate Freeze?; September 2004 — Review of Tax Implications of Corporate-Owned Life Insurance Buy-Sell Arrangements.

Tax Topics: No. 1971-72, 2009 Canadian Tax Foundation Conference: Wizards, Tiny Taxes and "Evil" Kirk; No. 1960, Control Premium — CRA Changes Policy on Freezes; No. 1910, Valuation and Family-Business Share Structures — Some Musings; No. 1635, Estate Planning in the Twenty-First Century; No. 1570, Estate Planning in the 21st Century.

Income Tax Technical News: Issue No. 44, Valuation of Special Voting Shares; Issue No. 38, Value of Company Attributable to Voting Non-Participating Shares.

Information Circulars: IC 72-25R4 Business equity valuations; IC 89-3 Policy statement on business equity valuations.

Interpretation Bulletins: *Primary* — IT-140R3 Buy-sell agreements; IT-416R3 Valuation of shares of a corporation receiving life insurance proceeds on death of a shareholder. *Secondary* — IT-278R2 Death of a partner or of a retired partner; IT-288R2 Gifts of capital properties to a charity and others; IT-349R3 Intergenerational transfers of farm property on death; IT-504R2 (Consolid.) Visual artists and writers; IT-522R Vehicle, travel and sales expenses of employees.

Tax Window Files: STEP 2018 – Q8 - Application of subsection 70(5), *May 29, 2018*, CRA Document No. 2018-0742141C6; Post-mortem pipeline, *17XXXX*, CRA Document No. 2016-0670871R3; Postmortem Hybrid/Partial Pipeline Planning, *15XXXX*, CRA Document No. 2015-0606721R3; Post-Mortem Pipeline Planning, *15XXXX*, CRA Document No. 2014-0545531R3; Postmortem Pipeline Planning, *15XXXX*, CRA Document No. 2014-0552071R3; Costs Incurred with Respect to Deemed Dispositions of Property, *2006 STEP Round Table, Question 5, September 11, 2006*, CRA Document No. 2006-0185591C6; Transfer Of Title To Joint Ownership With Child, *July 6, 2006*, CRA Document No. 2005-0152011E5; Property Inherited from Non-Resident, *Technical Interpretation, International and Trusts Division, June 3, 2003*, CRA Document No. 2002-0155735. Paragraph 70(5)(*b*) applicable to non-resident estate of deceased individual that acquires property upon the death of the individual.

Cases: A shareholders' agreement provided that, on a shareholder's death, his shares were deemed to have been redeemed by the corporation on the day preceding his death. This did not avoid the deemed disposition because, by its terms, the redemption could only operate once the taxpayer had died, by which time s. 70(5) would have already applied. *Nussey Estate v. The Queen*, 2001 DTC 5240 (F.C.A.), affirming 99 DTC 1211 (T.C.C.).

▶ 70(5.1) ◀

(5.1) Transfer or distribution — Class 14.1. Notwithstanding subsection (6), if property included in Class 14.1 of Schedule II to the *Income Tax Regulations* of the taxpayer in respect of a business carried on by the taxpayer immediately before the taxpayer's death that is a property to which subsection (5) would otherwise apply is, as a consequence of the death, transferred or distributed (otherwise than by way of a distribution of property by a trust that claimed a deduction under paragraph 20(1)(*a*) or (*b*) in respect of the property or in circumstances to which subsection 24(2) applies) to any person (in this subsection referred to as the "beneficiary"), the following rules apply:

(*a*) paragraphs (5)(*a*) and (*b*) do not apply in respect of the property;

(*b*) the taxpayer is deemed to have, immediately before the taxpayer's death, disposed of the property and received proceeds of disposition equal to the lesser of the capital cost and the cost amount to the taxpayer of the property immediately before the death;

(c) the beneficiary is deemed to have acquired the property at the time of the death at a cost equal to those proceeds; and

(d) paragraph (5)(c) applies as if the references to "paragraph (a)" were read as references to "paragraph (5.1)(b)" and the reference to "paragraph (b)" were read as reference to "paragraph (5.1)(c)".

Editorial Note: Subsection 70(5.1) of the Act sets out the rules for the transfer of a taxpayer's Class 14.1 property (eligible capital property prior to 2017) to a beneficiary on death. See the historical note for pre-2017 wording that applied to eligible capital property.

Subsection 70(5.1) does not apply where s. 24(2) applies. Subsection 24(2) provides a rollover similar to s. 70(5.1) if the deceased's spouse or common-law partner or controlled corporation carries on the business and acquires all of the property that was the deceased's eligible capital property in respect of the business and that had value.

History: S. 70(5.1) was replaced by S.C. 2016, c. 12, s. 20(2), in force January 1, 2017, and formerly read:

(5.1) *Eligible capital property of deceased.* Notwithstanding subsection 24(1), where at any time a taxpayer dies and any person (in this subsection referred to as the beneficiary), as a consequence of the taxpayer's death, acquires an eligible capital property of the taxpayer in respect of a business carried on by the taxpayer immediately before that time (otherwise than by way of a distribution of property by a trust that claimed a deduction under paragraph 20(1)(b) in respect of the property or in circumstances to which subsection 24(2) applies),

(a) the taxpayer shall be deemed to have disposed of the property, immediately before the taxpayer's death, for proceeds equal to $^4/_3$ of that proportion of the cumulative eligible capital of the taxpayer in respect of the business that the fair market value immediately before that time of the property is of the fair market value immediately before that time of all of the eligible capital property of the taxpayer in respect of the business;

(b) subject to paragraph (c), the beneficiary shall be deemed to have acquired a capital property at the time of the taxpayer's death at a cost equal to the proceeds referred to in paragraph (a);

(c) where the beneficiary continues to carry on the business previously carried on by the taxpayer, the beneficiary shall be deemed to have, at the time of the taxpayer's death, acquired an eligible capital property and made an eligible capital expenditure at a cost equal to the total of

(i) the proceeds referred to in paragraph (a), and

(ii) $^4/_3$ of that proportion of the amount, if any, determined for F in the definition "cumulative eligible capital" in subsection 14(5) in respect of the business of the taxpayer at that time that the fair market value immediately before that time of the particular property is of the fair market value immediately before that time of all eligible capital property of the taxpayer in respect of the business,

and, for the purposes of determining at any time the beneficiary's cumulative eligible capital in respect of the business, an amount equal to $^3/_4$ of the amount determined under subparagraph (ii) shall be added to the amount otherwise determined, in respect of the business, for P in the definition "cumulative eligible capital" in subsection 14(5); and

(d) for the purpose of determining, after that time, the amount required by paragraph 14(1)(b) to be included in computing the income of the beneficiary in respect of any subsequent disposition of the property of the business, there shall be added to the amount determined for Q in the definition "cumulative eligible capital" in subsection 14(5) the amount determined by the formula

$$A \times B/C$$

where

A is the amount, if any, determined for Q in that definition in respect of the business of the taxpayer immediately before that time,

B is the fair market value immediately before that time of the particular property, and

C is the fair market value immediately before that time of all eligible capital property of the taxpayer in respect of the business.

Related Sections: S. 24(2) Business carried on by spouse or controlled corporation; s. 54, "eligible capital property"; s. 248(1), "business".

Interpretation Bulletins: *Secondary* — IT-313R2 Eligible capital property — Rules where a taxpayer has ceased carrying on a business or has died.

► 70(5.2) ◄

(5.2) Resource property and land inventory. If in a taxation year a taxpayer dies,

(a) the taxpayer is deemed

(i) to have disposed, at the time that is immediately before the taxpayer's death, of each

(A) Canadian resource property of the taxpayer,

(B) foreign resource property of the taxpayer, and

(C) property that was land included in the inventory of a business of the taxpayer, and

(ii) subject to paragraph (c), to have received at that time proceeds of disposition for each such property equal to its fair market value at that time;

(b) any person who, as a consequence of the taxpayer's death, acquires a property that is deemed by paragraph (a) to have been disposed of by the taxpayer is, subject to paragraph (c), deemed to have acquired the property at the time of the death at a cost equal to its fair market value at the time that is immediately before the death; and

(c) where the taxpayer was resident in Canada at the time that is immediately before the taxpayer's death, a particular property described in clause (a)(i)(A), (B) or (C) is, on or after the death and as a consequence of the death, transferred or distributed to a spouse or common-law partner of the taxpayer described in paragraph (6)(a) or a trust described in paragraph (6)(b), and it can be shown within the period that ends 36 months after the death (or, where written application has been made to the Minister by the taxpayer's legal representative within that period, within any longer period that the Minister considers reasonable in the circumstances) that the particular property has, within that period, vested indefeasibly in the spouse, common-law partner or trust, as the case may be,

(i) the taxpayer is deemed to have received, at the time that is immediately before the taxpayer's death, proceeds of disposition of the particular property equal to

(A) if the particular property is Canadian resource property of the taxpayer or foreign resource property of the taxpayer, the amount specified by the taxpayer's legal representative in the taxpayer's return of income filed under paragraph 150(1)(b), not exceeding its fair market value at that time, and

(B) if the particular property was land included in the inventory of a business of the taxpayer, its cost amount to the taxpayer at that time, and

(ii) the spouse, common-law partner or trust, as the case may be, is deemed to have acquired at the time of the death the particular property at a cost equal to the amount determined under subparagraph (i) in respect of the disposition of it under paragraph (a).

Editorial Note: Subsection 70(5.2) of the Act provides rules with respect to the disposition of resource properties and land inventories on the death of an individual.

Paragraph 70(5.2)(c) provides an optional full or partial rollover for resource properties and s. 70(5.2)(d) provides an optional rollover for land inventory left to the deceased's spouse or common-law partner or qualifying trust.

Subsection 248(9.2) provides that the "vesting indefeasibly" requirement will not be met unless the property so vests prior to the spouse's or common-law partner's death.

See also s. 248(8) and (23.1) regarding the acquisition of property "as a consequence of" a taxpayer's death. See also s. 248(9.1), which provides that a trust created under dependant's' relief legislation can qualify as a trust "created by the taxpayer's will". Subsection 248(9.2) provides that the "vesting indefeasibly" requirement will not be met unless the property so vests prior to the spouse's or common-law partner's death.

History: S. 70(5.2) was replaced by S.C. 2013, c. 34, s. 209(2), applicable to taxation years that begin after 2006, and formerly read:

(5.2) *Resource properties and land inventories of a deceased taxpayer.* Where in a taxation year a taxpayer dies,

(*a*) the taxpayer is deemed to have, immediately before the taxpayer's death, disposed of each Canadian resource property and foreign resource property of the taxpayer and received proceeds of disposition for that property equal to its fair market value immediately before the death;

(*a*.1) subject to subparagraph (*b*)(ii), any particular person who as a consequence of the taxpayer's death acquires any property that is deemed by paragraph (*a*) to have been disposed of by the taxpayer is deemed to have acquired the property at the time of the death at a cost equal to the fair market value of the property immediately before the death;

(*b*) notwithstanding paragraph (*a*), where the taxpayer was resident in Canada immediately before the taxpayer's death, any Canadian resource property or foreign resource property of the taxpayer that is, on or after the death and as a consequence of the death, transferred or distributed to a spouse or common-law partner of the taxpayer described in paragraph (6)(*a*) or a trust described in paragraph (6)(*b*) and it can be shown within the period ending 36 months after the death or, where written application therefor has been made to the Minister by the taxpayer's legal representative within that period, within such longer period as the Minister considers reasonable in the circumstances, that the property vested indefeasibly in the spouse or common-law partner or trust, as the case may be,

(i) the taxpayer shall be deemed to have, immediately before the death, disposed of the property and received proceeds of disposition therefor equal to such amount as is specified by the taxpayer's legal representative in the return of income of the taxpayer filed under paragraph 150(1)(*b*), not exceeding its fair market value immediately before the death, and

(ii) the spouse, common-law partner or trust, as the case may be, is deemed to have acquired the property at the time of the death at a cost equal to the amount determined in respect of the disposition under subparagraph (i);

(*c*) the taxpayer is deemed to have, immediately before the taxpayer's death, disposed of each property that was land included in the inventory of a business of the taxpayer and received proceeds of disposition for that property equal to its fair market value immediately before the death;

(*c*.1) subject to subparagraph (*d*)(ii), any particular person who as a consequence of the taxpayer's death acquires any property that is deemed by paragraph (*c*) to have been disposed of by the taxpayer is deemed to have acquired the property at the time of the death at a cost equal to the fair market value of the property immediately before the death; and

(*d*) notwithstanding paragraph (*c*), where the taxpayer was resident in Canada immediately before the taxpayer's death, any property that is land included in the inventory of a business of the taxpayer is, on or after the death and as a consequence of the death, transferred or distributed to a spouse or common-law partner of the taxpayer described in paragraph (6)(*a*) or a trust described in paragraph (6)(*b*) and it can be shown within the period ending 36 months after the death of the taxpayer or, where written application therefor has been made to the Minister by the taxpayer's legal representative within that period, within such longer period as the Minister considers reasonable in the circumstances, that the property vested indefeasibly in the spouse or common-law partner or trust, as the case may be

(i) the taxpayer shall be deemed to have, immediately before the death, disposed of the land and received proceeds of disposition therefor equal to its cost amount to the taxpayer immediately before the death, and

(ii) the spouse or common-law partner or trust, as the case may be, shall be deemed to have acquired the property at the time of the death at a cost equal to those proceeds.

Related Sections: S. 59(1) Consideration for foreign resource property; s. 59(3.2)(*c*) Recovery of exploration and development expenses; s. 66(15), "Canadian resource property", "foreign resource property"; s. 66.2(1) Amount to be included in income; s. 66.2(5), "cumulative Canadian development expense"; s. 66.4(5), "cumulative Canadian oil and gas property expense"; s. 104(5.8) Trust transfers; s. 159(5) Election where certain provisions applicable.

Tax Profile: October 2007 — Important Changes Announced to the Canada — U.S. Income Tax Convention.

Interpretation Bulletins: *Primary* — IT-125R4 Disposition of resource properties. *Secondary* — IT-212R3 Income of deceased persons — Rights or things.

▶ 70(5.3) ◀

(5.3) Fair market value. For the purposes of subsections (5) and 104(4) and section 128.1, the fair market value at any time of any property deemed to have been disposed of at that time as a consequence of a particular individual's death or as a consequence of the particular individual becoming or ceasing to be resident in Canada shall be determined as though the fair market value at that time of any life insurance policy, under which the particular individual (or any other individual not dealing at arm's length with the particular individual at that time or at the time the policy was issued) was a person whose life was insured, were the cash surrender value (as defined in subsection 148(9)) of the policy immediately before the particular individual died or became or ceased to be resident in Canada, as the case may be.

Editorial Note: In the event that the property includes shares and there was a life insurance policy under which the taxpayer's life was insured, the fair market value of the shares is determined under s. 70(5.3) as if the value of the policy were the policy's cash surrender value immediately before the taxpayer's death. The purpose of s. 70(5.3) is to ensure that life insurance proceeds payable as a consequence of death are not reflected in share value and therefore do not give rise to a capital gain on death.

Related Sections: S. 110.6(15) Value of assets of corporations; s. 139.1(5) Fair market value of ownership rights.

Tax Profile: January 2010 — Shareholders' Agreements — A Survey of Income Tax Issues; September 2004 — Review of Tax Implications of Corporate-Owned Life Insurance Buy-Sell Arrangements.

Information Circulars: IC 72-25R4 Business equity valuations; IC 89-3 Policy statement on business equity valuations.

Interpretation Bulletins: *Primary* — IT-416R3 Valuation of shares of a corporation receiving life insurance proceeds on death of a shareholder.

Tax Window Files: Share Valuation and Policy Loans, *June 9, 2003,* CRA Document No. 2003-0004335.

▶ 70(5.31) ◀

(5.31) Fair market value. For the purposes of subsections (5) and 104(4), the fair market value at any time of any property deemed to have been disposed of at that time as a consequence of a particular individual's death is to be determined as though the fair market value at that time of any annuity contract were the total of all amounts each of which is the amount of a premium paid on or before that time under the contract if

(*a*) the contract is, in respect of an LIA policy, a contract referred to in subparagraph (*b*)(ii) of the definition "LIA policy" in subsection 248(1); and

(*b*) the particular individual is the individual, in respect of the LIA policy, referred to in that subparagraph.

History: S. 70(5.31) was added by S.C. 2013, c. 40, s. 34(1), applicable to taxation years that end after March 20, 2013.

▶ 70(5.4) ◀

(5.4) NISA on death. Where a taxpayer who dies has at the time of death a net income stabilization account, all amounts held for or on behalf of the taxpayer in the taxpayer's NISA Fund No. 2 shall be deemed to have been paid out of that fund to the taxpayer immediately before that time.

Editorial Note: See s. 70(6.1), which provides a rollover of a deceased taxpayer's NISA Fund No. 2 to a spouse, common-law partner or qualifying trust.

Related Sections: S. 12(10.2) NISA receipts; s. 248(1), "net income stabilization account", "NISA Fund No. 2".

► 70(6) ◄

(6) Where transfer or distribution to spouse or spouse trust. Where any property of a taxpayer who was resident in Canada immediately before the taxpayer's death that is a property to which subsection (5) would otherwise apply is, as a consequence of the death, transferred or distributed to

(*a*) the taxpayer's spouse or common-law partner who was resident in Canada immediately before the taxpayer's death, or

(*b*) a trust, created by the taxpayer's will, that was resident in Canada immediately after the time the property vested indefeasibly in the trust and under which

(i) the taxpayer's spouse or common-law partner is entitled to receive all of the income of the trust that arises before the spouse's or common-law partner's death, and

(ii) no person except the spouse or common-law partner may, before the spouse's or common-law partner's death, receive or otherwise obtain the use of any of the income or capital of the trust,

if it can be shown, within the period ending 36 months after the death of the taxpayer or, where written application therefor has been made to the Minister by the taxpayer's legal representative within that period, within such longer period as the Minister considers reasonable in the circumstances, that the property has become vested indefeasibly in the spouse or common-law partner or trust, as the case may be, the following rules apply:

(*c*) paragraphs (5)(*a*) and (*b*) do not apply in respect of the property,

(*d*) subject to paragraph (*d*.1), the taxpayer shall be deemed to have, immediately before the taxpayer's death, disposed of the property and received proceeds of disposition therefor equal to

(i) where the property was depreciable property of a prescribed class, the lesser of the capital cost and the cost amount to the taxpayer of the property immediately before the death, and

(ii) in any other case, its adjusted cost base to the taxpayer immediately before the death,

and the spouse or common-law partner or trust, as the case may be, shall be deemed to have acquired the property at the time of the death at a cost equal to those proceeds,

(*d*.1) where the property is an interest in a partnership (other than an interest in a partnership to which subsection 100(3) applies),

(i) the taxpayer shall, except for the purposes of paragraph 98(5)(*g*), be deemed not to have disposed of the property as a consequence of the taxpayer's death,

(ii) the spouse or common-law partner or the trust, as the case may be, shall be deemed to have acquired the property at the time of the death at a cost equal to its cost to the taxpayer, and

(iii) each amount added or deducted in computing the adjusted cost base to the taxpayer of the property shall be deemed to be required by subsection 53(1) or (2) to be added or deducted, as the case may be, in computing the adjusted cost base to the spouse or common-law partner or the trust, as the case may be, of the property; and

(*e*) where the property was depreciable property of the taxpayer of a prescribed class, paragraph (5)(*c*) applies as if the references therein to "paragraph (*a*)" and to "paragraph (*b*)" were read as references to "paragraph (6)(*d*)".

Editorial Note: S. 70(6) provides a rollover of capital property transferred or distributed to the spouse or common-law partner of the deceased taxpayer (paragraph (*a*)) or a qualifying spousal or common-law partner trust (paragraph (*b*)) as a consequence of the taxpayer's death. See ss. 248(8) and (23.1) regarding the requirement that the property be transferred or distributed "as a consequence of" a taxpayer's death. See also s. 248(9.1), which provides that a trust created under dependant's relief legislation can qualify as a trust "created by the taxpayer's will". S. 248(9.2) provides that the "vesting indefeasibly" requirement will not be met unless the property so vests prior to the spouse's or common-law partner's death.

For qualifying spousal trusts, the income to which the spouse beneficiary must be entitled (paragraph 70(6)(*b*)) is income under trust law, which does not include capital gains. However, no one else may receive any capital gains of the trust while the spouse beneficiary is alive.

S. 70(6.2) allows the deceased's legal representative to elect out of the s. 70(6) rollover on a property-by-property basis. Any resulting loss on the election out of the rollover will not be subject to the superficial loss rules, which do not apply upon death.

Related Regulations: 600(*b*).

Related Sections: S. 13(21), "depreciable property"; s. 40(4) Disposal of principal residence to spouse or trust for spouse; s. 70(9.1) When subsection (9.11) applies; s. 70(9.3) When subsection (9.31) applies; s. 70(13) Capital cost of certain depreciable property; s. 70(14) Order of disposal of depreciable property; s. 73(1) Inter vivos transfers by individuals; s. 73(1.01) Qualifying transfers; s. 104(4) Deemed disposition by trust; s. 104(5) Depreciable property; s. 108(3) Income of a trust in certain provisions; s. 108(4) Trust not disqualified; s. 248(1), "common-law partner", "cost amount", "depreciable property"; s. 248(8) Occurrences as a consequence of death; s. 248(9) Definitions; s. 248(9.1) How trust created; s. 248(9.2) Vested indefeasibly; s. 248(23.1) Transfers after death; s. 252(3) Extended meaning of "spouse" and "former spouse".

Canadian Tax Foundation: Infanti, *Trust's Payment of Insurance Premiums Disqualifies Spousal Trust Status*, 2016 Tax for the Owner-Manager 16(2):4; Wright, *Spousal Trust Trap: Waiving Entitlement to Income*, 2013 Canadian Tax Focus 3(1):7; Addison and Korn, *Interspousal Property Transfers: The Things They Don't Tell You at the Diamond Shop*, 2002 Canadian Tax Journal 2:728–757; Schusheim, *Trust Basics: An Overview*, 1998 Conference Report 32:1–31.

STEP Canada: Florence Marino, "Planning with Life Insurance – Part III," PowerPoint presentation to the 15th National Conference of STEP Canada, Toronto, June 10-11, 2013.

Tax Profile: January 2010 — Shareholders' Agreements — A Survey of Income Tax Issues; September 2004 — Review of Tax Implications of Corporate-Owned Life Insurance Buy-Sell Arrangements.

Forms: T1255 — Designation of a Property as a Principal Residence by the Legal Representative of a Deceased Individual.

Interpretation Bulletins: *Primary* — IT-305R4 Testamentary spouse trusts. *Secondary* — IT-125R4 Disposition of resource properties; IT-278R2 Death of a partner or of a retired partner; IT-522R Vehicle, travel and sales expenses of employees.

Tax Window Files: Delay in final distribution from spousal trust, *April 20, 2016*, CRA Document No. 2015-0601141E5; Spousal Trust — Requirement to Pay Life Insurance Premiums, *2006 STEP Round Table, Question 2, September 11, 2006*, CRA Document No. 2006-0185551C6; Testamentary Trust — Waiving Right to Income, *2005 APFF Conference — Round Table on Federal Taxation, Question 27, October 7, 2005*, CRA Document No. 2005-0141181C6; Testamentary Trust, *Technical Interpretation, International and Trusts Division, April 18, 2005*, CRA Document No. 2004-0093821E5. Beneficiary spouse renouncing right to income does not disqualify trust (see also Document No. 2003-0014515); but may affect testamentary trust status if renounced after income became payable; Spousal Rollover of Undivided

Share of Real Property, *Technical Interpretation, International and Trusts Division, January 26, 2004,* CRA Document No. 2003-0006025. Rollover available for undivided share in land left to spouse; Transfer of Property to Spouse or Common-Law Partner Trust, *Technical Interpretation, International and Trusts Division, September 4, 2003,* CRA Document No. 2002-016643A; Tainted Spousal Trust, *July 17, 2003,* CRA Document No. 2003-0019235; Payment of Trust Expenses by Beneficiary, *Technical Interpretation, International and Trusts Division, April 17, 2003,* CRA Document No. 2002-0154435; Spousal Trust, *February 4, 2003,* CRA Document No. 2002-0129655. Trust income cannot generally be accumulated for the benefit of the spouse to be received after being taxed to the trust.

Cases: After the taxpayer died intestate, his shares were transferred to his wife in August 1987 in her capacity as administratrix of his estate and on December 1, 1987 she purchased them for $10,260 in cash, with the balance of the price being set off against debts owing by the estate. The spousal rollover treatment was denied because such transfer did not fall within the purview of s. 70(6). *Husel Estate v. The Queen,* 94 DTC 1765 (T.C.C.)

After the death of her husband the taxpayer was not entitled to the benefit of the spousal rollover provisions because a buy-sell agreement compelled her to sell the shares she acquired to the remaining partner of the business. The shares were never "indefeasibly vested" in the taxpayer. *Parkes v. M.N.R.,* 86 DTC 1214 (T.C.C.). See also *Greenwood et al. v. The Queen,* 94 DTC 6190 (F.C.A.), affirming 90 DTC 6690 (F.C.T.D.).

► 70(6.1) ◄

(6.1) Transfer or distribution of NISA to spouse or trust. Where a property that is a net income stabilization account of a taxpayer is, on or after the taxpayer's death and as a consequence thereof, transferred or distributed to

(*a*) the taxpayer's spouse or common-law partner, or

(*b*) a trust, created by the taxpayer's will, under which

(i) the taxpayer's spouse or common-law partner is entitled to receive all of the income of the trust that arises before the spouse's or common-law partner's death, and

(ii) no person except the spouse or common-law partner may, before the spouse's or common-law partner's death, receive or otherwise obtain the use of any of the income or capital of the trust,

subsections (5.4) and 73(5) do not apply in respect of the taxpayer's NISA Fund No. 2 if it can be shown, within the period ending 36 months after the death of the taxpayer or, where written application therefor has been made to the Minister by the taxpayer's legal representative within that period, within such longer period as the Minister considers reasonable in the circumstances, that the property has vested indefeasibly in the spouse or common-law partner or trust, as the case may be.

Editorial Note: See s. 70(6.2) for the election out of the NISA fund rollover.

Related Sections: S. 104(1) Reference to trust or estate; s. 104(5.1) Interest in NISA Fund No. 2; s. 108(3) Income of a trust in certain provisions; s. 108(4) Trust not disqualified; s. 248(1), "common-law partner", "net income stabilization account", "NISA Fund No. 2", "trust"; s. 252(3) Extended meaning of "spouse" and "former spouse".

Interpretation Bulletins: *Secondary* — IT-305R4 Testamentary spouse trusts.

► 70(6.2) ◄

(6.2) Election. Subsection (5.1), (6) or (6.1) does not apply to any property of a deceased taxpayer in respect of which the taxpayer's legal representative elects, in the taxpayer's return of income under this Part (other than a return of income filed under subsection (2) or 104(23), paragraph 128(2)(*e*) or subsection 150(4)) for the year in which the taxpayer died, to have subsection (5) or (5.4), as the case may be, apply.

Editorial Note: The election out of the rollover under s. 70(6) may be beneficial if the property has an accrued loss (the superficial loss rules do not apply at death), if any accrued gain in respect of the property can be offset by the deceased's losses, or if any resulting gain qualifies for the capital gains exemption under s. 110.6. The election is made on a property-by-property basis.

History: S. 70(6.2) was replaced by S.C. 2016, c. 12, s. 20(3), in force January 1, 2017, and formerly read:

(6.2) *Election.* Subsection (6) or (6.1) does not apply to any property of a deceased taxpayer in respect of which the taxpayer's legal representative elects, in the taxpayer's return of income under this Part (other than a return of income filed under subsection (2) or 104(23), paragraph 128(2)(*e*) or subsection 150(4)) for the year in which the taxpayer died, to have subsection (5) or (5.4), as the case may be, apply.

Related Regulations: 600(*b*).

Related Sections: S. 159(5) Election where certain provisions applicable; s. 220(3.2) Late, amended or revoked elections.

Information Circulars: IC 07-1 Taxpayer Relief Provisions.

Interpretation Bulletins: *Secondary* — IT-305R4 Testamentary spouse trusts.

► 70(7) ◄

(7) Special rules applicable in respect of trust for benefit of spouse. Where a trust created by a taxpayer's will would, but for the payment of, or provision for payment of, any particular testamentary debts in respect of the taxpayer, be a trust to which subsection (6) or (6.1) applies,

(*a*) for the purpose of determining the day on or before which a return (in this subsection referred to as the "taxpayer's return") of the taxpayer's income for the taxation year in which the taxpayer died is required to be filed by the taxpayer's legal representatives, subsection 150(1) shall be read without reference to paragraph 150(1)(*b*) and as if paragraph 150(1)(*d*) read as follows:

"(*d*) in the case of any other person, by the person's legal representative within 18 months after the person's death; or;" and

(*b*) where the taxpayer's legal representative so elects in the taxpayer's return (other than a return of income filed under subsection (2) or 104(23), paragraph 128(2)(*e*) or subsection 150(4)) and lists therein one or more properties (other than a net income stabilization account) that were, on or after the taxpayer's death and as a consequence thereof, transferred or distributed to the trust, the total fair market value of which properties immediately after the taxpayer's death was not less than the total of the non-qualifying debts in respect of the taxpayer,

(i) subsection (6) does not apply in respect of the properties so listed, and

(ii) notwithstanding the payment of, or provision for payment of, any such particular testamentary debts, the trust shall be deemed to be a trust described in subsection (6),

except that, where the fair market value, immediately after the taxpayer's death, of all of the properties so listed exceeds the total of the non-qualifying debts in respect of the taxpayer (the amount of which excess is referred to in this subsection as the "listed value excess") and the taxpayer's legal representative designates in the taxpayer's return one property so listed (other than money) that is capital property other than depreciable property,

(iii) the amount of the taxpayer's capital gain or capital loss, as the case may be, from the disposition of that property deemed by subsection (5) to have been made by the taxpayer is that proportion of that capital gain or capital loss otherwise determined that

(A) the amount, if any, by which the fair market value of that property immediately after the taxpayer's death exceeds the listed value excess,

is of

(B) the fair market value of that property immediately after the taxpayer's death, and

(iv) the cost to the trust of that property is

(A) where the taxpayer has a capital gain from the disposition of that property deemed by subsection (5) to have been made by the taxpayer, the total of

(I) its adjusted cost base to the taxpayer immediately before the taxpayer's death, and

(II) the amount determined under subparagraph (iii) to be the taxpayer's capital gain from the disposition of that property, or

(B) where the taxpayer has a capital loss from the disposition of that property deemed by subsection (5) to have been made by the taxpayer, the amount by which

(I) its adjusted cost base to the taxpayer immediately before the taxpayer's death

exceeds

(II) the amount determined under subparagraph (iii) to be the taxpayer's capital loss from the disposition of that property.

Editorial Note: Subsection 70(7) of the Act provides rules under which certain "tainted" spousal trusts may be considered qualifying spousal trusts for the purposes of the rollover of capital property under s. 70(6). These rules apply where a spousal trust is not a qualifying spousal trust because of the payment of, or provision for payment of, certain testamentary debts. Essentially, these rules provide a mechanism by which such testamentary debts may be applied against certain property of the trust so listed by the legal representatives of the deceased taxpayer whose will created the trust. In these circumstances, s. 70(7)(*a*)provides that the terminal return of the deceased taxpayer whose will created the trust may be filed up to 18 months after the date of death.

Related Sections: S. 13(21), "depreciable property"; s. 54, "capital property"; s. 70(8) Meaning of certain expressions in s. (7); s. 104(1) Reference to trust or estate; s. 248(1), "net income stabilization account", "trust".

Tax Window Files: Transfer of Property to Spouse or Common-Law Partner Trust, *Technical Interpretation, International and Trusts Division, September 4, 2003*, CRA Document No. 2002-016643A; General Comments on 70(7), *June 3, 2003*, CRA Document No. 2002-016643.

► 70(8) ◄

(8) Meaning of certain expressions in s. (7). In subsection (7),

(*a*) the "fair market value" at any time of any property subject to a mortgage or hypothec is the amount, if any, by which the fair market value at that time of the property otherwise determined exceeds the amount outstanding at that time of the debt secured by the mortgage or hypothec, as the case may be;

(*b*) "non-qualifying debt" in respect of a taxpayer who has died and by whose will any trust has been created that would, but for the payment of, or provision for payment of, any particular testamentary debts in respect of the taxpayer, be a trust described in subsection (6), means any such particular testamentary debt in respect of the taxpayer other than

(i) any estate, legacy, succession or inheritance duty payable, in consequence of the taxpayer's death, in respect of any property of, or interest in, the trust, or

(ii) any debt secured by a mortgage or hypothec on property owned by the taxpayer immediately before the taxpayer's death; and

(*c*) "testamentary debt", in respect of a taxpayer who has died, means

(i) any debt owing by the taxpayer, or any other obligation of the taxpayer to pay an amount, that was outstanding immediately before the taxpayer's death, and

(ii) any amount payable (other than any amount payable to any person as a beneficiary of the taxpayer's estate) by the taxpayer's estate in consequence of the taxpayer's death,

including any income or profits tax payable by or in respect of the taxpayer for the taxation year in which the taxpayer died or for any previous taxation year, and any estate, legacy, succession or inheritance duty payable in consequence of the taxpayer's death.

► 70(9) ◄

(9) When subsection (9.01) applies. Subsection (9.01) applies to a taxpayer and a child of the taxpayer in respect of land in Canada or depreciable property in Canada of a prescribed class of the taxpayer in respect of which subsection (5) would, if this Act were read without reference to this subsection, apply if

(*a*) the property was, before the death of the taxpayer, used principally in a farming or fishing business carried on in Canada in which the taxpayer, the spouse or common-law partner of the taxpayer or a child or parent of the taxpayer was actively engaged on a regular and continuous basis (or, in the case of property used in the operation of a woodlot, was engaged to the extent required by a prescribed forest management plan in respect of that woodlot);

(*b*) the child of the taxpayer was resident in Canada immediately before the day on which the taxpayer died; and

(*c*) as a consequence of the death of the taxpayer, the property is transferred to and becomes vested indefeasibly in the child within the period ending 36 months after the death of the taxpayer or, if written application has been made to the Minister by the taxpayer's legal representative within that period, within any longer period that the Minister considers reasonable in the circumstances.

Editorial Note: The 2014 Federal Budget amended the rollover provisions for family farm or fishing property, essentially to include combinations of farm and fishing businesses. The amendments provide that the various tests relating to the "principal" or "all or substantially all" use of the property will now apply to uses in farming, fishing, or a combination of the two activities, rather than only one of the two activities. The amendments apply to dispositions in 2014 and subsequent years.

See also the extended definition of "child" in subsection 70(10).

History: S. 70(9)(*a*) was replaced by S.C. 2014, c. 39, s. 13(1), deemed to have come into force on January 1, 2014, and formerly read:

(*a*) the property was, before the death of the taxpayer, used principally in a fishing or farming business carried on in Canada in which the taxpayer, the spouse or common-law partner of the taxpayer or a child or a parent of the taxpayer was actively engaged on a regular and continuous basis (or, in the case of property used in the operation of a woodlot, was engaged to the extent required by a prescribed forest management plan in respect of that woodlot);

Related Regulations: 7400.

Related Sections: S. 13(21), "depreciable property"; s. 70(5) Capital property of a deceased taxpayer; s. 70(6) Where transfer or distribution to spouse or spouse trust; s. 70(10), "child"; s. 70(13) Capital cost of certain depreciable property; s. 70(14) Order of disposal of depreciable property; s. 248(1), "business", "common-law partner", "farming"; s. 252(1) Extended meaning of "child".

Information Circulars: IC 07-1 Taxpayer relief provisions.

Interpretation Bulletins: *Primary* — IT-349R3 Intergenerational transfers of farm property on death. *Secondary* — IT-373R2 (Consolid.) Woodlots.

► 70(9.01) ◄

(9.01) Transfer of farming and fishing property to child. If, because of subsection (9), this subsection applies to the taxpayer and a child of the taxpayer in respect of a property of the taxpayer that has been transferred to the child as a consequence of the death of the taxpayer, the following rules apply:

(*a*) where the taxpayer's legal representative does not elect in the taxpayer's return of income under this Part for the year in which the taxpayer died, to have paragraph (*b*) apply to the taxpayer and the child in respect of the property,

(i) paragraphs (5)(*a*) and (*b*) and section 69 do not apply to the taxpayer and the child in respect of the property,

(ii) the taxpayer is deemed to have

(A) disposed of the property immediately before the taxpayer's death, and

(B) received, at the time of the disposition of the property, proceeds of disposition in respect of that disposition of the property equal to

(I) where the property was depreciable property of a prescribed class, the lesser of

1. the capital cost to the taxpayer of the property, and

2. the amount, determined immediately before the time of the disposition of the property, that is that proportion of the undepreciated capital cost of property of that class to the taxpayer that the capital cost to the taxpayer of the property is of the capital cost to the taxpayer of all property of that class that had not, at or before that time, been disposed of, and

(II) where the property is land (other than land to which subclause (I) applies), the adjusted cost base to the taxpayer of the property immediately before the time of the disposition of the property,

(iii) the child is, immediately after the time of the disposition of the property, deemed to have acquired the property at a cost equal to the taxpayer's proceeds of disposition in respect of the disposition of the property determined under subparagraph (ii), and

(iv) where the property was depreciable property of a prescribed class, paragraphs (5)(*c*) and (*d*) apply to the taxpayer and the child in respect of the property as if the references in those paragraphs to "paragraph (*a*)" and "paragraph (*b*)" were read as "subparagraph (9.01)(*a*)(ii)" and "subparagraph (9.01)(*a*)(iii)", respectively; and

(*b*) where the taxpayer's legal representative elects, in the taxpayer's return of income under this Part for the taxation year in which the taxpayer died, to have this paragraph apply to the taxpayer in respect of the property,

(i) paragraphs (5)(*a*) and (*b*) and section 69 do not apply to the taxpayer and the child in respect of the property,

(ii) the taxpayer is deemed to have

(A) disposed of the property immediately before the taxpayer's death, and

(B) received, at the time of the disposition of the property, proceeds of disposition in respect of that disposition of the property equal to

(I) where the property was depreciable property of a prescribed class, the amount that the legal representative designates, which must not be greater than the greater of nor less than the lesser of

1. the fair market value of the property immediately before the time of the disposition of the property, and

2. the lesser of the capital cost to the taxpayer of the property and the amount, determined immediately before the time of the disposition of the property, that is that proportion of the undepreciated capital cost of property of that class to the taxpayer that the capital cost to the taxpayer of the property is of the capital cost to the taxpayer of all property of that class that had not, at or before that time, been disposed of, and

(II) where the property is land (other than land to which subclause (I) applies), the amount that the legal representative designates, which must not be greater than the greater of nor less than the lesser of

1. the fair market value of the property immediately before the time of the disposition of the property, and

2. the adjusted cost base to the taxpayer of the property immediately before the time of the disposition of the property,

(iii) the child is, immediately after the time of the disposition of the property, deemed to have acquired the property at a cost equal to the taxpayer's proceeds of disposition in respect of the disposition of the property determined under subparagraph (ii),

(iv) where the property was depreciable property of a prescribed class, paragraphs (5)(*c*) and (*d*) apply to the taxpayer in respect of the property as if the references in those paragraphs to "paragraph (*a*)" and "paragraph (*b*)" were read as "subparagraph (9.01)(*b*)(ii)" and "subparagraph (9.01)(*b*)(iii)", respectively,

(v) except for the purpose of this subparagraph,

(A) where the amount designated by the taxpayer's legal representative under subclause (ii)(B)(I), exceeds the greater of the amounts determined under sub-subclauses (ii)(B)(I)1 and 2 in respect of the property, the amount designated is deemed to be equal to the greater of those amounts, and

(B) where the amount designated by the taxpayer's legal representative under subclause (ii)(B)(II) exceeds the greater of the amounts determined under sub-subclauses (ii)(B)(II)1 and 2 in respect of the property, the amount designated is deemed to be equal to the greater of those amounts, and

(vi) except for the purpose of this subparagraph,

(A) where the amount designated by the taxpayer's legal representative under subclause (ii)(B)(I) is less than the lesser of the amounts determined under sub-subclauses (ii)(B)(I)1 and 2 in respect of the property, the amount designated is deemed to be equal to the lesser of those amounts, and

(B) where the amount designated by the taxpayer's legal representative under subclause (ii)(B)(II) is less than the lesser of the amounts determined under sub-subclauses (ii)(B)(II)1 and 2 in respect of the property, the amount designated is deemed to be equal to the lesser of those amounts.

Editorial Note: The farming and fishing property rollover applies automatically under s. 70(9.01)(*a*) unless the taxpayer's legal representative elects out of the rollover under s. 70(9.01)(*b*). A child of the taxpayer includes a grandchild and great-grandchild of the taxpayer, and a person who, while under the age of 19, was wholly dependent on and under the custody and control of the taxpayer (see s. 70(10)).

Related Regulations: 600(*b*).

Related Sections: S. 220(3.2) Late, amended or revoked elections.

► 70(9.1) ◄

(9.1) When subsection (9.11) applies. Subsection (9.11) applies to a trust and a child of the settlor of the trust in respect of a property in respect of which subsection 104(4) or (5) would, if this Act were read without reference to this subsection, apply to the trust as a consequence of the death of the beneficiary under the trust who was a spouse or a common-law partner of the settlor if

(*a*) the property (or property for which the property was substituted) was transferred to the trust by the settlor;

(*b*) subsection (6), subsection 73(1) (as that subsection applied to transfers before 2000) or subparagraph 73(1.01)(*c*)(i) applied to the settlor and the trust in respect of the transfer referred to in paragraph (*a*);

(*c*) the property is, immediately before the beneficiary's death, land or a depreciable property of a prescribed class of the trust that was used in a farming or fishing business carried on in Canada;

(*d*) the child of the settlor is, immediately before the beneficiary's death, resident in Canada; and

(*e*) as a consequence of the beneficiary's death, the property is transferred to and becomes vested indefeasibly in the child of the settlor within the period ending 36 months after that beneficiary's death or, if written application has been made to the Minister by the taxpayer's legal representative within that period, within any longer period that the Minister considers reasonable in the circumstances.

History: S. 70(9.1)(*c*) was replaced by S.C. 2014, c. 39, s. 13(2), deemed to have come into force on January 1, 2014, and formerly read:

(*c*) the property is, immediately before the beneficiary's death, land or a depreciable property of a prescribed class of the trust that was used in a fishing or farming business carried on in Canada;

Related Sections: 248(29) Farming or fishing business; S. 70(5) Capital property of a deceased taxpayer; s. 70(6) Where transfer or distribution to spouse or spouse trust; s. 70(13) Capital cost of certain depreciable property; s. 70(14) Order of disposal of depreciable property; s. 73(1) Inter vivos transfers by individuals; s. 104(1) Reference to trust or estate; s. 164(4) Interest on interest repaid; s. 164(5) Effect of carryback of loss, etc; s. 248(1), "cost amount", "trust".

Information Circulars: IC 07-1 Taxpayer Relief Provisions.

Interpretation Bulletins: *Secondary* — IT-349R3 Intergenerational transfers of farm property on death; IT-373R2 (Consolid.) Woodlots.

Cases: In determining the extent to which the lands passed to the deceased's children had been used "in the business of farming" at the time of his death, s. 70(9) must receive a large and liberal construction. Inasmuch as the test is expressed in the terms of the "business of farming", it should not be restricted to the portion of the property used for the tillage of soil or for the other agricultural operations. The deceased's use of the lands "in the business of farming" was therefore extended to 50%. *Bouchard Estate v. M.N.R.*, 93 DTC 1163 (T.C.C.)

► 70(9.11) ◄

(9.11) Transfer of farming and fishing property from trust to settlor's children. If, because of subsection (9.1), this subsection applies to the trust and a child of the settlor of the trust in respect of a property of the trust that has been distributed to the child as a consequence of the death of the beneficiary under the trust who was the spouse or common-law partner of the settlor, the following rules apply:

(*a*) where the trust does not elect, in its return of income under this Part for the taxation year in which the beneficiary died, to have paragraph (*b*) apply to the trust in respect of the property,

(i) subsections 104(4) and (5) and section 69 do not apply to the trust and the child in respect of the property,

(ii) the trust is deemed to have

(A) disposed of the property immediately before the beneficiary's death, and

(B) received, at the time of the disposition, proceeds of disposition in respect of that disposition equal to

(I) where the property was depreciable property of a prescribed class, the lesser of

1. the capital cost to the trust of the property, and

2. the amount, determined immediately before the time of the disposition of the property, that is that proportion of the undepreciated capital cost of property of that class to the trust that the capital cost to the trust of the property is of the capital cost to the trust of all property of that class that had not, at or before that time, been disposed of, and

(II) where the property is land (other than land to which subclause (I) applies), the adjusted cost base to the trust of the property immediately before the time of the disposition of the property, and

(iii) the child is, immediately after the time of the disposition of the property, deemed to have acquired the property at a cost equal to the trust's proceeds of disposition in respect of the disposition of the property determined under subparagraph (ii);

(*b*) where the trust elects, in the trust's return of income under this Part for the taxation year in which the beneficiary died, to have this paragraph apply to the trust in respect of the property,

(i) subsections 104(4) and (5) do not apply to the trust in respect of the property,

(ii) the trust is deemed to have

(A) disposed of the property immediately before the beneficiary's death, and

(B) received, at the time of the disposition of the property, proceeds of disposition in respect of the disposition of the property equal to

(I) where the property was depreciable property of a prescribed class, the amount that the trust designates, which must not be greater than the greater of nor less than the lesser of

1. the fair market value of the property immediately before the time of the disposition of the property, and

2. the lesser of the capital cost to the trust of the property and the amount, determined immediately before the time of the disposition of the property, that is that proportion of the undepreciated capital cost of property of that class to the trust that the capital cost to the trust of the property is of the capital cost to the trust of all property of that class that had not, at or before that time, been disposed of, and

(II) where the property is land (other than land to which subclause (I) applies), the amount that the trust designates, which must not be greater than the greater of nor less than the lesser of

1. the fair market value of the property immediately before the time of the disposition of the property, and

2. the adjusted cost base to the trust of the property immediately before the time of the disposition of the property,

(iii) the child is, immediately after the time of the disposition of the property, deemed to have acquired the property at a cost equal to the trust's proceeds of disposition in respect of the disposition of the property determined under subparagraph (ii),

(iv) except for the purpose of this subparagraph,

(A) where the amount designated by the trust under subclause (ii)(B)(I) exceeds the greater of the amounts determined under sub-subclauses (ii)(B)(I)1 and 2 in respect of the property, the amount designated is deemed to be equal to the greater of those amounts, and

(B) where the amount designated by the trust under subclause (ii)(B)(II) exceeds the greater of the amounts determined under sub-subclauses (ii)(B)(II)1 and 2 in respect of the property, the amount designated is deemed to be equal to the greater of those amounts, and

(v) except for the purpose of this subparagraph,

(A) where the amount designated by the trust under subclause (ii)(B)(I) is less than the lesser of the amounts determined under sub-subclauses (ii)(B)(I)1 and 2 in respect of the property, the amount designated is deemed to be equal to the lesser of those amounts, and

(B) where the amount designated by the trust under subclause (ii)(B)(II), is less than the lesser of the amounts determined under sub-subclauses (ii)(B)(II)1 and 2 in respect of the property, the amount designated is deemed to be equal to the lesser of those amounts;

(*c*) where paragraph (*a*) or (*b*) (each of which is referred to in this subsection as the "relevant provision") applied to the trust in respect of a property that was depreciable property of a prescribed class (other than where the trust's proceeds of disposition of the property under the relevant provision are redetermined under subsection 13(21.1)),

(i) the capital cost to the child of the property, immediately after the time of the disposition, is deemed to be the amount that was the capital cost to the trust of the property, immediately before the time of the disposition, and

(ii) the amount, if any, by which the capital cost to the trust of the property, immediately before the time of the disposition, exceeds the amount determined under the relevant provision to be the cost of the property to the child, immediately after the time of the disposition, is, for the purposes of sections 13 and 20 and any regulations made for the purpose of paragraph 20(1)(*a*), deemed to have been allowed to the child in respect of the property under regulations made for the purpose of paragraph 20(1)(*a*) in computing income for taxation years that ended before the child acquired the property; and

(*d*) where the relevant provision applied to the trust in respect of a property and the trust's proceeds of disposition in respect of the disposition of the property determined under the relevant provision are redetermined under subsection 13(21.1), notwithstanding the relevant provision,

(i) where the capital cost to the trust of the property, immediately before the time of the disposition, exceeds the amount redetermined under subsection 13(21.1), for the purposes of sections 13 and 20 and any regulations made for the purpose of paragraph 20(1)(*a*),

(A) the capital cost to the child of the property, immediately after the time of the disposition, is deemed to be the amount that was the capital cost to the trust of the property, immediately before the time of the disposition, and

(B) the amount, if any, by which the capital cost to the trust of the property, immediately before the time of the disposition, exceeds the amount redetermined under subsection 13(21.1) is deemed to have been allowed to the child in respect of the property under regulations made for the purpose of paragraph 20(1)(*a*) in computing income for taxation years that ended before the child acquired the property, and

(ii) where the property is land, the cost to the child of the property is deemed to be the amount that was the trust's proceeds of disposition as redetermined under subsection 13(21.1).

Editorial Note: The farming and fishing property rollover applies automatically under s. 70(9.11)(*a*) unless the trust elects out of the rollover under s. 70(9.11)(*b*). A child of the taxpayer includes a grandchild and great-grandchild of the taxpayer, and a person who, while under the age of 19, was wholly dependent on and under the custody and control of the taxpayer (see s. 70(10)).

Related Regulations: 600(*b*).

Related Sections: S. 220(3.2) Late, amended or revoked elections.

► 70(9.2) ◄

(9.2) When subsection (9.21) applies. Subsection (9.21) applies to a taxpayer and a child of the taxpayer in respect of a property of the taxpayer in respect of which subsection (5) would, if this Act were read without reference to this subsection, apply to the taxpayer and the child if

(*a*) the property was, immediately before the death of the taxpayer, a share of the capital stock of a family farm or fishing corporation of the taxpayer or an interest in a family farm or fishing partnership of the taxpayer;

(*b*) the child of the taxpayer was resident in Canada immediately before the day on which taxpayer died; and

(*c*) as a consequence of the death of the taxpayer, the property is transferred to and becomes vested indefeasibly in the child within the period ending 36 months after the death of the taxpayer or, if written application has been made to the Minister by the taxpayer's legal representative within that period, within any longer period that the Minister considers reasonable in the circumstances.

History: S. 70(9.2)(*a*) was replaced by S.C. 2014, c. 39, s. 13(3), deemed to have come into force on January 1, 2014, and formerly read:

(*a*) the property was, immediately before the death of the taxpayer, a share of the capital stock of a family fishing corporation of the taxpayer, an interest in a family fishing partnership of the taxpayer, a share of the capital stock of a family farm corporation of the taxpayer or an interest in a family farm partnership of the taxpayer;

Editorial Note: The 2014 Federal Budget amended the rollover provisions for family farm or fishing property to include combinations of farm and fishing businesses carried on by a corporations. The amendments provide that the various tests relating to the "principal" or "all or substantially all" use of the property will now apply to uses in farming, fishing, or a combination of the two activities, rather than only one of the two activities. The amendments apply to dispositions in 2014 and subsequent years.

See also the extended definition of "child" in subsection 70(10).

Related Sections: S. 70(5) Capital property of a deceased taxpayer; s. 70(10), "interest in a family farm or fishing partnership", "share of the capital stock of a family farm or fishing corporation"; s. 252(1) Extended meaning of "child"; s. 255 Canada.

Information Circulars: IC 07-1 Taxpayer relief provisions.

Interpretation Bulletins: *Secondary* — IT-349R3 Intergenerational transfers of farm property on death; IT-373R2 (Consolid.) Woodlots.

► 70(9.21) ◄

(9.21) Transfer of family farm and fishing corporations and partnerships. If, because of subsection (9.2), this subsection applies to the taxpayer and a child of the taxpayer in respect of a property of the taxpayer that has been transferred to the child as a consequence of the death of the taxpayer, the following rules apply:

(*a*) where the taxpayer's legal representative does not elect, in the taxpayer's return of income under this Part for the taxation year in which the taxpayer died, to have paragraph (*b*) apply to the taxpayer in respect of the property,

(i) paragraphs (5)(*a*) and (*b*) and section 69 do not apply to the taxpayer and the child in respect of the property,

(ii) where the property is, immediately before the death of the taxpayer, a share of the capital stock of a family farm or fishing corporation of the taxpayer,

(A) the taxpayer is deemed to have

(I) disposed of the property immediately before the taxpayer's death, and

(II) received proceeds of disposition in respect of that disposition equal to the adjusted cost base to the taxpayer, immediately before the time of that disposition, of the property, and

(B) the child is, immediately after the time of the disposition, deemed to have acquired the property at a cost equal to the taxpayer's proceeds of disposition in respect of that disposition determined under clause (A), and

(iii) where the property is, immediately before the death of the taxpayer, a partnership interest described in paragraph (9.2)(*a*) (other than a partnership interest to which subsection 100(3) applies),

(A) the taxpayer is, except for the purpose of paragraph 98(5)(*g*), deemed not to have disposed of the property as a consequence of the taxpayer's death,

(B) the child is deemed to have acquired the property at the time of the taxpayer's death at a cost equal to the cost to the taxpayer of the interest immediately before the time that is immediately before the time of the taxpayer's death, and

(C) each amount required by subsection 53(1) or (2) to be added or deducted in computing the adjusted cost base to the taxpayer, immediately before the time of the taxpayer's death, of the property is deemed to be an amount required by subsection 53(1) or (2) to be added or deducted in computing, at any time at or after the time of the taxpayer's death, the adjusted cost base to the child of the property; and

(*b*) where the taxpayer's legal representative elects, in the taxpayer's return of income under this Part for the taxation year in which the taxpayer died, to have this paragraph apply to the taxpayer in respect of the property,

(i) paragraphs (5)(*a*) and (*b*) and section 69 do not apply to the taxpayer and the child in respect of the property,

(ii) subject to subparagraph (iii), where the property is, immediately before the taxpayer's death, a share of the capital stock of a family farm or fishing corporation of the taxpayer or an interest in a family farm or fishing partnership of the taxpayer,

(A) the taxpayer is deemed to have

(I) disposed of the property immediately before the taxpayer's death, and

(II) received, at the time of the disposition of the property, proceeds of disposition in respect of the disposition of the property equal to the amount that the taxpayer's legal representative designates, which must not be greater than the greater of nor less than the lesser of

1. the fair market value of the property immediately before the taxpayer's death, and

2. the adjusted cost base to the taxpayer of the property immediately before the time of the disposition,

(B) the child is, immediately after the time of the disposition, deemed to have acquired the property at a cost equal to the taxpayer's proceeds of disposition in respect of the disposition of the property determined under clause (A),

(C) except for the purpose of this clause, where the amount designated by the taxpayer's legal representative under subclause (A)(II) exceeds the greater of the amounts determined under sub-subclauses (A)(II)1 and 2 in respect of the property, the amount designated is deemed to be equal to the greater of those amounts, and

(D) except for the purpose of this clause, where the amount designated by the taxpayer's legal representative under subclause (A)(II) is less than the lesser of the amounts determined under sub-subclauses (A)(II)1 and 2 in respect of the property, the amount designated is deemed to be equal to the lesser of those amounts, and

(iii) where the property is, immediately before the death of the taxpayer, a partnership interest described in paragraph (9.2)(*a*) (other than a partnership interest to which subsection 100(3) applies), and the taxpayer's legal representative further elects, in the taxpayer's return of income under this Part for the taxation year in which the taxpayer died, to have this subparagraph apply to the taxpayer in respect of the property,

(A) the taxpayer is, except for the purpose of paragraph 98(5)(*g*), deemed not to have disposed of the property as a consequence of the taxpayer's death,

(B) the child is deemed to have acquired the property at the time of the taxpayer's death at a cost equal to the cost to the taxpayer of the interest immediately before the time that is immediately before the death of the taxpayer, and

(C) each amount required by subsection 53(1) or (2) to be added or deducted in computing the adjusted cost base to the taxpayer, immediately before the time of the taxpayer's death, of the property is deemed to be an amount required by subsection 53(1) or (2) to be added or deducted in computing, at any time at or after the taxpayer's death, the adjusted cost base to the child of the property.

Editorial Note: The farming and fishing property rollover applies automatically under s. 70(9.21)(*a*) unless the taxpayer's legal representative elects out of the rollover under s. 70(9.21)(*b*). A child of the taxpayer includes a grandchild and great-grandchild of the taxpayer, and a person who, while under the age of 19, was wholly dependent on and under the custody and control of the taxpayer (see s. 70(10)).

History: S. 70(9.21)(*a*)(ii), the portion before clause (A) was replaced by S.C. 2014, c. 39, s. 13(4), deemed to have come into force on January 1, 2014, and formerly read:

> (ii) where the property is, immediately before the death of the taxpayer, a share of the capital stock of a family fishing corporation of the taxpayer, or a share of the capital stock of a family farm corporation of the taxpayer,

S. 70(9.21)(*b*)(ii), the portion before clause (A) was replaced by S.C. 2014, c. 39, s. 13(5), deemed to have come into force on January 1, 2014, and formerly read:

> (ii) subject to subparagraph (iii), where the property is, immediately before the taxpayer's death, a share of the capital stock of a family fishing corporation of the taxpayer, a share of the capital stock of a family farm corporation of the taxpayer, an interest in a family fishing partnership of the taxpayer or an interest in a family farm partnership of the taxpayer,

Related Regulations: 600(*b*).

Related Sections: S. 220(3.2) Late, amended or revoked elections.

▶ 70(9.3) ◀

(9.3) When subsection (9.31) applies. Subsection (9.31) applies to a trust and a child of the settlor of the trust in respect of a property in respect of which subsection 104(4) would, if this Act were read without reference to this subsection, apply to the trust as a consequence of the death of the beneficiary under the trust who was a spouse or a common-law partner of the settlor of the trust if

(*a*) the property (or property for which the property was substituted) was transferred to the trust by the settlor and was, immediately before that transfer, a share of the capital stock of a family farm or fishing corporation of the settlor or an interest in a family farm or fishing partnership of the settlor;

(*b*) subsection (6), subsection 73(1) (as that subsection applied to transfers before 2000) or subparagraph 73(1.01)(*c*)(i) applied to the settlor and the trust in respect of the transfer referred to in paragraph (*a*);

(*c*) the property is, immediately before the beneficiary's death,

(i) a share of the capital stock of a Canadian corporation that would, immediately before that beneficiary's death, be a share of the capital stock of a family farm or fishing corporation of the settlor, if the settlor owned the share at that time and paragraph (*a*) of the definition "share of the capital stock of a family farm or fishing corporation" in subsection (10) were read without the words "in which the individual, the individual's spouse or common-law partner, a child of the individual or a parent of the individual was actively engaged on a regular and continuous basis (or, in the case of property used in the operation of a woodlot, was engaged to the extent required by a prescribed forest management plan in respect of that woodlot)", or

(ii) (Repealed by S.C. 2014, c. 39, s. 13(7).)

(iii) a partnership interest in a partnership that carried on in Canada a farming or fishing business in which it used all or substantially all of the property;

(*d*) the child of the settlor was, immediately before that beneficiary's death, resident in Canada; and

(*e*) as a consequence of that beneficiary's death, the property is transferred to and becomes vested indefeasibly in the child within the period ending 36 months after that beneficiary's death or, if written application has been made to the Minister by the taxpayer's legal representative within that period, within any longer period that the Minister considers reasonable in the circumstances.

History: S. 70(9.3)(*a*) was replaced by S.C. 2014, c. 39, s. 13(6), deemed to have come into force on January 1, 2014, and formerly read:

(*a*) the property (or property for which the property was substituted) was transferred to the trust by the settlor and was, immediately before that transfer, a share of the capital stock of a family farm corporation of the settlor, a share of the capital stock of a family fishing corporation of the settlor, an interest in a family farm partnership of the settlor or an interest in a family fishing partnership of the settlor;

S. 70(9.3)(*c*)(i) was replaced and s. 70(9.3)(*c*)(ii) was repealed by S.C. 2014, c. 39, s. 13(7), deemed to have come into force on January 1, 2014, and formerly read:

(i) a share of the capital stock of a Canadian corporation that would, immediately before that beneficiary's death, be a share of the capital stock of a family farm corporation of the settlor, if the settlor owned the share at that time and paragraph (*a*) of the definition "share of the capital stock of a family farm corporation", in subsection (10) were read without the words "in which the person or a spouse, common-law partner, child or parent of the person was actively engaged on a regular and continuous basis (or, in the case of property used in the operation of a woodlot, was engaged to the extent required by a prescribed forest management plan in respect of that woodlot)",

(ii) a share of the capital stock of a Canadian corporation that would, immediately before the beneficiary's death, be a share of the capital stock of a family fishing corporation of the settlor, if the settlor owned the share at that time and paragraph (*a*) of the definition "share of the capital stock of a family fishing corporation" in subsection (10) were read without reference to the words "in which the individual, the individual's spouse or common-law partner, a child of the individual or a parent of the individual was actively engaged on a regular and continuous basis", or

S. 70(9.3)(*c*)(iii) was replaced by S.C. 2014, c. 39, s. 13(8), deemed to have come into force on January 1, 2014, and formerly read:

(iii) a partnership interest in a partnership that carried on the business of farming or fishing in Canada in which it used all or substantially all of the property;

Related Regulations: 7400.

Related Sections: S. 70(10), "share of the capital stock of a family farm or fishing corporation"; s. 89(1), "Canadian corporation"; s. 248(1), "Canadian corporation".

Information Circulars: IC 07-1 Taxpayer Relief Provisions.

Interpretation Bulletins: *Secondary* — IT-349R3 Intergenerational transfers of farm property on death; IT-373R2 (Consolid.) Woodlots.

► 70(9.31) ◄

(9.31) Transfer of family farm or fishing corporation or family farm or fishing partnership from trust to children of settlor. If, because of subsection (9.3), this subsection applies to the trust and a child of the settlor of the trust in respect of a property of the trust that has been distributed to the child as a consequence of the death of the beneficiary under the trust who was a spouse or common-law partner of the settlor of the trust, the following rules apply:

(*a*) where the trust does not elect, in its return of income under this Part for the taxation year in which the beneficiary died, to have paragraph (*b*) apply to the trust in respect of the property

(i) section 69 and subsection 104(4) do not apply to the trust and the child in respect of the property,

(ii) where the property is, immediately before the beneficiary's death, a share described in subparagraph (9.3)(*c*)(i),

(A) the trust is deemed to have

(I) disposed of the property immediately before the beneficiary's death, and

(II) received proceeds of disposition in respect of that disposition equal to the adjusted cost base to the trust of the property immediately before the time of that disposition, and

(B) the child is, immediately after the time of the disposition, deemed to have acquired the property at a cost equal to the trust's proceeds of disposition in respect of that disposition of the property determined under clause (A), and

(iii) where the property is, immediately before the beneficiary's death, a partnership interest described in subparagraph (9.3)(*c*)(iii) (other than a partnership interest to which subsection 100(3) applies),

(A) the trust is, except for the purpose of paragraph 98(5)(*g*), deemed not to have disposed of the property as a consequence of the beneficiary's death,

(B) the child is deemed to have acquired the property, at the time of the beneficiary's death, at a cost equal to the cost to the trust of the interest immediately before the time that is immediately before the time of the beneficiary's death, and

(C) each amount required by subsection 53(1) or (2) to be added or deducted in computing the adjusted cost base to the trust, immediately before the beneficiary's death, of the property is deemed to be an amount required by subsection 53(1) or (2) to be added or deducted in computing, at or after the time of the beneficiary's death, the adjusted cost base to the child of the property; and

(*b*) where the trust elects, in its return of income under this Part for the taxation year in which the beneficiary died, to have this paragraph apply to the trust in respect of the property

(i) subsection 104(4) does not apply to the trust in respect of the property and section 69 does not apply to the trust or the child in respect of the transfer of the property,

(ii) subject to subparagraph (iii), where the property is, immediately before the beneficiary's death, a share described in subparagraph (9.3)(*c*)(i) or a partnership interest described in subparagraph (9.3)(*c*)(iii),

(A) the trust is deemed to have

(I) disposed of the property immediately before the beneficiary's death, and

(II) received, at the time of the disposition of property, proceeds of disposition in respect of the disposition of the property equal to the amount that the trust designates, which must not be greater than the greater of nor less than the lesser of

1. the fair market value of the property immediately before the beneficiary's death, and

2. the adjusted cost base to the trust of the property immediately before the beneficiary's death, and

(B) the child is, immediately after the time of the disposition of the property, deemed to have acquired the property at a cost equal to the trust's proceeds of disposition in respect of that disposition of the property determined under clause (A),

(iii) where the property is, immediately before that beneficiary's death, a partnership interest described in subparagraph (9.3)(*c*)(iii) (other than a partnership interest to which subsection 100(3) applies), and the trust further elects, in its return of income under this Part for the taxation year in which the beneficiary died, to have this subparagraph apply to the trust in respect of the property,

(A) the trust is, except for the purpose of paragraph 98(5)(*g*), deemed not to have disposed of the property as a consequence of the beneficiary's death,

(B) the child is deemed to have acquired the property, at the time of the beneficiary's death, at a cost equal to the cost to the trust of the property immediately before the time that is immediately before the beneficiary's death, and

(C) each amount required by subsection 53(1) or (2) to be added or deducted in computing, immediately before the beneficiary's death, the adjusted cost base to the trust of the property is deemed to be an amount required by subsection 53(1) or (2) to be added or deducted in computing, at or after the time of the beneficiary's death, the adjusted cost base to the child of the property,

(iv) except for the purpose of this subparagraph, where the amount designated by the trust under subclause (ii)(A)(II) exceeds the greater of the amounts determined under sub-subclauses (ii)(A)(II)1 and 2 in respect of the property, the amount designated is deemed to be equal to the greater of those amounts, and

(v) except for the purpose of this subparagraph, where the amount designated by the trust under subclause (ii)(A)(II) is less than the lesser of the amounts determined under sub-subclauses (ii)(A)(II)1 and 2 in respect of the property, the amount designated is deemed to be equal to the lesser of those amounts.

Editorial Note: The farming and fishing property rollover applies automatically under s. 70(9.31)(*a*) unless the trust elects out of the rollover under s. 70(9.31)(*b*). A child of the taxpayer includes a grandchild and great-grandchild of the taxpayer, and a person who, while under the age of 19, was wholly dependent on and under the custody and control of the taxpayer (see s. 70(10)).

History: S. 70(9.31)(*a*)(ii), the portion before clause (A) was replaced by S.C. 2014, c. 39, s. 13(9), deemed to have come into force on January 1, 2014, and formerly read:

(ii) where the property is, immediately before the beneficiary's death, a share described in subparagraph (9.3)(*c*)(i) or (ii),

S. 70(9.31)(*b*)(ii), the portion before clause (A) was replaced by S.C. 2014, c. 39, s. 13(10), deemed to have come into force on January 1, 2014, and formerly read:

(ii) subject to subparagraph (iii), where the property is, immediately before the beneficiary's death, a share of the capital stock of a corporation described in subparagraph (9.3)(*c*)(i) or (ii) or a partnership interest described in subparagraph (9.3)(*c*)(iii),

Related Regulations: 600(*b*).

Related Sections: S. 220(3.2) Late, amended or revoked elections.

▶ 70(9.4) ◀

(9.4) Transfer of shares of small business corporation — (Repealed by 1986, c. 6, s. 33(3).)

▶ 70(9.5) ◀

(9.5) Transfer of share of capital stock of small business corporation from spouse's trust to children of settlor — (Repealed by 1986, c. 6, s. 33(3).)

▶ 70(9.6) ◀

(9.6) Transfer to a parent. Subsection (9.01) or (9.21), as the case may be, applies in respect of a transfer of a property as if the references in those subsections to "child" were read as references to "parent" if

(*a*) the property was acquired by a taxpayer in circumstances where any of subsections (9.01), (9.11), (9.21), (9.31) and 73(3.1) and (4.1) applied in respect of the acquisition;

(*b*) as a consequence of the death of the taxpayer the property is transferred to a parent of the taxpayer; and

(*c*) the taxpayer's legal representative has elected, in the taxpayer's return of income under this Part for the taxation year in which the taxpayer died, that this subsection apply in respect of the transfer.

Interpretation Bulletins: *Primary* — IT-349R3 Intergenerational transfers of farm property on death. *Secondary* — IT-268R4 Inter vivos transfer of farm property to child.

▶ 70(9.7) ◀

(9.7) Transfer to parent — (Repealed by 1986, c. 6, s. 33(4).)

▶ 70(9.8) ◀

(9.8) Leased farm or fishing property. For the purposes of subsections (9) and 73(3) and paragraph (*d*) of the definition "qualified farm or fishing property" in subsection 110.6(1), a property of an individual is, at a particular time, deemed to be used by the individual in a farming or fishing business carried on in Canada if, at that particular time, the property is being used, principally in the course of carrying on a farming or fishing business in Canada, by

(*a*) a corporation, a share of the capital stock of which is a share of the capital stock of a family farm or fishing corporation of the individual, the individual's spouse or common-law partner, a child of the individual or a parent of the individual; or

(*b*) a partnership, a partnership interest in which is an interest in a family farm or fishing partnership of the individual, the individual's spouse or common-law partner, a child of the individual or a parent of the individual.

History: S. 70(9.8), the portion before paragraph (*a*) was replaced by S.C. 2016, c. 12, s. 20(4), in force January 1, 2017, and formerly read:

(9.8) *Leased farm or fishing property.* For the purposes of subsections (9) and 14(1), paragraph 20(1)(*b*), subsection 73(3) and paragraph (*d*) of the definition "qualified farm or fishing property" in subsection 110.6(1), a property of an individual is, at a particular time, deemed to be used by the individual in a farming or fishing business carried on in Canada if, at that particular time, the property is being used, principally in the course of carrying on a farming or fishing business in Canada, by

S. 70(9.8) was replaced by S.C. 2014, c. 39, s. 13(11), applicable to dispositions and transfers that occur in the 2014 and subsequent taxation years, and formerly read:

(9.8) *Leased farm and fishing property.* For the purposes of subsections (9) and 14(1), paragraph 20(1)(*b*), subsection 73(3) and paragraph (*d*) of the definitions "qualified farm property" and "qualified fishing property" in subsection 110.6(1), a property of an individual is, at a particular time, deemed to be used by the individual in a fishing or farming business, as the case may be, carried on in Canada if, at that particular time, the property is being used, principally in the course of carrying on a fishing or farming business in Canada, by

(*a*) a corporation, a share of the capital stock of which is a share of the capital stock of a family fishing corporation, or a share of the capital stock of a family farm corporation, of the individual, the individual's spouse or common-law partner, a child of the individual or a parent of the individual; or

(*b*) a partnership, a partnership interest of which is an interest in a family fishing partnership, or an interest in a family farm partnership, of the individual, the individual's spouse or common-law partner, a child of the individual or a parent of the individual.

Related Sections: S. 14(1) Eligible capital property — inclusion in income from business; s. 20(1)(*b*) Cumulative eligible capital amount; s. 110.6(1), "qualified farm or fishing property".

Interpretation Bulletins: *Primary* — IT-349R3 Intergenerational transfers of farm property on death. *Secondary* — IT-268R4 Inter vivos transfer of farm property to child.

▶ 70(10) ◀

(10) Definitions. In this section,

Interpretation Bulletins: *Primary* — IT-349R3 Intergenerational transfers of farm property on death. *Secondary* — IT-268R4 Inter vivos transfer of farm property to child.

"child" — "child" of a taxpayer includes

(*a*) a child of the taxpayer's child,

(*b*) a child of the taxpayer's child's child,

(*b*.1) a person who was a child of the taxpayer immediately before the death of the person's spouse or common-law partner, and

(*c*) a person who, at any time before the person attained the age of 19 years, was wholly dependent on the taxpayer for support and of whom the taxpayer had, at that time, in law or in fact, the custody and control;

History: S. 70(10), paragraph (*b.1*) of the definition "child" was added by S.C. 2014, c. 39, s. 13(13), deemed to have come into force on January 1, 2014.

"interest in a family farm or fishing partnership" — "interest in a family farm or fishing partnership", of an individual at any time, means a partnership interest owned by the individual at that time if, at that time, all or substantially all of the fair market value of the property of the partnership was attributable to

(*a*) property that has been used principally in the course of carrying on a farming or fishing business in Canada in which the individual, the individual's spouse or common-law partner, a child of the individual or a parent of the individual was actively engaged on a regular and continuous basis (or, in the case of property used in the operation of a woodlot, was engaged to the extent required by a prescribed forest management plan in respect of that woodlot), by

(i) the partnership,

(ii) a corporation, a share of the capital stock of which was a share of the capital stock of a family farm or fishing corporation of the individual, the individual's spouse or common-law partner, a child of the individual or a parent of the individual,

(iii) a partnership, a partnership interest in which was an interest in a family farm or fishing partnership of the individual, the individual's spouse or common-law partner, a child of the individual or a parent of the individual, or

(iv) the individual, the individual's spouse or common-law partner, a child of the individual or a parent of the individual,

(*b*) shares of the capital stock or indebtedness of one or more corporations of which all or substantially all of the fair market value of the property was attributable to property described in paragraph (*d*),

(*c*) partnership interests or indebtedness of one or more partnerships of which all or substantially all of the fair market value of the property was attributable to property described in paragraph (*d*), or

(*d*) properties described in any of paragraphs (*a*) to (*c*);

Editorial Note: This definition, along with that of "share of the capital stock of a family farm or fishing corporation" replaced the former definitions relating to family farm partnerships/corporations and family fishing partnerships/corporations. The new definitions reflect changes announced in the 2014 Federal Budget, under which various tests relating to the "used principally" now apply to uses of property in farming, fishing, or a combination of the two activities, rather than only one of the two activities.

History: S. 70(10), the definition "interest in a family farm or fishing partnership" was added by S.C. 2014, c. 39, s. 13(14), deemed to have come into force on January 1, 2014.

"interest in a family farm partnership" — (Repealed by S.C. 2014, c. 39, s. 13(12).)

History: S. 70(10), the definition "interest in a family farm partnership" was repealed by S.C. 2014, c. 39, s. 13(12), deemed to have come into force on January 1, 2014, and formerly read:

"interest in a family farm partnership" — "interest in a family farm partnership" of an individual at any time means a partnership interest owned by the individual at that time if, at that time, all or substantially all of the fair market value of the property of the partnership was attributable to

(*a*) property that has been used principally in the course of carrying on a farming business in Canada in which the individual, the individual's spouse or common-law partner, a child of the individual or a parent of the individual was actively engaged on a regular and continuous basis (or, in the case of property used in the operation of a woodlot, was engaged to the extent required by a prescribed forest management plan in respect of that woodlot), by

(i) the partnership,

(ii) a corporation, a share of the capital stock of which is a share of the capital stock of a family farm corporation of the individual, the individual's spouse or common-law partner, a child of the individual or a parent of the individual,

(iii) a partnership, a partnership interest in which is an interest in a family farm partnership of the individual, the individual's spouse or common-law partner, a child of the individual or a parent of the individual, or

(iv) the individual, the individual's spouse or common-law partner, a child of the individual or a parent of the individual,

(*b*) shares of the capital stock or indebtedness of one or more corporations all or substantially all of the fair market value of the property of which was attributable to property described in paragraph (*d*),

(*c*) partnership interests or indebtedness of one or more partnerships all or substantially all of the fair market value of the property of which was attributable to property described in paragraph (*d*), or

(*d*) properties described in any of paragraphs (*a*) to (*c*);

"interest in a family fishing partnership" — (Repealed by S.C. 2014, c. 39, s. 13(12).)

History: S. 70(10), the definition "interest in a family fishing partnership" was repealed by S.C. 2014, c. 39, s. 13(12), deemed to have come into force on January 1, 2014, and formerly read:

"interest in a family fishing partnership" — "interest in a family fishing partnership" of an individual at any time means a partnership interest owned by the individual at that time if, at that time, all or substantially all of the fair market value of the property of the partnership was attributable to

(*a*) property that has been used principally in the course of carrying on a fishing business in Canada in which the individual, the individual's spouse or common-law partner, a child of the individual or a parent of the individual was actively engaged on a regular and continuous basis, by

(i) the partnership,

(ii) a corporation, a share of the capital stock of which is a share of the capital stock of a family fishing corporation of the individual, the individual's spouse or common-law partner, a child of the individual or a parent of the individual,

(iii) a partnership, a partnership interest in which is an interest in a family fishing partnership of the individual, the individual's spouse or common-law partner, a child of the individual or a parent of the individual, or

(iv) the individual, the individual's spouse or common-law partner, a child of the individual or a parent of the individual,

(*b*) shares of the capital stock or indebtedness of one or more corporations all or substantially all of the fair market value of the property of which was attributable to property described in paragraph (*d*),

(*c*) partnership interests or indebtedness of one or more partnerships all or substantially all of the fair market value of the property of which was attributable to property described in paragraph (*d*), or

(*d*) properties described in any of paragraphs (*a*) to (*c*);

"share of the capital stock of a family farm corporation" — (Repealed by S.C. 2014, c. 39, s. 13(12).)

History: S. 70(10), the definition "share of the capital stock of a family farm corporation" was repealed by S.C. 2014, c. 39, s. 13(12), deemed to have come into force on January 1, 2014, and formerly read:

"share of the capital stock of a family farm corporation" — "share of the capital stock of a family farm corporation" of a person at a particular time means a share of the capital stock of a corporation owned by the person at that time where, at that time, all or substantially all of the fair market value of the property owned by the corporation was attributable to

(*a*) property that has been used by

(i) the corporation or any other corporation, a share of the capital stock of which was a share of the capital stock of a family farm corporation of the person or of a spouse, common-law partner, child or parent of the person,

(i.1) a corporation controlled by a corporation referred to in subparagraph (i),

(ii) the person,

(iii) a spouse, common-law partner, child or parent of the person, or

(iv) a partnership, an interest in which was an interest in a family farm partnership of the person or of a spouse, common-law partner, child or parent of the person,

principally in the course of carrying on a farming business in Canada in which the person or a spouse, common-law partner, child or parent of the person was actively engaged on a regular and continuous basis (or, in the case of property used in the operation of a woodlot, was engaged to the extent required by a prescribed forest management plan in respect of that woodlot),

(*b*) shares of the capital stock or indebtedness of one or more corporations all or substantially all of the fair market value of the property of which was attributable to property described in paragraph (*c*), or

(*c*) properties described in paragraph (*a*) or (*b*).

"share of the capital stock of a family farm or fishing corporation" — "share of the capital stock of a family farm or fishing corporation", of an individual at any time, means a share of the capital stock of a corporation owned by the individual at that time if, at that time, all or substantially all of the fair market value of the property owned by the corporation was attributable to

(*a*) property that has been used principally in the course of carrying on a farming or fishing business in Canada in which the individual, the individual's spouse or common-law partner, a child of the individual or a parent of the individual was actively engaged on a regular and continuous basis (or, in the case of property used in the operation of a woodlot, was engaged to the extent required by a prescribed forest management plan in respect of that woodlot), by

(i) the corporation,

(ii) a corporation, a share of the capital stock of which was a share of the capital stock of a family farm or fishing corporation of the individual, the individual's spouse or common-law partner, a child of the individual or a parent of the individual,

(iii) a corporation controlled by a corporation described in subparagraph (i) or (ii),

(iv) a partnership, a partnership interest in which was an interest in a family farm or fishing partnership of the individual, the individual's spouse or common-law partner, a child of the individual or a parent of the individual, or

(v) the individual, the individual's spouse or common-law partner, a child of the individual or a parent of the individual,

(*b*) shares of the capital stock or indebtedness of one or more corporations of which all or substantially all of the fair market value of the property was attributable to property described in paragraph (*d*),

(*c*) partnership interests or indebtedness of one or more partnerships of which all or substantially all of the fair market value of the property was attributable to property described in paragraph (*d*), or

(*d*) properties described in any of paragraphs (*a*) to (*c*).

Editorial Note: This definition, along with that of "interest in a family farm or fishing partnership", replaced the former definitions relating to family farm partnerships/corporations and family fishing partnerships/corporations. The new definitions reflect changes announced in the 2014 Federal Budget, under which various tests relating to the "used principally" now apply to uses of property in farming, fishing, or a combination of the two activities, rather than only one of the two activities.

History: S. 70(10), the definition "share of the capital stock of a family farm or fishing corporation" was added by S.C. 2014, c. 39, s. 13(14), deemed to have come into force on January 1, 2014.

"share of the capital stock of a family fishing corporation" — (Repealed by S.C. 2014, c. 39, s. 13(12).)

History: S. 70(10), the definition "share of the capital stock of a family fishing corporation" was repealed by S.C. 2014, c. 39, s. 13(12), deemed to have come into force on January 1, 2014, and formerly read:

"share of the capital stock of a family fishing corporation"—"share of the capital stock of a family fishing corporation" of an individual at any time means a share of the capital stock of a corporation owned by the individual at that time if, at that time, all or substantially all of the fair market value of the property owned by the corporation was attributable to

(*a*) property that has been used principally in the course of carrying on a fishing business in Canada in which the individual, the individual's spouse or common-law partner, a child of the individual or a parent of the individual was actively engaged on a regular and continuous basis, by

(i) the corporation,

(ii) a corporation, a share of the capital stock of which is a share of the capital stock of a family fishing corporation of the individual, the individual's spouse or common-law partner, a child of the individual or a parent of the individual,

(iii) a corporation controlled by a corporation described in subparagraph (i) or (ii),

(iv) a partnership, a partnership interest in which is an interest in a family fishing partnership of the individual, the individual's spouse or common-law partner, a child of the individual or a parent of the individual, or

(v) the individual, the individual's spouse or common-law partner, a child of the individual or a parent of the individual,

(*b*) shares of the capital stock or indebtedness of one or more corporations all or substantially all of the fair market value of the property of which was attributable to property described in paragraph (*d*),

(*c*) partnership interests or indebtedness of one or more partnerships all or substantially all of the fair market value of the property of which was attributable to property described in paragraph (*d*), or

(*d*) properties described in any of paragraphs (*a*) to (*c*);

▶ 70(11) ◀

(11) Application of s. 138(12). The definitions in subsection 138(12) apply to this section.

▶ 70(12) ◀

(12) Value of NISA. For the purpose of the definition "share of the capital stock of a family farm or fishing corporation" in subsection (10), the fair market value of a net income stabilization account is deemed to be nil.

History: S. 70(12) was replaced by S.C. 2014, c. 39, s. 13(15), deemed to have come into force on January 1, 2014, and formerly read:

(12) *Value of NISA.* For the purpose of the definition "share of the capital stock of a family farm corporation" in subsection 10, the fair market value of a net income stabilization account shall be deemed to be nil.

Related Sections: S. 248(1), "net income stabilization account".

▶ 70(13) ◀

(13) Capital cost of certain depreciable property. For the purposes of this section and, where a provision of this section (other than this subsection) applies, for the purposes of sections 13 and 20 (but not for the purposes of any regulation made for the purpose of paragraph 20(1)(*a*)),

(*a*) the capital cost to a taxpayer of depreciable property of a prescribed class disposed of immediately before the taxpayer's death, or

(*b*) the capital cost to a trust, to which subsection (9.1) applies, of depreciable property of a prescribed class disposed of immediately before the death of the spouse or common-law partner described in that subsection,

shall, in respect of property that was not disposed of by the taxpayer or the trust before that time, be the amount that it would be if subsection 13(7) were read without reference to

(*c*) the expression "the lesser of" in paragraph (*b*) and clause (*d*)(i)(A) thereof, and

(*d*) subparagraph (*b*)(ii), subclause (*d*)(i)(A)(II), clause (*d*)(i)(B) and paragraph (*e*) thereof.

▶ 70(14) ◀

(14) Order of disposal of depreciable property. Where 2 or more depreciable properties of a prescribed class are disposed of at the same time as a consequence of a taxpayer's death, this section and paragraph (*a*) of the definition "cost amount" in subsection 248(1) apply as if each property so disposed of were separately disposed of in the order designated by the taxpayer's legal representative or, in the case of a trust described in subsection (9.1), by the trust and, where the taxpayer's legal representative or the trust, as the case may be, does not designate an order, in the order designated by the Minister.

SECTION 71: Application of para. 3(e) on death of taxpayer

(Repealed by 1986, c. 6, s. 34(1).)

SECTION 72: Reserves, etc., for year of death

▶ 72(1) ◀

(1) Reserves, etc., for year of death. Where in a taxation year a taxpayer has died,

(*a*) paragraph 20(1)(*n*) does not apply to allow, in computing the income of the taxpayer for the year from a business, the deduction of any amount as a reserve in respect of property sold in the course of the business;

(*b*) no amount is deductible under subsection 32(1) as a reserve in respect of unearned commissions in computing the taxpayer's income for the year;

(*c*) no amount may be claimed under subparagraph 40(1)(*a*)(iii), paragraph 40(1.01)(*c*) or subparagraph 44(1)(*e*)(iii) in computing any gain of the taxpayer for the year;

(*d*) subsection 64(1) does not apply to allow, in computing the income of the taxpayer for the year, the deduction of any amount as a reserve in respect of the disposition of any property; and

(*e*) subsection 64(1.1) does not apply to allow, in computing the income of the taxpayer for the year, the deduction of any amount as a reserve in respect of the disposition of any property.

Editorial Note: Since s. 72(1) denies the deduction of the reserves described therein, the underlying amounts are included in the deceased's income in the year of death. However, s. 72(2) allows the deduction of the reserves and effectively provides a "rollover" of the reserves where the right to the underlying amount is transferred to the deceased's spouse or common-law partner or qualifying trust.

Interpretation Bulletins: *Secondary* — IT-152R3 Special reserves — Sale of land; IT-154R Special reserves.

▶ 72(2) ◀

(2) Election by legal representative and transferee re reserves. Where property of a taxpayer that is a right to receive any amount has, on or after the death of the taxpayer and as a consequence thereof, been transferred or distributed to the taxpayer's spouse or common-law partner described in paragraph 70(6)(*a*) or to a trust described in paragraph 70(6)(*b*) (in this subsection referred to as the "transferee"), if the taxpayer was resident in Canada immediately before the taxpayer's death and the taxpayer's legal representative and the transferee have executed jointly an election in respect of the property in prescribed form,

(*a*) any amount in respect of the property that would, but for paragraph (1)(*a*), (*b*), (*d*) or (*e*), as the case may be, have been deductible as a reserve in computing the taxpayer's income for the taxation year in which the taxpayer died shall,

(i) notwithstanding subsection (1), be deducted in computing the taxpayer's income for the taxation year in which the taxpayer died,

(ii) be included in computing the transferee's income for the transferee's first taxation year ending after the death of the taxpayer, and

(iii) be deemed to be

(A) an amount that has been included in computing the transferee's income from a business for a previous year in respect of property sold in the course of the business,

(B) an amount that has been included in computing the transferee's income for a previous year as a commission in respect of an insurance contract, other than a life insurance contract,

(C) an amount that by virtue of subsection 59(1) has been included in computing the transferee's income for a preceding taxation year, or

(D) for the purposes of subsection 64(1.1), an amount that by virtue of paragraph 59(3.2)(*c*) has been included in computing the transferee's income for a preceding taxation year and to be an amount deducted by the transferee pursuant to paragraph 64(1.1)(*a*) in computing the transferee's income for the transferee's last taxation year ending before the death,

as the case may be;

(*b*) any amount in respect of the property that could, but for paragraph (1)(*c*), have been claimed under subparagraph 40(1)(*a*)(iii) or 44(1)(*e*)(iii) in computing the amount of any gain of the taxpayer for the year shall,

(i) notwithstanding paragraph (1)(*c*), be deemed to have been so claimed, and

(ii) for the purpose of computing the transferee's income for the transferee's first taxation year ending after the death of the taxpayer and any subsequent taxation year, be deemed to have been

(A) proceeds of the disposition of capital property disposed of by the transferee in that first taxation year, and

(B) the amount determined under subparagraph 40(1)(*a*)(i) or 44(1)(*e*)(i), as the case may be, in respect of the capital property referred to in clause (A); and

(*c*) notwithstanding paragraphs (*a*) and (*b*), where any property had been disposed of by the taxpayer, in computing the income of the transferee for any taxation year ending after the death of the taxpayer,

(i) the amount of the transferee's deduction under paragraph 20(1)(*n*) as a reserve in respect of the property sold in the course of business,

(ii) the amount of the transferee's claim under subparagraph 40(1)(*a*)(iii) or 44(1)(*e*)(iii) in respect of the disposition of the property, and

(iii) the amount of the transferee's deduction under section 64 as a reserve in respect of the disposition of the property

shall be computed as if the transferee were the taxpayer who had disposed of the property and as if the property were disposed of by the transferee at the time it was disposed of by the taxpayer.

Editorial Note: See the editorial note following s. 72(1). The effect of s. 72(2)(*c*) is that the deceased's three-year limit for the reserve in s. 20(1)(*n*) and five-year limit (10-year limit for certain property transferred to children) for the reserves in ss. 40(1)(*a*)(iii) and 44(1)(*e*)(iii) are effectively carried over to the transferee. In other words, the limitation periods do not start afresh for the transferee.

Related Regulations: 600(b).

Related Sections: S. 54, "capital property"; s. 220(3.2) Late, amended or revoked elections; s. 248(1), "amount", "business", "property".

Forms: T2069 — Election in Respect of Amounts Not Deductible as Reserves for the Year of Death.

Information Circulars: IC 07-1 Taxpayer relief provisions.

Interpretation Bulletins: *Secondary* — IT-152R3 Special reserves — Sale of land.

Cases: Amounts were properly included in a taxpayer's income where payments on a loan were enforceably due, but were waived. *Fontaine v. M.N.R.*, 88 DTC 1656 (T.C.C.)

SECTION 73: Inter vivos transfers by individuals

▶ 73(1) ◀

(1) Inter vivos transfers by individuals. For the purposes of this Part, where at any time any particular capital property of an individual (other than a trust) has been transferred in circumstances to which subsection (1.01) applies and both the individual and the transferee are resident in Canada at that time, unless the individual elects in the individual's return of income under this Part for the taxation year in which the property was transferred that the provisions of this subsection not apply, the particular property is deemed

(*a*) to have been disposed of at that time by the individual for proceeds equal to,

(i) where the particular property is depreciable property of a prescribed class, that proportion of the undepreciated capital cost to the individual immediately before that time of all property of that class that the fair market value immediately before that time of the particular property is of the fair market value immediately before that time of all of that property of that class, and

(ii) in any other case, the adjusted cost base to the individual of the particular property immediately before that time; and

(*b*) to have been acquired at that time by the transferee for an amount equal to those proceeds.

Editorial Note: Note that if the rollover applies to a property and the transferee is the transferor's spouse or common-law partner (or a trust in which such person is beneficially interested), the income attribution rules of ss. 74.1 and 74.2 will normally apply to any income or taxable capital gains realized in respect of the property. In order to avoid such attribution, among other things, the transferor must elect out of the rollover; see s. 74.5(1)(*c*).

If the transferor elects out of the rollover and the transfer is made for inadequate consideration, the deemed disposition rules of s. 69(1) will apply. Any loss on the transfer will be denied under the superficial loss rule of s. 40(2)(*g*)(i) unless the transfer is to a former spouse or former common-law partner (see also "superficial loss" in s. 54 and "affiliated persons" in s. 251.1(1)).

History: The application of the amendment to s. 73(1) by S.C. 2001, c. 17, s. 53(1) was amended by S.C. 2013, c. 34, s. 24(1), deemed in force June 14, 2001, to ensure that for transfers that occur after 1999 and before 2007, the residence of a transferee trust will be determined without reference to section 94 of the Act, as it reads in its application to taxation years that began before 2007. This 2001 amendment is not reproduced in print but is available in all CCH Canadian electronic versions of the Income Tax Act.

Related Regulations: 600(b); 6500(1).

Related Sections: S. 40(4) Disposal of principal residence to spouse or trust for spouse; s. 44.1(5) Special rule — re breakdown of relationships; s. 69(1) Inadequate considerations; s. 70(9.1) When subsection (9.11) applies; s. 70(9.3) When subsection (9.31) applies; s. 74.5(1)(*c*) Transfers for fair market consideration; s. 104(4) Deemed disposition by trust; s. 107(4.1) Where subsection 75(2) applicable to trust; s. 107.4(1) Qualifying disposition; s. 108(3) Income of a trust in certain provisions; s. 220(3.2) Late, amended or revoked elections; s. 252(3) Extended meaning of "spouse" and "former spouse"; ITAR s. 20(1.1) Where depreciable property disposed of to spouse, trust or child.

Canadian Tax Foundation: Gosselin, *TCC Shuts Down Strategy To Multiply Lifetime Capital Gains Exemption*, 2014 Tax for the Owner-Manager 14(3):4–5; Friedlan and Friedlan, *Principal and Cottage Residence Planning: A Review of Selected Issues — Part 1*, 2013 Ontario Tax Conference 8A:1–23; Freedman and Nakonechny, *The Tax Principles of Family Law*, 2012 Ontario Tax Conference 4:1–52; Laidlaw and Mah, *Trust After Marriage: Using a Trust To Satisfy Support Obligations*, 2010 Canadian Tax Journal 1:145–163; Addison and Korn, *Interspousal Property Transfers: The Things They Don't Tell You at the Diamond Shop*, 2002 Canadian Tax Journal 2:728–757; Stephenson, *Alter Ego and Joint Partner Trusts — A Case Study*, 2001 Prairie Provinces Tax Conference 3:1–45; Rajan and Brown, *Personal Trusts 2000: Taxation and Planning in the New Millennium*, 2000 Conference Report 28:1–40; Bratz, *Spouse Trusts: Tips and Traps — Part 2*, 2000 Canadian Tax Journal 2:477–497; Schusheim, *Spouse Trusts: Tips and Traps — Part 1*, 1999 Canadian Tax Journal 6:1525–1544; Schusheim, *Trust Basics: An Overview*, 1998 Conference Report 32:1–31.

Tax Profile: February 2008 — Income Splitting A–Z; July 2006 — Asset Protection Planning; December 2002 — Update on Current CCRA GAAR Activity.

Tax Topics: No. 1702, Income Tax Issues To Be Considered in Negotiating Marriage Contracts.

Information Circulars: IC 07-1 Taxpayer relief provisions.

Interpretation Bulletins: *Secondary* — IT-209R Inter-vivos gifts of capital property to individuals directly or through trusts; IT-325R2 Property transfers after separation, divorce and annulment.

Tax Window Files: Avantage imposable - maison habitée sans frais, *March 22, 2012*, CRA Document No. 2011-0425571E5; Transfer of Farm Property, *March 14, 2011*, CRA Document No. 2011-0394201M4; Alter Ego Trust, *December 17, 2009*, CRA Document No. 2009-0308611R3; Property Transfer — Common-Law Partners, *Technical Interpretation, Business and Partnerships Division, January 6, 2004*, CRA Document No. 2003-0031925; RRSP and Subsection 73(1) of the Act, *Technical Interpretation, Financial Industries Division, November 12, 2003*, CRA Document No. 2003-0032907. Rollover not applicable to transfers to spousal RRSP.

▶ 73(1.01) ◀

(1.01) Qualifying transfers. Subject to subsection (1.02), property is transferred by an individual in circumstances to which this subsection applies where it is transferred to

(*a*) the individual's spouse or common-law partner;

(*b*) a former spouse or common-law partner of the individual in settlement of rights arising out of their marriage or common-law partnership; or

(*c*) a trust created by the individual under which

(i) the individual's spouse or common-law partner is entitled to receive all of the income of the trust that arises before the spouse's or common-law partner's death and no person except the spouse or common-law partner may, before the spouse's or common-law partner's death, receive or otherwise obtain the use of any of the income or capital of the trust,

(ii) the individual is entitled to receive all of the income of the trust that arises before the individual's death and no person except the individual may, before the individual's death, receive or otherwise obtain the use of any of the income or capital of the trust, or

(iii) either

(A) the individual or the individual's spouse is, in combination with the other, entitled to receive all of the income of the trust that arises before the later of the death of the individual and the death of the spouse and no other person may, before the later of those deaths, receive or otherwise obtain the use of any of the income or capital of the trust, or

(B) the individual or the individual's common-law partner is, in combination with the other, entitled to receive all of the income of the trust that arises before the later of the death of the individual and the death of the common-law partner and no other person may, before the later of those deaths, receive or otherwise obtain the use of any of the income or capital of the trust.

Editorial Note: See the editorial note under s. 73(1) regarding the rollover. Note that the rollover to an alter ego trust (s. 73(1.01)(*c*)(ii)) does not apply if the trust elects under s. 104(4)(*a*)(ii.1) out of the deemed disposition rule that would otherwise apply at the time of the individual's death.

Related Sections: S. 70(9.1) When subsection (9.11) applies; s. 70(9.3) When subsection (9.31) applies; s. 104(4) Deemed disposition by trust; s. 107.4(1) Qualifying disposition; s. 108(3) Income of a trust in certain provisions; s. 108(4) Trust not disqualified; s. 248(1), "common-law partner", "joint spousal or common-law partner trust".

Canadian Tax Foundation: Infanti, *Trust's Payment of Insurance Premiums Disqualifies Spousal Trust Status*, 2016 Tax for the Owner-Manager 16(2):4; Main and McEachren, *Using Inter Vivos Trusts in Estate and Family Planning: Alter Ego and Joint Spousal and Common-Law Partner Trusts*, 2013 Ontario Tax Conference 9:3–29; Brown, *Alter Ego Joint Conjugal and Self-Benefit Trusts Revisited: Some Troubling Tax Issues and a Search for Better Alternatives*, 2005 Canadian Tax Journal 1:224–244; Hoffstein, *Alter Ego Trusts/Joint Partner Trusts — Tips, Traps & Planning*, 2004 Ontario Tax Conference 12A:1–47.

Tax Topics: No. 1702, Income Tax Issues To Be Considered in Negotiating Marriage Contracts.

Tax Window Files: Spousal trust & life insurance, *November 16, 2015*, CRA Document No. 2014-0529361E5; Transfer of Property to Former Common-Law Partner, *Technical Interpretation, Business and Partnerships Division, January 6, 2004*, CRA Document No. 2003-0031925.

▶ 73(1.02) ◀

(1.02) Exception for transfers. Subsection (1.01) applies to a transfer of property by an individual to a trust the terms of which satisfy the conditions in subparagraph (1.01)(*c*)(ii) or (iii) only where

(*a*) the trust was created after 1999;

(*b*) either

(i) the individual had attained 65 years of age at the time the trust was created, or

(ii) the transfer does not result in a change in beneficial ownership of the property and there is immediately after the transfer no absolute or contingent right of a person (other than the individual) or partnership as a beneficiary (determined with reference to subsection 104(1.1)) under the trust; and

(*c*) in the case of a trust the terms of which satisfy the conditions in subparagraph (1.01)(*c*)(ii), the trust does not make an election under subparagraph 104(4)(*a*)(ii.1).

Tax Profile: February 2002 — Transferring Property to a Trust After the Enactment of Bill C-22.

▶ 73(1.1) ◀

(1.1) Interpretation. For greater certainty, a property is, for the purposes of subsections (1) and (1.01), deemed to be property of the individual referred to in subsection (1) that has been transferred to a particular transferee where,

(*a*) under the laws of a province or because of a decree, order or judgment of a competent tribunal made in accordance with those laws, the property

(i) is acquired or is deemed to have been acquired by the particular transferee,

(ii) is deemed or declared to be property of, or is awarded to, the particular transferee, or

(iii) has vested in the particular transferee; and

(*b*) the property was or would, but for those laws, have been a capital property of the individual referred to in subsection (1).

Related Regulations: 6500(2).

Interpretation Bulletins: *Secondary* — IT-325R2 Property transfers after separation, divorce and annulment.

▶ 73(1.2) ◀

(1.2) Idem — (Repealed by 1980-81-82-83, c. 140, s. 41(1).)

▶ 73(2) ◀

(2) Capital cost and amount deemed allowed to spouse, etc., or trust. If a transferee is deemed by subsection (1) to have acquired any particular depreciable property of a prescribed class of a taxpayer for an amount determined under paragraph (1)(*b*) and the capital cost to the taxpayer of the particular property exceeds the amount determined under that paragraph, in applying sections 13 and 20 and any regulations made under paragraph 20(1)(*a*)

(*a*) the capital cost to the transferee of the particular property is deemed to be the amount that was the capital cost to the taxpayer of the particular property; and

(*b*) the excess is deemed to have been allowed to the transferee in respect of the particular property under regulations made under paragraph 20(1)(*a*) in computing income for taxation years before the acquisition of the particular property.

Editorial Note: The effect of s. 73(2) is to flow through to the transferee any potential recapture in respect of the depreciable property to the extent that it reflects capital cost allowance previously deducted by the transferor.

History: S. 73(2) was replaced by S.C. 2013, c. 34, s. 211(1), applicable to transfers that occur after 1999, and formerly read:

(2) *Capital cost and amount deemed allowed to spouse, etc., or trust.* Where a transferee is deemed by subsection (1) to have acquired any particular depreciable property of a prescribed class of a taxpayer for an amount determined under paragraph (1)(*e*) and the capital cost to the taxpayer of the particular property exceeds the amount determined under that paragraph, for the purposes of sections 13 and 20 and any regulations made under paragraph 20(1)(*a*)

(*a*) the capital cost to the transferee of the particular property shall be deemed to be the amount that was the capital cost to the taxpayer thereof; and

(*b*) the excess shall be deemed to have been allowed to the transferee in respect of the particular property under regulations made under paragraph 20(1)(*a*) in computing income for taxation years before the acquisition thereof.

Related Sections: S. 70(6)(*e*) Where transfer or distribution to spouse or spouse trust.

Interpretation Bulletins: *Secondary* — IT-209R Inter-vivos gifts of capital property to individuals directly or through trusts; IT-325R2 Property transfers after separation, divorce and annulment.

▶ 73(3) ◀

(3) When subsection (3.1) applies. Subsection (3.1) applies to a taxpayer and a child of the taxpayer in respect of property that has been transferred, at any time, by the taxpayer to the child, where

(*a*) the property was, before the transfer, land in Canada or depreciable property in Canada of a prescribed class, of the taxpayer;

(*b*) the child of the taxpayer was resident in Canada immediately before the transfer; and

(*c*) the property has been used principally in a farming or fishing business in which the taxpayer, the taxpayer's spouse or common-law partner, a child of the taxpayer or a parent of the taxpayer was actively engaged on a regular and continuous basis (or, in the case of property used in the operation of a woodlot, was engaged to the extent required by a prescribed forest management plan in respect of that woodlot).

History: S. 73(3)(*a*) was replaced by S.C. 2016, c. 12, s. 21(1), in force January 1, 2017, and formerly read:

(*a*) the property was, before the transfer, land in Canada or depreciable property in Canada of a prescribed class, of the taxpayer, or any eligible capital property in respect of a farming or fishing business carried on in Canada by the taxpayer;

S. 73(3)(*a*) was replaced by S.C. 2014, c. 39, s. 14(1), applicable to transfers that occur in the 2014 and subsequent taxation years, and formerly read:

(*a*) the property was, before the transfer, land in Canada or depreciable property in Canada of a prescribed class, of the taxpayer, or any eligible capital property in respect of a fishing or farming business carried on in Canada by the taxpayer;

S. 73(3)(*c*) was replaced by S.C. 2014, c. 39, s. 14(2), applicable to transfers that occur in the 2014 and subsequent taxation years, and formerly read:

(*c*) the property has been used principally in a fishing or farming business in which the taxpayer, the taxpayer's spouse or common-law partner, a child of the taxpayer or a parent of the taxpayer was actively engaged on a regular and continuous basis (or in the case of property used in the operation of a woodlot, was engaged to the extent required by a prescribed forest management plan in respect of that woodlot).

S. 73(3)(*a*) was replaced by S.C. 2013, c. 34, s. 211(2), applicable to dispositions of property that occur after May 1, 2006, other than a disposition in respect of which a taxpayer has made an election under subsection 11(5) of the *Budget Implementation Act, 2006, No. 2* (S.C. 2007, c. 2 — see below). S. 73(3)(*a*) formerly read:

(*a*) the property was, immediately before the transfer, land in Canada or depreciable property in Canada of a prescribed class, of the taxpayer, or any eligible capital property in respect of a fishing or farming business carried on in Canada by the taxpayer;

Related Regulations: 7400.

Related Sections: 248(29) Farming or fishing business; S. 13(21), "depreciable property"; s. 14(5), "cumulative eligible capital"; s. 54, "eligible capital property"; s. 70(9.6) Transfer to a parent; s. 75.1(1) Gain or loss deemed that of transferor; s. 248(1), "cumulative eligible capital", "depreciable property", "eligible capital property", "farming"; s. 252(1) Extended meaning of "child".

Interpretation Bulletins: *Primary* — IT-268R4 Inter vivos transfer of farm property to child. *Secondary* — IT-373R2 (Consolid.) Woodlots; IT-427R Livestock of Farmers.

▶ 73(3.1) ◀

(3.1) Inter vivos transfer of farm or fishing property to child. If, because of subsection (3), this subsection applies to the taxpayer and a child of the taxpayer in respect of a property transferred by the taxpayer to the child of the taxpayer, the following rules apply:

(*a*) where, immediately before the transfer, the property was depreciable property of a prescribed class, the taxpayer is deemed to have disposed of the property, at the time of the transfer, for proceeds of disposition equal to

(i) in any case to which neither subparagraph (ii) nor (iii) applies, the taxpayer's proceeds of disposition otherwise determined,

(ii) the greater of the amounts referred to in clauses (A) and (B), if the taxpayer's proceeds of disposition otherwise determined exceed the greater of

(A) the fair market value of the property immediately before the time of the transfer, and

(B) the lesser of

(I) the capital cost to the taxpayer of the property, and

(II) the amount, determined immediately before the time of the disposition of the property, that is that proportion of the undepreciated capital cost of property of that class to the taxpayer that the capital cost to the taxpayer of the property is of the capital cost to the taxpayer of all property of that class that had not, at or before that time, been disposed of, or

(iii) if the taxpayer's proceeds of disposition otherwise determined are less than the lesser of the amounts referred to in clauses (ii)(A) and (B), the lesser of those amounts;

(*b*) where the property transferred was land, the taxpayer is deemed to have disposed of the property at the time of the transfer for proceeds of disposition equal to,

(i) in any case to which neither subparagraph (ii) nor (iii) applies, the taxpayer's proceeds of disposition otherwise determined,

(ii) the greater of the amounts referred to in clauses (A) and (B), if the taxpayer's proceeds of disposition otherwise determined exceed the greater of

(A) the fair market value of the land immediately before the time of the transfer, and

(B) the adjusted cost base to the taxpayer of the land immediately before the time of the transfer, or

(iii) if the taxpayer's proceeds of disposition otherwise determined are less than the lesser of the amounts referred to in clauses (ii)(A) and (B), the lesser of those amounts;

(*c*) (Repealed by S.C. 2016, c. 12, s. 21(2).)

(*d*) subsection 69(1) does not apply to the taxpayer and the child in respect of the property;

(*e*) the child is deemed to have acquired the property at a cost equal to the taxpayer's proceeds of disposition in respect of the disposition of the property determined under

(i) where the property is depreciable property of the taxpayer, paragraph (*a*), and

(ii) where the property is land of the taxpayer, paragraph (*b*) and;

(*f*) (Repealed by S.C. 2016, c. 12, s. 21(3).)

(*g*) (Repealed by S.C. 2016, c. 12, s. 21(3).)

(*h*) where the property is depreciable property of a prescribed class of the taxpayer and the capital cost to the taxpayer of the property exceeds the cost to the child of the property, for the purposes of sections 13 and 20 and any regulations made under paragraph 20(1)(*a*),

(i) the capital cost to the child of the property is deemed to be the amount that was the capital cost to the taxpayer of the property immediately before the transfer, and

(ii) the excess is deemed to have been allowed to the child in respect of the property under regulations made under paragraph 20(1)(*a*) in computing income for taxation years that ended before the the [*sic*] child acquired the property.

Editorial Note: When land or depreciable property in Canada (or, prior to January 1, 2017, eligible capital property) in respect of a farming or fishing business carried on in Canada by a taxpayer, is rolled over by the taxpayer under ss. 73(3) and (3.1) to a child of the taxpayer, the rollover occurs on a tax-deferred basis, the same as when such property is passed upon the death of a taxpayer under s. 70(9) and (9.1). The taxpayer, the taxpayer's spouse or common-law partner, or a child or parent of the taxpayer must have been actively engaged in a farming or fishing business and the property so transferred must have been principally used in that business.

Under s. 70(10), a child includes a grandchild or great-grandchild of the taxpayer, as well as a person who, prior to turning age 19, was dependent on and under the custody and control of the taxpayer. The child must be a resident of Canada immediately before the transfer for the rollover provisions to apply. If the farming or fishing property rollover applies and the transferee child subsequently disposes of the property before attaining the age of 18, the attribution rules of s. 75.1 may apply.

History: S. 73(3.1)(*c*) was repealed by S.C. 2016, c. 12, s. 21(2), in force January 1, 2017, and formerly read:

(*c*) where, immediately before the transfer, the property was eligible capital property, the taxpayer is deemed to have disposed of the property, at the time of the transfer, for proceeds of disposition equal to,

(i) in any case to which neither subparagraph (ii) nor (iii) applies, the taxpayer's proceeds of disposition otherwise determined,

(ii) the greater of the amounts referred to in clauses (A) and (B), if the taxpayer's proceeds of disposition otherwise determined exceed the greater of

(A) the fair market value of the property immediately before the time of the transfer, and

(B) the amount determined by the formula

$$4/3 (A \times B/C)$$

where

A is the taxpayer's cumulative eligible capital in respect of the business,

B is the fair market value of the property immediately before the transfer, and

C is the fair market value immediately before the transfer of all the taxpayer's eligible capital property in respect of the business, or

(iii) if the taxpayer's proceeds of disposition otherwise determined are less than the lesser of the amounts referred to in clauses (ii)(A) and (B), the lesser of those amounts;

S. 73(3.1)(*f*) and (*g*) were repealed by S.C. 2016, c. 12, s. 21(3), in force January 1, 2017, and formerly read:

(*f*) if the property was, immediately before the transfer, an eligible capital property of the taxpayer in respect of a business, the child is deemed to have acquired

(i) where the child does not continue to carry on the business, a capital property, immediately after the transfer, at a cost equal to the taxpayer's proceeds of disposition in respect of the disposition of the property determined under paragraph (*c*),

(ii) where the child continues to carry on the business, an eligible capital property and to have made an eligible capital expenditure at a cost equal to the total of

(A) the taxpayer's proceeds of disposition referred to in paragraph (*c*), and

(B) $^4/_3$ of the amount determined by the formula

$$(A \times B/C) - D$$

where

A is the amount, if any, determined for F in the definition "cumulative eligible capital" in subsection 14(5) in respect of the business immediately before the transfer,

B is the fair market value of the property immediately before the transfer,

C is the fair market value immediately before the transfer of all the taxpayer's eligible capital property in respect of the business, and

D is the amount, if any, included under paragraph 14(1)(*a*) in computing the taxpayer's income as a result of the disposition, and

(iii) for the purpose of determining at any subsequent time the child's cumulative eligible capital in respect of the business, an amount equal to $^3/_4$ of the amount determined under subparagraph (ii) is to be added to the amount otherwise determined for P in the definition "cumulative eligible capital" in subsection 14(5);

(*g*) for the purpose of determining, in respect of any disposition of the property, after the time of the transfer, the amount deemed to be the child's taxable capital gain, and the amount to be included in computing the child's income, there shall be added to the amount otherwise determined for Q in respect of the business in the definition "cumulative eligible capital" in subsection 14(5), the amount determined by the formula,

$$A \times B/C$$

where

A is the amount, if any, determined for Q in that definition in respect of the business immediately before the time of the transfer,

B is the fair market value, immediately before that time, of the transferred property, and

C is the fair market value immediately before that time of all the taxpayer's eligible capital property in respect of the business; and

Tax Window Files: Inter vivos transfer of farm land to adult children, CRA Document No. 2015-0576961R3.

▶ 73(4) ◀

(4) When subsection (4.1) applies. Subsection (4.1) applies to a taxpayer and a child of the taxpayer in respect of property that has been transferred, at any time, to the child if

(*a*) the child was resident in Canada immediately before the transfer; and

(*b*) the property was, immediately before the transfer, a share of the capital stock of a family farm or fishing corporation of the taxpayer or an interest in a family farm or fishing partnership of the taxpayer (as defined in subsection 70(10)).

History: S. 73(4)(*b*) was replaced by S.C. 2014, c. 39, s. 14(3), applicable to transfers that occur in the 2014 and subsequent taxation years, and formerly read:

(*b*) the property was, immediately before the transfer, a share of the capital stock of a family fishing corporation of the taxpayer, a share of the capital stock of a family farm corporation of the taxpayer, an interest in a family fishing partnership of the taxpayer or an interest in a family farm partnership of the taxpayer (within the meaning assigned by subsection 70(10)).

Interpretation Bulletins: *Primary* — IT-268R4 Inter vivos transfer of farm property to child.

▶ 73(4.1) ◀

(4.1) Inter vivos transfer of family farm or fishing corporations and partnerships. If, because of subsection (4), this subsection applies to the taxpayer and the taxpayer's child in respect of the transfer of the property by the taxpayer to the child,

(*a*) subject to paragraph (*c*), where the property was, immediately before the transfer, a share of the capital stock of a family farm or fishing corporation of the taxpayer or an interest in a family farm or fishing partnership of the taxpayer, the taxpayer is deemed to have disposed of the property at the time of the transfer for proceeds of disposition equal to,

(i) in any case to which neither subparagraph (ii) nor (iii) applies, the taxpayer's proceeds of disposition otherwise determined,

(ii) the greater of the amounts referred to in clauses (A) and (B), if the taxpayer's proceeds of disposition otherwise determined exceed the greater of

(A) the fair market value of the property immediately before the time of the transfer, and

(B) the adjusted cost base to the taxpayer of the property immediately before the time of the transfer, or

(iii) if the taxpayer's proceeds of disposition otherwise determined are less than the lesser of the amounts referred to in clauses (ii)(A) and (B), the lesser of those amounts;

(*b*) subject to paragraph (*c*), where the property is, immediately before the transfer, a share of the capital stock of a family farm or fishing corporation of the taxpayer or an interest in a family farm or fishing partnership of the taxpayer, the child is deemed to have acquired the property for an amount equal to the taxpayer's proceeds of disposition in respect of the disposition of the property determined under paragraph (*a*);

(*c*) where the property is, immediately before the transfer, an interest in a family farm or fishing partnership of the taxpayer (other than a partnership interest to which subsection 100(3) applies), the taxpayer receives no consideration in respect of the transfer of the property and the taxpayer elects, in the taxpayer's return of income under this Part for the taxation year which includes the time of the transfer, to have this paragraph apply in respect of the transfer of the property,

(i) the taxpayer is, except for the purpose of paragraph 98(5)(*g*), deemed not to have disposed of the property at the time of the transfer,

(ii) the child is deemed to have acquired the property at the time of the transfer at a cost equal to the cost to the taxpayer of the interest immediately before the transfer, and

(iii) each amount required by subsection 53(1) or (2) to be added or deducted in computing the adjusted cost base to the taxpayer, immediately before the transfer, of the property is deemed to be an amount required by subsection 53(1) or (2) to be added or deducted in computing at any time at or after the time of the transfer, the adjusted cost base to the child of the property; and

(*d*) subsection 69(1) does not apply to the taxpayer and the child in respect of the property.

Editorial Note: Shares of a family farm or fishing corporation or an interest in a family farm or fishing partnership are allowed a tax-deferred rollover when they are transferred by a taxpayer to his or her child. Under s. 70(10), a child includes a grandchild or great-grandchild of the taxpayer, as well as a person who, prior to turning age 19, was dependent on and under the custody and control of the taxpayer. The child must be a resident of Canada immediately before the transfer for the rollover provisions to apply.

Subsection 70(10) also sets out the definitions of "share of the capital stock of a family farm corporation", "share of the capital stock of a family fishing corporation", "interest in a family fishing partnership", and "interest in a family farm partnership".

If the s. 73(4.1) rollover applies and the transferee child subsequently disposes of the property before attaining the age of 18, the attribution rules of s. 75.1 may apply.

Similar provisions apply when such property is transferred on a taxpayer's death to the taxpayer's child; see s. 70(9.2) to (9.21).

History: S. 73(4.1)(*a*), the portion before subparagraph (i) was replaced by S.C. 2014, c. 39, s. 14(4), applicable to transfers that occur in the 2014 and subsequent taxation years, and formerly read:

(*a*) subject to paragraph (*c*), where the property was, immediately before the transfer, a share of the capital stock of a family fishing corporation of the taxpayer, a share of the capital stock of a family farm corporation of the taxpayer, an interest in a family fishing partnership of the taxpayer or an interest in a family farm partnership of the taxpayer, the taxpayer is deemed to have disposed of the property at the time of the transfer for proceeds of disposition equal to,

S. 73(4.1)(*b*) was replaced by S.C. 2014, c. 39, s. 14(5), applicable to transfers that occur in the 2014 and subsequent taxation years, and formerly read:

(*b*) subject to paragraph (*c*), where the property is, immediately before the transfer, a share of the capital stock of a family fishing corporation of the taxpayer, a share of the capital stock of a family farm corporation of the taxpayer, an interest in a family fishing partnership of the taxpayer or an interest in a family farm partnership of the taxpayer, the child is deemed to have acquired the property for an amount equal to the taxpayer's proceeds of disposition in respect of the disposition of the property determined under paragraph (*a*);

S. 73(4.1)(*c*), the portion before subparagraph (i) was replaced by S.C. 2014, c. 39, s. 14(6), applicable to transfers that occur in the 2014 and subsequent taxation years, and formerly read:

(*c*) where the property is, immediately before the transfer, an interest in a family fishing partnership of the taxpayer, or an interest in a family farm partnership of the taxpayer (other than a partnership interest to which subsection 100(3) applies), the taxpayer receives no consideration in respect of the transfer of the property and the taxpayer elects, in the taxpayer's return of income under this Part for the taxation year which includes the time of the transfer, to have this paragraph apply in respect of the transfer of the property,

▶ 73(5) ◀

(5) Disposition of a NISA. Where at any time a taxpayer disposes of an interest in the taxpayer's NISA Fund No. 2, an amount equal to the balance in the fund so disposed of shall be deemed to have been paid out of the fund at that time to the taxpayer except that,

(*a*) where the interest is disposed of to the taxpayer's spouse or common-law partner, former spouse or common-law partner or an individual referred to in paragraph (1)(*d*) (as it applies to transfers of property that occurred before 1993) in settlement of rights arising out of their marriage or common-law partnership, on or after the breakdown of the marriage or common-law partnership, that amount shall not be deemed to have been paid to the taxpayer if

(i) the disposition is made under a decree, order or judgment of a competent tribunal or, in the case of a spouse or common-law partner or former spouse or common-law partner, a written separation agreement, and

(ii) the taxpayer elects in the taxpayer's return of income under this Part for the taxation year in which the property was disposed of to have this paragraph apply to the disposition; and

(*b*) where the interest is disposed of to a taxable Canadian corporation in a transaction in respect of which an election is made under section 85, an amount equal to the proceeds of disposition in respect of that interest shall be deemed to be paid, at that time, to the taxpayer out of the taxpayer's NISA Fund No. 2.

Related Sections: S. 13(21), "proceeds of disposition"; s. 54, "proceeds of disposition"; s. 89(1), "taxable Canadian corporation"; s. 248(1), "amount", "common-law partner", "property", "taxable Canadian corporation".

▶ 73(6) ◀

(6) Application of s. 70(10). The definitions in subsection 70(10) apply to this section.

SECTION 74: Transfers to spouse

(Repealed by 1986, c. 6, s. 37(1).)

SECTION 74.1: [Transfers and loans to spouse or common-law partner or minor]

▶ 74.1(1) ◀

(1) Transfers and loans to spouse or common-law partner. If an individual has transferred or lent property (otherwise than by an assignment of any portion of a retirement pension under section 65.1 of the *Canada Pension Plan* or a comparable provision of a provincial pension plan as defined in section 3 of that Act), either directly or indirectly, by means of a trust or by any other means whatever, to or for the benefit of a person who is the individual's spouse or common-law partner or who has since become the individual's spouse or common-law partner, any income or loss, as the case may be, of that person for a taxation year from the property or from property substituted therefor, that relates to the period in the year throughout which the individual is resident in Canada and that person is the individual's spouse or common-law partner, is deemed to be income or a loss, as the case may be, of the individual for the year and not of that person.

Editorial Note: The attribution rules in s. 74.1 apply to income or loss from property that was transferred (or loaned) directly or indirectly to a spouse or common-law partner (subsection (1)) or minor children or others who are non-arm's length with, or nieces or nephews of, the transferor (subsection (2)). The attribution rules in s. 74.2 apply to capital gains realized in respect of property that was transferred to the spouse or common-law partner; no attribution of capital gains applies in respect of transfers of property to minor children (except in the case of rolled-over farm or fishing property; see s. 75.1). S. 74.3 contains rules that apply for the purposes of the attribution rules of s. 74.1 or 74.2 where property is transferred to a trust in which the spouse, common-law partner, or minor child (etc.) is beneficially interested. S. 74.4 contains a corporate income attribution rule that can apply where the transfer of property is made to a corporation and the spouse, common-law partner, or minor child (etc.) is a specified shareholder of the corporation (an exception generally applies if the corporation is a small business corporation). S. 74.5 contains exceptions to the attribution rules, additional rules regarding their application, and certain definitions. Under s. 160(1)(*d*), joint and several liability is imposed on the recipient and transferor (or lender) for the transferor's liability as a result of the attribution rules in s. 74.1 to 75.1 (in addition to the general rules in s. 160(1)(*e*) where property is transferred for deficient consideration).

S. 74.1(1) applies to direct or indirect transfers (or loans) from an individual to a person who is or becomes a spouse or common-law partner. The provision (which is applicable to income or loss from the transferred or loaned property or substituted property) applies only to periods when the transferring or lending individual is both Canadian resident and the recipient is a spouse or common-law partner (e.g., the rules are inapplicable following death or during the period in which the transferor is non-resident e.g., see IT-511R, par. 18 (archived, as it doesn't meet current government web standards)). S. 74.1(1) may not apply to transferred property for fair market value consideration or loans for value (including prescribed-interest-rate loans — see ss. 74.5(1) and (2)). If a marriage or common-law relationship has broken down, see s. 74.5(3), by virtue of which the income attribution rules no longer apply and the parties may elect to have the capital gain attribution rules in 74.2 no longer apply. The CRA acknowledges that the income attribution rules do not apply to business income or loss; but see s. 96(1.8) by virtue of income/loss for a "specified member" of a partnership (per s. 248(1) — basically a limited or inactive partner) is deemed to be from property. See also s. 60.03 for eligible pension income splitting.

The income attribution rules do not apply to "second generation income" — i.e., income on previously attributed income (see, for example, paragraph 6 of IT-511R). The attribution rules continue to apply to income from capital gains realized from transferred or loaned property.

Note that these rules operate independently of the Tax On Split Income ("TOSI") rules in s. 120.4 which deal with the "split income" of family members. Previously these rules were referred to as the "kiddie tax" and applied only to minor children, but they now have a significantly expanded scope.

History: S. 74.1(1) was replaced by S.C. 2011, c. 24, s. 16(1), applicable to transfers and loans made after 2010. S. 74.1(1) formerly read:

(1) *Transfers and loans to spouse.* Where an individual has transferred or lent property (otherwise than by an assignment of any portion of a retirement pension pursuant to section 65.1 of the *Canada Pension Plan* or a comparable provision of a provincial pension plan as defined in section 3 of that Act or of a prescribed provincial pension plan), either directly or indirectly, by means of a trust or by any other means whatever, to or for the benefit of a person who is the individual's spouse or common-law partner or who has since become the individual's spouse or common-law partner, any income or loss, as the case may be, of that person for a taxation year from the property or from property substituted therefor, that relates to the period in the year throughout which the individual is resident in Canada and that person is the individual's spouse or common-law partner, shall be deemed to be income or a loss, as the case may be, of the individual for the year and not of that person.

Related Regulations: 7800(1).

Related Sections: S. 40(2)(*g*)(i) Limitations; s. 54, "superficial loss"; s. 56(2) Indirect payments; s. 56(4) Transfer of rights to income; s. 56(4.1) Interest free or low interest loans; s. 60.03 Definitions; s. 69(1) Inadequate considerations; s. 73(1) Inter vivos transfers by individuals; s. 74.3(1) Transfers or loans to a trust; s. 74.5 Exceptions; s. 75(2) Trusts; s. 82(2) Certain dividends received by taxpayer; s. 96(1.8) Loan of property; s. 108(5) Interpretation; s. 120.4 Tax on split income; s. 160(1) Tax liability re property transferred not at arm's length; s. 212(12) Deemed payments to spouse, etc; s. 248(5) Substituted property; s. 251.1 Arm's length.

Canadian Tax Foundation: Lee, *Subsection 74.5(11) and Professional Corporation Shares*, 2014 Tax for the Owner-Manager 14(3):3–4; Carreiro and Hoag, *Marriage Breakdown and the Division of Corporate Wealth*, 2012 British Columbia Tax Conference 5:1–26; Hoffstein and Lee, *Revisiting the Attribution Rules*, 2012 Ontario Tax Conference 9:1–40; Freedman and Nakonechny, *The Tax Principles of Family Law*, 2012 Ontario Tax Conference 4:1–52; Brown and Wiener, *A Practical Look at the Attribution Rules: Tips and Traps*, 2011 Conference Report 38:1–49; Jacob and Lee, *Income-Splitting Strategies: Selected Aspects*, 2010 Canadian Tax Journal 4:1005–1023; Templeton, *Current Cases: Supreme Court of Canada — The Supreme Court Revisits GAAR (Lipson v. Canada, 2009 SCC 1)*, 2009 Canadian Tax Journal 1:59–66; McDonnell, *Current Cases: Federal Court of Appeal — The Relevance of "Overall Purpose" in a GAAR Analysis (Lipson et al. v. The Queen, 2007 DTC 5172)*, 2007 Canadian Tax Journal 3:720–730; McDonnell, *Current Cases: Tax Court of Canada — GAAR Applied To Reverse Attribution Plan (Lipson et al. v. The Queen, 2006 DTC 148)*, 2006 Canadian Tax Journal 3:711–719; Rosenberg, *Inter Vivos Trusts: Their Utility and Tax Treatment in the Context of Estate Planning*, 2004 Prairie Provinces Tax Conference 15:1–45; Rochwerg, *Using Trusts as an Income-Splitting Tool*, 2003 Conference Report 18:1–28; Donnelly et al., *Income Splitting and the New Kiddie Tax: Major Changes for Minor Children*, 2000 Canadian Tax Journal 4:979–1018; Addison and Korn, *Interspousal Property Transfers: The Things They Don't Tell You at the Diamond Shop*, 2002 Canadian Tax Journal 2:728–757.

Tax Profile: February 2010 — Planning With Trusts; February 2009 — SCC on the GAAR — Taxpayer Loses in Lipson; February 2008 — Income Splitting A–Z; July 2007 — Canadian Tax Traps; July 2006 — Asset Protection Planning.

Tax Topics: No. 1924, Lipson (SCC) — A Unanimously Divided Supreme Court; No. 1702, Income Tax Issues To Be Considered in Negotiating Marriage Contracts.

Income Tax Folios: *Secondary* — S4-F3-C1 Price Adjustment Clauses.

Interpretation Bulletins: *Primary* — IT-511R Interspousal and certain other transfers and loans of property. *Secondary* — IT-295R4 Taxable dividends received after 1987 by a spouse; IT-394R2 Preferred beneficiary election.

Tax Window Files: Spousal Attribution Re: Joint Line of Credit, *Income Tax Rulings Directorate, Financial Sector and Exempt Entities Division, July 20, 2009*, CRA Document No. 2009-0317041E5; Attribution rules — spouses, *September 15, 2006*, CRA Document No. 2006-0199361E5; Attribution Rules — Separation of Common-Law Partners, *Technical Interpretation, Business and Partnerships Division, July 13, 2005*, CRA Document No. 2005-0131351E5; Allocation of Partnership Income Between Spouse Partners, *Technical Interpretation, Business and Partnerships Division, January 14, 2004*, CRA Document No. 2003-0029571E5; Transfer of Property to Trust Allows Capital Gains Exemption To Be Claimed, *Round Table on Federal Taxation — 2003 APFF Conference, Question 15, October 10, 2003*, CRA Document No. 2003-0030105; Transfer of Mutual Funds Into Joint Tenancy, *February 17, 2003*, CRA Document No. 2003-0182177.

Cases: The taxpayer's wife obtained a bank loan to purchase shares of a family corporation from him. He used the proceeds to buy a new house. They then took out a mortgage on the house and used it to pay off the bank loan. The mortgage interest was deducted from her dividend income and the resulting loss was attributed to him under s. 74.1(1). GAAR applied since this was an abuse of the attribution rules. *Lipson et al. v. The Queen*, 2009 DTC 5015 (S.C.C.), affirming 2007 DTC 5172 (F.C.A.), affirming 2006 DTC 2687 (T.C.C.)

► 74.1(2) ◄

(2) Transfers and loans to minors. If an individual has transferred or lent property, either directly or indirectly, by means of a trust or by any other means whatever, to or for the benefit of a person who was under 18 years of age (other than an amount received in respect of that person either as a consequence of the operation of subsection 122.61(1) or under section 4 of the *Universal Child Care Benefit Act*) and who

(*a*) does not deal with the individual at arm's length, or

(*b*) is the niece or nephew of the individual,

any income or loss, as the case may be, of that person for a taxation year from the property or from property substituted for that property, that relates to the period in the taxation year throughout which the individual is resident in Canada, is deemed to be income or a loss, as the case may be, of the individual and not of that person unless that person has, before the end of the taxation year, attained the age of 18 years.

Editorial Note: S. 74.1(2) extends the income attribution rules to direct or indirect transfers (or loans) from an individual to minors — i.e., a person who is under 18 and either is non-arm's length or a niece or nephew. Related persons (per s. 251(1)) are deemed not to be at arm's length; there is also a factual non-arm's length concept (determined under case law by whether there is a "common mind" directing both sides of a transaction, the parties are acting in concert without separate interests, or there is effective control by one party). See too, the editorial note under s. 74.1(1) for the application. See s. 56(4.1)–56(5) re attribution rules applying to loans to adults.

In the case of minors, there is no general attribution rule applying to capital gains — i.e., along the lines of s. 74.2 (except in the case of rolled-over farm or fishing property — see s. 75.1). However, changes in 2011 restricted the scope of capital gains splitting with minors by adding to the tax on split income under s. 120.4 to include taxable capital gains (including from a trust) included in the income of a minor from the disposition of shares after March 21, 2011 to a non-arm's length person, if taxable dividends on such shares would have been subject to the tax on split income (e.g., shares of a private corporation). As such gains are excluded from taxable capital gains, they will not qualify for the one-half inclusion rate for capital gains or the lifetime capital gains exemption (as indexed), nor will they be included under s. 74.1(2), by virtue of s. 74.5(13), which excludes split income tax under s. 120.4 from the attribution rules.

The income attribution rules do not apply to "second generation income" — i.e., income on previously attributed income (see, for example, paragraph 4 of IT-510). The attribution rules continue to apply to income from capital gains realized from transferred or loaned property.

Related Sections: S. 56(2) Indirect payments; s. 56(4) Transfer of rights to income; 56(4.1) Interest free or low interest loans; 56(4.2) Exception; 56(4.3) Repayment of existing indebtedness; 56(5) Exception for split income; s. 69(1) Inadequate considerations; s. 74.3(1) Transfers or loans to a trust; s. 74.5 Exceptions; s. 75(2) Trusts; s. 82(2) Certain dividends received by taxpayer; s. 96(1.8) Loan of property; s. 108(5) Interpretation; s. 120.4 Tax on split income; s. 160(1) Tax liability re property transferred not at arm's length; s. 212(12) Deemed payments to spouse, etc; s. 248(5) Substituted property; s. 251 Arm's length.

Canadian Tax Foundation: Hoffstein and Lee, *Revisiting the Attribution Rules*, 2012 Ontario Tax Conference 9:1–40; Brown and Wiener, *A Practical Look at the Attribution Rules: Tips and Traps*, 2011 Conference Report 38:1–49; Donnelly et al., *Income Splitting and the New Kiddie Tax: Major Changes for Minor Children*, 2000 Canadian Tax Journal 4:979–1018.

Tax Profile: February 2010 — Planning With Trusts; February 2008 — Income Splitting A–Z.

Income Tax Folios: *Secondary* — S4-F3-C1 Price Adjustment Clauses.

Interpretation Bulletins: *Primary* — IT-510 Transfers and loans of property made after May 22, 1985 to related minor.

Tax Window Files: RESP — Attribution Rules, *May 20, 2004*, CRA Document No. 2004-0064551E5.

► 74.1(3) ◄

(3) Repayment of existing indebtedness. For the purposes of subsections (1) and (2), where, at any time, an individual has lent or transferred property (in this subsection referred to as the "lent or transferred property") either directly or indirectly, by means of a trust or by any other means whatever, to or for the benefit of a person, and the lent or transferred property or property substituted therefor is used

(*a*) to repay, in whole or in part, borrowed money with which other property was acquired, or

(*b*) to reduce an amount payable for other property,

there shall be included in computing the income from the lent or transferred property, or from property substituted therefor, that is so used, that proportion of the income or loss, as the case may be, derived after that time from the other property or from property substituted therefor that the fair market value at that time of the lent or transferred property, or property substituted therefor, that is so used is of the cost to that person of the other property at the time of its acquisition, but for greater certainty nothing in this subsection shall affect the application of subsections (1) and (2) to any income or loss derived from the other property or from property substituted therefor.

Editorial Note: Subsection 74.1(3) extends the attribution rules in subsection 74.1(1) and (2) to potentially apply to transferred or loaned property which is used either to repay borrowed money that was used to acquire other property, or to reduce an amount payable for the other property. An example is a gift made by a spouse to pay down an arm's length debt of the transferee. Income from the other property is attributed back and included in the transferor's income, in the proportion that the fair market value of such (transferred or loaned) property is to the cost of the other property. S. 74.1(3) provides that nothing in this subsection shall affect the application of subsections (1) and (2).

See "Owner Manager Remuneration: Part I", Luvisotto, 2010 OC p.9A:8/9 for discussion of technical issues. (See also "Income-Splitting Strategies: Selected Aspects" Jacob and Lee, 2010 CTJ 4 p. 1008/9; the authors state that the term and value of the new loan should be different from the repaid loan, and that it is preferred that the lender not use the proceeds from the repaid loan for the new loan, so that the new loan will not be viewed as the same loan. A "rate reset" or advancing funds at the new prescribed rate to repay the original loans are problematic — see also Document No. 9336625. For the CRA comments on joint lines of credit, see 2009-0317041E5.

Interpretation Bulletins: *Secondary* — IT-510 Transfers and loans of property made after May 22, 1985 to related minor.

SECTION 74.2: Gain or loss deemed that of lender or transferor

► 74.2(1) ◄

(1) Gain or loss deemed that of lender or transferor. Where an individual has lent or transferred property (in this section referred to as "lent or transferred property"), either directly or indirectly, by means of a trust or by any other means whatever, to or for the benefit of a person (in this subsection referred to as the "recipient") who is the individual's spouse or common-law partner or who has since become the individual's spouse or common-law partner, the following rules apply for the purposes of computing the income of the individual and the recipient for a taxation year:

(*a*) the amount, if any, by which

(i) the total of the recipient's taxable capital gains for the year from dispositions of property (other than listed personal property) that is lent or transferred property or property substituted therefor occurring in the period (in this subsection referred to as the "attribution period") throughout which the individual is resident in Canada and the recipient is the individual's spouse or common-law partner

exceeds

(ii) the total of the recipient's allowable capital losses for the year from dispositions occurring in the attribution period of property (other than listed personal property) that is lent or transferred property or property substituted therefor

shall be deemed to be a taxable capital gain of the individual for the year from the disposition of property other than listed personal property;

(*b*) the amount, if any, by which the total determined under subparagraph (*a*)(ii) exceeds the total determined under subparagraph (*a*)(i) shall be deemed to be an allowable capital loss of the individual for the year from the disposition of property other than listed personal property;

(*c*) the amount, if any, by which

(i) the amount that the total of the recipient's gains for the year from dispositions occurring in the attribution period of listed personal property that is lent or transferred property or property substituted therefor would be if the recipient had at no time owned listed personal property other than listed personal property that was lent or transferred property or property substituted therefor

exceeds

(ii) the amount that the total of the recipient's losses for the year from dispositions of listed personal property that is lent or transferred property or property substituted therefor would be if the recipient had at no time owned listed personal property other than listed personal property that was lent or transferred property or property substituted therefor,

shall be deemed to be a gain of the individual for the year from the disposition of listed personal property;

(*d*) the amount, if any, by which the total determined under subparagraph (*c*)(ii) exceeds the total determined under subparagraph (*c*)(i) shall be deemed to be a loss of the individual for the year from the disposition of listed personal property; and

(*e*) any taxable capital gain or allowable capital loss or any gain or loss taken into account in computing an amount described in paragraph (*a*), (*b*), (*c*) or (*d*) shall, except for the purposes of those paragraphs and to the extent that the amount so described is deemed by virtue of this subsection to be a taxable capital gain or an allowable capital loss or a gain or loss of the individual, be deemed not to be a taxable capital gain or an allowable capital loss or a gain or loss, as the case may be, of the recipient.

Editorial Note: This provision extends the attribution rules to capital gains and losses, for direct or indirect transfers (or loans) from an individual to a person who is or becomes a spouse or common-law partner. S. 74.2(1)(*a*) attributes net capital gains from transfers or loans of property or substituted property (other than listed personal property) to the transferring (or lending) individual for dispositions in periods when the individual is both Canadian resident and the recipient is a spouse or common-law partner, with (*b*) similarly attributing such net capital losses; e.g., the rules are inapplicable following death or during the period in which the individual is non-resident e.g., see IT-511R, par. 18. (Note the provisions are based on dispositions rather than capital-gains accruals during such period.) S. 74.2(1)(*c*) and (*d*) contain similar rules applicable to listed personal property gains and losses. S. 74.2(1)(*e*) essentially eliminates double tax by deeming such gains or losses not to be gains or losses of the recipient spouse. As with other attribution rules, this rule may not apply to transferred property for fair market value consideration or loans for value (including prescribed-interest-rate loans — see ss. 74.5(1) and (2)). There is also an exception for deemed dispositions on emigration — see s. 74.2(3). See also the editorial comment under s. 74.1(1).

In *Zeitler v. Zeitler Estate*, 2010 DTC 5119, the BC Court of Appeal held that, in the circumstances, and notwithstanding the attribution rules which required the transferor spouse to pay tax on a subsequent disposition of property transferred to the transferee spouse, there was an implied obligation to the transferee spouse to defray these taxes. See "Estate Cases Raise Taxing Issues", Tax Notes No. 570, July 2010. See Document No. 2009-0327081C6 on the CRA's position in view of the *Lipson* case, 2009 DTC 5015 (S.C.C.), whether the transfer of latent capital losses between spouses is still acceptable.

Related Sections: S. 38 Taxable capital gain and allowable capital loss; s. 39(1) Meaning of capital gain and capital loss; s. 54, "listed personal property"; s. 69(1) Inadequate considerations; s. 73(1) Inter vivos transfers by individuals; s. 74.3(1) Transfers or loans to a trust; s. 74.5 Exceptions; s. 160(1) Tax liability re property transferred not at arm's length; s. 212(12) Deemed payments to spouse, etc; s. 248(5) Substituted property.

Canadian Tax Foundation: Gosselin, *TCC Shuts Down Strategy To Multiply Lifetime Capital Gains Exemption*, 2014 Tax for the Owner-Manager 14(3):4–5; Hoffstein and Lee, *Revisiting the Attribution Rules*, 2012 Ontario Tax Conference 9:1–40; Brown and Wiener, *A Practical Look at the Attribution Rules: Tips and Traps*, 2011 Conference Report 38:1–49.

Tax Profile: February 2010 — Planning With Trusts; February 2008 — Income Splitting A–Z.

Tax Topics: No. 1702, Income Tax Issues To Be Considered in Negotiating Marriage Contracts.

Income Tax Folios: *Secondary* — S4-F3-C1 Price Adjustment Clauses.

Interpretation Bulletins: *Primary* — IT-511R Interspousal and certain other transfers and loans of property. *Secondary* — IT-394R2 Preferred beneficiary election.

Tax Window Files: Attribution rules — spouses, *September 15, 2006*, CRA Document No. 2006-0199361E5.

Cases: There was a series of transactions involving tax avoidance. The husband's election to take advantage of the rollover provisions of s. 73(1) resulted in the application of s. 47(1) at the time that the wife sold 2 million shares. As a result, a portion of the taxable capital gain that would normally have been attributed to the husband accrued to the wife. Subsection 74.2(1) was intended to avoid this result, and the series of transactions constituted abusive tax avoidance. GAAR was used to attribute back to the husband the capital gain reported by his wife on the sale of the shares. *Gervais et al. v. The Queen*, 2016 DTC 1166 (CCI). [Under Appeal]

▶ 74.2(2) ◀

(2) Deemed gain or loss. Where an amount is deemed by subsection (1) or 75(2) or section 75.1 of this Act, or subsection 74(2) of the *Income Tax Act*, chapter 148 of the Revised Statutes of Canada, 1952, to be a taxable capital gain or an allowable capital loss of an individual for a taxation year,

(*a*) for the purposes of sections 3 and 111, as they apply for the purposes of section 110.6, such portion of the gain or loss as may reasonably be considered to relate to the disposition of a property by another person in the year shall be deemed to arise from the disposition of that property by the individual in the year; and

(*b*) for the purposes of section 110.6, that property shall be deemed to have been disposed of by the individual on the day on which it was disposed of by the other person.

Editorial Note: S. 74.2(2) effectively provides that any capital gain or loss attributed to a transferor in respect of qualified small business corporation shares or qualified farm or fishing property is eligible for the individual's lifetime capital gains exemption under s. 110.6.

Related Sections: S. 110.6 Capital gains exemption.

Interpretation Bulletins: *Primary* — IT-511R Interspousal and certain other transfers and loans of property. *Secondary* — IT-369R Attribution of trust income to settlor.

Tax Window Files: Qualified farm property — Attribution (Property Last Acquired), *Technical Interpretation, Business and Partnerships Division, June 25, 2004*, CRA Document No. 2004-0065501E5.

▶ 74.2(3) ◀

(3) Election for subsection (1) to apply. Subsection (1) does not apply to a disposition at any particular time (in this subsection referred to as the "emigration disposition") under paragraph 128.1(4)(*b*), by a taxpayer who is a recipient referred to in subsection (1), unless the recipient and the individual referred to in that subsection, in their returns of income for the taxation year that includes the first time, after the particular time, at which the recipient disposes of the property, jointly elect that subsection (1) apply to the emigration disposition.

Editorial Note: The attribution rules in s. 74.2(1) do not apply to the deemed disposition upon ceasing to be resident (i.e., under paragraph 128.1(4)(*b*)), unless the individual and the individual's spouse or common-law partner jointly elect in their returns for the relevant year. S. 74.2(4) deals with assessments necessary for the joint election; it provides that no such assessment shall affect the computation of interest or penalties.

Related Sections: S. 128.1(8) Post-emigration loss; s. 220(4.5) Security for departure tax.

▶ 74.2(4) ◀

(4) Application of subsection (3). For the purpose of applying subsection (3) and notwithstanding subsections 152(4) to (5), any assessment of tax payable under this Act by the recipient or the individual referred to in subsection (1) shall be made that is necessary to take an election under subsection (3) into account except that no such assessment shall affect the computation of

(*a*) interest payable under this Act to or by a taxpayer in respect of any period that is before the taxpayer's filing-due date for the taxation year that includes the first time, after the particular time referred to in subsection (3), at which the recipient disposes of the property referred to in that subsection; or

(*b*) any penalty payable under this Act.

Editorial Note: See the editorial note under s. 74.2(3).

Related Sections: S. 128.1(8) Post-emigration loss; s. 220(4.5) Security for departure tax.

SECTION 74.3: Transfers or loans to a trust

▶ 74.3(1) ◀

(1) Transfers or loans to a trust. Where an individual has lent or transferred property (in this section referred to as "lent or transferred property"), either directly or indirectly, by means of a trust or by any other means whatever, to a trust in which another individual who is at any time a designated person in respect of the individual is beneficially interested at any time, the following rules apply:

(*a*) for the purposes of section 74.1, the income of the designated person for a taxation year from the lent or transferred property shall be deemed to be an amount equal to the lesser of

(i) the amount in respect of the trust that was included by virtue of paragraph 12(1)(*m*) in computing the income for the year of the designated person, and

(ii) that proportion of the amount that would be the income of the trust for the year from the lent or transferred property or from property substituted therefor if no deduction were made under subsection 104(6) or (12) that

(A) the amount determined under subparagraph (i) in respect of the designated person for the year

is of

(B) the total of all amounts each of which is an amount determined under subparagraph (i) for the year in respect of the designated person or any other person who is throughout the year a designated person in respect of the individual; and

(*b*) for the purposes of section 74.2, an amount equal to the lesser of

(i) the amount that was designated under subsection 104(21) in respect of the designated person in the trust's return of income for the year, and

(ii) the amount, if any, by which

(A) the total of all amounts each of which is a taxable capital gain for the year from the disposition by the trust of the lent or transferred property or property substituted therefor

exceeds

(B) the total of all amounts each of which is an allowable capital loss for the year from the disposition by the trust of the lent or transferred property or property substituted therefor,

shall be deemed to be a taxable capital gain of the designated person for the year from the disposition of property (other than listed personal property) that is lent or transferred property.

Editorial Note: Section 74.3 sets out the method of calculating the amount of income and loss and the amount of capital gain and loss which is to be attributed to an individual under sections 74.1 and 74.2, respectively, where the individual has loaned or transferred property, directly or indirectly, by means of a trust or by any other means whatever, to a trust in which a "designated person" in respect of the individual is beneficially interested at any time. Pursuant to ss. 74.3(2) and 74.5(5), a designated person in respect of an individual means the individual's spouse or common-law partner, or a child (or other person not at arm's length with the individual), niece, or nephew of the individual who is under the age of 18. Subsection 74.3(1) ensures that income of the trust derived from such property or property substituted therefor is allocated first to beneficiaries of the trust who are designated persons in relation to the individual who transferred or lent the property, and is therefore subject to the attribution rules. Calculations are made separately for the income and capital gains attribution rules in s. 74.1 and 74.2 respectively (note that the latter is only applicable to spouses and common-law partners). The amount subject to the attribution rules cannot exceed the amount of the income of the designated person from the trust (under s. 12(1)(*m*) and 104(21) respectively). The attribution rules will not apply to the extent that income is accumulated by, and therefore taxed in, the trust. See also the editorial note under s. 74.1(1).

Related Sections: S. 69(1) Inadequate considerations; s. 73(1) Inter vivos transfers by individuals; s. 74.5 Exceptions; s. 74.5(5) Definition of "designated person"; s. 74.5(9) Transfers or loans to a trust; s. 75(2) Trusts; s. 96(1.8) Loan of property; s. 104(13) Income of beneficiary; s. 104(21) Taxable capital gains; s. 108(5) Interpretation; s. 212(12) Deemed payments to spouse, etc; s. 248(5) Substituted property.

Canadian Tax Foundation: Brown and Wiener, *A Practical Look at the Attribution Rules: Tips and Traps*, 2011 Conference Report 38:1–49.

Income Tax Folios: *Secondary* — S4-F3-C1 Price Adjustment Clauses.

Interpretation Bulletins: *Secondary* — IT-394R2 Preferred beneficiary election; IT-510 Transfers and loans of property made after May 22, 1985 to related minor; IT-511R Interspousal and certain other transfers and loans of property.

Tax Window Files: Attribution Where Property Transferred to Trust, *Technical Interpretation, Financial Industries Division, April 26, 2004*, CRA Document No. 2004-0064471E5. Allocation under subsection 74.3(1) where individual transfers property to trust in which his spouse is beneficiary; trust has other income and other beneficiaries.

▶ 74.3(2) ◀

(2) Definition of "designated person". In this section, "designated person", in respect of an individual, has the meaning assigned by subsection 74.5(5).

Editorial Note: See the editorial note under s. 74.3(1).

SECTION 74.4: [Transfers and loans to corporations]

► 74.4(1) ◄

(1) Definitions. In this section,

"designated person" —"designated person", in respect of an individual, has the meaning assigned by subsection 74.5(5);

"excluded consideration" —"excluded consideration", at any time, means consideration received by an individual that is

(*a*) indebtedness,

(*b*) a share of the capital stock of a corporation, or

(*c*) a right to receive indebtedness or a share of the capital stock of a corporation.

Editorial Note: See the editorial note under s. 74.4(3).

Related Sections: S. 74.5(5), "designated person"; s. 104(1) Reference to trust or estate; s. 248(1), "corporation", "principal amount", "share", "small business corporation", "taxable dividend".

Interpretation Bulletins: *Secondary* — IT-394R2 Preferred beneficiary election.

► 74.4(2) ◄

(2) Transfers and loans to corporations. Where an individual has transferred or lent property, either directly or indirectly, by means of a trust or by any other means whatever, to a corporation and one of the main purposes of the transfer or loan may reasonably be considered to be to reduce the income of the individual and to benefit, either directly or indirectly, by means of a trust or by any other means whatever, a person who is a designated person in respect of the individual, in computing the income of the individual for any taxation year that includes a period after the loan or transfer throughout which

(*a*) the person is a designated person in respect of the individual and would have been a specified shareholder of the corporation if the definition "specified shareholder" in subsection 248(1) were read without reference to paragraphs (*a*) and (*d*) of that definition and if the reference therein to "any other corporation that is related to the corporation" were read as a reference to "any other corporation (other than a small business corporation) that is related to the corporation",

(*b*) the individual was resident in Canada, and

(*c*) the corporation was not a small business corporation,

the individual shall be deemed to have received as interest in the year the amount, if any, by which

(*d*) the amount that would be interest on the outstanding amount of the loan or transfer of the property for such periods in the year if the interest were computed thereon at the prescribed rate of interest for such periods

exceeds the total of

(*e*) any interest received in the year by the individual in respect of the transfer or loan (other than amounts deemed by this subsection to be interest),

(*f*) all amounts included in the individual's income for the taxation year pursuant to subsection 82(1) or 90(1) in respect of taxable dividends received (other than dividends deemed by section 84 to have been received) by the individual in the year on shares that were received from the corporation as consideration for the transfer or as repayment for the loan that were excluded consideration at the time the dividends were received or on shares substituted therefor that were excluded consideration at that time, and

(*g*) where the designated person is a specified individual in relation to the year, the amount required to be included in computing the designated person's income for the year in respect of all taxable dividends received by the designated person that

(i) can reasonably be considered to be part of the benefit sought to be conferred, and

(ii) are included in computing the designated person's split income for any taxation year.

Editorial Note: The "corporate attribution rules" may apply to an individual who directly or indirectly transfers or loans property to a corporation, one of the main purposes being to reduce the transferor's income and benefit a "designated person", i.e., the transferor's spouse or common-law partner; or, if not 18, a child (or other non-arm's length person), or a niece or nephew (see s. 74.5(5)). Taxable benefits, based on prescribed interest rates applied to the "outstanding amount" (per s. 74.4(3)) of the loan or transfer, apply for periods throughout which (a) the person is a designated person and specified shareholder, (b) the transferor is a Canadian resident, and (c) the corporation is not a "small business corporation" (see the definition in s. 248(1), relating to corporations whose assets are devoted to Canadian active business activities). For these purposes, a specified shareholder includes a person who owns at least 10% of the shares of any class of the corporation, or a related corporation other than a small business corporation. A corporate reorganization can be classified as a transfer, e.g., where shares are transferred to a holding company, or exchanged for other shares of the company, including an estate freeze (see also s. 84(9)). If the small business corporation exception is to be relied on, purification mechanisms to jettison non-qualifying assets should be considered.

Related Regulations: 4301.

Related Sections: S. 51(1) Convertible property; s. 51(2) Limitation of rollover benefit; s. 69(1) Inadequate considerations; s. 74.5 Exceptions; s. 84(9) Shares disposed of on redemptions, etc; s. 85(1) Transfer of property to corporation by shareholders; s. 86(1) Exchange of shares by a shareholder in course of reorganization of capital; s. 86(2) Disposition of old shares and benefit; s. 87(2)(*j.7*) Certain transfers and loans; s. 120.4(1), "split income"; s. 212(12) Deemed payments to spouse, etc; s. 248(1), "specified shareholder", "small business corporation".

Canadian Tax Foundation: Kakkar et al., *Corporate Attribution: Refreeze May Cause Unsolvable Corporate Attribution Problem*, 2018 Tax for the Owner Manager 18(3):6–7; Gosselin, *Estate Freeze Plan Trips over Corporation Attribution Rules*, 2015 Tax for the Owner-Manager 15(2):1–2; Hudson and McCamis, *Refresher on Specific Anti-Avoidance Provisions*, 2014 Prairie Provinces Tax Conference 12:1–41; Ehinger, *Implementing an Estate Freeze Through a Stock Dividend*, 2014 Canadian Tax Focus 4(2):4–5; Jung and McIntyre, *Current Issues: Corporate Attribution Rule — Transfer to Corporation*, 2013 Ontario Tax Conference 1:24–26; Hoffstein and Lee, *Revisiting the Attribution Rules*, 2012 Ontario Tax Conference 9:1–40; Brown and Wiener, *A Practical Look at the Attribution Rules: Tips and Traps*, 2011 Conference Report 38:1–49; Laidlaw and Mah, *Trust After Marriage: Using a Trust To Satisfy Support Obligations*, 2010 Canadian Tax Journal 1:145–163; Marquette, *Estate Freezes Involving Trusts*, 2002 Canadian Tax Journal 1:335–356.

Tax Profile: February 2010 — Planning With Trusts; February 2008 — Income Splitting A–Z; September 2004 — Review of Tax Implications of Corporate-Owned Life Insurance Buy-Sell Arrangements.

Income Tax Folios: *Secondary* — S4-F3-C1 Price Adjustment Clauses.

Information Circulars: IC 88-2 General anti-avoidance rule — Section 245 of the Income Tax Act (para. 10).

► 74.4(3) ◄

(3) Outstanding amount. For the purposes of subsection (2), the outstanding amount of a transferred property or loan at a particular time is

(*a*) in the case of a transfer of property to a corporation, the amount, if any, by which the fair market value of the property at the time of the transfer exceeds the total of

(i) the fair market value, at the time of the transfer, of the consideration (other than consideration that is excluded consideration at the particular time) received by the transferor for the property, and

(ii) the fair market value, at the time of receipt, of any consideration (other than consideration that is excluded consideration at the particular time) received by the transferor at or before the particular time from the corporation or from a person with whom the transferor deals at arm's length, in exchange for excluded consideration previously received by the transferor as consideration for the property or for excluded consideration substituted for such consideration;

(*b*) in the case of a loan of money or property to a corporation, the amount, if any, by which

(i) the principal amount of the loan of money at the time the loan was made, or

(ii) the fair market value of the property lent at the time the loan was made,

as the case may be, exceeds the fair market value, at the time the repayment is received by the lender, of any repayment of the loan (other than a repayment that is excluded consideration at the particular time).

Editorial Note: As the prescribed rate is applied to the "outstanding amount" of a transfer or loan to a corporation, this forms the basis of the taxable benefit arising from the corporate attribution rules in s. 74.4(2). The fair market value of property transferred is reduced by amounts ("consideration") received by the transferor from the corporation (or a non-arm's length person); but "excluded consideration" (debt, shares or a right to receive them) doesn't count. Non-excluded consideration received in exchange for previously-excluded consideration also reduces the outstanding amount. In the case of a loan of money (or property), the outstanding amount is the principal (or fair market value of property lent), less the value of non-excluded repayments.

► 74.4(4) ◄

(4) Benefit not granted to a designated person. For the purposes of subsection (2), one of the main purposes of a transfer or loan by an individual to a corporation shall not be considered to be to benefit, either directly or indirectly, a designated person in respect of the individual, where

(*a*) the only interest that the designated person has in the corporation is a beneficial interest in shares of the corporation held by a trust;

(*b*) by the terms of the trust, the designated person may not receive or otherwise obtain the use of any of the income or capital of the trust while being a designated person in respect of the individual; and

(*c*) the designated person has not received or otherwise obtained the use of any of the income or capital of the trust, and no deduction has been made by the trust in computing its income under subsection 104(6) or (12) in respect of amounts paid or payable to, or included in the income of, that person while being a designated person in respect of the individual.

Editorial Note: The exception in s. 74.4(4) to the attribution rule of s. 74.4(2) generally contemplates a freeze using a family trust, but the exception is relatively narrow owing to the income and capital restrictions in s. 74.4(4) (*b*) and (*c*). A trust agreement seeking to utilize the s. 74.4(4) exception should contain a blanket prohibition on anyone's receipt or use of income or capital while a designated person, rather than limiting the prohibition to situations where the corporate attribution rules would otherwise apply (e.g., a trust agreement provision that the prohibition does not apply while the corporation is a small business corporation would not meet the criteria for the s. 74.4(4) exception should the corporation lose SBC status). See, for example, CRA Document No. 2005-0126381E5.

Related Sections: S. 74.5(5) Definition of "designated person".

Information Circulars: IC 88-2 General anti-avoidance rule — Section 245 of the Income Tax Act (para. 10).

Tax Window Files: Attribution — Property Transferred to a Corporation, *Technical Interpretation, Reorganizations and Resources Division, May 13, 2005*, CRA Document No. 2005-0126381E5. Subsection 74.4(4) exception not available if designated person can receive income or capital from trust, albeit only while the corporation is a small business corporation.

► 74.4(5) ◄

(5) Time of dividend — (Repealed by 1986, c. 55, s. 19(1).)

SECTION 74.5: Transfers for fair market consideration

► 74.5(1) ◄

(1) Transfers for fair market consideration. Notwithstanding any other provision of this Act, subsections 74.1(1) and (2) and section 74.2 do not apply to any income, gain or loss derived in a particular taxation year from transferred property or from property substituted therefor if

(*a*) at the time of the transfer the fair market value of the transferred property did not exceed the fair market value of the property received by the transferor as consideration for the transferred property;

(*b*) where the consideration received by the transferor included indebtedness,

(i) interest was charged on the indebtedness at a rate equal to or greater than the lesser of

(A) the prescribed rate that was in effect at the time the indebtedness was incurred, and

(B) the rate that would, having regard to all the circumstances, have been agreed on, at the time the indebtedness was incurred, between parties dealing with each other at arm's length,

(ii) the amount of interest that was payable in respect of the particular year in respect of the indebtedness was paid not later than 30 days after the end of the particular year, and

(iii) the amount of interest that was payable in respect of each taxation year preceding the particular year in respect of the indebtedness was paid not later than 30 days after the end of each such taxation year; and

(*c*) where the property was transferred to or for the benefit of the transferor's spouse or common-law partner, the transferor elected in the transferor's return of income under this Part for the taxation year in which the property was transferred not to have the provisions of subsection 73(1) apply.

Editorial Note: S. 74.5(1) provides an exception to the attribution rules applying to transferred property (i.e., in s. 74.1(1) and (2) and 74.2), provided that the following applies to the consideration received by the transferor: (a) fair market value or greater consideration is received for the transferred property; (b) interest on indebtedness (if any) is at prescribed rates in effect at the time the debt was incurred (or a "reasonable" rate, if less), provided that the amount of interest payable in respect of the taxation year (and preceding years) is paid within 30 days after year-end; and (c) the transferor opts out of the rollover rule (s. 73(1)) where the property is transferred to the transferor's spouse or common-law partner. The fair market value indebtedness exception (s. 74.5(1)(*b*)) ceases to apply if the interest payable in respect of any year is not paid within 30 days after the end of the year, even if the interest is subsequently paid. See also the editorial notes under s. 74.1(1) and 74.5(2) (FMV loans).

Related Regulations: 4301(*c*) ("prescribed rate").

Related Sections: S. 73(1) Inter vivos transfers by individuals; s. 87(2)(*j*.7) Certain transfers and loans; s. 120.4 Definitions; s. 248(5) Substituted property.

Tax Profile: July 2006 — Asset Protection Planning.

Tax Topics: No. 1702, Income Tax Issues To Be Considered in Negotiating Marriage Contracts.

Interpretation Bulletins: *Secondary* — IT-394R2 Preferred beneficiary election; IT-510 Transfers and loans of property made after May 22, 1985 to related minor; IT-511R Interspousal and certain other transfers and loans of property.

► 74.5(2) ◄

(2) Loans for value. Notwithstanding any other provision of this Act, subsections 74.1(1) and (2) and section 74.2 do not apply to any income, gain or loss derived in a particular taxation year from lent property or from property substituted therefor if

(*a*) interest was charged on the loan at a rate equal to or greater than the lesser of

(i) the prescribed rate that was in effect at the time the loan was made, and

(ii) the rate that would, having regard to all the circumstances, have been agreed on, at the time the loan was made, between parties dealing with each other at arm's length;

(*b*) the amount of interest that was payable in respect of the particular year in respect of the loan was paid not later than 30 days after the end of the particular year; and

(*c*) the amount of interest that was payable in respect of each taxation year preceding the particular year in respect of the loan was paid not later than 30 days after the end of each such taxation year.

Editorial Note: This provision is an exception to the attribution rules for lent property (i.e., in s. 74.1(1), 74.1(2), and 74.2), provided that interest on the loan is at prescribed rates in effect at the time the debt was incurred (or a "reasonable" rate, if less) and the amount of interest payable in respect of the taxation year (and preceding years) is paid within 30 days after year-end. If the interest payable on the loan in respect of any year is not paid within 30 days after the end of the year, the exception in s. 74.5(2) ceases to apply, even if the interest is subsequently paid. See also editorial comments under s. 74.1(3) for refinancing prescribed rate loans, and s. 74.1(1) and 74.5(1) (FMV transfers).

The CRA's position is that the 30-day deadline applies to interest accrued in the calendar year, even if it is not payable until a subsequent time — see Document No. 2009-0330081C6.

Related Regulations: 4301(*c*) ("prescribed rate").

Interpretation Bulletins: *Secondary* — IT-510 Transfers and loans of property made after May 22, 1985 to related minor; IT-511R Interspousal and certain other transfers and loans of property.

► 74.5(3) ◄

(3) Spouses or common-law partners living apart. Notwithstanding subsection 74.1(1) and section 74.2, where an individual has lent or transferred property, either directly or indirectly, by means of a trust or by any other means whatever, to or for the benefit of a person who is the individual's spouse or common-law partner or who has since become the individual's spouse or common-law partner,

(*a*) subsection 74.1(1) does not apply with respect to any income or loss from the property, or property substituted therefor, that relates to the period throughout which the individual is living separate and apart from that person by reason of a breakdown of their marriage or common-law partnership; and

(*b*) section 74.2 does not apply to a disposition of the property, or property substituted therefor, occurring at any time while the individual is living separate and apart from that person because of a breakdown of their marriage or common-law partnership, if an election completed jointly with that person not to have that section apply is filed with the individual's return of income under this Part for the taxation year that includes that time or for any preceding taxation year.

Editorial Note: If a marriage or common-law relationship has broken down, per s. 74.5(3)(*a*), the income attribution rules (s. 74.1(1)) no longer apply; this rule is automatic — no election is filed. See also s. 74.5(4) for the non-application of the corporate attribution rules (this provision is also automatic). Per s. 74.5(3)(*b*), the capital gain attribution rules in s. 74.2 will no longer apply (i.e., the attribution of capital gain or losses from loans or transfers), provided the parties have elected jointly in the particular year of disposition or a preceding year not to have this provision apply. (If the parties don't elect, the capital gain attribution rules continue to apply to dispositions prior to divorce, subject to the fair market value consideration exceptions in s. 74.5(1) and (2).) S. 74.5(3)(*a*) and (*b*) apply to individuals living separate and apart by reason of a breakdown of their marriage or common-law partnership. Also note that s. 73(1.01)(*b*) extends the s. 73(1) rollover of capital property to a former spouse or common-law partner in settlement of rights arising out of their marriage or partnership (see also s. 73(1.1)). S. 73(1) itself requires parties to be Canadian residents; the transferor can elect out of the rollover.

Related Sections: S. 73(1) Inter vivos transfers by individuals; s. 73(1.01)(*b*) Qualifying transfers; s. 73(1.1) Interpretation; s. 160(4) Special rules re transfer of property to spouse.

Canadian Tax Foundation: Freedman and Nakonechny, *The Tax Principles of Family Law*, 2012 Ontario Tax Conference 4:1–52.

Tax Topics: No. 1702, Income Tax Issues To Be Considered in Negotiating Marriage Contracts.

Interpretation Bulletins: *Secondary* — IT-511R Interspousal and certain other transfers and loans of property.

Tax Window Files: Attribution Rules — Separation of Common-Law Partners, *Technical Interpretation, Business and Partnerships Division, July 13, 2005*, CRA Document No. 2005-0131351E5; Separation — Transfer Capital Property to Spouse, *December 9, 2004*, CRA Document No. 2004-0089951E5.

► 74.5(4) ◄

(4) Idem. No amount shall be included in computing the income of an individual under subsection 74.4(2) in respect of a designated person in respect of the individual who is the spouse or common-law partner of the individual for any period throughout which the individual is living separate and apart from the designated person by reason of a breakdown of their marriage or common-law partnership.

Editorial Note: See the editorial comment under s. 74.5(3).

Related Sections: S. 74.5(5) Definition of "designated person".

► 74.5(5) ◄

(5) Definition of "designated person". For the purposes of this section, "designated person", in respect of an individual, means a person (*a*) who is the spouse or common-law partner of the individual; or

(*b*) who is under 18 years of age and who

(i) does not deal with the individual at arm's length, or

(ii) is the niece or nephew of the individual.

Editorial Note: A "designated person" is the individual's spouse or common-law partner; or, if not 18, a child (or other non-arm's length person), or a niece or nephew. Related persons (per s. 251(1)) are not at arm's length; there is also a factual non-arm's length concept (determined under case law by whether there is a "common mind" directing both sides of a transaction, the parties are acting in concert without separate interests, or there is effective control by one party).

Related Sections: S. 74.3 Transfers or loans to a trust; s. 251(1) Arm's length.

Interpretation Bulletins: *Secondary* — IT-511R Interspousal and certain other transfers and loans of property.

▶ 74.5(6) ◀

(6) Back to back loans and transfers. Where an individual has lent or transferred property

(*a*) to another person and that property, or property substituted therefor, is lent or transferred by any person (in this subsection referred to as a "third party") directly or indirectly to or for the benefit of a specified person with respect to the individual, or

(*b*) to another person on condition that property be lent or transferred by any person (in this subsection referred to as a "third party") directly or indirectly to or for the benefit of a specified person with respect to the individual,

the following rules apply:

(*c*) for the purposes of sections 74.1, 74.2, 74.3 and 74.4, the property lent or transferred by the third party shall be deemed to have been lent or transferred, as the case may be, by the individual to or for the benefit of the specified person, and

(*d*) for the purposes of subsection (1), the consideration received by the third party for the transfer of the property shall be deemed to have been received by the individual.

Editorial Note: S. 74.5(6) provides rules intended to ensure that the application of the attribution rules cannot be avoided through the use of intermediaries by an individual to effect a loan or transfer of property to or for the benefit of a specified person. S. 74.5(6)(*a*) applies where the individual loans or transfers property to "another person" (i.e., the original transfer or loan) and that property or property substituted is subsequently loaned or transferred (either by the other person or any other person — referred to in the provision as the "third party"), to or for the benefit of the specified person. There is no time limit on the subsequent loan or transfer, nor is there a "series of transactions" test. A specified person is defined in s. 74.5(8) as a "designated person" per 74.5(5) — i.e., who is the individual's spouse or common-law partner, or certain persons who under 18 years of age — or a corporation, other than a small business corporation, in which, generally speaking, such a person has a direct or indirect interest. The provision also applies where the individual loans or transfers property to another person on condition that any property be loaned or transferred by any person to the specified person. Where the provision applies, the property that is loaned or transferred to the specified person by the "third party" is treated as if it had been loaned or transferred by the individual (i.e., the original transferor or lender — s. 74.5(6)(*c*)); as well, the consideration received by the "third party" is deemed to have been received by the individual — s. 74.5(6)(*d*).

S. 74.5(6) appears to potentially apply to a reverse (or downstream) freeze in relation to the application of the corporate attribution rule in s. 74.4(2). Consider, for example, where an individual has transferred or lent property (i.e., the original transfer or loan) to Holdco — i.e., to "another person", and that property or substituted property is subsequently loaned or transferred (i.e., from Holdco to Newco on the reverse freeze) to or for the benefit of a "specified person" (Newco) with respect to the individual. If the rules apply, the individual who made the original transfer is deemed to have made the subsequent transfer (i.e., from Holdco to Newco on the reverse freeze — see paragraph 74.5(6)(*c*)), thus putting the corporate attribution rules into play. Presumably, the intention (purpose) required for the operation of the corporate attribution rules is to be applied to the individual who made the original transfer — but at the time of the subsequent transfer. See also Paul W. Festeryga, "Corporate Attribution: The 'Anti-Freeze' Rule" in "Personal Tax Planning," (2010), Vol. 58, No. 3, *Canadian Tax Journal*, 675-696 at 681.

Related Sections: S. 74.5(8) Definition of "specified person".

Interpretation Bulletins: *Secondary* — IT-510 Transfers and loans of property made after May 22, 1985 to related minor; IT-511R Interspousal and certain other transfers and loans of property.

▶ 74.5(7) ◀

(7) Guarantees. Where an individual is obligated, either absolutely or contingently, to effect any undertaking including any guarantee, covenant or agreement given to ensure the repayment, in whole or in part, of a loan made by any person (in this subsection referred to as the "third party") directly or indirectly to or for the benefit of a specified person with respect to the individual or the payment, in whole or in part, of any interest payable in respect of the loan, the following rules apply:

(*a*) for the purposes of sections 74.1, 74.2, 74.3 and 74.4, the property lent by the third party shall be deemed to have been lent by the individual to or for the benefit of the specified person; and

(*b*) for the purposes of paragraphs (2)(*b*) and (*c*), the amount of interest that is paid in respect of the loan shall be deemed not to include any amount paid by the individual to the third party as interest on the loan.

Related Sections: S. 74.5(8) Definition of "specified person".

Interpretation Bulletins: *Secondary* — IT-510 Transfers and loans of property made after May 22, 1985 to related minor; IT-511R Interspousal and certain other transfers and loans of property.

▶ 74.5(8) ◀

(8) Definition of "specified person". For the purposes of subsections (6) and (7), "specified person", with respect to an individual, means

(*a*) a designated person in respect of the individual; or

(*b*) a corporation, other than a small business corporation, of which a designated person in respect of the individual would have been a specified shareholder if the definition "specified shareholder" in subsection 248(1) were read without reference to paragraphs (*a*) and (*d*) of that definition.

Editorial Note: See the editorial note under s. 74.5(6).

Interpretation Bulletins: *Secondary* — IT-510 Transfers and loans of property made after May 22, 1985 to related minor; IT-511R Interspousal and certain other transfers and loans of property.

▶ 74.5(9) ◀

(9) Transfers or loans to a trust. Where a taxpayer has lent or transferred property, either directly or indirectly, by means of a trust or by any other means whatever, to a trust in which another taxpayer is beneficially interested, the taxpayer shall, for the purposes of this section and sections 74.1 to 74.4, be deemed to have lent or transferred the property, as the case may be, to or for the benefit of the other taxpayer.

Interpretation Bulletins: *Secondary* — IT-510 Transfers and loans of property made after May 22, 1985 to related minor; IT-511R Interspousal and certain other transfers and loans of property.

▶ 74.5(10) ◀

(10) Beneficially interested — (Repealed by S.C. 1994, c. 7 Sched. VIII, s. 30(1).)

▶ 74.5(11) ◀

(11) Artificial transactions. Notwithstanding any other provision of this Act, sections 74.1 to 74.4 do not apply to a transfer or loan of property where it may reasonably be concluded that one of the main reasons for the transfer or loan was to reduce the amount of tax that would, but for this subsection, be payable under this Part on the income and gains derived from the property or from property substituted therefor.

Canadian Tax Foundation: Hudson and McCamis, *Refresher on Specific Anti-Avoidance Provisions*, 2014 Prairie Provinces Tax Conference 12:1–41; Lee, *Subsection 74.5(11) and Professional Corporation Shares*, 2014 Tax for the Owner-Manager 14(3):3–4.

Interpretation Bulletins: *Secondary* — IT-510 Transfers and loans of property made after May 22, 1985 to related minor; IT-511R Interspousal and certain other transfers and loans of property.

Cases: The taxpayer carried on his dental practice through a professional corporation. Shares in the corporation were transferred from a family trust to the taxpayer's spouse and then to the taxpayer. Dividends were declared and those dividends were reported as income of the spouse, on the basis of the attribution rule in section 74.1. Subsection 74.5(11) applied to deny such attribution because one of the main reasons why the transaction was carried out in the manner it was implemented was to reduce the amount of tax payable on the dividend income. *Mady v. The Queen*, 2017 DTC 1065 (TCC)

The taxpayer sold shares in a family corporation to his spouse, which she paid for with borrowed funds. Interest and carrying costs on the loans resulted in losses. Subsection 74.5(11) would not have precluded attribution of the losses to him, as the transfers were made for creditor-proofing and not to reduce tax, but his claim for the losses was disallowed because the funds were not borrowed to earn income. *Swirsky v. The Queen*, 2014 DTC 5037 (F.C.A.), affirming 2013 DTC 1078 (T.C.C.)

▶ 74.5(12) ◀

(12) Where ss. 74.1 to 74.3 do not apply. Sections 74.1, 74.2 and 74.3 do not apply in respect of a transfer by an individual of property

(*a*) as a payment of a premium under a registered retirement savings plan under which the individual's spouse or common-law partner is, immediately after the transfer, the annuitant (within the meaning of subsection 146(1)) to the extent that the premium is deductible in computing the income of the individual for a taxation year;

(*a*.1) (Repealed.)

(*a*.2) as a payment of a contribution under a registered disability savings plan;

(*b*) as or on account of an amount paid by the individual to another individual who is the individual's spouse or common-law partner or a person who was under 18 years of age in a taxation year and who

(i) does not deal with the individual at arm's length, or

(ii) is the niece or nephew of the individual,

that is deductible in computing the individual's income for the year and is required to be included in computing the income of the other individual; or

(*c*) to the individual's spouse or common-law partner,

(i) while the property, or property substituted for it, is held under a TFSA of which the spouse or common-law partner is the holder, and

(ii) to the extent that the spouse or common-law partner does not, at the time of the contribution of the property under the TFSA, have an excess TFSA amount (as defined in subsection 207.01(1)).

Editorial Note: S. 74.5(12) provides various exceptions to the attribution rules (i.e., ss. 74.1, 74.2 and 74.3) re: deductible "spousal" RRSP contributions (i.e., for a spouse and common-law partner — s. 74.5(12)(*a*)); RDSP contributions (s. 74.5(12)(*a.2*)); and "spousal" TFSA contributions — while the transferred or substituted property remains in a TFSA and only to the extent that the contribution is made using the spouse or common-law partner's available TFSA contribution room (s. 74.5(12)(*c*)). S. 74.5(12)(*b*), exempts the attribution rules for amounts paid by an individual, which are deductible and included in computing the income of the recipient; for example, reasonable salaries/fees paid, or interest on a loan.

In Document No. 2010-0354491E5, the CRA indicated that paragraph 75.4(12)(*c*) provides that the attribution rules do not apply while the transferred (or substituted) property remains in a TFSA, and only to the extent that the contribution is made using the individual's spouse or common-law partner's available TFSA contribution room. The exception no longer applies when the transferred property (or any substituted property) is withdrawn from the TFSA. (See also Document No. 2008-030149.)

History: S. 74.5(12)(*a.1*) was repealed by S.C. 2011, c. 24, s. 17(1), applicable to transfers made after 2010. S. 74.5(12)(*a.1*) formerly read:

(*a*.1) as an amount contributed under a provincial pension plan prescribed for the purposes of paragraph 60(*v*) under which the individual's spouse or common-law partner is, immediately after the transfer, the annuitant (within the meaning assigned by subsection 146(1)) or the owner of the account under the plan to the extent that the amount does not exceed the amount by which the amount prescribed for the purposes of subparagraph 60(*v*)(ii) for the year in respect of the plan exceeds the total of all other contributions to the plan for the year to the account of the spouse or common-law partner under the plan;

Related Sections: S. 146(8.2) Amount deductible.

Interpretation Bulletins: *Secondary* — IT-510 Transfers and loans of property made after May 22, 1985 to related minor; IT-511R Interspousal and certain other transfers and loans of property.

Cases: The cash portion of the purchase price of shares was transferred from the taxpayer's bank account to a joint account with his former wife, from which she and her daughter received cash payments. The non-cash portion took the form of promissory notes payable to the taxpayer and his ex-wife. The interest on the promissory notes and the capital gains on the shares were attributed to the taxpayer. *Gosse v. The Queen*, 93 DTC 1017 (T.C.C.)

▶ 74.5(13) ◀

(13) Exception from attribution rules. Subsections 74.1(1) and (2), 74.3(1) and 75(2) of this Act and section 74 of the *Income Tax Act*, chapter 148 of the Revised Statutes of Canada, 1952, do not apply to any amount that is included in computing a specified individual's split income for a taxation year.

Editorial Note: The attribution rules do not apply to amounts subject to tax on split income (per s. 120.4).

Related Sections: S. 120.4(1), "specified individual", "split income".

SECTION 75: [Trusts — attribution rule]

▶ 75(1) ◀

(1) Transfers to minors — (Repealed by 1986, c. 6, s. 39(1).)

▶ 75(2) ◀

(2) Trusts. If a trust, that is resident in Canada and that was created in any manner whatever since 1934, holds property on condition

(*a*) that it or property substituted therefor may

(i) revert to the person from whom the property or property for which it was substituted was directly or indirectly received (in this subsection referred to as "the person"), or

(ii) pass to persons to be determined by the person at a time subsequent to the creation of the trust, or

(*b*) that, during the existence of the person, the property shall not be disposed of except with the person's consent or in accordance with the person's direction,

any income or loss from the property or from property substituted for the property, and any taxable capital gain or allowable capital loss from the disposition of the property or of property substituted for the property, shall, during the existence of the person while the person is resident in Canada, be deemed to be income or a loss, as the case may be, or a taxable capital gain or allowable capital loss, as the case may be, of the person.

Editorial Note: Where property or property which was substituted for that property is held by a trust can revert back to the settlor of a trust, pass to beneficiaries whom that settlor has the discretion to designate subsequent to the creation of the trust, or can only be disposed of with that settlor's consent, income or losses from that property and capital gains and losses resulting from the disposition of that property will be deemed to be taxable in the hands of the settlor rather than the trust. This attribution rule applies specifically to Canadian resident trusts, but see the discussion below regarding non-resident trusts. The Canada Revenue Agency has acknowledged that s. 75(2) does not apply to business income or "second-generation" income, but it continues to apply to non-business income from the disposition of property or substituted property (see IT-369R, paragraphs 5-7 (archived, as it doesn't meet current government web standards)). Capital gains attributed under this subsection will potentially be eligible for the capital gains exemption.

Reversion and Discretion: Provided that the property or substituted property can revert back to the settlor, income and capital gains respecting that property are attributed back to the settlor. Even where certain conditions must be met under the terms of the trust to enable the reversion of the property to the settlor, these conditions need not be met for the purpose of applying s. 75(2)(*a*)(i). Rather, the existence of a possibility of an unlikely outcome of future events which would cause a reversion to the settlor would satisfy this rule (see CRA Document No. 2002-0162855). If the trust's documentation grants the settlor's spouse the discretion to later designate the capital beneficiaries, s. 75(2) will apply on the grounds that the settlor could subsequently be appointed as a capital beneficiary. However, if the spouse has the discretion to appoint any capital beneficiary except for the settlor, s. 75(2) would not apply (see CRA Document No. 2004-0086951C6).

Paragraph 75(2)(*b*) will apply where the settlor has the ability to choose beneficiaries of the trust or has discretion over the distributions of the trust property to the beneficiaries. Attribution applies if the settlor is the sole trustee regardless of the fact that the trust is irrevocable and non-discretionary (see CRA Document No. 1999-0013055). The settlor would not be exercising discretion as defined under s. 75(2)(*b*) solely on the basis of being a co-trustee, but where the trustees require the settlor's permission to dispose of or distribute property, this paragraph will apply.

Loans to a Trust: The Tax Court of Canada held that this attribution rule does not apply to a loan of funds to a trust (*Howson*, 2007 DTC 141). This is contingent upon the fact that the loan to the trust is genuine, outside, and independent of the terms of the trust (see Interpretation Bulletin IT-369R). An interest-free loan would not be subject to attribution under s. 75(2) if the loan meets the aforementioned conditions. This said, s. 56(4.1) and 74.1(1) to (3) may still trigger undesirable tax consequences with respect to loans to a trust.

Sale to a Trust at FMV: The Federal Court of Appeal upheld the lower court's ruling that s. 75(2) does not apply where a trust acquires property from a beneficiary at fair market value ("FMV") (see *Sommerer*, 2012 DTC 5126). This decision was based upon two assumptions. First, the FCA held that s. 75(2) applies only to a settlor of the trust and subsequent contributors who are akin to a settlor; no other individual can be "the person" for the purpose of s. 75(2). Second, the beneficiary transferred property to a trust by means of a genuine sale. A transfer of property by a beneficiary to a trust at less than FMV may trigger attribution under s. 75(2), as it would not be a genuine sale.

Subsection 75(2) may still apply if property transferred is substituted property in respect of the contributor (e.g., a settlor, who settles a trust for $100, is also a capital beneficiary, and the trust uses those settlement funds to purchase property at FMV from the settlor (see CRA Document No. 2013-0480351C6).

Denial of Tax-Deferred Rollout: If property held by a trust is subject to attribution under s. 75(2), the tax-deferred rollout of the trust's property to its beneficiaries under s. 107(2) is denied. Subsection 107(2) is a beneficial provision with respect to tax-planning, since it allows a trust to distribute property to its beneficiaries without triggering capital gains or losses. However, s. 107(4.1) denies this rollout provision where the trust's property was subject to s. 75(2). Therefore, when the property is distributed to its beneficiaries, the trust will be deemed to have disposed of the property at its FMV.

This rollout denial applies to the distribution of all of the trust's property rather than just the property that is subject to attribution. If s. 75(2) ever applied to any of the trust's property, s. 107(4.1) will apply for the rest of the trust's existence. Subsection 107(4.1) does not apply with respect to distributions to "the person" or the person's spouse or common-law partner, so the trust can continue to distribute its property to those individuals without triggering capital gains or losses. Moreover, s. 107(4.1) does not apply after the person ceases to exist (*i.e.*, in the case of an individual who has died).

Non-resident trusts: Paragraph 94(4)(*h*) specifically excludes a trust deemed resident in Canada under subsection 94(3) from being subject to subsection 75(2). For property held by non-resident trusts, the 2013 federal Budget introduced subsections 94(8.1) and (8.2), which generally apply to non-resident trusts in the same circumstances as subsection 75(2) applies to resident trusts.

History: S. 75(2), the portion before paragraph (*a*) was replaced by S.C. 2013, c. 40, s. 35(1), applicable to taxation years that end after March 20, 2013, and formerly read:

(2) *Trusts.* Where, by a trust created in any manner whatever since 1934, property is held on condition

Related Sections: S. 74.4(2) Transfers and loans to corporations; s. 74.5(13) Exception from attribution rules; s. 75(3) Exceptions; s. 75.2 Rules applicable with respect to "qualifying trust annuity"; s. 82(2) Certain dividends received by taxpayer; s. 94(3) Liabilities of non-resident trusts and others; s. 94(4) Excluded provisions; s. 94(8.1) Application of subsection (8.2); s. 94(8.2) Deemed transfer of restricted property; s. 107(4.1) Where subsection 75(2) applicable to trust; s. 160(1) Tax liability re property transferred not at arm's length; s. 212(12) Deemed payments to spouse, etc; s. 256(1.2)(*f*) Control, etc.

Canadian Tax Foundation: Wen, *GAAR Applies to Deliberate Triggering of Subsection 75(2)*, 2017 Canadian Tax Focus 7(3):3; Korne and Côté, *Back to the GAAR Future: Can a Tax Benefit Arise Even if the Impugned Event Has Not?*, 2017 Canadian Tax Journal 4:993–1001; Bernstein and Atsaidis, *Subsection 75(2) and the 21-Year Rule*, 2015 Canadian Tax Highlights 23(10):4–5; Wright, *FMV Sale to a Trust: Sommerer Invoked*, 2014 Canadian Tax Focus 4(1):10; Thompson, *Revisiting the Attribution Rules*, 2013 British Columbia Tax Conference 12:1–24; Roth, *Including or Adding the Freezor as a Discretionary Trust Beneficiary*, 2013 Ontario Tax Conference 14C:1–25; Wang and Bernier, *Principal and Cottage Residence Planning: A Review of Selected Issues — Part 2*, 2013 Ontario Tax Conference 8B:1–20; Moody, *Owner Manager Remuneration — Current Trends, Strategies, and Challenges*, 2013 Prairie Provinces Tax Conference 7:1–49; Doobay, *Subsection 75(2) Post-Sommerer*, 2013 Canadian Tax Highlights 21(12):8; Hoffstein and Lee, *Revisiting the Attribution Rules*, 2012 Ontario Tax Conference 9:1–40; Brown and Wiener, *A Practical Look at the Attribution Rules: Tips and Traps*, 2011 Conference Report 38:1–49; Anderson, *Current Cases: The Tangled Web of Subsection 75(2) Unravelled*, 2011 Canadian Tax Journal 3:562–570; Roth and Youdan, *Subsection 75(2): Is the CRA's Interpretation Appropriate?*, 2010 Conference Report 34:1–45; Laidlaw and Mah, *Trust After Marriage: Using a Trust To Satisfy Support Obligations*, 2010 Canadian Tax Journal 1:145–163; Bueschkens, *A Practical Guide to Using and Maintaining Trusts Effectively*, 2010 Ontario Tax Conference 3:1–29; Caruk, *Trust Principles: Tax and General Trust Law Concepts*, 2010 Prairie Provinces Tax Conference 3:1–33; Hoffstein, *Tax Planning with Trusts — Current Issues*, 2007 Ontario Tax Conference 13A:1–45; Gill, *Application of Subsection 75(2) to Loans*, 2007 Tax for the Owner-Manager 7(1):3–4; Stacey, *Lending to Trusts: Subsection 75(2)*, 2007 Canadian Tax Highlights 15(1):1–2; Crockett, *Subsection 75(2): The Spoiler*, 2005 Canadian Tax Journal 3:806–830; Brown, *Alter Ego Joint Conjugal and Self-Benefit Trusts Revisited: Some Troubling Tax Issues and a Search for Better Alternatives*, 2005 Canadian Tax Journal 1:224–244; Matthews, *Water Runs Downhill: Interprovincial Tax Planning*, 2004 Conference Report 25:1–45; Hoffstein, *Alter Ego Trusts/Joint Partner Trusts — Tips, Traps & Planning*, 2004 Ontario Tax Conference 12A:1–47; Rochwerg, *Using Trusts as an Income-Splitting Tool*, 2003 Conference Report 18:1–28; Stephenson, *Alter Ego and Joint Partner Trusts — A Case Study*, 2001 Prairie Provinces Tax Conference 3:1–45.

STEP Canada: Elie Roth, "Adding and Deleting a Beneficiary to a Trust," PowerPoint presentation to the 15th National Conference of STEP Canada, Toronto, June 10-11, 2013.

Tax Profile: April 2013 — Canadian Estate Freezes in Favour of U.S. Citizens; January 2012 — The Top 10 Cases of 2011; August 2011 — *Sommerer v. R.*; June 2011 — Summary of Canada Revenue Agency Round Table Held at the 13th National STEP Canada Conference; February 2008 — Income Splitting A–Z; February 2002 — Transferring Property to a Trust After the Enactment of Bill C-22.

Tax Topics: No. 2112, Significant Taxpayer Win — A Useful Precedent for Domestic and International Tax Planners; No. 2049, Who Is "the person" in Subsection 75(2)?; No. 2023-24, 2010 Canadian Tax Foundation CRA Roundtable: Pipelines, Privilege and Working Papers (Again!).

Income Tax Folios: *Secondary* — S4-F3-C1 Price Adjustment Clauses; S6-F1-C1 Residence of a Trust or Estate.

Interpretation Bulletins: *Primary* — IT-369R Attribution of trust income to settlor. *Secondary* — IT-394R2 Preferred beneficiary election.

Tax Window Files: 2017 STEP - Q12 - 75(2) and T3 Reporting, *June 13, 2017*, CRA Document No. 2017-0693371C6; 75(2) applicability to trust, *February 16, 2017*, CRA Document No. 2016-0669881I7; 2006 STEP Conference — Question 14, Attribution of FAPI under Subsection 75(2), *2006 STEP Conference, Question 14, September 11, 2006*, CRA Document No. 2006-0185671C6; 2006 STEP Conference — Question 4, Application of subsection 75(2) to a Genuine Loan, *2006 STEP Conference, Question 4, September 11, 2006*, CRA Document No. 2006-0185571C6; Attribution of FAPI of a 94(1)(c) Trust, *April 19, 2006*, CRA Document No. 2004-0080731I7; Application of 75(2), *ROUND TABLE — 2004 APFF CONFERENCE, Question 26, October 8, 2004*, CRA Document No. 2004-0086941C6; Attribution of Trust Income — Charitable Annuity Contract, *Technical Interpretation, International and Trusts Division, August 3, 2004*, CRA Document No. 2004-0066431E5; Attribution Where Property May Revert to Transferor, *Technical Interpretation, International and Trusts Division, April 25, 2003*, CRA Document No. 2002-0162855. Subsection 75(2) applies where trust indenture confers a right to appoint any person (therefore including settlor) as a capital beneficiary of the trust.

Cases: A tax plan involving a discretionary trust was developed, predicated on the understanding that s. 75(2) would apply no matter how property was transferred to the trust and the trust would not be taxable on certain dividends it received. Following *Sommerer v. The Queen*, 2012 DTC 5126 (F.C.A.), the Minister determined s. 75(2) would not apply and proposed to reassess, taxing the trust at the highest possible rate on the dividends. The trust applied for and received an order rescinding the dividends. *Re Pallen Trust*, 2014 DTC 5039 (B.C.S.C.)

S. 75(2) did not apply because the taxpayer purchased the shares for valuable consideration from the operating company. The dividend was not attributable to the operating company but instead remained to the benefit and for the account of the taxpayer. *Brent Kern Family Trust v. The Queen*, 2015 DTC 5004 (F.C.A.), affirming 2013 DTC 1249 (T.C.C.)

The taxpayers sought a rectification order to correct a trust deed to account for their intention at the time it was drafted to allow for a tax-free rollover of assets to beneficiaries. The application was dismissed because they did not provide adequate proof of their purported intent. *Kanji v. A.G. of Canada*, 2013 DTC 5058 (Ont. S.C.J.)

Subsection 75(2) does not apply to a beneficiary of a trust who transfers property to the trust by means of a genuine sale. *The Queen v. Sommerer*, 2012 DTC 5126 (F.C.A.), affirming 2011 DTC 1162 (T.C.C.)

The s. 75(2) attribution rules did not apply to the taxpayer since funds she put into a family trust were in fact loans to the trust. *Bona fide* loans are not subject to reversion under the terms of the trust. They return to the lender by virtue of the loan itself, and through the law of creditors' rights. *Howson v. The Queen*, 2007 DTC 141 (T.C.C.)

► 75(3) ◄

(3) Exceptions. Subsection (2) does not apply to property held in a taxation year

(*a*) by a trust governed by a deferred profit sharing plan, an employee benefit plan, an employees profit sharing plan, a pooled registered pension plan, a registered disability savings plan, a registered education savings plan, a registered pension plan, a registered retirement income fund, a registered retirement savings plan, a registered supplementary unemployment benefit plan, a retirement compensation arrangement or a TFSA;

(*b*) by an employee life and health trust, an employee trust, a private foundation that is a registered charity, a related segregated fund trust (within the meaning assigned by paragraph 138.1(1)(*a*)), a trust described by paragraph (*a.1*) of the definition "trust" in subsection 108(1), or a trust described by paragraph 149(1)(*y*);

(*c*) by a qualifying environmental trust; or

(*d*) by a trust if

(i) the trust acquired the property, or other property for which the property is a substitute, from a particular individual,

(ii) the particular individual acquired the property or the other property, as the case may be, in respect of another individual as a consequence of the operation of subsection 122.61 (1) or under section 4 of the *Universal Child Care Benefit Act*, and

(iii) the trust has no *beneficiaries* (as defined in subsection 108(1)) who may for any reason receive directly from the trust any of the income or capital of the trust other than individuals in respect of whom the particular individual acquired property as a consequence of the operation of a provision described in subparagraph (ii).

Editorial Note: This subsection exempts certain trusts from the attribution rules of s. 75(2). The attribution rules do not apply to the following trusts governed by:

- a deferred profit sharing plan;
- an employee benefit plan;
- an employees profit sharing plan;
- a pooled registered pension plan;
- a registered disability savings plan;
- a registered education savings plan;
- a registered pension plan;
- a registered retirement income fund;
- a registered retirement savings plan;
- a registered supplementary unemployment benefit plan;
- a retirement compensation arrangement; or
- a TFSA.

The following trusts are also exempt from the attribution rules of s. 75(2):

- an employee life and health trust;
- an employee trust;
- a private foundation that is a registered charity;
- a related segregated fund trust (within the meaning assigned by paragraph 138.1(1)(a));
- a trust described by paragraph 75(2)(*a.1*) of the definition "trust" in subsection 108(1);
- a trust described by paragraph 149(1)(*y*);
- a qualifying environmental trust (applicable to taxation years that end after March 20, 2013); or
- for taxation years that end after September 15, 2016, a trust if
  - the trust acquired the property, or other property for which the property is a substitute, from a particular individual,
  - that individual acquired the property as a consequence of subsection 122.61(1) or section 4 of the *Universal Child Care Benefit Act*, and
  - the trust has no beneficiaries who may for any reason receive directly from the trust any income or capital of the trust, other than individuals in respect of whom the individual acquired property as a consequence of a provision described in the foregoing bullet point.

History: S. 75(3)(*d*) was replaced by S.C. 2017, c. 33, s. 21(1), applicable to taxation years that end after September 15, 2016, and formerly read:

(*d*) by a prescribed trust.

S. 75(3)(*c*) was replaced and (*c*.1) to (*c*.3) were repealed by S.C. 2013, c. 40, s. 35(2), applicable to taxation years that end after March 20, 2013, and formerly read:

(*c*) by a trust that

(i) is not resident in Canada,

(ii) is resident in a country under the laws of which an income tax is imposed,

(iii) is exempt under the laws referred to in subparagraph (ii) from the payment of income tax to the government of the country of which the trust is a resident, and

(iv) was established principally in connection with, or the principal purpose of which is to administer or provide benefits under, one or more superannuation, pension or retirement funds or plans or any funds or plans established to provide employee benefits;

(*c*.1) by a qualifying environmental trust;

(c.2) by a trust if the person from whom the trust acquired the property is, in respect of the trust, an electing contributor as defined in subsection 94(1);

(c.3) by a trust that is non-resident, but would be resident in Canada for the purpose of computing its income for the year if the definition "resident contributor" in subsection 94(1) were read without reference to its paragraph (a); or

S. 75(3)(*b*) was replaced by S.C. 2013, c. 34, s. 212(1), applicable to taxation years that begin after October 31, 2011, and formerly read:

(*b*) by an employee life and health trust, an employee trust, a related segregated fund trust (within the meaning assigned by paragraph 138.1(1)(*a*)), a trust described in paragraph (*a.1*) of the definition "trust" in subsection 108(1), or a trust described in paragraph 149(1)(*y*);

S. 75(3)(*c.2*) was added by S.C. 2013, c. 34, s. 5(1), applicable to taxation years that end after March 4, 2010.

S. 75(3)(*c.3*) was added by S.C. 2013, c. 34, s. 5(1), applicable to taxation years that begin after 2000 except that, for taxation years that end before 2007, it is to be read as follows:

"(c.3) by a trust that is non-resident, but would be resident in Canada for the purpose of computing its income for the year if section 94, as it reads in its application to the 2007 taxation year, had applied to the trust for the year and the definition "resident contributor" in that section were read without reference to its paragraph (*a*); or"

S. 75(3)(*a*) was replaced by S.C. 2012, c. 31, s. 15(1), in force December 14, 2012, and formerly read:

(*a*) by a trust governed by a deferred profit sharing plan, an employee benefit plan, an employees profit sharing plan, a registered disability savings plan, a registered education savings plan, a registered pension plan, a registered retirement income fund, a registered retirement savings plan, a registered supplementary unemployment benefit plan, a retirement compensation arrangement or a TFSA;

S. 75(3)(*b*) was replaced by S.C. 2010, c. 25, s. 14(1), applicable after 2009. S. 75(3)(*b*) formerly read:

(*b*) by an employee trust, a related segregated fund trust (within the meaning assigned by paragraph 138.1(1)(*a*)), a trust described in paragraph (*a*.1) of the definition "trust" in subsection 108(1), or a trust described in paragraph 149(1)(*y*);

Related Sections: S. 38 Taxable capital gain and allowable capital loss; s. 104(1) Reference to trust or estate; s. 107.3 Application of subsection (3.1); s. 146.4(1), "registered disability savings plan"; s. 149(1)(*z*) Qualifying environmental trust; s. 160(1) Tax liability re property transferred not at arm's length; s. 212(12) Deemed payments to spouse, etc.

Interpretation Bulletins: *Secondary* — IT-369R Attribution of trust income to settlor.

Tax Window Files: Non-Resident Health and Welfare Trusts: Barbados, Bermuda and Cayman Islands, *Technical Interpretation, International and Trusts Division, May 10, 2004*, CRA Document No. 2004-0057511I7.

SECTION 75.1: Gain or loss deemed that of transferor

► 75.1(1) ◄

(1) Gain or loss deemed that of transferor. Where

(*a*) subsection 73(3) or (4) applied to the transfer of property (in this subsection referred to as "transferred property") by a taxpayer to a child of the taxpayer,

(*b*) the transfer was made at less than the fair market value of the transferred property immediately before the time of the transfer, and

(*c*) in a taxation year, the transferee disposed of the transferred property and did not, before the end of that year, attain the age of 18 years,

the following rules apply:

(*d*) the amount, if any, by which

(i) the total of the transferee's taxable capital gains for the year from dispositions of transferred property

exceeds

(ii) the total of the transferee's allowable capital losses for the year from dispositions of transferred property,

shall, during the lifetime of the transferor while the transferor is resident in Canada, be deemed to be a taxable capital gain of the transferor for the year from the disposition of property,

(*e*) the amount, if any, by which the total determined under subparagraph (*d*)(ii) exceeds the total determined under subparagraph (*d*)(i) shall, during the lifetime of the transferor while the transferor is resident in Canada, be deemed to be an allowable capital loss of the transferor for the year from the disposition of property, and

(*f*) any taxable capital gain or allowable capital loss taken into account in computing an amount described in paragraph (*d*) or the amount described in paragraph (*e*) shall, except for the purposes of those paragraphs, to the extent that the amount so described is deemed by virtue of this subsection to be a taxable capital gain or an allowable capital loss of the transferor, be deemed not to be a taxable capital gain or an allowable capital loss, as the case may be, of the transferee.

Editorial Note: S. 75.1(1) provides an exception to the general rule that taxable capital gains of minor children are not subject to attribution.

Related Sections: S. 38 Taxable capital gain and allowable capital loss; s. 39(1) Meaning of capital gain and capital loss; s. 160(1) Tax liability re property transferred not at arm's length.

Interpretation Bulletins: *Secondary* — IT-268R4 Inter vivos transfer of farm property to child.

► 75.1(2) ◄

(2) Definition of "child". For the purposes of this section, "child" of a taxpayer includes a child of the taxpayer's child and a child of the taxpayer's child's child.

SECTION 75.2: Rules applicable with respect to "qualifying trust annuity"

If an amount paid to acquire a qualifying trust annuity with respect to a taxpayer was deductible under paragraph 60(*l*) in computing the taxpayer's income,

(*a*) any amount that is paid out of or under the annuity at any particular time after 2005 and before the death of the taxpayer is deemed to have been received out of or under the annuity at the particular time by the taxpayer, and not to have been received by any other taxpayer; and

(*b*) if the taxpayer dies after 2005

(i) an amount equal to the fair market value of the annuity at the time of the taxpayer's death is deemed to have been received, immediately before the taxpayer's death, by the taxpayer out of or under the annuity, and

(ii) for the purpose of subsection 70(5), the annuity is to be disregarded in determining the fair market value (immediately before the taxpayer's death) of the taxpayer's interest in the trust that is the annuitant under the annuity.

History: S. 75.2 was added by S.C. 2013, c. 34, s. 213(1), deemed to have come into force on January 1, 2006.

Related Sections: S. 56(1)(*d.2*) Annuity payments; s. 60.011(2) Meaning of "qualifying trust annuity"; s. 160.2(2.1) Joint and several liability in respect of a qualifying trust annuity.

SECTION 76: Security in satisfaction of income debt

▶ 76(1) ◀

(1) Security in satisfaction of income debt. Where a person receives a security or other right or a certificate of indebtedness or other evidence of indebtedness wholly or partially as payment of, in lieu of payment of or in satisfaction of, a debt that is then payable, the amount of which debt would be included in computing the person's income if it were paid, the value of the security, right or indebtedness or the applicable portion thereof shall, notwithstanding the form or legal effect of the transaction, be included in computing the person's income for the taxation year in which it is received.

Related Sections: S. 214(3) Deemed payments; s. 214(4) Securities.

Interpretation Bulletins: *Secondary* — IT-433R Farming or fishing — Use of cash method.

Tax Window Files: Sale of Farm Inventory, *June 18, 2004*, CRA Document No. 2004-007306117.

Cases: Where the taxpayers, members of a dairy products marketing association, received the profits from sale of their products partly in cash and partly in certificates redeemable for cash in the future, the amount of the certificates constituted income in their hands. Receipt of profits by the marketing association as the agent of the taxpayers constituted receipt by the taxpayers. *Pendray Farms Ltd. and Fortuna Farms Ltd. v. The Queen*, 80 DTC 6062 (F.C.T.D.)

▶ 76(2) ◀

(2) Idem. Where a security or other right or a certificate of indebtedness or other evidence of indebtedness is received by a person wholly or partially as payment of, in lieu of payment of or in satisfaction of, a debt before the debt is payable, but is not itself payable or redeemable before the day on which the debt is payable, it shall, for the purpose of subsection (1), be deemed to be received by the person holding it at that time when the debt becomes payable.

▶ 76(3) ◀

(3) Section enacted for greater certainty. This section is enacted for greater certainty and shall not be construed as limiting the generality of the other provisions of this Part by which amounts are required to be included in computing income.

▶ 76(4) ◀

(4) Debt deemed not to be income debt. Where a cash purchase ticket or other form of settlement prescribed pursuant to the *Canada Grain Act* or by the Minister is issued to a taxpayer in respect of grain delivered in a taxation year of a taxpayer to a primary elevator or process elevator and the ticket or other form of settlement entitles the holder thereof to payment by the operator of the elevator of the purchase price, without interest, stated in the ticket for the grain at a date that is after the end of that taxation year, the amount of the purchase price stated in the ticket or other form of settlement shall, notwithstanding any other provision of this section, be included in computing the income of the taxpayer to whom the ticket or other form of settlement was issued for the taxpayer's taxation year immediately following the taxation year in which the grain was delivered and not for the taxation year in which the grain was delivered.

Related Sections: S. 76(5) Definitions of certain expressions.

Canadian Tax Foundation: Kiefer and Miazga, *Section 76 and the Taxation of Cash Purchase Tickets*, 2018 Tax for the Owner Manager 18(4):4–5.

Interpretation Bulletins: *Primary* — IT-184R Deferred cash purchase tickets issued for grain.

▶ 76(5) ◀

(5) Definitions of certain expressions. In subsection (4), the expressions "cash purchase ticket", "operator", "primary elevator" and "process elevator" have the meanings assigned by the *Canada Grain Act*, and "grain" means wheat, oats, barley, rye, flaxseed, rapeseed and canola produced in Canada.

History: S. 76(5) was replaced by S.C. 2012, c. 19, s. 2(1), applicable in respect of cash purchase tickets and other forms of settlement issued to a taxpayer after December 14, 2011. S. 76(5) formerly read:

(5) *Definitions of certain expressions.* In subsection (4), the expressions "cash purchase ticket", "operator", "primary elevator" and "process elevator" have the meanings assigned by the *Canada Grain Act* and "grain" means wheat, oats, barley, rye, flaxseed and rapeseed produced in the designated area defined by the *Canadian Wheat Board Act*.

Related Sections: S. 248(1), "amount".

SECTION 76.1: Non-resident moving debt from Canadian business

▶ 76.1(1) ◀

(1) Non-resident moving debt from Canadian business. If at any time a debt obligation of a non-resident taxpayer that is denominated in a foreign currency ceases to be an obligation of the taxpayer in respect of a business or part of a business carried on by the taxpayer in Canada immediately before that time (other than an obligation in respect of which the taxpayer ceased to be indebted at that time), for the purpose of determining the amount of any income, loss, capital gain or capital loss due to the fluctuation in the value of the foreign currency relative to Canadian currency, the taxpayer is deemed to have settled the debt obligation immediately before that time at the amount outstanding on account of its principal amount.

Related Sections: S. 10(12) Removing property from inventory; s. 10(13) Adding property to inventory; s. 13(9) Meaning of "gaining or producing income"; s. 14(14) Ceasing to use property in Canadian business; s. 14(15) Beginning to use property in Canadian business; s. 142.6(2) Deemed disposition not applicable; s. 248(1), "foreign currency".

▶ 76.1(2) ◀

(2) Non-resident assuming debt. If at any time a debt obligation of a non-resident taxpayer that is denominated in a foreign currency becomes an obligation of the taxpayer in respect of a business or part of a business that the taxpayer carries on in Canada after that time (other than an obligation in respect of which the taxpayer became indebted at that time), the amount of any income, loss, capital gain or capital loss in respect of the obligation due to the fluctuation in the value of the foreign currency relative to Canadian currency shall be determined based on the amount of the obligation in Canadian currency at that time.

SECTION 77: Bond conversion

(Repealed by S.C. 1995, c. 21, s. 52(1).)

SECTION 78: Unpaid amounts

▶ 78(1) ◀

(1) Unpaid amounts. Where an amount in respect of a deductible outlay or expense that was owing by a taxpayer to a person with whom the taxpayer was not dealing at arm's length at the time the outlay or expense was incurred and at the end of the second taxation year following the taxation year in which the outlay or expense was incurred, is unpaid at the end of that second taxation year, either

(*a*) the amount so unpaid shall be included in computing the taxpayer's income for the third taxation year following the taxation year in which the outlay or expense was incurred, or

(*b*) where the taxpayer and that person have filed an agreement in prescribed form on or before the day on or before which the taxpayer is required by section 150 to file the taxpayer's return of income for the third succeeding taxation year, for the purposes of this Act the following rules apply:

(i) the amount so unpaid shall be deemed to have been paid by the taxpayer and received by that person on the first day of that third taxation year, and section 153, except subsection 153(3), is applicable to the extent that it would apply if that amount were being paid to that person by the taxpayer, and

(ii) that person shall be deemed to have made a loan to the taxpayer on the first day of that third taxation year in an amount equal to the amount so unpaid minus the amount, if any, deducted or withheld therefrom by the taxpayer on account of that person's tax for that third taxation year.

Related Sections: S. 12(1)(*i*) Sale of bill; s. 20(1)(*l*) Doubtful or impaired debts; s. 20(1)(*p*) Bad debts; s. 28(1) Farming or fishing business.

Forms: T2047 — Agreement in Respect of Unpaid Amounts.

Information Circulars: IC 88-2 General anti-avoidance rule — Section 245 of the Income Tax Act (para. 16).

Interpretation Bulletins: *Primary* — IT-109R2 Unpaid amounts. *Secondary* — IT-152R3 Special reserves — Sale of land; IT-293R Debtor's gain on settlement of debt.

Cases: The taxpayer was formed by amalgamation. One of its predecessor corporations had deducted $30,990,627 in unpaid interest accrued on a related company loan. The loan became the taxpayer's debt under s. 87(7). The unpaid amount was to be included in its income under s. 78(1) since the taxpayer was deemed to be related to its predecessor and to have been dealing at non-arm's length with the debtor at the time the obligation arose. *Dow Chemical Canada Inc. v. The Queen*, 2008 DTC 6544 (F.C.A.), reversing 2007 DTC 1701 (T.C.C.).

▶ 78(2) ◀

(2) Idem. Where an amount in respect of a deductible outlay or expense that was owing by a taxpayer that is a corporation to a person with whom the taxpayer was not dealing at arm's length is unpaid at the time when the taxpayer is wound up, and the taxpayer is wound up before the end of the second taxation year following the taxation year in which the outlay or expense was incurred, the amount so unpaid shall be included in computing the taxpayer's income for the taxation year in which it was wound up.

Related Sections: S. 78(5) Where s. (1) does not apply.

▶ 78(3) ◀

(3) Late filing. Where, in respect of an amount described in subsection (1) that was owing by a taxpayer to a person, an agreement in a form prescribed for the purposes of this section is filed after the day on or before which the agreement is required to be filed for the purposes of paragraph (1)(*b*), both paragraphs (1)(*a*) and (*b*) apply in respect of the said amount, except that paragraph (1)(*a*) shall be read and construed as requiring 25% only of the said amount to be included in computing the taxpayer's income.

▶ 78(4) ◀

(4) Unpaid remuneration and other amounts. Where an amount in respect of a taxpayer's expense that is a superannuation or pension benefit, a retiring allowance, salary, wages or other remuneration (other than reasonable vacation or holiday pay or a deferred amount under a salary deferral arrangement) in respect of an office or employment is unpaid on the day that is 180 days after the end of the taxation year in which the expense was incurred, for the purposes of this Act other than this subsection, the amount shall be deemed not to have been incurred as an expense in the year and shall be deemed to be incurred as an expense in the taxation year in which the amount is paid.

Editorial Note: The limitation in s. 78(4) prevents unlimited deferral — that is, without the limitation, the accrual-basis payer could deduct the remuneration in the year in which it became payable, while the recipient would normally include the remuneration in the year in which it was received. Effectively, owing to the 180-day limitation, this type of deferral is limited to one taxation year.

Related Regulations: 2900(9).

Related Sections: S. 37(11) Filing requirement s. 37(12) Misclassified expenditures; s. 127(9), "investment tax credit"; s. 127(13) Agreement to transfer qualified expenditures.

Income Tax Technical News: Issue No. 38, Subsection 78(4) — Liability Assumed by Third Party.

Tax Window Files: Unpaid Remuneration, *Technical Interpretation, Business and Partnerships Division, March 22, 2004*, CRA Document No. 2004-0060641E5.

▶ 78(5) ◀

(5) Where s. (1) does not apply. Subsection (1) does not apply in any case where subsection (4) applies.

Related Sections: S. 78(4) Unpaid remuneration and other amounts.

▶ 78(6) ◀

(6) Late filing — (Repealed by 1986, c. 55, s. 21(1).)

SECTION 79: [Surrender of property by debtor]

▶ 79(1) ◀

(1) Definitions. In this section,

Related Sections: S. 18(9.3)(*e*) Interest on debt obligations — extinguished obligations; s. 54, "adjusted cost base"; s. 80 Debt forgiveness rules; s. 248(1), "amount", "principal amount", "property".

Interpretation Bulletins: *Secondary* — IT-170R Sale of property — When included in income computation.

Cases: The taxpayers invested in realty, title to which was held on their behalf by trustees. Funding was provided by a group of financiers in exchange for a share of the property as of a certain date. The property was foreclosed upon prior to that date. In deducting the loss resulting from the foreclosure, the taxpayers were not restricted to the amount of their own investments, but were entitled to deduct the full amount. *Ward v. The Queen*, 88 DTC 6212 (F.C.T.D.)

"creditor" — "creditor" of a particular person includes a person to whom the particular person is obligated to pay an amount under a mortgage, hypothecary claim or similar obligation and, where property was sold to the particular person under a conditional sales agreement, the seller of the property (or any assignee with respect to the agreement) is deemed to be a creditor of the particular person in respect of that property;

"debt" — "debt" includes an obligation to pay an amount under a mortgage, hypothecary claim or similar obligation or under a conditional sales agreement;

"person" —"person" includes a partnership;

"property" —"property" does not include

(*a*) money, or

(*b*) indebtedness owed by or guaranteed by the government of a country, or a province, state, or other political subdivision of that country;

"specified amount" —"specified amount" at any time of a debt owed or assumed by a person means

(*a*) the unpaid principal amount of the debt at that time, and

(*b*) unpaid interest accrued to that time on the debt.

► 79(2) ◄

(2) Surrender of property. For the purposes of this section, a property is surrendered at any time by a person to another person where the beneficial ownership of the property is acquired or reacquired at that time from the person by the other person and the acquisition or reacquisition of the property was in consequence of the person's failure to pay all or part of one or more specified amounts of debts owed by the person to the other person immediately before that time.

Editorial Note: S. 79 — which results in deemed proceeds of an asset surrendered to a creditor based on applicable debt balances (see s. 79(3)) — is operative where there is a "surrender" of property by a person, which in ss. 79 and 79.1 includes a partnership. This occurs where beneficial ownership of the property is acquired (or reacquired) by another person — i.e., the creditor — in consequence of the person's — i.e., the debtor's — failure to pay all or part of one or more debts (which includes an obligation under conditional sales agreement) owed to the creditor immediately before the time the debt property is surrendered. The application of s. 79 generally "trumps" the debt forgiveness rules (see s. 80(2)) (unless s. 80 applied in a previous year under the debt parking provisions). Taking legal proceedings is not a prerequisite of the section. Because property must be acquired by the creditor, s. 79 will generally apply to a foreclosure, quit claim, or repossession under a conditional sales agreement, but generally not to a power of sale or judicial sale, so that these remedies may have very different tax effects. Also, s. 79 will not normally apply to the debtor if the creditor acquires the asset from a third party, e.g., a transferee of the debtor.

Related Sections: S. 13(21)(*h*) Definitions; s. 18(9.3) Interest on debt obligations — extinguished obligations; s. 54, "proceeds of disposition" (paragraph (*h*)); s. 79.1 Seizure of property by creditor; s. 80(1), "excluded obligation", "forgiven amount"; s. 80(2) Application of debt forgiveness rules; s. 87(2)(*h.1*) Debts; s. 118(2) Age credit; s. 122.5(1), "adjusted income"; s. 122.6, "adjusted income"; s. 122.7(1), "adjusted net income"; s. 127.2(1)(*d*) Share-purchase tax credit; s. 180.2(1), "adjusted income"; s. 261 Definitions.

Tax Notes: Issue No. 569, Family Trust Vulnerable to the CRA? More Warning Signs: Subsections 75(2)–107(4.1).

► 79(3) ◄

(3) Proceeds of disposition for debtor. Where a particular property is surrendered at any time by a person (in this subsection referred to as the "debtor") to a creditor of the debtor, the debtor's proceeds of disposition of the particular property shall be deemed to be the amount determined by the formula

$$(A + B + C + D + E - F) \times G/H$$

where

A is the total of all specified amounts of debts of the debtor that are in respect of properties surrendered at that time by the debtor to the creditor and that are owing immediately before that time to the creditor;

B is the total of all amounts each of which is a specified amount of a debt that is owed by the debtor immediately before that time to a person (other than the creditor), to the extent that the amount ceases to be owing by the debtor as a consequence of properties being surrendered at that time by the debtor to the creditor;

C is the total of all amounts each of which is a specified amount of a particular debt that is owed by the debtor immediately before that time to a person (other than a specified amount included in the amount determined for A or B as a consequence of properties being surrendered at that time by the debtor to the creditor), where

(*a*) any property surrendered at that time by the debtor to the creditor was security for

(i) the particular debt, and

(ii) another debt that is owed by the debtor immediately before that time to the creditor, and

(*b*) the other debt is subordinate to the particular debt in respect of that property;

D is

(*a*) where a specified amount of a debt owed by the debtor immediately before that time to a person (other than the creditor) ceases, as a consequence of the surrender at that time of properties by the debtor to the creditor, to be secured by all properties owned by the debtor immediately before that time, the lesser of

(i) the amount, if any, by which the total of all such specified amounts exceeds the portion of that total included in any of the amounts determined for B or C as a consequence of properties being surrendered at that time by the debtor to the creditor, and

(ii) the amount, if any, by which the total cost amount to the debtor of all properties surrendered at that time by the debtor to the creditor exceeds the total amount that would, but for this description and the description of F, be determined under this subsection as a consequence of the surrender, and

(*b*) in any other case, nil;

E is

(*a*) where the particular property is surrendered at that time by the debtor in circumstances in which paragraph 69(1)(*b*) would, but for this subsection, apply and the fair market value of all properties surrendered at that time by the debtor to the creditor exceeds the amount that would, but for this description and the description of F, be determined under this subsection as a consequence of the surrender, that excess, and

(*b*) in any other case, nil;

F is the total of all amounts each of which is the lesser of

(*a*) the portion of a particular specified amount of a particular debt included in the amount determined for A, B, C or D in computing the debtor's proceeds of disposition of the particular property, and

(*b*) the total of

(i) all amounts included under paragraph 6(1)(*a*) or subsection 15(1) in computing the income of any person because the particular debt was settled, or deemed by subsection 80.01(8) to have been settled, at or before the end of the taxation year that includes that time,

(ii) all amounts renounced under subsection 66(10), (10.1), (10.2) or (10.3) by the debtor in respect of the particular debt,

(iii) all amounts each of which is a forgiven amount (within the meaning assigned by subsection 80(1)) in respect of the debt at a previous time that the particular debt was deemed by subsection 80.01(8) to have been settled,

(iv) where the particular debt is an excluded obligation (within the meaning assigned by subsection 80(1)), the particular specified amount, and

(v) the lesser of

(A) the unpaid interest accrued to that time on the particular debt, and

(B) the total of

(I) the amount, if any, by which the total of all amounts included because of section 80.4 in computing the debtor's income for the taxation year that includes that time or for a preceding taxation year in respect of interest on the particular debt exceeds the total of all amounts paid before that time on account of interest on the particular debt, and

(II) such portion of that unpaid interest as would, if it were paid, be included in the amount determined under paragraph 28(1)(*e*) in respect of the debtor;

G is the fair market value at that time of the particular property; and

H is the fair market value at that time of all properties surrendered by the debtor to the creditor at that time.

Editorial Note: This provision determines the deemed proceeds of disposition of an asset surrendered to a creditor (but does not affect the tax cost of the surrendered asset or the nature of the gain or loss). Generally, the deemed proceeds are based on the "specified amounts" (unpaid principal and accrued interest) owing to the creditor/transferee in respect of the surrendered asset (the description of A); added to proceeds are specified amounts owing to others which cease to be owing as a consequence of the surrender (the description of B) or other debts having priority, e.g., a 1st mortgage, where property is surrendered to a second mortgagee (the description of C). Also added is a debt owing to a person other than the creditor/transferee which ceases to be secured by all assets owned by the debtor, e.g., a 2nd mortgage which continues to be owing when property is surrendered to a first mortgagee (the description of D — the addition is limited by the cost of the surrendered property). Subtracted are amounts otherwise included in proceeds, but which have been taken into account under other income tax provisions (the description of F). The deemed proceeds are prorated based on the fair market values of the surrendered assets (the descriptions of G and H). (Per s. 79(7), the amount of foreign currency debt is determined based on the foreign exchange rate at the time of issuance.)

The deemed proceeds may increase to the fair market value of the surrendered assets where the debtor and creditor are not at arm's length (the description of E). Gains from dispositions to which s. 79 apply are sometimes excluded from amounts elsewhere in the *Income Tax Act* which based on income, e.g., certain tax credits for low-income individuals. S. 79(4) provides relief where a debtor formerly subject to this subsection subsequently pays the debt.

Related Sections: S. 13(21)(*h*) Definitions; s. 18(9.3) Interest on debt obligations — extinguished obligations; s. 54, "proceeds of disposition" (paragraphs (*g*) and (*h*)); s. 79.1 Seizure of property by creditor; s. 80(1), "excluded obligation", "forgiven amount"; s. 80(2) Application of debt forgiveness rules; s. 87(2)(*h.1*) Debts; s. 118(2) Age credit; s. 122.5(1), "adjusted income"; s. 122.6 "adjusted income"; s. 122.7(1), "adjusted net income"; s. 127.2(1)(*d*) Share-purchase tax credit; s. 180.2(1), "adjusted income"; s. 261 Functional currency reporting.

Tax Profile: October 2008 — Tax Consequences of Debt Restructuring and Workouts in Canada.

▶ 79(4) ◀

(4) Subsequent payment by debtor. An amount paid at any time by a person as, on account of or in satisfaction of, a specified amount of a debt that can reasonably be considered to have been included in the amount determined for A, C or D in subsection (3) in respect of a property surrendered before that time by the person shall be deemed to be a repayment of assistance, at that time in respect of the property, to which

(*a*) subsection 39(13) applies, where the property was capital property (other than depreciable property) of the person immediately before its surrender;

(*b*) paragraph 20(1)(*hh*.1) applies, where the cost of the property to the person was an eligible capital expenditure at the time the property was acquired;

(*c*) the description of E in the definition "cumulative Canadian exploration expense" in subsection 66.1(6), the description of D in the definition "cumulative Canadian development expense" in subsection 66.2(5) or the description of D in the definition "cumulative Canadian oil and gas property expense" in subsection 66.4(5), as the case may be, applies, where the cost of the property to the person was a Canadian exploration expense, a Canadian development expense or a Canadian oil and gas property expense; or

(*d*) paragraph 20(1)(*hh*) applies, in any other case.

Editorial Note: S. 79(4) provides relief where a debtor formerly subject to s. 79(3) treatment (i.e., in respect of deemed proceeds for an asset surrendered to a creditor) subsequently pays the debt. The type of relief corresponds with the nature of the deemed proceeds. Such a payment is treated as a capital loss under s. 39(13) to the extent that it relates to previously-surrendered non-depreciable capital property, or added to the resource pool if it relates to property the cost of which was CEE, CDE or COGPE. In all other cases, the amount of the payment (or, prior to January 1, 2017, three-quarters of the payment where the property was eligible capital property at the time the expenditure was made) is deductible (under s. 20(1)(*hh*) or (*hh.1*).

History: S. 79(4)(*b*) was replaced by S.C. 2016, c. 12, s. 22(1), in force January 1, 2017, and formerly read:

(*b*) paragraph 20(1)(*hh*.1) applies, where the cost of the property to the person was an eligible capital expenditure;

▶ 79(5) ◀

(5) Subsequent application with respect to employee or shareholder debt. Any amount included under paragraph 6(1)(*a*) or subsection 15(1) in computing a person's income for a taxation year that can reasonably be considered to have been included in the amount determined for A, C or D in subsection (3) as a consequence of properties being surrendered before the year by the person shall be deemed to be a repayment by the person, immediately before the end of the year, of assistance to which subsection (4) applies.

▶ 79(6) ◀

(6) Surrender of property not payment or repayment by debtor. Where a specified amount of a debt is included in the amount determined at any time for A, B, C or D in subsection (3) in respect of a property surrendered at that time by a person to a creditor of the person, for the purpose of computing the person's income, no amount shall be considered to have been paid or repaid by the person as a consequence of the acquisition or reacquisition of the surrendered property by the creditor.

► 79(7) ◄

(7) Foreign exchange. Where a debt is denominated in a currency (other than Canadian currency), any amount determined for A, B, C or D in subsection (3) in respect of the debt shall be determined with reference to the relative value of that currency and Canadian currency at the time the debt was issued.

Editorial Note: See the editorial note to s. 79(3).

SECTION 79.1: [Seizure of property by creditor]

► 79.1(1) ◄

(1) Definitions. In this section,

"creditor" —"creditor" has the meaning assigned by subsection 79(1);

"debt" —"debt" has the meaning assigned by subsection 79(1);

"person" —"person" has the meaning assigned by subsection 79(1);

"property" —"property" has the meaning assigned by subsection 79(1);

"specified amount" —"specified amount" has the meaning assigned by subsection 79(1);

"specified cost" —"specified cost" to a person of a debt owing to the person means

(*a*) where the debt is capital property of the person, the adjusted cost base to the person of the debt, and

(*b*) in any other case, the amount, if any, by which

(i) the cost amount to the person of the debt

exceeds

(ii) such portion of that cost amount as would be deductible in computing the person's income (otherwise than in respect of the principal amount of the debt) if the debt were established by the person to have become a bad debt or to have become uncollectable.

► 79.1(2) ◄

(2) Seizure of property. Subject to subsection (2.1) and for the purpose of this section, a property is seized at any time by a person in respect of a debt where

(*a*) the beneficial ownership of the property is acquired or reacquired at that time by the person; and

(*b*) the acquisition or reacquisition of the property is in consequence of another person's failure to pay to the person all or part of the specified amount of the debt.

Editorial Note: S. 79.1 — which results in deemed cost to a creditor of a seized asset based in part on pre-existing debt balances (see s. 79.1(6)) — is operative where there is a "seizure" of property by a person, which in s. 79 and 79.1 includes a partnership. This occurs where beneficial ownership of the property is acquired (or reacquired) by a person — i.e., the creditor — in consequence of another person's — i.e., the debtor's — failure to pay all or part of a debt (which includes an obligation under a conditional sales agreement). Taking legal proceedings is not a pre-requisite of this section. Because property must be acquired by the creditor, s. 79 will generally apply to a foreclosure, quit claim, or repossession under a conditional sales agreement, but generally not to a power of sale or judicial sale. Also, it is not necessary that the property be seized from the debtor: subsection 79.1(2) could apply where the original debtor transfers the secured property to a third party and there is not a debtor-creditor relationship between the third party and the creditor.

Section 79.1 is not limited to the property which secured the debt; a creditor may seize other property as a result of the debtor's failure to pay the debt. However, the CRA's view is that the property must have previously been held by the debtor (even if transferred to a third party) and would not include an ownership interest in the debtor. See Document No. 2011-0427101C6 (Tax Executives Institute Canada — Canada Revenue Agency Liaison Meeting, December 6, 2011, Q.14).

► 79.1(2.1) ◄

(2.1) Exception. For the purpose of this section, foreign resource property is deemed not to be seized at any time from

(*a*) an individual or a corporation, if the individual or corporation is non-resident at that time; or

(*b*) a partnership (other than a partnership each member of which is resident in Canada at that time).

► 79.1(3) ◄

(3) Creditor's capital gains reserves. Where a property is seized at any time in a particular taxation year by a creditor in respect of a debt, for the purpose of computing the income of the creditor for the particular year, the amount claimed by the creditor under subparagraph 40(1)(*a*)(iii) or 44(1)(*e*)(iii) in computing the creditor's gain for the preceding taxation year from any disposition before the particular year of the property shall be deemed to be the amount, if any, by which the amount so claimed exceeds the total of all amounts each of which is an amount determined under paragraph (6)(*a*) or (*b*) in respect of the seizure.

Editorial Note: Where a property is seized, reserves for the preceding year are not added back to income, but instead reduce the cost of the seized property (per s. 79.1(6)). However, if the preceding year's reserve exceeds the creditor's cost of the seized property (per ss. 79.1(6)(*a*) and (*b*)), the excess is added to the creditor's income in the year of seizure.

► 79.1(4) ◄

(4) Creditor's inventory reserves. Where a property is seized at any time in a particular taxation year by a creditor in respect of a debt, for the purpose of computing the income of the creditor for the particular year, the amount deducted under paragraph 20(1)(*n*) in computing the income of the creditor for the preceding taxation year in respect of any disposition of the property before the particular year shall be deemed to be the amount, if any, by which the amount so deducted exceeds the total of all amounts each of which is an amount determined under paragraph (6)(*a*) or (*b*) in respect of the seizure.

Editorial Note: See the editorial note to s. 79.1(3).

► 79.1(5) ◄

(5) Adjustment where disposition and reacquisition of capital property in same year. Where a property is seized at any time in a taxation year by a creditor in respect of one or more debts and the property was capital property of the creditor that was disposed of by the creditor at a previous time in the year, the proceeds of disposition of the property to the creditor at the previous time shall be deemed to be the lesser of the amount of the proceeds (determined without reference to this subsection) and the amount that is the greater of

(*a*) the amount, if any, by which the amount of such proceeds (determined without reference to this subsection) exceeds such portion of the proceeds as is represented by the specified amounts of those debts immediately before that time, and

(*b*) the cost amount to the creditor of the property immediately before the previous time.

Editorial Note: S. 79.1(5) provides relief to a creditor who seizes capital property during the year of sale by the creditor, generally by reducing the creditor's proceeds of disposition by the unpaid portion of those proceeds at the time of the seizure (the deemed proceeds cannot be less than the creditor's previous tax cost). There is a corresponding reduction in the cost of the seized property to the creditor, under s. 79.1(6).

► 79.1(6) ◄

(6) Cost of seized properties for creditor. Where a particular property is seized at any time in a taxation year by a creditor in respect of one or more debts, the cost to the creditor of the particular property shall be deemed to be the amount, if any, by which the total of

(*a*) that proportion of the total specified costs immediately before that time to the creditor of those debts that

(i) the fair market value of the particular property immediately before that time

is of

(ii) the fair market value of all properties immediately before that time that were seized by the creditor at that time in respect of those debts, and

(*b*) all amounts each of which is an outlay or expense made or incurred, or a specified amount at that time of a debt that is assumed, by the creditor at or before that time to protect the creditor's interest, or for civil law the creditor's right, in the particular property, except to the extent the outlay or expense

(i) was included in the cost to the creditor of property other than the particular property,

(ii) was included before that time in computing, for the purposes of this Act, any balance of undeducted outlays, expenses or other amounts of the creditor, or

(iii) was deductible in computing the creditor's income for the year or a preceding taxation year

exceeds

(*c*) the amount, if any, claimed or deducted under paragraph 20(1)(*n*) or subparagraph 40(1)(*a*)(iii) or 44(1)(*e*)(iii), as the case may be, in respect of the particular property in computing the creditor's income or capital gain for the preceding taxation year or the amount by which the proceeds of disposition of the creditor of the particular property are reduced because of subsection (5) in respect of a disposition of the particular property by the creditor occurring before that time and in the year.

Editorial Note: This provision determines the deemed cost of an asset seized by a creditor, which is based on the tax balance of the pre-existing debt, plus amounts incurred to protect the creditor's interest, less reserves from a prior sale of the asset. More specifically, the deemed cost is based on the "specified cost" of the debt (as defined in s. 79.1(1)) — ACB in the case of debt which is capital property — prorated based on the fair market values of seized properties (s. 79.1(6)(*a*)). Added to this amount are outlays incurred not otherwise taken into account for tax purposes (that is, not included in other properties' cost, balances of undeducted outlays, or otherwise deductible), and the "specified amount" of debt assumed by the creditor at or before seizure to protect its interest in the asset (s. 79.1(6)(*b*)). Subtracted are the previous year's reserves in respect of a prior sale of the asset (which do not have to be added back to income, per ss. 79.1(3) and (4), and the special reduction of proceeds in s. 79.1(5) where property is sold and seized in the same year (s. 79.1(6)(*c*)). Where a creditor previously sold the seized asset to the debtor and a resale at an amount in excess of the cost determined above is not planned in the near future, it may be advantageous to seize the property early on, that is, when reserves are high. (Technical note: "specified amount" includes accrued but unpaid interest, whereas "specified cost" does not.)

History: S. 79.1(6)(*b*), the portion before subparagraph (i) was replaced by S.C. 2013, c. 34, s. 117, in force June 26, 2013, and formerly read:

(*b*) all amounts each of which is an outlay or expense made or incurred, or a specified amount at that time of a debt that is assumed, by the creditor at or before that time to protect the creditor's interest in the particular property, except to the extent the outlay or expense

Related Sections: S. 79 Surrender of property by debtor; s. 138(11.93) Property acquired on default in payment; s. 142.4(3) Rules applicable to disposition.

► 79.1(7) ◄

(7) Treatment of debt. Where a property is seized at any time in a taxation year by a creditor in respect of a particular debt,

(*a*) the creditor shall be deemed to have disposed of the particular debt at that time;

(*b*) the amount received on account of the particular debt as a consequence of the seizure shall be deemed

(i) to be received at that time, and

(ii) to be equal to

(A) where the particular debt is capital property, the adjusted cost base to the creditor of the particular debt, and

(B) in any other case, the cost amount to the creditor of the particular debt;

(*c*) where any portion of the particular debt is outstanding immediately after that time, the creditor shall be deemed to have reacquired that portion immediately after that time at a cost equal to

(i) where the particular debt is capital property, nil, and

(ii) in any other case, the amount, if any, by which

(A) the cost amount to the creditor of the particular debt

exceeds

(B) the specified cost to the creditor of the particular debt; and

(*d*) where no portion of the particular debt is outstanding immediately after that time and the particular debt is not capital property, the creditor may deduct as a bad debt in computing the creditor's income for the year the amount described in subparagraph (*c*)(ii) in respect of the seizure.

Editorial Note: While s. 79.1(6) deals with the tax cost of assets seized by a creditor, s. 79.1(7) deals with the tax treatment of the indebtedness held by the creditor in respect of the seizure. It is generally designed to ensure that there will be no gain or loss on the debt itself in respect of the seizure, unless the creditor subsequently recovers further amounts on the debt. More specifically: the debt is considered to have been disposed of at the time of seizure (s. 79.1(7)(*a*)); the amount received as a consequence of the seizure is deemed to equal the debt's adjusted cost base (or its cost amount, if not capital property) (s. 79.1(7)(*b*)). If any portion of the debt is still outstanding after the seizure, it is deemed to have been reacquired at a cost of nil, if capital property (s. 79.1(7)(*c*)(i)). (If the debt is not capital property, it is deemed to be reacquired at its cost amount less its "specified cost" (s. 79.1(7)(*c*)(ii)). In the event that no part of a debt remains outstanding after seizure, the excess may be deducted by the creditor as a bad debt (s. 79.1(7)(*d*)); this allows a deduction for unpaid interest.)

S. 79.1(8) ensures that, where an asset is seized, no amount in respect of the creditor's debt is deductible as a bad, doubtful or impaired debt (per the Explanatory Notes, this prohibition does not apply to unpaid interest); nor can any amount be included in computing any balances of undeducted outlays and the like.

Related Sections: S. 20(1)(*l*) Doubtful or impaired debts; s. 20(1)(*p*) Bad debts; s. 20(4) Bad debts from dispositions of depreciable property; s. 20(4.1) Bad debts re timber resource property s. 20(4.2) Bad debts re eligible capital property; s. 20(4.3) Deemed allowable capital loss; s. 50(1) Debts established to be bad debts and shares of bankrupt corporation.

► 79.1(8) ◄

(8) Claims for debts. Where a property is seized at any time in a taxation year by a creditor in respect of a debt, no amount in respect of the debt

(*a*) is deductible in computing the creditor's income for the year or a subsequent taxation year as a bad, doubtful or impaired debt; or

(*b*) shall be included after that time in computing, for the purposes of this Act, any balance of undeducted outlays, expenses or other amounts of the creditor as a bad, doubtful or impaired debt.

Editorial Note: See editorial note to s. 79.1(7).

Related Sections: S. 20(1)(*l*) Doubtful or impaired debts; s. 20(1)(*p*) Bad debts; s. 20(4) Bad debts from dispositions of depreciable property; s. 20(4.1) Bad debts re timber resource property; s. 20(4.2) Bad debts re eligible capital property; s. 20(4.3) Deemed allowable capital loss; s. 50(1) Debts established to be bad debts and shares of bankrupt corporation.

SECTION 80: [Debt forgiveness rules]

► 80(1) ◄

(1) Definitions. In this section,

Interpretation Bulletins: *Primary* — IT-293R Debtor's gain on settlement of debt. *Secondary* — IT-109R2 Unpaid amounts; IT-142R3 Settlement of debts on the winding-up of a corporation; IT-232R3 Non-capital losses, net capital losses, restricted farm losses, farm losses and limited partnership losses — Their composition and deductibility in computing taxable income; IT-268R4 Inter vivos transfer of farm property to child; IT-430R3 (Consolid.) — Life insurance proceeds received by a private corporation or a partnership as a consequence of death.

Tax Window Files: Whether s. 80 or s. 143.4 applies, *16XXXX*, CRA Document No. 2016-0661071R3; Employee Life and Health Trust, *July 14, 2011*, CRA Document No. 2010-0389651R3; ACB of Partnership Interest, *April 26, 2010*, CRA Document No. 2010-0358091E5; Debt parking and foreign currency, *December 8, 2009*, CRA Document No. 2009-0347661C6; Forgiveness of Accrued Interest, *Technical Interpretation, Financial Industries Division, July 15, 2009*, CRA Document No. 2008-0289731E5; Surrender of Property, *Income Tax Rulings Directorate, Policy and Legislation Branch, May 27, 2009*, CRA Document No. 2009-0305751E5; Cancellation of Debt Forgiveness, *Technical Interpretation, Financial Industries Division, March 22, 2005*, CRA Document No. 2005-0115451I7; Debt Forgiveness — Winding-Up of Wholly-Owned Subsidiary, *Technical Interpretation, Financial Industries Division, December 21, 2004*, CRA Document No. 2004-0096211I7; Housing Loan by a Corporation to its Sole Shareholder, *Technical Interpretation, Business and Partnerships Division, February 26, 2004*, CRA Document No. 2003-0045471E5; Application of Section 80, *Technical Interpretation, Financial Industries Division, August 8, 2003*, CRA Document No. 2003-0025837.

Cases: The taxpayer's predecessor benefited from the forgiveness of a loan. The loan was a "commercial debt obligation" and s. 80 applied despite the taxpayer's arguments to the contrary based on the concepts of retrospective application, release of debtor, novation, loan vs. debt and lack of REOP. *Gibralt Capital Corporation v. The Queen*, 2003 DTC 5270 (F.C.A.), affirming 2002 DTC 1601 (T.C.C.).

"commercial debt obligation" — "commercial debt obligation" issued by a debtor means a debt obligation issued by the debtor

(*a*) where interest was paid or payable by the debtor in respect of it pursuant to a legal obligation, or

(*b*) if interest had been paid or payable by the debtor in respect of it pursuant to a legal obligation,

an amount in respect of the interest was or would have been deductible in computing the debtor's income, taxable income or taxable income earned in Canada, as the case may be, if this Act were read without reference to subsections 15.1(2) and 15.2(2), paragraph 18(1)(*g*), subsections 18(2), (3.1) and (4) and section 21;

Tax Profile: October 2008 — Tax Consequences of Debt Restructuring and Workouts in Canada.

"commercial obligation" — "commercial obligation" issued by a debtor means

(*a*) a commercial debt obligation issued by the debtor, or

(*b*) a distress preferred share issued by the debtor;

Related Sections: S. 6(15.1) Forgiven amount; s. 15(1.21) Forgiven amount; s. 40(2)(e.2) Limitations.

Canadian Tax Foundation: Tunney, *Update on Debt Forgiveness*, 2003 Ontario Tax Conference 9:1–22; Glass, *Section 80: An Update*, 2002 British Columbia Tax Conference 16:1–37; Felesky and Sykora, *The Debt Forgiveness and Foreclosure Rules: Is There a Better Way?*, 1995 Canadian Tax Journal 5:1316–1342.

"debtor" — "debtor" includes any corporation that has issued a distress preferred share and any partnership;

"directed person" — "directed person" at any time in respect of a debtor means

(*a*) a taxable Canadian corporation or an eligible Canadian partnership by which the debtor is controlled at that time, or

(*b*) a taxable Canadian corporation or an eligible Canadian partnership that is controlled at that time by

(i) the debtor,

(ii) the debtor and one or more persons related to the debtor, or

(iii) a person or group of persons by which the debtor is controlled at that time;

Related Sections: S. 89(1), "taxable Canadian corporation"; s. 256(7) Acquiring control; s. 256(8) Deemed exercise of right.

"distress preferred share" — "distress preferred share" issued by a corporation means, at any time, a share issued after February 21, 1994 (other than a share issued pursuant to an agreement in writing entered into on or before that date) by the corporation that is a share described in paragraph (*e*) of the definition "term preferred share" in subsection 248(1) that would be a term preferred share at that time if that definition were read without reference to paragraphs (*e*) and (*f*);

"eligible Canadian partnership" — "eligible Canadian partnership" at any time means a Canadian partnership none of the members of which is, at that time,

(*a*) a non-resident owned investment corporation,

(*b*) a person exempt, because of subsection 149(1), from tax under this Part on all or part of the person's taxable income,

(*c*) a partnership, other than an eligible Canadian partnership, or

(*d*) a trust, other than a trust in which no non-resident person and no person described in paragraph (*a*), (*b*) or (*c*) is beneficially interested;

"excluded obligation" — "excluded obligation" means an obligation issued by a debtor where

(*a*) the proceeds from the issue of the obligation

(i) were included in computing the debtor's income or, but for the expression "other than a prescribed amount" in paragraph 12(1)(*x*), would have been so included,

(ii) were deducted in computing, for the purposes of this Act, any balance of undeducted outlays, expenses or other amounts, or

(iii) were deducted in computing the capital cost or cost amount to the debtor of any property of the debtor,

(*b*) an amount paid by the debtor in satisfaction of the entire principal amount of the obligation would be included in the amount determined under paragraph 28(1)(*e*) or section 30 in respect of the debtor,

(*c*) section 78 applies to the obligation, or

(*d*) the principal amount of the obligation would, if this Act were read without reference to sections 79 and 80 and the obligation were settled without any amount being paid in satisfaction of its principal amount, be included in computing the debtor's income because of the settlement of the obligation;

Canadian Tax Foundation: Ruby, *Section 80 and Unincorporated Entities*, 1997 Conference Report 19:1–37.

Cases: Where debt forgiveness pertains to a "trade debt", it will usually form part of the profit of the business. However, as in this case, where a forgiveness occurs in a borrower-lender relationship entered into to finance the operations of the business, it will usually be treated as an abatement of a capital liability. Hence, its forgiveness has no impact on the taxpayer's profit for the year is not required to be included in the taxpayer's income. *Queenswood Land Associates Limited v. The Queen*, 2000 DTC 6065 (F.C.A.), reversing 97 DTC 1048 (T.C.C.)

The taxpayer was indebted to a related company in relation to the purchase of certain chemicals from that company. The company later forgave a portion of the taxpayer's indebtedness. The forgiveness had the effect of reducing the taxpayer's cost of goods sold and therefore increasing profits. Accordingly, the taxpayer should pay tax on these profits. *M.N.R. v. Enjay Chemical Co. Limited*, 71 DTC 5293 (F.C.T.D.), reversing in part 70 DTC 1477 (T.A.B.)

An automobile dealership was overstocked with cars. Its supplier agreed to provide a rebate of $250 for each automobile in stock that the dealer subsequently sold. The rebate was applied against the outstanding debt owed by the dealer to the supplier. The rebates were included in the dealer's income, because their net effect was to add to the dealer's revenues. *Oxford Motors Limited v. M.N.R.*, 59 DTC 1119 (S.C.C.), affirming 58 DTC 1104 (Ex. Ct.).

"excluded property" —"excluded property" means property of a non-resident debtor that is treaty-protected property or that is not taxable Canadian property;

Related Sections: S. 248(1), "treaty-protected property".

"excluded security" —"excluded security" issued by a corporation to a person as consideration for the settlement of a debt means

(*a*) a distress preferred share issued by the corporation to the person, or

(*b*) a share issued by the corporation to the person under the terms of the debt, where the debt was a bond, debenture or note listed on a designated stock exchange in Canada and the terms for the conversion to the share were not established or substantially modified after the later of February 22, 1994 and the time that the bond, debenture or note was issued;

Related Sections: S. 262 Designated stock exchanges.

"forgiven amount" —"forgiven amount" at any time in respect of a commercial obligation issued by a debtor is the amount determined by the formula

$$A - B$$

where

A is the lesser of the amount for which the obligation was issued and the principal amount of the obligation, and

B is the total of

(*a*) the amount, if any, paid at that time in satisfaction of the principal amount of the obligation,

(*b*) the amount, if any, included under paragraph 6(1)(*a*) or subsection 15(1) in computing the income of any person because of the settlement of the obligation at that time,

(*c*) the amount, if any, deducted at that time under paragraph 18(9.3)(*f*) in computing the forgiven amount in respect of the obligation,

(*d*) the capital gain, if any, of the debtor resulting from the application of subsection 39(3) to the purchase at that time of the obligation by the debtor,

(*e*) such portion of the principal amount of the obligation as relates to an amount renounced under subsection 66(10), (10.1), (10.2) or (10.3) by the debtor,

(*f*) any portion of the principal amount of the obligation that is included in the amount determined for A, B, C or D in subsection 79(3) in respect of the debtor for the taxation year of the debtor that includes that time or for a preceding taxation year,

(*g*) the total of all amounts each of which is a forgiven amount at a previous time that the obligation was deemed by subsection 80.01(8) or (9) to have been settled,

(*h*) such portion of the principal amount of the obligation as can reasonably be considered to have been included under section 80.4 in computing the debtor's income for a taxation year that includes that time or for a preceding taxation year,

(*i*) where the debtor is a bankrupt at that time, the principal amount of the obligation,

(*j*) such portion of the principal amount of the obligation as represents the principal amount of an excluded obligation,

(*k*) where the debtor is a partnership and the obligation was, since the later of the creation of the partnership or the issue of the obligation, always payable to a member of the partnership actively engaged, on a regular, continuous and substantial basis, in those activities of the partnership that are other than the financing of the partnership business, the principal amount of the obligation, and

(*l*) the amount, if any, given at or before that time by the debtor to another person as consideration for the assumption by the other person of the obligation;

Related Sections: S. 6(15.1) Forgiven amount; s. 15(1.21) Forgiven amount; s. 87(2)(*h*.1) Debts.

Canadian Tax Foundation: Tunney, *Update on Debt Forgiveness*, 2003 Ontario Tax Conference 9:1–22; Glass, *Section 80: An Update*, 2002 British Columbia Tax Conference 16:1–37; Felesky and Sykora, *The Debt Forgiveness and Foreclosure Rules: Is There a Better Way?*, 1995 Canadian Tax Journal 5:1316–1342.

Tax Topics: No. 2023-24, 2010 Canadian Tax Foundation CRA Roundtable: Pipelines, Privilege and Working Papers (Again!).

"person" —"person" includes a partnership;

"relevant loss balance" —"relevant loss balance", at a particular time for a commercial obligation and in respect of a debtor's non-capital loss, farm loss, restricted farm loss or net capital loss, as the case may be, for a particular taxation year, is

(*a*) subject to paragraph (*b*), the amount of such loss that would be deductible in computing the debtor's taxable income or taxable income earned in Canada, as the case may be, for the taxation year that includes that time if

(i) the debtor had sufficient incomes from all sources and sufficient taxable capital gains,

(ii) subsections (3) and (4) did not apply to reduce such loss at or after that time, and

(iii) paragraph 111(4)(*a*) and subsection 111(5) did not apply to the debtor, and

(*b*) nil if the debtor is a taxpayer that was at a previous time subject to a loss restriction event and the particular year ended before the previous time, unless

(i) the obligation was issued by the debtor before, and not in contemplation of, the loss restriction event, or

(ii) all or substantially all of the proceeds from the issue of the obligation were used to satisfy the principal amount of another obligation to which subparagraph (i) or this subparagraph would apply if the other obligation were still outstanding;

History: S. 80(1), the definition "relevant loss balance" was replaced by S.C. 2013, c. 40, s. 36(1), deemed to have come into force on March 21, 2013, and formerly read:

"relevant loss balance"—"relevant loss balance" at a particular time for a commercial obligation and in respect of a debtor's non-capital loss, farm loss, restricted farm loss or net capital loss, as the case may be, for a particular taxation year means the amount of such loss that would be deductible in computing the debtor's taxable income or taxable income earned in Canada, as the case may be, for the taxation year that includes that time if

(*a*) the debtor had sufficient incomes from all sources and sufficient taxable capital gains,

(*b*) subsections (3) and (4) did not apply to reduce such loss at or after that time, and

(*c*) paragraph 111(4)(*a*) and subsection 111(5) did not apply to the debtor,

except that, where the debtor is a corporation the control of which was acquired at a previous time by a person or group of persons and the particular year ended before the previous time, the relevant loss balance at the particular time for the obligation and in respect of such loss for the particular year shall be deemed to be nil unless

(*d*) the obligation was issued by the debtor before, and not in contemplation of, the acquisition of control, or

(*e*) all or substantially all of the proceeds from the issue of the obligation were used to satisfy the principal amount of another obligation to which paragraph (*d*) or this paragraph would apply if the other obligation were still outstanding;

Related Sections: S. 31(1.1) Restricted farm loss; s. 111(8), "farm loss", "net capital loss", "non-capital loss"; s. 251.2(2) Loss restriction event.

"successor pool" —"successor pool" at any time for a commercial obligation and in respect of an amount determined in relation to a debtor means the portion of that amount that would be deductible under subsection 66.7(2), (2.3), (3), (4) or (5), as the case may be, in computing the debtor's income for the taxation year that includes that time, if

(*a*) the debtor had sufficient incomes from all sources,

(*b*) subsection (8) did not apply to reduce the amount so determined at that time,

(*c*) the year ended immediately after that time, and

(*d*) paragraphs 66.7(2.3)(*a*), (4)(*a*) and (5)(*a*) were read without reference to the expressions "30% of", "30% of" and "10% of", respectively,

except that the successor pool at that time for the obligation is deemed to be nil unless

(*e*) the obligation was issued by the debtor before, and not in contemplation of, the event described in paragraph (8)(*a*) that gives rise to the deductibility under subsection 66.7(2), (2.3), (3), (4) or (5), as the case may be, of all or part of that amount in computing the debtor's income, or

(*f*) all or substantially all of the proceeds from the issue of the obligation were used to satisfy the principal amount of another obligation to which paragraph (*e*) or this paragraph would apply if the other obligation were still outstanding;

Canadian Petroleum Tax Journal: Canada Customs and Revenue Agency 1999 Roundtable Questions and Answers, Question 6, 2000, Vol. 13, No. 1.

"unrecognized loss" —"unrecognized loss", at a particular time, in respect of an obligation issued by a debtor, from the disposition of a property, is the amount that would, but for subparagraph 40(2)(*g*)(ii), be a capital loss from the disposition by the debtor at or before the particular time of a debt or other right to receive an amount, except that if the debtor is a taxpayer that is subject to a loss restriction event before the particular time and after the time of the disposition, the unrecognized loss at the particular time in respect of the obligation is nil unless

(*a*) the obligation was issued by the debtor before, and not in contemplation of, the loss restriction event, or

(*b*) all or substantially all of the proceeds from the issue of the obligation were used to satisfy the principal amount of another obligation to which paragraph (*a*) or this paragraph would apply if the other obligation were still outstanding.

History: S. 80(1), the portion of the definition "unrecognized loss" before paragraph (*b*) was replaced by S.C. 2013, c. 40, s. 36(2), deemed to have come into force on March 21, 2013, and formerly read:

"unrecognized loss"—"unrecognized loss" at a particular time, in respect of an obligation issued by a debtor, from the disposition of a property means the amount that would, but for subparagraph 40(2)(*g*)(ii), be a capital loss from the disposition by the debtor at or before the particular time of a debt or other right to receive an amount, except that where the debtor is a corporation the control of which was acquired before the particular time and after the time of the disposition by a person or group of persons, the unrecognized loss at the particular time in respect of the obligation is deemed to be nil unless

(*a*) the obligation was issued by the debtor before, and not in contemplation of, the acquisition of control, or

Related Sections: S. 87(2)(*l*.21) Forgiven amount.

► 80(2) ◄

(2) Application of debt forgiveness rules. For the purposes of this section,

(*a*) an obligation issued by a debtor is settled at any time where the obligation is settled or extinguished at that time (otherwise than by way of a bequest or inheritance or as consideration for the issue of a share described in paragraph (*b*) of the definition "excluded security" in subsection (1));

(*b*) an amount of interest payable by a debtor in respect of an obligation issued by the debtor shall be deemed to be an obligation issued by the debtor that

(i) has a principal amount, and

(ii) was issued by the debtor for an amount,

equal to the portion of the amount of such interest that was deductible or would, but for subsection 18(2) or (3.1) or section 21, have been deductible in computing the debtor's income for a taxation year;

(*c*) subsections (3) to (5) and (8) to (13) apply in numerical order to the forgiven amount in respect of a commercial obligation;

(*d*) the applicable fraction of the unapplied portion of a forgiven amount at any time in respect of an obligation issued by the debtor is in respect of a loss for any other taxation year, the fraction required to be used under section 38 for that year;

(*e*) where an applicable fraction (as determined under paragraph (*d*)) of the unapplied portion of a forgiven amount is applied under subsection (4) to reduce at any time a loss for a taxation year, the portion of the forgiven amount so applied shall, except for the purpose of reducing the loss, be deemed to be the quotient obtained when the amount of the reduction is divided by the applicable fraction;

(*f*) (Repealed by S.C. 2016, c. 12, s. 23(2).)

(*g*) where a corporation issues a share (other than an excluded security) to a person as consideration for the settlement of a debt issued by the corporation and payable to the person, the amount paid in satisfaction of the debt because of the issue of the share is deemed to be equal to the fair market value of the share at the time it was issued;

(*g*.1) where a debt issued by a corporation and payable to a person is settled at any time, the amount, if any, that can reasonably be considered to be the increase, as a consequence of the settlement of the debt, in the fair market value of shares of the capital stock of the corporation owned by the person (other than any shares acquired by the person as consideration for the settlement of the debt) is deemed to be an amount paid at that time in satisfaction of the debt;

(*h*) where any part of the consideration given by a debtor to another person for the settlement at any time of a particular commercial debt obligation issued by the debtor and payable to the other person consists of a new commercial debt obligation issued by the debtor to the other person

(i) an amount equal to the principal amount of the new obligation shall be deemed to be paid by the debtor at that time, because of the issue of the new obligation, in satisfaction of the principal amount of the particular obligation, and

(ii) the new obligation shall be deemed to have been issued for an amount equal to the amount, if any, by which

(A) the principal amount of the new obligation

exceeds

(B) the amount, if any, by which the principal amount of the new obligation exceeds the amount for which the particular obligation was issued;

(*i*) where 2 or more commercial obligations issued by a debtor are settled at the same time, those obligations shall be treated as if they were settled at different times in the order designated by the debtor in a prescribed form filed with the debtor's return of income under this Part for the debtor's taxation year that includes that time or, if the debtor does not so designate any such order, in the order designated by the Minister;

(*j*) for the purpose of determining, at any time, whether 2 persons are related to each other or whether any person is controlled by any other person, it shall be assumed that

(i) each partnership and each trust is a corporation having a capital stock of a single class of voting shares divided into 100 issued shares,

(ii) each member of a partnership and each beneficiary under a trust owned at that time the number of issued shares of that class that is equal to the proportion of 100 that

(A) the fair market value at that time of the member's interest in the partnership or the beneficiary's interest in the trust, as the case may be

is of

(B) the fair market value at that time of all members' interests in the partnership or all beneficiaries' interests in the trust, as the case may be, and

(iii) where a beneficiary's share of the income or capital of a trust depends on the exercise by any person of, or the failure by any person to exercise, any discretionary power, the fair market value at any time of the beneficiary's interest in the trust is equal to

(A) where the beneficiary is not entitled to receive or otherwise obtain the use of any of the income or capital of the trust before the death after that time of one or more other beneficiaries under the trust, nil, and

(B) in any other case, the total fair market value at that time of all beneficiaries' interests under the trust;

(*k*) where an obligation is denominated in a currency (other than Canadian currency), the forgiven amount at any time in respect of the obligation shall be determined with reference to the relative value of that currency and Canadian currency at the time the obligation was issued;

(*l*) where an amount is paid in satisfaction of the principal amount of a particular commercial obligation issued by a debtor and, as a consequence of the payment, the debtor is legally obliged to pay that amount to another person, the obligation to pay that amount to the other person shall be deemed to be a commercial obligation that was issued by the debtor at the same time and in the same circumstances as the particular obligation;

(*m*) for greater certainty, the amount that can be applied under this section to reduce another amount may not exceed that other amount;

(*n*) except for the purposes of this paragraph, where

(i) a commercial debt obligation issued by a debtor is settled at any time,

(ii) the debtor is at that time a member of a partnership, and

(iii) the obligation was, under the agreement governing the obligation, treated immediately before that time as a debt owed by the partnership,

the obligation shall be considered to have been issued by the partnership and not by the debtor;

(*o*) notwithstanding paragraph (*n*), if a commercial debt obligation, for which a particular person is liable with one or more other persons, is settled at any time in respect of the particular person but not in respect of all of the other persons, the portion of the obligation that can reasonably be considered to be the particular person's share of the obligation shall be considered to have been issued by the particular person and settled at that time and not at any subsequent time;

(*p*) a commercial debt obligation issued by an individual that is outstanding at the time of the individual's death and settled at a subsequent time shall, if the estate of the individual was liable for the obligation immediately before the subsequent time, be deemed to have been issued by the estate at the same time and in the same circumstances as the obligation was issued by the individual; and

(*q*) where a commercial debt obligation issued by an individual would, but for this paragraph, be settled at any time in the period ending 6 months after the death of an individual (or within such longer period as is acceptable to the Minister and the estate of the individual) and the estate of the individual was liable immediately before that time for the obligation

(i) the obligation shall be deemed to have been settled at the beginning of the day on which the individual died and not at that time,

(ii) any amount paid at that time by the estate in satisfaction of the principal amount of the obligation shall be deemed to have been paid at the beginning of the day on which the individual died,

(iii) any amount given by the estate at or before that time to another person as consideration for assumption by the other person of the obligation shall be deemed to have been given at the beginning of the day on which the individual died, and

(iv) paragraph (*b*) shall not apply in respect of the settlement to interest that accrues within that period,

except that this paragraph does not apply in circumstances in which any amount is because of the settlement included under paragraph 6(1)(*a*) or subsection 15(1) in computing the income of any person or in which section 79 applies in respect of the obligation.

Editorial Note: When a "commercial obligation" (s. 80(1)) of a debtor (including deductible interest per s. 80(2)(*b*)) is settled or extinguished, s. 80(3) through (12) (excluding s. 80(7) as of January 1, 2017) apply in sequential order to reduce tax attributes of the debtor (including a partnership), such as non-capital loss and capital loss carryforwards and the cost of certain properties, to the extent of the "forgiven amount" (s. 80(1)) of the obligation. If there is a remaining unapplied forgiven amount after the application of s. 80(3) through (12), one-half of the unapplied forgiven amount is included in the debtor's income under s. 80(13). A reserve may be available to partially or wholly offset that income inclusion under s. 61.2, 61.3, or 61.4. Alternatively, the debtor can elect to transfer any unapplied forgiven amount to an "eligible transferee" (under the provisions of s. 80.04), which reduces the income inclusion under s. 80(13) for the debtor. The amount so transferred is effectively treated as a forgiven amount of a commercial obligation of the eligible transferee for the purposes of s. 80.

The debt forgiveness rules can apply on a s. 88(1) wind-up or amalgamation where indebtedness is between the parties, or if debt becomes "parked" or statute-barred (s. 80.01). A person may realize a capital gain on the "surrender" of a capital property that is a share, an interest in a partnership, or a capital interest in a trust, the adjusted cost base of which has been reduced as a result of the debt forgiveness rules. A surrender may occur in circumstances where a tax-free rollover would otherwise be available (s. 80.03).

The rules contain an exception for debts settled or extinguished by way of bequest or inheritance (see s. 80(2)(*a*)), but there is no similar exception for debts extinguished by *inter vivos* gift (see CRA Document No. 2012-0433941E5).

History: S. 80(2)(*c*) was replaced by S.C. 2016, c. 12, s. 23(1), in force January 1, 2017, and formerly read:

(*c*) subsections (3) to (5) and (7) to (13) apply in numerical order to the forgiven amount in respect of a commercial obligation;

S. 80(2)(*f*) was repealed by S.C. 2016, c. 12, s. 23(2), in force January 1, 2017, and formerly read:

(*f*) where $^3/_4$ of the unapplied portion of a forgiven amount is applied under subsection (7) to reduce cumulative eligible capital, except for the purpose of reducing the cumulative eligible capital, the portion of the forgiven amount so applied shall be deemed to be $^4/_3$ of the amount of the reduction;

S. 80(2)(*o*) was replaced by S.C. 2013, c. 34, s. 118, in force June 26, 2013, and formerly read:

(*o*) notwithstanding paragraph (*n*), where a commercial debt obligation for which a particular person is jointly liable with one or more other persons is settled at any time in respect of the particular person but not in respect of all of the other persons, the portion of the obligation that can reasonably be considered to be the particular person's share of the obligation shall be considered to have been issued by the particular person and settled at that time and not at any subsequent time;

Related Sections: S. 6(15) Forgiveness of employee debt; s. 6(15.1) Forgiven amount; s. 15(1.2) Forgiveness of shareholder debt; s. 15(1.21) Forgiven amount; s. 53(2)(g) Amounts to be deducted — Debt forgiveness; s. 79(3) Proceeds of disposition for debtor; s. 80.01 Debt forgiveness rules — Deemed settlement of debt; s. 80.02 Debt forgiveness rules — Distress preferred shares; s. 80.03 Surrender of capital property; s. 80.04 Debt forgiveness rules — Transfer of forgiven amount; s. 95(2)(g.1) Determination of certain components of foreign accrual property income; s. 139.1(18) Acquisition of control; s. 220(3.21) Designations and allocations; s. 248(26) Debt obligations; s. 248(27) Parts of debt obligations; s. 256(7) Acquiring control; s. 256(8) Deemed exercise of right.

Canadian Tax Foundation: Cepparo, *Debt Forgiveness and Bank Overdraft*, 2015 Canadian Tax Highlights 23(9):8; Vantil, *Corporate Debt Settlement and Forgiveness: The Technical Rules*, 2009 British Columbia Tax Conference 6:2–38; Hegedus, *Fond Memories of Section 80 and Distressed Preferred Share Rules*, 2009 Prairie Provinces Tax Conference 9:1–40; Bauer, *Restructuring Debt Obligations*, 2008 Conference Report 37:1–30; Baek, *Tax Planning for Recessionary Times*, 2003 Conference Report 53:1–29; Ahmed and Silverson, *The New Debt Forgiveness Rules: Planning Opportunities and Traps for the Unwary*, 1996 Conference Report 21:1–38; Arnold and Ward, *Dispositions — A Critique of Revenue Canada's Interpretation*, 1980 Canadian Tax Journal 5:559.

Tax Profile: October 2008 — Tax Consequences of Debt Restructuring and Workouts in Canada.

Forms: T2153 — Designations with Respect to Forgiven Debt Under Paragraph 80(2).

Information Circulars: IC 88-2 General anti-avoidance rule — Section 245 of the Income Tax Act (para. 23, Supp. 1, para. 6).

Cases: When the agreement reached during the course of a trial made no reference to a debenture held by the taxpayer's bank against all of its assets, the deduction by the taxpayer of interest on the debenture was disallowed on the ground that it had been "settled". *Central City Financial Services Ltd. v. The Queen*, 98 DTC 6645 (F.C.A.), affirming 98 DTC 1021 (T.C.C.).

► 80(3) ◄

(3) Reductions of non-capital losses. Where a commercial obligation issued by a debtor is settled at any time, the forgiven amount at that time in respect of the obligation shall be applied to reduce at that time, in the following order,

(*a*) the debtor's non-capital loss for each taxation year that ended before that time to the extent that the amount so applied

(i) does not exceed the amount (in subsection (4) referred to as the debtor's "ordinary non-capital loss at that time for the year") that would be the relevant loss balance at that time for the obligation and in respect of the debtor's non-capital loss for the year if the description of E in the definition "non-capital loss" in subsection 111(8) were read without reference to the expression "the taxpayer's allowable business investment loss for the year", and

(ii) does not, because of this subsection, reduce the debtor's non-capital loss for a preceding taxation year;

(*b*) the debtor's farm loss for each taxation year that ended before that time, to the extent that the amount so applied

(i) does not exceed the amount that is the relevant loss balance at that time for the obligation and in respect of the debtor's farm loss for the year, and

(ii) does not, because of this subsection, reduce the debtor's farm loss for a preceding taxation year; and

(*c*) the debtor's restricted farm loss for each taxation year that ended before that time, to the extent that the amount so applied

(i) does not exceed the amount that is the relevant loss balance at that time for the obligation and in respect of the debtor's restricted farm loss for the year, and

(ii) does not, because of this subsection, reduce the debtor's restricted farm loss for a preceding taxation year.

Editorial Note: The forgiven amount is first applied to reduce non-capital, farm, and restricted farm loss carryforwards, in that order (s. 80(3)), and then to reduce allowable business investment and net capital loss carryforwards, grossed up to reflect the full amount of such losses, in that order (s. 80(4)). The forgiven amount is applied to loss carryforwards arising in earlier years first. The application of the forgiven amount to loss carryforwards is mandatory.

The amount by which a loss for a year may be reduced is limited to the "relevant loss balance" (defined in s. 80(1)) for the obligation in respect of the loss. The relevant loss balance of a corporation (or a trust after March 20, 2013) for an obligation in respect of a non-capital, farm, restricted farm, or net capital loss is deemed to be nil for a taxation year that ended before a loss restriction event (e.g., an acquisition of control of a corporation), unless the obligation was issued before and not in contemplation of the loss restriction event or as a replacement for such an obligation.

(See also the editorial note for s. 80(2).)

Related Sections: S. 31(1.1) Restricted farm loss; s. 111(8), "farm loss" (the description of C); "non-capital loss" (the description of D.2).

Forms: T2027 — Election to Deem Amount of Settlement of a Debt or Obligation.

Interpretation Bulletins: *Primary* — IT-142R3 Settlement of debts on the winding-up of a corporation.

► 80(4) ◄

(4) Reductions of capital losses. Where a commercial obligation issued by a debtor is settled at any time, the applicable fraction of the remaining unapplied portion of a forgiven amount at that time in respect of the obligation shall be applied to reduce at that time, in the following order,

(*a*) the debtor's non-capital loss for each taxation year that ended before that time to the extent that the amount so applied

(i) does not exceed the amount, if any, by which

(A) the relevant loss balance at that time for the obligation and in respect of the debtor's non-capital loss for the year

exceeds

(B) the debtor's ordinary non-capital loss (within the meaning assigned by subparagraph (3)(*a*)(i)) at that time for the year, and

(ii) does not, because of this subsection, reduce the debtor's non-capital loss for a preceding taxation year; and

(*b*) the debtor's net capital loss for each taxation year that ended before that time, to the extent that the amount so applied

(i) does not exceed the relevant loss balance at that time for the obligation and in respect of the debtor's net capital loss for the year, and

(ii) does not, because of this subsection, reduce the debtor's net capital loss for a preceding taxation year.

Editorial Note: See the editorial note to s. 80(3).

Related Sections: S. 111(8), "net capital loss" (the description of D); "non-capital loss".

Interpretation Bulletins: *Secondary* — IT-142R3 Settlement of debts on the winding-up of a corporation.

▶ 80(5) ◀

(5) Reductions with respect to depreciable property. Where a commercial obligation issued by a debtor is settled at any time, the remaining unapplied portion of the forgiven amount at that time in respect of the obligation shall be applied, in such manner as is designated by the debtor in a prescribed form filed with the debtor's return of income under this Part for the taxation year that includes that time, to reduce immediately after that time the following amounts:

(*a*) the capital cost to the debtor of a depreciable property that is owned by the debtor immediately after that time; and

(*b*) the undepreciated capital cost to the debtor of depreciable property of a prescribed class immediately after that time.

Editorial Note: After the (mandatory) application of the forgiven amount to loss carryforwards, the remaining unapplied portion of the forgiven amount may be applied (i.e., if the debtor designates) to reduce the debtor's undepreciated capital cost ("UCC") of depreciable properties, cumulative eligible capital (prior to January 1, 2017), and resource expenditures, immediately after the time of forgiveness, under s. 80(5), (7) (prior to January 1, 2017), and (8), respectively. The application is elective, but if these tax attributes are not reduced to the maximum extent possible, the debtor cannot "move on" to later subsections, such as applying the forgiven amount to non-depreciable capital property or transferring unapplied forgiven amounts to an eligible transferee under s. 80.04. An income inclusion under s. 80(13) may therefore result to the extent that a portion of the forgiven amount remains. There is no requirement to designate these attributes in any order — e.g., resource pools can be designated instead of UCC, and low-rate rather than high-rate CCA classes can be designated.

See also the editorial note for s. 80(2).

Related Sections: S. 13(7.1) Deemed capital cost of certain property; s. 13(21), "depreciable property", "undepreciated capital cost"; s. 88(1) Winding-up; s. 96(3) Agreement or election of partnership members; s. 220(3.21) Designations and allocations.

Forms: T2154 — Application of Designated Forgiven Debt Under Section 80.

▶ 80(6) ◀

(6) Restriction with respect to depreciable property. Where a commercial obligation issued by a debtor is settled at any time,

(*a*) an amount may be applied under subsection (5) to reduce, immediately after that time, the capital cost to the debtor of a depreciable property of a prescribed class only to the extent that

(i) the undepreciated capital cost to the debtor of depreciable property of that class at that time

exceeds

(ii) the total of all other reductions immediately after that time to that undepreciated capital cost; and

(*b*) an amount may be applied under subsection (5) to reduce, immediately after that time, the capital cost to the debtor of a depreciable property (other than a depreciable property of a prescribed class) only to the extent that

(i) the capital cost to the debtor of the property at that time

exceeds

(ii) the amount that was allowed to the debtor before that time under Part XVII of the *Income Tax Regulations* in respect of the property.

▶ 80(7) ◀

(7) Reductions of cumulative eligible capital — (Repealed by S.C. 2016, c. 12, s. 23(3).)

Editorial Note: See the editorial note to s. 80(5).

History: S. 80(7) was repealed by S.C. 2016, c. 12, s. 23(3), in force January 1, 2017, and formerly read:

(7) *Reductions of cumulative eligible capital.* Where a commercial obligation issued by a debtor is settled at any time, $^3/_4$ of the remaining unapplied portion of the forgiven amount at that time in respect of the obligation shall be applied (to the extent designated in a prescribed form filed with the debtor's return of income under this Part for the taxation year that includes that time) to reduce immediately after that time the cumulative eligible capital of the debtor in respect of each business of the debtor (or, where the debtor is at that time non-resident, in respect of each business carried on in Canada by the debtor).

Related Sections: S. 14(5), "cumulative eligible capital"; s. 220(3.21) Designations and allocations.

Forms: T2154 — Application of Designated Forgiven Debt Under Section 80.

▶ 80(8) ◀

(8) Reductions of resource expenditures. Where a commercial obligation issued by a debtor is settled at any time, the remaining unapplied portion of the forgiven amount at that time in respect of the obligation shall be applied (to the extent designated in a prescribed form filed with the debtor's return of income under this Part for the taxation year that includes that time) to reduce immediately after that time the following amounts:

(*a*) where the debtor is a corporation resident in Canada throughout that year, each particular amount that would be determined in respect of the debtor under paragraph 66.7(2)(*a*), (2.3)(*a*), (3)(*a*), (4)(*a*) or (5)(*a*) if paragraphs 66.7(2.3)(*a*), (4)(*a*) and (5)(*a*) were read without reference to the expressions "30% of", "30% of" and "10% of", respectively, as a consequence of the acquisition of control of the debtor by a person or group of persons, the debtor ceasing to be exempt from tax under this Part on its taxable income or the acquisition of properties by the debtor by way of an amalgamation or merger, where the amount so applied does not exceed the successor pool immediately after that time for the obligation and in respect of the particular amount;

(*b*) the cumulative Canadian exploration expense (within the meaning assigned by subsection 66.1(6)) of the debtor;

(*c*) the cumulative Canadian development expense (within the meaning assigned by subsection 66.2(5)) of the debtor;

(*d*) the cumulative Canadian oil and gas property expense (within the meaning assigned by subsection 66.4(5)) of the debtor;

(*e*) the total determined under paragraph 66(4)(*a*) in respect of the debtor, where

(i) the debtor is resident in Canada throughout that year, and

(ii) the amount so applied does not exceed such portion of the total of the debtor's foreign exploration and development expenses (within the meaning assigned by subsection 66(15)) as were incurred by the debtor before that time and would be deductible under subsection 66(4) in computing the debtor's income for that year if the debtor had sufficient income described in subparagraph 66(4)(*b*)(ii) and if that year ended at that time; and

(*f*) the cumulative foreign resource expense (within the meaning assigned by subsection 66.21(1)) of the debtor in respect of a country.

Editorial Note: See the editorial note to s. 80(5).

Related Sections: S. 220(3.21) Designations and allocations.

Forms: T2154 — Application of Designated Forgiven Debt Under Section 80.

Tax Window Files: Debt parking and foreign currency, *December 8, 2009*, CRA Document No. 2009-0347661C6.

► 80(9) ◄

(9) Reductions of adjusted cost bases of capital properties. If a commercial obligation issued by a debtor is settled at any time and amounts have been designated under subsections (5) and (8) to the maximum extent permitted in respect of the settlement, subject to subsection (18)

(*a*) the remaining unapplied portion of the forgiven amount at that time in respect of the obligation shall be applied (to the extent designated in a prescribed form filed with the debtor's return of income under this Part for the taxation year that includes that time) to reduce immediately after that time the adjusted cost bases to the debtor of capital properties (other than shares of the capital stock of corporations of which the debtor is a specified shareholder at that time, debts issued by corporations of which the debtor is a specified shareholder at that time, interests in partnerships that are related to the debtor at that time, depreciable property that is not of a prescribed class, personal-use properties and excluded properties) that are owned by the debtor immediately after that time;

(*b*) an amount may be applied under this subsection to reduce, immediately after that time, the capital cost to the debtor of a depreciable property of a prescribed class only to the extent that

(i) the capital cost immediately after that time to the debtor of the property (determined without reference to the settlement of the obligation at that time)

exceeds

(ii) its capital cost immediately after that time to the debtor for the purposes of paragraphs 8(1)(*j*) and (*p*), sections 13 and 20 and any regulations made for the purpose of paragraph 20(1)(*a*) (determined without reference to the settlement of the obligation at that time); and

(*c*) for the purposes of paragraphs 8(1)(*j*) and (*p*), sections 13 and 20 and any regulations made for the purpose of paragraph 20(1)(*a*), no amount shall be considered to have been applied under this subsection.

Editorial Note: After the (mandatory) application of the forgiven amount to loss carryforwards (per s. 80(3) and 80(4)), and provided that the maximum designation is made to reduce the undepreciated cost of depreciable properties, cumulative eligible capital (prior to January 1, 2017), and resource pools (per s. 80(5) and (8); s. 80(7) only applied prior to January 1, 2017), the remaining unapplied portion of the forgiven amount may be applied (i.e., if the debtor designates) to reduce the debtor's adjusted cost base of capital properties owned immediately after the time of forgiveness, subject to certain exclusions including personal use properties, interests in related partnerships, and shares and debts of corporations of which the debtor is a "specified shareholder" ("specified shareholder property" and "related-partnership property" are covered in s. 80(10) and 80(11)). There is no specific requirement of a "nexus" to the investment or business in respect of which the debt was forgiven. The application is elective (presumably, the debtor would designate long-term holds), but if maximum claims are not made, the debtor cannot "move on", e.g., to transfer an unapplied forgiven amount to an eligible transferee under s. 80.04. An income inclusion under s. 80(13) may therefore result to the extent that a portion of the forgiven amount remains. Paragraphs 80(9)(*b*) and (*c*) apply where the capital cost of a depreciable property is restricted for capital cost allowance purposes, e.g., where there has been a change of use or non-arm's length transfer of the property subject to s. 13(7). In Document No. 2010-0371021E5, the CRA concluded that s. 80(9) could reduce debt from a related partnership. Note that special rules apply to partnerships (see s. 80(18)).

See also the editorial note for s. 80(2).

History: S. 80(9), the portion before paragraph (*a*) was replaced by S.C. 2016, c. 12, s. 23(4), in force January 1, 2017, and formerly read:

(9) *Reductions of adjusted cost bases of capital properties.* Where a commercial obligation issued by a debtor is settled at any time and amounts have been designated under subsections (5), (7) and (8) to the maximum extent permitted in respect of the settlement, subject to subsection (18)

Related Sections: S. 53(2)(*g*) Amounts to be deducted — Debt forgiveness; s. 53(2)(*g*.1) Amounts to be deducted — Debt forgiveness; s. 88(1) Winding-up; s. 96(3) Agreement or election of partnership members; s. 220(3.21) Designations and allocations.

Forms: T2154 — Application of Designated Forgiven Debt Under Section 80.

► 80(10) ◄

(10) Reduction of adjusted cost bases of certain shares and debts. If a commercial obligation issued by a debtor is settled at any time in a taxation year and amounts have been designated by the debtor under subsections (5), (8) and (9) to the maximum extent permitted in respect of the settlement, subject to subsection (18) the remaining unapplied portion of that forgiven amount shall be applied (to the extent that it is designated in a prescribed form filed with the debtor's return of income under this Part for the year) to reduce immediately after that time the adjusted cost bases to the debtor of capital properties, owned by the debtor immediately after that time, that are shares of the capital stock of corporations of which the debtor is a specified shareholder at that time and debts issued by corporations of which the debtor is a specified shareholder at that time (other than shares of the capital stock of corporations related to the debtor at that time, debts issued by corporations related to the debtor at that time and excluded properties).

Editorial Note: After the (mandatory) application of the forgiven amount to loss carryforwards (per s. 80(3) and (4)) and provided that the maximum designation is made to reduce the undepreciated capital cost of depreciable property, cumulative eligible capital (prior to January 1, 2017), and resource pools (per s. 80(5) and (8); s. 80(7) applied prior to January 1, 2017), and "general" capital property (per s. 80(9)), the remaining unapplied portion of the forgiven amount may be applied (i.e., if the debtor designates) to reduce the debtor's adjusted cost base of capital property that is shares or debt of a corporation in which the debtor is a "specified shareholder" at the time of forgiveness, other than corporations to which the debtor is related (covered in s. 80(11)). "Specified shareholder", per the definition in s. 248(1), refers to a debtor who owns 10% or more of the shares of any class of the corporation (or of another related corporation), counting shares owned by non-arm's length persons. Such shareholdings may often be long-term holds and therefore advantageous to designate, although the repayment of debt owing by such a corporation may trigger a gain, if designated. Special rules apply to partnerships (see s. 80(18)). Restrictions apply to non-residents' "excluded property".

(See also the editorial note for s. 80(2).)

History: S. 80(10) was replaced by S.C. 2016, c. 12, s. 23(5), in force January 1, 2017, and formerly read:

(10) *Reduction of adjusted cost bases of certain shares and debts.* Where a commercial obligation issued by a debtor is settled at any time in a taxation year and amounts have been designated by the debtor under subsections (5), (7), (8) and (9) to the maximum extent permitted in respect of the settlement, subject to subsection (18) the remaining unapplied portion of that forgiven amount shall be applied (to the extent that it is designated in a prescribed form filed with the debtor's return of income under this Part for the year) to reduce immediately after that time the adjusted cost bases to the debtor of capital properties, owned by the debtor immediately after that time, that are shares of the capital stock of corporations of which the debtor is a specified shareholder at that time and debts issued by corporations of which the debtor is a specified shareholder at that time (other than shares of the capital stock of corporations related to the debtor at that time, debts issued by corporations related to the debtor at that time and excluded properties).

Related Sections: S. 53(2)(*g*) Amounts to be deducted — Debt forgiveness; s. 53(2)(*g*.1) Amounts to be deducted — Debt forgiveness; s. 96(3) Agreement or election of partnership members; s. 220(3.21) Designations and allocations.

Forms: T2154 — Application of Designated Forgiven Debt Under Section 80.

▶ 80(11) ◀

(11) Reduction of adjusted cost bases of certain shares, debts and partnership interests. If a commercial obligation issued by a debtor is settled at any time in a taxation year and amounts have been designated by the debtor under subsections (5), (8), (9) and (10) to the maximum extent permitted in respect of the settlement, subject to subsection (18) the remaining unapplied portion of that forgiven amount shall be applied (to the extent that it is designated in a prescribed form filed with the debtor's return of income under this Part for the year) to reduce immediately after that time the adjusted cost bases to the debtor of

(*a*) shares and debts that are capital properties (other than excluded properties and properties the adjusted cost bases of which are reduced at that time under subsection (9) or (10)) of the debtor immediately after that time; and

(*b*) interests in partnerships that are related to the debtor at that time that are capital properties (other than excluded properties) of the debtor immediately after that time.

Editorial Note: After the (mandatory) application of the forgiven amount to loss carryforwards, and provided that the maximum designations are made under the preceding subsections, the remaining unapplied portion of the forgiven amount may be applied (i.e., if the debtor designates) to reduce the debtor's "related party property" — i.e., adjusted cost base of capital property that is shares or debts of related corporations or interests in related partnerships immediately after the time of forgiveness. (Per s. 80(2)(*j*), related partnership status is determined by assuming that the partnership is a corporation, and pro-rating the taxpayer's interest based on fair market value.) In most cases, such designations will not be advisable because , unless the forgiven amount has been applied to reduce the tax attributes of "directed persons" to the maximum extent possible under s. 80.04, such reductions will not alleviate the debtor's income inclusion under s. 80(13). Special rules apply to partnerships (see s. 80(18)). Restrictions apply to non-residents' "excluded property".

(See also the editorial note for s. 80(2).)

History: S. 80(11), the portion before paragraph (*a*) was replaced by S.C. 2016, c. 12, s. 23(6), in force January 1, 2017, and formerly read:

(11) *Reduction of adjusted cost bases of certain shares, debts and partnership interests.* Where a commercial obligation issued by a debtor is settled at any time in a taxation year and amounts have been designated by the debtor under subsections (5), (7), (8), (9) and (10) to the maximum extent permitted in respect of the settlement, subject to subsection (18) the remaining unapplied portion of that forgiven amount shall be applied (to the extent that it is designated in a prescribed form filed with the debtor's return of income under this Part for the year) to reduce immediately after that time the adjusted cost bases to the debtor of

Related Sections: S. 53(2)(*g*) Amounts to be deducted — Debt forgiveness; s. 53(2)(*g*.1) Amounts to be deducted — Debt forgiveness; s. 96(3) Agreement or election of partnership members; s. 220(3.21) Designations and allocations.

Forms: T2154 — Application of Designated Forgiven Debt Under Section 80.

Tax Window Files: Debt parking and foreign currency, *December 8, 2009*, CRA Document No. 2009-0347661C6.

▶ 80(12) ◀

(12) Capital gain where current year capital loss. If a commercial obligation issued by a debtor (other than a partnership) is settled at any time in a taxation year and amounts have been designated by the debtor under subsections (5), (8) and (9) to the maximum extent permitted in respect of the settlement,

(*a*) the debtor shall be deemed to have a capital gain for the year from the disposition of capital property (or, where the debtor is non-resident at the end of the year, taxable Canadian property), equal to the lesser of

(i) the remaining unapplied portion of the forgiven amount at that time in respect of the obligation, and

(ii) the amount, if any, by which the total of

(A) all of the debtor's capital losses for the year from the dispositions of properties (other than listed personal properties and excluded properties), and

(B) twice the amount that would, because of subsection 88(1.2), be deductible under paragraph 111(1)(*b*) in computing the debtor's taxable income for the year, if the debtor had sufficient income and taxable capital gains for the year,

exceeds the total of

(C) all of the debtor's capital gains for the year from the dispositions of such properties (determined without reference to this subsection), and

(D) all amounts each of which is an amount deemed by this subsection to be a capital gain of the debtor for the year as a consequence of the application of this subsection to other commercial obligations settled before that time; and

(*b*) the forgiven amount at that time in respect of the obligation shall be considered to have been applied under this subsection to the extent of the amount deemed by this subsection to be a capital gain of the debtor for the year as a consequence of the application of this subsection to the settlement of the obligation at that time.

Editorial Note: After the (mandatory) application of the forgiven amount to loss carryforwards (per s. 80(3) and (4)), and provided that the maximum designations are made to reduce the undepreciated capital cost of depreciable properties, cumulative eligible capital (prior to January 1, 2017), and resource pools (per s. 80(5) and (8); s. 80(7) applied prior to January 1, 2017), and "general" capital property (per s. 80(9)), the remaining unapplied portion of the forgiven amount is applied to reduce current year capital losses. This is done by deeming an amount of the unapplied portion equivalent to current year capital losses to be a capital gain. The application of this provision is mandatory and does not require a designation to be filed; however, it appears that it can be avoided by not making maximum designations for certain elective deductions (as described above). The debtor is not required to apply the forgiven amount to reduce the adjusted cost base of shares or debts of related corporations or interests in related partnerships under s. 80(11) before s. 80(12) will apply. The deemed capital gain is added to the corporation's capital dividend account at the end of the year (see Document No. 2011-0412541E5).

History: S. 80(12), the portion before paragraph (*a*) was replaced by S.C. 2016, c. 12, s. 23(7), in force January 1, 2017, and formerly read:

(12) *Capital gain where current year capital loss.* Where a commercial obligation issued by a debtor (other than a partnership) is settled at any time in a taxation year and amounts have been designated by the debtor under subsections (5), (7), (8) and (9) to the maximum extent permitted in respect of the settlement,

▶ 80(13) ◀

(13) Income inclusion. Where a commercial obligation issued by a debtor is settled at any time in a taxation year, there shall be added, in computing the debtor's income for the year from the source in connection with which the obligation was issued, the amount determined by the formula

$$(A + B - C - D) \times E$$

where

A is the remaining unapplied portion of the forgiven amount at that time in respect of the obligation,

B is the lesser of

(*a*) the total of all amounts designated under subsection (11) by the debtor in respect of the settlement of the obligation at that time, and

(*b*) the residual balance at that time in respect of the settlement of the obligation,

C is the total of all amounts each of which is an amount specified in an agreement filed under section 80.04 in respect of the settlement of the obligation at that time,

D is

(*a*) if the debtor has designated amounts under subsections (5), (8), (9) and (10) to the maximum extent permitted in respect of the settlement, the amount, if any, by which

(i) the total of all amounts each of which is an unrecognized loss at that time, in respect of the obligation, from the disposition of a property

exceeds

(ii) twice the total of all amounts each of which is an amount by which the amount determined before that time under this subsection in respect of a settlement of an obligation issued by the debtor has been reduced because of an amount determined under this paragraph, and

(*b*) in any other case, nil, and

E is

(*a*) where the debtor is a partnership, 1, and

(*b*) in any other case, $^1/_2$.

Editorial Note: S. 80(13) provides for an "income hit" based on 50% (100% for a partnership) of the remaining unapplied portion of the forgiven amount (the description of A), i.e., after the application of the previous subsections (s. 80(3)–(12), excluding s. 80(7) as of January 1, 2017). The income hit, which is subject to reserves/offsets in s. 61.2–61.4, is adjusted for certain items, notably transfers of forgiven amounts to eligible transferees under s. 80.04:

- Added are amounts applied under s. 80(11) to reduce ACB of "related party property" (i.e., capital property that is shares or debts of related corporations or interests in related partnerships) (the description of B).

  Note: this addback (and therefore the income hit) is reduced if the "residual balance" is less than amounts applied under s. 80(11). Basically, "residual balance" pertains to "gross tax attributes" (see below) available to persons within the debtor's Canadian control group ("directed persons", per the definition in s. 80(1)). This addback is designed to ensure that the debtor has maximized transfers of unapplied forgiven amounts to directed persons (under s. 80.04), before "related party property" can be designated by the debtor (under s. 80(11)) to reduce the income hit. Basically, "gross tax attributes" of directed persons refer to tax attributes other than "related party property" remaining after settlement, taking into account s. 80.04 transfers of unapplied forgiven amounts (see ss. 80(14) and (14.1)).

- Subtracted are transfers of unapplied forgiven amounts to eligible transferees under s. 80.04 — i.e., this can be done to reduce the income hit (the description of C).

- Subtracted are certain stopped losses (under s. 40(2)(*g*)(ii) — see the definition of "unrecognized loss" in s. 80(1)), provided that maximum designations other than under s. 80(11) have been made (the description of D).

See also the Editorial Note for s. 80(2).

History: S. 80(13), the portion of paragraph (*a*) before subparagraph (i) in the description of D, was replaced by S.C. 2016, c. 12, s. 23(8), in force January 1, 2017, and formerly read:

(*a*) where the debtor has designated amounts under subsections (5), (7), (8), (9) and (10) to the maximum extent permitted in respect of the settlement, the amount, if any, by which

Related Sections: S. 12(1)(z3) Debt forgiveness; s. 28(1) Farming or fishing business; s. 61.2 Reserve for debt forgiveness for resident individuals; s. 61.3(1) Deduction for insolvency with respect to resident corporations; s. 61.3(2) Reserve for insolvency with respect to non-resident corporations; s. 61.4 Reserve for debt forgiveness for corporations and others; s. 80(16) Designations by Minister; s. 95(1), "foreign accrual property income".

Tax Profile: October 2008 — Tax Consequences of Debt Restructuring and Workouts in Canada.

Information Circulars: IC 88-2 General anti-avoidance rule — Section 245 of the Income Tax Act (para. 23).

▶ 80(14) ◀

(14) Residual balance. For the purpose of subsection (13), the residual balance at any time in a taxation year in respect of the settlement of a particular commercial obligation issued by a debtor is the amount, if any, by which

(*a*) the gross tax attributes of directed persons at that time in respect of the debtor

exceeds the total of

(*b*) the value of A in subsection (13) in respect of the settlement of the particular obligation at that time,

(*c*) all amounts each of which is

(i) the amount, if any, by which the value of A in subsection (13) in respect of a settlement before that time and in the year of a commercial obligation issued by the debtor exceeds the value of C in that subsection in respect of the settlement,

(ii) the value of A in subsection (13) in respect of a settlement of a commercial obligation that is deemed by paragraph 80.04(4)(*e*) to have been issued by a directed person in respect of the debtor because of the filing of an agreement under section 80.04 in respect of a settlement before that time and in the year of a commercial obligation issued by the debtor, or

(iii) the amount specified in an agreement (other than an agreement with a directed person in respect of the debtor) filed under section 80.04 in respect of the settlement before that time and in the year of a commercial obligation issued by the debtor, and

(*d*) all amounts each of which is an amount in respect of a settlement at a particular time before that time and in the year of a commercial obligation issued by the debtor equal to the least of

(i) the total of all amounts designated under subsection (11) in respect of the settlement,

(ii) the residual balance of the debtor at the particular time, and

(iii) the amount, if any, by which the sum of the values of A and B in subsection (13) in respect of the settlement exceeds the value of C in that subsection in respect of the settlement.

► 80(14.1) ◄

(14.1) Gross tax attributes. The gross tax attributes of directed persons at any time in respect of a debtor means the total of all amounts each of which is an amount that would be applied under any of subsections (3) to (10) and (12) in respect of a settlement of a separate commercial obligation (in this subsection referred to as a "notional obligation") issued by directed persons at that time in respect of the debtor if the following assumptions were made:

(*a*) a notional obligation was issued immediately before that time by each of those directed persons and was settled at that time;

(*b*) the forgiven amount at that time in respect of each of those notional obligations was equal to the total of all amounts each of which is a forgiven amount at or before that time and in the year in respect of a commercial obligation issued by the debtor;

(*c*) amounts were designated under subsections (5), (8), (9) and (10) by each of those directed persons to the maximum extent permitted in respect of the settlement of each of those notional obligations; and

(*d*) no amounts were designated under subsection (11) by any of those directed persons in respect of the settlement of any of the notional obligations.

History: S. 80(14.1)(*c*) was replaced by S.C. 2016, c. 12, s. 23(9), in force January 1, 2017, and formerly read:

(*c*) amounts were designated under subsections (5), (7), (8), (9) and (10) by each of those directed persons to the maximum extent permitted in respect of the settlement of each of those notional obligations; and

► 80(15) ◄

(15) Members of partnerships. Where a commercial debt obligation issued by a partnership (in this subsection referred to as the "partnership obligation") is settled at any time in a fiscal period of the partnership that ends in a taxation year of a member of the partnership,

(*a*) the member may deduct, in computing the member's income for the year, such amount as the member claims not exceeding the relevant limit in respect of the partnership obligation;

(*b*) for the purpose of paragraph (*a*), the relevant limit in respect of the partnership obligation is the amount that would be included in computing the member's income for the year as a consequence of the application of subsection (13) and section 96 to the settlement of the partnership obligation if the partnership had designated amounts under subsections (5), (8), (9) and (10) to the maximum extent permitted in respect of each obligation settled in that fiscal period and if income arising from the application of subsection (13) were from a source of income separate from any other sources of partnership income; and

(*c*) for the purposes of this section and section 80.04,

(i) the member shall be deemed to have issued a commercial debt obligation that was settled at the end of that fiscal period,

(ii) the amount deducted under paragraph (*a*) in respect of the partnership obligation in computing the member's income shall be treated as if it were the forgiven amount at the end of that fiscal period in respect of the obligation referred to in subparagraph (i),

(iii) subject to subparagraph (iv), the obligation referred to in subparagraph (i) shall be deemed to have been issued at the same time at which, and in the same circumstances in which, the partnership obligation was issued,

(iv) if the member is a taxpayer that was subject to a loss restriction event at a particular time that is before the end of that fiscal period and before the taxpayer became a member of the partnership, and the partnership obligation was issued before the particular time,

(A) subject to the application of this subparagraph to the taxpayer after the particular time and before the end of that fiscal period, the obligation referred to in subparagraph (i) is deemed to have been issued by the member after the particular time, and

(B) subparagraph (*b*)(ii) of the definition "relevant loss balance" in subsection (1), paragraph (*f*) of the definition "successor pool" in that subsection and paragraph (*b*) of the definition "unrecognized loss" in that subsection do not apply in respect of the loss restriction event, and

(v) the source in connection with which the obligation referred to in subparagraph (i) was issued shall be deemed to be the source in connection with which the partnership obligation was issued.

Editorial Note: Where an amount would otherwise be included in a partner's income as a result of debt forgiveness to a partnership to which there is an income hit (i.e., s. 80(13) applies to the partnership), s. 80(15) allows a partner to claim an offsetting deduction (s. 80(15)(*a*)), which is treated as if it were a debt which was settled vis-à-vis the partner at the end of the partnership's fiscal period (s. 80(15)(*c*)(i)). Thus, it may be applied against the partner's tax accounts, etc. The deduction cannot exceed the "relevant limit" — the amount included in the partner's income assuming that the partnership made maximum designations under s. 80(5)–(10) (s. 80(15)(*b*)). (Note: under s. 80(18), the maximum designations in respect of non-depreciable capital property by a partnership cannot exceed the excess of the ACB over fair market value of the property at the time.)

It appears that the deduction does not prevent what would otherwise be the income of the partnership from increasing the partner's partnership ACB (the deduction under s. 80(15)(*a*) has no effect on the ACB of a partnership interest), and that the deemed forgiven debt can be applied to positive ACB which results from the income (see Document No. 2010-0358091E5). An important advantage of the election is that the "income hit" to a partner is 50% of the amount to a partnership (see description D of s. 80(13)).

History: S. 80(15)(*b*) was replaced by S.C. 2016, c. 12, s. 23(10), in force January 1, 2017, and formerly read:

(*b*) for the purpose of paragraph (*a*), the relevant limit in respect of the partnership obligation is the amount that would be included in computing the member's income for the year as a consequence of the application of subsection (13) and section 96 to the settlement of the partnership obligation if the partnership had designated amounts under subsections (5), (7), (8), (9) and (10) to the maximum extent permitted in respect of each obligation settled in that fiscal period and if income arising from the application of subsection (13) were from a source of income separate from any other sources of partnership income; and

S. 80(15)(*c*)(iv) was replaced by S.C. 2013, c. 40, s. 36(3), deemed to have come into force on March 21, 2013, and formerly read:

(iv) where the member is a corporation the control of which was acquired at a particular time that is before the end of that fiscal period and before the corporation became a member of the partnership and the partnership obligation was issued before the particular time,

(A) subject to the application of this subparagraph to an acquisition of control of the corporation after the particular time and before the end of that fiscal period, the obligation referred to in subparagraph (i) shall be deemed to have been issued by the member after the particular time, and

(B) paragraph (*e*) of the definition "relevant loss balance" in subsection (1), paragraph (*f*) of the definition "successor pool" in that subsection and paragraph (*b*) of the definition "unrecognized loss" in that subsection do not apply in respect of that acquisition of control, and

Related Sections: S. 20(1)(*uu*) Debt forgiveness; s. 61.2 Reserve for debt forgiveness for resident individuals; s. 61.3 Deduction for insolvency with respect to resident corporations; s. 61.4 Reserve for debt forgiveness for corporations and others; s. 80(18) Partnership designations; s. 80.04(4) Agreement respecting transfer of forgiven amount.

► 80(16) ◄

(16) Designations by Minister. Where a commercial obligation issued by a debtor is settled at any time in a taxation year and, as a consequence of the settlement an amount would, but for this subsection, be deducted under section 61.2 or 61.3 in computing the debtor's income for the year and the debtor has not designated amounts under subsections (5) to (11) to the maximum extent possible in respect of the settlement,

(*a*) the Minister may designate amounts under subsections (5) to (11) to the extent that the debtor would have been permitted to designate those amounts; and

(*b*) the amounts designated by the Minister shall, except for the purpose of this subsection, be deemed to have been designated by the debtor as required by subsections (5) to (11).

Editorial Note: This provision is operative where a debtor claims reserves/offsets against an "income hit" under s. 80(13) pursuant to s. 61.2 or 61.3, and the debtor has not made the maximum designations under ss. 80(5)–(11). It allows the CRA to designate such amounts on behalf of the debtor, to the extent that the debtor would have been permitted to designate such amounts.

► 80(17) ◄

(17) Income inclusion where residual balance a positive amount — (Repealed by S.C. 1998, c. 19, s. 111(5).)

Related Sections: S. 12(1)(*z*.3) Debt forgiveness; s. 34.2(4) Reserve.

► 80(18) ◄

(18) Partnership designations. Where a commercial obligation issued by a partnership is settled at any time after December 20, 1994, the amount designated under subsection (9), (10) or (11) in respect of the settlement by the partnership to reduce the adjusted cost base of a capital property acquired shall not exceed the amount, if any, by which the adjusted cost base at that time to the partnership of the property exceeds the fair market value at that time of the property.

Sec. 80(16)

Editorial Note: See the editorial note to s. 80(15).

SECTION 80.01: [Debt forgiveness rules — Deemed settlement of debt]

► 80.01(1) ◄

(1) Definitions. In this section,

"commercial debt obligation" — "commercial debt obligation" has the meaning assigned by subsection 80(1);

"commercial obligation" — "commercial obligation" has the meaning assigned by subsection 80(1);

"debtor" — "debtor" has the meaning assigned by subsection 80(1);

"distress preferred share" — "distress preferred share" has the meaning assigned by subsection 80(1);

"forgiven amount" — "forgiven amount" has the meaning assigned by subsection 80(1) except that, where an amount would be included in computing a person's income under paragraph 6(1)(*a*) or subsection 15(1) as a consequence of the settlement of an obligation if the obligation were settled without any payment being made in satisfaction of its principal amount, "forgiven amount" in respect of that obligation has the meaning assigned by subsection 6(15.1) or 15(1.21), as the case may be;

"person" — "person" has the meaning assigned by subsection 80(1);

"specified cost" — "specified cost" at any time to a person of an obligation means,

(*a*) where the obligation is capital property of the person at that time, the adjusted cost base at that time to the person of the obligation, and

(*b*) in any other case, the cost amount to the person of the obligation.

► 80.01(2) ◄

(2) Application. For the purposes of this section,

(*a*) paragraphs 80(2)(*a*), (*b*), (*j*), (*l*) and (*n*) apply; and

(*b*) a person has a significant interest in a corporation at any time if the person owned at that time

(i) shares of the capital stock of the corporation that would give the person 25% or more of the votes that could be cast under all circumstances at an annual meeting of shareholders of the corporation, or

(ii) shares of the capital stock of the corporation having a fair market value of 25% or more of the fair market value of all the issued shares of the capital stock of the corporation

and, for the purposes of this paragraph, a person shall be deemed to own at any time each share of the capital stock of a corporation that is owned, otherwise than because of this paragraph, at that time by another person with whom the person does not deal at arm's length.

Related Sections: S. 95(2)(*g*.1) Determination of certain components of foreign accrual property income.

▶ 80.01(3) ◀

(3) Deemed settlement on amalgamation. Where a commercial obligation or another obligation (in this subsection referred to as the "indebtedness") of a debtor that is a corporation to pay an amount to another corporation (in this subsection referred to as the "creditor") is settled on an amalgamation of the debtor and the creditor, the indebtedness shall be deemed to have been settled immediately before the time that is immediately before the amalgamation by a payment made by the debtor and received by the creditor of an amount equal to the amount that would have been the creditor's cost amount of the indebtedness at that time if

(*a*) the definition "cost amount" in subsection 248(1) were read without reference to paragraph (*e*) of that definition; and

(*b*) that cost amount included amounts added in computing the creditor's income in respect of the portion of the indebtedness representing unpaid interest, to the extent those amounts have not been deducted in computing the creditor's income as bad debts in respect of that unpaid interest.

▶ 80.01(4) ◀

(4) Deemed settlement on winding-up. Where there is a winding-up of a subsidiary to which the rules in subsection 88(1) apply and

(*a*) a debt or other obligation (in this subsection referred to as the "subsidiary's obligation") of the subsidiary to pay an amount to the parent, or

(*b*) a debt or other obligation (in this subsection referred to as the "parent's obligation") of the parent to pay an amount to the subsidiary

is, as a consequence of the winding-up, settled at a particular time without any payment of an amount or by the payment of an amount that is less than the principal amount of the subsidiary's obligation or the parent's obligation, as the case may be,

(*c*) where that payment is less than the amount that would have been the cost amount to the parent or subsidiary of the subsidiary's obligation or the parent's obligation immediately before the particular time if the definition "cost amount" in subsection 248(1) were read without reference to paragraph (*e*) of that definition and the parent so elects in a prescribed form on or before the day on or before which the parent is required to file a return of income pursuant to section 150 for the taxation year that includes the particular time, the amount paid at that time in satisfaction of the principal amount of the subsidiary's obligation or the parent's obligation shall be deemed to be equal to the amount that would be the cost amount to the parent or the subsidiary, as the case may be, of the subsidiary's obligation or the parent's obligation immediately before the particular time if

(i) the definition "cost amount" in subsection 248(1) were read without reference to paragraph (*e*) of that definition, and

(ii) that cost amount included amounts added in computing the parent's income or the subsidiary's income in respect of the portion of the indebtedness representing unpaid interest, to the extent that the parent or the subsidiary has not deducted any amounts as bad debts in respect of that unpaid interest, and

(*d*) for the purposes of applying section 80 to the subsidiary's obligation, where property is distributed at any time in circumstances to which paragraph 88(1)(*a*) or (*b*) applies and the subsidiary's obligation is settled as a consequence of the distribution, the subsidiary's obligation shall be deemed to have been settled immediately before the time that is immediately before the time of the distribution and not at any later time.

Related Regulations: 600(*c*).

Related Sections: S. 220(3.2) Late, amended or revoked elections.

Forms: T2027 — Election to Deem Amount of Settlement of a Debt or Obligation.

Information Circulars: IC 07-1 Taxpayer Relief Provisions.

▶ 80.01(5) ◀

(5) Deemed settlement on winding-up. Where there is a winding-up of a subsidiary to which the rules in subsection 88(1) apply and, as a consequence of the winding-up, a distress preferred share issued by the subsidiary and owned by the parent (or a distress preferred share issued by the parent and owned by the subsidiary) is settled at any time without any payment of an amount or by the payment of an amount that is less than the principal amount of the share,

(*a*) where the payment was less than the adjusted cost base of the share to the parent or the subsidiary, as the case may be, immediately before that time, for the purposes of applying the provisions of this Act to the issuer of the share, the amount paid at that time in satisfaction of the principal amount of the share shall be deemed to be equal to its adjusted cost base to the parent or to the subsidiary, as the case may be; and

(*b*) for the purposes of applying section 80 to the share, where property is distributed at any time in circumstances to which paragraph 88(1)(*a*) or (*b*) applies and the share is settled as a consequence of the distribution, the share shall be deemed to have been settled immediately before the time that is immediately before the time of the distribution and not at any later time.

▶ 80.01(5.1) ◀

(5.1) Deemed settlement on SIFT trust wind-up event. If a trust that is a SIFT wind-up entity is the only beneficiary under another trust (in this subsection referred to as the "subsidiary trust"), and a capital property that is a debt or other obligation (in this subsection referred to as the "subsidiary trust's obligation") of the subsidiary trust to pay an amount to the SIFT wind-up entity is, as a consequence of a distribution from the subsidiary trust that is a SIFT trust wind-up event, settled at a particular time without any payment of an amount or by the payment of an amount that is less than the principal amount of the subsidiary trust's obligation

(*a*) paragraph (*b*) applies if

(i) the payment is less than the amount that would have been the adjusted cost base to the SIFT wind-up entity of the subsidiary trust's obligation immediately before the particular time, and

(ii) the SIFT wind-up entity elects, in prescribed form on or before the SIFT wind-up entity's filing-due date for the taxation year that includes the particular time, to have paragraph (*b*) apply;

(*b*) if this paragraph applies, the amount paid at the particular time in satisfaction of the principal amount of the subsidiary trust's obligation is deemed to be equal to the amount that would be the adjusted cost base to the SIFT wind-up entity of the subsidiary trust's obligation immediately before the particular time if that adjusted cost base included amounts added in computing the SIFT wind-up entity's income in respect of the portion of the indebtedness representing unpaid interest, to the extent that the SIFT wind-up entity has not deducted any amounts as bad debts in respect of that unpaid interest; and

(*c*) for the purposes of applying section 80 to the subsidiary trust's obligation, the subsidiary trust's obligation is deemed to have been settled immediately before the time that is immediately before the distribution.

History: S. 80.01(5.1) was added by S.C. 2009, c. 2, s. 17(1), applicable after July 14, 2008.

▶ 80.01(6) ◀

(6) Specified obligation in relation to debt parking. For the purpose of subsection (7), an obligation issued by a debtor is, at a particular time, a specified obligation of the debtor where

(*a*) at any previous time (other than a time before the last time, if any, the obligation became a parked obligation before the particular time),

(i) a person who owned the obligation

(A) dealt at arm's length with the debtor, and

(B) where the debtor is a corporation, did not have a significant interest in the debtor, or

(ii) the obligation was acquired by the holder of the obligation from another person who was, at the time of that acquisition, not related to the holder or related to the holder only because of paragraph 251(5)(*b*); or

(*b*) the obligation is deemed by subsection 50(1) to be reacquired at the particular time.

Editorial Note: See the editorial note to s. 80.01(8).

▶ 80.01(7) ◀

(7) Parked obligation. For the purposes of this subsection and subsections (6), (8) and (10),

(*a*) an obligation issued by a debtor is a "parked obligation" at any time where at that time

(i) the obligation is a specified obligation of the debtor, and

(ii) the holder of the obligation

(A) does not deal at arm's length with the debtor, or

(B) where the debtor is a corporation and the holder acquired the obligation after July 12, 1994 (otherwise than pursuant to an agreement in writing entered into on or before July 12, 1994), has a significant interest in the debtor; and

(*b*) an obligation that is, at any time, acquired or reacquired in circumstances to which subparagraph (6)(*a*)(ii) or paragraph (6)(*b*) applies shall, if the obligation is a parked obligation immediately after that time, be deemed to have become a parked obligation at that time.

Editorial Note: See the editorial note to s. 80.01(8).

▶ 80.01(8) ◀

(8) Deemed settlement after debt parking. Where at any particular time after February 21, 1994 a commercial debt obligation that was issued by a debtor becomes a parked obligation (otherwise than pursuant to an agreement in writing entered into before February 22, 1994) and the specified cost at the particular time to the holder of the obligation is less than 80% of the principal amount of the obligation, for the purpose of applying the provisions of this Act to the debtor

(*a*) the obligation shall be deemed to have been settled at the particular time; and

(*b*) the forgiven amount at the particular time in respect of the obligation shall be determined as if the debtor had paid an amount at the particular time in satisfaction of the principal amount of the obligation equal to that specified cost.

Editorial Note: When a commercial debt obligation becomes a "parked obligation" (this may occur, for example, if the debt becomes held by persons who closely hold the debtor corporation) and the tax cost of the obligation is less than 80% of the principal amount, the debt forgiveness rules apply as if the debt was settled for an amount equal to the tax cost (s. 80.01(8)).

To be a "parked obligation", a debt must be a "specified obligation" (s. 80.01(7)(*a*)(i)). Per s. 80.01(6), a debt will be a specified obligation if:

- it was previously owned by a person at arm's length with the debtor and, if the debtor is a corporation, the person did not have a "significant interest" in the debtor (s. 80.01(6)(*a*)(i)). Basically, "significant interest" pertains to ownership of shares having at least 25% of either votes or value, counting ownership by non-arm's length persons — see s. 80.01(2);
- it was acquired from a non-related person or a person related only because of s. 251(5)(*b*) (s. 80.01(6)(*a*)(ii)); or
- the holder elected to claim the obligation as a bad debt under s. 50(1) (s. 80.01(6)(*b*)).

In addition, the debt must become "parked" — i.e., where the holder of the obligation is not at arm's length with the debtor (s. 80.01(7)(*a*)(ii)(A)) or has a "significant interest" (see above) in a corporate debtor (s. 80.01(7)(*a*)(ii)(B)).

Common situations in which the debt parking rules apply are where a creditor who is non-arm's length to the debtor (or holds a significant interest) claims a bad debt loss under s. 50(1) or where a corporation is taken over at significantly less than book value (i.e., debt is acquired for less than 80% of its principal amount).

Subsection 80.01(10) permits, in certain circumstances, a debtor to claim a deduction for a payment made in respect of the principal amount of a commercial debt obligation that was previously settled.

Technical Note: The specified obligation must "become" a parked obligation, normally requiring a change of status from "unparked" to "parked". However, in the case of s. 80.01(6)(*a*)(ii) and (*b*) (see above), s. 80.01(7)(*b*) deems a debt to have "become" parked if it is a parked debt immediately after an acquisition or reacquisition to which either of these sections applies. This may deem the debt parking rules to apply for certain simultaneous sales of shares and debt.

Related Sections: S. 79(3) Proceeds of disposition for debtor.

Canadian Tax Foundation: Ruby, *Section 80 and Unincorporated Entities*, 1997 Conference Report 19:1–37.

Tax Window Files: Debt parking and foreign currency, *December 8, 2009*, CRA Document No. 2009-0347661C6.

▶ 80.01(9) ◀

(9) Statute-barred debt. Where at any particular time after February 21, 1994 a commercial debt obligation issued by a debtor that is payable to a person (other than a person with whom the debtor is related at the particular time) becomes unenforceable in a court of competent jurisdiction because of a statutory limitation period and the obligation would, but for this subsection, not have been settled or extinguished at the particular time, for the purpose of applying the provisions of this Act to the debtor, the obligation shall be deemed to have been settled at the particular time.

▶ 80.01(10) ◀

(10) Subsequent payments in satisfaction of debt. Where a commercial debt obligation issued by a debtor is first deemed by subsection (8) or (9) to have been settled at a particular time, at a subsequent time a payment is made by the debtor of an amount in satisfaction of the principal amount of the obligation and it cannot reasonably be considered that one of the reasons the obligation became a parked obligation or became unenforceable, as the case may be, before the subsequent time was to have this subsection apply to the payment, in computing the debtor's income for the taxation year (in this subsection referred to as the "subsequent year") that includes the subsequent time from the source in connection with which the obligation was issued, there may be deducted the amount determined by the formula

$$0.5(A - B) - C$$

where

A is the amount of the payment,

B is the amount, if any, by which

(*a*) the principal amount of the obligation

exceeds the total of

(*b*) all amounts each of which is a forgiven amount at any time

(i) in the period that began at the particular time and ended immediately before the subsequent time, and

(ii) at which a particular portion of the obligation is deemed by subsection (8) or (9) to be settled

in respect of the particular portion, and

(*c*) all amounts paid in satisfaction of the principal amount of the obligation in the period that began at the particular time and ended immediately before the subsequent time, and

C is the amount, if any, by which the total of

(*a*) all amounts deducted under section 61.3 in computing the debtor's income for the subsequent year or a preceding taxation year,

(*b*) all amounts added because of subsection 80(13) in computing the debtor's income for the subsequent year or a preceding taxation year in respect of a settlement under subsection (8) or (9) in a period during which the debtor was exempt from tax under this Part on its taxable income, and

(*c*) all amounts added because of subsection 80(13) in computing the debtor's income for the subsequent year or a preceding taxation year in respect of a settlement under subsection (8) or (9) in a period during which the debtor was non-resident (other than any of those amounts added in computing the debtor's taxable income or taxable income earned in Canada)

exceeds the total of

(*d*) the amount, if any, deducted because of paragraph 37(1)(*f*.1) in determining the balance determined under subsection 37(1) in respect of the debtor immediately after the subsequent year, and

(*e*) all amounts by which the amount deductible under this subsection in respect of a payment made by the debtor before the subsequent time in computing the debtor's income for the subsequent year or a preceding year has been reduced because of this description.

History: [**Editorial Note**: The application of the amendment to s. 80.01(10) by S.C. 2001, c. 17, s. 59(1) was amended by S.C. 2013, c. 34, s. 372, to provide that, in computing a debtor's income for a particular taxation year, the fraction in paragraph 38(*a*) to be applied in respect of the settlement of a commercial debt obligation is the fraction in that paragraph that applied to the debtor in the debtor's taxation year in which the obligation was deemed to have been settled, instead of the fraction in that paragraph that applies to the debtor in the particular taxation year. This 2001 amendment is not reproduced in print but is available in all CCH Canadian electronic versions of the Income Tax Act.]

Related Sections: S. 20(1)(*uu*) Debt forgiveness; s. 87(2)(*l*.21) Forgiven amount.

▶ 80.01(11) ◀

(11) Foreign currency gains and losses. Where an obligation issued by a debtor is denominated in a currency (other than the Canadian currency) and the obligation is deemed by subsection (8) or (9) to have been settled, those subsections do not apply for the purpose of determining any gain or loss of the debtor on the settlement that is attributable to a fluctuation in the value of the currency relative to the value of Canadian currency.

Tax Window Files: Debt parking and foreign currency, *December 8, 2009*, CRA Document No. 2009-0347661C6.

SECTION 80.02: [Debt forgiveness rules — Distress preferred shares]

▶ 80.02(1) ◀

(1) Definitions. In this section, "commercial debt obligation", "commercial obligation", "distress preferred share" and "person" have the meanings assigned by subsection 80(1).

▶ 80.02(2) ◀

(2) General rules for distress preferred shares. For the purpose of applying the provisions of this Act to an issuer of a distress preferred share,

(*a*) the principal amount, at any time, of the share shall be deemed to be the amount (determined at that time) for which the share was issued;

(*b*) the amount for which the share was issued shall, at any time, be deemed to be the amount, if any, by which the total of

(i) the amount for which the share was issued, determined without reference to this paragraph, and

(ii) all amounts by which the paid-up capital in respect of the share increased after the share was issued and before that time

exceeds

(iii) the total of all amounts each of which is an amount paid before that time on a reduction of the paid-up capital in respect of the share, except to the extent that the amount is deemed by section 84 to have been paid as a dividend;

(*c*) the share shall be deemed to be settled at such time as it is redeemed, acquired or cancelled by the issuer; and

(*d*) a payment in satisfaction of the principal amount of the share is any payment made on a reduction of the paid-up capital in respect of the share to the extent that the payment would be proceeds of disposition of the share within the meaning that would be assigned by the definition "proceeds of disposition" in section 54 if that definition were read without reference to paragraph (*j*).

Related Sections: S. 95(2)(*g*.1) Determination of certain components of foreign accrual property income.

▶ 80.02(3) ◀

(3) Substitution of distress preferred share for debt. Where any part of the consideration given by a corporation to another person for the settlement or extinguishment at any time of a commercial debt obligation that was issued by the corporation and owned immediately before that time by the other person consists of a distress preferred share issued by the corporation to the other person,

(*a*) for the purposes of section 80, the amount paid at that time in satisfaction of the principal amount of the obligation because of the issue of that share shall be deemed to be equal to the lesser of

(i) the principal amount of the obligation, and

(ii) the amount by which the paid-up capital in respect of the class of shares that include that share increases because of the issue of that share; and

(*b*) for the purpose of subparagraph (2)(*b*)(i), the amount for which the share was issued shall be deemed to be equal to the amount deemed by paragraph (*a*) to have been paid at that time.

▶ 80.02(4) ◀

(4) Substitution of commercial debt obligation for distress preferred share. Where any part of the consideration given by a corporation to another person for the settlement at any time of a distress preferred share that was issued by the corporation and owned immediately before that time by the other person consists of a commercial debt obligation issued by the corporation to the other person, for the purposes of section 80

(*a*) the amount paid at that time in satisfaction of the principal amount of the share because of the issue of that obligation shall be deemed to be equal to the principal amount of the obligation; and

(*b*) the amount for which the obligation was issued shall be deemed to be equal to its principal amount.

▶ 80.02(5) ◀

(5) Substitution of distress preferred share for other distress preferred share. Where any part of the consideration given by a corporation to another person for the settlement at any time of a particular distress preferred share that was issued by the corporation and owned immediately before that time by the other person consists of another distress preferred share issued by the corporation to the other person, for the purposes of section 80

(*a*) the amount paid at that time in satisfaction of the principal amount of the particular share because of the issue of the other share shall be deemed to be equal to the amount by which the paid-up capital in respect of the class of shares that includes the other share increases because of the issue of the other share; and

(*b*) for the purpose of subparagraph (2)(*b*)(i), the amount for which the other share was issued shall be deemed to be equal to the amount deemed by paragraph (*a*) to have been paid at that time.

▶ 80.02(6) ◀

(6) Substitution of non-commercial obligation for distress preferred share. Where any part of the consideration given by a corporation to another person for the settlement at any time of a distress preferred share that was issued by the corporation and owned immediately before that time by the other person consists of another share (other than a distress preferred share) or an obligation (other than a commercial obligation) issued by the corporation to the other person, for the purposes of section 80, the amount paid at that time in satisfaction of the principal amount of the distress preferred share because of the issue of the other share or obligation shall be deemed to be equal to the fair market value of the other share or obligation, as the case may be, at that time.

▶ 80.02(7) ◀

(7) Deemed settlement on expiry of term. Where at any time a distress preferred share becomes a share that is not a distress preferred share, for the purposes of section 80

(*a*) the share shall be deemed to have been settled immediately before that time; and

(*b*) a payment equal to the fair market value of the share at that time shall be deemed to have been made immediately before that time in satisfaction of the principal amount of the share.

SECTION 80.03: [Surrender of capital property]

▶ 80.03(1) ◀

(1) Definitions. In this section, "commercial debt obligation", "commercial obligation", "distress preferred share", "forgiven amount" and "person" have the meanings assigned by subsection 80(1).

History: S. 80.03(1) was added by S.C. 2017, c. 33, s. 22(1), applicable to taxation years that end after February 21, 1994.

▶ 80.03(2) ◀

(2) Deferred recognition of debtor's gain on settlement of debt. Where at any time in a taxation year a person (in this subsection referred to as the "transferor") surrenders a particular capital property (other than a distress preferred share) that is a share, a capital interest in a trust or an interest in a partnership, the person shall be deemed to have a capital gain from the disposition at that time of another capital property (or, where the particular property is a taxable Canadian property, another taxable Canadian property) equal to the amount, if any, by which

(*a*) the total of all amounts deducted under paragraph 53(2)(*g*.1) in computing the adjusted cost base to the transferor of the particular property immediately before that time

exceeds the total of

(*b*) the amount that would be the transferor's capital gain for the year from the disposition of the particular property if this Act were read without reference to subsection 100(2), and

(*c*) where, at the end of the year, the transferor is resident in Canada or is a non-resident person who carries on business in Canada through a fixed place of business, the amount designated under subsection (7) by the transferor in respect of the disposition, at that time or immediately after that time, of the particular property.

Editorial Note: Subsection 80.03(2) is intended to prevent a person (including a partnership) from enjoying indefinite deferrals for capital properties whose adjusted cost base ("ACB") has been reduced under s. 80(9) to (11). It applies where a person "surrenders" certain capital property; such a surrender occurs in respect of:

- the disposition of shares of a subsidiary on a s. 88(1) winding-up (s. 80.03(3)(*a*)(i));
- shares of another corporation which merges with the corporate shareholder (s. 80.03(3)(*a*)(ii));
- a capital interest in a personal trust disposed of under an otherwise tax-deferred rollover pursuant to s. 107(2)(*c*) (s. 80.03(3)(*b*)); or
- a partnership interest disposed of under an otherwise tax-deferred rollover in respect of the dissolution of the partnership pursuant to s. 98(3)(*a*) or (5)(*a*) (s. 80.03(3)(*c*)).

In these four situations, the person is deemed to have a capital gain equal to the ACB reductions under s. 53(2)(*g.1*) in respect of the surrendered property; the ACM reductions are based on the application of s. 80(9)–80(11) (s. 80.03(2)(*a*)). This amount is reduced by any actual capital gain on the surrendered property, except to the extent the gain is the result of the disposition of a partnership interest with a negative ACB (s. 80.03(2)(*b*)), and the amount designated under s. 80.03(7), if the person is resident in Canada or is non-resident with a fixed place of business in Canada (s. 80.03(2)(*c*)). Paragraph 53(2)(*g.1*) maintains the record of ACB reductions pertaining to these four situations through various transactions; these include specified rollovers, non-arm's length transfers, and amalgamations (see s. 53(4) to (6), respectively).

Related Sections: S. 47(1)(*c*) Identical properties; s. 49(3.01)(*a*) Option to acquire specified property exercised; s. 51(1)(*d.1*) Convertible property; s. 53(2)(*g.1*) Amounts to be deducted — Debt forgiveness; 53(4) Recomputation of adjusted cost base on transfers and deemed dispositions; 53(5) Recomputation of adjusted cost base on other transfer; 53(6) Recomputation of adjusted cost base on amalgamation; s. 86(4)(*a*) Computation of adjusted cost base; s. 87(5.1)(*a*) Adjusted cost base of option; s. 87(6.1)(*a*) Adjusted cost base; s. 95(2)(*g*.1) Determination of certain components of foreign accrual property income.

▶ 80.03(3) ◀

(3) Surrender of capital property. For the purpose of subsection (2), a person shall be considered to have surrendered a property at any time only where

(*a*) in the case of a share of the capital stock of a particular corporation,

(i) the person is a corporation that disposed of the share at that time and the proceeds of disposition of the share are determined under paragraph 88(1)(*b*), or

(ii) the person is a corporation that owned the share at that time and, immediately after that time, amalgamates or merges with the particular corporation;

(*b*) in the case of a capital interest in a trust, the person disposed of the interest at that time and the proceeds of disposition are determined under paragraph 107(2)(*c*); and

(*c*) in the case of an interest in a partnership, the person disposed of the interest at that time and the proceeds of disposition are determined under paragraph 98(3)(*a*) or (5)(*a*).

Editorial Note: See the editorial note to s. 80.03(2).

▶ 80.03(4) ◀

(4) Dispositions by corporations — (Repealed by S.C. 1998, c. 19, s. 112(2).)

▶ 80.03(5) ◀

(5) Specified period — (Repealed by S.C. 1998, c. 19, s. 112(2).)

▶ 80.03(6) ◀

(6) When property acquired — (Repealed by S.C. 1998, c. 19, s. 112(2).)

▶ 80.03(7) ◀

(7) Alternative treatment. Where at any time in a taxation year a person disposes of a property, for the purposes of subsection (2) and section 80

(*a*) the person may designate an amount in a prescribed form filed with the person's return of income under this Part for the year; and

(*b*) where an amount is designated by the person under paragraph (*a*) in respect of the disposition,

(i) the person shall be deemed to have issued a commercial debt obligation at that time that is settled immediately after that time,

(ii) the lesser of the amount so designated and the amount that would, but for this subsection, be a capital gain determined in respect of the disposition because of subsection (2) shall be treated as if it were the forgiven amount at the time of the settlement in respect of the obligation referred to in subparagraph (i),

(iii) the source in connection with which the obligation referred to in subparagraph (i) was issued shall be deemed to be the business, if any, carried on by the person at the end of the year, and

(iv) where the person does not carry on a business at the end of the year, the person shall be deemed to carry on an active business at the end of the year and the source in connection with which the obligation referred to in subparagraph (i) was issued shall be deemed to be the business deemed by this subparagraph to be carried on.

Editorial Note: See the editorial note to s. 80.03(2).

Related Sections: S. 87(2)(*h*.1) Debts; s. 220(3.21) Designations and allocations.

Forms: T2155 — Alternative Treatment of Capital Gains Under Section 80.03 that Arise from a Forgiven Debt.

▶ 80.03(8) ◀

(8) Lifetime capital gains exemption. If, as a consequence of the disposition at any time by an individual of a property that is a qualified farm or fishing property of the individual or a qualified small business corporation share of the individual (as defined in subsection 110.6(1)), the individual is deemed by subsection (2) to have a capital gain at that time from the disposition of another property, for the purposes of sections 3, 74.3 and 111, as they apply for the purposes of section 110.6, the other property is deemed to be a qualified farm or fishing property of the individual or a qualified small business corporation share of the individual, as the case may be.

History: S. 80.03(8) was replaced by S.C. 2014, c. 39, s. 15(1), applicable to dispositions that occur in the 2014 and subsequent taxation years, and formerly read:

(8) *Lifetime capital gains exemption.* Where, as a consequence of the disposition at any time by an individual of a property that is a qualified farm property of the individual or a qualified small business corporation share of the individual (within the meanings assigned by subsection 110.6(1)), the individual is deemed by subsection (2) to have a capital gain at that time from the disposition of another property, for the purposes of sections 3, 74.3 and 111, as they apply for the purpose of section 110.6, the other property shall be deemed to be a qualified farm property of the individual or a qualified small business corporation share of the individual, as the case may be.

SECTION 80.04: [Debt forgiveness rules — Transfer of forgiven amount]

▶ 80.04(1) ◀

(1) Definitions. In this section, "commercial debt obligation", "commercial obligation", "debtor", "directed person", "eligible Canadian partnership", "forgiven amount" and "person" have the meanings assigned by subsection 80(1).

▶ 80.04(2) ◀

(2) Eligible transferee. For the purpose of this section, an "eligible transferee" of a debtor at any time is a directed person at that time in respect of the debtor or a taxable Canadian corporation or eligible Canadian partnership related (otherwise than because of a right referred to in paragraph 251(5)(*b*)) at that time to the debtor.

Related Sections: S. 87(2)(*h*.1) Debts.

▶ 80.04(3) ◀

(3) Application. Paragraphs 80(2)(*a*), (*b*), (*j*), (*l*) and (*n*) apply for the purpose of this section.

▶ 80.04(4) ◀

(4) Agreement respecting transfer of forgiven amount. Where

(*a*) a particular commercial obligation (other than an obligation deemed by paragraph (*e*) to have been issued) issued by a debtor is settled at a particular time,

(*b*) amounts have been designated by the debtor under subsections 80(5) to (10) to the maximum extent permitted in respect of the settlement of the particular obligation at the particular time,

(*c*) the debtor and an eligible transferee of the debtor at the particular time file under this section an agreement between them in respect of that settlement, and

(*d*) an amount is specified in that agreement

the following rules apply:

(*e*) except for the purposes of subsection 80(11), the transferee shall be deemed to have issued a commercial debt obligation that was settled at the particular time,

(*f*) the specified amount shall be deemed to be the forgiven amount at the particular time in respect of the obligation referred to in paragraph (*e*),

(*g*) subject to paragraph (*h*), the obligation referred to in paragraph (*e*) shall be deemed to have been issued at the same time (in paragraph (*h*) referred to as the "time of issue") at which, and in the same circumstances in which, the particular obligation was issued,

(*h*) if the transferee is a taxpayer that is subject to a loss restriction event after the time of issue and the transferee and the debtor were, if the transferee is a corporation, not related to each other — or, if the transferee is a trust, not affiliated with each other — immediately before the loss restriction event,

(i) the obligation referred to in paragraph (*e*) is deemed to have been issued after the loss restriction event, and

(ii) subparagraph (*b*)(ii) of the definition "relevant loss balance" in subsection 80(1), paragraph (*f*) of the definition "successor pool" in that subsection and paragraph (*b*) of the definition "unrecognized loss" in that subsection do not apply in respect of the loss restriction event,

(*i*) the source in connection with which the obligation referred to in paragraph (*e*) was issued shall be deemed to be the source in connection with which the particular obligation was issued, and

(*j*) for the purposes of sections 61.3 and 61.4, the amount included under subsection 80(13) in computing the income of the eligible transferee in respect of the settlement of the obligation referred to in paragraph (*e*) or deducted under paragraph 80(15)(*a*) in respect of such income shall be deemed to be nil.

History: S. 80.04(4)(*h*) was replaced by S.C. 2013, c. 40, s. 37(1), deemed to have come into force on March 21, 2013, and formerly read:

(*h*) where the transferee is a corporation the control of which was acquired by a person or group of persons after the time of issue and the transferee and the debtor were not related to each other immediately before that acquisition of control,

(i) the obligation referred to in paragraph (*e*) shall be deemed to have been issued after that acquisition of control, and

(ii) paragraph (*e*) of the definition "relevant loss balance" in subsection 80(1), paragraph (*f*) of the definition "successor pool" in that subsection and paragraph (*b*) of the definition "unrecognized loss" in that subsection do not apply in respect of that acquisition of control,

Related Sections: S. 96(3) Agreement or election of partnership members; s. 251.2(2) Loss restriction event.

▶ 80.04(5) ◀

(5) Consideration for agreement. For the purposes of this Part, where property is acquired at any time by an eligible transferee as consideration for entering into an agreement with a debtor that is filed under this section

(*a*) where the property was owned by the debtor immediately before that time,

(i) the debtor shall be deemed to have disposed of the property at that time for proceeds equal to the fair market value of the property at that time, and

(ii) no amount may be deducted in computing the debtor's income as a consequence of the transfer of the property, except any amount arising as a consequence of the application of subparagraph (i);

(*b*) the cost at which the property was acquired by the eligible transferee at that time shall be deemed to be equal to the fair market value of the property at that time; and

(*c*) the eligible transferee shall not be required to add an amount in computing income solely because of the acquisition at that time of the property;

(*d*) (Repealed by S.C. 1998, c. 19, s. 113(1).)

▶ 80.04(5.1) ◀

(5.1) No benefit conferred. For the purposes of this Part, where a debtor and an eligible transferee enter into an agreement that is filed under this section, no benefit shall be considered to have been conferred on the debtor as a consequence of the agreement.

▶ 80.04(6) ◀

(6) Manner of filing agreement. Subject to subsection (7), a particular agreement between a debtor and an eligible transferee in respect of an obligation issued by the debtor that was settled at any time shall be deemed not to have been filed under this section

(*a*) where it is not filed with the Minister in a prescribed form

(i) on or before the later of

(A) the day on or before which the debtor's return of income under this Part is required to be filed for the taxation year or fiscal period, as the case may be, that includes that time (or would be required to be filed if tax under this Part were payable by the debtor for the year), and

(B) the day on or before which the transferee's return of income under this Part is required to be filed for the taxation year or fiscal period, as the case may be, that includes that time, or

(ii) on or before the later of

(A) the expiry of the 90-day period commencing on the day of mailing of an assessment of tax payable under this Part or a notification that no tax is payable under this Part, as the case may be, for a taxation year or fiscal period described in clause (i)(A) or (B), as the case may be, and

(B) if the debtor is an individual (other than a trust) or a graduated rate estate, the day that is one year after the taxpayer's filing-due date for the year;

(*b*) where it is not accompanied by,

(i) where the debtor is a corporation and its directors are legally entitled to administer its affairs, a certified copy of their resolution authorizing the agreement to be made,

(ii) where the debtor is a corporation and its directors are not legally entitled to administer its affairs, a certified copy of the document by which the person legally entitled to administer its affairs authorized the agreement to be made,

(iii) where the transferee is a corporation and its directors are legally entitled to administer its affairs, a certified copy of their resolution authorizing the agreement to be made, and

(iv) where the transferee is a corporation and its directors are not legally entitled to administer its affairs, a certified copy of the document by which the person legally entitled to administer its affairs authorized the agreement to be made; or

(*c*) if an agreement amending the particular agreement has been filed in accordance with this section, except where subsection (8) applies to the particular agreement.

History: S. 80.04(6)(*a*)(ii)(B) was replaced by S.C. 2014, c. 39, s. 16(1), applicable to the 2016 and subsequent taxation years, and formerly read:

(B) if the debtor is an individual (other than a trust) or a testamentary trust, the day that is one year after the taxpayer's filing-due date for the year;

S. 80.04(6)(*a*)(ii) was replaced by S.C. 2013, c. 34, s. 214(1), applicable for taxation years that end after February 21, 1994, and formerly read:

(ii) within the period within which the debtor or the transferee may serve a notice of objection to an assessment of tax payable under this Part for a taxation year or fiscal period, as the case may be, described in clause (i)(A) or (B), as the case may be;

Forms: T2156 — Transfer Agreement for Transferor of Forgiven Debt Under Section 80.04.

► 80.04(7) ◄

(7) Filing by partnership. For the purpose of subsection (6), where an obligation is settled at any time in a fiscal period of a partnership, it shall be assumed that

(*a*) the partnership is required to file a return of income under this Part for the fiscal period on or before the latest day on or before which any member of the partnership during the fiscal period is required to file a return of income under this Part for the taxation year in which that fiscal period ends (or would be required to file such a return of income if tax under this Part were payable by the member for that year); and

(*b*) the partnership may serve a notice of objection described in subparagraph (6)(*a*)(ii) within each period within which any member of the partnership during the fiscal period may serve a notice of objection to tax payable under this Part for a taxation year in which that fiscal period ends.

► 80.04(8) ◄

(8) Related corporations. Where at any time a corporation becomes related to another corporation and it can reasonably be considered that the main purpose of the corporation becoming related to the other corporation is to enable the corporations to file an agreement under this section, the amount specified in the agreement shall be deemed to be nil for the purpose of the description of C in subsection 80(13).

► 80.04(9) ◄

(9) Assessment of taxpayers in respect of agreement. The Minister shall, notwithstanding subsections 152(4) to (5), assess or reassess the tax, interest and penalties payable under this Act by any taxpayer in order to take into account an agreement filed under this section.

► 80.04(10) ◄

(10) Liability of debtor. Without affecting the liability of any person under any other provision of this Act, where a debtor and an eligible transferee file an agreement between them under this section in respect of an obligation issued by the debtor that was settled at any time, the debtor is, to the extent of 30% of the amount specified in the agreement, liable to pay

(*a*) where the transferee is a corporation, all taxes payable under this Act by it for taxation years that end in the period that begins at that time and ends 4 calendar years after that time;

(*b*) where the transferee is a partnership, the total of all amounts each of which is the tax payable under this Act by a person for a taxation year

(i) that begins or ends in that period, and

(ii) that includes the end of a fiscal period of the partnership during which the person was a member of the partnership; and

(*c*) interest and penalties in respect of such taxes.

► 80.04(11) ◄

(11) Joint and several, or solidary, liability. If taxes, interest and penalties are payable under this Act by a person for a taxation year and those taxes, interest and penalties are payable by a debtor because of subsection (10), the debtor and the person are jointly and severally, or solidarily, liable to pay those amounts.

History: S. 80.04(11) was replaced by S.C. 2013, c. 34, s. 119, in force June 26, 2013, and formerly read:

(11) *Joint liability.* Where taxes, interest and penalties are payable under this Act by a person for a taxation year and those taxes, interest and penalties are payable by a debtor because of subsection (10), the debtor and the person are jointly and severally liable to pay those amounts.

▶ 80.04(12) ◀

(12) Assessments in respect of liability. Where a debtor and an eligible transferee file an agreement between them under this section in respect of an obligation issued by the debtor that was settled at a particular time,

(*a*) where the debtor is an individual or a corporation, the Minister may at any subsequent time assess the debtor in respect of taxes, interest and penalties for which the debtor is liable because of subsection (10); and

(*b*) where the debtor is a partnership, the Minister may at any subsequent time assess any person who has been a member of the partnership in respect of taxes, interest and penalties for which the partnership is liable because of subsection (10), to the extent that those amounts relate to taxation years of the transferee (or, where the transferee is another partnership, members of the other partnership) that end at or after

(i) where the person was not a member of the partnership at the particular time, the first subsequent time the person becomes a member of the partnership, and

(ii) in any other case, the particular time.

▶ 80.04(13) ◀

(13) Application of Division I. The provisions of Division I apply to an assessment under subsection (12) as though it had been made under section 152.

▶ 80.04(14) ◀

(14) Partnership members. For the purposes of paragraphs (10)(*b*) and (12)(*b*) and this subsection, where at any time a member of a particular partnership is another partnership, each member of the other partnership shall be deemed to be a member of the particular partnership at that time.

SECTION 80.1: [Expropriation assets]

▶ 80.1(1) ◀

(1) Expropriation assets acquired as compensation for, or as consideration for sale of, foreign property taken by or sold to foreign issuer. Where in a taxation year ending coincidentally with or after December 31, 1971 a taxpayer resident in Canada has acquired any bonds, debentures, mortgages, hypothecary claims, notes or similar obligations (in this section referred to as "expropriation assets") issued by the government of a country other than Canada or issued by a person resident in a country other than Canada and guaranteed by the government of that country,

(*a*) as compensation for

(i) shares owned by the taxpayer of the capital stock of a foreign affiliate of the taxpayer that carried on business in that country, or

(ii) all or substantially all of the property used by the taxpayer in carrying on business in that country,

(which shares or property, as the case may be, are referred to in this section as "foreign property"), taken, after June 18, 1971, from the taxpayer by the issuer under the authority of a law of that country, or

(*b*) as consideration for the sale of foreign property sold, after June 18, 1971, by the taxpayer to the issuer, if

(i) the sale was, by a law of that country, expressly required to be made, or

(ii) the sale was made after notice or other manifestation of an intention to take the foreign property,

if the taxpayer has so elected, in prescribed form and within prescribed time, in respect of all of the expropriation assets so acquired by the taxpayer, the following rule applies, namely, an amount in respect of each such expropriation asset, equal to

(*c*) the principal amount of the asset, or

(*d*) where the taxpayer has designated in the taxpayer's election an amount in respect of the asset that is less than the principal amount thereof, the amount so designated,

shall be deemed to be

(*e*) the cost to the taxpayer of the asset, and

(*f*) for the purpose of computing the taxpayer's proceeds of disposition of the foreign property so taken or sold, the amount received by the taxpayer by virtue of the taxpayer's acquisition of the asset,

except that in no case may the taxpayer designate an amount in respect of any expropriation asset so that the taxpayer's proceeds of disposition of the foreign property so taken or sold (computed having regard to the provisions of paragraph (*f*)) are less than the cost amount to the taxpayer of the foreign property immediately before it was so taken or sold.

Related Regulations: 600(*b*); 4500.

Related Sections: S. 53(1) Adjustments to cost base; s. 53(2) Amounts to be deducted; s. 80.1(4) Assets acquired from foreign affiliate of taxpayer as dividend in kind or as benefit to shareholder; s. 80.1(5) Assets acquired from foreign affiliate of taxpayer as consideration for settlement, etc., of debt; s. 80.1(6) Assets acquired from foreign affiliate of taxpayer on winding-up, etc; 90 [Dividends and loans from non-resident corporations]; 91 Amounts to be included in respect of share of foreign affiliate; 92 Adjusted cost base of share of foreign affiliate; 93 Election re disposition of share of foreign affiliate; 93.1 Shares held by partnership; 93.2 [Non-resident corporation without share capital]; 93.3 [Australian trust]; 94 [Non-resident trusts]; 94.1 Offshore investment fund property; 94.2 Investments in non-resident commercial trusts; 95 [Foreign accrual property income]; s. 220(3.2) Late, amended or revoked elections.

Forms: T2079 — Election Re: Expropriation Assets Acquired as Compensation for or a Consideration for Sale of Foreign Property Taken by or Sold to Foreign Issuer.

▶ 80.1(2) ◀

(2) Election re interest received or to be received on expropriation assets acquired by taxpayer. Where a taxpayer has elected in prescribed form and within prescribed time in respect of all amounts (each of which is referred to in this section as an "interest amount") received or to be received by the taxpayer as or on account of interest on all expropriation assets acquired by the taxpayer as compensation for, or as consideration for the sale of, foreign property taken by or sold to any particular issuer as described in subsection (1), the following rules apply in respect of each such asset so acquired by the taxpayer:

(*a*) in computing the taxpayer's income for a taxation year from the asset, there may be deducted, in respect of each interest amount received by the taxpayer in the year on the asset, the lesser of the interest amount and the total of

(i) the amount required by paragraph (*b*) to be added, by virtue of the receipt by the taxpayer of the interest amount, in computing the adjusted cost base to the taxpayer of the asset, and

(ii) the greater of

(A) the adjusted cost base to the taxpayer of the asset immediately before the interest amount was so received by the taxpayer, and

(B) the adjusted principal amount to the taxpayer of the asset immediately before the interest amount was so received by the taxpayer,

and there shall be included, in respect of each amount (in this paragraph referred to as a "capital amount") received by the taxpayer in the year as, on account or in lieu of payment of, or in satisfaction of,

(iii) any proceeds of disposition of the asset, or

(iv) the principal amount of the asset,

the amount, if any, by which the capital amount exceeds the greater of the adjusted cost base to the taxpayer of the asset immediately before the capital amount was received by the taxpayer and its adjusted principal amount to the taxpayer at that time;

(*b*) in computing, at any particular time, the adjusted cost base to the taxpayer of the asset, there shall be added, in respect of each interest amount received by the taxpayer on the asset before the particular time, an amount equal to the lesser of

(i) any income or profits tax paid by the taxpayer to the government of a country other than Canada in respect of the interest amount, and

(ii) that proportion of the tax referred to in subparagraph (i) that the adjusted cost base to the taxpayer of the asset immediately before the interest amount was received by the taxpayer is of the amount, if any, by which the interest amount exceeds the tax referred to in that subparagraph,

and there shall be deducted

(iii) each interest amount received by the taxpayer on the asset before the particular time, and

(iv) each amount received by the taxpayer before the particular time on account of the principal amount of the asset;

(*c*) the receipt by the taxpayer of an amount described in subparagraph (*b*)(iv) in respect of the asset shall be deemed not to be a partial disposition thereof; and

(*d*) for the purposes of section 126, notwithstanding the definition "non-business-income tax" in subsection 126(7), the "non-business-income tax" paid by a taxpayer does not include any tax, or any portion thereof, the amount of which is required by paragraph (*b*) to be added in computing the adjusted cost base to the taxpayer of the asset.

Related Regulations: 4500.

Related Sections: S. 80.1(3) Where interest amount and capital amount received at same time; s. 80.1(7) Definition of "adjusted principal amount"; s. 80.1(8) Currency in which adjusted principal amount to be computed or expressed; s. 80.1(9) Election in respect of two or more expropriation assets acquired by taxpayer.

Forms: T2079 — Election Re: Expropriation Assets Acquired as Compensation for or a Consideration for Sale of Foreign Property Taken by or Sold to Foreign Issuer.

▶ 80.1(3) ◀

(3) Where interest amount and capital amount received at same time. For the purposes of subsection (2), where an interest amount on an expropriation asset and a capital amount with respect to that asset are received by a taxpayer at the same time, the interest amount shall be deemed to have been received by the taxpayer immediately before the capital amount.

▶ 80.1(4) ◀

(4) Assets acquired from foreign affiliate of taxpayer as dividend in kind or as benefit to shareholder. Where a foreign affiliate of a taxpayer resident in Canada would, on the assumption that the foreign affiliate were resident in Canada and its only foreign affiliates were corporations that were foreign affiliates of the taxpayer, be entitled to make an election under subsection (1) in respect of assets acquired by it that would, on that assumption, be expropriation assets of the foreign affiliate, and all or any of those assets are subsequently acquired by the taxpayer from the foreign affiliate as a dividend payable in kind, or as a benefit received from the foreign affiliate that would otherwise be required by subsection 15(1) to be included in computing the income of the taxpayer, if the taxpayer has so elected, in prescribed form and within prescribed time, in respect of all assets so acquired by the taxpayer from the foreign affiliate, the following rules apply in respect of each asset so acquired by the taxpayer:

(*a*) an amount equal to

(i) the principal amount of the asset, or

(ii) where the taxpayer has designated in the taxpayer's election an amount in respect of the asset that is less than the principal amount thereof, the amount so designated,

shall be deemed to be,

(iii) notwithstanding subsection 52(2), the cost to the taxpayer of the asset, and

(iv) the amount of the dividend or benefit, as the case may be, received by the taxpayer by virtue of the acquisition by the taxpayer of the asset;

(*b*) where the asset was so acquired as such a benefit and the taxpayer has designated in the election a class of shares as described in this paragraph in respect of the asset, the amount of the benefit shall be deemed

(i) to have been received by the taxpayer as a dividend from the foreign affiliate in respect of such class of shares of the capital stock thereof as the taxpayer has designated in the election, and

(ii) not to be an amount required by subsection 15(1) to be included in computing the taxpayer's income;

(c) in computing the taxable income of the taxpayer for the taxation year in which the taxpayer acquired the asset, there may be deducted from the taxpayer's income for the year the amount, if any, by which the amount received by the taxpayer as a dividend by virtue of the acquisition by the taxpayer of the asset exceeds the total of amounts deductible in respect of the dividend under sections 91 and 113 in computing the taxpayer's income or taxable income, as the case may be, for the year;

(d) there shall be deducted in computing the adjusted cost base to the taxpayer of each share of the capital stock of the foreign affiliate that is a share of a class in respect of which an amount was received by the taxpayer as a dividend by virtue of the acquisition by the taxpayer of the asset, the quotient obtained by dividing the amount, if any, deducted by the taxpayer under paragraph (c) in respect of the dividend by the number of shares of that class owned by the taxpayer immediately before that amount was received by the taxpayer as a dividend;

(e) any capital loss of the taxpayer from the disposition, after the time when the asset was so acquired by the taxpayer, of a share of the capital stock of the foreign affiliate shall be deemed to be nil; and

(f) where the taxpayer has so elected in prescribed form and within prescribed time, subsection (2) applies as if the asset were an expropriation asset acquired by the taxpayer as compensation for foreign property taken by a particular issuer as described in subsection (1).

Related Regulations: 600(b); 4500.

Related Sections: S. 53(2)(b) Amounts to be deducted — Share of non-resident corporation; s. 220(3.2) Late, amended or revoked elections.

Forms: T2079 — Election Re: Expropriation Assets Acquired as Compensation for or a Consideration for Sale of Foreign Property Taken by or Sold to Foreign Issuer.

Information Circulars: IC 07-1 Taxpayer relief provisions.

► 80.1(5) ◄

(5) Assets acquired from foreign affiliate of taxpayer as consideration for settlement, etc., of debt. Where a foreign affiliate of a taxpayer resident in Canada would, on the assumption that the foreign affiliate were resident in Canada and its only foreign affiliates were corporations that were foreign affiliates of the taxpayer, be entitled to make an election under subsection (1) in respect of assets acquired by it that would, on that assumption, be expropriation assets of the foreign affiliate, and all or any of those assets are subsequently acquired by the taxpayer from the foreign affiliate as consideration for the settlement or extinguishment of a capital property of the taxpayer that was a debt payable by the foreign affiliate to the taxpayer or any other obligation of the foreign affiliate to pay an amount to the taxpayer (which debt or other obligation is referred to in this subsection as the "obligation"), if the taxpayer has so elected, in prescribed form and within prescribed time, in respect of all of the assets so acquired by the taxpayer from the foreign affiliate, the following rules apply in respect of each such asset so acquired by the taxpayer:

(a) paragraph (4)(a) applies in respect of the asset as if subparagraph (4)(a)(iv) were read as follows:

"(iv) the taxpayer's proceeds of the disposition of the obligation settled or extinguished by virtue of the acquisition by the taxpayer of the asset;";

(b) where the taxpayer has designated in the taxpayer's election a class of shares as described in this paragraph in respect of the asset,

(i) the amount, if any, by which the cost to the taxpayer of the asset (computed having regard to paragraph (a) and paragraph (4)(a)) exceeds the amount of the obligation settled or extinguished by virtue of the acquisition by the taxpayer of the asset shall be deemed to have been received by the taxpayer as a dividend from the foreign affiliate in respect of such class of shares of the capital stock thereof as the taxpayer has designated in the election, and

(ii) the taxpayer's gain, if any, from the disposition of the obligation shall be deemed to be nil;

(c) the taxpayer's loss, if any, from the disposition of the obligation shall be deemed to be nil; and

(d) paragraphs (4)(c) to (f) apply in respect of the asset.

Related Regulations: 4500.

Forms: T2079 — Election Re: Expropriation Assets Acquired as Compensation for or a Consideration for Sale of Foreign Property Taken by or Sold to Foreign Issuer.

► 80.1(6) ◄

(6) Assets acquired from foreign affiliate of taxpayer on winding-up, etc. Where a foreign affiliate of a taxpayer resident in Canada would, on the assumption that the foreign affiliate were resident in Canada and its only foreign affiliates were corporations that were foreign affiliates of the taxpayer, be entitled to make an election under subsection (1) in respect of assets acquired by it that would, on that assumption, be expropriation assets of the foreign affiliate, and all or any of those assets are subsequently acquired by the taxpayer from the foreign affiliate,

(a) on the winding-up, discontinuance or reorganization of the business of the foreign affiliate, or

(b) as consideration for the redemption, cancellation or acquisition by the foreign affiliate of shares of its capital stock,

if the taxpayer has so elected, in prescribed form and within prescribed time,

(c) in respect of all of the assets so acquired by the taxpayer from the foreign affiliate, subsection (1) applies in respect of each such asset, or

(d) in respect of all amounts received or to be received by the taxpayer as or on account of interest on all of the assets so acquired by the taxpayer from the foreign affiliate, subsection (2) applies in respect of each such asset,

as if the assets were expropriation assets acquired by the taxpayer as consideration for the sale of foreign property that consisted of shares of the capital stock of the foreign affiliate owned by the taxpayer immediately before the assets were so acquired and that was sold to a particular issuer as described in subsection (1).

Related Regulations: 4500.

Forms: T2079 — Election Re: Expropriation Assets Acquired as Compensation for or a Consideration for Sale of Foreign Property Taken by or Sold to Foreign Issuer.

► 80.1(7) ◄

(7) Definition of "adjusted principal amount". In this section, "adjusted principal amount" to a taxpayer of an expropriation asset at any particular time means the amount, if any, by which

(*a*) the total of the principal amount of the asset and, in respect of each interest amount received by the taxpayer on the asset before the particular time, the lesser of the tax referred to in subparagraph (2)(*b*)(i) in respect of that interest amount and the proportion determined under subparagraph (2)(*b*)(ii) in respect thereof,

exceeds

(*b*) the total of each amount received by the taxpayer before the particular time as an interest amount on the asset and each amount received by the taxpayer before the particular time as, on account or in lieu of payment of, or in satisfaction of, the principal amount of the asset.

Related Sections: S. 80.1(9) Election in respect of two or more expropriation assets acquired by taxpayer.

► 80.1(8) ◄

(8) Currency in which adjusted principal amount to be computed or expressed. For the purposes of this section, the adjusted principal amount, at any particular time, of an expropriation asset or of any asset assumed for the purposes of this section to be an expropriation asset shall be computed in the currency in which the principal amount of the asset is, under the terms thereof, payable, except that for greater certainty, for the purposes of paragraph (2)(*a*), the adjusted principal amount at any particular time of such an asset is its adjusted principal amount at that time computed as provided in this subsection but expressed in Canadian currency.

Related Sections: S. 80.1(9) Election in respect of two or more expropriation assets acquired by taxpayer.

► 80.1(9) ◄

(9) Election in respect of two or more expropriation assets acquired by taxpayer. For the purposes of subdivision c and subsection (2), and in applying subsections (7) and (8) for those purposes, where two or more expropriation assets that were

(*a*) issued by the government of a country other than Canada, or

(*b*) issued by a person resident in a country other than Canada and guaranteed by the government of that country

at the same time, or as compensation for, or consideration for the sale of, the same foreign property, have been acquired by a taxpayer and the taxpayer has so elected, in prescribed form and within prescribed time, in respect of all of the expropriation assets that were so issued or guaranteed by the government of that country and acquired by the taxpayer before the making of the election, all of those expropriation assets shall be considered to be a single expropriation asset that was issued or guaranteed by the government of that country and acquired by the taxpayer.

Related Regulations: 4500.

Forms: T2079 — Election Re: Expropriation Assets Acquired as Compensation for or a Consideration for Sale of Foreign Property Taken by or Sold to Foreign Issuer.

SECTION 80.2: [Reimbursement of Crown charges]

► 80.2(1) ◄

(1) Application. Subsections (2) to (13) apply if

(*a*) in a taxation year, a taxpayer, under the terms of a contract, pays to a person (referred to in this section as the "recipient") an amount (referred to in this section as the "specified amount") that may reasonably be considered to be received by the recipient as a reimbursement of, or a contribution or an allowance in respect of, an amount (referred to in this section as the "original amount")

(i) that was described by paragraph 18(1)(*m*) and was paid or payable by the recipient, or

(ii) that was, in respect of the recipient, an amount described by paragraph 12(1)(*o*);

(*b*) the original amount is paid or became payable or receivable in a taxation year or fiscal period of the recipient that begins before 2007; and

(*c*) the taxpayer is resident in Canada or carries on business in Canada when the specified amount is paid.

History: S. 80.2(1) was added by S.C. 2013, c. 34, s. 215(1), applicable in respect of specified amounts paid after 2001.

Where a person is liable to an amount of tax under Part I of the Act for a taxation year that exceeds the amount to which the person would be liable if section 80.2 of the Act applied as it read on December 31, 2001, the person is deemed, for the purpose of determining any interest or penalty payable by that person, to have paid the excess on that person's balance-due day, if

(*a*) the person's balance-due day for the taxation year was before September 17, 2004; and

(*b*) the excess was paid to the Receiver General before March 2005.

Notwithstanding subsections 152(4) to (5) of the Act, all assessments, determinations, and redeterminations may be made as necessary to give effect to the addition of section 80.2.

Interpretation Bulletins: *Secondary* — IT-438R2 Crown charges — Resource properties in Canada.

► 80.2(2) ◄

(2) Rules relating to time of payment. If the specified amount is paid in a taxation year of the taxpayer that begins before 2008, the eligible portion of the specified amount, referred to in subsection (11), is deemed to be a payment described by paragraph 18(1)(*m*). If, however, the specified amount is paid in a taxation year of the taxpayer that begins after 2007, the specified amount is deemed, for the purpose of applying this section to the taxpayer, to be nil.

History: S. 80.2(2) was added by S.C. 2013, c. 34, s. 215(1), applicable in respect of specified amounts paid after 2001.

See s. 80.2(1) for additional assessment provisions regarding tax liability under s. 80.2.

► 80.2(3) ◄

(3) Applying paragraph 18(1)(*m*). For the purpose of applying paragraph 18(1)(*m*) for the taxpayer's taxation year in which the specified amount was paid, the amount to which that paragraph applies is to be determined for that taxation year

(*a*) if the taxpayer was in existence at the time the original amount became receivable by a person referred to in subparagraph 12(1)(*o*)(i) or became payable to a person referred to in subparagraph 18(1)(*m*)(i), as if the specified amount were paid by the taxpayer at that time; and (*b*) in any other case, as if

(i) the taxpayer were in existence and had a calendar taxation year at the time the original amount became receivable by a person referred to in subparagraph 12(1)(*o*)(i) or became payable to a person referred to in subparagraph 18(1)(*m*)(i), and

(ii) the specified amount were paid by the taxpayer at that time.

History: S. 80.2(3) was added by S.C. 2013, c. 34, s. 215(1), applicable in respect of specified amounts paid after 2001.

See s. 80.2(1) for additional assessment provisions regarding tax liability under s. 80.2.

Related Sections: S. 18(1)(*m*) Limitation re employee stock option expenses.

▶ 80.2(4) ◀

(4) Exception for certain partnership reimbursements. Subsection (3) does not apply to a specified amount paid by a taxpayer if

(*a*) the recipient is a partnership;

(*b*) the original amount became receivable by a person referred to in subparagraph 12(1)(*o*)(i) or became payable to a person referred to in subparagraph 18(1)(*m*)(i), in a particular fiscal period of the partnership;

(*c*) the taxpayer is a member of the partnership at the end of the particular fiscal period; and

(*d*) the taxpayer paid the specified amount before the end of the taxation year of the taxpayer in which that particular fiscal period ends.

History: S. 80.2(4) was added by S.C. 2013, c. 34, s. 215(1), applicable in respect of specified amounts paid after 2001.

See s. 80.2(1) for additional assessment provisions regarding tax liability under s. 80.2.

▶ 80.2(5) ◀

(5) Specified amount deemed to be paid at end of taxation year. A specified amount paid by the taxpayer to a partnership is deemed to have been paid on the last day of a particular taxation year of the taxpayer, and not at the time it was paid, if

(*a*) the taxpayer paid an amount to the partnership in the particular taxation year (referred to in this subsection as the "initial payment");

(*b*) the initial payment was paid before September 17, 2004;

(*c*) the initial payment is an amount to which subsection (3) did not apply because of subsection (4);

(*d*) the taxpayer's share of the original amount in respect of the initial payment is greater than the initial payment;

(*e*) the specified amount is equal to or less than the difference between the taxpayer's share of the original amount in respect of the initial payment and the initial payment;

(*f*) the taxpayer elects in the taxpayer's return of income for the taxpayer's taxation year that includes the time at which the specified amount would, if this Act were read without reference to this subsection, have been paid, to have this subsection apply to the specified amount; and

(*g*) the specified amount is paid before 2006.

History: S. 80.2(5) was added by S.C. 2013, c. 34, s. 215(1), applicable in respect of specified amounts paid after 2001.

See s. 80.2(1) for additional assessment provisions regarding tax liability under s. 80.2.

▶ 80.2(6) ◀

(6) Inclusion in recipient's income. The recipient shall include in computing the recipient's income for the taxation year or fiscal period in which the original amount was paid or became payable or receivable, the amount, if any, by which the eligible portion of the specified amount exceeds the portion of the original amount that was included in computing the income of the recipient for the taxation year or fiscal period because of paragraph 12(1)(*o*) or that was not deductible in computing the income of the recipient for the taxation year or fiscal period because of paragraph 18(1)(*m*).

History: S. 80.2(6) was added by S.C. 2013, c. 34, s. 215(1), applicable in respect of specified amounts paid after 2001.

See s. 80.2(1) for additional assessment provisions regarding tax liability under s. 80.2.

▶ 80.2(7) ◀

(7) Interpretation — portion of the original amount. For the purpose of subsection (6), the portion of the original amount that was included in computing the income of the recipient or that was not deductible in computing the income of the recipient is the amount that would be included in computing the income of the recipient under paragraph 12(1)(*o*) or that would not be deductible in computing the income of the recipient under paragraph 18(1)(*m*), if the original amount were equal to the eligible portion of the specified amount.

History: S. 80.2(7) was added by S.C. 2013, c. 34, s. 215(1), applicable in respect of specified amounts paid after 2001.

See s. 80.2(1) for additional assessment provisions regarding tax liability under s. 80.2.

▶ 80.2(8) ◀

(8) Inclusion in recipient's income. The recipient shall include, in computing the recipient's income for its taxation year or fiscal period in which the original amount was paid or became payable or receivable, the amount, if any, by which the specified amount exceeds the eligible portion of the specified amount.

History: S. 80.2(8) was added by S.C. 2013, c. 34, s. 215(1), applicable in respect of specified amounts paid after 2001.

See s. 80.2(1) for additional assessment provisions regarding tax liability under s. 80.2.

▶ 80.2(9) ◀

(9) Deduction by taxpayer. Subject to paragraphs 18(1)(*a*) and (*b*), the taxpayer may deduct in computing the taxpayer's income for the taxpayer's taxation year in which the specified amount was paid, the amount, if any, by which the specified amount exceeds the eligible portion of the specified amount.

History: S. 80.2(9) was added by S.C. 2013, c. 34, s. 215(1), applicable in respect of specified amounts paid after 2001.

See s. 80.2(1) for additional assessment provisions regarding tax liability under s. 80.2.

▶ 80.2(10) ◀

(10) Specified amount deemed not to be payable or receivable. Except for the purposes of this section and subparagraph 53(1)(*e*)(iv.1),

(*a*) the taxpayer is deemed not to have paid, and not to have been obligated to pay, the specified amount; and (*b*) the recipient is deemed not to have received, and not to have been entitled to receive, the specified amount.

History: S. 80.2(10) was added by S.C. 2013, c. 34, s. 215(1), applicable in respect of specified amounts paid after 2001.

See s. 80.2(1) for additional assessment provisions regarding tax liability under s. 80.2.

▶ 80.2(11) ◀

(11) Eligible portion of a specified amount. The eligible portion of a specified amount is

(*a*) an amount equal to the specified amount if

(i) the specified amount was paid before September 17, 2004,

(ii) the original amount is a tax imposed under a provincial law on the production of

(A) petroleum, natural gas or related hydrocarbons from a natural accumulation of petroleum or natural gas (other than a mineral resource) located in Canada, or from an oil or gas well located in Canada if the petroleum, natural gas or related hydrocarbons are not, before extraction, owned by the Crown in right of Canada or a province, or

(B) metals, minerals or coal from a mineral resource located in Canada if the metals, minerals or coal are not, before extraction, owned by the Crown in right of Canada or a province,

(iii) the specified amount does not exceed the taxpayer's share of the original amount, or

(iv) the original amount is a prescribed amount; and

(*b*) the taxpayer's share of the original amount, in any other case.

History: S. 80.2(11) was added by S.C. 2013, c. 34, s. 215(1), applicable in respect of specified amounts paid after 2001.

See s. 80.2(1) for additional assessment provisions regarding tax liability under s. 80.2.

▶ 80.2(12) ◀

(12) Taxpayer's share of original amount. A taxpayer's share of an original amount in respect of a specified amount paid by the taxpayer to a recipient in respect of a property is the amount that may reasonably be considered to be the taxpayer's share of the total of all amounts described in paragraph 12(1)(*o*) or 18(1)(*m*) in respect of the property, which share may not exceed the total of

(*a*) that proportion of the total of all amounts described in paragraph 12(1)(*o*) or 18(1)(*m*) in respect of the property that the taxpayer's share of production from the property payable to the taxpayer as a royalty, which royalty is computed without reference to the costs of exploration or production, is of the total production from the property, and

(*b*) that proportion of the total of all amounts described in paragraph 12(1)(*o*) or 18(1)(*m*) in respect of the property (other than those amounts which the recipient has received or is entitled to receive as a reimbursement, contribution or allowance in respect of a royalty described in paragraph (*a*)) that the taxpayer's share of the income from the property is of the total income from the property.

History: S. 80.2(12) was added by S.C. 2013, c. 34, s. 215(1), applicable in respect of specified amounts paid after 2001.

See s. 80.2(1) for additional assessment provisions regarding tax liability under s. 80.2.

▶ 80.2(13) ◀

(13) Reduction in original amount for Part XII of the regulations. For the purpose of applying Part XII of the *Income Tax Regulations*, an original amount in respect of which a specified amount is received is deemed, for the taxation year in which the original amount was paid or became payable or receivable, not to include an amount equal to the eligible portion of the specified amount.

History: S. 80.2(13) was added by S.C. 2013, c. 34, s. 215(1), applicable in respect of specified amounts paid after 2001.

See s. 80.2(1) for additional assessment provisions regarding tax liability under s. 80.2.

SECTION 80.3: [Income deferral — Forced destruction of livestock or sale in drought or flood regions]

▶ 80.3(1) ◀

(1) Definitions. In this section,

"breeding animals" —"breeding animals" means deer, elk and other similar grazing ungulates, bovine cattle, bison, goats, sheep and horses that are over 12 months of age and are kept for breeding;

History: S. 80.3(1), the definition "breeding animals" was replaced by S.C. 2014, c. 39, s. 17(1), applicable to the 2014 and subsequent taxation years, and formerly read:

"breeding animals" —"breeding animals" means

(*a*) horses that are over 12 months of age and are kept for breeding in the commercial production of pregnant mares' urine, and

(*b*) deer, elk and other similar grazing ungulates, bovine cattle, bison, goats and sheep that are over 12 months of age and are kept for breeding;

Interpretation Bulletins: *Secondary* — IT-425 Miscellaneous farm income.

"breeding bees" —"breeding bees" means bees that are not used principally to pollinate plants in greenhouses and larvae of those bees;

History: S. 80.3(1), the definition "breeding bees" was added by S.C. 2014, c. 39, s. 17(2), applicable to the 2014 and subsequent taxation years.

"breeding bee stock" —"breeding bee stock", of a taxpayer at any time, means a reasonable estimate of the quantity of a taxpayer's breeding bees held at that time in the course of carrying on a farming business using a unit of measurement that is accepted as an industry standard;

History: S. 80.3(1), the definition "breeding bee stock" was added by S.C. 2014, c. 39, s. 17(2), applicable to the 2014 and subsequent taxation years.

"breeding herd" —"breeding herd" of a taxpayer at any time means the number determined by the formula

$$A - (B - C)$$

where

A is the total number of the taxpayer's breeding animals held in the course of carrying on a farming business at that time,

B is the total number of the taxpayer's breeding animals held in the business at that time that are female bovine cattle that have not given birth to calves, and

C is the lesser of the number determined as the value of B and one-half the total number of the taxpayer's breeding animals held in the business at that time that are female bovine cattle that have given birth to calves.

Interpretation Bulletins: *Secondary* — IT-425 Miscellaneous farm income.

▶ 80.3(2) ◀

(2) Income deferral from the destruction of livestock. Where a particular amount in respect of the forced destruction of livestock under statutory authority in a taxation year of a taxpayer is included in computing the income of the taxpayer for the year from a farming business, there may be deducted in computing that income such amount as the taxpayer claims not exceeding the particular amount.

Related Sections: S. 11(2) Reference to "taxation year".

▶ 80.3(3) ◀

(3) Inclusion of deferred amount. The amount deducted under subsection (2) in computing the income of a taxpayer from a farming business for a taxation year shall be deemed to be income of the taxpayer from the business for the taxpayer's immediately following taxation year.

▶ 80.3(4) ◀

(4) Income deferral for regions of drought, flood or excessive moisture. If in a taxation year a taxpayer carries on a farming business in a region that is at any time in the year a prescribed drought region or a prescribed region of flood or excessive moisture and the taxpayer's breeding herd at the end of the year in respect of the business does not exceed 85% of the taxpayer's breeding herd at the beginning of the year in respect of the business, there may be deducted in computing the taxpayer's income from the business for the year the amount that the taxpayer claims, not exceeding the amount, if any, determined by the formula

$$(A - B) \times C$$

where

A is the amount by which

(*a*) the total of all amounts included in computing the taxpayer's income for the year from the business in respect of the sale of breeding animals in the year

exceeds

(*b*) the total of all amounts deducted under paragraph 20(1)(*n*) in computing the taxpayer's income from the business for the year in respect of an amount referred to in paragraph (*a*) of this description;

B is the total of all amounts deducted in computing the taxpayer's income from the business for the year in respect of the acquisition of breeding animals; and

C is

(*a*) 30% where the taxpayer's breeding herd at the end of the year in respect of the business exceeds 70% of the taxpayer's breeding herd at the beginning of the year in respect of the business, and

(*b*) 90% where the taxpayer's breeding herd at the end of the year in respect of the business does not exceed 70% of the taxpayer's breeding herd at the beginning of the year in respect of the business.

History: S. 80.3(4), the portion before the formula was replaced by S.C. 2009, c. 31, s. 2(1), applicable to the 2008 and subsequent taxation years. S. 80.3(4), the portion before the formula formerly read:

(4) *Income deferral for sales in prescribed drought region.* Where in a taxation year a taxpayer carries on a farming business in a region that is a prescribed drought region at any time in the year and the taxpayer's breeding herd at the end of the year in respect of the business does not exceed 85% of the taxpayer's breeding herd at the beginning of the year in respect of the business, there may be deducted in computing the taxpayer's income from the business for the year such amount as the taxpayer claims, not exceeding the amount, if any, determined by the formula

Related Regulations: 7305; 7305.01; 7305.02.

Related Sections: 28(1) Farming or fishing business; S. 11(2) Reference to "taxation year".

▶ 80.3(4.1) ◀

(4.1) Income deferral. If in a taxation year a taxpayer carries on a farming business in a region that is at any time in the year a prescribed drought region or a prescribed region of flood or excessive moisture and the taxpayer's breeding bee stock at the end of the year in respect of the business does not exceed 85% of the taxpayer's breeding bee stock at the beginning of the year in respect of the business, there may be deducted in computing the taxpayer's income from the business for the year the amount that the taxpayer claims, not exceeding the amount, if any, determined by the formula

$$(A - B) \times C$$

where

A is the amount by which

(*a*) the total of all amounts included in computing the taxpayer's income from the business for the year in respect of the sale of breeding bees in the year

exceeds

(*b*) the total of all amounts deducted under paragraph 20(1)(*n*) in computing the taxpayer's income from the business for the year in respect of an amount referred to in paragraph (*a*);

B is the total of all amounts deducted in computing the taxpayer's income from the business for the year in respect of the acquisition of breeding bees; and

C is

(*a*) 30% if the taxpayer's breeding bee stock in respect of the business at the end of the year exceeds 70% of the taxpayer's breeding bee stock in respect of the business at the beginning of the year, and

(*b*) 90% if the taxpayer's breeding bee stock in respect of the business at the end of the year does not exceed 70% of the taxpayer's breeding bee stock in respect of the business at the beginning of the year.

History: S. 80.3(4.1) was added by S.C. 2014, c. 39, s. 17(3), applicable to the 2014 and subsequent taxation years.

Related Sections: 28(1) Farming or fishing business; 80.3(1) breeding bees; 80.3(1) breeding bee stock; 80.3(7) Measuring breeding bee stock.

▶ 80.3(5) ◀

(5) Inclusion of deferred amount. An amount deducted under subsection (4) or (4.1) in computing the income of a taxpayer for a particular taxation year from a farming business carried on in a region prescribed under those subsections may, to the extent that the taxpayer so elects, be included in computing the taxpayer's income from the business for a taxation year ending after the particular taxation year, and is, except to the extent that the amount has been included under this subsection in computing the taxpayer's income from the business for a preceding taxation year after the particular year, deemed to be income of the taxpayer from the business for the taxation year of the taxpayer that is the earliest of

(*a*) the first taxation year beginning after the end of the period or series of continuous periods, as the case may be, for which the region is prescribed under those subsections, (*b*) the first taxation year, following the particular taxation year, at the end of which the taxpayer is

(i) non-resident, and

(ii) not carrying on business through a fixed place of business in Canada, and

(*c*) the taxation year in which the taxpayer dies.

History: S. 80.3(5), the portion before paragraph (*b*) was replaced by S.C. 2014, c. 39, s. 17(4), applicable to the 2014 and subsequent taxation years, and formerly read:

(5) *Inclusion of deferred amount.* The amount deducted under subsection (4) in computing the income of a taxpayer for a particular taxation year from a farming business carried on in a region prescribed under that subsection may, to the extent that the taxpayer so elects, be included in computing the taxpayer's income from the business for a taxation year ending after the particular taxation year, and is, except to the extent that the amount has been included under this subsection in computing the taxpayer's income from the business for a preceding taxation year after the particular year, deemed to be income of the taxpayer from the business for the taxation year of the taxpayer that is the earliest of

(*a*) the first taxation year beginning after the end of the period or series of continuous periods, as the case may be, for which the region is prescribed under that subsection,

S. 80.3(5), the portion before paragraph (*b*) was replaced by S.C. 2009, c. 31, s. 2(2), applicable to the 2008 and subsequent taxation years. S. 80.3(5), the portion before paragraph (*b*) formerly read:

(5) *Inclusion of deferred amount.* The amount deducted under subsection (4) in computing the income of a taxpayer for a particular taxation year from a farming business carried on in a prescribed drought region may, to the extent that the taxpayer so elects, be included in computing the taxpayer's income from the business for a taxation year ending after the particular taxation year, and shall, except to the extent that the amount has been included under this subsection in computing the taxpayer's income from the business for a preceding taxation year after the particular year, be deemed to be income of the taxpayer from the business for the taxation year of the taxpayer that is the earliest of

(*a*) the first taxation year beginning after the end of the period or series of continuous periods, as the case may be, for which the region is a prescribed drought region,

► 80.3(6) ◄

(6) Subsections (2), (4) and (4.1) not applicable. Subsections (2), (4) and (4.1) do not apply to a taxpayer in respect of a farming business for a taxation year

(*a*) in which the taxpayer died; or

(*b*) where at the end of the year the taxpayer is non-resident and not carrying on the business through a fixed place of business in Canada.

History: S. 80.3(6), the portion before paragraph (*a*) was replaced by S.C. 2014, c. 39, s. 14(5), applicable to the 2014 and subsequent taxation years, and formerly read:

(6) *Where s. (2) and (4) do not apply.* Subsections (2) and (4) do not apply to a taxpayer in respect of a farming business for a taxation year

► 80.3(7) ◄

(7) Measuring breeding bee stock. In applying subsection (4.1) in respect of a taxation year, the unit of measurement used for estimating the quantity of a taxpayer's breeding bee stock held in the course of carrying on a farming business at the end of the year is to be the same as that used for the beginning of the year.

History: S. 80.3(7) was added by S.C. 2014, c. 39, s. 14(6), applicable to the 2014 and subsequent taxation years.

SECTION 80.4: Loans

► 80.4(1) ◄

(1) Loans. Where a person or partnership receives a loan or otherwise incurs a debt because of or as a consequence of a previous, the current or an intended office or employment of an individual, or because of the services performed or to be performed by a corporation carrying on a personal services business, the individual or corporation, as the case may be, shall be deemed to have received a benefit in a taxation year equal to the amount, if any, by which the total of

(*a*) all interest on all such loans and debts computed at the prescribed rate on each such loan and debt for the period in the year during which it was outstanding, and

(*b*) the total of all amounts each of which is an amount of interest that was paid or payable in respect of the year on such a loan or debt by

(i) a person or partnership (in this paragraph referred to as the "employer") that employed or intended to employ the individual,

(ii) a person (other than the debtor) related to the employer, or

(iii) a person or partnership to or for whom or which the services were or were to be provided or performed by the corporation or a person (other than the debtor) who does not deal at arm's length with that person or any member of that partnership,

exceeds the total of

(*c*) the amount of interest for the year paid on all such loans and debts not later than 30 days after the end of the year, and

(*d*) any portion of the total determined in respect of the year under paragraph (*b*) that is reimbursed in the year or within 30 days after the end of the year by the debtor to the person or entity who made the payment referred to in that paragraph.

Editorial Note: If the loan is used for income-earning purposes, an offsetting deduction is normally allowed under s. 80.5. See also the special treatment for home purchase loans (s. 80.4(4)) (and, prior to January 1, 2018, home relocation loans (s. 110(1)(*j*))).

Related Regulations: 4301.

Related Sections: S. 6(9) Amount in respect of interest on employee debt; s. 6(23) Employer-provided housing subsidies; s. 12(1)(*w*) S. 80.4(1) benefit; s. 15(9) Deemed benefit to shareholder by corporation; s. 79(3) Proceeds of disposition for debtor; s. 80(1), "forgiven amount"; s. 80.4(2) Loan or debt by virtue of shareholding; s. 80.5 Deemed interest; s. 110(1)(*j*) Home relocation loan; s. 125(7), "personal services business"; s. 248(1), "corporation", "employment", "home relocation loan", "individual", "office".

Canadian Petroleum Tax Journal: Attracting and Retaining Executives and Employees with Tax-Efficient Incentives, Julie Y. Lee, 2001, Vol. 14, No. 1.

Guides: T4130 Employers Guide to Payroll Deductions — Taxable Benefits.

Interpretation Bulletins: *Primary* — IT-421R2 Benefits to individuals, corporations and shareholders from loans or debt. *Secondary* — IT-73R6 The small business deduction.

Tax Window Files: Application of Subsection 80.4(1) — Group Housing Benefit, *April 20, 2006*, CRA Document No. 2005-0154531E5.

► 80.4(1.1) ◄

(1.1) Interpretation. A loan or debt is deemed to have been received or incurred because of an individual's office or employment, or because of services performed by a corporation that carries on a personal services business, as the case may be, if it is reasonable to conclude that, but for an individual's previous, current or intended office or employment, or the services performed or to be performed by the corporation,

(*a*) the terms of the loan or debt would have been different; or

(*b*) the loan would not have been received or the debt would not have been incurred.

Editorial Note: This provision was added in response to the *Siwik* decision (97 DTC 5444 (F.C.A.), affirming 96 DTC 1678 (T.C.C.)), where the court reasoned that s. 80.4(1) did not apply because the loan at issue was received by an employee from his employer for the purpose of purchasing a new home, and not because of or as a consequence of the employee's employment.

Related Sections: S. 6(23) Employer-provided housing subsidies; s. 62(1) Moving expenses; s. 110(1)(*j*) Home relocation loan; s. 248(1), "eligible relocation", "home relocation loan".

▶ 80.4(2) ◀

(2) Idem. Where a person (other than a corporation resident in Canada) or a partnership (other than a partnership each member of which is a corporation resident in Canada) was

(*a*) a shareholder of a corporation,

(*b*) connected with a shareholder of a corporation, or

(*c*) a member of a partnership, or a beneficiary of a trust, that was a shareholder of a corporation,

and by virtue of that shareholding that person or partnership received a loan from, or otherwise incurred a debt to, that corporation, any other corporation related thereto or a partnership of which that corporation or any corporation related thereto was a member, the person or partnership shall be deemed to have received a benefit in a taxation year equal to the amount, if any, by which

(*d*) all interest on all such loans and debts computed at the prescribed rate on each such loan and debt for the period in the year during which it was outstanding

exceeds

(*e*) the total of

(i) the amount of interest for the year paid on all such loans and debts (other than loans deemed to have been made under subsection 15(2.17)) not later than 30 days after the end of the year, and

(ii) the specified interest amounts, for the year, in respect of all such loans that are deemed to have been made under subsection 15(2.17).

Editorial Note: The imputed interest benefit under subsection 80.4(2) is reduced by the amount of interest actually paid on the loan or debt in the relevant year or by 30 days after the end of the year. Furthermore, for loans and debt incurred after March 21, 2016 and the portion of any previous loans outstanding on that date (which are treated as separate loans), the benefit is reduced by the "specified interest amounts" (subsection 80.4(7)) paid in the year or by 30 days after the end of the year. The specified interest amounts relate to the situation where the back-to-back loans provisions of subsection 15(2.17) apply. In general terms, those provisions can apply where a shareholder of a corporation borrows or becomes indebted to a third party "funder" ("shareholder debt"), and in turn that funder is indebted to (or receives security in respect of a property from) an "ultimate funder", where the ultimate funder is the corporation such that subsection 15(2) would have applied to the shareholder debt had the ultimate funder been the creditor of the shareholder debt.

If the loan is used for income-earning purposes, an offsetting deduction is normally allowed under s. 80.5.

See s. 80.4(8) to determine whether a person is "connected" with a shareholder.

History: S. 80.4(2)(*e*) was replaced by S.C. 2016, c. 12, s. 24(1), applicable in respect of

(*a*) loans received and indebtedness incurred after March 21, 2016; and

(*a*) any portion of a particular loan received or indebtedness incurred before March 22, 2016 that remains outstanding on that day, as if that portion were a separate loan or indebtedness that was received or incurred, as the case may be, on March 22, 2016 in the same manner and on the same terms as the particular loan or indebtedness.

The paragraph formerly read:

(*e*) the amount of interest for the year paid on all such loans and debts not later than 30 days after the later of the end of the year and December 31, 1982.

Related Regulations: 4301.

Related Sections: S. 15(2) Shareholder debt; s. 15(9) Deemed benefit to shareholder by corporation; s. 79(3) Proceeds of disposition for debtor; s. 80(1), "forgiven amount"; s. 80.5 Deemed interest.

Cases: A taxpayer cannot avoid having interest on a loan added to his income by purporting to set-off the debt by means of the *ex post facto* declaration of a dividend. *Wood v. M.N.R.*, 88 DTC 1180 (T.C.C.). Nor can a taxpayer avoid the possibility that the Minister will deem him to have received interest on a debt owed to him by a corporation by virtue of the indebtedness being set-off by drawings received from the corporation. *Gannon v. M.N.R.*, 88 DTC 1282 (T.C.C.) and *Wolf v. M.N.R.*, 92 DTC 1858 (T.C.C.). Similarly, a taxpayer cannot avoid the possibility that the Minister will deem him to have received interest on a loan by purporting to set off accrued but unpaid bonuses against it. *Austin v. M.N.R.*, 91 DTC 778 (T.C.C.)

▶ 80.4(3) ◀

(3) Where ss. (1) and (2) do not apply. Subsections (1) and (2) do not apply in respect of any loan or debt, or any part thereof,

(*a*) on which the rate of interest was equal to or greater than the rate that would, having regard to all the circumstances (including the terms and conditions of the loan or debt), have been agreed on, at the time the loan was received or the debt was incurred, between parties dealing with each other at arm's length if

(i) none of the parties received the loan or incurred the debt by virtue of an office or employment or by virtue of the shareholding of a person or partnership, and

(ii) the ordinary business of the creditor included the lending of money,

except where an amount is paid or payable in any taxation year to the creditor in respect of interest on the loan or debt by a party other than the debtor; or

(*b*) that was included in computing the income of a person or partnership under this Part.

Cases: S. 80.4(3) did not permit the market rate of interest on a portion of the taxpayer's loan to be blended with the rates (at less than market) paid by him on other portion of the loan, so as to reduce his taxable benefit. *Marchand v. The Queen*, 97 DTC 5272 (F.C.A.).

▶ 80.4(4) ◀

(4) Interest on loans for home purchase or relocation. For the purpose of computing the benefit under subsection (1) in a taxation year in respect of a home purchase loan or a home relocation loan, the amount of interest determined under paragraph (1)(*a*) shall not exceed the amount of interest that would have been determined thereunder if it had been computed at the prescribed rate in effect at the time the loan was received or the debt was incurred, as the case may be.

Editorial Note: S. 80.4(4) provides upside protection for employees subject to the deemed interest benefit rules if the prescribed rate of interest increases beyond the rate that was in effect at the time that a home purchase loan (s. 80.4(7)) or home relocation loan (s. 248(1)) was received. For these purposes, if the term of the loan is more than five years, the prescribed rate of interest on the fifth anniversary of the loan (and each subsequent fifth anniversary date) is deemed to be the rate in effect at the time the loan was received, by virtue of s. 80.4(6). In other words, the interest rate "cap" is reset every five years.

History: S. 80.4(4) was replaced by S.C. 2017, c. 20, s. 5(1), in force January 1, 2018, and previously read:

(4) *Interest on loans for home purchase or relocation.* For the purpose of computing the benefit under subsection (1) in a taxation year in respect of a home purchase loan or a home relocation loan and for the purpose of paragraph 110(1)(*j*), the amount of interest determined under paragraph (1)(*a*) shall not exceed the amount of interest that would have been determined thereunder if it had been computed at the prescribed rate in effect at the time the loan was received or the debt was incurred, as the case may be.

Related Regulations: 4301.

Related Sections: S. 80.4(7), "home purchase loan"; s. 248(1), "home relocation loan".

▶ 80.4(5) ◀

(5) Idem. Where an individual has, before November 13, 1981,

(*a*) received a housing loan, or

(*b*) made arrangements in writing in respect of a home purchase loan that would, if the loan were made before 1982, have been a housing loan,

for the purpose of computing the amount of interest referred to in paragraph (1)(*a*) on the loan, the amount of the loan may be reduced

(*c*) for the 1982 taxation year, by the amount, if any, by which $40,000 exceeds the total of

(i) all amounts claimed as a reduction under this subsection for the year by the individual's spouse or common-law partner with whom the individual resided in the year, and

(ii) all amounts claimed as a reduction under this subsection for the year by the individual on all other loans, and

(*d*) for the 1983 taxation year, by the amount, if any, by which $20,000 exceeds the total of

(i) all amounts claimed as a reduction under this subsection for the year by the individual's spouse or common-law partner with whom the individual resided in the year, and

(ii) all amounts claimed as a reduction under this subsection for the year by the individual on all other loans.

▶ 80.4(6) ◀

(6) Deemed new home purchase loans. For the purposes of this section, other than paragraph (3)(*a*) and subsection (5), where a home purchase loan or a home relocation loan of an individual has a term for repayment exceeding five years, the balance outstanding on the loan on the date that is five years from the day the loan was received or was last deemed by this subsection to have been received shall be deemed to be a new home purchase loan received by the individual on that date.

Editorial Note: See the editorial note under s. 80.4(4).

▶ 80.4(7) ◀

(7) Definitions. In this section,

"home purchase loan" —"home purchase loan" means that portion of any loan received or debt otherwise incurred by an individual in the circumstances described in subsection (1) that is used to acquire, or to repay a loan or debt that was received or incurred to acquire, a dwelling, or a share of the capital stock of a cooperative housing corporation acquired for the sole purpose of acquiring the right to inhabit a dwelling owned by the corporation, where the dwelling is for the habitation of

(*a*) the individual by virtue of whose office or employment the loan is received or the debt is incurred,

(*b*) a specified shareholder of the corporation by virtue of whose services the loan is received or the debt is incurred, or

(*c*) a person related to a person described in paragraph (*a*) or (*b*),

or that is used to repay a home purchase loan;

Tax Window Files: Employer Assisted Mortgage, *March 8, 2011*, CRA Document No. 2010-0384201E5.

"prescribed rate" —"prescribed rate" of interest means

(*a*) 6% per annum before 1978,

(*b*) 8% per annum for 1978, and

(*c*) for any year, or part thereof, after 1978, such rate of interest as is prescribed therefor except that, for the purpose of computing the benefit under subsection (1) in a taxation year on a home purchase loan received after November 12, 1981 and before 1982, the prescribed rate of interest at the time the loan was received shall be deemed to be 16% per annum;

Related Regulations: 4301.

"specified interest amount" —"specified interest amount" for a year, in respect of a loan (referred to in this definition as the "deemed loan") deemed to have been made under subsection 15(2.17) by an "ultimate funder" (as defined in subsection 15(2.192)), means the amount determined by the formula

$$A \times (B/C)$$

where

A is the amount of interest for the year paid not later than 30 days after the end of the year on all debts — owing by one or more "funders" (as defined in subsection 15(2.192), but excluding any funders that are "ultimate funders" as defined in subsection 15(2.192)) under one or more "funding arrangements" (as defined in subsection 15(2.192)) to the ultimate funder — that gave rise to the deemed loan;

B is the average amount outstanding for the year in respect of the deemed loan; and

C is the total of all amounts each of which is the average amount outstanding in the year as or on account of an amount owing under a debt described in A.

History: S. 80.4(7), the definition of "specified interest amount" was added by S.C. 2016, c. 12, s. 24(2), applicable in respect of

(*a*) loans received and indebtedness incurred after March 21, 2016; and

(*b*) any portion of a particular loan received or indebtedness incurred before March 22, 2016 that remains outstanding on that day, as if that portion were a separate loan or indebtedness that was received or incurred, as the case may be, on March 22, 2016 in the same manner and on the same terms as the particular loan or indebtedness.

▶ 80.4(8) ◀

(8) Meaning of connected. For the purposes of subsection (2), a person or partnership is connected with a shareholder of a corporation if that person or partnership does not deal at arm's length with, or is affiliated with, the shareholder, unless, in the case of a person, that person is

(*a*) a foreign affiliate of the corporation; or

(*b*) a foreign affiliate of a person resident in Canada with which the corporation does not deal at arm's length.

History: S. 80.4(8), the portion before paragraph (*a*) was replaced by S.C. 2013, c. 34, s. 216(1), applicable in respect of loans made and indebtedness arising after October 31, 2011, and formerly read:

(8) *Persons connected with a shareholder.* For the purposes of subsection (2), a person is connected with a shareholder of a corporation if that person does not deal at arm's length with the shareholder and if that person is a person other than

SECTION 80.5: Deemed interest

Where a benefit is deemed by section 80.4 to have been received in a taxation year by

(*a*) an individual or corporation under subsection 80.4(1), or

(*b*) a person or partnership under subsection 80.4(2),

the amount of the benefit shall, for the purposes of subparagraph 8(1)(*j*)(i) and paragraph 20(1)(*c*), be deemed to be interest paid in, and payable in respect of, the year by the debtor pursuant to a legal obligation to pay interest on borrowed money.

Editorial Note: S. 80.5 effectively provides that the deemed interest amounts under s. 80.4 will also be deductible, to the extent that the borrowed money is used for income-earning purposes as set out in either s. 8(1)(*j*) or 20(1)(*c*).

Interpretation Bulletins: *Primary* — IT-421R2 Benefits to Individuals, Corporations and Shareholders from Loans or Debt.

SECTION 80.6: [Synthetic disposition]

► 80.6(1) ◄

(1) Synthetic disposition. If a synthetic disposition arrangement is entered into in respect of a property owned by a taxpayer and the synthetic disposition period of the arrangement is one year or more, the taxpayer is deemed

(*a*) to have disposed of the property immediately before the beginning of the synthetic disposition period for proceeds equal to its fair market value at the beginning of the synthetic disposition period; and

(*b*) to have reacquired the property at the beginning of the synthetic disposition period at a cost equal to that fair market value.

Editorial Note: Section 80.6 provides that a taxpayer who owns property and enters into a "synthetic disposition arrangement" for a period of least one year is deemed to dispose of the property and reacquire the same property at fair market value immediately before the "synthetic disposition period," thus eliminating potential deferral of tax on a capital gain. A synthetic disposition arrangement is defined in s. 248(1) and includes a transaction, series of transactions, or arrangement designed to eliminate "all or substantially all" (administratively held to be 90% or more) of both the taxpayer's risk of loss and opportunity for gain or profit from a property (without selling the property). Examples of these types of arrangements can include certain put-call arrangements, secured loans, future sales, short sales, swaps, and other equity monetization arrangements. Subsection 80.6(2) sets out a number of exceptions to this deemed disposition rule for dispositions not resulting in capital gain or income, mark-to-market property, leases, convertible property, and property disposed of within a year.

History: S. 80.6(1) was added by S.C. 2013, c. 40, s. 38(1), applicable to agreements and arrangements entered into after March 20, 2013, and to an agreement or arrangement entered into before March 21, 2013, the term of which is extended after March 20, 2013, as if the agreement or arrangement were entered into at the time of the extension.

Related Sections: 112(8) Synthetic disposition — holding period; 126(4.5) Synthetic disposition — holding period; 248(1) synthetic disposition arrangement; 248(1) synthetic disposition period.

Canadian Tax Foundation: Miller and Milet, *Derivative Forward Agreements and Synthetic Disposition Arrangements*, 2013 Conference Report 10:1–50; Panasiuk, *Synthetic Dispositions: Get Cash Now, Pay Tax Later*, 2013 Canadian Tax Focus 13(2):10.

► 80.6(2) ◄

(2) Exception. Subsection (1) does not apply in respect of a property owned by a taxpayer if

(*a*) the disposition referred to in subsection (1) would not result in the realization of a capital gain or income;

(*b*) the property is a mark-to-market property (as defined in subsection 142.2(1)) of the taxpayer;

(*c*) the synthetic disposition arrangement referred to in subsection (1) is a lease of tangible property or, for civil law, corporeal property;

(*d*) the arrangement is an exchange of property to which subsection 51(1) applies; or

(*e*) the property is disposed of as part of the arrangement, within one year after the day on which the synthetic disposition period of the arrangement begins.

History: S. 80.6(2) was added by S.C. 2013, c. 40, s. 38(1), applicable to agreements and arrangements entered into after March 20, 2013, and to an agreement or arrangement entered into before March 21, 2013, the term of which is extended after March 20, 2013, as if the agreement or arrangement were entered into at the time of the extension.

Subdivision g — Amounts Not Included in Computing Income

SECTION 81: Amounts not included in income

► 81(1) ◄

(1) Amounts not included in income. There shall not be included in computing the income of a taxpayer for a taxation year,

► 81(1)(a) ◄

(a) Statutory exemptions — an amount that is declared to be exempt from income tax by any other enactment of Parliament, other than an amount received or receivable by an individual that is exempt by virtue of a provision contained in a tax convention or agreement with another country that has the force of law in Canada;

Related Sections: S. 126(3) Employees of international organizations; s. 212(1)(*h*) Pension benefits.

Interpretation Bulletins: *Primary* — IT-397R Amounts excluded from income — Statutory exemptions and certain service or RCMP pensions, allowances and compensation.

Tax Window Files: Indian Employment Income – Guideline 4, *February 19, 2019*, CRA Document No. 2018-0781651E5; Designated Airport Authorities, *August 8, 2016*, CRA Document No. 2016-0651841E5; Indian Tax Exemption and the Daniels Decision, *August 30, 2016*, CRA Document No. 2016-0656851E5; Indian Employment Income, *March 16, 2016*, CRA Document No. 2016-0629491E5; Indian Employment Income and Dividend Income, *February 10, 2016*, CRA Document No. 2015-0603891E5; Business Income of Self-employed Indian Fishers, *October 20, 2015*, CRA Document No. 2015-0585231E5; Indian Employment Income, *October 26, 2015*, CRA Document No. 2015-0585751E5; Indian Employment Income, *May 28, 2015*, CRA Document No. 2015-0568081E5; Indian Business Income XXXXXXXXXX, *June 16, 2015*, CRA Document No. 2014-0553331E5; First Nation's Land Claim Settlement Trust Income, *July 22, 2015*, CRA Document No. 2014-0528511I7.

Cases: Personal property of an Indian situated on a reserve is exempt from taxation. In determining whether employment income paid by a corporation owned and controlled by the employee is exempt, the particular business carried on by that company must be examined to determine the relevant connecting factors to the reserve rather than the connecting factors relating to employment income. *Bell v. The Queen*, 2018 DTC 5060 (FCA)

To succeed, the taxpayer had to show significant substantive connection between the bonuses and the reserve. The taxpayer's employment was not a strong connecting factor to the reserve, nor was the residence of the employer, the residence of the taxpayer, nor the location where she was paid. The bonuses did not qualify for exemption from tax. Moving the employer's offices to the reserve to take advantage of the s. 87 exemption was not abusive. *Bell v. The Queen*, 2016 DTC 1153 (TCC)

Locating a corporation on a reserve and having some corporate decisions made there are not strong enough factors to connect income to the reserve. The substantive aspects of the fishing business were all located off-reserve and the income earned was not exempt from tax. *Pilfold Estate v. The Queen*, 2014 DTC 5057 (FCA)

Non-physical property, such as benefits or income, can qualify as property situated on a reserve. The taxpayer's case was referred back to the Tax Court for a more comprehensive review of the connecting factors, including weight and relevance of each factor. Although he ran his business from his off-reserve home office, the question was whether his property (i.e., business income) was situated on a reserve, not whether he was situated on a reserve. *Kelly v. The Queen*, 2013 DTC 5129 (FCA), reversing 2009 DTC 1126 (TCC)

An Indian's interest income was exempt since it was derived from a contractual obligation entered into on a reserve, with a caisse populaire carrying on business there, to pay money on that reserve. The taxpayer's place of residence was given little weight and it didn't matter that he was not a member of the particular reserve where the caisse populaire was located. *Dubé v. The Queen et al.*, 2011 DTC 5120 (SCC), reversing 2009 DTC 5175 (FCA) and 2008 DTC 4022 (TCC)

An Indian's interest income from an on-reserve caisse populaire was exempt since all relevant factors connected it to a reserve, including the location of the caisse populaire and the taxpayer's residence. It was irrelevant whether it was integral to the life of the reserve or the preservation of a traditional Indian way of life, or whether the caisse populaire produced revenue in the "commercial mainstream" off-reserve. *Bastien Estate v. The Queen et al.*, 2011 DTC 5118 (SCC), reversing 2010 DTC 5054 (FCA) and 2008 DTC 4064 (TCC)

Treaty 8 did not include a promise of exemption from taxation for the Aboriginal signatories. *Benoit et al. v. The Queen*, 2003 DTC 5366 (F.C.A.), reversing 2002 DTC 6896 (FCTD)

Although the school and hospital they worked at were not on the reserve, status Indians' employment earnings were deemed to be situated on the reserve and tax exempt when their employers and the reserve were found to be intimately connected. *The Queen v. Poker et al.*, 94 DTC 6658 (FCTD), affirming (for this taxpayer) 92 DTC 2267 (TCC); and *Folster v. The Queen*, 97 DTC 5314 (FCA), reversing (for this taxpayer) 94 DTC 6658 (FCTD) [Editorial Note: Originally, the Court found for both taxpayers. The subsequent FCTD decision was in favour of only one of the taxpayers (employed by the school). The last appeal to the FCA was successful for the remaining taxpayer (employed by the hospital).]

Applying the relevant connecting factors, the unemployment insurance benefits received by an Indian on a reserve were not taxable. *Williams v. The Queen*, 92 DTC 6320 (SCC), reversing in part 90 DTC 6399 (FCA)

► 81(1)(b) ◄

(b) War Savings Certificate — an amount received under a War Savings Certificate issued by His Majesty in right of Canada or under a similar savings certificate issued by His Majesty in right of Newfoundland before April 1, 1949;

► 81(1)(c) ◄

(c) Ship or aircraft of non-residents — the income for the year of a non-resident person earned in Canada from international shipping or from the operation of aircraft in international traffic, if the country in which the person is resident grants substantially similar relief for the year to persons resident in Canada;

Editorial Note: Article 8 in most Canadian tax conventions provides that profits from shipping or aircraft operations in international traffic are taxable only in the country of the enterprise that derives them.

History: S. 81(1)(*c*) was replaced by S.C. 2014, c. 39, s. 18(1), applicable to taxation years that begin after July 12, 2013, and formerly read:

> (*c*) *Ship or aircraft of non-residents* — the income for the year of a non-resident person earned in Canada from the operation of a ship or aircraft in international traffic, if the country where that person resided grants substantially similar relief for the year to a person resident in Canada;

Related Sections: 248(1) international shipping; S. 18(8) Where s. (4) does not apply.

Forms: T2Sch97 — Additional Information on Non-Resident Corporations in Canada.

Interpretation Bulletins: *Secondary* — IT-494 Hire of ships and aircraft from non-residents.

Tax Window Files: International shipping, *December 24, 2015*, CRA Document No. 2014-0560831I7.

Cases: A U.K. shipping company operated its own ships besides controlling a large number of subsidiary shipping companies and having large investments in associated companies. Its six branch offices in Canada derived income by providing service to all these companies as well as outside companies. The Court held that the U.K. company was entitled to exemption for income earned by the Canadian branches from services rendered to ships owned or chartered by the U.K. company. Profits realized from services performed for affiliates, subsidiaries and outsiders were subject to tax with a deduction permitted for head office administration expenses attributable to operations in Canada. *Furness Withy & Co. Ltd. v. M.N.R.*, 68 DTC 5033 (S.C.C.), affirming 66 DTC 5358 (Ex. Ct.)

► 81(1)(d) ◄

(d) Service pension, allowance or compensation — a pension payment, an allowance or compensation that is received under or is subject to the *Pension Act*, the *Civilian War-related Benefits Act* or the *War Veterans Allowance Act*, an amount received under the Gallantry Awards Order or compensation received under the regulations made under section 9 of the *Aeronautics Act*;

Interpretation Bulletins: *Secondary* — IT-397R Amounts excluded from income — Statutory exemptions and certain service or RCMP pensions, allowances and compensation.

▶ 81(1)(d.1) ◀

(d.1) Canadian Forces members and veterans amounts — the total of all amounts received by the taxpayer in the year on account of

(i) a Canadian Forces income support benefit payable to the taxpayer under Part 2 of the *Veterans Well-being Act*,

(ii) pain and suffering compensation, additional pain and suffering compensation or a critical injury benefit, disability award, death benefit, clothing allowance or detention benefit payable to the taxpayer under Part 3 of the *Veterans Well-being Act*,

(iii) a family caregiver relief benefit or caregiver recognition benefit payable to the taxpayer under Part 3.1 of the *Veterans Well-being Act*, or

Amendment not yet in force

Budget Implementation Act, No. 1 [S.C. 2018, c. 12]

S. 81(1)(*d*.1)(iii) was replaced by S.C. 2018, c. 12, s. 5(2), and will read as follows:

(iii) a caregiver recognition benefit payable to the taxpayer under Part 3.1 of the *Veterans Well-being Act*, or

Applicable: To the 2020 and subsequent taxation years.

(iv) an amount payable to the taxpayer under subsection 132(1) of the *Veterans Well-being Act*;

History: S. 81(1)(*d*.1) was replaced by S.C. 2018, c. 12, s. 5(1), in force April 1, 2019, and formerly read:

(*d*.1) *Canadian Forces members and veterans amounts* — the total of all amounts received by the taxpayer in the year on account of a Canadian Forces income support benefit payable to the taxpayer under Part 2 of the *Veterans Well-being Act*, on account of a critical injury benefit, disability award, death benefit, clothing allowance or detention benefit payable to the taxpayer under Part 3 of that Act or on account of a family caregiver relief benefit or a caregiver recognition benefit payable to the taxpayer under Part 3.1 of that Act;

S. 81(1)(*d*.1) was replaced by S.C. 2017, c. 20, s. 6(2), applicable in respect of the 2020 and subsequent taxation years. However, this amendment was repealed by S.C. 2018, c. 12, s. 41. S. 81(1)(*d*.1), as it was replaced by S.C. 2017, c. 20, s. 6(2), read as follows:

(*d*.1) *Canadian Forces members and veterans amounts* — the total of all amounts received by the taxpayer in the year on account of a Canadian Forces income support benefit payable to the taxpayer under Part 2 of the *Veterans Well-being Act*, on account of a critical injury benefit, disability award, death benefit, clothing allowance or detention benefit payable to the taxpayer under Part 3 of that Act or on account of a caregiver recognition benefit payable to the taxpayer under Part 3.1 of that Act;

S. 81(1)(*d*.1) was replaced by S.C. 2017, c. 20, s. 6(1), in force April 1, 2018, and formerly read:

(*d*.1) *Canadian Forces members and veterans amounts* — the total of all amounts received by the taxpayer in the year on account of a Canadian Forces income support benefit payable to the taxpayer under Part 2 of the *Canadian Forces Members and Veterans Re-establishment and Compensation Act*, on account of a critical injury benefit, disability award, death benefit, clothing allowance or detention benefit payable to the taxpayer under Part 3 of that Act or on account of a family caregiver relief benefit payable to the taxpayer under Part 3.1 of that Act;

S. 81(1)(*d*.1) was replaced by S.C. 2015, c. 36, s. 3(1), applicable to the 2015 and subsequent taxation years, and formerly read:

(*d*.1) **Canadian Forces members and veterans amounts** — the total of all amounts received by the taxpayer in the year on account of a Canadian Forces income support benefit payable to the taxpayer under Part 2 of the *Canadian Forces Members and Veterans Re-establishment and Compensation Act* or on account of a disability award, death benefit, clothing allowance or detention benefit payable to the taxpayer under Part 3 of that Act;

▶ 81(1)(e) ◀

(e) War pensions — a pension payment received on account of disability or death arising out of a war from a country that was an ally of Canada at the time of the war, if that country grants substantially similar relief for the year to a person receiving a pension referred to in paragraph (*d*);

Interpretation Bulletins: *Secondary* — IT-397R Amounts excluded from income — Statutory exemptions and certain service or RCMP pensions, allowances and compensation.

▶ 81(1)(f) ◀

(f) Halifax disaster pensions, grants or allowances — a pension payment, a grant or an allowance in respect of death or injury sustained in the explosion in Halifax in 1917 and received from the Halifax Relief Commission the incorporation of which was confirmed by *An Act respecting the Halifax Relief Commission*, chapter 24 of the Statutes of Canada, 1918, or received pursuant to the *Halifax Relief Commission Pension Continuation Act*, chapter 88 of the Statutes of Canada, 1974-75-76;

▶ 81(1)(g) ◀

(g) Compensation by Federal Republic of Germany — a payment made by the Federal Republic of Germany or by a public body performing a function of government within that country as compensation to a victim of National Socialist persecution, where no tax is payable in respect of that payment under a law of the Federal Republic of Germany that imposes an income tax;

Related Sections: S. 56(1)(*a*) Pension benefits, unemployment insurance benefits, etc.

▶ 81(1)(g.1) ◀

(g.1) Income from personal injury award property — the income for the year from any property acquired by or on behalf of a person as an award of, or pursuant to an action for, damages in respect of physical or mental injury to that person, or from any property substituted therefor and any taxable capital gain for the year from the disposition of any such property,

(i) where the income was income from the property, if the income was earned in respect of a period before the end of the taxation year in which the person attained the age of 21 years, and

(ii) in any other case, if the person was less than 21 years of age during any part of the year;

Related Sections: S. 81(1)(*g*.2) Income from income exempt under para. (g.1); s. 81(5) Election.

Interpretation Bulletins: *Secondary* — IT-365R2 Damages, settlements, and similar receipts.

Tax Window Files: Interest income of a minor, *April 8, 2016*, CRA Document No. 2016-0628941E5.

▶ 81(1)(g.2) ◀

(g.2) Income from income exempt under para. (*g*.1) — any income for the year from any income that is by virtue of this paragraph or paragraph (*g*.1) not required to be included in computing the taxpayer's income (other than any income attributable to any period after the end of the taxation year in which the person on whose behalf the income was earned attained the age of 21 years);

Interpretation Bulletins: *Secondary* — IT-365R2 Damages, settlements, and similar receipts.

Tax Window Files: Interest income of a minor, *April 8, 2016*, CRA Document No. 2016-0628941E5.

▶ 81(1)(g.3) ◀

(g.3) Certain government funded trusts — the amount that, but for this paragraph, would be the income of the taxpayer for the year if

(i) the taxpayer is the trust established under

(A) the 1986-1990 Hepatitis C Settlement Agreement entered into by Her Majesty in right of Canada and Her Majesty in right of each of the provinces,

(B) the Pre-1986/Post-1990 Hepatitis C Settlement Agreement entered into by Her Majesty in right of Canada, or

(C) the Indian Residential Schools Settlement Agreement entered into by Her Majesty in right of Canada on May 8, 2006, and

(ii) the only contributions made to the taxpayer before the end of the year are those provided for under the relevant Agreement described in subparagraph (i);

History: S. 81(1)(*g*.3) was replaced by S.C. 2013, c. 34, s. 217(1), applicable to the 2006 and subsequent taxation years, except that for the 2006 taxation year, subparagraph 81(1)(*g*.3)(i) is to be read as follows:

"(i) the taxpayer is the trust established under

(A) the 1986-1990 Hepatitis C Settlement Agreement entered into by Her Majesty in right of Canada and Her Majesty in right of each of the provinces, or

(B) the Pre-1986/Post-1990 Hepatitis C Settlement Agreement entered into by Her Majesty in right of Canada, and"

S. 81(1)(*g*.3) formerly read:

(*g*.3) *Hepatitis C trust* — the amount that, but for this paragraph, would be the income of the taxpayer for the year where

(i) the taxpayer is the trust established under the 1986-1990 Hepatitis C Settlement Agreement entered into by Her Majesty in right of Canada and Her Majesty in right of each of the provinces, and

(ii) the only contributions made to the trust before the end of the year are those provided for under the Agreement;

▶ 81(1)(g.4) ◀

(g.4) Relief for increased heating expenses — an amount received pursuant to the *Order Authorizing Ex Gratia Payments for Increased Heating Expenses*;

▶ 81(1)(g.5) ◀

(g.5) Energy cost relief — an amount received pursuant to Part 1 of the *Energy Costs Assistance Measures Act*;

▶ 81(1)(g.6) ◀

(g.6) Ontario Electricity Support Program — an amount of rate assistance received under section 79.2 of the *Ontario Energy Board Act, 1998*, S.O. 1998, c. 15, Sch B, as amended from time to time;

History: S. 81(1)(*g*.6) was added by S.C. 2016, c. 7, s. 8(1), applicable to the 2016 and subsequent taxation years.

▶ 81(1)(h) ◀

(h) Social assistance — where the taxpayer is an individual (other than a trust), a social assistance payment (other than a prescribed payment) ordinarily made on the basis of a means, needs or income test under a program provided for by an Act of Parliament or a law of a province, to the extent that it is received directly or indirectly by the taxpayer for the benefit of another individual (other than the taxpayer's spouse or common-law partner or a person who is related to the taxpayer or to the taxpayer's spouse or common-law partner), if

(i) no family allowance under the *Family Allowances Act* or any similar allowance under a law of a province that provides for payment of an allowance similar to the family allowance provided under that Act is payable in respect of the other individual for the period in respect of which the social assistance payment is made, and

(ii) the other individual resides in the taxpayer's principal place of residence, or the taxpayer's principal place of residence is maintained for use as the residence of that other individual, throughout the period referred to in subparagraph (i);

Related Sections: S. 56(1)(*u*) Social assistance payments; s. 248(1), "common-law partner", "individual"; s. 251(6) Blood relationship, etc; s. 252(2) Relationships.

Income Tax Technical News: Issue No. 31R2, Application of Paragraph 81(1)(h).

▶ 81(1)(h.1) ◀

(h.1) Social assistance for informal care programs — if the taxpayer is an individual (other than a trust), a social assistance payment ordinarily made on the basis of a means, needs or income test provided for under a program of the Government of Canada or the government of a province, to the extent that it is received directly or indirectly by the taxpayer for the benefit of a particular individual, if

(i) payments to recipients under the program are made for the care and upbringing, on a temporary basis, of another individual in need of protection,

(ii) the particular individual is a child of the taxpayer because of paragraph 252(1)(*b*) (or would be a child of the taxpayer because of that paragraph if the taxpayer did not receive payments under the program), and

(iii) no special allowance under the *Children's Special Allowances Act* is payable in respect of the particular individual for the period in respect of which the social assistance payment is made;

History: S. 81(1)(*h*.1) was added by S.C. 2019, c. 29, s. 9(1), deemed to have come into force on January 1, 2009.

Related Sections: 252(1) Extended meaning of "child".

▶ 81(1)(i) ◀

(i) R.C.M.P. pension or compensation — a pension payment or compensation received under section 5, 31 or 45 of the *Royal Canadian Mounted Police Pension Continuation Act*, chapter R-10 of the Revised Statutes of Canada, 1970, or section 32 or 33 of the *Royal Canadian Mounted Police Superannuation Act*, in respect of an injury, disability or death;

Interpretation Bulletins: *Secondary* — IT-397R Amounts excluded from income — Statutory exemptions and certain service or RCMP pensions, allowances and compensation.

▶ 81(1)(j) ◀

(j) Memorial grant — an amount received under the Memorial Grant Program for First Responders established under the authority of the *Department of Public Safety and Emergency Preparedness Act* in respect of individuals who die in the course of, or as a result of, their duties or as a result of an occupational illness or psychological impairment;

History: S. 81(1)(*j*) was added by S.C. 2018, c. 12, s. 5(3), applicable in respect of amounts received after March 2018.

▶ 81(1)(k) ◀

(k) Employees profit sharing plan — a payment or part of a payment from an employees profit sharing plan that section 144 provides is not to be included;

▶ 81(1)(l) ◀

(l) Prospecting — an amount in respect of the receipt of a share that section 35 provides is not to be included;

▶ 81(1)(m) ◀

(m) Interest on certain obligations — interest that accrued to, became receivable or was received by, a corporation resident in Canada (in this paragraph referred to as the "parent corporation") on a bond, debenture, bill, note, mortgage or similar obligation received by it as consideration for the disposition by it, before June 18, 1971, of

(i) a business carried on by it in a country other than Canada, or

(ii) all of the shares of a corporation that carried on a business in a country other than Canada, and such of the debts and other obligations of that corporation as were, immediately before the disposition, owing to the parent corporation,

if

(iii) the business was of a public utility or public service nature,

(iv) the business or the property described in subparagraph (ii), as the case may be, was disposed of to a person or persons resident in that country, and

(v) the obligation received by the parent corporation was issued by or guaranteed by the government of that country or any agent thereof;

Related Sections: S. 12(1)(*c*) Interest; s. 40(2)(*d*) Limitations; s. 87(2)(*jj*) Interest on certain obligations; s. 212(1)(*b*) Interest.

▶ 81(1)(n) ◀

(n) Governor General — income from the office of Governor General of Canada, other than salary under the *Governor General's Act*;

History: S. 81(1)(*n*) was replaced by S.C. 2012, c. 19, s. 3(1), applicable to the 2013 and subsequent taxation years. S. 81(1)(*n*) formerly read:

(*n*) *Governor General* — income from the office of Governor General of Canada;

▶ 81(1)(o) ◀

(o) RESP refunds — (Repealed by S.C. 1998, c. 19, s. 14(1).)

▶ 81(1)(p) ◀

(p) Educational assistance payments — (Repealed by S.C. 1998, c. 19, s. 14(1).)

▶ 81(1)(q) ◀

(q) Provincial indemnities — an amount paid to an individual as an indemnity under a prescribed provision of the law of a province;

Related Regulations: 6501.

▶ 81(1)(r) ◀

(r) Foreign retirement arrangements — an amount that is credited or added to a deposit or account governed by a foreign retirement arrangement as interest or other income in respect of the deposit or account, where the amount would, but for this paragraph, be included in the taxpayer's income solely because of that crediting or adding; or

Related Sections: S. 248(1), "foreign retirement arrangement".

▶ 81(1)(s) ◀

(s) Salary deferral leave plans — an amount paid to the taxpayer in the year under an arrangement described in paragraph 6801(*a*) of the *Income Tax Regulations* to the extent that the amount may reasonably be considered to be attributable to amounts that

(i) were included in the taxpayer's income for a preceding taxation year and were income, interest or other additional amounts, described in subparagraph 6801(*a*)(iv) of the *Income Tax Regulations*, and

(ii) were re-contributed by the taxpayer under the arrangement in a preceding taxation year.

History: S. 81(1)(*s*) was added by S.C. 2013, c. 34, s. 217(2), applicable to the 2000 and subsequent taxation years.

▶ 81(1.1) ◀

(1.1) Interpretation — (Repealed by 1986, c. 2, s. 20(2).)

▶ 81(2) ◀

(2) M.L.A.'s expense allowance. (Repealed by S.C. 2017, c. 20, s. 6(3).)

History: S. 81(2) was repealed by S.C. 2017, c. 20, s. 6(3), in force on January 1, 2019, and formerly read:

(2) *M.L.A.'s expense allowance.* Where an elected member of a provincial legislative assembly has, under an Act of the provincial legislature, been paid an allowance in a taxation year for expenses incident to the discharge of the member's duties in that capacity, the allowance shall not be included in computing the member's income for the year unless it exceeds $^1/_2$ of the maximum fixed amount provided by law as payable to the member by way of salary, indemnity and other remuneration as a member in respect of attendance at a session of the legislature, in which event there shall be included in computing the member's income for the year only the amount by which the allowance exceeds $^1/_2$ of that maximum fixed amount.

Related Sections: S. 6(1)(*b*) Personal or living expenses; s. 8(3) Limitation re employment expense deduction.

▶ 81(3) ◀

(3) Municipal officers' expense allowance. (Repealed by S.C. 2017, c. 20, s. 6(3).)

History: S. 81(3) was repealed by S.C. 2017, c. 20, s. 6(3), in force on January 1, 2019, and formerly read:

(3) *Municipal officers' expense allowance.* Where a person who is

(*a*) an elected officer of an incorporated municipality,

(*b*) an officer of a municipal utilities board, commission or corporation or any other similar body, the incumbent of whose office as such an officer is elected by popular vote, or

(*c*) a member of a public or separate school board or similar body governing a school district,

has been paid by the municipal corporation or the body of which the person was such an officer or member (in this subsection referred to as the person's "employer") an amount as an allowance in a taxation year for expenses incident to the discharge of the person's duties as such an officer or member, the allowance shall not be included in computing the person's income for the year unless it exceeds 1/2 of the amount that was paid to the person in the year by the person's employer as salary or other remuneration as such an officer or member, in which event there shall be included in computing the person's income for the year only the amount by which the allowance exceeds 1/2 of the amount so paid to the person by way of salary or remuneration.

Related Sections: S. 6(1)(*b*) Personal or living expenses; s. 8(3) Limitation re employment expense deduction.

Interpretation Bulletins: *Primary* — IT-292 Taxation of elected officers of incorporated municipalities, school boards, municipal commissions and similar bodies.

► 81(3.1) ◄

(3.1) Travel expenses. There shall not be included in computing an individual's income for a taxation year an amount (not in excess of a reasonable amount) received by the individual from an employer with whom the individual was dealing at arm's length as an allowance for, or reimbursement of, travel expenses incurred by the individual in the year in respect of the individual's part-time employment in the year with the employer (other than expenses incurred in the performance of the duties of the individual's part-time employment) if

(*a*) throughout the period in which the expenses were incurred,

(i) the individual had other employment or was carrying on a business, or

(ii) where the employer is a designated educational institution (within the meaning assigned by subsection 118.6(1)), the duties of the individual's part-time employment were the provision in Canada of a service to the employer in the individual's capacity as a professor or teacher; and

(*b*) the duties of the individual's part-time employment were performed at a location not less than 80 kilometres from,

(i) where subparagraph (*a*)(i) applies, both the individual's ordinary place of residence and the place of the other employment or business referred to in that subparagraph, and

(ii) where subparagraph (*a*)(ii) applies, the individual's ordinary place of residence.

Editorial Note: A travel allowance paid to a part-time employee is not taxable as long as it meets the following conditions:

- the employment must be arm's length;
- the employee must have other employment or carry on another business;
- the amount reimbursed must be reasonable; and
- the employment must be conducted at least 80 kilometers from the employee's residence and the employer's other place of employment or place of business.

If the travel allowance is paid to a part-time teacher or professor, the only requirement that needs to be met to avoid tax on a travel allowance is the place of employment must be at least 80 kilometers from that individual's place of residence.

Related Sections: S. 6(1)(*b*) Personal or living expenses.

Income Tax Folios: S2-F3-C2 Benefits and Allowances Received from Employment.

Interpretation Bulletins: *Secondary* — IT-522R Vehicle, travel and sales expenses of employees.

Tax Window Files: Per Diem Amounts to Attend Committee Meetings, *Technical Interpretation, Business and Partnerships Division, August 26, 2008*, CRA Document No. 2008-0273351E5; Automobile Allowance — Travel Between Home and Place of Work, *Technical Interpretation, Business and Partnerships Division, April 15, 2008*, CRA Document No. 2006-0216791E5.

► 81(4) ◄

(4) Payments for volunteer services. Where

(*a*) an individual was employed or otherwise engaged in a taxation year by a government, municipality or public authority (in this subsection referred to as "the employer") and received in the year from the employer one or more amounts for the performance, as a volunteer, of the individual's duties as

(i) an ambulance technician,

(ii) a firefighter, or

(iii) a person who assists in the search or rescue of individuals or in other emergency situations, and

(*b*) if the Minister so demands, the employer has certified in writing that

(i) the individual was in the year a person described in paragraph (*a*), and

(ii) the individual was at no time in the year employed or otherwise engaged by the employer, otherwise than as a volunteer, in connection with the performance of any of the duties referred to in paragraph (*a*) or of similar duties,

there shall not be included in computing the individual's income derived from the performance of those duties the lesser of $1,000 and the total of those amounts, unless the individual makes a claim under section 118.06 or 118.07 for the year.

Editorial Note: Individuals who provide emergency services as a volunteer can deduct the first $1,000 paid for such voluntary services. This applies to amounts paid for volunteer services as ambulance technicians, search and rescue technicians, and firefighters; however, firefighters who claim the tax credit under s. 118.06 and search and rescue volunteers who claim the tax credit under s. 118.07 cannot also claim this deduction. This credit only applies to amounts paid voluntarily and not to earnings paid to an employee carrying out these duties.

History: S. 81(4), the portion after subparagraph (*b*)(ii) was replaced by S.C. 2014, c. 20, s. 4(1), applicable to the 2014 and subsequent taxation years, and formerly read:

> there shall not be included in computing the individual's income derived from the performance of those duties the lesser of $1,000 and the total of those amounts, other than, if the individual makes a claim under section 118.06 for the year, amounts received in respect of duties as a firefighter.

S. 81(4), the portion after paragraph (*b*) was replaced by S.C. 2011, c. 24, s. 18(1), applicable to the 2011 and subsequent taxation years. S. 81(4), the portion after paragraph (*b*) formerly read:

> there shall not be included in computing the individual's income derived from the performance of those duties the lesser of $1,000 and the total of those amounts.

Tax Window Files: Exemption amounts for volunteer emergency services, *June 9, 2017*, CRA Document No. 2017-0690251I7; $1,000 Volunteer Exemption — Meaning of the Term, *Technical Interpretation, Business and Partnerships Division, July 7, 2009*, CRA Document No. 2008-0267941E5.

► 81(5) ◄

(5) Election. Where a taxpayer or a person described in paragraph (1)(*g.1*) has acquired capital property under the circumstances described in that paragraph, the taxpayer or the person may, in the return of income of the taxpayer for the taxation year in which the taxpayer attains the age of 21 years, elect to treat any such capital property held by the taxpayer or person as having been disposed of on the day immediately preceding the day on which the taxpayer attained the age of 21 years for proceeds of disposition equal to the fair market value of the property on that day and the person or taxpayer making the election shall be deemed to have reacquired that property immediately thereafter at a cost equal to those proceeds.

Related Sections: S. 6(1)(*b*) Personal or living expenses; s. 248(1), "amount", "business", "corporation", "employer", "non-resident", "office", "prescribed", "property", "regulation", "share".

Subdivision h — Corporations Resident in Canada and Their Shareholders

SECTION 82: Taxable dividends received

► 82(1) ◄

(1) Taxable dividends received. In computing the income of a taxpayer for a taxation year, there shall be included the total of the following amounts:

(*a*) the amount, if any, by which

(i) the total of all amounts, other than eligible dividends and amounts described in paragraph (*c*), (*d*) or (*e*), received by the taxpayer in the taxation year from corporations resident in Canada as, on account of, in lieu of payment of or in satisfaction of, taxable dividends,

exceeds

(ii) if the taxpayer is an individual, the total of all amounts each of which is, or is deemed by paragraph 260(12)(*b*) to have been, paid by the taxpayer in the taxation year and deemed by subsection 260(5.1) to have been received by another person as a taxable dividend (other than an eligible dividend);

(*a*.1) the amount, if any, by which

(i) the total of all amounts, other than amounts included in computing the income of the taxpayer because of paragraph (*c*), (*d*) or (*e*), received by the taxpayer in the taxation year from corporations resident in Canada as, on account of, in lieu of payment of or in satisfaction of, eligible dividends,

exceeds

(ii) if the taxpayer is an individual, the total of all amounts each of which is, or is deemed by paragraph 260(12)(*b*) to have been, paid by the taxpayer in the taxation year and deemed by subsection 260(5.1) to have been received by another person as an eligible dividend;

(*b*) if the taxpayer is an individual, other than a trust that is a registered charity, the total of

(i) the product of the amount determined under paragraph (*a*) in respect of the taxpayer for the taxation year multiplied by

(A) for the 2018 taxation year, 16%, and

(B) for taxation years after 2018, 15%, and

(ii) the product of the amount determined under paragraph (*a.1*) in respect of the taxpayer for the taxation year multiplied by

(A) for taxation years that end after 2005 and before 2010, 45%,

(B) for the 2010 taxation year, 44%,

(C) for the 2011 taxation year, 41%, and

(D) for taxation years that end after 2011, 38%;

(*c*) all taxable dividends received by the taxpayer in the taxation year, from corporations resident in Canada, under dividend rental arrangements of the taxpayer;

(*d*) all taxable dividends (other than taxable dividends described in paragraph (*c*)) received by the taxpayer in the taxation year from corporations resident in Canada that are not taxable Canadian corporations; and

(*e*) if the taxpayer is a trust, all amounts each of which is all or part of a taxable dividend (other than a taxable dividend described in paragraph (*c*) or (*d*)) that was received by the trust in the taxation year on a share of the capital stock of a taxable Canadian corporation and that can reasonably be considered to have been included in computing the income of a beneficiary under the trust who was non-resident at the end of the taxation year.

Editorial Note: The amount under s. 82(1)(*b*) is the so-called gross-up in respect of taxable dividends received by individuals (other than trusts that are registered charities) from Canadian-resident corporations. For "eligible dividends" (see the definition in s. 89(1)), the gross-up is 38%. For non-eligible dividends, the gross-up factor is 17% for dividends paid after 2015 and before 2018, 16% for dividends paid in 2018, and 15% for subsequent taxation years. The federal dividend tax credit under s. 121 equals 6/11 of the gross-up for eligible dividends. The dividend tax credit for non-eligible dividends is 21/29 of the gross-up for non-eligible dividends paid after 2015 and before 2018, 8/11 of the gross-up for non-eligible dividends paid in 2018, and 9/13 of the gross-up for non-eligible dividends paid in subsequent years. Changes to the dividend tax credit rates are made in response to changes in the general or small business corporate tax rates to achieve tax integration between the corporate and personal tax systems. Regarding s. 82(1)(*c*), see the Editorial Note for s. 112(2.3).

History: S. 82(1)(*b*)(i) was replaced by S.C. 2018, c. 12, s. 6(1), applicable to the 2018 and subsequent taxation years, and formerly read:

> (i) the product of the amount determined under paragraph (*a*) in respect of the taxpayer for the taxation year multiplied by 17%, and

S. 82(1)(*b*)(i) was replaced by S.C. 2016, c. 7, s. 9(1), applicable to the 2016 and subsequent taxation years, and formerly read:

> (i) the product of the amount determined under paragraph (*a*) in respect of the taxpayer for the taxation year multiplied by
>
> (A) for the 2016 and 2017 taxation years, 17%,
>
> (B) for the 2018 taxation year, 16%, and
>
> (C) for taxation years after 2018, 15%, and

S. 82(1)(*b*)(i) was replaced by S.C. 2015, c. 36, s. 4(1), applicable to the 2016 and subsequent taxation years, and formerly read:

> (i) 18% of the amount determined under paragraph (*a*) in respect of the taxpayer for the taxation year, and

S. 82(1)(*b*)(i) was replaced by S.C. 2013, c. 33, s. 5(1), applicable to dividends paid after 2013, and formerly read:

> (i) 25% of the amount determined under paragraph (*a*) in respect of the taxpayer for the taxation year, and

S. 82(1), the portion before paragraph (*c*) was replaced by S.C. 2013, c. 34, s. 218(2), applicable to amounts received or paid after 2005, and formerly read:

> (1) *Taxable dividends received.* In computing the income of a taxpayer for a taxation year, there shall be included the total of the following amounts:
>
> (*a*) the amount, if any, by which
>
> (i) the total of all amounts, other than eligible dividends and amounts described in paragraph (*c*), (*d*) or (*e*), received by the taxpayer in the taxation year from corporations resident in Canada as, on account of, in lieu of payment of or in satisfaction of, taxable dividends,
>
> exceeds
>
> (ii) if the taxpayer is an individual, the total of all amounts paid by the taxpayer in the taxation year that are deemed by subsection 260(5) to have been received by another person as taxable dividends (other than eligible dividends);
>
> (*a*.1) the amount, if any, by which
>
> (i) the total of all amounts, other than amounts included in computing the income of the taxpayer because of paragraph (*c*), (*d*) or (*e*), received by the taxpayer in the taxation year from corporations resident in Canada as, on account of, in lieu of payment of or in satisfaction of, eligible dividends,
>
> exceeds
>
> (ii) if the taxpayer is an individual, the total of all amounts paid by the taxpayer in the taxation year that are deemed by subsection 260(5) to have been received by another person as eligible dividends;
>
> (*b*) if the taxpayer is an individual, other than a trust that is a registered charity, the total of

(i) 25% of the amount determined under paragraph (*a*) in respect of the taxpayer for the taxation year, and

(ii) the product of the amount determined under paragraph (*a.1*) in respect of the taxpayer for the taxation year multiplied by

(A) for the 2009 taxation year, 45%,

(B) for the 2010 taxation year, 44%,

(C) for the 2011 taxation year, 41%, and

(D) for taxation years after 2011, 38%;

Related Regulations: Part II.

Related Sections: S. 12(1)(*j*) Dividends from resident corporations; s. 104(19) Taxable dividends; s. 112(1) Deduction of taxable dividends received by corporation resident in Canada; s. 121 Deduction for taxable dividends; s. 127.5 Obligation to pay minimum tax.

Canadian Tax Foundation: Bleiwas and Ball, *Current Issues for Private Companies, Including Dividend Tax Credit Changes and Integration*, 2013 Conference Report 6:1–32.

Tax Profile: October 2006 — New Rules for the Taxation of Dividends; October 2004 — Taxation of Dividends: A Survey in the Context of Private Corporations and Their Shareholders.

Tax Topics: No. 1903, Tax Smart Investing; No. 1809, New Tax on Income Trusts and Public Partnerships, Trick or treat — a taxing announcement.

Forms: T5 Sum. — Return of Investment Income; T5 — Statement of Investment Income.

Interpretation Bulletins: *Secondary* — IT-67R3 Taxable dividends from corporations resident in Canada; IT-379R Employees profit sharing plans — Allocations to beneficiaries; IT-432R2 Benefits conferred on shareholders; IT-524 Trusts — Flow-through of taxable dividends to a beneficiary — After 1987.

► 82(1.1) ◄

(1.1) Limitation as to paragraph (1)(*c*). An amount shall be included in the amounts described in paragraph (1)(*c*) in respect of a taxable dividend received at any time as part of a dividend rental arrangement only if that dividend was received on a share acquired before that time and after April, 1989.

Editorial Note: "Dividend rental arrangement" is defined in s. 248(1).

History: S. 82(1.1) was replaced by S.C. 2013, c. 34, s. 218(3), applicable to amounts received or paid after 2005, and formerly read:

(1.1) *Limitation as to subparagraph (1)(a)*(i). An amount shall be included in the amounts described in subparagraph (1)(*a*)(i) in respect of a taxable dividend received at any time as part of a dividend rental arrangement only where that dividend was received on a share acquired before that time and after April, 1989.

► 82(2) ◄

(2) Certain dividends received by taxpayer. Where by reason of subsection 56(4) or (4.1) or sections 74.1 to 75 of this Act or section 74 of the *Income Tax Act*, chapter 148 of the Revised Statutes of Canada, 1952, there is included in computing a taxpayer's income for a taxation year a dividend received by another person, for the purposes of this Act, the dividend shall be deemed to have been received by the taxpayer.

Editorial Note: By deeming the dividend to be received by the taxpayer to whom one of the listed attribution rules applied, s. 82(2) ensures, among other things, that the taxpayer will be entitled to the dividend tax credit in the case of an individual (s. 121), or an intercorporate dividend deduction in the case of a corporation (s. 112 or 113).

Related Sections: S. 82(1) Taxable dividends received; s. 112(1) Deduction of taxable dividends received by corporation resident in Canada; s. 113(1) Deduction in respect of dividend received from foreign affiliate; s. 121 Deduction for taxable dividends.

Interpretation Bulletins: *Secondary* — IT-440R2 Transfer of rights to income.

► 82(3) ◄

(3) Dividends received by spouse or common-law partner. Where the amount that would, but for this subsection, be deductible under subsection 118(1) by reason of paragraph 118(1)(*a*) in computing a taxpayer's tax payable under this Part for a taxation year that is less than the amount that would be so deductible if no amount were required by subsection (1) to be included in computing the income for the year of the taxpayer's spouse or common-law partner and the taxpayer so elects in the taxpayer's return of income for the year under this Part, all amounts described in paragraph (1)(*a*) or (*a*.1) received in the year from taxable Canadian corporations by the taxpayer's spouse or common-law partner are deemed to have been so received by that taxpayer and not by the spouse or common-law partner.

Editorial Note: Where a taxpayer's spouse (or common-law partner) receives taxable dividends in a taxation year that if included in the spouse's income would result in a reduction in the taxpayer's married tax credit for the year (s. 118(1)(*a*)), s. 83(2) allows the taxpayer to elect to include the taxable dividends in his or her income instead. By doing so, the taxpayer can maximize the married tax credit and utilize the dividend tax credit (s. 121), which can result in less overall tax payable for the couple.

Related Regulations: 600(b).

Related Sections: S. 89(1), "Canadian corporation", "taxable Canadian corporation", "taxable dividends"; s. 104(19) Taxable dividends; s. 220(3.2) Late, amended or revoked elections; s. 248(1), "amount", "corporation", "dividend", "individual"; s. 255 Canada.

Tax Profile: October 2004 — Taxation of Dividends: A Survey in the Context of Private Corporations and Their Shareholders.

Information Circulars: IC 07-1 Taxpayer relief provisions.

Interpretation Bulletins: *Primary* — IT-295R4 Taxable dividends received after 1987 by a spouse.

Cases: When a taxpayer sought to deduct part of his spouse's dividend income before adding the grossed up balance to his own income the Minister assessed as if all the dividend income had been grossed up and added to the taxpayer's income. The Court ruled that either all or none of the spouse's dividend income must be added. Paragraph 109(1)(*a*) comes into operation only after the taxpayer's taxable income has been computed. *Gillis v. The Queen*, 77 DTC 5227 (F.C.T.D.)

SECTION 83: Qualifying dividends

► 83(1) ◄

(1) Qualifying dividends. Where a qualifying dividend has been paid by a public corporation to shareholders of a series of tax-deferred preferred shares of a class of the capital stock of the corporation that were outstanding on March 31, 1977, the following rules apply:

(*a*) no part of the qualifying dividend shall be included in computing the income of any shareholder of the corporation by virtue of this subdivision; and

(*b*) in computing the adjusted cost base to any shareholder of the corporation of any tax-deferred preferred share of the corporation owned by the shareholder, there shall be deducted in respect of the qualifying dividend an amount as provided by subparagraph 53(2)(*a*)(i).

Related Regulations: 2100.

Related Sections: S. 83(3) Late filed elections; s. 83(6) Definition of "qualifying dividend"; s. 89(1), "Canadian corporation"; s. 134 Non-resident-owned corporation not a Canadian corporation, etc.; s. 185(1) Assessment of tax; s. 185(2) Payment of tax and interest.

Interpretation Bulletins: *Secondary* — IT-67R3 Taxable dividends from corporations resident in Canada; IT-146R4 Shares entitling shareholders to choose taxable or capital dividends; IT-379R Employees Profit Sharing Plan — Allocations to Beneficiaries; IT-465R Non-resident beneficiaries of trusts.

► 83(2) ◄

(2) Capital dividend. Where at any particular time after 1971 a dividend becomes payable by a private corporation to shareholders of any class of shares of its capital stock and the corporation so elects in respect of the full amount of the dividend, in prescribed manner and prescribed form and at or before the particular time or the first day on which any part of the dividend was paid if that day is earlier than the particular time, the following rules apply:

(*a*) the dividend shall be deemed to be a capital dividend to the extent of the corporation's capital dividend account immediately before the particular time; and

(*b*) no part of the dividend shall be included in computing the income of any shareholder of the corporation.

Editorial Note: The full amount of the elected dividend payable by a private corporation is excluded from the income of each resident shareholder, even if the total dividend exceeds the corporation's capital dividend account ("CDA") (s. 89(1)) such that the excess is not a capital dividend (and therefore does not reduce the payer corporation's CDA — see Document No. 2011-0417511E5). However, the corporation may be subject to a penalty tax in respect of the excess under s. 184(2); alternatively, the corporation can elect under s. 184(3) to have the excess treated as a separate taxable dividend. A capital dividend paid to a non-resident is subject to withholding tax under s. 212(2). In the CRA's view, after validly declaring a dividend, the directors of the corporation cannot modify the dividend, e.g., to split an excessive dividend into two (Document No. 2011-0412071C6); also, a s. 84.1 deemed dividend to a non-shareholder cannot be the subject of a s. 83(2) election (Document No. 2011-0414731E5).

Anti-avoidance rules (s. 83(2.1), subject to exceptions in s. 83(2.1)–(2.4)) may apply to "trafficking" in CDA. CDA is eliminated when a private corporation controlled by non-residents becomes a CCPC (other than by reason of a shareholder's change of residence) or ceases to be exempt from Part I tax (see s. 89(1.1) and (1.2)).

Related Regulations: 600(*b*); 2101.

Related Sections: S. 14(1.01) Election re capital gain; s. 14(1.02) Election re property acquired with pre-1972 outlays or expenditures;, s. 83(2.1) Capital dividend — anti-avoidance rule–s. 83(5) Unpaid balance of penalty; s. 89(1), "capital dividend account"; s. 89(1.1) Capital dividend account where control acquired; s. 89(1.2) Capital dividend account of tax-exempt corporation; s. 89(3) Simultaneous dividends; s. 184(2) Tax on excessive elections; s. 184(3) Election to treat excess as separate dividend; s. 184(3.2) Election to treat dividend as loan — capital dividend; s. 185 Assessment of tax. s. 212(2) Tax on dividends; s. 220(2) Officers, clerks and employees; s. 220(3.2) Late, amended or revoked elections.

Canadian Tax Foundation: Hoegner, *The Best Things in Life are (Tax-) Free: A Current Look at the Capital Dividend Account*, 2002 Canadian Tax Journal 4:1426–1457.

Tax Profile: November 2009 — Purchase and Sale of a Canadian Business; July 2007 — Canadian Tax Traps; October 2004 — Taxation of Dividends: A Survey in the Context of Private Corporations and Their Shareholders; September 2004 — Review of Tax Implications of Corporate-Owned Life Insurance Buy-Sell Arrangements.

Tax Topics: No. 1857, Sham - As Bad As It Gets.

Forms: T2054 — Election for a Capital Dividend Under Subsection 83(2).

Income Tax Folios: *Primary* — S3-F2-C1 Capital Dividends.

Information Circulars: IC 07-1 Taxpayer Relief Provisions.

Interpretation Bulletins: *Secondary* — IT-149R4 Winding-up dividend.

Tax Window Files: 2016 CTF - Q4 - 55(2) and Part IV Tax, *November 29, 2016*, CRA Document No. 2016-0671491C6; Capital Dividend Received by Partnership, *Technical Interpretation, Business and Partnerships Division, December 4, 2003*, CRA Document No. 2003-0038595. Corporate partner can include, in computing its capital dividend account, its share of a capital dividend received by the partnership at the time the partner becomes entitled to a share of the dividend.

Cases: A directors' resolution declared a $298,000 capital dividend on December 31, 2015. The accountants missed subsection 89(1), which states that amounts may be added to the capital account only at the end of the company's taxation year. This would have been August 31, 2016. The CRA issued the shareholders a notice of assessment for $110,873, 60% of the amount the dividend exceeded the company's actual capital dividend account on December 31, 2015.The company was granted rectification of the directors' resolution in order to distribute the maximum amount distributable on a tax-free basis. *In the Matter of 5551928 Manitoba Ltd.*, 2018 DTC 5102 (BCSC)

► 83(2.1) ◄

(2.1) Idem. Notwithstanding subsection (2), where a dividend that, but for this subsection, would be a capital dividend is paid on a share of the capital stock of a corporation and the share (or another share for which the share was substituted) was acquired by its holder in a transaction or as part of a series of transactions one of the main purposes of which was to receive the dividend,

(*a*) the dividend shall, for the purposes of this Act (other than for the purposes of Part III and computing the capital dividend account of the corporation), be deemed to be received by the shareholder and paid by the corporation as a taxable dividend and not as a capital dividend; and

(*b*) paragraph (2)(*b*) does not apply in respect of the dividend.

Related Sections: S. 83(2.2) Capital dividend — exception to anti-avoidance rule; s. 83(2.3) Capital dividend — exception to anti-avoidance rule; s. 83(2.4) Capital dividend — exception to anti-avoidance rule; s. 87(2)(*x*) Taxable dividends.

Canadian Tax Foundation: Hudson and McCamis, *Refresher on Specific Anti-Avoidance Provisions*, 2014 Prairie Provinces Tax Conference 12:1–41.

Tax Profile: October 2004 — Taxation of Dividends: A Survey in the Context of Private Corporations and Their Shareholders.

Income Tax Folios: *Primary* — S3-F2-C1 Capital Dividends.

Interpretation Bulletins: *Secondary* — IT-149R4 Winding-up dividend.

Cases: Capital dividends declared following a corporate restructuring were deemed to be taxable dividends under s. 83(2.1) since declaring capital dividends was "one of the main purposes" for the series of transactions. *Groupe Honco Inc. v. The Queen*, 2013 DTC 5105 (F.C.A.), affirming 2013 DTC 1032 (T.C.C.)

► 83(2.2) ◄

(2.2) Where s. 83(2.1) does not apply. Subsection (2.1) does not apply in respect of a particular dividend, in respect of which an election is made under subsection (2), paid on a share of the capital stock of a particular corporation to an individual where it is reasonable to consider that all or substantially all of the capital dividend account of the particular corporation immediately before the particular dividend became payable consisted of amounts other than any amount

(*a*) added to that capital dividend account under paragraph (*b*) of the definition "capital dividend account" in subsection 89(1) in respect of a dividend received on a share of the capital stock of another corporation, which share (or another share for which the share was substituted) was acquired by the particular corporation in a transaction or as part of a series of transactions one of the main purposes of which was that the particular corporation receive the dividend, but not in respect of a dividend where it is reasonable to consider that the purpose of paying the dividend was to distribute an amount that was received by the other corporation and included in computing the other corporation's capital dividend account by reason of paragraph (*d*) of that definition;

(*b*) added to that capital dividend account under paragraph 87(2)(*z*.1) as a result of an amalgamation or winding-up or a series of transactions including the amalgamation or winding-up that would not have been so added had the amalgamation or winding-up occurred or the series of transactions been commenced after 4:00 p.m. Eastern Daylight Saving Time, September 25, 1987;

(*c*) added to that capital dividend account at a time when the particular corporation was controlled, directly or indirectly, in any manner whatever, by one or more non-resident persons; or

(*d*) in respect of a capital gain from a disposition of a property by the particular corporation or another corporation that may reasonably be considered as having accrued while the property (or another property for which it was substituted) was a property of a corporation that was controlled, directly or indirectly, in any manner whatever, by one or more non-resident persons.

Tax Profile: October 2004 — Taxation of Dividends: A Survey in the Context of Private Corporations and Their Shareholders.

► 83(2.3) ◄

(2.3) Idem. Subsection (2.1) does not apply in respect of a dividend, in respect of which an election is made under subsection (2), paid on a share of the capital stock of a corporation where it is reasonable to consider that the purpose of paying the dividend was to distribute an amount that was received by the corporation and included in computing its capital dividend account by reason of paragraph (*d*) of the definition "capital dividend account" in subsection 89(1).

Tax Profile: October 2004 — Taxation of Dividends: A Survey in the Context of Private Corporations and Their Shareholders.

► 83(2.4) ◄

(2.4) Idem. Subsection (2.1) does not apply in respect of a particular dividend, in respect of which an election is made under subsection (2), paid on a share of the capital stock of a particular corporation to a corporation (in this subsection referred to as the "related corporation") related (otherwise than by reason of a right referred to in paragraph 251(5)(*b*)) to the particular corporation where it is reasonable to consider that all or substantially all of the capital dividend account of the particular corporation immediately before the particular dividend became payable consisted of amounts other than any amount

(*a*) added to that capital dividend account under paragraph (*b*) of the definition "capital dividend account" in subsection 89(1) in respect of a dividend received on a share of the capital stock of another corporation if it is reasonable to consider that any portion of the capital dividend account of that other corporation immediately before that dividend became payable consisted of amounts added to that account under paragraph 87(2)(*z*.1) or paragraph (*b*) of that definition as a result of a transaction or a series of transactions that would not have been so added had the transaction occurred or the series of transactions been commenced after 4:00 p.m. Eastern Daylight Saving Time, September 25, 1987;

(*b*) that represented the capital dividend account of a corporation before it became related to the related corporation;

(*c*) added to the capital dividend account of the particular corporation at a time when that corporation was controlled, directly or indirectly, in any manner whatever, by one or more non-resident persons;

(*d*) in respect of a capital gain from a disposition of a property by the particular corporation or another corporation that may reasonably be considered as having accrued while the property (or another property for which it was substituted) was a property of a corporation that was controlled, directly or indirectly, in any manner whatever, by one or more non-resident persons; or

(*e*) in respect of a capital gain from a disposition of a property (or another property for which it was substituted) that may reasonably be considered as having accrued while the property or the other property was a property of a person that was not related to the related corporation.

Tax Profile: October 2004 — Taxation of Dividends: A Survey in the Context of Private Corporations and Their Shareholders.

► 83(3) ◄

(3) Late filed elections. Where at any particular time after 1974 a dividend has become payable by a corporation to shareholders of any class of shares of its capital stock, and subsection (1) or (2) would have applied to the dividend except that the election referred to therein was not made on or before the day on or before which the election was required by that subsection to be made, the election shall be deemed to have been made at the particular time or on the first day on which any part of the dividend was paid, whichever is the earlier, if

(*a*) the election is made in prescribed manner and prescribed form;

(*b*) an estimate of the penalty in respect of that election is paid by the corporation when that election is made; and

(*c*) the directors or other person or persons legally entitled to administer the affairs of the corporation have, before the time the election is made, authorized the election to be made.

Related Regulations: Part XXI.

Related Sections: S. 83(3.1) Request for election; s. 83(4) Penalty for late filed election; s. 83(5) Unpaid balance of penalty.

Income Tax Folios: *Primary* — S3-F2-C1 Capital Dividends.

► 83(3.1) ◄

(3.1) Request for election. The Minister may at any time, by written request served personally or by registered mail, request that an election referred to in subsection (3) be made by a taxpayer, and where the taxpayer on whom such a request is served does not comply therewith within 90 days of service thereof on the taxpayer, subsection (3) does not apply to such an election made by the taxpayer.

► 83(4) ◄

(4) Penalty for late filed election. For the purposes of this section, the penalty in respect of an election referred to in paragraph (3)(*a*) is an amount equal to the lesser of

(*a*) 1% per annum of the amount of the dividend referred to in the election for each month or part of a month during the period commencing with the time that the dividend became payable, or the first day on which any part of the dividend was paid if that day is earlier, and ending with the day on which that election was made, and

(*b*) the product obtained when $500 is multiplied by the proportion that the number of months or parts of months during the period referred to in paragraph (*a*) bears to 12.

Related Sections: S. 83(3) Late filed elections.

Income Tax Folios: *Primary* — S3-F2-C1 Capital Dividends.

▶ 83(5) ◀

(5) Unpaid balance of penalty. The Minister shall, with all due dispatch, examine each election referred to in paragraph (3)(*a*), assess the penalty payable and send a notice of assessment to the corporation and the corporation shall pay, forthwith to the Receiver General, the amount, if any, by which the penalty so assessed exceeds the total of all amounts previously paid on account of that penalty.

▶ 83(6) ◀

(6) Definition of "qualifying dividend". For the purposes of subsection (1), "qualifying dividend" means a dividend on shares of a series of a class of the capital stock of a public corporation that is prescribed to be a tax-deferred preferred series that became payable by the corporation after 1978 and not later than

(*a*) where the terms as at March 31, 1977 of the shares of that series entitled the holder of such a share to exchange it after a particular date for a share or shares of another series or class of preferred shares of the capital stock of the corporation, that particular date,

(*b*) where the terms as at March 31, 1977 of the shares of that series required the corporation to offer to purchase at a time not later than a particular date all of the shares of that series from all of the holders of those shares, that particular date, and

(*c*) in any other case, October 1, 1991,

whichever is applicable in respect of that series of shares, except that a dividend on shares of such a series that would otherwise be a qualifying dividend shall be deemed not to be a qualifying dividend if

(*d*) at the time that the dividend became payable, the terms of the shares of that series differ from the terms as at March 31, 1977 of the shares of that series, or

(*e*) after March 31, 1977 the corporation issued additional shares of that series.

Related Regulations: 2107.

▶ 83(7) ◀

(7) Amalgamation where there are tax-deferred preferred shares. For the purposes of this section, where, after March 31, 1977, there has been an amalgamation within the meaning of section 87 and one or more of the predecessor corporations had a series of shares outstanding on March 31, 1977 that was prescribed to be a tax-deferred preferred series, the following rules apply:

(*a*) the series of shares of the capital stock of the predecessor corporation that was prescribed to be a tax-deferred preferred series shall be deemed to have been continued in existence in the form of the new shares; and

(*b*) the new corporation shall be deemed to be the same corporation as, and a continuation of, each such predecessor corporation.

Related Sections: S. 54, "adjusted cost base"; s. 83(2), "capital dividends"; s. 89(1), "Canadian corporation", "capital dividend account", "private corporation", "taxable dividend"; s. 133(1) Computation of income; s. 184(2) Tax on excessive elections; s. 185(1) Assessment of tax; s. 185(2) Payment of tax and interest; s. 248(1), "corporation", "dividend", "prescribed", "share", "shareholders".

SECTION 84: Deemed dividend

▶ 84(1) ◀

(1) Deemed dividend. Where a corporation resident in Canada has at any time after 1971 increased the paid-up capital in respect of the shares of any particular class of its capital stock, otherwise than by

(*a*) payment of a stock dividend,

(*b*) a transaction by which

(i) the value of its assets less its liabilities has been increased, or

(ii) its liabilities less the value of its assets have been decreased,

by an amount not less than the amount of the increase in the paid-up capital in respect of the shares of the particular class,

(*c*) a transaction by which the paid-up capital in respect of the shares of all other classes of its capital stock has been reduced by an amount not less than the amount of the increase in the paid-up capital in respect of the shares of the particular class,

(*c*.1) if the corporation is an insurance corporation, any action by which it converts contributed surplus related to its insurance business (other than any portion of that contributed surplus that arose at a time when it was non-resident, or that arose in connection with a disposition to which subsection 212.1(1.1) applies or an *investment*, as defined in subsection 212.3(10), to which subsection 212.3(2) applies) into paid-up capital in respect of the shares of its capital stock,

(*c*.2) if the corporation is a bank, any action by which it converts any of its contributed surplus that arose on the issuance of shares of its capital stock (other than any portion of that contributed surplus that arose at a time when it was non-resident, or that arose in connection with a disposition to which subsection 212.1(1.1) applies or an *investment*, as defined in subsection 212.3(10), to which subsection 212.3(2) applies) into paid-up capital in respect of shares of its capital stock, or

(*c*.3) if the corporation is neither an insurance corporation nor a bank, any action by which it converts into paid-up capital in respect of a class of shares of its capital stock any of its contributed surplus that arose after March 31, 1977 (other than any portion of that contributed surplus that arose at a time when it was non-resident, or that arose in connection with a disposition to which subsection 212.1(1.1) applies or an *investment*, as defined in subsection 212.3(10), to which subsection 212.3(2) applies)

(i) on the issuance of shares of that class or shares of another class for which the shares of that class were substituted (other than an issuance to which section 51, 66.3, 84.1, 85, 85.1, 86 or 87 or subsection 192(4.1) or 194(4.1) applied),

(ii) on the acquisition of property by the corporation from a person who at the time of the acquisition held any of the issued shares of that class or shares of another class for which shares of that class were substituted for no consideration or for consideration that did not include shares of the capital stock of the corporation, or

(iii) as a result of any action by which the paid-up capital in respect of that class of shares or in respect of shares of another class for which shares of that class were substituted was reduced by the corporation, to the extent of the reduction in paid-up capital that resulted from the action,

the corporation shall be deemed to have paid at that time a dividend on the issued shares of the particular class equal to the amount, if any, by which the amount of the increase in the paid-up capital exceeds the total of

(*d*) the amount, if any, of the increase referred to in subparagraph (*b*)(i) or the decrease referred to in subparagraph (*b*)(ii), as the case may be,

(*e*) the amount, if any, of the reduction referred to in paragraph (*c*), and

(*f*) the amount, if any, of the increase in the paid-up capital that resulted from a conversion referred to in paragraph (*c*.1), (*c*.2) or (*c*.3),

and a dividend shall be deemed to have been received at that time by each person who held any of the issued shares of the particular class immediately after that time equal to that proportion of the dividend so deemed to have been paid by the corporation that the number of the shares of the particular class held by the person immediately after that time is of the number of the issued shares of that class outstanding immediately after that time.

Editorial Note: Deemed dividends under s. 84(1) in respect of a share are added in computing the adjusted cost base of the share under s. 53(1)(*b*). This ensures that the increases in paid-up capital referred to in s. 84(1) are not subsequently taxed in the form of capital gains.

History: S. 84(1)(*c*.3), the portion before subparagraph (ii) was replaced by S.C. 2018, c. 27, s. 5(2), applicable in respect of transactions or events that occur after February 26, 2018, and formerly read:

(*c*.3) if the corporation is neither an insurance corporation nor a bank, any action by which it converts into paid-up capital in respect of a class of shares of its capital stock any of its contributed surplus that arose after March 31, 1977 (other than any portion of that contributed surplus that arose in connection with an investment, as defined in subsection 212.3(10), to which subsection 212.3(2) applies)

(i) on the issuance of shares of that class or shares of another class for which the shares of that class were substituted (other than an issuance to which section 51, 66.3, 84.1, 85, 85.1, 86 or 87 or subsection 192(4.1), 194(4.1) or 212.1(1.1) applied),

S. 84(1)(*c*.1) and (*c*.2) were replaced by S.C. 2018, c. 27, s. 5(1), applicable in respect of transactions or events that occur after February 26, 2018, and formerly read:

(*c*.1) if the corporation is an insurance corporation, any action by which it converts contributed surplus related to its insurance business (other than any portion of that contributed surplus that arose in connection with an investment, as defined in subsection 212.3(10), to which subsection 212.3(2) applies) into paid-up capital in respect of the shares of its capital stock,

(*c*.2) if the corporation is a bank, any action by which it converts any of its contributed surplus that arose on the issuance of shares of its capital stock (other than any portion of that contributed surplus that arose in connection with an investment, as defined in subsection 212.3(10), to which subsection 212.3(2) applies) into paid-up capital in respect of shares of its capital stock, or

S. 84(1)(*c*.3)(i) was replaced by S.C. 2016, c. 12, s. 25(1), deemed to have come into force on March 22, 2016, and formerly read:

(i) on the issuance of shares of that class or shares of another class for which the shares of that class were substituted (other than an issuance to which section 51, 66.3, 84.1, 85, 85.1, 86 or 87, subsection 192(4.1) or 194(4.1) or section 212.1 applied),

S. 84(1)(*c*.1) and (*c*.2) were replaced by S.C. 2012, c. 31, s. 16(1), deemed to have come into force on March 29, 2012. S. 84(1)(*c*.1) and (*c*.2) formerly read:

(*c*.1) where the corporation is an insurance corporation, any action by which it converts contributed surplus related to its insurance business into paid-up capital in respect of the shares of its capital stock,

(*c*.2) where the corporation is a bank, any action by which it converts any of its contributed surplus that arose on the issuance of shares of its capital stock into paid-up capital in respect of shares of its capital stock, or

S. 84(1)(*c*.3), the portion before subparagraph (i) was replaced by S.C. 2012, c. 31, s. 16(2), deemed to have come into force on March 29, 2012. S. 84(1)(*c*.3), the portion before subparagraph (i) formerly read:

(*c*.3) where the corporation is neither an insurance corporation nor a bank, any action by which it converts into paid-up capital in respect of a class of shares of its capital stock any of its contributed surplus that arose after March 31, 1977

Related Regulations: Part II.

Related Sections: S. 15(1) Benefit conferred on shareholder; s. 53(1)(*b*) Adjustments to cost base — Deemed dividend; s. 53(1)(*c*) Adjustments to cost base — Contributions of capital; s. 84(6) Where s. (2) or (3) does not apply; s. 84(10) Reduction of contributed surplus; s. 84(11) Computation of contributed surplus; s. 85(2.1) Computing paid-up capital; s. 87(2)(*y*) Contributed surplus; s. 89(1), "paid-up capital"; s. 131(11) Rules respecting prescribed labour-sponsored venture capital corporations; s. 138(11.9) Computation of contributed surplus; s. 139.1(6) Paid-up capital — insurance corporation; s. 248(1), "bank", "insurance corporation".

Canadian Tax Foundation: Cardarelli, *Transactions Involving Paid-Up Capital*, 2004 Conference Report 26:1–22; Suarez and Ahmed, *Public Company Non-Butterfly Spinouts*, 2003 Conference Report 32:1–49; Smith and Devan, *Paid-Up Capital Planning*, 2003 Canadian Tax Journal 6:2296–2319; Lewin, *Tax Attributes: Cost or Capital Cost and Paid-Up Capital*, 1998 Conference Report 8:1–40; Durand and Freedman, *Dealing with Paid-Up Capital*, 1997 Corporate Management Tax Conference 17:1–42.

Tax Profile: September 2013 — Federal Court of Appeal Expands the Scope of Surplus-Stripping Rule in *MacDonald*; December 2004 — Taxation of Dividends: A Survey in the Context of Private Corporations and Their Shareholders — Part 2; October 2004 — Taxation of Dividends: A Survey in the Context of Private Corporations and Their Shareholders.

Tax Topics: No. 1820, Beware of Pitfalls in November 9, 2006 Technical Amendments When Crystallizing "Safe Income"!.

Forms: T5 Sum. — Return of Investment Income; T5 — Statement of Investment Income.

Income Tax Technical News: Issue No. 44, Paid-Up Capital Increase by an Unlimited Liability Company.

Interpretation Bulletins: *Secondary* — IT-67R3 Taxable dividends from corporations resident in Canada; IT-291R3 Transfer of property to a corporation under subsection 85(1); IT-432R2 Benefits conferred on shareholders; IT-463R2 Paid-up Capital.

Tax Window Files: Conversion of Contributed Surplus to PUC, *15XXXX*, CRA Document No. 2015-0584151R3; Application of Subsection 84(1)/Paid-Up Capital, *February 26, 2009*, CRA Document No. 2008-0293401E5; Capital loss reduction under 112(3.2) for estate, *Technical Interpretation, International and Trusts Division, May 30, 2007*, CRA Document No. 2007-0224371I7; Return of Contributed Surplus to Shareholder, *Technical Interpretation, Reorganizations and Resources Division, August 25, 2003*, CRA Document No. 2003-0031585. If contributed surplus is paid directly to a shareholder and is not converted into paid-up capital as per paragraph 84(1)(*c*.3), amount is included in shareholder's income either as dividend or benefit; Transfer of Shares, *Technical Interpretation, Reorganizations and Resources Division, February 17, 2003*, CRA Document No. 2002-0176455. Corporate reorganization in which the exception in subparagraph 84(1)(*b*)(i) could apply; increase in the value of the corporation's assets could offset the increase in its paid-up capital.

► 84(2) ◄

(2) Distribution on winding-up, etc. Where funds or property of a corporation resident in Canada have at any time after March 31, 1977 been distributed or otherwise appropriated in any manner whatever to or for the benefit of the shareholders of any class of shares in its capital stock, on the winding-up, discontinuance or reorganization of its business, the corporation shall be deemed to have paid at that time a dividend on the shares of that class equal to the amount, if any, by which

(*a*) the amount or value of the funds or property distributed or appropriated, as the case may be,

exceeds

(*b*) the amount, if any, by which the paid-up capital in respect of the shares of that class is reduced on the distribution or appropriation, as the case may be,

and a dividend shall be deemed to have been received at that time by each person who held any of the issued shares at that time equal to that proportion of the amount of the excess that the number of the shares of that class held by the person immediately before that time is of the number of the issued shares of that class outstanding immediately before that time.

Editorial Note: The amount of a deemed dividend arising under s. 84(2) or (3) on a redemption, acquisition, or cancellation of a shareholder's share is excluded from the proceeds of disposition of the share; see paragraph (*j*) of the definition of "proceeds of disposition" in s. 54. If the shareholder's adjusted cost base of the share exceeds the paid-up capital in respect of the share, the deemed dividend will generally be accompanied by a capital loss on the disposition of the share; however, the stop-loss rule of s. 40(3.6) (shareholder and corporation affiliated immediately after disposition) or the loss reduction rules in s. 112(3) and (3.2) (loss reduced by tax-free dividends received) may apply.

In contrast to s. 84(3), s. 84(2) can apply even if the share is not redeemed, acquired, or cancelled, such that there is no disposition of the share; see, for example, CRA Document No. 2006-0184821R3.

Related Sections: S. 40(3.6) Loss on shares; s. 53(2)(*a*) Amounts to be deducted — Share of the capital stock of a corporation; s. 54, "proceeds of disposition"; s. 55(2) Deemed proceeds or gain; s. 69(5) Winding-up of corporation; s. 83(2) Capital dividend; s. 84(9) Shares disposed of on redemptions, etc; s. 88(1)(*d.1*) Winding-up; s. 88(2)(*b*) Winding-up of Canadian corporation; s. 89(1), "paid-up capital"; s. 112(3) Loss on share that is capital property; s. 112(3.1) Loss on share held by partnership; s. 112(3.2) Loss on share held by trust; s. 135.1(8) Application of subsections 84(2) and (3); s. 137(4.2) Deemed interest not a dividend; s. 191(4) Deemed dividends; s. 248(1), "disposition".

Canadian Tax Foundation: Baxter et al., *Surplus Stripping — What's Acceptable, What's Not, and What Should Be?*, 2014 British Columbia Tax Conference 12:1–A5; Smith, *Pipeline and Bump Planning*, 2014 British Columbia Tax Conference 7A:1–7; Gilbert and Dolson, *Accessing Surplus: What Works, What Doesn't, What's Left*, 2014 Prairie Provinces Tax Conference 9:1–57; Bleiwas and Ball, *Current Issues for Private Companies, Including Dividend Tax Credit Changes and Integration*, 2013 Conference Report 6:1–32; Haney, *Current Cases: Federal Court of Appeal — Surplus-Stripping Plan Struck Down (Canada v. MacDonald, 2013 FCA 110)*, 2013 Canadian Tax Journal 3:739–745; Meredith and Fehr, *Surplus Stripping: In the Eye of the Beholder*, 2013 British Columbia Tax Conference 14:1–29; Rickards, *Hybrid Assets Share Planning when Selling Private Enterprises*, 2013 British Columbia Tax Conference 8:1–24; Fuller and Muise, *Recent Court Decisions: R. v. MacDonald, 2013 FCA 110*, 2013 Prairie Provinces Tax Conference 1:1–5; Bernstein and Gucciardo, *Surplus Stripping in MacDonald*, 2013 Canadian Tax Highlights 21(6):9–11; Moraitis and Kakkar, *Stopping the Pipeline — In Any Manner Whatever*, 2013 Tax for the Owner-Manager 13(3):2–3; Jang, *Post Mortem Pipeline Potentially Upset by FCA*, 2013 Canadian Tax Focus 3(3):9–10; Durand and Gwyer, *Surplus Stripping and Domestic Private Corporations*, 2012 Conference Report 13:1–20; Falk and Morand, *Current Issues Forum: Pipeline Planning; Subsection 164(6) Circularity Issue; Eligible Dividend Designations*, 2012 Ontario Tax Conference 1B:1–26; Bordeleau et al., *Post Mortem Estate Planning: Pipeline Transactions (Canada Revenue Agency and Revenu Québec Round Table, Question 22)*, 2011 Conference Report 4:16–17; Jadd and Brady, *Structuring the Purchase and Sale of a Business: Some Tips and Traps*, 2011 Ontario Tax Conference 11:1–33; Suarez and Ahmed, *Public Company Non-Butterfly Spinouts*, 2003 Conference Report 32:1–49; Smith and Devan, *Paid-Up Capital Planning*, 2003 Canadian Tax Journal 6:2296–2319; Roberts and Briggs, *Winding Up: Part 1*, 1996 Canadian Tax Journal 2:533–560.

Tax Profile: February 2015 — Canada-US Agreement to Implement FATCA Reporting Obligations Enters into Force; September 2013 — Federal Court of Appeal Expands the Scope of Surplus-Stripping Rule in *MacDonald*; February 2012 — Post-Mortem Planning — Double Taxation on Death; January 2012 — Highlights from the 2011 Ontario Tax Conference: Q&A with the Tax Administration Panel; June 2011 — Summary of Canada Revenue Agency Round Table Held at the 13th National STEP Canada Conference; October 2004 — Taxation of Dividends: A Survey in the Context of Private Corporations and Their Shareholders.

Tax Topics: No. 2150, Federal Court Of Appeal Strikes Down *Inter Vivos* Surplus Strip; No. 2104, Pipeline Planning Alive and Well After All?; No. 2075, 2011 Canadian Tax Foundation Roundtable; No. 2023-24, 2010 Canadian Tax Foundation CRA Roundtable: Pipelines, Privilege and Working Papers (Again!); No. 2005, Subsection 84(2) Did Not Apply — *The Queen v. Tremblay* (FCA).

Interpretation Bulletins: *Primary* — IT-126R2 Meaning of "winding-up". *Secondary* — IT-444R Corporations — Involuntary Dissolutions.

Tax Window Files: Reduction of Stated Capital of Public Corporation, *March 4, 2009*, CRA Document No. 2008-0289331R3; Meaning of "Reorganization" in 84(2), *October 5, 2007*, CRA Document No. 2007-0243221C6; PUC reduction by a public corporation, *October 18, 2006*, CRA Document No. 2006-0184821R3; Paid-Up Capital Reduction — Public Corporation, *April 26, 2006*, CRA Document No. 2005-0165091R3; Reorganization of a Business, *March 29, 2006*, CRA Document No. 2005-0149751R3; Distribution of Funds by a Public Corporation, *Tax Ruling, Reorganizations and Resources Division, August 31, 2005*, CRA Document No. 2004-0067531R3; Shareholder/Manager Remuneration, *Technical Interpretation, Business and Partnerships Division, May 31, 2005*, CRA Document No. 2004-0106951I7. Whether amounts paid to shareholders on winding-up are bonuses or deemed dividends; Surplus Stripping Post-Geransky, *Round Table on Federal Taxation, APFF — 2003 Conference Question 1, October 10, 2003*, CRA Document No. 2003-0029955.

Cases: A deemed dividend occurs when funds or property are distributed to shareholders on the winding-up or discontinuance of a corporation. The corporation stopped operating in 2006, and there were no funds in the company after the foreclosure. It had no retained earnings once it ceased operations and no funds or property were distributed or appropriated by the taxpayers. *Latham v. The Queen*, 2015 DTC 1104 (T.C.C.)

Subsection 84(2) contemplates only one single transaction or set of transactions by one corporation, and the Minister's reliance on it to support the reassessments under appeal was misplaced. *Descarries v. The Queen*, 2014 DTC 1081 (T.C.C.)

When a company owned by the taxpayers was wound up, its shares of V, a public corporation, were not distributed to the taxpayers, but to V itself, which retired those shares and issued new shares to the taxpayers. S. 84(2) did not apply since the new shares were never property of the wound-up company. *The Queen v. Vaillancourt-Tremblay et al.*, 2010 DTC 5079 (F.C.A.), affirming 2009 DTC 1204 (T.C.C.)

Where taxpayers through a complicated series of transactions effected a distribution of the surplus of a company wound-up although not formally liquidated, they were taxed as deemed dividends under then s. 81(1) and the Minister granted a dividend tax credit. This procedure was held a proper application of s. 81(1), and it was found unnecessary to express an opinion on s. 137(2), upon which the Minister had also relied. *Smythe et al. v. M.N.R.*, 69 DTC 5361 (S.C.C.), affirming 67 DTC 5334 (Ex. Ct.) as to the application of s. 81(1)

▶ 84(3) ◀

(3) Redemption, etc. Where at any time after December 31, 1977 a corporation resident in Canada has redeemed, acquired or cancelled in any manner whatever (otherwise than by way of a transaction described in subsection (2)) any of the shares of any class of its capital stock,

(*a*) the corporation shall be deemed to have paid at that time a dividend on a separate class of shares comprising the shares so redeemed, acquired or cancelled equal to the amount, if any, by which the amount paid by the corporation on the redemption, acquisition or cancellation, as the case may be, of those shares exceeds the paid-up capital in respect of those shares immediately before that time; and

(*b*) a dividend shall be deemed to have been received at that time by each person who held any of the shares of that separate class at that time equal to that portion of the amount of the excess determined under paragraph (*a*) that the number of those shares held by the person immediately before that time is of the total number of shares of that separate class that the corporation has redeemed, acquired or cancelled, at that time.

Editorial Note: See the editorial note for s. 84(2).

Related Sections: S. 40(3.6) Loss on shares; S. 51(1) Convertible property; s. 51(3) Computation of paid-up capital; s. 54, "proceeds of disposition"; s. 55(2) Deemed proceeds or gain; s. 66.3(2) Deductions from paid-up capital; s. 66.3(4) Paid-up capital; s. 84(9) Shares disposed of on redemptions, etc; s. 84.1(3) Addition to paid-up capital; s. 84.2(1) Computation of paid-up capital in respect of particular class of shares; s. 85(2.1) Computing paid-up capital; s. 85.1(2.1) Computation of paid-up capital; s. 86(1) Exchange of shares by a shareholder in course of reorganization of capital; s. 86(2.1) Computation of paid-up capital; s. 87(3) Computation of paid-up capital; s. 87(9) Rules applicable in respect of certain mergers; s. 89(1), "paid-up capital"; s. 112(3) Loss on share that is capital property; s. 112(3.1) Loss on share held by partnership; s. 112(3.2) Loss on share held by trust; s. 128.1(3) Paid-up capital adjustment; s. 137(4.2) Deemed interest not a dividend; s. 138(11.7) Computation of paid-up capital; s. 139.1(6) Paid-up capital — insurance corporation; s. 139.1(7) Paid-up capital — holding corporation; s. 212.1(2) Paid-up capital calculation after March 31, 1977.

Canadian Tax Foundation: Smith and Devan, *Paid-Up Capital Planning*, 2003 Canadian Tax Journal 6:2296–2319.

Tax Profile: April 2013 — Canadian Estate Freezes in Favour of U.S. Citizens; October 2012 — Exchangeable Shares in Canada; December 2004 — Taxation of Dividends: A Survey in the Context of Private Corporations and Their Shareholders — Part 2; October 2004 — Taxation of Dividends: A Survey in the Context of Private Corporations and Their Shareholders.

Income Tax Technical News: Issue No. 33, Income Earned or Realized — The Kruco Case.

Interpretation Bulletins: *Secondary* — IT-291R3 Transfer of property to a corporation under subsection 85(1).

Tax Window Files: 2015 CTF Q.6(d), Use of 84(3) Dividend, *November 24, 2015*, CRA Document No. 2015-0610681C6; Interaction Between Sections 89 and 55, *September 17, 2009*, CRA Document No. 2009-0310251E5; Redemption of Shares [Interplay between subsection 84(3) and subsection 116(5)], *June 12, 2009*, CRA Document No. 2008-0301701E5; Redemption of Shares — Balance of Purchase Price, *Technical Interpretation, Reorganizations and Resources Division, October 28, 2005*, CRA Document No. 2005-0145891E5; Interaction of 84(3) and 69(1)(b), *Round Table — 2004 APFF CONFERENCE, Question 15, October 8, 2004*, CRA Document No. 2004-0086821C6.

Cases: The corporate taxpayer was deemed by s. 84(3) to have received a dividend upon the redemption of shares of G corporation. The same shareholders owned all of the shares of both the taxpayer and G. They subsequently sold their shares of G at arm's length. The redemption by G of its shares, and the sale by the shareholders of their G shares were part of a series of transactions coming within s. 55(2). *Granite Bay Charters Ltd. v. The Queen*, 2001 DTC 615 (T.C.C.)

► 84(4) ◄

(4) Reduction of paid-up capital. Where at any time after March 31, 1977 a corporation resident in Canada has reduced the paid-up capital in respect of any class of shares of its capital stock otherwise than by way of a redemption, acquisition or cancellation of any shares of that class or a transaction described in subsection (2) or (4.1),

(*a*) the corporation shall be deemed to have paid at that time a dividend on shares of that class equal to the amount, if any, by which the amount paid by it on the reduction of the paid-up capital, exceeds the amount by which the paid-up capital in respect of that class of shares of the corporation has been so reduced; and

(*b*) a dividend shall be deemed to have been received at that time by each person who held any of the issued shares at that time equal to that proportion of the amount of the excess referred to in paragraph (*a*) that the number of the shares of that class held by the person immediately before that time is of the number of the issued shares of that class outstanding immediately before that time.

Editorial Note: An amount paid out on the reduction of the paid-up capital in respect of a class of shares is received tax-free to the extent it does not exceed the reduction of paid-up capital in respect of the class, but such amount reduces the shareholder's adjusted cost base of the shares (s. 53(2)(*a*)(ii)).

If the reduction causes the adjusted cost base of the share to become negative, the taxpayer will realize a capital gain (s. 40(3)) and the adjusted cost base will be readjusted to nil (s. 53(1)(*a*)). However, to the extent that the paid-up capital reduction results in a dividend under s. 84(4), the adjusted cost base is not reduced.

Related Sections: S. 53(2)(*a*)(ii) Amounts to be deducted; s. 84.1(3) Addition to paid-up capital; s. 84.2(1) Computation of paid-up capital in respect of particular class of shares; s. 87(9) Rules applicable in respect of certain mergers; s. 89(1), "paid-up capital"; s. 128.1(3) Paid-up capital adjustment; s. 137(4.2) Deemed interest not a dividend; s. 139.1(6) Paid-up capital — insurance corporation; s. 139.1(7) Paid-up capital — holding corporation; s. 212.1(2) Paid-up capital calculation after March 31, 1977.

Canadian Tax Foundation: Smith and Devan, *Paid-Up Capital Planning*, 2003 Canadian Tax Journal 6:2296–2319.

Tax Profile: October 2004 — Taxation of Dividends: A Survey in the Context of Private Corporations and Their Shareholders.

Tax Topics: No. 1949, GAAR in the Gaps: Collins & Aikman Products Co. et al. v. The Queen; No. 1894, Negative Paid-Up Capital and Subsection 84(4) Reduction.

Tax Window Files: Reduction of Stated Capital of Public Corporation, *March 4, 2009*, CRA Document No. 2008-0289331R3; Reduction of PUC, *February 28, 2008*, CRA Document No. 2008-0266181I7; Deemed Capital Gain on PUC Reduction, *Technical Interpretation, International and Trust Division, February 14, 2003*, CRA Document No. 2002-0168815. Where PUC reduction results in negative adjusted cost base.

► 84(4.1) ◄

(4.1) Deemed dividend on reduction of paid-up capital. Any amount paid by a public corporation on the reduction of the paid-up capital in respect of any class of shares of its capital stock, otherwise than by way of a redemption, acquisition or cancellation of any shares of that class or by way of a transaction described in subsection (2) or section 86, is deemed to have been paid by the corporation and received by the person to whom it was paid, as a dividend, unless

(*a*) the amount may reasonably be considered to be derived from proceeds of disposition realized by the public corporation, or by a person or partnership in which the public corporation had a direct or indirect interest at the time that the proceeds were realized, from a transaction that occurred

(i) outside the ordinary course of the business of the corporation, or of the person or partnership that realized the proceeds, and

(ii) within the period that commenced 24 months before the payment; and

(*b*) no amount that may reasonably be considered to be derived from those proceeds was paid by the public corporation on a previous reduction of the paid-up capital in respect of any class of shares of its capital stock.

History: S. 84(4.1) was replaced by S.C. 2013, c. 34, s. 219(1), applicable to amounts paid after 1996, except that in respect of those amounts paid before February 27, 2004, subsection 84(4.1) is to be read as follows:

"(4.1) Any amount paid by a public corporation on the reduction of the paid-up capital in respect of any class of shares of its capital stock, otherwise than by way of a redemption, acquisition or cancellation of any shares of that class or by way of a transaction described in subsection (2) or in section 86, is deemed to have been paid by the corporation and received by the person to whom it was paid, as a dividend, unless the amount may reasonably be considered to be derived from proceeds of disposition realized by the public corporation, or by a person or partnership in which the public corporation had a direct or indirect interest at the time that the proceeds were realized, from a transaction that occurred outside the ordinary course of the business of the public corporation, or of the person or partnership that realized the proceeds."

S. 84(4.1) formerly read:

(4.1) *Deemed dividend on reduction of paid-up capital.* Where at any time after April 10, 1978, a public corporation has reduced the paid-up capital in respect of any class of shares of its capital stock otherwise than by way of a redemption, acquisition or cancellation of any shares of that class or a transaction described in subsection (2) or section 86, any amount paid by it on the reduction of the paid-up capital shall be deemed to have been paid by the corporation and received by the person to whom it was paid, as a dividend.

Related Sections: S. 84.1(3) Addition to paid-up capital; s. 89(1), "paid-up capital"; s. 139.1(6) Paid-up capital — insurance corporation; s. 139.1(7) Paid-up capital — holding corporation; s. 212.1(2) Paid-up capital calculation after March 31, 1977.

Canadian Tax Foundation: Smith and Devan, *Paid-Up Capital Planning*, 2003 Canadian Tax Journal 6:2296–2319; Ahmed, *Corporate Distributions Other Than Butterfly Transactions*, 1998 Conference Report 15:1–38.

Tax Window Files: Reduction of Stated Capital of Public Corporation, *March 4, 2009*, CRA Document No. 2008-0289331R3.

▶ 84(4.2) ◀

(4.2) Deemed dividend on term preferred share. Where, at any time after November 16, 1978, the paid-up capital in respect of a term preferred share owned by a shareholder that is

(*a*) a specified financial institution, or

(*b*) a partnership or trust of which a specified financial institution or a person related to such an institution was a member or a beneficiary,

was reduced otherwise than by way of a redemption, acquisition or cancellation of the share or of a transaction described in subsection (2) or (4.1), the amount received by the shareholder on the reduction of the paid-up capital in respect of the share shall be deemed to be a dividend received by the shareholder at that time unless the share was not acquired in the ordinary course of the business carried on by the shareholder.

▶ 84(4.3) ◀

(4.3) Deemed dividend on guaranteed share. Where at any time after 1987 the paid-up capital in respect of a share of the capital stock of a particular corporation owned

(*a*) by a shareholder that is another corporation to which subsection 112(2.2) or (2.4) would, if the particular corporation were a taxable Canadian corporation, apply to deny the deduction under subsection 112(1) or (2) or 138(6) of a dividend received on the share, or

(*b*) by a partnership or trust of which the other corporation is a member or beneficiary, as the case may be,

was reduced otherwise than by way of a redemption, acquisition or cancellation of the share or of a transaction described in subsection (2) or (4.1), the amount received by the shareholder on the reduction of the paid-up capital in respect of the share shall be deemed to be a dividend received by the shareholder at that time.

▶ 84(5) ◀

(5) Amount distributed or paid where a share. Where

(*a*) the amount of property distributed by a corporation or otherwise appropriated to or for the benefit of its shareholders as described in paragraph (2)(*a*), or

(*b*) the amount paid by a corporation as described in paragraph (3)(*a*) or (4)(*a*),

includes a share of the capital stock of the corporation, for the purposes of subsections (2) to (4) the following rules apply:

(*c*) in computing the amount referred to in paragraph (*a*) at any time, the share shall be valued at an amount equal to its paid-up capital at that time, and

(*d*) in computing the amount referred to in paragraph (*b*) at any time, the share shall be valued at an amount equal to the amount by which the paid-up capital in respect of the class of shares to which it belongs has increased by virtue of its issue.

Related Sections: S. 51(3) Computation of paid-up capital; s. 85(2.1) Computing paid-up capital; s. 86(2.1) Computation of paid-up capital.

Interpretation Bulletins: *Secondary* — IT-291R3 Transfer of property to a corporation under subsection 85(1).

▶ 84(6) ◀

(6) Where s. (2) or (3) does not apply. Subsection (2) or (3), as the case may be, is not applicable

(*a*) in respect of any transaction or event, to the extent that subsection (1) is applicable in respect of that transaction or event; and

(*b*) in respect of any purchase by a corporation of any of its shares in the open market, if the corporation acquired those shares in the manner in which shares would normally be purchased by any member of the public in the open market.

Related Sections: S. 183.1(2) Tax payable.

▶ 84(7) ◀

(7) When dividend payable. A dividend that is deemed by this section or section 84.1, 128.1 or 212.1 to have been paid at a particular time is deemed, for the purposes of this subdivision and sections 131 and 133, to have become payable at that time.

History: S. 84(7) was replaced by S.C. 2013, c. 34, s. 219(2), applicable to dividends deemed to have been paid after February 23, 1998, and formerly read:

> (7) *When dividend payable.* A dividend that is deemed by this subsection or section 84.1, 128.1 or 212.1 to have been paid at a particular time is deemed, for the purposes of this subdivision and sections 131 and 133, to have become payable at that time.

▶ 84(8) ◀

(8) Where s. (3) does not apply. Subsection (3) does not apply to deem a dividend to have been received by a shareholder of a public corporation where the shareholder is an individual resident in Canada who deals at arm's length with the corporation and the shares redeemed, acquired or cancelled are prescribed shares of the capital stock of the corporation.

Related Regulations: 6206.

▶ 84(9) ◀

(9) Shares disposed of on redemptions, etc. For greater certainty it is declared that where a shareholder of a corporation has disposed of a share of the capital stock of the corporation as a result of the redemption, acquisition or cancellation of the share by the corporation, the shareholder shall, for the purposes of this Act, be deemed to have disposed of the share to the corporation.

Editorial Note: The main purpose of s. 84(9) is to ensure that where the shareholder and corporation do not deal at arm's length, the various provisions of the Act that deal with dispositions between non-arm's length persons will apply where the shareholder disposes of a share of the corporation as a result of the redemption, acquisition, or cancellation of the share. See also the stop-loss rule in s. 40(3.6) where the shareholder and corporation are affiliated immediately after the disposition. Subsection 84(9) does not expressly deem the corporation to have purchased or acquired the share; this issue may be relevant, for example, in respect of the potential application of s. 116(5) to the corporation if the shareholder is non-resident.

Related Sections: S. 40(3.6) Loss on shares; s. 69(1) Inadequate considerations; s. 84(2) Distribution on winding-up, etc; s. 84(3) Redemption, etc; s. 85(1) Transfer of property to corporation by shareholders; s. 86(1) Exchange of shares by a shareholder in course of reorganization of capital; s. 116(5) Liability of purchaser.

Income Tax Folios: S4-F8-C1 Business Investment Losses.

Tax Window Files: Redemption of Shares [Interplay between subsection 84(3) and subsection 116(5)], *June 12, 2009*, CRA Document No. 2008-0301701E5.

► 84(10) ◄

(10) Reduction of contributed surplus. For the purpose of paragraph (1)(*c*.3), there shall be deducted in determining at any time a corporation's contributed surplus that arose after March 31, 1977 in any manner described in that paragraph the lesser of

(*a*) the amount, if any, by which the amount of a dividend paid by the corporation at or before that time and after March 31, 1977 and when it was a public corporation exceeded its retained earnings immediately before the payment of the dividend, and

(*b*) the amount of its contributed surplus immediately before the payment of the dividend referred to in paragraph (*a*) that arose after March 31, 1977.

► 84(11) ◄

(11) Computation of contributed surplus. For the purpose of subparagraph (1)(*c*.3)(ii), where the property acquired by the corporation (in this subsection referred to as the "acquiring corporation") consists of shares (in this subsection referred to as the "subject shares") of any class of the capital stock of another corporation resident in Canada (in this subsection referred to as the "subject corporation") and, immediately after the acquisition of the subject shares, the subject corporation would be connected (within the meaning that would be assigned by subsection 186(4) if the references in that subsection to "payer corporation" and "particular corporation" were read as "subject corporation" and "acquiring corporation", respectively) with the acquiring corporation, the contributed surplus of the acquiring corporation that arose on the acquisition of the subject shares shall be deemed to be the lesser of

(*a*) the amount added to the contributed surplus of the acquiring corporation on the acquisition of the subject shares, and

(*b*) the amount, if any, by which the paid-up capital in respect of the subject shares at the time of the acquisition exceeded the fair market value of any consideration given by the acquiring corporation for the subject shares.

SECTION 84.1: Non-arm's length sale of shares

► 84.1(1) ◄

(1) Non-arm's length sale of shares. Where after May 22, 1985 a taxpayer resident in Canada (other than a corporation) disposes of shares that are capital property of the taxpayer (in this section referred to as the "subject shares") of any class of the capital stock of a corporation resident in Canada (in this section referred to as the "subject corporation") to another corporation (in this section referred to as the "purchaser corporation") with which the taxpayer does not deal at arm's length and, immediately after the disposition, the subject corporation would be connected (within the meaning assigned by subsection 186(4) if the references therein to "payer corporation" and to "particular corporation" were read as "subject corporation" and "purchaser corporation" respectively) with the purchaser corporation,

(*a*) where shares (in this section referred to as the "new shares") of the purchaser corporation have been issued as consideration for the subject shares, in computing the paid-up capital, at any particular time after the issue of the new shares, in respect of any particular class of shares of the capital stock of the purchaser corporation, there shall be deducted an amount determined by the formula

$$(A - B) \times C/A$$

where

A is the increase, if any, determined without reference to this section as it applies to the acquisition of the subject shares, in the paid-up capital in respect of all shares of the capital stock of the purchaser corporation as a result of the issue of the new shares,

B is the amount, if any, by which the greater of

(i) the paid-up capital, immediately before the disposition, in respect of the subject shares, and

(ii) subject to paragraphs (2)(*a*) and (*a*.1), the adjusted cost base to the taxpayer, immediately before the disposition, of the subject shares,

exceeds the fair market value, immediately after the disposition, of any consideration (other than the new shares) received by the taxpayer from the purchaser corporation for the subject shares, and

C is the increase, if any, determined without reference to this section as it applies to the acquisition of the subject shares, in the paid-up capital in respect of the particular class of shares as a result of the issue of the new shares; and

(*b*) for the purposes of this Act, a dividend shall be deemed to be paid to the taxpayer by the purchaser corporation and received by the taxpayer from the purchaser corporation at the time of the disposition in an amount determined by the formula

$$(A + D) - (E + F)$$

where

A is the increase, if any, determined without reference to this section as it applies to the acquisition of the subject shares, in the paid-up capital in respect of all shares of the capital stock of the purchaser corporation as a result of the issue of the new shares,

D is the fair market value, immediately after the disposition, of any consideration (other than the new shares) received by the taxpayer from the purchaser corporation for the subject shares,

E is the greater of

(i) the paid-up capital, immediately before the disposition, in respect of the subject shares, and

(ii) subject to paragraphs (2)(*a*) and (*a*.1), the adjusted cost base to the taxpayer, immediately before the disposition, of the subject shares, and

F is the total of all amounts each of which is an amount required to be deducted by the purchaser corporation under paragraph (*a*) in computing the paid-up capital in respect of any class of shares of its capital stock by virtue of the acquisition of the subject shares.

Editorial Note: Section 84.1 may limit the consideration a taxpayer (other than a corporation) can receive as proceeds of disposition on a non-arm's length sale of shares to a corporation. It applies only if the purchaser is connected after the purchase with the company acquired. Any amount received over the limit is deemed to be a dividend. The total cash, debt and paid-up capital of shares received cannot exceed the greater of the paid-up capital of the shares sold and an amount often referred to as the "arm's-length acquisition cost" (AAC) or "hard cost".

AAC is the adjusted cost base of the shares sold, reduced by the portion reflecting V-day value and any capital gains deduction previously claimed on a disposition of the shares by anyone not dealing at arm's length with the vendor. Thus, the maximum proceeds of disposition the vendor can receive on a sale to a non-arm's length corporation is what the vendor or non-arm's length parties have previously paid to acquire the shares from an arm's length party, (or the paid-up capital of the shares sold, if that is greater), and any additional amount received is a dividend.

Section 84.1 is commonly encountered in an individual's sale of shares in a family business corporation: the vendor can claim the capital gains deduction or the purchaser can use corporate funds to pay the purchase price, but not both.

Paid-up Capital Reduction: Paid-up capital is reduced to the extent total cash, debt and paid-up capital exceed the AAC of the shares sold (or their paid-up capital, if that is greater). If this rule is relevant, the paid-up capital reduction (in s. 85(2.1)) on a section 85 transfer does not apply, even if section 84.1 does not result in a paid-up capital reduction (see CRA Document No. 2011-0412121C6).

Designating the Deemed Dividend: If total cash and debt received, less the reduction in paid-up capital, exceeds the greater of the AAC and the paid-up capital of the shares sold, the transferor is deemed to have received a taxable dividend (s. 84.1(1)(*b*)). This deemed dividend can be designated as eligible even if the recipient does not own shares in the payer (see CRA Document No. 2012-0454091C6). It can also be designated as a capital dividend, but only where the vendor owns shares in the purchaser (see CRA Document No. 2006-0183851E5). If the dividend is uncollectible, it cannot be treated as a bad debt as s. 84.1 deems it to have been paid (see *Mills Estate*, 2011 DTC 5124 (F.C.A.)).

CRA's Administrative Position: Non-arm's Length: S. 84.1 can only apply if the vendor does not deal at arm's length with the purchasing corporation. The CRA will not rule on whether unrelated employees act at arm's length in buy-out situations (see Canadian Tax Highlights, January 2013, "CRA's GAAR Update"; CRA Document 2007-0243171C6: An unrelated employee was not acting arm's length in using corporate funds to buy into a corporation).

Partnership as Vendor: Section 84.1 applies to a "taxpayer", other than a corporation. As that term is defined to include any person, whether or not liable for tax, section 84.1 applies to a partnership (see CRA Document No. 9801695 and CRA Document No. 2003-0037425).

Related Sections: S. 54, "proceeds of disposition"; s. 82(1) Taxable dividends received; s. 89(1), "paid-up capital"; s. 212.1(1) Non-arm's length sales of shares by non-residents.

Canadian Tax Foundation: Hamelin, *Surplus Stripping: A New Approach?*, 2018 Tax for the Owner Manager 18(4):7–8; Halil and Kakkar, *Section 84.1 and Factual Non-Arm's-Length Considered*, 2017 Tax for the Owner Manager 17(1):4–5; Gilbert and Dolson, *Accessing Surplus: What Works, What Doesn't, What's Left*, 2014 Prairie Provinces Tax Conference 9:1–57; Desroches, *V-Day Surplus Stripping an Abuse of Section 84.1*, 2014 Canadian Tax Focus 4(3):12–13; Dergousoff, *Employee Buyco Transactions: Not Arm's-Length?*, 2013 Canadian Tax Focus 3(4):2–3; Meredith and Fehr, *Surplus Stripping: In the Eye of the Beholder*, 2013 British Columbia Tax Conference 14:1–29; Durand and Gwyer, *Surplus Stripping and Domestic Private Corporations*, 2012 Conference Report 13:1–20; Kraft and Kraft, *The Application of Section 84.1 — Tips and Traps*, 2012 Canadian Tax Journal 2:449–470; Diksic, *Selected Issues in Purchase and Sale Transactions: Section 84.1 and Restrictive Covenants*, 2005 Conference Report 43:1–12; Smith and Devan, *Paid-Up Capital Planning*, 2003 Canadian Tax Journal 6:2296–2319; Bienvenue, *Update on Section 84.1*, 2003 Tax for the Owner-Manager 3(1):9; Scaletta, *Section 84.1 and Succession Planning*, 2003 Tax for the Owner-Manager 3(1):2–3; Wilkenfeld, *Section 84.1 Update*, 2002 Tax for the Owner-Manager 2(1):6–7; Marquette, *Selected Income Tax Issues of Particular Relevance to Shareholders Agreements: Part 2*, 2001 Canadian Tax Journal 2:407–437; McDonnell, *Section 84.1: Dont Get Caught By It*, 2001 Tax for the Owner-Manager 1(1):4.

Tax Profile: February 2015 — Canada-US Agreement to Implement FATCA Reporting Obligations Enters into Force; February 2012 — Post-Mortem Planning — Double Taxation on Death; January 2012 — Highlights from the 2011 Ontario Tax Conference: Q&A with the Tax Administration Panel; January 2010 — Shareholders' Agreements — A Survey of Income Tax Issues; October 2004 — Taxation of Dividends: A Survey in the Context of Private Corporations and Their Shareholders.

Tax Topics: No. 2104, Pipeline Planning Alive and Well After All?.

No. 1780, Claude Desmarais: The Latest Float in the GAAR Parade.

Information Circulars: IC 88-2 General anti-avoidance rule — Section 245 of the Income Tax Act (para. 25, Supp. 1, paras. 4 and 9).

Interpretation Bulletins: *Primary* — IT-489R Non-arm's length sale of shares to a corporation.

Tax Window Files: Transfer to Corporations Owned by Brothers, *November 2, 2009*, CRA Document No. 2009-0317541E5; Interaction between 69(1)(b) and 84.1(1)(b), *Technical Interpretation, Reorganizations and Resources Division, November 30, 2007*, CRA Document No. 2007-0228281E5; Application of Par. 84.1(1)(b) on a Sale of Shares, *January 12, 2005*, CRA Document No. 2004-0106161E5; Surplus Strip — Capital Gains v. Dividend, *November 14, 2003*, CRA Document No. 2003-0035435.

Cases: The tax plan developed for the taxpayer circumvented section 84.1, violating its spirit and resulting in abusive tax avoidance. *Pomerleau v. The Queen*, 2018 DTC 5076 (FCA)

While the corporate reorganization changed the tax attributes of a class of preferred shares in a way which created the potential for a tax-free distribution of retained earnings, that potential had not, to date, been realized. Because the tax-free distribution of retained earnings which section 84.1 was intended to prevent had not occurred, there was no evidence that the section had been misused or abused and GAAR did not apply. *1245989 Alberta Ltd. et al v. Attorney General of Canada*, 2018 DTC 5067 (FCA)

The reference in s. 84.1 of the Act to s. 186(4) incorporates the definition of the word "control" as found in s. 186(2). *The Queen v. Olsen*, 2002 DTC 6770 (F.C.A.), reversing 2000 DTC 2121 (T.C.C.).

▶ 84.1(2) ◀

(2) Idem. For the purposes of this section,

(*a*) where a share disposed of by a taxpayer was acquired by the taxpayer before 1972, the adjusted cost base to the taxpayer of the share at any time shall be deemed to be the total of

(i) the amount that would be its adjusted cost base to the taxpayer if the *Income Tax Application Rules* were read without reference to subsections 26(3) and (7) of that Act, and

(ii) the total of all amounts each of which is an amount received by the taxpayer after 1971 and before that time as a dividend on the share and in respect of which the corporation that paid the dividend has made an election under subsection 83(1);

(*a*.1) where a share disposed of by a taxpayer was acquired by the taxpayer after 1971 from a person with whom the taxpayer was not dealing at arm's length, was a share substituted for such a share or was a share substituted for a share owned by the taxpayer at the end of 1971, the adjusted cost base to the taxpayer of the share at any time shall be deemed to be the amount, if any, by which its adjusted cost base to the taxpayer, otherwise determined, exceeds the total of

(i) where the share or a share for which the share was substituted was owned at the end of 1971 by the taxpayer or a person with whom the taxpayer did not deal at arm's length, the amount in respect of that share equal to the amount, if any, by which

(A) the fair market value of the share or the share for which it was substituted, as the case may be, on valuation day (within the meaning assigned by section 24 of the *Income Tax Application Rules*)

exceeds the total of

(B) the actual cost (within the meaning assigned by subsection 26(13) of that Act) of the share or the share for which it was substituted, as the case may be, on January 1, 1972, to the taxpayer or the person with whom the taxpayer did not deal at arm's length, and

(C) the total of all amounts each of which is an amount received by the taxpayer or the person with whom the taxpayer did not deal at arm's length after 1971 and before that time as a dividend on the share or the share for which it was substituted and in respect of which the corporation that paid the dividend has made an election under subsection 83(1), and

(ii) the total of all amounts each of which is an amount determined after 1984 under subparagraph 40(1)(*a*)(i) in respect of a previous disposition of the share or a share for which the share was substituted (or such lesser amount as is established by the taxpayer to be the amount in respect of which a deduction under section 110.6 was claimed) by the taxpayer or an individual with whom the taxpayer did not deal at arm's length;

(*a*.2) (Repealed by 1998, c. 19, s. 115(1).)

(*b*) in respect of any disposition described in subsection (1) by a taxpayer of shares of the capital stock of a subject corporation to a purchaser corporation, the taxpayer shall, for greater certainty, be deemed not to deal at arm's length with the purchaser corporation if the taxpayer

(i) was, immediately before the disposition, one of a group of fewer than 6 persons that controlled the subject corporation, and

(ii) was, immediately after the disposition, one of a group of fewer than 6 persons that controlled the purchaser corporation, each member of which was a member of the group referred to in subparagraph (i); and

(*c*) (Repealed by 1998, c. 19, s. 115(2).)

(*d*) a trust and a beneficiary of the trust or a person related to a beneficiary of the trust shall be deemed not to deal with each other at arm's length.

(*e*) (Repealed by 1998, c. 19, s. 115(3).)

Editorial Note: See also the deeming rules in ss. 84.1(2.01) through 84.1(2.2).

Tax Window Files: Subparagraph 84.1(2)(a.1)(ii) and Section 110.6, *Technical Interpretation, Reorganizations and Resources Division, August 9, 2006*, CRA Document No. 2005-0163621E5; Application of Sec 84.1 — Non-Arm's Length Sale of Shares, *Technical Interpretation, Reorganizations and Resources Division, March 7, 2005*, CRA Document No. 2005-0118291E5; Non Arm's Length Sale of Shares, *December 7, 2004*, CRA Document No. 2004-0104321E5; Deemed ACB Under 84.1(2)(a.1), *November 7, 2003*, CRA Document No. 2003-0006675; Non Arms Length Transfer of Shares, *October 31, 2003*, CRA Document No. 2003-0034757.

▶ 84.1(2.01) ◀

(2.01) Rules for par. 84.1(2)(a.1). For the purpose of paragraph (2)(*a*.1),

(*a*) where at any time a corporation issues a share of its capital stock to a taxpayer, the taxpayer and the corporation are deemed not to be dealing with each other at arm's length at that time;

(*b*) where a taxpayer is deemed by paragraph 110.6(19)(*a*) to have reacquired a share, the taxpayer is deemed to have acquired the share at the beginning of February 23, 1994 from a person with whom the taxpayer was not dealing at arm's length; and

(*c*) where a share owned by a particular person, or a share substituted for that share, has by one or more transactions or events between persons not dealing at arm's length become vested in another person, the particular person and the other person are deemed at all times not to be dealing at arm's length with each other whether or not the particular person and the other person coexisted.

▶ 84.1(2.1) ◀

(2.1) Idem. For the purposes of subparagraph (2)(*a*.1)(ii), where the taxpayer or an individual with whom the taxpayer did not deal at arm's length (in this subsection referred to as the "transferor") disposes of a share in a taxation year and claims an amount under subparagraph 40(1)(*a*)(iii) in computing the gain for the year from the disposition, the amount in respect of which a deduction under section 110.6 was claimed in respect of the transferor's gain from the disposition shall be deemed to be equal to the lesser of

(*a*) the total of

(i) the amount claimed under subparagraph 40(1)(*a*)(iii) by the transferor for the year in respect of the disposition, and

(ii) twice the amount deducted under section 110.6 in computing the taxable income of the transferor for the year in respect of the taxable capital gain from the disposition, and

(*b*) twice the maximum amount that could have been deducted under section 110.6 in computing the taxable income of the transferor for the year in respect of the taxable capital gain from the disposition if

(i) no amount had been claimed by the transferor under subparagraph 40(1)(*a*)(iii) in computing the gain for the year from the disposition, and

(ii) all amounts deducted under section 110.6 in computing the taxable income of the transferor for the year in respect of taxable capital gains from dispositions of property to which this subsection does not apply were deducted before determining the maximum amount that could have been deducted under section 110.6 in respect of the taxable capital gain from the disposition,

and, for the purposes of subparagraph (ii), $1/2$ of the total of all amounts determined under this subsection for the year in respect of other property disposed of before the disposition of the share shall be deemed to have been deducted under section 110.6 in computing the taxable income of the transferor for the year in respect of the taxable capital gain from the disposition of property to which this subsection does not apply,

and, for the purposes of this subsection, where more than one share to which this subsection applies is disposed of in the year, each such share shall be deemed to have been separately disposed of in the order designated by the taxpayer in the taxpayer's return of income under this Part for the year.

Canadian Tax Foundation: Wen and Dickinson, *Are Shares Tainted Forever Under Subsection 84.1(2.1)?*, 2018 Canadian Tax Focus 8(4):15–15.

Tax Window Files: Subsection 84.1(2.1), *April 28, 2016*, CRA Document No. 2015-0594461E5.

► 84.1(2.2) ◄

(2.2) Rules for par. 84.1(2)(b). For the purpose of paragraph (2)(*b*),

(*a*) in determining whether or not a taxpayer referred to in that paragraph was a member of a group of fewer than 6 persons that controlled a corporation at any time, any shares of the capital stock of that corporation owned at that time by

(i) the taxpayer's child (as defined in subsection 70(10)), who is under 18 years of age, or the taxpayer's spouse or common-law partner,

(ii) a trust of which the taxpayer, a person described in subparagraph (i) or a corporation described in subparagraph (iii), is a beneficiary, or

(iii) a corporation controlled by the taxpayer, by a person described in subparagraph (i) or (ii) or by any combination of those persons or trusts

are deemed to be owned at that time by the taxpayer and not by the person who actually owned the shares at that time;

(*b*) a group of persons in respect of a corporation means any 2 or more persons each of whom owns shares of the capital stock of the corporation;

(*c*) a corporation that is controlled by one or more members of a particular group of persons in respect of that corporation is considered to be controlled by that group of persons; and

(*d*) a corporation may be controlled by a person or a particular group of persons even though the corporation is also controlled or deemed to be controlled by another person or group of persons.

► 84.1(3) ◄

(3) Addition to paid-up capital. In computing the paid-up capital at any time after May 22, 1985 in respect of any class of shares of the capital stock of a corporation, there shall be added an amount equal to the lesser of

(*a*) the amount, if any, by which

(i) the total of all amounts each of which is an amount deemed by subsection 84(3), (4) or (4.1) to be a dividend on shares of the class paid after May 22, 1985 and before that time by the corporation

exceeds

(ii) the total of such dividends that would be determined under subparagraph (i) if this Act were read without reference to paragraph (1)(*a*), and

(*b*) the total of all amounts required by paragraph (1)(*a*) to be deducted in computing the paid-up capital in respect of that class of shares after May 22, 1985 and before that time.

Related Sections: S. 212.1(2) Paid-up capital calculation after March 31, 1977.

SECTION 84.2: Computation of paid-up capital in respect of particular class of shares

► 84.2(1) ◄

(1) Computation of paid-up capital in respect of particular class of shares. In computing the paid-up capital in respect of any particular class of shares of the capital stock of a corporation at any particular time after March 31, 1977,

(*a*) there shall be deducted that proportion of the amount, if any, by which the paid-up capital in respect of all of the issued shares of the capital stock of the corporation on April 1, 1977, determined without reference to this section, exceeds the greater of

(i) the amount that the paid-up capital limit of the corporation would have been on March 31, 1977 if paragraph 89(1)(*d*) of the *Income Tax Act*, chapter 148 of the Revised Statutes of Canada, 1952, as it read at that date, were read without reference to clause 89(1)(*d*)(iv.1)(F) of that Act and without reference to all subparagraphs of paragraph 89(1)(*d*) of that Act except subparagraphs 89(1)(*d*)(iv.1) and (vii) of that Act, and

(ii) the paid-up capital limit of the corporation on March 31, 1977,

that the paid-up capital on April 1, 1977, determined without reference to this section, in respect of the particular class of shares is of the paid-up capital on April 1, 1977, determined without reference to this section, in respect of all of the issued and outstanding shares of the capital stock of the corporation; and

(*b*) there shall be added an amount equal to the lesser of

(i) the amount, if any, by which

(A) the total of all amounts each of which is an amount deemed by subsection 84(3) or (4) to be a dividend on shares of the particular class paid by the corporation after March 31, 1977 and before the particular time

exceeds

(B) the total that would be determined under clause (A) if this Act were read without reference to paragraph (*a*), and

(ii) the amount required by paragraph (*a*) to be deducted in computing the paid-up capital of shares of the particular class.

Related Sections: S. 84.1(1) Non-arm's length sale of shares; s. 89(1) Capital dividend account.

Interpretation Bulletins: *Secondary* — IT-463R2 Paid-up capital.

► 84.2(2) ◄

(2) Debt deficiency. In computing, after March 31, 1977, the adjusted cost base to an individual of a debt that was owing to the individual by a corporation on March 31, 1977, there shall be deducted the amount of any dividend that would have been deemed to have been received by the individual on that day if the corporation had paid the debt in full on that day.

Related Sections: S. 53(2) Amounts to be deducted; s. 84.2(3) Conversion of debt into shares.

► 84.2(3) ◄

(3) Idem. Where, after March 31, 1977 and before 1979, any debt referred to in subsection (2) owing by a corporation and held by an individual on March 31, 1977 and continuously after that date until conversion, is converted into shares of a particular class of the capital stock of the corporation,

(*a*) subsection (2) shall not apply in respect of the debt; and

(*b*) in computing the paid-up capital in respect of the shares of the particular class at any particular time after the conversion,

(i) there shall be deducted the amount by which the adjusted cost base to the taxpayer of the debt would, but for paragraph (*a*), have been reduced by virtue of subsection (2), and

(ii) there shall be added an amount equal to the lesser of

(A) the amount, if any, by which

(I) the total of all amounts deemed by subsection 84(3), (4) or (4.1) to be a dividend on shares of the particular class paid by the corporation after the conversion and before the particular time,

exceeds

(II) the total that would be determined under subclause (I) if this Act were read without reference to subparagraph (i), and

(B) the amount required by subparagraph (i) to be deducted in computing the paid-up capital of shares of the particular class.

SECTION 85: Transfer of property to corporation by shareholders

► 85(1) ◄

(1) Transfer of property to corporation by shareholders. Where a taxpayer has, in a taxation year, disposed of any of the taxpayer's property that was eligible property to a taxable Canadian corporation for consideration that includes shares of the capital stock of the corporation, if the taxpayer and the corporation have jointly elected in prescribed form and in accordance with subsection (6), the following rules apply:

(*a*) the amount that the taxpayer and the corporation have agreed on in their election in respect of the property shall be deemed to be the taxpayer's proceeds of disposition of the property and the corporation's cost of the property;

(*b*) subject to paragraph (*c*), where the amount that the taxpayer and the corporation have agreed on in their election in respect of the property is less than the fair market value, at the time of the disposition, of the consideration therefor (other than any shares of the capital stock of the corporation or a right to receive any such shares) received by the taxpayer, the amount so agreed on shall, irrespective of the amount actually so agreed on by them, be deemed to be an amount equal to that fair market value;

(*c*) where the amount that the taxpayer and the corporation have agreed on in their election in respect of the property is greater than the fair market value, at the time of the disposition, of the property so disposed of, the amount so agreed on shall, irrespective of the amount actually so agreed on, be deemed to be an amount equal to that fair market value;

(*c*.1) where the property was inventory, capital property (other than depreciable property of a prescribed class), a NISA Fund No. 2 or a property that is eligible property because of paragraph (1.1)(*g*) or (*g*.1), and the amount that the taxpayer and corporation have agreed on in their election in respect of the property is less than the lesser of

(i) the fair market value of the property at the time of the disposition, and

(ii) the cost amount to the taxpayer of the property at the time of the disposition,

the amount so agreed on shall, irrespective of the amount actually so agreed on by them, be deemed to be an amount equal to the lesser of the amounts described in subparagraphs (i) and (ii);

(*c*.2) subject to paragraphs (*b*) and (*c*) and notwithstanding paragraph (*c*.1), where the taxpayer carries on a farming business the income from which is computed in accordance with the cash method and the property was inventory owned in connection with that business immediately before the particular time the property was disposed of to the corporation,

(i) the amount that the taxpayer and the corporation agreed on in their election in respect of inventory purchased by the taxpayer shall be deemed to be equal to the amount determined by the formula

$$(A \times B/C) + D$$

where

A is the amount that would be included because of paragraph 28(1)(*c*) in computing the taxpayer's income for the taxpayer's last taxation year beginning before the particular time if that year had ended immediately before the particular time,

B is the value (determined in accordance with subsection 28(1.2)) to the taxpayer immediately before the particular time of the purchased inventory in respect of which the election is made,

C is the value (determined in accordance with subsection 28(1.2)) of all of the inventory purchased by the taxpayer that was owned by the taxpayer in connection with that business immediately before the particular time, and

D is such additional amount as the taxpayer and the corporation designate in respect of the property,

(ii) for the purpose of subparagraph 28(1)(*a*)(i), the disposition of the property and the receipt of proceeds of disposition therefor shall be deemed to have occurred at the particular time and in the course of carrying on the business, and

(iii) where the property is owned by the corporation in connection with a farming business and the income from that business is computed in accordance with the cash method, for the purposes of section 28,

(A) an amount equal to the cost to the corporation of the property shall be deemed to have been paid by the corporation, and

(B) the corporation shall be deemed to have purchased the property for an amount equal to that cost,

at the particular time and in the course of carrying on that business;

(*d*) (Repealed by S.C. 2016, c. 12, s. 26(1).)

(*d*.1) (Repealed by S.C. 2016, c. 12, s. 26(1).)

(*d*.11) (Repealed by S.C. 2016, c. 12, s. 26(1).)

(*d*.12) (Repealed by S.C. 2016, c. 12, s. 26(1).)

(*e*) where the property was depreciable property of a prescribed class of the taxpayer and the amount that, but for this paragraph, would be the proceeds of disposition thereof is less than the least of

(i) the undepreciated capital cost to the taxpayer of all property of that class immediately before the disposition,

(ii) the cost to the taxpayer of the property, and

(iii) the fair market value of the property at the time of the disposition,

the amount agreed on by the taxpayer and the corporation in their election in respect of the property shall, irrespective of the amount actually so agreed on by them, be deemed to be the least of the amounts described in subparagraphs (i) to (iii);

(*e*.1) where two or more properties, each of which is a property described in paragraph (*e*), are disposed of at the same time, paragraph (*e*) applies as if each property so disposed of had been separately disposed of in the order designated by the taxpayer before the time referred to in subsection (6) for the filing of an election in respect of those properties or, if the taxpayer does not so designate any such order, in the order designated by the Minister;

(*e*.2) where the fair market value of the property immediately before the disposition exceeds the greater of

(i) the fair market value, immediately after the disposition, of the consideration received by the taxpayer for the property disposed of by the taxpayer, and

(ii) the amount that the taxpayer and the corporation have agreed on in their election in respect of the property, determined without reference to this paragraph,

and it is reasonable to regard any part of the excess as a benefit that the taxpayer desired to have conferred on a person related to the taxpayer (other than a corporation that was a wholly owned corporation of the taxpayer immediately after the disposition), the amount that the taxpayer and the corporation agreed on in their election in respect of the property shall, regardless of the amount actually so agreed on by them, be deemed (except for the purposes of paragraphs (*g*) and (*h*)) to be an amount equal to the total of the amount referred to in subparagraph (ii) and that part of the excess;

(*e*.3) where, under any of paragraphs (*c*.1) and (*e*), the amount that the taxpayer and the corporation have agreed on in their election in respect of the property (in this paragraph referred to as the "elected amount") would be deemed to be an amount that is greater or less than the amount that would be deemed, subject to paragraph (*c*), to be the elected amount under paragraph (*b*), the elected amount is deemed to be the greater of

(i) the amount deemed by paragraph (*c*.1) or (*e*), as the case may be, to be the elected amount, and

(ii) the amount deemed by paragraph (*b*) to be the elected amount;

(*e*.4) where

(i) the property is depreciable property of a prescribed class of the taxpayer and is a passenger vehicle the cost to the taxpayer of which was more than $20,000 or such other amount as may be prescribed, and

(ii) the taxpayer and the corporation do not deal at arm's length,

the amount that the taxpayer and the corporation have agreed on in their election in respect of the property shall be deemed to be an amount equal to the undepreciated capital cost to the taxpayer of the class immediately before the disposition, except that, for the purposes of subsection 6(2), the cost to the corporation of the vehicle shall be deemed to be an amount equal to its fair market value immediately before the disposition;

(*e*.5) if the property is depreciable property of a prescribed class of the taxpayer that is a zero-emission passenger vehicle to which paragraph 13(7)(*i*) applies and the taxpayer and the corporation do not deal at arm's length,

(i) the amount that the taxpayer and the corporation have agreed on in their election in respect of the vehicle is deemed to be an amount equal to the cost amount to the taxpayer of the vehicle immediately before the disposition, and

(ii) for the purposes of subsection 6(2), the cost to the corporation of the vehicle is deemed to be an amount equal to its fair market value immediately before the disposition;

(*f*) the cost to the taxpayer of any particular property (other than shares of the capital stock of the corporation or a right to receive any such shares) received by the taxpayer as consideration for the disposition shall be deemed to be an amount equal to the lesser of

(i) the fair market value of the particular property at the time of the disposition, and

(ii) that proportion of the fair market value, at the time of the disposition, of the property disposed of by the taxpayer to the corporation that

(A) the amount determined under subparagraph (i)

is of

(B) the fair market value, at the time of the disposition, of all properties (other than shares of the capital stock of the corporation or a right to receive any such shares) received by the taxpayer as consideration for the disposition;

(*g*) the cost to the taxpayer of any preferred shares of any class of the capital stock of the corporation receivable by the taxpayer as consideration for the disposition shall be deemed to be the lesser of the fair market value of those shares immediately after the disposition and that proportion of the amount, if any, by which the proceeds of the disposition exceed the fair market value of the consideration (other than shares of the capital stock of the corporation or a right to receive any such shares) received by the taxpayer for the disposition, that

(i) the fair market value, immediately after the disposition, of those preferred shares of that class,

is of

(ii) the fair market value, immediately after the disposition, of all preferred shares of the capital stock of the corporation receivable by the taxpayer as consideration for the disposition;

(*h*) the cost to the taxpayer of any common shares of any class of the capital stock of the corporation receivable by the taxpayer as consideration for the disposition shall be deemed to be that proportion of the amount, if any, by which the proceeds of the disposition exceed the total of the fair market value, at the time of the disposition, of the consideration (other than shares of the capital stock of the corporation or a right to receive any such shares) received by the taxpayer for the disposition and the cost to the taxpayer of all preferred shares of the capital stock of the corporation receivable by the taxpayer as consideration for the disposition, that

(i) the fair market value, immediately after the disposition, of those common shares of that class,

is of

(ii) the fair market value, immediately after the disposition, of all common shares of the capital stock of the corporation receivable by the taxpayer as consideration for the disposition; and

(*i*) where the property so disposed of is taxable Canadian property of the taxpayer, all of the shares of the capital stock of the Canadian corporation received by the taxpayer as consideration for the property are deemed to be, at any time that is within 60 months after the disposition, taxable Canadian property of the taxpayer.

Editorial Note: Subsection 85(1) provides the well-known "rollover" for the transfer of property to a taxable Canadian corporation for consideration that includes at least one share in the capital of the corporation. Property eligible for the rollover is described in s. 85(1.1) (see CRA Document No. 2011-0395501E5).

Elected Amount: The transferor and the corporation make a joint election and the elected amount becomes the transferor's proceeds of disposition of the transferred property and the corporation's cost of the property. Transfers to a corporation that was a wholly owned corporation of the taxpayer immediately after the disposition will not be subject to paragraph 85(1)(*e*.2). Property that has been transferred to a corporation under subsection 85(1), and sold immediately thereafter will not preclude capital gains treatment (both positions confirmed in CRA Document no. 2013-0500891I7).

The elected amount cannot be less than the lesser of the fair market value and the cost or cost amount of the transferred property (e.g. s. 85(1)(*c*.1), and (*e*) (and (*d*), prior to January 1, 2017), and cannot be less than the fair market value of the non-share consideration (s. 85(1)(*b*)); see s. 85(1)(*e*.3) regarding conflicts with the first-noted limitation, and IT-291R3, *Transfer of Property to a Corporation under Subsection 85(1)* (archived, as it doesn't meet current government web standards). A loss on the transfer may be subject to stop-loss rules, including s. 13(21.2), 14(12) (prior to 2017), or 40(3.4), or it may be a superficial loss (defined in s. 54).

Subsection 85(2) incorporates by reference the rules of s. 85(1) when property is transferred by a partnership to a taxable Canadian corporation. Subsection 97(2) incorporates by reference most of the provisions of s. 85(1), with changes as necessary, when property is transferred to a Canadian partnership by a person who is a member of the partnership immediately after the transfer. Property transferred to partnership which is then "rolled-over" to a corporation is valid (see *Loyens et al. v. The Queen*, 2003 DTC 355 (T.C.C.).

Anti-Avoidance Provision: Subsection 69(11) is an anti-avoidance provision that may apply to deny a tax-deferred transfer under s. 85(1). Where it applies, the transferor will be deemed to have disposed of the property for proceeds equal to its FMV at that time (see IT-291R3, *Transfer of Property to a Corporation* under s. 85(1)).

Errors and Failures to Elect: The CRA will assess tax on capital gain that could have been deferred if an election was not filed (see *Houweling v. The Queen*, 2007 DTC 5006 (F.C.A.), affirming 2006 DTC 2258 (T.C.C.)). The intention of the taxpayer is not sufficient where full information and agreements to the election are not provided (see *Deconinck v. The Queen*, 90 DTC 6617 (F.C.A.), affirming 88 DTC 6410 (F.C.T.D.). However, a rectification order may be obtained from a court if it is satisfied that the parties agreed and intended for the rollover to occur, but without the proper wording in the relevant documents. Taxpayers who made a transfer in exchange for a promissory note rather than shares in the transferee corporation were granted a rectification order that substituted shares for the consideration note, thus allowing a s. 85 rollover on a retroactive basis (*Juliar et al.*, 2000 DTC 6589 (O.C.A.)) (leave to appeal to the SCC denied). The SCC considered the scope of rectification as an equitable remedy in the cases of Canada (Attorney General) v. Fairmont Hotels Inc., 2016 DTC 5135, and Jean Coutu Group (PJC) Inc. v. Canada (Attorney General), 2016 DTC 5134. These cases held that rectification is available in situations where the parties have agreed on the terms of a contact, but the documentation does not accurately reflect these terms, returning the remedy to its original concept and significantly restricting its scope. .

Exchanges and Adjustments: A taxpayer would not have realized a disposition of a particular share of a corporation if, after an exchange of shares, the taxpayer possessed a share having the same rights, preferences, conditions and restrictions as those of the particular share (see CRA Document No. 2009-0330161C6). Common shares that have a nil FMV when exchanged for preferred shares under section 51, s. 85(1)(*c*) would deem the agreed amount (and consequently the proceeds of disposition) to also be nil, resulting in a capital loss to the extent of the ACB of the transferred shares (see CRA Document No. 2008-0300391C6).

Where property is transferred in a non-arm's-length transaction, the parties may include a price adjustment clause in the covering agreement (see Income Tax Folio S4-F3-C1, *Price Adjustment Clauses*). The requirements governing the recognition of a price adjustment clause that were established in the case of *Guilder News (1963) Ltd. v MNR*, 73 DTC 5048 (F.C.A.) are still applicable, with certain CRA administrative views reflected.

Deadlines: Under s. 85(7), an election can be made up to three years after the filing deadline. Subsection 85(7.1) provides that one can file an election more than three years after the original due date. In the absence of a Court Order rectifying a previous agreement, the CRA will not accept a late-filed election based on a contract that is modified after the fact to include share consideration for the transfer rather than non-share consideration (CRA document no. 2008-0296721E5). See the discussion regarding the possibility of obtaining a rectification order above.

History: S. 85(1)(*e*.5) was added by S.C. 2019, c. 29, s. 10(1), deemed to have come into force on March 19, 2019.

S. 85(1)(*d*) to (*d*.12) were repealed by S.C. 2016, c. 12, s. 26(1), in force January 1, 2017, and formerly read:

(*d*) where the property was eligible capital property in respect of a business of the taxpayer and the amount that, but for this paragraph, would be the proceeds of disposition of the property is less than the least of

(i) $^4/_3$ of the taxpayer's cumulative eligible capital in respect of the business immediately before the disposition,

(ii) the cost to the taxpayer of the property, and

(iii) the fair market value of the property at the time of the disposition,

the amount agreed on by the taxpayer and the corporation in their election in respect of the property shall, irrespective of the amount actually so agreed on by them, be deemed to be the least of the amounts described in subparagraphs (i) to (iii);

(*d*.1) for the purpose of determining after the disposition time the amount to be included under paragraph 14(1)(*b*) in computing the corporation's income, there shall be added to the amount otherwise determined for C in that paragraph the amount determined by the formula

$$1/2 \times [(A \times B/C) - 2(D - E)] + F + G$$

where

A is the amount, if any, determined for Q in the definition "cumulative eligible capital" in subsection 14(5) in respect of the taxpayer's business immediately before the disposition time,

B is the fair market value immediately before the disposition time of the eligible capital property disposed of to the corporation by the taxpayer,

C is the total of the fair market value immediately before the disposition time of all eligible capital property of the taxpayer in respect of the business and each amount that was described in B in respect of an earlier disposition made after the taxpayer's adjustment time,

D is the amount, if any, that would be included under subsection 14(1) in computing the taxpayer's income as a result of the disposition if the values determined for C and D in paragraph 14(1)(*b*) were zero,

E is the amount, if any, that would be included under subsection 14(1) in computing the taxpayer's income as a result of the disposition if the value determined for D in paragraph 14(1)(*b*) were zero,

F is the total of all amounts, each of which is an amount determined under this paragraph as it applied to the taxpayer in respect of a disposition to the corporation on or before the disposition time, and

G is the total of all amounts, each of which is an amount determined under subparagraph 88(1)(*c.1*)(ii) as it applied to the taxpayer in respect of a winding-up before the disposition time;

(*d*.11) for the purpose of determining after the time of the disposition (referred to in this paragraph and in paragraphs (*d.1*) and (*d.12*) as the "disposition time") the amount to be included under paragraph 14(1)(*a*) or (*b*) in computing the corporation's income, there shall be added to the amount otherwise determined for each of A and F in the definition "cumulative eligible capital" in subsection 14(5) the amount, if any, determined by the formula

$$(A \times B/C) + D + E$$

where

A is the amount, if any, that would be determined for F in that definition in respect of the taxpayer's business at the beginning of the taxpayer's following taxation year if the taxpayer's taxation year that includes the disposition time had ended immediately after the disposition time and if, in respect of the disposition, this Act were read without reference to paragraph (*d.12*),

B is the fair market value immediately before the disposition time of the eligible capital property disposed of to the corporation by the taxpayer,

C is the fair market value immediately before the disposition time of all eligible capital property of the taxpayer in respect of the business and each amount that was described in B in respect of an earlier disposition made after the taxpayer's adjustment time,

D is the total of all amounts, each of which is an amount determined under this paragraph as it applied to the taxpayer in respect of a disposition to the corporation on or before the disposition time, and

E is the total of all amounts, each of which is an amount determined under subparagraph 88(1)(*c.1*)(i) as it applied to the taxpayer in respect of a winding-up before the disposition time;

(*d*.12) for the purpose of determining after the disposition time the amount to be included under paragraph 14(1)(*a*) or (*b*) in computing the taxpayer's income, the amount, if any, determined by the formula in paragraph (*d.11*) in respect of the disposition is to be deducted from each of the amounts otherwise determined

(i) by subparagraph 14(1)(*a*)(ii), and

(ii) for the description of B in paragraph 14(1)(*b*);

S. 85(1)(*e*.1) was replaced by S.C. 2016, c. 12, s. 26(2), in force January 1, 2017, and formerly read:

(*e*.1) where two or more properties, each of which is a property described in paragraph (*d*) or each of which is a property described in paragraph (*e*), are disposed of at the same time, paragraph (*d*) or (*e*), as the case may be, applies as if each property so disposed of had been separately disposed of in the order designated by the taxpayer before the time referred to in subsection (6) for the filing of an election in respect of those properties or, if the taxpayer does not so designate any such order, in the order designated by the Minister;

S. 85(1)(*e*.3), the portion before subparagraph (ii) was replaced by S.C. 2016, c. 12, s. 26(3), in force January 1, 2017, and formerly read:

(*e*.3) where, under any of paragraphs (*c*.1), (*d*) and (*e*), the amount that the taxpayer and the corporation have agreed on in their election in respect of the property (in this paragraph referred to as "the elected amount") would be deemed to be an amount that is greater or less than the amount that would be deemed, subject to paragraph (*c*), to be the elected amount under paragraph (*b*), the elected amount shall be deemed to be the greater of

(i) the amount deemed by paragraph (*c*.1), (*d*) or (*e*), as the case may be, to be the elected amount, and

S. 85(1)(*d.1*) was replaced by S.C. 2013, c. 34, s. 220(1), applicable to taxation years of a corporation that end after December 20, 2002, and formerly read:

(*d*.1) for the purpose of determining after the time of the disposition the amount to be included under paragraph 14(1)(*b*) in computing the corporation's income, there shall be added to the amount otherwise determined for Q in the definition "cumulative eligible capital" in subsection 14(5) the amount determined by the formula

$$(A \times B/C) - 2(D - E)$$

where

A is the amount, if any, determined for Q in that definition in respect of the taxpayer's business immediately before the time of the disposition, ,

B is the fair market value immediately before that time of the eligible capital property disposed of to the corporation by the taxpayer,

C is the fair market value immediately before that time of all eligible capital property of the taxpayer in respect of the business,

D is the amount, if any, that would be included under subsection 14(1) in computing the taxpayer's income as a result of the disposition if the values determined for C and D in paragraph 14(1)(*b*) were zero, and

E is the amount, if any, that would be included under subsection 14(1) in computing the taxpayer's income as a result of the disposition if the value determined for D in paragraph 14(1)(b) were zero;

S. 85(1)(*d.11*) and (*d.12*) were added by S.C. 2013, c. 34, s. 220(2), applicable in respect of the disposition of an eligible capital property by a taxpayer to a corporation unless

(*a*) the disposition by the taxpayer occurred before December 21, 2002; and

(*b*) the corporation disposed of the eligible capital property, before June 7, 2007 and in a taxation year of the corporation ending after February 27, 2000, to a person with whom the corporation was dealing at arm's length at the time of that disposition by the corporation.

S. 85(1)(*i*) was replaced by S.C. 2010, c. 12, s. 6(1), applicable in determining after March 4, 2010 whether a property is taxable Canadian property of a taxpayer. S. 85(1)(*i*) formerly read:

(*i*) where the property so disposed of is taxable Canadian property of the taxpayer, all of the shares of the capital stock of the Canadian corporation received by the taxpayer as consideration for the property shall be deemed to be taxable Canadian property of the taxpayer.

Related Regulations: Part XI; Part LIII; 5905; 7307(1).

Related Sections: S. 6(2) Reasonable standby charge; s. 13(7)(*i*) Rules applicable; s. 13(21) Definitions; s. 13(21.2) Loss on certain transfers; s. 14(12) Loss on certain transfers; s. 15(1) Benefit conferred on shareholder; s. 18(15) Loss on certain properties; s. 24(1) Ceasing to carry on business; s. 24(2) Business carried on by spouse or controlled corporation; s. 40(2)(*g*) Limitations; s. 40(3.4) Loss on certain properties; s. 44.1(6) Special rule — re eligible small business corporation share exchanges; s. 44.1(7) Special rule — re active business corporation share exchanges; s. 51(4) Application; s. 53(1)(*c*) Adjustments to cost base — Contributions of capital; s. 53(1)(*f*) Adjustments to cost base — Substituted property; s. 53(4) Recomputation of adjusted cost base on transfers and deemed dispositions; s. 54, "capital property", "eligible capital property"; s. 54.2 Certain shares deemed to be capital property; s. 69(11) Deemed proceeds of disposition; s. 84.1(1)(*a*) Non-arm's length sale of shares; s. 85.1(2) Where s. (1) does not apply; s. 86(3) Application; s. 89(1), "taxable Canadian corporation"; s. 97(2) Rules where election by partners; s. 138(11.5) Transfer of insurance business by non-resident insurer; s. 142.6(6) Definition of "rollover transaction"; s. 142.7(3) Branch-establishment rollover; s. 248(1), "eligible capital property", "inventory", "taxable Canadian property". s. 248(4) Interest in real property; ITAR s. 20(1.2) Other transfers of depreciable property, s. 26(5.2) Transfer of capital property to a corporation.

Canadian Petroleum Tax Journal: The Recent Take-Over Phenomenon, D. Alan Ross and Stanley R. Ebel, 2001, Vol. 14, No. 1; A Comparative Study of Canadian and U.S. Rules Regarding the Taxation of Corporate Reorganizations, Firoz Talakshi and Christy Palmer, 2000, Vol. 13, No. 1.

Canadian Tax Foundation: Tollstam, *Rectification Denied for Missed Rollover Election*, 2015 Canadian Tax Highlights 23(11):1–2; Gosselin, *Estate*

Freeze Transactions: Big Accounting Shake-Up in the Works, 2015 Tax for the Owner-Manager 15(1):1–2; Gill, *Fixing Mistakes: Rectification & Rescission*, 2014 British Columbia Tax Conference 9:1–11; Truster, *The Challenges of Creditor Proofing*, 2014 Tax for the Owner-Manager 14(3):7; Manwaring, *Recent Developments in the Taxation of Shareholders and Their Business: Asset Protection and Tax Planning*, 2003 Ontario Tax Conference 15B:1–15; Truster, *A Close Look at Paragraph 85(1)(e.2)*, 2013 Tax for the Owner-Manager 13(2):5–6; Bernstein, *Valuation and Related Tax Issues, Part 1*, 2011 Conference Report 17:1–31; Ireland et al., *Disarming the Succession Time Bomb: The Role of Trusts, Insurance, and Shareholders' Agreements in the Transition of Family Businesses*, 2011 Conference Report 15:1–53; Lang and Taylor, *Tax Issues in Purchase and Sale Agreements*, 2011 Conference Report 14:1–52; Tabuchi, *Share Capital Reorganizations for Private Corporations*, 2003 Canadian Tax Journal 3:1340–1378; Moch and Ebel, *Basics of Corporate Reorganizations: Sections 51, 85, 85.1, and 86*, 2002 Prairie Provinces Tax Conference 10:1–32; Wilkenfeld, *Section 85 Rollovers: Checklist*, 2001 Tax for the Owner-Manager 1(3):17–18; Moch and Ebel, *Share Reorganizations and Corporate Takeover Transactions: Using Tax Rollover Provisions*, 2000 Conference Report 8:1–20.

STEP Canada: Christine Cauwenberghe, "Avoiding Family Law Fiascos in Family Estate Freezes," PowerPoint presentation to the 15th National Conference of STEP Canada, Toronto, June 10-11, 2013.

Tax Profile: April 2015 — Breaking the Link — Nature of a Forward Contract After a Section 85 Rollover; April 2013 — Canadian Estate Freezes in Favour of U.S. Citizens; February 2013 — The Purchase of US Businesses by Canadians; August 2012 — U.S. Purchases and Sales of Canadian Businesses: Tax and Corporate Issues; April 2012 — Price Adjustment Clauses; September 2011 — Acquisition of Canadian Business by Non-Residents; November 2009 — Purchase and Sale of a Canadian Business; September 2009 — Time To Refreeze?; March 2009 — Sale of Businesses to Employees: The Leveraged Buy-Out — Part I; October 2007 — Will Canadian Unlimited Liability Companies Survive?; July 2007 — Canadian Tax Traps; July 2006 — Asset Protection Planning.

Tax Topics: No. 1925, The Perils of "Rolling" Real Estate Inventory; No. 1690, Estate Planning In The 21st Century; No. 1525, Application of paragraph 85(1)(*b*); No. 1511, Changes in CCRA's position regarding paragraph 85(1)(*b*).

Forms: T2 SCH 44 — Non-Arm's Length Transaction; T2057 — Election on Disposition of Property by a Taxpayer to a Taxable Canadian Corporation.

Income Tax Folios: *Secondary* — S4-F3-C1 Price Adjustment Clauses.

Information Circulars: IC 76-19R3 Transfer of property to a corporation under section 85; IC 88-2 General anti-avoidance rule — Section 245 of the Income Tax Act (paras. 7, 9, 10, 13, 14, 22 and 23, Supp. 1, paras. 3 and 8); IC 89-3 Policy statement on business equity valuations.

Interpretation Bulletins: *Primary* — IT-291R3 Transfer of property to a corporation under subsection 85(1). *Secondary* — IT-457R Election by professionals to exclude work in progress from income; IT-489R Non-arm's length sale of shares to a corporation.

Tax Window Files: Late Filed Election 85(7) — Amending Transactions, *April 30, 2009*, CRA Document No. 2008-0296721E5; Price adjustment clause, *October 5, 2007*, CRA Document No. 2007-0243251C6; Erroneous Elections in Statute-Barred Years, *July 7, 2005*, CRA Document No. 2005-0122191E5; Transfer of Property - Partnership, *April 6, 2005*, CRA Document No. 2004-0104291E5; 85(1), 248(1) "Disposition", *November 10, 2004*, CRA Document No. 2004-0092561E5; Price Adjustment Clauses, *July 6, 2004*, CRA Document No. 2004-0081631E5; Replacement Property Rules, *May 28, 2004*, CRA Document No. 2004-0066251E5; Rollover For Contractors, *February 16, 2004*, CRA Document No. 2003-0054091E5.

Cases: To circumvent the prohibition against rolling over real estate inventory under s. 85, the real estate was rolled into a partnership under s. 97(2) and the partnership interest was then rolled over under s. 85. The s. 85 rollover was technically valid. *Loyens et al. v. The Queen*, 2003 DTC 355 (T.C.C.)

The applicants transferred their shares of a corporation to a second corporation, and took back a promissory note as consideration rather than shares of the second corporation. To avoid unintended tax consequences, a rectification order was granted to substitute shares of the second company for its promissory note. *A.G. Canada v. Juliar et al.*, 2000 DTC 6589 (Ont. CA), affirming 99 DTC 5743 (Ont. S.C.)

When a corporation's authorized capital had been amended retroactively to December 28, 1995, the shares issued thereafter for the transfer of an apartment building could be part of an election and of a capital dividend declaration. *Dale et al. v. The Queen*, 97 DTC 5252 (F.C.A.), reversing 94 DTC 1100 (T.C.C.)

A taxpayer transferred five properties to a taxable Canadian corporation and filed an election that rollover treatment apply. The election failed to mention four of the five properties, and the Minister assessed the taxpayer with a capital gain on the one property based on the full elected amount. The Court held that, although the failure to mention the four properties in the election was inadvertent, the rollover did not apply to them. The intention of the taxpayer was not sufficient where full information was not supplied. *Deconinck v. The Queen*, 90 DTC 6617 (F.C.A.), affirming 88 DTC 6410 (F.C.T.D.).

▶ 85(1.1) ◀

(1.1) Definition of "eligible property". For the purposes of subsection (1), "eligible property" means

(*a*) a capital property (other than real or immovable property, an option in respect of such property, or an interest in real property or a real right in an immovable, owned by a non-resident person);

(*b*) a capital property that is real or immovable property, an option in respect of such property, or an interest in real property or a real right in an immovable, owned by a non-resident insurer if that property and the property received as consideration for that property are designated insurance property for the year;

(*c*) a Canadian resource property;

(*d*) a foreign resource property;

(*e*) (Repealed by S.C. 2016, c. 12, s. 26(4).)

(*f*) an inventory (other than real or immovable property, an option in respect of such property, or an interest in real property or a real right in an immovable);

(*g*) a property that is a security or debt obligation used by the taxpayer in the year in, or held by it in the year in the course of, carrying on the business of insurance or lending money, other than

(i) a capital property,

(ii) inventory, or

(iii) where the taxpayer is a financial institution in the year, a mark-to-market property for the year;

(*g*.1) where the taxpayer is a financial institution in the year, a specified debt obligation (other than a mark-to-market property of the taxpayer for the year);

(*h*) a capital property that is real or immovable property, an option in respect of such property, or an interest in real property or a real right in an immovable, owned by a non-resident person (other than a non-resident insurer) and used in the year in a business carried on in Canada by that person; or

(*i*) a NISA Fund No. 2, if that property is owned by an individual.

Editorial Note: See s. 85(1.2) regarding property described in s. 85(1.1)(*h*).

History: S. 85(1.1)(*e*) was repealed by S.C. 2016, c. 12, s. 26(4), in force January 1, 2017, and formerly read:

(*e*) an eligible capital property;

S. 85(1.1)(*a*) and (*b*) were replaced by S.C. 2013, c. 34, s. 120(1), in force June 26, 2013, and formerly read:

(*a*) a capital property (other than real property, or an interest in or an option in respect of real property, owned by a non-resident person);

(*b*) a capital property that is real property, or an interest in or an option in respect of real property, owned by a non-resident insurer where that property and the property received as consideration for that property are designated insurance property for the year;

S. 85(1.1)(*f*) was replaced by S.C. 2013, c. 34, s. 120(2), in force June 26, 2013, and formerly read:

(*f*) an inventory (other than real property, an interest in real property or an option in respect of real property);

S. 85(1.1)(*h*) was replaced by S.C. 2013, c. 34, s. 120(3), in force June 26, 2013, and formerly read:

(*h*) a capital property that is real property, an interest in real property or an option in respect of real property, owned by a non-resident person (other than a non-resident insurer) and used in the year in a business carried on in Canada by that person; or

Related Sections: S. 54, "capital property", "eligible capital property"; s. 66(15), "Canadian resource property", "foreign resource property"; s. 85(1.4) Definitions; s. 138(12), "designated insurance property"; s. 248(1), "inventory"; "NISA Fund No. 2"; s. 248(4) Interest in real property.

Interpretation Bulletins: *Secondary* — IT-291R3 Transfer of property to a corporation under subsection 85(1).

▶ 85(1.11) ◀

(1.11) Exception. Notwithstanding subsection (1.1), a foreign resource property, or an interest in a partnership that derives all or part of its value from one or more foreign resource properties, is not an eligible property of a taxpayer in respect of a disposition by the taxpayer to a corporation where

(*a*) the taxpayer and the corporation do not deal with each other at arm's length; and

(*b*) it is reasonable to conclude that one of the purposes of the disposition, or a series of transactions or events of which the disposition is a part, is to increase the extent to which any person may claim a deduction under section 126.

Related Sections: S. 66(4) Foreign exploration and development expenses; s. 66.21(4) Deduction for cumulative foreign resource expense; s. 66.7(2) Successor of foreign exploration and development expenses; s. 66.7(2.3) Successor of foreign resource expenses; s. 126(9) Computation of qualifying incomes and losses.

Interpretation Bulletins: *Secondary* — IT-291R3 Transfer of property to a corporation under subsection 85(1).

▶ 85(1.12) ◀

(1.12) Eligible derivatives. Notwithstanding subsection (1.1), an *eligible derivative* (as defined in subsection 10.1 (5)) of a taxpayer to which subsection 10.1(6) applies is not an eligible property of the taxpayer in respect of a disposition by the taxpayer to a corporation.

History: S. 85(1.12) was added by S.C. 2017, c. 33, s. 23(1), applicable to taxation years that begin after March 21, 2017.

Related Sections: 10.1(5) Definition of eligible derivative.

▶ 85(1.2) ◀

(1.2) Application of subsection (1). Subsection (1) does not apply to a disposition by a taxpayer to a corporation of a property referred to in paragraph (1.1)(*h*) unless

(*a*) immediately after the disposition, the corporation is controlled by the taxpayer, a person or persons related (otherwise than because of a right referred to in paragraph 251(5)(*b*)) to the taxpayer or the taxpayer and a person or persons so related to the taxpayer;

(*b*) the disposition is part of a transaction or series of transactions in which all or substantially all of the property used in the business referred to in paragraph (1.1)(*h*) is disposed of by the taxpayer to the corporation; and

(*c*) the disposition is not part of a series of transactions that result in control of the corporation being acquired by a person or group of persons after the time that is immediately after the disposition.

Related Sections: S. 89(1), "taxable Canadian corporation", s. 256(7) Acquiring control.

Interpretation Bulletins: *Secondary* — IT-291R3 Transfer of property to a corporation under subsection 85(1).

▶ 85(1.3) ◀

(1.3) Meaning of "wholly owned corporation". For the purposes of this subsection and paragraph (1)(*e*.2), "wholly owned corporation" of a taxpayer means a corporation all the issued and outstanding shares of the capital stock of which (except directors' qualifying shares) belong to

(*a*) the taxpayer;

(*b*) a corporation that is a wholly owned corporation of the taxpayer; or

(*c*) any combination of persons described in paragraph (*a*) or (*b*).

Interpretation Bulletins: *Secondary* — IT-291R3 Transfer of property to a corporation under subsection 85(1).

▶ 85(1.4) ◀

(1.4) Definitions. For the purpose of subsection (1.1), "financial institution", "mark-to-market property" and "specified debt obligation" have the meanings assigned by subsection 142.2(1).

▶ 85(2) ◀

(2) Transfer of property to corporation from partnership. Where

(*a*) a partnership has disposed, to a taxable Canadian corporation for consideration that includes shares of the corporation's capital stock, of any partnership property (other than an *eligible derivative*, as defined in subsection 10.1(5), of the partnership if subsection 10.1(6) applies to the partnership) that was

(i) a capital property (other than real or immovable property, an option in respect of such property, or an interest in real property or a real right in an immovable, if the partnership was not a Canadian partnership at the time of the disposition),

(ii) a property described in any of paragraphs (1.1)(*c*) to (*f*), or

(iii) a property that would be described in paragraph (1.1)(*g*) or (*g*.1) if the references in those paragraphs to "taxpayer" were read as "partnership", and

(*b*) the corporation and all the members of the partnership have jointly so elected, in prescribed form and within the time referred to in subsection (6),

paragraphs (1)(*a*) to (*i*) are applicable, with such modifications as the circumstances require, in respect of the disposition as if the partnership were a taxpayer resident in Canada who had disposed of the property to the corporation.

Editorial Note: See the editorial note under s. 85(1). See s. 85(3) where the partnership is wound up within 60 days of the disposition that is subject to s. 85(2).

If a second partnership is a member of the partnership that disposes of the property to the corporation, for the purposes of s. 85(2)(*b*), the CRA allows one partner of the second partnership who is authorized to act for its partners to make the election; see paragraph 4 of IT-378R (archived, as it doesn't meet current government web standards).

History: S. 85(2)(*a*), the portion before subparagraph (i) was replaced by S.C. 2017, c. 33, s. 23(2), applicable to taxation years that begin after March 21, 2017, and formerly read:

(*a*) a partnership has disposed, to a taxable Canadian corporation for consideration that includes shares of the corporation's capital stock, of any partnership property that was

S. 85(2)(*a*)(i) was replaced by S.C. 2013, c. 34, s. 120(4), in force June 26, 2013, and formerly read:

(i) a capital property (other than real property, or an interest in or an option in respect of real property, where the partnership was not a Canadian partnership at the time of the disposition),

Related Regulations: Part XI; Part LIII.

Related Sections: 10.1(5) Definition of eligible derivative; S. 69(11) Deemed proceeds of disposition; s. 85(1.1) Definition of "eligible property"; s. 85(2.1) Computing paid-up capital; s. 85(3) Where partnership wound up; s. 85(5) Rules on transfers of depreciable property; s. 85(5.1) Acquisition of certain tools — capital cost and deemed depreciation; s. 86(3) Application; s. 102(1) Definition of "Canadian partnership"; ITAR s. 20(1.2) Other transfers of depreciable property.

Forms: T2 SCH 44 — Non-Arm's Length Transaction; T2058 — Election on Disposition of Property by a Partnership to a Taxable Canadian Corporation.

Information Circulars: IC 76-19R3 Transfer of property to a corporation under section 85.

Interpretation Bulletins: *Secondary* — IT-378R Winding-up of a partnership; IT-457R Election by professionals to exclude work in progress from income.

► 85(2.1) ◄

(2.1) Computing paid-up capital. Where subsection (1) or (2) applies to a disposition of property (other than a disposition of property to which section 84.1 or 212.1 applies) to a corporation by a person or partnership (in this subsection referred to as the "taxpayer"),

(*a*) in computing the paid-up capital in respect of any particular class of shares of the capital stock of the corporation at the time of, and at any time after, the issue of shares of the capital stock of the corporation in consideration for the disposition of the property, there shall be deducted an amount determined by the formula

$$(A - B) \times C/A$$

where

A is the increase, if any, determined without reference to this section as it applies to the disposition of the property, in the paid-up capital in respect of all the shares of the capital stock of the corporation as a result of the acquisition by the corporation of the property,

B is the amount, if any, by which the corporation's cost of the property, immediately after the acquisition, determined under subsection (1) or (2), as the case may be, exceeds the fair market value, immediately after the acquisition, of any consideration (other than shares of the capital stock of the corporation) received by the taxpayer from the corporation for the property, and

C is the increase, if any, determined without reference to this section as it applies to the disposition of the property, in the paid-up capital in respect of the particular class of shares as a result of the acquisition by the corporation of the property; and

(*b*) in computing the paid-up capital, at any time after November 21, 1985, in respect of any class of shares of the capital stock of a corporation, there shall be added an amount equal to the lesser of

(i) the amount, if any, by which

(A) the total of all amounts each of which is an amount deemed by subsection 84(3), (4) or (4.1) to be a dividend on shares of that class paid after November 21, 1985 and before that time by the corporation

exceeds

(B) the total of such dividends that would be determined under clause (A) if this Act were read without reference to paragraph (*a*), and

(ii) the total of all amounts required by paragraph (*a*) to be deducted in computing the paid-up capital in respect of that class of shares after November 21, 1985 and before that time.

Editorial Note: The paid-up capital grind in s. 85(2.1) effectively means that the increase in the paid-up capital as a result of the issuance of the shares as consideration for the property transferred to the corporation is limited to the amount, if any, by which the elected amount under s. 85(1) or (2) (the corporation's cost of the property) exceeds the fair market value of any non-share consideration received by the transferor from the corporation for the property. In the case of more than one class of shares, the paid-up capital grind occurs on a *pro-rata* basis (see the fraction C/A in the formula in paragraph (*a*)). Note that the paid-up capital adjustments under s. 84.1(1)(*a*) and 212.1(1)(*b*), if applicable, take precedence over s. 85(2.1).

Related Sections: S. 84(1) Deemed dividend; s. 84(5) Amount distributed or paid where a share; s. 89(1), "paid-up capital".

Interpretation Bulletins: *Secondary* — IT-291R3 Transfer of property to a corporation under subsection 85(1).

► 85(3) ◄

(3) Where partnership wound up. Where,

(*a*) in respect of any disposition of partnership property of a partnership to a corporation, subsection (2) applies,

(*b*) the affairs of the partnership were wound up within 60 days after the disposition, and

(*c*) immediately before the winding-up there was no partnership property other than money or property received from the corporation as consideration for the disposition,

the following rules apply:

(*d*) the cost to any member of the partnership of any property (other than shares of the capital stock of the corporation or a right to receive any such shares) received by the member as consideration for the disposition of the member's partnership interest on the winding-up shall be deemed to be the fair market value of the property at the time of the winding-up,

(*e*) the cost to any member of the partnership of any preferred shares of any class of the capital stock of the corporation receivable by the member as consideration for the disposition of the member's partnership interest on the winding-up shall be deemed to be

(i) where any common shares of the capital stock of the corporation were also receivable by the member as consideration for the disposition of the interest, the lesser of

(A) the fair market value, immediately after the winding-up, of the preferred shares of that class so receivable by the member, and

(B) that proportion of the amount, if any, by which the adjusted cost base to the member of the member's partnership interest immediately before the winding-up exceeds the total of the fair market value, at the time of the winding-up, of the consideration (other than shares of the capital stock of the corporation or a right to receive any such shares) received by the member for the disposition of the interest, that

(I) the fair market value, immediately after the winding-up, of the preferred shares of that class so receivable by the member,

is of

(II) the fair market value, immediately after the winding-up, of all preferred shares of the capital stock of the corporation receivable by the member as consideration for the disposition, and

(ii) in any other case, the amount determined under clause (i)(B),

(*f*) the cost to any member of the partnership of any common shares of any class of the capital stock of the corporation receivable by the member as consideration for the disposition of the member's partnership interest on the winding-up shall be deemed to be that proportion of the amount, if any, by which the adjusted cost base to the member of the member's partnership interest immediately before the winding-up exceeds the total of the fair market value, at the time of the winding-up, of the consideration (other than shares of the capital stock of the corporation or a right to receive any such shares) received by the member for the disposition of the interest and the cost to the member of all preferred shares of the capital stock of the corporation receivable by the member as consideration for the disposition of the interest, that

(i) the fair market value, immediately after the winding-up, of the common shares of that class so receivable by the member,

is of

(ii) the fair market value, immediately after the winding-up, of all common shares of the capital stock of the corporation so receivable by the member as consideration for the disposition,

(*g*) the proceeds of disposition of the partnership interest of any member of the partnership shall be deemed to be the cost to the member of all shares and property receivable or received by the member as consideration for the disposition of the interest plus the amount of any money received by the member as consideration for the disposition, and

(*h*) where the partnership has distributed partnership property referred to in paragraph (*c*) to a member of the partnership, the partnership shall be deemed to have disposed of that property for proceeds equal to the cost amount to the partnership of the property immediately before its distribution.

Editorial Note: The rollover under s. 85(3) ensures that the partnership will have no gain or loss in respect of property, including the shares of the corporation, that is received from the corporation on the s. 85(2) rollover and that is subsequently distributed to its partners on the winding-up of the partnership in consideration for the disposition of their partnership interests (s. 85(3)(*c*) and (*h*)). The results to each partner, owing to the cost allocation rules of s. 85(3)(*d*), (*e*) and (*f*) and the corresponding proceeds of disposition rules under paragraph (*g*), can be summarized as follows. If a partner receives only non-share property (property other than shares of the corporation) as consideration for the disposition of its partnership interest, the partner may realize a gain or loss, depending on whether the fair market value of the non-share property exceeds, or is less than, the partner's adjusted cost base of the partnership interest. A partner who receives non-share property plus any shares of the corporation may have a gain on the disposition of its partnership interest (if the fair market value of the non-share property exceeds the partner's adjusted cost base of the interest), but not a loss (since the proceeds of disposition will at least equal the partner's adjusted cost base of the interest). A partner who receives only shares of the corporation will have neither a gain nor a loss on the disposition of its partnership interest (since the proceeds of disposition will equal the partner's adjusted cost base of the interest).

When a partnership is incorporated, the shares of the corporation issued on the s. 85(2) rollover are sometimes issued in the names of the partners instead of the name of the partnership. The CRA's view is that this procedure does not invalidate the application of s. 85(2) or the subsequent application of s. 85(3) if the intent is that the shares beneficially belong to the partnership and not to the partners themselves. See para. 2 of IT-378R.

Subsection 98(3), which can otherwise apply where a partnership ceases to exist and its property is distributed to its former partners, does not apply where s. 85(3) applies (s. 98(4)).

Related Sections: S. 98(2) Deemed proceeds; s. 98.1(1) Residual interest in partnership; s. 98(4) Where s. (3) does not apply; ITAR s. 20(1.2) Other transfers of depreciable property.

Canadian Tax Foundation: Cepparo, *More Than 60 Days for Partnership Rollover*, 2015 Canadian Tax Highlights 23(8):8–9.

Interpretation Bulletins: *Primary* — IT-378R Winding-up of a partnership. *Secondary* — IT-457R Election by professionals to exclude work in progress from income.

Tax Window Files: 85(3) rollover, *January 14, 2015*, CRA Document No. 2014-0559731E5; Farm Inventory and Partnership Wind Up, *February 23, 2004*, CRA Document No. 2004-0056471E5.

▶ 85(4) ◀

(4) Loss from disposition to controlled corporation — (Repealed by S.C. 1998, c. 19, s. 116(3).)

▶ 85(5) ◀

(5) Rules on transfers of depreciable property. Where subsection (1) or (2) has applied to a disposition at any time of depreciable property to a person (in this subsection referred to as the "transferee") and the capital cost to the transferor of the property exceeds the transferor's proceeds of disposition of the property, for the purposes of sections 13 and 20 and any regulations made for the purpose of paragraph 20(1)(*a*),

(*a*) the capital cost to the transferee of the property is deemed to be the amount that was its capital cost to the transferor; and

(*b*) the excess is deemed to have been deducted by the transferee under paragraph 20(1)(*a*) in respect of the property in computing income for taxation years that ended before that time.

Editorial Note: Subsection 85(5) effectively ensures that any built-in recapture in respect of transferred depreciable property is not converted into a capital gain upon a disposition of the property by the transferee corporation.

Related Regulations: 1100(1).

Related Sections: S. 13(21), "undepreciated capital cost".

Interpretation Bulletins: *Secondary* — IT-291R3 Transfer of property to a corporation under subsection 85(1).

▶ 85(5.1) ◀

(5.1) Acquisition of certain tools — capital cost and deemed depreciation. If subsection (1) has applied in respect of the acquisition at any particular time of any depreciable property by a corporation from an individual, the cost of the property to the individual was included in computing an amount under paragraph 8(1)(*r*) or (*s*) in respect of the individual, and the amount that would be the cost of the property to the individual immediately before the transfer if this Act were read without reference to subsection 8(7) (which amount is in this subsection referred to as the "individual's original cost") exceeds the individual's proceeds of disposition of the property, (*a*) the capital cost to the corporation of the property is deemed to be equal to the individual's original cost; and

(*b*) the amount by which the individual's original cost exceeds the individual's proceeds of disposition in respect of the property is deemed to have been deducted by the corporation under paragraph 20(1)(*a*) in respect of the property in computing income for taxation years that ended before that particular time.

Related Regulations: Part XI.

Interpretation Bulletins: *Secondary* — IT-291R3 Transfer of property to a corporation under subsection 85(1).

▶ 85(6) ◀

(6) Time for election. Any election under subsection (1) or (2) shall be made on or before the day that is the earliest of the days on or before which any taxpayer making the election is required to file a return of income pursuant to section 150 for the taxation year in which the transaction to which the election relates occurred.

Editorial Note: Where s. 85(2) applies, the election is made by the corporation and all of the members of the transferor partnership, so that the filing deadlines of all of the partners must be taken into account under s. 85(6).

▶ 85(7) ◀

(7) Late filed election. Where the election referred to in subsection (6) was not made on or before the day on or before which the election was required by that subsection to be made and that day is after May 6, 1974, the election shall be deemed to have been made on that day if, on or before the day that is 3 years after that day,

(*a*) the election is made in prescribed form; and

(*b*) an estimate of the penalty in respect of that election is paid by the taxpayer or the partnership, as the case may be, when that election is made.

Canadian Tax Foundation: Tollstam, *Rectification Denied for Missed Rollover Election*, 2015 Canadian Tax Highlights 23(11):1–2.

Information Circulars: IC 76-1R3 Transfer of property to a corporation under section 85.

Tax Window Files: Late Filed Election 85(7) — Amending Transactions, *April 30, 2009*, CRA Document No. 2008-0296721E5.

▶ 85(7.1) ◀

(7.1) Special cases. Where, in the opinion of the Minister, the circumstances of a case are such that it would be just and equitable

(*a*) to permit an election under subsection (1) or (2) to be made after the day that is 3 years after the day on or before which the election was required by subsection (6) to be made, or

(*b*) to permit an election made under subsection (1) or (2) to be amended,

the election or amended election shall be deemed to have been made on the day on or before which the election was so required to be made if

(*c*) the election or amended election is made in prescribed form, and

(*d*) an estimate of the penalty in respect of the election or amended election is paid by the taxpayer or partnership, as the case may be, when the election or amended election is made,

and where this subsection applies to the amendment of an election, that election shall be deemed not to have been effective.

Canadian Tax Foundation: Gill, *Backdoor Amendment of the Elected Amount in Rollovers*, 2017 Canadian Tax Focus 7(3):1–2.

Information Circulars: IC 76-19R3 Transfer of property to a corporation under section 85.

Tax Window Files: Price Adjustment Clauses, *July 6, 2004*, CRA Document No. 2004-0081631E5.

▶ 85(8) ◀

(8) Penalty for late filed election. For the purposes of this section, the penalty in respect of an election or an amended election referred to in paragraph (7)(*a*) or (7.1)(*c*) is an amount equal to the lesser of

(*a*) 1/4 of 1% of the amount, if any, by which

(i) the fair market value of the property in respect of which that election or amended election was made, at the time the property was disposed of,

exceeds

(ii) the amount agreed on in the election or amended election by the taxpayer or partnership, as the case may be, and the corporation,

for each month or part of a month during the period commencing with the day on or before which the election is required by subsection (6) to be made and ending on the day the election or amended election is made, and

(*b*) an amount, not exceeding $8,000, equal to the product obtained by multiplying $100 by the number of months each of which is a month all or part of which is during the period referred to in paragraph (*a*).

▶ 85(9) ◀

(9) Unpaid balance of penalty. The Minister shall, with all due dispatch, examine each election and amended election referred to in paragraph (7)(*a*) or (7.1)(*c*), assess the penalty payable and send a notice of assessment to the taxpayer or partnership, as the case may be, and the taxpayer or partnership, as the case may be, shall pay forthwith to the Receiver General the amount, if any, by which the penalty so assessed exceeds the total of all amounts previously paid on account of that penalty.

SECTION 85.1: Share for share exchange

▶ 85.1(1) ◀

(1) Share for share exchange. Where shares of any particular class of the capital stock of a Canadian corporation (in this section referred to as the "purchaser") are issued to a taxpayer (in this section referred to as the "vendor") by the purchaser in exchange for a capital property of the vendor that is shares of any particular class of the capital stock (in this section referred to as the "exchanged shares") of another corporation that is a taxable Canadian corporation (in this section referred to as the "acquired corporation"), subject to subsection (2),

(*a*) except where the vendor has, in the vendor's return of income for the taxation year in which the exchange occurred, included in computing the vendor's income for that year any portion of the gain or loss, otherwise determined, from the disposition of the exchanged shares, the vendor shall be deemed

(i) to have disposed of the exchanged shares for proceeds of disposition equal to the adjusted cost base to the vendor of those shares immediately before the exchange, and

(ii) to have acquired the shares of the purchaser at a cost to the vendor equal to the adjusted cost base to the vendor of the exchanged shares immediately before the exchange,

and where the exchanged shares were taxable Canadian property of the vendor, the shares of the purchaser so acquired by the vendor are deemed to be, at any time that is within 60 months after the exchange, taxable Canadian property of the vendor; and

(*b*) the cost to the purchaser of each exchanged share, at any time up to and including the time the purchaser disposed of the share, shall be deemed to be the lesser of

(i) its fair market value immediately before the exchange, and

(ii) its paid-up capital immediately before the exchange.

Editorial Note: The rollover under s. 85.1(1)(*a*) is automatic for the vendor unless the vendor chooses to include any portion of the gain or loss otherwise determined. The deemed cost rule for the purchaser under s. 85.1(1)(*b*) applies regardless of whether the vendor claims the rollover or chooses to include a gain or loss. The provisions do not apply if the parties make a joint election under s. 85 (s. 85.1(2)(*c*)). A s. 85 rollover could provide the purchaser with a higher adjusted cost base of the exchanged share relative to a s. 85.1 rollover if the vendor's adjusted cost base of the share exceeded its paid-up capital.

History: S. 85.1(1)(*a*), the portion after subparagraph (ii) was replaced by S.C. 2010, c. 12, s. 7(1), applicable in determining after March 4, 2010 whether a property is taxable Canadian property of a taxpayer. S. 85.1(1)(*a*), the portion after subparagraph (ii) formerly read:

> and where the exchanged shares were taxable Canadian property of the vendor, the shares of the purchaser so acquired by the vendor shall be deemed to be taxable Canadian property of the vendor; and

Related Sections: S. 40(3.5) Deemed identical property; s. 89(1), "Canadian corporation", "paid-up capital"; s. 112(7) Rules where shares exchanged; s. 248(1), "Canadian corporation", "corporation", "taxable Canadian property"; ITAR 26(26).

Canadian Petroleum Tax Journal: The Recent Take-Over Phenomenon, D. Alan Ross and Stanley R. Ebel, 2001, Vol. 14, No. 1; A Comparative Study of Canadian and US Rules Regarding the Taxation of Corporate Reorganizations, Firoz Talakshi and Christy Palmer, 2000, Vol. 13, No. 1.

Canadian Tax Foundation: Moch and Ebel, *Basics of Corporate Reorganizations: Sections 51, 85, 85.1, and 86*, 2002 Prairie Provinces Tax Conference 10:1–32; Moch and Ebel, *Share Reorganizations and Corporate Takeover Transactions: Using Tax Rollover Provisions*, 2000 Conference Report 8:1–20.

Tax Profile: August 2012 — U.S. Purchases and Sales of Canadian Businesses: Tax and Corporate Issues; September 2011 — Acquisition of Canadian Business by Non-Residents.

Income Tax Folios: *Primary* — S4-F5-C1 Share for Share Exchange.

Interpretation Bulletins: *Primary* — IT-450R Share for share exchange. *Secondary* — IT-113R4 Benefits to employees — Stock options; IT-291R3 Transfer of property to a corporation under subsection 85(1).

► 85.1(2) ◄

(2) Where s. (1) does not apply. Subsection (1) does not apply where

(*a*) the vendor and purchaser were, immediately before the exchange, not dealing with each other at arm's length (otherwise than because of a right referred to in paragraph 251(5)(*b*) that is a right of the purchaser to acquire the exchanged shares);

(*b*) the vendor or persons with whom the vendor did not deal at arm's length, or the vendor together with persons with whom the vendor did not deal at arm's length,

(i) controlled the purchaser, or

(ii) beneficially owned shares of the capital stock of the purchaser having a fair market value of more than 50% of the fair market value of all of the outstanding shares of the capital stock of the purchaser,

immediately after the exchange;

(*c*) the vendor and the purchaser have filed an election under subsection 85(1) or (2) with respect to the exchanged shares;

(*d*) consideration other than shares of the particular class of the capital stock of the purchaser was received by the vendor for the exchanged shares, notwithstanding that the vendor may have disposed of shares of the capital stock of the acquired corporation (other than the exchanged shares) to the purchaser for consideration other than shares of one class of the capital stock of the purchaser; or

(*e*) the vendor

(i) is a foreign affiliate of a taxpayer resident in Canada at the end of the taxation year of the vendor in which the exchange occurred, and

(ii) has included any portion of the gain or loss, otherwise determined, from the disposition of the exchanged shares in computing its foreign accrual property income for the taxation year of the vendor in which the exchange occurred.

Editorial Note: If the vendor does not deal at arm's length with the purchaser, the s. 85.1(1) rollover does not apply (s. 85.1(2)(*a*)), although the parties could elect to use the s. 85 rollover, in which case the rules of s. 84.1 could also apply. S. 85 is also available if the parties deal at arm's length.

The requirement that no consideration other than shares of the purchaser be received by the vendor for the exchanged shares (s. 85.1(2)(*d*)) could be problematic where the vendor receives cash in lieu of a fractional share, or where the vendor receives shares and non-share consideration for the exchanged shares. However, in paragraph 1.7 of Income Tax Folio S4-F5-C1, the CRA indicates that s. 85.1 can be utilized in these situations to provide at least a partial rollover. Alternatively, if the s. 85 election is used, the vendor can claim a full rollover as long as the value of the non-share consideration does not exceed the vendor's adjusted cost base of the exchanged shares. However, the purchaser's cost of the exchanged shares under s. 85 (the elected amount) would likely differ from that determined under s. 85.1 (lesser of fair market value and paid-up capital immediately before the exchange; see s. 85.1(1)(*b*)).

Related Sections: S. 95(1), "foreign affiliate"; s. 251 Arm's length.

Income Tax Folios: *Primary* — S4-F5-C1 Share for Share Exchange.

► 85.1(2.1) ◄

(2.1) Computation of paid-up capital. Where, at any time, a purchaser has issued shares of its capital stock as a result of an exchange to which subsection (1) applied, in computing the paid-up capital in respect of any particular class of shares of its capital stock at any particular time after that time

(*a*) there shall be deducted that proportion of the amount, if any, by which

(i) the increase, if any, as a result of the issue, in the paid-up capital in respect of all the shares of the capital stock of the purchaser, computed without reference to this subsection as it applies to the issue,

exceeds

(ii) the paid-up capital in respect of all the exchanged shares received as a result of the exchange

that

(iii) the increase, if any, as a result of the issue, in the paid-up capital in respect of the particular class of shares, computed without reference to this subsection as it applies to the issue,

is of

(iv) the amount, if any, determined in subparagraph (i) in respect of the issue; and

(*b*) there shall be added an amount equal to the lesser of

(i) the amount, if any, by which

(A) the total of all amounts each of which is an amount deemed by subsection 84(3), (4) or (4.1) to be a dividend on shares of that class paid by the purchaser before the particular time

exceeds

(B) the total that would be determined under clause (A) if this Act were read without reference to paragraph (*a*), and

(ii) the total of all amounts required by paragraph (*a*) to be deducted in respect of that particular class of shares before the particular time.

Editorial Note: The paid-up capital grind in s. 85.1(2.1) effectively means that the increase in the paid-up capital as a result of the issuance of the shares by the purchaser corporation is limited to the paid-up capital in respect of the exchanged shares.

Related Sections: S. 89(1), "paid-up capital".

Information Circulars: IC 88-2 General anti-avoidance rule — Section 245 of the Income Tax Act (para. 25).

► 85.1(2.2) ◄

(2.2) Issuance deemed made to vendor. For the purposes of subsection (1), if a purchaser issues shares of a class of its capital stock (in this subsection referred to as "purchaser shares") to a trust under a court-approved plan or scheme of arrangement in consideration for which a vendor disposes of exchanged shares that trade on a designated stock exchange to the purchaser solely for purchaser shares that are widely traded on a designated stock exchange immediately after and as part of completion of the plan or scheme of arrangement, the issuance to the trust is deemed to be an issuance to the vendor.

History: S. 85.1(2.2) was added by S.C. 2013, c. 34, s. 221(1), applicable to share exchanges made after June 2005 except that subsection 85.1(2.2) does not apply to a particular share exchange of a taxpayer that occurs before November 5, 2010 if, within six months of being advised by the Minister of National Revenue that subsection 85.1(2.2) applies to the exchange, the taxpayer elects in writing not to have that subsection apply to the exchange.

► 85.1(3) ◄

(3) Disposition of shares of foreign affiliate. Where a taxpayer has disposed of capital property that was shares of the capital stock of a foreign affiliate of the taxpayer to any corporation that was, immediately following the disposition, a foreign affiliate of the taxpayer (in this subsection referred to as the "acquiring affiliate") for consideration including shares of the capital stock of the acquiring affiliate,

(*a*) the cost to the taxpayer of any property (other than shares of the capital stock of the acquiring affiliate) receivable by the taxpayer as consideration for the disposition shall be deemed to be the fair market value of the property at the time of the disposition;

(*b*) the cost to the taxpayer of any shares of any class of the capital stock of the acquiring affiliate receivable by the taxpayer as consideration for the disposition shall be deemed to be that proportion of the amount, if any, by which the total of the adjusted cost bases to the taxpayer, immediately before the disposition, of the shares disposed of exceeds the fair market value at that time of the consideration receivable for the disposition (other than shares of the capital stock of the acquiring affiliate) that

(i) the fair market value, immediately after the disposition, of those shares of the acquiring affiliate of that class

is of

(ii) the fair market value, immediately after the disposition, of all shares of the capital stock of the acquiring affiliate receivable by the taxpayer as consideration for the disposition;

(*c*) the taxpayer's proceeds of disposition of the shares shall be deemed to be an amount equal to the cost to the taxpayer of all shares and other property receivable by the taxpayer from the acquiring affiliate as consideration for the disposition; and

(*d*) the cost to the acquiring affiliate of the shares acquired from the taxpayer shall be deemed to be an amount equal to the taxpayer's proceeds of disposition referred to in paragraph (*c*).

Editorial Note: The CRA has indicated that s. 85.1(3) can apply where a foreign affiliate of a taxpayer issues shares to the taxpayer in consideration for the acquisition of its own shares (that is, the foreign affiliate is also the "acquiring affiliate"); see CRA Document no. 9M19020, question 3.6.

Related Sections: S. 53(1)(*c*) Adjustments to cost base — Contributions of capital; s. 95(1), "foreign affiliate".

Canadian Petroleum Tax Journal: A Comparative Study of Canadian and US Rules Regarding the Taxation of Corporate Reorganizations, Firoz Talakshi and Christy Palmer, 2000, Vol. 13, No. 1.

Tax Profile: July 2008 — International Tax Planning for the Owner-Manager.

► 85.1(4) ◄

(4) Exception. Subsection (3) does not apply in respect of a disposition at any time by a taxpayer of a share of the capital stock of a particular foreign affiliate of the taxpayer to another foreign affiliate of the taxpayer if

(*a*) both

(i) all or substantially all of the property of the particular affiliate was, immediately before that time, excluded property (within the meaning assigned by subsection 95(1)) of the particular affiliate, and

(ii) the disposition is part of a transaction or event or a series of transactions or events for the purpose of disposing of the share to a person or partnership that, immediately after the transaction, event or series, was a person or partnership (other than a foreign affiliate of the taxpayer in respect of which the taxpayer has a qualifying interest (within the meaning assigned by paragraph 95(2)(*m*)) at the time of the transaction or event or throughout the series, as the case may be) with whom the taxpayer was dealing at arm's length; or

(*b*) the adjusted cost base to the taxpayer of the share at that time is greater than the amount that would, in the absence of subsection (3), be the taxpayer's proceeds of disposition of the share in respect of the disposition.

History: S. 85.1(4) was replaced by S.C. 2013, c. 34, s. 63(1), applicable in respect of dispositions that occur after August 19, 2011.

Any assessment of a taxpayer's tax, interest and penalties payable under the Act for any taxation year that ends before June 26, 2013 that would, in the absence of this section, be precluded because of subsections 152(4) to (5) of the Act shall be made to the extent necessary to take into account the amendments by S.C. 2013, c. 34, s. 54 to 89.

S. 85.1(4) formerly read:

(4) *Exception.* Subsection (3) is not applicable in respect of a disposition at any time by a taxpayer of a share of the capital stock of a foreign affiliate, all or substantially all of the property of which at that time was excluded property (within the meaning assigned by subsection 95(1)), to another foreign affiliate of the taxpayer where the disposition is part of a series of transactions or events for the purpose of disposing of the share to a person who, immediately after the series of transactions or events, was a person (other than a foreign affiliate of the taxpayer) with whom the taxpayer was dealing at arm's length.

► 85.1(5) ◄

(5) Foreign share for foreign share exchange. Subject to subsections (3) and (6) and 95(2), where a corporation resident in a country other than Canada (in this section referred to as the "foreign purchaser") issues shares of its capital stock (in this section referred to as the "issued foreign shares") to a vendor in exchange for shares of the capital stock of another corporation resident in a country other than Canada (in this section referred to as the "exchanged foreign shares") that were immediately before the exchange capital property of the vendor, except where the vendor has, in the vendor's return of income for the taxation year in which the exchange occurred, included in computing the vendor's income for that year any portion of the gain or loss, otherwise determined, from the disposition of the exchanged foreign shares, the vendor is deemed

(*a*) to have disposed of the exchanged foreign shares for proceeds of disposition equal to the adjusted cost base to the vendor of those shares immediately before the exchange, and

(*b*) to have acquired the issued foreign shares at a cost to the vendor equal to the adjusted cost base to the vendor of the exchanged foreign shares immediately before the exchange,

and where the exchanged foreign shares were taxable Canadian property of the vendor, the issued foreign shares so acquired by the vendor are deemed to be, at any time that is within 60 months after the exchange, taxable Canadian property of the vendor.

Editorial Note: S. 85.1(5) effectively extends the subsection (1) tax-deferred rollover treatment to shareholders involved in foreign corporate takeovers, and in particular, where a shareholder-vendor disposes of shares of one foreign corporation to another foreign corporation (purchaser) in exchange for shares issued by the purchaser.

History: S. 85.1(5), the portion after paragraph (*b*) was replaced by S.C. 2010, c. 12, s. 7(2), applicable in determining after March 4, 2010 whether a property is taxable Canadian property of a taxpayer. S. 85.1(5), the portion after paragraph (*b*) formerly read:

and where the exchanged foreign shares were taxable Canadian property of the vendor, the issued foreign shares so acquired by the vendor are deemed to be taxable Canadian property of the vendor.

Related Sections: S. 248(1), "taxable Canadian property".

Canadian Tax Foundation: Steeves, *Foreign Share Exchanges and Foreign Spinoffs*, 2001 Canadian Tax Journal 4:1066–1074.

Tax Window Files: Foreign Share for share Exchange, *August 23, 2016*, CRA Document No. 2015-0614981E5.

► 85.1(6) ◄

(6) Where subsection (5) does not apply. Subsection (5) does not apply where

(*a*) the vendor and foreign purchaser were, immediately before the exchange, not dealing with each other at arm's length (otherwise than because of a right referred to in paragraph 251(5)(*b*) that is a right of the foreign purchaser to acquire the exchanged foreign shares);

(*b*) immediately after the exchange the vendor, persons with whom the vendor did not deal at arm's length or the vendor together with persons with whom the vendor did not deal at arm's length

(i) controlled the foreign purchaser, or

(ii) beneficially owned shares of the capital stock of the foreign purchaser having a fair market value of more than 50% of the fair market value of all of the outstanding shares of the capital stock of the foreign purchaser;

(*c*) consideration other than issued foreign shares was received by the vendor for the exchanged foreign shares, notwithstanding that the vendor may have disposed of shares of the capital stock of the other corporation referred to in subsection (5) (other than the exchanged foreign shares) to the foreign purchaser for consideration other than shares of the capital stock of the foreign purchaser;

(*d*) the vendor

(i) is a foreign affiliate of a taxpayer resident in Canada at the end of the taxation year of the vendor in which the exchange occurred, and

(ii) has included any portion of the gain or loss, otherwise determined, from the disposition of the exchanged foreign shares in computing its foreign accrual property income for the taxation year of the vendor in which the exchange occurred; or

(*e*) the vendor is a foreign affiliate of a taxpayer resident in Canada at the end of the taxation year of the vendor in which the exchange occurred and the exchanged foreign shares are excluded property (within the meaning assigned by subsection 95(1)) of the vendor.

Editorial Note: The CRA has indicated that its administrative position in paragraph 7 of IT-450R, which applies for the purposes of ss. 85.1(1) and (2) where the vendor receives both shares and non-share consideration from the purchaser corporation for the exchanged shares (see the editorial note to s. 85.1(2)), similarly applies for the purposes of ss. 85.1(5) and (6). See CRA Document No. 2000-0000765.

Related Sections: S. 95(1), "foreign accrual property income", "foreign affiliate"; s. 251(1) Arm's length.

Income Tax Folios: *Primary* — S4-F5-C1 Share for Share Exchange.

▶ 85.1(6.1) ◀

(6.1) Issuance deemed made to vendor. For the purposes of subsection (5), if a foreign purchaser issues shares of a class of its capital stock (in this subsection referred to as "foreign purchaser shares") to a trust under a court-approved plan or scheme of arrangement in consideration for which a vendor disposes of exchanged foreign shares that trade on a designated stock exchange to the purchaser solely for foreign purchaser shares that are widely traded on a designated stock exchange immediately after and as part of completion of the plan or scheme of arrangement, the issuance to the trust is deemed to be an issuance to the vendor.

History: S. 85.1(6.1) was added by S.C. 2013, c. 34, s. 221(2), applicable to share exchanges made after June 2005 except that subsection 85.1(6.1) does not apply to a particular share exchange of a taxpayer that occurs before November 5, 2010 if, within six months of being advised by the Minister of National Revenue that subsection 85.1(6.1) applies to the exchange, the taxpayer elects in writing not to have that subsection apply to the exchange.

▶ 85.1(7) ◀

(7) Application of subsection (8). Subsection (8) applies in respect of the disposition before 2013 by a taxpayer of SIFT wind-up entity equity (referred to in subsection (8) as the "particular unit") to a taxable Canadian corporation if

(*a*) the disposition occurs during a period (referred to in this subsection and subsection (8) as the "exchange period") of no more than 60 days at the end of which all of the equity in the SIFT wind-up entity is owned by the corporation;

(*b*) the taxpayer receives no consideration for the disposition other than a share (referred to in this subsection and subsection (8) as the "exchange share") of the capital stock of the corporation that is issued during the exchange period to the taxpayer by the corporation;

(*c*) neither of subsections 85(1) and (2) applies to the disposition; and

(*d*) all of the exchange shares issued to holders of equity in the SIFT wind-up entity are shares of a single class of the capital stock of the corporation.

History: S. 85.1(7), the portion before paragraph (*a*) was replaced by S.C. 2013, c. 34, s. 221(3), in force June 26, 2013, and formerly read:

(7) *Application of subsection (8).* Subsection (8) applies in respect of the disposition before 2013 by a taxpayer of SIFT wind-up entity equity (referred to [in] subsection (8) as the "particular unit") to a taxable Canadian corporation if

S. 85.1(7) was added by S.C. 2009, c. 2, s. 18(1), applicable to

(a) dispositions that occur on or after July 14, 2008; and

(b) a disposition, by a taxpayer to a corporation, that occurs on or after December 20, 2007 and before July 14, 2008, if the corporation (jointly with the taxpayer, if the taxpayer and the corporation have validly elected that subsection 85(1) or (2) apply to the disposition) elects in writing, filed with the Minister of National Revenue on or before the corporation's filing-due date for its taxation year that includes the day on which this Act is assented to [R.A. March 12, 2009], that s. 85.1(7) and (8) apply to the disposition.

Related Sections: S. 248(1), "SIFT wind-up entity", "SIFT wind-up entity equity".

▶ 85.1(8) ◀

(8) Rollover on SIFT unit for share exchange. If this subsection applies in respect of a disposition by a taxpayer of a particular unit of a SIFT wind-up entity to a corporation for consideration that is an exchange share, the following rules apply:

(*a*) the taxpayer's proceeds of disposition of the particular unit, and cost of the exchange share, are deemed to be equal to the cost amount to the taxpayer of the particular unit immediately before the disposition;

(*b*) if the particular unit was immediately before the disposition taxable Canadian property of the taxpayer, the exchange share is deemed to be, at any time that is within 60 months after the disposition, taxable Canadian property of the taxpayer;

(*c*) if the exchange share's fair market value immediately after the disposition exceeds the particular unit's fair market value at the time of the disposition, the excess is deemed to be an amount that section 15 requires to be included in computing the taxpayer's income for the taxpayer's taxation year in which the disposition occurs;

(*d*) if the particular unit's fair market value at the time of the disposition exceeds the exchange share's fair market value immediately after the disposition, and it is reasonable to regard any part of the excess as a benefit that the taxpayer desired to have conferred on a person, or partnership, with whom the taxpayer does not deal at arm's length, the excess is deemed to be an amount that section 15 requires to be included in computing the taxpayer's income for the taxpayer's taxation year in which the disposition occurs;

(*e*) the cost to the corporation of the particular unit is deemed to be the lesser of

(i) the fair market value of the particular unit immediately before the disposition, and

(ii) the amount determined for B in the formula in paragraph (*f*) in respect of the particular unit; and

(*f*) in computing the paid-up capital in respect of each class of shares of the capital stock of the corporation at any time after the disposition there shall be deducted the amount determined by the formula

$$(A - B) \times C/A$$

where

A is the increase, if any, as a result of the disposition, in the paid-up capital in respect of all the shares of the capital stock of the corporation, computed without reference to this paragraph as it applies to the disposition,

B is the amount determined by the formula

$$D - E$$

where

D is

(i) unless subparagraph (ii) applies, the total of all amounts each of which is

(A) if the SIFT wind-up entity is a trust, the fair market value of property received by the SIFT wind-up entity on the issuance of the particular unit, or

(B) if the SIFT wind-up entity is a partnership,

(I) an amount that has at any time been added, in computing the adjusted cost base to any taxpayer of the particular unit on or before the disposition, because of subparagraph 53(1)(*e*)(iv) or (x), or

(II) an amount that would at any time have been added, in computing the adjusted cost base to any taxpayer of the particular unit on or before the disposition, because of subparagraph 53(1)(*e*)(i) if subsection 96(1) were read without reference to its paragraph (*d*) and the partnership deducted all amounts otherwise deductible because of that paragraph, and

(ii) if the SIFT wind-up entity has on or after the end of the exchange period issued a unit, nil, and

E is the total of all amounts each of which

(i) if the SIFT wind-up entity is a trust, has become payable by the SIFT wind-up entity, in respect of the particular unit, to any holder of the unit on or before the disposition, other than an amount that has become payable out of its income (determined without reference to subsection 104(6)) or capital gains, and

(ii) if the SIFT wind-up entity is a partnership,

(A) has at any time been deducted, in computing the adjusted cost base to any taxpayer of the particular unit on or before the disposition, because of subparagraph 53(2)(*c*)(iv) or (v), or

(B) would have at any time been deducted, in computing the adjusted cost base to any taxpayer of the particular unit on or before the disposition, because of subparagraph 53(2)(*c*)(i) if subsection 96(1) were read without reference to its paragraph (*d*) and the partnership deducted all amounts otherwise deductible because of that paragraph, and

C is the increase, if any, as a result of the disposition, in the paid-up capital in respect of the class of shares, computed without reference to this paragraph as it applies to the disposition.

Editorial Note: Subsection 85.1(8) is intended to facilitate the tax-efficient disposition of a unit in a specified investment flow-through entity ("SIFT") where such a unit is exchanged for a share of a corporation. This provision (generally referred to as the "exchange method") permits a SIFT to effectively convert into a corporation while allowing unitholders tax-deferred rollover treatment similar to the treatment that would apply in respect of a share-for-share exchange under s. 85.1. The exchange method and the other SIFT "conversion" rules in s. 88.1 and 107(3.1) were introduced as a corollary to the rules in s. 122, which imposes an entity-level tax on a SIFT comparable to the general corporate tax rate that would apply if the SIFT were a corporation.

History: S. 85.1(8)(*f*), the portion before the first formula was replaced by S.C. 2013, c. 34, s. 221(4), in force June 26, 2013, and formerly read:

(*f*) in computing the paid up capital in respect of each class of shares of the capital stock of the corporation at any time after the disposition there shall be deducted the amount determined by the formula

S. 85.1(8)(*b*) was replaced by S.C. 2010, c. 12, s. 7(3), applicable in determining after March 4, 2010 whether a property is taxable Canadian property of a taxpayer. S. 85.1(8)(*b*) formerly read:

(*b*) if the particular unit was immediately before the disposition taxable Canadian property of the taxpayer, the exchange share is deemed to be taxable Canadian property of the taxpayer;

S. 85.1(8) was added by S.C. 2009, c. 2, s. 18(1), applicable to

(a) dispositions that occur on or after July 14, 2008; and

(b) a disposition, by a taxpayer to a corporation, that occurs on or after December 20, 2007 and before July 14, 2008, if the corporation (jointly with the taxpayer, if the taxpayer and the corporation have validly elected that subsection 85(1) or (2) apply to the disposition) elects in writing, filed with the Minister of National Revenue on or before the corporation's filing-due date for its taxation year that includes the day on which this Act is assented to [R.A. March 12, 2009], that s. 85.1(7) and (8) apply to the disposition.

Related Sections: S. 85(2.1) Computing paid-up capital; s. 85.1(7) Application of subsection (8); s. 88.1(2) SIFT trust wind-up event; s. 107(3.1) SIFT trust wind-up event; s. 122(1) Tax payable by *inter vivos* trust; s. 248(1), "SIFT wind-up entity", "SIFT wind-up entity equity".

Canadian Tax Foundation: Perry, *Income Trusts: Reorganizations and Planning for 2011*, 2008 Conference Report 8:1–33.

SECTION 86: Exchange of shares by a shareholder in course of reorganization of capital

► 86(1) ◄

(1) Exchange of shares by a shareholder in course of reorganization of capital. Where, at a particular time after May 6, 1974, in the course of a reorganization of the capital of a corporation, a taxpayer has disposed of capital property that was all the shares of any particular class of the capital stock of the corporation that were owned by the taxpayer at the particular time (in this section referred to as the "old shares"), and property is receivable from the corporation therefor that includes other shares of the capital stock of the corporation (in this section referred to as the "new shares"), the following rules apply:

(*a*) the cost to the taxpayer of any property (other than new shares) receivable by the taxpayer for the old shares shall be deemed to be its fair market value at the time of the disposition;

(*b*) the cost to the taxpayer of any new shares of any class of the capital stock of the corporation receivable by the taxpayer for the old shares shall be deemed to be that proportion of the amount, if any, by which the total of the adjusted cost bases to the taxpayer, immediately before the disposition, of the old shares exceeds the fair market value at that time of the consideration receivable for the old shares (other than new shares) that

(i) the fair market value, immediately after the disposition, of those new shares of that class,

is of

(ii) the fair market value, immediately after the disposition, of all new shares of the capital stock of the corporation receivable by the taxpayer for the old shares; and

(*c*) the taxpayer shall be deemed to have disposed of the old shares for proceeds of disposition equal to the cost to the taxpayer of all new shares and other property receivable by the taxpayer for the old shares.

Editorial Note: S. 86(1) allows a rollover where a taxpayer's shares in a corporation (old shares) are exchanged for other shares in the corporation (new shares) in the course of a reorganization of its capital. Note the requirement that all of the old shares of the class owned by the taxpayer must be exchanged. The taxpayer may receive non-share consideration as well as the new shares on the exchange. However, there will not be a complete rollover under s. 86(1) if the value of the non-share consideration exceeds the adjusted cost base of the old shares. If the value of the non-share consideration exceeds the paid-up capital of the old shares, the excess will be a deemed dividend (s. 84(3)), which will be excluded from the proceeds of disposition of the old shares (s. 54, s. (*j*) of "proceeds of disposition").

If the value of the new shares plus any non-share consideration is less than the value of the old shares, and it is reasonable to consider the difference as being a gift to a person related to the taxpayer, s. 86(2) may apply to limit the rollover and reduce the cost of the new shares. If the value of the non-share consideration and the new shares exceeds the value of the old shares, there may be a shareholder benefit under s. 15(1).

S. 86(1) does not apply where the rollover in s. 85(1) or (2) applies (s. 86(3)), but it does take precedence over the rollover provisions of s. 51 (s. 51(4)).

Related Sections: S. 15(1) Benefit conferred on shareholder; s. 51(4) Application; s. 54, "proceeds of disposition"; s. 55(1), "permitted exchange"; s. 84(3) Redemption, etc; s. 84(4.1) Deemed dividend on reduction of paid-up capital; s. 84(5) Amount distributed or paid where a share.

Canadian Petroleum Tax Journal: The Recent Take-Over Phenomenon, D. Alan Ross and Stanley R. Ebel, 2001, Vol. 14, No. 1; A Comparative Study of Canadian and US Rules Regarding the Taxation of Corporate Reorganizations, Firoz Talakshi and Christy Palmer, 2000, Vol. 13, No. 1.

Canadian Tax Foundation: Truster, *The Challenges of Creditor Proofing,* 2014 Tax for the Owner-Manager 14(3):7; Bernstein, *Valuation and Related Tax Issues, Part 1,* 2011 Conference Report 17:1–31; Ireland et al., *Disarming the Succession Time Bomb: The Role of Trusts, Insurance, and Shareholders' Agreements in the Transition of Family Businesses,* 2011 Conference Report 15:1–53; Tabuchi, *Share Capital Reorganizations for Private Corporations,* 2003 Canadian Tax Journal 3:1340–1378; Moch and Ebel, *Basics of Corporate Reorganizations: Sections 51, 85, 85.1, and 86,* 2002 Prairie Provinces Tax Conference 10:1–32; Penny et al., *Recent Developments in Exchangeable-Share Transactions,* 2000 Conference Report 25:1–27; Moch and Ebel, *Share Reorganizations and Corporate Takeover Transactions: Using Tax Rollover Provisions,* 2000 Conference Report 8:1–20; Ahmed, *Corporate Distributions Other Than Butterfly Transactions,* 1998 Conference Report 15:1–38.

STEP Canada: Christine Cauwenberghe, "Avoiding Family Law Fiascos in Family Estate Freezes," PowerPoint presentation to the 15th National Conference of STEP Canada, Toronto, June 10-11, 2013.

Tax Profile: April 2013 — Canadian Estate Freezes in Favour of U.S. Citizens; October 2012 — Exchangeable Shares in Canada; August 2012 — U.S. Purchases and Sales of Canadian Businesses: Tax and Corporate Issues; September 2011 — Acquisition of Canadian Business by Non-Residents; November 2009 — Purchase and Sale of a Canadian Business; September 2009 — Time To Refreeze?; October 2007 — Will Canadian Unlimited Liability Companies Survive?; July 2006 — Asset Protection Planning; July 2005 — Alberta Introduces Alberta Unlimited Liability Corporations.

Tax Topics: No. 2045, Rectification? In Quebec?.

Tax Window Files: Share Disposition, *October 9, 2009,* CRA Document No. 2009-0330161C6; 86(1) [Price adjustment clauses], *March 15, 2006,* CRA Document No. 2005-0113161R3.

Cases: The parties successfully requested amendments to the agreements to reflect their original intentions to reorganize the corporations and transfer interest in them without tax consequences. Courts have the power under Quebec civil law to correct agreements to give effect to the parties' true intention. *Québec (Agence du Revenu) v. Services Environnementaux AES Inc.,* 2013 DTC 5174 (S.C.C.)

► 86(2) ◄

(2) Idem. Notwithstanding paragraphs (1)(*b*) and (*c*), where a taxpayer has disposed of old shares in circumstances described in subsection (1) and the fair market value of the old shares immediately before the disposition exceeds the total of

(*a*) the cost to the taxpayer of the property (other than new shares) receivable by the taxpayer for the old shares as determined under paragraph (1)(*a*), and

(*b*) the fair market value of the new shares, immediately after the disposition,

and it is reasonable to regard any portion of the excess (in this subsection referred to as the "gift portion") as a benefit that the taxpayer desired to have conferred on a person related to the taxpayer, the following rules apply:

(*c*) the taxpayer shall be deemed to have disposed of the old shares for proceeds of disposition equal to the lesser of

(i) the total of the cost to the taxpayer of the property as determined under paragraph (1)(*a*) and the gift portion

and

(ii) the fair market value of the old shares immediately before the disposition,

(*d*) the taxpayer's capital loss from the disposition of the old shares shall be deemed to be nil, and

(*e*) the cost to the taxpayer of any new shares of any class of the capital stock of the corporation receivable by the taxpayer for the old shares shall be deemed to be that proportion of the amount, if any, by which the total of the adjusted cost bases to the taxpayer, immediately before the disposition, of the old shares exceeds the total determined under subparagraph (*c*)(i) that

(i) the fair market value, immediately after the disposition, of the new shares of that class,

is of

(ii) the fair market value, immediately after the disposition, of all new shares of the capital stock of the corporation receivable by the taxpayer for the old shares.

Tax Profile: April 2012 — Price Adjustment Clauses.

Income Tax Folios: *Secondary* — S4-F3-C1 Price Adjustment Clauses.

► 86(2.1) ◄

(2.1) Computation of paid-up capital. Where subsection (1) applies to a disposition of shares of the capital stock of a corporation (in this subsection referred to as the "exchange"), in computing the paid-up capital in respect of a particular class of shares of the capital stock of the corporation at any particular time that is the time of, or any time after, the exchange,

(*a*) there shall be deducted the amount determined by the formula

$$(A - B) \times C/A$$

where

A is the total of all amounts each of which is the increase, if any, as a result of the exchange, in the paid-up capital in respect of a class of shares of the capital stock of the corporation, computed without reference to this subsection as it applies to the exchange,

B is the amount, if any, by which the paid-up capital in respect of the old shares exceeds the fair market value of the consideration (other than shares of the capital stock of the corporation) given by the corporation for the old shares on the exchange, and

C is the increase, if any, as a result of the exchange, in the paid-up capital in respect of the particular class of shares, computed without reference to this subsection as it applies to the exchange; and

(*b*) there shall be added an amount equal to the lesser of

(i) the amount, if any, by which

(A) the total of all amounts deemed by subsection 84(3), (4) or (4.1) to be a dividend on shares of that class paid by the corporation before the particular time

exceeds

(B) the total that would be determined under clause (A) if this Act were read without reference to paragraph (*a*), and

(ii) the total of all amounts required by paragraph (*a*) to be deducted in respect of that particular class of shares before the particular time.

Editorial Note: See the editorial note under s. 86(1) regarding the rollover where old shares in the capital of a corporation are exchanged for new shares in the capital of the corporation. The paid-up capital grind under s. 86(2.1)(*a*) ensures that the increase in the paid-up capital as a result of the issuance of the new shares will not exceed the amount, if any, by which the paid-up capital in respect of the old shares exceeds the value of any non-share consideration received on the exchange. However, the CRA has indicated that the provision does not prevent the "shifting" of paid-up capital — for example, where the aggregate paid-up capital of the old shares is effectively allocated amongst different classes of the new shares; see CRA Document No. 9613115.

If s. 85(1) applies to the exchange instead of s. 86(1), the paid-up capital adjustment under s. 85(2.1) will apply instead of s. 86(2.1).

Tax Window Files: Application of Subsection 84(1)/Paid-Up Capital, *February 26, 2009*, CRA Document No. 2008-0293401E5.

▶ 86(3) ◀

(3) Application. Subsections (1) and (2) do not apply in any case where subsection 85(1) or (2) applies.

▶ 86(4) ◀

(4) Computation of adjusted cost base. Where a taxpayer has disposed of old shares in circumstances described in subsection (1),

(*a*) there shall be deducted after the disposition in computing the adjusted cost base to the taxpayer of each new share the amount determined by the formula

$$A \times B/C$$

where

A is the amount, if any, by which

(i) the total of all amounts deducted under paragraph 53(2)(*g*.1) in computing the adjusted cost base to the taxpayer of the old shares immediately before the disposition

exceeds

(ii) the amount that would be the taxpayer's capital gain for the taxation year that includes the time of the disposition from the disposition of the old shares if paragraph 40(1)(*a*) were read without reference to subparagraph (iii) of that paragraph,

B is the fair market value of the new share at the time it was acquired by the taxpayer in consideration for the disposition of the old shares, and

C is the total of all amounts each of which is the fair market value of a new share at the time it was acquired by the taxpayer in consideration for the disposition of the old shares; and

(*b*) the amount determined under paragraph (*a*) in respect of the acquisition shall be added in computing the adjusted cost base to the taxpayer of the new share after the disposition.

Related Sections: S. 53(1)(*q*) Adjustments to cost base — Debt forgiveness.

SECTION 86.1: Foreign spin-offs

▶ 86.1(1) ◀

(1) Eligible distribution not included in income. Notwithstanding any other provision of this Part,

(*a*) the amount of an eligible distribution received by a taxpayer shall not be included in computing the income of the taxpayer; and

(*b*) subsection 52(2) does not apply to the eligible distribution received by the taxpayer.

Editorial Note: In general terms, s. 86.1 allows a tax-deferred rollover where a non-resident corporation distributes its shares ("spin-off shares") in another corporation (typically a subsidiary) to its own shareholders. The rollover applies to a Canadian resident shareholder who receives the spin-off shares under an "eligible distribution" (s. 86.1(2)). Among other things, the class of the "original shares" (the shares in the distributing non-resident corporation owned by the shareholder) must be widely held and (i) are actively traded on a designated stock exchange, or (ii) are registered shares that were required to be registered under the U.S. *Securities Exchange Act*, and a rollover must be available in the country in which the corporation is resident. The rollover is elective at the shareholder's option, unless the taxpayer is a deferred income plan subject to Part XI.

Canadian Tax Foundation: Steeves, *Foreign Share Exchanges and Foreign Spinoffs*, 2001 Canadian Tax Journal 4:1066–1074; Fontaine and Kong, *The March 16, 2001 Draft Legislation: Thin Capitalization, Non-Resident-Owned Investment Corporations and Foreign Spinoff Relief*, 2001 Canadian Tax Journal 2:383–401.

Tax Topics: No. 2047, Foreign Reorganizations and Canadian Shareholders: Section 86.1, Stock Dividends, and Stock Splits; No. 1584, Foreign Spin-offs; No. 1572, Q&A Re Foreign Spin-offs; No. 1516, Foreign Spin-offs.

Income Tax Technical News: Issue No. 28, Section 86.1 — Foreign Spin-Offs with "Poison Pill" Shareholder Rights Plans.

Tax Window Files: Corporate Restructuring, *August 19, 2009*, CRA Document No. 2009-0326271E5; Foreign Spin-Off, *January 29, 2009*, CRA Document No. 2008-0285911E5; Distribution Ineligible for Benefits of Section 86.1, *Technical Interpretation, International and Trusts Division, November 21, 2003*, CRA Document No. 2003-0023925.

▶ 86.1(2) ◀

(2) Eligible distribution. For the purpose of this section, a distribution by a particular corporation that is received by a taxpayer is an eligible distribution if

(*a*) the distribution is with respect to all of the taxpayer's common shares of the capital stock of the particular corporation (in this section referred to as the "original shares");

(*b*) the distribution consists solely of common shares of the capital stock of another corporation that were owned by the particular corporation immediately before their distribution to the taxpayer (in this section referred to as the "spin-off shares");

(*c*) in the case of a distribution that is not prescribed,

(i) at the time of the distribution, both corporations are resident in the United States and were never resident in Canada,

(ii) at the time of the distribution, the shares of the class that includes the original shares are widely held and

(A) are actively traded on a designated stock exchange in the United States, or

(B) are required, under the *Securities Exchange Act of 1934* of the United States, as amended from time to time, to be registered with the Securities and Exchange Commission of the United States and are so registered, and

(iii) under the provisions of the *Internal Revenue Code of 1986* of the United States, as amended from time to time, that apply to the distribution, the shareholders of the particular corporation who are resident in the United States are not taxable in respect of the distribution;

(*d*) in the case of a distribution that is prescribed,

(i) at the time of the distribution, both corporations are resident in the same country, other than the United States, with which Canada has a tax treaty (in this section referred to as the "foreign country") and were never resident in Canada,

(ii) at the time of the distribution, the shares of the class that includes the original shares are widely held and actively traded on a designated stock exchange,

(iii) under the law of the foreign country, those shareholders of the particular corporation who are resident in that country are not taxable in respect of the distribution, and

(iv) the distribution is prescribed subject to such terms and conditions as are considered appropriate in the circumstances;

(*e*) before the end of the sixth month following the day on which the particular corporation first distributes a spin-off share in respect of the distribution, the particular corporation provides to the Minister information satisfactory to the Minister establishing

(i) that, at the time of the distribution, the shares of the class that includes the original shares are shares described in subparagraph (*c*)(ii) or (*d*)(ii),

(ii) that the particular corporation and the other corporation referred to in paragraph (*b*) were never resident in Canada,

(iii) the date of the distribution,

(iv) the type and fair market value of each property distributed to residents of Canada,

(v) the name and address of each resident of Canada that received property with respect to the distribution,

(vi) in the case of a distribution that is not prescribed, that the distribution is not taxable under the provisions of the *Internal Revenue Code of 1986* of the United States, as amended from time to time, that apply to the distribution,

(vii) in the case of a distribution that is prescribed, that the distribution is not taxable under the law of the foreign country, and

(viii) such other matters that are required, in prescribed form; and

(*f*) the taxpayer elects in writing filed with the taxpayer's return of income for the taxation year in which the distribution occurs that this section apply to the distribution and provides information satisfactory to the Minister

(i) of the number, cost amount (determined without reference to this section) and fair market value of the taxpayer's original shares immediately before the distribution,

(ii) of the number, and fair market value, of the taxpayer's original shares and the spin-off shares immediately after the distribution of the spin-off shares to the taxpayer,

(iii) except where the election is filed with the taxpayer's return of income for the year in which the distribution occurs, concerning the amount of the distribution, the manner in which the distribution was reported by the taxpayer and the details of any subsequent disposition of original shares or spin-off shares for the purpose of determining any gains or losses from those dispositions, and

(iv) of such other matters that are required, in prescribed form.

Department of Finance Comfort Letters

(April 30, 2018) [Prescribed distribution for 86.1 foreign spinoff rules: Svenska Cellulosa Aktiebolaget's distribution of Essity Aktiebolag shares]

Dear XXXX:

Re: Svenska Cellulosa Aktiebolaget SCA (pupl) – Spin-off of Common Shares of Essity Aktiebolag (pupl)

I am replying to your submission of December 11, 2017 to the Canada Revenue Agency (the "CRA") concerning your request on behalf of Svenska Cellulosa Aktiebolaget SCA (pupl) ("SCA") and the follow-up emails of February 16 and 26, 2018 by you and XXXX to XXXX of the Department of Finance. You ask that SCA's distribution of common shares of Essity Aktiebolag (publ) ("Essity") to SCA's common shareholders be "prescribed" for the purpose of the foreign spin-off tax-deferral rules in section 86.1 of the *Income Tax Act*.

The CRA has confirmed to the Department of Finance that SCA's pro rata distribution of Class A and Class B common shares of Essity to SCA's Class A and Class B common shareholders, respectively, satisfies the technical requirements of the foreign spin-off rules in section 86.1 of the *Income Tax Act*.

The Department of Finance understands that SCA's common shares were widely held and actively traded on the NASDAQ Stockholm Exchange at the time of the distribution, that SCA distributed all of its shares of Essity immediately before the distribution, and that SCA's distribution of common shares of Essity occurred on June 15, 2017. We note that the Swedish Tax Agency Notice indicates that the distribution is not taxable under Swedish law.

Based on our understanding of the information referred to above, we are prepared to recommend to the Minister of Finance that SCA's *pro rata* distribution to its shareholders of the common shares of Essity on June 15, 2017 be a prescribed distribution for the purpose of section 86.1 of the *Income Tax Act*. While we cannot offer any assurance that our recommendation will be accepted, we trust that this information is of assistance.

As per the separate written authorizations we received from SCA and Essity on March 21, 2018, the Government of Canada intends to release this letter under the *Access to Information Act* without redacting the names of the parties given that Canadian shareholders who held common shares of SCA at the time of the distribution may be interested in knowing the content of this letter.

Yours sincerely,

Brian Ernewein

General Director — Legislation

Tax Policy Branch

History: S. 86.1(2)(*c*)(ii) and (iii) were replaced by S.C. 2013, c. 34, s. 222(1), applicable to distributions made after 1999, except that

(*a*) with respect to a distribution in respect of original shares described in clause 86.1(2)(*c*)(ii)(B),

(i) information referred to in paragraph 86.1(2)(*e*) is deemed to be provided to the Minister of National Revenue on a timely basis if it is provided to that Minister before September 24, 2013 [the 90th day after royal assent]; and

(ii) an election referred to in paragraph 86.1(2)(*f*) of the Act is deemed to be filed on a timely basis if it is filed with the Minister of National Revenue before September 24, 2013 [the 90th day after royal assent]; and

(*b*) for the period before December 14, 2007, the reference to "designated stock exchange" in clause 86.1(2)(*c*)(ii)(A) is to be read as a reference to "prescribed stock exchange".

S. 86.1(2)(*c*)(ii) and (iii) formerly read:

(ii) at the time of the distribution, the shares of the class that includes the original shares are widely held and actively traded on a designated stock exchange in the United States, and

(iii) under the *United States Internal Revenue Code* applicable to the distribution, the shareholders of the particular corporation who are resident in the United States are not taxable in respect of the distribution;

S. 86.1(2)(*e*)(i) was replaced by S.C. 2013, c. 34, s. 222(2), applicable, subject to the application following the history note to the amendment to s. 86.1(2)(*c*)(i) and (ii) (above), to distributions made after 1999, and formerly read:

(i) that, at the time of the distribution, the shares of the class that includes the original shares are widely held and actively traded on a prescribed stock exchange,

S. 86.1(2)(*e*)(vi) was replaced by S.C. 2013, c. 34, s. 222(3), applicable, subject to the application following the history note to the amendment to s. 86.1(2)(*c*)(i) and (ii) (above), to distributions made after 1999, and formerly read:

(vi) in the case of a distribution that is not prescribed, that the distribution is not taxable under the *United States Internal Revenue Code* applicable to the distribution,

Related Regulations: 600(*c*); 5600.

Related Sections: S. 206(3.1) Acquisition of qualifying security; s. 206(3.2) Qualifying security; s. 220(3.2) Late, amended or revoked elections; s. 248(1), "cost amount"; s. 262 Designated stock exchange.

Tax Window Files: Foreign Spin-off & Foreign Merger, *Technical Interpretation, International and Trusts Division, June 20, 2007,* CRA Document No. 2006-0178941I7.

Cases: The taxpayer owned shares of a U.S. company. As a result of a reorganization, he received shares of a second U.S. company. Although this might have qualified as an "eligible distribution", the company failed to provide the CRA with sufficient information and the taxpayer failed to file an election. Since the statutory requirements weren't met, the value of the shares was included in his income. *Allen v. The Queen*, 2007 DTC 48 (T.C.C.).

► 86.1(3) ◄

(3) Cost adjustments. Where a spin-off share is distributed by a corporation to a taxpayer pursuant to an eligible distribution with respect to an original share of the taxpayer,

(*a*) there shall be deducted for the purpose of computing the cost amount to the taxpayer of the original share at any time the amount determined by the formula

$$A \times (B/C)$$

where

A is the cost amount, determined without reference to this section, to the taxpayer of the original share at the time that is immediately before the distribution or, if the original share is disposed of by the taxpayer, before the distribution, at the time that is immediately before its disposition,

B is the fair market value of the spin-off share immediately after its distribution to the taxpayer, and

C is the total of

(i) the fair market value of the original share immediately after the distribution of the spin-off share to the taxpayer, and

(ii) the fair market value of the spin-off share immediately after its distribution to the taxpayer; and

(*b*) the cost to the taxpayer of the spin-off share is the amount by which the cost amount of the taxpayer's original share was reduced as a result of paragraph (*a*).

Editorial Note: Essentially, under s. 86.1(3), the taxpayer's cost amount of each original share as it stood immediately before the distribution is allocated on a pro-rata basis to the original share and the spin-off share, based on their respective fair market values immediately after the distribution.

Related Sections: S. 248(1), "cost amount".

► 86.1(4) ◄

(4) Inventory. For the purpose of calculating the value of the property described in an inventory of a taxpayer's business,

(*a*) an eligible distribution to the taxpayer of a spin-off share that is included in the inventory is deemed not to be an acquisition of property in the fiscal period of the business in which the distribution occurs; and

(*b*) for greater certainty, the value of the spin-off share is to be included in computing the value of the inventory at the end of that fiscal period.

Editorial Note: The rules in s. 86.1(4) prevent the double-counting of cost that would occur if the cost of a spin-off share was added to the cost of inventory acquired in the year.

► 86.1(5) ◄

(5) Reassessments. Notwithstanding subsections 152(4) to (5), the Minister may make at any time such assessments, reassessments, determinations and redeterminations that are necessary where information is obtained that the conditions in subparagraph (2)(*c*)(iii) or (*d*)(iii) are not, or are no longer, satisfied.

SECTION 87: Amalgamations

► 87(1) ◄

(1) Amalgamations. In this section, an amalgamation means a merger of two or more corporations each of which was, immediately before the merger, a taxable Canadian corporation (each of which corporations is referred to in this section as a "predecessor corporation") to form one corporate entity (in this section referred to as the "new corporation") in such a manner that

(*a*) all of the property (except amounts receivable from any predecessor corporation or shares of the capital stock of any predecessor corporation) of the predecessor corporations immediately before the merger becomes property of the new corporation by virtue of the merger,

(*b*) all of the liabilities (except amounts payable to any predecessor corporation) of the predecessor corporations immediately before the merger become liabilities of the new corporation by virtue of the merger, and

(*c*) all of the shareholders (except any predecessor corporation), who owned shares of the capital stock of any predecessor corporation immediately before the merger, receive shares of the capital stock of the new corporation because of the merger,

otherwise than as a result of the acquisition of property of one corporation by another corporation, pursuant to the purchase of that property by the other corporation or as a result of the distribution of that property to the other corporation on the winding-up of the corporation.

Editorial Note: S. 87 provides rules that apply to an amalgamation of two or more predecessor taxable Canadian corporations. In general terms, s. 87 provides a tax-free rollover of each predecessor's property and a carryover of various tax attributes and pools to the amalgamated corporation, such as the cost of properties, reserves, deferred amounts, prepaid amounts, surplus accounts, and investment tax credits.

Although s. 87(1)(*c*) provides that all of the shareholders of the predecessor corporations (except any predecessor corporation) must receive shares of the amalgamated corporation, the CRA has historically taken the position that an amalgamation will not be disqualified by reason only of certain shareholders of predecessor corporations receiving consideration other than shares of the amalgamated corporation, such as cash, by virtue of exercising a statutory right to dissent to the amalgamation (paragraph 1.5 of S4-F7-C1). In other cases where cash is to be provided to shareholders of a predecessor corporation, it is acceptable to issue redeemable preferred shares of the amalgamated corporation to such shareholders, who then redeem the shares for cash immediately after the amalgamation. In this regard, the CRA has stated that it will not apply the general anti-avoidance rule where preferred shares are issued by the amalgamated corporation solely for the purpose of meeting the requirements of s. 87(1)(*c*) (paragraph 28 of IC 88-2).

Related Regulations: Part XI; 5905.

Related Sections: s. 69(11) Deemed proceeds of disposition; s. 83(7) Amalgamation where there are tax-deferred preferred shares; s. 87(1.1) Shares deemed to have been received by virtue of merger; s. 87(9) Rules applicable in respect of certain mergers; s. 89(1), "taxable Canadian corporation"; s. 112(7) Rules where shares exchanged; s. 127(9.1) Loss restriction event before end of year; s. 134 Non-resident-owned corporation not a Canadian corporation, etc; s. 248(1), "corporation"; 261(17) Amalgamations; ITAR s. 26(21) Shares received on amalgamation.

Canadian Petroleum Tax Journal: A Comparative Study of Canadian and US Rules Regarding the Taxation of Corporate Reorganizations, Firoz Talakshi and Christy Palmer, 2000, Vol. 13, No. 1.

Canadian Tax Foundation: Scheuerman, *Current Cases: Supreme Court of Canada — Like Two Rivers Flow: Some Things Are, Perhaps, Meant To Be (Envision Credit Union v. Canada, 2013 SCC 48)*, 2014 Canadian Tax Journal 1:175–183; Gosselin, *Many Different Approaches to Envision*, 2013 Canadian Tax Highlights 21(11):1–2; Crowe and Senyk, *Amalgamation and Windup: What's The Difference?*, 2003 Prairie Provinces Tax Conference 10:1–34; Trossman, *Triangular Amalgamations*, 2001 Conference Report 22:1–32; Brayley, *Merging Companies: A Practical Checklist for Amalgamations and Wind-Ups*, 2000 Conference Report 6:1–58; Richler, *Merger by Way of Partnership with a Comparison to Amalgamation*, 1999 Conference Report 25:1–30; Richards, *Amalgamations in The Taxation of Corporate Reorganizations*, 1996 Canadian Tax Journal 1:241–259.

Tax Topics: No. 2178, "Upon Amalgamation, Predecessor Corporations' PRA and UCC Balances Flowed through to Taxpayer as the Amalgamated Entity".

Forms: T2 SCH 24 — First Time Filer after Incorporation, Amalgamation, or Winding-up of a Subsidiary into a Parent.

Income Tax Folios: *Primary* — S4-F7-C1 Amalgamations of Canadian Corporations.

Information Circulars: IC 88-2 General anti-avoidance rule — Section 245 of the Income Tax Act (paras. 20, 21 and 28, Supp. 1, para. 9).

Interpretation Bulletins: *Secondary* — IT-302R3 Losses of a corporation — The effect on their deductibility of changes in control, amalgamation and winding-up; IT-427R Livestock of farmers.

Cases: A credit union argued that it was not formed by a "qualifying amalgamation" under s. 87(1)(a) since its predecessors sold surplus assets at the moment of amalgamation so that not "all" of their property passed to it. This would have reset its UCC to the original cost of assets, allowing it to claim CCA already claimed by its predecessors. However, under B.C. law, an amalgamated credit union automatically becomes the owner of all its predecessors' property. *Envision Credit Union v. The Queen*, 2013 DTC 5144 (S.C.C.), affirming 2012 DTC 5055 (F.C.A.) and 2010 DTC 1399 (T.C.C.)

► 87(1.1) ◄

(1.1) Shares deemed to have been received by virtue of merger. For the purposes of paragraph (1)(*c*) and the *Income Tax Application Rules*, where there is a merger of

(*a*) a corporation and one or more of its subsidiary wholly-owned corporations, or

(*b*) two or more corporations each of which is a subsidiary wholly-owned corporation of the same corporation

any shares of the capital stock of a predecessor corporation owned by a shareholder (except any predecessor corporation) immediately before the merger that were not cancelled on the merger shall be deemed to be shares of the capital stock of the new corporation received by the shareholder by virtue of the merger as consideration for the disposition of the shares of the capital stock of the predecessor corporations.

Editorial Note: Under corporate law statutes such as the *Canada Business Corporations Act*, a parent corporation may amalgamate with a subsidiary corporation (a vertical short-form amalgamation), and two or more subsidiary corporations of a parent corporation may amalgamate (a horizontal short-form amalgamation), without the issuance of new shares by the amalgamated corporation upon the amalgamation to persons who were shareholders of the predecessor corporations. S. 87(1.1) ensures that these types of short-form amalgamations can qualify under s. 87 by deeming shareholders (other than predecessor corporations) of the predecessor corporations to have received shares of the amalgamated corporation by virtue of the merger for the purposes of s. 87(1)(*c*).

Related Sections: S. 87(1.4), "subsidiary wholly owned corporation".

► 87(1.2) ◄

(1.2) New corporation continuation of a predecessor. Where there has been an amalgamation of corporations described in paragraph (1.1)(*a*) or of two or more corporations each of which is a subsidiary wholly-owned corporation of the same person, the new corporation is, for the purposes of section 29 of the *Income Tax Application Rules*, subsection 59(3.3) and sections 66, 66.1, 66.2, 66.21, 66.4 and 66.7, deemed to be the same corporation as, and a continuation of, each predecessor corporation, except that this subsection does not affect the determination of any predecessor corporation's fiscal period, taxable income or tax payable.

Related Regulations: 1214(1).

Related Sections: S. 87(1.4), "subsidiary wholly-owned corporation".

Interpretation Bulletins: *Secondary* — IT-125R4 Disposition of resource properties.

► 87(1.3) ◄

(1.3) Shareholder corporation — (Repealed by 1985, c. 45, s. 42(1).)

► 87(1.4) ◄

(1.4) Definition of "subsidiary wholly-owned corporation". Notwithstanding subsection 248(1), for the purposes of this subsection and subsections (1.1), (1.2) and (2.11), "subsidiary wholly-owned corporation" of a person (in this subsection referred to as the "parent") means a corporation all the issued and outstanding shares of the capital stock of which belong to

(*a*) the parent;

(*b*) a corporation that is a subsidiary wholly-owned corporation of the parent; or

(*c*) any combination of persons each of which is a person described in paragraph (*a*) or (*b*).

Editorial Note: The difference between the definition in s. 87(1.4) and the definition in s. 248(1) is that the former allows shares of the subsidiary to be owned by the parent or subsidiary wholly-owned corporations of the parent (or both), whereas the definition in s. 248(1) provides that all of the shares of the subsidiary (except qualifying directors' shares) must be owned by the parent.

► 87(1.5) ◄

(1.5) Definitions. For the purpose of this section, "financial institution", "mark-to-market property" and "specified debt obligation" have the meanings assigned by subsection 142.2(1).

► 87(2) ◄

(2) Rules applicable. Where there has been an amalgamation of two or more corporations after 1971 the following rules apply:

Editorial Note: In general terms, s. 87(2) provides that most of the assets and tax accounts of the predecessor corporations (including reserves, surplus accounts, deferred amounts, Eligible Refundable Dividend Tax On Hand (ERDTOH) and Non-Eligible Refundable Tax On Hand (NERDTOH) (for taxation years that begin after 2018), RDTOH (generally prior to 2019), and so on) pass to the amalgamated corporation and without immediate tax consequences.

Related Sections: S. 88(1) Winding-up.

Information Circulars: IC 88-2 General anti-avoidance rule — Section 245 of the Income Tax Act (para. 21).

► 87(2)(a) ◄

(a) Taxation year — for the purposes of this Act, the corporate entity formed as a result of the amalgamation shall be deemed to be a new corporation the first taxation year of which shall be deemed to have commenced at the time of the amalgamation, and a taxation year of a predecessor corporation that would otherwise have ended after the amalgamation shall be deemed to have ended immediately before the amalgamation;

Editorial Note: S. 87(2)(*a*) deems the amalgamated corporation to be a new corporation for the purposes of the Act, notwithstanding that under most corporate legislation the amalgamated corporation is considered a continuation of the predecessor corporations. However, the rest of s. 87(2) effectively flows through many of the tax costs of properties, and other tax attributes and pools of the predecessor corporations to the amalgamated corporation (often by deeming the amalgamated corporation to be the same corporation as, and a continuation of, each predecessor corporation with respect to those tax costs, tax attributes and pools). The amalgamation will result in each of the predecessors having a year end immediately before the amalgamation and the amalgamated corporation can select its own year end. It should be noted that administratively, the CRA permits the amalgamated corporation to file most elections on behalf of the predecessor corporations (e.g., s. 85 election — see CRA Document 2003-0046015).

Related Sections: S. 125(5) Special rules for business limit.

► 87(2)(b) ◄

(b) Inventory — for the purpose of computing the income of the new corporation, where the property described in the inventory, if any, of the new corporation at the beginning of its first taxation year includes property that was described in the inventory of a predecessor corporation at the end of the taxation year of the predecessor corporation that ended immediately before the amalgamation (which taxation year of a predecessor corporation is referred to in this section as its "last taxation year"), the property so included shall be deemed to have been acquired by the new corporation at the beginning of its first taxation year for an amount determined in accordance with section 10 as the value thereof for the purpose of computing the income of the predecessor corporation for its last taxation year, except that where the income of the predecessor corporation for its last taxation year from a farming business was computed in accordance with the cash method, the amount so determined in respect of inventory owned in connection with that business shall be deemed to be the total of all amounts each of which is an amount included because of paragraph 28(1)(*b*) or (*c*) in computing that income for that year and, where the income of the new corporation from a farming business is computed in accordance with the cash method, for the purpose of section 28,

(i) an amount equal to that total shall be deemed to have been paid by the new corporation, and

(ii) the new corporation shall be deemed to have purchased the property for an amount equal to that total,

in its first taxation year and in the course of carrying on that business;

► 87(2)(c) ◄

(c) Method adopted for computing income — in computing the income of the new corporation for a taxation year from a business or property

(i) there shall be included any amount received or receivable (depending on the method followed by the new corporation in computing its income for that year) by it in that year that would, if it had been received or receivable (depending on the method followed by the predecessor corporation in computing its income for its last taxation year) by the predecessor corporation in its last taxation year, have been included in computing the income of the predecessor corporation for that year, and

(ii) there may be deducted any amount paid or payable (depending on the method followed by the new corporation in computing its income for that year) by it in that year that would, if it had been paid or payable (depending on the method followed by the predecessor corporation in computing its income for its last taxation year) by the predecessor corporation in its last taxation year, have been deductible in computing the income of the predecessor corporation for that year;

► 87(2)(d) ◄

(d) Depreciable property — for the purposes of sections 13 and 20 and any regulations made under paragraph 20(1)(*a*),

(i) where depreciable property of a prescribed class has been acquired by the new corporation from a predecessor corporation, the capital cost of the property to the new corporation shall be deemed to be the amount that was the capital cost of the property to the predecessor corporation, and

(ii) in determining the undepreciated capital cost to the new corporation of depreciable property of a prescribed class at any time,

(A) there shall be added to the capital cost to the new corporation of depreciable property of the class acquired before that time the cost amount, immediately before the amalgamation, to a predecessor corporation of each property included in that class by the new corporation,

(B) there shall be subtracted from the capital cost to the new corporation of depreciable property of that class acquired before that time the capital cost to the new corporation of property of that class acquired by virtue of the amalgamation,

(C) a reference in subparagraph 13(5)(*b*)(ii) to amounts that would have been deducted in respect of property in computing a taxpayer's income shall be construed as including a reference to amounts that would have been deducted in respect of that property in computing a predecessor corporation's income, and

(D) where depreciable property that is deemed by subsection 37(6) to be a separate prescribed class has been acquired by the new corporation from a predecessor corporation, the property shall continue to be deemed to be of that same separate prescribed class;

▶ 87(2)(d.1) ◀

(d.1) Depreciable property acquired from predecessor corporation — for the purposes of this Act, where depreciable property (other than property of a prescribed class) has been acquired by the new corporation from a predecessor corporation, the new corporation shall be deemed to have acquired the property before 1972 at an actual cost equal to the actual cost of the property to the predecessor corporation, and the new corporation shall be deemed to have been allowed the total of all amounts allowed to the predecessor corporation in respect of the property, under regulations made under paragraph 20(1)(*a*), in computing the income of the predecessor corporation;

Related Sections: S. 13(21) Definitions; s. 20(1)(*a*) Capital cost of property.

▶ 87(2)(e) ◀

(e) Capital property — subject to paragraph (*e*.4) and subsection 142.6(5), where a capital property (other than depreciable property or an interest in a partnership) has been acquired by the new corporation from a predecessor corporation, the cost of the property to the new corporation shall be deemed to be the amount that was the adjusted cost base of the property to the predecessor corporation immediately before the amalgamation;

▶ 87(2)(e.1) ◀

(e.1) Partnership interest — where a partnership interest that is capital property has been acquired from a predecessor corporation to which the new corporation was related, for the purposes of this Act, the cost of that partnership interest to the new corporation shall be deemed to be the amount that was the cost of that interest to the predecessor corporation and, in respect of that partnership interest, the new corporation shall be deemed to be the same corporation as and a continuation of the predecessor corporation;

▶ 87(2)(e.2) ◀

(e.2) Security or debt obligation — subject to paragraphs (*e*.3) and (*e*.4) and subsection 142.6(5), where a property that is a security or debt obligation (other than a capital property or an inventory) of a predecessor corporation used by it in the year in, or held by it in the year in the course of, carrying on the business of insurance or lending money in the taxation year ending immediately before the amalgamation has been acquired by the new corporation from the predecessor corporation, the cost of the property to the new corporation shall be deemed to be the amount that was the cost amount of the property to the predecessor corporation immediately before the amalgamation;

▶ 87(2)(e.3) ◀

(e.3) Financial institutions — specified debt obligation — where the new corporation is a financial institution in its first taxation year, it shall be deemed, in respect of a specified debt obligation (other than a mark-to-market property) acquired from a predecessor corporation that was a financial institution in its last taxation year, to be the same corporation as, and a continuation of, the predecessor corporation;

▶ 87(2)(e.4) ◀

(e.4) Financial institutions — mark-to-market property — where

(i) the new corporation is a financial institution in its first taxation year and a property acquired by the new corporation from a predecessor corporation is a mark-to-market property of the new corporation for the year, or

(ii) a predecessor corporation was a financial institution in its last taxation year and a property acquired by the new corporation from the predecessor corporation was a mark-to-market property of the predecessor corporation for the year,

the cost of the property to the new corporation shall be deemed to be the amount that was the fair market value of the property immediately before the amalgamation;

► 87(2)(e.41) ◄

(e.41) [Eligible derivative — cost amount] — if subsection 10.1(6) applied to a predecessor corporation in its last taxation year, each *eligible derivative* (as defined in subsection 10.1(5)) of the predecessor corporation immediately before the end of its last taxation year is deemed to have been reacquired, or reissued or renewed, as the case may be, by the new corporation at its fair market value immediately before the amalgamation;

History: 87(2)(*e*.41) was added by S.C. 2017, c. 33, s. 24(1), applicable to taxation years that begin after March 21, 2017.

Related Sections: 10.1(6) Deemed disposition.

► 87(2)(e.42) ◄

(e.42) [Continuation of predecessor corporation — eligible derivative] — for the purposes of subsection 10.1(7), the new corporation is deemed to be the same corporation as, and a continuation of, each predecessor corporation;

History: 87(2)(*e*.42) was added by S.C. 2017, c. 33, s. 24(1), applicable to taxation years that begin after March 21, 2017.

Related Sections: 10.1(6) Deemed disposition; 88(1)(e.2) [Winding-up — Application of amalgamation provisions].

► 87(2)(e.5) ◄

(e.5) Financial institutions — mark-to-market property — for the purposes of subsections 112(5) to (5.2) and (5.4) and the definition "mark-to-market property" in subsection 142.2(1), the new corporation shall be deemed to be the same corporation as, and a continuation of, each predecessor corporation;

► 87(2)(f) ◄

(f) Eligible capital property — (Repealed by S.C. 2016, c. 12, s. 27(1).)

History: S. 87(2)(*f*) was repealed by S.C. 2016, c. 12, s. 27(1), in force January 1, 2017, and formerly read:

(*f*) *Eligible capital property* — for the purposes of determining under this Act any amount relating to cumulative eligible capital, an eligible capital amount, an eligible capital expenditure or eligible capital property, the new corporation shall be deemed to be the same corporation as, and a continuation of, each predecessor corporation;

Related Sections: S. 14(1) Eligible capital property — inclusion in income from business; s. 14(5), "cumulative eligible capital", "eligible capital expenditure"; s. 54, "eligible capital property"; s. 248(1), "eligible capital amount".

► 87(2)(f.1) ◄

(f.1) Idem — (Repealed by S.C. 1994, c. 7, Sched. VIII, s. 37(3).)

► 87(2)(g) ◄

(g) Reserves — for the purpose of computing the income of the new corporation for a taxation year,

(i) any amount that has been deducted as a reserve in computing the income of a predecessor corporation for its last taxation year shall be deemed to have been deducted as a reserve in computing the income of the new corporation for a taxation year immediately preceding its first taxation year, and

(ii) any amount deducted under paragraph 20(1)(*p*) in computing the income of a predecessor corporation for its last taxation year or a previous taxation year shall be deemed to have been deducted under that paragraph in computing the income of the new corporation for a taxation year immediately preceding its first taxation year;

► 87(2)(g.1) ◄

(g.1) Continuation — for the purposes of sections 12.4 and 26, subsection 97(3) and section 256.1, the new corporation is deemed to be the same corporation as, and a continuation of, each predecessor corporation;

History: S. 87(2)(*g.1*) was replaced by S.C. 2013, c. 40, s. 39(1), deemed to have come into force on March 21, 2013, and formerly read:

(*g*.1) *Continuation* — for the purposes of sections 12.4 and 26 and subsection 97(3), the new corporation is deemed to be the same corporation as, and a continuation of, each predecessor corporation;

S. 87(2)(*g.1*) was replaced by S.C. 2012, c. 31, s.17(1), applicable in respect of amalgamations that occur, and windings-up that begin, after March 28, 2012. S. 87(2)(*g.1*) formerly read:

(*g*.1) *Continuation* — for the purposes of sections 12.3 and 12.4, subsection 20(26) and section 26, the new corporation shall be deemed to be the same corporation as, and a continuation of, each predecessor corporation;

► 87(2)(g.2) ◄

(g.2) Financial institution rules — for the purposes of paragraphs 142.4(4)(*c*) and (*d*) and subsections 142.51(11) and 142.6(1), the new corporation is deemed to be the same corporation as, and a continuation of, each predecessor corporation;

History: S. 87(2)(*g.2*) was replaced by S.C. 2013, c. 34, s. 223(1), applicable to taxation years that begin after October 31, 2011, and formerly read:

(*g*.2) *Financial institution rules* — for the purposes of paragraphs 142.4(4)(*c*) and (*d*) and subsections 142.5(5) and (7), 142.51(11) and 142.6(1), the new corporation is deemed to be the same corporation as, and a continuation of, each predecessor corporation;

S. 87(2)(*g.2*) was replaced by S.C. 2009, c. 2, s. 19(1), applicable to taxation years that begin after September 2006. S. 87(2)(*g.2*) formerly read:

(*g*.2) *Financial institution rules* — for the purposes of paragraphs 142.4(4)(*c*) and (*d*) and subsections 142.5(5) and (7) and 142.6(1), the new corporation shall be deemed to be the same corporation as, and a continuation of, each predecessor corporation;

► 87(2)(g.3) ◄

(g.3) Superficial losses — for the purposes of applying subsections 13(21.2), 18(15) and 40(3.4) to any property that was disposed of by a predecessor corporation before the amalgamation, the new corporation is deemed to be the same corporation as, and a continuation of, each predecessor corporation;

History: S. 87(2)(*g*.3) was replaced by S.C. 2016, c. 12, s. 27(2), in force January 1, 2017, and formerly read:

(*g*.3) *Superficial losses* — for the purposes of applying subsections 13(21.2), 14(12), 18(15) and 40(3.4) to any property that was disposed of by a predecessor corporation before the amalgamation, the new corporation is deemed to be the same corporation as, and a continuation of, each predecessor corporation;

► 87(2)(g.4) ◄

(g.4) Superficial losses — capital property — for the purpose of applying paragraph 40(3.5)(*c*) in respect of any share that was acquired by a predecessor corporation, the new corporation is deemed to be the same corporation as, and a continuation of, each predecessor corporation;

► 87(2)(g.5) ◄

(g.5) Patronage dividends — for the purposes of section 135, the new corporation is deemed to be the same corporation as, and a continuation of, each predecessor corporation;

History: S. 87(2)(*g.5*) was added by S.C. 2013, c. 34, s. 223(2), applicable to amalgamations that occur, and windings-up that begin, after 1997.

► 87(2)(h) ◄

(h) Debts — for the purpose of computing a deduction from the income of the new corporation for a taxation year under paragraph 20(1)(*l*), (*l*.1) or (*p*)

(i) any debt owing to a predecessor corporation that was included in computing the income of the predecessor corporation for its last taxation year or a preceding taxation year,

(ii) where a predecessor corporation was an insurer or a corporation the ordinary business of which included the lending of money, any loan or lending asset made or acquired by the predecessor corporation in the ordinary course of its business of insurance or the lending of money, or

(iii) where a predecessor corporation was an insurer or a corporation the ordinary business of which included the lending of money, any instrument or commitment described in paragraph 20(1)(*l*.1) that was issued, made or assumed by the predecessor corporation in the ordinary course of its business of insurance or the lending of money,

and that by reason of the amalgamation, has been acquired by the new corporation, shall be deemed to be a debt owing to the new corporation that was included in computing its income for a preceding taxation year, a loan or lending asset made or acquired or an instrument or commitment that was issued, made or assumed by the new corporation in a preceding taxation year in the ordinary course of its business of insurance or the lending of money, as the case may be;

► 87(2)(h.1) ◄

(h.1) Debts — for the purposes of section 61.4, the description of F in subsection 79(3), the definition "forgiven amount" in subsection 80(1), subsection 80.03(7) and section 80.04, the new corporation shall be deemed to be the same corporation as, and a continuation of, each predecessor corporation;

► 87(2)(i) ◄

(i) Special reserve — for the purpose of computing a deduction from the income of the new corporation for a taxation year under paragraph 20(1)(*n*), any amount included in computing the income of a predecessor corporation from a business for its last taxation year or a previous taxation year in respect of property sold in the course of the business shall be deemed to have been included in computing the income of the new corporation from the business for a previous year in respect of that property;

Interpretation Bulletins: *Secondary* — IT-154R Special reserves.

► 87(2)(j) ◄

(j) Special reserves — for the purposes of paragraphs 20(1)(*m*), (*m*.1) and (*m*.2), subsection 20(24) and section 34.2, the new corporation is deemed to be the same corporation as, and a continuation of, each predecessor corporation;

Interpretation Bulletins: *Secondary* — IT-154R Special reserves.

► 87(2)(j.1) ◄

(j.1) Inventory adjustment — for the purposes of paragraph 20(1)(*ii*), an amount required by paragraph 12(1)(*r*) to be included in computing the income of a predecessor corporation for its last taxation year shall be deemed to be an amount required by paragraph 12(1)(*r*) to be included in computing the income of the new corporation for a taxation year immediately preceding its first taxation year;

► 87(2)(j.2) ◄

(j.2) Prepaid expenses and matchable expenditures — for the purposes of subsections 18(9) and (9.01), section 18.1 and paragraph 20(1)(*mm*), the new corporation is deemed to be the same corporation as, and a continuation of, each predecessor corporation;

► 87(2)(j.3) ◄

(j.3) Employee benefit plans etc. — for the purposes of paragraphs 12(1)(*n.1*) to (*n.3*) and 20(1)(*r*), (*s*), (*oo*) and (*pp*), section 32.1, paragraph 104(13)(*b*), subsections 144.1(4) to (7) and Part XI.3, the new corporation is deemed to be the same corporation as, and a continuation of, each predecessor corporation;

History: S. 87(2)(*j.3*) was replaced by S.C. 2010, c. 25, s. 15(1), applicable after 2009. S. 87(2)(*j.3*) formerly read:

(*j.3*) *Employee benefit plans, etc.* — for the purposes of paragraphs 12(1)(*n*.1), (*n*.2) and (*n*.3) and 20(1)(*r*), (*oo*) and (*pp*), section 32.1, paragraph 104(13)(*b*) and Part XI.3, the new corporation shall be deemed to be the same corporation as, and a continuation of, each predecessor corporation;

Interpretation Bulletins: *Secondary* — IT-502 Employee benefit plans and employee trusts.

► 87(2)(j.4) ◄

(j.4) Accrual rules — for the purposes of subsections 12(3) and (9), section 12.2, subsection 20(19) and the definition "adjusted cost basis" in subsection 148(9) of this Act, and subsections 12(5) and (6) and paragraph 56(1)(*d*.1) of the *Income Tax Act*, chapter 148 of the Revised Statutes of Canada, 1952, the new corporation shall be deemed to be the same corporation as, and a continuation of, each predecessor corporation;

► 87(2)(j.5) ◄

(j.5) Cancellation of lease — for the purposes of paragraphs 20(1)(*z*) and (*z*.1), the new corporation shall be deemed to be the same corporation as, and a continuation of, each predecessor corporation;

► 87(2)(j.6) ◄

(j.6) Continuing corporation — for the purposes of paragraphs 12(1)(*t*) and (*x*), subsections 12(2.2) and 13(7.1), (7.4) and (24), paragraphs 13(27)(*b*) and (28)(*c*), subsections 13(29) and 18(9.1), paragraphs 20(1)(*e*), (*e*.1) and (*hh*), sections 20.1 and 32, paragraph 37(1)(*c*), subsection 39(13), subparagraphs 53(2)(*c*)(vi) and (*h*)(ii), paragraph 53(2)(*s*), subsections 53(2.1), 66(11.4), 66.7(11) and 127(10.2), section 139.1, subsection 152(4.3), the determination of D in the definition "undepreciated capital cost" in subsection 13(21) and the determination of L in the definition "cumulative Canadian exploration expense" in subsection 66.1(6), the new corporation is deemed to be the same corporation as, and a continuation of, each predecessor corporation;

History: S. 87(2)(*j.6*) was replaced by S.C. 2019, c. 29, s. 11(1), applicable to taxation years that end after March 18, 2019. S. 87(2)(*j.6*) formerly read:

(*j.6*) *Continuing corporation* — for the purposes of paragraphs 12(1)(*t*) and (*x*), subsections 12(2.2) and 13(7.1), (7.4) and (24), paragraphs 13(27)(*b*) and (28)(*c*), subsections 13(29) and 18(9.1), paragraphs 20(1)(*e*), (*e*.1) and (*hh*), sections 20.1 and 32, paragraph 37(1)(*c*), subsection 39(13), subparagraphs 53(2)(*c*)(vi) and (*h*)(ii), paragraph 53(2)(*s*), subsections 53(2.1), 66(11.4) and 66.7(11), section 139.1, subsection 152(4.3), the determination of D in the definition "undepreciated capital cost" in subsection 13(21) and the determination of L in the definition "cumulative Canadian exploration expense" in subsection 66.1(6), the new corporation is deemed to be the same corporation as, and a continuation of, each predecessor corporation;

Related Sections: 127(10.2) Expenditure limit.

▶ 87(2)(j.7) ◀

(j.7) Certain transfers and loans — for the purposes of sections 74.4 and 74.5, the new corporation shall be deemed to be the same corporation as, and a continuation of, each predecessor corporation;

▶ 87(2)(j.8) ◀

(j.8) International banking centre business — (Repealed by S.C. 2013, c. 33, s. 6(1).)

History: S. 87(2)(*j.8*) was repealed by S.C. 2013, c. 33, s. 6(1), applicable to taxation years that begin after March 20, 2013, and formerly read:

(*j.8*) *International banking centre business* — for the purposes of section 33.1, the new corporation shall be deemed to be the same corporation as, and a continuation of, each predecessor corporation;

▶ 87(2)(j.9) ◀

(j.9) Part I.3 tax — for the purpose of determining the amount deductible by the new corporation for any taxation year under section 125.3, the new corporation is deemed to be the same corporation as, and a continuation of, each predecessor corporation;

History: S. 87(2)(*j.9*) was replaced by S.C. 2013, c. 34, s. 223(3), applicable to taxation years that begin after October 31, 2011, and formerly read:

(*j.9*) *Part VI and Part I.3 tax* — for the purposes of determining the amount deductible by the new corporation for any taxation year under section 125.2 or 125.3, the new corporation shall be deemed to be the same corporation as, and a continuation of, each predecessor corporation;

▶ 87(2)(j.91) ◀

(j.91) Part I.3 and Part VI tax — for the purpose of determining the amount deductible under subsection 181.1(4) or 190.1(3) by the new corporation for any taxation year, the new corporation is deemed to be the same corporation as, and a continuation of, each predecessor corporation, except that this paragraph does not affect the determination of the fiscal period of any corporation or the tax payable by any corporation for any taxation year that ends before the amalgamation;

History: S. 87(2)(*j.91*) was replaced by S.C. 2013, c. 34, s. 223(3), applicable to amalgamations that occur, and windings-up that begin, after December 20, 2002, and formerly read:

(*j.91*) *Part I.3 and Part VI tax* — for the purpose of determining the amount deductible under subsection 181.1(4) or 190.1(3) by the new corporation for any taxation year, the new corporation is deemed to be the same corporation as, and a continuation of, each predecessor corporation, except that this paragraph does not affect the determination of the fiscal period of any corporation or the tax payable by any predecessor corporation;

▶ 87(2)(j.92) ◀

(j.92) Subsections 125(5.1) and 157.1(1) — for the purposes of subsection 125(5.1) and the definition "eligible corporation" in subsection 157.1(1), the new corporation is deemed to be the same corporation as, and a continuation of, each predecessor corporation;

▶ 87(2)(j.93) ◀

(j.93) Mining reclamation trusts — for the purposes of paragraphs 12(1)(*z*.1) and (*z*.2) and 20(1)(*ss*) and (*tt*) and sections 107.3 and 127.41, the new corporation shall be deemed to be the same corporation as, and a continuation of, each predecessor corporation;

▶ 87(2)(j.94) ◀

(j.94) Film or video productions — for the purposes of sections 125.4 and 125.5, the new corporation is deemed to be the same corporation as, and a continuation of, each predecessor corporation;

Related Sections: S. 125.4 Canadian Film or Video Production Tax Credit.

▶ 87(2)(j.95) ◀

(j.95) Non-resident entities — for the purposes of sections 94 to 94.2, the new corporation is deemed to be the same corporation as, and a continuation of, each predecessor corporation;

History: S. 87(2)(*j.95*) was added by S.C. 2013, c. 34, s. 6(1), applicable to taxation years that end after 2000.

▶ 87(2)(j.96) ◀

(j.96) Journalism organizations — for the purposes of section 125.6, the new corporation is deemed to be the same corporation as, and a continuation of, each predecessor corporation;

History: S. 87(2)(*j.96*) was added by S.C. 2019, c. 29, s. 11(2), deemed to have come into force on January 1, 2019.

Related Sections: 125.6(1) Definitions.

▶ 87(2)(k) ◀

(k) Certain payments to employees — for the purpose of subsection 6(3), any amount received by a person from the new corporation that would, if received by the person from a predecessor corporation, be deemed for the purpose of section 5 to be remuneration for that person's services rendered as an officer or during a period of employment, shall be deemed for the purposes of section 5 to be remuneration for services so rendered by the person;

▶ 87(2)(l) ◀

(l) Scientific research and experimental development — for the purposes of section 37 and Part VIII, the new corporation shall be deemed to be the same corporation as, and a continuation of, each predecessor corporation;

► 87(2)(l.1) ◄

(l.1) Idem — for the purposes of this paragraph, paragraph (*l*.2) and section 37.1,

(i) the base period for a particular taxation year of a new corporation that has fewer than 3 preceding taxation years shall be deemed to be the period

(A) commencing on the day that

(I) is the earliest of all days each of which is a day immediately before the commencement of a taxation year of a predecessor corporation in respect of the new corporation that ended after 1976, and

(II) is in the 3 year period ending on the day immediately before the commencement of the particular year, and

(B) ending immediately before the first day of the particular taxation year,

(ii) where subparagraph (i) applies,

(A) in determining the qualified expenditures made by the new corporation in its base period, there shall be included the total of all amounts each of which is the qualified expenditure made by a predecessor corporation in a taxation year that commenced in the base period of the new corporation, and

(B) in determining the total of the amounts paid to the new corporation by persons referred to in subparagraphs (*b*)(i) to (iii) of the definition "expenditure base" in subsection 37.1(5) in its base period, there shall be included the total of all such amounts paid to a predecessor corporation by a person referred to in those subparagraphs in a taxation year that commenced in the base period of the new corporation,

(iii) the capital cost to the new corporation of any property that was a research property of a predecessor corporation acquired by it from the predecessor corporation shall be deemed to be the capital cost thereof to the predecessor corporation and the property shall be deemed to be a research property of the new corporation, and

(iv) each amount determined in respect of the new corporation under subparagraph 37.1(3)(*b*)(i) or (iii), as the case may be, shall be deemed to be the total of the amount otherwise determined and the total of amounts each of which is the amount determined under subparagraph 37.1(3)(*b*)(i) or (iii), as the case may be, in respect of a predecessor corporation;

► 87(2)(l.2) ◄

(l.2) Definition of "predecessor corporation" — for the purposes of this paragraph and paragraph (*l*.1), "predecessor corporation" includes any corporation in respect of which a predecessor corporation was a new corporation;

► 87(2)(l.21) ◄

(l.21) Forgiven amount — for the purposes of section 61.3, the definition "unrecognized loss" in subsection 80(1) and subsection 80.01(10), the new corporation is deemed to be the same corporation as, and a continuation of, each predecessor corporation;

Related Sections: 88(1)(e.2) [Winding-up — Application of amalgamation provisions].

► 87(2)(l.3) ◄

(l.3) Replacement property — where before the amalgamation property of a predecessor corporation was unlawfully taken, lost, destroyed or taken under statutory authority, or was a former business property of the predecessor corporation, for the purposes of applying sections 13 and 44 and the definition "former business property" in subsection 248(1) to the new corporation in respect of the property and any replacement property acquired therefor, the new corporation shall be deemed to be the same corporation as, and a continuation of, the predecessor corporation;

Related Sections: S. 248(1), "former business property".

Interpretation Bulletins: *Secondary* — IT-259R4 Exchange of property.

► 87(2)(l.4) ◄

(l.4) Subsection 13(4.2) election — for the purposes of subsection 13(4.3) and paragraph 20(16.1)(*b*), the new corporation is deemed to be the same corporation as, and a continuation of, each predecessor corporation;

History: S. 87(2)(*l.4*) was added by S.C. 2013, c. 34, s. 223(4), applicable to amalgamations that occur, and windings-up that begin, after December 20, 2002.

► 87(2)(l.5) ◄

(l.5) Contingent amount — section 143.4 — for the purposes of section 143.4, the new corporation is deemed to be the same corporation as, and a continuation of, each predecessor corporation;

History: S. 87(2)(*l.5*) was added by S.C. 2013, c. 34, s. 223(4), applicable in respect of taxation years that end on or after March 16, 2011.

► 87(2)(m) ◄

(m) Reserves — for the purpose of computing the income of the new corporation for a taxation year, any amount claimed under subparagraph 40(1)(*a*)(iii) or 44(1)(*e*)(iii) in computing a predecessor corporation's gain for its last taxation year from the disposition of any property shall be deemed

(i) to have been claimed under subparagraph 40(1)(*a*)(iii) or 44(1)(*e*)(iii), as the case may be, in computing the new corporation's gain for a taxation year immediately preceding its first taxation year from the disposition of that property by it before its first taxation year, and

(ii) to be the amount determined under subparagraph 40(1)(*a*)(i) or 44(1)(*e*)(i), as the case may be, in respect of that property;

► 87(2)(m.1) ◄

(m.1) Gift of non-qualifying security — for the purpose of computing the new corporation's gain under subsection 40(1.01) for any taxation year from the disposition of a property, the new corporation is deemed to be the same corporation as, and a continuation of, each predecessor corporation;

▶ 87(2)(m.2) ◀

(m.2) Gift of predecessor's property — for the purpose of computing the fair market value of property under subsection 248(35), the new corporation is deemed to be the same corporation as, and a continuation of, each predecessor corporation;

History: S. 87(2)(*m.2*) was added by S.C. 2013, c. 34, s. 223(5), applicable in respect of gifts of property made after 6:00 p.m. (Eastern Standard Time) on December 4, 2003.

▶ 87(2)(n) ◀

(n) Outlays made pursuant to warranty — for the purpose of section 42, any outlay or expense made or incurred by the new corporation in a taxation year, pursuant to or by virtue of an obligation described in that section incurred by a predecessor corporation, that would, if the outlay or expense had been made or incurred by the predecessor corporation in that year, have been deemed to be a loss of the predecessor corporation for that year from the disposition of a capital property shall be deemed to be a loss of the new corporation for that year from the disposition of a capital property;

▶ 87(2)(o) ◀

(o) Expiration of options previously granted — for the purpose of subsection 49(2),

(i) any option granted by a predecessor corporation that expires after the amalgamation is deemed to have been granted by the new corporation, and any proceeds received by the predecessor corporation for the granting of the option is deemed to have been received by the new corporation,

(ii) any person to whom the option was granted who was not dealing at arm's length with the predecessor corporation at the time that the option was granted is deemed to have been dealing with the new corporation not at arm's length at the time that the option was granted, and

(iii) any person to whom the option was granted who was dealing at arm's length with the predecessor corporation at the time that the option was granted is deemed to have been dealing with the new corporation at arm's length at the time that the option was granted;

History: S. 87(2)(*o*) was replaced by S.C. 2013, c. 34, s. 223(6), applicable to options issued after October 24, 2012, and formerly read:

(*o*) *Expiration of options previously granted* — for the purpose of subsection 49(2), any option granted by a predecessor corporation that expires after the amalgamation shall be deemed to have been granted by the new corporation, and any proceeds received by the predecessor corporation for the granting of the option shall be deemed to have been received by the new corporation therefor;

▶ 87(2)(p) ◀

(p) Consideration for resource property disposition — for the purpose of computing a deduction from the income of the new corporation for a taxation year under section 64 of the *Income Tax Act*, chapter 148 of the Revised Statutes of Canada, 1952, any amount that has been included in computing the income of a predecessor corporation for its last taxation year or a previous taxation year by reason of subsection 59(1) or paragraph 59(3.2)(*c*) of this Act, of subsection 59(3) of the *Income Tax Act*, chapter 148 of the Revised Statutes of Canada, 1952, or of subsection 83A(5ba) or (5c) of that Act as it read in its application to a taxation year before the 1972 taxation year, shall be deemed to have been included in computing the income of the new corporation for a previous year by virtue thereof;

▶ 87(2)(q) ◀

(q) Registered plans — for the purposes of sections 147, 147.1 and 147.2 and any regulations made under subsection 147.1(18), the new corporation shall be deemed to be the same corporation as, and a continuation of, each predecessor corporation;

▶ 87(2)(r) ◀

(r) Employees profit sharing plan — an election made under subsection 144(10) by a predecessor corporation is deemed to be an election made by the new corporation;

History: S. 87(2)(*r*) was added by S.C. 2013, c. 34, s. 223(7), applicable to amalgamations that occur, and windings-up that begin, after 1994.

▶ 87(2)(s) ◀

(s) Tax deferred cooperative shares — for the purpose of section 135.1, if the new corporation is, at the beginning of its first taxation year, an agricultural cooperative corporation (within the meaning assigned by subsection 135.1(1)),

(i) the new corporation is deemed to be the same corporation as, and a continuation of, each predecessor corporation that was an agricultural cooperative corporation at the end of the predecessor corporation's last taxation year, and

(ii) if, on the amalgamation, the new corporation issues a share (in this subparagraph and subsection 135.1(10) referred to as the "new share") that is described in all of paragraphs (*b*) to (*d*) of the definition "tax deferred cooperative share" in subsection 135.1(1) to a taxpayer in exchange for a share of a predecessor corporation (in this subparagraph and subsection 135.1(10) referred to as the "old share") that was, at the end of the predecessor corporation's last taxation year, a tax deferred cooperative share within the meaning assigned by that definition, and the amount of paid-up capital, and the amount, if any, that the taxpayer is entitled to receive on a redemption, acquisition or cancellation, of the new share are equal to those amounts, respectively, in respect of the old share, subsection 135.1(10) applies in respect of the exchange;

History: S. 87(2)(*s*)(ii) was replaced by S.C. 2013, c. 34, s. 223(8), deemed to have come into force on September 29, 2009, and formerly read:

(ii) if, on the amalgamation, the new corporation issues a share (in this subparagraph referred to as the "new share") that is described in all of paragraphs (*b*) to (*d*) of the definition "tax deferred cooperative share" in subsection 135.1(1) to a taxpayer in exchange for a share of a predecessor corporation (in this subparagraph referred to as the "old share") that was, at the end of the predecessor corporation's last taxation year, a tax deferred cooperative share within the meaning assigned by that definition, and the amount of paid-up capital, and the amount, if any, that the taxpayer is entitled to receive on a redemption, acquisition or cancellation, of the new share are equal to those amounts, respectively, in respect of the old share,

(A) the new share is deemed to have been issued at the time the old share was issued, and

(B) in applying subsection 135.1(2), the taxpayer is deemed to have disposed of the old share for nil proceeds;

▶ 87(2)(s.1) ◀

(s.1) Deemed SIFT wind-up corporation — if a predecessor corporation was a SIFT wind-up corporation immediately before the amalgamation, the new corporation is deemed to be a SIFT wind-up corporation;

History: S. 87(2)(*s.1*) was added by S.C. 2009, c. 2, s. 19(2), applicable after December 19, 2007.

Related Sections: S. 88.1 SIFT trust wind-up event; s. 248(1), "SIFT trust wind-up event", "SIFT wind-up corporation".

▶ 87(2)(t) ◀

(t) Pre-1972 capital surplus on hand — for the purpose of subsection 88(2.1), any capital property owned by a predecessor corporation on December 31, 1971 that was acquired by the new corporation by virtue of the amalgamation shall be deemed to have been acquired by the new corporation before 1972 at an actual cost to it equal to the actual cost of the property to the predecessor corporation;

▶ 87(2)(u) ◀

(u) Shares of foreign affiliate — where one or more shares of the capital stock of a foreign affiliate of a predecessor corporation have, by virtue of the amalgamation, been acquired by the new corporation and as a result of the acquisition the affiliate has become a foreign affiliate of the new corporation,

(i) for the purposes of subsection 91(5) and paragraph 92(1)(*b*), any amount required by section 92 to be added or deducted, as the case may be, in computing the adjusted cost base of any such share to the predecessor corporation before the amalgamation shall be deemed to have been so required to be added or deducted, as the case may be, in computing the adjusted cost base of the share to the new corporation, and

(ii) for the purposes of subsections 93(2.01), (2.11), (2.21) and (2.31), any exempt dividend received by the predecessor corporation on any such share is deemed to be an exempt dividend received by the new corporation on the share;

History: S. 87(2)(*u*)(ii) was replaced by S.C. 2013, c. 34, s. 64(1), applicable if subsection 93(2.01) applies, except that, if subsection 93(2.01) applies but subsection 93(2.11) does not apply, subparagraph 87(2)(*u*)(ii) is to be read as follows:

"(ii) for the purposes of subsection 93(2.01), any exempt dividend received by the predecessor corporation on any such share is deemed to be an exempt dividend received by the new corporation on the share;"

Any assessment of a taxpayer's tax, interest and penalties payable under the Act for any taxation year that ends before June 26, 2013 that would, in the absence of this section, be precluded because of subsections 152(4) to (5) of the Act shall be made to the extent necessary to take into account the amendments by S.C. 2013, c. 34 s. 54 to 89.

S. 87(2)(*u*)(ii) formerly read:

(ii) for the purposes of subsections 93(2) to (2.3), any exempt dividend received by the predecessor corporation on any such share is deemed to be an exempt dividend received by the new corporation on the share;

▶ 87(2)(v) ◀

(v) Gifts — for the purposes of section 110.1, the new corporation shall be deemed to be the same corporation as, and a continuation of, each predecessor corporation with respect to gifts;

▶ 87(2)(w) ◀

(w) Losses — (Repealed by 1983-84, c. 1, s. 38(3).)

▶ 87(2)(x) ◀

(x) Taxable dividends — for the purposes of subsections 112(3) to (4.22),

(i) any taxable dividend received on a share that was deductible from the predecessor corporation's income for a taxation year under section 112 or subsection 138(6) is deemed to be a taxable dividend received on the share by the new corporation that was deductible from the new corporation's income under section 112 or subsection 138(6), as the case may be,

(ii) any dividend (other than a taxable dividend) received on a share by the predecessor corporation is deemed to have been received on the share by the new corporation, and

(iii) a share acquired by the new corporation from a predecessor corporation is deemed to have been owned by the new corporation throughout any period of time throughout which it was owned by a predecessor corporation;

▶ 87(2)(y) ◀

(y) Contributed surplus — for the purposes of subsections 84(1) and (10), the new corporation shall be deemed to be the same corporation as, and a continuation of, each predecessor corporation;

▶ 87(2)(y.1) ◀

(y.1) Preferred-earnings amount — (Repealed by S.C. 1998, c. 19, s. 117(7).)

▶ 87(2)(z) ◀

(z) Foreign tax carryover — for the purposes of determining the new corporation's unused foreign tax credit (within the meaning of subsection 126(7)) in respect of a country for any taxation year and determining the extent to which subsection 126(2.3) applies to reduce the amount that may be claimed by the new corporation under paragraph 126(2)(*a*) in respect of an unused foreign tax credit in respect of a country for a taxation year, the new corporation shall be deemed to be the same corporation as, and a continuation of, each predecessor corporation, except that this paragraph shall in no respect affect the determination of

(i) the fiscal period of the new corporation or any of its predecessor corporations, or

(ii) the tax payable under this Act by any predecessor corporation;

Income Tax Folios: *Secondary* — S5-F2-C1 Foreign Tax Credit.

▶ 87(2)(z.1) ◀

(z.1) Capital dividend account — for the purposes of computing the capital dividend account of the new corporation, it shall be deemed to be the same corporation as, and a continuation of, each predecessor corporation, other than a predecessor corporation to which subsection 83(2.1) would, if a dividend were paid immediately before the amalgamation and an election were made under subsection 83(2) in respect of the full amount of that dividend, apply to deem any portion of the dividend to be paid by the predecessor corporation as a taxable dividend;

Related Sections: S. 89(1), "capital dividend account".

▶ 87(2)(z.2) ◀

(z.2) Application of Parts III and III.1 — for the purposes of Parts III and III.1, the new corporation is deemed to be the same corporation as, and a continuation of, each predecessor corporation;

Tax Window Files: Excessive Capital Dividend and 87(2)(z.2), *Reorganizations and Resources Division, Income Tax Rulings Directorate, January 7, 2009*, CRA Document No. 2008-0303091E5.

▶ 87(2)(aa) ◀

(aa) Refundable dividend tax on hand — if the new corporation was a private corporation immediately after the amalgamation, the following rules apply:

(i) for the purpose of computing the "eligible refundable dividend tax on hand" and "non-eligible refundable dividend tax on hand" (as defined in subsection 129(4)) of the new corporation at the end of its first taxation year there shall be added to the total determined under those definitions in respect of the new corporation for the year

(A) in respect of the new corporation's eligible refundable dividend tax on hand, the total of all amounts each of which is the amount, if any, by which the eligible refundable dividend tax on hand of a predecessor corporation at the end of its last taxation year exceeds the total of all amounts each of which is the portion, if any, of its dividend refund for its last taxation year from its eligible refundable dividend tax on hand determined under subparagraph 129(1)(*a*)(i) or clause 129(1)(*a*)(ii)(B), and

(B) in respect of the new corporation's non-eligible refundable dividend tax on hand, the total of all amounts each of which is the amount, if any, by which the non-eligible refundable dividend tax on hand of a predecessor corporation at the end of its last taxation year exceeds the portion, if any, of its dividend refund for its last taxation year from its non-eligible refundable dividend tax on hand determined under clause 129(1)(*a*)(ii)(A), and

(ii) no amount shall be added under this paragraph in respect of a predecessor corporation

(A) that was not a private corporation at the end of its last taxation year, or

(B) where subsection 129(1.2) would have applied to deem a dividend paid by the predecessor corporation immediately before the amalgamation not to be a taxable dividend for the purpose of subsection 129(1);

History: S. 87(2)(*aa*) was replaced by S.C. 2018, c. 12, s. 7(1), applicable to taxation years that begin after 2018, and also to a taxation year of a corporation that begins before 2019 and ends after 2018 if

(a) the corporation's preceding taxation year was, because of a transaction or event or a series of transactions or events, shorter than it would have been in the absence of that transaction, event or series; and

(b) one of the reasons for the transaction, event or series was to defer the application of subsections 20(2) and (3) or 22(1) to (5) [of the *Budget Implementation Act, 2018, No. 1*] to the corporation.

S. 87(2)(*aa*) formerly read:

(*aa*) *Refundable dividend tax on hand* — where the new corporation was a private corporation immediately after the amalgamation, for the purpose of computing the refundable dividend tax on hand (within the meaning assigned by subsection 129(3)) of the new corporation at the end of its first taxation year there shall be added to the total determined under subsection 129(3) in respect of the new corporation for the year the total of all amounts each of which is the amount, if any, by which the refundable dividend tax on hand of a predecessor corporation at the end of its last taxation year exceeds its dividend refund (within the meaning assigned by subsection 129(1)) for its last taxation year, except that no amount shall be added under this paragraph in respect of a predecessor corporation

(i) that was not a private corporation at the end of its last taxation year, or

(ii) where subsection 129(1.2) would have applied to deem a dividend paid by the predecessor corporation immediately before the amalgamation not to be a taxable dividend for the purpose of subsection 129(1);

Related Sections: s. 129(1) Dividend refund to private corporation; s. 129(3) Definition of "refundable dividend tax on hand"; s. 131(5) Dividend refund to mutual fund corporation; s. 186(5) Deemed private corporation.

▶ 87(2)(bb) ◀

(bb) Mutual fund and investment corporations — where the new corporation is a mutual fund corporation or an investment corporation, there shall be added to

(i) the amount determined under each of paragraphs (*a*) and (*b*) of the definition "capital gains dividend account" in subsection 131(6), and

(ii) the values of A and B in the definition "refundable capital gains tax on hand" in that subsection

in respect of the new corporation at any time the amounts so determined and the values of those factors immediately before the amalgamation, in respect of each predecessor corporation that was, immediately before the amalgamation, a mutual fund corporation or an investment corporation;

▶ 87(2)(bb.1) ◀

(bb.1) Flow-through entities — where a predecessor corporation was, immediately before the amalgamation, an investment corporation, a mortgage investment corporation or a mutual fund corporation and the new corporation is an investment corporation, a mortgage investment corporation or a mutual fund corporation, as the case may be, for the purpose of section 39.1, the new corporation is deemed to be the same corporation as, and a continuation of, the predecessor corporation;

Related Sections: S. 110.6(19) Election for property owned on February 22, 1994.

▶ 87(2)(cc) ◀

(cc) Non-resident-owned investment corporation — in the case of a new corporation that is a non-resident-owned investment corporation,

(i) for the purpose of computing its allowable refundable tax on hand (within the meaning assigned by subsection 133(9)) at any time, where a predecessor corporation had allowable refundable tax on hand immediately before the amalgamation, the amount thereof shall be added to the total determined for A in the definition "allowable refundable tax on hand" in subsection 133(9),

(ii) for the purpose of computing its capital gains dividend account (within the meaning assigned by subsection 133(8)) at any time, where a predecessor corporation had an amount in its capital gains dividend account immediately before the amalgamation, that amount shall be added to the amount determined under paragraph (*a*) of the description of A in the definition "capital gains dividend account" in subsection 133(8), and

(iii) for the purpose of computing its cumulative taxable income (within the meaning assigned by subsection 133(9)) at any time, where a predecessor corporation had cumulative taxable income immediately before the amalgamation, the amount thereof shall be added to the total determined for A in the definition "cumulative taxable income" in subsection 133(9);

Related Sections: S. 133(8) Definitions; s. 133(9) Definitions relating to definition of "allowable refund"; s. 248(1), "non-resident-owned investment corporation".

▶ 87(2)(dd) ◀

(dd) Tax in respect of ineligible investments — (Repealed by 1973-74, c. 14, s. 26(3).)

▶ 87(2)(ee) ◀

(ee) Preferred-rate amount — (Repealed by 1984, c. 45, s. 27(5).)

▶ 87(2)(ff) ◀

(ff) Application of Part VII — (Repealed by 1977-78, c. 1, s. 42(5).)

▶ 87(2)(gg) ◀

(gg) Designated surplus — (Repealed by 1977-78, c. 1, s. 42(5).)

▶ 87(2)(hh) ◀

(hh) 1971 undistributed income on hand — (Repealed by 1977-78, c. 1, s. 42(5).)

▶ 87(2)(ii) ◀

(ii) Public corporation — where a predecessor corporation was a public corporation immediately before the amalgamation, the new corporation shall be deemed to have been a public corporation at the commencement of its first taxation year;

▶ 87(2)(jj) ◀

(jj) Interest on certain obligations — for the purposes of paragraph 81(1)(*m*), the new corporation shall be deemed to be the same corporation as, and a continuation of, each predecessor corporation;

▶ 87(2)(kk) ◀

(kk) Disposition of shares of controlled corporation — for the purposes of paragraph 40(2)(*h*),

(i) where a corporation was controlled, directly or indirectly in any manner whatever, by a predecessor corporation immediately before the amalgamation and has, by reason of the amalgamation, become controlled, directly or indirectly in any manner whatever, by the new corporation, the new corporation shall be deemed to have acquired control of the corporation so controlled at the time control thereof was acquired by the predecessor corporation, and

(ii) where a predecessor corporation was immediately before the amalgamation controlled, directly or indirectly in any manner whatever, by a corporation that, immediately after the amalgamation, controlled, directly or indirectly in any manner whatever, the new corporation, the new corporation shall be deemed to be the same corporation as, and a continuation of, each predecessor corporation;

Related Sections: S. 256(5.1) Control in fact.

▶ 87(2)(ll) ◀

(ll) Para. 20(1)(n) and subpara. 40(1)(a)(iii) amounts — notwithstanding any other provision of this Act, where any property was disposed of by a predecessor corporation, the new corporation shall, in computing

(i) the amount of any deduction under paragraph 20(1)(*n*) as a reserve in respect of the property sold in the course of business, and

(ii) the amount of its claim under subparagraph 40(1)(*a*)(iii) or 44(1)(*e*)(iii) in respect of the disposition of the property,

be deemed to be the same corporation as, and a continuation of, the predecessor corporation;

▶ 87(2)(mm) ◀

(mm) Idem — (Repealed by S.C. 2013, c. 34, s. 223(9).)

History: S. 87(2)(*mm*) was repealed by S.C. 2013, c. 34, s. 223(9), applicable to amalgamations that occur after March 20, 2003, and formerly read:

> (*mm*) *Idem* — for the purposes of section 126.1, the new corporation shall be deemed to be the same corporation as, and a continuation of, each predecessor corporation;

▶ 87(2)(nn) ◀

(nn) Refundable Part VII tax on hand — for the purpose of computing the refundable Part VII tax on hand of the new corporation at the end of any taxation year, there shall be added to the total determined under paragraph 192(3)(*a*) the total of all amounts each of which is the amount, if any, by which

(i) a predecessor corporation's refundable Part VII tax on hand at the end of its last taxation year exceeds

(ii) the predecessor corporation's Part VII refund for its last taxation year;

▶ 87(2)(oo) ◀

(oo) Investment tax credit — (Repealed by S.C. 2019, c. 29, s. 11(3).)

History: S. 87(2)(*oo*) was repealed by S.C. 2019, c. 29, s. 11(3), applicable to taxation years that end after March 18, 2019. S. 87(2)(*oo*) formerly read:

(*oo*) *Investment tax credit* — for the purpose of applying subsection 127(10.2) to any corporation, the new corporation is deemed to have had

(i) a particular taxation year that

(A) where it was associated with another corporation in the new corporation's first taxation year, ended in the calendar year that precedes the calendar year in which that first year ends, and

(B) in any other case, immediately precedes that first year, and

(ii) taxable income for the particular year (determined before taking into consideration the specified future tax consequences for the particular year) equal to the total of all amounts each of which is a predecessor corporation's taxable income for its taxation year that ended immediately before the amalgamation (determined before taking into consideration the specified future tax consequences for that year);

Related Sections: S. 127(10.1) Additions to investment tax credit; s. 127(10.2) Expenditure limit determined; s. 127.1(2) Definitions.

▶ 87(2)(oo.1) ◀

(oo.1) Refundable investment tax credit and balance-due day — for the purpose of applying the definition "qualifying corporation" in subsection 127.1(2), and subparagraph (*d*)(i) of the definition "balance-due day" in subsection 248(1), to any corporation, the new corporation is deemed to have had

(i) a particular taxation year that

(A) where it was associated with another corporation in the new corporation's first taxation year, ended in the calendar year that precedes the calendar year in which that first year ends, and

(B) where clause (A) does not apply, immediately precedes that first year,

(ii) taxable income for the particular year (determined before taking into consideration the specified future tax consequences for the particular year) equal to the total of all amounts each of which is a predecessor corporation's taxable income for its taxation year that ended immediately before the amalgamation (determined before taking into consideration the specified future tax consequences for that year),

(iii) a business limit for the particular year equal to the total of all amounts each of which is a predecessor corporation's business limit for its taxation year that ended immediately before the amalgamation, and

(iv) a qualifying income limit for the particular year equal to the total of all amounts each of which is a predecessor corporation's qualifying income limit for its taxation year that ended immediately before the amalgamation;

History: S. 87(2)(*oo.1*)(iv) was added by S.C. 2013, c. 40, s. 39(2), applicable to amalgamations that occur after February 25, 2008.

Related Sections: S. 248(1), "specified future tax consequences".

▶ 87(2)(pp) ◀

(pp) Cumulative offset account computation — for the purpose of computing the cumulative offset account (within the meaning assigned by subsection 66.5(2)) of the new corporation at any time, there shall be added to the total otherwise determined under paragraph 66.5(2)(*a*) the total of all amounts each of which is the amount, if any, by which

(i) a predecessor corporation's cumulative offset account at the end of its last taxation year

exceeds

(ii) the amount deducted under subsection 66.5(1) in computing the predecessor corporation's income for its last taxation year;

▶ 87(2)(qq) ◀

(qq) Continuation of corporation — for the purpose of computing the new corporation's investment tax credit at the end of any taxation year, the new corporation is deemed to be the same corporation as, and a continuation of, each predecessor corporation, except that this paragraph does not affect the determination of the fiscal period of any corporation or the tax payable by any predecessor corporation;

Related Sections: S. 127(5) Investment tax credit.

▶ 87(2)(rr) ◀

(rr) Tax on taxable preferred shares — for the purposes of subsections 112(2.9), 191(4), and 191.1(2) and (4), the new corporation shall be deemed to be the same corporation as, and a continuation of, each predecessor corporation;

▶ 87(2)(ss) ◀

(ss) Transferred liability for Part VI.1 tax — for the purposes of section 191.3, the new corporation shall be deemed to be the same corporation as, and a continuation of, each predecessor corporation;

▶ 87(2)(tt) ◀

(tt) Livestock — inclusion of deferred amount — for the purposes of subsections 80.3(3) and (5), the new corporation shall be deemed to be the same corporation as, and a continuation of, each predecessor corporation;

▶ 87(2)(uu) ◀

(uu) Fuel tax rebates — for the purposes of paragraph 12(1)(*x.1*), the description of D.1 in the definition "non-capital loss" in subsection 111(8), and subsections 111(10) and (11), the new corporation is deemed to be the same corporation as, and a continuation of, each predecessor corporation;

▶ 87(2)(vv) ◀

(vv) General rate income pool — if the new corporation is a Canadian-controlled private corporation or a deposit insurance corporation in its first taxation year, in computing its general rate income pool at the end of that first taxation year there shall be added the total of all amounts determined under subsection 89(5) in respect of the corporation for that first taxation year; and

▶ 87(2)(ww) ◀

(ww) Low rate income pool — if the new corporation is neither a Canadian-controlled private corporation nor a deposit insurance corporation in its first taxation year, there shall be added in computing its low rate income pool at any time in that first taxation year the total of all amounts determined under subsection 89(9) in respect of the corporation for that first taxation year.

▶ 87(2.01) ◀

(2.01) Application of s. 37.1(5). The definitions in subsection 37.1(5) apply to subsection (2).

▶ 87(2.1) ◀

(2.1) Non-capital losses, etc., of predecessor corporations. Where there has been an amalgamation of two or more corporations, for the purposes only of

(*a*) determining the new corporation's non-capital loss, net capital loss, restricted farm loss, farm loss or limited partnership loss, as the case may be, for any taxation year, and

(*b*) determining the extent to which subsections 111(3) to (5.4) and paragraph 149(10)(*c*) apply to restrict the deductibility by the new corporation of any non-capital loss, net capital loss, restricted farm loss, farm loss or limited partnership loss, as the case may be,

the new corporation shall be deemed to be the same corporation as, and a continuation of, each predecessor corporation, except that this subsection shall in no respect affect the determination of

(*c*) the fiscal period of the new corporation or any of its predecessors,

(*d*) the income of the new corporation or any of its predecessors, or

(*e*) the taxable income of, or the tax payable under this Act by, any predecessor corporation.

Editorial Note: In general terms, s. 87(2.1) permits non-capital losses, net capital losses, restricted farm losses, farm losses, and limited partnership losses of a predecessor corporation to be carried forward and utilized by the amalgamated corporation, subject to the restrictions in s. 111(3) to (5.4) and s. 149(10)(*c*) dealing with the ordering of losses and the use of losses where there is a change of control or in tax-exempt status. This provision does not allow losses of the amalgamated corporation to be carried back to a predecessor's taxation year. However, s. 87(2.11) allows an amalgamated corporation's losses to be carried back to reduce a particular predecessor's taxable income under s. 111 (certain unused tax credits may also be carried back) where the particular predecessor was a parent corporation that amalgamated with one or more of its wholly owned subsidiaries.

Related Sections: S. 111(1) Losses deductible; s. 256(7) Acquiring control.

Interpretation Bulletins: *Primary* — IT-302R3 Losses of a corporation — The effect on their deductibility of changes in control, amalgamation and winding-up. *Secondary* — IT-232R3 Non-capital losses, net capital losses, restricted farm losses, farm losses and limited partnership losses — Their composition and deductibility in computing taxable income.

Cases: By bringing two corporations under common control prior to their amalgamation, the taxpayer had successfully avoided the acquisition of control restrictions and was able to transfer non-capital losses from one to the other. *Duha Printers (Western) Ltd. v. The Queen*, 98 DTC 6334 (S.C.C.), reversing 96 DTC 6323 (F.C.A.) and affirming 95 DTC 828 (T.C.C.).

▶ 87(2.11) ◀

(2.11) Vertical amalgamations. Where a new corporation is formed by the amalgamation of a particular corporation and one or more of its subsidiary wholly-owned corporations, the new corporation is deemed to be the same corporation as, and a continuation of, the particular corporation for the purposes of applying sections 111 and 126, subsections 127(5) to (26) and 181.1(4) to (7), Part IV and subsections 190.1(3) to (6) in respect of the particular corporation.

Editorial Note: See the editorial note following s. 87(2.1).

Related Sections: S. 87(1.4) Definition of "subsidiary wholly-owned corporation"; s. 248(1), "corporation".

▶ 87(2.2) ◀

(2.2) Amalgamation of insurers. Where there has been an amalgamation and one or more of the predecessor corporations was an insurer, the new corporation is, notwithstanding subsection (2), deemed, for the purposes of paragraphs 12(1)(*d*), (*e*), (*e.1*), (*i*) and (*s*), subsection 12.5(8), paragraphs 20(1)(*l*), (*l.1*), (*p*) and (*jj*) and 20(7)(*c*), subsections 20(22) and 20.4(4), sections 138, 138.1, 140, 142 and 148 and Part XII.3, to be the same corporation as, and a continuation of, each of those predecessor corporations.

History: S. 87(2.2) was replaced by S.C. 2009, c. 2, s. 19(3), applicable to taxation years that begin after September 2006. S. 87(2.2) formerly read:

> (2.2) *Amalgamation of insurers.* Where there has been an amalgamation and one or more of the predecessor corporations was an insurer, the new corporation is, notwithstanding subsection (2), deemed, for the purposes of paragraphs 12(1)(*d*), (*e*), (*e.1*), (*i*) and (*s*) and 20(1)(*l*), (*l.1*), (*p*) and (*jj*) and 20(7)(*c*), subsection 20(22), sections 138, 138.1, 140, 142 and 148 and Part XII.3, to be the same corporation as, and a continuation of, each of those predecessor corporations.

▶ 87(2.3) ◀

(2.3) Quebec credit unions. For the purpose of applying this section to an amalgamation governed by section 689 of *An Act respecting financial services cooperatives*, R.S.Q., c. C-67.3, an investment deposit of a credit union is deemed to be a share of a separate class of the capital stock of a predecessor corporation in respect of the amalgamation the adjusted cost base and paid up capital of which to the credit union is equal to the adjusted cost base to the credit union of the investment deposit immediately before the amalgamation if

(*a*) immediately before the amalgamation, the investment deposit is an investment deposit to which section 425 of the *Savings and Credit Unions Act*, R.S.Q., c. C-4.1, applies to the investment fund of that predecessor corporation; and

(*b*) on the amalgamation the credit union disposes of the investment deposit for consideration that consists solely of shares of a class of the capital stock of the new corporation.

History: S. 87(2.3) was added by S.C. 2013, c. 34, s. 223(10), applicable to amalgamations that occur after June 2001.

▶ 87(3) ◀

(3) Computation of paid-up capital. Subject to subsection (3.1), where there is an amalgamation or a merger of 2 or more Canadian corporations, in computing at any particular time the paid-up capital in respect of any particular class of shares of the capital stock of the new corporation,

(*a*) there shall be deducted that proportion of the amount, if any, by which the paid-up capital, determined without reference to this subsection, in respect of all the shares of the capital stock of the new corporation immediately after the amalgamation or merger exceeds the total of all amounts each of which is the paid-up capital in respect of a share (except a share held by any other predecessor corporation) of the capital stock of a predecessor corporation immediately before the amalgamation or merger, that

(i) the paid-up capital, determined without reference to this subsection, of the particular class of shares of the capital stock of the new corporation immediately after the amalgamation or merger

is of

(ii) the paid-up capital, determined without reference to this subsection, in respect of all of the issued and outstanding shares of the capital stock of the new corporation immediately after the amalgamation or merger; and

(*b*) there shall be added an amount equal to the lesser of

(i) the amount, if any, by which

(A) the total of all amounts each of which is an amount deemed by subsection 84(3), (4) or (4.1) to be a dividend on shares of the particular class paid by the new corporation before the particular time

exceeds

(B) the total that would be determined under clause (A) if this Act were read without reference to paragraph (*a*), and

(ii) the amount required by paragraph (*a*) to be deducted in computing the paid-up capital of shares of the particular class.

Editorial Note: Although the paid-up capital reduction under s. 87(3)(*a*), if any, ensures that the aggregate paid-up capital ("PUC") in respect of the shares of the amalgamated corporation does not exceed the aggregate PUC in respect of the shares of all of the predecessor corporations (except those shares owned by predecessor corporations), the provision does not prevent the "shifting" of PUC from the previous shareholders of one predecessor corporation to the previous shareholders of another predecessor corporation. While the CRA had traditionally condoned such "shifting" of PUC, the Supreme Court of Canada found that a series of transactions whereby two corporations that had been parent-subsidiary became subsidiaries of the same corporation and then amalgamated (thus effectively "doubling-up" the same PUC) was an abuse of s. 87(3), particularly the parenthetical part of s. 87(3)(*a*), and GAAR applied: *Copthorne Holdings Ltd. v. The Queen* [2012 DTC 5007].

Related Sections: S. 89(1), "paid-up capital".

► 87(3.1) ◄

(3.1) Election for non-application of subsection (3). Where,

(*a*) there is an amalgamation of 2 or more corporations,

(*b*) all of the issued shares, immediately before the amalgamation, of each class of shares (other than a class of shares all of the issued shares of which were cancelled on the amalgamation) of the capital stock of each predecessor corporation (in this subsection referred to as the "exchanged class") are converted into all of the issued shares, immediately after the amalgamation, of a separate class of shares of the capital stock of the new corporation (in this subsection referred to as the "substituted class"),

(*c*) immediately after the amalgamation, the number of shareholders of each substituted class, the number of shares of each substituted class owned by each shareholder, the number of issued shares of each substituted class, the terms and conditions of each share of a substituted class, and the paid-up capital of each substituted class determined without reference to the provisions of this Act are identical to the number of shareholders of the exchanged class from which the substituted class was converted, the number of shares of each such exchanged class owned by each shareholder, the number of issued shares of each such exchanged class, the terms and conditions of each share of such exchanged class, and the paid-up capital of each such exchanged class determined without reference to the provisions of this Act, respectively, immediately before the amalgamation, and

(*d*) the new corporation elects in its return of income filed in accordance with section 150 for its first taxation year to have the provisions of this subsection apply,

for the purpose of computing at any particular time the paid-up capital in respect of any particular class of shares of the capital stock of the new corporation,

(*e*) subsection (3) does not apply in respect of the amalgamation, and

(*f*) each substituted class shall be deemed to be the same as, and a continuation of, the exchanged class from which it was converted.

Editorial Note: In contrast to the "shifting" of PUC that can occur when s. 87(3) applies, s. 87(3.1) ensures that the PUC in respect of each class of shares of a predecessor corporation flows through to the class of shares of the amalgamated corporation into which it is converted.

Related Sections: S. 89(1), "paid-up capital".

► 87(4) ◄

(4) Shares of predecessor corporation. Where there has been an amalgamation of two or more corporations after May 6, 1974, each shareholder (except any predecessor corporation) who, immediately before the amalgamation, owned shares of the capital stock of a predecessor corporation (in this subsection referred to as the "old shares") that were capital property to the shareholder and who received no consideration for the disposition of those shares on the amalgamation, other than shares of the capital stock of the new corporation (in this subsection referred to as the "new shares"), shall be deemed

(*a*) to have disposed of the old shares for proceeds equal to the total of the adjusted cost bases to the shareholder of those shares immediately before the amalgamation, and

(*b*) to have acquired the new shares of any particular class of the capital stock of the new corporation at a cost to the shareholder equal to that proportion of the proceeds described in paragraph (*a*) that

(i) the fair market value, immediately after the amalgamation, of all new shares of that particular class so acquired by the shareholder,

is of

(ii) the fair market value, immediately after the amalgamation, of all new shares so acquired by the shareholder,

except that, where the fair market value of the old shares immediately before the amalgamation exceeds the fair market value of the new shares immediately after the amalgamation and it is reasonable to regard any portion of the excess (in this subsection referred to as the "gift portion") as a benefit that the shareholder desired to have conferred on a person related to the shareholder, the following rules apply:

(*c*) the shareholder shall be deemed to have disposed of the old shares for proceeds of disposition equal to the lesser of

(i) the total of the adjusted cost bases to the shareholder, immediately before the amalgamation, of the old shares and the gift portion, and

(ii) the fair market value of the old shares immediately before the amalgamation,

(*d*) the shareholder's capital loss from the disposition of the old shares shall be deemed to be nil, and

(*e*) the cost to the shareholder of any new shares of any class of the capital stock of the new corporation acquired by the shareholder on the amalgamation shall be deemed to be that proportion of the lesser of

(i) the total of the adjusted cost bases to the shareholder, immediately before the amalgamation, of the old shares, and

(ii) the total of the fair market value, immediately after the amalgamation, of all new shares so acquired by the shareholder and the amount that, but for paragraph (*d*), would have been the shareholder's capital loss from the disposition of the old shares

that

(iii) the fair market value, immediately after the amalgamation, of the new shares of that class so acquired by the shareholder

is of

(iv) the fair market value, immediately after the amalgamation, of all new shares so acquired by the shareholder,

and where the old shares were taxable Canadian property of the shareholder, the new shares are deemed to be, at any time that is within 60 months after the amalgamation, taxable Canadian property of the shareholder.

Editorial Note: A conversion of shares of a predecessor corporation ("old shares") into shares of the amalgamated corporation ("new shares") will normally be considered a disposition of the old shares; see subparagraph (*b*)(iii) of the definition of "disposition" in s. 248(1). S. 87(4) provides a rollover (deemed disposition for proceeds equal to the adjusted cost base of the old shares) where the shareholder of a predecessor corporation (other than a predecessor corporation) receives only new shares as consideration for the disposition of its old shares. The old shares must be capital property of the shareholder. The CRA has stated that it will not deny the rollover merely because the shareholder is required to receive cash or other consideration in lieu of a fraction of a new share of the amalgamated corporation; see paragraph 1.65 of S4-F7-C1 and CRA Document No. 2003-0013315. The rollover may be limited under s. 87(1)(*c*) if the fair market value of the shareholder's new shares is less than the fair market value of the shareholder's old shares and it is reasonable to regard the difference as a benefit that the shareholder desired to have conferred on a related person.

Paragraph (*n*) of the definition of "disposition" in s. 248(1) generally excludes from that definition the cancellation, upon the amalgamation, of a share of a predecessor corporation held by another predecessor corporation. Therefore, there will be no proceeds of disposition of the share in such case. (See paragraph 1.76 of S4-F7-C1 regarding the CRA position prior to the introduction of paragraph (*n*) referred to above.) However, if the other corporation is a parent corporation and the amalgamation is a vertical amalgamation subject to s. 87(11), the cancellation of the shares of the predecessor corporation held by the parent corporation is considered a disposition of those shares, and the deemed proceeds of disposition are determined under s. 88(1)(*b*). See the editorial note to s. 87(11).

See also s. 7(1.5), which can apply if the old shares were acquired under an employee stock option and the resulting stock option benefit was deferred under s. 7(1.1). For the purposes of the stock option rules, the employee/shareholder is deemed not to have disposed of the old shares, and the new shares are generally deemed to be the same as, and a continuation of, the old shares.

History: S. 87(4), the portion following paragraph (*e*) was replaced by S.C. 2010, c. 12, s. 8(1), applicable in determining after March 4, 2010 whether a property is taxable Canadian property of a taxpayer. S. 87(4), the portion following paragraph (*e*) formerly read:

> and where the old shares were taxable Canadian property of the shareholder, the new shares shall be deemed to be taxable Canadian property of the shareholder.

Related Sections: S. 7(1.5) Rules where securities exchanged; s. 54, "adjusted cost base", "capital property"; s. 87(5) Options to acquire shares of predecessor corporation; s. 87(8) Foreign merger; s. 87(9) Rules applicable in respect of certain mergers; ITAR s. 26(21) Shares received on amalgamation.

Tax Topics: No. 1870, CRA Reverts to Its Original Position in IT-474R2; No. 1869, Happy New Year! How the CRA Has Lengthened the Wait Time for Section 116 Clearance Certificates.

Tax Window Files: Absorptive merger-exchange of shares, *July 8, 2015*, CRA Document No. 2014-0550641E5.

Cases: When a subsidiary amalgamated with an unrelated company, its parent company exchanged its shares for preferred shares of the amalgamated company, redeemable for a promissory note due in 25 years. This may have shifted value to the amalgamated company, but the s. 87(4)(*b*) rollover exception did not apply since no person related to the parent benefited, although it was part of a series of transactions allowing a related company to acquire the parent. *Husky Oil Limited v. The Queen*, 2010 DTC 5089 (F.C.A.), reversing 2009 DTC 1094 (T.C.C.).

► 87(4.1) ◄

(4.1) Exchanged shares. For the purposes of the definition "term preferred share" in subsection 248(1), where there has been an amalgamation of two or more corporations after November 16, 1978 and a share of any class of the capital stock of the new corporation (in this subsection referred to as the "new share") was issued in consideration for the disposition of a share of any class of the capital stock of a predecessor corporation (in this subsection referred to as the "exchanged share") and the terms and conditions of the new share were the same as, or substantially the same as, the terms and conditions of the exchanged share,

(*a*) the new share shall be deemed to have been issued at the time the exchanged share was issued;

(*b*) if the exchanged share was issued under an agreement in writing, the new share shall be deemed to have been issued under that agreement; and

(*c*) the new corporation shall be deemed to be the same corporation as, and a continuation of, each such predecessor corporation.

Related Sections: S. 248(1), "term preferred share".

► 87(4.2) ◄

(4.2) Idem. Where there has been an amalgamation or merger of two or more corporations after November 27, 1986 and a share of any class of the capital stock of the new corporation (in this subsection referred to as the "new share") was issued to a shareholder in consideration for the disposition of a share by that shareholder of any class of the capital stock of a predecessor corporation (in this subsection referred to as the "exchanged share") and the terms and conditions of the new share were the same as, or substantially the same as, the terms and conditions of the exchanged share, for the purposes of applying the provisions of this subsection, subsections 112(2.2) and (2.4), Parts IV.1 and VI.1, section 258 and the definitions "grandfathered share", "short-term preferred share", "taxable preferred share" and "taxable RFI share" in subsection 248(1) to the new share, the following rules apply:

(*a*) the new share shall be deemed to have been issued at the time the exchanged share was issued;

(*b*) where the exchanged share was a share described in paragraph (*a*), (*b*), (*c*) or (*d*) of the definition "grandfathered share" in subsection 248(1), the new share shall be deemed to be the same share as the exchanged share for the purposes of that definition;

(*c*) the new share shall be deemed to have been acquired by the shareholder at the time the exchanged share was acquired by the shareholder;

(*d*) the new corporation shall be deemed to be the same corporation as, and a continuation of, each predecessor corporation;

(*e*) an election made under subsection 191.2(1) by a predecessor corporation with respect to the class of shares of its capital stock to which the exchanged share belonged shall be deemed to be an election made by the new corporation with respect to the class of shares of its capital stock to which the new share belongs; and

(*f*) where the terms or conditions of the exchanged share or an agreement in respect of the exchanged share specify an amount in respect of the exchanged share for the purposes of subsection 191(4) and an amount equal to the amount so specified in respect of the exchanged share is specified in respect of the new share for the purposes of subsection 191(4),

(i) for the purposes of subparagraphs 191(4)(*d*)(i) and (*e*)(i), the new share shall be deemed to have been issued for the same consideration as that for which the exchanged share was issued and to have been issued for the purpose for which the exchanged share was issued,

(ii) for the purposes of subparagraphs 191(4)(*d*)(ii) and (*e*)(ii), the new share shall be deemed to be the same share as the exchanged share and to have been issued for the purpose for which the exchanged share was issued, and

(iii) where the shareholder received no consideration for the disposition of the exchanged share other than the new share, for the purposes of subsection 191(4),

(A) in the case of an exchanged share to which subsection 191(4) applies because of paragraph 191(4)(*a*), the new share shall be deemed to have been issued for consideration having a fair market value equal to the consideration for which the exchanged share was issued, and

(B) in the case of an exchanged share to which subsection 191(4) applies because of an event described in paragraph 191(4)(*b*) or (*c*), the consideration for which the new share was issued shall be deemed to have a fair market value equal to the fair market value of the exchanged share immediately before the time that event occurred.

▶ 87(4.3) ◀

(4.3) Exchanged rights. Where there has been an amalgamation or merger of two or more corporations after June 18, 1987 and a right listed on a designated stock exchange to acquire a share of any class of the capital stock of the new corporation (in this subsection referred to as the "new right") was acquired by a shareholder in consideration for the disposition of a right described in paragraph (*d*) of the definition "grandfathered share" in subsection 248(1) to acquire a share of any class of the capital stock of a predecessor corporation (in this subsection referred to as the "exchanged right"), the new right shall be deemed to be the same right as the exchanged right for the purposes of paragraph (*d*) of the definition "grandfathered share" in subsection 248(1) where the terms and conditions of the new right were the same as, or substantially the same as, the terms and conditions of the exchanged right and the terms and conditions of the share receivable on an exercise of the new right were the same as, or substantially the same as, the terms and conditions of the share that would have been received on an exercise of the exchanged right.

Related Sections: S. 262 Designated stock exchanges.

▶ 87(4.4) ◀

(4.4) Flow-through shares. Where

(*a*) there is an amalgamation of two or more corporations each of which is a principal-business corporation (within the meaning assigned by subsection 66(15)) or a corporation that at no time carried on business,

(*b*) a predecessor corporation entered into an agreement with a person at a particular time for consideration given by the person to the predecessor corporation,

(*c*) for the consideration under the agreement

(i) a share (in this subsection referred to as the "old share") of the predecessor corporation that was a flow-through share (other than a right to acquire a share) was issued to the person before the amalgamation, or

(ii) a right was issued to the person before the amalgamation to acquire a share that would, if it were issued, be a flow-through share, and

(*d*) the new corporation

(i) issues, on the amalgamation and in consideration for the disposition of the old share, a share (in this subsection referred to as a "new share") of any class of its capital stock to the person (or to any person or partnership that subsequently acquired the old share) and the terms and conditions of the new share are the same as, or substantially the same as, the terms and conditions of the old share, or

(ii) is, because of the right referred to in subparagraph (*c*)(ii), obliged after the amalgamation to issue to the person a share of any class of the new corporation's capital stock that would, if it were issued, be a flow-through share,

for the purposes of subsection 66(12.66) and Part XII.6 and for the purposes of renouncing an amount under subsection 66(12.6), (12.601) or (12.62) in respect of Canadian exploration expenses or Canadian development expenses that would, but for the renunciation, be incurred by the new corporation after the amalgamation,

(*e*) the person shall be deemed to have given the consideration under the agreement to the new corporation for the issue of the new share,

(*f*) the agreement shall be deemed to have been entered into between the new corporation and the person at the particular time,

(*g*) the new share shall be deemed to be a flow-through share of the new corporation, and

(*h*) the new corporation shall be deemed to be the same corporation as, and a continuation of, the predecessor corporation.

History: S. 87(4.4)(*c*) and (*d*) were replaced by S.C. 2013, c. 34, s. 223(11), applicable to amalgamations that occur after 1997, and formerly read:

(*c*) a share of the predecessor corporation

(i) that was a flow-through share (in this subsection having the meaning that would be assigned by subsection 66(15) if the definition "flow-through share" in that subsection were read without reference to the portion after paragraph (*b*) of that definition) was issued to the person before the amalgamation, or

(ii) that would (if it were issued) be a flow-through share, was to be issued to the person

for the consideration under the agreement, and

(*d*) the new corporation

(i) issues a share (in this subsection referred to as a "new share") of any class of its capital stock on the amalgamation to the person in consideration for the disposition of the flow-through share of the predecessor corporation and the terms and conditions of the new share are the same as, or substantially the same as, the terms and conditions of the flow-through share, or

(ii) is obliged after the amalgamation to issue a new share of any class of its capital stock to the person under the obligation of the predecessor corporation to issue a flow-through share of the predecessor corporation to the person and the new share would not, if issued, be a prescribed share referred to in the definition "flow-through share" in subsection 66(15),

Related Sections: 66 [Exploration and development expenses].

► 87(5) ◄

(5) Options to acquire shares of predecessor corporation. Where there has been an amalgamation of two or more corporations after May 6, 1974, each taxpayer (except any predecessor corporation) who immediately before the amalgamation owned a capital property that was an option to acquire shares of the capital stock of a predecessor corporation (in this subsection referred to as the "old option") and who received no consideration for the disposition of that option on the amalgamation, other than an option to acquire shares of the capital stock of the new corporation (in this subsection referred to as the "new option"), shall be deemed

(*a*) to have disposed of the old option for proceeds equal to the adjusted cost base to the taxpayer of that option immediately before the amalgamation, and

(*b*) to have acquired the new option at a cost to the taxpayer equal to the proceeds described in paragraph (*a*),

and where the old option was taxable Canadian property of the taxpayer, the new option is deemed to be, at any time that is within 60 months after the amalgamation, taxable Canadian property of the taxpayer.

Editorial Note: See also s. 7(1.4), which can apply if the "old option" is an option acquired under an employee stock option agreement referred to in s. 7(1). Where s. 7(1.4) applies, for the purposes of the stock option rules, the shareholder is deemed not to have disposed of the old option, and the "new option" is deemed to be the same as, and a continuation of, the old option.

History: S. 87(5), the portion following paragraph (*b*) was replaced by S.C. 2010, c. 12, s. 8(2), applicable in determining after March 4, 2010 whether a property is taxable Canadian property of a taxpayer. S. 87(5), the portion following paragraph (*b*) formerly read:

and where the old option was taxable Canadian property of the taxpayer, the new option shall be deemed to be taxable Canadian property of the taxpayer.

Related Sections: S. 7(1.4) Exchange of options; s. 54, "adjusted cost base", "capital property".

► 87(5.1) ◄

(5.1) Adjusted cost base of option. Where the cost to a taxpayer of a new option is determined at any time under subsection (5),

(*a*) there shall be deducted after that time in computing the adjusted cost base to the taxpayer of the new option the total of all amounts deducted under paragraph 53(2)(g.1) in computing, immediately before that time, the adjusted cost base to the taxpayer of the old option; and

(*b*) the amount determined under paragraph (*a*) shall be added after that time in computing the adjusted cost base to the taxpayer of the new option.

► 87(6) ◄

(6) Obligations of predecessor corporation. Notwithstanding subsection (7), where there has been an amalgamation of two or more corporations after May 6, 1974, each taxpayer (except any predecessor corporation) who, immediately before the amalgamation, owned a capital property that was a bond, debenture, mortgage, hypothecary claim, note or other similar obligation of a predecessor corporation (in this subsection referred to as the "old property") and who received no consideration for the disposition of the old property on the amalgamation other than a bond, debenture, mortgage, hypothecary claim, note or other similar obligation respectively, of the new corporation (in this subsection referred to as the "new property") is, if the amount payable to the holder of the new property on its maturity is the same as the amount that would have been payable to the holder of the old property on its maturity, deemed

(*a*) to have disposed of the old property for proceeds equal to the adjusted cost base to the taxpayer of that property immediately before the amalgamation; and

(*b*) to have acquired the new property at a cost to the taxpayer equal to the proceeds described in paragraph (*a*).

Related Sections: S. 54, "adjusted cost base", "capital property"; s. 87(7) Obligations of predecessor corporation — position of amalgamated corporation; s. 88(1) Winding-up.

▶ 87(6.1) ◀

(6.1) Adjusted cost base. Where the cost to a taxpayer of a particular property that is a bond, debenture or note is determined at any time under subsection (6) and the terms of the bond, debenture or note conferred upon the holder the right to exchange that bond, debenture or note for shares,

(*a*) there shall be deducted after that time in computing the adjusted cost base to the taxpayer of the bond, debenture or note the total of all amounts deducted under paragraph 53(2)(*g*.1) in computing, immediately before that time, the adjusted cost base to the taxpayer of the property for which the particular property was exchanged at that time; and

(*b*) the amount determined under paragraph (*a*) in respect of the particular property shall be added after that time in computing the adjusted cost base to the taxpayer of the particular property.

▶ 87(7) ◀

(7) Idem. Where there has been an amalgamation of two or more corporations after May 6, 1974 and

(*a*) a debt or other obligation of a predecessor corporation that was outstanding immediately before the amalgamation became a debt or other obligation of the new corporation on the amalgamation, and

(*b*) the amount payable by the new corporation on the maturity of the debt or other obligation, as the case may be, is the same as the amount that would have been payable by the predecessor corporation on its maturity,

the provisions of this Act

(*c*) shall not apply in respect of the transfer of the debt or other obligation to the new corporation, and

(*d*) shall apply as if the new corporation had incurred or issued the debt or other obligation at the time it was incurred or issued by the predecessor corporation under the agreement made on the day on which the predecessor corporation made an agreement under which the debt or other obligation was issued,

except that, for the purposes of the definition "income bond" or "income debenture" in subsection 248(1), paragraph (*d*) shall not apply to any debt or other obligation of the new corporation unless the terms and conditions thereof immediately after the amalgamation are the same as, or substantially the same as, the terms and conditions of the debt or obligation that was an income bond or income debenture of the predecessor corporation immediately before the amalgamation.

Editorial Note: To qualify as an amalgamation under s. 87, the amalgamated corporation must assume all liabilities of the predecessor corporations (except for liabilities between predecessors). Subsection 87(6) provides for a rollover when the predecessors' obligations are exchanged for obligations of the amalgamated corporation. Subsection 87(7) looks to the position of the amalgamated corporation and generally deems it to have incurred the debt at the time the predecessor incurred the debt so that the rules in the Act in respect to the issuance of debt apply to the amalgamated corporation. Subsection 87(7) was considered in *Dow Chemical*, 2008 DTC 6544 (F.C.A.), which dealt with the applicability of s. 78(1)(*a*) in respect of unpaid amounts between non-arm's length parties and the requirement to include in income certain amounts which are unpaid at the end of the second taxation year following the taxation year in which the expense arose, where one of the corporations had amalgamated at the end of the second taxation year. Although s. 87(7) does not expressly deem the amalgamated corporation to be the same corporation as a predecessor corporation, it was held that s. 87 provides generally for the continuation of the rights and obligations of predecessor corporations to the amalgamated corporation.

Related Sections: S. 87(6) Obligations of predecessor corporation — position of debtholder; s. 88(1) Winding-up.

▶ 87(8) ◀

(8) Foreign merger. Subject to subsection 95(2), where there has been a foreign merger in which a taxpayer's shares or options to acquire shares of the capital stock of a corporation that was a predecessor foreign corporation immediately before the merger were exchanged for or became shares or options to acquire shares of the capital stock of the new foreign corporation or the foreign parent corporation, unless the taxpayer elects in the taxpayer's return of income for the taxation year in which the foreign merger took place not to have this subsection apply, subsections (4) and (5) apply to the taxpayer as if the references in those subsections to

(*a*) "amalgamation" were read as "foreign merger";

(*b*) "predecessor corporation" were read as "predecessor foreign corporation"; and

(*c*) "new corporation" were read as "new foreign corporation or the foreign parent corporation".

Editorial Note: Subsection 87(8) provides a tax-free rollover where the shares of a non-resident corporation have been disposed of on a foreign merger as defined in s. 87(8.1). It should be noted that an election to have the provisions of this subsection not apply may be made in the year in which the foreign merger takes place. If no election is made and the criteria set out in the provisions are met, then the provisions of s. 87(4) and (5) apply so that the disposition of shares and options on shares in the predecessor corporation is effected on a tax-deferred basis. Other provisions of the Act apply on a foreign merger. For example, s. 95(2)(*d.1*) applies in respect of capital property acquired on a foreign merger of two or more non-resident corporations by a non-resident amalgamated corporation. In addition, Regulation 5905(3) provides for the effect of a foreign merger on the exempt surplus, taxable surplus and the underlying foreign tax of a merged foreign corporation.

Related Sections: S. 95(1), "foreign affiliate"; s. 133(8), "non-resident-owned investment corporation"; s. 134 Non-resident-owned corporation not a Canadian corporation, etc.

Canadian Petroleum Tax Journal: A Comparative Study of Canadian and US Rules Regarding the Taxation of Corporate Reorganizations, Firoz Talakshi and Christy Palmer, 2000, Vol. 13, No. 1.

Canadian Tax Foundation: Marley and Slaats, *Foreign Affiliate Reorganizations — Recent Amendments to the Rules*, 2012 Conference Report 27:1–25; Swiderski and Lau, *Canadian Foreign Affiliate Implications of Common U.S. Asset Transfers*, 2000 Conference Report 15:1–46.

Tax Profile: July 2008 — International Tax Planning for the Owner-Manager.

Tax Window Files: Absorptive merger-exchange of shares, *July 8, 2015*, CRA Document No. 2014-0550641E5; Foreign Spin-off & Foreign Merger, *Technical Interpretation, International and Trusts Division, June 20, 2007*, CRA Document No. 2006-0178941I7.

▶ 87(8.1) ◀

(8.1) Definition of "foreign merger". For the purposes of this section, "foreign merger" means a merger or combination of two or more corporations each of which was, immediately before the merger or combination, resident in a country other than Canada (each of which is in this section referred to as a "predecessor foreign corporation") to form one corporate entity resident in a country other than Canada (in this section referred to as the "new foreign corporation") in such a manner that, and otherwise than as a result of the distribution of property to one corporation on the winding-up of another corporation,

(*a*) all or substantially all the property (except amounts receivable from any predecessor foreign corporation or shares of the capital stock of any predecessor foreign corporation) of the predecessor foreign corporations immediately before the merger or combination becomes property of the new foreign corporation as a consequence of the merger or combination;

(*b*) all or substantially all the liabilities (except amounts payable to any predecessor foreign corporation) of the predecessor foreign corporations immediately before the merger or combination become liabilities of the new foreign corporation as a consequence of the merger or combination; and

(*c*) all or substantially all of the shares of the capital stock of the predecessor foreign corporations (except any shares or options owned by any predecessor foreign corporation) are exchanged for or become, because of the merger or combination,

(i) shares of the capital stock of the new foreign corporation, or

(ii) if, immediately after the merger, the new foreign corporation was controlled by another corporation (in this section referred to as the "foreign parent corporation") that was resident in a country other than Canada, shares of the capital stock of the foreign parent corporation.

Editorial Note: "Foreign merger" is defined to mean a merger or combination of any two corporations, each of which is not resident in Canada, to form one corporate entity resident in a country other than Canada, in a manner other than a distribution of property to one corporation on the winding-up of another corporation. In addition, (a) substantially all the property (except for intercorporate receivables or shares) of predecessor foreign corporations immediately before the merger or combination must become the property of the new foreign amalgamated corporation, (b) substantially all the liabilities (except intercorporate amounts payable) of the predecessor foreign corporations immediately before the merger or combination must become liabilities of the new foreign corporation; and (c) substantially all of the shares of the capital stock of the predecessor foreign corporations (except any shares or options owned by any predecessor foreign corporation) must be exchanged for or become shares of the new foreign amalgamated corporation, or if immediately after the merger, the new amalgamated foreign corporation was controlled by another corporation that was not resident in Canada, shares of the capital stock of such other foreign corporation.

The CRA generally takes the position that "substantially all" means 90% or more. It should be noted that the definition of "foreign merger" is broader than the domestic provisions and in certain situations will cover a merger or combination as a result of the acquisition of property of one corporation by another foreign corporation that is not the result of a winding-up. The concept of "merger" was considered in *Allendale Mutual Insurance*, 73 DTC 5382 (F.C.T.D.).

Related Sections: 87(8.4) Taxable Canadian property — conditions for rollover.

Tax Profile: July 2008 — International Tax Planning for the Owner-Manager.

Tax Window Files: Absorptive merger-exchange of shares, *July 8, 2015*, CRA Document No. 2014-0550641E5.

► 87(8.2) ◄

(8.2) Absorptive mergers. For the purposes of the definition "foreign merger" in subsection (8.1), if there is a merger or combination, otherwise than as a result of the distribution of property to one corporation on the winding-up of another corporation, of two or more non-resident corporations (each of which is referred to in this subsection as a "predecessor foreign corporation"), as a result of which one or more predecessor foreign corporations ceases to exist and, immediately after the merger or combination, another predecessor foreign corporation (referred to in this subsection as the "survivor corporation") owns properties (except amounts receivable from, or shares of the capital stock of, any predecessor foreign corporation) representing all or substantially all of the fair market value of all such properties owned by each predecessor foreign corporation immediately before the merger or combination, then

(*a*) the merger or combination is deemed to be a merger or combination of the predecessor foreign corporations to form one non-resident corporation;

(*b*) the survivor corporation is deemed to be the non-resident corporation so formed;

(*c*) all of the properties of the survivor corporation immediately before the merger or combination that are properties of the survivor corporation immediately after the merger or combination are deemed to become properties of the survivor corporation as a consequence of the merger or combination;

(*d*) all of the liabilities of the survivor corporation immediately before the merger or combination that are liabilities of the survivor corporation immediately after the merger or combination are deemed to become liabilities of the survivor corporation as a consequence of the merger or combination;

(*e*) all of the shares of the capital stock of the survivor corporation that were outstanding immediately before the merger or combination that are shares of the capital stock of the survivor corporation immediately after the merger or combination are deemed to become shares of the capital stock of the survivor corporation as a consequence of the merger or combination; and

(*f*) all of the shares of the capital stock of each predecessor foreign corporation (other than the survivor corporation) that were outstanding immediately before the merger or combination and that cease to exist as a consequence of the merger or combination are deemed to be exchanged by the shareholders of each such predecessor corporation for shares of the survivor corporation as a consequence of the merger or combination.

History: S. 87(8.2) was added by S.C. 2013, c. 34, s. 64(2), applicable in respect of mergers or combinations in respect of a taxpayer that occur after 1994. However, new s. 87(8.2) does not apply in respect of all mergers or combinations in respect of the taxpayer that occur on or before August 19, 2011 if the taxpayer elects in writing under this subsection and files the election with the Minister of National Revenue on or before the day that is the later of the taxpayer's filing-due date for the taxpayer's taxation year that includes June 26, 2013 and June 26, 2014 [the day that is one year after royal assent].

Any assessment of a taxpayer's tax, interest and penalties payable under the Act for any taxation year that ends before June 26, 2013 that would, in the absence of this section, be precluded because of subsections 152(4) to (5) of the Act shall be made to the extent necessary to take into account the amendments by S.C. 2013, c. 34, s. 54 to 89.

Related Sections: 87(8.4) Taxable Canadian property — conditions for rollover.

Tax Window Files: Absorptive merger-exchange of shares, *July 8, 2015*, CRA Document No. 2014-0550641E5.

► 87(8.3) ◄

(8.3) Anti-avoidance. Subsection (8) does not apply in respect of a taxpayer's shares of the capital stock of a predecessor foreign corporation that are exchanged for or become, on a foreign merger, shares of the capital stock of the new foreign corporation or the foreign parent corporation, if (*a*) the new foreign corporation is, at the time that is immediately after the foreign merger, a foreign affiliate of the taxpayer;

(*b*) shares of the capital stock of the new foreign corporation are, at that time, excluded property (as defined in subsection 95(1)) of another foreign affiliate of the taxpayer; and

(*c*) the foreign merger is part of a transaction or event or a series of transactions or events that includes a disposition of shares of the capital stock of the new foreign corporation, or property substituted for the shares, to

(i) a person (other than a foreign affiliate of the taxpayer in respect of which the taxpayer has a qualifying interest (within the meaning assigned by paragraph 95(2)(*m*)) at the time of the transaction or event or throughout the series, as the case may be) with whom the taxpayer was dealing at arm's length immediately after the transaction, event or series, or

(ii) a partnership a member of which is, immediately after the transaction, event or series, a person described in subparagraph (i).

History: S. 87(8.3) was added by S.C. 2014, c. 39, s. 19(1), applicable to foreign mergers that occur after July 12, 2013.

Canadian Tax Foundation: Nijhawan and Richards, *Corporate Combinations: An Update on Canadian Mergers*, 2013 Conference Report 8:1–87; O'Hagan and Buttenham, *Foreign Affiliate Reorganizations: Where Are We Now?*, 2013 Conference Report 20:1–56.

▶ 87(8.4) ◀

(8.4) Taxable Canadian property — conditions for rollover. Subsection (8.5) applies at any time if

(*a*) there is at that time a foreign merger of two or more predecessor foreign corporations (within the meaning assigned by subsection (8.1), if that subsection and subsection (8.2) were read without reference to the expression "otherwise than as a result of the distribution of property to one corporation on the winding-up of another corporation") that were, immediately before that time,

(i) resident in the same country, and

(ii) related to each other (determined without reference to paragraph 251(5)(*b*));

(*b*) because of the foreign merger,

(i) a predecessor foreign corporation (referred to in this subsection and subsection (8.5) as the "disposing predecessor foreign corporation") disposes of a property (referred to in this subsection and subsection (8.5) as the "subject property") that is, at that time,

(A) a taxable Canadian property (other than treaty-protected property) of the disposing predecessor foreign corporation, and

(B) any of the following:

(I) a share of the capital stock of a corporation,

(II) an interest in a partnership, and

(III) an interest in a trust, and

(ii) the subject property becomes property of a corporation that is a new foreign corporation for the purposes of subsection (8.1);

(*c*) no shareholder (except any predecessor foreign corporation) that owned shares of the capital stock of a predecessor foreign corporation immediately before the foreign merger received consideration for the disposition of those shares on the foreign merger, other than shares of the capital stock of the new foreign corporation;

(*d*) if the subject property is a share of the capital stock of a corporation or an interest in a trust, the corporation or trust is not, at any time in the 24-month period beginning at that time, as part of a transaction or event, or series of transactions or events including the foreign merger, subject to a loss restriction event; and

(*e*) the new foreign corporation and the disposing predecessor foreign corporation jointly elect in writing under this paragraph in respect of the foreign merger and file the election with the Minister on or before the filing-due date of the disposing predecessor foreign corporation (or the date that would be its filing-due date, if subsection (8.5) did not apply in respect of the disposition of the subject property) for the taxation year that includes that time.

History: 87(8.4) was added by S.C. 2017, c. 33, s. 24(2), applicable to foreign mergers that occur after September 15, 2016, except that an election referred to in paragraph 87(8.4)(*e*) is deemed to have been filed on a timely basis if it is filed on or before June 14, 2018 (the day that is six months after the day on which this Act receives royal assent (December 14, 2017)).

Related Sections: 87(8.1) Definition of "foreign merger"; 87(8.2) Absorptive mergers; 248(1) taxable Canadian property.

▶ 87(8.5) ◀

(8.5) Foreign merger — taxable Canadian property rollover. If this subsection applies at any time,

(*a*) if the subject property is an interest in a partnership,

(i) the disposing predecessor foreign corporation is deemed not to dispose of the subject property (other than for the purposes of subsection (8.4)), and

(ii) the new foreign corporation is deemed

(A) to have acquired the subject property at a cost equal to the cost of the subject property to the disposing predecessor foreign corporation, and

(B) to be the same corporation as, and a continuation of, the disposing predecessor foreign corporation in respect of the subject property; and

(*b*) if the subject property is a share of the capital stock of a corporation or an interest in a trust,

(i) the subject property is deemed to have been disposed of at that time by the disposing predecessor foreign corporation to the new foreign corporation (that is referred to in subparagraph (8.4)(*b*)(ii)) for proceeds of disposition equal to the adjusted cost base of the subject property to the disposing predecessor foreign corporation immediately before that time, and

(ii) the cost of the subject property to the new foreign corporation is deemed to be the amount that is deemed by subparagraph (i) to be the proceeds of disposition of the subject property.

History: 87(8.5) was added by S.C. 2017, c. 33, s. 24(2), applicable to foreign mergers that occur after September 15, 2016, except that an election referred to in paragraph 87(8.4)(*e*) is deemed to have been filed on a timely basis if it is filed on or before June 14, 2018 (the day that is six months after the day on which this Act receives royal assent (December 14, 2017)).

► 87(9) ◄

(9) Rules applicable in respect of certain mergers. Where there has been a merger of two or more taxable Canadian corporations to form a new corporation that was controlled, immediately after the merger, by a taxable Canadian corporation (in this subsection referred to as the "parent") and, on the merger, shares of the capital stock of the parent (in this subsection referred to as "parent shares") were issued by the parent to persons who were, immediately before the merger, shareholders of a predecessor corporation, the following rules apply:

(*a*) for the purposes of paragraph (1)(*c*), subsection (4) and the *Income Tax Application Rules*, any parent shares received by a shareholder of a predecessor corporation shall be deemed to be shares of the capital stock of the new corporation received by the shareholder by virtue of the merger;

(*a*.1) for the purposes of subsections (4.1) and (4.2), a parent share issued to a shareholder in consideration for the disposition of a share of a class of the capital stock of a predecessor corporation shall be deemed to be a share of a class of the capital stock of the new corporation that was issued in consideration for the disposition of a share of a class of the capital stock of a predecessor corporation by that shareholder;

(*a*.2) for the purposes of subsection (4.3), a right listed on a designated stock exchange to acquire a share of a class of the capital stock of the parent shall be deemed to be a right listed on a designated stock exchange to acquire a share of a class of the capital stock of the new corporation;

(*a*.21) for the purpose of paragraph (4.4)(*d*)

(i) each parent share received by a shareholder of a predecessor corporation is deemed to be a share of the capital stock of the new corporation issued to the shareholder by the new corporation on the merger, and

(ii) any obligation of the parent to issue a share of any class of its capital stock to a person in circumstances described in subparagraph (4.4)(*d*)(ii) is deemed to be an obligation of the new corporation to issue a share to the person;

(*a*.3) for the purpose of applying subsection (5) in respect of the merger, the reference in that subsection to "the new corporation" shall be read as a reference to "the parent";

(*a*.4) for the purpose of paragraph (*c*), any shares of the new corporation acquired by the parent on the merger shall be deemed to be new shares;

(*a*.5) for the purpose of applying subsection (10) in respect of the merger,

(i) the reference in paragraph (10)(*b*) to "the new corporation" shall be read as a reference to "the new corporation or the parent, within the meaning assigned by subsection (9)", and

(ii) the references in paragraphs (10)(*c*) and (*f*) to "the new corporation" shall be read as references to "the public corporation described in paragraph (*b*)";

(*b*) in computing, at any particular time, the paid-up capital in respect of any particular class of shares of the capital stock of the parent that included parent shares immediately after the merger

(i) there shall be deducted that proportion of the amount, if any, by which the paid-up capital, determined without reference to this paragraph, in respect of all the shares of the capital stock of the parent immediately after the merger exceeds the total of all amounts each of which is the paid-up capital in respect of a share of the capital stock of the parent or a predecessor corporation (other than any share of a predecessor corporation owned by the parent or by another predecessor corporation and any share of a predecessor corporation owned by a shareholder other than the parent or another predecessor corporation that was not exchanged on the merger for parent shares) immediately before the merger that

(A) the paid-up capital, determined without reference to this paragraph, in respect of that particular class of shares of the capital stock of the parent immediately after the merger

is of

(B) the paid-up capital, determined without reference to this paragraph, in respect of all the issued and outstanding shares of the classes of the capital stock of the parent that included parent shares immediately after the merger, and

(ii) there shall be added an amount equal to the lesser of

(A) the amount, if any, by which

(I) the total of all amounts each of which is an amount deemed by subsection 84(3), (4) or (4.1) to be a dividend on shares of the particular class paid by the parent before the particular time

exceeds

(II) the total that would be determined under subclause (I) if this Act were read without reference to subparagraph (i), and

(B) the amount required by subparagraph (i) to be deducted in computing the paid-up capital of shares of the particular class; and

(*c*) notwithstanding paragraph (4)(*b*), the parent shall be deemed to have acquired the new shares of any particular class of the capital stock of the new corporation at a cost equal to the total of

(i) the amount otherwise determined under paragraph (4)(*b*) to be the cost of those shares, and

(ii) in any case where the parent owned, immediately after the merger, all the issued shares of the capital stock of the new corporation, such portion of

(A) the amount, if any, by which

(I) the amount by which the total of the money on hand of the new corporation and all amounts each of which is the cost amount to the new corporation of a property owned by it, immediately after the merger, exceeds the total of all amounts each of which is the amount of any debt owing by the new corporation, or of any other obligation of the new corporation to pay any amount, that was outstanding immediately after the merger,

exceeds

(II) the total of the adjusted cost bases to the parent of all shares of the capital stock of each predecessor corporation beneficially owned by it immediately before the merger

as is designated by the parent in respect of the shares of that particular class in its return of income under this Part for its taxation year in which the merger occurred, except that

(B) in no case shall the amount so designated in respect of the shares of a particular class exceed the amount, if any, by which the total fair market value, immediately after the merger, of the shares of that particular class issued by virtue of the merger exceeds the cost of those shares to the parent determined without reference to this paragraph, and

(C) in no case shall the total of the amounts so designated in respect of the shares of each class of the capital stock of the new corporation exceed the amount determined under clause (A).

Editorial Note: S. 87(9) applies to so-called triangular amalgamations, and effectively ensures that such amalgamations can qualify for the various rollovers provided under s. 87. The type of triangular amalgamation contemplated by the provision is one in which two or more predecessor corporations are amalgamated, and upon the amalgamation (at least some) shareholders of the predecessor corporations are issued shares in the parent corporation that controls the amalgamated corporation immediately after the amalgamation. As an example, a parent corporation would own shares in each of predecessors Corporation X and Corporation Y, which would amalgamate such that their shareholders, other than the parent corporation, would acquire newly issued shares of the parent corporation on the amalgamation. The parent corporation would acquire shares of the amalgamated corporation on the amalgamation.

By deeming the shares of the parent received by persons who were shareholders of the predecessor corporations to be shares of the amalgamated corporation for the purposes of s. 87(1)(*c*) and s. 87(4), s. 87(9)(*a*) ensures that the amalgamation qualifies as an amalgamation for the purposes of s. 87, and that such persons can qualify for the s. 87(4) rollover in respect of the disposition of their shares in the predecessor corporations. The parent can also qualify for the s. 87(4) rollover in respect of the disposition of its shares in the predecessor corporations, and further, may qualify for a "bump" in the cost of its shares in the amalgamated corporation under s. 87(9)(*c*)(ii).

Note that the parent corporation does not have to own all of the shares of the amalgamated corporation in order for s. 87(9) to apply; as noted, it only has to control the amalgamated corporation immediately after the amalgamation. However, in order for the parent to qualify for the "bump" under s. 87(9)(*c*)(ii), the parent must own all of the shares of the amalgamated corporation immediately after the amalgamation.

History: S. 87(9)(*a.21*) was added by S.C. 2013, c. 34, s. 223(12), applicable to amalgamations that occur after 1997.

Canadian Tax Foundation: Trossman, *Triangular Amalgamations*, 2001 Conference Report 22:1–32.

Tax Window Files: 2018 CTF – Q13 - 20(1)(c) & Triangular Amalgamation, *November 27, 2018*, CRA Document No. 2018-0779991C6.

► 87(10) ◄

(10) Share deemed listed. Where

(*a*) a new corporation is formed as a result of an amalgamation,

(*b*) the new corporation is a public corporation,

(*c*) the new corporation issues a share (in this subsection referred to as the "new share") of its capital stock,

(*d*) the new share is issued in exchange for a share (in this subsection referred to as the "old share") of the capital stock of a predecessor corporation,

(*e*) immediately before the amalgamation, the old share was listed on a designated stock exchange, and

(*f*) the new share is redeemed, acquired or cancelled by the new corporation within 60 days after the amalgamation,

the new share is deemed, for the purposes of subsection 116(6), the definitions *qualified investment* in subsections 146(1), 146.1(1), 146.3(1) and 146.4(1), in section 204 and in subsection 207.01(1), and the definition *taxable Canadian property* in subsection 248(1), to be listed on the exchange until the earliest time at which it is so redeemed, acquired or cancelled.

Editorial Note: In certain amalgamations involving predecessor corporations that had shares listed on a designated stock exchange, the amalgamated corporation may issue "temporary" shares that are not listed on an exchange. S. 87(10) provides that such shares are deemed to be listed on the exchange if the amalgamated corporation is a public corporation and the new shares are redeemed, acquired or cancelled by the amalgamated corporation within 60 days after the amalgamation. This deeming rule applies for the purpose of determining whether the shares of the amalgamated corporation are taxable Canadian property under s. 248(1), excluded property under s. 116(6) and qualified investments for the purposes of certain registered plans such as RRSPs.

History: 87(10), the portion following paragraph (*f*) was replaced by S.C. 2017, c. 33, s. 24(3), deemed to have come into force on March 23, 2017, and formerly read:

> the new share is deemed, for the purposes of subsection 116(6), the definitions "qualified investment" in subsections 146(1), 146.1(1) and 146.3(1), in section 204 and in subsections 205(1) and 207.01(1), and the definition "taxable Canadian property" in subsection 248(1), to be listed on the exchange until the earliest time at which it is so redeemed, acquired or cancelled.

Related Sections: S. 262 Designated stock exchanges.

► 87(11) ◄

(11) Vertical amalgamations. Where at any time there is an amalgamation of a corporation (in this subsection referred to as the "parent") and one or more other corporations (each of which in this subsection is referred to as the "subsidiary") each of which is a subsidiary wholly-owned corporation of the parent,

(*a*) the shares of the subsidiary are deemed to have been disposed of by the parent immediately before the amalgamation for proceeds equal to the proceeds that would be determined under paragraph 88(1)(*b*) if subsections 88(1) and (1.7) applied, with any modifications that the circumstances require, to the amalgamation; and

(*b*) the cost to the new corporation of each capital property of the subsidiary acquired on the amalgamation is deemed to be the amount that would have been the cost to the parent of the property if the property had been distributed at that time to the parent on a winding-up of the subsidiary and subsections 88(1) and (1.7) had applied to the winding-up.

Editorial Note: S. 87(11) applies to a vertical amalgamation, that is an amalgamation between a parent corporation and one or more of its subsidiaries each of which is a "subsidiary wholly-owned corporation" (defined in s. 248(1)). S. 87(11)(*a*) provides that the parent is deemed to have disposed of its shares in each subsidiary for proceeds determined under s. 88(1)(*b*). Therefore, if the lesser of the paid-up capital in respect of those shares and the parent's cost amount of the subsidiary's net assets (more particularly, the amount determined under s. 88(1)(*d*)(i)) exceeds the parent's adjusted cost base of the shares, the parent will realize a capital gain. If there is a possibility of a capital gain, consideration should be given to reducing the paid-up capital of the shares of the subsidiaries to a nominal amount without any payment being made before the amalgamation, so that a gain cannot arise on the vertical amalgamation. Otherwise, the disposition of the shares will result in a tax-free rollover. There can be no loss on the disposition.

S. 87(11)(*b*) incorporates by reference the "bump" rule in s. 88(1), which otherwise applies to a winding-up of a subsidiary into its parent corporation. The bump rule can apply to increase the parent's cost of non-depreciable capital properties of the subsidiary acquired by the parent on the amalgamation. The "bump" rule is summarized in the editorial note following s. 88(1).

Tax Window Files: Clarification of Application of 87(11), *Reorganizations Division, Income Tax Rulings Directorate, December 9, 2011*, CRA Document No. 2011-0428071E5.

Cases: Three subsidiaries of the corporate taxpayer amalgamated under provincial corporations legislation with the intent of creating a tax "bump". The manner in which the transactions were structured failed to achieve that objective. The corporate taxpayer sought and obtained a rectification order with respect to that amalgamation transaction, and the order was upheld on appeal. *Slate Management Corporation v. Attorney General of Canada*, 2017 DTC 5120 (ONCA)

SECTION 88: Winding-up

► 88(1) ◄

(1) Winding-up. Where a taxable Canadian corporation (in this subsection referred to as the "subsidiary") has been wound up after May 6, 1974 and not less than 90% of the issued shares of each class of the capital stock of the subsidiary were, immediately before the winding-up, owned by another taxable Canadian corporation (in this subsection referred to as the "parent") and all of the shares of the subsidiary that were not owned by the parent immediately before the winding-up were owned at that time by persons with whom the parent was dealing at arm's length, notwithstanding any other provision of this Act other than subsection 69(11), the following rules apply:

Editorial Note: Subsection 88(1) governs the winding-up of a taxable Canadian corporation (referred to therein as the "subsidiary"), where not less than 90% of the issued shares of each class of the subsidiary are held by another taxable Canadian corporation (referred to therein as the "parent"), and all the remaining shares of the subsidiary are owned by persons who deal at arm's length with the parent. Generally speaking, these rules provide a tax-free rollover upon the winding-up, including a carryover of most of the subsidiary's tax accounts, such as reserves, deferred amounts, prepaid amounts, investment tax credits, and so on, to the parent. On a winding-up to which s. 88(1) applies, the parent is deemed to have disposed of the shares in a subsidiary for the greater of: (a) the lesser of the paid-up capital in respect of those shares and the parent's cost amount of the subsidiary's net assets (i.e., the amount determined under s. 88(1)(*d*)(i)); and (b) the total of the parent's adjusted cost base of the shares. If both the amounts in (a) exceed the parent's adjusted cost base of the shares, the parent will realize a capital gain. If there is a possibility of a capital gain, consideration should be given to reducing the paid-up capital of the shares of the subsidiary to a nominal amount, without any payment being made before the winding-up, so that a gain cannot arise on the winding-up. Many of the amalgamation provisions are incorporated by reference for the purposes of the winding-up rules (s. 88(1)(*e*.2)).

One of the significant provisions of s. 88(1) is the so-called "bump" rule of paragraph (*d*), which allows the parent to add certain amounts to the cost of the subsidiary's former capital property distributed to the parent on the winding-up (other than depreciable property and other "ineligible property", a lengthy definition of which is found in paragraph (*c*)). The total bump for all such properties is generally limited to the amount by which the adjusted cost base of the parent's former shares in the subsidiary exceeds the total of the subsidiary's cost amounts of its properties and the money owned immediately before the winding-up net of the subsidiary's debts and other obligations outstanding immediately before the winding-up (with certain further adjustments, as set out in s. 88(1)(*d*)). Among other restrictions, the parent can bump up the cost of a particular capital property only to the extent that the fair market value of the property at the time the parent last acquired control of the subsidiary exceeds the greater of the cost amount of the property immediately before the winding-up and (applicable to windings-up that begin and amalgamations that occur after December 20, 2012, with certain grandfathering provisions) the cost amount at the time the parent last acquired control of the subsidiary (plus, in the case of a foreign affiliate, the prescribed amount). Furthermore, the property must have been owned by the subsidiary at the time the parent last acquired control of the subsidiary and thereafter without interruption until it was distributed to the parent on the winding-up (s. 88(1)(*c*)).

Applicable to amalgamations that occur and windings-up that begin after March 28, 2012, with certain grandfathering provisions, s. 88(1)(*d*)(ii.1) applies to reduce the fair market value of a subsidiary's interest in a partnership at the time the parent last acquired control of the subsidiary to the extent that the accrued gain of the interest at that time was attributable to accrued gains of depreciable property, Canadian or foreign resource property, or accrued gains of inventory or other property (other than capital property or resource property) that was held directly by the partnership or indirectly through one or more partnerships. Since the amount by which the fair market value of the partnership interest exceeds the cost of the interest to the subsidiary will be thus reduced, the amount by which the parent can bump up the cost of the partnership interest will also be reduced. The purpose of s. 88(1)(*d*)(ii.1) is to ensure that the bump is not available in respect of a subsidiary's interest in a partnership to the extent that the fair market value of the interest reflects unrealized gains and income that would not be eligible for the bump if held directly by the subsidiary.

Related Regulations: Part XI; Part LIII; 5905.

Related Sections: S. 12(1)(*e*.1) Negative reserves; s. 13(21), "proceeds of disposition"; s. 20(22) Deduction for negative reserves; s. 54, "adjusted cost base", "eligible capital property", "proceeds of disposition"; s. 55(3.3) Interpretation of "specified shareholder" changed; s. 59(2) Deduction under former s. 64 in preceding year; s. 66(15), "Canadian resource property", "foreign resource property"; s. 69(11) Deemed proceeds of disposition; s. 87(7) Obligations of predecessor corporation — position of amalgamated corporation; s. 89(1) Capital dividend account; s. 127(5) Investment tax credit; s. 127(9.1) Loss restriction event before end of year; s. 127(10.2) Expenditure limit determined; s. 127.1(2) Definitions; s. 129(1) Dividend refund to private corporation; s. 129(3) Definition of "refundable dividend tax on hand"; s. 186(2) When corporation controlled; s. 186(5) Deemed private corporation; s. 248(1), "dividend", "private corporation", "share", "specified future tax consequences", "taxable dividend"; s. 251 Arm's length; s. 252(2) Relationships.

Canadian Petroleum Tax Journal: The Recent Take-Over Phenomenon, D. Alan Ross and Stanley R. Ebel, 2001, Vol. 14, No. 1; Recent Developments in Corporate Reorganizations and International Transactions, Doug Richardson and Edward Rowe, 2000, Vol. 13, No. 1; A Comparative Study of Canadian and US Rules Regarding the Taxation of Corporate Reorganizations, Firoz Talakshi and Christy Palmer, 2000, Vol. 13, No. 1; Canada Customs and Revenue Agency 1999 Roundtable Questions and Answers, Question 4, , 2000, Vol. 13, No. 1.

Canadian Tax Foundation: Yip, *Recent Legislation Affecting Partnerships and Foreign Affiliates — Subsection 88(1) and Section 100*, 2013 Canadian Tax Journal 1:229–256; Talakshi, *The Foreign Affiliate Proposals — An Update*, 2005 Conference Report 14:1–20; Ireland, *Selected Developments in Post-Mortem Planning*, 2005 Conference Report 13:1–34; Heine and Legge, *Merger Building Blocks: Amalgamations and Windups*, 2004 Conference Report 37:1–50; Singh, *An Introduction to the "Bump" Rules*, 2003 Conference Report 51:1–27; Ton-That, *The Bump Denial Rules: In History and in Practice*, 2000 Conference Report 27:1–61; Brayley, *Merging Companies: A Practical Checklist for Amalgamations and Wind-Ups*, 2000 Conference Report 6:1–58; Addison and Korn, *Employee Stock Options: An Update*, 2000 Canadian Tax Journal 3:778–811; Woods and Wortsman, *The Bump Denial Rule in Subparagraph 88(1)(c)(vi)*, 1998 Conference Report 14:1–40; Richards, *Takeovers and Subsection 88(1); Hybrids: Update on LLCs/ULCs*, 1996 Conference Report 6:1–27; Sandler, *Character Rolls: Property Transfers and Characterization Issues*, 1996 Canadian Tax Journal 3:605–679; Roberts and Briggs, *Winding Up: Part 1*, 1996 Canadian Tax Journal 2:533–560.

Tax Profile: August 2012 — U.S. Purchases and Sales of Canadian Businesses: Tax and Corporate Issues; September 2011 — Acquisition of Canadian Business by Non-Residents; November 2009 — Purchase and Sale of a Canadian Business; February 2009 — Voting Shares — Premium for Control on Estate Freeze?; August 2005 — The Bump Denial Rules in Practice: Getting Comfort for Problems You Didn't Know You Had?; June 2003 — The December 20, 2002 Technical Amendments to the Income Tax Act.

Tax Topics: No. 1798, Bumping Foreign Affiliate Shares under the February 27, 2004 Proposals; No. 1701, "Bumping" Cost of Real Estate Inventory; No. 1690, Estate Planning In The 21st Century; No. 1635, Estate Planning in the Twenty-First Century; No. 1626, Estate Planning in the 21st Century; No. 1609, Estate Planning in the 21st Century; No. 1570, Estate Planning in the 21st Century.

Forms: T2 SCH 24 — First Time Filer after Incorporation, Amalgamation, or Winding-up of a Subsidiary into a Parent.

Income Tax Folios: *Secondary* — S5-F2-C1 Foreign Tax Credit. *Secondary* — S4-F7-C1 Amalgamations of Canadian Corporations.

Information Circulars: IC 88-2 General anti-avoidance rule — Section 245 of the Income Tax Act (Supp. 1, para. 8).

Interpretation Bulletins: *Primary* — IT-126R2 Meaning of "winding-up". *Secondary* — IT-142R3 Settlement of debts on the winding-up of a corporation; IT-259R4 Exchange of property.

Tax Window Files: Due date for subparagraph 88.1(1)(d)(ii) election, *February 9, 2011*, CRA Document No. 2011-0394271I7; Treaty Exemption, *January 28, 2003*, CRA Document No. 2003-0048443.

Cases: The taxpayer failed to discharge the burden in establishing that the conditions for granting rectification have been met. As such, rectification is not an appropriate remedy for the taxpayer's "bump mistake". *Harvest Operations Corp v. Canada (Attorney General)*, 2015 DTC 5067 (Alta. Q.B.)

Land acquired by a real estate developer upon the winding-up of its subsidiary formed part of the developer's trading inventory. The developer was accordingly entitled to apply the deemed cost amount of the land to the subsidiary against its proceeds of disposition, and to claim the resulting loss. Ss. 9(1) and 18(1)(*a*) did not preclude it from using the rollover provisions of s. 88(1). S. 88(1) operates notwithstanding any other provisions of the Act. *Mara Properties Ltd. v. The Queen*, 96 DTC 6309 (S.C.C.), reversing 95 DTC 5168 (F.C.A.)

▶ 88(1)(a) ◀

(a) **[Winding-up — Proceeds of disposition of subsidiary's property]** — subject to paragraphs (*a*.1) and (*a*.3), each property (other than an interest in a partnership) of the subsidiary that was distributed to the parent on the winding-up shall be deemed to have been disposed of by the subsidiary for proceeds equal to

(i) in the case of a Canadian resource property, a foreign resource property or a right to receive production (as defined in subsection 18.1(1)) to which a matchable expenditure (as defined in subsection 18.1(1)) relates, nil, and

(ii) (Repealed by 1994, c. 7, Sched. VIII, S. 38(1).)

(iii) in the case of any other property, the cost amount to the subsidiary of the property immediately before the winding-up;

▶ 88(1)(a.1) ◀

(a.1) **[Winding-up — Pre-1972 capital surplus of subsidiary]** — each property of the subsidiary that was distributed to the parent on the winding-up shall, for the purpose of paragraph (2.1)(*b*) or (*e*), be deemed not to have been disposed of;

▶ 88(1)(a.2) ◀

(a.2) **[Winding-up — Partnership interest of subsidiary]** — each interest of the subsidiary in a partnership that was distributed to the parent on the winding-up shall, except for the purpose of paragraph 98(5)(*g*), be deemed not to have been disposed of by the subsidiary;

▶ 88(1)(a.3) ◀

(a.3) **[Winding-up — Specified debt obligations of financial institutions]** — where

(i) the subsidiary was a financial institution in its taxation year in which its assets were distributed to the parent on the winding up, and

(ii) the parent was a financial institution in its taxation year in which it received the assets of the subsidiary on the winding up,

each specified debt obligation (other than a mark-to-market property) of the subsidiary that was distributed to the parent on the winding-up shall, except for the purpose of subsection 69(11), be deemed not to have been disposed of, and for the purpose of this paragraph, "financial institution", "mark-to-market property" and "specified debt obligation" have the meanings assigned by subsection 142.2(1);

▶ 88(1)(b) ◀

(b) **[Winding-up — Disposition of shares of subsidiary]** — the shares of the capital stock of the subsidiary owned by the parent immediately before the winding-up shall be deemed to have been disposed of by the parent on the winding-up for proceeds equal to the greater of

(i) the lesser of the paid-up capital in respect of those shares immediately before the winding-up and the amount determined under subparagraph (*d*)(i), and

(ii) the total of all amounts each of which is an amount in respect of any share of the capital stock of the subsidiary so disposed of by the parent on the winding-up, equal to the adjusted cost base to the parent of the share immediately before the winding-up;

Tax Window Files: 2018 CTF - Q5 - GAAR on PUC reduction, *November 27, 2018*, CRA Document No. 2018-0780041C6.

▶ 88(1)(c) ◀

(c) **[Winding-up — Cost of property received by parent]** — subject to paragraph 87(2)(*e*.3) (as modified by paragraph (*e*.2)), and notwithstanding paragraph 87(2)(*e*.1) (as modified by paragraph (*e*.2)), the cost to the parent of each property of the subsidiary distributed to the parent on the winding-up shall be deemed to be

(i) in the case of a property that is an interest in a partnership, the amount that but for this paragraph would be the cost to the parent of the property, and

(ii) in any other case, the amount, if any, by which

(A) the amount that would, but for subsection 69(11), be deemed by paragraph (*a*) to be the proceeds of disposition of the property

exceeds

(B) any reduction of the cost amount to the subsidiary of the property made because of section 80 on the winding-up,

plus, where the property was a capital property (other than an ineligible property) of the subsidiary at the time that the parent last acquired control of the subsidiary and was owned by the subsidiary thereafter without interruption until such time as it was distributed to the parent on the winding-up, the amount determined under paragraph (*d*) in respect of the property and, for the purposes of this paragraph, "ineligible property" means

(iii) depreciable property,

(iv) property transferred to the parent on the winding-up where the transfer is part of a distribution (within the meaning assigned by subsection 55(1)) made in the course of a reorganization in which a dividend was received to which subsection 55(2) would, but for paragraph 55(3)(*b*), apply,

(v) property acquired by the subsidiary from the parent or from any person or partnership that was not (otherwise than because of a right referred to in paragraph 251(5)(*b*)) dealing at arm's length with the parent, or any other property acquired by the subsidiary in substitution for it, where the acquisition was part of the series of transactions or events in which the parent last acquired control of the subsidiary, and

(vi) property distributed to the parent on the winding-up where, as part of the series of transactions or events that includes the winding-up,

(A) the parent acquired control of the subsidiary, and

(B) any property distributed to the parent on the winding-up or any other property acquired by any person in substitution therefor is acquired by

(I) a particular person (other than a specified person) that, at any time during the course of the series and before control of the subsidiary was last acquired by the parent, was a specified shareholder of the subsidiary,

(II) 2 or more persons (other than specified persons), if a particular person would have been, at any time during the course of the series and before control of the subsidiary was last acquired by the parent, a specified shareholder of the subsidiary if all the shares that were then owned by those 2 or more persons were owned at that time by the particular person, or

(III) a corporation (other than a specified person or the subsidiary)

1. of which a particular person referred to in subclause (I) is, at any time during the course of the series and after control of the subsidiary was last acquired by the parent, a specified shareholder, or

2. of which a particular person would be, at any time during the course of the series and after control of the subsidiary was last acquired by the parent, a specified shareholder if all the shares then owned by persons (other than specified persons) referred to in subclause (II) and acquired by those persons as part of the series were owned at that time by the particular person;

Canadian Tax Foundation: Nikolakakis and Léonard, *The Acquisition of Canadian Corporations by Non-Residents*, 2005 Conference Report 21:1–45.

► 88(1)(c.1) ◄

(c.1) [Winding-up — Eligible capital property] — (Repealed by S.C. 2016, c. 12, s. 28(1).)

History: S. 88(1)(*c*.1) was repealed by S.C. 2016, c. 12, s. 28(1), in force January 1, 2017, and formerly read:

(*c*.1) *[Winding-up — Eligible capital property]* — for the purpose of determining after the winding-up the amount to be included under subsection 14(1) in computing the parent's income in respect of the business carried on by the subsidiary immediately before the winding-up

(i) there shall be added to the amount otherwise determined for each of the descriptions of A and F in the definition "cumulative eligible capital" in subsection 14(5), the total of all amounts, each of which is the amount, if any,

(A) determined for the description of F in that definition in respect of that business immediately before the winding up,

(B) determined under this subparagraph as it applied to the subsidiary in respect of a winding-up before that time, or

(C) determined under paragraph 85(1)(*d*.11) as it applied to the subsidiary in respect of a disposition to the subsidiary before that time, and

(ii) there shall be added to the amount determined for the description of C in the formula in paragraph 14(1)(*b*), the total of all amounts, each of which is an amount that is

(A) one-half of the amount, if any, determined for the description of Q in that definition in respect of that business immediately before the winding up,

(B) determined under this subparagraph as it applied to the subsidiary in respect of a winding-up before that time, or

(C) determined under paragraph 85(1)(*d*.1) as it applied to the subsidiary in respect of a disposition to the subsidiary before that time;

S. 88(1)(*c*.1) was replaced by S.C. 2013, c. 34, s. 224(1), applicable in respect of the disposition of an eligible capital property by a subsidiary to a parent unless

(*a*) the disposition by the subsidiary occurred before December 21, 2002; and

(*b*) the parent disposed of the eligible capital property, before November 9, 2006, and in a taxation year of the parent ending after February 27, 2000, to a person with whom the parent did not deal at arm's length at the time of that disposition by the parent.

S. 88(1)(*c*.1) formerly read:

(*c*.1) *[Winding-up — Eligible capital property]* — for the purpose of determining after the winding-up the amount to be included under paragraph 14(1)(*b*) in computing the parent's income in respect of the business carried on by the subsidiary immediately before the winding-up, there shall be added to the amount otherwise determined for Q in the definition "cumulative eligible capital" in subsection 14(5) the amount, if any, determined for Q in that definition in respect of that business immediately before the disposition;

► 88(1)(c.2) ◄

(c.2) [Winding-up — Specified person and specified shareholder] — for the purposes of this paragraph and subparagraph (*c*)(vi),

(i) "specified person", at any time, means

(A) the parent,

(B) each person who would be related to the parent at that time if

(I) this Act were read without reference to paragraph 251(5)(*b*), and

(II) each person who is the child of a deceased individual were related to each brother or sister of the individual and to each child of a deceased brother or sister of the individual, and

(C) if the time is before the incorporation of the parent, each person who is described in clause (B) throughout the period that begins at the time the parent is incorporated and ends at the time that is immediately before the beginning of the winding-up,

(i.1) a person described in clause (i)(B) or (C) is deemed not to be a specified person if it can reasonably be considered that one of the main purposes of one or more transactions or events is to cause the person to be a specified person so as to prevent a property that is distributed to the parent on the winding-up from being an ineligible property for the purposes of paragraph (*c*),

(ii) where at any time a property is owned or acquired by a partnership or a trust,

(A) the partnership or the trust, as the case may be, shall be deemed to be a person that is a corporation having one class of issued shares, which shares have full voting rights under all circumstances,

(B) each member of the partnership or beneficiary under the trust, as the case may be, shall be deemed to own at that time the proportion of the number of issued shares of the capital stock of the corporation that

(I) the fair market value at that time of that member's interest in the partnership or that beneficiary's interest in the trust, as the case may be,

is of

(II) the fair market value at that time of all the members' interests in the partnership or beneficiaries' interests in the trust, as the case may be, and

(C) the property shall be deemed to have been owned or acquired at that time by the corporation;

(iii) in determining whether a person is a specified shareholder of a corporation,

(A) the reference in the definition "specified shareholder" in subsection 248(1) to "the issued shares of any class of the capital stock of the corporation or of any other corporation that is related to the corporation" shall be read as "the issued shares of any class (other than a specified class) of the capital stock of the corporation or of any other corporation that is related to the corporation and that has a significant direct or indirect interest in any issued shares of the capital stock of the corporation",

(A.1) a corporation controlled by another corporation is, at any time, deemed not to own any shares of the capital stock of the other corporation if, at that time, the corporation does not have a direct or an indirect interest in any of the shares of the capital stock of the other corporation,

(A.2) the definition "specified shareholder" in subsection 248(1) is to be read without reference to its paragraph (*a*) in respect of any share of the capital stock of the subsidiary that the person would, but for this clause, be deemed to own solely because the person has a right described in paragraph 251(5)(*b*) to acquire shares of the capital stock of a corporation that

(I) is controlled by the subsidiary, and

(II) does not have a direct or an indirect interest in any of the shares of the capital stock of the subsidiary, and

(B) a corporation is deemed not to be a specified shareholder of itself; and

(iv) property that is distributed to the parent on the winding-up is deemed not to be acquired by a person if the person acquired the property before the acquisition of control referred to in clause (*c*)(vi)(A) and the property is not owned by the person at any time after that acquisition of control;

History: S. 88(1)(*c*.2)(i) was replaced and s. 88(1)(*c*.2)(i.1) was added by S.C. 2013, c. 40, s. 40(1), applicable to windings-up that begin, and amalgamations that occur, after 2001. S. 88(1)(*c*.2)(i) formerly read:

(i) "specified person" at any time means the parent and each person that would, if this Act were read without reference to paragraph 251(5)(*b*), be related to the parent at that time and, for this purpose, a person shall be deemed not to be related to the parent where it can reasonably be considered that one of the main purposes of one or more transactions or events was to cause the person to be related to the parent so as to prevent a property that was distributed to the parent on the winding-up from being an ineligible property for the purpose of paragraph (*c*),

S. 88(1)(*c*.2)(iii)(A.1) and (A.2) were added by S.C. 2013, c. 40, s. 40(2), applicable to windings-up that begin, and amalgamations that occur, after 2001.

S. 88(1)(*c*.2)(iv) was added by S.C. 2013, c. 40, s. 40(3), applicable to windings-up that begin, and amalgamations that occur, after 2001.

► 88(1)(c.3) ◄

(c.3) [Winding-up — Substituted property] — for the purpose of clause (*c*)(vi)(B), property acquired by any person in substitution for particular property or properties distributed to the parent on the winding-up includes

(i) property (other than a specified property) owned by the person at any time after the acquisition of control referred to in clause (*c*)(vi)(A) more than 10% of the fair market value of which is, at that time, attributable to the particular property or properties, and

(ii) property owned by the person at any time after the acquisition of control referred to in clause (*c*)(vi)(A) the fair market value of which is, at that time, determinable primarily by reference to the fair market value of, or to any proceeds from a disposition of, the particular property or properties

but does not include

(iii) money,

(iv) property that was not owned by the person at any time after the acquisition of control referred to in clause (*c*)(vi)(A), or

(v) property described in subparagraph (i) if the only reason the property is described in that subparagraph is because a specified property described in any of subparagraphs (*c*.4)(i) to (iv) was received as consideration for the acquisition of a share of the capital stock of the subsidiary in the circumstances described in subparagraphs (*c*.4)(i) to (iv);

(vi) a share of the capital stock of the subsidiary or a debt owing by it, if the share or debt, as the case may be, was owned by the parent immediately before the winding-up, or

(vii) a share of the capital stock of a corporation or a debt owing by a corporation, if the fair market value of the share or debt, as the case may be, was not, at any time after the beginning of the winding-up, wholly or partly attributable to property distributed to the parent on the winding-up;

History: S. 88(1)(*c*.3)(i) was replaced by S.C. 2013, c. 40, s. 40(4), applicable to windings-up that begin, and amalgamations that occur, after December 20, 2012, and formerly read:

(i) property (other than a specified property) owned by the person at any time after the acquisition of control referred to in clause (*c*)(vi)(A) the fair market value of which is, at that time, wholly or partly attributable to the particular property or properties, and

S. 88(1)(*c*.3)(vi) and (vii) were added by S.C. 2013, c. 34, s. 224(2), applicable to windings-up that begin, and amalgamations that occur, after 1997.

► 88(1)(c.4) ◄

(c.4) [Winding-up — Specified property] — for the purposes of subparagraphs (*c*.3)(i) and (v), a specified property is

(i) a share of the capital stock of the parent that was

(A) received as consideration for the acquisition of a share of the capital stock of the subsidiary by the parent or by a corporation that was a specified subsidiary corporation of the parent immediately before the acquisition, or

(B) issued for consideration that consists solely of money,

(ii) an indebtedness that was issued

(A) by the parent as consideration for the acquisition of a share of the capital stock of the subsidiary by the parent, or

(B) for consideration that consists solely of money,

(iii) a share of the capital stock of a taxable Canadian corporation that was received as consideration for the acquisition of a share of the capital stock of the subsidiary by the taxable Canadian corporation or by the parent where the parent was a specified subsidiary corporation of the taxable Canadian corporation immediately before the acquisition,

(iv) an indebtedness of a taxable Canadian corporation that was issued by it as consideration for the acquisition of a share of the capital stock of the subsidiary by the taxable Canadian corporation or by the parent where the parent was a specified subsidiary corporation of the taxable Canadian corporation immediately before the acquisition, and

(v) if the subsidiary was formed on the amalgamation of two or more predecessor corporations at least one of which was a subsidiary wholly-owned corporation of the parent,

(A) a share of the capital stock of the subsidiary that was issued on the amalgamation and that is, before the beginning of the winding-up,

(I) redeemed, acquired or cancelled by the subsidiary for consideration that consists solely of money or shares of the capital stock of the parent, or of any combination of the two, or

(II) exchanged for shares of the capital stock of the parent, or

(B) a share of the capital stock of the parent issued on the amalgamation in exchange for a share of the capital stock of a predecessor corporation;

(vi) (Repealed.)

History: S. 88(1)(*c*.4)(ii) was replaced by S.C. 2013, c. 40, s. 40(5), applicable to windings-up that begin, and amalgamations that occur, after 2001, and formerly read:

(ii) an indebtedness that was issued by the parent as consideration for the acquisition of a share of the capital stock of the subsidiary by the parent,

S. 88(1)(*c*.4)(v) and (vi) were replaced by S.C. 2013, c. 40, s. 40(6), applicable to windings-up that begin, and amalgamations that occur, after 2001, and formerly read:

(v) where the subsidiary was formed on the amalgamation of 2 or more predecessor corporations at least one of which was a subsidiary wholly-owned corporation of the parent, a share of the capital stock of the subsidiary

(A) that was issued on the amalgamation in exchange for a share of the capital stock of a predecessor corporation, and

(B) that was, immediately after the amalgamation, redeemed, acquired or cancelled by the subsidiary for money, and

(vi) where the subsidiary was formed on the amalgamation of 2 or more predecessor corporations at least one of which was a subsidiary wholly-owned corporation of the parent, a share of the capital stock of the parent

(A) that was issued on the amalgamation in exchange for a share of the capital stock of a predecessor corporation, and

(B) that was, immediately after the amalgamation, redeemed, acquired or cancelled by the parent for money;

S. 88(1)(*c*.4)(vi) was repealed by S.C. 2013, c. 40, s. 40(7), applicable to windings-up that begin, and amalgamations that occur, after December 20, 2012 other than — if a taxable Canadian corporation (in this application referred to as the "parent corporation") has acquired control of another taxable Canadian corporation (in this application referred to as the "subsidiary corporation") — an amalgamation of the parent corporation and the subsidiary corporation that occurs, or a winding-up of the subsidiary corporation into the parent corporation that begins, before July 2013 if

(*a*) the parent corporation acquired control of the subsidiary corporation before December 21, 2012, or was obligated as evidenced in writing before December 21, 2012 to acquire control of the subsidiary corporation (except that the parent corporation shall not be considered to be obligated if, as a result of amendments to the Act, it may be excused from the obligation to acquire control); and

(*b*) the parent corporation had the intention as evidenced in writing before December 21, 2012 to amalgamate with, or wind up, the subsidiary corporation. S. 88(1)(*c*.4)(vi) formerly read:

(vi) a share of the capital stock of a corporation issued to a person described in clause (*c*)(vi)(B) if all the shares of the capital stock of the subsidiary were acquired by the parent for consideration that consists solely of money;

S. 88(1)(*c*.4)(i) was replaced by S.C. 2013, c. 34, s. 224(3), applicable to windings-up that begin, and amalgamations that occur, after 1997, and formerly read:

(i) a share of the capital stock of the parent that was received as consideration for the acquisition of a share of the capital stock of the subsidiary by the parent or by a corporation that was a specified subsidiary corporation of the parent immediately before the acquisition,

► 88(1)(c.5) ◄

(c.5) [Winding-up — Specified subsidiary corporation] — for the purpose of paragraph (*c*.4), a corporation is a specified subsidiary corporation of another corporation, at any time, where the other corporation holds, at that time, shares of the corporation

(i) that give the shareholder 90% or more of the votes that could be cast under all circumstances at an annual meeting of shareholders of the corporation, and

(ii) having a fair market value of 90% or more of the fair market value of all the issued shares of the capital stock of the corporation;

▶ 88(1)(c.6) ◀

(c.6) [Winding-up — Control acquired by way of articles of arrangement] — for the purpose of paragraph (*c*.3) and notwithstanding subsection 256(9), where control of a corporation is acquired by way of articles of arrangement, that control is deemed to have been acquired at the end of the day on which the arrangement becomes effective;

▶ 88(1)(c.7) ◀

(c.7) [Winding-up — Leasehold interests in and options for depreciable property] — for the purpose of subparagraph (*c*)(iii), a leasehold interest in a depreciable property and an option to acquire a depreciable property are depreciable properties;

▶ 88(1)(c.8) ◀

(c.8) [Winding-up — Specified class of capital stock] — for the purpose of clause (*c*.2)(iii)(A), a specified class of the capital stock of a corporation is a class of shares of the capital stock of the corporation where

(i) the paid-up capital in respect of the class was not, at any time, less than the fair market value of the consideration for which the shares of that class then outstanding were issued,

(ii) the shares are non-voting in respect of the election of the board of directors of the corporation, except in the event of a failure or default under the terms or conditions of the shares,

(iii) under neither the terms and conditions of the shares nor any agreement in respect of the shares are the shares convertible into or exchangeable for shares other than shares of a specified class of the capital stock of the corporation, and

(iv) under neither the terms and conditions of the shares nor any agreement in respect of the shares is any holder of the shares entitled to receive on the redemption, cancellation or acquisition of the shares by the corporation or by any person with whom the corporation does not deal at arm's length an amount (excluding any premium for early redemption) greater than the total of the fair market value of the consideration for which the shares were issued and the amount of any unpaid dividends on the shares;

▶ 88(1)(c.9) ◀

(c.9) [Winding-up — Right to acquire share] — for the purposes of paragraph (*c*.4), a reference to a share of the capital stock of a corporation includes a right to acquire a share of the capital stock of the corporation;

History: S. 88(1)(*c*.9) was added by S.C. 2013, c. 40, s. 40(8), applicable to windings-up that begin, and amalgamations that occur, after 2001.

▶ 88(1)(d) ◀

(d) [Winding-up — Addition to cost of property acquired by parent (the "bump")] — the amount determined under this paragraph in respect of each property of the subsidiary distributed to the parent on the winding-up is such portion of the amount, if any, by which the total determined under subparagraph (*b*)(ii) exceeds the total of

(i) the amount, if any, by which

(A) the total of all amounts each of which is an amount in respect of any property owned by the subsidiary immediately before the winding-up, equal to the cost amount to the subsidiary of the property immediately before the winding-up, plus the amount of any money of the subsidiary on hand immediately before the winding-up,

exceeds the total of

(B) all amounts each of which is the amount of any debt owing by the subsidiary, or of any other obligation of the subsidiary to pay any amount, that was outstanding immediately before the winding-up, and

(C) the amount of any reserve (other than a reserve referred to in paragraph 20(1)(*n*), subparagraph 40(1)(*a*)(iii) or 44(1)(*e*)(iii) of this Act or in subsection 64(1) or (1.1) of the *Income Tax Act*, chapter 148 of the Revised Statutes of Canada, 1952, as those two provisions read immediately before November 3, 1981) deducted in computing the subsidiary's income for its taxation year during which its assets were distributed to the parent on the winding-up, and

(i.1) the total of all amounts each of which is an amount in respect of any share of the capital stock of the subsidiary disposed of by the parent on the winding-up or in contemplation of the winding-up, equal to the total of all amounts received by the parent or by a corporation with which the parent was not dealing at arm's length (otherwise than because of a right referred to in paragraph 251(5)(*b*) in respect of the subsidiary) in respect of

(A) taxable dividends on the share or on any share (in this subparagraph referred to as a "replaced share") for which the share or a replaced share was substituted or exchanged to the extent that the amounts thereof were deductible from the recipient's income for any taxation year by virtue of section 112 or subsection 138(6) and were not amounts on which the recipient was required to pay tax under Part VII of the *Income Tax Act*, chapter 148 of the Revised Statutes of Canada, 1952, as it read on March 31, 1977, or

(B) capital dividends and life insurance capital dividends on the share or on any share (in this subparagraph referred to as a "replaced share")

for which a share or a replaced share was substituted or exchanged,

as is designated by the parent in respect of that capital property in its return of income under this Part for its taxation year in which the subsidiary was so wound up, except that

(ii) the amount designated in respect of any such capital property may not exceed the amount determined by the formula

A - (B + C)

where

A is the fair market value of the property at the time the parent last acquired control of the subsidiary,

B is the greater of the cost amount to the subsidiary of the property at the time the parent last acquired control of the subsidiary and the cost amount to the subsidiary of the property immediately before the winding-up, and

C is the prescribed amount, and

(ii.1) for the purpose of calculating the amount in subparagraph (ii) in respect of an interest of the subsidiary in a partnership, the fair market value of the interest at the time the parent last acquired control of the subsidiary is deemed to be the amount determined by the formula

A - B

where

A is the fair market value (determined without reference to this subparagraph) of the interest at that time, and

B is the portion of the amount by which the fair market value (determined without reference to this subparagraph) of the interest at that time exceeds its cost amount at that time as may reasonably be regarded as being attributable at that time to the total of all amounts each of which is

(A) in the case of a depreciable property held directly by the partnership or held indirectly by the partnership through one or more other partnerships, the amount by which the fair market value (determined without reference to liabilities) of the property exceeds its cost amount,

(B) in the case of a Canadian resource property or a foreign resource property held directly by the partnership or held indirectly by the partnership through one or more other partnerships, the fair market value (determined without reference to liabilities) of the property, or

(C) in the case of a property that is not a capital property, a Canadian resource property or a foreign resource property and that is held directly by the partnership or held indirectly through one or more other partnerships, the amount by which the fair market value (determined without reference to liabilities) of the property exceeds its cost amount, and

(iii) in no case shall the total of amounts so designated in respect of all such capital properties exceed the amount, if any, by which the total determined under subparagraph (*b*)(ii) exceeds the total of the amounts determined under subparagraphs (i) and (i.1),

History: S. 88(1)(*d*)(ii) was replaced by S.C. 2013, c. 40, s. 40(9), applicable to windings-up that begin, and amalgamations that occur, after December 20, 2012 other than — if a taxable Canadian corporation (in this application referred to as the "parent corporation") has acquired control of another taxable Canadian corporation (in this application referred to as the "subsidiary corporation") — an amalgamation of the parent corporation and the subsidiary corporation that occurs, or a winding-up of the subsidiary corporation into the parent corporation that begins, before July 2013 if

(*a*) the parent corporation acquired control of the subsidiary corporation before December 21, 2012, or was obligated as evidenced in writing before December 21, 2012 to acquire control of the subsidiary corporation (except that the parent corporation shall not be considered to be obligated if, as a result of amendments to the Act, it may be excused from the obligation to acquire control); and

(*b*) the parent corporation had the intention as evidenced in writing before December 21, 2012 to amalgamate with, or wind up, the subsidiary corporation. S. 88(1)(*d*)(ii) formerly read:

(ii) in no case shall the amount so designated in respect of any such capital property exceed the amount, if any, by which the fair market value of the property at the time the parent last acquired control of the subsidiary exceeds the total of

(A) the cost amount to the subsidiary of the property immediately before the winding-up, and

(B) the prescribed amount, and

S. 88(1)(*d*)(ii) was replaced by S.C. 2013, c. 34, s. 30(1), in respect of windings-up that begin, and amalgamations that occur, after February 27, 2004.

However, any assessment of a taxpayer's tax, interest and penalties payable under the Act for any taxation year that ends before June 26, 2013 that would, in the absence of this section, be precluded because of subsections 152(4) to (5) of the Act, shall be made to the extent necessary to take into account this amendment, if the taxpayer

(i) elects in writing in respect of all of its foreign affiliates that this section apply in respect of that provision, and

(ii) files that election with the Minister of National Revenue on or before December 26, 2013 [the day that is six months after royal assent].

S. 88(1)(*d*)(ii) formerly read:

(ii) in no case shall the amount so designated in respect of any such capital property exceed the amount, if any, by which the fair market value of the property at the time the parent last acquired control of the subsidiary exceeds the cost amount to the subsidiary of the property immediately before the winding-up,

S. 88(1)(*d*)(ii.1) was added by S.C. 2012, c. 31, s. 18(1), applicable to amalgamations that occur and windings-up that begin after March 28, 2012, other than — if a taxable Canadian corporation (in this subsection referred to as the "parent corporation") has acquired control of another taxable Canadian corporation (in this subsection referred to as the "subsidiary corporation") — an amalgamation of the parent corporation and the subsidiary corporation that occurs before 2013, or a winding-up of the subsidiary corporation into the parent corporation that begins before 2013, if

(a) the parent corporation acquired control of the subsidiary corporation before March 29, 2012 or was obligated as evidenced in writing before March 29, 2012 to acquire control of the subsidiary (except that the parent corporation shall not be considered to be obligated if, as a result of amendments to the Act, it may be excused from the obligation to acquire control); and

(b) the parent corporation had the intention as evidenced in writing before March 29, 2012 to amalgamate with, or wind up, the subsidiary corporation.

Canadian Tax Foundation: Carr and Colden, *The Bump Denial Rules Revisited*, 2014 Canadian Tax Journal 1:273–299; Smith, *Pipeline and Bump Planning*, 2014 British Columbia Tax Conference 7A:1–7; Stepak and Xiao, *The Paragraph 88(1)(d) Bump: An Update*, 2013 Conference Report 13:1–60; Oldewening et al., *An Update on Amendments Affecting Partnerships*, 2013 Ontario Tax Conference 3:1–23; Frydberg, *Top Technical Bill Issues for Owner-Managers*, 2013 Prairie Provinces Tax Conference 11:1–26; Yip, *Recent Legislation Affecting Partnerships and Foreign Affiliates — Subsection 88(1) and Section 100*, 2013 Canadian Tax Journal 1:229–256; Blanchet, *The Impact of the 2012 Budget on Transactions Involving Interests in Partnerships*, 2012 Conference Report 10:1–17; Truster, *The Windup*

Bump, 2006 Tax for the Owner-Manager 6(2):1–2; Barnett et al., *Post Mortem Planning for Private Company Shares: The New Regime*, 2002 Conference Report 32:1–86; Barnett et al., *Post Mortem Planning for Private Company Shares — The New Regime: Alternatives For Minimizing The Tax Exposure Arising On The Death Of The Owner Of Private Company Shares*, 2002 British Columbia Tax Conference 19:1–91.

Tax Profile: February 2012 — Post-Mortem Planning — Double Taxation on Death; October 2011 — Donations of Real Estate and Shares of Real Estate Companies.

Tax Topics: No. 2026, The Acquisition of Control Surplus/ACB Trade-Off in the August 27, 2010 Foreign Affiliate Proposals.

Cases: The transactions involved rolling three real estate properties through a tiered partnership structure, increasing the adjusted cost base of the partnership interests. Those interests were then sold to tax-exempt entities without tax being paid on the latent recapture and accrued gains in the property held by the partnerships. The elimination of the capital gain on the sale of the partnership interests to exempt entities by the use of "bumps" under sections 88 and 98, and the consequential avoidance of recapture under section 100, frustrated those provisions and were abusive. *The Queen v. Oxford Properties*, 2018 DTC 5017 (FCA)

▶ 88(1)(d.1) ◀

(d.1) [Winding-up — Provisions not applicable] — subsection 84(2) and section 21 of the *Income Tax Application Rules* do not apply to the winding-up of the subsidiary, and subsection 13(21.2) does not apply to the winding-up of the subsidiary with respect to property acquired by the parent on the winding-up;

History: S. 88(1)(*d*.1) was replaced by S.C. 2016, c. 12, s. 28(2), in force January 1, 2017, and formerly read:

(*d*.1) *[Winding-up — Provisions not applicable]* — subsection 84(2) and section 21 of the *Income Tax Application Rules* do not apply to the winding-up of the subsidiary, and subsections 13(21.2) and 14(12) do not apply to the winding-up of the subsidiary with respect to property acquired by the parent on the winding-up;

Tax Topics: No. 2104, Pipeline Planning Alive and Well After All?.

▶ 88(1)(d.2) ◀

(d.2) [Winding-up — Timing of acquisition of control] — in determining, for the purposes of this paragraph and paragraphs (*c*) and (*d*), the time at which a person or group of persons (in this paragraph and paragraph (*d*.3) referred to as the "acquirer") last acquired control of the subsidiary, where control of the subsidiary was acquired from another person or group of persons (in this paragraph referred to as the "vendor") with whom the acquirer was not (otherwise than solely because of a right referred to in paragraph 251(5)(*b*)) dealing at arm's length, the acquirer is deemed to have last acquired control of the subsidiary at the earlier of

(i) the time at which the vendor last acquired control (within the meaning that would be assigned by subsection 186(2) if the reference in that subsection to "another corporation" were read as "a person" and the references in that subsection to "the other corporation" were read as "the person") of the subsidiary, and

(ii) the time at which the vendor was deemed for the purpose of this paragraph to have last acquired control of the subsidiary;

▶ 88(1)(d.3) ◀

(d.3) [Winding-up — Control acquired as consequence of death] — for the purposes of paragraphs (*c*), (*d*) and (*d*.2), where at any time control of a corporation is last acquired by an acquirer because of an acquisition of shares of the capital stock of the corporation as a consequence of the death of an individual, the acquirer is deemed to have last acquired control of the corporation immediately after the death from a person who dealt at arm's length with the acquirer;

▶ 88(1)(e) ◀

(e) [Winding-up — Fair market value of interest in partnership] — for the purposes of the description of A in subparagraph (d)(ii.1), the fair market value of an interest in a particular partnership held by the subsidiary at the time the parent last acquired control of the subsidiary is deemed not to include the amount that is the total of each amount that is the fair market value of a property that would otherwise be included in the fair market value of the interest, if

(i) as part of the transaction or event or series of transactions or events in which control of the subsidiary is last acquired by the parent and on or before the acquisition of control,

(A) the subsidiary disposes of the property to the particular partnership or any other partnership and subsection 97(2) applies to the disposition, or

(B) where the property is an interest in a partnership, the subsidiary acquires the interest in the particular partnership or any other partnership from a person or partnership with whom the subsidiary does not deal at arm's length (otherwise than because of a right referred to in paragraph 251(5)(*b*)) and section 85 applies in respect of the acquisition of the interest, and

(ii) at the time of the acquisition of control, the particular partnership holds directly, or indirectly through one or more other partnerships, property described in clauses (A) to (C) of the description of B in subparagraph (*d*)(ii.1);

History: S. 88(1)(*e*) was added by S.C. 2012, c. 31, s. 18(2), applicable to dispositions made after August 13, 2012 other than a disposition made before 2013 pursuant to an obligation under a written agreement entered into before August 14, 2012 by parties that deal with each other at arm's length. The parties shall not be considered to be obligated if any party may be excused from the obligation as a result of amendments to the Act.

▶ 88(1)(e.1) ◀

(e.1) [Winding-up — Reserves for subsidiary] — the subsidiary may, for the purposes of computing its income for its taxation year during which its assets were transferred to, and its obligations were assumed by, the parent on the winding-up, claim any reserve that would have been allowed under this Part if its assets had not been transferred to, or its obligations had not been assumed by, the parent on the winding-up and notwithstanding any other provision of this Part, no amount shall be included in respect of any reserve so claimed in computing the income of the subsidiary for its taxation year, if any, following the year in which its assets were transferred to or its obligations were assumed by the parent;

► 88(1)(e.2) ◄

(e.2) [Winding-up — Application of amalgamation provisions] — paragraphs 87(2)(*c*), (*d*.1), (*e*.1), (*e*.3), (*e*.42), (*g*) to (*l*), (*l*.21) to (*u*), (*x*), (*z*.1), (*z*.2), (*aa*), (*cc*), (*ll*), (*nn*), (*pp*), (*rr*) and (*tt*) to (*ww*), subsection 87(6) and, subject to section 78, subsection 87(7) apply to the winding-up as if the references in those provisions to

(i) "amalgamation" were read as "winding-up",

(ii) "predecessor corporation" were read as "subsidiary",

(iii) "new corporation" were read as "parent",

(iv) "its first taxation year" were read as "its taxation year during which it received the assets of the subsidiary on the winding-up",

(v) "its last taxation year" were read as "its taxation year during which its assets were distributed to the parent on the winding-up",

(vi) "predecessor corporation's gain" were read as "subsidiary's gain",

(vii) "predecessor corporation's income" were read as "subsidiary's income",

(viii) "new corporation's income" were read as "parent's income",

(ix) "subsection 89(5)" and "subsection 89(9)" were read as "subsection 89(6)" and "subsection 89(10)", respectively,

(x) "any predecessor private corporation" were read as "the subsidiary (if it was a private corporation at the time of the winding-up)",

(xi) (Repealed by 1994, c. 7, Sched. II, S. 66(8).)

(xii) (Repealed by 1994, c. 7, Sched. II, S. 66(8).)

(xiii) "two or more corporations" were read as "a subsidiary",

(xiv) (Repealed by 1998, c. 19, S. 118(11).)

(xv) (Repealed by 1998, c. 19, S. 118(11).)

(xvi) "the life insurance capital dividend account of any predecessor corporation immediately before the amalgamation" were read as "the life insurance capital dividend account of the subsidiary at the time the subsidiary was wound-up",

(xvii) "predecessor corporation's refundable Part VII tax on hand" were read as "subsidiary's refundable Part VII tax on hand",

(xviii) "predecessor corporation's Part VII refund" were read as "subsidiary's Part VII refund",

(xix) "predecessor corporation's refundable Part VIII tax on hand" were read as "subsidiary's refundable Part VIII tax on hand",

(xx) "predecessor corporation's Part VIII refund" were read as "subsidiary's Part VIII refund", and

(xxi) "predecessor corporation's cumulative offset account" were read as "subsidiary's cumulative offset account";

History: S. 88(1)(*e*.2), the portion before subparagraph (i) was replaced by S.C. 2017, c. 33, s. 25(2), applicable to taxation years that begin after March 21, 2017, and formerly read:

(*e*.2) *[Winding-up — Application of amalgamation provisions]* — paragraphs 87(2)(*c*), (*d*.1), (*e*.1), (*e*.3), (*g*) to (*l*), (*l*.21) to (*u*), (*x*), (*z*.1), (*z*.2), (*aa*), (*cc*), (*ll*), (*nn*), (*pp*), (*rr*) and (*tt*) to (*ww*), subsection 87(6) and, subject to section 78, subsection 87(7) apply to the winding-up as if the references in those provisions to

S. 88(1)(*e*.2), the portion before subparagraph (i) was replaced by S.C. 2017, c. 33, s. 25(1), applicable to taxation years that end after 2001, and formerly read:

(*e*.2) *[Winding-up — Application of amalgamation provisions]* — paragraphs 87(2)(*c*), (*d*.1), (*e*.1), (*e*.3), (*g*) to (*l*), (*l*.3) to (*u*), (*x*), (*z*.1), (*z*.2), (*aa*), (*cc*), (*ll*), (*nn*), (*pp*), (*rr*) and (*tt*) to (*ww*), subsection 87(6) and, subject to section 78, subsection 87(7) apply to the winding-up as if the references in those provisions to

Related Sections: 87(2)(e.42) [Continuation of predecessor corporation — eligible derivative]; 87(2)(l.21) Forgiven amount.

► 88(1)(e.3) ◄

(e.3) [Winding-up — Investment tax credit] — for the purpose of computing the parent's investment tax credit at the end of any particular taxation year ending after the subsidiary was wound up,

(i) property acquired or expenditures made by the subsidiary or an amount included in the investment tax credit of the subsidiary by virtue of paragraph (*b*) of the definition "investment tax credit" in subsection 127(9) in a taxation year (in this paragraph referred to as the "expenditure year") shall be deemed to have been acquired, made or included, as the case may be, by the parent in its taxation year in which the expenditure year of the subsidiary ended, and

(ii) there shall be added to the amounts otherwise determined for the purposes of paragraphs (*f*) to (*k*) of the definition "investment tax credit" in subsection 127(9) in respect of the parent for the particular year

(A) the amounts that would have been determined in respect of the subsidiary for the purposes of paragraph (*f*) of the definition "investment tax credit" in subsection 127(9) for its taxation year in which it was wound up if the reference therein to "a preceding taxation year" were read as a reference to "the year or a preceding taxation year",

(B) the amounts determined in respect of the subsidiary for the purposes of paragraphs (*g*) to (*i*) and (*k*) of the definition "investment tax credit" in subsection 127(9) for its taxation year in which it was wound up, and

(C) the amount determined in respect of the subsidiary for the purposes of paragraph (*j*) of the definition "investment tax credit" in subsection 127(9) for its taxation year in which it was wound up except that, for the purpose of the calculation in this clause, where control of the subsidiary has been acquired by a person or group of persons (each of whom is referred to in this clause as the "purchaser") at any time (in this clause referred to as "that time") before the end of the taxation year in which the subsidiary was wound up, there may be added to the amount determined under subparagraph 127(9.1)(*d*)(i) in respect of the subsidiary the amount, if any, by which that proportion of the amount that, but for subsections 127(3) and (5) and sections 126, 127.2 and 127.3, would be the parent's tax payable under this Part for the particular year, that,

(I) where the subsidiary carried on a particular business in the course of which a property was acquired, or an expenditure was made, before that time in respect of which an amount was included in computing the subsidiary's investment tax credit for its taxation year in which it was wound up, and the parent carried on the particular business throughout the particular year, the amount, if any, by which the total of all amounts each of which is the parent's income for the particular year from the particular business, or the parent's income for the particular year from any other business substantially all the income of which was derived from the sale, leasing, rental or development of properties or the rendering of services similar to the properties sold, leased, rented or developed, or the services rendered, as the case may be, by the subsidiary in carrying on the particular business before that time, exceeds the total of the amounts, if any, deducted for the particular year under paragraph 111(1)(*a*) or (*d*) by the parent in respect of a non-capital loss or a farm loss, as the case may be, for a taxation year in respect of the particular business

is of the greater of

(II) the amount determined under subclause (I), and

(III) the parent's taxable income for the particular year

exceeds the amount, if any, calculated under subparagraph 127(9.1)(*d*)(i) in respect of the particular business or the other business, as the case may be, in respect of the parent at the end of the particular year

to the extent that those amounts determined in respect of the subsidiary may reasonably be considered to have been included in computing the parent's investment tax credit at the end of the particular year by virtue of subparagraph (i);

and, for the purposes of the definitions "first term shared-use-equipment" and "second term shared-use-equipment" in subsection 127(9), the parent shall be deemed to be the same corporation as, and a continuation of, the subsidiary;

▶ 88(1)(e.4) ◀

(e.4) [Winding-up — Employment tax credit] — for the purpose of computing the parent's employment tax credit at the end of any particular taxation year ending after the subsidiary was wound up,

(i) the subsidiary's taxpayer employment credits for any taxation year (in this paragraph referred to as the "employment year") and any amounts required to be added by virtue of subsection 127(15) of the *Income Tax Act*, chapter 148 of the Revised Statutes of Canada, 1952, in computing the subsidiary's employment tax credit at the end of the employment year shall be deemed to be taxpayer employment credits of the parent for, and amounts required to be added by virtue of that subsection in computing the parent's employment tax credit at the end of, its taxation year in which the employment year of the subsidiary ended, and

(ii) there shall be added to the amounts otherwise determined under paragraphs 127(16)(*c*) and (*d*) of the *Income Tax Act*, chapter 148 of the Revised Statutes of Canada, 1952, in respect of the parent for the particular taxation year, the amounts that would have been determined under those paragraphs in respect of the subsidiary for its taxation year in which it was wound-up if the reference in paragraph 127(16)(*c*) of that Act to "the five immediately preceding taxation years" were read as a reference to "that taxation year or the five immediately preceding taxation years" to the extent that those amounts determined in respect of the subsidiary may reasonably be considered to be in respect of a taxpayer employment credit or an amount required to be added by virtue of subsection 127(15) of that Act that is included in computing the parent's employment tax credit at the end of the particular year by virtue of subparagraph (i);

▶ 88(1)(e.5) ◀

(e.5) [Winding-up — Refundable dividend tax on hand] — (Repealed by S.C. 1996, c. 21, s. 16(2).)

▶ 88(1)(e.6) ◀

(e.6) [Winding-up — Charitable gifts] — if a subsidiary has made a gift in a taxation year (in this section referred to as the "gift year"), for the purposes of computing the amount deductible under section 110.1 by the parent for its taxation years that end after the subsidiary was wound up, the parent is deemed to have made a gift, in each of its taxation years in which a gift year of the subsidiary ended, equal to the amount, if any, by which the total of all amounts, each of which is the amount of a gift or, in the case of a gift made after December 20, 2002, the eligible amount of the gift, made by the subsidiary in the gift year exceeds the total of all amounts deducted under section 110.1 by the subsidiary in respect of those gifts;

History: S. 88(1)(*e.6*) was replaced by S.C. 2013, c. 34, s. 224(4), applicable to windings-up that begin, and amalgamations that occur, after December 20, 2002, and formerly read:

(*e.6*) *[Winding-up — Charitable gifts]* — where a subsidiary has made a gift in a taxation year (in this section referred to as the "gift year"), for the purposes of computing the amount deductible under section 110.1 by the parent for its taxation years ending after the subsidiary was wound up, the parent shall be deemed to have made a gift in each of its taxation years in which a gift year of the subsidiary ended equal to the amount, if any, by which the total of all gifts made by the subsidiary in the gift year exceeds the total of all amounts deducted by the subsidiary under section 110.1 of this Act or paragraph 110(1)(*a*), (*b*) or (*b.1*) of the *Income Tax Act*, chapter 148 of the Revised Statutes of Canada, 1952, in respect of those gifts;

► 88(1)(e.61) ◄

(e.61) [Winding-up — Donation of non-qualifying securities] — the parent is deemed for the purpose of section 110.1 to have made any gift deemed by subsection 118.1(13) to have been made by the subsidiary after the subsidiary ceased to exist;

► 88(1)(e.7) ◄

(e.7) [Winding-up — Unused foreign tax credits of subsidiary] — for the purposes of

(i) determining the amount deductible by the parent under subsection 126(2) for any taxation year commencing after the commencement of the winding-up, and

(ii) determining the extent to which subsection 126(2.3) applies to reduce the amount that may be claimed by the parent under paragraph 126(2)(*a*),

any unused foreign tax credit (within the meaning of subsection 126(7)) of the subsidiary in respect of a country for a particular taxation year (in this section referred to as the "foreign tax year"), to the extent that it exceeds the total of all amounts each of which is claimed in respect thereof under paragraph 126(2)(*a*) in computing the tax payable by the subsidiary under this Part for any taxation year, shall be deemed to be an unused foreign tax credit of the parent for its taxation year in which the subsidiary's foreign tax year ended;

► 88(1)(e.8) ◄

(e.8) [Winding-up — Expenditure limit of parent or associated corporation] — (Repealed by 2019, c. 29, S. 12(1).)

History: S. 88(1)(e.8) was repealed by S.C. 2019, c. 29, s. 12(1), applicable to taxation years that end after March 18, 2019. S. 88(1)(e.8) formerly read:

(e.8) *[Winding-up — Expenditure limit of parent or associated corporation]* — for the purpose of applying subsection 127(10.2) to any corporation (other than the subsidiary)

(i) where the parent is associated with another corporation in a taxation year (in this paragraph referred to as the "current year") of the parent that begins after the parent received an asset of the subsidiary on the winding-up and that ends in a calendar year,

(A) the parent's taxable income for its last taxation year that ended in the preceding calendar year (determined before taking into consideration the specified future tax consequences for that last year) is deemed to be the total of

(I) its taxable income for that last year (determined before applying this paragraph to the winding-up and before taking into consideration the specified future tax consequences for that last year), and

(II) the total of the subsidiary's taxable incomes for its taxation years that ended in that preceding calendar year (determined without reference to clause (B) and before taking into consideration the specified future tax consequences for those years), and

(B) the subsidiary's taxable income for each of its taxation years that ends after the first time that the parent receives an asset of the subsidiary on the winding-up of the subsidiary is deemed to be nil, and

(ii) where the parent received an asset of the subsidiary on the winding-up before the current year and is not associated with any corporation in the current year, the parent's taxable income for its immediately preceding taxation year (determined before taking into consideration the specified future tax consequences for that preceding year) is deemed to be the total of

(A) its taxable income for that preceding taxation year (determined before applying this paragraph to the winding-up and before taking into consideration the specified future tax consequences for that preceding taxation year), and

(B) the total of the subsidiary's taxable incomes for its taxation years that ended in the calendar year in which that preceding taxation year ended (determined before taking into consideration the specified future tax consequences for those years);

► 88(1)(e.9) ◄

(e.9) [Winding-up — Business limit and balance-due day of parent] — for the purpose of applying the definition "qualifying corporation" in subsection 127.1(2), and subparagraph (*d*)(i) of the definition "balance-due day" in subsection 248(1), to any corporation (other than the subsidiary)

(i) where the parent is associated with another corporation in a taxation year (in this paragraph referred to as the "current year") of the parent that begins after the parent received an asset of the subsidiary on the winding-up and ends in a calendar year,

(A) the parent's taxable income for its last taxation year that ended in the preceding calendar year (determined before taking into consideration the specified future tax consequences for that last year) is deemed to be the total of

(I) its taxable income for that last year (determined before applying this paragraph to the winding-up and before taking into consideration the specified future tax consequences for that last year), and

(II) the total of the subsidiary's taxable incomes for its taxation years that ended in that preceding calendar year (determined without reference to subparagraph (iii) and before taking into consideration the specified future tax consequences for those years),

(B) the parent's business limit for that last year is deemed to be the total of

(I) its business limit (determined before applying this paragraph to the winding-up) for that last year, and

(II) the total of the subsidiary's business limits (determined without reference to subparagraph (iii)) for its taxation years that ended in that preceding calendar year, and

(C) the parent's qualifying income limit for that last year is deemed to be the total of

(I) its qualifying income limit (determined before applying this paragraph to the winding-up) for that last year, and

(II) the total of the subsidiary's qualifying income limits (determined without reference to subparagraph (iii)) for its taxation years that ended in that preceding calendar year,

(ii) where the parent received an asset of the subsidiary on the winding-up before the current year and subparagraph (i) does not apply,

(A) the parent's taxable income for its immediately preceding taxation year (determined before taking into consideration the specified future tax consequences for that preceding year) is deemed to be the total of

(I) its taxable income for that preceding taxation year (determined before applying this paragraph to the winding-up and before taking into consideration the specified future tax consequences for that preceding taxation year), and

(II) the total of the subsidiary's taxable incomes for the subsidiary's taxation years that end in the calendar year in which that preceding taxation year ended (determined before taking into consideration the specified future tax consequences for those years),

(B) the parent's business limit for that preceding taxation year is deemed to be the total of

(I) its business limit (determined before applying this paragraph to the winding-up) for that preceding taxation year, and

(II) the total of the subsidiary's business limits (determined without reference to subparagraph (iii)) for the subsidiary's taxation years that end in the calendar year in which that preceding taxation year ended, and

(C) the parent's qualifying income limit for that preceding taxation year is deemed to be the total of

(I) its qualifying income limit (determined before applying this paragraph to the winding-up) for that preceding taxation year, and

(II) the total of the subsidiary's qualifying income limits (determined without reference to subparagraph (iii)) for the subsidiary's taxation years that end in the calendar year in which that preceding taxation year ended, and

(iii) where the parent and the subsidiary are associated with each other in the current year, the subsidiary's taxable income, the subsidiary's business limit and the subsidiary's qualifying income limit for each taxation year that ends after the first time that the parent receives an asset of the subsidiary on the winding-up are deemed to be nil;

History: S. 88(1)(*e.9*)(i)(C) was added by S.C. 2013, c. 40, s. 40(10), applicable to windings-up that begin after February 25, 2008.

S. 88(1)(*e.9*)(ii)(C) was added by S.C. 2013, c. 40, s. 40(11), applicable to windings-up that begin after February 25, 2008.

S. 88(1)(*e.9*)(iii) was replaced by S.C. 2013, c. 40, s. 40(12), applicable to windings-up that begin after February 25, 2008, and formerly read:

(iii) where the parent and the subsidiary are associated with each other in the current year, the subsidiary's taxable income and the subsidiary's business limit for each taxation year that ends after the first time that the parent receives an asset of the subsidiary on the winding-up are deemed to be nil;

▶ 88(1)(f) ◀

(f) [Winding-up — Depreciable property] — where property that was depreciable property of a prescribed class of the subsidiary has been distributed to the parent on the winding-up and the capital cost to the subsidiary of the property exceeds the amount deemed by paragraph (*a*) to be the subsidiary's proceeds of disposition of the property, for the purposes of sections 13 and 20 and any regulations made under paragraph 20(1)(*a*),

(i) notwithstanding paragraph (*c*), the capital cost to the parent of the property shall be deemed to be the amount that was the capital cost of the property to the subsidiary, and

(ii) the excess shall be deemed to have been allowed to the parent in respect of the property under regulations made under paragraph 20(1)(*a*) in computing income for taxation years before the acquisition by the parent of the property;

▶ 88(1)(g) ◀

(g) [Winding-up — Insurance corporations] — where the subsidiary was an insurance corporation,

(i) for the purposes of paragraphs 12(1)(*d*), (*e*), (*e.1*), (*i*) and (*s*), subsection 12.5(8), paragraphs 20(1)(*l*), (*l.1*), (*p*) and (*jj*) and 20(7)(*c*), subsections 20(22) and 20.4(4), sections 138, 138.1, 140, 142 and 148 and Part XII.3, the parent is deemed to be the same corporation as, and a continuation of, the subsidiary, and

(ii) for the purpose of determining the amount of the gross investment revenue required to be included under subsection 138(9) in the income of the subsidiary and the parent and the amount of gains and losses of the subsidiary and the parent from property used by them in the year or held by them in the year in the course of carrying on an insurance business in Canada

(A) the subsidiary and the parent shall, in addition to their normal taxation years, be deemed to have had a taxation year ending immediately before the time when the property of the subsidiary was transferred to, and the obligations of the subsidiary were assumed by, the parent on the winding-up, and

(B) for the taxation years of the subsidiary and the parent following the time referred to in clause (A), the property transferred to, and the obligations assumed by, the parent on the winding-up shall be deemed to have been transferred or assumed, as the case may be, on the last day of the taxation year ending immediately before that time and the parent shall be deemed to be the same corporation as and a continuation of the subsidiary with respect to that property, those obligations and the insurance businesses carried on by the subsidiary;

History: S. 88(1)(*g*)(i) was replaced by S.C. 2009, c. 2, s. 20(1), applicable to taxation years that begin after September 2006. S. 88(1)(*g*)(i) formerly read:

(i) for the purposes of paragraphs 12(1)(*d*), (*e*), (*e.1*), (*i*) and (*s*) and 20(1)(*l*), (*l.1*), (*p*) and (*jj*) and 20(7)(*c*), subsection 20(22), sections 138, 138.1, 140, 142 and 148 and Part XII.3, the parent is deemed to be the same corporation as, and a continuation of, the subsidiary, and

Related Sections: S. 12.5(8) Ceasing to carry on business; s. 138(9) Computation on income; s. 248(1), "insurance corporations".

▶ 88(1)(h) ◀

(h) [Winding-up — Stop-loss rules and mark-to-market property] — for the purposes of subsections 112(5) to (5.2) and (5.4) and the definition "mark-to-market property" in subsection 142.2(1), the parent shall be deemed, in respect of each property distributed to it on the winding-up, to be the same corporation as, and a continuation of, the subsidiary;

▶ 88(1)(i) ◀

(i) [Winding-up — Mark-to-market property] — for the purpose of subsection 142.5(2), the subsidiary's taxation year in which its assets were distributed to the parent on the winding-up shall be deemed to have ended immediately before the time when the assets were distributed; and

▶ 88(1)(j) ◀

(j) [Winding-up — eligible derivative] — for the purposes of subsection 10.1(6), the subsidiary's taxation year in which an *eligible derivative* (as defined in subsection 10.1(5)) was distributed to, or assumed by, the parent on the winding-up is deemed to have ended immediately before the time when the eligible derivative was distributed or assumed.

History: S. 88(1)(*j*) was added by S.C. 2017, c. 33, s. 25(3), applicable to taxation years that begin after March 21, 2017.

▶ 88(1.1) ◀

(1.1) Non-capital losses, etc., of subsidiary. Where a Canadian corporation (in this subsection referred to as the "subsidiary") has been wound up and not less than 90% of the issued shares of each class of the capital stock of the subsidiary were, immediately before the winding-up, owned by another Canadian corporation (in this subsection referred to as the "parent") and all the shares of the subsidiary that were not owned by the parent immediately before the winding-up were owned at that time by a person or persons with whom the parent was dealing at arm's length, for the purpose of computing the taxable income of the parent under this Part and the tax payable under Part IV by the parent for any taxation year commencing after the commencement of the winding-up, such portion of any non-capital loss, restricted farm loss, farm loss or limited partnership loss of the subsidiary as may reasonably be regarded as its loss from carrying on a particular business (in this subsection referred to as the "subsidiary's loss business") and any other portion of any non-capital loss or limited partnership loss of the subsidiary as may reasonably be regarded as being derived from any other source or being in respect of a claim made under section 110.5 for any particular taxation year of the subsidiary (in this subsection referred to as the "subsidiary's loss year"), to the extent that it

(*a*) was not deducted in computing the taxable income of the subsidiary for any taxation year of the subsidiary, and

(*b*) would have been deductible in computing the taxable income of the subsidiary for any taxation year beginning after the commencement of the winding-up, on the assumption that it had such a taxation year and that it had sufficient income for that year,

shall, for the purposes of this subsection, paragraphs 111(1)(*a*), (*c*), (*d*) and (*e*), subsection 111(3) and Part IV,

(*c*) in the case of such portion of any non-capital loss, restricted farm loss, farm loss or limited partnership loss of the subsidiary as may reasonably be regarded as its loss from carrying on the subsidiary's loss business, be deemed, for the taxation year of the parent in which the subsidiary's loss year ended, to be a non-capital loss, restricted farm loss, farm loss or limited partnership loss, respectively, of the parent from carrying on the subsidiary's loss business, that was not deductible by the parent in computing its taxable income for any taxation year that commenced before the commencement of the winding-up,

(*d*) in the case of any other portion of any non-capital loss or limited partnership loss of the subsidiary as may reasonably be regarded as being derived from any other source, be deemed, for the taxation year of the parent in which the subsidiary's loss year ended, to be a non-capital loss or a limited partnership loss, respectively, of the parent that was derived from the source from which the subsidiary derived the loss and that was not deductible by the parent in computing its taxable income for any taxation year that commenced before the commencement of the winding-up, and

(*d*.1) in the case of any other portion of any non-capital loss of the subsidiary as may reasonably be regarded as being in respect of a claim made under section 110.5, be deemed, for the taxation year of the parent in which the subsidiary's loss year ended, to be a non-capital loss of the parent in respect of a claim made under section 110.5 that was not deductible by the parent in computing its taxable income for any taxation year that commenced before the commencement of the winding-up,

except that

(*e*) if control of the parent has been acquired by a person or group of persons at any time after the commencement of the winding-up, or control of the subsidiary has been acquired by a person or group of persons at any time whatever, no amount in respect of the subsidiary's non-capital loss or farm loss for a taxation year ending before that time is deductible in computing the taxable income of the parent for a particular taxation year ending after that time, except that such portion of the subsidiary's non-capital loss or farm loss as may reasonably be regarded as its loss from carrying on a business and, where a business was carried on by the subsidiary in that year, such portion of the non-capital loss as may reasonably be regarded as being in respect of an amount deductible under paragraph 110(1)(*k*) in computing its taxable income for the year is deductible only

(i) if that business is carried on by the subsidiary or the parent for profit or with a reasonable expectation of profit throughout the particular year, and

(ii) to the extent of the total of the parent's income for the particular year from that business and, where properties were sold, leased, rented or developed or services rendered in the course of carrying on that business before that time, from any other business substantially all of the income of which was derived from the sale, leasing, rental or development, as the case may be, of similar properties or the rendering of similar services

and, for the purpose of this paragraph, where this subsection applied to the winding-up of another corporation in respect of which the subsidiary was the parent and this paragraph applied in respect of losses of that other corporation, the subsidiary shall be deemed to be the same corporation as, and a continuation of, that other corporation with respect to those losses, and

(*f*) any portion of a loss of the subsidiary that would otherwise be deemed by paragraph (*c*), (*d*) or (*d*.1) to be a loss of the parent for a particular taxation year beginning after the commencement of the winding-up shall be deemed, for the purpose of computing the parent's taxable income for taxation years beginning after the commencement of the winding-up, to be such a loss of the parent for its immediately preceding taxation year and not for the particular year, where the parent so elects in its return of income under this Part for the particular year.

History: S. 88(1.1)(*e*), the portion before subparagraph (i) was replaced by S.C. 2013, c. 34, s. 224(5), applicable to windings-up that begin after May 1996, and formerly read:

(*e*) where at any time control of the parent or subsidiary has been acquired by a person or group of persons, no amount in respect of the subsidiary's non-capital loss or farm loss for a taxation year ending before that time is deductible in computing the taxable income of the parent for a particular taxation year ending after that time, except that such portion of the subsidiary's non-capital loss or farm loss as may reasonably be regarded as its loss from carrying on a business and, where a business was carried on by the subsidiary in that year, such portion of the non-capital loss as may reasonably be regarded as being in respect of an amount deductible under paragraph 110(1)(*k*) in computing its taxable income for the year is deductible only

Related Sections: S. 10(11) Loss restriction event; s. 88(1.3) Computation of income and tax of parent; s. 256(7) Acquiring control; s. 256.1 [Corporate tax-attribute trading].

Tax Topics: No. 2033, Deduction of Losses by Non-Resident — *Saipem UK Limited v. The Queen.*

Interpretation Bulletins: *Primary* — IT-302R3 Losses of a corporation — The effect on their deductibility of changes in control, amalgamation and winding-up. *Secondary* — IT-232R3 Non-capital losses, net capital losses, restricted farm losses, farm losses and limited partnership losses — Their composition and deductibility in computing taxable income.

Tax Window Files: Utilization of Non-Capital Losses — Amalgamation or Winding-Up, *Technical Interpretation, Reorganizations and Resources Division, February 2, 2006*, CRA Document No. 2005-0152431E5; Carry-forward of Losses — Wind-up of Subsidiary, *Technical Interpretation, Reorganizations and Resources Division, January 10, 2006*, CRA Document No. 2005-0144591E5; Non-Capital Losses of Subsidiary, *Technical Interpretation, Reorganizations and Resources Division, November 1, 2004*, CRA Document No. 2004-0064951E5.

▶ 88(1.2) ◀

(1.2) Net capital losses of subsidiary. Where the winding-up of a Canadian corporation (in this subsection referred to as the "subsidiary") commenced after March 31, 1977 and not less than 90% of the issued shares of each class of the capital stock of the subsidiary were, immediately before the winding-up, owned by another Canadian corporation (in this subsection referred to as the "parent") and all the shares of the subsidiary that were not owned by the parent immediately before the winding-up were owned at that time by persons with whom the parent was dealing at arm's length, for the purposes of computing the taxable income of the parent for any taxation year commencing after the commencement of the winding-up, any net capital loss of the subsidiary for any particular taxation year of the subsidiary (in this subsection referred to as the "subsidiary's loss year"), to the extent that it

(*a*) was not deducted in computing the taxable income of the subsidiary for any taxation year of the subsidiary, and

(*b*) would have been deductible in computing the taxable income of the subsidiary for any taxation year beginning after the commencement of the winding-up, on the assumption that it had such a taxation year and that it had sufficient income and taxable capital gains for that year,

shall, for the purposes of this subsection, paragraph 111(1)(*b*) and subsection 111(3), be deemed to be a net capital loss of the parent for its taxation year in which the particular taxation year of the subsidiary ended, except that

(*c*) where at any time control of the parent or subsidiary has been acquired by a person or group of persons, no amount in respect of the subsidiary's net capital loss for a taxation year ending before that time is deductible in computing the parent's taxable income for a taxation year ending after that time, and

(*d*) any portion of a net capital loss of the subsidiary that would otherwise be deemed by this subsection to be a loss of the parent for a particular taxation year beginning after the commencement of the winding-up shall be deemed, for the purposes of computing its taxable income for taxation years beginning after the commencement of the winding-up, to be a net capital loss of the parent for its immediately preceding taxation year and not for the particular year, where the parent so elects in its return of income under this Part for the particular year.

Related Sections: S. 88(1.3) Computation of income and tax of parent; s. 111(1)(*b*) Net capital losses; s. 256(7) Acquiring control; s. 256.1 [Corporate tax-attribute trading].

Interpretation Bulletins: *Primary* — IT-302R3 Losses of a corporation — The effect on their deductibility of changes in control, amalgamation and winding-up. *Secondary* — IT-232R3 Non-capital losses, net capital losses, restricted farm losses, farm losses and limited partnership losses — Their composition and deductibility in computing taxable income.

Tax Window Files: Subsections 88(1.1) and 88(1.2), *February 17, 2016*, CRA Document No. 2015-0618211E5.

▶ 88(1.3) ◀

(1.3) Computation of income and tax of parent. For the purpose of paragraphs (1)(*e*.3), (*e*.6) and (*e*.7), subsections (1.1) and (1.2), section 110.1, subsections 111(1) and (3) and Part IV, where a parent corporation has been incorporated or otherwise formed after the end of an expenditure year, gift year, foreign tax year or loss year, as the case may be, of a subsidiary of the parent, for the purpose of computing the taxable income of, and the tax payable under this Part and Part IV by, the parent for any taxation year,

(*a*) it shall be deemed to have been in existence during the particular period beginning immediately before the end of the subsidiary's first expenditure year, gift year, foreign tax year or loss year, as the case may be, and ending immediately after it was incorporated or otherwise formed;

(*b*) it shall be deemed to have had, throughout the particular period, fiscal periods ending on the day of the year on which its first fiscal period ended; and (*c*) it shall be deemed to have been controlled, throughout the particular period, by the person or persons who controlled it immediately after it was incorporated or otherwise formed.

Related Sections: S. 88(1.1) Non-capital losses, etc., of subsidiary; s. 88(1.2) Net capital losses of subsidiary; s. 111(1)(*b*) Net capital losses.

▶ 88(1.4) ◀

(1.4) Qualified expenditure of subsidiary. For the purposes of this subsection and section 37.1, where the rules in subsection (1) applied to the winding-up of a subsidiary, for the purpose of computing the income of its parent for any taxation year commencing after the subsidiary has been wound up, the following rules apply:

(*a*) where the parent's base period consists of fewer than three taxation years, its base period shall be determined on the assumption that it had taxation years in each of the calendar years preceding the year in which it was incorporated, each of which commenced on the same day of the year as the day of its incorporation;

(*b*) the qualified expenditure made by the parent in a particular taxation year in its base period shall be deemed to be the total of the amount thereof otherwise determined and the qualified expenditure made by the subsidiary in its taxation year ending in the same calendar year as the particular year;

(*c*) the total of the amounts paid to the parent by persons referred to in subparagraphs (*b*)(i) to (iii) of the definition "expenditure base" in subsection 37.1(5) in a particular taxation year in its base period shall be deemed to be the total otherwise determined and all those amounts paid to the subsidiary by a person referred to in those subparagraphs in the subsidiary's taxation year ending in the same calendar year as the particular year; and

(*d*) there shall be added to the total of the amounts otherwise determined in respect of the parent under subparagraphs 37.1(3)(*b*)(i) and (iii) respectively, the total of the amounts determined under those subparagraphs in respect of the subsidiary.

▶ 88(1.41) ◀

(1.41) Application of s. 37.1(5). The definitions in subsection 37.1(5) apply to subsection (1.4).

▶ 88(1.5) ◀

(1.5) Parent continuation of subsidiary. For the purposes of section 29 of the *Income Tax Application Rules*, subsection 59(3.3) and sections 66, 66.1, 66.2, 66.21, 66.4 and 66.7, where the rules in subsection (1) applied to the winding-up of a subsidiary, its parent is deemed to be the same corporation as, and a continuation of, the subsidiary.

Related Regulations: 1214(1).

Interpretation Bulletins: *Secondary* — IT-125R4 Disposition of resource properties.

▶ 88(1.6) ◀

(1.6) Idem. Where a corporation that carries on a farming business and computes its income from that business in accordance with the cash method is wound up in circumstances to which subsection (1) applies and, at the time that is immediately before the winding-up of the corporation, owned inventory that was used in connection with that business,

(*a*) for the purposes of subparagraph (1)(*a*)(iii), the cost amount to the corporation at that time of property purchased by it that is included in that inventory shall be deemed to be the amount determined by the formula

$$(A \times B/C) + D$$

where

A is the amount, if any, that would be included under paragraph 28(1)(*c*) in computing the corporation's income for its last taxation year beginning before that time if that year had ended at that time,

B is the value (determined in accordance with subsection 28(1.2)) to the corporation at that time of the purchased inventory that is distributed to the parent on the winding-up,

C is the value (determined in accordance with subsection 28(1.2)) of all of the inventory purchased by the corporation that was owned by it in connection with that business at that time, and

D is the lesser of

(i) such additional amount as the corporation designates in respect of the property, and

(ii) the amount, if any, by which the fair market value of the property at that time exceeds the amount determined for A in respect of the property;

(*b*) for the purpose of subparagraph 28(1)(*a*)(i), the disposition of the inventory and the receipt of the proceeds of disposition therefor shall be deemed to have occurred at that time and in the course of carrying on the business; and

(*c*) where the parent carries on a farming business and computes its income therefrom in accordance with the cash method, for the purposes of section 28,

(i) an amount equal to the cost to the parent of the inventory shall be deemed to have been paid by it, and

(ii) the parent shall be deemed to have purchased the inventory for an amount equal to that cost,

in the course of carrying on that business and at the time it acquired the inventory.

▶ 88(1.7) ◀

(1.7) Interpretation. For the purposes of paragraphs (1)(*c*) and (*d*), where a parent of a subsidiary did not deal at arm's length with another person (other than a corporation the control of which was acquired by the parent from a person with whom the parent dealt at arm's length) at any time before the winding-up of the subsidiary, the parent and the other person are deemed never to have dealt with each other at arm's length, whether or not the parent and the other person coexisted.

► 88(1.8) ◄

(1.8) Application of subsection (1.9). Subsection (1.9) applies if

(*a*) a corporation has made a designation (referred to in this subsection and subsection (1.9) as the "initial designation") under paragraph (1)(*d*) in respect of a share of the capital stock of a foreign affiliate of the corporation, or an interest in a partnership that, based on the assumptions contained in paragraph 96(1)(*c*), owns a share of the capital stock of a foreign affiliate of the corporation, on or before the filing-due date for its return of income under this Part for the taxation year in which a disposition of the share or the partnership interest, as the case may be, occurred in the course of a winding-up referred to in subsection (1) or an amalgamation referred to in subsection 87(11);

(*b*) the corporation made reasonable efforts to determine the foreign affiliate's tax-free surplus balance (within the meaning assigned by subsection 5905(5.5) of the *Income Tax Regulations*), in respect of the corporation, that was relevant in the computation of the maximum amount available under subparagraph (1)(*d*)(ii) to be designated in respect of that disposition; and

(*c*) the corporation amends the initial designation on or before the day that is 10 years after the filing-due date referred to in paragraph (*a*).

History: S. 88(1.8) was added by S.C. 2013, c. 34, s. 30(3), deemed to have come into force on December 19, 2009.

However, any assessment of a taxpayer's tax, interest and penalties payable under the Act for any taxation year that ends before June 26, 2013 that would, in the absence of this section, be precluded because of subsections 152(4) to (5) of the Act, shall be made to the extent necessary to take into account this amendment, if the taxpayer

(i) elects in writing in respect of all of its foreign affiliates that this section apply in respect of that provision, and

(ii) files that election with the Minister of National Revenue on or before December 26, 2013 [the day that is six months after royal assent].

► 88(1.9) ◄

(1.9) Amended designation. If this subsection applies and, in the opinion of the Minister, the circumstances are such that it would be just and equitable to permit the initial designation to be amended, the amended designation under paragraph (1.8)(*c*) is deemed to have been made on the day on which the initial designation was made and the initial designation is deemed not to have been made.

History: S. 88(1.9) was added by S.C. 2013, c. 34, s. 30(3), deemed to have come into force on December 19, 2009.

See the Application Provision in the history note for s. 88(1.8) regarding the override of the statute-barring rules for assessments for taxation years that end before June 26, 2013.

► 88(2) ◄

(2) Winding-up of Canadian corporation. Where a Canadian corporation (other than a subsidiary to the winding-up of which the rules in subsection (1) applied) has been wound up after 1978 and, at a particular time in the course of the winding-up, all or substantially all of the property owned by the corporation immediately before that time was distributed to the shareholders of the corporation,

(*a*) for the purposes of computing the corporation's

(i) capital dividend account,

(i.1) capital gains dividend account (within the meaning assigned by subsection 131(6), where the corporation is an investment corporation,

(ii) capital gains dividend account (within the meaning assigned by section 133), and

(iii) pre-1972 capital surplus on hand,

at the time (in this paragraph referred to as the "time of computation") immediately before the particular time,

(iv) the taxation year of the corporation that otherwise would have included the particular time shall be deemed to have ended immediately before the time of computation, and a new taxation year shall be deemed to have commenced at that time, and

(v) each property of the corporation that was so distributed at the particular time shall be deemed to have been disposed of by the corporation immediately before the end of the taxation year so deemed to have ended for proceeds equal to the fair market value of the property immediately before the particular time,

(vi) (Repealed by S.C. 1994, c. 7, Sched. II, s. 66(16).)

(*b*) where the corporation is, by virtue of subsection 84(2), deemed to have paid at the particular time a dividend (in this paragraph referred to as the "winding-up dividend") on shares of any class of its capital stock, the following rules apply:

(i) such portion of the winding-up dividend as does not exceed the corporation's capital dividend account immediately before that time or capital gains dividend account immediately before that time, as the case may be, shall be deemed, for the purposes of an election in respect thereof under subsection 83(2), 131(1) (as that subsection applies for the purposes of section 130) or 133(7.1), as the case may be, and where the corporation has so elected, for all other purposes, to be the full amount of a separate dividend,

(ii) the portion of the winding-up dividend equal to the lesser of the corporation's pre-1972 capital surplus on hand immediately before that time and the amount by which the winding-up dividend exceeds

(A) the portion thereof in respect of which the corporation has made an election under subsection 83(2), or

(B) the portion thereof in respect of which the corporation has made an election under subsection 133(7.1),

as the case may be, shall be deemed not to be a dividend,

(iii) notwithstanding the definition "taxable dividend" in subsection 89(1), the winding-up dividend, to the extent that it exceeds the total of the portion thereof deemed by subparagraph (i) to be a separate dividend for all purposes and the portion deemed by subparagraph (ii) not to be a dividend, shall be deemed to be a separate dividend that is a taxable dividend, and

(iv) each person who held any of the issued shares of that class at the particular time shall be deemed to have received that proportion of any separate dividend determined under subparagraph (i) or (iii) that the number of shares of that class held by the person immediately before the particular time is of the number of issued shares of that class outstanding immediately before that time, and

(*c*) for the purpose of computing the income of the corporation for its taxation year that includes the particular time, paragraph 12(1)(*t*) shall be read as follows:

"(*t*) the amount deducted under subsection 127(5) or (6) in computing the taxpayer's tax payable for the year or a preceding taxation year to the extent that it was not included under this paragraph in computing the taxpayer's income for a preceding taxation year or is not included in an amount determined under paragraph 13(7.1)(*e*) or 37(1)(*e*) or subparagraph 53(2)(*c*)(vi) or (*h*)(ii) or the amount determined for I in the definition "undepreciated capital cost" in subsection 13(21) or L in the definition "cumulative Canadian exploration expense" in subsection 66.1(6);".

Editorial Note: Subsection 88(1) contains a complete set of rules for winding up a taxable Canadian corporation into its parent where the parent is a taxable Canadian corporation and owns at least 90% of the issued shares of the subsidiary. This provision does not apply where one of the corporations is not a taxable Canadian corporation or the corporation being wound up is not owned at least 90% by the parent.

Subsection 88(2) applies to situations which are not covered by s. 88(1). Various other provisions in the Act also apply to wind-ups which are not covered by s. 88(1), including s. 69(5), which deems a disposition of property to occur at fair market value, and s. 84(2), which provides that a corporation will be deemed to pay a dividend on its shares on a winding-up. Note that the nature and amount of the deemed dividend is modified by the special rules in s. 88(2).

Subsection 88(2) also deals with the computation and distribution of capital surplus on hand, the capital dividend account, and the capital gains dividend account. The provision deems a year end immediately before the winding-up for the purposes of computing these accounts.

Related Sections: S. 88(2.1) Definition of "pre-1972 capital surplus on hand"; s. 134 Non-resident-owned corporation not a Canadian corporation, etc.

Canadian Tax Foundation: Ross, *Taxable Windup: A Practical Approach to Capital Dividends*, 2018 Tax for the Owner Manager 18(3):3–4; Roberts and Briggs, *Winding Up: Part 2*, 1996 Canadian Tax Journal 3:943–954.

Interpretation Bulletins: *Primary* — IT-149R4 Winding-up dividend. *Secondary* — IT-126R2 Meaning of "winding-up"; IT-444R Corporations — Involuntary dissolutions.

▶ 88(2.1) ◀

(2.1) Definition of "pre-1972 capital surplus on hand". For the purposes of subsection (2), "pre-1972 capital surplus on hand" of a particular corporation at a particular time means the amount, if any, by which the total of

(*a*) the corporation's 1971 capital surplus on hand on December 31, 1978 within the meaning of the *Income Tax Act*, chapter 148 of the Revised Statutes of Canada, 1952, as it read on that date,

(*b*) the total of all amounts each of which is an amount in respect of a capital property of the corporation owned by it on December 31, 1971 and disposed of by it after 1978 and before the particular time, equal to the amount, if any, by which the lesser of its fair market value on valuation day (within the meaning assigned by section 24 of the *Income Tax Application Rules*) and the corporation's proceeds of disposition of that capital property exceeds its actual cost to the corporation determined without reference to the *Income Tax Application Rules* other than subsections 26(15), (17) and (21) to (27) of that Act,

(*c*) where before the particular time a subsidiary (to the winding-up of which the rules in subsection (1) applied) of the particular corporation has been wound up after 1978, an amount equal to the pre-1972 capital surplus on hand of the subsidiary immediately before the commencement of the winding-up, and

(*d*) where the particular corporation is a new corporation formed as a result of an amalgamation (within the meaning of section 87) after 1978 and before the particular time, the total of all amounts each of which is an amount in respect of a predecessor corporation, equal to the predecessor corporation's pre-1972 capital surplus on hand immediately before the amalgamation

exceeds

(*e*) the total of all amounts each of which is an amount in respect of a capital property (other than depreciable property) of the corporation owned by it on December 31, 1971 and disposed of by it after 1978 and before the particular time equal to the amount, if any, by which its actual cost to the corporation determined without reference to the *Income Tax Application Rules*, other than subsections 26(15), (17) and (21) to (27) of that Act, exceeds the greater of the fair market value of the property on valuation day (within the meaning assigned by section 24 of that Act) and the corporation's proceeds of disposition of the property.

Related Sections: S. 87(2)(*t*) Pre-1972 capital surplus on hand; s. 88(2.2) Determination of pre-1972 capital surplus on hand; s. 88(2.3) Actual cost of certain depreciable property.

▶ 88(2.2) ◀

(2.2) Determination of pre-1972 capital surplus on hand. For the purposes of determining the pre-1972 capital surplus on hand of any corporation at a particular time after 1978, the following rules apply:

(*a*) an amount referred to in paragraphs (2.1)(*b*) and (*e*) in respect of the corporation shall be deemed to be nil, where the property disposed of is

(i) a share of the capital stock of a subsidiary, within the meaning of subsection (1), that was disposed of on the winding-up of the subsidiary where that winding-up commenced after 1978,

(ii) a share of the capital stock of another Canadian corporation that was controlled, within the meaning assigned by subsection 186(2), by the corporation immediately before the disposition and that was disposed of by the corporation after 1978 to a person with whom the corporation was not dealing at arm's length immediately after the disposition, other than by a disposition referred to in paragraph (*b*), or

(iii) subject to subsection 26(21) of the *Income Tax Application Rules*, a share of the capital stock of a particular corporation that was disposed of by the corporation after 1978, on an amalgamation, within the meaning assigned by subsection 87(1), where the corporation controlled, within the meaning assigned by subsection 186(2), both the particular corporation immediately before the amalgamation and the new corporation immediately after the amalgamation; and

(*b*) where another corporation that is a Canadian corporation owned a capital property on December 31, 1971 and subsequently disposed of it to the corporation in a transaction to which section 85 applied, the other corporation shall be deemed not to have disposed of that property in the transaction and the corporation shall be deemed to have owned that property on December 31, 1971 and to have acquired it at an actual cost equal to the actual cost of that property to the other corporation.

▶ 88(2.3) ◀

(2.3) Actual cost of certain depreciable property. For the purpose of subsection (2.1), the actual cost of the depreciable property that was acquired by a corporation before the commencement of its 1949 taxation year that is capital property referred to in that subsection shall be deemed to be the capital cost of that property to the corporation (within the meaning assigned by section 144 of the *Income Tax Act*, chapter 148 of the Revised Statutes of Canada, 1952, as it read in its application to the 1971 taxation year).

▶ 88(3) ◀

(3) Liquidation and dissolution of foreign affiliate. Notwithstanding subsection 69(5), if at any time a taxpayer receives a property (referred to in this subsection as the "distributed property") from a foreign affiliate (referred to in this subsection as the "disposing affiliate") of the taxpayer on a liquidation and dissolution of the disposing affiliate and the distributed property is received in respect of shares of the capital stock of the disposing affiliate that are disposed of on the liquidation and dissolution,

(*a*) subject to subsections (3.3) and (3.5), the distributed property is deemed to have been disposed of at that time by the disposing affiliate to the taxpayer for proceeds of disposition equal to the relevant cost base (within the meaning assigned by subsection 95(4)) to the disposing affiliate of the distributed property in respect of the taxpayer, immediately before that time, if

(i) the liquidation and dissolution is a qualifying liquidation and dissolution of the disposing affiliate, or

(ii) the distributed property is a share of the capital stock of another foreign affiliate of the taxpayer that was, immediately before that time, excluded property (within the meaning assigned by subsection 95(1)) of the disposing affiliate;

(*b*) if paragraph (*a*) does not apply to the distributed property, the distributed property is deemed to have been disposed of at that time by the disposing affiliate to the taxpayer for proceeds of disposition equal to the distributed property's fair market value at that time;

(*c*) the distributed property is deemed to have been acquired, at that time, by the taxpayer at a cost equal to the amount determined under paragraph (*a*) or (*b*) to be the disposing affiliate's proceeds of disposition of the distributed property;

(*d*) each share (referred to in paragraph (*e*) and subsections (3.3) and (3.4) as a "disposed share") of a class of the capital stock of the disposing affiliate that is disposed of by the taxpayer on the liquidation and dissolution is deemed to be disposed of for proceeds of disposition equal to the amount determined by the formula

$$A/B$$

where

A is the total of all amounts each of which is the net distribution amount in respect of a distribution of distributed property made, at any time, in respect of the class, and

B is the total number of issued and outstanding shares of the class that are owned by the taxpayer during the liquidation and dissolution; and

(*e*) if the liquidation and dissolution is a qualifying liquidation and dissolution of the disposing affiliate, any loss of the taxpayer in respect of the disposition of a disposed share is deemed to be nil.

Editorial Note: S. 88(3) applies to a taxpayer who has received property from a foreign affiliate on the liquidation and dissolution of the disposing affiliate. If the liquidation and dissolution is a "qualifying liquidation and dissolution" (a "QLAD"), as defined in s. 88(3.1), the rules generally provide for a rollover of the distributed property received by the taxpayer. In order to have a QLAD, the taxpayer must make an election (under Regulation 5911) and either: (i) own at least 90% of the shares of the affiliate throughout the liquidation and dissolution, or (ii) have received at least 90% of the assets of the affiliate and have at least 90% of the votes in the affiliate. For shares of another foreign affiliate that are received, there is an automatic rollover provided that the shares are "excluded property" as defined in s. 95(1).

History: S. 88(3) was replaced by S.C. 2013, c. 34, s. 65(1), applicable in respect of liquidations and dissolutions of foreign affiliates of a taxpayer that begin after February 27, 2004. However, if the taxpayer elects in writing under this subsection in respect of all of its foreign affiliates and files the election with the Minister of National Revenue on or before the day that is the later of the taxpayer's filing-due date for the taxpayer's taxation year that includes June 26, 2013 and June 26, 2014 [the day that is one year after royal assent],

(*a*) subsection 88(3) also applies to property received by the taxpayer after February 27, 2004 and before August 19, 2011 on a redemption, acquisition or cancellation of shares of the capital stock of, on a payment of a dividend by, or on a reduction of the paid-up capital of, a foreign affiliate of the taxpayer; and

(*b*) in respect of property described in paragraph (*a*) and property received by the taxpayer on a liquidation and dissolution of a foreign affiliate of the taxpayer that began after February 27, 2004 and before August 19, 2011,

(i) subsection 88(3) is to be read as follows:

"(3) Notwithstanding subsection 69(5), if at any time a taxpayer receives a property (referred to in this subsection as the "distributed property") from a foreign affiliate (referred to in this subsection as the "disposing affiliate") of the taxpayer, on a liquidation and dissolution of the disposing affiliate, on a redemption, acquisition or cancellation of shares of the capital stock of the disposing affiliate, on a payment of a dividend by the disposing affiliate, or on a reduction of the paid-up capital of the disposing affiliate,

(*a*) subject to subsections (3.3) and (3.5), the distributed property is deemed to have been disposed of at that time by the disposing affiliate to the taxpayer for proceeds of disposition equal to the relevant cost base (within the meaning assigned by subsection 95(4)) to the disposing affiliate of the distributed property in respect of the taxpayer, immediately before that time, if the distributed property

(i) was received on a liquidation and dissolution of the disposing affiliate that is a qualifying liquidation and dissolution of the disposing affiliate, or

(ii) was a share of the capital stock of another foreign affiliate of the taxpayer that was, immediately before that time, excluded property (within the meaning assigned by subsection 95(1)) of the disposing affiliate;

(*b*) if paragraph (*a*) does not apply to the distributed property, the distributed property is deemed to have been disposed of at that time by the disposing affiliate to the taxpayer for proceeds of disposition equal to the distributed property's fair market value at that time;

(*c*) the distributed property is deemed to have been acquired, at that time, by the taxpayer at a cost equal to the amount determined under paragraph (*a*) or (*b*) to be the disposing affiliate's proceeds of disposition of the distributed property;

(*d*) if the taxpayer disposed of shares of the capital stock of the disposing affiliate on a liquidation and dissolution of the disposing affiliate (each such share being referred to in paragraph (*f*) and subsections (3.3) and (3.4) as a "disposed share") or on a redemption, acquisition or cancellation of shares of the capital stock of the disposing affiliate, the taxpayer's proceeds of disposition of the shares are deemed to be the amount determined by the formula

$$A - B$$

where

A is the total of all amounts each of which is the cost to the taxpayer of a distributed property, as determined under paragraph (*c*), and

B is the total of all amounts each of which is an amount owing (other than an unpaid dividend) by, or an obligation of, the disposing affiliate that was assumed or cancelled by the taxpayer because of the liquidation and dissolution or the redemption, acquisition or cancellation;

(*e*) if the taxpayer received the distributed property as a dividend or a reduction of paid-up capital, the amount of the dividend paid by the disposing affiliate or the amount of the reduction of the paid-up capital of the disposing affiliate, as the case may be, is deemed to be the amount determined by the formula

$$C - D$$

where

C is the total of all amounts each of which is the cost to the taxpayer of a distributed property, as determined under paragraph (*c*), and

D is the total of all amounts each of which is an amount owing (other than an unpaid dividend) by, or an obligation of, the disposing affiliate that was assumed or cancelled by the taxpayer because of the payment of the dividend or the reduction of paid-up capital; and

(*f*) if the distributed property was received on a liquidation and dissolution of the disposing affiliate that is a qualifying liquidation and dissolution of the disposing affiliate, any loss of the taxpayer in respect of the disposition of a disposed share is deemed to be nil."

(ii) section 88 is to be read without reference to its subsection (3.2).

Any assessment of a taxpayer's tax, interest and penalties payable under the Act for any taxation year that ends before June 26, 2013 that would, in the absence of this section, be precluded because of subsections 152(4) to (5) of the Act shall be made to the extent necessary to take into account the amendments by S.C. 2013, c. 34, s. 54 to 89.

S. 88(3) formerly read:

(3) *Dissolution of foreign affiliate.* Where on the dissolution of a controlled foreign affiliate (within the meaning assigned by subsection 95(1)) of a taxpayer (in this subsection referred to as the "disposing affiliate") one or more shares of the capital stock of another foreign affiliate of the taxpayer have been disposed of to the taxpayer,

(*a*) the disposing affiliate's proceeds of disposition of each such share and the cost thereof to the taxpayer shall be deemed to be an amount equal to the adjusted cost base to the disposing affiliate of the share immediately before the dissolution, or such greater amount as the taxpayer claims not exceeding the fair market value of the share immediately before the dissolution; and

(*b*) the taxpayer's proceeds of disposition of the shares of the disposing affiliate shall be deemed to be the amount, if any, by which the total of

(i) the cost to the taxpayer of the shares of the other foreign affiliate, as determined in paragraph (*a*), and

(ii) the fair market value of any property (other than the shares referred to in subparagraph (i)) disposed of by the disposing affiliate to the taxpayer on the dissolution,

exceeds

(iii) the total of all debts owing by the disposing affiliate, and of all amounts of other obligations of the disposing affiliate to pay amounts, otherwise than as or on account of a dividend owing by the disposing affiliate to the taxpayer or to persons with whom the taxpayer was not dealing at arm's length, that were outstanding immediately before the dissolution and that were assumed or cancelled by the taxpayer on the dissolution.

Related Sections: S. 54, "adjusted cost base", "proceeds of disposition".

Canadian Tax Foundation: Lockwood and Lopes, *Subsection 88(3): Deferring Gains on Liquidation and Dissolution*, 2013 Canadian Tax Journal 1:209–228; Pham and Feness, *CFA Suppression Election: Potential Risks*, 2013 Canadian Tax Focus 3(3):2; Marley and Slaats, *Foreign Affiliate Reorganizations — Recent Amendments to the Rules*, 2012 Conference Report 27:1–25; Woolford and Favre, *The Latest Foreign Affiliate Proposals: Selected Aspects*, 2010 Canadian Tax Journal 4:791–843; Talakshi, *The Foreign Affiliate Proposals — An Update*, 2005 Conference Report 14:1–20; Slaats, *Repatriation from Foreign Affiliates: Selected Issues*, 2005 Canadian Tax Journal 3:858–884; Turner, *Foreign Affiliate Liquidation and Merger Rollovers: Where Are We Now and Where Should We Be?*, 2005 Canadian Tax Journal 3:640–684.

Tax Topics: No. 2195, June 2014 Election Deadlines for Retroactive Application of New Foreign Affiliate Reorganization Rules.

Tax Window Files: Dissolution of Foreign Affiliate — Loan to Taxpayer, *Technical Interpretation, International and Trusts Division, October 26, 2007*, CRA Document No. 2005-0137641E5; Dissolution of Foreign Affiliate, *Technical Interpretation, International and Trusts Division, January 9, 2003*, CRA Document No. 2002-0178147.

► 88(3.1) ◄

(3.1) Qualifying liquidation and dissolution. For the purposes of subsections (3), (3.3) and (3.5), a "qualifying liquidation and dissolution" of a foreign affiliate (referred to in this subsection as the "disposing affiliate") of a taxpayer means a liquidation and dissolution of the disposing affiliate in respect of which the taxpayer elects in accordance with prescribed rules and

(*a*) the taxpayer owns not less than 90% of the issued and outstanding shares of each class of the capital stock of the disposing affiliate throughout the liquidation and dissolution; or

(*b*) both

(i) the percentage determined by the following formula is greater than or equal to 90%:

$$A/B$$

where

A is the amount, if any, by which

(A) the total of all amounts each of which is the fair market value, at the time at which it is distributed, of a property that is distributed by the disposing affiliate to the taxpayer in the course of the liquidation and dissolution in respect of shares of the capital stock of the disposing affiliate

exceeds

(B) the total of all amounts each of which is an amount owing (other than an unpaid dividend) by, or an obligation of, the disposing affiliate that was assumed or cancelled by the taxpayer in consideration for a property referred to in clause (A), and

B is the amount, if any, by which

(A) the total of all amounts each of which is the fair market value, at the time at which it is distributed, of a property that is distributed by the disposing affiliate to a shareholder of the disposing affiliate in the course of the liquidation and dissolution in respect of shares of the capital stock of the disposing affiliate

exceeds

(B) the total of all amounts each of which is an amount owing (other than an unpaid dividend) by, or an obligation of, the disposing affiliate that was assumed or cancelled by a shareholder of the disposing affiliate in consideration for a property referred to in clause (A), and

(ii) at the time of each distribution of property by the disposing affiliate in the course of the liquidation and dissolution in respect of shares of the capital stock of the disposing affiliate, the taxpayer holds shares of that capital stock that would, if an annual general meeting of the shareholders of the disposing affiliate were held at that time, entitle it to 90% or more of the votes that could be cast under all circumstances at the meeting.

History: S. 88(3.1) was added by S.C. 2013, c. 34, s. 65(1), applicable in respect of liquidations and dissolutions of foreign affiliates of a taxpayer that begin after February 27, 2004.

See the application provision following the amendment to s. 88(3) for the extension of assessment periods to take into account the amendments by S.C. 2013, c. 34, s. 54 to 89.

► 88(3.2) ◄

(3.2) Net distribution amount. For the purposes of the description of A in paragraph (3)(*d*), "net distribution amount" in respect of a distribution of distributed property means the amount determined by the formula

A - B

where

A is the cost to the taxpayer of the distributed property as determined under paragraph (3)(*c*), and

B is the total of all amounts each of which is an amount owing (other than an unpaid dividend) by, or an obligation of, the disposing affiliate that was assumed or cancelled by the taxpayer in consideration for the distribution of the distributed property.

History: S. 88(3.2) was added by S.C. 2013, c. 34, s. 65(1), applicable in respect of liquidations and dissolutions of foreign affiliates of a taxpayer that begin after February 27, 2004.

See the application provision following the amendment to s. 88(3) for the extension of assessment periods to take into account the amendments by S.C. 2013, c. 34, s. 54 to 89.

► 88(3.3) ◄

(3.3) Suppression election. For the purposes of paragraph (3)(*a*), if the liquidation and dissolution is a qualifying liquidation and dissolution of the disposing affiliate and the taxpayer would, in the absence of this subsection and, for greater certainty, after taking into account any election under subsection 93(1), realize a capital gain (the amount of which is referred to in subsection (3.4) as the "capital gain amount") from the disposition of a disposed share, the taxpayer may elect, in accordance with prescribed rules, that distributed property that was, immediately before the disposition, capital property of the disposing affiliate be deemed to have been disposed of by the disposing affiliate to the taxpayer for proceeds of disposition equal to the amount claimed (referred to in subsection (3.4) as the "claimed amount") by the taxpayer in the election.

Editorial Note: S. 88(3.3) and (3.4) provide a taxpayer with the ability to suppress the gain that might otherwise result on a distribution by a liquidating foreign affiliate of capital property where a valid QLAD election has been made.

History: S. 88(3.3) was added by S.C. 2013, c. 34, s. 65(1), applicable in respect of liquidations and dissolutions of foreign affiliates of a taxpayer that begin after February 27, 2004.

See the application provision following the amendment to s. 88(3) for the extension of assessment periods to take into account the amendments by S.C. 2013, c. 34, s. 54 to 89.

Canadian Tax Foundation: Pham and Feness, *CFA Suppression Election: Potential Risks*, 2013 Canadian Tax Focus 3(3):2.

► 88(3.4) ◄

(3.4) Conditions for subsection (3.3) election. An election under subsection (3.3) in respect of distributed property disposed of in the course of the liquidation and dissolution is not valid unless

(*a*) the claimed amount in respect of each distributed property does not exceed the amount that would, in the absence of subsection (3.3), be determined under paragraph (3)(*a*) in respect of the distributed property; and

(*b*) the amount determined by the following formula does not exceed the total of all amounts each of which is the capital gain amount in respect of a disposed share:

A - B

where

A is the total of all amounts that would, in the absence of subsection (3.3), be determined under paragraph (3)(*a*) to be the proceeds of disposition of a distributed property in respect of which an election under subsection (3.3) is made by the taxpayer, and

B is the total of all amounts each of which is the claimed amount in respect of a distributed property referred to in the description of A.

History: S. 88(3.4) was added by S.C. 2013, c. 34, s. 65(1), applicable in respect of liquidations and dissolutions of foreign affiliates of a taxpayer that begin after February 27, 2004.

See the application provision following the amendment to s. 88(3) for the extension of assessment periods to take into account the amendments by S.C. 2013, c. 34, s. 54 to 89.

► 88(3.5) ◄

(3.5) Taxable Canadian property. For the purposes of paragraph (3)(*a*), the distributed property is deemed to have been disposed of by the disposing affiliate to the taxpayer for proceeds of disposition equal to the adjusted cost base of the distributed property to the disposing affiliate immediately before the time of its disposition, if

(*a*) the liquidation and dissolution is a qualifying liquidation and dissolution of the disposing affiliate;

(*b*) the distributed property is, at the time of its disposition, taxable Canadian property (other than treaty-protected property) of the disposing affiliate that is a share of the capital stock of a corporation resident in Canada; and

(*c*) the taxpayer and the disposing affiliate have jointly elected in accordance with prescribed rules.

Editorial Note: Under s. 88(3.5), a taxpayer and the disposing foreign affiliate may elect to deem a disposition of non-treaty protected taxable Canadian property that is a share of a corporation resident in Canada to occur at the affiliate's "adjusted cost base" rather than at its "relevant cost base" in order to prevent a taxable capital gain from arising in circumstances where the latter is greater than the former.

History: S. 88(3.5) was added by S.C. 2013, c. 34, s. 65(1), applicable in respect of liquidations and dissolutions of foreign affiliates of a taxpayer that begin after February 27, 2004.

See the application provision following the amendment to s. 88(3) for the extension of assessment periods to take into account the amendments by S.C. 2013, c. 34, s. 54 to 89.

▶ 88(4) ◀

(4) Amalgamation deemed not to be acquisition of control. For the purposes of paragraphs (1)(*c*), (*c*.2), (*d*) and (*d*.2) and, for greater certainty, paragraphs (*c*.3) to (*c*.8) and (*d*.3),

(*a*) subject to paragraph (*c*), control of any corporation shall be deemed not to have been acquired because of an amalgamation;

(*b*) any corporation formed as a result of an amalgamation shall be deemed to be the same corporation as, and a continuation of, each predecessor corporation; and

(*c*) in the case of an amalgamation described in subsection 87(9), control of a predecessor corporation that was not controlled by the parent before the amalgamation shall be deemed to have been acquired by the parent immediately before the amalgamation.

Related Sections: S. 13(21), "depreciable property"; s. 15(1) Benefit conferred on shareholder; s. 54, "capital property"; s. 84(2) Distribution on winding-up, etc; s. 89(1), "Canadian corporation", "capital dividend account"; s. 248(1), "adjusted cost base", "amount", "corporation", "cost amount", "insurance corporation", "property", "share"; s. 256(1.2) Control, etc.; ITAR s. 20(1.2) Other transfers of depreciable property.

Tax Window Files: 88(1)(c) Bump After Acquisition of Control, *Tax Ruling, Reorganizations and Resources Division, June 25, 2008*, CRA Document No. 2007-0240271R3.

SECTION 88.1: [SIFT trust wind-up event]

▶ 88.1(1) ◀

(1) Application. Subsection (2) applies to a trust's distribution of property to a taxpayer if

(*a*) the distribution is a SIFT trust wind-up event;

(*b*) the trust is

(i) a SIFT wind-up entity whose only beneficiary, at all times at which the trust makes a distribution that is a SIFT trust wind-up event, is a taxable Canadian corporation, or

(ii) a trust whose only beneficiary, at all times at which the trust makes a distribution that is a SIFT trust wind-up event, is another trust described by subparagraph (i);

(*c*) where the trust is a SIFT wind-up entity, the distribution occurs no more than 60 days after the earlier of

(i) the first SIFT trust wind-up event of the trust, and

(ii) the first distribution to the trust that is a SIFT trust wind-up event of another trust; and

(*d*) if the property is shares of the capital stock of a taxable Canadian corporation,

(i) the property was not acquired by the trust on a distribution to which subsection 107(3.1) applies, and

(ii) the trust elects in writing, filed with the Minister on or before the trust's filing-due date for its taxation year that includes the time of the distribution, that this section apply to the distribution.

History: S. 88.1(1) was added by S.C. 2009, c. 2, s. 21(1), applicable after July 14, 2008, except that subsection 88.1(1) is to be read without reference to its paragraph (*c*) in its application to a trust's distribution of property, if the distribution occurs no more than 60 days after this Act is assented to [R.A. March 12, 2009].

Related Sections: S. 85.1(8) Rollover on SIFT unit for share exchange; s. 107(3.1) SIFT trust wind-up event; s. 122(1) Tax payable by *inter vivos* trust; s. 248(1), "SIFT trust wind-up event", "SIFT wind-up entity".

Tax Window Files: Due date for subparagraph 88.1(1)(d)(ii) election, *February 9, 2011*, CRA Document No. 2011-0394271I7; Conversion SIFT Trust to Corporation, *October 29, 2009*, CRA Document No. 2009-0317211E5.

▶ 88.1(2) ◀

(2) SIFT trust wind-up event. If this subsection applies to a trust's distribution of property to a taxpayer, subsections 88(1) to (1.7), and section 87 and paragraphs 256(7)(*a*) to (*e*) as they apply for the purposes of those subsections, apply, with any modifications that the circumstances require, as if

(*a*) the trust were a taxable Canadian corporation (in this subsection referred to as the "subsidiary") that is not a private corporation;

(*b*) where the taxpayer is a SIFT wind-up entity, the taxpayer were a taxable Canadian corporation that is not a private corporation;

(*c*) the distribution were a winding-up of the subsidiary;

(*d*) the taxpayer's interest as a beneficiary under the trust were shares of a single class of shares of the capital stock of the subsidiary owned by the taxpayer;

(*e*) paragraph 88(1)(*b*) deemed the taxpayer's proceeds of disposition of the shares described in paragraph (*d*) and owned by the taxpayer immediately before the distribution to be equal to the adjusted cost base to the taxpayer of the taxpayer's interest as a beneficiary under the trust immediately before the distribution;

(*f*) each trust, a majority-interest beneficiary (in this subsection, within the meaning assigned by section 251.1) of which is another trust that is by operation of this subsection treated as if it were a corporation, were a corporation; and

(*g*) except for the purposes of subsections 88(1.1) and (1.2), the taxpayer last acquired control of the subsidiary and of each corporation (including a trust that is by operation of this subsection treated as if it were a corporation) controlled by the subsidiary at the time, if any, at which the taxpayer last became a majority-interest beneficiary of the trust.

Editorial Note: Section 88.1 was intended to facilitate the tax-effective liquidation of a SIFT trust by allowing the liquidation to qualify for the same general tax-deferred treatment that applies to the wind-up of a taxable Canadian corporation under ss. 88(1) to 88(1.7). Section 88.1 applies only in respect of liquidations occurring before 2013. This liquidation mechanism, along with the other SIFT "conversion" rules in ss. 85.1(7) and (8) and 107(3.1), were introduced as a corollary to the rules in s. 122, which impose an entity-level tax on a SIFT trust comparable to the general corporate tax rate that would otherwise apply if the SIFT were a public corporation. S. 88.1 generally facilitated the collapse of SIFT structures in circumstances where the SIFT was "converted" into a corporation.

History: S. 88.1(2) was added by S.C. 2009, c. 2, s. 21(1), applicable after July 14, 2008.

Related Sections: S. 80.01(5.1) Deemed settlement on SIFT trust wind-up event; s. 85.1(8) Rollover on SIFT unit for share exchange; s. 87 Amalgamations; s. 107(2) Distribution by personal trust; s. 107(3), s. 107(3.1) SIFT trust wind-up event; s. 122(1) Tax payable by *inter vivos* trust; s. 248(1), "SIFT trust wind-up event", "SIFT wind-up entity".

Canadian Tax Foundation: Perry, *Income Trusts: Reorganizations and Planning for 2011*, 2008 Conference Report 8:1–33.

SECTION 89: [Dividends]

▶ 89(1) ◀

(1) Definitions. In this subdivision,

"adjusted taxable income" — "adjusted taxable income" of a corporation for a taxation year is the amount determined by the formula

A - B - C

where

A is

(*a*) unless paragraph (*b*) applies, the corporation's taxable income for the taxation year, and

(*b*) if the corporation is a deposit insurance corporation in the taxation year, nil,

B is the amount determined by multiplying the amount, if any, deducted by the corporation under subsection 125(1) for the taxation year by the quotient obtained by dividing 100 by the rate of the deduction provided under that subsection for the taxation year, and

C is

(*a*) if the corporation is a Canadian-controlled private corporation in the taxation year, the lesser of the corporation's aggregate investment income for the taxation year and the corporation's taxable income for the taxation year, and

(*b*) in any other case, nil;

Editorial Note: "Adjusted taxable income" is a component in determining a corporation's general rate income pool ("GRIP") that is intended to reflect a corporation's before-tax earnings that are subject to the non-preferential general rate of tax (e.g., earnings not eligible for the small business deduction). A corporation's adjusted taxable income is the corporation's taxable income for the year, (or nil, if the corporation is a deposit insurance corporation (the description of A)), less income that has benefitted from the small business deduction (the description of B) and the lesser of the corporation's aggregate investment income for the year and the corporation's taxable income for the year, (or nil, if the corporation is not a Canadian-controlled private corporation (the description of C)). A corporation's adjusted taxable income is multiplied by its "general rate factor" in order to generate an amount that represents the after-tax earnings of the corporation. This amount increases the corporation's GRIP for the year (see the description of D in the definition of "general rate income pool" in s. 89(1)).

History: S. 89(1), the definition "adjusted taxable income" was added by S.C. 2009, c. 2, s. 22(3), applicable to the 2006 and subsequent taxation years.

Related Sections: S. 89(1), "general rate income pool"; s. 89(15) Meaning of expression "deposit insurance corporation"; s. 125(7) "Canadian-controlled private corporation".

"Canadian corporation" — "Canadian corporation" at any time means a corporation that is resident in Canada at that time and was

(*a*) incorporated in Canada, or

(*b*) resident in Canada throughout the period that began on June 18, 1971 and that ends at that time,

and, for greater certainty, a corporation formed at any particular time by the amalgamation or merger of, or by a plan of arrangement or other corporate reorganization in respect of, 2 or more corporations (otherwise than as a result of the acquisition of property of one corporation by another corporation, pursuant to the purchase of the property by the other corporation or as a result of the distribution of the property to the other corporation on the winding-up of the corporation) is a Canadian corporation because of paragraph (*a*) only if

(*c*) that reorganization took place under the laws of Canada or a province, and

(*d*) each of those corporations was, immediately before the particular time, a Canadian corporation;

Editorial Note: "Canadian corporation" status is a prerequisite for "Canadian-controlled private corporation" and "taxable Canadian corporation" status. A Canadian corporation must generally be resident in Canada at the particular time, and have been incorporated in Canada (or have been continuously resident in Canada since 1971). Subsection 250(4) deems a corporation to be resident in Canada throughout a taxation year in certain circumstances, including if it was incorporated in Canada after April 26, 1965; see, however, s. 250(5) (residence under a treaty) and (5.1) (continuance and residence).

Related Regulations: Part XIII; 4900.

Related Sections: S. 85.1(1) Share for share exchange; s. 88 Winding-up; s. 89(1), "taxable Canadian corporation"; s. 125(7), "Canadian-controlled private corporation"; s. 248(1), "Canadian corporation"; s. 250 Person deemed resident.

Income Tax Folios: *Secondary* — S4-F7-C1 Amalgamations of Canadian Corporations.

Interpretation Bulletins: *Secondary* — IT-291R3 Transfer of property to a corporation under subsection 85(1); IT-458R2 Canadian-controlled private corporation.

"capital dividend account" — "capital dividend account" of a corporation at any particular time means the amount, if any, by which the total of

(*a*) the amount, if any, by which the total of

(i) the total of all amounts each of which is the amount if any, by which

(A) the amount of the corporation's capital gain — computed without reference to subclause 52(3)(*a*)(ii)(A)(II) and subparagraph 53(1)(*b*)(ii) — from the disposition (other than a disposition under paragraph 40(3.1)(*a*) or subsection 40(12) or a disposition that is the making of a gift after December 8, 1997 that is not a gift described in subsection 110.1(1)) of a property in the period beginning at the beginning of its first taxation year that began after the corporation last became a private corporation and that ended after 1971 and ending immediately before the particular time (in this definition referred to as the *period*)

exceeds the total of

(B) the portion of the capital gain referred to in clause (A) that is the corporation's taxable capital gain,

(B.1) the corporation's taxable capital gain from a disposition in the period under subsection 40(12), and

(C) the portion of the amount, if any, by which the amount determined under clause (A) exceeds the amount determined under clause (B) from the disposition by it of a property that can reasonably be regarded as having accrued while the property, or a property for which it was substituted,

(I) except in the case of a disposition of a designated property, was a property of a corporation (other than a private corporation, an investment corporation, a mortgage investment corporation or a mutual fund corporation),

(II) where, after November 26, 1987, the property became a property of a Canadian-controlled private corporation (otherwise than by reason of a change in the residence of one or more shareholders of the corporation), was a property of a corporation controlled directly or indirectly in any manner whatever by one or more non-resident persons, or

(III) where, after November 26, 1987, the property became a property of a private corporation that was not exempt from tax under this Part on its taxable income, was a property of a corporation exempt from tax under this Part on its taxable income, and

(*i*.1) all amounts each of which is an amount in respect of a distribution made, in the period and after September 15, 2016, by a trust to the corporation in respect of capital gains of the trust equal to the lesser of

(A) the amount, if any, by which

(I) the amount of the distribution

exceeds

(II) the amount designated under subsection 104(21) by the trust in respect of the net taxable capital gains of the trust attributable to those capital gains, and

(B) the amount determined by the formula

$$A \times B$$

where

A is the fraction or whole number determined when 1 is subtracted from the reciprocal of the fraction under paragraph 38(*a*) applicable to the trust for the year, and

B is the amount referred to in subclause (A)(II),

exceeds

(ii) the total of all amounts each of which is the amount, if any, by which

(A) the amount of the corporation's capital loss — computed without reference to subclause 52(3)(*a*)(ii)(A)(II) and subparagraph 53(1)(*b*)(ii) — from the disposition (other than a disposition under subsection 40(3.12) or a disposition that is the making of a gift after December 8, 1997 that is not a gift described in subsection 110.1(1)) of a property in the period

exceeds the total of

(B) the part of the capital loss referred to in clause (A) that is the corporation's allowable capital loss, and

(C) the portion of the amount, if any, by which the amount determined under clause (A) exceeds the amount determined under clause (B) from the disposition by it of a property that can reasonably be regarded as having accrued while the property, or a property for which it was substituted,

(I) except in the case of a disposition of a designated property, was a property of a corporation (other than a private corporation, an investment corporation, a mortgage investment corporation or a mutual fund corporation),

(II) where, after November 26, 1987, the property became a property of a Canadian-controlled private corporation (otherwise than by reason of a change in the residence of one or more shareholders of the corporation), was a property of a corporation controlled directly or indirectly in any manner whatever by one or more non-resident persons, or

(III) where, after November 26, 1987, the property became a property of a private corporation that was not exempt from tax under this Part on its taxable income, was a property of a corporation exempt from tax under this Part on its taxable income,

(*b*) all amounts each of which is an amount in respect of a dividend received by the corporation on a share of the capital stock of another corporation in the period, which amount was, by virtue of subsection 83(2), not included in computing the income of the corporation,

(*c*) the total of all amounts each of which is an amount required to have been included under this paragraph as it read in its application to a taxation year that ended before February 28, 2000,

(*c*.1) the amount, if any, by which

(i) $^1/_2$ of the total of all amounts each of which is an amount required by paragraph 14(1)(*b*) (as it read before 2017) to be included in computing the corporation's income in respect of a business carried on by the corporation for a taxation year that is included in the period and that ended after February 27, 2000 and before October 18, 2000,

exceeds

(ii) where the corporation has deducted an amount under subsection 20(4.2) in respect of a debt established by it to have become a bad debt in a taxation year that is included in the period and that ended after February 27, 2000 and before October 18, 2000, or has an allowable capital loss for such a year because of the application of subsection 20(4.3), the amount determined by the formula

$$V + W$$

where

V is $^1/_2$ of the value determined for A under subsection 20(4.2) in respect of the corporation for the last such taxation year that ended in the period, and

W is $^1/_3$ of the value determined for B under subsection 20(4.2) in respect of the corporation for the last such taxation year that ended in the period, and

(iii) in any other case, nil,

(*c*.2) the amount, if any, by which

(i) the total of all amounts each of which is an amount required by paragraph 14(1)(*b*) (as it read before 2017) or subparagraph 13(38)(*d*)(iii) to be included in computing the corporation's income in respect of a business carried on by the corporation for a taxation year that is included in the period and that ends after October 17, 2000,

exceeds

(ii) where the corporation has deducted an amount under subsection 20(4.2) in respect of a debt established by it to have become a bad debt in a taxation year that is included in the period and that ends after October 17, 2000, or has an allowable capital loss for such a year because of the application of subsection 20(4.3), the amount determined by the formula

$$X + Y$$

where

X is the value determined for A under subsection 20(4.2) in respect of the corporation for the last such taxation year that ended in the period, and

Y is $\frac{1}{3}$ of the value determined for B under subsection 20(4.2) in respect of the corporation for the last such taxation year that ended in the period, and

(iii) in any other case, nil,

(*d*) the amount, if any, by which the total of

(i) all amounts each of which is the proceeds of a life insurance policy of which the corporation was a beneficiary on or before June 28, 1982 received by the corporation in the period and after 1971 in consequence of the death of any person, and

(ii) all amounts each of which is the proceeds of a life insurance policy (other than an LIA policy) of which the corporation was not a beneficiary on or before June 28, 1982 received by the corporation in the period and after May 23, 1985 in consequence of the death of any person

exceeds the total of all amounts each of which is

(iii) the "adjusted cost basis" (in this paragraph as defined in subsection 148(9)), immediately before the death, of

(A) if the death occurs before March 22, 2016, a policy referred to in subparagraph (i) or (ii) to the corporation, and

(B) if the death occurs after March 21, 2016, a policyholder's interest in a policy referred to in subparagraph (i) or (ii),

(iv) if the policy is a 10/8 policy immediately before the death and the death occurs after 2013, the amount outstanding, immediately before the death, of the borrowing that is described in subparagraph (*a*)(i) of the definition "10/8 policy" in subsection 248(1) in respect of the policy,

(v) if the death occurs after March 21, 2016, an interest in the policy was disposed of by a policyholder (other than a taxable Canadian corporation) after 1999 and before March 22, 2016 and subsection 148(7) applied to the disposition, the total of

(A) the amount, if any, by which the fair market value of consideration given in respect of the disposition exceeds the total of

(I) the greater of the amount determined under subparagraph 148(7)(*a*)(i) in respect of the disposition and the adjusted cost basis to the policyholder of the interest immediately before the disposition, and

(II) the amount by which the paid-up capital of any class of the capital stock of a corporation resulting from the disposition is reduced at the beginning of March 22, 2016 because of the application of paragraphs 148(7)(*c*) and (*f*) in respect of the disposition, and

(B) if the paid-up capital in respect of a class of shares of the capital stock of a corporation was increased before March 22, 2016 as described in subparagraph 148(7)(*f*)(iii) in respect of the disposition, the amount, if any, by which the total reduction in the paid-up capital in respect of that class — not exceeding the amount of that increase — after that increase and before March 22, 2016 (except to the extent that the amount of the reduction was deemed by subsection 84(4) or (4.1) to be a dividend received by a taxpayer) exceeds the amount determined under subparagraph 148(7)(*a*)(i) in respect of the disposition, or

(vi) if the death occurs after March 21, 2016, an interest in the policy was disposed of by a policyholder (other than a taxable Canadian corporation) after 1999 and before March 22, 2016 and subsection 148(7) applied to the disposition, the amount, if any, determined by the formula

$$A - B$$

where

A is the amount, if any, by which the lesser of the adjusted cost basis to the policyholder of the interest immediately before the disposition and the fair market value of consideration given in respect of the disposition exceeds the amount determined under subparagraph 148(7)(*a*)(i) in respect of the disposition, and

B is the absolute value of the negative amount, if any, that would be, in the absence of section 257, the adjusted cost basis, immediately before the death, of the interest in the policy,

(*e*) the amount of the corporation's life insurance capital dividend account immediately before May 24, 1985,

(*f*) all amounts each of which is an amount in respect of a distribution made, in the period and before September 16, 2016, by a trust to the corporation in respect of capital gains of the trust equal to the lesser of

(i) the amount, if any, by which

(A) the amount of the distribution,

exceeds

(B) the amount designated under subsection 104(21) by the trust (other than a designation to which subsection 104(21.4), as it read in its application to the corporation's last taxation year that began before November 2011, applied) in respect of the net taxable capital gains of the trust attributable to those capital gains, and

(ii) the amount determined by the formula

$$A \times B$$

where

A is the fraction or whole number determined when 1 is subtracted from the reciprocal of the fraction under paragraph 38(*a*) applicable to the trust for the year, and

B is the amount referred to in clause (i) (B), and

(*g*) all amounts each of which is an amount in respect of a distribution made by a trust to the corporation in the period in respect of a dividend (other than a taxable dividend) paid on a share of the capital stock of another corporation resident in Canada to the trust during a taxation year of the trust throughout which the trust was resident in Canada equal to the lesser of

(i) the amount of the distribution, and

(ii) the amount designated under subsection 104(20) by the trust in respect of the corporation in respect of that dividend,

exceeds the total of all capital dividends that became payable by the corporation after the commencement of the period and before the particular time;

Editorial Note: The "capital dividend account" ("CDA") of a corporation represents the tax-free portion of qualifying amounts and is relevant for the purposes of making an election under s. 83(2) to classify a dividend of a corporation as a capital dividend. The significance of a dividend being classified as a capital dividend is that it is not included in the income of any recipient resident shareholder (see s. 83(2)(*b*); note that withholding tax under s. 212(2) applies if the shareholder is non-resident).

CDA is calculated on a cumulative basis for a particular period of a corporation beginning on the first day of the first taxation year that started after the corporation last became a private corporation and ended after 1971 and ending immediately prior to the calculation.

The primary components of the CDA are, generally: (i) the total of the non-taxable portion of capital gains realized by the corporation and effective on or after September 16, 2016, the non-taxable portions of capital gains distributed from a trust to the corporation, minus the non-allowable portion of the corporation's capital losses (paragraph (*a*)); (ii) intercorporate capital dividends (paragraph (*b*)); (iii) the non-taxable portion of gains on dispositions of eligible capital property (paragraph (*c.2*)); (iv) insurance proceeds (to the extent such proceeds exceed the adjusted cost basis of the policy) (paragraph (*d*)); (v) the non-taxable portion of capital gains distributed to the corporation by a trust (paragraph (*f*)) (this is now incorporated into item (i)); and (vi) capital dividends distributed by a trust (paragraph (*g*)); less (vii) capital dividends payable by the corporation during the period (per the post-amble).

For proceeds of life insurance received by the corporation in respect of deaths occurring after March 21, 2016, the amount of such proceeds which are added to the CDA are reduced by certain other amounts, including the following:

(1) If an interest in the policy was disposed of after 1999 and before March 22, 2016, by a policy holder (other than a taxable Canadian corporation) to a non-arm's length person such that subsection 148(7) applied, the amount, if any, by which the fair market value of consideration given on the non-arm's length disposition exceeds the total of two amounts. The first amount ((A)(I) in subparagraph (v) of the CDA definition) is the greater of the adjusted cost base of the interest to the policy holder and the value of the interest (e.g., its cash surrender value) at the time of the disposition. The second amount ((A)(II)) applies where the disposition was made to a corporation as a contribution of capital, and equals the amount by which the paid-up capital of the corporation is reduced on March 22, 2016, under paragraphs 148(7)(*c*) and (*f*) (typically, this is the amount by which the increase in the paid-up capital as a result of the capital contribution exceeded the value — e.g., the cash surrender value — of the interest at the time of the disposition); and

(2) If an interest in the policy was disposed of after 1999 and before March 22, 2016, by a policyholder (other than a taxable Canadian corporation) to a non-arm's length person such that subsection 148(7) applied, the amount determined by the formula A – B (in subparagraph (vi) of the CDA definition). A is the amount, if any, by which the lesser of the adjusted cost base to the policyholder of the interest and the fair market value consideration given in respect of the disposition exceeds the value of the interest at the time of the disposition (e.g., its cash surrender value). B only applies if the adjusted cost basis of the interest immediately before the death of the person would have been negative but for the rule in section 257. In such case, amount B is the absolute value of that negative amount.

Note that since under s. 38(*a.1*) and (*a.2*) no part of the gain arising from a donation of a listed security is taxable, it appears that the entire untaxed gain would be added to the corporation's CDA.

Since income from eligible capital property is a year-end calculation, CDA from eligible capital property sales will materialize at year end rather than at the time of sale unless an election is made under s. 14(1.01) (now repealed) with the s. 83(2) election to treat the sale as a sale of ordinary capital property. However, this election will not be available in many cases, including sales of goodwill. (See the editorial note for s. 14(1.01).) Beginning in 2017, the concept of eligible capital property is repealed. The types of property formerly contained in this category are now depreciable capital property (new Class 14.1).

The CRA has indicated that, for purposes of calculating CDA, the portion of a capital gains reserve of a corporation claimed under s. 40(1)(*a*)(iii) that is considered to be included in income of the corporation for a particular year is deemed to be included in the corporation's income on the first day of the corporation's taxation year (see CRA Document No. 2004-0090461E5). For the CRA's view on the timing of s. 55(2) and the CDA, see Document No. 2011-0412131C6.

Per CRA Document No. 2010-0363191C6, the CDA of a corporate beneficiary which receives capital dividends from a trust is not increased until the end of the trust's taxation year. For the CRA's view on the timing of sources of CDA earned by corporate partners, see Document Nos. 2003-0038595 (capital dividends) and 2006-0215001E5 (eligible capital property).

In *Innovative Installation Inc.*, 2010 DTC 5175, the FCA allowed a creditor to add to its CDA the proceeds of a life insurance policy assigned to the creditor to discharge a debt of the life insured. Per Document No. 2011-0401431C6, the CRA accepts the decision effective as of October 27, 2010 (the date of the FCA's decision), but this is limited to "fact situations that are similar or identical to the *Innovative Installation* decision" (for a differing fact situation, see Document No. 2011-0399771C6; for a discussion of the CRA's views of payments of life insurance proceeds to a bare trustee, see Document No. 2012-0435641C6).

History: S. 89(1), the portion of paragraph (*f*) before subparagraph (i) of the definition "capital dividend account" was replaced by S.C. 2017, c. 33, s. 26(3), in force December 14, 2017, and formerly read:

(*f*) all amounts each of which is an amount in respect of a distribution made in the period by a trust to the corporation in respect of capital gains of the trust equal to the lesser of

S. 89(1), paragraph (*i.1*) of the definition "capital dividend account" was added by S.C. 2017, c. 33, s. 26(2), in force December 14, 2017.

S. 89(1), the portion of paragraph (*a*) before subparagraph (i) of the definition "capital dividend account" was replaced by S.C. 2017, c. 33, s. 26(1), in force December 14, 2017, and formerly read:

(*a*) the amount, if any, by which

S. 89(1), subparagraph (*c.1*)(i) of the definition "capital dividend account" was replaced by S.C. 2016, c. 12, s. 29(1), in force January 1, 2017, and formerly read:

(i) $^1/_2$ of the total of all amounts each of which is an amount required by paragraph 14(1)(*b*) to be included in computing the corporation's income in respect of a business carried on by the corporation for a taxation year that is included in the period and that ended after February 27, 2000 and before October 18, 2000,

S. 89(1), subparagraph (*c.2*)(i) of the definition "capital dividend account" was replaced by S.C. 2016, c. 12, s. 29(2), in force January 1, 2017, and formerly read:

(i) the total of all amounts each of which is an amount required by paragraph 14(1)(*b*) to be included in computing the corporation's income in respect of a business carried on by the corporation for a taxation year that is included in the period and that ends after October 17, 2000,

S. 89(1), subparagraph (*d*)(iii) of the definition "capital dividend account" was replaced by S.C. 2016, c. 12, s. 29(3), in force December 15, 2016, and formerly read:

(iii) the adjusted cost basis (within the meaning assigned by subsection 148(9)) of a policy referred to in subparagraph (i) or (ii) to the corporation immediately before the death, or

S. 89(1), subparagraphs (*d*)(v) and (vi) of the definition "capital dividend account" were added by S.C. 2016, c. 12, s. 29(4), in force December 15, 2016.

S. 89(1), clause (*a*)(i)(A) of the definition "capital dividend account" was replaced by S.C. 2016, c. 7, s. 10(1), applicable to dispositions made after April 20, 2015, and formerly read:

(A) the amount of the corporation's capital gain — computed without reference to subparagraphs 52(3)(*a*)(ii) and 53(1)(*b*)(ii) — from the disposition (other than a disposition under paragraph 40(3.1)(*a*) or subsection 40(12) or a disposition that is the making of a gift after December 8, 1997 that is not a gift described in subsection 110.1(1)) of a property in the period beginning at the beginning of its first taxation year that began after the corporation last became a private corporation and that ended after 1971 and ending immediately before the particular time (in this definition referred to as "the period")

S. 89(1), clause (*a*)(ii)(A) of the definition "capital dividend account" was replaced by S.C. 2016, c. 7, s. 10(2), applicable to dispositions made after April 20, 2015, and formerly read:

(A) the amount of the corporation's capital loss — computed without reference to subparagraphs 52(3)(*a*)(ii) and 53(1)(*b*)(ii) — from the disposition (other than a disposition under subsection 40(3.12) or a disposition that is the making of a gift after December 8, 1997 that is not a gift described in subsection 110.1(1)) of a property in the period

S. 89(1), the portion of paragraph (*d*) of the definition "capital dividend account" after subparagraph (i) was replaced by S.C. 2013, c. 40, s. 41(1), applicable to taxation years that end after March 20, 2013, and formerly read:

(ii) all amounts each of which is the proceeds of a life insurance policy of which the corporation was not a beneficiary on or before June 28, 1982 received by the corporation in the period and after May 23, 1985 in consequence of the death of any person

exceeds the total of all amounts each of which is the adjusted cost basis (within the meaning assigned by subsection 148(9)) of a policy referred to in subparagraph (i) or (ii) to the corporation immediately before that person's death,

S. 89(1), clause (*f*)(i)(B) of the definition "capital dividend account" was replaced by S.C. 2013, c. 34, s. 225(7), applicable to taxation years that begin after October 31, 2011, and formerly read:

(B) the amount designated under subsection 104(21) by the trust (other than a designation to which subsection 104(21.4) applies) in respect of the net taxable capital gains of the trust attributable to those capital gains, and

S. 89(1), clause (*a*)(ii)(A) of the definition "capital dividend account" was replaced by S.C. 2013, c. 34, s. 225(5), applicable to dispositions under subsection 40(3.12) that occur after October 31, 2011, other than dispositions that relate to amounts deemed under subsection 40(3.1) to have been a gain from a disposition that occurred before November 1, 2011. S. 89(1), clause (*a*)(ii)(A) of the definition "capital dividend account" formerly read:

(A) the amount of the corporation's capital loss — computed without reference to subparagraphs 52(3)(*a*)(ii) and 53(1)(*b*)(ii) — from the disposition (other than a disposition that is the making of a gift after December 8, 1997 that is not a gift described in subsection 110.1(1)) of a property in the period

S. 89(1), clause (*a*)(ii)(A) of the definition "capital dividend account" was replaced by S.C. 2013, c. 34, s. 225(4), applicable in respect of dispositions that occur on or after November 9, 2006, and formerly read:

(A) the amount of the corporation's capital loss from a disposition (other than a disposition that is the making of a gift after December 8, 1997 that is not a gift described in subsection 110.1(1)) of a property in that period

S. 89(1), clause (*a*)(i)(A) of the definition "capital dividend account" was replaced by S.C. 2013, c. 34, s. 225(3), applicable to dispositions under paragraph 40(3.1)(*a*) of the Act that occur after October 31, 2011, and formerly read:

(A) the amount of the corporation's capital gain — computed without reference to subparagraphs 52(3)(*a*)(ii) and 53(1)(*b*)(ii) — from the disposition (other than a disposition under subsection 40(12) or that is the making of a gift after December 8, 1997 that is not a gift described in subsection 110.1(1)) of a property in the period beginning at the beginning of its first taxation year (that began after the corporation last became a private corporation and that ended after 1971) and ending immediately before the particular time (in this definition referred to as "the period")

S. 89(1), clause (*a*)(i)(A) of the definition "capital dividend account" was replaced by S.C. 2013, c. 34, s. 225(2), applicable to dispositions that occur on or after March 22, 2011, and formerly read:

(A) the amount of the corporation's capital gain — computed without reference to subparagraphs 52(3)(*a*)(ii) and 53(1)(*b*)(ii) — from the disposition (other than a disposition that is the making of a gift after December 8, 1997 that is not a gift described in subsection 110.1(1)) of a property in the period beginning at the beginning of its first taxation year that began after the corporation last became a private corporation and that ended after 1971 and ending immediately before the particular time (in this definition referred to as "the period")

S. 89(1), clause (*a*)(i)(A) of the definition "capital dividend account" was replaced by S.C. 2013, c. 34, s. 225(1), applicable in respect of dispositions that occur on or after November 9, 2006, and formerly read:

(A) the amount of the corporation's capital gain from the disposition (other than a disposition under subsection 40(12) or that is the making of a gift after December 8, 1997 that is not a gift described in subsection 110.1(1)) of a property in the period beginning at the beginning of its first taxation year (that began after the corporation last became a private corporation and that ended after 1971) and ending immediately before the particular time (in this definition referred to as "the period")

S. 89(1), clause (*a*)(i)(A) of the definition "capital dividend account" was replaced by S.C. 2011, c. 24, s. 19(1), applicable to dispositions that occur on or after March 22, 2011. S. 89(1), clause (*a*)(i)(A) of the definition "capital dividend account" formerly read:

(A) the amount of the corporation's capital gain from a disposition (other than a disposition that is the making of a gift after December 8, 1997 that is not a gift described in subsection 110.1(1)) of a property in the period beginning at the beginning of its first taxation year (that began after the corporation last became a private corporation and that ended after 1971) and ending immediately before the particular time (in this definition referred to as "the period")

S. 89(1), clause (*a*)(i)(B.1) of the definition "capital dividend account" was added by S.C. 2011, c. 24, s. 19(2), applicable to dispositions that occur on or after March 22, 2011.

Related Regulations: 600.

Related Sections: S. 14(1.01) Election re capital gain; s. 83(2) Capital dividend; s. 83(2.1) Capital dividend — anti-avoidance rule; s. 83(2.2) Capital dividend — exception to anti-avoidance rule; s. 83(2.3) Capital dividend — exception to anti-avoidance rule; s. 83(2.4) Capital dividend — exception to anti-avoidance rule; s. 87(2)(z.1) Capital dividend account; s. 88(2) Winding-up of Canadian corporation; s. 89(1.1) Capital dividend account where control acquired; s. 111(4) Acquisition of control; s. 184 Tax on excess of dividend paid over portion payable out of tax-paid undistributed surplus or 1971 capital surplus; s. 185 Assessment of tax; ITAR s. 57(9) Capital dividend account.

Canadian Tax Foundation: Korhonen, *Reverse Earnouts and the CDA*, 2015 Canadian Tax Focus 4(2):4–5.

Tax Profile: October 2004 — Taxation of Dividends: A Survey in the Context of Private Corporations and Their Shareholders.

Tax Topics: No. 2441-42, Rectification Granted for Miscalculated Capital Dividend Account Balance; No. 1975, Creditor Insurance — Where Are We Now?.

Income Tax Folios: *Primary* — S3-F2-C1 Capital Dividends. S4-F8-C1 Business Investment Losses.

Interpretation Bulletins: *Secondary* — IT-123R6 Transactions involving eligible capital property; IT-430R3 (Consolid.) — Life insurance proceeds received by a private corporation or a partnership as a consequence of death.

Tax Window Files: Capital Dividend Account and 149(1)(n), *August 17, 2016*, CRA Document No. 2016-0639251I7; Compte de dividendes en capital, *March 28, 2012*, CRA Document No. 2011-0412541E5; Capital dividend account - beneficiary of a trust, *June 8, 2010*, CRA Document No. 2010-0363191C6; Surrender of Property, *Income Tax Rulings Directorate, Policy and Legislation Branch, May 27, 2009*, CRA Document No. 2009-0305751E5.

"designated property" — "designated property" means

(*a*) any property of a private corporation that last became a private corporation before November 13, 1981 and that was acquired by it

(i) before November 13, 1981, or

(ii) after November 12, 1981 pursuant to an agreement in writing entered into on or before that date,

(*b*) any property of a private corporation that was acquired by it from another private corporation with which the private corporation was not dealing at arm's length (otherwise than by virtue of a right referred to in paragraph 251(5)(*b*)) at the time the property was acquired, where the property was a designated property of the other private corporation,

(*c*) a share acquired by a private corporation in a transaction to which section 51, subsection 85(1) or section 85.1, 86 or 87 applied in exchange for another share that was a designated property of the corporation, or

(*d*) a replacement property (within the meaning assigned by section 44) for a designated property disposed of by virtue of an event referred to in paragraph (*b*), (*c*) or (*d*) of the definition "proceeds of disposition" in section 54;

Income Tax Folios: *Primary* — S3-F2-C1 Capital Dividends.

"eligible dividend" —"eligible dividend" means

(*a*) an amount that is equal to the portion of a taxable dividend that is received by a person resident in Canada, paid by a corporation resident in Canada and designated under subsection (14) to be an eligible dividend, and

(*b*) in respect of a person resident in Canada, an amount that is deemed by subsection 96(1.11) or 104(16) to be a taxable dividend that is received by the person;

Editorial Note: Eligible dividends qualify for a 38% gross-up and a dividend tax credit of $6/11$ of that amount. Prior to 2012, more generous gross-up and tax credit rates applied (see s. 82(1) and 121). Canadian-controlled private corporations ("CCPCs") and deposit insurance corporations can generally pay eligible dividends without penalties to the extent of their general rate income pool. Other corporations resident in Canada (as well as SIFT partnerships and trusts) can pay eligible dividends without penalties after they have exhausted their low rate income pool by paying ineligible dividends. Eligible dividends must be designated, per s. 89(14). Applicable after March 28, 2012, a portion of a dividend may be designated as an eligible dividend (see the editorial note for s. 89(14)). An eligible dividend must be received by a person resident in Canada. See also the editorial notes for s. 89(1), "excessive eligible dividend designation", "general rate income pool", "low rate income pool", s. 89(11), and s. 249(3.1) (regarding a change of status to or from a CCPC).

History: S. 89(1), paragraph (*a*) of the definition "eligible dividend" was replaced by S.C. 2012, c. 19, s. 4(1), applicable to dividends paid after March 28, 2012. S. 89(1), paragraph (*a*) of the definition "eligible dividend" formerly read:

(*a*) a taxable dividend that is received by a person resident in Canada, paid after 2005 by a corporation resident in Canada and designated, as provided under subsection (14), to be an eligible dividend, and

Related Sections: S. 82(1) Taxable dividends received; s. 82(3) Dividends received by spouse or common-law partner; s. 87(2)(*z.2*) Application of Parts III and III.1; s. 87(2)(*vv*) Losses; s. 87(2)(*ww*) Low rate income pool; s. 88(1)(*e.2*) Windings-up; s. 89(1), "excessive eligible dividend designation", "general rate income pool", "low rate income pool"; 89(4) GRIP addition — becoming CCPC; 89(5) GRIP addition — post-amalgamation; 89(6) GRIP addition — post-winding-up; 89(7) GRIP addition for 2006; 89(8) LRIP addition — ceasing to be CCPC; 89(9) LRIP addition — amalgamation; 89(10) LRIP addition — winding-up; 89(11) Election: non-CCPC; 89(12) Revoking election; 89(13) Repeated elections — consent required; 89(14) Dividend designation; 89(14.1) Late designation; 89(15) Meaning of expression "deposit insurance corporation"; s. 96(1.11)(*b*) Deemed dividend of SIFT partnership; s. 104(16) SIFT deemed dividend; s. 121 Deduction for taxable dividends; s. 125(7), "Canadian-controlled private corporation", paragraph (*d*); s. 185.1 Tax on excessive eligible dividend designations; s. 185.2 Return; s. 248(1), "eligible dividend", "excessive eligible dividend designation", "general rate income pool", "low rate income pool"; s. 249(3.1) Year end on status change; s. 260(1.1) Eligible dividend; s. 260(5) Deemed dividend.

Canadian Tax Foundation: Moody, *Owner Manager Remuneration — Current Trends, Strategies, and Challenges*, 2013 Prairie Provinces Tax Conference 7:1–49.

Tax Profile: January 2007 — Update on New Rules for the Taxation of Dividends; December 2006 — Major Changes to the Taxation of Income Trusts and Certain Flow-Through Entities.

Tax Topics: No. 1795, Eligible Dividends — The Good, the Bad, and the Ugly.

No. 2102, Eligible Dividends and Subsection 55(2); No. 1903, Tax Smart Investing.

Income Tax Technical News: Issue No. 41, Eligible Dividend Designation — Subsection 89(14).

Tax Window Files: Foreign Currency Denominated Dividends, *November 20, 2015*, CRA Document No. 2014-0539951E5.

"excessive eligible dividend designation" —"excessive eligible dividend designation", made by a corporation in respect of an eligible dividend paid by the corporation at any time in a taxation year, means

(*a*) unless paragraph (*c*) applies to the dividend, if the corporation is in the taxation year a Canadian-controlled private corporation or a deposit insurance corporation, the amount, if any, determined by the formula

$$(A - B) \times C/A$$

where

A is the total of all amounts each of which is the amount of an eligible dividend paid by the corporation in the taxation year,

B is the greater of nil and the corporation's general rate income pool at the end of the taxation year, and

C is the amount of the eligible dividend,

(*b*) unless paragraph (*c*) applies to the dividend, if the corporation is not a corporation described in paragraph (*a*), the amount, if any, determined by the formula

$$A \times B/C$$

where

A is the lesser of

(i) the total of all amounts each of which is an eligible dividend paid by the corporation at that time, and

(ii) the corporation's low rate income pool at that time,

B is the amount of the eligible dividend, and

C is the amount determined under subparagraph (i) of the description of A, and

(*c*) an amount equal to the amount of the eligible dividend, if it is reasonable to consider that the eligible dividend was paid in a transaction, or as part of a series of transactions, one of the main purposes of which was to artificially maintain or increase the corporation's general rate income pool, or to artificially maintain or decrease the corporation's low rate income pool;

Editorial Note: Part III.1 of the Act imposes penalties on "excessive eligible dividend designations". For Canadian-controlled private corporations and deposit insurance corporations, per paragraph (*a*) of the definition, this is the amount by which the total of eligible dividends paid in a taxation year exceeds the corporation's general rate income pool ("GRIP") at the end of the year. For other corporations (including public corporations), per paragraph (*b*), this amount is based on the lesser of the corporation's low rate income pool ("LRIP") at the particular time and eligible dividends if paid at that time (i.e., LRIP effectively "blocks" eligible dividend benefits, such that a qualifying corporation with no LRIP can pay unlimited eligible dividends). In order to determine the excessive eligible dividend designation in respect of a particular eligible dividend, the total amount of excessive eligible dividend designations is prorated. Per paragraph (*c*), however, a corporation's excessive eligible dividend designation in respect of a dividend is equal to the entire amount of the eligible dividend if it is reasonable to consider that the eligible dividend was paid in a transaction, or as part of a series of transactions, one of the main purposes of which was to artificially maintain or increase the corporation's GRIP, or maintain or decrease its LRIP; severe penalties then apply (see CRA Document Nos. 2011-0395121E5 and 2007-0231521R3 for examples of the CRA's views on the application of this paragraph). The recipient can still treat an excessive dividend as eligible. See also the editorial note for s. 185.1(1).

Related Sections: S. 87(2)(*z.2*) Application of Parts III and III.1; s. 88(1)(*e.2*) Winding-up; s. 89(1), "eligible dividend", "general rate income pool", "low rate income pool"; 89(4) GRIP addition — becoming CCPC; 89(5) GRIP addition — post-amalgamation; 89(6) GRIP addition — post-winding-up; 89(7) GRIP addition for 2006; 89(8) LRIP addition — ceasing to be CCPC; 89(9) LRIP addition — amalgamation; 89(10) LRIP addition — winding-up; 89(11) Election: non-CCPC; 89(12) Revoking election; 89(13) Repeated elections — consent required; 89(14) Dividend designation; 89(14.1) Late designation; 89(15) Meaning of expression "deposit insurance corporation"; s. 125(7), "Canadian-controlled private corporation", paragraph (*d*); s. 137.1, "deposit insurance corporation"; s. 185.1 Tax on excessive eligible dividend designations; s. 185.2 Return; s. 248(1), "eligible dividend", "excessive eligible dividend designation".

Forms: T2 Schedule 55 — Part III.1 Tax on Excessive Eligible Dividend Designations.

Tax Window Files: Eligible Dividends and LRIP, *May 5, 2010*, CRA Document No. 2010-0363851C6.

"general rate factor" —"general rate factor" of a corporation for a taxation year is the total of

(*a*) that proportion of 0.68 that the number of days in the taxation year that are before 2010 is of the number of days in the taxation year,

(*b*) that proportion of 0.69 that the number of days in the taxation year that are in 2010 is of the number of days in the taxation year,

(*c*) that proportion of 0.70 that the number of days in the taxation year that are in 2011 is of the number of days in the taxation year, and

(*d*) that proportion of 0.72 that the number of days in the taxation year that are after 2011 is of the number of days in the taxation year;

Editorial Note: A corporation's "general rate factor" is relevant to determining the corporation's general rate income pool ("GRIP"). The general rate factor is 72% for taxation years after 2011, 70% for 2011, 69% for 2010, and 68% before 2010. This percentage is applied to the corporation's "adjusted taxable income" in order to generate an amount that represents the after-tax earnings of the corporation. This amount increases the corporation's GRIP for the year (see the description of D in the "general rate income pool" definition in s. 89(1).)

History: S. 89(1), the definition "general rate factor" was added by S.C. 2009, c. 2, s. 22(3), applicable to the 2006 and subsequent taxation years.

"general rate income pool" —"general rate income pool" at the end of a particular taxation year, of a taxable Canadian corporation that is a Canadian-controlled private corporation or a deposit insurance corporation in the particular taxation year, is the positive or negative amount determined by the formula

$$A - B$$

where

A is the positive or negative amount that would, before taking into consideration the specified future tax consequences for the particular taxation year, be determined by the formula

$$C + D + E + F - G$$

where

C is the corporation's general rate income pool at the end of its preceding taxation year,

D is the amount, if any, that is the product of the corporation's general rate factor for the particular taxation year multiplied by its adjusted taxable income for the particular taxation year,

E is the total of all amounts each of which is

(*a*) an eligible dividend received by the corporation in the particular taxation year, or

(*b*) an amount deductible under section 113 in computing the taxable income of the corporation for the particular taxation year,

F is the total of all amounts determined under subsections (4) to (6) in respect of the corporation for the particular taxation year, and

G is

(*a*) unless paragraph (*b*) applies, the amount, if any, by which

(i) the total of all amounts each of which is the amount of an eligible dividend paid by the corporation in its preceding taxation year

exceeds

(ii) the total of all amounts each of which is an excessive eligible dividend designation made by the corporation in its preceding taxation year, or

(*b*) if subsection (4) applies to the corporation in the particular taxation year, nil, and

B is the amount determined by the formula

$$H \times (I - J)$$

where

H is the corporation's general rate factor for the particular taxation year,

I is the total of the corporation's full rate taxable incomes (as would be defined in the definition "full rate taxable income" in subsection 123.4(1), if that definition were read without reference to its subparagraphs (*a*)(i) to (iii)) for the corporation's preceding three taxation years, determined without taking into consideration the specified future tax consequences, for those preceding taxation years, that arise in respect of the particular taxation year, and

J is the total of the corporation's full rate taxable incomes (as would be defined in the definition "full rate taxable income" in subsection 123.4(1), if that definition were read without reference to its subparagraphs (*a*)(i) to (iii)) for those preceding taxation years;

Editorial Note: This tax account (applicable to taxation years after 2005) is relevant to eligible dividends paid by Canadian-controlled private corporations ("CCPCs") and deposit insurance corporations. If eligible dividends exceed the corporation's general rate income pool ("GRIP"), the "excessive eligible dividend designation" penalty regime will apply. GRIP is a year-end calculation whereby eligible dividends can be paid without penalties at a time when there is insufficient GRIP, provided that by year end there is enough GRIP to cover the dividends. Generally, and in simplified form, the following are components of the GRIP account:

The description of A:

- GRIP at the end of the preceding taxation year (the description of C).
- Add "adjusted taxable income" times the corporation's "general rate factor" for the year (the description of D). (See definitions in s. 89(1).)
- Add eligible dividends received by the corporation (paragraph (a) of the description of E), dividends deductible under s. 113 (e.g., dividends from exempt surplus) (paragraph (*b*) of the description of E), and GRIP addi-

tions on becoming a CCPC or in respect of amalgamation or winding-up (the description of F).

- Subtract eligible dividends paid in the preceding taxation year, net of excessive eligible dividend designations in the preceding taxation year (nil if the corporation has become a CCPC so that s. 89(4) applies in the year — see the description of G.)

Per the description of B, subsequent years' losses that are carried back to a particular year (and other "specified future tax consequences"), do not reduce that year's GRIP, but instead reduce GRIP at the end of the year in which the loss arises. See CRA Document No. 2007-0243091C6 for the effect of losses on the GRIP calculation.

A CCPC may qualify for an addition to GRIP in respect of years prior to its 2006 taxation year by virtue of s. 89(7). Separate calculations apply upon becoming a CCPC (s. 89(4)), to amalgamations, and to windings-up (s. 89(5) and (6)). Dividends deemed to be capital gains to the recipient under s. 55(2) nonetheless deplete the GRIP of the payer — see CRA Document Nos. 2007-0233771C6 and 2008-0271401E5. Dividends received by non-residents are not eligible dividends and therefore do not reduce GRIP — see CRA Document No. 2008-0284951C6 (see Document No. 2009-0330141C6 for dividends paid to a partnership with non-resident partners). Dividends received (per paragraph (*a*) of the description of E) must be based on the taxation year, not the calendar year; see Document No. 2009-0330151C6.

History: S. 89(1), the definition "general rate income pool" was replaced by S.C. 2009, c. 2, s. 22(1), applicable to the 2006 and subsequent taxation years. S. 89(1), the definition "general rate income pool" formerly read:

"general rate income pool"—"general rate income pool" at the end of a particular taxation year, of a taxable Canadian corporation that is a Canadian-controlled private corporation or a deposit insurance corporation in the particular taxation year, is the positive or negative amount determined by the formula

$$A - B$$

where

A is the positive or negative amount that would, before taking into consideration the specified future tax consequences for the particular taxation year, be determined by the formula

$$C + 0.68(D - E - F) + G + H - I$$

where

C is the corporation's general rate income pool at the end of its preceding taxation year,

D is

(*a*) unless paragraph (*b*) applies, the corporation's taxable income for the particular taxation year, and

(*b*) if the corporation is a deposit insurance corporation in the particular taxation year, nil,

E is the amount determined by multiplying the amount, if any, deducted by the corporation under subsection 125(1) for the particular taxation year by the quotient obtained by dividing 100 by the rate of the deduction provided under that subsection for the particular taxation year,

F is

(*a*) if the corporation is a Canadian-controlled private corporation in the particular taxation year, the lesser of the corporation's aggregate investment income for the particular taxation year and the corporation's taxable income for the particular taxation year, and

(*b*) in any other case, nil,

G is the total of all amounts each of which is

(*a*) an eligible dividend received by the corporation in the particular taxation year, or

(*b*) an amount deductible under section 113 in computing the taxable income of the corporation for the particular taxation year,

H is the total of all amounts determined under subsections (4) to (6) in respect of the corporation for the particular taxation year, and

I is

(*a*) unless paragraph (*b*) applies, the amount, if any, by which

(i) the total of all amounts each of which is the amount of an eligible dividend paid by the corporation in its preceding taxation year

exceeds

(ii) the total of all amounts each of which is an excessive eligible dividend designation made by the corporation in its preceding taxation year, or

(*b*) if subsection (4) applies to the corporation in the particular taxation year, nil, and

B is 68% of the amount, if any, by which

(*a*) the total of the corporation's full rate taxable incomes (as would be defined in the definition "full rate taxable income" in subsection 123.4(1), if that definition were read without reference to its subparagraphs (*a*)(i) to (iii)) for the corporation's preceding three taxation years, determined without taking into consideration the specified future tax consequences, for those preceding taxation years, that arise in respect of the particular taxation year,

exceeds

(*b*) the total of the corporation's full rate taxable incomes (as would be defined in the definition "full rate taxable income" in subsection 123.4(1), if that definition were read without reference to its subparagraphs (*a*)(i) to (iii)) for those preceding taxation years;

Related Sections: S. 87(2)(*vv*) General rate income pool; s. 88(1)(*e.2*) Winding-up; s. 89(1), "eligible dividend", "excessive eligible dividend designation", "general rate factor" "low rate income pool"; 89(4) GRIP addition — becoming CCPC; 89(5) GRIP addition — post-amalgamation; 89(6) GRIP addition — post-winding-up; 89(7) GRIP addition for 2006; 89(8) LRIP addition — ceasing to be CCPC; 89(9) LRIP addition — amalgamation; 89(10) LRIP addition — winding-up; 89(11) Election: non-CCPC; 89(12) Revoking election; 89(13) Repeated elections — consent required; 89(14) Dividend designation; 89(14.1) Late designation; 89(15) Meaning of expression "deposit insurance corporation"; s. 125(7), "Canadian-controlled private corporation", paragraph (*d*); s. 248(1), "general rate income pool", "specified future tax consequences".

Tax Profile: January 2007 — Update on New Rules for the Taxation of Dividends.

Forms: T2 Schedule 53 — General Rate Income Pool (GRIP) Calculation (2009 and Later Tax Years).

"Life insurance capital dividend account" — (Repealed by 1986, c. 6, s. 48(2).)

"low rate income pool" —"low rate income pool", at any particular time in a particular taxation year, of a corporation (in this definition referred to as the "non-CCPC") that is resident in Canada and is in the particular taxation year neither a Canadian-controlled private corporation nor a deposit insurance corporation, is the amount determined by the formula

$$(A + B + C + D + E + F) - (G + H)$$

where

A is the non-CCPC's low rate income pool at the end of its preceding taxation year,

B is the total of all amounts each of which is an amount deductible under section 112 in computing the non-CCPC's taxable income for the year in respect of a taxable dividend (other than an eligible dividend) that became payable, in the particular taxation year but before the particular time, to the non-CCPC by a corporation resident in Canada,

C is the total of all amounts determined under subsections (8) to (10) in respect of the non-CCPC for the particular taxation year,

D is

(*a*) if the non-CCPC would, but for paragraph (*d*) of the definition "Canadian-controlled private corporation" in subsection 125(7), be a Canadian-controlled private corporation in its preceding taxation year, 80% of its aggregate investment income for its preceding taxation year, and

(*b*) in any other case, nil,

E is

(*a*) if the non-CCPC was not a Canadian-controlled private corporation in its preceding taxation year, 80% of the amount determined by multiplying the amount, if any, deducted by the corporation under subsection 125(1) for that preceding taxation year by the quotient obtained by dividing 100 by the rate of the deduction provided under that subsection for that preceding taxation year, and

(*b*) in any other case, nil,

F is

(*a*) if the non-CCPC was an investment corporation in its preceding taxation year, four times the amount, if any, deducted by it under subsection 130(1) for its preceding taxation year, and

(*b*) in any other case, nil,

G is the total of all amounts each of which is a taxable dividend (other than an eligible dividend, a capital gains dividend within the meaning assigned by subsection 130.1(4) or 131(1) or a taxable dividend deductible by the non-CCPC under subsection 130.1(1) in computing its income for the particular taxation year or for its preceding taxation year) that became payable, in the particular taxation year but before the particular time, by the non-CCPC, and

H is the total of all amounts each of which is an excessive eligible dividend designation made by the non-CCPC in the particular taxation year but before the particular time;

Editorial Note: This tax account, which generally applies to corporations other than Canadian-controlled private corporations ("CCPCs") and deposit insurance corporations, must be "cleared-out" before such corporations can pay eligible dividends without penalties under the "excessive eligible dividend designation" regime. Unlike the general rate income pool ("GRIP"), which is a year-end calculation applying to CCPCs, the low rate income pool ("LRIP") is a point-in-time calculation.

Generally, and in simplified form, the following are the components of LRIP (applicable to taxation years that end after 2005):

- LRIP at the end of the preceding taxation year (the description of A);
- Add ineligible dividends payable before the particular time to the corporation from a corporation resident in Canada (the description of B);
- Add LRIP additions on ceasing to be a CCPC or in respect of an amalgamation or winding-up (the description of C);
- Add 80% of aggregate investment income for the preceding tax year if the corporation would be a CCPC for that year but for a change-of-status election (paragraph (*a*) of the description of D);
- Subtract taxable dividends (other than eligible dividends and certain other dividends) payable in the taxation year before the particular time and excessive eligible dividend designations made in the taxation year but before the particular time (the descriptions of G and H — the descriptions of E and F apply to special status corporations).

Separate calculations apply upon ceasing to be a CCPC (s. 89(8)), to amalgamations, and to windings-up (s. 89(9) and 89(10)). Dividends received by non-residents are not eligible dividends, but reduce the payer corporation's LRIP (see, for example, Document No. 2009-0308511E5).

Related Sections: S. 87(2)(*ww*) Low rate income pool; s. 88(1)(*e.2*) Winding-up; s. 89(1), "eligible dividend", "excessive eligible dividend designation", "general rate income pool"; 89(4) GRIP addition — becoming CCPC; 89(5) GRIP addition — post-amalgamation; 89(6) GRIP addition — post-winding-up; 89(7) GRIP addition for 2006; 89(8) LRIP addition — ceasing to be CCPC; 89(9) LRIP addition — amalgamation; 89(10) LRIP addition — winding-up; 89(11) Election: non-CCPC; 89(12) Revoking election; 89(13) Repeated elections — consent required; 89(14) Dividend designation; 89(14.1) Late designation; 89(15) Meaning of expression "deposit insurance corporation"; s. 125(7), "Canadian-controlled private corporation", paragraph (*d*); s. 248(1), "low rate income pool".

Tax Profile: January 2007 — Update on New Rules for the Taxation of Dividends.

Forms: T2 Schedule 54 — Low Rate Income Pool (LRIP) Calculation (2006 and Later Tax Years).

"paid-up capital" — "paid-up capital" at any particular time means,

(*a*) in respect of a share of any class of the capital stock of a corporation, an amount equal to the paid-up capital at that time, in respect of the class of shares of the capital stock of the corporation to which that share belongs, divided by the number of issued shares of that class outstanding at that time,

(*b*) in respect of a class of shares of the capital stock of a corporation,

(i) where the particular time is before May 7, 1974, an amount equal to the paid-up capital in respect of that class of shares at the particular time, computed without reference to the provisions of this Act,

(ii) where the particular time is after May 6, 1974, and before April 1, 1977, an amount equal to the paid-up capital in respect of that class of shares at the particular time, computed in accordance with the *Income Tax Act*, chapter 148 of the Revised Statutes of Canada, 1952, as it read on March 31, 1977, and

(iii) if the particular time is after March 31, 1977, an amount equal to the paid-up capital in respect of that class of shares at the particular time, computed without reference to the provisions of this Act except subsections 51(3) and 66.3(2) and (4), sections 84.1 and 84.2, subsections 85(2.1), 85.1(2.1) and (8), 86(2.1), 87(3) and (9), paragraph 128.1(1)(*c.3*), subsections 128.1(2) and (3), section 135.2, subsections 138(11.7), 139.1(6) and (7), 148(7), 192(4.1) and 194(4.1) and sections 212.1 and 212.3,

except that, where the corporation is a cooperative corporation (within the meaning assigned by subsection 136(2)) or a credit union and the statute by or under which it was incorporated does not provide for paid-up capital in respect of a class of shares, the paid-up capital in respect of that class of shares at the particular time, computed without reference to the provisions of this Act, shall be deemed to be the amount, if any, by which

(iv) the total of the amounts received by the corporation in respect of shares of that class issued and outstanding at that time

exceeds

(v) the total of all amounts each of which is an amount or part thereof described in subparagraph (iv) repaid by the corporation to persons who held any of the issued shares of that class before that time, and

(*c*) in respect of all the shares of the capital stock of a corporation, an amount equal to the total of all amounts each of which is an amount equal to the paid-up capital in respect of any class of shares of the capital stock of the corporation at the particular time;

Editorial Note: The paid-up capital of a class of shares is initially computed "without reference to the provisions of this Act", which is understood to mean the amount determined for corporate law purposes (the amount determined under corporate law is often referred to as the "stated capital" of the class of shares). The paid-up capital of the class of shares is then subject to adjustments under specific provisions of the Act as set out in paragraph (*b*) of the definition.

History: S. 89(1), subparagraph (*b*)(iii) of the definition "paid-up capital" was replaced by S.C. 2016, c. 12, s. 29(5), in force December 15, 2016, and formerly read:

(iii) where the particular time is after March 31, 1977, an amount equal to the paid-up capital in respect of that class of shares at the particular time, computed without reference to the provisions of this Act except subsections 51(3) and 66.3(2) and (4), sections 84.1 and 84.2, subsections 85(2.1), 85.1(2.1) and (8), 86(2.1), 87(3) and (9), paragraph 128.1(1)(*c.3*), subsections 128.1(2) and (3), section 135.2, subsections 138(11.7), 139.1(6) and (7), 192(4.1) and 194(4.1) and sections 212.1 and 212.3,

S. 89(1), subparagraph (*b*)(iii) of the definition "paid-up capital" was replaced by S.C. 2016, c. 7, s. 10(3), deemed to have come into force on July 1, 2015, and formerly read:

(iii) where the particular time is after March 31, 1977, an amount equal to the paid-up capital in respect of that class of shares at the particular time, computed without reference to the provisions of this Act except subsections 51(3) and 66.3(2) and (4), sections 84.1 and 84.2, subsections 85(2.1), 85.1(2.1) and (8), 86(2.1), 87(3) and (9), paragraph 128.1(1)(*c.3*), subsections 128.1(2) and (3), 138(11.7), 139.1(6) and (7), 192(4.1) and 194(4.1) and sections 212.1 and 212.3,

S. 89(1), subparagraph (*b*)(iii) of the definition "paid-up capital" was replaced by S.C. 2012, c. 31, s. 19(1), deemed to have come into force on March 29, 2012. S. 89(1), subparagraph (*b*)(iii) of the definition "paid-up capital" formerly read:

(iii) where the particular time is after March 31, 1977, an amount equal to the paid-up capital in respect of that class of shares at the particular time, computed without reference to the provisions of this Act except subsections 51(3) and 66.3(2) and (4), sections 84.1 and 84.2, subsections 85(2.1), 85.1(2.1) and (8), 86(2.1), 87(3) and (9), 128.1(2) and (3), 138(11.7), 139.1(6) and (7), 192(4.1) and 194(4.1) and section 212.1,

S. 89(1), subparagraph (*b*)(iii) of the definition "paid-up capital" was replaced by S.C. 2009, c. 2, s. 22(2), applicable after December 19, 2007. S. 89(1), subparagraph (*b*)(iii) of the definition "paid-up capital" formerly read:

(iii) where the particular time is after March 31, 1977, an amount equal to the paid-up capital in respect of that class of shares at the particular time, computed without reference to the provisions of this Act except subsections 51(3) and 66.3(2) and (4), sections 84.1 and 84.2, subsections 85(2.1), 85.1(2.1), 86(2.1), 87(3) and (9), 128.1(2) and (3), 138(11.7), 139.1(6) and (7), 192(4.1) and 194(4.1) and section 212.1,

Related Sections: S. 84(1) Deemed dividend.

Canadian Tax Foundation: Wach, *Paid-Up Capital of Shares Held by a Functional-Currency Reporter: How Do We Resolve the Conflicts?*, 2017 Canadian Tax Journal 4:1001–1020; Nobrega, *Paid-Up Capital Planning*, 2015 Canadian Tax Journal 1:315–336; Cardarelli, *Transactions Involving Paid-Up Capital*, 2004 Conference Report 26:1–22; Smith and Devan, *Paid-Up Capital Planning*, 2003 Canadian Tax Journal 6:2296–2319; Lewin, *Tax Attributes: Cost or Capital Cost and Paid-Up Capital*, 1998 Conference Report 8:1–40; Durand and Freedman, *Dealing with Paid-Up Capital*, 1997 Corporate Management Tax Conference 17:1–42.

Tax Topics: No. 2357, 1245989 Alberta Ltd.: Tax Court Applies GAAR to PUC Averaging Transaction; No. 1894, Negative Paid-Up Capital and Subsection 84(4) Reduction.

Interpretation Bulletins: *Primary* — IT-463R2 Paid-up capital.

Tax Window Files: IFA 2016 Q3: PUC of Shares of a FC Reporter, *May 26, 2016*, CRA Document No. 2016-0642111C6; Stock dividend from CFA & PUC , *December 12, 2010*, CRA Document No. 2010-0374141R3.

"private corporation" —"private corporation" at any particular time means a corporation that, at the particular time, is resident in Canada, is not a public corporation and is not controlled by one or more public corporations (other than prescribed venture capital corporations) or prescribed federal Crown corporations or by any combination thereof and, for greater certainty, for the purposes of determining at any particular time when a corporation last became a private corporation,

(*a*) a corporation that was a private corporation at the commencement of its 1972 taxation year and thereafter without interruption until the particular time shall be deemed to have last become a private corporation at the end of its 1971 taxation year, and

(*b*) a corporation incorporated after 1971 that was a private corporation at the time of its incorporation and thereafter without interruption until the particular time shall be deemed to have last become a private corporation immediately before the time of its incorporation;

Editorial Note: "Private corporation" status is a prerequisite for "Canadian-controlled private corporation" status, as well as obtaining dividend refunds and capital dividend elections. A private corporation must be resident in Canada, and cannot be a public corporation or a corporation controlled by one or more public corporations (other than prescribed venture capital corporations), prescribed federal Crown corporations, or a combination. (A private corporation may be controlled by a non-resident.) S. 250(4) deems a corporation to be resident in Canada throughout a taxation year in certain circumstances, including if it was incorporated in Canada after April 26, 1965; see, however, ss. 250(5) (re residence under a treaty) and (5.1) (re continuance and residence).

Related Regulations: 2101; 6700; 7100.

Related Sections: S. 15(2.5) When s. 15(2) not to apply — certain trusts; s. 55(5)(*b*) Applicable rules; s. 83(2) Capital dividend; s. 87(2)(*aa*) Refundable dividend tax on hand; s. 88(1)(*e.2*)(x) Winding-up; s. 89(1), "capital dividend account", "designated property", "public corporation"; s. 89(1.1) Capital dividend account where control acquired; s. 125(7), "Canadian-controlled private corporation"; s. 129 Dividend refund to private corporation; s. 186 Tax on assessable dividends; s. 187.1(1), "excepted dividend"; s. 248(1), "private corporation"; 250 Person deemed resident; ITAR s. 50(3) Designation by Minister.

Interpretation Bulletins: *Primary* — IT-391R Status of corporations. *Secondary* — IT-73R6 The small business deduction; IT-458R2 Canadian-controlled private corporation.

"public corporation" —"public corporation" at any particular time means

(*a*) a corporation that is resident in Canada at the particular time if at that time a class of shares of the capital stock of the corporation is listed on a designated stock exchange in Canada,

(*b*) a corporation (other than a prescribed labour-sponsored venture capital corporation) that is resident in Canada at the particular time if at any time after June 18, 1971 and

(i) before the particular time, it elected in prescribed manner to be a public corporation, and at the time of the election it complied with prescribed conditions relating to the number of its shareholders, the dispersal of ownership of its shares and the public trading of its shares, or

(ii) before the day that is 30 days before the day that includes the particular time it was, by notice in writing to the corporation, designated by the Minister to be a public corporation and at the time it was so designated it complied with the conditions referred to in subparagraph (i),

unless, after the election or designation, as the case may be, was made and before the particular time, it ceased to be a public corporation because of an election or designation under paragraph (*c*), or

(*c*) a corporation (other than a prescribed labour-sponsored venture capital corporation) that is resident in Canada at the particular time if, at any time after June 18, 1971 and before the particular time it was a public corporation, unless after the time it last became a public corporation and

(i) before the particular time, it elected in prescribed manner not to be a public corporation, and at the time it so elected it complied with prescribed conditions relating to the number of its shareholders, the dispersal of ownership of its shares and the public trading of its shares, or

(ii) before the day that is 30 days before the day that includes the particular time, it was, by notice in writing to the corporation, designated by the Minister not to be a public corporation and at the time it was so designated it complied with the conditions referred to in subparagraph (i),

and where a corporation has, on or before its filing-due date for its first taxation year, become a public corporation, it is, if it so elects in its return of income for the year, deemed to have been a public corporation from the beginning of the year until the time when it so became a public corporation;

Related Regulations: 4800; 6700; 6701.

Related Sections: S. 250 Person deemed resident; ITAR s. 50(3) Designation by Minister; s. 262 Designated stock exchanges.

Forms: T2067 — Election Not To Be A Public Corporation; T2073 — Election to be a Public Corporation.

Interpretation Bulletins: *Secondary* — IT-73R6 The small business deduction; IT-391R Status of corporations; IT-458R2 Canadian-controlled private corporation.

"taxable Canadian corporation" —"taxable Canadian corporation" means a corporation that, at the time the expression is relevant,

(*a*) was a Canadian corporation, and

(*b*) was not, by reason of a statutory provision, exempt from tax under this Part;

Editorial Note: "Taxable Canadian corporation" status (i.e., a non-tax-exempt "Canadian corporation") is a prerequisite for many provisions including: the dividend tax credit (s. 82(1) and s. 121), a number of rollovers, including amalgamations (s. 87(1)), wind-ups (s. 88(1)), s. 85 transfers (the transferee must have this status), and the s. 112(1) deduction for intercorporate dividends (the payor must have this status unless it is controlled by the recipient).

History: S. 89(1), paragraph (*b*) of the definition "taxable Canadian corporation" was replaced by S.C. 2017, c. 20, s. 7(1), applicable to taxation years that begin after 2018, and formerly read:

(*b*) was not, by reason of a statutory provision other than paragraph 149(1)(*t*), exempt from tax under this Part;

S. 89(1), paragraph (*b*) of the definition "taxable Canadian corporation" was replaced by S.C. 2013, c. 34, s. 225(9), applicable in respect of taxation years that end after 1999, and formerly read:

(*b*) was not, by virtue of a statutory provision, exempt from tax under this Part;

Related Regulations: Part LI; 5905(5); 6203(1).

Related Sections: S. 44.1 Reserve — property disposed of to a child; s. 53(1)(*f.1*) Adjustments to cost base — Previously denied capital loss; s. 80(1), "directed person"; s. 80.04(2) Eligible transferee; s. 82(1) Taxable dividends received; s. 85(1) Transfer of property to corporation by shareholders; s. 85(2) Transfer of property to corporation from partnership; s. 85.1 Share for share exchange; s. 87(1) Amalgamations; s. 87(9) Rules applicable in respect of certain mergers; s. 88(1) Winding-up; s. 89(1), "general rate income pool"; s. 91(6) Amounts deductible in respect of dividends received — shares acquired from another corporation; s. 96(1.11) Deemed dividend of SIFT partnership; s. 104(16) SIFT deemed dividend; s. 104(19) Taxable dividends; s. 112 Deduction of taxable dividends received by corporation resident in Canada; s. 121 Deduction for taxable dividends; s. 144 Definitions; s. 187.1 Definition of "excepted dividend"; s. 191 Definitions; s. 191.1 Tax on taxable dividends; s. 191.2 Election; s. 191.3 Agreement respecting liability for tax; s. 258 Deemed dividend on term preferred share.

"taxable dividend" —"taxable dividend" means a dividend other than

(*a*) a dividend in respect of which the corporation paying the dividend has elected in accordance with subsection 83(1) as it read prior to 1979 or in accordance with subsection 83(2), and

(*b*) a qualifying dividend paid by a public corporation to shareholders of a prescribed class of tax-deferred preferred shares of the corporation within the meaning of subsection 83(1).

Interpretation Bulletins: *Secondary* — IT-67R3 Taxable dividends from corporations resident in Canada.

▶ 89(1.01) ◀

(1.01) Application of s. 138(12). The definitions in subsection 138(12) apply to this section.

▶ 89(1.1) ◀

(1.1) Capital dividend account where control acquired. Where at any particular time after March 31, 1977 a corporation that was, at a previous time, a private corporation controlled directly or indirectly in any manner whatever by one or more non-resident persons becomes a Canadian-controlled private corporation (otherwise than by reason of a change in the residence of one or more of its shareholders), in computing the corporation's capital dividend account at and after the particular time there shall be deducted the amount of the corporation's capital dividend account immediately before the particular time.

Related Sections: S. 89(1), "capital dividend account", "private corporation"; s. 256(5.1) Control in fact.

▶ 89(1.2) ◀

(1.2) Capital dividend account of tax-exempt corporation. Where at any particular time after November 26, 1987 a corporation ceases to be exempt from tax under this Part on its taxable income, in computing the corporation's capital dividend account at and after the particular time there shall be deducted the amount of the corporation's capital dividend account (computed without reference to this subsection) immediately after the particular time.

Tax Window Files: Capital Dividend Account and 149(1)(n), *August 17, 2016*, CRA Document No. 2016-0639251I7.

▶ 89(2) ◀

(2) Where corporation is beneficiary. For the purposes of this section,

(*a*) where a corporation was a beneficiary under a life insurance policy on June 28, 1982, it shall be deemed not to have been a beneficiary under such a policy on or before June 28, 1982 where at any time after December 1, 1982 a prescribed premium has been paid under the policy or there has been a prescribed increase in any benefit on death under the policy; and

(*b*) where a corporation becomes a beneficiary under a life insurance policy by virtue of an amalgamation or a winding-up to which subsection 87(1) or 88(1) applies, it shall be deemed to have been a beneficiary under the policy throughout the period during which its predecessor or subsidiary, as the case may be, was a beneficiary under the policy.

Related Regulations: 309.

Income Tax Folios: *Primary* — S3-F2-C1 Capital Dividends.

Interpretation Bulletins: *Secondary* — IT-87R2 Policyholders' income from life insurance policies.

▶ 89(3) ◀

(3) Simultaneous dividends. Where a dividend becomes payable at the same time on more than one class of shares of the capital stock of a corporation, for the purposes of sections 83, 84 and 88, the dividend on any such class of shares shall be deemed to become payable at a different time than the dividend on the other class or classes of shares and to become payable in the order designated

(*a*) by the corporation on or before the day on or before which its return of income for its taxation year in which such dividends become payable is required to be filed; or

(*b*) in any other case, by the Minister.

Related Sections: S. 13(21), "depreciable property"; s. 14(5), "cumulative eligible capital", "eligible capital expenditure"; s. 39, "capital loss"; s. 54, "capital property"; s. 83(2), "capital dividends"; s. 89(1), "Canadian corporation"; s. 125(7), "Canadian-controlled private corporation"; s. 248(1), "amount", "business", "corporation", "mortgage investment corporation", "mutual fund corporation", "prescribed", "property", "share", "shareholder"; s. 255 Canada.

► 89(4) ◄

(4) GRIP addition — becoming CCPC. If, in a particular taxation year, a corporation is a Canadian-controlled private corporation or a deposit insurance corporation but was, in its preceding taxation year, a corporation resident in Canada other than a Canadian-controlled private corporation or a deposit insurance corporation, there may be included in computing the corporation's general rate income pool at the end of the particular taxation year, the amount determined by the formula

$$A + B + C - D - E - F - G - H$$

where

A is the total of all amounts each of which is the cost amount to the corporation of a property immediately before the end of its preceding taxation year;

B is the amount of any money of the corporation on hand immediately before the end of its preceding taxation year;

C is the amount, if any, by which

(*a*) the total of all amounts that, if the corporation had had unlimited income for its preceding taxation year from each business carried on, and from each property held, by it in that preceding taxation year and had realized an unlimited amount of capital gains for that preceding taxation year, would have been deductible under subsection 111(1) in computing its taxable income for that preceding taxation year

exceeds

(*b*) the total of all amounts deducted under subsection 111(1) in computing the corporation's taxable income for that preceding taxation year;

D is the total of all amounts each of which is the amount of any debt owing by the corporation, or of any other obligation of the corporation to pay any amount, that was outstanding immediately before the end of its preceding taxation year;

E is the paid up capital, immediately before the end of its preceding taxation year, of all of the issued and outstanding shares of the capital stock of the corporation;

F is the total of all amounts each of which is a reserve deducted in computing the corporation's income for its preceding taxation year;

G is the corporation's capital dividend account, if any, immediately before the end of its preceding taxation year; and

H is the corporation's low rate income pool immediately before the end of its preceding taxation year.

Forms: T2 Schedule 53 — General Rate Income Pool (GRIP) Calculation (2009 and Later Tax Years).

► 89(5) ◄

(5) GRIP addition — post-amalgamation. If a Canadian-controlled private corporation or a deposit insurance corporation (in this subsection referred to as the "new corporation") is formed as a result of an amalgamation (within the meaning assigned by subsection 87(1)), there shall be included in computing the new corporation's general rate income pool at the end of its first taxation year the total of all amounts each of which is

(*a*) in respect of a predecessor corporation that was, in its taxation year that ended immediately before the amalgamation (in this paragraph referred to as its "last taxation year"), a Canadian-controlled private corporation or a deposit insurance corporation, the positive or negative amount determined in respect of the predecessor corporation by the formula

$$A - B$$

where

A is the predecessor corporation's general rate income pool at the end of its last taxation year, and

B is the amount, if any, by which

(i) the total of all amounts each of which is an eligible dividend paid by the predecessor corporation in its last taxation year

exceeds

(ii) the total of all amounts each of which is an excessive eligible dividend designation made by the predecessor corporation in its last taxation year; or

(*b*) in respect of a predecessor corporation (in this paragraph referred to as the "non-CCPC predecessor") that was, in its taxation year that ended immediately before the amalgamation (in this paragraph referred to as its "last taxation year"), not a Canadian-controlled private corporation or a deposit insurance corporation, the amount determined by the formula

$$A + B + C - D - E - F - G - H$$

where

A is the total of all amounts each of which is the cost amount to the non-CCPC predecessor of a property immediately before the end of its last taxation year,

B is the amount of any money of the non-CCPC predecessor on hand immediately before the end of its last taxation year,

C is the amount, if any, by which

(i) the total of all amounts that, if the non-CCPC predecessor had had unlimited income for its last taxation year from each business carried on, and from each property held, by it in that last taxation year and had realized an unlimited amount of capital gains for that last taxation year, would have been deductible under subsection 111(1) in computing its taxable income for that last taxation year

exceeds

(ii) the total of all amounts deducted under subsection 111(1) in computing the non-CCPC predecessor's taxable income for its last taxation year,

D is the total of all amounts each of which is the amount of any debt owing by the non-CCPC predecessor, or of any other obligation of the non-CCPC predecessor to pay any amount, that was outstanding immediately before the end of its last taxation year,

E is the paid up capital, immediately before the end of its last taxation year, of all of the issued and outstanding shares of the capital stock of the non-CCPC predecessor,

F is the total of all amounts each of which is a reserve deducted in computing the non-CCPC predecessor's income for its last taxation year,

G is the non-CCPC predecessor's capital dividend account, if any, immediately before the end of its last taxation year, and

H is the non-CCPC predecessor's low rate income pool immediately before the end of its last taxation year.

Forms: T2 Schedule 53 — General Rate Income Pool (GRIP) Calculation (2009 and Later Tax Years).

▶ 89(6) ◀

(6) GRIP addition — post-winding-up. If subsection 88(1) applies to the winding-up of a subsidiary into a parent (within the meanings assigned by that subsection) that is a Canadian-controlled private corporation or a deposit insurance corporation, there shall be included in computing the parent's general rate income pool at the end of its taxation year that immediately follows the taxation year during which it receives the assets of the subsidiary on the winding-up

(*a*) if the subsidiary was, in its taxation year during which its assets were distributed to the parent on the winding-up (in this paragraph referred to as its "last taxation year"), a Canadian-controlled private corporation or a deposit insurance corporation, the positive or negative amount determined by the formula

$$A - B$$

where

A is the subsidiary's general rate income pool at the end of its last taxation year, and

B is the amount, if any, by which

(i) the total of all amounts each of which is an eligible dividend paid by the subsidiary in its last taxation year

exceeds

(ii) the total of all amounts each of which is an excessive eligible dividend designation made by the subsidiary in its last taxation year; and

(*b*) in any other case, the amount determined by the formula

$$A + B + C - D - E - F - G - H$$

where

A is the total of all amounts each of which is the cost amount to the subsidiary of a property immediately before the end of its taxation year during which its assets were distributed to the parent on the winding-up (in this paragraph referred to as its "last taxation year"),

B is the amount of any money of the subsidiary on hand immediately before the end of its last taxation year,

C is the amount, if any, by which

(i) the total of all amounts that, if the subsidiary had had unlimited income for its last taxation year from each business carried on, and from each property held, by it in that last taxation year and had realized an unlimited amount of capital gains for that last taxation year, would have been deductible under subsection 111(1) in computing its taxable income for that last taxation year

exceeds

(ii) the total of all amounts deducted under subsection 111(1) in computing the subsidiary's taxable income for its last taxation year,

D is the total of all amounts each of which is the amount of any debt owing by the subsidiary, or of any other obligation of the subsidiary to pay any amount, that was outstanding immediately before the end of its last taxation year,

E is the paid up capital, immediately before the end of its last taxation year, of all of the issued and outstanding shares of the capital stock of the subsidiary,

F is the total of all amounts each of which is a reserve deducted in computing the subsidiary's income for its last taxation year,

G is the subsidiary's capital dividend account, if any, immediately before the end of its last taxation year, and

H is the subsidiary's low rate income pool immediately before the end of its last taxation year.

Forms: T2 Schedule 53 — General Rate Income Pool (GRIP) Calculation (2009 and Later Tax Years).

▶ 89(7) ◀

(7) GRIP addition for 2006. If a corporation was (or, but for an election under subsection (11), would have been), throughout its first taxation year that includes any part of January 1, 2006, a Canadian-controlled private corporation, its general rate income pool at the end of its immediately preceding taxation year is deemed to be the greater of nil and the amount determined by the formula

$$A - B$$

where

A is the total of

(*a*) 63% of the total of all amounts each of which is the corporation's full rate taxable income (as defined in subsection 123.4(1)), for a taxation year of the corporation that ended after 2000 and before 2004, determined before taking into consideration the specified future tax consequences for that taxation year,

(*b*) 63% of the total of all amounts each of which is the corporation's full rate taxable income (as would be defined in subsection 123.4(1), if that definition were read without reference to its subparagraphs (*a*)(i) and (ii)), for a taxation year of the corporation that ended after 2003 and before 2006, determined before taking into consideration the specified future tax consequences for that taxation year, and

(*c*) all amounts each of which was deductible under subsection 112(1) in computing the corporation's taxable income for a taxation year of the corporation (in this paragraph referred to as the "particular corporation") that ended after 2000 and before 2006, and is in respect of a dividend received from a corporation (in this paragraph referred to as the "payer corporation") that was, at the time it paid the dividend, connected (within the meaning assigned by subsection 186(4)) with the particular corporation, to the extent that it is reasonable to consider, having regard to all the circumstances (including but not limited to other shareholders having received dividends from the payer corporation), that the dividend was attributable to an amount that is, or if this subsection applied to the payer corporation would be, described in this paragraph or in paragraph (*a*) or (*b*) in respect of the payer corporation; and

B is the total of all amounts each of which is a taxable dividend paid by the corporation in those taxation years.

Editorial Note: Although the general rate income pool ("GRIP") generally pertains to taxation years ending after 2005, a special addition applies to corporations that were Canadian-controlled private corporations ("CCPCs") (or that would have been, but for an election under s. 87(11)) throughout their first taxation year that includes January 1, 2006. This is based on 63% of earnings subject to the general corporate tax rate for years ending after 2000 and before 2006 (ignoring loss carry backs and other "specified future tax consequences"), less taxable dividends paid during this period (the description of B). Income qualifying for the manufacturing and processing or electrical energy and steam deduction for taxation years ending after 2000 and before 2004 will not qualify for the addition (paragraph (*a*) of the description of A), but will after 2003 and before 2006 (paragraph (*b*) of the description of A). Taxable dividends deductible under s. 112(1) received by the corporation enlarge the addition, if received from a connected corporation (defined in s. 186(4)) and reasonably attributable to amounts described in paragraphs (*a*), (*b*), or (*c*) of the description of A (generally, full rate taxable income and dividends deductible under s. 112(1) for a taxation year that ended after 2000 and before 2006 (the "period")) (paragraph (*c*) of the description of A). Dividends deductible under s. 113 (i.e., dividends from foreign affiliates) or "portfolio dividends" are ignored. The "reasonably attributable" test is on a cumulative, and not a year-by-year, basis; e.g., a dividend paid early in the period might exceed the accumulated full-rate income of the payer for the year in which the dividend is paid, but fully increase the recipient's GRIP if the payer's cumulative high-rate income for the period exceeds the dividend; see CRA Document No. 2007-0243051C6. GRIP on an amalgamation or winding-up of a corporation within the stub period is lost. Dividends paid/received after a corporation's 2005 taxation year but before 2006 appear to be ignored (see, for example, CRA Document No. 2007-0257721E5).

Related Sections: S. 89(1), "general rate income pool; s. 89(11) Election: non-CCPC; s. 112(1) Deduction of taxable dividends received by corporation resident in Canada; s. 123.4(1) Definitions; s. 125(7), "Canadian-controlled private corporation"; s. 248(1), "specified future tax consequences".

Forms: T2 Schedule 53 — General Rate Income Pool (GRIP) Calculation (2009 and Later Tax Years).

► 89(8) ◄

(8) LRIP addition — ceasing to be CCPC. If, in a particular taxation year, a corporation is neither a Canadian-controlled private corporation nor a deposit insurance corporation but was, in its preceding taxation year, a Canadian-controlled private corporation or a deposit insurance corporation, there shall be included in computing the corporation's low rate income pool at any time in the particular taxation year the amount determined by the formula

$$A + B + C - D - E - F - G - H$$

where

A is the total of all amounts each of which is the cost amount to the corporation of a property immediately before the end of its preceding taxation year;

B is the amount of any money of the corporation on hand immediately before the end of its preceding taxation year;

C is the amount, if any, by which

(*a*) the total of all amounts that, if the corporation had had unlimited income for its preceding taxation year from each business carried on, and from each property held, by it in that preceding taxation year and had realized an unlimited amount of capital gains for that preceding taxation year, would have been deductible under subsection 111(1) in computing its taxable income for that preceding taxation year

exceeds

(*b*) the total of all amounts deducted under subsection 111(1) in computing the corporation's taxable income for its preceding taxation year;

D is the total of all amounts each of which is the amount of any debt owing by the corporation, or of any other obligation of the corporation to pay any amount, that was outstanding immediately before the end of its preceding taxation year;

E is the paid up capital, immediately before the end of its preceding taxation year, of all of the issued and outstanding shares of the capital stock of the corporation;

F is the total of all amounts each of which is a reserve deducted in computing the corporation's income for its preceding taxation year;

G is

(*a*) if the corporation is not a private corporation in the particular taxation year, the corporation's capital dividend account, if any, immediately before the end of its preceding taxation year, and

(*b*) in any other case, nil; and

H is the positive or negative amount determined by the formula

$$I - J$$

where

I is the corporation's general rate income pool at the end of its preceding taxation year, and

J is the amount, if any, by which

(*a*) the total of all amounts each of which is an eligible dividend paid by the corporation in its preceding taxation year

exceeds

(*b*) the total of all amounts each of which is an excessive eligible dividend designation made by the corporation in its preceding taxation year.

Forms: T2 Schedule 54 — Low Rate Income Pool (LRIP) Calculation (2006 and Later Tax Years).

Income Tax Technical News: Issue No. 44, Calculating LRIP for Cash-Basis Taxpayers.

► 89(9) ◄

(9) LRIP addition — amalgamation. If a corporation that is resident in Canada and that is neither a Canadian-controlled private corporation nor a deposit insurance corporation (in this subsection referred to as the "new corporation") is formed as a result of the amalgamation or merger of two or more corporations one or more of which is a taxable Canadian corporation, there shall be included in computing the new corporation's low rate income pool at any time in its first taxation year the total of all amounts each of which is

(*a*) in respect of a predecessor corporation that was, in its taxation year that ended immediately before the amalgamation, neither a Canadian-controlled private corporation nor a deposit insurance corporation, the predecessor corporation's low rate income pool at the end of that taxation year; and

(*b*) in respect of a predecessor corporation (in this paragraph referred to as the "CCPC predecessor") that was, throughout its taxation year that ended immediately before the amalgamation (in this paragraph referred to as its "last taxation year"), a Canadian-controlled private corporation or a deposit insurance corporation, the amount determined by the formula

$$A + B + C - D - E - F - G - H$$

where

A is the total of all amounts each of which is the cost amount to the CCPC predecessor of a property immediately before the end of its last taxation year,

B is the amount of any money of the CCPC predecessor on hand immediately before the end of its last taxation year,

C is the amount, if any, by which

(i) the total of all amounts that, if the CCPC predecessor had had unlimited income for its last taxation year from each business carried on, and from each property held, by it in that last taxation year and had realized an unlimited amount of capital gains for that last taxation year, would have been deductible under subsection 111(1) in computing its taxable income for that last taxation year

exceeds

(ii) the total of all amounts deducted under subsection 111(1) in computing the CCPC predecessor's taxable income for its last taxation year,

D is the total of all amounts each of which is the amount of any debt owing by the CCPC predecessor, or of any other obligation of the CCPC predecessor to pay any amount, that was outstanding immediately before the end of its last taxation year,

E is the paid up capital, immediately before the end of its last taxation year, of all of the issued and outstanding shares of the capital stock of the CCPC predecessor,

F is the total of all amounts each of which is a reserve deducted in computing the CCPC predecessor's income for its last taxation year,

G is

(i) if the new corporation is not a private corporation in its first taxation year, the CCPC predecessor's capital dividend account, if any, immediately before the end of its last taxation year, and

(ii) in any other case, nil, and

H is the positive or negative amount determined by the formula

$$I - J$$

where

I is the CCPC predecessor's general rate income pool at the end of its last taxation year, and

J is the amount, if any, by which

(i) the total of all amounts each of which is an eligible dividend paid by the CCPC predecessor in its last taxation year

exceeds

(ii) the total of all amounts each of which is an excessive eligible dividend designation made by the CCPC predecessor in its last taxation year.

Forms: T2 Schedule 54 — Low Rate Income Pool (LRIP) Calculation (2006 and Later Tax Years).

► 89(10) ◄

(10) LRIP addition — winding-up. If, in a particular taxation year, a corporation (in this subsection referred to as the "parent") is neither a Canadian-controlled private corporation nor a deposit insurance corporation and in the particular taxation year all or substantially all of the assets of another corporation (in this subsection referred to as the "subsidiary") were distributed to the parent on a dissolution or winding-up of the subsidiary, there shall be included in computing the parent's low rate income pool at any time in the particular taxation year that is at or after the end of the subsidiary's taxation year (in this subsection referred to as the subsidiary's "last taxation year") during which its assets were distributed to the parent on the winding-up,

(*a*) if the subsidiary was, in its last taxation year, neither a Canadian-controlled private corporation nor a deposit insurance corporation, the subsidiary's low rate income pool immediately before the end of that taxation year; and (*b*) in any other case, the amount determined by the formula

$$A + B + C - D - E - F - G - H$$

where

A is the total of all amounts each of which is the cost amount to the subsidiary of a property immediately before the end of its last taxation year,

B is the amount of any money of the subsidiary on hand immediately before the end of its last taxation year,

C is the amount, if any, by which

(i) the total of all amounts that, if the subsidiary had had unlimited income for its last taxation year from each business carried on, and from each property held, by it in that last taxation year and had realized an unlimited amount of capital gains for that last taxation year, would have been deductible under subsection 111(1) in computing its taxable income for that last taxation year

exceeds

(ii) the total of all amounts deducted under subsection 111(1) in computing the subsidiary's taxable income for its last taxation year,

D is the total of all amounts each of which is the amount of any debt owing by the subsidiary, or of any other obligation of the subsidiary to pay any amount, that was outstanding immediately before the end of its last taxation year,

E is the paid up capital, immediately before the end of its last taxation year, of all of the issued and outstanding shares of the capital stock of the subsidiary,

F is the total of all amounts each of which is a reserve deducted in computing the subsidiary's income for its last taxation year,

G is

(i) if the parent is not a private corporation in the particular taxation year, the subsidiary's capital dividend account, if any, immediately before the end of its last taxation year, and

(ii) in any other case, nil, and

H is the positive or negative amount determined by the formula

$$I - J$$

where

I is the subsidiary's general rate income pool at the end of its last taxation year, and

J is the amount, if any, by which

(i) the total of all amounts each of which is an eligible dividend paid by the subsidiary in its last taxation year

exceeds

(ii) the total of all amounts each of which is an excessive eligible dividend designation made by the subsidiary in its last taxation year.

Forms: T2 Schedule 54 — Low Rate Income Pool (LRIP) Calculation (2006 and Later Tax Years).

► 89(11) ◄

(11) Election: non-CCPC. Subject to subsection (12), a corporation that files with the Minister on or before its filing-due date for a particular taxation year an election in prescribed form to have this subsection apply is deemed for the purposes described in paragraph (*d*) of the definition "Canadian-controlled private corporation" in subsection 125(7) not to be a Canadian-controlled private corporation at any time in or after the particular taxation year.

Editorial Note: This provision allows a corporation to elect to give up its Canadian-controlled private corporation ("CCPC") status for certain purposes — notably, eligibility for the small business deduction (see paragraph (*d*) of the definition of "Canadian-controlled private corporation" in s. 125(7)). This will enable the corporation to pay eligible dividends by default, provided it does not have a balance in its low rate income pool account ("LRIP") (i.e., a corporation must deplete its LRIP account before it can pay eligible dividends without penalties).

The election, which must be filed on or before the corporation's filing-due date for the particular taxation year, does not change the year-end of the corporation; opening LRIP is calculated at the end of the preceding year (in essence, this account is calculated on a "tax balance sheet" approach). It is possible to revoke this election under s. 89(12) but repeated elections and revocations require ministerial consent (see s. 89(13)). A late-filed election will not be accepted under the "taxpayer relief provisions" (see s. 220(3.2) and Reg. 600). In Document No. 2009-0329981C6, the CRA was of the view that a s. 89(11) election is a transaction for the purposes of GAAR.

Document No. 2010-0377251E5 considered the deadline for filing a s. 89(11) election where there is a deemed year-end due to would-be change of status which would be eliminated by the s. 89(11) election (so that assuming the validity of the s. 89(11) election, the year-end would be deferred). In the CRA's view, the filing deadline for the s. 89(11) election is the would-be year-end that would exist but for the s. 89(11) election (see also Document No. 2011-0396281E5).

Related Regulations: 600.

Related Sections: S. 89(1), "general rate income pool", "low rate income pool"; 89(4) GRIP addition — becoming CCPC; 89(5) GRIP addition — post-amalgamation; 89(6) GRIP addition — post-winding-up; 89(7) GRIP addition for 2006; 89(8) LRIP addition — ceasing to be CCPC; 89(9) LRIP addition — amalgamation; 89(10) LRIP addition — winding-up; 89(12) Revoking election; 89(13) Repeated elections — consent required; 89(14) Dividend designation; 89(14.1) Late designation; 89(15) Meaning of expression "deposit insurance corporation"; s. 125(7), "Canadian-controlled private corporation", paragraph (*d*); s. 249(3.1) Year end on status change.

Tax Profile: January 2007 — Update on New Rules for the Taxation of Dividends.

Forms: T2002 — Election or Revocation of an election not to be a Canadian controlled private corporation (2006 and later tax year).

► 89(12) ◄

(12) Revoking election. If a corporation files with the Minister on or before its filing-due date for a particular taxation year a notice in prescribed form revoking, as of the end of the particular taxation year, an election described in subsection (11), the election ceases to apply to the corporation at the end of the particular taxation year.

Forms: T2002 — T002 Election or Revocation of an election not to be a Canadian controlled private corporation (2006 and later tax year).

► 89(13) ◄

(13) Repeated elections — consent required. If a corporation has, under subsection (12), revoked an election, any subsequent election under subsection (11) or subsequent revocation under subsection (12) is invalid unless

(*a*) the Minister consents in writing to the subsequent election or the subsequent revocation, as the case may be; and

(*b*) the corporation complies with any conditions imposed by the Minister.

▶ 89(14) ◀

(14) Dividend designation. A corporation designates a portion of a dividend it pays at any time to be an eligible dividend by notifying in writing at that time each person or partnership to whom the dividend is paid that the portion of the dividend is an eligible dividend.

Editorial Note: A corporation designates a portion of a dividend to be an eligible dividend by notifying in writing, at that time the dividend is paid, the person or partnership to whom the dividend is paid that the portion of the dividend is an eligible dividend. Before March 29, 2012, a portion of a dividend could not be designated to be an eligible dividend; rather, a corporation wishing to make an eligible dividend designation was required to make the designation in respect of the full amount of the dividend paid.

Although the designation must generally be made separately for each dividend at the time the dividend is paid, s. 89(14.1) allows a corporation to make an eligible dividend designation within the three-year period immediately following payment of the dividend if, in the opinion of the Minister, the circumstances are such that it would be just and equitable to permit the late designation. A late designation cannot be made in respect of dividends paid before March 29, 2012.

Notification of designation of an eligible dividend by a Canadian-controlled private corporation must include the quantum of the dividend (see CRA Document No. 2007-0249941E5). In contrast, the CRA has extended administrative relief in respect of the notification requirement to public companies permitting them to, before or at the time dividends are paid, make a designation stating that all dividends are eligible dividends unless otherwise indicated (see CRA Document Nos. 2012-0449821E5, 2008-0300381C6, and 2009-0347491C6). See *Income Tax Technical News* No. 41, where several situations are addressed: where the holder is a nominee, eligible dividends flowed through trusts, reorganizations into two classes of shares, etc. See also Document No. 2010-0373281C6, where the particulars of a designation in respect of a s. 84(3) deemed dividend are discussed.

History: S. 89(14) was replaced by S.C. 2012, c. 19, s. 4(2), applicable to dividends paid after March 28, 2012. S. 89(14) formerly read:

(14) *Dividend designation.* A corporation designates a dividend it pays at any time to be an eligible dividend by notifying in writing at that time each person or partnership to whom it pays all or any part of the dividend that the dividend is an eligible dividend.

Related Sections: S. 82(1) Taxable dividends received; s. 82(3) Dividends received by spouse or common-law partner; s. 87(2)(*z.2*) Application of Parts III and III.1; s. 87(2)(*vv*) General rate income pool; s. 87(2)(*ww*) Low rate income pool; s. 88(1)(*e.2*) Winding-up; s. 89(1), "excessive eligible dividend designation", "general rate income pool", "low rate income pool"; 89(4) GRIP addition — becoming CCPC; 89(5) GRIP addition — post-amalgamation; 89(6) GRIP addition — post-winding-up; 89(7) GRIP addition for 2006; 89(8) LRIP addition — ceasing to be CCPC; 89(9) LRIP addition — amalgamation; 89(10) LRIP addition — winding-up; 89(11) Election: non-CCPC; 89(12) Revoking election; 89(13) Repeated elections — consent required; 89(14.1) Late designation; 89(15) Meaning of expression "deposit insurance corporation"; s. 96(1.11)(*b*) Deemed dividend of SIFT partnership; s. 104(16) SIFT deemed dividend; s. 121 Deduction for taxable dividends; s. 125(7), "Canadian-controlled private corporation", paragraph (*d*); s. 185.1 Tax on excessive eligible dividend designations; s. 185.2 Return; s. 248(1), "eligible dividend", "excessive eligible dividend designation", "general rate income pool", "low rate income pool"; s. 249(3.1) Year end on status change; s. 260(1.1) Eligible dividend; s. 260(5) Deemed dividend.

Canadian Tax Foundation: Gosselin, *Late-Filed Eligible-Dividend Designations Subject to Strict Three-Year Window*, 2015 Tax for the Owner-Manager 15(3):4–5; Gosselin, *CRA Confirms GRIP Trap When Dividend Not Paid Out of Safe Income*, 2014 Tax for the Owner-Manager 14(3):1–2; Tremblay, *Deemed Timing of a Dividend Receipt by a Trust Beneficiary*, 2014 Canadian Tax Focus 4(1):5.

Tax Profile: January 2007 — Update on New Rules for the Taxation of Dividends.

Tax Topics: No. 1919-20, 2008 Canadian Tax Foundation Annual Conference — Department of Finance Presentation and CRA Round Table; No. 1814, 2006 Canadian Tax Foundation Annual Conference CRA Round Table.

Income Tax Technical News: Issue No. 41, Eligible Dividend Designation — Subsection 89(14).

▶ 89(14.1) ◀

(14.1) Late designation. If, in the opinion of the Minister, the circumstances are such that it would be just and equitable to permit a designation under subsection (14) to be made before the day that is three years after the day on which the designation was required to be made, the designation is deemed to have been made at the time the designation was required to be made.

Editorial Note: This provision allows a corporation to make a late eligible dividend designation within the three-year period immediately following the date on which the designation was first required to be made (i.e., the date the dividend was paid). The CRA must be of the opinion that permitting the late designation would be "just and equitable in the circumstances" (taking into account the interests of affected shareholders and the extent to which the corporation actually had income tax at general corporate tax rates when the dividend was paid — per the explanatory notes to s. 89(14.1)). In contrast, relief will not be granted where it is reasonable to conclude that the request was for retroactive tax-planning purposes (see CRA Document Nos. 2012-0445661C6 and 2013-0475261E5). This provision applies to dividends paid after March 28, 2012.

History: S. 89(14.1) was added by S.C. 2012, c. 19, s. 4(2), applicable to dividends paid after March 28, 2012.

Canadian Tax Foundation: Gosselin, *Late-Filed Eligible-Dividend Designations Subject to Strict Three-Year Window*, 2015 Tax for the Owner-Manager 15(3):4–5; Gosselin, *CRA Confirms GRIP Trap When Dividend Not Paid Out of Safe Income*, 2014 Tax for the Owner-Manager 14(3):1–2.

Tax Topics: No. 2265, Late Eligible Dividend Election Following an Appeal.

Tax Window Files: Eligible Dividend - Late Filing 89(14.1) & 184(3), *August 2, 2013*, CRA Document No. 2013-0475261E5.

▶ 89(15) ◀

(15) Meaning of expression "deposit insurance corporation". For the purposes of paragraphs 87(2)(*vv*) and (*ww*) (including, for greater certainty, in applying those paragraphs as provided under paragraph 88(1)(*e.2*)), the definitions "excessive eligible dividend designation", "general rate income pool", and "low rate income pool" in subsection (1) and subsections (4) to (6) and (8) to (10), a corporation is a deposit insurance corporation if it would be a deposit insurance corporation as defined in the definition "deposit insurance corporation" in subsection 137.1(5) were that definition read without reference to its paragraph (*b*) and were this Act read without reference to subsection 137.1(5.1).

SECTION 89.1: Paid-up capital

(Repealed by 1977-78, c. 1, s. 45(1).)

Subdivision i — Shareholders of Corporations Not Resident in Canada

SECTION 90: [Dividends and loans from non-resident corporations]

► 90(1) ◄

(1) Dividend from non-resident corporation. In computing the income for a taxation year of a taxpayer resident in Canada, there is to be included any amount received by the taxpayer at any time in the year as, on account or in lieu of payment of, or in satisfaction of, a dividend on a share owned by the taxpayer of the capital stock of a non-resident corporation.

Editorial Note: S. 90 provides that dividends received by a Canadian-resident taxpayer from a corporation that is not a resident of Canada are included in computing the taxpayer's income for the taxation year in which the dividends are received. A deduction in computing taxable income in respect of the dividend may be available under s. 113(1)(*a*) (dividends prescribed to be paid from exempt surplus, s. 113(1)(*b*) (underlying foreign tax applicable to dividends prescribed to be paid from taxable surplus), s. 113(1)(*c*) (non-business income tax applicable to dividends prescribed to be paid from taxable surplus), s. 113(1)(*d*) (dividends prescribed to be paid from pre-acquisition surplus) and s. 113(2) (certain foreign shares held by taxpayer at the end of 1975) where the dividends are paid by a foreign affiliate of a taxpayer that is a corporation resident in Canada. In any other case, the taxpayer may be entitled to a deduction under s. 20(11) or (12) or a foreign tax credit under s. 126(1) or (2).

History: S. 90(1) was replaced by S.C. 2013, c. 34, s. 66(1), applicable after August 19, 2011. However, if a taxpayer has elected under section 79(2)(*a*) of the *Technical Tax Amendments Act, 2012* (Bill C-48), subsection 90(1) also applies after December 20, 2002 and on or before August 19, 2011 in respect of the taxpayer.

If the taxpayer referred to in any election dealing with various foreign affiliate amendments is a partnership, any reference in those elections to "the taxpayer's filing-due date" is to be read as a reference to "the earliest of the filing-due dates of any member of the taxpayer".

Any assessment of a taxpayer's tax, interest and penalties payable under the Act for any taxation year that ends before June 26, 2013 that would, in the absence of this section, be precluded because of subsections 152(4) to (5) of the Act shall be made to the extent necessary to take into account the amendments by S.C. 2013, c. 34, s. 54 to 89.

S. 90(1) formerly read:

(1) *Dividends received from non-resident corporation.* In computing the income for a taxation year of a taxpayer resident in Canada, there shall be included any amounts received by the taxpayer in the year as, on account or in lieu of payment of, or in satisfaction of, dividends on a share owned by the taxpayer of the capital stock of a corporation not resident in Canada.

Related Sections: S. 12(1)(*k*) Dividends from other corporations; s. 20(11) Foreign taxes on income from property exceeding 15%; s. 20(12) Foreign non-business income tax; s. 20(12.1) Foreign tax where no economic profit; s. 20(13) Dividend on share from foreign affiliate of taxpayer; s. 53(2)(*b*) Amounts to be deducted — Share of non-resident corporation; s. 74.4(2)(*f*) Amounts included under s. 90(1) decreases deemed interest on a transfer or loan to a corporation in certain circumstances; s. 91(5) Amounts deductible in respect of dividends received; s. 91(6) Amounts deductible in respect of dividends received — shares acquired from another corporation; s. 91(7) Shares acquired from a partnership; s. 92(1)(*b*) Adjusted cost base decrease to the extent of s. 91(5) deduction for dividends from controlled foreign affiliate; s. 93(1) Election re disposition of share in foreign affiliate; s. 112(2) Dividends received from non-resident corporation; s. 113(1)(*a*) Exempt surplus deduction; s. 113(1)(*b*) Deduction for underlying foreign tax applicable to taxable surplus; s. 113(1)(*c*) Deduction for non-business income tax applicable to taxable surplus; s. 113(1)(*d*) Pre-acquisition surplus deduction; s. 113(2) Additional deduction; s. 126(1) Foreign tax deduction — non-business income; s. 126(2) Foreign tax deduction — business income; s. 139.1(4)(*f*) Deemed dividends arising on de-mutualization; s. 139.1(4)(*g*) Deemed dividends arising on de-mutualization; s. 139.2 Mutual holding corporations; s. 248(1), "amount", "corporation", "dividend", "resident in Canada", "share", "taxpayer"; s. 249 Definition of "taxation year"; s. 255 Canada.

Canadian Tax Foundation: McDowell et al., *Upstream Loans, Hybrid Surplus, and Other Technical Changes Affecting the Taxation of Foreign Affiliates*, 2012 Conference Report 21:1–28; Boidman and Kandev, *Foreign Entity Classification and the Meaning of "Corporation"/"Société" in the Income Tax Act*, 2009 Canadian Tax Journal 4:880–904.

Tax Profile: December 2012 — Taxpayer's Equity Characterization of Hybrid Instruments — Canadian Implications; February 2007 — U.S. Limited Liability Companies — The Good, the Bad and the Ugly; January 2006 — Foreign Source Income: Outbound Structures and Foreign Tax Credit Planning — Part I; February 2006 — Foreign Source Income: Outbound Structures and Foreign Tax Credit Planning — Part II.

Tax Topics: No. 1884, Amounts Received by Shareholders from Foreign Corporations in the Course of Winding Up.

Interpretation Bulletins: *Secondary* — IT-451R Deemed disposition and acquisition on ceasing to be or becoming resident in Canada.

Tax Window Files: 2011 TEI Q#5 - Distributions from Foreign Corp., *December 6, 2012*, CRA Document No. 2011-0427001C6; 2011 STEP Conf - Q12 - CG from foreign mutual fund, *June 3, 2011*, CRA Document No. 2011-0405261C6.

► 90(2) ◄

(2) Dividend from foreign affiliate. For the purposes of this Act, an amount is deemed to be a dividend paid or received, as the case may be, at any time on a share of a class of the capital stock of a non-resident corporation that is a foreign affiliate of a taxpayer if the amount is the share's portion of a pro rata distribution (other than a distribution made in the course of a liquidation and dissolution of the corporation, on a redemption, acquisition or cancellation of the share by the corporation, or on a qualifying return of capital in respect of the share) made at that time by the corporation in respect of all the shares of that class.

History: S. 90(2) was added by S.C. 2013, c. 34, s. 66(1), applicable after August 19, 2011. However, if a taxpayer has elected under section 79(2)(*a*) of the *Technical Tax Amendments Act, 2012* (Bill C-48), subsection 90(2) also applies after December 20, 2002 and on or before August 19, 2011 in respect of the taxpayer, except that, on or before August 19, 2011, subsection 90(2) is, in respect of the taxpayer, to be read as follows:

"(2) For the purposes of this Act, an amount is deemed to be a dividend paid or received, as the case may be, at any time on a share of a class of the capital stock of a non-resident corporation that is a foreign affiliate of a taxpayer if the amount is the share's portion of a pro rata distribution (other than a distribution made in the course of a liquidation and dissolution of the corporation, on a redemption, acquisition or cancellation of the share by the corporation, or on a reduction of the paid-up capital of the corporation in respect of the share) made at that time by the corporation in respect of all the shares of that class."

If the taxpayer referred to in any election dealing with various foreign affiliate amendments] is a partnership, any reference in those elections to "the taxpayer's filing-due date" is to be read as a reference to "the earliest of the filing-due dates of any member of the taxpayer".

See the application for s. 90(1) for the extension of assessment periods to take into account the amendments by S.C. 2013, c. 34, s. 54 to 89.

Tax Topics: No. 2193, June 2014 Election Deadlines for Retroactive Application of New Foreign Affiliate Reorganization Rules; No. 2133, New Foreign Affiliate Capital Distribution Elections: QROCs and Regulation 5901(2)(b) Dividends; No. 2079, UpEnding the Surplus Ordering Rules: Implications of the New Regulation 5901(2)(B) Election.

Tax Window Files: Payments under a German profit transfer agreement "PTA", *16XXXX*, CRA Document No. 2015-0617351R3.

► 90(3) ◄

(3) Qualifying return of capital. For the purposes of subsection (2), a distribution made at any time by a foreign affiliate of a taxpayer in respect of a share of the capital stock of the affiliate that is a reduction of the paid-up capital of the affiliate in respect of the share and that would, in the absence of this subsection, be deemed under subsection (2) to be a dividend paid or received, at that time, on the share is a qualifying return of capital, at that time, in respect of the share if an election is made under this subsection, in respect of the distribution and in accordance with prescribed rules,

(*a*) by the taxpayer, where there is no person or partnership that meets the conditions in subparagraphs (*b*)(i) and (ii); or (*b*) jointly by the taxpayer and each person or partnership that is, at that time,

(i) a connected person or partnership in respect of the taxpayer, and

(ii) a person or partnership of which the affiliate would, at that time, be a foreign affiliate if paragraph (*b*) of the definition "equity percentage" in subsection 95(4) were read as if the reference in that paragraph to "any corporation" were a reference to "any corporation other than a corporation resident in Canada".

History: S. 90(3) was added by S.C. 2013, c. 34, s. 66(1), applicable after August 19, 2011. However, if a taxpayer has elected under section 79(2)(*a*) of the *Technical Tax Amendments Act, 2012* (Bill C-48), subsection 90(3) also applies after December 20, 2002 and on or before August 19, 2011 in respect of the taxpayer, except that, on or before August 19, 2011, section 90 is to be read without reference to its subsections (3) and (4).

If the taxpayer referred to in any election dealing with various foreign affiliate amendments is a partnership, any reference in those elections to "the taxpayer's filing-due date" is to be read as a reference to "the earliest of the filing-due dates of any member of the taxpayer".

See the application for s. 90(1) for the extension of assessment periods to take into account the amendments by S.C. 2013, c. 34, s. 54 to 89.

Related Regulations: 5911(6).

Tax Topics: No. 2133, New Foreign Affiliate Capital Distribution Elections: QROCs and Regulation 5901(2)(b) Dividends.

▶ 90(4) ◀

(4) Connected person or partnership. For the purposes of subsection (3), a "connected person or partnership" in respect of a taxpayer, at any time, is

(*a*) a person that is, at that time, related to the taxpayer, and

(*b*) a partnership a member of which is, at that time,

(i) the taxpayer, or

(ii) a person that is related to the taxpayer.

History: S. 90(4) was added by S.C. 2013, c. 34, s. 66(1), applicable after August 19, 2011. However, if a taxpayer has elected under section 79(2)(*a*) of the *Technical Tax Amendments Act, 2012* (Bill C-48), subsection 90(4) also applies after December 20, 2002 and on or before August 19, 2011 in respect of the taxpayer, except that, on or before August 19, 2011, section 90 is to be read without reference to its subsections (3) and (4).

If the taxpayer referred to in any election dealing with various foreign affiliate amendments is a partnership, any reference in those elections to "the taxpayer's filing-due date" is to be read as a reference to "the earliest of the filing-due dates of any member of the taxpayer".

See the application for s. 90(1) for the extension of assessment periods to take into account the amendments by S.C. 2013, c. 34, s. 54 to 89.

▶ 90(5) ◀

(5) Exclusion. No amount paid or received at any time is, for the purposes of this Act, a dividend paid or received on a share of the capital stock of a non-resident corporation that is a foreign affiliate of a taxpayer unless it is so deemed under this Part.

History: S. 90(5) was added by S.C. 2013, c. 34, s. 66(1), applicable after August 19, 2011. However, if a taxpayer has elected under section 79(2)(*a*) of the *Technical Tax Amendments Act, 2012* (Bill C-48), subsection 90(5) also applies after December 20, 2002 and on or before August 19, 2011 in respect of the taxpayer.

If the taxpayer referred to in any election dealing with various foreign affiliate amendments is a partnership, any reference in those elections to "the taxpayer's filing-due date" is to be read as a reference to "the earliest of the filing-due dates of any member of the taxpayer".

See the application for s. 90(1) for the extension of assessment periods to take into account the amendments by S.C. 2013, c. 34, s. 54 to 89.

▶ 90(6) ◀

(6) Loan from foreign affiliate. Except where subsection 15(2) applies, if a person or partnership receives at any time a loan from, or becomes at that time indebted to, a creditor that is at that time a foreign affiliate (referred to in subsections (9), (11) and (15) as the "creditor affiliate") of a taxpayer resident in Canada or that is at that time a partnership (referred to in subsections (9), (11) and (15) as the "creditor partnership") of which such an affiliate is a member and the person or partnership is at that time a specified debtor in respect of the taxpayer, then the specified amount in respect of the loan or indebtedness is to be included in computing the income of the taxpayer for the taxpayer's taxation year that includes that time.

Department of Finance Comfort Letters

(May 1, 2018) [Upstream loan rules in ss. 90(6)-(15)]

Dear XXXX,

I am writing in response to your recent letter to, and subsequent discussions with, officials of the Tax Legislation Division concerning an issue you have identified in respect of the "upstream loan" rules in subsections 90(6) to (15) of the Income Tax Act (the "Act"). This issue arises in the context of impending refinancing transactions involving a Bermuda-resident foreign affiliate ("FA 1") or your client, XXXX ("Canco").

You have described the following financing structure involving FA 1 and other members of Canco's XXXX-parented group. FA 1 has made loans (the "FA 1 Loans") to XXXX ("Forco 1"), which, in turn, has made loans (the "Forco 1 Loans") to XXXX ("Forco 2"). Forco 1 and Forco 2 are specified debtors, as defined in subsection 90(15), in respect of Canco and are not foreign affiliates of Canco. The FA 1 Loans and the Forco 1 Loans are back-to-back loans described in subsection 90(7), with the result that, for the purposes of subsections 90(6) to (15), paragraph 90(7)(*a*) has deemed the Forco 1 Loans to have been made by FA 1 to Forco 2 (each a "Deemed Loan"), and paragraph 90(7)(*b*) has deemed each actual FA 1 Loan and Force 1 Loan not to have been made.

For each taxation year in which a Deemed Loan has been deemed to be made, subsection 90(6) has applied to include a specified amount in respect of the Deemed Loan in Canco's income and Canco has claimed an offsetting deduction under subsection 90(9) in respect of FA 1's exempt surplus. In each subsequent year, the amount so deducted has been brought back into Canco's income under subsection 90(12) and another offsetting deduction has been claimed under subsection 90(9).

As part of the impending refinancing transactions, Forco 1 will repay the FA 1 Loans and FA 1 will use the proceeds of such repayments to make loans to another specified debtor in respect of Canco (the "FA 1-New Specified Debtor Loans").

You note that there are no provisions in the Act that provide, for the purposes of paragraph 90(8)(a) and subsection 90(14), for the repayment of a loan that is deemed to have been made under subsection 90(7). You are therefore concerned that the repayment of the FA 1 Loans as part of the refinancing transactions may not be considered to result in the repayment of the Deemed Loans. In that case, the repayment, combined with the subsequent redeployment of the proceeds in the FA 1-New Specified Debtor Loans, could result in a double income inclusion to Canco for the year, with subsection 90(12) applying to bring into income the amount claimed in the previous year as a deduction in respect of each Deemed Loan under subsection 90(9), and subsection 90(6) applying to bring the amount of each FA 1-New Specified Debtor Loan into Canco's income for the year. This would be an adverse result since FA 1 does not have sufficient exempt surplus to support a deduction by Canco under subsection 90(9) equal to the amount of the two income inclusions.

Our Comments

We agree that, in policy terms, the transactions described above ought not to give rise to two concurrent upstream loans, and two related income inclusions under the upstream loan rules. We are therefore prepared to recommend to the Minister of Finance that the Act be amended to introduce rules —

similar to the deemed repayment rules in subsections 15(2.18) and (2.19) (which apply for the purposes of the back-to-back shareholder loan rules in subsections 15(2.16) and (2.17)), but with such modifications as are required by the context of the upstream loan rules — that would deem all or a portion of a loan that is deemed to be made under subsection 90(7) to be repaid for the purposes of paragraph 90(8)(*a*) and subsection 90(14) if certain conditions are met.

These conditions would be similar to those in subsection 15(2.18). In general terms, a loan deemed to have been made under subsection 90(7) would be deemed to be repaid, in whole or in part, as a result of certain repayments, in whole or in part, of one or both of the loans between the "initial lender" and the "intermediate lender", and the "intermediate lender" and the "intended borrower" (as those terms are defined in subsection 90(7)).

As in the case of a deemed repayment under subsection 15(2.19), the determination whether a deemed repayment is part of a series of loans or other transactions or repayments for purposes of paragraph 90(8)(*a*) and subsection 90(14) would need to be made on a case-by-case basis, having regard to all of the facts and circumstances.

We will recommend that this proposed amendment apply to repayments occurring aer April 10, 2018.

While we cannot offer any assurance that either the Minister of Finance or Parliament will agree with our recommendations in respect of this matter, we hope that this statement of our intentions is helpful.

Yours sincerely,
Brian Ernewein
General Director — Legislation
Tax Policy Branch

History: S. 90(6) was added by S.C. 2013, c. 34, s. 66(1), applicable in respect of loans received and indebtedness incurred after August 19, 2011. However, subsection 90(6) also applies in respect of any portion of a particular loan received or a particular indebtedness incurred on or before August 19, 2011 that remains outstanding on August 19, 2014 as if that portion were a separate loan or indebtedness that was received or incurred, as the case may be, on August 20, 2014 in the same manner and on the same terms as the particular loan or indebtedness.

If the taxpayer referred to in any election dealing with various foreign affiliate amendments is a partnership, any reference in those elections to "the taxpayer's filing-due date" is to be read as a reference to "the earliest of the filing-due dates of any member of the taxpayer".

See the application for s. 90(1) for the extension of assessment periods to take into account the amendments by S.C. 2013, c. 34, s. 54 to 89.

Canadian Tax Foundation: Zabarylo, *Emerging Issues in Tax Accounting: Implications of Foreign Affiliate Changes in Bill C-48*, 2013 Conference Report 34:1–7; Buttenham, *Are You Ready for the Upstream Loan Rules?*, 2013 Canadian Tax Journal 3:747–768; Barnicke and Huynh, *Upstream Loans: CRA Update*, 2013 Canadian Tax Highlights 21(12):3–4.

Tax Window Files: 90(6) & sale of creditor affiliate, *August 4, 2016*, CRA Document No. 2016-0645521I7.

► 90(6.1) ◄

(6.1) Upstream loan continuity — reorganizations. Subsection (6.11) applies at any time if

(*a*) immediately before that time, a person or partnership (referred to in this subsection and subsection (6.11) as the "original debtor") owes an amount in respect of a loan or indebtedness (referred to in this subsection and subsection (6.11) as the "pre-transaction loan") to another person or partnership (referred to in this subsection and subsection (6.11) as the "original creditor");

(*b*) the pre-transaction loan was, at the time it was made or entered into, a loan or indebtedness that is described in subsection (6); and

(*c*) in the course of an amalgamation, a merger, a winding-up or a liquidation and dissolution,

(i) the amount owing in respect of the pre-transaction loan becomes owing at that time by another person or partnership (the amount owing after that time and the other person or partnership are referred to in subsection (6.11) as the "post-transaction loan payable" and the "new debtor", respectively),

(ii) the amount owing in respect of the pre-transaction loan becomes owing at that time to another person or partnership (the amount owing after that time and the other person or partnership are referred to in subsection (6.11) as the "post-transaction loan receivable" and the "new creditor", respectively), or

(iii) the taxpayer in respect of which the original debtor was a specified debtor at the time referred to in paragraph (*b*)

(A) ceases to exist, or

(B) merges with one or more corporations to form one corporate entity (referred to in subsection (6.11) as the "new corporation").

History: S. 90(6.1) was added by S.C. 2017, c. 33, s. 27(1), applicable to transactions and events that occur after September 15, 2016. However, if a taxpayer files an election with the Minister before 2017, s. 90(6.1) applies in respect of the taxpayer as of August 20, 2011.

► 90(6.11) ◄

(6.11) Upstream loan continuity — reorganizations. If this subsection applies at any time, for the purposes of subsections (6) and (7) to (15) and 39(2.1) and (2.2) and paragraph 95(2)(*g*.04),

(*a*) if the condition in subparagraph (6.1)(*c*)(i) is met,

(i) the post-transaction loan payable is deemed to be the same loan or indebtedness as the pre-transaction loan, and

(ii) the new debtor is deemed to be same debtor as, and a continuation of, the original debtor;

(*b*) if the condition in subparagraph (6.1)(*c*)(ii) is met,

(i) the post-transaction loan receivable is deemed to be the same loan or indebtedness as the pre-transaction loan, and

(ii) the new creditor is deemed to be same creditor as, and a continuation of, the original creditor;

(*c*) if the condition in clause (6.1)(*c*)(iii)(A) is met,

(i) subject to subparagraph (ii), each entity that held an equity interest in the taxpayer immediately before the winding-up (referred to in this paragraph as a "successor entity") is deemed to be the same entity as, and a continuation of, the taxpayer, and

(ii) for the purposes of applying subsection (13) and the description of A in subsection (14), an amount is deemed, in respect of a loan or indebtedness, to have been included under subsection (6) in computing the income of each successor entity equal to

(A) if the taxpayer is a partnership, the amount that may reasonably be considered to be the successor entity's share (determined in a manner consistent with the determination of the successor entity's share of the income of the partnership under subsection 96(1) for the taxpayer's final fiscal period) of the specified amount that was required to be included in computing the income of the taxpayer under subsection (6) in respect of the loan or indebtedness, and

(B) in any other case, the proportion of the specified amount included in computing the taxpayer's income under subsection (6), in respect of the loan or indebtedness, that the fair market value of the successor entity's equity interest in the taxpayer, immediately before the distribution of the taxpayer's assets on the winding-up, is of the total fair market value of all equity interests in the taxpayer at that time; and

(*d*) if the condition in clause (6.1)(*c*)(iii)(B) is met, the new corporation is deemed to be the same corporation as, and a continuation of, the taxpayer.

History: S. 90(6.11) was added by S.C. 2017, c. 33, s. 27(1), applicable to transactions and events that occur after September 15, 2016. However, if a taxpayer files an election with the Minister before 2017, s. 90(6.11) applies in respect of the taxpayer as of August 20, 2011.

▶ 90(7) ◀

(7) Back-to-back loans. For the purposes of this subsection and subsections (6), (8) to (15) and 39(2.1) and (2.2) and paragraph 95(2)(*g*.04), if at any time a person or partnership (referred to in this subsection as the "intermediate lender") makes a loan to another person or partnership (in this subsection referred to as the "intended borrower") because the intermediate lender received a loan from another person or partnership (in this subsection referred to as the "initial lender")

(*a*) the loan made by the intermediate lender to the intended borrower is deemed, at that time, to have been made by the initial lender to the intended borrower (to the extent of the lesser of the amount of the loan made by the initial lender to the intermediate lender and the amount of the loan made by the intermediate lender to the intended borrower) under the same terms and conditions and at the same time as it was made by the intermediate lender; and

(*b*) the loan made by the initial lender to the intermediate lender and the loan made by the intermediate lender to the intended borrower are deemed not to have been made to the extent of the amount of the loan deemed to have been made under paragraph (*a*).

History: S. 90(7), the portion before paragraph (*a*) was replaced by S.C. 2017, c. 33, s. 27(2), applicable in respect of loans received and indebtedness incurred after August 19, 2011. However, subsection 90(7) also applies in respect of any portion of a particular loan received or a particular indebtedness incurred before August 20, 2011 that remains outstanding on August 19, 2014 as if that portion were a separate loan or indebtedness that was received or incurred, as the case may be, on August 20, 2014 in the same manner and on the same terms as the particular loan or indebtedness. S. 90(7), the portion before paragraph (*a*) formerly read:

(7) *Back-to-back loans.* For the purposes of this subsection and subsections (6) and (8) to (15), if at any time a person or partnership (referred to in this subsection as the "intermediate lender") makes a loan to another person or partnership (in this subsection referred to as the "intended borrower") because the intermediate lender received a loan from another person or partnership (in this subsection referred to as the "initial lender")

S. 90(7) was added by S.C. 2013, c. 34, s. 66(1), applicable in respect of loans received and indebtedness incurred after August 19, 2011. However,

(*a*) subsections 90(7) also applies in respect of any portion of a particular loan received or a particular indebtedness incurred on or before August 19, 2011 that remains outstanding on August 19, 2014 as if that portion were a separate loan or indebtedness that was received or incurred, as the case may be, on August 20, 2014 in the same manner and on the same terms as the particular loan or indebtedness; and

(*b*) if the taxpayer so elects in writing under this paragraph and files the election with the Minister of National Revenue on or before the day that is the later of the taxpayer's filing-due date for the taxpayer's taxation year that includes June 26, 2013 and June 26, 2014 [the day that is one year after royal assent], section 90 is, in respect of the taxpayer, to be read without reference to its subsection (7) in respect of all loans received and indebtedness incurred on or before October 24, 2012.

If the taxpayer referred to in any election dealing with various foreign affiliate amendments is a partnership, any reference in those elections to "the taxpayer's filing-due date" is to be read as a reference to "the earliest of the filing-due dates of any member of the taxpayer".

See the application for s. 90(1) for the extension of assessment periods to take into account the amendments by S.C. 2013, c. 34, s. 54 to 89.

Tax Window Files: IFA 2016 Q.5: Upstream loans: 90(7) and 90(9), *May 26, 2016*, CRA Document No. 2016-0642091C6.

▶ 90(8) ◀

(8) Exceptions to subsection (6). Subsection (6) does not apply to

(*a*) a loan or indebtedness that is repaid, other than as part of a series of loans or other transactions and repayments, within two years of the day the loan was made or the indebtedness arose;

(*b*) indebtedness that arose in the ordinary course of the business of the creditor or a loan made in the ordinary course of the creditor's ordinary business of lending money if, at the time the indebtedness arose or the loan was made, *bona fide* arrangements were made for repayment of the indebtedness or loan within a reasonable time;

(*c*) a loan that was made, or indebtedness that arose, in the ordinary course of carrying on a life insurance business outside Canada if

(i) the loan or indebtedness is owed by the taxpayer or by a subsidiary wholly-owned corporation of the taxpayer,

(ii) the taxpayer, or the subsidiary wholly-owned corporation, as the case may be, is a life insurance corporation resident in Canada,

(iii) the loan or indebtedness directly relates to a business of the taxpayer, or of the subsidiary wholly-owned corporation, that is carried on outside Canada, and

(iv) the interest on the loan or indebtedness is, or would be if it were otherwise income from property, included in the active business income of the creditor, or if the creditor is a partnership, a member of the partnership, under clause 95(2)(*a*)(ii)(A); and

(*d*) subject to subsection (8.1), an upstream deposit owing to an eligible bank affiliate.

History: S. 90(8)(*d*) was added by S.C. 2014, c. 39, s. 20(1), applicable in respect of taxation years of a foreign affiliate of a taxpayer that begin after February 27, 2014.

S. 90(8) was added by S.C. 2013, c. 34, s. 66(1), applicable in respect of loans received and indebtedness incurred after August 19, 2011. However, subsection 90(8) also applies in respect of any portion of a particular loan received or a particular indebtedness incurred on or before August 19, 2011 that remains outstanding on August 19, 2014 as if that portion were a separate loan or indebtedness that was received or incurred, as the case may be, on August 20, 2014 in the same manner and on the same terms as the particular loan or indebtedness.

If the taxpayer referred to in any election dealing with various foreign affiliate amendments is a partnership, any reference in those elections to "the taxpayer's filing-due date" is to be read as a reference to "the earliest of the filing-due dates of any member of the taxpayer".

See the application for s. 90(1) for the extension of assessment periods to take into account the amendments by S.C. 2013, c. 34, s. 54 to 89.

Tax Topics: No. 2179, 2013 Canadian Tax Foundation Roundtable – Part I; No. 2073, December 01, 2011, Upstream Loan Rules — Why Now?.

Tax Window Files: 90(6) & sale of creditor affiliate, *August 4, 2016*, CRA Document No. 2016-0645521I7; IFA 2014 Question 3b – Upstream Loan, *May 22, 2014*, CRA Document No. 2014-0526731C6; Upstream loans and set-off, *November 24-26, 2013*, CRA Document No. 2013-0508141C6; Upstream Loans, *May 22, 2013*, CRA Document No. 2013-0483791C6.

► 90(8.1) ◄

(8.1) Upstream deposit — eligible bank affiliate. For the purposes of this section, if a taxpayer is an eligible Canadian bank and an eligible bank affiliate of the taxpayer is owed, at any time in a particular taxation year of the affiliate or the immediately preceding taxation year, an upstream deposit,

(*a*) the affiliate is deemed to make a loan to the taxpayer immediately before the end of the particular year equal to the amount determined by the following formula, where all amounts referred to in the formula are to be determined using Canadian currency:

$$A - B - C$$

where

A is 90% of the average of all amounts each of which is, in respect of a calendar month that ends in the particular year, the greatest total amount at any time in the month of the upstream deposits owing to the affiliate,

B is the lesser of

(i) the amount, if any, by which the affiliate's excess liquidity for the particular year exceeds the average of all amounts each of which is, in respect of a calendar month that ends in the particular year, the greatest total amount at any time in the month of eligible Canadian indebtedness owing to the affiliate, and

(ii) the amount determined for A, and

C is the amount, if any, by which the amount determined for A for the immediately preceding year exceeds the amount determined for B for the immediately preceding year; and

(*b*) if the formula in paragraph (*a*) would, in the absence of section 257, result in a negative amount for the particular year,

(i) the taxpayer is deemed to repay immediately before the end of the particular year — in an amount equal to the absolute value of the negative amount and in the order in which they arose — loans made by the affiliate under paragraph (*a*) in a prior taxation year and not previously repaid, and

(ii) the repayment is deemed to not be part of a series of loans or other transactions and repayments.

History: S. 90(8.1) was added by S.C. 2014, c. 39, s. 20(2), applicable in respect of taxation years of a foreign affiliate of a taxpayer that begin after February 27, 2014.

► 90(9) ◄

(9) Corporations: deduction for amounts included under subsection (6) or (12). There may be deducted in computing the income for a taxation year of a corporation resident in Canada a particular amount, in respect of a specified amount included under subsection (6), or an amount included under subsection (12), in computing the corporation's income for the taxation year in respect of a particular loan or indebtedness, if

(*a*) the corporation demonstrates that the particular amount is the total of all amounts (not to exceed the amount so included) each of which would — if the specified amount in respect of the particular loan or indebtedness were, at the time (referred to in subparagraph (i) and subsection (11) as the "lending time") the particular loan was made or the particular indebtedness was incurred, instead paid by the creditor affiliate, or the creditor partnership, as the case may be, to the corporation directly as part of one dividend, or indirectly as part of one or more dividends and, if applicable, partnership distributions — reasonably be considered to have been deductible, in respect of the payment, for the corporation's taxation year in which the specified amount was included in its income under subsection (6), in computing

(i) the taxable income of the corporation under any of

(A) paragraph 113(1)(*a*), in respect of the exempt surplus — at the lending time, in respect of the corporation — of a foreign affiliate of the corporation,

(B) paragraph 113(1)(*a.1*), in respect of the hybrid surplus — at the lending time, in respect of the corporation — of a foreign affiliate of the corporation, if the amount of that hybrid surplus is less than or equal to the amount determined by the formula

$$[A \times (B - 0.5)] + (C \times 0.5)$$

where

A is the affiliate's hybrid underlying tax in respect of the corporation at the lending time,

B is the corporation's relevant tax factor (within the meaning assigned by subsection 95(1)) for the corporation's taxation year that includes the lending time, and

C is the affiliate's hybrid surplus in respect of the corporation at the lending time,

(C) paragraph 113(1)(*b*), in respect of the taxable surplus — at the lending time, in respect of the corporation — of a foreign affiliate of the corporation, and

(D) paragraph 113(1)(*d*), in respect of the pre-acquisition surplus — at the lending time, in respect of the corporation — of a foreign affiliate of the corporation to the extent of the adjusted cost base to the corporation, at the lending time, of the shares of the capital stock of the affiliate, and except if the specified debtor is

(I) a non-resident person with which the corporation does not deal at arm's length, or

(II) a partnership any member of which is a person described in subclause (I), or

(ii) the income of the corporation under subsection 91(5), in respect of the taxable surplus of a foreign affiliate of the corporation, unless the specified debtor is a person or partnership described in subclause (i)(D)(I) or (II);

(*b*) that exempt surplus, hybrid surplus, taxable surplus, or adjusted cost base is not relevant in applying this subsection in respect of any other loan made or indebtedness incurred, or in respect of any deduction claimed under subsection 91(5) or 113(1) in respect of a dividend paid, during the period in which the particular loan or indebtedness is outstanding; and

(*c*) that adjusted cost base is not relevant in determining the taxability of any other distribution made during the period in which the particular loan or indebtedness is outstanding.

History: S. 90(9)(*a*)(ii) was replaced by S.C. 2017, c. 33, s. 27(3), applicable in respect of loans received and indebtedness incurred after August 19, 2011; however, subparagraph 90(9)(*a*)(ii) also applies in respect of any portion of a particular loan received or a particular indebtedness incurred before August 20, 2011 that remains outstanding on August 19, 2014 as if that portion were a separate loan or indebtedness that was received or incurred, as the case may be, on August 20, 2014 in the same manner and on the same terms as the particular loan or indebtedness. In respect of loans received and indebtedness incurred prior to September 16, 2016, subparagraph 90(9)(*a*)(ii) is to be read without reference to "unless the specified debtor is a person or partnership described in subclause (i)(D)(I) or (II)". S. 90(9)(*a*)(ii) formerly read:

> (ii) the income of the corporation under subsection 91(5), in respect of the taxable surplus of a foreign affiliate of the corporation, if the specified debtor is a person or partnership described in subclause (i)(D)(I) or (II);

S. 90(9) was added by S.C. 2013, c. 34, s. 66(1), applicable in respect of loans received and indebtedness incurred after August 19, 2011. However, subsection 90(9) also applies in respect of any portion of a particular loan received or a particular indebtedness incurred on or before August 19, 2011 that remains outstanding on August 19, 2014 as if that portion were a separate loan or indebtedness that was received or incurred, as the case may be, on August 20, 2014 in the same manner and on the same terms as the particular loan or indebtedness.

If the taxpayer referred to in any election dealing with various foreign affiliate amendments is a partnership, any reference in those elections to "the taxpayer's filing-due date" is to be read as a reference to "the earliest of the filing-due dates of any member of the taxpayer".

See the application for s. 90(1) for the extension of assessment periods to take into account the amendments by S.C. 2013, c. 34, s. 54 to 89.

Tax Window Files: IFA 2016 Q.5: Upstream loans: 90(7) and 90(9), *May 26, 2016*, CRA Document No. 2016-0642091C6.

▶ 90(10) ◀

(10) Corporate partners: application of subsection (9). In applying subsection (9) to a corporation resident in Canada that is a member of a partnership at the end of a fiscal period of the partnership,

(*a*) each amount that may reasonably be considered to be the corporation's share (determined in a manner consistent with the determination of the corporation's share of the income of the partnership under subsection 96(1)) of each specified amount that is required to be included in computing the income of the partnership for that fiscal period under subsection (6), in respect of a particular loan or indebtedness, is deemed to be a specified amount in respect of the particular loan or indebtedness that was included in the corporation's income, for its taxation year that includes the last day of that fiscal period, under subsection (6);

(*b*) subparagraph (9)(*a*)(i) is to be read without reference to its clause (D);

(*c*) subparagraph (9)(*a*)(ii) is to be read as follows:

> (ii) the income of the partnership, referred to in subsection (10), under subsection 91(5), in respect of the taxable surplus of a foreign affiliate of the partnership, to the extent of the amount that may reasonably be considered to be the corporation's share of that deduction (determined in a manner consistent with the determination of the corporation's share of the income of the partnership under subsection 96(1));

(*d*) paragraph (9)(*b*) is to be read as follows:

> (*b*) that exempt surplus, hybrid surplus, or taxable surplus is not relevant in applying this subsection in respect of any other loan made or indebtedness incurred, or in respect of any deduction claimed under subsection 91(5) or 113(1) in respect of a dividend paid, during the period in which the particular loan or indebtedness is outstanding; and

(*e*) subsection (9) is to be read without reference to its paragraph (*c*).

History: S. 90(10) was added by S.C. 2013, c. 34, s. 66(1), applicable in respect of loans received and indebtedness incurred after August 19, 2011. However, subsection 90(10) also applies in respect of any portion of a particular loan received or a particular indebtedness incurred on or before August 19, 2011 that remains outstanding on August 19, 2014 as if that portion were a separate loan or indebtedness that was received or incurred, as the case may be, on August 20, 2014 in the same manner and on the same terms as the particular loan or indebtedness.

If the taxpayer referred to in any election dealing with various foreign affiliate amendments is a partnership, any reference in those elections to "the taxpayer's filing-due date" is to be read as a reference to "the earliest of the filing-due dates of any member of the taxpayer".

See the application for s. 90(1) for the extension of assessment periods to take into account the amendments by S.C. 2013, c. 34, s. 54 to 89.

Canadian Tax Foundation: Spinelli et al., *Upstream Loans Disadvantage Corporate Members of a Partnership*, 2018 Canadian Tax Focus 8(4):4–5.

▶ 90(11) ◀

(11) Downstream surplus. For the purposes of subparagraph (9)(*a*)(i), the amounts of exempt surplus or exempt deficit, hybrid surplus or hybrid deficit, hybrid underlying tax, taxable surplus or taxable deficit, and underlying foreign tax of the creditor affiliate, or of each foreign affiliate of the corporation that is a member of the creditor partnership, as the case may be, in respect of the corporation, at the lending time are deemed to be the amounts that would be determined, at the lending time, under subparagraph 5902(1)(*a*)(i) of the *Income Tax Regulations* if that subparagraph were applicable at the lending time and the references in that subparagraph to "the dividend time" were references to the lending time.

History: S. 90(11) was added by S.C. 2013, c. 34, s. 66(1), applicable in respect of loans received and indebtedness incurred after August 19, 2011. However, subsection 90(11) also applies in respect of any portion of a particular loan received or a particular indebtedness incurred on or before August 19, 2011 that remains outstanding on August 19, 2014 as if that portion were a separate loan or indebtedness that was received or incurred, as the case may be, on August 20, 2014 in the same manner and on the same terms as the particular loan or indebtedness.

If the taxpayer referred to in any election dealing with various foreign affiliate amendments is a partnership, any reference in those elections to "the taxpayer's filing-due date" is to be read as a reference to "the earliest of the filing-due dates of any member of the taxpayer".

See the application for s. 90(1) for the extension of assessment periods to take into account the amendments by S.C. 2013, c. 34, s. 54 to 89.

▶ 90(12) ◀

(12) Add-back for subsection (9) deduction. There is to be included in computing the income of a corporation resident in Canada for a particular taxation year any amount deducted by the corporation under subsection (9) in computing the corporation's income for the taxation year that immediately precedes the particular year.

History: S. 90(12) was added by S.C. 2013, c. 34, s. 66(1), applicable in respect of loans received and indebtedness incurred after August 19, 2011. However, subsection 90(12) also applies in respect of any portion of a particular loan received or a particular indebtedness incurred on or before August 19, 2011 that remains outstanding on August 19, 2014 as if that portion were a separate loan or indebtedness that was received or incurred, as the case may be, on August 20, 2014 in the same manner and on the same terms as the particular loan or indebtedness.

If the taxpayer referred to in any election dealing with various foreign affiliate amendments is a partnership, any reference in those elections to "the taxpayer's filing-due date" is to be read as a reference to "the earliest of the filing-due dates of any member of the taxpayer".

See the application for s. 90(1) for the extension of assessment periods to take into account the amendments by S.C. 2013, c. 34, s. 54 to 89.

▶ 90(13) ◀

(13) No double deduction. A corporation may not claim a deduction for a taxation year under subsection (9) in respect of the same portion of the specified amount in respect of a loan or indebtedness for which a deduction is claimed for that year or a preceding year by the corporation, or by a partnership of which the corporation is a member, under subsection (14).

History: S. 90(13) was added by S.C. 2013, c. 34, s. 66(1), applicable in respect of loans received and indebtedness incurred after August 19, 2011. However, subsection 90(13) also applies in respect of any portion of a particular loan received or a particular indebtedness incurred on or before August 19, 2011 that remains outstanding on August 19, 2014 as if that portion were a separate loan or indebtedness that was received or incurred, as the case may be, on August 20, 2014 in the same manner and on the same terms as the particular loan or indebtedness.

If the taxpayer referred to in any election dealing with various foreign affiliate amendments is a partnership, any reference in those elections to "the taxpayer's filing-due date" is to be read as a reference to "the earliest of the filing-due dates of any member of the taxpayer".

See the application for s. 90(1) for the extension of assessment periods to take into account the amendments by S.C. 2013, c. 34, s. 54 to 89.

▶ 90(14) ◀

(14) Repayment of loan. There may be deducted in computing the income of a taxpayer for a particular taxation year the amount determined by the formula

$$A \times B/C$$

where

A is the specified amount, in respect of a loan or indebtedness, that is included under subsection (6) in computing the taxpayer's income for a preceding taxation year,

B is the portion of the loan or indebtedness that was repaid in the particular year, to the extent it is established, by subsequent events or otherwise, that the repayment was not part of a series of loans or other transactions and repayments, and

C is the amount, in respect of the loan or indebtedness, that is referred to in the description of A in the definition "specified amount" in subsection (15).

History: S. 90(14) was added by S.C. 2013, c. 34, s. 66(1), applicable in respect of loans received and indebtedness incurred after August 19, 2011. However, subsection 90(14) also applies in respect of any portion of a particular loan received or a particular indebtedness incurred on or before August 19, 2011 that remains outstanding on August 19, 2014 as if that portion were a separate loan or indebtedness that was received or incurred, as the case may be, on August 20, 2014 in the same manner and on the same terms as the particular loan or indebtedness.

If the taxpayer referred to in any election dealing with various foreign affiliate amendments is a partnership, any reference in those elections to "the taxpayer's filing-due date" is to be read as a reference to "the earliest of the filing-due dates of any member of the taxpayer".

See the application for s. 90(1) for the extension of assessment periods to take into account the amendments by S.C. 2013, c. 34, s. 54 to 89.

Tax Window Files: 2015 CTF Q.8 - FA Liquidation and upstream loans, *November 24, 2015*, CRA Document No. 2015-0610621C6.

▶ 90(15) ◀

(15) Definitions. The following definitions apply in this section.

History: S. 90(15) was added by S.C. 2013, c. 34, s. 66(1), applicable in respect of loans received and indebtedness incurred after August 19, 2011. However, subsection 90(15) also applies in respect of any portion of a particular loan received or a particular indebtedness incurred on or before August 19, 2011 that remains outstanding on August 19, 2014 as if that portion were a separate loan or indebtedness that was received or incurred, as the case may be, on August 20, 2014 in the same manner and on the same terms as the particular loan or indebtedness.

If the taxpayer referred to in any election dealing with various foreign affiliate amendments is a partnership, any reference in those elections to "the taxpayer's filing-due date" is to be read as a reference to "the earliest of the filing-due dates of any member of the taxpayer".

See the application for s. 90(1) for the extension of assessment periods to take into account the amendments by S.C. 2013, c. 34, s. 54 to 89.

"eligible bank affiliate" —"eligible bank affiliate" has the same meaning as in subsection 95(2.43).

History: S. 90(15), the definition "eligible bank affiliate" was added by S.C. 2014, c. 39, s. 20(3), applicable in respect of taxation years of a foreign affiliate of a taxpayer that begin after February 27, 2014.

"eligible Canadian bank" —"eligible Canadian bank" has the same meaning as in subsection 95(2.43).

History: S. 90(15), the definition "eligible Canadian bank" was added by S.C. 2014, c. 39, s. 20(3), applicable in respect of taxation years of a foreign affiliate of a taxpayer that begin after February 27, 2014.

"eligible Canadian indebtedness" —"eligible Canadian indebtedness" has the same meaning as in subsection 95(2.43).

History: S. 90(15), the definition "eligible Canadian indebtedness" was added by S.C. 2014, c. 39, s. 20(3), applicable in respect of taxation years of a foreign affiliate of a taxpayer that begin after February 27, 2014.

"excess liquidity" — "excess liquidity" has the same meaning as in subsection 95(2.43).

History: S. 90(15), the definition "excess liquidity" was added by S.C. 2014, c. 39, s. 20(3), applicable in respect of taxation years of a foreign affiliate of a taxpayer that begin after February 27, 2014.

"specified amount" — "specified amount", in respect of a loan or indebtedness that is required by subsection (6) to be included in computing the income of a taxpayer for a taxation year, means the amount determined by the formula

$$A \times (B - C)$$

where

A is the amount of the loan or indebtedness, and

B is, in the case of

(*a*) a creditor affiliate of the taxpayer, the percentage that is or would be, if the taxpayer referred to in subsection (6) were a corporation resident in Canada, the taxpayer's surplus entitlement percentage (in this definition determined without reference to subsection 5908(1) of the *Income Tax Regulations*) in respect of the creditor affiliate at the time (referred to in this definition as the "determination time") referred to in subsection (6), or

(*b*) a creditor partnership of which a foreign affiliate of the taxpayer is a member, the total of each percentage determined, in respect of a member (referred to in this paragraph as a "member affiliate") of the creditor partnership that is a foreign affiliate of the taxpayer, by the formula

$$D \times E/F$$

where

D is the percentage that is or would be, if the taxpayer were a corporation resident in Canada, the taxpayer's surplus entitlement percentage in respect of a particular member affiliate at the determination time,

E is the fair market value, at the determination time, of the particular member affiliate's direct or indirect interest in the creditor partnership, and

F is the fair market value, at the determination time, of all interests in the creditor partnership, and

C is,

(*a*) if the debtor under the loan or indebtedness is

(i) another foreign affiliate of the taxpayer, the percentage that is or would be, if the taxpayer were a corporation resident in Canada, the taxpayer's surplus entitlement percentage in respect of the other affiliate at the determination time, or

(ii) a partnership (referred to in this paragraph as the "borrower partnership") of which one or more other foreign affiliates of the taxpayer are members, the total of each percentage that is determined by the following formula in respect of each such member

$$G \times H/I$$

where

G is the percentage that is or would be, if the taxpayer were a corporation resident in Canada, the taxpayer's surplus entitlement percentage in respect of a particular member of the borrower partnership at the determination time,

H is the fair market value, at the determination time, of the particular member's direct or indirect interest in the borrower partnership, and

I is the fair market value, at the determination time, of all interests in the borrower partnership, and

(*b*) in any other case, nil.

"specified debtor" — "specified debtor", in respect of a taxpayer resident in Canada, at any time, means

(*a*) the taxpayer;

(*b*) a person with which the taxpayer does not, at that time, deal at arm's length, other than

(i) a non-resident corporation that is at that time a *controlled foreign affiliate*, within the meaning assigned by section 17, of the taxpayer, or

(ii) a non-resident corporation (other than a corporation that is described in subparagraph (i)) that is, at that time, a foreign affiliate of the taxpayer, if each share of the capital stock of the affiliate is owned at that time by any of

(A) the taxpayer,

(B) persons resident in Canada,

(C) non-resident persons that deal at arm's length with the taxpayer,

(D) persons described in subparagraph (i),

(E) partnerships, each member of which is described in any of clauses (A) to (F), and

(F) a corporation each shareholder of which is described in any of clauses (A) to (F);

(*c*) a partnership a member of which is at that time a person or partnership that is a specified debtor in respect of the taxpayer because of paragraph (*a*) or (*b*); and

(*d*) if the taxpayer is a partnership,

(i) any member of the partnership that is a corporation resident in Canada if the creditor affiliate, or member of the creditor partnership, as the case may be, is, at that time, a foreign affiliate of the corporation,

(ii) a person with which a corporation referred to in subparagraph (i) does not, at that time, deal at arm's length, other than a controlled foreign affiliate, within the meaning assigned by section 17, of the partnership or of a member of the partnership that owns, directly or indirectly, an interest in the partnership representing at least 90% of the fair market value of all such interests, or

(iii) a partnership a member of which is at that time a person that is a specified debtor in respect of the taxpayer because of subparagraph (i) or (ii).

History: S. 90(15), paragraph (*b*) of the definition "specified debtor" was replaced by S.C. 2017, c. 33, s. 27(4), applicable in respect of loans received and indebtedness incurred after August 19, 2011 and in respect of any portion of a particular loan received or indebtedness incurred before August 20, 2011 that remained outstanding on August 19, 2014. S. 90(15), paragraph (*b*) of the definition "specified debtor" formerly read:

(*b*) a person with which the taxpayer does not, at that time, deal at arm's length, other than a non-resident corporation that is at that time a controlled foreign affiliate, within the meaning assigned by section 17, of the taxpayer;

"upstream deposit" — "upstream deposit" has the same meaning as in subsection 95(2.43).

History: S. 90(15), the definition "upstream deposit" was added by S.C. 2014, c. 39, s. 20(3), applicable in respect of taxation years of a foreign affiliate of a taxpayer that begin after February 27, 2014.

SECTION 91: Amounts to be included in respect of share of foreign affiliate

► 91(1) ◄

(1) Amounts to be included in respect of share of foreign affiliate. In computing the income for a taxation year of a taxpayer resident in Canada, there shall be included, in respect of each share owned by the taxpayer of the capital stock of a controlled foreign affiliate of the taxpayer, as income from the share, the percentage of the foreign accrual property income of any controlled foreign affiliate of the taxpayer, for each taxation year of the affiliate ending in the taxation year of the taxpayer, equal to that share's participating percentage in respect of the affiliate, determined at the end of each such taxation year of the affiliate.

Editorial Note: S. 91(1) is the cornerstone of the foreign accrual property income (FAPI) rules in the Act. Generally speaking, FAPI is comprised of passive income and active business income that erodes the Canadian tax base. The FAPI rules eliminate the deferral of Canadian tax that would otherwise arise on income earned by a foreign corporation that is resident in a low tax jurisdiction by imputing FAPI earned by the affiliate to the Canadian resident shareholder. More particularly, in computing a Canadian resident taxpayer's income for a taxation year, s. 91(1) includes, in respect of each share of a controlled foreign affiliate that is owned by the taxpayer, the percentage of the affiliate's FAPI for the affiliate's taxation years ending in the particular taxation year of the shareholder that is equal to the share's participating percentage in respect of the affiliate determined at the end of the affiliate's taxation year. See the editorial note accompanying the definition of "participating percentage" in s. 95(1).

S. 91(1) is accompanied by a number of mechanical rules in s. 91 and s. 92 that, in very general terms, operate to eliminate double taxation of FAPI under the Act. In brief, the amount of a controlled foreign affiliate's FAPI included in a taxpayer's income in respect of a share of the affiliate for a particular year under s. 91(1) is added to the taxpayer's adjusted cost base of that share under s. 92(1)(*a*). If foreign accrual tax is applicable to the income then s. 91(4) provides that the taxpayer may deduct an amount in respect of the foreign accrual tax, which provides an indirect foreign tax credit for the foreign tax paid. Any amount deducted under s. 91(4) is deducted from the taxpayer's adjusted cost base of the shares of the affiliate. Where an affiliate pays a dividend, the taxpayer may be entitled to a deduction under s. 91(5) which, in effect, allows the repatriation of FAPI that was previously included in the taxpayer's income and added to the taxpayer's adjusted cost base of the affiliate's shares.

Related Sections: S. 12(1)(*k*) Dividends from other corporations; s. 17(1)(*b*)(iii); s. 17(1) inclusion reduced by FAPI attributable to interest on amount owing; s. 53(1)(*d*) Adjustments to cost base — Share of foreign affiliate; s. 53(2)(*b*) Amounts to be deducted — Share of non-resident corporation; s. 91(2) Reserve where foreign exchange restriction; s. 91(3) Reserve for preceding year to be included; s. 91(4) Amounts deductible in respect of foreign taxes; s. 91(5) Amounts deductible in respect of dividends received; s. 91(6) Amounts deductible in respect of dividends received — shares acquired from another corporation; s. 91(7) Shares acquired from a partnership; s. 92(1)(*a*) Adjusted cost base increase to the extent of FAPI and foreign exchange reserve inclusion; s. 92(1)(*b*) Adjusted cost base decreased by deduction for foreign accrual tax, foreign exchange reserve and dividends paid by affiliate; s. 95(1), "controlled foreign affiliate", "foreign accrual property income", "participating percentage", "taxation year"; s. 152(6.1) Reassessment where amount included in income under subsection 91(1) is reduced; s. 248(1), "resident in Canada", "share", "taxpayer"; s. 249 Definition of "taxation year"; s. 255 Canada.

Canadian Petroleum Tax Journal: Moving Forward With Mobile Income, Chris Roberge, CA, CPA, 2001, Vol. 14, No. 1.

Canadian Tax Foundation: Morier and Juneja, *Foreign Affiliates: An Updated Primer*, 2012 Conference Report 28:1–48; Lanthier and Meek, *Canadian Foreign Affiliate Rules*, 1997 Conference Report 31:1–42.

Tax Profile: November 2010 — Canadian Acquisition of U.S. Real Estate; January 2009 — Enhancing Canada's International Tax Advantage; January 2006 — Foreign Source Income: Outbound Structures and Foreign Tax Credit Planning — Part I; February 2006 — Foreign Source Income: Outbound Structures and Foreign Tax Credit Planning — Part II.

Tax Topics: No. 1930, Budget 2009 Provides Initial Response to Final Report Issued by the Advisory Panel on Canada's System of International Taxation; No. 1810, FAPI and Tax Treaty Interpretation: *Canwest Mediaworks Inc. v. Her Majesty the Queen*.

Information Circulars: IC 77-9R Books, records and other requirements for taxpayers having foreign affiliates.

Interpretation Bulletins: *Secondary* — IT-451R Deemed disposition and acquisition on ceasing to be or becoming resident in Canada.

Cases: The wholly-owned foreign subsidiary of the taxpayer received dividend income which was not taxable according to the foreign law. The taxpayer included the dividend as "foreign accrual property income" but was not allowed a deduction based on s. 91(4). The tax treaty with the foreign country provided that the treaty was not to be construed as preventing Canada from imposing tax on amounts included in the income of a Canadian resident according to s. 91. *Canada–Israel Development Ltd. v. M.N.R.*, 85 DTC 718 (T.C.C.)

► 91(1.1) ◄

(1.1) Conditions for application of subsection (1.2). Subsection (1.2) applies at a particular time in respect of a particular foreign affiliate of a taxpayer resident in Canada if

(*a*) an amount would be included under subsection (1) in computing the income of the taxpayer, in respect of a share of the particular affiliate or another foreign affiliate of the taxpayer that has an *equity percentage* (as defined in subsection 95(4)) in the particular affiliate, for the taxation year of the particular affiliate (determined without reference to subsection (1.2)) that includes the particular time (referred to in this subsection and subsection (1.3) as the "ordinary taxation year" of the particular affiliate), if the ordinary taxation year of the particular affiliate ended at the particular time;

(*b*) immediately after the particular time, there is

(i) an acquisition of control of the taxpayer, or

(ii) a triggering event that can reasonably be considered to result in a change in the aggregate participating percentage of the taxpayer in respect of the particular affiliate for the ordinary taxation year of the particular affiliate;

(*c*) if subparagraph (*b*)(i) applies, all or a portion of an amount described in paragraph 95(2)(*f*) that accrued to the particular affiliate during the portion of the ordinary taxation year of the particular affiliate before the particular time is excluded in computing the income of another taxpayer because paragraph 95(2)(*f*.1) applies as a result of the taxpayer being, at a time before the acquisition of control, a designated acquired corporation of the other taxpayer; and

(*d*) if subparagraph (*b*)(ii) applies, none of the following is the case:

(i) the change referred to in that subparagraph

(A) is a decrease, and

(B) is equal to the total of all amounts each of which is the increase — that can reasonably be considered to result from the triggering event — in the aggregate participating percentage of another taxpayer, in respect of the particular affiliate for the ordinary taxation year of the particular affiliate, if the other taxpayer

(I) is a person resident in Canada, other than a person that is — or a trust, any of the beneficiaries under which is — by reason of a statutory provision, exempt from tax under this Part, and

(II) is related to the taxpayer,

1 if the triggering event results from a winding-up of the taxpayer to which subsection 88(1) applies, at the particular time, and

2 in any other case, immediately after the particular time,

(ii) the triggering event is on an *amalgamation* as defined in subsection 87(1),

(iii) the triggering event is an excluded acquisition or disposition, in respect of the ordinary taxation year of the particular affiliate, and

(iv) if one or more triggering events — all of which are described in subparagraph (*b*)(ii) and in respect of which none of the conditions in subparagraphs (i) to (iii) are satisfied — occur in the ordinary taxation year of the particular affiliate, the percentage determined by the following formula is not greater than 5%:

$$A - B$$

where

A is the total of all amounts each of which is the decrease — which can reasonably be considered to result from a triggering event described in subparagraph (*b*)(ii) (other than a triggering event that satisfies the conditions in subparagraph (i) or (ii)) — in the aggregate participating percentage of the taxpayer in respect of the particular affiliate for the ordinary taxation year of the particular affiliate, and

B is the total of all amounts each of which is the increase — which can reasonably be considered to result from a triggering event described in subparagraph (*b*)(ii) (other than a triggering event that satisfies the conditions in subparagraph (i) or (ii)) — in the aggregate participating percentage of the taxpayer in respect of the particular affiliate for the ordinary taxation year of the particular affiliate.

History: S. 91(1.1) was added by S.C. 2017, c. 33, s. 28(1), deemed to have come into force on July 12, 2013, except that

(a) an election referred to in subsection 91(1.4), as enacted, is deemed to have been filed by the particular taxpayer and all specified corporations (within the meaning assigned by subsection 91(1.4)) referred to in that subsection on a timely basis if the election is filed on or before the earliest filing-due date, for all taxpayers making the election, for the respective taxation year that includes the day on which this Act receives Royal Assent (December 14, 2017);

(b) an election referred to in subsection 91(1.5), as enacted, is deemed to have been filed by the particular taxpayer referred to in that subsection on a timely basis if the election is filed on or before the filing-due date for the particular taxpayer for its taxation year that includes the day on which this Act receives Royal Assent (December 14, 2017);

(c) subject to paragraph (d), for the purpose of applying subsections 91(1.1) to (1.4), as enacted, if the particular time referred to in subsection 91(1.1), as enacted, is before September 8, 2017, those subsections are to be read as follows:

(1.1) *Conditions for application of subsection (1.2).* Subsection (1.2) applies at a particular time in respect of a particular foreign affiliate of a taxpayer resident in Canada if

(*a*) an amount would be included under subsection (1) in computing the income of the taxpayer, in respect of a share of the particular affiliate or another foreign affiliate of the taxpayer that has an equity percentage (as defined in subsection 95(4)) in the particular affiliate, for the taxation year of the particular affiliate (determined without reference to subsection (1.2)) that includes the particular time, if that taxation year ended at the particular time; and

(*b*) immediately after the particular time, there is an acquisition or disposition of shares of the capital stock of a foreign affiliate of the taxpayer that results in a change to the surplus entitlement percentage of the taxpayer in respect of the particular affiliate (determined as if the taxpayer were a corporation resident in Canada), unless

(i) the change is a decrease in the surplus entitlement percentage of the taxpayer (determined as if the taxpayer were a corporation resident in Canada) in respect of the particular affiliate and, as a result of the acquisition or disposition, one or more taxpayers, each of which is a taxable Canadian corporation that does not deal at arm's length with the taxpayer immediately after the particular time, have increases to their surplus entitlement percentages in respect of the particular affiliate that are, in total, equal to the reduction in the taxpayer's surplus entitlement percentage in respect of the particular affiliate immediately after the particular time,

(ii) the acquisition or disposition is on an "amalgamation" as defined in subsection 87(1), or

(iii) if one or more such acquisitions or dispositions in respect of which the conditions in subparagraphs (i) and (ii) are not satisfied occur in a particular taxation year of the particular affiliate (determined without reference to this subsection and subsection (1.2)), the percentage determined by the following formula is not greater than 5%:

$$A - B$$

where

A is the total of all amounts each of which is the decrease in the surplus entitlement percentage of the taxpayer in respect of the particular affiliate resulting from such acquisition or disposition in the particular year (other than an acquisition or disposition described in subparagraph (i) or (ii)), and

B is the total of all amounts each of which is the increase in the surplus entitlement percentage of the taxpayer in respect of the particular affiliate resulting from such acquisition or disposition in the particular year (other than an acquisition from a person that does not deal at arm's length with the taxpayer).

(1.2) *Deemed year-end.* If this subsection applies at a particular time in respect of a foreign affiliate of a particular taxpayer resident in Canada, then for the purposes of this section and section 92,

(*a*) in respect of the particular taxpayer and each corporation or partnership that is connected to the particular taxpayer, the affiliate's taxation year that would, in the absence of this subsection, have included the particular time is deemed to have ended at the time (referred to in this section as the "stub-period end time") that is immediately before the particular time;

(*b*) if the affiliate is, immediately after the particular time, a foreign affiliate of the particular taxpayer or a corporation or partnership that is connected to the particular taxpayer, the affiliate's next taxation year after the stub-period end time is deemed, in respect of the taxpayer or the connected corporation or partnership, as the case may be, to begin immediately after the particular time; and

(*c*) in determining the foreign accrual property income of the affiliate for that taxation year in respect of the particular taxpayer or a corporation or partnership that is connected to the particular taxpayer, all transactions or events that occur at the particular time are deemed to occur at the stub-period end time.

(1.3) *Connected — meaning.* For the purposes of subsection (1.2),

(*a*) a corporation is connected to the particular taxpayer if, at or immediately after the particular time, it is resident in Canada and does not deal at arm's length with the taxpayer; and

(*b*) a partnership is connected to the particular taxpayer if, at or immediately after the particular time, the particular taxpayer or a corporation described in paragraph (*a*) is, directly or indirectly through one or more partnerships, a member of the partnership.

(1.4) *Election for application of subsection (1.2).* If the conditions in subsection (1.1) are not met at a particular time in respect of a particular foreign affiliate of a taxpayer resident in Canada, subsection (1.2) applies in respect of the particular affiliate at that time if

(*a*) the conditions in paragraph (1.1)(*a*) are met in respect of the particular affiliate at the particular time;

(*b*) immediately after the particular time there is a disposition of shares of the capital stock of the particular affiliate or another foreign affiliate of the taxpayer that had an *equity percentage* (as defined in subsection 95(4)) in the particular affiliate by

(i) the taxpayer, or

(ii) a controlled foreign affiliate of the taxpayer, if the shares are not excluded property of the controlled foreign affiliate immediately after the particular time; and

(*c*) the taxpayer and all specified corporations jointly elect, by filing with the Minister in prescribed manner a form containing prescribed information on or before the day that is the earliest filing-due date for all taxpayers making the election in respect of the taxation year in which the transaction to which the election relates occurred, and for this purpose, a *specified corporation* means a corporation that at or immediately after the particular time meets the following conditions:

(i) the corporation is resident in Canada,

(ii) the corporation does not deal at arm's length with the taxpayer, and

(iii) the particular affiliate is a foreign affiliate of the corporation, or of a partnership of which the corporation is, directly or indirectly through one or more partnerships, a member.

(d) paragraph (c) does not apply in respect of a taxpayer if

(i) the taxpayer and all connected persons and connected partnerships (within the meanings assigned by subsection 91(1.3), as enacted) in respect of the taxpayer jointly elect in writing, and

(ii) the election is filed with the Minister by the later of the taxpayer's filing-due date for its taxation year that includes September 8, 2017 and six months after the day on which this Act receives royal assent; and

(e) if paragraph (c) does not apply in respect of a taxpayer because of paragraph (d),

(i) section 91, as amended, shall be read without reference to its subsection (1.5), and

(ii) subsection 91(1.1), as enacted, shall be read without reference to its subparagraph (*b*)(i) and paragraph (*c*) in respect of any acquisition of control of the taxpayer that occurs before September 8, 2017.

Related Sections: 95(1) designated acquired corporation; 95(2)(f.1) [Determination of FAPI — Exclusion of amounts].

► 91(1.2) ◄

(1.2) Deemed year-end. If this subsection applies at a particular time in respect of a foreign affiliate of a particular taxpayer resident in Canada, then for the purposes of this section and section 92,

(*a*) in respect of the particular taxpayer and each connected person, or connected partnership, in respect of the particular taxpayer, the affiliate's taxation year that would, in the absence of this subsection, have included the particular time is deemed to have ended at the time (referred to in this section as the "stub-period end time") that is immediately before the particular time;

(*b*) if the affiliate is, immediately after the particular time, a foreign affiliate of the particular taxpayer or a connected person, or connected partnership, in respect of the particular taxpayer, the affiliate's next taxation year after the stub-period end time is deemed, in respect of the particular taxpayer or the connected person or connected partnership, as the case may be, to begin immediately after the particular time; and

(*c*) in determining the foreign accrual property income of the affiliate for the taxation year referred to in paragraph (*a*) in respect of the particular taxpayer or a connected person or connected partnership, in respect of the particular taxpayer, all transactions or events that occur at the particular time are deemed to occur at the stub-period end time.

History: S. 91(1.2) was added by S.C. 2017, c. 33, s. 28(1). For the application of this subsection, please see the history note following s. 91(1.1).

► 91(1.3) ◄

(1.3) Definitions. The following definitions apply in this subsection and subsections (1.1) and (1.2).

"aggregate participating percentage" — "aggregate participating percentage", of a taxpayer in respect of a foreign affiliate of the taxpayer for a taxation year of the affiliate, means the total of all amounts, each of which is the participating percentage, in respect of the affiliate, of a share of the capital stock of a corporation that is owned by the taxpayer at the end of the taxation year.

"connected person" — "connected person", in respect of a particular taxpayer, means a person that — at or immediately after the particular time at which subsection (1.2) applies in respect of a foreign affiliate of the particular taxpayer — is resident in Canada and

(*a*) does not deal at arm's length with the particular taxpayer; or

(*b*) deals at arm's length with the particular taxpayer, if

(i) the foreign affiliate is a foreign affiliate of the person at the particular time, and

(ii) the aggregate participating percentage of the person in respect of the foreign affiliate for the affiliate's ordinary taxation year may reasonably be considered to have increased as a result of the triggering event that gave rise to the application of subsection (1.2).

"connected partnership" — "connected partnership", in respect of a particular taxpayer, means a partnership if, at or immediately after the particular time at which subsection (1.2) applies in respect of a foreign affiliate of the particular taxpayer,

(*a*) the particular taxpayer or a connected person in respect of the particular taxpayer is, directly or indirectly through one or more partnerships, a member of the partnership; or

(*b*) if paragraph (*a*) does not apply,

(i) the foreign affiliate is a foreign affiliate of the partnership at the particular time, and

(ii) the aggregate participating percentage of the partnership in respect of the foreign affiliate for the affiliate's ordinary taxation year may reasonably be considered to have increased as a result of the triggering event that gave rise to the application of subsection (1.2).

"excluded acquisition or disposition" — "excluded acquisition or disposition", in respect of a taxation year of a foreign affiliate of a taxpayer, means an acquisition or disposition of an equity interest in a corporation, partnership or trust that can reasonably be considered to result in a change in the aggregate participating percentage of the taxpayer in respect of the affiliate for the taxation year of the affiliate, if

(*a*) the change is less than 1%; and

(*b*) it cannot reasonably be considered that one of the main reasons the acquisition or disposition occurs as a separate acquisition or disposition from one or more other acquisitions or dispositions is to avoid the application of subsection (1.2).

"triggering event" — "triggering event" means

(*a*) an acquisition or disposition of an equity interest in a corporation, partnership or trust;

(*b*) a change in the terms or conditions of a share of the capital stock of a corporation or the rights as a member of a partnership or as a beneficiary under a trust; and

(*c*) a disposition or change of a right referred to in paragraph 95(6)(*a*).

History: S. 91(1.3) was added by S.C. 2017, c. 33, s. 28(1). For the application of this subsection, please see the history note following s. 91(1.1).

► 91(1.4) ◄

(1.4) Election for application of subsection (1.2). If the conditions in subsection (1.1) are not met at a particular time in respect of a particular foreign affiliate of a taxpayer resident in Canada, subsection (1.2) applies in respect of the particular affiliate at that time if

(*a*) the conditions in paragraph (1.1)(*a*) are met in respect of the particular affiliate at the particular time;

(*b*) immediately after the particular time there is a disposition of shares of the capital stock of the particular affiliate or another foreign affiliate of the taxpayer that had an *equity percentage* (as defined in subsection 95(4)) in the particular affiliate by

(i) the taxpayer, or

(ii) a controlled foreign affiliate of the taxpayer; and

(*c*) the taxpayer and all specified corporations jointly elect in writing to apply subsection (1.2) in respect of the disposition and file the election with the Minister on or before the day that is the earliest filing-due date for all taxpayers making the election in respect of the taxation year in which the transaction to which the election relates occurred, and for this purpose, a *specified corporation* means a corporation that at or immediately after the particular time meets the following conditions:

(i) the corporation is resident in Canada,

(ii) the corporation does not deal at arm's length with the taxpayer, and

(iii) the particular affiliate is a foreign affiliate of the corporation, or of a partnership of which the corporation is, directly or indirectly through one or more partnerships, a member.

History: S. 91(1.4) was added by S.C. 2017, c. 33, s. 28(1). For the application of this subsection, please see the history note following s. 91(1.1).

Related Regulations: 600(b).

► 91(1.5) ◄

(1.5) Election for application of subsection (1.2) — (Repealed by S.C. 2017, c. 33, s. 28(2).)

History: S. 91(1.5) was repealed by S.C. 2017, c. 33, s. 28(2), applicable to taxation years that begin after September 7, 2017, and formerly read:

(1.5) *Election for application of subsection (1.2).* A particular taxpayer resident in Canada may elect, by filing with the Minister in prescribed manner a form containing prescribed information on or before the particular taxpayer's filing-due date for its taxation year that includes a particular time, to have subsection (1.2) apply at the particular time in respect of a particular foreign affiliate of the particular taxpayer if

(*a*) immediately after the particular time, there is an acquisition or disposition of shares of the capital stock of a foreign affiliate of another taxpayer that results in a decrease to the surplus entitlement percentage of the other taxpayer in respect of the particular affiliate;

(*b*) as a result of the acquisition or disposition described in paragraph (*a*), subsection (1.2) applies to the other taxpayer resident in Canada in respect of the particular affiliate;

(*c*) the surplus entitlement percentage of the particular taxpayer in respect of the particular affiliate increases as a result of the acquisition or disposition described in paragraph (*a*);

(*d*) subsection (1.2) does not apply, in the absence of this subsection, to the particular taxpayer in respect of the acquisition or disposition; and

(*e*) the particular affiliate is a foreign affiliate of the particular taxpayer at the particular time.

S. 91(1.5) was added by S.C. 2017, c. 33, s. 28(1). For the application of this subsection, please see the history note following s. 91(1.1).

► 91(2) ◄

(2) Reserve where foreign exchange restriction. Where an amount in respect of a share has been included in computing the income of a taxpayer for a taxation year by virtue of subsection (1) or (3) and the Minister is satisfied that, by reason of the operation of monetary or exchange restrictions of a country other than Canada, the inclusion of the whole amount with no deduction for a reserve in respect thereof would impose undue hardship on the taxpayer, there may be deducted in computing the taxpayer's income for the year such amount as a reserve in respect of the amount so included as the Minister deems reasonable in the circumstances.

Editorial Note: S. 91(2) permits the taxpayer to deduct in computing income for the year an amount in respect of a reserve that the Minister considers reasonable where the Minister is satisfied that the inclusion in income of the whole amount of FAPI under s. 91(1) (or the s. 91(2) exchange reserve for a prior year) would impose hardship on the taxpayer because of monetary exchange controls in a foreign country. A deduction under s. 92(2) results in a corresponding deduction from the taxpayer's adjusted cost base of the affiliate's shares under s. 92(1)(*b*)(i) and s. 53(2)(*b*). The amount of the s. 91(2) reserve deducted in a particular year is included in the following taxation year by s. 91(3), which results in a corresponding addition to the taxpayer's adjusted cost base of the affiliate's shares under s. 92(1)(*a*) and s. 53(1)(*d*).

Related Sections: S. 12(1)(*k*) Dividends from other corporations; s. 53(2)(*b*) Amounts to be deducted — Share of non-resident corporation; s. 91(1) Amounts to be included in respect of share of foreign affiliate; s. 91(3) Reserve for preceding year to be included; s. 91(6) Amounts deductible in respect of dividends received — shares acquired from another corporation; s. 91(7) Shares acquired from a partnership; s. 92(1)(*b*) Adjusted cost base decreased by deduction for foreign accrual tax, foreign exchange reserve and dividends paid by affiliate; s. 248(1), "amount", "Minister", "share", "taxpayer"; s. 249 Definition of "taxation year"; s. 255 Canada.

► 91(3) ◄

(3) Reserve for preceding year to be included. In computing the income of a taxpayer for a taxation year, there shall be included each amount in respect of a share that was deducted by virtue of subsection (2) in computing the taxpayer's income for the immediately preceding year.

Editorial Note: S. 91(3) includes in income the amount of a s. 91(2) foreign exchange reserve that was deducted in computing the taxpayer's income in the immediately preceding taxation year. Where an amount is included in income under s. 91(3), an equivalent amount is added to the taxpayer's adjusted cost base of the shares of the affiliate under s. 92(1)(*a*) and s. 53(1)(*d*).

Related Sections: S. 12(1)(*k*) Dividends from other corporations; s. 53(1)(*d*) Adjustments to cost base — Share of foreign affiliate; s. 91(2) Reserve where foreign exchange restriction; s. 91(6) Amounts deductible in respect of dividends received — shares acquired from another corporation; s. 91(7) Shares acquired from a partnership; s. 92(1)(*a*) Adjusted cost base increase to the extent of FAPI and foreign exchange reserve inclusion; s. 92(1)(*b*) Adjusted cost base decreased by deduction for foreign accrual tax, foreign exchange reserve and dividends paid by affiliates; s. 248(1), "amount", "share", "taxpayer"; s. 249 Definition of "taxation year".

▶ 91(4) ◀

(4) Amounts deductible in respect of foreign taxes. Where, by virtue of subsection (1), an amount in respect of a share has been included in computing the income of a taxpayer for a taxation year or for any of the 5 immediately preceding taxation years (in this subsection referred to as the "income amount"), there may be deducted in computing the taxpayer's income for the year the lesser of

(*a*) the product obtained when

(i) the portion of the foreign accrual tax applicable to the income amount that was not deductible under this subsection in any previous year

is multiplied by

(ii) the taxpayer's relevant tax factor for the year, and

(*b*) the amount, if any, by which the income amount exceeds the total of the amounts in respect of that share deductible under this subsection in any of the 5 immediately preceding taxation years in respect of the income amount.

Editorial Note: S. 91(4) provides an indirect foreign tax credit for foreign taxes paid (foreign accrual tax) in respect of FAPI included in computing the taxpayer's income under s. 91(1) in the year or the five preceding taxation years. The indirect credit provided by s. 91(4) is in the form of a deduction in computing income equal to the lesser of: (i) a "grossed-up" amount of the foreign accrual tax applicable to the relevant amount included under s. 91(1); and (ii) the amount by which the amount included income under s. 91(1) in the year (or the previous five taxation years) exceeds the amounts deductible under s. 91(4) in the five preceding taxation years. The "grossed-up" amount is the amount that results from multiplying the foreign accrual tax by the relevant tax factor. The relevant tax factor limits the indirect credit available to the federal tax rate that is assumed would apply to the amount included in income under s. 91(1).

Where an amount is deducted under s. 91(4) a corresponding amount is deducted from the taxpayer's adjusted cost base of the share of the affiliate under s. 92(1)(*b*)(i) and s. 53(2)(*b*).

History: S. 91(4)(*a*)(ii) was replaced by S.C. 2013, c. 34, s. 226(1), applicable to the 2002 and subsequent taxation years, and formerly read:

(ii) the relevant tax factor, and

Related Sections: S. 53(2)(*b*) Amounts to be deducted — Share of non-resident corporation; s. 91(1) Amounts to be included in respect of share of foreign affiliate; s. 91(6) Amounts deductible in respect of dividends received — shares acquired from another corporation; s. 91(7) Shares acquired from a partnership; s. 92(1)(*b*) Adjusted cost base decrease to the extent of foreign accrual tax deduction; s. 95(1), "foreign accrual tax", "relevant tax factor"; s. 248(1), "amount", "share", "taxpayer"; s. 249 Definition of "taxation year".

Tax Profile: June 2008 — International Tax Planning for the Owner-Manager; February 2007 — U.S. Limited Liability Companies — The Good, the Bad and the Ugly; January 2006 — Foreign Source Income: Outbound Structures and Foreign Tax Credit Planning — Part I; February 2006 — Foreign Source Income: Outbound Structures and Foreign Tax Credit Planning — Part II.

▶ 91(4.1) ◀

(4.1) Denial of foreign accrual tax. For the purposes of the definition "foreign accrual tax" in subsection 95(1), foreign accrual tax applicable to a particular amount included in computing a taxpayer's income under subsection (1) for a taxation year of the taxpayer in respect of a particular foreign affiliate of the taxpayer is not to include the amount that would, in the absence of this subsection, be foreign accrual tax applicable to the particular amount if, at any time in the taxation year (referred to in this subsection as the "affiliate year") of the particular affiliate that ends in the taxation year of the taxpayer,

(*a*) a specified owner in respect of the taxpayer is considered,

(i) under the income tax laws (referred to in subsections (4.5) and (4.6) as the "relevant foreign tax law") of any country other than Canada under the laws of which any income of a particular corporation — that is, at any time in the affiliate year, a pertinent person or partnership in respect of the particular affiliate — is subject to income taxation, to own less than all of the shares of the capital stock of the particular corporation that are considered to be owned by the specified owner for the purposes of this Act, or

(ii) under the income tax laws (referred to in subsections (4.5) and (4.6) as the "relevant foreign tax law") of any country other than Canada under the laws of which any income of a particular partnership — that is, at any time in the affiliate year, a pertinent person or partnership in respect of the particular affiliate — is subject to income taxation, to have a lesser direct or indirect share of the income of the particular partnership than the specified owner is considered to have for the purposes of this Act; or

(*b*) where the taxpayer is a partnership, the direct or indirect share of the income of the partnership of any member of the partnership that is, at any time in the affiliate year, a person resident in Canada or a foreign affiliate of such a person is, under the income tax laws (referred to in subsection (4.6) as the "relevant foreign tax law") of any country other than Canada under the laws of which any income of the partnership is subject to income taxation, less than the member's direct or indirect share of that income for the purposes of this Act.

History: S. 91(4.1) was added by S.C. 2013, c. 34, s. 226(2), applicable in respect of the computation of foreign accrual tax applicable to an amount included in computing a taxpayer's income under subsection 91(1), for a taxation year of the taxpayer that ends after March 4, 2010, in respect of a foreign affiliate of the taxpayer. However, for taxation years of the taxpayer that end on or before October 24, 2012, subsection 91(4.1) is to be read as follows:

"(4.1) For the purposes of the definition "foreign accrual tax" in subsection 95(1), foreign accrual tax applicable to a particular amount included in computing a taxpayer's income under subsection (1) for a taxation year in respect of a particular foreign affiliate of the taxpayer shall not include the amount that would, in the absence of this subsection, be foreign accrual tax applicable to the particular amount if the particular amount is earned during a period in which

(*a*) if the taxpayer is a partnership, the share of the income of any member of the partnership that is a person resident in Canada is, under the income tax laws (referred to in subsection (4.6) as the "relevant foreign tax law") of any country, other than Canada, under the laws of which the income of the partnership is subject to income taxation, less than its share of the income for the purposes of this Act; or

(*b*) in any other case, the taxpayer is considered, under the income tax laws (referred to in subsection (4.5) as the "relevant foreign tax law") of any country, other than Canada, under the laws of which the income of the particular affiliate is subject to income taxation, to own less than all of the shares of the capital stock of the particular affiliate, of another foreign affiliate of the taxpayer in which the particular affiliate has an equity percentage, or of another foreign affiliate of the taxpayer that has an equity percentage in the particular affiliate, that are considered to be owned by the taxpayer for the purposes of this Act."

▶ 91(4.2) ◀

(4.2) Specified owner. For the purposes of subsections (4.1) and (4.5), a "specified owner", at any time, in respect of a taxpayer means the taxpayer or a person or partnership that is, at that time,

(*a*) a partnership of which the taxpayer is a member;

(*b*) a foreign affiliate of the taxpayer;

(*c*) a partnership a member of which is a foreign affiliate of the taxpayer; or

(*d*) a person or partnership referred to in any of subparagraphs (4.4)(*a*)(i) to (iii).

History: S. 91(4.2) was added by S.C. 2013, c. 34, s. 226(2), applicable in respect of the computation of foreign accrual tax applicable to an amount included in computing a taxpayer's income under subsection 91(1), for a taxation year of the taxpayer that ends after March 4, 2010, in respect of a foreign affiliate of the taxpayer. However, for taxation years of the taxpayer that end on or before October 24, 2012, section 91 is to be read without reference to its subsection (4.2).

▶ 91(4.3) ◀

(4.3) Pertinent person or partnership. For the purposes of this subsection and subsection (4.1), a "pertinent person or partnership", at any time, in respect of a particular foreign affiliate of a taxpayer means the particular affiliate or a person or partnership that is, at that time,

(*a*) another foreign affiliate of the taxpayer

(i) in which the particular affiliate has an equity percentage, or

(ii) that has an equity percentage in the particular affiliate;

(*b*) a partnership a member of which is at that time a pertinent person or partnership in respect of the particular affiliate under this subsection; or

(*c*) a person or partnership referred to in any of subparagraphs (4.4)(*b*)(i) to (iii).

History: S. 91(4.3) was added by S.C. 2013, c. 34, s. 226(2), applicable in respect of the computation of foreign accrual tax applicable to an amount included in computing a taxpayer's income under subsection 91(1), for a taxation year of the taxpayer that ends after March 4, 2010, in respect of a foreign affiliate of the taxpayer. However, for taxation years of the taxpayer that end on or before October 24, 2012, section 91 is to be read without reference to its subsection (4.3).

▶ 91(4.4) ◀

(4.4) Series of transactions. For the purposes of subsections (4.2) and (4.3), if, as part of a series of transactions or events that includes the earning of the foreign accrual property income that gave rise to the particular amount referred to in subsection (4.1), a foreign affiliate (referred to in this subsection as the "funding affiliate") of the taxpayer or of a person (referred to in this subsection as the "related person") resident in Canada that is related to the taxpayer, or a partnership (referred to in this subsection as the "funding partnership") of which such an affiliate is a member, directly or indirectly provided funding to the particular affiliate, or a partnership of which the particular affiliate is a member, otherwise than by way of loans or other indebtedness that are subject to terms or conditions made or imposed, in respect of the loans or other indebtedness, that do not differ from those that would be made or imposed between persons dealing at arm's length or by way of an acquisition of shares of the capital stock of any corporation, then

(*a*) if the funding affiliate is, or the funding partnership has a member that is, a foreign affiliate of the related person, the following persons and partnerships are deemed, at all times during which the foreign accrual property income is earned by the particular affiliate, to be specified owners in respect of the taxpayer:

(i) the related person,

(ii) each foreign affiliate of the related person, and

(iii) each partnership a member of which is a person referred to in subparagraph (i) or (ii); and

(*b*) the following persons and partnerships are deemed, at all times during which the foreign accrual property income is earned by the particular affiliate, to be pertinent persons or partnerships in respect of the particular affiliate:

(i) the funding affiliate or the funding partnership,

(ii) a non-resident corporation

(A) in which the funding affiliate has an equity percentage, or

(B) that has an equity percentage in the funding affiliate, and

(iii) a partnership a member of which is a person or partnership referred to in subparagraph (i) or (ii).

History: S. 91(4.4) was added by S.C. 2013, c. 34, s. 226(2), applicable in respect of the computation of foreign accrual tax applicable to an amount included in computing a taxpayer's income under subsection 91(1), for a taxation year of the taxpayer that ends after March 4, 2010, in respect of a foreign affiliate of the taxpayer, However, for taxation years of the taxpayer that end on or before October 24, 2012, section 91 is to be read without reference to its subsection (4.4).

▶ 91(4.5) ◀

(4.5) Exception — hybrid entities. For the purposes of subparagraph (4.1)(*a*)(i), a specified owner in respect of the taxpayer is not to be considered, under the relevant foreign tax law, to own less than all of the shares of the capital stock of a corporation that are considered to be owned for the purposes of this Act solely because the specified owner or the corporation is not treated as a corporation under the relevant foreign tax law.

History: S. 91(4.5) was replaced by S.C. 2017, c. 33, s. 28(3), applicable in respect of the computation of foreign accrual tax applicable to an amount included in computing a taxpayer's income under subsection 91(1), for a taxation year of the taxpayer that ends after October 24, 2012, in respect of a foreign affiliate of the taxpayer, and formerly read:

(4.5) *Exception — hybrid entities.* For the purposes of subparagraph (4.1)(*a*)(i), a specified owner in respect of the taxpayer is not to be considered, under the relevant foreign tax law, to own less than all of the shares of the capital stock of a corporation that are considered to be owned for the purposes of this Act solely because the specified owner is not treated as a corporation under the relevant foreign tax law.

S. 91(4.5) was added by S.C. 2013, c. 34, s. 226(2), applicable in respect of the computation of foreign accrual tax applicable to an amount included in computing a taxpayer's income under subsection 91(1), for a taxation year of the taxpayer that ends after March 4, 2010, in respect of a foreign affiliate of the taxpayer. However, for taxation years of the taxpayer that end on or before October 24, 2012, subsection 91(4.5) is to be read as follows:

"(4.5) For the purposes of paragraph (4.1)(*b*), a taxpayer is not to be considered, under the relevant foreign tax law, to own less than all of the shares of the capital stock of a foreign affiliate of the taxpayer that are considered to be owned by the taxpayer for the purposes of this Act solely because the taxpayer or the foreign affiliate is not treated as a corporation under the relevant foreign tax law."

Related Regulations: 5907(1.07).

▶ 91(4.6) ◀

(4.6) Exceptions — partnerships. For the purposes of subparagraph (4.1)(*a*)(ii) and paragraph (4.1)(*b*), a member of a partnership is not to be considered to have a lesser direct or indirect share of the income of the partnership under the relevant foreign tax law than for the purposes of this Act solely because of one or more of the following:

(*a*) a difference between the relevant foreign tax law and this Act in the manner of

(i) computing the income of the partnership, or

(ii) allocating the income of the partnership because of the admission to, or withdrawal from, the partnership of any of its members;

(*b*) the treatment of the partnership as a corporation under the relevant foreign tax law; or

(*c*) the fact that the member is not treated as a corporation under the relevant foreign tax law.

History: S. 91(4.6) was added by S.C. 2013, c. 34, s. 226(2), applicable in respect of the computation of foreign accrual tax applicable to an amount included in computing a taxpayer's income under subsection 91(1), for a taxation year of the taxpayer that ends after March 4, 2010, in respect of a foreign affiliate of the taxpayer. However, for taxation years of the taxpayer that end on or before October 24, 2012, the portion of subsection 91(4.6) before paragraph (*a*) is to be read as follows:

"(4.6) For the purposes of paragraph (4.1)(*a*), a member of a partnership is not to be considered to have a lesser share of the income of the partnership under the relevant foreign tax law than for the purposes of this Act solely because of one or more of the following:"

▶ 91(4.7) ◀

(4.7) Deemed ownership. For the purposes of subsection (4.1), if a specified owner owns, for the purposes of this Act, shares of the capital stock of a corporation and the dividends, or similar amounts, in respect of those shares are treated under the income tax laws of any country other than Canada under the laws of which any income of the corporation is subject to income taxation as interest or another form of deductible payment, the specified owner is deemed to be considered, under those tax laws, to own less than all of the shares of the capital stock of the corporation that are considered to be owned by the specified owner for the purposes of this Act.

History: S. 91(4.7) was added by S.C. 2013, c. 34, s. 226(2), applicable in respect of the computation of foreign accrual tax applicable to an amount included in computing a taxpayer's income under subsection 91(1), for a taxation year of the taxpayer that ends after March 4, 2010, in respect of a foreign affiliate of the taxpayer. However, for taxation years of the taxpayer that end on or before October 24, 2012, section 91 is to be read without reference to its subsection (4.7).

▶ 91(5) ◀

(5) Amounts deductible in respect of dividends received. Where in a taxation year a taxpayer resident in Canada has received a dividend on a share of the capital stock of a corporation that was at any time a controlled foreign affiliate of the taxpayer, there may be deducted, in respect of such portion of the dividend as is prescribed to have been paid out of the taxable surplus of the affiliate, in computing the taxpayer's income for the year, the lesser of

(*a*) the amount by which that portion of the dividend exceeds the amount, if any, deductible in respect thereof under paragraph 113(1)(*b*), and

(*b*) the amount, if any, by which

(i) the total of all amounts required by paragraph 92(1)(*a*) to be added in computing the adjusted cost base to the taxpayer of the share before the dividend was so received by the taxpayer

exceeds

(ii) the total of all amounts required by paragraph 92(1)(*b*) to be deducted in computing the adjusted cost base to the taxpayer of the share before the dividend was so received by the taxpayer.

Editorial Note: S. 91(5) provides a deduction in respect of a dividend received from a controlled foreign affiliate to the extent that the dividend relates to FAPI included in income in respect of a share of the affiliate under s. 91(1). Specifically, a deduction is available where the dividend is prescribed to be paid from taxable surplus, and is limited to the lesser of: (i) the dividend less the amount deductible in respect of the dividend under s. 113(1)(*b*) (underlying foreign tax applicable to taxable surplus dividend); and (ii) the amount by which the total of all amounts added to the adjusted cost base of the taxpayer's shares of the affiliate under s. 92(1)(*a*) exceeds the amounts deducted from the adjusted cost base of those shares under s. 92(1)(*b*). Note that in the case of an individual taxpayer, regulation 5900(3) provides that the amount of the dividend is the amount prescribed to be paid from taxable surplus.

Where an amount is deducted under s. 91(5), a corresponding amount is deducted from the taxpayer's adjusted cost base of the shares of the affiliate under s. 92(1)(*b*)(ii) and s. 53(2)(*b*).

Related Regulations: 5900(3).

Related Sections: S. 12(1)(*k*) Dividends from other corporations; s. 20(13) Dividend on share from foreign affiliate of taxpayer; s. 53(2)(*b*) Amounts to be deducted — Share of non-resident corporation; s. 90 Dividends received from non-resident corporation; s. 91(6) Amounts deductible in respect of dividends received — shares acquired from another corporation; s. 91(7) Shares acquired from a partnership; s. 92(1)(*a*) Adjusted cost base increase to the extent of FAPI and foreign exchange reserve inclusion; s. 92(1)(*b*) Adjusted cost base decreased by deduction for foreign accrual tax, foreign exchange reserve and dividends paid by affiliate; s. 95(1), "controlled foreign affiliate"; s. 113(1)(*b*) Deduction for underlying foreign tax applicable to taxable surplus; s. 248(1), "resident in Canada", "share", "taxpayer"; s. 249 Definition of "taxation year".

Tax Profile: February 2007 — U.S. Limited Liability Companies — The Good, the Bad and the Ugly; January 2006 — Foreign Source Income: Outbound Structures and Foreign Tax Credit Planning — Part I; February 2006 — Foreign Source Income: Outbound Structures and Foreign Tax Credit Planning — Part II.

▶ 91(5.1) ◀

(5.1) Deduction of dividend by shareholder — (Repealed by S.C. 2009, c. 2, s. 23(1).)

History: S. 91(5.1) was repealed by S.C. 2009, c. 2, s. 23(1), applicable after 2011. S. 91(5.1) was previously added by S.C. 2007, c. 35, s. 24(1), applicable after 2011. This subsection was consequential to s. 18.2, which was added and repealed for the same period. See the editorial note following s. 18.2. S. 91(5.1) formerly read:

(5.1) *Deduction of dividend by shareholder.* Where in a taxation year a corporation resident in Canada receives a dividend on a share of the capital stock of a corporation that was at any time a foreign affiliate of the corporation and subsection (5) does not apply in respect of that dividend, there may be deducted, in respect of such portion of the dividend as is prescribed to have been paid out of the taxable surplus of the affiliate, in computing the corporation's income for the year, the lesser of

(*a*) the amount, if any, by which that portion of the dividend exceeds the amount, if any, deductible in respect of the dividend under paragraph 113(1)(*b*), and

(*b*) the amount, if any, by which

(i) the total of all amounts required under subparagraph 92(1)(*a*)(ii) to be added in computing the adjusted cost base to the taxpayer of the share before the dividend was so received by the corporation

exceeds

(ii) the total of all amounts required under paragraph 92(1)(*b*) to be deducted in computing the adjusted cost base to the taxpayer of the share before the dividend was so received by the taxpayer.

► 91(5.2) ◄

(5.2) Deduction of dividend by member of partnership — (Repealed by S.C. 2009, c. 2, s. 23(1).)

History: S. 91(5.2) was repealed by S.C. 2009, c. 2, s. 23(1), applicable after 2011. S. 91(5.2) was previously added by S.C. 2007, c. 35, s. 24(1), applicable after 2011. This subsection was consequential to s. 18.2, which was added and repealed for the same period. See the editorial note following s. 18.2. S. 91(5.2) formerly read:

(5.2) *Deduction of dividend by member of partnership.* Where in a taxation year a corporation is deemed under section 93.1 to have received a dividend from a foreign affiliate, there may be deducted, in respect of such portion of the dividend as is prescribed to have been paid out of the taxable surplus of the affiliate, in computing the corporation's income for the year, the lesser of

(*a*) the amount, if any, by which that portion of the dividend exceeds the amount, if any, deductible in respect of the dividend under paragraph 113(1)(*b*), and

(*b*) the amount, if any, by which

(i) the total of all amounts required under subparagraph 53(1)(*e*)(xiv) to be added in computing the adjusted cost base to the taxpayer of the partnership interest that are reasonably attributable to a share in respect of which the dividend was paid

exceeds

(ii) the total of all amounts required under subparagraph 53(2)(*c*)(xiii) to be deducted in computing the adjusted cost base to the taxpayer of the partnership interest that are reasonably attributable to a share in respect of which the dividend was paid.

► 91(5.3) ◄

(5.3) Deduction of capital gain by member of partnership — (Repealed by S.C. 2009, c. 2, s. 23(1).)

History: S. 91(5.3) was repealed by S.C. 2009, c. 2, s. 23(1), applicable after 2011. S. 91(5.3) was previously added by S.C. 2007, c. 35, s. 24(1), applicable after 2011. This subsection was consequential to s. 18.2, which was added and repealed for the same period. See the editorial note following s. 18.2. S. 91(5.3) formerly read:

(5.3) *Deduction of capital gain by member of partnership.* Where in a taxation year a taxpayer is a member of a partnership, there may be deducted from the taxpayer's income for the taxation year an amount equal to the lesser of

(*a*) $^{1}/_{2}$ the amount of the taxpayer's specified proportion (within the meaning of paragraph 18.2(10)(*b*)) of any capital gain that is attributable to a disposition by the partnership of a share of the capital stock of a corporation, and

(*b*) the amount, if any, by which

(i) the total of all amounts required under subparagraph 53(1)(*e*)(xiv) to be added in computing the adjusted cost base to the taxpayer of its interest in the partnership that are reasonably attributable to the share

exceeds

(ii) the total of all amounts required under subparagraph 53(2)(*c*)(xiii) to be deducted in computing the adjusted cost base to the taxpayer of the partnership interest that are reasonably attributable to the share.

► 91(6) ◄

(6) Idem. Where a share of the capital stock of a foreign affiliate of a taxpayer that is a taxable Canadian corporation is acquired by the taxpayer from another corporation resident in Canada with which the taxpayer is not dealing at arm's length, for the purpose of subsection (5), any amount required by section 92 to be added or deducted, as the case may be, in computing the adjusted cost base to the other corporation of the share shall be deemed to have been so required to be added or deducted, as the case may be, in computing the adjusted cost base to the taxpayer of the share.

Editorial Note: Where a taxpayer that is a taxable Canadian corporation acquires shares of a foreign affiliate from a non-arm's length Canadian-resident corporation, s. 91(6) provides that all amounts required by s. 92 to be added or deducted from the transferor's adjusted cost base of a share of a foreign affiliate are deemed to be required to be added or deducted by s. 92 to the adjusted cost base of the taxpayer. S. 91(6) applies for the limited purpose of the dividend deduction rule in s. 91(5).

► 91(7) ◄

(7) Shares acquired from a partnership. For the purpose of subsection (5), where a taxpayer resident in Canada acquires a share of the capital stock of a corporation that is immediately after the acquisition a foreign affiliate of the taxpayer from a partnership of which the taxpayer, or a corporation resident in Canada with which the taxpayer was not dealing at arm's length at the time the share was acquired, was a member (each such person referred to in this subsection as the "member") at any time during any fiscal period of the partnership that began before the acquisition,

(*a*) that portion of any amount required by subsection 92(1) to be added to the adjusted cost base to the partnership of the share of the capital stock of the foreign affiliate equal to the amount included in the income of the member because of subsection 96(1) in respect of the amount that was included in the income of the partnership because of subsection (1) or (3) in respect of the foreign affiliate and added to that adjusted cost base, and

(*b*) that portion of any amount required by subsection 92(1) to be deducted from the adjusted cost base to the partnership of the share of the capital stock of the foreign affiliate equal to the amount by which the income of the member from the partnership under subsection 96(1) was reduced because of the amount deducted in computing the income of the partnership under subsection (2), (4) or (5) and deducted from that adjusted cost base

is deemed to be an amount required by subsection 92(1) to be added or deducted, as the case may be, in computing the adjusted cost base to the taxpayer of the share.

Related Sections: S. 54, "adjusted cost base"; s. 95(1), "foreign affiliate"; s. 248(1), "foreign affiliate"; s. 251(1) Arm's length.

SECTION 92: Adjusted cost base of share of foreign affiliate

► 92(1) ◄

(1) Adjusted cost base of share of foreign affiliate. In computing, at any time in a taxation year, the adjusted cost base to a taxpayer resident in Canada of any share owned by the taxpayer of the capital stock of a foreign affiliate of the taxpayer,

(*a*) there shall be added in respect of that share any amount included in respect of that share under subsection 91(1) or (3) in computing the taxpayer's income for the year or any preceding taxation year (or that would have been required to have been so included in computing the taxpayer's income but for subsection 56(4.1) and sections 74.1 to 75 of this Act and section 74 of the *Income Tax Act*, chapter 148 of the Revised Statutes of Canada, 1952); and

(*b*) there shall be deducted in respect of that share

(i) any amount deducted by the taxpayer under subsection 91(2) or (4), and

(ii) any dividend received by the taxpayer before that time, to the extent of the amount deducted by the taxpayer, in respect of the dividend, under subsection 91(5)

in computing the taxpayer's income for the year or any preceding taxation year (or that would have been deductible by the taxpayer but for subsection 56(4.1) and sections 74.1 to 75 of this Act and section 74 of the *Income Tax Act*, chapter 148 of the Revised Statutes of Canada, 1952).

Editorial Note: Amounts included in a taxpayer's FAPI in respect of a share of a controlled foreign affiliate (including prior year foreign currency reserves brought into income under s. 91(3)) are added to the adjusted cost base of the share as provided by s. 53(1)(*d*) and s. 92(1)(*a*). Amounts deducted by the taxpayer under s. 91(4) (FAT) or s. 91(5) (dividends to the extent they are derived from FAPI included in income) are deducted from the adjusted cost base of the share pursuant to s. 53(2)(*b*) and s. 92(1)(*b*).

History: Application Provision, S.C. 2013, c. 34, s. 51 [Consolidated Net Surplus Election] Subject to the Modified Consolidated Net Surplus Election (below), if a corporation resident in Canada elects in writing in respect of all of its foreign affiliates and files the election with the Minister of National Revenue on or before the day that is the later of the corporation's filing-due date for the corporation's taxation year that includes June 26, 2013 and June 26, 2014 [the day that is one year after royal assent], the following rules apply:

(*a*) if there is an election (referred to in this section as a "designated section 93 election") made by the corporation under subsection 93(1) or (1.2) of the *Income Tax Act* in respect of a disposition of shares (referred to in this section as the "designated shares") of the capital stock of a foreign affiliate of the corporation that occurs after December 20, 2002 and before December 19, 2009, other than a disposition that is required to be made under an agreement in writing made by the vendor before December 21, 2002, section 92 is, in respect of the designated shares, to be read as if it also contained the following subsections :

"(1.2) Subsection (1.4) applies to a holder of a share (referred to in this subsection and subsections (1.3) and (1.4) as the "relevant share") of a foreign affiliate (referred to in subsection (1.3) as the "relevant foreign affiliate") of a particular corporation resident in Canada in computing at any time (referred to in this subsection and subsection (1.3) as the "computation time") the adjusted cost base to the holder of the relevant share, if, at the computation time, there is a specified section 93 election related to the relevant share.

(1.3) An election made by the particular corporation resident in Canada under subsection 93(1) or (1.2), as the case may be, in respect of a share of a particular foreign affiliate of the particular corporation that is disposed of at a time (referred to in this subsection and subsection (1.4) as the "election time") before the computation time is, at the computation time, a specified section 93 election related to the relevant share if

(*a*) the particular foreign affiliate has, at the election time, an equity percentage in the relevant foreign affiliate;

(*b*) the relevant foreign affiliate was, at the election time, a foreign affiliate of the particular corporation;

(*c*) throughout the period that begins at the election time and ends at the computation time,

(i) the holder held the relevant share, and

(ii) the holder was

(A) a foreign affiliate of the particular corporation,

(B) a foreign affiliate of a corporation resident in Canada that was related to the particular corporation,

(C) a partnership of which a foreign affiliate of the particular corporation was a member, or

(D) a partnership of which a foreign affiliate, of a corporation resident in Canada that was related to the particular corporation, was a member;

(*d*) the relevant share was, at the election time, excluded property of the holder (or would have been, at the election time, excluded property of the holder if the holder had been a foreign affiliate of the particular corporation); and

(*e*) the relevant share is, at the computation time, excluded property of the holder (or would have been, at the computation time, excluded property of the holder if the holder had been a foreign affiliate of the particular corporation or of a corporation resident in Canada that is related to the particular corporation).

(1.4) If this subsection applies, for the purposes of computing, at any time after the election time, the exempt surplus or deficit, the taxable surplus or deficit, and the underlying foreign tax, of the holder, in respect of the particular corporation resident in Canada or in respect of any other person that would, at the time after the election time, be a designated person in respect of the particular corporation, the following rules apply in determining the adjusted cost base to the holder of the relevant share:

(*a*) there shall be added, to the adjusted cost base to the holder of the relevant share, the amount prescribed in respect of the relevant share in respect of the specified section 93 election, and

(*b*) there shall be deducted, from the adjusted cost base to the holder of the relevant share, the amount prescribed in respect of the relevant share in respect of the specified section 93 election.

(1.5) For the purposes of subsection (1.4), a designated person, in respect of a particular corporation, at any time means

(*a*) any person with whom the particular corporation was not dealing at arm's length;

(*b*) any person with whom the particular corporation would not have been dealing at arm's length if the person had been in existence after the particular corporation came into existence;

(*c*) any predecessor corporation (within the meaning assigned by subsection 87(1)) of a person described in paragraph (*a*) or (*b*); or

(*d*) any predecessor corporation (within the meaning assigned by paragraph 87(2)(*l.2*)) of a person described in paragraph (*a*) or (*b*)."

Application Provision, S.C. 2013, c. 34, s. 52 [Modified Consolidated Net Surplus Election.]

(1) The application in subsection (2) (below) applies if

(*a*) a corporation has made the election above; and

(*b*) the corporation has made an election under subsection 93(1) or (1.2) of the Income Tax Act in respect of a disposition of a share of the capital stock of a foreign affiliate of the corporation that occurs after December 20, 2002 and on or before February 27, 2004 (other than a disposition required to be made under an agreement in writing made by a vendor on or before December 20, 2002), or in respect of a disposition that occurs after February 27, 2004 and that is required to be made under an agreement in writing made by a vendor after December 20, 2002 and before February 28, 2004; and

(*c*) the corporation elects in writing to apply paragraph (*d*) (below) in respect of all of its foreign affiliates and files the election with the Minister of National Revenue on or before the day that is the later of the corporation's filing-due date for the corporation's taxation year that includes June 26, 2013 and June 26, 2014 [the day that is one year after royal assent];

(2) then the Consolidated Net Surplus Election above does not apply in respect of dispositions referred to in paragraph (*b*).

S. 92(1) was replaced by S.C. 2009, c. 2, s. 24(1), applicable after 2011. S. 92(1) had been replaced by S.C. 2007, c. 35, applicable after 2011, pursuant to the addition of s. 18.2. S.C. 2009, c. 2 replaced s. 92(1) to delete the reference to s. 18.2 (pursuant to the repeal of s. 18.2) and to revise the wording in paragraph (*a*) slightly. S. 92(1) formerly read:

(1) *Adjusted cost base of share of foreign affiliate.* In computing, at any time in a taxation year, the adjusted cost base to a taxpayer resident in Canada of any share owned by the taxpayer of the capital stock of a foreign affiliate of the taxpayer,

(*a*) there shall be added any amount required to be included in respect of that share by reason of subsection 91(1) or (3) in computing the taxpayer's income for the year or any preceding taxation year (or that would have been so required to be included but for subsection 56(4.1) and sections 74.1 to 75 of this Act and section 74 of the *Income Tax Act*, chapter 148 of the Revised Statutes of Canada, 1952); and

(*b*) there shall be deducted in respect of that share

(i) any amount deducted by the taxpayer by reason of subsection 91(2) or (4), and

(ii) any dividend received by the taxpayer before that time to the extent of the amount deducted by the taxpayer in respect thereof by reason of subsection 91(5)

in computing the taxpayer's income for the year or any preceding taxation year (or that would have been deductible by the taxpayer but for subsection 56(4.1) and sections 74.1 to 75 of this Act and section 74 of the *Income Tax Act*, chapter 148 of the Revised Statutes of Canada, 1952).

Related Sections: S. 53(1) Adjustments to cost base; s. 53(2) Amounts to be deducted.

Information Circulars: IC 77-9R Books, records and other requirements for taxpayers having foreign affiliates.

Interpretation Bulletins: *Secondary* — IT-451R Deemed disposition and acquisition on ceasing to be or becoming resident in Canada.

► 92(1.1) ◄

(1.1) Adjustment for prescribed amount. The prescribed amount shall be added in computing the adjusted cost base of a share of the capital stock of a foreign affiliate of a corporation resident in Canada to

(*a*) another foreign affiliate of the corporation; or

(*b*) a partnership of which another foreign affiliate of the corporation is a member.

History: S. 92(1.1) was added by S.C. 2013, c. 34, s. 31(1), deemed to have come into force on December 19, 2009. See also the Consolidated Net Surplus Elections following s. 92(1).

Any assessment of a taxpayer's tax, interest and penalties payable under the Act for any taxation year that ends before June 26, 2013 that would, in the absence of this section, be precluded because of subsections 152(4) to (5) of the Act, shall be made to the extent necessary to take into account this amendment, if the taxpayer

(i) elects in writing in respect of all of its foreign affiliates that this section apply in respect of that provision, and

(ii) files that election with the Minister of National Revenue on or before December 26, 2013 [the day that is six months after royal assent].

Related Regulations: 5907(7.6); 5908(11).

► 92(1.2) ◄

(1.2) Adjustment re adjusted cost base. There is to be added in computing the adjusted cost base to a taxpayer of a share of the capital stock of a foreign affiliate of the taxpayer any amount required by paragraph 93(4)(*b*) to be so added.

History: S. 92(1.2) was added by S.C. 2013, c. 34, s. 67(1), deemed to have come into force on February 28, 2004.

Any assessment of a taxpayer's tax, interest and penalties payable under the Act for any taxation year that ends before June 26, 2013 that would, in the absence of this section, be precluded because of subsections 152(4) to (5) of the Act shall be made to the extent necessary to take into account the amendments by S.C. 2013, c. 34, s. 54 to 89.

► 92(2) ◄

(2) Deduction in computing adjusted cost base. In computing, at any time in a taxation year,

(*a*) the adjusted cost base to a corporation resident in Canada (in this subsection referred to as an "owner") of any share of the capital stock of a foreign affiliate of the corporation, or

(*b*) the adjusted cost base to a foreign affiliate (in this subsection referred to as an "owner") of a person resident in Canada of any share of the capital stock of another foreign affiliate of that person,

there shall be deducted, in respect of any dividend received on the share before that time by the owner of the share, an amount equal to the amount, if any, by which

(*c*) such portion of the amount of the dividend so received as was deductible by virtue of paragraph 113(1)(*d*) from the income of the owner for the year in computing the owner's taxable income for the year or as would have been so deductible if the owner had been a corporation resident in Canada,

exceeds

(*d*) such portion of any income or profits tax paid by the owner to the government of a country other than Canada as may reasonably be regarded as having been paid in respect of the portion described in paragraph (*c*).

Editorial Note: S. 92(2) and s. 53(2)(*b*) provide that a corporation that receives a dividend on a share of a foreign affiliate that is prescribed to be paid from pre-acquisition surplus must reduce the adjusted cost base of the share of the affiliate by the amount of the dividend less any foreign withholding tax on the dividend. The rule also applies where the foreign affiliate's shares are owned by another foreign affiliate of a person resident in Canada.

Related Sections: S. 113(1)(*d*) Deduction in respect of dividend received from foreign affiliate.

► 92(3) ◄

(3) Idem. In computing, at any time in a taxation year, the adjusted cost base to a corporation resident in Canada of any share of the capital stock of a foreign affiliate of the corporation, there shall be deducted an amount in respect of any dividend received on the share by the corporation before that time equal to such portion of the amount so received as was deducted under subsection 113(2) from the income of the corporation for the year or any preceding year in computing its taxable income.

Editorial Note: S. 92(3) reduces the adjusted cost base of a share of a foreign affiliate on which a dividend has been received to the extent of a s. 113(2) deduction in respect of the dividend. This is relevant only where the foreign affiliate was owned by the corporation at the end of its 1975 taxation year.

Related Sections: S. 2(2) Taxable income; s. 53(2) Amounts to be deducted; s. 54, "adjusted cost base"; s. 95(1), "foreign affiliate"; s. 248(1), "amount", "corporation", "dividend", "share"; s. 255 Canada.

► 92(4) ◄

(4) Disposition of a partnership interest. Where a corporation resident in Canada or a foreign affiliate of a corporation resident in Canada has at any time disposed of all or a portion of an interest in a partnership of which it was a member, there shall be added, in computing the proceeds of disposition of that interest, the amount determined by the formula

$$(A - B) \times (C/D)$$

where

A is the amount, if any, by which

(*a*) the total of all amounts each of which is an amount that was deductible under paragraph 113(1)(*d*) by the member from its income in computing its taxable income for any taxation year of the member that began before that time in respect of any portion of a dividend received by the partnership, or would have been so deductible if the member were a corporation resident in Canada,

exceeds

(*b*) the total of all amounts each of which is the portion of any income or profits tax paid by the partnership or the member of the partnership to a government of a country other than Canada that can reasonably be considered as having been paid in respect of the member's share of the dividend described in paragraph (*a*);

B is the total of

(*a*) the total of all amounts each of which was an amount added under this subsection in computing the member's proceeds of a disposition before that time of another interest in the partnership, and

(*b*) the total of all amounts each of which was an amount deemed by subsection (5) to be a gain of the member from a disposition before that time of a share by the partnership;

C is the adjusted cost base, immediately before that time, of the portion of the member's interest in the partnership disposed of by the member at that time; and

D is the adjusted cost base, immediately before that time, of the member's interest in the partnership immediately before that time.

Editorial Note: Where a Canadian-resident corporation or a foreign affiliate of the corporation disposes of an interest in a partnership, s. 92(4) increases the proceeds of disposition of the partnership interest by the amount by which (i) any dividends prescribed to be paid from pre-acquisition surplus that were deductible by the disposing corporation pursuant to s. 113(1)(*d*) (or dividends that would have been deductible if the member were resident in Canada) exceed (ii) foreign withholding taxes paid in respect of the dividend. This amount does not include amounts previously added under s. 92(5).

Related Sections: S. 54, "adjusted cost base"; s. 95(1), "foreign affiliate"; s. 248(1), "foreign affiliate".

► 92(5) ◄

(5) Deemed gain from the disposition of a share. Where a partnership has, at any time in a fiscal period of the partnership at the end of which a corporation resident in Canada or a foreign affiliate of a corporation resident in Canada was a member, disposed of a share of the capital stock of a corporation, the amount determined under subsection (6) in respect of such a member is deemed to be a gain of the member from the disposition of the share by the partnership for the member's taxation year in which the fiscal period of the partnership ends.

Editorial Note: Where a partnership disposes of a share of a corporation and at the end of the fiscal period in which the disposition occurred a corporation resident in Canada or a foreign affiliate of a corporation resident in Canada was a member of the partnership, s. 92(5) provides that the amount determined by s. 92(6) will be deemed to be a gain of the member from the disposition of the share for the member's taxation year in which the fiscal period of the partnership ends.

► 92(6) ◄

(6) Formula. The amount determined for the purposes of subsection (5) is the amount determined by the formula

$$A - B$$

where

A is the amount, if any, by which

(*a*) the total of all amounts each of which is an amount that was deductible under paragraph 113(1)(*d*) by the member from its income in computing its taxable income for a taxation year in respect of any portion of a dividend received by the partnership on the share in a fiscal period of the partnership that began before the time referred to in subsection (5) and ends in the member's taxation year, or would have been so deductible if the member were a corporation resident in Canada,

exceeds

(*b*) the total of all amounts each of which is the portion of any income or profits tax paid by the partnership or the member to a government of a country other than Canada that can reasonably be considered as having been paid in respect of the member's share of the dividend described in paragraph (*a*); and

B is the total of all amounts each of which is an amount that was added under subsection (4) in computing the member's proceeds of a disposition before the time referred to in subsection (5) of an interest in the partnership.

Editorial Note: S. 92(6) provides the amount of the deemed gain for the purposes of s. 92(5). The s. 92(6) amount is the amount that was deductible (or that would have been deductible by the member if it were a corporation resident in Canada) by the particular member of the partnership in respect of pre-acquisition surplus dividends less the total of all income or profits taxes paid by the partnership or by the member to a government of a country other than Canada that can reasonably be considered as having been paid in respect of the member's share of the pre-acquisition surplus dividends.

SECTION 93: Election re disposition of share of foreign affiliate

► 93(1) ◄

(1) Election re disposition of share of foreign affiliate. For the purposes of this Act, if a corporation resident in Canada elects, in accordance with prescribed rules, in respect of any share of the capital stock of a particular foreign affiliate of the corporation that is disposed of, at any time, by the corporation (referred to in this subsection as the "disposing corporation") or by another foreign affiliate (referred to in this subsection as the "disposing affiliate") of the corporation,

(*a*) the amount (referred to in this subsection as the "elected amount") designated by the corporation in its election not exceeding the amount that would, in the absence of this subsection, be the gain of the disposing corporation or disposing affiliate, as the case may be, from the disposition of the share, is deemed

(i) to have been a dividend received on the share from the particular affiliate by the disposing corporation or disposing affiliate, as the case may be, immediately before that time, and

(ii) not to have been received by the disposing corporation or disposing affiliate, as the case may be, as proceeds of disposition in respect of the disposition of the share; and

(*b*) if subsection 40(3) applies to the disposing corporation or disposing affiliate, as the case may be, in respect of the share, the amount deemed by that subsection to be the gain of the disposing corporation or disposing affiliate, as the case may be, from the disposition of the share is, except for the purposes of paragraph 53(1)(*a*), deemed to be equal to the amount, if any, by which

(i) the amount deemed by that subsection to be the gain from the disposition of the share determined without reference to this paragraph

exceeds

(ii) the elected amount.

Editorial Note: S. 93(1) provides a discretionary election that may be made in respect of a disposition of a share of a foreign affiliate of a corporation resident in Canada by that corporation or by a foreign affiliate of that corporation. The amount elected is treated as a dividend received by the corporation and not as proceeds of disposition. This is beneficial where there is exempt surplus or taxable surplus with supporting underlying foreign tax available in the foreign affiliate.

History: S. 93(1)(*b*) was replaced by S.C. 2013, c. 34, s. 32(1), in respect of elections made in respect of dispositions that occur after December 18, 2009.

Any assessment of a taxpayer's tax, interest and penalties payable under the Act for any taxation year that ends before June 26, 2013 that would, in the absence of this section, be precluded because of subsections 152(4) to (5) of the Act, shall be made to the extent necessary to take into account this amendment, if the taxpayer

(i) elects in writing in respect of all of its foreign affiliates that this section apply in respect of that provision, and

(ii) files that election with the Minister of National Revenue on or before December 26, 2013 [the day that is six months after royal assent].

S. 93(1)(*b*) formerly read:

(*b*) where subsection 40(3) applies to the disposing corporation or disposing affiliate, as the case may be, in respect of the share,

(i) the amount deemed by that subsection to be the gain of the disposing corporation or disposing affiliate, as the case may be, from the disposition of the share shall, except for the purposes of paragraph 53(1)(*a*), be deemed to be equal to the amount, if any, by which

(A) the amount deemed by that subsection to be the gain from the disposition of the share determined without reference to this subparagraph

exceeds

(B) the elected amount, and

(ii) for the purposes of determining the exempt surplus, exempt deficit, taxable surplus, taxable deficit and underlying foreign tax of the affiliate in respect of the corporation resident in Canada (within the meanings assigned by Part LIX of the Income Tax Regulations), the affiliate is deemed to have redeemed at the time of the disposition shares of a class of its capital stock.

S. 93(1), the portion before paragraph (*b*) was replaced by S.C. 2013, c. 34, s. 68(1), applicable in respect of elections in respect of dispositions that occur after August 19, 2011. However, the amendment to the portion of subsection 93(1) before paragraph (*b*) does not apply in respect of the determination of the income earned or realized of a foreign affiliate of a corporation under paragraph 55(5)(*d*) unless paragraph 55(5)(*d*) applies in respect of that determination.

Any assessment of a taxpayer's tax, interest and penalties payable under the Act for any taxation year that ends before June 26, 2013 that would, in the absence of this section, be precluded because of subsections 152(4) to (5) of the Act shall be made to the extent necessary to take into account the amendments by S.C. 2013, c. 34, s. 54 to 89.

S. 93(1), the portion before paragraph (*b*) formerly read:

(1) *Election re disposition of share in foreign affiliate.* For the purposes of this Act, where a corporation resident in Canada so elects, in prescribed manner and within the prescribed time, in respect of any share of the capital stock of a foreign affiliate of the corporation disposed of by it or by another foreign affiliate of the corporation,

(*a*) the amount (in this subsection referred to as the "elected amount") designated by the corporation in its election not exceeding the proceeds of disposition of the share shall be deemed to have been a dividend received on the share from the affiliate by the disposing corporation or disposing affiliate, as the case may be, immediately before the disposition and not to have been proceeds of disposition; and

Related Regulations: 5902.

Related Sections: S. 53(2) Amounts to be deducted; s. 54, "adjusted cost base", "proceeds of disposition"; s. 87(2)(*u*) Shares of foreign affiliate; s. 95(1), "foreign affiliate".

Canadian Petroleum Tax Journal: Foreign Affiliate Surplus: Got Enough?, Talakshi and Samuel, 2005, Vol. 18, No. 1.

Canadian Tax Foundation: Colborne and McLaren, *Section 93 Elections*, 2007 Canadian Tax Journal 4:855–893; Grosman and Manin, *A Comparison of the Earnings and Profits and Surplus Concepts: Selected Issues*, 2004 Canadian Tax Journal 2:574–601; Nikolakakis et al., *Foreign Affiliates: A Review of the Proposed Rules*, 2003 Conference Report 24:1–14; Hayre and Kroeker, *Foreign Affiliate Rules — The 2002 Amendments*, 2003 British Columbia Tax Conference 11:1–26; Nikolakakis, *The 1999-2000 Foreign Affiliate Amendments: Partnerships, Foreign Exchange Issues, and the Use of Losses*, 2000 Conference Report 14:1–60.

Tax Profile: February 2013 — The Purchase of US Businesses by Canadians; December 2012 — Taxpayer's Equity Characterization of Hybrid Instruments — Canadian Implications; November 2010 — Canadian Acquisition of U.S. Real Estate; December 2004 — Taxation of Dividends: A Survey in the Context of Private Corporations and Their Shareholders — Part 2; June 2003 — The December 20, 2002 Technical Amendments to the Income Tax Act; April 2002 — Tax Considerations for Canadian Businesses Expanding to the U.S.

Forms: T2107 — Election in Respect of a Share Disposition in a Foreign Affiliate.

Information Circulars: IC 76-19R3 Transfer of property to a corporation under section 85; IC 77-9R Books, records and other requirements for taxpayers having foreign affiliates.

Tax Window Files: Foreign affiliate share redemption, *April 11, 2017*, CRA Document No. 2016-0670541I7.

▶ 93(1.1) ◀

(1.1) Application of subsection (1.11). Subsection (1.11) applies if

(*a*) a particular foreign affiliate of a corporation resident in Canada disposes at any time of a share (referred to in this paragraph and subsection (1.11) as the "disposed share") of the capital stock of another foreign affiliate of the corporation and the particular affiliate would, in the absence of subsections (1) and (1.11), have a capital gain from the disposition of the disposed share; or

(*b*) a corporation resident in Canada would, in the absence of subsections (1) and (1.11), be deemed under subsection 40(3), because of an election under subsection 90(3) or subparagraph 5901(2)(*b*)(i) of the *Income Tax Regulations*, to have realized a gain from a disposition at any time of a share (referred to in subsection (1.11) as the "disposed share") of the capital stock of a foreign affiliate of the corporation.

Editorial Note: S. 93(1.1) deems an election to have been made under s. 93(1) in respect of dispositions by a foreign affiliate of a foreign affiliate share that constitutes excluded property.

History: S. 93(1.1) was replaced by S.C. 2013, c. 34, s. 68(3), applicable to dispositions of shares of the capital stock of a foreign affiliate of a corporation that occur after August 19, 2011. However, if the corporation

(*a*) has elected under the application to section 5901(2) of the *Income Tax Regulations*, then subsection 93(1.1) also applies to dispositions of shares of the capital stock of all foreign affiliates of the corporation that occur after December 20, 2002 and on or before August 19, 2011 as if paragraph 93(1.1)(*b*) were read as follows:

"(*b*) a corporation resident in Canada would, in the absence of subsections (1) and (1.11), be deemed under subsection 40(3), because of an election under subparagraph 5901(2)(*b*)(i) of the *Income Tax Regulations*, to have realized a gain from a disposition at any time of a share (referred to in subsection (1.11) as the "disposed share") of the capital stock of a foreign affiliate of the corporation."

(*b*) has not elected under the application to section 5901(2) of the *Income Tax Regulations*, but elects in writing and files the election with the Minister of National Revenue on or before the day that is the later of the corporation's filing-due date for the corporation's taxation year that includes June 26, 2013 and June 26, 2014 [the day that is one year after royal assent], then subsection 93(1.1) is to be read as follows in respect of any disposition of shares of the capital stock of a foreign affiliate of the corporation that occurs after February 27, 2004 and on or before August 19, 2011:

"(1.1) If at any time shares of the capital stock of a foreign affiliate of a corporation resident in Canada are disposed of by another foreign affiliate of the corporation, the corporation is deemed

(*a*) to have made an election at that time under subsection (1) in respect of each of those shares; and

(*b*) to have designated, in the election, the amount prescribed in respect of each of those shares."

Any assessment of a taxpayer's tax, interest and penalties payable under the Act for any taxation year that ends before June 26, 2013 that would, in the absence of this section, be precluded because of subsections 152(4) to (5) of the Act shall be made to the extent necessary to take into account the amendments by S.C. 2013, c. 34, s. 54 to 89.

S. 93(1.1) formerly read:

(1.1) *Idem.* Where at any time shares of the capital stock of a foreign affiliate of a corporation resident in Canada that are excluded property are disposed of by another foreign affiliate of the corporation (other than a disposition to which paragraph 95(2)(*c*), (*d*) or (*e*) applies), the corporation shall be deemed to have made an election at that time under subsection (1) in respect of each such share disposed of and in the election to have designated an amount equal to such amount as is prescribed.

▶ 93(1.11) ◀

(1.11) Deemed election. If this subsection applies, the corporation resident in Canada referred to in subsection (1.1) is deemed

(*a*) to have made an election, at the time referred to in subsection (1.1), under subsection (1) in respect of the disposition of the disposed share; and (*b*) to have designated, in the election, the prescribed amount in respect of the disposition of the disposed share.

History: S. 93(1.11) was added by S.C. 2013, c. 34, s. 68(3), applicable to dispositions of shares of the capital stock of a foreign affiliate of a corporation that occur after August 19, 2011.

See the application for the amendment to s. 93(1.1) for the extension of assessment periods to take into account the amendments by S.C. 2013, c. 34, s. 54 to 89.

► 93(1.2) ◄

(1.2) Disposition of shares of a foreign affiliate held by a partnership. Where a particular corporation resident in Canada or a foreign affiliate of the particular corporation (each of which is referred to in this subsection as the "disposing corporation") would, but for this subsection, have a taxable capital gain from a disposition by a partnership, at any time, of shares of a class of the capital stock of a foreign affiliate of the particular corporation and the particular corporation so elects in prescribed manner in respect of the disposition,

(*a*) twice

(i) the amount designated by the particular corporation (which amount shall not exceed the amount that is equal to the proportion of the taxable capital gain of the partnership that the number of shares of that class of the capital stock of the foreign affiliate, determined as the amount, if any, by which the number of those shares that were deemed to have been owned by the disposing corporation for the purposes of subsection 93.1(1) immediately before the disposition exceeds the number of those shares that were deemed to have been owned for those purposes by the disposing corporation immediately after the disposition, is of the number of those shares of the foreign affiliate that were owned by the partnership immediately before the disposition), or

(ii) if subsection (1.3) applies, the prescribed amount

in respect of those shares is deemed to have been a dividend received immediately before that time on the number of those shares of the foreign affiliate which shall be determined as the amount, if any, by which the number of those shares that the disposing corporation was deemed to own for the purpose of subsection 93.1(1) immediately before the disposition exceeds the number of those shares of the foreign affiliate that the disposing corporation was deemed to own for the purposes of subsection 93.1 (1) immediately after the disposition;

(*b*) notwithstanding section 96, the disposing corporation's taxable capital gain from the disposition of those shares is deemed to be the amount, if any, by which the disposing corporation's taxable capital gain from the disposition of the shares otherwise determined exceeds the amount designated by the particular corporation in respect of the shares;

(*c*) for the purpose of any regulation made under this subsection, the disposing corporation is deemed to have disposed of the number of those shares of the foreign affiliate which shall be determined as the amount, if any, by which the number of those shares that the disposing corporation was deemed to own for the purposes of subsection 93.1(1) immediately before the disposition exceeds the number of those shares that the disposing corporation was deemed to own for those purposes immediately after the disposition;

(*d*) for the purposes of section 113 in respect of the dividend referred to in paragraph (*a*), the disposing corporation is deemed to have owned the shares on which that dividend was received; and

(*e*) where the disposing corporation has a taxable capital gain from the partnership because of the application of subsection 40(3) to the partnership in respect of those shares, for the purposes of this subsection, the shares are deemed to have been disposed of by the partnership.

Editorial Note: S. 93(1.2) provides an election in connection with taxable capital gains arising from dispositions of foreign affiliate shares by a partnership of which a Canadian-resident corporation or a foreign affiliate of such a corporation is a member. In concept, s. 93(1.2), in concert with s. 93.1, is intended to allow the disposing corporation to look-through a partnership for the purpose of accessing surplus of the affiliate disposed of in a manner similar to that provided by the s. 93(1) election. Note that no similar rules exist in connection with the disposition of partnership interests.

History: [**Editorial Note**: The application to the amendment to s. 93(1.2) by S.C. 2001, c. 17, s. 70(4) was amended by S.C. 2013, c. 34, s. 373, to correct a technical deficiency. The wording was modified to ensure that, for a taxation year of a taxpayer that includes either February 28, 2000 or October 17, 2000 or began after February 28, 2000 and ended before October 17, 2000, the reference to the word "twice" is to read as references to the reciprocal of the capital gains inclusion rate applicable to the corporation resident in Canada or to the foreign affiliate for the taxation year. This 2001 amendment is not reproduced in print but is available in all CCH Canadian electronic versions of the Income Tax Act.]

S. 93(1.2)(*a*)(ii) was replaced by S.C. 2013, c. 34, s. 32(2), applicable in respect of elections made under subsection 93(1.2) in respect of dispositions that occur after November 1999.

See the application following s. 93(1) regarding the override of the statute-barring rules for assessments for taxation years that end before June 26, 2013.

S. 93(1.2)(*a*)(ii) formerly read:

> (ii) where subsection (1.3) applies, the amount prescribed for the purpose of that subsection

Related Regulations: 5908(8).

► 93(1.3) ◄

(1.3) Deemed election. Where a foreign affiliate of a particular corporation resident in Canada has a gain from the disposition by a partnership at any time of shares of a class of the capital stock of a foreign affiliate of the particular corporation that are excluded property, the particular corporation is deemed to have made an election under subsection (1.2) in respect of the number of shares of the foreign affiliate which shall be determined as the amount, if any, by which the number of those shares that the disposing corporation was deemed to own for the purposes of subsection 93.1(1) immediately before the disposition exceeds the number of those shares that the disposing corporation was deemed to own for those purposes immediately after the disposition.

Editorial Note: S. 93(1.3) deems a s. 93(1.2) election to have been made in respect of gains realized by a foreign affiliate from the disposition of foreign affiliate shares that constitute excluded property by a partnership of which the disposing affiliate is a member.

► 93(2) ◄

(2) Application of subsection (2.01). Subsection (2.01) applies if

(*a*) a particular corporation (referred to in subparagraph (2.01)(*b*)(ii) as the "vendor", as the context requires) resident in Canada has a particular loss, determined without reference to this section, from the disposition by it at any time (referred to in subsection (2.01) as the "disposition time") of a share (referred to in subsection (2.01) as the "affiliate share") of the capital stock of a foreign affiliate of the particular corporation; or

(*b*) a foreign affiliate (referred to in subparagraph (2.01)(*b*)(ii) as the "vendor") of a particular corporation resident in Canada has a particular loss, determined without reference to this section, from the disposition by it at any time (referred to in subsection (2.01) as the "disposition time") of a share (referred to in subsection (2.01) as the "affiliate share") of the capital stock of another foreign affiliate of the particular corporation that is not excluded property.

History: [Editorial Note: The application to the amendment to s. 93(2) by S.C. 2001, c. 17, s. 70(5) was amended by S.C. 2013, c. 34, s. 373, to make minor modifications to the wording of the amendment. This 2001 amendment is not reproduced in print but is available in all CCH Canadian electronic versions of the Income Tax Act.]

S. 93(2) was amended by S.C. 2013, c. 34, s. 68(4), applicable in respect of losses of a corporation resident in Canada, or of foreign affiliates of such a corporation, in respect of dispositions of shares and partnership interests that occur after February 27, 2004.

However, if the corporation elects in writing in respect of all losses of the corporation, and of all foreign affiliates of the corporation, in respect of dispositions (referred to in this paragraph as "pertinent dispositions" in respect of the corporation) of shares and partnership interests that occur on or before February 27, 2004 and files the election with the Minister of National Revenue on or before the day that is the later of the corporation's filing-due date for the corporation's taxation year that includes June 26, 2013 and June 26, 2014 [the day that is one year after royal assent], subsection 93(2) also applies in respect of all pertinent dispositions in respect of the corporation that occur after 1994 and on or before February 27, 2004.

See the application for the amendment to s. 93(1.1) for the extension of assessment periods to take into account the amendments by S.C. 2013, c. 34, s. 54 to 89.

S. 93(2) formerly read:

(2) *Loss limitation on disposition of share.* Where

(*a*) a corporation resident in Canada has a loss from the disposition by it at any time of a share of the capital stock of a foreign affiliate of the corporation (in this subsection referred to as the "affiliate share"), or

(*b*) a foreign affiliate of a corporation resident in Canada has a loss from the disposition by it at any time of a share of the capital stock of another foreign affiliate of the corporation resident in Canada that is not excluded property (in this subsection referred to as the "affiliate share"),

the amount of the loss is deemed to be the amount determined by the formula

$$A - (B - C)$$

where

A is the amount of the loss determined without reference to this subsection,

B is the total of all amounts each of which is an amount received before that time, in respect of an exempt dividend on the affiliate share or on a share for which the affiliate share was substituted, by

(*a*) the corporation resident in Canada,

(*b*) a corporation related to the corporation resident in Canada,

(*c*) a foreign affiliate of the corporation resident in Canada, or

(*d*) a foreign affiliate of a corporation related to the corporation resident in Canada, and

C is the total of

(*a*) the total of all amounts each of which is the amount by which a loss (determined without reference to this section), from another disposition at or before that time by a corporation or foreign affiliate described in the description of B of the affiliate share or a share for which the affiliate share was substituted, was reduced under this subsection in respect of the exempt dividends referred to in the description of B,

(*b*) the total of all amounts each of which is twice the amount by which an allowable capital loss (determined without reference to this section), of a corporation or foreign affiliate described in the description of B from a previous disposition by a partnership of the affiliate share or a share for which the affiliate share was substituted, was reduced under subsection (2.1) in respect of the exempt dividends referred to in the description of B,

(*c*) the total of all amounts each of which is the amount by which a loss (determined without reference to this section), from a disposition at or before that time by a corporation or foreign affiliate described in the description of B of an interest in a partnership, was reduced under subsection (2.2) in respect of the exempt dividends referred to in the description of B, and

(*d*) the total of all amounts each of which is twice the amount by which an allowable capital loss (determined without reference to this section), of a corporation or foreign affiliate described in the description of B from a disposition at or before that time by a partnership of an interest in another partnership, was reduced under subsection (2.3) in respect of the exempt dividends referred to in the description of B.

Related Sections: S. 87(2)(*u*) Shares of foreign affiliate; s. 93(3) Exempt dividends; s. 93(5) Late filed elections.

Canadian Tax Foundation: Samuel, *Stopping The Losses: The Application Of Stop-Loss Rules To Transactions Involving Foreign Affiliates*, 2010 Canadian Tax Journal 4:897–925; Lockwood et al., *Proposed Technical Amendments to the FAPI and Foreign Affiliate Rules*, 2000 Canadian Tax Journal 2:456–476.

► 93(2.01) ◄

(2.01) Loss limitation on disposition of share of foreign affiliate. If this subsection applies, the amount of the particular loss referred to in paragraph (2)(*a*) or (*b*) is deemed to be the greater of

(*a*) the amount determined by the formula

$$A - (B - C)$$

where

A is the amount of the particular loss determined without reference to this section,

B is the total of all amounts each of which is an amount received before the disposition time, in respect of an exempt dividend on the affiliate share or on a share for which the affiliate share was substituted, by

(i) the particular corporation referred to in subsection (2),

(ii) another corporation that is related to the particular corporation,

(iii) a foreign affiliate of the particular corporation, or

(iv) a foreign affiliate of another corporation that is related to the particular corporation, and

C is the total of

(i) the total of all amounts each of which is the amount by which a loss (determined without reference to this section), from a previous disposition by a corporation, or a foreign affiliate described in the description of B, of the affiliate share or a share for which the affiliate share was substituted, was reduced under this paragraph in respect of the exempt dividends referred to in the description of B,

(ii) the total of all amounts each of which is twice the amount by which an allowable capital loss (determined without reference to this section), of a corporation or a foreign affiliate described in the description of B, from a previous disposition by a partnership of the affiliate share or a share for which the affiliate share was substituted, was reduced under paragraph (2.11)(*a*) in respect of the exempt dividends referred to in the description of B,

(iii) the total of all amounts each of which is the amount by which a loss (determined without reference to this section), from a previous disposition by a corporation, or a foreign affiliate described in the description of B, of an interest in a partnership, was reduced under paragraph (2.21)(*a*) in respect of the exempt dividends referred to in the description of B, and

(iv) the total of all amounts each of which is twice the amount by which an allowable capital loss (determined without reference to this section), of a corporation, or a foreign affiliate described in the description of B, from a previous disposition by a partnership of an interest in another partnership, was reduced under paragraph (2.31)(*a*) in respect of the exempt dividends referred to in the description of B, and

(*b*) the lesser of

(i) the portion of the particular loss, determined without reference to this section, that can reasonably be considered to be attributable to a fluctuation in the value of a currency other than Canadian currency relative to Canadian currency, and

(ii) the amount determined in respect of the vendor that is

(A) if the particular loss is a capital loss, the amount of a gain (other than a specified gain) that

(I) was made within 30 days before or after the disposition time by the vendor and that

1. is deemed under subsection 39(2) to be a capital gain of the vendor for the taxation year that includes the time the gain was made from the disposition of currency other than Canadian currency, and

2. is in respect of the settlement or extinguishment of a foreign currency debt that was issued or incurred by the vendor within 30 days before or after the acquisition of the affiliate share by the vendor and that was, at all times at which it was a debt obligation of the vendor owing to a person or partnership that dealt, at all times during which the foreign currency debt was outstanding, at arm's length with the particular corporation and can reasonably be considered to have been issued or incurred in relation to the acquisition of the affiliate share, or

(II) is a capital gain realized within 30 days before or after the disposition time by the vendor under an agreement that

1. was entered into by the vendor within 30 days before or after the acquisition of the affiliate share by the vendor with a person or partnership that dealt, at all times during which the agreement was in force, at arm's length with the particular corporation,

2. provides for the purchase, sale or exchange of currency, and

3. can reasonably be considered to have been entered into by the vendor for the principal purpose of hedging the foreign exchange exposure arising in connection with the acquisition of the affiliate share, or

(B) in any other case, the amount of a gain (other than a specified gain or a capital gain) that was realized within 30 days before or after the disposition time by the vendor that is included in computing the income of the vendor for the taxation year that includes the time the gain was realized and

(I) that is in respect of the settlement or extinguishment of a foreign currency debt that

1. was issued or incurred by the vendor within 30 days before or after the acquisition of the affiliate share by the vendor,

2. was, at all times at which it was a debt obligation of the vendor owing to a person or partnership that dealt, at all times during which the foreign currency debt was outstanding, at arm's length with the particular corporation, and

3. can reasonably be considered to have been issued or incurred in relation to the acquisition of the affiliate share, or

(II) under an agreement that

1. was entered into by the vendor within 30 days before or after the acquisition of the affiliate share by the vendor with a person or partnership that dealt, at all times during which the agreement was in force, at arm's length with the particular corporation,

2. provides for the purchase, sale or exchange of currency, and

3. can reasonably be considered to have been entered into by the vendor for the principal purpose of hedging the foreign exchange exposure arising in connection with the acquisition of the affiliate share.

History: S. 93(2.01) was added by S.C. 2013, c. 34, s. 68(4), applicable in respect of losses of a corporation resident in Canada, or of foreign affiliates of such a corporation, in respect of dispositions (referred to in paragraphs (*a*) and (*c*) below as "relevant dispositions" in respect of the corporation) of shares and partnership interests that occur after February 27, 2004. However,

(a) subject to paragraph (c), in respect of relevant dispositions in respect of the corporation that occur before August 19, 2012, the Act is to be read without reference to its subsections 93(2.02), (2.12), (2.22) and (2.32), and

(i) if the corporation does not elect under subparagraph (ii) [below],

(A) paragraph 93(2.01)(b) is to be read as follows:

"(b) the total of the following amounts determined in respect of the particular corporation, or the foreign affiliate (that is referred to in paragraph (2)(b)) of the particular corporation, as the case may be,

(i) the amount of the gain that is included in the determination made under subsection 39(2) of the capital gain or capital loss of the particular corporation or the foreign affiliate, as the case may be, for the taxation year that includes the time the gain was made from the disposition of currency of a country other than Canada if the gain is in respect of

(A) the settlement or extinguishment of an obligation of the particular corporation or the foreign affiliate, as the case may be, that can reasonably be considered to have been issued or incurred in relation to the acquisition of the affiliate share by the particular corporation or the foreign affiliate, as the case may be, or

(B) if that taxation year began on or before August 19, 2011 (in the case of the particular corporation) or ended on or before August 19, 2011 (in the case of the foreign affiliate), the redemption, acquisition or cancellation of a share of the capital stock of the particular corporation or the foreign affiliate, as the case may be, that can reasonably be considered to have been issued in relation to the acquisition of the affiliate share by the particular corporation or the foreign affiliate, as the case may be, and

(ii) the amount of any gain realized by the particular corporation or the foreign affiliate, as the case may be, under an agreement that provides for the purchase, sale or exchange of currency, or from the disposition of a currency, which agreement or currency, as the case may be, can reasonably be considered to have been entered into or acquired, by the particular corporation or the foreign affiliate, as the case may be, for the principal purpose of hedging the foreign exchange exposure arising in connection with the acquisition of the affiliate share."

(E) if the corporation has made an election in respect of the application of s. 95(2)(f.11) to (g.02), the reference to "August 19, 2011" in clause 93(2.01)(b)(i)(B) in the read-as text in clause (A) [above], is, in respect of the foreign affiliates referred to in that clause, to be read as references to "June 30, 2011",

(ii) if the corporation elects in writing in respect of all relevant dispositions in respect of the corporation and files the election with the Minister of National Revenue on or before the day that is the later of the corporation's filing-due date for the corporation's taxation year that includes June 26, 2013 and June 26, 2014 [the day that is one year after royal assent],

(A) in respect of subsection 93(2.01),

(I) the formula in paragraph (a) of subsection 93(2.01) is, in respect of all relevant dispositions in respect of the corporation, to be read as follows:

"A – (B – C) + D"

(II) paragraph (a) of subsection 93(2.01) is, in respect of all relevant dispositions in respect of the corporation, to be read as if it contained a description of D that reads as follows:

"D is the lesser of

(i) the amount, if any, by which the amount determined for B exceeds the amount determined for C, and

(ii) the total of the following amounts determined in respect of the particular corporation, or the foreign affiliate (that is referred to in paragraph (2)(b)) of the particular corporation, as the case may be,

(A) the amount of the gain that is included in the determination made under subsection 39(2) of the capital gain or capital loss of the particular corporation or the foreign affiliate, as the case may be, for the taxation year that includes the time the gain was made from the disposition of currency of a country other than Canada if the gain is in respect of

(I) the settlement or extinguishment of an obligation of the particular corporation or the foreign affiliate, as the case may be, that can reasonably be considered to have been issued or incurred in relation to the acquisition of the affiliate share by the particular corporation or the foreign affiliate, as the case may be, or

(II) if that taxation year began on or before August 19, 2011 (in the case of the particular corporation) or ended on or before August 19, 2011 (in the case of the foreign affiliate), the redemption, acquisition or cancellation of a share of the capital stock of the particular corporation or the foreign affiliate, as the case may be, that can reasonably be considered to have been issued in relation to the acquisition of the affiliate share by the particular corporation or the foreign affiliate, as the case may be, and

(B) the amount of any gain realized by the particular corporation or the foreign affiliate, as the case may be, under an agreement that provides for the purchase, sale or exchange of currency, or from the disposition of a currency, which agreement or currency, as the case may be, can reasonably be considered to have been entered into or acquired, by the particular corporation or the foreign affiliate, as the case may be, for the principal purpose of hedging the foreign exchange exposure arising in connection with the acquisition of the affiliate share."

(III) if the corporation has made an election in respect of the application of s. 95(2)(f.11) to (g.02), the reference to "August 19, 2011" in subclause (ii)(A)(II) of that description of D is, in respect of the foreign affiliate referred to in that subclause, to be read as a reference to "June 30, 2011",

(IV) paragraph (b) of subsection 93(2.01) is, in respect of all relevant dispositions in respect of the corporation, to be read as follows:

"(b) nil."

(b) if the corporation elects in writing in respect of all losses of the corporation, and of all foreign affiliates of the corporation, in respect of dispositions (referred to in this paragraph as "pertinent dispositions" in respect of the corporation) of shares and partnership interests that occur on or before February 27, 2004 and files the election with the Minister of National Revenue on or before the day that is the later of the corporation's filing-due date for the corporation's taxation year that includes June 26, 2013 and June 26, 2014 [the day that is one year after royal assent],

(i) subsection (2.01) with the modifications described in paragraph (a) (if applicable) being taken into account, also applies in respect of all pertinent dispositions in respect of the corporation that occur after 1994 and on or before February 27, 2004, except that the references to "twice" in subsection 93(2.01), are,

(A) for taxation years of the corporation that end before February 28, 2000, to be read as references to "4/3 of", and

(B) for taxation years of the corporation that include February 28, 2000 or October 17, 2000 or that begin after February 28, 2000 and end before October 17, 2000, to be read as references to "the fraction that is the reciprocal of the fraction in paragraph 38(a), as amended by S.C. 2001, c. 17, that applies to the taxpayer for the year, multiplied by", and

(c) if the corporation elects in writing in respect of all relevant dispositions in respect of the corporation that occur before August 19, 2012 and files the election with the Minister of National Revenue on or before the day that is the later of the corporation's filing-due date for the corporation's taxation year that includes June 26, 2013 and June 26, 2014 [the day that is one year after royal assent], paragraph (a) does not apply in respect of all those relevant dispositions.

See the application for the amendment to s. 93(1.1) for the extension of assessment periods to take into account the amendments by S.C. 2013, c. 34, s. 54 to 89.

Tax Window Files: IFA 2016 Q.7: 93(2.01) & Capital Contribution, *May 26, 2016*, CRA Document No. 2016-0642121C6.

► 93(2.02) ◄

(2.02) Specified gain. For the purposes of clauses (2.01)(b)(ii)(A) and (B), a "specified gain" means a gain in respect of the settlement or extinguishment of a foreign currency debt referred to in sub-subclause (2.01)(*b*)(ii)(A)(I)2 or subclause (2.01)(*b*)(ii)(B)(I), as the case may be, or that arises under a particular agreement referred to in subclause (2.01)(*b*)(ii)(A)(II) or (B)(II), if the particular corporation, or any person or partnership with which the particular corporation was not — at any time during which the foreign currency debt was outstanding or the particular agreement was in force, as the case may be — dealing at arm's length, entered into an agreement that may reasonably be considered to have been entered into for the principal purpose of hedging any foreign exchange exposure arising in connection with the foreign currency debt or the particular agreement.

History: S. 93(2.02) was added by S.C. 2013, c. 34, s. 68(4), applicable in respect of losses of a corporation resident in Canada, or of foreign affiliates of such a corporation, in respect of dispositions (referred to in paragraphs (*a*) and (*c*) below as "relevant dispositions" in respect of the corporation) of shares and partnership interests that occur after February 27, 2004. However,

(*a*) subject to paragraph (*c*) [below], in respect of relevant dispositions in respect of the corporation that occur before August 19, 2012, the Act is to be read without reference to its subsections 93(2.02),

(*b*) if the corporation elects in writing in respect of all losses of the corporation, and of all foreign affiliates of the corporation, in respect of dispositions (referred to in this paragraph as "pertinent dispositions" in respect of the corporation) of shares and partnership interests that occur on or before February 27, 2004 and files the election with the Minister of National Revenue on or before the day that is the later of the corporation's filing-due date for the corporation's taxation year that includes June 26, 2013 and June 26, 2014 [the day that is one year after royal assent],

(i) if paragraph (*c*) [below] applies, subsection 93(2.02), with the modifications described in paragraph (*a*) (if applicable) being taken into account, also applies in respect of all pertinent dispositions in respect of the corporation that occur after 1994 and on or before February 27, 2004, and

(*c*) if the corporation elects in writing in respect of all relevant dispositions in respect of the corporation that occur before August 19, 2012 and files the election with the Minister of National Revenue on or before the day that is the later of the corporation's filing-due date for the corporation's taxation year that includes June 26, 2013 and June 26, 2014 [the day that is one year after royal assent], paragraph (a) does not apply in respect of all those relevant dispositions.

See the application for the amendment to s. 93(1.1) for the extension of assessment periods to take into account the amendments by S.C. 2013, c. 34, s. 54 to 89.

► 93(2.1) ◄

(2.1) Application of subsection (2.11). Subsection (2.11) applies if

(*a*) a particular corporation resident in Canada has a particular allowable capital loss, determined without reference to this section, from the disposition at any time (referred to in subsection (2.11) as the "disposition time") by a partnership (referred to in subsections (2.11) and (2.12) as the "disposing partnership") of a share (referred to in subsection (2.11) as the "affiliate share") of the capital stock of a foreign affiliate of the particular corporation; or

(*b*) a foreign affiliate of a particular corporation resident in Canada has a particular allowable capital loss, determined without reference to this section, from the disposition at any time (referred to in subsection (2.11) as the "disposition time") by a partnership (referred to in subsections (2.11) and (2.12) as the "disposing partnership") of a share (referred to in subsection (2.11) as the "affiliate share") of the capital stock of another foreign affiliate of the particular corporation that would not be excluded property of the affiliate if the affiliate had owned the share immediately before the disposition time.

History: S. 93(2.1) was replaced by S.C. 2013, c. 34, s. 68(4), applicable in respect of losses of a corporation resident in Canada, or of foreign affiliates of such a corporation, in respect of dispositions of shares and partnership interests that occur after February 27, 2004. However,

(*b*) if the corporation elects in writing in respect of all losses of the corporation, and of all foreign affiliates of the corporation, in respect of dispositions (referred to in this paragraph as "pertinent dispositions" in respect of the corporation) of shares and partnership interests that occur on or before February 27, 2004 and files the election with the Minister of National Revenue on or before the day that is the later of the corporation's filing-due date for the corporation's taxation year that includes June 26, 2013 and June 26, 2014 [the day that is one year after royal assent], subsection 93(2.1) also applies in respect of all pertinent dispositions in respect of the corporation that occur after November 1999 and on or before February 27, 2004.

See the application for the amendment to s. 93(1.1) for the extension of assessment periods to take into account the amendments by S.C. 2013, c. 34, s. 54 to 89.

s. 93(2.1) formerly read:

(2.1) *Loss limitation — disposition of share by partnership.* Where

(*a*) a corporation resident in Canada has an allowable capital loss from a disposition at any time by a partnership of a share of the capital stock of a foreign affiliate of the corporation (in this subsection referred to as the "affiliate share"), or

(*b*) a foreign affiliate of a corporation resident in Canada has an allowable capital loss from a disposition at any time by a partnership of a share of the capital stock of another foreign affiliate of the corporation resident in Canada that would not be excluded property of the affiliate if the affiliate owned the share immediately before it was disposed of (in this subsection referred to as the "affiliate share"),

the amount of the allowable capital loss is deemed to be the amount determined by the formula

$$A - (B - C)$$

where

A is the amount of the allowable capital loss determined without reference to this subsection,

B is $1/2$ of the total of all amounts each of which was received before that time, in respect of an exempt dividend on the affiliate share or on a share for which the affiliate share was substituted, by

(*a*) the corporation resident in Canada,

(*b*) a corporation related to the corporation resident in Canada,

(*c*) a foreign affiliate of the corporation resident in Canada, or

(*d*) a foreign affiliate of a corporation related to the corporation resident in Canada, and

C is the total of

(*a*) the total of all amounts each of which is the amount by which an allowable capital loss (determined without reference to this section), of a corporation or foreign affiliate described in the description of B from a disposition at or before that time by a partnership of the affiliate share or a share for which the affiliate share was substituted, was reduced under this subsection in respect of the exempt dividends referred to in the description of B,

(*b*) the total of all amounts each of which is $1/2$ of the amount by which a loss (determined without reference to this section), of a corporation or foreign affiliate described in the description of B from another disposition at or before that time of the affiliate share or a share for which the affiliate share was substituted, was reduced under subsection (2) in respect of the exempt dividends referred to in the description of B,

(*c*) the total of all amounts each of which is $1/2$ of the amount by which a loss (determined without reference to this section), from a disposition at or before that time by a corporation or foreign affiliate described in the description of B of an interest in a partnership, was reduced under subsection (2.2) in respect of the exempt dividends referred to in the description of B, and

(*d*) the total of all amounts each of which is the amount by which an allowable capital loss (determined without reference to this section), of a corporation or foreign affiliate described in the description of B from a disposition at or before that time by a partnership of an interest in another partnership, was reduced under subsection (2.3) in respect of exempt dividends referred to in the description of B.

► 93(2.11) ◄

(2.11) Loss limitation on disposition of foreign affiliate share by a partnership. If this subsection applies, the amount of the particular allowable capital loss referred to in paragraph (2.1)(*a*) or (*b*) is deemed to be the greater of

(*a*) the amount determined by the formula

$$A - (B - C)$$

where

A is the amount of the particular allowable capital loss determined without reference to this section,

B is $^1/_2$ of the total of all amounts each of which is an amount received before the disposition time, in respect of an exempt dividend on the affiliate share or on a share for which the affiliate share was substituted, by

(i) the particular corporation referred to in subsection (2.1),

(ii) another corporation that is related to the particular corporation,

(iii) a foreign affiliate of the particular corporation, or

(iv) a foreign affiliate of another corporation that is related to the particular corporation, and

C is the total of

(i) the total of all amounts each of which is $^1/_2$ of the amount by which a loss (determined without reference to this section), from a previous disposition by a corporation, or a foreign affiliate described in the description of B, of the affiliate share or a share for which the affiliate share was substituted, was reduced under paragraph (2.01)(*a*) in respect of the exempt dividends referred to in the description of B,

(ii) the total of all amounts each of which is the amount by which an allowable capital loss (determined without reference to this section), of a corporation or a foreign affiliate described in the description of B, from a previous disposition by a partnership of the affiliate share or a share for which the affiliate share was substituted, was reduced under this paragraph in respect of the exempt dividends referred to in the description of B,

(iii) the total of all amounts each of which is $^1/_2$ of the amount by which a loss (determined without reference to this section), from a previous disposition by a corporation, or a foreign affiliate described in the description of B, of an interest in a partnership, was reduced under paragraph (2.21)(*a*) in respect of the exempt dividends referred to in the description of B, and

(iv) the total of all amounts each of which is the amount by which an allowable capital loss (determined without reference to this section), of a corporation, or a foreign affiliate described in the description of B, from a previous disposition by a partnership of an interest in another partnership, was reduced under paragraph (2.31)(*a*) in respect of the exempt dividends referred to in the description of B, and

(*b*) the lesser of

(i) the portion of the particular allowable capital loss, determined without reference to this section, that can reasonably be considered to be attributable to a fluctuation in the value of a currency other than Canadian currency relative to Canadian currency, and

(ii) $^1/_2$ of the amount determined in respect of the particular corporation, or the foreign affiliate (that is referred to in paragraph (2.1)(*b*)) of the particular corporation, that is the amount of a gain (other than a specified gain) that

(A) was made within 30 days before or after the disposition time by the disposing partnership to the extent that the gain is reasonably attributable to the particular corporation or the foreign affiliate, as the case may be, and that

(I) is deemed under subsection 39(2) to be a capital gain of the disposing partnership for the taxation year that includes the time the gain was made from the disposition of currency other than Canadian currency, and

(II) is in respect of the settlement or extinguishment of a foreign currency debt that

1. was issued or incurred by the disposing partnership within 30 days before or after the acquisition of the affiliate share by the disposing partnership,

2. was, at all times at which it was a debt obligation of the disposing partnership, owing to a person or partnership that dealt, at all times during which the foreign currency debt was outstanding, at arm's length with the particular corporation, and

3. can reasonably be considered to have been issued or incurred in relation to the acquisition of the affiliate share, or

(B) is a capital gain (to the extent that the capital gain is reasonably attributable to the particular corporation or the foreign affiliate, as the case may be) realized within 30 days before or after the disposition time by the disposing partnership under an agreement that

(I) was entered into by the disposing partnership, within 30 days before or after the acquisition of the affiliate share by the disposing partnership, with a person or partnership that dealt, at all times during which the agreement was in force, at arm's length with the particular corporation,

(II) provides for the purchase, sale or exchange of currency, and

(III) can reasonably be considered to have been entered into by the disposing partnership for the principal purpose of hedging the foreign exchange exposure arising in connection with the acquisition of the affiliate share.

History: S. 93(2.11) was added by S.C. 2013, c. 34, s. 68(4), applicable in respect of losses of a corporation resident in Canada, or of foreign affiliates of such a corporation, in respect of dispositions (referred to below as "relevant dispositions" in respect of the corporation) of shares and partnership interests that occur after February 27, 2004. However,

(*a*) subject to paragraph (*c*), in respect of relevant dispositions in respect of the corporation that occur before August 19, 2012, the Act is to be read without reference to its subsections 93(2.02), (2.12), (2.22) and (2.32), and

(i) if the corporation does not elect under subparagraph (ii) [below],

(B) paragraph 93(2.11)(*b*) is to be read as follows:

"(*b*) 1/2 of the total of the following amounts determined in respect of the particular corporation, or the foreign affiliate (that is referred to in paragraph (2.1)(*b*)) of the particular corporation, as the case may be:

(i) the amount of the gain of the particular corporation, the foreign affiliate or the disposing partnership (to the extent that the gain is reasonably attributable to the particular corporation or the foreign affiliate, as the case may be) that is included in the determination made under subsection 39(2) of the capital gain or capital loss of the particular corporation, the foreign affiliate or the disposing partnership, as the case may be, for the taxation year that includes the time the gain was made from the disposition of currency of a country other than Canada if the gain is in respect of

(A) the settlement or extinguishment of an obligation of the particular corporation, the foreign affiliate or the disposing partnership, as the case may be, that can reasonably be considered to have been issued or incurred in relation to the acquisition of the affiliate share by the disposing partnership, or

(B) if that taxation year began on or before August 19, 2011 (in the case of the particular corporation) or ended on or before August 19, 2011 (in the case of the foreign affiliate), the redemption, acquisition or cancellation of a share of the capital stock of the particular corporation or the foreign affiliate, as the case may be, that can reasonably be considered to have been issued in relation to the acquisition of the affiliate share by the disposing partnership, and

(ii) the amount of any gain realized by the disposing partnership (to the extent that the gain is reasonably attributable to the particular corporation or the foreign affiliate, as the case may be), the particular corporation or the foreign affiliate, as the case may be, under an agreement that provides for the purchase, sale or exchange of currency, or from the disposition of a currency, which agreement or currency, as the case may be, can reasonably be considered to have been entered into or acquired, by the disposing partnership, the particular corporation or the foreign affiliate, as the case may be, for the principal purpose of hedging the foreign exchange exposure arising in connection with the acquisition of the affiliate share."

(E) if the corporation has made an election in respect of the application of s. 95(2)(*f.11*) to (*g.02*), the reference to "August 19, 2011" in clause (2.11)(*b*)(i)(B) in the read-as text in clause (B) [above], is, in respect of the foreign affiliates referred to in that clause, to be read as references to "June 30, 2011",

(ii) if the corporation elects in writing in respect of all relevant dispositions in respect of the corporation and files the election with the Minister of National Revenue on or before the day that is the later of the corporation's filing-due date for the corporation's taxation year that includes June 26, 2013 and June 26, 2014 [the day that is one year after royal assent],

(B) in respect of subsection 93(2.11),

(I) the formula in paragraph (*a*) of subsection 93(2.11) is, in respect of all relevant dispositions in respect of the corporation, to be read as follows:

"A – (B – C) + D"

(II) paragraph (*a*) of subsection 93(2.11) is, in respect of all relevant dispositions in respect of the corporation, to be read as if it contained a description of D that reads as follows:

"D is the lesser of

(i) the amount, if any, by which the amount determined for B exceeds the amount determined for C, and

(ii) 1/2 of the total of the following amounts determined in respect of the particular corporation, or the foreign affiliate (that is referred to in paragraph (2.1)(*b*)) of the particular corporation, as the case may be:

(A) the amount of the gain of the particular corporation, the foreign affiliate or the disposing partnership (to the extent that the gain is reasonably attributable to the particular corporation or the foreign affiliate, as the case may be) that is included in the determination made under subsection 39(2) of the capital gain or capital loss of the particular corporation, the foreign affiliate or the disposing partnership, as the case may be, for the taxation year that includes the time the gain was made from the disposition of currency of a country other than Canada if the gain is in respect of

(I) the settlement or extinguishment of an obligation of the particular corporation, the foreign affiliate or the disposing partnership, as the case may be, that can reasonably be considered to have been issued or incurred in relation to the acquisition of the affiliate share by the disposing partnership, or

(II) if that taxation year began on or before August 19, 2011 (in the case of the particular corporation) or ended on or before August 19, 2011 (in the case of the foreign affiliate), the redemption, acquisition or cancellation of a share of the capital stock of the particular corporation or the foreign affiliate, as the case may be, that can reasonably be considered to have been issued in relation to the acquisition of the affiliate share by the disposing partnership, and

(B) the amount of any gain realized by the disposing partnership (to the extent that the gain is reasonably attributable to the particular corporation or the foreign affiliate, as the case may be), the particular corporation or the foreign affiliate, as the case may be, under an agreement that provides for the purchase, sale or exchange of currency, or from the disposition of a currency, which agreement or currency, as the case may be, can reasonably be considered to have been entered into or acquired, by the disposing partnership, the particular corporation or the foreign affiliate, as the case may be, for the principal purpose of hedging the foreign exchange exposure arising in connection with the acquisition of the affiliate share."

(III) if the corporation has made an election in respect of the application of s. 95(2)(*f.11*) to (*g.02*), the reference to "August 19, 2011" in subclause (ii)(A)(II) of that description of D is, in respect of the foreign affiliate referred to in that subclause, to be read as a reference to "June 30, 2011", and

(IV) paragraph (*b*) of subsection 93(2.11) is, in respect of all relevant dispositions in respect of the corporation, to be read as follows:

"(*b*) nil."

(*b*) if the corporation elects in writing in respect of all losses of the corporation, and of all foreign affiliates of the corporation, in respect of dispositions (referred to in this paragraph as "pertinent dispositions" in respect of the corporation) of shares and partnership interests that occur on or before February 27, 2004 and files the election with the Minister of National Revenue on or before the day that is the later of the corporation's filing-due date for the corporation's taxation year that includes June 26, 2013 and June 26, 2014 [the day that is one year after royal assent],

(ii) subsection 93(2.11), with the modifications described in paragraph (*a*) (if applicable) being taken into account, also applies in respect of all pertinent dispositions in respect of the corporation that occur after November 1999 and on or before February 27, 2004, except that the reference to "twice" in subsection 93(2.11) is,

(A) for taxation years of the corporation that end before February 28, 2000, to be read as references to "4/3 of", and

(B) for taxation years of the corporation that include February 28, 2000 or October 17, 2000 or that begin after February 28, 2000 and end before October 17, 2000, to be read as references to "the fraction that is the reciprocal of the fraction in paragraph 38(*a*), as amended by S.C. 2001, c. 17, that applies to the taxpayer for the year, multiplied by": and

(*c*) if the corporation elects in writing in respect of all relevant dispositions in respect of the corporation that occur before August 19, 2012 and files the election with the Minister of National Revenue on or before the day that is the later of the corporation's filing-due date for the corporation's taxation year that includes June 26, 2013 and June 26, 2014 [the day that is one year after royal assent], paragraph (*a*) does not apply in respect of all those relevant dispositions.

See the application for the amendment to s. 93(1.1) for the extension of assessment periods to take into account the amendments by S.C. 2013, c. 34, s. 54 to 89.

► 93(2.12) ◄

(2.12) Specified gain. For the purposes of subparagraph (2.11)(*b*)(ii), a "specified gain" means a gain in respect of the settlement or extinguishment of a foreign currency debt referred to in subclause (2.11)(*b*)(ii)(A)(II), or that arises under a particular agreement referred to in clause (2.11)(*b*)(ii)(B), if the disposing partnership, or any person or partnership with which the particular corporation was not — at any time during which the foreign currency debt was outstanding or the particular agreement was in force, as the case may be — dealing at arm's length, entered into an agreement that may reasonably be considered to have been entered into for the principal purpose of hedging any foreign exchange exposure arising in connection with the foreign currency debt or the particular agreement.

History: s. 93(2.12) was added by S.C. 2013, c. 34, s. 68(4), applicable in respect of losses of a corporation resident in Canada, or of foreign affiliates of such a corporation, in respect of dispositions (referred to in paragraphs (*a*) and (*c*) as "relevant dispositions" in respect of the corporation) of shares and partnership interests that occur after February 27, 2004. However,

(*a*) subject to paragraph (*c*) [below], in respect of relevant dispositions in respect of the corporation that occur before August 19, 2012, the Act is to be read without reference to its subsection 93(2.12),

(*b*) if the corporation elects in writing in respect of all losses of the corporation, and of all foreign affiliates of the corporation, in respect of dispositions (referred to in this paragraph as "pertinent dispositions" in respect of the corporation) of shares and partnership interests that occur on or before February 27, 2004 and files the election with the Minister of National Revenue on or before the day that is the later of the corporation's filing-due date for the corporation's taxation year that includes June 26, 2013 and June 26, 2014 [the day that is one year after royal assent],

(ii) if paragraph (*c*) [below] applies, subsection 93(2.12) with the modifications described in paragraph (*a*) (if applicable) being taken into account, also applies in respect of all pertinent dispositions in respect of the corporation that occur after November 1999 and on or before February 27, 2004, and

(*c*) if the corporation elects in writing in respect of all relevant dispositions in respect of the corporation that occur before August 19, 2012 and files the election with the Minister of National Revenue on or before the day that is the later of the corporation's filing-due date for the corporation's taxation year that includes June 26, 2013 and June 26, 2014 [the day that is one year after royal assent], paragraph (*a*) does not apply in respect of all those relevant dispositions.

See the application for the amendment to s. 93(1.1) for the extension of assessment periods to take into account the amendments by S.C. 2013, c. 34, s. 54 to 89.

► 93(2.2) ◄

(2.2) Application of subsection (2.21). Subsection (2.21) applies if

(*a*) a particular corporation (referred to in subparagraph (2.21)(*b*)(ii) as the "vendor", as the context requires) resident in Canada has a particular loss, determined without reference to this section, from the disposition by it at any time (referred to in subsection (2.21) as the "disposition time") of an interest (referred to in subsection (2.21) as the "partnership interest") in a partnership that has a direct or indirect interest, or, for civil law, a direct or indirect right, in shares (referred to in subsection (2.21) as the "affiliate shares") of the capital stock of a foreign affiliate of the particular corporation; or

(*b*) a foreign affiliate (referred to in subparagraph (2.21)(*b*)(ii) as the "vendor") of a particular corporation resident in Canada has a particular loss, determined without reference to this section, from the disposition by it at any time (referred to in subsection (2.21) as the "disposition time") of an interest (referred to in subsection (2.21) as the "partnership interest") in a partnership that has a direct or indirect interest, or, for civil law, a direct or indirect right, in shares (referred to in subsection (2.21) as the "affiliate shares") of the capital stock of another foreign affiliate of the particular corporation that would not be excluded property of the affiliate if the affiliate had owned the shares immediately before the disposition time.

History: [**Editorial Note**: The application to the amendment to s. 93(2.2) by S.C. 2001, c. 17, s. 70(7) was amended by S.C. 2013, c. 34, s. 373, to make minor modifications to the wording of the amendment. This 2001 amendment is not reproduced in print but is available in all CCH Canadian electronic versions of the Income Tax Act.]

S. 93(2.2) was replaced by S.C. 2013, c. 34, s. 68(4), applicable in respect of losses of a corporation resident in Canada, or of foreign affiliates of such a corporation, in respect of dispositions (referred to in paragraphs (*a*) and (*c*) as "relevant dispositions" in respect of the corporation) of shares and partnership interests that occur after February 27, 2004. However,

(*b*) if the corporation elects in writing in respect of all losses of the corporation, and of all foreign affiliates of the corporation, in respect of dispositions of shares and partnership interests that occur on or before February 27, 2004 and files the election with the Minister of National Revenue on or before the day that is the later of the corporation's filing-due date for the corporation's taxation year that includes June 26, 2013 and June 26, 2014 [the day that is one year after royal assent],

(ii) subsection 93(2.2) also applies in respect of all pertinent dispositions in respect of the corporation that occur after November 1999 and on or before February 27, 2004.

See the application for the amendment to s. 93(1.1) for the extension of assessment periods to take into account the amendments by S.C. 2013, c. 34, s. 54 to 89.

S. 93(2.2) formerly read:

(2.2) *Loss limitation — disposition of partnership interest.* Where

(*a*) a corporation resident in Canada has a loss from the disposition by it at any time of an interest in a partnership (in this subsection referred to as the "partnership interest"), which has a direct or indirect interest in shares of the capital stock of a foreign affiliate of the corporation resident in Canada (in this subsection referred to as "affiliate shares"), or

(*b*) a foreign affiliate of a corporation resident in Canada has a loss from the disposition by it at any time of an interest in a partnership (in this subsection referred to as the "partnership interest"), which has a direct or indirect interest in shares of the capital stock of another foreign affiliate of the corporation resident in Canada that would not be excluded property if the shares were owned by the affiliate (in this subsection referred to as "affiliate shares")

the amount of the loss is deemed to be the amount determined by the formula

$$A - (B - C)$$

where

A is the amount of the loss determined without reference to this subsection,

B is the total of all amounts each of which was received before that time, in respect of an exempt dividend on affiliate shares or on shares for which affiliate shares were substituted, by

(*a*) the corporation resident in Canada,

(b) a corporation related to the corporation resident in Canada,

(c) a foreign affiliate of the corporation resident in Canada, or

(d) a foreign affiliate of a corporation related to the corporation resident in Canada, and

C is the total of

(a) the total of all amounts each of which is the amount by which a loss (determined without reference to this section), from another disposition at or before that time by a corporation or foreign affiliate described in the description of B of affiliate shares or shares for which affiliate shares were substituted, was reduced under subsection (2) in respect of the exempt dividends referred to in the description of B,

(b) the total of all amounts each of which is twice the amount by which an allowable capital loss (determined without reference to this section), of a corporation or foreign affiliate described in the description of B from another disposition at or before that time by a partnership of affiliate shares or shares for which affiliate shares were substituted, was reduced under subsection (2.1) in respect of the exempt dividends referred to in the description of B,

(c) the total of all amounts each of which is the amount by which a loss (determined without reference to this section), from a disposition at or before that time by a corporation or foreign affiliate described in the description of B of an interest in a partnership, was reduced under this subsection in respect of the exempt dividends referred to in the description of B, and

(d) the total of all amounts each of which is twice the amount by which an allowable capital loss (determined without reference to this section), of a corporation or foreign affiliate described in the description of B from a disposition at or before that time by a partnership of an interest in another partnership, was reduced under subsection (2.3) in respect of the exempt dividends referred to in the description of B.

► 93(2.21) ◄

(2.21) Loss limitation on disposition of partnership that has foreign affiliate shares. If this subsection applies, the amount of the particular loss referred to in paragraph (2.2)(a) or (b) is deemed to be the greater of

(a) the amount determined by the formula

$$A - (B - C)$$

where

A is the amount of the particular loss determined without reference to this section,

B is the total of all amounts each of which is an amount received before the disposition time, in respect of an exempt dividend on affiliate shares or on shares for which affiliate shares were substituted, by

(i) the particular corporation referred to in subsection (2.2),

(ii) another corporation that is related to the particular corporation,

(iii) a foreign affiliate of the particular corporation, or

(iv) a foreign affiliate of another corporation that is related to the particular corporation, and

C is the total of

(i) the total of all amounts each of which is the amount by which a loss (determined without reference to this section), from a previous disposition by a corporation, or a foreign affiliate described in the description of B, of the affiliate shares or shares for which the affiliate shares were substituted, was reduced under paragraph (2.01)(a) in respect of the exempt dividends referred to in the description of B,

(ii) the total of all amounts each of which is twice the amount by which an allowable capital loss (determined without reference to this section), of a corporation or a foreign affiliate described in the description of B, from a previous disposition by a partnership of the affiliate shares or shares for which the affiliate shares were substituted, was reduced under paragraph (2.11)(a) in respect of the exempt dividends referred to in the description of B,

(iii) the total of all amounts each of which is the amount by which a loss (determined without reference to this section), from a previous disposition by a corporation, or a foreign affiliate described in the description of B, of an interest in a partnership, was reduced under this paragraph in respect of the exempt dividends referred to in the description of B, and

(iv) the total of all amounts each of which is twice the amount by which an allowable capital loss (determined without reference to this section), of a corporation, or a foreign affiliate described in the description of B, from a previous disposition by a partnership of an interest in another partnership, was reduced under paragraph (2.31)(a) in respect of the exempt dividends referred to in the description of B, and

(b) the lesser of

(i) the portion of the particular loss, determined without reference to this section, that can reasonably be considered to be attributable to a fluctuation in the value of a currency other than Canadian currency relative to Canadian currency, and

(ii) the amount determined in respect of the vendor that is

(A) if the particular loss is a capital loss, the amount of a gain (other than a specified gain) that

(I) was made within 30 days before or after the disposition time by the vendor and that

1. is deemed under subsection 39(2) to be a capital gain of the vendor for the taxation year that includes the time the gain was made from the disposition of currency other than Canadian currency, and

2. is in respect of the settlement or extinguishment of a foreign currency debt that was issued or incurred by the vendor within 30 days before or after the acquisition of the partnership interest by the vendor and that was, at all times at which it was a debt obligation of the vendor owing to a person or partnership that dealt, at all times during which the foreign currency debt was outstanding, at arm's length with the particular corporation and can reason-

ably be considered to have been issued or incurred in relation to the acquisition of the partnership interest, or

(II) is a capital gain realized within 30 days before or after the disposition time by the vendor under an agreement that

1. was entered into by the vendor within 30 days before or after the acquisition of the partnership interest by the vendor with a person or partnership that dealt, at all times during which the agreement was in force, at arm's length with the particular corporation,

2. provides for the purchase, sale or exchange of currency, and

3. can reasonably be considered to have been entered into by the vendor for the principal purpose of hedging the foreign exchange exposure arising in connection with the acquisition of the partnership interest, or

(B) in any other case, the amount of a gain (other than a specified gain or a capital gain) that was realized within 30 days before or after the disposition time by the vendor that is included in computing the income of the vendor for the taxation year that includes the time the gain was realized and

(I) that is in respect of the settlement or extinguishment of a foreign currency debt that

1. was issued or incurred by the vendor within 30 days before or after the acquisition of the partnership interest by the vendor,

2. was, at all times at which it was a debt obligation of the vendor owing to a person or partnership that dealt, at all times during which the foreign currency debt was outstanding, at arm's length with the particular corporation, and

3. can reasonably be considered to have been issued or incurred in relation to the acquisition of the partnership interest, or

(II) under an agreement that

1. was entered into by the vendor within 30 days before or after the acquisition of the partnership interest by the vendor with a person or partnership that dealt, at all times during which the agreement was in force, at arm's length with the particular corporation,

2. provides for the purchase, sale or exchange of currency, and

3. can reasonably be considered to have been entered into by the vendor for the principal purpose of hedging the foreign exchange exposure arising in connection with the acquisition of the partnership interest.

History: S. 93(2.21) was added by S.C. 2013, c. 34, s. 68(4), applicable in respect of losses of a corporation resident in Canada, or of foreign affiliates of such a corporation, in respect of dispositions (referred to in paragraphs (*a*) and (*c*) as "relevant dispositions" in respect of the corporation) of shares and partnership interests that occur after February 27, 2004. However,

(*a*) subject to paragraph (*c*), in respect of relevant dispositions in respect of the corporation that occur before August 19, 2012, the Act is to be read without reference to its subsections 93(2.02), (2.12), (2.22) and (2.32), and

(i) if the corporation does not elect under subparagraph (ii) [below],

(C) paragraph 93(2.21)(*b*) is to be read as follows:

"(*b*) the total of the following amounts determined in respect of the particular corporation, or the foreign affiliate (that is referred to in paragraph (2.2)(*b*)) of the particular corporation, as the case may be:

(i) the amount of the gain of the particular corporation, the foreign affiliate or the partnership (to the extent that the gain is reasonably attributable to the particular corporation or the foreign affiliate, as the case may be) that is included in the determination made under subsection 39(2) of the capital gain or capital loss of the particular corporation, the foreign affiliate or the partnership, as the case may be, for the taxation year that includes the time the gain was made from the disposition of currency of a country other than Canada if the gain is in respect of

(A) the settlement or extinguishment of an obligation of the particular corporation, the foreign affiliate or the partnership, as the case may be, that can reasonably be considered to have been issued or incurred in relation to the acquisition of the affiliate shares, or

(B) if that taxation year began on or before August 19, 2011 (in the case of the particular corporation) or ended on or before August 19, 2011 (in the case of the foreign affiliate), the redemption, acquisition or cancellation of a share of the particular corporation or the foreign affiliate, as the case may be, or of an interest in the partnership that can reasonably be considered to have been issued in relation to the acquisition of the affiliate shares, and

(ii) the amount of any gain realized by the particular corporation or the foreign affiliate, as the case may be, under an agreement that provides for the purchase, sale or exchange of currency, or from the disposition of a currency, which agreement or currency, as the case may be, can reasonably be considered to have been entered into or acquired by the particular corporation, the foreign affiliate or the partnership, as the case may be, for the principal purpose of hedging the foreign exchange exposure arising in connection with the acquisition of the affiliate shares."

(E) if the corporation has made an election in respect of the application of s. 95(2)(*f.11*) to (*g.02*), the reference to "August 19, 2011" in clause 93(2.21)(*b*)(i)(B) in the read-as text in clause (C) [above], is, in respect of the foreign affiliates referred to in that clause, to be read as reference to "June 30, 2011",

(ii) if the corporation elects in writing in respect of all relevant dispositions in respect of the corporation and files the election with the Minister of National Revenue on or before the day that is the later of the corporation's filing-due date for the corporation's taxation year that includes June 26, 2013 and June 26, 2014 [the day that is one year after royal assent],

(C) in respect of subsection 93(2.21),

(I) the formula in paragraph (*a*) of subsection 93(2.21) is, in respect of all relevant dispositions in respect of the corporation, to be read as follows:

"A – (B – C) + D"

(II) paragraph (*a*) of subsection 93(2.21) is, in respect of all relevant dispositions in respect of the corporation, to be read as if it contained a description of D that reads as follows:

"D is the lesser of

(i) the amount, if any, by which the amount determined for B exceeds the amount determined for C, and

(ii) the total of the following amounts determined in respect of the particular corporation, or the foreign affiliate (that is referred to in paragraph (2.2)(*b*)) of the particular corporation, as the case may be:

(A) the amount of the gain of the particular corporation, the foreign affiliate or the partnership (to the extent that the gain is reasonably attributable to the particular corporation or the foreign affiliate, as the case may be) that is included in the determination made under subsection 39(2) of the capital gain or capital loss of the particular corporation, the foreign affiliate or the partnership, as the case may be, for the taxation year that includes the time the gain was made from the disposition of currency of a country other than Canada if the gain is in respect of

(I) the settlement or extinguishment of an obligation of the particular corporation, the foreign affiliate or the partnership, as the case may be, that can reasonably be considered to have been issued or incurred in relation to the acquisition of the affiliate shares, or

(II) if that taxation year began on or before August 19, 2011 (in the case of the particular corporation) or ended on or before August 19, 2011 (in the case of the foreign affiliate), the redemption, acquisition or cancellation of a share of the particular corporation or the foreign affiliate, as the case may be, or of an interest in the partnership that can reasonably be considered to have been issued in relation to the acquisition of the affiliate shares, and

(B) the amount of any gain realized by the particular corporation or the foreign affiliate, as the case may be, under an agreement that provides for the purchase, sale or exchange of currency, or from the disposition of a currency, which agreement or currency, as the case may be, can reasonably be considered to have been entered into or acquired by the particular corporation, the foreign affiliate or the partnership, as the case may be, for the principal purpose of hedging the foreign exchange exposure arising in connection with the acquisition of the affiliate shares."

(III) if the corporation has elected in respect of the application of s. 95(2)(*f.11*) to (*g.02*), the reference to "August 19, 2011" in subclause (ii)(A)(II) of that description of D is, in respect of the foreign affiliate referred to in that subclause, to be read as a reference to "June 30, 2011", and

(IV) paragraph (*b*) of subsection 93(2.21) is, in respect of all relevant dispositions in respect of the corporation, to be read as follows:

"(*b*) nil."

(*b*) if the corporation elects in writing in respect of all losses of the corporation, and of all foreign affiliates of the corporation, in respect of dispositions (referred to in this paragraph as "pertinent dispositions" in respect of the corporation) of shares and partnership interests that occur on or before February 27, 2004 and files the election with the Minister of National Revenue on or before the day that is the later of the corporation's filing-due date for the corporation's taxation year that includes June 26, 2013 and June 26, 2014 [the day that is one year after royal assent],

(ii) subsection 93(2.21) with the modifications described in paragraph (*a*) (if applicable) being taken into account, also applies in respect of all pertinent dispositions in respect of the corporation that occur after November 1999 and on or before February 27, 2004, except that the reference to "twice" in subsection 93(2.21) is,

(A) for taxation years of the corporation that end before February 28, 2000, to be read as references to "4/3 of", and

(B) for taxation years of the corporation that include February 28, 2000 or October 17, 2000 or that begin after February 28, 2000 and end before October 17, 2000, to be read as references to "the fraction that is the reciprocal of the fraction in paragraph 38(*a*), as amended by S.C. 2001, c. 17, that applies to the taxpayer for the year, multiplied by"; and

(*c*) if the corporation elects in writing in respect of all relevant dispositions in respect of the corporation that occur before August 19, 2012 and files the election with the Minister of National Revenue on or before the day that is the later of the corporation's filing-due date for the corporation's taxation year that includes June 26, 2013 and June 26, 2014 [the day that is one year after royal assent], paragraph (*a*) does not apply in respect of all those relevant dispositions.

See the application for the amendment to s. 93(1.1) for the extension of assessment periods to take into account the amendments by S.C. 2013, c. 34, s. 54 to 89.

▶ 93(2.22) ◀

(2.22) Specified gain. For the purposes of clauses (2.21)(*b*)(ii)(A) and (B), a "specified gain" means a gain in respect of the settlement or extinguishment of a foreign currency debt referred to in sub-subclause (2.21)(*b*)(ii)(A)(I)2 or subclause (2.21)(*b*)(ii)(B)(I), as the case may be, or that arises under a particular agreement referred to in subclause (2.21)(*b*)(ii)(A)(II) or (B)(II), if the particular corporation, or any person or partnership with which the particular corporation was not — at any time during which the foreign currency debt was outstanding or the particular agreement was in force, as the case may be — dealing at arm's length, entered into an agreement that may reasonably be considered to have been entered into for the principal purpose of hedging any foreign exchange exposure arising in connection with the foreign currency debt or the particular agreement.

History: S. 93(2.22) was added by S.C. 2013, c. 34, s. 68(4), applicable in respect of losses of a corporation resident in Canada, or of foreign affiliates of such a corporation, in respect of dispositions (referred to in paragraphs (*a*) and (*c*) as "relevant dispositions" in respect of the corporation) of shares and partnership interests that occur after February 27, 2004. However,

(*a*) subject to paragraph (*c*) [below], in respect of relevant dispositions in respect of the corporation that occur before August 19, 2012, the Act is to be read without reference to its subsection 93(2.22),

(*b*) if the corporation elects in writing in respect of all losses of the corporation, and of all foreign affiliates of the corporation, in respect of dispositions (referred to in this paragraph as "pertinent dispositions" in respect of the corporation) of shares and partnership interests that occur on or before February 27, 2004 and files the election with the Minister of National Revenue on or before the day that is the later of the corporation's filing-due date for the corporation's taxation year that includes June 26, 2013 and June 26, 2014 [the day that is one year after royal assent],

(ii) subsection 93(2.2), with the modifications described in paragraph (*a*) (if applicable) being taken into account, also applies in respect of all pertinent dispositions in respect of the corporation that occur after November 1999 and on or before February 27, 2004

(*c*) if the corporation elects in writing in respect of all relevant dispositions in respect of the corporation that occur before August 19, 2012 and files the election with the Minister of National Revenue on or before the day that is the later of the corporation's filing-due date for the corporation's taxation year that includes June 26, 2013 and June 26, 2014 [the day that is one year after royal assent], paragraph (*a*) does not apply in respect of all those relevant dispositions.

See the application for the amendment to s. 93(1.1) for the extension of assessment periods to take into account the amendments by S.C. 2013, c. 34, s. 54 to 89.

▶ 93(2.3) ◀

(2.3) Application of subsection (2.31). Subsection (2.31) applies if

(*a*) a particular corporation resident in Canada has a particular allowable capital loss, determined without reference to this section, from the disposition at any time (referred to in subsection (2.31) as the "disposition time") by a particular partnership of an interest (referred to in subsection (2.31) as the "partnership interest") in another partnership that has a direct or indirect interest, or, for civil law, a direct or indirect right, in shares (referred to in subsection (2.31) as the "affiliate shares") of the capital stock of a foreign affiliate of the particular corporation; or

(*b*) a foreign affiliate of a particular corporation resident in Canada has a particular allowable capital loss, determined without reference to this section, from the disposition at any time (referred to in subsection (2.31) as the "disposition time") by a particular partnership of an interest (referred to in subsection (2.31) as the "partnership interest") in another partnership that has a direct or indirect interest, or, for civil law, a direct or indirect right, in shares (referred to in subsection (2.31) as the "affiliate shares") of the capital stock of a foreign affiliate of the particular corporation that would not be excluded property of the affiliate if the affiliate had owned the shares immediately before the disposition time.

History: S. 93(2.3) was replaced by S.C. 2013, c. 34, s. 68(4), applicable in respect of losses of a corporation resident in Canada, or of foreign affiliates of such a corporation, in respect of dispositions (referred to in paragraphs (*a*) and (*c*) as "relevant dispositions" in respect of the corporation) of shares and partnership interests that occur after February 27, 2004. However,

(*b*) if the corporation elects in writing in respect of all losses of the corporation, and of all foreign affiliates of the corporation, in respect of dispositions of shares and partnership interests that occur on or before February 27, 2004 and files the election with the Minister of National Revenue on or before the day that is the later of the corporation's filing-due date for the corporation's taxation year that includes June 26, 2013 and June 26, 2014 [the day that is one year after royal assent],

(ii) subsection 93(2.3) also applies in respect of all pertinent dispositions in respect of the corporation that occur after November 1999 and on or before February 27, 2004.

See the application for the amendment to s. 93(1.1) for the extension of assessment periods to take into account the amendments by S.C. 2013, c. 34, s. 54 to 89.

S. 93(2.3) formerly read:

(2.3) *Loss limitation — disposition of partnership interest.* Where

(*a*) a corporation resident in Canada has an allowable capital loss from a partnership from a disposition at any time of an interest in another partnership that has a direct or indirect interest in shares of the capital stock of a foreign affiliate of the corporation resident in Canada (in this subsection referred to as "affiliate shares"), or

(*b*) a foreign affiliate of a corporation resident in Canada has an allowable capital loss from a partnership from a disposition at any time by a partnership of an interest in another partnership that has a direct or indirect interest in shares of the capital stock of a foreign affiliate of the corporation resident in Canada that would not be excluded property of the affiliate if the affiliate owned the shares immediately before the disposition (in this subsection referred to as "affiliate shares"),

the amount of the allowable capital loss is deemed to be the amount determined by the formula

A - (B - C)

where

A is the amount of the allowable capital loss determined without reference to this subsection,

B is $1/2$ of the total of all amounts each of which was received before that time, in respect of an exempt dividend on affiliate shares or on shares for which affiliate shares were substituted, by

(*a*) the corporation resident in Canada,

(*b*) a corporation related to the corporation resident in Canada,

(*c*) a foreign affiliate of the corporation resident in Canada, or

(*d*) a foreign affiliate of a corporation related to the corporation resident in Canada, and

C is the total of

(*a*) the total of all amounts each of which is $1/2$ of the amount by which a loss (determined without reference to this section), of a corporation or foreign affiliate described in the description of B from another disposition at or before that time of affiliate shares or shares for which affiliate shares were substituted, was reduced under subsection (2) in respect of the exempt dividends referred to in the description of B,

(*b*) the total of all amounts each of which is the amount by which an allowable capital loss (determined without reference to this section), of a corporation or foreign affiliate described in the description of B from a disposition at or before that time by a partnership of affiliate shares or shares for which affiliate shares were substituted, was reduced under subsection (2.1) in respect of the exempt dividends referred to in the description of B,

(*c*) the total of all amounts each of which is $1/2$ of the amount by which a loss (determined without reference to this section), from a disposition at or before that time by a corporation or foreign affiliate described in the description of B of an interest in a partnership, was reduced under subsection (2.2) in respect of the exempt dividends referred to in the description of B, and

(*d*) the total of all amounts each of which is the amount by which an allowable capital loss (determined without reference to this section), of a corporation or foreign affiliate described in the description of B from a disposition at or before that time by a partnership of an interest in another partnership, was reduced under this subsection in respect of the exempt dividends referred to in the description of B.

▶ 93(2.31) ◀

(2.31) Loss limitation on disposition by a partnership of an indirect interest in foreign affiliate shares. If this subsection applies, the amount of the particular allowable capital loss referred to in paragraph (2.3)(*a*) or (*b*) is deemed to be the greater of

(*a*) the amount determined by the formula

A – (B – C)

where

A is the amount of the particular allowable capital loss determined without reference to this section,

B is $1/2$ of the total of all amounts each of which is an amount received before the disposition time, in respect of an exempt dividend on the affiliate shares or on shares for which the affiliate shares were substituted, by

(i) the particular corporation referred to in subsection (2.3),

(ii) another corporation that is related to the particular corporation,

(iii) a foreign affiliate of the particular corporation, or

(iv) a foreign affiliate of another corporation that is related to the particular corporation, and

C is the total of

(i) the total of all amounts each of which is $1/2$ of the amount by which a loss (determined without reference to this section), from a previous disposition by a corporation, or a foreign affiliate described in the description of B, of the affiliate shares or shares for which the affiliate shares were substituted, was reduced under paragraph (2.01)(*a*) in respect of the exempt dividends referred to in the description of B,

(ii) the total of all amounts each of which is the amount by which an allowable capital loss (determined without reference to this section), of a corporation or a foreign affiliate described in the description of B, from a previous disposition by a partnership of the affiliate shares or shares for which the affiliate shares were substituted, was reduced under paragraph (2.11)(*a*) in respect of the exempt dividends referred to in the description of B,

(iii) the total of all amounts each of which is $1/2$ of the amount by which a loss (determined without reference to this section), from a previous disposition by a corporation, or a foreign affiliate described in the description of B, of an interest in a partnership, was reduced under paragraph (2.21)(*a*) in respect of the exempt dividends referred to in the description of B, and

(iv) the total of all amounts each of which is the amount by which an allowable capital loss (determined without reference to this section), of a corporation, or a foreign affiliate described in the description of B, from a previous disposition by a partnership of an interest in another partnership, was reduced under this paragraph in respect of the exempt dividends referred to in the description of B, and

(*b*) the lesser of

(i) the portion of the particular allowable capital loss, determined without reference to this section, that can reasonably be considered to be attributable to a fluctuation in the value of a currency other than Canadian currency relative to Canadian currency, and

(ii) $^1/_2$ of the amount determined in respect of the particular corporation, or the foreign affiliate (that is referred to in paragraph (2.3)(*b*)), of the particular corporation, that is the amount of a gain (other than a specified gain) that

(A) was made within 30 days before or after the disposition time by the particular partnership to the extent that the gain is reasonably attributable to the particular corporation or the foreign affiliate, as the case may be, and that

(I) is deemed under subsection 39(2) to be a capital gain of the particular partnership for the taxation year that includes the time the gain was made from the disposition of currency other than Canadian currency, and

(II) is in respect of the settlement or extinguishment of a foreign currency debt that

1. was issued or incurred by the particular partnership within 30 days before or after the acquisition of the partnership interest by the particular partnership,

2. was, at all times at which it was a debt obligation of the particular partnership, owing to a person or partnership that dealt, at all times during which the foreign currency debt was outstanding, at arm's length with the particular corporation, and

3. can reasonably be considered to have been issued or incurred in relation to the acquisition of the partnership interest, or

(B) is a capital gain (to the extent that the capital gain is reasonably attributable to the particular corporation or the foreign affiliate, as the case may be) realized within 30 days before or after the disposition time by the particular partnership under an agreement that

(I) was entered into by the particular partnership, within 30 days before or after the acquisition of the partnership interest by the particular partnership, with a person or partnership that dealt, at all times during which the agreement was in force, at arm's length with the particular corporation,

(II) provides for the purchase, sale or exchange of currency, and

(III) can reasonably be considered to have been entered into by the particular partnership for the principal purpose of hedging the foreign exchange exposure arising in connection with the acquisition of the partnership interest.

History: S. 93(2.31) was added by S.C. 2013, c. 34, s. 68(4), applicable in respect of losses of a corporation resident in Canada, or of foreign affiliates of such a corporation, in respect of dispositions (referred to below as "relevant dispositions" in respect of the corporation) of shares and partnership interests that occur after February 27, 2004. However,

(*a*) subject to paragraph (*c*), in respect of relevant dispositions in respect of the corporation that occur before August 19, 2012, the Act is to be read without reference to its subsections 93(2.02), (2.12), (2.22) and (2.32), and

(i) if the corporation does not elect under subparagraph (ii) [below],

(D) paragraph 93(2.31)(*b*) is to be read as follows:

"(*b*) $^1/_2$ of the total of the following amounts determined in respect of the particular corporation, or the foreign affiliate (that is referred to in paragraph (2.3)(*b*)) of the particular corporation, as the case may be:

(i) the amount of the gain of the particular corporation, the foreign affiliate or the particular partnership (to the extent that the gain is reasonably attributable to the particular corporation or the foreign affiliate, as the case may be) that is included in the determination made under subsection 39(2) of the capital gain or capital loss of the particular corporation, the foreign affiliate or the particular partnership, as the case may be, for the taxation year that includes the time the gain was made from the disposition of currency of a country other than Canada if the gain is in respect of

(A) the settlement or extinguishment of an obligation of the particular corporation, the foreign affiliate, the particular partnership or the other partnership, as the case may be, that can reasonably be considered to have been issued or incurred in relation to the acquisition of the affiliate shares, or

(B) if that taxation year began on or before August 19, 2011 (in the case of the particular corporation) or ended on or before August 19, 2011 (in the case of the foreign affiliate), the redemption, acquisition or cancellation of a share of the particular corporation or the foreign affiliate, as the case may be, or an interest in the particular partnership or the other partnership, as the case may be, that can reasonably be considered to have been issued in relation to the acquisition of the affiliate shares, and

(ii) the amount of any gain realized by a partnership (to the extent that the gain is reasonably attributable to the particular corporation or the foreign affiliate, as the case may be), by the particular corporation or the foreign affiliate, as the case may be, under an agreement that provides for the purchase, sale or exchange of currency, or from the disposition of a currency, which agreement or currency, as the case may be, can reasonably be considered to have been entered into or acquired by the partnership, the particular corporation or the foreign affiliate, as the case may be, for the principal purpose of hedging the foreign exchange exposure arising in connection with the acquisition of the affiliate shares."

(E) if the corporation has made an election in respect of the application of s. 95(2)(*f.11*) to (*g.02*), the reference to "August 19, 2011" in clause 93(2.31)(*b*)(i)(B) in the read-as text in clause (D) [above], is, in respect of the foreign affiliates referred to in that clause, to be read as a reference to "June 30, 2011",

(ii) if the corporation elects in writing in respect of all relevant dispositions in respect of the corporation and files the election with the Minister of National Revenue on or before the day that is the later of the corporation's filing-due date for the corporation's taxation year that includes June 26, 2013 and June 26, 2014 [the day that is one year after royal assent],

(D) in respect of subsection 93(2.31),

(I) the formula in paragraph (*a*) of subsection 93(2.31) is, in respect of all relevant dispositions in respect of the corporation, to be read as follows:

"A – (B – C) + D"

(II) paragraph (*a*) of subsection 93(2.31) is, in respect of all relevant dispositions in respect of the corporation, to be read as if it contained a description of D that reads as follows:

"D is the lesser of

(i) the amount, if any, by which the amount determined for B exceeds the amount determined for C, and

(ii) 1/2 of the total of the following amounts determined in respect of the particular corporation, or the foreign affiliate (that is referred to in paragraph (2.3)(*b*)) of the particular corporation, as the case may be:

(A) the amount of the gain of the particular corporation, the foreign affiliate or the particular partnership (to the extent that the gain is reasonably attributable to the particular corporation or the foreign affiliate, as the case may be) that is included in the determination made under subsection 39(2) of the capital gain or capital loss of the particular corporation, the foreign affiliate or the particular partnership, as the case may be, for the taxation year that includes the time the gain was made from the disposition of currency of a country other than Canada if the gain is in respect of

(I) the settlement or extinguishment of an obligation of the particular corporation, the foreign affiliate, the particular partnership or the other partnership, as the case may be, that can reasonably be considered to have been issued or incurred in relation to the acquisition of the affiliate shares, or

(II) if that taxation year began on or before August 19, 2011 (in the case of the particular corporation) or ended on or before August 19, 2011 (in the case of the foreign affiliate), the redemption, acquisition or cancellation of a share of the particular corporation or the foreign affiliate, as the case may be, or an interest in the particular partnership or the other partnership, as the case may be, that can reasonably be considered to have been issued in relation to the acquisition of the affiliate shares, and

(B) the amount of any gain realized by a partnership (to the extent that the gain is reasonably attributable to the particular corporation or the foreign affiliate, as the case may be), by the particular corporation or the foreign affiliate, as the case may be, under an agreement that provides for the purchase, sale or exchange of currency, or from the disposition of a currency, which agreement or currency, as the case may be, can reasonably be considered to have been entered into or acquired by the partnership, the particular corporation or the foreign affiliate, as the case may be, for the principal purpose of hedging the foreign exchange exposure arising in connection with the acquisition of the affiliate shares."

(III) if the corporation has elected in respect of the application s. 95(2)(*f.11*) to (*g.02*), the reference to "August 19, 2011" in subclause (ii)(A)(II) of that description of D is, in respect of the foreign affiliate referred to in that subclause, to be read as a reference to "June 30, 2011", and

(IV) paragraph (*b*) of subsection 93(2.31) is, in respect of all relevant dispositions in respect of the corporation, to be read as follows:

"(*b*) nil."

(*b*) if the corporation elects in writing in respect of all losses of the corporation, and of all foreign affiliates of the corporation, in respect of dispositions (referred to in this paragraph as "pertinent dispositions" in respect of the corporation) of shares and partnership interests that occur on or before February 27, 2004 and files the election with the Minister of National Revenue on or before the day that is the later of the corporation's filing-due date for the corporation's taxation year that includes June 26, 2013 and June 26, 2014 [the day that is one year after royal assent],

(ii) subsections 93(2.31), with the modifications described in paragraph (*a*) (if applicable) being taken into account, also applies in respect of all pertinent dispositions in respect of the corporation that occur after November 1999 and on or before February 27, 2004, except that the reference to "twice" in subsection 93(2.31), is,

(A) for taxation years of the corporation that end before February 28, 2000, to be read as references to "4/3 of", and

(B) for taxation years of the corporation that include February 28, 2000 or October 17, 2000 or that begin after February 28, 2000 and end before October 17, 2000, to be read as references to "the fraction that is the reciprocal of the fraction in paragraph 38(*a*), as amended by S.C. 2001, c. 17, that applies to the taxpayer for the year, multiplied by": and

(*c*) if the corporation elects in writing in respect of all relevant dispositions in respect of the corporation that occur before August 19, 2012 and files the election with the Minister of National Revenue on or before the day that is the later of the corporation's filing-due date for the corporation's taxation year that includes June 26, 2013 and June 26, 2014 [the day that is one year after royal assent], paragraph (*a*) does not apply in respect of all those relevant dispositions.

See the application for the amendment to s. 93(1.1) for the extension of assessment periods to take into account the amendments by S.C. 2013, c. 34, s. 54 to 89.

► 93(2.32) ◄

(2.32) Specified gain. For the purposes of subparagraph (2.31)(*b*)(ii), a "specified gain" means a gain in respect of the settlement or extinguishment of a foreign currency debt referred to in subclause (2.31)(*b*)(ii)(A)(II), or that arises under a particular agreement referred to in clause (2.31)(*b*)(ii)(B), if the particular partnership, or any person or partnership with which the particular corporation was not — at any time during which the foreign currency debt was outstanding or the particular agreement was in force, as the case may be — dealing at arm's length, entered into an agreement that may reasonably be considered to have been entered into for the principal purpose of hedging any foreign exchange exposure arising in connection with the foreign currency debt or the particular agreement.

History: S. 93(2.32) was added by S.C. 2013, c. 34, s. 68(4), applicable in respect of losses of a corporation resident in Canada, or of foreign affiliates of such a corporation, in respect of dispositions (referred to below as "relevant dispositions" in respect of the corporation) of shares and partnership interests that occur after February 27, 2004. However,

(*a*) subject to paragraph (*c*) [below], in respect of relevant dispositions in respect of the corporation that occur before August 19, 2012, the Act is to be read without reference to its subsection 93(2.32), and

(*b*) if the corporation elects in writing in respect of all losses of the corporation, and of all foreign affiliates of the corporation, in respect of dispositions (referred to in this paragraph as "pertinent dispositions" in respect of the corporation) of shares and partnership interests that occur on or before February 27, 2004 and files the election with the Minister of National Revenue on or before the day that is the later of the corporation's filing-due date for the corporation's taxation year that includes June 26, 2013 and June 26, 2014 [the day that is one year after royal assent],

(ii) if paragraph (*c*) [below] applies, subsection 93(2.32), with the modifications described in paragraph (*a*) (if applicable) being taken into account, also applies in respect of all pertinent dispositions in respect of the corporation that occur after November 1999 and on or before February 27, 2004, and

(*c*) if the corporation elects in writing in respect of all relevant dispositions in respect of the corporation that occur before August 19, 2012 and files the election with the Minister of National Revenue on or before the day that is the later of the corporation's filing-due date for the corporation's taxation year that includes June 26, 2013 and June 26, 2014 [the day that is one year after royal assent], paragraph (*a*) does not apply in respect of all those relevant dispositions.

See the application for the amendment to s. 93(1.1) for the extension of assessment periods to take into account the amendments by S.C. 2013, c. 34, s. 54 to 89.

► 93(3) ◄

(3) Exempt dividends. For the purposes of subsections (2.01), (2.11), (2.21) and (2.31), (*a*) a dividend received by a corporation resident in Canada is an exempt dividend to the extent of the amount in respect of the dividend that is deductible from the income of the corporation for the purpose of computing the taxable income of the corporation because of any of paragraphs 113(1)(*a*) to (*c*); and

(*b*) a dividend received by a particular foreign affiliate of a corporation resident in Canada from another foreign affiliate of the corporation is an exempt dividend to the extent of the amount, if any, by which the portion of the dividend that was not prescribed to have been paid out of the pre-acquisition surplus of the other affiliate exceeds the total of such portion of the income or profits tax that can reasonably be considered to have been paid in respect of that portion of the dividend by the particular affiliate or by a partnership in which the particular affiliate had, at the time of the payment of the income or profits tax, a partnership interest, either directly or indirectly; and

(*c*) the prescribed amount is deemed to be an amount that is received, at the adjustment time referred to in subsection 5905(7.7) of the *Income Tax Regulations*, by a particular foreign affiliate of a corporation resident in Canada from another foreign affiliate of the corporation and that is in respect of an exempt dividend on a share of the capital stock of the other affiliate.

History: S. 93(3)(*c*) was added by S.C. 2013, c. 34, s. 32(3), deemed to have come into force on December 19, 2009.

See the application following s. 93(1) regarding the override of the statute-barring rules for assessments for taxation years that end before June 26, 2013.

S. 93(3), the portion before paragraph (*b*) was replaced by S.C. 2013, c. 34, s. 68(5), applicable if subsection 93(2.01) applies, except that,

(*a*) where subsection 93(2.01) applies but subsection 93(2.11) does not apply, the portion of subsection 93(3) before paragraph (*a*) is to be read as follows:

"(3) For the purposes of subsection (2.01),"

(*b*) in respect of dispositions that occur on or before August 19, 2011, paragraph 93(3)(*a*) is to be read as follows:

"(*a*) a dividend received by a corporation resident in Canada is an exempt dividend to the extent of the amount in respect of the dividend that is deductible from the income of the corporation for the purposes of computing the taxable income of the corporation because of paragraph 113(1)(*a*), (*b*) or (*c*); and"

See the application for the amendment to s. 93(1.1) for the extension of assessment periods to take into account the amendments by S.C. 2013, c. 34, s. 54 to 89.

S. 93(3), the portion before paragraph (*b*) formerly read:

(3) *Exempt dividends.* For the purposes of subsections (2) to (2.3),

(*a*) a dividend received by a corporation resident in Canada is an exempt dividend to the extent of the amount in respect of the dividend that is deductible from the income of the corporation for the purpose of computing the taxable income of the corporation because of paragraph 113(1)(*a*), (*b*) or (*c*);

▶ 93(4) ◀

(4) Loss on disposition of shares of foreign affiliate. If a taxpayer resident in Canada or a foreign affiliate (which taxpayer or foreign affiliate is referred to in this subsection as the "transferee") of the taxpayer has acquired shares of the capital stock of one or more foreign affiliates (each referred to in this subsection as an "acquired affiliate") of the taxpayer on a disposition of shares (such shares disposed of being referred to in this subsection as the "disposed shares") of the capital stock of any other foreign affiliate of the taxpayer (other than, where the transferee is a foreign affiliate of the taxpayer, a disposition of shares that are, immediately before the acquisition, excluded property of the transferee or a disposition to which subsection 40(3.4) applies), the following rules apply:

(*a*) the capital loss, if any, of the transferee from the disposition, is deemed to be nil; and

(*b*) in computing the adjusted cost base to the transferee of a share of a particular class of the capital stock of an acquired affiliate that is owned by the transferee immediately after the disposition, there is to be added the amount determined by the formula

$$[(A - B) \times C/D] / E$$

where

A is the total of all amounts each of which is the cost amount to the transferee, immediately before the disposition, of a disposed share,

B is the total of

(i) the total of all amounts each of which is the proceeds of disposition of a disposed share, and

(ii) the total of all amounts in respect of the computation of losses of the transferee from the dispositions of the disposed shares, each of which is, in respect of the disposition of a disposed share, the amount by which the amount for A in the formula in paragraph (2.01)(*a*) exceeds the amount determined by that formula,

C is the fair market value, immediately after the disposition, of all shares of the particular class owned, immediately after the disposition, by the transferee,

D is the fair market value, immediately after the disposition, of all shares owned, immediately after the disposition, by the transferee of the capital stock of all acquired affiliates, and

E is the number of shares of the particular class that are owned by the transferee immediately after the disposition.

History: S. 93(4) was replaced by S.C. 2013, c. 34, s. 68(6), applicable to acquisitions of shares of the capital stock of a foreign affiliate of a taxpayer that occur after February 27, 2004. However, if

(*a*) the acquisition occurs on or before August 19, 2011, the portion of subsection 93(4) before paragraph (*a*) is to be read as follows:

"(4) If a taxpayer resident in Canada or a foreign affiliate (which taxpayer or foreign affiliate is referred to in this subsection as the "transferee") of the taxpayer has acquired shares of the capital stock of one or more foreign affiliates (each referred to in this subsection as an "acquired affiliate") of the taxpayer on a disposition of shares (such shares disposed of being referred to in this subsection as the "disposed shares") of the capital stock of any other foreign affiliate of the taxpayer (other than a disposition to which subsection 40(3.4) applies), the following rules apply:"

(*b*) the taxpayer has elected under paragraph (*b*) of the application provision for the addition of subsections 93(2) to (2.32), subsection 93(4), the portion before paragraph (*a*), being read as required by the application in paragraph (*a*) above, applies to all acquisitions of shares of the capital stock of all foreign affiliates of the taxpayer that occur after 1994.

See the application for the amendment to s. 93(1.1) for the extension of assessment periods to take into account the amendments by S.C. 2013, c. 34, s. 54 to 89.

S. 93(4) formerly read:

(4) *Loss on disposition of shares of foreign affiliate.* Where a taxpayer resident in Canada or a foreign affiliate of the taxpayer (in this subsection referred to as the "vendor") has acquired shares of a foreign affiliate of the taxpayer (in this subsection referred to as the "acquired affiliate") on the disposition of shares of any other foreign affiliate of the taxpayer (other than a disposition to which subsection 40(3.4) applies), the following rules apply:

(*a*) the capital loss therefrom otherwise determined shall be deemed to be nil; and

(*b*) in computing the adjusted cost base to the vendor of all shares of any particular class of the capital stock of the acquired affiliate owned by the vendor immediately after the disposition, there shall be added an amount determined by the formula

$$(A - B) \times C/D$$

where

A is the cost amount to the vendor immediately before the disposition of the shares disposed of,

B is the total of

(i) the proceeds of disposition of the shares disposed of, and

(ii) the total of all amounts deducted under paragraph (2)(*d*) in computing losses of the vendor from the dispositions of the shares disposed of,

C is the fair market value, immediately after the disposition, of all shares of that particular class owned by it at that time, and

D is the fair market value, immediately after the disposition, of all shares of the capital stock of the acquired affiliate owned by it at that time.

Tax Window Files: Interpretation of subsection 93(4), *September 5, 2018*, CRA Document No. 2017-0698241I7.

▶ 93(5) ◀

(5) Late filed elections. Where the election referred to in subsection (1) was not made on or before the day on or before which the election was required by that subsection to be made, the election shall be deemed to have been made on that day if, on or before the day that is 3 years after that day,

(*a*) the election is made in prescribed manner; and

(*b*) an estimate of the penalty in respect of that election is paid by the corporation when that election is made.

Forms: T2107 — Election in Respect of a Share Disposition in a Foreign Affiliate.

▶ 93(5.1) ◀

(5.1) Special cases. Where, in the opinion of the Minister, the circumstances of a case are such that it would be just and equitable

(*a*) to permit an election under subsection (1) to be made after the day that is 3 years after the day on or before which the election was required by that subsection to be made, or

(*b*) to permit an election made under subsection (1) to be amended,

the election or amended election shall be deemed to have been made on the day on or before which the election was so required to be made if

(*c*) the election or amended election is made in prescribed form, and

(*d*) an estimate of the penalty in respect of the election or amended election is paid by the corporation when the election or amended election is made,

and where this subsection applies to the amendment of an election, that election shall be deemed not to have been effective.

▶ 93(5.2) ◀

(5.2) Amended election. An election (referred to in this subsection as the "amended election") by a taxpayer under subsection (1) in respect of a disposition of shares of the capital stock of a foreign affiliate of the taxpayer is deemed to have been made on the day on or before which the election was required to be made and any previous election (referred to in this subsection as the "old election") under subsection (1) in respect of that disposition is deemed not to have been made if

(*a*) the taxpayer has not elected under section 51 of the *Technical Tax Amendments Act, 2012*;

(*b*) the taxpayer made the old election on or before December 18, 2009;

(*c*) in the opinion of the Minister, the circumstances are such that it would be just and equitable to permit the old election to be amended; and

(*d*) the amended election is made in prescribed form on or before December 31, 2013.

History: S. 93(5.2) was added by S.C. 2013, c. 34, s. 32(4), deemed to have come into force on December 19, 2009.

See the application following s. 92(1) regarding the election under section 51 of the *Technical Tax Amendments Act, 2012* [S.C. 2013, c. 34.]

▶ 93(6) ◀

(6) Penalty for late filed election. For the purposes of this section, the penalty in respect of an election or amended election referred to in paragraph (5)(*a*) or (5.1)(*c*) is an amount equal to the lesser of

(*a*) 1/4 of 1% of the amount designated in the election or amended election for each month or part of a month during the period commencing with the day on or before which the election is required by subsection (1) to be made and ending on the day the election is made, and

(*b*) an amount, not exceeding $8,000, equal to the product obtained by multiplying $100 by the number of months each of which is a month all or part of which is during the period referred to in paragraph (*a*).

▶ 93(7) ◀

(7) Unpaid balance of penalty. The Minister shall, with all due dispatch, examine each election and amended election referred to in paragraph (5)(*a*) or (5.1)(*c*), assess the penalty payable and send a notice of assessment to the corporation, and the corporation shall pay forthwith to the Receiver General the amount, if any, by which the penalty so assessed exceeds the total of all amounts previously paid on account of that penalty.

Related Sections: S. 39, "capital gain", "capital loss"; s. 54, "adjusted cost base", "proceeds of disposition"; s. 95(1), "foreign affiliate"; s. 248(1), "amount", "corporation", "dividend", "prescribed", "share"; s. 255 Canada.

SECTION 93.1: Shares held by partnership

► 93.1(1) ◄

(1) Shares held by partnership. For the purpose of determining whether a non-resident corporation is a foreign affiliate of a corporation resident in Canada for the purposes of a specified provision, if, based on the assumptions contained in paragraph 96(1)(*c*), at any time shares of a class of the capital stock of a corporation are owned by a partnership or are deemed under this subsection to be owned by a partnership, then each member of the partnership is deemed to own at that time the number of those shares that is equal to the proportion of all those shares that

(*a*) the fair market value of the member's interest in the partnership at that time

is of

(*b*) the fair market value of all members' interests in the partnership at that time.

Editorial Note: Where a Canadian–resident corporation owns shares of a non-resident corporation through a partnership, section 93.1 determines whether the non-resident corporation is a foreign affiliate of the Canadian-resident corporation for various provisions of the Act. In these cases, subsection 93.1(1) provides a look-through rule that deems the Canadian corporation to own its proportionate number of the non-resident's corporation's shares based on the relative fair market value of its interest in the partnership.

Subsection 93.1(1) is divided in to two subsections. Subsection 93.1(1.1) lists the provisions for which the look-through rule applies, including provisions in subsections 93.1(1.1), 93.1(5), and 95(2.2) and section 233.4. The addition of subsection 93.1(5) is consequential to the addition of subsections 93.1(5) and 93.1(6), which require the determination of foreign affiliate status through a partnership.

The addition of subsection 95(2.2) addresses a concern identified in an April 19, 2006 comfort letter issued by the Department of Finance. The concern in the letter was the application of subsection 95(2.2) in situations where the shares of a non-resident corporation are acquired by the partnership. If it applies, subsection 95(2.2) deems a non-resident corporation to be a foreign affiliate of a taxpayer in respect of which the taxpayer has a qualifying interest throughout the year for the purposes of paragraphs 95(2)(*a*) and (*g*). In some cases, subsection 95(2.2) requires the determination of foreign affiliate status through a partnership.

A reference to section 233.4 is added so the partnership look-through rule applies for the purpose of determining whether a non-resident corporation or trust is a foreign affiliate of a taxpayer or partnership for the purposes of subsection 233.4(4) reporting requirements.

The amendments in subsections 93.1(1) and 93.1(1.1) are effective July 12, 2013, subject to an election to have them effective as of January 1, 2010, except the reference to subsection 95(2.2), which is effective for year ends after 1999.

History: S. 93.1(1), the portion before paragraph (*a*) was replaced by S.C. 2014, c. 39, s. 21(4), deemed to have come into force on July 12, 2013. However, if a taxpayer elects in writing under s. 21(15) of the *Economic Action Plan 2014 Act, No. 2* [S.C. 2014, c. 39] , then in respect of the taxpayer, this amendment is deemed to have come into force on January 1, 2010.

In addition, any assessment of a taxpayer's tax, interest and penalties payable under the Act for any taxation year that ends before the day on which this amendment receives royal assent [December 16, 2014] that would, in the absence of this section, be precluded because of the time references in subsection 152(4) of the Act is to be made to the extent necessary to take into account this amendment.

S. 93.1(1), the portion before paragraph (*a*) formerly read:

(1) *Shares held by partnership.* For the purpose of determining whether a non-resident corporation is a foreign affiliate of a corporation resident in Canada for the purposes of subsections (2), 20(12) and 39(2.1), sections 90, 93 and 113, paragraphs 128.1(1)(*c.3*) and (*d*), section 212.3 and subsection 219.1(2), (and any regulations made for the purposes of those provisions), section 95 (to the extent that it is applied for the purposes of those provisions), paragraph 95(2)(*g.04*), subsection 95(2.2) and section 126, if, based on the assumptions contained in paragraph 96(1)(*c*), at any time shares of a class of the capital stock of a corporation are owned by a partnership or are deemed under this subsection to be owned by a partnership, then each member of the partnership is deemed to own at that time the number of those shares that is equal to the proportion of all those shares that

S. 93.1(1), the portion before paragraph (*a*) was replaced by S.C. 2014, c. 39, s. 21(3), deemed to have come into force on March 29, 2012.

In addition, any assessment of a taxpayer's tax, interest and penalties payable under the Act for any taxation year that ends before the day on which this amendment receives royal assent [December 16, 2014] that would, in the absence of this section, be precluded because of the time references in subsection 152(4) of the Act is to be made to the extent necessary to take into account this amendment.

S. 93.1(1), the portion before paragraph (*a*) formerly read:

(1) *Shares held by partnership.* For the purpose of determining whether a non-resident corporation is a foreign affiliate of a corporation resident in Canada for the purposes of subsections (2), 20(12) and 39(2.1), sections 90, 93 and 113, paragraph 128.1(1)(*d*), (and any regulations made for the purposes of those provisions), section 95 (to the extent that it is applied for the purposes of those provisions), paragraph 95(2)(*g.04*), subsection 95(2.2) and section 126, if, based on the assumptions contained in paragraph 96(1)(*c*), at any time shares of a class of the capital stock of a corporation are owned by a partnership or are deemed under this subsection to be owned by a partnership, then each member of the partnership is deemed to own at that time the number of those shares that is equal to the proportion of all those shares that

S. 93.1(1), the portion before paragraph (*a*) was replaced by S.C. 2014, c. 39, s. 21(2), deemed to have come into force on August 20, 2011.

In addition, any assessment of a taxpayer's tax, interest and penalties payable under the Act for any taxation year that ends before the day on which this amendment receives royal assent [December 16, 2014] that would, in the absence of this section, be precluded because of the time references in subsection 152(4) of the Act is to be made to the extent necessary to take into account this amendment.

S. 93.1(1), the portion before paragraph (*a*) formerly read:

(1) *Shares held by partnership.* For the purpose of determining whether a non-resident corporation is a foreign affiliate of a corporation resident in Canada for the purposes of subsections (2) and 20(12), sections 93 and 113, paragraph 128.1(1)(*d*), (and any regulations made for the purposes of those provisions), section 95 (to the extent that it is applied for the purposes of those provisions), subsection 95(2.2) and section 126, if, based on the assumptions contained in paragraph 96(1)(*c*), at any time shares of a class of the capital stock of a corporation are owned by a partnership or are deemed under this subsection to be owned by a partnership, then each member of the partnership is deemed to own at that time the number of those shares that is equal to the proportion of all those shares that

S. 93.1(1), the portion before paragraph (*a*) was replaced by S.C. 2014, c. 39, s. 21(1), applicable to taxation years of a foreign affiliate of a taxpayer that end after 1999.

In addition, any assessment of a taxpayer's tax, interest and penalties payable under the Act for any taxation year that ends before the day on which this amendment receives royal assent [December 16, 2014] that would, in the absence of this section, be precluded because of the time references in subsection 152(4) of the Act is to be made to the extent necessary to take into account this amendment.

S. 93.1(1), the portion before paragraph (*a*) formerly read:

(1) *Shares held by a partnership.* For the purposes of determining whether a non-resident corporation is a foreign affiliate of a corporation resident in Canada for the purposes of subsections (2), 20(12) and 39(2.1), sections 90, 93 and 113, paragraphs 128.1(1)(*c.3*) and (*d*), section 212.3 and subsection 219.1(2), (and any regulations made for the purposes of those provisions), section 95 (to the extent that it is applied for the purposes of those provisions), paragraph 95(2)(*g.04*) and section 126, if, based on the assumptions contained in paragraph 96(1)(*c*), at any time shares of a class of the capital stock of a corporation are owned by a partnership or are deemed under this subsection to be owned by a partnership, then each member of the partnership is deemed to own at that time the number of those shares that is equal to the proportion of all those shares that

S. 93.1(1), the portion before paragraph (*a*) was replaced by S.C. 2013, c. 34, s. 427(2)(*c*), deemed to have come into force on August 20, 2011, except that before March 29, 2012, the portion of subsection 93.1(1) paragraph (*a*) is to be read as follows:

"(1) **Shares held by partnership.** For the purposes of determining whether a non-resident corporation is a foreign affiliate of a corporation resident in Canada for the purposes of subsections (2), 20(12) and 39(2.1), sections 90, 93 and 113, paragraph 128.1(1)(*d*), (and any regulations made for the purposes of those provisions), section 95 (to the extent that it is applied for the purposes of those provisions), paragraph 95(2)(*g.04*) and section 126, if, based on the assumptions contained in paragraph 96(1)(*c*), at any time shares of a class of the capital stock of a corporation are owned by a partnership or are deemed under this subsection to be owned by a partnership, then each member of the partnership is deemed to own at that time the number of those shares that is equal to the proportion of all those shares that"

S. 93.1(1), the portion before paragraph (*a*) formerly read:

(1) *Shares held by a partnership.* For the purposes of determining whether a non-resident corporation is a foreign affiliate of a corporation resident in Canada for the purposes of subsections (2), 20(12) and 39(2.1), sections 90, 93 and 113, paragraph 128.1(1)(*d*), (and any regulations made for the purposes of those provisions), section 95 (to the extent that it is applied for the purposes of those provisions), paragraph 95(2)(*g.04*) and section 126, if, based on the assumptions contained in paragraph 96(1)(*c*), at any time shares of a class of the capital stock of a corporation are owned by a partnership or are deemed under this subsection to be owned by a partnership, then each member of the partnership is deemed to own at that time the number of those shares that is equal to the proportion of all those shares that

S. 93.1(1), the portion before paragraph (*a*) was replaced by S.C. 2013, c. 34, s. 69(1), deemed to have come into force on August 20, 2011, and formerly read:

(1) *Shares held by a partnership.* For the purposes of determining whether a non-resident corporation is a foreign affiliate of a corporation resident in Canada for the purposes of subsections (2) and 20(12), sections 93 and 113, paragraphs 128.1(1)(*c.3*) and (*d*), section 212.3 and subsection 219.1(2), (and any regulations made for the purposes of those provisions), section 95 (to the extent that it is applied for the purposes of those provisions) and section 126, if, based on the assumptions contained in paragraph 96(1)(*c*), at any time shares of a class of the capital stock of a corporation are owned by a partnership or are deemed under this subsection to be owned by a partnership, then each member of the partnership is deemed to own at that time the number of those shares that is equal to the proportion of all those shares that

S. 93.1(1), the portion before paragraph (*a*) was replaced by S.C. 2012, c. 31, s. 69(1), deemed to have come into force on March 29, 2012. S. 93.1(1), the portion before paragraph (*a*) formerly read:

(1) *Shares held by a partnership.* For the purpose of determining whether a non-resident corporation is a foreign affiliate of a corporation resident in Canada for the purposes of subsections (2) and 20(12), sections 93 and 113, paragraph 128.1(1)(*d*), (and any regulations made for the purposes of those provisions), section 95 (to the extent that that section is applied for the purposes of those provisions) and section 126, where based on the assumptions contained in paragraph 96(1)(*c*), at any time shares of a class of the capital stock of a corporation are owned by a partnership or are deemed under this subsection to be owned by a partnership, each member of the partnership is deemed to own at that time that number of those shares that is equal to the proportion of all those shares that

Canadian Tax Foundation: Nikolakakis, *The 1999-2000 Foreign Affiliate Amendments: Partnerships, Foreign Exchange Issues, and the Use of Losses*, 2000 Conference Report 14:1–60.

▶ 93.1(1.1) ◀

(1.1) Specified provisions for subsection (1). For the purposes of subsection (1), the specified provisions are

(*a*) subsections (2), (5), 20(12) and 39(2.1), sections 90, 93, 93.3 and 113, paragraphs 128.1(1)(*c.3*) and (*d*), section 212.3, subsection 219.1(2) and section 233.4;

(*b*) section 95 to the extent that section is applied for the purposes of the provisions referred to in paragraph (*a*);

(*c*) any regulations made for the purposes of the provisions referred to in paragraph (*a*); and

(*d*) paragraph 95(2)(*g*.04), subsections 95(2.2) and (8) to (12) and section 126.

History: S. 93.1(1.1)(*d*) was replaced by S.C. 2018, c. 27, s. 6(1), deemed to have come into force on February 27, 2018, and formerly read:

(*d*) paragraph 95(2)(*g.04*), subsection 95(2.2) and section 126.

S. 93.1(1.1) was added by S.C. 2014, c. 39, s. 21(5), deemed to have come into force on July 12, 2013. However, if a taxpayer elects in writing under s. 21(15) of the *Economic Action Plan 2014 Act, No. 2* [S.C. 2014, c. 39], then in respect of the taxpayer, this amendment is deemed to have come into force on January 1, 2010, and s. 93.1(1.1) is to be read

(*a*) in respect of any time that is after 2009 and before August 20, 2011 as follows:

"(1.1) For the purposes of subsection (1), the specified provisions are

(*a*) subsections (2), (5) and 20(12), sections 93 and 113 and paragraph 128.1(1)(*d*);

(*b*) section 95 to the extent that section is applied for the purposes of the provisions referred to in paragraph (*a*);

(*c*) any regulations made for the purposes of the provisions referred to in paragraph (*a*); and

(*d*) subsection 95(2.2) and section 126."

(*b*) in respect of any time that is after August 19, 2011 and before March 29, 2012 as follows:

"(1.1) For the purposes of subsection (1), the specified provisions are

(*a*) subsections (2), (5), 20(12) and 39(2.1), sections 90, 93 and 113 and paragraph 128.1(1)(*d*),

(*b*) section 95 to the extent that section is applied for the purposes of the provisions referred to in paragraph (*a*);

(*c*) any regulations made for the purposes of the provisions referred to in paragraph (*a*); and

(*d*) paragraph 95(2)(*g.04*), subsection 95(2.2) and section 126."

(*c*) in respect of any time that is after March 28, 2012 and before July 12, 2013 as follows:

"(1.1) For the purposes of subsection (1), the specified provisions are

(*a*) subsections (2), (5), 20(12) and 39(2.1), sections 90, 93 and 113, paragraphs 128.1(1)(*c.3*) and (*d*), section 212.3 and subsection 219.1(2);

(*b*) section 95 to the extent that section is applied for the purposes of the provisions referred to in paragraph (*a*);

(*c*) any regulations made for the purposes of the provisions referred to in paragraph (*a*); and

(*d*) paragraph 95(2)(*g.04*), subsection 95(2.2) and section 126."

In addition, any assessment of a taxpayer's tax, interest and penalties payable under the Act for any taxation year that ends before the day on which this amendment receives royal assent [December 16, 2014] that would, in the absence of this section, be precluded because of the time references in subsection 152(4) of the Act is to be made to the extent necessary to take into account this amendment.

▶ 93.1(2) ◀

(2) Where dividends received by a partnership. Where, based on the assumptions contained in paragraph 96(1)(*c*), at any time shares of a class of the capital stock of a foreign affiliate of a corporation resident in Canada (in this subsection referred to as "affiliate shares") are owned by a partnership and at that time the affiliate pays a dividend on affiliate shares to the partnership (in this subsection referred to as the "partnership dividend"),

(*a*) for the purposes of sections 93 and 113 and any regulations made for the purposes of those sections, each member of the partnership (other than another partnership) is deemed to have received the proportion of the partnership dividend that

(i) the fair market value of the member's interest held, directly or indirectly through one or more other partnerships, in the partnership at that time

is of

(ii) the fair market value of all the interests in the partnership held directly by members of the partnership at that time;

(*b*) for the purposes of sections 93 and 113 and any regulations made for the purposes of those sections, the proportion of the partnership dividend deemed by paragraph (*a*) to have been received by a member of the partnership at that time is deemed to have been received by the member in equal proportions on each affiliate share that is property of the partnership at that time;

(*c*) for the purpose of applying section 113, in respect of the dividend referred to in paragraph (*a*), each affiliate share referred to in paragraph (*b*) is deemed to be owned by each member of the partnership; and

(*d*) notwithstanding paragraphs (*a*) to (*c*),

(i) where the corporation resident in Canada is a member of the partnership, the amount deductible by it under section 113 in respect of the dividend referred to in paragraph (*a*) shall not exceed the portion of the amount of the dividend included in its income pursuant to subsection 96(1), and

(ii) where another foreign affiliate of the corporation resident in Canada is a member of the partnership, the amount included in that other affiliate's income in respect of the dividend referred to in paragraph (*a*) shall not exceed the amount that would be included in its income pursuant to subsection 96(1) in respect of the partnership dividend received by the partnership if the value for H in the definition "foreign accrual property income" in subsection 95(1) were nil and this Act were read without reference to this subsection.

Editorial Note: Subsection 93.1(2) provides a look-through rule for the purposes of sections 93 and 113 and related regulations, of dividends paid by a foreign affiliate to a partnership of which either a corporation resident in Canada or another foreign affiliate is a member.

Subsection 93.1(1) is divided in to two subsections. Subsection 93.1(1.1) lists the provisions for which the look-through rule applies, including provisions in subsections 93.1(1.1), 93.1(5), and 95(2.2) and section 233.4. The addition of subsection 93.1(5) is consequential to the addition of subsections 93.1(5) and 93.1(6), which require the determination of foreign affiliate status through a partnership.

The addition of subsection 95(2.2) addresses a concern identified in an April 19, 2006 comfort letter issued by the Department of Finance. The concern in the letter was the application of subsection 95(2.2) in situations where the shares of a non-resident corporation are acquired by the partnership. If it applies, subsection 95(2.2) deems a non-resident corporation to be a foreign affiliate of a taxpayer in respect of which the taxpayer has a qualifying interest throughout the year for the purposes of paragraphs 95(2)(*a*) and (*g*). In some cases, subsection 95(2.2) requires the determination of foreign affiliate status through a partnership.

History: S. 93.1(2)(*a*) was replaced by S.C. 2014, c. 39, s. 21(6), applicable to dividends received after November 1999.

In addition, any assessment of a taxpayer's tax, interest and penalties payable under the Act for any taxation year that ends before the day on which this amendment receives royal assent [December 16, 2014] that would, in the absence of this section, be precluded because of the time references in subsection 152(4) of the Act is to be made to the extent necessary to take into account this amendment.

S. 93.1(2)(*a*) formerly read:

(*a*) for the purposes of sections 93 and 113 and any regulations made for the purposes of those sections, each member of the partnership is deemed to have received the proportion of the partnership dividend that

(i) the fair market value of the member's interest in the partnership at that time

is of

(ii) the fair market value of all members' interests in the partnership at that time;

► 93.1(3) ◄

(3) Tiered partnerships. A person or partnership that is (or is deemed by this subsection to be) a member of a particular partnership that is a member of another partnership is deemed to be a member of the other partnership, and the person or partnership is deemed to have, directly, rights to the income or capital of the other partnership to the extent of the person or partnership's direct and indirect rights to that income or capital, for the purposes of applying

(*a*) except to the extent that the context otherwise requires, a provision of this subdivision;

(*b*) any of paragraphs 13(21.2)(*a*), 14(12)(*a*), 18(13)(*a*), 40(2)(*e.1*), (*e.3*) and (*g*) and (3.3)(*a*); and

(*c*) subsections 39(2.1), 40(3.6) and 87(8.3).

Editorial Note: Subsection 93.1(3) provides a look-through rule for tiered partnerships that applies to certain provisions of the Act. Subsection 93.1(3) was amended to add a reference to subsection 87(8.3).The amendment applies in respect of taxation years of a foreign affiliate that end after July 12, 2013. For further details please see the commentary for subsection 87(8.3).

History: S. 93.1(3)(*c*) was replaced by S.C. 2014, c. 39, s. 21(7), applicable in respect of taxation years of a foreign affiliate of a taxpayer that end after July 12, 2013.

In addition, any assessment of a taxpayer's tax, interest and penalties payable under the Act for any taxation year that ends before the day on which this amendment receives royal assent [December 16, 2014] that would, in the absence of this section, be precluded because of the time references in subsection 152(4) of the Act is to be made to the extent necessary to take into account this amendment.

S. 93.1(3)(*c*) formerly read:

(*c*) subsections 39(2.1) and 40(3.6).

S. 93.1(3) was added by S.C. 2013, c. 34, s. 69(2), applicable in respect of taxation years of a foreign affiliate of a taxpayer that end after August 19, 2011.

► 93.1(4) ◄

(4) Partnership deemed to be corporation. For the purpose of applying clause 95(2)(*a*)(ii)(D) in respect of an amount paid or payable by a partnership to a foreign affiliate, of a taxpayer, that is a member of the partnership or to another foreign affiliate of the taxpayer,

(*a*) if, at any time, all the members (in this subsection referred to as "member affiliates") of the partnership are foreign affiliates of the taxpayer,

(i) the partnership is deemed to be, at that time in respect of the taxpayer and the member affiliates, a non-resident corporation without share capital, and

(ii) all the membership interests in the partnership are deemed to be, at that time, equity interests in the corporation held by the member affiliates; and

(*b*) if, at any time, all the member affiliates are resident in a particular country and the partnership does not carry on business outside the particular country, the partnership is deemed to be, at that time, resident in the particular country.

Editorial Note: Subsection 93.1(4) deems, in certain circumstances, a partnership to be a corporation, and to be resident in a particular country for the purposes of clause 95(2)(*a*)(ii)(D). This allows the recharacterization of interest and other deductible payments received by a financing affiliate from a partnership as active business income if the partnership is the owner of the "third affiliate" as contemplated in that clause.

Under paragraph 93.1(4)(*a*), where all members of a partnership are foreign affiliates of a taxpayer, the partnership is deemed to be a non-resident corporation without share capital, and the membership interests in the partnership are deemed to be equity interests in the corporation. In conjunction with section 93.2 for non-resident corporations without share capital, this allows the corporation to be considered a "foreign affiliate" of the taxpayer if the relevant equity holding thresholds are met. Subsection 93.1(4), together with section 93.2, allows for the application of the "equity percentage" and "direct equity percentage" concepts found in subsection 95(4).

Paragraph 93.1(4)(*b*) deems a partnership to be resident in a particular country if all of the members of the partnership are resident in that country and the partnership carries on business only in that country. If this results in the partnership being resident in a designated treaty country, this can potentially allow an amount paid or payable by the partnership that is deemed active business income of the payee foreign affiliate to be included in the exempt earnings of the payee foreign affiliate (subsection 5907(1) of the *Income Tax Regulations*).

Subsection 93.1(4) applies in respect of taxation years of a foreign affiliate of a taxpayer that end after July 12, 2013.

History: S. 93.1(4) was added by S.C. 2014, c. 39, s. 21(8), applicable in respect of taxation years of a foreign affiliate of a taxpayer that end after July 12, 2013.

In addition, any assessment of a taxpayer's tax, interest and penalties payable under the Act for any taxation year that ends before the day on which this amendment receives royal assent [December 16, 2014] that would, in the absence of this section, be precluded because of the time references in subsection 152(4) of the Act is to be made to the extent necessary to take into account this amendment.

▶ 93.1(5) ◀

(5) Computing FAPI in respect of partnership. For the purpose of applying a relevant provision in respect of a foreign affiliate of a taxpayer resident in Canada, if at any time the taxpayer is a partnership of which a particular corporation resident in Canada, or a foreign affiliate of the particular corporation, is a member and if, based on the relevant assumptions, the particular corporation and the taxpayer would be related, then

(*a*) a non-resident corporation that is, at that time, a foreign affiliate of the particular corporation is deemed to be, at that time, a foreign affiliate of the taxpayer; and

(*b*) the taxpayer is deemed to have, at that time, a qualifying interest in respect of that foreign affiliate if the particular corporation has, at that time, a qualifying interest in respect of the non-resident corporation.

History: S. 93.1(5) was added by S.C. 2014, c. 39, s. 21(8), applicable in respect of taxation years of foreign affiliates of a taxpayer that end after July 12, 2013. However, if the taxpayer elects in writing under s. 21(15) of the *Economic Action Plan 2014 Act, No. 2* [S.C. 2014, c. 39] in respect of all its foreign affiliates and files the election with the Minister of National Revenue on or before the day that is the later of the day that an information return referred to in subsection 229(1) of the *Income Tax Regulations* is required (or would be required if the taxpayer were a Canadian partnership), pursuant to subsections 229(5) and (6) of the *Income Tax Regulations*, to be filed in respect of the fiscal period of the taxpayer that includes the day on which the *Economic Action Plan 2014 Act, No. 2* [S.C. 2014, c. 39] receives royal assent [December 16, 2014] and the day that is one year after the day on which the *Economic Action Plan 2014 Act, No. 2* [S.C. 2014, c. 39] receives royal assent [December 16, 2015], then subsection 93.1(5) is deemed to have come into force on January 1, 2010.

In addition, any assessment of a taxpayer's tax, interest and penalties payable under the Act for any taxation year that ends before the day on which this amendment receives royal assent [December 16, 2014] that would, in the absence of this section, be precluded because of the time references in subsection 152(4) of the Act is to be made to the extent necessary to take into account this amendment.

▶ 93.1(6) ◀

(6) Relevant provisions and assumptions. For the purposes of subsection (5),

(*a*) the relevant provisions are

(i) paragraph (*b*) of the description of A in the definition "foreign accrual property income" in subsection 95(1),

(ii) in determining whether a property of a foreign affiliate of a taxpayer is excluded property of the affiliate, the description of B in the definition "foreign accrual property income" in subsection 95(1),

(iii) paragraphs 95(2)(*a*) and (*g*), and

(iv) subsections 95(2.2) and (2.21); and

(*b*) the relevant assumptions are that

(i) the partnership is a non-resident corporation having capital stock of a single class divided into 100 issued shares that each have full voting rights, and

(ii) each member of the partnership (other than another partnership) owns, at any time, the proportion of the issued shares of that class that

(A) the fair market value of the member's interest held, directly or indirectly through one or more partnerships, in the partnership at that time

is of

(B) the fair market value of all the interests in the partnership held directly by members of the partnership at that time.

History: S. 93.1(6) was added by S.C. 2014, c. 39, s. 21(8), applicable in respect of taxation years of foreign affiliates of a taxpayer that end after July 12, 2013. However, if the taxpayer elects in writing under s. 21(15) of the *Economic Action Plan 2014 Act, No. 2* [S.C. 2014, c. 39] in respect of all its foreign affiliates and files the election with the Minister of National Revenue on or before the day that is the later of the day that an information return referred to in subsection 229(1) of the *Income Tax Regulations* is required (or would be required if the taxpayer were a Canadian partnership), pursuant to subsections 229(5) and (6) of the *Income Tax Regulations*, to be filed in respect of the fiscal period of the taxpayer that includes the day on which the *Economic Action Plan 2014 Act, No. 2* [S.C. 2014, c. 39] receives royal assent [December 16, 2014] and the day that is one year after the day on which the *Economic Action Plan 2014 Act, No. 2* [S.C. 2014, c. 39] receives royal assent [December 16, 2015], then subsection 93.1(6) is deemed to have come into force on January 1, 2010.

In addition, any assessment of a taxpayer's tax, interest and penalties payable under the Act for any taxation year that ends before the day on which this amendment receives royal assent [December 16, 2014] that would, in the absence of this section, be precluded because of the time references in subsection 152(4) of the Act is to be made to the extent necessary to take into account this amendment.

SECTION 93.2: [Non-resident corporation without share capital]

▶ 93.2(1) ◀

(1) Definitions. The definitions in this subsection apply in this section.

History: S. 93.2(1) was added by S.C. 2014, c. 39, s. 22(1), applicable in respect of taxation years of non-resident corporations that end after 1994 except that if a taxpayer elects in writing under s. 22(2) of the *Economic Action Plan 2014 Act, No. 2* [S.C. 2014, c. 39] and files the election with the Minister of National Revenue on or before the day that is the later of the taxpayer's filing-due date for the taxpayer's taxation year that includes the day on which the *Economic Action Plan 2014 Act, No. 2* [S.C. 2014, c. 39] receives royal assent [December 16, 2014] and the day that is one year after the day on which the *Economic Action Plan 2014 Act, No. 2* [S.C. 2014, c. 39] receives royal assent [December 16, 2015], then section 93.2 applies, in respect of the taxpayer, in respect of taxation years of non-resident corporations that end after July 12, 2013.

In addition, any assessment of a taxpayer's tax, interest and penalties payable under the Act for any taxation year that ends before the day on which this amendment receives royal assent [December 16, 2014] that would, in the absence of this section, be precluded because of the time references in subsection 152(4) of the Act is to be made to the extent necessary to take into account this amendment.

"equity interest" —"equity interest", in a non-resident corporation without share capital, means any right, whether absolute or contingent, conferred by the non-resident corporation to receive, either immediately or in the future, an amount that can reasonably be regarded as all or any part of the capital, revenue or income of the non-resident corporation, but does not include a right as creditor.

"non-resident corporation without share capital" —"non-resident corporation without share capital" means a non-resident corporation that, determined without reference to this section, does not have capital divided into shares.

► 93.2(2) ◄

(2) Non-resident corporation without share capital. For the purposes of this Act,

(*a*) equity interests in a non-resident corporation without share capital that have identical rights and obligations, determined without reference to proportionate differences in all of those rights and obligations, are deemed to be shares of a separate class of the capital stock of the corporation;

(*b*) the corporation is deemed to have 100 issued and outstanding shares of each class of its capital stock;

(*c*) each person or partnership that holds, at any time, an equity interest in a particular class of the capital stock of the corporation is deemed to own, at that time, that number of shares of the particular class that is equal to the proportion of 100 that

(i) the fair market value, at that time, of all the equity interests of the particular class held by the person or partnership

is of

(ii) the fair market value, at that time, of all the equity interests of the particular class; and

(*d*) shares of a particular class of the capital stock of the corporation are deemed to have rights and obligations that are the same as those of the corresponding equity interests.

History: S. 93.2(2) was added by S.C. 2014, c. 39, s. 22(1), applicable in respect of taxation years of non-resident corporations that end after 1994 except that if a taxpayer elects in writing under s. 22(2) of the *Economic Action Plan 2014 Act, No. 2* [S.C. 2014, c. 39] and files the election with the Minister of National Revenue on or before the day that is the later of the taxpayer's filing-due date for the taxpayer's taxation year that includes the day on which the *Economic Action Plan 2014 Act, No. 2* [S.C. 2014, c. 39] receives royal assent [December 16, 2014] and the day that is one year after the day on which the *Economic Action Plan 2014 Act, No. 2* [S.C. 2014, c. 39] receives royal assent [December 16, 2015], then section 93.2 applies, in respect of the taxpayer, in respect of taxation years of non-resident corporations that end after July 12, 2013.

In addition, any assessment of a taxpayer's tax, interest and penalties payable under the Act for any taxation year that ends before the day on which this amendment receives royal assent [December 16, 2014] that would, in the absence of this section, be precluded because of the time references in subsection 152(4) of the Act is to be made to the extent necessary to take into account this amendment.

► 93.2(3) ◄

(3) Non-resident corporation without share capital. For the purposes of section 51, subsection 85.1(3), section 86 and paragraph 95(2)(*c*),

(*a*) subject to paragraph (*b*), if at any time a taxpayer resident in Canada or a foreign affiliate of the taxpayer (in this subsection referred to as the "vendor") disposes of capital property that is shares of the capital stock of a foreign affiliate of the taxpayer, or a debt obligation owing to the taxpayer by the affiliate, to — or exchanges the shares or debt for shares of the capital stock of — a non-resident corporation without share capital, that is immediately after that time a foreign affiliate of the taxpayer, in a manner that increases the fair market value of a class of shares of the capital stock of the non-resident corporation, the non-resident corporation is deemed to have issued, and the vendor is deemed to have received, new shares of the class as consideration in respect of the disposition or exchange; and

(*b*) if the taxpayer elects under this paragraph and files the election in writing with the Minister on or before its filing-due date for the taxation year that includes the day on which the disposition or exchange occurs, paragraph (*a*) does not apply to the disposition or exchange.

History: S. 93.2(3) was added by S.C. 2014, c. 39, s. 22(1), applicable in respect of taxation years of non-resident corporations that end after 1994 except that

(*a*) if a taxpayer elects in writing under s. 22(2) of the *Economic Action Plan 2014 Act, No. 2* [S.C. 2014, c. 39] and files the election with the Minister of National Revenue on or before the day that is the later of the taxpayer's filing-due date for the taxpayer's taxation year that includes the day on which the *Economic Action Plan 2014 Act, No. 2* [S.C. 2014, c. 39] receives royal assent [December 16, 2014] and the day that is one year after the day on which the *Economic Action Plan 2014 Act, No. 2* [S.C. 2014, c. 39] receives royal assent [December 16, 2015], then section 93.2 applies, in respect of the taxpayer, in respect of taxation years of non-resident corporations that end after July 12, 2013;

(*b*) in respect of dispositions that occur before July 12, 2013, section 93.2 of the Act is to be read without reference to its subsection (3); and

(*c*) in respect of dispositions that occur after July 11, 2013 and before October 10, 2014, the reference in paragraph 93.2(3)(*b*) to the taxpayer's "filing-due date" is to be read as the filing-due date for the taxpayer's taxation year that includes the day on which the *Economic Action Plan 2014 Act, No. 2* [S.C. 2014, c. 39] receives royal assent [December 16, 2014].

In addition, any assessment of a taxpayer's tax, interest and penalties payable under the Act for any taxation year that ends before the day on which this amendment receives royal assent [December 16, 2014] that would, in the absence of this section, be precluded because of the time references in subsection 152(4) of the Act is to be made to the extent necessary to take into account this amendment.

SECTION 93.3: [Australian trust]

► 93.3(1) ◄

(1) Definition of "Australian trust". In this section, "Australian trust", at any time, means a trust in respect of which the following apply at that time:

(*a*) in the absence of subsection (3), the trust would be described in paragraph (*h*) of the definition "exempt foreign trust" in subsection 94(1);

(*b*) the trust is resident in Australia;

(*c*) the interest of each beneficiary under the trust is described by reference to units of the trust; and

(*d*) the liability of each beneficiary under the trust is limited by the operation of any law governing the trust.

History: S. 93.3(1) was added by S.C. 2014, c. 39, s. 22(1), deemed to have come into force on July 12, 2013. However, if a corporation resident in Canada and each other corporation resident in Canada that, at any time after 2005 and before July 12, 2013, was both related to the corporation and had a foreign affiliate (determined as if the reference in paragraph (*b*) of the definition "equity percentage" in subsection 95(4) to "any corporation" were a reference to "any corporation other than a corporation resident in Canada") that was beneficially interested in an Australian trust (as defined in subsection 93.3(1)), jointly elect in writing under s. 22(3) of the *Economic Action Plan 2014 Act, No. 2* [S.C. 2014, c. 39] and file the election with the Minister of National Revenue on or before the day that is one year after the day on which the *Economic Action Plan 2014 Act, No. 2* [S.C. 2014, c. 39] receives royal assent [December 16, 2015], then in respect of each corporation that has elected under s. 22(3) of the *Economic Action Plan 2014 Act, No. 2* [S.C. 2014, c. 39], s. 93.3(1) is deemed to have come into force on January 1, 2006.

In addition, any assessment of a taxpayer's tax, interest and penalties payable under the Act for any taxation year that ends before the day on which this amendment receives royal assent [December 16, 2014] that would, in the absence of this section, be precluded because of the time references in subsection 152(4) of the Act is to be made to the extent necessary to take into account this amendment.

▶ 93.3(2) ◀

(2) Conditions for subsection (3). Subsection (3) applies at any time to a taxpayer resident in Canada in respect of a trust if

(*a*) a non-resident corporation is at that time beneficially interested in the trust;

(*b*) the non-resident corporation is at that time a foreign affiliate of the taxpayer in respect of which the taxpayer has a qualifying interest;

(*c*) the trust is at that time an Australian trust;

(*d*) the total fair market value at that time of all fixed interests (in this section as defined in subsection 94(1)) of a class in the trust held by the non-resident corporation, or persons or partnerships that do not deal at arm's length with the non-resident corporation, is at least 10% of the total fair market value at that time of all fixed interests of the class; and

(*e*) unless the non-resident corporation first acquires a beneficial interest in the trust at that time, immediately before that time (referred to in this paragraph as the "preceding time") subsection (3) applied

(i) to the taxpayer in respect of the trust, or

(ii) to a corporation resident in Canada, that at the preceding time did not deal at arm's length with the taxpayer, in respect of the trust.

History: S. 93.3(2) was added by S.C. 2014, c. 39, s. 22(1), deemed to have come into force on July 12, 2013. However, if a corporation resident in Canada and each other corporation resident in Canada that, at any time after 2005 and before July 12, 2013, was both related to the corporation and had a foreign affiliate (determined as if the reference in paragraph (*b*) of the definition "equity percentage" in subsection 95(4) to "any corporation" were a reference to "any corporation other than a corporation resident in Canada") that was beneficially interested in an Australian trust (as defined in subsection 93.3(1)), jointly elect in writing under s. 22(3) of the *Economic Action Plan 2014 Act, No. 2* [S.C. 2014, c. 39] and file the election with the Minister of National Revenue on or before the day that is one year after the day on which the *Economic Action Plan 2014 Act, No. 2* [S.C. 2014, c. 39] receives royal assent [December 16, 2015], then in respect of each corporation that has elected under s. 22(3) of the *Economic Action Plan 2014 Act, No. 2* [S.C. 2014, c. 39], s. 93.3(2) is deemed to have come into force on January 1, 2006.

In addition, any assessment of a taxpayer's tax, interest and penalties payable under the Act for any taxation year that ends before the day on which this amendment receives royal assent [December 16, 2014] that would, in the absence of this section, be precluded because of the time references in subsection 152(4) of the Act is to be made to the extent necessary to take into account this amendment.

▶ 93.3(3) ◀

(3) Australian trusts. If this subsection applies at any time to a taxpayer resident in Canada in respect of a trust, the following rules apply at that time for the specified purposes:

(*a*) the trust is deemed to be a non-resident corporation that is resident in Australia and not to be a trust;

(*b*) each particular class of fixed interests in the trust is deemed to be a separate class of 100 issued shares, of the capital stock of the non-resident corporation, that have the same attributes as the interests of the particular class;

(*c*) each beneficiary under the trust is deemed to hold the number of shares of each separate class described in paragraph (*b*) equal to the proportion of 100 that the fair market value at that time of that beneficiary's fixed interests in the corresponding particular class of fixed interests in the trust is of the fair market value at that time of all fixed interests in the particular class;

(*d*) the non-resident corporation is deemed to be controlled by the taxpayer resident in Canada — a foreign affiliate of which is referred to in paragraph (2)(*b*) and is beneficially interested in the trust — that has the greatest equity percentage in the non-resident corporation;

(*e*) a particular foreign affiliate of the taxpayer in which the taxpayer has a direct equity percentage (as defined in subsection 95(4)) at a particular time, and that is not a controlled foreign affiliate of the taxpayer at that time, is deemed to be a controlled foreign affiliate of the taxpayer at that time if, at that time,

(i) the particular affiliate has an equity percentage (as defined in subsection 95(4)) in the foreign affiliate referred to in paragraph (2)(*b*), or

(ii) the particular affiliate is the foreign affiliate referred to in paragraph (2)(*b*); and

(*f*) section 94.2 does not apply to the taxpayer in respect of the trust.

History: S. 93.3(3) was added by S.C. 2014, c. 39, s. 22(1), deemed to have come into force on July 12, 2013. However, if a corporation resident in Canada and each other corporation resident in Canada that, at any time after 2005 and before July 12, 2013, was both related to the corporation and had a foreign affiliate (determined as if the reference in paragraph (*b*) of the definition "equity percentage" in subsection 95(4) to "any corporation" were a reference to "any corporation other than a corporation resident in Canada") that was beneficially interested in an Australian trust (as defined in subsection 93.3(1)), jointly elect in writing under s. 22(3) of the *Economic Action Plan 2014 Act, No. 2* [S.C. 2014, c. 39] and file the election with the Minister of National Revenue on or before the day that is one year after the day on which the *Economic Action Plan 2014 Act, No. 2* [S.C. 2014, c. 39] receives royal assent [December 16, 2015], then in respect of each corporation that has elected under s. 22(3) of the *Economic Action Plan 2014 Act, No. 2* [S.C. 2014, c. 39], s. 93.3(3) is deemed to have come into force on January 1, 2006.

In addition, any assessment of a taxpayer's tax, interest and penalties payable under the Act for any taxation year that ends before the day on which this amendment receives royal assent [December 16, 2014] that would, in the absence of this section, be precluded because of the time references in subsection 152(4) of the Act is to be made to the extent necessary to take into account this amendment.

▶ 93.3(4) ◀

(4) Specified purposes. For the purposes of subsection (3), the specified purposes are

(*a*) the determination, in respect of an interest in an Australian trust, of the Canadian tax results (as defined in subsection 261(1)) of the taxpayer resident in Canada referred to in subsection (3) for a taxation year in respect of shares of the capital stock of a foreign affiliate of the taxpayer;

(*b*) the filing obligations of the taxpayer under section 233.4; and

(*c*) if the taxpayer is a corporation resident in Canada, the application of section 212.3 in respect of an investment (as defined in subsection 212.3(10)) by the taxpayer.

History: S. 93.3(4) was added by S.C. 2014, c. 39, s. 22(1), deemed to have come into force on July 12, 2013. However, if a corporation resident in Canada and each other corporation resident in Canada that, at any time after 2005 and before July 12, 2013, was both related to the corporation and had a foreign affiliate (determined as if the reference in paragraph (*b*) of the definition "equity percentage" in subsection 95(4) to "any corporation" were a reference to "any corporation other than a corporation resident in Canada") that was beneficially interested in an Australian trust (as defined in subsection 93.3(1)), jointly elect in writing under s. 22(3) of the *Economic Action Plan 2014 Act, No. 2* [S.C. 2014, c. 39] and file the election with the Minister of National Revenue on or before the day that is one year after the day on which the *Economic Action Plan 2014 Act, No. 2* [S.C. 2014, c. 39] receives royal assent [December 16, 2015], then in respect of each corporation that has elected under s. 22(3) of the *Economic Action Plan 2014 Act, No. 2* [S.C. 2014, c. 39], s. 93.3(4) is deemed to have come into force on January 1, 2006.

In addition, any assessment of a taxpayer's tax, interest and penalties payable under the Act for any taxation year that ends before the day on which this amendment receives royal assent [December 16, 2014] that would, in the absence of this section, be precluded because of the time references in subsection 152(4) of the Act is to be made to the extent necessary to take into account this amendment.

► 93.3(5) ◄

(5) Mergers. For the purposes of this section,

(*a*) if there has been an amalgamation to which subsection 87(1) applies, the new corporation referred to in that subsection is deemed to be the same corporation as, and a continuation of, each predecessor corporation referred to in that subsection; and

(*b*) if there has been a winding-up to which subsection 88(1) applies, the parent referred to in that subsection is deemed to be the same corporation as, and a continuation of, the subsidiary referred to in that subsection.

History: S. 93.3(5) was added by S.C. 2014, c. 39, s. 22(1), deemed to have come into force on July 12, 2013. However, if a corporation resident in Canada and each other corporation resident in Canada that, at any time after 2005 and before July 12, 2013, was both related to the corporation and had a foreign affiliate (determined as if the reference in paragraph (*b*) of the definition "equity percentage" in subsection 95(4) to "any corporation" were a reference to "any corporation other than a corporation resident in Canada") that was beneficially interested in an Australian trust (as defined in subsection 93.3(1)), jointly elect in writing under s. 22(3) of the *Economic Action Plan 2014 Act, No. 2* [S.C. 2014, c. 39] and file the election with the Minister of National Revenue on or before the day that is one year after the day on which the *Economic Action Plan 2014 Act, No. 2* [S.C. 2014, c. 39] receives royal assent [December 16, 2015], then in respect of each corporation that has elected under s. 22(3) of the *Economic Action Plan 2014 Act, No. 2* [S.C. 2014, c. 39], s. 93.3(5)

(*a*) is deemed to have come into force on January 1, 2006; and

(*b*) before July 12, 2013, s. 93.3 is to be read as if it contained the following after subsection (5):

"(6) For the purpose of determining whether a non-resident corporation is a foreign affiliate of a corporation resident in Canada for the purposes of this section, if, based on the assumptions contained in paragraph 96(1)(*c*), at any time shares of a class of the capital stock of a corporation are owned by a partnership or are deemed under this subsection to be owned by a partnership, then each member of the partnership is deemed to own at that time the number of those shares that is equal to the proportion of all those shares that

(*a*) the fair market value of the member's interest in the partnership at that time

is of

(*b*) the fair market value of all members' interests in the partnership at that time."

In addition, any assessment of a taxpayer's tax, interest and penalties payable under the Act for any taxation year that ends before the day on which this amendment receives royal assent [December 16, 2014] that would, in the absence of this section, be precluded because of the time references in subsection 152(4) of the Act is to be made to the extent necessary to take into account this amendment.

SECTION 94: [Non-resident trusts]

► 94(1) ◄

(1) Definitions. The following definitions apply in this section and section 94.2.

History: S. 94(1) was replaced by S.C. 2013, c. 34, s. 7(1), applicable to taxation years that end after 2006, except that subsections 94(1) to (15) also apply to the particular taxation year of a trust that ends after 2000 and before 2007, and to each subsequent taxation year of the trust that ends before 2007, and to each taxation year of the beneficiaries under, and contributors to, the trust in which such a trust taxation year ends, if the trust elects to have section 94 apply to the particular taxation year by filing the election in writing with the Minister of National Revenue on or before the trust's filing-due date for the trust's taxation year that includes June 26, 2013.

If

(i) an election or form referred to in section 94 would otherwise be required to be filed before October 24, 2013 [120 days after royal assent], it is deemed to have been filed with the Minister of National Revenue on a timely basis if it is filed with the Minister of National Revenue within 365 days after June 26, 2013, and

(ii) a trust's return of income for a taxation year throughout which it was deemed by subsection 94(3) to be resident in Canada for the purpose of computing its income (or was deemed by paragraph 94(3)(*f*) to exist) would otherwise be required to be filed before October 24, 2013 [120 days after royal assent] it is deemed to have been filed, for the purposes of section 162 of the Act, with the Minister of National Revenue on a timely basis if it is filed with the Minister of National Revenue within 365 days after June 26, 2013 (however, this subparagraph does not apply in respect of a return of income for a taxation year that ends before June 26, 2013 and for which the trust was deemed resident in Canada by section 94 of the Act as it read before the amendments by S.C. 2013, c. 34, s. 7).

Notwithstanding subsection 152(4) of the Act, the Minister of National Revenue may reassess a trust for its particular taxation year in respect of which it elects under the election above and in respect of each of its subsequent taxation years that ends before 2007, tax, interest or penalties payable under Part I of the Act by the trust if

(*a*) the trust is deemed by subsection 94(3) to be resident in Canada for the purpose of computing its income for the particular taxation year; and

(*b*) on or before June 26, 2014 [the day that is 365 days after royal assent], the trust files with the Minister of National Revenue a prescribed form amending, as necessary, each of its returns for taxation years to which that election applies.

S. 94(1) formerly read:

(1) *Application of certain provisions to trusts not resident in Canada.* Where,

(*a*) at any time in a taxation year of a trust that is not resident in Canada or that, but for paragraph (*c*), would not be so resident, a person beneficially interested in the trust (in this section referred to as a "beneficiary") was

(i) a person resident in Canada,

(ii) a corporation or trust with which a person resident in Canada was not dealing at arm's length, or

(iii) a controlled foreign affiliate of a person resident in Canada, and

(*b*) at any time in or before the taxation year of the trust,

(i) the trust, or a non-resident corporation that would, if the trust were resident in Canada, be a controlled foreign affiliate of the trust, has, other than in prescribed circumstances, acquired property, directly or indirectly in any manner whatever, from

(A) a particular person who

(I) was the beneficiary referred to in paragraph (*a*), was related to that beneficiary or was the uncle, aunt, nephew or niece of that beneficiary,

(II) was resident in Canada at any time in the 18 month period before the end of that year or, in the case of a person who has ceased to exist, was resident in Canada at any time in the 18 month period before the person ceased to exist, and

(III) in the case of an individual, had before the end of that year been resident in Canada for a period of, or periods the total of which is, more than 60 months, or

(B) a trust or corporation that acquired the property, directly or indirectly in any manner whatever, from a particular person described in clause (A) with whom it was not dealing at arm's length

and the trust was not

(C) an *inter vivos* trust created at any time before 1960 by a person who at that time was a non-resident person,

(D) a testamentary trust that arose as a consequence of the death of an individual before 1976, or

(E) governed by a foreign retirement arrangement, or

(ii) all or any part of the interest of the beneficiary in the trust was acquired directly or indirectly by the beneficiary by way of

(A) purchase,

(B) gift, bequest or inheritance from a person referred to in clause (i)(A) or (B), or

(C) the exercise of a power of appointment by a person referred to in clause (i)(A) or (B),

the following rules apply for that taxation year of the trust:

(*c*) where the amount of the income or capital of the trust to be distributed at any time to any beneficiary of the trust depends on the exercise by any person of, or the failure by any person to exercise, any discretionary power,

(i) the trust is deemed for the purposes of this Part and sections 233.3 and 233.4 to be a person resident in Canada no part of whose taxable income is exempt because of section 149 from tax under this Part and whose taxable income for the year is the amount, if any, by which the total of

(A) the amount, if any, that would but for this subparagraph be its taxable income earned in Canada for the year,

(B) the amount that would be its foreign accrual property income for the year if

(I) except for the purpose of applying subsections 104(4) to (5.2) to days after 1998 that are determined under subsection 104(4), the trust were a non-resident corporation all the shares of which were owned by a person who was resident in Canada,

(II) the description of A in the definition "foreign accrual property income" in subsection 95(1) were, in respect of dividends received after 1998, read without reference to paragraph (*b*) of that description,

(III) the descriptions of B and E in that definition were, in respect of dispositions that occur after 1998, read without reference to "other than dispositions of excluded property to which none of paragraphs (2)(*c*), (*d*) and (*e*) apply",

(IV) the value of C in that definition were nil, and

(V) for the purposes of computing the trust's foreign accrual property income, the consequences of the application of subsections 104(4) to (5.2) applied in respect of days after 1998 that are determined under subsection 104(4),

(C) the amount, if any, by which the total of all amounts each of which is an amount required by subsection 91(1) or (3) to be included in computing its income for the year exceeds the total of all amounts each of which is an amount deducted by it for that year under subsection 91(2), (4) or (5), and

(D) the amount, if any, required by section 94.1 to be included in computing its income for the year,

exceeds

(E) the amount, if any, by which the total of all amounts each of which is an amount deducted by it under subsection 91(2), (4) or (5) in computing its income for the year exceeds the total of all amounts each of which is an amount included in computing its income for the year because of subsection 91(1) or (3), and

(ii) for the purposes of section 126,

(A) the amount that would be determined under subparagraph (i) in respect of the trust for the year, if that subparagraph were read without reference to clause (i)(A), is deemed to be income of the trust for the year from sources in the country other than Canada in which the trust would, but for subparagraph (i), be resident, and

(B) any income or profits tax paid by the trust for the year (other than any tax paid because of this section), to the extent that it can reasonably be regarded as having been paid in respect of that income, is deemed to be non-business income tax paid by the trust to the government of that country, and

(*d*) in any other case, for the purposes of subsections 91(1) to (4) and sections 95 and 233.4,

(i) the trust shall, with respect to any beneficiary under the trust the fair market value of whose beneficial interest in the trust is not less than 10% of the total fair market value of all beneficial interests in the trust, be deemed to be a non-resident corporation that is controlled by the beneficiary,

(ii) the trust shall be deemed to be a non-resident corporation having a capital stock of a single class divided into 100 issued shares, and

(iii) each beneficiary under the trust shall be deemed to own at any time the number of the issued shares that is equal to the proportion of 100 that

(A) the fair market value at that time of the beneficiary's beneficial interest in the trust

is of

(B) the fair market value at that time of all beneficial interests in the trust.

Related Sections: S. 233.3 Reporting requirements; s. 233.4 Reporting entity.

Canadian Tax Foundation: Harris et al., *The Long and Winding Road: Sections 94, 94.1, and 94.2*, 2013 Conference Report 23:1–60; Haney, *Current Cases: Tax Court of Canada — Trust Residence: A Significant Departure or a Cautionary Tale? Garron Family Trust et al. v. The Queen (2009 DTC 1287)*, 2009 Canadian Tax Journal 4:864–870; Gagnon, *The New Non-Resident Trust Rules*, 2007 Conference Report 21:1–25; Innes and Dobrev, *Observations on Section 94*, 2006 Conference Report 29:1–54; Roth, *Canadian Taxation of Non-Resident Trusts: A Critical Review of Section 94 of the Income Tax Act*, 2004 Canadian Tax Journal 2:329–427; Bowman, *Non-Resident Trusts Update: Living with the New Section 94*, 2003 Conference Report 19:1–60; Emes, *The New Non-Resident Trust Rules*, 2002 Prairie Provinces Tax Conference 13:1–48; Cadesky et al., *Amendments to Taxation of Non-Resident Trusts: An Update*, 2001 Conference Report 20:1–43; Cadesky and Chow, *Amendments to Taxation of Non-Resident Trusts*, 2000 Conference Report 34:1–72; Fortin, *Strangers in Strange Lands: The Hidden Traps of Offshore Trusts*, 1999 Conference Report 40:1–68; Goodman, *Offshore Tax Planning: Beyond the Basics*, 1996 Conference Report 57:1–12.

"arm's length transfer" — "arm's length transfer", at any time by a person or partnership (referred to in this definition as the "transferor") means a transfer or loan (which transfer or loan is referred to in this definition as the "transfer") of property (other than restricted property) that is made at that time (referred to in this definition as the "transfer time") by the transferor to a particular person or partnership (referred to in this definition as the "recipient") if

(*a*) it is reasonable to conclude that none of the reasons (determined by reference to all the circumstances including the terms of a trust, an intention, the laws of a country or the existence of an agreement, a memorandum, a letter of wishes or any other arrangement) for the transfer is the acquisition at any time by any person or partnership of an interest as a beneficiary under a non-resident trust; and

(*b*) the transfer is

(i) a payment of interest, of a dividend, of rent, of a royalty or of any other return on investment, or any substitute for such a return on investment, in respect of a particular property held by the recipient, if the amount of the payment is not more than the amount that the transferor would have paid if the transferor dealt at arm's length with the recipient,

(ii) a payment made by a corporation on a reduction of the paid-up capital in respect of shares of a class of its capital stock held by the recipient, if the amount of the payment is not more than the lesser of the amount of the reduction in the paid-up capital and the consideration for which the shares were issued,

(iii) a transfer in exchange for which the recipient transfers or loans property to the transferor, or becomes obligated to transfer or loan property to the transferor, and for which it is reasonable to conclude

(A) having regard only to the transfer and the exchange, that the transferor would have been willing to make the transfer if the transferor dealt at arm's length with the recipient, and

(B) that the terms and conditions, and circumstances, under which the transfer was made would have been acceptable to the transferor if the transferor dealt at arm's length with the recipient,

(iv) a transfer made in satisfaction of an obligation referred to in subparagraph (iii) and for which it is reasonable to conclude

(A) having regard only to the transfer and the obligation, that the transferor would have been willing to make the transfer if the transferor dealt at arm's length with the recipient, and

(B) that the terms and conditions, and circumstances, under which the transfer was made would have been acceptable to the transferor if the transferor dealt at arm's length with the recipient,

(v) a payment of an amount owing by the transferor under a written agreement the terms and conditions of which, when entered into, were terms and conditions that, having regard only to the amount owing and the agreement, would have been acceptable to the transferor if the transferor dealt at arm's length with the recipient of the payment,

(vi) a payment made before 2002 to a trust, to a corporation controlled by a trust or to a partnership of which a trust is a majority-interest partner in repayment of or otherwise in respect of a loan made by a trust, corporation or partnership to the transferor, or

(vii) a payment made after 2001 to a trust, to a corporation controlled by the trust or to a partnership of which the trust is a majority-interest partner, in repayment of or otherwise in respect of a particular loan made by the trust, corporation or partnership to the transferor and either

(A) the payment is made before 2011 and they would have been willing to enter into the particular loan if they dealt at arm's length with each other, or

(B) the payment is made before 2005 in accordance with fixed repayment terms agreed to before June 23, 2000.

Editorial Note: The definition of arm's length transfer lists transactions which are considered to be arm's length transfers provided in all cases that it is reasonable to conclude that none of the reasons for the transfer is the acquisition of an interest in a non-resident trust. An arm's length transfer is not a contribution to a trust unless the transfer is in respect of restricted property.

The receipt of a return on an investment in the form of interest, dividends, rent or royalties is an arm's length transfer if the amount of the payment is not more than the recipient would have received if the transferor and the recipient dealt with each other on an arm's length basis. Payment by a corporation to a shareholder on the reduction of its paid-up capital will also constitute an arm's length transfer if the amount is not more than the lesser of the amount paid for the shares and the amount of the reduction in the paid-up capital.

An exchange of property is considered to be an "arm's length transfer" provided that it is reasonable to conclude that the exchange would have been made if the parties were dealing with each other on an arm's length basis.

Subparagraph *(b)*(v) of the definition enables a person to enter into ordinary commercial agreements without the person being a contributor for purposes of these rules.

History: S. 94(1), subparagraph *(b)*(vi) of the definition "arm's length transfer" was replaced by S.C. 2013, c. 40, s. 42(1), in force December 12, 2013, and formerly read:

(vi) a payment made before 2002 to a trust, to a corporation controlled by a trust or to a partnership of which a trust is a majority interest partner in repayment of or otherwise in respect of a loan made by a trust, corporation or partnership to the transferor, or

S. 94(1), the portion of subparagraph *(b)*(vii) of the definition "arm's length transfer" before clause (A) was replaced by S.C. 2013, c. 40, s. 42(2), in force December 12, 2013, and formerly read:

(vii) a payment made after 2001 to a trust, to a corporation controlled by the trust or to a partnership of which the trust is a majority interest partner, in repayment of or otherwise in respect of a particular loan made by the trust, corporation or partnership to the transferor and either

S. 94(1), the definition "arm's length transfer" was added by S.C. 2013, c. 34, s. 7(1), applicable to taxation years that end after 2006, except that if a trust elects, by notifying the Minister of National Revenue in writing on or before its filing-due date for its taxation year that includes June 26, 2013, in applying section 94 in respect of the trust, the definition "arm's length transfer" in subsection 94(1) does not include a loan or other transfer of property that is identified in the election and that is made in a taxation year that begins before 2003.

"beneficiary" —"beneficiary" under a trust includes

(*a*) a person or partnership that is beneficially interested in the trust; and

(*b*) a person or partnership that would be beneficially interested in the trust if the reference in subparagraph 248(25)(*b*)(ii) to

(i) "any arrangement in respect of the particular trust" were read as a reference to "any arrangement (including, for greater certainty, the terms or conditions of a share, or any arrangement in respect of a share, of the capital stock of a corporation that is beneficially interested in the particular trust) in respect of the particular trust", and

(ii) "the particular person or partnership might" were read as a reference to "the particular person or partnership becomes (or could become on the exercise of any discretion by any person or partnership), directly or indirectly, entitled to any amount derived, directly or indirectly, from the income or capital of the particular trust or might".

History: S. 94(1), the definition "beneficiary" was added by S.C. 2013, c. 34, s. 7(1), applicable to taxation years that end after 2006.

"closely held corporation" —"closely held corporation" at any time means a corporation, other than a corporation in respect of which

(*a*) there is at least one class of shares of its capital stock that includes shares prescribed for the purpose of paragraph 110(1)(*d*);

(*b*) it is reasonable to conclude that at that time, in respect of each class of shares described in paragraph (*a*), shares of the class are held by at least 150 shareholders each of whom holds shares of the class that have a total fair market value of at least $500; and

(*c*) it is reasonable to conclude that at that time in no case does a particular shareholder (or particular shareholder together with any other shareholder with whom the particular shareholder does not deal at arm's length) hold shares of the corporation

(i) that would give the particular shareholder (or the particular shareholder together with those other shareholders referred to in this paragraph) 10% or more of the votes that could be cast under any circumstance at an annual meeting of shareholders of the corporation if the meeting were held at that time, or

(ii) that have a fair market value of 10% or more of the fair market value of all of the issued and outstanding shares of the corporation.

History: S. 94(1), the definition "closely held corporation" was added by S.C. 2013, c. 34, s. 7(1), applicable to taxation years that end after 2006.

"connected contributor" —"connected contributor", to a trust at a particular time, means a contributor to the trust at the particular time, other than a person all of whose contributions to the trust made at or before the particular time were made at a non-resident time of the person.

Editorial Note: A non-resident trust is subject to the rules in s. 94 if there is either a "resident contributor" or a "resident beneficiary" of the trust. The definition of "connected contributor" is relevant in determining whether there is a resident beneficiary of the trust. The test in determining whether there is a "resident beneficiary" to the trust is twofold (see definition of resident beneficiary below). The first part of the test is the determination of whether there is a beneficiary who is resident in Canada. If it is established that there is a beneficiary who is resident in Canada, it is necessary to determine whether there is a connected contributor to the trust. A connected contributor to a trust is a "contributor" to the trust other than an individual whose contributions to the trust were made at a "non-resident time" of the person. If there is no connected contributor, the non-resident trust rules are not applicable. See, however, the editorial note to s. 94(10), which applies where a contributor becomes resident in Canada within 60 months after making a contribution. Amendments pursuant to the 2014 federal Budget eliminated the exception for immigration trusts for taxation years ending after Feb. 10, 2014 (with limited transitional provisions).

History: S. 94(1), the definition "connected contributor" was replaced by S.C. 2014, c. 39, s. 23(1), applicable to taxation years that end after February 10, 2014, except that the amendment to the definition "connected contributor" does not apply in respect of a trust to taxation years that end before 2015 if the following conditions are satisfied:

(a) no contributions are made to the trust after February 10, 2014 and before 2015; and

(b) if the trust were to have a particular taxation year that ended after 2013 and before February 11, 2014,

(i) the trust would be non-resident for the purpose of computing its income for the particular year, and

(ii) if the definitions "connected contributor" and "resident contributor" in subsection 94(1) were read for the particular year without reference to their paragraphs (*a*), the trust would be resident in Canada for the purpose of computing its income for the particular year.

The definition "connected contributor" formerly read:

"connected contributor"—"connected contributor" to a trust at a particular time means a contributor to the trust at the particular time, other than

(*a*) an individual (other than a trust) who was, at or before the particular time, resident in Canada for a period of, or periods the total of which is, not more than 60 months (but not including an individual who, before the particular time, was never non-resident); or

(*b*) a person all of whose contributions to the trust made at or before the particular time were made at a non-resident time of the person.

S. 94(1), the definition "connected contributor" was added by S.C. 2013, c. 34, s. 7(1), applicable to taxation years that end after 2006.

"contribution" —"contribution" to a trust by a particular person or partnership means

(*a*) a transfer or loan (other than an arm's length transfer) of property to the trust by the particular person or partnership;

(*b*) if a particular transfer or loan (other than an arm's length transfer) of property is made by the particular person or partnership as part of a series of transactions that includes another transfer or loan (other than an arm's length transfer) of property to the trust by another person or partnership, that other transfer or loan to the extent that it can reasonably be considered to have been made in respect of the particular transfer or loan; and

(*c*) if the particular person or partnership becomes obligated to make a particular transfer or loan (other than a transfer or loan that would, if it were made, be an arm's length transfer) of property as part of a series of transactions that includes another transfer or loan (other than an arm's length transfer) of property to the trust by another person or partnership, that other transfer or loan to the extent that it can reasonably be considered to have been made in respect of the obligation.

History: S. 94(1), the definition "contribution" was added by S.C. 2013, c. 34, s. 7(1), applicable to taxation years that end after 2006.

"contributor" —"contributor" to a trust at any time means a person (other than an exempt person but including a person that has ceased to exist) that, at or before that time, has made a contribution to the trust.

History: S. 94(1), the definition "contributor" was added by S.C. 2013, c. 34, s. 7(1), applicable to taxation years that end after 2006.

"electing contributor" —"electing contributor" at any time in respect of a trust means a resident contributor, to the trust, who has elected to have subsection (16) apply in respect of the contributor and the trust for a taxation year of the contributor that includes that time or that ends before that time and for all subsequent taxation years, if

(*a*) the election was in writing filed with the Minister on or before the contributor's filing-due date for the first taxation year of the contributor for which the election was to take effect (referred to in this definition as the "initial year"); and

(*b*) the election included both the trust's account number as assigned by the Minister and evidence that the contributor notified, no later than 30 days after the end of the trust's taxation year that ends in the initial year, the trust that the election would be made.

History: S. 94(1), the definition "electing contributor" was added by S.C. 2013, c. 34, s. 7(1), applicable to taxation years that end after 2006.

"electing trust" —"electing trust" in respect of a trust's particular taxation year means the trust, if the trust

(*a*) holds at any time in the particular taxation year, or in a prior taxation year of the trust throughout which it was deemed by subsection (3) to be resident in Canada for the purpose of computing its income, property that is at that time part of its non-resident portion;

(*b*) elects to have paragraph (3)(*f*) apply to it for

(i) its first taxation year

(A) throughout which it is deemed by subsection (3) to be resident in Canada for the purpose of computing its income, and

(B) in which it holds property that is at a time in the year part of its non-resident portion, and

(ii) all of its taxation years that end after its taxation year described in subparagraph (i); and

(*c*) files the election described in paragraph (*b*) in writing filed with the Minister with the trust's return of income for its taxation year described in subparagraph (*b*)(i).

Editorial Note: A trust may elect to be treated as though the non-resident portion of its property is, in effect, held in a separate trust. Upon such election, the property forming the non-resident portion is not subject to the deemed resident trust rules. An election has to be filed for the first taxation year throughout which the trust is deemed resident in Canada and in which it holds property that would form its non-resident portion. The election has to be filed in writing with the trust's income tax return for the relevant taxation year. It appears there is no mechanism for late filing or revoking the election.

History: S. 94(1), the definition "electing trust" was added by S.C. 2013, c. 34, s. 7(1), applicable to taxation years that end after 2006.

"exempt amount" —"exempt amount" in respect of a trust's particular taxation year means an amount that is

(*a*) paid or credited (in this definition within the meaning assigned by Part XIII) by the trust before 2004;

(*b*) paid or credited by the trust and referred to in paragraph 104(7.01)(*b*) in respect of the trust for the particular taxation year; or

(*c*) paid in the particular taxation year (or within 60 days after the end of the particular taxation year) by the trust directly to a beneficiary (determined without reference to subsection 248(25)) under the trust if

(i) the beneficiary is a natural person none of whose interests as a beneficiary under the trust was ever acquired for consideration,

(ii) the amount is described in subparagraph 212(1)(*c*)(i) and is not included in computing an exempt amount in respect of any other taxation year of the trust,

(iii) the trust was created before October 30, 2003, and

(iv) no contribution has been made to the trust on or after July 18, 2005.

History: S. 94(1), the definition "exempt amount" was added by S.C. 2013, c. 34, s. 7(1), applicable to taxation years that end after 2006.

Related Sections: S. 108(7) Interests acquired for consideration.

"exempt foreign trust" —"exempt foreign trust" at a particular time means

(*a*) a non-resident trust if

(i) each beneficiary under the trust at the particular time is

(A) an individual who, at the time that the trust was created, was, because of mental or physical infirmity, dependent on an individual who is a contributor to the trust or on an individual related to such a contributor (which beneficiary is referred to in this paragraph as an "infirm beneficiary"), or

(B) a person who is entitled, only after the particular time, to receive or otherwise obtain the use of any of the trust's income or capital,

(ii) at the particular time there is at least one infirm beneficiary who suffers from a mental or physical infirmity that causes the beneficiary to be dependent on a person,

(iii) each infirm beneficiary is, at all times that the infirm beneficiary is a beneficiary under the trust during the trust's taxation year that includes the particular time, non-resident, and

(iv) each contribution to the trust made at or before the particular time can reasonably be considered to have been, at the time that the contribution was made, made to provide for the maintenance of an infirm beneficiary during the expected period of the beneficiary's infirmity;

(*b*) a non-resident trust if

(i) the trust was created as a consequence of the breakdown of a marriage or common-law partnership of two particular individuals to provide for the maintenance of a beneficiary under the trust who was, during that marriage or common-law partnership,

(A) a child of both of those particular individuals (which beneficiary is referred to in this paragraph as a "child beneficiary"), or

(B) one of those particular individuals (which beneficiary is referred to in this paragraph as the "adult beneficiary"),

(ii) each beneficiary under the trust at the particular time is

(A) a child beneficiary under 21 years of age,

(B) a child beneficiary under 31 years of age who is enrolled at any time in the trust's taxation year that includes the particular time at an educational institution that is described in subclause (iv)(B)(I) or (II),

(C) the adult beneficiary, or

(D) a person who is entitled, only after the particular time, to receive or otherwise obtain the use of any of the trust's income or capital,

(iii) each beneficiary described in any of clauses (ii)(A) to (C) is, at all times that the beneficiary is a beneficiary under the trust during the trust's taxation year that includes the particular time, non-resident, and

(iv) each contribution to the trust, at the time that the contribution was made, was

(A) an amount paid by the particular individual other than the adult beneficiary that would be a support amount as defined in subsection 56.1(4) if it had been paid by that particular individual directly to the adult beneficiary, or

(B) made by one of those particular individuals or a person related to one of those particular individuals to provide for the maintenance of a child beneficiary while the child was either under 21 years of age or was under 31 years of age and enrolled at an educational institution located outside Canada that is

(I) a university, college or other educational institution that provides courses at a post-secondary school level, or

(II) an educational institution that provides courses designed to furnish a person with skills for, or improve a person's skills in, an occupation;

(*c*) a non-resident trust if

(i) at the particular time the trust is an agency of the United Nations,

(ii) at the particular time the trust owns and administers a university described in subparagraph (*a*)(iv) of the definition "qualified donee" in subsection 149.1(1),

(iii) at any time in the trust's taxation year that includes the particular time or at any time in the preceding calendar year Her Majesty in right of Canada has made a gift to the trust, or

(iv) the trust is established under the International Convention on the Establishment of an International Fund for Compensation for Oil Pollution Damage, 1992, or any protocol to it that has been ratified by the Government of Canada;

(*d*) a non-resident trust

(i) that throughout the particular period that began at the time it was created and ends at the particular time would be non-resident if this Act were read without reference to subsection (1) as that subsection read in its application to taxation years that include December 31, 2000,

(ii) that was created exclusively for charitable purposes and has been operated throughout the particular period exclusively for charitable purposes,

(iii) if the particular time is more than 24 months after the day on which the trust was created, in respect of which, there are at the particular time at least 20 persons (other than trusts) each of whom at the particular time

(A) is a contributor to the trust,

(B) exists, and

(C) deals at arm's length with at least 19 other contributors to the trust,

(iv) the income of which (determined in accordance with the laws described in subparagraph (v)) for each of its taxation years that ends at or before the particular time would, if the income were not distributed and the laws described in subparagraph (v) did not apply, be subject to an income or profits tax in the country in which it was resident in each of those taxation years, and

(v) that was, for each of its taxation years that ends at or before the particular time, exempt under the laws of the country in which it was resident from the payment of income or profits tax to the government of that country in recognition of the charitable purposes for which the trust is operated;

(*e*) a non-resident trust that throughout the trust's taxation year that includes the particular time is a trust governed by an employees profit sharing plan, a retirement compensation arrangement or a foreign retirement arrangement;

(*f*) a non-resident trust if

(i) throughout the particular period that began when it was created and ends at the particular time it has been operated exclusively for the purpose of administering or providing employee benefits in respect of employees or former employees, and

(ii) throughout the trust's taxation year that includes the particular time

(A) the trust is a trust governed by an employee benefit plan or is a trust described in paragraph (*a.1*) of the definition "trust" in subsection 108(1),

(B) the trust is maintained for the benefit of natural persons the majority of whom are non-resident, and

(C) no benefits are provided under the trust other than benefits in respect of qualifying services;

(*g*) a non-resident trust (other than a prescribed trust or a trust described in paragraph (*a.1*) of the definition "trust" in subsection 108(1)) that throughout the particular period that began when it was created and ends at the particular time

(i) has been resident in a particular country (other than Canada) the laws of which have, throughout the particular period,

(A) imposed an income or profits tax, and

(B) exempted the trust from the payment of all income tax, and all profits tax, to the government of that particular country in recognition of the purposes for which the trust is operated, and

(ii) has been operated exclusively for the purpose of administering or providing superannuation or pension benefits that are primarily in respect of services rendered in the particular country by natural persons who were non-resident at the time those services were rendered;

(*h*) a non-resident trust (other than a trust that elects, in writing filed with the Minister on or before the trust's filing-due date for the trust's taxation year that includes the particular time, not to be an exempt foreign trust under this paragraph for the taxation year in which the election is made and for each subsequent taxation year), if at the particular time

(i) the only beneficiaries who may for any reason receive, at or after the particular time and directly from the trust, any of the income or capital of the trust are beneficiaries that hold fixed interests in the trust, and

(ii) any of the following applies:

(A) there are at least 150 beneficiaries described in subparagraph (i) under the trust each of whose fixed interests in the trust have at the particular time a total fair market value of at least $500,

(B) all fixed interests in the trust are listed on a designated stock exchange and in the 30 days immediately preceding the particular time fixed interests in the trust were traded on a designated stock exchange on at least 10 days,

(C) each outstanding fixed interest in the trust

(I) was issued by the trust in exchange for consideration that was not less than 90% of the interest's proportionate share of the net asset value of the trust's property at the time of its issuance, or

(II) was acquired in exchange for consideration equal to the fair market value of the interest at the time of its acquisition, or

(D) the trust is governed by

(I) a Roth IRA, within the meaning of section 408A of the *Internal Revenue Code* of the United States, or

(II) a plan or arrangement that was created after September 21, 2007, that is subject to that Code and that the Minister agrees is substantially similar to a Roth IRA; or

(*i*) a trust that is at the particular time a prescribed trust.

History: S. 94(1), the definition "exempt foreign trust" was added by S.C. 2013, c. 34, s. 7(1), applicable to taxation years that end after 2006, except that

(*a*) clause (*f*)(ii)(C) of the definition "exempt foreign trust" in subsection 94(1) is, in respect of a trust for its taxation years that end before 2009, to be read as follows:

"(C) no benefits are provided under the trust, other than benefits in respect of

(I) qualifying services,

(II) particular services rendered before November 9, 2006, to an employer by an employee of the employer if the employee had on November 8, 2006, a right (whether immediate or future or whether absolute or contingent) to receive the benefits in respect of the particular services under an agreement in writing

1. that was entered into before November 9, 2006, and

2. if the employee was resident in Canada on November 9, 2006, a copy of which was filed with a prescribed form with the Minister by or on behalf of the employer no later than April 30 of the first calendar year that begins after November 9, 2006, or

(III) any combination of services that are described in subclause (I) or (II);"

(*b*) Subparagraph (*c*)(ii) of the definition "exempt foreign trust" in subsection 94(1) is, before January 1, 2012, to be read as follows:

"(ii) at the particular time the trust owns and administers a university described in paragraph (*f*) of the definition "total charitable gifts" in subsection 118.1(1),"

Related Sections: S. 108(3) Income of a trust in certain provisions.

"exempt person" — "exempt person" at any time means

(*a*) Her Majesty in right of Canada or a province;

(*b*) a person whose taxable income for the taxation year that includes that time is exempt from tax under this Part because of subsection 149(1);

(*c*) a trust resident in Canada or a Canadian corporation

(i) that was established by or arises under an Act of Parliament or of the legislature of a province, and

(ii) the principal activities of which at that time are to administer, manage or invest the monies of one or more pension funds or plans established under an Act of Parliament or of the legislature of a province;

(*d*) a trust or corporation established by or arising by reason of an Act of Parliament or the legislature of a province in connection with a scheme or program for the compensation of workers injured in an accident arising out of or in the course of their employment;

(*e*) a trust resident in Canada all the beneficiaries under which are at that time exempt persons;

(*f*) a Canadian corporation all the shares, or rights to shares, of which are held at that time by exempt persons;

(*g*) a Canadian corporation without share capital all the property of which is held at that time exclusively for the benefit of exempt persons;

(*h*) a partnership all the members of which are at that time exempt persons; and

(*i*) a trust or corporation that is at that time a mutual fund.

History: S. 94(1), the definition "exempt person" was added by S.C. 2013, c. 34, s. 7(1), applicable to taxation years that end after 2006.

"exempt service" — "exempt service" means a service rendered at any time by a person or partnership (referred to in this definition as the "service provider") to, for or on behalf of, another person or partnership (referred to in this definition as the "recipient") if

(*a*) the recipient is a trust and the service relates to the administration of the trust; or

(*b*) the following conditions apply in respect of the service, namely,

(i) the service is rendered in the service provider's capacity at that time as an employee or agent of the recipient,

(ii) in exchange for the service, the recipient transfers or loans property or becomes obligated to transfer or loan property, and

(iii) it is reasonable to conclude

(A) having regard only to the service and the exchange, that the service provider would be willing to carry out the service if the service provider were dealing at arm's length with the recipient, and

(B) that the terms, conditions and circumstances under which the service is provided would be acceptable to the service provider if the service provider were dealing at arm's length with the recipient.

History: S. 94(1), the definition "exempt service" was added by S.C. 2013, c. 34, s. 7(1), applicable to taxation years that end after 2006.

"fixed interest" —"fixed interest" at any time of a person or partnership in a trust means an interest of the person or partnership as a beneficiary (in this definition, determined without reference to subsection 248(25)) under the trust provided that no amount of the income or capital of the trust to be distributed at any time in respect of any interest in the trust depends on the exercise by any person or partnership of, or the failure by any person or partnership to exercise, any discretionary power, other than a power in respect of which it is reasonable to conclude that

(*a*) the power is consistent with normal commercial practice;

(*b*) the power is consistent with terms that would be acceptable to the beneficiaries under the trust if the beneficiaries were dealing with each other at arm's length; and

(*c*) the exercise of, or failure to exercise, the power will not materially affect the value of an interest as a beneficiary under the trust relative to the value of other such interests under the trust.

History: S. 94(1), the definition "fixed interest" was added by S.C. 2013, c. 34, s. 7(1), applicable to taxation years that end after 2006.

"joint contributor" —"joint contributor" at any time in respect of a contribution to a trust means, if more than one contributor has made the contribution, each of those contributors that is at that time a resident contributor to the trust.

History: S. 94(1), the definition "joint contributor" was added by S.C. 2013, c. 34, s. 7(1), applicable to taxation years that end after 2006.

"mutual fund" —"mutual fund" at a particular time means a mutual fund trust or mutual fund corporation (referred to in this definition as the "fund"), but does not include a fund in respect of which statements or representations have been made at or before the particular time — by the fund, or by a promoter or other representative of the fund, in respect of the acquisition or offering of an interest in the fund — that the taxes, if any, under this Part on the income, profit or gains for any particular year — in respect of property that is held by the fund and that is, or derives its value from, an interest in a trust — are less than, or are expected to be less than, the tax that would have been applicable under this Part if the income, profits or gains from the property had been earned directly by a person who acquires an interest in the fund.

History: S. 94(1), the definition "mutual fund" was added by S.C. 2013, c. 34, s. 7(1), applicable to taxation years that end after 2006.

"non-resident portion" —"non-resident portion" of a trust at any time means all property held by the trust to the extent that it is not at that time part of the resident portion of the trust.

History: S. 94(1), the definition "non-resident portion" was added by S.C. 2013, c. 34, s. 7(1), applicable to taxation years that end after 2006.

"non-resident time" —"non-resident time" of a person in respect of a contribution to a trust and a particular time means a time (referred to in this definition as the "contribution time") at which the person made a contribution to a trust that is before the particular time and at which the person was non-resident (or, if the person is not in existence at the contribution time, the person was non-resident throughout the 18 months before ceasing to exist), if the person was non-resident or not in existence throughout the period that began 60 months before the contribution time (or, if the person is an individual and the trust arose on and as a consequence of the death of the individual, 18 months before the contribution time) and ends at the earlier of

(*a*) the time that is 60 months after the contribution time, and

(*b*) the particular time.

Editorial Note: "Non-resident time" is relevant in determining whether there is a "connected contributor" to a trust. Generally, a non-resident time means a time at which a person was non-resident and made a contribution to a trust, if the person was non-resident throughout the period that began 60 months before the contribution and that ends 60 months after the contribution (see also the editorial note to s. 94(10)). For example, if A has been a non-resident of Canada for 60 months and makes a contribution to the trust at that time and remains a non-resident for a further 60 months, then that contribution would have been made during A's "non-resident time". If A makes the contribution to the trust having been a non-resident of Canada for 60 months, but subsequently establishes residence in Canada within 60 months of the date of contribution, the trust will be a deemed resident of Canada from the time of the contribution. The "non-resident time" is reduced to 18 months in certain circumstances, in particular if the contributor has ceased to exist (e.g., has died or been wound up).

History: S. 94(1), the definition "non-resident time" was added by S.C. 2013, c. 34, s. 7(1), applicable to taxation years that end after 2006, except that the expression "if the person is an individual and the trust arose on and as a consequence of the death of the individual, 18 months before the contribution time" in the definition "non-resident time" in subsection 94(1) is, in respect of contributions made before June 23, 2000, to be read as the expression "if the contribution time is before June 23, 2000, 18 months before the end of the trust's taxation year that includes the contribution time".

"promoter" —"promoter" of a trust or corporation at any time means

(*a*) a person or partnership that at or before that time establishes, organizes or substantially reorganizes the undertakings of the trust or corporation, as the case may be; and

(*b*) for the purposes of the definition "mutual fund" in this subsection, a person or partnership described by paragraph (*a*) and a person or partnership who in the course of a business

(i) sells or issues, or promotes the sale, issuance or acquisition of, an interest in a mutual fund corporation or mutual fund trust,

(ii) acts as an agent or advisor in respect of the sale or issuance, or the promotion of the sale, issuance or acquisition of, an interest in a mutual fund corporation or mutual fund trust, or

(iii) accepts, whether as a principal or agent, consideration in respect of an interest in a mutual fund corporation or mutual fund trust.

History: S. 94(1), the definition "promoter" was added by S.C. 2013, c. 34, s. 7(1), applicable to taxation years that end after 2006.

"qualifying services" —"qualifying services" means services that are

(*a*) rendered to an employer by an employee of the employer, which employee was non-resident throughout the period during which the services were rendered;

(*b*) rendered to an employer by an employee of the employer, other than services that were

(i) rendered primarily in Canada,

(ii) rendered primarily in connection with a business carried on by the employer in Canada, or

(iii) a combination of services described in subparagraphs (i) and (ii);

(*c*) rendered in a particular calendar month to an employer by an employee of the employer, which employee

(i) was resident in Canada throughout no more than 60 months during the 72-month period that ends at the end of the particular month, and

(ii) became a member of, or a beneficiary under, the plan or trust under which benefits in respect of the services may be provided (or a similar plan or trust for which the plan or the trust was substituted) before the end of the calendar month following the month in which the employee became resident in Canada; or

(*d*) any combination of services that are qualifying services determined without reference to this paragraph.

History: S. 94(1), the definition "qualifying services" was added by S.C. 2013, c. 34, s. 7(1), applicable to taxation years that end after 2006.

"resident beneficiary" —"resident beneficiary" under a trust at any time means a person (other than a person that is at that time a successor beneficiary under the trust or an exempt person) that is, at that time, a beneficiary under the trust if, at that time,

(*a*) the person is resident in Canada; and

(*b*) there is a connected contributor to the trust.

Editorial Note: Under s. 94(3), a non-resident trust is subject to the rules in s. 94 if the trust has a resident beneficiary. A resident beneficiary means a person who is a beneficiary of the trust and is resident in Canada, if, at the relevant time, there is a "connected contributor" to the trust (see the editorial note to the definition of "connected contributor"). A resident beneficiary excludes a "successor beneficiary" or an "exempt person". A successor beneficiary is a person who is a beneficiary under the trust if that person may only receive income or capital after the death of an individual who contributed to the trust or is related to a contributor to the trust (including an aunt, uncle or niece or nephew of the contributor). Exempt persons include Her Majesty in right of Canada or a province, persons whose income is exempt under s. 149(1) and certain trusts created in order to manage pension funds and workers' compensation.

History: S. 94(1), the definition "resident beneficiary" was added by S.C. 2013, c. 34, s. 7(1), applicable to taxation years that end after 2006.

"resident contributor" —"resident contributor", to a trust at any time, means a person that is, at that time, resident in Canada and a contributor to the trust, but — if the trust was created before 1960 by a person who was non-resident when the trust was created — does not include an individual (other than a trust) who has not, after 1959, made a contribution to the trust.

Editorial Note: A trust will be deemed to be resident in Canada under s. 94(3) if there is resident contributor to the trust. A resident contributor is, generally, a person who is resident in Canada and is a contributor to the trust. An individual will cease to be a resident contributor when the individual dies. Prior to 2014, an individual who had not been a resident of Canada for more than 60 months in aggregate was excluded from the definition of resident contributor, thus providing for so-called "immigration trusts". Pursuant to the 2014 federal Budget, the exception for immigration trusts was repealed for taxation years ending after Feb. 10, 2014 (with limited transitional provisions).

History: S. 94(1), the definition "resident contributor" was replaced by S.C. 2014, c. 39, s. 23(1), applicable to taxation years that end after February 10, 2014, except that the amendment to the definition "resident contributor" does not apply in respect of a trust to taxation years that end before 2015 if the following conditions are satisfied:

(a) no contributions are made to the trust after February 10, 2014 and before 2015; and

(b) if the trust were to have a particular taxation year that ended after 2013 and before February 11, 2014,

(i) the trust would be non-resident for the purpose of computing its income for the particular year, and

(ii) if the definitions "connected contributor" and "resident contributor" in subsection 94(1) were read for the particular year without reference to their paragraphs (*a*), the trust would be resident in Canada for the purpose of computing its income for the particular year.

The definition "resident contributor" formerly read:

"resident contributor" —"resident contributor" to a trust at any time means a person that is, at that time, resident in Canada and a contributor to the trust, but does not include

(*a*) an individual (other than a trust) who has not, at that time, been resident in Canada for a period of, or periods the total of which is, more than 60 months (other than an individual who, before that time, was never non-resident); or

(*b*) an individual (other than a trust) if

(i) the trust is an *inter vivos* trust that was created before 1960 by a person who was non-resident when the trust was created, and

(ii) the individual has not, after 1959, made a contribution to the trust.

S. 94(1), the definition "resident contributor" was added by S.C. 2013, c. 34, s. 7(1), applicable to taxation years that end after 2006.

"resident portion" —"resident portion" of a trust at a particular time means all of the trust's property that is

(*a*) property in respect of which a contribution has been made at or before the particular time to the trust by a contributor that is at the particular time a resident contributor, or if there is at the particular time a resident beneficiary under the trust a connected contributor, to the trust and, for the purposes of this paragraph,

(i) if a property is held by a contributor in common or in partnership immediately before the property is contributed to the trust, it is contributed by the contributor only to the extent that the contributor so held the property, and

(ii) if the contribution is a transfer described by any of paragraphs (2)(*a*), (*c*), (*d*) or (*f*), the property in respect of which the contribution has been made is deemed to be

(A) in respect of a transfer under paragraph (2)(*a*), property

(I) if clause (2)(*a*)(ii)(A) applies, the fair market value of which has increased because of a transfer or loan described by subparagraph (2)(*a*)(i), or

(II) if clause (2)(*a*)(ii)(B) applies, that would not otherwise be included in the resident portion of the trust, that is selected by the trust (or, failing which, is selected by the Minister) and that has a fair market value at least equal to the absolute value of a decrease in a liability or potential liability of the trust that arose because of a transfer or loan described by subparagraph (2)(*a*)(i),

(B) in respect of a transfer under paragraph (2)(*c*), property described by subparagraph (2)(*c*)(ii),

(C) in respect of a transfer under paragraph (2)(*d*), property acquired as a result of any undertaking including a guarantee, covenant or agreement given by a person or partnership other than the trust to ensure the repayment, in whole or in part, of a loan or other indebtedness incurred by the trust as described by paragraph (2)(*d*), and

(D) in respect of a transfer under paragraph (2)(*f*), property selected by the trust (or, failing which, is selected by the Minister) that has a fair market value at least equal to the fair market value of property deemed to be transferred to the trust as described by paragraph (2)(*f*);

(*b*) property that is acquired, at or before the particular time, by way of indebtedness incurred by the trust (referred to in this paragraph as the "subject property"), if

(i) all or part of the indebtedness is secured on property (other than the subject property) that is held in the trust's resident portion,

(ii) it was reasonable to conclude, at the time that the indebtedness was incurred, that the indebtedness would be repaid with recourse to any property (other than the subject property) held at any time in the trust's resident portion, or

(iii) a person resident in Canada or partnership of which a person resident in Canada is a member has become obligated, either absolutely or contingently, to effect any undertaking including a guarantee, covenant or agreement given to ensure the repayment, in whole or in part, of the indebtedness, or provided any other financial assistance in respect of the indebtedness;

(*c*) property to the extent that it is derived, directly or indirectly, in any manner whatever, from property described by any of paragraphs (*a*), (*b*) and (*d*), and, without limiting the generality of the foregoing, including property derived from the income (computed without reference to paragraph (16)(*f*) and subsections 104(6) and (12)) of the trust for a taxation year of the trust that ends at or before the particular time and property in respect of which an amount would be described at the particular time in respect of the trust by the definition "capital dividend account" in subsection 89(1) if the trust were at the particular time a corporation; and

(*d*) property to the extent that it is at the particular time substituted for a property described by any of paragraphs (*a*) to (*c*).

Editorial Note: On an elective basis, only the "resident portion" of a deemed resident trust is subject to these rules. In general terms, the property contributed to the trust by one or more residents of Canada is considered to be the resident portion of the trust property. This is contrasted with the "non-resident portion" of the trust property, which is property contributed by non-residents of Canada and in respect of which a trust has filed an election (an "electing trust"). If a non-resident contributor to a trust subsequently becomes a resident of Canada, then the formerly non-resident portion of the trust property may form part of the resident portion of the trust property. See also s. 94(10), which applies where a contributor becomes resident in Canada within 60 months after making a contribution.

History: S. 94(1), the definition "resident portion" was added by S.C. 2013, c. 34, s. 7(1), applicable to taxation years that end after 2006.

"restricted property" —"restricted property" of a person or partnership means property that the person or partnership holds and that is

(*a*) a share (or a right to acquire a share) of the capital stock of a closely held corporation if the share or right, or a property for which the share or right was substituted, was at any time acquired by the person or partnership as part of a transaction or series of transactions under which

(i) a specified share of the capital stock of a closely held corporation was acquired by any person or partnership in exchange for, as consideration for or upon the conversion of any property and the cost of the specified share to the person who acquired it was less than the fair market value of the specified share at the time of the acquisition, or

(ii) a share (other than a specified share) of the capital stock of a closely held corporation becomes a specified share of the capital stock of the corporation;

(*b*) an indebtedness or other obligation, or a right to acquire an indebtedness or other obligation, of a closely held corporation if

(i) the indebtedness, obligation or right, or property for which the indebtedness, obligation or right was substituted, became property of the person or partnership as part of a transaction or series of transactions under which

(A) a specified share of the capital stock of a closely held corporation was acquired by any person or partnership in exchange for, as consideration for or upon the conversion of any property and the cost of the specified share to the person who acquired it was less than the fair market value of the specified share at the time of the acquisition, or

(B) a share (other than a specified share) of a closely held corporation becomes a specified share of the capital stock of the corporation, and

(ii) the amount of any payment under the indebtedness, obligation or right (whether the right to the amount is immediate or future, absolute or contingent or conditional on or subject to the exercise of any discretion by any person or partnership) is, directly or indirectly, determined primarily by one or more of the following criteria:

(A) the fair market value of, production from or use of any of the property of the closely held corporation,

(B) gains or profits from the disposition of any of the property of the closely held corporation,

(C) income, profits, revenue or cash flow of the closely held corporation, or

(D) any other criterion similar to a criterion referred to in any of clauses (A) to (C); and

(*c*) property

(i) that the person or partnership acquired as part of a series of transactions described in paragraph (*a*) or (*b*) in respect of another property, and

(ii) the fair market value of which is derived in whole or in part, directly or indirectly, from that other property.

Editorial Note: Generally any contribution of "restricted property" to a non-resident trust, results in the application of the deemed resident trust rules. In general terms, restricted property includes shares and indebtedness of closely held corporations, and other property deriving its value from such property, acquired in the course of certain corporate reorganizations.

History: S. 94(1), the definition "restricted property" was added by S.C. 2013, c. 34, s. 7(1), applicable to taxation years that end after 2006.

"specified party" —"specified party" in respect of a particular person at any time means

(*a*) the particular person's spouse or common-law partner at that time;

(*b*) a corporation that at that time

(i) is a controlled foreign affiliate of the particular person or their spouse or common-law partner, or

(ii) would be a controlled foreign affiliate of a partnership, of which the particular person is a majority-interest partner, if the partnership were a person resident in Canada at that time;

(*c*) a person, or a partnership of which the particular person is a majority-interest partner, for which it is reasonable to conclude that the benefit referred to in subparagraph (8)(*a*)(iv) was conferred

(i) in contemplation of the person becoming after that time a corporation described by paragraph (*b*), or

(ii) to avoid or minimize a liability that arose, or that would otherwise have arisen, under this Part with respect to the particular person; or

(*d*) a corporation in which the particular person, or partnership of which the particular person is a majority-interest partner, is a shareholder if

(i) the corporation is at or before that time a beneficiary under a trust, and

(ii) the particular person or the partnership is a beneficiary under the trust solely because of the application of paragraph (*b*) of the definition "beneficiary" in this subsection to the particular person or the partnership in respect of the corporation.

History: S. 94(1), subparagraph (*b*)(ii) of the definition "specified party" was replaced by S.C. 2013, c. 40, s. 42(3), in force December 12, 2013, and formerly read:

(ii) would be a controlled foreign affiliate of a partnership, of which the particular person is a majority interest partner, if the partnership were a person resident in Canada at that time;

S. 94(1), the portion of paragraph (*c*) of the definition "specified party" before subparagraph (i) was replaced by S.C. 2013, c. 40, s. 42(4), in force December 12, 2013, and formerly read:

(*c*) a person, or a partnership of which the particular person is a majority interest partner, for which it is reasonable to conclude that the benefit referred to in subparagraph (8)(*a*)(iv) was conferred

S. 94(1), the portion of paragraph (*d*) of the definition "specified party" before subparagraph (i) was replaced by S.C. 2013, c. 40, s. 42(5), in force December 12, 2013, and formerly read:

(*d*) a corporation in which the particular person, or partnership of which the particular person is a majority interest partner, is a shareholder if

S. 94(1), the definition "specified party" was added by S.C. 2013, c. 34, s. 7(1), applicable to taxation years that end after 2006.

"specified share" —"specified share" means a share of the capital stock of a corporation other than a share that is a prescribed share for the purpose of paragraph 110(1)(*d*).

History: S. 94(1), the definition "specified share" was added by S.C. 2013, c. 34, s. 7(1), applicable to taxation years that end after 2006.

"specified time" —"specified time" in respect of a trust for a taxation year of the trust means

(*a*) if the trust exists at the end of the taxation year, the time that is the end of that taxation year; and

(*b*) in any other case, the time in that taxation year that is immediately before the time at which the trust ceases to exist.

History: S. 94(1), the definition "specified time" was added by S.C. 2013, c. 34, s. 7(1), applicable to taxation years that end after 2006.

"successor beneficiary" —"successor beneficiary" at any time under a trust means a person that is a beneficiary under the trust solely because of a right of the person to receive any of the trust's income or capital, if under that right the person may so receive that income or capital only on or after the death after that time of an individual who, at that time, is alive and

(*a*) is a contributor to the trust;

(*b*) is related to (in this definition including an uncle, aunt, niece or nephew of) a contributor to the trust; or

(*c*) would have been related to a contributor to the trust if every individual who was alive before that time were alive at that time.

History: S. 94(1), the definition "successor beneficiary" was added by S.C. 2013, c. 34, s. 7(1), applicable to taxation years that end after 2006.

"transaction" —"transaction" includes an arrangement or event.

History: S. 94(1), the definition "transaction" was added by S.C. 2013, c. 34, s. 7(1), applicable to taxation years that end after 2006.

"trust" —"trust" includes, for greater certainty, an estate.

History: S. 94(1), the definition "trust" was added by S.C. 2013, c. 34, s. 7(1), applicable to taxation years that end after 2006.

▶ 94(2) ◀

(2) Rules of application. In this section and section 94.2,

(*a*) a person or partnership is deemed to have transferred, at any time, a property to a trust if

(i) at that time the person or partnership transfers or loans property (other than by way of an arm's length transfer) to another person or partnership, and

(ii) because of that transfer or loan

(A) the fair market value of one or more properties held by the trust increases at that time, or

(B) a liability or potential liability of the trust decreases at that time;

(*b*) the fair market value, at any time, of a property deemed by paragraph (*a*) to be transferred at that time by a person or partnership is deemed to be the amount of the absolute value of the increase or decrease, as the case may be, referred to in subparagraph (*a*)(ii) in respect of the property, and if that time is after August 27, 2010, and the property that the person or partnership transfers or loans at that time is restricted property of the person or partnership, the property deemed by paragraph (*a*) to be transferred at that time to a trust is deemed to be restricted property transferred at that time to the trust;

(*c*) a person or partnership is deemed to have transferred, at any time, property to a trust if

(i) at that time the person or partnership transfers restricted property, or loans property other than by way of an arm's length transfer, to another person (referred to in this paragraph and paragraph (*c.1*) as the "intermediary"),

(ii) at or after that time, the trust holds property (other than property described by paragraph (14)(*b*)) the fair market value of which is derived in whole or in part, directly or indirectly, from property held by the intermediary, and

(iii) it is reasonable to conclude that one of the reasons the transfer or loan is made is to avoid or minimize a liability under this Part;

(*c*.1) the fair market value, at any time, of a property deemed by paragraph (*c*) to be transferred at that time by a person or partnership is deemed to be the fair market value of the property referred to in subparagraph (*c*)(i), and if that time is after October 24, 2012 and the property that the person or partnership transfers or loans to the intermediary is restricted property of the intermediary, the property deemed by paragraph (*c*) to be transferred at that time by the person or partnership to a trust is deemed to be restricted property transferred at that time to the trust throughout the period in which the intermediary holds the restricted property;

(*d*) if, at any time, a particular person or partnership becomes obligated, either absolutely or contingently, to effect any undertaking including a guarantee, covenant or agreement given to ensure the repayment, in whole or in part, of a loan or other indebtedness incurred by another person or partnership, or has provided any other financial assistance to another person or partnership,

(i) the particular person or partnership is deemed to have transferred, at that time, property to that other person or partnership, and

(ii) the property, if any, transferred to the particular person or partnership from the other person or partnership in exchange for the guarantee or other financial assistance is deemed to have been transferred to the particular person or partnership in exchange for the property deemed by subparagraph (i) to have been transferred;

(*e*) the fair market value at any time of a property deemed by subparagraph (*d*)(i) to have been transferred at that time to another person or partnership is deemed to be the amount at that time of the loan or indebtedness incurred by the other person or partnership to which the property relates;

(*f*) if, at any time after June 22, 2000, a particular person or partnership renders any service (other than an exempt service) to, for or on behalf of another person or partnership,

(i) the particular person or partnership is deemed to have transferred, at that time, property to that other person or partnership, and

(ii) the property, if any, transferred to the particular person or partnership from the other person or partnership in exchange for the service is deemed to have been transferred to the particular person or partnership in exchange for the property deemed by subparagraph (i) to have been transferred;

(*g*) each of the following acquisitions of property by a particular person or partnership is deemed to be a transfer of the property, at the time of the acquisition of the property, to the particular person or partnership from the person or partnership from which the property was acquired, namely, the acquisition by the particular person or partnership of

(i) a share of a corporation from the corporation,

(ii) an interest as a beneficiary under a trust (otherwise than from a beneficiary under the trust),

(iii) an interest in a partnership (otherwise than from a member of the partnership),

(iv) a debt owing by a person or partnership from the person or partnership, and

(v) a right (granted after June 22, 2000, by the person or partnership from which the right was acquired) to acquire or to be loaned property;

(*h*) the fair market value at any time of a property deemed by subparagraph (*f*)(i) to have been transferred at that time is deemed to be the fair market value at that time of the service to which the property relates;

(*i*) a person or partnership that at any time becomes obligated to do an act that would, if done, constitute the transfer or loan of a property to another person or partnership is deemed to have become obligated at that time to transfer or loan, as the case may be, property to that other person or partnership;

(*j*) in applying at any time the definition "non-resident time" in subsection (1), if a trust acquires property of an individual as a consequence of the death of the individual and the individual was immediately before death resident in Canada, the individual is deemed to have transferred the property to the trust immediately before the individual's death;

(*k*) a transfer or loan of property at any time is deemed to be made at that time jointly by a particular person or partnership and a second person or partnership (referred to in this paragraph as the "specified person") if

(i) the particular person or partnership transfers or loans property at that time to another person or partnership,

(ii) the transfer or loan is made at the direction, or with the acquiescence, of the specified person, and

(iii) it is reasonable to conclude that one of the reasons the transfer or loan is made is to avoid or minimize the liability, of any person or partnership, under this Part that arose, or that would otherwise have arisen, because of the application of this section;

(*k*.1) a transfer or loan of property made at any time on or after November 9, 2006, is deemed to be made at that time jointly by a particular person or partnership and a second person or partnership (referred to in this paragraph as the "specified person") if

(i) the particular person or partnership transfers or loans property at that time to another person or partnership, and

(ii) a purpose or effect of the transfer or loan may reasonably be considered to be to provide benefits in respect of services rendered by a person as an employee of the specified person (whether the provision of the benefits is because of a right that is immediate or future, absolute or contingent, or conditional on or subject to the exercise of any discretion by any person or partnership);

(*l*) a transfer or loan of property at any time is deemed to be made at that time jointly by a corporation and a person or partnership (referred to in this paragraph as the "specified person") if

(i) the corporation transfers or loans property at that time to another person or partnership,

(ii) the transfer or loan is made at the direction, or with the acquiescence, of the specified person,

(iii) that time is not, or would not be if the transfer or loan were a contribution of the specified person,

(A) a non-resident time of the specified person, or

(B) if the specified person is a partnership, a non-resident time of one or more members of the partnership, and

(iv) either

(A) the corporation is, at that time, a controlled foreign affiliate of the specified person, or would at that time be a controlled foreign affiliate of the specified person if the specified person were at that time resident in Canada, or

(B) it is reasonable to conclude that the transfer or loan was made in contemplation of the corporation becoming after that time a corporation described in clause (A);

(*m*) a particular person or partnership is deemed to have transferred, at a particular time, a particular property or particular part of it, as the case may be, to a corporation described in subparagraph (i) or a second person or partnership described in subparagraph (ii) if

(i) the particular property is a share of the capital stock of a corporation held at the particular time by the particular person or partnership, and as consideration for the disposition at or before the particular time of the share, the particular person or partnership received at the particular time (or became entitled at the particular time to receive) from the corporation a share of the capital stock of the corporation, or

(ii) the particular property (or property for which the particular property is substituted) was acquired, before the particular time, from the second person or partnership by any person or partnership, in circumstances that are described by any of subparagraphs (*g*)(i) to (v) (or would be so described if it applied at the time of that acquisition) and at the particular time,

(A) the terms or conditions of the particular property change,

(B) the second person or partnership redeems, acquires or cancels the particular property or the particular part of it,

(C) if the particular property is a debt owing by the second person or partnership, the debt or the particular part of it is settled or cancelled, or

(D) if the particular property is a right to acquire or to be loaned property, the particular person or partnership exercises the right;

(*n*) a contribution made at any time by a particular trust to another trust is deemed to have been made at that time jointly by the particular trust and by each person or partnership that is at that time a contributor to the particular trust;

(*o*) a contribution made at any time by a particular partnership to a trust is deemed to have been made at that time jointly by the particular partnership and by each person or partnership that is at that time a member of the particular partnership;

(*p*) subject to paragraph (*q*) and subsection (9), the amount of a contribution to a trust at the time it was made is deemed to be the fair market value, at that time, of the property that was the subject of the contribution;

(*q*) a person or partnership that at any time acquires a fixed interest in a trust (or a right, issued by the trust, to acquire a fixed interest in the trust) from another person or partnership (other than from the trust that issued the interest or the right) is deemed to have made at that time a contribution to the trust and the amount of the contribution is deemed to be equal to the fair market value at that time of the interest or right, as the case may be;

(*r*) a particular person or partnership that has acquired a fixed interest in a trust as a consequence of making a contribution to the trust — or that has made a contribution to the trust as a consequence of having acquired a fixed interest in the trust or a right described in paragraph (*q*) — is, for the purpose of applying this section at any time after the time that the particular person or partnership transfers the fixed interest or the right, as the case may be, to another person or partnership (which transfer is referred to in this paragraph as the "sale"), deemed not to have made the contribution in respect of the fixed interest, or right, that is the subject of the sale if

(i) in exchange for the sale, the other person or partnership transfers or loans, or becomes obligated to transfer or loan, property (which property is referred to in subparagraph (ii) as the "consideration") to the particular person or partnership, and

(ii) it is reasonable to conclude

(A) having regard only to the sale and the consideration that the particular person or partnership would be willing to make the sale if the particular person or partnership were dealing at arm's length with the other person or partnership, and

(B) that the terms and conditions made or imposed in respect of the exchange would be acceptable to the particular person or partnership if the particular person or partnership were dealing at arm's length with the other person or partnership;

(*s*) a transfer to a trust by a particular person or partnership is deemed not to be, at a particular time, a contribution to the trust if

(i) the particular person or partnership has transferred, at or before the particular time and in the ordinary course of business of the particular person or partnership, property to the trust,

(ii) the transfer is not an arm's length transfer, but would be an arm's length transfer if the definition "arm's length transfer" in subsection (1) were read without reference to paragraph (*a*) and subparagraphs (*b*)(i), (ii) and (iv) to (vii) of that definition,

(iii) it is reasonable to conclude that the particular person or partnership was the only person or partnership that acquired, in respect of the transfer, an interest as a beneficiary under the trust,

(iv) the particular person or partnership was required, under the securities law of a country or of a political subdivision of the country in respect of the issuance by the trust of interests as a beneficiary under the trust, to acquire an interest because of the particular person or partnership's status at the time of the transfer as a manager or promoter of the trust,

(v) at the particular time the trust is not an exempt foreign trust, but would be at that time an exempt foreign trust if it had not made an election under paragraph (*h*) of the definition "exempt foreign trust" in subsection (1), and

(vi) the particular time is before the earliest of

(A) the first time at which the trust becomes an exempt foreign trust,

(B) the first time at which the particular person or partnership ceases to be a manager or promoter of the trust, and

(C) the time that is 24 months after the first time at which the total fair market value of consideration received by the trust in exchange for interests as a beneficiary (other than the particular person or partnership's interest referred to in subparagraph (iii)) under the trust is greater than $500,000;

(*t*) a transfer, by a Canadian corporation of particular property, that is at a particular time a contribution by the Canadian corporation to a trust, is deemed not to be, after the particular time, a contribution by the Canadian corporation to the trust if

(i) the trust acquired the property before the particular time from the Canadian corporation in circumstances described in subparagraph (*g*)(i) or (iv),

(ii) as a result of a transfer (which transfer is referred to in this paragraph as the "sale") at the particular time by any person or partnership (referred to in this paragraph as the "seller") to another person or partnership (referred to in this paragraph as the "buyer") the trust

(A) no longer holds any property that is shares of the capital stock of, or debt issued by, the Canadian corporation, and

(B) no longer holds any property that is property the fair market value of which is derived in whole or in part, directly or indirectly, from shares of the capital stock of, or debt issued by, the Canadian corporation,

(iii) the buyer deals at arm's length immediately before the particular time with the Canadian corporation, the trust and the seller,

(iv) in exchange for the sale, the buyer transfers or becomes obligated to transfer property (which property is referred to in this paragraph as the "consideration") to the seller, and

(v) it is reasonable to conclude

(A) having regard only to the sale and the consideration that the seller would be willing to make the sale if the seller were dealing at arm's length with the buyer,

(B) that the terms and conditions made or imposed in respect of the exchange would be acceptable to the seller if the seller were dealing at arm's length with the buyer, and

(C) that the value of the consideration is not, at or after the particular time, determined in whole or in part, directly or indirectly, by reference to shares of the capital stock of, or debt issued by, the Canadian corporation;

(*u*) a transfer, before October 11, 2002, to a personal trust by an individual (other than a trust) of particular property is deemed not to be a contribution of the particular property by the individual to the trust if

(i) the individual identifies the trust in prescribed form filed with the Minister on or before the individual's filing-due date for the individual's 2003 taxation year (or a later date that is acceptable to the Minister), and

(ii) the Minister is satisfied that

(A) the individual (and any person or partnership not dealing at any time at arm's length with the individual) has never loaned or transferred, directly or indirectly, restricted property to the trust,

(B) in respect of each contribution (determined without reference to this paragraph) made before October 11, 2002, by the individual to the trust, none of the reasons (determined by reference to all the circumstances including the terms of the trust, an intention, the laws of a country or the existence of an agreement, a memorandum, a letter of wishes or any other arrangement) for the contribution was to permit or facilitate, directly or indirectly, the conferral at any time of a benefit (for greater certainty, including an interest as a beneficiary under the trust) on

(I) the individual,

(II) a descendant of the individual, or

(III) any person or partnership with whom the individual or descendant does not, at any time, deal at arm's length, and

(C) the total of all amounts each of which is the amount of a contribution (determined without reference to this paragraph) made before October 11, 2002, by the individual to the trust does not exceed the greater of

(I) 1% of the total of all amounts each of which is the amount of a contribution (determined without reference to this paragraph) made to the trust before October 11, 2002, and

(II) $500; and

(*v*) a loan made by a particular specified financial institution to a trust is deemed not to be a contribution to the trust if

(i) the loan is made on terms and conditions that would have been agreed to by persons dealing at arm's length, and

(ii) the loan is made by the specified financial institution in the ordinary course of the business carried on by it.

History: S. 94(2) was replaced by S.C. 2013, c. 34, s. 7(1), applicable to taxation years that end after 2006, except that paragraph 94(2)(*o*) is, in its application to a transfer that occurred before August 27, 2010 to be read as follows:

"(*o*) a contribution made at any time by a particular partnership to a trust is deemed to have been made at that time jointly by the particular partnership and by each person or partnership that is at that time a member of the particular partnership (other than a member of the particular partnership if the liability of the member as a member of the particular partnership is limited by operation of any law governing the partnership arrangement);"

S. 94(2) formerly read:

(2) *Rights and obligations.* Where paragraph (1)(*c*) is applicable to a trust, each person described in clause (1)(*b*)(i)(A) or (B) shall jointly and severally with the trust have the rights and obligations of the trust by virtue of Divisions I and J and shall be subject to the provisions of Part XV, but no amount in respect of taxes, penalties, costs and other amounts payable under this Act shall be recoverable from any such person except to the extent of

(*a*) amounts paid to the person by the trust or the payment of which from the trust the person is entitled to enforce; and

(*b*) amounts received by the person on the disposition of an interest in the trust.

Related Sections: S. 162(10.1) Additional penalty; s. 163(2.4) False statement or omission; s. 233.2 [Reporting for loans or transfers to non-resident trusts].

Tax Topics: No. 1705, NRT Rules: Harsher Than You Think.

▶ 94(3) ◀

(3) Liabilities of non-resident trusts and others. If at a specified time in a trust's particular taxation year (other than a trust that is, at that time, an exempt foreign trust) the trust is non-resident (determined without reference to this subsection) and, at that time, there is a resident contributor to the trust or a resident beneficiary under the trust,

(*a*) the trust is deemed to be resident in Canada throughout the particular taxation year for the purposes of

(i) section 2,

(ii) computing the trust's income for the particular taxation year,

(iii) applying subsections 104(13.1) to (28) and 107(2.1), in respect of the trust and a beneficiary under the trust,

(iv) applying clause 53(2)(*h*)(i.1)(B), the definition "non-resident entity" in subsection 94.1(2), subsection 107(2.002) and section 115, in respect of a beneficiary under the trust,

(v) paragraph (*c*) and subsection 111(9),

(vi) determining an obligation of the trust to file a return under section 233.3 or 233.4,

(vii) determining the rights and obligations of the trust under Divisions I and J,

(viii) determining the liability of the trust for tax under Part I, and under Part XIII on amounts paid or credited (in this paragraph having the meaning assigned by Part XIII) to the trust,

(ix) applying Part XIII in respect of an amount (other than an exempt amount) paid or credited by the trust to any person, and

(x) determining whether a foreign affiliate of a taxpayer (other than the trust) is a controlled foreign affiliate of the taxpayer;

(*b*) no deduction shall be made under subsection 20(11) by the trust in computing its income for the particular taxation year, and for the purposes of applying subsection 20(12) and section 126 to the trust for the particular taxation year

(i) in determining the non-business-income tax (in this paragraph as defined by subsection 126(7)) paid by the trust for the particular taxation year, paragraph (*b*) of the definition "non-business-income tax" does not apply, and

(ii) if, at that specified time, the trust is resident in a country other than Canada,

(A) the trust's income for the particular taxation year (other than income — not including dividends or interest — from sources in Canada) is deemed to be from sources in that country and not to be from any other source, and

(B) the business-income tax (in this paragraph as defined by subsection 126(7)), and the non-business-income tax, paid by the trust for the particular taxation year are deemed to have been paid by the trust to the government of that country and not to any other government;

Related Sections: 94(16) Attribution to electing contributors; 104(22) Designation in respect of foreign source income; 104(22.1) Foreign tax deemed paid by beneficiary; 104(22.2) Recalculation of trust's foreign source income; 104(22.3) Recalculation of trust's foreign tax.

(*c*) if the trust was non-resident throughout its taxation year (referred to in this paragraph as the "preceding year") immediately preceding the particular taxation year, the trust is deemed to have

(i) immediately before the end of the preceding year, disposed of each property (other than property described in any of subparagraphs 128.1(1)(*b*)(i) to (iv)) held by the trust at that time for proceeds of disposition equal to its fair market value at that time, and

(ii) at the beginning of the particular taxation year, acquired each of those properties so disposed of at a cost equal to its proceeds of disposition;

(*d*) each person that at any time in the particular taxation year is a resident contributor to the trust (other than an electing contributor in respect of the trust at the specified time) or a resident beneficiary under the trust

(i) has jointly and severally, or solidarily, with the trust and with each other such person, the rights and obligations of the trust in respect of the particular taxation year under Divisions I and J, and

(ii) is subject to Part XV in respect of those rights and obligations;

(*e*) each person that at any time in the particular taxation year is a beneficiary under the trust and was a person from whom an amount would be recoverable at the end of the trust's 2006 taxation year under subsection (2) (as it read in its application to taxation years that end before 2007) in respect of the trust if the person had received before the trust's 2007 taxation year amounts described under paragraph (2)(*a*) or (*b*) in respect of the trust (as those paragraphs read in their application to taxation years that end before 2007)

(i) has, to the extent of the person's recovery limit for the year, jointly and severally, or solidarily, with the trust and with each other such person, the rights and obligations of the trust in respect of the taxation years, of the trust, that end before 2007 under Divisions I and J, and

(ii) is, to the extent of the person's recovery limit for the year, subject to Part XV in respect of those rights and obligations;

(*f*) if the trust (referred to in this paragraph as the "particular trust") is an electing trust in respect of the particular taxation year,

(i) an *inter vivos* trust (in this paragraph referred to as the "non-resident portion trust") is deemed for the purposes of this Act (other than for the purposes of subsection 104(2))

(A) to be created at the first time at which the particular trust exists in its first taxation year in respect of which the particular trust is an electing trust, and

(B) to continue in existence until the earliest of

(I) the time at which the particular trust ceases to be resident in Canada because of subsection (5) or (5.1),

(II) the time at which the particular trust ceases to exist, and

(III) the time at which the particular trust becomes resident in Canada otherwise than because of this subsection,

(ii) all of the particular trust's property that is part of the particular trust's non-resident portion is deemed to be the property of the non-resident portion trust and not to be, except for the purposes of this paragraph and the definition "electing trust" in subsection (1), the particular trust's property,

(iii) the terms and conditions of, and rights and obligations of beneficiaries under, the particular trust (determined by reference to all the circumstances including the terms of a trust, an intention, the laws of a country or the existence of an agreement, a memorandum, a letter of wishes or any other arrangement) are deemed to be the terms and conditions of, and rights and obligations of beneficiaries under, the non-resident portion trust,

(iv) for greater certainty

(A) the trustees of the particular trust are deemed to be the trustees of the non-resident portion trust,

(B) the beneficiaries under the particular trust are deemed to be the beneficiaries under the non-resident portion trust, and

(C) the non-resident portion trust is deemed not to have a resident contributor or connected contributor to it,

(v) the non-resident portion trust is deemed to be, without affecting the liability of its trustees for their own income tax, in respect of its property an individual,

(vi) if all or part of a property becomes at a particular time part of the particular trust's non-resident portion and immediately before that time the property or that part, as the case may be, was part of its resident portion, the particular trust is deemed to have transferred at the particular time the property or that part, as the case may be, to the non-resident portion trust,

(vii) if all or part of a property becomes at a particular time part of the particular trust's resident portion and immediately before that time the property or that part, as the case may be, was part of its non-resident portion, the non-resident portion trust is deemed to have transferred at the particular time the property or that part, as the case may be, to the particular trust,

(viii) the particular trust and the non-resident portion trust are deemed at all times to be affiliated with each other and to not deal with each other at arm's length,

(ix) the particular trust

(A) has jointly and severally, or solidarily, with the non-resident portion trust, the rights and obligations of the non-resident portion trust in respect of any taxation year under Divisions I and J, and

(B) is subject to Part XV in respect of those rights and obligations, and

(x) if the non-resident portion trust ceases to exist at a particular time (for greater certainty, as determined by clause (i)(B))

(A) the non-resident portion trust is deemed, at the time (referred to in this subparagraph as the "disposition time") that is immediately before the time that is immediately before the particular time, to have

(I) in the case of each property of the non-resident portion trust that is property described in any of subparagraphs 128.1(1)(*b*)(i) to (iv), disposed of the property for proceeds of disposition equal to the cost amount to it of the property at the disposition time, and

(II) in the case of each other property of the non-resident portion trust, disposed of the property for proceeds of disposition equal to its fair market value of the property at the disposition time,

(B) the particular trust is deemed to have acquired, at the time that is immediately before the particular time, each property described in subclause (A)(I) or (II) at a cost equal to the proceeds determined under that subclause in respect of the property, and

(C) each person or partnership that is at the time immediately before the particular time a beneficiary under the non-resident portion trust is deemed

(I) at the disposition time to have disposed of the beneficiary's interest as a beneficiary under the non-resident portion trust for proceeds equal to the beneficiary's cost amount in the interest at the disposition time, and

(II) at the disposition time, to have ceased to be, other than for purposes of this clause, a beneficiary under the non-resident portion trust; and

(*g*) if a person deducts or withholds any amount (referred to in this paragraph as the "withholding amount") as required by section 215 from a particular amount paid or credited or deemed to have been paid or credited to the trust, and the particular amount has been included in the trust's income for the particular taxation year, the withholding amount is deemed to have been paid on account of the trust's tax under this Part for the particular taxation year.

Editorial Note: Subsection 94(3) is the main charging provision of s. 94. In general terms, s. 94(3) applies to a trust if there is a resident contributor to the trust or a resident beneficiary under the trust, unless that trust is an exempt foreign trust. Exempt foreign trusts (defined in s. 94(1)) include trusts established for beneficiaries who suffer from mental or physical infirmities, trusts created as a consequence of a breakdown of marriage or common law partnership, certain trusts to which her Majesty in Right of Canada has made a gift, as well as trusts created for certain charitable purposes. Exempt foreign trusts also include trusts created for certain employee profit sharing and compensation plans, as well as those trusts where there are at least 150 direct beneficiaries each of whom holds fixed interest worth at least $500 and such fixed interests are listed or traded on designated stock exchanges (see, however, the anti-avoidance rules in s. 94(15)). Beneficiaries of the latter such trusts, however, may be subject to the provisions of s. 94.1 or s. 94.2, as the case may be.

Where subsection 94(3) applies, the trust is deemed to be resident in Canada throughout the tax year for the purposes listed therein, including computing the trust's income for the year. Subsection 94(4) provides for greater certainty a list of provisions of the Act for which the trust is not deemed to be a resident of Canada.

To the extent that a trust becomes subject to the provisions of s. 94(3), there will be a bump in the cost base of the assets of the trust under s. 94(3)(*c*) to the fair market value immediately prior to the year in which the trust is deemed to be a resident of Canada. Pursuant to s. 94(3)(*d*) a resident contributor and resident beneficiary are jointly and severally, and solidarily, liable together with the trust for the trust's income tax.

See also the application for a trust with a taxation year that ends after 2000 and before 2007 in the history note before the definitions in s. 94(1).

History: S. 94(3)(*b*)(ii)(A) was replaced by S.C. 2017, c. 33, s. 29(1), applicable to taxation years that end after September 15, 2016, and formerly read:

(A) the trust's income for the particular taxation year is deemed to be from sources in that country and not to be from any other source, and

S. 94(3) was replaced by S.C. 2013, c. 34, s. 7(1), applicable to taxation years that end after 2006, except that

(*a*) subparagraph 94(3)(*a*)(x) does not apply in determining, on or before July 18, 2005, whether a foreign affiliate is a controlled foreign affiliate of a taxpayer; and

(*b*) the reference to "(28)" in subparagraph 94(3)(*a*)(iii) is, for taxation years that begin before 2007, to be read as a reference to "(29)".

S. 94(3) formerly read:

(3) *Deduction in computing taxable income.* In computing the amount of taxable income of a trust to which paragraph (1)(*c*) applies for any taxation year, there may be deducted such portion of the amount that would, but for this subsection, be included in computing the taxable income of the trust for the year by virtue of clauses (1)(*c*)(i)(B) and (C) as may reasonably be consid-

ered as having become an amount payable in the year within the meaning of subsection 104(24) to a beneficiary.

Related Regulations: 202(6.1).

Related Sections: S. 104(7.01) Trusts deemed to be resident in Canada; s. 160(2.1) Assessment; s. 160(3) Discharge of liability; s. 216(4.1) Optional method of payment.

Canadian Tax Foundation: Ouelette and Warner, *Estate Planning: US-Resident Beneficiaries of a Canadian Estate — Part 1*, 2014 Canadian Tax Journal 1:197–219; Schweitzer and Brodlieb, *Canadian Taxation of Income Earned and Distributed by a Subsection 94(3) Trust*, 2013 Canadian Tax Journal 2:461–478.

STEP Canada: Bruce Harris and Beth Webel, "Offshore Funds and Non-Resident Trusts: Update 2013," PowerPoint presentation to the 15th National Conference of STEP Canada, Toronto, June 10-11, 2013.

Tax Profile: April 2012 — Residency of Trusts Particularly in the Context of Estates; March 2011 — Canada 2010 — Year in Review; January 2011 — FCA Confirms Trust Residency to be Based on Central Management and Control; October 2009 — Corporate Management and Control Extended to Trust Residency: A New and Novel Approach; February 2004 — Non-Resident Trust Rules and Investment Funds; December 2003 — Non-Resident Trust Rules To Apply To Usufructs And Foundations; January 2003 — Non-Resident Trust Update; December 2002 — Update on Current CCRA GAAR Activity.

Tax Topics: No. 1962, Another NRT seeks Judicial Review: *Morris and Smith v. M.N.R.*; No. 1915, Too Late and Too Early: No Relief for NRTs; No. 1867-68, 2007 Canadian Tax Foundation Annual Conference CRA Round Table; No. 1678, FEE, FIE, FOE, FUM: I Smell the Blood of a NERT.

Forms: T2 SCH 22 — Non-resident Discretionary Trust.

Income Tax Folios: *Secondary* — S6-F1-C1 Residence of a Trust or Estate.

Income Tax Technical News: Issue No. 43, Taxation of Roth IRAs; Issue No. 38, Canada-U.S. Treaty's Competent Authority Provision.

Information Circulars: IC 77-9R Books, records and other requirements for taxpayers having foreign affiliates.

Interpretation Bulletins: *Secondary* — IT-342R Trusts — Income payable to beneficiaries.

Tax Window Files: 2016 STEP–Q7 Deemed Resident Trust and CCPC Status, *June 10, 2016*, CRA Document No. 2016-0634911C6; Residence of a trust, *June 26, 2014*, CRA Document No. 2013-0514771E5; Deemed Resident Trusts & Foreign Tax Credit, *May 28, 2013*, CRA Document No. 2013-0476381I7; Classification of a Foreign Entity — Anstalt, *Income Tax Rulings Directorate, International and Trusts Division, September 28, 2009*, CRA Document No. 2008-0300511I7; Status of Liechtenstein Foundation, *Technical Interpretation, International and Trusts Division, April 15, 2008*, CRA Document No. 2008-0266251I7; Distribution by Deemed Resident Trust, *Technical Interpretation, International & Trusts Division, November 13, 2007*, CRA Document No. 2007-0250731E5; Treatment of Roth IRA, *Technical Interpretation, International and Trusts Division and Minister's Correspondence, December 11, 2002 and July 11, 2006*, CRA Document No. 2006-0186661M4; Attribution of Trust Income, *Technical Interpretation, International & Trusts Division, April 19, 2006*, CRA Document No. 2004-0080731I7; Non-Resident Trusts, *Technical Interpretation, International & Trusts Division, September 12, 2005*, CRA Document No. 2005-0143901I7; Immigration of Non-Resident Discretionary Trust, *Technical Interpretation, International & Trusts Division, January 5, 2005*, CRA Document No. 2004-0083551E5; Non-resident Health and Welfare Type Trust, *Technical Interpretation, International and Trusts Division, August 26, 2004*, CRA Document No. 2004-0060281I7; Distribution of Gain by Deemed Resident Trust, *Technical Interpretation, International and Trusts Division, March 5, 2004*, CRA Document No. 2003-0024621I7; Immigration of a Discretionary Trust — Loss on Disposition of Trust Property, *Technical Interpretation, International and Trusts Division, February 6, 2004*, CRA Document No. 2003-0054041E5; Immigration of a Discretionary Trust — Application of sections 94 and 128.1, *Technical Interpretation, International and Trusts Division, November 14, 2003*, CRA Document No. 2003-0013445; Distribution by Non-Resident Trust, *Technical Interpretation, International and Trusts Division, June 6, 2003*, CRA Document No. 2003-0183437.

Cases: A trustee of a non-resident trust requested a determination of the trust's residence under Article IV(4) of the Canada–U.S. Tax Treaty, on the basis that it might be a deemed Canadian resident under s. 94(1) of the Act. The application was premature since it was based on a proposed amendment to s. 94. The trust was not a deemed Canadian resident under the existing s. 94(1), so there was no dual residency issue to settle. *Perry v. M.N.R. et al.*, 2008 DTC 6623 (F.C.A.), affirming 2007 DTC 5625 (F.C.).

► 94(4) ◄

(4) Excluded provisions. For greater certainty, paragraph (3)(*a*) does not deem a trust to be resident in Canada for the purposes of

(*a*) the definitions "arm's length transfer" and "exempt foreign trust" in subsection (1);

(*b*) subsections (8.1) and (8.2), paragraph (14)(*a*), subsections 70(6) and 73(1), the definition "Canadian partnership" in subsection 102(1), paragraph 107.4(1)(*c*), the definition "qualified disability trust" in subsection 122(3), paragraph (*a*) of the definition "mutual fund trust" in subsection 132(6), the definition "eligible trust" in subsection 135.2(1) and subparagraph (*b*)(i) of the definition "investment fund" in subsection 251.2(1);

(*c*) determining the liability of a person (other than the trust) that would arise under section 215;

(*d*) determining whether, in applying subsection 128.1(1), the trust becomes resident in Canada at a particular time;

(*e*) determining whether, in applying subsection 128.1(4), the trust ceases to be resident in Canada at a particular time;

(*f*) subparagraph (*f*)(i) of the definition "disposition" in subsection 248(1);

(*g*) determining whether subsection 107(5) applies to a distribution on or after July 18, 2005, of property to the trust; and

(*h*) determining whether subsection 75(2) applies.

Editorial Note: Subsection 94(4) is the converse of s. 94(3); excluding a non-resident trust from being deemed to be resident in Canada for specific enumerated provisions. Notably, s. 94(4)(*c*) provides that a non-resident trust that is deemed to be a person resident in Canada under s. 94(3) is not deemed to be resident in Canada for purposes of determining another person's withholding obligation under s. 215. As a result, payments from a Canadian person to such a trust which are subject to Part XIII withholding tax will be subject to withholding by the payer, despite no actual Part XIII tax liability for the trust. The trust will be able to claim such withholding tax on account of its tax liability, if any, and may receive a refund of tax if the tax withheld exceeds its tax liability.

History: S. 94(4)(*b*) was replaced by S.C. 2016, c. 12, s. 30(1), deemed to have come into force on March 21, 2013, except that paragraph 94(4)(*b*) is to be read without reference to

(a) before July 1, 2015, "the definition *eligible trust in* subsection 135.2(1)"; and

(b) for taxation years that end before 2016, "the definition *qualified disability trust* in subsection 122(3),".

S. 94(4)(*b*) formerly read:

(*b*) subsections (8.1) and (8.2), paragraph (14)(*a*), subsections 70(6) and 73(1), the definition *Canadian partnership* in subsection 102(1), paragraph 107.4(1)(*c*), the definition *qualified disability trust* in subsection 122(3), paragraph (*a*) of the definition *mutual fund trust* in subsection 132(6) and the definition *eligible trust* in subsection 135.2(1);

S. 94(4)(*b*) was replaced by S.C. 2016, c. 7, s. 11(1), deemed to have come into force on July 1, 2015, except that, for taxation years that end before 2016, paragraph 94(4)(*b*) is to be read without reference to "the definition *qualified disability trust* in subsection 122(3),". S. 94(4)(*b*) formerly read:

(*b*) subsections (8.1) and (8.2), paragraph (14)(*a*), subsections 70(6) and 73(1), the definition "Canadian partnership" in subsection 102(1), paragraph 107.4(1)(*c*), the definition "qualified disability trust" in subsection 122(3) and paragraph (*a*) of the definition "mutual fund trust" in subsection 132(6);

S. 94(4)(*b*) was replaced by S.C. 2014, c. 39, s. 23(2), applicable to the 2016 and subsequent taxation years, and formerly read:

(*b*) subsections (8.1) and (8.2), paragraph (14)(*a*), subsections 70(6) and 73(1), the definition "Canadian partnership" in subsection 102(1), paragraph 107.4(1)(*c*) and paragraph (*a*) of the definition "mutual fund trust" in subsection 132(6);

S. 94(4)(*b*) was replaced by S.C. 2013, c. 40, s. 42(6), applicable to taxation years that end after March 20, 2013, and formerly read:

(*b*) paragraph (14)(*a*), subsections 70(6) and 73(1), the definition "Canadian partnership" in subsection 102(1), paragraph 107.4(1)(*c*) and paragraph (*a*) of the definition "mutual fund trust" in subsection 132(6);

S. 94(4)(*h*) was replaced by S.C. 2013, c. 40, s. 42(7), applicable to taxation years that end after March 20, 2013, and formerly read:

(*h*) determining whether subsection 75(2) applies to deem an amount to be an income, loss, taxable capital gain or allowable capital loss of the trust.

S. 94(4) was replaced by S.C. 2013, c. 34, s. 7(1), applicable to taxation years that end after 2006, except that

(*a*) paragraph 94(4)(*b*) is

(i) subject to subparagraph (ii), for taxation years that begin on or before July 18, 2005, to be read without reference to "the definition "Canadian partnership" in subsection 102(1),", and

(ii) to be read as follows in its application to a transfer, by a trust, that occurred before February 28, 2004:

"(*b*) subsections 70(6) and 73(1), paragraph 107.4(1)(*c*) other than subparagraph (i) of that paragraph and paragraph (*a*) of the definition "mutual fund trust" in subsection 132(6);".

(*b*) Paragraph 94(4)(*f*), is, in its application to a transfer by a trust that occurred before February 28, 2004, to be read as follows:

"(*f*) determining the residency of the transferee in applying subparagraph (*f*)(ii) of the definition "disposition" in subsection 248(1);".

(*c*) If a trust was, for its last taxation year that ends before 2007, deemed by paragraph 94(1)(*c*) (as it read in its application to that taxation year) to be resident in Canada, paragraphs 94(4)(*d*) and (*e*) do not apply to the trust for the period that starts immediately before the end of that last taxation year and that ends immediately after the beginning of its first taxation year that ends after 2006, unless during that period a change in the trustees of the trust occurred.

S. 94(4) formerly read:

(4) *Deduction from foreign accrual property income.* In computing the foreign accrual property income of a trust to which paragraph (1)(*d*) applies for any taxation year, there may be deducted such portion of the amount that would, but for this subsection, be the foreign accrual property income of the trust as may reasonably be considered as having become an amount payable in the year within the meaning of subsection 104(24) to a beneficiary.

▶ 94(5) ◀

(5) Deemed cessation of residence — loss of resident contributor or resident beneficiary. A trust is deemed to cease to be resident in Canada at the earliest time at which there is neither a resident contributor to the trust nor a resident beneficiary under the trust in a taxation year (determined without reference to subsection 128.1(4)) of the trust

(*a*) that immediately follows a taxation year of the trust throughout which it was deemed by subsection (3) to be resident in Canada for the purpose of computing its income; and

(*b*) at a specified time in which the trust

(i) is non-resident,

(ii) is not an exempt foreign trust, and

(iii) has no resident contributor to it or resident beneficiary under it.

History: S. 94(5) was replaced by S.C. 2013, c. 34, s. 7(1), applicable to taxation years that end after 2006, except that if a trust elects, by notifying the Minister of National Revenue in writing on or before its filing-due date for its taxation year that includes June 26, 2013, subsection 94(5) is, for the trust's taxation years that end on or before October 24, 2012, to be read as follows:

"(5) A trust is deemed to cease to be resident in Canada at the earliest time at which there is neither a resident contributor to the trust nor a resident beneficiary under the trust in a period that would, if this Act were read without reference to subsection 128.1(4), be a taxation year of the trust

(*a*) that immediately follows a taxation year of the trust throughout which it was resident in Canada;

(*b*) at the beginning of which there was a resident contributor to the trust or a resident beneficiary under the trust; and

(*c*) at the end of which the trust is non-resident."

S. 94(5) formerly read:

(5) *Adjusted cost base of capital interest in trust.* In computing, at any time in a taxation year, the adjusted cost base to a taxpayer resident in Canada of a capital interest in a trust to which paragraph (1)(*d*) applies,

(*a*) there shall be added any amount required by subsection 91(1) or (3) to be included in computing the taxpayer's income for the year or any preceding taxation year (or that would have been so required to be included but for subsection 56(4.1) and sections 74.1 to 75 of this Act and section 74 of the *Income Tax Act*, chapter 148 of the Revised Statutes of Canada, 1952) in respect of that interest; and

(*b*) there shall be deducted any amount deducted by the taxpayer by reason of subsection 91(2) or (4) in computing the taxpayer's income for the year or any preceding taxation year (or that would have been so deductible by the taxpayer but for subsection 56(4.1) and sections 74.1 to 75 of this Act and section 74 of the *Income Tax Act*, chapter 148 of the Revised Statutes of Canada, 1952) in respect of that interest.

▶ 94(5.1) ◀

(5.1) Deemed cessation of residence — becoming an exempt foreign trust. A trust is deemed to cease to be resident in Canada at the earliest time at which the trust becomes an exempt foreign trust in a taxation year (determined without reference to subsection 128.1(4)) of the trust

(*a*) that immediately follows a taxation year of the trust throughout which it was deemed by subsection (3) to be resident in Canada for the purpose of computing its income; and

(*b*) at a specified time in which

(i) there is a resident contributor to the trust or a resident beneficiary under the trust, and

(ii) the trust is an exempt foreign trust.

History: S. 94(5.1) was added by S.C. 2013, c. 34, s. 7(1), applicable to taxation years that end after 2006.

▶ 94(5.2) ◀

(5.2) Administrative relief — changes in status. If a trust is deemed by subsection (5) or (5.1) to cease to be resident in Canada at a particular time, the following rules apply to the trust in respect of the particular taxation year that is, as a result of that cessation of residence, deemed by subparagraph 128.1(4)(*a*)(i) to end immediately before the particular time:

(*a*) the trust's return of income for the particular taxation year is deemed to be filed with the Minister on a timely basis if it is filed with the Minister within 90 days from the end of the trust's taxation year that is deemed by subparagraph 128.1(4)(*a*)(i) to start at the particular time; and

(*b*) an amount that is included in the trust's income (determined without reference to subsections 104(6) and (12)) for the particular taxation year but that became payable (determined without regard to this paragraph) by the trust in the period after the particular taxation year and before the end of the trust's taxation year that is deemed by subparagraph 128.1(4)(*a*)(i) to start at the particular time, is deemed to have become payable by the trust immediately before the end of the particular taxation year and not at any other time.

History: S. 94(5.2) was added by S.C. 2013, c. 34, s. 7(1), applicable to taxation years that end after 2006.

Related Sections: S. 104(24) Amount payable.

▶ 94(6) ◀

(6) Ceasing to be an exempt foreign trust. If at a specified time in a trust's taxation year it is an exempt foreign trust, at a particular time in the immediately following taxation year (determined without reference to this subsection) the trust ceases to be an exempt foreign trust (otherwise than because of becoming resident in Canada), and at the particular time there is a resident contributor to, or resident beneficiary under, the trust,

(*a*) the trust's taxation year (determined without reference to this subsection) that includes the particular time is deemed to have ended immediately before the particular time and a new taxation year of the trust is deemed to begin at the particular time; and

(*b*) for the purpose of determining the trust's fiscal period after the particular time, the trust is deemed not to have established a fiscal period before the particular time.

History: S. 94(6) was replaced by S.C. 2013, c. 34, s. 7(1), applicable to taxation years that end after 2006, except that if a trust elects, by notifying the Minister of National Revenue in writing on or before its filing-due date for its taxation year that includes June 26, 2013, subsection 94(6) is, for the trust's taxation years that end on or before October 24, 2012, to be read as follows:

"(6) If at any time a trust becomes or ceases to be an exempt foreign trust (otherwise than because of becoming resident in Canada),

(*a*) its taxation year that would otherwise include that time is deemed to have ended immediately before that time and a new taxation year of the trust is deemed to begin at that time; and

(*b*) for the purpose of determining the trust's fiscal period after that time, the trust is deemed not to have established a fiscal period before that time."

S. 94(6) formerly read:

(6) *Where financial assistance given.* For the purposes of paragraph (1)(*b*), a trust or a non-resident corporation shall be deemed to have acquired property from any person who has given a guarantee on its behalf or from whom it has received any other financial assistance whatever.

▶ 94(7) ◀

(7) Limit to amount recoverable. The maximum amount recoverable under the provisions referred to in paragraph (3)(*d*) at any particular time from a person in respect of a trust (other than a person that is deemed, under subsection (12) or (13), to be a contributor or a resident contributor to the trust) and a particular taxation year of the trust is the person's recovery limit at the particular time in respect of the trust and the particular year if

(*a*) either

(i) the person is liable under a provision referred to in paragraph (3)(*d*) in respect of the trust and the particular year solely because the person was a resident beneficiary under the trust at a specified time in respect of the trust in the particular year, or

(ii) at a specified time in respect of the trust in the particular year, the total of all amounts each of which is the amount, at the time it was made, of a contribution to the trust made before the specified time by the person or by another person or partnership not dealing at arm's length with the person, is not more than the greater of

(A) $10,000, and

(B) 10% of the total of all amounts each of which was the amount, at the time it was made, of a contribution made to the trust before the specified time;

(*b*) except if the total determined in subparagraph (*a*)(ii) in respect of the person and all persons or partnerships not dealing at arm's length with the person is $10,000 or less, the person has filed on a timely basis under section 233.2 all information returns required to be filed by the person before the particular time in respect of the trust (or on any later day that is acceptable to the Minister); and

(*c*) it is reasonable to conclude that for each transaction that occurred before the end of the particular year at the direction of, or with the acquiescence of, the person

(i) none of the purposes of the transaction was to enable the person to avoid or minimize any liability under a provision referred to in paragraph (3)(*d*) in respect of the trust, and

(ii) the transaction was not part of a series of transactions any of the purposes of which was to enable the person to avoid or minimize any liability under a provision referred to in paragraph (3)(*d*) in respect of the trust.

Editorial Note: Under s. 94(7), a limit is imposed on the amount that is otherwise recoverable under s. 94(3)(*d*), which generally makes resident contributors and resident beneficiaries jointly and severally, or solidarily, liable for a deemed resident trust's taxes. This limit does not apply if the person is deemed to be a contributor or resident contributor under s. 94(12) or (13). Generally, the limitation applies only to resident beneficiaries or certain contributors who have contributed no more than $10,000 or 10% of the contributions made to the trust. In addition, foreign reporting in respect of contributions made to the trust must be current (except where the person has made less than $10,000 in contributions to the trust). As well, there is an anti-avoidance element to the test. Where s. 94(7) applies, s. 94(8) provides a complex formula for determining the extent of the contributor or beneficiary's recovery limit. Very generally, the recovery limit is equal to payments received out of the trust, minus amounts previously recovered by the CRA, subject to various adjustments to deal with the fact that the legislation has changed since initially proposed.

History: S. 94(7) was added by S.C. 2013, c. 34, s. 7(1), applicable to taxation years that end after 2006.

▶ 94(8) ◀

(8) Recovery limit. The recovery limit referred to in paragraph (3)(*e*) and subsection (7) at a particular time of a particular person in respect of a trust and a particular taxation year of the trust is the amount, if any, by which the greater of

(*a*) the total of all amounts each of which is

(i) an amount received or receivable after 2000 and before the particular time

(A) by the particular person on the disposition of all or part of the person's interest as a beneficiary under the trust, or

(B) by a person or partnership (that was, when the amount became receivable, a specified party in respect of the particular person) on the disposition of all or part of the specified party's interest as a beneficiary under the trust,

(ii) an amount (other than an amount described in subparagraph (i)) made payable by the trust after 2000 and before the particular time to

(A) the particular person because of the interest of the particular person as a beneficiary under the trust, or

(B) a person or partnership (that was, when the amount became payable, a specified party in respect of the particular person) because of the interest of the specified party as a beneficiary under the trust,

(iii) an amount received after August 27, 2010, by the particular person, or a person or partnership (that was, when the amount was received, a specified party in respect of the particular person), as a loan from the trust to the extent that the amount has not been repaid,

(iv) an amount (other than an amount described in any of subparagraphs (i) to (iii)) that is the fair market value of a benefit received or enjoyed, after 2000 and before the particular time, from or under the trust by

(A) the particular person, or

(B) a person or partnership that was, when the benefit was received or enjoyed, a specified party in respect of the particular person, or

(v) the maximum amount that would be recoverable from the particular person at the end of the trust's 2006 taxation year under subsection (2) (as it read in its application to taxation years that end before 2007) if the trust had tax payable under this Part at the end of the trust's 2006 taxation year and that tax payable exceeded the total of the amounts described in respect of the particular person under paragraphs (2)(*a*) and (*b*) (as they read in their application to taxation years that end before 2007), except to the extent that the amount so recoverable is in respect of an amount that is included in the particular person's recovery limit because of subparagraph (i) or (ii), and

(*b*) the total of all amounts each of which is the amount, when made, of a contribution to the trust before the particular time by the particular person,

exceeds the total of all amounts each of which is

(*c*) an amount recovered before the particular time from the particular person in connection with a liability of the particular person (in respect of the trust and the particular year or a preceding taxation year of the trust) that arose because of the application of subsection (3) (or the application of this section as it read in its application to taxation years that end before 2007),

(*d*) an amount (other than an amount in respect of which this paragraph has applied in respect of any other person) recovered before the particular time from a specified party in respect of the particular person in connection with a liability of the particular person (in respect of the trust and the particular year or a preceding taxation year of the trust) that arose because of the application of subsection (3) (or the application of this section as it read in its application to taxation years that end before 2007), or

(*e*) the amount, if any, by which the particular person's tax payable under this Part for any taxation year in which an amount described in any of subparagraphs (*a*)(i) to (iv) was paid, became payable, was received, became receivable or was enjoyed by the particular person exceeds the amount that would have been the particular person's tax payable under this Part for that taxation year if no such amount were paid, became payable, were received, became receivable or were enjoyed by the particular person in that taxation year.

History: S. 94(8) was added by S.C. 2013, c. 34, s. 7(1), applicable to taxation years that end after 2006.

Related Sections: S. 104(24) Amount payable.

► 94(8.1) ◄

(8.1) Application of subsection (8.2). Subsection (8.2) applies at any time to a particular person, and to a particular property, in respect of a non-resident trust, if at that time

(*a*) the particular person is resident in Canada; and

(*b*) the trust holds the particular property on condition that the particular property or property substituted for the particular property

(i) may

(A) revert to the particular person, or

(B) pass to one or more persons or partnerships to be determined by the particular person, or

(ii) shall not be disposed of by the trust during the existence of the particular person, except with the particular person's consent or in accordance with the particular person's direction.

History: S. 94(8.1) was added by S.C. 2013, c. 40, s. 42(8), applicable to taxation years that end after March 20, 2013.

► 94(8.2) ◄

(8.2) Deemed transfer of restricted property. If this subsection applies at any time to a particular person, and to a particular property, in respect of a non-resident trust, then in applying this section in respect of the trust for a taxation year of the trust that includes that time

(*a*) every transfer or loan made at or before that time by the particular person (or by a trust or partnership of which the particular person was a beneficiary or member, as the case may be) of the particular property, of another property for which the particular property is a substitute, or of property from which the particular property derives, or the other property derived, its value in whole or in part, directly or indirectly, is deemed to be a transfer or loan, as the case may be, by the particular person

(i) that is not an arm's length transfer, and

(ii) that is, for the purposes of paragraph (2)(*c*) and subsection (9), a transfer or loan of restricted property; and

(*b*) paragraph (2)(*c*) is to be read without reference to subparagraph (2)(*c*)(iii) in its application to each transfer and loan described in paragraph (*a*).

History: S. 94(8.2) was added by S.C. 2013, c. 40, s. 42(8), applicable to taxation years that end after March 20, 2013.

Related Sections: S. 107(4.1) Where subsection 75(2) applicable to trust.

► 94(9) ◄

(9) Determination of contribution amount — restricted property. If a person or partnership contributes at any time restricted property to a trust, the amount of the contribution at that time is deemed, for the purposes of this section, to be the greater of

(*a*) the amount, determined without reference to this subsection, of the contribution at that time, and

(*b*) the amount that is the greatest fair market value of the restricted property, or property substituted for it, in the period that begins immediately after that time and ends at the end of the third calendar year that ends after that time.

History: S. 94(9) was added by S.C. 2013, c. 34, s. 7(1), applicable to taxation years that end after 2006.

▶ 94(10) ◀

(10) Contributor — resident in Canada within 60 months after contribution. In applying this section at each specified time, in respect of a trust's taxation year, that is before the particular time at which a contributor to the trust becomes resident in Canada within 60 months after making a contribution to the trust, the contribution is deemed to have been made at a time other than a non-resident time of the contributor if

(*a*) in applying the definition "non-resident time" in subsection (1) at each of those specified times, the contribution was made at a non-resident time of the contributor; and

(*b*) in applying the definition "non-resident time" in subsection (1) immediately after the particular time, the contribution is made at a time other than a non-resident time of the contributor.

Editorial Note: Subsection 94(10) applies for the purpose of determining whether there is a "connected contributor". Subsection 94(1) effectively provides that a trust can be retroactively deemed resident in Canada to the date of a contribution by a non-resident where the non-resident contributor to the trust becomes a resident of Canada within 60 months of the contribution.

History: S. 94(10) was added by S.C. 2013, c. 34, s. 7(1), applicable to taxation years that end after 2006.

Related Sections: S. 152(4) Assessment

▶ 94(11) ◀

(11) Application of subsections (12) and (13). Subsections (12) and (13) apply to a trust or a person in respect of a trust if

(*a*) at any time property of a trust (referred to in this subsection and subsections (12) and (13) as the "original trust") is transferred or loaned, directly or indirectly, in any manner, to another trust (referred to in this subsection and subsections (12) and (13) as the "transferee trust");

(*b*) the original trust

(i) is deemed to be resident in Canada immediately before that time because of paragraph (3)(*a*),

(ii) would be deemed to be resident in Canada immediately before that time because of paragraph (3)(*a*) if this section, as it read in its application to the 2013 taxation year, were read without reference to paragraph (*a*) of the definition "connected contributor" in subsection (1) and paragraph (*a*) of the definition "resident contributor" in that subsection,

(iii) was deemed to be resident in Canada immediately before that time because of subsection (1) as it read in its application to taxation years that end before 2007, or

(iv) would have been deemed to be resident in Canada immediately before that time because of subsection (1) as it read in its application to taxation years that end before 2007 if that subsection were read in that application without reference to subclause (*b*)(i)(A)(III) of that subsection; and

(*c*) it is reasonable to conclude that one of the reasons the transfer or loan is made is to avoid or minimize a liability under this Part that arose, or that would otherwise have arisen, because of the application of this section (or the application of this section as it read in its application to taxation years that end before 2007).

History: S. 94(11)(*b*)(ii) was replaced by S.C. 2014, c. 39, s. 23(3), applicable to taxation years that end after February 10, 2014, except that the amendment does not apply in respect of a trust to taxation years that end before 2015 if the following conditions are satisfied:

(a) no contributions are made to the trust after February 10, 2014 and before 2015; and

(b) if the trust were to have a particular taxation year that ended after 2013 and before February 11, 2014,

(i) the trust would be non-resident for the purpose of computing its income for the particular year, and

(ii) if the definitions "connected contributor" and "resident contributor" in subsection 94(1) were read for the particular year without reference to their paragraphs (*a*), the trust would be resident in Canada for the purpose of computing its income for the particular year.

S. 94(11)(*b*)(ii) formerly read:

(ii) would be deemed to be resident in Canada immediately before that time because of paragraph (3)(*a*) if this section were read without reference to paragraph (*a*) of the definition "connected contributor" in subsection (1) and paragraph (*a*) of the definition "resident contributor" in that subsection,

S. 94(11) was added by S.C. 2013, c. 34, s. 7(1), applicable to taxation years that end after 2006.

▶ 94(12) ◀

(12) Deemed resident contributor. The original trust described in subsection (11) (including a trust that has ceased to exist) is deemed to be, at and after the time of the transfer or loan referred to in that subsection, a resident contributor to the transferee trust for the purpose of applying this section in respect of the transferee trust.

History: S. 94(12) was added by S.C. 2013, c. 34, s. 7(1), applicable to taxation years that end after 2006.

▶ 94(13) ◀

(13) Deemed contributor. A person (including any person that has ceased to exist) that is, at the time of the transfer or loan referred to in subsection (11), a contributor to the original trust, is deemed to be at and after that time

(*a*) a contributor to the transferee trust; and

(*b*) a connected contributor to the transferee trust, if at that time the person is a connected contributor to the original trust.

History: S. 94(13) was added by S.C. 2013, c. 34, s. 7(1), applicable to taxation years that end after 2006.

▶ 94(14) ◀

(14) Restricted property — exception. A particular property that is, or will be, at any time held, loaned or transferred, as the case may be, by a particular person or partnership is not restricted property held, loaned or transferred, as the case may be, at that time by the particular person or partnership if

(*a*) the following conditions are met:

(i) the particular property (and property, if any, for which it is, or is to be, substituted) was not, and will not be, at any time acquired, held, loaned or transferred by the particular person or partnership (or any person or partnership with whom the particular person or partnership does not at any time deal at arm's length) in whole or in part for the purpose of permitting any change in the value of the property of a corporation (that is, at any time, a closely held corporation) to accrue directly or indirectly in any manner whatever to the value of property held by a non-resident trust,

(ii) the Minister is satisfied that the particular property (and property, if any, for which it is, or is to be, substituted) is described by subparagraph (i), and

(iii) the particular property is identified in prescribed form, containing prescribed information, filed, by or on behalf of the particular person or partnership, with the Minister on or before

(A) in the case of a person, the particular person's filing-due date for the particular person's taxation year that includes that time,

(B) in the case of a partnership, the day on or before which a return is required by section 229 of the *Income Tax Regulations* to be filed in respect of the fiscal period of the particular partnership or would be required to be so filed if that section applied to the partnership, or

(C) another date that is acceptable to the Minister; or

(*b*) at that time

(i) the particular property is

(A) a share of the capital stock of a corporation,

(B) a fixed interest in a trust, or

(C) an interest, as a member of a partnership, under which, by operation of any law governing the arrangement in respect of the partnership, the liability of the member as a member of the partnership is limited,

(ii) there are at least 150 persons each of whom holds at that time property that at that time

(A) is identical to the particular property, and

(B) has a total fair market value of at least $500,

(iii) the total of all amounts each of which is the fair market value, at that time, of the particular property (or of identical property that is held, at that time, by the particular person or partnership or a person or partnership with whom the particular person or partnership does not deal at arm's length) does not exceed 10% of the total of all amounts each of which is the fair market value, at that time, of the particular property or of identical property held by any person or partnership,

(iv) property that is identical to the particular property can normally be acquired by and sold by members of the public in the open market, and

(v) the particular property, or identical property, is listed on a designated stock exchange.

History: S. 94(14) was added by S.C. 2013, c. 34, s. 7(1), applicable to taxation years that end after 2006, except that the reference to "designated stock exchange" in subparagraph 94(14)(*b*)(v) is, before December 14, 2007, to be read as a reference to "prescribed stock exchange".

► 94(15) ◄

(15) Anti-avoidance. In applying this section,

(*a*) if it can reasonably be considered that one of the main reasons that a person or partnership

(i) is at any time a shareholder of a corporation is to cause the condition in paragraph (*b*) of the definition "closely held corporation" in subsection (1) to be satisfied in respect of the corporation, the condition is deemed not to have been satisfied at that time in respect of the corporation,

(ii) holds at any time an interest in a trust is to cause the condition in clause (*h*)(ii)(A) of the definition "exempt foreign trust" in subsection (1) to be satisfied in respect of the trust, the condition is deemed not to have been satisfied at that time in respect of the trust, and

(iii) holds at any time a property is to cause the condition described in subparagraph (14)(*b*)(ii) to be satisfied in respect of the property or an identical property held by any person, the condition is deemed not to have been satisfied at that time in respect of the property or the identical property;

(*b*) if at any time at or before a specified time in a trust's taxation year, a resident contributor to the trust contributes to the trust property that is restricted property of the trust, or property for which restricted property of the trust is substituted, and the trust is at that specified time an exempt foreign trust by reason of paragraph (*f*) of the definition "exempt foreign trust" in subsection (1), the amount of the trust's income for the taxation year from the restricted property, and the amount of any taxable capital gain from the disposition in the taxation year by the trust of the restricted property, shall be included in computing the income of the resident contributor for its taxation year in which that taxation year of the trust ends and not in computing the income of the trust for that taxation year of the trust; and

(*c*) if at a specified time in a trust's taxation year it is an exempt foreign trust by reason of paragraph (*h*) of the definition "exempt foreign trust" in subsection (1), at a time immediately before a particular time in the immediately following taxation year (determined without reference to subsection (6)) there is a resident contributor to, or resident beneficiary under, the trust, at the time that is immediately before the particular time a beneficiary holds a fixed interest in the trust, and at the particular time the interest ceases to be a fixed interest in the trust,

(i) the trust is deemed, other than for purposes of subsection (6), not to be an exempt foreign trust at any time in the trust's taxation year (referred to in this paragraph as its "assessment year") that ends (for greater certainty as determined under paragraph (6)(*a*)) at the time that is immediately before the particular time,

(ii) the trust shall include in computing its income for its assessment year an amount equal to the amount determined by the formula

$$A - B - C$$

where

A is the amount by which the total of all amounts each of which is the fair market value of a property held by the trust at the end of its assessment year exceeds the total of all amounts each of which is the principal amount outstanding at the end of its assessment year of a liability of the trust,

B is the amount by which the total of all amounts each of which is the fair market value of a property held by the trust at the earliest time at which there is a resident contributor to, or resident beneficiary under, the trust and at which the trust is an exempt foreign trust (referred to in this paragraph as the "initial time") exceeds the total of all amounts each of which is the principal amount outstanding at the initial time of a liability of the trust, and

C is the total of all amounts each of which is the amount of a contribution made to the trust in the period that begins at the initial time and ends at the end of its assessment year (in this paragraph referred to as the "interest gross-up period"), and

(iii) if the trust is liable for tax for its assessment year, then throughout the period that begins at the trust's balance-due day for each taxation year that ends in the interest gross-up period and ends at the balance-due day for its assessment year, the trust is (in addition to any excess otherwise determined in respect of the trust under that subsection) deemed to have an excess for the purposes of subsection 161(1) equal to the amount determined by the formula

$$A/B \times 42.92\%$$

where

A is the amount determined under subparagraph (ii) in respect of the trust for the particular taxation year, and

B is the number of the trust's taxation years that end in the interest gross-up period.

History: S. 94(15) was added by S.C. 2013, c. 34, s. 7(1), applicable to taxation years that end after 2006.

▶ 94(16) ◀

(16) Attribution to electing contributors. If at a specified time in respect of a trust for a taxation year of the trust (referred to in this subsection as the "trust's year"), there is an electing contributor in respect of the trust, the following rules apply:

(*a*) the electing contributor is required to include in computing their income for their taxation year (referred to in this subsection as the "contributor's year") in which the trust's year ends, the amount determined by the formula

$$A/B \times (C - D)$$

where

A is the total of all amounts each of which is

(i) if at or before the specified time the electing contributor has made a contribution to the trust and is not a joint contributor in respect of the trust and the contribution, the amount of the contribution, or

(ii) if at or before the specified time the electing contributor has made a contribution to the trust and is a joint contributor in respect of the trust and the contribution, the amount obtained when the amount of the contribution is divided by the number of joint contributors in respect of the contribution,

B is the total of all amounts each of which is the amount that would be determined under A for each resident contributor, or connected contributor, to the trust at the specified time if all of those contributors were electing contributors in respect of the trust,

C is the trust's income, computed without reference to paragraph (*f*), for the trust's year, and

D is the amount deducted by the trust under section 111 in computing its taxable income for the trust's year;

(*b*) subject to paragraph (*c*), the amount, if any, required by paragraph (*a*) to be included in the electing contributor's income for the contributor's year is deemed to be income from property from a source in Canada;

(*c*) for the purposes of this paragraph, paragraph (*d*) and section 126, an amount in respect of the trust's income for the trust's year from a source in a country other than Canada is deemed to be income of the electing contributor for the contributor's year from that source if

(i) the amount is designated by the trust, in respect of the electing contributor, in the trust's return of income under this Part for the trust's year,

(ii) the amount may reasonably be considered (having regard to all the circumstances including the terms and conditions of the trust) to be part of the amount that because of paragraph (*a*) was included in computing the income of the electing contributor for the contributor's year, and

(iii) the total of all amounts designated by the trust, under this paragraph or subsection 104(22) in respect of that source, in the trust's return of income under this Part for the trust's year is not greater than the trust's income for the trust's year from that source;

(*d*) for the purposes of this paragraph and section 126, the electing contributor is deemed to have paid as business-income tax (in this subsection as defined by subsection 126(7)) or non-business-income tax (in this subsection as defined by subsection 126(7)), as the case may be, for the contributor's year in respect of a source the amount determined by the formula

$$A \times B/C$$

where

A is the amount that, in the absence of subparagraph (*e*)(i), would be the business-income tax or non-business-income tax, as the case may be, paid by the trust in respect of that source for the trust's year,

B is the total of all amounts each of which is an amount designated under paragraph (*c*) in respect of that source by the trust in respect of the electing contributor in the trust's return of income under this Part for the trust's year, and

C is the trust's income for the trust's year from that source;

(*e*) in applying subsection 20(12) and section 126 in respect of the trust's year there shall be deducted

(i) in computing the trust's income from a source for the trust's year the total of all amounts each of which is an amount deemed by paragraph (*c*) to be income from that source of the electing contributor for the contributor's year, and

(ii) in computing the business-income tax or non-business-income tax paid by the trust for the trust's year in respect of a source the total of all amounts in respect of that source each of which is an amount deemed by paragraph (*d*) to be paid by the electing contributor as business-income tax or non-business-income tax, as the case may be, in respect of that source;

(*f*) in computing the trust's income for the trust's year there may be deducted the amount that does not exceed the amount included by reason of paragraph (*a*) in the electing contributor's income for the contributor's year; and

(*g*) if before the specified time the electing contributor made a contribution to the trust as part of a series of transactions in which another person made the same contribution, in applying paragraphs (*a*) to (*f*) in respect of the electing contributor and the other person, the other person is deemed not to be a joint contributor in respect of the contribution if it can reasonably be considered that one of the main purposes of the series was to obtain the benefit of any deduction in computing income, taxable income or tax payable under this Act or any balance of undeducted outlays, expenses or other amounts available to the other person or any exemption available to the other person from tax payable under this Act.

History: S. 94(16) was added by S.C. 2013, c. 34, s. 7(1), applicable only to taxation years that end after March 4, 2010.

Related Sections: 94(3) Liabilities of non-resident trusts and others.

▶ 94(17) ◀

(17) Liability for joint contribution. If, at or before a specified time in a trust's taxation year (referred to in this subsection as the "trust's year"), there is an electing contributor in respect of the trust who is a joint contributor in respect of a contribution to the trust,

(*a*) each person who is a joint contributor in respect of the contribution

(i) has, in respect of the contribution, jointly and severally, or solidarily, the rights and obligations under Divisions I and J of each other person (referred to in this subsection as the "specified person") who is, at or before the specified time, a joint contributor in respect of that contribution, for the specified person's taxation year in which the trust's year ends, and

(ii) is subject to Part XV in respect of those rights and obligations; and

(*b*) the maximum amount recoverable under the provisions referred to in paragraph (*a*) at a particular time from the person in respect of the contribution and a taxation year, of another person who is the specified person, in which the trust's year ends is the amount determined by the formula

$$A - B - C$$

where

A is the total of the amounts payable by the specified person under this Part for the specified person's taxation year in which the trust's year ends,

B is the amount that would be determined for A if the total of the amounts payable by the specified person under this Part for the particular specified person's taxation year in which the trust's year ends were computed without reference to the contribution, and

C is the amount recovered before the particular time from the specified person, and any other joint contributor in respect of the trust and the contribution, in connection with the liability of the specified person in respect of the contribution.

History: S. 94(17) was added by S.C. 2013, c. 34, s. 7(1), applicable only to taxation years that end after March 4, 2010.

Related Sections: S. 160(2.1) Assessment; S. 160(3) Discharge of liability.

SECTION 94.1: Offshore investment fund property

▶ 94.1(1) ◀

(1) Offshore investment fund property. If in a taxation year a taxpayer holds or has an interest in property (referred to in this section as an "offshore investment fund property")

(*a*) that is a share of the capital stock of, an interest in, or a debt of, a non-resident entity (other than a controlled foreign affiliate of the taxpayer or a prescribed non-resident entity) or an interest in or a right or option to acquire such a share, interest or debt, and

(*b*) that may reasonably be considered to derive its value, directly or indirectly, primarily from portfolio investments of that or any other non-resident entity in

(i) shares of the capital stock of one or more corporations,

(ii) indebtedness or annuities,

(iii) interests in one or more corporations, trusts, partnerships, organizations, funds or entities,

(iv) commodities,

(v) real estate,

(vi) Canadian or foreign resource properties,

(vii) currency of a country other than Canada,

(viii) rights or options to acquire or dispose of any of the foregoing, or

(ix) any combination of the foregoing,

and it may reasonably be concluded, having regard to all the circumstances, including

(*c*) the nature, organization and operation of any non-resident entity and the form of, and the terms and conditions governing, the taxpayer's interest in, or connection with, any non-resident entity,

(*d*) the extent to which any income, profits and gains that may reasonably be considered to be earned or accrued, whether directly or indirectly, for the benefit of any non-resident entity are subject to an income or profits tax that is significantly less than the income tax that would be applicable to such income, profits and gains if they were earned directly by the taxpayer, and

(*e*) the extent to which the income, profits and gains of any non-resident entity for any fiscal period are distributed in that or the immediately following fiscal period,

that one of the main reasons for the taxpayer acquiring, holding or having the interest in such property was to derive a benefit from portfolio investments in assets described in any of subparagraphs (*b*)(i) to (ix) in such a manner that the taxes, if any, on the income, profits and gains from such assets for any particular year are significantly less than the tax that would have been applicable under this Part if the income, profits and gains had been earned directly by the taxpayer, there shall be included in computing the taxpayer's income for the year the amount, if any, by which

(*f*) the total of all amounts each of which is the product obtained when

(i) the designated cost to the taxpayer of the offshore investment fund property at the end of a month in the year

is multiplied by

(ii) 1/12 of the total of

(A) the prescribed rate of interest for the period that includes that month, and

(B) two per cent

exceeds

(*g*) the taxpayer's income for the year (other than a capital gain) from the offshore investment fund property determined without reference to this subsection.

Editorial Note: Section 94.1 is an anti-avoidance provision which applies when a taxpayer has an interest in an offshore investment fund property and one of the main reasons for the taxpayer having the interest is to reduce tax under the Act. Where it applies, the taxpayer must include a specified amount of income in respect of the property each year. Generally the amount required to be included is the prescribed interest rate under Regulation 4301(*c*) plus two percent times the taxpayer's "designated" cost (defined in s. 94.1(2)) of the property. The taxpayer's income for the year (other than a capital gain) from the property otherwise determined is subtracted from this amount.

History: S. 94.1(1), the portion before paragraph (*a*) was replaced by S.C. 2013, c. 34, s. 8(1), applicable to taxation years that end after March 4, 2010. The amendment to the portion of section 94.1(1) before paragraph (*a*) also applies to each taxation year of a beneficiary under a trust that ends before March 5, 2010 if subsection 94(1) applies to the trust for a taxation year of the trust that ends in that earlier taxation year of the beneficiary.

S. 94.1(1), the portion before paragraph (*a*), formerly read:

(1) *Offshore investment fund property.* Where in a taxation year a taxpayer, other than a non-resident-owned investment corporation, holds or has an interest in property (in this section referred to as an "offshore investment fund property")

S. 94.1(1)(*f*)(ii) was replaced by S.C. 2013, c. 34, s. 8(2), applicable to taxation years that end after March 4, 2010, and formerly read:

(ii) the quotient obtained when the prescribed rate of interest for the period including that month is divided by 12

[Transitional Rules]

(5) Subsection (6) [below] applies to a taxpayer for each taxation year that ends in the period that begins on January 1, 2001 and ends on March 4, 2010 (referred to in this subsection and subsections (7), (8) and (10) [below] as the "relevant period"), if

(*a*) in the return of income for the year the taxpayer has, in respect of one or more participating interests held by the taxpayer during the relevant period, in this subsection and subsections (6) to (10) [below] having the meaning of "participating interest" as set out in the provisions of sections 94.1 to 94.4 of the Act contained in section 18 of Bill C-10 of the second session of the 39th Parliament as passed by the House of Commons on October 29, 2007, included or deducted an amount (referred to in this subsection and subsections (6) to (8) and (10) [below] as the "reported inclusion" or "reported deduction" as the case may be) under those provisions in computing income for the year; and

(*b*) the taxpayer files a prescribed form on or before the taxpayer's filing-due date for the taxpayer's taxation year which includes June 26, 2013

(i) identifying each participating interest of the taxpayer for which a reported inclusion or reported deduction described in paragraph (*a*) [above] has been included, or deducted, in computing the taxpayer's income for a taxation year ending in the relevant period, and

(ii) providing sufficient detail of each of those participating interests, including any reported inclusions, reported deductions, and any taxable capital gains or allowable capital losses realized on the participating interests described in subparagraph (i).

(6) If this subsection applies to a taxpayer for a taxation year,

(*a*) the taxpayer's reported inclusion and any taxable capital gains for the year in respect of a participating interest is deemed to be the amount required to be included under the Act in computing the taxpayer's income for that year in respect of that participating interest; and

(*b*) the taxpayer's reported deduction and any allowable capital loss for the year in respect of a participating interest is deemed to be the amount deductible under the Act in computing the taxpayer's income, or the allowable capital loss, respectively, for that year in respect of that participating interest.

(7) If subsection (6) [above] applies to a taxpayer for one or more taxation years, in computing the taxpayer's income for the first taxation year that ends after the relevant period, there may be deducted the amount that does not exceed the amount, if any, determined by the formula

$$(A - B) - (C - D)$$

where

A is the total of all amounts each of which is a reported inclusion for a year in respect of a participating interest, or a taxable capital gain for a taxation year that ends in the relevant period from the disposition of a participating interest of the taxpayer described in paragraph (5)(*a*) [above];

B is the total of all amounts each of which is a reported deduction for a year in respect of a participating interest, or an allowable capital loss for a taxation year that ends in the relevant period from the disposition of a participating interest of the taxpayer described in paragraph (5)(*a*) [above];

C is the total of all amounts each of which is

(*a*) an amount that would be required to be included under the provisions of the Act, read without reference to this Act, in the taxpayer's income for a taxation year that ends in the relevant period in respect of a property that is a participating interest of the taxpayer described in paragraph (5)(*a*) [above], or

(*b*) a taxable capital gain computed without reference to this Act for a taxation year that ends in the relevant period from the disposition of a participating interest of the taxpayer described in paragraph (5)(a) [above]; and

D is the total of all amounts each of which is an allowable capital loss computed without reference to this Act for a taxation year that ends in the relevant period from the disposition of a participating interest of the taxpayer described in paragraph (5)(*a*) [above].

(8) Subsection (9) [below] applies to a taxpayer in respect of a participating interest described in paragraph (5)(*a*) [above] for the first taxation year that ends after the relevant period if

(*a*) at the start of the year the taxpayer holds the participating interest;

(*b*) the total of all amounts each of which is a reported deduction for a year in respect of the participating interest exceeds the total of all amounts each of which is a reported inclusion for a year in respect of the participating interest; and

(*c*) the amount determined for B in applying the formula in subsection (7) [above] in computing the taxpayer's income for that year exceeds the amount, if any, that is the amount determined for A in so applying that formula.

(9) If this subsection applies to a taxpayer in respect of a participating interest for a taxation year, in computing the adjusted cost base to the taxpayer of the participating interest at any time after the start of the taxation year, there is to be deducted an amount equal to the excess determined in respect of the participating interest under paragraph (8)(*b*) [above].

(10) Notwithstanding subsection 152(4) of the Act, the Minister of National Revenue may reassess tax, interest or penalties payable under Part I of the Act by the taxpayer, in respect of each of the taxpayer's participating interests for each of the taxpayer's taxation years that ends in the relevant period to give effect to the application of the Act as read in respect of each of those years without regard to this Part if

(*a*) subsection (6) [above] does not apply to the taxpayer;

(*b*) the taxpayer has a reported inclusion or a reported deduction in respect of those participating interests for one or more of those years; and

(*c*) at any time that is on or before June 26, 2014 [the day that is 365 days after royal assent] , the taxpayer files with the Minister of National Revenue a prescribed form amending, as necessary, each of the returns for those taxation years.

Related Regulations: 4301.

Canadian Tax Foundation: Barnicke and Huynh, *Section 94.1 and Gerbro Holdings*, 2016 Canadian Tax Highlights 24(8):1; Harris et al., *The Long and Winding Road: Sections 94, 94.1, and 94.2*, 2013 Conference Report 23:1–60; Baker, *Dealing with FIEs in Practice*, 2007 Conference Report 20:1–23; Lockwood, *Foreign Affiliates and the New Foreign Investment Entity Rules, Revisited*, 2004 Canadian Tax Journal 4:1186–1216; Lockwood and Pantaleo, *Foreign Affiliates and the New Foreign Investment Entity Rules*, 2003 Canadian Tax Journal 1:539–568; Emes, *The New Non-Resident Trust Rules*, 2002 Prairie Provinces Tax Conference 13:1–48; Spindler and Wilkie, *The Revised Foreign Investment Entity Rules*, 2001 Conference Report 23:1–22; Cadesky et al., *Amendments to Taxation of Non-Resident Trusts: An Update*, 2001 Conference Report 20:1–43; Bauer, *Fie, Fi, Fo, Fum — The Foreign Investment Entity Rules*, 2001 British Columbia Tax Conference 14:1–32; Cadesky and Chow, *Amendments to Taxation of Non-Resident Trusts*, 2000 Conference Report 34:1–72; Lorito and Kraus, *The Proposed Foreign Investment Entity Rules*, 2000 Conference Report 32:1–77.

International Tax: No. 90, The Wait Is Finally Over: The Tax Court's Analysis of Section 94.1.

STEP Canada: Bruce Harris and Beth Webel, "Offshore Funds and Non-Resident Trusts: Update 2013," PowerPoint presentation to the 15th National Conference of STEP Canada, Toronto, June 10-11, 2013.

Tax Profile: October 2011 — Hedge Funds and Private Equity Funds in Canada; March 2008 — International Tax Planning for the Owner-Manager; November 2006 — Structuring and Taxation of Canadian Hedge Funds; January 2006 — Foreign Source Income: Outbound Structures and Foreign Tax Credit Planning — Part I; December 2003 — The Foreign Investment Entity Rules: Round Four; March 2003 — Memorandum: Revised Foreign Investment Entities Proposals.

Tax Topics: No. 1678, FEE, FIE, FOE, FUM: I Smell the Blood of a NERT; No. 1655, New Rules for Foreign Investment Entities; No. 1604, FIE-ASCO Rules? - Part II; No. 1603, FIE-ASCO Rules? - Part I.

Interpretation Bulletins: *Secondary* — IT-451R Deemed disposition and acquisition on ceasing to be or becoming resident in Canada.

Tax Window Files: Aggregate Investment Income, *July 20, 2011*, CRA Document No. 2011-0397961I7.

Cases: For purposes of the taxpayer's appeals, the two Notes held by the non-resident entity constituted debt for purposes of paragraph 94.1(1)(*a*). *Barejo Holdings ULC v. The Queen*, 2018 DTC 1144 (TCC) [under appeal]

The imputed income rules applied when one of the main reasons for interposing a Bermudian corporation between the taxpayer and the investments it held in two Bermudian open-ended investment corporations was to avoid the tax that would have been imposed had the taxpayer held those investments directly. *Walton v. The Queen*, 98 DTC 1780 (T.C.C.).

► 94.1(2) ◄

(2) Definitions. In this section,

International Tax: No. 90, The Wait Is Finally Over: The Tax Court's Analysis of Section 94.1.

"designated cost" —"designated cost" to a taxpayer at any time in a taxation year of an offshore investment fund property that the taxpayer holds or has an interest in means the amount determined by the formula

$$A + B + C + D$$

where

A is the cost amount to the taxpayer of the property at that time (determined without reference to paragraphs 53(1)(*m*) and (*q*), subparagraph 53(2)(*c*)(i.3), paragraphs 53(2)(*g*) and (g.1) and section 143.2),

B is, where an additional amount has been made available by a person to another person after 1984 and before that time, whether by way of gift, loan, payment for a share, transfer of property at less than its fair market value or otherwise, in circumstances such that it may reasonably be concluded that one of the main reasons for so making the additional amount available to the other person was to increase the value of the property, the total of all amounts each of which is the amount, if any, by which such an additional amount exceeds any increase in the cost amount to the taxpayer of the property by virtue of that additional amount,

C is the total of all amounts each of which is an amount included in respect of the offshore investment fund property by virtue of this section in computing the taxpayer's income for a preceding taxation year, and

D is

(*a*) where the taxpayer has held or has had the interest in the property at all times since the end of 1984, the amount, if any, by which the fair market value of the property at the end of

1984 exceeds the cost amount to the taxpayer of the property at the end of 1984, or

(*b*) in any other case, the total of

(i) the amount, if any, by which the fair market value of the property at the particular time the taxpayer acquired the property exceeds the cost amount to the taxpayer of the property at the particular time, and

(ii) the amount, if any, by which

(A) the total of all amounts each of which is an amount that would have been included in respect of the property because of this section in computing the taxpayer's income for a taxation year that began before June 20, 1996 if the cost to the taxpayer of the property were equal to the fair market value of the property at the particular time

exceeds

(B) the total of all amounts each of which is an amount that was included in respect of the property because of this section in computing the taxpayer's income for a taxation year that began before June 20, 1996,

except that the designated cost of an offshore investment fund property that is a prescribed offshore investment fund property is nil;

Related Regulations: 6900.

"non-resident entity" —"non-resident entity" at any time means

(*a*) a corporation that is at that time non-resident,

(*b*) a partnership, organization, fund or entity that is at that time non-resident or is not at that time situated in Canada, or

(*c*) an exempt foreign trust (other than a trust described in any of paragraphs (*a*) to (*g*) of the definition "exempt foreign trust" in subsection 94(1)).

History: S. 94.1(2), the definition "non-resident entity" was amended by S.C. 2013, c. 34, s. 8(3), applicable to taxation years that end after March 4, 2010. The definition "non-resident entity" also applies to each taxation year of a beneficiary under a trust that ends before March 5, 2010 if subsection 94(1) applies to the trust for a taxation year of the trust that ends in that earlier taxation year of the beneficiary.

S. 94.1(2), the definition "non-resident entity", formerly read:

"non-resident entity"—"non-resident entity" means a corporation that is not resident in Canada, a partnership, organization, fund or entity that is not resident or is not situated in Canada or a trust with respect to which the rules in paragraph 94(1)(*c*) or (*d*) apply.

► 94.1(3) ◄

(3) Interpretation. Where subsection (1) is applied with respect to an offshore investment fund property that was

(*a*) held by the taxpayer on February 15, 1984,

(*b*) received as a stock dividend in respect of a share of the capital stock of a non-resident entity held by the taxpayer on February 15, 1984,

(*c*) received as a stock dividend in respect of a share of the capital stock of a non-resident entity that the taxpayer had previously received as described in paragraph (*b*), or

(*d*) substituted for a property held by the taxpayer on February 15, 1984 pursuant to an arrangement that existed on that date,

the reference to "1984" in the descriptions of B and D in the definition "designated cost" in subsection (2) shall be read as a reference to "1985".

SECTION 94.2: Investments in non-resident commercial trusts

► 94.2(1) ◄

(1) Investments in non-resident commercial trusts. Subsection (2) applies to a beneficiary under a trust, and to any particular person of which any such beneficiary is a controlled foreign affiliate, at any time if

(*a*) the trust is at that time an exempt foreign trust (other than a trust described in any of paragraphs (*a*) to (*g*) of the definition "exempt foreign trust" in subsection 94(1));

(*b*) either

(i) the total fair market value at that time of all fixed interests of a particular class in the trust held by the beneficiary, persons or partnerships not dealing at arm's length with the beneficiary, or persons or partnerships that acquired their interests in the trust in exchange for consideration given to the trust by the beneficiary, is at least 10% of the total fair market value at that time of all fixed interests of the particular class, or

(ii) the beneficiary or the particular person has at or before that time contributed restricted property to the trust; and

(*c*) the beneficiary is at that time a

(i) resident beneficiary,

(ii) mutual fund,

(iii) controlled foreign affiliate of the particular person, or

(iv) partnership of which a person described in any of subparagraphs (i) to (iii) is a member.

Editorial Note: Under s. 94.2, a Canadian resident who, together with non-arm's length persons, owns at least 10% of a non-resident trust that is an "exempt foreign trust" for purposes of s. 94(1) under paragraph (*h*) or (*l*) of that definition, will be subject to current tax on the income of that trust in accordance with the "controlled foreign affiliate" regime in s. 95. Paragraph (*h*) of the exempt foreign trust definition will catch most widely-held foreign commercial trusts. Under paragraph (*l*) of the definition, the government can prescribe particular trusts to be caught by these rules, although no trusts have been prescribed to date. Under s. 94.2(1)(*b*)(ii), if the beneficiary has contributed restricted property to the trust, s. 94.2 will also apply.

Where s. 94.2 applies, the foreign trust is deemed to be a non-resident corporation with 100 shares that is controlled by the Canadian resident. The Canadian resident will be deemed to hold a proportionate number of those shares relative to his, her or its "fixed interest" in the trust. As a result of the application of the controlled foreign affiliate regime, the taxpayer will be required to accrue "foreign accrual property income" (as defined in s. 95(1)) on an annual basis. This rule is a slightly broader version of the rule in "old" s. 94(1)(*d*) that applied to non-discretionary non-resident trusts for pre-2007 taxation years.

Amendments pursuant to the 2014 federal Budget eliminated the exception for immigration trusts for taxation years ending after Feb. 10, 2014 (with limited transitional provision).

History: S. 94.2(1), the portion before paragraph (*a*) was replaced by S.C. 2014, c. 39, s. 24(1), applicable to taxation years that end after February 10, 2014, except that it does not apply in respect of a trust to taxation years that end before 2015 if the following conditions are satisfied:

(a) no contributions are made to the trust after February 10, 2014 and before 2015; and

(b) if the trust were to have a particular taxation year that ended after 2013 and before February 11, 2014,

(i) the trust would be non-resident for the purpose of computing its income for the particular year, and

(ii) if the definitions "resident contributor" and "connected contributor" in subsection 94(1) were read for the particular year without reference to their paragraphs (*a*), the trust would be resident in Canada for the purpose of computing its income for the particular year.

S. 94.2(1), the portion before paragraph (*a*) formerly read:

(1) *Investments in non-resident commercial trusts.* Subsection (2) applies to a beneficiary under a trust, and to any particular person (other than an individual described in paragraph (*a*) of the definition "connected contributor" in subsection 94(1)) of which any such beneficiary is a controlled foreign affiliate, at any time if

S. 94.2(1) was added by S.C. 2013, c. 34, s. 9(1), applicable to taxation years that end after March 4, 2010, except that

(*a*) for taxation years that end before October 24, 2012, paragraph 94.2(1)(*c*) is to be read as follows:

"(*c*) the beneficiary is at that time a resident beneficiary or a mutual fund."

(*b*) if subsection 94(1) applies to a trust for a taxation year that ends before March 5, 2010, then section 94.2 applies to each beneficiary under the trust, and to each person of which a beneficiary under the trust is a controlled foreign affiliate, for a taxation year of the beneficiary or person in which the earlier taxation year of the trust ends and, for those earlier taxation years, section 94.2 is to be read as follows:

S. 94.2 **Investments in non-resident commercial trusts.** Where,

(*a*) at any time in a taxation year of a trust that is an exempt foreign trust (other than a trust described in any of paragraphs (*a*) to (*g*) of the definition "exempt foreign trust" in subsection 94(1)), a person beneficially interested in the trust (referred to in this section as a "beneficiary") was

(i) a person resident in Canada,

(ii) a corporation or trust with which a person resident in Canada was not dealing at arm's length, or

(iii) a controlled foreign affiliate of a person resident in Canada, and

(*b*) at any time in or before the taxation year of the trust,

(i) the trust, or a non-resident corporation that would, if the trust were resident in Canada, be a controlled foreign affiliate of the trust, has, other than by virtue of the repayment of a loan, acquired property, directly or indirectly in any manner whatever, from

(A) a particular person who

(I) was the beneficiary referred to in paragraph (*a*), was related to that beneficiary or was the uncle, aunt, nephew or niece of that beneficiary,

(II) was resident in Canada at any time in the 18-month period before the end of that year or, in the case of a person who has ceased to exist, was resident in Canada at any time in the 18-month period before the person ceased to exist, and

(III) in the case of an individual, had before the end of that year been resident in Canada for a period of, or periods the total of which is, more than 60 months, or

(B) a trust or corporation that acquired the property, directly or indirectly in any manner whatever, from a particular person described in clause (A) with whom it was not dealing at arm's length

and the trust was not

(C) an *inter vivos* trust created at any time before 1960 by a person who at that time was a non-resident person,

(D) a testamentary trust that arose as a consequence of the death of an individual before 1976, or

(E) governed by a foreign retirement arrangement, or

(ii) all or any part of the interest of the beneficiary in the trust was acquired directly or indirectly by the beneficiary by way of

(A) purchase,

(B) gift, bequest or inheritance from a person referred to in clause (i)(A) or (B), or

(C) the exercise of a power of appointment by a person referred to in clause (i)(A) or (B),

the following rules apply for that taxation year of the trust:

(*c*) for the purposes of subsections 91(1) to (4) and sections 95 and 233.4,

(i) the trust shall, with respect to any beneficiary under the trust whose beneficial interest in the trust has a fair market value that is not less than 10% of the aggregate fair market value of all beneficial interests in the trust, be deemed to be a non-resident corporation that is controlled by the beneficiary,

(ii) the trust shall be deemed to be a non-resident corporation having a capital stock of a single class divided into 100 issued shares, and

(iii) each beneficiary under the trust shall be deemed to own at any time the number of the issued shares that is equal to the proportion of 100 that

(A) the fair market value at that time of the beneficiary's beneficial interest in the trust

is of

(B) the fair market value at that time of all beneficial interests in the trust, and

(*d*) in computing the foreign accrual property income of the trust for that taxation year, there may be deducted such portion of the amount that would, but for this paragraph, be the foreign accrual property income of the trust as may reasonably be considered as having been included in computing a beneficiary's income under subsection 104(13) for a taxation year in which that taxation year of the trust ends."

Canadian Tax Foundation: Harris et al., *The Long and Winding Road: Sections 94, 94.1, and 94.2*, 2013 Conference Report 23:1–60.

▶ 94.2(2) ◀

(2) Deemed corporation. If this subsection applies at any time to a beneficiary under, or a particular person in respect of, a trust, then for the purposes of applying this section, subsections 91(1) to (4), paragraph 94.1(1)(*a*) and sections 95 and 233.4 to the beneficiary under, and, if applicable, to the particular person in respect of, the trust

(*a*) the trust is deemed to be at that time a non-resident corporation

(i) controlled by each of the beneficiary and the particular person, and

(ii) having, for each particular class of fixed interests in the trust, a separate class of capital stock of 100 issued shares that have the same attributes as the interests of the particular class; and

(*b*) each beneficiary under the trust is deemed to hold at that time the number of shares of each separate class described in subparagraph (*a*)(ii) equal to the proportion of 100 that the fair market value at that time of that beneficiary's fixed interests in the corresponding particular class of fixed interests in the trust is of the fair market value at that time of all fixed interests in the particular class.

History: S. 94.2(2) was added by S.C. 2013, c. 34, s. 9(1), applicable to taxation years that end after March 4, 2010. [**Editorial Note:** See the application for a trust with a taxation year that ends before March 5, 2010 in the history note following s. 94.2(1).]

Canadian Tax Foundation: Harris et al., *The Long and Winding Road: Sections 94, 94.1, and 94.2*, 2013 Conference Report 23:1–60.

▶ 94.2(3) ◀

(3) Relief from double tax. For the purposes of applying subsection 91(1) to the beneficiary, and, if applicable, to the particular person, to whom subsection (2) applies

(*a*) there may be deducted in computing the foreign accrual property income of the trust referred to in paragraph (2)(*a*) (in this subsection referred to as the "entity") for a particular taxation year of the entity the amount that would, in the absence of this paragraph, be the portion of the entity's foreign accrual property income that would reasonably be considered to have been if this Part were applicable to all beneficiaries of the entity, included under subsection 104(13) in computing the income of any beneficiary of the entity for the taxation year in which the particular taxation year of the entity ends; and

(*b*) subsection 5904(2) of the *Income Tax Regulations* is to be read without reference to its paragraph (*a*) in determining the distribution entitlement of all the shares of a class of the capital stock of the entity at the end of the particular taxation year.

History: S. 94.2(3) was added by S.C. 2013, c. 34, s. 9(1), applicable to taxation years that end after March 4, 2010. [**Editorial Note:** See the application for a trust with a taxation year that ends before March 5, 2010 in the history note following s. 94.2(1).]

► 94.2(4) ◄

(4) Request for information. If the Minister sends a written request, served personally or by registered mail, to a taxpayer requesting additional information for the purpose of enabling the Minister to determine the fair market value of interests in a trust for the purpose of determining the application of subsections (1) to (3) for a taxation year to the taxpayer, and information that may reasonably be considered to be sufficient to make the determination is not received by the Minister within 120 days (or within any longer period that is acceptable to the Minister) after the Minister sends the request, then in applying this section for the taxation year to the taxpayer the fair market value of those interests is deemed to be the fair market value as reasonably determined by the Minister based on the information received by the Minister within 120 days (or within any longer period that is acceptable to the Minister) after the Minister sends the request and any other information the Minister considers reasonable.

History: S. 94.2(4) was added by S.C. 2013, c. 34, s. 9(1), applicable to taxation years that end after March 4, 2010. [**Editorial Note:** See the application for a trust with a taxation year that ends before March 5, 2010 in the history note following s. 94.2(1).]

SECTION 95: [Foreign accrual property income]

► 95(1) ◄

(1) Definitions for this subdivision. In this subdivision,

Related Regulations: 5905; 5907.

Related Sections: 91(4.1) Denial of foreign accrual tax.

Interpretation Bulletins: *Secondary* — IT-451R Deemed disposition and acquisition on ceasing to be or becoming resident in Canada.

"active business" —"active business" of a foreign affiliate of a taxpayer means any business carried on by the foreign affiliate other than

(*a*) an investment business carried on by the foreign affiliate,

(*b*) a business that is deemed by subsection (2) to be a business other than an active business carried on by the foreign affiliate, or

(*c*) a non-qualifying business of the foreign affiliate;

Editorial Note: The term "active business" as defined in s. 95(1) is central to the application of the foreign affiliate rules contained in Subdivision i of the Act and the supporting rules in Part LIX of the Regulations. In particular, income earned by a foreign affiliate that is sourced from an active business will not be included in a foreign affiliate's foreign accrual property income (FAPI) and therefore such income will not be subject to Canadian taxation as earned by the affiliate. In addition, income earned by a foreign affiliate that is sourced from an active business will be included in the affiliate's "exempt earnings" or "taxable earnings" and therefore "exempt surplus" or "taxable surplus", respectively (see the definitions in regulation 5907(1)) depending on the affiliate's residence and the location of the business from which the income was earned.

Related Regulations: 5906(1) Where active business carried on; 5907(1), "active business" — Meaning assigned by s. 95(1), "earnings", "exempt earnings", "exempt loss", "loss", "net earnings", "net loss", "taxable earnings", "taxable loss"; 5907(2) Adjustment to earnings; 5907(2.1), (2.2), (2.3) and (2.6) Election for depreciable property; 5907(2.7), (2.8) and (2.9) Adjustment to earnings; 5907(5.1) Earnings computation on disposition of capital property; 5907(10) Tax sparing.

Related Sections: S. 17(8) Exception; s. 95(1), "excluded property", "foreign accrual property income", "income from an active business", "income from property"; s. 95(2) Determination of certain components of foreign accrual property income; s. 248(1), "business", "taxpayer".

Cases: Where the taxpayer's commercial undertakings went beyond mere passive investment in property, interest was held to be income from active business which did not constitute FAPI under s. 95(1)(b), as it then read. *The Queen v. Canada Trustco Mortgage Company*, 99 DTC 5094 (F.C.T.D.), affirming 91 DTC 1312 (T.C.C.)

"antecedent corporation" —"antecedent corporation" of a particular corporation means

(*a*) a predecessor corporation (within the meaning assigned by subsection 87(1)) in respect of an amalgamation to which subsection 87(11) applied and by which the particular corporation was formed,

(*b*) a predecessor corporation (within the meaning of subsection 87(1)) of the corporation (referred to in this definition as the "first amalco") that was formed on an amalgamation of the predecessor corporation and another corporation, where

(i) shares of the capital stock of the predecessor corporation that were not owned by the other corporation, or by a corporation of which the other corporation is a subsidiary wholly-owned corporation, were exchanged on the amalgamation for shares of the capital stock of the first amalco that were, during the series of transactions or events that includes the amalgamation, redeemed, acquired or cancelled by the first amalco for money,

(ii) the first amalco was a predecessor corporation (within the meaning assigned by subsection 87(1)) in respect of an amalgamation to which subsection 87(11) applied and by which the particular corporation was formed, and

(iii) the amalgamation referred to in subparagraph (i) occurred in a series of transactions or events that included the amalgamation referred to in subparagraph (ii),

(*c*) a corporation that was wound-up into the particular corporation in a winding-up to which subsection 88(1) applied, or

(*d*) an antecedent corporation of an antecedent corporation of the particular corporation;

Editorial Note: The term "antecedent corporation" is used in the definition of "designated acquired corporation", which in turn is used in the definition of "specified person or partnership" which is the integral defined term used in the s. 95(2)(*f.1*) carve-out rule. All of these terms are defined in s. 95(1).

History: S. 95(1), the definition "antecedent corporation" was added by S.C. 2009, c. 2, s. 25(1), applicable to taxation years of a foreign affiliate of a taxpayer that begin after October 2, 2007. However, if the taxpayer elects in writing in respect of all of its foreign affiliates and files the election with the Minister of National Revenue on or before the taxpayer's election day, the definition "antecedent corporation" also applies to taxation years of a foreign affiliate of the taxpayer that begin before October 2, 2007 and after the date chosen by the taxpayer as described below.

The taxpayer's election day is the later of (i) the taxpayer's filing-due date for the taxpayer's taxation year that includes the day on which this Act is assented to [R.A. March 12, 2009] and (ii) the day that is one year after the day on which this Act is assented to [March 12, 2010].

To be valid, an election [described above] must include the identification by the taxpayer of its choice of one of the following dates:

(i) December 31, 1994,

(ii) December 20, 2002, or

(iii) February 27, 2004.

Notwithstanding subsections 152(4) to (5) of the Act, any assessment of a taxpayer's tax, interest and penalties payable under the Act for any taxation year shall be made that is necessary to take into account this provision and any election made with respect to it.

Related Sections: S. 87(1) Amalgamations; s. 87(11) Vertical amalgamations; s. 88(1) Winding-up; s. 95(1), "designated acquired corporation"; s. 248(10) Series of transactions.

"calculating currency" —"calculating currency" for a taxation year of a foreign affiliate of a taxpayer means

(*a*) the currency of the country in which the foreign affiliate is resident at the end of the taxation year, or

(*b*) any currency that the taxpayer demonstrates to be reasonable in the circumstances;

Editorial Note: The term "calculating currency" is relevant to the determination of the amounts referred to in s. 95(2)(*f*); that is, (1) capital gains, capital losses, taxable capital gains and allowable capital losses from the disposition of property, and (2) income and losses from property, from non-active businesses and from non-qualifying businesses.

Pursuant to s. 95(2)(*f.12*), 95(2)(*f.13*) and 95(2)(*f.15*) the computation of these amounts is made having regard to a foreign affiliate's calculating currency.

History: S. 95(1), the definition "calculating currency" was added by S.C. 2009, c. 2, s. 25(1), applicable to taxation years of a foreign affiliate of a taxpayer that begin after October 2, 2007. However, if the taxpayer elects in writing in respect of all of its foreign affiliates and files the election with the Minister of National Revenue on or before the taxpayer's election day, the definition "calculating currency" also applies to taxation years of a foreign affiliate of the taxpayer that begin before October 2, 2007 and after the date chosen by the taxpayer as described below.

The taxpayer's election day is the later of (i) the taxpayer's filing-due date for the taxpayer's taxation year that includes the day on which this Act is assented to [R.A. March 12, 2009] and (ii) the day that is one year after the day on which this Act is assented to [March 12, 2010].

To be valid, an election [described above] must include the identification by the taxpayer of its choice of one of the following dates:

(i) December 31, 1994,

(ii) December 20, 2002, or

(iii) February 27, 2004.

Notwithstanding subsections 152(4) to (5) of the Act, any assessment of a taxpayer's tax, interest and penalties payable under the Act for any taxation year shall be made that is necessary to take into account this provision and any election made with respect to it.

Related Sections: S. 95(1), "foreign affiliate"; s. 95(2)(*f.12*) [Determination of FAPI — Use of calculating currency]; s. 95(2)(*f.13*) [Determination of FAPI — Conversion to Canadian currency]; s. 95(2)(*f.15*) [Determination of FAPI — Currency for S. 39(2)].

"controlled foreign affiliate" —"controlled foreign affiliate", at any time, of a taxpayer resident in Canada, means

(*a*) a foreign affiliate of the taxpayer that is, at that time, controlled by the taxpayer, or

(*b*) a foreign affiliate of the taxpayer that would, at that time, be controlled by the taxpayer if the taxpayer owned

(i) all of the shares of the capital stock of the foreign affiliate that are owned at that time by the taxpayer,

(ii) all of the shares of the capital stock of the foreign affiliate that are owned at that time by persons who do not deal at arm's length with the taxpayer,

(iii) all of the shares of the capital stock of the foreign affiliate that are owned at that time by the persons (each of whom is referred to in this definition as a "relevant Canadian shareholder"), in any set of persons not exceeding four (which set of persons shall be determined without reference to the existence of or the absence of any relationship, connection or action in concert between those persons), who

(A) are resident in Canada,

(B) are not the taxpayer or a person described in subparagraph (ii), and

(C) own, at that time, shares of the capital stock of the foreign affiliate, and

(iv) all of the shares of the capital stock of the foreign affiliate that are owned at that time by persons who do not deal at arm's length with any relevant Canadian shareholder;

Editorial Note: A Canadian-resident taxpayer is required to include an amount in income pursuant to s. 91(1) in respect of the "foreign accrual property income" (FAPI) as defined in s. 95(1) earned by a "controlled foreign affiliate" of the taxpayer. See the editorial note accompanying s. 91(1) for a discussion of the amount to be included in income. Generally, a foreign affiliate of a Canadian-resident taxpayer will be a controlled foreign affiliate of the taxpayer where the taxpayer is able to exercise *de jure* control over the affiliate. For the purposes of determining *de jure* control the definition of "controlled foreign affiliate" contains rules that deem the taxpayer to own shares of the affiliate held by other persons.

Related Regulations: 5903(1) and (2) Deductible loss computation; 5904(1), (2) and (3) Determination of participating percentage; 5907(1), "controlled foreign affiliate" — Meaning assigned by s. 95(1).

Related Sections: S. 17(3) Exception to anti-avoidance rule — indirect loan; s. 17(8) Exception; s. 17(8.1) Borrowed money; s. 17(8.2) Deemed use; s. 17(10) Determination of whether related and controlled foreign affiliate status; s. 17(12) Determination of controlled foreign affiliate status; s. 17(13) Extended definition of controlled foreign affiliate; s. 17(15) Definitions; s. 53(1)(*m*) Adjustments to cost base — Offshore investment fund property; s. 88(3) Dissolution of foreign affiliate; s. 91(1) Amounts to be included in respect of share of foreign affiliate; s. 91(5) Amounts deductible in respect of dividends received; s. 94(3) Liabilities of non-resident trusts and others; s. 94.1(1)(*a*) Exclusion from offshore investment fund rules; s. 95(1), "foreign accrual property income" element C, "participating percentage"; s. 95(2)(*a*) FAPI recharacterization; s. 95(2)(*f*)(i) Computation of capital gains and capital losses; s. 95(2)(*g*) Determination of foreign exchange gains and losses; s. 95(2)(*g.2*) Foreign spin-off election; s. 95(2)(*z*) Foreign affiliate as a partner; s. 95(2.01) Rules for the definition "controlled foreign affiliate"; s. 95(2.02) Rule against double-counting; s. 128.1(1)(*d*) Foreign affiliate; s. 162(10.2) Shares or debt owned by controlled foreign affiliate; s. 162(10.3) Application to partnerships; s. 162(10.4) Application to non-resident trusts; s. 163(2.5) Shares or debt owned by controlled foreign affiliate; s. 163(2.6) Application to partnerships; s. 163(2.91) Application to non-resident trusts; s. 233.2 Non-resident trust reporting; s. 233.4 Reporting entity; s. 233.5 Due diligence exception; s. 247(7) Exclusion for loans to certain controlled foreign affiliates; s. 248(1), "controlled foreign affiliate", "taxpayer"; s. 248(25)(*b*)(iii)(A)(IV) and (V) Meaning of "beneficially interested"; s. 256(6) Saving provision — controlled corporations; s. 256(6.1) Simultaneous control; Canada–US Income Tax Convention Article XXIX(5)(a)–US S-corporation deemed to be a controlled foreign affiliate.

Canadian Petroleum Tax Journal: Selected Income Tax Considerations When Structuring Foreign Resource Ventures, William A. Brebber, 2002, Vol. 15, No. 1.

Tax Profile: March 2008 — International Tax Planning for the Owner-Manager.

"designated acquired corporation" —"designated acquired corporation" of a taxpayer means a particular antecedent corporation of the taxpayer if

(*a*) the taxpayer or another antecedent corporation of the taxpayer acquired control of

(i) the particular antecedent corporation, or

(ii) a corporation (referred to in this definition as a "successor corporation") of which the particular antecedent corporation is an antecedent corporation, and

(*b*) immediately before the acquisition of control or a series of transactions or events that includes the acquisition of control, the taxpayer, the other antecedent corporation or a corporation resident in Canada of which the taxpayer or the other antecedent corporation is a subsidiary wholly-owned corporation, as the case may be, dealt at arm's length (otherwise than because of a right referred to in paragraph 251(5)(*b*)) with the particular antecedent corporation or the successor corporation, as the case may be;

Editorial Note: The term "designated acquired corporation" is used in the definition of "specified person or partnership" (itself defined in s. 95(1)) which is the integral defined term used in the s. 95(2)(*f.1*) carve-out rule.

History: S. 95(1), the definition "designated acquired corporation" was added by S.C. 2009, c. 2, s. 25(1), applicable to taxation years of a foreign affiliate of a taxpayer that begin after October 2, 2007. However, if the taxpayer elects in writing in respect of all of its foreign affiliates and files the election with the Minister of National Revenue on or before the taxpayer's election day, the definition "designated acquired corporation" also applies to taxation years of a foreign affiliate of the taxpayer that begin before October 2, 2007 and after the date chosen by the taxpayer as described below.

The taxpayer's election day is the later of (i) the taxpayer's filing-due date for the taxpayer's taxation year that includes the day on which this Act is assented to [R.A. March 12, 2009] and (ii) the day that is one year after the day on which this Act is assented to [March 12, 2010].

To be valid, an election [described above] must include the identification by the taxpayer of its choice of one of the following dates:

(i) December 31, 1994,

(ii) December 20, 2002, or

(iii) February 27, 2004.

Notwithstanding subsections 152(4) to (5) of the Act, any assessment of a taxpayer's tax, interest and penalties payable under the Act for any taxation year shall be made that is necessary to take into account this provision and any election made with respect to it.

Related Sections: S. 95(1), "antecedent corporation"; s. 248(10) Series of transactions; s. 256(6.1) Simultaneous control.

"designated liquidation and dissolution" —"designated liquidation and dissolution", of a foreign affiliate (referred to in this definition as the "disposing affiliate") of a taxpayer, means a liquidation and dissolution of the disposing affiliate in respect of which

(*a*) the taxpayer had, immediately before the time of the earliest distribution of property by the disposing affiliate in the course of the liquidation and dissolution, a surplus entitlement percentage in respect of the disposing affiliate of not less than 90%,

(*b*) both

(i) the percentage determined by the following formula is greater than or equal to 90%:

$$A/B$$

where

A is the amount, if any, by which

(A) the total of all amounts each of which is the fair market value, at the time at which it is distributed, of a property that is distributed by the disposing affiliate, in respect of shares of the capital stock of the disposing affiliate, in the course of the liquidation and dissolution to one particular shareholder of the disposing affiliate that was, immediately before the time of the distribution, a foreign affiliate of the taxpayer

exceeds

(B) the total of all amounts each of which is an amount owing (other than an unpaid dividend) by, or an obligation of, the disposing affiliate that was assumed or cancelled by the particular shareholder in consideration for a property referred to in clause (A), and

B is the amount, if any, by which

(A) the total of all amounts each of which is the fair market value, at the time at which it is distributed, of a property that is distributed by the disposing affiliate, in respect of shares of the capital stock of the disposing affiliate, to a shareholder of the disposing affiliate in the course of the liquidation and dissolution

exceeds

(B) the total of all amounts each of which is an amount owing (other than an unpaid dividend) by, or an obligation of, the disposing affiliate that was assumed or cancelled by a shareholder of the disposing affiliate in consideration for a property referred to in clause (A), and

(ii) at the time of each distribution of property by the disposing affiliate in the course of the liquidation and dissolution in respect of shares of the capital stock of the disposing affiliate, the particular shareholder holds shares of that capital stock that would, if an annual general meeting of the shareholders of the disposing affiliate were held at that time, entitle it to 90% or more of the votes that could be cast under all circumstances at the meeting, or

(*c*) one particular shareholder of the disposing affiliate that was, throughout the liquidation and dissolution, a foreign affiliate of the taxpayer owns not less than 90% of the issued shares of each class of the capital stock of the disposing affiliate throughout the liquidation and dissolution;

History: S. 95(1), the definition "designated liquidation and dissolution" was added by S.C. 2013, c. 34, s. 70(7), applicable in respect of liquidations and dissolutions of foreign affiliates of a taxpayer that begin after August 19, 2011. However, if the taxpayer elects in writing in respect of all of its foreign affiliates and files the election with the Minister of National Revenue on or before the day that is the later of the taxpayer's filing-due date for the taxpayer's taxation year that includes June 26, 2013 and June 26, 2014 [the day that is one year after royal assent], then

(*a*) the definition "designated liquidation and dissolution" in subsection 95(1) applies to liquidations and dissolutions of all foreign affiliates of the taxpayer that begin after December 20, 2002; and

(*b*) in respect of liquidations and dissolutions of all foreign affiliates of the taxpayer that begin on or before August 19, 2011, the definition "designated liquidation and dissolution" in subsection 95(1) is to be read without reference to its subparagraph (*b*)(ii).

If the taxpayer referred to in any election dealing with various foreign affiliate amendments is a partnership, any reference in those elections to "the taxpayer's filing-due date" is to be read as a reference to "the earliest of the filing-due dates of any member of the taxpayer".

Any assessment of a taxpayer's tax, interest and penalties payable under the Act for any taxation year that ends before June 26, 2013 that would otherwise be precluded because of subsections 152(4) to (5) of the Act shall be made to the extent necessary to take into account the amendments by S.C. 2013, c. 34, s. 54 to 89.

"eligible trust" —"eligible trust", at any time, means a trust, other than a trust

(*a*) created or maintained for charitable purposes,

(*b*) governed by an employee benefit plan,

(*c*) described in paragraph (*a.1*) of the definition "trust" in subsection 108(1),

(*d*) governed by a salary deferral arrangement,

(*e*) operated for the purpose of administering or providing superannuation, pension, retirement or employee benefits, or

(*f*) where the amount of income or capital that any entity may receive directly from the trust at any time as a beneficiary under the trust depends on the exercise by any entity of, or the failure by any entity to exercise, a discretionary power;

Editorial Note: The term "eligible trust" is relevant to the definition of "exempt trust" in s. 95(1). See the editorial note accompanying the definition of "exempt trust". Generally, an "eligible trust" is a trust other than certain enumerated trusts, including a trust: maintained for charitable purposes; governed by an employee benefit plan or a salary deferral arrangement; operated to administer pension and retirement benefits; or that is a discretionary trust.

Related Sections: S. 95(1), "entity", "exempt trust" para. (*a*) — Requirement to be an exempt trust; s. 108(1), "trust" para. (*a.1*); s. 248(1), "employee benefit plan", "salary deferral arrangement".

"entity" —"entity" includes an association, a corporation, a fund, a natural person, a joint venture, an organization, a partnership, a syndicate and a trust;

Related Sections: S. 95(1), "eligible trust", "foreign bank", "specified fixed interest", "specified purchaser"; s. 95(2)(*u*) Tiers of partnerships.

"excluded property" —"excluded property", at a particular time, of a foreign affiliate of a taxpayer means any property of the foreign affiliate that is

(*a*) used or held by the foreign affiliate principally for the purpose of gaining or producing income from an active business carried on by it,

(*b*) shares of the capital stock of another foreign affiliate of the taxpayer where all or substantially all of the fair market value of the property of the other foreign affiliate is attributable to property, of that other foreign affiliate, that is excluded property,

(*c*) property all or substantially all of the income from which is, or would be, if there were income from the property, income from an active business (which, for this purpose, includes income that would be deemed to be income from an active business by paragraph (2)(*a*) if that paragraph were read without reference to subparagraph (v)), or

(*c*.1) property arising under or as a result of an agreement that

(i) provides for the purchase, sale or exchange of currency, and

(ii) either

(A) can reasonably be considered to have been made by the affiliate to reduce its risk, with respect to an amount that was receivable under an agreement that relates to the sale of excluded property or with respect to an amount that was receivable and was a property described in paragraph (*c*), of fluctuations in the value of the currency in which the amount receivable was denominated, or

(B) can reasonably be considered to have been made by the affiliate to reduce its risk, with respect to any of the following amounts, of fluctuations in the value of the currency in which that amount was denominated:

(I) an amount that was payable under an agreement that relates to the purchase of property that (at all times between the time of the acquisition of the property and the particular time) is excluded property of the affiliate,

(II) an amount of indebtedness, to the extent that the proceeds derived from the issuance or incurring of the indebtedness can reasonably be considered to have been used to acquire property that (at all times between the time of the acquisition of that property and the particular time) is excluded property of the affiliate, or

(III) an amount of indebtedness, to the extent that the proceeds derived from the issuance or incurring of the indebtedness can reasonably be considered to have been used to repay the outstanding balance of

1. an amount that, immediately before the time of that repayment, is described by subclause (I),

2. an amount of indebtedness of the affiliate that, immediately before the time of that repayment, is described by subclause (II), or

3. an amount of indebtedness of the affiliate that, immediately before the time of that repayment, is described by this subclause,

and, for the purposes of the definitions "foreign affiliate" in this subsection and "direct equity percentage" in subsection (4) as they apply to this definition, where at any time a foreign affiliate of a taxpayer has an interest in a partnership,

(*d*) the partnership shall be deemed to be a non-resident corporation having capital stock of a single class divided into 100 issued shares, and

(*e*) the affiliate shall be deemed to own at that time that proportion of the issued shares of that class that

(i) the fair market value of the affiliate's interest in the partnership at that time

is of

(ii) the fair market value of all interests in the partnership at that time;

Editorial Note: The classification of property held by a foreign affiliate as "excluded property" is relevant for the purposes of computing the affiliate's "foreign accrual property income" (FAPI), if any, realized on the disposition of the property. Generally, taxable capital gains realized, and allowable capital losses incurred, on the disposition of excluded property are not included in the computation of a foreign affiliate's FAPI. More specifically, taxable capital gains realized by a foreign affiliate on the disposition of property are included in the affiliate's FAPI unless the property is excluded property and none of the foreign affiliate reorganization rules in ss. 95(2)(*c*), (*d*) and (*e*) apply to the disposition (see element B of the definition of "FAPI" in subsection 95(1)). Similarly, allowable capital losses incurred by a foreign affiliate on the disposition of property are deducted in computing the affiliate's FAPI unless the property is excluded property (see element E of the definition of "FAPI"). In either case, taxable capital gains and allowable capital losses will only be included in the computation of the foreign affiliate's FAPI to the extent that the gains and losses can reasonably be considered to have accrued after the affiliate's 1975 taxation year.

Related Regulations: 5907(1), "exempt earnings" clause (d)(ii)(H), "net earnings" para. (d), "net loss" para. (d), "taxable earnings" subpara. (b)(v), "taxable loss" subpara. (b)(iv).

Related Sections: S. 85.1(4) Exception; s. 85.1(6) Where subsection (5) does not apply; s. 93(1.1) Deemed s. 93(1) election; s. 93(1.3) Deemed s. 93(1) election; s. 93(2) Loss limitation on disposition of share; s. 93(2.1) Loss limitation — disposition of share by partnership; s. 93(2.2) Loss limitation — disposition of partnership interest; s. 93(2.3) Loss limitation — disposition of partnership interest; s. 95(1), "foreign accrual property income" (elements B and E), "investment property"; s. 95(2)(*a*)(ii)(D) and s. 95(2)(*a*)(v) FAPI recharacterization; s. 95(2)(*f*)(i) Computation of capital gains and capital losses; s. 95(2)(*g.02*) Foreign exchange gains and losses; s. 95(2)(*i*) Deemed gain or loss from the disposition of excluded property; s. 248(1), "taxpayer".

Canadian Tax Foundation: Barnicke and Huynh, *FA's LP Interest: Excluded Property?*, 2015 Canadian Tax Highlights 23(4):4–5.

International Tax: No. 103, Now It's "Excluded Property", Now It's Not.

"exempt trust" — "exempt trust", at a particular time in respect of a taxpayer resident in Canada, means a trust that, at that time, is a trust under which the interest of each beneficiary under the trust is, at all times that the interest exists during the trust's taxation year that includes the particular time, a specified fixed interest of the beneficiary in the trust, if at the particular time

(*a*) the trust is an eligible trust,

(*b*) there are at least 150 beneficiaries each of whom holds a specified fixed interest, in the trust, that has a fair market value of at least $500, and

(*c*) the total of all amounts each of which is the fair market value of an interest as a beneficiary under the trust held by a specified purchaser in respect of the taxpayer is not more than 10% of the total fair market value of all interests as a beneficiary under the trust;

Editorial Note: The term "exempt trust" is relevant for s. 95(2.01). Generally, an "exempt trust" is defined as an "eligible trust" under which the interest of each beneficiary is a "specified fixed interest" if the trust has at least 150 beneficiaries each of whom owns a specified fixed interest in the trust with a fair market value of at least $500. Even if a trust would otherwise be an exempt trust, such a trust will not be an exempt trust if the total fair market value of all beneficial interests in the trust held by a "specified purchaser" exceeds 10% of the fair market value of all beneficial interests in the trust. Each of "eligible trust", "specified fixed interest" and "specified purchaser" is defined in s. 95(1).

Related Sections: S. 95(1), "eligible trust", "specified purchaser" para. (*d*) — Exclusion; s. 95(2.01)(*c*) and (*d*) Determination of controlled foreign affiliate status where shares held by trust; s. 248(1), "taxpayer".

"foreign accrual property income" — "foreign accrual property income" of a foreign affiliate of a taxpayer, for any taxation year of the affiliate, means the amount determined by the formula

$$(A + A.1 + A.2 + B + C) - (D + E + F + F.1 + G + H)$$

where

A is the amount that would, if section 80 did not apply to the affiliate for the year or a preceding taxation year, be the total of all amounts, each of which is the affiliate's income for the year from property, the affiliate's income for the year from a business other than an active business or the affiliate's income for the year from a non-qualifying business of the affiliate, in each case that amount being determined as if each amount described in clause (2)(*a*)(ii)(D) that was paid or payable, directly or indirectly, by the affiliate to another foreign affiliate of the taxpayer or of a person with whom the taxpayer does not deal at arm's length were nil where an amount in respect of the income derived by the other foreign affiliate from that amount that was paid or payable to it by the affiliate was added in computing its income from an active business, other than

(*a*) interest that would, by virtue of paragraph 81(1)(*m*), not be included in computing the income of the affiliate if it were resident in Canada,

(*b*) a dividend from another foreign affiliate of the taxpayer,

(*c*) a taxable dividend to the extent that the amount thereof would, if the dividend were received by the taxpayer, be deductible by the taxpayer under section 112, or

(*d*) any amount included because of subsection 80.4(2) in the affiliate's income in respect of indebtedness to another corporation that is a foreign affiliate of the taxpayer or of a person resident in Canada with whom the taxpayer does not deal at arm's length,

A.1 is twice the total of all amounts included in computing the affiliate's income from property or businesses (other than active businesses) for the year because of subsection 80(13),

A.2 is the amount determined for G in respect of the affiliate for the preceding taxation year,

B is the total of all amounts each of which is the portion of the affiliate's income (to the extent that the income is not included under the description of A) for the year, or of the affiliate's taxable capital gain for the year that can reasonably be considered to have accrued after its 1975 taxation year, from a disposition of property

(*a*) that is not, at the time of disposition, excluded property of the affiliate, or

(*b*) that is, at the time of disposition, excluded property of the affiliate, if any of paragraphs (2)(*c*), (*d*) and (*d.1*), subparagraph (2)(*e*)(i) and paragraph 88(3)(*a*) applies to the disposition,

C is, where the affiliate is a controlled foreign affiliate of the taxpayer, the amount that would be required to be included in computing its income for the year if

(*a*) subsection 94.1(1) were applicable in computing that income,

(*b*) the words "earned directly by the taxpayer" in that subsection were replaced by the words "earned by the person resident in Canada in respect of whom the taxpayer is a foreign affiliate",

(*c*) the words "other than a controlled foreign affiliate of the taxpayer or a prescribed non-resident entity" in paragraph 94.1(1)(*a*) were replaced by the words "other than a prescribed non-resident entity or a controlled foreign affiliate of a person resident in Canada of whom the taxpayer is a controlled foreign affiliate", and

(*d*) the words "other than a capital gain" in paragraph 94.1(1)(*g*) were replaced by the words "other than any income that would not be included in the taxpayer's foreign accrual property income for the year if the value of C in the definition 'foreign accrual property income' in subsection 95(1) were nil and other than a capital gain",

D is the total of all amounts, each of which is the affiliate's loss for the year from property, the affiliate's loss for the year from a business other than an active business of the affiliate or the affiliate's loss for the year from a non-qualifying business of the affiliate, in each case that amount being determined as if there were not included in the affiliate's income any amount described in any of paragraphs (*a*) to (*d*) of the description of A and as if each amount described in clause (2)(*a*)(ii)(D) that was paid or payable, directly or indirectly, by the affiliate to another foreign affiliate of the taxpayer or of a person with whom the taxpayer does not deal at arm's length were nil where an amount in respect of the income derived by the other foreign affiliate from that amount that was paid or payable to it by the affiliate was added in computing its income from an active business,

E is the lesser of

(*a*) the amount of the affiliate's allowable capital losses for the year from dispositions of property (other than excluded property and property in respect of which an election is made by the taxpayer under subsection 88(3.3)) that can reasonably be considered to have accrued after its 1975 taxation year, and

(*b*) the total of all amounts each of which is the portion of a taxable capital gain of the affiliate that is included in the amount determined for B in respect of the affiliate for the year,

F is the prescribed amount for the year,

F.1 is the lesser of

(*a*) the prescribed amount for the year, and

(*b*) the amount, if any, by which

(i) the total of all amounts each of which is the portion of a taxable capital gain of the affiliate that is included in the amount determined for B in respect of the affiliate for the year

exceeds

(ii) the amount determined for E in respect of the affiliate for the year,

G is the amount, if any, by which

(*a*) the total of amounts determined for A.1 and A.2 in respect of the affiliate for the year

exceeds

(*b*) the total of all amounts determined for D to F.1 in respect of the affiliate for the year, and

H is

(*a*) if the affiliate was a member of a partnership at the end of the fiscal period of the partnership that ended in the year and the partnership received a dividend at a particular time in that fiscal period from a corporation that would be, if the reference in subsection 93.1(1) to "corporation resident in Canada" were a reference to "taxpayer resident in Canada", a foreign affiliate of the taxpayer for the purposes of sections 93 and 113 at that particular time, then the portion of the amount of that dividend that is included in the value determined for A in respect of the affiliate for the year and that would be, if the reference in subsection 93.1(2) to "corporation resident in Canada" were a reference to "taxpayer resident in Canada", deemed by paragraph 93.1(2)(*a*) to have been received by the affiliate for the purposes of sections 93 and 113, and

(*b*) in any other case, nil;

Editorial Note: A Canadian-resident taxpayer is required to include an amount in income pursuant to s. 91(1) in respect of the "foreign accrual property income" (FAPI) earned by a controlled foreign affiliate of the taxpayer. See the editorial note accompanying s. 91(1) for a discussion of the amount to be included in income. The additions to a foreign affiliate's FAPI that are most commonly encountered include income from property under general principles, "income from property" as defined in s. 95(1), income deemed by s. 95(2) to be from a business other than an active business, and certain taxable capital gains. Other additions are also present.

History: S. 95(1), paragraph (*a*) of the description of H in the definition "foreign accrual property income" was replaced by S.C. 2014, c. 39, s. 25(3), applicable in respect of taxation years of a foreign affiliate of a taxpayer that end after 2006.

In addition, any assessment of a taxpayer's tax, interest and penalties payable under the Act for any taxation year that ends before the day on which this amendment receives royal assent [December 16, 2014] that would, in the absence of this section, be precluded because of the time references in subsection 152(4) of the Act is to be made to the extent necessary to take into account this amendment.

S. 95(1), paragraph (*a*) of the description of H in the definition "foreign accrual property income" formerly read:

(*a*) where the affiliate was a member of a partnership at the end of the fiscal period of the partnership that ended in the year and the partnership received a dividend at a particular time in that fiscal period from a corporation that was, for the purposes of sections 93 and 113, a foreign affiliate of the taxpayer at that particular time, the portion of the amount of that dividend that is included in the value of A in respect of the affiliate for the year and that is deemed by paragraph 93.1(2)(a) to have been received by the affiliate for the purposes of sections 93 and 113, and

S. 95(1), the description of F in the definition "foreign accrual property income" was replaced by S.C. 2013, c. 34, s. 33(1), applicable to taxation years of a foreign affiliate of a taxpayer that begin after November 1999.

Any assessment of a taxpayer's tax, interest and penalties payable under the Act for any taxation year that ends before June 26, 2013 that would otherwise be precluded because of subsections 152(4) to (5) of the Act, shall be made to the extent necessary to take into account this amendment, if the taxpayer

(i) elects in writing in respect of all of its foreign affiliates that this section apply in respect of that provision, and

(ii) files that election with the Minister of National Revenue on or before December 26, 2013 [the day that is six months after royal assent].

The description of F in the definition "foreign accrual property income" formerly read:

F is the amount claimed by the taxpayer, which amount may not be greater than the amount prescribed to be the deductible loss of the affiliate for the year,

S. 95(1), the formula in the definition "foreign accrual property income" was replaced by S.C. 2013, c. 34, s. 70(1), applicable in respect of taxation years of a foreign affiliate of a taxpayer that end after August 19, 2011.

Any assessment of a taxpayer's tax, interest and penalties payable under the Act for any taxation year that ends before June 26, 2013 that would otherwise be precluded because of subsections 152(4) to (5) of the Act shall be made to the extent necessary to take into account the amendments by S.C. 2013, c. 34, s. 54 to 89.

S. 95(1), the formula in the definition "foreign accrual property income" formerly read:

(A + A.1 + A.2 + B + C) - (D + E + F + G + H)

S. 95(1), The description of B in the definition "foreign accrual property income" was replaced by S.C. 2013, c. 34, s. 70(2), applicable in respect of taxation years of a foreign affiliate of a taxpayer that end after December 19, 2002. However,

(a) if the taxpayer has made the election under the application to the definition "designated liquidation and dissolution" in s. 95(1) but has not made the election under the application to s. 95(2)(*d.1*), then paragraph (*b*) of the definition "foreign accrual property income" in s. 95(1) is to be read as follows:

"(*b*) that is, at the time of disposition, excluded property of the affiliate, if any of paragraphs (2)(*c*) and (*d*), subparagraph (2)(*e*)(i) and paragraph 88(3)(*a*) applies to the disposition,"

(b) if the taxpayer has made the election under the application to s. 95(2)(*d.1*) but has not made the election under the the application to definition "designated liquidation and dissolution" in s. 95(1), then paragraph (*b*) of the definition "foreign accrual property income" in s. 95(1) is to be read as follows:

"(*b*) that is, at the time of disposition, excluded property of the affiliate, if any of paragraphs (2)(*c*) to (*e*) and 88(3)(*a*) applies to the disposition,"

(c) if the taxpayer has not made the election under the application to definition "designated liquidation and dissolution" in s. 95(1) and has also not made the election under the application to s. 95(2)(*d.1*), then paragraph (*b*) of the definition "foreign accrual property income" in s. 95(1) is to be read as follows:

"(*b*) that is, at the time of disposition, excluded property of the affiliate, if any of paragraphs (2)(*c*), (*d*), (*e*) and 88(3)(*a*) applies to the disposition,"

S. 95(1), the description of B in the definition "foreign accrual property income" formerly read:

B is such portion of the affiliate's taxable capital gains for the year from dispositions of property, other than dispositions of excluded property to which none of paragraphs (2)(*c*), (*d*) and (*e*) apply, as may reasonably be considered to have accrued after its 1975 taxation year,

S. 95(1), the description of E in the definition "foreign accrual property income" was replaced by S.C. 2013, c. 34, s. 70(3), applicable to dispositions of property by a foreign affiliate of a taxpayer that occur after February 27, 2004, except that, in respect of such dispositions of property that occur in taxation years of the foreign affiliate that end on or before August 19, 2011, the description of E in the definition "foreign accrual property income" in subsection 95(1) is to be read as follows:

"E is the amount of the affiliate's allowable capital losses for the year from dispositions of property (other than excluded property and property in respect of which an election is made by the taxpayer under subsection 88(3.3)) that can reasonably be considered to have accrued after its 1975 taxation year,"

S. 95(1), the description of E in the definition "foreign accrual property income" formerly read:

E is the amount of the affiliate's allowable capital losses for the year from dispositions of property (other than excluded property) that can reasonably be considered to have accrued after its 1975 taxation year,

S. 95(1), the description of F.1 in the definition "foreign accrual property income" was added by S.C. 2013, c. 34, s. 70(4), applicable in respect of taxation years of a foreign affiliate of a taxpayer that end after August 19, 2011.

See the application following the amendment to the formula in the definition "foreign accrual property income", above, for the extension of assessment periods to take into account the amendments in S.C. 2013, c. 34, s. 54 to 89.

S. 95(1), paragraph (*b*) of the description of G in the definition "foreign accrual property income" was replaced by S.C. 2013, c. 34, s. 70(5), applicable In respect of taxation years of a foreign affiliate of a taxpayer that end after August 19, 2011.

See the application following the amendment to the formula in the definition "foreign accrual property income", above, for the extension of assessment periods to take into account the amendments in S.C. 2013, c. 34, s. 54 to 89.

S. 95(1), paragraph (*b*) of the description of G in the definition "foreign accrual property income" formerly read:

(*b*) the total of all amounts determined for D to F in respect of the affiliate for the year,

Related Regulations: 1102(3) Capital cost allowance rules; 5903 Prescribed deductible loss for FAPI (element F); 5907(1), "exempt earnings" subpara. (a)(i), "exempt loss" subparas. (a)(i),(b)(ii), "net earnings" para. (b), "net loss" para. (b), "taxable earnings" subpara. (b)(ii), "taxable loss" subpara. (b)(ii); 5907(2)(*c*) and (*i*) Adjustment to earnings; 5907(12) Adjusted cost base of partnership interest; 5907(13) Prescribed amount on immigration.

Related Sections: S. 17(3) Exception to anti-avoidance rule — indirect loan; s. 17(8) Exception; s. 40(3)(*d*) Deemed gain where adjusted cost base is reduced below nil; s. 53(1)(*m*) Adjustments to cost base — Offshore investment fund property; s. 85.1(2)(*e*) Limitation to s. 85.1(1) tax-deferred share exchange; s. 85.1(6) Where subsection (5) does not apply; s. 91(1) Amounts to be included in respect of share of foreign affiliate; s. 93.1(2)(*d*)(ii) Dividends received by partnerships; s. 95(1), "participating percentage"; s. 95(2)(*b*)(i)(B) Recharacterization rules; s. 95(2)(*d.1*)(ii) Foreign merger; s. 95(2)(*e.1*)(ii) Winding-up; s. 95(2)(*g.1*) FAPI and the debt forgiveness rules; s. 95(2)(*g.2*) FAPI and s. 86.1(2)(*f*) election; s. 95(2)(*n*) Meaning of "qualifying interest"; s. 95(2)(*z*) Foreign affiliate as a partner; s. 128.1(1)(*d*) Foreign affiliate; s. 152(6.1) Reassessment where amount included in income under subsection 91(1) is reduced; s. 248(1), " foreign accrual property income", "taxpayer"; s. 257 Negative amounts; Canada–U.S. Income Tax Convention Article XXIX(5)(b) — Income of U.S. S-corporation deemed to be FAPI.

Canadian Tax Foundation: Zabarylo, *Emerging Issues in Tax Accounting: Implications of Foreign Affiliate Changes in Bill C-48*, 2013 Conference Report 34:1–7; O'Hagan and Buttenham, *Foreign Affiliate Reorganizations: Where Are We Now?*, 2013 Conference Report 20:1–56; Morier and Juneja, *Foreign Affiliates: An Updated Primer*, 2012 Conference Report 28:1–48; Marley and Slaats, *Foreign Affiliate Reorganizations — Recent Amendments to the Rules*, 2012 Conference Report 27:1–25; Landry and Talbot, *Proposed Foreign Affiliate Amendments*, 2011 Atlantic Provinces Tax Conference 1C:1–5; Lagios and Minassian, *Foreign Accrual Property Income: Pitfalls for the Unwary*, 1999 Conference Report 3:1–53; Lockwood and Maikawa, *Foreign Affiliates and FAPI: Problems and Tax-Planning Opportunities Resulting from the 1995 Changes*, 1998 Canadian Tax Journal 2:377–414; Lanthier and Meek, *Canadian Foreign Affiliate Rules*, 1997 Conference Report 31:1–42.

Tax Profile: January 2009 — Enhancing Canada's International Tax Advantage; March 2008 — International Tax Planning for the Owner-Manager; February 2007 — U.S. Limited Liability Companies — The Good, the Bad and the Ugly.

Tax Topics: No. 1930, Budget 2009 Provides Initial Response to Final Report Issued by the Advisory Panel on Canada's System of International Taxation.

"foreign accrual tax" — "foreign accrual tax" applicable to any amount included under subsection 91(1) in computing a taxpayer's income for a taxation year of the taxpayer in respect of a particular foreign affiliate of the taxpayer means, subject to subsection 91(4.1),

(*a*) the portion of any income or profits tax that may reasonably be regarded as applicable to that amount and that is paid by

(i) the particular affiliate,

(ii) another foreign affiliate (in paragraph (*b*) referred to as the "shareholder affiliate") of the taxpayer where

(A) the other affiliate has an equity percentage in the particular affiliate,

(B) the income or profits tax is paid to a country other than Canada, and

(C) the other affiliate, and not the particular affiliate, is liable for that tax under the laws of that country, or

(iii) another foreign affiliate of the taxpayer in respect of a dividend received, directly or indirectly, from the particular affiliate, if that other affiliate has an equity percentage in the particular affiliate, and

(*b*) any amount prescribed in respect of the particular affiliate or the shareholder affiliate, as the case may be, to be foreign accrual tax applicable to that amount;

Editorial Note: The term "foreign accrual tax" is relevant for the s. 91(4) deduction in respect of foreign taxes applicable to an amount included in a Canadian-resident taxpayer's income pursuant to s. 91(1) (i.e., current imputation of "foreign accrual property income" ("FAPI") earned by a "controlled foreign affiliate", each as defined in s. 95(1). See the editorial notes for s. 91(1) and (4). Generally, the foreign accrual tax applicable to an amount included in income pursuant to s. 91(1) is the income or profits tax paid by the affiliate that earned the FAPI or paid by another foreign affiliate of the taxpayer in respect of a dividend paid by the affiliate that earned the FAPI. Application rules aid the determination where the affiliate that earned the FAPI is a member of a consolidated group or a party to a loss consolidation arrangement.

History: S. 95(1), the definition "foreign accrual tax" was replaced by S.C. 2014, c. 39, s. 25(1), applicable in respect of taxation years of a foreign affiliate of a taxpayer that end after 2010.

In addition, any assessment of a taxpayer's tax, interest and penalties payable under the Act for any taxation year that ends before the day on which this amendment receives royal assent [December 16, 2014] that would, in the absence of this section, be precluded because of the time references in subsection 152(4) of the Act is to be made to the extent necessary to take into account this amendment.

The definition "foreign accrual tax" formerly read:

"foreign accrual tax"—"foreign accrual tax" applicable to any amount included in computing a taxpayer's income under subsection 91(1) for a taxation year in respect of a particular foreign affiliate of the taxpayer means, subject to subsection 91(4.1),

(*a*) the portion of any income or profits tax that was paid by

(i) the particular affiliate, or

(ii) any other foreign affiliate of the taxpayer in respect of a dividend received from the particular affiliate

and that may reasonably be regarded as applicable to that amount, and

(*b*) any amount prescribed in respect of the particular affiliate to be foreign accrual tax applicable to that amount;

S. 95(1), the portion of the definition "foreign accrual tax" before paragraph (*a*) was amended by S.C. 2013, c. 34, s. 227(2), applicable to taxation years of a taxpayer that end after March 4, 2010, and formerly read:

"foreign accrual tax"—"foreign accrual tax" applicable to any amount included in computing a taxpayer's income by virtue of subsection 91(1) for a taxation year in respect of a particular foreign affiliate of the taxpayer means

Related Regulations: 5907(1.3) Prescribed amount.

Related Sections: S. 91(1) Amounts to be included in respect of share of foreign affiliate; s. 91(4) Amounts deductible in respect of foreign taxes; s. 248(1), "taxpayer".

"foreign affiliate"—"foreign affiliate", at any time, of a taxpayer resident in Canada means a non-resident corporation in which, at that time,

(*a*) the taxpayer's equity percentage is not less than 1%, and

(*b*) the total of the equity percentages in the corporation of the taxpayer and of each person related to the taxpayer (where each such equity percentage is determined as if the determinations under paragraph (*b*) of the definition "equity percentage" in subsection (4) were made without reference to the equity percentage of any person in the taxpayer or in any person related to the taxpayer) is not less than 10%,

except that a corporation is not a foreign affiliate of a non-resident-owned investment corporation;

Editorial Note: The term "foreign affiliate" has significance for three broadly stated reasons. First, "foreign accrual property income" (FAPI) earned by a foreign affiliate of a Canadian-resident taxpayer that is a "controlled foreign affiliate" of the taxpayer will be subject to current imputation pursuant to s. 91(1) (see the editorial notes accompanying the definition of "controlled foreign affiliate" and s. 91(1); each of "FAPI" and "controlled foreign affiliate" are defined in s. 95(1)). Second, dividends received by a Canadian-resident corporate taxpayer from a foreign affiliate of the taxpayer are eligible for the deductions in paragraph 113(1)(*a*) (dividends prescribed to be paid from exempt surplus), ss. 113(1)(*b*) and (*c*) (dividends prescribed to be paid from taxable surplus) and s. 113(1)(*d*) (dividends prescribed to be paid from pre-acquisition surplus). Finally, certain tax-deferred reorganization rules will be available to a non-resident corporation that is a foreign affiliate of a Canadian-resident taxpayer (see s. 85.1(3), s. 88(3), ss. 95(2)(*c*), (*d*), (*d.1*), (*e*) and (*e.1*)).

Related Regulations: 1408(1), "reported reserve"; 5900(1) Dividends paid from exempt surplus, taxable surplus and pre-acquisition surplus; 5900(2) Election to treat dividend from exempt surplus as dividend from taxable surplus; 5900(3) Application of s. 91(5) to individual; 5901(1) Order of surplus distributions; 5901(2) 90-day rule; 5901(3) Interaction of 5900(2) and 5901(1); 5902 Application rules where s. 93(1) election; 5903 Deductible loss computation; 5904 Determination of participating percentage; 5905 Surplus adjustment rules; 5906 Location of foreign affiliate business; 5907(1) Definitions; 5907(2), (2.1), (2.2), (2.3), (2.4), (2.6), (2.7) and (2.8) Adjustment to earnings; 5907(2.9) Fresh start rules; 5907(3) Foreign affiliate on January 1, 1972; 5907(4) Meaning of "government of a country"; 5907(5) Computation of capital gains and losses; 5907(5.1) No gain or loss recognized by foreign country; 5907(6) Calculating currency; 5907(7) Amount of stock dividend; 5907(7.1); 5907(8) Deemed year end on foreign merger; 5907(9) Dissolution of foreign affiliate; 5907(10) Tax sparing; 5907(11) and (11.1) Meaning of "designated treaty country"; 5907(11.2) Residence of foreign affiliate; 5907(12) Adjusted cost base of partnership interest; 5907(13) Prescribed amount on immigration.

Related Sections: S. 12(1)(*k*) Dividends from other corporations; s. 15(2.1) Persons connected with a shareholder; s. 17(3) Exception to anti-avoidance rule — indirect loan; s. 17(8) Exception; s. 17(15), "controlled foreign affiliate", "exempt loan or transfer"; s. 20(12) Foreign non-business income tax; s. 20(12.1) Foreign tax where no economic profit; s. 20(13) Dividend on share from foreign affiliate of taxpayer; s. 53(1)(*c*) Adjustments to cost base — Contributions of capital; s. 53(1)(*d*) Adjustments to cost base — Share of foreign affiliate; s. 53(1)(*m*) Adjustments to cost base — Offshore investment fund property; s. 55(5)(*d*) Safe income of foreign affiliate; s. 80.1(1)(*a*) Expropriation of foreign affiliate shares; s. 80.1(4) Assets acquired from foreign affiliate of taxpayer as dividend in kind or as benefit to shareholder; s. 80.1(5) Assets acquired from foreign affiliate of taxpayer as consideration for settlement, etc., of debt; s. 80.1(6) Assets acquired from foreign affiliate of taxpayer on winding-up, etc; s. 80.4(8) Persons connected with a shareholder; s. 85.1(2)(*e*) Limitation to s. 85.1(1) tax-deferred exchange; s. 85.1(3) Disposition of shares of foreign affiliate; s. 85.1(4) Exception; s. 85.1(6) Where subsection (5) does not apply; s. 87(2)(*u*) Shares of foreign affiliate; s. 87(8) Foreign merger; s. 87(8.1) Definition of "foreign merger"; s. 90(1) Dividends received from non-resident corporation; s. 91(1) Amounts to be included in respect of share of foreign affiliate; s. 91(5) Amounts deductible in respect of dividends received; s. 91(5.1) Deduction of dividend by shareholder [effective 2012]; s. 91(5.2) Deduction of dividend by member of partnership [effective 2012]; s. 91(6) Amounts deductible in respect of dividends received — shares acquired from another corporation; s. 91(7) Shares acquired from a partnership; s. 92 Adjusted cost base of share of foreign affiliate; s. 93(1) Election re disposition of share in foreign affiliate; s. 93(1.1) No election necessary re disposition of excluded property; s. 93(1.2) Disposition of shares of a foreign affiliate held by a partnership; s. 93(1.3) Deemed election; s. 93(2) Loss limitation on disposition of share; s. 93(2.1) Loss limitation — disposition of share by partnership; s. 93(2.2) Loss limitation — disposition of partnership interest; s. 93(2.3) Loss limitation — disposition of partnership interest; s. 93(3) Exempt dividends; s. 93(4) Loss on disposition of shares of foreign affiliate; s. 93.1(1) Shares held by a partnership; s. 93.1(2) Where dividends received by a partnership; s. 95(1), "calculating currency", "controlled foreign affiliate", "foreign affiliate"; s. 95(2)(*a*), (*a.1*), (*a.2*), (*a.3*), (*a.4*), and (*b*) FAPI recharacterization rules; s. 95(2)(*c*) Foreign affiliate share exchange; s. 95(2)(*d*) and (*d.1*) Foreign merger; s. 95(2)(*e*) and (*e.1*) Winding-up of foreign affiliate; s. 95(2)(*f*) Capital gains and losses; s. 95(2)(*f.1*) Income computation; s. 95(2)(*f.12*) [Determination of FAPI — Use of calculating currency]; s. 95(2)(*g*) Foreign exchange gains and losses of foreign affiliate; s. 95(2)(*g.01*), (*g.02*) and (*g.03*) Foreign exchange gains and losses of foreign affiliate; s. 95(2)(*g.1*) Debt forgiveness and foreign affiliate; s. 95(2)(*g.2*) FAPI and s.86.1(2)(*f*) election; s. 95(2)(*i*) Deemed gain or loss from the disposition of excluded property; s. 95(2)(*j*) Adjusted cost base of interest in partnership held by foreign affiliate; s. 95(2)(*k*) Fresh start rules; s. 95(2)(*l*) FAPI recharacterization rules; s. 95(2)(*m*) and (*n*) Meaning of "qualifying interest"; s. 95(2)(*r*) Foreign affiliate as a "qualifying member" of a partnership; s. 95(2)(*s*) Meaning of "designated corporation"; s. 95(2)(*t*) Meaning of "designated partnership"; s. 95(2)(*w*) [effective 2009] Location of foreign affiliate business; s. 95(2)(*x*) [effective 2009] Computation of loss; s. 95(2)(*y*) Shares held by partnership; s. 95(2)(*z*) Foreign affiliate as partner; s. 95(2.02) Rule against double-counting; s. 95(2.1) Rule for definition "investment business"; s. 95(2.2) Qualifying interest throughout year [effective 2009]; s. 95(2.21) Rule re subsection (2.2) [effective 2009]; s. 95(2.3) Application of paragraph (2)(a.1); s. 95(2.4) Application of paragraph (2)(a.3); s. 95(2.41) Application of paragraph (2)(a.3); s. 95(2.42) Exception re paragraph (2)(a.3); s. 95(2.5) Definitions for paragraph (2)(a.3); s. 95(2.6) Rule for the definition "specified person or partnership"; s. 95(3.1) Designated property — subparagraph (2)(a.1)(i); s. 95(4), "relevant cost base"; s. 95(7) Stock dividends from foreign affiliates; s. 108(1), "cost amount"; s. 112(2) Dividends received from non-resident corporation; s. 113(1) Deduction in respect of dividend received from foreign affiliate; s. 113(2) Additional deduction; s. 113(4) Portion of dividend deemed paid out of exempt surplus; s. 115(2)(*e*)(i)(B) Taxation of non-resident person; s. 122.3(2), "specified employer"; s. 126(1) Foreign tax deduction — non-business income; s. 128.1(1)(*c.2*) Deemed dividend to shareholder of immigrating corporation; s. 128.1(1)(*d*) Foreign affiliate; s. 133(8), "non-resident-owned investment corporation"; s. 152(6.1) Reassessment where amount included in income under subsection 91(1) is reduced; s. 162(10.1)(*f*) Penalties; s. 162(10.2) Shares or debt owned by controlled foreign affiliate; s. 162(10.3) Application to partnerships; s. 162(10.4) Application to non-resident trusts; s. 163(2.4)(*d*) Penalties; s. 163(2.5) Shares or debt owned by controlled foreign affiliate; s. 163(2.6) Application to partnerships; s. 163(2.91) Application to non-resident trusts; s. 187.1 Definition of "excepted dividend" para. (a); s. 233.2 Non-resident trust reporting; s. 233.4 Reporting entity; s. 233.5 Due diligence exception; s. 248(1), "foreign affiliate" — Meaning assigned by s. 95(1), taxpayer"; s. 249(4) Year end on change of control; s. 261(4)(*g*) Functional currency reporting; ITAR s. 26(8.3) Foreign affiliate shares owned on June 18 and December 31, 1971; s. 26(8.4) Foreign affiliate shares acquired after June 18, 1971 and owned on December 31, 1971; s. 26(11.1) Fair market value of share of foreign affiliate s. 26(11.2) Fair market value of share of foreign affiliate; s. 35 Foreign affiliates; s. 59(2) Non-resident-owned investment corporation.

Canadian Petroleum Tax Journal: Selected Income Tax Considerations When Structuring Foreign Resource Ventures, William A. Brebber, 2002, Vol. 15, No. 1.

Canadian Tax Foundation: Barchichat, *Quirk in Definition of FA for Partnership Interest Gives Rise to FAPI*, 2015 Canadian Tax Focus 2(3):4.

Tax Profile: March 2008 — International Tax Planning for the Owner-Manager.

Interpretation Bulletins: *Primary* — IT-343R Meaning of the term corporation.

Tax Window Files: Netherlands Antilles private foundation, *October 4, 2010*, CRA Document No. 2008-0289461I7.

"foreign bank" —"foreign bank" means an entity that would be a foreign bank within the meaning assigned by the definition of that expression in section 2 of the *Bank Act* if

(*a*) that definition were read without reference to the portion thereof after paragraph (*g*) thereof, and

(*b*) the entity had not been exempt under section 12 of that Act from being a foreign bank;

Editorial Note: The term "foreign bank" is relevant for the determination of whether a business carried on by a foreign affiliate constitutes an "investment business" as defined in s. 95(1). See the editorial note accompanying the definition of the term "investment business". The term "foreign bank" is also relevant for the foreign accrual property income recharacterization rules in s. 95(2)(*a.1*), (*a.3*) and (*l*).

Related Sections: S. 94.1(1), "exempt business" para. (a); s. 95(1), "investment business" subpara. (a)(i); s. 95(2)(*l*)(iii) FAPI recharacterization; s. 95(2.3)(*b*) Application of s. 95(2)(a.1); s. 95(2.4) Application of paragraph (2)(a.3); s. 95(2.5), "indebtedness" subpara. (c)(ii).

"income from an active business" —"income from an active business" of a foreign affiliate of a taxpayer for a taxation year includes the foreign affiliate's income for the taxation year that pertains to or is incident to that active business but does not include

(*a*) the foreign affiliate's income from property for the taxation year,

(*b*) the foreign affiliate's income for the taxation year from a business that is deemed by subsection (2) to be a business other than an active business of the foreign affiliate, or

(*c*) the foreign affiliate's income from a non-qualifying business of the foreign affiliate for the taxation year;

Editorial Note: See the editorial note accompanying the definition of the expression "active business" in s. 95(1).

Related Regulations: 5907(1), "exempt earnings" para. (d), "net earnings" para. (c), "net loss" para. (c), "taxable earnings" subpara. (b)(iv), "taxable loss" subpara. (b)(iii); 5907(2.8) Computations where s. 95(2)(a)(ii)(D) applies; 5907(5.1) Earnings computation on disposition of capital property.

Related Sections: S. 17(8) Exception; s. 95(1), "excluded property", "foreign accrual property income", "income from property"; s. 95(2) Determination of certain components of foreign accrual property income; s. 95(2.5), "specified deposit"; s. 248(1), "taxpayer".

Tax Profile: April 2008 — International Tax Planning for the Owner-Manager.

"income from a non-qualifying business" —"income from a non-qualifying business" of a foreign affiliate of a taxpayer resident in Canada for a taxation year includes the foreign affiliate's income for the taxation year that pertains to or is incident to that non-qualifying business, but does not include

(*a*) the foreign affiliate's income from property for the taxation year, or

(*b*) the foreign affiliate's income for the taxation year from a business that is deemed by subsection (2) to be a business other than an active business of the foreign affiliate;

Editorial Note: The expression "income from a non-qualifying business" is effective for taxation years beginning after 2008. See the editorial note accompanying the definition of the expression "non-qualifying business" in s. 95(1). A foreign affiliate's income from a non-qualifying business will be included in the affiliate's "foreign accrual property income" (FAPI) (see element A of the definition of "FAPI") and will not be considered "income from an active business". (Each of "FAPI" and "income from an active business" is defined in s. 95(1)).

Related Sections: S. 95(1), "foreign accrual property income" (description of A), "income from an active business" para. (c), "income from property"; s. 248(1), "taxpayer".

"income from property" —"income from property" of a foreign affiliate of a taxpayer for a taxation year includes the foreign affiliate's income for the taxation year from an investment business and the foreign affiliate's income for the taxation year from an adventure or concern in the nature of trade, but does not include

(*a*) the foreign affiliate's income for the taxation year from a business that is deemed by subsection (2) to be a business other than an active business of the foreign affiliate, or

(*b*) the foreign affiliate's income for the taxation year that pertains to or is incident to

(i) an active business of the foreign affiliate, or

(ii) a non-qualifying business of the foreign affiliate;

Editorial Note: The expression "income from property" as defined in s. 95(1) is relevant in determining the "foreign accrual property income" (FAPI) as defined in s. 95(1) earned by a foreign affiliate. In particular, a foreign affiliate's income from property will be included in the affiliate's FAPI (see element A of the definition of "FAPI") and will not be considered "income from an active business" as defined in s. 95(1). Subject to specific exclusions intended to prevent duplication of amounts added to a foreign affiliate's FAPI, "income from property" is defined to include income from an "investment business" as defined in s. 95(1) and income from an adventure or concern in the nature of trade. Note that the definition of "income from property" is inclusive, and therefore, income from a source that is property under common law principles will be included.

Related Sections: S. 9(1) Income; s. 95(1), "foreign accrual property income", "income from an active business", "income from a non-qualifying business", "investment business"; s. 95(2)(*l*) Income from trading or dealing in debt; s. 95(2.5), "specified deposit"; s. 248(1), "business", "taxpayer".

"investment business" —"investment business" of a foreign affiliate of a taxpayer means a business carried on by the foreign affiliate in a taxation year (other than a business deemed by subsection (2) to be a business other than an active business carried on by the foreign affiliate and other than a non-qualifying business of the foreign affiliate) the principal purpose of which is to derive income from property (including interest, dividends, rents, royalties or any similar returns or substitutes for such interest, dividends, rents, royalties or returns), income from the insurance or reinsurance of risks, income from the factoring of trade accounts receivable, or profits from the disposition of investment property, unless it is established by the taxpayer or the foreign affiliate that, throughout the period in the taxation year during which the business was carried on by the foreign affiliate,

(*a*) the business (other than any business conducted principally with persons with whom the affiliate does not deal at arm's length) is

(i) a business carried on by it as a foreign bank, a trust company, a credit union, an insurance corporation or a trader or dealer in securities or commodities, the activities of which are regulated under the laws

(A) of each country in which the business is carried on through a permanent establishment in that country and of the country under whose laws the affiliate is governed and any of exists, was (unless the affiliate was continued in any jurisdiction) formed or organized, or was last continued,

(B) of the country in which the business is principally carried on, or

(C) if the affiliate is related to a non-resident corporation, of the country under whose laws that non-resident corporation is governed and any of exists, was (unless that non-resident corporation was continued in any jurisdiction) formed or organized, or was last continued, if those regulating laws are recognized under the laws of the country in which the business is principally carried on and all of those countries are members of the European Union, or

(ii) the development of real property or immovables for sale, the lending of money, the leasing or licensing of property or the insurance or reinsurance of risks,

(*b*) either

(i) the affiliate (otherwise than as a member of a partnership) carries on the business (the affiliate being, in respect of those times, in that period of the year, that it so carries on the business, referred to in paragraph (*c*) as the "operator"), or

(ii) the affiliate carries on the business as a qualifying member of a partnership (the partnership being, in respect of those times, in that period of the year, that the affiliate so carries on the business, referred to in paragraph (*c*) as the "operator"), and

(*c*) the operator employs

(i) more than five employees full time in the active conduct of the business, or

(ii) the equivalent of more than five employees full time in the active conduct of the business taking into consideration only

(A) the services provided by employees of the operator, and

(B) the services provided outside Canada to the operator by any one or more persons each of whom is, during the time at which the services were performed by the person, an employee of

(I) a corporation related to the affiliate (otherwise than because of a right referred to in paragraph 251(5)(*b*)),

(II) in the case where the operator is the affiliate,

1. a corporation (referred to in this subparagraph as a "providing shareholder") that is a qualifying shareholder of the affiliate,

2. a designated corporation in respect of the affiliate, or

3. a designated partnership in respect of the affiliate, and

(III) in the case where the operator is the partnership described in subparagraph (*b*)(ii),

1. any person (referred to in this subparagraph as a "providing member") who is a qualifying member of that partnership,

2. a designated corporation in respect of the affiliate, or

3. a designated partnership in respect of the affiliate,

if the corporations referred to in subclause (B)(I) and the designated corporations, designated partnerships, providing shareholders or providing members referred to in subclauses (B)(II) and (III) receive compensation from the operator for the services provided to the operator by those employees the value of which is not less than the cost to those corporations, partnerships, shareholders or members of the compensation paid or accruing to the benefit of those employees that performed the services during the time at which the services were performed by those employees;

Editorial Note: Income earned by a foreign affiliate from a business that is considered an "investment business" will be included in the affiliate's "income from property" and therefore, its "foreign accrual property income", each as defined in s. 95(1). An investment business is, generally, any business the principal purpose of which is to derive income from property, income from the disposition of "investment property" as defined in s. 95(1) and income from other enumerated passive sources. However, the definition of "investment business" excludes a business that would otherwise be included if two conditions are met. The first condition requires that the business be carried on by an entity that is regulated under the laws of a specific jurisdiction, or that the business is one of an enumerated list (i.e., development of real estate for sale, "lending of money" as defined in s. 95(1), leasing or "licensing of property" as defined in s. 95(1), or insurance or reinsurance of risks). The second condition requires more than five full-time employees actively engaged in the conduct of the business. See CRA Document No. 2008-0299161I7, December 14, 2008, confirming that the CRA will apply the decision in *489599 B.C. Ltd.* (2008 DTC 4107 (T.C.C.)) to allow five full-time and one part-time employee to meet this second condition. Many international financing structures plan into the exception to the definition of "investment business" in s. 95(1).

One of the structures that appeared to fall within the exception would involve multiple taxpayers pooling their financial assets and employees in one foreign affiliate for the purpose of meeting the second condition discussed above regarding more than five full-time employees. Under the terms of the arrangement or the shares of the affiliate, each of the taxpayers effectively retained the right to its returns from its contributed assets; this type of arrangement was referred to as a "tracking arrangement". The 2018 federal Budget introduced rules that effectively treat each taxpayer in a tracking arrangement as having a separate business, such that the separate business must meet the condition of more than five full-time employees on its own. More specifically, under s. 95(9), where a person or partnership holds a "tracking interest" in respect of the foreign affiliate of a taxpayer, the "tracked property and activities" in respect of the tracking interest (terms defined in s. 95(8)) are deemed to be a separate investment business carried on by the affiliate and not to be part of any other business of the affiliate. The separate business will have to meet the more than five full-time employees test in order to fall within the exception.

Related Sections: S. 95(1), "active business", "income from property", "non-qualifying business"; s. 95(2)(*k*) Fresh start rules; s. 95(2)(*l*) Income from trading or dealing in debt; s. 95(2)(*s*) Meaning of "designated corporation"; s. 95(2)(*t*) Meaning of "designated partnership"; s. 95(2)(*u*) Tiers of partnerships; s. 95(2.1) Rule for definition "investment business"; s. 248(1), "taxpayer".

Canadian Tax Foundation: Padilla, *FAPI: The Definition of "Investment Business"*, 2018 Canadian Tax Focus 8(4):11–11.

Tax Profile: March 2008 — International Tax Planning for the Owner-Manager.

Cases: FAPI, which is taxable in the hands of a parent company, includes income from an investment business. "Investment business" exempts a business, other than a business conducted principally with non-arm's length persons, of a regulated foreign bank with more than five full-time employees or the equivalent. The taxpayer was conducting business principally with its parent company, a non-arm's length person, and could not avail itself of the financial institution exemption. However, in calculating the FAPI, the financial exchange gains and losses should be treated as income rather than capital account. *Loblaw Financial Holdings Inc. v. The Queen*, 2018 DTC 1128 (TCC) [under appeal]

"investment property" — "investment property" of a foreign affiliate of a taxpayer includes

(*a*) a share of the capital stock of a corporation other than a share of another foreign affiliate of the taxpayer that is excluded property of the affiliate,

(*b*) an interest in a partnership other than an interest in a partnership that is excluded property of the affiliate,

(*c*) an interest in a trust other than an interest in a trust that is excluded property of the affiliate,

(*d*) indebtedness or annuities,

(*e*) commodities or commodities futures purchased or sold, directly or indirectly in any manner whatever, on a commodities or commodities futures exchange (except commodities manufactured, produced, grown, extracted or processed by the affiliate or a person to whom the affiliate is related (otherwise than because of a right referred to in paragraph 251(5)(*b*)) or commodities futures in respect of such commodities),

(*f*) currency,

(*g*) real property or immovables,

(*h*) Canadian and foreign resource properties,

(*i*) interests in funds or entities other than corporations, partnerships and trusts, and

(*j*) interests in, or for civil law rights in, or options in respect of, property that is included in any of paragraphs (*a*) to (*i*);

Editorial Note: The expression "investment property" is relevant in determining whether a foreign affiliate carries on an "investment business" as defined in s. 95(1). See the editorial note accompanying the definition of "investment business".

History: S. 95(1), paragraph (*g*) of the definition "investment property" was replaced by S.C. 2013, c. 34, s. 121(2), in force June 26, 2013, and formerly read:

(*g*) real estate,

S. 95(1), paragraph (*j*) of the definition "investment property" was replaced by S.C. 2013, c. 34, s. 121(3), in force June 26, 2013, and formerly read:

(*j*) interests or options in respect of property that is included in any of paragraphs (*a*) to (*i*);

Related Sections: S. 66(15), "Canadian resource property", "foreign resource property"; s. 95(1), "investment business"; s. 95(2.5), "specified deposit"; s. 248(1), "foreign resource property", "taxpayer".

"lease obligation" — "lease obligation" of a person includes an obligation under an agreement that authorizes the use of or the production or reproduction of property including information or any other thing;

Editorial Note: The term "lease obligation" is relevant for s. 95(2)(*a.3*).

Related Sections: S. 95(2)(*a.3*) Foreign accrual property income recharacterization; s. 95(2.42) Exception re paragraph (2)(a.3); s. 95(2.5), "excluded income", "excluded revenue"; s. 248(1), "person".

"lending of money" — "lending of money" by a person (for the purpose of this definition referred to as the "lender") includes

(*a*) the acquisition by the lender of trade accounts receivable (other than trade accounts receivable owing by a person with whom the lender does not deal at arm's length) from another person or the acquisition by the lender of any interest in any such accounts receivable,

(*b*) the acquisition by the lender of loans made by and lending assets (other than loans or lending assets owing by a person with whom the lender does not deal at arm's length) of another person or the acquisition by the lender of any interest in such a loan or lending asset,

(*c*) the acquisition by the lender of a foreign resource property (other than a foreign resource property that is a rental or royalty payable by a person with whom the lender does not deal at arm's length) of another person, and

(*d*) the sale by the lender of loans or lending assets (other than loans or lending assets owing by a person with whom the lender does not deal at arm's length) or the sale by the lender of any interest in such loans or lending assets;

and for the purpose of this definition, the definition "lending asset" in subsection 248(1) shall be read without the words "but does not include a prescribed property";

Editorial Note: The term "lending of money" is relevant in determining whether a foreign affiliate carries on an "investment business" as defined in s. 95(1). See the editorial note accompanying the definition of "investment property".

Related Sections: S. 66(15), "foreign resource property"; s. 95(1), "investment business" subpara. (*a*)(ii); s. 248(1), "foreign resource property", "lending asset", "person".

"licensing of property" — "licensing of property" includes authorizing the use of or the production or reproduction of property including information or any other thing;

Editorial Note: The term "licensing of property" is relevant in determining whether a foreign affiliate carries on an "investment business" as defined in s. 95(1). See the editorial note accompanying the definition of "investment property" in s. 95(1).

Related Sections: S. 95(1), "investment business" subpara. (*a*)(ii).

"non-qualifying business" — "non-qualifying business" of a foreign affiliate of a taxpayer at any time means a business carried on by the foreign affiliate through a permanent establishment in a jurisdiction that, at the end of the foreign affiliate's taxation year that includes that time, is a non-qualifying country, other than

(*a*) an investment business of the foreign affiliate, or

(*b*) a business that is deemed by subsection (2) to be a business other than an active business of the foreign affiliate;

Editorial Note: For taxation years that begin after 2008, the expression "non-qualifying business" is relevant in determining whether income earned by a foreign affiliate constitutes "foreign accrual property income" (FAPI) as defined in s. 95(1). More specifically, a foreign affiliate's "income from a non-qualifying business" as defined in s. 95(1) will be included in the affiliate's FAPI. See the editorial note accompanying the definition of "income from a non-qualifying business". Subject to specific exclusions intended to prevent duplication of amounts added to a foreign affiliate's FAPI, a "non-qualifying business" is defined to be a business carried on by a foreign affiliate through a permanent establishment in a "non-qualifying country" as defined in s. 95(1).

Related Sections: S. 95(1), "income from a non-qualifying business", investment business", "non-qualifying country"; s. 95(2) Determination of certain components of foreign accrual property income; s. 248(1), "taxpayer".

"non-qualifying country"—"non-qualifying country", at any time, means a country or other jurisdiction

(*a*) with which Canada neither has a tax treaty at that time nor has, before that time, signed an agreement that will, on coming into effect, be a tax treaty,

(*a*.1) for which, if the time is after February 2014, the Convention on Mutual Administrative Assistance in Tax Matters — concluded at Strasbourg on January 25, 1988, as amended from time to time by a protocol, or other international instrument, as ratified by Canada — is at that time not in force and does not have effect,

(*b*) with which Canada does not have a comprehensive tax information exchange agreement that is in force and has effect at that time, and

(*c*) with which Canada has, more than 60 months before that time, either

(i) begun negotiations for a comprehensive tax information exchange agreement (unless that time is before 2014 and Canada was, on March 19, 2007, in the course of negotiating a comprehensive tax information exchange agreement with that jurisdiction), or

(ii) sought, by written invitation, to enter into negotiations for a comprehensive tax information exchange agreement (unless that time is before 2014 and Canada was, on March 19, 2007, in the course of negotiating a comprehensive tax information exchange agreement with that jurisdiction);

Editorial Note: For taxation years that begin after 2008, the term "non-qualifying country" is relevant in determining whether a foreign affiliate carries on a "non-qualifying business" as defined in s. 95(1). See the editorial note accompanying the definition of "non-qualifying business". Generally, a non-qualifying country is a country that has not entered into a tax treaty with Canada and has not entered into a tax information exchange agreement within Canada within five years after being invited to do so.

History: S. 95(1), the definition "non-qualifying country" was replaced by S.C. 2014, c. 39, s. 25(2), deemed to have come into force on January 1, 2014, and formerly read:

"non-qualifying country"—"non-qualifying country" at any time means a country or other jurisdiction with which

(*a*) Canada neither has a tax treaty at that time nor has, before that time, signed an agreement that will, on coming into effect, be a tax treaty,

(*b*) Canada does not have a comprehensive tax information exchange agreement that is in force and has effect at that time, and

(*c*) Canada has, more than 60 months before that time, either

(i) begun negotiations for a comprehensive tax information exchange agreement (unless that time is before 2014 and Canada was, on March 19, 2007, in the course of negotiating a comprehensive tax information exchange agreement with that jurisdiction), or

(ii) sought, by written invitation, to enter into negotiations for a comprehensive tax information exchange agreement (unless that time is before 2014 and Canada was, on March 19, 2007, in the course of negotiating a comprehensive tax information exchange agreement with that jurisdiction);

Related Sections: S. 95(1), "non-qualifying business".

"participating percentage"—"participating percentage" of a particular share owned by a taxpayer of the capital stock of a corporation in respect of any foreign affiliate of the taxpayer that was, at the end of its taxation year, a controlled foreign affiliate of the taxpayer is

(*a*) where the foreign accrual property income of the affiliate for that year is $5,000 or less, nil, and

(*b*) where the foreign accrual property income of the affiliate for that year exceeds $5,000,

(i) the percentage that would be the taxpayer's equity percentage in the affiliate at the end of that taxation year on the assumption that the taxpayer owned no shares other than the particular share (but in no case shall that assumption be made for the purpose of determining whether or not a corporation is a foreign affiliate of the taxpayer) if

(A) the affiliate and each corporation that is relevant to the determination of the taxpayer's equity percentage in the affiliate have, at that time, only one class of issued shares, and

(B) no foreign affiliate (referred to in this clause as the "upper-tier affiliate") of the taxpayer that is relevant to the determination of the taxpayer's equity percentage in the affiliate has, at that time, an equity percentage in a foreign affiliate (including, for greater certainty, the affiliate) of the taxpayer that has an equity percentage in the upper-tier affiliate, and

(ii) in any other case, the percentage determined in prescribed manner;

Editorial Note: The term "participating percentage" is relevant to the s. 91(1) imputation of "foreign accrual property income" (FAPI) earned by a "controlled foreign affiliate" of a Canadian-resident taxpayer. (Each of "FAPI" and "controlled foreign affiliate" is defined in s. 95(1)). See the editorial note accompanying s. 91(1). Four observations pertaining to the definition of "participating percentage" should be made. First, the participating percentage of a share of a non-resident corporation held by a Canadian-resident taxpayer is determined in respect of a foreign affiliate of the taxpayer (which is consistent with the imputation regime in s. 91(1) which attributes in respect of a share of a first-tier affiliate the FAPI earned by each controlled foreign affiliate in which the first tier affiliate has an "equity percentage" as defined in s. 95(4)). Second, the participating percentage of a share in respect of a particular foreign affiliate will not be determinable unless the foreign affiliate is a controlled foreign affiliate of the Canadian-resident taxpayer at the end of the affiliate's taxation year that ends in the taxation year of the taxpayer. Third, the definition of "participating percentage" contains a $5,000 *de minimis* threshold. Finally, the determination of a share's participating percentage is dependent on the number of classes of issued shares.

History: S. 95(1), subparagraph (*b*)(i) of the definition "participating percentage" was replaced by S.C. 2013, c. 34, s. 70(6), applicable in respect of taxation years of a foreign affiliate of a taxpayer that begin after August 19, 2011.

See the application following the amendment to the formula in the definition "foreign accrual property income", above, for the extension of assessment periods to take into account the amendments in S.C. 2013, c. 34, s. 54 to 89.

S. 95(1), subparagraph (*b*)(i) of the definition "participating percentage" formerly read:

(i) where the affiliate and each corporation that is relevant to the determination of the taxpayer's equity percentage in the affiliate has only one class of issued shares at the end of that taxation year of the affiliate, the percentage that would be the taxpayer's equity percentage in the affiliate at that time on the assumption that the taxpayer owned no shares other than the particular share (but in no case shall that assumption be made for the purpose of determining whether or not a corporation is a foreign affiliate of the taxpayer), and

Related Regulations: 5904 Prescribed participating percentage (where more than one issued class of shares).

Related Sections: S. 91(1) Amounts to be included in respect of share of foreign affiliate; s. 95(1), "foreign accrual property income", "foreign affiliate"; s. 95(4), "equity percentage"; s. 248(1), "taxpayer".

"permanent establishment" —"permanent establishment" has the meaning assigned by regulation;

History: S. 95(1), the definition "permanent establishment" was added by S.C. 2013, c. 34, s. 33(3), applicable to taxation years of a foreign affiliate of a taxpayer that begin after 1999.

See the application following the amendment to the description of F in the definition of "foreign accrual property income" in s. 95(1) regarding the override of the statute-barring rules for assessments for taxation years that end before June 26, 2013.

Related Regulations: 5906(2).

"relevant tax factor" —"relevant tax factor", of a person or partnership for a taxation year, means

(*a*) in the case of a corporation, or of a partnership all the members of which, other than non-resident persons, are corporations, the quotient obtained by the formula

$$1/(A - B)$$

where

A is the percentage set out in paragraph 123(1)(*a*), and

B is

(i) in the case of a corporation, the percentage that is the corporation's general rate reduction percentage (as defined by section 123.4) for the taxation year, and

(ii) in the case of a partnership, the percentage that would be determined under subparagraph (i) in respect of the partnership if the partnership were a corporation whose taxation year is the partnership's fiscal period, and

(*b*) in any other case, 1.9;

Editorial Note: The term "relevant tax factor" is relevant for the s. 91(4) deduction in respect of foreign taxes paid on foreign accrual property income (FAPI); see the editorial note accompanying s. 91(4) for a discussion. The relevant tax factor is currently 1.9 (2.2 from 2002 through 2015) where the taxpayer is an individual and, where the taxpayer is a corporation, it is based on the reciprocal amount of the Canadian corporate tax rate. The Canadian corporate tax rate for purposes of the determination of the relevant tax factor takes into account the rate reductions provided for in s. 123.4, which has been 13 percentage points since 2011. As a result, the relevant tax factor (for 2012 and subsequent years) for a corporation is 4 [1/(0.38–0.13)].

History: S. 95(1), paragraph (*b*) of the definition "relevant tax factor" was replaced by S.C. 2016, c. 7, s. 62(2), applicable to the 2016 and subsequent taxation years, and formerly read:

(*b*) in any other case, 2.2;

S. 95(1), the definition "relevant tax factor" was replaced by S.C. 2013, c. 34, s. 227(1), applicable to the 2002 and subsequent taxation years, and formerly read:

"relevant tax factor"—"relevant tax factor" means

(*a*) where the taxpayer is an individual, 2, or

(*b*) where the taxpayer is a corporation, the quotient obtained when one is divided by the percentage set out in paragraph 123(1)(*a*);

Related Regulations: 5907(13) Prescribed amount on immigration.

Related Sections: S. 91(4) Amounts deductible in respect of foreign taxes; s. 113(1)(*b*), (*c*) Deduction in respect of dividends prescribed to be paid from taxable surplus; s. 113(3), "relevant tax factor"; s. 123(1)(*a*) Corporate tax rate; s. 248(1), "taxpayer".

"specified fixed interest" —"specified fixed interest", at any time, of an entity in a trust, means an interest of the entity as a beneficiary under the trust if

(*a*) the interest includes, at that time, rights of the entity as a beneficiary under the trust to receive, at or after that time and directly from the trust, income and capital of the trust,

(*b*) the interest was issued by the trust, at or before that time, to an entity, in exchange for consideration and the fair market value, at the time at which the interest was issued, of that consideration was equal to the fair market value, at the time at which it was issued, of the interest,

(*c*) the only manner in which any part of the interest may cease to be the entity's is by way of a disposition (determined without reference to paragraph (*i*) of the definition "disposition" in subsection 248(1) and paragraph 248(8)(*c*)) by the entity of that part, and

(*d*) no amount of income or capital of the trust that any entity may receive directly from the trust at any time as a beneficiary under the trust depends on the exercise by any entity of, or the failure by any entity to exercise, a discretionary power;

Editorial Note: The expression "specified fixed interest" is relevant for the definition of "exempt trust" in s. 95(1). See the editorial note accompanying the definition of "exempt trust". Generally, an interest in a trust will be a specified fixed interest if the interest was issued by the trust for fair market value consideration; the holder of the interest controls its disposition; and the interest provides the holder with a right to receive income and capital from the trust which right is not dependent on the exercise of, or the failure to exercise, a discretionary power.

Related Sections: S. 95(1), "entity", "exempt trust".

"specified person or partnership" —"specified person or partnership", in respect of a taxpayer, at any time means the taxpayer or a person (other than a designated acquired corporation of the taxpayer), or a partnership, that is at that time

(*a*) a person (other than a partnership) that is resident in Canada and does not, at that time, deal at arm's length with the taxpayer,

(*b*) a specified predecessor corporation of the taxpayer or of a specified person or partnership in respect of the taxpayer,

(*c*) a foreign affiliate of

(i) the taxpayer,

(ii) a person that is at that time a specified person or partnership in respect of the taxpayer under this definition because of paragraph (*a*) or (*b*), or

(iii) a partnership that is at that time a specified person or partnership in respect of the taxpayer under this definition because of paragraph (*d*), or

(*d*) a partnership a member of which is at that time a specified person or partnership in respect of the taxpayer under this definition;

Editorial Note: The term "specified person or partnership" is the integral defined term used in the s. 95(2)(*f.1*) carve-out rule relating to the computation of (1) capital gains, capital losses, taxable capital gains and allowable capital losses of a foreign affiliate of a taxpayer from the disposition of property, and (2) income and losses of the foreign affiliate from property, from non-active businesses and from non-qualifying businesses.

See the commentary to s. 95(2)(*f.1*) or a description of the carve-out rule.

History: S. 95(1), the definition "specified person or partnership" was added by S.C. 2009, c. 2, s. 25(1), applicable to taxation years of a foreign affiliate of a taxpayer that begin after October 2, 2007. However, if the taxpayer elects in writing in respect of all of its foreign affiliates and files the election with the Minister of National Revenue on or before the taxpayer's election day, the definition "specified person or partnership" also applies to taxation years of a foreign affiliate of the taxpayer that begin before October 2, 2007 and after the date chosen by the taxpayer as described below.

The taxpayer's election day is the later of (i) the taxpayer's filing-due date for the taxpayer's taxation year that includes the day on which this Act is assented to [R.A. March 12, 2009] and (ii) the day that is one year after the day on which this Act is assented to [March 12, 2010].

To be valid, an election [described above] must include the identification by the taxpayer of its choice of one of the following dates:

(i) December 31, 1994,

(ii) December 20, 2002, or

(iii) February 27, 2004.

Notwithstanding subsections 152(4) to (5) of the Act, any assessment of a taxpayer's tax, interest and penalties payable under the Act for any taxation year shall be made that is necessary to take into account this provision and any election made with respect to it.

Related Sections: S. 95(1), "antecedent corporation", "designated acquired corporation", "foreign affiliate"; s. 95(2)(*f.1*) [Determination of FAPI — Exclusion of amounts]; s. 248(10) Series of transactions; s. 256(6.1) Simultaneous control.

"specified predecessor corporation" —"specified predecessor corporation" of a particular corporation means

(*a*) an antecedent corporation of the particular corporation,

(*b*) a predecessor corporation (within the meaning assigned by subsection 87(1)) in respect of an amalgamation by which the particular corporation was formed, or

(*c*) a specified predecessor corporation of a specified predecessor corporation of the particular corporation;

Editorial Note: The term "specified predecessor corporation" is used in the definition of "specified person or partnership" (itself defined in s. 95(1)) which is the integral defined term used in the s. 95(2)(*f.1*) carve-out rule.

History: S. 95(1), the definition "specified predecessor corporation" was added by S.C. 2009, c. 2, s. 25(1), applicable to taxation years of a foreign affiliate of a taxpayer that begin after October 2, 2007. However, if the taxpayer elects in writing in respect of all of its foreign affiliates and files the election with the Minister of National Revenue on or before the taxpayer's election day, the definition "specified predecessor corporation" also applies to taxation years of a foreign affiliate of the taxpayer that begin before October 2, 2007 and after the date chosen by the taxpayer as described below.

The taxpayer's election day is the later of (i) the taxpayer's filing-due date for the taxpayer's taxation year that includes the day on which this Act is assented to [R.A. March 12, 2009] and (ii) the day that is one year after the day on which this Act is assented to [March 12, 2010].

To be valid, an election [described above] must include the identification by the taxpayer of its choice of one of the following dates:

(i) December 31, 1994,

(ii) December 20, 2002, or

(iii) February 27, 2004.

Notwithstanding subsections 152(4) to (5) of the Act, any assessment of a taxpayer's tax, interest and penalties payable under the Act for any taxation year shall be made that is necessary to take into account this provision and any election made with respect to it.

Related Sections: S. 87(1) Amalgamations; s. 95(1), "antecedent corporation".

"specified purchaser" —"specified purchaser", at any time, in respect of a particular taxpayer resident in Canada, means an entity that is, at that time,

(*a*) the particular taxpayer,

(*b*) an entity resident in Canada with which the particular taxpayer does not deal at arm's length,

(*c*) a foreign affiliate of an entity described in any of paragraphs (*a*) and (*b*) and (*d*) to (*f*),

(*d*) a trust (other than an exempt trust) in which an entity described in any of paragraphs (*a*) to (*c*) and (*e*) and (*f*) is beneficially interested,

(*e*) a partnership of which an entity described in any of paragraphs (*a*) to (*d*) and (*f*) is a member, or

(*f*) an entity (other than an entity described in any of paragraphs (*a*) to (*e*)) with which an entity described in any of paragraphs (*a*) to (*e*) does not deal at arm's length;

Editorial Note: The expression "specified purchaser" is relevant for the definition of "exempt trust" in s. 95(1). See the editorial note accompanying the definition of "exempt trust". Generally, a specified purchaser in respect of a Canadian-resident taxpayer includes the taxpayer; an "entity" as defined in s. 95(1) that does not deal at arm's length with the taxpayer; and certain other entities, trusts and partnerships.

Related Sections: S. 95(1), "entity", "exempt trust"; s. 248(1), "taxpayer".

"surplus entitlement percentage" —"surplus entitlement percentage", at any time, of a taxpayer in respect of a foreign affiliate has the meaning assigned by regulation;

Editorial Note: The definition of the term "surplus entitlement percentage" (SEP) has the meaning prescribed by Regulation. See, in this regard, regulations 5905(10) to (13) which provide a set of rules to determine the SEP of a Canadian-resident corporate taxpayer in respect of a foreign affiliate. SEP is only relevant to a Canadian-resident taxpayer that is a corporation.

Where a foreign affiliate and each corporation that is relevant to the determination of the Canadian-resident corporate taxpayer's "equity percentage" (as defined in s. 95(4)) in the affiliate have only one class of issued shares, the SEP of the taxpayer in respect of the affiliate is the taxpayer's equity percentage in the affiliate.

In any other case, the determination is more complicated. Generally, in any other case, the SEP of a Canadian-resident corporate taxpayer in respect of a foreign affiliate (the "particular affiliate") represents the percentage of the "net surplus" (as defined in regulation 5907(1)) of the particular affiliate in respect of the taxpayer that would be received by the taxpayer if the particular affiliate paid dividends equal to its net surplus. For the purpose of determining the particular affiliate's net surplus in respect of the taxpayer it is assumed that each foreign affiliate of the taxpayer in which the particular affiliate held an equity percentage had paid a dividend equal to its particular net surplus in respect of the taxpayer immediately before its immediate shareholder paid such a dividend. The effect of the regulations is that the lowest-tier affiliate is assumed to pay a dividend equal to its net surplus in respect of the taxpayer before its shareholder is assumed to pay such a dividend, and so on. In the result, for the purposes of determining the taxpayer's SEP of the particular affiliate, the net surplus of the particular affiliate in respect of the taxpayer will represent the net surplus of the group of affiliates in which the particular affiliate holds an interest.

The determination of a taxpayer's SEP in respect of a particular foreign affiliate is important for two reasons. First, the tax deferred reorganization rules in ss. 95(2)(*d.1*) and (*e.1*) will only apply to reorganizations of affiliates in respect of which the taxpayer's SEP is not less than 90%. Second, if the taxpayer's SEP of a Canadian corporation in respect of a particular affiliate changes, the surplus, deficit and underlying foreign tax accounts of the affiliate and all other affiliates in which the particular affiliate has an equity percentage may have to be adjusted. See, in this regard, regulation 5905.

Related Regulations: 5903(3) Deductible loss computation; 5905(1), (2), (3), (4), (6), (8), (9) and (13) Surplus adjustment rules; 5907(1), "underlying foreign tax applicable".

Related Sections: S. 95(2)(*d.1*) Foreign merger; s. 95(2)(*e.1*) Winding-up; s. 248(1), "taxpayer".

"taxable Canadian business" —"taxable Canadian business", at any time, of a foreign affiliate of a taxpayer resident in Canada or of a partnership of which a foreign affiliate of a taxpayer resident in Canada is a member (which foreign affiliate or partnership is referred to in this definition as the "operator"), means a business the income from which (*a*) is, or would be if there were income from the business for the operator's taxation year or fiscal period that includes that time, included in computing the foreign affiliate's taxable income earned in Canada for a taxation year under subparagraph 115(1)(*a*)(ii), and

(*b*) is not, or would not be if there were income from the business for the operator's taxation year or fiscal period that includes that time, exempt, because of a tax treaty with a country, from tax under this Part;

History: S. 95(1), the definition of "taxable Canadian business" was added by S.C. 2013, c. 34, s. 70(7), applicable in respect of taxation years of a foreign affiliate of a taxpayer that begin after December 20, 2002. However,

(*a*) if the taxpayer elects in writing in respect of all of its foreign affiliates and files the election with the Minister of National Revenue on or before the day that is the later of the taxpayer's filing-due date for the taxpayer's taxation year that includes June 26, 2013 and June 26, 2014 [the day that is one year after royal assent],

(i) the definition "taxable Canadian business" in subsection 95(1) also applies in respect of taxation years of all foreign affiliates of the taxpayer that begin after 1994 and before December 21, 2002,

(ii) in applying paragraph (*b*) of the definition "taxable Canadian business" in subsection 95(1), in respect of the 1997 and preceding taxation years of all foreign affiliates of the taxpayer, that paragraph is to be read as follows:

"(*b*) is not, or would not be if there were income from the business for the operator's taxation year or fiscal period that includes that time, exempt — because of a comprehensive agreement or convention for the elimination of double taxation on income, between the Government of Canada and the government of another country, which has the force of law in Canada at that time — from tax under this Part:"

If the taxpayer referred to in any election dealing with various foreign affiliate amendments is a partnership, any reference in those elections to "the taxpayer's filing-due date" is to be read as a reference to "the earliest of the filing-due dates of any member of the taxpayer".

See the application following the addition of the definition "designated liquidation and dissolution" for the extension of assessment periods to take into account the amendments in S.C. 2013, c. 34, s. 54 to 89.

"taxation year" —"taxation year" in relation to a foreign affiliate of a taxpayer means the period for which the accounts of the foreign affiliate have been ordinarily made up, but no such period may exceed 53 weeks;

Editorial Note: The "taxation year" of a foreign affiliate of a taxpayer is defined to mean the period for which the affiliate's accounts are made up (no period to exceed 53 weeks).

Related Regulations: 5900(2) Election to treat dividend from exempt surplus as dividend from taxable surplus; 5901(1) Order of surplus distributions; 5901(2) 90-day rule; 5902(5) Application rules where s. 93(1) election made; 5903(1) and 5903(2) Deductible loss computation; 5904(1), 5904(2) and 5904(3) Determination of participating percentage; 5905(1), 5905(3), 5905(7), and 5905(12) Surplus adjustment rules; 5907(1), "earnings", "exempt earnings", "exempt loss", "exempt surplus", "loss", "net earnings", "net loss", "taxable earnings", "taxable loss", "taxable surplus", "underlying foreign tax", "underlying foreign tax applicable"; 5907(1.02), "meaning of "qualifying interest"", "related"; 5907(1.1) Foreign affiliate as a member of consolidated group; 5907(1.2) Loss transfer regime; 5907(1.3) Prescribed amount for the purposes of "foreign accrual tax"; 5907(2) Adjustment to earnings; 5907(2.1), 5907(2.2), 5907(2.3) and 5907(2.6) Election for depreciable property; 5907(2.7), 5907(2.8) and 5907(2.9) Adjustment to earnings; 5907(7.1); 5907(8) Deemed year end on foreign merger; 5907(9) Dissolution of foreign affiliate; 5907(10) Tax sparing; 5907(11) and 5907(11.1) Meaning of "designated treaty country"; 5907(12) Adjusted cost base of partnership interest; 5907(13) Prescribed amount on immigration.

Related Sections: S. 90(1) Dividends received from non-resident corporation; s. 91 Amounts to be included in respect of share of foreign affiliate; s. 92(1) Adjusted cost base of share of foreign affiliate; s. 92(2) Deduction in computing adjusted cost base; s. 92(3) Computation of adjusted cost base; s. 92(4) Disposition of a partnership interest; s. 92(5) Deemed gain from the disposition of a share; s. 92(6) Formula; s. 94 Non-resident trust rules; s. 94.1 Offshore investment fund rules; s. 95(1), "calculating currency", "exempt trust", "foreign accrual property income", "foreign accrual tax", "income from an active business", "income from a non-qualifying business", "income from property", "investment business", "non-qualifying business", "participating percentage"; s. 95(2)(*a*), (*a.1*), (*a.2*), (*a.3*) and (*a.4*) FAPI recharacterization; s. 95(2)(*g*) Determination of foreign exchange gains and losses; s. 95(2)(*g.2*) Foreign spin-off election; s. 95(2)(*i*) Deemed gain or loss from the disposition of excluded property; s. 95(2)(*k*) Fresh start rules; s. 95(2)(*l*) FAPI recharacterization; s. 95(2)(*m*) Meaning of "qualifying interest"; s. 95(2)(*p*) Meaning of "qualifying shareholder"; s. 95(2)(*t*) Meaning of "designated partnership"; s. 95(2)(*x*) [effective 2009] Computation of loss; s. 95(2)(*z*) Foreign affiliate as a partner; s. 95(2.2) Qualifying interest throughout year [effective 2009]; s. 95(2.21) Rule re subsection (2.2) [effective 2009] s. 95(2.41) Application of paragraph (2)(a.3); s. 95(2.42) Exception re paragraph (2)(a.3); s. 95(2.5), "excluded income", "excluded revenue".

Tax Topics: No. 1889, Taxation Year of a Foreign Affiliate.

"trust company" —"trust company" includes a corporation that is resident in Canada and that is a *loan company* as defined in subsection 2(1) of the *Canadian Payments Act*.

Editorial Note: The term "trust company" is relevant for the determination of whether a business carried on by a foreign affiliate constitutes an "investment business" as defined in s. 95(1). See the editorial note accompanying the definition of the term "investment business". The term "trust company" is also relevant for the foreign accrual property income recharacterization rules in ss. 95(2)(*a.1*), (*a.3*) and (*l*).

History: S. 95(1), the definition of "trust company" was replaced by S.C. 2017, c. 33, s. 30(1), deemed to have come into force on October 24, 2001, and formerly read:

"trust company" —"trust company" includes a corporation that is resident in Canada and that is a loan company as defined in subsection 2(1) of the *Canadian Payments Association Act*.

Related Sections: S. 95(2)(*l*)(iii) and (iv) Exclusion from "foreign accrual property income" (FAPI) recharacterization rule; s. 95(2.1) Rule for definition "investment business"; s. 95(2.3)(*a*) Application of s. 95(2)(*a.1*); s. 95(2.4)(*a*) Application of s. 95(2)(*a.3*); s. 95(2.5), "indebtedness" paras. (*b*),(*c*).

▶ 95(1.1) ◀

(1.1) British Virgin Islands. For the purposes of paragraph (*b*) of the definition "non-qualifying country" in subsection (1), the British Overseas Territory of the British Virgin Islands is deemed to have a comprehensive tax information exchange agreement with Canada that is in force and has effect after 2013 and before March 11, 2014.

History: S. 95(1.1) was added by S.C. 2014, c. 39, s. 25(4), deemed to have come into force on January 1, 2014.

▶ 95(2) ◀

(2) Determination of certain components of foreign accrual property income. For the purposes of this subdivision,

▶ 95(2)(a) ◀

(a) [Determination of FAPI — Property income deemed active business income] — in computing the income or loss from an active business for a taxation year of a particular foreign affiliate of a taxpayer in respect of which the taxpayer has a qualifying interest throughout the year or that is a controlled foreign affiliate of the taxpayer throughout the year, there shall be included any income or loss of the particular foreign affiliate for the year from sources in a country other than Canada that would otherwise be income or loss from property of the particular foreign affiliate for the year to the extent that

(i) the income or loss

(A) is derived by the particular foreign affiliate from activities of the particular foreign affiliate, or of a particular partnership of which the particular foreign affiliate is a member, to the extent that the activities occur while the particular affiliate is a qualifying member of the particular partnership that can reasonably be considered to be directly related to active business activities carried on in a country other than Canada by

(I) another foreign affiliate of the taxpayer in respect of which the taxpayer has a qualifying interest throughout the year,

(II) a life insurance corporation that is resident in Canada throughout the year and that is

1. the taxpayer,

2. a person who controls the taxpayer,

3. a person controlled by the taxpayer, or

4. a person controlled by a person who controls the taxpayer,

(III) the particular foreign affiliate or a partnership of which the particular foreign affiliate is a member, to the extent that the activities occur while the particular affiliate is a qualifying member of the partnership, or

(IV) a partnership of which another foreign affiliate of the taxpayer, in respect of which the taxpayer has a qualifying interest throughout the year, is a member, to the extent that the activities occur while the other affiliate is a qualifying member of the partnership, and

(B) if any of subclauses (A)(I), (II) and (IV) applies, would be included in computing the amount prescribed to be the earnings or loss, from an active business carried on in a country other than Canada, of

(I) that other foreign affiliate referred to in subclause (A)(I) or (IV), if the income were earned by it, or

(II) the life insurance corporation referred to in subclause (A)(II), if that life insurance corporation were a foreign affiliate of the taxpayer and the income were earned by it,

(ii) the income or loss is derived from amounts that were paid or payable, directly or indirectly, to the particular foreign affiliate or a partnership of which the particular foreign affiliate was a member

(A) by a life insurance corporation that is resident in Canada and that is the taxpayer, a person who controls the taxpayer, a person controlled by the taxpayer or a person controlled by a person who controls the taxpayer, to the extent that those amounts that were paid or payable were for expenditures that are deductible in a taxation year of the life insurance corporation by the life insurance corporation in computing its income or loss for a taxation year from carrying on its life insurance business outside Canada and are not deductible in computing its income or loss for a taxation year from carrying on its life insurance business in Canada,

(B) by

(I) another foreign affiliate of the taxpayer in respect of which the taxpayer has a qualifying interest throughout the year, to the extent that those amounts that were paid or payable are for expenditures that were deductible by that other foreign affiliate in computing the amounts prescribed to be its earnings or loss for a taxation year from an active business (other than an active business carried on in Canada), or

(II) a partnership of which another foreign affiliate of the taxpayer (in respect of which other foreign affiliate the taxpayer has a qualifying interest throughout the year) is a qualifying member throughout each period, in the fiscal period of the partnership that ends in the year, in which that other foreign affiliate was a member of the partnership, to the extent that those amounts that were paid or payable are for expenditures that are deductible by the partnership in computing that other foreign affiliate's share of any income or loss of the partnership, for a fiscal period, that is included in computing the amounts prescribed to be that other foreign affiliate's earnings or loss for a taxation year from an active business (other than an active business carried on in Canada),

(C) by a partnership of which the particular foreign affiliate is a qualifying member throughout each period, in the fiscal period of the partnership that ends in the year, in which the particular foreign affiliate was a member of the partnership, to the extent that those amounts that were paid or payable are for expenditures that are deductible by the partnership in computing the particular foreign affiliate's share of any income or loss of the partnership, for a fiscal period, that is included in computing the amounts prescribed to be the particular foreign affiliate's earnings or loss for a taxation year from an active business (other than an active business carried on in Canada), or

(D) by another foreign affiliate (referred to in this clause as the "second affiliate") of the taxpayer — in respect of which the taxpayer has a qualifying interest throughout the year — to the extent that the amounts are paid or payable by the second affiliate, in respect of any particular period in the year,

(I) under a legal obligation to pay interest on borrowed money used for the purpose of earning income from property, or

(II) on an amount payable for property acquired for the purpose of gaining or producing income from property

where

(III) the property is, throughout the particular period, excluded property of the second affiliate that is shares of the capital stock of a corporation (referred to in this clause as the "third affiliate") which is, throughout the particular period, a foreign affiliate (other than the particular foreign affiliate) of the taxpayer in respect of which the taxpayer has a qualifying interest, and

(IV) in respect of each of the second affiliate and the third affiliate, for each of their taxation years (each of which is referred to in this subclause as a "relevant taxation year") that end in the year, either

1. that affiliate is subject to income taxation in a country other than Canada in that relevant taxation year, or

2. the members or shareholders of that affiliate (which, for the purposes of this sub-subclause, includes a person that has, directly or indirectly, an interest, or for civil law a right, in a share of the capital stock of, or in an equity interest in, the affiliate) at the end of that relevant taxation year are subject to income taxation in a country other than Canada on, in aggregate, all or substantially all of the income of that affiliate for that relevant taxation year in their taxation years in which that relevant taxation year ends,

(V) (Repealed by S.C. 2014, c. 39, s. 25(6).)

(iii) the income or loss is derived by the particular foreign affiliate from the factoring of trade accounts receivable acquired by the particular foreign affiliate, or a partnership of which the particular foreign affiliate was a member, from another foreign affiliate of the taxpayer in respect of which the taxpayer has a qualifying interest throughout the year to the extent that the accounts receivable arose in the course of an active business carried on in a country other than Canada by that other foreign affiliate,

(iv) the income or loss is derived by the particular foreign affiliate from loans or lending assets acquired by the particular foreign affiliate, or a partnership of which the particular foreign affiliate was a member, from another foreign affiliate of the taxpayer in respect of which the taxpayer has a qualifying interest throughout the year, to the extent that the loans or lending assets arose in the course of an active business carried on in a country other than Canada by that other foreign affiliate,

(v) the income or loss is derived by the particular foreign affiliate from the disposition of excluded property that is not capital property, or

(vi) the income or loss is derived by the particular foreign affiliate under or as a result of an agreement that provides for the purchase, sale or exchange of currency and that can reasonably be considered to have been made by the particular foreign affiliate to reduce

(A) its risk — with respect to an amount that increases the amount required by this paragraph to be included in computing the particular foreign affiliate's income for a taxation year from an active business or that decreases the amount required by this paragraph to be included in computing the particular foreign affiliate's loss for a taxation year from an active business — of fluctuations in the value of the currency in which the amount was denominated, or

(B) its risk — with respect to an amount that decreases the amount required by this paragraph to be included in computing the particular foreign affiliate's income for a taxation year from an active business or that increases the amount required by this paragraph to be included in computing the particular foreign affiliate's loss for a taxation year from an active business — of fluctuations in the value of the currency in which the amount was denominated;

Editorial Note: Paragraph 95(2)(*a*) is an income recharacterization rule that applies for the purposes of the foreign affiliate rules in Subdivision i and the supporting rules in Part LIX of the Regulations.

Generally, where s. 95(2)(*a*) applies, it will, in effect, deem non-Canadian-source income (or loss) from property earned by a foreign affiliate of a Canadian-resident taxpayer to be income (or loss) from an active business of that affiliate. See the editorial notes for the definitions of "income from property" and "income from an active business" in s. 95(1). Where s. 95(2)(*a*) applies, the recharacterized income will not be included in an affiliate's foreign accrual property income ("FAPI") and therefore will not be subject to the FAPI imputation regime in s. 91(1). See the editorial notes for s. 91(1) and the definition of FAPI in s. 95(1).

Paragraph 95(2)(*a*) will apply to recharacterize non-Canadian-source income (or loss) from property earned by a foreign affiliate of a Canadian-resident taxpayer to be income (or loss) from an active business of that affiliate only if: (i) the taxpayer has a "qualifying interest" (as defined in s. 95(2)(*m*)) in that affiliate throughout the affiliate's taxation year or if the affiliate is a controlled foreign affiliate of the taxpayer throughout that taxation year (see s. 95(2.2) and (2.21)); and (ii) the income (or loss) is derived in the manner set out in any of s. 95(2)(*a*)(i) through (vi).

Note that where the rule applies, it only deems the income to be income from an active business. The rule does not deem the business itself to be an active business.

Any income (or loss) from property earned by a foreign affiliate of a Canadian-resident taxpayer that is deemed by s. 95(2)(*a*) to be income (or loss) from an active business of that affiliate will also be included in the affiliate's "earnings" (see paragraph (*b*) of the definition of "earnings" in Regulation 5907(1)). In consequence, the income will be included in the affiliate's "exempt earnings" or "taxable earnings" and therefore "exempt surplus" or "taxable surplus", respectively (see the definitions in regulation 5907(1)).

History: S. 95(2)(*a*)(i) was replaced by S.C. 2014, c. 39, s. 25(5), applicable in respect of taxation years of a foreign affiliate of a taxpayer that begin after July 12, 2013. However, if the taxpayer elects in writing under s. 25(31) of the *Economic Action Plan 2014 Act, No. 2* [S.C. 2014, c. 39] in respect of all its foreign affiliates and files the election with the Minister of National Revenue on or before the day that is the later of the taxpayer's filing-due date for the taxpayer's taxation year that includes the day on which the *Economic Action Plan 2014 Act, No. 2* [S.C. 2014, c. 39] receives royal assent [December 16, 2014] and the day that is one year after the day on which the *Economic Action Plan 2014 Act, No. 2* [S.C. 2014, c. 39] receives royal assent [December 16, 2015],

(*a*) s. 95(2)(*a*)(i) applies in respect of taxation years of all foreign affiliates of the taxpayer that end after 2007; and

(*b*) s. 95(2)(*a*)(i) of the Act is to be read as follows in respect of taxation years of foreign affiliates of the taxpayer that end after 2007 and begin before 2009:

"(i) the income or loss

(A) is derived by the particular foreign affiliate from activities of the particular foreign affiliate, or of a particular partnership of which the particular foreign affiliate is a member, to the extent that the activities occur while the particular affiliate is a qualifying member of the particular partnership, that can reasonably be considered to be directly related to active business activities carried on in a country other than Canada by

(I) another corporation

1. that is a non-resident corporation to which the particular foreign affiliate and the taxpayer are related throughout the year, or
2. that is another foreign affiliate of the taxpayer in respect of which the taxpayer has a qualifying interest throughout the year,

(II) a life insurance corporation that is resident in Canada throughout the year and that is

1. the taxpayer,
2. a person who controls the taxpayer,
3. a person controlled by the taxpayer, or
4. a person controlled by a person who controls the taxpayer,

(III) the particular foreign affiliate or a partnership of which the particular foreign affiliate is a member, to the extent that the activities occur while the particular affiliate is a qualifying member of the partnership, or

(IV) a partnership of which another foreign affiliate of the taxpayer, in respect of which the taxpayer has a qualifying interest throughout the year, is a member, to the extent that the activities occur while the other affiliate is a qualifying member of the partnership, and

(B) if any of subclauses (A)(I), (II) and (IV) applies, would be included in computing the amount prescribed to be the earnings or loss, from an active business carried on in a country other than Canada, of

(I) that other foreign affiliate referred to in sub-subclause (A)(I)2 or subclause (A)(IV), if the income were earned by it, or

(II) the non-resident corporation referred to in sub-subclause (A)(I)1 or the life insurance corporation referred to in subclause (A)(II), if that non-resident corporation or that life insurance corporation were a foreign affiliate of the taxpayer and the income were earned by it,"

In addition, any assessment of a taxpayer's tax, interest and penalties payable under the Act for any taxation year that ends before the day on which this amendment receives royal assent [December 16, 2014] that would, in the absence of this section, be precluded because of the time references in subsection 152(4) of the Act is to be made to the extent necessary to take into account this amendment.

S. 95(2)(*a*)(i) formerly read:

(i) the income or loss

(A) is derived by the particular foreign affiliate from activities that can reasonably be considered to be directly related to active business activities carried on in a country other than Canada by

(I) another foreign affiliate of the taxpayer in respect of which the taxpayer has a qualifying interest throughout the year, or

(II) a life insurance corporation that is resident in Canada throughout the year and that is

1. the taxpayer,
2. a person who controls the taxpayer,
3. a person controlled by the taxpayer, or
4. a person controlled by a person who controls the taxpayer, and

(B) would be included in computing the amount prescribed to be the earnings or loss, from an active business carried on in a country other than Canada, of

(I) that other foreign affiliate referred to in subclause (A)(I) if the income were earned by it, or

(II) the life insurance corporation referred to in subclause (A)(II) if that life insurance corporation were a foreign affiliate of the taxpayer and the income were earned by it,

S. 95(2)(*a*)(ii)(D)(IV) was replaced and s. 95(2)(*a*)(ii)(D)(V) was repealed by S.C. 2014, c. 39, s. 25(6), applicable in respect of taxation years of a foreign affiliate of a taxpayer that end after July 12, 2013, and formerly read:

(IV) the second affiliate and the third affiliate are resident in the same country for each of their taxation years (each of which taxation years is referred to in subclause (V) as a "relevant taxation year" of the second affiliate or of the third affiliate, as the case may be) that end in the year, and

(V) in respect of each of the second affiliate and the third affiliate for each relevant taxation year of that affiliate, either

1. that affiliate is subject to income taxation in that country in that relevant taxation year, or
2. the members or shareholders of that affiliate (which, for the purpose of this sub-subclause, includes a person that has, directly or indirectly, an interest, or for civil law a right, in a share of the capital stock of, or in an equity interest in, the affiliate) at the end of that relevant taxation year are subject to income taxation in that country on, in aggregate, all or substantially all of the income of that affiliate for that relevant taxation year in their taxation years in which that relevant taxation year ends,

Related Regulations: 5906 Location of foreign affiliate business; 5907(1), "earnings", "exempt earnings", "taxable earnings"; 5907(1.02) Qualifying interest; 5907(2.7), (2.8) Adjustment to earnings.

Related Sections: S. 20(3) Borrowed money; s. 95(1), "active business", "foreign accrual property income", "foreign affiliate", "income from an active business", "income from property"; 95(2)(f.1) [Determination of FAPI — Exclusion of amounts]; 95(2)(f.11) [Determination of FAPI — Application of other provisions]; 95(2)(f.12) [Determination of FAPI — Use of calculating currency]; 95(2)(f.13) [Determination of FAPI — Conversion to Canadian currency]; 95(2)(f.14) [Determination of FAPI — Use of Canadian currency]; 95(2)(f.15) [Determination of FAPI — Currency for s. 39(2)]; 95(2)(g) [Determination of FAPI — Foreign currency fluctuations]; 95(2)(g.01) [Determination of FAPI — Currency hedging agreements]; 95(2)(g.03) [Determination of FAPI — Foreign currency fluctuations where member of partnership]; 95(2)(g.04) [Determination of FAPI — Upstream loans]; 95(2)(g.1) [Determination of FAPI — Debt forgiveness rules]; 95(2)(g.2) [Determination of FAPI — Elections for foreign spin-off rules]; 95(2)(i) [Determination of FAPI — Settlement of debt or currency hedging agreement]; 95(2)(j) [Determination of FAPI — ACB of partnership interest]; 95(2)(j.1) [Determination of FAPI — Insurance business]; 95(2)(j.2) [Determination of FAPI — life insurance business]; 95(2)(k) [Determination of FAPI — Fresh start rules]; 95(2)(k.1) [Determination of FAPI — Fresh start rules]; 95(2)(k.2) [Determination of FAPI — Deemed separate business]; 95(2)(l) [Determination of FAPI — Trading or dealing in indebtedness]; 95(2)(m) [Determination of FAPI — Qualifying interest in foreign affiliate]; 95(2)(n) [Determination of FAPI — Foreign affiliate and qualifying interest]; 95(2)(o) [Determination of FAPI — Qualifying member of partnership]; 95(2)(q) [Determination of FAPI — Look-through rules]; 95(2)(r) [Determination of FAPI — Deemed qualifying member of partnership]; 95(2)(u) [Determination of FAPI — Tiered partnerships]; 95(2)(x) [Determination of FAPI — Determination of losses]; 95(2)(y) [Determination of FAPI — Qualifying interest in foreign affiliate — property of partnership]; 95(2.2) Qualifying interest throughout year; 95(2.21) Rule re subsection (2.2); 95(6) Where rights or shares issued, acquired or disposed of to avoid tax; s. 248(1), "business", "taxpayer"; s. 249(1) Definition of "taxation year"; s. 253 Extended meaning of "carrying on business".

Canadian Petroleum Tax Journal: Selected Income Tax Considerations When Structuring Foreign Resource Ventures, William A. Brebber, 2002, Vol. 15, No. 1; Moving Forward With Mobile Income, Chris Roberge, CA, CPA, 2001, Vol. 14, No. 1; High Tech in the Oil Patch: Planning Considerations For Transferring Technology Offshore, Derek A. Kurrant, 2000, Vol. 13, No. 1.

Canadian Tax Foundation: Khazam, *CRA Confirms Interpretation of Cap B in Partnership Context*, 2018 Canadian Tax Focus 8(1):6; Pham, *FAPI Recharacterization and LLCs*, 2013 Canadian Tax Focus 3(1):9–10; Morier and Juneja, *Foreign Affiliates: An Updated Primer*, 2012 Conference Report 28:1–48; Samuel, *Stopping The Losses: The Application Of Stop-Loss Rules To Transactions Involving Foreign Affiliates*, 2010 Canadian Tax Journal 4:897–925; Huynh and Lockwood, *Foreign Affiliates and Adjusted Cost Base*, 2007 Canadian Tax Journal 1:141–159; Maikawa and Martin, *Foreign Exchange and Foreign Affiliates: Continuing Problems and Possible Solutions*, 2006 Canadian Tax Journal 1:241–261; Juneja and Morier, *Foreign Affiliates: A Primer*, 2005 Conference Report 40:1–41; Talakshi, *The Foreign Affiliate Proposals — An Update*, 2005 Conference Report 14:1–20; Slaats, *Repatriation from Foreign Affiliates: Selected Issues*, 2005 Canadian Tax Journal 3:858–884; Turner, *Foreign Affiliate Liquidation and Merger Rollovers: Where Are We Now and Where Should We Be?*, 2005 Canadian Tax Journal 3:640–684; Tremblay and Wilkie, *The Canadian Triangle: Tax Policy Reflections on the Uneasy Interaction of 15(2), 17 and 95(2)*, 2002 Conference Report 18:1–16; Berwick et al., *The Upcoming Foreign Affiliate Amendments*, 2001 Conference Report 12:1–22; Swiderski and Lau, *Canadian Foreign Affiliate Implications of Common U.S. Asset Transfers*, 2000 Conference Report 15:1–46; Nikolakakis, *The 1999-2000 Foreign Affiliate Amendments: Partnerships, Foreign Exchange Issues, and the Use of Losses* , 2000 Conference Report 14:1–60; Huynh And Lockwood, *Foreign Accrual Property Income: A Practical Perspective*, 2000 Canadian Tax Journal 3:752–777; Lagios and Minassian, *Foreign Accrual Property Income: Pitfalls for the Unwary*, 1999 Conference Report 3:1–53; Bourgeois, *Canadian Taxation of Offshore Income: A Primer*, 1999 Conference Report 2:1–32; Lockwood and Maikawa, *Foreign Affiliates and FAPI: Problems and Tax-Planning Opportunities Resulting from the 1995 Changes*, 1998 Canadian Tax Journal 2:377–414; Bronstetter et al., *Loans Between Foreign Affiliates*, 1997 Canadian Tax Journal 3:560–583.

Tax Profile: July 2013 — CRA Rules that an Investment in a MRPS of Luxembourg Corporation Was a Share Investment; February 2013 — The Purchase of US Businesses by Canadians; April 2008 — International Tax Planning for the Owner-Manager; March 2008 — International Tax Planning for the Owner-Manager; September 2006 — Canadian Acquisition of U.S. Real Estate; June 2003 — The December 20, 2002 Technical Amendments to the Income Tax Act; April 2002 — Tax Considerations for Canadian Businesses Expanding to the U.S..

Tax Topics: No. 1614, New FAPI "Fresh Start" Rules Released - Wording Re Capital Gains Less Than Clear; Change of Business Pitfall Added.

Forms: T2SCH25 Investment in Foreign Affiliates (1998 and later taxation years).

Tax Window Files: IFA 2016 Q.8: s. 95(2)(a)(ii)(B) and borrowing to return capital, *May 26, 2016*, CRA Document No. 2016-0642041C6; 2015 CTF Q.9 - s. 95(2)(a)(ii)(D)(IV)(2), *November 24, 2015*, CRA Document No. 2015-0610561C6; Subparagraph 95(2)(a)(i), *15XXXX*, CRA Document No. 2015-0573141R3.

▶ 95(2)(a.1) ◀

(a.1) [Determination of FAPI — Income from sale of property] — in computing the income from a business other than an active business for a taxation year of a foreign affiliate of a taxpayer there shall be included the income of the affiliate for the year from the sale of property (which, for the purposes of this paragraph, includes the income of the affiliate for the year from the performance of services as an agent in relation to a purchase or sale of property) where

(i) it is reasonable to conclude that the cost to any person of the property (other than property that is designated property) is relevant in computing the income from a business carried on by the taxpayer or by a person resident in Canada with whom the taxpayer does not deal at arm's length or is relevant in computing the income from a business carried on in Canada by a non-resident person with whom the taxpayer does not deal at arm's length, and

(ii) the property was not

(A) manufactured, produced, grown, extracted or processed in the country

(I) under whose laws the affiliate is governed and any of exists, was (unless the affiliate was continued in any jurisdiction) formed or organized, or was last continued, and

(II) in which the affiliate's business is principally carried on,

(B) an interest in real property, or a real right in an immovable, located in, or a foreign resource property in respect of, the country

(I) under whose laws the affiliate is governed and any of exists, was (unless the affiliate was continued in any jurisdiction) formed or organized, or was last continued, and

(II) in which the affiliate's business is principally carried on, or

(C) an indebtedness, or a lease obligation, of a person resident in Canada or in respect of a business carried on in Canada, that was purchased and sold by the affiliate on its own account,

unless more than 90% of the gross revenue of the affiliate for the year from the sale of property (other than a property the income from the sale of which is not included in computing the income from a business other than an active business of the affiliate under this paragraph because of subsection (2.31)) is derived from the sale of such property (other than a property described in subparagraph (ii) the cost of which to any person is a cost referred to in subparagraph (i)) to persons with whom the affiliate deals at arm's length (which, for this purpose, includes a sale of property to a non-resident corporation with which the affiliate does not deal at arm's length for sale to persons with whom the affiliate deals at arm's length) and, where this paragraph applies to include income of the affiliate from the sale of property in the income of the affiliate from a business other than an active business,

(iii) the sale of such property shall be deemed to be a separate business, other than an active business, carried on by the affiliate, and

(iv) any income of the affiliate that pertains to or is incident to that business shall be deemed to be income from a business other than an active business;

Editorial Note: S. 95(2)(*a.1*) is an income recharacterization rule that applies for the purposes of the foreign affiliate rules in Subdivision i and the supporting rules in Part LIX of the Regulations.

S. 95(2)(*a.1*) deems certain income earned by a foreign affiliate of a Canadian-resident taxpayer from a business consisting of the sale of property (including the provision of services as an agent in relation to the purchase or sale of property) to be income from a separate business other than an active business. Where s. 95(2)(*a.1*) applies the recharacterized income will be included in an affiliate's foreign accrual property income (FAPI) and will, if the affiliate is a controlled foreign affiliate, be subject to the FAPI imputation regime in s. 91(1). See the editorial notes accompanying s. 91(1) and the definition of FAPI (specifically element A) in s. 95(1).

Any income earned by a foreign affiliate that is deemed by s. 95(2)(*a.1*) to be income from a business other than an active business will be included in the affiliate's "net earnings" from FAPI (see paragraph (*b*) of the definition of "net earnings" in regulation 5907(1)). In consequence, the income will be included in the affiliate's "taxable earnings" and therefore "taxable surplus" (see the definitions in regulation 5907(1)).

History: S. 95(2)(*a.1*), the portion after subparagraph (ii) and before subparagraph (iii) was replaced by S.C. 2017, c. 33, s. 30(2), applicable in respect of taxation years of a foreign affiliate of a taxpayer that end after October 2012, and formerly read:

> unless more than 90% of the gross revenue of the affiliate for the year from the sale of property is derived from the sale of such property (other than a property described in subparagraph (ii) the cost of which to any person is a cost referred to in subparagraph (i) or a property the income from the sale of which is not included in computing the income from a business other than an active business of the affiliate under this paragraph because of subsection (2.31)) to persons with whom the affiliate deals at arm's length (which, for this purpose, includes a sale of property to a non-resident corporation with which the affiliate does not deal at arm's length for sale to persons with whom the affiliate deals at arm's length) and, where this paragraph applies to include income of the affiliate from the sale of property in the income of the affiliate from a business other than an active business,

S. 95(2)(*a.1*)(ii), the portion before clause (A) was replaced by S.C. 2014, c. 39, s. 25(7), applicable in respect of taxation years of a foreign affiliate of a taxpayer that begin after October 2012, and formerly read:

> (ii) the property was neither

S. 95(2)(*a.1*)(ii)(C) was added by S.C. 2014, c. 39, s. 25(8), applicable in respect of taxation years of a foreign affiliate of a taxpayer that begin after October 2012.

S. 95(2)(*a.1*), the portion after subparagraph (ii) and before subparagraph (iii) was replaced by S.C. 2014, c. 39, s. 25(9), applicable in respect of taxation years of a foreign affiliate of a taxpayer that begin after October 2012, and formerly read:

> unless more than 90% of the gross revenue of the affiliate for the year from the sale of property is derived from the sale of such property (other than a property described in subparagraph (ii) the cost of which to any person is a cost referred to in subparagraph (i)) to persons with whom the affiliate

deals at arm's length (which, for this purpose, includes a sale of property to a non-resident corporation with which the affiliate does not deal at arm's length for sale to persons with whom the affiliate deals at arm's length) and, where this paragraph applies to include income of the affiliate from the sale of property in the income of the affiliate from a business other than an active business,

Related Regulations: 5907(1), "net earnings", "taxable earnings".

Related Sections: S. 66(15), "foreign resource property"; s. 95(1), "active business", "foreign accrual property income", "foreign affiliate", "income from an active business"; s. 95(2)(*k*) Fresh start rules; s. 95(2)(*u*) Partnership look through rule; s. 95(2.3) Application of paragraph (2)(a.1); s. 95(3.1) Designated property — subparagraph (2)(a.1)(i); s. 248(1), "business", "foreign resource property", "gross revenue", "taxpayer"; s. 249(1) Definition of "taxation year" s. 251 Arm's length; s. 253 Extended meaning of "carrying on business".

► 95(2)(a.2) ◄

(a.2) [Determination of FAPI — Income from insurance of Canadian risks] — in computing the income from a business other than an active business for a taxation year of a foreign affiliate of a taxpayer

(i) there shall be included the income of the affiliate for the year from the insurance of specified Canadian risks (which, for the purposes of this paragraph, includes income for the year from the reinsurance of specified Canadian risks), unless more than 90% of the gross premium revenue of the affiliate for the year from the insurance of risks (net of reinsurance ceded) was in respect of the insurance of risks (other than specified Canadian risks) of persons with whom the affiliate deals at arm's length,

(ii) if subparagraph (i) applies to include income of the affiliate from the insurance of specified Canadian risks,

(A) the insurance of those risks is deemed to be a separate business, other than an active business, carried on by the affiliate, and

(B) any income of the affiliate that pertains to or is incident to that business is deemed to be income from a business other than an active business,

(iii) there shall be included the income of the affiliate for the year in respect of the ceding of specified Canadian risks — except to the extent that the income is included because of subparagraph (i) or (ii) — which, for the purposes of this paragraph, includes

(A) income of the affiliate from services in respect of the ceding of specified Canadian risks, and

(B) except to the extent the amount is included under clause (A), the amount, if any, by which the fair market value of the consideration provided in respect of the ceding of the specified Canadian risks exceeds the affiliate's cost in respect of those specified Canadian risks, and

(iv) if subparagraph (iii) applies to include income of the affiliate in respect of the ceding of specified Canadian risks,

(A) the ceding of those risks is deemed to be a separate business, other than an active business, carried on by the affiliate, and

(B) any income of the affiliate that pertains to or is incident to that business is deemed to be income from a business other than an active business;

Editorial Note: S. 95(2)(*a.2*) is an income recharacterization rule that applies for the purposes of the foreign affiliate rules in Subdivision i and the supporting rules in Part LIX of the Regulations.

S. 95(2)(*a.2*) deems certain income earned by a foreign affiliate of a Canadian-resident taxpayer from the insurance and reinsurance of Canadian-source risks to be income from a separate business other than an active business. Pursuant to the 2014 Budget, paragraphs 95(2)(*a.21*) and 95(2)(*a.22*) were enacted to address application of this rule regarding insurance swaps or similar arrangements involving Canadian-source risks.

The 2016 Budget added subparagraphs 95(2)(*a.2*)(iii) and (iv), effective for taxation years that begin after April 20, 2015. Subparagraph 95(2)(*a.2*)(iii) provides that, to the extent that income in respect of the ceding of specified Canadian risks is not already included in a foreign affiliate's income from non-active business because of subparagraph 95(2)(*a.2*)(i) or (ii), it is to be so included. For these purposes, an affiliate's income in respect of the ceding of specified Canadian risks includes, but is not limited to, income of the affiliate from services in respect of the ceding of specified Canadian risks, and the amount, if any, by which the fair market value of the consideration provided in respect of the ceding of the specified Canadian risks exceeds the affiliate's cost in respect of those risks.

Subparagraph 95(2)(*a.2*)(iv) is analogous to subparagraph 95(2)(*a.2*)(ii). Where subparagraph 95(2)(*a.2*)(iii) above applies, it deems the ceding of specified Canadian risks to be income from a separate business other than an active business.

The application of s. 95(2)(*a.2*) gives rise to the same result as that which occurs where s. 95(2)(*a.1*) applies. See the editorial notes accompanying s. 95(2)(*a.1*).

History: S. 95(2)(*a.2*) was replaced by S.C. 2016, c. 7, s. 12(1), applicable to taxation years of a taxpayer that begin after April 20, 2015, and formerly read:

(a.2) *[Determination of FAPI — Income from insurance of Canadian risks]* — in computing the income from a business other than an active business for a taxation year of a foreign affiliate of a taxpayer there shall be included the income of the affiliate for the year from the insurance of a risk (which, for the purposes of this paragraph, includes income of the affiliate for the year from the reinsurance of a risk) where the risk was in respect of

(i) a person resident in Canada,

(ii) a property situated in Canada, or

(iii) a business carried on in Canada

unless more than 90% of the gross premium revenue of the affiliate for the year from the insurance of risks (net of reinsurance ceded) was in respect of the insurance of risks (other than risks in respect of a person, a property or a business described in subparagraphs (i) to (iii)) of persons with whom the affiliate deals at arm's length and, where this paragraph applies to include income of the affiliate from the insurance of risks in the income of the affiliate from a business other than an active business,

(iv) the insurance of those risks shall be deemed to be a separate business, other than an active business, carried on by the affiliate, and

(v) any income of the affiliate that pertains to or is incident to that business shall be deemed to be income from a business other than an active business;

Related Regulations: 5907(1), "net earnings", "taxable earnings".

Related Sections: S. 95(1), "active business", "foreign accrual property income", "foreign affiliate", "income from an active business"; s. 95(2)(*k*) Fresh start rules; s. 95(2)(*u*) Partnership look through rule; s. 95(2.41) Application of paragraph (2)(a.3); s. 248(1), "business", "gross revenue", "taxpayer"; s. 249(1) Definition of "taxation year"; s. 251 Arm's length; s. 253 Extended meaning of "carrying on business".

► 95(2)(a.21) ◄

(a.21) [Determination of FAPI — Income from insurance of Canadian risks] — for the purposes of paragraph (*a.2*), one or more risks insured by a foreign affiliate of a taxpayer that, if this Act were read without reference to this paragraph, would not be specified Canadian risks (in this paragraph referred to as the foreign *policy pool*) are deemed to be specified Canadian risks if

(i) the affiliate, or a person or partnership that does not deal at arm's length with the affiliate, enters into one or more agreements or arrangements in respect of the foreign policy pool,

(ii) the affiliate's risk of loss or opportunity for gain or profit in respect of the foreign policy pool, in combination with its risk of loss or opportunity for gain in respect of the agreements or arrangements, can reasonably be considered to be — or could reasonably be considered to be if the affiliate had entered into the agreements or arrangements entered into by the person or partnership — determined, in whole or in part, by reference to one or more criteria in respect of one or more risks insured by another person or partnership (in this paragraph referred to as the *tracked policy pool*), which criteria are

(A) the fair market value of the tracked policy pool,

(B) the revenue, income, loss or cash flow from the tracked policy pool, or

(C) any other similar criteria, and

(iii) 10% or more of the tracked policy pool consists of specified Canadian risks;

History: S. 95(2)(*a*.21) was replaced by S.C. 2016, c. 7, s. 12(1), applicable to taxation years of a taxpayer that begin after April 20, 2015, and formerly read:

(*a*.21) *[Determination of FAPI — Income from insurance of Canadian risks]* — for the purposes of paragraph (*a*.2), one or more risks insured by a foreign affiliate of a taxpayer that, if this Act were read without reference to this paragraph, would not be risks in respect of a person, property or business described in any of subparagraphs (*a*.2)(i) to (iii) (in this paragraph referred to as the "foreign policy pool") are deemed to be risks in respect of a person resident in Canada if

(i) the affiliate, or a person or partnership that does not deal at arm's length with the affiliate, enters into one or more agreements or arrangements in respect of the foreign policy pool,

(ii) the affiliate's risk of loss or opportunity for gain or profit in respect of the foreign policy pool, in combination with its risk of loss or opportunity for gain or profit in respect of the agreements or arrangements, can reasonably be considered to be — or could reasonably be considered to be if the affiliate had entered into the agreements or arrangements entered into by the person or partnership — determined, in whole or in part, by reference to one or more criteria in respect of one or more risks insured by another person or partnership (in this paragraph referred to as the "tracked policy pool"), which criteria are

(A) the fair market value of the tracked policy pool,

(B) the revenue, income, loss or cash flow from the tracked policy pool, or

(C) any other similar criteria, and

(iii) 10% or more of the tracked policy pool consists of risks in respect of a person, property or business described in any of subparagraphs (*a*.2)(i) to (iii);

S. 95(2)(*a*.21) was added by S.C. 2014, c. 39, s. 25(10), applicable to taxation years of a taxpayer that begin after February 10, 2014.

▶ 95(2)(a.22) ◀

(a.22) [Determination of FAPI — Income from insurance of Canadian risks] — if the conditions in paragraph (*a.21*) are satisfied in respect of a foreign affiliate of a taxpayer, or a foreign affiliate of another taxpayer if that other taxpayer does not deal at arm's length with the taxpayer, and a particular foreign affiliate of the taxpayer, or a partnership of which the particular affiliate is a member, has entered into one or more agreements or arrangements described in that paragraph,

(i) activities performed in connection with those agreements or arrangements are deemed to be a separate business, other than an active business, carried on by the particular affiliate to the extent that those activities can reasonably be considered to be performed for the purpose of obtaining the result described in subparagraph (*a.21*)(ii), and

(ii) any income of the particular affiliate from the business (including income that pertains to or is incident to the business) is deemed to be income from a business other than an active business;

History: S. 95(2)(*a*.22) was added by S.C. 2014, c. 39, s. 25(10), in respect of taxation years of a foreign affiliate of a taxpayer that begin after October 2012.

▶ 95(2)(a.23) ◀

(a.23) [Determination of FAPI — Income from insurance of Canadian risks] — for the purposes of paragraphs (*a*.2), (*a*.21) and (*a*.24), *specified Canadian risk* means a risk in respect of

(i) a person resident in Canada,

(ii) a property situated in Canada, or

(iii) a business carried on in Canada;

History: S. 95(2)(*a*.23), the portion before subparagraph (i) was replaced by S.C. 2017, c. 33, s. 30(3), applicable to transactions that occur after March 21, 2017, and formerly read:

(*a*.23) *[Determination of FAPI — Income from insurance of Canadian risks]* — for the purposes of paragraphs (*a*.2) and (*a*.21), *specified Canadian risk* means a risk in respect of

S. 95(2)(*a*.23) was added by S.C. 2016, c. 7, s. 12(2), applicable to taxation years of a taxpayer that begin after April 20, 2015.

▶ 95(2)(a.24) ◀

(a.24) [Determination of FAPI — deemed specified Canadian risk] — for the purposes of paragraph (*a*.2),

(i) a risk is deemed to be a specified Canadian risk of a particular foreign affiliate of a taxpayer if

(A) as part of a transaction or series of transactions, the particular affiliate insured or reinsured the risk,

(B) the risk would not be a specified Canadian risk if this Act were read without reference to this paragraph, and

(C) it can reasonably be concluded that one of the purposes of the transaction or series of transactions was to avoid the application of any of paragraphs (*a*.2) to (*a*.22), and

(ii) if the particular affiliate — or a foreign affiliate of another taxpayer, if that other taxpayer or affiliate, or a partnership of which that other taxpayer or affiliate is a member, does not deal at arm's length with the particular affiliate — enters into one or more agreements or arrangements in respect of the risk,

(A) activities performed in connection with those agreements or arrangements are deemed to be a separate business, other than an active business, carried on by the particular affiliate or other affiliate, as the case may be, and

(B) any income of the particular affiliate or other affiliate, as the case may be, from the business (including income that pertains to or is incident to the business) is deemed to be income from a business other than an active business;

History: S. 95(2)(*a.24*) was added by S.C. 2017, c. 33, s. 30(4), applicable to transactions that occur after March 21, 2017.

▶ 95(2)(a.3) ◀

(a.3) [Determination of FAPI — Income from indebtedness and lease obligations] — in computing the income from a business other than an active business for a taxation year of a foreign affiliate of a taxpayer there shall be included the income of the affiliate for the year derived directly or indirectly from indebtedness and lease obligations (which, for the purposes of this paragraph, includes the income of the affiliate for the year from the purchase and sale of indebtedness and lease obligations on its own account, but does not include excluded income)

(i) of persons resident in Canada, or

(ii) in respect of businesses carried on in Canada

unless more than 90% of the gross revenue of the affiliate derived directly or indirectly from indebtedness and lease obligations (other than excluded revenue or revenue that is not included in computing the income from a business other than an active business of the affiliate under this paragraph because of subsection (2.31)) was derived directly or indirectly from indebtedness and lease obligations of non-resident persons with whom the affiliate deals at arm's length and, where this paragraph applies to include income of the affiliate for the year in the income of the affiliate from a business other than an active business,

(iii) those activities carried out to earn such income shall be deemed to be a separate business, other than an active business, carried on by the affiliate, and

(iv) any income of the affiliate that pertains to or is incident to that business shall be deemed to be income from a business other than an active business;

Editorial Note: S. 95(2)(*a*.3) is an income recharacterization rule that applies for the purposes of the foreign affiliate rules in Subdivision i and the supporting rules in Part LIX of the Regulations.

S. 95(2)(*a*.3) deems certain income earned by a foreign affiliate of a Canadian-resident taxpayer derived from "indebtedness" and "lease obligations" (including income from the purchase and sale of indebtedness and lease obligations) to be income from a separate business other than an active business. See the editorial notes accompanying the definition of "indebtedness" in s. 95(2.5) and the definition of "lease obligation" in s. 95(1). The application of s. 95(2)(*a*.3) gives rise to the same result as that which occurs where s. 95(2)(*a*.1) applies. See the editorial notes accompanying s. 95(2)(*a*.1).

History: S. 95(2)(*a*.3), the portion after subparagraph (ii) and before subparagraph (iii) was replaced by S.C. 2014, c. 39, s. 25(11), applicable in respect of taxation years of a foreign affiliate of a taxpayer that begin after October 2012, and formerly read:

> unless more than 90% of the gross revenue of the affiliate derived directly or indirectly from indebtedness and lease obligations (other than excluded revenue) was derived directly or indirectly from indebtedness and lease obligations of non-resident persons with whom the affiliate deals at arm's length and, where this paragraph applies to include income of the affiliate for the year in the income of the affiliate from a business other than an active business,

Related Regulations: 5907(1), "net earnings", "taxable earnings"; 7900 Meaning of "prescribed financial institution".

Related Sections: S. 95(1), "active business", "foreign accrual property income", "foreign affiliate", "income from an active business", "lease obligation"; s. 95(2)(*k*) Fresh start rules; s. 95(2)(*u*) Partnership look through rule; ss. 95(2.4), (2.41) Application rules; s. 95(2.5) Definitions for paragraph (2)(a.3); s. 248(1), "business", "gross revenue", taxpayer"; s. 249(1) Definition of "taxation year"; s. 251 Arm's length; s. 253 Extended meaning of "carrying on business".

▶ 95(2)(a.4) ◀

(a.4) [Determination of FAPI — Income from indebtedness and lease obligations in respect of partnership business] — in computing the income from a business other than an active business for a taxation year of a foreign affiliate of a taxpayer there shall be included (to the extent not included under paragraph (*a*.3) in such income of the affiliate for the year) that proportion of the income of the affiliate for the year derived directly or indirectly from indebtedness and lease obligations (which, for the purposes of this paragraph, includes the income of the affiliate for the year from the purchase and sale of indebtedness and lease obligations on its own account) in respect of a business carried on outside Canada by a partnership (any portion of the income or loss of which for fiscal periods of the partnership that end in the year is included or would, if the partnership had an income or loss for such fiscal periods, be included directly or indirectly in computing the income or loss of the taxpayer or a person resident in Canada with whom the taxpayer does not deal at arm's length) that

(i) the total of all amounts each of which is the income or loss of the partnership for fiscal periods of the partnership that end in the year that are included directly or indirectly in computing the income or loss of the taxpayer or a person resident in Canada with whom the taxpayer does not deal at arm's length

is of

(ii) the total of all amounts each of which is the income or loss of the partnership for fiscal periods of the partnership that end in the year

unless more than 90% of the gross revenue of the affiliate derived directly or indirectly from indebtedness and lease obligations was derived directly or indirectly from indebtedness and lease obligations of non-resident persons with whom the affiliate deals at arm's length (other than indebtedness and lease obligations of a partnership described in this paragraph) and where this paragraph applies to include a proportion of the income of the affiliate for the year in the income of the affiliate from a business other than an active business

(iii) those activities carried out to earn such income of the affiliate for the year shall be deemed to be a separate business, other than an active business, carried on by the affiliate, and

(iv) any income of the affiliate that pertains to or is incident to that business shall be deemed to be income from a business other than an active business

and for the purpose of this paragraph, where the income or loss of a partnership for a fiscal period that ends in the year is nil, the proportion of the income of the affiliate that is to be included in the income of the affiliate for the year from a business other than an active business shall be determined as if the partnership had income of $1,000,000 for that fiscal period;

Editorial Note: S. 95(2)(*a.4*) is an income recharacterization rule that applies for the purposes of the foreign affiliate rules in Subdivision i and the supporting rules in Part LIX of the Regulations.

S. 95(2)(*a.4*) deems certain income earned by a foreign affiliate of a Canadian-resident taxpayer derived from "indebtedness" and "lease obligations" (including income from the purchase and sale of indebtedness and lease obligations) in respect of a business carried on outside Canada by a partnership to be income from a separate business other than an active business. See the editorial notes accompanying the definition of "indebtedness" in s. 95(2.5) and the definition of "lease obligation" in s. 95(1). The application of s. 95(2)(*a.4*) gives rise to the same result as that which occurs where s. 95(2)(*a.1*) applies. See the editorial notes accompanying s. 95(2)(*a.1*).

Related Regulations: 5907(1), "net earnings", "taxable earnings".

Related Sections: S. 95(1), "active business", "foreign accrual property income", "foreign affiliate", "income from an active business", "lease obligation"; s. 95(2)(*k*) Fresh start rules; s. 95(2)(*u*) Partnership look through rule; s. 95(2.4) Application of paragraph (2)(a.3); (2.41) Application rules; s. 95(2.5) Definitions for paragraph (2)(a.3); s. 96 Partnerships — General rules; s. 248(1), "business", "gross revenue", taxpayer"; s. 249(1) Definition of "taxation year"; s. 249.1 Definition of "fiscal period" s. 251 Arm's length; s. 253 Extended meaning of "carrying on business".

▶ 95(2)(b) ◀

(b) [Determination of FAPI — Provision of services] — the provision, by a foreign affiliate of a taxpayer, of services or of an undertaking to provide services

(i) is deemed to be a separate business, other than an active business, carried on by the affiliate, and any income from that business or that pertains to or is incident to that business is deemed to be income from a business other than an active business, to the extent that the amounts paid or payable in consideration for those services or for the undertaking to provide services

(A) are deductible, or can reasonably be considered to relate to amounts that are deductible, in computing the income from a business carried on in Canada, by

(I) any taxpayer of whom the affiliate is a foreign affiliate, or

(II) another taxpayer who does not deal at arm's length with

1. the affiliate, or

2. any taxpayer of whom the affiliate is a foreign affiliate, or

(B) are deductible, or can reasonably be considered to relate to an amount that is deductible, in computing the foreign accrual property income of a foreign affiliate of

(I) any taxpayer of whom the affiliate is a foreign affiliate, or

(II) another taxpayer who does not deal at arm's length with

1. the affiliate, or

2. any taxpayer of whom the affiliate is a foreign affiliate, and

(ii) is deemed to be a separate business, other than an active business, carried on by the affiliate, and any income from that business or that pertains to or is incident to that business is deemed to be income from a business other than an active business, to the extent that the services are, or are to be, performed by

(A) any taxpayer of whom the affiliate is a foreign affiliate,

(B) a relevant person who does not deal at arm's length with

(I) the affiliate, or

(II) any taxpayer of whom the affiliate is a foreign affiliate,

(C) a partnership any member of which is a person described in clause (A) or (B), or

(D) a partnership in which any person or partnership described in any of clauses (A) to (C) has, directly or indirectly, a partnership interest;

Department of Finance Comfort Letters

(June 12, 2017) Foreign accrual property income resulting from the application of paragraph 95(2)(b) of the Income Tax Act to inter-affiliate payments for services

2017FIN454948

XXXX

Dear XXXX:

SUBJECT: Foreign accrual property income resulting from the application of paragraph 95(2)(*b*) of the *Income Tax Act* to inter-affiliate payments for services

I am writing in response to your correspondence to the Tax Legislation Division, and various related communications, concerning your request for an amendment to the *Income Tax Act* (the "Act") to ensure that paragraph 95(2)(*b*) of the Act applies appropriately to certain services fees paid by one foreign affiliate of the XXXX ("Canco") to another foreign affiliate of Canco.

Paragraph 95(2)(*b*) is one of the "base erosion" rules in the Act. Your request relates, in particular, to clause 95(2)(*b*)(i)(B). In general terms, that clause deems the provision of services by a particular foreign affiliate of a taxpayer to be a separate business, other than an active business, of the particular foreign affiliate — and includes any income from that business in the particular foreign affiliate's foreign accrual property income ("FAPI") (as defined in subsection 95(1) of the Act) — to the extent that amounts paid or payable in consideration for those services are deductible in computing the FAPI of:

- another foreign affiliate of the taxpayer,
- a foreign affiliate of any other taxpayer of which the particular foreign affiliate is a foreign affiliate, or
- a foreign affiliate of another taxpayer that does not deal at arm's length with either the particular foreign affiliate, or a taxpayer of which the particular foreign affiliate is a foreign affiliate.

The issue that you have raised arises from the application of sub-clause 95(2)(*b*)(i)(B)(I) in the following factual situation, described in your letter. Canco, a corporation resident in Canada, carries on a foreign asset management business through its foreign subsidiaries. Typically, in the course of business, an investment fund (the "Fund") is established in the form of a non-resident corporation, and equity interests in the Fund are marketed and sold to arm's length investors. A non-resident wholly-owned subsidiary of Canco ("Manager") provides asset management services in respect of the Fund in consideration for a fee that is payable by the Fund. We understand that Canco and Manager each have a taxation year-end of XXXX and typically the Fund will have a taxation year-end of XXXX.

Although the Fund is generally owned primarily by arm's length non-resident investors, Manager or a related Canco group entity may hold a small equity interest in the Fund. For example, Manager may make an initial "seed capital" investment when the Fund is established, which may subsequently be redeemed once the Fund has attracted sufficient investment from arm's length investors.

In the investment structure described above, Manager is a "foreign affiliate" of Canco (as defined in subsection 95(1)). If Canco's "equity percentage" (as defined in subsection 95(4)) in the Fund is not less than 10 per cent, the Fund is also a foreign affiliate of Canco. Assuming the services fees paid or payable by the Fund to Manager are deductible in computing the Fund's FAPI (e.g., in computing its income from carrying on an "investment business", as defined in subsection 95(1)), then sub-clause 95(2)(*b*)(i)(B)(I) applies with the result that 100 per cent of the services fees paid by the Fund is included in computing Manager's FAPI.

You have submitted to us that this is a disproportionate result. In your view, if paragraph 95(2)(*b*) is to apply in these circumstances, clause 95(2)(*b*)(i)(B) should be amended such that the services fees are included in computing Manager's FAPI only in proportion to Canco's economic interest in the Fund's FAPI.

Our Comments:

We agree that, in policy terms, the application of paragraph 95(2)(*b*) in the circumstances described above can be refined so that less than 100 per cent of the services fees paid or payable to Manager by the Fund is included in computing Manager's FAPI. It would be consistent with the policy of paragraph 95(2)(*b*) that the proportion of the services fees so included be determined having regard to Canco's economic interest in the Fund's FAPI.

We are therefore prepared to recommend to the Minister of Finance that, effective for taxation years of foreign affiliates beginning after 2015, the Act be amended such that the clause 95(2)(*b*)(i)(B) deems the provision of services (or an undertaking to provide services) by a foreign affiliate of a taxpayer (the "first affiliate") to be a separate business, other than an active business, of the first affiliate — and includes any income from that business in the first affiliate's FAPI — to the extent of the portion of the amounts paid or payable in consideration for the services (or for the undertaking) determined by the formula A X B, where:

A is and amount paid or payable in consideration for the services or for the undertaking that is deductible, or can reasonably be considered to relate to an amount that is deductible, in computing the FAPI of a foreign affiliate of any of the taxpayers described in sub-clause 95(2)(*b*)(i)(B)(I) or (II) (the "second affiliate"); and

B is the total of the participating percentages (as defined in subsection 95(1)), in respect of the second affiliate of shares of corporations that are owned by any taxpayer resident in Canada of which the second affiliate is a foreign affiliate, at the end of the second affiliate's tax year in which that amount is deductible. For this purpose, the definition of "participating percentage" is to be read as though it applies to all foreign affiliates, and not only controlled foreign affiliates.

While we cannot offer any assurance that either the Minister of Finance or Parliament will agree with our recommendations in respect of this matter, we hope that this statement of our intention is helpful.

Yours sincerely,

Brian Ernewein

General Director - Legislation

Tax Policy Branch

Department of Finance Comfort Letters

(December 23, 2016) [Foreign Accrual Property Income ought not to result from payment for services between two foreign affiliates if certain conditions are met]

2016FIN444340

XXXX

Dear Mr. XXXX:

SUBJECT: Foreign accrual property income resulting from the application of paragraph 95(2)(*b*) of the Income Tax Act to inter-affiliate payments for services

I am writing in response to your correspondence to the Tax Legislation Division, and your various related communications, concerning your request for an amendment to the *Income Tax Act* (the "Act") to ensure that paragraph 95(2)(*b*) of the Act does not apply to certain services fees paid by one foreign affiliate of XXXX ("XXXX") to another foreign affiliate of XXXX.

Paragraph 95(2)(*b*) is one of the "base erosion" rules in the Act. Your request relates, in particular, to subclause 95(2)(*b*)(i)(B)(I). That subclause provides that, if a particular foreign affiliate of a taxpayer provides services to another foreign affiliate of the taxpayer, then, to the extent that amounts paid by the other foreign affiliate in consideration for the services are deductible in computing its foreign accrual properly income ("FAPI") (as defined in subsection 95(1) of the Act), these amounts are deemed to be income of the particular foreign affiliate from a business other than an active business - and are therefore included in the particular foreign affiliate's FAPI.

The issue that you have raised arises from the application of subclause 95(2)(*b*)(i)(B)(I) in the following factual situation, described in your letter. XXXX, a corporation resident in Canada, and its subsidiaries establish and invest in certain investment funds. In structuring such investments, a non-resident holding corporation ("Holdco") is formed to acquire shares of a non-resident operating company ("Opco") that carries on an active business (as defined in subsection 95(1) of the Act). XXXX (or a controlled foreign affiliate of XXXX) and a group of arm's length investors contribute capital to Holdco to fund the acquisition of Opco. A wholly-owned, non-resident subsidiary corporation of XXXX ("Manager") provides asset management and investment advisory services in respect of Opco in consideration for a management fee. Holdco, rather than Opco, pays the management fee to Manager because (among other reasons) Holdco is not the sole shareholder of Opco and Opco's other shareholders are unwilling to bear the fee.

In the investment structure described above, Holdco, Opco and Manager are all "foreign affiliates" of XXXX (as defined in subsection 95(1)). You note that, since Holdco does not carry on an active business (its sole activity being the holding of shares of Opco), the services fees paid by Holdco to Manager are deductible in computing Holdco's FAPI, resulting in a foreign accrual property loss ("FAPL"). Accordingly, subclause 95(2)(*b*)(i)(B)(I) applies with the result that the services income is included in Manager's FAPI.

You have submitted to us that this result is inappropriate in policy terms. In this regard, you note that neither Opco nor Holdco earns FAPI. In addition, Manager's services are provided in respect of Opco, a subsidiary of Holdco that carries on an active business and the shares of which are "excluded property" of Holdco (as defined in subsection 95(1)); if the services fees were paid by Opco out of its active business income, instead of by Holdco, paragraph 95(2)(*b*) would not apply.

Our Comments:

We agree that, in policy terms, paragraph 95(2)(*b*) ought not to apply to cause the services fees received by Manager from Holdco to be FAPI in the circumstances described above.

We are therefore prepared to recommend to the Minister of Finance that the Act be amended to provide that, effective for taxation years of foreign affiliates ending after 2016, subclause 95(2)(*b*)(i)(B)(I) does not apply in respect of income of a foreign affiliate ("FA1") of a taxpayer from the provision of services, to the extent that conditions generally analogous to those in clause

95(2)(*a*)(ii)(D) are satisfied, including in particular the following conditions:

- The income derives from amounts paid or payable by another foreign affiliate ("FA2") of the taxpayer in consideration for the services;
- The amounts paid or payable are for expenditures incurred by FA2 for the purpose of gaining or producing income from property;
- The property is shares of another foreign affiliate ("FA3") that are "excluded property" of FA2 (as defined in subsection 95(1)); and
- The Canadian taxpayer has a "qualifying interest" (as defined in paragraph 95(2)(*m*) of the Act) in FA1, FA2 and FA3.

We will also recommend that, to the extent that subclause 95(2)(*b*)(i)(B)(I) does not apply in respect of FA1's income from services because of the above recommended amendment, any FAPL of FA2 otherwise resulting from its corresponding expenditures for those services be eliminated.

While we cannot offer any assurance that either the Minister of Finance or Parliament will agree with our recommendations in respect of this matter, we hope that this statement of our intentions is helpful.

Yours sincerely,

Brian Ernewein

General Director - Legislation

Tax Policy Branch

Editorial Note: Paragraph 95(2)(*b*) is an income recharacterization rule that applies for the purposes of the foreign affiliate rules in Subdivision i and the supporting rules in Part LIX of the Regulations.

Paragraph 95(2)(*b*) deems certain income earned by a foreign affiliate of a Canadian-resident taxpayer from the provision of services to be income from a business other than an active business. For this purpose, "services" is defined in s. 95(3). See the editorial notes for the definition of "services" in s. 95(3). The application of s. 95(2)(*b*) gives rise to the same result as that which occurs where s. 95(2)(*a.1*) applies. See the editorial notes for s. 95(2)(*a.1*).

History: S. 95(2)(*b*)(ii)(B), the portion before subclause (I) was replaced by S.C. 2014, c. 39, s. 25(12), applicable in respect of taxation years of a foreign affiliate of a taxpayer that begin after July 12, 2013. However, if a taxpayer elects in writing under s. 25(34) of the *Economic Action Plan 2014 Act, No. 2* [S.C. 2014, c. 39] in respect of all its foreign affiliates and files the election with the Minister of National Revenue on or before the day that is the later of the taxpayer's filing-due date for the taxpayer's taxation year that includes the day on which the *Economic Action Plan 2014 Act, No. 2* [S.C. 2014, c. 39] receives royal assent [December 16, 2014] and the day that is one year after the day on which the *Economic Action Plan 2014 Act, No. 2* [S.C. 2014, c. 39] receives royal assent [December 16, 2015], then the amendment to the portion of s. 95(2)(*b*)(ii)(B) before subclause (I) applies in respect of taxation years of all foreign affiliates of the taxpayer that begin after February 27, 2004.

In addition, any assessment of a taxpayer's tax, interest and penalties payable under the Act for any taxation year that ends before the day on which this amendment receives royal assent [December 16, 2014] that would, in the absence of this section, be precluded because of the time references in subsection 152(4) of the Act is to be made to the extent necessary to take into account this amendment.

S. 95(2)(*b*)(ii)(B), the portion before subclause (I) formerly read:

(B) another taxpayer who does not deal at arm's length with

Related Regulations: 5907(1), "net earnings", "taxable earnings".

Related Sections: S. 95(1), "active business", "foreign accrual property income", "foreign affiliate", "income from an active business", "lease obligation"; s. 95(2)(*u*) Partnership look through rule; s. 95(3) Definition of "services"; s. 96 Partnerships — General rules; s. 248(1), "business", taxpayer"; s. 249(1) Definition of "taxation year" s. 249.1 Definition of "fiscal period" s. 251 Arm's length; s. 253 Extended meaning of "carrying on business".

Tax Profile: February 2013 — The Purchase of US Businesses by Canadians.

Cases: FAPI, which is taxable in the hands of a parent company, includes income from an investment business. "Investment business" exempts a business, other than a business conducted principally with non-arm's length persons, of a regulated foreign bank with more than five full-time employees or the equivalent. The taxpayer was conducting business principally with its parent company, a non-arm's length person, and could not avail itself of the financial institution exemption. However, in calculating the FAPI, the financial exchange gains and losses should be treated as income rather than capital account. *Loblaw Financial Holdings Inc. v. The Queen*, 2018 DTC 1128 (TCC) [under appeal]

▶ 95(2)(c) ◀

(c) [Determination of FAPI — Transfer of shares] — if a foreign affiliate (referred to in this paragraph as the "disposing affiliate") of a taxpayer has, at any time, disposed of capital property (other than property the adjusted cost base of which, at that time, is greater than the amount that would, in the absence of this paragraph, be the disposing affiliate's proceeds of disposition of the property in respect of the disposition) that was shares (referred to in this paragraph as the "shares disposed of") of the capital stock of another foreign affiliate of the taxpayer to any other corporation that was, immediately after that time, a foreign affiliate (referred to in this paragraph as the "acquiring affiliate") of the taxpayer for consideration that includes shares of the capital stock of the acquiring affiliate,

(i) the cost to the disposing affiliate of any property (other than shares of the capital stock of the acquiring affiliate) receivable by the disposing affiliate as consideration for the disposition is deemed to be the fair market value of the property at that time,

(ii) the cost to the disposing affiliate of each share of a class of the capital stock of the acquiring affiliate that is receivable by the disposing affiliate as consideration for the disposition is deemed to be the amount determined by the formula

$$(A - B) \times C/D$$

where

A is the total of all amounts each of which is the relevant cost base to the disposing affiliate at that time, in respect of the taxpayer, of a share disposed of,

B is the fair market value at that time of the consideration receivable for the disposition (other than shares of the capital stock of the acquiring affiliate),

C is the fair market value, immediately after that time, of the share, and

D is the fair market value, immediately after that time, of all shares of the capital stock of the acquiring affiliate receivable by the disposing affiliate as consideration for the disposition,

(iii) the disposing affiliate's proceeds of disposition of the shares are deemed to be an amount equal to the cost to it of all shares and other property receivable by it from the acquiring affiliate as consideration for the disposition, and

(iv) the cost to the acquiring affiliate of the shares acquired from the disposing affiliate is deemed to be an amount equal to the disposing affiliate's proceeds of disposition referred to in subparagraph (iii);

Editorial Note: S. 95(2)(*c*) is a foreign affiliate reorganization rule that is the foreign affiliate equivalent of the domestic share for share exchange rollover rule in s. 85.1(3).

S. 95(2)(*c*) applies where a foreign affiliate of a Canadian-resident taxpayer (FA1) transfers capital property that is a share of another foreign affiliate of the taxpayer (FA2) to any corporation that is, immediately after the disposition, a foreign affiliate of the taxpayer (FA3) for consideration including shares of FA3.

Similar to its domestic counterpart in s. 85.1(3), s. 95(2)(*c*) will permit FA1 to transfer the FA2 share to FA3 in a tax-deferred manner provided that the fair market value of the property other than shares received by FA1 in consideration for the transfer does not exceed the adjusted cost base to FA1 of the share of FA2.

History: S. 95(2)(*c*) was replaced by S.C. 2013, c. 34, s. 70(8), applicable to dispositions that occur after August 19, 2011.

See the application following the addition of the definition "designated liquidation and dissolution" for the extension of assessment periods to take into account the amendments in S.C. 2013, c. 34, s. 54 to 89.

S. 95(2)(*c*) formerly read:

(*c*) *[Determination of FAPI — Transfer of shares]* — where a foreign affiliate of a taxpayer (in this paragraph referred to as the "disposing affiliate") has disposed of capital property that was shares of the capital stock of another foreign affiliate of the taxpayer (in this paragraph referred to as the "shares disposed of") to any corporation that was, immediately following the disposition, a foreign affiliate of the taxpayer (in this paragraph referred to as the "acquiring affiliate") for consideration including shares of the capital stock of the acquiring affiliate,

(i) the cost to the disposing affiliate of any property (other than shares of the capital stock of the acquiring affiliate) receivable by the disposing affiliate as consideration for the disposition shall be deemed to be the fair market value of the property at the time of the disposition,

(ii) the cost to the disposing affiliate of any shares of any class of the capital stock of the acquiring affiliate receivable by the disposing affiliate as consideration for the disposition shall be deemed to be that proportion of the amount, if any, by which the total of the relevant cost bases to it, immediately before the disposition, of the shares disposed of exceeds the fair market value at that time of the consideration receivable for the disposition (other than shares of the capital stock of the acquiring affiliate) that

(A) the fair market value, immediately after the disposition, of those shares of the acquiring affiliate of that class

is of

(B) the fair market value, immediately after the disposition, of all shares of the capital stock of the acquiring affiliate receivable by the disposing affiliate as consideration for the disposition,

(iii) the disposing affiliate's proceeds of disposition of the shares shall be deemed to be an amount equal to the cost to it of all shares and other property receivable by it from the acquiring affiliate as consideration for the disposition, and

(iv) the cost to the acquiring affiliate of the shares acquired from the disposing affiliate shall be deemed to be an amount equal to the disposing affiliate's proceeds of disposition referred to in subparagraph (iii);

Related Regulations: 5907(1), "net earnings", "net loss", "taxable earnings", "taxable loss"; s. 5907(5) Capital gain and loss computation rule.

Related Sections: S. 53(1)(*c*) Adjustments to cost base — Contributions of capital; s. 93(1.1) No election necessary re disposition of excluded property; s. 95(1), "foreign accrual property income"; "foreign affiliate", s. 95(2)(*u*) Partnership look through rule; s. 248(1), "business", "taxpayer"; s. 249(1) Definition of "taxation year"; s. 251 Arm's length; s. 253 Extended meaning of "carrying on business".

Tax Window Files: IFA 2016 Q.10: 93.2 & 95(2)(c), *May 26, 2016*, CRA Document No. 2016-0642101C6.

► 95(2)(d) ◄

(d) [Determination of FAPI — Foreign merger] — where there has been a foreign merger in which the shares owned by a foreign affiliate of a taxpayer of the capital stock of a corporation that was a predecessor foreign corporation immediately before the merger were exchanged for or became shares of the capital stock of the new foreign corporation or the foreign parent corporation, subsection 87(4) applies to the foreign affiliate as if the references in that subsection to

(i) "amalgamation" were read as "foreign merger",

(ii) "predecessor corporation" were read as "predecessor foreign corporation",

(iii) "new corporation" were read as "new foreign corporation or the foreign parent corporation", and

(iv) "adjusted cost bases" were read as "relevant cost bases, in respect of the taxpayer,";

Editorial Note: S. 95(2)(*d*) is a foreign affiliate reorganization rule that is the foreign affiliate equivalent of the domestic foreign merger rollover rule in s. 87(8).

S. 95(2)(*d*) applies where there has been a foreign merger (as defined in s. 87(8.1)) in which the shares of a foreign corporation (NR) held by a foreign affiliate of the taxpayer (FA) were exchanged for or became shares of the new foreign corporation or the foreign parent corporation, thus permitting foreign triangular mergers.

Similar to its domestic counterpart in s. 87(8) s. 95(2)(*d*) provides that s. 87(4) applies to FA, with necessary modifications, to provide FA with the opportunity for the same rollover treatment available in the domestic context; that is, FA may be deemed to dispose of the NR shares for proceeds of disposition equal to the adjusted cost base of those shares to FA.

One of the modifications to the application of s. 87(4) provided by s. 95(2)(*d*) is that the reference to "adjusted cost base" in s. 87(4) should be read as a reference to "relevant cost base", itself an expression defined in s. 95(4). This reference provides FA with the ability to elect to realize a gain as a result of the foreign merger. Any such gain will be included in FA's FAPI pursuant to element B of the definition of FAPI in s. 95(1).

History: S. 95(2)(*d*)(iv) was replaced by S.C. 2013, c. 34, s. 70(9), applicable in respect of mergers or combinations in respect of a foreign affiliate of a taxpayer that occur after August 19, 2011.

See the application following the addition of the definition "designated liquidation and dissolution" for the extension of assessment periods to take into account the amendments in S.C. 2013, c. 34, s. 54 to 89.

S. 95(2)(*d*)(iv) formerly read:

(iv) "adjusted cost base" were read as "relevant cost base";

Related Regulations: 5905(3), (4) Surplus adjustments on foreign merger; 5907(1), "net earnings", "net loss", "taxable earnings", "taxable loss"; 5907(5) Capital gain and loss computation rule.

Related Sections: S. 87(4) Shares of predecessor corporation; s. 87(8.1) Definition of "foreign merger"; s. 95(1), "foreign accrual property income", "foreign affiliate"; s. 95(4), "relevant cost base"; s. 95(4.1) Application of s. 87(8.1).

Canadian Tax Foundation: Marley and Slaats, *Foreign Affiliate Reorganizations — Recent Amendments to the Rules,* 2012 Conference Report 27:1–25.

► 95(2)(d.1) ◄

(d.1) [Determination of FAPI — Foreign merger — surplus entitlement percentage of 90% or more] — if there has been a foreign merger of two or more predecessor foreign corporations to form a new foreign corporation that is, immediately after the merger, a foreign affiliate of a taxpayer and one or more of the predecessor foreign corporations (each being referred to in this paragraph as a "foreign affiliate predecessor") was, immediately before the merger, a foreign affiliate of the taxpayer,

(i) each property of the new foreign corporation that was a property of a foreign affiliate predecessor immediately before the merger is deemed to have been

(A) disposed of by the foreign affiliate predecessor immediately before the merger for proceeds of disposition equal to the relevant cost base of the property to the foreign affiliate predecessor, in respect of the taxpayer, at that time, and

(B) acquired by the new foreign corporation, at that time, at a cost equal to the amount determined under clause (A),

(ii) the new foreign corporation is deemed to be the same corporation as, and a continuation of, each foreign affiliate predecessor for the purposes of applying

(A) this subsection and the definition "foreign accrual property income" in subsection (1) with respect to any disposition by the new foreign corporation of any property to which subparagraph (i) applied,

(B) subsections 13(21.2), 18(15) and 40(3.4) in respect of any property that was disposed of, at any time before the merger, by a foreign affiliate predecessor, and

(C) paragraph 40(3.5)(*c*) in respect of any share that was deemed under that paragraph to be owned, at any time before the merger, by a foreign affiliate predecessor, and

(iii) for the purposes of the description of A.2 in the definition "foreign accrual property income" in subsection (1), the total of all amounts each of which is the amount determined for G in respect of a foreign affiliate predecessor for its last taxation year that ends on or before the time of the merger is deemed to be the amount determined for G in respect of the new foreign corporation for its taxation year that immediately precedes its first taxation year;

Editorial Note: S. 95(2)(*d.1*) is a foreign affiliate reorganization rule that applies to determine the "asset level" tax consequences to a foreign affiliate of a taxpayer arising on a foreign merger.

S. 95(2)(*d.1*) applies where: (a) there has been a foreign merger of two or more foreign corporations in respect of each of which the taxpayer's surplus entitlement percentage was not less than 90% immediately before the merger; (b) the taxpayer's surplus entitlement percentage in respect of the corporation formed on the foreign merger is not less than 90% immediately after the merger; and (c) no gain or loss is recognized under local foreign law.

Where s. 95(2)(*d.1*) applies each property disposed of by the predecessor foreign corporations is deemed to be disposed of for proceeds of disposition equal to the cost amount of the property and, for certain purposes, the corporation formed on the merger is deemed to be the continuation of the predecessors.

S. 95(2)(*d.1*) provides that, for greater certainty, the deemed disposition of property for the purposes of the Act on foreign mergers described in s. 95(2)(*d.1*) does not affect the determination of whether any property of a predecessor foreign corporation is disposed of on a foreign merger to which s. 95(2)(*d.1*) does not apply. If the assets of any predecessor corporation are considered to have been disposed of under the applicable foreign law, FAPI could result if those assets are not excluded property and there is an accrued gain.

History: S. 95(2)(*d.1*)(ii)(B) was replaced by S.C. 2016, c. 12, s. 31(1), in force January 1, 2017, and formerly read:

(B) subsections 13(21.2), 14(12), 18(15) and 40(3.4) in respect of any property that was disposed of, at any time before the merger, by a foreign affiliate predecessor, and

S. 95(2)(*d.1*) was replaced by S.C. 2013, c. 34, s. 70(10), applicable in respect of mergers or combinations in respect of a foreign affiliate of a taxpayer that occur after August 19, 2011. However, if the taxpayer elects in writing in respect of all of its foreign affiliates and files the election with the Minister of National Revenue on or before the day that is the later of the taxpayer's filing-due date for the taxpayer's taxation year that includes June 26, 2013 and June 26, 2014 [the day that is one year after royal assent],

(*a*) paragraph 95(2)(*d.1*) applies to mergers or combinations in respect of all foreign affiliates of the taxpayer that occur after December 20, 2002; and

(*b*) in respect of such mergers or combinations that occur before August 19, 2011, the portion of paragraph 95(2)(*d.1*) after subparagraph (i) is to be read as follows:

"(ii) for the purposes of this subsection and the definition "foreign accrual property income" in subsection (1), the new foreign corporation is, with respect to any disposition by it of any property to which subparagraph (i) applied, deemed to be the same corporation as, and a continuation of, the foreign affiliate predecessor that owned the property immediately before the merger;"

See the application following the addition of the definition "designated liquidation and dissolution" for the extension of assessment periods to take into account the amendments in S.C. 2013, c. 34, s. 54 to 89.

S. 95(2)(*d.1*) formerly read:

(*d.1*) *[Determination of FAPI — Foreign merger — surplus entitlement percentage of 90% or more]* — where there has been a foreign merger of two or more predecessor foreign corporations, in respect of each of which a taxpayer's surplus entitlement percentage was not less than 90% immediately before the merger, to form a new foreign corporation in respect of which the taxpayer's surplus entitlement percentage immediately after the merger was not less than 90%, other than a foreign merger where, under the income tax law of the country in which the predecessor foreign corporations were resident immediately before the merger, a gain or loss was recognized in respect of any capital property of a predecessor foreign corporation that became capital property of the new foreign corporation in the course of the merger,

(i) each capital property of the new foreign corporation that was a capital property of a predecessor foreign corporation immediately before the merger shall be deemed to have been disposed of by the predecessor foreign corporation immediately before the merger for proceeds of disposition equal to the cost amount of the property to the predecessor foreign corporation at that time, and

(ii) for the purposes of this subsection and the definition "foreign accrual property income" in subsection (1), the new foreign corporation shall, with respect to any disposition by it of any capital property to which subparagraph (i) applied, be deemed to be the same corporation as, and a continuation of, the predecessor foreign corporation that owned the property immediately before the merger,

but for greater certainty nothing in this paragraph shall affect the determination of whether any property of a predecessor foreign corporation is disposed of on a foreign merger other than one to which this paragraph applies;

Related Regulations: 5905(3), 5905(10), 5905(11), 5905(12), 5905(13) Surplus entitlement percentage determination; 5907(1), "net earnings", "net loss", "taxable earnings", "taxable loss"; 5907(5) Capital gain and loss computation rule.

Related Sections: S. 54, "capital property", "proceeds of disposition"; s. 87(8.1), "foreign merger"; s. 95(1), "foreign affiliate", "surplus entitlement percentage"; s. 248(1), "cost amount".

Tax Topics: No. 2193, June 2014 Election Deadlines for Retroactive Application of New Foreign Affiliate Reorganization Rules.

▶ 95(2)(e) ◀

(e) **[Determination of FAPI — Dissolution of foreign affiliate]** — notwithstanding subsection 69(5), if at any time a foreign affiliate (referred to in this paragraph as the "shareholder affiliate") of a taxpayer receives a property (referred to in this paragraph as the "distributed property") from another foreign affiliate (referred to in this paragraph as the "disposing affiliate") of the taxpayer on a liquidation and dissolution of the disposing affiliate and the distributed property is received in respect of shares of the capital stock of the disposing affiliate that are disposed of on the liquidation and dissolution,

(i) the distributed property is deemed to have been disposed of at that time by the disposing affiliate to the shareholder affiliate for proceeds of disposition equal to the relevant cost base to the disposing affiliate of the distributed property in respect of the taxpayer, immediately before that time, if

(A) the liquidation and dissolution is a designated liquidation and dissolution of the disposing affiliate, or

(B) the distributed property is a share of the capital stock of another foreign affiliate of the taxpayer that was, immediately before that time, excluded property of the disposing affiliate,

(ii) if subparagraph (i) does not apply to the distributed property, the distributed property is deemed to have been disposed of at that time by the disposing affiliate to the shareholder affiliate for proceeds of disposition equal to the distributed property's fair market value at that time,

(iii) the distributed property is deemed to have been acquired, at that time, by the shareholder affiliate at a cost equal to the amount determined under subparagraph (i) or (ii) to be the disposing affiliate's proceeds of disposition of the distributed property,

(iv) each share of a class of the capital stock of the disposing affiliate that is disposed of by the shareholder affiliate on the liquidation and dissolution of the disposing affiliate is deemed to be disposed of for proceeds of disposition equal to

(A) if the liquidation and dissolution is a designated liquidation and dissolution of the disposing affiliate

(I) where the amount that would, if clause (B) applied, be determined under that clause in respect of the share is greater than or equal to the adjusted cost base of the share to the shareholder affiliate immediately before the disposition, that adjusted cost base, or

(II) where the adjusted cost base of the share to the shareholder affiliate immediately before the disposition exceeds the amount that would, if clause (B) applied, be determined under that clause in respect of the share

1. if the share is not excluded property of the shareholder affiliate, that adjusted cost base, and

2. in any other case, the amount that would be determined under clause (B), and

(B) in any other case, the amount determined by the formula

$$(A - B)/C$$

where

A is the total of all amounts each of which is the cost to the shareholder affiliate of a distributed property, as determined under subparagraph (iii), received, at any time, in respect of the class,

B is the total of all amounts each of which is an amount owing (other than an unpaid dividend) by, or an obligation of, the disposing affiliate that was assumed or cancelled by the shareholder affiliate in consideration for the distribution of a distributed property referred to in the description of A, and

C is the total number of issued and outstanding shares of the class that are owned by the shareholder affiliate during the liquidation and dissolution, and

(v) if the liquidation and dissolution is a designated liquidation and dissolution of the disposing affiliate,

(A) the shareholder affiliate is deemed to be the same corporation as, and a continuation of, the disposing affiliate for the purposes of applying

(I) this subsection and the definition "foreign accrual property income" in subsection (1) with respect to any disposition by the shareholder affiliate of any property to which clause (i)(A) applied,

(II) subsections 13(21.2), 18(15) and 40(3.4) in respect of any property that was disposed of, at any time before the liquidation and dissolution, by the disposing affiliate, and

(III) paragraph 40(3.5)(*c*) in respect of any share that was deemed under that paragraph to be owned, at any time before the liquidation and dissolution, by the disposing affiliate, and

(B) for the purposes of the description of A.2 in the definition "foreign accrual property income" in subsection (1), the amount, if any, determined for G in respect of the disposing affiliate for its first taxation year that ends after the beginning of the liquidation and dissolution is to be added to the amount otherwise determined for G in respect of the shareholder affiliate for its taxation year that immediately precedes its taxation year that includes the time at which the liquidation and dissolution began;

Editorial Note: S. 95(2)(*e*) is a foreign affiliate reorganization rule that applies where on the dissolution of a foreign affiliate of a taxpayer (FA2) shares of another foreign affiliate of the taxpayer (FA3) are disposed of to a shareholder of FA2 that is another foreign affiliate of the taxpayer (FA1). S. 95(2)(*e*) is specifically made subject to the foreign affiliate reorganization rule in s.95(2)(e.1).

Where s. 95(2)(*e*) applies it determines the tax consequences to both FA2 (i.e., asset level consequences) and FA1 (i.e., shareholder level consequences).

FA2's proceeds of disposition of each share of FA3, and the cost of the FA3 share to FA1, will be equal to the relevant cost base to FA2 immediately before the dissolution. Similar to s. 95(2)(*d*), this reference to relevant cost base provides FA2 with the ability to elect to realize a gain as a result of the dissolution. Any such gain will be included in FA2's FAPI pursuant to element B of the definition of FAPI in s. 95(1).

FA1's proceeds of disposition of the FA2 shares will be determined by reference to the cost of the FA3 shares (determined having regard to the relevant cost base election, if any), the fair market value of all other property distributed on FA2's dissolution and the amount of debt owed by FA2.

History: S. 95(2)(*e*)(v)(A)(II) was replaced by S.C. 2016, c. 12, s. 31(2), in force January 1, 2017, and formerly read:

(II) subsections 13(21.2), (14.12), 18(15) and 40(3.4) in respect of any property that was disposed of, at any time before the liquidation and dissolution, by the disposing affiliate, and

S. 95(2)(*e*) was replaced by S.C. 2013, c. 34, s. 70(10), applicable in respect of liquidations and dissolutions of foreign affiliates of a taxpayer that begin after August 19, 2011. However, if the taxpayer elects in writing in respect of all of its foreign affiliates and files the election with the Minister of National

Revenue on or before the day that is the later of the taxpayer's filing-due date for the taxpayer's taxation year that includes June 26, 2013 and June 26, 2014 [the day that is one year after royal assent], then paragraph 95(2)(*e*) applies

(*a*) to liquidations and dissolutions of all foreign affiliates of the taxpayer that begin after December 20, 2002; and

(*b*) in respect of liquidations and dissolutions of all foreign affiliates of the taxpayer that begin on or before August 19, 2011, subparagraphs 95(2)(*e*)(iv) and (v) are to be read as follows:

"(iv) each share of a class of the capital stock of the disposing affiliate that is disposed of by the shareholder affiliate on the liquidation and dissolution of the disposing affiliate is deemed to be disposed of for proceeds of disposition equal to

(A) if the liquidation and dissolution is a designated liquidation and dissolution of the disposing affiliate, the adjusted cost base of the share to the shareholder affiliate immediately before the disposition, and

(B) in any other case, the amount determined by the formula

$$(A - B)/C$$

where

A is the total of all amounts each of which is the cost to the shareholder affiliate of a distributed property, as determined under subparagraph (iii), received in respect of the class,

B is the total of all amounts each of which is an amount owing (other than an unpaid dividend) by, or an obligation of, the disposing affiliate that was assumed or cancelled by the shareholder affiliate in consideration for the distribution of a distributed property referred to in the description of A, and

C is the total number of issued and outstanding shares of the class that are owned by the shareholder affiliate during the liquidation and dissolution, and

(v) if the liquidation and dissolution is a designated liquidation and dissolution of the disposing affiliate, for the purposes of this subsection and the definition "foreign accrual property income" in subsection (1), the shareholder affiliate is, with respect to any disposition by it of any property to which clause (i)(A) applied, deemed to be the same corporation as, and a continuation of, the disposing affiliate;"

If the taxpayer referred to in any election dealing with various foreign affiliate amendments is a partnership, any reference in those elections to "the taxpayer's filing-due date" is to be read as a reference to "the earliest of the filing-due dates of any member of the taxpayer".

See the application following the addition of the definition "designated liquidation and dissolution" for the extension of assessment periods to take into account the amendments in S.C. 2013, c. 34, s. 54 to 89.

S. 95(2)(*e*) formerly read:

(*e*) *[Determination of FAPI — Dissolution of foreign affiliate]* — except as otherwise provided in paragraph (*e*.1), where on the dissolution of a foreign affiliate of a taxpayer (in this paragraph referred to as the "disposing affiliate") one or more shares of the capital stock of another foreign affiliate of the taxpayer have been disposed of to a shareholder that is another foreign affiliate of the taxpayer,

(i) the disposing affiliate's proceeds of disposition of each such share and the cost thereof to the shareholder shall be deemed to be an amount equal to the relevant cost base to the disposing affiliate of the share immediately before the dissolution, and

(ii) the shareholder's proceeds of disposition of the shares of the disposing affiliate shall be deemed to be the amount, if any, by which the total of

(A) the cost to the shareholder of the shares of the other foreign affiliate, as determined in subparagraph (i), and

(B) the fair market value of any property (other than the shares referred to in clause (A)) disposed of by the disposing affiliate to the shareholder on the dissolution,

exceeds

(C) the total of all amounts each of which is the amount of any debt owing by the disposing affiliate, or of any other obligation of the disposing affiliate to pay any amount, that was outstanding immediately before the dissolution and that was assumed or cancelled by the shareholder on the dissolution;

Related Regulations: 5907(1), "net earnings", "net loss", "taxable earnings", "taxable loss"; 5907(5) Capital gain and loss computation rule; 5907(9) Dissolution of foreign affiliate.

Related Sections: S. 54, "proceeds of disposition"; s. 95(1), "foreign accrual property income", "foreign affiliate"; s. 95(2)(*e.1*) Dissolution of foreign affiliate; s. 95(4), "relevant cost base".

Canadian Tax Foundation: Marley and Slaats, *Foreign Affiliate Reorganizations — Recent Amendments to the Rules*, 2012 Conference Report 27:1–25.

Tax Topics: No. 2195, June 2014 Election Deadlines for Retroactive Application of New Foreign Affiliate Reorganization Rules.

► 95(2)(e.1) ◄

(e.1) [Determination of FAPI — Dissolution of foreign affiliate — surplus entitlement percentage of 90% or more] — (Repealed by S.C. 2013, c. 34, s. 70(10).)

Editorial Note: S. 95(2)(*e.1*) was a foreign affiliate reorganization rule that applied on the dissolution of a foreign affiliate of a taxpayer (FA2) where the taxpayer's surplus entitlement percentage in respect of FA1 was not less than 90% immediately before the liquidation and no gain or loss was recognized under local foreign law.

Where s. 95(2)(*e.1*) applied each capital property (note that it was restricted to capital property) disposed of by FA2 to another foreign affiliate of the taxpayer (FA1) was deemed to be disposed of for proceeds of disposition equal to the cost amount of the property to FA2 and, for certain purposes, FA1 was deemed to be the continuation of FA2.

FA1's proceeds of disposition of the FA2 shares in the course of the liquidation of FA2 was deemed to be equal to the adjusted cost base of those shares to FA1 immediately before the disposition.

History: S. 95(2)(*e.1*) was repealed by S.C. 2013, c. 34, s. 70(10), applicable in respect of liquidations and dissolutions of foreign affiliates of a taxpayer that begin after August 19, 2011. However, if the taxpayer elects in writing in respect of all of its foreign affiliates and files the election with the Minister of National Revenue on or before the day that is the later of the taxpayer's filing-due date for the taxpayer's taxation year that includes June 26, 2013 and June 26, 2014 [the day that is one year after royal assent], then the repeal of paragraph 95(2)(*e.1*) applies to liquidations and dissolutions of all foreign affiliates of the taxpayer that begin after December 20, 2002.

See the application following the addition of the definition "designated liquidation and dissolution" for the extension of assessment periods to take into account the amendments in S.C. 2013, c. 34, s. 54 to 89.

S. 95(2)(*e.1*) formerly read:

(*e*.1) *[Determination of FAPI — Dissolution of foreign affiliate — surplus entitlement percentage of 90% or more]* — where there has been a liquidation and a dissolution of a foreign affiliate (in this paragraph referred to as the "disposing affiliate") of a taxpayer in respect of which, immediately before the liquidation, the taxpayer's surplus entitlement percentage was not less than 90%, other than a liquidation and a dissolution where, under the income tax law of the country in which the disposing affiliate was resident immediately before the liquidation, a gain or loss was recognized by the disposing affiliate in respect of any capital property distributed by it in the course of the liquidation to another foreign affiliate of the taxpayer resident in that country, the following rules apply:

(i) each capital property of the disposing affiliate that was so distributed to another foreign affiliate of the taxpayer shall be deemed to have been disposed of by the disposing affiliate for proceeds of disposition equal to the cost amount of the property to the disposing affiliate immediately before the distribution,

(ii) for the purposes of this subsection and the definition "foreign accrual property income" in subsection (1), the other affiliate shall, with respect to any disposition by it of capital property to which subparagraph (i) applied, be deemed to be the same corporation as, and a continuation of, the disposing affiliate, and

(iii) the other affiliate's proceeds of disposition of the shares of the capital stock of the disposing affiliate disposed of in the course of the liquidation shall be deemed to be the adjusted cost base of those shares to the other affiliate immediately before the disposition;

Related Regulations: 5905(7) Surplus adjustments on foreign merger; 5905(10), 5905(11), 5905(12), 5905(13) Surplus entitlement percentage determination; 5907(1), "net earnings", "net loss", "taxable earnings", "taxable loss"; 5907(5) Capital gain and loss computation rule.

Related Sections: S. 54, "capital property", "proceeds of disposition"; s.87(8.1), "foreign merger"; s. 95(1), "foreign affiliate", "surplus entitlement percentage"; s. 95(2)(*c.1*); s. 95(2)(*e*) [Determination of FAPI — Dissolution of foreign affiliate]; s. 248(1), "cost amount.

► 95(2)(f) ◄

(f) [Determination of FAPI — Deemed residence in Canada] — except as otherwise provided in this subdivision and except to the extent that the context otherwise requires, a foreign affiliate of a taxpayer is deemed to be at all times resident in Canada for the purposes of determining, in respect of the taxpayer for a taxation year of the foreign affiliate, each amount that is the foreign affiliate's

(i) capital gain, capital loss, taxable capital gain or allowable capital loss from a disposition of a property, or

(ii) income or loss from a property, from a business other than an active business or from a non-qualifying business;

Editorial Note: S. 95(2)(*f*) contains rules regarding the determination of (1) capital gains, capital losses, taxable capital gains and allowable capital losses from the disposition of property, and (2) income and losses from property, from non-active businesses and from non-qualifying businesses.

For the purposes of determining those amounts, s. 95(2)(*f*) provides that a foreign affiliate of a taxpayer is deemed to be at all times resident in Canada. This rule applies except as otherwise provided in subdivision i and except to the extent that the context otherwise requires.

History: S. 95(2)(*f*) was replaced by S.C. 2009, c. 2, s. 25(2), applicable to taxation years of a foreign affiliate of a taxpayer that begin after October 2, 2007. However, for taxation years of a foreign affiliate that begin before 2009, subparagraph 95(2)(*f*)(ii) shall be read as follows:

"(ii) income or loss from a property or from a business other than an active business;"

If the taxpayer elects in writing in respect of all of its foreign affiliates and files the election with the Minister of National Revenue on or before the taxpayer's election day, s. 95(2)(*f*) also applies to taxation years of a foreign affiliate of the taxpayer that begin before October 2, 2007 and after the date chosen by the taxpayer as described below, except that subparagraph 95(2)(*f*)(ii) shall be read in its application to those taxation years in the manner described above.

The taxpayer's election day is (i) the taxpayer's filing-due date for the taxpayer's taxation year that includes the day on which this Act is assented to [R.A. March 12, 2009] and (ii) the day that is one year after the day on which this Act is assented to [March 12, 2010].

To be valid, an election [described above] must include the identification by the taxpayer of its choice of one of the following dates:

(i) December 31, 1994,

(ii) December 20, 2002, or

(iii) February 27, 2004.

Notwithstanding subsections 152(4) to (5) of the Act, any assessment of a taxpayer's tax, interest and penalties payable under the Act for any taxation year shall be made that is necessary to take into account this provision and any election made with respect to it.

S. 95(2)(*f*) formerly read:

(*f*) *[Determination of FAPI — Capital gains and losses]* — except as otherwise provided in this subsection, each taxable capital gain and each allowable capital loss of a foreign affiliate of a taxpayer from the disposition of property shall be computed in accordance with Part I, read without reference to section 26 of the *Income Tax Application Rules*, as though the affiliate were resident in Canada

(i) where that gain or loss is the gain or loss of a controlled foreign affiliate from the disposition of property to which paragraph (*c*), (*d*) or (*e*) or 88(3)(*a*) applies or from any other disposition of property (other than excluded property), in Canadian currency, and

(ii) in any other case, on the assumption that the currency of the country in which the affiliate is resident or such other currency as is reasonable in the circumstances (in this subparagraph referred to as the "calculating currency") were the currency of Canada and, where subsection 39(2) is applicable, on the further assumptions that

(A) the reference in that subsection to "the currency or currencies of one or more countries other than Canada relative to Canadian currency" were read as a reference to "one or more currencies other than the calculating currency relative to the calculating currency", and

(B) the references therein to "of a country other than Canada" were read as references to "of a country other than the country of the calculating currency",

except that in computing any such gain or loss from the disposition of property owned by the affiliate at the time it last became a foreign affiliate of the taxpayer there shall not be included such portion of the gain or loss, as the case may be, as may reasonably be considered to have accrued during the period that the affiliate was not a foreign affiliate of

(iii) the taxpayer,

(iv) any person with whom the taxpayer was not dealing at arm's length,

(v) any person with whom the taxpayer would not have been dealing at arm's length if the person had been in existence after the taxpayer came into existence,

(vi) any predecessor corporation (within the meaning assigned by subsection 87(1)) of the taxpayer or of a person described in subparagraph (iv) or (v), or

(vii) any predecessor corporation (within the meaning assigned by paragraph 87(2)(*l.2*)) of the taxpayer or of a person described in subparagraph (iv) or (v);

Related Regulations: S. 5903 Deductible loss rules; 5907(5) Capital gain and loss computation rule.

Related Sections: S. 38 Taxable capital gain and allowable capital loss; s. 39 Meaning of capital gain and capital loss; s. 40 General rules; s. 95(1), "foreign affiliate", "income from a non-qualifying business", "non-qualifying business", "income from property"; s. 95(2)(*f.1*), s. 95(2)(*f.11*) Computation rules; s. 95(2)(*f.12*), s. 95(2)(*f.13*),(*f.14*) , s. 95(2)(*f.15*) Currency computation rules; s. 95(2)(*g*), s. 95(2)(*g.01*), s. 95(2)(*g.02*), s. 95(2)(*g.03*) Currency fluctuation; s. 261 Functional currency reporting.

Canadian Tax Foundation: Barnicke and Huynh, *Stub Period FAPI on Disposition*, 2013 Canadian Tax Highlights 21(8):6–7.

Tax Window Files: Subsection 247(2), surplus, and FAPI, *October 27, 2017*, CRA Document No. 2017-0694231I7.

► 95(2)(f.1) ◄

(f.1) [Determination of FAPI — Exclusion of amounts] — in computing an amount described in paragraph (*f*) in respect of a property or a business, there is not to be included any portion of that amount that can reasonably be considered to have accrued, in respect of the property (including for the purposes of this paragraph any property for which the property was substituted) or the business, while no person or partnership that held the property or carried on the business was a specified person or partnership in respect of the taxpayer referred to in paragraph (*f*);

Editorial Note: S. 95(2)(*f.1*) contains a carve-out rule to be applied when computing the amounts referred to in s. 95(2)(*f*) and is intended to exclude from the computation of such amounts any portion that can reasonably be considered to have accrued in respect of the property or the business while no person that held the property or carried on the business was a specified person or partnership (defined in s. 95(1)) in respect of the taxpayer.

History: S. 95(2)(*f.1*) was added by S.C. 2009, c. 2, s. 25(2), applicable to taxation years of a foreign affiliate of a taxpayer that begin after October 2, 2007. However, if the taxpayer elects in writing in respect of all of its foreign affiliates and files the election with the Minister of National Revenue on or before the taxpayer's election day, s. 95(2)(*f.1*) also applies to taxation years of a foreign affiliate of the taxpayer that begin before October 2, 2007 and after the date chosen by the taxpayer as described below.

The taxpayer's election day is (i) the taxpayer's filing-due date for the taxpayer's taxation year that includes the day on which this Act is assented to [R.A. March 12, 2009] and (ii) the day that is one year after the day on which this Act is assented to [March 12, 2010].

To be valid, an election [described above] must include the identification by the taxpayer of its choice of one of the following dates:

(i) December 31, 1994,

(ii) December 20, 2002, or

(iii) February 27, 2004.

Notwithstanding subsections 152(4) to (5) of the Act, any assessment of a taxpayer's tax, interest and penalties payable under the Act for any taxation year shall be made that is necessary to take into account this provision and any election made with respect to it.

Related Sections: S. 95(1), "specified person or partnership"; s. 95(2)(*f*) Computation of capital gains and losses.

Canadian Tax Foundation: Barnicke and Huynh, *Stub Period FAPI on Disposition*, 2013 Canadian Tax Highlights 21(8):6–7.

Tax Topics: No. 1974, The New 95(2)(f.1) Carve-Out Rule — Election Deadline Approaching.

► 95(2)(f.11) ◄

(f.11) [Determination of FAPI — Application of other provisions] — in determining an amount described in paragraph (f) for a taxation year of a foreign affiliate of a taxpayer,

(i) if the amount is described in subparagraph (f)(i), this Act is to be

(A) read without reference to section 26 of the *Income Tax Application Rules*, and

(B) applied as if, in respect of any debt obligation owing by the foreign affiliate or a partnership of which the foreign affiliate is a member (which foreign affiliate or partnership is referred to in this clause as the "debtor"), each capital gain or loss of the debtor that is deemed to arise under subsection 39(2) or (3) in respect of the debt obligation were from a disposition of property that was held by the debtor throughout the period during which the debt obligation was owed by the debtor and, for greater certainty, at the time of the disposition,

(ii) if the amount is described in subparagraph (f)(ii),

(A) this Act is to be read without reference to subsections 17(1) and 18(4) and section 91, except that, where the foreign affiliate is a member of a partnership, section 91 is to be applied to determine the income or loss of the partnership and for that purpose subsection 96(1) is to be applied to determine the foreign affiliate's share of that income or loss of the partnership,

(B) if the foreign affiliate has, in the taxation year, disposed of a foreign resource property in respect of a country, it is deemed to have designated, in respect of the disposition and in accordance with subparagraph 59(1)(b)(ii) for the taxation year, the amount, if any, by which

(I) the amount determined under paragraph 59(1)(a) in respect of the disposition

exceeds

(II) the amount determined under subparagraph 59(1)(b)(i) in respect of the disposition, and

(C) this Act is to be applied as if, in respect of any debt obligation owing by the foreign affiliate or a partnership of which the foreign affiliate is a member (which foreign affiliate or partnership is referred to in this clause as the "debtor"), each amount of income or loss of the debtor — from a property, from a business other than an active business or from a non-qualifying business — in respect of the debt obligation were from such a property that was held, or such a business that was carried on, as the case may be, by the debtor throughout the period during which the debt obligation was owed by the debtor and at the time at which the debt obligation was settled or extinguished;

History: S. 95(2)(f.11)(ii)(A) was replaced by S.C. 2016, c. 12, s. 31(3), in force January 1, 2017, and formerly read:

(A) this Act is to be read without reference to subsections 14(1.01) to (1.03), 17(1) and 18(4) and section 91, except that, where the foreign affiliate is a member of a partnership, section 91 is to be applied to determine the income or loss of the partnership and for that purpose subsection 96(1) is to be applied to determine the foreign affiliate's share of that income or loss of the partnership,

S. 95(2)(f.11)(i) was replaced by S.C. 2013, c. 34, s. 70(11), applicable, subject to the application below, in respect of taxation years of a foreign affiliate of a taxpayer that end after August 19, 2011, and formerly read:

(i) if the amount is described in subparagraph (f)(i), this Act is to be read without reference to section 26 of the *Income Tax Application Rules*, and

S. 95(2)(f.11)(ii)(C) was added by S.C. 2013, c. 34, s. 70(12), applicable, subject to the application below, in respect of taxation years of a foreign affiliate of a taxpayer that end after August 19, 2011.

If the taxpayer so elects in writing in respect of all of its foreign affiliates and files the election with the Minister of National Revenue on or before the day that is the later of the taxpayer's filing-due date for the taxpayer's taxation year that includes June 26, 2013 and June 26, 2014 [the day that is one year after royal assent] then subparagraph 95(2)(f.11)(i) and new clause (C) in subparagraph 95(2)(f.11)(ii) applies in respect of taxation years of all foreign affiliates of the taxpayer that end after June 2011.

If the taxpayer referred to in any election dealing with various foreign affiliate amendments is a partnership, any reference in those elections to "the taxpayer's filing-due date" is to be read as a reference to "the earliest of the filing-due dates of any member of the taxpayer".

See the application following the addition of the definition "designated liquidation and dissolution" for the extension of assessment periods to take into account the amendments in S.C. 2013, c. 34, s. 54 to 89.

S. 95(2)(f.11) was added by S.C. 2009, c. 2, s. 25(2), applicable to taxation years of a foreign affiliate of a taxpayer that begin after October 2, 2007. However, if the taxpayer elects in writing in respect of all of its foreign affiliates and files the election with the Minister of National Revenue on or before the taxpayer's election day, s. 95(2)(f.11) also applies to taxation years of a foreign affiliate of the taxpayer that begin before October 2, 2007 and after the date chosen by the taxpayer as described below.

The taxpayer's election day is the later of (i) the taxpayer's filing-due date for the taxpayer's taxation year that includes the day on which this Act is assented to [R.A. March 12, 2009] and (ii) the day that is one year after the day on which this Act is assented to [March 12, 2010].

To be valid, an election [described above] must include the identification by the taxpayer of its choice of one of the following dates:

(i) December 31, 1994,

(ii) December 20, 2002, or

(iii) February 27, 2004.

Notwithstanding subsections 152(4) to (5) of the Act, any assessment of a taxpayer's tax, interest and penalties payable under the Act for any taxation year shall be made that is necessary to take into account this provision and any election made with respect to it.

► 95(2)(f.12) ◄

(f.12) [Determination of FAPI — Use of calculating currency] — a foreign affiliate of a taxpayer shall determine each of the following amounts using its calculating currency for a taxation year:

(i) subject to paragraph (f.13), each capital gain, capital loss, taxable capital gain and allowable capital loss (other than a gain or loss in respect of a debt referred to in subparagraph (i)(i) or (ii)) of the foreign affiliate for the taxation year from the disposition, at any time, of a property that, at that time, was an excluded property of the foreign affiliate,

(ii) its income or loss for the taxation year from each active business carried on by it in the taxation year in a country, and

(iii) its income or loss that is included in computing its income or loss from an active business for the taxation year because of paragraph (a);

History: S. 95(2)(f.12)(i) was replaced by S.C. 2013, c. 34, s. 70(13), applicable in respect of taxation years of a foreign affiliate of a taxpayer that end after August 19, 2011. However, if the taxpayer so elects in writing in respect of all of its foreign affiliates and files the election with the Minister of National

Revenue on or before the day that is the later of the taxpayer's filing-due date for the taxpayer's taxation year that includes June 26, 2013 and June 26, 2014 [the day that is one year after the day on which this Act receives royal assent], then subparagraph 95(2)(*f.12*)(i) applies in respect of taxation years of all foreign affiliates of the taxpayer that end after June 2011.

If the taxpayer referred to in any election dealing with various foreign affiliate amendments is a partnership, any reference in those elections to "the taxpayer's filing-due date" is to be read as a reference to "the earliest of the filing-due dates of any member of the taxpayer".

See the application following the addition of the definition "designated liquidation and dissolution" for the extension of assessment periods to take into account the amendments in S.C. 2013, c. 34, s. 54 to 89.

S. 95(2)(*f.12*)(i) formerly read:

> (i) subject to paragraph (*f.13*), each capital gain, capital loss, taxable capital gain and allowable capital loss of the foreign affiliate for the taxation year from the disposition, at any time, of a property that, at that time, was an excluded property of the foreign affiliate,

S. 95(2)(*f.12*) was added by S.C. 2009, c. 2, s. 25(2), applicable to taxation years of a foreign affiliate of a taxpayer that begin after October 2, 2007. However, if the taxpayer elects in writing in respect of all of its foreign affiliates and files the election with the Minister of National Revenue on or before the taxpayer's election day, s. 95(2)(*f.12*) also applies to taxation years of a foreign affiliate of the taxpayer that begin before October 2, 2007 and after the date chosen by the taxpayer as described below.

The taxpayer's election day is the later of (i) the taxpayer's filing-due date for the taxpayer's taxation year that includes the day on which this Act is assented to [R.A. March 12, 2009] and (ii) the day that is one year after the day on which this Act is assented to [March 12, 2010].

To be valid, an election [described above] must include the identification by the taxpayer of its choice of one of the following dates:

(i) December 31, 1994,

(ii) December 20, 2002, or

(iii) February 27, 2004.

Notwithstanding subsections 152(4) to (5) of the Act, any assessment of a taxpayer's tax, interest and penalties payable under the Act for any taxation year shall be made that is necessary to take into account this provision and any election made with respect to it.

▶ 95(2)(f.13) ◀

(f.13) [Determination of FAPI — Conversion to Canadian currency] — where the calculating currency of a foreign affiliate of a taxpayer is a currency other than Canadian currency, the foreign affiliate shall determine the amount included in computing its foreign accrual property income, in respect of the taxpayer for a taxation year of the foreign affiliate, attributable to its capital gain or taxable capital gain, from the disposition of an excluded property in the taxation year, in Canadian currency by converting the amount of the capital gain, or taxable capital gain, otherwise determined under subparagraph (*f*.12)(i) using its calculating currency for the taxation year into Canadian currency using the rate of exchange quoted by the Bank of Canada on the day on which the disposition was made, or another rate of exchange that is acceptable to the Minister;

History: S. 95(2)(*f.13*) was replaced by S.C. 2017, c. 33, s. 30(5), deemed to have come into force on March 1, 2017, and formerly read:

> (*f.*13) *[Determination of FAPI — Conversion to Canadian currency]* — where the calculating currency of a foreign affiliate of a taxpayer is a currency other than Canadian currency, the foreign affiliate shall determine the amount included in computing its foreign accrual property income, in respect of the taxpayer for a taxation year of the foreign affiliate, attributable to its capital gain or taxable capital gain, from the disposition of an excluded property in the taxation year, in Canadian currency by converting the amount of the capital gain, or taxable capital gain, otherwise determined under subparagraph (*f.12*)(i) using its calculating currency for the taxation year into Canadian currency using the rate of exchange quoted by the Bank of Canada at noon on the day on which the disposition was made;

S. 95(2)(*f.13*) was added by S.C. 2009, c. 2, s. 25(2), applicable to taxation years of a foreign affiliate of a taxpayer that begin after October 2, 2007. However, if the taxpayer elects in writing in respect of all of its foreign affiliates and files the election with the Minister of National Revenue on or before the taxpayer's election day, s. 95(2)(*f.13*) also applies to taxation years of a foreign affiliate of the taxpayer that begin before October 2, 2007 and after the date chosen by the taxpayer as described below.

The taxpayer's election day is the later of (i) the taxpayer's filing-due date for the taxpayer's taxation year that includes the day on which this Act is assented to [R.A. March 12, 2009] and (ii) the day that is one year after the day on which this Act is assented to [March 12, 2010].

To be valid, an election [described above] must include the identification by the taxpayer of its choice of one of the following dates:

(i) December 31, 1994,

(ii) December 20, 2002, or

(iii) February 27, 2004.

Notwithstanding subsections 152(4) to (5) of the Act, any assessment of a taxpayer's tax, interest and penalties payable under the Act for any taxation year shall be made that is necessary to take into account this provision and any election made with respect to it.

▶ 95(2)(f.14) ◀

(f.14) [Determination of FAPI — Use of Canadian currency] — a foreign affiliate of a taxpayer is to determine using Canadian currency each amount of its income, loss, capital gain, capital loss, taxable capital gain or allowable capital loss for a taxation year, other than an amount to which paragraph (*f*.12), (*f*.13) or (*f*.15) applies;

History: S. 95(2)(*f.14*) was replaced by S.C. 2013, c. 34, s. 70(14), applicable in respect of taxation years of a foreign affiliate of a taxpayer that end after August 19, 2011. However, if the taxpayer so elects in writing in respect of all of its foreign affiliates and files the election with the Minister of National Revenue on or before the day that is the later of the taxpayer's filing-due date for the taxpayer's taxation year that includes June 26, 2013 and June 26, 2014 [the day that is one year after the day on which this Act receives royal assent], then paragraphs 95(2)(*f.14*) applies in respect of taxation years of all foreign affiliates of the taxpayer that end after June 2011.

If the taxpayer referred to in any election dealing with various foreign affiliate amendments is a partnership, any reference in those elections to "the taxpayer's filing-due date" is to be read as a reference to "the earliest of the filing-due dates of any member of the taxpayer".

See the application following the addition of the definition "designated liquidation and dissolution" for the extension of assessment periods to take into account the amendments in S.C. 2013, c. 34, s. 54 to 89.

S. 95(2)(*f.14*) formerly read:

> (*f.*14) *[Determination of FAPI — Use of Canadian currency]* — a foreign affiliate of a taxpayer shall determine using Canadian currency each amount of its income, loss, capital gain, capital loss, taxable capital gain or allowable capital loss for a taxation year, other than an amount to which paragraph (*f.12*) or (*f.13*) applies;

S. 95(2)(*f.14*) was added by S.C. 2009, c. 2, s. 25(2), applicable to taxation years of a foreign affiliate of a taxpayer that begin after October 2, 2007. However, if the taxpayer elects in writing in respect of all of its foreign affiliates and files the election with the Minister of National Revenue on or before the taxpayer's election day, s. 95(2)(*f.14*) also applies to taxation years of a foreign affiliate of the taxpayer that begin before October 2, 2007 and after the date chosen by the taxpayer as described below.

The taxpayer's election day is the later of (i) the taxpayer's filing-due date for the taxpayer's taxation year that includes the day on which this Act is assented to [R.A. March 12, 2009] and (ii) the day that is one year after the day on which this Act is assented to [March 12, 2010].

To be valid, an election [described above] must include the identification by the taxpayer of its choice of one of the following dates:

(i) December 31, 1994,

(ii) December 20, 2002, or

(iii) February 27, 2004.

Notwithstanding subsections 152(4) to (5) of the Act, any assessment of a taxpayer's tax, interest and penalties payable under the Act for any taxation year shall be made that is necessary to take into account this provision and any election made with respect to it.

▶ 95(2)(f.15) ◀

(f.15) [Determination of FAPI — Currency for s. 39(2)] — for the purposes of applying subparagraph (*f*)(i), the references in subsection 39(2) to "Canadian currency" are to be read as "the taxpayer's calculating currency"

(i) in respect of a debt obligation owing by a foreign affiliate of a taxpayer, or a partnership of which the foreign affiliate is a member, that is a debt referred to in subparagraph (*i*)(i) or (ii), and

(ii) in respect of an agreement described in subparagraph (*i*)(iii) entered into by a foreign affiliate of a taxpayer, or a partnership of which the foreign affiliate is a member;

History: S. 95(2)(*f.15*) was replaced by S.C. 2017, c. 33, s. 30(6), applicable in respect of taxation years of a foreign affiliate that begin after October 2, 2007, and formerly read:

(*f.*15) *[Determination of FAPI — Currency for s. 39(2)]* — for the purposes of applying subparagraph (*f*)(i) in respect of a debt obligation owing by a foreign affiliate of a taxpayer, or a partnership of which the foreign affiliate is a member, that is a debt referred to in subparagraph (*i*)(i) or (ii), the references in subsection 39(2) to "Canadian currency" are to be read as references to "the taxpayer's calculating currency";

S. 95(2)(*f.15*) was replaced by S.C. 2013, c. 34, s. 70(14), applicable in respect of taxation years of a foreign affiliate of a taxpayer that end after August 19, 2011. However, if the taxpayer so elects in writing in respect of all of its foreign affiliates and files the election with the Minister of National Revenue on or before the day that is the later of the taxpayer's filing-due date for the taxpayer's taxation year that includes June 26, 2013 and June 26, 2014 [the day that is one year after the day on which this Act receives royal assent], then paragraphs 95(2)(*f.15*) applies in respect of taxation years of all foreign affiliates of the taxpayer that end after June 2011.

If the taxpayer referred to in any election dealing with various foreign affiliate amendments is a partnership, any reference in those elections to "the taxpayer's filing-due date" is to be read as a reference to "the earliest of the filing-due dates of any member of the taxpayer".

See the application following the addition of the definition "designated liquidation and dissolution" for the extension of assessment periods to take into account the amendments in S.C. 2013, c. 34, s. 54 to 89.

S. 95(2)(*f.15*) formerly read:

(*f.*15) *[Determination of FAPI — Currency for s. 39(2)]* — for the purpose of applying subparagraph (*f.12*)(i), the reference in subsection 39(2) to "the currency or currencies of one or more countries other than Canada relative to Canadian currency" is to be read as a reference to "one or more currencies other than the calculating currency relative to the calculating currency" and the references in that subsection to "of a country other than Canada" are to be read as references to "other than the calculating currency";

S. 95(2)(*f.15*) was added by S.C. 2009, c. 2, s. 25(2), applicable to taxation years of a foreign affiliate of a taxpayer that begin after October 2, 2007. However, if the taxpayer elects in writing in respect of all of its foreign affiliates and files the election with the Minister of National Revenue on or before the taxpayer's election day, s. 95(2)(*f.15*) also applies to taxation years of a foreign affiliate of the taxpayer that begin before October 2, 2007 and after the date chosen by the taxpayer as described below.

The taxpayer's election day is the later of (i) the taxpayer's filing-due date for the taxpayer's taxation year that includes the day on which this Act is assented to [R.A. March 12, 2009] and (ii) the day that is one year after the day on which this Act is assented to [March 12, 2010].

To be valid, an election [described above] must include the identification by the taxpayer of its choice of one of the following dates:

(i) December 31, 1994,

(ii) December 20, 2002, or

(iii) February 27, 2004.

Notwithstanding subsections 152(4) to (5) of the Act, any assessment of a taxpayer's tax, interest and penalties payable under the Act for any taxation year shall be made that is necessary to take into account this provision and any election made with respect to it.

▶ 95(2)(g) ◀

(g) [Determination of FAPI — Foreign currency fluctuations] — income earned, a loss incurred or a capital gain or capital loss realized, as the case may be, in a taxation year by a particular foreign affiliate of a taxpayer in respect of which the taxpayer has a qualifying interest throughout the taxation year or a particular foreign affiliate of a taxpayer that is a controlled foreign affiliate of the taxpayer throughout the taxation year, because of a fluctuation in the value of the currency of a country other than Canada relative to the value of Canadian currency, is deemed to be nil if it is earned, incurred or realized in reference to any of the following sources:

(i) a debt obligation that was owing to

(A) another foreign affiliate of the taxpayer in respect of which the taxpayer has a qualifying interest throughout the year (which other foreign affiliate is referred to in this paragraph as a "qualified foreign affiliate") by the particular affiliate, or

(B) the particular affiliate by a qualified foreign affiliate,

(ii) the redemption, acquisition or cancellation of, or a qualifying return of capital (within the meaning assigned by subsection 90(3)) in respect of, a share of the capital stock of a qualified foreign affiliate by the qualified foreign affiliate, or

(iii) the disposition to a qualified foreign affiliate of a share of the capital stock of another qualified foreign affiliate;

History: S. 95(2)(*g*)(ii) was replaced by S.C. 2013, c. 34, s. 70(15), applicable in respect of taxation years of a foreign affiliate of a taxpayer that end after August 19, 2011. However, if the taxpayer so elects in writing in respect of all of its foreign affiliates and files the election with the Minister of National Revenue on or before the day that is the later of the taxpayer's filing-due date for the taxpayer's taxation year that includes June 26, 2013 and June 26, 2014 [the day that is one year after the day on which this Act receives royal assent], then subparagraph 95(2)(*g*)(ii) applies in respect of taxation years of all foreign affiliates of the taxpayer that end after June 2011.

If the taxpayer referred to in any election dealing with various foreign affiliate amendments is a partnership, any reference in those elections to "the taxpayer's filing-due date" is to be read as a reference to "the earliest of the filing-due dates of any member of the taxpayer".

See the application following the addition of the definition "designated liquidation and dissolution" for the extension of assessment periods to take into account the amendments in S.C. 2013, c. 34, s. 54 to 89.

S. 95(2)(*g*)(ii) formerly read:

(ii) the redemption, cancellation or acquisition of a share of the capital stock of, or the reduction of the capital of, the particular affiliate or a qualified foreign affiliate (which particular affiliate or which qualified foreign affiliate is referred to in this subparagraph as the "issuing corporation") by the issuing corporation, or

S. 95(2)(*g*) was replaced by S.C. 2007, c. 35, s. 26(13), applicable, subject to the application below, to taxation years, of a foreign affiliate of a taxpayer, that begin after December 20, 2002, except that, for taxation years, of a foreign affiliate of a taxpayer, that begin after December 20, 2002 and before 2009, paragraph 95(2)(*g*) shall be read as follows:

"(*g*) income earned, a loss incurred or a capital gain or capital loss realized, as the case may be, in a taxation year by a particular foreign affiliate of a taxpayer in respect of which the taxpayer has a qualifying interest throughout the taxation year or that is a controlled foreign affiliate of the taxpayer throughout the taxation year, because of a fluctuation in the value of the currency of a country other than Canada relative to the value of Canadian currency, is deemed to be nil if it is earned, incurred or realized in reference to any of the following sources:

(i) a debt obligation that was owing to

(A) another foreign affiliate of the taxpayer in respect of which the taxpayer has a qualifying interest throughout the year or any other non-resident corporation to which the particular affiliate and the taxpayer are related throughout the year (which other foreign affiliate or other non-resident corporation is referred to in this paragraph as a 'qualified foreign corporation'), or

(B) the particular affiliate by a qualified foreign corporation,

(ii) the redemption, cancellation or acquisition of a share of the capital stock of, or the reduction of the capital of, the particular affiliate or a qualified foreign corporation (which particular affiliate or which qualified foreign affiliate is referred to in this subparagraph as the 'issuing corporation') by the issuing corporation, or

(iii) the disposition to a qualified foreign corporation of a share of the capital stock of another qualified foreign corporation;"

[Global Section 95 Election] If a taxpayer so elects in writing and files the election with the Minister of National Revenue on or before the day that is 18 months after the taxpayer's filing-due date for the taxpayer's taxation year that includes December 14, 2007, paragraph 95(2)(*g*) being read in the manner described in the application above, applies to taxation years, of all foreign affiliates of the taxpayer, that begin after 1994 and before December 21, 2002. This election deadline was extended by 18 months by S.C. 2013, c. 34, s. 39(8), deemed in force December 14, 2007.

If a taxpayer has made what would be a valid Global Section 95 Election described above, and the taxpayer has, on or before the taxpayer's filing-due date for the taxpayer's taxation year that includes December 14, 2010, filed with the Minister of National Revenue a notice in writing to revoke the election, the election is deemed, otherwise than for the purpose of this revocation, never to have been made.

Any assessment of a taxpayer's tax, interest and penalties payable under the Act for any taxation year that ends before December 14, 2007 and would otherwise be precluded because of subsections 152(4) to (5) of the Act shall be made to the extent necessary to take into account an election or revocation referred to above.

S. 95(2)(*g*) formerly read:

(*g*) where, because of a fluctuation in the value of the currency of a country other than Canada relative to the value of Canadian currency, a particular foreign affiliate of a taxpayer in respect of which the taxpayer has a qualifying interest throughout a taxation year of the particular affiliate has earned income or incurred a loss or realized a capital gain or a capital loss in the year, in reference to

(i) a debt obligation that was owing to

(A) another foreign affiliate of the taxpayer in respect of which the taxpayer has a qualifying interest throughout the year or any other non-resident corporation to which the particular affiliate and the taxpayer are related throughout the year (referred to in this paragraph as a "qualified foreign corporation"), or

(B) the particular affiliate by a qualified foreign corporation,

(ii) the redemption, cancellation or acquisition of a share of the capital stock of, or the reduction of the capital of, the particular affiliate or another foreign affiliate of the taxpayer in respect of which the taxpayer has a qualifying interest throughout the year, or

(iii) the disposition to a qualified foreign corporation of a share of the capital stock of another foreign affiliate of the taxpayer in respect of which the taxpayer has a qualifying interest throughout the year,

that income, gain or loss, as the case may be, is deemed to be nil;

► 95(2)(g.01) ◄

(g.01) [Determination of FAPI — Currency hedging agreements] — any income, loss, capital gain or capital loss, derived by a foreign affiliate of a taxpayer under or as a result of an agreement that provides for the purchase, sale or exchange of currency and that can reasonably be considered to have been made by the foreign affiliate to reduce its risk (with respect to any source, any particular income, gain or loss determined in reference to which is deemed by paragraph (*g*) to be nil) of fluctuations in the value of currency, is, to the extent of the absolute value of the particular income, gain or loss, deemed to be nil;

► 95(2)(g.02) ◄

(g.02) [Determination of FAPI — Application of s. 39(2)] — (Repealed by S.C. 2013, c. 34, s. 70(16).)

History: S. 95(2)(*g*.02) was repealed by S.C. 2013, c. 34, s. 70(16), applicable in respect of taxation years of a foreign affiliate of a taxpayer that end after August 19, 2011. However, if the taxpayer so elects in writing in respect of all of its foreign affiliates and files the election with the Minister of National Revenue on or before the day that is the later of the taxpayer's filing-due date for the taxpayer's taxation year that includes June 26, 2013 and June 26, 2014 [the day that is one year after this Act receives royal assent], then the repeal of paragraph 95(2)(*g.02*) applies in respect of taxation years of all foreign affiliates of the taxpayer that end after June 2011.

If the taxpayer referred to in any election dealing with various foreign affiliate amendments is a partnership, any reference in those elections to "the taxpayer's filing-due date" is to be read as a reference to "the earliest of the filing-due dates of any member of the taxpayer".

See the application following the addition of the definition "designated liquidation and dissolution" for the extension of assessment periods to take into account the amendments in S.C. 2013, c. 34, s. 54 to 89.

S. 95(2)(*g*.02) formerly read:

(*g*.02) *[Determination of FAPI — Application of s. 39(2)]* — in applying subsection 39(2) for the purpose of this subdivision (other than sections 94 and 94.1), the gains and losses of a foreign affiliate of a taxpayer in respect of excluded property are to be computed in respect of the taxpayer separately from the gains and losses of the foreign affiliate in respect of property that is not excluded property;

S. 95(2)(*g*.02) was added by S.C. 2007, c. 35, s. 26(13), applicable, subject to the application below (which has been amended by S.C. 2013, c. 34, s. 39(8) to (10), deemed to have come into force on December 14, 2007), to taxation years, of a foreign affiliate of a taxpayer, that begin after December 20, 2002.

[Global Section 95 Election] If a taxpayer so elects in writing and files the election with the Minister of National Revenue on or before the day that is 18 months after the taxpayer's filing-due date for the taxpayer's taxation year that includes December 14, 2007, paragraph 95(2)(*g.02*) applies to taxation years, of all foreign affiliates of the taxpayer, that begin after 1994. This election deadline was extended by 18 months by S.C. 2013, c. 34, s. 39(8), deemed in force December 14, 2007.

If a taxpayer has made what would be a valid Global Section 95 Election described above, and the taxpayer has, on or before the taxpayer's filing-due date for the taxpayer's taxation year that includes December 14, 2010, filed with the Minister of National Revenue a notice in writing to revoke the election, the election is deemed, otherwise than for the purpose of this revocation, never to have been made.

Any assessment of a taxpayer's tax, interest and penalties payable under the Act for any taxation year that ends before December 14, 2007 and would otherwise be precluded because of subsections 152(4) to (5) of the Act shall be made to the extent necessary to take into account an election or revocation referred to above.

► 95(2)(g.03) ◄

(g.03) [Determination of FAPI — Foreign currency fluctuations where member of partnership] — if at any time a particular foreign affiliate referred to in paragraph (g) is a member of a partnership or a qualified foreign affiliate referred to in that paragraph is a member of a partnership,

(i) in applying this paragraph, where a debt obligation is owing at that time by a debtor to the partnership of which the particular foreign affiliate is a member, the debt obligation is deemed to be owing at that time by the debtor to the particular foreign affiliate in the proportion that the particular foreign affiliate shared in any income earned, loss incurred or capital gain or capital loss realized by the partnership in respect of the debt obligation,

(ii) in applying this paragraph, where a debt obligation is owing at that time to a creditor by the partnership of which the particular foreign affiliate is a member, the debt obligation is deemed to be owing at that time to the creditor by the particular foreign affiliate in the proportion that the particular foreign affiliate shared in any income earned, loss incurred or capital gain or capital loss realized by the partnership in respect of the debt obligation,

(iii) in applying paragraph (*g*) and this paragraph, where a debt obligation is owing at that time by a debtor to the partnership of which the qualified foreign affiliate is a member, the debt obligation is deemed to be owing at that time by the debtor to the qualified foreign affiliate in the proportion that the qualified foreign affiliate shared in any income earned, loss incurred or capital gain or capital loss realized by the partnership in respect of the debt obligation,

(iv) in applying paragraph (*g*) and this paragraph, where a debt obligation is owing at that time to a creditor by the partnership of which the qualified foreign affiliate is a member, the debt obligation is deemed to be owing at that time to the creditor by the qualified foreign affiliate in the proportion that the qualified foreign affiliate shared in any income earned, loss incurred or capital gain or capital loss realized by the partnership in respect of the debt obligation, and

(v) in computing the particular foreign affiliate's income or loss from a partnership, any income earned, loss incurred or capital gain or capital loss realized, as the case may be, by the partnership — in respect of the portion of a debt obligation owing to or owing by the partnership that is deemed by any of subparagraphs (i) to (iv) to be a debt obligation owing to or owing by the particular foreign affiliate (referred to in this subparagraph as the "allocated debt obligation") — because of a fluctuation in the value of the currency of a country other than Canada relative to the value of Canadian currency, that is attributable to the allocated debt obligation is deemed to be nil to the extent that paragraph (*g*) would, if the rules in subparagraphs (i) to (iv) were applied, have applied to the particular foreign affiliate, to deem to be nil the income earned, loss incurred or capital gain or capital loss realized, as the case may be, by the particular foreign affiliate in respect of the allocated debt obligation, because of a fluctuation in the value of the currency of a country other than Canada relative to the value of Canadian currency;

► 95(2)(g.04) ◄

(g.04) [Determination of FAPI — Upstream loans] — if at any time a corporation resident in Canada or a partnership of which such a corporation is a member (such corporation or partnership referred to in this paragraph as the "borrowing party") has received a loan from, or become indebted to, a creditor that is a foreign affiliate (referred to in this paragraph as a "creditor affiliate") of a *qualifying entity* (in this paragraph within the meaning assigned by subsection 39(2.2)), or that is a partnership (referred to in this paragraph as a "creditor partnership") of which such an affiliate is a member, and the loan or indebtedness is at a later time repaid, in whole or in part, then the amount of the creditor affiliate's or creditor partnership's capital gain or capital loss, as the case may be, determined in the absence of this paragraph, in respect of the repayment, is to be reduced

(i) in the case of a capital loss

(A) if the creditor is a creditor affiliate, by an amount, not exceeding the amount of that capital loss so determined, that is determined by the formula

$$A/B$$

where

A is the amount by which the borrowing party's capital gain is reduced under paragraph 39(2.1)(*a*) in respect of that repayment, and

B is the total of all participating percentages, determined at the end of the taxation year of the creditor affiliate that includes the later time, of shares of the capital stock of a foreign affiliate that are owned by qualifying entities and on which an amount would be included under subsection 91(1), on the assumptions that

(I) the capital loss of the creditor affiliate, determined in the absence of this paragraph, in respect of the repayment of the loan or indebtedness were a capital gain of the creditor affiliate, and

(II) neither the creditor affiliate nor any other foreign affiliate of a qualifying entity had any other income, gain or loss for any taxation year, and

(B) if the creditor is a creditor partnership, by an amount, not exceeding the capital loss so determined, that is equal to the amount determined by the formula

$$A/(B \times C)$$

where

A is the amount by which the borrowing party's capital gain is reduced under paragraph 39(2.1)(*a*) in respect of that repayment,

B is the proportion that the amount of the capital loss of the creditor partnership in respect of the repayment of the loan or indebtedness, determined in the absence of this paragraph, that would be included in the determination of the income, gain or loss of the members of the creditor partnership that are foreign affiliates of qualifying entities is of the amount of the capital loss so determined, and

C is the total of all participating percentages, each of which is the participating percentage in respect of a share of the capital stock of a foreign affiliate of a qualifying entity, and that is owned by a qualifying entity, that is relevant in determining the amount that would be included in computing a qualifying entity's income under subsection 91(1), on the assumptions that

(I) the capital loss of the creditor partnership, determined in the absence of this paragraph, in respect of the repayment of the loan or indebtedness were a capital gain of the creditor partnership, and

(II) neither the creditor partnership nor any foreign affiliate of a qualifying entity had any other income, gain or loss for any taxation year, and

(ii) in the case of a capital gain,

(A) if the creditor is a creditor affiliate, by an amount, not exceeding that capital gain so determined, that is equal to the amount determined by the formula

$$A/B$$

where

A is the amount by which the borrowing party is required to reduce its capital loss under paragraph 39(2.1)(*b*) in respect of that repayment, and

B is the total of all participating percentages, determined at the end of the taxation year of the creditor affiliate that includes the later time, of shares of the capital stock of a foreign affiliate that are owned by qualifying entities and on which an amount would be included under subsection 91(1), on the assumption that neither the creditor affiliate nor any foreign affiliate of a qualifying entity had any other income, gain or loss for any taxation year other than its capital gain, determined in the absence of this paragraph, in respect of the repayment of the loan or indebtedness, and

(B) if the creditor is a creditor partnership, by an amount, not exceeding the capital loss so determined, that is equal to the amount determined by the following formula

$$A/(B \times C)$$

where

A is the amount by which the borrowing party is required to reduce its capital loss under paragraph 39(2.1)(*b*) in respect of that repayment,

B is the proportion that the amount of the capital gain of the creditor partnership in respect of the repayment of the loan or indebtedness, determined in the absence of this paragraph, that would be included in the determination of the income, gain or loss of the members of the creditor partnership that are foreign affiliates of qualifying entities is of the amount of the capital gain so determined, and

C is the total of all participating percentages, each of which is the participating percentage in respect of a share of the capital stock of a foreign affiliate of a qualifying entity, and that is owned by a qualifying entity, that is relevant in determining the amount that would be included in computing a qualifying entity's income under subsection 91(1), on the assumption that neither the creditor partnership nor any foreign affiliate of a qualifying entity had any other income, gain or loss for any taxation year;

History: S. 95(2)(*g.04*) was replaced by S.C. 2017, c. 33, s. 30(7), applicable in respect of portions of loans received and indebtedness incurred before August 20, 2011 that remain outstanding on August 19, 2011 and that are repaid, in whole or in part, before August 20, 2016, and formerly read:

(*g*.04) *[Determination of FAPI — Upstream loans]* — if at any time a corporation resident in Canada or a partnership of which such a corporation is a member (such corporation or partnership referred to in this paragraph as the "borrowing party") has received a loan from, or become indebted to, a creditor that is a foreign affiliate (referred to in this paragraph as a "creditor affiliate") of the borrowing party or that is a partnership (referred to in this paragraph as a "creditor partnership") of which such an affiliate is a member, the loan or indebtedness is at a later time repaid, in whole or in part, and the amount of the borrowing party's capital gain or capital loss determined, in the absence of subsection 39(2.1), under subsection 39(2) in respect of the repayment is equal to the amount of the creditor affiliate's or creditor partnership's capital loss or capital gain, as the case may be, determined, in respect of the borrowing party and in the absence of this paragraph, in respect of the repayment, then that capital loss or capital gain is deemed to be nil;

S. 95(2)(*g*.04) was added by S.C. 2013, c. 34, s., 70(17), applicable in respect of the portions of loans received and indebtedness incurred on or before August 19, 2011 that remain outstanding on that date and that are repaid, in whole or in part, on or before August 19, 2016.

See the application following the addition of the definition "designated liquidation and dissolution" for the extension of assessment periods to take into account the amendments in S.C. 2013, c. 34, s. 54 to 89.

▶ 95(2)(g.1) ◀

(g.1) [Determination of FAPI — Debt forgiveness rules] — in computing the foreign accrual property income of a foreign affiliate of a taxpayer the Act shall be read

(i) as if the expression "income, taxable income or taxable income earned in Canada, as the case may be" in the definition "commercial debt obligation" in subsection 80(1) were read as "foreign accrual property income (within the meaning assigned by subsection 95(1))", and

(ii) without reference to subsections 80(3) to (12) and (15) and 80.01(5) to (11) and sections 80.02 to 80.04;

▶ 95(2)(g.2) ◀

(g.2) [Determination of FAPI — Elections for foreign spin-off rules] — for the purpose of computing the foreign accrual property income of a foreign affiliate of any taxpayer resident in Canada for a taxation year of the affiliate, an election made pursuant to paragraph 86.1(2)(*f*) in respect of a distribution received by the affiliate in a particular taxation year of the affiliate is deemed to have been filed under that paragraph by the affiliate if

(i) where there is only one taxpayer resident in Canada in respect of whom the affiliate is a controlled foreign affiliate, the election is filed by the taxpayer with the taxpayer's return of income for the taxpayer's taxation year in which the particular year of the affiliate ends, and

(ii) where there is more than one taxpayer resident in Canada in respect of whom the affiliate is a controlled foreign affiliate, all of those taxpayers jointly elect in writing and each of them files the joint election with the Minister with their return of income for their taxation year in which the particular year of the affiliate ends;

▶ 95(2)(h) ◀

(h) [Gain or loss on currency fluctuations] — (Repealed by S.C. 2001, c. 17, s. 73(8).)

▶ 95(2)(i) ◀

(i) [Determination of FAPI — Settlement of debt or currency hedging agreement] — any income, gain or loss of a foreign affiliate of a taxpayer or of a partnership of which a foreign affiliate of a taxpayer is a member (which foreign affiliate or partnership is referred to in this paragraph as the "debtor"), for a taxation year or fiscal period of the debtor, as the case may be, is deemed to be income, a gain or a loss, as the case may be, from the disposition of an excluded property of the debtor, if the income, gain or loss is

(i) derived from the settlement or extinguishment of a debt of the debtor all or substantially all of the proceeds from which

(A) were used to acquire property, if at all times after the time at which the debt became debt of the debtor and before the time of that settlement or extinguishment, the property (or property substituted for the property) was property of the debtor and was, or would if the debtor were a foreign affiliate of the taxpayer be, excluded property of the debtor,

(B) were used at all times to earn income from an active business carried on by the debtor, or

(C) were used by the debtor for a combination of the uses described in clause (A) or (B),

(ii) derived from the settlement or extinguishment of a debt of the debtor all or substantially all of the proceeds from which were used to settle or extinguish a debt referred to in subparagraph (i) or in this subparagraph, or

(iii) derived under or as a result of an agreement that provides for the purchase, sale or exchange of currency and that can reasonably be considered to have been made by the debtor to reduce its risk, with respect to a debt referred to in subparagraph (i) or (ii), of fluctuations in the value of the currency in which the debt was denominated;

▶ 95(2)(j) ◀

(j) [Determination of FAPI — ACB of partnership interest] — the adjusted cost base to a foreign affiliate of a taxpayer of an interest in a partnership at any time shall be such amount as is prescribed by regulation;

Related Regulations: S. 5908(10).

▶ 95(2)(j.1) ◀

(j.1) [Determination of FAPI — Insurance business] — paragraph (*j.2*) applies if, in a particular taxation year of a foreign affiliate of a taxpayer or in a particular fiscal period of a partnership (which foreign affiliate or partnership is referred to in this paragraph and paragraph (*j.2*) as the "operator" and which particular taxation year or particular fiscal period is referred to in this paragraph and paragraph (*j.2*) as the "specified taxation year") a member of which is, at the end of the period, a foreign affiliate of a taxpayer,

(i) the operator carries on a business,

(ii) the business includes the insuring of risks,

(iii) the business is not, at any time, a taxable Canadian business,

(iv) the business is

(A) an investment business,

(B) a non-qualifying business, or

(C) a business whose activities include activities deemed by paragraph (*a.2*) or (*b*) to be a separate business, other than an active business, carried on by the affiliate, and

(v) in respect of the investment business, non-qualifying business or separate business (each of these businesses being referred to in this subparagraph and paragraph (*j.2*) as a "foreign business"), as the case may be, the operator would, if it were a corporation carrying on the foreign business in Canada, be required by law to report to, and be subject to the supervision of, a regulatory authority that is the Superintendent of Financial Institutions or is a similar authority of a province;

History: S. 95(2)(*j.1*) was added by S.C. 2013, c. 34, s. 70(19), applicable in respect of taxation years of a foreign affiliate of a taxpayer that begin after December 20, 2002. However,

(*a*) in respect of taxation years of a foreign affiliate of the taxpayer that begin before August 19, 2011,

(i) subparagraph 95(2)(*j.1*)(iv) is to be read without reference to its clause (B),

(ii) subparagraph 95(2)(*j.1*)(v) is to be read as follows:

"(v) in respect of the investment business or separate business (each of these businesses being referred to in this subparagraph and paragraph (*j.2*) as a "foreign business"), as the case may be, the operator would, if it were a corporation carrying on the foreign business in Canada, be required by law to report to, and be subject to the supervision of, a regulatory authority that is the Superintendent of Financial Institutions or a similar authority of a province;"

(*b*) if the taxpayer elects in writing in respect of all of its foreign affiliates and files the election with the Minister of National Revenue on or before the day that is the later of the taxpayer's filing-due date for the taxpayer's taxation year that includes June 26, 2013 and June 26, 2014 [the day that is one year after royal assent],

(i) paragraphs 95(2)(*j.1*), being read as required by subparagraphs (*a*)(i) and (ii) [in the application above], also applies in respect of taxation years of all foreign affiliates of the taxpayer that begin after 1994 and before December 21, 2002.

If the taxpayer referred to in any election dealing with various foreign affiliate amendments is a partnership, any reference in those elections to "the taxpayer's filing-due date" is to be read as a reference to "the earliest of the filing-due dates of any member of the taxpayer".

See the application following the addition of the definition "designated liquidation and dissolution" for the extension of assessment periods to take into account the amendments in S.C. 2013, c. 34, s. 54 to 89.

▶ 95(2)(j.2) ◀

(j.2) [Determination of FAPI — life insurance business] — if this paragraph applies, in computing the operator's income or loss from the foreign business for the specified taxation year and each subsequent taxation year or fiscal period in which the foreign business is carried on by the operator

(i) the operator is deemed to carry on the foreign business in Canada throughout that part of the specified taxation year, and of each of those subsequent taxation years or fiscal periods, in which the foreign business is carried on by the operator, and

(ii) for the purposes of Part XIV of the *Income Tax Regulations*,

(A) the operator is deemed to be required by law to report to, and to be subject to the supervision of, the regulatory authority referred to in subparagraph (*j.1*)(v), and

(B) if the operator is a life insurer and the foreign business is part of a life insurance business, the life insurance policies issued in the conduct of the foreign business are deemed to be life insurance policies in Canada;

History: S. 95(2)(*j.2*) was added by S.C. 2013, c. 34, s. 70(19), applicable in respect of taxation years of a foreign affiliate of a taxpayer that begin after December 20, 2002. However, if the taxpayer elects in writing in respect of all of its foreign affiliates and files the election with the Minister of National Revenue on or before the day that is the later of the taxpayer's filing-due date for the taxpayer's taxation year that includes June 26, 2013 and June 26, 2014 [the day that is one year after royal assent], paragraph 95(2)(*j.2*) also applies in respect of taxation years of all foreign affiliates of the taxpayer that begin after 1994 and before December 21, 2002.

See the application following the addition of the definition "designated liquidation and dissolution" for the extension of assessment periods to take into account the amendments in S.C. 2013, c. 34, s. 54 to 89.

► 95(2)(k) ◄

(k) [Determination of FAPI — Fresh start rules] — paragraph (*k.1*) applies if

(i) in a particular taxation year of a foreign affiliate of a taxpayer or in a particular fiscal period of a partnership (which foreign affiliate or partnership is referred to in this paragraph and paragraph (*k.1*) as the "operator" and which particular taxation year or particular fiscal period is referred to in this paragraph and paragraph (*k.1*) as the "specified taxation year") a member of which is, at the end of the period, a foreign affiliate of a taxpayer,

(A) the operator carries on a business,

(B) the business is not, at any time, a taxable Canadian business, and

(C) the business is

(I) an investment business,

(II) a non-qualifying business,

(III) a business whose activities include activities deemed by any of paragraphs (*a.1*) to (*b*) to be a separate business, other than an active business, carried on by the affiliate, or

(IV) a business the income from which is included by paragraph (*l*) in computing the affiliate's income from property for the specified taxation year, and

(ii) in the taxation year of the affiliate or the fiscal period of the partnership that includes the day that is immediately before the beginning of the specified taxation year,

(A) the affiliate or partnership carried on the business, or the activities so deemed to be a separate business, as the case may be,

(B) the business was not, or the activities were not, as the case may be, at any time, part of a taxable Canadian business, and

(C) the business was not described in any of subclauses (i)(C)(I), (II) and (IV), or the activities were not described in subclause (i)(C)(III), as the case may be;

History: S. 95(2)(*k*) was replaced by S.C. 2013, c. 34, s. 70(19), applicable in respect of taxation years of a foreign affiliate of a taxpayer that begin after December 20, 2002. However,

(*a*) in respect of taxation years of a foreign affiliate of the taxpayer that begin before August 19, 2011,

(iii) clause 95(2)(*k*)(i)(C) is to be read without reference to its subclause (II),

(iv) clause 95(2)(*k*)(ii)(C) is to be read as follows:

"(C) the business was not described in subclause (i)(C)(I) or (IV) or the activities were not described in subclause (i)(C)(III);"

(*b*) if the taxpayer elects in writing in respect of all of its foreign affiliates and files the election with the Minister of National Revenue on or before the day that is the later of the taxpayer's filing-due date for the taxpayer's taxation year that includes June 26, 2013 and June 26, 2014 [the day that is one year after royal assent],

(i) paragraph 95(2)(*k*), being read as required by subparagraphs (*a*)(iii) and (iv) [in the application above], also apply in respect of taxation years of all foreign affiliates of the taxpayer that begin after 1994 and before December 21, 2002,

(ii) in applying subparagraph 95(2)(*k*)(ii), in respect of taxation years of all foreign affiliates of the taxpayer that begin after 1994 and before December 21, 2002, subparagraph 95(2)(*k*)(ii) is to be read as follows:

"(ii) both

(A) in the taxation year of the affiliate or the fiscal period of the partnership that includes the day that is immediately before the beginning of the specified taxation year,

(I) the affiliate or partnership carried on the business, or the activities deemed to be a separate business, as the case may be,

(II) the business was not, or the activities were not, as the case may be, at any time, part of a taxable Canadian business, and

(III) the business was not described in subclause (i)(C)(IV), or the activities were not described in subclause (i)(C)(III), as the case may be, and

(B) in the case of the business, if any,

(I) the business was not described in subclause (i)(C)(I) in that taxation year or fiscal period, or

(II) the definition "investment business" in subsection (1) did not apply in respect of that taxation year or fiscal period;"

See the application following the addition of the definition "designated liquidation and dissolution" for the extension of assessment periods to take into account the amendments in S.C. 2013, c. 34, s. 54 to 89.

S. 95(2)(*k*) formerly read:

(*k*) *[Determination of FAPI — Fresh start rules]* — where, in a particular taxation year, a foreign affiliate of a taxpayer

(i) carries on an investment business outside Canada and, in the preceding taxation year, that business was not an investment business of the affiliate (or the definition "investment business" in subsection (1) did not apply in respect of the business in the preceding taxation year), or

(ii) is deemed by paragraph (*a*.1), (*a*.2), (*a*.3) or (*a*.4) to carry on a separate business, other than an active business, and, in the preceding taxation year, that paragraph did not apply to deem the affiliate to be carrying on that separate business,

for the purpose of computing the income of the affiliate from the investment business or the separate business as the case may be (in this subsection referred to as the "foreign business") for the particular year and each subsequent taxation year in which the foreign business is carried on,

(iii) the affiliate shall be deemed

(A) to have begun to carry on the foreign business in Canada at the later of the time the particular year began or the time that it began to carry on the foreign business, and

(B) to have carried on the foreign business in Canada throughout that part of the particular year and each such subsequent taxation year in which the foreign business was carried on by it,

(iv) if the foreign business of the affiliate is a business in respect of which the affiliate would, if the foreign business were carried on in Canada, be required by law to report to a regulating authority in Canada such as the Superintendent of Financial Institutions or a similar authority of a province,

(A) the affiliate is deemed to be required by law to report to and to be subject to the supervision of such regulating authority, and

(B) if the affiliate is a life insurer and the foreign business of the affiliate is a life insurance business, the life insurance policies issued in the conduct of that business are deemed to be life insurance policies in Canada, and

(v) paragraphs 138(11.91)(*c*) to (*f*) apply to the affiliate for the particular year in respect of the foreign business as if

(A) the affiliate were the insurer referred to in subsection 138(11.91),

(B) the particular year of the affiliate were the particular year of the insurer referred to in that subsection, and

(C) the foreign business of the affiliate were the business of the insurer referred to in that subsection;

S. 95(2)(*k*)(iv) was replaced by S.C. 2013, c. 34, s. 70(18), applicable in respect of taxation years of a foreign affiliate of a taxpayer that end after 1999.

Any assessment of a taxpayer's tax, interest and penalties payable under the Act for any taxation year that ends before June 26, 2013 that would otherwise be precluded because of subsections 152(4) to (5) of the Act shall be made to the extent necessary to take into account the amendments by S.C. 2013, c. 34, s. 54 to 89.

S. 95(2)(*k*)(iv) formerly read:

(iv) where the foreign business of the affiliate is a business in respect of which, if the foreign business were carried on in Canada, the affiliate would be required by law to report to a regulating authority in Canada such as the Superintendent of Financial Institutions or a similar authority of a province, the affiliate shall be deemed to have been required by law to report to and to have been subject to the supervision of such regulating authority, and

▶ 95(2)(k.1) ◀

(k.1) [Determination of FAPI — Fresh start rules] — if this paragraph applies, in computing the operator's income or loss from the investment business, non-qualifying business, separate business or business described in paragraph (*l*) (each of these businesses being referred to in this paragraph as a "foreign business"), as the case may be, and the operator's capital gain or capital loss from the disposition of property used or held in the course of carrying on the foreign business, for the specified taxation year and each subsequent taxation year or fiscal period in which the foreign business is carried on by the operator

(i) the operator is deemed

(A) to begin to carry on the foreign business in Canada at the beginning of the specified taxation year, and

(B) to carry on the foreign business in Canada throughout that part of the specified taxation year, and of each of those subsequent taxation years or fiscal periods, in which the foreign business is carried on by the operator,

(ii) where, in respect of the foreign business, the operator would, if it were a corporation carrying on the foreign business in Canada, be required by law to report to, and be subject to the supervision of, a regulatory authority that is the Superintendent of Financial Institutions or a similar authority of a province,

(A) the operator is deemed to be required by law to report to, and to be subject to the supervision of, the regulatory authority, and

(B) if the operator is a life insurer and the foreign business is part of a life insurance business, the life insurance policies issued in the conduct of the foreign business are deemed to be life insurance policies in Canada, and

(iii) paragraphs 138(11.91)(*c*) to (*e*) apply to the operator for the specified taxation year in respect of the foreign business as if

(A) the operator were the insurer referred to in subsection 138(11.91),

(B) the specified taxation year of the operator were the particular taxation year of the insurer referred to in that subsection,

(C) the foreign business of the operator were the business of the insurer referred to in that subsection, and

(D) the reference in paragraph 138(11.91)(*e*) to "property owned by it at that time that is designated insurance property in respect of the business" were read as a reference to "property owned or held by it at that time that is used or held by it in the particular taxation year in the course of carrying on the insurance business";

History: S. 95(2)(*k.1*) was added by S.C. 2013, c. 34, s. 70(19), applicable in respect of taxation years of a foreign affiliate of a taxpayer that begin after December 20, 2002. However,

(*a*) in respect of taxation years of a foreign affiliate of the taxpayer that begin before August 19, 2011,

(v) the portion of paragraph 95(2)(*k.1*) before subparagraph (i) is to be read as follows:

"(*k.1*) if this paragraph applies, in computing the operator's income or loss from the investment business, separate business or business referred to in paragraph (*l*) (each of these businesses being referred to in this paragraph as a "foreign business"), as the case may be, and the operator's capital gain or capital loss from the disposition of property used or held in the course of carrying on the foreign business, for the specified taxation year and each subsequent taxation year or fiscal period in which the foreign business is carried on by the operator"

(*b*) if the taxpayer elects in writing in respect of all of its foreign affiliates and files the election with the Minister of National Revenue on or before the day that is the later of the taxpayer's filing-due date for the taxpayer's taxation year that includes June 26, 2013 and June 26, 2014 [the day that is one year after royal assent], paragraph 95(2)(*k.1*), being read as required by subparagraphs (*a*)(v) [in the application above], also applies in respect of taxation years of all foreign affiliates of the taxpayer that begin after 1994 and before December 21, 2002.

See the application following the addition of the definition "designated liquidation and dissolution" for the extension of assessment periods to take into account the amendments in S.C. 2013, c. 34, s. 54 to 89.

▶ 95(2)(k.2) ◀

(k.2) [Determination of FAPI — Deemed separate business] — for the purposes of paragraphs (*j.1*) to (*k.1*) and the definition "taxable Canadian business" in subsection (1), any portion of a business carried on by a person or partnership that is carried on in Canada is deemed to be a business that is separate from any other portion of the business carried on by the person or partnership;

History: S. 95(2)(*k.2*) was added by S.C. 2013, c. 34, s. 70(19), applicable in respect of taxation years of a foreign affiliate of a taxpayer that begin after December 20, 2002.

See the application following the addition of the definition "designated liquidation and dissolution" for the extension of assessment periods to take into account the amendments in S.C. 2013, c. 34, s. 54 to 89.

▶ 95(2)(l) ◀

(l) [Determination of FAPI — Trading or dealing in indebtedness] — in computing the income from property for a taxation year of a foreign affiliate of a taxpayer there shall be included the income of the affiliate for the year from a business (other than an investment business of the affiliate) the principal purpose of which is to derive income from trading or dealing in indebtedness (which for the purpose of this paragraph includes the earning of interest on indebtedness) other than

(i) indebtedness owing by persons with whom the affiliate deals at arm's length who are resident in the country in which the affiliate was formed or continued and exists and is governed and in which the business is principally carried on, or

(ii) trade accounts receivable owing by persons with whom the affiliate deals at arm's length,

unless it is established by the taxpayer or the foreign affiliate that, throughout the period in the taxation year during which the business was carried on by the affiliate,

(iii) the business (other than any business conducted principally with persons with whom the affiliate does not deal at arm's length) is carried on by the affiliate as a foreign bank, a trust company, a credit union, an insurance corporation or a trader or dealer in securities or commodities, the activities of which are regulated under the laws

(A) of each country in which the business is carried on through a permanent establishment in that country and of the country under whose laws the affiliate is governed and any of exists, was (unless the affiliate was continued in any jurisdiction) formed or organized, or was last continued,

(B) of the country in which the business is principally carried on, or

(C) if the affiliate is related to a non-resident corporation, of the country under whose laws that non-resident corporation is governed and any of exists, was (unless that non-resident corporation was continued in any jurisdiction) formed or organized, or was last continued, if those regulating laws are recognized under the laws of the country in which the business is principally carried on and all of those countries are members of the European Union.

(iv) (Repealed by S.C. 2018, c. 27, s. 7(3).)

History: S. 95(2)(l)(iv) was repealed by S.C. 2018, c. 27, s. 7(3), applicable to taxation years of a foreign affiliate of a taxpayer that begin after February 26, 2018, and formerly read:

(iv) the taxpayer is

(A) a bank, a trust company, a credit union, an insurance corporation or a trader or dealer in securities or commodities resident in Canada, the business activities of which are subject by law to the supervision of a regulating authority such as the Superintendent of Financial Institutions or a similar authority of a province,

(B) a subsidiary wholly-owned corporation of a corporation described in clause (A),

(C) a corporation of which a corporation described in clause (A) is a subsidiary wholly-owned corporation, or

(D) a partnership each member of which is a corporation described in any of clauses (A) to (C);

S. 95(2)(l)(iii), the portion before clause (A) was replaced by S.C. 2018, c. 27, s. 7(2), applicable to taxation years of a foreign affiliate of a taxpayer that begin after February 26, 2018, and formerly read:

(iii) the business is carried on by the affiliate as a foreign bank, a trust company, a credit union, an insurance corporation or a trader or dealer in securities or commodities, the activities of which are regulated under the laws

S. 95(2)(l), the portion after subparagraph (ii) and before subparagraph (iii) was replaced by S.C. 2018, c. 27, s. 7(1), applicable to taxation years of a foreign affiliate of a taxpayer that begin after February 26, 2018, and formerly read:

unless

S. 95(2)(l)(iv)(D) was added by S.C. 2014, c. 39, s. 25(13), applicable to taxation years of a taxpayer that begin after 2014.

S. 95(2)(l)(iii)(A) was replaced by S.C. 2013, c. 34, s. 33(4), applicable to taxation years of a foreign affiliate of a taxpayer that begin after 1999.

See the application following the amendment to the description of F in the definition of "foreign accrual property income" in s. 95(1) regarding the override of the statute-barring rules for assessments for taxation years that end before June 26, 2013.

S. 95(2)(l)(iii)(A) formerly read:

(A) of each country in which the business is carried on through a permanent establishment (as defined by regulation) in that country and of the country under whose laws the affiliate is governed and any of exists, was (unless the affiliate was continued in any jurisdiction) formed or organized, or was last continued,

Canadian Tax Foundation: Yeung, *Trading Or Dealing In Indebtedness Offshore: Paragraph 95(2)(l) Revisited*, 2011 Canadian Tax Journal 1:85–101.

▶ 95(2)(m) ◀

(m) [Determination of FAPI — Qualifying interest in foreign affiliate] — a taxpayer has a qualifying interest in respect of a foreign affiliate of the taxpayer at any time if, at that time, the taxpayer owned

(i) not less than 10% of the issued and outstanding shares (having full voting rights under all circumstances) of the affiliate, and

(ii) shares of the affiliate having a fair market value of not less than 10% of the fair market value of all the issued and outstanding shares of the affiliate

and for the purpose of this paragraph

(iii) where, at any time, shares of a corporation are owned or are deemed for the purposes of this paragraph to be owned by another corporation (in this paragraph referred to as the "holding corporation"), those shares shall be deemed to be owned at that time by each shareholder of the holding corporation in a proportion equal to the proportion of all such shares that

(A) the fair market value of the shares of the holding corporation owned at that time by the shareholder

is of

(B) the fair market value of all the issued shares of the holding corporation outstanding at that time,

(iv) where, at any time, shares of a corporation are property of a partnership or are deemed for the purposes of this paragraph to be property of a partnership, those shares shall be deemed to be owned at that time by each member of the partnership in a proportion equal to the proportion of all such shares that

(A) the member's share of the income or loss of the partnership for its fiscal period that includes that time

is of

(B) the income or loss of the partnership for its fiscal period that includes that time

and for the purpose of this subparagraph, where the income and loss of the partnership for its fiscal period that includes that time are nil, that proportion shall be computed as if the partnership had income for the period in the amount of $1,000,000, and

(v) where, at any time, a person is a holder of convertible property issued by the affiliate before June 23, 1994 the terms of which confer on the holder the right to exchange the convertible property for shares of the affiliate and the taxpayer elects in its return of income for its first taxation year that ends after 1994 to have the provisions of this subparagraph apply to the taxpayer in respect of all the convertible property issued by the affiliate and outstanding at that time, each holder shall, in respect of the convertible property held by it at that time, be deemed to have, immediately before that time,

(A) exchanged the convertible property for shares of the affiliate, and

(B) acquired shares of the affiliate in accordance with the terms and conditions of the convertible property;

▶ 95(2)(n) ◀

(n) [Determination of FAPI — Foreign affiliate and qualifying interest] — in applying paragraphs (*a*) and (*g*), paragraph (*b*) of the description of A in the formula in the definition "foreign accrual property income" in subsection (1), subsections (2.2), (2.21) and 93.1(5) and paragraph (*d*) of the definition "exempt earnings", and paragraph (*c*) of the definition "exempt loss", in subsection 5907(1) of the *Income Tax Regulations*, a non-resident corporation is deemed to be, at any time, a foreign affiliate of a particular corporation resident in Canada, and a foreign affiliate of the particular corporation in respect of which the particular corporation has a qualifying interest, if at that time

(i) the non-resident corporation is a foreign affiliate of another corporation that is resident in Canada and that is related (otherwise than because of a right referred to in paragraph 251(5)(*b*)) to the particular corporation, and

(ii) that other corporation has a qualifying interest in respect of the non-resident corporation;

History: S. 95(2)(*n*), the portion before subparagaph (i) was replaced by S.C. 2014, c. 39, s. 25(14), applicable in respect of taxation years of a foreign affiliate of a taxpayer that end after July 12, 2013. However, if a taxpayer elects under subsection 21(15) of the *Economic Action Plan 2014 Act, No. 2* [S.C. 2014, c. 39], the amendment to s. 95(2)(*n*) before subparagaph (i) applies in respect of taxation years of all foreign affiliates of the taxpayer that end after 2010.

In addition, any assessment of a taxpayer's tax, interest and penalties payable under the Act for any taxation year that ends before the day on which this amendment receives royal assent [December 16, 2014] that would, in the absence of this section, be precluded because of the time references in subsection 152(4) of the Act is to be made to the extent necessary to take into account this amendment.

S. 95(2)(*n*), the portion before subparagaph (i) formerly read:

(*n*) *[Determination of FAPI — Foreign affiliate and qualifying interest]* — in applying paragraphs (*a*) and (*g*) and subsections (2.2) and (2.21), in applying paragraph (*b*) of the description of A in the formula in the definition "foreign accrual property income" in subsection (1) and in applying paragraph (*d*) of the definition "exempt earnings", and paragraph (*c*) of the definition "exempt loss", in subsection 5907(1) of the Regulations, a non-resident corporation is deemed to be, at any time, a foreign affiliate of a particular corporation resident in Canada, and a foreign affiliate of the particular corporation in respect of which the particular corporation has a qualifying interest, if at that time

▶ 95(2)(o) ◀

(o) [Determination of FAPI — Qualifying member of partnership] — a particular person is a qualifying member of a partnership at a particular time if, at that time, the particular person is a member of the partnership and

(i) throughout the period, in the fiscal period of the partnership that includes the particular time, during which the member was a member of the partnership, the particular person is, on a regular, continuous and substantial basis

(A) actively engaged in those activities, of the principal business of the partnership carried on in that fiscal period by the partnership, that are other than activities connected with the provision of or the acquisition of funds required for the operation of that principal business, or

(B) actively engaged in those activities, of a particular business carried on in that fiscal period by the particular person (otherwise than as a member of a partnership) that is similar to the principal business carried on in that fiscal period by the partnership, that are other than activities connected with the provision of or the acquisition of funds required for the operation of the particular business, or

(ii) throughout the period, in the fiscal period of the partnership that includes the particular time, during which the particular person was a member of the partnership

(A) the total of the fair market value of all partnership interests in the partnership owned by the particular person was equal to or greater than 1% of the total of the fair market value of all partnership interests in the partnership owned by all members of the partnership, and

(B) the total of the fair market value of all partnership interests in the partnership owned by the particular person or persons (other than trusts) related to the particular person was equal to or greater than 10% of the total of the fair market value of all partnership interests in the partnership owned by all members of the partnership;

▶ 95(2)(p) ◀

(p) [Determination of FAPI — Qualifying shareholder] — a particular person is a qualifying shareholder of a corporation at any time if throughout the period, in the taxation year of the corporation that includes that time, during which the particular person was a shareholder of the corporation

(i) the particular person owned 1% or more of the issued and outstanding shares (having full voting rights under all circumstances) of the capital stock of the corporation,

(ii) the particular person, or the particular person and persons (other than trusts) related to the particular person, owned 10% or more of the issued and outstanding shares (having full voting rights under all circumstances) of the capital stock of the corporation,

(iii) the total of the fair market value of all the issued and outstanding shares of the capital stock of the corporation owned by the particular person is 1% or more of the total fair market value of all the issued and outstanding shares of the capital stock of the corporation, and

(iv) the total of the fair market value of all the issued and outstanding shares of the capital stock of the corporation owned by the particular person or by persons (other than trusts) related to the particular person is 10% or more of the total fair market value of all the issued and outstanding shares of the capital stock of the corporation;

▶ 95(2)(q) ◀

(q) [Determination of FAPI — Look-through rules] — in applying paragraphs (*o*) and (*p*),

(i) where interests in any partnership or shares of the capital stock of any corporation (which interests or shares are referred to in this subparagraph as "equity interests") are, at any time, property of a particular partnership or are deemed under this paragraph to be, at any time, property of the particular partnership, the equity interests are deemed to be owned at that time by each member of the particular partnership in a proportion equal to the proportion of the equity interests that

(A) the fair market value, at that time, of the member's partnership interest in the particular partnership

is of

(B) the fair market value, at that time, of all members' partnership interests in the particular partnership, and

(ii) where interests in a partnership or shares of the capital stock of a corporation (which interests or shares are referred to in this subparagraph as "equity interests") are, at any time, property of a non-discretionary trust (within the meaning assigned by subsection 17(15)) or are deemed under this paragraph to be, at any time, property of such a non-discretionary trust, the equity interests are deemed to be owned at that time by each beneficiary under that trust in a proportion equal to that proportion of the equity interests that

(A) the fair market value, at that time, of the beneficiary's beneficial interest in the trust

is of

(B) the fair market value, at that time, of all beneficial interests in the trust;

▶ 95(2)(r) ◀

(r) [Determination of FAPI — Deemed qualifying member of partnership] — in applying paragraph (*a*) and in applying paragraph (*d*) of the definition "exempt earnings", and paragraph (*c*) of the definition "exempt loss", in subsection 5907(1) of the Regulations, a partnership is deemed to be, at any time, a partnership of which a foreign affiliate — of a particular corporation resident in Canada and in respect of which foreign affiliate the particular corporation has a qualifying interest — is a qualifying member, if at that time

(i) a particular foreign affiliate — of another corporation that is resident in Canada and that is related (otherwise than because of a right referred to in paragraph 251(5)(*b*)) to the particular corporation — is a member of the partnership,

(ii) that other corporation has a qualifying interest in respect of the particular foreign affiliate, and

(iii) the particular foreign affiliate is a qualifying member of the partnership;

▶ 95(2)(s) ◀

(s) [Determination of FAPI — Designated corporation] — in applying the definition "investment business" in subsection (1), a particular corporation is, at any time, a designated corporation in respect of a foreign affiliate of a taxpayer, if at that time

(i) a qualifying shareholder of the foreign affiliate or a person related to such a qualifying shareholder is a qualifying shareholder of the particular corporation,

(ii) the particular corporation

(A) is controlled by a qualifying shareholder of the foreign affiliate, or

(B) would be controlled by a particular qualifying shareholder of the foreign affiliate if the particular qualifying shareholder of the foreign affiliate owned each share of the capital stock of the particular corporation that is owned by a qualifying shareholder of the foreign affiliate or by a person related to a qualifying shareholder of the foreign affiliate, and

(iii) the total of all amounts each of which is the fair market value of a share of the capital stock of the particular corporation owned by a qualifying shareholder of the foreign affiliate or by a person related to a qualifying shareholder of the foreign affiliate is greater than 50% of the total fair market value of all the issued and outstanding shares of the capital stock of the particular corporation;

▶ 95(2)(t) ◀

(t) [Determination of FAPI — Designated partnership] — in applying the definition "investment business" in subsection (1) in respect of a business carried on by a foreign affiliate of a taxpayer in a taxation year, a particular partnership is, at any time, a designated partnership in respect of the foreign affiliate of the taxpayer, if at that time

(i) the foreign affiliate or a person related to the foreign affiliate is a qualifying member of the particular partnership, and

(ii) the total of all amounts — each of which is the fair market value of a partnership interest in the particular partnership held by the foreign affiliate, by a person related to the foreign affiliate or (where the foreign affiliate carries on, at that time, the business as a qualifying member of another partnership) by a qualifying member of the other partnership — is greater than 50% of the total fair market value of all partnership interests in the particular partnership owned by all members of the particular partnership;

▶ 95(2)(u) ◀

(u) [Determination of FAPI — Tiered partnerships] — (Repealed by S.C. 2014, c. 39, s. 25(16).)

History: S. 95(2)(*u*)(i), as it read immediately before it was repealed by subsection 70(21) of the *Technical Tax Amendments Act, 2012* [S.C. 2012, c. 34], was replaced by S.C. 2014, c. 39, s. 25(15) to read as follows:

(i) the entity is deemed to be a member of the other partnership for the purposes of

(A) subparagraph (ii),

(B) applying the reference, in paragraph (*a*), to "a member" of a partnership,

(C) paragraphs (*a.1*) to (*b*), (*g.03*), (*j.1*) to (*k.1*) and (*o*),

(D) paragraphs (*b*) and (*c*) of the definition "investment business" in subsection (1),

(E) the definition "taxable Canadian business" in subsection (1), and

(F) subsection 93.1(2), and

This amendment is applicable in respect of taxation years of a foreign affiliate of a taxpayer that end after 1999. However, if a taxpayer has not elected under paragraph 70(29)(*b*) of the *Technical Tax Amendments Act, 2012* [S.C. 2012, c. 34], then subparagraph 95(2)(*u*)(i) of the Act is to be read as follows in respect of taxation years of the foreign affiliate that end after 1999 and begin before December 21, 2002:

"(i) the entity is deemed to be a member of the other partnership for the purposes of

(A) subparagraph (ii),

(B) applying the reference, in paragraph (*a*), to "a member" of a partnership,

(C) paragraphs (*a.1*) to (*b*), (*g.03*) and (*o*),

(D) paragraphs (*b*) and (*c*) of the definition "investment business" in subsection (1), and

(E) subsection 93.1(2), and"

S. 95(2)(*u*)(i), as amended above, was repealed by S.C. 2014, c. 39, s. 16, applicable in respect of taxation years of a foreign affiliate of a taxpayer that end after August 19, 2011.

In addition, any assessment of a taxpayer's tax, interest and penalties payable under the Act for any taxation year that ends before the day on which this amendment receives royal assent [December 16, 2014] that would, in the absence of this section, be precluded because of the time references in subsection 152(4) of the Act is to be made to the extent necessary to take into account this amendment.

S. 95(2)(*u*) was repealed by S.C. 2013, c. 34, s. 70(21), applicable in respect of taxation years of a foreign affiliate of a taxpayer that end after August 19, 2011.

S. 95(2)(*u*) formerly read:

(*u*) *[Determination of FAPI — Tiered partnerships]* — if any entity is (or is deemed by this paragraph to be) a member of a particular partnership that is a member of another partnership,

(i) the entity is deemed to be a member of the other partnership for the purposes of

(A) subparagraph (ii),

(B) applying the reference, in paragraph (*a*), to "a member" of a partnership,

(C) paragraphs (*a.1*) to (*b*), (*g.03*), (*j.1*) to (*k.1*) and (*o*),

(D) paragraphs (*b*) and (*c*) of the definition "investment business" in subsection (1), and

(E) the definition "taxable Canadian business" in subsection (1), and

(ii) in applying paragraph (*g.03*) and the definition "taxable Canadian business" in subsection (1), the entity is deemed to have, directly, rights to the income or capital of the other partnership to the extent of the entity's direct and indirect rights to that income or capital;

S. 95(2)(*u*) was replaced by S.C. 2013, c. 34, s. 70(20), applicable in respect of taxation years of a foreign affiliate of a taxpayer that begin after December 20, 2002. However, if the taxpayer has made the election under the definition "taxable Canadian business" in s. 95(1), the amended paragraph 95(2)(*u*) also applies in respect of taxation years of all foreign affiliates of the taxpayer that begin after 1994 and before December 21, 2002, except that, if the taxpayer has not elected on or before the taxpayer's filing due date for the taxpayer's taxation year that includes December 14, 2007, paragraph 95(2)(*u*) is, in respect of taxation years of all foreign affiliates of the taxpayer that end before 2000, to be read as follows:

"(*u*) if any entity is, or is deemed by this paragraph to be, a member of a particular partnership that is a member of another partnership,

(i) the entity is deemed to be a member of the other partnership for the purposes of

(A) paragraphs (*j.1*) to (*k.1*), and

(B) the definition "taxable Canadian business" in subsection (1), and

(ii) in applying the definition "taxable Canadian business" in subsection (1), the entity is deemed to have, directly, rights to the income or capital of the other partnership to the extent of the entity's direct and indirect rights to that income or capital;"

See the application following the addition of the definition "designated liquidation and dissolution" for the extension of assessment periods to take into account the amendments in S.C. 2013, c. 34, s. 54 to 89.

S. 95(*u*) formerly read:

(*u*) *[Determination of FAPI — Tiered partnerships]* — if any entity is (or is deemed by this paragraph to be) a member of a particular partnership that is a member of another partnership,

(i) the entity is deemed to be a member of the other partnership for the purpose of

(A) subparagraph (ii),

(B) applying the reference, in paragraph (*a*), to "a member" of a partnership,

(C) paragraphs (*a.1*) to (*b*), (*g.03*) and (*o*), and

(D) paragraphs (*b*) and (*c*) of the definition "investment business" in subsection (1), and

(ii) in applying paragraph (*g.03*), the entity is deemed to have, directly, rights to the income or capital of the other partnership, to the extent of the entity's direct and indirect rights to that income or capital;

S. 95(2)(*u*) was added by S.C. 2007, c. 35, s. 26(16), applicable, subject to the election below, in respect of taxation years, of foreign affiliates of a taxpayer, that end after 1999.

However, if a taxpayer so elects in writing and files the election with the Minister of National Revenue on or before the day that is 18 months after the taxpayer's filing-due date for the taxpayer's taxation year that includes December 14, 2007, paragraph 95(2)(*u*) applies to taxation years, of all foreign affiliates of the taxpayer, that begin after 1994. This election deadline was extended by 18 months by S.C. 2013, c. 34, s. 39(5), deemed in force December 14, 2007.

If a taxpayer has made what would otherwise be a valid election and the taxpayer has, on or before the taxpayer's filing-due date for the taxpayer's taxation year that includes December 14, 2010, filed with the Minister of National Revenue a notice in writing to revoke the election, the election is deemed, otherwise than for the purpose of this revocation, never to have been made. The option to revoke this election was added by S.C. 2013, c. 34, s. 39(9), deemed in force December 14, 2007.

Any assessment of a taxpayer's tax, interest and penalties payable under the Act for any taxation year that ends before December 14, 2007 and would otherwise be precluded because of subsections 152(4) to (5) of the Act shall be made to the extent necessary to take into account an election or revocation referred to above.

▶ 95(2)(v) ◀

(v) [Determination of FAPI — Look-through rule for s. 95(2)(p)] — in applying paragraph (*p*),

(i) where shares of the capital stock of any corporation (referred to in this paragraph as the "issuing corporation") are, at any time, owned by a corporation (referred to in this paragraph as the "holding corporation") or are deemed under this paragraph to be, at any time, owned by a corporation (referred to in this paragraph as the "holding corporation"), those shares are deemed to be owned at that time by each shareholder of the holding corporation in a proportion equal to the proportion of those shares that

(A) the fair market value, at that time, of the shares of the capital stock of the issuing corporation that are owned by the shareholder

is of

(B) the fair market value, at that time, of all the issued and outstanding shares of the capital stock of the issuing corporation, and

(ii) a person who is deemed by subparagraph (i) to own, at any time, shares of the capital stock of a corporation is deemed to be, at that time, a shareholder of the corporation;

▶ 95(2)(w) ◀

(w) [Determination of FAPI — Where business carried on] — where a foreign affiliate of a corporation resident in Canada carries on an active business in more than one country,

(i) where the business is carried on in a country other than Canada, it is deemed to carry on that business in that country only to the extent that the profit or loss from that business can reasonably be attributed to a permanent establishment situated in that country, and

(ii) where the business is carried on in Canada, it is deemed to carry on that business in Canada only to the extent that the income from the active business is subject to tax under this Part;

▶ 95(2)(x) ◀

(x) [Determination of FAPI — Determination of losses] — the loss from an active business, from a non-qualifying business or from property (as the case may be) of a foreign affiliate of a taxpayer resident in Canada for a taxation year is the amount of that loss, if any, that is computed by applying the provisions in this subdivision with respect to the computation of income from the active business, from the non-qualifying business or from property (as the case may be) of the foreign affiliate for the taxation year with any modifications that the circumstances require;

▶ 95(2)(y) ◀

(y) [Determination of FAPI — Qualifying interest in foreign affiliate — property of partnership] — in determining — for the purpose of paragraph (*a*) and for the purpose of applying subsections (2.2) and (2.21) for the purpose of applying that paragraph — whether a non-resident corporation is, at any time, a foreign affiliate of a taxpayer in respect of which the taxpayer has a qualifying interest, where interests in any partnership or shares of the capital stock of any corporation (which interests or shares are referred to in this paragraph as "equity interests") are, at that time, property of a particular partnership or are deemed under this paragraph to be, at any time, property of the particular partnership, the equity interests are deemed to be owned at that time by each member of the particular partnership in a proportion equal to the proportion of the equity interests that

(i) the fair market value, at that time, of the member's partnership interest in the particular partnership

is of

(ii) the fair market value, at that time, of all members' partnership interests in the particular partnership; and

▶ 95(2)(z) ◀

(z) [Determination of FAPI — Member of partnership] — where a particular foreign affiliate of a taxpayer — in respect of which the taxpayer has a qualifying interest or that is a controlled foreign affiliate of the taxpayer — is a member of a partnership, the particular foreign affiliate's foreign accrual property income or loss in respect of the taxpayer for a taxation year shall not include any income or loss of the partnership to the extent that the income or loss

(i) is attributable to the foreign accrual property income or loss of a foreign affiliate of the partnership that is also a foreign affiliate of the taxpayer (referred to in this paragraph as the "second foreign affiliate") in respect of which the taxpayer has a qualifying interest or that is a controlled foreign affiliate of the taxpayer, and

(ii) is, because of paragraph (*a*) as applied in respect of the taxpayer, included in computing the income or loss from an active business of the second foreign affiliate for a taxation year.

▶ 95(2.01) ◀

(2.01) Rules for the definition "controlled foreign affiliate". In applying paragraph (*b*) of the definition "controlled foreign affiliate" in subsection (1) and in applying this subsection,

(*a*) shares of the capital stock of a corporation that are at any time owned by, or that are deemed by this subsection to be at any time owned by, another corporation are deemed to be, at that time, owned by, or property of, as the case may be, each shareholder of the other corporation in the proportion that

(i) the fair market value at that time of the shares of the capital stock of the other corporation that, at that time, are owned by, or are property of, the shareholder

is of

(ii) the fair market value at that time of all the issued and outstanding shares of the capital stock of the other corporation;

(*b*) shares of the capital stock of a corporation that are, or are deemed by this subsection to be, at any time, property of a partnership, are deemed to be, at that time, owned by, or property of, as the case may be, each member of the partnership in the proportion that

(i) the fair market value at that time of the member's partnership interest in the partnership

is of

(ii) the fair market value at that time of all partnership interests in the partnership;

(*c*) shares of the capital stock of a corporation that are at any time owned by, or that are deemed by this subsection to be at any time owned by, a non-discretionary trust (within the meaning assigned by subsection 17(15)) other than an exempt trust (within the meaning assigned by subsection (1)) are deemed to be, at that time, owned by, or property of, as the case may be, each beneficiary of the trust in the proportion that

(i) the fair market value at that time of the beneficiary's beneficial interest in the trust

is of

(ii) the fair market value at that time of all beneficial interests in the trust; and

(*d*) all of the shares of the capital stock of a corporation that are at any time owned by, or that are deemed by this subsection to be at any time owned by, a particular trust (other than an exempt trust within the meaning assigned by subsection (1) or a non-discretionary trust within the meaning assigned by subsection 17(15)) are deemed to be, at that time, owned by, or property of, as the case may be,

(i) each beneficiary of the particular trust at that time, and

(ii) each settlor (within the meaning assigned by subsection 17(15)) in respect of the particular trust at that time.

Tax Profile: March 2008 — International Tax Planning for the Owner-Manager.

► 95(2.02) ◄

(2.02) Rule against double-counting. In applying the assumption in paragraph (*b*) of the definition "controlled foreign affiliate" in subsection (1) in respect of a taxpayer resident in Canada to determine whether a foreign affiliate of the taxpayer is at any time a controlled foreign affiliate of the taxpayer, nothing in that paragraph or in subsection (2.01) is to be read or construed as requiring an interest, or for civil law a right, in a share of the capital stock of the foreign affiliate of the taxpayer owned at that time by the taxpayer to be taken into account more than once.

► 95(2.1) ◄

(2.1) Rule for definition "investment business". For the purposes of the definition "investment business" in subsection (1), a foreign affiliate of a taxpayer, the taxpayer and, where the taxpayer is a corporation all the issued shares of which are owned by a corporation described in subparagraph (*a*)(i), such corporation described in subparagraph (*a*)(i) shall be considered to be dealing with each other at arm's length in respect of the entering into of agreements that provide for the purchase, sale or exchange of currency and the execution of such agreements where

(*a*) the taxpayer is

(i) a bank, a trust company, a credit union, an insurance corporation or a trader or dealer in securities or commodities resident in Canada, the business activities of which are subject by law to the supervision of a regulating authority such as the Superintendent of Financial Institutions or a similar authority of a province, or

(ii) a subsidiary wholly-owned corporation of a corporation described in subparagraph (i);

(*b*) the agreements are swap agreements, forward purchase or sale agreements, forward rate agreements, futures agreements, options or rights agreements or similar agreements;

(*c*) the affiliate entered into the agreements in the course of a business carried on by the affiliate, if

(i) the business is carried on by the affiliate principally in a country (other than Canada) and principally with persons with whom the affiliate deals at arm's length, and

(ii) the business activities of the affiliate are regulated in that country; and

(*d*) the terms and conditions of such agreements are substantially the same as the terms and conditions of similar agreements made by persons dealing at arm's length.

Tax Profile: March 2008 — International Tax Planning for the Owner-Manager.

► 95(2.11) ◄

(2.11) Rule for *investment business* definition and paragraph (2)(*l*). A taxpayer or a foreign affiliate of the taxpayer, as the case may be, is deemed not to have established that the conditions in subparagraph (*a*)(i) of the definition *investment business* in subsection (1), or in subparagraph (2)(*l*)(iii), have been satisfied throughout a period in a particular taxation year of the affiliate unless

(*a*) throughout the period the taxpayer is

(i) a particular corporation resident in Canada

(A) that is a bank listed in Schedule I to the *Bank Act*, a trust company, a credit union, an insurance corporation or a trader or dealer in securities or commodities that is a registered securities dealer, the business activities of which are subject to the supervision of a regulating authority such as the Superintendent of Financial Institutions, a similar regulating authority of a province or an authority of, or approved by, a province to regulate traders or dealers in securities or commodities, and

(B) that is not a corporation the fair market value of any share of the capital stock of which is determined primarily by reference to one or more of the fair market value of, any revenue, income or cash flow from, any profits or gains from the disposition of, or any other similar criteria in respect of, property the fair market value of which is less than 90% of the fair market value of all of the property of the corporation,

(ii) a corporation resident in Canada

(A) of which

(I) the particular corporation described in subparagraph (i) is a subsidiary controlled corporation, or

(II) a corporation described in this subparagraph is a subsidiary wholly-owned corporation, and

(B) that is not a corporation the fair market value of any share of the capital stock of which is determined primarily by reference to one or more of the fair market value of, any revenue, income or cash flow from, any profits or gains from the disposition of, or any other similar criteria in respect of, property the fair market value of which is less than 90% of the fair market value of all of the property of the corporation,

(iii) a corporation resident in Canada each of the shares of the capital stock of which is owned by a corporation that is described in this subparagraph or in subparagraph (i) or (ii), or

(iv) a partnership

(A) each member of which is a corporation described in any of subparagraphs (i) to (iii), or another partnership described in this subparagraph, or

(B) in respect of which the following conditions are satisfied:

(I) the partnership is a registered securities dealer, the business activities of which are subject to the supervision of a regulating authority described in clause (a)(i)(A), and

(II) the share of the total income or loss of the partnership of a majority- interest partner of the partnership that is either a corporation resident in Canada or a Canadian partnership — together with the share of each corporation resident in Canada that is affiliated with the majority-interest partner — is equal to all or substantially all of the total income or loss of the partnership; and

(*b*) either

(i) throughout the period the particular corporation described in subparagraph (*a*)(i) has, or is deemed for certain purposes to have, $2 billion or more of equity

(A) if the particular corporation is a bank, under the *Bank Act*,

(B) if the particular corporation is a trust company, under the *Trust and Loan Companies Act*, or

(C) if the particular corporation is an insurance corporation, under the *Insurance Companies Act*, or

(ii) more than 50% of the total of all amounts each of which is an amount of taxable capital employed in Canada (within the meaning assigned by Part I.3) of the taxpayer — or of a corporation resident in Canada that is affiliated with the taxpayer — for the taxation year of the taxpayer or of the affiliated corporation, as the case may be, that ends in the particular year is attributable to a business carried on in Canada, the activities of which are subject to the supervision of a regulating authority such as the Superintendent of Financial Institutions, a similar regulating authority of a province or an authority of, or approved by, a province to regulate traders or dealers in securities or commodities.

History: S. 95(2.11), the portion before paragraph (*a*) was replaced by S.C. 2018, c. 27, s. 7(4), applicable to taxation years of a foreign affiliate of a taxpayer that begin after February 26, 2018, and formerly read:

(2.11) *Rule for definition "investment business".* A taxpayer or a foreign affiliate of the taxpayer, as the case may be, is deemed not to have established that the conditions in subparagraph (*a*)(i) of the definition "investment business" in subsection (1) have been satisfied throughout a period in a particular taxation year of the affiliate unless

S. 95(2.11) was added by S.C. 2014, c. 39, s. 25(17), applicable to taxation years of a taxpayer that begin after 2014.

▶ 95(2.2) ◀

(2.2) Qualifying interest throughout year. For the purposes of paragraphs (2)(*a*) and (*g*), a non-resident corporation that is not a foreign affiliate of a taxpayer in respect of which the taxpayer has a qualifying interest throughout a particular taxation year is deemed to be a foreign affiliate of the taxpayer in respect of which the taxpayer has a qualifying interest throughout that particular taxation year if

(*a*) a person or partnership has, in that particular taxation year, acquired or disposed of shares of the capital stock of that non-resident corporation or of any other corporation and, because of that acquisition or disposition, that non-resident corporation becomes or ceases to be a foreign affiliate of the taxpayer in respect of which the taxpayer has a qualifying interest, and

(*b*) at the beginning of that particular taxation year or at the end of that particular taxation year, the non-resident corporation is a foreign affiliate of the taxpayer in respect of which the taxpayer has a qualifying interest.

History: S. 95(2.2), the portion before paragraph (*a*) was replaced by S.C. 2009, c. 2, s. 25(3), applicable to taxation years of a foreign affiliate of a taxpayer that begin after 1994. However, the portion of s. 95(2.2) before paragraph (*a*) shall, in its application to taxation years of a foreign affiliate that begin after 1994 and before 2009, be read as follows:

"(2.2) For the purposes of paragraphs (2)(*a*) and (*g*),"

[Editorial Note: See the application above for s. 95(2.2) as enacted by S.C. 2007, c. 35, s. 26(19) for the reading of s. 95(2.2) for years that end after 1999 and begin before 2009, both where an election is not made and where an election is made.]

Notwithstanding subsections 152(4) to (5) of the Act, any assessment of a taxpayer's tax, interest and penalties payable under the Act for any taxation year shall be made that is necessary to take into account this amendment.

S. 95(2.2), the portion before paragraph (*a*) formerly read:

(2.2) *Rule re subsection (2).* For the purpose of subsection (2), other than paragraph (2)(*f*), a non-resident corporation that is not a foreign affiliate of a taxpayer in respect of which the taxpayer had a qualifying interest throughout a particular taxation year is deemed to be a foreign affiliate of the taxpayer in respect of which the taxpayer has a qualifying interest throughout that particular taxation year if

Related Regulations: 1104(2); 7500.

▶ 95(2.201) ◀

(2.201) Controlled foreign affiliate throughout year. For the purposes of paragraphs (2)(*a*) and (*g*), a non-resident corporation is deemed to be a controlled foreign affiliate of a taxpayer throughout a taxation year of the non-resident corporation if

(*a*) in the taxation year, a person or partnership acquires or disposes of shares of the capital stock of a corporation and, because of the acquisition or disposition, the non-resident corporation becomes or ceases to be a controlled foreign affiliate of the taxpayer; and

(*b*) at either or both of the beginning and end of the taxation year, the non-resident corporation is a controlled foreign affiliate of the taxpayer.

History: S. 95(2.201) was added by S.C. 2009, c. 2, s. 25(4), applicable to taxation years of a foreign affiliate of a taxpayer that end after 1999. However,

(a) subject to paragraph (*b*) [below], for taxation years of a foreign affiliate that begin before December 21, 2002, the reference to "for the purposes of paragraphs (2)(*a*) and (*g*)" in subsection 95(2.201) shall be read as a reference to "for the purpose of paragraph (2)(*a*)"; and

(b) if the taxpayer has made a valid Global Section 95 Election subsection 95(2.201) applies to taxation years of a foreign affiliate of the taxpayer that begin after 1994. This election deadline was extended by 18 months by S.C. 2013, c. 34, s. 39(8), deemed in force December 14, 2007.

Notwithstanding subsections 152(4) to (5) of the Act, any assessment of a taxpayer's tax, interest and penalties payable under the Act for any taxation year shall be made that is necessary to take into account this provision and any election made with respect to it.

▶ 95(2.21) ◀

(2.21) Rule re subsection (2.2). Subsection (2.2) does not apply for the purpose of paragraph (2)(*a*) in respect of any income or loss referred to in that paragraph, of a particular foreign affiliate of the taxpayer, to the extent that that income or loss can reasonably be considered to have been realized or to have accrued before the earlier of

(*a*) the time at which the particular affiliate became, as determined without reference to subsection (2.2), a foreign affiliate of the taxpayer in respect of which the taxpayer had a qualifying interest, and

(*b*) the time at which the particular affiliate became, as determined without reference to subsection (2.2), a foreign affiliate of another person resident in Canada in respect of which the other person resident in Canada had a qualifying interest, where

(i) the taxpayer is a corporation,

(ii) the taxpayer did not exist at the beginning of the taxation year,

(iii) the particular affiliate became a foreign affiliate of the taxpayer in the taxation year because of a disposition, in the taxation year, of shares of the capital stock of the particular affiliate to the taxpayer by the other person resident in Canada, and

(iv) the other person resident in Canada was, immediately before that disposition, related to the taxpayer.

▶ 95(2.3) ◀

(2.3) Application of paragraph (2)(*a.1*). Paragraph (2)(*a*.1) does not apply to a foreign affiliate of a taxpayer in respect of a sale or exchange of property that is currency or a right to purchase, sell or exchange currency where

(*a*) the taxpayer is

(i) a bank, a trust company, a credit union, an insurance corporation or a trader or dealer in securities or commodities resident in Canada, the business activities of which are subject by law to the supervision of a regulating authority such as the Superintendent of Financial Institutions or a similar authority of a province, or

(ii) a subsidiary wholly-owned corporation of a corporation described in subparagraph (i);

(*b*) the sale or exchange was made by the affiliate in the course of a business conducted principally with persons with whom the affiliate deals at arm's length, if

(i) the business is principally carried on in the country (other than Canada) under whose laws the affiliate is governed and any of exists, was (unless the affiliate was continued in any jurisdiction) formed or organized, or was last continued, or

(ii) the affiliate is a foreign bank, a trust company, a credit union, an insurance corporation or a trader or dealer in securities or commodities and the activities of the business are regulated

(A) under the laws of the country under whose laws the affiliate is governed and any of exists, was (unless the affiliate was continued in any jurisdiction) formed or organized, or was last continued, and under the laws of each country in which the business is carried on through a permanent establishment in that country,

(B) under the laws of the country (other than Canada) in which the business is principally carried on, or

(C) if the affiliate is related to a corporation, under the laws of the country under the laws of which that related corporation is governed and any of exists, was (unless that related corporation was continued in any jurisdiction) formed or organized, or was last continued, if those regulating laws are recognized under the laws of the country in which the business is principally carried on and all of those countries are members of the European Union; and

(*c*) the terms and conditions of the sale or exchange of such property are substantially the same as the terms and conditions of similar sales or exchanges of such property by persons dealing at arm's length.

History: S. 95(2.3)(*b*)(ii)(A) was replaced by S.C. 2013, c. 34, s. 33(5), applicable to taxation years of a foreign affiliate of a taxpayer that begin after 1999.

See the application following the amendment to the description of F in the definition of "foreign accrual property income" in s. 95(1) regarding the override of the statute-barring rules for assessments for taxation years that end before June 26, 2013.

S. 95(2.3)(*b*)(ii)(A) formerly read:

(A) under the laws of the country under whose laws the affiliate is governed and any of exists, was (unless the affiliate was continued in any jurisdiction) formed or organized, or was last continued, and under the laws of each country in which the business is carried on through a permanent establishment (as defined by regulation) in that country,

► 95(2.31) ◄

(2.31) Application of paragraphs (2)(*a.1*) and (*a.3*). Paragraphs (2)(*a.1*) and (*a.3*) do not apply to a controlled foreign affiliate (for the purposes of section 17) of an eligible Canadian bank (as defined in subsection (2.43)) in respect of activities carried out to earn income from a property, other than a specified property of the affiliate, if

(*a*) the affiliate sells the property, or performs services as an agent in relation to a purchase or sale of the property, and it is reasonable to conclude that the cost to any person of the property is relevant in computing the income from

(i) a business carried on by the bank or a person resident in Canada with whom the bank does not deal at arm's length, or

(ii) a business carried on in Canada by a non-resident person with whom the bank does not deal at arm's length;

(*b*) the property has a readily available fair market value and

(i) is listed on a recognized stock exchange,

(ii) would be a mark-to-market property (as defined in subsection 142.2(1)) of the bank if it were owned by the bank, or

(iii) is a debt obligation owing by the bank that would be a mark-to-market property (as defined in subsection 142.2(1)) of the affiliate if

(A) the affiliate were the taxpayer referred to in that definition, and

(B) the definition "specified debt obligation" in subsection 142.2(1) were read without reference to its paragraph (*d*);

(*c*) the purchase and sale of the property by the affiliate, or services performed by the affiliate as agent in respect of the purchase or sale, are made

(i) on terms and conditions that are substantially the same as the terms and conditions of similar purchases or sales of, or services performed in respect of the purchase or sale of, such property by persons dealing at arm's length,

(ii) in the course of a business

(A) that regularly includes trading or dealing in securities principally with persons with whom the affiliate deals at arm's length, and

(B) that is principally carried on through a permanent establishment in a country other than Canada, and

(iii) for the purpose of enabling the purchase or sale of the property by a particular person who deals at arm's length with the affiliate and the bank; and

(*d*) the affiliate is a foreign bank or a trader or dealer in securities and the activities of the business are regulated

(i) under the laws of the country under whose laws the affiliate is governed and any of exists, was (unless the affiliate was continued in any jurisdiction) formed or organized, or was last continued, and under the laws of each country in which the business is carried on through a permanent establishment in that country,

(ii) under the laws of the country (other than Canada) in which the business is principally carried on, or

(iii) if the affiliate is related to a corporation, under the laws of the country under whose laws that related corporation is governed and any of exists, was (unless that related corporation was continued in any jurisdiction) formed or organized, or was last continued, if those regulating laws are recognized under the laws of the country in which the business is principally carried on and all those countries are members of the European Union.

History: S. 95(2.31) was added by S.C. 2014, c. 39, s. 25(18), applicable in respect of taxation years of a foreign affiliate of a taxpayer that begin after October 2012.

► 95(2.32) ◄

(2.32) Definition of "specified property". For the purposes of subsection (2.31), "specified property", of a foreign affiliate, means a property that is owned by the affiliate for more than 10 days and that is

(*a*) a share of the capital stock of a corporation resident in Canada;

(*b*) a property traded on a stock exchange located in Canada and not traded on a stock exchange located in the jurisdiction in which the affiliate is resident; or

(*c*) a debt obligation

(i) of a corporation resident in Canada,

(ii) of a trust or partnership, units of which are traded on a stock exchange located in Canada, or

(iii) of, or guaranteed by, the Government of Canada, the government of a province, an agent of a province, a municipality in Canada or a municipal or public body performing a function of government in Canada.

History: S. 95(2.32) was added by S.C. 2014, c. 39, s. 25(18), applicable in respect of taxation years of a foreign affiliate of a taxpayer that begin after October 2012.

► 95(2.4) ◄

(2.4) Application of paragraph (2)(*a.3*). Paragraph (2)(*a.3*) does not apply to a foreign affiliate of a taxpayer in respect of its income derived directly or indirectly from indebtedness to the extent that

(*a*) the income is derived by the affiliate in the course of a business conducted principally with persons with whom the affiliate deals at arm's length carried on by it as a foreign bank, a trust company, a credit union, an insurance corporation or a trader or dealer in securities or commodities, the activities of which are regulated under the laws

(i) of the country under whose laws the affiliate is governed and any of exists, was (unless the affiliate was continued in any jurisdiction) formed or organized, or was last continued and of each country in which the business is carried on through a permanent establishment in that country,

(ii) of the country in which the business is principally carried on, or

(iii) if the affiliate is related to a corporation, of the country under the laws of which that related corporation is governed and any of exists, was (unless that related corporation was continued in any jurisdiction) formed or organized, or was last continued, if those regulating laws are recognized under the laws of the country in which the business is principally carried on and all of those countries are members of the European Union, and

(*b*) all the following conditions are satisfied:

(i) the income is derived by the affiliate from trading or dealing in the indebtedness (which, for this purpose, consists of income from the actual trading or dealing in the indebtedness and interest earned by the affiliate during a short term holding period on indebtedness acquired by it for the purpose of the trading or dealing) directly or indirectly with persons (in this subsection referred to as "regular customers") that

(A) deal at arm's length with the affiliate, and

(B) are resident, or carry on business through a permanent establishment, in a country other than Canada,

(ii) the affiliate has a substantial market presence in the country, and

(iii) one or more persons that deal at arm's length with the affiliate and are resident, or carry on business through a permanent establishment, in the country

(A) carry on a business

(I) that competes in the country with the business of the affiliate, and

(II) the activities of which are regulated under the laws of the country or, where the country is a member of the European Union, any country that is a member of the European Union, in the same manner as are the activities of the business of the affiliate, and

(B) have a substantial market presence in the country,

and, for the purpose of this subsection, an acquisition of indebtedness from the taxpayer shall be deemed to be part of the trading or dealing in indebtedness described in paragraph (*b*) where the indebtedness is acquired by the affiliate and sold to regular customers and the terms and conditions of the acquisition and the sale are substantially the same as the terms and conditions of similar acquisitions and sales made by the affiliate in transactions with persons with whom it deals at arm's length.

History: S. 95(2.4)(*b*) was replaced by S.C. 2014, c. 39, s. 25(20), applicable in respect of taxation years of a foreign affiliate of a taxpayer that begin after October 2012, and formerly read:

(*b*) the income is derived by the affiliate from trading or dealing in the indebtedness (which, for this purpose, consists of income from the actual trading or dealing in the indebtedness and interest earned by the affiliate during a short term holding period on indebtedness acquired by it for the purpose of the trading or dealing) with persons (in this subsection referred to as "regular customers") with whom it deals at arm's length who were resident in a country other than Canada in which it and any competitor (which is resident in the country in which the affiliate is resident and regulated in the same manner the affiliate is regulated in the country under whose laws the affiliate was formed or continued and exists and is governed and in which its business is principally carried on) compete and have a substantial market presence,

S. 95(2.4)(*a*)(i) was replaced by S.C. 2013, c. 34, s. 33(6), applicable to taxation years of a foreign affiliate of a taxpayer that begin after 1999.

See the application following the amendment to the description of F in the definition of "foreign accrual property income" in s. 95(1) regarding the override of the statute-barring rules for assessments for taxation years that end before June 26, 2013.

S. 95(2.4)(*a*)(i) formerly read:

(i) of the country under whose laws the affiliate is governed and any of exists, was (unless the affiliate was continued in any jurisdiction) formed or organized, or was last continued and of each country in which the business is carried on through a permanent establishment (as defined by regulation) in that country,

► 95(2.41) ◄

(2.41) Application of paragraph (2)(*a.3*). Paragraph (2)(*a.3*) does not apply to a foreign affiliate of a taxpayer resident in Canada in respect of the foreign affiliate's income for a taxation year derived, directly or indirectly, from indebtedness of persons resident in Canada or from indebtedness in respect of businesses carried on in Canada (referred to in this subsection as the "Canadian indebtedness") if

(*a*) the taxpayer is, at the end of the foreign affiliate's taxation year

(i) a life insurance corporation resident in Canada, the business activities of which are subject by law to the supervision of the Superintendent of Financial Institutions or a similar authority of a province, or

(ii) a corporation resident in Canada that is a subsidiary controlled corporation of a corporation described in subparagraph (i);

(*b*) the Canadian indebtedness is used or held by the foreign affiliate, throughout the period in the taxation year that that Canadian indebtedness was used or held by the foreign affiliate, in the course of carrying on a business (referred to in this subsection as the "foreign life insurance business") that is a life insurance business carried on outside Canada (other than a business deemed by paragraph (2)(*a.2*) to be a separate business other than an active business), the activities of which are regulated

(i) under the laws of the country under whose laws the foreign affiliate is governed and any of exists, was (unless the foreign affiliate was continued in any jurisdiction) formed or organized, or was last continued, and

(ii) under the laws of the country, if any, in which the business is principally carried on;

(*c*) more than 90% of the gross premium revenue of the foreign affiliate for the taxation year in respect of the foreign life insurance business was derived from the insurance or reinsurance of risks (net of reinsurance ceded) in respect of persons

(i) that were non-resident at the time at which the policies in respect of those risks were issued or effected, and

(ii) that were at that time dealing at arm's length with the foreign affiliate, the taxpayer and all persons that were related at that time to the foreign affiliate or the taxpayer; and

(*d*) it is reasonable to conclude that the foreign affiliate used or held the Canadian indebtedness

(i) to fund a liability or reserve of the foreign life insurance business, or

(ii) as capital that can reasonably be considered to have been required for the foreign life insurance business.

▶ 95(2.42) ◀

(2.42) Exception re paragraph (2)(*a.3*). If, at any time in a taxation year of a foreign affiliate of a taxpayer referred to in paragraph (2)(*a.3*), a life insurance corporation resident in Canada is the taxpayer referred to in paragraph (2)(*a.3*) or is a person who controls, or is controlled by, such a taxpayer, a particular indebtedness or a particular lease obligation of the life insurance corporation is, for the purposes of that paragraph, deemed, at that time, not to be an indebtedness or a lease obligation of a person resident in Canada, to the extent of the portion of the particular indebtedness or lease obligation that can reasonably be considered to have been issued by the life insurance corporation to the foreign affiliate

(*a*) in respect of the life insurance corporation's life insurance business carried on outside Canada; and

(*b*) not in respect of

(i) the life insurance corporation's life insurance business carried on in Canada, or

(ii) any other use.

▶ 95(2.43) ◀

(2.43) Definitions — subsections (2.43) to (2.45). The following definitions apply in this subsection and subsections (2.44) and (2.45).

History: S. 95(2.43) was added by S.C. 2014, c. 39, s. 25(21), applicable in respect of taxation years of a foreign affiliate of a taxpayer that begin after October 2012.

"Canadian indebtedness" — "Canadian indebtedness" means indebtedness (other than upstream deposits) owed by persons resident in Canada or in respect of businesses carried on in Canada.

"eligible bank affiliate" — "eligible bank affiliate", of an eligible Canadian bank at any time, means a foreign bank that, at that time, is a controlled foreign affiliate (for the purposes of section 17) of the eligible Canadian bank and is described in subparagraph (*a*)(i) of the definition "investment business" in subsection (1).

"eligible Canadian bank" — "eligible Canadian bank" means a bank listed in Schedule I to the *Bank Act*.

"eligible Canadian indebtedness" — "eligible Canadian indebtedness", owing to an eligible bank affiliate of an eligible Canadian bank, means bonds, debentures, notes or similar obligations of the Government of Canada, the government of a province, an agent of a province, a municipality in Canada or a municipal or public body performing a function of government in Canada, that are owing to the affiliate, other than property in respect of which paragraph (2)(*a.3*) does not apply because of subsection (2.31).

"eligible currency hedge" — "eligible currency hedge", of an eligible bank affiliate of an eligible Canadian bank, means an agreement that provides for the purchase, sale or exchange of currency and that

(*a*) can reasonably be considered to have been made by the affiliate to reduce its risk of fluctuations in the value of currency with respect to eligible Canadian indebtedness and upstream deposits owing to the affiliate; and

(*b*) cannot reasonably be considered to have been made by the affiliate to reduce its risk with respect to property other than eligible Canadian indebtedness and upstream deposits owing to the affiliate.

"excess liquidity" — "excess liquidity", of an eligible bank affiliate of an eligible Canadian bank for a taxation year of the affiliate, means the amount, if any, by which

(*a*) the average of all amounts each of which is, in respect of a month that ends in the 12-month period that begins 60 days prior to the beginning of the year — or, if the affiliate was formed after the beginning of the period, in respect of a month that ends in the year — the amount of the affiliate's relationship deposits for the month, expressed in the affiliate's calculating currency for the year unless the context requires otherwise,

exceeds

(*b*) the average of all amounts each of which is, in respect of a month that ends in the period — or, if the affiliate was formed after the beginning of the period, in respect of a month that ends in the year — the amount of the affiliate's organic assets for the month, expressed in the affiliate's calculating currency for the year unless the context requires otherwise.

"organic assets" — "organic assets", of an eligible bank affiliate of an eligible Canadian bank for a month, means the total of all amounts in respect of the affiliate each of which is (*a*) included in the amounts reported as loans in the assets section of the consolidated monthly balance sheet accepted by the Superintendent of Financial Institutions that is filed for the month by the bank, or another corporation resident in Canada that is related to the bank at the end of the month, or

(*b*) an amount owing to the affiliate by a person that is related to the affiliate (other than an amount described in paragraph (*a*))

but does not include the amount of an eligible Canadian indebtedness or upstream deposit owing to the affiliate.

"qualifying indebtedness" —"qualifying indebtedness", owing to an eligible bank affiliate of an eligible Canadian bank, means an upstream deposit owing to, or an eligible Canadian indebtedness of, the affiliate, to the extent that it can reasonably be considered that

(*a*) the upstream deposit or the acquisition of eligible Canadian indebtedness, as the case may be, is funded by

(i) property transferred or lent by a person other than the bank or a person resident in Canada that was not, at the time of the transfer or loan, dealing at arm's length with the bank,

(ii) a repayment of all or part of an upstream deposit owing to the affiliate, or

(iii) the purchase of eligible Canadian indebtedness by the bank or a person resident in Canada that was not, at the time of the transfer or loan, dealing at arm's length with the bank; and

(*b*) the proceeds of the upstream deposit or the proceeds received by the vendor of the eligible Canadian indebtedness, as the case may be, are used for a purpose other than to fund a transfer or loan of property by the bank — or another person resident in Canada that was not, at the time of the transfer or loan, dealing at arm's length with the bank — to the affiliate or another foreign affiliate of the bank or of the other person.

"relationship deposits" —"relationship deposits", of an eligible bank affiliate of an eligible Canadian bank for a month, means the total of all amounts included in the amounts reported as demand and notice deposits, and fixed-term deposits in the liabilities section of the consolidated monthly balance sheet accepted by the Superintendent of Financial Institutions that is filed for the month by the bank, or another corporation resident in Canada that is related to the bank at the end of the month, that are deposits (other than of a temporary nature) of the affiliate made by a person who at the end of the month

(*a*) deals at arm's length with the affiliate; and

(*b*) is not resident in Canada.

"total specified indebtedness" —"total specified indebtedness", owing to an eligible bank affiliate of an eligible Canadian bank for a taxation year of the affiliate, means the average of all amounts each of which is, in respect of a month that ends in the year, the greatest total amount at any time in the month that is the total of all amounts each of which is

(*a*) the amount of an upstream deposit owing to the affiliate;

(*b*) the amount of an eligible Canadian indebtedness owing to the affiliate; or

(*c*) the positive or negative fair market value of an eligible currency hedge of the affiliate.

"upstream deposit" —"upstream deposit", owing to an eligible bank affiliate of an eligible Canadian bank, means indebtedness owing by the bank to the affiliate.

► 95(2.44) ◄

(2.44) FAPI adjustment — eligible bank affiliate. If a non-resident corporation (in this subsection referred to as the "affiliate") is, throughout a taxation year of the affiliate, an eligible bank affiliate of an eligible Canadian bank, and the bank elects in writing under this subsection, in respect of the affiliate for the year, and files the election with the Minister on or before the filing-due date of the bank for the particular taxation year of the bank in which the year ends,

(*a*) there is to be deducted in computing the amount determined for A in the definition "foreign accrual property income" in subsection (1) in respect of the affiliate for the year, the lesser of

(i) the amount determined, without reference to this paragraph, for A in that definition in respect of the affiliate for the year, and

(ii) the amount determined by the following formula, where each amount referred to in the formula is to be determined using Canadian currency:

$$A - B - C - D$$

where

A is the total of all amounts each of which is the affiliate's income for the year that is from a qualifying indebtedness owing to, or an eligible currency hedge of, the affiliate and that would, in the absence of this subsection, be included in computing the income of the affiliate from a business other than an active business of the affiliate,

B is the total of all amounts each of which is the affiliate's loss for the year that is from a qualifying indebtedness owing to, or an eligible currency hedge of, the affiliate and that would, in the absence of this subsection, be deducted in computing the income of the affiliate from a business other than an active business of the affiliate,

C is the total of all amounts each of which is the amount, if any, by which an amount included in computing the amount determined for A or B in respect of an upstream deposit exceeds the amount that would be the affiliate's income, or is less than the amount that would be the affiliate's loss, as the case may be, for the year from the upstream deposit if the interest received or receivable by the affiliate in respect of the upstream deposit were computed at an interest rate equal to the lesser of

(A) the rate of interest in respect of the upstream deposit, and

(B) the benchmark rate of interest, acceptable to the Minister, that is

(I) if the upstream deposit is denominated in a qualifying currency (as defined in subsection 261(1)), the average, for the year, of a daily interbank offered rate for loans denominated in that currency with a term to maturity of three months, or

(II) in any other case, the average, for the year, of a daily rate for Canadian dollar denominated bankers' acceptances with a term to maturity of three months, and

D is the amount determined by the formula

$$E \times F/G$$

where

E is the amount, if any, by which the amount determined for A exceeds the total of the amounts determined for B and C,

F is the amount, if any, by which the total specified indebtedness owing to the affiliate for the year exceeds the affiliate's excess liquidity for the year, and

G is the total specified indebtedness owing to the affiliate for the year; and

(*b*) there is to be included, in computing the income of the affiliate from an active business for the year, an amount equal to the proportion of the amount computed under the formula in subparagraph (*a*)(ii), computed as if each amount referred to in that formula were determined using the affiliate's calculating currency, that the amount that is required to be deducted under paragraph (*a*) for the year is of the amount described in subparagraph (*a*)(ii).

History: S. 95(2.44) was added by S.C. 2014, c. 39, s. 25(21), applicable in respect of taxation years of a foreign affiliate of a taxpayer that begin after October 2012.

► 95(2.45) ◄

(2.45) Investment business and excluded property. If an election is made under subsection (2.44) in respect of an eligible bank affiliate of an eligible Canadian bank for a taxation year of the affiliate,

(*a*) for the purposes of the definition "investment business" in subsection (1), the bank, and any other person resident in Canada that does not deal at arm's length with the bank, are deemed to deal at arm's length with the affiliate in respect of the making of upstream deposits, and acquisitions of Canadian indebtedness from the bank or the other person, by the affiliate in the course of a business carried on by the affiliate in the year if the affiliate's excess liquidity for the year is at least 90% of the total specified indebtedness owing to the affiliate for the year; and

(*b*) for the purposes of paragraph (*b*) of the definition "excluded property" in subsection (1),

(i) the fair market value of each upstream deposit and Canadian indebtedness owing to, and eligible currency hedge of, the affiliate is deemed to be nil,

(ii) at any particular time, the lesser of the following amounts is deemed to be the fair market value of a property of the affiliate that is excluded property at that particular time:

(A) the total of all amounts each of which is the fair market value of an upstream deposit or Canadian indebtedness owing to, or an eligible currency hedge of, the affiliate, and

(B) the amount, if any, by which

(I) the affiliate's relationship deposits for the calendar month that is two months prior to the particular time (or if the affiliate was formed less than two months prior to the particular time, for the calendar month that includes the particular time)

exceeds

(II) the amount of the affiliate's organic assets for the calendar month that is two months prior to the particular time (or if the affiliate was formed less than two months prior to the particular time, for the calendar month that includes the particular time), and

(iii) the amount, if any, by which the amount in clause (ii)(A) exceeds the amount in subparagraph (ii) is deemed to be the fair market value of a property of the eligible bank affiliate that is not excluded property at that time.

History: S. 95(2.45) was added by S.C. 2014, c. 39, s. 25(21), applicable in respect of taxation years of a foreign affiliate of a taxpayer that begin after October 2012.

► 95(2.5) ◄

(2.5) Definitions for paragraph (2)(*a.3*). For the purpose of paragraph (2)(*a.3*),

"excluded income" and "excluded revenue" — "excluded income" and "excluded revenue" for a taxation year in respect of a foreign affiliate of a taxpayer mean, respectively, income or revenue, that is

(*a*) derived directly or indirectly from a specified deposit with a prescribed financial institution,

(*b*) derived directly or indirectly from a lease obligation of a person (other than the taxpayer or a person that does not deal at arm's length with the taxpayer) resident in Canada relating to property used by the person in the course of carrying on a business through a permanent establishment outside Canada,

(*c*) included in computing the affiliate's income for the year from carrying on a business through a permanent establishment in Canada, or (*d*) included in computing the affiliate's income or loss from an active business for the year because of subparagraph (2)(*a*)(ii);

History: S. 95(2.5), paragraph (*b*) of the definition "excluded income" and "excluded revenue" was replaced by S.C. 2014, c. 39, s. 25(22), applicable in respect of taxation years of a foreign affiliate of a taxpayer that begin after July 12, 2013. However, if a taxpayer elects in writing under s. 25(40) of the *Economic Action Plan 2014 Act, No. 2* [S.C. 2014, c. 39] in respect of all its foreign affiliates and files the election with the Minister of National Revenue on or before the day that is the later of the taxpayer's filing-due date for the taxpayer's taxation year that includes the day on which the *Economic Action Plan 2014 Act, No. 2* [S.C. 2014, c. 39] receives royal assent [December 16, 2014] and the day that is one year after the day on which the *Economic Action Plan 2014 Act, No. 2* [S.C. 2014, c. 39] receives royal assent [December 16, 2014], then this amendment applies in respect of taxation years of foreign affiliates of the taxpayer,

(*a*) if the taxpayer has elected under subsection 73(17) of the *Income Tax Amendments Act, 2000* [S.C. 2001, c. 17], that begin after 1994, or

(*b*) in any other case, that begin after 1999.

In addition, any assessment of a taxpayer's tax, interest and penalties payable under the Act for any taxation year that ends before the day on which this amendment receives royal assent [December 16, 2014] that would, in the absence of this section, be precluded because of the time references in subsection 152(4) of the Act is to be made to the extent necessary to take into account this amendment.

Paragraph (*b*) of the definition "excluded income" and "excluded revenue" formerly read:

(*b*) derived directly or indirectly from a lease obligation of a person (other than the taxpayer or a person that does not deal at arm's length with the taxpayer) relating to the use of property outside Canada, or

S. 95(2.5), paragraph (*d*) of the definition "excluded income" and "excluded revenue" was added by S.C. 2014, c. 39, s. 25(23), applicable in respect of taxation years of a foreign affiliate of a taxpayer that end after February 27, 2004.

In addition, any assessment of a taxpayer's tax, interest and penalties payable under the Act for any taxation year that ends before the day on which this amendment receives royal assent [December 16, 2014] that would, in the absence of this section, be precluded because of the time references in subsection 152(4) of the Act is to be made to the extent necessary to take into account this amendment.

"indebtedness" —"indebtedness" does not include obligations of a particular person under agreements with non-resident corporations providing for the purchase, sale or exchange of currency where

(*a*) the agreements are swap agreements, forward purchase or sale agreements, forward rate agreements, futures agreements, options or rights agreements, or similar agreements,

(*b*) the particular person is a bank, a trust company, a credit union, an insurance corporation or a trader or dealer in securities or commodities resident in Canada, the business activities of which are subject by law to the supervision of a regulating authority in Canada such as the Superintendent of Financial Institutions or a similar authority of a province,

(*c*) the agreements are entered into by the non-resident corporation in the course of a business conducted principally with persons with whom the non-resident corporation deals at arm's length, if

(i) the business is principally carried on in the country (other than Canada) under whose laws the non-resident corporation is governed and any of exists, was (unless the non-resident corporation was continued in any jurisdiction) formed or organized, or was last continued, or

(ii) the non-resident corporation is a foreign affiliate of the particular person, or of a person related to the particular person, and

(A) the non-resident corporation is a foreign bank, a trust company, a credit union, an insurance corporation or a trader or dealer in securities or commodities, and

(B) the activities of the business are regulated

(I) under the laws of the country under whose laws the non-resident corporation is governed and any of exists, was (unless the non-resident corporation was continued in any jurisdiction) formed or organized, or was last continued and under the laws of each country in which the business is carried on through a permanent establishment in that country,

(II) under the laws of the country (other than Canada) in which the business is principally carried, or

(III) if the affiliate is related to a corporation, under the laws of the country under the laws of which a corporation related to the non-resident corporation is governed and any of exists, was (unless that related corporation was continued in any jurisdiction) formed or organized, or was last continued, if those regulating laws are recognized under the laws of the country in which the business is principally carried on and all of those countries are members of the European Union, and

(*d*) the terms and conditions of such agreements are substantially the same as the terms and conditions of similar agreements made by persons dealings (*sic*) at arm's length;

History: S. 95(2.5), subclause (*c*)(ii)(B)(I) of the definition "indebtedness" was replaced by S.C. 2013, c. 34, s. 33(7), applicable to taxation years of a foreign affiliate of a taxpayer that begin after 1999.

See the application following the amendment to the description of F in the definition of "foreign accrual property income" in s. 95(1) regarding the override of the statute-barring rules for assessments for taxation years that end before June 26, 2013.

S. 95(2.5), subclause (*c*)(ii)(B)(I) of the definition "indebtedness" formerly read:

(I) under the laws of the country under whose laws the non-resident corporation is governed and any of exists, was (unless the non-resident corporation was continued in any jurisdiction) formed or organized, or was last continued and under the laws of each country in which the business is carried on through a permanent establishment (as defined by regulation) in that country,

"specified deposit" —"specified deposit", of a foreign affiliate of a taxpayer, means a deposit of the affiliate made with a permanent establishment in a country other than Canada of a prescribed financial institution resident in Canada if the income from the deposit is income of the affiliate for the year that would, in the absence of paragraph (2)(*a.3*), be income from an active business carried on by the affiliate in a country other than Canada, other than a business the principal purpose of which is to derive income from property (including any interest, dividends, rents, royalties or similar returns, or any substitutes for any of those) or profits from the disposition of investment property.

History: S. 95(2.5), the definition "specified deposit" was replaced by S.C. 2014, c. 39, s. 25(24), applicable in respect of taxation years of a foreign affiliate of a taxpayer that begin after October 2012, and formerly read:

"specified deposit"—"specified deposit" means a deposit of a foreign affiliate of a taxpayer resident in Canada with a prescribed financial institution resident in Canada where

(*a*) the income from the deposit is income of the affiliate for the year that would, but for paragraph (2)(*a*.3), be income from an active business carried on by it in a country other than Canada (other than a business the principal purpose of which is to derive income from property including interest, dividends, rents, royalties or similar returns or substitutes therefor or profits from the disposition of investment property), or

(*b*) the income from the deposit is income of the affiliate for the year that would, but for paragraph (2)(*a*.3), be income from an active business carried on by the affiliate principally with persons with whom the affiliate deals at arm's length in the country under whose laws the affiliate was formed or continued and exists and is governed and in which the business is principally carried on by it and the deposit was held by the affiliate in the course of carrying on that part of the business conducted with non-resident persons with whom the affiliate deals at arm's length or that part of the business conducted with a person with whom the affiliate was related where it can be demonstrated that the related person used or held the funds deposited in the course of a business carried on by the related person with non-resident persons with whom the related person and the affiliate deal at arm's length.

Related Sections: S. 125(7), "specified investment business".

▶ 95(2.6) ◀

(2.6) Rule for the definition "specified person or partnership". For the purposes of paragraphs (*a*) to (*d*) of the definition "specified person or partnership" in subsection (1), if a person or partnership (referred to in this subsection as the "taxpayer") is not dealing at arm's length with another person or partnership (referred to in this subsection as the "particular person") at a particular time, the taxpayer is deemed to have existed and not to have dealt at arm's length with the particular person, nor with each specified predecessor corporation of the particular person, throughout the period that began when the particular person or the specified predecessor corporation, as the case may be, came into existence and that ends at the particular time.

History: S. 95(2.6) was added by S.C. 2009, c. 2, s. 25(5), applicable to taxation years of a foreign affiliate of a taxpayer that begin after October 2, 2007. However, if the taxpayer elects in writing in respect of all of its foreign affiliates and files the election with the Minister of National Revenue on or before the day (referred to as the taxpayer's "election day") that is the later of (i) the taxpayer's filing-due date for the taxpayer's taxation year that includes the day on which this Act is assented to [R.A. March 12, 2009] and (ii) the day that is one year after the day on which this Act is assented to [March 12, 2010], s. 95(2.6) shall, in its application to a taxation year of a foreign affiliate of the taxpayer that begins after October 2, 2007 and before July 14, 2008, be read as follows:

"(2.6) For the purposes of paragraphs (*a*) to (*d*) of the definition "specified person or partnership" in subsection (1), in determining whether, at a particular time, a person was not, at a time (referred to in this subsection as the "prior time") that is before the particular time and at which that person did not exist, dealing at arm's length with another person, where the person exists at the particular time but did not exist at the prior time

(*a*) the person is deemed to exist at the prior time; and

(*b*) where the person is related to another person at the particular time, the person is deemed to have been related to that other person at the prior time."

If the taxpayer elects in writing in respect of all of its foreign affiliates and files the election with the Minister of National Revenue on or before the taxpayer's election day, s. 95(2.6) also applies to taxation years of a foreign affiliate of the taxpayer that begin before October 2, 2007 and after the date chosen by the taxpayer as described below.

To be valid, an election [described above] must include the identification by the taxpayer of its choice of one of the following dates:

(i) December 31, 1994,

(ii) December 20, 2002, or

(iii) February 27, 2004.

Notwithstanding subsections 152(4) to (5) of the Act, any assessment of a taxpayer's tax, interest and penalties payable under the Act for any taxation year shall be made that is necessary to take into account this provision and any election made with respect to it.

▶ 95(3) ◀

(3) Definition of "services". For the purposes of paragraph (2)(*b*), "services" includes the insurance of Canadian risks but does not include

(*a*) the transportation of persons or goods;

(*b*) services performed in connection with the purchase or sale of goods;

(*c*) the transmission of electronic signals or electricity along a transmission system located outside Canada; or

(*d*) the manufacturing or processing outside Canada, in accordance with the taxpayer's specifications and under a contract between the taxpayer and the affiliate, of tangible property, or for civil law corporeal property, that is owned by the taxpayer if the property resulting from the manufacturing or processing is used or held by the taxpayer in the ordinary course of the taxpayer's business carried on in Canada.

Related Sections: S. 95(2) Determination of certain components of foreign accrual property income.

▶ 95(3.01) ◀

(3.01) Application of paragraph (2)(*b*) — eligible Canadian bank. Paragraph (2)(*b*) does not apply to a controlled foreign affiliate (for the purposes of section 17) of an eligible Canadian bank (as defined in subsection (2.43)) in respect of services performed in connection with the purchase or sale of a property described in paragraph (2.31)(*b*) if

(*a*) the services have been performed by the affiliate

(i) under terms and conditions that are substantially the same as the terms and conditions that would have been made between persons who deal at arm's length with each other,

(ii) in the course of a business

(A) that regularly includes trading or dealing in securities principally with persons with whom the affiliate deals at arm's length, and

(B) that is principally carried on through a permanent establishment in a country other than Canada, and

(iii) for the purpose of enabling the acquisition or disposition of the property by a person who, at the time of the acquisition or disposition, deals at arm's length with the affiliate and the eligible Canadian bank; and

(*b*) the affiliate is a foreign bank or a trader or dealer in securities and the activities of the business are regulated

(i) under the laws of the country under whose laws the affiliate is governed and any of exists, was (unless the affiliate was continued in any jurisdiction) formed or organized, or was last continued, and under the laws of each country in which the business is carried on through a permanent establishment in that country,

(ii) under the laws of the country (other than Canada) in which the business is principally carried on, or

(iii) if the affiliate is related to a corporation, under the laws of the country under whose laws that related corporation is governed and any of exists, was (unless that related corporation was continued in any jurisdiction) formed or organized, or was last continued, if those regulating laws are recognized under the laws of the country in which the business is principally carried on and all those countries are members of the European Union.

History: S. 95(3.01) was added by S.C. 2014, c. 39, s. 25(25), applicable in respect of taxation years of a foreign affiliate of a taxpayer that begin after October 2012.

▶ 95(3.02) ◀

(3.02) Rules for clause (2)(*b*)(ii)(B). For the purposes of clause (2)(*b*)(ii)(B),

(*a*) a relevant person is

(i) a person resident in Canada, or

(ii) a non-resident person if the non-resident person performs the services referred to in subparagraph (2)(*b*)(ii) in the course of a business (other than a treaty-protected business) carried on in Canada; and

(*b*) any portion of a business carried on by a non-resident person that is carried on in Canada is deemed to be a business that is separate from any other portion of the business carried on by the person.

History: S. 95(3.02) was added by S.C. 2014, c. 39, s. 25(26), applicable in respect of taxation years of a foreign affiliate of a taxpayer that begin after July 12, 2013. However, if a taxpayer elects in writing under s. 25(34) of the *Economic Action Plan 2014 Act, No. 2* [S.C. 2014, c. 39] in respect of all its foreign affiliates and files the election with the Minister of National Revenue on or before the day that is the later of the taxpayer's filing-due date for the taxpayer's taxation year that includes the day on which the *Economic Action Plan 2014 Act, No. 2* [S.C. 2014, c. 39] receives royal assent [December 16, 2014] and the day that is one year after the day on which the *Economic Action Plan 2014 Act, No. 2* [S.C. 2014, c. 39] receives royal assent [December 16, 2015], then s. 95(3.02) applies in respect of taxation years of all foreign affiliates of the taxpayer that begin after February 27, 2004.

In addition, any assessment of a taxpayer's tax, interest and penalties payable under the Act for any taxation year that ends before the day on which this amendment receives royal assent [December 16, 2014] that would, in the absence of this section, be precluded because of the time references in subsection 152(4) of the Act is to be made to the extent necessary to take into account this amendment.

▶ 95(3.1) ◀

(3.1) Designated property — subparagraph (2)(*a.1*)(i). Designated property referred to in subparagraph (2)(*a.1*)(i) is property that is described in the portion of paragraph (2)(*a.1*) that is before subparagraph (i) that is

(*a*) property that was sold to non-resident persons other than the affiliate, or sold to the affiliate for sale to non-resident persons, and

(i) that

(A) was — in the course of carrying on a business in Canada — manufactured, produced, grown, extracted or processed in Canada by the taxpayer, or by a person with whom the taxpayer does not deal at arm's length, or

(B) was — in the course of a business carried on by a foreign affiliate of the taxpayer outside Canada — manufactured or processed from tangible property, or for civil law corporeal property, that, at the time of the manufacturing or processing, was owned by the taxpayer or by a person related to the taxpayer and used or held by the owner in the course of carrying on a business in Canada, if the manufacturing or processing was in accordance with the specifications of the owner of that tangible or corporeal property and under a contract between that owner and that foreign affiliate,

(ii) that was acquired, in the course of carrying on a business in Canada, by a purchaser from a vendor, if

(A) the purchaser is the taxpayer or is a person resident in Canada with whom the taxpayer does not deal at arm's length, and

(B) the vendor is a person

(I) with whom the taxpayer deals at arm's length,

(II) who is not a foreign affiliate of the taxpayer, and

(III) who is not a foreign affiliate of a person resident in Canada with whom the taxpayer does not deal at arm's length, or

(iii) that was acquired by a purchaser from a vendor, if

(A) the purchaser is the taxpayer or is a person resident in Canada with whom the taxpayer does not deal at arm's length,

(B) the vendor is a foreign affiliate of

(I) the taxpayer, or

(II) a person resident in Canada with whom the taxpayer does not deal at arm's length, and

(C) that property was manufactured, produced, grown, extracted or processed in the country

(I) under whose laws the vendor is governed and any of exists, was (unless the vendor was continued in any jurisdiction) formed or organized, or was last continued, and

(II) in which the vendor's business is principally carried on; or

(*b*) property that is an interest in real property, or a real right in an immovable, located in, or a foreign resource property in respect of, the country

(i) under whose laws the affiliate is governed and any of exists, was (unless the affiliate was continued in any jurisdiction) formed or organized, or was last continued, and

(ii) in which the affiliate's business is principally carried on.

► 95(3.2) ◄

(3.2) Contract manufacturing. For the purposes of clause (2)(*a.1*)(ii)(A), property of a particular foreign affiliate of a taxpayer is deemed to have been manufactured by the particular affiliate in a particular country if the property is

(*a*) developed and designed by the particular affiliate in the particular country in the course of an active business carried on by the particular affiliate in the particular country; and

(*b*) manufactured, produced or processed outside the particular country by another foreign affiliate of the taxpayer, during a period throughout which the taxpayer has a qualifying interest in the other affiliate,

(i) under a contract between the particular affiliate and the other affiliate, and

(ii) in accordance with specifications provided by the particular affiliate.

History: S. 95(3.2) was added by S.C. 2014, c. 39, s. 25(27), applicable in respect of taxation years of a foreign affiliate of a taxpayer that end after 2008.

In addition, any assessment of a taxpayer's tax, interest and penalties payable under the Act for any taxation year that ends before the day on which this amendment receives royal assent [December 16, 2014] that would, in the absence of this section, be precluded because of the time references in subsection 152(4) of the Act is to be made to the extent necessary to take into account this amendment.

► 95(4) ◄

(4) Definitions. In this section,

"direct equity percentage" —"direct equity percentage" at any time of any person in a corporation is the percentage determined by the following rules:

(*a*) for each class of the issued shares of the capital stock of the corporation, determine the proportion of 100 that the number of shares of that class owned by that person at that time is of the total number of issued shares of that class at that time, and

(*b*) select the proportion determined under paragraph (*a*) for that person in respect of the corporation that is not less than any other proportion so determined for that person in respect of the corporation at that time,

and the proportion selected under paragraph (*b*), when expressed as a percentage, is that person's direct equity percentage in the corporation at that time;

"eligible controlled foreign affiliate" —"eligible controlled foreign affiliate", of a taxpayer, at any time, means a foreign affiliate at that time of the taxpayer in respect of which the following conditions are met:

(*a*) the affiliate is a controlled foreign affiliate of the taxpayer at that time and at the end of the affiliate's taxation year that includes that time, and

(*b*) the total of all amounts each of which would be, if this definition were read without reference to this paragraph, the participating percentage (determined at the end of the taxation year) of a share owned by the taxpayer of the capital stock of a corporation, in respect of the affiliate, is not less than 90%;

History: S. 95(4), the definition "eligible controlled foreign affiliate" was added by S.C. 2013, c. 34, s. 70(23), applicable in respect of determinations made after February 27, 2004 in respect of property of a foreign affiliate of a taxpayer. However,

(*a*) if the taxpayer has made the election under the application of the definition "designated liquidation and dissolution" in s. 95(1) or under the application of s. 95(2)(*d.1*), the definition "eligible controlled foreign affiliate" in s. 95(4) also applies to such determinations made after December 20, 2002 and before February 28, 2004 but only in respect of

(i) where an election is made under the application of the definition "designated liquidation and dissolution" in s. 95(1) but no election is made under the application of s. 95(2)(*d.1*), property that is subject to the application of paragraph 95(2)(*e*),

(ii) where no election is made under the application of the definition "designated liquidation and dissolution" in s. 95(1) but an election is made under the application of s. 95(2)(*d.1*), property that is subject to the application of paragraph 95(2)(*d.1*), and

(iii) where elections are made under the application of the definition "designated liquidation and dissolution" in s. 95(1) and under the application of s. 95(2)(*d.1*), property that is subject to the application of paragraph 95(2)(*d.1*) or (*e*);

(*b*) in respect of any such determinations made for the purposes of paragraph 88(3)(*a*), if the determination is made on or before August 19, 2011 and is in respect of property received in the course of a qualifying liquidation and dissolution of the disposing affiliate, the definition "eligible controlled foreign affiliate" in subsection 95(4) is to be read as follows:

"'eligible controlled foreign affiliate', of a taxpayer at any time, means a controlled foreign affiliate of the taxpayer at that time."

(*c*) if the taxpayer has elected under the application of s. 95(2)(*d.1*), in respect of any such determinations made on or before August 19, 2011 for the purposes of paragraph 95(2)(*d.1*), the definition "eligible controlled foreign affiliate" in subsection 95(4) is to be read in the manner specified in paragraph (*b*) in the application above; and

(*e*) if the taxpayer has elected under the application of the definition "designated liquidation and dissolution" in s. 95(1), in respect of any such determinations made on or before August 19, 2011 for the purposes of paragraph 95(2)(*e*), the definition "eligible controlled foreign affiliate" in subsection 95(4) is to be read in the manner specified in paragraph (*b*) in the application above.

Any assessment of a taxpayer's tax, interest and penalties payable under the Act for any taxation year that ends before June 26, 2013 that would otherwise be precluded because of subsections 152(4) to (5) of the Act shall be made to the extent necessary to take into account the amendments by S.C. 2013, c. 34, s. 54 to 89.

"equity percentage" —"equity percentage" at any time of a person, in any particular corporation, is the total of

(*a*) the person's direct equity percentage at that time in the particular corporation, and

(*b*) all percentages each of which is the product obtained when the person's equity percentage at that time in any corporation is multiplied by that corporation's direct equity percentage at that time in the particular corporation

except that for the purposes of the definition "participating percentage" in subsection (1), paragraph (*b*) shall be read as if the reference to "any corporation" were a reference to "any corporation other than a corporation resident in Canada";

"relevant cost base" —"relevant cost base", of a property at any time to a foreign affiliate of a taxpayer, in respect of the taxpayer, means the greater of

(*a*) the amount determined — or, if the taxpayer is not a corporation, the amount that would be determined if the taxpayer were a corporation resident in Canada — by the formula

$$A + B - C$$

where

A is the amount for which the property could be disposed of at that time that would not, in the absence of paragraph (2)(*f.1*), result in any amount being added to, or deducted from, any of the affiliate's

(i) exempt earnings, exempt loss, taxable earnings and taxable loss (all within the meaning of subsection 5907(1) of the *Income Tax Regulations*), in respect of the taxpayer, for the taxation year of the affiliate that includes that time, and

(ii) hybrid surplus and hybrid deficit, in respect of the taxpayer, at that time,

B is the amount, if any, by which any income or gain from a disposition of the property would, if the property were disposed of at that time for proceeds of disposition equal to its fair market value at that time be reduced under paragraph (2)(*f.1*), and

C is the amount, if any, by which any loss from a disposition of the property would, if the property were disposed of at that time for proceeds of disposition equal to its fair market value at that time be reduced under paragraph (2)(*f.1*), and

(*b*) either

(i) if the affiliate is an eligible controlled foreign affiliate of the taxpayer at that time, the amount that the taxpayer elects, in accordance with prescribed rules, in respect of the property not exceeding the fair market value at that time of the property, or

(ii) in any other case, nil.

History: S. 95(4), the definition "relevant cost base" was replaced by S.C. 2013, c. 34, s. 70(22), applicable In respect of determinations made after February 27, 2004 in respect of property of a foreign affiliate of a taxpayer. However,

(*a*) if the taxpayer has made the election under the application of the definition "designated liquidation and dissolution" in s. 95(1) or under the application of s. 95(2)(*d.1*) the definition "relevant cost base" in s. 95(4) also applies to such determinations made after December 20, 2002 and before February 28, 2004 but only in respect of

(i) where an election is made under the application of the definition "designated liquidation and dissolution" in s. 95(1) but no election is made under the application of s. 95(2)(*d.1*), property that is subject to the application of paragraph 95(2)(*e*),

(ii) where no election is made under the application of the definition "designated liquidation and dissolution" in s. 95(1) but an election is made under the application of s. 95(2)(*d.1*), property that is subject to the application of paragraph 95(2)(*d.1*), and

(iii) where elections are made under the application of the definition "designated liquidation and dissolution" in s. 95(1) and under the application of s. 95(2)(*d.1*), property that is subject to the application of paragraph 95(2)(*d.1*) or (*e*);

(*b*) in respect of any such determinations made for the purposes of paragraph 88(3)(*a*), if the determination is made on or before August 19, 2011 and is in respect of property that is a share of the capital stock of a foreign affiliate of the taxpayer that is excluded property (within the meaning assigned by subsection 95(1)) of the disposing affiliate, the definition "relevant cost base" in subsection 95(4) is to be read as follows:

"'relevant cost base', of a property at any time to a foreign affiliate of a taxpayer, means the adjusted cost base to the affiliate of the property at that time or such greater amount as the taxpayer elects, in accordance with prescribed rules, in respect of the property not exceeding the fair market value at that time of the property."

(*c*) in respect of any such determinations made on or before August 19, 2011 for the purposes of paragraph 95(2)(*c*), (*d*) or, if the taxpayer has not elected under the application of the definition "designated liquidation and dissolution" in s. 95(1), paragraph 95(2)(*e*), the definition "relevant cost base" in subsection 95(4) is to be read in the manner specified in subparagraph (*b*)(i) in the application above.

See the application following the addition of the definition "designated liquidation and dissolution" for the extension of assessment periods to take into account the amendments in S.C. 2013, c. 34, s. 54 to 89.

S. 95(4), the definition "relevant cost base" formerly read:

"relevant cost base"—"relevant cost base" to a foreign affiliate of property at any time means the adjusted cost base to the affiliate of the property at that time or such greater amount as the taxpayer claims not exceeding the fair market value of the property at that time.

Related Sections: S. 95(5) Income bonds or debentures issued by foreign affiliates.

▶ 95(4.1) ◀

(4.1) Application of s. 87(8.1). In this section, the expressions "foreign merger", "predecessor foreign corporation", "new foreign corporation" and "foreign parent corporation" have the meanings assigned by subsection 87(8.1).

▶ 95(5) ◀

(5) Income bonds or debentures issued by foreign affiliates. For the purposes of this subdivision, an income bond or income debenture issued by a corporation (other than a corporation resident in Canada) shall be deemed to be a share of the capital stock of the corporation unless any interest or other similar periodic amount paid by the corporation on or in respect of the bond or debenture was, under the laws of the country in which the corporation was resident, deductible in computing the amount for the year on which the corporation was liable to pay income or profits tax imposed by the government of that country.

Related Sections: S. 95(6) Where rights or shares issued, acquired or disposed of to avoid tax.

▶ 95(6) ◀

(6) Where rights or shares issued, acquired or disposed of to avoid tax. For the purposes of this subdivision (other than section 90),

(*a*) where any person or partnership has a right under a contract, in equity or otherwise, either immediately or in the future and either absolutely or contingently, to, or to acquire, shares of the capital stock of a corporation or interests in a partnership and

(i) it can reasonably be considered that the principal purpose for the existence of the right is to cause 2 or more corporations to be related for the purpose of paragraph (2)(*a*), those corporations shall be deemed not to be related for that purpose, or

(ii) it can reasonably be considered that the principal purpose for the existence of the right is to permit any person to avoid, reduce or defer the payment of tax or any other amount that would otherwise be payable under this Act, those shares or partnership interests, as the case may be, are deemed to be owned by that person or partnership; and

(*b*) where a person or partnership acquires or disposes of shares of the capital stock of a corporation or interests in a partnership, either directly or indirectly, and it can reasonably be considered that the principal purpose for the acquisition or disposition is to permit a person to avoid, reduce or defer the payment of tax or any other amount that would otherwise be payable under this Act, that acquisition or disposition is deemed not to have taken place, and where the shares or partnership interests were unissued by the corporation or partnership immediately before the acquisition, those shares or partnership interests, as the case may be, are deemed not to have been issued.

Related Sections: S. 95(5) Income bonds or debentures issued by foreign affiliates.

Canadian Tax Foundation: Hudson and McCamis, *Refresher on Specific Anti-Avoidance Provisions*, 2014 Prairie Provinces Tax Conference 12:1–41; Baker and Slaats, *Lehigh: Paragraph 95(6)(b) Restricted*, 2014 Canadian Tax Highlights 22(5):1–2; Wang, *Current Cases: Tax Court of Canada — Searching for Purpose (Lehigh Cement Limited v. The Queen, 2013 TCC 176)*, 2013 Canadian Tax Journal 4:1139–1145; Barnicke and Huynh, *Lehigh and Paragraph 95(6)(b)*, 2013 Canadian Tax Highlights 21(6):1–2.

Tax Profile: July 2008 — International Tax Planning for the Owner-Manager; May 2007 — The CRA's Newest Weapon: S. 95(6)(b); November 2004 — Subsection 95(6) — Scope of Application.

Tax Topics: No. 1867-68, 2007 Canadian Tax Foundation Annual Conference CRA Round Table; No. 1814, 2006 Canadian Tax Foundation Annual Conference CRA Round Table; No. 1700, 2004 Canadian Tax Foundation Conference - CRA Round Table.

Income Tax Technical News: Issue No. 38, Application of Paragraph 95(6)(b); Issue No. 36, Paragraph 95(6)(b); Issue No. 34, Update on Subsection 95(6); Issue No. 32, Subsection 95(6): Scope of Application.

Cases: For s. 95 to apply, obtaining the tax benefit must be the principle purpose of the share acquisition. The taxpayers successfully showed that their main purpose in acquiring shares in their foreign affiliate was not to avoid Canadian taxes but to achieve overall U.S. tax savings. *The Queen v. Lehigh Cement Limited*, 2014 DTC 5058 (F.C.A.), affirming 2013 DTC 1139 (T.C.C.)

The taxpayer, Univar, was a subsidiary of UC. Univar incorporated B, a Barbadian subsidiary. B used the money received from Univar's share subscription to purchase a debt from UC. After paying 2.5% Barbadian tax on interest received on this debt, B paid dividends to Univar. The Minister could not use s. 95(6) and s. 245 to re-characterize these dividends as interest since his premise that the debt was purchased by Univar, rather than by B, was not true. *Univar Canada Ltd. v. The Queen*, 2005 DTC 1478 (T.C.C.).

▶ 95(7) ◀

(7) Stock dividends from foreign affiliates. For the purposes of this subdivision and subsection 52(3), the amount of any stock dividend paid by a foreign affiliate of a corporation resident in Canada shall, in respect of the corporation, be deemed to be nil.

Related Sections: S. 52(3) Cost of stock dividend; s. 54, "adjusted cost base"; s. 95(1), "foreign affiliate"; s. 248(1), "amount", "corporation", "business", "dividend", "income bond", "prescribed", "principal amount", "property", "share", "shareholder", "stock dividend"; s. 255 Canada.

Canadian Tax Foundation: Mahnger and McKilligan, *The Foreign Affiliate Fresh Start Rules*, 2009 Canadian Tax Journal 2:319–337; Nikolakakis, *The Taxation of Foreign Affiliates in the Resource Sectors*, 2008 Conference Report 29:1–60; Talakshi and Samuel, *Foreign Affiliate Surplus: What You See Isn't Always What You Get*, 2008 Conference Report 28:1–27; Goguen and Jack, *Selected Recent Legislative and Administrative Developments in the Foreign Affiliate Regime*, 2007 Conference Report 19:1–59; Huynh et al., *The Anti-Tax-Haven Initiative and the Foreign Affiliate Rules*, 2007 Canadian Tax Journal 3:655–675; Huynh and Lockwood, *Foreign Affiliates and Adjusted Cost Base*, 2007 Canadian Tax Journal 1:141–159; Barnicke, *ITTN No. 36: Paragraph 95(6)(b)*, 2007 Canadian Tax Highlights 15(8):4–5; Monaghan and Juneja, *Selected Issues in Cross-Border Debt Financing*, 2006 Conference Report 16:1–58; Holms and Shields, *Foreign Affiliate Rules: The Effect of the Investment Business Definition on Real Estate Developers*, 2006 Canadian Tax Journal 4:937–967; Johnson et al., *A Reasoned Response to the CRA's Views on the Scope and Interpretation of Paragraph 95(6)(b)*, 2006 Canadian Tax Journal 3:571–632; Maikawa and Martin, *Foreign Exchange and Foreign Affiliates: Continuing Problems and Possible Solutions*, 2006 Canadian Tax Journal 1:241–261; Juneja and Morier, *Foreign Affiliates: A Primer*, 2005 Conference Report 40:1–41; Slaats, *Repatriation from Foreign Affiliates: Selected Issues*, 2005 Canadian Tax Journal 3:858–884; Turner, *Foreign Affiliate Liquidation and Merger Rollovers: Where Are We Now and Where Should We Be?*, 2005 Canadian Tax Journal 3:640–684; Bouthillier, *Residence-Based Taxation and FAPI: A World of Fictions*, 2005 Canadian Tax Journal 1:179–204; Talakshi, *The Foreign Affiliate Proposals — An Update*, 2005 Conference Report 14:1–20; Jack et al., *Update on Subsection 95(6) (Canada Revenue Agency Round Table)*, 2005 Conference Report 6A:35–36; Jack et al., *International Taxation: The February 27, 2004 Draft Proposals on Foreign Affiliates* , 2004 Conference Report 20:1–105; Lockwood, *Foreign Affiliates and the New Foreign Investment Entity Rules, Revisited*, 2004 Canadian Tax Journal 4:1186–1216; Lockwood and Pantaleo, *Foreign Affiliates and the New Foreign Investment Entity Rules*, 2003 Canadian Tax Journal 1:539–568; Tremblay and Wilkie, *The Canadian Triangle: Tax Policy Reflections on the Uneasy Interaction of 15(2), 17 and 95(2)*, 2002 Conference Report 18:1–16; Berwick et al., *The Upcoming Foreign Affiliate Amendments*, 2001 Conference Report 12:1–22; Holms and Charpentier, *Financing Foreign Affiliates: Some Things Old and Some Things New*, 2001 British Columbia Tax Conference 12:1–32; Swiderski and Lau, *Canadian Foreign Affiliate Implications of Common U.S. Asset Transfers*, 2000 Conference Report 15:1–46; Nikolakakis, *The 1999-2000 Foreign Affiliate Amendments: Partnerships, Foreign Exchange Issues, and the Use of Losses* , 2000 Conference Report 14:1–60; Huynh and Lockwood, *Foreign Accrual Property Income: A Practical Perspective*, 2000 Canadian Tax Journal 3:752–777; Lockwood et al., *Proposed Technical Amendments to the FAPI and Foreign Affiliate Rules*, 2000 Canadian Tax Journal 2:456–476; Moskowitz, *Financing of Non-Residents and the Recent Amendments to Section 17*, 1999 Conference Report 43:1–61; Lagios and Minassian, *Foreign Accrual Property Income: Pitfalls for the Unwary*, 1999 Conference Report 3:1–53; Bourgeois, *Canadian Taxation of Offshore Income: A Primer*, 1999 Conference Report 2:1–32; Pantaleo, *Foreign Affiliates Under Siege: An Update*, 1999 Canadian Tax Journal 2:291–304; Schreiner, *Canadian Tax Implications of Foreign Divisive Reorganizations*, 1999 Canadian Tax Journal 1:115–133; Champoux and Nucciarone, *International Distribution of Intellectual Property*, 1998 Conference Report 42:1–44; Bourque and Bronstetter, *Foreign Affiliate Reporting: The First Filing*, 1998 Conference Report 19:1–25; Lockwood and Maikawa, *Foreign Affiliates and FAPI: Problems and Tax-Planning Opportunities Resulting from the 1995 Changes*, 1998 Canadian Tax Journal 2:377–414; Macdonald and Tiu, *Foreign Affiliate Reporting — The Inaugural Update*, 1998 British Columbia Tax Conference 22:1–35; Lanthier and Meek, *Canadian Foreign Affiliate Rules*, 1997 Conference Report 31:1–42; Bronstetter et al., *Loans Between Foreign Affiliates*, 1997 Canadian Tax Journal 3:560–583.

Interpretation Bulletins: *Secondary* — IT-88R2 Stock dividends.

▶ 95(8) ◀

(8) Tracking interests — interpretation. For the purposes of subsections (9) to (12), a particular property is a tracking interest in respect of a person or partnership (referred to in this subsection as the "tracked entity") if

(*a*) all or part of the fair market value of the particular property — or of any payment or right to receive an amount in respect of the particular property — can reasonably be considered to be determined, directly or indirectly, by reference to one or more of the following criteria in respect of property or activities of the tracked entity (referred to in this subsection and subsections (9) to (11) as the "tracked property and activities"):

(i) the fair market value of property of the tracked entity,

(ii) any revenue, income or cash flow from property or activities of the tracked entity,

(iii) any profits or gains from the disposition of property of the tracked entity, and

(iv) any similar criteria in respect of property or activities of the tracked entity; and

(*b*) the tracked property and activities in respect of the particular property represent less than all of the property and activities of the tracked entity.

Editorial Note: The definitions in s. 95(8) apply for two main purposes. First, they apply to determine whether a foreign affiliate has a separate investment business under the deeming rules of s. 95(9). Second, they apply to determine whether an affiliate will be a controlled foreign affiliate ("CFA") under s. 95(11) dealing specifically with the FAPI income inclusions under s. 91(1) and deductions under s. 91(4), or a CFA more generally under s. 95(12). The rules are meant to combat the use of so-called "tracking arrangements", under which multiple taxpayers pool their assets in one corporation, but effectively retain a right to the returns from the assets which they contributed. Tracking arrangements have been used to get around the FAPI investment business rules (see the editorial note to s. 95(9)), and to attempt to avoid CFA status and therefore the application of the FAPI rules more generally.

History: S. 95(8) was added by S.C. 2018, c. 27, s. 7(5), applicable to taxation years of a foreign affiliate of a taxpayer that begin after February 26, 2018, except that, notwithstanding subsection 95(10), subsection 95(11) shall not apply in respect of a foreign affiliate of the taxpayer in respect of taxation years of the affiliate that begin after February 26, 2018 and before [October 25, 2018], if the taxpayer

(a) elects in writing under this subsection in respect of all of its foreign affiliates; and

(b) files the election with the Minister of National Revenue on or before the day that is the later of

(i) the day that is six months after the day on which this Act receives royal assent [June 13, 2019], and

(ii) the taxpayer's filing-due date for its taxation year that includes [October 25, 2018].

International Tax: No. 103, The Tracking Interest Rules.

▶ 95(9) ◀

(9) Tracking interests — *investment business* definition. For the purposes of the definition *investment business* in subsection (1), if, at any time in a taxation year of a foreign affiliate of a taxpayer, a person or partnership holds a tracking interest in respect of the affiliate or a partnership of which the affiliate is a member, the tracked property and activities in respect of the tracking interest are, to the extent they would not otherwise be part of an investment business of the affiliate, deemed, in respect of the taxpayer,

(*a*) to be a separate business carried on by the affiliate throughout the year; and

(*b*) not to be part of any other business of the affiliate.

Editorial Note: Under s. 95(9), where a person or partnership holds a "tracking interest" in respect of the foreign affiliate of a taxpayer, the "tracked property and activities" in respect of the tracking interest (both terms defined in s. 95(8)) are deemed to be a separate investment business carried on by the affiliate and not to be part of any other business of the affiliate. An "investment business" (s. 95(1)) is not considered an active business such that income from the investment business is normally subject to the FAPI rules. One exception, where a business of investing is not considered an investment business, applies where the business employs throughout the relevant year more than five full-time employees. Any deemed separate investment business under s. 95(9) will have to meet that employee test in order to fall within the exception. The provision applies to taxation years of a foreign affiliate of a taxpayer that begin after February 26, 2018.

History: S. 95(9) was added by S.C. 2018, c. 27, s. 7(5), applicable to taxation years of a foreign affiliate of a taxpayer that begin after February 26, 2018, except that, notwithstanding subsection 95(10), subsection 95(11) shall not apply in respect of a foreign affiliate of the taxpayer in respect of taxation years of the affiliate that begin after February 26, 2018 and before [October 25, 2018], if the taxpayer

(a) elects in writing under this subsection in respect of all of its foreign affiliates; and

(b) files the election with the Minister of National Revenue on or before the day that is the later of

(i) the day that is six months after the day on which this Act receives royal assent [June 13, 2019], and

(ii) the taxpayer's filing-due date for its taxation year that includes [October 25, 2018].

International Tax: No. 103, The Tracking Interest Rules.

▶ 95(10) ◀

(10) Conditions for subsection (11). Subsection (11) applies in respect of a foreign affiliate of a taxpayer for a taxation year of the affiliate if, at any time in the year,

(*a*) the taxpayer holds a property that is a tracking interest in respect of the affiliate; and

(*b*) shares of a class of the capital stock of the affiliate the fair market value of which can reasonably be considered to be determined by reference to the tracked property and activities in respect of the tracking interest (referred to in subsection (11) as a "tracking class") are held by the taxpayer or a foreign affiliate of the taxpayer.

History: S. 95(10) was added by S.C. 2018, c. 27, s. 7(5), applicable to taxation years of a foreign affiliate of a taxpayer that begin after February 26, 2018, except that, notwithstanding subsection 95(10), subsection 95(11) shall not apply in respect of a foreign affiliate of the taxpayer in respect of taxation years of the affiliate that begin after February 26, 2018 and before [October 25, 2018], if the taxpayer

(a) elects in writing under this subsection in respect of all of its foreign affiliates; and

(b) files the election with the Minister of National Revenue on or before the day that is the later of

(i) the day that is six months after the day on which this Act receives royal assent [June 13, 2019], and

(ii) the taxpayer's filing-due date for its taxation year that includes [October 25, 2018].

▶ 95(11) ◀

(11) Tracking class — separate corporation. If this subsection applies in respect of a foreign affiliate (referred to in this subsection as the "actual affiliate") of a taxpayer for a taxation year of the actual affiliate, the following rules apply for the purpose of determining the amounts, if any, to be included under subsection 91(1), and to be deducted under subsection 91(4), by the taxpayer in respect of the year and for the purpose of applying section 233.4 in respect of the year:

(*a*) the tracked property and activities of the actual affiliate are deemed to be property and activities of a non-resident corporation (referred to in this subsection as the "separate corporation") that is separate from the actual affiliate and not to be property or activities of the actual affiliate;

(*b*) any income, losses or gains for the year in respect of the property and activities described in paragraph (*a*) are deemed to be income, losses or gains of the separate corporation and not of the actual affiliate;

(*c*) all rights and obligations of the actual affiliate in respect of the property and activities described in paragraph (*a*) are deemed to be rights and obligations of the separate corporation and not of the actual affiliate;

(*d*) the separate corporation is deemed to have, at the end of the year, 100 issued and outstanding shares of a single class (referred to in this subsection as the "single class") of its capital stock, having full voting rights under all circumstances;

(*e*) each shareholder of the actual affiliate is deemed to own, at the end of the year, that number of shares of the single class that is equal to the product of 100 and the amount that would be the *aggregate participating percentage* (as defined in subsection 91(1.3)) of that shareholder in respect of the actual affiliate for the year if

(i) the actual affiliate were a controlled foreign affiliate of that shareholder at the end of the year,

(ii) the only shares of the capital stock of the actual affiliate issued and outstanding at the end of the year were shares of tracking classes in respect of the tracked properties and activities, and

(iii) the only income, losses and gains of the actual affiliate for the year were those referred to in paragraph (*b*); and

(*f*) any amounts included under subsection 91(1), or deducted under subsection 91(4), by the taxpayer in respect of shares of the separate corporation are deemed to be amounts included under subsection 91(1), or deducted under subsection 91(4), as the case may be, by the taxpayer in respect of shares of tracking classes held by the taxpayer or a foreign affiliate of the taxpayer, as the case may be.

Editorial Note: By virtue of s. 95(10), s. 95(11) applies where a taxpayer holds a "tracking interest" (s. 95(8)) in respect of a foreign affiliate, and either the taxpayer or another foreign affiliate of the taxpayer holds shares of a "tracking class" of shares in the foreign affiliate. A tracking class of shares of an affiliate means a class of shares, the fair market value of which can reasonably be considered to be determined by reference to the "tracked property and activities" (s. 95 (8)(*a*)) of the affiliate in respect of the tracking interest. Where a taxpayer holds a tracking interest but neither the taxpayer nor a foreign affiliate of the taxpayer holds a tracking class of shares, s. 95(12) can apply rather than s. 95(11).

Effectively, s.95(11) deems the tracked property and activities of the foreign affiliate of a taxpayer to be that of a separate non-resident corporation whose income or loss is from the tracked property and activities. Paragraphs 95(11)(*d*) and (*e*) provide the deemed shareholdings of the separate corporation for shareholders of the foreign affiliate. The deeming rules apply for the purpose of determining whether the separate corporation is a controlled foreign affiliate ("CFA") of the taxpayer and thus subject to the FAPI inclusion and deduction rules of s. 95(1) and (4), respectively, and for the purposes of the foreign affiliate reporting rules of s. 233.4. Subsection 95(11) applies to taxation years of a foreign affiliate of a taxpayer that begin after February 26, 2018.

See also the editorial note to s. 95(8).

History: S. 95(11) was added by S.C. 2018, c. 27, s. 7(5), applicable to taxation years of a foreign affiliate of a taxpayer that begin after February 26, 2018, except that, notwithstanding subsection 95(10), subsection 95(11) shall not apply in respect of a foreign affiliate of the taxpayer in respect of taxation years of the affiliate that begin after February 26, 2018 and before [October 25, 2018], if the taxpayer

(a) elects in writing under this subsection in respect of all of its foreign affiliates; and

(b) files the election with the Minister of National Revenue on or before the day that is the later of

(i) the day that is six months after the day on which this Act receives royal assent [June 13, 2019], and

(ii) the taxpayer's filing-due date for its taxation year that includes [October 25, 2018].

► 95(12) ◄

(12) Tracking interests — controlled foreign affiliate. If subsection (11) does not apply in respect of a foreign affiliate of the taxpayer for a taxation year of the affiliate, the affiliate is deemed to be a controlled foreign affiliate of the taxpayer throughout the taxation year if, at any time in the year, a tracking interest in respect of the affiliate, or a partnership of which the affiliate is a member, is held by

(*a*) the taxpayer; or

(*b*) a person or partnership (each referred to in this paragraph as a "holder"), if

(i) the holder does not deal at arm's length with the taxpayer at that time,

(ii) where either the taxpayer or the holder is a partnership and the other party is not, any member of the partnership does not deal at arm's length, at that time, with the other party, or

(iii) where both the taxpayer and the holder are partnerships, the taxpayer or any member of the taxpayer does not deal at arm's length, at that time, with the holder or any member of the holder.

Editorial Note: See the editorial note to s. 95(8) regarding so-called "tracking arrangements". Subsection 95(11) generally applies where a taxpayer holds a "tracking interest" in respect of a foreign affiliate and a "tracking class" of shares of the affiliate, whereas s. 95(12) is the default provision that applies where the taxpayer does not own a tracking class but the taxpayer (or a non-arm's length party described in s. 95(12)(*b*)) holds a tracking interest. The default provision may apply, for example, where the taxpayer's tracking interest is effected through contractual arrangements rather than specific share conditions.

History: S. 95(12) was added by S.C. 2018, c. 27, s. 7(5), applicable to taxation years of a foreign affiliate of a taxpayer that begin after February 26, 2018, except that, notwithstanding subsection 95(10), subsection 95(11) shall not apply in respect of a foreign affiliate of the taxpayer in respect of taxation years of the affiliate that begin after February 26, 2018 and before [October 25, 2018], if the taxpayer

(a) elects in writing under this subsection in respect of all of its foreign affiliates; and

(b) files the election with the Minister of National Revenue on or before the day that is the later of

(i) the day that is six months after the day on which this Act receives royal assent [June 13, 2019], and

(ii) the taxpayer's filing-due date for its taxation year that includes [October 25, 2018].

Subdivision j — Partnerships and their Members

SECTION 96: General rules

▶ 96(1) ◀

(1) General rules. Where a taxpayer is a member of a partnership, the taxpayer's income, non-capital loss, net capital loss, restricted farm loss and farm loss, if any, for a taxation year, or the taxpayer's taxable income earned in Canada for a taxation year, as the case may be, shall be computed as if

(*a*) the partnership were a separate person resident in Canada;

(*b*) the taxation year of the partnership were its fiscal period;

(*c*) each partnership activity (including the ownership of property) were carried on by the partnership as a separate person, and a computation were made of the amount of

(i) each taxable capital gain and allowable capital loss of the partnership from the disposition of property, and

(ii) each income and loss of the partnership from each other source or from sources in a particular place,

for each taxation year of the partnership;

(*d*) each income or loss of the partnership for a taxation year were computed as if

(i) this Act were read without reference to sections 34.1 and 34.2, subsection 59(1), paragraph 59(3.2)(*c.1*) and subsections 66.1(1), 66.2(1) and 66.4(1), and

(ii) no deduction were permitted under any of section 29 of the *Income Tax Application Rules*, subsection 65(1) and sections 66, 66.1, 66.2, 66.21 and 66.4;

(*e*) each gain of the partnership from the disposition of land used in a farming business of the partnership were computed as if this Act were read without reference to paragraph 53(1)(*i*);

(*e*.1) the amount, if any, by which

(i) the total of all amounts determined under paragraphs 37(1)(*a*) to (*c*.1) in respect of the partnership at the end of the taxation year

exceeds

(ii) the total of all amounts determined under paragraphs 37(1)(*d*) to (*g*) in respect of the partnership at the end of the year

were deducted under subsection 37(1) by the partnership in computing its income for the year;

(*f*) the amount of the income of the partnership for a taxation year from any source or from sources in a particular place were the income of the taxpayer from that source or from sources in that particular place, as the case may be, for the taxation year of the taxpayer in which the partnership's taxation year ends, to the extent of the taxpayer's share thereof; and

(*g*) the amount, if any, by which

(i) the loss of the partnership for a taxation year from any source or sources in a particular place,

exceeds

(ii) in the case of a specified member (within the meaning of the definition "specified member" in subsection 248(1) if that definition were read without reference to paragraph (*b*) thereof) of the partnership in the year, the amount, if any, deducted by the partnership by virtue of section 37 in calculating its income for the taxation year from that source or sources in the particular place, as the case may be, and

(iii) in any other case, nil

were the loss of the taxpayer from that source or from sources in that particular place, as the case may be, for the taxation year of the taxpayer in which the partnership's taxation year ends, to the extent of the taxpayer's share thereof.

Editorial Note: Partnerships are not taxable entities. In general terms, partnership income or loss is computed at the partnership level for its fiscal period, and the income or loss, including its source, flows through to the partners who report such amounts in their taxation year in which the fiscal period ends. Amounts included in a partner's income are generally added to the adjusted cost base of the partner's interest (including the whole amount of any capital gain), and losses claimed by the partner are generally deducted from the adjusted cost base of the partner's interest (including the whole amount of any capital loss). (See also ss. 53(1)(*e*) and 53(2)(*c*)). Tax credits are generally claimed at the partner level (see, for example, s. 127(8), regarding the investment tax credit). Losses may be restricted for limited partners under s. 96(2.1).

History: S. 96(1)(*d*)(i) and (ii) were replaced by S.C. 2011, c. 24, s. 20(1), applicable to the 2011 and subsequent taxation years. S. 96(1)(*d*)(i) and (ii) formerly read:

> (i) this Act were read without reference to section 34.1, subsection 59(1), paragraph 59(3.2)(c.1) and subsections 66.1(1), 66.2(1) and 66.4(1), and
>
> (ii) no deduction were permitted under any of section 29 of the *Income Tax Application Rules*, subsections 34.2(4) and 65(1) and sections 66, 66.1, 66.2, 66.21 and 66.4;

Related Sections: S. 12(1)(*l*) Partnership income; s. 12(1)(*z*.5) TFSA amounts; s. 20(1)(*v*.1) Resource allowance; s. 34.1 Alternative method of reporting income; s. 34.2 and 34.3 Additions to income when corporate partner and partnership have different fiscal year-ends; s. 37(1) Scientific research and experimental development; s. 53(1)(*e*) Adjustments to cost base — Interest in a partnership; s. 53(2)(*c*) Amounts to be deducted — Interest in a partnership; s. 59(1) Consideration for foreign resource property; s. 59(1.1) Partnerships; s. 59(3.2)(*c*.1) Recovery of exploration and development expenses; s. 65(1) Allowance for oil or gas well, mine or timber limit; s. 66.1 Cumulative Canadian exploration expenses; s. 66.2 Cumulative Canadian development expenses; s. 66.21 Cumulative foreign resource expense; s. 66.4 Canadian oil and gas property expense; s. 66.8 Resource expenses of limited partner; s. 96(1.1) Allocation of share of income to retiring partner; s. 96(2.1) Limited partnership losses; s. 98(1) Disposition of partnership property; s. 98.1(1) Residual interest in partnership; s. 103(1) Agreement to share income, etc., so as to reduce or postpone tax otherwise payable; s. 103(1.1) Agreement to share income, etc., in unreasonable proportions; s. 120.4 Tax on split income; s. 212(13.1) Application of Part XIII tax where payer or payee is a partnership; s. 248(1), "specified member"; s. 249 Definition of "taxation year"; s. 249.1 Definition of "fiscal period".

Canadian Petroleum Tax Journal: Partnerships and other Dangerous Liaisons, Mar and Rowe, 2008, Vol. 171, No. 1; Recent Developments in Corporate Reorganizations and International Transactions, Doug Richardson and Edward Rowe, 2000, Vol. 13, No. 1; Recent Developments in Relation to Partnerships, Michael J. Flatters, 1997, Vol. 10, No. 1.

Canadian Tax Foundation: Fabbro, *Proving the Existence of a Spousal Partnership*, 2014 Canadian Tax Focus 4(2):8; Oldewening and Carr, *Limitation on Deferral of Partnership Income by a Corporation*, 2012 Canadian Tax Journal 1:219–256; Lille and Johnson, *Partnerships: An Update*, 2010 Conference Report 36:1–62; Monaghan and Juneja, *Selected Issues in Cross-Border Debt Financing*, 2006 Conference Report 16:1–58; Beiles, *Partnerships: A Review of Tax Planning Strategies*, 2006 British Columbia Tax Conference 11:1–31; Maclagan, *Partnerships: An Update*, 2005 Conference Report 37:1–39; Cherniawsky, *Use of Partnerships and Joint Ventures for Owner-Manager Businesses*, 2005 Prairie Provinces Tax Conference 14:1–24; MacKnight, *Tax Planning Using Partnerships*, 2003 Ontario Tax Conference 12:1–42; Kakkar and Rule, *Partnerships Versus Joint Ventures: The "Separate Person" Concept*, 2003 Tax for the Owner-Manager 3(2):6–7; McQuillan, *Some Important Issues in Partnerships in the Past Year*, 2002 Conference Report 1:1–25; Manoochehri and Nurmohamed, *Increasing Taxpayer Certainty in Using Partnerships*, 2002 Canadian Tax Journal 1:387–406; McQuillan, *Partnerships: The Most Significant Developments of The Past 12 Months*, 2001 Conference Report 4:1–15; Krahn, *Taxation of Partners*, 2001 British Columbia Tax Conference 7:1–27; Templeton, *Current Cases: The Federal Court of Appeal — What's a Partnership Without a View to Profit?*, 2000 Canadian Tax Journal 4:1252–1260; Richler, *Merger by Way of Partnership with a Comparison to Amalgamation*, 1999 Conference Report 25:1–30; Ewens, *Tax Issues Affecting Partnerships*, 1997 Conference Report 8:1–85.

Tax Profile: June 2012 — Use of Canadian Partnerships by Non-Residents; December 2011 — Partnership Taxation; September 2006 — Canadian Acquisition of U.S. Real Estate; July 2002 — Doing Business in Canada.

Tax Topics: No. 1932, The Thin Blue Line Between Expressions of Interest and True Partnerships; No. 1657, Can a Partnership Pay a Salary to a Partner? *Archbold* Revisited.

Income Tax Folios: *Primary* — S4-F16-C1 What is a Partnership?.

Income Tax Technical News: Issue No. 30, Computation/Allocation of Partnership Income and Losses; Issue No. 25, Partnership Issues.

Information Circulars: IC 73-13 Investment clubs.

Interpretation Bulletins: *Primary* — IT-81R Partnerships — Income of non-resident partners. *Secondary* — IT-259R4 Exchange of property; IT-278R2 Death of a partner or of a retired partner; IT-346R Commodity futures and certain commodities.

SR&ED Publications: SR&ED Claims for Partnerships Policy.

Tax Window Files: Application of Article V(9) to a partnership, *December 14, 2015*, CRA Document No. 2014-0558661I7; Partnership Income — Preference Units, *Technical Interpretation, Business and Partnerships Division, January 10, 2008*, CRA Document No. 2007-0227191E5; Foreign Exchange Gains and Losses — Conversion of Advances into Partnership Interests, *Technical Interpretation, International and Trust Division, August 29, 2007*, CRA Document No. 2007-0219931I7; Gift of Life Insurance Policies to Limited Partnerships, *Technical Interpretation, Financial Sector and Exempt Entities, June 5, 2007*, CRA Document No. 2007-0237291I7; Wind-Up of Partnership — Flow-Through Shares, *Technical Interpretation, Business and Partnerships Division, June 27, 2006*, CRA Document No. 2006-0174191I7; Roll-Over Provisions and Partnership, *December 16, 2005*, CRA Document No. 2005-0150411E5; Interest Incurred by U.S. Limited Partnership, *Technical Interpretation, International and Trusts Division, May 25, 2004*, CRA Document No. 2003-0039231E5. Canadian partners of U.S. limited partnership may be considered to be the payers of interest paid by the partnership to a non-resident person; Limited Partnership Losses of Tier Partnership, *Technical Interpretation, Business and Partnerships Division, May 14, 2004*, CRA Document No. 2004-0062801E5. Allocation of losses of limited partnership unavailable to members of top partnership that is partner of limited partnership; Capital Dividend Received by Partnership, *Technical Interpretation, Business and Partnerships Division, December 4, 2003*, CRA Document No. 2003-0038595. Corporate partner can include, in computing its capital dividend account, its share of a capital dividend received by the partnership at the time the partner becomes entitled to a share of the dividend; Allocation of Income — Deceased Partner, *Technical Interpretation, Business and Partnerships Division, October 30, 2003*, CRA Document No. 2003-0020545. Partnership had income up to the date of partner's death but nil income for the entire year; allocation of income to the deceased partner would be nil.

Cases: It is contrary to the object, spirit, or purposes of subsection 96(1) to use that provision to allocate taxable income in a manner that does not assist the organizational structure of the partnership or the efficient conduct of the partnership business. The taxpayer's actions amounted to abusive tax avoidance. *The Queen v. 594710 British Columbia Ltd.*, 2018 DTC 5111 (FCA)

The taxpayer was a retired partner in a national accounting firm with offices in Quebec. Although he had never lived or worked in Quebec, his retirement benefits represented a share of partnership profits and were subject to tax under the deeming provisions of the Quebec *Taxation Act*. *Dunne v. Quebec (Dep. Min. Revenue)*, 2007 DTC 5248 (S.C.C.), affirming 2007 DTC 5237 (Que. C.A.), reversing 2007 DTC 5234 (Court of Quebec)

Through a series of transactions, the taxpayers effectively paid $1.2 million to acquire $10.4 million in tax losses along with an apartment complex which they managed profitably after its acquisition. They were allowed to deduct partnership losses because, although the primary purpose in acquiring the partnership interest was to obtain a tax loss, they did have a secondary intention to acquire and retain an income-producing asset, by which they could continue to carry on business in common with a view to profit. *Spire Freezers Ltd. et al. v. The Queen*, 2001 DTC 5158 (S.C.C.), reversing 99 DTC 5297 (F.C.A.) and 98 DTC 1287 (T.C.C.)

The taxpayers acquired partnership interests for the sole purpose of acquiring potential tax losses. They also purchased interests in two other ventures but spent only nominal time, attention and labour on them. The partnership losses were denied since the taxpayers were not carrying on a business with a view to a profit. Also, they could not claim to be partners by assignment, because the criteria for a valid partnership must be reaffirmed in order for the partnership to continue in its new form. *Backman v. The Queen*, 2001 DTC 5149 (S.C.C.), affirming 99 DTC 5602 (F.C.A.) and 97 DTC 1468 (T.C.C.)

Nine taxpayers paid $320,000 for somewhat less than full ownership of a partnership whose only asset was a computer which had a value of $7,000, and a large historical cost. The partnership losses were denied since the taxpayers did not intend to carry on any business involving the computer. They simply intended to create a large tax loss. In addition, the partnership could not suffer a terminal loss since the partnership came to an end when the majority interest was transferred to new partners. *Duncan et al. v. The Queen*, 2001 DTC 96 (T.C.C.)

The fact that the taxpayer had sought tax benefits as its predominant purpose for the creation of a partnership did not negate the fact that the parties also had the ancillary purpose of sharing profit and therefore met the requirements for a partnership. *Continental Bank Leasing Corporation v. The Queen et al.*, 98 DTC 6505 (S.C.C.), reversing 96 DTC 6355 (F.C.A.), which reversed 94 DTC 1858 (T.C.C.).

► 96(1.01) ◄

(1.01) Income allocation to former member. If, at any time in a fiscal period of a partnership, a taxpayer ceases to be a member of the partnership

(*a*) for the purposes of subsection (1), sections 34.1, 101 and 103 and paragraph 249.1(1)(*b*), and notwithstanding paragraph 98.1(1)(*d*), the taxpayer is deemed to be a member of the partnership at the end of the fiscal period; and

(*b*) for the purposes of the application of paragraph (2.1)(*b*), subsection 40(3.12) and subparagraphs 53(1)(*e*)(i) and (viii) and (2)(*c*)(i) to the taxpayer, the fiscal period of the partnership is deemed to end

(i) immediately before the time at which the taxpayer is deemed by subsection 70(5) to have disposed of the interest in the partnership, where the taxpayer ceased to be a member of the partnership because of the taxpayer's death, and

(ii) immediately before the time that is immediately before the time that the taxpayer ceased to be a member of the partnership, in any other case.

Editorial Note: Where a partner ceases to be a member of a continuing partnership, the allocation of net income or loss for the year is usually after the cessation. Subsection 96(1.01) deems a former partner to be a partnership member at the end of the tax year in the year they left the partnership. The effect is that the adjusted cost base at the time of disposition for the partner includes their share of stub period net income or loss.

History: S. 96(1.01)(*a*) was replaced by S.C. 2013, c. 34, s. 228(2), applicable in respect of a taxpayer to taxation years that end after March 22, 2011, and formerly read:

(*a*) for the purposes of subsection (1) and sections 34.1, 34.2, 101, 103 and 249.1, and notwithstanding paragraph 98.1(1)(*d*), the taxpayer is deemed to be a member of the partnership at the end of the fiscal period; and

S. 96(1.01)(*b*), the portion before subparagraph (i) was replaced by S.C. 2013, c. 34, s. 228(3), applicable in respect of a taxpayer to taxation years that end after October 31, 2011, and formerly read:

(*b*) for the purposes of the application of paragraph (2.1)(*b*) and subparagraphs 53(1)(*e*)(i) and (viii) and (2)(*c*)(i) to the taxpayer, the fiscal period of the partnership is deemed to end

S. 96(1.01) was added by S.C. 2013, c. 34, s. 228(1), applicable in respect of a taxpayer

(*a*) in the case where the taxpayer ceases to be a member of a partnership because of the taxpayer's death, to the 2003 and subsequent taxation years; and *(b)* in any other case, to the 1995 and subsequent taxation years.

▶ 96(1.1) ◀

(1.1) Allocation of share of income to retiring partner. For the purposes of subsection (1) and sections 34.1, 34.2, 101, 103 and 249.1,

(*a*) where the principal activity of a partnership is carrying on a business in Canada and its members have entered into an agreement to allocate a share of the income or loss of the partnership from any source or from sources in a particular place, as the case may be, to any taxpayer who at any time ceased to be a member of

(i) the partnership, or

(ii) a partnership that at any time has ceased to exist or would, but for subsection 98(1), have ceased to exist, and either

(A) the members of that partnership, or

(B) the members of another partnership in which, immediately after that time, any of the members referred to in clause (A) became members

have agreed to make such an allocation

or to the taxpayer's spouse, common-law partner, estate or heirs or to any person referred to in subsection (1.3), the taxpayer, spouse, common-law partner, estate, heirs or person, as the case may be, shall be deemed to be a member of the partnership; and

(*b*) all amounts each of which is an amount equal to the share of the income or loss referred to in this subsection allocated to a taxpayer from a partnership in respect of a particular fiscal period of the partnership shall, notwithstanding any other provision of this Act, be included in computing the taxpayer's income for the taxation year in which that fiscal period of the partnership ends.

Editorial Note: Although s. 96(1.1) generally applies to taxpayers who are retired or former partners, it can also apply to the former partner's spouse, common-law partner, estate or heir. The amount allocated to the taxpayer (or spouse etc.) of the partnership income or loss is included in computing the taxpayer's income in the taxation year in which the partnership fiscal period ends. Where a partner ceases to be a member of a continuing partnership, the allocation of net income or loss for the year is usually after the cessation. For tax years after March 22, 2011, s. 96(1.01) deems a former partner to be a partnership member at the end of the tax year in the year they left the partnership. The effect is that the adjusted cost base at the time of disposition for the partner includes their share of stub period net income or loss. The amount of the income or loss is not subject to the addition or deduction rules of ss. 53(1)(*e*) and 53(2)(*c*) (which otherwise apply to the adjusted cost base of a partner's interest).

Related Sections: S. 98.1(1) Residual interest in partnership.

Tax Topics: No. 1967, Conversion of Partnership Interests into Income and Capital Components.

Interpretation Bulletins: *Secondary* — IT-242R Retired partners; IT-278R2 Death of a partner or of a retired partner.

Tax Window Files: Payments to Widow of Retired Partner, *Technical Interpretation, International & Trusts Division, November 29, 2006*, CRA Document No. 2005-0140621E5; Allocation of Income to Retired Partners, *Technical Interpretation, Business and Partnerships Division, May 29, 2006*, CRA Document No. 2005-0160581E5; Arrangement to Satisfy SEC, *November 9, 2005*, CRA Document No. 2003-0011341R3. Arrangement did not result in partnership assets funding retirement benefits, subsection 96(1.1) not applicable; Late Filing Penalty, *Technical Interpretation, Individual, Business and Partnerships Section, November 30, 2004*, CRA Document No. 2004-0095511I7; Allocation of Income to Retiring Partner's Spouse, *Technical Interpretation, Business and Partnerships Division, April 29, 2003*, CRA Document No. 2003-0006465. Subsection 96(1.1) permits retired partner to direct some or all of the allocation of income to spouse.

Cases: The taxpayer ceased to be a member of an accounting partnership in November of 1972. The remaining partners allocated to him a share of partnership profits for the fiscal period ended in January of 1973, which share the Minister included in 1973 income. The inclusion was overturned by the Court on the basis that there was no evidence supporting the allocation of partnership profits. *Dacen v. The Queen*, 89 DTC 5297 (F.C.T.D.), reversing 79 DTC 732 (T.R.B.)

▶ 96(1.11) ◀

(1.11) Deemed dividend of SIFT partnership. If a SIFT partnership is liable to tax for a taxation year under Part IX.1,

(*a*) paragraph (1)(*f*) is to be read as if the expression "the amount of the income of the partnership for a taxation year from any source or from sources in a particular place" were read as "the amount, if any, by which the income of the partnership for a taxation year from any source or from sources in a particular place exceeds, in respect of each such source, the portion of the partnership's taxable non-portfolio earnings for the taxation year that is applicable to that source"; and

(*b*) the partnership is deemed to have received a dividend in the taxation year from a taxable Canadian corporation equal to the amount by which the partnership's taxable non-portfolio earnings for the taxation year exceeds the tax payable by the partnership for the taxation year under Part IX.1.

Editorial Note: Part IX.1 imposes a tax on the "taxable non-portfolio earnings" of a "SIFT partnership" or specified investment flow-through partnership (defined in s. 197(1)) at a rate that approximates the general corporate tax rate. S. 96(1.11)(*b*) provides that the SIFT partnership is deemed to have received a taxable dividend in the taxation year from a taxable Canadian corporation equal to the amount by which the partnership's taxable non-portfolio earnings for the year exceeds the partnership's Part IX.1 tax payable for the year. The taxable dividend is included as an eligible dividend in the income of the partners under the general provisions of s. 96(1).

Related Sections: S. 89(1), "eligible dividend", "taxable dividend"; s. 197(1), "non-portfolio earnings", "SIFT partnership", "taxable non-portfolio earnings"; s. 197(2) Tax on partnership income.

▶ 96(1.2) ◀

(1.2) Disposal of right to share in income, etc. Where in a taxation year a taxpayer who has a right to a share of the income or loss of a partnership under an agreement referred to in subsection (1.1) disposes of that right,

(*a*) there shall be included in computing the taxpayer's income for the year the proceeds of the disposition; and

(*b*) for greater certainty, the cost to the taxpayer of each property received by the taxpayer as consideration for the disposition is the fair market value of the property at the time of the disposition.

Editorial Note: The amount included under s. 96(1.2) (net of any deduction under subsection (1.3)) is not a capital gain, but rather ordinary income; see also s. 96(1.4) which provides that the right is deemed not to be capital property.

Related Sections: S. 54, "proceeds of disposition".

▶ 96(1.3) ◀

(1.3) Deductions. Where, by virtue of subsection (1.1) or (1.2), an amount has been included in computing a taxpayer's income for a taxation year, there may be deducted in computing the taxpayer's income for the year the lesser of

(*a*) the amount so included in computing the taxpayer's income for the year, and

(*b*) the amount, if any, by which the cost to the taxpayer of the right to a share of the income or loss of a partnership under an agreement referred to in subsection (1.1) exceeds the total of all amounts in respect of that right that were deductible by virtue of this subsection in computing the taxpayer's income for previous taxation years.

Editorial Note: See the note under s. 96(1.5) regarding the CRA position on the cost of the right to a beneficiary of a deceased former partner.

Interpretation Bulletins: *Secondary* — IT-278R2 Death of a partner or of a retired partner.

► 96(1.4) ◄

(1.4) Right deemed not to be capital property. For the purposes of this Act, a right to a share of the income or loss of a partnership under an agreement referred to in subsection (1.1) shall be deemed not to be capital property.

Related Sections: S. 54, "capital property".

► 96(1.5) ◄

(1.5) Disposition by virtue of death of taxpayer. Where, at the time of a taxpayer's death, the taxpayer has a right to a share of the income or loss of a partnership under an agreement referred to in subsection (1.1), subsections 70(2) to (4) apply.

Editorial Note: The right is considered a "right or thing", and therefore, either included in the deceased taxpayer's income under s. 70(2) or the taxpayer's beneficiary's income under s. 70(3). In the latter case, the CRA takes the position that the amount so included is considered to be the beneficiary's cost of the interest, such that it may be deducted under s. 96(1.3) from the s. 96(1.1) inclusion, so as to prevent double taxation; see paragraph 15 of Interpretation Bulletin IT-278R2 (archived, as it doesn't meet current government web standards).

Related Sections: 70(2) Amounts receivable; 70(3) Rights or things transferred to beneficiaries; 70(3.1) Exception; 70(4) Revocation of election.

Interpretation Bulletins: *Secondary* — IT-212R3 Income of deceased persons — Rights or things; IT-278R2 Death of a partner or of a retired partner.

► 96(1.6) ◄

(1.6) Members deemed carrying on business. If a partnership carries on a business in Canada at any time, each taxpayer who is deemed by paragraph (1.1)(*a*) to be a member of the partnership at that time is deemed to carry on the business in Canada at that time for the purposes of subsection 2(3), sections 34.1 and 150 and (subject to subsection 34.2(18)) section 34.2.

History: S. 96(1.6) was replaced by S.C. 2013, c. 40, s. 43(1), applicable to taxation years that end after March 22, 2011, and formerly read:

(1.6) *Members of partnership deemed to be carrying on business in Canada.* Where a partnership carries on a business in Canada at any time, each taxpayer who is deemed by paragraph (1.1)(*a*) to be a member of the partnership at that time is deemed to carry on the business in Canada at that time for the purposes of subsection 2(3), sections 34.1 and 150 and (subject to subsection 34.2(7)) section 34.2.

Related Sections: S. 2(3) Tax payable by non-resident persons; s. 96(1.1) Allocation of share of income to retiring partner; s. 249.1(4) Alternative method.

Tax Window Files: Payment to Widow of Retired Partner, *Technical Interpretation, International & Trusts Division, November 29, 2006*, CRA Document No. 2005-0140621E5.

► 96(1.7) ◄

(1.7) Gains and losses. Notwithstanding subsection (1) or section 38, if in a particular taxation year of a taxpayer, the taxpayer is a member of a partnership with a fiscal period that ends in the particular year, the amount of a taxable capital gain, allowable capital loss or allowable business investment loss of the taxpayer for the particular year determined in respect of the partnership is the amount determined by the formula

$$A \times B/C$$

where

A is the amount of the taxpayer's taxable capital gain, allowable capital loss or allowable business investment loss, as the case may be, for the particular year otherwise determined under this section in respect of the partnership;

B is the relevant fraction that applies under paragraph 38(*a*), (*a*.1), (*a*.2), (*b*) or (*c*) for the particular year in respect of the taxpayer; and

C is the fraction that was used under section 38 for the fiscal period of the partnership.

History: S. 96(1.7), the portion before the formula was replaced by S.C. 2016, c. 12, s. 32(1), in force January 1, 2017, and formerly read:

(1.7) *Gains and losses.* Notwithstanding subsection (1) or section 38, where in a particular taxation year of a taxpayer, the taxpayer is a member of a partnership with a fiscal period that ends in the particular year, the amount of a taxable capital gain (other than that part of the amount that can reasonably be attributed to an amount deemed under subsection 14(1.1) to be a taxable capital gain of the partnership), allowable capital loss or allowable business investment loss of the taxpayer for the particular year determined in respect of the partnership is the amount determined by the formula

S. 96(1.7), the description of A was replaced by S.C. 2016, c. 12, s. 32(2), in force January 1, 2017, and formerly read:

A is the amount of the taxpayer's taxable capital gain (other than that part of the amount that can be attributed to an amount deemed under subsection 14(1.1) to be a taxable capital gain of the partnership), allowable capital loss or allowable business investment loss, as the case may be, for the particular year otherwise determined under this section in respect of the partnership;

[**Election for 2000 Taxation Year**] If a taxpayer, who is a member of a partnership at the end of a particular fiscal period, of the partnership, that ends in the taxpayer's 2000 taxation year, so elects in writing and files the election with the Minister of National Revenue on or before the taxpayer's filing-due date for the taxpayer's taxation year which includes June 26, 2013,

(*a*) subsection 96(1.7) of the Act does not apply to the taxpayer's 2000 taxation year;

(*b*) the taxpayer is deemed to have a capital gain, a capital loss or a business investment loss in respect of the partnership for the particular fiscal period equal to the amount of the taxable capital gain, the allowable capital loss or the allowable business investment loss in respect of the partnership for the particular fiscal period, as the case may be, multiplied by the reciprocal of the fraction in paragraph 38(*a*) of the Act that applies to the partnership for the particular fiscal period;

(*c*) the amount of a capital gain, a capital loss or a business investment loss determined under paragraph (*b*) is deemed to be a capital gain, a capital loss or a business investment loss, as the case may be, of the taxpayer from a disposition of a capital property on the day that the particular fiscal period ends; and

(*d*) except as provided by this subsection, no amount shall be included in computing the taxpayer's taxable capital gains, allowable capital losses and allowable business investment losses in respect of the taxable capital gains, allowable capital losses and allowable business investment losses of the partnership for the particular fiscal period. This application was added by 2013, c. 34, s. 228(11).

Related Sections: S. 108(1), "testamentary trust".

► 96(1.71) ◄

(1.71) Application. Where the fraction referred to in the description of C in subsection (1.7) cannot be determined by a taxpayer in respect of a fiscal period of a partnership that ended before February 28, 2000, or includes February 28, 2000 or October 17, 2000, for the purposes of subsection (1.7), the fraction is deemed to be (*a*) where the fiscal period ended before or began before February 28, 2000, 3/4;

(*b*) where the fiscal period began after February 27, 2000 and before October 18, 2000, 2/3; and

(*c*) in any other case, 1/2.

► 96(1.8) ◄

(1.8) Loan of property. For the purposes of subsection 56(4.1) and sections 74.1 and 74.3, where an individual has transferred or lent property, either directly or indirectly, by means of a trust or by any other means whatever, to a person and the property or property substituted therefor is an interest in a partnership, the person's share of the amount of any income or loss of the partnership for a fiscal period in which the person was a specified member of the partnership shall be deemed to be income or loss, as the case may be, from the property or substituted property.

Editorial Note: S. 96(1.8) effectively provides that the income attribution rules can apply to income or loss from a transferred or lent partnership interest, by deeming the income or loss therefrom to be from the property rather than the underlying partnership source.

Related Sections: S. 249.1(1) Definition of "fiscal period".

► 96(2) ◄

(2) Construction. The provisions of this subdivision shall be read and construed as if each of the assumptions in paragraphs (1)(*a*) to (g) were made.

► 96(2.01) ◄

(2.01) Tiered partnerships. For the purposes of this section, a taxpayer includes a partnership.

History: S. 96(2.01) was added by S.C. 2018, c. 27, s. 8(1), applicable to taxation years that end after February 26, 2018.

► 96(2.1) ◄

(2.1) Limited partnership losses. Notwithstanding subsection (1), where a taxpayer is, at any time in a taxation year, a limited partner of a partnership, the amount, if any, by which

(*a*) the total of all amounts each of which is the taxpayer's share of the amount of any loss of the partnership, determined in accordance with subsection (1), for a fiscal period of the partnership ending in the taxation year from a business (other than a farming business) or from property

exceeds

(*b*) the amount, if any, by which

(i) the taxpayer's at-risk amount in respect of the partnership at the end of the fiscal period

exceeds the total of

(ii) the amount required by subsection 127(8) in respect of the partnership to be added in computing the investment tax credit of the taxpayer for the taxation year,

(iii) the taxpayer's share of any losses of the partnership for the fiscal period from a farming business, and

(iv) the taxpayer's share of

(A) the foreign resource pool expenses, if any, incurred by the partnership in the fiscal period,

(B) the Canadian exploration expense, if any, incurred by the partnership in the fiscal period,

(C) the Canadian development expense, if any, incurred by the partnership in the fiscal period, and

(D) the Canadian oil and gas property expense, if any, incurred by the partnership in the fiscal period,

shall

(*c*) not be deducted in computing the taxpayer's income for the year,

(*d*) not be included in computing the taxpayer's non-capital loss for the year,

(*e*) if the taxpayer is not a partnership, be deemed to be the taxpayer's limited partnership loss in respect of the partnership for the year, and

(*f*) if the taxpayer is a partnership, reduce the taxpayer's share of any loss of the partnership for a fiscal period of the partnership ending in the taxation year of the taxpayer from a business (other than a farming business) or from property.

Editorial Note: See s. 96(2.2) regarding the calculation of the at-risk amount and s. 96(2.4) regarding the definition of "limited partner". The non-deductible portion of the loss under s. 96(2.1) is deemed to be the taxpayer's limited partnership loss, which can be carried forward indefinitely to future taxation years under s. 111(1)(*e*), subject again to the taxpayer's at-risk amount in the future year. Unlike regular losses, the non-deductible portion of the loss does not reduce the adjusted cost base of the taxpayer's interest in the partnership, unless and until it is deducted in the future year.

Historically, it was not clear whether the at-risk rules applied where a partnership was a limited partner ("upper partnership") of another partnership ("lower partnership"), such as in a tiered partnership structure. The 2018 Federal Budget "clarified" that the at-risk rules apply to an upper partnership that is itself a limited partner of a lower partnership. Accordingly, for taxation years that end after February 26, 2018, a partnership is deemed to be a taxpayer for the purposes of section 96, and therefore also for the provisions of subsection 96(2.1). The excess losses as described above, which continue to be limited partnership losses for other partners, will instead reduce the upper partnership's share of the losses of the lower partnership (other than farming business losses). Effectively, this means that the upper partnership's share of the losses of the lower partnership that can be allocated to the upper partnership's partners are limited to the upper partnership's at-risk amount in respect of the lower partnership. The non-deductible portion remains reflected in the upper partnership's adjusted cost base of its interest in the lower partnership.

History: S. 96(2.1)(*e*) was replaced and (*f*) was added by S.C. 2018, c. 27, s. 8(2), applicable to taxation years that end after February 26, 2018, and formerly read:

(*e*) be deemed to be the taxpayer's limited partnership loss in respect of the partnership for the year.

Related Sections: S. 40(3.1) Deemed gain for certain partners; s. 66.8(1) Resource expenses of limited partner; s. 96(2.2) At-risk amount; s. 96(2.4) Limited partner; s. 111(1)(*e*) Limited partnership losses; s. 127(8.1) Investment tax credit of limited partner; s. 143.2(6) Amount of expenditure; s. 249.1(1) Definition of "fiscal period".

Canadian Tax Foundation: Cheung and Chelstowska, *A Taxpayer Win on At-Risk Rules*, 2017 Canadian Tax Focus 7(3):4–5; Reid and Davies, *Tiered Partnership Losses*, 2016 Tax for the Owner-Manager 16(2):4–5; Fyfe, *The Taxation of Renewable Energy Investments in Canada*, 2011 Conference Report 42:1–42.

Tax Profile: December 2011 — Partnership Taxation; October 2011 — Hedge Funds and Private Equity Funds in Canada.

Tax Topics: No. 2418, Treatment of Limited Partnership Losses in Multi-Tier Partnership Structures Post-*Canada v. Green*; No. 2383, The Losses That Flow?; No. 1921, Ontario Limited Liability Partnerships — A Hidden Danger for Many Inventory.

Interpretation Bulletins: *Secondary* — IT-232R3 Losses — Their deductibility in the loss year or in other years.

Tax Window Files: Limited partnership losses and dissolution, *January 6, 2014*, CRA Document No. 2013-0477711E5; Limited Partnership Losses of Tier Partnership, *Technical Interpretation, Business and Partnerships Division, May 14, 2004*, CRA Document No. 2004-0062801E5. Allocation of losses of limited partnership unavailable to members of top partnership that was member of limited partnership.

Cases: Losses from a business incurred by a lower-tier partnership would still be losses from a business in the top-tier partnership and may be allocated to the partners of that top-tier partnership as losses from that business. *The Queen v. Green et al*, 2017 DTC 5068 (FCA)

Business losses of a bottom-tier partnership that exceed the top-tier partnership's at-risk amount in respect of the limited partnership do not cease to be business losses and are available to be flowed out to the partners of the top-tier partnership. *Green et al. v. The Queen*, 2017 DTC 5068 (FCA) [Subject to the Budget 2018 proposed amendments at clause 26(2)]

A limited partner was entitled to deduct its proportionate share of partnership losses without restriction as to its capital contribution where such losses were incurred in 1974 and 1975 prior to the introduction of provisions restricting such losses. *Signum Communications Inc. v. The Queen*, 91 DTC 5360 (F.C.A.), affirming 88 DTC 6427 (F.C.T.D.)

▶ 96(2.11) ◀

(2.11) Tiered partnerships — adjustments. The following rules apply to taxation years of a taxpayer that end after February 26, 2018:

(*a*) for the purpose of applying section 111, the taxpayer's non-capital loss, or limited partnership loss in respect of a partnership, for a preceding taxation year shall be determined as if subsection (2.01) and paragraph (2.1)(*f*) applied in respect of taxation years that end before February 27, 2018; and

(*b*) in computing the adjusted cost base to the taxpayer of the taxpayer's interest in a partnership after February 26, 2018, there shall be added an amount equal to the portion of the amount of any reduction because of paragraph (*a*) in a non-capital loss of the taxpayer that can reasonably be considered to relate to the amount of a loss deducted under subparagraph 53(2)(*c*)(i) in computing the adjusted cost base of that interest.

History: S. 96(2.11) was added by S.C. 2018, c. 27, s. 8(3), in force December 13, 2018.

▶ 96(2.2) ◀

(2.2) At-risk amount. For the purposes of this section and sections 111 and 127, the at-risk amount of a taxpayer, in respect of a partnership of which the taxpayer is a limited partner, at any particular time is the amount, if any, by which the total of

(*a*) the adjusted cost base to the taxpayer of the taxpayer's partnership interest at that time, computed in accordance with subsection (2.3) where applicable,

(*b*) where the particular time is the end of the fiscal period of the partnership, the taxpayer's share of the income of the partnership from a source for that fiscal period computed under the method described in subparagraph 53(1)(*e*)(i), and

(*b*.1) where the particular time is the end of the fiscal period of the partnership, the amount referred to in subparagraph 53(1)(*e*)(viii) in respect of the taxpayer for that fiscal period

exceeds the total of

(*c*) all amounts each of which is an amount owing at that time to the partnership, or to a person or partnership not dealing at arm's length with the partnership, by the taxpayer or by a person or partnership not dealing at arm's length with the taxpayer, other than any amount deducted under subparagraph 53(2)(*c*)(i.3) in computing the adjusted cost base, or under section 143.2 in computing the cost, to the taxpayer of the taxpayer's partnership interest at that time, and

(*d*) any amount or benefit that the taxpayer or a person not dealing at arm's length with the taxpayer is entitled, either immediately or in the future and either absolutely or contingently, to receive or to obtain, whether by way of reimbursement, compensation, revenue guarantee, proceeds of disposition, loan or any other form of indebtedness or in any other form or manner whatever, granted or to be granted for the purpose of reducing the impact, in whole or in part, of any loss that the taxpayer may sustain because the taxpayer is a member of the partnership or holds or disposes of an interest in the partnership, except to the extent that the amount or benefit is included in the determination of the value of J in the definition "cumulative Canadian exploration expense" in subsection 66.1(6), of M in the definition "cumulative Canadian development expense" in subsection 66.2(5) or of I in the definition "cumulative Canadian oil and gas property expense" in subsection 66.4(5) in respect of the taxpayer, or the entitlement arises

(i) by virtue of a contract of insurance with an insurance corporation dealing at arm's length with each member of the partnership under which the taxpayer is insured against any claim arising as a result of a liability incurred in the ordinary course of carrying on the partnership business,

(ii) (Repealed by S.C. 1996, c. 21, s. 17(4).)

(iii) as a consequence of the death of the taxpayer,

(iv) (Repealed by S.C. 1998, c. 19, s. 123(3).)

(v) (Repealed by S.C. 1998, c. 19, s. 123(3).)

(vi) in respect of an amount not included in the at-risk amount of the taxpayer determined without reference to this paragraph, or

(vii) because of an excluded obligation (as defined in subsection 6202.1(5) of the *Income Tax Regulations*) in relation to a share issued to the partnership by a corporation,

and, for the purposes of this subsection,

(*e*) where the amount or benefit to which the taxpayer or the person is entitled at any time is provided by way of an agreement or other arrangement under which the taxpayer or the person has a right, either immediately or in the future and either absolutely or contingently (otherwise than as a consequence of the death of the taxpayer), to acquire other property in exchange for all or any part of the partnership interest, for greater certainty the amount or benefit to which the taxpayer or the person is entitled under the agreement or arrangement is considered to be not less than the fair market value of the other property at that time, and

(*f*) where the amount or benefit to which the taxpayer or the person is entitled at any time is provided by way of a guarantee, security or similar indemnity or covenant in respect of any loan or other obligation of the taxpayer or the person, for greater certainty the amount or benefit to which the taxpayer or the person is entitled under the guarantee or indemnity at any particular time is considered to be not less than the total of the unpaid amount of the loan or obligation at that time and all other amounts outstanding in respect of the loan or obligation at that time.

Related Regulations: Part LXXV.

Related Sections: S. 40(3.1) Deemed gain for certain partners; s. 53(1)(*e*) Adjustments to cost base — Interest in a partnership; s. 53(2)(*c*) Amounts to be deducted — Interest in a partnership; s. 54 Definitions; s. 143.2(2) At-risk adjustment.

Tax Profile: December 2011 — Partnership Taxation; July 2003 — New Law for Software Tax Shelters.

Cases: The taxpayer's contribution to a partnership consisted of a cash payment of $4000 per unit and assumption of a proportionate share of a promissory note in the amount of $6000 per unit. However, since an amending agreement provided for the retraction of the taxpayer's partnership units for $8,000 each, only $2000 per unit was at risk. *Brown v. The Queen*, 2003 DTC 5298 (F.C.A.), affirming, in part, unreported (T.C.C.)

► 96(2.3) ◄

(2.3) Idem. For the purposes of subsection (2.2), where a taxpayer has acquired the taxpayer's partnership interest at any time from a transferor other than the partnership, the adjusted cost base to the taxpayer of that interest shall be computed as if the cost to the taxpayer of the interest were the lesser of

(*a*) the taxpayer's cost otherwise determined, and

(*b*) the greater of

(i) the adjusted cost base of that interest to the transferor immediately before that time, and

(ii) nil,

and where the adjusted cost base of the transferor cannot be determined, it shall be deemed to be equal to the total of the amounts determined in respect of the taxpayer under paragraphs (2.2)(*c*) and (*d*) immediately after that time.

► 96(2.4) ◄

(2.4) Limited partner. For the purposes of this section and sections 111 and 127, a taxpayer who is a member of a partnership at a particular time is a limited partner of the partnership at that time if the member's partnership interest is not an exempt interest (within the meaning assigned by subsection (2.5)) at that time and if, at that time or within 3 years after that time,

(*a*) by operation of any law governing the partnership arrangement, the liability of the member as a member of the partnership is limited (except by operation of a provision of a statute of Canada or a province that limits the member's liability only for debts, obligations and liabilities of the partnership, or any member of the partnership, arising from negligent acts or omissions, from misconduct or from fault of another member of the partnership or an employee, an agent or a representative of the partnership in the course of the partnership business while the partnership is a limited liability partnership);

(*b*) the member or a person not dealing at arm's length with the member is entitled, either immediately or in the future and either absolutely or contingently, to receive an amount or to obtain a benefit that would be described in paragraph (2.2)(*d*) if that paragraph were read without reference to subparagraphs (ii) and (vi);

(*c*) one of the reasons for the existence of the member who owns the interest

(i) can reasonably be considered to be to limit the liability of any person with respect to that interest, and

(ii) cannot reasonably be considered to be to permit any person who has an interest in the member to carry on that person's business (other than an investment business) in the most effective manner; or

(*d*) there is an agreement or other arrangement for the disposition of an interest in the partnership and one of the main reasons for the agreement or arrangement can reasonably be considered to be to attempt to avoid the application of this subsection to the member.

History: S. 96(2.4)(*a*) was replaced by S.C. 2013, c. 34, s. 228(4), deemed to have come into force on June 21, 2001, and formerly read:

(*a*) by operation of any law governing the partnership arrangement, the liability of the member as a member of the partnership is limited (except by operation of a provision of a statute of Canada or a province that limits the member's liability only for debts, obligations and liabilities of the partnership, or any member of the partnership, arising from negligent acts or omissions or misconduct that another member of the partnership or an employee, agent or representative of the partnership commits in the course of the partnership business while the partnership is a limited liability partnership);

Related Sections: S. 40(3,14) Limited partner; s. 96(2.5) Exempt interest.

Canadian Tax Foundation: Tollstam, *Limited Partnership Loss in a Trust*, 2014 Canadian Tax Highlights 22(7):10–11.

Tax Topics: No. 1921, Ontario Limited Liability Partnerships — A Hidden Danger for Many Inventory.

Interpretation Bulletins: *Secondary* — IT-232R3 Losses — Their deductibility in the loss year or in other years.

Cases: An amending agreement which provided partners with the right to redeem partnership units for $8000 per unit came into effect within the three-year period after the taxpayer sought to deduct his partnership losses. Hence, the taxpayer was a deemed limited partner to whom the at risk rules applied. *Brown v. The Queen*, 2003 DTC 5298 (F.C.A.), affirming, in part, unreported (T.C.C.)

► 96(2.5) ◄

(2.5) Exempt interest. For the purposes of subsection (2.4), an exempt interest in a partnership at any time means a prescribed partnership interest or an interest in a partnership that was actively carrying on business on a regular and a continuous basis immediately before February 26, 1986 and continuously thereafter until that time or that was earning income from the rental or leasing of property immediately before February 26, 1986 and continuously thereafter until that time, where there has not after February 25, 1986 and before that time been a substantial contribution of capital to the partnership or a substantial increase in the indebtedness of the partnership and, for this purpose, an amount will not be considered to be substantial where

(*a*) the amount was used by the partnership to make an expenditure required to be made pursuant to the terms of a written agreement entered into by it before February 26, 1986, or to repay a loan, debt or contribution of capital that had been received or incurred in respect of any such expenditure, (*b*) the amount was raised pursuant to the terms of a prospectus, preliminary prospectus or registration statement filed before February 26, 1986 with a public authority in Canada pursuant to and in accordance with the securities legislation of Canada or of any province, and, where required by law, accepted for filing by that public authority, or

(*c*) the amount was used for the activity that was carried on by the partnership on February 25, 1986 but was not used for a significant expansion of the activity

and, for the purposes of this subsection,

(*d*) a partnership in respect of which paragraph (*b*) applies shall be considered to have been actively carrying on a business on a regular and a continuous basis immediately before February 26, 1986 and continuously thereafter until the earlier of the closing date, if any, stipulated in the document referred to in that paragraph and January 1, 1987, and

(*e*) an expenditure shall not be considered to have been required to be made pursuant to the terms of an agreement where the obligation to make the expenditure is conditional in any way on the consequences under this Act relating to the expenditure and the condition has not been satisfied or waived before June 12, 1986.

▶ 96(2.6) ◀

(2.6) Artificial transactions. For the purposes of paragraph (2.2)(*c*), where at any time an amount owing by a taxpayer or a person with whom the taxpayer does not deal at arm's length is repaid and it is established, by subsequent events or otherwise, that the repayment was made as part of a series of loans or other transactions and repayments, the amount owing shall be deemed not to have been repaid.

▶ 96(2.7) ◀

(2.7) Idem. For the purposes of paragraph (2.2)(*a*), where at any time a taxpayer makes a contribution of capital to a partnership and the partnership or a person or partnership with whom or which the partnership does not deal at arm's length makes a loan to the taxpayer or to a person with whom the taxpayer does not deal at arm's length or repays the contribution of capital, and it is established, by subsequent events or otherwise, that the loan or repayment, as the case may be, was made as part of a series of loans or other transactions and repayments, the contribution of capital shall be deemed not to have been made to the extent of the loan or repayment, as the case may be.

▶ 96(3) ◀

(3) Agreement or election of partnership members. If a taxpayer who was a member of a partnership at any time in a fiscal period has, for any purpose relevant to the computation of the taxpayer's income from the partnership for the fiscal period, made or executed an agreement, designation or election under or in respect of the application of any of subsections 10.1(1), 13(4), (4.2) and (16), section 15.2, subsections 20(9) and 21(1) to (4), section 22, subsection 29(1), section 34, clause 37(8)(*a*)(ii)(B), subsections 44(1) and (6), 50(1) and 80(5) and (9) to (11), section 80.04, subsections 86.1(2), 88(3.1), (3.3) and (3.5) and 90(3), the definition *relevant cost base* in subsection 95(4) and subsections 97(2), 139.1(16) and (17) and 249.1(4) and (6) that, if this Act were read without reference to this subsection, would be a valid agreement, designation or election,

(*a*) the agreement, designation or election is not valid unless

(i) it was made or executed on behalf of the taxpayer and each other person who was a member of the partnership during the fiscal period, and

(ii) the taxpayer had authority to act for the partnership;

(*b*) unless the agreement, designation or election is invalid because of paragraph (*a*), each other person who was a member of the partnership during the fiscal period shall be deemed to have made or executed the agreement, designation or election; and

(*c*) notwithstanding paragraph (*a*), any agreement, designation or election deemed by paragraph (*b*) to have been made or executed by any person shall be deemed to be a valid agreement, designation or election made or executed by that person.

History: S. 96(3), the portion before paragraph (*a*) was replaced by S.C. 2017, c. 33, s. 31(1), applicable to taxation years that begin after March 21, 2017, and formerly read:

(3) *Agreement or election of partnership members.* If a taxpayer who was a member of a partnership at any time in a fiscal period has, for any purpose relevant to the computation of the taxpayer's income from the partnership for the fiscal period, made or executed an agreement, designation or election under or in respect of the application of any of subsections 13(4), (4.2) and (16), section 15.2, subsections 20(9) and 21(1) to (4), section 22, subsection 29(1), section 34, clause 37(8)(*a*)(ii)(B), subsections 44(1) and (6), 50(1) and 80(5) and (9) to (11), section 80.04, subsections 86.1(2), 88(3.1), (3.3) and (3.5) and 90(3), the definition "relevant cost base" in subsection 95(4) and subsections 97(2), 139.1(16) and (17) and 249.1(4) and (6) that, if this Act were read without reference to this subsection, would be a valid agreement, designation or election,

S. 96(3), the portion before paragraph (*a*) was replaced by S.C. 2016, c. 12, s. 32(3), in force January 1, 2017, and formerly read:

S. (3) *Agreement or election of partnership members.* If a taxpayer who was a member of a partnership at any time in a fiscal period has, for any purpose relevant to the computation of the taxpayer's income from the partnership for the fiscal period, made or executed an agreement, designation or election under or in respect of the application of any of subsections 13(4), (4.2) and (16) and 14(1.01), (1.02) and (6), section 15.2, subsections 20(9) and 21(1) to (4), section 22, subsection 29(1), section 34, clause 37(8)(*a*)(ii)(B), subsections 44(1) and (6), 50(1) and 80(5) and (9) to (11), section 80.04, subsections 86.1(2), 88(3.1), (3.3) and (3.5) and 90(3), the definition "relevant cost base" in subsection 95(4) and subsections 97(2), 139.1(16) and (17) and 249.1(4) and (6) that, if this Act were read without reference to this subsection, would be a valid agreement, designation or election,

S. 96(3), the portion before paragraph (*a*) was replaced by S.C. 2013, c. 34, s. 71(1), applicable to agreements, designations and elections made or executed after August 19, 2011.

Any assessment of a taxpayer's tax, interest and penalties payable under the Act for any taxation year that ends before June 26, 2013 that would, in the absence of this section, be precluded because of subsections 152(4) to (5) of the Act shall be made to the extent necessary to take into account the amendments by S.C. 2013, c. 34, s. 54 to 89.

S. 96(3), the portion before paragraph (*a*) formerly read:

(3) *Agreement or election of partnership members.* If a taxpayer who was a member of a partnership at any time in a fiscal period has, for any purpose relevant to the computation of the taxpayer's income from the partnership for the fiscal period, made or executed an agreement, designation or election under or in respect of the application of any of subsections 13(4), (4.2) and (16) and 14(1.01), (1.02) and (6), section 15.2, subsections 20(9) and 21(1) to (4), section 22, subsection 29(1), section 34, clause 37(8)(*a*)(ii)(B), subsections 44(1) and (6), 50(1) and 80(5) and (9) to (11), section 80.04 and subsections 86.1(2), 97(2), 139.1(16) and (17) and

249.1(4) and (6) that, if this Act were read without reference to this subsection, would be a valid agreement, designation or election,

S. 96(3), the portion before paragraph (*a*) was replaced by S.C. 2013, c. 34, s. 228(5), applicable to taxation years that end after February 27, 2000. However, subsection 96(3) is before December 21, 2002 to be read without reference to ", (4.2)" and ", (1.02)". S. 96(3), the portion before paragraph (*a*) formerly read:

(3) *Agreement or election of partnership members.* Where a taxpayer who was a member of a partnership at any time in a fiscal period has, for any purpose relevant to the computation of the taxpayer's income from the partnership for the fiscal period, made or executed an agreement, designation or election under or in respect of the application of any of subsections 13(4) and (16) and 14(6), section 15.2, subsections 20(9) and 21(1) to (4), section 22, subsection 29(1), section 34, clause 37(8)(*a*)(ii)(B), subsections 44(1) and (6), 50(1) and 80(5), (9), (10) and (11), section 80.04, subsections 86.1(2), 97(2), 139.1(16) and (17) and 249.1(4) and (6) that, but for this subsection, would be a valid agreement, designation or election,

Related Sections: S. 14(1) Eligible capital property — inclusion in income from business; s. 14(5), "cumulative eligible capital", "eligible capital expenditure"; s. 24(3) Where partnership has ceased to exist; s. 54, "eligible capital property"; s. 248(1), "business", "cost amount", "cumulative eligible capital", "eligible capital amount", "eligible capital expenditure", "eligible capital property", "property"; s. 249.1(4) Alternative method.

Interpretation Bulletins: *Primary* — IT-413R Election by members of a partnership under subsection 97(2). *Secondary* — IT-278R2 Death of a partner or of a retired partner; IT-457R Election by professionals to exclude work in progress from income.

▶ 96(4) ◀

(4) Election. Any election under subsection 97(2) or 98(3) shall be made on or before the day that is the earliest of the days on or before which any taxpayer making the election is required to file a return of income pursuant to section 150 for the taxpayer's taxation year in which the transaction to which the election relates occurred.

Forms: T2059 Election on Disposition of Property by a Taxpayer to a Canadian Partnership; T2060 Election for Disposition of Property Upon Cessation of Partnership.

Interpretation Bulletins: *Secondary* — IT-413R Election by members of a partnership under subsection 97(2).

▶ 96(5) ◀

(5) Late filing. Where an election referred to in subsection (4) was not made on or before the day on or before which the election was required by that subsection to be made and that day was after May 6, 1974, the election shall be deemed to have been made on that day if, on or before the day that is 3 years after that day,

(*a*) the election is made in prescribed form; and

(*b*) an estimate of the penalty in respect of that election is paid by the taxpayer referred to in subsection 97(2) or by the persons referred to in subsection 98(3), as the case may be, when that election is made.

Related Sections: S. 14(5), "cumulative eligible capital"; s. 24(3) Where partnership has ceased to exist; s. 54, "eligible capital property"; s. 96(4) Election; s. 97(2) Rules where election by partners; s. 98(3) Rules applicable where partnership ceases to exist; s. 248(1), "amount", "business", "cost amount", "cumulative eligible capital", "eligible capital property", "property".

Interpretation Bulletins: *Secondary* — IT-413R Election by members of a partnership under subsection 97(2).

▶ 96(5.1) ◀

(5.1) Special cases. Where, in the opinion of the Minister, the circumstances of a case are such that it would be just and equitable

(*a*) to permit an election under subsection 97(2) or 98(3) to be made after the day that is 3 years after the day on or before which the election was required by subsection (4) to be made, or

(*b*) to permit an election made under subsection 97(2) to be amended,

the election or amended election shall be deemed to have been made on the day on or before which the election was so required to be made if

(*c*) the election or amended election is made in prescribed form, and

(*d*) an estimate of the penalty in respect of the election or amended election is paid by the taxpayer referred to in subsection 97(2) or by the persons referred to in subsection 98(3), as the case may be, when the election or amended election is made,

and where this subsection applies to the amendment of an election, that election shall be deemed not to have been effective.

Canadian Tax Foundation: Gill, *Backdoor Amendment of the Elected Amount in Rollovers*, 2017 Canadian Tax Focus 7(3):1–2.

Interpretation Bulletins: *Secondary* — IT-413R Election by members of a partnership under subsection 97(2).

▶ 96(6) ◀

(6) Penalty for late-filed election. For the purposes of this section, the penalty in respect of an election or an amended election referred to in paragraph (5)(*a*) or (5.1)(*c*) is

(*a*) where the election or amended election is made under subsection 97(2), an amount equal to the lesser of

(i) 1/4 of 1% of the amount by which the fair market value of the property disposed of by the taxpayer referred to therein at the time of disposition exceeds the amount agreed on by the taxpayer and the members of the partnership in the election or amended election, for each month or part of a month during the period commencing with the day on or before which the election is required by subsection (4) to be made and ending on the day the election or amended election is made, and

(ii) an amount, not exceeding $8,000, equal to the product obtained by multiplying $100 by the number of months each of which is a month all or part of which is during the period referred to in subparagraph (i); and

(*b*) where the election is made under subsection 98(3), an amount equal to the lesser of

(i) 1/4 of 1% of the amount by which

(A) the total of all amounts of money and the fair market value of partnership property received by the persons referred to therein as consideration for their interests in the partnership at the time that the partnership ceased to exist

exceeds

(B) the total of each such person's proceeds of disposition of that person's interest in the partnership as determined under paragraph 98(3)(*a*),

for each month or part of a month during the period commencing with the day on or before which the election is required by subsection (4) to be made and ending on the day the election or amended election is made, and

(ii) an amount, not exceeding $8,000, equal to the product obtained by multiplying $100 by the number of months each of which is a month all or part of which is during the period referred to in subparagraph (i).

Related Sections: S. 96(5) Late filing; s. 97(2) Rules where election by partners; s. 98(3) Rules applicable where partnership ceases to exist.

Interpretation Bulletins: *Secondary* — IT-413R Election by members of a partnership under subsection 97(2).

Tax Window Files: Price Adjustment Clauses, *Technical Interpretation, Reorganizations and Resources Division, July 6, 2004,* CRA Document No. 2004-0081631E5.

▶ 96(7) ◀

(7) Unpaid balance of penalty. The Minister shall, with all due dispatch, examine each election and amended election referred to in paragraph (5)(*a*) or (5.1)(*c*), assess the penalty payable and send a notice of assessment to the taxpayer or persons, as the case may be, and the taxpayer or persons, as the case may be, shall pay forthwith to the Receiver General the amount, if any, by which the penalty so assessed exceeds the total of all amounts previously paid on account of that penalty.

Related Sections: S. 96(5) Late filing; s. 111(8), "net capital loss", "non-capital loss".

▶ 96(8) ◀

(8) Foreign partnerships. For the purposes of this Act, where at a particular time a person resident in Canada becomes a member of a partnership, or a person who is a member of a partnership becomes resident in Canada, and immediately before the particular time no member of the partnership is resident in Canada, the following rules apply for the purpose of computing the partnership's income for fiscal periods ending after the particular time:

(*a*) where, at or before the particular time, the partnership held depreciable property of a prescribed class (other than taxable Canadian property),

(i) no amount shall be included in determining the amounts for any of A, C, D and F to I in the definition "undepreciated capital cost" in subsection 13(21) in respect of the acquisition or disposition before the particular time of the property, and

(ii) where the property is the partnership's property at the particular time, the property shall be deemed to have been acquired, immediately after the particular time, by the partnership at a capital cost equal to the lesser of its fair market value and its capital cost to the partnership otherwise determined;

(*b*) in the case of the partnership's property that is inventory (other than inventory of a business carried on in Canada) or non-depreciable capital property (other than taxable Canadian property) of the partnership at the particular time, its cost to the partnership shall be deemed to be, immediately after the particular time, equal to the lesser of its fair market value and its cost to the partnership otherwise determined; and

(*c*) any loss in respect of the disposition of a property (other than inventory of a business carried on in Canada or taxable Canadian property) by the partnership before the particular time shall be deemed to be nil.

(*d*) (Repealed by S.C. 2016, c. 12, s. 32(4).)

History: S. 96(8)(*d*) was repealed by S.C. 2016, c. 12, s. 32(4), in force January 1, 2017, and formerly read:

(*d*) where $^4/_3$ of the cumulative eligible capital in respect of a business carried on at the particular time outside Canada by the partnership exceeds the total of the fair market value of each eligible capital property in respect of the business at that time, the partnership shall be deemed to have, immediately after that time, disposed of an eligible capital property in respect of the business for proceeds equal to the excess and to have received those proceeds.

▶ 96(9) ◀

(9) Application of foreign partnership rule. For the purposes of applying subsection (8) and this subsection,

(*a*) where it can reasonably be considered that one of the main reasons that a member of a partnership is resident in Canada is to avoid the application of subsection (8), the member is deemed not to be resident in Canada; and

(*b*) where at any time a particular partnership is a member of another partnership,

(i) each person or partnership that is, at that time, a member of the particular partnership is deemed to be a member of the other partnership at that time,

(ii) each person or partnership that becomes a member of the particular partnership at that time is deemed to become a member of the other partnership at that time, and

(iii) each person or partnership that ceases to be a member of the particular partnership at that time is deemed to cease to be a member of the other partnership at that time.

History: S. 96(9) was replaced by S.C. 2013, c. 34, s. 228(6), applicable to fiscal periods that begin after June 22, 2000, and formerly read:

(9) *Idem.* For the purpose of applying subsection (8), where it can reasonably be considered that one of the main reasons that there is a member of the partnership who is resident in Canada is to avoid the application of that subsection, the member shall be deemed not to be resident in Canada.

SECTION 97: Contribution of property to partnership

▶ 97(1) ◀

(1) Contribution of property to partnership. Where at any time after 1971 a partnership has acquired property from a taxpayer who was, immediately after that time, a member of the partnership, the partnership shall be deemed to have acquired the property at an amount equal to its fair market value at that time and the taxpayer shall be deemed to have disposed of the property for proceeds equal to that fair market value.

Editorial Note: The rule in s. 97(1) is subject to the rollover provisions of s. 97(2).

Canadian Tax Foundation: Yip, *Recent Legislation Affecting Partnerships and Foreign Affiliates — Subsection 88(1) and Section 100,* 2013 Canadian Tax Journal 1:229–256.

Interpretation Bulletins: *Secondary* — IT-457R Election by professionals to exclude work in progress from income.

▶ 97(2) ◀

(2) Rules if election by partners. Notwithstanding any other provision of this Act other than subsections (3) and 13(21.2), where a taxpayer at any time disposes of any property (other than an *eligible derivative*, as defined in subsection 10.1(5), of the taxpayer if subsection 10.1(6) applies to the taxpayer) that is a capital property, Canadian resource property, foreign resource property or inventory of the taxpayer to a partnership that immediately after that time is a Canadian partnership of which the taxpayer is a member, if the taxpayer and all the other members of the partnership jointly so elect in prescribed form within the time referred to in subsection 96(4),

(*a*) the provisions of paragraphs 85(1)(*a*) to (*f*) apply to the disposition as if

(i) the reference therein to "corporation's cost" were read as a reference to "partnership's cost",

(ii) the references therein to "other than any shares of the capital stock of the corporation or a right to receive any such shares" and to "other than shares of the capital stock of the corporation or a right to receive any such shares" were read as references to "other than an interest in the partnership",

(iii) the references therein to "shareholder of the corporation" were read as references to "member of the partnership",

(iv) the references therein to "the corporation" were read as references to "all the other members of the partnership", and

(v) the references therein to "to the corporation" were read as references to "to the partnership";

(*b*) in computing, at any time after the disposition, the adjusted cost base to the taxpayer of the taxpayer's interest in the partnership immediately after the disposition,

(i) there shall be added the amount, if any, by which the taxpayer's proceeds of disposition of the property exceed the fair market value, at the time of the disposition, of the consideration (other than an interest in the partnership) received by the taxpayer for the property, and

(ii) there shall be deducted the amount, if any, by which the fair market value, at the time of the disposition, of the consideration (other than an interest in the partnership) received by the taxpayer for the property so disposed of by the taxpayer exceeds the fair market value of the property at the time of the disposition; and

(*c*) where the property so disposed of by the taxpayer to the partnership is taxable Canadian property of the taxpayer, the interest in the partnership received by the taxpayer as consideration for the property is deemed to be, at any time that is within 60 months after the disposition, taxable Canadian property of the taxpayer.

Editorial Note: S. 97(2) provides an elective rollover where property is transferred by an existing or new member of a partnership to the partnership. The provision incorporates by reference the rollover provisions of s. 85(1), which otherwise applies to transfers of property by an existing or new shareholder to a corporation. Subject to certain limits (see the editorial note to s. 85(1)), the elective rollover can be a full rollover, such that no gain arises on the transfer, or a partial rollover, such some gain arises on the transfer.

History: S. 97(2), the portion before paragraph (*a*) was replaced by S.C. 2017, c. 33, s. 32(1), applicable to taxation years that begin after March 21, 2017, and formerly read:

(2) *Rules if election by partners.* Notwithstanding any other provision of this Act other than subsections (3) and 13(21.2), where a taxpayer at any time disposes of any property that is a capital property, Canadian resource property, foreign resource property or inventory of the taxpayer to a partnership that immediately after that time is a Canadian partnership of which the taxpayer is a member, if the taxpayer and all the other members of the partnership jointly so elect in prescribed form within the time referred to in subsection 96(4),

S. 97(2), the portion before paragraph (*a*) was replaced by S.C. 2016, c. 12, s. 33(1), in force January 1, 2017, and formerly read:

(2) *Rules if election by partners.* Notwithstanding any other provision of this Act other than subsections (3) and 13(21.2), where a taxpayer at any time disposes of any property that is a capital property, Canadian resource property, foreign resource property, eligible capital property or inventory of the taxpayer to a partnership that immediately after that time is a Canadian partnership of which the taxpayer is a member, if the taxpayer and all the other members of the partnership jointly so elect in prescribed form within the time referred to in subsection 96(4),

S. 97(2), the portion before paragraph (*a*) was replaced by S.C. 2012, c. 31, s. 21(1), applicable in respect of dispositions made after March 28, 2012. S. 97(2), the portion before paragraph (*a*) formerly read:

(2) *Rules where election by partners.* Notwithstanding any other provision of this Act other than subsection 13(21.2), where a taxpayer at any time disposes of any property that is a capital property, Canadian resource property, foreign resource property, eligible capital property or inventory of the taxpayer to a partnership that immediately after that time is a Canadian partnership of which the taxpayer is a member, if the taxpayer and all the other members of the partnership jointly so elect in prescribed form within the time referred to in subsection 96(4), the following rules apply:

S. 97(2)(*c*) was replaced by S.C. 2010, c. 12, s. 9(1), applicable in determining after March 4, 2010 whether a property is taxable Canadian property of a taxpayer. S. 97(2)(*c*) formerly read:

(*c*) where the property so disposed of by the taxpayer to the partnership is taxable Canadian property of the taxpayer, the interest in the partnership received by the taxpayer as consideration therefor shall be deemed to be taxable Canadian property of the taxpayer.

Related Regulations: Part XI.

Related Sections: S. 40(3.3) When subsection (3.4) applies; s. 54, "superficial loss"; s. 69(11) Deemed proceeds of disposition; s. 85(1) Transfer of property to corporation by shareholders; s. 85(2) Transfer of property to corporation from partnership; s. 85(3) Where partnership wound up; s. 96(5) Late filing; s. 96(5.1) Special cases; s. 97(4) Where capital cost to partner exceeds proceeds of disposition; s. 102(1) Definition of "Canadian partnership"; ITAR s. 20(1.2) Other transfers of depreciable property.

Canadian Tax Foundation: Ewens, *Tax Issues Affecting Partnerships*, 1997 Conference Report 8:1–85.

Tax Profile: December 2011 — Partnership Taxation; May 2011 — Partnership as a Holding Vehicle; March 2009 — Sale of Businesses to Employees: The Leveraged Buy-Out — Part I.

Tax Topics: No. 1967, Conversion of Partnership Interests into Income and Capital Components; No. 1925, The Perils of "Rolling" Real Estate Inventory.

Forms: T2059 — Election on Disposition of Property by a Taxpayer to a Canadian Partnership.

Information Circulars: IC 76-19R3 Transfer of property to a corporation under section 85; IC 88-2 General anti-avoidance rule — Section 245 of the Income Tax Act (paras. 12 and 22).

Interpretation Bulletins: *Primary* — IT-413R Election by members of a partnership under subsection 97(2). *Secondary* — IT-457R Election by professionals to exclude work in progress from income; IT-471R Merger of partnerships.

Tax Window Files: Transfer of Property — Partnership, *Technical Interpretation, Business and Partnerships Division, April 6, 2005*, CRA Document No. 2004-0104291E5; 97(2) and Retired Partners, *Technical Interpretation, Business and Partnerships Division, June 30, 2004*, CRA Document No. 2004-0073351E5; Assumption of Mortgages by Partnership, *Technical Interpretation, Reorganizations and Resources Division, March 10, 2004*, CRA Document No. 2003-0047905. Assumption of excess mortgages by a general partnership was consideration for properties transferred under an election pursuant to subsection 97(2); Transfer of Property to Partnership, *Technical Interpretation, Business and Partnerships Division, June 9, 2003*, CRA Document No. 2003-0004835. Partnership not considered a person related to taxpayer solely because the taxpayer is a majority interest partner; paragraph 85(1)(*e.2*) (see paragraph 97(2)(*a*)) not applicable if taxpayer contributes assets to the partnership in exchange for a nominal incremental partnership interest; Exchange of Partnership Units, *Technical Interpretation, Business and Partnerships Division, March 21, 2003*, CRA Document No. 2002-0180005. Subsection 97(2) could apply to exchange of limited partnership units for general partnership units of the same partnership.

Cases: There was no clear suggestion in subsection 97(2) that the more general rules regarding ACB found in section 54 should apply to give a cost equal to the fair market value where subsection 97(2) applied. *Iberville Developments Limited v. The Queen*, 2018 DTC 1078 (TCC) [under appeal]

The fact that the taxpayer had sought the tax benefits as its predominant purpose for the creation of a partnership did not negate the fact that the parties also had the ancillary purpose of sharing profit and there was otherwise a "partnership" under provincial law into which the taxpayer could rollover its assets under s. 97(2). *Continental Bank Leasing Corporation v. The Queen*, 98 DTC 6505 (S.C.C.), reversing 96 DTC 6355 (F.C.A.). See also *The Queen v. Continental Bank of Canada*, 98 DTC 6501 (S.C.C.) for the Crown's appeal on the capital gains versus income issue

Since the amounts credited to the taxpayer's capital account comprised proceeds of disposition of the assets rolled over to its partnership, the taxpayer's elected amount was revised upwards to reflect the fair market value of the consideration paid for the rollover. *Vantem Holdings Ltd. et al. v. The Queen*, 98 DTC 1335 (T.C.C.).

► 97(3) ◄

(3) Election not available — section 88. Subsection (2) does not apply to a disposition of a property by a taxpayer to a particular partnership if

(*a*) as part of a transaction or event or series of transactions or events that includes the disposition

(i) control of a taxable Canadian corporation (in this subsection referred to as the "subsidiary") is acquired by another taxable Canadian corporation (in this paragraph referred to as the "parent"),

(ii) the subsidiary is wound up under subsection 88(1) or amalgamated with one or more other corporations under subsection 87(11), and

(iii) the parent makes a designation under paragraph 88(1)(*d*) in respect of an interest in a partnership;

(*b*) the disposition occurs after the acquisition of control of the subsidiary;

(*c*) the property

(i) is referred to in clauses (A) to (C) of the description of B in subparagraph 88(1)(*d*)(ii.1), or

(ii) is an interest in a partnership that holds, directly or indirectly through one or more partnerships, property referred to in clauses (A) to (C) of the description of B in subparagraph 88(1)(*d*)(ii.1); and

(*d*) the subsidiary is the taxpayer or has, before the disposition of the property, directly or indirectly in any manner whatever, an interest in the taxpayer.

History: S. 97(3) was added by S.C. 2012, c. 31, s. 21(2), applicable in respect of dispositions made after March 28, 2012.

Related Sections: S. 97(3) Where property acquired from majority interest partner; s. 98(5) Where partnership business carried on as sole proprietorship.

► 97(3.1) ◄

(3.1) Deemed majority interest partner — (Repealed by S.C. 1998, c. 19, s. 124(2).)

► 97(4) ◄

(4) Where capital cost to partner exceeds proceeds of disposition. Where subsection (2) has been applicable in respect of the acquisition of any depreciable property by a partnership from a taxpayer who was, immediately after the taxpayer disposed of the property, a member of the partnership and the capital cost to the taxpayer of the property exceeds the taxpayer's proceeds of the disposition, for the purposes of sections 13 and 20 and any regulations made under paragraph 20(1)(*a*)

(*a*) the capital cost to the partnership of the property shall be deemed to be the amount that was the capital cost thereof to the taxpayer; and

(*b*) the excess shall be deemed to have been allowed to the partnership in respect of the property under regulations made under paragraph 20(1)(*a*) in computing income for taxation years before the acquisition by the partnership of the property.

Editorial Note: S. 97(4) ensures that any inherent recapture is preserved on a rollover of depreciable property to a partnership under s. 97(2), namely where the partnership's deemed cost of the property is less than the transferor's capital cost of the property.

Related Regulations: 1100(1).

Related Sections: S. 13(21), "depreciable property"; s. 85(5) Rules on transfers of depreciable property; s. 111(8), "net capital loss", "non-capital loss".

► 97(5) ◄

(5) Acquisition of certain tools — capital cost and deemed depreciation. If subsection (2) has applied in respect of the acquisition at any particular time of any depreciable property by a partnership from an individual, the cost of the property to the individual was included in computing an amount under paragraph 8(1)(*r*) or (*s*) in respect of the individual, and the amount that would be the cost of the property to the individual immediately before the transfer if this Act were read without reference to subsection 8(7) (which amount is in this subsection referred to as the "individual's original cost") exceeds the individual's proceeds of disposition of the property,

(*a*) the capital cost to the partnership of the property is deemed to be equal to the individual's original cost; and

(*b*) the amount by which the individual's original cost exceeds the individual's proceeds of disposition in respect of the property is deemed to have been deducted by the partnership under paragraph 20(1)(*a*) in respect of the property in computing income for taxation years that ended before that particular time.

SECTION 98: Disposition of partnership property

► 98(1) ◄

(1) Disposition of partnership property. For the purposes of this Act, where, but for this subsection, at any time after 1971 a partnership would be regarded as having ceased to exist, the following rules apply:

(*a*) until such time as all the partnership property and any property substituted therefor has been distributed to the persons entitled by law to receive it, the partnership shall be deemed not to have ceased to exist, and each person who was a partner shall be deemed not to have ceased to be a partner, (*b*) the right of each such person to share in that property shall be deemed to be an interest in the partnership, and

(*c*) notwithstanding subsection 40(3), where at the end of a fiscal period of the partnership, in respect of an interest in the partnership,

(i) the total of all amounts required by subsection 53(2) to be deducted in computing the adjusted cost base to the taxpayer of the interest at that time

exceeds

(ii) the total of the cost to the taxpayer of the interest determined for the purpose of computing the adjusted cost base to the taxpayer of that interest at that time and all amounts required by subsection 53(1) to be added to the cost to the taxpayer of the interest in computing the adjusted cost base to the taxpayer of that interest at that time,

the amount of the excess shall be deemed to be a gain of the taxpayer for the taxpayer's taxation year that includes that time from a disposition at that time of that interest.

Related Sections: S. 98.1(2) Continuation of original partnership; s. 99(1) Fiscal period of terminated partnership; s. 99(2) Fiscal period of terminated partnership for individual member; s. 249.1(1) Definition of "fiscal period".

Income Tax Folios: *Secondary* — S4-F7-C1 Amalgamations of Canadian Corporations.

Tax Window Files: Time Partnership Ceases to Exist, *November 5, 2003*, CRA Document No. 2003-0037485.

Cases: A taxpayer partner remaining in possession of farming property following termination of a farming partnership was not a partner, and had no partnership income after 1978 where it was the intention of the partners to terminate the business in 1978. *Howatt v. M.N.R.*, 89 DTC 215 (T.C.C.)

▶ 98(1.1) ◀

(1.1) Continuing partnership interest — (Repealed by 1974-75-76, c. 26, s. 62(1).)

▶ 98(2) ◀

(2) Deemed proceeds. Subject to subsections (3) and (5) and 85(3), where at any time after 1971 a partnership has disposed of property to a taxpayer who was, immediately before that time, a member of the partnership, the partnership shall be deemed to have disposed of the property for proceeds equal to its fair market value at that time and the taxpayer shall be deemed to have acquired the property at an amount equal to that fair market value.

Interpretation Bulletins: *Secondary* — IT-457R Election by professionals to exclude work in progress from income.

▶ 98(3) ◀

(3) Rules applicable if partnership ceases to exist. If at any particular time after 1971 a Canadian partnership has ceased to exist and all the partnership property has been distributed to persons who were members of the partnership immediately before that time so that immediately after that time each such person has, in each such property, an undivided interest, or for civil law an undivided right (which undivided interest or undivided right is referred to in this subsection as an "undivided interest or right", as the case may be) that, when expressed as a percentage (referred to in this subsection as that person's "percentage") of all undivided interests or rights in the property, is equal to the person's undivided interest or right, when so expressed, in each other such property, if each such person has jointly so elected in respect of the property in prescribed form and within the time referred to in subsection 96(4), the following rules apply:

(*a*) each such person's proceeds of the disposition of the person's interest in the partnership shall be deemed to be an amount equal to the greater of

(i) the adjusted cost base to the person, immediately before the particular time, of the person's interest in the partnership, and

(ii) the amount of any money received by the person on the cessation of the partnership's existence, plus the person's percentage of the total of amounts each of which is the cost amount to the partnership of each such property immediately before its distribution;

(*b*) the cost to each such person of that person's undivided interest or right in each such property is deemed to be an amount equal to the total of

(i) that person's percentage of the cost amount to the partnership of the property immediately before its distribution, and

(i.1) (Repealed by S.C. 2016, c. 12, s. 34(1).)

(ii) where the amount determined under subparagraph (*a*)(i) exceeds the amount determined under subparagraph (*a*)(ii), the amount determined under paragraph (*c*) in respect of the person's undivided interest or right in the property;

(*c*) the amount determined under this paragraph in respect of each such person's undivided interest or right in each such property that was a capital property (other than depreciable property) of the partnership is such portion of the excess, if any, described in subparagraph (*b*)(ii) as is designated by the person in respect of the property, except that

(i) in no case shall the amount so designated in respect of the person's undivided interest or right in any such property exceed the amount, if any, by which the person's percentage of the fair market value of the property immediately after its distribution exceeds the person's percentage of the cost amount to the partnership of the property immediately before its distribution, and

(ii) in no case shall the total of amounts so designated in respect of the person's undivided interest or right in all such capital properties (other than depreciable property) exceed the excess, if any, described in subparagraph (*b*)(ii);

(*d*) (Repealed by 1986, c. 55, s. 26(2).)

(*e*) if the property so distributed by the partnership was depreciable property of the partnership of a prescribed class and any such person's percentage of the amount that was the capital cost to the partnership of that property exceeds the amount determined under paragraph (*b*) to be the cost to the person of the person's undivided interest or right in the property, for the purposes of sections 13 and 20 and any regulations made under paragraph 20(1)(*a*)

(i) the capital cost to the person of the person's undivided interest or right in the property is deemed to be the person's percentage of the amount that was the capital cost to the partnership of the property, and

(ii) the excess is deemed to have been allowed to the person in respect of the property under regulations made under paragraph 20(1)(*a*) in computing income for taxation years before the acquisition by the person of the undivided interest or right; and

(*f*) the partnership shall be deemed to have disposed of each such property for proceeds equal to the cost amount to the partnership of the property immediately before its distribution.

(*g*) (Repealed by S.C. 2016, c. 12, s. 34(2).)

History: S. 98(3)(*b*)(i.1) was repealed by S.C. 2016, c. 12, s. 34(1), in force January 1, 2017, and formerly read:

(i.1) where the property is eligible capital property, that person's percentage of $^4/_3$ of the amount, if any, determined for F in the definition "cumulative eligible capital" in subsection 14(5) in respect of the partnership's business immediately before the particular time, and

S. 98(3)(*g*) was repealed by S.C. 2016, c. 12, s. 34(2), in force January 1, 2017, and formerly read:

(*g*) where the property so distributed by the partnership was eligible capital property in respect of the business,

(i) for the purposes of determining under this Act any amount relating to cumulative eligible capital, an eligible capital amount, an eligible capital expenditure or eligible capital property, each such person is deemed to have continued to carry on the business, in respect of which the property was eligible capital property and that was previously carried on by the partnership, until the time that the person disposes of the person's undivided interest or right in the property,

(ii) for the purposes of determining the person's cumulative eligible capital in respect of the business, an amount equal to $^3/_4$ of the amount determined under subparagraph (*b*)(i.1) in respect of the business shall be added to the amount otherwise determined in respect thereof for P in the definition "cumulative eligible capital" in subsection 14(5), and

(iii) for the purpose of determining after the particular time the amount required by paragraph 14(1)(*b*) to be included in computing the person's income in respect of any subsequent disposition of property of the business, the value determined for Q in the definition "cumulative eligible capital" in subsection 14(5) is deemed to be the amount, if any, of that person's percentage of the value determined for Q in that definition in respect of the partnership's business immediately before the particular time.

S. 98(3), the portion before paragraph (*a*) was replaced by S.C. 2013, c. 34, s. 122(1), in force June 26, 2013, and formerly read:

(3) *Rules applicable where partnership ceases to exist.* Where at any particular time after 1971 a Canadian partnership has ceased to exist and all the partnership property has been distributed to persons who were members of the partnership immediately before that time so that immediately after that time each such person has, in each such property, an undivided interest that, when expressed as a percentage (in this subsection referred to as that person's "percentage") of all undivided interests in the property, is equal to the person's undivided interest, when so expressed, in each other such property, if each such person has jointly so elected in respect of the property in prescribed form and within the time referred to in subsection 96(4), the following rules apply:

S. 98(3)(*b*), the portion before subparagraph (i) was replaced by S.C. 2013, c. 34, s. 122(2), in force June 26, 2013, and formerly read:

(*b*) the cost to each such person of that person's undivided interest in each such property shall be deemed to be an amount equal to the total of

S. 98(3)(*b*)(ii) was replaced by S.C. 2013, c. 34, s. 122(3), in force June 26, 2013, and formerly read:

(ii) where the amount determined under subparagraph (*a*)(i) exceeds the amount determined under subparagraph (*a*)(ii), the amount determined under paragraph (*c*) in respect of the person's undivided interest in the property;

S. 98(3)(*c*) was replaced by S.C. 2013, c. 34, s. 122(4), in force June 26, 2013, and formerly read:

(*c*) the amount determined under this paragraph in respect of each such person's undivided interest in each such property that was a capital property (other than depreciable property) of the partnership is such portion of the excess, if any, described in subparagraph (*b*)(ii) as is designated by the person in respect of the property, except that

(i) in no case shall the amount so designated in respect of the person's undivided interest in any such property exceed the amount, if any, by which the person's percentage of the fair market value of the property immediately after its distribution exceeds the person's percentage of the cost amount to the partnership of the property immediately before its distribution, and

(ii) in no case shall the total of amounts so designated in respect of the person's undivided interests in all such capital properties (other than depreciable property) exceed the excess, if any, described in subparagraph (*b*)(ii);

S. 98(3)(*e*) was replaced by S.C. 2013, c. 34, s. 122(5), in force June 26, 2013, and formerly read:

(*e*) where the property so distributed by the partnership was depreciable property of the partnership of a prescribed class and any such person's percentage of the amount that was the capital cost to the partnership of that property exceeds the amount determined under paragraph (*b*) to be the cost to the person of the person's undivided interest in the property, for the purposes of sections 13 and 20 and any regulations made under paragraph 20(1)(*a*)

(i) the capital cost to the person of the person's undivided interest in the property shall be deemed to be the person's percentage of the amount that was the capital cost to the partnership of the property, and

(ii) the excess shall be deemed to have been allowed to the person in respect of the property under regulations made under paragraph 20(1)(*a*) in computing income for taxation years before the acquisition by the person of the undivided interest;

S. 98(3)(*g*)(i) was replaced by S.C. 2013, c. 34, s. 122(6), applicable on June 26, 2013, and formerly read:

(i) for the purposes of determining under this Act any amount relating to cumulative eligible capital, an eligible capital amount, an eligible capital expenditure or eligible capital property, each such person shall be deemed to have continued to carry on the business, in respect of which the property was eligible capital property and that was previously carried on by the partnership, until the time that the person disposes of the person's undivided interest in the property,

Related Regulations: Part XI; Part XLVI.

Related Sections: S. 24(3) Where partnership has ceased to exist; s. 53(4) Recomputation of adjusted cost base on transfers and deemed dispositions; s. 69(11) Deemed proceeds of disposition; s. 80.03(3)(*c*) Surrender of capital property; s. 85(3) Where partnership wound up; s. 88(1)(*a*.2) Winding-up; s. 96(4) Election; s. 96(5) Late filing; s. 96(5.1) Special cases; s. 96(6) Penalty for late-filed election; s. 96(7) Unpaid balance of penalty; s. 98(2) Deemed proceeds; s. 98(4) Where s. (3) does not apply; ITAR s. 20(1.2) Other transfers of depreciable property.

Canadian Tax Foundation: Truster, *Windup-Bump Comparison: Subsections 98(3) and (5)*, 2015 Tax for the Owner-Manager 15(1):8–9.

Tax Profile: December 2011 — Partnership Taxation.

Forms: T2060 — Election in Respect of Disposition of Property Upon Cessation of Partnership.

Information Circulars: IC 76-19R3 Transfer of property to a corporation under section 85.

Interpretation Bulletins: *Primary* — IT-471R Merger of partnerships. *Secondary* — IT-442R Bad Debts and Reserves for Doubtful Bad Debts; IT-457R Election by professionals to exclude work in progress from income.

Tax Window Files: Application of Subsection 98(3), *February 14, 2006*, CRA Document No. 2005-0141981E5. Election not revocable.

Cases: The transactions involved rolling three real estate properties through a tiered partnership structure, increasing the adjusted cost base of the partnership interests. Those interests were then sold to tax-exempt entities without tax being paid on the latent recapture and accrued gains in the property held by the partnerships. The elimination of the capital gain on the sale of the partnership interests to exempt entities by the use of "bumps" under sections 88 and 98, and the consequential avoidance of recapture under section 100, frustrated those provisions and were abusive. *The Queen v. Oxford Properties*, 2018 DTC 5017 (FCA)

► 98(4) ◄

(4) Where s. (3) does not apply. Subsection (3) is not applicable in any case in which subsection (5) or 85(3) is applicable.

Related Sections: S. 85(3) Where partnership wound up; s. 98(5) Where partnership business carried on as sole proprietorship.

► 98(5) ◄

(5) Where partnership business carried on as sole proprietorship. Where at any particular time after 1971 a Canadian partnership has ceased to exist and within 3 months after the particular time one, but not more than one, of the persons who were, immediately before the particular time, members of the partnership (which person is in this subsection referred to as the "proprietor", whether an individual, a trust or a corporation) carries on alone the business that was the business of the partnership and continues to use, in the course of the business, any property that was, immediately before the particular time, partnership property and that was received by the proprietor as proceeds of disposition of the proprietor's interest in the partnership, the following rules apply:

(*a*) the proprietor's proceeds of disposition of the proprietor's interest in the partnership shall be deemed to be an amount equal to the greater of

(i) the total of the adjusted cost base to the proprietor, immediately before the particular time, of the proprietor's interest in the partnership, and the adjusted cost base to the proprietor of each other interest in the partnership deemed by paragraph (*g*) to have been acquired by the proprietor at the particular time, and

(ii) the total of

(A) the cost amount to the partnership, immediately before the particular time, of each such property so received by the proprietor, and

(B) the amount of any other proceeds of the disposition of the proprietor's interest in the partnership received by the proprietor;

(*b*) the cost to the proprietor of each such property shall be deemed to be an amount equal to the total of

(i) the cost amount to the partnership of the property immediately before that time, and

(i.1) (Repealed by S.C. 2016, c. 12, s. 34(3).)

(ii) where the amount determined under subparagraph (*a*)(i) exceeds the amount determined under subparagraph (*a*)(ii), the amount determined under paragraph (*c*) in respect of the property;

(*c*) the amount determined under this paragraph in respect of each such property so received by the proprietor that is a capital property (other than depreciable property) of the proprietor is such portion of the excess, if any, described in subparagraph (*b*)(ii) as is designated by the proprietor in respect of the property, except that

(i) in no case shall the amount so designated in respect of any such property exceed the amount, if any, by which the fair market value of the property immediately after the particular time exceeds the cost amount to the partnership of the property immediately before that time, and

(ii) in no case shall the total of amounts so designated in respect of all such capital properties (other than depreciable property) exceed the excess, if any, described in subparagraph (*b*)(ii);

(*d*) (Repealed by 1986, c. 55, s. 26(4).)

(*e*) where any such property so received by the proprietor was depreciable property of a prescribed class of the partnership and the amount that was the capital cost to the partnership of that property exceeds the amount determined under paragraph (*b*) to be the cost to the proprietor of the property, for the purposes of sections 13 and 20 and any regulations made under paragraph 20(1)(*a*)

(i) the capital cost to the proprietor of the property shall be deemed to be the amount that was the capital cost to the partnership of the property, and

(ii) the excess shall be deemed to have been allowed to the proprietor in respect of the property under regulations made under paragraph 20(1)(*a*) in computing income for taxation years before the acquisition by the proprietor of the property;

(*f*) the partnership shall be deemed to have disposed of each such property for proceeds equal to the cost amount to the partnership of the property immediately before the particular time; and

(*g*) where, at the particular time, all other persons who were members of the partnership immediately before that time have disposed of their interests in the partnership to the proprietor, the proprietor shall be deemed at that time to have acquired partnership interests from those other persons and not to have acquired any property that was property of the partnership.

(*h*) (Repealed by S.C. 2016, c. 12, s. 34(4).)

History: S. 98(5)(*b*)(i.1) was repealed by S.C. 2016, c. 12, s. 34(3), in force January 1, 2017, and formerly read:

(i.1) where the property is eligible capital property, $^4/_3$ of the amount, if any, determined for F in the definition "cumulative eligible capital" in subsection 14(5) in respect of the partnership's business immediately before the particular time, and

S. 98(5)(*h*) was repealed by S.C. 2016, c. 12, s. 34(4), in force January 1, 2017, and formerly read:

(*h*) where the property so received by the proprietor is eligible capital property in respect of the business,

(i) for the purpose of determining the proprietor's cumulative eligible capital in respect of the business, an amount equal to $^3/_4$ of the amount determined under subparagraph (*b*)(i.1) in respect of the business shall be added to the amount otherwise determined in respect thereof for P in the definition "cumulative eligible capital" in subsection 14(5), and

(ii) for the purpose of determining after the particular time the amount required by paragraph 14(1)(*b*) to be included in computing the proprietor's income in respect of any subsequent disposition of property of the business, the value determined for Q in the definition "cumulative eligible capital" in subsection 14(5) is deemed to be the value, if any, determined for Q in that definition in respect of the partnership's business immediately before the particular time.

Related Regulations: Part XI.

Related Sections: S. 24(3) Where partnership has ceased to exist; s. 53(4) Recomputation of adjusted cost base on transfers and deemed dispositions; s. 69(11) Deemed proceeds of disposition; s. 80.03(3)(*c*) Surrender of capital property; s. 88(1)(*a*.2) Winding-up; s. 98(2) Deemed proceeds; ITAR s. 20(1.2) Other transfers of depreciable property.

Tax Profile: December 2011 — Partnership Taxation.

Information Circulars: IC 88-2 General Anti-Avoidance Rule (para. 22).

Interpretation Bulletins: *Secondary* — IT-457R Election by professionals to exclude work in progress from income.

Tax Window Files: Winding-up of a partnership, *January 15, 2018*, CRA Document No. 2017-0722961E5; Partnership to Sole Proprietorship, *September 8, 2014*, CRA Document No. 2014-0529231E5; Partnerships —

Property Rollover to Former Partner, *Technical Interpretation, Business and Partnerships Division, February 17, 2004*, CRA Document No. 2003-0046981I7. General comments on whether subsection 98(5) would apply in different scenarios.

► 98(6) ◄

(6) Continuation of predecessor partnership by new partnership. Where a Canadian partnership (in this subsection referred to as the "predecessor partnership") has ceased to exist at any particular time after 1971 and, at or before that time, all of the property of the predecessor partnership has been transferred to another Canadian partnership (in this subsection referred to as the "new partnership") the only members of which were members of the predecessor partnership, the new partnership shall be deemed to be a continuation of the predecessor partnership and any member's partnership interest in the new partnership shall be deemed to be a continuation of the member's partnership interest in the predecessor partnership.

Related Sections: S. 54, "capital property", "proceeds of disposition"; s. 102 Definition of "Canadian partnership"; s. 248(1), "amount", "cost amount", "property".

Interpretation Bulletins: *Secondary* — IT-457R Election by professionals to exclude work in progress from income.

► 98(7) ◄

(7) Depreciable property — leasehold interests and options. For the purposes of paragraphs (3)(*c*) and (5)(*c*), a leasehold interest in a depreciable property and an option to acquire a depreciable property are depreciable properties.

History: S. 98(7) was added by S.C. 2017, c. 33, s. 33(1), applicable in respect of partnerships that cease to exist after September 15, 2016.

SECTION 98.1: Residual interest in partnership

► 98.1(1) ◄

(1) Residual interest in partnership. Where, but for this subsection, at any time after 1971 a taxpayer has ceased to be a member of a partnership of which the taxpayer was a member immediately before that time, the following rules apply:

(*a*) until such time as all the taxpayer's rights (other than a right to a share of the income or loss of the partnership under an agreement referred to in subsection 96(1.1)) to receive any property of or from the partnership in satisfaction of the taxpayer's interest in the partnership immediately before the time at which the taxpayer ceased to be a member of the partnership are satisfied in full, that interest (in this section referred to as a "residual interest") is, subject to sections 70, 110.6 and 128.1 but notwithstanding any other section of this Act, deemed not to have been disposed of by the taxpayer and to continue to be an interest in the partnership;

(*b*) where all of the taxpayer's rights described in paragraph (*a*) are satisfied in full before the end of the fiscal period of the partnership in which the taxpayer ceased to be a member thereof, the taxpayer shall, notwithstanding paragraph (*a*), be deemed not to have disposed of the taxpayer's residual interest until the end of that fiscal period;

(*c*) notwithstanding subsection 40(3), where at the end of a fiscal period of the partnership, in respect of a residual interest in the partnership,

(i) the total of all amounts required by subsection 53(2) to be deducted in computing the adjusted cost base to the taxpayer of the residual interest at that time

exceeds

(ii) the total of the cost to the taxpayer of the residual interest determined for the purpose of computing the adjusted cost base to the taxpayer of that interest at that time and all amounts required by subsection 53(1) to be added to the cost to the taxpayer of the residual interest in computing the adjusted cost base to the taxpayer of that interest at that time

the amount of the excess shall be deemed to be a gain of the taxpayer, for the taxpayer's taxation year that includes that time, from a disposition at that time of that residual interest; and

(*d*) where a taxpayer has a residual interest

(i) by reason of paragraph (*b*), the taxpayer shall, except for the purposes of subsections 110.1(4) and 118.1(8), be deemed not to be a member of the partnership, and

(ii) in any other case, the taxpayer shall, except for the purposes of subsection 85(3), be deemed not to be a member of the partnership.

Related Sections: S. 98.2 Transfer of interest on death; s. 250(5.1) Continued corporation.

Interpretation Bulletins: *Primary* — IT-242R Retired partners; IT-278R2 Death of a partner or of a retired partner.

Tax Window Files: Late Filing Penalty, *Technical Interpretation, Individual, Business and Partnerships Section, November 30, 2004*, CRA Document No. 2004-0095511I7.

► 98.1(2) ◄

(2) Continuation of original partnership. Where a partnership (in this subsection referred to as the "original partnership") has or would but for subsection 98(1) have ceased to exist at a time when a taxpayer had rights described in paragraph (1)(*a*) in respect of that partnership and the members of another partnership agree to satisfy all or part of those rights, that other partnership shall, for the purposes of that paragraph, be deemed to be a continuation of the original partnership.

SECTION 98.2: Transfer of interest on death

Where by virtue of the death of an individual a taxpayer has acquired a property that was an interest in a partnership to which, immediately before the individual's death, section 98.1 applied,

(*a*) the taxpayer shall be deemed to have acquired a right to receive partnership property and not to have acquired an interest in a partnership;

(*b*) the taxpayer shall be deemed to have acquired the right referred to in paragraph (*a*) at a cost equal to the amount determined to be the proceeds of disposition of the interest in the partnership to the deceased individual by virtue of paragraph 70(5)(*a*) or (6)(*d*), as the case may be; and

(*c*) section 43 is not applicable to the right.

Related Sections: S. 70(5)(*a*) Capital property of a deceased taxpayer; s. 70(6)(d) Where transfer or distribution to spouse or spouse trust; s. 98.1 Residual interest in partnership.

Interpretation Bulletins: *Secondary* — IT-242R Retired partners; IT-278R2 Death of a partner or of a retired partner; IT-349R3 Intergenerational transfers of farm property on death.

SECTION 99: Fiscal period of terminated partnership

▶ 99(1) ◀

(1) Fiscal period of terminated partnership. Subject to subsection (2), if, at any particular time in a fiscal period of a partnership, the partnership would, if this Act were read without reference to subsection 98(1), have ceased to exist, the fiscal period is deemed to have ended immediately before the time that is immediately before that particular time.

History: S. 99(1) was replaced by S.C. 2013, c. 34, s. 229, in force June 26, 2013, and formerly read:

(1) *Fiscal period of terminated partnership.* Except as provided in subsection (2), where, at any time in a fiscal period of a partnership, the partnership would, but for subsection 98(1), have ceased to exist, the fiscal period shall be deemed to have ended immediately before that time.

Related Sections: S. 249 Definition of "taxation year"; s. 249.1 Definition of "fiscal period".

Canadian Tax Foundation: Papale, *No Double Taxation When a Partnership Ceases To Exist*, 2018 Canadian Tax Focus 8(1):9.

Tax Profile: December 2011 — Partnership Taxation.

▶ 99(2) ◀

(2) Fiscal period of terminated partnership for individual member. Where an individual was a member of a partnership that, at any time in a fiscal period of a partnership, has or would have, but for subsection 98(1), ceased to exist, for the purposes of computing the individual's income for a taxation year the partnership's fiscal period may, if the individual so elects and subsection 249.1(4) does not apply in respect of the partnership, be deemed to have ended immediately before the time when the fiscal period of the partnership would have ended if the partnership had not so ceased to exist.

Related Sections: S. 249 Definition of "taxation year"; s. 249.1 Definition of "fiscal period".

Information Circulars: IC 76-19R3 Transfer of property to a corporation under section 85.

Interpretation Bulletins: *Secondary* — IT-287R2 Sale of inventory.

▶ 99(3) ◀

(3) Validity of election. An election under subsection (2) is not valid unless the individual was resident in Canada at the time when the fiscal period of the partnership would, if the election were valid, be deemed to have ended.

▶ 99(4) ◀

(4) Idem. An election under subsection (2) is not valid if, for the individual's taxation year in which a fiscal period of the partnership would not, if the election were valid, be deemed to have ended but in which it would otherwise have ended, the individual elects to have applicable the rules set out in the *Income Tax Application Rules* that apply when two or more fiscal periods of a partnership end in the same taxation year.

Related Sections: S. 248(1), "individual"; s. 249.1(1) Definition of "fiscal period"; s. 255 Canada.

SECTION 100: Disposition of interest in partnership

▶ 100(1) ◀

(1) Disposition of interest in partnership. If, as part of a transaction or event or series of transactions or events, a taxpayer disposes of an interest in a partnership and an interest in the partnership is acquired by a person or partnership described in any of paragraphs (1.1)(*a*) to (*d*), then notwithstanding paragraph 38(*a*), the taxpayer's taxable capital gain for a taxation year from the disposition of the interest is deemed to be the total of

(*a*) 1/2 of such portion of the taxpayer's capital gain for the year from the disposition as may reasonably be regarded as attributable to increases in the value of any partnership property of the partnership that is capital property (other than depreciable property) held directly by the partnership or held indirectly by the partnership through one or more other partnerships, and

(*b*) the whole of the remaining portion of that capital gain.

Editorial Note: In general terms, subsection 100(1) ensures that accrued recapture from depreciable property, or accrued gains from inventory or other income property, where the property is sold to a partnership, is subject to tax if an interest in the partnership is sold to a person exempt from tax under section 149. Subsection 100(1) provides that a taxpayer's taxable capital gain for a year from the disposition of an interest in a partnership to a tax-exempt person is 1/2 of the portion of the capital gain that can reasonably be attributed to increases in value of non-depreciable capital property of the partnership, plus the whole of the remaining portion of such capital gain (i.e., the amount that would be attributable to recapture or other ordinary income of the property in the partnership). The 2012 federal Budget extended the application of subsection 100(1) to sales of partnership interests to non-resident persons, with certain look-through rules where the acquirer is itself a partnership or a trust (subsection 100(1.1)).

History: S. 100(1)(*a*) was replaced by S.C. 2017, c. 33, s. 34(1), applicable in respect of dispositions made after August 13, 2012, and formerly read:

(*a*) 1/2 of such portion of the taxpayer's capital gain for the year from the disposition as may reasonably be regarded as attributable to increases in the value of any partnership property of the partnership that is capital property other than depreciable property held directly by the partnership or held indirectly by the partnership through one or more other partnerships, and

S. 100(1), the portion before paragraph (*b*) was replaced by S.C. 2012, c. 31, s. 22(1), applicable in respect of any disposition made after March 28, 2012, except that

(a) in respect of any disposition made before August 14, 2012, the portion of subsection 100(1) of the Act before paragraph (*b*) is to be read as follows:

"(1) *Disposition of an interest in a partnership.* If, as part of a transaction or event or series of transactions or events, a taxpayer disposes of an interest in a partnership and that interest is acquired by a person exempt from tax under section 149 or by a non-resident person, notwithstanding paragraph 38(*a*), the taxpayer's taxable capital gain for a taxation year from the disposition of the interest is deemed to be

(*a*) 1/2 of such portion of the taxpayer's capital gain for the year therefrom as may reasonably be regarded as attributable to increases in the value of any partnership property of the partnership that is capital property other than depreciable property,

plus"

(b) the amendment to s. 100(1) before paragraph (*b*) does not apply in respect of a disposition of an interest in a partnership by a taxpayer before 2013 to a person with whom the taxpayer deals at arm's length if the taxpayer is obligated to dispose of the interest to the person pursuant to a written agreement entered into by the taxpayer before March 29, 2012. A taxpayer is not considered to be obligated if, as a result of amendments to the Act, the taxpayer may be excused from the obligation.

S. 100(1) before paragraph (*b*) formerly read:

(1) *Disposition of interest in partnership.* Notwithstanding paragraph 38(*a*), a taxpayer's taxable capital gain for a taxation year from the disposition of an interest in a partnership to any person exempt from tax under section 149 shall be deemed to be

(*a*) 1/2 of such portion of the taxpayer's capital gain for the year therefrom as may reasonably be regarded as attributable to increases in the value of any partnership property of the partnership that is capital property other than depreciable property,

plus

Related Sections: S. 13(21), "depreciable property"; s. 38, "taxable capital gain"; s. 39, "capital gain"; s. 54, "adjusted cost base", "capital property"; s. 100(2) Gain from disposition of interest in partnership; s. 248(1), "amount".

Canadian Tax Foundation: Yip, *Recent Legislation Affecting Partnerships and Foreign Affiliates — Subsection 88(1) and Section 100*, 2013 Canadian Tax Journal 1:229–256; Blanchet, *The Impact of the 2012 Budget on Transactions Involving Interests in Partnerships*, 2012 Conference Report 10:1–17.

Tax Profile: June 2012 — Use of Canadian Partnerships by Non-Residents.

Tax Topics: No. 2162, Dispositions Of Partnership Interests — Navigating the Amendments to Section 100 of the *Income Tax Act*.

▶ 100(1.1) ◀

(1.1) Acquisition by certain persons or partnerships. Subject to subsection (1.2), subsection (1) applies in respect of a disposition of a partnership interest by a taxpayer if the interest is acquired by

(*a*) a person exempt from tax under section 149;

(*b*) a non-resident person;

(*c*) another partnership to the extent that the interest can reasonably be considered to be held, at the time of its acquisition by the other partnership, indirectly through one or more partnerships, by a person that is

(i) exempt from tax under section 149,

(ii) a non-resident, or

(iii) a trust resident in Canada (other than a mutual fund trust) if

(A) an interest as a beneficiary (in this subsection and subsection (1.2) having the meaning assigned by subsection 108(1)) under the trust is held, directly or indirectly through one or more other partnerships, by a person that is exempt from tax under section 149 or that is a trust (other than a mutual fund trust), and

(B) the total fair market value of the interests as beneficiaries under the trust held by persons referred to in clause (A) exceeds 10% of the fair market value of all the interests as beneficiaries under the trust; or

(*d*) a trust resident in Canada (other than a mutual fund trust) to the extent that the trust can reasonably be considered to have a beneficiary that is

(i) exempt from tax under section 149,

(ii) a partnership, if

(A) an interest in the partnership is held, whether directly or indirectly through one or more other partnerships, by one or more persons that are exempt from tax under section 149 or are trusts (other than mutual fund trusts), and

(B) the total fair market value of the interests held by persons referred to in clause (A) exceeds 10% of the fair market value of all the interests in the partnership, or

(iii) another trust (other than a mutual fund trust), if

(A) one or more beneficiaries under the other trust are a person exempt from tax under section 149, a partnership or a trust (other than a mutual fund trust), and

(B) the total fair market value of the interests as beneficiaries under the other trust held by the beneficiaries referred to in clause (A) exceeds 10% of the fair market value of all the interests as beneficiaries under the other trust.

History: S. 100(1.1) was added by S.C. 2012, c. 31, s. 22(2), deemed to have come into force on March 29, 2012, except that subsection 100(1.1) does not apply

(a) before August 14, 2012; or

(b) in respect of a disposition, dilution, reduction or alteration of an interest in a partnership if the disposition, dilution, reduction or alteration occurs before 2013 pursuant to an obligation under a written agreement entered into before August 14, 2012 by parties that deal with each other at arm's length and no party to the agreement may be excused from the obligation as a result of amendments to the Act.

▶ 100(1.2) ◀

(1.2) De minimis. Subsection (1) does not apply to a taxpayer's disposition of a partnership interest to a partnership or trust described in paragraph (1.1)(*c*) or (*d*) — other than a trust under which the amount of the income or capital to be distributed at any time in respect of any interest as a beneficiary under the trust depends on the exercise by any person or partnership of, or the failure by any person or partnership to exercise, any discretionary power — if the extent to which subsection (1) would, but for this subsection, apply to the taxpayer's disposition of the interest because of subsection (1.1) does not exceed 10% of the taxpayer's interest.

History: S. 100(1.2) was added by S.C. 2012, c. 31, s. 22(2), deemed to have come into force on March 29, 2012, except that subsection 100(1.2) does not apply

(a) before August 14, 2012; or

(b) in respect of a disposition, dilution, reduction or alteration of an interest in a partnership if the disposition, dilution, reduction or alteration occurs before 2013 pursuant to an obligation under a written agreement entered into before August 14, 2012 by parties that deal with each other at arm's length and no party to the agreement may be excused from the obligation as a result of amendments to the Act.

▶ 100(1.3) ◀

(1.3) Exception — non-resident person. Subsection (1) does not apply in respect of a disposition of an interest in a partnership by a taxpayer to a person referred to in paragraph (1.1)(*b*) if

(*a*) property of the partnership is used, immediately before and immediately after the acquisition of the interest by the non-resident person, in carrying on business through one or more permanent establishments in Canada; and

(*b*) the total fair market value of the property referred to in paragraph (*a*) equals at least 90% of the total fair market value of all property of the partnership.

History: S. 100(1.3) was added by S.C. 2012, c. 31, s. 22(2), deemed to have come into force on March 29, 2012.

▶ 100(1.4) ◀

(1.4) Anti-avoidance — dilution. Subsection (1.5) applies in respect of a taxpayer's interest in a partnership if (*a*) it is reasonable to conclude that one of the purposes of a dilution, reduction or alteration of the interest was to avoid the application of subsection (1) in respect of the interest; and

(*b*) as part of a transaction or event or series of transactions or events that includes the dilution, reduction or alteration, there is

(i) an acquisition of an interest in the partnership by a person or partnership described in any of paragraphs (1.1)(*a*) to (*d*), or

(ii) an increase in, or alteration of, an interest in the partnership held by a person or partnership described in any of paragraphs (1.1)(*a*) to (*d*).

History: S. 100(1.4) was added by S.C. 2012, c. 31, s. 22(2), deemed to have come into force on March 29, 2012, except that subsection 100(1.4) does not apply

(a) before August 14, 2012; or

(b) in respect of a disposition, dilution, reduction or alteration of an interest in a partnership if the disposition, dilution, reduction or alteration occurs before 2013 pursuant to an obligation under a written agreement entered into before August 14, 2012 by parties that deal with each other at arm's length and no party to the agreement may be excused from the obligation as a result of amendments to the Act.

▶ 100(1.5) ◀

(1.5) Deemed gain — dilution. If this subsection applies in respect of a particular interest in a partnership of a taxpayer, then for the purposes of subsection (1),

(*a*) the taxpayer is deemed to have disposed of an interest in the partnership at the time of the dilution, reduction or alteration;

(*b*) the taxpayer is deemed to have a capital gain from the disposition equal to the amount by which the fair market value of the particular interest immediately before the dilution, reduction or alteration exceeds its fair market value immediately thereafter; and

(*c*) the person or partnership referred to in paragraph (1.4)(*b*) is deemed to have acquired an interest in the partnership as part of the transaction or event or series of transactions or events that includes the disposition referred to in paragraph (*a*).

History: S. 100(1.5) was added by S.C. 2012, c. 31, s. 22(2), deemed to have come into force on March 29, 2012, except that subsection 100(1.5) does not apply

(a) before August 14, 2012; or

(b) in respect of a disposition, dilution, reduction or alteration of an interest in a partnership if the disposition, dilution, reduction or alteration occurs before 2013 pursuant to an obligation under a written agreement entered into before August 14, 2012 by parties that deal with each other at arm's length and no party to the agreement may be excused from the obligation as a result of amendments to the Act.

▶ 100(2) ◀

(2) Gain from disposition of interest in partnership. In computing a taxpayer's gain for a taxation year from the disposition of an interest in a partnership, there shall be included, in addition to the amount thereof determined under subsection 40(1), the amount, if any, by which

(*a*) the total of all amounts required by subsection 53(2) to be deducted in computing the adjusted cost base to the taxpayer, immediately before the disposition, of the interest in the partnership,

exceeds

(*b*) the total of

(i) the cost to the taxpayer of the interest in the partnership determined for the purpose of computing the adjusted cost base to the taxpayer of that interest at that time, and

(ii) all amounts required by subsection 53(1) to be added to the cost to the taxpayer of that interest in computing the adjusted cost base to the taxpayer of that interest at that time.

Interpretation Bulletins: *Secondary* — IT-268R4 Inter vivos transfer of farm property to child; IT-278R2 Death of a partner or of a retired partner.

Tax Window Files: Capital Gains Reserve, *Technical Interpretation, Financial Sector and Exempt Entities Division, June 23, 2005*, CRA Document No. 2005-0116081E5.

▶ 100(2.1) ◀

(2.1) Idem. Where, as a result of an amalgamation or merger, an interest in a partnership owned by a predecessor corporation has become property of the new corporation formed as a result of the amalgamation or merger and the predecessor corporation was not related to the new corporation, the predecessor corporation shall be deemed to have disposed of the interest in the partnership to the new corporation immediately before the amalgamation or merger for proceeds of disposition equal to the adjusted cost base to the predecessor corporation of the interest in the partnership at the time of the disposition and the new corporation shall be deemed to have acquired the interest in the partnership from the predecessor corporation immediately after that time at a cost equal to the proceeds of disposition.

Income Tax Folios: *Secondary* — S4-F7-C1 Amalgamations of Canadian Corporations.

▶ 100(3) ◀

(3) Transfer of interest on death. Where by virtue of the death of an individual a taxpayer has acquired a property that was an interest in a partnership immediately before the individual's death (other than an interest to which, immediately before the individual's death, section 98.1 applied) and the taxpayer is not a member of the partnership and does not become a member of the partnership by reason of that acquisition,

(*a*) the taxpayer shall be deemed to have acquired a right to receive partnership property and not to have acquired an interest in a partnership;

(*b*) the taxpayer shall be deemed to have acquired the right referred to in paragraph (*a*) at a cost equal to the amount determined to be the proceeds of disposition of the interest in the partnership to the deceased individual by virtue of paragraph 70(5)(*a*) or (6)(*d*), as the case may be; and

(*c*) section 43 is not applicable to the right.

Interpretation Bulletins: *Secondary* — IT-349R2 Intergenerational transfers of farm property on death; IT-278R2 Death of a partner or of a retired partner.

▶ 100(4) ◀

(4) Loss re interest in partnership. Notwithstanding paragraph 39(1)(*b*), the capital loss of a taxpayer from the disposition at any time of an interest in a partnership is deemed to be the amount of the loss otherwise determined minus the total of all amounts each of which is the amount by which the taxpayer's share of the partnership's loss, in respect of a share of the capital stock of a corporation that was property of a particular partnership at that time, would have been reduced under subsection 112(3.1) if the fiscal period of every partnership that includes that time had ended immediately before that time and the particular partnership had disposed of the share immediately before the end of that fiscal period for proceeds equal to its fair market value at that time.

▶ 100(5) ◀

(5) Replacement of partnership capital. A taxpayer who pays an amount at any time in a taxation year is deemed to have a capital loss from a disposition of property for the year if

(*a*) the taxpayer disposed of an interest in a partnership before that time or, because of subsection (3), acquired before that time a right to receive property of a partnership;

(*b*) that time is after the disposition or acquisition, as the case may be;

(*c*) the amount would have been described in subparagraph 53(1)(*e*)(iv) had the taxpayer been a member of the partnership at that time; and

(*d*) the amount is paid pursuant to a legal obligation of the taxpayer to pay the amount.

Editorial Note: A former member of a partnership or an heir of a deceased partner may in some circumstances be required to pay an amount to the partnership to cover a deficit in the former member's capital account. One case where this situation might arise is where the partnership has a net loss for the partnership's fiscal period in which the former partner ceased to be a member. The former partner may have been deemed to realize a capital gain under s. 100(2) upon the disposition of their partnership interest if the partner's capital account had a negative adjusted cost base at the time under s. 54. Subsection 100(5) deems the required payment by the former member or the deceased heir to be a capital loss provided that the payment would have been considered a capital contribution if it was made when the partner was a member of the partnership. The capital loss is available to the former partner or to an heir who has been deemed by s. 100(3) to have acquired a right to acquire partnership property.

History: S. 100(5) was added by S.C. 2013, c. 34, s. 230(1), applicable to the 1995 and subsequent taxation years.

SECTION 101: Disposition of farmland by partnership

Where a taxpayer was a member of a partnership at the end of a taxation year of the partnership in which the partnership disposed of land used in a farming business of the partnership, there may be deducted in computing the taxpayer's income for the taxpayer's taxation year in which the taxation year of the partnership ended, 1/2 of the total of all amounts each of which is an amount in respect of that taxation year of the taxpayer or any preceding taxation year of the taxpayer ending after 1971, equal to the taxpayer's loss, if any, for the year from the farming business, to the extent that the loss

(*a*) was, by virtue of section 31, not deductible in computing the taxpayer's income for the year;

(*b*) was not deducted for the purpose of computing the taxpayer's taxable income for the taxpayer's taxation year in which the partnership's taxation year in which the land was disposed of ended, or for any preceding taxation year of the taxpayer;

(*c*) did not exceed that proportion of the total of

(i) taxes (other than income or profits taxes or taxes imposed by reference to the transfer of the property) paid by the partnership in its taxation year ending in the year or payable by it in respect of that taxation year to a province or a Canadian municipality in respect of the property, and

(ii) interest paid by the partnership in its taxation year ending in the year or payable by it in respect of that taxation year, pursuant to a legal obligation to pay interest on borrowed money used to acquire the property or on any amount as consideration payable for the property,

(to the extent that the taxes and interest were included in computing the loss of the partnership for that taxation year from the farming business), that

(iii) the taxpayer's loss from the farming business for the year

is of

(iv) the partnership's loss from the farming business for its taxation year ending in the year; and

(*d*) did not exceed the remainder obtained when

(i) the total of each of the taxpayer's losses from the farming business for taxation years preceding the year (to the extent that those losses are included in computing the amount determined under this section in respect of the taxpayer)

is deducted from

(ii) twice the amount of the taxpayer's taxable capital gain from the disposition of the land.

Related Sections: S. 53(1)(i) Adjustments to cost base — Land used in farming; s. 96(1.1) Allocation of share of income to retiring partner; s. 111(7) Loss (from farming business) deemed not to be a loss in certain cases; s. 248(1), "amount", "business", "farming", "property", "province", "taxable income"; s. 249 Definition of "taxation year".

SECTION 102: Definition of "Canadian partnership"

▶ 102(1) ◀

(1) Definition of "Canadian partnership". In this subdivision, "Canadian partnership" means a partnership all of the members of which were, at any time in respect of which the expression is relevant, resident in Canada.

Canadian Tax Foundation: Tollstam, *Certificate of Partnership Residence*, 2015 Canadian Tax Highlights 23(1):6.

Tax Profile: December 2011 — Partnership Taxation; September 2006 — Canadian Acquisition of U.S. Real Estate.

Tax Topics: No. 1802, Non-Resident Partners and Canadian Real Estate.

▶ 102(2) ◀

(2) Member of a partnership. In this subdivision, a reference to a person or a taxpayer who is a member of a particular partnership shall include a reference to another partnership that is a member of the particular partnership.

Related Sections: S. 255 Canada.

Interpretation Bulletins: *Secondary* — IT-413R Election by members of a partnership under subsection 97(2).

Cases: Losses from a business incurred by a lower-tier partnership would still be losses from a business in the top-tier partnership and may be allocated to the partners of that top-tier partnership as losses from that business. *The Queen v. Green et al*, 2017 DTC 5068 (FCA)

SECTION 103: Agreement to share income, etc., so as to reduce or postpone tax otherwise payable

► 103(1) ◄

(1) Agreement to share income, etc., so as to reduce or postpone tax otherwise payable. Where the members of a partnership have agreed to share, in a specified proportion, any income or loss of the partnership from any source or from sources in a particular place, as the case may be, or any other amount in respect of any activity of the partnership that is relevant to the computation of the income or taxable income of any of the members thereof, and the principal reason for the agreement may reasonably be considered to be the reduction or postponement of the tax that might otherwise have been or become payable under this Act, the share of each member of the partnership in the income or loss, as the case may be, or in that other amount, is the amount that is reasonable having regard to all the circumstances including the proportions in which the members have agreed to share profits and losses of the partnership from other sources or from sources in other places.

Canadian Petroleum Tax Journal: Partnerships and other Dangerous Liaisons, Mar and Rowe, 2008, Vol. 171, No. 1; Recent Developments in Relation to Partnerships, Michael J. Flatters, 1997, Vol. 10, No. 1.

Canadian Tax Foundation: Fyfe, *The Taxation of Renewable Energy Investments in Canada*, 2011 Conference Report 42:1–42; Beiles, *Partnerships: A Review of Tax Planning Strategies*, 2006 British Columbia Tax Conference 11:1–31; Hickey, *Partnership Income Allocated*, 2006 Canadian Tax Highlights 14(1):4–5; van Banning, *Reasonable Remedies for Anti-Avoidance*, 2006 Tax for the Owner-Manager 6(1):3–4; Skingle, *The GAAR — Be Careful Out There!*, 2004 Prairie Provinces Tax Conference 3:1–38; Tunney, *Estate Freeze with Partnership*, 2004 Canadian Tax Highlights 12(10):7–8; MacKnight, *Tax Planning Using Partnerships*, 2003 Ontario Tax Conference 12:1–42; Leenstra, *Allocation of Partnership Income: Section 103 Issues*, 2003 Tax for the Owner-Manager 3(1):8.

Tax Profile: December 2011 — Partnership Taxation; February 2010 — Partnership Estate Freezes; August 2009 — Structuring a Services Business; November 2003 — Revenue Canada Round Table.

Tax Topics: No. 1967, Conversion of Partnership Interests into Income and Capital Components; No. 1841, Recent Decisions Affecting Allocations in Partnerships — Part 2; No. 1840, Recent Decisions Affecting Allocations in Partnerships — Part 1; No. 1657, Can a Partnership Pay a Salary to a Partner? *Archbold* Revisited.

Income Tax Technical News: Issue No. 30, Computation/Allocation of Partnership Income and Losses.

Tax Window Files: Répartitions des revenus et pertes entre associés, *March 12, 2012*, CRA Document No. 2011-0431171E5; Société de personnes - partage d'une perte, *September 7, 2010*, CRA Document No. 2010-037219117; Estate Freeze and Partnerships, *STEP Conference — Round Table, Topic 9, June 28, 2004*, CRA Document No. 2004-0070001C6.

Cases: Two companies owned by the taxpayer's spouse formed a partnership and incurred $7.5 million in losses. When the taxpayer purchased one partner's 80% interest for $1.1 million, a valid partnership was formed since he had a view to profit. He claimed 80% of the losses, which was not reduced under s. 103 since it was reasonable in the circumstances. *Stow v. The Queen*, 2010 DTC 1275 (T.C.C.)

W, a company with significant accumulated losses, joined the taxpayers' existing partnership in March 1992. In July 1992, the partnership sold one of its properties for over $10 million and allocated 80% of the profits to W. Most of this amount was reallocated to the taxpayers since the 80% allocation was unreasonable and the principal reason for bringing W into the partnership was the reduction of tax. *XCO Investments Ltd. et al. v. The Queen*, 2007 DTC 5146 (F.C.A.), affirming 2005 DTC 1731 (T.C.C.)

The way in which G and M shared their workload in 1979, together with their testimony as to what had transpired during that year, led to the conclusion that G's partnership share was 70% and that M's was 30%, such that the 1979 losses were apportioned between them in these proportions. *Graves et al. v. The Queen*, 90 DTC 6300 (F.C.T.D.), reversing in part 83 DTC 548 (T.C.C.)

► 103(1.1) ◄

(1.1) Agreement to share income, etc., in unreasonable proportions. Where two or more members of a partnership who are not dealing with each other at arm's length agree to share any income or loss of the partnership or any other amount in respect of any activity of the partnership that is relevant to the computation of the income or taxable income of those members and the share of any such member of that income, loss or other amount is not reasonable in the circumstances having regard to the capital invested in or work performed for the partnership by the members thereof or such other factors as may be relevant, that share shall, notwithstanding any agreement, be deemed to be the amount that is reasonable in the circumstances.

Canadian Tax Foundation: Ewens, *Tax Issues Affecting Partnerships*, 1997 Conference Report 8:1–85.

Tax Profile: February 2010 — Partnership Estate Freezes.

Interpretation Bulletins: *Primary* — IT-231R2 Partnerships — Partners not dealing at arm's length.

Tax Window Files: Allocation of Partnership Income Between Spouse Partners, *Technical Interpretation, Business and Partnerships Division, January 14, 2004*, CRA Document No. 2003-0029571E5. Partnership income allocation method did not appear to be reasonable considering the amount of net capital invested and work performed by each spouse/partner.

► 103(2) ◄

(2) Definition of "losses". For the purposes of this section, the word "losses" when used in the expression "profits and losses" means losses determined without reference to other provisions of this Act.

Related Sections: S. 4, "income or loss from a source in a place"; s. 103(1) Agreement to share income, etc., so as to reduce or postpone tax otherwise payable; s. 248(1), "amount", "assessment".

Subdivision k — Trusts and their Beneficiaries

SECTION 104: Reference to trust or estate

▶ 104(1) ◀

(1) Reference to trust or estate. In this Act, a reference to a trust or estate (in this subdivision referred to as a "trust") shall, unless the context otherwise requires, be read to include a reference to the trustee, executor, administrator, liquidator of a succession, heir or other legal representative having ownership or control of the trust property, but, except for the purposes of this subsection, subsection (1.1), subparagraph (*b*)(v) of the definition "disposition" in subsection 248(1) and paragraph (*k*) of that definition, a trust is deemed not to include an arrangement under which the trust can reasonably be considered to act as agent for all the beneficiaries under the trust with respect to all dealings with all of the trust's property unless the trust is described in any of paragraphs (*a*) to (*e*.1) of the definition "trust" in subsection 108(1).

Editorial Note: The definition of "trust" in s. 104(1) is not helpful in determining whether a trust exists — this must be determined by reference to the laws of equity (or civil law, in Quebec). The reference to an agency arrangement in s. 104(1) is meant to exclude so-called bare trusts from the trust provisions of the Act. Under s. 104(1), a reference to a trust includes a reference to the trustee, executor, and the other persons described therein. Under s. 104(2), a trust is deemed to be, in respect of the trust property, an individual. Accordingly, the CRA takes the position (s. 251(2)(*a*)) that the trust and the beneficiary will be related persons for the purpose of the Act if a beneficiary is connected to the trustee by blood relationship, marriage or common-law partnership, or adoption. (CRA document no. 2009-0311891I7, June 30, 2009).

Related Sections: S. 75(2) Trusts; s. 94(1) Application of certain provisions to trusts not resident in Canada; s. 108(1), "accumulating income", "beneficiary", "inter vivos trust", "testamentary trust"; "trust"; s. 122(1) Tax payable by inter vivos trust; s. 132(6) Meaning of "mutual fund trust"; s. 149(5) Exception re investment income of certain clubs; s. 248(1) "graduated rate estate"; s. 249 Definition of "taxation year"; s. 251(1)(*b*) Arm's length; 251.2 [Loss restriction events]; s. 256(7) Acquiring control.

Canadian Tax Foundation: MacKnight, *Brogan Family Trust: To Boldly Go, or Not?*, 2015 Tax for the Owner-Manager 15(1):6–8; Friedlan and Friedlan, *Rectification and the Mistake of "Unintended Interpretations"*, 2015 Tax for the Owner-Manager 15(1):3–4; Ma, *Estate Plans Involving Trusts Require Review*, 2015 Canadian Tax Focus 5(1):9–10; Dolson, *Trust Residence After Garron: Provincial Considerations*, 2014 Canadian Tax Journal 3:671–699; Dueck and Daniels, *Update and Review of the Related, Affiliated, and Associated Rules: Overlaps, Differences, and Their Significance*, 2014 British Columbia Tax Conference 10:1–77; Cruickshank, *Trusts: Recent Developments*, 2010 Conference Report 29:1–41; Stephan and van der Wissel, *Advising the Personal Representative of a Deceased Taxpayer: Selected Post Mortem Issues*, 2004 Conference Report 36:1–45; Hoffstein, *Alter Ego Trusts/Joint Partner Trusts — Tips, Traps & Planning*, 2004 Ontario Tax Conference 12A:1–47; Schusheim, *Trust Basics: An Overview*, 1998 Conference Report 32:1–31.

Tax Profile: May 2012 — Supreme Court Confirms Central Management and Control Test for Trust Residency; January 2011 — Barbados Trust Found to be Improperly Constituted and a Sham; October 2009 — Corporate Management and Control Extended to Trust Residency: A New and Novel Approach.

Tax Topics: No. 2278, The Challenge of Determining Residency of a Trust: Comparing Discovery Trust and Boettger; No. 2087, Is an Estate Not a Trust For All Purposes of the Income Tax Act?; No. 1980, *Garron v. The Queen:* Missing the Trees for the Forest?; No. 1969, Does the *Garron Family Trust* Decision Change Anything?; No. 1966, Case Comment — *Garron Family Trust*.

Income Tax Folios: *Primary* — S2-F1-C1 Health and Welfare Trusts. *Secondary* — S6-F1-C1 Residence of a Trust or Estate.

Interpretation Bulletins: *Secondary* — IT-502 Employee benefit plans and employee trusts.

Tax Window Files: 2016 STEP - Q10 - US Revocable Living Trusts, *June 10, 2016*, CRA Document No. 2016-0645781C6; 2015 CTF Q. 3 Provincial residency of a Trust, *November 24, 2015*, CRA Document No. 2015-0610791C6; Netherlands Antilles private foundation, *October 4, 2010*, CRA Document No. 2008-0289461I7; Existence of trust, *November 7, 2007*, CRA Document No. 2007-0256521E5. Whether trust exists where trustee and beneficiary same person; question of fact, but probably not; Distribution from bare trust, *September 11, 2006*, CRA Document No. 2006-0185601C6 . No disposition arises on the distribution of the trust's property to the contributor who is the beneficiary of the bare trust; Estates — Affiliated Persons, *March 30, 2006*, CRA Document No. 2004-0105471E5. Deceased person not affiliated with his or her estate; Acquisition of Control — Replacement of Trustees, *Technical Interpretations, Reorganizations and Resources Division, May 24, 2005*, CRA Document No. 2004-0087761E5. Whether control of corporation acquired when trustee of trust holding the shares of the corporation is replaced; Trusts — Ownership and Control of Trust Property, *Technical Interpretation, International and Trusts Division, April 28, 2004*, CRA Document No. 2004-0071191I7. Expression "having ownership or control of the trust property" relates to all parties listed in subsection 104(1) and not just legal representative; In Trust Accounts, *International and Trusts Division, Income Tax Rulings Directorate Policy and Legislation Branch, July 21, 2003*, CRA Document No. 2002-017676. Legal nature of "in trust" accounts depends on the facts.

Cases: The Court reviewed the series of events by which the impugned trust was created and property transferred to it and concluded there was no sham. There was no deceit regarding the legal relationships created, and the relevant documentation reflected the legal rights and obligations intended by the parties. The trust had been validly and effectively created under the laws of Quebec. *Lee v. The Queen*, 2018 DTC 1165 (TCC)

A central management and control test was applied to find a trust resident in Canada since its decisions were made by Canadian beneficiaries and not by the Barbados-resident trustee. *St. Michael Trust Corp. v. The Queen*, 2012 DTC 5063 (S.C.C.), affirming 2010 DTC 5189 (F.C.A.) and 2009 DTC 1287 (T.C.C.)

An offshore spousal trust, established by a resident taxpayer to hold and dispose of Canadian shares, was not validly created, because it lacked certainty of intention and subject matter. It was also a sham since both the taxpayer and the trustee gave a false impression of their rights and obligations. *Antle et al. v. The Queen*, 2010 DTC 5172 (F.C.A.), affirming 2009 DTC 1305 (T.C.C.)

Thibodeau Family Trust v. The Queen, 78 DTC 6376 (F.C.T.D.) is the leading case on the determination of the residence of a trust. The Court held that the trust was a resident in Bermuda because the majority of the trustees were resident in Bermuda and the trust document permitted a majority decision on all matters of trustee discretion. In *Holden v. M.N.R.*, 1 DTC 243 (T.C.C.), the Privy Council agreed with the Supreme Court of Canada that the residence of the beneficiaries of an estate was irrelevant in determining residence of the estate

An express trust must manifest the "three certainties": certainty of intent; certainty of subject matter; and certainty of objects. There have been several instances where the courts have looked at trust arrangements and disregarded them because of a lack of one of the three certainties. See *Kingsdale Securities Co. Limited v. M.N.R.*, 74 DTC 6674 (F.C.A.); *Atinco Paper Products Limited v. The Queen*, 78 DTC 6387 (F.C.A.); *Ablan Leon (1964) Limited v. M.N.R.*, 76 DTC 6280 (F.C.A.). It remains true that the courts may uphold undocumented trusts — see, for instance, *Joseph Blum v. M.N.R.*, 99 DTC 290 (T.C.C.) and *Koons v. Quibell* (1998) 164 Sask. R. 149. In *Fraser v. The Queen*, 95 DTC 5684 (F.C.A.), affirming 91 DTC 5123 (F.C.T.D.) a pooled mortgage fund was held to possess the three certainties

The courts will be inclined to disregard a trust established for tax planning purposes if the paperwork and accounting are "sloppy" — see *Romkey et al. v. The Queen*, 2000 DTC 6047 (F.C.A.), affirming 97 DTC 719 (T.C.C.)

The beneficial tax treatment of an estate as a testamentary trust cannot be prolonged artificially. When the administration of an estate (and the distribution of its assets) ought to be complete, the estate will lose its status as a testamentary trust — see *Grayson v. M.N.R.*, 90 DTC 1108 (T.C.C.)

▶ 104(1.1) ◀

(1.1) Restricted meaning of "beneficiary". Notwithstanding subsection 248(25), for the purposes of subsection (1), paragraph (4)(*a.4*), subparagraph 73(1.02)(*b*)(ii) and paragraph 107.4(1)(*e*), a person or partnership is deemed not to be a beneficiary under a trust at a particular time if the person or partnership is beneficially interested in the trust at the particular time solely because of

(*a*) a right that may arise as a consequence of the terms of the will or other testamentary instrument of an individual who, at the particular time, is a beneficiary under the trust;

(*b*) a right that may arise as a consequence of the law governing the intestacy of an individual who, at that time, is a beneficiary under the trust;

(*c*) a right as a shareholder under the terms of the shares of the capital stock of a corporation that, at the particular time, is a beneficiary under the trust;

(*d*) a right as a member of a partnership under the terms of the partnership agreement, where, at the particular time, the partnership is a beneficiary under the trust; or

(*e*) any combination of rights described in paragraphs (*a*) to (*d*).

Editorial Note: The restricted meaning of "beneficiary" in s. 104(1.1) applies mainly for the purposes of a trust to which property is transferred without a change in the beneficial ownership of the property and in which no one but the settlor has a right as a beneficiary. The provision ensures that so-called self-benefit trusts and protective trusts can qualify for the rollover in s. 73(1) (or in some cases s. 107.4(3)) where a person other than the settlor holds only a right or potential right in the trust as described in paragraphs (*a*) through (*e*) of the provision.

History: S. 104(1.1), the portion before paragraph (*a*) was replaced by S.C. 2013, c. 34, s. 231(1), applicable to the 1998 and subsequent taxation years, and formerly read:

(1.1) *Restricted meaning of "beneficiary"*. Notwithstanding subsection 248(25.1) and for the purposes of subsection (1), paragraph (4)(*a*.4), subparagraph 73(1.02)(*b*)(ii) and paragraph 107.4(1)(*e*), a person or partnership is deemed not to be a beneficiary under a trust at a particular time where the person or partnership is beneficially interested in the trust at the particular time solely because of

Related Sections: S. 73(1.02) Exception for transfers; s. 107.4(1) Qualifying disposition; s. 107.4(4) Fair market value of vested interest in trust; s. 248(25) Beneficially interested.

Tax Profile: February 2002 — Transferring Property to a Trust After the Enactment of Bill C-22.

▶ 104(2) ◀

(2) Taxed as individual. A trust shall, for the purposes of this Act, and without affecting the liability of the trustee or legal representative for that person's own income tax, be deemed to be in respect of the trust property an individual, but where there is more than one trust and

(*a*) substantially all of the property of the various trusts has been received from one person, and

(*b*) the various trusts are conditioned so that the income thereof accrues or will ultimately accrue to the same beneficiary, or group or class of beneficiaries,

such of the trustees as the Minister may designate shall, for the purposes of this Act, be deemed to be in respect of all the trusts an individual whose property is the property of all the trusts and whose income is the income of all the trusts.

Editorial Note: Notwithstanding that a trust is not a legal entity in our legal system, s. 104(2) deems a trust (which includes an estate) to be an individual and therefore a separate taxpayer. Pursuant to s. 117(2), testamentary trusts in taxation years prior to 2016 were taxed according to the same progressive marginal tax rates applicable to natural individuals. Accordingly, creating multiple testamentary trusts could result in advantageous post-mortem income-splitting for those taxation years. However, even this planning could be subject to the provision in s. 104(2), which provides that the Minister may, given certain circumstances, tax several trusts as a single taxpayer.

The CRA's administrative position has been that it is not necessary for each trust to have the same beneficiaries for s. 104(2) to apply; rather, it is sufficient that the beneficiaries of each trust are of the same group or class (see CRA Document No. 2011-0430261E5). However, the CRA's administrative position has also been that the discretion accorded the Minister under s. 104(2) will not be exercised where a testator creates a separate trust for each of his or her children (see CRA Document No. 9304865).

The CRA's position is that "substantially all" means 90% or more.

The 2014 federal Budget eliminated graduated rate taxation for testamentary trusts for the 2016 and later taxation years. Exceptions are provided for "graduated rate estates", of which there can only be one per deceased, for the 36 months following death, (see definition at 248(1)) and "qualified disability trusts" (see definition at 122(3)).

Related Regulations: Part II.

Related Sections: S. 7(1.11) Non-arm's length relationship with trusts; s. 12(1)(*m*) Benefits from trusts; s. 127.54(2) Foreign tax credit; s. 149(5) Exception re investment income of certain clubs; s. 150(1)(*c*) Filing returns of income — general rule; s. 248(1), "individual".

Canadian Tax Foundation: Reiss, *Testamentary Trust Planning: Dying is Harder Than You Think*, 2004 Prairie Provinces Tax Conference 16:1–29.

Tax Profile: December 2009 — Income Tax Consequences of Income Distributions by a Canadian Trust.

Forms: T3 — Statement of Trust Income Allocations or Designations.

Guides: T4013 T3 Guide and Trust Return.

Income Tax Folios: *Secondary* — S6-F1-C1 Residence of a Trust or Estate.

Interpretation Bulletins: *Secondary* — IT-406R2 Tax payable by an inter vivos trust.

Tax Window Files: Multiple Trusts, *April 26, 2013*, CRA Document No. 2013-0486211E5; Application of 104(2), *International and Trusts Division. Income Tax Rulings Directorate, December 13, 2005*, CRA Document No. 2004-0090941E5. Members of the same family may constitute a "group or class of beneficiaries" for purposes of s. 104(2).

Cases: The trustees chose not to allocate income to a beneficiary in a taxation year because the CRA had assessed other years and treated the trust and the beneficiary (which was also a trust) as one trust under subsection 104(2); the trustees felt that in light of the CRA assessments, an allocation in the taxation year at issue might be invalid. Subsequently, the dispute in respect of the subsection 104(2) was resolved, after which the trustees sought a rectification order to allocate income to the beneficiary for the taxation year. The Court held that the decision not to allocate income was not a mistake that ought to be remedied either by application of the doctrine of rectification or by the inherent jurisdiction of the court. There was no evidence that the trustees had a contrary intention at the time of that decision. *BC Trust v. Attorney General of Canada*, 2017 DTC 5017 (BCSC)

S. 104(2) was not applicable regarding four trusts where the beneficiary of each trust was a different child of the settlor. *Mitchell v. M.N.R.*, 56 DTC 521 (T.A.B.)

▶ 104(3) ◀

(3) Deduction not permitted — (Repealed by 1988, c. 55, s. 71(1).)

▶ 104(4) ◀

(4) Deemed disposition by trust. Every trust is, at the end of each of the following days, deemed to have disposed of each property of the trust (other than exempt property) that was capital property (other than depreciable property) or land included in the inventory of a business of the trust for proceeds equal to its fair market value (determined with reference to subsection 70(5.3)) at the end of that day and to have reacquired the property immediately after that day for an amount equal to that fair market value, and for the purposes of this Act those days are

(*a*) where the trust

(i) is a trust that was created by the will of a taxpayer who died after 1971 and that, at the time it was created, was a trust,

(i.1) is a trust that was created by the will of a taxpayer who died after 1971 to which property was transferred in circumstances to which paragraph 70(5.2)(*c*) (or, in the case of a transfer that occurred in a taxation year before 2007, (*b*) or (*d*), as those paragraphs read in their application to that taxation year) or (6)(*d*) applied, and that, immediately after any such property vested indefeasibly in the trust as a consequence of the death of the taxpayer, was a trust,

(ii) is a trust that was created after June 17, 1971 by a taxpayer during the taxpayer's lifetime that, at any time after 1971, was a trust, or

(ii.1) is a trust (other than a trust the terms of which are described in clause (iv)(A) that elects in its return of income under this Part for its first taxation year that this subparagraph not apply) that was created after 1999 by a taxpayer during the taxpayer's lifetime and that, at any time after 1999, was a trust

under which

(iii) the taxpayer's spouse or common-law partner was entitled to receive all of the income of the trust that arose before the spouse's or common-law partner's death and no person except the spouse or common-law partner could, before the spouse's or common-law partner's death, receive or otherwise obtain the use of any of the income or capital of the trust, or

(iv) in the case of a trust described in subparagraph (ii.1) created by a taxpayer who had attained 65 years of age at the time the trust was created,

(A) the taxpayer was entitled to receive all of the income of the trust that arose before the taxpayer's death and no person except the taxpayer could, before the taxpayer's death, receive or otherwise obtain the use of any of the income or capital of the trust,

(B) the taxpayer or the taxpayer's spouse was, in combination with the spouse or the taxpayer, as the case may be, entitled to receive all of the income of the trust that arose before the later of the death of the taxpayer and the death of the spouse and no other person could, before the later of those deaths, receive or otherwise obtain the use of any of the income or capital of the trust, or

(C) the taxpayer or the taxpayer's common-law partner was, in combination with the common-law partner or the taxpayer, as the case may be, entitled to receive all of the income of the trust that arose before the later of the death of the taxpayer and the death of the common-law partner and no other person could, before the later of those deaths, receive or otherwise obtain the use of any of the income or capital of the trust,

the day on which the death or the later death, as the case may be, occurs;

(*a*.1) where the trust is a pre-1972 spousal trust on January 1, 1993 and the spouse or common-law partner referred to in the definition "pre-1972 spousal trust" in subsection 108(1) in respect of the trust was

(i) in the case of a trust created by the will of a taxpayer, alive on January 1, 1976, and

(ii) in the case of a trust created by a taxpayer during the taxpayer's lifetime, alive on May 26, 1976,

the day that is the later of

(iii) the day on which that spouse or common-law partner dies, and

(iv) January 1, 1993;

(*a*.2) where the trust makes a distribution to a beneficiary in respect of the beneficiary's capital interest in the trust, it is reasonable to conclude that the distribution was financed by a liability of the trust and one of the purposes of incurring the liability was to avoid taxes otherwise payable under this Part as a consequence of the death of any individual, the day on which the distribution is made (determined as if a day ends for the trust immediately after the time at which each distribution is made by the trust to a beneficiary in respect of the beneficiary's capital interest in the trust);

(*a*.3) where property (other than property described in any of subparagraphs 128.1(4)(*b*)(i) to (iii)) has been transferred by a taxpayer after December 17, 1999 to the trust in circumstances to which subsection 73(1) applied, it is reasonable to conclude that the property was so transferred in anticipation that the taxpayer would subsequently cease to reside in Canada and the taxpayer subsequently ceases to reside in Canada, the first day after that transfer during which the taxpayer ceases to reside in Canada (determined as if a day ends for the trust immediately after each time at which the taxpayer ceases to be resident in Canada);

(*a*.4) where the trust is a trust to which property was transferred by a taxpayer who is an individual (other than a trust) in circumstances in which section 73 or subsection 107.4(3) applied, the transfer did not result in a change in beneficial ownership of that property and no person (other than the taxpayer) or partnership has any absolute or contingent right as a beneficiary under the trust (determined with reference to subsection (1.1)), the day on which the death of the taxpayer occurs;

(*b*) the day that is 21 years after the latest of

(i) January 1, 1972,

(ii) the day on which the trust was created, and

(iii) where applicable, the day determined under paragraph (*a*), (*a*.1) or (*a*.4) as those paragraphs applied from time to time after 1971; and

(*c*) the day that is 21 years after any day (other than a day determined under any of paragraphs (*a*) to (*a*.4)) that is, because of this subsection, a day on which the trust is deemed to have disposed of each such property.

Editorial Note: Subsection 104(4) provides the so-called 21-year deemed disposition rule for trusts, generally ensuring that the recognition of accrued capital gains of a trust cannot be deferred beyond 21 years after the creation of the trust. Trusts excepted from the initial 21-year deemed disposition include post-1971 spousal or common-law partner trusts, whose initial deemed disposition takes place at the death of the spouse or common-law partner beneficiary under the trust. Depreciable property is subject to a similar deemed disposition rule under s. 104(5); see also s. 104(5.2) regarding resource properties.

The deemed disposition of the trust's property can be avoided by distributing the trust property to its capital beneficiary prior to the deemed disposition date. Generally, this can be done on a rollover basis by virtue of s. 107(2). Such a distribution may require a variation of the terms of the trust which may require an application to be brought under the appropriate provincial legislation; therefore, planning for the trust's 21st anniversary should commence well in advance of the actual anniversary date. See also s. 107(4) through (5), which deny the rollover in certain circumstances.

The 21-year deemed disposition rule is often conflated with the common-law rule against perpetuities. There is, however, no connection between the two rules. The rule against perpetuities provides that an interest in a trust must vest within a life or lives in being at the time the trust is created, plus 21 years. If, at the time the trust is created, there is any possibility that the interest will not vest within the perpetuity period, the interest is void from the outset. By contrast, the 21-year deemed disposition rule has no bearing on the validity of a trust or interests therein.

Note that the deemed disposition rules in ss. 104(4), (5), and (5.2) do not apply to properties other than those specifically identified in these subsections. Not caught by these rules are eligible capital property (prior to 2017), inventory that is not land inventory, and depreciable property not of a prescribed class.

History: S. 104(4), the portion before paragraph (*a*) was replaced by S.C. 2017, c. 33, s. 35(1), applicable to taxation years that begin after 2016, and formerly read:

(4) *Deemed disposition by trust.* Every trust is, at the end of each of the following days, deemed to have disposed of each property of the trust (other

than exempt property) that was capital property (other than excluded property or depreciable property) or land included in the inventory of a business of the trust for proceeds equal to its fair market value (determined with reference to subsection 70(5.3)) at the end of that day and to have reacquired the property immediately after that day for an amount equal to that fair market value, and for the purposes of this Act those days are

S. 104(4)(*a*)(i.1) was replaced by S.C. 2013, c. 34, s. 231(2), applicable to trust taxation years that begin after 2006, and formerly read:

(i.1) is a trust that was created by the will of a taxpayer who died after 1971 to which property was transferred in circumstances to which paragraph 70(5.2)(*b*) or (*d*) or (6)(*d*) applied and that, immediately after any such property vested indefeasibly in the trust as a consequence of the death of the taxpayer, was a trust,

Related Sections: 104(13.4) Death of beneficiary — spousal and similar trusts; S. 13(21) Definitions; s. 54 Definitions; s. 70(5.31) Fair market value; s. 70(6.1) Transfer or distribution of NISA to spouse or trust; s. 104(1) Reference to trust or estate; s. 104(5) Depreciable property; s. 104(15) Allocable amount for preferred beneficiary; s. 107(4) Trusts in favour of spouse, common-law partner or self; s. 108(1), "exempt property", "excluded property", "pre-1972 spousal trust", "trust"; s. 108(3) Income of a trust in certain provisions; s. 108(4) Trust not disqualified; s. 108(6) Variation of trusts; s. 110.6(12) Trust deduction; s. 139.1(4)(*h*) Consequences of demutualization; s. 139.1(5) Fair market value of ownership rights; s. 248(1), "amount", "common-law partner", "depreciable property", "property", "trust"; s. 248(9.2) Vested indefeasibly; s. 252(3) Extended meaning of "spouse" and "former spouse".

Canadian Tax Foundation: Hoffstein and Weigl, *Overview of the Twenty-One Year Rule — A Trust Lawyer's Perspective*, 2014 Ontario Tax Conference 7:1–62; Baxter and Miedema, *Trusts — The 21-Year Rule*, 2013 Atlantic Provinces Tax Conference 4:1–20; Kandev and Purkey, *Practical Applications of Trusts*, 2004 Conference Report 40:1–39; Rajan and Brown, *Personal Trusts 2000: Taxation and Planning in the New Millennium*, 2000 Conference Report 28:1–40.

STEP Canada: Elie Roth, "Adding and Deleting a Beneficiary to a Trust," PowerPoint presentation to the 15th National Conference of STEP Canada, Toronto, June 10-11, 2013.

Forms: T1055 — Summary of Deemed Realizations.

Income Tax Folios: *Secondary* — S1-F3-C2 Principal Residence.

Interpretation Bulletins: *Secondary* — IT-286R2 Trusts — Amount payable; IT-381R3 Trusts — Deduction of amounts paid or payable to beneficiaries and flow-through of taxable capital gains to beneficiaries; IT-394R2 Preferred beneficiary election; IT-465R Non-resident beneficiaries of trusts.

Tax Window Files: 2017 STEP - Q2 - GAAR and 21-year planning, *June 13, 2017*, CRA Document No. 2017-0693321C6; 2016 STEP - Q11 - Tainting of a Spousal Trust, *June 10, 2016*, CRA Document No. 2016-0645821C6; Resettlement of a Trust, *August 9, 2016*, CRA Document No. 2014-0526171I7; 2014 STEP CRA Roundtable Question, *June 16, 2014*, CRA Document No. 2014-0523031C6; Joint Spousal or Common-Law Partner Trust Status, *March 22, 2013*, CRA Document No. 2012-0473661E5; First Deemed Disposition for a Spousal Trust, *Technical Interpretation, International & Trusts Division, April 17, 2007*, CRA Document No. 2006-0187741E5. First deemed disposition of a post-71 spousal or common law partner trust will be the date on which the primary beneficiary dies (rather than 21 years after creation) regardless of whether the property was received on a rollover basis; Carry Back of a Capital Loss, *Technical Interpretation, International and Trusts Division, December 21, 2006*, CRA Document No. 2006-0216261I7.

▶ 104(5) ◀

(5) Depreciable property. Every trust is, at the end of each day determined under subsection (4) in respect of the trust, deemed to have disposed of each property of the trust (other than exempt property) that was a depreciable property of a prescribed class of the trust for proceeds equal to its fair market value at the end of that day and to have reacquired the property immediately after that day at a capital cost (in this subsection referred to as the "deemed capital cost") equal to that fair market value, except that

(*a*) where the amount that was the capital cost to the trust of the property immediately before the end of the day (in this paragraph referred to as the "actual capital cost") exceeds the deemed capital cost to the trust of the property, for the purpose of sections 13 and 20 and any regulations made for the purpose of paragraph 20(1)(*a*) as they apply in respect of the property at any subsequent time,

(i) the capital cost to the trust of the property on its reacquisition shall be deemed to be the amount that was the actual capital cost to the trust of the property, and

(ii) the excess shall be deemed to have been allowed under paragraph 20(1)(*a*) to the trust in respect of the property in computing its income for taxation years that ended before the trust reacquired the property;

(*b*) for the purposes of this subsection, the reference to "at the end of a taxation year" in subsection 13(1) shall be read as a reference to "at the particular time a trust is deemed by subsection 104(5) to have disposed of depreciable property of a prescribed class"; and

(*c*) for the purpose of computing the excess, if any, referred to in subsection 13(1) at the end of the taxation year of a trust that included a day on which the trust is deemed by this subsection to have disposed of a depreciable property of a prescribed class, any amount that, on that day, was included in the trust's income for the year under subsection 13(1) as it reads because of paragraph (*b*), shall be deemed to be an amount included under section 13 in the trust's income for a preceding taxation year.

Editorial Note: The deemed disposition of depreciable property is covered by s. 104(5) rather than by s. 104(4). Subsection 104(5) deems each trust (other than certain trusts described in the definition of "trust" in s. 108(1)) to have realized a deemed disposition at the end of each day determined under s. 104(4) in respect of that trust. On deemed disposition day, a trust is deemed to have disposed of each property (other than exempt property) that was depreciable property of a prescribed class for proceeds equal to fair market value and to have re-acquired it generally at a capital cost equal to the same amount. On the deemed disposition day, the trust may realize capital gains or recapture. No capital loss may be realized on a deemed disposition of depreciable property.

Related Sections: S. 13(21) Definitions; s. 104(1) Reference to trust or estate; s. 104(6) Deduction in computing income of trust; s. 104(15) Allocable amount for preferred beneficiary; s. 108(1), "exempt property", "trust"; s. 108(6) Variation of trusts; s. 248(1), "amount", "depreciable property", "property", "trust".

Interpretation Bulletins: *Secondary* — IT-286R2 Trusts — Amount payable; IT-381R3 Trusts — Capital gains and losses and the flow-through of taxable capital gains to beneficiaries; IT-394R3 Preferred beneficiary election; IT-465R Non-resident beneficiaries of trusts.

Tax Window Files: 104(4)(a.3) & 104(5) Pertains to Depreciable Property, *International & Trusts Division Income Tax Rulings Directorate Policy and Planning Branch, November 4, 2005*, CRA Document No. 2004-0104951E5. Whether there is a deemed disposition on depreciable property used in a business by a trust where the business has been transferred to a spousal trust in anticipation of the emigration of the settlor and his spouse.

▶ 104(5.1) ◀

(5.1) NISA Fund No. 2. Every trust that holds an interest in a NISA Fund No. 2 that was transferred to it in circumstances to which paragraph 70(6.1)(*b*) applied is deemed, at the end of the day on which the spouse or common-law partner referred to in that paragraph dies, to have been paid an amount out of the fund equal to the balance at the end of that day in the fund so transferred.

History: S. 104(5.1) was replaced by S.C. 2014, c. 39, s. 26(1), applicable to the 2016 and subsequent taxation years, and formerly read:

(5.1) *Idem.* Every trust that holds an interest in a NISA Fund No. 2 that was transferred to it in circumstances to which paragraph 70(6.1)(*b*) applied shall be deemed, at the end of the day on which the spouse or common-law partner referred to in that paragraph dies (in this subsection referred to as the "spouse or common-law partner"), to have been paid an amount out of the fund equal to the amount, if any, by which

(*a*) the balance at the end of that day in the fund so transferred exceeds

(*b*) such portion of the amount described in paragraph (*a*) as is deemed by subsection (14.1) to have been paid to the spouse or common-law partner.

Related Sections: S. 104(1) Reference to trust or estate; s. 248(1), "amount", "common-law partner", "NISA Fund No. 2", "trust"; s. 252(3) Extended meaning of "spouse" and "former spouse".

► 104(5.2) ◄

(5.2) Resource property. Where at the end of a day determined under subsection (4) in respect of a trust, the trust owns a Canadian resource property (other than an exempt property) or a foreign resource property (other than an exempt property),

(*a*) for the purposes of determining the amounts under subsection 59(1), paragraphs 59(3.2)(*c*) and (*c*.1), subsections 66(4) and 66.2(1), the definition "cumulative Canadian development expense" in subsection 66.2(5), the definition "cumulative foreign resource expense" in subsection 66.21(1), subsection 66.4(1) and the definition "cumulative Canadian oil and gas property expense" in subsection 66.4(5), the trust is deemed

(i) to have a taxation year (in this subsection referred to as the "old taxation year") that ended at the end of that day and a new taxation year that begins immediately after that day, and

(ii) to have disposed, immediately before the end of the old taxation year, of each of those properties for proceeds that became receivable at that time equal to its fair market value at that time and to have reacquired, at the beginning of the new taxation year, each such property for an amount equal to that fair market value; and

(*b*) for the particular taxation year of the trust that included that day, the trust shall

(i) include in computing its income for the particular taxation year the amount, if any, determined under paragraph 59(3.2)(*c*) in respect of the old taxation year and the amount so included shall, for the purposes of the determination of B in the definition "cumulative Canadian development expense" in subsection 66.2(5), be deemed to have been included in computing its income for a preceding taxation year,

(i.1) include in computing its income for the particular taxation year the amount, if any, determined under paragraph 59(3.2)(*c*.1) in respect of the old taxation year and the amount so included is, for the purpose of determining the value of B in the definition "cumulative foreign resource expense" in subsection 66.21(1), deemed to have been included in computing its income for a preceding taxation year, and

(ii) deduct in computing its income for the particular taxation year the amount, if any, determined under subsection 66(4) in respect of the old taxation year and the amount so deducted shall, for the purposes of paragraph 66(4)(*a*), be deemed to have been deducted for a preceding taxation year.

Related Sections: S. 104(6) Deduction in computing income of trust; s. 108(1), "exempt property"; s. 108(6) Variation of trusts; s. 248(1), "Canadian resource property", "foreign resource property".

Interpretation Bulletins: *Secondary* — IT-381R3 Trusts — Deduction of amounts paid or payable to beneficiaries and flow-through of taxable capital gains to beneficiaries; IT-394R2 Preferred beneficiary election.

► 104(5.3) ◄

(5.3) Election — (Repealed by S.C. 2013, c. 34, s. 231(4).)

Editorial Note: S. 104(5.3) allowed the 21-year deemed disposition date for certain family trusts to be deferred, by means of an election, to January 1, 1999. Given that this election is no longer available, recourse is typically made to a roll-out of trust assets under s. 107(2) as a means of addressing the 21-year deemed disposition rule.

History: S. 104(5.3) was repealed by S.C. 2013, c. 34, s. 231(4), applicable to taxation years that begin after October 31, 2011, and formerly read:

(5.3) *Election.* Where a trust files an election under this subsection in prescribed form with the Minister within 6 months after the end of a taxation year of the trust that includes a day before 1999 (in this subsection referred to as the "disposition day") that would, but for this subsection, be determined in respect of the trust under paragraph (4)(*a*.1) in the case of a trust described in that paragraph, or under paragraph (4)(*b*) in any other case, and there is an exempt beneficiary under the trust on the disposition day,

(*a*) for the purposes of subsections (4) to (5.2), paragraph (6)(*b*) and subsection 159(6.1), the day determined under paragraph (4)(*a*.1) or (*b*), as the case may be, in respect of the trust is deemed to be the earlier of

(i) January 1, 1999, and

(ii) the first day of the trust's first taxation year that begins after the first day after the disposition day throughout which there is no exempt beneficiary under the trust;

(*b*) subsection 107(2) does not apply to a distribution made by the trust during the period

(i) beginning immediately after the disposition day, and

(ii) ending at the end of the first day after the disposition day that is determined in respect of the trust under subsection (4)

to any beneficiary (other than an individual who is an exempt beneficiary under the trust immediately before the time of the distribution);

(*b*.1) where the trust filed the form before March 1995, paragraph (*b*) does not apply to distributions made by the trust after February 1995; and

(*c*) subsection 107.4(3) does not apply to a disposition by the trust during the period

(i) beginning immediately after the disposition day, and

(ii) ending at the end of the first day after the disposition day that is determined in respect of the trust under subsection (4); and

(*d*) (Repealed.)

Related Regulations: 600(b).

Related Sections: S. 104(1) Reference to trust or estate; s. 104(5.31) Revocation of election; s. 104(5.4) Exempt beneficiary; s. 107(2) Distribution by personal trust; s. 220(3.2) Late, amended or revoked elections; s. 248(1), "individual", "property", "trust".

Information Circulars: IC 07-1 Taxpayer Relief Provisions.

Interpretation Bulletins: *Secondary* — IT-394R2, Preferred beneficiary election.

► 104(5.31) ◄

(5.31) Revocation of election — (Repealed by S.C. 2013, c. 34, s. 231(4).)

History: S. 104(5.31) was repealed by S.C. 2013, c. 34, s. 231(4), applicable to taxation years that begin after October 31, 2011, and formerly read:

(5.31) *Revocation of election.* Where a trust that has filed an election under subsection (5.3) before July 1995 applies before 1997 to the Minister in writing for permission to revoke the election and the Minister grants permission to revoke the election,

(*a*) the election is deemed, otherwise than for the purposes of this subsection, never to have been made;

(*b*) the trust is not liable to any penalty under this Act to the extent that the liability would, but for this paragraph, have increased because of the revocation of the election; and

(*c*) notwithstanding subsections 152(4) to (5), such assessments of tax, interest and penalties under this Act shall be made as are necessary to take into account the consequences of the revocation of the election.

► 104(5.4) ◄

(5.4) Exempt beneficiary — (Repealed by S.C. 2013, c. 34, s. 231(4).)

History: S. 104(5.4) was repealed by S.C. 2013, c. 34, s. 231(4), applicable to taxation years that begin after October 31, 2011, and formerly read:

(5.4) *Exempt beneficiary.* For the purpose of subsection (5.3), an "exempt beneficiary" under a trust at a particular time is an individual who is alive and a beneficiary under the trust at the particular time, where

(*a*) in the case of a trust that was created after February 11, 1991, the individual, or an individual who, otherwise than because of subsection 252(2), is the brother or sister of the individual, was alive at the earlier of

(i) the time the trust was created, and

(ii) the earliest of all times each of which is the time that another trust was created that, before the particular time and the end of the day that would, but for subsection (5.3), be determined in respect of the trust under paragraph (4)(*a*.1) or (*b*), transferred property to the trust either

(A) directly, or

(B) indirectly through one or more trusts,

in circumstances in which subsection (5.8) applies; and

(*b*) the individual or the individual's spouse or common-law partner or former spouse or common-law partner was

(i) the designated contributor in respect of the trust, or

(ii) a grandparent, parent, brother, sister, child, niece or nephew

(A) of the designated contributor in respect of the trust, or

(B) of the spouse or common-law partner or former spouse or common-law partner of the designated contributor in respect of the trust.

Related Sections: S. 248(1), "common-law partner", "individual"; s. 252(1) Extended meaning of "child"; s. 252(2) Relationships; s. 252(3) Extended meaning of "spouse" and "former spouse".

▶ 104(5.5) ◀

(5.5) Beneficiary — (Repealed by S.C. 2013, c. 34, s. 231(4).)

History: S. 104(5.5) was repealed by S.C. 2013, c. 34, s. 231(4), applicable to taxation years that begin after October 31, 2011, and formerly read:

(5.5) *Beneficiary.* For the purpose of subsection (5.4), a beneficiary under a trust is an individual who is beneficially interested in the trust, except that an individual shall be deemed not to be a beneficiary under a trust at a particular time

(*a*) where

(i) the interests in the trust at the particular time of all individuals who would, if this Act were read without reference to this paragraph, be exempt beneficiaries under the trust are conditional on or subject to the exercise of a discretionary power by a person,

(ii) by the exercise of (or the failure to exercise) such power under the terms of the trust after the particular time, all interests in the trust of

(A) those individuals, and

(B) other individuals who are children of deceased individuals who, if this Act were read without reference to this paragraph, would have been exempt beneficiaries under the trust at any time before the particular time

may terminate before the time at which the last of those individuals and the other individuals dies and without any of those individuals or the other individuals enjoying any benefit under the trust after the particular time, and

(iii) the trust was created after February 11, 1991 or subparagraph (ii) applies in respect of the trust because of a variation of the terms of the trust occurring after February 11, 1991; or

(*b*) where it is reasonable to consider that one of the main purposes for the creation of the interest of the individual in the trust was to defer the day determined under paragraph (4)(*a*.1) or (*b*) in respect of the trust.

Related Sections: S. 104(1) Reference to trust or estate; s. 104(5.3) Election; s. 248(1), "individual", "trust"; s. 252(1) Extended meaning of "child".

▶ 104(5.6) ◀

(5.6) Designated contributor — (Repealed by S.C. 2013, c. 34, s. 231(4).)

History: S. 104(5.6) was repealed by S.C. 2013, c. 34, s. 231(4), applicable to taxation years that begin after October 31, 2011, and formerly read:

(5.6) *Designated contributor.* For the purpose of subsection (5.4), a designated contributor in respect of a trust is

(*a*) where the trust is described in paragraph (4)(*a*) or was, on December 20, 1991, a pre-1972 spousal trust, the individual who created (or whose will created) the trust;

(*b*) where paragraph (*a*) does not apply and the trust is a testamentary trust at the end of the taxation year for which it makes an election under subsection (5.3), the individual as a consequence of whose death the trust was created; and

(*c*) in the case of any other trust, the individual who was, or who was related to, an individual beneficially interested in the trust and who is designated by the trust in its election under subsection (5.3)

(i) where, at each time in the relevant period, the total amount of property transferred or loaned before that time by the designated individual (either directly or through another trust) to the trust

(A) exceeded the total amount of property so transferred or loaned before that time by each other individual who was born before the designated individual and who, at any time, was related to any individual beneficially interested in the trust, and

(B) was not less than the total amount of property so transferred or loaned before that time by each other individual who was born after the designated individual and who, at any time, was related to any individual beneficially interested in the trust,

(ii) where

(A) no individual may be designated in respect of the trust because of subparagraph (i),

(B) the designated individual transferred or loaned property (either directly or through another trust) to the trust at any time before the end of the relevant period, and

(C) the designated individual was born before all other individuals who

(I) at any time were related to any individual beneficially interested in the trust or to any individual who transferred or loaned property to the trust before the end of the relevant period, and

(II) transferred or loaned property (either directly or through another trust) to the trust at any time before the end of the relevant period, or

(iii) where throughout the relevant period the property of the trust consisted primarily of

(A) shares of the capital stock of a corporation

(I) controlled, on the day that the trust was created or at the beginning of the relevant period, by the designated individual or by the designated individual and one or more other individuals born after, and related to, the designated individual, or

(II) all or substantially all of the value of which throughout the relevant period derived from property transferred to the corporation by the designated individual or by the designated individual and one or more other individuals born after, and related to, the designated individual,

(B) shares of the capital stock of a corporation all or substantially all of the value of which, throughout the part of the relevant period throughout which the shares were held by the trust, derived from shares described in clause (A),

(C) property substituted for the shares described in clause (A) or (B),

(D) property attributable to profits, gains or distributions in respect of property described in clause (A), (B) or (C), or

(E) any combination of the properties described in clauses (A) to (D).

Related Sections: S. 104(1) Reference to trust or estate; s. 248(1), "amount", "corporation", "individual", "property", "trust".

▶ 104(5.7) ◀

(5.7) Idem — (Repealed by S.C. 2013, c. 34, s. 231(4).)

History: S. 104(5.7) was repealed by S.C. 2013, c. 34, s. 231(4), applicable to taxation years that begin after October 31, 2011, and formerly read:

(5.7) *Idem.* For the purpose of subsection (5.6),

(*a*) the relevant period in respect of a trust is the period that begins one year after the day on which the trust was created and ends at the end of the day that would, but for the election of the trust under subsection (5.3), be determined in respect of the trust under paragraph (4)(*a*.1) or (*b*), as the case may be;

(*b*) 2 individuals shall be deemed to be related to each other where one of them is the aunt, great aunt, uncle or great uncle of the other individual;

(*c*) an individual shall be deemed not to be a designated contributor in respect of a trust where it is reasonable to consider that one of the main purposes of a series of transactions or events that includes

(i) an individual becoming a trustee in respect of trust property, or

(ii) an acquisition of property or a borrowing by any individual

was to defer the day determined under paragraph (4)(*b*) in respect of the trust; and

(*d*) in determining whether all or substantially all of the value of shares of the capital stock of a corporation is derived from other property, the other property shall be deemed to include property substituted for the other property and property attributable to profits, gains or distributions in respect of the other property and the substituted property.

Related Sections: S. 104(1) Reference to trust or estate; s. 248(1), "individual", "property", "share", "trust"; s. 252(2) Relationships.

▶ 104(5.8) ◀

(5.8) Trust transfers. Where capital property, land included in inventory, Canadian resource property or foreign resource property is transferred at a particular time by a trust (in this subsection referred to as the "transferor trust") to another trust (in this subsection referred to as the "transferee trust") in circumstances in which subsection 107(2) or 107.4(3) or paragraph (*f*) of the definition *disposition* in subsection 248(1) applies,

(*a*) for the purposes of applying subsections (4) to (5.2) after the particular time,

(i) subject to paragraphs (*b*) to (*b*.3), the first day (in this subsection referred to as the "disposition day") that ends at or after the particular time that would, if this section were read without reference to paragraphs (4)(*a*.2) and (*a*.3), be determined in respect of the transferee trust is deemed to be the earliest of

(A) the first day ending at or after the particular time that would be determined under subsection (4) in respect of the transferor trust without regard to the transfer and any transaction or event occurring after the particular time,

(B) the first day ending at or after the particular time that would otherwise be determined under subsection (4) in respect of the transferee trust without regard to any transaction or event occurring after the particular time,

(C) the first day that ends at or after the particular time, where

(I) the transferor trust is a joint spousal or common-law partner trust, a post-1971 spousal or common-law partner trust or a trust described in the definition "pre- 1972 spousal trust" in subsection 108(1), and

(II) the spouse or common-law partner referred to in paragraph (4)(*a*) or in the definition "pre-1972 spousal trust" in subsection 108(1) is alive at the particular time,

(C.1) the first day that ends at or after the particular time, where

(I) the transferor trust is an *alter ego*trust, a trust to which paragraph (4)(*a*.4) applies or a joint spousal or common-law partner trust, and

(II) the taxpayer referred to in paragraph (4)(*a*) or (*a*.4), as the case may be, is alive at the particular time, and

(D) where

(I) the disposition day would, but for the application of this subsection to the transfer, be determined under paragraph (5.3)(*a*) in respect of the transferee trust, and

(II) the particular time is after the day that would, but for subsection (5.3), be determined under paragraph (4)(*b*) in respect of the transferee trust,

the first day ending at or after the particular time, and

(ii) where the disposition day determined in respect of the transferee trust under subparagraph (i) is earlier than the day referred to in clause (i)(B) in respect of the transferee trust, subsections (4) to (5.2) do not apply to the transferee trust on the day referred to in clause (i)(B) in respect of the transferee trust;

(*b*) paragraph (*a*) does not apply in respect of the transfer where

(i) the transferor trust is a post-1971 spousal or common-law partner trust or a trust described in the definition "pre-1972 spousal trust" in subsection 108(1),

(ii) the spouse or common-law partner referred to in paragraph (4)(*a*) or in the definition "pre-1972 spousal trust" in subsection 108(1) is alive at the particular time, and

(iii) the transferee trust is a post-1971 spousal or common-law partner trust or a trust described in the definition "pre-1972 spousal trust" in subsection 108(1);

(*b*.1) paragraph (*a*) does not apply in respect of the transfer where

(i) the transferor trust is an *alter ego*trust,

(ii) the taxpayer referred to in paragraph (4)(*a*) is alive at the particular time, and

(iii) the transferee trust is an *alter ego*trust;

(*b*.2) paragraph (*a*) does not apply in respect of the transfer where

(i) the transferor trust is a joint spousal or common-law partner trust,

(ii) either the taxpayer referred to in paragraph (4)(*a*), or the spouse or common-law partner referred to in that paragraph, is alive at the particular time, and

(iii) the transferee trust is a joint spousal or common-law partner trust;

(*b*.3) paragraph (*a*) does not apply in respect of the transfer where

(i) the transferor trust is a trust to which paragraph (4)(*a*.4) applies,

(ii) the taxpayer referred to in paragraph (4)(*a*.4) is alive at the particular time, and

(iii) the transferee trust is a trust to which paragraph (4)(*a*.4) applies; and

(*c*) for the purposes of subsection (5.3), unless a day ending before the particular time has been determined under paragraph (4)(*a*.1) or (*b*) or would, but for subsection (5.3), have been so determined, a day determined under subparagraph (*a*)(i) shall be deemed to be a day determined under paragraph (4)(*a*.1) or (*b*), as the case may be, in respect of the transferee trust.

Editorial Note: S. 104(5.8) is designed to prevent the avoidance of the 21-year deemed disposition rule by the use of trust-to-trust transfers that do not involve dispositions of property at fair market value (e.g., where there is no change in beneficial ownership). Essentially, this provision provides for a transferee trust to assume the next deemed disposition day of the transferor, if that day is earlier than the transferee's next deemed disposition day. With regard to *alter ego* trusts, where the settlor of an *alter ego* trust is still alive, or, in the case of a joint partner trust, where the settlor or the spouse or partner is still alive, a deemed disposition may occur as soon as the transfer is completed, unless the transferee trust also qualifies as an *alter ego* trust or a joint partner trust, as the case may be, and the settlor, or, in the case of a joint partner trust, either the settlor or the spouse or partner, is alive.

History: S. 104(5.8), the portion before paragraph (*a*) was replaced by S.C. 2017, c. 33, s. 35(2), applicable to taxation years that begin after 2016, and formerly read:

(5.8) *Trust transfers.* Where capital property (other than excluded property), land included in inventory, Canadian resource property or foreign resource property is transferred at a particular time by a trust (in this subsection referred to as the "transferor trust") to another trust (in this subsection referred to as the "transferee trust") in circumstances in which subsection 107(2) or 107.4(3) or paragraph (*f*) of the definition "disposition" in subsection 248(1) applies,

Related Sections: S. 54, "capital property"; s. 66(15), "Canadian resource property", "foreign resource property"; s. 104(1) Reference to trust or estate; s. 108(1), "excluded property"; s. 248(1), "Canadian resource property", "capital property", "common-law partner", "foreign resource property", "inventory", "trust"; s. 248(25.1) Trust-to-trust transfers.

Tax Window Files: Creation of Testamentary Trust, *2007 STEP Round Table Q.3, June 8, 2007*, CRA Document No. 2007-0233721C6. While successive trusts established in the will of the decedent may qualify as testamentary, the deemed disposition date of the new trusts under the 21-year deemed disposition rule will be determined in accordance with the rules set out in subsection 104(5.8); Divide Family Trust Into Separate Trusts, *International and Trusts Division Income Tax Rulings Directorate Policy and Legislation Branch, June 4, 2003,* CRA Document No. 2002-0180473. Application of s. 104(5.8) to division of family trust into separate trusts.

▶ 104(6) ◀

(6) Deduction in computing income of trust. Subject to subsections (7) to (7.1), for the purposes of this Part, there may be deducted in computing the income of a trust for a taxation year

(*a*) in the case of an employee trust, the amount by which the amount that would, but for this subsection, be its income for the year exceeds the amount, if any, by which

(i) the total of all amounts each of which is its income for the year from a business

exceeds

(ii) the total of all amounts each of which is its loss for the year from a business;

(*a*.1) in the case of a trust governed by an employee benefit plan, such part of the amount that would, but for this subsection, be its income for the year as was paid in the year to a beneficiary;

(*a*.2) where the taxable income of the trust for the year is subject to tax under this Part because of paragraph 146(4)(*c*) or subsection 146.3(3.1), the part of the amount that, but for this subsection, would be the income of the trust for the year that was paid in the year to a beneficiary;

(*a*.3) in the case of a trust deemed by subsection 143(1) to exist in respect of a congregation that is a constituent part of a religious organization, such part of its income for the year as became payable in the year to a beneficiary;

(*a*.4) in the case of an employee life and health trust, an amount that became payable by the trust in the year as a designated employee benefit (as defined in subsection 144.1(1)); and

(*b*) in any other case, the amount that the trust claims not exceeding the amount, if any, determined by the formula

$$A - B$$

where

A is the part of its income (determined without reference to this subsection and subsection (12)) for the year that became payable in the year to, or that was included under subsection 105(2) in computing the income of, a beneficiary, and

B is

(i) if the trust is a trust for which a day is to be determined under paragraph (4)(*a*) or (*a*.4) by reference to a death or later death, as the case may be, that has not occurred before the beginning of the year, the total of

(A) the part of its income (determined without reference to this subsection and subsection (12)) for the year that became payable in the year to, or that was included under subsection 105(2) in computing the income of, a beneficiary (other than an individual whose death is that death or later death, as the case may be), and

(B) the total of all amounts each of which

(I) is included in its income (determined without reference to this subsection and subsection (12)) for the year — if the year is the year in which that death or later death, as the case may be, occurs and paragraph (13.4)(*b*) does not apply in respect of the trust for the year — because of the application of subsection (4), (5), (5.1) or (5.2) or 12(10.2), and

(II) is not included in the amount determined for clause (A) for the year, and

(ii) if the trust is a SIFT trust for the year, the amount, if any, by which

(A) the amount determined for A for the trust for the year

exceeds

(B) the amount, if any, by which the amount determined for A for the trust for the year exceeds its non-portfolio earnings for the year.

Editorial Note: S. 104(6) enables a trust to deduct from its income certain amounts that would otherwise be included in its income for a year and that become payable in the year to a beneficiary in accordance with the terms of the trust agreement.

S. 104(24) states that, for purposes of s. 104(6), an amount shall be deemed not to have become payable to a beneficiary in a taxation year unless it was paid in the year to the beneficiary or the beneficiary was entitled in the year to enforce payment of the amount. Subsection 104(24) is overruled by 104(18) (trusts for minors) where certain conditions are met.

For many amounts paid or payable to a beneficiary that are not deductible by the trust owing to the restrictions in s. 104(6)(*b*), an election is available under either s. 104(13.1) or (13.2) to have the amount taxed in the trust and avoid the inclusion of such amounts in the beneficiary's income.

A similar election under subsection 107(2.11) is provided in respect of income or gains resulting from the distribution of properties to beneficiaries of a trust.

For a spousal or common-law partner trust, joint spousal or common-law partner trust, alter ego trust, or self-benefit trust (each of which is a trust for which a day is determined under amount B in paragraph 104(6)(*b*)), income in the taxation year of the trust that ends upon the death of the relevant life beneficiary under the trust that is payable to a person other than the life beneficiary is not deductible for the trust by virtue of the restriction in paragraph 104(6)(*b*). (The relevant life beneficiary is the settlor in the case of an alter ego or self-benefit trust; the settlor's spouse or common-law partner in the case of a spousal or common-law partner trust; and both the settlor and spouse or common-law partner in the case of a joint spousal trust.) Furthermore, any income resulting from the deemed disposition of the trust property upon the death of the relevant life beneficiary cannot be deducted by the trust. In certain limited circumstances, the income of the trust for the taxation year ending upon the death of the life beneficiary of a testamentary spousal or common-law partner trust will be included in the beneficiary's income; see paragraphs 104(13.4)(*b*) and (*b*.1).

History: Subparagraph (i) of the description of B in s. 104(6)(*b*) was replaced by S.C. 2016, c. 12, s. 35(1), applicable to the 2016 and subsequent taxation years, and formerly read:

(i) if the trust is a trust for which a day is to be determined under paragraph (4)(*a*) or (*a.4*) by reference to a death or later death, as the case may be, that has not occurred before the end of the year, the part of its income (determined without reference to this subsection and subsection (12)) for the year that became payable in the year to, or that was included under subsection 105(2) in computing the income of, a beneficiary (other than an individual whose death is that death or later death, as the case may be), and

S. 104(6)(*a.3*) was replaced by S.C. 2014, c. 39, s. 26(2), applicable to the 2016 and subsequent taxation years, and formerly read:

(*a*.3) in the case of an *inter vivos* trust deemed by subsection 143(1) to exist in respect of a congregation that is a constituent part of a religious organization, such part of its income for the year as became payable in the year to a beneficiary;

S. 104(6)(*b*) was replaced by S.C. 2014, c. 39, s. 26(3), applicable to the 2016 and subsequent taxation years, and formerly read:

(*b*) in any other case, such amount as the trust claims not exceeding the amount, if any, by which

(i) such part (in this section referred to as the trust's "adjusted distributions amount" for the taxation year) of the amount that, but for

(A) this subsection,

(B) subsections (5.1), (12), and 107(4),

(C) the application of subsections (4), (5) and (5.2) in respect of a day determined under paragraph (4)(*a*), and

(D) subsection 12(10.2), except to the extent that that subsection applies to amounts paid to a trust described in paragraph 70(6.1)(*b*) and before the death of the spouse or common-law partner referred to in that paragraph,

would be its income for the year as became payable in the year to a beneficiary or was included under subsection 105(2) in computing the income of a beneficiary

exceeds

(ii) where the trust

(A) is a post-1971 spousal or common-law partner trust that was created after December 20, 1991, or

(B) would be a post-1971 spousal or common-law partner trust if the reference in paragraph (4)(*a*) to "at the time it was created" were read as "on December 20, 1991",

and the spouse or common-law partner referred to in paragraph (4)(*a*) in respect of the trust is alive throughout the year, such part of the amount that, but for

(C) this subsection,

(D) subsections (12) and 107(4), and

(E) subsection 12(10.2), except to the extent that that subsection applies to an amount paid to a trust described in paragraph 70(6.1)(*b*) and before the death of the spouse or common-law partner referred to in that paragraph,

would be its income for the year as became payable in the year to a beneficiary (other than the spouse or common-law partner) or was included under subsection 105(2) in computing the income of a beneficiary (other than the spouse or common-law partner),

(ii.1) where the trust is an *alter ego* trust or a joint spousal or common-law partner trust and the death or later death, as the case may be, referred to in subparagraph (4)(*a*)(iv) has not occurred before the end of the year, such part of the amount that, but for this subsection and subsections (12), 12(10.2) and 107(4), would be its income as became payable in the year to a beneficiary (other than a taxpayer, spouse or common-law partner referred to in clause (4)(*a*)(iv)(A), (B) or (C)) or was included under subsection 105(2) in computing the income of a beneficiary (other than such a taxpayer, spouse or common-law partner),

(iii) where the trust is an *alter ego* trust, a joint spousal or common-law partner trust, a trust to which paragraph (4)(*a*.4) applies or a post-1971 spousal or common-law partner trust and the death or the later death, as the case may be, referred to in paragraph (4)(*a*) or (*a*.4) in respect of the trust occurred on a day in the year, the amount, if any, by which

(A) the maximum amount that would be deductible under this subsection in computing the trust's income for the year if this subsection were read without reference to this subparagraph

exceeds the total of

(B) the amount that, but for this subsection and subsections (12), 12(10.2) and 107(4), would be its income that became payable in the year to the taxpayer, spouse or common-law partner referred to in subparagraph (4)(*a*)(iii), clause (4)(*a*)(iv)(A), (B) or (C) or paragraph (4)(*a*.4), as the case may be, and

(C) the amount that would be the trust's income for the year if that income were computed without reference to this subsection and subsection (12) and as if the year began immediately after the end of the day, and

(iv) where the trust is a SIFT trust for the taxation year, the amount, if any, by which

(A) its adjusted distributions amount for the taxation year

exceeds

(B) the amount, if any, by which

(I) the amount that would, if this Act were read without reference to this subsection, be its income for the taxation year

exceeds

(II) its non-portfolio earnings for the taxation year.

S. 104(6), the portion before paragraph (*a*) was amended by S.C. 2013, c. 34, s. 10(1), applicable to taxation years that end after 2006. The portion of subsection 104(6) before paragraph (*a*) also applies to each earlier taxation year of a trust to which subsection 94(1) [should be 94(3) – CCH] applies and each taxation year of a beneficiary under the trust in which one of those earlier taxation years of the trust ends.

S. 104(6), the portion before (*a*), formerly read:

(6) *Deduction in computing income of trust.* For the purposes of this Part, there may be deducted in computing the income of a trust for a taxation year

S. 104(6)(*a.4*) was added by S.C. 2010, c. 25, s. 16(1), applicable after 2009.

Related Sections: S. 6(1)(*h*) Employee trust; s. 104(1) Reference to trust or estate; s. 104(4) Deemed disposition by trust; s. 104(5) Depreciable property; s. 104(5.1) Interest in NISA Fund No. 2; s. 104(5.2) Resource property; s. 104(12) Deduction of amounts included in preferred beneficiaries' incomes; s. 104(13.4) Death of beneficiary — spousal and similar trusts; s. 104(16) SIFT deemed dividend; s. 104(18) Trust for minor; s. 104(24) Amount payable; s. 105(2) Upkeep, etc; s. 107(4) Trusts in favour of spouse, common-law partner or self; s. 107.1 Distribution by certain employment-related trusts; s. 122.1(1), "SIFT trust", "non-portfolio earnings"; s. 143(1) Communal organizations; s. 143(2) Election in respect of income; s. 248(1), "amount", "common-law partner", "trust".

Canadian Tax Foundation: Christian, *Trust Planning: Documentation Requirements*, 2004 Tax for the Owner-Manager 4(3):2–4.

Tax Profile: December 2009 — Income Tax Consequences of Income Distributions by a Canadian Trust.

Forms: T3 SCH 9 — Income Allocations and Designations to Beneficiaries.

Interpretation Bulletins: *Primary* — IT-381R3 Trusts — Deduction of amounts paid or payable to beneficiaries and flow-through of taxable capital gains to beneficiaries. *Secondary* — IT-286R2 Trusts — Amount payable; IT-342R Trusts — Income payable to beneficiaries; IT-394R2 Preferred beneficiary election; IT-465R Non-resident beneficiaries of trusts; IT-500R Registered retirement savings plans — Death of an annuitant.

Tax Window Files: Deemed resident trust under subsection 94(3), *July 25, 2014*, CRA Document No. 2013-0513641I7; Innovative Instrument, *Financial Sector and Exempt Entities Division, Income Tax Rulings Directorate, Legislative Policy and Regulatory Affairs Branch, April 19, 2006*, CRA Document No. 2005-0145921R3. S. 104(7.1) not applying to deny a deduction to the Trust under s. 104(6)(*b*) of amounts payable to its unit holders; Distribution of Gain by Deemed Resident Trust, *Technical Interpretation, International and Trusts Division, March 5, 2004*, CRA Document No. 2003-0024621I7. Non-resident trust deemed resident in Canada under paragraph 94(1)(*c*) not entitled to a deduction in computing income under 104(6) for an amount payable to a non-resident beneficiary in respect of a taxable capital gain on taxable Canadian property.

Cases: The trustees chose not to allocate income to a beneficiary in a taxation year because the CRA had assessed other years and treated the trust and the beneficiary (which was also a trust) as one trust under subsection 104(2); the trustees felt that in light of the CRA assessments, an allocation in the taxation year at issue might be invalid. Subsequently, the dispute in respect of the subsection 104(2) was resolved, after which the trustees sought a rectification order to allocate income to the beneficiary for the taxation year. The Court held that the decision not to allocate income was not a mistake that ought to be remedied either by application of the doctrine of rectification or by the inherent jurisdiction of the court. There was no evidence that the trustees had a contrary intention at the time of that decision. *BC Trust v. Attorney General of Canada*, 2017 DTC 5017 (BCSC)

Notwithstanding certain comments in *Langer Family Trust v. MNR*, 2002 DTC 1055 (T.C.C.) suggesting payments to third parties may not be deductible, in *Cockeram et al. v. The Queen*, 2004 DTC 2829 (T.C.C.), aff'd. 2005 DTC 5707 (F.C.A.), the Court suggested that it would not disallow payments to third parties : "If I had concluded that the property was or had become an asset of the Trust ... I see no reason ... why payments to third parties which benefit beneficiaries by preserving an asset of the Trust, may not be deducted pursuant to these provisions, where properly documented."

► 104(7) ◄

(7) Non-resident beneficiary. No deduction may be made under subsection (6) in computing the income for a taxation year of a trust in respect of such part of an amount that would otherwise be its income for the year as became payable in the year to a beneficiary who was, at any time in the year, a designated beneficiary of the trust (as that expression applies for the purposes of section 210.3) unless, throughout the year, the trust was resident in Canada.

Editorial Note: The main intent of s. 104(7) is to prevent a non-resident trust from earning income from sources in Canada and in turn flowing out the income to its non-resident beneficiary (or other "designated beneficiary") without the imposition of the appropriate amount of Canadian tax.

Related Sections: S. 104(24) Amount payable; s. 210, "designated beneficiary".

Tax Window Files: Deemed Resident Trust-Deductions, *International and Trusts Division, Income Tax Rulings Directorate, Policy and Planning Branch,, March 5, 2004*, CRA Document No. 2003-0024621I7. Non-resident trust deemed resident in Canada under s. 94(1)(*c*) not entitled to a deduction in computing income under s. 104(6) for an amount payable to a non-resident beneficiary re a taxable capital gain on taxable Canadian property.

▶ 104(7.01) ◀

(7.01) Trusts deemed to be resident in Canada. If a trust is deemed by subsection 94(3) to be resident in Canada for a taxation year for the purpose of computing the trust's income for the year, the maximum amount deductible under subsection (6) in computing its income for the year is the amount, if any, by which

(*a*) the maximum amount that, if this Act were read without reference to this subsection, would be deductible under subsection (6) in computing its income for the year,

exceeds

(*b*) the total of

(i) the portion of the trust's designated income for the year (within the meaning assigned by section 210) that became payable in the year to a non-resident beneficiary under the trust in respect of an interest of the non-resident as a beneficiary under the trust, and

(ii) all amounts each of which is determined by the formula

$$A \times B$$

where

A is an amount (other than an amount described in subparagraph (i)) that

(A) is paid or credited (having the meaning assigned by Part XIII) in the year to the trust,

(B) would, if this Act were read without reference to subparagraph 94(3)(*a*)(viii), paragraph 212(2)(*b*) and sections 216 and 217, be an amount as a consequence of the payment or crediting of which the trust would have been liable to tax under Part XIII, and

(C) becomes payable in the year by the trust to a non-resident beneficiary under the trust in respect of an interest of the non-resident as a beneficiary under the trust, and

B is

(A) 0.35, if the trust can establish to the satisfaction of the Minister that the non-resident beneficiary to whom the amount described in the description of A is payable is resident in a country with which Canada has a tax treaty under which the income tax that Canada may impose on the beneficiary in respect of the amount is limited, and

(B) 0.6, in any other case.

Editorial Note: Subsection 104(7.01) acts as a proxy for Part XIII withholding tax and Part XII.2 tax on designated income on amounts distributed by a trust deemed resident in Canada under s. 94(3) where the income distributed by the trust came from a Canadian source (such as a corporation resident in Canada) and is distributed to a non-resident beneficiary. Generally, the provision operates by reducing the deduction otherwise available under s. 104(6) from the trust's income.

With respect to Part XIII withholding tax, the amount of the reduction is intended to replicate the withholding tax that would apply to a trust resident in Canada under common law principles. The use of .35 of the factor in determining the limitation on the deduction where the beneficiary is resident in a treaty country results in approximately 15% of tax on the Canadian source income, which is generally the rate under s. 212(1)(*c*) after reduction by treaty. Where the .6 factor must be used, the trust will pay 25% tax on the income, which is the general withholding tax rate.

History: S. 104(7.01) was added by S.C. 2013, c. 34, s. 10(2), applicable to taxation years that end after 2006. Subsection 104(7.01) also applies to each earlier taxation year of a trust to which subsection 94(1) [should be 94(3) – CCH] applies and each taxation year of a beneficiary under the trust in which one of those earlier taxation years of the trust ends.

Canadian Tax Foundation: Ouelette and Warner, *Estate Planning: US-Resident Beneficiaries of a Canadian Estate — Part 1,* 2014 Canadian Tax Journal 1:197–219.

▶ 104(7.02) ◀

(7.02) Limitation — amount claimed as gift. No deduction may be made under subsection (6) in computing the income for a taxation year of an estate that arose on and as a consequence of an individual's death in respect of a payment to the extent that the payment is a gift in respect of which an amount is deducted under section 118.1 for any taxation year in computing the individual's tax payable under this Part.

Editorial Note: Beginning in 2016, the donations credit for gifts made as a consequence of death can be claimed by either the deceased in the year of death or the preceding year, or by the deceased's estate in the year of the donation or a previous year. Subsection 104(7.02) provides that the estate cannot deduct the amount payable to the donee if the deceased individual claims the tax credit.

History: S. 104(7.02) was added by S.C. 2014, c. 39, s. 26(4), applicable to taxation years that end after August 28, 2014.

Related Sections: 104(6) Deduction in computing income of trust.

▶ 104(7.1) ◀

(7.1) Capital interest greater than income interest. Where it is reasonable to consider that one of the main purposes for the existence of any term, condition, right or other attribute of an interest in a trust (other than a personal trust) is to give a beneficiary a percentage interest in the property of the trust that is greater than the beneficiary's percentage interest in the income of the trust, no amount may be deducted under paragraph (6)(*b*) in computing the income of the trust.

Related Sections: S. 104(7.2) Avoidance of s. (7.1).

Interpretation Bulletins: *Secondary* — IT-381R3 Trusts — Deduction of amounts paid or payable to beneficiaries and flow-through of taxable capital gains to beneficiaries.

Tax Window Files: Allocation of Gains to Redeeming Unitholders, *Resources, Partnerships and Trusts Division Income Tax Rulings Directorate, Policy and Legislation Branch, May 23, 2001,* CRA Document No. 2000-0041363. S. 104(7.1) may deny a trust a deduction under s. 104(6)(*b*) where the main purpose of the existence of any term, condition, right or other attribute of the trust is to give a beneficiary a percentage interest in the property of the trust that is greater than the beneficiary's percentage interest in the income of the trust. See also Document no. 9820753, May 10, 1999 — Reclassification; Document no. 9700733, September 19, 1997 — Pension fund — Pooling vehicles; Document no. 2004-0075461R3, October 6, 2004 — Amendment of Mutual Fund Trust Agreements.

▶ 104(7.2) ◀

(7.2) Avoidance of s. (7.1). Notwithstanding any other provision of this Act, where

(*a*) a taxpayer has acquired a right to or to acquire an interest in a trust, or a right to or to acquire a property of a trust, and

(*b*) it is reasonable to consider that one of the main purposes of the acquisition was to avoid the application of subsection (7.1) in respect of the trust,

on a disposition of the right (other than pursuant to the exercise thereof), the interest or the property, there shall be included in computing the income of the taxpayer for the taxation year in which the disposition occurs the amount, if any, by which

(*c*) the proceeds of disposition of the right, interest or property, as the case may be,

exceed

(*d*) the cost amount to the taxpayer of the right, interest or property, as the case may be.

▶ 104(8) ◀

(8) Limitation on deduction — (Repealed by 1988, c. 55, s. 71(4).)

▶ 104(9) ◀

(9) Idem — (Repealed by 1974-75-76, c. 26, s. 65(1).)

▶ 104(10) ◀

(10) Where property owned for non-residents — (Repealed by S.C. 2013, c. 34, s. 231(5).)

History: S. 104(10) was repealed by S.C. 2013, c. 34, s. 231(5), applicable to the 2005 and subsequent taxation years, and formerly read:

(10) *Where property owned for non-residents.* Where all the property of a trust is owned by the trustee for the benefit of non-resident persons or their unborn issue, in addition to the amount that may be deducted under subsection (6), there may be deducted in computing the income of the trust for a taxation year for the purposes of this Part, such part of the dividends and interest received by the trust in a year from a non-resident-owned investment corporation as are not deductible under that subsection in computing the income of the trust for the year.

Related Sections: S. 104(11) Dividend received from non-resident-owned investment corporation.

▶ 104(11) ◀

(11) Dividend received from non-resident-owned investment corporation — (Repealed by S.C. 2013, c. 34, s. 231(5).)

History: S. 104(11) was repealed by S.C. 2013, c. 34, s. 231(5), applicable to the 2005 and subsequent taxation years, and formerly read:

(11) *Dividend received from non-resident-owned investment corporation.* Where any part of the dividends received in a taxation year by a trust described in subsection (10) from a non-resident-owned investment corporation are deductible under that subsection in computing the income of the trust for the year, for the purposes of Part XIII the trust shall be deemed to have paid to a non-resident person on the last day of the year an amount equal to that part, as income of the non-resident person from the trust.

▶ 104(12) ◀

(12) Deduction of amounts included in preferred beneficiaries' incomes. There may be deducted in computing the income of a trust for a taxation year the lesser of

(*a*) the total of all amounts designated under subsection (14) by the trust in respect of the year, and

(*b*) the accumulating income of the trust for the year.

Related Sections: S. 104(6) Deduction in computing income of trust; s. 104(8) Limitation on deduction; s. 104(13) Income of beneficiary; s. 104(22) Designation of foreign source income by trust; s. 108(1) Definitions.

Interpretation Bulletins: *Secondary* — IT-381R3 Trusts — Deduction of amounts paid or payable to beneficiaries and flow-through of taxable capital gains to beneficiaries; IT-394R2 Preferred beneficiary election; IT-465R Non-resident beneficiaries of trusts.

▶ 104(13) ◀

(13) Income of beneficiary. There shall be included in computing the income for a particular taxation year of a beneficiary under a trust such of the following amounts as are applicable:

(*a*) in the case of a trust (other than a trust referred to in paragraph (*a*) of the definition "trust" in subsection 108(1)), such part of the amount that, but for subsections (6) and (12), would be the trust's income for the trust's taxation year that ended in the particular year as became payable in the trust's year to the beneficiary; and

(*b*) in the case of a trust governed by an employee benefit plan to which the beneficiary has contributed as an employer, such part of the amount that, but for subsections (6) and (12), would be the trust's income for the trust's taxation year that ended in the particular year as was paid in the trust's year to the beneficiary.

Editorial Note: Subsection 104(13) requires that a beneficiary of a trust shall include in computing his/her income for a particular year such part of the trust's income that was paid or payable to him/her in the trust's tax year that ended in the particular year. The trust may elect under s. 104(6) to deduct from its taxable income all or part of the amounts payable to beneficiaries.

The election under s. 104(6) is discretionary; the trust may claim an amount that is less than the full amount available under the subsection. Where the elected amount is less than the amount of income payable to beneficiaries, the trust may, pursuant to ss. 104(13.1) (income) and (13.2) (capital gains), designate an amount that is deemed not to have been payable to a beneficiary. Where the trust makes this designation, the beneficiary is not required to include such amount in his income. The designation allows the trust to be taxed on the income even if the income was paid or payable to a beneficiary. The result is that s. 104(13.1), for example, allows a trust to apply non-capital losses of other years, which may not be allocated to a beneficiary, against the trust income for the year. Additionally, the taxation of income in a testamentary trust may result in a tax saving where the trust's marginal tax rate is lower than the rate paid by the recipient beneficiary. Note that the graduated rate taxation for testamentary trusts was mostly eliminated for the 2016 and later taxation years. An exception is provided for estates for a period of 36 months after the death, i.e., for "graduated rate estates", to allow for administration.

See ss. 104(18) and (24) regarding the "payable" requirement.

Related Sections: S. 6(1)(*h*) Employee trust; s. 104(13.1) Amounts deemed not paid; s. 104(13.2) Amounts designated by trust; s. 104(16) SIFT deemed dividend; s. 104(18) Trust for minor; s. 104(19) Taxable dividends; s. 104(21) Taxable capital gains; s. 104(22) Designation of foreign source income by trust; s. 105(1) Benefits under trust; s. 105(2) Upkeep, etc; s. 106(1) Income interest in trust; s. 107.1 Distribution by certain employment-related trusts; s. 108(5) Interpretation; s. 120.4 Tax on split income; s. 143(2) Election in respect of income; s. 212(1)(*c*) Estate or trust income; s. 214(3) Deemed payments.

Interpretation Bulletins: *Primary* — IT-342R Trusts — Income payable to beneficiaries. *Secondary* — IT-286R2 Trusts — Amount payable; IT-381R3 Trusts — Deduction of amounts paid or payable to beneficiaries and flow-through of taxable capital gains to beneficiaries; IT-465R Non-resident beneficiaries of trusts; IT-500R Registered retirement savings plans — Death of an annuitant; IT-524 Trusts — Flow-through of taxable dividends to a beneficiary — After 1987.

Tax Window Files: 2017 CPA Alberta Q25: Estates – Income Paid or Payable, *September 14, 2017*, CRA Document No. 2017-0703921C6; Timing of Income Inclusion For Trust Beneficiary, *March 6, 2006*, CRA Document No. 2005-0159081I7. Income amounts must be recognized by the beneficiary in the beneficiary's taxation year in which the relevant trust taxation year ends; the relevant trust taxation year being that in which the amounts became payable by the trust to the beneficiary; Allocation of Income Earned by an Estate, *January 16, 2006*, CRA Document No. 2005-0116041E5. Where the will is silent on the matter, the even-hand principle would suggest that, to the extent that the income can be distributed to the beneficiaries, it must be distributed proportionately, according to each beneficiary's share.

▶ 104(13.1) ◀

(13.1) Amounts deemed not paid. Where a trust, in its return of income under this Part for a taxation year throughout which it was resident in Canada and not exempt from tax under Part I by reason of subsection 149(1), designates an amount in respect of a beneficiary under the trust, not exceeding the amount determined by the formula

$$A/B \times (C - D - E)$$

where

A is the beneficiary's share of the income of the trust for the year computed without reference to this Act,

B is the total of all amounts each of which is a beneficiary's share of the income of the trust for the year computed without reference to this Act,

C is the total of all amounts each of which is an amount that, but for this subsection or subsection (13.2), would be included in computing the income of a beneficiary under the trust by reason of subsection (13) or 105(2) for the year,

D is the amount deducted under subsection (6) in computing the income of the trust for the year, and

E is equal to the amount determined by the trust for the year and used as the value of C for the purposes of the formula in subsection (13.2) or, if no amount is so determined, nil,

the amount so designated shall be deemed, for the purposes of subsections (13) and 105(2), not to have been paid or to have become payable in the year to or for the benefit of the beneficiary or out of income of the trust.

Editorial Note: Subsection 104(13.1) allows the trust to include in its income such amounts that are paid or payable to a beneficiary and that would otherwise be included in the beneficiary's income. Historically, the purpose of the provision has been two-fold. First, it has allowed the trust to include such income at the trust level for the purpose of utilizing the trust's losses, or, in the case of a testamentary trust prior to 2016, to save tax in those cases where the trust's marginal rate of tax is lower than the beneficiary's rate. For 2016 and subsequent years, only "graduated rate estates" (subsection 248(1)) and "qualified disability trusts" (subsection 122(3)) are taxed at graduated tax rates, with all other testamentary trusts being subject to a flat tax at the highest marginal rate. Second, it avoided double taxation in those cases where the trust is denied a deduction of such amounts (for example, owing to the restrictions found in paragraph 104(6)(*b*)). Subsection 104(13.2) has served a similar purpose for the trust's taxable capital gains paid or payable to a beneficiary.

Additionally, the designation under subsection 104(13.1) (or (13.2)) may have been beneficial where a trust was set up in a province that had lower tax rates than the beneficiary's province of residence.

Effective for 2016 and subsequent taxation years, the designations under subsections 104(13.1) and (13.2) are restricted. The designations will be invalid if the trust's taxable income otherwise determined for the year is greater than nil (subsection (13.3)).

Basically, this means that the designations will be allowed only to the extent that they are offset by loss carryovers that are deductible in computing taxable income.

There is no prescribed form for making a designation pursuant to s. 104(13.1). The designation is made by indicating the designated amount on line 472 of the trust return and by attaching a statement to the T3 return showing the income designated and the amount designated for each beneficiary. The fact that the income is taxed in the hands of the trust is not evidence of a designation (see CRA document no. 2012-0437171E5).

Related Sections: S. 53(2)(*h*) Amounts to be deducted — Capital interest in a trust; s. 104(13.3) Invalid designation; s. 111(4) Loss restriction event — capital losses; s. 111(5) Loss restriction event — non-capital losses and farm losses; s. 220(3.2) Late, amended or revoked elections; s. 248(1) "graduated rate estate".

Canadian Tax Foundation: Chan and Morin, *Distributions by Canadian Testamentary Trusts*, 2005 Canadian Tax Journal 4:1090–1110.

Tax Profile: February 2010 — Planning With Trusts; July 2009 — Residency of Trusts — Under Attack?; February 2008 — Income Splitting A–Z.

Interpretation Bulletins: *Secondary* — IT-342R Trusts — Income payable to beneficiaries; IT-381R3 Trusts — Deduction of amounts paid or payable to beneficiaries and flow-through of taxable capital gains to beneficiaries; IT-394R2 Preferred beneficiary election.

Tax Window Files: 2016 STEP - Q5 - Subsection 104(13.3), *June 10, 2016*, CRA Document No. 2016-0634901C6; Income designation under subsection 104(13.1), *October 17, 2013*, CRA Document No. 2012-0437171E5.

Cases: There is no time limit for making a designation under s. 104(13.1); it may be made retroactively on an amended return. *Lussier v. The Queen*, 2000 DTC 1677 (T.C.C.)

▶ 104(13.2) ◀

(13.2) Idem. Where a trust, in its return of income under this Part for a taxation year throughout which it was resident in Canada and not exempt from tax under Part I by reason of subsection 149(1), designates an amount in respect of a beneficiary under the trust, not exceeding the amount determined by the formula

$$A/B \times C$$

where

A is the amount designated by the trust for the year in respect of the beneficiary under subsection (21),

B is the total of all amounts each of which has been designated for the year in respect of a beneficiary of the trust under subsection (21), and

C is the amount determined by the trust and used in computing all amounts each of which is designated by the trust for the year under this subsection, not exceeding the amount by which

(i) the total of all amounts each of which is an amount that, but for this subsection or subsection (13.1), would be included in computing the income of a beneficiary under the trust by reason of subsection (13) or 105(2) for the year

exceeds

(ii) the amount deducted under subsection (6) in computing the income of the trust for the year,

the amount so designated shall

(*a*) for the purposes of subsections (13) and 105(2) (except in the application of subsection (13) for the purposes of subsection (21)), be deemed not to have been paid or to have become payable in the year to or for the benefit of the beneficiary or out of income of the trust; and

(*b*) except for the purposes of subsection (21) as it applies for the purposes of subsections (21.1) and (21.2), reduce the amount of the taxable capital gains of the beneficiary otherwise included in computing the beneficiary's income for the year by reason of subsection (21).

Editorial Note: See the editorial note following s. 104(13.1).

History: S. 104(13.2)(*a*) was replaced by S.C. 2013, c. 34, s. 231(6), in force June 26, 2013, and formerly read:

(*a*) for the purposes of subsections (13) and 105(2) (except in the application of subsection (13) for the purposes of subsection (21)), be deemed not to have been paid or to have become payable in the year to or for the benefit of the beneficiaries or out of income of the trust; and

Related Sections: S. 53(2)(*h*) Amounts to be deducted — Capital interest in a trust; s. 104(13.3) Invalid designation; s. 111(4) Loss restriction event — capital losses; s. 111(5) Loss restriction event — non-capital losses and farm losses; s. 248(1) "graduated rate estate".

Canadian Tax Foundation: Chan and Morin, *Distributions by Canadian Testamentary Trusts*, 2005 Canadian Tax Journal 4:1090–1110.

Tax Profile: July 2009 — Residency of Trusts — Under Attack?.

Interpretation Bulletins: *Secondary* — IT-342R Trusts — Income payable to beneficiaries; IT-381R3 Trusts — Deduction of amounts paid or payable to beneficiaries and flow-through of taxable capital gains to beneficiaries.

Tax Window Files: 2016 STEP - Q5 - Subsection 104(13.3), *June 10, 2016*, CRA Document No. 2016-0634901C6.

▶ 104(13.3) ◀

(13.3) Invalid designation. Any designation made under subsection (13.1) or (13.2) by a trust in its return of income under this Part for a taxation year is invalid if the trust's taxable income for the year, determined without reference to this subsection, is greater than nil.

History: S. 104(13.3) was added by S.C. 2014, c. 39, s. 26(5), applicable to the 2016 and subsequent taxation years.

▶ 104(13.4) ◀

(13.4) Death of beneficiary — spousal and similar trusts. If an individual's death occurs on a day in a particular taxation year of a trust and the death is the death or later death, as the case may be, referred to in paragraph (4)(*a*), (*a.1*) or (*a.4*) in respect of the trust,

(*a*) the particular year is deemed to end at the end of that day, a new taxation year of the trust is deemed to begin immediately after that day and, for the purpose of determining the trust's fiscal period after the new taxation year began, the trust is deemed not to have established a fiscal period before the new taxation year began;

(*b*) subject to paragraph (*b*.1), the trust's income (determined without reference to subsections (6) and (12)) for the particular year is, notwithstanding subsection (24), deemed

(i) to have become payable in the year to the individual, and

(ii) not

(A) to have become payable to another beneficiary, or

(B) to be included under subsection 105(2) in computing the individual's income;

(*b*.1) paragraph (*b*) does not apply in respect of the trust for the particular year, unless

(i) the individual is resident in Canada immediately before the death,

(ii) the trust is, immediately before the death, a testamentary trust that

(A) is a post-1971 spousal or common-law partner trust, and

(B) was created by the will of a taxpayer who died before 2017, and

(iii) an election — made jointly between the trust and the legal representative administering the individual's graduated rate estate in prescribed form — that paragraph (*b*) applies is filed with

(A) the individual's return of income under this Part for the individual's year, and

(B) the trust's return of income under this Part for the particular year; and

(*c*) in respect of the particular year

(i) the references in paragraph 150(1)(*c*) to "year" and in subparagraph (*a*)(ii) of the definition "balance-due day" in subsection 248(1) to "taxation year" are to be read as "calendar year in which the taxation year ends", and

(ii) the reference in subsection 204(2) of the *Income Tax Regulations* to "end of the taxation year" is to be read as "end of the calendar year in which the taxation year ends".

Editorial Note: Beginning in 2016, a spousal or common-law partner trust, joint spousal or common-law partner trust, alter ego trust, or self-benefit trust (each of which is a trust in respect of which a beneficiary's death is referred to in the preamble to subsection 104(13.4)) is deemed to have a taxation year end at the end of the day on which the relevant life beneficiary dies. (The relevant life beneficiary is the settlor in the case of an alter ego or self-benefit trust; the settlor's spouse or common-law partner in the case of a spousal or common-law partner trust; and both the settlor and spouse or common-law partner in the case of a joint spousal trust.) The income of the trust for that taxation year that is not payable to the relevant life beneficiary is included in the trust's income and cannot be deducted even if payable to another beneficiary. In the limited circumstances in which paragraph 104(13.4)(*b*) applies (see paragraph (13.4)(*b*.1)), all of the income of the trust for that year is deemed to be payable to the life beneficiary and therefore included in that beneficiary's income rather than the trust's income.

History: S. 104(13.4)(*b*), the portion before subparagraph (i) was replaced by S.C. 2016, c. 12, s. 35(2), applicable to the 2016 and subsequent taxation years, and formerly read:

(*b*) the trust's income (determined without reference to subsections (6) and (12)) for the particular year is, notwithstanding subsection (24), deemed

S. 104(13.4)(*b*.1) was added by S.C. 2016, c. 12, s. 35(3), applicable to the 2016 and subsequent taxation years.

S. 104(13.4)(*c*)(i) was replaced by S.C. 2016, c. 12, s. 35(4), applicable to the 2016 and subsequent taxation years, and formerly read:

(i) the references in paragraphs 150(1)(*c*) and (*a*) of the definition "balance-due day" in subsection 248(1) to "year" are to be read as "calendar year in which the year ends", and

S. 104(13.4) was added by S.C. 2014, c. 39, s. 26(5), applicable to the 2016 and subsequent taxation years.

Related Sections: 104(4) Deemed disposition by trust; 104(6) Deduction in computing income of trust; 160(1.4) Joint liability — spousal and similar trusts.

Tax Window Files: 2015 STEP - Q6 - Subsection 104(13.4), *June 18, 2015*, CRA Document No. 2015-0572121C6.

► 104(14) ◄

(14) Election by trust and preferred beneficiary. Where a trust and a preferred beneficiary under the trust for a particular taxation year of the trust jointly so elect in respect of the particular year in prescribed manner, such part of the accumulating income of the trust for the particular year as is designated in the election, not exceeding the allocable amount for the preferred beneficiary in respect of the trust for the particular year, shall be included in computing the income of the preferred beneficiary for the beneficiary's taxation year in which the particular year ended and shall not be included in computing the income of any beneficiary of the trust for a subsequent taxation year.

Editorial Note: The preferred beneficiary election allows a trust to retain any of its accumulating income in a particular year while shifting the tax liability thereon to a preferred beneficiary. When that same income is ultimately distributed to a beneficiary (which need not be the preferred beneficiary), there is no further tax payable by the recipient beneficiary. Thus, the election allows income splitting. The amount designated in an election under s. 104(14) must be part of the accumulating income of the trust and may not exceed the allocable amount for the preferred beneficiary. The accumulating income of a trust is defined in s. 108(1) and the allocable amount for a preferred beneficiary is determined under s. 104(15).

The term "preferred beneficiary" is defined in s. 108(1).

Related Regulations: 600(b); 2800(1), (2), (2.1).

Related Sections: S. 104(12) Deduction of amounts included in preferred beneficiaries' incomes; s. 104(15) Allocable amount for preferred beneficiary; s. 104(16) SIFT deemed dividend; s. 104(19) Taxable dividends; s. 104(21) Taxable capital gains; s. 104(22) Designation of foreign source income by trust; s. 108(1), "trust"; s. 220(3.2) Late, amended or revoked elections.

Information Circulars: IC 07-1 Taxpayer Relief Provisions.

Interpretation Bulletins: *Primary* — IT-394R2 Preferred beneficiary election. *Secondary* — IT-381R3 Trusts — Deduction of amounts paid or payable to beneficiaries and flow-through of taxable capital gains to beneficiaries; IT-500R Registered retirement savings plans — Death of an annuitant; IT-524 Trusts — Flow-through of taxable dividends to a beneficiary — After 1987.

Tax Window Files: Tax on split income & preferred beneficiary, *July 6, 2018*, CRA Document No. 2018-0759521E5; 2016 STEP - Q4 - QDT & pref beneficiary election, *June 10, 2016*, CRA Document No. 2016-0645801C6.

Cases: A preferred beneficiary election filed 9 days late, not signed by the trustees or any beneficiary and not disclosing any information concerning the provisions of the trust and its administration was held to be invalid. *Muzich Family Trust v. M.N.R.*, 93 DTC 314 (T.C.C.). See also *Degrace Family Trust v. The Queen*, 99 DTC 453 (T.C.C.).

► 104(14.01) ◄

(14.01) Late, amended or revoked election — (Repealed by S.C. 2014, c. 39, s. 26(6).)

History: S. 104(14.01) was repealed by S.C. 2014, c. 39, s. 26(6), applicable to the 2016 and subsequent taxation years, and formerly read:

(14.01) *Late, amended or revoked election.* A trust and a preferred beneficiary under the trust may jointly make an election, or amend or revoke an election made, under subsection (14) where the election, amendment or revocation

(*a*) is made solely because of an election or revocation to which subsection 110.6(25), (26) or (27) applies; and

(*b*) is filed in prescribed manner with the Minister when the election or revocation referred to in paragraph (*a*) is filed.

► 104(14.02) ◄

(14.02) Late, amended or revoked election — (Repealed by S.C. 2014, c. 39, s. 26(6).)

History: S. 104(14.02) was repealed by S.C. 2014, c. 39, s. 26(6), applicable to the 2016 and subsequent taxation years, and formerly read:

(14.02) *Late, amended or revoked election.* Where a trust and a preferred beneficiary under the trust have made an election or amended or revoked an election in accordance with subsection (14.01), (*a*) the election or the amended election, as the case may be, is deemed to have been made on time for the purpose of subsection (14); and

(*b*) the election that was revoked is deemed, otherwise than for the purposes of this subsection and subsection (14.01), never to have been made.

▶ 104(14.1) ◀

(14.1) NISA election — (Repealed by S.C. 2014, c. 39, s. 26(6).)

History: S. 104(14.1) was repealed by S.C. 2014, c. 39, s. 26(6), applicable to the 2016 and subsequent taxation years, and formerly read:

(14.1) *NISA election.* Where, at the end of the day on which a taxpayer dies and as a consequence of the death, an amount would, but for this subsection, be deemed by subsection (5.1) to have been paid to a trust out of the trust's interest in a NISA Fund No. 2 and the trust and the legal representative of the taxpayer so elect in prescribed manner, such portion of the amount as is designated in the election shall be deemed to have been paid to the taxpayer out of a NISA Fund No. 2 of the taxpayer immediately before the end of the day and, for the purpose of paragraph (*a*) of the description of B in subsection 12(10.2) in respect of the trust, the amount shall be deemed to have been paid out of the trust's NISA Fund No. 2 immediately before the end of the day.

▶ 104(15) ◀

(15) Allocable amount for preferred beneficiary. For the purpose of subsection (14), the allocable amount for a preferred beneficiary under a trust in respect of the trust for a taxation year is

(*a*) where the trust is an *alter ego* trust, a joint spousal or common-law partner trust, a post-1971 spousal or common-law partner trust or a trust described in the definition "pre-1972 spousal trust" in subsection 108(1) at the end of the year and a beneficiary, referred to in paragraph (4)(*a*) or in that definition, is alive at the end of the year, an amount equal to

(i) if the preferred beneficiary is a beneficiary so referred to, the trust's accumulating income for the year, and

(ii) in any other case, nil;

(*b*) where paragraph (*a*) does not apply and the preferred beneficiary's interest in the trust is not solely contingent on the death of another beneficiary who has a capital interest in the trust and who does not have an income interest in the trust, the trust's accumulating income for the year; and

(*c*) in any other case, nil.

Related Regulations: 2800(3), (4).

Related Sections: S. 104(1) Reference to trust or estate; s. 104(4) Deemed disposition by trust; s. 104(12) Deduction of amounts included in preferred beneficiaries' incomes; s. 108(1), "common-law partner", "pre-1972 spousal trust", "trust"; s. 248(1), "trust".

Interpretation Bulletins: *Secondary* — IT-394R2 Preferred beneficiary election.

▶ 104(16) ◀

(16) SIFT deemed dividend. If an amount (in this subsection and section 122 referred to as the trust's "non-deductible distributions amount" for the taxation year) is determined under subparagraph (ii) of the description of B in paragraph (6)(*b*) in respect of a SIFT trust for a taxation year

(*a*) each beneficiary under the SIFT trust to whom at any time in the taxation year an amount became payable by the trust is deemed to have received at that time a taxable dividend that was paid at that time by a taxable Canadian corporation;

(*b*) the amount of a dividend described in paragraph (a) as having been received by a beneficiary at any time in a taxation year is equal to the amount determined by the formula

$$A/B \times C$$

where

A is the amount that became payable at that time by the SIFT trust to the beneficiary,

B is the total of all amounts, each of which became payable in the taxation year by the SIFT trust to a beneficiary under the SIFT trust, and

C is the SIFT trust's non-deductible distributions amount for the taxation year;

(*c*) the amount of a dividend described in paragraph (*a*) in respect of a beneficiary under the SIFT trust is deemed for the purpose of subsection (13) not to be an amount payable to the beneficiary; and

(*d*) for the purposes of applying Part XIII in respect of each dividend described in paragraph (*a*), the SIFT trust is deemed to be a corporation resident in Canada that paid the dividend.

Editorial Note: The amount of the dividend deemed to have been received by a beneficiary of the SIFT trust under s. 104(16) is considered an "eligible dividend" (s. 89(1)). As such, if the beneficiary is a Canadian resident individual, the beneficiary will be entitled to the enhanced dividend tax credit under s. 121(*b*). If the beneficiary is a Canadian corporation, it will be eligible for the intercorporate dividend deduction under s. 112(1). If the beneficiary is non-resident, s. 104(16)(*d*) provides that the deemed dividend is treated as a taxable dividend received from a corporation resident in Canada for the purposes of the Part XIII withholding tax, which may be reduced by income tax treaty.

History: S. 104(16), the portion before paragraph (*a*) was replaced by S.C. 2014, c. 39, s. 26(7), applicable to the 2016 and subsequent taxation years, and formerly read:

(16) *SIFT deemed dividend.* If an amount (in this subsection and section 122 referred to as the trust's "non-deductible distributions amount" for the taxation year) is determined under subparagraph (6)(*b*)(iv) in respect of a SIFT trust for a taxation year

Related Sections: S. 89(1), "eligible dividend", "taxable dividend"; s. 112(1) Deduction of taxable dividends received by corporation resident in Canada; s. 122.1(1), "SIFT trust", "non-portfolio earnings".

Tax Profile: September 2007 — U.S. and Canadian Tax Considerations in Acquiring Canadian Income Trusts; June 2007 — Canadian Income Trusts for Sale.

▶ 104(17) ◀

(17) Depletion allowance — (Repealed by 1988, c. 55, s. 71(6).)

▶ 104(17.1) ◀

(17.1) Determination, etc., ineffective — (Repealed by 1988, c. 55, s. 71(6).)

▶ 104(17.2) ◀

(17.2) Idem — (Repealed by 1988, c. 55, s. 71(6).)

▶ 104(18) ◀

(18) Trust for minor. Where any part of the amount that, but for subsections (6) and (12), would be the income of a trust for a taxation year throughout which it was resident in Canada

(*a*) has not become payable in the year,

(*b*) was held in trust for an individual who did not attain 21 years of age before the end of the year,

(*c*) the right to which vested at or before the end of the year otherwise than because of the exercise by any person of, or the failure of any person to exercise, any discretionary power, and (*d*) the right to which is not subject to any future condition (other than a condition that the individual survive to an age not exceeding 40 years),

notwithstanding subsection (24), that part of the amount is, for the purposes of subsections (6) and (13), deemed to have become payable to the individual in the year.

Editorial Note: Income of a trust subject to s. 104(18) is taxed to the beneficiary notwithstanding that it remains in the trust in the relevant taxation year. The beneficiary's right to the income must have vested other than because of a discretionary power, and without any condition other than a condition that the beneficiary reach an age not exceeding 40 (such trusts are sometimes referred to as "Age 40 Trusts"). An "Age 40 Trust" may be testamentary or *inter vivos*; however, the ability to have trust income taxed in the hands of the beneficiary (until he or she reaches age 21) will be particularly significant in the case of *inter vivos* trusts, which are subject to a flat tax at the highest marginal rate. Note that most testamentary trusts will be taxed at the highest marginal rate as well, beginning in the 2016 taxation year. An exception is provided for estates for a period of 36 months after the death, i.e., for "graduated rate estates", to allow for administration.

Canadian Tax Foundation: Rosenberg, *Inter Vivos Trusts: Their Utility and Tax Treatment in the Context of Estate Planning*, 2004 Prairie Provinces Tax Conference 15:1–45.

Tax Profile: December 2009 — Income Tax Consequences of Income Distributions by a Canadian Trust.

Interpretation Bulletins: *Secondary* — IT-286R2 Trusts — Amount payable; IT-342R Trusts — Income payable to beneficiaries; IT-381R3 Trusts — Deduction of amounts paid or payable to beneficiaries and flow-through of taxable capital gains to beneficiaries; IT-394R2 Preferred beneficiary election.

Tax Window Files: Trust for Benefit of Minor, *November 2, 2005*, CRA Document No. 2004-0093601E5 (in French only). The CRA commented on the interpretation of s 104(18) when a trust has certain characteristics regarding the distribution of its capital and the allocation or payment of its income.

► 104(19) ◄

(19) Designation in respect of taxable dividends. A portion of a taxable dividend received by a trust, in a particular taxation year of the trust, on a share of the capital stock of a taxable Canadian corporation is, for the purposes of this Act other than Part XIII, deemed to be a taxable dividend on the share received by a taxpayer, in the taxpayer's taxation year in which the particular taxation year ends, and is, for the purposes of paragraphs 82(1)(*b*) and 107(1)(*c*) and (*d*) and section 112, deemed not to have been received by the trust, if

(*a*) an amount equal to that portion

(i) is designated by the trust, in respect of the taxpayer, in the trust's return of income under this Part for the particular taxation year, and

(ii) may reasonably be considered (having regard to all the circumstances including the terms and conditions of the trust) to be part of the amount that, because of paragraph (13)(*a*), subsection (14) or section 105, was included in computing the income for that taxation year of the taxpayer;

(*b*) the taxpayer is in the particular taxation year a beneficiary under the trust;

(*c*) the trust is, throughout the particular taxation year, resident in Canada; and

(*d*) the total of all amounts each of which is an amount designated, under this subsection, by the trust in respect of a beneficiary under the trust in the trust's return of income under this Part for the particular taxation year is not greater than the total of all amounts each of which is the amount of a taxable dividend, received by the trust in the particular taxation year, on a share of the capital stock of a taxable Canadian corporation.

Editorial Note: The designation under s. 104(19) will allow a beneficiary who is a Canadian resident individual to claim the dividend tax credit in respect of the amount designated and deemed to be a taxable dividend received from the taxable Canadian corporation. If the beneficiary is a Canadian resident corporation, it will be eligible for the intercorporate dividend deduction under s. 112(1). If the beneficiary is another Canadian resident trust, it can either claim the dividend tax credit or pay out and designate the amount under s. 104(19) to its own beneficiaries. The designation is not relevant where the beneficiary is a non-resident of Canada since the dividend income will lose its character in the hands of the non-resident beneficiary.

History: S. 104(19) was replaced by S.C. 2013, c. 34, s. 231(7), applicable to taxation years that end after February 27, 2004, except that, for taxation years that end on or before July 18, 2005, the reference to "paragraph (13)(*a*)" in subparagraph 104(19)(*a*)(ii) is to be read as a reference to "subsection (13)". S. 104(19) formerly read:

(19) *Taxable dividends.* Such portion of a taxable dividend received by a trust in a taxation year throughout which it was resident in Canada on a share of the capital stock of a taxable Canadian corporation as

(*a*) may reasonably be considered (having regard to all the circumstances including the terms and conditions of the trust arrangement) to be part of the amount that, by reason of subsection (13) or (14) or section 105, as the case may be, was included in computing the income for a particular taxation year of a beneficiary under the trust, and

(*b*) was not designated by the trust in respect of any other beneficiary under the trust

is, if so designated by the trust in respect of the beneficiary in its return of income for the year, deemed, for the purposes of paragraphs 82(1)(*b*) and 107(1)(*c*) and (*d*) and section 112, not to have been received by the trust, and for the purposes of this Act (other than Part XIII), to be a taxable dividend on the share received by the beneficiary in the particular year from the corporation.

Related Sections: S. 82(1) Taxable dividends received; s. 107(1)(*c*) Disposition by taxpayer of capital interest; s. 112(3.2) Loss on share held by trust; s. 112(4.3) Loss on share that is not capital property of trust.

Canadian Tax Foundation: Tremblay, *Deemed Timing of a Dividend Receipt by a Trust Beneficiary*, 2014 Canadian Tax Focus 4(1):5; Jung and McIntyre, *Current Issues: Dividend Designation from a Trust*, 2013 Ontario Tax Conference 1:26–27.

Tax Profile: December 2009 — Income Tax Consequences of Income Distributions by a Canadian Trust.

Interpretation Bulletins: *Primary* — IT-524 Trusts — Flow-through of taxable dividends to a beneficiary — After 1987. *Secondary* — IT-328R3 Losses on shares on which dividends have been received.

► 104(20) ◄

(20) Designation in respect of non-taxable dividends. The portion of the total of all amounts, each of which is the amount of a dividend (other than a taxable dividend) paid on a share of the capital stock of a corporation resident in Canada to a trust during a taxation year of the trust throughout which the trust was resident in Canada, that can reasonably be considered (having regard to all the circumstances including the terms and conditions of the trust arrangement) to be part of an amount that became payable in the year to a particular beneficiary under the trust shall be designated by the trust in respect of the particular beneficiary in the return of the trust's income for the year for the purposes of subclause 53(2)(*h*)(i.1)(B)(II), paragraphs 107(1)(*c*) and (*d*) and subsections 112(3.1), (3.2), (3.31) and (4.2).

Editorial Note: A trust resident in Canada must designate a reasonable portion of non-taxable dividends (namely, capital dividends) received from a corporation resident in Canada as part of an amount payable to a particular beneficiary. This portion of a dividend is then excluded by the beneficiary in computing income.

Related Sections: S. 83(2) Capital dividend; s. 104(24) Amount payable; s. 105(1) Benefits under trust; s. 132(3) Application of s. 104(20).

Canadian Tax Foundation: Jung and McIntyre, *Current Issues: Capital Dividend received by a trust and CDA*, 2013 Ontario Tax Conference 1:27–28; Tollstam, *CDA Trapped in Trust*, 2013 Canadian Tax Highlights 21(8):12.

Tax Profile: December 2009 — Income Tax Consequences of Income Distributions by a Canadian Trust.

Interpretation Bulletins: *Secondary* — IT-328R3 Losses on shares on which dividends have been received.

► 104(21) ◄

(21) Designation in respect of taxable capital gains. For the purposes of sections 3 and 111, except as they apply for the purposes of section 110.6, and subject to paragraph 132(5.1)(*b*), an amount in respect of a trust's net taxable capital gains for a particular taxation year of the trust is deemed to be a taxable capital gain, for the taxation year of a taxpayer in which the particular taxation year ends, from the disposition by the taxpayer of capital property if

(*a*) the amount

(i) is designated by the trust, in respect of the taxpayer, in the trust's return of income under this Part for the particular taxation year, and

(ii) may reasonably be considered (having regard to all the circumstances including the terms and conditions of the trust) to be part of the amount that, because of paragraph (13)(*a*), subsection (14) or section 105, was included in computing the income for that taxation year of the taxpayer;

(*b*) the taxpayer is

(i) in the particular taxation year, a beneficiary under the trust, and

(ii) resident in Canada, unless the trust is, throughout the particular taxation year, a mutual fund trust;

(*c*) the trust is, throughout the particular taxation year, resident in Canada; and

(*d*) the total of all amounts each of which is an amount designated, under this subsection, by the trust in respect of a beneficiary under the trust in the trust's return of income under this Part for the particular taxation year is not greater than the trust's net taxable capital gains for the particular taxation year.

Editorial Note: S. 104(21) allows the net taxable capital gains of a Canadian resident trust (being its taxable capital gains for the year net of its allowable capital losses for the year and its capital loss carryovers deducted in the year) to be allocated to trust beneficiaries. This designation can be made in favour of a beneficiary only to the extent that it is reasonable to consider that the taxable capital gain realized by the trust was part of the income included in the income of the beneficiary. As a result, in the absence of trust terms to the contrary, since a taxable capital gain is capital for trust law purposes, the designation cannot be made in favour of a beneficiary who is entitled only to income in the trust law sense and not to capital of the trust. Any amount designated under s. 104(21) does not automatically qualify for the capital gains exemption under s. 110.6. A separate additional designation subject to special rules must be made under s. 104(21.2) to designate capital gains eligible for the capital gains exemption. The s. 104(21) designation can be made in respect of a non-resident beneficiary only if the trust is a mutual fund trust.

Note that, for trust taxation years beginning after 2000, allowable business investment losses (ABILs) will be disregarded in the computation of a trust's allowable capital losses. As a result, ABILs will not result in a reduction of taxable capital gains which may be flowed through to beneficiaries under trusts and against which allowable capital losses can be claimed.

History: S. 104(21) was replaced by S.C. 2013, c. 34, s. 231(8), applicable to taxation years that end after February 27, 2004, except that, for taxation years that end on or before July 18, 2005, the reference to "paragraph (13)(*a*)" in subparagraph 104(21)(*a*)(ii) is to be read as a reference to "subsection (13)". S. 104(21) formerly read:

(21) *Taxable capital gains.* Such portion of the net taxable capital gains of a trust for a taxation year throughout which it was resident in Canada as

(*a*) may reasonably be considered (having regard to all the circumstances including the terms and conditions of the trust arrangement) to be part of the amount that, by virtue of subsection (13) or (14) or section 105, as the case may be, was included in computing the income for the taxation year of

(i) a particular beneficiary under the trust, if the trust is a mutual fund trust, or

(ii) a particular beneficiary under the trust who is resident in Canada, if the trust is not a mutual fund trust, and

(*b*) was not designated by the trust in respect of any other beneficiary under the trust,

shall, if so designated by the trust in respect of the particular beneficiary in the return of its income for the year under this Part, be deemed, for the purposes of sections 3 and 111, except as they apply for the purpose of section 110.6, and subject to paragraph 132(5.1)(*b*), to be a taxable capital gain for the year of the particular beneficiary from the disposition by that beneficiary of capital property.

Related Sections: S. 38 Taxable capital gain and allowable capital loss; s. 104(21.2) Beneficiaries' taxable capital gain; s. 104(21.3) Net taxable capital gains of trust determined; s. 127.52(1)(*g*) Adjusted taxable income determined; s. 212(1)(*c*) Estate or trust income.

Tax Profile: December 2009 — Income Tax Consequences of Income Distributions by a Canadian Trust.

Forms: T3 SCH 4 — Cumulative Net Investment Loss.

Interpretation Bulletins: *Primary* — IT-381R3 Trusts — Deduction of amounts paid or payable to beneficiaries and flow-through of taxable capital gains to beneficiaries. *Secondary* — IT-342R Trusts — Income payable to beneficiaries; IT-394R2 Preferred beneficiary election; IT-465R Non-resident beneficiaries of trusts.

▶ 104(21.01) ◀

(21.01) Late, amended or revoked designation. A trust that has filed its return of income for its taxation year that includes February 22, 1994 may subsequently designate an amount under subsection (21), or amend or revoke a designation made under that subsection where the designation, amendment or revocation

(*a*) is made solely because of an increase or decrease in the net taxable capital gains of the trust for the year that results from an election or revocation to which subsection 110.6(25), (26) or (27) applies; and

(*b*) is filed with the Minister, with an amended return of income for the year, when the election or revocation referred to in paragraph (*a*) is filed with the Minister.

▶ 104(21.02) ◀

(21.02) Late, amended or revoked designation. A designation, amendment or revocation under subsection (21.01) that affects an amount determined in respect of a beneficiary under subsection (21.2) may be made only where the trust

(*a*) designates an amount, or amends or revokes a designation made, under subsection (21.2) in respect of the beneficiary; and

(*b*) files the designation, amendment or revocation referred to in paragraph (*a*) with the Minister when required by paragraph (21.01)(*b*).

▶ 104(21.03) ◀

(21.03) Late, amended or revoked designation. Where a trust designates an amount, or amends or revokes a designation, under subsection (21) or (21.2) in accordance with subsection (21.01),

(*a*) the designation or amended designation, as the case may be, is deemed to have been made in the trust's return of income for the trust's taxation year that includes February 22, 1994; and

(*b*) the designation that was revoked is deemed, other than for the purposes of this subsection and subsections (21.01) and (21.02), never to have been made.

▶ 104(21.1) ◀

(21.1) Beneficiary's taxable capital gain — (Repealed by S.C. 2013, c. 34, s. 231(9).)

History: S. 104(21.1) was repealed by S.C. 2013, c. 34, s. 231(9), applicable to taxation years that begin after October 31, 2011, and formerly read:

(21.1) *Beneficiary's taxable capital gain.* Notwithstanding subsection (21) or section 38, where in a particular taxation year, commencing before 1990, of a taxpayer (other than an individual who is not a testamentary trust) the taxpayer is a beneficiary of a trust with a taxation year ending in the particular year, the amount (other than that part of the amount that can be attributed to an amount deemed under subsection 14(1) to be a taxable capital gain of the trust) deemed by subsection (21) to be a taxable capital gain of the taxpayer for the particular year in respect of the trust shall be the amount determined by the formula

$$A \times B/C$$

where

A is the amount, if any, by which the amount (other than that part of the amount that can be attributed to an amount deemed under subsection 14(1) to be a taxable capital gain of the trust) deemed by subsection (21) to be the taxpayer's taxable capital gain for the particular year in respect of the trust exceeds the amount (other than that part of the amount that can be attributed to an amount deemed under subsection 14(1) to be a taxable capital gain of the trust) designated by the trust for the particular year in respect of the taxpayer under subsection (13.2);

B is the fraction that would be used under section 38 for the particular year in respect of the taxpayer if the taxpayer had a capital gain for the particular year; and

C is the fraction that is used under section 38 for the year of the trust.

Forms: T3 SCH 3 — Eligible Taxable Capital Gains.

Interpretation Bulletins: *Secondary* — IT-381R3 Trusts — Deduction of amounts paid or payable to beneficiaries and flow-through of taxable capital gains to beneficiaries.

▶ 104(21.2) ◀

(21.2) Beneficiaries' taxable capital gain. Where, for the purposes of subsection (21), a personal trust or a trust referred to in subsection 7(2) designates an amount in respect of a beneficiary in respect of its net taxable capital gains for a taxation year (in this subsection referred to as the "designation year"),

(*a*) the trust shall in its return of income under this Part for the designation year designate an amount in respect of its eligible taxable capital gains, if any, for the designation year in respect of the beneficiary equal to the amount determined in respect of the beneficiary under each of subparagraphs (*b*)(i) and (ii); and

(*b*) the beneficiary is, for the purposes of section 120.4 and for the purposes of sections 3, 74.3 and 111 as they apply for the purposes of section 110.6,

(i) deemed to have disposed of the capital property referred to in clause (ii)(A), (B) or (C) if a taxable capital gain is determined in respect of the beneficiary for the beneficiary's taxation year in which the designation year ends under those clauses, and

(ii) deemed to have a taxable capital gain for the beneficiary's taxation year in which the designation year ends

(A) from a disposition of a capital property that is qualified farm or fishing property (as defined for the purpose of section 110.6) of the beneficiary equal to the amount determined by the formula

$$(A \times B \times C)/(D \times E)$$

and

(B) from a disposition of a capital property that is a qualified small business corporation share (as defined for the purpose of section 110.6) of the beneficiary equal to the amount determined by the formula

$$(A \times B \times F)/(D \times E)$$

(C) (Repealed.)

where

A is the lesser of

(I) the amount determined by the formula

$$G - H$$

where

G is the total of amounts designated under subsection (21) for the designation year by the trust, and

H is the total of amounts designated under subsection (13.2) for the designation year by the trust, and

(II) the trust's eligible taxable capital gains for the designation year,

B is the amount, if any, by which the amount designated under subsection (21) for the designation year by the trust in respect of the beneficiary exceeds the amount designated under subsection (13.2) for the year by the trust in respect of the beneficiary for the taxation year,

C is the amount, if any, that would be determined under paragraph 3(*b*) for the designation year in respect of the trust's capital gains and capital losses if the only properties referred to in that paragraph were properties that, at the time they were disposed of, were qualified farm properties, qualified fishing properties or qualified farm or fishing properties of the trust,

D is the total of all amounts each of which is the amount determined for B for the designation year in respect of a beneficiary under the trust,

E is the total of the amounts determined for C and F for the designation year in respect of the beneficiary, and

F is the amount, if any, that would be determined under paragraph 3(*b*) for the designation year in respect of the trust's capital gains and capital losses if the only properties referred to in that paragraph were properties that, at the time they were disposed of, were qualified small business corporation shares of the trust, other than qualified farm property, qualified fishing property or qualified farm or fishing property,

I (Repealed.)

and for the purposes of section 110.6, those capital properties shall be deemed to have been disposed of by the beneficiary in that taxation year of the beneficiary.

History: S. 104(21.2)(*b*), the portion before subparagraph (i) was replaced by S.C. 2018, c. 12, s. 8(1), applicable to the 2018 and subsequent taxation years, and formerly read:

> (*b*) the beneficiary is, for the purposes of sections 3, 74.3 and 111 as they apply for the purposes of section 110.6,

S. 104(21.2)(*b*)(ii)(A), the portion before the formula was replaced by S.C. 2014, c. 39, s. 26(8), applicable to dispositions that occur in the 2014 and subsequent taxation years, and formerly read:

> (A) from a disposition of a capital property that is qualified farm property (as defined for the purpose of section 110.6) of the beneficiary equal to the amount determined by the formula

S. 104(21.2)(*b*)(ii)(C) was repealed by S.C. 2014, c. 39, s. 26(9), applicable to dispositions that occur in the 2014 and subsequent taxation years, and formerly read:

> (C) from a disposition of a capital property that is a qualified fishing property (as defined for the purpose of section 110.6) of the beneficiary equal to the amount determined by the formula
>
> $$(A \times B \times I)/(D \times E)$$

S. 104(21.2)(*b*)(ii), the description of C was replaced by S.C. 2014, c. 39, s. 26(10), applicable to dispositions that occur in the 2014 and subsequent taxation years, and formerly read:

C is the amount, if any, that would be determined under paragraph 3(*b*) for the designation year in respect of the trust's capital gains and capital losses if the only properties referred to in that paragraph were qualified farm properties of the trust disposed of by it after 1984,

S. 104(21.2)(*b*)(ii), the descriptions of E and F were replaced and the description of I was repealed by S.C. 2014, c. 39, s. 26(11), applicable to dispositions that occur in the 2014 and subsequent taxation years, and formerly read:

E is the total of the amounts determined for C, F and I for the designation year in respect of the beneficiary,

F is the amount, if any, that would be determined under paragraph 3(*b*) for the designation year in respect of the trust's capital gains and capital losses if the only properties referred to in that paragraph were qualified small business corporation shares of the trust, other than qualified farm property, disposed of by it after June 17, 1987, and

I is the amount, if any, that would be determined under paragraph 3(*b*) for the designation year in respect of the trust's capital gains and capital losses if the only properties referred to in that paragraph were qualified fishing properties of the trust disposed of by it on or after May 2, 2006,

Related Sections: S. 38 Taxable capital gain and allowable capital loss; s. 39 Meaning of capital gain and capital loss; s. 104(1) Reference to trust or estate; s. 104(21.3) Net taxable capital gains of trust determined; s. 108(1), "eligible real property gain", "eligible taxable capital gains", "non-qualifying real property", "qualified farm property", "qualified small business corporation share"; s. 110.6(1), "eligible real property gain", "non-qualifying real property", "qualified farm or fishing property", "qualified small business corporation share"; s. 248(1), "amount", "property", "trust".

Income Tax Folios: S4-F8-C1 Business Investment Losses.

Interpretation Bulletins: *Primary* — IT-381R3 Trusts — Deduction of amounts paid or payable to beneficiaries and flow-through of taxable capital gains to beneficiaries.

► 104(21.21) ◄

(21.21) Beneficiaries QFFP taxable capital gain. If clause (21.2)(*b*)(ii)(A) applies to deem, for the purposes of section 110.6, the beneficiary under a trust to have a taxable capital gain (referred to in this subsection as the "QFFP taxable capital gain") from a disposition of capital property that is qualified farm or fishing property of the beneficiary, for the beneficiary's taxation year that ends on or after April 21, 2015, and in which the designation year of the trust ends, for the purposes of subsection 110.6(2.2), the beneficiary is, if the trust complies with the requirements of subsection (21.22), deemed to have a taxable capital gain from the disposition of qualified farm or fishing property of the beneficiary on or after April 21, 2015 equal to the amount determined by the formula

$$A \times B/C$$

where

A is the amount of the QFFP taxable capital gain;

B is, if the designation year of the trust ends on or after April 21, 2015, the amount that would be determined in respect of the trust for the designation year under paragraph 3(*b*) in respect of capital gains and capital losses if the only properties referred to in that paragraph were qualified farm or fishing properties of the trust that were disposed of by the trust on or after April 21, 2015; and

C is, if the designation year of the trust ends on or after April 21, 2015, the amount that would be determined in respect of the trust for the designation year under paragraph 3(*b*) in respect of capital gains and capital losses if the only properties referred to in that paragraph were qualified farm or fishing properties.

Editorial Note: A gain on qualified farm or fishing property realized after April 20, 2015 qualifies for an enhanced capital gains deduction. Subsections 104(21.21) and 104(21.22) provide for a trust to designate such a gain in which case the beneficiary to whom the gain is paid or payable is deemed to have realized the gain and may claim his or her capital gains deduction.

History: S. 104(21.21) was added by S.C. 2015, c. 36, s. 5(1), applicable in respect of taxation years that end after April 20, 2015.

S. 104(21.21) was repealed by S.C. 2014, c. 39, s. 26(12), applicable to dispositions that occur in the 2014 and subsequent taxation years, and formerly read:

(21.21) *Beneficiaries' taxable capital gain — QFP taxable capital gain.* If clause (21.2)(*b*)(ii)(A) applies to deem, for the purpose of section 110.6, the beneficiary to have a taxable capital gain (referred to in this subsection as the "QFP taxable capital gain") from a disposition of capital property that is qualified farm property of the beneficiary, for the beneficiary's taxation year that includes March 19, 2007 and in which the designation year of the trust ends, for the purpose of subsection 110.6(2.3), the beneficiary is, where the trust complies with the requirements of subsection (21.24), deemed to have a taxable capital gain from the disposition of qualified farm property of the beneficiary on or after March 19, 2007 equal to the amount determined by the formula

$$A \times B/C$$

where

A is the amount of the QFP taxable capital gain;

B is, where the designation year of the trust includes March 19, 2007, the amount that would be determined in respect of the trust for the designation year under paragraph 3(*b*) in respect of capital gains and capital losses if the only properties referred to in paragraph 3(*b*) were qualified farm property of the trust that were disposed of by the trust on or after March 19, 2007; and

C is, where the designation year of the trust includes March 19, 2007, the amount that would be determined in respect of the trust for the designation year under paragraph 3(*b*) in respect of capital gains and capital losses if the only properties referred to in paragraph 3(*b*) were qualified farm property.

Related Sections: 104(21.2) Beneficiaries' taxable capital gain; 110.6(1) qualified farm or fishing property; 110.6(2.2) Additional deduction — qualified farm or fishing property.

► 104(21.22) ◄

(21.22) Trusts to designate amounts. A trust shall determine and designate, in its return of income under this Part for a designation year of the trust, the amount that is determined under subsection (21.21) to be the beneficiary's taxable capital gain from the disposition on or after April 21, 2015 of qualified farm or fishing property of the beneficiary.

History: S. 104(21.22) was added by S.C. 2015, c. 36, s. 5(1), applicable in respect of taxation years that end after April 20, 2015.

S. 104(2.22) was repealed by S.C. 2014, c. 39, s. 26(12), applicable to dispositions that occur in the 2014 and subsequent taxation years, and formerly read:

(21.22) *Beneficiaries' taxable capital gain — QSBC taxable capital gain.* If clause (21.2)(*b*)(ii)(B) applies to deem, for the purpose of section 110.6, the beneficiary to have a taxable capital gain (referred to in this subsection as the "QSBC taxable capital gain") from a disposition of capital property that is a qualified small business corporation share of the beneficiary, for the beneficiary's taxation year in which the designation year of the trust ends, for the purpose of subsection 110.6(2.3), the beneficiary, where the trust complies with requirements of subsection (21.24), is deemed to have a taxable capital gain from the disposition of a qualified small business corporation share of the beneficiary on or after March 19, 2007 equal to the amount determined by the formula

$$A \times B/C$$

where

A is the amount of the QSBC taxable capital gain;

B is, where the designation year of the trust includes March 19, 2007, the amount that would be determined in respect of the trust for the designation year under paragraph 3(*b*) in respect of capital gains and capital losses if the only properties referred to in paragraph 3(*b*) were qualified small business corporation shares of the trust that were disposed of by the trust on or after March 19, 2007; and

C is, where the designation year of the trust includes March 19, 2007, the amount that would be determined in respect of the trust for the designation year under paragraph 3(*b*) in respect of capital gains and capital losses if the only properties referred to in paragraph 3(*b*) were qualified small business corporation shares of the trust.

Related Sections: 104(21.2) Beneficiaries' taxable capital gain; 110.6(1) qualified farm or fishing property; 110.6(2.2) Additional deduction — qualified farm or fishing property.

► 104(21.23) ◄

(21.23) Beneficiaries' taxable capital gain — QFFP taxable capital gain — (Repealed by S.C. 2014, c. 39, s. 26(12).)

History: S. 104(2.23) was repealed by S.C. 2014, c. 39, s. 26(12), applicable to dispositions that occur in the 2014 and subsequent taxation years, and formerly read:

(21.23) *Beneficiaries' taxable capital gain — QFFP taxable capital gain.* If clause (21.2)(*b*)(ii)(C) applies to deem, for the purpose of section 110.6, the beneficiary to have a taxable capital gain (referred to in this subsection as the "QFFP taxable capital gain"), from a disposition of capital property that is qualified fishing property of the beneficiary, for the beneficiary's taxation year in which the designation year of the trust ends, for the purpose of subsection 110.6(2.3), the beneficiary, where the trust complies with requirements of subsection (21.24), is deemed to have a taxable capital gain from the disposition of qualified fishing property on or after March 19, 2007 equal to the amount determined by the formula

$$A \times B/C$$

where

A is the amount of the QFFP taxable capital gain;

B is, where the designation year of the trust includes March 19, 2007, the amount that would be determined in respect of the trust for the designation year under paragraph 3(*b*) in respect of capital gains and capital losses if the only properties referred to in paragraph 3(*b*) were qualified fishing property that were disposed of by the trust on or after March 19, 2007; and

C is, where the designation year of the trust includes March 19, 2007, the amount that would be determined in respect of the trust for the designation year under paragraph 3(*b*) in respect of capital gains and capital losses if the only properties referred to in paragraph 3(*b*) were qualified fishing property of the trust.

▶ 104(21.24) ◀

(21.24) Trusts to designate amounts — (Repealed by S.C. 2014, c. 39, s. 26(12).)

History: S. 104(2.24) was repealed by S.C. 2014, c. 39, s. 26(12), applicable to dispositions that occur in the 2014 and subsequent taxation years, and formerly read:

(21.24) *Trusts to designate amounts.* A trust shall determine and designate, in its return of income under this part for a designation year of the trust, the following amounts in respect of a beneficiary:

(*a*) the amount that is, under subsection (21.21), determined to be the beneficiary's taxable capital gain from the disposition, on or after March 19, 2007, of qualified farm property of the beneficiary,

(*b*) the amount that is, under subsection (21.22), determined to be the beneficiary's taxable capital gain from the disposition, on or after March 19, 2007, of qualified small business corporation share of the beneficiary, and

(*c*) the amount that is, under subsection (21.23), determined to be the beneficiary's taxable capital gain from the disposition, on or after March 19, 2007, of qualified fishing property of the beneficiary.

▶ 104(21.3) ◀

(21.3) Net taxable capital gains of trust determined. For the purposes of this section, the net taxable capital gains of a trust for a taxation year is the amount, if any, determined by the formula

$$A + B - C - D$$

where

A is the total of all amounts each of which is a taxable capital gain of the trust for the year from the disposition of a capital property that was held by the trust immediately before the disposition,

B is the total of all amounts each of which is deemed by subsection (21) to be a taxable capital gain of the trust for the year,

C is the total of all amounts each of which is an allowable capital loss (other than an allowable business investment loss) of the trust for the year from the disposition of a capital property, and

D is the amount, if any, deducted under paragraph 111(1)(*b*) in computing the trust's taxable income for the year.

History: S. 104(21.3) was replaced by S.C. 2013, c. 34, s. 231(11), applicable to taxation years that begin after October 31, 2011, and formerly read:

(21.3) *Net taxable capital gains of trust determined.* For the purposes of this section, the net taxable capital gains of a trust for a taxation year is the amount, if any, by which the total of the taxable capital gains of the trust for the year exceeds the total of

(*a*) the total of all amounts each of which is an allowable capital loss (other than an allowable business investment loss) of the trust for the year from the disposition of a capital property, and

(*b*) the amount, if any, deducted under paragraph 111(1)(*b*) in computing its taxable income for the year.

S. 104(21.3)(*a*) was replaced by S.C. 2013, c. 34, s. 231(10), applicable to trust taxation years that begin after 2000, and formerly read:

(*a*) its allowable capital losses for the year, and

Interpretation Bulletins: *Primary* — IT-381R3 Trusts — Deduction of amounts paid or payable to beneficiaries and flow-through of taxable capital gains to beneficiaries.

▶ 104(21.4) ◀

(21.4) Deemed gains — (Repealed by S.C. 2013, c. 34, s. 231(12).)

History: S. 104(21.4) was repealed by S.C. 2013, c. 34, s. 231(12), applicable to taxation years that begin after October 31, 2011, and formerly read:

(21.4) *Deemed gains.* Where an amount is designated in respect of a beneficiary by a trust for a particular taxation year of the trust that includes February 28, 2000 or October 17, 2000 and that amount is, because of subsection (21), deemed to be a taxable capital gain of the beneficiary from the disposition of capital property for the taxation year of the beneficiary in which the particular taxation year of the trust ends (in this subsection referred to as the "allocated gain"),

(*a*) the beneficiary is deemed to have realized capital gains (in this subsection referred to as the "deemed gains") from the disposition of capital property in the beneficiary's taxation year in which the particular taxation year ends equal to the amount, if any, by which

(i) the amount determined when the amount of the allocated gain is divided by the fraction in paragraph 38(*a*) that applies to the trust for the particular taxation year

exceeds

(ii) the amount claimed by the beneficiary not exceeding the beneficiary's exempt capital gains balance for the year in respect of the trust;

(*b*) notwithstanding subsection (21) and except as a consequence of the application of paragraph (*a*), the amount of the allocated gain shall not be included in computing the beneficiary's income for the beneficiary's taxation year in which the particular taxation year ends;

(*c*) the trust shall disclose to the beneficiary in prescribed form the portion of the deemed gains that are in respect of capital gains realized on dispositions of property that occurred before February 28, 2000, after February 27, 2000 and before October 18, 2000, and after October 17, 2000 and, if it does not do so, the deemed gains are deemed to be in respect of capital gains realized on dispositions of property that occurred before February 28, 2000; and

(*d*) where a trust so elects under this paragraph in its return of income for the year,

(i) the portion of the deemed gains that are in respect of capital gains from dispositions of property that occurred before February 28, 2000 is deemed to be that proportion of the deemed gains that the number of days that are in the particular year and before February 28, 2000 is of the number of days that are in the particular year,

(ii) the portion of the deemed gains that are in respect of capital gains from dispositions of property that occurred in the year and in the period that began at the beginning of February 28, 2000 and ended at the end of October 17, 2000, is deemed to be that proportion of the deemed gains that the number of days that are in the year and in that period is of the number of days that are in the particular year, and

(iii) the portion of the deemed gains that are in respect of capital gains from dispositions of property that occurred in the year and in the period that begins at the beginning of October 18, 2000 and ends at the end of the particular year, is deemed to be that proportion of the deemed gains that the number of days that are in the year and in that period is of the number of days that are in the particular year; and

(*e*) no amount may be claimed by the beneficiary under subsection 39.1(3) in respect of the allocated gain.

Interpretation Bulletins: *Secondary* — IT-381R3 Deduction of amounts paid or payable to beneficiaries and flow-through of taxable capital gains to beneficiaries.

▶ 104(21.5) ◀

(21.5) Deemed gains — (Repealed by S.C. 2013, c. 34, s. 231(12).)

History: S. 104(21.5) was repealed by S.C. 2013, c. 34, s. 231(12), applicable to taxation years that begin after October 31, 2011, and formerly read:

(21.5) *Deemed gains.* Where no amount is designated by a trust under subsection (21) in respect of its net taxable capital gains for a taxation year that includes February 28, 2000 or October 17, 2000, the trust has net capital gains or net capital losses from the disposition of property in the year, and the trust so elects under this subsection in its return of income for the year

(a) the portion of the net capital gains or net capital losses that are in respect of capital gains and losses from dispositions of property that occurred before February 28, 2000 is deemed to be that proportion of the net capital gains or net capital losses, as the case may be, that the number of days that are in the year and before February 28, 2000 is of the number of days that are in the year,

(b) the portion of the net capital gains or net capital losses that are in respect of capital gains and losses from dispositions of property that occurred in the year and in the period that began at the beginning of February 28, 2000 and ended at the end of October 17, 2000, is deemed to be that proportion of the net capital gains or net capital losses, as the case may be, that the number of days that are in the year and in that period is of the number of days that are in the year, and

(c) the portion of the net capital gains or net capital losses that are in respect of capital gains and losses from dispositions of property that occurred in the year and in the period that began at the beginning of October 18, 2000 and ended at the end of the year, is deemed to be that proportion of the net capital gains or net capital losses, as the case may be, that the number of days that are in the year and in that period is of the number of days that are in the year,

and, for the purpose of this subsection,

(d) the net capital gains of a trust from dispositions of property in a year is the amount, if any, by which the trust's capital gains from dispositions of property in the year exceeds the trust's capital losses from dispositions of property in the year, and

(e) the net capital losses of a trust from dispositions of property in a year is the amount, if any, by which the trust's capital losses from dispositions of property in the year exceeds the trust's capital gains from dispositions of property in the year.

▶ 104(21.6) ◀

(21.6) Deemed gains — subsection (21.4) applies — (Repealed by S.C. 2013, c. 34, s. 231(14).)

History: S. 104(21.6) was repealed by S.C. 2013, c. 34, s. 231(14), applicable to taxation years that begin after October 31, 2011, and formerly read:

(21.6) *Deemed gains — subsection (21.4) applies.* Where a taxpayer is deemed by subsection (21.4) to have realized capital gains from the disposition of capital property in a taxation year of the taxpayer in respect of dispositions of property by a trust of which the taxpayer is a beneficiary,

(a) if the deemed gains are in respect of capital gains of the trust from dispositions of property before February 28, 2000 and the taxation year of the taxpayer includes February 27, 2000, the deemed gains are deemed to be a capital gain of the taxpayer from the disposition by the taxpayer of capital property in the taxpayer's taxation year and before February 28, 2000;

(b) if the deemed gains are in respect of capital gains of the trust from dispositions of property before February 28, 2000 and the taxation year of the taxpayer began after February 27, 2000 and ended before October 18, 2000, 9/8 of the deemed gains is deemed to be a capital gain of the taxpayer from the disposition by the taxpayer of capital property in the taxpayer's taxation year;

(c) if the deemed gains are in respect of capital gains of the trust from dispositions of property before February 28, 2000 and the taxation year of the taxpayer began after February 27, 2000 and ended after October 17, 2000, 9/8 of the deemed gains is deemed to be a capital gain of the taxpayer from the disposition by the taxpayer of capital property in the taxpayer's taxation year and before October 18, 2000;

(d) if the deemed gains are in respect of capital gains of the trust from dispositions of property before February 28, 2000 and the taxation year of the taxpayer began after October 17, 2000, 3/2 of the deemed gains is deemed to be a capital gain of the taxpayer from the disposition by the taxpayer of capital property in the taxpayer's taxation year;

(e) if the deemed gains are in respect of capital gains of the trust from dispositions of property after February 27, 2000 and before October 18, 2000, and the taxation year of the taxpayer began after October 17, 2000, 4/3 of the deemed gains is deemed to be a capital gain of the taxpayer from the disposition by the taxpayer of capital property in the taxpayer's taxation year;

(f) if the deemed gains are in respect of capital gains of the trust from dispositions of property after February 27, 2000 and before October 18, 2000 and the taxation year of the taxpayer includes February 28, 2000 and October 17, 2000, the deemed gains are deemed to be a capital gain of the taxpayer from the disposition by the taxpayer of capital property in the taxpayer's taxation year and in the period that began after February 27, 2000 and ended before October 18, 2000;

(f.1) if the deemed gains are in respect of capital gains of the trust from dispositions of property after February 27, 2000 and before October 17, 2000 and the taxation year of the taxpayer began after February 27, 2000 and ended after October 17, 2000, the deemed gains are deemed to be a capital gain of the taxpayer from the disposition by the taxpayer of capital property in the taxpayer's taxation year and in the period that began after February 27, 2000 and ended before October 18, 2000;

(g) if the deemed gains are in respect of capital gains of the trust from dispositions of property after February 27, 2000 and before October 17, 2000 and the taxation year of the taxpayer began after February 27, 2000 and ended before October 18, 2000, the deemed gains are deemed to be a capital gain of the taxpayer from the disposition by the taxpayer of capital property in the taxpayer's taxation year; and

(h) in any other case, the deemed gains are deemed to be a capital gain of the taxpayer from the disposition of capital property by the taxpayer in the taxpayer's taxation year and after October 17, 2000.

S. 104(21.6)(f.1) was added by S.C. 2013, c. 34, s. 231(13), applicable to taxation years that end after February 27, 2000.

S. 104(21.6)(g) was replaced by S.C. 2013, c. 34, s. 231(13), applicable to trust taxation years that end after December 20, 2002, and formerly read:

(g) if the deemed gains are in respect of capital gains of the trust from dispositions of property after February 27, 2000 and before October 17, 2000 and the taxation year of the taxpayer began after February 27, 2000 and ended before October 17, 2000, the deemed gains are deemed to be a capital gain of the taxpayer from the disposition by the taxpayer of capital property in the taxpayer's taxation year; and

▶ 104(21.7) ◀

(21.7) Deemed gains — subsection (21.4) does not apply — (Repealed by S.C. 2013, c. 34, s. 231(14).)

History: S. 104(21.7) was repealed by S.C. 2013, c. 34, s. 231(14), applicable to taxation years that begin after October 31, 2011, and formerly read:

(21.7) *Deemed gains — subsection (21.4) does not apply.* Where an amount is designated under subsection (21) in respect of a beneficiary by a trust for a particular taxation year of the trust that ends in a taxation year of the beneficiary that includes February 28, 2000 or October 17, 2000 and subsection (21.4) does not apply in respect of the designated amount,

(a) notwithstanding subsection (21) and except as a consequence of the application of paragraph (b), the designated amount shall not be included in computing the beneficiary's income;

(b) the beneficiary is deemed to have a capital gain from the disposition by the beneficiary of capital property on the day on which the particular taxation year ends equal to the amount, if any, by which

(i) the amount determined by dividing the designated amount by the fraction in paragraph 38(a) that applies to the trust for the particular taxation year

exceeds

(ii) the amount claimed by the beneficiary, which amount may not be greater than the beneficiary's exempt capital gains balance for the year in respect of the trust; and

(c) no amount may be claimed under subsection 39.1(3) by the beneficiary in respect of the designated amount.

▶ 104(22) ◀

(22) Designation in respect of foreign source income. For the purposes of this subsection, subsection (22.1) and section 126, an amount in respect of a trust's income for a particular taxation year of the trust from a source in a country other than Canada is deemed to be income of a taxpayer, for the taxation year of the taxpayer in which the particular taxation year ends, from that source if

(a) the amount

(i) is designated by the trust, in respect of the taxpayer, in the trust's return of income under this Part for the particular taxation year, and

(ii) may reasonably be considered (having regard to all the circumstances including the terms and conditions of the trust) to be part of the amount that, because of paragraph (13)(a) or subsection (14), was included in computing the income for that taxation year of the taxpayer;

(b) the taxpayer is in the particular taxation year a beneficiary under the trust;

(c) the trust is, throughout the particular taxation year, resident in Canada; and

(d) the total of all amounts each of which is an amount designated, under this subsection in respect of that source, by the trust in respect of a beneficiary under the trust in the trust's return of income under this Part for the particular taxation year is not greater than the trust's income for the particular taxation year from that source.

Editorial Note: S. 104(22) allows a Canadian resident trust to designate its foreign source income that may reasonably be considered to be part of the amount included in a beneficiary's income under either s. 104(13) or (14). The designated amount is deemed to be income of the beneficiary from the foreign source for the purposes of the foreign tax credit provisions. The beneficiary is similarly deemed to have paid the tax paid by the trust on the designated amount for the purposes of the foreign tax credit (see also ss. 104(22.1) through (22.3)).

History: S. 104(22) was replaced by S.C. 2013, c. 34, s. 231(15), applicable to taxation years that end after February 27, 2004, except that, for taxation years that end on or before July 18, 2005, the reference to "paragraph (13)(*a*)" in subparagraph 104(22)(*a*)(ii) is to be read as a reference to "subsection (13)". S. 104(22) formerly read:

(22) *Designation of foreign source income by trust.* For the purposes of this subsection, subsection (22.1) and section 126, such portion of a trust's income for a taxation year (in this subsection referred to as "that year") throughout which it is resident in Canada from a source in a country other than Canada as

(*a*) can reasonably be considered (having regard to all the circumstances including the terms and conditions of the trust arrangement) to be part of the income that, because of subsection (13) or (14), was included in computing the income for a particular taxation year of a particular beneficiary under the trust, and

(*b*) is not designated by the trust in respect of any other beneficiary thereunder

shall, if so designated by the trust in respect of the particular beneficiary in its return of income under this Part for that year, be deemed to be the particular beneficiary's income for the particular year from that source.

Related Sections: 94(3) Liabilities of non-resident trusts and others; S. 126(1) Foreign tax deduction — non-business income; Canada–United States Income Tax Convention, Article XXI, s. 6.

Tax Profile: December 2009 — Income Tax Consequences of Income Distributions by a Canadian Trust.

Interpretation Bulletins: *Primary* — IT-201R2 Foreign tax credit — Trust and beneficiaries. *Secondary* — IT-506 Foreign income taxes as a deduction from income.

▶ 104(22.1) ◀

(22.1) Foreign tax deemed paid by beneficiary. Where a taxpayer is a beneficiary under a trust, for the purposes of this subsection and section 126, the taxpayer shall be deemed to have paid as business-income tax or non-business-income tax, as the case may be, for a particular taxation year in respect of a source the amount determined by the formula

$$A \times B/C$$

where

A is the amount that, but for subsection (22.3), would be the business-income tax or non-business-income tax, as the case may be, paid by the trust in respect of the source for a taxation year (in this subsection referred to as "that year") of the trust that ends in the particular year;

B is the amount deemed, because of a designation under subsection (22) for that year by the trust, to be the taxpayer's income from the source; and

C is the trust's income for that year from the source.

Related Sections: 94(3) Liabilities of non-resident trusts and others.

▶ 104(22.2) ◀

(22.2) Recalculation of trust's foreign source income. For the purpose of section 126, there shall be deducted in computing a trust's income from a source for a taxation year the total of all amounts deemed, because of designations under subsection (22) by the trust for the year, to be income of beneficiaries under the trust from that source.

Related Sections: 94(3) Liabilities of non-resident trusts and others.

▶ 104(22.3) ◀

(22.3) Recalculation of trust's foreign tax. For the purpose of section 126, there shall be deducted in computing the business-income tax or non-business-income tax paid by a trust for a taxation year in respect of a source the total of all amounts deemed, because of designations under subsection (22) by the trust for the year, to be paid by beneficiaries under the trust as business-income tax or non-business-income tax, as the case may be, in respect of the source.

Related Sections: 94(3) Liabilities of non-resident trusts and others.

▶ 104(22.4) ◀

(22.4) Definitions. For the purposes of subsections (22) to (22.3), the expressions "business-income tax" and "non-business-income tax" have the meanings assigned by subsection 126(7).

▶ 104(23) ◀

(23) Deceased beneficiary of graduated rate estate. In the case of a trust that is a graduated rate estate,

(*a*) (Repealed by S.C. 2013, c. 34, s. 231(16).)

(*b*) (Repealed by S.C. 2013, c. 34, s. 231(16).)

(*c*) the income of a person for a taxation year from the trust shall be deemed to be the person's benefits from or under the trust for the taxation year or years of the trust that ended in the year determined as provided by this section and section 105; and

(*d*) where an individual having income from the trust died after the end of a taxation year of the trust but before the end of the calendar year in which the taxation year ended, the individual's income from the trust for the period commencing immediately after the end of the taxation year and ending at the time of death shall be included in computing the individual's income for the individual's taxation year in which the individual died unless the individual's legal representative has elected otherwise, in which case the legal representative shall file a separate return of income for the period under this Part and pay the tax for the period under this Part as if

(i) the individual were another person,

(ii) the period were a taxation year,

(iii) that other person's only income for the period were the individual's income from the trust for that period, and

(iv) subject to sections 114.2 and 118.93, that other person were entitled to the deductions to which the individual was entitled under sections 110, 118 to 118.7 and 118.9 for the period in computing the individual's taxable income or tax payable under this Part, as the case may be, for the period.

(*e*) (Repealed by S.C. 2014, c. 39, s. 26(14).)

Editorial Note: In taxation years prior to 2016, trusts other than testamentary trusts were required by s. 249(1)(*b*) to have a taxation year that coincides with the calendar year. However, s. 249(5) in conjunction with s. 249(1)(*c*) permitted a testamentary trust (including an estate) prior to 2016 to choose any date for its first year end, provided that the taxation year was not more than 12 months long (this rule was formerly found in s. 104(23)(*a*)). Therefore, for example, if a person died on February 1, 2011, the date of January 31, 2012 could have been chosen as the estate's taxation year end. Paragraph 104(23)(*c*) provides that a beneficiary's income from a trust for a year is the beneficiary's benefits from the trust for the taxation year of the trust ending in the year. Therefore, if the trust/estate in the above example designated income payable to individual beneficiaries during its first taxation year, such amounts would have been taxable to the beneficiaries in their taxation year ending December 31, 2012. However, the flexibility to select a short first taxation year could also have been useful, for example, where a large sum of income was expected at a future date which was within the 12-month period following the date of death. By choosing an appropriate fiscal year end for the estate, the personal representative could have deferred taxation of that income until the estate's next taxation year.

These rules have now been changed. Subsection 249(1) provides that beginning in the 2016 taxation year, testamentary trusts, other than "graduated rate estates" (defined in subsection 248(1) but essentially testamentary trusts that are estates and are in their first 36 months following death) and "qualified disability trusts", are no longer permitted to choose their year end. To bring these new rules into effect, subsection 249(4.1) provided that testamentary trusts and estates (other than graduated rate estates and qualified disability trusts) existing on December 31, 2015 had a deemed year end at that time.

Under s. 104(23)(*d*), if a beneficiary of a graduated rate estate dies after the end of a trust taxation year but before the end of the calendar year in which the trust taxation year ends, the beneficiary's income for the period from the end of the trust taxation year to the time of death ("stub period") is included in the beneficiary's income for the year of death. However, the beneficiary's personal representative can elect to include the stub period income in a separate tax return as if the beneficiary were a separate person, thus allowing for some income splitting and doubling-up of some personal credits (see also s. 114.2 and 118.93). Graduated rate estates are exempt from instalments by virtue of subsection 156.1(2), while all other testamentary trusts will not have to make such payments starting in 2016.

History: S. 104(23), the portion before paragraph (*c*) was replaced by S.C. 2014, c. 39, s. 26(13), applicable to the 2016 and subsequent taxation years, and formerly read:

(23) *Testamentary trusts.* In the case of a testamentary trust, notwithstanding any other provision of this Act, the following rules apply:

S. 104(23)(*e*) was repealed by S.C. 2014, c. 39, s. 26(14), applicable to the 2016 and subsequent taxation years, and formerly read:

(*e*) in lieu of making the payments required by sections 155, 156 and 156.1, the trust shall pay to the Receiver General within 90 days after the end of each taxation year, the tax payable under this Part by it for the year.

S. 104(23)(*a*) was repealed by S.C. 2013, c. 34, s. 231(16), deemed to have come into force on December 21, 2002, and formerly read:

(*a*) the taxation year of the trust is the period for which the accounts of the trust are made up for purposes of assessment under this Act, but no such period may exceed 12 months and no change in the time when such a period ends may be made for the purposes of this Act without the concurrence of the Minister;

S. 104(23)(*b*) was repealed by S.C. 2013, c. 34, s. 231(16), deemed to have come into force on December 21, 2002, and formerly read:

(*b*) when a taxation year is referred to by reference to a calendar year, the reference is to the taxation year or years coinciding with, or ending in, that year;

Related Sections: 248(1) graduated rate estate; S. 114.2 Deductions in separate returns; s. 118.93 Credits in separate returns; s. 127.55 Application of s. 127.5; s. 249(1)(*c*) Definition of "taxation year"; s. 249(5) Testamentary trusts.

Canadian Tax Foundation: Gray, *Review of Tax Filings Required as a Result of the Death of a Taxpayer*, 2003 British Columbia Tax Conference 8:3–30.

Interpretation Bulletins: *Secondary* — IT-326R3 Returns of deceased persons as "another person".

▶ 104(24) ◀

(24) Amount payable. For the purposes of subsections (6), (7), (7.01), (13), (16) and (20), subparagraph 53(2)(*h*)(i.1) and subsections 94(5.2) and (8), an amount is deemed not to have become payable to a beneficiary in a taxation year unless it was paid in the year to the beneficiary or the beneficiary was entitled in the year to enforce payment of it.

Editorial Note: Where a trust is discretionary, a beneficiary will normally be entitled to enforce payment of an amount of the trust's income in a year if the trustees exercise their discretion in the year and provide notice of the exercise to the beneficiary. Payment of that amount by a cheque cashable on the date of issue or a demand promissory note payable on demand without restriction should be made by the trust once the amount is known. Note that a trust may elect under s. 104(13.1) or s. 104(13.2) to have an amount treated as not having been paid or become payable to a beneficiary for certain purposes. And, where its conditions are met, s. 104(18) overrides s. 104(24).

History: S. 104(24) was amended by S.C. 2013, c. 34, s. 10(3), applicable to taxation years that end after 2006. Subsection 104(24) also applies to each earlier taxation year of a trust to which subsection 94(1) [should be 94(3) – CCH] applies and each taxation year of a beneficiary under the trust in which one of those earlier taxation years of the trust ends, except that subsection 104(24) is to be read as follows in its application before October 31, 2006:

"(24) For the purposes of subsections (6), (7), (7.01), (13) and (20), subparagraph 53(2)(*h*)(i.1) and subsections 94(5.2) and (8), an amount is deemed not to have become payable to a beneficiary in a taxation year unless it was paid in the year to the beneficiary or the beneficiary was entitled in the year to enforce payment of it."

S. 104(24) formerly read:

(24) *Amount payable.* For the purposes of subsections (6), (7), (13), (16) and (20) and subparagraph 53(2)(*h*)(i.1), an amount is deemed not to have become payable to a beneficiary in a taxation year unless it was paid in the year to the beneficiary or the beneficiary was entitled in the year to enforce payment of it.

Canadian Tax Foundation: Rodrigo, *Interpretation of Deeming Rules: Subsection 104(24)*, 2017 Canadian Tax Focus 7(3):3–4; Monaco et al., *Trust Payment to a Minor (CRA Roundtable, Question 19)*, 2012 Ontario Tax Conference 14:29–31.

Tax Profile: June 2011 — Summary of Canada Revenue Agency Round Table Held at the 13th National STEP Canada Conference.

Interpretation Bulletins: *Primary* — IT-286R2 Trusts — Amount payable. *Secondary* — IT-342R Trusts — Income payable to beneficiaries; IT-381R3 Trusts — Deduction of amounts paid or payable to beneficiaries and flow-through of taxable capital gains to beneficiaries.

Tax Window Files: Phantom Income, *STEP Round Table — 2004 Annual Conference, Question 3, June 21, 2004*, CRA Document No. 2004-0069951C6. "Phantom income" (e.g., resulting from a deemed disposition) cannot be defined as income for trust law purposes, therefore, unless, under the terms of the trust, income is defined as income under the Act, or authorizes the trustee to allocate a deemed receipt as if it were an actual receipt, the deemed receipt cannot be allocated to a beneficiary; Post-1971 Spousal or Common-Law Partner Trust — Entitlement to Income, *Technical Interpretation, International and Trusts Division, June 2, 2003*, CRA Document No. 2003-0014515. Spouse beneficiary of spousal trust directs that income of the trust remain in the trust for a particular year; trust income still payable to the spouse in the year within the meaning of subsection 104(24).

Cases: A trust kept no records, made no regular reconciliations of its income and maintained no bank accounts. Accordingly, there was no way in which to prove that certain of the amounts which it had sought to deduct were ever "paid" or "payable" and such amounts were not deductible. *The Howard Langer Family Trust v. M.N.R.*, 92 DTC 1055 (T.C.C.); appealed to F.C.T.D. (April 16, 1992), File T-907-92

▶ 104(25) ◀

(25) Excess amount — (Repealed by 1988, c. 55, s. 71(15).)

▶ 104(25.1) ◀

(25.1) Idem — (Repealed by 1988, c. 55, s. 71(15).)

▶ 104(26) ◀

(26) Portion of interest deemed interest of beneficiary — (Repealed by 1988, c. 55, s. 71(16).)

▶ 104(27) ◀

(27) Pension benefits. If a trust, in a taxation year in which it is resident in Canada and is the graduated rate estate of an individual, receives a superannuation or pension benefit or a benefit out of or under a foreign retirement arrangement and designates, in its return of income for the year under this Part, an amount in respect of a beneficiary under the trust equal to the portion (in this subsection referred to as the "beneficiary's share") of the benefit that

(*a*) may reasonably be considered (having regard to all the circumstances including the terms and conditions of the trust arrangement) to be part of the amount that, by reason of subsection (13), was included in computing the income for a particular taxation year of the beneficiary, and

(*b*) was not designated by the trust in respect of any other beneficiary under the trust,

the following rules apply:

(*c*) where

(i) the benefit is an amount described in subparagraph (*a*)(i) of the definition "pension income" in subsection 118(7), and

(ii) the beneficiary was a spouse or common-law partner of the individual, the beneficiary's share of the benefit shall be deemed, for the purposes of subsections 118(3) and (7), to be a payment described in subparagraph (*a*)(i) of the definition "pension income" in subsection 118(7) that is included in computing the beneficiary's income for the particular year,

(*d*) where the benefit

(i) is a single amount (as defined in subsection 147.1(1)), other than an amount that relates to an actuarial surplus, paid by a registered pension plan to the trust as a consequence of the individual's death and the individual was, at the time of death, a spouse or common-law partner of the beneficiary, or

(ii) would be an amount included in the total determined under paragraph 60(*j*) in respect of the beneficiary for the taxation year of the beneficiary in which the benefit was received by the trust if the benefit had been received by the beneficiary at the time it was received by the trust,

the beneficiary's share of the benefit is, for the purposes of paragraph 60(*j*), an eligible amount in respect of the beneficiary for the particular year, and

(*e*) where the benefit is a single amount (as defined in subsection 147.1(1)) paid by a registered pension plan to the trust as a consequence of the individual's death,

(i) if the beneficiary was, immediately before the death, a child or grandchild of the individual who, because of mental or physical infirmity, was financially dependent on the individual for support, the beneficiary's share of the benefit (other than any portion of it that relates to an actuarial surplus) is deemed, for the purposes of paragraph 60(*l*), to be an amount from a registered pension plan included in computing the beneficiary's income for the particular year as a payment described in clause 60(*l*)(v)(B.01), and

(ii) if the beneficiary was, at the time of the death, under 18 years of age and a child or grandchild of the individual, the beneficiary's share of the benefit (other than any portion of it that relates to an actuarial surplus) is deemed, for the purposes of paragraph 60(*l*), to be an amount from a registered pension plan included in computing the beneficiary's income for the particular year as a payment described in subclause 60(*l*)(v)(B.1)(II).

Editorial Note: S. 104(27) permits superannuation, pension and foreign retirement arrangement benefits received by a testamentary trust resident in Canada to be treated as superannuation or pension benefits received by a beneficiary of the testamentary trust for certain purposes where it is reasonable to consider that these amounts were part of the amounts included in the income of the beneficiary under s. 104(13). As a result, for example, if such pension benefits qualify as pension income (as described in s. 118(7)), the beneficiary may be able to claim a tax credit under s. 118(3). The trust must make a designation in its income tax return under Part I.

Effective for the 2016 and subsequent taxation years, the designation under subsection 104(27) applies only to graduated rate estates and not to other testamentary trusts. A graduated rate estate is basically an estate of a deceased individual for up to 36 after the individual's death, although only one estate can qualify as such (subsection 248(1) "graduated rate estate").

History: S. 104(27), the portion before paragraph (*a*) was replaced by S.C. 2014, c. 39, s. 26(15), applicable to the 2016 and subsequent taxation years, and formerly read:

(27) *Pension benefits.* Where a testamentary trust has, in a taxation year throughout which it was resident in Canada, received a superannuation or pension benefit or a benefit out of or under a foreign retirement arrangement and has designated, in the return of its income for the year under this Part, an amount in respect of a beneficiary under the trust equal to such portion (in this subsection referred to as the "beneficiary's share") of the benefit as

S. 104(27)(*c*)(ii) was replaced by S.C. 2014, c. 39, s. 26(16), applicable to the 2016 and subsequent taxation years, and formerly read:

(ii) the beneficiary was a spouse or common-law partner of the settlor of the trust,

S. 104(27)(*d*)(i) was replaced by S.C. 2014, c. 39, s. 26(17), applicable to the 2016 and subsequent taxation years, and formerly read:

(i) is a single amount (within the meaning assigned by subsection 147.1(1)), other than an amount that relates to an actuarial surplus, paid by a registered pension plan to the trust as a consequence of the death of the settlor of the trust who was, at the time of death, a spouse or common-law partner of the beneficiary, or

S. 104(27)(*e*) was replaced by S.C. 2014, c. 39, s. 26(18), applicable to the 2016 and subsequent taxation years, and formerly read:

(*e*) where the benefit is a single amount (within the meaning assigned by subsection 147.1(1)) paid by a registered pension plan to the trust as a consequence of the death of the settlor of the trust,

(i) if the beneficiary was, immediately before the settlor's death, a child or grandchild of the settlor who, because of mental or physical infirmity, was financially dependent on the settlor for support, the beneficiary's share of the benefit (other than any portion of it that relates to an actuarial surplus) is deemed, for the purposes of paragraph 60(*l*), to be an amount from a registered pension plan included in computing the beneficiary's income for the particular year as a payment described in clause 60(*l*)(v)(B.01), and

(ii) if the beneficiary was, at the time of the settlor's death, under 18 years of age and a child or grandchild of the settlor, the beneficiary's share of the benefit (other than any portion of it that relates to an actuarial surplus) is deemed, for the purposes of paragraph 60(*l*), to be an amount from a registered pension plan included in computing the beneficiary's income for the particular year as a payment described in subclause 60(*l*)(v)(B.1)(II).

Related Sections: 248(1) graduated rate estate; S. 60(*j*) Transfer of superannuation benefits; s. 104(1) Reference to trust or estate; s. 118(7), "pension income"; s. 146(1.1) Restriction — financially dependent; s. 147.1(1), "single amount"; s. 248(1), "amount", "common-law partner", "registered pension plan", "trust".

Forms: T3 SCH 7 — Pension Income Allocations and Designations.

Interpretation Bulletins: *Primary* — IT-528 Transfers of funds between registered plans. *Secondary* — IT-124R6 Contributions to registered retirement savings plans.

► 104(27.1) ◄

(27.1) DPSP benefits. Where

(*a*) a trust, in a taxation year (in this subsection referred to as the "trust year") in which it is resident in Canada and is the graduated rate estate of an individual, receives an amount from a deferred profit sharing plan as a consequence of the individual's death,

(*b*) the individual was an employee of an employer who participated in the plan on behalf of the individual, and

(*c*) the amount is not part of a series of periodic payments,

such portion of the amount as

(*d*) is included under subsection 147(10) in computing the income of the trust for the trust year,

(*e*) can reasonably be considered (having regard to all the circumstances including the terms and conditions of the trust arrangement) to be part of the amount that was included under subsection (13) in computing the income for a particular taxation year of a beneficiary under the trust who was, at the time of the death, the individual's spouse or common-law partner, and

(*f*) is designated by the trust in respect of the beneficiary in the trust's return of income under this Part for the trust year is, for the purposes of paragraph 60(*j*), an eligible amount in respect of the beneficiary for the particular year.

Editorial Note: Analogous to s. 104(27), s. 104(27.1) permits a flow-through of amounts received by a testamentary trust from a DPSP as a consequence of the death of the settlor. Where it may reasonably be considered to be part of the amount that was included in the income of a beneficiary pursuant to s. 104(13) who was the spouse or common-law partner of the settlor, then such amounts will be eligible for a rollover by the spouse or common-law partner pursuant to s. 60(*j*). The trust must make a designation of the amounts in respect of the spouse or common-law partner in its income return for the year in which it receives the amounts.

Effective as of the 2016 taxation year, the designation under subsection 104(27.1) applies only to graduated rate estates and not to other testamentary trusts. A graduated rate estate is basically an estate of a deceased individual for up to 36 after the individual's death, although only one estate can qualify as such (subsection 248(1) "graduated rate estate").

History: S. 104(27.1)(*a*) and (*b*) were replaced by S.C. 2014, c. 39, s. 26(19), applicable to the 2016 and subsequent taxation years, and formerly read:

(*a*) a testamentary trust has received in a taxation year (in this subsection referred to as the "trust year") throughout which it was resident in Canada an amount from a deferred profit sharing plan as a consequence of the death of the settlor of the trust,

(*b*) the settlor was an employee of an employer who participated in the plan on behalf of the settlor, and

S. 104(27.1)(*e*) was replaced by S.C. 2014, c. 39, s. 26(20), applicable to the 2016 and subsequent taxation years, and formerly read:

(*e*) can reasonably be considered (having regard to all the circumstances including the terms and conditions of the trust arrangement) to be part of the amount that was included under subsection (13) in computing the income for a particular taxation year of a beneficiary under the trust who was, at the time of the settlor's death, a spouse or common-law partner of the settlor, and

Related Sections: 248(1) graduated rate estate; S. 60(*j*) Transfer of superannuation benefits; s. 248(1), "amount", "common-law partner", "trust"; s. 252(4) Extended meaning of spouse.

Interpretation Bulletins: *Primary* — IT-528 Transfers of funds between registered plans. *Secondary* — IT-124R6 Contributions to registered retirement savings plans.

▶ 104(28) ◀

(28) Death benefit. If the graduated rate estate of an individual receives an amount on or after the individual's death in recognition of the individual's service in an office or employment, the portion of the amount that can reasonably be considered (having regard to all the circumstances including the terms and conditions of the trust arrangement) to be paid or payable at any time to a beneficiary under the estate is deemed

(*a*) to be an amount received by the beneficiary at that time on or after the death in recognition of the individual's service in an office or employment; and

(*b*) except for purposes of this subsection, not to have been received by the estate.

Editorial Note: Under s. 104(28), a death benefit received by a testamentary trust, which is paid or payable to a beneficiary, is deemed to be received by the beneficiary and not by the trust. Where s. 104(28) applies, the death benefit is included in the beneficiary's income under s. 56(1)(*a*)(iii) (note that, pursuant to the definition of "death benefit" in s. 248(1), the first $10,000 of a death benefit is exempt from tax). There is no requirement that the trust designate the amount as payable to a beneficiary for the death benefit to retain its character.

Where a death benefit is paid or payable to a beneficiary such that s. 104(28) applies, the trust does not have the option of designating the amount for the purposes of s. 104(13.1). Subsection 104(13.1) allows the trust to designate amounts which have been included in the income of the trust and have been paid or are payable to beneficiaries of the trust. Where s. 104(28) applies, the death benefit is not included in the income of the trust.

Effective as of the 2016 taxation year, the designation under subsection 104(28) applies only to graduated rate estates and not to other testamentary trusts. A graduated rate estate is basically an estate of a deceased individual for up to 36 after the individual's death, although only one estate can qualify as such (subsection 248(1) "graduated rate estate").

History: S. 104(28) was replaced by S.C. 2014, c. 39, s. 26(21), applicable to the 2016 and subsequent taxation years, and formerly read:

(28) *Idem.* Such portion of any amount received by a testamentary trust in a taxation year on or after the death of an employee in recognition of the employee's service in an office or employment as may reasonably be considered (having regard to all the circumstances including the terms and conditions of the trust arrangement) to be paid or payable at a particular time to a particular beneficiary under the trust shall be deemed to be an amount received by the particular beneficiary at the particular time on or after the death of the employee in recognition of the employee's service in an office or employment and not to have been received by the trust.

Related Sections: 248(1) graduated rate estate; S. 56(1)(*a*)(iii) Amounts to be included in income for year; s. 104(13.1) Amounts deemed not paid; s. 248(1), "death benefit".

▶ 104(29) ◀

(29) Amounts deemed payable to beneficiaries — (Repealed by S.C. 2003, c. 28, s. 11(2).)

▶ 104(30) ◀

(30) Tax under Part XII.2. For the purposes of this Part, there shall be deducted in computing the income of a trust for a taxation year the tax paid by the trust for the year under Part XII.2.

Editorial Note: S. 104(30) requires the trust to deduct its Part XII.2 tax liability in computing its income for Part I purposes. S. 104(31) requires beneficiaries taxable under Part I to include in computing income the amount of Part XII.2 tax deemed to have been paid by them under s. 210.2(3). In combination with s. 104(30), s. 104(31) produces the same result that would transpire if the amount of the trust's Part XII.2 tax that is deemed to have been paid by beneficiaries had been trust income payable to them for the purposes of ss. 104(6) and 104(13).

Interpretation Bulletins: *Secondary* — IT-342R Trusts — Income payable to beneficiaries.

▶ 104(31) ◀

(31) Idem. The amount in respect of a taxation year of a trust that is deemed under subsection 210.2(3) to have been paid by a beneficiary under the trust on account of the beneficiary's tax under this Part shall, for the purposes of subsection (13), be deemed to be an amount in respect of the income of the trust for the year that has become payable by the trust to the beneficiary at the end of the year.

Interpretation Bulletins: *Secondary* — IT-342R Trusts — Income payable to beneficiaries.

SECTION 105: Benefits under trust

▶ 105(1) ◀

(1) Benefits under trust. The value of all benefits to a taxpayer during a taxation year from or under a trust, irrespective of when created, shall, subject to subsection (2), be included in computing the taxpayer's income for the year except to the extent that the value

(*a*) is otherwise required to be included in computing the taxpayer's income for a taxation year; or

(*b*) has been deducted under paragraph 53(2)(*h*) in computing the adjusted cost base of the taxpayer's interest in the trust or would be so deducted if that paragraph

(i) applied in respect of the taxpayer's interest in the trust, and

(ii) were read without reference to clause 53(2)(*h*)(i.1)(B).

Editorial Note: Basically, s. 105(1) provides that the value of all benefits (other than a distribution or payment of capital) to a taxpayer during a taxation year from or under a trust shall be included in computing the income of the taxpayer for the year. "Benefit" is not defined in the Act, therefore, its ordinary (very broad) usage applies. However, it is the CRA's administrative policy that a taxable benefit from a trust under s. 105(1) is not assessed on personal-use property (including real property) owned by the trust primarily for the use and enjoyment of a beneficiary or a person related thereto (CRA Document No. 2006-0173261I7).

S. 105(1) does not apply to amounts otherwise required to be included in the beneficiary's income, including under s. 104(13) or (14) or 105(2), which is significant because these latter amounts are deductible in computing the trust's income whereas amounts included in a beneficiary's income under s. 105(1) are not deductible. By virtue of s. 105(1)(*b*)(ii), amounts such as capital dividends and the one-half non-taxable portion of capital gains paid out to a beneficiary are not included as benefits.

Related Sections: S. 53(2)(*h*) Amounts to be deducted — Capital interest in a trust; s. 104(1) Reference to trust or estate; s. 104(6) Deduction in computing income of trust; s. 104(19) Taxable dividends; s. 104(21) Taxable capital gains; s. 108(1), "beneficiary", "income interest", "trust"; s. 248(1), "amount", "property".

Tax Profile: December 2009 — Income Tax Consequences of Income Distributions by a Canadian Trust.

Forms: T3 — Statement of Trust Income Allocations and Designations; T3SUM — Summary of Trust Income Allocations and Designations.

Interpretation Bulletins: *Secondary* — IT-342R Trusts — Income payable to beneficiaries; IT-381R3 Trusts — Deduction of amounts paid or payable to beneficiaries and flow-through of taxable capital gains to beneficiaries; IT-524 Trusts — Flow-through of taxable dividends to a beneficiary — After 1987.

Tax Window Files: Payment by a Trustee of Income Taxes Owed by a Trust, *Technical Interpretation, International and Trusts Division, March 20, 2007*, CRA Document No. 2006-0173711E5. S. 105(1) judged not to apply re payment of trust taxes by trustee; Advantage Conferred by Trust, *October 19, 2006*, CRA Document No. 2006-0173261I7. CRA policy is not to assess re personal-use of trust.

Cases: An interest-free loan made to a beneficiary of a testamentary trust to enable him to purchase a house was not a taxable benefit. *Cooper v. M.N.R.*, 88 DTC 6525 (F.C.T.D.), reversing 87 DTC 194 (T.C.C.)

► 105(2) ◄

(2) Upkeep, etc. Such part of an amount paid by a trust out of income of the trust for the upkeep, maintenance or taxes of or in respect of property that, under the terms of the trust arrangement, is required to be maintained for the use of a tenant for life or a beneficiary as is reasonable in the circumstances shall be included in computing the income of the tenant for life or other beneficiary from the trust for the taxation year for which it was paid.

Editorial Note: Subsection 105(2) requires a beneficiary to include in his or her income that portion of the trust's annual income paid by the trust for the upkeep and maintenance of, or taxes on, property to the extent that the trust is required under the terms of the trust arrangements to make those payments for the use of that property by the beneficiary. Subsection 104(6) provides a deduction to the trust for any such amounts. Note that mortgage payments do not constitute payments for "upkeep, maintenance or taxes".

Related Sections: S. 104(6) Deduction in computing income of trust; s. 105(1) Benefits under trust; s. 120.4 Tax on split income.

Tax Profile: December 2009 — Income Tax Consequences of Income Distributions by a Canadian Trust.

Interpretation Bulletins: *Secondary* — IT-342R Trusts — Income payable to beneficiaries; IT-465R Non-resident beneficiaries of trusts; IT-524 Trusts — Flow-through of taxable dividends to a beneficiary — After 1987.

Cases: For s. 105(2) to apply, the trust instrument must stipulate that the property is to be maintained for the use of the life tenant or other beneficiary; it is not sufficient if this is done in some other instrument or contract. *Blackstein v. the Queen*, 98 DTC 3371 (T.C.C.).

SECTION 106: Income interest in trust

► 106(1) ◄

(1) Income interest in trust. Where an amount in respect of a taxpayer's income interest in a trust has been included in computing the taxpayer's income for a taxation year by reason of subsection (2) or 104(13), except to the extent that an amount in respect of that income interest has been deducted in computing the taxpayer's taxable income pursuant to subsection 112(1) or 138(6), there may be deducted in computing the taxpayer's income for the year the lesser of

(*a*) the amount so included in computing the taxpayer's income for the year, and

(*b*) the amount, if any, by which the cost to the taxpayer of the income interest exceeds the total of all amounts in respect of the interest that were deductible under this subsection in computing the taxpayer's income for previous taxation years.

Editorial Note: If the beneficiary has a "hard" cost of the income interest (see s. 106(1.1)), the beneficiary can deduct the cost from any trust income included in the beneficiary's income under s. 104(13), or, alternatively, in computing the income inclusion under s. 106(2) upon a disposition of the interest to a third party.

Related Sections: S. 108(1), "trust"; s. 115(1) Non-resident's taxable income in Canada.

► 106(1.1) ◄

(1.1) Cost of income interest in a trust. The cost to a taxpayer of an income interest of the taxpayer in a trust is deemed to be nil unless

(*a*) any part of the interest was acquired by the taxpayer from a person who was the beneficiary in respect of the interest immediately before that acquisition; or

(*b*) the cost of any part of the interest would otherwise be determined not to be nil under paragraph 128.1(1)(*c*) or (4)(*c*).

Editorial Note: Pursuant to s. 106(1.1), the cost to a beneficiary of an income interest in a trust is nil, except where the interest was acquired from a beneficiary under the trust, or where the cost of any part of the interest was ever determined not to be nil under the taxpayer migration rules in s. 128.1.

► 106(2) ◄

(2) Disposition by taxpayer of income interest. Where in a taxation year a taxpayer disposes of an income interest in a trust,

(*a*) except where subsection (3) applies to the disposition, there shall be included in computing the taxpayer's income for the year the amount, if any, by which

(i) the proceeds of disposition

exceed

(ii) where that interest includes a right to enforce payment of an amount by the trust, the amount in respect of that right that has been included in computing the taxpayer's income for a taxation year because of subsection 104(13);

(*b*) any taxable capital gain or allowable capital loss of the taxpayer from the disposition shall be deemed to be nil; and

(*c*) for greater certainty, the cost to the taxpayer of each property received by the taxpayer as consideration for the disposition is the fair market value of the property at the time of the disposition.

Editorial Note: A taxpayer who assigns or disposes of an income interest in a trust in favour of another person will be subject to s. 106(2) and must include in income the proceeds of disposition. If the transaction is not at arm's length and the proceeds are less than fair market value, the taxpayer will be deemed by s. 69(1)(*b*) to have received proceeds of disposition equal to the fair market value of the interest. Similarly, where the taxpayer disposes of an income interest by gift *inter vivos*, the proceeds of disposition are deemed to be the fair market value of the income interest.

If the disposition of the interest results from a distribution of trust property in satisfaction of the interest (see also s. 106(3)), there is no income inclusion in respect of the disposition under s. 106(2).

Related Sections: S. 61(2) Income-averaging annuity — eligible income; s. 106(1) Income interest in trust; s. 115(1) Non-resident's taxable income in Canada.

Canadian Tax Foundation: Rajan and Brown, *Personal Trusts 2000: Taxation and Planning in the New Millennium*, 2000 Conference Report 28:1–40.

Income Tax Folios: *Primary* — S6-F2-C1 Disposition of an Income Interest in a Trust.

Tax Window Files: Renunciation of Testamentary Spouse Trust Income and Capital, *Technical Interpretation, International and Trust Division, May 9, 2007*, CRA Document No. 2006-0189931E5. S. 69(1) and s. 106(2) not applicable re renunciation of interest in testamentary spousal trust.

► 106(3) ◄

(3) Proceeds of disposition of income interest. For greater certainty, where at any time any property of a trust has been distributed by the trust to a taxpayer who was a beneficiary under the trust in satisfaction of all or any part of the taxpayer's income interest in the trust, the trust shall be deemed to have disposed of the property for proceeds of disposition equal to the fair market value of the property at that time.

Editorial Note: See the editorial note to s. 106(2).

Related Sections: S. 38 Taxable capital gain and allowable capital loss; s. 104(1) Reference to trust or estate; s. 106(2) Disposition by taxpayer of income interest; s. 108(1), "beneficiary", "income interest", "trust"; s. 248(1), "amount", "property".

Income Tax Folios: *Secondary*— S6-F2-C1 Disposition of an Income Interest in a Trust.

Information Circulars: IC 82-6R10 Clearance certificate.

SECTION 107: Disposition by taxpayer of capital interest

▶ 107(1) ◀

(1) Disposition by taxpayer of capital interest. Where a taxpayer has disposed of all or any part of the taxpayer's capital interest in a trust,

(*a*) where the trust is a personal trust or a prescribed trust, for the purpose of computing the taxpayer's capital gain, if any, from the disposition, the adjusted cost base to the taxpayer of the interest or the part of the interest, as the case may be, immediately before the disposition is, unless any part of the interest has ever been acquired for consideration and, at the time of the disposition, the trust is non-resident, deemed to be the greater of

(i) its adjusted cost base, otherwise determined, to the taxpayer immediately before the disposition, and

(ii) the amount, if any, by which

(A) its cost amount to the taxpayer immediately before the disposition

exceeds

(B) the total of all amounts deducted under paragraph 53(2)(*g*.1) in computing its adjusted cost base to the taxpayer immediately before the disposition;

(*b*) (Repealed by S.C. 2001, c. 17, s. 80(2).)

(*c*) where the taxpayer is not a mutual fund trust, the taxpayer's loss from the disposition is deemed to be the amount, if any, by which the amount of that loss otherwise determined exceeds the amount, if any, by which

(i) the total of all amounts each of which was received or would, but for subsection 104(19), have been received by the trust on a share of the capital stock of a corporation before the disposition (and, where the trust is a unit trust, after 1987) and

(A) where the taxpayer is a corporation,

(I) was a taxable dividend designated under subsection 104(19) by the trust in respect of the taxpayer, to the extent of the amount of the dividend that was deductible under section 112 or subsection 115(1) or 138(6) in computing the taxpayer's taxable income or taxable income earned in Canada for any taxation year, or

(II) was an amount designated under subsection 104(20) by the trust in respect of the taxpayer,

(B) where the taxpayer is another trust, was an amount designated under subsection 104(19) or (20) by the trust in respect of the taxpayer, and

(C) where the taxpayer is not a corporation, trust or partnership, was an amount designated under subsection 104(20) by the trust in respect of the taxpayer

exceeds

(ii) the portion of the total determined under subparagraph (i) that can reasonably be considered to have resulted in a reduction, under this paragraph, of the taxpayer's loss otherwise determined from a previous disposition of an interest in the trust;

(*d*) where the taxpayer is a partnership, the share of a person (other than another partnership or a mutual fund trust) of any loss of the partnership from the disposition is deemed to be the amount, if any, by which that loss otherwise determined exceeds the amount, if any, by which

(i) the total of all amounts each of which is a dividend that was received or would, but for subsection 104(19), have been received by the trust on a share of the capital stock of a corporation before the disposition (and, where the trust is a unit trust, after 1987) and

(A) where the person is a corporation,

(I) was a taxable dividend that was designated under subsection 104(19) by the trust in respect of the taxpayer, to the extent of the amount of the dividend that was deductible under section 112 or subsection 115(1) or 138(6) in computing the person's taxable income or taxable income earned in Canada for any taxation year, or

(II) was a dividend designated under subsection 104(20) by the trust in respect of the taxpayer and was an amount received by the person,

(B) where the person is an individual other than a trust, was a dividend designated under subsection 104(20) by the trust in respect of the taxpayer and was an amount received by the person, and

(C) where the person is another trust, was a dividend designated under subsection 104(19) or (20) by the trust in respect of the taxpayer and was an amount received by the person (or that would have been received by the person if this Act were read without reference to subsection 104(19)),

exceeds

(ii) the portion of the total determined under subparagraph (i) that can reasonably be considered to have resulted in a reduction, under this paragraph, of the person's loss otherwise determined from a previous disposition of an interest in the trust; and

(*e*) if the capital interest is not a capital property of the taxpayer, notwithstanding the definition "cost amount" in subsection 108(1), its cost amount is deemed to be the amount, if any, by which

(i) the amount that would, if this Act were read without reference to this paragraph and the definition "cost amount" in subsection 108(1), be its cost amount

exceeds

(ii) the total of all amounts, each of which is an amount in respect of the capital interest that has become payable to the taxpayer before the disposition and that would be described in subparagraph 53(2)(*h*)(i.1) if that subparagraph were read without reference to its subclause (B)(I).

Editorial Note: Where s. 107(1)(*a*) applies, the adjusted cost base to the taxpayer of a trust capital interest for capital gains purposes is generally equal to the greater of the adjusted cost base otherwise determined (see also s. 107(1.1)) and the cost amount of the interest. In the case of a disposition of the capital interest to a third party, the cost amount of the interest is generally determined based on a *pro rata* portion of the amount of the trust's money and the cost amount of the trust's other property. In the case of a disposition of an interest in the trust in exchange for property distributed by the trust, the cost amount of the interest is equal to the total cost amounts of the distributed property. See s. 108(1), "cost amount".

History: S. 107(1)(*e*) was added by S.C. 2013, c. 34, s. 233(1), applicable to dispositions that occur, and valuations made,

(*a*) after 2001 in respect of qualified trust units, as defined in subsection 260(1) in respect of which an amount described in paragraph 260(5.1)(*b*), or that would have been so described had no election been made under s. 260(5.1), is paid after 2001 and before February 28, 2004, except that subparagraph 107(1)(*e*)(ii) is, with respect to amounts described in subclause 53(2)(*h*)(i.1)(B)(I) that were payable on or before 2002, to be read without reference to the words "if that subparagraph were read without reference to its subclause (B)(I)"; and

(*b*) in any other case, after February 27, 2004, except that, subject to paragraph (*a*),

(i) paragraph 107(1)(*e*) does not apply to a disposition by a taxpayer after February 27, 2004 and before 2005 pursuant to an agreement in writing made by the taxpayer on or before February 27, 2004, and

(ii) subparagraph 107(1)(*e*)(ii) is, with respect to amounts described in subclause 53(2)(*h*)(i.1)(B)(I) that were payable on or before February 27, 2004, to be read without reference to the words "if that subparagraph were read without reference to its subclause (B)(I)".

[**Editorial Note**: The applications to the amendment to s. 107(1)(*a*), the portion before subparagraph (i) by S.C. 2001, c. 17, s. 80(1), the repeal of s. 107(1)(*b*) by S.C. 2001, c. 17, s. 80(2), and the repeal of s. 107(1), the portion after paragraph (*d*) by S.C. 2001, c. 17, s. 80(3), were amended by S.C. 2013, c. 34, s. 25(1), deemed to have come into force on June 14, 2001. This amendment was made to ensure that transfers that occur after 1999 and before 2007, the residence of a transferee trust will be determined without reference to section 94 of the Act, as it reads in its application to taxation years that began before 2007. These 2001 amendments are not reproduced in print but are available in all CCH Canadian electronic versions of the Income Tax Act.]

Related Regulations: 4800.1.

Related Sections: S. 13(21), "depreciable property"; s. 38 Taxable capital gain and allowable capital loss; s. 53(2)(*h*)(i) Amounts to be deducted — Capital interest in a trust; s. 54, "adjusted cost base", "capital property"; s. 104(1) Reference to trust or estate; s. 107(1.1) Cost of capital interest in a trust; s. 107(2) Distribution by personal trust; s. 108(1), "beneficiary", "capital interest", "cost amount", "inter vivos trust", "trust"; s. 112(4) Loss on share that is not capital property; s. 115(1), "taxable Canadian property"; s. 248(1), "amount", "insurance corporation", "non-resident", "prescribed", "property", "regulation"; s. 255 Canada.

Canadian Tax Foundation: Brown, *Alter Ego Joint Conjugal and Self-Benefit Trusts Revisited: Some Troubling Tax Issues and a Search for Better Alternatives*, 2005 Canadian Tax Journal 1:224–244; Rajan and Brown, *Personal Trusts 2000: Taxation and Planning in the New Millennium*, 2000 Conference Report 28:1–40.

Tax Profile: February 2002 — Transferring Property to a Trust After the Enactment of Bill C-22.

Tax Window Files: Deemed Disposition of Interest in Trust on Emigration from Canada, *Technical Interpretation, International & Trusts Division, February 27, 2004*, CRA Document No. 2004-0061841E5. Calculation of capital gain upon deemed disposition of interest in trust on emigration from Canada; Deemed Disposition of Interest in Trust on Emigration from Canada, *Technical Interpretation, International & Trusts Division, February 27, 2004*, CRA Document No. 2004-0061841E5. Calculation of capital gain upon deemed disposition of interest in trust on emigration from Canada.

▶ 107(1.1) ◀

(1.1) Cost of capital interest in a trust. The cost to a taxpayer of a capital interest of the taxpayer in a personal trust or a prescribed trust is deemed to be,

(*a*) where the taxpayer elected under subsection 110.6(19) in respect of the interest and the trust does not elect under that subsection in respect of any property of the trust, the taxpayer's cost of the interest determined under paragraph 110.6(19)(*a*); and

(*b*) in any other case, nil, unless

(i) any part of the interest was acquired by the taxpayer from a person who was the beneficiary in respect of the interest immediately before that acquisition, or

(ii) the cost of any part of the interest would otherwise be determined not to be nil under section 48 as it read in its application before 1993 or under paragraph 111(4)(*e*) or 128.1(1)(*c*) or (4)(*c*).

Editorial Note: The cost of a capital interest in a personal or prescribed trust (regulation 4800.1) is deemed to be nil unless the beneficiary acquired the interest from another beneficiary or the interest was subject to the deemed disposition and acquisition provisions of s. 128.1.

Related Regulations: 4800.1.

Related Sections: S. 70(5) Capital property of a deceased taxpayer; s. 107(1) Disposition by taxpayer of capital interest.

▶ 107(1.2) ◀

(1.2) Deemed fair market value — non-capital property. For the purpose of section 10, the fair market value at any time of a capital interest in a trust is deemed to be equal to the amount that is the total of

(*a*) the amount that would, if this Act were read without reference to this subsection, be its fair market value at that time, and

(*b*) the total of all amounts, each of which is an amount that would be described, in respect of the capital interest, in subparagraph 53(2)(*h*)(i.1) if that subparagraph were read without reference to its subclause (B)(I), that has become payable to the taxpayer before that time.

History: S. 107(1.2) was added by S.C. 2013, c. 34, s. 233(2), applicable to dispositions that occur, and valuations made,

(*a*) after 2001 in respect of qualified trust units, as defined in subsection 260(1) in respect of which an amount described in paragraph 260(5.1)(*b*), or that would have been so described had no election been made under s. 260(5.1), is paid after 2001 and before February 28, 2004, except that paragraph 107(1.2)(*b*)(ii) is, with respect to amounts described in subclause 53(2)(*h*)(i.1)(B)(I) that were payable on or before 2002, to be read without reference to the words "if that subparagraph were read without reference to its subclause (B)(I)"; and

(*b*) in any other case, after February 27, 2004, except that paragraph 107(1.2)(*b*) is, with respect to amounts described in subclause 53(2)(*h*)(i.1)(B)(I) that were payable on or before February 27, 2004, to be read without reference to the words "if that subparagraph were read without reference to its subclause (B)(I)".

▶ 107(2) ◀

(2) Distribution by personal trust. Subject to subsections (2.001), (2.002) and (4) to (5), if at any time a property of a personal trust or a prescribed trust is distributed (otherwise than as a SIFT trust wind-up event) by the trust to a taxpayer who was a beneficiary under the trust and there is a resulting disposition of all or any part of the taxpayer's capital interest in the trust, (*a*) the trust shall be deemed to have disposed of the property for proceeds of disposition equal to its cost amount to the trust immediately before that time;

(*b*) subject to subsection (2.2), the taxpayer is deemed to have acquired the property at a cost equal to the total of its cost amount to the trust immediately before that time and the specified percentage of the amount, if any, by which

(i) the adjusted cost base to the taxpayer of the capital interest or part of it, as the case may be, immediately before that time (determined without reference to paragraph (1)(*a*))

exceeds

(ii) the cost amount to the taxpayer of the capital interest or part of it, as the case may be, immediately before that time;

(*b*.1) for the purpose of paragraph (*b*), the specified percentage is,

(i) where the property is capital property (other than depreciable property), 100%, and

(ii) (Repealed.)

(iii) in any other case, 50%;

(*c*) the taxpayer's proceeds of disposition of the capital interest in the trust (or of the part of it) disposed of by the taxpayer on the distribution are deemed to be equal to the amount, if any, by which

(i) the cost at which the taxpayer would be deemed by paragraph (*b*) to have acquired the property if the specified percentage referred to in that paragraph were 100%

exceeds

(ii) the total of all amounts each of which is an eligible offset at that time of the taxpayer in respect of the capital interest or the part of it;

(*d*) where the property so distributed was depreciable property of a prescribed class of the trust and the amount that was the capital cost to the trust of that property exceeds the cost at which the taxpayer is deemed by this section to have acquired the property, for the purposes of sections 13 and 20 and any regulations made under paragraph 20(1)(*a*)

(i) the capital cost to the taxpayer of the property shall be deemed to be the amount that was the capital cost of the property to the trust, and

(ii) the excess shall be deemed to have been allowed to the taxpayer in respect of the property under regulations made under paragraph 20(1)(*a*) in computing income for taxation years before the acquisition by the taxpayer of the property.

(*d*.1) (Repealed by S.C. 2010, c. 12, s.10(2).)

(*e*) (Repealed by S.C. 1994, c. 7, Sched. VIII, s. 43(1).)

(*f*) (Repealed by S.C. 2016, c. 12, s. 36(2).)

Editorial Note: In general terms, s. 107(2) provides a tax-deferred rollover where property is distributed from a personal or prescribed trust to a beneficiary in satisfaction of all or part of the beneficiary's capital interest. The beneficiary will not realize a capital gain and normally will not realize a capital loss, although under certain circumstances a capital loss may be realized (a loss may be realized if there is an "eligible offset" — see s. 107(2)(*c*)(ii)). If the beneficiary's adjusted cost base of the capital interest (with regard to s. 107(1.1) but not s. 107(1)(*a*)) exceeds the cost amount of the distributed property, the cost of the property to the beneficiary will normally be bumped up (s. 107(2)(*b*)).

S. 107(2.1) applies, and the rollover under s. 107(2) does not apply, if the trust or beneficiary elects out of the rollover under s. 107(2.001) or (2.002), or if any of ss. 107(4), (4.1) or (5) apply.

History: S. 107(2)(*b*.1)(ii) was repealed by S.C. 2016, c. 12, s. 36(1), in force January 1, 2017, and formerly read:

(ii) where the property is eligible capital property in respect of a business of the trust, 100%, and

S. 107(2)(*f*) was repealed by S.C. 2016, c. 12, s. 36(2), in force January 1, 2017, and formerly read:

(*f*) where the property so distributed was eligible capital property of the trust in respect of a business of the trust,

(i) where the eligible capital expenditure of the trust in respect of the property exceeds the cost at which the taxpayer is deemed by this subsection to have acquired the property, for the purposes of sections 14, 20 and 24,

(A) the eligible capital expenditure of the taxpayer in respect of the property shall be deemed to be the amount that was the eligible capital expenditure of the trust in respect of the property, and

(B) $^3/_4$ of the excess shall be deemed to have been allowed under paragraph 20(1)(*b*) to the taxpayer in respect of the property in computing income for taxation years ending

(I) before the acquisition by the taxpayer of the property, and

(II) after the adjustment time of the taxpayer in respect of the business, and

(ii) for the purpose of determining after that time the amount required by paragraph 14(1)(*b*) to be included in computing the taxpayer's income in respect of any subsequent disposition of property of the business, there shall be added to the value otherwise determined for Q in the definition "cumulative eligible capital" in subsection 14(5) the amount determined by the formula

$$A \times B/C$$

where

A is the amount, if any, determined for Q in that definition in respect of the business of the trust immediately before the distribution,

B is the fair market value of the property so distributed immediately before the distribution, and

C is the fair market value immediately before the distribution of all eligible capital property of the trust in respect of the business.

S. 107(2)(*b.1*)(iii) was replaced by S.C. 2013, c. 34, s. 233(3), applicable to distributions made after December 20, 2002, and formerly read:

(iii) in any other case, 75%;

S. 107(2)(*c*), before subparagraph (i) was replaced by S.C. 2013, c. 34, s. 233(4), applicable to distributions made after 1999, and formerly read:

(*c*) the taxpayer is deemed to have disposed of all or part, as the case may be, of the capital interest for proceeds equal to the amount, if any, by which

S. 107(2)(*d.1*) was repealed by S.C. 2010, c. 12, s. 10(2), applicable in determining after March 4, 2010 whether a property is taxable Canadian property of a taxpayer. S. 107(2)(*d.1*) formerly read:

(*d*.1) the property is deemed to be taxable Canadian property of the taxpayer where

(i) the taxpayer is non-resident at that time,

(ii) that time is before October 2, 1996, and

(iii) the property was deemed by paragraph 51(1)(*f*), 85(1)(*i*) or 85.1(1)(*a*), subsection 85.1(5) or 87(4) or (5) or paragraph 97(2)(*c*) to be taxable Canadian property of the trust; and

S. 107(2)(*d.1*)(iii) was replaced by S.C. 2010, c. 12, s. 10(1), applicable in determining after October 1, 1996 whether a property is taxable Canadian property of a taxpayer. S. 107(2)(*d.1*)(iii) formerly read:

(iii) the property was deemed by paragraph 51(1)(*f*), 85(1)(*i*) or 85.1(1)(*a*), subsection 87(4) or (5) or paragraph 97(2)(*c*) to be taxable Canadian property of the trust; and

S. 107(2), the portion before paragraph (*a*) was replaced by S.C. 2009, c. 2, s. 26(1), applicable after July 14, 2008. S. 107(2), the portion before paragraph (*a*) formerly read:

(2) *Distribution by personal trust.* Subject to subsections (2.001), (2.002) and (4) to (5), where at any time a property of a personal trust or a prescribed trust is distributed by the trust to a taxpayer who was a beneficiary under the trust and there is a resulting disposition of all or any part of the taxpayer's capital interest in the trust,

Related Regulations: 4800.1.

Related Sections: S. 14(1) Eligible capital property — inclusion in income from business; s. 20(1)(*b*) Cumulative eligible capital amount; s. 54, "eligible capital property"; s. 107(1) Disposition by taxpayer of capital interest; s. 107(3) Application of subsection (3.1); s. 107(4) Trusts in favour of spouse, common-law partner or self; s. 107(5) Distribution to non-resident; s. 108(1), "cost amount"; s. 248(1), "amount", "business", "disposition", "eligible capital expenditure", "eligible capital property", "property", "trust"; ITAR s. 20(1.2)

Other transfers of depreciable property; s. 36 Application of paras. 107(2)(b) and (d) of amended Act.

Canadian Tax Foundation: Wang and Bernier, *Principal and Cottage Residence Planning: A Review of Selected Issues — Part 2*, 2013 Ontario Tax Conference 8B:1–20; Baxter and Miedema, *Trusts — The 21-Year Rule*, 2013 Atlantic Provinces Tax Conference 4:1–20; Chan and Morin, *Distributions by Canadian Testamentary Trusts*, 2005 Canadian Tax Journal 4:1090–1110; Rajan and Brown, *Personal Trusts 2000: Taxation and Planning in the New Millennium*, 2000 Conference Report 28:1–40; Webb, *The New Proposals For Trust Distributions And Related Issues*, 1999 Conference Report 34:1–24.

STEP Canada: Elie Roth, "Adding and Deleting a Beneficiary to a Trust," PowerPoint presentation to the 15th National Conference of STEP Canada, Toronto, June 10-11, 2013.

Tax Profile: April 2013 — Canadian Estate Freezes in Favour of U.S. Citizens; February 2002 — Transferring Property to a Trust After the Enactment of Bill C-22.

Interpretation Bulletins: *Secondary* — IT-209R Inter-vivos gifts of capital property to individuals directly or through trusts; IT-349R3 Intergenerational transfers of farm property on death.

Tax Window Files: 107(2) distribution, *July 2, 2013*, CRA Document No. 2013-0488381E5; Bargain Purchase Under a Will, *August 1, 2007*, CRA Document No. 2007-0232421R3. S. 107(2) applied where a beneficiary of an estate acquired property from the estate at less than fair market value; Trust Roll-Out Trust Roll-Out, *June 22, 2004*, CRA Document No. 2004-0069901C6 . S. 107(2) will generally apply to a distribution of property to a beneficiary of a discretionary personal trust; Assumption of Liability in Connection with Distribution of Property By Trust, *Technical Interpretation, International and Trusts Division, April 30, 2003*, CRA Document No. 2002-0156045. Assumption of trust's debt by beneficiary not contribution to trust, may qualify as eligible offset; Property Inherited From Non-Resident, *Technical Interpretation, International and Trusts Division, January 23, 2003*, CRA Document No. 2002-0133410. Relationship between subsections 70(5) and 107(2) when property received by beneficiary from estate.

Cases: The taxpayer sued the trustees of a trust of which he was the beneficiary. He accepted a cash settlement and disclaimed his beneficial interest in the trust property. The taxpayer failed to demonstrate that the cash he received had come out of the trust. As a result, there was no evidence that trust property had been distributed to the taxpayer so as to allow him to invoke the provisions of s. 107(2). *Chan v. The Queen*, 2001 DTC 5570 (F.C.A.), affirming 99 DTC 1215 (T.C.C.).

► 107(2.001) ◄

(2.001) No rollover on election by a trust. Where a trust makes a distribution of a property to a beneficiary of the trust in full or partial satisfaction of the beneficiary's capital interest in the trust and so elects in prescribed form filed with the Minister with the trust's return of income for its taxation year in which the distribution occurred, subsection (2) does not apply to the distribution if

(*a*) the trust is resident in Canada at the time of the distribution;

(*b*) the property is taxable Canadian property; or

(*c*) the property is capital property used in, or property described in the inventory of, a business carried on by the trust through a "permanent establishment" (as defined by regulation) in Canada immediately before the time of the distribution.

Editorial Note: S. 107(2.001) may be useful if the distributed property has an accrued loss that can be utilized at the trust level, or an accrued gain that can be offset by the trust's losses (an election under s. 107(2.11) or s. 104(13.2) may be necessary to ensure that any resulting gain is included in the trust's income on the distribution). Where the election is made, the tax consequences of the distribution are determined pursuant to s. 107(2.1), and the trust will realize proceeds of distribution equal to the fair market value of the distributed property.

History: S. 107(2.001)(*c*) was replaced by S.C. 2016, c. 12, s. 36(3), in force January 1, 2017, and formerly read:

> (*c*) the property is capital property used in, eligible capital property in respect of, or property described in the inventory of, a business carried on by the trust through a permanent establishment (as defined by regulation) in Canada immediately before the time of the distribution.

Related Regulations: 400(2); 600(*b*).

Related Sections: S. 54, "capital property", "eligible capital property"; s. 107(2.1) Other distributions; s. 108(1), "beneficiary", "capital interest", "trust"; s. 220(3.2) Late, amended or revoked elections. s. 248(1), "inventory", "property" "taxable Canadian property"; s. 250 Person deemed resident.

Tax Topics: No. 1690, Estate Planning In The 21st Century; No. 1582, Estate Planning in the 21st Century; No. 1573, Non-rollover Distributions to Capital Beneficiaries of Trusts.

Income Tax Folios: *Primary* — S6-F1-C1 Residence of a Trust or Estate.

Tax Window Files: Subsection 107(2.001) election, *July 11, 2013*, CRA Document No. 2012-0471061E5.

► 107(2.002) ◄

(2.002) No rollover on election by a beneficiary. Where a non-resident trust makes a distribution of a property (other than a property described in paragraph (2.001)(*b*) or (*c*)) to a beneficiary of the trust in full or partial satisfaction of the beneficiary's capital interest in the trust and the beneficiary makes an election under this subsection in prescribed form filed with the Minister with the beneficiary's return of income for the beneficiary's taxation year in which the distribution occurred,

(*a*) subsection (2) does not apply to the distribution; and

(*b*) for the purpose of subparagraph (1)(*a*)(ii), the cost amount of the interest to the beneficiary is deemed to be nil.

Editorial Note: The election under s. 107(2.002) may be useful to provide a stepped-up cost of the distributed property in the hands of a Canadian resident beneficiary, particularly if the beneficiary has losses that can offset any resulting gain owing to the application of s. 107(2.1).

Related Sections: S. 107(2.1) Other distributions; s. 108(1), "beneficiary", "capital interest", "cost amount", "trust"; s. 233.6(1) Returns respecting distributions from non-resident trusts; s. 248(1), "non-resident", "property.

Income Tax Folios: *Primary* — S6-F1-C1 Residence of a Trust or Estate.

Tax Window Files: Subsection 107(2.002) election, *October 11, 2013*, CRA Document No. 2013-0496431E5; Property Inherited From Non-Resident, *Technical Interpretation, International and Trusts Division, January 23, 2003*, CRA Document No. 2002-0133410. Absent an election under s. 107(2.002), the cost of a property acquired by a non-resident estate, as a consequence of the death of a non-resident individual would be determined in accordance with s. 70(5)(*b*).

► 107(2.01) ◄

(2.01) Distribution of principal residence. Where property that would, if a personal trust had designated the property under paragraph (*c*.1) of the definition "principal residence" in section 54, be a principal residence (within the meaning of that definition) of the trust for a taxation year, is at any time (in this subsection referred to as "that time") distributed by the trust to a taxpayer in circumstances in which subsection (2) applies and the trust so elects in its return of income for the taxation year that includes that time,

(*a*) the trust shall be deemed to have disposed of the property immediately before the particular time that is immediately before that time for proceeds of disposition equal to the fair market value of the property at that time; and

(*b*) the trust shall be deemed to have reacquired the property at the particular time at a cost equal to that fair market value.

Editorial Note: The deemed disposition and reacquisition of the residence at fair market value under s. 107(2.01) occur immediately before the subsequent distribution under s. 107(2), meaning that the rollover under s. 107(2) takes place at the stepped-up cost (the fair market value) of the residence. The purpose of the s. 107(2.01) election is to allow the trust to claim its available principal residence exemption in respect of the gain accruing up to the time of the distribution of the residence to the beneficiary. If an election is made under s. 107(2.01), the look-back ownership rule in s. 40(7) will have no practical consequence because the beneficiary will be deemed to have owned the home only from the time of the deemed reacquisition by the trust. The election must be made in the trust's return of income for the taxation year that includes the time of the distribution.

Related Sections: S. 54, "principal residence"; s. 104(1) Reference to trust or estate; s. 248(1), "property", "trust".

Income Tax Folios: *Secondary*— S1-F3-C2 Principal Residence.

▶ 107(2.1) ◀

(2.1) Other distributions. Where at any time a property of a trust is distributed by the trust to a beneficiary under the trust, there would, if this Act were read without reference to paragraphs (*h*) and (*i*) of the definition "disposition" in subsection 248(1), be a resulting disposition of all or any part of the beneficiary's capital interest in the trust (which interest or part, as the case may be, is in this subsection referred to as the "former interest") and the rules in subsections (2) and (3.1) and sections 88.1 and 132.2 do not apply in respect of the distribution,

(*a*) the trust is deemed to have disposed of the property for proceeds equal to its fair market value at that time;

(*b*) the beneficiary is deemed to have acquired the property at a cost equal to the proceeds determined under paragraph (*a*);

(*c*) subject to paragraph (*e*), the beneficiary's proceeds of disposition of the portion of the former interest disposed of by the beneficiary on the distribution are deemed to be equal to the amount, if any, by which

(i) the proceeds determined under paragraph (*a*) (other than the portion, if any, of the proceeds that is a payment to which paragraph (*h*) or (*i*) of the definition "disposition" in subsection 248(1) applies)

exceed the total of

(ii) where the property is not a Canadian resource property or foreign resource property, the amount, if any, by which

(A) the fair market value of the property at that time

exceeds the total of

(B) the cost amount to the trust of the property immediately before that time, and

(C) the portion, if any, of the excess that would be determined under this subparagraph if this subparagraph were read without reference to this clause that represents a payment to which paragraph (*h*) or (*i*) of the definition "disposition" in subsection 248(1) applies, and

(iii) all amounts each of which is an eligible offset at that time of the taxpayer in respect of the former interest;

(*d*) notwithstanding paragraphs (*a*) to (*c*), where the trust is non-resident at that time, the property is not described in paragraph (2.001)(*b*) or (*c*) and, if this Act were read without reference to this paragraph, there would be no income, loss, taxable capital gain or allowable capital loss of a taxpayer in respect of the property because of the application of subsection 75(2) to the disposition at that time of the property,

(i) the trust is deemed to have disposed of the property for proceeds equal to the cost amount of the property,

(ii) the beneficiary is deemed to have acquired the property at a cost equal to the fair market value of the property, and

(iii) the beneficiary's proceeds of disposition of the portion of the former interest disposed of by the beneficiary on the distribution are deemed to be equal to the amount, if any, by which

(A) the fair market value of the property

exceeds the total of

(B) the portion, if any, of the amount of the distribution that is a payment to which paragraph (*h*) or (*i*) of the definition "disposition" in subsection 248(1) applies, and

(C) all amounts each of which is an eligible offset at that time of the taxpayer in respect of the former interest; and

(*e*) where the trust is a mutual fund trust, the distribution occurs in a taxation year of the trust before its 2003 taxation year, the trust has elected under subsection (2.11) in respect of the year and the trust so elects in respect of the distribution in prescribed form filed with the trust's return of income for the year,

(i) this subsection shall be read without reference to paragraph (*c*), and

(ii) the beneficiary's proceeds of disposition of the portion of the former interest disposed of by the beneficiary on the distribution are deemed to be equal to the amount determined under paragraph (*a*).

Editorial Note: S. 107(2.1) is an exception to the rollover rule in s. 107(2) that otherwise applies to distributions of property by a personal or prescribed trust to a beneficiary in satisfaction of the beneficiary's capital interest in the trust. S. 107(2.1) also applies to distributions of property by a trust other than a personal or prescribed trust. Under s. 107(2.1), a distribution of property from a trust to a beneficiary is deemed to take place for proceeds equal to the fair market value of the property, and the beneficiary is deemed to acquire the property at the same fair market value. However, in the case of a non-resident trust subject to s. 107(2.1)(*d*), the distribution is a rollover for the trust, although the beneficiary may realize a gain on the accompanying disposition of the capital interest in the trust.

History: S. 107(2.1), the portion before paragraph (*a*) was replaced by S.C. 2009, c. 2, s. 26(2), applicable after July 14, 2008. S. 107(2.1), the portion before paragraph (*a*) formerly read:

(2.1) *Other distributions.* Where at any time a property of a trust is distributed by the trust to a beneficiary under the trust, there would, if this Act were read without reference to paragraphs (*h*) and (*i*) of the definition "disposition" in subsection 248(1), be a resulting disposition of all or any part of the beneficiary's capital interest in the trust (which interest or part, as the case may be, is in this subsection referred to as the "former interest") and the rules in subsection (2) and section 132.2 do not apply in respect of the distribution,

Related Sections: S. 13(21), "proceeds of disposition"; s. 54, "capital property", "proceeds of disposition"; s. 66(15), "Canadian resource property", "foreign resource property"; s. 104(1) Reference to trust or estate; s. 104(4) Deemed disposition by trust; s. 107(5) Distribution to non-resident; s. 248(1), "Canadian resource property", "capital property", "foreign resource property", "inventory", "property", "trust".

Canadian Tax Foundation: Chan and Morin, *Distributions by Canadian Testamentary Trusts*, 2005 Canadian Tax Journal 4:1090–1110.

Tax Topics: No. 1911, Estate Distributions to Non-Residents; No. 1573, Non-rollover Distributions to Capital Beneficiaries of Trusts.

▶ 107(2.11) ◀

(2.11) Gains not distributed to beneficiaries. If a trust that is resident in Canada for a taxation year makes in the taxation year one or more distributions to which subsection (2.1) applies and the trust elects in prescribed form filed with the trust's return for the year or a preceding taxation year to have one of the following paragraphs apply, the income of the trust for the year (determined without reference to subsection 104(6)) shall, for the purposes of subsections 104(6) and (13), be computed without regard

(*a*) if the election is to have this paragraph apply, to all of those distributions (other than distributions of cash denominated in Canadian dollars) to non-resident persons (including a partnership other than a Canadian partnership); and

(*b*) if the election is to have this paragraph apply, to all of those distributions (other than distributions of cash denominated in Canadian dollars).

Editorial Note: The main purpose of s. 107(2.11) is to ensure that any accrued gains in respect of distributed trust property under s. 107(2.1) are included in the trust's income, and are not "payable" to the beneficiary to whom the property is distributed for the purposes of s. 104(13). Under the election in paragraph (*a*), the rule applies to all distributions made to non-resident beneficiaries in the year that are subject to subsection 107(2.1). Under the election in paragraph (*b*), the rule applies to all distributions made in the year to beneficiaries that are subject to subsection 107(2.1).

History: S. 107(2.11) was replaced by S.C. 2013, c. 34, s. 233(14), applicable to the 2002 and subsequent taxation years. It also applies to the 2000 and 2001 taxation years of a trust if the trust so elects, by notifying the Minister of National Revenue in writing on or before its filing-due date for its taxation year that includes June 26, 2013, in which case the portion of subsection 107(2.11), before paragraph (*a*), is to be read as follows for the 2000 and 2001 taxation years of the trust:

"(2.11) If a trust that is resident in Canada for a taxation year makes in the taxation year one or more distributions to which subsection (2.1) applies (or, in the case of property distributed after October 1, 1996 and before 2000, in circumstances in which subsection (5) applied) and the trust elects in prescribed form filed with the trust's return for the year or a preceding taxation year, the income of the trust for the year (determined without reference to subsection 104(6)) shall, for the purposes of subsections 104(6) and (13), be computed without regard"

S. 107(2.11) formerly read:

(2.11) *Gains not distributed to beneficiaries.* Where a trust makes one or more distributions of property in a taxation year in circumstances in which subsection (2.1) applies (or, in the case of property distributed after October 1, 1996 and before 2000, in circumstances in which subsection (5) applied)

(*a*) where the trust is resident in Canada at the time of each of those distributions and has so elected in prescribed form filed with the trust's return for the year or a preceding taxation year, the income of the trust for the year (determined without reference to subsection 104(6)) shall, for the purposes of subsections 104(6) and (13), be computed without regard to all of those distributions to non-resident persons (including a partnership other than a Canadian partnership); and

(*b*) where the trust is resident in Canada at the time of each of those distributions and has so elected in prescribed form filed with the trust's return for the year or a preceding taxation year, the income of the trust for the year (determined without reference to subsection 104(6)) shall, for the purposes of subsections 104(6) and (13), be computed without regard to all of those distributions.

Related Sections: S. 102(1), "Canadian partnership"; 104(23) Deceased beneficiary of graduated rate estate; s. 108(1), "trust"; s. 248(1), "non-resident", "property"; s. 249(1) Definition of "taxation year"; 250 Person deemed resident.

Tax Topics: No. 1573, Non-rollover Distributions to Capital Beneficiaries of Trusts.

Interpretation Bulletins: *Primary* — IT-465R Non-resident beneficiaries of trusts.

Tax Window Files: Capital Distribution to Non-Resident Beneficiary, *Technical Interpretation, International and Trusts Division, June 24, 2003*, CRA Document No. 2003-0000695. In the absence of an election under s. 107(2.11), the accrued gain realized by a trust on the distribution of property to non-resident beneficiary is considered payable to that beneficiary.

► 107(2.12) ◄

(2.12) Election — Subsection (2.11). An election made under subsection (2.11) by a mutual fund trust is deemed, for the trust's 2003 and subsequent taxation years, not to have been made if

(*a*) the election is made after December 20, 2000 and applies to any taxation year that ends before 2003; and

(*b*) the proceeds of disposition of a beneficiary's interest in the trust have been determined under paragraph (2.1)(*e*).

Related Sections: 54 Definitions; 104(23) Deceased beneficiary of graduated rate estate; s. 108(1), "trust"; s. 132(6) Meaning of "mutual fund trust"; s. 248(1), "mutual fund trust"; s. 249(1) Definition of "taxation year".

► 107(2.2) ◄

(2.2) Flow-through entity. Where at any time before 2005 a beneficiary under a trust described in paragraph (*h*), (*i*) or (*j*) of the definition "flow-through entity" in subsection 39.1(1) received a distribution of property from the trust in satisfaction of all or a portion of the beneficiary's interests in the trust and the beneficiary files with the Minister on or before the beneficiary's filing-due date for the taxation year that includes that time an election in respect of the property in prescribed form, there shall be included in the cost to the beneficiary of a particular property (other than money) received by the beneficiary as part of the distribution of property the least of

(*a*) the amount, if any, by which the beneficiary's exempt capital gains balance (as defined in subsection 39.1(1)) in respect of the trust for the beneficiary's taxation year that includes that time exceeds the total of all amounts each of which is

(i) an amount by which a capital gain is reduced under section 39.1 in the year because of the beneficiary's exempt capital gains balance in respect of the trust,

(ii) twice an amount by which a taxable capital gain is reduced under section 39.1 in the year because of the beneficiary's exempt capital gains balance in respect of the trust, or

(iii) an amount included in the cost to the beneficiary of another property received by the beneficiary at or before that time in the year because of this subsection,

(*b*) the amount by which the fair market value of the particular property at that time exceeds the adjusted cost base to the trust of the particular property immediately before that time, and

(*c*) the amount designated in respect of the particular property in the election.

Related Sections: S. 53(1)(*p*) Adjustments to cost base — Flow-through entity, after 2004; s. 53(1)(*r*) Adjustments to cost base — Flow-through entity, before 2005; s. 110.6(19) Election for property owned on February 22, 1994.

► 107(3) ◄

(3) Application of subsection (3.1). Subsection (3.1) applies to a trust's distribution of property to a taxpayer if

(*a*) the distribution is a SIFT trust wind-up event to which section 88.1 does not apply;

(*b*) the property is a share and the only shares distributed on any SIFT trust wind-up event of the trust are of a single class of the capital stock of a taxable Canadian corporation; and

(*c*) where the trust is a SIFT wind-up entity, the distribution occurs no more than 60 days after the earlier of

(i) the first SIFT trust wind-up event of the trust, and

(ii) the first distribution to the trust that is a SIFT trust wind-up event of another trust.

History: S. 107(3) was added by S.C. 2009, c. 2, s. 26(3), applicable after July 14, 2008, except that

(a) paragraph 107(3)(*b*) is to be read without reference to "of a single class" in its application to a trust's distribution of property before February 3, 2009; and

(b) subsection 107(3) is to be read without reference to its paragraph (*c*) in its application to a trust's distribution of property, if the distribution occurs no more than 60 days after the day on which this Act is assented to [R.A. March 12, 2009].

Related Sections: S. 122.1(1), "real estate investment trust", "SIFT trust"; s. 248(1), "SIFT wind-up entity", "SIFT trust wind-up event".

► 107(3.1) ◄

(3.1) SIFT trust wind-up event. If this subsection applies to a trust's distribution of property, the following rules apply:

(*a*) the trust is deemed to have disposed of the property for proceeds of disposition equal to the adjusted cost base to the trust of the property immediately before the distribution;

(*b*) the taxpayer is deemed to have disposed of the taxpayer's interest as a beneficiary under the trust for proceeds of disposition equal to the cost amount to the taxpayer of the interest immediately before the distribution;

(*c*) the taxpayer is deemed to have acquired the property at a cost equal to

(i) if, at all times at which the trust makes a distribution that is a SIFT trust wind-up event, the taxpayer is the only beneficiary under the trust and is a SIFT wind-up entity or a taxable Canadian corporation, the adjusted cost base to the trust of the property immediately before the distribution, and

(ii) in any other case, the cost amount to the taxpayer of the taxpayer's interest as a beneficiary under the trust immediately before the distribution;

(*d*) if the taxpayer's interest as a beneficiary under the trust was immediately before the disposition taxable Canadian property of the taxpayer, the property is deemed to be, at any time that is within 60 months after the distribution, taxable Canadian property of the taxpayer; and

(*e*) if a liability of the trust becomes as a consequence of the distribution a liability of the corporation described in paragraph (3)(*b*) in respect of the distribution, and the amount payable by the corporation on the maturity of the liability is the same as the amount that would have been payable by the trust on its maturity,

(i) the transfer of the liability by the trust to the corporation is deemed not to have occurred, and

(ii) the liability is deemed

(A) to have been incurred or issued by the corporation at the time at which, and under the agreement under which, it was incurred or issued by the trust, and

(B) not to have been incurred or issued by the trust.

Editorial Note: S. 107(3.1) effectively allows SIFT trusts (also known as income trusts) to make a "conversion" into corporations on a tax-free basis. The provision, which applies when the conditions of s. 107(3) are met, allows the tax-free distribution by the trust of its shares in a taxable Canadian corporation to its beneficiaries on the redemption of the beneficiaries' units or interests in the trust (often, the SIFT trust or income trust structure involves the trust owning shares in a taxable Canadian corporation that carries on the underlying business). See also s. 85.1(8), which provides an alternative "conversion" method, under which units of a trust can be exchanged on a tax-free basis for shares in a taxable Canadian corporation.

History: S. 107(3.1)(*d*) was replaced by S.C. 2010, c. 12, s. 10(3), applicable in determining after March 4, 2010 whether a property is taxable Canadian property of a taxpayer. S. 107(3.1)(*d*) formerly read:

(*d*) if the taxpayer's interest as a beneficiary under the trust was immediately before the disposition taxable Canadian property of the taxpayer, the property is deemed to be taxable Canadian property of the taxpayer; and

S. 107(3.1) was added by S.C. 2009, c. 2, s. 26(3), applicable after July 14, 2008.

Related Sections: S. 85.1(8) Rollover on SIFT unit for share exchange; s. 88.1(1) Application; s. 107(2.1) Other distributions; s. 248(1), "cost amount", "SIFT wind-up entity", "SIFT trust wind-up event".

Canadian Tax Foundation: Perry, *Income Trusts: Reorganizations and Planning for 2011*, 2008 Conference Report 8:1–33.

► 107(4) ◄

(4) Trusts in favour of spouse, common-law partner or self. Subsection (2.1) applies (and subsection (2) does not apply) at any time to property distributed to a beneficiary by a trust described in paragraph 104(4)(*a*) where

(*a*) the beneficiary is not

(i) in the case of a post-1971 spousal or common-law partner trust, the spouse or common-law partner referred to in paragraph 104(4)(*a*),

(ii) in the case of an alter ego trust, the taxpayer referred to in paragraph 104(4)(*a*), and

(iii) in the case of a joint spousal or common-law partner trust, the taxpayer, spouse or common-law partner referred to in paragraph 104(4)(*a*); and

(*b*) the distribution of the property occurs on or before the earlier of

(i) a reacquisition, in respect of any property of the trust, that occurs immediately after the day described by paragraph 104(4)(*a*), and

(ii) the cessation of the trust's existence.

Editorial Note: S. 107(4) denies the s. 107(2) rollover (in that s. 107(2.1) applies) where a distribution of property is made by a spousal or common-law partner trust to a beneficiary other than the spouse or common-law partner beneficiary while the latter is alive, by a joint spousal or common-law partner trust to a beneficiary other than the settlor or spouse or common-law partner beneficiary while one of the latter is alive, or by an alter ego trust to a beneficiary other than the settler/beneficiary while the latter is alive.

History: S. 107(4)(*b*) was replaced by S.C. 2013, c. 34, s. 233(17), applicable to distributions made after October 31, 2011, and formerly read:

(*b*) a taxpayer, spouse or common-law partner referred to in subparagraph (*a*)(i), (ii) or (iii), as the case may be, is alive on the day of the distribution.

Related Sections: S. 73(1) Inter vivos transfers by individuals; s. 73(1.01) Qualifying transfers; s. 70(6) Where transfer or distribution to spouse or spouse trust; s. 248(1), "alter ego trust", "joint spousal or common-law partner trust", "post-1971 spousal or common-law partner trust".

Canadian Tax Foundation: Kakkar, *Trust Rollouts: Subsection 107(4.1)*, 2013 Tax for the Owner-Manager 13(2):1.

Information Circulars: IC 82-6R10 Clearance certificate.

Interpretation Bulletins: *Secondary* — IT-286R2 Trusts — Amount payable; IT-381R3 Trusts — Deduction of amounts paid or payable to beneficiaries and flow-through of taxable capital gains to beneficiaries; IT-394R2 Preferred beneficiary election; IT-465R Non-resident beneficiaries of trusts.

► 107(4.1) ◄

(4.1) Where subsection 75(2) applicable to trust. Subsection (2.1) applies (and subsection (2) does not apply) in respect of a distribution of any property of a particular personal trust or prescribed trust (other than an excluded property of the particular trust) by the particular trust to a taxpayer who was a beneficiary under the particular trust where (*a*) the distribution was in satisfaction of all or any part of the taxpayer's capital interest in the particular trust;

(*b*) subsection 75(2) was applicable (determined without its reference to "while the person is resident in Canada" and as if subsection 75(3) as it read before March 21, 2013 were read without reference to its paragraph (*c.2*)), or subsection 94(8.2) was applicable (determined without reference to paragraph 94(8.1)(*a*)), at a particular time in respect of any property of

(i) the particular trust, or

(ii) a trust the property of which included a property that, through one or more dispositions to which subsection 107.4(3) applied, became a property of the particular trust, and the property was not, at any time after the particular time and before the distribution, the subject of a disposition for proceeds of disposition equal to the fair market value of the property at the time of the disposition;

(*c*) the taxpayer was neither

(i) the person (other than a trust described in subparagraph (*b*)(ii)) from whom the particular trust directly or indirectly received the property, or property for which the property was substituted, nor

(ii) an individual in respect of whom subsection 73(1) would be applicable on the transfer of capital property from the person described in subparagraph (i); and

(*d*) the person described in subparagraph (*c*)(i) was in existence at the time the property was distributed.

Editorial Note: Note that s. 107(4.1) continues to apply even if s. 75(2) no longer applies to the trust, and it applies to all the property of the trust and not just that to which s. 75(2) applies (or had applied). The provision does not apply to a distribution made to the person who contributed the property that was subject to s. 75(2) or to that person's spouse or common-law partner. It does not apply after the death of the contributor.

Where s. 107(4.1) applies to exclude s. 107(2), s. 107(2.1) applies instead, with the result that: (i) The trust is deemed to have disposed of the property distributed to the beneficiary for proceeds equal to its fair market value at the time of distribution. As a result, there may be a capital gain or loss at the time of distribution. (ii) The beneficiary is deemed to have acquired the trust property at a cost equal to its fair market value.

History: S. 107(4.1), the portion before paragraph (*a*) was replaced by S.C. 2017, c. 33, s. 36(1), applicable to taxation years that begin after 2016, and formerly read:

(4.1) *Where subsection 75(2) applicable to trust.* Subsection (2.1) applies (and subsection (2) does not apply) in respect of a distribution of any property of a particular personal trust or prescribed trust by the particular trust to a taxpayer who was a beneficiary under the particular trust where

S. 107(4.1)(*b*), the portion before subparagraph (i) was replaced by S.C. 2013, c. 40, applicable to taxation years that end after March 20, 2013, and formerly read:

(*b*) subsection 75(2) was applicable, or would have been applicable if it were read without reference to the phrase "while the person is resident in Canada" and subsection 75(3) were read without reference to paragraph (*c.2*), at a particular time in respect of any property of

S. 107(4.1)(*b*), the portion before subparagraph (i) was replaced by S.C. 2013, c. 34, s. 233(19), applicable to distributions made after October 31, 2011, and formerly read:

(*b*) subsection 75(2) was applicable, or would have been applicable if subsection 75(3) were read without reference to its paragraph (*c.2*), at a particular time in respect of any property of

S. 107(4.1)(*b*), the portion before subparagraph (i) was amended by S.C. 2013, c. 34, s. 11(1), applicable to distributions made after August 27, 2010, and formerly read:

(*b*) subsection 75(2) was applicable at a particular time in respect of any property of

[**Editorial Note**: The application to the amendment to s. 107(4.1) by S.C. 2001, c. 17, s. 80(17) was amended by S.C. 2013, c. 34, s. 374, to add two conditions where s. 107(4.1) is to be read without reference to its subparagraph (*b*)(ii). This 2001 amendment is not reproduced in print but is available in all CCH Canadian electronic versions of the Income Tax Act.]

Related Regulations: 4800.1.

Related Sections: 108(1) excluded property.

Canadian Tax Foundation: Bernstein and Santia, *Principal-Residence Exemption: Trusts and Non-Residents*, 2017 Canadian Tax Highlights 25(1):6–7; Thompson, *Revisiting the Attribution Rules*, 2013 British Columbia Tax Conference 12:1–24; Roth, *Including or Adding the Freezor as a Discretionary Trust Beneficiary*, 2013 Ontario Tax Conference 14C:1–25; Kakkar, *Trust Rollouts: Subsection 107(4.1)*, 2013 Tax for the Owner-Manager 13(2):1; Hoffstein and Lee, *Revisiting the Attribution Rules*, 2012 Ontario Tax Conference 9:1–40; Rajan and Brown, *Personal Trusts 2000: Taxation and Planning in the New Millennium*, 2000 Conference Report 28:1–40.

STEP Canada: Elie Roth, "Adding and Deleting a Beneficiary to a Trust," PowerPoint presentation to the 15th National Conference of STEP Canada, Toronto, June 10-11, 2013.

Tax Window Files: Subsection 107(4.1), *May 12, 2016*, CRA Document No. 2014-0552341E5.

► 107(4.2) ◄

(4.2) Distribution of property received on qualifying disposition. Subsection (2.1) applies (and subsection (2) does not apply) at any time to property distributed after December 20, 2002 to a beneficiary by a personal trust or a trust prescribed for the purpose of subsection (2), if

(*a*) at a particular time before December 21, 2002 there was a qualifying disposition (within the meaning assigned by subsection 107.4(1)) of the property, or of other property for which the property is substituted, by a particular partnership or a particular corporation, as the case may be, to a trust; and

(*b*) the beneficiary is neither the particular partnership nor the particular corporation.

History: S. 107(4.2) was added by S.C. 2013, c. 34, s. 233(22), applicable to distributions made after December 20, 2002.

► 107(5) ◄

(5) Distribution to non-resident. Subsection (2.1) applies (and subsection (2) does not apply) in respect of a distribution of a property (other than a share of the capital stock of a non-resident-owned investment corporation or property described in any of subparagraphs 128.1(4)(*b*)(i) to (iii)) by a trust to a non-resident taxpayer (including a partnership other than a Canadian partnership) in satisfaction of all or part of the taxpayer's capital interest in the trust.

Editorial Note: S. 107(5) provides that where a trust resident in Canada makes a distribution of property (other than the property described in parentheses in the provision) to a non-resident taxpayer in satisfaction of all or part of the taxpayer's capital interest in the trust, the "rollover" under s. 107(2) is not available and the Canadian tax consequences to both the trust and the non-resident taxpayer will be determined by s. 107(2.1).

History: S. 107(5) was replaced by S.C. 2013, c. 34, s. 233(22), applicable to distributions made after February 27, 2004, and formerly read:

(5) *Distribution to non-resident.* Subsection (2.1) applies (and subsection (2) does not apply) in respect of a distribution of a property (other than a share of the capital stock of a non-resident-owned investment corporation or property described in any of subparagraphs 128.1(4)(*b*)(i) to (iii)) by a trust resident in Canada to a non-resident taxpayer (including a partnership other than a Canadian partnership) in satisfaction of all or part of the taxpayer's capital interest in the trust.

Related Sections: S. 66(15), "Canadian resource property"; s. 104(1) Reference to trust or estate; s. 108(1), "excluded property"; s. 212(10) Trust beneficiaries residing outside of Canada; s. 248(1), "Canadian resource property", "property", "taxable Canadian property", "trust".

Canadian Tax Foundation: Rajan and Brown, *Personal Trusts 2000: Taxation and Planning in the New Millennium*, 2000 Conference Report 28:1–40; Webb, *The New Proposals For Trust Distributions And Related Issues*, 1999 Conference Report 34:1–24.

Tax Profile: October 2007 — Will Canadian Unlimited Liability Companies Survive?; July 2005 — Alberta Introduces Alberta Unlimited Liability Corporations.

Tax Topics: No. 1911, Estate Distributions to Non-Residents.

▶ 107(5.1) ◀

(5.1) Instalment interest. If, solely because of the application of subsection (5), paragraphs (2)(*a*) to (*c*) do not apply to a distribution in a taxation year of taxable Canadian property by a trust, in applying sections 155 and 156 and subsections 156.1(1) to (3) and 161(2), (4) and (4.01) and any regulations made for the purposes of those provisions, the trust's tax payable under this Part for the year is deemed to be the lesser of

(*a*) the trust's tax payable under this Part for the year, determined before taking into consideration the specified future tax consequences for the year, and

(*b*) the amount that would be determined under paragraph (*a*) if subsection (5) did not apply to each distribution in the year of taxable Canadian property to which the rules in subsection (2) do not apply solely because of the application of subsection (5).

History: S. 107(5.1), the portion before paragraph (*b*) was replaced by S.C. 2013, c. 34, s. 233(23), applicable to distributions made after October 31, 2011, and formerly read:

(5.1) *Instalment interest.* Where, solely because of the application of subsection (5), paragraphs (2)(*a*) to (*c*) do not apply to a distribution in a taxation year of taxable Canadian property by a trust, in applying sections 155, 156 and 156.1 and subsections 161(2), (4) and (4.01) and any regulations made for the purpose of those provisions, the trust's total taxes payable under this Part and Part I.1 for the year are deemed to be the lesser of

(*a*) the trust's total taxes payable under this Part and Part I.1 for the year, determined before taking into consideration the specified future tax consequences for the year, and

Related Sections: 104(23) Deceased beneficiary of graduated rate estate; s. 108(1), "trust"; 220(4.6) Security for tax on distributions of taxable Canadian property to non-resident beneficiaries; 220(4.61) Limit; 220(4.62) Inadequate security; 220(4.63) Extension of time; s. 248(1), "taxable Canadian property", "specified future tax consequences"; s. 249(1) Definition of "taxation year".

▶ 107(6) ◀

(6) Loss reduction. Notwithstanding any other provision of this Act, where a person or partnership (in this subsection referred to as the "vendor") has disposed of property and would, but for this subsection, have had a loss from the disposition, the vendor's loss otherwise determined in respect of the disposition shall be reduced by such portion of that loss as may reasonably be considered to have accrued during a period in which

(*a*) the property or property for which it was substituted was held by a trust; and

(*b*) either

(i) the trust was non-resident and the property (or property for which it was substituted) was not taxable Canadian property of the trust, or

(ii) neither the vendor — nor a person that would, if section 251.1 were read without reference to the definition "controlled" in subsection 251.1(3), be affiliated with the vendor — had a capital interest in the trust.

History: S. 107(6)(*a*) and (*b*) were replaced by S.C. 2013, c. 34, s. 233(25), applicable to dispositions made after October 31, 2011, and formerly read:

(*a*) the property or property for which it was substituted was owned by a trust; and

(*b*) neither the vendor nor a person that would, if section 251.1 were read without reference to the definition "controlled" in subsection 251.1(3), be affiliated with the vendor had a capital interest in the trust.

Related Sections: S. 13(21.2) Loss on certain transfers; s. 14(12) Loss on certain transfers; s. 14(13) Deemed identical property; s. 40(3.3) When subsection (3.4) applies; s. 40(3.4) Loss on certain properties.

SECTION 107.1: Distribution by certain employment-related trusts

If at any time any property of an employee life and health trust, an employee trust, a trust governed by an employee benefit plan or a trust described in paragraph (*a.1*) of the definition "trust" in subsection 108(1) has been distributed by the trust to a taxpayer who was a beneficiary under the trust in satisfaction of all or any part of the taxpayer's interest in the trust, the following rules apply:

(*a*) in the case of an employee life and health trust, an employee trust or a trust described in paragraph (*a.1*) of the definition "trust" in subsection 108(1),

(i) the trust shall be deemed to have disposed of the property immediately before that time for proceeds of disposition equal to its fair market value at that time, and

(ii) the taxpayer shall be deemed to have acquired the property at a cost equal to its fair market value at that time;

(*b*) in the case of a trust governed by an employee benefit plan,

(i) the trust shall be deemed to have disposed of the property for proceeds of disposition equal to its cost amount to the trust immediately before that time, and

(ii) the taxpayer shall be deemed to have acquired the property at a cost equal to the greater of

(A) its fair market value at that time, and

(B) the adjusted cost base to the taxpayer of the taxpayer's interest or part thereof, as the case may be, immediately before that time;

(*c*) the taxpayer shall be deemed to have disposed of the taxpayer's interest or part thereof, as the case may be, for proceeds of disposition equal to the adjusted cost base to the taxpayer of that interest or part thereof immediately before that time; and

(*d*) where the property was depreciable property of a prescribed class of the trust and the amount that was the capital cost to the trust of that property exceeds the cost at which the taxpayer is deemed by this section to have acquired the property, for the purposes of sections 13 and 20 and any regulations made under paragraph 20(1)(*a*),

(i) the capital cost to the taxpayer of the property shall be deemed to be the amount that was the capital cost of the property to the trust, and

(ii) the excess shall be deemed to have been allowed to the taxpayer in respect of the property under regulations made under paragraph 20(1)(*a*) in computing income for taxation years before the acquisition by the taxpayer of the property.

History: S. 107.1, the portion before subparagraph (*a*)(i) was replaced by S.C. 2010, c. 25, s. 17(1), applicable after 2009. S. 107.1, the portion before subparagraph (*a*)(i) formerly read:

S. 107.1 *Distribution by employee trust, employee benefit plan or similar trust.* Where at any time any property of an employee trust, a trust governed by an employee benefit plan or a trust described in paragraph (*a*.1) of the definition "trust" in subsection 108(1) has been distributed by the trust to a taxpayer who was a beneficiary under the trust in satisfaction of all or any part of the taxpayer's interest in the trust, the following rules apply:

(*a*) in the case of an employee trust or a trust described in paragraph (*a*.1) of the definition "trust" in subsection 108(1),

Related Sections: S. 6(1)(*h*) Employee trust; s. 12(1)(*n*) Employees profit sharing plan; s. 18(1)(*o*) Employee benefit plan contributions; s. 32.1 Employee benefit plan contributions; s. 104(6) Deduction in computing income of trust; s. 104(13) Income of beneficiary; s. 248(1), "employee benefit plan", "employee trust".

Interpretation Bulletins: *Secondary* — IT-502 Employee benefit plans and employee trusts.

SECTION 107.2: Distribution by a retirement compensation arrangement

Where, at any time, any property of a trust governed by a retirement compensation arrangement has been distributed by the trust to a taxpayer who was a beneficiary under the trust in satisfaction of all or any part of the taxpayer's interest in the trust, for the purposes of this Part and Part XI.3, the following rules apply:

(*a*) the trust shall be deemed to have disposed of the property for proceeds of disposition equal to its fair market value at that time;

(*b*) the trust shall be deemed to have paid to the taxpayer as a distribution an amount equal to that fair market value;

(*c*) the taxpayer shall be deemed to have acquired the property at a cost equal to that fair market value;

(*d*) the taxpayer shall be deemed to have disposed of the taxpayer's interest or part thereof, as the case may be, for proceeds of disposition equal to the adjusted cost base to the taxpayer of that interest or part thereof immediately before that time; and

(*e*) where the property was depreciable property of a prescribed class of the trust and the amount that was the capital cost to the trust of that property exceeds the cost at which the taxpayer is deemed by this section to have acquired the property, for the purposes of sections 13 and 20 and any regulations made under paragraph 20(1)(*a*),

(i) the capital cost to the taxpayer of the property shall be deemed to be the amount that was the capital cost of the property to the trust, and

(ii) the excess shall be deemed to have been allowed to the taxpayer in respect of the property under regulations made under paragraph 20(1)(*a*) in computing the taxpayer's income for taxation years before the acquisition by the taxpayer of the property.

Related Sections: S. 56(1)(*x*) Retirement compensation arrangement — employee recipient; s. 56(2) Indirect payments; s. 248(1), "retirement compensation arrangement".

Guides: T4041 Retirement Compensation Arrangements Guide.

SECTION 107.3: Treatment of beneficiaries under qualifying environmental trusts

► 107.3(1) ◄

(1) Treatment of beneficiaries under qualifying environmental trusts. Where a taxpayer is a beneficiary under a qualifying environmental trust in a taxation year of the trust (in this subsection referred to as the "trust's year") that ends in a particular taxation year of the taxpayer,

(*a*) subject to paragraph (*b*), the taxpayer's income, non-capital loss and net capital loss for the particular year shall be computed as if the amount of the income or loss of the trust for the trust's year from any source or from sources in a particular place were the income or loss of the taxpayer from that source or from sources in that particular place for the particular year, to the extent of the portion thereof that can reasonably be considered to be the taxpayer's share of such income or loss; and

(*b*) if the taxpayer is non-resident at any time in the particular year and an income or loss described in paragraph (*a*) or an amount to which paragraph 12(1)(*z*.1) or (*z*.2) applies would not otherwise be included in computing the taxpayer's taxable income or taxable income earned in Canada, as the case may be, notwithstanding any other provision of this Act, the income, the loss or the amount shall be attributed to the carrying on of business in Canada by the taxpayer through a fixed place of business located in the province in which the site to which the trust relates is situated.

Editorial Note: The beneficiary will generally be eligible for a credit under s. 127.41 in respect of the tax paid by the trust under s. 211.6.

Related Sections: S. 12(1)(*z*.1) Qualifying environmental trusts; s. 20(1)(*ss*) Qualifying environmental trusts; s. 20(1)(*tt*) Acquisition of interests in qualifying environmental trusts; s. 75(3) Exceptions; s. 127.41 Part XII.4 tax credit; s. 211.6(1) Tax on qualifying environmental trusts; s. 149(1)(*z*) Qualifying environmental trust; s. 248(1), "qualifying environmental trust"; s. 250(7) Residence of a qualifying environmental trust.

Canadian Tax Foundation: Frankovic, *The Case for "Reverse Depreciation" of Reclamation Costs*, 2004 Canadian Tax Journal 1:1–58.

► 107.3(2) ◄

(2) Transfers to beneficiaries. Where property of a qualifying environmental trust is transferred at any time to a beneficiary under the trust in satisfaction of all or any part of the beneficiary's interest as a beneficiary under the trust,

(*a*) the trust shall be deemed to have disposed of the property at that time for proceeds of disposition equal to its fair market value at that time; and

(*b*) the beneficiary shall be deemed to have acquired the property at that time at a cost equal to its fair market value at that time.

► 107.3(3) ◄

(3) Ceasing to be qualifying environmental trust. If at any time a trust ceases to be a qualifying environmental trust,

(*a*) for the purposes of subsections 111(5.5) and 149(10), the trust is deemed to cease at that time to be exempt from tax under this Part on its taxable income;

(*b*) each beneficiary under the trust immediately before that time is deemed to receive at that time from the trust an amount equal to the percentage of the fair market value of the properties of the trust immediately after that time that can reasonably be considered to be the beneficiary's interest in the trust; and

(*c*) each beneficiary under the trust is deemed to acquire immediately after that time an interest in the trust at a cost equal to the amount deemed by paragraph (*b*) to be received by the beneficiary from the trust.

History: S. 107.3(3) was replaced by S.C. 2013, c. 40, s. 45(1), deemed to have come into force on March 21, 2013, and formerly read:

(3) *Ceasing to be a qualifying environmental trust.* Where a trust ceases at any time to be a qualifying environmental trust,

(*a*) the taxation year of the trust that would otherwise have included that time is deemed to have ended immediately before that time and a new taxation year of the trust is deemed to have begun at that time;

(*b*) the trust shall be deemed to have disposed immediately before that time of each property held by the trust immediately after that time for proceeds of disposition equal to its fair market value at that time and to have reacquired immediately after that time each such property for an amount equal to that fair market value;

(*c*) each beneficiary under the trust immediately before that time shall be deemed to have received at that time from the trust an amount equal to the percentage of the fair market value of the properties of the trust immediately after that time that can reasonably be considered to be the beneficiary's interest in the trust; and

(*d*) each beneficiary under the trust shall be deemed to have acquired immediately after that time an interest in the trust at a cost equal to the amount deemed by paragraph (*c*) to have been received by the beneficiary from the trust.

► 107.3(4) ◄

(4) Application. Subsection 104(13) and sections 105 to 107 do not apply to a trust with respect to a taxation year during which it is a qualifying environmental trust.

SECTION 107.4: Qualifying disposition

► 107.4(1) ◄

(1) Qualifying disposition. In this section, a "qualifying disposition" of a property means a disposition of the property before December 21, 2002 by a person or partnership, and a disposition of property after December 20, 2002 by an individual, (which person, partnership or individual is referred to in this subsection as the "contributor") as a result of a transfer of the property to a particular trust where

(*a*) the disposition does not result in a change in the beneficial ownership of the property;

(*b*) the proceeds of disposition would, if this Act were read without reference to this section and sections 69 and 73, not be determined under any provision of this Act;

(*c*) the particular trust is resident in Canada at the time of the transfer;

(*d*) (Repealed by S.C. 2013, c. 34, s. 235(3).)

(*e*) unless the contributor is a trust, there is immediately after the disposition no absolute or contingent right of a person or partnership (other than the contributor or, where the property was co-owned, each of the joint contributors) as a beneficiary (determined with reference to subsection 104(1.1)) under the particular trust;

(*f*) the contributor is not an individual (other than a trust described in any of paragraphs (*a*) to (*e*.1) of the definition "trust" in subsection 108(1)), if the particular trust is described in any of paragraphs (*a*) to (*e*.1) of the definition "trust" in subsection 108(1);

(*g*) the disposition is not part of a series of transactions or events

(i) that begins after December 17, 1999 and that includes the subsequent acquisition, for consideration given to a personal trust, of a capital interest or an income interest in the trust,

(ii) that begins after December 17, 1999 and that includes the disposition of all or part of a capital interest or an income interest in a personal trust, other than a disposition solely as a consequence of a distribution from a trust to a person or partnership in satisfaction of all or part of that interest, or

(iii) that begins after June 5, 2000 and that includes the transfer to the particular trust of particular property as consideration for the acquisition of a capital interest in the particular trust, if the particular property can reasonably be considered to have been received by the particular trust in order to fund a distribution (other than a distribution that is proceeds of disposition of a capital interest in the particular trust);

(*h*) the disposition is not, and is not part of, a transaction

(i) that occurs after December 17, 1999, and

(ii) that includes the giving to the contributor, for the disposition, of any consideration (other than consideration that is an interest of the contributor as a beneficiary under the particular trust or that is the assumption by the particular trust of debt for which the property can, at the time of the disposition, reasonably be considered to be security);

(*i*) subsection 73(1) does not apply to the disposition and would not apply to the disposition if

(i) no election had been made under that subsection, and

(ii) section 73 were read without reference to subsection 73(1.02); and

(*j*) if the contributor is an amateur athlete trust, a cemetery care trust, an employee life and health trust, an employee trust, a trust deemed by subsection 143(1) to exist in respect of a congregation that is a constituent part of a religious organization, a related segregated fund trust (within the meaning assigned by paragraph 138.1(1)(*a*)), a trust described in paragraph 149(1)(*o*.4) or a trust governed by an eligible funeral arrangement, an employees profit sharing plan, a registered disability savings plan, a registered education savings plan, a registered supplementary unemployment benefit plan or a TFSA, the particular trust is the same type of trust.

History: S. 107.4(1)(*j*) was replaced by S.C. 2014, c. 39, s. 27(1), applicable to the 2016 and subsequent taxation years, and formerly read:

(*j*) if the contributor is an amateur athlete trust, a cemetery care trust, an employee life and health trust, an employee trust, an *inter vivos* trust deemed by subsection 143(1) to exist in respect of a congregation that is a constituent part of a religious organization, a related segregated fund trust (within the meaning assigned by paragraph 138.1(1)(*a*)), a trust described in paragraph 149(1)(*o*.4) or a trust governed by an eligible funeral arrangement, an employees profit sharing plan, a registered disability savings plan, a registered education savings plan, a registered supplementary unemployment benefit plan or a TFSA, the particular trust is the same type of trust.

S. 107.4(1), the portion before paragraph (*a*) was replaced by S.C. 2013, c. 34, s. 235(1), deemed to have come into force on December 20, 2002, and formerly read:

(1) *Qualifying disposition.* For the purpose of this section, a "qualifying disposition" of a property means a disposition of the property by a person or partnership (in this subsection referred to as the "contributor") as a result of a transfer of the property to a particular trust where

S. 107.4(1)(*c*) was replaced by S.C. 2013, c. 34, s. 235(2), applicable to dispositions that occur after February 27, 2004, and formerly read:

(*c*) if the particular trust is non-resident, the disposition is not

(i) by a person resident in Canada or by a partnership (other than a partnership each member of which is non-resident), or

(ii) a transfer of taxable Canadian property from a non-resident person who was resident in Canada in any of the ten calendar years preceding the transfer;

S. 107.4(1)(*d*) was repealed by S.C. 2013, c. 34, s. 235(3), deemed to have come into force on December 20, 2002, and formerly read:

(*d*) the contributor is not a partnership, if the disposition is part of a series of transactions or events that begin after December 17, 1999 that includes the cessation of the partnership's existence and a subsequent distribution from a personal trust to a former member of the partnership in circumstances to which subsection 107(2) applies;

S. 107.4(1)(*j*) was replaced by S.C. 2010, c. 25, s. 18(1), applicable after 2009. S. 107.4(1)(*j*) formerly read:

(*j*) if the contributor is an amateur athlete trust, a cemetery care trust, an employee trust, an *inter vivos* trust deemed by subsection 143(1) to exist in respect of a congregation that is a constituent part of a religious organization, a related segregated fund trust (as defined by section 138.1), a trust described in paragraph 149(1)(*o.4*) or a trust governed by an eligible funeral arrangement, an employees profit sharing plan, a registered disability savings plan, a registered education savings plan, a registered supplementary unemployment benefit plan or a TFSA, the particular trust is the same type of trust; and

Related Sections: S. 54, "proceeds of disposition"; s. 69(1)(*b*) Inadequate considerations; s. 104(1.1), "beneficiary"; s. 106(2) Disposition by taxpayer of income interest; s. 106(3) Proceeds of disposition of income interest; s. 107(1) Disposition by taxpayer of capital interest; s. 108(1), "beneficiary", "capital interest", "income interest", "trust"; s. 143.1(1), "amateur athlete trust"; s. 144(1), "employees profit sharing plan"; s. 145(1), "registered supplementary unemployment benefit plan"; s. 146(1), "annuitant", "registered education savings plan"; s. 146.1(1), "registered education savings plan"; s. 146.3(1), "annuitant", "registered retirement income fund"; s. 146.4(1), "registered disability savings plan"; s. 148.1(1), "cemetery care trust", "eligible funeral arrangement"; s. 248(1), "disposition", "employee trust", "individual", "non-resident", "property", "taxable Canadian property"; s. 248(25.2) Trusts to ensure obligations fulfilled; s. 248(25.4) Where acquisition by another of right to enforce.

Canadian Tax Foundation: Brown, *Alter Ego Joint Conjugal and Self-Benefit Trusts Revisited: Some Troubling Tax Issues and a Search for Better Alternatives*, 2005 Canadian Tax Journal 1:224–244.

Tax Profile: February 2002 — Transferring Property to a Trust After the Enactment of Bill C-22.

Tax Window Files: Transfer of Debt as Qualifying Disposition, *18XXXX*, CRA Document No. 2018-0752811R3; qualifying disposition -mutual fund trust, *13XXXX*, CRA Document No. 2013-0492731R3.

Cases: Very broad interpretation given to meaning of "beneficial ownership"; among other things, the fact that a "self-benefit trust" could be amended to allow for a distribution to persons other than the settlor did not mean there had been a change in beneficial ownership. *Williams v. the Queen*, 2005 DTC 1228 (T.C.C.).

▶ 107.4(2) ◀

(2) Application of paragraph (1)(a). For the purpose of paragraph (1)(*a*),

(*a*) except where paragraph (*b*) applies, where a trust (in this paragraph and subsection (2.1) referred to as the "transferor trust"), in a period that does not exceed one day, disposes of one or more properties in the period to one or more other trusts, there is deemed to be no resulting change in the beneficial ownership of those properties if

(i) the transferor trust receives no consideration for the disposition, and

(ii) as a consequence of the disposition, the value of each beneficiary's beneficial ownership at the beginning of the period under the transferor trust in each particular property of the transferor trust (or group of two or more properties of the transferor trust that are identical to each other) is the same as the value of the beneficiary's beneficial ownership at the end of the period under the transferor trust and the other trust or trusts in each particular property (or in property that was immediately before the disposition included in the group of identical properties referred to above); and

(*b*) where a trust (in this paragraph referred to as the "transferor") governed by a registered retirement savings plan or by a registered retirement income fund transfers a property to a trust (in this paragraph referred to as the "transferee") governed by a registered retirement savings plan or by a registered retirement income fund, the transfer is deemed not to result in a change in the beneficial ownership of the property if the annuitant of the plan or fund that governs the transferor is also the annuitant of the plan or fund that governs the transferee.

Related Sections: S. 104(1.1), "beneficiary"; s. 108(1), "beneficiary", "trust"; s. 146(1), "annuitant", "registered retirement savings plan"; s. 146.3(1), "annuitant", "registered retirement income fund"; s. 248(1), "property", "disposition".

Tax Profile: February 2002 — Transferring Property to a Trust After the Enactment of Bill C-22.

Tax Window Files: Merging of 3 identical family trusts, *November 1, 2006*, CRA Document No. 2006-019143R3. On the merging of three trusts into one single trust where the terms of each trust were virtually identical, s. 107.4(2)(*a*) applied ensure that there was no change in beneficial ownership and the transfer was a qualifying disposition. See also, "Split assets of 3 trusts into 5 separate trusts", November 1, 2006, Document No. 2005-0143361R3 and "Divide Family Trust Into Separate Trusts", June 4, 2003, Document no. 2002-0180473.

▶ 107.4(2.1) ◀

(2.1) Fractional interests. For the purpose of applying paragraph (2)(*a*) in respect of a transfer by a transferor trust of property that includes a share and money, the other trust or trusts referred to in that paragraph may receive, in lieu of a transfer of a fractional interest in a share that would otherwise be required, a disproportionate amount of money or interest in the share (the value of which does not exceed the lesser of $200 and the fair market value of the fractional interest).

Related Sections: S. 108(1), "trust"; s. 248(1), "amount", "property", "share".

▶ 107.4(3) ◀

(3) Tax consequences of qualifying dispositions. Where at a particular time there is a qualifying disposition of a property by a person or partnership (in this subsection referred to as the "transferor") to a trust (in this subsection referred to as the "transferee trust"),

(*a*) the transferor's proceeds of disposition of the property are deemed to be

(i) where the transferor so elects in writing and files the election with the Minister on or before the transferor's filing-due date for its taxation year that includes the particular time, or at any later time that is acceptable to the Minister, the amount specified in the election that is not less than the cost amount to the transferor of the property immediately before the particular time and not more than the fair market value of the property at the particular time, and

(ii) in any other case, the cost amount to the transferor of the property immediately before the particular time;

(*b*) the transferee trust's cost of the property is deemed to be the amount, if any, by which

(i) the proceeds determined under paragraph (*a*) in respect of the qualifying disposition

exceed

(ii) the amount by which the transferor's loss otherwise determined from the qualifying disposition would be reduced because of subsection 100(4), paragraph 107(1)(*c*) or (*d*) or any of subsections 112(3) to (4.2), if the proceeds determined under paragraph (*a*) were equal to the fair market value of the property at the particular time;

(*c*) (Repealed.)

(*d*) if the property was depreciable property of a prescribed class of the transferor and its capital cost to the transferor exceeds the cost at which the transferee trust is deemed by this subsection to have acquired the property, for the purposes of sections 13 and 20 and any regulations made for the purpose of paragraph 20(1)(*a*),

(i) the capital cost of the property to the transferee trust is deemed to be the amount that was the capital cost of the property to the transferor, and

(ii) the excess is deemed to have been allowed to the transferee trust in respect of the property under regulations made for the purpose of paragraph 20(1)(*a*) in computing income for taxation years that ended before the particular time;

(*e*) (Repealed by S.C. 2016, c. 12, s. 37(1).)

(*f*) if, as a result of a transaction or event, the property was deemed to be taxable Canadian property of the transferor by this paragraph or any of paragraphs 44.1(2)(*c*), 51(1)(*f*), 85(1)(*i*) and 85.1(1)(*a*), subsection 85.1(5), paragraph 85.1(8)(*b*), subsections 87(4) and (5) and paragraphs 97(2)(*c*) and 107(3.1)(*d*), the property is also deemed to be, at any time that is within 60 months after the transaction or event, taxable Canadian property of the transferee trust;

(*g*) where the transferor is a related segregated fund trust (in this paragraph having the meaning assigned by section 138.1),

(i) paragraph 138.1(1)(*i*) does not apply in respect of a disposition of an interest in the transferor that occurs in connection with the qualifying disposition, and

(ii) in computing the amount determined under paragraph 138.1(1)(*i*) in respect of a subsequent disposition of an interest in the transferee trust where the interest is deemed to exist in connection with a particular life insurance policy, the acquisition fee (as defined by subsection 138.1(6)) in respect of the particular policy shall be determined as if each amount determined under any of paragraphs 138.1(6)(*a*) to (*d*) in respect of the policyholder's interest in the transferor had been determined in respect of the policyholder's interest in the transferee trust;

(*h*) if the transferor is a trust to which property had been transferred by an individual (other than a trust),

(i) where subsection 73(1) applied in respect of the property so transferred and it is reasonable to consider that the property was so transferred in anticipation of the individual ceasing to be resident in Canada, for the purposes of paragraph 104(4)(*a*.3) and the application of this paragraph to a disposition by the transferee trust after the particular time, the transferee trust is deemed after the particular time to be a trust to which the individual had transferred property in anticipation of the individual ceasing to reside in Canada and in circumstances to which subsection 73(1) applied, and

(ii) for the purposes of paragraph (*j*) of the definition "excluded right or interest" in subsection 128.1(10) and the application of this paragraph to a disposition by the transferee trust after the particular time, where the property so transferred was transferred in circumstances to which this subsection would apply if subsection (1) were read without reference to paragraphs (1)(*h*) and (*i*), the transferee trust is deemed after the particular time to be a trust an interest in which was acquired by the individual as a consequence of a qualifying disposition;

(*i*) if the transferor is a trust (other than a personal trust or a trust prescribed for the purposes of subsection 107(2)), the transferee trust is deemed to be neither a personal trust nor a trust prescribed for the purposes of subsection 107(2);

(*j*) if the transferor is a trust and a taxpayer disposes of all or part of a capital interest in the transferor because of the qualifying disposition and, as a consequence, acquires a capital interest or part of it in the transferee trust

(i) the taxpayer is deemed to dispose of the capital interest or part of it in the transferor for proceeds equal to the cost amount to the taxpayer of that interest or part of it immediately before the particular time, and

(ii) the taxpayer is deemed to acquire the capital interest or part of it in the transferee trust at a cost equal to the amount, if any, by which

(A) that cost amount

exceeds

(B) the amount by which the taxpayer's loss otherwise determined from the disposition referred to in subparagraph (i) would be reduced because of paragraph 107(1)(*c*) or (*d*) if the proceeds under that subparagraph were equal to the fair market value of the capital interest or part of it in the transferor immediately before the particular time;

(*k*) where the transferor is a trust, a taxpayer's beneficial ownership in the property ceases to be derived from the taxpayer's capital interest in the transferor because of the qualifying disposition and no part of the taxpayer's capital interest in the transferor was disposed of because of the qualifying disposition, there shall, immediately after the particular time, be added to the cost otherwise determined of the taxpayer's capital interest in the transferee trust, the amount determined by the formula

$$A \times [(B - C)/B] - D$$

where

A is the cost amount to the taxpayer of the taxpayer's capital interest in the transferor immediately before the particular time,

B is the fair market value immediately before the particular time of the taxpayer's capital interest in the transferor,

C is the fair market value at the particular time of the taxpayer's capital interest in the transferor (determined as if the only property disposed of at the particular time were the particular property), and

D is the lesser of

(i) the amount, if any, by which the cost amount to the taxpayer of the taxpayer's capital interest in the transferor immediately before the particular time exceeds the fair market value of the taxpayer's capital interest in the transferor immediately before the particular time, and

(ii) the maximum amount by which the taxpayer's loss from a disposition of a capital interest otherwise determined could have been reduced because of paragraph 107(1)(*c*) or (*d*) if the taxpayer's capital interest in the transferor had been disposed of immediately before the particular time;

(*l*) where paragraph (*k*) applies to the qualifying disposition in respect of a taxpayer, the amount that would be determined under that paragraph in respect of the qualifying disposition if the amount determined for D in that paragraph were nil shall, immediately after the particular time, be deducted in computing the cost otherwise determined of the taxpayer's capital interest in the transferor;

(*m*) where paragraphs (*j*) and (*k*) do not apply in respect of the qualifying disposition, the transferor is deemed to acquire the capital interest or part of it in the transferee trust that is acquired as a consequence of the qualifying disposition

(i) where the transferee trust is a personal trust, at a cost equal to nil, and

(ii) in any other case, at a cost equal to the excess determined under paragraph (*b*) in respect of the qualifying disposition; and

(*n*) if the transferor is a trust and a taxpayer disposes of all or part of an income interest in the transferor because of the qualifying disposition and, as a consequence, acquires an income interest or a part of an income interest in the transferee trust, for the purpose of subsection 106(2), the taxpayer is deemed not to dispose of any part of the income interest in the transferor at the particular time.

History: S. 107.4(3)(*e*) was repealed by S.C. 2016, c. 12, s. 37(1), in force January 1, 2017, and formerly read:

(*e*) if the property was eligible capital property of the transferor in respect of a business of the transferor,

(i) where the eligible capital expenditure of the transferor in respect of the property exceeds the cost at which the transferee trust is deemed by this subsection to have acquired the property, for the purposes of sections 14, 20 and 24,

(A) the eligible capital expenditure of the transferee trust in respect of the property is deemed to be the amount that was the eligible capital expenditure of the transferor in respect of the property, and

(B) $^3/_4$ of the excess is deemed to have been allowed under paragraph 20(1)(*b*) to the transferee trust in respect of the property in computing income for taxation years that ended

(I) before the particular time, and

(II) after the adjustment time of the transferee trust in respect of the business, and

(ii) for the purpose of determining after the particular time the amount required by paragraph 14(1)(*b*) to be included in computing the transferee trust's income in respect of any subsequent disposition of the property of the business, there shall be added to the value otherwise determined for Q in the definition "cumulative eligible capital" in subsection 14(5) the amount determined by the formula

$$A \times (B/C)$$

where

A is the amount, if any, determined for Q in that definition in respect of the business of the transferor immediately before the particular time,

B is the fair market value of the property immediately before the particular time, and

C is the fair market value immediately before the particular time of all eligible capital property of the transferor in respect of the business;

S. 107.4(3)(*f*) was replaced by S.C. 2010, c. 12, s. 11(1), applicable in determining after March 4, 2010 whether a property is taxable Canadian property of a taxpayer. S. 107.4(3)(*f*) formerly read:

(*f*) if the property was deemed to be taxable Canadian property of the transferor by this paragraph or paragraph 44.1(2)(*c*), 51(1)(*f*), 85(1)(*i*) or 85.1(1)(*a*) or (8)(*b*), subsection 85.1(5) or 87(4) or (5) or paragraph 97(2)(*c*) or 107(2)(*d.1*) or (3.1)(*d*), the property is deemed to be taxable Canadian property of the transferee trust;

S. 107.4(3)(*f*) was replaced by S.C. 2009, c. 2, s. 27(1), applicable

(a) to dispositions that occur after December 23, 1998; and

(b) in respect of the 1996 and subsequent taxation years, to transfers of capital property that occurred before December 24, 1998.

S. 107.4(3)(*f*) formerly read:

(*f*) if the property was deemed to be taxable Canadian property of the transferor by this paragraph or paragraph 51(1)(*f*), 85(1)(*i*) or 85.1(1)(*a*), subsection 87(4) or (5) or paragraph 97(2)(*c*) or 107(2)(*d.1*), the property is deemed to be taxable Canadian property of the transferee trust;

Related Regulations: 1105; Schedule II.

Related Sections: S. 13(21), "depreciable property"; s. 14(5), "adjustment time", "eligible capital expenditure"; s. 53(4) Recomputation of adjusted cost base on transfers and deemed dispositions; s. 54, "eligible capital property", "proceeds of disposition"; s. 104(4)(*a.4*) Deemed disposition by trust; s. 104(5.8) Trust transfers; s. 104(6) Deduction in computing income of trust; s. 104(23)(*a*) Testamentary trusts; s. 107(4.1) Where subsection 75(2) applicable to trust; s. 107.4(1), "qualifying disposition"; s. 108(1), "capital interest", "cost amount", "trust"; s. 128.1(10) Definitions; s. 138(12), "life insurance policy"; s. 146(1), "registered retirement savings plan"; s. 146.3(1), "registered retirement income fund"; s. 248(1), "amount", "cost amount", "disposition", "filing-due date", "property", "taxable Canadian property"; s. 248(9.2) Vested indefeasibly; s. 249(1)(*b*) Definition of "taxation year".

Tax Profile: February 2002 — Transferring Property to a Trust After the Enactment of Bill C-22.

► 107.4(4) ◄

(4) Fair market value of vested interest in trust. Where

(*a*) a particular capital interest in a trust is held by a beneficiary at any time,

(*b*) the particular interest is vested indefeasibly at that time,

(*c*) the trust is not described in any of paragraphs (*a*) to (*e.1*) of the definition "trust" in subsection 108(1), and

(*d*) interests under the trust are not ordinarily disposed of for consideration that reflects the fair market value of the net assets of the trust,

the fair market value of the particular interest at that time is deemed to be not less than the amount determined by the formula

$$(A - B) \times (C/D)$$

where

A is the total fair market value at that time of all properties of the trust,

B is the total of all amounts each of which is the amount of a debt owing by the trust at that time or the amount of any other obligation of the trust to pay any amount that is outstanding at that time,

C is the fair market value at that time of the particular interest (determined without reference to this subsection), and

D is the total fair market value at that time of all interests as beneficiaries under the trust (determined without reference to this subsection).

Related Sections: S. 104(1.1), "beneficiary"; s. 108(1), "beneficiary", "capital interest", "trust"; s. 248(1), "amount", "property"; s. 248(9.2) Vested indefeasibly.

SECTION 108: [Trusts]

▶ 108(1) ◀

(1) Definitions. In this subdivision,

Related Sections: S. 70(6.1) Transfer or distribution of NISA to spouse or trust; s. 104(1) Reference to trust or estate; s. 104(4) Deemed disposition by trust; s. 104(5) Depreciable property; s. 104(5.1) Interest in NISA Fund No. 2; s. 104(5.2) Resource property; s. 104(12) Deduction of amounts included in preferred beneficiaries' incomes; s. 107(4) Trusts in favour of spouse, common-law partner or self; s. 108(1), "pre-1972 spousal trust"; s. 144(1), "employees profit sharing plan"; s. 145(1), "registered supplementary unemployment benefit plan"; s. 146(1), "registered retirement savings plan"; s. 146.1(1), "registered education savings plan"; s. 146.3(1), "registered retirement income fund"; s. 147(1), "deferred profit sharing plan"; s. 248(1), "amount", "employee benefit plan", "employee trust", "individual", "property", "trust".

Tax Window Files: Prolonged administration of assets/Will, *March 26, 2012*, CRA Document No. 2011-0422471E5; TCP distributed by N/R trust to N/R beneficiary, *June 2, 2011*, CRA Document No. 2011-0399501E5; Testamentary Insurance Trust, *January 6, 2011*, CRA Document No. 2009-0350811E5; Spousal Trusts, *December 15, 2010*, CRA Document No. 2010-0358461E5; Respecting Distributions from Non-Resident Trusts, *March 23, 2010*, CRA Document No. 2009-0332521I7; Testamentary Trust — Agreement Signed by the Heirs of a Deceased Person, *Technical Interpretation, International and Trust Division, October 20, 2009*, CRA Document No. 2009-0328441E5; Renunciation of Spousal Trust Income, *Technical Interpretation, International and Trusts Division, February 26, 2007*, CRA Document No. 2005-0159431E5; Disposition of a Beneficiary's Capital Interest in an Estate to Another Beneficiary, *Technical Interpretation, International and Trust Division, March 6, 2006*, CRA Document No. 2005-0155271E5; Testamentary Trust, *Technical Interpretation, International and Trusts Division, April 18, 2005*, CRA Document No. 2004-0093821E5. If the direction by the beneficiary spouse occurs before the trust income becomes payable to the spouse, the direction will not result in a contribution of property and therefore will not result in the trust losing its testamentary trust status.

"accumulating income" —"accumulating income" of a trust for a taxation year means the amount that would be the income of the trust for the year if that amount were computed

(*a*) without reference to paragraphs 104(4)(*a*) and (*a*.1) and subsections 104(5.1), (5.2) and (12) and 107(4),

(*b*) as if the greatest amount that the trust was entitled to claim under subsection 104(6) in computing its income for the year were so claimed, and

(*c*) without reference to subsection 12(10.2), except to the extent that that subsection applies to amounts paid to a trust to which paragraph 70(6.1)(*b*) applies and before the death of the spouse or common-law partner referred to in that paragraph;

Editorial Note: The definition of "accumulating income" is relevant to the preferred beneficiary election in s. 104(14). Accumulating income generally means a trust's income (including net capital gains) for the taxation year after the maximum amount of deductions available under s. 104(6) (even if such deductions are not actually claimed by the trust), but without regard to certain specified provisions. Income held by a trust for a minor beneficiary deemed to be "payable" under s. 104(18) is deductible by the trust under s. 104(6) and thus reduces its accumulating income.

Interpretation Bulletins: *Secondary* — IT-381R3 Trusts — Deduction of amounts paid or payable to beneficiaries and flow-through of taxable capital gains to beneficiaries; IT-394R2 Preferred beneficiary election.

"beneficiary" —"beneficiary" under a trust includes a person beneficially interested therein;

Related Sections: S. 104(1.1) Restricted meaning of "beneficiary"; s. 248(25) Beneficially interested.

"capital interest" —"capital interest" of a taxpayer in a trust means all rights of the taxpayer as a beneficiary under the trust, and after 1999 includes a right (other than a right acquired before 2000 and disposed of before March 2000) to enforce payment of an amount by the trust that arises as a consequence of any such right, but does not include an income interest in the trust;

Related Regulations: 4800.1.

"cost amount" —"cost amount" to a taxpayer at any time of a capital interest or part of it, as the case may be, in a trust, means (notwithstanding subsection 248(1) and except for the purposes of subsection 107(3.1) and section 107.4 and except in respect of a capital interest in a trust that is at that time a foreign affiliate of the taxpayer),

(*a*) where any money or other property of the trust has been distributed by the trust to the taxpayer in satisfaction of all or part of the taxpayer's capital interest (whether on the winding-up of the trust or otherwise), the total of

(i) the money so distributed, and

(ii) all amounts each of which is the cost amount to the trust, immediately before the distribution, of each such other property,

(*a*.1) where that time (in this paragraph referred to as the "particular time") is immediately before the time that is immediately before the time of the death of the taxpayer and subsection 104(4) or (5) deems the trust to dispose of property at the end of the day that includes the particular time, the amount that would be determined under paragraph (*b*) if the taxpayer had died on a day that ended immediately before the time that is immediately before the particular time, and

(*b*) in any other case, the amount determined by the formula

$$(A - B) \times C/D$$

where

A is the total of

(i) all money of the trust on hand immediately before that time, and

(ii) all amounts each of which is the cost amount to the trust, immediately before that time, of each other property of the trust,

B is the total of all amounts each of which is the amount of any debt owing by the trust, or of any other obligation of the trust to pay any amount, that was outstanding immediately before that time,

C is the fair market value at that time of the capital interest or part thereof, as the case may be, in the trust, and

D is the fair market value at that time of all capital interests in the trust;

History: S. 108(1), paragraph (*a.1*) of the definition "cost amount" was replaced by S.C. 2013, c. 34, s. 236(1), in force June 26, 2013, and formerly read:

(*a*.1) where that time is immediately before the time of the death of the taxpayer and subsection 104(4) or (5) deems the trust to dispose of property at the end of the day that includes that time, the amount that would be determined under paragraph (*b*) if the taxpayer had died on a day that ended immediately before that time, and

S. 108(1), the portion of the definition "cost amount" before paragraph (*a*) was replaced by S.C. 2009, c. 2, s. 28(1), applicable after July 14, 2008. S. 108(1), the portion of the definition "cost amount" before paragraph (*a*) formerly read:

"cost amount"—"cost amount" to a taxpayer at any time of a capital interest or part of the interest, as the case may be, in a trust (other than a trust that

is a foreign affiliate of the taxpayer) means, except for the purposes of section 107.4 and notwithstanding subsection 248(1),

"eligible offset" —"eligible offset" at any time of a taxpayer in respect of all or part of the taxpayer's capital interest in a trust is the portion of any debt or obligation that is assumed by the taxpayer and that can reasonably be considered to be applicable to property distributed at that time in satisfaction of the interest or part of the interest, as the case may be, if the distribution is conditional upon the assumption by the taxpayer of the portion of the debt or obligation;

"eligible real property gain" — (Repealed by S.C. 1995, c. 3, s. 31(1).)

"eligible real property loss" — (Repealed by S.C. 1995, c. 3, s. 31(1).)

"eligible taxable capital gains" —"eligible taxable capital gains", of a trust for a taxation year, means the lesser of

(*a*) its annual gains limit (within the meaning assigned by subsection 110.6(1)) for the year, and

(*b*) the amount determined by the formula

$$A - B$$

where

A is its cumulative gains limit (within the meaning assigned by subsection 110.6(1)) at the end of the year, and

B is the total of all amounts designated under subsection 104(21.2) by the trust in respect of beneficiaries for taxation years before that year;

History: S. 108(1), the portion of the definition "eligible taxable capital gains" before paragraph (*a*) was replaced by S.C. 2017, c. 33, s. 37(2), in force December 14, 2017 (Royal Assent), and formerly read:

"eligible taxable capital gains"—"eligible taxable capital gains" of a personal trust for a taxation year means the lesser of

Related Sections: S. 110.6(1) Definitions — fair market value of NISA.

Interpretation Bulletins: *Secondary* — IT-381R3 Trusts — Deduction of amounts paid or payable to beneficiaries and flow-through of taxable capital gains to beneficiaries.

"excluded property" —"excluded property", of a trust, means property owned by the trust at, and distributed by the trust after, the end of 2016, if

(*a*) the trust is not in its first taxation year that begins after 2016 a trust described in subparagraph (*c*.1)(iii.1) of the definition *principal residence* in section 54, and

(*b*) the property is a property that would be the trust's *principal residence* (as defined in section 54) for the taxation year in which the distribution occurs if

(i) that definition were read without reference to its subparagraph (*c*. 1)(iii.1), and

(ii) the trust designated the property under that definition as its principal residence for the taxation year;

History: S. 108(1), the definition "excluded property" was replaced by S.C. 2017, c. 33, s. 37(1), applicable to taxation years that begin after 2016, and formerly read:

"excluded property"—"excluded property" means a share of the capital stock of a non-resident-owned investment corporation that is not taxable Canadian property;

Related Sections: 107(4.1) Where subsection 75(2) applicable to trust.

"exempt property" —"exempt property" of a taxpayer at any time means property any income or gain from the disposition of which by the taxpayer at that time would, because the taxpayer is non-resident or because of a provision contained in a tax treaty, not cause an increase in the taxpayer's tax payable under this Part;

"income interest" —"income interest" of a taxpayer in a trust means a right (whether immediate or future and whether absolute or contingent) of the taxpayer as a beneficiary under a personal trust to, or to receive, all or any part of the income of the trust and, after 1999, includes a right (other than a right acquired before 2000 and disposed of before March 2000) to enforce payment of an amount by the trust that arises as a consequence of any such right;

Related Sections: S. 108(3) Income of a trust in certain provisions.

Income Tax Folios: *Secondary*— S6-F2-C1 Disposition of an Income Interest in a Trust.

"inter vivos trust" —"inter vivos trust" means a trust other than a testamentary trust;

"non-qualifying real property" — (Repealed by S.C. 1995, c. 3, s. 31(1).)

Related Sections: S. 104(1) Reference to trust or estate; s. 131(6) Definitions relating to mutual fund corporations; s. 248(1), "trust".

"pre-1972 spousal trust" —"pre-1972 spousal trust" at a particular time means a trust that was

(*a*) created by the will of a taxpayer who died before 1972, or

(*b*) created before June 18, 1971 by a taxpayer during the taxpayer's lifetime

that, throughout the period beginning at the time it was created and ending at the earliest of January 1, 1993, the day on which the taxpayer's spouse or common-law partner died and the particular time, was a trust under which the taxpayer's spouse or common-law partner was entitled to receive all of the income of the trust that arose before the spouse's or common-law partner's death, unless a person other than the spouse or common-law partner received or otherwise obtained the use of any of the income or capital of the trust before the end of that period;

Related Sections: S. 104(1) Reference to trust or estate; s. 104(4) Deemed disposition by trust; s. 104(15) Allocable amount for preferred beneficiary; s. 108(3) Income of a trust in certain provisions; s. 108(4) Trust not disqualified; s. 248(1), "common-law partner", "trust"; s. 252(3) Extended meaning of "spouse" and "former spouse".

"preferred beneficiary" —"preferred beneficiary" under a trust for a particular taxation year of the trust means a beneficiary under the trust at the end of the particular year who is resident in Canada at that time if

(*a*) the beneficiary is

(i) an individual in respect of whom paragraphs 118.3(1)(*a*) to (*b*) apply for the individual's taxation year (in this definition referred to as the "beneficiary's year") that ends in the particular year, or

(ii) an individual

(A) who attained the age of 18 years before the end of the beneficiary's year, was a dependant (within the meaning assigned by subsection 118(6)) of another individual for the beneficiary's year and was dependent on the other individual because of mental or physical infirmity, and

(B) whose income (computed without reference to subsection 104(14)) for the beneficiary's year does not exceed the amount used under paragraph (*c*) of the description of B in subsection 118(1) for the year, and

(*b*) the beneficiary is

(i) the settlor of the trust,

(ii) the spouse or common-law partner or former spouse or common-law partner of the settlor of the trust, or

(iii) a child, grandchild or great grandchild of the settlor of the trust or the spouse or common-law partner of any such person;

Editorial Note: To be a "preferred beneficiary", a beneficiary must be the settlor of the trust, the spouse, common-law partner, or former spouse or common-law partner of the settlor, or the child, grandchild, or great-grandchild of the settlor, or the spouse or common-law partner of any such person. The beneficiary must be entitled to the disability tax credit under s. 118.3(1), or be 18 years old or older and dependent upon another individual by reason of physical or mental infirmity and have income less than the basic personal credit amount.

Interpretation Bulletins: *Secondary* — IT-394R2 Preferred beneficiary election.

"qualified farm property" — (Repealed by S.C. 2014, c. 39, s. 28(1).)

History: S. 108(1), the definition "qualified farm property" was repealed by S.C. 2014, c. 39, s. 28(1), applicable to dispositions that occur in the 2014 and subsequent taxation years, and formerly read:

"qualified farm property"—"qualified farm property" of an individual has the meaning assigned by subsection 110.6(1);

"qualified fishing property" — (Repealed by S.C. 2014, c. 39, s. 28(1).)

Editorial Note: The trust's "income computed without reference to the provisions of this Act" is understood to mean the trust's income for trust law purposes. Under trust law, capital gains are not income.

History: S. 108(1), the definition "qualified fishing property" was repealed by S.C. 2014, c. 39, s. 28(1), applicable to dispositions that occur in the 2014 and subsequent taxation years, and formerly read:

"qualified fishing property"—"qualified fishing property" of an individual has the meaning assigned by subsection 110.6(1);

"qualified small business corporation share" — (Repealed by S.C. 2014, c. 39, s. 28(1).)

History: S. 108(1), the definition "qualified small business corporation share" was repealed by S.C. 2014, c. 39, s. 28(1), applicable to dispositions that occur in the 2014 and subsequent taxation years, and formerly read:

"qualified small business corporation share"—"qualified small business corporation share" of an individual has the meaning assigned by subsection 110.6(1);

"settlor" —"settlor",

(*a*) in relation to a testamentary trust, means the individual referred to in the definition "testamentary trust" in this subsection, and

(*b*) in relation to an *inter vivos*trust,

(i) if the trust was created by the transfer, assignment or other disposition of property thereto (in this definition referred to as property "contributed") by not more than one individual and the fair market value of such of the property of the trust as was contributed by the individual at the time of the creation of the trust or at any subsequent time exceeds the fair market value of such of the property of the trust as was contributed by any other person or persons at any subsequent time (such fair market values being determined at the time of the making of any such contribution), means that individual, and

(ii) if the trust was created by the contribution of property thereto jointly by an individual and the individual's spouse or common-law partner and by no other person and the fair market value of such of the property of the trust as was contributed by them at the time of the creation of the trust or at any subsequent time exceeds the fair market value of such of the property of the trust as was contributed by any other person or persons at any subsequent time (such fair market values being determined at the time of the making of any such contribution), means that individual and the spouse or common-law partner;

Editorial Note: The definition of "settlor" is relevant in the context of the preferred beneficiary election because a "preferred beneficiary" is defined in relation to the settlor.

Related Sections: S. 104(5.6) Designated contributor; s. 108(1), "preferred beneficiary".

Interpretation Bulletins: *Secondary* — IT-394R2 Preferred beneficiary election.

"testamentary trust" —"testamentary trust", in a taxation year, means a trust that arose on and as a consequence of the death of an individual (including a trust referred to in subsection 248(9.1)), other than

(*a*) a trust created by a person other than the individual,

(*b*) a trust created after November 12, 1981 if, before the end of the taxation year, property has been contributed to the trust otherwise than by an individual on or after the individual's death and as a consequence thereof,

(*c*) a trust created before November 13, 1981 if

(i) after June 28, 1982 property has been contributed to the trust otherwise than by an individual on or after the individual's death and as a consequence thereof, or

(ii) before the end of the taxation year, the total fair market value of the property owned by the trust that was contributed to the trust otherwise than by an individual on or after the individual's death and as a consequence thereof and the property owned by the trust that was substituted for such property exceeds the total fair market value of the property owned by the trust that was contributed by an individual on or after the individual's death and as a consequence thereof and the property owned by the trust that was substituted for such property, and for the purposes of this subparagraph the fair market value of any property shall be determined as at the time it was acquired by the trust, and

(*d*) a trust that, at any time after December 20, 2002 and before the end of the taxation year, incurs a debt or any other obligation owed to, or guaranteed by, a beneficiary or any other person or partnership (which beneficiary, person or partnership is referred to in this paragraph as the "specified party") with whom any beneficiary of the trust does not deal at arm's length, other than a debt or other obligation

(i) incurred by the trust in satisfaction of the specified party's right as a beneficiary under the trust

(A) to enforce payment of an amount of the trust's income or capital gains payable at or before that time by the trust to the specified party, or

(B) to otherwise receive any part of the capital of the trust,

(ii) owed to the specified party, if the debt or other obligation arose because of a service (for greater certainty, not including any transfer or loan of property) rendered by the specified party to, for or on behalf of the trust,

(iii) owed to the specified party, if

(A) the debt or other obligation arose because of a payment made by the specified party for or on behalf of the trust,

(B) in exchange for the payment (and in full settlement of the debt or other obligation), the trust transfers property, the fair market value of which is not less than the principal amount of the debt or other obligation, to the specified party within 12 months after the payment was made (or, if written application has been made to the Minister by the trust within that 12-month period, within any longer period that the Minister considers reasonable in the circumstances), and

(C) it is reasonable to conclude that the specified party would have been willing to make the payment if the specified party dealt at arm's length with the trust, except where the trust is the individual's estate and that payment was made within the first 12 months after the individual's death (or, if written application has been made to the Minister by the estate within that 12-month period, within any longer period that the Minister considers reasonable in the circumstances), or

(iv) incurred by the trust before October 24, 2012 if, in full settlement of the debt or other obligation the trust transfers property, the fair market value of which is not less than the principal amount of the debt or other obligation, to the person or partnership to whom the debt or other obligation is owed within 12 months after the day on which the *Technical Tax Amendments Act, 2012* receives royal assent (or if written application has been made to the Minister by the trust within that 12-month period, within any longer period that the Minister considers reasonable in the circumstances);

Editorial Note: Basically, a testamentary trust is a trust or estate created as a consequence of a person's death. The terms of a testamentary trust are typically established in the will of the deceased. (A testamentary trust may also be created by means of a court order under provincial or territorial dependant's relief or support statutes.) Generally, a testamentary trust does not include a trust if any property was contributed to it other than by a deceased. Furthermore, for taxation years ending after December 20, 2002, if the trust incurs a debt or other obligation to pay an amount to, or guaranteed by, a beneficiary or other person or partnership with whom any beneficiary of the trust does not deal at arm's length (all of whom will be referred to here as the beneficiary), the testamentary trust may become an *inter vivos* trust. If the assets are not distributed to the beneficiaries according to the terms of the will, a testamentary trust may become an *inter vivos* trust.

A trust that is not a testamentary trust is an *inter vivos* trust. The death of the settlor of an *inter vivos* trust does not cause it to become a testamentary trust. A testamentary trust is a personal trust (as defined in s. 248(1)). S. 122(1.1) precludes a personal trust from claiming the tax credits set out in s. 118. On the other hand, paragraph (*c*.1) of the definition of "principal residence" in s. 54 allows the exemption in regard thereto to be claimed by a personal trust.

A testamentary trust (but not an *inter vivos* trust) is subject to the graduated tax rates applicable to natural individuals. Instalments of tax are not required. The testamentary trust can have a fiscal period and taxation year that does not coincide with the calendar year end. However, note that the graduated rate taxation for testamentary trusts is mostly eliminated for the 2016 and later taxation years. An exception is provided for estates for a period of 36 months after the death, i.e., for "graduated rate estates", to allow for administration. Further, testamentary trusts, other than graduated rate estates, will be required to have a fiscal period that coincides with the calendar year beginning in the 2016 taxation year. Finally, effective for the 2016 and subsequent taxation years, testamentary trusts, including estates, will be required to pay instalments.

History: S. 108(1), the portion before paragraph (*a*) of the definition "testamentary trust" was replaced by S.C. 2013, c. 34, s. 236(2), applicable to taxation years that end after December 20, 2002, and formerly read:

"testamentary trust" — "testamentary trust" in a taxation year means a trust or estate that arose on and as a consequence of the death of an individual (including a trust referred to in subsection 248(9.1)), other than

S. 108(1), paragraph (*d*) of the definition "testamentary trust" was added by S.C. 2013, c. 34, s. 236(3), applicable to taxation years that end after December 20, 2002, except that

(*a*) a transfer that is required, by clause (*d*)(iii)(B) of the definition "testamentary trust" in subsection 108(1), to be made within 12 months after a payment was made is deemed to be made in a timely manner if it is made no later than June 26, 2014 [12 months after June 26, 2013]; and

(*b*) for those taxation years that end before June 26, 2013, the reference to "within the first 12 months after the individual's death" in clause (*d*)(iii)(C) of the definition "testamentary trust" in subsection 108(1) is to be read as a reference to "after the individual's death and no later than 12 months after the day on which the *Technical Tax Amendments Act, 2012* receives royal assent".

Related Sections: 122(3) qualified disability trust; 248(1) graduated rate estate; S. 104(1) Reference to trust or estate; s. 104(2) Taxed as individual; 104(23) Deceased beneficiary of graduated rate estate; s. 117(2) Rates for taxation years after 2008; s. 152(4.2) Reassessment with taxpayer's consent; s. 248(8) Occurrences as a consequence of death; s. 249.1(1) Definition of "fiscal period".

Canadian Tax Foundation: Chan and Morin, *Distributions by Canadian Testamentary Trusts*, 2005 Canadian Tax Journal 4:1090–1110; Reiss, *Testamentary Trust Planning: Dying is Harder Than You Think*, 2004 Prairie Provinces Tax Conference 16:1–29.

Tax Profile: June 2004 — Planning For Aging Parents.

Tax Topics: No. 1684, Testamentary Trusts — Not a Dead Issue — Use Them But Don't Abuse Them.

Interpretation Bulletins: *Secondary* — IT-381R3 Trusts — Capital gains and losses and the flow-through of taxable capital gains to beneficiaries.

Tax Window Files: Testamentary Trust, *Technical Interpretation, International and Trusts Division, April 18, 2005*, CRA Document No. 2004-0093821E5. If the direction by the beneficiary spouse occurs before the trust income becomes payable to the spouse, the direction will not result in a contribution of property and therefore will not result in the trust losing its testamentary trust status; Designation of Testamentary Trust as RRSP Beneficiary, *Technical Interpretation, Financial Industries Division, April 6, 2005*, CRA Document No. 2005-0116491E5. A testamentary trust may be funded by proceeds from the deceased's RRSP (or RRIF) provided certain conditions are met; Retention of Income by Spousal Trust, *Technical Interpretation, International and Trusts Division, December 1, 2004*, CRA Document No. 2003-0046171E5. If the direction by the beneficiary spouse occurs before the trust income becomes payable to the spouse, the direction will not result in a contribution of property and therefore will not result in the trust losing its testamentary trust status.

Cases: Voluntary transfer by beneficiary aimed at increasing the trust's capital resulted in loss of status as testamentary trust. *Greenberg Estate v. The Queen*, 97 DTC 1380 (T.C.C.).

"trust" — "trust" includes an *inter vivos* trust and a testamentary trust but in subsections 104(4), (5), (5.2), (12),

(13.1), (13.2), (14) and (15) and sections 105 to 107 does not include

(*a*) an amateur athlete trust, an employee life and health trust, an employee trust, a trust described in paragraph 149(1)(*o.4*) or a trust governed by a deferred profit sharing plan, an employee benefit plan, an employees profit sharing plan, a foreign retirement arrangement, a pooled registered pension plan, a registered disability savings plan, a registered education savings plan, a registered pension plan, a registered retirement income fund, a registered retirement savings plan, a registered supplementary unemployment benefit plan or a TFSA,

(*a*.1) a trust (other than a trust described in paragraph (*a*) or (*d*), a trust to which subsection 7(2) or (6) applies or a trust prescribed for the purpose of subsection 107(2)) all or substantially all of the property of which is held for the purpose of providing benefits to individuals each of whom is provided with benefits in respect of, or because of, an office or employment or former office or employment of any individual,

(*b*) a related segregated fund trust (within the meaning assigned by section 138.1),

(*c*) a trust deemed by subsection 143(1) to exist in respect of a congregation that is a constituent part of a religious organization,

(*d*) an RCA trust (within the meaning assigned by subsection 207.5(1)),

(*e*) a trust each of the beneficiaries under which was at all times after it was created a trust referred to in paragraph (*a*), (*b*) or (*d*) or a person who is a beneficiary of the trust only because of being a beneficiary under a trust referred to in any of those paragraphs, or

(*e*.1) a cemetery care trust or a trust governed by an eligible funeral arrangement,

and, in applying subsections 104(4), (5), (5.2), (12), (14) and (15) at any time, does not include

(*f*) a trust that, at that time, is a unit trust, or

(*g*) a trust all interests in which, at that time, have vested indefeasibly, other than

(i) an *alter ego*trust, a joint spousal or common-law partner trust, a post-1971 spousal or common-law partner trust or a trust to which paragraph 104(4)(*a*.4) applies,

(ii) (Repealed by S.C. 2013, c. 34, s. 236(6).)

(iii) a trust that has, in its return of income under this Part for its first taxation year that ends after 1992, elected that this paragraph not apply,

(iv) a trust that is at that time resident in Canada where the total fair market value at that time of all interests in the trust held at that time by beneficiaries under the trust who at that time are non-resident is more than 20% of the total fair market value at that time of all interests in the trust held at that time by beneficiaries under the trust,

(v) a trust under the terms of which, at that time, all or part of a person's interest in the trust is to be terminated with reference to a period of time (including a period of time determined with reference to the person's death), otherwise than as a consequence of terms of the trust under which an interest in the trust is to be terminated as a consequence of a distribution to the person (or the person's estate) of property of the trust if the fair market value of the property to be distributed is required to be commensurate with the fair market value of that interest immediately before the distribution, or

(vi) a trust that, before that time and after December 17, 1999, has made a distribution to a beneficiary in respect of the beneficiary's capital interest in the trust, if the distribution can reasonably be considered to have been financed by a liability of the trust and one of the purposes of incurring the liability was to avoid taxes otherwise payable under this Part as a consequence of the death of any individual.

Editorial Note: The Act contains no definition as to what constitutes a "trust" *per se*; accordingly, recourse is made to the common law (or, in Quebec, to the fourth book of the *Civil Code of Québec*). In essence, a trust is created where a settlor transfers property to a trustee in circumstances such that the property is to be held for the benefit of others. The general exclusion of agency relations from qualifying as trusts does not apply to the trusts listed in paragraphs (*a*) to (*e*.1) of the definition of "trust" in s. 108(1); these include amateur athlete trusts, certain employee trusts, related segregated fund trusts, certain trusts for religious organizations, retirement compensation arrangement trusts, cemetery care trusts, and trusts governing an eligible funeral arrangement. Certain specified provisions are not applicable to these trusts. For example, the income designations under ss. 104(13.1) and (13.2) are not available to these trusts; and s. 105 and s. 107 dealing with benefits under trusts and distributions from trusts are also not applicable.

History: S. 108(1), paragraph (*c*) of the definition "trust" was replaced by S.C. 2014, c. 39, s. 28(2), applicable to the 2016 and subsequent taxation years, and formerly read:

(*c*) an *inter vivos* trust deemed by subsection 143(1) to exist in respect of a congregation that is a constituent part of a religious organization,

S. 108(1), paragraph (*a.1*) of the definition "trust" was replaced by S.C. 2013, c. 34, s. 236(4), applicable to trust taxation years that begin after 2006, and formerly read:

(*a*.1) a trust, other than a trust described in paragraph (*a*) or (*d*), all or substantially all of the property of which is held for the purpose of providing benefits to individuals each of whom is provided with benefits in respect of, or because of, an office or employment or former office or employment of any individual,

S. 108(1), the portion after paragraph (*e.1*) and before paragraph (*f*) of the definition "trust" was replaced by S.C. 2013, c. 34, s. 236(5), applicable to the 1998 and subsequent taxation years, and formerly read:

and, in applying subsections 104(4), (5), (5.2), (12), (14) and (15) and section 106 at any time, does not include

S. 108(1), paragraph (*g*)(ii) of the definition "trust" was repealed by S.C. 2013, c. 34, s. 236(6), applicable to taxation years that begin after October 31, 2011, and formerly read:

(ii) a trust that has elected under subsection 104(5.3),

S. 108(1), paragraph (*a*) of the definition "trust" was replaced by S.C. 2012, c. 31, s. 23(1), in force December 14, 2012, and formerly read:

(*a*) an amateur athlete trust, an employee life and health trust, an employee trust, a trust described in paragraph 149(1)(*o.4*) or a trust governed by a deferred profit sharing plan, an employee benefit plan, an employees profit sharing plan, a foreign retirement arrangement, a registered disability savings plan, a registered education savings plan, a registered pension plan, a registered retirement income fund, a registered retirement savings plan, a registered supplementary unemployment benefit plan or a TFSA,

S. 108(1), paragraph (*a*) of the definition "trust" was replaced by S.C. 2010, c. 25, s. 19(1), applicable after 2009. S. 108(1), paragraph (*a*) of the definition "trust" formerly read:

(*a*) an amateur athlete trust, an employee trust, a trust described in paragraph 149(1)(*o.4*) or a trust governed by a deferred profit sharing plan, an employee benefit plan, an employees profit sharing plan, a foreign retirement arrangement, a registered disability savings plan, a registered education savings plan, a registered pension plan, a registered retirement income fund, a registered retirement savings plan, a registered supplementary unemployment benefit plan or a TFSA,

Related Sections: S. 146.2(3) Paragraphs (2)(a), (b) and (e) not applicable; s. 148.1(1), "Cemetery care trust", "eligible funeral arrangement"; s. 149(1)(s.2) Cemetery care trust; s. 248(1), "foreign retirement arrangement", "cemetery care trust".

Canadian Tax Foundation: Pappin, *December 20, 2002 Draft Technical Changes — Charitable Donations, Charities and Trusts*, 2003 Ontario Tax Conference 5:1–32.

Interpretation Bulletins: *Secondary* — IT-394R2 Preferred beneficiary election; IT-502 Employee benefit plans and employee trusts.

Cases: *Meade v. M.N.R.*, 63 DTC 997-33 (T.A.B.); *Andrews Estate v. M.N.R.*, 66 DTC 798 (T.A.B.); *Kingsdale Securities Co. Limited v. M.N.R.*, 74 DTC 6674 (F.C.A.); *Atinco Paper Products Limited v. The Queen*, 78 DTC 6387 (F.C.A.).

► 108(1.1) ◄

(1.1) Testamentary trust not disqualified. For the purpose of the definition "testamentary trust" in subsection (1), a contribution to a particular trust does not include

(*a*) a "qualifying expenditure" (within the meaning of section 118.04 or 118.041) of a beneficiary under the trust; or

(*b*) an amount paid to, or on behalf of, the trust by another trust if

(i) the trust is an individual's graduated rate estate (determined without regard to the payment and this subsection),

(ii) paragraph 104(13.4)(*b*) applies to the other trust, for a taxation year that ends at a time determined by reference to the individual's death, because of a joint election made under subparagraph 104(13.4)(*b*.1)(iii) by the other trust and the legal representative administering the estate,

(iii) the payment is on account of the tax payable by the individual, for the individual's taxation year that includes the day on which the individual dies, under

(A) this Part, or

(B) the law of the province, in which the individual was resident immediately before the individual's death, that imposes a tax on the taxable income of individuals resident in that province, and

(iv) the amount of the payment does not exceed the amount by which that tax payable is greater than it would have been if paragraph 104(13.4)(*b*) did not apply to the other trust in respect of the taxation year referred to in subparagraph (ii).

History: S. 108(1.1) was replaced by S.C. 2016, c. 12, s. 38(1), applicable to the 2016 and subsequent taxation years, and formerly read:

(1.1) *Credits — home renovation.* For the purpose of the definition "testamentary trust" in subsection (1), a contribution to a trust does not include a qualifying expenditure (within the meaning of section 118.04 or 118.041) of a beneficiary under the trust.

S. 108(1.1) was replaced by S.C. 2015, c. 36, s. 6(1), applicable to the 2016 and subsequent taxation years, and formerly read:

(1.1) *Home renovation tax credit.* For the purpose of the definition "testamentary trust" in subsection (1), a contribution to a trust does not include a qualifying expenditure (within the meaning of section 118.04) of a beneficiary under the trust.

S. 108(1.1) was added by S.C. 2009, c. 31, s. 3(1), applicable to the 2009 and subsequent taxation years.

Related Sections: 108.041(3).

► 108(2) ◄

(2) When trust is a unit trust. For the purposes of this Act, a trust is a unit trust at any particular time if, at that time, it was an *inter vivos* trust the interest of each beneficiary under which was described by reference to units of the trust, and

(*a*) the issued units of the trust included

(i) units having conditions attached thereto that included conditions requiring the trust to accept, at the demand of the holder thereof and at prices determined and payable in accordance with the conditions, the surrender of the units, or fractions or parts thereof, that are fully paid, or

(ii) units qualified in accordance with prescribed conditions relating to the redemption of the units by the trust,

and the fair market value of such of the units as had conditions attached thereto that included such conditions or as were so qualified, as the case may be, was not less than 95% of the fair market value of all of the issued units of the trust (such fair market values being determined without regard to any voting rights attaching to units of the trust);

(*b*) each of the following conditions was satisfied:

(i) throughout the taxation year that includes the particular time (in this paragraph referred to as the "current year"), the trust was resident in Canada,

(ii) throughout the period or periods (in this paragraph referred to as the "relevant periods") that are in the current year and throughout which the conditions in paragraph (*a*) are not satisfied in respect of the trust, its only undertaking was

(A) the investing of its funds in property (other than real property or an interest in real property or an immovable or a real right in an immovable),

(B) the acquiring, holding, maintaining, improving, leasing or managing of any real property or an interest in real property, or of any immovable or a real right in immovables, that is capital property of the trust, or

(C) any combination of the activities described in clauses (A) and (B),

(iii) throughout the relevant periods at least 80% of its property consisted of any combination of

(A) shares,

(B) any property that, under the terms or conditions of which or under an agreement, is convertible into, is exchangeable for or confers a right to acquire, shares,

(C) cash,

(D) bonds, debentures, mortgages, hypothecary claims, notes and other similar obligations,

(E) marketable securities,

(F) real property situated in Canada, and interests in such real property, or immovables situated in Canada and real rights in such immovables, and

(G) rights to and interests in — or, for civil law, rights in or to — any rental or royalty computed by reference to the amount or value of production from a natural accumulation of petroleum or natural gas in Canada, from an oil or gas well in Canada or from a mineral resource in Canada,

(iv) either

(A) not less than 95% of its income for the current year (computed without regard to subsections 39(2), 49(2.1) and 104(6)) was derived from, or from the disposition of, investments described in subparagraph (iii), or

(B) not less than 95% of its income for each of the relevant periods (computed without regard to subsections 39(2), 49(2.1) and 104(6) and as though each of those periods were a taxation year) was derived from, or from the disposition of, investments described in subparagraph (iii),

(v) throughout the relevant periods, not more than 10% of its property consisted of bonds, securities or shares in the capital stock of any one corporation or debtor other than Her Majesty in right of Canada or a province or a Canadian municipality, and

(vi) where the trust would not be a unit trust at the particular time if this paragraph were read without reference to this subparagraph and subparagraph (iii) were read without reference to clause (F), the units of the trust are listed at any time in the current year or in the following taxation year on a designated stock exchange in Canada, or

(*c*) the fair market value of the property of the trust at the end of 1993 was primarily attributable to real property or an interest in real property — or to immovables or a real right in immovables — and the trust was a unit trust throughout any calendar year that ended before 1994 and the fair market value of the property of the trust at the particular time is primarily attributable to property described in paragraph (*a*) or (*b*) of the definition "qualified investment" in section 204, real property or an interest in real property — or immovables or a real right in immovables — or any combination of those properties.

History: S. 108(2)(*b*)(ii)(A) and (B) were replaced by S.C. 2013, c. 34, s. 123(1), in force June 26, 2013, and formerly read:

(A) the investing of its funds in property (other than real property or an interest in real property),

(B) the acquiring, holding, maintaining, improving, leasing or managing of any real property or an interest in real property, that is capital property of the trust, or

S. 108(2)(*b*)(iii)(F) and (G) were replaced by S.C. 2013, c. 34, s. 123(2), in force June 26, 2013, and formerly read:

(F) real property situated in Canada and interests in real property situated in Canada, and

(G) rights to and interests in any rental or royalty computed by reference to the amount or value of production from a natural accumulation of petroleum or natural gas in Canada, from an oil or gas well in Canada or from a mineral resource in Canada,

S. 108(2)(*c*) was replaced by S.C. 2013, c. 34, s. 123(3), in force June 26, 2013, and formerly read:

(*c*) the fair market value of the property of the trust at the end of 1993 was primarily attributable to real property (or an interest in real property), the trust was a unit trust throughout any calendar year that ended before 1994 and the fair market value of the property of the trust at the particular time is primarily attributable to property described in paragraph (*a*) or (*b*) of the definition "qualified investment" in section 204, real property (or an interest in real property) or any combination of those properties.

S. 108(2)(*b*)(iv)(A) and (B) were replaced by S.C. 2013, c. 34, s. 236(10), applicable to the 2003 and subsequent taxation years, and formerly read:

(A) not less than 95% of its income for the current year (computed without regard to subsections 49(2.1) and 104(6)) was derived from, or from the disposition of, investments described in subparagraph (iii), or

(B) not less than 95% of its income for each of the relevant periods (computed without regard to subsections 49(2.1) and 104(6) and as though each of those periods were a taxation year) was derived from, or from the disposition of, investments described in subparagraph (iii),

Related Sections: S. 131(8) Meaning of "mutual fund corporation"; s. 132(6) Meaning of "mutual fund trust"; s. 248(4) Interest in real property; s. 253.1 Investments in limited partnerships.

Canadian Petroleum Tax Journal: Taxation Issues Relating to Royalty Trusts and Income Funds, Robert D. Penner, 1997, Vol. 10, No. 1.

Canadian Tax Foundation: Bernstein, *Methods of Owning Real Estate: Joint Ventures, Partnerships & Trusts*, 1998 Ontario Tax Conference 3:1–32; Williamson, *Real Estate Investment Trust*, 1997 Corporate Management Tax Conference 5:1–19; McMullen, *Real Estate Investment Trusts: The Latest in the Series?*, 1997 Prairie Provinces Tax Conference 13:1–29.

Tax Profile: April 2004 — 2004 Budget Imposes Restrictions on Pension Funds Investing in Business Income Trusts; April 2004 — Cross-Border Income Trusts — New Variations.

Tax Window Files: Unit Trust — Suspension of Redemption Rights, *Tax Ruling, International & Trusts Division, January 11, 2006*, CRA Document No. 2005-0152491R3. Suspension of Redemption Rights — the trust would not cease to qualify as a unit trust as a result of the temporary suspension of the right to redeem the units of the trust.

▶ 108(3) ◀

(3) Income of a trust in certain provisions. For the purposes of the definitions "income interest" in subsection (1), "lifetime benefit trust" in subsection 60.011(1) and "exempt foreign trust" in subsection 94(1), the income of a trust is its income computed without reference to the provisions of this Act and, for the purposes of the definition "pre-1972 spousal trust" in subsection (1) and paragraphs 70(6)(*b*) and (6.1)(*b*), 73(1.01)(*c*) and 104(4)(*a*), the income of a trust is its income computed without reference to the provisions of this Act, minus any dividends included in that income

(*a*) that are amounts not included by reason of section 83 in computing the income of the trust for the purposes of the other provisions of this Act;

(*b*) that are described in subsection 131(1); or

(*c*) to which subsection 131(1) applies by reason of subsection 130(2).

Editorial Note: The trust's "income computed without reference to the provisions of this Act" is understood to mean the trust's income for trust law purposes. Under trust law, capital gains are not income.

History: S. 108(3), the portion before paragraph (*a*) was amended by S.C. 2013, c. 34, s. 12(1), applicable to trust taxation years that begin after 2000, and formerly read:

(3) *Income of a trust in certain provisions.* For the purposes of the definition "income interest" in subsection (1), the income of a trust is its income computed without reference to the provisions of this Act and, for the purposes of the definition "pre-1972 spousal trust" in subsection (1) and paragraphs 70(6)(*b*) and (6.1)(*b*), 73(1.01)(*c*) and 104(4)(*a*), the income of a

trust is its income computed without reference to the provisions of this Act, minus any dividends included in that income

Related Sections: S. 104(1) Reference to trust or estate; s. 248(1), "dividend", "trust".

Canadian Tax Foundation: Chan and Morin, *Distributions by Canadian Testamentary Trusts*, 2005 Canadian Tax Journal 4:1090–1110; Hoffstein, *Selected Non-Tax Considerations in Estate Planning*, 2000 Conference Report 31:1–68.

Interpretation Bulletins: *Secondary* — IT-305R4 Testamentary spouse trusts.

Tax Window Files: Capital Dividend Received by a Spousal Trust, *Technical Interpretation, International & Trusts Division, September 17, 2004*, CRA Document No. 2004-0060161E5. Dividends: distinguishing income from capital.

Cases: In determining whether a corporate distribution is to be considered income or capital by the trust receiving it, "form is substance". *Waters v. Toronto General Trusts Corporation et al.*, 56 DTC 1113 [1956] S.C.R. 889 (S.C.C.).

▶ 108(4) ◀

(4) Trust not disqualified. For the purposes of the definition "pre-1972 spousal trust" in subsection (1), subparagraphs 70(6)(*b*)(ii) and (6.1)(*b*)(ii) and paragraphs 73(1.01)(*c*) and 104(4)(*a*), if a trust was created by a taxpayer whether by the taxpayer's will or otherwise, no person is deemed to have received or otherwise obtained or to be entitled to receive or otherwise obtain the use of any income or capital of the trust solely because of

(*a*) the payment, or provision for payment, as the case may be, by the trust of

(i) any estate, legacy, succession or inheritance duty payable, in consequence of the death of the taxpayer, or a spouse or common-law partner of the taxpayer who is a beneficiary under the trust, in respect of any property of, or interest in, the trust, or

(ii) any income or profits tax payable by the trust in respect of any income of the trust; or

(*b*) the inhabiting at any time by an individual of a housing unit that is, or is in respect of, property that is owned at that time by the trust, if

(i) the property is described in the definition "principal residence" in section 54 in respect of the trust for the trust's taxation year that includes that time, and

(ii) the individual is

(A) the taxpayer, or

(B) the taxpayer's

(I) spouse or common-law partner,

(II) former spouse or common-law partner, or

(III) child.

Editorial Note: S. 108(4) ensures that a spousal trust, *alter ego* trust, spousal or common-law partner trust, joint spousal or common-law partner trust, or a self-benefit trust will not be disqualified as such solely because of a provision in the trust instrument for payment of any estate, legacy, succession or inheritance duty or any income or profits tax. Beginning in 2016, the provision also ensures that the trust will not be disqualified as such if property of the trust is inhabited by the taxpayer that created the trust, or the taxpayer's spouse or common-law partner, former spouse or common-law partner, or child.

History: S. 108(4) was replaced by S.C. 2017, c. 33, s. 37(3), applicable to taxation years that begin after 2016, and formerly read:

(4) *Trust not disqualified.* For the purposes of the definition "pre-1972 spousal trust" in subsection (1), subparagraphs 70(6)(*b*)(ii) and (6.1)(*b*)(ii) and paragraphs 73(1.01)(*c*) and 104(4)(*a*), where a trust was created by a taxpayer whether by the taxpayer's will or otherwise, no person is deemed to have received or otherwise obtained or to be entitled to receive or otherwise obtain the use of any income or capital of the trust solely because of the payment, or provision for payment, as the case may be, by the trust of

(*a*) any estate, legacy, succession or inheritance duty payable, in consequence of the death of the taxpayer, or a spouse or common-law partner of the taxpayer who is a beneficiary under the trust, in respect of any property of, or interest in, the trust; or

(*b*) any income or profits tax payable by the trust in respect of any income of the trust.

Related Sections: S. 104(1) Reference to trust or estate; s. 248(1), "common-law partner", "trust", s. 248(8) Occurrences as a consequence of death; s. 248(9) Definitions.

Interpretation Bulletins: *Secondary* — IT-305R4 Testamentary spouse trust.

▶ 108(5) ◀

(5) Interpretation. Except as otherwise provided in this Part,

(*a*) an amount included in computing the income for a taxation year of a beneficiary of a trust under subsection 104(13) or (14) or section 105 shall be deemed to be income of the beneficiary for the year from a property that is an interest in the trust and not from any other source, and

(*b*) an amount deductible in computing the amount that would, but for subsections 104(6) and (12), be the income of a trust for a taxation year shall not be deducted by a beneficiary of the trust in computing the beneficiary's income for a taxation year,

but, for greater certainty, nothing in this subsection shall affect the application of subsection 56(4.1), sections 74.1 to 75 and 120.4 and subsection 160(1.2) of this Act and section 74 of the *Income Tax Act*, chapter 148 of the Revised Statutes of Canada, 1952.

Editorial Note: Except as otherwise provided in Part I, s. 108(5) deems amounts received by a beneficiary from a trust to be income from property. Thus, generally, an amount received by a beneficiary of a trust loses its original character and identity as a particular type of income. There are several exceptions to s. 108(5)(*a*) which allow the income of the trust resident in Canada to retain its character. These exceptions can be found in s. 104(19) (taxable dividend), s. 104(20) (dividend other than taxable dividend), s. 104(21) (taxable capital gains), s. 104(22) (foreign source income), s. 104(27) (pension benefits), and s. 127(7) (investment tax credit), etc. These provisions are generally referred to as the flow-through provisions.

S. 108(5) does not affect the attribution rules in ss. 74.1 to 75; so, income from property (i.e., interest and dividend income) and the capital gains of the trust keep their nature for the purposes of these rules. Similarly, s. 108(5) does not affect the tax on split income of minor children imposed under s. 120.4.

Interpretation Bulletins: *Secondary* — IT-243R4, Dividend refund to private corporations.

Tax Window Files: Property Held in Trust for Corporation, *ROUND TABLE — 2004 APFF CONFERENCE, Question 25, October 8, 2004*, CRA Document No. 2004-0086931C6. Income from the rental property held by the trust would be included in Holdco's income under s. 104(13) and would be deemed by s. 108(5) to be income from property that is an interest in the trust.

▶ 108(6) ◀

(6) Variation of trusts. Where at any time the terms of a trust are varied

(*a*) for the purposes of subsections 104(4), (5) and (5.2) and subject to paragraph (*b*), the trust is, at and after that time, deemed to be the same trust as, and a continuation of, the trust immediately before that time;

(*b*) for greater certainty, paragraph (*a*) does not affect the application of paragraph 104(4)(*a.1*); and

(*c*) for the purposes of paragraph 53(2)(*h*), subsection 107(1), paragraph (*j*) of the definition "excluded right or interest" in subsection 128.1(10) and the definition "personal trust" in subsection 248(1), no interest of a beneficiary under the trust before it was varied is considered to be consideration for the interest of the beneficiary in the trust as varied.

Editorial Note: Essentially, the anti-avoidance rule in s. 108(6)(*a*) provides that, for purposes of the 21-year deemed realization rules, a trust will not be treated as a separate trust by reason of a variation of its terms. The purpose of this provision is to ensure that a trust may not delay the application of the deemed realization rules by means of a variation of its terms.

Related Sections: S. 104(1) Reference to trust or estate; s. 248(1), "trust".

► 108(7) ◄

(7) Interests acquired for consideration. For the purposes of paragraph 53(2)(*h*), subparagraph (*c*)(i) of the definition "exempt amount" in subsection 94(1), subsection 107(1), paragraph (*j*) of the definition "excluded right or interest" in subsection 128.1(10) and paragraph (*b*) of the definition "personal trust" in subsection 248(1),

(*a*) an interest in a trust is deemed not to be acquired for consideration solely because it was acquired in satisfaction of any right as a beneficiary under the trust to enforce payment of an amount by the trust; and

(*b*) if all the beneficial interests in a particular trust acquired by way of the transfer, assignment or other disposition of property to the particular trust were acquired by

(i) one person, or

(ii) two or more persons who would be related to each other if

(A) a trust and another person were related to each other, where the other person is a beneficiary under the trust or is related to a beneficiary under the trust, and

(B) a trust and another trust were related to each other, where a beneficiary under the trust is a beneficiary under the other trust or is related to a beneficiary under the other trust,

any beneficial interest in the particular trust acquired by such a person is deemed to have been acquired for no consideration.

History: S. 108(7)(*b*), the portion before subparagraph (i), was replaced by S.C. 2014, c. 39, s. 28(3), applicable to the 2016 and subsequent taxation years, and formerly read:

(*b*) where all the beneficial interests in a particular *inter vivos* trust acquired by way of the transfer, assignment or other disposition of property to the particular trust were acquired by

S. 108(7), the portion before paragraph (*a*) was amended by S.C. 2013, c. 34, s. 12(2), applicable to taxation years that end after 2006. The portion of s. 108(7) before paragraph (*a*) also applies to each earlier taxation year of a trust to which subsection 94(1) applies [should be 94(3) – CCH] and each taxation year of a beneficiary under the trust in which one of those earlier taxation years of the trust ends.

S. 108(7), the portion before (*a*), formerly read:

(7) *Interests acquired for consideration.* For the purposes of paragraph 53(2)(*h*), subsection 107(1), paragraph (*j*) of the definition "excluded right or interest" in subsection 128.1(10) and the definition "personal trust" in subsection 248(1),

Related Sections: S. 108(1), "beneficiary", "inter vivos trust", "trust"; s. 248(1), "amount", "disposition", "property"; s. 251(2) Definition of "related persons"; s. 251(3) Corporations related through a third corporation; s. 251(3.1) Relation where amalgamation or merger; s. 251(3.2) Amalgamation of related corporations; s. 251(4) Definitions concerning groups; s. 251(5) Control by related groups, options, etc; s. 251(6) Blood relationship, etc.

Division C — Computation of Taxable Income

SECTION 109: Deductions permitted by individuals

[Section 109 (except as noted below) was repealed by 1988, c. 55, s. 76. Paragraph 109(1)(*i*) was repealed by 1976-77, c. 4, s. 42(2). Subsection 109(3) was repealed by S.C. 1985, c. 45, s. 53(3)].

SECTION 110: Deductions permitted

Proposed Amendment

Notice of Ways and Means Motion to amend the Income Tax Act (June 17, 2019)

Section 110 of the Act is amended by adding the following before subsection (1):

SECTION 110 Definitions.

(0.1) The following definitions apply in this section.

specified person —*specified person* means a qualifying person other than a qualifying person that

(*a*) is a Canadian-controlled private corporation; or

(*b*) meets prescribed conditions.

vesting year —*vesting year*, of a security to be acquired under an agreement, means

(*a*) if the agreement specifies the calendar year in which the taxpayer's right to acquire the security first becomes exercisable (otherwise than as a consequence of an event that is not reasonably foreseeable at the time the agreement is entered into), that calendar year; and

(*b*) in any other case, the first calendar year in which the right to acquire the security can reasonably be expected to be exercised.

Applicable: On January 1, 2020.

▶ 110(1) ◀

(1) Deductions permitted. For the purpose of computing the taxable income of a taxpayer for a taxation year, there may be deducted such of the following amounts as are applicable:

Related Sections: S. 111.1 Order of applying provisions; s. 127.5 Obligation to pay minimum tax.

▶ 110(1)(a) ◀

(a) Charitable gifts — (Repealed by 1988, c. 55, s. 77(1).)

▶ 110(1)(b) ◀

(b) Gifts to Her Majesty — (Repealed by 1988, c. 55, s. 77(1).)

▶ 110(1)(b.1) ◀

(b.1) Gifts to institutions — (Repealed by 1988, c. 55, s. 77(1).)

▶ 110(1)(c) ◀

(c) Medical expenses — (Repealed by 1988, c. 55, s. 77(1).)

▶ 110(1)(d) ◀

(d) Employee options — an amount equal to 1/2 of the amount of the benefit deemed by subsection 7(1) to have been received by the taxpayer in the year in respect of a security that a particular qualifying person has agreed after February 15, 1984 to sell or issue under an agreement, in respect of the transfer or other disposition of rights under the agreement or as a result of the death of the taxpayer because the taxpayer immediately before death owned a right to acquire the security under the agreement, if

Proposed Amendment

Notice of Ways and Means Motion to amend the Income Tax Act (June 17, 2019)

The portion of paragraph 110(1)(*d*) of the Act before subparagraph (i) is replaced by the following:

(d) Employee options — an amount equal to 1/2 of the amount of the benefit deemed by subsection 7(1) to have been received by the taxpayer in the year in respect of a security (other than a security that is a non-qualified security) that a particular qualifying person has agreed after February 15, 1984 to sell or issue under an agreement, in respect of the transfer or other disposition of rights under the agreement or as a result of the death of the taxpayer because the taxpayer immediately before death owned a right to acquire the security under the agreement, if

Applicable: On January 1, 2020.

(i) the security was acquired under the agreement

(A) by the taxpayer or a person not dealing at arm's length with the taxpayer in circumstances described in paragraph 7(1)(*c*), or

(B) in the case of a benefit deemed by paragraph 7(1)(*e*) to have been received by the taxpayer, within the first taxation year of the graduated rate estate of the taxpayer, by

(I) the graduated rate estate of the taxpayer,

(II) a person who is a "beneficiary" (as defined in subsection 108(1)) under the graduated rate estate of the taxpayer, or

(III) a person in whom the rights of the taxpayer under the agreement have vested as a result of the death,

(i.1) the security

(A) is a prescribed share at the time of its sale or issue, as the case may be,

(B) would have been a prescribed share if it were issued or sold to the taxpayer at the time the taxpayer disposed of rights under the agreement,

(B.1) in the case of a benefit deemed by paragraph 7(1)(*e*) to have been received by the taxpayer, would have been a prescribed share if it were issued or sold to the taxpayer immediately before the death of the taxpayer,

(C) would have been a unit of a mutual fund trust at the time of its sale or issue if those units issued by the trust that were not identical to the security had not been issued,

(D) would have been a unit of a mutual fund trust if

(I) it were issued or sold to the taxpayer at the time the taxpayer disposed of rights under the agreement, and

(II) those units issued by the trust that were not identical to the security had not been issued, or

(E) in the case of a benefit deemed by paragraph 7(1)(*e*) to have been received by the taxpayer, would have been a unit of a mutual fund trust if

(I) it were issued or sold to the taxpayer immediately before the death of the taxpayer, and

(II) those units issued by the trust that were not identical to the security had not been issued,

(ii) where rights under the agreement were not acquired by the taxpayer as a result of a disposition of rights to which subsection 7(1.4) applied,

(A) the amount payable by the taxpayer to acquire the security under the agreement is not less than the amount by which

(I) the fair market value of the security at the time the agreement was made

exceeds

(II) the amount, if any, paid by the taxpayer to acquire the right to acquire the security, and

(B) at the time immediately after the agreement was made, the taxpayer was dealing at arm's length with

(I) the particular qualifying person,

(II) each other qualifying person that, at the time, was an employer of the taxpayer and was not dealing at arm's length with the particular qualifying person, and

(III) the qualifying person of which the taxpayer had, under the agreement, a right to acquire a security, and

(iii) where rights under the agreement were acquired by the taxpayer as a result of one or more dispositions to which subsection 7(1.4) applied,

(A) the amount payable by the taxpayer to acquire the security under the agreement is not less than the amount that was included, in respect of the security, in the amount determined under subparagraph 7(1.4)(*c*)(ii) with respect to the most recent of those dispositions,

(B) at the time immediately after the agreement the rights under which were the subject of the first of those dispositions (in this subparagraph referred to as the "original agreement") was made, the taxpayer was dealing at arm's length with

(I) the qualifying person that made the original agreement,

(II) each other qualifying person that, at the time, was an employer of the taxpayer and was not dealing at arm's length with the qualifying person that made the original agreement, and

(III) the qualifying person of which the taxpayer had, under the original agreement, a right to acquire a security,

(C) the amount that was included, in respect of each particular security that the taxpayer had a right to acquire under the original agreement, in the amount determined under subparagraph 7(1.4)(*c*)(iv) with respect to the first of those dispositions was not less than the amount by which

(I) the fair market value of the particular security at the time the original agreement was made

exceeded

(II) the amount, if any, paid by the taxpayer to acquire the right to acquire the security, and

(D) for the purpose of determining if the condition in paragraph 7(1.4)(*c*) was satisfied with respect to each of the particular dispositions following the first of those dispositions,

(I) the amount that was included, in respect of each particular security that could be acquired under the agreement the rights under which were the subject of the particular disposition, in the amount determined under subparagraph 7(1.4)(*c*)(iv) with respect to the particular disposition

was not less than

(II) the amount that was included, in respect of the particular security, in the amount determined under subparagraph 7(1.4)(*c*)(ii) with respect to the last of those dispositions preceding the particular disposition;

Editorial Note: The deduction under s. 110(1)(*d*) effectively means the security option benefit is taxed at the capital gains inclusion rate. Typically, the deduction is allowed if the security is a prescribed share or a unit of a mutual fund trust, the option exercise price (plus the amount paid to acquire the option, if any) was not less than the fair market value of the security at the time the option was granted, and the employee was dealing at arm's length with the employer (and the corporation or mutual fund that granted the option, if it was not the employer).

For acquisitions of securities and dispositions of options after 4 PM EST on March 4, 2010, the one-half deduction under s. 110(1)(*d*) is generally not allowed unless the employee or a person not dealing at arm's length with the employee acquires the securities, such that employees receiving employer "cash-outs" of options are not eligible for the deduction. An exception is provided under s. 110(1.1), which effectively provides that the employee need not acquire the securities, if the employer elects that it and any non-arm's length person will not deduct any amount in respect of a payment made to or for the benefit of the employee for the employee's transfer or disposition of the option (other than a "designated amount", which is generally a payment made to an arm's length person for the purpose of managing the qualifying person's financial risk in respect of the option agreement), the employer provides the employee with evidence in writing of such election, and the employee files such evidence with his or her return of income for the year in which the stock option deduction is claimed.

Paragraph 110(1)(*d*) was amended for acquisitions of securities and transfers or dispositions of rights occurring after 4 PM EST on March 4, 2010, to permit the one-half deduction in computing the taxable income of a deceased taxpayer who is deemed by paragraph 7(1)(*e*) to have received a benefit because he or she owned a right to acquire a security under an employee stock option plan immediately before death.

For more information regarding claiming the s. 110(1)(*d*) deduction where an option's exercise price is subsequently reduced after having been granted, see the editorial notes for s. 110(1.7) and (1.8).

History: S. 110(1)(*d*), the portion before subparagraph (ii) was replaced by S.C. 2017, c. 33, s. 38(1), applicable in respect of acquisitions of securities and transfers or dispositions of rights occurring after 4:00 pm Eastern Standard Time on March 4, 2010, except that for taxation years ending before 2016, the references to "graduated rate estate" in paragraph 110(1)(*d*) are to be read as "estate". S. 110(1)(*d*), the portion before subparagraph (ii) formerly read:

(*d*) *Employee options* — an amount equal to 1/2 of the amount of the benefit deemed by subsection 7(1) to have been received by the taxpayer in the year in respect of a security that a particular qualifying person has agreed after February 15, 1984 to sell or issue under an agreement, or in respect of the transfer or other disposition of rights under the agreement, if

(i) the security was acquired under the agreement by the taxpayer or a person not dealing at arm's length with the taxpayer in circumstances described in paragraph 7(1)(*c*),

(i.1) the security

(A) is a prescribed share at the time of its sale or issue, as the case may be,

(B) would have been a prescribed share if it were issued or sold to the taxpayer at the time the taxpayer disposed of rights under the agreement,

(C) would have been a unit of a mutual fund trust at the time of its sale or issue if those units issued by the trust that were not identical to the security had not been issued, or

(D) would have been a unit of a mutual fund trust if

(I) it were issued or sold to the taxpayer at the time the taxpayer disposed of rights under the agreement, and

(II) those units issued by the trust that were not identical to the security had not been issued,

S. 110(1)(*d*)(i) was replaced, and subparagraph (i.1) was added, by S.C. 2010, c. 25, s. 20(1), applicable in respect of acquisitions of securities and transfers or dispositions of rights occurring after 4:00 p.m. Eastern Standard Time, March 4, 2010. S. 110(1)(*d*)(i) formerly read:

(i) the security

(A) is a prescribed share at the time of its sale or issue, as the case may be,

(B) would have been a prescribed share if it were issued or sold to the taxpayer at the time the taxpayer disposed of rights under the agreement,

(C) would have been a unit of a mutual fund trust at the time of its sale or issue if those units issued by the trust that were not identical to the security had not been issued, or

(D) would have been a unit of a mutual fund trust if

(I) it were issued or sold to the taxpayer at the time the taxpayer disposed of rights under the agreement, and

(II) those units issued by the trust that were not identical to the security had not been issued,

Related Regulations: 6204.

Related Sections: 7(1) Agreement to issue securities to employees; S. 7(1.4) Exchange of options; s. 7(1.5) Rules where securities exchanged; s. 7(9) Meaning of "qualifying acquisition"; s. 7(14) Deferral deemed valid; s. 110(1)(*d*.01) Charitable donation of employee option securities; s. 110(1)(*d*.1) Employee options for CCPC shares; s. 110(1.5) Determination of amounts relating to employee security options; s. 110(2.1) Charitable donation — proceeds of disposition of employee option securities; s. 115(1) Non-resident's taxable income in Canada; s. 127.52(1)(*h*) Adjusted taxable income determined; s. 164(6.1) Realization of deceased employees' options.

Canadian Petroleum Tax Journal: Attracting and Retaining Executives and Employees with Tax-Efficient Incentives, Julie Y. Lee, 2001, Vol. 14, No. 1.

Canadian Tax Foundation: Heakes, *Employee Share Ownership and Similar Arrangements for CCPCs*, 2017 Ontario Tax Conference 14:1–13; Coburn, *Stock Options, With a Focus on Start-Ups*, 2017 British Columbia Tax Conference 13:1–23; Carbone, *The Stock Option Deduction and Prescribed Shares*, 2017 Canadian Tax Focus 7(4):5; Infanti, *Employee Stock Option Rules and Legally Binding Agreements*, 2017 Tax for the Owner Manager 17(2):1–2; Wen, *Stock Options in Merger and Acquisition Transactions*, 2016 Canadian Tax Focus 6(2):9; Morreale, *Stock Option Deduction Is Available on Death*, 2015 Canadian Tax Focus 2(3):13; Nijhawan and Sieker, *Topical Issues in Equity-Based Employee Compensation*, 2008 Conference Report 15:1–36; Colquhoun et al., *Executive Compensation: Current and Deferred Remuneration Strategies — "Is Aligning Just a Line?"*, 2003 Conference Report 15:1–26; Ebel and Stewart, *Update on Employee Stock Options and Employee Benefits*, 2002 Conference Report 27:1–39; Robinson and Hoeven, *Repricing Stock Options: An Update*, 2002 Tax for the Owner-Manager 2(4):28–29; Sandler, *The Tax Treatment of Employee Stock Options: Generous to a Fault*, 2001 Canadian Tax Journal 2:259–302; Van Cauwenberghe, *Taxation of Employee Stock Options — A Review and Update*, 2001 Prairie Provinces Tax Conference 2:1–53; Addison and Korn, *Employee Stock Options: An Update*, 2000 Canadian Tax Journal 3:778–811.

Tax Profile: July 2010 — Employee Compensation Planning: Stock-Based Incentive Compensation Plans; March 2006 — Some Tax Considerations for Investing in Silicon Valley North.

Tax Topics: No. 1613, Technical Amendments Allow Reduction in Exercise Price of Employee Stock Options.

Interpretation Bulletins: *Secondary* — IT-113R4 Benefits to employees — Stock options.

Tax Window Files: Employee Stock Option — Prescribed Shares, *Technical Interpretation, Financial Sector and Exempt Entities Division, October 12, 2007*, CRA Document No. 2007-0251101E5; Employee Stock Option Deduction — Prescribed Shares, *Technical Interpretation, Financial Sector and Exempt Entities Division, August 29, 2005*, CRA Document No. 2005-0125811E5; Employee Share Purchase Plan (ESPP), *Technical Interpretation, Financial Industries Division, April 25, 2005*, CRA Document No. 2005-0112901E5; Stock Options — Exchange, *December 1, 2004*, CRA Document No. 2004-0058171R3; Reduction in Exercise Price of Security Options, *Technical Interpretation, Financial Industries Division, October 29, 2004*, CRA Document No. 2004-0093241E5; Employee Stock Option Deduction, *Technical Interpretation, Financial Industries Division, May 31, 2004*, CRA Document No. 2004-0077341I7; Employee Stock Option — Election To Receive/Pay Cash, *Technical Interpretation, Income Tax Rulings Directorate, December 23, 2003*, CRA Document No. 2003-0049927.

Cases: In December 2001, the taxpayers were granted options to acquire shares of Cybectec, a CCPC. On January 26, 2007, Cooper Inc. acquired practically all Cybectec's assets and two days later the taxpayers took up their options to acquire Cybectec shares at the option price of 20 cents per share. They resold these the same day to Cybectec's parent corporation for $1.2583 per share, subsequently reporting as income for tax benefit purposes the difference between the option take up price and the proceeds of disposition of the shares. Regulation 6204(1) did not invalidate their claim, and the taxpayers were allowed a stock option deduction under paragraph 110(1)(*d*). *Montminy et al v. The Queen*, 2017 DTC 5091 (CAF)

► 110(1)(d.01) ◄

(d.01) Charitable donation of employee option securities — subject to subsection (2.1), if the taxpayer disposes of a security acquired in the year by the taxpayer under an agreement referred to in subsection 7(1) by making a gift of the security to a qualified donee, an amount in respect of the disposition of the security equal to 1/2 of the lesser of the benefit deemed by paragraph 7(1)(*a*) to have been received by the taxpayer in the year in respect of the acquisition of the security and the amount that would have been that benefit had the value of the security at the time of its acquisition by the taxpayer been equal to the value of the security at the time of the disposition, if

(i) the security is a security described in subparagraph 38(*a*.1)(i),

(ii) (Repealed by S.C. 2002, c. 9, S. 33(1).)

(iii) the gift is made in the year and on or before the day that is 30 days after the day on which the taxpayer acquired the security, and

(iv) the taxpayer is entitled to a deduction under paragraph (*d*) in respect of the acquisition of the security;

Editorial Note: S. 110(1)(*d*.01) provides a deduction from the employee benefit in s. 7(1) where an employee makes a charitable donation of a security acquired under an employee stock option agreement. The combination of this deduction and the deduction under s. 110(1)(*d*) provides that the employment benefit is taxed at the reduced capital gains inclusion rate for donations of employee stock option securities (s. 38(*a*.1)). For such a donation, the inclusion rate is zero for gifts made after May 1, 2006.

Related Sections: S. 7(1.3) Order of disposition of securities; s. 7(1.5) Rules where securities exchanged; s. 7(2) Securities held by trustee; s. 7(6) Sale to trustee for employees; s. 7(7) Definitions; s. 110(1)(*d*) Employee options; s. 110(2.1) Charitable donation — proceeds of disposition of employee option securities; s. 127.52(1)(*h*) Adjusted taxable income determined.

Tax Profile: May 2002 — Update on Charitable Giving.

► 110(1)(d.1) ◄

(d.1) Idem — where the taxpayer

(i) is deemed, under paragraph 7(1)(*a*) by virtue of subsection 7(1.1), to have received a benefit in the year in respect of a share acquired by the taxpayer after May 22, 1985,

(ii) has not disposed of the share (otherwise than as a consequence of the taxpayer's death) or exchanged the share within two years after the date the taxpayer acquired it, and

(iii) has not deducted an amount under paragraph (*d*) in respect of the benefit in computing the taxpayer's taxable income for the year,

an amount equal to 1/2 of the amount of the benefit;

Editorial Note: Unlike the deduction under s. 110(1)(*d*), there is no requirement under s. 110(1)(*d*.1) that the option exercise price be equal to or greater than the fair market value of the securities at the time the option was granted. Note that the two-year holding period is waived in the case of a deemed disposition upon the taxpayer's death (which will occur under s. 70(5) or (6)).

Related Sections: S. 7(1.1) Employee stock options; s. 7(1.3) Order of disposition of securities; s. 7(1.5) Rules where securities exchanged; s. 7(1.6) Emigrant; s. 7(2) Securities held by trustee; s. 7(6) Sale to trustee for employees; s. 8(12) Forfeiture of securities by employee.

Canadian Petroleum Tax Journal: Attracting and Retaining Executives and Employees with Tax-Efficient Incentives, Julie Y. Lee, 2001, Vol. 14, No. 1.

Canadian Tax Foundation: Coburn, *Stock Options, With a Focus on Start-Ups*, 2017 British Columbia Tax Conference 13:1–23.

Tax Profile: March 2006 — Some Tax Considerations for Investing in Silicon Valley North.

Interpretation Bulletins: *Secondary* — IT-113R4 Benefits to employees — Stock options.

▶ 110(1)(d.2) ◀

(d.2) Prospector's and grubstaker's shares — where the taxpayer has, under paragraph 35(1)(*d*), included an amount in the taxpayer's income for the year in respect of a share received after May 22, 1985, an amount equal to 1/2 of that amount unless that amount is exempt from income tax in Canada by reason of a provision contained in a tax convention or agreement with another country that has the force of law in Canada;

Editorial Note: Where a prospector or grubstaker has utilized s. 35(1) to transfer (roll over) mining property to a corporation in exchange for shares of that company and then disposes of those shares, s. 110(1)(*d.2*) provides a deduction equal to 1/2 of the amount that — unless exempt by tax treaty — was upon disposal included in income under s. 35(1)(*d*). This has the effect of reducing the amount included in income to the same amount as the inclusion rates for capital gains.

▶ 110(1)(d.3) ◀

(d.3) Employer's shares — where the taxpayer has, under subsection 147(10.4), included an amount in computing the taxpayer's income for the year, an amount equal to 1/2 of that amount;

▶ 110(1)(e) ◀

(e) Mental or physical impairment — (Repealed by 1988, c. 55, s. 77(6).)

Proposed Amendment

Notice of Ways and Means Motion to amend the Income Tax Act (June 17, 2019)

Subsection 110(1) of the Act is amended by adding the following after paragraph (*d*.3):

(e) Employer deduction — non-qualified securities — an amount equal to the amount of the benefit deemed by subsection 7(1) to have been received by an individual in the year in respect of a non-qualified security that the taxpayer has agreed to sell or issue under an agreement with the individual, if

(i) the taxpayer is a specified person,

(ii) at the time the agreement was entered into, the taxpayer was the employer of the individual,

(iii) an amount would have been deductible in computing the taxable income of the individual under paragraph (*d*) if the security were not a nonqualifying security, and

(iv) the conditions in subsection (1.9) are met in respect of the security;

Applicable: In respect of agreements to sell or issue securities entered into after 2019.

▶ 110(1)(e.1) ◀

(e.1) Dependant having impairment — (Repealed by 1988, c. 55, s. 77(6).)

▶ 110(1)(e.2) ◀

(e.2) Deduction transfer — (Repealed by 1986, c. 6, s. 55(5).)

▶ 110(1)(f) ◀

(f) Deductions for payments — any social assistance payment made on the basis of a means, needs or income test and included because of clause 56(1)(*a*)(i)(A) or paragraph 56(1)(*u*) in computing the taxpayer's income for the year or any amount that is

(i) an amount exempt from income tax in Canada because of a provision contained in a tax convention or agreement with another country that has the force of law in Canada,

(ii) compensation received under an employees' or workers' compensation law of Canada or a province in respect of an injury, disability or death, except any such compensation received by a person as the employer or former employer of the person in respect of whose injury, disability or death the compensation was paid,

(iii) income from employment with a prescribed international organization,

(iv) the taxpayer's income from employment with a prescribed international non-governmental organization, where the taxpayer

(A) was not, at any time in the year, a Canadian citizen,

(B) was a non-resident person immediately before beginning that employment in Canada, and

(C) if the taxpayer is resident in Canada, became resident in Canada solely for the purpose of that employment, or

(v) the lesser of

(A) the employment income earned by the taxpayer as a member of the Canadian Forces, or as a police officer, while serving on a deployed international operational mission (as determined by the Minister of National Defence, the Minister of Public Safety and Emergency Preparedness or by a person designated by either Minister), and

(B) the employment income that would have been so earned by the taxpayer if the taxpayer had been paid at the maximum rate of pay that applied, from time to time during the mission, to a Lieutenant-Colonel (General Service Officers) of the Canadian Forces,

to the extent that it is included in computing the taxpayer's income for the year;

History: S. 110(1)(*f*)(v)(A) was replaced by S.C. 2018, c. 27, s. 9(2), applicable to the 2017 and subsequent taxation years, and formerly read:

(A) the employment income earned by the taxpayer as a member of the Canadian Forces, or as a police officer, while serving on a deployed operational mission (as determined by the Department of National Defence or the Department of Public Safety and Emergency Preparedness) that is

(I) assessed for risk allowance at level 3 or higher (as determined by the Department of National Defence), or

(II) assessed at a risk score greater than 1.99 and less than 2.50 (as determined by the Department of National Defence) and designated by the Minister of Finance, and

S. 110(1)(*f*)(v)(A) was replaced by S.C. 2018, c. 27, s. 9(1), applicable in respect of missions initiated after September 2012 and in respect of missions initiated before October 2012 that were not prescribed under Part LXXV of the *Income Tax Regulations* as that Part read on February 28, 2013. S. 110(1)(*f*)(v)(A) formerly read:

(A) the employment income earned by the taxpayer as a member of the Canadian Forces, or as a police officer, while serving on a deployed international operational mission (as determined by the Minister of National Defence or by a person designated by that Minister), and

S. 110(1)(*f*)(v)(A) and (B) were replaced by S.C. 2018, c. 12, s. 9(1), applicable to the 2017 and subsequent taxation years, and formerly read:

(A) the employment income earned by the taxpayer as a member of the Canadian Forces, or as a police officer, while serving on a deployed operational mission (as determined by the Department of National Defence) that is

(I) assessed for risk allowance at level 3 or higher (as determined by the Department of National Defence), or

(II) assessed at a risk score greater than 1.99 and less than 2.50 (as determined by the Department of National Defence) and designated by the Minister of Finance, and

(B) the employment income that would have been so earned by the taxpayer if the taxpayer had been paid at the maximum rate of pay that applied, from time to time during the mission, to a non-commissioned member of the Canadian Forces;

S. 110(1)(*f*)(v)(A) was replaced by S.C. 2013, c. 33, s. 7(1), applicable in respect of missions initiated after September 2012 and in respect of missions initiated before October 2012 that were not prescribed under Part LXXV of the *Income Tax Regulations* as that Part read on February 28, 2013.

S. 110(1)(*f*)(v)(A) formerly read:

(A) the employment income earned by the taxpayer as a member of the Canadian Forces, or as a police officer, while serving on

(I) a deployed operational mission (as determined by the Department of National Defence) that is assessed for risk allowance at level 3 or higher (as determined by the Department of National Defence),

(II) a prescribed mission that is assessed for risk allowance at level 2 (as determined by the Department of National Defence), or

(III) any other mission that is prescribed, and

Related Regulations: 232; 7500; 8900.

Related Sections: S. 56(1)(*u*) Social assistance payments; s. 56(1)(*v*) Worker's compensation; s. 126(3) Employees of international organizations; s. 127.52(1)(*h*) Adjusted taxable income determined; s. 212(1)(*h*) Pension benefits.

Income Tax Technical News: Issue No. 35, Treaty Residence — Resident of Convenience.

Interpretation Bulletins: *Primary* — IT-202R2 Employees' or workers' compensation. *Secondary* — IT-528 Transfers of funds between registered plans.

Cases: The taxpayer, a federal employee, was injured while engaged in his employment duties. Pursuant to the terms of the applicable Collective Agreement, he made a claim to the provincial workers' compensation board, which approved his claim. He was then granted injury-on-duty leave and received his full salary and a T4 was issued. 85% of that income constituted workers' compensation payments "received under an employees' or workers' compensation law" that were reportable as income under paragraph 56(1)(*v*) and consequently was deductible under subparagraph 110(1)(*f*)(ii). *McCarthy v. The Queen*, 2019 DTC 1054 (TCC)

The corporate taxpayer, a resident of Luxembourg, received a capital gain from the sale of its shares of a wholly-owned Canadian subsidiary and claimed the gain was exempt from tax under Article 13(5) of the *Canada-Luxembourg Income Tax Convention* (1999). Canada has the right to tax capital gains from the disposition of shares where those shares derive their value principally from immovable property located in Canada, except for excluded property where the business of the corporation is carried on in the property. A resource property qualifies as excluded property when developed in accordance with the industry's best practices. The taxpayer used the best practices of the industry to develop its reserves at each stage of development. All of the taxpayer's interest in the Canadian resource property qualified as excluded property, and GAAR did not apply to preclude the taxpayer from claiming the available treaty exemption. *Alta Energy Luxembourg S.A.R.L. v. The Queen*, 2018 DTC 1120 (TCC) [under appeal]

The day on which the exempt amount arose determines the appropriate exchange rate that should be used to convert the US dollar amount into Canadian dollars. The exempt amount arises on the date of receipt of each benefit payment, and the Minister's use of the annual average exchange rate for 2010 was appropriate for converting the deductible amount. *Korfage v. The Queen*, 2016 DTC 1054 (TCC)

An RCMP officer who volunteered to participate in a U.N. peace mission in Haiti was denied a s. 110(1)(*f*) deduction since he was employed by the RCMP, not the U.N., during the mission. *Lalancette v. The Queen*, 2002 DTC 7391 (F.C.A.), affirming 2001 DTC 352 (T.C.C.).

► 110(1)(g) ◄

(g) Financial assistance — any amount that

(i) is received by the taxpayer in the year under a program referred to in subparagraph 56(1)(*r*)(ii) or (iii), a program established under the authority of the *Department of Employment and Social Development Act* or a prescribed program,

(ii) is financial assistance for the payment of tuition fees of the taxpayer that are not included in computing an amount deductible under subsection 118.5(1) in computing the taxpayer's tax payable under this Part for any taxation year,

(iii) is included in computing the taxpayer's income for the year, and

(iv) is not otherwise deductible in computing the taxpayer's taxable income for the year;

Editorial Note: Paragraph 110(1)(*g*) provides a deduction for certain financial assistance payments received by an individual in respect of tuition fees that do not qualify for the tuition tax credit.

History: S. 110(1)(*g*)(i) was amended by S.C. 2013, c. 40, s. 236(1)(*e*)(ii), by replacing "*Department of Human Resources and Skills Development Act*" with "*Department of Employment and Social Development Act*", in force December 12, 2013.

Related Sections: S. 60(*n*) Repayment of pension or benefits.

Income Tax Folios: *Secondary* — S1-F2-C3 Scholarships, Research Grants and Other Education Assistance.

Tax Window Files: Training assistance for ABE, *August 9, 2016*, CRA Document No. 2016-0644171E5.

► 110(1)(h) ◄

(h) [U.S. social security benefits] — 35 per cent of the total of all benefits (in this paragraph referred to as "U.S. social security benefits") that are received by the taxpayer in the taxation year and to which paragraph 5 of Article XVIII of the *Convention between Canada and the United States of America with respect to Taxes on Income and on Capital* as set out in Schedule I to the *Canada–United States Tax Convention Act, 1984*, S.C. 1984, c. 20, applies, if

(i) the taxpayer has continuously during a period that begins before 1996 and ends in the taxation year, been resident in Canada, and has received U.S. social security benefits in each taxation year that ends in that period, or

(ii) in the case where the benefits are payable to the taxpayer in respect of a deceased individual,

(A) the taxpayer was, immediately before the deceased individual's death, the deceased individual's spouse or common-law partner,

(B) the taxpayer has continuously during a period that begins at the time of the deceased individual's death and ends in the taxation year, been resident in Canada,

(C) the deceased individual was, in respect of the taxation year in which the deceased individual died, a taxpayer described in subparagraph (i), and

(D) in each taxation year that ends in a period that begins before 1996 and that ends in the taxation year, the taxpayer, the deceased individual, or both of them, received U.S. social security benefits.

History: S. 110(1)(*h*) was added by S.C. 2010, c. 12, s. 12(1), applicable to the 2010 and subsequent taxation years.

► 110(1)(i) ◄

(i) Unemployment insurance benefit repayment — (Repealed by S.C. 1994, c. 7, Sched. II, s. 78(3).)

► 110(1)(j) ◄

(j) Home relocation loan — (Repealed by S.C. 2017, c. 20, s. 8(1).)

History: S. 110(1)(*j*) was repealed by S.C. 2017, c. 20, s. 8(1), in force January 1, 2018, and formerly read:

(*j*) *Home relocation loan* — where the taxpayer has, by virtue of section 80.4, included an amount in the taxpayer's income for the year in respect of a benefit received by the taxpayer in respect of a home relocation loan, the least of

(i) the amount of the benefit that would have been deemed to have been received by the taxpayer under section 80.4 in the year if that section had applied only in respect of the home relocation loan,

(ii) the amount of interest for the year that would be computed under paragraph 80.4(1)(*a*) in respect of the home relocation loan if that loan were in the amount of $25,000 and were extinguished on the earlier of

(A) the day that is five years after the day on which the home relocation loan was made, and

(B) the day on which the home relocation loan was extinguished, and

(iii) the amount of the benefit deemed to have been received by the taxpayer under section 80.4 in the year; and

▶ 110(1)(k) ◀

(k) Part VI.1 tax — the amount determined by multiplying the taxpayer's tax payable under subsection 191.1(1) for the year by

(i) if the taxation year ends before 2010, 3,

(ii) if the taxation year ends after 2009 and before 2012, 3.2, and

(iii) if the taxation year ends after 2011, 3.5.

Editorial Note: The s. 110(1)(*k*) deduction is intended to effectively offset the Part VI.1 tax payable against corporation income tax payable for the year, or for another year through the non-capital loss carryback and carryforward mechanism. The credit may be effectively greater or less than the Part VI.1 tax, depending on the actual corporate tax rate.

History: S. 110(1)(*k*) was replaced by S.C. 2013, c. 34, s. 237(1), applicable to the 2003 and subsequent taxation years, and formerly read:

(*k*) *Part VI.1 tax* — $^{9}/_{4}$ of the tax payable under subsection 191.1(1) by the taxpayer for the year.

Related Sections: S. 111(5) Deduction of non-capital or farm losses.

Tax Profile: June 2003 — The December 20, 2002 Technical Amendments to the *Income Tax Act*.

▶ 110(1.1) ◀

(1.1) Election by particular qualifying person. For the purpose of computing the taxable income of a taxpayer for a taxation year, paragraph (1)(*d*) shall be read without reference to its subparagraph (i) in respect of all rights granted to the taxpayer under an agreement to sell or issue securities referred to in subsection 7(1) if

(*a*) the particular qualifying person elects in prescribed form that neither the particular qualifying person nor any person not dealing at arm's length with the particular qualifying person will deduct in computing its income for a taxation year any amount (other than a designated amount described in subsection (1.2)) in respect of a payment to or for the benefit of a taxpayer for the taxpayer's transfer or disposition of rights under the agreement;

(*b*) the particular qualifying person files the election with the Minister;

(*c*) the particular qualifying person provides the taxpayer or, if the taxpayer is deceased, the graduated rate estate of the taxpayer, with evidence in writing of the election; and

(*d*) the taxpayer or, if the taxpayer is deceased, the graduated rate estate of the taxpayer, files the evidence with the Minister with the taxpayer's return of income for the year in which a deduction under paragraph (1)(*d*) is claimed.

Editorial Note: For acquisitions of securities and dispositions of options after 4 PM EST on March 4, 2010, either the taxpayer, or a person described in s. 7(1)(*c*), must actually acquire the securities specified under the agreement. While this would generally preclude eligibility of so-called employer "cash-outs of options" for the s. 110(1)(*d*) deduction, the deduction will still be allowed to a qualifying person who elects under s. 110(1.1) that no payments in consideration for the release or surrender of the option — in excess of the s. 110(1.2) "designated amount" — will be deducted from income.

Subsection 110(1.1) has been amended effective 4 PM EST on March 4, 2010, to provide for situations where the taxpayer is deceased and his or her terminal return is handled by the taxpayer's graduated rate estate, or, for taxation years before 2016, the taxpayer's estate.

History: S. 110(1.1)(*c*) and (*d*) were replaced by S.C. 2017, c. 33, s. 38(2), applicable in respect of acquisitions of securities and transfers or dispositions of rights occurring after 4:00 pm Eastern Standard Time on March 4, 2010, except that for taxation years ending before 2016, the references to "graduated rate estate" in paragraphs (1.1)(*c*) and (*d*) are to be read as "estate". S. 110(1.1)(*c*) and (*d*) formerly read:

(*c*) the particular qualifying person provides the taxpayer with evidence in writing of the election; and

(*d*) the taxpayer files the evidence with the Minister with the taxpayer's return of income for the year in which a deduction under paragraph (1)(*d*) is claimed.

S. 110(1.1) was added by S.C. 2010, c. 25, s. 20(2), applicable in respect of acquisitions of securities and transfers or dispositions of rights occurring after 4:00 p.m. Eastern Standard Time, March 4, 2010.

Canadian Tax Foundation: Wen, *Stock Options in Merger and Acquisition Transactions*, 2016 Canadian Tax Focus 6(2):9; Forgie et al., *Structuring Stock Options in Light of the 2010 Budget and Other Current Issues in Executive Compensation*, 2011 Conference Report 13:1–29.

Tax Window Files: Election under 110(1.1), *November 1, 2017*, CRA Document No. 2016-0674411E5.

▶ 110(1.2) ◀

(1.2) Designated amount. For the purposes of subsection (1.1), an amount is a designated amount if the following conditions are met:

(*a*) the amount would otherwise be deductible in computing the income of the particular qualifying person in the absence of subsection (1.1);

(*b*) the amount is payable to a person

(i) with whom the particular qualifying person deals at arm's length, and

(ii) who is neither an employee of the particular qualifying person nor of any person not dealing at arm's length with the particular qualifying person; and

(*c*) the amount is payable in respect of an arrangement entered into for the purpose of managing the particular qualifying person's financial risk associated with a potential increase in value of the securities under the agreement described in subsection (1.1).

Editorial Note: See the editorial note for s. 110(1.1).

History: S. 110(1.2) was added by S.C. 2010, c. 25, s. 20(2), applicable in respect of acquisitions of securities and transfers or dispositions of rights occurring after 4:00 p.m. Eastern Standard Time, March 4, 2010.

▶ 110(1.3) ◀

(1.3) Designated mission — (Repealed by S.C. 2018, c. 12, s. 9(2).)

Proposed Amendment

Notice of Ways and Means Motion to amend the Income Tax Act (June 17, 2019)

Section 110 of the Act is amended by adding the following after subsection (1.2):

(1.3) Determination of non-qualified securities. Subsection (1.31) applies to a taxpayer in respect of an agreement if

(*a*) a particular specified person agrees to sell or issue securities of the particular specified person (or another specified person that does not deal at arm's length with the particular specified person) to the taxpayer under the agreement; and

(*b*) at the time the agreement is entered into (in subsection (1.31) referred to as the "relevant time") the taxpayer is an employee of the particular specified person (or another specified person that does not deal at arm's length with the particular specified person).

(1.31) Annual vesting limit. If this subsection applies to a taxpayer in respect of an agreement, the securities to be sold or issued under the agreement, for each vesting year of those securities, are deemed to be non-qualified securities for the purposes of this section in the proportion determined by the formula

$$A/B$$

where

A is the amount determined by the formula

$$C + D - \$200{,}000$$

where

C is the total of all amounts each of which is the fair market value at the relevant time of each security under the agreement that has that same vesting year, and

D is the lesser of

(i) $200,000, and

(ii) the total of all amounts each of which is an amount determined for C in respect of securities that have that same vesting year to be acquired under agreements (other than the agreement) entered into at or before the relevant time with the particular specified person referred to in subsection (1.3) (or another specified person that does not deal at arm's length with the particular specified person); and

B is the amount determined for C.

Applicable: In respect of agreements to sell or issue securities entered into after 2019.

History: S. 110(1.3) was repealed by S.C. 2018, c. 12, s. 9(2), applicable to the 2017 and subsequent taxation years, and formerly read:

(1.3) *Designated mission.* The Minister of Finance may, on the recommendation of the Minister of National Defence (in respect of members of the Canadian Forces) or the Minister of Public Safety (in respect of police officers), designate a deployed operational mission for the purposes of subclause (1)(*f*)(v)(A)(II). The designation shall specify the day on which it comes into effect, which may precede the day on which the designation is made.

S. 110(1.3) was added by S.C. 2013, c. 33, s. 7(2), applicable in respect of missions initiated after September 2012 and in respect of missions initiated before October 2012 that were not prescribed under Part LXXV of the *Income Tax Regulations* as that Part read on February 28, 2013.

▶ 110(1.4) ◀

(1.4) Replacement of home relocation loan — (Repealed by S.C. 2017, c. 20, s. 8(2).)

Proposed Amendment

Notice of Ways and Means Motion to amend the Income Tax Act (June 17, 2019)

Section 110 of the Act is amended by adding the following after subsection (1.2):

(1.4) Non-qualified security designation. If a particular specified person agrees, at any time, to sell or issue one or more securities of the particular specified person (or of another specified person with which the particular specified person does not deal at arm's length) to an employee of the particular specified person and the particular specified person designates one or more securities to be sold or issued under the agreement as non-qualified securities in the agreement, those securities are deemed to be non-qualified securities for the purposes of this section.

(1.41) Ordering of acquisition of securities. If a taxpayer acquires a security under an agreement and the acquired security could be a security that is not a non-qualified security, the security is to be considered a security that is not a non-qualified security for the purposes of this section.

Applicable: In respect of agreements to sell or issue securities entered into after 2019.

History: S. 110(1.4) was repealed by S.C. 2017, c. 20, s. 8(2), in force January 1, 2018, and formerly read:

(1.4) *Replacement of home relocation loan.* For the purposes of paragraph (1)(*j*), a loan received by a taxpayer that is used to repay a home relocation loan shall be deemed to be the same loan as the relocation loan and to have been made on the same day as the relocation loan.

▶ 110(1.5) ◀

(1.5) Determination of amounts relating to employee security options. For the purpose of paragraph (1)(*d*),

(*a*) the amount payable by a taxpayer to acquire a security under an agreement referred to in subsection 7(1) shall be determined without reference to any change in the value of a currency of a country other than Canada, relative to Canadian currency, occurring after the agreement was made;

(*b*) the fair market value of a security at the time an agreement in respect of the security was made shall be determined on the assumption that all specified events associated with the security that occurred after the agreement was made and before the sale or issue of the security or the disposition of the taxpayer's rights under the agreement in respect of the security, as the case may be, had occurred immediately before the agreement was made; and

(*c*) in determining the amount that was included, in respect of a security that a qualifying person has agreed to sell or issue to a taxpayer, in the amount determined under subparagraph 7(1.4)(*c*)(ii) for the purpose of determining if the condition in paragraph 7(1.4)(*c*) was satisfied with respect to a particular disposition, an assumption shall be made that all specified events associated with the security that occurred after the particular disposition and before the sale or issue of the security or the taxpayer's subsequent disposition of rights under the agreement in respect of the security, as the case may be, had occurred immediately before the particular disposition.

Related Sections: S. 7(7) Definitions; s. 110(1.6) Meaning of "specified event".

Canadian Tax Foundation: Frydberg, *Top Technical Bill Issues for Owner-Managers*, 2013 Prairie Provinces Tax Conference 11:1–26.

▶ 110(1.6) ◀

(1.6) Meaning of "specified event". For the purpose of subsection (1.5), a specified event associated with a security is

(*a*) where the security is a share of the capital stock of a corporation,

(i) a subdivision or consolidation of shares of the capital stock of the corporation,

(ii) a reorganization of share capital of the corporation, and

(iii) a stock dividend of the corporation; and

(*b*) where the security is a unit of a mutual fund trust,

(i) a subdivision or consolidation of the units of the trust, and

(ii) an issuance of units of the trust as payment, or in satisfaction of a person's right to enforce payment, out of the trust's income (determined before the application of subsection 104(6)) or out of the trust's capital gains.

Related Sections: S. 7(7) Definitions.

▶ 110(1.7) ◀

(1.7) Reduction in exercise price. If the amount payable by a taxpayer to acquire securities under an agreement referred to in subsection 7(1) is reduced at any particular time and the conditions in subsection (1.8) are satisfied in respect of the reduction,

(*a*) the rights (referred to in this subsection and subsection (1.8) as the "old rights") that the taxpayer had under the agreement immediately before the particular time are deemed to have been disposed of by the taxpayer immediately before the particular time;

(*b*) the rights (referred to in this subsection and subsection (1.8) as the "new rights") that the taxpayer has under the agreement at the particular time are deemed to be acquired by the taxpayer at the particular time; and (*c*) the taxpayer is deemed to receive the new rights as consideration for the disposition of the old rights.

Editorial Note: Subsection 110(1.7) — subject to conditions in s. 110(1.8) — enables employees to claim the s. 110(1)(*d*) deduction even where the options' exercise price is subsequently reduced to a point lower than the fair market value of the optioned securities at the time the options were originally granted.

History: S. 110(1.7) was replaced by S.C. 2013, c. 34, s. 237(2), applicable to reductions that occur after 1998.

[Extended Deadline for Deferral Election] An election by a taxpayer under subsection 7(10) of the *Income Tax Act*, as it read immediately before its repeal by S.C. 2010, c. 25, s. 3(10), to have subsection 7(8) apply, as it read immediately before its repeal by S.C. 2010, c. 25, s. 3(8), is deemed to have been filed in a timely manner if

(*a*) it is filed on or before August 25, 2013 [the 60th day after royal assent];

(*b*) it is in respect of a security acquired by the taxpayer before June 26, 2013;

(*c*) the taxpayer is entitled to a deduction under paragraph 110(1)(*d*) of the Act in respect of the acquisition; and

(*d*) the taxpayer would not have been so entitled if subsection 110(1.7), as enacted by S.C. 2013, c. 34, s. 237(2) did not apply.

S. 110(1.7) formerly read:

(1.7) *Definitions in subsection 7(7).* The definitions in subsection 7(7) apply for the purposes of subsections (1.5) and (1.6).

Canadian Tax Foundation: Frydberg, *Top Technical Bill Issues for Owner-Managers*, 2013 Prairie Provinces Tax Conference 11:1-26.

Income Tax Technical News: Issue No. 38, Employee Stock Option Deduction.

▶ 110(1.8) ◀

(1.8) Conditions for subsection (1.7) to apply. The following are the conditions in respect of the reduction:

(*a*) that the taxpayer would not be entitled to a deduction under paragraph (1)(*d*) if the taxpayer acquired securities under the agreement immediately after the particular time and this section were read without reference to subsection (1.7); and

(*b*) that the taxpayer would be entitled to a deduction under paragraph (1)(*d*) if the taxpayer

(i) disposed of the old rights immediately before the particular time,

(ii) acquired the new rights at the particular time as consideration for the disposition, and

(iii) acquired securities under the agreement immediately after the particular time.

Proposed Amendment

Notice of Ways and Means Motion to amend the Income Tax Act (June 17, 2019)

Section 110 of the Act is amended by adding the following after subsection (1.8):

(1.9) Notification — non-qualified security. If a security to be issued or sold under an agreement between an employee and a specified person is a non-qualified security, the specified person shall

(*a*) notify the employee in writing that the security is a non-qualified security on the day that the agreement is entered into, if the security is deemed to be a nonqualified security because of subsection (1.31); and

(*b*) notify the Minister that the security is a non-qualified security in prescribed form filed with its return of income under this Part for the taxation year that includes the time that the agreement is entered into.

Applicable: In respect of agreements to sell or issue securities entered into after 2019.

History: S. 110(1.8) was added by S.C. 2013, c. 34, s. 237(2), applicable to reductions that occur after 1998. **Editorial Note:** See the application provision under s. 110(1.7) in respect of an extended deadline for a deferral election.

▶ 110(2) ◀

(2) Charitable gifts. Where an individual is, during a taxation year, a member of a religious order and has, as such, taken a vow of perpetual poverty, the individual may deduct in computing the individual's taxable income for the year an amount equal to the total of the individual's superannuation or pension benefits and the individual's earned income for the year (within the meaning assigned by section 63) if, of the individual's income, that amount is paid in the year to the order.

Related Sections: S. 63(3), "earned income"; s. 117.1(1) Annual adjustment; s. 143(2) Election in respect of income.

Interpretation Bulletins: *Primary* — IT-86R Vow of perpetual poverty.

Cases: Where a taxpayer gave only part of his income to the Society of Jesus under a vow of poverty, he was held not entitled to a deduction under the former s. 27(2) [now s. 110(2)]. *Aubry v. The Queen*, 76 DTC 6343 (F.C.T.D.)

▶ 110(2.1) ◀

(2.1) Charitable donation — proceeds of disposition of employee option securities. Where a taxpayer, in exercising a right to acquire a security that a particular qualifying person has agreed to sell or issue to the taxpayer under an agreement referred to in subsection 7(1), directs a broker or dealer appointed or approved by the particular qualifying person (or by a qualifying person that does not deal at arm's length with the particular qualifying person) to immediately dispose of the security and pay all or a portion of the proceeds of disposition of the security to a qualified donee,

(*a*) if the payment is a gift, the taxpayer is deemed, for the purpose of paragraph (1)(*d*.01), to have disposed of the security by making a gift of the security to the qualified donee at the time the payment is made; and

(*b*) the amount deductible under paragraph (1)(*d*.01) by the taxpayer in respect of the disposition of the security is the amount determined by the formula

$$A \times B/C$$

where

A is the amount that would be deductible under paragraph (1)(*d*.01) in respect of the disposition of the security if this subsection were read without reference to this paragraph,

B is the amount of the payment, and

C is the amount of the proceeds of disposition of the security.

Editorial Note: In order to qualify for the deduction under s. 110(1)(*d*.01), the payment of the proceeds of disposition must be made to the qualified donee within 30 days of the acquisition of the security (see the timing rule in s. 110(1)(*d*.01)). The deduction is prorated if less than all of the proceeds are donated (s. 110(2.1)(*b*)).

Related Sections: S. 7(1.3) Order of disposition of securities; s. 7(7) Definitions.

▶ 110(2.2)-(9) ◀

(2.2)-(9) — (Repealed by 1985, c. 45, s. 54(8) and 1988, c. 55, s.77(12).)

SECTION 110.1: Deduction for gifts

▶ 110.1(1) ◀

(1) Deduction for gifts. For the purpose of computing the taxable income of a corporation for a taxation year, there may be deducted such of the following amounts as the corporation claims:

► 110.1(1)(a) ◄

(a) Charitable gifts — the total of all amounts each of which is the eligible amount of a gift (other than a gift described in paragraph (*c*) or (*d*)) made by the corporation in the year or in any of the five preceding taxation years to a qualified donee, not exceeding the lesser of the corporation's income for the year and the amount determined by the formula

$$0.75A + 0.25(B + C + D)$$

where

A is the corporation's income for the year computed without reference to subsection 137(2),

B is the total of all amounts, each of which is that proportion of the corporation's taxable capital gain for the taxation year in respect of a gift made by the corporation in the taxation year (in respect of which gift an eligible amount is described in this paragraph for the taxation year) that the eligible amount of the gift is of the corporation's proceeds of disposition in respect of the gift,

C is the total of all amounts each of which is a taxable capital gain of the corporation for the year, because of subsection 40(1.01), from a disposition of a property in a preceding taxation year, and

D is the total of all amounts each of which is determined in respect of the corporation's depreciable property of a prescribed class and equal to the lesser of

(A) the amount included under subsection 13(1) in respect of the class in computing the corporation's income for the year, and

(B) the total of all amounts each of which is determined in respect of a disposition that is the making of a gift of property of the class by the corporation in the year (in respect of which gift an eligible amount is described in this paragraph for the taxation year) equal to the lesser of

(I) that proportion, of the amount by which the proceeds of disposition of the property exceeds any outlays and expenses, to the extent that they were made or incurred by the corporation for the purpose of making the disposition, that the eligible amount of the gift is of the corporation's proceeds of disposition in respect of the gift, and

(II) that proportion, of the capital cost to the corporation of the property, that the eligible amount of the gift is of the corporation's proceeds of disposition in respect of the gift;

Editorial Note: Paragraph 110.1(1)(*a*) provides that a corporation will be allowed to claim a deduction in respect of the eligible amount of a gift made in the year or the five preceding taxation years to a "qualified donee" as defined in s. 149.1. The deduction limit is 75% of the corporation's income plus, for gifts of capital property, (i) 25% of the taxable capital gain arising from the gift and taken into income in the year and (ii) 25% of the lesser of any recapture of capital cost allowance on the property included in the taxpayer's income in the year and the property's capital cost or proceeds of disposition (whichever is less). The "eligible amount" of a gift is defined in subsections 248(30) though (41), and in general terms is the fair market value of the gift reduced by the amount of any advantage received by the donor in the form of compensation or other benefits.

Paragraphs (*c*) and (*d*) provide for corporate deductions in respect of the eligible portion of gifts of cultural property, and gifts of ecologically sensitive land. Prior to March 22, 2017, paragraph 110.1(1)(*a.1*) provided for corporate deductions in respect of gifts of medicine. Prior to 2016, paragraph 110.1(1)(*b*) provided a deduction for gifts (other than a gift described in paragraph (*c*) or (*d*)) made by a corporation to Her Majesty in right of Canada or of a province.

Similar deductions for individuals in the form of tax credits are set out under section 118.1.

History: S. 110.1(1)(*a*), the portion before the formula was replaced by S.C. 2014, c. 39, s. 29(1), applicable to the 2016 and subsequent taxation years, and formerly read:

(*a*) *Charitable gifts* — the total of all amounts each of which is the eligible amount of a gift (other than a gift described in paragraph (*b*), (*c*) or (*d*)) made by the corporation in the year or in any of the five preceding taxation years to a qualified donee, not exceeding the lesser of the corporation's income for the year and the amount determined by the formula

S. 110.1(1)(*a*), the portion before the formula was replaced by S.C. 2013, c. 34, s. 238(2), deemed to have come into force on January 1, 2012, and formerly read:

(*a*) *Charitable gifts* — the total of all amounts each of which is the eligible amount of a gift (other than a gift described in paragraph (*b*), (*c*) or (*d*)) made by the corporation in the year or in any of the five preceding taxation years to

(i) a registered charity,

(ii) a registered Canadian amateur athletic association,

(iii) a corporation resident in Canada and described in paragraph 149(1)(*i*),

(iv) a municipality in Canada,

(iv.1) a municipal or public body performing the function of government in Canada,

(v) the United Nations or an agency thereof,

(vi) a university outside Canada that is prescribed to be a university the student body of which ordinarily includes students from Canada,

(vii) a charitable organization outside Canada to which Her Majesty in right of Canada has made a gift in the year or in the 12-month period preceding the year, or

(viii) Her Majesty in right of Canada or a province,; not exceeding the lesser of the corporation's income for the year and the amount determined by the formula

S. 110.1(1)(*a*), the portion before the formula was replaced by S.C. 2013, c. 34, s. 238(1), applicable to gifts made after December 20, 2002, and formerly read:

(*a*) *Charitable gifts* — the total of all amounts each of which is the fair market value of a gift (other than a gift described in paragraph (*b*), (*c*) or (*d*)) made by the corporation in the year or in any of the five preceding taxation years to a qualified donee, not exceeding the lesser of the corporation's income for the year and the amount determined by the formula

S. 110.1(1)(*a*), the description of B was replaced by S.C. 2013, c. 34, s. 238(3), applicable to gifts made after December 20, 2002, and formerly read:

B is the total of all amounts each of which is a taxable capital gain of the corporation for the year from a disposition that is the making of a gift made by the corporation in the year and described in this paragraph,

S. 110.1(1)(*a*), clause (B) in the description of D was replaced by S.C. 2013, c. 34, s. 238(4), applicable to gifts made after December 20, 2002, and formerly read:

(B) the total of all amounts each of which is determined in respect of a disposition that is the making of a gift of property of the class made by the corporation in the year that is described in this paragraph and equal to the lesser of

(I) the proceeds of disposition of the property minus any outlays and expenses to the extent that they were made or incurred by the corporation for the purpose of making the disposition, and

(II) the capital cost to the corporation of the property;

S. 110.1(1)(*a*), the portion before the formula was replaced by S.C. 2011, c. 24, s. 21(2), in force January 1, 2012. S. 110.1(1)(*a*), the portion before the formula formerly read:

(*a*) *Charitable gifts* — the total of all amounts each of which is the fair market value of a gift (other than a gift described in paragraph (*b*), (*c*) or (*d*)) made by the corporation in the year or in any of the 5 preceding taxation years to

(i) a registered charity,

(ii) a registered Canadian amateur athletic association,

(iii) a corporation resident in Canada and described in paragraph 149(l)(*i*),

(iv) a municipality in Canada,

(iv.1) a municipal or public body performing a function of government in Canada,

(v) the United Nations or an agency thereof,

(vi) a university outside Canada that is prescribed to be a university the student body of which ordinarily includes students from Canada,

(vii) a charitable organization outside Canada to which Her Majesty in right of Canada has made a gift in the year or in the 12-month period preceding the year, or

(viii) Her Majesty in right of Canada or a province,

not exceeding the lesser of the corporation's income for the year and the amount determined by the formula

S. 110.1(1)(*a*)(iv.1) was added by S.C. 2011, c. 24, s. 21(1), applicable to gifts made after May 8, 2000.

Related Regulations: Part XXXV.

3501(1.1); 3503; Schedule VIII.

Related Sections: S. 37(5) Where no deduction allowed under ss. 110.1 and 118.1; s. 54, "adjusted cost base", "capital property"; s. 118.1(1), "total gifts"; s. 127.52(1)(*d*) Adjusted taxable income determined; s. 149.1(6.4) National arts service organizations; s. 248(1), "registered Canadian amateur athletic association", "registered charity"; s. 248(31) Eligible amount of gift or monetary contribution; s. 249 Definition of "taxation year".

S. 110.1(1)(*b*) Gifts to Her Majesty; s. 110.1(1)(*c*) Gifts to institutions; s. 110.1(3) Gifts of capital property; s. 149.1(1), "qualified donee".

Tax Profile: May 2002 — Update on Charitable Giving.

December 2005 — Fair Market Value — What the Appraiser Thinks Doesn't Matter; June 2004 — Planning For Aging Parents; April 2004 — The Battle of the Art Donation Cases Continues.

Tax Topics: No. 1970, Charitable Gifting — *Russell et al. v. The Queen* and *Maréchaux v. The Queen*; No. 1654, Tax Shelters - Past, Present and Future.

Forms: T2 SCH 2 — T2SCH2 Charitable Donations and Gifts (1998 and later taxation years).

Income Tax Technical News: Issue No. 26, Proposed Guidelines on Split-Receipting.

Interpretation Bulletins: *Primary* — IT-110R3 Deductible gifts and official donation receipts; IT-226R Gift to a charity of a residual interest in real property or an equitable interest in a trust; IT-297R2 Gifts in kind to charity and others. *Secondary* — IT-232R3 Losses — Their deductibility in the loss year or in other years; IT-288R2 Gifts of capital properties to a charity and others.

Tax Window Files: 2015 TEI Meeting Q7 Donations to qualifying US charity, *November 17, 2015*, CRA Document No. 2015-0614251C6; Charity's interest in a taxable corporation, *2012*, CRA Document No. 2011-0431051R3; Donation of depreciable property, *August 01, 2012*, CRA Document No. 2012-0446631E5; Donation to a U.S. charity, *November 4, 2010*, CRA Document No. 2010-0380811E5; Financial Assistance to Employees' Extended Family, *May 20, 2010*, CRA Document No. 2009-0349581E5; Directed Gift to Municipality, *Income Tax Rulings Directorate, March 16, 2009*, CRA Document No. 2008-0304471E5; Deductibility of Legal Fees and Penalties, *Income Tax Rulings Directorate, February 20, 2009*, CRA Document No. 2008-0294701E5; Ecological Gift — Capital or Inventory Property, *Technical Interpretation, Financial Sector and Exempt Entities Division, September 12, 2008*, CRA Document No. 2008-0275041E5; Charitable Donations to University Outside Canada, *Technical Interpretation, Income Tax Rulings Directorate, April 30, 2008*, CRA Document No. 2008-0275391C6; Gift to Charity — Transfer of Property, *Technical Interpretation, Financial Sector and Exempt Entities Division, March 26, 2007*, CRA Document No. 2007-0228391E5; Charitable Gift — Meal at Fund-Raising Event, *Technical Interpretation, Financial Industries Division, January 22, 2004*, CRA Document No. 2003-0054781I7.

Cases: The taxpayers each purchased a group of limited edition prints, donated them to charities and received donation receipts for approximately three times the purchase price. Since the prints were acquired and donated in groups, FMV should be determined on a group basis and was equal to the highest price that the art vendor charged for each group of prints. *A.G. of Canada v. Nash et al.*, 2005 DTC 5696 (F.C.A.), reversing 2004 DTC 3391 (T.C.C.), 2004 DTC 3328 and 2004 DTC 3360.

► 110.1(1)(a.1) ◄

(a.1) Gifts of medicine — (Repealed by S.C. 2017, c. 20, s. 9(1).)

History: S. 110.1(1)(*a.1*) was repealed by S.C. 2017, c. 20, s. 9(1), applicable in respect of gifts made after March 21, 2017, and formerly read:

(*a*.1) *Gifts of medicine* — the total of all amounts each of which is an amount, in respect of property that is the subject of an eligible medical gift made by the corporation in the taxation year or in any of the five preceding taxation years, determined by the formula

$$A \times B/C$$

where

A is the lesser of

(*a*) the cost to the corporation of the property, and

(*b*) 50 per cent of the amount, if any, by which the corporation's proceeds of disposition of the property in respect of the gift exceeds the cost to the corporation of the property;

B is the eligible amount of the gift; and

C is the corporation's proceeds of disposition of the property in respect of the gift.

S. 110.1(1)(*a.1*) was replaced by S.C. 2013, c. 34, s. 238(5), applicable to gifts made after March 18, 2007, and formerly read:

(*a*.1) *Gifts of medicine* — the total of all amounts in respect of property that is the subject of an eligible medical gift made by the corporation in the taxation year or in any of the five preceding taxation years, each of which is the lesser of

(i) the cost to the corporation of the property, and

(ii) 50% of the amount, if any, by which the corporation's proceeds of disposition of the property in respect of the gift exceeds the cost to the corporation of the property.

► 110.1(1)(b) ◄

(b) Gifts to Her Majesty — (Repealed by S.C. 2014, c. 39, s. 29(2).)

History: S. 110.1(1)(*b*) was repealed by S.C. 2014, c. 39, s. 29(2), applicable to the 2016 and subsequent taxation years, and formerly read:

(*b*) *Gifts to Her Majesty* — the total of all amounts each of which is the eligible amount of a gift (other than a gift described in paragraph (*c*) or (*d*)) made by the corporation to Her Majesty in right of Canada or of a province

(i) in the year or in any of the 5 preceding taxation years, and

(ii) before February 19, 1997 or under a written agreement made before that day;

S. 110.1(1)(*b*), the portion before subparagraph (i) was replaced by S.C. 2013, c. 34, s. 238(6), applicable to gifts made after December 20, 2002, and formerly read:

(*b*) *Gifts to Her Majesty* — the total of all amounts each of which is the fair market value of a gift (other than a gift described in paragraph (*c*) or (*d*)) made by the corporation to Her Majesty in right of Canada or a province

Related Regulations: 3501(1.1).

► 110.1(1)(c) ◄

(c) Gifts to institutions — the total of all amounts each of which is the eligible amount of a gift (other than a gift described in paragraph (*d*)) of an object that the Canadian Cultural Property Export Review Board has determined meets the criterion set out in paragraph 29(3)(*b*) of the *Cultural Property Export and Import Act*, which gift was made by the corporation in the year or in any of the five preceding taxation years to an institution or a public authority in Canada that was, at the time the gift was made, designated under subsection 32(2) of that Act either generally or for a specified purpose related to that object; and

History: S. 110.1(1)(*c*) was replaced by S.C. 2019, c. 29, s. 13(1), deemed to have come into force on March 19, 2019. S. 110.1(1)(*c*) formerly read:

(*c*) *Gifts to institutions* — the total of all amounts each of which is the eligible amount of a gift (other than a gift described in paragraph (*d*)) of an object that the Canadian Cultural Property Export Review Board has determined meets the criteria set out in paragraphs 29(3)(*b*) and (*c*) of the *Cultural Property Export and Import Act*, which gift was made by the corporation in the year or in any of the five preceding taxation years to an institution or a public authority in Canada that was, at the time the gift was made, designated under subsection 32(2) of that Act either generally or for a specified purpose related to that object; and

S. 110.1(1)(*c*) was replaced by S.C. 2013, c. 34, s. 238(7), applicable to gifts made after December 20, 2002, and formerly read:

(*c*) *Gifts to institutions* — the total of all amounts each of which is the fair market value of a gift (other than a gift described in paragraph (*d*)) of an object that the Canadian Cultural Property Export Review Board has determined meets the criteria set out in paragraphs 29(3)(*b*) and (*c*) of the *Cultural Property Export and Import Act*, which gift was made by the corporation in the year or in any of the 5 preceding taxation years to an institution or a public authority in Canada that was, at the time the gift was made, designated under subsection 32(2) of that Act either generally or for a specified purpose related to that object; and

Related Regulations: 3501(1.1).

Related Sections: S. 118.1(7.1) Gifts of cultural property.

Interpretation Bulletins: *Secondary* — IT-407R4 (Consolid.) Dispositions of cultural property to designated Canadian institutions.

► 110.1(1)(d) ◄

(d) Ecological gifts — the total of all amounts each of which is the eligible amount of a gift of land (including a covenant or an easement to which land is subject or, in the case of land in the Province of Quebec, a personal servitude (the rights to which the land is subject and which has a term of not less than 100 years) or a real servitude) if

(i) the fair market value of the gift is certified by the Minister of the Environment,

(ii) the land is certified by that Minister, or by a person designated by that Minister, to be ecologically sensitive land, the conservation and protection of which is, in the opinion of that Minister or the designated person, important to the preservation of Canada's environmental heritage, and

(iii) the gift was made by the corporation in the year or in any of the 10 preceding taxation years to a qualified donee that is

(A) Her Majesty in right of Canada or of a province,

(B) a municipality in Canada that is approved by that Minister or the designated person in respect of the gift,

(C) a municipal or public body performing a function of government in Canada that is approved by that Minister or the designated person in respect of the gift, or

(D) a registered charity (other than a private foundation) one of the main purposes of which is, in the opinion of that Minister, the conservation and protection of Canada's environmental heritage, and that is approved by that Minister or the designated person in respect of the gift.

Editorial Note: Paragraph 110.1(1)(*d*) allows a corporation to deduct from taxable income the eligible amount (as defined in s. 248(31)) of a gift of ecologically sensitive land; there is an explicit requirement that eligible gifts after February 10, 2014 must be made to a qualified donee (see 149.1(1)). Effective for gifts made after March 21, 2017, private foundations are no longer qualified donees. This deduction is not subject to the 75% income limit applicable to charitable donations. Gifts of land must be certified by the Ministry of Environment, which will determine the fair market value of the gift (see 110.1(5)). Any unused deduction may be carried forward for up to 10 years (five years prior to February 10, 2014). Section 207.31 imposes a special tax on a recipient who subsequently and without approval disposes of, or changes the use of, donated land. Effective for dispositions or changes of use made after March 21, 2017, the penalty tax will apply to a qualified donee even if the property was not donated — for example, a charity or municipality to which the property was transferred by the original recipient donee. The Minister of the Environment and Climate Change is granted the ability to determine whether changes to the use of the property have occurred.

History: S. 110.1(1)(*d*), the portion before subparagraph (i) was replaced by S.C. 2017, c. 33, s. 39(1), applicable in respect of gifts made after March 21, 2017, and formerly read:

(*d*) *Ecological gifts* — the total of all amounts each of which is the eligible amount of a gift of land (including a covenant or an easement to which land is subject or, in the case of land in the Province of Quebec, a real servitude) if

S. 110.1(1)(*d*)(iii)(B) to (D) were replaced by S.C. 2017, c. 33, s. 39(2), applicable in respect of gifts made after March 21, 2017, and formerly read:

(B) a municipality in Canada,

(C) a municipal or public body performing a function of government in Canada, or

(D) a registered charity one of the main purposes of which is, in the opinion of that Minister, the conservation and protection of Canada's environmental heritage, and that is approved by that Minister or the designated person in respect of the gift.

S. 110.1(1)(*d*)(iii), the portion before clause (A) was replaced by S.C. 2014, c. 39, s. 29(3), applicable to gifts made after February 10, 2014, and formerly read:

(iii) the gift was made by the corporation in the year or in any of the 10 preceding taxation years to

S. 110.1(1)(*d*)(iii), the portion before clause (A) was replaced by S.C. 2014, c. 20, s. 5(1), applicable to gifts made after February 10, 2014, and formerly read:

(iii) the gift was made by the corporation in the year or in any of the five preceding taxation years to

S. 110.1(1)(*d*) was replaced by S.C. 2013, c. 34, s. 238(9), applicable to gifts made after December 20, 2002, and formerly read:

(*d*) *Ecological gifts* — the total of all amounts each of which is the fair market value of a gift of land, including a servitude for the use and benefit of a dominant land, a covenant or an easement, the fair market value of which is certified by the Minister of the Environment and that is certified by that Minister, or by a person designated by that Minister, to be ecologically sensitive land, the conservation and protection of which is, in the opinion of that Minister, or that person, important to the preservation of Canada's environmental heritage, which gift was made by the corporation in the year or in any of the five preceding taxation years to

(i) Her Majesty in right of Canada or of a province, a municipality in Canada or a municipal or public body performing a function of government in Canada, or

(ii) a registered charity one of the main purposes of which is, in the opinion of that Minister, the conservation and protection of Canada's environmental heritage, and that is approved by that Minister or that person in respect of the gift.

S. 110.1(1)(*d*)(i) was replaced by S.C. 2013, c. 34, s. 238(8), applicable to gifts made after May 8, 2000, and formerly read:

(i) Her Majesty in right of Canada or a province or a municipality in Canada, or

Related Sections: S. 110.1(5) Ecological gifts; s. 118.1(1), "total ecological gifts"; s. 118.1(10.2) Request for determination by the Minister of the Environment; s. 118.1(10.3) Duty of Minister of the Environment; s. 118.1(10.4) Ecological gifts — redetermination; s. 118.1(10.5) Certificate of Fair Market Value; s. 169(1.1) Ecological gifts; s. 207.31 Tax payable by recipient of an ecological gift; s. 207.4(1) Return and payment of tax.

► 110.1(1.1) ◄

(1.1) Limitation on deductibility. For the purpose of determining the amount deductible under subsection (1) in computing a corporation's taxable income for a taxation year,

(*a*) an amount in respect of a gift is deductible only to the extent that it exceeds amounts in respect of the gift deducted under that subsection in computing the corporation's taxable income for preceding taxation years; and

(*b*) no amount in respect of a gift made in a particular taxation year is deductible under any of paragraphs (1)(*a*) to (*d*) until amounts deductible under that paragraph in respect of gifts made in taxation years preceding the particular year have been deducted.

Editorial Note: Deductions made pursuant to the terms of this section are made in the order the gifts were made. No gift in a subsequent taxation year may be utilized while previous year gifts remain outstanding.

Related Sections: S. 118.1(2.1) Ordering.

► 110.1(1.2) ◄

(1.2) Where control acquired. Notwithstanding paragraph 88(1)(*e.6*), if control of a particular corporation is acquired at any time by a person or group of persons,

(*a*) no amount is deductible under any of paragraphs (1)(*a*) to (*d*) in computing any corporation's taxable income for a taxation year that ends on or after that time in respect of a gift made by the particular corporation before that time; and

(*b*) no amount is deductible under any of paragraphs (1)(*a*) to (*d*) in computing any corporation's taxable income for a taxation year that ends on or after that time in respect of a gift made by any corporation on or after that time if the property that is the subject of the gift was acquired by the particular corporation under an arrangement under which it was expected that control of the particular corporation would be so acquired by a person or group of persons, other than a qualified donee that received the gift, and the gift would be so made.

Editorial Note: Where there is a change of control of a corporation, charitable deductions that were not previously used will be disallowed going forward.

► 110.1(2) ◄

(2) Proof of gift. An eligible amount of a gift shall not be included for the purpose of determining a deduction under subsection (1) unless the making of the gift is evidenced by filing with the Minister (*a*) a receipt for the gift that contains prescribed information;

(*b*) in the case of a gift described in paragraph (1)(*c*), the certificate issued under subsection 33(1) of the *Cultural Property Export and Import Act*; and

(*c*) in the case of a gift described in paragraph (1)(*d*), both certificates referred to in that paragraph.

Editorial Note: For gifts to be deducted, the necessary filings must be provided to the Minister, namely, a receipt with the prescribed information as well as the necessary certificates in the case of a gift of cultural property or ecologically sensitive land.

History: S. 110.1(2), the portion before paragraph (*a*) was replaced by S.C. 2013, c. 34, s. 238(10), applicable to gifts made after December 20, 2002, and formerly read:

(2) *Proof of gift.* A gift shall not be included for the purpose of determining a deduction under subsection (1) unless the making of the gift is proven by filing with the Minister

Related Regulations: 3501(1).

Income Tax Technical News: Issue No. 26, Proposed Guidelines on Split Receipting.

▶ 110.1(2.1) ◀

(2.1) Where subsection (3) applies. Subsection (3) applies in circumstances where

(*a*) a corporation makes a gift at any time of

(i) capital property to a qualified donee, or

(ii) in the case of a corporation not resident in Canada, real or immovable property situated in Canada to a prescribed donee who provides an undertaking, in a form satisfactory to the Minister, to the effect that the property will be held for use in the public interest; and

(*b*) the fair market value of the property otherwise determined at that time exceeds

(i) in the case of depreciable property of a prescribed class, the lesser of the undepreciated capital cost of that class at the end of the taxation year of the corporation that includes that time (determined without reference to the proceeds of disposition designated in respect of the property under subsection (3)) and the adjusted cost base to the corporation of the property immediately before that time, and

(ii) in any other case, the adjusted cost base to the corporation of the property immediately before that time.

Editorial Note: Together with s. 110.1(3), this subsection provides that corporations that make gifts of capital property to a qualified donee (or in the case of a non-resident corporation, a gift of real or immovable property in Canada to a prescribed donee who undertakes to retain the real property for the public interest) may elect a value between the adjusted cost base and the fair market value of such donated property, and such elected value will be treated as the amount of the proceeds of disposition (for determination of the capital gain) and the value of the gift for the purposes of the deduction under s. 110.1(1) (subject to the advantage rules in s. 248(31) to (34)). In particular, the designated amount cannot be less than the greater of (i) the amount of the advantage if any, and (ii) the adjusted cost base of the property (or in the case of depreciable property, the undepreciated capital cost of such property at the end of the taxation year of the gift).

History: S. 110.1(2.1)(*a*)(i) was replaced by S.C. 2013, c. 34, s. 238(12), deemed to have come into force on January 1, 2012, and formerly read:

(i) capital property to a donee described in paragraph (1)(*a*), (*b*) or (*d*), or

S. 110.1(2.1) was added by S.C. 2013, c. 34, s. 238(11), applicable to gifts made after 1999.

Related Sections: S. 248(35) Deemed fair market value.

▶ 110.1(3) ◀

(3) Gifts of capital property. If this subsection applies in respect of a gift by a corporation of property, and the corporation designates an amount in respect of the gift in its return of income under section 150 for the year in which the gift is made, the amount so designated is deemed to be its proceeds of disposition of the property and, for the purpose of subsection 248(31), the fair market value of the gift, but the amount so designated may not exceed the fair market value of the property otherwise determined and may not be less than the greater of

(*a*) in the case of a gift made after December 20, 2002, the amount of the advantage, if any, in respect of the gift, and

(*b*) the amount determined under subparagraph (2.1)(*b*)(i) or (ii), as the case may be, in respect of the property.

Editorial Note: See the editorial note under s. 110.1(2.1).

History: S. 110.1(3) was replaced by S.C. 2013, c. 34, s. 238(11), applicable to gifts made after 1999, except that, for gifts made after 1999 and before December 21, 2002, the reference to "subsection 248(31)" in subsection 110.1(3) is to be read as a reference to "subsection (1)". S. 110.1(3) formerly read:

(3) *Gifts of capital property.* Where at any time

(*a*) a corporation makes a gift of

(i) capital property to a qualified donee, or

(ii) in the case of a corporation not resident in Canada, real property situated in Canada to a prescribed donee who provides an undertaking, in a form satisfactory to the Minister, to the effect that the property will be held for use in the public interest, and

(*b*) the fair market value of the property at that time exceeds its adjusted cost base to the corporation,

such amount, not greater than the fair market value otherwise determined and not less than the adjusted cost base to the corporation of the property at that time, as the corporation designates in its return of income under section 150 for the year in which the gift is made is, if the making of the gift is proven by filing with the Minister a receipt containing prescribed information, deemed to be its proceeds of disposition of the property and, for the purposes of subsection (1), the fair market value of the gift made by the corporation.

S. 110.1(3)(*a*)(i) was replaced by S.C. 2011, c. 24, s. 21(3), in force January 1, 2012. S. 110.1(3)(*a*)(i) formerly read:

(i) capital property to a donee described in paragraph (1)(*a*), (*b*) or (*d*), or

Related Regulations: 3501(1), (1.1); 3504.

Related Sections: S. 13(21), "proceeds of disposition"; s. 54, "proceeds of disposition"; s. 248(35) Deemed fair market value.

Interpretation Bulletins: *Primary* — IT-288R2 Gifts of capital properties to a charity and others.

▶ 110.1(4) ◀

(4) Gifts made by partnership. If at the end of a fiscal period of a partnership a corporation is a member of the partnership, its share of any amount that would, if the partnership were a person, be the eligible amount of a gift made by the partnership to any donee is, for the purpose of this section, deemed to be the eligible amount of a gift made to that donee by the corporation in its taxation year in which the fiscal period of the partnership ends.

Editorial Note: A corporate partner is deemed pursuant to this subsection to have made a gift equal to its share of the corporate partnership. The corporate partner is deemed to have made the gift in the taxation year in which the fiscal period of the partnership ends. For example, where a company has a June 30 year end and that company belongs to a partnership with a December 31 year end, a donation by the partnership in its year ending December 31 of year 1 will be recognized by the corporation in its year ended June 30 of year 2.

History: S. 110.1(4) was replaced by S.C. 2013, c. 34, s. 238(13), applicable to gifts made after December 20, 2002, and formerly read:

(4) *Gifts made by partnership.* Where a corporation is, at the end of a fiscal period of a partnership, a member of the partnership, its share of any amount that would, if the partnership were a person, be a gift made by the partnership to any donee shall, for the purposes of this section, be deemed to be a gift made to that donee by the corporation in its taxation year in which the fiscal period of the partnership ends.

▶ 110.1(5) ◀

(5) Ecological gifts. For the purposes of applying subparagraph 69(1)(*b*)(ii), this section and section 207.31 in respect of a gift described in paragraph (1)(*d*) that is made by a taxpayer, the amount that is the fair market value (or, for the purpose of subsection (3), the fair market value otherwise determined) of the gift at the time the gift was made and, subject to subsection (3), the taxpayer's proceeds of disposition of the gift, is deemed to be the amount determined by the Minister of the Environment to be

(*a*) where the gift is land, the fair market value of the gift; or

(*b*) where the gift is a covenant or an easement to which land is subject or, in the case of land in the Province of Quebec, a real or personal servitude, the greater of

(i) the fair market value otherwise determined of the gift, and

(ii) the amount by which the fair market value of the land is reduced as a result of the making of the gift.

Editorial Note: Where ecologically sensitive land is gifted, the fair market value of the gift is the amount determined by the Minister of the Environment.

History: S. 110.1(5)(*b*), the portion before subparagraph (i) was replaced by S.C. 2017, c. 33, s. 39(3), applicable in respect of gifts made after March 21, 2017, and formerly read:

(*b*) where the gift is a covenant or an easement to which land is subject or, in the case of land in the Province of Quebec, a real servitude, the greater of

S. 110.1(5)(*b*), the portion before subparagraph (i) was replaced by S.C. 2013, c. 34, s. 238(14), applicable to gifts made after December 20, 2002, and formerly read:

(*b*) where the gift is a servitude, covenant or easement to which land is subject, the greater of

Related Sections: S. 118.1(10.2) Request for determination by the Minister of the Environment; s. 118.1(10.3) Duty of Minister of the Environment; s. 118.1(10.4) Ecological gifts — redetermination; s. 118.1(10.5) Certificate of Fair Market Value; s. 118.1(12) Ecological gifts; s. 169(1.1) Ecological gifts; s. 207.31 Tax payable by recipient of an ecological gift.

► 110.1(6) ◄

(6) Non-qualifying securities. Subsections 118.1(13) to (14) and (16) to (20) apply to a corporation as if the references in those subsections to an individual were read as references to a corporation and as if a non-qualifying security of a corporation included a share (other than a share listed on a designated stock exchange) of the capital stock of the corporation.

Editorial Note: See editorial notes to s. 118.1(13) through (14) and (16) through (20).

History: S. 110.1(6) was replaced by S.C. 2011, c. 24, s. 21(4), deemed to have come into force on March 22, 2011. S. 110.1(6) formerly read:

(6) *Non-qualifying securities.* Subsections 118.1(13), and (14) and (16) to (20) apply to a corporation as if the references in those subsections to an individual were read as references to a corporation and as if a non-qualifying security of a corporation included a share (other than a share listed on a designated stock exchange) of the capital stock of the corporation.

► 110.1(7) ◄

(7) Corporation ceasing to exist. If, but for this subsection, a corporation (other than a corporation that was a predecessor corporation in an amalgamation to which subsection 87(1) applied or a corporation that was wound up in a winding-up to which subsection 88(1) applied) would be deemed by subsection 118.1(13) to have made a gift after the corporation ceased to exist, for the purpose of this section, the corporation is deemed to have made the gift in its last taxation year, except that the amount of interest payable under any provision of this Act is the amount that it would be if this subsection did not apply to the gift.

Editorial Note: If as a result of the rules relating to non-qualifying securities in s. 110(6) a corporation is deemed to have made the gift in a year after it has ceased to exist, the gift is deemed to be made in the last taxation year of the corporation. However, if the corporation ceased to exist as a result of an amalgamation or winding-up, then the new corporation will be treated as having made the gift at the time determined under the non-qualifying securities rules.

► 110.1(8) ◄

(8) Eligible medical gift — (Repealed by S.C. 2017, c. 20, s. 9(2).)

History: S. 110.1(8) was repealed by S.C. 2017, c. 20, s. 9(2), applicable in respect of gifts made after March 21, 2017, and formerly read:

(8) *Eligible medical gift.* For the purpose of paragraph (1)(*a.1*), a gift referred to in paragraph (1)(*a*) is an eligible medical gift of a corporation if

(*a*) the corporation has directed the donee to apply the gift to charitable activities outside of Canada;

(*b*) the property that is the subject of the gift is a medicine that is available for the donee's use at least six months prior to its expiration date, within the meaning of the *Food and Drug Regulations*;

(*c*) the medicine qualifies as a drug, within the meaning of the *Food and Drugs Act*, and the drug

(i) meets the requirements of that Act, or would meet those requirements if that Act were read without reference to its subsection 37(1), and

(ii) is not a food, cosmetic or device (as those terms are defined in that Act), a natural health product (as defined in the *Natural Health Products Regulations*) or a veterinary drug;

(*d*) the property was, immediately before the making of the gift, described in an inventory in respect of a business of the corporation; and

(*e*) the donee is a registered charity that, in the opinion of the Minister for International Development (or, if there is no such Minister, the Minister of Foreign Affairs) meets conditions prescribed by regulation.

S. 110.1(8)(*e*) was amended by S.C. 2013, c. 33, s. 196(1), by replacing "Minister for International Cooperation" with "Minister for International Development", in force June 26, 2013.

S. 110.1(8)(*e*) was amended by S.C. 2013, c. 33, s. 198, by replacing "Minister responsible for the Canadian International Development Agency" with "Minister of Foreign Affairs", in force June 26, 2013.

S. 110.1(8)(*e*) was replaced by S.C. 2009, c. 2, s. 29(1), applicable in respect of gifts made after June 2008. S. 110.1(8)(*e*) formerly read:

(*e*) the donee is a registered charity that, in the opinion of the Minister of International Cooperation (or, if there is no such Minister, the Minister responsible for the Canadian International Development Agency) meets prescribed conditions.

Related Regulations: 3505.

Related Sections: S. 149.1(15) Information may be communicated.

► 110.1(9) ◄

(9) Rules governing international medical charities — (Repealed by S.C. 2017, c. 20, s. 9(2).)

History: S. 110.1(9) was repealed by S.C. 2017, c. 20, s. 9(2), applicable in respect of gifts made after March 21, 2017, and formerly read:

(9) *Rules governing international medical charities.* For the purpose of paragraph (8)(*e*),

(*a*) for greater certainty, nothing in paragraph (8)(*b*) modifies the application to a registered charity of the prescribed conditions referred to in paragraph (8)(*e*);

(*b*) if, in respect of a registered charity, the Minister referred to in paragraph (8)(*e*) is of the opinion described in that paragraph

(i) that Minister may also designate a period of time during which that opinion is valid, and

(ii) notwithstanding subparagraph (i), the opinion may be revoked at any time by that Minister if

(A) that Minister is of the opinion that the registered charity no longer meets prescribed conditions referred to in paragraph (8)(*e*), or

(B) any person has made any misrepresentation that is attributable to neglect, carelessness or wilful default for the purpose of obtaining the opinion; and

(*c*) a revocation referred to in subparagraph (*b*)(ii) is effective as of the time that notice, in writing, of the revocation is issued by that Minister to the registered charity.

S. 110.1(9) was added by S.C. 2009, c. 2, s. 29(2), applicable in respect of gifts made after June 2008.

► 110.1(10) ◄

(10) Options. Subject to subsections (12) and (13), if a corporation has granted an option to a qualified donee in a taxation year, no amount in respect of the option is to be included in computing an amount under any of paragraphs (1)(*a*) to (*d*) in respect of the corporation for any year.

Editorial Note: Subsections 110.1(10) to (13) provide that a deduction under any of paragraphs 110.1(1)(*a*) to (*d*) is not available to a corporate donor in respect of the granting by the donor of an option to acquire a particular property of the donor. In certain circumstances, the deduction may become available at the time the option is exercised by the donee and the property is acquired by the donee. Rules also exist to cover the situation where the donee disposes of the option before it is exercised. Analogous rules apply to the granting of options by individuals (see s. 118.1(21)–(24)).

History: S. 110.1(10) was added by S.C. 2011, c. 24, s. 21(5), applicable to options granted on or after March 22, 2011.

Related Sections: S. 110.1(11) Application of subsection (12); s. 110.1(12) Granting of an option; s. 110.1(13) Disposition of an option.

► 110.1(11) ◄

(11) Application of subsection (12). Subsection (12) applies if

(*a*) an option to acquire a property of a corporation is granted to a qualified donee;

(*b*) the option is exercised so that the property is disposed of by the corporation and acquired by the qualified donee at a particular time; and

(*c*) either

(i) the amount that is 80% of the fair market value of the property at the particular time is greater than or equal to the total of

(A) the consideration received by the corporation from the qualified donee for the property, and

(B) the consideration received by the corporation from the qualified donee for the option, or

(ii) the corporation establishes to the satisfaction of the Minister that the granting of the option or the disposition of the property was made by the corporation with the intention to make a gift to the qualified donee.

Editorial Note: See notes to s. 110.1(10).

History: S. 110.1(11) was added by S.C. 2011, c. 24, s. 21(5), applicable to options granted on or after March 22, 2011.

Related Sections: S. 110.1(10) Options; s. 110.1(12) Granting of an option; s. 110.1(13) Disposition of an option.

► 110.1(12) ◄

(12) Granting of an option. If this subsection applies, notwithstanding subsection 49(3),

(*a*) the corporation is deemed to have received proceeds of disposition of the property equal to the property's fair market value at the particular time; and

(*b*) there shall be included in the total referred to in paragraph (1)(*a*), for the corporation's taxation year that includes the particular time, the amount by which the property's fair market value exceeds the total described in subparagraph (11)(*c*)(i).

Editorial Note: See notes to s. 110.1(10).

History: S. 110.1(12) was added by S.C. 2011, c. 24, s. 21(5), applicable to options granted on or after March 22, 2011.

Related Sections: S. 110.1(10) Options; s. 110.1(11) Application of subsection (12); s. 110.1(13) Disposition of an option.

► 110.1(13) ◄

(13) Disposition of an option. If an option to acquire a particular property of a corporation is granted to a qualified donee and the option is disposed of by the qualified donee (otherwise than by the exercise of the option) at a particular time

(*a*) the corporation is deemed to have disposed of a property at the particular time

(i) the adjusted cost base of which to the corporation immediately before the particular time is equal to the consideration, if any, paid by the qualified donee for the option, and

(ii) the proceeds of disposition of which are equal to the lesser of the fair market value of the particular property at the particular time and the fair market value of any consideration (other than a non-qualifying security of any person) received by the qualified donee for the option; and

(*b*) there shall be included in the total referred to in paragraph (1)(*a*) for the corporation's taxation year that includes the particular time the amount, if any, by which the proceeds of disposition as determined by paragraph (*a*) exceed the consideration, if any, paid by the qualified donee for the option.

Editorial Note: See notes to s. 110.1(10).

History: S. 110.1(13) was added by S.C. 2011, c. 24, s. 21(5), applicable to options granted on or after March 22, 2011.

Related Sections: S. 110.1(10) Options; s. 110.1(11) Application of subsection (12); s. 110.1(12) Granting of an option.

► 110.1(14) ◄

(14) Returned property. Subsection (15) applies if a qualified donee has issued to a corporation a receipt referred to in subsection (2) in respect of a transfer of a property (in this subsection and subsection (15) referred to as the "original property") and a particular property that is

(*a*) the original property is later transferred to the corporation (unless that later transfer is reasonable consideration or remuneration for property acquired by or services rendered to a person); or

(*b*) any other property that may reasonably be considered compensation for or a substitute for, in whole or in part, the original property, is later transferred to the corporation.

Editorial Note: Subsections 110.1(14) to (17) allow the Minister to reassess a donor where property donated to a "qualified donee" (and in respect of which a receipt was issued to the donor under subsection 110.1(2)) is subsequently returned to the donor. Specifically, if the donated property, an identical property or other property that may be reasonably considered to be transferred in substitution for, or compensation for, the donated property is transferred by the qualified donee to the donor, the original gift is deemed not to have been made and the Minister of National Revenue has the authority to reassess any person whose income would reasonably be regarded as relating to the return of property. These rules do not, however, apply if the property is returned to the donor as reasonable consideration or remuneration for property or services. See CRA Charities Guidance Document CG-016, *Qualified donees — Consequences of returning donated property.*

If the returned property is not the original property, the donor is deemed to have disposed of the original property at the time it receives the returned property for proceeds of disposition equal to the greater of the fair market value of the returned property at that time and the fair market value of the original property at the time it was originally transferred by the donor to the donee. In such a case, if the fair market value of the original property at the time of the original donation exceeds the fair market value of the returned property at the time it is returned to the donor, the excess will be considered a gift made by the donor at the time of the gift of the original property.

If the value of the returned property is greater than $50.00, the transferor must file an information return containing prescribed information with the Minister not later than 90 days after the day on which the property was returned and a copy must be provided to the donor.

History: S. 110.1(14) was added by S.C. 2011, c. 24, s. 21(5), applicable to transfers of property made on or after March 22, 2011.

Related Sections: S. 110.1(15) Returned property; s. 110.1(16) Information return; s. 110.1(17) Reassessment.

► 110.1(15) ◄

(15) Returned property. If this subsection applies, then

(*a*) irrespective of whether the transfer of the original property by the corporation to the qualified donee referred to in subsection (14) was a gift, the corporation is deemed not to have disposed of the original property at the time of that transfer nor to have made a gift;

(*b*) if the particular property is identical to the original property, the particular property is deemed to be the original property; and

(*c*) if the particular property is not the original property, then

(i) the corporation is deemed to have disposed of the original property at the time that the particular property is transferred to the corporation for proceeds of disposition equal to the greater of the fair market value of the particular property at that time and the fair market value of the original property at the time that it was transferred by the corporation to the donee, and

(ii) if the transfer of the original property by the corporation would be a gift if this section were read without reference to paragraph (*a*), the corporation is deemed to have, at the time of that transfer, transferred to the donee a property that is the subject of a gift having a fair market value equal to the amount, if any, by which the fair market value of the original property at the time of that transfer exceeds the fair market value of the particular property at the time that it is transferred to the corporation.

Editorial Note: See notes to s. 110.1(14).

History: S. 110.1(15) was added by S.C. 2011, c. 24, s. 21(5), applicable to transfers of property made on or after March 22, 2011.

Related Sections: S. 110.1(14) Returned property; s. 110.1(16) Information return; s. 110.1(17) Reassessment.

▶ 110.1(16) ◀

(16) Information return. If subsection (15) applies in respect of a transfer of property to a corporation and that property has a fair market value greater than $50, the transferor must file an information return containing prescribed information with the Minister not later than 90 days after the day on which the property was transferred and provide a copy of the return to the corporation.

Editorial Note: See notes to s. 110.1(14).

History: S. 110.1(16) was added by S.C. 2011, c. 24, s. 21(5), applicable to transfers of property made on or after March 22, 2011, except that an information return required to be filed under subsection 110.1(16) that is filed before November 16, 2011 is deemed to have been filed on time.

Related Regulations: 3501.1.

Related Sections: S. 110.1(14) Returned property; s. 110.1(15) Returned property; s. 110.1(17) Reassessment.

▶ 110.1(17) ◀

(17) Reassessment. If subsection (15) applies in respect of a transfer of property to a corporation, the Minister may reassess a return of income of any person to the extent that the reassessment can reasonably be regarded as relating to the transfer.

Editorial Note: See notes to s. 110.1(14).

History: S. 110.1(17) was added by S.C. 2011, c. 24, s. 21(5), applicable to transfers of property made on or after March 22, 2011.

Related Sections: S. 110.1(14) Returned property; s. 110.1(15) Returned property; s. 110.1(16) Information return.

SECTION 110.2: Lump-sum payments

▶ 110.2(1) ◀

(1) Definitions. The definitions in this subsection apply in this section and section 120.31.

Tax Window Files: Ajustements salariaux rétroactifs, *March 3, 2011*, CRA Document No. 2010-0381851E5; Lump-Sum Payments — Retroactive Pay Equity Adjustments, *Technical Interpretation, Business and Partnerships Division, February 6, 2008*, CRA Document No. 2008-0265661I7; Lump-Sum Payments — Workers' Compensation, *Technical Interpretation, Business and Partnerships Division, May 12, 2006*, CRA Document No. 2006-0184781I7; Retroactive Lump-Sum Payment of Old Age Security Benefits, *Technical Interpretation, Financial Industries Division, September 7, 2004*, CRA Document No. 2004-0073081E5.

"eligible taxation year" — "eligible taxation year" in respect of a qualifying amount received by an individual, means a taxation year

(*a*) that ended after 1977 and before the year in which the individual received the qualifying amount;

(*b*) throughout which the individual was resident in Canada;

(*c*) that did not end in a calendar year in which the individual became a bankrupt; and

(*d*) that was not included in an averaging period, within the meaning assigned by section 119 (as it read in its application to the 1987 taxation year), pursuant to an election that was made and not revoked by the individual under that section.

"qualifying amount" — "qualifying amount" received by an individual in a taxation year means an amount (other than the portion of the amount that can reasonably be considered to be received as, on account of, in lieu of payment of or in satisfaction of, interest) that is included in computing the individual's income for the year and is

(*a*) an amount

(i) that is received pursuant to an order or judgment of a competent tribunal, an arbitration award or a contract by which the payor and the individual terminate a legal proceeding, and

(ii) that is

(A) included in computing the individual's income from an office or employment, or

(B) received as, on account of, in lieu of payment of or in satisfaction of, damages in respect of the individual's loss of an office or employment,

(*b*) a superannuation or pension benefit (other than a benefit referred to in clause 56(1)(*a*)(i)(B)) received on account of, in lieu of payment of or in satisfaction of, a series of periodic payments (other than payments that would have otherwise been made in the year or in a subsequent taxation year),

(*c*) an amount described in paragraph 6(1)(*f*) or (*f.1*), subparagraph 56(1)(*a*)(iv) or paragraph 56(1)(*b*), or

(*d*) a prescribed amount or benefit,

except to the extent that the individual may deduct for the year an amount under paragraph 8(1)(*b*), (*n*) or (*n*.1), 60(*n*) or (*o*.1) or 110(1)(*f*) in respect of the amount so included.

History: S. 110.2(1), paragraph (*c*) of the definition "qualifying amount" was replaced by S.C. 2013, c. 34, s. 239(1), deemed to have come into force on April 1, 2006, and formerly read:

(*c*) an amount described in paragraph 6(1)(*f*), subparagraph 56(1)(*a*)(iv) or paragraph 56(1)(*b*), or

"specified portion" — "specified portion", in relation to an eligible taxation year, of a qualifying amount received by an individual means the portion of the qualifying amount that relates to the year, to the extent that the individual's eligibility to receive the portion existed in the year.

▶ 110.2(2) ◀

(2) Deduction for lump-sum payments. There may be deducted in computing the taxable income of an individual (other than a trust) for a particular taxation year the total of all amounts each of which is a specified portion of a qualifying amount received by the individual in the particular year, if that total is $3,000 or more.

Editorial Note: Because income is generally taxable in the year it is received, the tax payable on lump-sum payments may be significantly higher than it would have been if payment had been received and taxed on an ongoing basis. Section 110.2 provides relief to individuals (other than trusts) by allowing them to deduct in computing their taxable income for a year the specified portion of a qualifying amount received by the individual in that year.

Related Sections: S. 111.1 Order of applying provisions; s. 120.31(2) Addition to tax payable.

Canadian Tax Foundation: Frankovic, *The Taxation of Retroactive Lump-Sum Payments: The Practice and the Policy*, 2010 Canadian Tax Journal 1:1–23.

Forms: T1198 — Statement of Qualifying Retroactive Lump-Sum Payment.

Tax Window Files: QRLSP through arbitration, *March 14, 2019*, CRA Document No. 2019-0796871E5; Settlement amount for disability benefits, *August 11, 2015*, CRA Document No. 2015-0580521E5.

SECTION 110.3: Transfer of unused deductions

(Repealed by 1988, c. 55, s. 79(1).)

SECTION 110.4: Forward averaging

[Subsections 110.4(1), (3) and (6) were repealed by 1988, c. 55, s. 80; subsections 110.4(2), (4), (5), (6.1) and (8) were repealed by 2000, c. 19, s. 18(1); and subsection 110.4(7) was repealed by 1985, c. 45, s. 55(2).]

SECTION 110.5: Additions for foreign tax deductions

There shall be added to a corporation's taxable income otherwise determined for a taxation year such amount as the corporation may claim to the extent that the addition thereof

(*a*) increases any amount deductible by the corporation under subsection 126(1) or (2) for the year; and

(*b*) does not increase an amount deductible by the corporation under any of sections 125, 125.1, 127, 127.2 and 127.3 for the year.

Related Sections: S. 88(1.1) Non-capital losses, etc., of subsidiary; s. 127.5 Obligation to pay minimum tax.

Tax Profile: February 2013 — The Purchase of US Businesses by Canadians; January 2006 — Foreign Source Income: Outbound Structures and Foreign Tax Credit Planning — Part I.

Income Tax Folios: *Secondary* — S5-F2-C1 Foreign Tax Credit.

Interpretation Bulletins: *Secondary* — IT-232R3 Losses — Their deductibility in the loss year or in other years; IT-302R3 Losses of a corporation — The effect that acquisitions of control, amalgamations, and windings-up have on their deductibility — After January 15, 1987.

Tax Window Files: Clarification of 2013-0481151I7, *February 7, 2014*, CRA Document No. 2013-0512601I7; Application of 152(4)(b)(iv) and 110.5, *July 16, 2013*, CRA Document No. 2013-0481151I7.

SECTION 110.6: [Capital gains exemption]

► 110.6(1) ◄

(1) Definitions. For the purposes of this section,

Canadian Tax Foundation: Truster, *Gervais and Selling a Professional Practice*, 2015 Tax for the Owner-Manager 15(2):7–8; Tollstam, *FIFO Derails QSBC Planning*, 2013 Canadian Tax Highlights 21(9):9–10; Beswick and Young, *The Use of Holding Companies in the Private Business Context*, 2012 Canadian Tax Journal 1:169–191; Kakkar and Yan, *Practical Considerations in Claiming an ABIL or the Capital Gains Exemption*, 2012 Ontario Tax Conference 5:1–28; Hermann, *The Capital Gains Exemption: A Comprehensive Review*, 2000 Conference Report 29:1–54.

Tax Window Files: QSBCS deduction by the beneficiary, *June 4, 2012*, CRA Document No. 2012-0439271E5; Biens agricoles admissibles, *March 29, 2012*, CRA Document No. 2011-0427821E5; Avantage imposable - maison habitée sans frais, *March 22, 2012*, CRA Document No. 2011-0425571E5; Bien agricole admissible, *March 8, 2012*, CRA Document No. 2011-0426061E5; QSBC Shares, *January 16, 2012*, CRA Document No. 2011-0423951E5; Usufruit de terres boisées acquises avant 1987, *January 12, 2012*, CRA Document No. 2011-0421791E5; ITA 110.6(14)(f), *November 21, 2011*, CRA Document No. 2011-0424331E5; Providing a Statement of Account to a Bankrupt, *September 27, 2011*, CRA Document No. 2010-0385281I7; Purification - Small Business Corporation, *August 22, 2011*, CRA Document No. 2011-0415161E5; CGE - Qualified Small Business Corporation Shares, *August 15, 2011*, CRA Document No. 2011-0410871E5; Qualified Farm Property (Acq. before June 18, 87), *July 7, 2011*, CRA Document No. 2011-0396391E5; Active business, *April 11, 2011*, CRA Document No. 2011-0398011E5; Transfer of Farm Property, *March 14, 2011*, CRA Document No. 2011-0394201M4; Capital Gains and Farm Property, *November 24, 2010*, CRA Document No. 2010-0381321E5; Capital Gains Deduction, *October 20, 2010*, CRA Document No. 2010-0382651E5; Beneficial Ownership - Farm, *September 2, 2010*, CRA Document No. 2010-0367961E5; Qualified Small Business Corporation Share, *July 13, 2010*, CRA Document No. 2010-0359781E5; QSBCS - 24 Month Holding Period, *June 24, 2010*, CRA Document No. 2010-0367031E5; Qualified Farm Property, *June 18, 2010*, CRA Document No. 2010-0356961E5; Qualified Farm Property, *February 18, 2010*, CRA Document No. 2009-0344851E5; Asset Used Principally in an Active Business, *Income Tax Rulings Directorate, Business and Partnerships Division, November 5, 2009*, CRA Document No. 2009-0307931E5; Actions admissibles de petite entreprise, *October 9, 2009*, CRA Document No. 2009-0330071C6; Qualified Farm Property, *Income Tax Rulings Directorate, Business and Partnerships Division, October 7, 2009*, CRA Document No. 2009-0332871I7; Qualified Farm Property — Family Farm Corporation, *Income Tax Rulings Directorate, March 16, 2009*, CRA Document No. 2008-0299741I7; Quebec Servitude, *2006 APFF Conference Round Table on the Federal Taxation, Question 39, October 6, 2006*, CRA Document No. 2006-0196071C6; Specified Investment Business — Full-Time Employee Test, *Technical Interpretation, Business and Partnerships Division, June 7, 2006*, CRA Document No. 2005-0139641E5; Deemed Dividend on Sale of Shares to Unrelated Person, *Technical Interpretation, Reorganizations and Resources Division, December 30, 2003*, CRA Document No. 2003-0049105.

"annual gains limit" — "annual gains limit" of an individual for a taxation year means the amount determined by the formula

$$A - B$$

where

A is the lesser of

(*a*) the amount determined in respect of the individual for the year under paragraph 3(*b*) in respect of capital gains and capital losses, and

(*b*) the amount that would be determined in respect of the individual for the year under paragraph 3(*b*) in respect of capital gains and losses if the only properties referred to in that paragraph were properties that, at the time they were disposed of, were qualified farm properties, qualified fishing properties, qualified farm or fishing properties and qualified small business corporation shares, and

B is the total of

(*a*) the amount, if any, by which

(i) the individual's net capital losses for other taxation years deducted under paragraph 111(1)(*b*) in computing the individual's taxable income for the year

exceeds

(ii) the amount, if any, by which the amount determined in respect of the individual for the year under paragraph 3(*b*) in respect of capital gains and capital losses exceeds the amount determined for A in respect of the individual for the year, and

(*b*) all of the individual's allowable business investment losses for the year;

History: S. 110.6(1), paragraph (*b*) of the description of A in the definition "annual gains limit" was replaced by S.C. 2014, c. 39, s. 30(2), applicable to dispositions and transfers that occur in the 2014 and subsequent taxation years, and formerly read:

(*b*) the amount that would be determined in respect of the individual for the year under paragraph 3(*b*) in respect of capital gains and losses if the only properties referred to in that paragraph were qualified farm properties disposed of by the individual after 1984, qualified small business corporation shares disposed of by the individual after June 17, 1987 and qualified fishing properties disposed of by the individual on or after May 2, 2006, and

Related Sections: S. 3 Income for taxation year; s. 38 Taxable capital gain and allowable capital loss; s. 39(1) Meaning of capital gain and capital loss; s. 110.6(1), "eligible real property gain", "eligible real property loss", "non-qualifying real property"; s. 111(1)(*b*) Net capital losses; s. 248(1), "amount", "individual", "property".

Interpretation Bulletins: *Secondary* — IT-278R2 Death of a partner or of a retired partner; IT-373R2 (Consolid.) Woodlots.

"child" — "child" has the meaning assigned by subsection 70(10);

"cumulative gains limit" — "cumulative gains limit" of an individual at the end of a taxation year means the amount, if any, by which

(*a*) the total of all amounts determined in respect of the individual for the year or preceding taxation years that end after 1984 for A in the definition "annual gains limit"

exceeds the total of

(*b*) all amounts determined in respect of the individual for the year or preceding taxation years that end after 1984 for B in the definition "annual gains limit",

(*c*) the amount, if any, deducted under paragraph 3(*e*) in computing the individual's income for the 1985 taxation year,

(*d*) all amounts deducted under this section in computing the individual's taxable incomes for preceding taxation years, and

(*e*) the individual's cumulative net investment loss at the end of the year;

Related Sections: S. 3 Income for taxation year; s. 110.6(1), "annual gains limit", "Cumulative net investment loss"; s. 248(1), "amount", "individual".

"cumulative net investment loss" —"cumulative net investment loss" of an individual at the end of a taxation year means the amount, if any, by which

(*a*) the total of all amounts each of which is the investment expense of the individual for the year or a preceding taxation year ending after 1987

exceeds

(*b*) the total of all amounts each of which is the investment income of the individual for the year or a preceding taxation year ending after 1987;

Forms: T936 Calculation of Cumulative Net Investment Loss (CNIL) to December 31, 2018.

"eligible real property gain" — (Repealed by 1995, c. 3, s. 32(1).)

"eligible real property loss" — (Repealed by 1995, c. 3, s. 32(1).)

"interest in a family farm or fishing partnership" — "interest in a family farm or fishing partnership", of an individual (other than a trust that is not a personal trust) at any time, means a partnership interest owned by the individual at that time if

(*a*) throughout any 24-month period ending before that time, more than 50% of the fair market value of the property of the partnership was attributable to

(i) property that was used principally in the course of carrying on a farming or fishing business in Canada in which the individual, a beneficiary referred to in clause (C) or a spouse, common-law partner, child or parent of the individual or of a beneficiary referred to in clause (C) was actively engaged on a regular and continuous basis, by

(A) the partnership,

(B) the individual,

(C) if the individual is a personal trust, a beneficiary of the trust,

(D) a spouse, common-law partner, child or parent of the individual or of a beneficiary referred to in clause (C),

(E) a corporation, a share of the capital stock of which was a share of the capital stock of a family farm or fishing corporation of the individual, a beneficiary referred to in clause (C) or a spouse, common-law partner, child or parent of the individual or of a beneficiary referred to in clause (C), or

(F) a partnership, a partnership interest in which was an interest in a family farm or fishing partnership of the individual, a beneficiary referred to in clause (C) or a spouse, common-law partner, child or parent of the individual or of a beneficiary referred to in clause (C),

(ii) shares of the capital stock or indebtedness of one or more corporations of which all or substantially all of the fair market value of the property was attributable to properties described in subparagraph (iv),

(iii) a partnership interest in or indebtedness of one or more partnerships of which all or substantially all of the fair market value of the property was attributable to properties described in subparagraph (iv), or

(iv) properties described in any of subparagraphs (i) to (iii), and

(*b*) at that time, all or substantially all of the fair market value of the property of the partnership was attributable to property described in subparagraph (*a*)(iv);

History: S. 110.6(1), the definition "interest in a family farm or fishing partnership" was added by S.C. 2014, c. 39, s. 30(3), applicable to dispositions and transfers that occur in the 2014 and subsequent taxation years.

"interest in a family farm partnership" — (Repealed by S.C. 2014, c. 39, s. 30(1).)

History: S. 110.6(1), the definition "interest in a family farm partnership" was repealed by S.C. 2014, c. 39, s. 30(1), applicable to dispositions and transfers that occur in the 2014 and subsequent taxation years, and formerly read:

"interest in a family farm partnership"—"interest in a family farm partnership" of an individual (other than a trust that is not a personal trust) at any time means a partnership interest owned by the individual at that time if

(*a*) throughout any 24-month period ending before that time, more than 50% of the fair market value of the property of the partnership was attributable to

(i) property that was used principally in the course of carrying on the business of farming in Canada in which the individual, a beneficiary referred to in clause (C) or a spouse, common-law partner, child or parent of the individual or of a beneficiary referred to in clause (C) was actively engaged on a regular and continuous basis, by

(A) the partnership,

(B) the individual,

(C) where the individual is a personal trust, a beneficiary of the trust,

(D) a spouse, common-law partner, child or parent of the individual or of a beneficiary referred to in clause (C),

(E) a corporation, a share of the capital stock of which was a share of the capital stock of a family farm corporation of the individual, a beneficiary referred to in clause (C) or a spouse, common-law partner, child or parent of the individual or of a beneficiary referred to in clause (C), or

(F) a partnership, a partnership interest of which was an interest in a family farm partnership of the individual, a beneficiary referred to in clause (C) or a spouse, common-law partner, child or parent of the individual or of a beneficiary referred to in clause (C),

(ii) shares of the capital stock or indebtedness of one or more corporations all or substantially all of the fair market value of the property of which was attributable to properties described in subparagraph (iv),

(iii) a partnership interest in or indebtedness of one or more partnerships all or substantially all of the fair market value of the property of which was attributable to properties described in subparagraph (iv), or

(iv) properties described in any of subparagraph [*sic*] (i) to (iii), and

(*b*) at that time, all or substantially all of the fair market value of the property of the partnership was attributable to property described in subparagraph (*a*)(iv);

Related Sections: S. 104(1) Reference to trust or estate; s. 248(1), "business", "common-law partner", "corporation", "farming", "individual", "property", "trust"; s. 252(1) Extended meaning of "child"; s. 252(2) Relationships.

"interest in a family fishing partnership" — (Repealed by S.C. 2014, c. 39, s. 30(1).)

History: S. 110.6(1), the definition "interest in a family fishing partnership" was repealed by S.C. 2014, c. 39, s. 30(1), applicable to dispositions and transfers that occur in the 2014 and subsequent taxation years, and formerly read:

"interest in a family fishing partnership"—"interest in a family fishing partnership" of an individual (other than a trust that is not a personal trust) at any time means a partnership interest owned by the individual at that time if

(a) throughout any 24-month period ending before that time, more than 50% of the fair market value of the property of the partnership was attributable to

(i) property that was used principally in the course of carrying on the business of fishing in Canada in which the individual, a beneficiary referred to in clause (C) or a spouse or common-law partner, child or parent of the individual or of a beneficiary referred to in clause (C) was actively engaged on a regular and continuous basis, by

(A) the partnership,

(B) the individual,

(C) where the individual is a personal trust, a beneficiary of the trust,

(D) a spouse, common-law partner, child or parent of the individual or of a beneficiary referred to in clause (C),

(E) a corporation, a share of the capital stock of which was a share of the capital stock of a family fishing corporation of the individual, a beneficiary referred to in clause (C) or a spouse, common-law partner, child or parent of the individual or of a beneficiary referred to in clause (C), or

(F) a partnership, a partnership interest of which was an interest in a family fishing partnership of the individual, a beneficiary referred to in clause (C) or a spouse, common-law partner, child or parent of the individual or of a beneficiary referred to in clause (C),

(ii) shares of the capital stock or indebtedness of one or more corporations all or substantially all of the fair market value of the property of which was attributable to properties described in subparagraph (iv),

(iii) a partnership interest in or indebtedness of one or more partnerships all or substantially all of the fair market value of the property of which was attributable to properties described in subparagraph (iv), or

(iv) properties described in any of subparagraph (i) to (iii), and

(b) at that time, all or substantially all of the fair market value of the property of the partnership was attributable to property described in subparagraph (a)(iv);

"investment expense" —"investment expense" of an individual for a taxation year means the total of

(a) all amounts deducted in computing the individual's income for the year from property (except to the extent that the amounts were otherwise taken into account in computing the individual's investment expense or investment income for the year) other than any amounts deducted under

(i) paragraph 20(1)(c), (d), (e) or (e.1) of this Act or paragraph 20(1)(k) of the *Income Tax Act*, chapter 148 of the Revised Statutes of Canada, 1952, in respect of borrowed money that was used by the individual, or that was used to acquire property that was used by the individual,

(A) to make a payment as consideration for an income-averaging annuity contract,

(B) to pay a premium under a registered retirement savings plan, or

(C) to make a contribution to a pooled registered pension plan, registered pension plan or deferred profit sharing plan, or

(ii) paragraph 20(1)(j) or subsection 65(1), 66(4), 66.1(3), 66.2(2), 66.21(4) or 66.4(2),

(b) the total of

(i) all amounts deducted under paragraph 20(1)(c), (d), (e), (e.1), (f) or (bb) of this Act or paragraph 20(1)(k) of the *Income Tax Act*, chapter 148 of the Revised Statutes of Canada, 1952 in computing the individual's income for the year from a partnership of which the individual was a specified member in the fiscal period of the partnership ending in the year, and

(ii) all amounts deducted under subparagraph 20(1)(e)(vi) in computing the individual's income for the year in respect of an expense incurred by a partnership of which the individual was a specified member in the fiscal period of the partnership ending immediately before it ceased to exist,

(c) the total of

(i) all amounts (other than allowable capital losses) deducted in computing the individual's income for the year in respect of the individual's share of the amount of any loss of a partnership of which the individual was a specified member in the partnership's fiscal period ending in the year, and

(ii) all amounts each of which is an amount deducted under paragraph 111(1)(e) in computing the individual's taxable income for the year,

(d) 50% of the total of all amounts each of which is an amount deducted under subsection 66(4), 66.1(3), 66.2(2), 66.21(4) or 66.4(2) in computing the individual's income for the year in respect of expenses

(i) incurred and renounced under subsection 66(12.6), (12.601), (12.62) or (12.64) by a corporation, or

(ii) incurred by a partnership of which the individual was a specified member in the fiscal period of the partnership in which the expense was incurred, and

(e) the total of all amounts each of which is the amount of the individual's loss for the year from

(i) property, or

(ii) renting or leasing a rental property (within the meaning assigned by subsection 1100(14) of the *Income Tax Regulations*) or a property described in Class 31 or 32 of Schedule II to the *Income Tax Regulations*

owned by the individual or by a partnership of which the individual was a member, other than a partnership of which the individual was a specified member in the partnership's fiscal period ending in the year, and

(f) the amount, if any, by which the total of the individual's net capital losses for other taxation years deducted under paragraph 111(1)(b) in computing the individual's taxable income for the year exceeds the amount determined in respect of the individual for the year under paragraph (a) of the description of B in the definition "annual gains limit";

History: S. 110.6(1), clause (a)(i)(C) of the definition "investment expense" was replaced by S.C. 2012, c. 31, s. 24(1), in force December 14, 2012, and formerly read:

(C) to make a contribution to a registered pension plan or a deferred profit sharing plan, or

Related Sections: S. 110.6(1), "annual gains limit"; s. 111(1)(b) Net capital losses; s. 248(1), "amount", "individual".

"investment income" —"investment income" of an individual for a taxation year means the total of

(a) all amounts included in computing the individual's income for the year from property (other than an amount included under subsection 15(2) or paragraph 56(1)(d) of this Act or paragraph 56(1)(d.1) of the *Income Tax Act*, chapter 148 of the Revised Statutes of Canada 1952), including, for greater certainty, any amount so included under subsection 13(1) in respect of a property any income from which would be income from property (except to the extent that the amount was otherwise taken into account in computing the individual's investment income or investment expense for the year),

(b) all amounts (other than taxable capital gains) included in computing the individual's income for the year in respect of the individual's share of the income of a partnership of which the individual was a specified member in the partnership's fiscal period ending in the year, including, for greater certainty, the individual's share of all amounts included under subsection 13(1) in computing the income of the partnership,

(*c*) 50% of all amounts included under subsection 59(3.2) in computing the individual's income for the year,

(*d*) all amounts each of which is the amount of the individual's income for the year from

(i) a property, or

(ii) renting or leasing a rental property (within the meaning assigned by subsection 1100(14) of the *Income Tax Regulations*) or a property described in Class 31 or 32 of Schedule II to the *Income Tax Regulations*

owned by the individual or by a partnership of which the individual was a member (other than a partnership of which the individual was a specified member in the partnership's fiscal period ending in the year), including, for greater certainty, any amount included under subsection 13(1) in computing the individual's income for the year in respect of a rental property of the individual or the partnership or in respect of a property any income from which would be income from property,

(*e*) the amount, if any, by which

(i) the total of all amounts (other than amounts in respect of income-averaging annuity contracts or annuity contracts purchased under deferred profit sharing plans or plans referred to in subsection 147(15) as revoked plans) included under paragraph 56(1)(*d*) of this Act or paragraph 56(1)(*d*.1) of the *Income Tax Act*, chapter 148 of the Revised Statutes of Canada, 1952, in computing the individual's income for the year

exceeds

(ii) the total of all amounts deducted under paragraph 60(*a*) in computing the individual's income for the year, and

(*f*) the amount, if any, by which the total of all amounts included under paragraph 3(*b*) in respect of capital gains and capital losses in computing the individual's income for the year exceeds the amount determined in respect of the individual for the year for A in the definition "annual gains limit";

Related Sections: S. 3 Income for taxation year; s. 110.6(1), "annual gains limit"; s. 248(1), "amount".

"non-qualifying real property" — (Repealed by S.C. 1995, c. 3, s. 32(1).)

"qualified farm property" — (Repealed by S.C. 2014, c. 39, s. 30(1).)

History: S. 110.6(1), the definition "qualified farm property" was repealed by S.C. 2014, c. 39, s. 30(1), applicable to dispositions and transfers that occur in the 2014 and subsequent taxation years, and formerly read:

"qualified farm property"—"qualified farm property" of an individual (other than a trust that is not a personal trust) at any time means a property owned at that time by the individual, the spouse or common-law partner of the individual or a partnership, an interest in which is an interest in a family farm partnership of the individual or the individual's spouse or common-law partner that is

(*a*) real or immovable property that was used in the course of carrying on the business of farming in Canada by,

(i) the individual,

(ii) if the individual is a personal trust, a beneficiary of the trust that is entitled to receive directly from the trust any income or capital of the trust,

(iii) a spouse, common-law partner, child or parent of a person referred to in subparagraph (i) or (ii),

(iv) a corporation, a share of the capital stock of which is a share of the capital stock of a family farm corporation of an individual referred to in any of subparagraphs (i) to (iii), or

(v) a partnership, an interest in which is an interest in a family farm partnership of an individual referred to in any of subparagraphs (i) to (iii),

(*b*) a share of the capital stock of a family farm corporation of the individual or the individual's spouse or common-law partner,

(*c*) an interest in a family farm partnership of the individual or the individual's spouse or common-law partner, or

(*d*) an eligible capital property (which is deemed to include capital property to which paragraph 70(5.1)(*b*) or 73(3.1)(*f*) applies) used by a person or partnership referred to in any of subparagraphs (*a*)(i) to (v), or by a personal trust from which the individual acquired the property, in the course of carrying on the business of farming in Canada;

S. 110.6(1), the portion of paragraph (*a*) before subparagraph (i) of the definition "qualified farm property" was replaced by S.C. 2013, c. 34, s. 240(1), applicable to dispositions of property that occur after May 1, 2006, and formerly read:

(*a*) real or immovable property that was used principally in the course of carrying on the business of farming in Canada by,

Tax Window Files: Farm Property Inherited by Children — Capital Gains Exemption under Subsection 110.6(2) — Inter Vivos Transfer under Subsection 73(3), *Technical Interpretation, Business and Partnerships Division, March 1, 2004*, CRA Document No. 2003-0017861E5.

"qualified farm or fishing property" —"qualified farm or fishing property", of an individual (other than a trust that is not a personal trust) at any time, means a property that is owned at that time by the individual, the spouse or common-law partner of the individual or a partnership, an interest in which is an interest in a family farm or fishing partnership of the individual or the individual's spouse or common-law partner and that is

(*a*) real or immovable property or a fishing vessel that was used in the course of carrying on a farming or fishing business in Canada by,

(i) the individual,

(ii) if the individual is a personal trust, a beneficiary of the trust that is entitled to receive directly from the trust any income or capital of the trust,

(iii) a spouse, common-law partner, child or parent of an individual referred to in subparagraph (i) or (ii),

(iv) a corporation, a share of the capital stock of which is a share of the capital stock of a family farm or fishing corporation of an individual referred to in any of subparagraphs (i) to (iii), or

(v) a partnership, an interest in which is an interest in a family farm or fishing partnership of an individual referred to in any of subparagraphs (i) to (iii),

(*b*) a share of the capital stock of a family farm or fishing corporation of the individual or the individual's spouse or common-law partner,

(*c*) an interest in a family farm or fishing partnership of the individual or the individual's spouse or common-law partner, or

(*d*) a property included in Class 14.1 of Schedule II to the *Income Tax Regulations*, used by a person or partnership referred to in any of subparagraphs (*a*)(i) to (v), or by a personal trust from which the individual acquired the property, in the course of carrying on a farming or fishing business in Canada;

History: S. 110(1), paragraph (*d*) of the definition "qualified farm or fishing property" was replaced by S.C. 2016, c. 12, s. 39(1), in force January 1, 2017, and formerly read:

(*d*) an eligible capital property (which is deemed to include capital property to which paragraph 70(5.1)(*b*) or 73(3.1)(*f*) applies) used by a person or partnership referred to in any of subparagraphs (*a*)(i) to (v), or by a personal trust from which the individual acquired the property, in the course of carrying on a farming or fishing business in Canada;

S. 110.6(1), the definition "qualified farm or fishing property" was added by S.C. 2014, c. 39, s. 30(3), applicable to dispositions and transfers that occur in the 2014 and subsequent taxation years.

Related Sections: 110.6(1) share of the capital stock of a family farm or fishing corporation; interest in a family farm or fishing partnership.

Canadian Tax Foundation: Friedley and Leenstra, *Opportunities, Pitfalls, and Traps Accessing the Capital Gains Exemption on Qualified Farm Property*, 2018 Prairie Provinces Tax Conference 12:0.

"qualified fishing property" — (Repealed by S.C. 2014, c. 39, s. 30(1).)

History: S. 110.6(1), the definition "qualified fishing property" was repealed by S.C. 2014, c. 39, s. 30(1), applicable to dispositions and transfers that occur in the 2014 and subsequent taxation years, and formerly read:

"qualified fishing property" — "qualified fishing property" of an individual (other than a trust that is not a personal trust) at any time means a property owned at that time by the individual, the spouse or common-law partner of the individual or a partnership, an interest in which is an interest in a family fishing partnership of the individual or the individual's spouse or common-law partner that is

(*a*) real or immovable property or a fishing vessel that was used in the course of carrying on the business of fishing in Canada by,

(i) the individual,

(ii) if the individual is a personal trust, a beneficiary of the trust that is entitled to receive directly from the trust any income or capital of the trust,

(iii) a spouse, common-law partner, child or parent of a person referred to in subparagraph (i) or (ii),

(iv) a corporation, a share of the capital stock of which is a share of the capital stock of a family fishing corporation of an individual referred to in any of subparagraphs (i) to (iii), or

(v) a partnership, an interest in which is an interest in a family fishing partnership of an individual referred to in any of subparagraphs (i) to (iii),

(*b*) a share of the capital stock of a family fishing corporation of the individual or the individual's spouse or common-law partner,

(*c*) an interest in a family fishing partnership of the individual or the individual's spouse or common-law partner, or

(*d*) an eligible capital property (which is deemed to include capital property to which paragraph 70(5.1)(*b*) or 73(3.1)(*f*) applies) used by a person or partnership referred to in any of subparagraphs (*a*)(i) to (v), or by a personal trust from which the individual acquired the property, in the course of carrying on the business of fishing in Canada;

S. 110.6(1), the portion of paragraph (*a*) before subparagraph (i) of the definition "qualified fishing property" was replaced by S.C. 2013, c. 34, s. 240(2), applicable to dispositions of property that occur after May 1, 2006, and formerly read:

(*a*) real or immovable property or a fishing vessel that was used principally in the course of carrying on the business of fishing in Canada by,

"qualified small business corporation share" — "qualified small business corporation share" of an individual (other than a trust that is not a personal trust) at any time (in this definition referred to as the "determination time") means a share of the capital stock of a corporation that,

(*a*) at the determination time, is a share of the capital stock of a small business corporation owned by the individual, the individual's spouse or common-law partner or a partnership related to the individual,

(*b*) throughout the 24 months immediately preceding the determination time, was not owned by anyone other than the individual or a person or partnership related to the individual, and

(*c*) throughout that part of the 24 months immediately preceding the determination time while it was owned by the individual or a person or partnership related to the individual, was a share of the capital stock of a Canadian-controlled private corporation more than 50% of the fair market value of the assets of which was attributable to

(i) assets used principally in an active business carried on primarily in Canada by the corporation or by a corporation related to it,

(ii) shares of the capital stock or indebtedness of one or more other corporations that were connected (within the meaning of subsection 186(4) on the assumption that each of the other corporations was a "payer corporation" within the meaning of that subsection) with the corporation where

(A) throughout that part of the 24 months immediately preceding the determination time that ends at the time the corporation acquired such a share or indebtedness, the share or indebtedness was not owned by anyone other than the corporation, a person or partnership related to the corporation or a person or partnership related to such a person or partnership, and

(B) throughout that part of the 24 months immediately preceding the determination time while such a share or indebtedness was owned by the corporation, a person or partnership related to the corporation or a person or partnership related to such a person or partnership, it was a share or indebtedness of a Canadian-controlled private corporation more than 50% of the fair market value of the assets of which was attributable to assets described in subparagraph (iii), or

(iii) assets described in either of subparagraph (i) or (ii)

except that

(*d*) where, for any particular period of time in the 24-month period ending at the determination time, all or substantially all of the fair market value of the assets of a particular corporation that is the corporation or another corporation that was connected with the corporation cannot be attributed to assets described in subparagraph (*c*)(i), shares or indebtedness of corporations described in clause (*c*)(ii)(B), or any combination thereof, the reference in clause (*c*)(ii)(B) to "more than 50%" shall, for the particular period of time, be read as a reference to "all or substantially all" in respect of each other corporation that was connected with the particular corporation and, for the purpose of this paragraph, a corporation is connected with another corporation only where

(i) the corporation is connected (within the meaning of subsection 186(4) on the assumption that the corporation was a "payer corporation" within the meaning of that subsection) with the other corporation, and

(ii) the other corporation owns shares of the capital stock of the corporation and, for the purpose of this subparagraph, the other corporation shall be deemed to own the shares of the capital stock of any corporation that are owned by a corporation any shares of the capital stock of which are owned or are deemed by this subparagraph to be owned by the other corporation,

(*e*) where, at any time in the 24-month period ending at the determination time, the share was substituted for another share, the share shall be considered to have met the requirements of this definition only where the other share

(i) was not owned by any person or partnership other than a person or partnership described in paragraph (*b*) throughout the period beginning 24 months before the determination time and ending at the time of substitution, and

(ii) was a share of the capital stock of a corporation described in paragraph (*c*) throughout that part of the period referred to in subparagraph (i) during which such share was owned by a person or partnership described in paragraph (*b*), and

(*f*) where, at any time in the 24-month period ending at the determination time, a share referred to in subparagraph (*c*)(ii) is substituted for another share, that share shall be considered to meet the requirements of subparagraph (*c*)(ii) only where the other share

(i) was not owned by any person or partnership other than a person or partnership described in clause (*c*)(ii)(A) throughout the period beginning 24 months before the determination time and ending at the time of substitution, and

(ii) was a share of the capital stock of a corporation described in paragraph (*c*) throughout that part of the period referred to in subparagraph (i) during which the share was owned by a person or partnership described in clause (*c*)(ii)(A);

Editorial Note: The definition of qualified small business corporation ("QSBC") share is relevant for the purposes of the $400,000 capital gains deduction in s. 110.6(2) (indexed after 2014). The lifetime deduction is allowed for Canadian resident individuals, and the lifetime limit applies to gains from QSBC shares and qualified farm or fishing property (aggregate gains from all such properties).

Hold period: To qualify as a QSBC share of an individual, throughout the period of 24 months immediately preceding the time of disposition, the share must not have been owned by anyone other than the individual or a person or partnership related to the individual. Subsection 110.6(14) provides special rules for determining when a person or partnership is related to the individual for this purpose, which may permit shareholders of new small business corporations (e.g., incorporating a business as long as all or substantially all of the business assets are transferred in) to have access to the capital gains exemption.

Although the individual shareholder must have been resident in Canada throughout the year of disposition, the individual need not be resident throughout the 24-month hold period (CRA Document No. 2010-0359781E5).

90% or more asset test: At the time of the disposition, the corporation must be a "small business corporation" ("SBC") (s. 248(1)). It therefore must meet the "all or substantially all" requirement in terms of its business assets or shares or debt in other connected small business corporations (generally 90% or more) at the time of the disposition. Note that the 12-month grace period allowed prior to the disposition (for the all or substantially all test) applies only for the purposes of the ABIL rules in s. 39(1)(*c*), and not for the purposes of the capital gains deduction.

An "active business" (s. 248(1)) does not include a personal services business or a specified investment business.

In one case where the term deposits maintained by a corporation were not an integral aspect of its business operations, the corporation did not meet the "all or substantially all" test, and hence was not a qualified small business corporation for the purpose of the capital gains deduction (see *Skidmore et al. v. The Queen*, 2000 DTC 6186 (F.C.A.)).

According to the Canada Revenue Agency ("CRA"), a "future income tax asset is not an asset for the purposes of the definition of SBC and of the definition of QSBC" (CRA Document No. 2014-0537611C6).

50% or more asset test: In addition, in general terms, the corporation must have been a Canadian-controlled private corporation ("CCPC") and must have had more than 50% of the fair market value ("FMV") of its assets used in an active business carried on primarily in Canada throughout the 24-month period prior to the disposition of the share. Where the corporation held shares or debt of a connected corporation (as defined in s. 186(4)), the following conditions can fulfill the 50% asset requirement: (1) the shares or debt of the connected corporation were not held by anyone other than specified related parties throughout the relevant part (described in clause (*c*)(ii)(A) of the definition) of the 24-month period; and (2) throughout the relevant part (described in clause (*c*)(ii)(B)) of the 24-month period, the connected corporation was a CCPC that used more than 50% of the FMV of its assets in an active business as defined above. However, during any time where all or substantially all of the corporation's assets were neither assets used in an active business carried on primarily in Canada by the corporation or a related corporation, nor are shares or debt of connected corporations that meet the 50% active business test, the connected corporations must meet the all or substantially all test for their assets during that time (90% or more).

Related Sections: 110.6(1.1) Value of NISA; 110.6(2.1) Capital gains deduction — qualified small business corporation shares; 110.6(16) Personal trust; 125(7) Canadian-controlled private corporation; 248(1) small business corporation.

Canadian Tax Foundation: Mammola and Youn, *The Capital Gains Exemption: Selected Planning Issues Related to Qualified Small Business Corporation Shares*, 2017 Canadian Tax Journal 1:191–214.

Information Circulars: IC 88-2 General anti-avoidance rule — Section 245 of the Income Tax Act (para. 15).

Tax Window Files: Undivided Interest in Shares, *Technical Interpretation, Business and Partnerships Division, June 9, 2005*, CRA Document No. 2004-0092001E5. Undivided interest in shares could qualify for the capital gains exemption; Capital Gains Exemption — Qualified Small Business Corporation Shares, *Technical Interpretation, Business and Partnerships Division, October 18, 2004*, CRA Document No. 2004-0077151E5. Purported unfairness of 24-month ownership rule for newly issued QSBC shares when compared to exception in paragraph 110.6(14), where rule waived if unincorporated business transferred to corporation for newly issued shares; Assets Used in Active Business — Vacant Land Held for Resale, *Technical Interpretation, Business and Partnerships Division, July 20, 2004*, CRA Document No. 2004-0062031E5. Whether holding vacant land for resale is active business carried on by corporation.

Cases: Throughout the 24-month period preceding the taxpayers' disposition of their shares of the corporation, it was not a qualified small business corporation because not more than 50% of its assets were attributable to assets used principally in an active business carried on primarily in Canada by it. The corporation was a holding company and not carrying on a business. In addition, throughout the same 24 months, the shares of the subsidiary owned by the corporation also were not shares of a qualified small business corporation, inasmuch as not more than 50% of the fair market value of its assets were attributable to assets used principally in an active business carried out primarily in Canada by it or a corporation related or connected to it. *Durocher et al v. The Queen*, 2016 DTC 1013 (TCC), appeal dismissed 2017 DTC 5050 (FCA)

Despite the applicant being less than 24 months old, he still met the 24-month share ownership requirement governing entitlement to the capital gains deduction. *Pellerin v. The Queen*, 2015 DTC 1125 (T.C.C.)

A corporation spent several years trying to develop a river's hydro-electric potential. The fact that they were never able to reach an agreement for the sale of the electricity did not mean that they were not carrying on an active business during the years of preparation. Accordingly, its shares were eligible for a QSBC deduction. *Hudon et al. v. The Queen*, 2001 DTC 5630 (F.C.A.), reversing *Harquail v. The Queen*, 99 DTC 1318 (T.C.C.)

Since the term deposits it maintained were not required as a form of self insurance in the event of crop failure and it was not relying on them as an integral aspect of its business operations, a corporation did not meet the "all or substantially all" test and hence was not a qualified small business corporation for the purpose of the capital gains deduction. *Skidmore et al. v. The Queen*, 2000 DTC 6186 (F.C.A.), affirming 98 DTC 1135 (T.C.C.).

"share of the capital stock of a family farm corporation" — (Repealed by S.C. 2014, c. 39, s. 30(1).)

History: S. 110.6(1), the definition "share of the capital stock of a family farm corporation" was repealed by S.C. 2014, c. 39, s. 30(1), applicable to dispositions and transfers that occur in the 2014 and subsequent taxation years, and formerly read:

"share of the capital stock of a family farm corporation" — "share of the capital stock of a family farm corporation" of an individual (other than a trust that is not a personal trust) at any time means a share of the capital stock of a corporation owned by the individual at that time if

(*a*) throughout any 24-month period ending before that time, more than 50% of the fair market value of the property owned by the corporation was attributable to

(i) property that was used principally in the course of carrying on the business of farming in Canada in which the individual, a beneficiary referred to in clause (C) or a spouse or common-law partner, child or parent of the individual or of a beneficiary referred to in clause (C) was actively engaged on a regular and continuous basis, by

(A) the corporation,

(B) the individual,

(C) where the individual is a personal trust, a beneficiary of the trust,

(D) a spouse, common-law partner, child or parent of the individual or of a beneficiary referred to in clause (C),

(D.1) [Spent. Applicable before May, 2, 2006.]

(E) another corporation that is related to the corporation and of which a share of the capital stock was a share of the capital stock of a family farm corporation of the individual, a beneficiary referred to in clause (C) or a spouse, common-law partner, child or parent of the individual or of a beneficiary referred to in clause (C), or

(F) a partnership, an interest in which was an interest in a family farm partnership of the individual, a beneficiary referred to in clause (C) or a spouse, common-law partner, child or parent of the individual or of such a beneficiary,

(ii) shares of the capital stock or indebtedness of one or more corporations all or substantially all of the fair market value of the property of which was attributable to property described in subparagraph (iv),

(iii) a partnership interest in or indebtedness of one or more partnerships all or substantially all of the fair market value of the property of which was attributable to properties described in subparagraph (iv), or

(iv) properties described in any of subparagraphs (i) to (iii), and

(*b*) at that time, all or substantially all of the fair market value of the property owned by the corporation was attributable to property described in subparagraph (*a*)(iv);

Related Sections: 39(1) capital gain; 39(1) capital loss; 70(9.8) Leased farm or fishing property; 70(10) share of the capital stock of a family farm corporation; 110.6(1.1) Value of NISA; 110.6(2) Capital gains deduction — qualified farm or fishing property; s. 248(1), "active business", "Canadian-controlled private corporation", "farming", "property", "small business corporation", "specified member"; 251 Arm's length.

Forms: T657 — Calculation of Capital Gains Deduction for 1999; T936 — Calculation of Cumulative Net Investment Loss (CNIL) to December 31, 1999.

Interpretation Bulletins: *Secondary* — IT-232R3 Losses — Their deductibility in the loss year or in other years; IT-268R4 Inter vivos transfer of farm property to child; IT-268R3 Inter vivos transfer of farm property to child; IT-369R Attribution of trust income to settlor; IT-381R3 Trusts — Deduction of amounts paid or payable to beneficiaries and flow-through of taxable capital gains to beneficiaries; IT-451R Deemed disposition and acquisition on ceasing to be or becoming resident in Canada; IT-504R2 (Consolid.) Visual artists and writers.

"share of the capital stock of a family farm or fishing corporation" — "share of the capital stock of a family farm or fishing corporation", of an individual (other than a trust that is not a personal trust) at any time, means a share of the capital stock of a corporation owned by the individual at that time if

(*a*) throughout any 24-month period ending before that time, more than 50% of the fair market value of the property owned by the corporation was attributable to

(i) property that was used principally in the course of carrying on a farming or fishing business in Canada in which the individual, a beneficiary referred to in clause (C) or a spouse or common-law partner, child or parent of the individual or of a beneficiary referred to in clause (C), was actively engaged on a regular and continuous basis, by

(A) the corporation,

(B) the individual,

(C) if the individual is a personal trust, a beneficiary of the trust,

(D) a spouse, common-law partner, child or parent of the individual or of a beneficiary referred to in clause (C),

(E) another corporation that is related to the corporation and of which a share of the capital stock was a share of the capital stock of a family farm or fishing corporation of the individual, a beneficiary referred to in clause (C) or a spouse, common-law partner, child or parent of the individual or of a beneficiary referred to in clause (C), or

(F) a partnership, an interest in which was an interest in a family farm or fishing partnership of the individual, a beneficiary referred to in clause (C) or a spouse, common-law partner, child or parent of the individual or of such a beneficiary,

(ii) shares of the capital stock or indebtedness of one or more corporations of which all or substantially all of the fair market value of the property was attributable to property described in subparagraph (iv),

(iii) a partnership interest in or indebtedness of one or more partnerships of which all or substantially all of the fair market value of the property was attributable to properties described in subparagraph (iv), or

(iv) properties described in any of subparagraphs (i) to (iii), and

(*b*) at that time, all or substantially all of the fair market value of the property owned by the corporation was attributable to property described in subparagraph (*a*)(iv).

History: S. 110.6(1), the definition "share of the capital stock of a family farm or fishing corporation" was added by S.C. 2014, c. 39, s. 30(3), applicable to dispositions and transfers that occur in the 2014 and subsequent taxation years.

Income Tax Folios: S4-F8-C1 Business Investment Losses.

"share of the capital stock of a family fishing corporation" — (Repealed by S.C. 2014, c. 39, s. 30(1).)

History: S. 110.6(1), the definition "share of the capital stock of a family fishing corporation" was repealed by S.C. 2014, c. 39, s. 30(1), applicable to dispositions and transfers that occur in the 2014 and subsequent taxation years, and formerly read:

"share of the capital stock of a family fishing corporation" — "share of the capital stock of a family fishing corporation" of an individual (other than a trust that is not a personal trust) at any time means a share of the capital stock of a corporation owned by the individual at that time if

(*a*) throughout any 24-month period ending before that time, more than 50% of the fair market value of the property owned by the corporation was attributable to

(i) property that was used principally in the course of carrying on the business of fishing in Canada in which the individual, a beneficiary referred to in clause (C) or a spouse or common-law partner, child or parent of the individual or of a beneficiary referred to in clause (C), was actively engaged on a regular and continuous basis, by

(A) the corporation,

(B) the individual,

(C) where the individual is a personal trust, a beneficiary of the trust,

(D) a spouse, common-law partner, child or parent of the individual or of a beneficiary referred to in clause (C),

(E) another corporation that is related to the corporation and of which a share of the capital stock was a share of the capital stock of a family fishing corporation of the individual, a beneficiary referred to in clause (C) or a spouse, common-law partner, child or parent of the individual or of a beneficiary referred to in clause (C), or

(F) a partnership, an interest in which was an interest in a family fishing partnership of the individual, a beneficiary referred to in clause (C) or a spouse, common-law partner, child or parent of the individual or of such a beneficiary,

(ii) shares of the capital stock or indebtedness of one or more corporations all or substantially all of the fair market value of the property of which was attributable to property described in subparagraph (iv),

(iii) a partnership interest in or indebtedness of one or more partnerships all or substantially all of the fair market value of the property of which was attributable to properties described in subparagraph (iv), or

(iv) properties described in any of subparagraphs (i) to (iii), and

(*b*) at that time, all or substantially all of the fair market value of the property owned by the corporation was attributable to property described in subparagraph (*a*)(iv).

► 110.6(1.1) ◄

(1.1) Value of NISA. For the purposes of the definitions "qualified small business corporation share" and "share of the capital stock of a family farm or fishing corporation" in subsection (1), the fair market value of a net income stabilization account is deemed to be nil.

History: S. 110.6(1.1) was replaced by S.C. 2014, c. 39, s. 30(4), applicable to dispositions and transfers that occur in the 2014 and subsequent taxation years, and formerly read:

(1.1) *Idem.* For the purposes of the definitions "qualified small business corporation share" and "share of the capital stock of a family farm corporation" in subsection (1), the fair market value of a net income stabilization account shall be deemed to be nil.

► 110.6(1.2) ◄

(1.2) Property used in a fishing business — (Repealed by S.C. 2014, c. 39, s. 30(4).)

History: S. 110.6(1.2) was repealed by S.C. 2014, c. 39, s. 30(4), applicable to dispositions and transfers that occur in the 2014 and subsequent taxation years, and formerly read:

(1.2) *Property used in a fishing business.* For the purposes of applying the definition "qualified fishing property", in subsection (1), of an individual, at any time, a property owned at that time by the individual, the spouse or common-law partner of the individual, or a partnership, an interest in which is an interest in a family fishing partnership of the individual or of the individual's spouse or common-law partner, will not be considered to have been used in the course of carrying on the business of fishing in Canada, unless

(*a*) throughout the period of at least 24 months immediately preceding that time, the property or property for which the property was substituted (in this paragraph referred to as "the property") was owned, by any one or more of

(i) the individual, or a spouse, common-law partner, child or parent of the individual,

(ii) a partnership, an interest in which is an interest in a family fishing partnership of the individual or of the individual's spouse or common-law partner,

(iii) if the individual is a personal trust, the individual from whom the trust acquired the property or a spouse, common-law partner, child or parent of that individual, or

(iv) a personal trust from which the individual or a child or parent of the individual acquired the property; and

(*b*) either

(i) in at least two years while the property was owned by the one or more persons referred to in paragraph (*a*),

(A) the gross revenue of a person (in this clause referred to as the "operator") referred to in paragraph (*a*) from the fishing business referred to in clause (B) for the period during which the property was owned by a person described in paragraph (*a*) exceeded the income of the operator from all other sources for that period, and

(B) the property was used principally in a fishing business carried on in Canada in which an individual referred to in paragraph (*a*), or where the individual is a personal trust, a beneficiary of the trust, was actively engaged on a regular and continuous basis, or

(ii) throughout a period of at least 24 months while the property was owned by one or more persons referred to in paragraph (*a*), the property was used by a corporation referred to in subparagraph (*a*)(iv) of the definition "qualified fishing property" in subsection (1) or by a partnership referred to in paragraph (*a*)(v) of that definition in a fishing business in which an individual referred to in any of subparagraphs (*a*)(i) to (iii) of that definition was actively engaged on a regular and continuous basis.

► 110.6(1.3) ◄

(1.3) Farming or fishing property — conditions. For the purpose of applying the definition "qualified farm or fishing property", in subsection (1), of an individual, at any time, a property owned at that time by the individual, the spouse or common-law partner of the individual, or a partnership, an interest in which is an interest in a family farm or fishing partnership of the individual or of the individual's spouse or common-law partner, will not be considered to have been used in the course of carrying on a farming or fishing business in Canada, unless

(*a*) the following apply in respect of the property or property for which the property was substituted (in this paragraph referred to as "the property"),

(i) the property was owned throughout the period of at least 24 months immediately preceding that time by one or more of

(A) the individual, or a spouse, common-law partner, child or parent of the individual,

(B) a partnership, an interest in which is an interest in a family farm or fishing partnership of the individual or of the individual's spouse or common-law partner,

(C) if the individual is a personal trust, the individual from whom the trust acquired the property or a spouse, common-law partner, child or parent of that individual, or

(D) a personal trust from which the individual or a child or parent of the individual acquired the property, and

(ii) either

(A) in at least two years while the property was owned by one or more persons or partnerships referred to in subparagraph (i),

(I) the gross revenue of a person (in this subclause referred to as the "operator") referred to in subparagraph (i) from the farming or fishing business referred to in subclause (II) for the period during which the property was owned by a person or partnership described in subparagraph (i) exceeded the income of the operator from all other sources for that period, and

(II) the property was used principally in a farming or fishing business carried on in Canada in which an individual referred to in subparagraph (i), or where the individual is a personal trust, a beneficiary of the trust, was actively engaged on a regular and continuous basis, or

(B) throughout a period of at least 24 months while the property was owned by one or more persons or partnerships referred to in subparagraph (i), the property was used by a corporation referred to in subparagraph (*a*)(iv) of the definition "qualified farm or fishing property" in subsection (1) or by a partnership referred to in subparagraph (*a*)(v) of that definition in a farming or fishing business in which an individual referred to in any of subparagraphs (*a*)(i) to (iii) of that definition was actively engaged on a regular and continuous basis; or

(*b*) (Repealed by S.C. 2013, c. 34, s. 240(3).)

(*c*) if the property or property for which the property was substituted was last acquired by the individual or partnership before June 18, 1987 or after June 17, 1987 under an agreement in writing entered into before that date,

(i) in the year the property was disposed of by the individual, the property was used principally in the course of carrying on the business of farming in Canada by

(A) the individual, or a spouse, common-law partner, child or parent of the individual,

(B) a beneficiary referred to in subparagraph (*a*)(ii) of the definition "qualified farm or fishing property" in subsection (1) or a spouse, common-law partner, child or parent of that beneficiary,

(C) a corporation referred to in subparagraph (*a*)(iv) of the definition "qualified farm or fishing property" in subsection (1),

(D) a partnership referred to in subparagraph (*a*)(v) of the definition "qualified farm or fishing property" in subsection (1), or

(E) a personal trust from which the individual acquired the property, or

(ii) in at least five years during which the property was owned by a person described in any of clauses (A) to (E), the property was used principally in the course of carrying on the business of farming in Canada by

(A) the individual, or a spouse, common-law partner, child or parent of the individual,

(B) a beneficiary referred to in subparagraph (*a*)(ii) of the definition "qualified farm or fishing property" in subsection (1) or a spouse, common-law partner, child or parent of that beneficiary,

(C) a corporation referred to in subparagraph (*a*)(iv) of the definition "qualified farm or fishing property" in subsection (1),

(D) a partnership referred to in subparagraph (*a*)(v) of the definition "qualified farm or fishing property" in subsection (1), or

(E) a personal trust from which the individual acquired the property.

History: S. 110.6(1.3), the portion before paragraph (*c*) was replaced by S.C. 2014, c. 39, s. 30(5), applicable to dispositions and transfers that occur in the 2014 and subsequent taxation years, and formerly read:

(1.3) *Property used in a farming business.* For the purposes of applying the definition "qualified farm property", in subsection (1), of an individual, at any time, a property owned at that time by the individual, the spouse or common-law partner of the individual, or a partnership, an interest in which is an interest in a family farm partnership of the individual or of the individual's spouse or common-law partner, will not be considered to have been used in the course of carrying on the business of farming in Canada, unless

(*a*) the following apply in respect of the property or property for which the property was substituted (in this paragraph referred to as "the property"),

(i) the property was owned throughout the period of at least 24 months immediately preceding that time by one or more of

(A) the individual, or a spouse, common-law partner, child or parent of the individual,

(B) a partnership, an interest in which is an interest in a family farm partnership of the individual or of the individual's spouse or common-law partner,

(C) if the individual is a personal trust, the individual from whom the trust acquired the property or a spouse, common-law partner, child or parent of that individual, or

(D) a personal trust from which the individual or a child or parent of the individual acquired the property, and

(ii) either

(A) in at least two years while the property was owned by one or more persons referred to in subparagraph (i),

(I) the gross revenue of a person (in this subclause referred to as the "operator") referred to in subparagraph (i) from the farming business referred to in subclause (II) for the period during which the property was owned by a person described in subparagraph (i) exceeded the income of the operator from all other sources for that period, and

(II) the property was used principally in a farming business carried on in Canada in which an individual referred to in subparagraph (i), or where the individual is a personal trust, a beneficiary of the trust, was actively engaged on a regular and continuous basis, or

(B) throughout a period of at least 24 months while the property was owned by one or more persons or partnerships referred to in subparagraph (i), the property was used by a corporation referred to in subparagraph (*a*)(iv) of the definition "qualified farm property" in subsection (1) or by a partnership referred to in subparagraph (*a*)(v) of that definition in a farming business in which an individual referred to in any of subparagraphs (*a*)(i) to (iii) of that definition was actively engaged on a regular and continuous basis; or

(*b*) (Repealed.)

S. 110.6(1.3)(*c*) was replaced by S.C. 2014, c. 39, s. 30(6), applicable to dispositions and transfers that occur in the 2014 and subsequent taxation years, and formerly read:

(*c*) if the property or property for which the property was substituted was last acquired by the individual or partnership before June 18, 1987 or after June 17, 1987 under an agreement in writing entered into before that date,

(i) in the year the property was disposed of by the individual, the property was used principally in the course of carrying on the business of farming in Canada by

(A) the individual, or a spouse, common-law partner, child or parent of the individual,

(B) a beneficiary referred to in subparagraph (*a*)(ii) in the definition "qualified farm property" in subsection (1) or a spouse, common-law partner, child or parent of that beneficiary,

(C) a corporation referred to in subparagraph (*a*)(iv) in the definition "qualified farm property" in subsection (1),

(D) a partnership referred to in subparagraph (*a*)(v) in the definition "qualified farm property" in subsection (1), or

(E) a personal trust from which the individual acquired the property, or

(ii) in at least five years during which the property was owned by a person described in clauses (A) to (E), the property was used principally in the course of carrying on the business of farming in Canada by

(A) the individual, or a spouse, common-law partner, child or parent of the individual,

(B) a beneficiary referred to in subparagraph (*a*)(ii) in the definition "qualified farm property" in subsection (1) or a spouse, common-law partner, child or parent of that beneficiary,

(C) a corporation referred to in subparagraph (*a*)(iv) in the definition "qualified farm property" in subsection (1),

(D) a partnership referred to in subparagraph (*a*)(v) in the definition "qualified farm property" in subsection (1), or

(E) a personal trust from which the individual acquired the property.

S. 110.6(1.3)(*a*) and (*b*) were replaced by S.C. 2013, c. 34, s. 240(3), applicable to dispositions of property that occur after November 5, 2010, and formerly read:

(*a*) throughout the period of at least 24 months immediately preceding that time, the property or property for which the property was substituted (in this paragraph referred to as "the property") was owned, by any one or more of

(i) the individual, or a spouse, common-law partner, child or parent of the individual,

(ii) a partnership, an interest in which is an interest in a family farm partnership of the individual or of the individual's spouse or common-law partner,

(iii) if the individual is a personal trust, the individual from whom the trust acquired the property or a spouse, common-law partner, child or parent of that individual, or

(iv) a personal trust from which the individual or a child or parent of the individual acquired the property;

(*b*) if paragraph (*c*) does not apply, either

(i) in at least two years while the property was owned by the one or more persons referred to in paragraph (*a*),

(A) the gross revenue of a person (in this clause referred to as the "operator") referred to in paragraph (*a*) from the farming business referred to in clause (B) for the period during which the property was owned by a person described in paragraph (*a*) exceeded the income of the operator from all other sources for that period, and

(B) the property was used principally in a farming business carried on in Canada in which an individual referred to in paragraph (*a*), or where the individual is a personal trust, a beneficiary of the trust, was actively engaged on a regular and continuous basis, or

(ii) throughout a period of at least 24 months while the property was owned by one or more persons or partnerships referred to in paragraph (*a*), the property was used by a corporation referred to in subparagraph (*a*)(iv) of the definition "qualified farm property" in subsection (1) or by a partnership referred to in subparagraph (*a*)(v) of that definition in a farming business in which an individual referred to in any of subparagraphs (*a*)(i) to (iii) of that definition was actively engaged on a regular and continuous basis; or

Related Sections: 248(29) Farming or fishing business.

▶ 110.6(2) ◀

(2) Capital gains deduction — qualified farm or fishing property. In computing the taxable income for a taxation year of an individual (other than a trust) who was resident in Canada throughout the year and who disposed of qualified farm or fishing property in the year or a preceding taxation year (or who disposed of before 2014 property that was qualified farm property or qualified fishing property at the time of disposition), there may be deducted such amount as the individual may claim not exceeding the least of

(*a*) the amount determined by the formula

$$[\$400{,}000 - (A + B + C + D)] \times E$$

where

A is the total of all amounts each of which is an amount deducted under this section in computing the individual's taxable income for a preceding taxation year that ended

(i) before 1988, or

(ii) after October 17, 2000,

B is the total of all amounts each of which is

(i) 3/4 of an amount deducted under this section in computing the individual's taxable income for a preceding taxation year that ended after 1987 and before 1990 (other than amounts deducted under this section for a taxation year in respect of an amount that was included in computing an individual's income for that year because of subparagraph 14(1)(*a*)(v) as that subparagraph applied for taxation years that ended before February 28, 2000), or

(ii) 3/4 of an amount deducted under this section in computing the individual's taxable income for a preceding taxation year that began after February 27, 2000 and ended before October 18, 2000,

C is 2/3 of the total of all amounts each of which is an amount deducted under this section in computing the individual's taxable income

(i) for a preceding taxation year that ended after 1989 and before February 28, 2000, or

(ii) in respect of an amount that was included because of subparagraph 14(1)(*a*)(v) (as that subparagraph applied for taxation years that ended before February 28, 2000) in computing the individual's income for a taxation year that began after 1987 and ended before 1990,

D is the product obtained when the reciprocal of the fraction determined for E that applied to the taxpayer for a preceding taxation year that began before and included February 28, 2000 or October 17, 2000 is multiplied by the amount deducted under this subsection in computing the individual's taxable income for that preceding year,

E is

(i) in the case of a taxation year that includes February 28, 2000 or October 17, 2000, the amount determined by the formula

$$2 \times (F + G)/H$$

where

F is the amount deemed by subsection 14(1.1) to be a taxable capital gain of the taxpayer for the taxation year;

G is the amount by which the amount determined in respect of the taxpayer for the year under paragraph 3(*b*) exceeds the amount determined for F; and

H is the total of

(A) the amount deemed by subsection 14(1.1) to be a taxable capital gain of the taxpayer for the taxation year multiplied by

(I) where that amount is determined by reference to paragraph 14(1.1)(*a*), the reciprocal of the fraction obtained by multiplying the fraction 3/4 by the fraction in paragraph 14(1)(*b*) that applies to the taxpayer for the taxation year,

(II) where that amount is determined by reference to paragraph 14(1.1)(*b*), and the taxation year does not end after February 27, 2000 and before October 18, 2000, 2, and

(III) where that amount is determined by reference to paragraph 14(1.1)(*b*), and the taxation year ends after February 27, 2000 and before October 18, 2000, 3/2, and

(B) the amount determined for G multiplied by the reciprocal of the fraction in paragraph 38(*a*) that applies to the taxpayer for the taxation year; and

(ii) in any other case, 1,

(*b*) the individual's cumulative gains limit at the end of the year,

(*c*) the individual's annual gains limit for the year, and

(*d*) the amount that would be determined in respect of the individual for the year under paragraph 3(*b*) in respect of capital gains and capital losses if the only properties referred to in that paragraph were properties that, at the time they were disposed of, were qualified farm properties, qualified fishing properties or qualified farm or fishing properties.

CRA News Release

2.2% Indexation Factor for 2019

See the CRA Fact Sheet, dated November 16, 2018, that is reproduced following subsection117.1(1). This release announces a 2.2% indexation factor applicable for 2019 tax bracket thresholds, personal amounts and other amounts relating to non-refundable credits, as well as the refundable medical expense supplement, Old Age Security repayment threshold, certain board and lodging allowances, and the tradesperson's tools deduction. Increases to tax bracket thresholds, amounts relating to non-refundable credits, and most other amounts will take effect on January 1, 2019. However, increases in amounts for certain income-tested benefits (for example, the goods and services tax credit) will take effect on July 1, 2019.

Editorial Note: S. 110.6 provides for a lifetime $800,000 exemption for capital gains realized on the disposition of qualified farm or fishing property (s. 110.6(2)) and qualified small business corporation shares (s. 110.6(2.1)). Pursuant to changes announced in the 2013 Federal Budget, the lifetime limit was increased from $750,000 to $800,000 beginning in 2014, and is indexed for inflation for subsequent years (for gains after April 20, 2015, s. 110.6(2.2) provides an additional deduction for qualified farm or fishing property). The exemption may be claimed by Canadian-resident individuals, including, prior to 2016 and in limited circumstances, trusts (see s. 110.6(12)). A special rule in s. 110.6(5) applies where an individual ceases to be a resident in the year.

The terms "qualified farm or fishing property" and "qualified small business corporation share", as well as other terms, are defined in s. 110.6(1). The definition of "qualified farm or fishing property" imposes a use test and a holding period test which are critical to whether or not the property qualifies for the exemption (see also s. (1.3)). Although the person who claims the exemption is not required to carry on the farming or fishing business, he or she must generally be related to the person who did carry on the business. Similarly, the definition of a qualified small business corporation share requires the assets of the corporation to be used in an active business, and generally imposes a 24-month holding period test for the shares.

The exemption is limited by the individual's annual gain limit, as defined, which takes into account the capital gains realized in the current year on QFP and QSBC shares, the net capital losses claimed, and the allowable business investment losses. The exemption is also limited by the taxpayer's cumulative gains limit, as defined, which tracks the annual gains limit from prior years, the exemption previously claimed, and the taxpayer's cumulative net investment loss (investment expenses in excess of investment income). Various anti-avoidance rules also apply to restrict the exemption.

History: S. 110.6(2), the portion before paragraph (*a*) was replaced by S.C. 2014, c. 39, s. 30(7), applicable to dispositions and transfers that occur in the 2014 and subsequent taxation years, and formerly read:

(2) *Capital gains deduction — qualified farm property.* In computing the taxable income for a taxation year of an individual (other than a trust) who was resident in Canada throughout the year and who disposed of qualified farm property in the year or a preceding taxation year ending after 1984, there may be deducted such amount as the individual may claim not exceeding the least of

S. 110.6(2)(*d*) was replaced by S.C. 2014, c. 39, s. 30(8), applicable to dispositions and transfers that occur in the 2014 and subsequent taxation years, and formerly read:

(*d*) the amount that would be determined in respect of the individual for the year under paragraph 3(*b*) in respect of capital gains and capital losses if the only properties referred to in that paragraph were qualified farm properties of the individual disposed of after June 17, 1987.

S. 110.6(2)(*a*), the formula was replaced by S.C. 2013, c. 40, s. 46(1), applicable to the 2014 and subsequent taxation years, and formerly read:

[$375,000 - (A + B + C + D)] × E

Related Sections: S. 14(1) Eligible capital property — inclusion in income from business; s. 38 Taxable capital gain and allowable capital loss; s. 39 Meaning of capital gain and capital loss; s. 110.6(4) Maximum capital gains deduction; 110.6(6) Failure to report capital gain; 110.6(7) Deduction not permitted; 110.6(8) Deduction not permitted; s. 111.1 Order of applying provisions; s. 126(5.1) Deductions for specified capital gains; s. 248(1), "amount", "individual".

Canadian Tax Foundation: Shew and Wong, *Multi-Level Farming Structures and the Capital Gains Exemption*, 2016 Canadian Tax Focus 6(3):10–11.

Forms: T3 SK (CG) — Saskatchewan Farm and Small Business Capital Gains Tax Credit (Trusts); T1237 — Saskatchewan Farm and Small Business Capital Gains Tax Credit; T657 — Calculation of Capital Gains Deduction.

Interpretation Bulletins: *Secondary* — IT-426R Shares sold subject to an earnout agreement.

Tax Window Files: Farm Property Inherited by Children — Capital Gains Exemption under Subsection 110.6(2) — Inter Vivos Transfer under Subsection 73(3), *Technical Interpretation, Business and Partnerships Division, March 1, 2004*, CRA Document No. 2003-0017861E5.

► 110.6(2.1) ◄

(2.1) Capital gains deduction — qualified small business corporation shares. In computing the taxable income for a taxation year of an individual (other than a trust) who was resident in Canada throughout the year and who disposed of a share of a corporation in the year or a preceding taxation year and after June 17, 1987 that, at the time of disposition, was a qualified small business corporation share of the individual, there may be deducted such amount as the individual may claim not exceeding the least of

(*a*) the amount determined by the formula in paragraph (2)(*a*) in respect of the individual for the year,

(*b*) the amount, if any, by which the individual's cumulative gains limit at the end of the year exceeds the amount deducted under subsection (2) in computing the individual's taxable income for the year,

(*c*) the amount, if any, by which the individual's annual gains limit for the year exceeds the amount deducted under subsection (2) in computing the individual's taxable income for the year, and

(*d*) the amount that would be determined in respect of the individual for the year under paragraph 3(*b*) (to the extent that that amount is not included in computing the amount determined under paragraph (2)(*d*) in respect of the individual) in respect of capital gains and capital losses if the only properties referred to in paragraph 3(*b*) were qualified small business corporation shares of the individual.

Editorial Note: To qualify for this exemption (normally available only to Canadian-resident individuals other than trusts), shares must be those of a "small business corporation" (per s. 248(1)) at the time of disposition and be "qualified small business corporation shares", which entails the corporation meeting certain requirements with respect to assets in the preceding 24 months (see definition in s. 110.6(1) for further comments). The exemption is limited to the amount in excess of cumulative net investment losses. If ABILs have been incurred in the year or in a previous year, the exemption is limited to the excess of such amounts; conversely the exemption limits future year claims. The exemption may be reduced to the extent that deductions are claimed under the former $100,000 exemption or the qualifying farm property exemption and/or to the extent the lifetime capital gains exemption was previously claimed.

Circumstances in which the exemption may be denied include where the taxpayer did not report the gain or failed to file a return within one year of its deadline (knowingly or under gross negligence — s. 110.6(6)); where the exemption is part of a series of transactions involving a proportional butterfly or asset acquisition by a corporation or partnership at less than fair market value (s. 110.6(7)); where the corporation issued "low-dividend preferred shares" (ss. 110.6(8) and (9)); or where a flow-through entity has allocated a qualifying gain which is disproportionately large relative to the individual's income interest (s. 110.6(11)). A non-proportional tax deferred "spin-out" of some of the corporation's assets will generally not be available as part of a series of transactions where the exemption is claimed on a sale or other disposition of assets to an unrelated purchaser or a transaction that increases such person's interest in a corporation.

The 2011 federal Budget restricted the scope of s. 110.6(2.1) by adding to the tax on split income rules under s. 120.4 to include taxable capital gains (including from a trust) included in the income of a minor from the disposition of shares to a non-arm's length person, if taxable dividends on such shares would have been subject to the tax on split income. Accordingly, as such gains are excluded from taxable capital gains, they will not qualify for the 1/2 inclusion rate for capital gains, nor will they qualify for the lifetime capital gains exemption.

History: S. 110.6(2.1)(*d*) was replaced by S.C. 2014, c. 39, s. 30(9), applicable to dispositions and transfers that occur in the 2014 and subsequent taxation years, and formerly read:

(*d*) the amount that would be determined in respect of the individual for the year under paragraph 3(*b*) (to the extent that that amount is not included in computing the amount determined under paragraph (2)(*d*) or (2.2)(*d*) in respect of the individual) in respect of capital gains and capital losses if the only properties referred to in paragraph 3(*b*) were qualified small business corporation shares of the individual disposed of after June 17, 1987.

Related Sections: S. 38 Taxable capital gain and allowable capital loss; s. 39 Meaning of capital gain and capital loss; s. 48.1 Gain when small business corporation becomes public; s. 84.1 Non-arm's length sale of shares; 110.6(4) Maximum capital gains deduction; 110.6(5) Deemed resident in Canada; 110.6(6) Failure to report capital gain; 110.6(7) Deduction not permitted; 110.6(8) Deduction not permitted; s. 111.1 Order of applying provisions; s. 126(5.1) Deductions for specified capital gains; s. 248(1), "small business corporation".

Canadian Petroleum Tax Journal: A Practical Guide to the Flow-Through Share Rules, Greg Johnson, 2002, Vol. 15, No. 1.

Canadian Tax Foundation: Truster, *Gervais and Selling a Professional Practice*, 2015 Tax for the Owner-Manager 15(2):7–8; Tollstam, *FIFO Derails QSBC Planning*, 2013 Canadian Tax Highlights 21(9):9–10; Beswick and Young, *The Use of Holding Companies in the Private Business Context*, 2012 Canadian Tax Journal 1:169–191; Kakkar and Yan, *Practical Considerations in Claiming an ABIL or the Capital Gains Exemption*, 2012 Ontario Tax Conference 5:1–28; Hermann, *The Capital Gains Exemption: A Comprehensive Review*, 2000 Conference Report 29:1–54.

Tax Profile: April 2013 — Canadian Estate Freezes in Favour of U.S. Citizens; August 2012 — U.S. Purchases and Sales of Canadian Businesses: Tax and Corporate Issues; September 2011 — Acquisition of Canadian Business by Non-Residents; May 2011 — Partnership as a Holding Vehicle; November 2009 — Purchase and Sale of a Canadian Business; October 2007 — Will Canadian Unlimited Liability Companies Survive?; July 2005 — Alberta Introduces Alberta Unlimited Liability Corporations.

Tax Topics: No. 1881, Parallel Universe: La Survivance and the Capital Gains Exemption; No. 1879, Interaction of Subsections 110.6(2.1) and 256(9).

Information Circulars: IC 88-2 General anti-avoidance rule — Section 245 of the Income Tax Act (para. 15; Supp. 1, paras. 3 and 4).

Interpretation Bulletins: *Secondary* — IT-426R Shares sold subject to an earnout agreement.

Tax Window Files: Undivided Interest in Shares, *Technical Interpretation, Business and Partnerships Division, June 9, 2005*, CRA Document No. 2004-0092001E5. Undivided interest in shares could qualify for the capital gains exemption; Capital Loss Realized by Estate, *Technical Interpretation, Business and Partnerships Division, November 24, 2004*, CRA Document No. 2004-0088061I7. Capital losses on QSBC shares of an estate carried back under subsection 164(6) netted against the deceased's capital gains on QSBC shares in terminal year.

► 110.6(2.2) ◄

(2.2) Additional deduction — qualified farm or fishing property. In computing the taxable income for a taxation year of an individual (other than a trust) who was resident in Canada throughout the year and who disposed of qualified farm or fishing property in the year or a preceding taxation year and after April 20, 2015, there may be deducted an amount claimed by the individual that does not exceed the least of

(*a*) the amount, if any, by which $500,000 exceeds the total of

(i) $400,000 adjusted for each year after 2014 in the manner set out by section 117.1, and

(ii) the total of all amounts each of which is an amount deducted under this subsection in computing the individual's taxable income for a preceding taxation year that ended after 2014,

(*b*) the amount, if any, by which the individual's cumulative gains limit at the end of the year exceeds the total of all amounts each of which is an amount deducted by the individual under subsection (2) or (2.1) in computing the individual's taxable income for the year,

(*c*) the amount, if any, by which the individual's annual gains limit for the year exceeds the total of all amounts each of which is an amount deducted by the individual under subsection (2) or (2.1) in computing the individual's taxable income for the year, and

(*d*) the amount that would be determined in respect of the individual for the year under paragraph 3(*b*) in respect of capital gains and capital losses if the only properties referred to in that paragraph were qualified farm or fishing properties disposed of by the individual after April 20, 2015.

Editorial Note: Subsection 110.6(2.2) provides an enhanced capital gains exemption for gains after April 20, 2015 on the disposition of qualified farm or fishing property. The lifetime exemption limit for such gains is the greater of $400,000 (which is indexed) and $500,000 (which is not), so that the additional exemption will be available until the indexed amount exceeds $500,000.

History: S. 110.6(2.2) was added by S.C. 2015, c. 36, s. 7(1), applicable to taxation years that end after April 20, 2015.

S. 110.6(2.2) was repealed by S.C. 2014, c. 39, s. 30(10), applicable to dispositions and transfers that occur in the 2014 and subsequent taxation years, and formerly read:

(2.2) *Capital gains deduction — qualified fishing property.* In computing the taxable income for a taxation year of an individual (other than a trust) who was resident in Canada throughout the year and who, in the year or a preceding year, disposed of a property that was, at the time of disposition, a qualified fishing property of the individual, there may be deducted the amount that the individual claims not exceeding the least of

(*a*) the amount determined by the formula in paragraph (2)(*a*) in respect of the individual for the year;

(*b*) the amount, if any, by which the individual's cumulative gains limit at the end of that year exceeds the total of all amounts each of which is an amount deducted under subsection (2) or (2.1) in computing the individual's taxable income for the year;

(*c*) the amount, if any, by which the individual's annual gains limit for the year exceeds the total of all amounts each of which is an amount deducted under subsection (2) or (2.1) in computing the individual's taxable income for the year; and

(*d*) the amount that would be determined in respect of the individual for the year under paragraph 3(*b*) in respect of capital gains and capital losses if the only properties referred to in that paragraph were qualified fishing properties of the individual disposed of on or after May 2, 2006.

Related Sections: 104(21.21) Beneficiaries QFFP taxable capital gain; 110.6(2) Capital gains deduction — qualified farm or fishing property.

Canadian Tax Foundation: Shew and Wong, *Multi-Level Farming Structures and the Capital Gains Exemption*, 2016 Canadian Tax Focus 6(3):10–11.

▶ 110.6(2.3) ◀

(2.3) Additional deduction — ordering rule. Subsection (2.2) does not apply in computing the taxable income for a taxation year of an individual unless the individual has claimed the maximum amount that could be claimed under subsections (2) and (2.1) for the taxation year.

History: S. 110.6(2.3) was added by S.C. 2015, c. 36, s. 7(1), applicable to taxation years that end after April 20, 2015.

S. 110.6(2.3) was repealed by S.C. 2014, c. 39, s. 30(10), applicable to dispositions and transfers that occur in the 2014 and subsequent taxation years, and formerly read:

(2.3) *Additional capital gains deduction — taxation year that includes March 19, 2007.* In computing the taxable income of an individual (other than a trust) for the individual's taxation year that includes March 19, 2007 (referred to in this subsection as the "transition year"), there may be deducted, where that individual was resident in Canada throughout the transition year and that individual disposed of in the transition year, and on or after March 19, 2007, a qualified small business corporation share of the individual, a qualified farm property of the individual, or a qualified fishing property of the individual, such amount as the individual may claim not exceeding the least of

(*a*) $125,000,

(*b*) the amount, if any, by which the individual's cumulative gains limit at the end of the transition year exceeds the total of all amounts each of which is an amount deducted by the individual under subsection (2), (2.1) or (2.2) in computing the individual's taxable income for the transition year,

(*c*) the amount, if any, by which the individual's annual gains limit for the transition year exceeds the total of all amounts each of which is an amount deducted by the individual under subsection (2), (2.1) or (2.2) in computing the individual's taxable income for the transition year, and

(*d*) the amount that would be determined in respect of the individual for the transition year under paragraph 3(*b*) in respect of capital gains and capital losses if the only properties referred to in that paragraph were qualified small business corporation shares of the individual, qualified farm properties of the individual, and qualified fishing properties of the individual, disposed of by the individual on or after March 19, 2007.

Related Sections: 110.6(2) Capital gains deduction — qualified farm or fishing property; 110.6(2.1) Capital gains deduction — qualified small business corporation shares.

▶ 110.6(3) ◀

(3) Capital gains deduction — other property — (Repealed by S.C. 1995, c. 3, s. 32(3).)

▶ 110.6(4) ◀

(4) Maximum capital gains deduction. Notwithstanding subsections (2) and (2.1), the total amount that may be deducted under this section in computing an individual's income for a taxation year shall not exceed the total of the amount determined by the formula in paragraph (2)(*a*) and the amount that may be deducted under subsection (2.2), in respect of the individual for the year.

History: S. 110.6(4) was replaced by S.C. 2015, c. 36, s. 7(2), applicable to taxation years that end after April 20, 2015, and formerly read:

(4) **Maximum capital gains deduction.** Notwithstanding subsections (2) and (2.1), the total amount that may be deducted under this section in computing an individual's income for a taxation year shall not exceed the amount determined by the formula in paragraph (2)(*a*) in respect of the individual for the year.

S. 110.6(4) was replaced by S.C. 2014, c. 39, s. 30(10), applicable to dispositions and transfers that occur in the 2014 and subsequent taxation years, and formerly read:

(4) *Maximum capital gains deduction.* Notwithstanding subsections (2), (2.1) and (2.2), the total amount that may be deducted under this section in computing an individual's income for a taxation year shall not exceed the total of the amount determined by the formula in paragraph 2(*a*) and the amount that may be deducted under subsection (2.3), in respect of the individual for the year.

▶ 110.6(5) ◀

(5) Deemed resident in Canada. For the purposes of subsections (2) to (2.2), an individual is deemed to have been resident in Canada throughout a particular taxation year if

(*a*) the individual was resident in Canada at any time in the particular taxation year; and

(*b*) the individual was resident in Canada throughout the immediately preceding taxation year or throughout the immediately following taxation year.

History: S. 110.6(5), the portion before paragraph (*a*), was replaced by S.C. 2015, c. 36, s. 7(3), applicable to taxation years that end after April 20, 2015, and formerly read:

(5) **Deemed resident in Canada.** For the purposes of subsections (2) and (2.1), an individual is deemed to have been resident in Canada throughout a particular taxation year if

(*a*) the individual was resident in Canada at any time in the particular taxation year; and (*b*) the individual was resident in Canada throughout the immediately preceding taxation year or throughout the immediately following taxation year.

S. 110.6(5), the portion before paragraph (*a*) was replaced by S.C. 2014, c. 39, s. 30(11), applicable to dispositions and transfers that occur in the 2014 and subsequent taxation years, and formerly read:

(5) *Deemed resident in Canada.* For the purposes of subsections (2) to (2.3), an individual is deemed to have been resident in Canada throughout a particular taxation year if

Related Sections: S. 110.6(13) Determination under paragraph 3(b).

► 110.6(6) ◄

(6) Failure to report capital gain. Notwithstanding subsections (2) to (2.2), no amount may be deducted under this section in respect of a capital gain of an individual for a particular taxation year in computing the individual's taxable income for the particular taxation year or any subsequent year, if

(*a*) the individual knowingly or under circumstances amounting to gross negligence

(i) fails to file the individual's return of income for the particular taxation year within one year after the taxpayer's filing-due date for the particular taxation year, or

(ii) fails to report the capital gain in the individual's return of income for the particular taxation year; and

(*b*) the Minister establishes the facts justifying the denial of such an amount under this section.

History: S. 110.6(6), the portion before paragraph (*a*), was replaced by S.C. 2015, c. 36, s. 7(4), applicable to taxation years that end after April 20, 2015, and formerly read:

(6) **Failure to report capital gain.** Notwithstanding subsections (2) and (2.1), no amount may be deducted under this section in respect of a capital gain of an individual for a particular taxation year in computing the individual's taxable income for the particular taxation year or any subsequent year, if

(*a*) the individual knowingly or under circumstances amounting to gross negligence

(i) fails to file the individual's return of income for the particular taxation year within one year after the taxpayer's filing-due date for the particular taxation year, or

(ii) fails to report the capital gain in the individual's return of income for the particular taxation year; and

(*b*) the Minister establishes the facts justifying the denial of such an amount under this section.

S. 110.6(6), the portion before paragraph (*a*) was replaced by S.C. 2014, c. 39, s. 30(12), applicable to dispositions and transfers that occur in the 2014 and subsequent taxation years, and formerly read:

(6) *Failure to report capital gain.* Notwithstanding subsections (2) to (2.3), no amount may be deducted under this section in respect of a capital gain of an individual for a particular taxation year in computing the individual's taxable income for the particular taxation year or any subsequent year, if

S. 110.6(6), the portion before paragraph (*a*) was replaced by S.C. 2013, c. 34, s. 240(4), applicable to any taxation year for which a return of income has not been filed before October 31, 2011, except in respect of gains realized in another taxation year for which a return of income was filed before October 31, 2011. S. 110.6(6), the portion before paragraph (*a*) formerly read:

(6) *Failure to report capital gain.* Notwithstanding subsections (2) to (2.3), no amount may be deducted under this section in respect of a capital gain of an individual for a particular taxation year in computing the individual's taxable income for the particular taxation year, if

Forms: T657 — Calculation of Capital Gains Deduction.

► 110.6(7) ◄

(7) Deduction not permitted. Notwithstanding subsections (2) to (2.2), no amount may be deducted under this section in computing an individual's taxable income for a taxation year in respect of a capital gain of the individual for the taxation year if the capital gain is from a disposition of property which disposition is part of a series of transactions or events

(*a*) that includes a dividend received by a corporation to which dividend subsection 55(2) does not apply but would apply if this Act were read without reference to paragraph 55(3)(*b*); or

(*b*) in which any property is acquired by a corporation or partnership for consideration that is significantly less than the fair market value of the property at the time of acquisition (other than an acquisition as the result of an amalgamation or merger of corporations or the winding-up of a corporation or partnership or a distribution of property of a trust in satisfaction of all or part of a corporation's capital interest in the trust).

History: S. 110.6(7), the portion before paragraph (*a*), was replaced by S.C. 2015, c. 36, s. 7(5), applicable to taxation years that end after April 20, 2015, and formerly read:

(7) **Deduction not permitted.** Notwithstanding subsections (2) and (2.1), no amount may be deducted under this section in computing an individual's taxable income for a taxation year in respect of a capital gain of the individual for the taxation year if the capital gain is from a disposition of property which disposition is part of a series of transactions or events

(*a*) that includes a dividend received by a corporation to which dividend subsection 55(2) does not apply but would apply if this Act were read without reference to paragraph 55(3)(*b*); or

(*b*) in which any property is acquired by a corporation or partnership for consideration that is significantly less than the fair market value of the property at the time of acquisition (other than an acquisition as the result of an amalgamation or merger of corporations or the winding-up of a corporation or partnership or a distribution of property of a trust in satisfaction of all or part of a corporation's capital interest in the trust).

S. 110.6(7), the portion before paragraph (*a*) was replaced by S.C. 2014, c. 39, s. 30(13), applicable to dispositions and transfers that occur in the 2014 and subsequent taxation years, and formerly read:

(7) *Deduction not permitted.* Notwithstanding subsections (2) to (2.3), no amount may be deducted under this section in computing an individual's taxable income for a taxation year in respect of a capital gain of the individual for the taxation year if the capital gain is from a disposition of property which disposition is part of a series of transactions or events

► 110.6(8) ◄

(8) Deduction not permitted. Notwithstanding subsections (2) to (2.2), if an individual has a capital gain for a taxation year from the disposition of a property and it can reasonably be concluded, having regard to all the circumstances, that a significant part of the capital gain is attributable to the fact that dividends were not paid on a share (other than a prescribed share) or that dividends paid on such a share in the taxation year or in any preceding taxation year were less than 90% of the average annual rate of return on that share for that year, no amount in respect of that capital gain shall be deducted under this section in computing the individual's taxable income for the year.

Editorial Note: S. 110.6(8) — pertaining to "deficient dividends" — is operative to deny the capital gains exemption where it may reasonably be considered that either a significant portion of the capital gain is attributable to dividends not being paid on a share, or dividends paid on such a share were less than 90% of an amount determined by s. 110.6(9) — based on the return a "knowledgeable and prudent investor" would expect to receive. Conceptually, at least, these provisions can potentially apply in a very wide range of circumstances, and are not explicitly premised on an intent to enlarge capital gains exemption claims. Regulation 6205 contains detailed provisions that deal with the requirements for a "prescribed share", which is exempt from the provisions. Among other things, the regulations potentially enable shares in typical freeze structures to qualify.

History: S. 110.6(8) was replaced by S.C. 2015, c. 36, s. 7(6), applicable to taxation years that end after April 20, 2015, and formerly read:

(8) **Deduction not permitted.** Notwithstanding subsections (2) and (2.1), if an individual has a capital gain for a taxation year from the disposition of a property and it can reasonably be concluded, having regard to all the circumstances, that a significant part of the capital gain is attributable to the fact that dividends were not paid on a share (other than a prescribed share) or that dividends paid on such a share in the taxation year or in any preceding taxation year were less than 90% of the average annual rate of return on that share for that year, no amount in respect of that capital gain shall be deducted under this section in computing the individual's taxable income for the year.

S. 110.6(8) was replaced by S.C. 2014, c. 39, s. 30(14), applicable to dispositions and transfers that occur in the 2014 and subsequent taxation years, and formerly read:

(8) *Deduction not permitted.* Notwithstanding subsections (2) to (2.3), where an individual has a capital gain for a taxation year from the disposition of a property and it can reasonably be concluded, having regard to all the circumstances, that a significant part of the capital gain is attributable to the fact that dividends were not paid on a share (other than a prescribed share) or that dividends paid on such a share in the taxation year or in any preceding taxation year were less than 90% of the average annual rate of return on that share for that year, no amount in respect of that capital gain shall be deducted under this section in computing the individual's taxable income for the year.

Related Regulations: 6205.

Related Sections: S. 110.6(9) Average annual rate of return; s. 183.1(7) Where s. 110.6(8) does not apply.

Canadian Tax Foundation: Hudson and McCamis, *Refresher on Specific Anti-Avoidance Provisions*, 2014 Prairie Provinces Tax Conference 12:1–41.

► 110.6(9) ◄

(9) Average annual rate of return. For the purpose of subsection (8), the average annual rate of return on a share (other than a prescribed share) of a corporation for a taxation year is the annual rate of return by way of dividends that a knowledgeable and prudent investor who purchased the share on the day it was issued would expect to receive in that year, other than the first year after the issue, in respect of the share if

(*a*) there was no delay or postponement of the payment of dividends and no failure to pay dividends in respect of the share;

(*b*) there was no variation from year to year in the amount of dividends payable in respect of the share (other than where the amount of dividends payable is expressed as an invariant percentage of or by reference to an invariant difference between the dividend expressed as a rate of interest and a generally quoted market interest rate); and

(*c*) the proceeds to be received by the investor on the disposition of the share are the same amount the corporation received as consideration on the issue of the share.

Related Regulations: 6205.

► 110.6(10) ◄

(10) Gain from extension or renewal of option — (Repealed by 1988, c. 55, s. 81(13).)

► 110.6(11) ◄

(11) Where deduction not permitted. Where it is reasonable to consider that one of the main reasons for an individual acquiring, holding or having an interest in a partnership or trust (other than an interest in a personal trust) or a share of an investment corporation, mortgage investment corporation or mutual fund corporation, or for the existence of any terms, conditions, rights or other attributes of the interest or share, is to enable the individual to receive or have allocated to the individual a percentage of any capital gain or taxable capital gain of the partnership, trust or corporation that is larger than the individual's percentage of the income of the partnership, trust or corporation, as the case may be, notwithstanding any other provision of this Act,

(*a*) no amount may be deducted under this section by the individual in respect of any such gain allocated or distributed to the individual after November 21, 1985; and

(*b*) where the individual is a trust, any such gain allocated or distributed to it after November 21, 1985 shall not be included in computing its eligible taxable capital gain (within the meaning assigned by subsection 108(1)).

► 110.6(12) ◄

(12) Trust deduction — death of spouse or common-law partner — (Repealed by S.C. 2014, c. 39, s. 30(16).)

Editorial Note: Prior to 2016, s. 110.6(12) was an exception to the general exclusions in ss. 110.6(2), (2.1), and (2.2) that otherwise would prevent trusts from claiming the capital gains exemption. Under s. 110.6(12), the exemption might generally be claimed by a trust for the benefit of a spouse or common-law partner for the year of the trust in which the spouse or common-law partner dies. The exemption claimed by the trust could not exceed the unused exemption of the deceased spouse or common-law partner beneficiary.

History: S. 110.6(12) was repealed by S.C. 2014, c. 39, s. 30(16), applicable to the 2016 and subsequent taxation years, and formerly read:

(12) *Trust deduction — death of spouse or common-law partner.* Notwithstanding any other provision of this Act, a trust (other than an *alter ego* trust or a joint spousal or common-law partner trust) that is described in paragraph 104(4)(*a*) or (*a.1*) may, in computing its taxable income for its taxation year that includes the day determined under paragraph 104(4)(*a*) or (*a.1*), as the case may be, in respect of the trust, deduct under this section an amount equal to the least of

(*a*) the amount, if any, by which the eligible taxable capital gains (within the meaning assigned by subsection 108(1)) of the trust for that year exceeds the amount, if any, by which

(i) the total of all amounts each of which is the amount, if any, determined under paragraph (*b*) or (*d*) of the definition "cumulative gains limit" in subsection (1) in respect of the taxpayer's spouse or common-law partner at the end of the taxation year in which the spouse or common-law partner died

exceeds

(ii) the amount if any, determined under paragraph (*a*) of the definition "cumulative gains limit" in subsection (1) in respect of the taxpayer's spouse or common-law partner at the end of the taxation year in which the spouse or common-law partner died,

(*b*) the amount, if any, that would be determined in respect of the trust for that year under paragraph 3(*b*) in respect of capital gains and capital losses if the only properties referred to in that paragraph were properties that, at the time they were disposed of, were qualified farm or fishing properties, qualified small business corporation shares, qualified farm properties or qualified fishing properties, and

(*c*) the amount, if any, by which the amount determined by the formula in paragraph (2)(*a*) in respect of the taxpayer's spouse or common-law partner for the taxation year in which that spouse or common-law partner died exceeds the amount deducted under this section for that taxation year by that spouse or common-law partner.

S. 110.6(12)(*b*) was replaced by S.C. 2014, c. 39, s. 30(15), applicable to dispositions and transfers that occur in the 2014 and subsequent taxation years, and formerly read:

(*b*) the amount, if any, that would be determined in respect of the trust for that year under paragraph 3(*b*) in respect of capital gains and capital losses if the only properties referred to in that paragraph were qualified farm properties disposed of by it after 1984, qualified small business corporation shares disposed of by it after June 17, 1987 and qualified fishing properties disposed of by it on or after May 2, 2006, and

S. 110.6(12), the portion before paragraph (*a*) was replaced by S.C. 2013, c. 34, s. 240(6), applicable to taxation years that begin after October 31, 2011, and formerly read:

(12) *Trust deduction.* Notwithstanding any other provision of this Act, a trust described in paragraph 104(4)(*a*) or (*a*.1) (other than a trust that elected under subsection 104(5.3), an *alter ego* trust or a joint spousal or common-law partner trust) may, in computing its taxable income for its taxation year that includes the day determined under paragraph 104(4)(*a*) or (*a*.1), as the case may be, in respect of the trust, deduct under this section an amount equal to the least of

Related Sections: S. 3(*b*) Net taxable capital gains; s. 39 Meaning of capital gain and capital loss; s. 54, "disposition of property"; s. 104(4) Deemed disposition by trust; s. 104(5.3) Election; s. 110.6(1), "eligible real property gain", "eligible real property loss", "non-qualifying real property"; s. 248(1), "amount", "property".

Forms: T3 SCH 4 — Cumulative Net Investment Loss; T3 SCH 5 — Beneficiary Spouse or Common-Law Partner Information and Spousal or Common-Law Partner Trust's Capital Gains Deduction.

► 110.6(13) ◄

(13) Determination under paragraph 3(*b*). For the purposes of this section, the amount determined under paragraph 3(*b*) in respect of an individual for a period throughout which the individual was not resident in Canada is nil.

► 110.6(14) ◄

(14) Related persons, etc. For the purposes of the definition "qualified small business corporation share" in subsection (1),

(*a*) a taxpayer shall be deemed to have disposed of shares that are identical properties in the order in which the taxpayer acquired them;

(*b*) in determining whether a corporation is a small business corporation or a Canadian-controlled private corporation at any time, a right referred to in paragraph 251(5)(*b*) shall not include a right under a purchase and sale agreement relating to a share of the capital stock of a corporation;

(*c*) a personal trust shall be deemed

(i) to be related to a person or partnership for any period throughout which the person or partnership was a beneficiary of the trust, and

(ii) in respect of shares of the capital stock of a corporation, to be related to the person from whom it acquired those shares where, at the time the trust disposed of the shares, all of the beneficiaries (other than registered charities) of the trust were related to that person or would have been so related if that person were living at that time;

(*d*) a partnership shall be deemed to be related to a person for any period throughout which the person was a member of the partnership;

(*d*.1) a person who is a member of a partnership that is a member of another partnership is deemed to be a member of the other partnership;

(*e*) where a corporation acquires shares of a class of the capital stock of another corporation from any person, it shall be deemed in respect of those shares to be related to the person where all or substantially all the consideration received by that person from the corporation in respect of those shares was common shares of the capital stock of the corporation;

(*f*) shares issued after June 13, 1988 by a corporation to a particular person or partnership shall be deemed to have been owned immediately before their issue by a person who was not related to the particular person or partnership unless the shares were issued

(i) as consideration for other shares,

(ii) as part of a transaction or series of transactions in which the person or partnership disposed of property to the corporation that consisted of

(A) all or substantially all the assets used in an active business carried on by that person or the members of that partnership, or

(B) an interest in a partnership all or substantially all the assets of which were used in an active business carried on by the members of the partnership, or

(iii) as payment of a stock dividend; and

(*g*) where, immediately before the death of an individual, or, in the case of a deemed transfer under subsection 248(23), immediately before the time that is immediately before the death of an individual, a share would, but for paragraph (*a*) of the definition "qualified small business corporation share" in subsection (1), be a qualified small business corporation share of the individual, the share shall be deemed to be a qualified small business corporation share of the individual if it was a qualified small business corporation share of the individual at any time in the 12-month period immediately preceding the death of the individual.

History: S. 110.6(14)(*d.1*) was added by S.C. 2013, c. 34, s. 240(7), applicable

(*a*) to dispositions that occur after December 20, 2002; and

(*b*) to dispositions made by a taxpayer after 1999, if the taxpayer so elects in writing and files the election with the Minister of National Revenue on or before the taxpayer's filing-due date for the taxpayer's taxation year which includes June 26, 2013.

Related Sections: S. 110.6(16) Personal trust.

Tax Window Files: Capital Gains Exemption — Qualified Small Business Corporation Shares, *Technical Interpretation, Business and Partnerships Division, October 18, 2004*, CRA Document No. 2004-0077151E5. Purported unfairness of 24-month ownership rule for newly issued QSBC shares when compared to exception in paragraph 110.6(14), where rule waived if unincorporated business transferred to corporation for newly issued shares; Qualified Small Business Corporation Share — Holding Period Test, *Technical Interpretation, Business and Partnerships Division, April 23, 2003*, CRA Document No. 2003-0012695. Paragraph 110.6(14)(*g*) exception not applicable where unincorporated business split up and assets transferred to various separate corporations.

Cases: A Canadian resident is entitled to claim an enhanced capital gains deduction to offset capital gains arising on the disposition of shares of a small business corporation, subject to a 24-month holding requirement. For treasury shares issued by a small business corporation, an anti-avoidance rule requires that property disposed of to the corporation in exchange for such shares be all or substantially all of the assets used in an active business carried on by the person or the members of a partnership making the disposition. The limited partnership was formed on December 7, 2007; it acquired the assets in issue on the same day and then immediately sold those assets to the purchaser corporation. It could not be said the limited partnership used those assets in an active business; the limited partnership did not dispose of all or substantially all of the assets it used in an active business. *Gillen v. The Queen*, 2017 DTC 1099 (TCC)

► 110.6(15) ◄

(15) Value of assets of corporations. For the purposes of the definitions "qualified small business corporation share" and "share of the capital stock of a family farm or fishing corporation" in subsection (1), the definition "share of the capital stock of a family farm or fishing corporation" in subsection 70(10) and the definition "small business corporation" in subsection 248(1),

(*a*) where a person (in this subsection referred to as the "insured"), whose life was insured under an insurance policy owned by a particular corporation, owned shares of the capital stock (in this subsection referred to as the "subject shares") of the particular corporation, any corporation connected with the particular corporation or with which the particular corporation is connected or any corporation connected with any such corporation or with which any such corporation is connected (within the meaning of subsection 186(4) on the assumption that the corporation referred to in this subsection was a payer corporation within the meaning of that subsection),

(i) the fair market value of the life insurance policy shall, at any time before the death of the insured, be deemed to be its cash surrender value (within the meaning assigned by subsection 148(9)) at that time, and

(ii) the total fair market value of assets — other than assets described in any of subparagraphs (*c*)(i) to (iii) of the definition "qualified small business corporation share" in subsection (1), any of subparagraphs (*a*)(i) to (iii) of the definition "share of the capital stock of a family farm or fishing corporation" in subsection (1) or any of paragraphs (*a*) to (*c*) of the definition "small business corporation" in subsection 248(1), as the case may be — of any of those corporations that are

(A) the proceeds, the right to receive the proceeds or attributable to the proceeds, of the life insurance policy of which the particular corporation was a beneficiary, and

(B) used, directly or indirectly, within the 24-month period beginning at the time of the death of the insured or, where written application therefor is made by the particular corporation within that period, within such longer period as the Minister considers reasonable in the circumstances, to redeem, acquire or cancel the subject shares owned by the insured immediately before the death of the insured,

not in excess of the fair market value of the assets immediately after the death of the insured, shall, until the later of

(C) the redemption, acquisition or cancellation, and

(D) the day that is 60 days after the payment of the proceeds under the policy,

be deemed not to exceed the cash surrender value (within the meaning assigned by subsection 148(9)) of the policy immediately before the death of the insured; and

(*b*) the fair market value of an asset of a particular corporation that is a share of the capital stock or indebtedness of another corporation with which the particular corporation is connected shall be deemed to be nil and, for the purpose of this paragraph, a particular corporation is connected with another corporation only where

(i) the particular corporation is connected (within the meaning assigned by paragraph (*d*) of the definition "qualified small business corporation share" in subsection (1)) with the other corporation, and

(ii) the other corporation is not connected (within the meaning of subsection 186(4) as determined without reference to subsection 186(2) and on the assumption that the other corporation is a payer corporation within the meaning of subsection 186(4)) with the particular corporation,

except that this paragraph applies only in determining whether a share of the capital stock of another corporation with which the particular corporation is connected is a qualified small business corporation share or a share of the capital stock of a family farm or fishing corporation and in determining whether the other corporation is a small business corporation.

History: S. 110.6(15), the portion before paragraph (*a*) was replaced by S.C. 2014, c. 39, s. 30(17), applicable to dispositions and transfers that occur in the 2014 and subsequent taxation years, and formerly read:

(15) *Value of assets of corporations.* For the purposes of the definitions "qualified small business corporation share" and "share of the capital stock of a family farm corporation" in subsection (1), the definition "share of the capital stock of a family farm corporation" in subsection 70(10) and the definition "small business corporation" in subsection 248(1),

S. 110.6(15)(*a*)(ii), the portion before clause (A) was replaced by S.C. 2014, c. 39, s. 30(18), applicable to dispositions and transfers that occur in the 2014 and subsequent taxation years, and formerly read:

(ii) the total fair market value of assets (other than assets described in subparagraph (*c*)(i), (ii) or (iii) of the definition "qualified small business corporation share" in subsection (1), subparagraph (*b*)(i), (ii) or (iii) of the definition "share of the capital stock of a family farm corporation" in subsection (1) or paragraph (*a*), (*b*) or (*c*) of the definition "small business corporation" in subsection 248(1), as the case may be) of any of those corporations that are

S. 110.6(15)(*b*), the portion after subparagraph (ii) was replaced by S.C. 2014, c. 39, s. 30(19), applicable to dispositions and transfers that occur in the 2014 and subsequent taxation years, and formerly read:

except that this paragraph applies only in determining whether a share of the capital stock of another corporation with which the particular corporation is connected is a qualified small business corporation share or a share of the capital stock of a family farm corporation and in determining whether the other corporation is a small business corporation.

Tax Profile: January 2010 — Shareholders' Agreements — A Survey of Income Tax Issues; September 2004 — Review of Tax Implications of Corporate-Owned Life Insurance Buy-Sell Arrangements.

▶ 110.6(16) ◀

(16) Personal trust. For the purposes of the definition "qualified small business corporation share" in subsection (1) and of paragraph (14)(*c*), a personal trust shall be deemed to include a trust described in subsection 7(2).

Related Sections: S. 7(2) Securities held by trustee; s. 110.6(1), "qualified small business corporation share"; s. 110.6(14) Related persons, etc; s. 248(1) "personal trust".

▶ 110.6(17) ◀

(17) Order of deduction. For the purpose of clause (2)(*a*)(iii)(A), amounts deducted under this section in computing an individual's taxable income for a taxation year that ended before 1990 shall be deemed to have first been deducted in respect of amounts that were included in computing the individual's income under this Part for the year because of subparagraph 14(1)(*a*)(v) before being deducted in respect of any other amounts that were included in computing the individual's income under this Part for the year.

Related Sections: S. 14(1) Eligible capital property — inclusion in income from business; s. 248(1), "amount", "individual".

▶ 110.6(18) ◀

(18) Eligible real property gains and losses — (Repealed by S.C. 1995, c. 3, s. 32(11).)

▶ 110.6(19) ◀

(19) Election for property owned on February 22, 1994. Subject to subsection (20), where an individual (other than a trust) or a personal trust (each of which is referred to in this subsection and subsections (20) to (29) as the "elector"), elects in prescribed form to have the provisions of this subsection apply in respect of

(*a*) a capital property (other than an interest in a trust referred to in any of paragraphs (*f*) to (*j*) of the definition "flow-through entity" in subsection 39.1(1)) owned at the end of February 22, 1994 by the elector, the property shall be deemed, except for the purposes of sections 7 and 35 and subparagraph 110(1)(*d*.1)(ii),

(i) to have been disposed of by the elector at that time for proceeds of disposition equal to the greater of

(A) the amount determined by the formula

$$A - B$$

where

A is the amount designated in respect of the property in the election, and

B is the amount, if any, that would, if the disposition were a disposition for the purpose of section 7 or 35, be included under that section as a result of the disposition in computing the income of the elector, and

(B) the adjusted cost base to the elector of the property immediately before the disposition, and

(ii) to have been reacquired by the elector immediately after that time at a cost equal to

(A) where the property is an interest in or a share of the capital stock of a flow-through entity (within the meaning assigned by subsection 39.1(1)) of the elector, the cost to the elector of the property immediately before the disposition referred to in subparagraph (i),

(B) where an amount would, if the disposition referred to in subparagraph (i) were a disposition for the purpose of section 7 or 35, be included under that section as a result of the disposition in computing the income of the elector, the lesser of

(I) the elector's proceeds of disposition of the property determined under subparagraph (i), and

(II) the amount determined by the formula

A - B

where

A is the amount, if any, by which the fair market value of the property at that time exceeds the amount that would, if the disposition referred to in subparagraph (i) were a disposition for the purpose of section 7 or 35, be included under that section as a result of the disposition in computing the income of the elector, and

B is the amount that would be determined by the formula in subclause (C)(II) in respect of the property if clause (C) applied to the property, and

(C) in any other case, the lesser of

(I) the designated amount, and

(II) the amount, if any, by which the fair market value of the property at that time exceeds the amount determined by the formula

A - 1.1B

where

A is the designated amount, and

B is the fair market value of the property at that time;

(*b*) a business carried on by the elector (otherwise than as a member of a partnership) on February 22, 1994,

(i) the amount that would be determined under subparagraph 14(1)(*a*)(v) at the end of that day in respect of the elector if

(A) all the eligible capital property owned at that time by the elector in respect of the business were disposed of by the elector immediately before that time for proceeds of disposition equal to the amount designated in the election in respect of the business, and

(B) the fiscal period of the business ended at that time

shall be deemed to be a taxable capital gain of the elector for the taxation year in which the fiscal period of the business that includes that time ends from the disposition of a particular property and, for the purposes of this section, the particular property shall be deemed to have been disposed of by the elector at that time, and

(ii) for the purpose of paragraph 14(3)(*b*), the amount of the taxable capital gain determined under subparagraph (i) shall be deemed to have been claimed, by a person who does not deal at arm's length with each person or partnership that does not deal at arm's length with the elector, as a deduction under this section in respect of a disposition at that time of the eligible capital property; and

(*c*) an interest owned at the end of February 22, 1994 by the elector in a trust referred to in any of paragraphs (*f*) to (*j*) of the definition "flow-through entity" in subsection 39.1(1), the elector shall be deemed to have a capital gain for the year from the disposition on February 22, 1994 of property equal to the lesser of

(i) the total of amounts designated in elections made under this subsection by the elector in respect of interests in the trust, and

(ii) $^4/_3$ of the amount that would, if all of the trust's capital properties were disposed of at the end of February 22, 1994 for proceeds of disposition equal to their fair market value at that time and that portion of the trust's capital gains and capital losses or its net taxable capital gains, as the case may be, arising from the dispositions as can reasonably be considered to represent the elector's share thereof were allocated to or designated in respect of the elector, be the increase in the annual gains limit of the elector for the 1994 taxation year as a result of the dispositions.

Editorial Note: The special election under s. 110.6(19) was available for properties held on February 22, 1994. The provision allowed the taxpayer to trigger gain on properties held on that date in order to claim the exemption.

Related Sections: S. 53(1)(*p*) Adjustments to cost base — Flow-through entity, after 2004; s. 53(1)(*r*) Adjustments to cost base — Flow-through entity, before 2005; s. 87(2)(*bb*.1) Flow-through entities; s. 107(2.2) Flow-through entity; s. 144(1), "unused portion of a beneficiary's exempt capital gains balance".

Income Tax Folios: *Secondary* — S1-F3-C2 Principal Residence.

Interpretation Bulletins: *Secondary* — IT-379R Employees profit sharing plans — Allocations to beneficiaries.

Tax Window Files: Farm Property Inherited by Children — Capital Gains Exemption under Subsection 110.6(2) — Inter Vivos Transfer under Subsection 73(3), *Technical Interpretation, Business and Partnerships Division, March 1, 2004,* CRA Document No. 2003-0017861E5.

► 110.6(20) ◄

(20) Application of subsection (19). Subsection (19) applies to a property or to a business, as the case may be, of an elector only if

(*a*) where the elector is an individual (other than a trust),

(i) its application to all of the properties in respect of which elections were made under that subsection by the elector or a spouse or common-law partner of the elector and to all the businesses in respect of which elections were made under that subsection by the elector

(A) would result in an increase in the amount deductible under subsection (3) in computing the taxable income of the elector or a spouse or common-law partner of the elector, and

(B) in respect of each of the 1994 and 1995 taxation years,

(I) where no part of the taxable capital gain resulting from an election by the elector is included in computing the income of a spouse or common-law partner of the elector, would not result in the amount determined under paragraph (3)(*a*) for the year in respect of the elector being exceeded by the lesser of the amounts determined under paragraphs (3)(*b*) and (*c*) for the year in respect of the elector, and

(II) where no part of the taxable capital gain resulting from an election by the elector is included in computing the income of the elector, would not result in the amount determined under paragraph (3)(*a*) for the year in respect of a spouse or common-law partner of the elector being exceeded by the lesser of the amounts determined under paragraphs (3)(*b*) and (*c*) for the year in respect of the spouse or common-law partner,

(ii) the amount designated in the election in respect of the property exceeds $^{11}/_{10}$ of its fair market value at the end of February 22, 1994, or

(iii) the amount designated in the election in respect of the business is $1.00 or exceeds $^{11}/_{10}$ of the fair market value at the end of February 22, 1994 of all the eligible capital property owned at that time by the elector in respect of the business; and

(*b*) where the elector is a personal trust, its application to all of the properties in respect of which an election was made under that subsection by the elector would result in

(i) an increase in the amount deemed by subsection 104(21.2) to be a taxable capital gain of an individual (other than a trust) who was a beneficiary under the trust at the end of February 22, 1994 and resident in Canada at any time in the individual's taxation year in which the trust's taxation year that includes that day ends, or

(ii) where subsection (12) applies to the trust for the trust's taxation year that includes that day, an increase in the amount deductible under that subsection in computing the trust's taxable income for that year.

▶ 110.6(21) ◀

(21) Effect of election on non-qualifying real property. Where an elector is deemed by subsection (19) to have disposed of a non-qualifying real property,

(*a*) in computing the elector's taxable capital gain from the disposition, there shall be deducted the amount determined by the formula

$$0.75(A - B)$$

where

A is the elector's capital gain from the disposition, and

B is the elector's eligible real property gain from the disposition; and

(*b*) in determining at any time after the disposition the capital cost to the elector of the property where it is a depreciable property and the adjusted cost base to the elector of the property in any other case (other than where the property was at the end of February 22, 1994 an interest in or a share of the capital stock of a flow-through entity within the meaning assigned by subsection 39.1(1)), there shall be deducted $^{4}/_{3}$ of the amount determined under paragraph (*a*) in respect of the property.

▶ 110.6(22) ◀

(22) Adjusted cost base. Where an elector is deemed by paragraph (19)(*a*) to have reacquired a property, there shall be deducted in computing the adjusted cost base to the elector of the property at any time after the reacquisition the amount, if any, by which

(*a*) the amount determined by the formula

$$A - 1.1B$$

where

A is the amount designated in the election under subsection (19) in respect of the property, and

B is the fair market value of the property at the end of February 22, 1994

exceeds

(*b*) where the property is an interest in or a share of the capital stock of a flow-through entity (within the meaning assigned by subsection 39.1(1)), $^{4}/_{3}$ of the taxable capital gain that would have resulted from the election if the amount designated in the election were equal to the fair market value of the property at the end of February 22, 1994 and, in any other case, the fair market value of the property at the end of February 22, 1994.

▶ 110.6(23) ◀

(23) Disposition of partnership interest. Where an elector is deemed by subsection (19) to have disposed of an interest in a partnership, in computing the adjusted cost base to the elector of the interest immediately before the disposition

(*a*) there shall be added the amount determined by the formula

$$(A - B) \times C/D + E$$

where

A is the total of all amounts each of which is the elector's share of the partnership's income (other than a taxable capital gain from the disposition of a property) from a source or from sources in a particular place for its fiscal period that includes February 22, 1994,

B is the total of all amounts each of which is the elector's share of the partnership's loss (other than an allowable capital loss from the disposition of a property) from a source or from sources in a particular place for that fiscal period,

C is the number of days in the period that begins the first day of that fiscal period and ends February 22, 1994,

D is the number of days in that fiscal period, and

E is $^{4}/_{3}$ of the amount that would be determined under paragraph 3(*b*) in computing the elector's income for the taxation year in which that fiscal period ends if the elector had no taxable capital gains or allowable capital losses other than those arising from dispositions of property by the partnership that occurred before February 23, 1994; and (*b*) there shall be deducted the amount that would be determined under paragraph (*a*) if the formula in that paragraph were read as

"(B - A) × C/D - E"

► 110.6(24) ◄

(24) Time for election. An election made under subsection (19) shall be filed with the Minister

(*a*) where the elector is an individual (other than a trust),

(i) if the election is in respect of a business of the elector, on or before the individual's filing-due date for the taxation year in which the fiscal period of the business that includes February 22, 1994 ends, and

(ii) in any other case, on or before the individual's balance-due day for the 1994 taxation year; and

(*b*) where the elector is a personal trust, on or before March 31 of the calendar year following the calendar year in which the taxation year of the trust that includes February 22, 1994 ends.

Related Sections: S. 248(1), "filing-due date".

► 110.6(25) ◄

(25) Revocation of election. Subject to subsection (28), an elector may revoke an election made under subsection (19) by filing a written notice of the revocation with the Minister before 1998.

► 110.6(26) ◄

(26) Late election. Where an election made under subsection (19) is filed with the Minister after the day (referred to in this subsection and subsections (27) and (29) as the "election filing date") on or before which the election is required by subsection (24) to have been filed and on or before the day that is 2 years after the election filing date, the election shall be deemed for the purposes of this section (other than subsection (29)) to have been filed on the election filing date if an estimate of the penalty in respect of the election is paid by the elector when the election is filed with the Minister.

► 110.6(27) ◄

(27) Amended election. Subject to subsection (28), an election under subsection (19) in respect of a property or a business is deemed to be amended and the election, as amended, is deemed for the purpose of this section (other than subsection (29)) to have been filed on the election filing date if

(*a*) an amended election in prescribed form in respect of the property or the business is filed with the Minister before 1998; and

(*b*) an estimate of the penalty, if any, in respect of the amended election is paid by the elector when the amended election is filed with the Minister.

► 110.6(28) ◄

(28) Election that cannot be revoked or amended. An election under subsection (19) cannot be revoked or amended where the amount designated in the election exceeds $^{11}/_{10}$ of

(*a*) if the election is in respect of a property other than an interest in a partnership, the fair market value of the property at the end of February 22, 1994;

(*b*) if the election is in respect of an interest in a partnership, the greater of $1 and the fair market value of the property at the end of February 22, 1994; and

(*c*) if the election is in respect of a business, the greater of $1 and the fair market value at the end of February 22, 1994 of all the eligible capital property owned at that time by the elector in respect of the business.

► 110.6(29) ◄

(29) Amount of penalty. The penalty in respect of an election to which subsection (26) or (27) applies is the amount determined by the formula

(A × B)/300

where

A is the number of months each of which is a month all or part of which is during the period that begins the day after the election filing date and ends the day the election or amended election is filed with the Minister; and

B is the total of all amounts each of which is the taxable capital gain of the elector or a spouse or common-law partner of the elector that results from the application of subsection (19) to the property or the business in respect of which the election is made less, where subsection (27) applies to the election, the total of all amounts each of which would, if the Act were read without reference to subsections (20) and (27), be the taxable capital gain of the elector or a spouse or common-law partner of the elector that resulted from the application of subsection (19) to the property or the business.

► 110.6(30) ◄

(30) Unpaid balance of penalty. The Minister shall, with all due dispatch, examine each election to which subsection (26) or (27) applies, assess the penalty payable and send a notice of assessment to the elector who made the election, and the elector shall pay forthwith to the Receiver General the amount, if any, by which the penalty so assessed exceeds the total of all amounts previously paid on account of that penalty.

► 110.6(31) ◄

(31) Reserve limit. If an amount is included in an individual's income for a particular taxation year because of subparagraph 40(1)(*a*)(ii) in respect of a disposition of property in a preceding taxation year that, at the time of the disposition, is qualified farm or fishing property, a qualified small business corporation share, qualified farm property or qualified fishing property, the total of all amounts deductible by the individual for the particular year under this section is reduced by the amount, if any, determined by the formula

A - B

where

A is the total of all amounts each of which is an amount deductible under this section by the individual for the particular year or a preceding taxation year, computed without reference to this subsection; and

B is the total of all amounts each of which is an amount that would be deductible under this section by the individual for the particular year or a preceding taxation year if the individual had not for any preceding taxation year claimed a reserve under subparagraph 40(1)(*a*)(iii) and had claimed, for each taxation year ending before the particular year, the amount that would have been deductible under this section.

History: S. 110.6(31), the portion before the formula was replaced by S.C. 2014, c. 39, s. 30(20), applicable to dispositions and transfers that occur in the 2014 and subsequent taxation years, and formerly read:

(31) *Reserve limit.* If an amount is included in an individual's income for a particular taxation year because of subparagraph 40(1)(*a*)(ii) in respect of a disposition of property in a preceding taxation year that is qualified farm property, qualified fishing property or a qualified small business corporation share, the total of all amounts deductible by the individual for the particular year under this section is reduced by the amount, if any, determined by the formula

S. 110.6(31) was replaced by S.C. 2013, c. 40, s. 46(2), applicable to taxation years that begin after March 19, 2007, and formerly read:

(31) *Conditions for the application of subsection (32).* Subsection (32) applies to an individual for a taxation year that begins after March 19, 2007 if

(*a*) in the taxation year the individual has a taxable capital gain from the disposition, before March 19, 2007, of a qualified small business corporation share of the individual, a qualified farm property of the individual or a qualified fishing property of the individual; and

(*b*) the total of all amounts each of which is an amount of a taxable capital gain of the individual described in paragraph (*a*) exceeds the amount that would be determined under paragraph (2)(*a*) in respect of the individual for the taxation year were the reference to "$375,000" in that paragraph read as a reference to "$250,000" (the amount of which excess is referred to in subsection (32) as the "denied excess").

► 110.6(32) ◄

(32) Deduction denied — (Repealed by S.C. 2013, c. 40, s. 46(2).)

History: S. 110.6(32) was repealed by S.C. 2013, c. 40, s. 46(2), applicable to taxation years that begin after March 19, 2007, and formerly read:

(32) *Deduction denied.* Notwithstanding subsections (2) to (2.3), if this subsection applies to an individual for a taxation year, no amount may be deducted under this section for the taxation year by the individual in respect of the individual's taxable capital gains for the year described in paragraph (31)(*a*) to the extent of the denied excess.

SECTION 110.7: Residing in prescribed zone

► 110.7(1) ◄

(1) Residing in prescribed zone. Where, throughout a period (in this section referred to as the "qualifying period") of not less than 6 consecutive months beginning or ending in a taxation year, a taxpayer who is an individual has resided in one or more particular areas each of which is a prescribed northern zone or prescribed intermediate zone for the year and files for the year a claim in prescribed form, there may be deducted in computing the taxpayer's taxable income for the year

(*a*) the total of all amounts each of which is the product obtained by multiplying the specified percentage for a particular area for the year in which the taxpayer so resided by an amount received, or the value of a benefit received or enjoyed, in the year by the taxpayer in respect of the taxpayer's employment in the particular area by a person with whom the taxpayer was dealing at arm's length in respect of travel expenses incurred by the taxpayer or another individual who was a member of the taxpayer's household during the part of the year in which the taxpayer resided in the particular area, to the extent that

(i) the amount received or the value of the benefit, as the case may be,

(A) does not exceed a prescribed amount in respect of the taxpayer for the period in the year in which the taxpayer resided in the particular area,

(B) is included and is not otherwise deducted in computing the taxpayer's income for the year or any other taxation year, and

(C) is not included in determining an amount deducted under subsection 118.2(1) for the year or any other taxation year,

(ii) the travel expenses were incurred in respect of trips made in the year by the taxpayer or another individual who was a member of the taxpayer's household during the part of the year in which the taxpayer resided in the particular area, and

(iii) neither the taxpayer nor a member of the taxpayer's household is at any time entitled to a reimbursement or any form of assistance (other than a reimbursement or assistance included in computing the income of the taxpayer or the member) in respect of travel expenses to which subparagraph (ii) applies; and

(*b*) the lesser of

(i) 20% of the taxpayer's income for the year, and

(ii) the total of all amounts each of which is the product obtained by multiplying the specified percentage for a particular area for the year in which the taxpayer so resided by the total of

(A) $11.00 multiplied by the number of days in the year included in the qualifying period in which the taxpayer resided in the particular area, and

(B) $11.00 multiplied by the number of days in the year included in that portion of the qualifying period throughout which the taxpayer maintained and resided in a self-contained domestic establishment in the particular area (except any day included in computing a deduction claimed under this paragraph by another person who resided on that day in the establishment).

Editorial Note: Individuals residing in a prescribed northern zone or a prescribed intermediate zone (see the definition in Regulation 7303.1) for a period of at least six consecutive months beginning or ending in the taxation year may enclose a Form T2222 with their tax return to claim a northern residents deduction in respect of the period. The deduction has two components:

(1) A travel deduction for travel benefits received from an arm's length employer in respect of trips for obtaining medical services not available locally or a maximum of two annual non-medical trips provided the following conditions are met: (i) the trips are taken by the individual or by members of the individual's household, and (ii) the travel benefits are included in the individual's income, are not deductible from income, are not taken into account to calculate the medical expenses tax credit, and do not exceed prescribed amounts described in Regulation 7304.

(2) A residency deduction for living expenses incurred by the individual and his or her family in the prescribed zone that would include the lesser of: (i) 20% of the individual's annual income, and (ii) the total of $11 per day of residence in the prescribed zone, and an extra $11 for each day for which they resided in a self-contained domestic establishment and no other individual claimed the basic $11 deduction.

Residents of the prescribed northern zone may claim the full northern residents deduction while residents of the prescribed intermediate zone may claim only 50% of it. Individuals with their principal place residence located outside the prescribed zones but residing at a special work site located in one of them may not claim both the exemption in s. 6(6) and the northern residents deduction in s. 110.7(1).

History: S. 110.7(1)(*b*)(ii)(A) and (B) were replaced by S.C. 2016, c. 7, s. 13(1), applicable to the 2016 and subsequent taxation years, and formerly read:

(A) $8.25 multiplied by the number of days in the year included in the qualifying period in which the taxpayer resided in the particular area, and

(B) $8.25 multiplied by the number of days in the year included in that portion of the qualifying period throughout which the taxpayer maintained and resided in a self-contained domestic establishment in the particular area (except any day included in computing a deduction claimed under this paragraph by another person who resided on that day in the establishment).

Related Regulations: 7303.1; 7304.

Related Sections: S. 111.1 Order of applying provisions; s. 248(1), "self-contained domestic establishment".

Tax Topics: No. 2429, A Prescribed Zone Sojourn and the Northern Residents Deduction.

Forms: T2222 — Northern Residents Deductions.

Guides: RC4054 Ceiling Amounts for Housing Benefits Paid in Prescribed Zones; T4039 Northern Residents Deductions; T4130 Employers Guide to Payroll Deductions — Taxable Benefits.

Cases: The taxpayer only "sojourned" in a northern zone. He intermittently stayed at the work site and did not establish a "residence". His employer would provide him with a room but when he was off, he gave his room to a colleague and went to his residence in Québec City. *Talbot v. The Queen*, 2018 DTC 1074 (TCC)

▶ 110.7(2) ◀

(2) Specified percentage. For the purpose of subsection (1), the specified percentage for a particular area for a taxation year is

(*a*) where the area is a prescribed northern zone for the year, 100%; and

(*b*) where the area is a prescribed intermediate zone for the year, 50%.

▶ 110.7(3) ◀

(3) Restriction. The total determined under paragraph (1)(*a*) for a taxpayer in respect of travel expenses incurred in a taxation year in respect of an individual shall not be in respect of more than 2 trips made by the individual in the year, other than trips to obtain medical services that are not available in the locality in which the taxpayer resided.

▶ 110.7(4) ◀

(4) Board and lodging allowances, etc. The amount determined under subparagraph (1)(*b*)(ii) for a particular area for a taxpayer for a taxation year shall not exceed the amount by which the amount otherwise determined under that subparagraph for the particular area for the year exceeds the value of, or an allowance in respect of expenses incurred by the taxpayer for, the taxpayer's board and lodging in the particular area (other than at a work site described in paragraph 67.1(2)(*e*)) that

(*a*) would, but for subparagraph 6(6)(*a*)(i), be included in computing the taxpayer's income for the year; and

(*b*) can reasonably be considered to be attributable to that portion of the qualifying period that is in the year and during which the taxpayer maintained a self-contained domestic establishment as the taxpayer's principal place of residence in an area other than a prescribed northern zone or a prescribed intermediate zone for the year.

▶ 110.7(5) ◀

(5) Idem. Where on any day an individual resides in more than one particular area referred to in subsection (1), for the purpose of that subsection, the individual shall be deemed to reside in only one such area on that day.

Cases: Even if the words "prescribed area" could in 1988 refer to the new concepts of "prescribed northern zone" or "prescribed intermediate zone", the taxpayers had not lived in such an area and their claims for the deduction had to be disallowed despite the fact that the Minister had allowed it in 1987. *Catton et al. v. The Queen*, 93 DTC 117 (T.C.C.)

SECTION 111: Losses deductible

▶ 111(1) ◀

(1) Losses deductible. For the purpose of computing the taxable income of a taxpayer for a taxation year, there may be deducted such portion as the taxpayer may claim of the taxpayer's

Related Sections: S. 2(2) Taxable income; s. 2(3) Tax payable by non-resident persons; s. 3 Income for taxation year; s. 9 Income or loss from business or property; s. 31 Loss from farming where chief source of income not farming; s. 87(2.1) Non-capital losses, etc., of predecessor corporations; s. 87(2.11) Vertical amalgamations; s. 88(1.1) Non-capital losses, etc., of subsidiary; s. 88(1.2) Net capital losses of subsidiary; s. 88(1.3) Computation of income and tax of parent; s. 89(4) GRIP addition — becoming CCPC; s. 89(5) GRIP addition — post-amalgamation; s. 89(6) GRIP addition — post-winding-up; s. 89(7) GRIP addition for 2006; s. 89(8) LRIP addition — ceasing to be CCPC; s. 89(9) LRIP addition — amalgamation; s. 89(10) LRIP addition — winding-up; s. 89(11) Election: non-CCPC; s. 96(2.2) At-risk amount; s. 111(3) Limitation on deductibility; s. 111(8) Definitions; s. 111.1 Order of applying provisions; s. 114 Individual resident in Canada for only part of year; s. 115(1) Non-resident's taxable income in Canada; s. 164(5) Effect of carryback of loss, etc. s. 256(7) Acquiring control; s. 256(8) Deemed exercise of right; s. 256.1 [Corporate tax-attribute trading].

Forms: T1A — Request for Loss Carryback; T2 SCH 4 — Corporation Loss Continuity and Application; T3A — Request for Loss Carry-Back by a Trust.

Income Tax Folios: *Secondary* — S4-F11-C1 Meaning of Farming and Farming Business; S4-F7-C1 Amalgamations of Canadian Corporations.

Income Tax Technical News: Issue No. 30, Corporate Loss Utilization Transactions.

Interpretation Bulletins: *Primary* — IT-232R3 Losses — Their deductibility in the loss year or in other years. *Secondary* — IT-262R2 Losses of non-residents and part-year residents; IT-302R3 Losses of a corporation — The effect that acquisitions of control, amalgamations, and windings-up have on their deductibility — After January 15, 1987; IT-322R Farm losses; IT-381R3 Trusts — Deduction of amounts paid or payable to beneficiaries and flow-through of taxable capital gains to beneficiaries.

▶ 111(1)(a) ◀

(a) Non-capital losses — non-capital losses for the 20 taxation years immediately preceding and the 3 taxation years immediately following the year;

Editorial Note: Historically, allowable business investment losses (ABILs) formed part of a taxpayer's non-capital loss until the expiration of the carryforward period in s. 111(1)(*a*). However, for the 2006 and subsequent taxation years, the non-capital loss carryforward period was extended from 10 years to 20 years, while the corresponding ABIL carryforward period was not extended beyond 10 years (s. 111(8) "non-capital loss"). Therefore, ABILs remain part of a taxpayer's non-capital losses in the year in which they are sustained and in the following 10 years to the extent they are not utilized. If they are not utilized within the 10-year period, they become net capital losses subject to the indefinite carryforward period in s. 111(1)(*b*), although in such case they are only deductible against taxable capital gains (subject to the year of death rules in s. 111(2)).

Related Sections: S. 80(3) Reductions of non-capital losses; s. 80(4) Reductions of capital losses; s. 87(2.1) Non-capital losses, etc., of predecessor corporations; s. 87(2.11) Vertical amalgamations; s. 88(1.1) Non-capital losses, etc., of subsidiary; s. 88(1.2) Net capital losses of subsidiary; s. 88(1.3) Computation of income and tax of parent; s. 111(3) Limitation on deductibility; s. 111(5) Deduction of non-capital or farm losses; s. 111(5.4) Non-capital loss; s. 111(8), "non-capital loss"; s. 111(9) Exception; s. 111(7.2) Non-capital loss of life insurer; s. 111(8) Definitions; s. 125.3(3) Acquisition of control; s. 127(9.1) Loss restriction event before end of year; s. 127(9.2) Loss restriction event after end of year; s. 152(1.1) Determination of losses; s. 152(1.2) Provisions applicable; s. 152(1.3) Determination binding; s. 186(1) Tax on assessable dividends; s. 190.1(6) Acquisition of control; s. 256(7) Acquiring control; s. 256(8) Deemed exercise of right.

Canadian Tax Foundation: Burghardt and Chiu, *"Loss" Is Just a Four-Letter Word: Policy, Practice, and Proposals*, 2013 Conference Report 14:1–43; Wharram, *Loss Utilization*, 2013 Ontario Tax Conference 4:1–33.

Tax Profile: March 2004 — Loss Planning.

Forms: T3A — Request for Loss Carry-Back by a Trust.

Information Circulars: IC 88-2 General anti-avoidance rule — Section 245 of the Income Tax Act (para. 8).

Interpretation Bulletins: *Secondary* — IT-484R Business investment losses.

Tax Window Files: Application of 111(1)(a) and 152(4.2), *January 14, 2014*, CRA Document No. 2013-0514331I7; Consequential Assessments — Non-Capital Loss Carryover, *Technical Interpretation, Reorganizations and Resources Division, February 7, 2006*, CRA Document No. 2005-0122381E5; Bonus to Shareholder/Manager — Loss Carryback, *July 21, 2004*, CRA Document No. 2004-0072741R3.

▶ 111(1)(b) ◀

(b) Net capital losses — net capital losses for taxation years preceding and the three taxation years immediately following the year;

Editorial Note: Allowable business investment losses (ABILs) that are not utilized as non-capital losses in the year in which they are sustained or in the following 10 years become net capital losses; see the definitions of "net capital loss" and "non-capital loss" in s. 111(8). Net capital losses can be carried back or forward but only to offset taxable capital gains in other years. An exception applies in the year of an individual's death and the preceding year, in which case unapplied net capital losses can offset other sources of income (see s. 111(2)).

Related Sections: S. 3(*b*) Income for taxation year; s. 38 Taxable capital gain and allowable capital loss; s. 41(2) Determination of net gain; s. 80(4) Reductions of capital losses; s. 87(2.1) Non-capital losses, etc., of predecessor corporations; s. 87(2.11) Vertical amalgamations; s. 88(1.2) Net capital losses of subsidiary; s. 88(1.3) Computation of income and tax of parent; s. 104(21.3) Net taxable capital gains of trust determined; s. 110.6(1), "annual gains limit; s. 111(1.1) Net capital losses; s. 111(2) Year of death; s. 111(3) Limitation on deductibility; s. 111(4) Loss restriction event — capital losses; s. 111(8) Definitions; s. 111(9) Exception; s. 126(1) Foreign tax deduction — non-business income; s. 129(3) Definition of "refundable dividend tax on hand"; s. 129(4), "aggregate investment income"; s. 152(1.1) Determination of losses; s. 152(1.2) Provisions applicable; s. 152(1.3) Determination binding; s. 164(6) Where disposition of property by legal representative of deceased taxpayer; s. 256(7) Acquiring control; s. 256(8) Deemed exercise of right.

Forms: T3A — Request for Loss Carry-Back by a Trust.

Income Tax Folios: *Secondary* — S5-F2-C1 Foreign Tax Credit.

Tax Window Files: Carry Back of Capital Losses by Estate, *Technical Interpretation, International and Trusts Division, December 21, 2006*, CRA Document No. 2006-0216261I7.

► 111(1)(c) ◄

(c) **Restricted farm losses** — restricted farm losses for the 20 taxation years immediately preceding and the 3 taxation years immediately following the year, but no amount is deductible for the year in respect of restricted farm losses except to the extent of the taxpayer's incomes for the year from all farming businesses carried on by the taxpayer;

Editorial Note: "Restricted farm loss" is defined in s. 31(1.1).

Related Sections: S. 31 Loss from farming where chief source of income not farming; s. 80(3) Reductions of non-capital losses; s. 87(2.1) Non-capital losses, etc., of predecessor corporations; s. 88(1.1) Non-capital losses, etc., of subsidiary; s. 111(3) Limitation on deductibility; s. 111(5) Deduction of non-capital or farm losses; s. 111(9) Exception; s. 152(1.1) Determination of losses; s. 152(1.2) Provisions applicable; s. 152(1.3) Determination binding; s. 256(7) Acquiring control; s. 256(8) Deemed exercise of right.

Forms: T3A — Request for Loss Carry-Back by a Trust.

Guides: RC4408 Farming Income and the AgriStability and AgriInvest Programs Harmonized Guide.

► 111(1)(d) ◄

(d) **Farm losses** — farm losses for the 20 taxation years immediately preceding and the 3 taxation years immediately following the year; and

Related Sections: S. 28(1) Farming or fishing business; s. 80(3) Reductions of non-capital losses; s. 87(2.1) Non-capital losses, etc., of predecessor corporations; s. 88(1.1) Non-capital losses, etc., of subsidiary; s. 111(3) Limitation on deductibility; s. 111(5) Deduction of non-capital or farm losses; s. 111(8), "farm loss"; s. 111(9) Exception; s. 152(1.1) Determination of losses; s. 152(1.2) Provisions applicable; s. 152(1.3) Determination binding; s. 186(1) Tax on assessable dividends; s. 256(7) Acquiring control; s. 256(8) Deemed exercise of right.

Forms: T3A — Request for Loss Carry-Back by a Trust.

Guides: RC4408 Farming Income and the AgriStability and AgriInvest Programs Harmonized Guide.

► 111(1)(e) ◄

(e) **Limited partnership losses** — limited partnership losses in respect of a partnership for taxation years preceding the year, but no amount is deductible for the year in respect of a limited partnership loss except to the extent of the amount by which

(i) the taxpayer's at-risk amount in respect of the partnership (within the meaning assigned by subsection 96(2.2)) at the end of the last fiscal period of the partnership ending in the taxation year

exceeds

(ii) the total of all amounts each of which is

(A) the amount required by subsection 127(8) in respect of the partnership to be added in computing the investment tax credit of the taxpayer for the taxation year,

(B) the taxpayer's share of any losses of the partnership for that fiscal period from a business or property, or

(C) the taxpayer's share of

(I) the foreign resource pool expenses, if any, incurred by the partnership in that fiscal period,

(II) the Canadian exploration expense, if any, incurred by the partnership in that fiscal period,

(III) the Canadian development expense, if any, incurred by the partnership in that fiscal period, and

(IV) the Canadian oil and gas property expense, if any, incurred by the partnership in that fiscal period.

Editorial Note: Limited partnership losses can be carried forward indefinitely but are subject to the taxpayer's at-risk amount in respect of the partnership that gave rise to the losses. Limited partnership losses cannot be carried back.

Related Sections: S. 53(2)(*c*) Amounts to be deducted — Interest in a partnership; s. 87(2.1) Non-capital losses, etc., of predecessor corporations; s. 88(1.1) Non-capital losses, etc., of subsidiary; s. 96(2.1) Limited partnership losses; s. 96(2.2) At-risk amount; s. 96(2.4) Limited partner; s. 111(3) Limitation on deductibility; s. 111(9) Exception; s. 127.52(1)(i) Adjusted taxable income determined; s. 152(1.1) Determination of losses; s. 152(1.2) Provisions applicable; s. 152(1.3) Determination binding; s. 248(1), "foreign resource pool expenses".

Tax Topics: No. 2383, The Losses That Flow?.

Tax Window Files: Limited Partnership Losses of Tier Partnership, *Technical Interpretation, Business and Partnerships Division, May 14, 2004*, CRA Document No. 2004-0062801E5.

► 111(1.1) ◄

(1.1) **Net capital losses.** Notwithstanding paragraph (1)(*b*), the amount that may be deducted under that paragraph in computing a taxpayer's taxable income for a particular taxation year is the total of

(*a*) the lesser of

(i) the amount, if any, determined under paragraph 3(*b*) in respect of the taxpayer for the particular year, and

(ii) the total of all amounts each of which is an amount determined by the formula

$$A \times B/C$$

where

A is the amount claimed under paragraph (1)(*b*) for the particular year by the taxpayer in respect of a net capital loss for a taxation year (in this paragraph referred to as the "loss year"),

B is the fraction that would be used for the particular year under section 38 in respect of the taxpayer if the taxpayer had a capital loss for the particular year, and

C is the fraction required to be used under section 38 in respect of the taxpayer for the loss year;

(*b*) where the taxpayer is an individual, the least of

(i) $2,000,

(ii) the taxpayer's pre-1986 capital loss balance for the particular year, and

(iii) the amount, if any, by which

(A) the amount claimed under paragraph (1)(*b*) in respect of the taxpayer's net capital losses for the particular year

exceeds

(B) the total of the amounts in respect of the taxpayer's net capital losses that, using the formula in subparagraph (*a*)(ii), would be required to be claimed under paragraph (1)(*b*) for the particular year to produce the amount determined under paragraph (*a*) for the particular year; and

(*c*) the amount, if any, that the Minister determines to be reasonable in the circumstances for the particular year and after considering the application to the taxpayer of subsections 104(21.6), 130.1(4), 131(1) and 138.1(3.2) as they read in their application to the taxpayer's last taxation year that began before November 2011.

Editorial Note: If a taxpayer's ordinary loss for a year would otherwise be deducted under s. 3(*d*) against the taxpayer's taxable capital gains for the year, and the taxpayer has a net capital loss carryforward available, the taxpayer can instead utilize the net capital loss carryforward to offset the taxable capital gains, which will have the effect of preserving the unused ordinary loss as a non-capital loss; see also amounts E and F in s. 111(8)"non-capital loss", and paragraph 25 of IT-232R3 for an example of this scenario.

History: S. 111(1.1)(*c*) was replaced by S.C. 2013, c. 34, s. 241(2), applicable to taxation years that begin after October 31, 2011, and formerly read:

(*c*) the amount, if any, that the Minister determines to be reasonable in the circumstances, after considering the application of subsections 104(21.6), 130.1(4), 131(1) and 138.1(3.2) to the taxpayer for the particular year.

S. 111(1.1)(*c*) was added by S.C. 2013, c. 34, s. 241(1), applicable to the 2000 and subsequent taxation years.

Related Sections: S. 3 Income for taxation year; s. 70(5) Capital property of a deceased taxpayer; s. 111(2) Year of death; s. 111(8), "non-capital loss".

▶ 111(2) ◀

(2) Year of death. Where a taxpayer dies in a taxation year, for the purpose of computing the taxpayer's taxable income for that year and the immediately preceding taxation year, the following rules apply:

(*a*) paragraph (1)(*b*) shall be read as follows:

"(*b*) the taxpayer's net capital losses for all taxation years not claimed for the purpose of computing the taxpayer's taxable income for any other taxation year;"; and

(*b*) paragraph (1.1)(*b*) shall be read as follows:

"(*b*) the amount, if any, by which

(i) the amount claimed under paragraph (1)(*b*) in respect of the taxpayer's net capital losses for the particular year

exceeds the total of

(ii) all amounts in respect of the taxpayer's net capital losses that, using the formula in subparagraph (*a*)(ii), would be required to be claimed under paragraph (1)(*b*) for the particular year to produce the amount determined under paragraph (*a*) for the particular year, and

(iii) all amounts each of which is an amount deducted under section 110.6 in computing the taxpayer's taxable income for a taxation year, except to the extent that, where the particular year is the year in which the taxpayer died, the amount, if any, by which the amount determined under subparagraph (i) in respect of the taxpayer for the immediately preceding taxation year exceeds the amount so determined under subparagraph (ii)."

Editorial Note: S. 111(2) provides an exception to the general rule that net capital losses can only be deducted against taxable capital gains. The provision allows net capital losses, after they are utilized to offset taxable capital gains, and net of any capital gains exemption claimed for any taxation year, to be deducted against all forms of income in the year of an individual's death and the immediately preceding year.

▶ 111(3) ◀

(3) Limitation on deductibility. For the purposes of subsection (1),

(*a*) an amount in respect of a non-capital loss, restricted farm loss, farm loss or limited partnership loss, as the case may be, for a taxation year is deductible, and an amount in respect of a net capital loss for a taxation year may be claimed, in computing the taxable income of a taxpayer for a particular taxation year only to the extent that it exceeds the total of

(i) amounts deducted under this section in respect of that non-capital loss, restricted farm loss, farm loss or limited partnership loss in computing taxable income for taxation years preceding the particular taxation year,

(i.1) the amount that was claimed under paragraph (1)(*b*) in respect of that net capital loss for taxation years preceding the particular taxation year, and

(ii) amounts claimed in respect of that loss under paragraph 186(1)(*c*) for the year in which the loss was incurred or under paragraph 186(1)(*d*) for the particular taxation year and taxation years preceding the particular taxation year, and

(*b*) no amount is deductible in respect of a non-capital loss, net capital loss, restricted farm loss, farm loss or limited partnership loss, as the case may be, for a taxation year until

(i) in the case of a non-capital loss, the deductible non-capital losses,

(ii) in the case of a net capital loss, the deductible net capital losses,

(iii) in the case of a restricted farm loss, the deductible restricted farm losses,

(iv) in the case of a farm loss, the deductible farm losses, and

(v) in the case of a limited partnership loss, the deductible limited partnership losses,

for preceding taxation years have been deducted.

Editorial Note: The ordering rule in s. 111(3) provides that losses of a particular category must be utilized in the order in which they arose (i.e. prior years' losses must be deducted first). However, there is no similar rule that dictates the order of years to which the losses must be carried forward or back.

Related Sections: S. 41(2) Determination of net gain; s. 46(4) Decrease in value of personal-use property of corporation, etc; s. 87(2.1) Non-capital losses, etc., of predecessor corporations; s. 88(1.1) Non-capital losses, etc., of subsidiary; s. 88(1.2) Net capital losses of subsidiary; s. 88(1.3) Computation of income and tax of parent; s. 111(8) Definitions; s. 245 General anti-avoidance rule.

Interpretation Bulletins: *Primary* — IT-302R3 Losses of a corporation — The effect that acquisitions of control, amalgamations, and windings-up have on their deductibility — After January 15, 1987.

▶ 111(4) ◀

(4) Loss restriction event — capital losses. Notwithstanding subsection (1), and subject to subsection (5.5), if at any time (in this subsection referred to as "that time") a taxpayer is subject to a loss restriction event,

(*a*) no amount in respect of a net capital loss for a taxation year that ended before that time is deductible in computing the taxpayer's taxable income for a taxation year that ends after that time;

(*b*) no amount in respect of a net capital loss for a taxation year that ends after that time is deductible in computing the taxpayer's taxable income for a taxation year that ends before that time;

(*c*) in computing the adjusted cost base to the taxpayer at and after that time of each capital property, other than a depreciable property, of the taxpayer immediately before that time, there is to be deducted the amount, if any, by which the adjusted cost base to the taxpayer of the property immediately before that time exceeds its fair market value immediately before that time;

(*d*) each amount required by paragraph (*c*) to be deducted in computing the adjusted cost base to the taxpayer of a property is deemed to be a capital loss of the taxpayer for the taxation year that ended immediately before that time from the disposition of the property;

(*e*) if the taxpayer designates — in its return of income under this Part for the taxation year that ended immediately before that time or in a prescribed form filed with the Minister on or before the day that is 90 days after the day on which a notice of assessment of tax payable for the year or notification that no tax is payable for the year is sent to the taxpayer — a property that was a capital property of the taxpayer immediately before that time (other than a property in respect of which an amount would, but for this paragraph, be required by paragraph (*c*) to be deducted in computing its adjusted cost base to the taxpayer or a depreciable property of a prescribed class to which, but for this paragraph, subsection (5.1) would apply),

(i) the taxpayer is deemed to have disposed of the property at the time that is immediately before the time that is immediately before that time for proceeds of disposition equal to the lesser of

(A) the fair market value of the property immediately before that time, and

(B) the greater of the adjusted cost base to the taxpayer of the property immediately before the disposition and such amount as is designated by the taxpayer in respect of the property,

(ii) subject to subparagraph (iii), the taxpayer is deemed to have reacquired the property at that time at a cost equal to those proceeds of disposition, and

(iii) if the property is depreciable property of the taxpayer the capital cost of which to the taxpayer immediately before the disposition exceeds those proceeds of disposition, for the purposes of sections 13 and 20 and any regulations made for the purposes of paragraph 20(1)(*a*),

(A) the capital cost of the property to the taxpayer at that time is deemed to be the amount that was its capital cost immediately before the disposition, and

(B) the excess is deemed to have been allowed to the taxpayer in respect of the property under regulations made for the purposes of paragraph 20(1)(*a*) in computing the taxpayer's income for taxation years that ended before that time; and

(*f*) for the purposes of the definition "capital dividend account" in subsection 89(1), each amount that because of paragraph (*d*) or (*e*) is a capital loss or gain of the taxpayer from a disposition of a property for the taxation year that ended immediately before that time is deemed to be a capital loss or gain, as the case may be, of the taxpayer from the disposition of the property immediately before the time that a capital property of the taxpayer in respect of which paragraph (*e*) would be applicable would be deemed by that paragraph to have been disposed of by the taxpayer.

Editorial Note: S. 111(4) ensures that net capital losses of a corporation or trust cannot be carried forward or back after a change of control of the corporation or a "loss restriction event" of a trust. Similarly, accrued capital losses cannot be utilized beyond the change of control or loss restriction event, owing to the "write-down" of cost to fair market value under s. 111(4)(*c*). This write-down will generate capital losses in the year ending immediately before the change of control or loss restriction event (paragraph (*d*)). The corporation or trust can elect under paragraph (*e*) to generate a deemed disposition of other capital property — for example, for the purpose of generating capital gains that can be offset by the capital losses triggered by the write-down. See s. 111(5.1) regarding accrued terminal losses in respect of depreciable property. See also the editorial note under s. 249(4).

For the above purposes, a "loss restriction event" of a trust occurs when a person becomes a majority-interest beneficiary or a group becomes a majority-interest group of beneficiaries. See subsection 251.2(2).

History: S. 111(4) was replaced by S.C. 2013, c. 40, s. 47(1), deemed to have come into force on March 21, 2013, and formerly read:

(4) *Acquisition of control.* Notwithstanding subsection (1), where, at any time (in this subsection referred to as "that time"), control of a corporation has been acquired by a person or group of persons

(*a*) no amount in respect of a net capital loss for a taxation year ending before that time is deductible in computing the corporation's taxable income for a taxation year ending after that time, and

(*b*) no amount in respect of a net capital loss for a taxation year ending after that time is deductible in computing the corporation's taxable income for a taxation year ending before that time,

and where, at that time, the corporation neither became nor ceased to be exempt from tax under this Part on its taxable income,

(*c*) in computing the adjusted cost base to the corporation at and after that time of each capital property, other than a depreciable property, owned by the corporation immediately before that time, there shall be deducted the amount, if any, by which the adjusted cost base to the corporation of the property immediately before that time exceeds its fair market value immediately before that time,

(*d*) each amount required by paragraph (*c*) to be deducted in computing the adjusted cost base to the corporation of a property shall be deemed to be a capital loss of the corporation for the taxation year that ended immediately before that time from the disposition of the property,

(*e*) each capital property owned by the corporation immediately before that time (other than a property in respect of which an amount would, but for this paragraph, be required by paragraph (*c*) to be deducted in computing its adjusted cost base to the corporation or a depreciable property of a prescribed class to which, but for this paragraph, subsection (5.1) would apply) as is designated by the corporation in its return of income under this Part for the taxation year that ended immediately before that time or in a prescribed form filed with the Minister on or before the day that is 90 days after the day on which a notice of assessment of tax payable for the year or notification that no tax is payable for the year is sent to the corporation, is deemed to have been disposed of by the corporation immediately before the time that is immediately before that time for proceeds of disposition equal to the lesser of

(i) the fair market value of the property immediately before that time, and

(ii) the greater of the adjusted cost base to the corporation of the property immediately before the disposition and such amount as is designated by the corporation in respect of the property,

and shall be deemed to have been reacquired by it at that time at a cost equal to the proceeds of disposition thereof, except that, where the property is depreciable property of the corporation the capital cost of which to the corporation immediately before the disposition time exceeds those proceeds of disposition, for the purposes of sections 13 and 20 and any regulations made for the purpose of paragraph 20(1)(*a*),

(iii) the capital cost of the property to the corporation at that time shall be deemed to be the amount that was its capital cost immediately before the disposition, and

(iv) the excess shall be deemed to have been allowed to the corporation in respect of the property under regulations made for the purpose of paragraph 20(1)(*a*) in computing its income for taxation years ending before that time, and

(*f*) each amount that by virtue of paragraph (*d*) or (*e*) is a capital loss or gain of the corporation from a disposition of a property for the taxation year that ended immediately before that time shall, for the purposes of the definition "capital dividend account" in subsection 89(1), be deemed to be a capital loss or gain, as the case may be, of the corporation from the disposition of the property immediately before the time that a capital property of the corporation in respect of which paragraph (*e*) would be applicable would be deemed by that paragraph to have been disposed of by the corporation.

S. 111(4)(*e*), the portion before subparagraph (i) was replaced by S.C. 2010, c. 25, s. 21(1), in force on Royal Assent, December 15, 2010. S. 111(4)(*e*), the portion before subparagraph (i) formerly read:

(*e*) each capital property owned by the corporation immediately before that time (other than a property in respect of which an amount would, but for this paragraph, be required by paragraph (*c*) to be deducted in computing its adjusted cost base to the corporation or a depreciable property of a prescribed class to which, but for this paragraph, subsection (5.1) would apply) as is designated by the corporation in its return of income under this Part for the taxation year that ended immediately before that time or in a prescribed form filed with the Minister on or before the day that is 90 days after the day on which a notice of assessment of tax payable for the year or notification that no tax is payable for the year is mailed to the corporation, shall be deemed to have been disposed of by the corporation immediately before the time that is immediately before that time for proceeds of disposition equal to the lesser of

See the applications for s. 111(8), "exchange rate" and "foreign currency debt" and s. 111(12), enacted by S.C. 2009, c. 2, regarding a timely designation under s. 111(4)(*e*).

Related Sections: S. 13(7)(*f*) Rules applicable; s. 53(2)(*b.2*) Amounts to be deducted — Non-depreciable capital property of a corporation; s. 53(4) Recomputation of adjusted cost base on transfers and deemed dispositions; s. 87(2.1) Non-capital losses, etc., of predecessor corporations; s. 107(1.1) Cost of capital interest in a trust; s. 111(5.1) Computation of undepreciated capital cost; s. 111(8) Definitions; s. 249(4) Loss restriction event – year end; s. 251.2(2) Loss restriction event.

Tax Profile: August 2012 — U.S. Purchases and Sales of Canadian Businesses: Tax and Corporate Issues.

November 2011 — Corporate Control: An Evolving Canadian Concept; September 2011 — Acquisition of Canadian Business by Non-Residents; November 2009 — Purchase and Sale of a Canadian Business; March 2009 — Sale of Businesses to Employees: The Leveraged Buy-Out — Part I; March 2004 — Loss Planning.

Tax Topics: No. 1798, Bumping Foreign Affiliate Shares under the February 27, 2004 Proposals.

Forms: T2 SCH 6 — Summary of Dispositions of Capital Property.

Interpretation Bulletins: *Primary* — IT-302R3 Losses of a corporation — The effect that acquisitions of control, amalgamations, and windings-up have on their deductibility — After January 15, 1987.

▶ 111(5) ◀

(5) Loss restriction event — non-capital losses and farm losses. If at any time a taxpayer is subject to a loss restriction event,

(*a*) no amount in respect of the taxpayer's non-capital loss or farm loss for a taxation year that ended before that time is deductible by the taxpayer for a taxation year that ends after that time, except that the portion of the taxpayer's non-capital loss or farm loss, as the case may be, for a taxation year that ended before that time as may reasonably be regarded as the taxpayer's loss from carrying on a business and, if a business was carried on by the taxpayer in that year, the portion of the non-capital loss as may reasonably be regarded as being in respect of an amount deductible under paragraph 110(1)(*k*) in computing the taxpayer's taxable income for that year is deductible by the taxpayer for a particular taxation year that ends after that time

(i) only if that business was carried on by the taxpayer for profit or with a reasonable expectation of profit throughout the particular year, and

(ii) only to the extent of the total of the taxpayer's income for the particular year from

(A) that business, and

(B) if properties were sold, leased, rented or developed or services rendered in the course of carrying on that business before that time, any other business substantially all the income of which was derived from the sale, leasing, rental or development, as the case may be, of similar properties or the rendering of similar services; and

(*b*) no amount in respect of the taxpayer's non-capital loss or farm loss for a taxation year that ends after that time is deductible by the taxpayer for a taxation year that ended before that time, except that the portion of the taxpayer's non-capital loss or farm loss, as the case may be, for a taxation year that ended after that time as may reasonably be regarded as the taxpayer's loss from carrying on a business and, if a business was carried on by the taxpayer in that year, the portion of the non-capital loss as may reasonably be regarded as being in respect of an amount deductible under paragraph 110(1)(*k*) in computing the taxpayer's taxable income for that year is deductible by the taxpayer for a particular taxation year that ends before that time

(i) only if throughout the taxation year and in the particular year that business was carried on by the taxpayer for profit or with a reasonable expectation of profit, and

(ii) only to the extent of the taxpayer's income for the particular year from

(A) that business, and

(B) if properties were sold, leased, rented or developed or services rendered in the course of carrying on that business before that time, any other business substantially all the income of which was derived from the sale, leasing, rental or development, as the case may be, of similar properties or the rendering of similar services.

Editorial Note: S. 111(5) prohibits the carryforward or carryback of non-capital losses and farm losses of a corporation after a change in the control. An exception is made under the "streaming rules" under paragraphs (*a*) and (*b*), which can apply to allow the losses if the corporation continues to carry on the pre-change of control business for profit or with a reasonable expectation of profit, and generally to the extent of income from that business and similar businesses in the year in which the loss is claimed. Effective March 21, 2013, the same prohibition applies to a trust that is subject to a "loss restriction event", which occurs when a person becomes a majority-interest beneficiary or a group becomes a majority-interest group of beneficiaries. See subsection 251.2(2).

History: S. 111(5) was replaced by S.C. 2013, c. 40, s. 47(1), deemed to have come into force on March 21, 2013, and formerly read:

(5) *Idem.* Where, at any time, control of a corporation has been acquired by a person or group of persons, no amount in respect of its non-capital loss or farm loss for a taxation year ending before that time is deductible by the corporation for a taxation year ending after that time and no amount in respect of its non-capital loss or farm loss for a taxation year ending after that time is deductible by the corporation for a taxation year ending before that time except that

(*a*) such portion of the corporation's non-capital loss or farm loss, as the case may be, for a taxation year ending before that time as may reasonably be regarded as its loss from carrying on a business and, where a business was carried on by the corporation in that year, such portion of the non-capital loss as may reasonably be regarded as being in respect of an amount deductible under paragraph 110(1)(*k*) in computing its taxable income for the year is deductible by the corporation for a particular taxation year ending after that time

(i) only if that business was carried on by the corporation for profit or with a reasonable expectation of profit throughout the particular year, and

(ii) only to the extent of the total of the corporation's income for the particular year from that business and, where properties were sold, leased, rented or developed or services rendered in the course of carrying on that business before that time, from any other business substantially all the income of which was derived from the sale, leasing, rental or development, as the case may be, of similar properties or the rendering of similar services; and

(*b*) such portion of the corporation's non-capital loss or farm loss, as the case may be, for a taxation year ending after that time as may reasonably be regarded as its loss from carrying on a business and, where a business was carried on by the corporation in that year, such portion of the non-capital loss as may reasonably be regarded as being in respect of an amount deductible under paragraph 110(1)(*k*) in computing its taxable income for the year is deductible by the corporation for a particular year ending before that time

(i) only if throughout the taxation year and in the particular year that business was carried on by the corporation for profit or with a reasonable expectation of profit, and

(ii) only to the extent of the corporation's income for the particular year from that business and, where properties were sold, leased, rented or developed or services rendered in the course of carrying on that business before that time, from any other business substantially all the income of which was derived from the sale, leasing, rental or development, as the case may be, of similar properties or the rendering of similar services.

Related Sections: S. 10(11) Loss restriction event; s. 87(2.1) Non-capital losses, etc., of predecessor corporations; s. 111(8) Definitions; s. 249(4) Loss restriction event – year end; s. 251.2(2) Loss restriction event.

Canadian Tax Foundation: Bodie and Novotny, *Acquisitions of Control Under the Income Tax Act — Recent Developments*, 2013 Prairie Provinces Tax Conference 6:1–27; Friedlan, *Deductibility of Losses After an Acquisition of Control: A Stricter Test?*, 2013 Tax for the Owner-Manager 13(2):2–3; Munoz, *Loss Utilizations in Arm's Length Business Combinations*, 2009 Canadian Tax Journal 3:660–698; Courage, *Utilization of Tax Losses and Debt Restructuring*, 2006 Ontario Tax Conference 9:1–86; Finkelstein and Nixon, *Takeovers*, 2004 Conference Report 21:1–48.

Tax Profile: November 2009 — Purchase and Sale of a Canadian Business; March 2009 — Sale of Businesses to Employees: The Leveraged Buy-Out — Part I; March 2004 — Loss Planning.

Income Tax Technical News: Issue No. 34, Loss Consolidation — Unanimous Shareholder Agreements; Issue No. 34, Sale of Tax Losses; Issue No. 34, Loss Consolidation — Provincial Tax; Issue No. 25, Refreshing Losses.

Interpretation Bulletins: *Primary* — IT-302R3 Losses of a corporation — The effect that acquisitions of control, amalgamations, and windings-up have on their deductibility — After January 15, 1987. *Secondary* — IT-206R Separate businesses.

Cases: Subsection 111(5) limits the ability to deduct unused business losses where there has been a change of control of the corporation. There is no change of control as a result of an amalgamation unless one of subparagraphs 256(7)(*b*)(ii) or (iii) deems it. Neither applied in this case. However, the series of transactions involved in the amalgamation was not undertaken primarily for purposes other than to obtain a tax benefit in the form of the losses being claimed, which made it an "avoidance transaction". The insertion of the short-lived Class B shares, whose only purpose was to be converted into common shares, constituted the manipulation of the shareholdings of a predecessor contrary to subsection 256(7). This constituted an abuse of that provision. The solution was to ignore the Class B shares, with the result that there was a change of control immediately before the amalgamation, which justified the refusal to permit the taxpayer to deduct pre-amalgamation accumulated non-capital losses. *Birchcliff Energy Ltd. v. The Queen*, 2017 DTC 1151 (TCC)

The explosives division sold by the taxpayer was not a separate business, therefore, the taxpayer was not subject to recapture of capital cost allowance or an increased s. 14(1) income inclusion. Indicators of integration included centralized financing and credit management, centralized purchasing, and common research facilities. *Du Pont Canada Inc. v. The Queen*, 2001 DTC 5269 (F.C.A.), reversing 99 DTC 1132 (T.C.C.)

A corporation acquired a competitor for the purpose of eliminating competition and then amalgamated the two corporations to form the corporate taxpayer. The successor corporation was not entitled to deduct the predecessor corporation's losses since the successor did not continue to carry on any significant portion of the predecessor's business "for profit or with a reasonable expectation of profit". *Garage Montplaisir Inc. v. The Queen*, 2000 DTC 6216 (F.C.A.), affirming 96 DTC 6557 (F.C.T.D.) and 92 DTC 2317 (T.C.C.)

Although the parent company did not have *de facto* over both corporations, it did have *de jure* control, and that was sufficient to allow the non-capital losses to be transferred from one corporation to the other. *Duha Printers (Western) Ltd.*, 98 DTC 6334 (S.C.C.), reversing 96 DTC 6323 (F.C.A.), which reversed 95 DTC 828 (T.C.C.)

Although its predecessor corporation's panels were used in the trailers sold by the taxpayer, they were not "similar" properties under the "substantially all" income test so that the taxpayer was not entitled to carryforward its predecessor's non-capital losses after their merger. *Manac Inc. Corp. v. The Queen*, 98 DTC 6352 (F.C.A.), affirming 97 DTC 1715 (T.C.C.).

► 111(5.1) ◄

(5.1) Loss restriction event — UCC computation. Subject to subsection (5.5), if at any time a taxpayer is subject to a loss restriction event and, if this Act were read without reference to subsection 13(24), the undepreciated capital cost to the taxpayer of depreciable property of a prescribed class immediately before that time would have exceeded the total of

(*a*) the fair market value of all the property of that class immediately before that time, and

(*b*) the amount in respect of property of that class otherwise allowed under regulations made under paragraph 20(1)(*a*) or deductible under subsection 20(16) in computing the taxpayer's income for the taxation year that ended immediately before that time,

the excess is to be deducted in computing the taxpayer's income for the taxation year that ended immediately before that time and is deemed to have been allowed in respect of property of that class under regulations made under paragraph 20(1)(*a*).

Editorial Note: S. 111(4)(*e*) allows an elective "write-up" for depreciable property, generally where the fair market value of the property exceeds the cost amount of the property. The election could be advisable if any resulting recapture could be offset by the deduction in respect of accrued losses under s. 111(5.1).

History: S. 111(5.1) was replaced by S.C. 2013, c. 40, s. 47(1), deemed to have come into force on March 21, 2013, and formerly read:

(5.1) *Computation of undepreciated capital cost.* Where, at any time, control of a corporation (other than a corporation that at that time became or ceased to be exempt from tax under this Part on its taxable income) has been acquired by a person or group of persons and, if this Act were read without reference to subsection 13(24), the undepreciated capital cost to the corporation of depreciable property of a prescribed class immediately before that time would have exceeded the total of

(*a*) the fair market value of all the property of that class immediately before that time, and

(*b*) the amount in respect of property of that class otherwise allowed under regulations made under paragraph 20(1)(*a*) or deductible under subsection 20(16) in computing the corporation's income for the taxation year ending immediately before that time,

the excess shall be deducted in computing the income of the corporation for the taxation year ending immediately before that time and shall be deemed to have been allowed in respect of property of that class under regulations made under paragraph 20(1)(*a*).

Related Sections: S. 111(4)(*e*) Loss restriction event — capital losses; s. 249(4) Loss restriction event – year end; s. 251.2(2) Loss restriction event.

Interpretation Bulletins: *Secondary* — IT-302R3 Losses of a corporation — The effect that acquisitions of control, amalgamations, and windings-up have on their deductibility — After January 15, 1987.

► 111(5.2) ◄

(5.2) Loss restriction event — CEC computation — (Repealed by S.C. 2016, c. 12, s. 40(1).)

History: S. 111(5.2) was repealed by S.C. 2016, c. 12, s. 40(1), in force January 1, 2017, and formerly read:

(5.2) *Loss restriction event — CEC computation.* Subject to subsection (5.5), if at any time a taxpayer is subject to a loss restriction event and immediately before that time the taxpayer's cumulative eligible capital in respect of a business exceeds the total of

(*a*) 3/4 of the fair market value of the eligible capital property in respect of the business, and

(*b*) the amount otherwise deducted under paragraph 20(1)(*b*) in computing the taxpayer's income from the business for the taxation year that ended immediately before that time,

the excess is to be deducted under paragraph 20(1)(*b*) in computing the taxpayer's income for the taxation year that ended immediately before that time.

S. 111(5.2) was replaced by S.C. 2013, c. 40, s. 47(1), deemed to have come into force on March 21, 2013, and formerly read:

(5.2) *Computation of cumulative eligible capital.* Where, at any time, control of a corporation (other than a corporation that at that time became or ceased to be exempt from tax under this Part on its taxable income) has been acquired by a person or group of persons and immediately before that time the corporation's cumulative eligible capital in respect of a business exceeded the total of

(*a*) $^{3}/_{4}$ of the fair market value of the eligible capital property in respect of the business, and

(*b*) the amount otherwise deducted under paragraph 20(1)(*b*) in computing the corporation's income from the business for the taxation year ending immediately before that time,

the excess shall be deducted under paragraph 20(1)(*b*) in computing the corporation's income from the business for the taxation year ending immediately before that time.

Related Sections: S. 249(4) Loss restriction event – year end; s. 251.2(2) Loss restriction event.

Interpretation Bulletins: *Secondary* — IT-302R3 Losses of a corporation — The effect that acquisitions of control, amalgamations, and windings-up have on their deductibility — After January 15, 1987.

▶ 111(5.3) ◀

(5.3) Loss restriction event — doubtful debts and bad debts. Subject to subsection (5.5), if at any time a taxpayer is subject to a loss restriction event,

(*a*) no amount may be deducted under paragraph 20(1)(*l*) in computing the taxpayer's income for the taxation year that ended immediately before that time; and

(*b*) in respect of each debt owing to the taxpayer immediately before that time

(i) the amount that is the greatest amount that would, but for this subsection and subsection 26(2) of this Act and subsection 33(1) of the *Income Tax Act*, chapter 148 of the Revised Statutes of Canada, 1952, have been deductible under paragraph 20(1)(*l*)

(A) is deemed to be a separate debt, and

(B) notwithstanding any other provision of this Act, is to be deducted as a bad debt under paragraph 20(1)(*p*) in computing the taxpayer's income for its taxation year that ended immediately before that time, and

(ii) the amount by which the debt exceeds that separate debt is deemed to be a separate debt incurred at the same time and under the same circumstances as the debt was incurred.

Editorial Note: Subsection 111(5.3) provides that, in the taxation year deemed to have ended immediately before an acquisition of control or loss restriction event, a corporation or trust must deduct the full amount of its doubtful debts — including the "doubtful portions" of its debts that are otherwise neither doubtful nor bad — as bad debts under s. 20(1)(*p*). Any amounts recovered by the corporation or trust on account of such debts thereafter are required by s. 12(1)(*i*) to be included in income in the year of receipt.

History: S. 111(5.3) was replaced by S.C. 2013, c. 40, s. 47(1), deemed to have come into force on March 21, 2013, and formerly read:

(5.3) *Doubtful debts and bad debts.* Where, at any time, control of a corporation (other than a corporation that at that time became or ceased to be exempt from tax under this Part on its taxable income) has been acquired by a person or group of persons, no amount may be deducted under paragraph 20(1)(*l*) in computing the corporation's income for its taxation year ending immediately before that time and each amount that is the greatest amount that would, but for this subsection and subsection 26(2) of this Act and subsection 33(1) of the *Income Tax Act*, chapter 148 of the Revised Statutes of Canada, 1952, have been deductible under paragraph 20(1)(*l*) in respect of a debt owing to the corporation immediately before that time shall be deemed to be a separate debt and shall, notwithstanding any other provision of this Act, be deducted as a bad debt under paragraph 20(1)(*p*) in computing the corporation's income for the year and the amount by which the debt exceeds that separate debt shall be deemed to be a separate debt incurred at the same time and under the same circumstances as the debt was incurred.

Related Sections: S. 12(1)(*i*) Bad debts recovered; s. 249(4) Loss restriction event – year end; s. 251.2(2) Loss restriction event.

Interpretation Bulletins: *Secondary* — IT-302R3 Losses of a corporation — The effect that acquisitions of control, amalgamations, and windings-up have on their deductibility — After January 15, 1987.

▶ 111(5.4) ◀

(5.4) Non-capital loss. Where, at any time, control of a corporation has been acquired by a person or persons, such portion of the corporation's non-capital loss for a taxation year ending before that time as

(*a*) was not deductible in computing the corporation's income for a taxation year ending before that time, and

(*b*) can reasonably be considered to be a non-capital loss of a subsidiary corporation (in this subsection referred to as the "former subsidiary corporation") from carrying on a particular business (in this subsection referred to as the "former subsidiary corporation's loss business") that was deemed by subsection 88(1.1) of the *Income Tax Act*, chapter 148 of the Revised Statutes of Canada, 1952, as it read on November 12, 1981 to be the non-capital loss of the corporation for the taxation year of the corporation in which the former subsidiary corporation's loss year ended

shall be deemed to be a non-capital loss of the corporation from carrying on the former subsidiary corporation's loss business.

Interpretation Bulletins: *Primary* — IT-302R3 Losses of a corporation — The effect that acquisitions of control, amalgamations, and windings-up have on their deductibility — After January 15, 1987.

▶ 111(5.5) ◀

(5.5) Loss restriction event — special rules. If at any time a taxpayer is subject to a loss restriction event,

(*a*) paragraphs (4)(*c*) to (*f*) and subsections (5.1) to (5.3) do not apply to the taxpayer in respect of the loss restriction event if at that time the taxpayer becomes or ceases to be exempt from tax under this Part on its taxable income; and

(*b*) if it can reasonably be considered that the main reason that the taxpayer is subject to the loss restriction event is to cause paragraph (4)(*d*) or any of subsections (5.1) to (5.3) to apply with respect to the loss restriction event, the following do not apply with respect to the loss restriction event:

(i) that provision and paragraph (4)(*e*), and

(ii) if that provision is paragraph (4)(*d*), paragraph (4)(*c*).

History: S. 111(5.5) was replaced by S.C. 2013, c. 40, s. 47(2), deemed to have come into force on March 21, 2013, and formerly read:

(5.5) *Restriction.* Where control of a corporation has been acquired by a person or group of persons and it may reasonably be considered that the main reason for the acquisition of control was to cause paragraph (4)(*d*) or subsection (5.1), (5.2) or (5.3) to apply with respect to the acquisition,

(*a*) that provision and paragraph (4)(*e*), and

(*b*) where that provision is paragraph (4)(*d*), paragraph (4)(*c*)

shall not apply with respect to the acquisition.

Tax Profile: March 2004 — Loss Planning.

▶ 111(6) ◀

(6) Limitation. For the purposes of this section and paragraph 53(1)(*i*), any loss of a taxpayer for a taxation year from a farming business shall, after the taxpayer disposes of the land used in that farming business and to the extent that the amount of the loss is required by paragraph 53(1)(*i*) to be added in computing the adjusted cost base to the taxpayer of the land immediately before the disposition, be deemed not to be a loss.

Editorial Note: Paragraph 53(1)(*i*) allows certain unused farm losses to be added to a hobby farm's adjusted cost base. Subsection 111(6) prevents any loss thus utilized from also being available to reduce income from other farming businesses.

▶ 111(7) ◀

(7) Idem. For the purposes of this section, any loss of a taxpayer for a taxation year from a farming business shall, to the extent that the loss is included in the amount of any deduction permitted by section 101 in computing the taxpayer's income for any subsequent taxation year, be deemed not to be a loss of the taxpayer for the purpose of computing the taxpayer's taxable income for that subsequent year or any taxation year subsequent thereto.

Editorial Note: Similar to s. 53(1)(*i*), the combined effect of s. 101 and 96(1)(*e*) is to "transform" restricted (i.e., undeducted) farm losses into increased farming business partnership adjusted cost base. Subsection 111(7) prevents any loss thus transformed from also being available to reduce income from other farming businesses.

▶ 111(7.1) ◀

(7.1) Effect of election by insurer under s. 138(9) in respect of 1975 taxation year — (Repealed by S.C. 2013, c. 34, s. 241(3).)

History: S. 111(7.1) was repealed by S.C. 2013, c. 34, s. 241(3), applicable to taxation years that begin after October 31, 2011, and formerly read:

(7.1) *Effect of election by insurer under s. 138(9) in respect of 1975 taxation year.* Where an insurer has made an election under subsection 138(9) in respect of its 1975 taxation year, for the purpose of determining the amount deductible in computing its taxable income for its 1977 and subsequent taxation years in respect of the non-capital loss, if any, for the 1972 and each subsequent taxation year ending before 1977, a portion of the non-capital loss for each such year equal to the lesser of

(*a*) the portion of the non-capital loss for the year (determined without reference to this subsection) that would be deductible in computing the insurer's taxable income for its 1977 taxation year if the insurer had sufficient income for that year, and

(*b*) the amount, if any, by which

(i) its 1975 branch accounting election deficiency

exceeds

(ii) the total of

(A) the amount determined under subparagraph 138(4.1)(*d*)(ii) in respect of the insurer,

(B) the total of all amounts each of which is an amount determined under paragraph 13(22)(*b*) with respect to depreciable property of a prescribed class of the insurer, and

(C) the total of all amounts each of which is the portion determined under this subsection in respect of the non-capital loss for a taxation year after 1971 and preceding the year

shall, for the purposes of this section, be deemed to have been deductible under this section in computing the insurer's taxable income for a taxation year ending before 1977.

Related Sections: S. 138(12) Definitions.

▶ 111(7.11) ◀

(7.11) Application of s. 138(12) — (Repealed by S.C. 2013, c. 34, s. 241(3).)

History: S. 111(7.11) was repealed by S.C. 2013, c. 34, s. 241(3), applicable to taxation years that begin after October 31, 2011, and formerly read:

(7.11) *Application of s. 138(12).* The definitions in subsection 138(12) apply to subsection (7.1).

▶ 111(7.2) ◀

(7.2) Non-capital loss of life insurer — (Repealed by S.C. 2013, c. 34, s. 241(3).)

History: S. 111(7.2) was repealed by S.C. 2013, c. 34, s. 241(3), applicable to taxation years that begin after October 31, 2011, and formerly read:

(7.2) *Non-capital loss of life insurer.* Notwithstanding paragraph (1)(*a*), in the case of a life insurer the amount deductible in computing its taxable income for its 1978 and subsequent taxation years,

(*a*) in respect of its non-capital loss for each taxation year ending before 1977 shall be deemed to be nil; and

(*b*) in respect of its non-capital loss for its 1977 taxation year shall be deemed to be the amount, if any, by which

(i) the amount referred to in subparagraph 138(4.2)(*a*)(iv)

exceeds the total of

(ii) the amount of the reserve determined for the purpose of subparagraph 138(4.2)(*a*)(i),

(iii) in any case where subparagraph 138(4.2)(*a*)(ii) applies, the total of amounts referred to in that subparagraph, and

(iv) in any case where subparagraph 138(4.2)(*a*)(iii) applies, the amount referred to in that subparagraph.

▶ 111(7.3) ◀

(7.3) Non-capital losses of employee life and health trusts. Paragraph (1)(*a*) does not apply in computing the taxable income of a trust for a taxation year if the trust is, in the year, an employee life and health trust.

History: S. 111(7.3) was added by S.C. 2010, c. 25, s. 21(2), applicable after 2009.

▶ 111(7.4) ◀

(7.4) Non-capital losses of employee life and health trusts. For the purposes of computing the taxable income of an employee life and health trust for a taxation year, there may be deducted such portion as the trust may claim of the trust's non-capital losses for the three taxation years immediately preceding and the three taxation years immediately following the year.

Editorial Note: Note that s. 104(6)(*a.4*) allows an employee life and health trust to deduct amounts that became payable in a year as designated employee benefits, regardless of whether those amounts exceed the revenues of the trust. In other words, the payment of designated employee benefits out of the trust's capital can create a non-capital loss, which will be subject to the carryover rules of s. 111(7.4).

History: S. 111(7.4) was added by S.C. 2010, c. 25, s. 21(2), applicable after 2009.

Related Sections: S. 104(6)(*a.4*) Deduction in computing income of trust, s. 144.1(2) Employee life and health trust; s. 144.1(13) Non-capital losses.

▶ 111(7.5) ◀

(7.5) Non-capital losses of employee life and health trusts. Notwithstanding paragraph (1)(*a*) and subsection (7.4), no amount in respect of the trust's non-capital losses for a taxation year in which the trust was an employee life and health trust may be deducted in computing the trust's taxable income for another taxation year (referred to in this subsection as the "specified year") if

(*a*) the trust was not an employee life and health trust for the specified year; or

(*b*) the trust is an employee life and health trust that, because of the application of subsection 144.1(3), is not permitted to deduct any amount under subsection 104(6) for the specified year.

History: S. 111(7.5) was added by S.C. 2010, c. 25, s. 21(2), applicable after 2009.

▶ 111(8) ◀

(8) Definitions. In this section,

"exchange rate" — "exchange rate", at any time in respect of a currency of a country other than Canada, means the rate of exchange between that currency and Canadian currency quoted by the Bank of Canada on the day that includes that time or, if that day is not a business day, on the day that immediately precedes that day, or a rate of exchange acceptable to the Minister;

History: S. 111(8), the definition "exchange rate" was replaced by S.C. 2017, c. 33, s. 40(1), deemed to have come into force on March 1, 2017, and formerly read:

"exchange rate" — "exchange rate" at any time in respect of a currency of a country other than Canada means the rate of exchange between that currency and Canadian currency quoted by the Bank of Canada at noon on the day that includes that time or, if that day is not a business day, on the day that immediately precedes that day, or a rate of exchange acceptable to the Minister;

S. 111(8), the definition "exchange rate" was added by S.C. 2009, c. 2, s. 30(1), applicable to any acquisition of control of a corporation that occurs

(a) after March 7, 2008, other than an acquisition of control that occurs before 2009 under the terms of an agreement made in writing on or before March 7, 2008; or

(b) after 2005, if the corporation so elects in writing and files the election with the Minister of National Revenue on or before the corporation's filing-due date for the corporation's taxation year that includes the day on which this Act is assented to [R.A. March 12, 2009].

If an election under paragraph (*b*) [above] is made by the corporation in respect of an acquisition of control, a designation under paragraph 111(4)(*e*) by the corporation for its taxation year that ended immediately before the acquisition of control is deemed to have been made in a timely manner if that designation is made on or before the corporation's filing-due date for its taxation year that includes the day on which this Act is assented to [R.A. March 12, 2009].

"farm loss" — "farm loss" of a taxpayer for a taxation year means the amount determined by the formula

$$A - C$$

where

A is the lesser of

(*a*) the amount, if any, by which

(i) the total of all amounts each of which is the taxpayer's loss for the year from a farming or fishing business

exceeds

(ii) the total of all amounts each of which is the taxpayer's income for the year from a farming or fishing business, and

(*b*) the amount that would be the taxpayer's non-capital loss for the year if the amount determined for D in the definition "non-capital loss" in this subsection were nil, and

C is the total of all amounts by which the farm loss of the taxpayer for the year is required to be reduced because of section 80;

History: S. 111(8), paragraph (*b*) of the description of A in the definition "farm loss" was replaced by S.C. 2013, c. 40, s. 47(3), in force December 12, 2013, and formerly read:

(*b*) the amount that would be the taxpayer's non-capital loss for the year if each of the amounts determined for C and D in the definition "non-capital loss" in this subsection were zero, and

Related Sections: S. 111(1)(*d*) Farm losses.

Interpretation Bulletins: *Secondary* — IT-302R3 Losses of a corporation — The effect that acquisitions of control, amalgamations, and windings-up have on their deductibility — After January 15, 1987.

"foreign currency debt" —"foreign currency debt" means a debt obligation denominated in a currency of a country other than Canada;

History: S. 111(8), the definition "foreign currency debt" was added by S.C. 2009, c. 2, s. 30(1), applicable to any acquisition of control of a corporation that occurs

(a) after March 7, 2008, other than an acquisition of control that occurs before 2009 under the terms of an agreement made in writing on or before March 7, 2008; or

(b) after 2005, if the corporation so elects in writing and files the election with the Minister of National Revenue on or before the corporation's filing-due date for the corporation's taxation year that includes the day on which this Act is assented to [R.A. March 12, 2009].

If an election under paragraph (*b*) [above] is made by the corporation in respect of an acquisition of control, a designation under paragraph 111(4)(*e*) by the corporation for its taxation year that ended immediately before the acquisition of control is deemed to have been made in a timely manner if that designation is made on or before the corporation's filing-due date for its taxation year that includes the day on which this Act is assented to [R.A. March 12, 2009].

"net capital loss" —"net capital loss" of a taxpayer for a taxation year means the amount determined by the formula

$$A - B + C - D$$

where

A is the amount, if any, determined under subparagraph 3(*b*)(ii) in respect of the taxpayer for the year,

B is the lesser of the total determined under subparagraph 3(*b*)(i) in respect of the taxpayer for the year and the amount determined for A in respect of the taxpayer for the year,

C is the least of

(*a*) the amount of the allowable business investment losses of the taxpayer for the taxpayer's tenth preceding taxation year,

(*b*) the amount, if any, by which the amount of the non-capital loss of the taxpayer for the taxpayer's tenth preceding taxation year exceeds the total of all amounts in respect of that non-capital loss deducted in computing the taxpayer's taxable income or claimed by the taxpayer under paragraph 186(1)(*c*) or (*d*) for the year or for any preceding taxation year, and

(*c*) if the taxpayer was subject to a loss restriction event before the end of the year and after the end of the taxpayer's tenth preceding taxation year, nil, and

D is the total of all amounts by which the net capital loss of the taxpayer for the year is required to be reduced because of section 80;

History: S. 111(8), paragraph (*c*) of the description of C in the definition "net capital loss" was replaced by S.C. 2013, c. 40, s. 47(4), deemed to have come into force on March 21, 2013, and formerly read:

(*c*) if the taxpayer is a corporation the control of which was acquired by a person or group of persons before the end of the year and after the end of the taxpayer's tenth preceding taxation year, nil, and

Related Sections: S. 111(1)(*b*) Net capital losses.

Interpretation Bulletins: *Secondary* — IT-302R3 Losses of a corporation — The effect that acquisitions of control, amalgamations, and windings-up have on their deductibility — After January 15, 1987.

"non-capital loss" —"non-capital loss" of a taxpayer for a taxation year means, at any time, the amount determined by the formula

$$(A + B) - (D + D.1 + D.2)$$

where

A is the amount determined by the formula

$$E - F$$

where

E is the total of all amounts each of which is

(*a*) the taxpayer's loss for the year from an office, employment, business or property,

(*a*.1) an amount deductible under paragraph 104(6)(*a*.4) in computing the taxpayer's income for the year,

(*b*) an amount deducted under paragraph (1)(*b*) or section 110.6, or deductible under any of paragraphs 110(1)(*d*) to (*d*.3), (*f*), (*g*) and (*k*), section 112 and subsections 113(1) and 138(6), in computing the taxpayer's taxable income for the year, or

Proposed Amendment

Notice of Ways and Means Motion to amend the Income Tax Act (June 17, 2019)

Paragraph (*b*) of the description of E in the definition *non-capital loss* in subsection 111(8) of the Act is replaced by the following:

(*b*) an amount deducted under paragraph (1)(*b*) or section 110.6, or deductible under any of paragraphs 110(1)(*d*) to (*g*) and (*k*), section 112 and subsections 113(1) and 138(6), in computing the taxpayer's taxable income for the year, or

Applicable: On January 1, 2020.

(*c*) if that time is before the taxpayer's eleventh following taxation year, the taxpayer's allowable business investment loss for the year, and

F is the amount determined under paragraph 3(*c*) in respect of the taxpayer for the year,

B is the amount, if any, determined in respect of the taxpayer for the year under section 110.5 or subparagraph 115(1)(*a*)(vii),

D is the amount that would be the taxpayer's farm loss for the year if the amount determined for B in the definition "farm loss" in this subsection were zero,

D.1 is the total of all amounts deducted under subsection (10) in respect of the taxpayer for the year, and

D.2 is the total of all amounts by which the non-capital loss of the taxpayer for the year is required to be reduced because of section 80;

History: S. 111(8), paragraph (*b*) of the description of E in the definition "non-capital loss" was replaced by S.C. 2017, c. 20, s. 10(1), in force January 1, 2018, and formerly read:

(*b*) an amount deducted under paragraph (1)(*b*) or section 110.6, or deductible under any of paragraphs 110(1)(*d*) to (*d.3*), (*f*), (*g*), (*j*) and (*k*), section 112 and subsections 113(1) and 138(6), in computing the taxpayer's taxable income for the year, or

S. 111(8), subparagraph (*a.1*) of the description of E in the definition "non-capital loss" was added by S.C. 2010, c. 25, s. 21(3), applicable after 2009.

Related Sections: S. 3 Income for taxation year; s. 9(2) Loss; s. 38 Taxable capital gain and allowable capital loss; s. 111(1)(*a*) Non-capital losses. s. 248(1), "allowable business investment loss".

Income Tax Folios: S4-F8-C1 Business Investment Losses.

Interpretation Bulletins: *Secondary* — IT-232R3 Losses — Their Deductibility in the Loss Year or in Other Years; IT-302R3 Losses of a corporation — The effect that acquisitions of control, amalgamations, and windings-up have on their deductibility — After January 15, 1987.

"pre-1986 capital loss balance" — "pre-1986 capital loss balance" of an individual for a particular taxation year means the amount determined by the formula

$$(A + B) - (C + D + E + E.1)$$

where

A is the total of all amounts each of which is an amount determined by the formula

$$F - G$$

where

F is the individual's net capital loss for a taxation year ending before 1985, and

G is the total of all amounts claimed under this section by the individual in respect of that loss in computing the individual's taxable income for taxation years preceding the particular taxation year, and

B is the amount determined by the formula

$$H - I$$

where

H is the lesser of

(*a*) the amount of the individual's net capital loss for the 1985 taxation year, and

(*b*) the amount, if any, by which the amount determined under subparagraph 3(*e*)(ii) of the *Income Tax Act*, chapter 148 of the Revised Statutes of Canada, 1952, in respect of the individual for the 1985 taxation year exceeds the amount deductible by reason of paragraph 3(*e*) of that Act in computing the individual's taxable income for the 1985 taxation year, and

I is the total of all amounts claimed under this section by the individual in respect of the individual's net capital loss for the 1985 taxation year in computing the individual's taxable income for taxation years preceding the particular taxation year,

C is the total of all amounts deducted under section 110.6 in computing the individual's taxable income for taxation years that ended before 1988 or begin after October 17, 2000,

D is 3/4 of the total of all amounts each of which is an amount deducted under section 110.6 in computing the individual's taxable income for a taxation year, preceding the particular year, that

(*a*) ended after 1987 and before 1990, or

(*b*) began after February 27, 2000 and ended before October 18, 2000,

E is 2/3 of the total of all amounts deducted under section 110.6 in computing the individual's taxable income for taxation years, preceding the particular year, that ended after 1989 and before February 28, 2000, and

E.1 is the amount determined by the formula

$$J \times (0.5/K)$$

where

J is the amount deducted by the individual under section 110.6 for a taxation year of the individual, preceding the particular year, that includes February 28, 2000 or October 17, 2000, and

K is the fraction in paragraph 38(*a*) that applies to the individual for the individual's taxation year referred to in the description of J.

History: S. 111(8), the description of C in the definition "pre-1986 capital loss balance" was replaced by S.C. 2013, c. 34, s. 241(4), applicable to the 2000 and subsequent taxation years, and formerly read:

C is the total of all amounts deducted under section 110.6 in computing the individual's taxable income for taxation years that end before 1988 or after October 17, 2000,

► 111(9) ◄

(9) Exception. In this section, a taxpayer's non-capital loss, net capital loss, restricted farm loss, farm loss and limited partnership loss for a taxation year during which the taxpayer was not resident in Canada shall be determined as if

(*a*) in the part of the year throughout which the taxpayer was non-resident, if section 114 applies to the taxpayer in respect of the year, and

(*b*) throughout the year, in any other case,

the taxpayer had no income other than income described in any of subparagraphs 115(1)(*a*)(i) to (vi), the taxpayer's only taxable capital gains, allowable capital losses and allowable business investment losses were from dispositions of taxable Canadian property (other than treaty-protected property) and the taxpayer's only other losses were losses from the duties of an office or employment performed by the taxpayer in Canada and businesses (other than treaty-protected businesses) carried on by the taxpayer in Canada.

Editorial Note: Essentially, s. 111(9) ensures that only Canadian-source losses can be carried forward or back to offset Canadian-source gains or income. Losses from "treaty-protected" property or business cannot be carried back or forward to offset Canadian-source income that is subject to Canadian tax.

Related Sections: S. 2(3) Tax payable by non-resident persons; s. 111(1)(*a*) Non-capital losses; s. 111(1)(*b*) Net capital losses; s. 111(1)(*c*) Restricted farm losses; s. 111(1)(*d*) Farm losses; s. 111(1)(*e*) Limited partnership losses; s. 248(1), "taxable Canadian property", "treaty-protected business", "treaty-protected property".

Tax Window Files: Losses of Non-resident, *Technical Interpretation, International and Trusts Division, July 2, 2003*, CRA Document No. 2003-0007967.

► 111(10) ◄

(10) Fuel tax rebate loss abatement. Where in a particular taxation year a taxpayer received an amount (in this subsection referred to as a "rebate") as a fuel tax rebate under subsection 68.4(2) or (3.1) of the *Excise Tax Act*, in computing the taxpayer's non-capital loss for a taxation year (in this subsection referred to as the "loss year") that is one of the 7 taxation years preceding the particular year, there shall be deducted the lesser of

(*a*) the amount determined by the formula

$$10(A - B) - C$$

where

A is the total of all rebates received by the taxpayer in the particular year,

B is the total of all amounts, in respect of rebates received by the taxpayer in the particular year, repaid by the taxpayer under subsection 68.4(7) of that Act, and

C is the total of all amounts, in respect of rebates received in the particular year, deducted under this subsection in computing the taxpayer's non-capital losses for other taxation years; and

(*b*) such amount as the taxpayer claims, not exceeding the portion of the taxpayer's non-capital loss for the loss year (determined without reference to this subsection) that would be deductible in computing the taxpayer's taxable income for the particular year if the taxpayer had sufficient income for the particular year from businesses carried on by the taxpayer in the particular year.

► 111(11) ◄

(11) Fuel tax rebate — partnerships. Where a taxpayer was a member of a partnership at any time in a fiscal period of the partnership during which it received a fuel tax rebate under subsection 68.4(2), (3) or (3.1) of the *Excise Tax Act*, the taxpayer is deemed

(*a*) to have received at that time as a rebate under subsection 68.4(2), (3) or (3.1), as the case may be, of that Act an amount equal to that proportion of the amount of the rebate received by the partnership that the member's share of the partnership's income or loss for that fiscal period is of the whole of that income or loss, determined without reference to any rebate under section 68.4 of that Act; and

(*b*) to have paid as a repayment under subsection 68.4(7) of that Act an amount equal to that proportion of all amounts repaid under subsection 68.4(7) of that Act in respect of the rebate that the member's share of the partnership's income or loss for that fiscal period is of the whole of that income or loss, determined without reference to any rebate under section 68.4 of that Act.

► 111(12) ◄

(12) Foreign currency debt on loss restriction event. For the purposes of subsection (4), if at any time a taxpayer owes a foreign currency debt in respect of which the taxpayer would have had, if the foreign currency debt had been repaid at that time, a capital loss or gain, the taxpayer is deemed to own at the time (in this subsection referred to as the "measurement time") that is immediately before that time a property

(*a*) the adjusted cost base of which at the measurement time is the amount determined by the formula

$$A + B - C$$

where

A is the amount of principal owed by the taxpayer under the foreign currency debt at the measurement time, calculated, for greater certainty, using the exchange rate applicable at the measurement time,

B is the portion of any gain, previously recognized in respect of the foreign currency debt because of this section, that is reasonably attributable to the amount described in A, and

C is the portion of any capital loss previously recognized in respect of the foreign currency debt because of this section, that is reasonably attributable to the amount described in A; and

(*b*) the fair market value of which is the amount that would be the amount of the principal owed by the taxpayer under the foreign currency debt at the measurement time if that amount were calculated using the exchange rate applicable at the time of the original borrowing.

Editorial Note: S. 111(12) provides that a foreign currency debt owed by a taxpayer at any time that would otherwise generate a capital gain or loss if repaid at that time (a foreign currency capital gain or loss) is deemed to a property owned by the taxpayer for the purposes of the accrued loss write-down rules of s. 111(4) that apply upon an acquisition of control of the taxpayer corporation. Accordingly, a foreign currency debt with an accrued loss will be subject to the write-down rule, and the loss will be realized by the taxpayer in its taxation year ending immediately before the acquisition of control. Effective March 21, 2013, the provision similarly applies to a trust that is subject to a "loss restriction event" (subsection 251.2(2)), generally occurring when a person has become a majority-interest beneficiary, or a group of persons has become a majority-interest group of beneficiaries, of the trust. The election in s. 111(4)(*e*) can apply to a foreign currency debt obligation of the taxpayer with an accrued foreign exchange gain immediately before the acquisition of control, for the purpose of realizing the gain (which can be offset by the accrued losses owing to the write-down rule); the gain will then serve to reduce any further gain on the repayment of the debt under subsection 40(11).

History: S. 111(12) was replaced by S.C. 2013, c. 40, s. 47(5), deemed to have come into force on March 21, 2013, and formerly read:

(12) *Foreign currency debt on acquisition of control.* For the purposes of subsection (4), if at any time a corporation owes a foreign currency debt in respect of which the corporation would have had, if the foreign currency debt had been repaid at that time, a capital loss or gain, the corporation is deemed to own at the time (in this subsection referred to as the "measurement time") that is immediately before that time a property

(*a*) the adjusted cost base of which at the measurement time is the amount determined by the formula

$$A + B - C$$

where

A is the amount of principal owed by the corporation under the foreign currency debt at the measurement time, calculated, for greater certainty, using the exchange rate applicable at the measurement time,

B is the portion of any gain, previously recognized in respect of the foreign currency debt because of this section, that is reasonably attributable to the amount described in A, and

C is the portion of any capital loss previously recognized in respect of the foreign currency debt because of this section, that is reasonably attributable to the amount described in A; and

(*b*) the fair market value of which is the amount that would be the amount of the principal owed by the corporation under the foreign currency debt at the measurement time if that amount were calculated using the exchange rate applicable at the time of the original borrowing.

S. 111(12) was added by S.C. 2009, c. 2, s. 30(2), applicable to any acquisition of control of a corporation that occurs

(a) after March 7, 2008, other than an acquisition of control that occurs before 2009 under the terms of an agreement made in writing on or before March 7, 2008; or

(b) after 2005, if the corporation so elects in writing and files the election with the Minister of National Revenue on or before the corporation's filing-due date for the corporation's taxation year that includes the day on which this Act is assented to [R.A. March 12, 2009].

If an election under paragraph (*b*) [above] is made by the corporation in respect of an acquisition of control, a designation under paragraph 111(4)(*e*) by the corporation for its taxation year that ended immediately before the acquisition of control is deemed to have been made in a timely manner if that designation is made on or before the corporation's filing-due date for its taxation year that includes the day on which this Act is assented to [R.A. March 12, 2009].

Related Sections: S. 40(10) Application; s. 40(11) Gain or loss on foreign currency debt; s. 111(4) Loss restriction event — capital losses; s. 111(8), "exchange rate", "foreign currency debt".

International Tax: No. 92, Foreign Currency Debts and Acquisitions of Control: Beware the Unexpected Gain.

SECTION 111.1: Order of applying provisions

In computing an individual's taxable income for a taxation year, the provisions of this Division shall be applied in the following order: sections 110, 110.2, 111, 110.6 and 110.7.

Interpretation Bulletins: *Primary* — IT-523 Order of provisions applicable in computing an individual's taxable income and tax payable. *Secondary* — IT-232R3 Losses — Their deductibility in the loss year or in other years.

SECTION 112: Deduction of taxable dividends received by corporation resident in Canada

► 112(1) ◄

(1) Deduction of taxable dividends received by corporation resident in Canada. Where a corporation in a taxation year has received a taxable dividend from

(*a*) a taxable Canadian corporation, or

(*b*) a corporation resident in Canada (other than a non-resident-owned investment corporation or a corporation exempt from tax under this Part) and controlled by it,

an amount equal to the dividend may be deducted from the income of the receiving corporation for the year for the purpose of computing its taxable income.

Related Sections: S. 55(2) Deemed proceeds or gain; s. 112(2.1) Where no deduction permitted; s. 112(2.2) Guaranteed shares; s. 138(6) Deduction for dividends from taxable corporations; s. 186(1) Tax on assessable dividends; s. 192(1) Corporation to pay tax.

Canadian Tax Foundation: Welters et al., *When is an Inter-Corporate Dividend Not Tax-Free?*, 2015 British Columbia Tax Conference 6:1–36.

Tax Profile: October 2004 — Taxation of Dividends: A Survey in the Context of Private Corporations and Their Shareholders.

Information Circulars: IC 88-2 General anti-avoidance rule — Section 245 of the Income Tax Act (para. 13).

Interpretation Bulletins: *Secondary* — IT-232R3 Losses — Their deductibility in the loss year or in other years; IT-269R4 Part IV tax on taxable dividends received by a private corporation or a subject corporation; IT-524 Trusts — Flow-through of taxable dividends to a beneficiary — After 1987.

► 112(2) ◄

(2) Dividends received from non-resident corporation. Where a taxpayer that is a corporation has, in a taxation year, received a dividend from a corporation (other than a foreign affiliate of the taxpayer) that was taxable under subsection 2(3) for the year and that has, throughout the period from June 18, 1971 to the time when the dividend was received, carried on a business in Canada through a permanent establishment as defined by regulation, an amount equal to that proportion of the dividend that the paying corporation's taxable income earned in Canada for the immediately preceding year is of the whole of the amount that its taxable income for that year would have been if it had been resident in Canada throughout that year, may be deducted from the income of the receiving corporation for the taxation year for the purpose of computing its taxable income.

Editorial Note: Subsection 112(2) applies to dividends received from certain non-resident corporations that are not foreign affiliates. Where a foreign affiliate pays a dividend, a portion thereof may be deducted in computing the recipient's taxable income according to rules set out in s. 113.

Related Regulations: Part LI; 400(2); 8201.

Related Sections: S. 55(2) Deemed proceeds or gain; s. 95(1), "foreign affiliate"; s. 112(2.1) Where no deduction permitted; s. 112(2.2) Guaranteed shares; s. 247(1) Transfer pricing — definitions.

► 112(2.1) ◄

(2.1) No deduction permitted. No deduction may be made under subsection (1) or (2) in computing the taxable income of a specified financial institution in respect of a dividend received by it on a share that was, at the time the dividend was received, a term preferred share, other than a dividend on a share of the capital stock of a corporation that was not acquired in the ordinary course of the business carried on by the institution, and for the purposes of this subsection, if a restricted financial institution received the dividend on a share of the capital stock of a mutual fund corporation or an investment corporation at any time after the mutual fund or investment corporation has elected under subsection 131(10) not to be a restricted financial institution, the share is deemed to be a term preferred share acquired in the ordinary course of business.

Editorial Note: This provision, which may deny normal deductions for intercorporate dividends, applies to a specified financial institution ("SFI") which acquires a term preferred share (both terms being defined in s. 248(1)) outside the ordinary course of business. An SFI includes a corporation whose principal business is arm's length money lending and/or purchasing of debt obligations, as well as related corporations. Because of this surprisingly wide definition, it may be necessary to rely on the outside-the-ordinary-course-of-business exception, a concept on which there has been comparatively little authority in Canadian tax law.

History: S. 112(2.1) was replaced by S.C. 2013, c. 34, s. 242(1), applicable to dividends received on or after November 5, 2010, and formerly read:

(2.1) *Where no deduction permitted.* No deduction may be made under subsection (1) or (2) in computing the taxable income of a specified financial institution in respect of a dividend received by it on a share that was, at the time the dividend was paid, a term preferred share, other than a dividend paid on a share of the capital stock of a corporation that was not acquired in the ordinary course of the business carried on by the institution, and for the purposes of this subsection, where a restricted financial institution received the dividend on a share of the capital stock of a mutual fund corporation or an investment corporation at any time after that mutual fund corporation or investment corporation has elected pursuant to subsection 131(10) not to be a restricted financial institution, the share shall be deemed to be a term preferred share acquired in the ordinary course of business.

Related Sections: S. 191(4) Deemed dividends; s. 248(1), "amount", "term preferred share"; s. 248(14) Related corporations; s. 258(2) Deemed dividend on term preferred share.

Canadian Tax Foundation: Moskowitz, *The Preferred Share Rules: Yes They Can Apply to You!*, 1997 Conference Report 9:1–47.

Tax Profile: October 2004 — Taxation of Dividends: A Survey in the Context of Private Corporations and Their Shareholders.

Cases: The taxpayer acquired preferred shares that included the right to convert to common shares at a ratio determined at the time of conversion. The conversion right did not constitute a "form of guarantee, security or similar indemnity or covenant". Therefore the shares were not "term preferred shares" and the taxpayer was entitled to deduct the dividends received thereon. *The Queen v. Citibank Canada*, 2002 DTC 6876 (F.C.A.), affirming 2001 DTC 111 (T.C.C.)

The taxpayer's philosophy had been to acquire investments in ordinary shares in order to perform what it saw to be its role as an active partner in the management of a limited number of development businesses. The term preferred shares in issue were acquired upon the conversion of its original debenture holding. This was an exceptional situation not occurring within the "ordinary course" of its business. *Société d'Investissement Desjardins v. M.N.R.*, 91 DTC 393 (T.C.C.)

► 112(2.2) ◄

(2.2) Guaranteed shares. No deduction may be made under subsection (1), (2) or 138(6) in computing the taxable income of a particular corporation in respect of a dividend received on a share of the capital stock of a corporation that was issued after 8:00 p.m. Eastern Daylight Saving Time, June 18, 1987 where

(*a*) a person or partnership (in this subsection and subsection (2.21) referred to as the "guarantor") that is a specified financial institution or a specified person in relation to a specified financial institution, but that is not the issuer of the share or an individual other than a trust, is, at or immediately before the time the dividend was received, obligated, either absolutely or contingently and either immediately or in the future, to effect any undertaking (in this subsection and subsections (2.21) and (2.22) referred to as a "guarantee agreement"), including any guarantee, covenant or agreement to purchase or repurchase the share and including the lending of funds to or the placing of amounts on deposit with, or on behalf of, the particular corporation or any specified person in relation to the particular corporation given to ensure that

(i) any loss that the particular corporation or a specified person in relation to the particular corporation may sustain by reason of the ownership, holding or disposition of the share or any other property is limited in any respect, or

(ii) the particular corporation or a specified person in relation to the particular corporation will derive earnings by reason of the ownership, holding or disposition of the share or any other property; and

(*b*) the guarantee agreement was given as part of a transaction or event or a series of transactions or events that included the issuance of the share.

Editorial Note: This provision, which may deny normal deductions for intercorporate dividends, applies where, as part of the series of transactions involving the issuance of shares, a specified financial institution ("SFI") or a "specified person" in relation thereto enters into certain arrangements (referred to as "guarantee agreements") to ensure earnings or limit losses in respect thereof. An SFI, per s. 248(1), includes a corporation whose principal business is arm's length money lending and/or purchasing of debt obligations, as well as related corporations. "Specified person" (per paragraph (*h*) of the taxable preferred share definition in s. 248(1)) includes a person who is non-arm's length with the SFI or with certain associated partnerships or trusts. An exclusion will apply where the share and guarantee agreement are acquired/given in the ordinary course of business and the issuer is related to the particular corporation.

History: S. 112(2.2)(*a*), the portion before subparagraph (i) was replaced by S.C. 2013, c. 34, s. 242(2), applicable to dividends received on or after November 5, 2010, and formerly read:

(*a*) a person or partnership (in this subsection and subsection (2.21) referred to as the "guarantor") that is a specified financial institution or a specified person in relation to any such institution, but that is not the issuer of the share or an individual other than a trust, is, at or immediately before the time the dividend is paid, obligated, either absolutely or contingently and either immediately or in the future, to effect any undertaking (in this subsection and subsections (2.21) and (2.22) referred to as a "guarantee agreement"), including any guarantee, covenant or agreement to purchase or repurchase the share and including the lending of funds to or the placing of amounts on deposit with, or on behalf of, the particular corporation or any specified person in relation to the particular corporation given to ensure that

Related Regulations: 6201(3); 6201(8).

Related Sections: S. 84(4.3) Deemed dividend on guaranteed share; s. 87(4.2) Exchanged shares — amalgamations after November 27, 1986; s. 112(2.21) Exceptions; s. 112(2.22) Interpretation; s. 187.1 Definition of "excepted dividend"; s. 191(1), "private holding corporation"; s. 248(1), "amount"; "specified financial institution"; s. 248(10) Series of transactions; s. 248(14) Related corporations; s. 258(3) Deemed interest on preferred shares; s. 258(5) Deemed interest on certain shares; s. 262 Designated stock exchanges.

Tax Profile: October 2004 — Taxation of Dividends: A Survey in the Context of Private Corporations and Their Shareholders.

▶ 112(2.21) ◀

(2.21) Exceptions. Subsection (2.2) does not apply to a dividend received by a particular corporation on

(*a*) a share that is at the time the dividend is received a share described in paragraph (*e*) of the definition "term preferred share" in subsection 248(1);

(*b*) a grandfathered share, a taxable preferred share issued before December 16, 1987 or a prescribed share;

(*c*) a taxable preferred share issued after December 15, 1987 and of a class of the capital stock of a corporation that is listed on a designated stock exchange where all guarantee agreements in respect of the share were given by one or more of the issuer of the share and persons that are related (otherwise than because of a right referred to in paragraph 251(5)(*b*)) to the issuer unless, at the time the dividend is paid to the particular corporation, dividends in respect of more than 10 per cent of the issued and outstanding shares to which the guarantee agreement applies are paid to the particular corporation or the particular corporation and specified persons in relation to the particular corporation; or

(*d*) a share

(i) that was not acquired by the particular corporation in the ordinary course of its business,

(ii) in respect of which the guarantee agreement was not given in the ordinary course of the guarantor's business, and

(iii) the issuer of which is, at the time the dividend is paid, related (otherwise than because of a right referred to in paragraph 251(5)(*b*)) to both the particular corporation and the guarantor.

Related Sections: S. 248(1), "grandfathered share".

▶ 112(2.22) ◀

(2.22) Interpretation. For the purposes of subsections (2.2) and (2.21),

(*a*) where a guarantee agreement in respect of a share is given at any particular time after 8:00 p.m. Eastern Daylight Saving Time, June 18, 1987, otherwise than under a written arrangement to do so entered into before 8:00 p.m. Eastern Daylight Saving Time, June 18, 1987, the share is deemed to have been issued at the particular time and the guarantee agreement is deemed to have been given as part of a series of transactions that included the issuance of the share; and

(*b*) "specified person" has the meaning assigned by paragraph (*h*) of the definition "taxable preferred share" in subsection 248(1).

▶ 112(2.3) ◀

(2.3) Where no deduction permitted. No deduction may be made under subsection (1) or (2) or 138(6) in computing the taxable income of a particular corporation in respect of a dividend received on a share of the capital stock of a corporation where there is, in respect of the share, a dividend rental arrangement of the particular corporation, a partnership of which the particular corporation is directly or indirectly a member or a trust under which the particular corporation is a beneficiary.

Editorial Note: Subsection 112(2.3) denies the deduction for intercorporate dividends in those cases where the dividend is received on a share that is subject to a "dividend rental arrangement" (s. 248(1)). A dividend rental arrangement includes an arrangement where it can reasonably be considered that the main reason for entering into the arrangement was to enable a corporate person or partnership to receive a dividend, and under the arrangement someone other than that dividend-receiving person or partnership bears the risk of loss or enjoys the opportunity for gain or profit with respect to the share in any material respect. This wide definition can potentially apply to many situations (including those involving a non-corporate "person" or partnership; see the s. 82(1)(*c*) provision) where there is short-lived ownership of a share on which dividends are received.

The rules were subsequently broadened such that a dividend rental arrangement now can include a "synthetic equity arrangement" (s. 248(1)). Generally speaking, this is an arrangement involving derivative contracts or similar arrangements under which the taxpayer retains legal title to the underlying shares while effectively transferring the opportunity for profit or risk for loss with respect to the shares to another party. The synthetic equity arrangement provisions generally apply to dividends paid or payable after April 2017, or paid or payable at any particular time after October 2015 for arrangements that were entered into, acquired, extended, or renewed after April 21, 2015, and before the particular time.

History: S. 112(2.3) was replaced by S.C. 2016, c. 7, s. 14(1), applicable to

(*a*) dividends that are paid or become payable after April 2017; and

(*b*) dividends that are paid or become payable at any time after October 2015 and before May 2017 on a share if

(i) there is a synthetic equity arrangement, or one or more agreements or arrangements described by paragraph (*d*) of the definition *dividend rental arrangement* in subsection 248(1) of the Act, as enacted by subsection 48(1) of this Act, in respect of the share at that time, and

(ii) after April 21, 2015 and before that time, all or any part of the synthetic equity arrangement, or the agreements or arrangements, referred to in subparagraph (i) — including an option, swap, futures contract, forward contract or other financial or commodity contract or instrument as well as a right or obligation under the terms of such a contract or instrument — that contributes or could contribute to the effect of providing all or substantially all of the risk of loss and opportunity for gain or profit, in respect of the share, to one or more persons or partnerships is

(A) entered into, acquired, extended or renewed after April 21, 2015, or

(B) in the case of a right to increase the notional amount under an agreement that is or is part of the synthetic equity arrangement, is exercised or acquired after April 21, 2015.

S. 112(2.3) formerly read:

(2.3) *Idem.* No deduction may be made under subsection (1) or (2) or 138(6) in computing the taxable income of a particular corporation in respect of a dividend received on a share of the capital stock of a corporation as part of a dividend rental arrangement of the particular corporation.

Related Sections: 112(2.31) Dividend rental arrangements – exception; S. 248(1), "dividend rental arrangement", "synthetic equity arrangement".

Tax Profile: October 2004 — Taxation of Dividends: A Survey in the Context of Private Corporations and Their Shareholders.

► 112(2.31) ◄

(2.31) Dividend rental arrangements – exception. Subsection (2.3) does not apply to a dividend received on a share where there is, in respect of the share, a dividend rental arrangement of a person or partnership (referred to in this subsection and subsection (2.32) as the *taxpayer*) throughout a particular period during which the synthetic equity arrangement referred to in paragraph (*c*) of the definition *dividend rental arrangement* in subsection 248(1) is in effect if

(*a*) the dividend rental arrangement is a dividend rental arrangement because of that paragraph; and

(*b*) the taxpayer establishes that, throughout the particular period, no tax-indifferent investor or group of tax-indifferent investors, each member of which is affiliated with every other member, has all or substantially all of the risk of loss and opportunity for gain or profit in respect of the share.

Editorial Note: Subsection 112(2.31) provides that an arrangement that is a dividend rental arrangement of a taxpayer because it is a "synthetic equity arrangement" (s. 248(1)) will not be subject to the subsection 112(2.3) denial of the intercorporate dividend deduction if the taxpayer establishes that, throughout the period, no tax-indifferent investor or affiliated group of tax-indifferent investors has all or substantially all of the risk of loss and opportunity for gain or profit in respect of the share. This condition can be satisfied by any of the four methods described in paragraphs 112(2.32)(*a*) through (*d*).

History: S. 112(2.31)(*b*) was replaced by S.C. 2018, c. 27, s. 10(1), applicable in respect of dividends that are paid or become payable after February 26, 2018, and formerly read:

(*b*) the taxpayer establishes that, throughout the particular period, no tax-indifferent investor or group of tax-indifferent investors, each member of which is affiliated with every other member, has all or substantially all of the risk of loss and opportunity for gain or profit in respect of the share because of the synthetic equity arrangement or a specified synthetic equity arrangement.

S. 112(2.31) was added by S.C. 2016, c. 7, s. 14(1), applicable to

(*a*) dividends that are paid or become payable after April 2017; and

(*b*) dividends that are paid or become payable at any time after October 2015 and before May 2017 on a share if

(i) there is a synthetic equity arrangement, or one or more agreements or arrangements described by paragraph (*d*) of the definition *dividend rental arrangement* in subsection 248(1) of the Act, as enacted by subsection 48(1) of this Act, in respect of the share at that time, and

(ii) after April 21, 2015 and before that time, all or any part of the synthetic equity arrangement, or the agreements or arrangements, referred to in subparagraph (i) — including an option, swap, futures contract, forward contract or other financial or commodity contract or instrument as well as a right or obligation under the terms of such a contract or instrument — that contributes or could contribute to the effect of providing all or substantially all of the risk of loss and opportunity for gain or profit, in respect of the share, to one or more persons or partnerships is

(A) entered into, acquired, extended or renewed after April 21, 2015, or

(B) in the case of a right to increase the notional amount under an agreement that is or is part of the synthetic equity arrangement, is exercised or acquired after April 21, 2015.

Related Sections: S. 248(1), "dividend rental arrangement", "synthetic equity arrangement".

► 112(2.32) ◄

(2.32) Representations. A taxpayer is considered to have satisfied the condition described in paragraph (2.31)(*b*) in respect of a share if

(*a*) the taxpayer or the connected person referred to in paragraph (*a*) of the definition *synthetic equity arrangement* in subsection 248(1) (either of which is referred to in this subsection as the *synthetic equity arrangement party*) obtains accurate representations in writing from its counterparty, or from each member of a group comprised of all its counterparties each of which is affiliated with each other (each member of this group of counterparties is referred to in this subsection as an *affiliated counterparty*), with respect to the synthetic equity arrangement, as appropriate, that

(i) it is not a tax-indifferent investor and it does not reasonably expect to become a tax-indifferent investor during the particular period referred to in subsection (2.31), and

(ii) all or substantially all of its risk of loss and opportunity for gain or profit in respect of the share during the particular period referred to in subsection (2.31) has not been eliminated and cannot reasonably be expected by it to be eliminated;

(*b*) the synthetic equity arrangement party obtains accurate representations in writing from its counterparty, or from each affiliated counterparty, with respect to the synthetic equity arrangement that the counterparty, or each affiliated counterparty, as appropriate

(i) is not a tax-indifferent investor and does not reasonably expect to become a tax-indifferent investor during the particular period referred to in subsection (2.31),

(ii) has entered into one or more specified synthetic equity arrangements that have the effect of eliminating all or substantially all of its risk of loss and opportunity for gain or profit, in respect of the share, in one of the following circumstances:

(A) in the case of a counterparty, that counterparty

(I) has entered into a specified synthetic equity arrangement with its own counterparty (a counterparty of a counterparty or of an affiliated counterparty is referred to in this subsection as a *specified counterparty*), or

(II) has entered into a specified synthetic equity arrangement with each member of a group of its own counterparties each member of which is affiliated with each other member (each member of this group of counterparties is referred to in this subsection as an *affiliated specified counterparty*), or

(B) in the case of an affiliated counterparty, each affiliated counterparty

(I) has entered into a specified synthetic equity arrangement with the same specified counterparty, or

(II) has entered into a specified synthetic equity arrangement with an affiliated specified counterparty that is part of the same group of affiliated specified counterparties, and

(iii) has obtained accurate representations in writing from each of its specified counterparties, or from each member of the group of affiliated specified counterparties referred to in subclause (A)(II) or (B)(II), as appropriate, that

(A) it is not a tax-indifferent investor and it does not reasonably expect to become a tax-indifferent investor during the particular period referred to in subsection (2.31), and

(B) all or substantially all of its risk of loss and opportunity for gain or profit in respect of the share during the particular period referred to in subsection (2.31) has not been eliminated and cannot reasonably be expected by it to be eliminated;

(*c*) the synthetic equity arrangement party obtains accurate representations in writing from its counterparty, or from each affiliated counterparty, with respect to the synthetic equity arrangement that the counterparty, or each affiliated counterparty, as appropriate

(i) is not a tax-indifferent investor and does not reasonably expect to become a tax-indifferent investor during the particular period referred to in subsection (2.31),

(ii) has entered into specified synthetic equity arrangements

(A) that have the effect of eliminating all or substantially all of its risk of loss and opportunity for gain or profit in respect of the share,

(B) where no single specified counterparty or group of affiliated specified counterparties has been provided with all or substantially all of the risk of loss and opportunity for gain or profit in respect of the share, and

(C) where each specified counterparty or affiliated specified counterparty deals at arm's length with each other (other than in the case of affiliated specified counterparties, within the same group, of affiliated specified counterparties), and

(iii) has obtained accurate representations in writing from each of its specified counterparties, or from each of its affiliated specified counterparties, that

(A) it is a person resident in Canada and it does not reasonably expect to cease to be resident in Canada during the particular period referred to in subsection (2.31), and

(B) all or substantially all of its risk of loss and opportunity for gain or profit in respect of the share during the particular period referred to in subsection (2.31) has not been eliminated and cannot reasonably be expected by it to be eliminated; or

(*d*) where a person or partnership is a party to a synthetic equity arrangement chain in respect of the share, the person or partnership

(i) has obtained all or substantially all of the risk of loss and opportunity for gain or profit in respect of the share under the synthetic equity arrangement chain,

(ii) has entered into one or more specified synthetic equity arrangements that have the effect of eliminating all or substantially all of its risk of loss and opportunity for gain or profit in respect of the share, and

(iii) obtains accurate representations in writing of the type described in paragraph (*a*), (*b*) or (*c*), as if it were a synthetic equity arrangement party, from each of its counterparties where each such counterparty deals at arm's length with that person or partnership.

History: S. 112(2.32)(*c*)(iii)(B) was replaced by S.C. 2018, c. 27, s. 10(4), applicable in respect of dividends that are paid or become payable after February 26, 2018, and formerly read:

(B) it has not eliminated and it does not reasonably expect to eliminate all or substantially all of its risk of loss and opportunity for gain or profit in respect of the share during the particular period referred to in subsection (2.31); or

S. 112(2.32)(*b*)(iii)(B) was replaced by S.C. 2018, c. 27, s. 10(3), applicable in respect of dividends that are paid or become payable after February 26, 2018, and formerly read:

(B) it has not eliminated and it does not reasonably expect to eliminate all or substantially all of its risk of loss and opportunity for gain or profit in respect of the share during the particular period referred to in subsection (2.31);

S. 112(2.32)(*a*)(ii) was replaced by S.C. 2018, c. 27, s. 10(2), applicable in respect of dividends that are paid or become payable after February 26, 2018, and formerly read:

(ii) it has not eliminated and it does not reasonably expect to eliminate all or substantially all of its risk of loss and opportunity for gain or profit in respect of the share during the particular period referred to in subsection (2.31);

S. 112(2.32) was added by S.C. 2016, c. 7, s. 14(1), applicable to

(*a*) dividends that are paid or become payable after April 2017; and

(*b*) dividends that are paid or become payable at any time after October 2015 and before May 2017 on a share if

(i) there is a synthetic equity arrangement, or one or more agreements or arrangements described by paragraph (*d*) of the definition *dividend rental arrangement* in subsection 248(1) of the Act, as enacted by subsection 48(1) of this Act, in respect of the share at that time, and

(ii) after April 21, 2015 and before that time, all or any part of the synthetic equity arrangement, or the agreements or arrangements, referred to in subparagraph (i) — including an option, swap, futures contract, forward contract or other financial or commodity contract or instrument as well as a right or obligation under the terms of such a contract or instrument — that contributes or could contribute to the effect of providing all or substantially all of the risk of loss and opportunity for gain or profit, in respect of the share, to one or more persons or partnerships is

(A) entered into, acquired, extended or renewed after April 21, 2015, or

(B) in the case of a right to increase the notional amount under an agreement that is or is part of the synthetic equity arrangement, is exercised or acquired after April 21, 2015.

► 112(2.33) ◄

(2.33) End of particular period. If, at a time during a particular period referred to in subsection (2.31), a counterparty, specified counterparty, affiliated counterparty or affiliated specified counterparty reasonably expects to become a tax-indifferent investor or — if it has provided a representation described by subparagraph (2.32)(*a*)(ii) or clause (2.32)(*b*)(iii)(B) or (*c*)(iii)(B) in respect of a share — that all or substantially all of its risk of loss and opportunity for gain or profit in respect of the share will be eliminated, the particular period for which it has provided a representation in respect of the share is deemed to end at that time.

History: S. 112(2.33) was replaced by S.C. 2018, c. 27, s. 10(5), applicable in respect of dividends that are paid or become payable after February 26, 2018, and formerly read:

(2.33) *End of particular period.* If, at a time during a particular period referred to in subsection (2.31), a counterparty, specified counterparty, affiliated counterparty or affiliated specified counterparty reasonably expects to become a tax-indifferent investor or, if it has provided a representation described by subparagraph (2.32)(*a*)(ii) or clause (2.32)(*b*)(iii)(B) or (*c*)(iii)(B) in respect of a share, to eliminate all or substantially all of its risk of loss and opportunity for gain or profit in respect of the share, the particular period for which it has provided a representation in respect of the share is deemed to end at that time.

S. 112(2.33) was added by S.C. 2016, c. 7, s. 14(1), applicable to

(*a*) dividends that are paid or become payable after April 2017; and

(*b*) dividends that are paid or become payable at any time after October 2015 and before May 2017 on a share if

(i) there is a synthetic equity arrangement, or one or more agreements or arrangements described by paragraph (*d*) of the definition *dividend rental arrangement* in subsection 248(1) of the Act, as enacted by subsection 48(1) of this Act, in respect of the share at that time, and

(ii) after April 21, 2015 and before that time, all or any part of the synthetic equity arrangement, or the agreements or arrangements, referred to in subparagraph (i) — including an option, swap, futures contract, forward contract or other financial or commodity contract or instrument as well as a right or obligation under the terms of such a contract or instrument — that contributes or could contribute to the effect of providing all or substantially all of the risk of loss and opportunity for gain or profit, in respect of the share, to one or more persons or partnerships is

(A) entered into, acquired, extended or renewed after April 21, 2015, or

(B) in the case of a right to increase the notional amount under an agreement that is or is part of the synthetic equity arrangement, is exercised or acquired after April 21, 2015.

▶ 112(2.34) ◀

(2.34) Interpretation. For greater certainty, each reference in subsection (2.32) to a "counterparty", a "specified counterparty", an "affiliated counterparty" or an "affiliated specified counterparty" is to be read as referring only to a person or partnership that obtains all or any portion of the risk of loss or opportunity for gain or profit in respect of the share.

History: S. 112(2.34) was added by S.C. 2016, c. 7, s. 14(1), applicable to

(*a*) dividends that are paid or become payable after April 2017; and

(*b*) dividends that are paid or become payable at any time after October 2015 and before May 2017 on a share if

(i) there is a synthetic equity arrangement, or one or more agreements or arrangements described by paragraph (*d*) of the definition *dividend rental arrangement* in subsection 248(1) of the Act, as enacted by subsection 48(1) of this Act, in respect of the share at that time, and

(ii) after April 21, 2015 and before that time, all or any part of the synthetic equity arrangement, or the agreements or arrangements, referred to in subparagraph (i) — including an option, swap, futures contract, forward contract or other financial or commodity contract or instrument as well as a right or obligation under the terms of such a contract or instrument — that contributes or could contribute to the effect of providing all or substantially all of the risk of loss and opportunity for gain or profit, in respect of the share, to one or more persons or partnerships is

(A) entered into, acquired, extended or renewed after April 21, 2015, or

(B) in the case of a right to increase the notional amount under an agreement that is or is part of the synthetic equity arrangement, is exercised or acquired after April 21, 2015.

▶ 112(2.4) ◀

(2.4) Where no deduction permitted. No deduction may be made under subsection (1) or (2) or subsection 138(6) in computing the taxable income of a particular corporation in respect of a dividend received on a share (in this subsection referred to as the "subject share"), other than an exempt share, of the capital stock of another corporation where

(*a*) any person or partnership was obligated, either absolutely or contingently, to effect an undertaking, including any guarantee, covenant or agreement to purchase or repurchase the subject share, under which an investor is entitled, either immediately or in the future, to receive or obtain any amount or benefit for the purpose of reducing the impact, in whole or in part, of any loss that an investor may sustain by virtue of the ownership, holding or disposition of the subject share, and any property is used, in whole or in part, either directly or indirectly in any manner whatever, to secure the undertaking; or

(*b*) the consideration for which the subject share was issued or any other property received, either directly or indirectly, by an issuer from an investor, or any property substituted therefor, is or includes

(i) an obligation of an investor to make payments that are required to be included, in whole or in part, in computing the income of the issuer, other than an obligation of a corporation that, immediately before the subject share was issued, would be related to the corporation that issued the subject share if this Act were read without reference to paragraph 251(5)(*b*), or

(ii) any right to receive payments that are required to be included, in whole or in part, in computing the income of the issuer where that right is held on condition that it or property substituted therefor may revert or pass to an investor or a person or partnership to be determined by an investor,

where that obligation or right was acquired by the issuer as part of a transaction or event or a series of transactions or events that included the issuance or acquisition of the subject share, or a share for which the subject share was substituted.

Editorial Note: This provision, which may deny normal deductions for intercorporate dividends, is directed against arrangements designed to protect share investments in corporations with undeducted balances (e.g., where an investor corporation injects investment income into a "Lossco", and expects to receive tax-free dividends on shares taken back from the Lossco/issuer). It is therefore reminiscent of s. 69(11).

The provision may apply where the investor may be entitled to obtain an amount or benefit from the issuer or a third party for the purpose of reducing the impact of any loss that it may sustain from the shares (including any guarantee, covenant or agreement to purchase the share), and the undertaking is secured (see paragraph (a)). Alternatively, s. 112(2.4) may apply where (as part of the series involving the issuance or acquisition of the share or substituted share) consideration for the share includes either an obligation of an investor to make payments included in the issuer's income, or the right to receive payments included in the issuer's income with reversionary rights relating to the investor (see paragraph (b)).

Per 112(2.5), the denial will apply only where the share was issued in a transaction that enabled any corporation (usually the issuer) to earn "investment income" or "substituted" income, and as a result, the taxes of the corporation were lower than if this were its only income (e.g., it did not have loss balances).

Related Sections: S. 69(11) Deemed proceeds of disposition; 112(2.5) Application of s. (2.4); 112(2.6) Definitions; 112(2.7) Change in agreement or condition; 112(2.8) Loss sustained by investor; 112(2.9) Related corporations; s. 258(5) Deemed interest on certain shares.

Tax Profile: October 2004 — Taxation of Dividends: A Survey in the Context of Private Corporations and Their Shareholders.

▶ 112(2.5) ◀

(2.5) Application of s. (2.4). Subsection (2.4) applies only in respect of a dividend on a share where, having regard to all the circumstances, it may reasonably be considered that the share was issued or acquired as part of a transaction or event or a series of transactions or events that enabled any corporation to earn investment income, or any income substituted therefor, and, as a result, the amount of its taxes payable under this Act for a taxation year is less than the amount that its taxes payable under this Act would be for the year if that investment income were the only income of the corporation for the year and all other taxation years and no amount were deductible under subsections 127(5) and 127.2(1) in computing its taxes payable under this Act.

▶ 112(2.6) ◀

(2.6) Definitions. For the purposes of this subsection and subsection (2.4),

"exempt share"—"exempt share" means

(*a*) a prescribed share,

(*b*) a share of the capital stock of a corporation issued before 5:00 p.m. Eastern Standard Time, November 27, 1986, other than a share held at that time

(i) by the issuer, or

(ii) by any person or partnership where the issuer may become entitled to receive any amount after that time by way of subscription proceeds or contribution of capital with respect to that share pursuant to an agreement made before that time, or

(*c*) a share that was, at the time the dividend referred to in subsection (2.4) was received, a share described in paragraph (*e*) of the definition "term preferred share" in subsection 248(1) during the applicable period referred to in that paragraph;

"investor"—"investor" means the particular corporation referred to in subsection (2.4) and a person with whom that corporation does not deal at arm's length and any partnership or trust of which that corporation, or a person with whom that corporation does not deal at arm's length, is a member or beneficiary, but does not include the other corporation referred to in that subsection;

"issuer"—"issuer" means the other corporation referred to in subsection (2.4) and a person with whom that corporation does not deal at arm's length and any partnership or trust of which that corporation, or a person with whom that corporation does not deal at arm's length, is a member or beneficiary, but does not include the particular corporation referred to in that subsection.

▶ 112(2.7) ◀

(2.7) Change in agreement or condition. For the purposes of the definition "exempt share" in subsection (2.6), where at any time after 5:00 p.m. Eastern Standard Time, November 27, 1986 the terms or conditions of a share of the capital stock of a corporation have been changed or any agreement in respect of the share has been changed or entered into by the corporation, the share shall be deemed to have been issued at that time.

▶ 112(2.8) ◀

(2.8) Loss sustained by investor. For the purposes of paragraph (2.4)(*a*), any loss that an investor may sustain by virtue of the ownership, holding or disposition of the subject share referred to in that paragraph shall be deemed to include any loss with respect to an obligation or share that was issued or acquired as part of a transaction or event or a series of transactions or events that included the issuance or acquisition of the subject share, or a share for which the subject share was substituted.

▶ 112(2.9) ◀

(2.9) Related corporations. For the purposes of subparagraph (2.4)(*b*)(i), where it may reasonably be considered having regard to all the circumstances that a corporation has become related to any other corporation for the purpose of avoiding any limitation on the deduction of a dividend under subsection (1), (2) or 138(6), the corporation shall be deemed not to be related to the other corporation.

▶ 112(3) ◀

(3) Loss on share that is capital property. Subject to subsections (5.5) and (5.6), the amount of any loss of a taxpayer (other than a trust) from the disposition of a share that is capital property of the taxpayer (other than a share that is property of a partnership) is deemed to be the amount of the loss determined without reference to this subsection minus,

(*a*) where the taxpayer is an individual, the lesser of

(i) the total of all amounts each of which is a dividend received by the taxpayer on the share in respect of which an election was made under subsection 83(2) where subsection 83(2.1) does not deem the dividend to be a taxable dividend, and

(ii) the loss determined without reference to this subsection minus all taxable dividends received by the taxpayer on the share; and

(*b*) where the taxpayer is a corporation, the total of all amounts received by the taxpayer on the share each of which is

(i) a taxable dividend, to the extent of the amount of the dividend that was deductible under this section or subsection 115(1) or 138(6) in computing the taxpayer's taxable income or taxable income earned in Canada for any taxation year,

(ii) a dividend in respect of which an election was made under subsection 83(2) where subsection 83(2.1) does not deem the dividend to be a taxable dividend, or

(iii) a life insurance capital dividend.

Editorial Note: S. 112(3) is a stop-loss rule which may deny a portion of a capital loss on the disposition of a share of a corporation by a natural person (i.e., an individual other than a trust, to which separate provisions apply), or by a corporation, as a result of the receipt of tax-advantaged dividends (including by virtue of deemed dividends on a share redemption, which may trigger the loss itself).

In the case of a natural person, the loss is reduced by the total amount of capital dividends received on the share (more precisely, a dividend on which a capital dividend election has been made including excessive elections, but not including a separate taxable dividend per a s. 184(3) election or a would-be capital dividend subject to the capital dividend anti-avoidance rules in s. 83(2.1)). However, the amount subject to the stop-loss is reduced if the loss otherwise determined, less taxable dividends received on the share, is less than this amount; in other words, taxable dividends can enlarge the loss that can be claimed (s. 112(3)(*a*)).

In the case of a corporation, the capital loss on a disposition of a share in another corporation is reduced by: (i) tax-free intercorporate dividends (e.g., dividends deductible under s. 112, but not under s. 113); (ii) capital dividends (as described above); and (iii) life insurance capital dividends received on the share (s. 112(3)(*b*)).

Dividends which would otherwise enlarge the disallowed loss are ignored in computing the amount of the denied losses, per a "5/365 exception" (per s. 112(3.01)), which applies if the dividend was received when the shareholder and non-arm's length persons did not own more than 5% of the shares of any class (or series) in the corporation, and the shares were owned throughout the 365-day period before the disposition (s. 112(3.01)). This means that the stop-loss rules will not apply if a taxpayer and non-arm's length persons did not hold more than 5% of the class (or series) of shares, if held for the 365-day period. For dispositions after March 21, 2011, such dividends must be "qualified dividends" as defined in s. 112(6.1). The net effect of these changes is that any deemed dividend under s. 84(3) received on the redemption of shares held by a corporation do not qualify for the exception, unless the corporation is a private corporation and the payer corporation is also a private corporation.

S. 112(7) preserves the continuity of the stop-loss rules through specified reorganizations; s. 112(6) contains some definitions relevant to s. 112.

Fairly similar stop-loss rules apply to shares held by partnerships (s. 112(3.1)), trusts (ss. 112(3.2)–(3.32)), shares that are not capital property (ss. 112(4)–(4.22)) and shares held by financial institutions (ss. 112(5)–(5.6)). Where a shareholder and the corporation redeeming its shares are affiliated immediately afterward, s. 40(3.6) potentially applies as well; while the denied loss per this provision is added to the cost base of the shareholder per s. 53(1)(*f.2*), this is calculated after the effect of s. 112(3).

Related Sections: S. 40(1) General rules; s. 40(3.6) Loss on shares; s. 40(3.7) Losses of non-resident; s. 53(1)(*f*) Adjustments to cost base — Substituted property; s. 53(1)(*f.2*) Adjustments to cost base — Denied loss on transfer of shares to corporation; s. 54, "capital property"; s. 83(2) Capital dividend; s. 83(2.1) Capital dividend — anti-avoidance rule; s. 87(2)(*x*) Taxable dividends; s. 89(1), "capital dividend account"; s. 112(3.01) Loss on share that is capital property — excluded dividends; s. 112(3.1) Loss on share held by partnership; s. 112(3.2) Loss on share held by trust; s. 112(3.3) Loss on share held by trust — special cases; s. 112(3.31) Loss on share held by trust — excluded dividends; s. 112(3.32) Loss on share held by trust — excluded dividends; s. 112(4) Loss on share that is not capital property; s. 112(4.01) Loss on share that is not capital property — excluded dividends; s. 112(4.1) Fair market value of shares held as inventory; s. 112(4.11) Fair market value of shares held as inventory — excluded dividends; s. 112(4.2) Loss on share held by trust; s. 112(4.21) Loss on share held by trust — excluded dividends; s. 112(4.22) Loss on share held by trust — excluded dividends; s. 112(5) Disposition of share by financial institution; s. 112(5.1) Share held for less than one year; s. 112(5.2) Adjustment re dividends; s. 112(5.21) Subsection (5.2) — excluded dividends; s. 112(5.3) Adjustment not applicable; s. 112(5.4) Deemed dispositions; s. 112(5.5) Stop-loss rules not applicable; s. 112(5.6) Stop-loss rules restricted; s. 112(6) Meaning of certain expressions; s. 112(7) Rules where shares exchanged; s. 115(1) Non-resident's taxable income in Canada; s. 138(6) Deduction for dividends from taxable corporations; s. 248(6) "Class" of shares issued in series; s. 251 Arm's length.

Canadian Tax Foundation: Suarez, *The Capital Property Dividend Stop-Loss Rules*, 2005 Canadian Tax Journal 1:269–291; Squire and Halil, *Shareholder Agreements — Selected Tax Issues*, 2005 Prairie Provinces Tax Conference 7:1–28; Kakkar, *Section 112 Stop-Loss Rules Prevail*, 2005 Tax for the Owner-Manager 5(3):3–4; Carson and Watson, *Affiliated Person Rules: A Review of Recent Technical Amendments and Practical Issues Relating to Stop-Loss Rules*, 2004 British Columbia Tax Conference 13:2–41; De Angelis, *Stop-Loss Rules: Pitfalls and Opportunities*, 2003 Conference Report 50:1–16; Barnett et al., *Post Mortem Planning for Private Company Shares — The New Regime: Alternatives for Minimizing the Tax Exposure Arising on the Death of the Owner of Private Company Shares*, 2002 British Columbia Tax Conference 19:1–91; Barnett et al., *Post Mortem Planning for Private Company Shares: The New Regime*, 2002 Conference Report 32:1–86; Creasy, *The Stop-Loss Rules: 1*, 2002 Tax for the Owner-Manager 2(4):25–26; Sibson, *Private Companies: The Most Significant Tax Issue of the Last 12 Months*, 2001 Conference Report 5:1–8; Cuperfain, *Got Me Those "Low Capital Gain, High Dividend Tax, Stop-loss Rules, Estate Planning" Blues*, 2001 Canadian Tax Journal 3:764–794; Burpee, *The New Stop-Loss Rules: Grandfathered Shares*, 1998 Canadian Tax Journal 3:678–695; Everett and Ireland, *Impact of the Proposed New Stop-Loss Rules*, 1997 Conference Report 17:1–26.

Tax Profile: October 2004 — Taxation of Dividends: A Survey in the Context of Private Corporations and Their Shareholders; May 2004 — The Stop-Loss Rules.

Interpretation Bulletins: *Primary* — IT-328R3 Losses on shares from which dividends have been received.

► 112(3.01) ◄

(3.01) Loss on share that is capital property — excluded dividends. A qualified dividend shall not be included in the total determined under subparagraph (3)(*a*)(i) or paragraph (3)(*b*) if the taxpayer establishes that

(*a*) it was received when the taxpayer and persons with whom the taxpayer was not dealing at arm's length did not own in total more than 5% of the issued shares of any class of the capital stock of the corporation from which the dividend was received; and

(*b*) it was received on a share that the taxpayer owned throughout the 365-day period that ended immediately before the disposition.

Editorial Note: See the editorial note to s. 112(3).

History: S. 112(3.01), the portion before paragraph (*a*) was replaced by S.C. 2011, c. 24, s. 22(1), applicable to dispositions occurring on or after March 22, 2011. S. 112(3.01), the portion before paragraph (*a*) formerly read:

(3.01) *Loss on share that is capital property — excluded dividends.* A dividend shall not be included in the total determined under subparagraph (3)(*a*)(i) or paragraph (3)(*b*) where the taxpayer establishes that

Related Sections: S. 112(3.11) Loss on share held by partnership — excluded dividends; s. 112(3.31) Loss on share held by trust — excluded dividends; s. 112(3.32) Loss on share held by trust — excluded dividends; s. 112(4.01) Loss on share that is not capital property — excluded dividends; s. 112(4.11) Fair market value of shares held as inventory — excluded dividends; s. 112(4.21) Loss on share held by trust — excluded dividends; s. 112(4.22) Loss on share held by trust — excluded dividends; s. 112(5.21) Subsection (5.2) — excluded dividends; s. 251 Arm's length.

► 112(3.1) ◄

(3.1) Loss on share held by partnership. Subject to subsections (5.5) and (5.6), where a taxpayer (other than a partnership or a mutual fund trust) is a member of a partnership, the taxpayer's share of any loss of the partnership from the disposition of a share that is held by a particular partnership as capital property is deemed to be that share of the loss determined without reference to this subsection minus,

(*a*) where the taxpayer is an individual, the lesser of

(i) the total of all amounts each of which is a dividend received by the taxpayer on the share in respect of which an election was made under subsection 83(2) where subsection 83(2.1) does not deem the dividend to be a taxable dividend, and

(ii) that share of the loss determined without reference to this subsection minus all taxable dividends received by the taxpayer on the share;

(*b*) where the taxpayer is a corporation, the total of all amounts received by the taxpayer on the share each of which is

(i) a taxable dividend, to the extent of the amount of the dividend that was deductible under this section or subsection 115(1) or 138(6) in computing the taxpayer's taxable income or taxable income earned in Canada for any taxation year,

(ii) a dividend in respect of which an election was made under subsection 83(2) where subsection 83(2.1) does not deem the dividend to be a taxable dividend, or

(iii) a life insurance capital dividend; and

(*c*) where the taxpayer is a trust, the total of all amounts each of which is

(i) a taxable dividend, or

(ii) a life insurance capital dividend

received on the share and designated under subsection 104(19) or (20) by the trust in respect of a beneficiary that was a corporation, partnership or trust.

Editorial Note: This provision may deny a portion of a capital loss from the disposition of a share held by a partnership in respect of taxpayers (other than partnerships and mutual fund trusts) who are partners. The determination of the amount of the denied loss is made at the partner level, including through multiple-tier partnerships. The loss is based on the partner's share of the loss, less the following amounts:

- In the case of an individual, including a trust, the total amount of capital dividends received on the share (more precisely, a dividend on which a capital dividend election has been made, including excessive elections, but not including a separate taxable dividend per a s. 184(3) election or a would-be capital dividend subject to the capital dividend anti-avoidance rules in s. 83(2.1)). However, the amount subject to the stop-loss is reduced if the individual's share of the loss otherwise determined, less taxable dividends received on the share, is less than this amount; in other words, taxable dividends can enlarge the loss that can be claimed (s. 112(3.1)(*a*)).
- In the case of a corporation: (i) tax-free intercorporate dividends (e.g., dividends deductible under s. 112, but not under s. 113); (ii) capital dividends (as described above); and (iii) life insurance capital dividends received on the share (s. 112(3.1)(*b*)).
- Where the partner is a trust, the loss will be further reduced by the total amounts of taxable or life insurance capital dividends designated by the trust to flow through to a beneficiary that is a corporation, partnership or trust (s. 112(3)(*c*)). (There is an exception in the last two cases where the dividend is established to be ultimately received by a natural person (see s. 112(3.12)).

As is the case with s. 112(3), dividends which would otherwise enlarge the disallowed loss are ignored under a "5/365 exception": very basically, if holdings of a class (or series) of shares do not exceed 5% at the time received, and the shares were held throughout the 365-day period before the disposition — see s. 112(3.11). For dispositions after March 21, 2011, any dividend deemed under s. 84(3) received on the redemption of shares held by a partnership and allocated to a corporate partner does not qualify for this exception, unless the corporate partner is a private corporation and the payer corporation is also a private corporation (see the definition of "qualified dividend" in s. 112(6.1)).

S. 53(2)(*c*)(i)(C) reduces the ACB of a partnership interest to include the disallowed loss per s. 112(3.1). S. 100(4) is a complimentary provision which reduces the loss from the disposition of a partnership interest by the amount by which the partner's share of the partnership's loss in respect of a share held by the partnership would have been reduced under s. 112(3.1) (on the assumption that the partnership's year had ended immediately before the time of disposition and the partnership had disposed of the shares immediately before the end of the fiscal period).

Related Sections: S. 40(1) General rules; s. 53(2)(*c*)(i)(C) Amounts to be deducted — Interest in a partnership; s. 100(4) Loss re interest in partnership; s. 104(20) Designation in respect of non-taxable dividends; s. 112(3) Loss on share that is capital property; s. 112(3.11) Loss on share held by partnership — excluded dividends; s. 112(3.12) Loss on share held by partnership — excluded dividends; s. 112(4) Loss on share that is not capital property; s. 112(6) Meaning of certain expressions; s. 112(7) Rules where shares exchanged; s. 251 Arm's length.

Canadian Tax Foundation: Suarez, *The Capital Property Dividend Stop-Loss Rules*, 2005 Canadian Tax Journal 1:269–291.

Interpretation Bulletins: *Primary* — IT-328R3 Losses on shares from which dividends have been received.

► 112(3.11) ◄

(3.11) Loss on share held by partnership — excluded dividends. A qualified dividend shall not be included in the total determined under subparagraph (3.1)(*a*)(i) or paragraph (3.1)(*b*) or (*c*) if the taxpayer establishes that

(*a*) it was received when the particular partnership, the taxpayer and persons with whom the taxpayer was not dealing at arm's length did not hold in total more than 5% of the issued shares of any class of the capital stock of the corporation from which the dividend was received; and

(*b*) it was received on a share that the particular partnership held throughout the 365-day period that ended immediately before the disposition.

History: S. 112(3.11), the portion before paragraph (*a*) was replaced by S.C. 2011, c. 24, s. 22(2), applicable to dispositions occurring on or after March 22, 2011. S. 112(3.11), the portion before paragraph (*a*) formerly read:

(3.11) *Loss on share held by partnership — excluded dividends.* A dividend shall not be included in the total determined under subparagraph (3.1)(*a*)(i) or paragraph (3.1)(*b*) or (*c*) where the taxpayer establishes that

► 112(3.12) ◄

(3.12) Loss on share held by partnership — excluded dividends. A taxable dividend received on a share and designated under subsection 104(19) by a particular trust in respect of a beneficiary that was a partnership or trust shall not be included in the total determined under paragraph (3.1)(*c*) where the particular trust establishes that the dividend was received by an individual (other than a trust).

► 112(3.2) ◄

(3.2) Loss on share held by trust. Subject to subsections (5.5) and (5.6), the amount of any loss of a trust (other than a mutual fund trust) from the disposition of a share of the capital stock of a corporation that is capital property of the trust is deemed to be the amount of the loss determined without reference to this subsection minus the total of

(*a*) the amount, if any, by which the lesser of

(i) the total of all amounts each of which is a dividend received by the trust on the share in respect of which an election was made under subsection 83(2) where subsection 83(2.1) does not deem the dividend to be a taxable dividend, and

(ii) the loss determined without reference to this subsection minus the total of all amounts each of which is the amount of a taxable dividend

(A) received by the trust on the share,

(B) received on the share and designated under subsection 104(19) by the trust in respect of a beneficiary who is an individual (other than a trust), or

(C) that is a qualified dividend received on the share and designated under subsection 104(19) by the trust in respect of a beneficiary that was a corporation, partnership or another trust where the trust establishes that

(I) it owned the share throughout the 365-day period that ended immediately before the disposition, and

(II) the dividend was received while the trust, the beneficiary and persons not dealing at arm's length with the beneficiary owned in total less than 5% of the issued shares of any class of the capital stock of the corporation from which the dividend was received

exceeds

(iii) if the trust is an individual's graduated rate estate, the share was acquired as a consequence of the individual's death and the disposition occurs during the trust's first taxation year, 1/2 of the lesser of

(A) the loss determined without reference to this subsection, and

(B) the individual's capital gain from the disposition of the share immediately before the individual's death, and

(*b*) the total of all amounts each of which is

(i) a taxable dividend, or

(ii) a life insurance capital dividend

received on the share and designated under subsection 104(19) or (20) by the trust in respect of a beneficiary that was a corporation, partnership or trust.

Editorial Note: Subsection 112(3.2) is a stop-loss rule, which may deny a portion of a capital loss on the disposition of a share in a corporation by a trust as a result of the receipt of tax-advantaged dividends (including by virtue of deemed dividends on a redemption of the share which may trigger the loss itself). The loss is reduced to the extent of dividends the trust received on which a capital dividend election has been made (s. 112(3.2)(*a*)(i) — see also editorial note to s. 112(3)). A lesser reduction will apply if the loss otherwise determined, less qualifying taxable dividends received by the trust (see below), is less than this amount; in other words, qualifying taxable dividends may increase the loss that can be claimed (s. 112(3.2)(*a*)(ii)). However, the amount of the loss will be reduced further by the total amounts of taxable dividends or life insurance capital dividends designated by the trust in respect of a beneficiary that is a corporation, partnership or trust — see s. 112(3.2)(*b*) (certain exceptions apply — see s. 112(3.32)). As is the case for s. 112(3), dividends which would otherwise reduce the loss are ignored under a "5/365 exception": very basically, the exception applies if holdings do not exceed 5% of a class (or series) of shares at the time of the dividend, and the shares were held throughout the 365-day period before the disposition (s. 112(3.31)). S. 107(1)(*c*) and (*d*) provide somewhat similar stop-loss rules in respect of dispositions of capital interests in trusts at a loss. (The "qualifying taxable dividends" referred to above are those: received and taxed in the trust; designated to a beneficiary who is a natural person; or that are qualified dividends designated to a beneficiary that is a corporation, partnership or trust and a "5/365 exception" is met (s. 112(3.2)(*a*)(ii)(C).)

In the case of an individual's estate, if the share is acquired as a consequence of the individual's death and the disposition occurs during the estate's first taxation year, the amount of the disallowed loss determined under s. 112(3.2)(*a*) will be reduced, based on one-half of the lesser of the loss otherwise determined, or the terminal-period gain (s. 112(3.2)(*a*)(iii)). This usually means that the full amount of the loss may be applied against the terminal period gain as long as the amount of the capital dividend received by the estate does not exceed these limits. Beginning in 2016, this one-half loss reduction applies only if the estate is the individual's graduated rate estate – the main significance of this rule change is that an individual may have only one graduated rate estate.

Where a shareholder and the corporation redeeming its shares are affiliated immediately afterward, s. 40(3.6) potentially applies as well. However, in the case of an estate which triggers a loss to be applied to a terminal period return under s. 164(6), s. 40(3.61) may override s. 40(3.6), to the extent of the loss so applied.

History: S. 112(3.2)(*a*)(iii), the portion before clause (A) was replaced by S.C. 2014, c. 39, s. 31(1), applicable to the 2016 and subsequent taxation years, and formerly read:

> (iii) where the trust is an individual's estate, the share was acquired as a consequence of the individual's death and the disposition occurs during the trust's first taxation year, 1/2 of the lesser of

S. 112(3.2)(*a*)(ii)(C), the portion before subclause (I) was replaced by S.C. 2011, c. 24, s. 22(3), applicable to dispositions occurring on or after March 22, 2011. S. 112(3.2)(*a*)(ii)(C), the portion before subclause (I) formerly read:

> (C) received on the share and designated under subsection 104(19) by the trust in respect of a beneficiary that was a corporation, partnership or another trust where the trust establishes that

Related Sections: S. 40(1) General rules; s. 40(3.6) Loss on shares; s. 40(3.61) Exception — estate loss carried back; S. 40(3.7) Losses of non-resident; s. 53(1)(*f*) Adjustments to cost base — Substituted property; s. 53(1)(*f.2*) Adjustments to cost base — Denied loss on transfer of shares to corporation; s. 70(5) Capital property of a deceased taxpayer; s. 83(2) Capital dividend; s. 83(2.1) Capital dividend — anti-avoidance rule; s. 87(2)(*x*) Taxable dividends; 107(1)(c); 107(1)(d); s. 107.4(3)(*b*)(ii) Tax consequences of qualifying dispositions; s. 112(3.3) Loss on share held by trust — special cases; s. 112(3.31) Loss on share held by trust — excluded dividends; s. 112(3.32) Loss on share held by trust — excluded dividends; s. 112(4) Loss on share that is not capital property; s. 112(4.01) Loss on share that is not capital property — excluded dividends; s. 112(4.1) Fair market value of shares held as inventory; s. 112(4.11) Fair market value of shares held as inventory — excluded dividends; s. 112(4.2) Loss on share held by trust; s. 112(4.21) Loss on share held by trust — excluded dividends; 112(4.22) Loss on share held by trust — excluded dividends; 112(4.5); s. 112(5.1) Share held for less than one year; s. 112(5.2) Adjustment re dividends; s. 112(5.21) Subsection (5.2) — excluded dividends; s. 112(5.3) Adjustment not applicable; s. 112(5.4) Deemed dispositions; s. 112(5.5) Stop-loss rules not applicable; s. 112(5.6) Stop-loss rules restricted; s. 112(6) Meaning of certain expressions; s. 112(7) Rules where shares exchanged; s. 164(6) Where disposition of property by legal representative of deceased taxpayer; s. 248(1) "graduated rate estate"; s. 251 Arm's length.

Canadian Tax Foundation: Suarez, *The Capital Property Dividend Stop-Loss Rules*, 2005 Canadian Tax Journal 1:269–291; Sibson, *Private Companies: The Most Significant Tax Issue of the Last 12 Months*, 2001 Conference Report 5:1–8; Cuperfain, *Got Me Those "Low Capital Gain, High Dividend Tax, Stop-loss Rules, Estate Planning" Blues*, 2001 Canadian Tax Journal 3:764–794.

Tax Profile: February 2012 — Post-Mortem Planning — Double Taxation on Death; January 2010 — Shareholders' Agreements — A Survey of Income Tax Issues; September 2004 — Review of Tax Implications of Corporate-Owned Life Insurance Buy-Sell Arrangements.

Tax Topics: No. 1690, Estate Planning In The 21st Century; No. 1682, Life Insurance: Exploring the Corporate Edge — Part II; No. 1681, Life Insurance: Exploring the Corporate Edge — Part I; No. 1582, Estate Planning in the 21st Century.

Interpretation Bulletins: *Primary* — IT-328R3 Losses on shares from which dividends have been received.

Tax Window Files: Trust audit issues, *June 16, 2014*, CRA Document No. 2014-0523061C6.

▶ 112(3.3) ◀

(3.3) Loss on share held by trust — special cases. Notwithstanding subsection (3.2), where a trust has at any time acquired a share of the capital stock of a corporation because of subsection 104(4), the amount of any loss of the trust from a disposition after that time is deemed to be the amount of the loss determined without reference to subsection (3.2) and this subsection minus the total of

(*a*) the amount, if any, by which the lesser of

(i) the total of all amounts each of which is a dividend received after that time by the trust on the share in respect of which an election was made under subsection 83(2) where subsection 83(2.1) does not deem the dividend to be a taxable dividend, and

(ii) the loss determined without reference to subsection (3.2) and this subsection minus the total of all amounts each of which is the amount of a taxable dividend

(A) received by the trust on the share after that time,

(B) received on the share after that time and designated under subsection 104(19) by the trust in respect of a beneficiary who is an individual (other than a trust), or

(C) that is a qualified dividend received on the share after that time and designated under subsection 104(19) by the trust in respect of a beneficiary that was a corporation, partnership or another trust where the trust establishes that

(I) it owned the share throughout the 365-day period that ended immediately before the disposition, and

(II) the dividend was received when the trust, the beneficiary and persons not dealing at arm's length with the beneficiary owned in total less than 5% of the issued shares of any class of the capital stock of the corporation from which the dividend was received

exceeds

(iii) 1/2 of the lesser of

(A) the loss from the disposition, determined without reference to subsection (3.2) and this subsection, and

(B) the trust's capital gain from the disposition immediately before that time of the share because of subsection 104(4), and

(*b*) the total of all amounts each of which is a taxable dividend received on the share after that time and designated under subsection 104(19) by the trust in respect of a beneficiary that was a corporation, partnership or trust.

Editorial Note: S. 112(3.3) is a variation of the stop-loss rule in s. 112(3.2) applying to a trust (including an estate), which applies where there has previously been a deemed disposition/acquisition by the trust under s. 104(4), generally on the death of a spouse who was the beneficiary under a spouse trust or by virtue of the 21st anniversary of a trust. The provision is similar to s. 112(3.2), a notable exception being that dividends are relevant in the determination of the denied losses only after the time of the deemed acquisition.

Like s. 112(3.2), the provision also contains a "50% safe-harbour" rule which is based on one-half of the lesser of the loss otherwise determined and the capital gain pursuant to s. 104(4). Subject to the foregoing, the post-deemed-disposition capital loss from a redemption or other disposition by the trust can be applied (including within the normal three-year carry-back period) to the trust's year in which the deemed disposition occurs. However, in order to obtain the loss, the shares in question must remain in the trust or estate, rather than being distributed to beneficiaries.

Where a shareholder and the corporation redeeming its shares are affiliated immediately afterward, s. 40(3.6) potentially applies as well; while the denied loss per this provision is added to the cost base of the shareholder per s. 53(1)(*f.2*), it appears that this is calculated after the effect of s. 112(3.3). (Where there is a deemed disposition by virtue of s. 104(4), s. 40(3.61) does not override s. 40(3.6).)

History: S. 112(3.3)(*a*)(ii)(C), the portion before subclause (I) was replaced by S.C. 2011, c. 24, s. 22(4), applicable to dispositions occurring on or after March 22, 2011. S. 112(3.3)(*a*)(ii)(C), the portion before subclause (I) formerly read:

> (C) received on the share after that time and designated under subsection 104(19) by the trust in respect of a beneficiary that was a corporation, partnership or another trust where the trust establishes that

Related Sections: S. 40(1) General rules; s. 40(3.6) Loss on shares; s. 40(3.61) Exception — estate loss carried back; s. 40(3.7) Losses of non-resident; s. 53(1)(*f*) Adjustments to cost base — Substituted property; s. 53(1)(*f.2*) Adjustments to cost base — Denied loss on transfer of shares to corporation; s. 70(6) Where transfer or distribution to spouse or spouse trust;

s. 73(1.01)(*c*) Qualifying transfers; s. 83(2) Capital dividend; s. 83(2.1) Capital dividend — anti-avoidance rule; s. 87(2)(*x*) Taxable dividends; s. 104(4) Deemed disposition by trust; s. 107.4(3)(*b*)(ii) Tax consequences of qualifying dispositions; s. 112(3.2) Loss on share held by trust; s. 112(3.31) Loss on share held by trust — excluded dividends; s. 112(3.32) Loss on share held by trust — excluded dividends; s. 112(4) Loss on share that is not capital property; s. 112(4.01) Loss on share that is not capital property — excluded dividends; s. 112(4.1) Fair market value of shares held as inventory; s. 112(4.11) Fair market value of shares held as inventory — excluded dividends; s. 112(4.2) Loss on share held by trust; s. 112(4.21) Loss on share held by trust — excluded dividends; s. 112(4.22) Loss on share held by trust — excluded dividends; s. 112(5) Disposition of share by financial institution; s. 112(5.1) Share held for less than one year; s. 112(5.2) Adjustment re dividends; s. 112(5.21) Subsection (5.2) — excluded dividends; s. 112(5.3) Adjustment not applicable; s. 112(5.4) Deemed dispositions; s. 112(5.5) Stop-loss rules not applicable; s. 112(5.6) Stop-loss rules restricted; s. 112(6) Meaning of certain expressions; s. 112(7) Rules where shares exchanged; s. 251 Arm's length.

Tax Topics: No. 1690, Estate Planning In The 21st Century.

▶ 112(3.31) ◀

(3.31) Loss on share held by trust — excluded dividends. A qualified dividend received by a trust shall not be included under subparagraph (3.2)(*a*)(i) or (*b*)(ii) or (3.3)(*a*)(i) if the trust establishes that the dividend

(*a*) was received,

(i) in any case where the dividend was designated under subsection 104(19) or (20) by the trust, when the trust, the beneficiary and persons with whom the beneficiary was not dealing at arm's length did not own in total more than 5% of the issued shares of any class of the capital stock of the corporation from which the dividend was received, or

(ii) in any other case, when the trust and persons with whom the trust was not dealing at arm's length did not own in total more than 5% of the issued shares of any class of the capital stock of the corporation from which the dividend was received, and

(*b*) was received on a share that the trust owned throughout the 365-day period that ended immediately before the disposition.

Editorial Note: S. (3.32) is a stop-loss rule which may deny a portion of a capital loss on the disposition of a share in a corporation by a trust as a result of the receipt of tax-advantaged dividends (including by virtue of deemed dividends on a redemption of the share which may trigger the loss itself). The loss is reduced to the extent of dividends received by the trust on which a capital dividend election has been made (s. 112(3.2)(*a*)(i) — see also editorial note to s. 112(3)). A lesser reduction will apply if the loss otherwise determined, less qualifying taxable dividends received by the trust (see below), is less than this amount; in other words, qualifying taxable dividends may increase the loss that can be claimed (s. 112(3.2)(*a*)(ii)). However, the amount of the loss will be reduced further by the total amounts of taxable or life insurance capital dividends designated by the trust in respect of a beneficiary that is a corporation, partnership or trust — see s. 112(3.2)(*b*) (certain exceptions apply — see s. 112(3.32)). As is the case for s. 112(3), dividends which would otherwise reduce the loss are ignored under a "5/365 exception": very basically, the exception applies if holdings do not exceed 5% of a class (or series) of shares at the time of the dividend, and the shares were held throughout the 365 day period before the disposition (s. 112(3.31)). S. 107(1)(*c*) and (*d*) provide somewhat similar stop-loss rules in respect of dispositions of capital interests in trusts at a loss. (The "qualifying taxable dividends" referred to above are those: received and taxed in the trust; designated to a beneficiary who is a natural person; or that are qualified dividends designated to a beneficiary that is a corporation, partnership or trust and a "5/365 exception" is met (s. 112(3.2)(*a*)(ii)(C)).)

In the case of an individual's estate, if the share is acquired as a consequence of the individual's death and the disposition occurs during the estate's first taxation year, the amount of the disallowed loss determined under s. 112(3.2)(*a*) will be reduced, based on one-half of the lesser of the loss otherwise determined, or the terminal-period gain (s. 112(3.2)(*a*)(iii)). This usually means that the full amount of the loss may be applied against the terminal period gain as long as the amount of the capital dividend received by the estate does not exceed these limits. Beginning in 2016, this one-half loss reduction applies only if the estate is the individual's graduated rate estate – the main significance of this rule change is that an individual may have only one graduated rate estate.

Where a shareholder and the corporation redeeming its shares are affiliated immediately afterward, s. 40(3.6) potentially applies as well. However, in the case of an estate which triggers a loss to be applied to a terminal period return under s. 164(6), s. 40(3.61) may override s. 40(3.6), to the extent of the loss so applied.

History: S. 112(3.31), the portion before paragraph (*a*) was replaced by S.C. 2011, c. 24, s. 22(5), applicable to dispositions occurring on or after March 22, 2011. S. 112(3.31), the portion before paragraph (*a*) formerly read:

(3.31) *Loss on share held by trust — excluded dividends.* No dividend received by a trust shall be included under subparagraph (3.2)(*a*)(i) or (*b*)(ii) or (3.3)(*a*)(i) where the trust establishes that the dividend

Related Sections: S. 112(3.01) Loss on share that is capital property — excluded dividends; s. 112(3.11) Loss on share held by partnership — excluded dividends; s. 112(3.32) Loss on share held by trust — excluded dividends; s. 112(4.01) Loss on share that is not capital property — excluded dividends; s. 112(4.11) Fair market value of shares held as inventory — excluded dividends; s. 112(4.21) Loss on share held by trust — excluded dividends; s. 112(4.22) Loss on share held by trust — excluded dividends; s. 112(5.21) Subsection (5.2) — excluded dividends; s. 251 Arm's length.

▶ 112(3.32) ◀

(3.32) Loss on share held by trust — excluded dividends. A qualified dividend that is a taxable dividend received on the share and that is designated under subsection 104(19) by the trust in respect of a beneficiary that was a corporation, partnership or trust, shall not be included under paragraph (3.2)(*b*) or (3.3)(*b*) if the trust establishes that the dividend was received by an individual (other than a trust), or

(*a*) was received when the trust, the beneficiary and persons with whom the beneficiary was not dealing at arm's length did not own in total more than 5% of the issued shares of any class of the capital stock of the corporation from which the dividend was received; and

(*b*) was received on a share that the trust owned throughout the 365-day period that ended immediately before the disposition.

Editorial Note: See the editorial note to s. 112(3.31).

History: S. 112(3.32), the portion before paragraph (*a*) was replaced by S.C. 2011, c. 24, s. 22(6), applicable to dispositions occurring on or after March 22, 2011. S. 112(3.32), the portion before paragraph (*a*) formerly read:

(3.32) *Loss on share held by trust — excluded dividends.* No taxable dividend received on the share and designated under subsection 104(19) by the trust in respect of a beneficiary that was a corporation, partnership or trust shall be included under paragraph (3.2)(*b*) or (3.3)(*b*) where the trust establishes that the dividend was received by an individual (other than a trust), or

Related Sections: S. 112(3.01) Loss on share that is capital property — excluded dividends; s. 112(3.11) Loss on share held by partnership — excluded dividends; s. 112(3.31) Loss on share held by trust — excluded dividends; s. 112(4.01) Loss on share that is not capital property — excluded dividends; s. 112(4.11) Fair market value of shares held as inventory — excluded dividends; s. 112(4.21) Loss on share held by trust — excluded dividends; s. 112(4.22) Loss on share held by trust — excluded dividends; s. 112(5.21) Subsection (5.2) — excluded dividends; s. 251 Arm's length.

▶ 112(4) ◀

(4) Loss on share that is not capital property. Subject to subsections (5.5) and (5.6), the amount of any loss of a taxpayer (other than a trust) from the disposition of a share of the capital stock of a corporation that is property (other than capital property) of the taxpayer is deemed to be the amount of the loss determined without reference to this subsection minus,

(*a*) where the taxpayer is an individual and the corporation is resident in Canada, the total of all dividends received by the individual on the share;

(*b*) where the taxpayer is a partnership, the total of all dividends received by the partnership on the share; and

(*c*) where the taxpayer is a corporation, the total of all amounts received by the taxpayer on the share each of which is

(i) a taxable dividend, to the extent of the amount of the dividend that was deductible under this section, section 113 or subsection 115(1) or 138(6) in computing the taxpayer's taxable income or taxable income earned in Canada for any taxation year, or

(ii) a dividend (other than a taxable dividend).

Editorial Note: S. 112(4) is a stop-loss rule which applies to a share that is not capital property, if held by a taxpayer other than a trust. For an individual, the loss will be reduced by all dividends received, taxable or otherwise, from the corporation, if resident in Canada. For a partnership, the loss is reduced by all dividends received, taxable or otherwise. (Note that the loss restriction is made at the partnership level; this differs from the stop-loss rule applying to shares which are capital property — see s. 112(3.1).) For a corporation, the loss is reduced by dividends which are deductible in computing taxable income (e.g., under s. 112 or 113) as well as non-taxable dividends. A "5/365 exception" for dividends applies by virtue of s. 112(4.01). However, for non-capital property, the 365-day hold requirement may often not be met. Furthermore, for dispositions after March 21, 2011, such dividends must be "qualified dividends" as defined in s. 112(6.1). The net effect of these changes is that any dividend deemed under s. 84(3) received on the redemption of shares held by a corporation (whether the shares are held directly or indirectly through a partnership or trust) do not qualify for the exception, unless the corporation is a private corporation and the payer corporation is also a private corporation.

For rules applicable to trusts that hold shares that are not capital property, see s. 112(4.2)–(4.22). To prevent the avoidance of these rules through the application of the lower of cost and market rule, s. 112(4.1) and (4.11) impose rules similar to the foregoing applicable to shares held as inventory, i.e., for the purpose of s. 10, which adds the amount of dividends specified in s. 112(4.1) to the value of shares held as closing inventory, so as to eliminate the recognition of accrued losses to the extent attributable to such dividends.

Related Sections: 53(2) Amounts to be deducted; S. 54, "capital property"; s. 87(2)(*x*) Taxable dividends; s. 107(1)(*d*) Disposition by taxpayer of capital interest; s. 112(4.01) Loss on share that is not capital property — excluded dividends; s. 112(4.1) Fair market value of shares held as inventory; s. 112(4.11) Fair market value of shares held as inventory — excluded dividends; s. 112(4.2) Loss on share held by trust; s. 112(4.21) Loss on share held by trust — excluded dividends; s. 112(4.22) Loss on share held by trust — excluded dividends; s. 112(5) Disposition of share by financial institution; s. 112(5.1) Share held for less than one year; s. 112(5.2) Adjustment re dividends; s. 112(5.21) Subsection (5.2) — excluded dividends; s. 112(5.3) Adjustment not applicable; s. 112(5.4) Deemed dispositions; s. 112(5.5) Stop-loss rules not applicable; s. 112(5.6) Stop-loss rules restricted; s. 112(6) Meaning of certain expressions; s. 112(7) Rules where shares exchanged; s. 251 Arm's length.

Interpretation Bulletins: *Primary* — IT-328R3 Losses on shares from which dividends have been received.

► 112(4.01) ◄

(4.01) Loss on share that is not capital property — excluded dividends. A qualified dividend shall not be included in the total determined under paragraph (4)(*a*), (*b*) or (*c*) if the taxpayer establishes that

(*a*) it was received when the taxpayer and persons with whom the taxpayer was not dealing at arm's length did not own in total more than 5% of the issued shares of any class of the capital stock of the corporation from which the dividend was received; and

(*b*) it was received on a share that the taxpayer owned throughout the 365-day period that ended immediately before the disposition.

History: S. 112(4.01), the portion before paragraph (*a*) was replaced by S.C. 2011, c. 24, s. 22(7), applicable to dispositions occurring on or after March 22, 2011. S. 112(4.01), the portion before paragraph (*a*) formerly read:

(4.01) *Loss on share that is not capital property — excluded dividends.* A dividend shall not be included in the total determined under paragraph (4)(*a*), (*b*) or (*c*) where the taxpayer establishes that

► 112(4.1) ◄

(4.1) Fair market value of shares held as inventory. For the purpose of section 10, the fair market value at any time of a share of the capital stock of a corporation is deemed to be equal to the fair market value of the share at that time, plus

(*a*) where the shareholder is a corporation, the total of all amounts received by the shareholder on the share before that time each of which is

(i) a taxable dividend, to the extent of the amount of the dividend that was deductible under this section, section 113 or subsection 115(1) or 138(6) in computing the shareholder's taxable income or taxable income earned in Canada for any taxation year, or

(ii) a dividend (other than a taxable dividend);

(*b*) where the shareholder is a partnership, the total of all amounts each of which is a dividend received by the shareholder on the share before that time; and

(*c*) where the shareholder is an individual and the corporation is resident in Canada, the total of all amounts each of which is a dividend received by the shareholder on the share before that time (or, where the shareholder is a trust, that would have been so received if this Act were read without reference to subsection 104(19)).

Editorial Note: See the editorial note to s. 112(4).

Related Sections: S. 54, "capital property".

Interpretation Bulletins: *Primary* — IT-328R3 Losses on shares from which dividends have been received.

► 112(4.11) ◄

(4.11) Fair market value of shares held as inventory — excluded dividends. A qualified dividend shall not be included in the total determined under paragraph (4.1)(*a*), (*b*) or (*c*) if the shareholder establishes that

(*a*) it was received while the shareholder and persons with whom the shareholder was not dealing at arm's length did not hold in total more than 5% of the issued shares of any class of the capital stock of the corporation from which the dividend was received; and

(*b*) it was received on a share that the shareholder held throughout the 365-day period that ended at the time referred to in subsection (4.1).

History: S. 112(4.11), the portion before paragraph (*a*) was replaced by S.C. 2011, c. 24, s. 22(8), applicable to dispositions occurring on or after March 22, 2011. S. 112(4.11), the portion before paragraph (*a*) formerly read:

(4.11) *Fair market value of shares held as inventory — excluded dividends.* A dividend shall not be included in the total determined under paragraph (4.1)(*a*), (*b*) or (*c*) where the shareholder establishes that

► 112(4.2) ◄

(4.2) Loss on share held by trust. Subject to subsections (5.5) and (5.6), the amount of any loss of a trust from the disposition of a share that is property (other than capital property) of the trust is deemed to be the amount of the loss determined without reference to this subsection minus

(*a*) the total of all amounts each of which is a dividend received by the trust on the share, to the extent that the amount was not designated under subsection 104(20) in respect of a beneficiary of the trust; and

(*b*) the total of all amounts each of which is a dividend received on the share that was designated under subsection 104(19) or (20) by the trust in respect of a beneficiary of the trust.

Editorial Note: S. 112(4.2) is a stop-loss rule which applies to a share that is not capital property held by a trust (including an estate). The loss is reduced by all dividends (whether or not taxable) either if taxable to the trust or flowed-through to beneficiaries. A "5/365 exemption" applies to dividends received — very basically, if holdings do not exceed 5% of a class (or series) of shares at the time, and the shares were held throughout the 365-day period before the disposition — see ss. 112(4.21) and (4.22). For dispositions after March 21, 2011, any dividend deemed under s. 84(3) received on the redemption of shares held by the trust and allocated to a corporate beneficiary under s. 104(19) do not qualify for this exception, unless both the corporation paying the dividend and the corporate beneficiary are private corporations.

Related Sections: S. 107(1)(*c*) and (*d*) Disposition by taxpayer of capital interest; s. 112(4) Loss on share that is not capital property; s. 112(4.21) Loss on share held by trust — excluded dividends; s. 112(4.22) Loss on share held by trust — excluded dividends; s. 251 Arm's length.

Interpretation Bulletins: *Primary* — IT-328R3 Losses on shares from which dividends have been received.

► 112(4.21) ◄

(4.21) Loss on share held by trust — excluded dividends. A qualified dividend shall not be included in the total determined under paragraph (4.2)(*a*) if the taxpayer establishes that

(*a*) it was received when the trust and persons with whom the trust was not dealing at arm's length did not own in total more than 5% of the issued shares of any class of the capital stock of the corporation from which the dividend was received; and

(*b*) it was received on a share that the trust owned throughout the 365-day period that ended immediately before the disposition.

History: S. 112(4.21), the portion before paragraph (*a*) was replaced by S.C. 2011, c. 24, s. 22(9), applicable to dispositions occurring on or after March 22, 2011. S. 112(4.21), the portion before paragraph (*a*) formerly read:

(4.21) *Loss on share held by trust — excluded dividends.* A dividend shall not be included in the total determined under paragraph (4.2)(*a*) where the taxpayer establishes that

► 112(4.22) ◄

(4.22) Loss on share held by trust — excluded dividends. A qualified dividend shall not be included in the total determined under paragraph (4.2)(*b*) if the taxpayer establishes that

(*a*) it was received when the trust, the beneficiary and persons with whom the beneficiary was not dealing at arm's length did not own in total more than 5% of the issued shares of any class of the capital stock of the corporation from which the dividend was received; and

(*b*) it was received on a share that the trust owned throughout the 365-day period that ended immediately before the disposition.

History: S. 112(4.22), the portion before paragraph (*a*) was replaced by S.C. 2011, c. 24, s. 22(10), applicable to dispositions occurring on or after March 22, 2011. S. 112(4.22), the portion before paragraph (*a*) formerly read:

(4.22) *Loss on share held by trust — excluded dividends.* A dividend shall not be included in the total determined under paragraph (4.2)(*b*) where the taxpayer establishes that

► 112(4.3) ◄

(4.3) Loss on share that is not capital property of trust — (Repealed by S.C. 1998, c. 19, s. 131(2).)

► 112(5) ◄

(5) Disposition of share by financial institution. Subsection (5.2) applies to the disposition of a share by a taxpayer in a taxation year where

(*a*) the taxpayer is a financial institution in the year;

(*b*) the share is a mark-to-market property for the year; and

(*c*) the taxpayer received

(i) a dividend on the share at a time when the taxpayer and persons with whom the taxpayer was not dealing at arm's length held in total more than 5% of the issued shares of any class of the capital stock of the corporation from which the dividend was received, or

(ii) a dividend on the share under subsection 84(3).

History: S. 112(5)(*c*) was replaced by S.C. 2011, c. 24, s. 22(11), applicable to dispositions occurring on or after March 22, 2011. S. 112(5)(*c*) formerly read:

(*c*) the taxpayer received a dividend on the share at a time when the taxpayer and persons with whom the taxpayer was not dealing at arm's length held in total more than 5% of the issued shares of any class of the capital stock of the corporation from which the dividend was received.

► 112(5.1) ◄

(5.1) Share held for less than one year. Subsection (5.2) applies to the disposition of a share by a taxpayer in a taxation year where

(*a*) the disposition is an actual disposition;

(*b*) the taxpayer did not hold the share throughout the 365-day period that ended immediately before the disposition; and

(*c*) the share was a mark-to-market property of the taxpayer for a taxation year that begins after October 1994 and in which the taxpayer was a financial institution.

► 112(5.2) ◄

(5.2) Adjustment re dividends. Subject to subsection (5.3), where subsection (5) or (5.1) provides that this subsection applies to the disposition of a share by a taxpayer at any time, the taxpayer's proceeds of disposition shall be deemed to be the amount determined by the formula

$$A + B - (C - D)$$

where

A is the taxpayer's proceeds determined without reference to this subsection,

B is

(*a*) if the taxpayer received a dividend under subsection 84(3) in respect of the share, the total determined under subparagraph (b)(ii), and

(*b*) in any other case, the lesser of

(i) the loss, if any, from the disposition of the share that would be determined before the application of this subsection if the cost of the share to any taxpayer were determined without reference to

(A) paragraphs 87(2)(*e*.2) and (*e*.4), 88(1)(*c*), 138(11.5)(*e*) and 142.5(2)(*b*),

(B) subsection 85(1), where the provisions of that subsection are required by paragraph 138(11.5)(*e*) to be applied, and

(C) paragraph 142.6(1)(*d*), and

(ii) the total of all amounts each of which is

(A) where the taxpayer is a corporation, a taxable dividend received by the taxpayer on the share, to the extent of the amount that was deductible under this section or subsection 115(1) or 138(6) in computing the taxpayer's taxable income or taxable income earned in Canada for any taxation year,

(B) where the taxpayer is a partnership, a taxable dividend received by the taxpayer on the share, to the extent of the amount that was deductible under this section or subsection 115(1) or 138(6) in computing the taxable income or taxable income earned in Canada for any taxation year of members of the partnership,

(C) where the taxpayer is a trust, an amount designated under subsection 104(19) in respect of a taxable dividend on the share, or

(D) a dividend (other than a taxable dividend) received by the taxpayer on the share,

C is the total of all amounts each of which is the amount by which

(*a*) the taxpayer's proceeds of disposition on a deemed disposition of the share before that time were increased because of this subsection,

(*b*) where the taxpayer is a corporation or trust, a loss of the taxpayer on a deemed disposition of the share before that time was reduced because of subsection (3), (3.2), (4) or (4.2), or

(*c*) where the taxpayer is a partnership, a loss of a member of the partnership on a deemed disposition of the share before that time was reduced because of subsection (3.1) or (4), and

D is the total of all amounts each of which is the amount by which the taxpayer's proceeds of disposition on a deemed disposition of the share before that time were decreased because of this subsection.

History: S. 112(5.2), paragraph (*c*) of the description of C was replaced by S.C. 2018, c. 27, s. 10(7), applicable in respect of dispositions that occur after February 26, 2018, and formerly read:

(*c*) where the taxpayer is a partnership, a loss of a member of the partnership on a deemed disposition of the share before that time was reduced because of subsection (3.1) or (4.2), and

S. 112(5.2), the description of B was replaced by S.C. 2018, c. 27, s. 10(6), applicable in respect of dispositions that occur after February 26, 2018, and formerly read:

B is the lesser of

(*a*) the loss, if any, from the disposition of the share that would be determined before the application of this subsection if the cost of the share to any taxpayer were determined without reference to

(i) paragraphs 87(2)(*e*.2) and (*e*.4), 88(1)(*c*), 138(11.5)(*e*) and 142.5(2)(*b*),

(ii) subsection 85(1), where the provisions of that subsection are required by paragraph 138(11.5)(*e*) to be applied, and

(iii) paragraph 142.6(1)(*d*), and

(*b*) the total of all amounts each of which is

(i) where the taxpayer is a corporation, a taxable dividend received by the taxpayer on the share, to the extent of the amount that was deductible under this section or subsection 115(1) or 138(6) in computing the taxpayer's taxable income or taxable income earned in Canada for any taxation year,

(ii) where the taxpayer is a partnership, a taxable dividend received by the taxpayer on the share, to the extent of the amount that was deductible under this section or subsection 115(1) or 138(6) in computing the taxable income or taxable income earned in Canada for any taxation year of members of the partnership,

(iii) where the taxpayer is a trust, an amount designated under subsection 104(19) in respect of a taxable dividend on the share, or

(iv) a dividend (other than a taxable dividend) received by the taxpayer on the share,

Related Sections: 53(2) Amounts to be deducted.

▶ 112(5.21) ◀

(5.21) Subsection (5.2) — excluded dividends. A dividend, other than a dividend received under subsection 84(3), shall not be included in the total determined under subparagraph (*b*)(ii) of the description of B in subsection (5.2) unless

(*a*) the dividend was received when the taxpayer and persons with whom the taxpayer did not deal at arm's length held in total more than 5% of the issued shares of any class of the capital stock of the corporation from which the dividend was received; or

(*b*) the share was not held by the taxpayer throughout the 365-day period that ended immediately before the disposition.

History: S. 112(5.21), the portion before paragraph (*a*) was replaced by S.C. 2018, c. 27, s. 10(8), applicable in respect of dispositions that occur after February 26, 2018, and formerly read:

(5.21) *Subsection (5.2) — excluded dividends.* A dividend, other than a dividend received under subsection 84(3), shall not be included in the total determined under paragraph (*b*) of the description of B in subsection (5.2) unless

S. 112(5.21), the portion before paragraph (*a*) was replaced by S.C. 2011, c. 24, s. 22(12), applicable to dispositions occurring on or after March 22, 2011. S. 112(5.21), the portion before paragraph (*a*) formerly read:

(5.21) *Subsection (5.2) — excluded dividends.* A dividend shall not be included in the total determined under paragraph (*b*) of the description of B in subsection (5.2) unless

Related Sections: S. 112(3.01) Loss on share that is capital property — excluded dividends; s. 112(3.11) Loss on share held by partnership — excluded dividends; s. 112(3.31) Loss on share held by trust — excluded dividends; s. 112(3.32) Loss on share held by trust — excluded dividends; s. 112(4.01) Loss on share that is not capital property — excluded dividends; s. 112(4.11) Fair market value of shares held as inventory — excluded dividends; s. 112(4.21) Loss on share held by trust — excluded dividends; s. 112(4.22) Loss on share held by trust — excluded dividends.

▶ 112(5.3) ◀

(5.3) Adjustment not applicable. For the purpose of determining the cost of a share to a taxpayer on a deemed reacquisition of the share after a deemed disposition of the share, the taxpayer's proceeds of disposition shall be determined without regard to subsection (5.2).

▶ 112(5.4) ◀

(5.4) Deemed dispositions. Where a taxpayer disposes of a share at any time,

(*a*) for the purpose of determining whether subsection (5.2) applies to the disposition, the conditions in subsections (5) and (5.1) shall be applied without regard to a deemed disposition and reacquisition of the share before that time; and

(*b*) total amounts under subsection (5.2) in respect of the disposition shall be determined from the time when the taxpayer actually acquired the share.

▶ 112(5.5) ◀

(5.5) Stop-loss rules not applicable. Subsections (3) to (4) and (4.2) do not apply to the disposition of a share by a taxpayer in a taxation year that begins after October 1994 where

(*a*) the share is a mark-to-market property for the year and the taxpayer is a financial institution in the year; or

(*b*) subsection (5.2) applies to the disposition.

▶ 112(5.6) ◀

(5.6) Stop-loss rules restricted. In determining whether any of subsections (3) to (4) and (4.2) apply to reduce a loss of a taxpayer from the disposition of a share, this Act shall be read without reference to paragraphs (3.01)(*b*) and (3.11)(*b*), subclauses (3.2)(*a*)(ii)(C)(I) and (3.3)(*a*)(ii)(C)(I) and paragraphs (3.31)(*b*), (3.32)(*b*), (4.01)(*b*), (4.21)(*b*) and (4.22)(*b*) where

(*a*) the disposition occurs

(i) because of subsection 142.5(2) in a taxation year that includes October 31, 1994, or

(ii) because of paragraph 142.6(1)(*b*) after October 30, 1994; or

(*b*) the share was a mark-to-market property of the taxpayer for a taxation year that begins after October 1994 in which the taxpayer was a financial institution.

▶ 112(6) ◀

(6) Meaning of certain expressions. For the purposes of this section,

(*a*) "dividend" and "taxable dividend" do not include a capital gains dividend (within the meaning assigned by subsection 131(1)) or any dividend received by a taxpayer on which the taxpayer was required to pay tax under Part VII of the *Income Tax Act*, chapter 148 of the Revised Statutes of Canada, 1952, as it read on March 31, 1977;

(*b*) one corporation is controlled by another corporation if more than 50% of its issued share capital (having full voting rights under all circumstances) belongs to the other corporation, to persons with whom the other corporation does not deal at arm's length, or to the other corporation and persons with whom the other corporation does not deal at arm's length; and

(*c*) "financial institution" and "mark-to-market property" have the meanings assigned by subsection 142.2(1).

Editorial Note: This provision provides for the meaning of certain expressions in s. 112. In particular, a dividend or taxable dividend does not include a capital gains dividend or dividend from designated surplus.

Related Sections: S. 131(1) Election re capital gains dividend; s. 251(1) Arm's length.

► 112(6.1) ◄

(6.1) Interpretation — qualified dividend. For the purposes of this section, a dividend on a share is a qualified dividend to the extent that

(*a*) it is a dividend other than a dividend received under subsection 84(3); or

(*b*) it is received under subsection 84(3) and,

(i) if the share is held by an individual other than a trust, the dividend is received by the individual,

(ii) if the share is held by a corporation, the dividend is received by the corporation while it is a private corporation, and is paid by another private corporation,

(iii) if the share is held by a trust,

(A) the dividend is received by the trust,

(B) the dividend is designated under subsection 104(19) by the trust in respect of a beneficiary and

(I) the beneficiary is an individual other than a trust,

(II) the beneficiary is a private corporation when the dividend is received by it and the dividend is paid by another private corporation,

(III) the beneficiary is another trust that does not designate the dividend under subsection 104(19), or

(IV) the beneficiary is a partnership all of the members of which are, when the dividend is received, a person described by any of subclauses (I) to (III), or

(C) the dividend is designated by the trust under subsection 104(19) in respect of a beneficiary that is another trust or a partnership and the trust establishes that the dividend is received by a person described by any of subclauses (B)(I) to (III), and

(iv) if the share is held by a partnership,

(A) the dividend is included in the income of a member of a partnership and

(I) the member is an individual, or

(II) the member is a private corporation when the dividend is received by it and the dividend is paid by another private corporation, or

(B) the dividend is designated under subsection 104(19) by a member of a partnership that is a trust in respect of a beneficiary described by any of subclauses (iii)(B)(I) to (IV) or is described by clause (iii)(C).

Editorial Note: The provisions of subsection 112(3) through (5) are stop-loss rules that effectively reduce the amount of a loss realized on the disposition of a share by the amount of tax-free dividends (or in some cases taxable dividends) previously received or deemed to have been received on the shares. There is an exception from the stop-loss rules that generally applies where (i) the share is held by the (disposing) shareholder for 365 days or more; and (ii) the shareholder (together with all persons who do not deal at arm's length with the shareholder) owns 5% or less of the class of shares in respect of which the dividend is received. For dispositions that occur on or after March 22, 2011, only a "qualified dividend" as defined in section 54 is eligible for this exception. In general terms, a qualified dividend is any dividend other than a deemed dividend under subsection 84(3) arising on the redemption of a share of a corporation directly or indirectly held by another corporation (whether the shares are held directly or indirectly through a partnership or trust) unless both corporations are private corporations.

History: S. 112(6.1) was added by S.C. 2011, c. 24, s. 22(13), applicable to dispositions occurring on or after March 22, 2011.

► 112(7) ◄

(7) Rules where shares exchanged. Where a share (in this subsection referred to as the "new share") has been acquired in exchange for another share (in this subsection referred to as the "old share") in a transaction to which section 51, 85.1, 86 or 87 applies, for the purposes of the application of any of subsections (3) to (3.32) in respect of a disposition of the new share, the new share is deemed to be the same share as the old share, except that

(*a*) any dividend received on the old share is deemed for those purposes to have been received on the new share only to the extent of the proportion of the dividend that

(i) the shareholder's adjusted cost base of the new share immediately after the exchange

is of

(ii) the shareholder's adjusted cost base of all new shares immediately after the exchange acquired in exchange for the old share; and

(*b*) the amount, if any, by which a loss from the disposition of the new share is reduced because of the application of this subsection shall not exceed the proportion of the shareholder's adjusted cost base of the old share immediately before the exchange that

(i) the shareholder's adjusted cost base of the new share immediately after the exchange

is of

(ii) the shareholder's adjusted cost base of all new shares, immediately after the exchange, acquired in exchange for the old share.

Editorial Note: S. 112(7) provides continuity of the stop-loss rules in ss. 112(3) to (3.2) through reorganizations (conversions, share exchanges, capital reorganizations and amalgamations) by deeming "new" shares received on such a reorganization to be the "old" shares. Dividends received on the old shares therefore carry over (s. 112(7)(*a*)), as does the cost base of the old shares (s. 112(7)(*b*)), both pro-rated based on ACB of shares. The provision also applies to preserve the grandfathering rules in respect of corporate-owned life insurance notwithstanding such reorganizations (i.e., in determining whether the taxpayer owned the share on April 26th, 1995 and whether a main purpose of life insurance policy was intended to fund a redemption — see the editorial note to s. 112(3.2)).

Related Sections: S. 112(3) Loss on share that is capital property; s. 112(3.1) Loss on share held by partnership; s. 112(3.2) Loss on share held by trust.

Interpretation Bulletins: *Primary* — IT-328R3 Losses on shares from which dividends have been received.

► 112(8) ◄

(8) Synthetic disposition — holding period. If a synthetic disposition arrangement is entered into in respect of a property owned by a taxpayer and the synthetic disposition period of the arrangement is 30 days or more, for the purposes of paragraphs (3.01)(*b*) and (3.11)(*b*), subclauses (3.2)(*a*)(ii)(C)(I) and (3.3)(*a*)(ii)(C)(I) and paragraphs (3.31)(*b*), (3.32)(*b*), (4.01)(*b*), (4.11)(*b*), (4.21)(*b*), (4.22)(*b*), (5.1)(*b*) and (5.21)(*b*) and subsection (9), the taxpayer is deemed not to own the property during the synthetic disposition period.

Editorial Note: Any period of time in which a taxpayer's property is considered subject to a synthetic disposition arrangement cannot constitute part of the 365-day period of ownership necessary to avoid the s.112 stop-loss provisions, as the property is deemed not to have been owned by the taxpayer during that time.

History: S. 112(8) was added by S.C. 2013, c. 40, s. 48(1), applicable to:

(*a*) an agreement or arrangement entered into after March 20, 2013; and

(*b*) an agreement or arrangement entered into before March 21, 2013, the term of which is extended after March 20, 2013, as if the agreement or arrangement were entered into at the time of the extension.

► 112(9) ◄

(9) Exception. Subsection (8) does not apply in respect of a property owned by a taxpayer in respect of a synthetic disposition arrangement if the taxpayer owned the property throughout the 365-day period (determined without reference to this subsection) that ended immediately before the synthetic disposition period of the arrangement.

History: S. 112(9) was added by S.C. 2013, c. 40, s. 48(1), applicable, subject to the application below, to:

(*a*) an agreement or arrangement entered into after March 20, 2013; and

(*b*) an agreement or arrangement entered into before March 21, 2013, the term of which is extended after March 20, 2013, as if the agreement or arrangement were entered into at the time of the extension.

In respect of an agreement or arrangement referred to above that is entered into before September 13, 2013 and the term of which is not extended after September 12, 2013, subsection 112(9) is to be read as follows:

"(9) Subsection (8) does not apply in respect of a property owned by a taxpayer in respect of a synthetic disposition arrangement if the taxpayer owned the property throughout the 365-day period that ended immediately before the synthetic disposition period of the arrangement."

► 112(9.1) ◄

(9.1) Exception. Subsection (8) does not apply for the purpose of paragraph (5.21)(*b*) in respect of a dividend received on a share, referred to in paragraph (*a*) of the description of B in subsection (5.2), during a synthetic disposition period of a synthetic disposition arrangement in respect of that share.

History: S. 112(9.1) was added by S.C. 2018, c. 27, s. 10(9), applicable in respect of dispositions that occur after February 26, 2018.

► 112(10) ◄

(10) Synthetic equity arrangements — ordering. For the purposes of subsections (3), (3.1), (4), (4.1) and (5.2), if a synthetic equity arrangement is in respect of a number of shares that are identical properties (referred to in this subsection as *identical shares*) that is less than the total number of such identical shares owned by a person or partnership at that time and in respect of which there is no other synthetic equity arrangement, the synthetic equity arrangement is deemed to be in respect of those identical shares in the order in which the person or partnership acquired them.

Editorial Note: Subsection 112(2.3) denies the intercorporate dividend deduction for a recipient corporation where the dividend is received as part of a dividend rental arrangement, including a synthetic equity arrangement. Subsection 112(10) provides an ordering rule that applies where the number of shares subject to a synthetic equity arrangement at a particular time is less than the total number of identical shares owned by a person (or partnership) at that time. In such a case, the synthetic equity arrangement is deemed to be in respect of those identical shares in the order in which the person or partnership acquired them.

History: S. 112(10) was added by S.C. 2016, c. 7, s. 14(2), deemed to have come into force on April 22, 2015.

Related Sections: S. 248(1) "dividend rental arrangement", "synthetic equity arrangement".

► 112(11) ◄

(11) Interest in a partnership — cost reduction. In computing the cost to a taxpayer, at any time, of an interest in a partnership that is property (other than capital property) of the taxpayer, there is to be deducted an amount equal to the total of all amounts each of which is the taxpayer's share of any loss of the partnership from the disposition by the partnership, or another partnership of which the partnership is directly or indirectly a member, of a share of the capital stock of a corporation (referred to in this subsection and subsection (12) as the "partnership loss") in a fiscal period of the partnership that includes that time or a prior fiscal period, computed without reference to subsections (3.1), (4) and (5.2), to the extent that the taxpayer's share of the partnership loss has not previously reduced the taxpayer's cost of the interest in the partnership because of the application of this subsection.

Editorial Note: Subsections 112(11) to (13), deemed in force September 16, 2016, are intended to ensure that taxpayers cannot circumvent the dividend stop-loss rules in subsections 112(3) to (7) by holding shares through a partnership, as opposed to holding them directly. Subsection 112(11) is the substantive provision that provides for a reduction in the cost of the partner's partnership interest equal to the share of the partner's loss from the disposition of a share of a corporation held by the partnership (or by another partnership of which the partnership is a direct or indirect member). The loss is to be determined without reference to subsections 112(3.1), (4), and (5.2).

Subsections 112(12) and (13) provide the application rules for subsection 112(11).

History: S. 112(11) was added by S.C. 2017, c. 33, s. 41(1), deemed to have come into force on September 16, 2016.

► 112(12) ◄

(12) Application. For the purposes of subsection (11), if a taxpayer disposes of an interest in a partnership at any particular time, the taxpayer's share of a partnership loss is to be computed as if

(*a*) the fiscal period of each partnership of which the taxpayer is directly or indirectly a member had ended immediately before the time that is immediately before the particular time;

(*b*) any share of the capital stock of a corporation that was property of a partnership referred to in paragraph (*a*) at the particular time had been disposed of by the relevant partnership immediately before the end of that fiscal period for proceeds equal to its fair market value at the particular time; and

(*c*) each member of a partnership referred to in paragraph (*a*) were allocated a share of any loss (computed without reference to subsections (3.1), (4) and (5.2)) in respect of dispositions described in paragraph (*b*) determined by reference to the member's specified proportion for the fiscal period referred to in paragraph (*a*).

Editorial Note: Subsection 112(12) provides application rules for subsection 112(11) relating to the computation of the partner's share of a partnership loss where the partner disposes of his or her interest in the partnership.

History: S. 112(12) was added by S.C. 2017, c. 33, s. 41(1), deemed to have come into force on September 16, 2016.

► 112(13) ◄

(13) Application. For the purposes of subsection (11), if a taxpayer (referred to as the "transferee" in this subsection) acquires an interest in a partnership at any time from another taxpayer (referred to as the "transferor" in this subsection), in computing the cost of the partnership interest to the transferee there is to be added an amount equal to the total of all amounts each of which is an amount deducted from the transferor's cost of the partnership interest because of subsection (11), other than an amount to which subsection (3.1) would apply.

Editorial Note: Subsection 112(13) provides application rules for subsection 112(11) to determine the cost of a partnership interest that a taxpayer acquires from another taxpayer where subsection 112(11) previously applied to reduce the cost of the partnership interest to that other taxpayer.

History: S. 112(13) was added by S.C. 2017, c. 33, s. 41(1), deemed to have come into force on September 16, 2016.

SECTION 113: Deduction in respect of dividend received from foreign affiliate

► 113(1) ◄

(1) Deduction in respect of dividend received from foreign affiliate. Where in a taxation year a corporation resident in Canada has received a dividend on a share owned by it of the capital stock of a foreign affiliate of the corporation, there may be deducted from the income for the year of the corporation for the purpose of computing its taxable income for the year, an amount equal to the total of

(*a*) an amount equal to such portion of the dividend as is prescribed to have been paid out of the exempt surplus, as defined by regulation (in this Part referred to as "exempt surplus") of the affiliate,

(*a*.1) an amount equal to the total of

(i) one-half of the portion of the dividend that is prescribed to have been paid out of the hybrid surplus, as defined by regulation (in this Part referred to as "hybrid surplus"), of the affiliate, and

(ii) the lesser of

(A) the total of

(I) the product obtained when the foreign tax prescribed to be applicable to the portion of the dividend referred to in subparagraph (i) is multiplied by the amount by which

1. the corporation's relevant tax factor for the year

exceeds

2. one-half, and

(II) the product obtained when

1. the non-business-income tax paid by the corporation applicable to the portion of the dividend referred to in subparagraph (i)

is multiplied by

2. the corporation's relevant tax factor for the year, and

(B) the amount determined under subparagraph (i),

(*b*) an amount equal to the lesser of

(i) the product obtained when the foreign tax prescribed to be applicable to such portion of the dividend as is prescribed to have been paid out of the taxable surplus, as defined by regulation (in this Part referred to as "taxable surplus") of the affiliate is multiplied by the amount by which

(A) the corporation's relevant tax factor for the year

exceeds

(B) one, and

(ii) that portion of the dividend,

(*c*) an amount equal to the lesser of

(i) the product obtained when

(A) the non-business-income tax paid by the corporation applicable to such portion of the dividend as is prescribed to have been paid out of the taxable surplus of the affiliate

is multiplied by

(B) the corporation's relevant tax factor for the year, and

(ii) the amount by which such portion of the dividend as is prescribed to have been paid out of the taxable surplus of the affiliate exceeds the deduction in respect thereof referred to in paragraph (*b*), and

(*d*) an amount equal to such portion of the dividend as is prescribed to have been paid out of the pre-acquisition surplus of the affiliate,

and for the purposes of this subsection and subdivision i of Division B, the corporation may make such elections as may be prescribed.

History: S. 113(1)(*a.1*) was added by S.C. 2013, c. 34, s. 72(1), applicable in respect of dividends received after August 19, 2011.

Any assessment of a taxpayer's tax, interest and penalties payable under the Act for any taxation year that ends before June 26, 2013 that would, in the absence of this section, be precluded because of subsections 152(4) to (5) of the Act shall be made to the extent necessary to take into account the amendments by S.C. 2013, c. 34, s. 54 to 89.

S. 113(1)(*b*)(i)(A) was replaced by S.C. 2013, c. 34, s. 243(1), deemed to have come into force on January 1, 2001, and formerly read:

(A) the relevant tax factor

S. 113(1)(*c*)(i)(B) was replaced by S.C. 2013, c. 34, s. 243(2), deemed to have come into force on January 1, 2001, and formerly read:

(B) the relevant tax factor, and

Related Regulations: 5900(1), (2); 5907.

Related Sections: S. 93(3) Exempt dividends; s. 95(1) Foreign affiliate; s. 111(8) Definitions; s. 125(6) Corporate partnerships; s. 126(7) Definitions; s. 143(1) Communal organizations; s. 186(1) Tax on assessable dividends.

Canadian Petroleum Tax Journal: Foreign Affiliate Surplus: Got Enough?, Talakshi and Samuel, 2005, Vol. 18, No. 1; High Tech in the Oil Patch: Planning Considerations For Transferring Technology Offshore, Derek A. Kurrant, 2000, Vol. 13, No. 1.

Canadian Tax Foundation: Lanthier, *FAPI or Taxable Surplus Dividend*, 2015 Canadian Tax Highlights 23(2):4–5; Zabarylo, *Emerging Issues in Tax Accounting: Implications of Foreign Affiliate Changes in Bill C-48*, 2013 Conference Report 34:1–7; O'Hagan and Buttenham, *Foreign Affiliate Reorganizations: Where Are We Now?*, 2013 Conference Report 20:1–56; Morier and Juneja, *Foreign Affiliates: An Updated Primer*, 2012 Conference Report 28:1–48; Talakshi and Samuel, *Foreign Affiliate Surplus: What You See Isn't Always What You Get*, 2008 Conference Report 28:1–27; Minassian and Selby, *Computation of Surplus Accounts*, 2002 Conference Report 43:1–19.

Tax Profile: December 2012 — Taxpayer's Equity Characterization of Hybrid Instruments — Canadian Implications; November 2010 — Canadian Acquisition of U.S. Real Estate; January 2009 — Enhancing Canada's International Tax Advantage; June 2008 — International Tax Planning for the Owner-Manager; July 2008 — International Tax Planning for the Owner-Manager; April 2008 — International Tax Planning for the Owner-Manager; May 2007 — Impact of 2007 Federal Budget on Cross-Border Transactions; February 2007 — U.S. Limited Liability Companies — The Good, the Bad and the Ugly; February 2006 — Foreign Source Income: Outbound Structures and Foreign Tax Credit Planning — Part II; December 2004 — Taxation of Dividends: A Survey in the Context of Private Corporations and Their Shareholders — Part 2.

Tax Topics: No. 1930, Budget 2009 Provides Initial Response to Final Report Issued by the Advisory Panel on Canada's System of International Taxation.

Information Circulars: IC 77-9R Books, records and other requirements for taxpayers having foreign affiliates.

Interpretation Bulletins: *Secondary* — IT-232R3 Non-capital losses, net capital losses, restricted farm losses, farm losses and limited partnership losses — Their composition and deductibility in computing taxable income; IT-269R4 Part IV tax on taxable dividends received by a private corporation or a subject corporation.

Tax Window Files: Interpretation of paragraph 5907(2.01) of the Regulations, *April 22, 2015*, CRA Document No. 2014-0550451E5.

► 113(2) ◄

(2) Additional deduction. Where, at any particular time in a taxation year ending after 1975, a corporation resident in Canada has received a dividend on a share owned by it at the end of its 1975 taxation year of the capital stock of a foreign affiliate of the corporation, there may be deducted from the income for the year of the corporation for the purpose of computing its taxable income for the year, an amount in respect of the dividend equal to the lesser of

(*a*) the amount, if any, by which the amount of the dividend so received exceeds the total of

(i) the deduction in respect of the dividend permitted by subsection 91(5) in computing the corporation's income for the year, and

(ii) the deduction in respect of the dividend permitted by subsection (1) from the income for the year of the corporation for the purpose of computing its taxable income, and

(*b*) the amount, if any, by which

(i) the adjusted cost base to the corporation of the share at the end of its 1975 taxation year

exceeds the total of

(ii) (Repealed.)

(iii) such amounts in respect of dividends received by the corporation on the share after the end of its 1975 taxation year and before the particular time as are deductible under paragraph (1)(*d*) in computing the taxable income of the corporation for taxation years ending after 1975,

(iii.1) the total of all amounts received by the corporation on the share after the end of its 1975 taxation year and before the particular time

(A) on a reduction, before August 20, 2011, of the paid-up capital of the foreign affiliate in respect of the share, or

(B) on a reduction, after August 19, 2011, of the paid-up capital of the foreign affiliate in respect of the share that is a qualifying return of capital (within the meaning assigned by subsection 90(3)) in respect of the share, and

(iv) the total of all amounts deducted under this subsection in respect of dividends received by the corporation on the share before the particular time.

History: S. 113(2)(*b*)(iii.1) was replaced by S.C. 2013, c. 34, s. 72(2), deemed to have come into force on August 20, 2011.

Any assessment of a taxpayer's tax, interest and penalties payable under the Act for any taxation year that ends before June 26, 2013 that would, in the absence of this section, be precluded because of subsections 152(4) to (5) of the Act shall be made to the extent necessary to take into account the amendments by S.C. 2013, c. 34, s. 54 to 89.

S. 113(2)(*b*)(iii.1) formerly read:

(iii.1) the total of all amounts received by the corporation on the share after the end of its 1975 taxation year and before the particular time on a reduction of the paid-up capital of the foreign affiliate in respect of the share, and

Related Sections: S. 92(1) Adjusted cost base of share of foreign affiliate; s. 92(3) Computation of adjusted cost base; s. 113(1) Deduction in respect of dividend received from foreign affiliate.

Tax Profile: December 2004 — Taxation of Dividends: A Survey in the Context of Private Corporations and Their Shareholders — Part 2.

▶ 113(3) ◀

(3) Definitions. In this section,

"non-business-income tax" — "non-business-income tax" paid by a taxpayer has the meaning assigned by subsection 126(7);

"relevant tax factor" — "relevant tax factor" has the meaning assigned by subsection 95(1).

▶ 113(4) ◀

(4) Portion of dividend deemed paid out of exempt surplus. Such portion of any dividend received at any time in a taxation year by a corporation resident in Canada on a share owned by it of the capital stock of a foreign affiliate of the corporation, that was received after the 1971 taxation year of the affiliate and before the affiliate's 1976 taxation year, as exceeds the amount deductible in respect of the dividend under paragraph (1)(*d*) in computing the corporation's taxable income for the year shall, for the purposes of paragraph (1)(*a*), be deemed to be the portion of the dividend prescribed to have been paid out of the exempt surplus of the affiliate.

Related Regulations: 5900.

Related Sections: S. 95(1)(*b*) Foreign affiliate; s. 113(1) Deduction in respect of dividend received from foreign affiliate.

Cases: Considering the distinction between "listed" and "unlisted" countries and the fact that Puerto Rico had to be taken as being distinct from the U.S., a tax exemption received by the taxpayer's foreign affiliate from the Puerto Rican government was an "export incentive" so that its dividends did not qualify for the deduction under s. 113(1)(*a*). *The Queen v. Old HW-GW Ltd.*, 93 DTC 5199 (F.C.A.), reversing 91 DTC 5327 (F.C.T.D.).

▶ 113(5) ◀

(5) Limitation on foreign accrual tax where treaty — (Repealed by 1974-75-76, c. 26, s. 73(4).)

▶ 113(6) ◀

(6) Construction of other provisions — (Repealed by 1974-75-76, c. 26, s. 73(4).)

▶ 113(7) ◀

(7) Meaning of "foreign accrual tax applicable" — (Repealed by 1974-75-76, c. 26, s. 73(4).)

SECTION 114: Individual resident in Canada for only part of year

Notwithstanding subsection 2(2), the taxable income for a taxation year of an individual who is resident in Canada throughout part of the year and non-resident throughout another part of the year is the amount, if any, by which

(*a*) the amount that would be the individual's income for the year if the individual had no income or losses, for the part of the year throughout which the individual was non-resident, other than

(i) income or losses described in paragraphs 115(1)(*a*) to (*c*), and

(ii) income that would have been included in the individual's taxable income earned in Canada for the year under subparagraph 115(1)(*a*)(v) if the part of the year throughout which the individual was non-resident were the whole taxation year,

exceeds the total of

(*b*) the deductions permitted by subsection 111(1) and, to the extent that they relate to amounts included in computing the amount determined under paragraph (*a*), the deductions permitted by any of paragraphs 110(1)(*d*) to (*d*.2) and (*f*), and

(*c*) any other deduction permitted for the purpose of computing taxable income to the extent that

(i) it can reasonably be considered to be applicable to the part of the year throughout which the individual was resident in Canada, or

(ii) if all or substantially all of the individual's income for the part of the year throughout which the individual was non-resident is included in the amount determined under paragraph (*a*), it can reasonably be considered to be applicable to that part of the year.

Related Regulations: 2606; 2606(2).

Related Sections: S. 2(2) Taxable income; s. 8(10) Certificate of employer; s. 28(4) Non-resident; s. 111(8) Definitions; s. 120(3) Definition of "the individual's income for the year"; s. 122.3 Deduction from tax payable where employment out of Canada; s. 126(1) Foreign tax deduction — non-business income; s. 126(2) Foreign tax deduction — business income; s. 126(3) Employees of international organizations; s. 248(1), "amount", "business", "individual", "property", "taxable income earned in Canada"; s. 249 Definition of "taxation year"; s. 255 Canada.

Tax Profile: December 2008 — Tax Planning for Emigration from Canada to the United States.

Guides: T4055 Newcomers to Canada; T4056 Emigrants and Income Tax.

Income Tax Folios: *Secondary* — S5-F1-C1 Determining an Individual's Residence Status.

Interpretation Bulletins: *Primary* — IT-262R2 Losses of non-residents and part-year residents. *Secondary* — IT-420R3 Non-residents — Income earned in Canada; IT-497R4 Overseas employment tax credit.

Cases: Days before emigrating from Canada, the taxpayers executed a departure trade designed to create a $1.7 million interest deduction. Since the interest was payable one day after they became non-residents, it couldn't be deducted under s. 114(*a*). It wasn't deductible under s. 114(*c*) either since the phrase, "any other deduction permitted for the purpose of computing taxable income" is restricted to Division C deductions, which excludes a s. 20(1)(*c*) interest deduction. *Grant et al. v. The Queen*, 2007 DTC 5351 (F.C.A.), affirming 2006 DTC 3071 (T.C.C.)

A taxpayer was not resident in Canada for a certain period although his family was temporarily resident there, and although he visited them on several occasions. *Kallos v. M.N.R.*, 72 DTC 1099 (T.R.B.). Similarly, a taxpayer living in France for 246 days while training for a position with a Canadian subsidiary was held resident in Canada. *Queen v. Reeder*, 75 DTC 5160 (F.C.T.D.), reversing 75 DTC 17 (T.R.B.).

SECTION 114.1: Application of s. 115(2)

(Repealed by S.C. 2001, c. 17, s. 89(1).)

SECTION 114.2: Deductions in separate returns

Where a separate return of income with respect to a taxpayer is filed under subsection 70(2), 104(23) or 150(4) for a particular period and another return of income under this Part with respect to the taxpayer is filed for a period ending in the calendar year in which the particular period ends, for the purpose of computing the taxable income under this Part of the taxpayer in those returns, the total of all deductions claimed in all those returns under section 110 shall not exceed the total that could be deducted under that section for the year with respect to the taxpayer if no separate returns were filed under subsections 70(2), 104(23) and 150(4).

Interpretation Bulletins: *Primary* — IT-326R3 Returns of deceased persons as "another person". *Secondary* — IT-212R3 Income of deceased persons — Rights or things.

Division D — Taxable Income Earned in Canada by Non-Residents

SECTION 115: Non-resident's taxable income in Canada

▶ 115(1) ◀

(1) Non-resident's taxable income in Canada. For the purposes of this Act, the taxable income earned in Canada for a taxation year of a person who at no time in the year is resident in Canada is the amount, if any, by which the amount that would be the non-resident person's income for the year under section 3 if

(*a*) the non-resident person had no income other than

(i) incomes from the duties of offices and employments performed by the non-resident person in Canada and, if the person was resident in Canada at the time the person performed the duties, outside Canada,

(ii) incomes from businesses carried on by the non-resident person in Canada which, in the case of the Canadian banking business of an authorized foreign bank, is, subject to this Part, the profit from that business computed using the bank's branch financial statements (within the meaning assigned by subsection 20.2(1),

(iii) taxable capital gains from dispositions described in paragraph (*b*),

(iii.1) the amount by which the amount required by paragraph 59(3.2)(*c*) to be included in computing the non-resident person's income for the year exceeds any portion of that amount that was included in computing the non-resident person's income from a business carried on by the non-resident person in Canada,

(iii.2) amounts required by section 13 to be included in computing the non-resident person's income for the year in respect of dispositions of properties to the extent that those amounts were not included in computing the non-resident person's income from a business carried on by the non-resident person in Canada,

(iii.21) the total of all amounts, each of which is an amount included under subparagraph 56(1)(*r*)(v) or section 56.3 in computing the non-resident person's income for the year,

(iii.3) in any case where, in the year, the non-resident person carried on a business in Canada described in any of paragraphs (*a*) to (*g*) of the definition "principal-business corporation" in subsection 66(15), all amounts in respect of a Canadian resource property that would be required to be included in computing the non-resident person's income for the year under this Part if the non-resident person were resident in Canada at any time in the year, to the extent that those amounts are not included in computing the non-resident person's income by virtue of subparagraph (ii) or (iii.1),

(iv) the amount, if any, by which any amount required by subsection 106(2) to be included in computing the non-resident person's income for the year as proceeds of the disposition of an income interest in a trust resident in Canada exceeds the amount in respect of that income interest that would, if the non-resident person had been resident in Canada throughout the year, be deductible under subsection 106(1) in computing the non-resident person's income for the year,

(iv.1) the amount, if any, by which any amount required by subsection 96(1.2) to be included in computing the non-resident person's income for the year as proceeds of the disposition of a right to a share of the income or loss under an agreement referred to in paragraph 96(1.1)(*a*) exceeds the amount in respect of that right that would, if the non-resident person had been resident in Canada throughout the year, be deductible under subsection 96(1.3) in computing the non-resident person's income for the year,

(v) in the case of a non-resident person described in subsection (2), the total determined under paragraph (2)(*e*) in respect of the non-resident person,

(vi) the amount that would have been required to be included in computing the non-resident person's income in respect of a life insurance policy in Canada by virtue of subsection 148(1) or (1.1) if the non-resident person had been resident in Canada throughout the year, and

(vii) in the case of an authorized foreign bank, the amount claimed by the bank to the extent that the inclusion of the amount in income

(A) increases any amount deductible by the bank under subsection 126(1) for the year, and

(B) does not increase an amount deductible by the bank under section 127 for the year,

(*b*) the only taxable capital gains and allowable capital losses referred to in paragraph 3(*b*) were taxable capital gains and allowable capital losses from dispositions, other than dispositions deemed under subsection 218.3(2), of taxable Canadian properties (other than treaty-protected properties), and

(*b*.1) (Repealed by S.C. 2001, c. 17, s. 90(4).)

(*c*) the only losses for the year referred to in paragraph 3(*d*) were losses from duties of an office or employment performed by the person in Canada and businesses (other than treaty-protected businesses) carried on by the person in Canada and allowable business investment losses in respect of property any gain from the disposition of which would, because of this subsection, be included in computing the person's taxable income earned in Canada,

exceeds the total of

(*d*) the deductions permitted by subsection 111(1) and, to the extent that they relate to amounts included in computing the amount determined under any of paragraphs (*a*) to (*c*), the deductions permitted by any of paragraphs 110(1)(*d*) to (*d*.2) and (*f*) and subsection 110.1(1),

(*d*.1) (Repealed by S.C. 1999, c. 22, s. 29(2).)

(*e*) the deductions permitted by any of subsections 112(1) and (2) and 138(6) in respect of a dividend received by the non-resident person, to the extent that the dividend is included in computing the non-resident person's taxable income earned in Canada for the year,

(*e*.1) the deduction permitted by subsection (4.1), and

(*f*) where all or substantially all of the non-resident person's income for the year is included in computing the non-resident person's taxable income earned in Canada for the year, such of the other deductions permitted for the purpose of computing taxable income as may reasonably be considered wholly applicable.

Editorial Note: A non-resident's taxable income earned in Canada may be exempt or reduced by an income tax treaty (see also s. 110(1)(*f*)). Most forms of Canadian-sourced passive investment income received by a non-resident (including interest, dividends, royalties and rent that is income from property) do not constitute taxable income earned in Canada, and are instead subject to Part XIII withholding tax.

History: S. 115(1)(*a*)(iii.21) was replaced by S.C. 2009, c. 2, s. 31(1), applicable to the 2008 and subsequent taxation years. S. 115(1)(*a*)(iii.21) formerly read:

(iii.21) the amount, if any, included under section 56.3 in computing the non-resident person's income for the year,

Related Regulations: Part VIII; Part XXVI.

Related Sections: S. 13(21) Definitions; s. 38 Taxable capital gain and allowable capital loss; s. 39(1)(*c*) Meaning of capital gain and capital loss; s. 40(9) Additions to taxable Canadian property; s. 116(1) Disposition by non-resident person of certain property; s. 116(3) Notice to Minister; s. 116(5) Liability of purchaser; s. 141(5) Exclusion from taxable Canadian property; s. 216 Alternatives re rents and timber royalties; s. 217 Alternative re Canadian benefits; s. 248(1), "business", "disposition", "employment", "office", "property", "taxable income earned in Canada", "treaty-protected business", "treaty-protected property"; s. 250 Person deemed resident; s. 251(1) Arm's length; s. 255 Canada.

Canadian Petroleum Tax Journal: Taxable Canadian Property, Tony Van Rooyen, 2000, Vol. 13, No. 1.

Canadian Tax Foundation: Nitikman, *More on Services PEs — What Is a Connected Project?*, 2014 Canadian Tax Journal 2:317–382; Chiu, *Taxation of Non-Resident Investors in Canadian Investment Funds*, 2010 Canadian Tax Journal 1:117–143; Spadorcia and Diles, *Compensating the Cross-Border Executive: Stock Option Plans*, 2000 Conference Report 30:1–32; Raizenne and Nikolakakis, *Taxable Canadian Property* , 1996 Conference Report 46:1–72.

Tax Profile: October 2009 — New Rules under the Canada-U.S. Treaty and Canadian Withholding Taxes on Cross-Border Services; August 2007 — Professionals and Other Service Providers Beware — A Canadian Trap.

Forms: T2Sch97 — T2 Sch. 97 Additional Information on Non-Resident Corporations in Canada; T1248 — Information About Your Residency Status; T2061A — Election by an Emigrant to Report Deemed Dispositions of Taxable Canadian Property and Capital Gains and/or Losses Thereon.

Guides: T4058 Non-Residents and Income Tax.

Income Tax Folios: *Secondary* — S5-F1-C1 Determining an Individual's Residence Status.

Income Tax Technical News: Issue No. 35, Treaty Residence — Resident of Convenience.

Information Circulars: IC 72-17R6 Procedures concerning the disposition of taxable Canadian property by non-residents of Canada — Section 116; IC 88-2 General anti-avoidance rule — Section 245 of the Income Tax Act.

Interpretation Bulletins: *Primary* — IT-176R2 Taxable Canadian property — Interests in and options on real property and shares; IT-262R2 Losses of non-residents and part-year residents; IT-420R3 Non-residents — Income earned in Canada. *Secondary* — IT-81R Partnerships — Income of non-resident partners; IT-168R3 Athletes and players employed by football, hockey and similar clubs; IT-393R2 Election re tax on rents and timber royalties — Non-residents; IT-434R Rental of real property by individual; IT-451R Deemed disposition and acquisition on ceasing to be or becoming resident in Canada; IT-465R Non-resident beneficiaries of trusts.

Cases: Interest income was "income from a business carried on in Canada", rather than income from property since the taxpayer's core activity was the operation of an investment holding business and earning interest income was its major business activity. *Inter-Leasing Inc. v. Ontario (Revenue)*, 2013 DTC 5124 (Ont. S.C.J.)

Rental income derived by a non-resident from a single family dwelling in Canada was income from property and not income from a business. There was no merit in the taxpayer's argument that inconsistency existed between the Minister's assessments under s. 155 and Part XIII. The onus was on the taxpayer to demonstrate that these two assessments cover the same income and he failed to do so. *Gupta v. The Queen*, 2000 DTC 6326 (F.C.A.), affirming 99 DTC 224 (T.C.C.)

A U.S. resident performing services in Canada under contract was not subject to Canadian tax under Article XIV of the Convention because he did not have a "fixed base" in Canada. The expression "fixed base" is to be given a liberal interpretation. However, there is little difference in meaning between a "fixed base" and a "permanent establishment". *Dudney v. The Queen*, 2000 DTC 6169 (F.C.A.), affirming 99 DTC 147 (T.C.C.)

Since the capital gain from the deemed disposition by a U.S. resident of an Ontario cottage first began to accrue on Valuation Day, its exempt portion under the Canada-U.S. Convention could not take into account any months prior to December 31, 1971. *A. G. of Canada v. Estate of W.F. Kubicek*, 97 DTC 5454 (F.C.A.), reversing 97 DTC 1551 (T.C.C.)

A non-resident was precluded under ss. 115(1)(*c*) and (*e*) from deducting the rental loss he had not incurred "from carrying on a business in Canada" when he was merely collecting rental income from a passive investment in a condominium and was performing the activities of a simple owner. *Matlas v. The Queen*, 94 DTC 1591 (T.C.C.)

Although the taxpayer was a non-resident of Canada, he was not entitled to the protection of article 15(1) of the *Canada–U.K. Tax Convention*, since the amounts in issue — (i) money realized from the exercise of share purchase option rights under an executive share option plan he had while employed in Canada and (ii) director's fees received in Canada — did not fall within the purview of the expression "salaries, wages, and other remuneration" appearing in that article. *Hale v. The Queen*, 92 DTC 6473 (F.C.A.), affirming 90 DTC 6481 (F.C.T.D.).

▶ 115(2) ◀

(2) Idem. Where, in a taxation year, a non-resident person was

(*a*) a student in full-time attendance at an educational institution in Canada that is a university, college or other educational institution providing courses at a post-secondary school level in Canada,

(*b*) a student attending, or a teacher teaching at, an educational institution outside Canada that is a university, college or other educational institution providing courses at a post-secondary school level, who in any preceding taxation year ceased to be resident in Canada in the course of or subsequent to moving to attend or to teach at the institution,

(*b*.1) an individual who in any preceding taxation year ceased to be resident in Canada in the course of or subsequent to moving to carry on research or any similar work under a grant received by the individual to enable the individual to carry on the research or work,

(*c*) an individual

(i) who had, in any previous year, ceased to be resident in Canada,

(ii) who received, in the taxation year, salary or wages or other remuneration in respect of an office or employment that was paid to the individual directly or indirectly by a person resident in Canada, and

(iii) who was, under an agreement or a convention with one or more countries that has the force of law in Canada, entitled to an exemption from an income tax otherwise payable in any of those countries in respect of the salary or wages or other remuneration, or

(*c*.1) a person who received in the year an amount, under a contract, that was or will be deductible in computing the income of a taxpayer subject to tax under this Part and the amount can, irrespective of when the contract was entered into or the form or legal effect of the contract, reasonably be regarded as having been received, in whole or in part,

(i) as consideration or partial consideration for entering into a contract of service or an agreement to perform a service where any such service is to be performed in Canada, or for undertaking not to enter into such a contract or agreement with another party, or

(ii) as remuneration or partial remuneration from the duties of an office or employment or as compensation or partial compensation for services to be performed in Canada,

the following rules apply:

(*d*) for the purposes of subsection 2(3) the non-resident person shall be deemed to have been employed in Canada in the year,

(*e*) for the purposes of subparagraph (1)(*a*)(v), the total determined under this paragraph in respect of the non-resident person is the total of

(i) any remuneration in respect of an office or employment that was paid to the non-resident person directly or indirectly by a person resident in Canada and was received by the non-resident person in the year, except to the extent that the remuneration is attributable to the duties of an office or employment performed by the non-resident person anywhere outside Canada and

(A) is subject to an income or profits tax imposed by the government of a country other than Canada, or

(B) is paid in connection with the selling of property, the negotiating of contracts or the rendering of services for the non-resident person's employer, or a foreign affiliate of the employer, or any other person with whom the employer does not deal at arm's length, in the ordinary course of a business carried on by the employer, that foreign affiliate or that person,

(ii) amounts that would be required by paragraph 56(1)(*n*) or (*o*) to be included in computing the non-resident person's income for the year if the non-resident person were resident in Canada throughout the year and the reference in the applicable paragraph to "received by the taxpayer in the year" were read as a reference to "received by the taxpayer in the year from a source in Canada",

(iii) [Repealed by S.C. 1994, c. 7, Sched. VII, s. 5(2).]

(iv) amounts that would be required by paragraph 56(1)(*q*) to be included in computing the non-resident person's income for the year if the non-resident person were resident in Canada throughout the year, and

(v) amounts described in paragraph (*c*.1) received by the non-resident person in the year, except to the extent that they are otherwise required to be included in computing the non-resident person's taxable income earned in Canada for the year, and

(*f*) there may be deducted in computing the taxable income of the non-resident person for the year the amount that would be deductible in computing the non-resident person's income for the year by virtue of section 62 if

(i) the definition "eligible relocation" in subsection 248(1) were read without reference to subparagraph (*a*)(i) of that definition, and

(ii) the amounts described in subparagraph 62(1)(*c*)(ii) were the amounts described in subparagraph (*e*)(ii) of this subsection.

(iii) (Repealed.)

Editorial Note: Subparagraph 115(1)(*a*)(v) and s. 115(2) extend the provisions of s. 2(3) to certain non-resident employees, students, and researchers and, in effect, subject certain amounts received by them to Part I tax. The net amount calculated as a result of the provisions in s. 115(2) is included in "taxable income earned in Canada" under s. 115(1), and by reason of s. 2(3), this amount is subject to Part I tax.

Related Regulations: 104; Part XXVI.

Income Tax Folios: *Secondary* — S1-F3-C4 Moving Expenses; S1-F2-C3 Scholarships, Research Grants and Other Education Assistance.

Interpretation Bulletins: *Primary* — IT-161R3 Non-residents — Exemption from tax deductions at source on employment income.

Cases: A bursary of $14,749 granted by McGill University to a Chinese student who had entered Canada on a visitor's visa but had applied for and received a landed immigrant status sometime in 1990 after his marriage to a Canadian was included in his income for 1990 and was not tax exempt under the Tax Agreement with China since his presence in Canada was no longer a temporary one. *Li v. The Queen*, 94 DTC 6059 (F.C.A.)

► 115(2.1) ◄

(2.1) Non-resident actors. Notwithstanding subsection (1), where a non-resident person is liable to tax under subsection 212(5.1), or would if this Act were read without reference to subsection 212(5.2) be so liable, in respect of an amount paid, credited or provided in a particular taxation year, the amount shall not be included in computing the non-resident person's taxable income earned in Canada for any taxation year unless a valid election is made under subsection 216.1(1) in respect of the non-resident person for the particular year.

Editorial Note: Subsections 115(2.1) and (2.2) should be read in conjunction with s. 212(5.1), which applies a 23% withholding tax on certain payments made to (a) non-resident film and video actors, and (b) corporations related to such individuals. Subsections 115(2.1) and (2.2) provide that amounts received for acting services rendered in Canada will not under s. 115(1) be included in the non-resident person's — or related corporation's — "taxable income earned in Canada", unless a Part I tax return is filed and an election is made under s. 216.1 to include under Part I the amounts received in computing taxable income earned in Canada.

► 115(2.2) ◄

(2.2) Deferred payment by actor's corporation. Where a corporation is liable to tax under subsection 212(5.1) in respect of a corporation payment (within the meaning assigned by subsection 212(5.2)) made in a taxation year in respect of an actor and, in a subsequent year, the corporation makes an actor payment (within the meaning assigned by subsection 212(5.2)) to or for the benefit of the actor, the amount of the actor payment is not deductible in computing the income of the corporation for any taxation year and is not included in computing the taxable income earned in Canada of the actor for any taxation year.

Editorial Note: See the editorial note for s. 115(2.1).

► 115(2.3) ◄

(2.3) Non-resident persons — 2010 Olympic and Paralympic Winter Games. Notwithstanding subsection (1), no amount is to be included in computing the taxable income earned in Canada for any taxation year of a non-resident person, in respect of any amount paid or payable to that person in respect of activities performed in Canada by that person in connection with the 2010

Olympic Winter Games or the 2010 Paralympic Winter Games, after 2009 and before April 2010, if that person is

(*a*) an athlete who represents a country other than Canada;

(*b*) a member of an officially registered support staff associated with a team from a country other than Canada;

(*c*) a person who serves as a games official;

(*d*) the International Olympic Committee;

(*e*) the International Paralympic Committee;

(*f*) an international sports federation that is a member of the General Association of International Sports Federations;

(*g*) an accredited foreign media organization; or

(*h*) an individual, other than a trust, who is an employee, an officer or a member of a person described in any one or more of paragraphs (*a*) to (*g*), or who provides services under contract with one or more persons described in those paragraphs.

▶ 115(3) ◀

(3) Non-resident employed as aircraft pilot. For the purpose of applying subparagraph (1)(*a*)(i) to a non-resident person employed as an aircraft pilot, income of the non-resident person that is attributable to a flight (including a leg of a flight) and paid directly or indirectly by a person resident in Canada is attributable to duties performed in Canada in the following proportions:

(*a*) all of the income attributable to the flight if the flight departs from a location in Canada and arrives at a location in Canada;

(*b*) one-half of the income attributable to the flight if the flight departs from a location in Canada and arrives at a location outside Canada;

(*c*) one-half of the income attributable to the flight if the flight departs from a location outside Canada and arrives at a location in Canada; and

(*d*) none of the income attributable to the flight if the flight departs from a location outside Canada and arrives at a location outside Canada.

Editorial Note: Applicable to the 2013 and subsequent years, s. 115(3) provides that each leg of a "flight" (i.e., a take-off and landing) will constitute a flight in calculating non-resident pilots' income subject to Part I tax. For each departure from or arrival in a location in Canada, one-half of a non-resident pilot's income from the flight is to be considered taxable income earned in Canada. Income not attributable to any specific flight but received for services performed in Canada will be considered Canadian source.

History: S. 115(3) was added by S.C. 2013, c. 33, s. 8(1), applicable to the 2013 and subsequent taxation years.

Tax Window Files: Subsection 115(3), *September 7, 2016*, CRA Document No. 2014-0559751E5.

▶ 115(4) ◀

(4) Non-resident's income from Canadian resource property. Where a non-resident person ceases at any particular time in a taxation year to carry on such of the businesses described in any of paragraphs (*a*) to (*g*) of the definition "principal business corporation" in subsection 66(15) as were carried on by the non-resident person immediately before that time at one or more fixed places of business in Canada and either does not commence after that time and during the year to carry on any business so described at a fixed place of business in Canada or disposes of Canadian resource property at any time in the year during which the non-resident person was not carrying on any business so described at a fixed place of business in Canada, the following rules apply:

(*a*) the taxation year of the non-resident person that would otherwise have included the particular time shall be deemed to have ended at that time and a new taxation year shall be deemed to have commenced immediately thereafter;

(*b*) the non-resident person or any partnership of which the non-resident person was a member immediately after the particular time shall be deemed, for the purpose only of computing the non-resident person's income earned in Canada for the taxation year that is deemed to have ended, to have disposed immediately before the particular time of each Canadian resource property that was owned by the non-resident person or by the partnership immediately after the particular time and to have received therefor immediately before the particular time proceeds of disposition equal to the fair market value thereof at the particular time; and

(*c*) the non-resident person or any partnership of which the non-resident person was a member immediately after the particular time shall be deemed, for the purpose only of computing the non-resident person's income earned in Canada for a taxation year commencing after the particular time, to have reacquired immediately after the particular time, at a cost equal to the amount deemed by paragraph (*b*) to have been received by the non-resident person or the partnership as the proceeds of disposition therefor, each property deemed by that paragraph to have been disposed of.

Editorial Note: Where a non-resident person who has carried on certain resource business in Canada ceases to carry on that business, the deeming provisions in s. 115(4) will effectively negate or restrict the non-resident person's access to those income tax conventions that — by virtue of the non-resident person no longer having a permanent establishment in Canada — would otherwise have operated to limit the non-resident person's Canadian tax.

Related Regulations: Part XXVI.

Related Sections: S. 66.2(7) Exception; s. 66.4(7) Exception; s. 115(5) Interpretation of "partnership".

Interpretation Bulletins: *Secondary* — IT-125R4 Disposition of resource properties.

▶ 115(4.1) ◀

(4.1) Foreign resource pool expenses. Where a taxpayer ceases at any time after February 27, 2000 to be resident in Canada, a particular taxation year of the taxpayer ends after that time and the taxpayer was non-resident throughout the period (in this subsection referred to as the "non-resident period") that begins at that time and ends at the end of the particular year,

(*a*) in computing the taxpayer's taxable income earned in Canada for the particular year, there may be deducted each amount that would be permitted to be deducted in computing the taxpayer's income for the particular year under subsection 66(4) or 66.21(4) if

(i) subsection 66(4) were read without reference to the words "who is resident throughout a taxation year in Canada" and as if the amount determined under subparagraph 66(4)(*b*)(ii) were nil, and

(ii) subsection 66.21(4) were read without reference to the words "throughout which the taxpayer is resident in Canada" and as if the amounts determined under subparagraph 66.21(4)(*a*)(ii) and paragraph 66.21(4)(*b*) were nil; and

(*b*) an amount deducted under this subsection in computing the taxpayer's taxable income earned in Canada for the particular year is deemed, for the purpose of applying subsection 66(4) or 66.21(4), as the case may be, to a subsequent taxation year, to have been deducted in computing the taxpayer's income for the particular year.

Editorial Note: A non-resident taxpayer is precluded under s. 66(4) and 66.21(4) of the Act from claiming deductions for foreign exploration expenses and foreign resource expenses in a country in computing income. Subsection 115(4.1) permits a non-resident taxpayer to claim a deduction in computing taxable income earned in Canada with reference to the rules in those subsections.

► 115(5) ◄

(5) Interpretation of "partnership". For the purposes of subsection (4), "partnership" does not include a prescribed partnership.

Related Sections: S. 2(2) Taxable income; s. 4(1) Income or loss from a source or from sources in a place; s. 4(3) Deductions applicable; s. 38, "allowable capital losses", "taxable capital gains"; s. 54, "capital property"; s. 89(1), "public corporation"; s. 102 Definition of "Canadian partnership"; s. 104(1) Reference to trust or estate; s. 108(1), "capital interest", "income interest"; s. 108(2) When trust is a unit trust; s. 115(1) Non-resident's taxable income in Canada; s. 120(3) Definition of "the individual's income for the year"; s. 132(6) Meaning of "mutual fund trust"; s. 248(1), "amount", "business", "corporation", "employment", "individual", "non-resident", "office", "property", "taxable Canadian property"; s. 249 Definition of "taxation year"; s. 255 Canada.

► 115(6) ◄

(6) Application of s. 138(12). The definitions in subsection 138(12) apply to this section.

SECTION 115.1: Competent authority agreements

► 115.1(1) ◄

(1) Competent authority agreements. Notwithstanding any other provision of this Act, where the Minister and another person have, under a provision contained in a tax convention or agreement with another country that has the force of law in Canada, entered into an agreement with respect to the taxation of the other person, all determinations made in accordance with the terms and conditions of the agreement shall be deemed to be in accordance with this Act.

Related Sections: S. 255 Canada.

Canadian Petroleum Tax Journal: Taxable Canadian Property, Tony Van Rooyen, 2000, Vol. 13, No. 1.

Income Tax Folios: *Secondary* — S5-F2-C1 Foreign Tax Credit.

Interpretation Bulletins: *Secondary* — IT-173R2 Capital gains derived in Canada by residents of the United States.

► 115.1(2) ◄

(2) Transfer of rights and obligations. Where rights and obligations under an agreement described in subsection (1) have been transferred to another person with the concurrence of the Minister, that other person shall be deemed, for the purpose of subsection (1), to have entered into the agreement with the Minister.

Information Circulars: IC 71-17R5 Guidance on competent authority assistance under Canada's tax conventions.

SECTION 115.2: Non-Residents with Canadian Investment Service Providers

► 115.2(1) ◄

(1) Definitions. The definitions in this subsection apply in this section.

"Canadian investor" —"Canadian investor", at any time in respect of a non-resident person, means a person that the non-resident person knows, or ought to know after reasonable inquiry, is at that time resident in Canada.

"Canadian service provider" —"Canadian service provider" means a corporation resident in Canada, a trust resident in Canada or a Canadian partnership.

Related Sections: S. 102 Definition of "Canadian partnership".

"designated investment services" —"designated investment services" provided to a person or partnership means any one or more of the services described in the following paragraphs:

(*a*) investment management and advice with respect to qualified investments, regardless of whether the manager has discretionary authority to buy or sell;

(*b*) purchasing and selling qualified investments, exercising rights incidental to the ownership of qualified investments such as voting, conversion and exchange, and entering into and executing agreements with respect to such purchasing and selling and the exercising of such rights;

(*c*) investment administration services, such as receiving, delivering and having custody of investments, calculating and reporting investment values, receiving subscription amounts from, and paying distributions and proceeds of disposition to, investors in and beneficiaries of the person or partnership, record keeping, accounting and reporting to the person or partnership and its investors and beneficiaries; and

(*d*) in the case of a corporation, trust or partnership the only undertaking of which is the investing of its funds in qualified investments, marketing investments in the corporation, trust or partnership to non-resident investors.

"promoter" —"promoter" of a corporation, trust or partnership means a particular person or partnership that initiates or directs the founding, organization or substantial reorganization of the corporation, trust or partnership, and a person or partnership that is affiliated with the particular person or partnership.

"qualified investment" —"qualified investment" of a person or partnership means

(*a*) a share of the capital stock of a corporation, or an interest in a partnership, trust, entity, fund or organization, other than a share or an interest

(i) that is either

(A) not listed on a designated stock exchange, or

(B) listed on a designated stock exchange, if the person or partnership, together with all persons with whom the person or partnership does not deal at arm's length, owns 25% or more of the issued shares of any class of the capital stock of the corporation or of the total value of interests in the partnership, entity, trust, fund or organization, as the case may be, and

(ii) of which more than 50% of the fair market value is derived from one or more of

(A) real or immovable property situated in Canada,

(B) Canadian resource property, and

(C) timber resource property;

(*b*) indebtedness;

(*c*) annuities;

(*d*) commodities or commodities futures purchased or sold, directly or indirectly in any manner whatever, on a commodities or commodities futures exchange;

(*e*) currency; and

(*f*) options, interests, rights and forward and futures agreements in respect of property described in any of paragraphs (*a*) to (*e*) or this paragraph, and agreements under which obligations are derived from interest rates, from the price of property described in any of those paragraphs, from payments made in respect of such a property by its issuer to holders of the property, or from an index reflecting a composite measure of such rates, prices or payments, whether or not the agreement creates any rights in or obligations regarding the referenced property itself.

History: S. 115.2(1), clause (*a*)(ii)(A) of the definition "qualified investment" was replaced by S.C. 2013, c. 34, s. 124, in force June 26, 2013, and formerly read:

(A) real property situated in Canada,

Related Sections: S. 13(21), "timber resource property"; s. 66(15), "Canadian resource property"; s. 248(1), "annuity"; s. 262 Designated stock exchange.

"qualified non-resident" — (Repealed by S.C. 2002, c. 9, s. 35(1).)

► 115.2(2) ◄

(2) Not carrying on business in Canada. For the purposes of subsections 115(1) and 150(1) and Part XIV, a non-resident person is not considered to be carrying on business in Canada at any particular time solely because of the provision to the person, or to a partnership of which the person is a member, at the particular time of designated investment services by a Canadian service provider if

(*a*) in the case of services provided to a non-resident individual other than a trust, the individual is not affiliated at the particular time with the Canadian service provider;

(*b*) in the case of services provided to a non-resident person that is a corporation or trust,

(i) the person has not, before the particular time, directly or through its agents,

(A) directed any promotion of investments in itself principally at Canadian investors, or

(B) sold an investment in itself that is outstanding at the particular time to a person who was a Canadian investor at the time of the sale and who is a Canadian investor at the particular time,

(ii) the person has not, before the particular time, directly or through its agents, filed any document with a public authority in Canada in accordance with the securities legislation of Canada or of any province in order to permit the distribution of interests in the person to persons resident in Canada, and

(iii) when the particular time is more than one year after the time at which the person was created, the total of the fair market value, at the particular time, of investments in the person that are beneficially owned by persons and partnerships (other than a designated entity in respect of the Canadian service provider) that are affiliated with the Canadian service provider does not exceed 25% of the fair market value, at the particular time, of all investments in the person; and

(*c*) in the case of services provided to a partnership of which the non-resident person is a member,

(i) the particular time is not more than one year after the partnership was formed,

(ii) where the non-resident person is, or is affiliated with, a person or partnership described in clause (A) or (B), the total of the fair market value of all investments in the partnership at the particular time is not less than four times the total of the fair market value of each investment in the partnership beneficially owned at the particular time by

(A) a person or partnership (other than a designated entity in respect of the Canadian service provider), more than 25% of the total of the fair market value, at the particular time, of investments in which are beneficially owned by persons and partnerships (other than a designated entity in respect of the Canadian service provider) that are affiliated with the Canadian service provider, or

(B) a person or partnership (other than a designated entity in respect of the Canadian service provider) that is affiliated with the Canadian service provider, or

(iii) at the particular time, the non-resident person is not affiliated with the Canadian service provider and is not affiliated with any person or partnership (other than the partnership to which the services are provided) described in clause (ii)(A) or (B).

History: S. 115.2(2), before paragraph (*a*) was replaced by S.C. 2013, c. 34, s. 244(1), applicable to the 1999 and subsequent taxation years, and formerly read:

(2) *Not carrying on business in Canada.* For the purposes of subsection 115(1) and Part XIV, a non-resident person is not considered to be carrying on business in Canada at any particular time solely because of the provision to the person, or to a partnership of which the person is a member, at the particular time of designated investment services by a Canadian service provider if

S. 115.2(2)(*c*)(ii) was replaced and s. 115.2(2)(*c*)(iii) was added by S.C. 2013, c. 34, s. 244(2), applicable to the 2002 and subsequent taxation years, except that for the period that begins at the beginning of the 2002 taxation year of a taxpayer and that ends on October 31, 2011, paragraph 115.2(2)(*c*) does not apply to the taxpayer if the taxpayer so elects and files the election in writing with the Minister of National Revenue on or before the taxpayer's filing-due date for the taxpayer's taxation year that includes October 31, 2011.

S. 115.2(2)(c)(ii) formerly read:

(ii) the total of the fair market value, at the particular time, of investments in the partnership that are beneficially owned by persons and partnerships (other than a designated entity in respect of the Canadian service provider) that are affiliated with the Canadian service provider does not exceed 25% of the fair market value, at the particular time, of all investments in the partnership.

Related Sections: S. 115.2(3) Interpretation; s. 251.1(1) Definition of "affiliated persons"; s. 251.1(2) Affiliation where amalgamation or merger; s. 251.1(3) Definitions; s. 251.1(4) Interpretation.

Tax Profile: October 2011 — Hedge Funds and Private Equity Funds in Canada.

▶ 115.2(3) ◀

(3) Interpretation. For the purposes of this subsection and subparagraphs (2)(*b*)(iii) and (*c*)(ii),

(*a*) the fair market value of an investment in a corporation, trust or partnership shall be determined without regard to any voting rights attaching to that investment; and

(*b*) a person or partnership is, at a particular time, a designated entity in respect of a Canadian service provider if the total of the fair market value at the particular time, of investments in the entity that are beneficially owned by persons and partnerships (other than another designated entity in respect of the Canadian service provider) that are affiliated with the Canadian service provider does not exceed 25% of the fair market value, at the particular time, of all investments in the entity.

History: S. 115.2(3), the portion before paragraph (*a*) was replaced by S.C. 2013, c. 34, s. 244(3), applicable to the 2002 and subsequent taxation years, and formerly read:

(3) *Interpretation.* For the purpose of subparagraph (2)(*b*)(iii) and this subsection,

▶ 115.2(4) ◀

(4) Transfer pricing. For the purpose of section 247, where subsection (2) applies in respect of services provided to a person that is a corporation or trust or to a partnership, if the Canadian service provider referred to in that subsection does not deal at arm's length with the promoter of the person or of the partnership, the service provider is deemed not to deal at arm's length with the person or partnership.

▶ 115.2(5) ◀

(5) [Property of a Partnership] — (Repealed by S.C. 2013, c. 34, s. 244(5).)

History: S. 115.2(5) was repealed by S.C. 2013, c. 34, s. 244(5), deemed to have come into force on March 5, 2010, and formerly read:

(5) *Property of a partnership.* For the purpose of determining whether a non-resident person's interest in a partnership is, at any particular time before March 5, 2010, a taxable Canadian property, property of the partnership shall not be considered to be used or held by the partnership in a business carried on in Canada, if because of subsection (2) the non-resident person is not considered to be carrying on business in Canada at the particular time.

S. 115.2(5) was added by S.C. 2013, c. 34, s. 244(4), applicable to the 2008 and subsequent taxation years.

SECTION 116: Disposition by non-resident person of certain property

▶ 116(1) ◀

(1) Disposition by non-resident person of certain property. If a non-resident person proposes to dispose of any taxable Canadian property (other than property described in subsection (5.2) and excluded property) the non-resident person may, at any time before the disposition, send to the Minister a notice setting out

(*a*) the name and address of the person to whom he proposes to dispose of the property (in this section referred to as the "proposed purchaser");

(*b*) a description of the property sufficient to identify it;

(*c*) the estimated amount of the proceeds of disposition to be received by the non-resident person for the property; and

(*d*) the amount of the adjusted cost base to the non-resident person of the property at the time of the sending of the notice.

Editorial Note: Non-resident vendors of taxable Canadian property (other than property described in s. 116(5.2) or excluded property as defined in s. 116(6)) have two options under s. 116. First, they may file a prescribed form with the CRA before the disposition under s. 116(1), and upon paying the 25% tax on the estimated gain (or providing adequate security), will be issued the certificate under subsection (2). Alternatively, they may file a prescribed form within 10 days after the disposition under s. 116(3), and upon paying the 25% tax on the actual gain (or providing adequate security), will be issued the certificate under subsection (4). (The s. 116(3) filing is not required if the s. 116(1) route was chosen, generally if the estimated gain was equal to or greater than the actual gain.) Failure to obtain the certificate will normally result in the purchaser being liable to pay the tax on behalf of the non-resident vendor under s. 116(5) and being entitled to withhold such amount from the purchase price of the property. If the capital gain is treaty-exempt, the CRA will normally waive the requirement that the tax be paid or the security provided; see paragraphs 29 to 35 of Information Circular 72-17R6. For transfers of taxable Canadian property to a corporation under the rollover provisions of s. 85, see paragraphs 37 and 38 of the same circular. See ss. 116(5.2) and (5.3) for similar provisions dealing with a non-resident's disposition of a life insurance policy in Canada, a Canadian resource property, land inventory in Canada, a timber resource property, or a depreciable property that is a taxable Canadian property.

Related Sections: S. 115(1)(*b*) Non-resident's taxable income in Canada; s. 227(9) Penalty; s. 248(1), "taxable Canadian property".

Canadian Petroleum Tax Journal: Taxable Canadian Property, Tony Van Rooyen, 2000, Vol. 13, No. 1.

Canadian Tax Foundation: Oakey, *Non-Residents Owning Canadian Real Property*, 2013 Atlantic Provinces Tax Conference 2B:1–20; Choudhury and Connell, *Select Issues in the Purchase and Sale of a Business*, 2012 Ontario Tax Conference 11:1–31; Di Maio and Hutchinson, *Cross-Border Potpourri Issues for Small and Mid-Sized Businesses (Canada-U.S. Tax Treaty Update)*, 2012 Ontario Tax Conference 3:1–49; Bernstein and Choudhury, *Section 116 Notice*, 2011 Canadian Tax Highlights 19(3):2–3; Falk and Morand, *Section 116 Clearance Certificates*, 2010 British Columbia Tax Conference 12:1–41; Bernstein, *New Section 116 Certificates*, 2009 Canadian Tax Highlights 17(2):4–5; Sieker and Mercier, *Estate Planning Update*, 2008 Prairie Provinces Tax Conference 16:1–25; Bernstein, *Section 116 Certificates*, 2007 Canadian Tax Highlights 15(10):6–7; Moffat et al., *Certificate of Compliance and Waivers (Questions 4 to 6)*, 2005 British Columbia Tax Conference 19:3–5; Bernstein, *Section 116: Part 2*, 2005 Canadian Tax Highlights 13(11):8; Bernstein, *Section 116 Certificates*, 2005 Canadian Tax Highlights 13(10):7–8; Hickey, *Section 116 Applications*, 2004 Canadian Tax Highlights 12(11):6–7; Kakkar, *Partnerships: Compliance Issues — The Section 116 Requirements of a Non-Resident Partner*, 2003 Tax for the Owner-Manager 3(4):6–7; Lerman, *Hot Issues in Tax Compliance: Section 116 — Disposition of Canadian Property by Non-Residents*, 2002 Ontario Tax Conference 16:27–42; Marquette, *Selected Income Tax Issues of Particular Relevance to Shareholders Agreements: Part 2*, 2001 Canadian Tax Journal 2:407–437.

Tax Profile: March 2013 — Non-Resident Investment in Canadian Real Estate; October 2012 — Exchangeable Shares in Canada; September 2012 — Canadian Refundable Withholding Taxes — Traps; August 2012 — U.S. Purchases and Sales of Canadian Businesses: Tax and Corporate Issues; June 2012 — Use of Canadian Partnerships by Non-Residents; August 2011 — Canadian Share Dispositions by a Non-Resident — Taxable in Canada?; February 2009 — Section 116 Certificates — New Legislation Enacted; January 2009 — Enhancing Canada's International Tax Advantage; November 2008 — 2008 Cross-Border Developments in Canada; August 2008 — Fifth Protocol to the Canada–U.S. Tax Convention: A Canadian Perspective; January 2008 — Tax Ramifications of Non-Resident Purchases of Canadian Businesses; November 2007 — Section 116 Certificates — A Canadian Nightmare; May 2007 — Why Canada Should End Roadblock to Foreign Private Equity; December 2005 — Sales of Shares of Real Estate Companies by a Non-Resident of Canada — Canadian Tax Consequences.

Tax Topics: No. 2350, Section 116: Tips and Traps for the Unsuspecting Non-Resident; No. 2176, Escrow Arrangements in Acquisition Agreements: What Are You Creating?; No. 1911, Estate Distributions to Non-Residents; No. 1870, CRA Reverts to Its Original Position in IT-474R2; No. 1869, Happy New Year! How the CRA Has Lengthened the Wait Time for Section 116

Clearance Certificates; No. 1802, Non-Resident Partners and Canadian Real Estate; No. 1779, Application of Section 116 to Distributions by Canadian Resident Trusts to Non-Resident Beneficiaries; No. 1576, CCRA's Comments on Section 116 Issues.

Forms: NR301 — Declaration of Eligibility for Benefits under a Tax Treaty for a Non-Resident Taxpayer; NR302 — Declaration of Eligibility for Benefits under a Tax Treaty for a Partnership with Non-Resident Partner; NR303 — Declaration of Eligibility for Benefits under a Tax Treaty for a Hybrid Entity; T2 SCH 97 — Additional Information on Non-Resident Corporations in Canada; T1248 — Information About Your Residency Status; T1261 — Application for a Canada Revenue Agency Individual Tax Number (ITN) for Non-Residents; T2062 — Notice by a Non-Resident of Canada Concerning the Disposition or Proposed Disposition of Canadian Taxable Property; T2062A — Notice by a Non-Resident of Canada Concerning the Disposition or Proposed Disposition of Canadian Depreciable and/or Canadian Resource Properties; T2062A SCH 1 — Disposition of Canadian Resource Property by Non-Residents.

Guides: T4058 Non-Residents and Income Tax.

Income Tax Folios: *Secondary*— S4-F7-C1 Amalgamations of Canadian Corporations.

Income Tax Technical News: Issue No. 38, Anti-Discrimination Provisions.

Information Circulars: IC 72-17R6 Procedures concerning the disposition of taxable Canadian property by non-residents of Canada — Section 116.

Tax Window Files: Deemed Disposition of Property By Non-Resident, *Technical Interpretation, Reorganizations and Resources Division, June 13, 2005*, CRA Document No. 2005-0113981E5. Section 116 certificate not required for conversion by non-resident of personal-use property to income-earning property if subsection 45(2) or (3) election made; if no election, deemed disposition and certificate required; Distribution of Property by Non-Resident Estate, *Technical Interpretation, International and Trusts Division, February 1, 2005*, CRA Document No. 2004-0083201E5. Section 116 certificate required for distribution of taxable Canadian property from non-resident trust to non-resident beneficiary.

Cases: The non-resident taxpayer sold its shares of a Canadian corporation and the purchaser paid $5,350,603 to the Receiver General in escrow under s. 116. The taxpayer's assessment (and refund) was delayed by a GAAR audit. The taxpayer's application for an order of *mandamus* requiring such assessment together with the release of the $5,350,603 was dismissed because the GAAR audit constituted "special circumstances" justifying the Minister's delay in issuing the assessment. *Merlis Investments Limited v. The Queen*, 2000 DTC 6634 (F.C.T.D.).

► 116(2) ◄

(2) Certificate in respect of proposed disposition. Where a non-resident person who has sent to the Minister a notice under subsection (1) in respect of a proposed disposition of any property has

(*a*) paid to the Receiver General, as or on account of tax under this Part payable by the non-resident person for the year, 25% of the amount, if any, by which the estimated amount set out in the notice in accordance with paragraph (1)(*c*) exceeds the amount set out in the notice in accordance with paragraph (1)(*d*), or

(*b*) furnished the Minister with security acceptable to the Minister in respect of the proposed disposition of the property,

the Minister shall forthwith issue to the non-resident person and the proposed purchaser a certificate in prescribed form in respect of the proposed disposition, fixing therein an amount (in this section referred to as the "certificate limit") equal to the estimated amount set out in the notice in accordance with paragraph (1)(*c*).

Tax Topics: No. 2350, Section 116: Tips and Traps for the Unsuspecting Non-Resident.

► 116(3) ◄

(3) Notice to Minister. Every non-resident person who in a taxation year disposes of any taxable Canadian property of that person (other than property described in subsection (5.2) and excluded property) shall, not later than 10 days after the disposition, send to the Minister, by registered mail, a notice setting out

(*a*) the name and address of the person to whom the non-resident person disposed of the property (in this section referred to as the "purchaser"),

(*b*) a description of the property sufficient to identify it, and

(*c*) a statement of the proceeds of disposition of the property and the amount of its adjusted cost base to the non-resident person immediately before the disposition,

unless the non-resident person has, at any time before the disposition, sent to the Minister a notice under subsection (1) in respect of any proposed disposition of that property and

(*d*) the purchaser was the proposed purchaser referred to in that notice,

(*e*) the estimated amount set out in that notice in accordance with paragraph (1)(*c*) is equal to or greater than the proceeds of disposition of the property, and

(*f*) the amount set out in that notice in accordance with paragraph (1)(*d*) does not exceed the adjusted cost base to the non-resident person of the property immediately before the disposition.

Editorial Note: Paragraphs 116(3)(*d*) to (*f*) become relevant when a certificate was applied for prior to the property's disposition but the transaction is completed in a manner different to that originally reported by the non-resident. Where a second notice to the Minister is required, s. 116(3) requires that it be sent by registered mail no later than 10 days after the disposition.

Related Sections: S. 54, "adjusted cost base", "proceeds of disposition"; s. 238(1) Offences and punishment.

Tax Profile: March 2013 — Non-Resident Investment in Canadian Real Estate; August 2011 — Canadian Share Dispositions by a Non-Resident — Taxable in Canada?; February 2009 — Section 116 Certificates — New Legislation Enacted; January 2009 — Enhancing Canada's International Tax Advantage; November 2008 — 2008 Cross-Border Developments in Canada; August 2008 — Fifth Protocol to the Canada–U.S. Tax Convention: A Canadian Perspective; November 2007 — Section 116 Certificates — A Canadian Nightmare; December 2005 — Sales of Shares of Real Estate Companies by a Non-Resident of Canada — Canadian Tax Consequences.

Tax Topics: No. 2087, Is an Estate Not a Trust For All Purposes of the Income Tax Act?; No. 1911, Estate Distributions to Non-Residents.

Forms: T2062 — Notice by a Non-Resident of Canada Concerning the Disposition or Proposed Disposition of Canadian Taxable Property; T2062A — Notice by a Non-Resident of Canada Concerning the Disposition or Proposed Disposition of Canadian Depreciable and/or Canadian Resource Properties; T2062A SCH 1 — Disposition of Canadian Resource Property by Non-Residents.

Income Tax Technical News: Issue No. 38, Anti-Discrimination Provisions.

Information Circulars: IC 72-17R6 Procedures concerning the disposition of taxable Canadian property by non-residents of Canada — Section 116.

Tax Window Files: Deemed Disposition of Property By Non-Resident, *Technical Interpretation, Reorganizations and Resources Division, June 13, 2005*, CRA Document No. 2005-0113981E5. Section 116 certificate not required for conversion by non-resident of personal-use property to income-earning property if subsection 45(2) or (3) election made; if no election, deemed disposition and certificate required; Distribution of Property by Non-Resident Estate, *Technical Interpretation, International and Trusts Division, February 1, 2005*, CRA Document No. 2004-0083201E5. Section 116 certificate required for distribution of taxable Canadian property from non-resident trust to non-resident beneficiary.

Cases: The corporate taxpayer was a trust company acting as the trustee of self-administered RRSPs. It acquired shares from a non-resident vendor without obtaining a s. 116 clearance or remitting the non-resident's deemed tax. Despite arguments it was not the beneficial owner but merely a bare trustee, the taxpayer was indeed the "purchaser" as contemplated in s. 116(3). *Olympia Trust Company v. The Queen*, 2015 DTC 5134 (F.C.A.).

► 116(4) ◄

(4) Certificate in respect of property disposed of. Where a non-resident person who has sent to the Minister a notice under subsection (3) in respect of a disposition of any property has

(*a*) paid to the Receiver General, as or on account of tax under this Part payable by the non-resident person for the year, 25% of the amount, if any, by which the proceeds of disposition of the property exceed the adjusted cost base to the non-resident person of the property immediately before the disposition, or

(*b*) furnished the Minister with security acceptable to the Minister in respect of the disposition of the property,

the Minister shall forthwith issue to the non-resident person and the purchaser a certificate in prescribed form in respect of the disposition.

Editorial Note: Where s. 116(3) requires that a second notice be sent to the Minister, the non-resident *per* s. 116(4) can remit an amount (or post security for it) so that — together with any earlier remittance — the total amount paid to the Receiver General is 25% of the excess of the taxpayer's actual proceeds of disposition over the taxpayer's adjusted cost base at the time of disposition.

Information Circulars: IC 72-17R6 Procedures concerning the disposition of taxable Canadian property by non-residents of Canada — Section 116.

Cases: Furnishing the Minister with security did not constitute the actual payment of tax. *King v. M.N.R.*, 91 DTC 651 (T.C.C.)

► 116(5) ◄

(5) Liability of purchaser. Where in a taxation year a purchaser has acquired from a non-resident person any taxable Canadian property (other than depreciable property or excluded property) of the non-resident person, the purchaser, unless

(*a*) after reasonable inquiry the purchaser had no reason to believe that the non-resident person was not resident in Canada,

Tax Window Files: Paragraph 116(5)(a) - reasonable inquiry, *August 25, 2017*, CRA Document No. 2017-0703351E5.

(*a*.1) subsection (5.01) applies to the acquisition, or

(*b*) a certificate under subsection (4) has been issued to the purchaser by the Minister in respect of the property,

is liable to pay, and shall remit to the Receiver General within 30 days after the end of the month in which the purchaser acquired the property, as tax under this Part for the year on behalf of the non-resident person, 25% of the amount, if any, by which

(*c*) the cost to the purchaser of the property so acquired

exceeds

(*d*) the certificate limit fixed by the certificate, if any, issued under subsection (2) in respect of the disposition of the property by the non-resident person to the purchaser,

and is entitled to deduct or withhold from any amount paid or credited by the purchaser to the non-resident person or otherwise recover from the non-resident person any amount paid by the purchaser as such a tax.

Related Sections: S. 227(9) Penalty.

Canadian Tax Foundation: MacArthur, *Current Cases — Trustee Liability Under Subsection 116(5)*, 2017 Canadian Tax Journal 2:444–453.

Tax Topics: No. 2438, An Unsworn Declaration That a Vendor Was Not a Resident in Canada Was Not a "Reasonable Inquiry" Under Paragraph 116(5)(*a*) Given Red Flags; No. 2350, Section 116: Tips and Traps for the Unsuspecting Non-Resident; No. 1892, Proposed Changes to Section 116 of the *Income Tax Act*; No. 1779, Application of Section 116 to Distributions by Canadian Resident Trusts to Non-Resident Beneficiaries.

Information Circulars: IC 72-17R6 Procedures concerning the disposition of taxable Canadian property by non-residents of Canada — Section 116.

► 116(5.01) ◄

(5.01) Treaty-protected property. This subsection applies to the acquisition of a property by a person (referred to in this subsection as the "purchaser") from a non-resident person if

(*a*) the purchaser concludes after reasonable inquiry that the non-resident person is, under a tax treaty that Canada has with a particular country, resident in the particular country;

(*b*) the property would be treaty-protected property of the non-resident person if the non-resident person were, under the tax treaty referred to in paragraph (*a*), resident in the particular country; and

(*c*) the purchaser provides notice under subsection (5.02) in respect of the acquisition.

Editorial Note: A purchaser is not required to remit 25% of the purchase price to the Receiver General if s. 116(5.01) applies to the acquisition of taxable Canadian property. S. 116(5.01) applies to such acquisition if (a) the purchaser concludes after reasonable inquiry that the vendor is resident in a treaty jurisdiction; (b) the property would be treaty-protected property of the non-resident person if the non-resident person were resident in the treaty jurisdiction; and (c) the purchaser provides notice under s. 116(5.02). There is little guidance about what will constitute a reasonable inquiry as to whether the vendor is resident in a country with which Canada has a tax treaty. If the purchaser incorrectly concludes that the property is treaty-protected property, the purchaser may be liable for the 25% tax. In most cases, it may be unlikely that an arm's length purchaser would be able to verify that the property is treaty-protected property. As such, it is doubtful that an arm's length purchaser would be willing to assume this risk and therefore, would most likely withhold the 25% tax. The effect of this provision may be to reduce the number of applications for s. 116 clearance certificates for transfers of taxable Canadian property between non-arm's length parties but that the effect on the number of applications between arm's length parties will likely be minimal.

Tax Profile: August 2011 — Canadian Share Dispositions by a Non-Resident — Taxable in Canada?; September 2009 — Is It Necessary To Comply with Section 116 of the *Income Tax Act* if the Property is Treaty-Exempt Property?.

Tax Topics: No. 2044, No Section 116 Safe Harbour; No. 1962, Another NRT seeks Judicial Review: *Morris and Smith v. M.N.R.*.

Forms: T2062C — Notification of an Acquisition of Treaty-Protected Property from a Non-Resident Vendor.

► 116(5.02) ◄

(5.02) Notice by purchaser in respect of an acquisition of property. A person (referred to in this subsection as the "purchaser") who acquires property from a non-resident person provides notice under this subsection in respect of the acquisition if the purchaser sends to the Minister, on or before the day that is 30 days after the date of the acquisition, a notice setting out

(*a*) the date of the acquisition;

(*b*) the name and address of the non-resident person;

(*c*) a description of the property sufficient to identify it;

(*d*) the amount paid or payable, as the case may be, by the purchaser for the property; and

(*e*) the name of the country with which Canada has concluded a tax treaty under which the property is a treaty-protected property for the purposes of subsection (5.01) or (6.1), as the case may be.

Tax Profile: September 2009 — Is It Necessary To Comply with Section 116 of the *Income Tax Act* if the Property is Treaty-Exempt Property?.

Tax Topics: No. 2044, No Section 116 Safe Harbour.

▶ 116(5.1) ◀

(5.1) Gifts, etc. If a non-resident person has disposed of or proposes to dispose of a life insurance policy in Canada, a Canadian resource property or a taxable Canadian property other than

(*a*) excluded property, or

(*b*) property that has been transferred or distributed on or after the non-resident person's death and as a consequence thereof

to any person by way of gift *inter vivos* or to a person with whom the non-resident person was not dealing at arm's length for no proceeds of disposition or for proceeds of disposition less than the fair market value of the property at the time the non-resident person so disposed of it or proposes to dispose of it, as the case may be, the following rules apply:

(*c*) the reference in paragraph (1)(*c*) to "the proceeds of disposition to be received by the non-resident person for the property" shall be read as a reference to "the fair market value of the property at the time the non-resident person proposes to dispose of it",

(*d*) the references in subsections (3) and (4) to "the proceeds of disposition of the property" shall be read as references to "the fair market value of the property immediately before the disposition",

(*e*) the references in subsection (5) to "the cost to the purchaser of the property so acquired" shall be read as references to "the fair market value of the property at the time it was so acquired", and

(*f*) the reference in subsection (5.3) to "the amount payable by the taxpayer for the property so acquired" shall be read as a reference to "the fair market value of the property at the time it was so acquired".

Editorial Note: S. 116(5.1) provides special rules for *inter vivos* gifts and non-arm's length transactions which take place at less than fair market value. Where the property is a life insurance policy in Canada, a Canadian resource property or any taxable Canadian property, the transferor is required to report the fair market value of the property rather than the actual proceeds of disposition and the liability for taxes payable under s. 116(4) or 116(5) is based on the fair market value of the property and not the actual proceeds of disposition. These rules do not apply when the property transferred is excluded property as defined in s. 116(6) or where property is transferred or distributed on or as a consequence of a person's death.

Related Sections: S. 54, "proceeds of disposition"; s. 248(1), "non-resident", "taxable Canadian property"; s. 251(1) Arm's length.

Tax Topics: No. 1962, Another NRT seeks Judicial Review: *Morris and Smith v. M.N.R.*

Forms: T2062B — Notice of Dispositions of Life Insurance Policies in Canada by a Non-Resident of Canada; T2062B SCH 1 — Certification and Remittance Notice.

▶ 116(5.2) ◀

(5.2) Certificates for dispositions. If a non-resident person has, in respect of a disposition, or a proposed disposition, in a taxation year to a taxpayer of property (other than excluded property) that is a life insurance policy in Canada, a Canadian resource property, a property (other than capital property) that is real property, or an immovable, situated in Canada, a timber resource property, depreciable property that is a taxable Canadian property or any interest in, or for civil law any right in, or any option in respect of, a property to which this subsection applies (whether or not that property exists),

(*a*) paid to the Receiver General, as or on account of tax under this Part payable by the non-resident person for the year, such amount as is acceptable to the Minister in respect of the disposition or proposed disposition of the property, or

(*b*) furnished the Minister with security acceptable to the Minister in respect of the disposition or proposed disposition of the property,

the Minister shall forthwith issue to the non-resident person and to the taxpayer a certificate in prescribed form in respect of the disposition or proposed disposition fixing therein an amount equal to the proceeds of disposition, proposed proceeds of disposition or such other amount as is reasonable in the circumstances.

History: S. 116(5.2), the portion before paragraph (*a*) was replaced by S.C. 2016, c. 12, s. 41(1), in force January 1, 2017, and formerly read:

(5.2) *Certificates for dispositions.* If a non-resident person has, in respect of a disposition, or a proposed disposition, in a taxation year to a taxpayer of property (other than excluded property) that is a life insurance policy in Canada, a Canadian resource property, a property (other than capital property) that is real property, or an immovable, situated in Canada, a timber resource property, depreciable property that is a taxable Canadian property, eligible capital property that is a taxable Canadian property or any interest in, or for civil law any right in, or any option in respect of, a property to which this subsection applies (whether or not that property exists),

S. 116(5.2), the portion before paragraph (*a*) was replaced by S.C. 2013, c. 34, s. 245(1), deemed to have come into force on December 24, 1998, and formerly read:

(5.2) *Certificates for dispositions.* If a non-resident person has, in respect of a disposition or proposed disposition to a taxpayer in a taxation year of property (other than excluded property) that is a life insurance policy in Canada, a Canadian resource property, a property (other than capital property) that is real property situated in Canada, a timber resource property, depreciable property that is a taxable Canadian property or any interest in or option in respect of a property to which this subsection applies (whether or not that property exists),

▶ 116(5.3) ◀

(5.3) Liability of purchaser in certain cases. Where in a taxation year a taxpayer has acquired from a non-resident person property referred to in subsection (5.2),

(*a*) the taxpayer, unless subsection (5.01) applies to the acquisition or unless after reasonable inquiry the taxpayer had no reason to believe that the non-resident person was not resident in Canada, is liable to pay, as tax under this Part for the year on behalf of the non-resident person, 50% of the amount, if any, by which

(i) the amount payable by the taxpayer for the property so acquired

exceeds

(ii) the amount fixed in the certificate, if any, issued under subsection (5.2) in respect of the disposition of the property by the non-resident person to the taxpayer

and is entitled to deduct or withhold from any amount paid or credited by the taxpayer to the non-resident person or to otherwise recover from the non-resident person any amount paid by the taxpayer as such a tax; and

(*b*) the taxpayer shall, within 30 days after the end of the month in which the taxpayer acquired the property, remit to the Receiver General the tax for which the taxpayer is liable under paragraph (*a*).

Tax Topics: No. 1892, Proposed Changes to Section 116 of the *Income Tax Act*

Information Circulars: IC 72-17R6 Procedures concerning the disposition of taxable Canadian property by non-residents of Canada — Section 116.

► 116(5.4) ◄

(5.4) Presumption. Where there has been a disposition by a non-resident of a life insurance policy in Canada by virtue of subsection 148(2) or any of paragraphs (*a*) to (*c*) and (*e*) of the definition "disposition" in subsection 148(9), the insurer under the policy shall, for the purposes of subsections (5.2) and (5.3) be deemed to be the taxpayer who acquired the property for an amount equal to the proceeds of disposition as determined under section 148.

► 116(6) ◄

(6) Definition of "excluded property". For the purposes of this section, "excluded property" of a non-resident person means

(*a*) a property that is a taxable Canadian property solely because a provision of this Act deems it to be a taxable Canadian property;

(*a*.1) a property (other than real or immovable property situated in Canada, a Canadian resource property or a timber resource property) that is described in an inventory of a business carried on in Canada by the person;

(*b*) a security that is

(i) listed on a recognized stock exchange, and

(ii) either

(A) a share of the capital stock of a corporation, or

(B) SIFT wind-up entity equity;

(*c*) a unit of a mutual fund trust;

(*d*) a bond, debenture, bill, note, mortgage, hypothecary claim or similar obligation;

(*e*) property of a non-resident insurer that

(i) is licensed or otherwise authorized under the laws of Canada or a province to carry on an insurance business in Canada, and

(ii) carries on an insurance business, within the meaning of subsection 138(1) of the Act, in Canada;

(*f*) property of an authorized foreign bank that carries on a Canadian banking business;

(*g*) an option in respect of property referred to in any of paragraphs (*a*) to (*f*) whether or not such property is in existence;

(*h*) an interest, or for civil law a right, in property referred to in any of paragraphs (*a*) to (*g*); and

(*i*) a property that is, at the time of its disposition, a treaty-exempt property of the person.

History: S. 116(6)(*a*.1) was replaced by S.C. 2013, c. 34, s. 125(1), in force June 26, 2013, and formerly read:

(*a*.1) a property (other than real property situated in Canada, a Canadian resource property or a timber resource property) that is described in an inventory of a business carried on in Canada by the person;

S. 116(6)(*h*) was amended by S.C. 2013, c. 34, s. 125(2), in force June 26, 2013, and formerly read:

(*h*) an interest in property referred to in any of paragraphs (*a*) to (*g*); and

S. 116(6)(*f*) was replaced by S.C. 2013, c. 34, s. 245(2), deemed to have come into force on June 28, 1999, and formerly read:

(*f*) property of an authorized foreign bank that is used or held in the course of the bank's Canadian banking business;

S. 116(6)(*b*) was replaced by S.C. 2009, c. 2, s. 32(1), applicable after July 14, 2008. S. 116(6)(*b*) formerly read:

(*b*) a share of a class of shares of the capital stock of a corporation that is listed on a recognized stock exchange;

Related Regulations: 810.

Related Sections: 40(3) Deemed gain where amounts to be deducted from adjusted cost base exceed cost plus amounts to be added to adjusted cost base; 40(3.1) Deemed gain for certain partners; S. 54, "adjusted cost base"; S. 55(6) Unlisted shares deemed listed; s. 248(1), "non-resident", "property", "taxable Canadian property"; s. 249 Definition of "taxation year"; s. 255 Canada.

Tax Profile: November 2008 — 2008 Cross-Border Developments in Canada.

Tax Topics: No. 1892, Proposed Changes to Section 116 of the *Income Tax Act*.

► 116(6.1) ◄

(6.1) Treaty-exempt property. For the purpose of subsection (6), a property is a treaty-exempt property of a non-resident person, at the time of the non-resident person's disposition of the property to another person (referred to in this subsection as the "purchaser"), if

(*a*) it is, at that time, a treaty-protected property of the non-resident person; and

(*b*) where the purchaser and the non-resident person are related at that time, the purchaser provides notice under subsection (5.02) in respect of the disposition.

Editorial Note: S. 116(6.1), effective beginning after 2008, provides that property is a "treaty-exempt property" of a non-resident person if it is a "treaty-protected property" (defined in s. 248(1)) of the non-resident person. Where the vendor and the purchaser are related, a property will be a treaty-exempt property if it is a "treaty-protected property" and the purchaser provides notice under s. (5.02) in respect of the disposition.

Related Sections: 40(3) Deemed gain where amounts to be deducted from adjusted cost base exceed cost plus amounts to be added to adjusted cost base; 40(3.1) Deemed gain for certain partners.

► 116(7) ◄

(7) Application of s. 138(12). The definitions in subsection 138(12) apply to this section.

Division E — Computation of Tax

Subdivision a — Rules Applicable to Individuals

SECTION 117: Tax payable under this Part

► 117(1) ◄

(1) Tax payable under this Part. For the purposes of this Division, except section 120 (other than subparagraph (*a*)(ii) of the definition "tax otherwise payable under this Part" in subsection 120(4)), tax payable under this Part, tax otherwise payable under this Part and tax under this Part shall be computed as if this Part were read without reference to Division E.1.

► 117(2) ◄

(2) Rates for taxation years after 2015. The tax payable under this Part by an individual on the individual's taxable income or taxable income earned in Canada, as the case may be (in this subdivision referred to as the "amount taxable") for a taxation year is

(*a*) 15% of the amount taxable, if the amount taxable is equal to or less than the amount determined for the taxation year in respect of $45,282;

(*b*) if the amount taxable is greater than $45,282, but is equal to or less than $90,563, the maximum amount determinable in respect of the taxation year under paragraph (*a*), plus 20.5% of the amount by which the amount taxable exceeds $45,282 for the year;

(*c*) if the amount taxable is greater than $90,563, but is equal to or less than $140,388, the maximum amount determinable in respect of the taxation year under paragraph (*b*), plus 26% of the amount by which the amount taxable exceeds $90,563 for the year;

(*d*) if the amount taxable is greater than $140,388, but is equal to or less than $200,000, the maximum amount determinable in respect of the taxation year under paragraph (*c*), plus 29% of the amount by which the amount taxable exceeds $140,388 for the year; and

(*e*) if the amount taxable is greater than $200,000, the maximum amount determinable in respect of the taxation year under paragraph (*d*), plus 33% of the amount by which the amount taxable exceeds $200,000 for the year.

CRA News Release

2.2% Indexation Factor for 2019

See the CRA Fact Sheet, dated November 16, 2018, that is reproduced following subsection117.1(1). This release announces a 2.2% indexation factor applicable for 2019 tax bracket thresholds, personal amounts and other amounts relating to non-refundable credits, as well as the refundable medical expense supplement, Old Age Security repayment threshold, certain board and lodging allowances, and the tradesperson's tools deduction. Increases to tax bracket thresholds, amounts relating to non-refundable credits, and most other amounts will take effect on January 1, 2019. However, increases in amounts for certain income-tested benefits (for example, the goods and services tax credit) will take effect on July 1, 2019.

History: S. 117(2) was replaced by S.C. 2016, c. 11, s. 1(1), applicable to the 2016 and subsequent taxation years, and formerly read:

(2) *Rates for taxation years after 2008.* The tax payable under this Part by an individual on the individual's taxable income or taxable income earned in Canada, as the case may be (in this subdivision referred to as the "amount taxable") for a taxation year is

(*a*) 15% of the amount taxable, if the amount taxable is equal to or less than the amount determined for the taxation year in respect of $40,726;

(*b*) if the amount taxable is greater than $40,726 and is equal to or less than $81,452, the maximum amount determinable in respect of the taxation year under paragraph (*a*), plus 22% of the amount by which the amount taxable exceeds $40,726 for the year;

(*c*) if the amount taxable is greater than $81,452, but is equal to or less than $126,264, the maximum amount determinable in respect of the taxation year under paragraph (*b*), plus 26% of the amount by which the amount taxable exceeds $81,452 for the year; and

(*d*) if the amount taxable is greater than $126,264, the maximum amount determinable in respect of the taxation year under paragraph (*c*), plus 29% of the amount by which the amount taxable exceeds $126,264 for the year.

S. 117(2) was replaced by S.C. 2009, c. 2, s. 33(1), applicable to the 2009 and subsequent taxation years. S. 117(2) formerly read:

(2) *Rates for taxation years after 2006.* The tax payable under this Part by an individual on the individual's taxable income or taxable income earned in Canada, as the case may be (in this subdivision referred to as the "amount taxable") for a taxation year is

(*a*) 15% of the amount taxable, if the amount taxable is equal to or less than the amount determined for the taxation year in respect of $36,378;

(*b*) if the amount taxable is greater than the amount determined for the year in respect of $36,378 and is equal to or less than the amount determined for the year in respect of $72,756, the amount determined in respect of the taxation year under paragraph (*a*) plus 22% of the amount by which the amount taxable exceeds the amount determined in respect of $36,378 for the year;

(*c*) if the amount taxable is greater than the amount determined for the year in respect of $72,756, but is equal to or less than the amount determined for the year in respect of $118,285, the total of the amounts determined in respect of the taxation year under paragraphs (*a*) and (*b*) plus 26% of the amount by which the amount taxable exceeds the amount determined in respect of $72,756; and

(*d*) if the amount taxable is greater than the amount that would be determined for the year in respect of $118,285, the total of the amounts determined in respect of the taxation year under paragraphs (*a*), (*b*) and (*c*) plus 29% of the amount by which the amount taxable exceeds the amount determined in respect of $118,285.

Related Sections: 117.1(1) Annual adjustment.

► 117(2.1) ◄

(2.1) Tax payable — WITB advance payment. The tax payable under this Part on the individual's taxable income for a taxation year, as computed under subsection (2), is deemed to be the total of the amount otherwise computed under that subsection and, except for the purposes of sections 118 to 118.9, 120.2, 121, 122.3 and subdivision c, the total of all amounts received by the individual in respect of the taxation year under subsection 122.7(7).

Editorial Note: The working income tax benefit (WITB) advance payments received by a taxpayer for a taxation year are deemed under s. 117(2.1) to be included in the individual's tax payable for the year. The individual is required to file a tax return for the year, and to pay interest on the tax payable on the advance payments. For example, if the individual ceases to qualify for a WITB after having filed an application with the CRA, he or she may have to refund and to pay interest on a portion of those advance payments. The advance payments are not part of the tax payable for the purpose of calculating the minimum tax carryover and most tax credits claimed on the tax return.

Related Sections: S. 150(1) Filing returns of income — general rule s. 150(1.1)(*b*)(i) Exception; s. 161(1) Interest.

Guides: RC4227 Working Income Tax Benefit.

► 117(3) ◄

(3) Minimum thresholds for 2004. Each of the amounts of $30,754, $61,509 and $100,000 referred to in subsection (2) is deemed, for the purposes of applying subsection (2) to the 2004 taxation year, to be the greater of

(*a*) the amount that would be used for the 2004 taxation year if this section were read without reference to this subsection; and

(*b*) in the case of

(i) the amount of $30,754, $35,000,

(ii) the amount of $61,509, $70,000, and

(iii) the amount of $100,000, $113,804.

► 117(4)-(5.1) ◄

(4)-(5.1) — (Repealed by 1985, c. 45, s. 62(1).)

► 117(5.2) ◄

(5.2) 1982 and subsequent taxation years rates — (Repealed by 1988, c. 55, s. 90(3).)

► 117(6) ◄

(6) Special table — (Repealed by S.C. 2000, c. 19, s. 22(2).)

Related Regulations: 2500; 2501.

► 117(7) ◄

(7) Notch provision — (Repealed by S.C. 1994, c. 7, Sched. VII, s. 6(1)).)

SECTION 117.1: Annual adjustment

► 117.1(1) ◄

(1) Annual adjustment. The amount of $1,000 referred to in the formula in paragraph 8(1)(*s*), each of the amounts expressed in dollars in subparagraph 6(1)(*b*)(v.1), subsection 117(2), the description of B in subsection 118(1), subsection 118(2), paragraph (*a*) of the description of B in subsection 118(10), subsection 118.01(2), the descriptions of C and F in subsection 118.2(1) and subsections 118.3(1), 122.5(3) and 122.51(1) and (2), the amount of $400,000 referred to in the formula in paragraph 110.6(2)(*a*), the amounts of $925 and $1,680 referred to in the description of A, and the amounts of $10,500 and $14,500 referred to in the description of B, in the formula in subsection 122.7(2), the amount of $462.50 referred to in the description of C, and the amounts of $16,667 and $25,700 referred to in the description of D, in the formula in subsection 122.7(3), and each of the amounts expressed in dollars in Part I.2 in relation to tax payable under this Part or Part I.2 for a taxation year shall be adjusted so that the amount to be used under those provisions for the year is the total of

Amendment not yet in force

Budget Implementation Act, 2019, No. 1 [S.C. 2019, c. 29]

S. 117.1(1), the portion before paragraph (*a*) was replaced by S.C. 2019, c. 29, s. 14(1), and will read as follows:

SECTION 117.1 (1) Annual adjustment. The amount of $1,000 referred to in the formula in paragraph 8(1)(*s*), each of the amounts expressed in dollars in subparagraph 6(1)(*b*)(v.1), subsection 117(2), the description of B in subsection 118(1), subsection 118(2), paragraph (*a*) of the description of B in subsection 118(10), subsection 118.01(2), the descriptions of C and F in subsection 118.2(1) and subsections 118.3(1), 122.5(3) and 122.51(1) and (2), the amount of $400,000 referred to in the formula in paragraph 110.6(2)(*a*), the amounts of $1,355 and $2,335 referred to in the description of A, and the amounts of $12,820 and $ 17,025 referred to in the description of B, in the formula in subsection 122.7(2), the amount of $700 referred to in the description of C, and the amounts of $24,111 and $36,483 referred to in the description of D, in the formula in subsection 122.7(3), the amount of $10,000 referred to in the description of B in the formula in subsection 122.91(2), and each of the amounts expressed in dollars in Part I.2 in relation to tax payable under this Part or Part I.2 for a taxation year shall be adjusted so that the amount to be used under those provisions for the year is the total of

Applicable: To the 2020 and subsequent taxation years, except that the adjustment provided for in subsection 117.1(1) does not apply for the 2020 taxation year in respect of the amount of $10,000.

(*a*) the amount that would, but for subsection (3), be the amount to be used under those provisions for the preceding taxation year, and

(*b*) the product obtained by multiplying

(i) the amount referred to in paragraph (*a*)

by

(ii) the amount, adjusted in such manner as may be prescribed and rounded to the nearest one-thousandth, or, where the result obtained is equidistant from two consecutive one-thousandths, to the higher thereof, that is determined by the formula

$$(A/B) - 1$$

where

A is the Consumer Price Index for the 12 month period that ended on September 30 next before that year, and

B is the Consumer Price Index for the 12 month period immediately preceding the period mentioned in the description of A.

CRA News Release

2.2% Indexation Factor for 2019

[Reproduced below is a CRA Fact Sheet, released on November 16, 2018, that sets out a 2.2% indexation factor for various figures relating to personal income tax, including the 2019 income tax thresholds, personal credit amounts, the Canada child benefit and the GST/HST Credit. Although the Fact Sheet does not list the indexed amounts relating to the Working Income Tax Benefit in subsections 122.7(2) and (3), indexing also applies to these amounts as set out in subsection 117.1(1) in the Act.]

Increases to tax bracket thresholds, amounts relating to non-refundable credits, and most other amounts below take effect on January 1 of the applicable year.

Increases in amounts for certain income-tested benefits like the goods and services tax credit, the Canada child benefit[4] and Child disability benefit,[5] take effect on July 1 to coincide with the beginning of the program year for payments of these benefits.

[4] Under changes announced by the Government on October 24, 2017, the Canada child benefit is indexed starting July 2018 using the 2017 as the base year.

[5] Changes announced in the 2016 Federal Budget to the Child disability benefit were effective July 1, 2016. Under changes announced by the Government on October 24, 2017, the Child disability benefit is indexed starting July 2018.

The following chart provides the indexed amounts for four tax years.

Indexation amounts in $

Description	2019	2018	2017	2016
Indexation increase	2.2%	1.5%	1.4%	1.3%
Tax bracket thresholds				
Taxable income above which the 20.5% bracket begins	47,630	46,605	45,916	45,282
Taxable income above which the 26% bracket begins	95,259	93,208	91,831	90,563
Taxable income above which the 29% bracket begins	147,667	144,489	142,353	140,388
Taxable income above which the 33% bracket begins	210,371	205,842	202,800	200,000
Amounts relating to non-refundable tax credits				
Basic personal amount	12,069	11,809	11,635	11,474
Age amount	7,494	7,333	7,225	7,125
Net income threshold for age amount	37,790	36,976	36,430	35,927
Spouse or common-law partner amount (maximum)	12,069	11,809	11,635	11,474
Spouse or common-law partner amount (maximum if dependant eligible for the Canada caregiver amount)[1]	14,299	13,991	13,785	13,595
Amount for an eligible dependant (maximum)	12,069	11,809	11,635	11,474
Amount for an eligible dependant (maximum if dependant eligible for the Canada caregiver amount)[1]	14,299	13,991	13,785	13,595
Canada caregiver amount for children under age 18[1]	2,230	2,182	2,150	2,121
Canada employment amount (maximum)	1,222	1,195	1,178	1,161
Infirm dependant amount (maximum per dependant)[1]	NA	NA	NA	6,788
Net income threshold for infirm dependant amount[1]	NA	NA	NA	6,807
Caregiver amount (maximum per dependant)[1]	NA	NA	NA	4,667
Caregiver amount (maximum per dependant eligible for the family caregiver amount)[1]	NA	NA	NA	6,788
Net income threshold for caregiver amount	NA	NA	NA	15,940
Canada caregiver amount for other infirm dependants age 18 or older (maximum amount)[1]	7,140	6,986	6,883	NA
Net income threshold for Canada caregiver amount[1]	16,766	16,405	16,163	NA
Disability amount	8,416	8,235	8,113	8,001
Supplement for children with disabilities (maximum)	4,909	4,804	4,733	4,667
Threshold relating to allowable child care and attendant care expenses	2,875	2,814	2,772	2,734
Adoption expenses (maximum per adoption)	16,255	15,905	15,670	15,453
Medical expense tax credit (3% of net income ceiling)	2,352	2,302	2,268	2,237
Refundable medical expense supplement				
Maximum supplement	1,248	1,222	1,203	1,187
Minimum earnings threshold	3,645	3,566	3,514	3,465
Family net income threshold	27,639	27,044	26,644	26,277
Old age security repayment				
Old age security repayment threshold	77,580	75,910	74,788	73,756
Certain board and lodging allowances paid to players on sports teams or members of recreation programs				
Income exclusion (maximum per month)	366	359	353	348
Tradesperson's tools deduction				
Threshold amount relating to cost of eligible tools	1,222	1,195	1,178	1,161
Goods and services tax/harmonized sales tax credit				
Adult maximum	290	284	280	276
Child maximum	153	149	147	145
Single supplement	153	149	147	145
Phase-in threshold for the single supplement	9,412	9,209	9,073	8,948
Family net income at which credit begins to phase out	37,789	36,976	36,429	35,926
Tax-free savings account				
Annual TFSA dollar limit[2]	6,000	5,500	5,500	5,500

[1] As of 2017, the new Canada caregiver amount has replaced the family caregiver amount, the amount for infirm dependants age 18 or older and the caregiver amount.

[2] Under changes announced by the Government in a Department of Finance news release on December 7, 2015, for 2016 and each subsequent year, the annual TFSA dollar limit is fixed at 5,000, indexed to inflation for each year after 2009, and rounded to the nearest $500.

Lifetime capital gains exemption for qualified farm or fishing property and qualified small business corporation shares[3]				
Exemption limit	866,912	848,252	835,716	824,176
Deduction limit (since 1/2 of the capital gain is taxable)	433,456	424,126	417,858	412,088
Additional exemption amount for qualified farm or fishing property	133,088	151,748	164,284	175,824
Additional deduction amount for qualified farm or fishing property (since 1/2 of the capital gain is taxable)	66,544	75,874	82,142	87,912
Canada child benefit (CCB)[4]				
CCB (base benefit, child under age 6)	6,639	6,496	6,400	6,400
CCB (base benefit, child aged 6 to 17)	5,602	5,481	5,400	5,400
Adjusted family net income at which phase out begins	31,120	30,450	30,000	30,000
Second phase out threshold	67,426	65,975	65,000	65,000
Base phase out amount for one eligible child	2,541	2,487	2,450	2,450
Base phase out amount for two eligible children	4,901	4,796	4,725	4,725
Base phase out amount for three eligible children	6,898	6,750	6,650	6,650
Base phase out amount for four or more eligible children	8,351	8,171	8,050	8,050
Child disability benefit (CDB)[5]				
Maximum benefit	2,832	2771	2730	2730
Family net income threshold for phase out	67,426	65,975	65,000	65,000
Children's special allowance (CSA)[6]				
CSA base amount	[6]	[6]	[6]	[6]

History: S. 117.1(1), the portion before paragraph *(a)*, was replaced by S.C. 2018, c. 12, s. 10(1), applicable to the 2019 and subsequent taxation years, except that the adjustment provided for in subsection 117.1(1) does not apply for the 2019 taxation year in respect of the amounts of $1,355, $2,335, $12,820, $17,025, $700, $24,111 and $36,483. S. 117.1(1), the portion before paragraph *(a)* formerly read:

(1) *Annual adjustment.* The amount of $1,000 referred to in the formula in paragraph 8(1)*(s)*, each of the amounts expressed in dollars in subparagraph 6(1)*(b)*(v.1), subsection 117(2), the description of B in subsection 118(1), subsection 118(2), paragraph *(a)* of the description of B in subsection 118(10), subsection 118.01(2), the descriptions of C and F in subsection 118.2(1) and subsections 118.3(1), 122.5(3) and 122.51(1) and (2), the amount of $400,000 referred to in the formula in paragraph 110.6(2)*(a)*, the amounts of $1,355 and $2,335 referred to in the description of A, and the amounts of $12,820 and $17,025 referred to in the description of B, in the formula in subsection 122.7(2), the amount of $700 referred to in the description of C, and the amounts of $24,111 and $36,483 referred to in the description of D, in the formula in subsection 122.7(3), and each of the amounts expressed in dollars in Part I.2 in relation to tax payable under this Part or Part I.2 for a taxation year shall be adjusted so that the amount to be used under those provisions for the year is the total of

S. 117.1(1) was replaced by S.C. 2016, c. 14, s. 67(1), applicable to 2019 and subsequent taxation years, except that the adjustment provided for in subsection 117.1(1) does not apply for the 2019 taxation year in respect of the amounts of $1,192, $2,165, $20,844 and $32,491. However, this amendment was repealed by S.C. 2018, c. 12, s. 39. S. 117.1(1), as it was replaced by S.C. 2016, c. 14, s. 67(1), read as follows:

117.1(1) *Annual adjustment.* The amount of $1,000 referred to in the formula in paragraph 8(1)*(s)*, each of the amounts expressed in dollars in subparagraph 6(1)*(b)*(v.1), subsection 117(2), the description of B in subsection 118(1), subsection 118(2), paragraph *(a)* of the description of B in subsection 118(10), subsection 118.01(2), the descriptions of C and F in subsection 118.2(1) and subsections 118.3(1), 122.5(3) and 122.51(1) and (2), the amount of $400,000 referred to in the formula in paragraph 110.6(2)*(a)*, the amounts of $1,192 and $2,165 referred to in the description of A, and the amounts of $10,500 and $14,500 referred to in the description of B, in the formula in subsection 122.7(2), the amount of $462.50 referred to in the description of C, and the amounts of $20,844 and $32,491 referred to in the description of D, in the formula in subsection 122.7(3), and each of the amounts expressed in dollars in Part I.2 in relation to tax payable under this Part or Part I.2 for a taxation year shall be adjusted so that the amount to be used under those provisions for the year is the total of

S. 117.1(1), the portion before paragraph *(a)* was replaced by S.C. 2013, c. 40, s. 49(1), applicable to the 2015 and subsequent taxation years, and formerly read:

(1) *Annual adjustment.* The amount of $1,000 referred to in the formula in paragraph 8(1)*(s)*, each of the amounts expressed in dollars in subparagraph 6(1)*(b)*(v.1), subsection 117(2), the description of B in subsection 118(1), subsection 118(2), paragraph *(a)* of the description of B in subsection 118(10), subsection 118.01(2), the descriptions of C and F in subsection 118.2(1), subsections 118.3(1), 122.5(3) and 122.51(1) and (2), the amounts of $925 and $1,680 referred to in the description of A, and the amounts of $10,500 and $14,500 referred to in the description of B, in the formula in subsection 122.7(2), the amount of $462.50 referred to in the description of C, and the amounts of $16,667 and $25,700 referred to in the description of D, in the formula in subsection 122.7(3), and each of the amounts expressed in dollars in Part I.2 in relation to tax payable under this Part or Part I.2 for a taxation year shall be adjusted so that the amount to be used under those provisions for the year is the total of

S. 117.1(1), the portion before paragraph *(a)* was replaced by S.C. 2010, c. 25, s. 22(1), applicable to the 2009 and subsequent taxation years. S. 117.1(1), the portion before paragraph *(a)* formerly read:

S. 117.1 *Annual Adjustment of Deductions and Other Amounts.* (1) *Annual adjustment.* The amount of $1,000 referred to in the formula in paragraph 8(1)*(s)*, each of the amounts expressed in dollars in subparagraph 6(1)*(b)*(v.1), subsection 117(2), the description of B in subsection 118(1), subsection 118(2), paragraph *(a)* of the description of B in subsection 118(10), subsection 118.01(2), the descriptions of C and F in subsection 118.2(1), subsections 118.3(1), 122.5(3) and 122.51(1) and (2), the amounts of $500 and $1,000 referred to in the description of A, and the amounts of $9,500 and $14,500 referred to in the description of B, in the formula in subsection 122.7(2), the amount of $250 referred to in the description of C, and the amounts of $12,833 and $21,167 referred to in the description of D, in the formula in subsection 122.7(3), and each of the amounts expressed in dollars in Part I.2 in relation to tax payable under this Part or Part I.2 for a taxation year shall be adjusted so that the amount to be used under those provisions for the year is the total of

Related Sections: S. 117.1(4) Consumer Price Index; s. 122.91(2) Training amount limit; s. 249(1) Definition of "taxation year".

► 117.1(1.1) ◄

(1.1) Adjustment of certain amounts — (Repealed by S.C. 2017, c. 20, s. 11(1).)

History: S. 117.1(1.1) was repealed by S.C. 2017, c. 20, s. 11(1), applicable to the 2017 and subsequent taxation years, and formerly read:

(1.1) *Adjustment of certain amounts.* Notwithstanding any other provision of this section, for the purpose of making the adjustment provided under

[3] Under changes announced in the 2015 Federal Budget, the lifetime capital gains exemption applicable to capital gains realized on the disposition of qualified farm or fishing property, disposed of after April 20, 2015, is the greater of (1) $1 million and (2) the indexed lifetime capital gains exemption applicable to capital gains realized on the disposition of qualified small business corporation shares.

[6] Under changes announced in the 2016 Federal Budget, the Children's special allowance is based on the Canada child benefit, effective July 1, 2016. The benefit is the same as the Canada child benefit plus the Child disability benefit (where applicable). However there is no phase out for the Children's special allowance. See the Canada child benefit amounts for the two age groups. Under changes announced by the Government on October 24, 2017, the Canada child benefit and the Child disability benefit are indexed starting July 2018, therefore the Children's special allowance is indexed starting then as well.

subsection (1) for the 2000 taxation year, the amounts used for the 1999 taxation year

(*a*) in respect of the amounts of $6,000, $5,000 and $500 referred to in paragraphs (*a*), (*b*) and (*c*) of the description of B in subsection 118(1) and the amount of $625 referred to in subparagraph 180.2(4)(*a*)(ii) are deemed to be $7,131, $6,055, $606 and $665, respectively; and

(*b*) in respect of the amounts of $6,456 and $4,103 referred to in paragraph (*d*) of the description of B in subsection 118(1) are deemed to be $7,131 and $4,778, respectively.

▶ 117.1(2) ◀

(2) Idem — (Repealed by S.C. 2000, c. 19, s. 23(2).)

Related Sections: S. 117.1(1) Annual adjustment (indexing).

▶ 117.1(3) ◀

(3) Rounding. Where an amount referred to in this section, when adjusted as provided in this section, is not a multiple of one dollar, it shall be rounded to the nearest multiple of one dollar or, where it is equidistant from two such consecutive multiples, to the higher thereof.

▶ 117.1(4) ◀

(4) Consumer Price Index. In this section, the Consumer Price Index for any 12 month period is the result arrived at by

(*a*) aggregating the Consumer Price Index for Canada, as published by Statistics Canada under the authority of the *Statistics Act*, adjusted in such manner as is prescribed, for each month in that period;

(*b*) dividing the aggregate obtained under paragraph (*a*) by twelve; and

(*c*) rounding the result obtained under paragraph (*b*) to the nearest one-thousandth or, where the result obtained is equidistant from two consecutive one-thousandths, to the higher thereof.

▶ 117.1(5) ◀

(5) Idem — (Repealed by 1986, c. 6, s. 65(5).)

▶ 117.1(6) ◀

(6) Rounding of amounts — (Repealed by 1988, c. 55, s. 91(1).)

▶ 117.1(7) ◀

(7) Determination of "Consumer Price Index for a 12 month period" — (Repealed by 1988, c. 55, s. 91(1).)

▶ 117.1(7.1) ◀

(7.1) Annual adjustment of amounts expressed in dollars — (Repealed by 1985, c. 45, s. 63(3).)

▶ 117.1(8) ◀

(8) Limitation — (Repealed by 1986, c. 6, s. 65(7).)

SECTION 118: Personal credits

▶ 118(1) ◀

(1) Personal credits. For the purpose of computing the tax payable under this Part by an individual for a taxation year, there may be deducted an amount determined by the formula

$$A \times B$$

where

A is the appropriate percentage for the year, and

B is the total of,

▶ 118(1)(a) ◀

(a) Married or common-law partnership status — in the case of an individual who at any time in the year is a married person or a person who is in a common-law partnership who supports the individual's spouse or common-law partner and is not living separate and apart from the spouse or common-law partner by reason of a breakdown of their marriage or common-law partnership, an amount equal to the total of

(i) $10,527, and

(ii) the amount determined by the formula

$$\$10{,}527 + C - C.1$$

where

C is

(A) $2,150 if the spouse or common-law partner is dependent on the individual by reason of mental or physical infirmity, and

(B) in any other case, nil, and

C.1 is the income of the individual's spouse or common-law partner for the year or, if the individual and the individual's spouse or common-law partner are living separate and apart at the end of the year because of a breakdown of their marriage or common-law partnership, the spouse's or common-law partner's income for the year while married to, or in a common-law partnership with, the individual and not so separated,

CRA News Release

2.2% Indexation Factor for 2019

See the CRA Fact Sheet, dated November 16, 2018, that is reproduced following subsection117.1(1). This release announces a 2.2% indexation factor applicable for 2019 tax bracket thresholds, personal amounts and other amounts relating to non-refundable credits, as well as the refundable medical expense supplement, Old Age Security repayment threshold, certain board and lodging allowances, and the tradesperson's tools deduction. Increases to tax bracket thresholds, amounts relating to non-refundable credits, and most other amounts will take effect on January 1, 2019. However, increases in amounts for certain income-tested benefits (for example, the goods and services tax credit) will take effect on July 1, 2019.

Editorial Note: Paragraph 118(1)(*a*) allows an individual who is married or in a common-law partnership at any time during a year to claim a personal tax credit, but only if he/she actually supports his/her spouse or common-law partner at any time in the year. The term "support" means the payment of expenses like utilities, taxes, insurance, and repairs for the maintenance of a household. A full credit may be claimed even if the partner is supported for only part of the year (e.g., if they got married or if the other partner died during the year). The higher income spouse is normally considered to support the lower income spouse. To qualify for the credit, the partners could not be living separately because of a breakdown in their relationship but could be living separately because of illness or out-of-town employment. The credit is non-refundable, which means that it cannot be claimed if the individual has no tax payable before claiming it. If the spouse or common-law partner is disabled, an additional Canada caregiver tax credit may be claimed.

History: S. 118(1), clause (A) of the description of C in subparagraph (*a*)(ii) of the description of B was replaced by S.C. 2017, c. 20, s. 12(1), applicable to the 2017 and subsequent taxation years. However, for the 2017 taxation year, subsection 117.1(1) does not apply in respect of amounts expressed in dollars in clause (A) of the description of C in subparagraph (*a*)(ii) of the description of B in subsection 118(1). Clause (A) of the description of C in subparagraph (*a*)(ii) of the description of B formerly read:

(A) $2,000 if the spouse or common-law partner is dependent on the individual by reason of mental or physical infirmity, and

S. 118(1), subparagraphs (*a*)(i) and (ii) of the description of B were replaced by S.C. 2011, c. 24, s. 23(1), applicable to the 2011 and subsequent taxation years, except that

(a) for the 2011 taxation year, the reference to "$2,000" is to be read as a reference to "nil";

(b) for the 2011 taxation year, subsection 117.1(1) does not apply for the purposes of computing the amounts to be used under paragraphs (*a*), (*b*), (*b.1*), (*c.1*) and (*d*) of the description of B in subsection 118(1) [No indexing of these amounts for 2011];

(c) for the 2012 taxation year, subsection 117.1(1) does not apply in respect of the amount of $2,000 referred to in paragraphs (*a*), (*b*), (*b.1*), (*c.1*) and (*d*) of the description of B in subsection 118(1) [No indexing of $2,000 amount for 2012].

S. 118(1), subparagraphs (*a*)(i) and (ii) of the description of B formerly read:

(i) $10,320, and

(ii) the amount determined by the formula

$$10,320 - C$$

where

C is the income of the individual's spouse or common-law partner for the year or, where the individual and the individual's spouse or common-law partner are living separate and apart at the end of the year because of a breakdown of their marriage or common-law partnership, the spouse's or common-law partner's income for the year while married to, or in a common-law partnership with, the individual and not so separated,

S. 118(1), the portion of paragraph (*a*) of the description of B before the description of C was replaced by S.C. 2009, c. 2, s. 34(1), applicable to the 2009 and subsequent taxation years. S. 118(1), the portion of paragraph (*a*) of the description of B before the description of C formerly read:

(*a*) *Married or common-law partnership status* — in the case of an individual who at any time in the year is a married person or a person who is in a common-law partnership who supports the individual's spouse or common-law partner and is not living separate and apart from the spouse or common-law partner by reason of a breakdown of their marriage or common-law partnership, an amount equal to the total of

(i) $7,131, and

(ii) the amount determined by the formula

$$6,055 - C$$

where

S. 118(1), the description of C in subparagraph (*a*)(ii) of the description of B was replaced by S.C. 2009, c. 2, s. 34(2), applicable to the 2009 and subsequent taxation years. S. 118(1), the description of C in subparagraph (*a*)(ii) of the description of B formerly read:

C is the income of the individual's spouse or common-law partner for the year or, where the individual and the individual's spouse or common-law partner are living separate and apart at the end of the year because of a breakdown of their marriage or common-law partnership, the spouse's income for the year while married to, or in a common-law partnership with, the individual and not so separated,

Related Sections: S. 60(*b*) Support; s. 60(*c*) Pension income reallocation; s. 82(3) Dividends received by spouse or common-law partner; s. 118(3.1) Additions to personal credits — basic personal amount; s. 118(3.2) Additions to personal credits — spouse or common-law partner or wholly dependent person; s. 118(4) Limitations re s. (1); s. 118(5) Support; s. 118(5.1) Where subsection (5) does not apply; s. 248(1), "common-law partner", and "common-law partnership".

Income Tax Folios: *Primary* — S1-F4-C1 Basic Personal and Dependant Tax Credits.

Cases: Prior to 1993, common-law spouses were not considered married for purposes of the *Income Tax Act*. See *No. 673 v. M.N.R.*, 60 DTC 21 (T.A.B.); *Schapira v. M.N.R.*, 66 DTC 157 (T.A.B.); and *Sokil v. M.N.R.*, 68 DTC 314 (T.A.B.)

► 118(1)(b) ◄

(b) Wholly dependent person — in the case of an individual who does not claim a deduction for the year because of paragraph (*a*) and who, at any time in the year,

(i) is

(A) a person who is unmarried and who does not live in a common-law partnership, or

(B) a person who is married or in a common-law partnership, who neither supported nor lived with their spouse or common law-partner and who is not supported by that spouse or common-law partner, and

(ii) whether alone or jointly with one or more other persons, maintains a self-contained domestic establishment (in which the individual lives) and actually supports in that establishment a person who, at that time, is

(A) except in the case of a child of the individual, resident in Canada,

(B) wholly dependent for support on the individual, or the individual and the other person or persons, as the case may be,

(C) related to the individual, and

(D) except in the case of a parent or grandparent of the individual, either under 18 years of age or so dependent by reason of mental or physical infirmity,

an amount equal to the total of

(iii) $10,527, and

(iv) the amount determined by the formula

$$10,527 + D - D.1$$

where

D is

(A) $2,150 if

(I) the dependent person is, at the end of the taxation year, 18 years of age or older and is, at any time in the year, dependent on the individual by reason of mental or physical infirmity, or

(II) the dependent person is a person, other than a child of the individual in respect of whom paragraph (*b.1*) applies, who, at the end of the taxation year, is under the age of 18 years and who, by reason of mental or physical infirmity, is likely to be, for a long and continuous period of indefinite duration, dependent on others for significantly more assistance in attending to the dependent person's personal needs and care, when compared to persons of the same age, and is so dependent on the individual at any time in the year, and

(B) in any other case, nil, and

D.1 is the dependent person's income for the year,

> **CRA News Release**
>
> **2.2% Indexation Factor for 2019**
>
> **See the CRA Fact Sheet, dated November 16, 2018, that is reproduced following subsection117.1(1). This release announces a 2.2% indexation factor applicable for 2019 tax bracket thresholds, personal amounts and other amounts relating to non-refundable credits, as well as the refundable medical expense supplement, Old Age Security repayment threshold, certain board and lodging allowances, and the tradesperson's tools deduction. Increases to tax bracket thresholds, amounts relating to non-refundable credits, and most other amounts will take effect on January 1, 2019. However, increases in amounts for certain income-tested benefits (for example, the goods and services tax credit) will take effect on July 1, 2019.**

Editorial Note: Paragraph 118(1)(*b*) allows an individual who is single, separated, divorced, or widowed at any time in the year or who has a spouse or common-law partner whom he/she does not support and does not live with during that year to claim a personal tax credit for an eligible dependant provided he/she maintains a self-contained domestic establishment in which he/she lives with that dependant. The establishment may be a dwelling house, apartment, or similar place of residence owned or rented where he/she eats and sleeps. A hotel room or boarding house where an individual sleeps but does not eat would not qualify for the credit. An eligible dependant would include a Canadian-resident parent or grandparent, another Canadian-resident relative infirm or under 18, or a child infirm or under 18 regardless of his/her residence. The credit is non-refundable, which means that it cannot be claimed if the individual has no tax payable before claiming it. If the eligible dependant is disabled, an additional Canada caregiver tax credit may be claimed.

History: S. 118(1), the portion of clause (A) before subclause (I) of the description of D in subparagraph (*b*)(iv) of the description of B was replaced by S.C. 2017, c. 20, s. 12(2), applicable to the 2017 and subsequent taxation years. However, for the 2017 taxation year, subsection 117.1(1) does not apply in respect of amounts expressed in dollars in clause (A) of the description of D in subparagraph (*b*)(iv) of the description of B in subsection 118(1). The portion of clause (A) before subclause (I) of the description of D in subparagraph (*b*)(iv) of the description of B formerly read:

(A) $2,000 if

S. 118(1), subparagraphs (*b*)(iii) and (iv) of the description of B was replaced by S.C. 2011, c. 24, s. 23(2), applicable to the 2011 and subsequent taxation years, except that

(a) for the 2011 taxation year, the reference to "$2,000" is to be read as a reference to "nil"

(b) for the 2011 taxation year, subsection 117.1(1) of the Act does not apply for the purposes of computing the amounts to be used under paragraphs (*a*), (*b*), (*b.1*), (*c.1*) and (*d*) of the description of B in subsection 118(1) [No indexing of these amounts for 2011];

(c) for the 2012 taxation year, subsection 117.1(1) of the Act does not apply in respect of the amount of $2,000 referred to in paragraphs (*a*), (*b*), (*b.1*), (*c.1*) and (*d*) of the description of B in subsection 118(1) [No indexing of $2,000 amount for 2012].

S. 118(1), subparagraphs (*b*)(iii) and (iv) of the description of B formerly read:

(iii) $10,320, and

(iv) the amount determined by the formula

$10,320 - D

where

D is the dependent person's income for the year,

S. 118(1), subparagraphs (*b*)(iii) and (iv) of the description of B were replaced by S.C. 2009, c. 2, s. 34(4), applicable to the 2009 and subsequent taxation years. S. 118(1), subparagraphs (*b*)(iii) and (iv) of the description of B formerly read:

(iii) $7,131, and

(iv) the amount determined by the formula

$6,055 - D

where

D is the dependent person's income for the year,

Related Sections: S. 118(1)(*e*) Additional amount; s. 118(3.1) Additions to personal credits — basic personal amount; s. 118(3.2) Additions to personal credits — spouse or common-law partner or wholly dependent person; s. 118(4) Limitations re s. (1); s. 118(5) Support; s. 118(5.1) Where subsection (5) does not apply; s. 248(1), "self-contained domestic establishment"; s. 252(1) Extended meaning of "child"; s. 252(2) Relationships.

Forms: T1 SCH 5 — Amounts for Spouse or Common-law Partner and Dependants.

Income Tax Folios: *Primary* — S1-F4-C1 Basic Personal and Dependant Tax Credits.

Tax Window Files: Eligibility: caregiver amount for infirm child, *July 26, 2018*, CRA Document No. 2017-0721711E5.

► 118(1)(b.1) ◄

(b.1) Caregiver amount for infirm child — $2,150 for each child, who is under the age of 18 years at the end of the taxation year, of the individual and who, by reason of mental or physical infirmity, is likely to be, for a long and continuous period of indefinite duration, dependent on others for significantly more assistance in attending to the child's personal needs and care, when compared to children of the same age if

(i) the child ordinarily resides throughout the taxation year with the individual together with another parent of the child, or

(ii) except if subparagraph (i) applies, the individual

(A) may deduct an amount under paragraph (*b*) in respect of the child, or

(B) could deduct an amount under paragraph (*b*) in respect of the child if

(I) paragraph (4)(*a*) and the reference in paragraph (4)(*b*) to "or the same domestic establishment" did not apply to the individual for the taxation year, and

(II) the child had no income for the year,

CRA News Release

2.2% Indexation Factor for 2019

See the CRA Fact Sheet, dated November 16, 2018, that is reproduced following subsection117.1(1). This release announces a 2.2% indexation factor applicable for 2019 tax bracket thresholds, personal amounts and other amounts relating to non-refundable credits, as well as the refundable medical expense supplement, Old Age Security repayment threshold, certain board and lodging allowances, and the tradesperson's tools deduction. Increases to tax bracket thresholds, amounts relating to non-refundable credits, and most other amounts will take effect on January 1, 2019. However, increases in amounts for certain income-tested benefits (for example, the goods and services tax credit) will take effect on July 1, 2019.

Editorial Note: Since 2015, the child tax credit can no longer be claimed for a non-disabled child but the family caregiver tax credit (before 2017) or Canada caregiver tax credit (after 2016) may continue to be claimed for a physically or mentally disabled child.

History: S. 118(1), the portion of paragraph (*b.1*) before subparagraph (i) of the description of B was replaced by S.C. 2017, c. 20, s. 12(3), applicable to the 2017 and subsequent taxation years. However, for the 2017 taxation year, subsection 117.1(1) does not apply in respect of amounts expressed in dollars in paragraph (*b.1*) of the description of B in subsection 118(1). The portion of paragraph (*b.1*) before subparagraph (i) of the description of B formerly read:

(*b.1*) *Family caregiver amount for child* — $2,000 for each child, who is under the age of 18 years at the end of the taxation year, of the individual and who, by reason of mental or physical infirmity, is likely to be, for a long and continuous period of indefinite duration, dependent on others for significantly more assistance in attending to the child's personal needs and care, when compared to children of the same age if

S. 118(1), paragraph (*b.1*) of the description of B was replaced by S.C. 2015, c. 36, s. 30(1), applicable to the 2015 and subsequent taxation years. For the purpose of making the adjustment provided under subsection 117.1(1) of the Act as it applies to paragraph (*b.1*) of the description of B in subsection 118(1) of the Act, as enacted by this amendment, the amount to be used in the 2015 taxation year for the preceding taxation year is the amount under clause (*b.1*)(i)(B) of the description of B in subsection 118(1) of the Act that would, but for subsection 117.1(3) of the Act, be the amount to be used under that clause for the 2014 taxation year.

S. 118(1), paragraph (*b.1*) of the description of B formerly read:

(*b.1*) **Child amount** — if

(i) a child, who is under the age of 18 years at the end of the taxation year, of the individual ordinarily resides throughout the taxation year with the individual together with another parent of the child, the total of

(A) $2,131 for each such child, and

(B) $2,000 for each such child who, by reason of mental or physical infirmity, is likely to be, for a long and continuous period of indefinite duration, dependent on others for significantly more assistance in attending to the child's personal needs and care, when compared to children of the same age, or

(ii) except where subparagraph (i) applies, the individual may deduct an amount under paragraph (*b*) in respect of the individual's child who is under the age of 18 years at the end of the taxation year, or could deduct such an amount in respect of that child if paragraph (4)(*a*) and the reference in paragraph (4)(*b*) to "or the same domestic establishment" did not apply to the individual for the taxation year and if the child had no income for the year, the total of

(A) $2,131 for each such child, and

(B) $2,000 for each such child who, by reason of mental or physical infirmity, is likely to be, for a long and continuous period of indefinite duration, dependent on others for significantly more assistance in attending to the child's personal needs and care, when compared to children of the same age,

S. 118(1), paragraph (*b.1*) of the description of B was replaced by S.C. 2011, c. 24, s. 23(3), applicable to the 2011 and subsequent taxation years, except that

(a) for the 2011 taxation year, the reference to "$2,000" is to be read as a reference to "nil";

(b) for the 2011 taxation year, subsection 117.1(1) of the Act does not apply for the purposes of computing the amounts to be used under paragraphs (*a*), (*b*), (*b.1*), (*c.1*) and (*d*) of the description of B in subsection 118(1) [No indexing of these amounts for 2011];

(c) for the 2012 taxation year, subsection 117.1(1) of the Act does not apply in respect of the amount of $2,000 referred to in paragraphs (*a*), (*b*), (*b.1*), (*c.1*) and (*d*) of the description of B in subsection 118(1) [No indexing of $2,000 amount for 2012].

S. 118(1), paragraph (*b.1*) of the description of B formerly read:

(*b.1*) *Child amount* — where

(i) a child of the individual ordinarily resides throughout the taxation year with the individual together with another parent of the child, $2,000 for each such child who is under the age of 18 years at the end of the taxation year, or

(ii) except where subparagraph (i) applies, the individual may deduct an amount under paragraph (*b*) in respect of the individual's child who is under the age of 18 years at the end of the taxation year, or could deduct such an amount in respect of that child if paragraph 118(4)(*a*) did not apply to the individual for the taxation year and if the child had no income for the year, $2,000 for each such child.

Related Sections: S. 117.1(1) Annual adjustment (indexing); s. 118(3.1) Additions to personal credits — basic personal amount; s. 118(4) Limitations re s. (1); s. 118(5) Support; s. 118(5.1) Where subsection (5) does not apply; s. 118.8 Transfer of unused credits to spouse or common-law partner. s. 118(9.1) Child tax credit.

Income Tax Folios: *Primary* — S1-F4-C1 Basic Personal and Dependant Tax Credits.

Tax Window Files: Eligibility: caregiver amount for infirm child, *July 26, 2018*, CRA Document No. 2017-0721711E5.

► 118(1)(c) ◄

(c) Single status — except in the case of an individual entitled to a deduction because of paragraph (*a*) or (*b*), $10,320,

CRA News Release

2.2% Indexation Factor for 2019

See the CRA Fact Sheet, dated November 16, 2018, that is reproduced following subsection117.1(1). This release announces a 2.2% indexation factor applicable for 2019 tax bracket thresholds, personal amounts and other amounts relating to non-refundable credits, as well as the refundable medical expense supplement, Old Age Security repayment threshold, certain board and lodging allowances, and the tradesperson's tools deduction. Increases to tax bracket thresholds, amounts relating to non-refundable credits, and most other amounts will take effect on January 1, 2019. However, increases in amounts for certain income-tested benefits (for example, the goods and services tax credit) will take effect on July 1, 2019.

Editorial Note: Paragraph 118(1)(*c*) allows an individual who is single, separated, divorced, or widowed and does not qualify for a credit under s. 118(1)(*a*) or (*b*) to claim a personal tax credit equal to 15% of the annually indexed value of the amount described in paragraph (c). Individuals using the formulas in paragraphs (*a*) or (*b*) to determine their spousal, common-law partner, or eligible dependant amount could not use the amount in paragraph (*c*) since the formulas already include a basic personal amount for individuals supporting their dependants. The amount shown in paragraph (*c*) is indexed every year under s. 117.1(1) by reference to the Consumer Price Index. A mentally or physically infirm individual could not increase his/her basic personal amount with the family caregiver amount (as for certain other credits) but could claim a credit for mental or physical impairment under s. 118.3 provided certain conditions were met.

History: S. 118(1), paragraph (*c*) of the description of B was replaced by S.C. 2009, c. 2, s. 34(5), applicable to the 2009 and subsequent taxation years. S. 118(1), paragraph (*c*) of the description of B formerly read:

(*c*) *Single status* — except in the case of an individual entitled to a deduction because of paragraph (*a*) or (*b*), $7,131,

Related Sections: S. 118(3.1) Additions to personal credits — basic personal amount.

Income Tax Folios: *Primary* — S1-F4-C1 Basic Personal and Dependant Tax Credits.

► 118(1)(c.1) ◄

(c.1) In-home care of relative — (Repealed by S.C. 2017, c. 20, s. 12(4).)

History: S. 118(1), paragraph (c.1) of the description of B was repealed by S.C. 2017, c. 20, s. 12(4), applicable to the 2017 and subsequent taxation years, and formerly read:

(c.1) *In-home care of relative* — in the case of an individual who, at any time in the year alone or jointly with one or more persons, maintains a self-contained domestic establishment which is the ordinary place of residence of the individual and of a particular person

(i) who has attained the age of 18 years before that time,

(ii) who is

(A) the individual's child or grandchild, or

(B) resident in Canada and is the parent, grandparent, brother, sister, aunt, uncle, nephew or niece of the individual or of the individual's spouse or common-law partner, and

(iii) who is

(A) the individual's parent or grandparent and has attained the age of 65 years before that time, or

(B) dependent on the individual because of the particular person's mental or physical infirmity,

the amount determined by the formula

$$18,906 + E - E.1$$

where

E is

(I) $2,000 if the particular person is dependent on the individual by reason of mental or physical infirmity, and

(II) in any other case, nil, and

E.1 is the greater of $14,624 and the particular person's income for the year,

S. 118(1), the portion of paragraph (*c.1*) of the description of B after subparagraph (iii) was replaced by S.C. 2011, c. 24, s. 23(4), applicable to the 2011 and subsequent taxation years, except that

(a) for the 2011 taxation year, the reference to "$2,000"is to be read as a reference to "nil";

(b) for the 2011 taxation year, subsection 117.1(1) of the Act does not apply for the purposes of computing the amounts to be used under paragraphs (*a*), (*b*), (*b.1*), (*c.1*) and (*d*) of the description of B in subsection 118(1) [No indexing of these amounts for 2011];

(c) for the 2012 taxation year, subsection 117.1(1) of the Act does not apply in respect of the amount of $2,000 referred to in paragraphs (*a*), (*b*), (*b.1*), (*c.1*) and (*d*) of the description of B in subsection 118(1) [No indexing of $2,000 amount for 2012].

S. 118(1), the portion of paragraph (*c.1*) of the description of B after subparagraph (iii) formerly read:

the amount determined by the formula

$$15,453 - D.1$$

where

D.1 is the greater of $11,953 and the particular person's income for the year,

Related Sections: S. 118(1)(*e*) Additional amount; s. 118(4) Limitations re s. (1); s. 248(1), "self-contained domestic establishment".

Forms: T1 SCH 5 — Amounts for Spouse or Common-law Partner and Dependants.

Income Tax Folios: *Primary* — S1-F4-C1 Basic Personal and Dependant Tax Credits.

► 118(1)(d) ◄

(d) Canada caregiver credit — for each person who, at any time in the year,

(i) is dependent on the individual because of mental or physical infirmity, and

(ii) either

(A) is a spouse or common-law partner of the individual, or

(B) has attained the age of 18 years and is a dependant of the individual,

the amount determined by the formula

$$6,883 - E$$

where

E is the amount, if any, by which the dependant's income for the year exceeds $16,163, and

CRA News Release

2.2% Indexation Factor for 2019

See the CRA Fact Sheet, dated November 16, 2018, that is reproduced following subsection117.1(1). This release announces a 2.2% indexation factor applicable for 2019 tax bracket thresholds, personal amounts and other amounts relating to non-refundable credits, as well as the refundable medical expense supplement, Old Age Security repayment threshold, certain board and lodging allowances, and the tradesperson's tools deduction. Increases to tax bracket thresholds, amounts relating to non-refundable credits, and most other amounts will take effect on January 1, 2019. However, increases

in amounts for certain income-tested benefits (for example, the goods and services tax credit) will take effect on July 1, 2019.

Editorial Note: Paragraph 118(1)(*d*) allows an individual to claim a Canada caregiver tax credit for a person that is a parent, grandparent, brother, sister, aunt, uncle, niece, nephew or adult child (excluding a spouse or common-law partner or child under 18) and who is mentally or physically disabled and dependent on the individual for support. To qualify for the Canada caregiver tax credit, the relative must be 18 and resident in Canada at any time in the year. The amount used to calculate the credit is reduced dollar-for-dollar by the dependant's net income threshold. The credit can be claimed even if the individual does not live with the dependant but cannot be claimed for a non-disabled relative over 65 even if the individual lives with him/her. A lower Canada caregiver tax credit can be claimed for a disabled child under 18, disabled spouse or common-law partner, or eligible dependant (i.e., in addition to the regular spousal or common-law partner tax credit or eligible dependant tax credit).

If an individual can claim both the Canada caregiver tax credit and spouse or common-law partner tax credit or both the Canada caregiver tax credit and eligible dependant tax credit, and the Canada caregiver amount (net of the dependant's income over the income threshold) is greater than the spouse or common-law partner amount or eligible dependant amount (net of the dependant's income), the difference between the Canada caregiver amount and the other amount may be used to claim an additional top-up tax credit.

History: S. 118(1), paragraph (*d*) of the description of B were replaced by S.C. 2017, c. 20, s. 12(4), applicable to the 2017 and subsequent taxation years. However, for the 2017 taxation year, subsection 117.1(1) does not apply in respect of amounts expressed in dollars in paragraph (*d*) of the description of B in subsection 118(1). Paragraph (*d*) of the description of B formerly read:

(*d*) *Dependants* — for each dependant of the individual for the year who

(i) attained the age of 18 years before the end of the year, and

(ii) was dependent on the individual because of mental or physical infirmity,

the amount determined by the formula

$$\$10,358 + \$2,000 - F$$

where

F is the greater of $6,076 and the dependant's income for the year, and

S. 118(1), the portion of paragraph (*d*) of the description of B after subparagraph (ii) was replaced by S.C. 2011, c. 24, s. 23(5), applicable to the 2011 and subsequent taxation years, except that

(a) for the 2011 taxation year, the reference to "$2,000" is to be read as a reference to "nil";

(b) for the 2011 taxation year, subsection 117.1(1) does not apply for the purposes of computing the amounts to be used under paragraphs (*a*), (*b*), (*b.1*), (*c.1*) and (*d*) of the description of B in subsection 118(1) [No indexing of these amounts for 2011];

(c) for the 2012 taxation year, for the purpose of making the adjustment provided under subsection 117.1(1) as it applies to paragraph (*d*) of the description of B in subsection 118(1) in lieu of the amounts of $10,358 and $6,076, the amounts to be used for the preceding year are $10,527 and $6,245, respectively; and

(d) for the 2012 taxation year, subsection 117.1(1) does not apply in respect of the amount of $2,000 referred to in paragraphs (*a*), (*b*), (*b.1*), (*c.1*) and (*d*) of the description of B in subsection 118(1) [No indexing of $2,000 amount for 2012].

S. 118(1), the portion of paragraph (*d*) of the description of B after subparagraph (ii) formerly read:

the amount determined by the formula

$$\$8,466 - E$$

where

E is the greater of $4,966 and the dependant's income for the year, and

Related Sections: S. 118(1)(*e*) Additional amount; s. 118(4) Limitations re s. (1); s. 118(5) Support; s. 118(6) Definition of dependant; s. 252(1) Extended meaning of "child"; s. 252(2) Relationships.

Forms: T1 SCH 5 — Amounts for Spouse or Common-law Partner and Dependants.

Income Tax Folios: *Primary* — S1-F4-C1 Basic Personal and Dependant Tax Credits.

Cases: The age limit for the dependant credit was held not to constitute discrimination based on age, contrary to subsection 15(1) of the Charter. *Mercier v. M.N.R.*, 97 DTC 5081 (F.C.T.D.), reversing 92 DTC 1693 (T.C.C.)

► 118(1)(e) ◄

(e) Additional amount — in the case of an individual entitled to a deduction in respect of a person because of paragraph (*a*) or (*b*) and who would also be entitled, but for paragraph (4)(*c*), to a deduction because of paragraph (*d*) in respect of the person, the amount by which the amount that would be determined under paragraph (*d*) exceeds the amount determined under paragraph (*a*) or (*b*), as the case may be, in respect of the person.

Editorial Note: An individual taxpayer may claim the top-up amount under s. 118(1)(*e*) in addition to the spouse or common-law partner amount claimed under s. 118(1)(*a*) or the eligible dependant amount claimed under s. 118(1)(*b*) if he or she would qualify for a Canada caregiver amount under s. 118(1)(*d*) but is prevented by s. 118(4)(*c*) from claiming it. The top-up amount is equal to the difference between two figures:

- the excess of the Canada caregiver amount over the dependant's net income exceeding a net income threshold; and
- the excess of the spouse or common-law partner amount over the dependant's net income, or the excess of the eligible dependant amount over the dependant's net income.

The adjustment is required when the dependant's net income exceeds the difference between the spouse or common-law partner amount and the Canada caregiver amount or between the eligible dependant amount and the Canada caregiver amount. When a dependant has no or very little net income, the adjustment is not required. The principal reason for the adjustment is that the spouse or common-law partner amount or the eligible dependant amount is reduced by any net income earned by the dependant and the Canada caregiver amount is only reduced by the dependant's net income exceeding an indexed threshold.

History: S. 118(1), paragraph (*e*) of the description of B were replaced by S.C. 2017, c. 20, s. 12(4), applicable to the 2017 and subsequent taxation years. However, for the 2017 taxation year, subsection 117.1(1) does not apply in respect of amounts expressed in dollars in paragraph (*d*) of the description of B in subsection 118(1). Paragraph (*e*) of the description of B formerly read:

(*e*) *Additional amount* — in the case of an individual entitled to a deduction in respect of a person because of paragraph (*b*) and who would also be entitled, but for paragraph (4)(*c*), to a deduction because of paragraph (*c.1*) or (*d*) in respect of the person, the amount by which the amount that would be determined under paragraph (*c.1*) or (*d*), as the case may be, exceeds the amount determined under paragraph (*b*) in respect of the person.

Related Sections: S. 117 Annual adjustment; s. 117.1(1) Annual adjustment (indexing); s. 118(6) Definition of dependant; s. 248(1), "amount", "appropriate percentage", "self-contained domestic establishment"; s. 249 Definition of "taxation year".

Forms: TD1 — Personal Tax Credits Return; TD1-WS — Worksheet for the __ Personal Tax Credits Return.

Income Tax Folios: *Primary* — S1-F4-C1 Basic Personal and Dependant Tax Credits.

Information Circulars: IC 07-1 Taxpayer relief provisions.

Interpretation Bulletins: *Secondary* — IT-295R4 Taxable dividends received after 1987 by a spouse; IT-394R2 Preferred beneficiary election.

Cases: Although s. 118(1) provides a greater benefit to a tax-paying couple with a child cohabiting common-law than to a married couple, such benefit cannot be characterized as discrimination based on religion. Nor could the inequality in benefit be said to have arisen simply by reason of the taxpayer's marital status. A finding of discrimination under s. 15 of the Charter requires the existence of a discrete and insular minority and it was not possible in the context of s. 118(1) to define the discrete and insular minority in terms of women. *Schachtschneider v. The Queen*, 93 DTC 5298 (F.C.A.)

Tax Window Files: Taxability of Support Payments, *February 9, 2012*, CRA Document No. 2011-0406701E5; Personal Credits Claimed for Disabled Child, *Technical Interpretation, Business and Partnerships Division, June 24, 2005*, CRA Document No. 2005-0126251E5; Pension Credit — Payments from a Life Income Fund, *Technical Interpretation, Financial Industries Division, July 8, 2004*, CRA Document No. 2004-0079771E5; Donations — Gifts by Direct Designation, *Technical Interpretation, Financial Industries Division, January 16, 2003*, CRA Document No. 2002-0133545.

► 118(2) ◄

(2) Age credit. For the purpose of computing the tax payable under this Part for a taxation year by an individual who, before the end of the year, has attained the age of 65 years, there may be deducted the amount determined by the formula

$$A \times (\$6,408 - B)$$

where

A is the appropriate percentage for the year; and

B is 15% of the amount, if any, by which the individual's income for the year would exceed $ 25,921 if, in computing that income, no amount were included in respect of a gain from a disposition of property to which section 79 applies and no amount were deductible under paragraph 20(1)(*ww*).

CRA News Release

2.2% Indexation Factor for 2019

See the CRA Fact Sheet, dated November 16, 2018, that is reproduced following subsection117.1(1). This release announces a 2.2% indexation factor applicable for 2019 tax bracket thresholds, personal amounts and other amounts relating to non-refundable credits, as well as the refundable medical expense supplement, Old Age Security repayment threshold, certain board and lodging allowances, and the tradesperson's tools deduction. Increases to tax bracket thresholds, amounts relating to non-refundable credits, and most other amounts will take effect on January 1, 2019. However, increases in amounts for certain income-tested benefits (for example, the goods and services tax credit) will take effect on July 1, 2019.

Editorial Note: An individual taxpayer who is at least 65 years of age at year end may claim an age amount (indexed every year), but must then reduce the amount by the excess of his or her net income for the year over an annually indexed threshold amount. If the taxpayer defaulted on a mortgage, conditional sale, or other debt obligation and realized a capital gain under s. 79 on the property acquired or reacquired by the creditor, the gain must be excluded from the taxpayer's net income for the purpose of calculating the above reduction. Beginning in 2018, the taxpayer's income will not take into account the amount of split income of the taxpayer otherwise deductible under paragraph 20(1)(*ww*), meaning that the split income will be included for the purposes of computing the taxpayer's age credit.

History: S. 118(2), the description of B was replaced by S.C. 2018, c. 12, s. 11(1), applicable to the 2018 and subsequent taxation years, and formerly read:

B is 15% of the amount, if any, by which the individual's income for the year would exceed $25,921 if no amount were included in respect of a gain from a disposition of property to which section 79 applies in computing that income.

The formula in s. 118(2) was replaced by S.C. 2009, c. 2, s. 34(6), applicable to the 2009 and subsequent taxation years. The formula in s. 118(2) formerly read:

A × ($5,066 - B)

Related Sections: S. 117.1(1) Annual adjustment (indexing); s. 118.8 Transfer of unused credits to spouse or common-law partner.

Information Circulars: IC 07-1 Taxpayer relief provisions.

Cases: While the legislation established legal distinctions based on age, the legal distinctions were not discriminatory within the context of the test laid down by the Supreme Court of Canada in *Andrews v. The Law Society of British Columbia*, [1989] 1 S.C.R. 143. *Tiberio et al. v. M.N.R.*, 91 DTC 17 (T.C.C.)

► 118(3) ◄

(3) Pension credit. For the purpose of computing the tax payable under this Part by an individual for a taxation year, there may be deducted an amount determined by the formula

A x B

where

A is the appropriate percentage for the year; and

B is the lesser of

(*a*) $2,000, and

(*b*) the total of

(i) the eligible pension income of the individual for the taxation year,

(ii) the total of all amounts received by the individual in the year on account of a retirement income security benefit under Part 2 of the *Veterans Well-being Act*, and

(iii) the total of all amounts received by the individual in the year on account of an income replacement benefit payable to the individual under Part 2 of the *Veterans Well-being Act*, if the amount is determined under subsection 19.1(1), paragraph 23(1)(*b*) or subsection 26.1(1) of that Act (as modified, where applicable, under Part 5 of that Act).

Editorial Note: An individual taxpayer having received eligible pension income during the year may claim a pension amount not exceeding the lesser of the above income and $2,000. Effective for the 2015 and subsequent taxation years, all amounts received on account of a retirement income security benefit (RISB amount) will be eligible for the non-refundable credit. Effective April 1, 2019, all amounts received on account of income replacement benefits (IRB) paid in respect of a Canadian Forces veteran are also eligible. Specifically, the credit will be calculated by reference to up to $2,000 of the combined eligible pension income, RISB, and IRB amounts for the year, multiplied by the appropriate percentage for the year. For an individual under 65 years of age, the eligible pension income would include his or her RPP/SPP lifetime annuities, and the following amounts if they were paid as a result of his or her spouse's or common-law partner's death: RRSP annuities; amounts paid under a RRIF, DPSP, or pooled RPP; and periodic payments received under a money purchase RPP. For an individual who is 65 years of age or more, the eligible pension income would include any of the above amounts paid or not paid as a result of his or her spouse's or common-law partner's death. Death benefits and payments or supplements paid under the CPP, QPP, or OAS would not qualify for the pension credit.

History: S. 118(3), in the description of B, subparagraph (*b*)(ii) was replaced and subparagraph (*b*)(iii) was added by S.C. 2018, c. 12, s. 11(2), in force April 1, 2019. S. 118(3), subparagraph (*b*)(ii) of the description of B formerly read:

(ii) the total of all amounts received by the individual in the year on account of a retirement income security benefit payable to the individual under Part 2 of the *Canadian Forces Members and Veterans Re-establishment and Compensation Act*.

S. 118(3), the description of B was replaced by S.C. 2017, c. 33, s. 42(1), applicable to the 2015 and subsequent taxation years, and formerly read:

B is the lesser of $2,000 and the eligible pension income of the individual for the taxation year.

Related Regulations: 7800(1).

Related Sections: S. 60.03(2) Effect of pension income split; s. 104(27) Pension benefits; s. 118(7) Definitions; s. 118(8) Interpretation; s. 118.8 Transfer of unused credits to spouse or common-law partner; s. 248(1), "amount", "individual".

► 118(3.1) ◄

(3.1) Additions to personal credits — basic personal amount — (Repealed by S.C. 2009, c. 2, s. 34(7).)

History: S. 118(3.1) was repealed by S.C. 2009, c. 2, s. 34(7), applicable to the 2009 and subsequent taxation years. S. 118(3.1) formerly read:

(3.1) *Additions to personal credits — basic personal amount.* The amount of $7,131 referred to in paragraphs (*a*) to (*c*) of the description of B in subsection (1) (in this subsection referred to as the "particular amount") that is to be used for the purpose of determining the amount of that description is

(*a*) for the 2005 taxation year, to be replaced by $8,648;

(*b*) for the 2006 taxation year, to be replaced by $8,839, except that, for the purpose of determining the particular amount for the 2007 taxation year, the particular amount for 2006 is deemed to be $8,639;

(*c*) for the 2007 and 2008 taxation years, to be replaced by $9,600;

(*d*) for the 2009 taxation year, to be replaced by $10,100; and

(*e*) for each of the 2010 and subsequent taxation years, to be replaced by the amount that is the amount that would be determined for that description for those years in respect of the particular amount by applying section 117.1 (without reference to subsection 117.1(3)) to the amount determined under this subsection in respect of the amount for the immediately preceding taxation year.

(*f*) (Repealed.)

Related Sections: S. 117.1(1) Annual adjustment (indexing).

► 118(3.2) ◄

(3.2) Additions to personal credits — spouse or common-law partner or wholly dependent person — (Repealed by S.C. 2009, c. 2, s. 34(7).)

History: S. 118(3.2) was repealed by S.C. 2009, c. 2, s. 34(7), applicable to the 2009 and subsequent taxation years. S. 118(3.2) formerly read:

(3.2) *Additions to personal credits — spouse or common-law partner or wholly dependent person.* The amount of $6,055 referred to in subparagraphs (*a*)(ii) and (*b*)(iv) of the description of B in subsection (1) (in this subsection referred to as the "particular amount") that is to be used for the purpose of determining the amount of that description is

(*a*) for the 2005 taxation year, to be replaced by $7,344;

(*b*) for the 2006 taxation year, to be replaced by $7,505, except that, for the purpose of determining the particular amount for the 2007 taxation year, the particular amount for 2006 is deemed to be $7,335;

(*c*) for the 2007 and 2008 taxation years, to be replaced by $9,600;

(*d*) for the 2009 taxation year, to be replaced by $10,100; and

(*e*) for each of the 2010 and subsequent taxation years, to be replaced by the amount that is the amount that would be determined for that description for those years in respect of the particular amount by applying section 117.1 (without reference to subsection 117.1(3)) to the amount determined under this subsection in respect of the amount for the immediately preceding taxation year.

(*f*) (Repealed.)

▶ 118(3.3) ◀

(3.3) Additions to personal credits — net income threshold — (Repealed by S.C. 2007, c. 29, s. 9(8).)

▶ 118(4) ◀

(4) Limitations re s. (1). For the purposes of subsection (1), the following rules apply:

(*a*) no amount may be deducted under subsection (1) because of paragraphs (*a*) and (*b*) of the description of B in subsection (1) by an individual in a taxation year for more than one other person;

(*a*.1) no amount may be deducted under subsection (1) because of paragraph (*b*) of the description of B in subsection (1) by an individual for a taxation year for a person in respect of whom an amount is deducted because of paragraph (*a*) of that description by another individual for the year if, throughout the year, the person and that other individual are married to each other or in a common-law partnership with each other and are not living separate and apart because of a breakdown of their marriage or the common-law partnership, as the case may be;

(*a*.2) a reference to income for a year is to be read as a reference to that income determined as if, in computing that income, no amount were deductible under paragraph 20(1)(*ww*);

(*b*) not more than one individual is entitled to a deduction under subsection (1) because of paragraph (*b*) of the description of B in that subsection for a taxation year in respect of the same person or the same domestic establishment and where two or more individuals otherwise entitled to such a deduction fail to agree as to the individual by whom the deduction may be made, no such deduction for the year shall be allowed to either or any of them;

(*b*.1) not more than one individual is entitled to a deduction under subsection (1) because of paragraph (*b.1*) of the description of B in that subsection for a taxation year in respect of the same child and where two or more individuals otherwise entitled to such a deduction fail to agree as to the individual by whom the deduction may be made, no such deduction for the year shall be allowed to either or any of them;

(*c*) if an individual is entitled to a deduction under subsection (1) because of paragraph (*a*) or (*b*) of the description of B in subsection (1) for a taxation year in respect of any person, no amount may be deducted because of paragraph (*d*) of that description by any individual for the year in respect of the person; and

(*d*) if more than one individual is entitled to a deduction under subsection (1) because of paragraph (*d*) of the description of B in subsection (1) for a taxation year in respect of the same person,

(i) the total of all amounts so deductible for the year shall not exceed the maximum amount that would be so deductible for the year by any one of those individuals for that person if that individual were the only individual entitled to deduct an amount for the year because of that paragraph for that person, and

(ii) if the individuals cannot agree as to what portion of the amount each can so deduct, the Minister may fix the portions.

(*e*) (Repealed by S.C. 2017, c. 20, s. 12(5).)

Editorial Note: Subsection 118(4) includes several restrictions on the personal tax credits claimable by a taxpayer. A taxpayer claiming a spouse or common-law partner credit cannot claim an eligible dependant credit for another person. Income for the purposes of the income thresholds includes income that is split income under section 120.4. If a taxpayer claims a spouse or common-law partner credit for a person with whom he or she lives and is not separated from in the year, nobody else can claim the eligible dependant credit for that spouse or common-law partner. If two individuals are entitled to claim an eligible dependant credit or caregiver for infirm child credit for the same person, they must agree on how to share the credit or lose it entirely. A taxpayer already claiming a spouse or common-law partner credit or an eligible dependant credit for a person cannot also claim a regular Canada caregiver credit for the same person. Where more than one individual claims a Canada caregiver credit for the same person, the total credit cannot exceed the maximum claimable if only one taxpayer claimed it.

History: S. 118(4)(*a*.2) was added by S.C. 2018, c. 12, s. 11(3), applicable to the 2018 and subsequent taxation years.

S. 118(4)(*c*) and (*d*) were replaced by S.C. 2017, c. 20, s. 12(5), applicable to the 2017 and subsequent taxation years, and formerly read:

(*c*) where an individual is entitled to a deduction under subsection (1) because of paragraph (*b*) of the description of B in subsection (1) for a taxation year in respect of any person, no amount may be deducted because of paragraph (*c*.1) or (*d*) of that description by any individual for the year in respect of the person;

(*d*) where an individual is entitled to a deduction under subsection (1) because of paragraph (*c*.1) of the description of B in subsection (1) for a taxation year in respect of any person, the person is deemed not to be a dependant of any individual for the year for the purpose of paragraph (*d*) of that description; and

S. 118(4)(*e*) was repealed by S.C. 2017, c. 20, s. 12(5), applicable to the 2017 and subsequent taxation years, and formerly read:

(*e*) where more than one individual is entitled to a deduction under subsection (1) because of paragraph (*c*.1) or (*d*) of the description of B in subsection (1) for a taxation year in respect of the same person,

(i) the total of all amounts so deductible for the year shall not exceed the maximum amount that would be so deductible for the year by any one of those individuals for that person if that individual were the only individual entitled to deduct an amount for the year because of that paragraph for that person, and

(ii) if the individuals cannot agree as to what portion of the amount each can so deduct, the Minister may fix the portions.

S. 118(4)(*b*) was replaced, and paragraph (*b.1*) was added, by S.C. 2011, c. 24, s. 23(6), applicable to the 2011 and subsequent taxation years. S. 118(4)(*b*) formerly read:

(*b*) not more than one individual is entitled to a deduction under subsection (1) because of paragraph (*b*) or (*b*.1) of the description of B in that subsection for a taxation year in respect of the same person or the same domestic establishment and where two or more individuals otherwise entitled to such a deduction fail to agree as to the individual by whom the deduction may be made, no such deduction for the year shall be allowed to either or any of them;

Related Sections: S. 118(1)(*e*) Additional amount; s. 118(6) Definition of dependant; s. 248(1), "common-law partner", "common-law partnership".

Income Tax Folios: *Primary* — S1-F4-C1 Basic Personal and Dependant Tax Credits.

Tax Window Files: Eligibility: caregiver amount for infirm child, *July 26, 2018*, CRA Document No. 2017-0721711E5.

▶ 118(5) ◀

(5) Support. No amount may be deducted under subsection (1) in computing an individual's tax payable under this Part for a taxation year in respect of a person where the individual is required to pay a support amount (within the meaning assigned by subsection 56.1(4)) to the individual's spouse or common-law partner or former spouse or common-law partner in respect of the person and the individual

(*a*) lives separate and apart from the spouse or common-law partner or former spouse or common-law partner throughout the year because of the breakdown of their marriage or common-law partnership; or

(*b*) claims a deduction for the year because of section 60 in respect of a support amount paid to the spouse or common-law partner or former spouse or common-law partner.

Editorial Note: An individual taxpayer having to pay support to a current or former spouse, common-law partner, or children and living separate from him or her cannot claim personal credits for them even if he or she did not actually make the support payments or did not claim a tax deduction for those payments. If he or she must make support payments and claims a tax deduction for the payments, he or she will not be able to claim personal credits for his or her spouse or common-law partner and children even if he or she still lives with them. If he or she pays support to his or her spouse or common-law partner but does not live with him or her, he or she has two options:

- claim a tax deduction for the support payments under s. 60(*b*) and not claim the spouse or common-law partner tax credit under s. 118(1)(*a*); or
- not claim a tax deduction for the support payments under s. 60(b) and, instead, claim the spouse or common-law partner tax credit under s. 118(1)(*a*).

Related Sections: s. 248(1), "common-law partner", "common-law partnership".

Income Tax Folios: *Primary* — S1-F4-C1 Basic Personal and Dependant Tax Credits. *Secondary* — S1-F3-C3 Support Payments.

Information Circulars: IC 07-1 Taxpayer Relief Provisions.

Cases: The taxpayer is the only parent making a child support payment in virtue of an order of a competent tribunal or an agreement and, accordingly, cannot claim the dependant tax credit. The taxpayer's argument based on the fairness of s. 118(5) is untenable, as is the "set-off" argument that his former spouse pays *him* a form of child support because she has imputed income factored into the support amount he pays. *Sauve v. The Queen*, 2014 DTC 1115 (T.C.C.)

► 118(5.1) ◄

(5.1) Where subsection (5) does not apply. Where, if this Act were read without reference to this subsection, solely because of the application of subsection (5), no individual is entitled to a deduction under paragraph (*b*) or (*b.1*) of the description of B in subsection (1) for a taxation year in respect of a child, subsection (5) shall not apply in respect of that child for that taxation year.

Editorial Note: A taxpayer required to pay a support amount for a former spouse/common-law partner or child is not allowed under s. 118(5) to claim a personal tax credit for them in a particular taxation year if he/she also claims a deduction for the payment in that year or lives separately from that former spouse/common-law partner throughout the year due to a breakdown of their marriage or common-law partnership. If both parents pay a support amount for their child, one of them will be allowed under s. 118(5.1) to claim a wholly dependent person or child tax credit in respect of that child. Before the adoption of that provision, neither parent was allowed under s. 118(5) to claim the credit.

Cases: A parent who pays support for a dependent cannot claim a dependent deduction for that person. The exception in s. 118(5.1) prevents loss of the deduction where each parent factually pays to the other child support. A factual payment requires that each parent pay an amount pursuant to a court order or formal agreement, together with evidence of the payment. It does not include the use of offsetting inputs resulting in the unilateral payment of support by only one parent to the other. The taxpayer was the only spouse to factually pay support and the exception was not available. *Harder v. The Queen*, 2016 DTC 1167 (TCC)

► 118(6) ◄

(6) Definition of "dependant". For the purposes of paragraph (*d*) of the description of B in subsection (1), "dependant", of an individual for a taxation year, means a person who at any time in the year is dependent on the individual for support and is

(*a*) the child or grandchild of the individual or of the individual's spouse or common-law partner; or

(*b*) the parent, grandparent, brother, sister, uncle, aunt, niece or nephew, if resident in Canada at any time in the year, of the individual or of the individual's spouse or common-law partner.

History: S. 118(6), the portion before paragraph (*a*) was replaced by S.C. 2017, c. 20, s. 12(6), applicable to the 2017 and subsequent taxation years, and formerly read:

(6) *Definition of dependant.* For the purposes of paragraphs (*d*) and (*e*) of the description of B in subsection (1) and paragraph (4)(*e*), "dependant" of an individual for a taxation year means a person who at any time in the year is dependent on the individual for support and is

Related Sections: S. 248(1), "common-law partner", "common-law partnership".

Income Tax Folios: *Primary* — S1-F4-C1 Basic Personal and Dependant Tax Credits. *Secondary* — S1-F1-C1 Medical Expense Tax Credit.

Interpretation Bulletins: *Secondary* — IT-394R2 Preferred beneficiary election.

► 118(7) ◄

(7) Definitions. Subject to subsections (8) and (8.1), for the purposes of this subsection and subsection (3),

Tax Window Files: Pension Splitting - Supplemental Pensions, *December 7, 2011*, CRA Document No. 2011-0425871E5; US Annuities, *August 18, 2010*, CRA Document No. 2010-0371161E5; Taxation of annuity received from Switzerland, *August 11, 2010*, CRA Document No. 2010-0375511E5; Pension Split of Spousal RRIF Payments, *March 18, 2009*, CRA Document No. 2007-0257001E5; Unfunded Supplemental Plan — 118(8)(f), *March 9, 2009*, CRA Document No. 2008-0299941E5; Splitting Pension Income in Case of Death, *September 17, 2008*, CRA Document No. 2008-0275731E5.

"eligible pension income" —"eligible pension income" of an individual for a taxation year means

(*a*) if the individual has attained the age of 65 years before the end of the taxation year, the pension income received by the individual in the taxation year, and

(*b*) if the individual has not attained the age of 65 years before the end of the taxation year, the qualified pension income received by the individual in the taxation year;

"pension income" —"pension income" received by an individual in a taxation year means the total of

(*a*) the total of all amounts each of which is an amount included in computing the individual's income for the year that is

(i) a payment in respect of a life annuity out of or under a superannuation or pension plan (other than a pooled registered pension plan) or a specified pension plan,

(ii) an annuity payment under a registered retirement savings plan, under an "amended plan" as referred to in subsection 146(12) or under an annuity in respect of which an amount is included in computing the individual's income by reason of paragraph 56(1)(*d.*2),

(iii) a payment out of or under a registered retirement income fund or under an "amended fund" as referred to in subsection 146.3(11),

(iii.1) a payment (other than a payment described in subparagraph (i)) payable on a periodic basis under a money purchase provision (within the meaning assigned by subsection 147.1(1)) of a registered pension plan,

(iii.2) an amount included under section 147.5,

(iv) an annuity payment under a deferred profit sharing plan or under a "revoked plan" as referred to in subsection 147(15),

(v) a payment described in subparagraph 147(2)(*k*)(v), or

(vi) the amount by which an annuity payment included in computing the individual's income for the year by reason of paragraph 56(1)(*d*) exceeds the capital element of that payment as determined or established under paragraph 60(*a*), and

(*b*) the total of all amounts each of which is an amount included in computing the individual's income for the year by reason of section 12.2 of this Act or paragraph 56(1)(*d.*1) of the *Income Tax Act*, chapter 148 of the Revised Statutes of Canada, 1952;

Department of Finance Comfort Letters

(May 11, 2018) [Saskatchewan Pension Plan – Tax Treatment of Variable Benefit Option]

Dear XXXX:

I am writing in response to your letter of December 21, 2017 in which you request amendments to the *Income Tax Act* (the Act) to ensure that variable benefits paid from the Saskatchewan Pension Plan will be eligible for the pension income credit and for pension income splitting.

Officials from Finance Canada have had ongoing discussions with Saskatchewan Finance officials regarding the use of the existing tax framework for registered pension variable benefits as a model for tax accommodation of variable benefits paid out of the Saskatchewan Pension Plan. In conjunction with these discussions, we note that *The Saskatchewan Pension Plan Amendment Regulations, 2018* introduced variable benefits options for members and surviving spouses. We understand that the variable benefit option will become available under the Saskatchewan Pension Plan beginning in 2019.

These changes included references to pertinent sections of the *Income Tax Regulations* in order to ensure that variable benefits paid out of the Saskatchewan Pension Plan will satisfy the tax rules (including "minimum amount" withdrawals) that apply to variable benefits paid out of money purchase registered pension plans. However, as the Saskatchewan Pension Plan is not a registered plan *per se*, but rather is prescribed as a "specified pension plan", the Act would need to be amended to deem the tax provisions applicable to money purchase variable benefits to also apply to the Saskatchewan Pension Plan's variable benefits.

Given those recent changes to your regulations and the fact that the Act currently permits registered pension plans to offer variable benefits to members, we believe that your request is supported to income tax policy terms. We do note, however, that any amendments to the Act would need to include conditions with respect to variable benefits that are consistent with the conditions applicable to benefits paid out of these registered plans.

Consequently, we are prepared to recommend to the Minister of Finance that the Act be amended such that variable benefits paid out of a specified pension plan to a taxpayer:

i. would qualify for the pension income credit and pension income splitting after the taxpayer attains age 65; and

ii. would be subject to the rules in section 8506 of the *Income Tax Regulations* that apply to variable benefits paid out of money purchase registered pension plans.

If our recommendations are accepted, we would also recommend that these proposed amendments apply in respect of any variable benefit payments made from a specified pension plan after 2018. While I cannot offer any assurance that our recommendations with respect to this matter will be accepted, I hope this statement of our intention is helpful to you.

Thank you for writing to us on this matter.

Yours sincerely,

Brian Ernewein

General Director — Legislation

Tax Policy Branch

History: S. 118(7), subparagraph (*a*)(iii.1) of the definition "pension income" was added by S.C. 2013, c. 34, s. 246(1), applicable to the 2004 and subsequent taxation years.

S. 118(7), subparagraph (*a*)(i) of the definition "pension income" was replaced by S.C. 2012, c. 31, s. 25(1), in force December 14, 2012, and formerly read:

> (i) a payment in respect of a life annuity out of or under a superannuation plan, a pension plan or a specified pension plan,

S. 118(7), subparagraph (*a*)(iii.2) of the definition "pension income" was added by S.C. 2012, c. 31, s. 25(2), in force December 14, 2012.

S. 118(7), subparagraph (*a*)(i) of the definition "pension income" was replaced by S.C. 2011, c. 24, s. 23(7), applicable after 2009. S. 118(7), subparagraph (*a*)(i) of the definition "pension income" formerly read:

> (i) a payment in respect of a life annuity out of or under a superannuation or pension plan,

"qualified pension income" — "qualified pension income" received by an individual in a taxation year means the total of all amounts each of which is an amount included in computing the individual's income for the year and described in

(*a*) subparagraph (*a*)(i) of the definition "pension income" in this subsection, or

(*b*) any of subparagraphs (*a*)(ii) to (vi) or paragraph (*b*) of the definition "pension income" in this subsection received by the individual as a consequence of the death of a spouse or common-law partner of the individual.

Related Sections: S. 104(27) Pension benefits; s. 248(1), "common-law partner", "individual".

► 118(8) ◄

(8) Interpretation. For the purposes of subsection (7), "pension income" and "qualified pension income" received by an individual in a taxation year do not include any amount that is

(*a*) the amount of a pension or supplement under the *Old Age Security Act* or of any similar payment under a law of a province;

(*b*) the amount of a benefit under the *Canada Pension Plan* or under a provincial pension plan as defined in section 3 of that Act;

(*c*) a death benefit;

(*d*) the amount, if any, by which

(i) an amount required to be included in computing the individual's income for the year

exceeds

(ii) the amount, if any, by which the amount referred to in subparagraph (i) exceeds the total of all amounts deducted (other than under paragraph 60(*c*)) by the individual for the year in respect of that amount;

(*e*) a payment received out of or under a salary deferral arrangement, a retirement compensation arrangement, an employee benefit plan or an employee trust; or

(*f*) a payment (other than a payment under the *Judges Act* or the *Lieutenant Governors Superannuation Act*) received out of or under an unfunded supplemental plan or arrangement, being a plan or arrangement where

(i) the payment was in respect of services rendered to an employer by the individual or the individual's spouse or common-law partner or former spouse or common-law partner as an employee, and

(ii) the plan or arrangement would have been a retirement compensation arrangement or an employee benefit plan had the employer made a contribution in respect of the payment to a trust governed by the plan or arrangement.

History: S. 118(8)(*e*) was replaced by S.C. 2011, c. 24, s. 23(8), applicable after 2009. S. 118(8)(*e*) formerly read:

> (*e*) a payment received out of or under a salary deferral arrangement, a retirement compensation arrangement, an employee benefit plan, an employee trust or a prescribed provincial pension plan; or

Related Regulations: 7800(1).

Interpretation Bulletins: *Secondary* — IT-517R Pension tax credit.

► 118(8.1) ◄

(8.1) Bridging benefits. For the purposes of subsection (7), a payment in respect of a life annuity under a superannuation or pension plan is deemed to include a payment in respect of bridging benefits, being benefits payable under a registered pension plan on a periodic basis and not less frequently than annually to an individual where

(*a*) the individual or the individual's spouse or common-law partner or former spouse or common-law partner was a member (as defined in subsection 147.1(1)) of the registered pension plan;

(*b*) the benefits are payable for a period ending no later than the end of the month following the month in which the member attains 65 years of age or would have attained that age if the member had survived to that day; and

(*c*) the amount (expressed on an annualized basis) of the benefits payable to the individual for a calendar year does not exceed the total of the maximum amount of benefits payable for that year under Part I of the *Old Age Security Act* and the maximum amount of benefits (other than disability, death or survivor benefits) payable for that year under either the *Canada Pension Plan* or a provincial pension plan as defined in section 3 of that Act.

▶ 118(9) ◀

(9) Rounding — (Repealed by S.C. 2009, c. 2, s. 34(7).)

History: S. 118(9) was repealed by S.C. 2009, c. 2, s. 34(7), applicable to the 2009 and subsequent taxation years. S. 118(9) formerly read:

(9) *Rounding.* If an amount determined under any of paragraphs (3.1)(*a*) to (*f*) and (3.2)(*a*) to (*f*) is not a multiple of one dollar, it shall be rounded to the nearest multiple of one dollar or, where it is equidistant from two such consecutive multiples, to the greater multiple.

Related Sections: S. 67.1(1) Expenses for food, etc; s. 117.1(1) Annual adjustment (indexing).

▶ 118(9.1) ◀

(9.1) Child tax credit. For greater certainty, in the case of a child who in a taxation year is born, adopted or dies, the reference to "throughout the taxation year" in subparagraph 118(1)(*b*.1)(i) is to be read as a reference to "throughout the portion of the taxation year that is after the child's birth or adoption or before the child's death".

▶ 118(10) ◀

(10) Canada Employment Credit. For the purpose of computing the tax payable under this Part by an individual for a taxation year, there may be deducted the amount determined by the formula

$$A \times B$$

where

A is the appropriate percentage for the taxation year; and

B is the lesser of

(*a*) $1,000, and

(*b*) the total of all amounts, each of which is an amount included in computing the individual's income for the taxation year from an office or employment or an amount included in the taxpayer's income for the taxation year because of subparagraph 56(1)(*r*)(v).

CRA News Release

2.2% Indexation Factor for 2019

See the CRA Fact Sheet, dated November 16, 2018, that is reproduced following subsection117.1(1). This release announces a 2.2% indexation factor applicable for 2019 tax bracket thresholds, personal amounts and other amounts relating to non-refundable credits, as well as the refundable medical expense supplement, Old Age Security repayment threshold, certain board and lodging allowances, and the tradesperson's tools deduction. Increases to tax bracket thresholds, amounts relating to non-refundable credits, and most other amounts will take effect on January 1, 2019. However, increases in amounts for certain income-tested benefits (for example, the goods and services tax credit) will take effect on July 1, 2019.

History: S. 118(10), paragraph (*b*) of the description of B was replaced by S.C. 2009, c. 2, s. 34(8), applicable to the 2008 and subsequent taxation years. S. 118(10), paragraph (*b*) of the description of B formerly read:

(*b*) the amount that would be the individual's income for the taxation year from all offices and employments if this Act were read without reference to section 8.

SECTION 118.01: [Adoption expense tax credit]

▶ 118.01(1) ◀

(1) Definitions. The following definitions apply in this section.

"adoption period" — "adoption period", in respect of an eligible child of an individual, means the period that

(*a*) begins at the earlier of the time that an application is made for registration with a provincial ministry responsible for adoption (or with an adoption agency licensed by a provincial government) and the time, if any, that an application related to the adoption is made to a Canadian court; and

(*b*) ends at the later of the time an adoption order is issued by, or recognized by, a government in Canada in respect of that child, and the time that the child first begins to reside permanently with the individual.

History: S. 118.01(1), paragraph (*a*) of the definition "adoption period" was replaced by S.C. 2013, c. 33, s. 9(1), applicable to the 2013 and subsequent taxation years, and formerly read:

(*a*) begins at the earlier of the time that the eligible child's adoption file is opened with a provincial ministry responsible for adoption (or with an adoption agency licensed by a provincial government) and the time, if any, that an application related to the adoption is made to a Canadian court; and

"eligible adoption expense" — "eligible adoption expense", in respect of an eligible child of an individual, means an amount paid for expenses incurred during the adoption period in respect of the adoption of that child, including

(*a*) fees paid to an adoption agency licensed by a provincial government;

(*b*) court costs and legal and administrative expenses related to an adoption order in respect of that child;

(*c*) reasonable and necessary travel and living expenses of that child and the adoptive parents;

(*d*) document translation fees;

(*e*) mandatory fees paid to a foreign institution;

(*f*) mandatory expenses paid in respect of the immigration of that child; and

(*g*) any other reasonable expenses related to the adoption required by a provincial government or an adoption agency licensed by a provincial government.

"eligible child" — "eligible child", of an individual, means a child who has not attained the age of 18 years at the time that an adoption order is issued or recognized by a government in Canada in respect of the adoption of that child by that individual.

▶ 118.01(2) ◀

(2) Adoption expense tax credit. For the purpose of computing the tax payable under this Part by an individual for the taxation year that includes the end of the adoption period in respect of an eligible child of the individual, there may be deducted the amount determined by the formula

$$A \times B$$

where

A is the appropriate percentage for the taxation year; and

B is the lesser of

(*a*) $15,000, and

(*b*) the amount determined by the formula

$$C - D$$

where

C is the total of all eligible adoption expenses in respect of the eligible child, and

D is the total of all amounts each of which is the amount of a reimbursement or any other form of assistance (other than an amount that is included in computing the individual's income and that is not deductible in computing the individual's taxable income) that any individual is or was entitled to receive in respect of an amount included in computing the value of C.

CRA News Release

2.2% Indexation Factor for 2019

See the CRA Fact Sheet, dated November 16, 2018, that is reproduced following subsection117.1(1). This release announces a 2.2% indexation factor applicable for 2019 tax bracket thresholds, personal amounts and other amounts relating to non-refundable credits, as well as the refundable medical expense supplement, Old Age Security repayment threshold, certain board and lodging allowances, and the tradesperson's tools deduction. Increases to tax bracket thresholds, amounts relating to non-refundable credits, and most other amounts will take effect on January 1, 2019. However, increases in amounts for certain income-tested benefits (for example, the goods and services tax credit) will take effect on July 1, 2019.

History: S. 118.01(2), paragraph (*a*) of the description of B was replaced by S.C. 2014, c. 20, s. 6(1), applicable to the 2014 and subsequent taxation years. However, s. 117.1(1) does not apply in respect of s. 118.01(2) for the 2014 taxation year. S. 118.01(2), paragraph (*a*) of the description of B formerly read:

(*a*) $10,000, and

Tax Window Files: adoption expense tax credit, *February 21, 2018*, CRA Document No. 2017-0692561E5; Adoption Expense Tax Credit, *April 30, 2014*, CRA Document No. 2013-0515791E5.

► 118.01(3) ◄

(3) Apportionment of credit. Where more than one individual is entitled to a deduction under this section for a taxation year in respect of the adoption of an eligible child, the total of all amounts so deductible shall not exceed the maximum amount that would be so deductible for the year by any one of those individuals for that child if that individual were the only individual entitled to deduct an amount for the year under this section, and if the individuals cannot agree as to what portion of the amount each can so deduct, the Minister may fix the portions.

SECTION 118.02: [Transit pass tax credit]

► 118.02(1) ◄

(1) Definitions. (Repealed.)

"eligible electronic payment card" — (Repealed by S.C. 2017, c. 20, s. 13(2).)

History: S. 118.02(1), the definition "eligible electronic payment card" was repealed by S.C. 2017, c. 20, s. 13(2), applicable to the 2018 and subsequent taxation years, and formerly read:

S. 118.02 *[Transit pass tax credit].*

(1) *Definitions.* The following definitions apply in this section.

"eligible electronic payment card" — "eligible electronic payment card" means an electronic payment card that is

(*a*) used by an individual for at least 32 one-way trips, between the place of origin of the trip and its termination, during an uninterrupted period not exceeding 31 days, and

(*b*) issued by or on behalf of a qualified Canadian transit organization, which organization records and receipts the cost and usage of the electronic payment card and identifies the right, of the individual who is the holder or owner of such a card, to use public commuter transit services of that qualified Canadian transit organization.

"eligible public transit pass" — (Repealed by S.C. 2017, c. 20, s. 13(2).)

History: S. 118.02(1), the definition "eligible public transit pass" was repealed by S.C. 2017, c. 20, s. 13(2), applicable to the 2018 and subsequent taxation years, and formerly read:

"eligible public transit pass" — "eligible public transit pass" means a document

(*a*) issued by or on behalf of a qualified Canadian transit organization; and

(*b*) identifying the right of an individual who is the holder or owner of the document to use public commuter transit services of that qualified Canadian transit organization

(i) on an unlimited number of occasions and on any day on which the public commuter transit services are offered during an uninterrupted period of at least 28 days, or

(ii) on an unlimited number of occasions during an uninterrupted period of at least five consecutive days, if the combination of that document and one or more other such documents gives the right to the individual to use those public commuter transit services on at least 20 days in a 28-day period.

"public commuter transit services" — (Repealed by S.C. 2017, c. 20, s. 13(2).)

History: S. 118.02(1), the definition "public commuter transit services" was repealed by S.C. 2017, c. 20, s. 13(2), applicable to the 2018 and subsequent taxation years, and formerly read:

"public commuter transit services" — "public commuter transit services" means services offered to the general public, ordinarily for a period of at least five days per week, of transporting individuals, from a place in Canada to another place in Canada, by means of bus, ferry, subway, train or tram, and in respect of which it can reasonably be expected that those individuals would return daily to the place of their departure.

"qualified Canadian transit organization" — (Repealed by S.C. 2017, c. 20, s. 13(2).)

History: S. 118.02(1), the definition "qualified Canadian transit organization" was repealed by S.C. 2017, c. 20, s. 13(2), applicable to the 2018 and subsequent taxation years, and formerly read:

"qualified Canadian transit organization" — "qualified Canadian transit organization" means a person authorised, under a law of Canada or a province, to carry on in Canada a business that is the provision of public commuter transit services, which is carried on through a permanent establishment (as defined by regulation) in Canada.

S. 118.02(1), the definition "qualified Canadian transit organization" was replaced by S.C. 2013, c. 34, s. 247(1), applicable to the 2009 and subsequent taxation years, and formerly read:

"qualified Canadian transit organization" — "qualified Canadian transit organization" means a person authorised, under a law of Canada or a province, to carry on in Canada a business that is the provision of public commuter transit services, which is carried on through a permanent establishment in Canada.

"qualifying relation" — (Repealed by S.C. 2017, c. 20, s. 13(2).)

History: S. 118.02(1), the definition "qualifying relation" was repealed by S.C. 2017, c. 20, s. 13(2), applicable to the 2018 and subsequent taxation years, and formerly read:

"qualifying relation" — "qualifying relation" of an individual for a taxation year means a person who is

(*a*) the individual's spouse or common-law partner at any time in the taxation year; or

(*b*) a child of the individual who has not, during the taxation year, attained the age of 19 years.

► 118.02(2) ◄

(2) Transit pass tax credit — (Repealed by S.C. 2017, c. 20, s. 13(2).)

Editorial Note: The non-refundable digital news subscription tax credit is available for the taxation years 2020 through 2024. The credit equals 15% of the lesser of $500 and the individual's "qualifying subscription expense" for the year. As such, the maximum amount of the federal credit is $75 per year.

A "qualifying subscription expense" is an amount paid to a "qualified Canadian journalism organization" (subsection 248(1)) for a "digital news subscription" (subsection 118.02(1)). If the qualified Canadian journalism organization provides content in a non-digital form or content other than content of qualified Canadian journalism organizations ("extra content"), the maximum amount that qualifies for the credit, regardless of the amount actually paid, is the cost of a comparable digital news subscription with the particular organization without the extra content, or, if there is no comparable subscription, 50% of the amount actually paid.

History: S. 118.02(2) was repealed by S.C. 2017, c. 20, s. 13(2), applicable to the 2018 and subsequent taxation years, and formerly read:

(2) *Transit pass tax credit.* For the purpose of computing the tax payable under this Part by an individual for a taxation year, there may be deducted the amount determined by the formula

$$A \times B$$

where

A is the appropriate percentage for the taxation year; and
B is the amount determined by the formula

C - D

where

C is the total of all amounts each of which is the portion of the cost of an eligible public transit pass or of an eligible electronic payment card, attributable to the use of public commuter transit services in the taxation year and before July 2017 by the individual or by a person who is in the taxation year a qualifying relation of the individual, and

D is the total of all amounts each of which is the amount of a reimbursement, allowance or any other form of assistance that any person is or was entitled to receive in respect of an amount included in computing the value of C (other than an amount that is included in computing the income for any taxation year of that person and that is not deductible in computing the taxable income of that person).

S. 118.02(2), the description of C in the description of B was replaced by S.C. 2017, c. 20, s. 13(1), applicable to the 2017 taxation year, and formerly read:

C is the total of all amounts each of which is the portion of the cost of an eligible public transit pass or of an eligible electronic payment card, attributable to the use of public commuter transit services in the taxation year by the individual or by a person who is in the taxation year a qualifying relation of the individual, and

► 118.02(3) ◄

(3) Apportionment of credit — (Repealed by S.C. 2017, c. 20, s. 13(2).)

History: S. 118.02(3) was repealed by S.C. 2017, c. 20, s. 13(2), applicable to the 2018 and subsequent taxation years, and formerly read:

(3) *Apportionment of credit.* If more than one individual is entitled to a deduction under this section for a taxation year in respect of an eligible public transit pass or of an eligible electronic payment card, the total of all amounts so deductible shall not exceed the maximum amount that would be so deductible for the year by any one of those individuals for that eligible public transit pass or eligible electronic payment card if that individual were the only individual entitled to deduct an amount for the year under this section, and if the individuals cannot agree as to what portion of the amount each can so deduct, the Minister may fix the portions.

Amendment not yet in force

Budget Implementation Act, 2019, No. 1 [S.C. 2019, c. 29]

S. 118.02 was added by S.C. 2019, c. 29, s. 15(1), and will read as follows:

SECTION 118.02 Definitions.

(1) Definitions. The following definitions apply in this section.

digital news subscription —"digital news subscription", of an individual with a qualified Canadian journalism organization, means an agreement entered into between the individual and the qualified Canadian journalism organization, if

(*a*) the agreement entitles an individual to access content of the qualified Canadian journalism organization in digital form; and

(*b*) the qualified Canadian journalism organization is primarily engaged in the production of original written news content and is not engaged in a *broadcasting undertaking* as defined in subsection 2(1) of the *Broadcasting Act*.

qualifying subscription expense —"qualifying subscription expense", for a taxation year, means the amount paid in the year for a digital news subscription of an individual with a qualified Canadian journalism organization and, for this purpose, if the digital news subscription provides access to content in non-digital form or content other than content of qualified Canadian journalism organizations, the amount considered to be paid for the digital news subscription shall not exceed

(*a*) the cost of a comparable digital news subscription with the qualified Canadian journalism organization that solely provides access to content of qualified Canadian journalism organizations in digital form; and

(*b*) if there is no such comparable digital news subscription, 1/2 of the amount actually paid.

(2) Digital news subscription tax credit. For the purpose of computing the tax payable under this Part by an individual for a taxation year that is before 2025, there may be deducted the amount determined by the formula

$$A \times B$$

where

A is the appropriate percentage for the year; and

B is the lesser of

(*a*) $500, and

(*b*) the total of all amounts each of which is a qualifying subscription expense of the individual for the year.

(3) Apportionment of credit. If more than one individual is entitled to a deduction under this section for a taxation year in respect of a qualifying subscription expense, the total of all amounts so deductible shall not exceed the maximum amount that would be so deductible for the year by any one of those individuals in respect of the qualifying subscription expense, if that individual were the only individual entitled to deduct an amount for the year under this section, and if the individuals cannot agree as to what portion of the amount each can so deduct, the Minister may fix the portions.

Applicable: To the 2020 and subsequent taxation years.

SECTION 118.03: [Child fitness tax credit]

► 118.03(1) ◄

(1) Definitions.

Canadian Tax Foundation: Fisher et al., *Awareness and Use of Canada's Children's Fitness Tax Credit*, 2013 Canadian Tax Journal 3:599-632.

"eligible fitness expense" — (Repealed by S.C. 2014, c. 39, s. 32(2).)

History: S. 118.03(1), the definition "eligible fitness expense" was repealed by S.C. 2014, c. 39, s. 32(2), applicable to the 2015 and subsequent taxation years, and formerly read:

"eligible fitness expense"—"eligible fitness expense" in respect of a qualifying child of an individual for a taxation year means the amount of a fee paid to a qualifying entity (other than an amount paid to a person that is, at the time the amount is paid, the individual's spouse or common-law partner or another individual who is under 18 years of age) to the extent that the fee is attributable to the cost of registration or membership of the qualifying child in a prescribed program of physical activity and, for the purposes of this section, that cost

(*a*) includes the cost to the qualifying entity of the program in respect of its administration, instruction, rental of required facilities, and uniforms and equipment that are not available to be acquired by a participant in the program for an amount less than their fair market value at the time, if any, they are so acquired; and

(*b*) does not include

(i) the cost of accommodation, travel, food or beverages, or

(ii) any amount deductible under section 63 in computing any person's income for any taxation year.

Related Regulations: 9400.

"qualifying child" — (Repealed by S.C. 2014, c. 39, s. 32(2).)

History: S. 118.03(1), the definition "qualifying child" was repealed by S.C. 2014, c. 39, s. 32(2), applicable to the 2015 and subsequent taxation years, and formerly read:

"qualifying child"—"qualifying child" of an individual for a taxation year means a child of the individual who is, at the beginning of the taxation year,

(*a*) under 16 years of age; or

(*b*) in the case where an amount is deductible under section 118.3 in computing any person's tax payable under this Part for the taxation year in respect of that child, under 18 years of age.

"qualifying entity" — (Repealed by S.C. 2014, c. 39, s. 32(2).)

History: S. 118.03(1), the definition "qualifying entity" was repealed by S.C. 2014, c. 39, s. 32(2), applicable to the 2015 and subsequent taxation years, and formerly read:

"qualifying entity"—"qualifying entity" means a person or partnership that offers one or more prescribed programs of physical activity.

► 118.03(2) ◄

(2) Child fitness tax credit — (Repealed by S.C. 2014, c. 39, s. 32(2).)

History: S. 118.03(2), was repealed by S.C. 2014, c. 39, s. 32(2), applicable to the 2015 and subsequent taxation years, and formerly read:

(2) *Child fitness tax credit.* For the purpose of computing the tax payable under this Part by an individual for a taxation year, there may be deducted the amount determined by the formula

$$A \times B$$

where

A is the appropriate percentage for the taxation year; and

B is the total of all amounts each of which is, in respect of a qualifying child of the individual for the taxation year, the lesser of $1,000 and the amount determined by the formula

C - D

where

C is total of all amounts each of which is an amount paid in the taxation year by the individual, or by the individual's spouse or common law partner, that is an eligible fitness expense in respect of the qualifying child of the individual, and

D is the total of all amounts that any person is or was entitled to receive, each of which relates to an amount included in computing the value of C in respect of the qualifying child that is the amount of a reimbursement, allowance or any other form of assistance (other than an amount that is included in computing the income for any taxation year of that person and that is not deductible in computing the taxable income of that person).

S. 118.03(2), the portion of the description of B before the formula was replaced by S.C. 2014, c. 39, s. 32(1), applicable to the 2014 taxation year, and formerly read:

B is the total of all amounts each of which is, in respect of a qualifying child of the individual for the taxation year, the lesser of $500 and the amount determined by the formula

Related Regulations: 9400.

Canadian Tax Foundation: Fisher et al., *Awareness and Use of Canada's Children's Fitness Tax Credit*, 2013 Canadian Tax Journal 3:599–632.

Income Tax Folios: *Secondary*— S1-F3-C1 Child Care Expense Deduction.

► 118.03(2.1) ◄

(2.1) Child fitness tax credit — child with disability — (Repealed by S.C. 2014, c. 39, s. 32(2).)

History: S. 118.03(2.1), was repealed by S.C. 2014, c. 39, s. 32(2), applicable to the 2015 and subsequent taxation years, and formerly read:

(2.1) *Child fitness tax credit — child with disability.* For the purpose of computing the tax payable under this Part by an individual for a taxation year there may be deducted in respect of a qualifying child of the individual an amount equal to $500 multiplied by the appropriate percentage for the taxation year if

(*a*) the amount referred to in the description of B in subsection (2) is $100 or more; and

(*b*) an amount is deductible in respect of the qualifying child under section 118.3 in computing any person's tax payable under this Part for the taxation year.

► 118.03(3) ◄

(3) Apportionment of credit — (Repealed by S.C. 2014, c. 39, s. 32(2).)

History: S. 118.03(3), was repealed by S.C. 2014, c. 39, s. 32(2), applicable to the 2015 and subsequent taxation years, and formerly read:

(3) *Apportionment of credit.* If more than one individual is entitled to a deduction under this section for a taxation year in respect of a qualifying child, the total of all amounts so deductible shall not exceed the maximum amount that would be so deductible for the year by any one of those individuals in respect of that qualifying child if that individual were the only individual entitled to deduct an amount for the year under this section in respect of that qualifying child, and if the individuals cannot agree as to what portion of the amount each can so deduct, the Minister may fix the portions.

SECTION 118.031: [Children's arts tax credit]

► 118.031(1) ◄

(1) Definitions. (Repealed by S.C. 2016, c. 7, s. 15(2).)

History: S. 118.031 was repealed by S.C. 2016, c. 7, s. 15(2), in force January 1, 2017, and formerly read:

S. 118.031 *[Children's arts tax credit]*

(1) *Definitions.* The following definitions apply in this section.

"eligible expense"—"eligible expense" in respect of a qualifying child of an individual for a taxation year means the amount of a fee paid to a qualifying entity (other than an amount paid to a person who is, at the time the amount is paid, the individual's spouse or common-law partner or another individual who is under 18 years of age) to the extent that the fee is attributable to the cost of registration or membership of the qualifying child in a prescribed program of artistic, cultural, recreational or developmental activity and, for the purposes of this section, that cost

(*a*) includes the cost to the qualifying entity of the program in respect of its administration, instruction, rental of required facilities, and uniforms and equipment that are not available to be acquired by a participant in the program for an amount less than their fair market value at the time, if any, they are so acquired; and

(*b*) does not include

(i) the cost of accommodation, travel, food or beverages,

(ii) any amount deductible in computing any person's income for any taxation year, or

(iii) any amount included in computing a deduction from any person's tax payable under any Part of this Act, for any taxation year.

"qualifying child"—"qualifying child" of an individual has the meaning assigned by subsection 122.8(1).

"qualifying entity"—"qualifying entity" means a person or partnership that offers one or more programs of artistic, cultural, recreational or developmental activity prescribed for the purposes of the definition "eligible expense".

S. 118.031(1), the definition "qualifying child" was replaced by S.C. 2014, c. 39, s. 33(1), applicable to the 2015 and subsequent taxation years, and formerly read:

"qualifying child"—"qualifying child" of an individual has the meaning assigned by subsection 118.03(1).

S. 118.031(1) was added by S.C. 2011, c. 24, s. 24(1), applicable to the 2011 and subsequent taxation years.

Tax Window Files: CATC - Fees paid for an optional school trip, *May 24, 2012*, CRA Document No. 2012-0441061M4; Children's Arts & Fitness Tax Credits, *May 2, 2012*, CRA Document No. 2012-0438981M4; Crédit pour la condition physique, *April 24, 2012*, CRA Document No. 2012-0439611M4; CIAAE, *April 16, 2012*, CRA Document No. 2012-0437491M4; children's arts tax credit, *April 11, 2012*, CRA Document No. 2012-0438041M4; Children's Arts Tax Credit, *April 5, 2012*, CRA Document No. 2012-0437311M4; children's arts tax credit, *November 7, 2011*, CRA Document No. 2011-0423081M4; children's arts tax credit, *October 28, 2011*, CRA Document No. 2011-0422861M4.

► 118.031(2) ◄

(2) Children's arts tax credit. (Repealed by S.C. 2016, c. 7, s. 15(2).)

History: S. 118.031(2) was repealed by S.C. 2016, c. 7, s. 15(2), in force January 1, 2017, and formerly read:

(2) *Children's arts tax credit.* For the purpose of computing the tax payable under this Part by an individual for a taxation year, there may be deducted the amount determined by the formula

$$A \times B$$

where

A is the appropriate percentage for the taxation year; and

B is the total of all amounts each of which is, in respect of a qualifying child of the individual for the taxation year, the lesser of $250 and the amount determined by the formula

$$C - D$$

where

C is total of all amounts each of which is an amount paid in the taxation year by the individual, or by the individual's spouse or common-law partner, that is an eligible expense in respect of the qualifying child of the individual, and

D is the total of all amounts that any person is or was entitled to receive, each of which relates to an amount included in computing the value determined for C in respect of the qualifying child that is the amount of a reimbursement, allowance or any other form of assistance (other than an amount that is included in computing the income for any taxation year of that person and that is not deductible in computing the taxable income of that person).

S.118.031(2), the portion of the description of B before the formula was replaced by S.C. 2016, c. 7, s. 15(1), applicable to the 2016 taxation year, and formerly read:

B is the total of all amounts each of which is, in respect of a qualifying child of the individual for the taxation year, the lesser of $500 and the amount determined by the formula

S. 118.031(2) was added by S.C. 2011, c. 24, s. 24(1), applicable to the 2011 and subsequent taxation years.

Related Regulations: 9401.

► 118.031(3) ◄

(3) Children's arts tax credit — child with disability. (Repealed by S.C. 2016, c. 7, s. 15(2).)

History: S. 118.031(3) was repealed by S.C. 2016, c. 7, s. 15(2), in force January 1, 2017, and formerly read:

(3) *Children's arts tax credit — child with disability.* For the purpose of computing the tax payable under this Part by an individual for a taxation year there may be deducted in respect of a qualifying child of the individual an amount equal to $500 multiplied by the appropriate percentage for the taxation year if

(*a*) the amount referred to in the description of B in subsection (2) is $100 or more; and

(*b*) an amount is deductible in respect of the qualifying child under section 118.3 in computing any person's tax payable under this Part for the taxation year.

S. 118.031(3) was added by S.C. 2011, c. 24, s. 24(1), applicable to the 2011 and subsequent taxation years.

► 118.031(4) ◄

(4) Apportionment of credit. (Repealed by S.C. 2016, c. 7, s. 15(2).)

History: S. 118.031(4) was repealed by S.C. 2016, c. 7, s. 15(2), in force January 1, 2017, and formerly read:

(4) *Apportionment of credit.* If more than one individual is entitled to a deduction under this section for a taxation year in respect of a qualifying child, the total of all amounts so deductible shall not exceed the maximum amount that would be so deductible for the year by any one of those individuals in respect of that qualifying child if that individual were the only individual entitled to deduct an amount for the year under this section in respect of that qualifying child, and if the individuals cannot agree as to what portion of the amount each can so deduct, the Minister may fix the portions.

S. 118.031(4) was added by S.C. 2011, c. 24, s. 24(1), applicable to the 2011 and subsequent taxation years.

SECTION 118.04: [Home renovation tax credit — Applicable to individuals' 2009 taxation year]

► 118.04(1) ◄

(1) Definitions. The following definitions apply in this section.

Tax Window Files: CIRD-date de l'entente, *January 26, 2010*, CRA Document No. 2010-0354221M4.

"eligible dwelling" —"eligible dwelling" of an individual, at any time, means a housing unit (including the land subjacent to the housing unit and the immediately contiguous land, but not including the portion of such land that exceeds the greater of ½ hectare and the portion of such land that the individual establishes is necessary for the use and enjoyment of the housing unit as a residence) located in Canada if

(*a*) the individual (or a trust under which the individual is a beneficiary) owns, whether jointly with another person or otherwise, at that time, the housing unit or a share of the capital stock of a co-operative housing corporation acquired for the sole purpose of acquiring the right to inhabit the housing unit owned by the corporation; and

(*b*) the housing unit is ordinarily inhabited at any time during the eligible period by the individual, by the individual's spouse or common-law partner or former spouse or common-law partner or by a child of the individual.

History: S. 118.04(1), the definition "eligible dwelling" was added by S.C. 2009, c. 31, s. 4(1), applicable to the 2009 and subsequent taxation years.

"eligible period" —"eligible period" means the period that begins on January 28, 2009 and that ends on January 31, 2010.

History: S. 118.04(1), the definition "eligible period" was added by S.C. 2009, c. 31, s. 4(1), applicable to the 2009 and subsequent taxation years.

"individual" —"individual" does not include a trust.

History: S. 118.04(1), the definition "individual" was added by S.C. 2009, c. 31, s. 4(1), applicable to the 2009 and subsequent taxation years.

"qualifying expenditure" —"qualifying expenditure" of an individual means an outlay or expense that is made or incurred, by the individual or by a qualifying relation in respect of the individual during the eligible period, that is directly attributable to a qualifying renovation by the individual and that is the cost of goods acquired or services received during the eligible period and includes such an outlay or expense for permits required for, or for the rental of equipment used in the course of, the qualifying renovation, but does not include such an outlay or expense

(*a*) to acquire goods that have been used, or acquired for use or lease, by the individual or by a qualifying relation in respect of the individual, for any purpose whatever before they were acquired by the individual or the qualifying relation in respect of the individual;

(*b*) made or incurred under the terms of an agreement entered into before the eligible period;

(*c*) to acquire a property that can be used independently of the qualifying renovation;

(*d*) that is the cost of annual, recurring or routine repair or maintenance;

(*e*) to acquire a household appliance;

(*f*) to acquire an electronic home-entertainment device;

(*g*) for financing costs in respect of the qualifying renovation;

(*h*) made or incurred for the purpose of gaining or producing income from a business or property; or

(*i*) in respect of goods or services provided by a person not dealing at arm's length with the individual, unless the person is registered for the purposes of Part IX of the *Excise Tax Act*.

History: S. 118.04(1), the definition "qualifying expenditure" was added by S.C. 2009, c. 31, s. 4(1), applicable to the 2009 and subsequent taxation years.

Related Sections: S. 108(1.1) Home renovation tax credit.

Forms: T1 SCH 12 — Resource-Related Deductions (2006 and later taxation years).

"qualifying relation" —"qualifying relation" in respect of an individual means a person who is the individual's spouse or common-law partner, or a child of the individual who has not attained the age of 18 years before the end of 2009 (other than a child who was, at any time during the eligible period, a married person, a person who is in a common-law partnership or a person who has a child).

History: S. 118.04(1), the definition "qualifying relation" was added by S.C. 2009, c. 31, s. 4(1), applicable to the 2009 and subsequent taxation years.

"qualifying renovation" —"qualifying renovation" by an individual, at any time, means a renovation or alteration, of a property that is at that time an eligible dwelling of the individual or of a qualifying relation in respect of the individual, that is of an enduring nature and that is integral to the eligible dwelling.

History: S. 118.04(1), the definition "qualifying renovation" was added by S.C. 2009, c. 31, s. 4(1), applicable to the 2009 and subsequent taxation years.

► 118.04(2) ◄

(2) Rules of application. For the purposes of this section,

(*a*) a qualifying expenditure of an individual includes an outlay or expense made or incurred by a co-operative housing corporation, a condominium corporation (or, for civil law, a syndicate of co-owners) or a similar entity (in this paragraph referred to as the "corporation"), in respect of a property that is owned, administered or managed by that corporation, and that includes an eligible dwelling of the individual, to the extent of the individual's share of that outlay or expense, if

(i) the outlay or expense would be a qualifying expenditure of the corporation if the corporation were a natural person and the property were an eligible dwelling of that natural person, and

(ii) the corporation has notified the individual, in writing, of the individual's share of the outlay or expense; and

(*b*) a qualifying expenditure of an individual includes an outlay or expense made or incurred by a trust, in respect of a property owned by the trust that includes an eligible dwelling of the individual, to the extent of the share of that outlay or expense that is reasonably attributable to the individual, having regard to the amount of the outlays or expenses made or incurred in respect of the eligible dwelling of the individual (including, for this purpose, common areas relevant to more than one eligible dwelling), if

(i) the outlay or expense would be a qualifying expenditure of the trust if the trust were a natural person and the property were an eligible dwelling of that natural person, and

(ii) the trust has notified the individual, in writing, of the individual's share of the outlay or expense.

History: S. 118.04(2) was added by S.C. 2009, c. 31, s. 4(1), applicable to the 2009 and subsequent taxation years.

► 118.04(3) ◄

(3) Home renovation tax credit. For the purposes of computing the tax payable under this Part by an individual for the individual's 2009 taxation year, there may be deducted the amount determined by the formula

$$A \times (B - \$1{,}000)$$

where

A is the appropriate percentage for the taxation year; and

B is the lesser of $10,000 and the total of all amounts, each of which is a qualifying expenditure of the individual.

Editorial Note: S. 118.04 allows an individual and his or her family to claim a tax credit not exceeding $1,350 in respect of renovation expenses of an enduring nature made to their principal residence from January 28, 2009 to January 31, 2010 under an agreement made after January 27, 2009. This credit is temporary and may be claimed only on a 2009 tax return.

History: S. 118.04(3) was added by S.C. 2009, c. 31, s. 4(1), applicable to the 2009 and subsequent taxation years.

► 118.04(4) ◄

(4) Interaction with medical expense credit. Notwithstanding paragraph 248(28)(*b*), an amount may be included in determining both an amount under subsection (3) and under section 118.2 if those amounts otherwise qualify to be included for the purposes of those provisions.

History: S. 118.04(4) was added by S.C. 2009, c. 31, s. 4(1), applicable to the 2009 and subsequent taxation years.

► 118.04(5) ◄

(5) Apportionment of credit. If more than one individual is entitled to a deduction under this section for a taxation year in respect of a qualifying expenditure of an individual, the total of all amounts so deductible shall not exceed the maximum amount that would be so deductible for the year by any one of those individuals in respect of the qualifying expenditure, if that individual were the only individual entitled to deduct an amount for the year under this section, and if the individuals cannot agree as to what portion of the amount each can so deduct, the Minister may fix the portions.

History: S. 118.04(5) was added by S.C. 2009, c. 31, s. 4(1), applicable to the 2009 and subsequent taxation years.

SECTION 118.041: [Home Accessibility Tax Credit]

► 118.041(1) ◄

(1) Definitions. The following definitions apply in this section.

eligible dwelling — "eligible dwelling" of an individual, at any time in a taxation year, means a housing unit (including the land subjacent to the housing unit and the immediately contiguous land, but not including the portion of that land that exceeds the greater of ½ hectare and the portion of that land that the individual establishes is necessary for the use and enjoyment of the housing unit as a residence) located in Canada if

(*a*) the individual (or a trust under which the individual is a beneficiary) owns — whether jointly with another person or otherwise — at that time, the housing unit or a share of the capital stock of a cooperative housing corporation acquired for the sole purpose of acquiring the right to inhabit the housing unit owned by the corporation; and

(*b*) the housing unit is ordinarily inhabited, or is reasonably expected to be ordinarily inhabited, at any time in the taxation year

(i) by the individual, if the individual is a qualifying individual, or

(ii) by the individual and a qualifying individual, if

(A) the individual is an eligible individual in respect of the qualifying individual, and

(B) the qualifying individual does not, throughout the taxation year, own — whether jointly with another person or otherwise — and ordinarily inhabit another housing unit in Canada.

eligible individual — "eligible individual", in respect of a qualifying individual for a taxation year, means

(*a*) an individual who is the qualifying individual's spouse or common-law partner in the year;

(*b*) except if paragraph (*c*) applies, an individual who is entitled to deduct an amount under subsection 118.3(2) for the year in respect of the qualifying individual or would be if no amount was claimed for the year by the qualifying individual under subsection 118.3(1) or by the qualifying individual's spouse or common-law partner under section 118.8; or

(*c*) in the case of a qualifying individual who has attained the age of 65 before the end of the year, an individual who

(i) claimed for the year a deduction under subsection 118(1) in respect of the qualifying individual because of

(A) paragraph (*b*) of the description of B in that subsection, or

(B) paragraph (*d*) of the description of B in that subsection where the qualifying individual is a parent, grandparent, child, grandchild, brother, sister, aunt, uncle, nephew or niece of the individual, or of the individual's spouse or common-law partner, or

(ii) could have claimed for the year a deduction referred to in subparagraph (i) in respect of the qualifying individual if

(A) the qualifying individual had no income for the year,

(B) in the case of a deduction referred to in clause (i)(A), the individual were not married and not in a common-law partnership, and

(C) in the case of a deduction under subsection 118(1) because of paragraph (*d*) of the description of B in that subsection in respect of a qualifying individual who is a dependant (within the meaning of subsection 118(6)) of the individual, the qualifying individual was dependent on the individual because of mental or physical infirmity.

History: S. 118.041(1), clause (*c*)(i)(B) of the definition "eligible individual" was replaced by S.C. 2017, c. 20, s. 14(1), applicable to the 2017 and subsequent taxation years, and formerly read:

> (B) paragraph (*c.1*) or (*d*) of the description of B in that subsection where the qualifying individual is a parent, grandparent, child, grandchild, brother, sister, aunt, uncle, nephew or niece of the individual, or of the individual's spouse or common-law partner, or

individual —"individual" does not include a trust.

qualifying expenditure —"qualifying expenditure" of an individual means an outlay or expense that is made or incurred, during a taxation year, that is directly attributable to a qualifying renovation — of an eligible dwelling of a qualifying individual or an eligible individual in respect of a qualifying individual — and that is the cost of goods acquired or services received during the year and includes an outlay or expense for permits required for, or for the rental of equipment used in the course of, the qualifying renovation, but does not include an outlay or expense

(*a*) to acquire a property that can be used independently of the qualifying renovation;

(*b*) that is the cost of annual, recurring or routine repair or maintenance;

(*c*) to acquire a household appliance;

(*d*) to acquire an electronic home-entertainment device;

(*e*) that is the cost of housekeeping, security monitoring, gardening, outdoor maintenance or similar services;

(*f*) for financing costs in respect of the qualifying renovation;

(*g*) made or incurred primarily for the purpose of increasing or maintaining the value of the eligible dwelling;

(*h*) made or incurred for the purpose of gaining or producing income from a business or property;

(*i*) in respect of goods or services provided by a person not dealing at arm's length with the qualifying individual or the eligible individual, unless the person is registered for the purposes of Part IX of the *Excise Tax Act;* or

(*j*) to the extent that the outlay or expense can reasonably be considered to have been reimbursed, otherwise than as assistance from the federal or a provincial government including a grant, subsidy, forgivable loan or a deduction from tax.

qualifying individual —"qualifying individual", in respect of a taxation year, means an individual

(*a*) who has attained the age of 65 years before the end of the taxation year; or

(*b*) in respect of whom an amount is deductible, or would be deductible if this Act were read without reference to paragraph 118.3(1)(*c*), under section 118.3 in computing a taxpayer's tax payable under this Part for the taxation year.

qualifying renovation —"qualifying renovation" means a renovation or alteration of an eligible dwelling of a qualifying individual or an eligible individual in respect of a qualifying individual that

(*a*) is of an enduring nature and integral to the eligible dwelling; and

(*b*) is undertaken to

(i) enable the qualifying individual to gain access to, or to be mobile or functional within, the eligible dwelling, or

(ii) reduce the risk of harm to the qualifying individual within the eligible dwelling or in gaining access to the dwelling.

► 118.041(2) ◄

(2) Qualifying expenditure rules. For the purpose of this section,

(*a*) a qualifying expenditure in respect of an eligible dwelling of a particular individual — who is a qualifying individual or an eligible individual in respect of a qualifying individual — includes an outlay or expense made or incurred by a cooperative housing corporation, a condominium corporation (or, for civil law, a syndicate of co-owners) or a similar entity (in this paragraph referred to as the "corporation"), in respect of a property that is owned, administered or managed by that corporation and that includes the eligible dwelling, to the extent of the share of that outlay or expense that is reasonably attributable to the eligible dwelling, if

(i) the outlay or expense would be a qualifying expenditure of the corporation if the corporation were an individual and the property were an eligible dwelling of that individual, and

(ii) the corporation has notified, in writing, either the particular individual or, if the particular individual is an eligible individual in respect of a qualifying individual, the qualifying individual, of the share of the outlay or expense that is attributable to the eligible dwelling; and

(*b*) a qualifying expenditure in respect of an eligible dwelling of a particular individual — who is a qualifying individual or an eligible individual in respect of a qualifying individual — includes an outlay or expense made or incurred by a trust, in respect of a property owned by the trust that includes the eligible dwelling, to the extent of the share of that outlay or expense that is reasonably attributable to the eligible dwelling, having regard to the amount of the outlays or expenses made or incurred in respect of the eligible dwelling (including, for this purpose, common areas relevant to more than one eligible dwelling), if

(i) the outlay or expense would be a qualifying expenditure of the trust if the trust were an individual and the property were an eligible dwelling of that individual, and

(ii) the trust has notified, in writing, either the particular individual or, if the particular individual is an eligible individual in respect of a qualifying individual, the qualifying individual, of the share of the outlay or expense that is attributable to the eligible dwelling.

► 118.041(3) ◄

(3) Home accessibility tax credit. For the purpose of computing the tax payable under this Part by a qualifying individual or an eligible individual, in respect of an eligible dwelling for a taxation year, there may be deducted the amount determined by the formula

$$A \times B$$

where

A is the appropriate percentage for the taxation year; and

B is the lesser of

(*a*) $10,000, and

(*b*) the total of all amounts, each of which is a qualifying expenditure of the individual in respect of the eligible dwelling for the taxation year.

Tax Window Files: METC & HATC for a dependant, *May 6, 2019*, CRA Document No. 2019-0791601E5.

► 118.041(4) ◄

(4) Interaction with medical expense credit. Despite paragraph 248(28)(*b*), an amount may be included in determining both an amount under subsection (3) and under section 118.2 if those amounts otherwise qualify to be included for the purposes of those provisions.

Related Sections: 118.2(1) Medical expense credit.

► 118.041(5) ◄

(5) Limits. For the purpose of this section,

(*a*) a maximum of $10,000 of qualifying expenditures for a taxation year in respect of a qualifying individual can be claimed under subsection (3) by the qualifying individual and all eligible individuals in respect of the qualifying individual;

(*b*) if there is more than one qualifying individual in respect of an eligible dwelling, a maximum of $10,000 of qualifying expenditures for a taxation year in respect of the eligible dwelling can be claimed under subsection (3) by the qualifying individuals and all eligible individuals in respect of the qualifying individuals; and

(*c*) if more than one individual is entitled to a deduction under subsection (3) for a taxation year in respect of the same qualifying individual or the same eligible dwelling and the individuals cannot agree as to what portion of the amount each can so deduct, the Minister may fix the portions.

► 118.041(6) ◄

(6) Effect of bankruptcy. For the purpose of subsection (5), if an individual becomes bankrupt in a particular calendar year, despite subsection 128(2), any reference to the taxation year of the individual is deemed to be a reference to the particular calendar year.

Related Sections: 128(2) Where individual bankrupt.

► 118.041(7) ◄

(7) In the event of death and bankruptcy. For the purpose of this section,

(*a*) if an individual dies during a calendar year and would have attained 65 years of age if the individual were alive at the end of the year, the individual is deemed to have attained 65 years of age at the beginning of the year;

(*b*) if an individual becomes a qualifying individual during a calendar year and becomes bankrupt in that year, the individual is deemed to be a qualifying individual at the beginning of that year; and

(*c*) if an individual becomes a qualifying individual during a calendar year and an eligible individual in respect of the qualifying individual becomes bankrupt in that year, the individual is deemed to be a qualifying individual at the beginning of the year.

History: S. 118.041 was added by S.C. 2015, c. 36, s. 8(1), applicable to the 2016 and subsequent taxation years.

SECTION 118.05: [First-time home buyers' tax credit]

► 118.05(1) ◄

(1) Definitions. The following definitions apply in this section.

"qualifying home"—"qualifying home" in respect of an individual, means a "qualifying home" as defined in subsection 146.01(1) that is acquired, whether jointly or otherwise, after January 27, 2009 if

(*a*) the home is acquired by the individual, or by the individual's spouse or common-law partner, and

(i) the individual intends to inhabit the home as a principal place of residence not later than one year after its acquisition,

(ii) the individual did not own, whether jointly or otherwise, a home that was occupied by the individual in the period

(A) that began at the beginning of the fourth preceding calendar year that ended before the acquisition, and

(B) that ended on the day before the acquisition, and

(iii) the individual's spouse or common-law partner did not, in the period referred to in subparagraph (ii), own, whether jointly or otherwise, a home

(A) that was inhabited by the individual during the marriage to or common-law partnership with the individual, or

(B) that was a share of the capital stock of a cooperative housing corporation that relates to a housing unit inhabited by the individual during the marriage to or common-law partnership with the individual; or

(*b*) the home is acquired by the individual for the benefit of a specified person in respect of the individual, and

(i) the individual intends that the home be inhabited by the specified person as a principal place of residence not later than one year after its acquisition by the individual, and

(ii) the purpose of the acquisition of the home by the individual is to enable the specified person to live in

(A) a home that is more accessible by the specified person or in which the specified person is more mobile or functional, or

(B) an environment better suited to the specified person's personal needs and care.

Editorial Note: A qualifying home would include a single-family house, a semi-detached house, a townhouse, a mobile home, a condominium unit, or an apartment. Any share in a co-operative housing corporation giving its owner an equity interest in the housing unit would qualify for the credit. A home does not have to be purchased to qualify for the credit. It could be built by the taxpayer even if the land on which it is constructed was acquired before January 27, 2009.

History: S. 118.05(1), the definition "qualifying home" was added by S.C. 2009, c. 31, s. 4(1), applicable to the 2009 and subsequent taxation years.

"specified person"—"specified person" in respect of an individual, at any time, means a person who

(*a*) is the individual or is related at that time to the individual; and

(*b*) would be entitled to a deduction under subsection 118.3(1) in computing tax payable under this Part for the person's taxation year that includes that time if that subsection were read without reference to paragraph (*c*) of that subsection.

History: S. 118.05(1), the definition "specified person" was added by S.C. 2009, c. 31, s. 4(1), applicable to the 2009 and subsequent taxation years.

► 118.05(2) ◄

(2) Rules of application. For the purposes of this section, an individual is considered to have acquired a qualifying home only if the individual's interest (or for civil law, right) in it is registered in accordance with the land registration system or other similar system applicable where it is located.

History: S. 118.05(2) was added by S.C. 2009, c. 31, s. 4(1), applicable to the 2009 and subsequent taxation years.

► 118.05(3) ◄

(3) First-time home buyers' tax credit. In computing the tax payable under this Part by an individual for a taxation year in which a qualifying home in respect of the individual is acquired, there may be deducted the amount determined by multiplying $5,000 by the appropriate percentage for the taxation year.

Editorial Note: S. 118.05 allows an individual buying or building a qualifying home after January 27, 2009 to claim a tax credit not exceeding $750 in the year of acquisition if neither the individual nor his/her spouse or common-law partner had owned or lived in another home in the year of acquisition or the four preceding calendar years. The credit is non-recurring and calculated at a rate of 15% on an amount of $5,000. If two spouses or common-law partners share the credit, the total claim cannot exceed $750. To qualify for the credit, the home must be located in Canada, be registered in the name of the taxpayer or his/her spouse or common-law partner, and the taxpayer or his/her spouse or common-law partner must intend to inhabit the home as a principal residence within one year from the date of acquisition. The same credit may be claimed by a disabled person or a relative of a disabled person entitled to claim the disability tax credit under s. 118.3 if the purpose of the home acquisition is to allow the disabled person to live in a home that is more accessible or better suited for his/her personal needs or care.

History: S. 118.05(3) was added by S.C. 2009, c. 31, s. 4(1), applicable to the 2009 and subsequent taxation years.

Related Sections: S. 118.61(1) Unused tuition, textbook and education tax credits; s. 118.61(2) Deduction of carryforward; s. 118.8 Transfer of unused credits to spouse or common-law partner; s. 118.81 Tuition, textbook and education tax credits transferred; s. 118.91; s. 118.92 Ordering of credits; s. 118.94 Tax payable by non-residents (credits restricted); s. 118.95 Credits in year of bankruptcy; s. 127.531 Basic minimum tax credit determined; s. 128(2)(iii)(A) Where individual bankrupt.

► 118.05(4) ◄

(4) Apportionment of credit. If more than one individual is entitled to a deduction under this section for a taxation year in respect of a particular qualifying home, the total of all amounts so deductible shall not exceed the maximum amount that would be so deductible for the year by any one of those individuals in respect of the qualifying home, if that individual were the only individual entitled to deduct an amount for the year under this section, and if the individuals cannot agree as to what portion of the amount each can so deduct, the Minister may fix the portions.

History: S. 118.05(4) was added by S.C. 2009, c. 31, s. 4(1), applicable to the 2009 and subsequent taxation years.

SECTION 118.06: [Volunteer firefighter tax credit]

► 118.06(1) ◄

(1) Definition of "eligible volunteer firefighting services". In this section and section 118.07, "eligible volunteer firefighting services" means services provided by an individual in the individual's capacity as a volunteer firefighter to a fire department that consist primarily of responding to and being on call for firefighting and related emergency calls, attending meetings held by the fire department and participating in required training related to the prevention or suppression of fires, but does not include services provided to a particular fire department if the individual provides firefighting services to the department otherwise than as a volunteer.

History: S. 118.06(1) was replaced by S.C. 2014, c. 20, s. 7(1), applicable to the 2014 and subsequent taxation years, and formerly read:

(1) *Definition of "eligible volunteer firefighting services".* In this section, "eligible volunteer firefighting services" means services provided by an individual in the individual's capacity as a volunteer firefighter to a fire department that consist primarily of responding to and being on call for firefighting and related emergency calls, attending meetings held by the fire department and participating in required training related to the prevention or suppression of fires, but does not include services provided to a particular fire department if the individual provides firefighting services to the department otherwise than as a volunteer.

S. 118.06(1) was added by S.C. 2011, c. 24, s. 25(1), applicable to the 2011 and subsequent taxation years.

► 118.06(2) ◄

(2) Volunteer firefighter tax credit. For the purpose of computing the tax payable under this Part for a taxation year by an individual who performs eligible volunteer firefighting services in the year, there may be deducted the amount determined by multiplying $3,000 by the appropriate percentage for the taxation year if the individual

(*a*) performs in the year not less than 200 hours of service each of which is an hour of

(i) eligible volunteer firefighting service for a fire department, or

(ii) eligible search and rescue volunteer service for an eligible search and rescue organization; and

(*b*) provides the certificates referred to in subsections (3) and 118.07(3) as and when requested by the Minister.

History: S. 118.06(2) was replaced by S.C. 2014, c. 20, s. 7(1), applicable to the 2014 and subsequent taxation years, and formerly read:

(2) *Volunteer firefighter tax credit.* For the purpose of computing the tax payable under this Part for a taxation year by an individual, there may be deducted the amount determined by multiplying $3,000 by the appropriate percentage for the taxation year if the individual

(*a*) performs not less than 200 hours of eligible volunteer firefighting services in the taxation year for one or more fire departments; and

(*b*) provides the certificates referred to in subsection (3) as and when requested by the Minister.

S. 118.06(2) was added by S.C. 2011, c. 24, s. 25(1), applicable to the 2011 and subsequent taxation years.

Related Sections: S. 81(4) Payments for volunteer services.

► 118.06(3) ◄

(3) Certificate. If the Minister so demands, an individual making a claim under this section in respect of a taxation year shall provide to the Minister a written certificate from the fire chief or a delegated official of each fire department to which the individual provided eligible volunteer firefighting services for the year, attesting to the number of hours of eligible volunteer firefighting services performed in the year by the individual for the particular fire department.

History: S. 118.06(3) was added by S.C. 2011, c. 24, s. 25(1), applicable to the 2011 and subsequent taxation years.

SECTION 118.07: [Search and rescue volunteers tax credit]

► 118.07(1) ◄

(1) Definitions. The following definitions apply in this section and section 118.06.

History: S. 118.07(1) was added by S.C. 2014, c. 20, s. 8(1), applicable to the 2014 and subsequent taxation years.

"eligible search and rescue organization" — "eligible search and rescue organization" means a search and rescue organization

(*a*) that is a member of the Search and Rescue Volunteer Association of Canada, the Civil Air Search and Rescue Association or the Canadian Coast Guard Auxiliary; or

(*b*) whose status as a search and rescue organization is recognized by a provincial, municipal or public authority.

"eligible search and rescue volunteer services" — "eligible search and rescue volunteer services" means services, other than eligible volunteer firefighting services, provided by an individual in the individual's capacity as a volunteer to an eligible search and rescue organization that consist primarily of responding to and being on call for search and rescue and related emergency calls, attending meetings held by the organization and participating in required training related to search and rescue services, but does not include services provided to an organization if the individual provides search and rescue services to the organization otherwise than as a volunteer.

▶ 118.07(2) ◀

(2) Search and rescue volunteer tax credit. For the purpose of computing the tax payable under this Part for a taxation year by an individual who performs eligible search and rescue volunteer services in the year, there may be deducted the amount determined by multiplying $3,000 by the appropriate percentage for the taxation year if the individual

(*a*) performs in the year not less than 200 hours of service each of which is an hour of

(i) eligible search and rescue volunteer service for an eligible search and rescue organization, or

(ii) eligible volunteer firefighting services for a fire department;

(*b*) provides the certificates referred to in subsections (3) and 118.06(3) as and when requested by the Minister; and

(*c*) has not deducted an amount under section 118.06 for the year.

History: S. 118.07(2) was added by S.C. 2014, c. 20, s. 8(1), applicable to the 2014 and subsequent taxation years.

Related Sections: S. 81(4) Payments for volunteer services.

▶ 118.07(3) ◀

(3) Certificate. If the Minister so demands, an individual making a claim under this section in respect of a taxation year shall provide to the Minister a written certificate from the team president, or other individual who fulfils a similar role, of each eligible search and rescue organization to which the individual provided eligible search and rescue volunteer services for the year, attesting to the number of hours of eligible search and rescue volunteer services performed in the year by the individual for the particular organization.

History: S. 118.07(3) was added by S.C. 2014, c. 20, s. 8(1), applicable to the 2014 and subsequent taxation years.

SECTION 118.1: [Charitable and other gifts]

▶ 118.1(1) ◀

(1) Definitions. In this section,

Related Sections: S. 110.1(1) Deduction for gifts.

Tax Topics: No. 1654, Tax Shelters — Past, Present and Future.

Interpretation Bulletins: *Secondary* — IT-407R4 (Consolid.) Dispositions of cultural property to designated Canadian institutions.

Tax Window Files: Alter Ego Trust, *December 17, 2009,* CRA Document No. 2009-0308611R3.

Canadian Tax Foundation: Studniberg, *Current Cases: Tax Court of Canada — Distinguishing Between a Charitable Motive and the Rationale for a Gift (Kossow v. The Queen, 2012 TCC 325),* 2013 Canadian Tax Journal 1:198–208; Zweibel and Cooper, *Charitable Gifts of Conservation Easements: Lessons from the US Experience in Enhancing the Tax Incentive,* 2010 Canadian Tax Journal 1:25–62; Cooper and Man, *Planned Giving for High Net Worth Clients,* 2006 Ontario Tax Conference 6:1–34; Pappin, *December 20, 2002 Draft Technical Changes — Charitable Donations, Charities and Trusts,* 2003 Ontario Tax Conference 5:1–32; Belley, *Eco-Gifts: Administrative Policies and Statutory Amendments,* 2003 Tax for the Owner-Manager 3(2):2–3.

"first-time donor" — (Repealed by S.C. 2013, c. 33, s. 10(2).)

History: S. 118.1(1), the definition "first-time donor" was repealed by S.C. 2013, c. 33, s. 10(2), applicable to the 2018 and subsequent taxation years, and formerly read:

"first-time donor" —"first-time donor", for a taxation year, means an individual (other than a trust)

(*a*) who has not deducted an amount under subsection (3) for a preceding taxation year that ends after 2007, and

(*b*) who is not, at the end of the year, married to a person (other than a person who was at that time separated from the individual by reason of a breakdown of their marriage), or in a common-law partnership with a person, who has deducted an amount under subsection (3) for a preceding taxation year that ends after 2007;

S. 118.1(1), the definition "first-time donor" was added by S.C. 2013, c. 33, s. 10(1), applicable in respect of gifts made after March 20, 2013.

"total charitable gifts" —"total charitable gifts", of an individual for a particular taxation year, means the total of all amounts each of which is the eligible amount — to the extent it is not otherwise included in determining an amount that is deducted under this section in computing any individual's tax payable under this Part for any taxation year — of a gift (other than a gift any part of the eligible amount of which is included in the total cultural gifts or the total ecological gifts of any individual for any taxation year) that is made

(*a*) to a qualified donee,

(*b*) in a taxation year that is not a year for which an amount is deducted under subsection 110(2) in computing the individual's taxable income, and

(*c*) if the individual is

(i) not a trust,

(A) by the individual, or the individual's spouse or common-law partner, in the particular year or any of the five preceding taxation years,

(B) by the individual in the year in which the individual dies if the particular year is the taxation year that precedes the taxation year in which the individual dies, or

(C) by the individual's estate if subsection (5.1) applies to the gift and the particular year is the taxation year in which the individual dies or the preceding taxation year, or

(ii) a trust

(A) by the trust in the particular year or any of the five preceding taxation years,

(B) by the trust if

(I) the trust is an individual's estate,

(II) subsection (5.1) applies to the gift, and

(III) the particular year is a taxation year

1. in which the estate is the individual's graduated rate estate, and

2. that precedes the taxation year in which the gift is made, or

(C) by the trust if

(I) the end of the particular year is determined by paragraph 104(13.4)(*a*) because of an individual's death,

(II) the gift is made after the particular year and on or before the trust's filing-due date for the particular year, and

(III) the subject of the gift is property that is held by the trust at the time of the individual's death or is property that was substituted for that property;

Editorial Note: Subsection 118.1(3) allows an individual to claim a tax credit for eligible amounts of "total gifts" for a taxation year; total gifts includes the individual's total charitable gifts, total cultural gifts, and total ecological gifts (all defined in subsection (1)). See the editorial note to subsection 118.1(3) regarding the credit rates for gifts.

The definition of "total gifts" in subsection 118.1(1) sets out the maximum amount that an individual may claim for charitable gifts and Crown gifts (prior to 2016). The limit is 75% of the individual's income for the year plus for gifts of capital property, (i) 25% of the taxable capital gain arising from the gift (to the extent that the gain was not excluded from the individual's taxable income by the lifetime capital gains exemption in subsection 110.6), and (ii) 25% of the lesser of any recapture of capital cost allowance on the property included in the taxpayer's income in the year and the property's capital cost or proceeds of disposition (whichever is less). This effectively enables an individual to claim a full credit for a donation of a capital property to the extent that the capital gains have been included in the individual's income.

For 2016 and subsequent years the definition of "total charitable gifts" in subsection 118.1(1) is amended to extend the conditions where the eligible amount of a gift is included in the individual's total charitable gifts for a given year. Paragraph (*c*) of the definition is introduced so the individual's total charitable gifts for a particular taxation year (subject to the definition's other conditions) includes the eligible amount of a gift:

- made by the individual's spouse or common law partner in the year or any of the five preceding taxation years (consistent with the CRA's current administrative practice);
- made by the individual in the taxation year in which the individual dies if the particular year is the immediately preceding year (this maintains the carryback provision that was previously contained in subsection 118.1(4)); or
- made by the individual's estate, if subsection 118.1(5.1) applies and the particular year is the year of death or the immediately preceding year. This allows the individual's legal representative to claim a charitable donations tax credit in respect of the eligible amount in those taxation years of the individual, as otherwise permitted in section 118.1.

The foregoing conditions found in paragraph (*c*) of the definition are also found in the definitions of "total ecological gifts" and "total cultural gifts"; in other words, the same requirements apply to those categories of gifts.

History: S. 118.1(1), clause (*c*)(i)(C) of the definition "total charitable gifts" was replaced by S.C. 2016, c. 12, s. 42(1), applicable to the 2016 and subsequent taxation years, and formerly read:

(C) by the individual's graduated rate estate if subsection (5.1) applies to the gift and the particular year is the taxation year in which the individual dies or the preceding taxation year, or

S. 118.1(1), clause (*c*)(ii)(B) of the definition "total charitable gifts" was replaced by S.C. 2016, c. 12, s. 42(2), applicable to the 2016 and subsequent taxation years, and formerly read:

(B) by the individual's graduated rate estate if subsection (5.1) applies to the gift and the particular year is the taxation year in which the individual dies or the preceding taxation year, or

S. 118.1(1), clause (*c*)(ii)(C) of the definition "total charitable gifts" was added by S.C. 2016, c. 12, s. 42(2), applicable to the 2016 and subsequent taxation years.

S. 118.1(1), the definition "total charitable gifts" was replaced by S.C. 2014, c. 39, s. 34(2), applicable to the 2016 and subsequent taxation years, and formerly read:

"total charitable gifts"—"total charitable gifts", of an individual for a taxation year, means the total of all amounts each of which is the eligible amount of a gift (other than a gift the eligible amount of which is included in the total Crown gifts, the total cultural gifts or the total ecological gifts of the individual for the year) made by the individual in the year or in any of the five preceding taxation years (other than in a year for which a deduction under subsection 110(2) was claimed in computing the individual's taxable income) to a qualified donee, to the extent that the amount was not included in determining an amount that was deducted under this section in computing the individual's tax payable under this Part for a preceding taxation year;

S. 118.1(1), the definition "total charitable gifts" was replaced by S.C. 2013, c. 34, s. 248(2), deemed to have come into force on January 1, 2012, and formerly read:

"total charitable gifts"—"total charitable gifts", of an individual for a taxation year, means the total of all amounts each of which is the eligible amount of a gift (other than a gift described in the definition "total Crown gifts", "total cultural gifts" or "total ecological gifts") made by the individual in the year or in any of the five preceding taxation years (other than in a year for which a deduction under subsection 110(2) was claimed in computing the individual's taxable income) to

(*a*) a registered charity,

(*b*) a registered Canadian amateur athletic association,

(*c*) a housing corporation resident in Canada and exempt from tax under this Part because of paragraph 149(1)(*i*),

(*d*) a municipality in Canada,

(*d*.1) a municipal or public body performing a function of government in Canada,

(*e*) the United Nations or an agency thereof,

(*f*) a university outside Canada that is prescribed to be a university the student body of which ordinarily includes students from Canada,

(*g*) a charitable organization outside Canada to which her Majesty in right of Canada has made a gift during the individual's taxation year or the 12 months immediately preceding that taxation year, or

(*g*.1) Her Majesty in right of Canada or a province,

to the extent that those amounts were

(*h*) not deducted in computing the individual's taxable income for a taxation year ending before 1988, and

(*i*) not included in determining an amount that was deducted under this section in computing the individual's tax payable under this Part for a preceding taxation year;

S. 118.1(1), the definition "total charitable gifts" was replaced by S.C. 2013, c. 34, s. 248(1), applicable to gifts made after December 20, 2002, and formerly read:

"total charitable gifts"—"total charitable gifts", of an individual for a taxation year, means the total of all amounts each of which is the fair market value of a gift (other than a gift the fair market value of which is included in the total Crown gifts, the total cultural gifts or the total ecological gifts of the individual for the year) made by the individual in the year or in any of the five preceding taxation years (other than in a year for which a deduction under subsection 110(2) was claimed in computing the individual's taxable income) to a qualified donee, to the extent that the amount was not included in determining an amount that was deducted under this section in computing the individual's tax payable under this Part for a preceding taxation year;

S. 118.1(1), the definition "total charitable gifts" was replaced by S.C. 2011, c. 24, s. 26(3), in force January 1, 2012. S. 118.1(1), the definition "total charitable gifts" formerly read:

"total charitable gifts"—"total charitable gifts" of an individual for a taxation year means the total of all amounts each of which is the fair market value of a gift (other than a gift the fair market value of which is included in the total Crown gifts, the total cultural gifts or the total ecological gifts of the individual for the year) made by the individual in the year or in any of the 5 immediately preceding taxation years (other than in a year for which a deduction under subsection 110(2) was claimed in computing the individual's taxable income) to

(*a*) a registered charity,

(*b*) a registered Canadian amateur athletic association,

(*c*) a housing corporation resident in Canada and exempt from tax under this Part because of paragraph 149(1)(*i*),

(*d*) a municipality in Canada,

(*d*.1) a municipal or public body performing a function of government in Canada,

(*e*) the United Nations or an agency thereof,

(*f*) a university outside Canada that is prescribed to be a university the student body of which ordinarily includes students from Canada,

(*g*) a charitable organization outside Canada to which Her Majesty in right of Canada has made a gift during the individual's taxation year or the 12 months immediately preceding that taxation year, or

(*g*.1) Her Majesty in right of Canada or a province,

to the extent that those amounts were

(*h*) not deducted in computing the individual's taxable income for a taxation year ending before 1988, and

(*i*) not included in determining an amount that was deducted under this section in computing the individual's tax payable under this Part for a preceding taxation year;

S. 118.1(1), paragraph (*d*) of the definition "total charitable gifts" was replaced by S.C. 2011, c. 24, s. 26(1), applicable to gifts made after May 8, 2000. S. 118.1(1), paragraph (*d*) of the definition "total charitable gifts" formerly read:

(*d*) a Canadian municipality,

S. 118.1(1), paragraph (*d*.1) of the definition "total charitable gifts" was added by S.C. 2011, c. 24, s. 26(2), applicable to gifts made after May 8, 2000.

Related Regulations: 3501(1.1); 3503; Schedule VIII.

Related Sections: S. 143(3.1) Election in respect of gifts; s. 149.1(1), "qualified donee"; s. 248(31) Eligible amount of gift or monetary contribution.

Tax Profile: December 2005 — Fair Market Value — What the Appraiser Thinks Doesn't Matter.

Tax Topics: No. 2297, Changes to Tax Rules for Donations Upon or After Death.

Information Circulars: IC 75-23 Tuition fees and charitable donations paid to privately supported secular and religious schools; IC 84-3R6 Gifts to certain charitable organizations outside Canada.

Tax Window Files: Charitable Gifts – Meaning of the Term "Gift", *External Technical Interpretation, Financial Industries and Trusts Division, April 16, 2013,* CRA Document No. 2013-0477981E5; Ordering of Tax Credits and Charitable Gifts, *Technical Interpretation, Financial Industries Division, January 11, 2012,* CRA Document No. 2011-0410641E5; Charitable Donation, *Technical Interpretation, Ontario Corporate Tax Division, September 13, 2010,* CRA Document No. 2010-0377811E5.

Other Publications: CG-010 Qualified Donees; CG-015 Charitable Organizations Outside Canada that Have Received a Gift from Her Majesty in Right of Canada.

"total Crown gifts" — (Repealed by 2014, c. 39, s. 34(1).)

History: S. 118.1(1), the definition "total Crown gifts" was repealed by S.C. 2014, c. 39, s. 34(1), applicable to the 2016 and subsequent taxation years, and formerly read:

"total Crown gifts"—"total Crown gifts", of an individual for a taxation year, means the total of all amounts each of which is the eligible amount of a gift (other than a gift described in the definition "total cultural gifts" or "total ecological gifts") made by the individual in the year or in any of the five preceding taxation years to Her Majesty in right of Canada or of a province, to the extent that those amounts were

(*a*) not deducted in computing the individual's taxable income for a taxation year ending before 1988,

(*b*) not included in determining an amount that was deducted under this section in computing the individual's tax payable under this Part for a preceding taxation year; and

(*c*) in respect of gifts made before February 19, 1997 or under agreements in writing made before that day;

S. 118.1(1), the portion before paragraph (*a*) of the definition "total Crown gifts" was replaced by S.C. 2013, c. 34, s. 248(5), applicable to gifts made after December 20, 2002, and formerly read:

"total Crown gifts"—"total Crown gifts" of an individual for a taxation year means the total of all amounts each of which is the fair market value of a gift (other than a gift the fair market value of which is included in the total cultural gifts or the total ecological gifts of the individual for the year)

made by the individual in the year or in any of the 5 immediately preceding taxation years to Her Majesty in right of Canada or a province, to the extent that those amounts were

Related Regulations: 3501(1.1).

"total cultural gifts" —"total cultural gifts", of an individual for a particular taxation year, means the total of all amounts each of which is the eligible amount — to the extent it is not otherwise included in determining an amount that is deducted under this section in computing any individual's tax payable under this Part for any taxation year — of a gift

(*a*) of an object that the Canadian Cultural Property Export Review Board has determined meets the criterion set out in paragraph 29(3)(*b*) of the *Cultural Property Export and Import Act*,

(*b*) that is made to an institution or a public authority in Canada that is, at the time the gift is made, designated under subsection 32(2) of the *Cultural Property Export and Import Act* either generally or for a specified purpose related to that object, and

(*c*) that is made

(i) if the individual is not a trust,

(A) by the individual, or the individual's spouse or common-law partner, in the particular year or any of the five preceding taxation years,

(B) by the individual in the year in which the individual dies if the particular year is the taxation year that precedes the taxation year in which the individual dies, or

(C) by the individual's estate if subsection (5.1) applies to the gift and the particular year is the taxation year in which the individual dies or the preceding taxation year, or

(ii) if the individual is a trust,

(A) by the trust in the particular year or any of the five preceding taxation years,

(B) by the trust if

(I) the trust is an individual's estate,

(II) subsection (5.1) applies to the gift, and

(III) the particular year is a taxation year

1. in which the estate is the individual's graduated rate estate, and

2. that precedes the taxation year in which the gift is made, or

(C) by the trust if

(I) the end of the particular year is determined by paragraph 104(13.4)(*a*) because of an individual's death,

(II) the gift is made after the particular year and on or before the trust's filing-due date for the particular year, and

(III) the subject of the gift is property that is held by the trust at the time of the individual's death or is property that was substituted for that property;

(*d*) (Repealed by S.C. 2014, c. 39, s. 34(4).)

History: S. 118.1(1), paragraph (*a*) of the definition "total cultural gifts" was replaced by S.C. 2019, c. 29, s. 16(1), deemed to have come into force on March 19, 2019, and formerly read:

(*a*) of an object that the Canadian Cultural Property Export Review Board has determined meets the criteria set out in paragraphs 29(3)(*b*) and (*c*) of the *Cultural Property Export and Import Act*,

S. 118.1(1), clause (*c*)(i)(C) of the definition "total cultural gifts" was replaced by S.C. 2016, c. 12, s. 42(3), applicable to the 2016 and subsequent taxation years, and formerly read:

(C) by the individual's graduated rate estate if subsection (5.1) applies to the gift and the particular year is the taxation year in which the individual dies or the preceding taxation year, or

S. 118.1(1), subparagraph (*c*)(ii)(B) of the definition "total cultural gifts" was replaced by S.C. 2016, c. 12, s. 42(4), applicable to the 2016 and subsequent taxation years, and formerly read:

(B) by the trust if the trust is a graduated rate estate, subsection (5.1) applies to the gift and the particular year is the taxation year in which the gift is made or a preceding taxation year of the estate;

S. 118.1(1), clause (*c*)(ii)(C) of the definition "total cultural gifts" was added by S.C. 2016, c. 12, s. 42(4), applicable to the 2016 and subsequent taxation years.

S. 118.1(1), the portion of the definition "total cultural gifts" before paragraph (*a*) was replaced by S.C. 2014, c. 39, s. 34(3), applicable to the 2016 and subsequent taxation years, and formerly read:

"total cultural gifts"—"total cultural gifts", of an individual for a taxation year, means the total of all amounts each of which is the eligible amount of a gift

S. 118.1(1), the portion of the definition "total cultural gifts" after paragraph (*a*) was replaced by S.C. 2014, c. 39, s. 34(4), applicable to the 2016 and subsequent taxation years, and formerly read:

(*b*) that was made by the individual in the year or in any of the 5 immediately preceding taxation years to an institution or a public authority in Canada that was, at the time the gift was made, designated under subsection 32(2) of the *Cultural Property Export and Import Act* either generally or for a specified purpose related to that object,

to the extent that those amounts were

(*c*) not deducted in computing the individual's taxable income for a taxation year ending before 1988, and

(*d*) not included in determining an amount that was deducted under this section in computing the individual's tax payable under this Part for a preceding taxation year;

S. 118.1(1), the portion before paragraph (*a*) of the definition "total cultural gifts" was replaced by S.C. 2013, c. 34, s. 248(6), applicable to gifts made after December 20, 2002, and formerly read:

"total cultural gifts"—"total cultural gifts" of an individual for a taxation year means the total of all amounts each of which is the fair market value of a gift

Related Regulations: 3501(1.1).

Related Sections: S. 143(3.1) Election in respect of gifts; s. 248(31) Eligible amount of gift or monetary contribution.

"total ecological gifts" —"total ecological gifts", of an individual for a particular taxation year, means the total of all amounts each of which is the eligible amount — to the extent it is not otherwise included in determining an amount that is deducted under this section in computing any individual's tax payable under this Part for any taxation year — of a gift (other than a gift any part of the eligible amount of which is included in the total cultural gifts of any individual for any taxation year)

(*a*) of land (including a covenant or an easement to which land is subject or, in the case of land in the Province of Quebec, a personal servitude (the rights to which the land is subject and which has a term of not less than 100 years) or a real servitude)

(i) the fair market value of which is certified by the Minister of the Environment, and

(ii) that is certified by that Minister, or by a person designated by that Minister, to be ecologically sensitive land, the conservation and protection of which is, in the opinion of that Minister or the designated person, important to the preservation of Canada's environmental heritage,

(*b*) that is made to a qualified donee that is

(i) Her Majesty in right of Canada or of a province,

(i.1) a municipality in Canada, or a municipal or public body performing a function of government in Canada, that is approved by that Minister or the designated person in respect of the gift, or

(ii) a registered charity (other than a private foundation) one of the main purposes of which is, in the opinion of that Minister, the conservation and protection of Canada's environmental heritage, and that is approved by that Minister or the designated person in respect of the gift, and

(*c*) that is made

(i) if the individual is not a trust,

(A) by the individual, or the individual's spouse or common-law partner, in the particular year or any of the 10 preceding taxation years,

(B) by the individual in the year in which the individual dies if the particular year is the taxation year that precedes the taxation year in which the individual dies, or

(C) by the individual's estate if subsection (5.1) applies to the gift and the particular year is the taxation year in which the individual dies or the preceding taxation year, or

(ii) if the individual is a trust,

(A) by the trust in the particular year or any of the 10 preceding taxation years,

(B) by the trust if

(I) the trust is an individual's estate,

(II) subsection (5.1) applies to the gift, and

(III) the particular year is a taxation year

1. in which the estate is the individual's graduated rate estate, and

2. that precedes the taxation year in which the gift is made, or

(C) by the trust if

(I) the end of the particular year is determined by paragraph 104(13.4)(*a*) because of an individual's death,

(II) the gift is made after the particular year and on or before the trust's filing-due date for the particular year, and

(III) the subject of the gift is property that is held by the trust at the time of the individual's death or is property that was substituted for that property;

History: S. 118.1(1), the portion of paragraph (*a*) before subparagraph (i) of the definition "total ecological gifts" was replaced by S.C. 2017, c. 33, s. 43(1), applicable in respect of gifts made after March 21, 2017, and formerly read:

(*a*) of land (including a covenant or an easement to which land is subject or, in the case of land in the Province of Quebec, a real servitude)

S. 118.1(1), subparagraphs (*b*)(i) and (ii) of the definition "total ecological gifts" were replaced and subparagraph (*b*)(i.1) was added by S.C. 2017, c. 33, s. 43(2), applicable in respect of gifts made after March 21, 2017. Subparagraphs (*b*)(i) and (ii) of the definition "total ecological gifts" formerly read:

(i) Her Majesty in right of Canada or of a province, a municipality in Canada or a municipal or public body performing a function of government in Canada, or

(ii) a registered charity one of the main purposes of which is, in the opinion of that Minister, the conservation and protection of Canada's environmental heritage, and that is approved by that Minister or the designated person in respect of the gift, and

S. 118.1(1), clause (*c*)(i)(A) of the definition "total ecological gifts" was replaced by S.C. 2016, c. 12, s. 42(5), applicable to the 2016 and subsequent taxation years, and formerly read:

(A) by the individual, or the individual's spouse or common-law partner, in the particular year or any of the five preceding taxation years,

S. 118.1(1), clause (*c*)(i)(C) of the definition "total ecological gifts" was replaced by S.C. 2016, c. 12, s. 42(6), applicable to the 2016 and subsequent taxation years, and formerly read:

(C) by the individual's graduated rate estate if subsection (5.1) applies to the gift and the particular year is the taxation year in which the individual dies or the preceding taxation year, or

S. 118.1(1), subparagraph (*c*)(ii)(B) of the definition "total ecological gifts" was replaced by S.C. 2016, c. 12, s. 42(7), applicable to the 2016 and subsequent taxation years, and formerly read:

(B) by the trust if the trust is a graduated rate estate, subsection (5.1) applies to the gift and the particular year is the taxation year in which the gift is made or a preceding taxation year of the estate;

S. 118.1(1), clause (*c*)(ii)(C) of the definition "total ecological gifts" was added by S.C. 2016, c. 12, s. 42(7), applicable to the 2016 and subsequent taxation years.

S. 118.1(1), the definition "total ecological gifts" was replaced by S.C. 2014, c. 39, s. 34(6), applicable to the 2016 and taxation years, and formerly read:

"total ecological gifts"—"total ecological gifts", of an individual for a taxation year, means the total of all amounts each of which is the eligible amount of a gift (other than a gift described in the definition "total cultural gifts") of land (including a covenant or an easement to which land is subject or, in the case of land in the Province of Quebec, a real servitude) if

(*a*) the fair market value of the gift is certified by the Minister of the Environment,

(*b*) the land is certified by that Minister, or by a person designated by that Minister, to be ecologically sensitive land, the conservation and protection of which is, in the opinion of that Minister or the designated person, important to the preservation of Canada's environmental heritage, and

(*c*) the gift was made by the individual in the year or in any of the 10 preceding taxation years to a qualified donee that is

(i) Her Majesty in right of Canada or of a province,

(ii) a municipality in Canada,

(iii) a municipal or public body performing a function of government in Canada, or

(iv) a registered charity one of the main purposes of which is, in the opinion of that Minister, the conservation and protection of Canada's environmental heritage, and that is approved by that Minister or the designated person in respect of the gift,

to the extent that those amounts were not included in determining an amount that was deducted under this section in computing the individual's tax payable under this Part for a preceding taxation year;

S. 118.1(1), the portion of paragraph (*c*) of the definition "total ecological gifts" before subparagraph (i) was replaced by S.C. 2014, c. 39, s. 34(5), applicable to gifts made after February 10, 2014, and formerly read:

(*c*) the gift was made by the individual in the year or in any of the 10 preceding taxation years to

S. 118.1(1), the portion of paragraph (*c*) of the definition "total ecological gifts" before subparagraph (i) was replaced by S.C. 2014, c. 20, s. 9(1), applicable to gifts made after February 10, 2014, and formerly read:

(*c*) the gift was made by the individual in the year or in any of the five preceding taxation years to

S. 118.1(1), the definition "total ecological gifts" was replaced by S.C. 2013, c. 34, s. 248(4), applicable to gifts made after December 20, 2002, and formerly read:

"total ecological gifts"—"total ecological gifts" of an individual for a taxation year means the total of all amounts each of which is the fair market value of a gift (other than a gift the fair market value of which is included in the total cultural gifts of the individual for the year) of land, including a servitude for the use and benefit of a dominant land, a covenant or an easement, the fair market value of which is certified by the Minister of the Environment and that is certified by that Minister, or a person designated by that Minister, to be ecologically sensitive land, the conservation and protection of which is, in the opinion of that Minister, or that person, important to the preservation of Canada's environmental heritage, which gift was made by the individual in the year or in any of the five immediately preceding taxation years to

(*a*) Her Majesty in right of Canada or of a province, a municipality in Canada or a municipal or public body performing a function of government in Canada, or

(*b*) a registered charity one of the main purposes of which is, in the opinion of the Minister of the Environment, the conservation and protection of Canada's environmental heritage, and that is approved by that Minister, or that person, in respect of that gift,

to the extent that those amounts were not included in determining an amount that was deducted under this section in computing the individual's tax payable under this Part for a preceding taxation year;

S. 118.1(1), paragraph (*a*) of the definition "total ecological gifts" was replaced by S.C. 2013, c. 34, s. 248(3), applicable to gifts made after May 8, 2000, and formerly read:

(*a*) Her Majesty in right of Canada or a province or a municipality in Canada, or

Related Sections: S. 143(3.1) Election in respect of gifts; s. 207.31 Tax payable by recipient of an ecological gift; s. 207.4(1) Return and payment of tax; s. 248(31) Eligible amount of gift or monetary contribution.

Tax Window Files: Ecogifts, *External Technical Interpretation, Financial Industries and Trusts Division,March 4, 2014,* CRA Document No. 2013-0513251E5.

"total gifts"—"total gifts" of an individual for a taxation year means the total of

(*a*) the least of

(i) the individual's total charitable gifts for the year,

(ii) the individual's income for the year where the individual dies in the year or in the following taxation year, and

(iii) in any other case, the lesser of the individual's income for the year and the amount determined by the formula

$$0.75A + 0.25 (B + C + D - E)$$

where

A is the individual's income for the year,

B is the total of all amounts, each of which is that proportion of the individual's taxable capital gain for the taxation year in respect of a gift made by the individual in the taxation year (in respect of which gift an eligible amount is included in the individual's total charitable gifts for the taxation year) that the eligible amount of the gift is of the individual's proceeds of disposition in respect of the gift,

C is the total of all amounts each of which is a taxable capital gain of the individual for the year, because of subsection 40(1.01), from a disposition of a property in a preceding taxation year,

D is the total of all amounts each of which is determined in respect of the individual's depreciable property of a prescribed class and equal to the lesser of

(A) the amount included under subsection 13(1) in respect of the class in computing the individual's income for the year, and

(B) the total of all amounts each of which is determined in respect of a disposition that is the making of a gift of property of the class made by the individual in the year (in respect of which gift an eligible amount is included in the individual's total charitable gifts for the taxation year) equal to the lesser of

(I) that proportion, of the amount by which the proceeds of disposition of the property exceed any outlays and expenses, to the extent that they were made or incurred by the individual for the purpose of making the disposition, that the eligible amount of the gift is of the individual's proceeds of disposition in respect of the gift, and

(II) that proportion, of the capital cost to the individual of the property, that the eligible amount of the gift is of the individual's proceeds of disposition in respect of the gift, and

E is the total of all amounts each of which is the portion of an amount deducted under section 110.6 in computing the individual's taxable income for the year that can reasonably be considered to be in respect of a gift referred to in the description of B or C,

(*b*) (Repealed by S.C. 2014, c. 39, s. 34(7).)

(*c*) the individual's total cultural gifts for the year, and

(*d*) the individual's total ecological gifts for the year.

History: S. 118.1(1), paragraph (*b*) of the definition "total gifts" was repealed by S.C. 2014, c. 39, s. 34(7), applicable to the 2016 and subsequent taxation years, and formerly read:

(*b*) the individual's total Crown gifts for the year,

S. 118.1(1), the description of B in subparagraph (*a*)(iii) of the definition "total gifts" was replaced by S.C. 2013, c. 34, s. 248(7), applicable to gifts made after December 20, 2002, and formerly read:

B is the total of all amounts each of which is a taxable capital gain of the individual for the year from a disposition that is the making of a gift made by the individual in the year, which gift is included in the individual's total charitable gifts for the year,

S. 118.1(1), clause (B) in the description of D in subparagraph (*a*)(iii) of the definition "total gifts" was replaced by S.C. 2013, c. 34, s. 248(8), applicable to gifts made after December 20, 2002, and formerly read:

(B) the total of all amounts each of which is determined in respect of a disposition that is the making of a gift of property of the class made by the individual in the year that is included in the individual's total charitable gifts for the year and equal to the lesser of

(I) the proceeds of disposition of the property minus any outlays and expenses to the extent that they were made or incurred by the individual for the purpose of making the disposition, and

(II) the capital cost to the individual of the property, and

Related Regulations: Part XXXV; Sched. VIII; 3503.

Related Sections: S. 110.1(1) Deduction for gifts; s. 118.1(2) Proof of gift; 118.1(5) Gifts — deaths after 2015; 118.1(5.1) Gifts by graduated rate estate; s. 118.1(6) Gift of capital property; s. 118.1(7) Gifts of art; s. 118.1(9) Commuter's charitable donations; s. 127.52(1)(*d*) Adjusted taxable income determined; s. 149.1(6.4) National arts service organizations; s. 207.31 Tax payable by recipient of an ecological gift; s. 248, "amount", "individual", "registered Canadian amateur athletic association", "registered charity", "taxable income".

Interpretation Bulletins: *Primary* — IT-110R3 Deductible gifts and official donation receipts; IT-297R2 Gifts in kind to charity and others. *Secondary* — IT-226R Gift to a charity of a residual interest in real property or an equitable interest in a trust; IT-288R2 Gifts of capital properties to a charity and others; IT-407R4 (Consolid.) Dispositions of cultural property to designated Canadian institutions; IT-504R2 (Consolid.) Visual artists and writers.

Other Publications: CG-010 Qualified Donees; CG-015 Charitable Organizations Outside Canada that Have Received a Gift from Her Majesty in Right of Canada.

► 118.1(2) ◄

(2) Proof of gift. An eligible amount of a gift is not to be included in the total charitable gifts, total cultural gifts or total ecological gifts of an individual unless the making of the gift is evidenced by filing with the Minister

(*a*) a receipt for the gift that contains prescribed information;

(*b*) in the case of a gift described in the definition "total cultural gifts" in subsection (1), the certificate issued under subsection 33(1) of the *Cultural Property Export and Import Act*; and

(*c*) in the case of a gift described in the definition "total ecological gifts" in subsection (1), both certificates referred to in that definition.

Editorial Note: Subsection 118.1(2) provides that tax credits for charitable, cultural, and ecological gifts may only be claimed if proven by filing a prescribed receipt with the Minister. For 2016 and subsequent taxation years, the reference in subsection 118.1(2) to Crown gifts is removed consequential to the repeal of the definition of "total Crown gifts" in subsection 118.1(1). Regulations 3500, 3501, and 3502 prescribe the details for receipts for purposes of this tax credit. In addition to filing a receipt, a certificate issued under the *Cultural Property Export and Import Act* must also be filed in respect of gifts of cultural property. For ecological gifts, a certificate issued by the Minister of Environment confirming the ecological sensitivity and fair market value of the land must also be filed.

History: S. 118.1(2), the portion before paragraph (*a*) was replaced by S.C. 2014, c. 39, s. 34(8), applicable to the 2016 and subsequent taxation years, and formerly read:

(2) *Proof of gift.* An eligible amount of a gift shall not be included in the total charitable gifts, total Crown gifts, total cultural gifts or total ecological gifts of an individual unless the making of the gift is evidenced by filing with the Minister

S. 118.1(2), the portion before paragraph (*a*) was replaced by S.C. 2013, c. 34, s. 248(9), applicable to gifts made after December 20, 2002, and formerly read:

(2) *Proof of gift.* A gift shall not be included in the total charitable gifts, total Crown gifts, total cultural gifts or total ecological gifts of an individual unless the making of the gift is proven by filing with the Minister

Related Regulations: 3501(1).

Related Sections: S. 118.1(1) Definitions.

Income Tax Technical News: Issue No. 26, Proposed Guidelines on Split Receipting.

Interpretation Bulletins: *Secondary* — IT-407R4 (Consolid.) Dispositions of cultural property to designated Canadian institutions.

Cases: The eligible amount of a gift must be proven by filing a receipt that contains prescribed information. The prescribed information includes a requirement that the exact amount of any cash gift must be included, failing which the receipt is deemed to be spoiled. The amount stated on the receipt was not the amount of the actual cash donation made by the taxpayers, and the receipt was therefore spoiled. The taxpayer was denied any tax credit. *The Queen v. Castro et al.*, 2015 DTC 5113 (FCA) [Leave to appeal to SCC refused]

▶ 118.1(2.1) ◀

(2.1) Ordering of gifts. For the purpose of determining an individual's total charitable gifts, total cultural gifts and total ecological gifts for a taxation year, no amount in respect of a gift described in any of the definitions of those expressions and made in a particular taxation year is to be considered to have been included in determining an amount that was deducted under this section in computing the individual's tax payable under this Part for a taxation year until amounts in respect of such gifts made in taxation years preceding the particular year that can be so considered are so considered.

History: S. 118.1(2.1) was replaced by S.C. 2014, c. 39, s. 34(9), applicable to the 2016 and subsequent taxation years, and formerly read:

(2.1) *Ordering.* For the purposes of determining the total charitable gifts, total Crown gifts, total cultural gifts and total ecological gifts of an individual for a taxation year, no amount in respect of a gift described in any of the definitions of those expressions and made in a particular taxation year shall be considered to have been included in determining an amount that was deducted under this section in computing the individual's tax payable under this Part for a taxation year until amounts in respect of such gifts made in taxation years preceding the particular year that can be so considered are so considered.

Related Sections: S. 110.1(1.1) Limitation on deductibility.

Interpretation Bulletins: *Secondary* — IT-407R4 (Consolid.) Dispositions of cultural property to designated Canadian institutions.

▶ 118.1(3) ◀

(3) Deduction by individuals for gifts. For the purpose of computing the tax payable under this Part by an individual for a taxation year, there may be deducted such amount as the individual claims not exceeding the amount determined by the formula

$$A \times B + C \times D + E \times F$$

where

A is the appropriate percentage for the year;

B is the lesser of $200 and the individual's total gifts for the year;

C is the highest individual percentage for the year;

D is

(*a*) in the case of a trust (other than a graduated rate estate or a "qualified disability trust" as defined in subsection 122(3)), the amount, if any, by which its total gifts for the year exceeds $200, and

(*b*) in any other case, the lesser of

(i) the amount, if any, by which the individual's total gifts for the year exceeds $200, and

(ii) the amount, if any, by which the individual's amount taxable for the year for the purposes of subsection 117(2) exceeds the first dollar amount for the year referred to in paragraph 117(2)(*e*);

E is 29%; and

F is the amount, if any, by which the individual's total gifts for the year exceed the total of $200 and the amount determined for D.

Editorial Note: Section 118.1 allows an individual to claim a tax credit for charitable gifts, cultural gifts, and ecological gifts made to qualified donees during a taxation year or carried forward from any of the five previous years. The credit is calculated at the lowest personal tax rate for gifts of up to $200. For individuals (including graduated rate estates and qualified disability trusts) a 29% credit rate applies to gifts over the $200 amount if the individual does not have taxable income in excess of a certain threshold ($200,000 for 2016, and indexed thereafter). If taxable income is greater than the threshold, the tax credit rate is 33% of total gifts in excess of $200, to the extent the individual has taxable income above the threshold. For trusts other than graduated rate estates and qualified disability trusts, the 33% credit rate applies to all gifts above the $200 amount.

For gifts made by a deceased's will or by the deceased's estate, see the editorial note to subsection 118.1(5.1).

History: S. 118.1(3) was replaced by S.C. 2016, c. 7, s. 62(3), applicable to the 2016 and subsequent taxation years and, for the purpose of calculating the amount determined for D in subsection 118.1(3), an individual's total gifts for the year are determined without reference to gifts made before the 2016 taxation year. S. 118.1(3) formerly read:

(3) *Deduction by individuals for gifts.* For the purpose of computing the tax payable under this Part by an individual for a taxation year, there may be deducted such amount as the individual claims not exceeding the amount determined by the formula

$$A \times B + C \times D + E \times F$$

where

A is the appropriate percentage for the year;

B is the lesser of $200 and the individual's total gifts for the year;

C is the highest individual percentage for the year;

D is the lesser of

(*a*) the amount, if any, by which the individual's total gifts for the year exceeds $200, and

(*b*) the amount, if any, by which the individual's amount taxable for the year for the purposes of subsection 117(2) exceeds the first dollar amount (as adjusted for the year in accordance with section 117.1) referred to in paragraph 117(2)(*e*);

E is 29%; and

F is the amount, if any, by which the individual's total gifts for the year exceed the total of $200 and the amount determined for D.

The formula in s. 118.1(3) was replaced by S.C. 2016, c. 11, s. 2(1), applicable to gifts made after 2015, and formerly read:

$$(A \times B) + [C \times (D - B)]$$

S. 118.1(3), the descriptions of C and D in the formula were replaced by S.C. 2016, c. 11, s. 2(2), applicable to gifts made after 2015, and formerly read:

C is the highest percentage referred to in subsection 117(2) that applies in determining tax that might be payable under this Part for the year; and

D is the individual's total gifts for the year.

Related Sections: 118.1(5.1) Gifts by graduated rate estate; 118.1(4.1) Gifts — deaths after 2015; S. 37(5) Where no deduction allowed under ss. 110.1 and 118.1; s. 38(*a.1*) Taxable capital gain — donation of listed securities; s. 38(*a.2*) Taxable capital gain — donation of ecological gift; s. 110(2) Charitable gifts; 118.1(4) Gifts — deaths before 2016; 118.1(4.1) Gifts — deaths after 2015; 118.1(5) Gifts — deaths after 2015; s. 118.1(6) Gift of capital property; s. 118.1(7) Gift of art [by artist]; 13 Recaptured depreciation; 13.1; 13.2; 13.3; 14 [Eligible capital property]; 14.1; 15 Benefit conferred on shareholder; 16 Income and capital combined; 17 Amount owing by non-resident; 18 General limitations; 19 Limitation re advertising expense — newspapers; 20 Deductions permitted in computing income from business or property; 21 Cost of borrowed money; 22 Sale of accounts receivable; 23 Sale of inventory; 24 Ceasing to carry on business.

Canadian Tax Foundation: Studniberg, *Current Cases: Tax Court of Canada — Distinguishing Between a Charitable Motive and the Rationale for a Gift (Kossow v. The Queen, 2012 TCC 325)*, 2013 Canadian Tax Journal 1:198–208; Bromley, *Devising Without Denial: Charitable Gift Planning In Revocationland*, 2013 British Columbia Tax Conference 13:1–23; Ball and Dietrich, *Rewards for the Generous: A Review of Recent Tax Changes for Charitable Donations*, 1998 Canadian Tax Journal 2:415–441.

Tax Profile: January 2012 — The Top 10 Cases of 2011; April 2004 — The Battle of the Art Donation Cases Continues; May 2002 — Update on Charitable Giving.

Tax Topics: No. 2297, Changes to Tax Rules for Donations Upon or After Death; No. 2023-24, 2010 Canadian Tax Foundation CRA Roundtable: Pipelines, Privilege and Working Papers (Again!); No. 1970, Charitable Gifting — *Russell et al. v. The Queen* and *Maréchaux v. The Queen*.

Forms: T1 SCH 9 — Donations and Gifts.

Guides: RC4142 Tax Advantages of Donating to Charity; P113 Gifts and Income tax.

Income Tax Technical News: Issue No. 26, Proposed Guidelines on Split-Receipting.

Information Circulars: IC 75-23 Tuition fees and charitable donations paid to privately supported secular and religious schools; IC 07-1 Taxpayer relief provisions.

Interpretation Bulletins: *Primary* — IT-226R Gift to a charity of a residual interest in real property or an equitable interest in a trust. *Secondary* — IT-407R4 (Consolid.) Dispositions of cultural property to designated Canadian institutions.

Cases: The amounts transferred to the charity were paid part in cash and part through borrowings from subsidiaries of the promoter (which had been set up for that sole purpose). Eighty to 85% of the total pledged was borrowed, but the receipts were for the full amount. The taxpayers received a non-tax benefit in the form of indebtedness not repayable for 20 or 25 years, without interest, which could be extinguished through a put option. These terms created significant benefit to the recipients. This was not a gift and the taxpayers were not entitled to the credit, even for the cash portion of their donation. *Markou et al v. The Queen*, 2018 DTC 1056 (TCC)

It could not be said with certainty that the meaning of "gift" prior to the 2002 amendments excluded the concept of split gifts in the common law provinces. *French et al. v. The Queen*, 2016 DTC 5035 (FCA)

For a gift to be eligible for a tax donation receipt there must be a donative intent. The taxpayers participated in a leveraged donation scheme in which they expected to receive inflated tax receipts and profit from their donations. There was no donative intent. Furthermore, the taxpayers could not identify the number or type of software licenses donated, and one cannot voluntarily give away property that cannot be identified. The program was a sham and participation in such was enough to invalidate the gifts. *Mariano v. The Queen*, 2015 DTC 1209 (TCC)

A gift is a voluntary transfer of property for which the donor receives no benefit. The taxpayer's donations were conditional on receiving a long-term interest-free loan. Since the loan was a benefit, no gift was made and a charitable donation tax credit cannot be claimed. *Kossow v. The Queen*, 2014 DTC 5017 (F.C.A.)

The taxpayer claimed to have donated $5,996 under a "Charitable Technology Gifting Program" ($1,872 cash and $4,124 in software licences). A tax credit for the entire $5,996 was disallowed since he had no donative intent and CRA registration of the program as a tax shelter was no guarantee of the credit. *Bandi v. The Queen*, 2013 DTC 1192 (T.C.C.)

Donations to a charity were not eligible for tax credits since they were made in expectation that they would result in the donors' children or grandchildren obtaining bursaries or scholarships from the charity. *Ballard et al. v. The Queen*, 2011 DTC 5040 (F.C.A.), affirming *Coleman et al. v. The Queen*, 2010 DTC 1096 (T.C.C.)

The taxpayers each purchased a group of limited edition prints, donated them to charities and received donation receipts for approximately three times the purchase price. Since the prints were acquired and donated in groups, FMV should be determined on a group basis and was equal to the highest price that the art vendor charged for each group of prints. *A.G. of Canada v. Nash et al.*, 2005 DTC 5696 (F.C.A.), reversing 2004 DTC 3391, 2004 DTC 3328 and 2004 DTC 3360 (T.C.C.)

The taxpayer arranged for the owner of an art gallery to purchase works of art in his name, and to donate them to charitable organizations in return for a tax receipt. The taxpayer never saw or took possession of the art. The taxpayer was denied a charitable donations tax credit because the supporting documentation was inadequate. The taxpayer had failed to prove that he was the owner of the works in issue, that he had donated them, or that the values shown in the receipts represented true fair market values. *Chabot v. The Queen*, 2002 DTC 6708 (F.C.A.), affirming in the main 2000 DTC 1795 (T.C.C.)

Taxpayers entitled to credit for donation of art to registered charitable organizations even though the taxpayers never had physical possession of the art. However, the taxpayers had demonstrated gross negligence by obtaining receipts for the art showing the value to be four times fair market value. *The Queen v. Côté*, 2000 DTC 6615 (F.C.A.), affirming 99 DTC 72 (T.C.C.)

Payments made to the Canadian Ski Association, a registered amateur athletic association, were not true "gifts". The donor believed he was paying for his daughter's ski training. He, therefore, did not have the *animus donandi* or liberal intent to make the gift without expecting to receive a benefit in return. *Dr. Burns v. The Queen*, 90 DTC 6335 (F.C.A.), affirming 88 DTC 6101 (F.C.T.D.)

The taxpayer could not deduct contributions to religious schools which were attended by his children. Although the schools were registered charities and although the taxpayer was not bound to pay tuition fees, financial contribution was expected where possible and the taxpayer was well aware of this. *The Queen v. McBurney*, 85 DTC 5433 (F.C.A.), reversing 84 DTC 6494 (F.C.T.D.)

The maximum must be calculated on total income received, even where the taxpayer was permitted to report a reduced amount because he had two fiscal periods in the same taxation year. *The Queen v. Goodman*, 75 DTC 5022 (F.C.T.D.)

The cash surrender value of a life insurance policy designating a university as beneficiary was held to qualify as a charitable donation. *Konrad v. M.N.R.*, 75 DTC 199 (T.R.B.)

Since the Act specifically speaks about charitable organizations in Canada, no deduction could be allowed with respect of a gift sent direct to England for flood relief. *Merrill v. M.N.R.*, 55 DTC 421 (T.A.B.)

► 118.1(3.1) ◄

(3.1) First-time donor credit — (Repealed by S.C. 2013, c. 33, s. 10(4).)

Editorial Note: The 2013 Budget introduced the First-Time Donor Super Credit, which was repealed at the end of 2017. A person qualified as a "first-time donor" if neither the person nor the person's spouse (including common-law relationships) had deducted an amount under s. 118(3) for any taxation year after 2007 and before the current taxation year. Where a person qualified as a first-time donor, he or she was able to utilize this credit, which effectively added 25% to the rates used in the calculation of the charitable donations tax credit for the first $1,000 of monetary donations. As a result, a first-time donor was allowed a 40% federal credit for donations of $200 or less and a 54% federal credit for the portion of donations over $200 but not exceeding $1,000. Spouses could only claim $1,000 in the aggregate for the super credit.

History: S. 118.1(3.1) was repealed by S.C. 2013, c. 33, s. 10(4), applicable to the 2018 and subsequent taxation years, and formerly read:

(3.1) *First-time donor credit.* For the purpose of computing the tax payable under this Part by a first-time donor for a taxation year that begins after 2012 and ends before 2018, the first-time donor may deduct an amount not exceeding the lesser of $250 and the amount that is 25% of the total of all amounts, each of which is an eligible amount of a gift of money in the year or in any of the four preceding taxation years and in respect of which the first-time donor — or a person who is, at the end of the year, the first-time donor's spouse (other than a person who was at that time separated from the first-time donor by reason of a breakdown of their marriage) or common-law partner — has deducted an amount for the year under subsection (3).

S. 118.1(3.1) was added by S.C. 2013, c. 33, s. 10(3), applicable in respect of gifts made after March 20, 2013.

Canadian Tax Foundation: Parachin, *Policy Forum: Reflections on the First-Time Donor Credit — The Link Between Donation Incentives and the Regulation of Legal Charity*, 2013 Canadian Tax Journal 4:1109–1122; Laforest, *Policy Forum: Assessing the First-Time Donor Credit — Can It Increase the Charitable Donation Levels of First-Time Donors?*, 2013 Canadian Tax Journal 4:1103–1108; Payne, *Policy Forum: The First-Time Donor Credit — Sound Policy or Short-Term Fix?*, 2013 Canadian Tax Journal 4:1091–1101.

► 118.1(3.2) ◄

(3.2) Apportionment of credit — (Repealed by S.C. 2013, c. 33, s. 10(4).)

History: S. 118.1(3.2) was repealed by S.C. 2013, c. 33, s. 10(4), applicable to the 2018 and subsequent taxation years, and formerly read:

(3.2) *Apportionment of credit.* If, at the end of a taxation year, both an individual and a person with whom the individual is married (other than a person who was at that time separated from the individual by reason of a breakdown of their marriage) or is in a common-law partnership may deduct an amount under subsection (3.1) for the year, the total of all amounts so deductible by the individual and the other person shall not exceed the maximum amount that would be deductible for the year by either person if the individual were the only one entitled to deduct an amount under subsection (3.1), and where the individual and the other person cannot agree as to what portion of the amount each can deduct, the Minister may fix the portions.

S. 118.1(3.2) was added by S.C. 2013, c. 33, s. 10(3), applicable in respect of gifts made after March 20, 2013.

► 118.1(4) ◄

(4) Gifts — deaths before 2016. If an individual dies before 2016 and any of this subsection and subsections (5), (5.2), (5.3), (7) and (7.1) (as they read for the taxation year in which the death occurred) applied to deem the individual to have made a gift at a time before the death, then for the purposes of this section the gift is deemed not to have been made by any other taxpayer or at any other time.

Editorial Note: Subsection 118.1(4), prior to 2016, provides that a gift made in an individual's year of death but not claimed in that year may be carried back and claimed in the year preceding death as if it had been made in that year (subject to certain exceptions where a gift of a non-qualifying security is made in the year of death). Charitable gifts of up to 100% of the individual's income may be claimed in the year of death.

For deaths that occur after 2015, subsection 118.1(4) is replaced by new rules. The revised 118.1(4) applies to deaths that occur before 2016. Essentially, if subsections 118.1(4), (5), (5.2), (5.3), (7) or (7.1), as they read in the taxation year of the individual's death, applied to treat a gift (whether made by the individual's will or as a consequence of the individual's death) to have been made by the individual at a time before the individual's death, the gift is deemed made by the individual at that time and not at any other time or by any other taxpayer. See subsection 118.1(4.1) for the rules for deaths after 2015.

History: S. 118.1(4) was replaced by S.C. 2014, c. 39, s. 34(10), applicable to the 2016 and subsequent taxation years, and formerly read:

(4) *Gift in year of death.* Subject to subsection (13), a gift made by an individual in the particular taxation year in which the individual dies (including, for greater certainty, a gift otherwise deemed by subsection (5), (5.2), (5.3), (7), (7.1), (13) or (15) to have been so made) is deemed, for the purpose of this section other than this subsection, to have been made by the individual in the preceding taxation year, and not in the particular year, to the extent that an amount in respect of the gift is not deducted in computing the individual's tax payable under this Part for the particular year.

Related Sections: 118.1(4.1) Gifts — deaths after 2015.

Canadian Tax Foundation: Ball and Dietrich, *Charitable Bequests and Estate Planning*, 2011 Canadian Tax Journal 1:103–124.

Interpretation Bulletins: *Secondary* — IT-288R2 Gifts of capital properties to a charity and others; IT-407R4 (Consolid.) Dispositions of cultural property to designated Canadian institutions.

► 118.1(4.1) ◄

(4.1) Gifts — deaths after 2015. Subsection (5) applies to a gift if an estate arises on and as a consequence of the death after 2015 of an individual and the gift is

(*a*) made by the individual by the individual's will;

(*b*) deemed by subsection (5.2) to have been made in respect of the death; or

(*c*) made by the estate.

History: S. 118.1(4.1) was added by S.C. 2014, c. 39, s. 34(10), applicable to the 2016 and subsequent taxation years.

Related Sections: 118.1(5) Gifts — deaths after 2015.

Tax Topics: No. 2297, Changes to Tax Rules for Donations Upon or After Death.

▶ 118.1(5) ◀

(5) Gifts — deaths after 2015. If this subsection applies to a gift, then for the purposes of the Act (other than subsections (4.1) and (5.2)) the gift is deemed to be made

(*a*) by the estate referred to in subsection (4.1) and not by any other taxpayer; and

(*b*) subject to subsection (13), at the time that the property that is the subject of the gift is transferred to the donee and not at any other time.

Editorial Note: ***Pre-2016 Rules:*** Under subsection 118.1(5) of the Act, a donation or gift to a qualified donee that is made by an individual's will is deemed to be made by the individual immediately before the individual's death. Similarly, certain designations of life insurance proceeds or the deceased's RRSP, RRIF, or TFSA to a qualified donee are also deemed to be gifts made immediately before the individual's death ("designation donations") (see ss. 118.1(5.1)–(5.3)). Under either scenario, the donation tax credit may be applied only against the individual's income tax otherwise payable. Charitable donations made by an individual's estate may be applied only against the estate's income tax otherwise payable.

Whether or not a particular bequest qualifies as a gift by will is a question of fact. According to the Canada Revenue Agency (the "CRA"), a gift is made under an individual's will if the amount that the charity (or other eligible recipient) is entitled to receive can be determined by reference to the will at the time of death. If the amount cannot be so determined, it likely will not be considered as having been made under the will.

If the executors of the deceased's estate have full discretion to choose charities and to determine how much each charity will receive out of the estate, the donations will not be considered as having been made under the will. (See CRA Document No. 1999-0006625, dated February 15, 2000.) Similarly, if a spousal trust or other testamentary trust is set up under the will and the trustees have discretion to make charitable donations out of the trust income or capital, the donations will not be considered as having been made under the will.

If a charity is specified by the deceased's will and a dollar range for the amount of the gift is provided, the CRA takes the view that the deceased is entitled to the charitable tax credit for the lowest amount in the dollar range, with the estate being entitled to a credit in respect of the donation in excess of that lowest amount (see position 3 in CRA Document No. 9918215, dated December 1, 1999).

In the case of a gift of a residual interest in an estate (the amount left over after paying testamentary debts, other bequests, etc.) to one or more charities, the CRA has indicated that the gift will be considered to have been made under the will if the terms of the will indicate: (i) that the deceased taxpayer intended to make donations to one or more specific registered charities; (ii) the amount of the donation to be made to each charity, stipulated as a specific percentage or amount of the residual of the estate; (iii) how to determine the amount of the residual amount of the estate; and (iv) that no discretionary capital encroachments will be made by the trustees of the estate or others (see CRA Document No. 9918215, dated December 1, 1999).

It is the CRA's position that where the gift is not completed until some period after the date of death, the amount to be receipted is its value immediately before death (see Registered Charities Newsletter No. 27).

Rules for 2016 and Subsequent Years: Donations made by an individual's will after 2015 are no longer deemed to have been made immediately before the individual's death. Instead, these donations are deemed to have been made by the estate in the year in which the property is transferred to the qualified donee. A gift is considered to be made by the estate of the taxpayer if the gift is made by the estate or by the taxpayer by the taxpayer's will. Subject to the time limits in the next paragraph, the trustee of the estate may allocate the available donation among any of the taxation year of the estate in which the donation is made, an earlier taxation year of the estate, or the last two taxation years of the individual. The limits that apply in determining the total donations that are creditable in a year continue to apply for 2016 and subsequent taxation years (i.e., the 100% income limitation for the deceased individual for donations made in the year of death or the preceding year, and the 75% income limit that otherwise applies to individuals (including estates)).

The above rules apply if the property is donated by the estate to the qualified donee while the estate is a graduated rate estate ("GRE") — it can qualify as such for up to 36 months after the individual's death — or if the donation is made within 60 months after the death if the estate would qualify as a GRE but for the fact that more than 36 months have passed since the death (s. 118.1(5.1)). The donated property is required to have been acquired by the estate on and as a consequence of the individual's death (or to have been substituted for such property). A similar 36-month rule exists for transfers from an RRSP, RRIF, TFSA, or insurer (s. 118.1(5.2)). Alternatively, an estate can carry forward the credits for up to five years, assuming it remains in existence.

Consequential amendments ensure that capital gains on gifts of publicly listed securities, ecological gifts, and certified cultural property arising because of the deemed disposition upon an individual's death under s. 70 will remain non-taxable if the property is donated in the manner described above (see ss. 38(*a*.1)(ii) and (*a*.2)(ii) and 39(1)(*a*)(i.1).

History: S. 118.1(5) was replaced by S.C. 2014, c. 39, s. 34(10), applicable to the 2016 and subsequent taxation years, and formerly read:

(5) *Gift by will.* Subject to subsection (13), where an individual by the individual's will makes a gift, the gift is, for the purpose of this section, deemed to have been made by the individual immediately before the individual died.

Related Sections: 118.1(4.1) Gifts — deaths after 2015.

Canadian Tax Foundation: Tollstam, *Estate Cannot Double Up on Donation*, 2015 Canadian Tax Highlights 23(7):3–4; Wen, *New Rules for Donations by Will*, 2015 Canadian Tax Focus 5(2):6.

STEP Canada: Angela M. Ross and Sandra Enticknap, "Giving So it Doesn't Hurt – Maximizing Credits When Gifting by Will and Trusts," PowerPoint presentation to the 15th National Conference of STEP Canada, Toronto, June 10-11, 2013.

Tax Profile: October 2011 — Donations of Real Estate and Shares of Real Estate Companies.

Tax Topics: No. 2297, Changes to Tax Rules for Donations Upon or After Death; No. 2249, Dying to Donate — Determining Charitable Donation Tax Credits on Death After 2015.

Interpretation Bulletins: *Secondary* — IT-226R Gift to a charity of a residual interest in real property or an equitable interest in a trust; IT-407R4 (Consolid.) Dispositions of cultural property to designated Canadian institutions.

▶ 118.1(5.1) ◀

(5.1) Gifts by graduated rate estate. This subsection applies to a gift made by an individual's graduated rate estate (determined without reference to paragraph (*a*) of the definition "graduated rate estate" in subsection 248(1)) if the gift is made no more than 60 months after the individual's death, the death occurs after 2015 and either

(*a*) the gift is deemed by subsection (5.2) to have been made in respect of the death, or

(*b*) the subject of the gift is property that was acquired by the estate on and as a consequence of the death or is property that was substituted for that property.

Editorial Note: For deaths that occur after 2015, the transfer rules in the pre-2016 subsections 118.1(5.1) to (5.3) are found in the revised subsection 118.1(5.2).

Subsection 118.1(5.1) after 2015 applies to a gift made by the individual's graduated rate estate and either the gift is an eligible transfer to which subsection 118.1(5.2) applies or the gift property is acquired by the estate as a consequence of the death (or property substituted for the gift property).

For 2016 and subsequent years, if subsection 118.1(5.1) applies to the gift, all or a portion of the gift's eligible amount may be included in the individual's total charitable gifts, total cultural gifts, and total ecological gifts for:

1) that taxation year;
2) the preceding taxation year; or
3) a taxation year of the individual's estate that precedes the year in which the estate makes the gift.

Also, if paragraph 118.1(5.1)(*b*) applies to the gift, subparagraphs 38(*a*.1)(ii) and (*a*.2)(ii) and 39(1)(*a*)(1.1) could apply so no portion of a section 70 gain on disposition of the property is included in the deceased individual's final personal tax return. Also see editorial note to s. 118.1(5) and the proposed amendment following s. 118.1(5.3).

History: S. 118.1(5.1), the portion before paragraph (*a*) was replaced by S.C. 2016, c. 12, s. 42(8), applicable to the 2016 and subsequent taxation years, and formerly read:

(5.1) *Gifts by graduated rate estate.* This subsection applies to a gift made by the graduated rate estate of an individual if the individual's death occurs after 2015 and either

S. 118.1(5.1) was replaced by S.C. 2014, c. 39, s. 34(10), applicable to the 2016 and subsequent taxation years, and formerly read:

(5.1) *Direct designation — insurance proceeds.* Subsection (5.2) applies to an individual in respect of a life insurance policy where

(*a*) the policy is a life insurance policy under which, immediately before the individual's death, the individual's life was insured;

(*b*) a transfer of money, or a transfer by means of a negotiable instrument, is made as a consequence of the individual's death and solely because of the obligations under the policy, from an insurer to a qualified donee (other than a transfer the amount of which is not included in computing the income of the individual or the individual's estate for any taxation year but would have been included in computing the income of the individual or the individual's estate for a taxation year if the transfer had been made to the individual's legal representative for the benefit of the individual's estate and this Act were read without reference to subsection 70(3));

(c) immediately before the individual's death,

(i) the individual's consent would have been required to change the recipient of the transfer described in paragraph (b), and

(ii) the donee was neither a policyholder under the policy, nor an assignee of the individual's interest under the policy; and

(d) the transfer occurs within the 36 month period that begins at the time of the death (or, where written application to extend the period has been made to the Minister by the individual's legal representative, within such longer period as the Minister considers reasonable in the circumstances).

Related Sections: 248(1) graduated rate estate.

Tax Profile: May 2002 — Update on Charitable Giving.

Tax Window Files: Gifts by graduated rate estates, *March 22, 2017*, CRA Document No. 2017-0684481E5.

► 118.1(5.2) ◄

(5.2) Deemed gifts — eligible transfers. For the purposes of this section, money or a negotiable instrument transferred to a qualified donee is deemed to be property that is the subject of a gift, in respect of an individual's death, made to the qualified donee, if the death occurs after 2015 and the transfer is

(a) a transfer — other than a transfer the amount of which is not included in computing the income of the individual or the individual's estate for any taxation year but would have been included in computing the income of the individual or the estate for a taxation year if the transfer had been made to the individual's legal representative for the estate's benefit and this Act were read without reference to subsection 70(3) — made

(i) as a consequence of the death,

(ii) solely because of the obligations under a life insurance policy under which, immediately before the death, the individual's life was insured, and the individual's consent would have been required to change the recipient of the transfer, and

(iii) from an insurer to a person that is the qualified donee and that was, immediately before the death, neither a policyholder under the policy nor an assignee of the individual's interest under the policy; or

(b) a transfer made

(i) as a consequence of the death,

(ii) solely because of the qualified donee's interest or, for civil law a right, as a beneficiary under an arrangement (other than an arrangement of which a licensed annuities provider is the issuer or carrier)

(A) that is a registered retirement savings plan or registered retirement income fund or that was, immediately before the death, a TFSA, and

(B) under which the individual was, immediately before the death, the annuitant or holder, and

(iii) from the arrangement to the qualified donee.

Editorial Note: For deaths that occur after 2015, the transfer rules in the pre-2016 subsections 118.1(5.1) to (5.3) are found in the revised subsection 118.1(5.2). For 2016 and later years the previous subsection 118.1(5.3) is repealed. The post-2015 subsection 118.1(5.2) applies to treat the transfer as a gift made in respect of the individual's death. In turn, subsections 118.1(4.1) and (5) deem the gift to have been made by the estate that arose on or as a consequence of the individual's death and not by any other taxpayer. Also see the editorial note to s. 118.1(5) and the proposed amendment following subsection 118.1(5.3).

History: S. 118.1(5.2) was replaced by S.C. 2014, c. 39, s. 34(10), applicable to the 2016 and subsequent taxation years, and formerly read:

(5.2) *Deemed gift — subsection (5.1).* Where this subsection applies,

(a) for the purpose of this section (other than subsection (5.1) and this paragraph) and section 149.1, the transfer described in subsection (5.1) is deemed to be a gift made, immediately before the individual's death, by the individual to the qualified donee referred to in subsection (5.1); and

(b) the fair market value of the gift is deemed to be the fair market value, at the time of the individual's death, of the right to that transfer (determined without reference to any risk of default with regard to obligations of the insurer).

► 118.1(5.3) ◄

(5.3) Direct designation — RRSPs, RRIFs and TFSAs — (Repealed by 2014, c. 39, s. 34(10).)

Editorial Note: For deaths that occur after 2015, the transfer rules in the pre-2016 subsections 118.1(5.1) to (5.3) are found in the revised subsection 118.1(5.2). For 2016 and later years the previous subsection 118.1(5.3) is repealed. The post-2015 subsection 118.1(5.2) applies to treat the transfer as a gift made in respect of the individual's death. In turn, subsections 118.1(4.1) and (5) deem the gift to have been made by the estate that arose on or as a consequence of the individual's death and not by any other taxpayer.

History: S. 118.1(5.3) was repealed by S.C. 2014, c. 39, s. 34(10), applicable to the 2016 and subsequent taxation years, and formerly read:

(5.3) *Direct designation — RRSPs, RRIFs and TFSAs.* If as a consequence of an individual's death, a transfer of money, or a transfer by means of a negotiable instrument, is made, from an arrangement (other than an arrangement of which a licensed annuities provider is the issuer or carrier) that is a registered retirement savings plan or registered retirement income fund or that was, immediately before the individual's death, a TFSA to a qualified donee, solely because of the donee's interest or, for civil law, a right as a beneficiary under the arrangement, the individual was the annuitant under, or the holder of, the arrangement immediately before the individual's death and the transfer occurs within the 36-month period that begins at the time of the death (or, where written application to extend the period has been made to the Minister by the individual's legal representative, within such longer period as the Minister considers reasonable in the circumstances),

(a) for the purposes of this section (other than this paragraph) and section 149.1, the transfer is deemed to be a gift made, immediately before the individual's death, by the individual to the donee; and

(b) the fair market value of the gift is deemed to be the fair market value, at the time of the individual's death, of the right to the transfer (determined without reference to any risk of default with regard to the obligations of the issuer or carrier of the arrangement).

S. 118.1(5.3), the portion before paragraph (a) was replaced by S.C. 2009, c. 2, s. 35(1), applicable to the 2009 and subsequent taxation years. S. 118.1(5.3), the portion before paragraph (a) formerly read:

(5.3) *Direct designation — RRSPs, RRIFs and TFSAs.* If as a consequence of an individual's death, a transfer of money, or a transfer by means of a negotiable instrument, is made, from an arrangement that is a registered retirement savings plan, registered retirement income fund or TFSA (other than an arrangement of which a licensed annuities provider is the issuer or carrier) to a qualified donee, solely because of the donee's interest or, for civil law, a right as a beneficiary under the arrangement, the individual was the annuitant under, or the holder of, the arrangement immediately before the individual's death and the transfer occurs within the 36-month period that begins at the time of the death (or, where written application to extend the period has been made to the Minister by the individual's legal representative, within such longer period as the Minister considers reasonable in the circumstances),

► 118.1(5.4) ◄

(5.4) Where subsection (6) applies. Subsection (6) applies in circumstances where

(a) an individual

(i) makes a gift at any time of capital property to a qualified donee, or

(ii) who is non-resident, makes a gift at any time of real or immovable property situated in Canada to a prescribed donee who provides an undertaking, in a form satisfactory to the Minister, to the effect that the property will be held for use in the public interest; and

(b) the fair market value of the property otherwise determined at that time exceeds

(i) in the case of depreciable property of a prescribed class, the lesser of the undepreciated capital cost of that class at the end of the taxation year of the individual that includes that time (determined without reference to proceeds of disposition designated in respect of the property under subsection (6)) and the adjusted cost base to the individual of the property immediately before that time, and

(ii) in any other case, the adjusted cost base to the individual of the property immediately before that time.

Editorial Note: This provision, applicable to gifts made by individuals, parallels rules for corporate gifts in ss. 110.1(2.1) and (3) — see the editorial notes to those subsections. Also see the editorial note to s. 38(*a.1*) regarding donations of listed securities.

History: S. 118.1(5.4)(*a*)(i) and (ii) were replaced by S.C. 2014, c. 39, s. 34(11), applicable to the 2016 and subsequent taxation years, and formerly read:

(i) makes a gift (by the individual's will or otherwise) at any time of capital property to a qualified donee, or

(ii) who is non-resident, makes a gift (by the individual's will or otherwise) at any time of real or immovable property situated in Canada to a prescribed donee who provides an undertaking, in a form satisfactory to the Minister, to the effect that the property will be held for use in the public interest; and

S. 118.1(5.4)(*a*)(i) was replaced by S.C. 2013, c. 34, s. 248(11), deemed to have come into force on January 1, 2012, and formerly read:

(i) makes a gift (by the individual's will or otherwise) at any time of capital property to a donee described in the definition "total charitable gifts", "total Crown gifts" or "total ecological gifts" in subsection (1), or

S. 118.1(5.4) was added by S.C. 2013, c. 34, s. 248(10), applicable to gifts made after 1999.

► 118.1(6) ◄

(6) Gifts of capital property. If this subsection applies in respect of a gift by an individual of property, and the individual or the individual's legal representative designates an amount in respect of the gift in the individual's return of income under section 150 for the year in which the gift is made, the amount so designated is deemed to be the individual's proceeds of disposition of the property and, for the purpose of subsection 248(31), the fair market value of the gift, but the amount so designated may not exceed the fair market value of the property otherwise determined and may not be less than the greater of

(*a*) in the case of a gift made after December 20, 2002, the amount of the advantage, if any, in respect of the gift, and

(*b*) the amount determined under subparagraph (5.4)(*b*)(i) or (ii), as the case may be, in respect of the property.

Editorial Note: This provision, applicable to gifts made by individuals, parallels rules for corporate gifts in ss. 110.1(2.1) and (3) — see the editorial notes to those subsections. Also see editorial note to s. 38(*a.1*) regarding donations of listed securities.

History: S. 118.1(6) was replaced by S.C. 2013, c. 34, s. 248(10), applicable to gifts made after 1999, except that, for gifts made before December 21, 2002, the reference to "subsection 248(31)" in subsection 118.1(6) is to be read as a reference to "subsection (1)". S. 118.1(6) formerly read:

(6) *Gift of capital property.* Where, at any time, whether by the individual's will or otherwise, an individual makes a gift of

(*a*) capital property to a qualified donee, or

(*b*) in the case of an individual who is a non-resident person, real property situated in Canada to a prescribed donee who provides an undertaking, in a form satisfactory to the Minister, to the effect that the property will be held for use in the public interest,

and the fair market value of the property otherwise determined at that time exceeds its adjusted cost base to the individual, such amount, not greater than the fair market value and not less than the adjusted cost base to the individual of the property at that time, as the individual or the individual's legal representative designates in the individual's return of income under section 150 for the year in which the gift is made is, if the making of the gift is proven by filing with the Minister a receipt containing prescribed information, deemed to be the individual's proceeds of disposition of the property and, for the purposes of subsection (1), the fair market value of the gift made by the individual.

S. 118.1(6)(*a*) was replaced by S.C. 2011, c. 24, s. 26(4), in force January 1, 2012. S. 118.1(6)(*a*) formerly read:

(*a*) capital property to a donee described in the definition "total charitable gifts", "total Crown gifts" or "total ecological gifts" in subsection (1), or

Related Regulations: 3501(1), (1.1); 3504.

Related Sections: S. 54, "proceeds of disposition"; s. 248(1), "adjusted cost base", "amount", "individual", "property"; s. 248(35) Deemed fair market value.

Tax Profile: October 2011 — Donations of Real Estate and Shares of Real Estate Companies.

Interpretation Bulletins: *Primary* — IT-288R2 Gifts of capital properties to a charity and others. *Secondary* — IT-226R Gift to a charity of a residual interest in real property or an equitable interest in a trust; IT-504R2 (Consolid.) Visual artists and writers.

► 118.1(7) ◄

(7) Gift of art. Subsection (7.1) applies to a gift made by an individual if the gift is described in the definition "total charitable gifts" or "total cultural gifts" in subsection (1) and the property that is the subject of the gift is a work of art that

(*a*) was created by the individual and is in the individual's inventory;

(*b*) was acquired by the individual under circumstances where subsection 70(3) applies; or

(*c*) if the individual is an estate that arose on and as a consequence of the death of a particular individual who created the work of art, was in the particular individual's inventory immediately before the death.

Editorial Note: Except where subsection 118.1(7.1) applies, subsection 118.1(7) allows an artist to designate an amount (not greater than the item's fair market value and not less than its cost amount or the amount of any advantage under 248(32)) as the proceeds of disposition. The designation is available for a gift of art that was property included in the artist's inventory and produced by the artist. The taxpayer or his/her legal representative must designate the deemed amount in the taxpayer's return for the year in which the gift is made. As well, the donation must be supported by a receipt containing prescribed information.

For deaths prior to 2016, where the gift is made as a consequence of death, it is deemed to have been made immediately before death.

For 2016 and subsequent years subsections 118.1(7) and 118.1(7.1) no longer treat as gift made as a consequence of the artist's death to be made by the artist immediately before death. Instead subsection 118.1(7.1) is applicable where the gift is made by the artist's graduated rate estate out of the artist's inventory. Where a gift under subsection 118.1(7.1) is made by an individual other than a graduated rate estate, subparagraphs 118.1(7.1)(*a*)(i) and (*b*)(i) and (ii) preserve the pre-2016 rules for cultural and charitable gifts that were in paragraphs 118.1(7)(*d*) and (*d.1*).

Where a gift of artwork made by an artist's graduated rate estate under subsection 118.1(7.1) and immediately before death the fair market value of the artwork exceeds the artist's cost, subparagraphs 118.1(7.1)(*a*)(ii) and (*b*)(iii) and (*b*)(iv) apply. Subparagraph 118.1(7.1)(*a*)(ii) deems the artist to immediately before death receive proceeds of disposition equal to the artist's cost amount at that time. The result is that under section 70 no income is recognized by the artist for the artwork in the taxation year of the artist's death. The graduated rate estate is deemed to have acquired the artwork at a cost equal to those deemed proceeds.

Under paragraph 118.1(7.1)(*b*), if the artwork is a charitable gift, the artist's legal representative may designate a value between the artwork's cost and fair market value to be used in determining the artist's income from this art in the year of death. The graduated rate estate is deemed to acquire the artwork for a cost equal to the deemed proceeds.

Subsections 118.1(5) to (5.2) apply to determine the tax treatment of the gift. This is done in conjunction with paragraphs (c) of the 118.1(1) definitions "total charitable gifts" and "total cultural gifts" to determine whether any portion of the gift's eligible amount can be included in the artist's total charitable gifts or total cultural gifts in the year of death or the preceding year.

History: S. 118.1(7) was replaced by S.C. 2014, c. 39, s. 34(12), applicable to the 2016 and subsequent taxation years, and formerly read:

(7) *Gifts of art.* Except where subsection (7.1) applies, where at any time, whether by the individual's will or otherwise, an individual makes a gift described in the definition "total charitable gifts" or "total Crown gifts" in subsection (1) of a work of art that was

(*a*) created by the individual and that is property in the individual's inventory, or

(*b*) acquired under circumstances where subsection 70(3) applied,

and at that time the fair market value of the work of art exceeds its cost amount to the individual, the following rules apply:

(*c*) where the gift is made as a consequence of the death of the individual, the gift is deemed to have been made immediately before the death, and

(*d*) the amount that the individual or the individual's legal representative designates in the individual's return of income under section 150 for the year in which the gift is made is deemed to be the individual's proceeds of disposition of the work of art and, for the purpose of subsection 248(31), the fair market value of the work of art, but the amount so designated may not exceed the fair market value otherwise determined of the work of art and may not be less than the greater of

(i) the amount of the advantage, if any, in respect of the gift, and

(ii) the cost amount to the individual of the work of art.

S. 118.1(7)(*d*) was replaced by S.C. 2013, c. 34, s. 248(13), applicable to gifts made after December 20, 2002, and formerly read:

(*d*) the amount, not greater than that fair market value at the time the gift is made and not less than the cost amount of the property to the individual, that is designated in the individual's return of income under section 150 for the year in which the gift is made is, if the making of the gift is proven by filing with the Minister a receipt containing prescribed information, deemed to be the individual's proceeds of disposition of the work of art and, for the purposes of subsection (1), the fair market value of the gift made by the individual.

Related Regulations: 3501(1).

Related Sections: 118.1(7.1) Gift of art.

Tax Profile: May 2002 — Update on Charitable Giving.

Interpretation Bulletins: *Secondary* — IT-288R2 Gifts of capital properties to a charity and others; IT-504R2 (Consolid.) Visual artists and writers.

► 118.1(7.1) ◄

(7.1) Gift of art. If this subsection applies to a gift made by an individual, the following rules apply:

(*a*) in the case of a gift described in the definition "total cultural gifts" in subsection (1),

(i) if at the time the gift is made the fair market value of the work of art that is the subject of the gift exceeds its cost amount to the individual, the individual is deemed to receive at that time proceeds of disposition in respect of the work of art equal to the greater of its cost amount to the individual at that time and the amount of the advantage, if any, in respect of the gift, and

(ii) if the individual is the graduated rate estate of a particular individual who created the work of art that is the subject of the gift and at the time immediately before the particular individual's death the fair market value of the work of art exceeds its cost amount to the particular individual, the particular individual is deemed to receive at that time proceeds of disposition in respect of the work of art equal to the cost amount to the particular individual at that time and the estate is deemed to have acquired the work of art at a cost equal to those proceeds; and

(*b*) in the case of a gift described in the definition "total charitable gifts" in subsection (1),

(i) if at the time the gift is made the fair market value of the work of art that is the subject of the gift exceeds its cost amount to the individual, then the amount designated in the individual's return of income under section 150 for the taxation year that includes that time is deemed to be

(A) the individual's proceeds of disposition in respect of the work of art, and

(B) the fair market value of the work of art for the purposes of subsection 248(31),

(ii) a designation under subparagraph (i) is of no effect to the extent that the amount designated

(A) exceeds the fair market value of the work of art otherwise determined, or

(B) is less than the greater of the amount of the advantage, if any, in respect of the gift, and the cost amount to the individual of the work of art,

(iii) if the individual is the graduated rate estate of a particular individual who created the work of art that is the subject of the gift and at the time immediately before the particular individual's death the fair market value of the work of art exceeds its cost amount to the particular individual,

(A) the amount designated in the particular individual's return of income under section 150 for the taxation year that includes that time is deemed to be the value of the work of art at the time of the death, and

(B) the estate is deemed to have acquired the work of art at a cost equal to that value, and

(iv) a designation under subparagraph (iii) is of no effect to the extent that the amount designated

(A) exceeds the fair market value of the work of art otherwise determined, or

(B) is less than the cost amount to the particular individual of the work of art.

Editorial Note: Where the gift of an artist's inventory qualifies as cultural property, the gift is deemed to have proceeds of disposition equal to the greater of the cost amount of the property or the amount of any advantage received (see s. 248(32)).

For 2016 and subsequent years subsection 118.1(7.1) no longer treats a gift made as a consequence of the artist's death to be made by the artist immediately before death. See the editorial note for subsection 118.1(7) for full details of these changes and the revised tax effects.

History: S. 118.1(7.1) was replaced by S.C. 2014, c. 39, s. 34(12), applicable to the 2016 and subsequent taxation years, and formerly read:

(7.1) *Gifts of cultural property.* Where at any particular time, whether by the individual's will or otherwise, an individual makes a gift described in the definition "total cultural gifts" in subsection (1) of a work of art that was

(*a*) created by the individual and that is property in the individual's inventory, or

(*b*) acquired under circumstances where subsection 70(3) applied,

and at that time the fair market value of the work of art exceeds its cost amount to the individual, the following rules apply:

(*c*) where the gift is made as a consequence of the death of the individual, the individual is deemed to have made the gift immediately before the death, and

(*d*) the individual is deemed to have received at the particular time proceeds of disposition in respect of the work of art equal to the greater of its cost amount to the individual at that time and the amount of the advantage, if any, in respect of the gift.

S. 118.1(7.1)(*d*) was replaced by S.C. 2013, c. 34, s. 248(15), applicable to gifts made after December 20, 2002, and formerly read:

(*d*) the individual is deemed to have received at the particular time proceeds of disposition in respect of the gift equal to its cost amount to the individual at that time.

Related Sections: S. 110.1(1)(*c*) Gifts to institutions; s. 118.1(7) Gifts of art; s. 248(32) Amount of advantage.

Interpretation Bulletins: *Secondary* — IT-407R4 (Consolid.) Dispositions of cultural property to designated Canadian institutions.

► 118.1(8) ◄

(8) Gifts made by partnership. If at the end of a fiscal period of a partnership an individual is a member of the partnership, the individual's share of any amount that would, if the partnership were a person, be the eligible amount of a gift made by the partnership to any donee is, for the purpose of this section, deemed to be the eligible amount of a gift made to that donee by the individual in the individual's taxation year in which the fiscal period of the partnership ends.

Editorial Note: See commentary to parallel rule for donation by corporate partner — s. 110.1(4).

History: S. 118.1(8) was replaced by S.C. 2013, c. 34, s. 248(16), applicable to gifts made after December 20, 2002, and formerly read:

(8) *Gifts made by partnership.* Where an individual is, at the end of a fiscal period of a partnership, a member of the partnership, the individual's share of any amount that would, if the partnership were a person, be a gift made by the partnership to any donee shall, for the purposes of this section, be deemed to be a gift made by the individual to that donee in the individual's taxation year in which the fiscal period of the partnership ends.

► 118.1(9) ◄

(9) Commuter's charitable donations. Where throughout a taxation year an individual resided in Canada near the boundary between Canada and the United States, if

(*a*) the individual commuted to the individual's principal place of employment or business in the United States, and

(*b*) the individual's chief source of income for the year was that employment or business,

a gift made by the individual in the year to a religious, charitable, scientific, literary or educational organization created or organized in or under the laws of the United States that would be allowed as a deduction under the *United States Internal Revenue Code* shall, for the purpose of the definition "total charitable gifts" in subsection (1), be deemed to have been made to a registered charity.

Editorial Note: An individual resident in Canada who lives near the Canada and U.S. border and who has his/her principal place of business or employment in the U.S. may, if the individual's chief source of income for the year was from that employment or business, be entitled to include in his/her "total charitable gifts" those gifts made to certain U.S. organizations. To qualify, the organization must be a religious, charitable, scientific, literary, or educational organization created or organized under U.S. law. Further, gifts to the entity must qualify for deduction under the U.S. *Internal Revenue Code*.

► 118.1(10) ◄

(10) Determination of fair market value. For the purposes of paragraph 110.1(1)(*c*) and the definition "total cultural gifts" in subsection (1), the fair market value of an object is deemed to be the fair market value determined by the Canadian Cultural Property Export Review Board.

Editorial Note: The fair market value of a qualified cultural gift is determined by the Canadian Cultural Export Review Board. This determination will be deemed to be the fair market value of such a gift for a period of two years subsequent to the date of determination and for all provisions of the Act relating to charitable donations and gifts of property (see 118.1(10.1). This rule ties in with s. 39(1)(*a*)(i.1), which provides that cultural property gifts may be exempt from capital gains tax.

Interpretation Bulletins: *Secondary* — IT-407R4 (Consolid.) Dispositions of cultural property to designated Canadian institutions.

► 118.1(10.1) ◄

(10.1) Determination of fair market value. For the purposes of this section, subparagraph 69(1)(*b*)(ii), subsection 70(5) and sections 110.1 and 207.31, if at any time the Canadian Cultural Property Export Review Board or the Minister of the Environment determines or redetermines an amount to be the fair market value of a property that is the subject of a gift described in paragraph 110.1(1)(*a*), or in the definition "total charitable gifts" in subsection (1), made by a taxpayer within the two-year period that begins at that time, an amount equal to the last amount so determined or redetermined within the period is deemed to be the fair market value of the gift at the time the gift was made and, subject to subsections (6), (7.1) and 110.1(3), to be the taxpayer's proceeds of disposition of the gift.

Editorial Note: Subsection 118.1(10.1) provides that where the fair market value of a gift has been determined or redetermined by the Canadian Cultural Property Export Review Board or the Minister of the Environment, that value will apply to the property for purposes related to charitable donations and gifts for a period of two years from the date of determination.

The application of subsection 118.1(10.1) to determine the taxpayer's proceeds of disposition is subject to the provisions in subsections 110.1(3) and 118.1(6), (7) and (7.1). For 2016 and subsequent taxation years, subsection 118.1(10.1) is amended to remove references to subsection 118.1(7) consequential to amendments to subsections 118.1(7) and (7.1).

History: S. 118.1(10.1) was replaced by S.C. 2014, c. 39, s. 34(13), applicable to the 2016 and subsequent taxation years, and formerly read:

(10.1) *Determination of fair market value.* For the purposes of subparagraph 69(1)(*b*)(ii), subsection 70(5) and sections 110.1, 207.31 and this section, where at any time the Canadian Cultural Property Export Review Board or the Minister of the Environment determines or redetermines an amount to be the fair market value of a property that is the subject of a gift described in paragraph 110.1(1)(*a*), or in the definition "total charitable gifts" in subsection (1), made by a taxpayer within the two-year period that begins at that time, an amount equal to the last amount so determined or redetermined within the period is deemed to be the fair market value of the gift at the time the gift was made and, subject to subsections (6), (7), (7.1) and 110.1(3), to be the taxpayer's proceeds of disposition of the gift.

► 118.1(10.2) ◄

(10.2) Request for determination by the Minister of the Environment. Where a person disposes or proposes to dispose of a property that would, if the disposition were made and the certificates described in paragraph 110.1(1)(*d*) or in the definition "total ecological gifts" in subsection (1) were issued by the Minister of the Environment, be a gift described in those provisions, the person may request, by notice in writing to that Minister, a determination of the fair market value of the property.

Editorial Note: Subsections 118.1(10.2) to (10.5) set out the administrative procedures regarding the request for a determination of fair market value of ecological gifts, which require that fair market value determinations of ecologically sensitive land must be certified by the Minister of the Environment.

► 118.1(10.3) ◄

(10.3) Duty of Minister of the Environment. In response to a request made under subsection (10.2), the Minister of the Environment shall with all due dispatch make a determination in accordance with subsection (12) or 110.1(5), as the case may be, of the fair market value of the property referred to in that request and give notice of the determination in writing to the person who has disposed of, or who proposes to dispose of, the property, except that no such determination shall be made if the request is received by that Minister after three years after the end of the person's taxation year in which the disposition occurred.

► 118.1(10.4) ◄

(10.4) Ecological gifts — redetermination. Where the Minister of the Environment has, under subsection (10.3), notified a person of the amount determined by that Minister to be the fair market value of a property in respect of its disposition or proposed disposition,

(*a*) that Minister shall, on receipt of a written request made by the person on or before the day that is 90 days after the day that the person was so notified of the first such determination, with all due dispatch confirm or redetermine the fair market value;

(*b*) that Minister may, on that Minister's own initiative, at any time redetermine the fair market value;

(*c*) that Minister shall in either case notify the person in writing of that Minister's confirmation or redetermination; and

(*d*) any such redetermination is deemed to replace all preceding determinations and redeterminations of the fair market value of that property from the time at which the first such determination was made.

► 118.1(10.5) ◄

(10.5) Certificate of Fair Market Value. Where the Minister of the Environment determines under subsection (10.3) the fair market value of a property, or redetermines that value under subsection (10.4), and the property has been disposed of to a qualified donee described in paragraph 110.1(1)(*d*) or in the definition "total ecological gifts" in subsection (1), that Minister shall issue to the person who made the disposition a certificate that states the fair market value of the property so determined or redetermined and, where more than one certificate has been so issued, the last certificate is deemed to replace all preceding certificates from the time at which the first certificate was issued.

► 118.1(11) ◄

(11) Assessments. Notwithstanding subsections 152(4) to (5), such assessments or reassessments of a taxpayer's tax, interest or penalties payable under this Act for any taxation year shall be made as are necessary to give effect

(*a*) to a certificate issued under subsection 33(1) of the *Cultural Property Export and Import Act* or to a decision of a court resulting from an appeal made pursuant to section 33.1 of that Act; or

(*b*) to a certificate issued under subsection (10.5) or to a decision of a court resulting from an appeal made pursuant to subsection 169(1.1).

Editorial Note: A taxpayer may be assessed beyond the normal time period allowed in subsections 152(4) and (5) for amounts arising from a redetermination of fair market value pursuant to either a certificate issued under subsection 33(1) of the *Cultural Property Export and Import Act* or a court decision pursuant to section 33.1 of that Act.

▶ 118.1(12) ◀

(12) Ecological gifts. For the purposes of applying subparagraph 69(1)(*b*)(ii), subsection 70(5), this section and section 207.31 in respect of a gift described in the definition "total ecological gifts" in subsection (1) that is made by an individual, the amount that is the fair market value (or, for the purpose of subsection (6), the fair market value otherwise determined) of the gift at the time the gift was made and, subject to subsection (6), the individual's proceeds of disposition of the gift, is deemed to be the amount determined by the Minister of the Environment to be

(*a*) where the gift is land, the fair market value of the gift; or

(*b*) where the gift is a servitude, covenant or easement to which land is subject, the greater of

(i) the fair market value otherwise determined of the gift, and

(ii) the amount by which the fair market value of the land is reduced as a result of the making of the gift.

Related Sections: S. 110.1(5) Ecological gifts.

▶ 118.1(13) ◀

(13) Non-qualifying securities. For the purposes of this section (other than this subsection), if at any particular time an individual makes a gift (including a gift that, but for this subsection, would be deemed by subsection (5) to be made at the particular time) of a non-qualifying security of the individual and the gift is not an excepted gift,

(*a*) except for the purpose of applying subsection (6) to determine the individual's proceeds of disposition of the security, the gift is deemed not to have been made;

(*b*) if the security ceases to be a non-qualifying security of the individual at a subsequent time that is within 60 months after the particular time and the donee has not disposed of the security at or before the subsequent time, the individual is deemed to have made a gift to the donee of property at the subsequent time and the fair market value of that property is deemed to be the lesser of the fair market value of the security at the subsequent time and the fair market value of the security at the particular time that would, if this Act were read without reference to this subsection, have been included in calculating the individual's total charitable gifts for a taxation year;

(*c*) if the security is disposed of by the donee within 60 months after the particular time and paragraph (*b*) does not apply to the security, the individual is deemed to have made a gift to the donee of property at the time of the disposition and the fair market value of that property is deemed to be the lesser of the fair market value of any consideration (other than a non-qualifying security of any person) received by the donee for the disposition and the fair market value of the security at the particular time that would, if this Act were read without reference to this subsection, have been included in calculating the individual's total charitable gifts for a taxation year; and

(*d*) a designation under subsection (6) or 110.1(3) in respect of the gift made at the particular time may be made in the individual's return of income for the year that includes the subsequent time referred to in paragraph (*b*) or the time of the disposition referred to in paragraph (*c*).

Editorial Note: Subsections 118.1(13) to (20) provide rules which defer the recognition of certain types of non-arm's length gifts (gifts of non-qualifying securities which include shares and debt of a non-arm's length person) to a charity and thus, deny the charitable donation tax credit unless certain events occur within five years of the making of the gift. Where the gift ceases to be a non-qualifying security or the donee disposes of the gift within five years, the donor will be treated as having made the gift (and thus, will be eligible for the tax credit) at this later time. Charitable donation treatment is also restricted in loanback arrangements whereby taxpayers donated property to a charity which was not at arm's length and received a loan in return or were permitted to use the property donated to the charity. These arrangements are caught by subsection 118.1(16).

Where a security is deemed to be gifted at a later time, the fair market value of that gift is deemed to be the lesser of (i) the fair market value of the security at that subsequent time, and (ii) the fair market value at the time of the original gift. Similarly, by virtue of paragraph 118.1(13)(*c*), if the donee disposes of the security within five years after the gift, the individual donor will be treated as having made a gift at this subsequent time. The fair market value of the gift at this subsequent time will be the lesser of (i) the consideration received by the donee for the disposition (except to the extent that the consideration is another non-qualifying security of the individual), and (ii) the fair market value of the gift at the time it was originally donated.

Subsection 118.1(13) does not apply to "excepted gifts" as defined by subsection 118.1(19), which in general refers to arm's length gifts of shares to a charitable organization or public foundation.

For subsection 118.1(13) purposes where a gift is made by an individual's will, the gift is considered to be made immediately before the individual's death (determined under subsection 118.1(5) without regard to subsection 118.1(4)). This rule is effective for deaths prior to 2016. For deaths after 2015, the reference to subsection 118.1(4) is removed. Also for deaths after 2015 amended subsection 118.1(5) indicates that where a gift is made by an individual's will (or otherwise deemed in that subsection to be made by the individual's estate) the gift is considered to be made at the time the gift property is transferred to the donee. Subsection 118.1(13) refers to that particular time. Paragraph 118.1(13)(*a*) deems the gift not to be made for charitable donation tax credit purposes.

For taxation years after 2015, paragraphs 118.1(13)(*b*) and (*c*) are amended to remove references to total Crown gifts as result of the repeal of the definition in subsection 118.1(1) of "total Crown gifts".

Subsections 118.1(13.1), (13.2), and (13.3) are anti-avoidance rules that apply generally in "back-to-back" circumstances where, as a part of a series of transactions, (i) an individual has made a gift to a qualified donee; (ii) a particular person holds a non-qualifying security of the individual; and (iii) the qualified donee acquires a non-qualifying security of the individual or of the particular person. For example, this could arise if, as part of a series of transactions, a charity uses cash that it received as a gift to purchase a promissory note owing by a person that in turn owes an amount to the person that originally made the cash gift to the charity.

A "non-qualifying security" of an individual means an obligation of the individual or the individual's estate (or of a non-arm's length person or partnership to the individual or estate), a share of a corporation with which the individual or estate does not deal at arm's length, or any other security issued by the individual or estate or non-arm's length person or partnership. Specifically excluded from the definition are obligations, shares, and other securities listed on a designated stock exchange. If the individual is a trust, a non-qualifying security further includes a share of a corporation with which a person affiliated with the trust does not deal at arm's length.

History: S. 118.1(13), the portion before paragraph (*a*) was replaced by S.C. 2014, c. 39, s. 34(14), applicable to the 2016 and subsequent taxation years, and formerly read:

(13) *Non-qualifying securities.* For the purpose of this section (other than this subsection), where at any particular time an individual makes a gift (including a gift that, but for this subsection and subsection (4), would be deemed by subsection (5) to be made at the particular time) of a non-qualifying security of the individual and the gift is not an excepted gift,

S. 118.1(13)(*b*) and (*c*) were replaced by S.C. 2014, c. 39, s. 34(15), applicable to the 2016 and subsequent taxation years, and formerly read:

(*b*) if the security ceases to be a non-qualifying security of the individual at a subsequent time that is within 60 months after the particular time and the donee has not disposed of the security at or before the subsequent time, the individual is deemed to have made a gift to the donee of property at the subsequent time and the fair market value of that property is deemed to be the lesser of the fair market value of the security at the subsequent time and the fair market value of the security at the particular time that would, if this Act were read without reference to this subsection, have been included in calculating the individual's total charitable gifts or total Crown gifts for a taxation year;

(*c*) if the security is disposed of by the donee within 60 months after the particular time and paragraph (*b*) does not apply to the security, the individual is deemed to have made a gift to the donee of property at the time of the disposition and the fair market value of that property is deemed to be the lesser of the fair market value of any consideration (other than a non-qualifying security of any person) received by the donee for the disposition and the fair market value of the security at the particular time that would, if this Act were read without reference to this subsection, have been included in calculating the individual's total charitable gifts or total Crown gifts for a taxation year; and

S. 118.1(13)(*c*) was replaced by S.C. 2013, c. 34, s. 248(18), deemed to have come into force on March 22, 2011, and formerly read:

(*c*) if the security is disposed of by the donee within 60 months after the particular time and paragraph (*b*) does not apply to the security, the individual is deemed to have made a gift to the donee of property at the time of the disposition and the fair market value of that property is deemed to be the lesser of the fair market value of any consideration (other than a non-qualifying security of the individual or a property that would be a non-qualifying security of the individual if the individual were alive at that time) received by the donee for the disposition and the fair market value of the security at the particular time that would, if this Act were read without reference to this subsection, have been included in calculating the individual's total charitable gifts or total Crown gifts for a taxation year; and

S. 118.1(13)(*b*) and (*c*) were replaced by S.C. 2013, c. 34, s. 248(17), applicable to gifts made after December 20, 2002, and formerly read:

(*b*) if the security ceases to be a non-qualifying security of the individual at a subsequent time that is within 60 months after the particular time and the donee has not disposed of the security at or before the subsequent time, the individual is deemed to have made a gift to the donee of property at the subsequent time and the fair market value of that gift is deemed to be the lesser of the fair market value of the security at the subsequent time and the amount of the gift made at the particular time that would, but for this subsection, have been included in the individual's total charitable gifts or total Crown gifts for a taxation year;

(*c*) if the security is disposed of by the donee within 60 months after the particular time and paragraph (*b*) does not apply to the security, the individual is deemed to have made a gift to the donee of property at the time of the disposition and the fair market value of that gift is deemed to be the lesser of the fair market value of any consideration (other than a non-qualifying security of any person) received by the donee for the disposition and the amount of the gift made at the particular time that would, but for this subsection, have been included in the individual's total charitable gifts or total Crown gifts for a taxation year; and

S. 118.1(13)(*c*) was replaced by S.C. 2011, c. 24, s. 26(5), deemed to have come into force on March 22, 2011. S. 118.1(13)(*c*) formerly read:

(*c*) if the security is disposed of by the donee within 60 months after the particular time and paragraph (*b*) does not apply to the security, the individual is deemed to have made a gift to the donee of property at the time of the disposition and the fair market value of that gift is deemed to be the lesser of the fair market value of any consideration (other than a non-qualifying security of the individual or a property that would be a non-qualifying security of the individual if the individual were alive at that time) received by the donee for the disposition and the amount of the gift made at the particular time that would, but for this subsection, have been included in the individual's total charitable gifts or total Crown gifts for a taxation year; and

Related Sections: S. 40(1.01) [Reserve on] Gift of non-qualifying security; s. 118.1(13.1) Application of subsection (13.2); s. 118.1(13.2) Non-qualifying securities — third-party accommodation [indirect gift]; s. 118.1(13.3) Non-qualifying securities — anti-avoidance; s. 118.1(14) Exchanged security; s. 118.1(14.1) Exchange in beneficial interest in a trust; s. 118.1(15) Death of donor; s. 118.1(16) Loanbacks; s. 118.1(17) Ordering rule; s. 118.1(18) Non-qualifying security defined; s. 118.1(19) Excepted gift; s. 118.1(20) Financial institution defined.

► 118.1(13.1) ◄

(13.1) Application of subsection (13.2). Subsection (13.2) applies if, as part of a series of transactions,

(*a*) an individual makes, at a particular time, a gift of a particular property to a qualified donee;

(*b*) a particular person holds a non-qualifying security of the individual; and

(*c*) the qualified donee acquires, directly or indirectly, a non-qualifying security of the individual or of the particular person.

Editorial Note: See note to s. 118.1(13).

History: S. 118.1(13.1) was added by S.C. 2011, c. 24, s. 26(6), deemed to have come into force on March 22, 2011.

Related Sections: See related sections in s. 118.1(13).

► 118.1(13.2) ◄

(13.2) Non-qualifying securities — third-party accommodation. If this subsection applies,

(*a*) for the purposes of this section, the fair market value of the particular property is deemed to be reduced by an amount equal to the fair market value of the non-qualifying security acquired by the qualified donee; and

(*b*) for the purposes of subsection (13),

(i) if the non-qualifying security acquired by the qualified donee is a non-qualifying security of the particular person, it is deemed to be a non-qualifying security of the individual,

(ii) the individual is deemed to have made, at the particular time referred to in subsection (13.1), a gift of the non-qualifying security acquired by the qualified donee, the fair market value of which does not exceed the amount, if any, by which

(A) the fair market value of the particular property determined without reference to paragraph (*a*)

exceeds

(B) the fair market value of the particular property determined under paragraph (*a*), and

(iii) paragraph (13)(*b*) does not apply in respect of the gift.

Editorial Note: See editorial note to s. 118.1(13).

History: S. 118.1(13.2) was added by S.C. 2011, c. 24, s. 26(6), deemed to have come into force on March 22, 2011.

Related Sections: See related sections in s. 118.1(13).

► 118.1(13.3) ◄

(13.3) Non-qualifying securities — anti-avoidance. For the purposes of subsections (13.1) and (13.2), if, as part of a series of transactions, an individual makes a gift to a qualified donee and the qualified donee acquires a non-qualifying security of a person (other than the individual or particular person referred to in subsection (13.1)) and it may reasonably be considered, having regard to all the circumstances, that one of the purposes or results of the acquisition of the non-qualifying security by the qualified donee was to facilitate, directly or indirectly, the making of the gift by the individual, then the non-qualifying security acquired by the qualified donee is deemed to be a non-qualifying security of the individual.

Editorial Note: See editorial note to s. 118.1(13).

History: S. 118.1(13.3) was added by S.C. 2011, c. 24, s. 26(6), deemed to have come into force on March 22, 2011.

Related Sections: See related sections in s. 118.1(13).

► 118.1(14) ◄

(14) Exchanged security. Where a share (in this subsection referred to as the "new share") that is a non-qualifying security of an individual has been acquired by a donee referred to in subsection (13) in exchange for another share (in this subsection referred to as the "original share") that is a non-qualifying security of the individual by means of a transaction to which section 51, subparagraphs 85.1(1)(*a*)(i) and (ii) or section 86 or 87 applies, the new share is deemed for the purposes of this subsection and subsection (13) to be the same share as the original share.

Editorial Note: See editorial note to s. 118.1(13).

Related Sections: See related sections in s. 118.1(13).

► 118.1(14.1) ◄

(14.1) Exchange of beneficial interest in trust. Where a donee disposes of a beneficial interest in a trust that is a non-qualifying security of an individual in circumstances where paragraph (13)(*c*) would, but for this subsection, apply in respect of the disposition, and in respect of which the donee receives no consideration other than other non-qualifying securities of the individual, for the purpose of subsection (13) the gift referred to in that subsection is to be read as a reference to a gift of those other non-qualifying securities.

Editorial Note: See editorial note to s. 118.1(13).

Related Sections: See related sections in s. 118.1(13).

▶ 118.1(15) ◀

(15) Death of donor. If, but for this subsection, an individual would be deemed by subsection (13) to have made a gift after the individual's death, for the purpose of this section the individual is deemed to have made the gift in the taxation year in which the individual died, except that the amount of interest payable under any provision of this Act is the amount that it would be if this subsection did not apply to the gift.

Editorial Note: Where an individual makes a gift of non-qualifying securities but dies prior to the disposition of the securities by the donee or prior to the securities ceasing to be non-qualifying, either of which occurs within five years of the individual's gift (as provided by subsection 118.1(13)), subsection 118.1(15) deems the gift to have been made in the year in which the individual died.

Related Sections: See related sections in s. 118.1(13).

▶ 118.1(16) ◀

(16) Loanbacks. For the purpose of this section, where

(*a*) at any particular time an individual makes a gift of property,

(*b*) if the property is a non-qualifying security of the individual, the gift is an excepted gift, and

(*c*) within 60 months after the particular time

(i) the donee holds a non-qualifying security of the individual that was acquired by the donee after the time that is 60 months before the particular time, or

(ii) the individual or any person or partnership with which the individual does not deal at arm's length uses property of the donee under an agreement that was made or modified after the time that is 60 months before the particular time, and the property was not used in the carrying on of the donee's charitable activities,

the fair market value of the gift is deemed to be that value otherwise determined minus the total of all amounts each of which is the fair market value of the consideration given by the donee to so acquire a non-qualifying security so held or the fair market value of such a property so used, as the case may be.

Editorial Note: See note to s. 118.1(13).

Related Sections: See related sections in s. 118.1(13).

▶ 118.1(17) ◀

(17) Ordering rule. For the purpose of applying subsection (16) to determine the fair market value of a gift made at any time by a taxpayer, the fair market value of consideration given to acquire property described in subparagraph (16)(*c*)(i) or of property described in subparagraph (16)(*c*)(ii) is deemed to be that value otherwise determined minus any portion of it that has been applied under that subsection to reduce the fair market value of another gift made before that time by the taxpayer.

Editorial Note: An ordering rule in s. 118.1(17) is provided for the purposes of determining the order of the reduction in tax credits where s. 118.1(16) applies. The technical Notes to s. 118.1(17) indicate that ordering is done on a "first in, first out" basis, and give the following example: if, in each of years 1 to 3, a donor makes a gift of $100, and in year 4, the donee acquires a non-qualifying security of the donor for $130, s. 118.1(16) and (17) will be triggered to eliminate the gift in year 1 and reduce the gift in year 2 to $70.

Related Sections: See related sections in s. 118.1(13).

▶ 118.1(18) ◀

(18) Non-qualifying security defined. For the purposes of this section, "non-qualifying security" of an individual at any time means

(*a*) an obligation (other than an obligation of a financial institution to repay an amount deposited with the institution or an obligation listed on a designated stock exchange) of the individual or the individual's estate or of any person or partnership with which the individual or the estate does not deal at arm's length immediately after that time;

(*b*) a share (other than a share listed on a designated stock exchange) of the capital stock of a corporation with which the individual or the estate or, where the individual is a trust, a person affiliated with the trust, does not deal at arm's length immediately after that time;

(*b*.1) a beneficial interest of the individual or the estate in a trust that

(i) immediately after that time is affiliated with the individual or the estate, or

(ii) holds, immediately after that time, a non-qualifying security of the individual or estate, or held, at or before that time, a share described in paragraph (*b*) that is, after that time, held by the donee; or

(*c*) any other security (other than a security listed on a designated stock exchange) issued by the individual or the estate or by any person or partnership with which the individual or the estate does not deal at arm's length (or, in the case where the person is a trust, with which the individual or estate is affiliated) immediately after that time.

Editorial Note: See note to s. 118.1(13).

Related Sections: See related sections in s. 118.1(13).

Tax Profile: October 2011 — Donations of Real Estate and Shares of Real Estate Companies.

Tax Topics: No. 1977, Whether Parties Were At Arm's Length.

▶ 118.1(19) ◀

(19) Excepted gift. For the purposes of this section, a gift made by a taxpayer is an excepted gift if

(*a*) the security is a share;

(*b*) the donee is not a private foundation;

(*c*) either,

(i) if the taxpayer is an individual's graduated rate estate,

(A) the individual dealt at arm's length with the donee immediately before the individual's death, and

(B) the graduated rate estate deals at arm's length with the donee (determined without reference to paragraph 251(1)(*b*)), or

(ii) if subparagraph (i) does not apply, the taxpayer deals at arm's length with the donee; and

(*d*) where the donee is a charitable organization or a public foundation, the taxpayer deals at arm's length with each director, trustee, officer and like official of the donee.

Editorial Note: An excepted gift is not subject to the non-qualifying security rules in s. 118.1(13). However, it may be subject to the loan-back rules in s. 118.1(16). See editorial note for s. 118.1(13).

History: S. 118.1(19)(*c*) was replaced by S.C. 2016, c. 12, s. 42(9), applicable to the 2016 and subsequent taxation years, and formerly read:

(*c*) the taxpayer deals at arm's length with the donee; and

Related Sections: See related sections in s. 118.1(13).

▶ 118.1(20) ◀

(20) Financial institution defined. For the purpose of subsection (18), "financial institution" means a corporation that is (*a*) a member of the Canadian Payments Association; or

(*b*) a credit union that is a shareholder or member of a body corporate or organization that is a central for the purposes of the *Canadian Payments Act*.

Editorial Note: See note to s. 118.1(13).

History: S. 118.1(20)(*b*) was replaced by S.C. 2017, c. 33, s. 43(3), deemed to have come into force on October 24, 2001, and formerly read:

(*b*) a credit union that is a shareholder or member of a body corporate or organization that is a central for the purposes of the "Canadian Payments Association Act".

Related Sections: See related sections in s. 118.1(13).

► 118.1(21) ◄

(21) Options. Subject to subsections (23) and (24), if an individual has granted an option to a qualified donee in a taxation year, no amount in respect of the option is to be included in computing the total charitable gifts, total cultural gifts or total ecological gifts in respect of any taxpayer for any taxation year.

Editorial Note: Subsections 118.1(21) to (24) provide that a charitable donations tax credit under subsection 118.1(3) is not available to an individual in respect of the granting by the donor of an option to acquire a particular property of the donor. An exception is available in certain cases where either (i) the amount paid by the donee for the option plus the amount paid to acquire the property pursuant to the option is less than or equal to 80% of the fair market value of the property at the time the underlying property is acquired by the donee; or (ii) the Minister of National Revenue is satisfied that the granting of the option was made with the intention to make a gift to the qualified donee. In certain circumstances, the tax credit may become available at the time the option is exercised by the donee and the property is acquired by the donee.

History: S. 118.1(21) was replaced by S.C. 2014, c. 39, s. 34(16), applicable to the 2016 and subsequent taxation years, and formerly read:

(21) *Options.* Subject to subsections (23) and (24), if an individual has granted an option to a qualified donee in a taxation year, no amount in respect of the option is to be included in computing the total charitable gifts, total Crown gifts, total cultural gifts or total ecological gifts in respect of the individual for any year.

S. 118.1(21) was added by S.C. 2011, c. 24, s. 26(7), applicable in respect of options granted on or after March 22, 2011.

Related Sections: S. 118.1(22) Application of subsection (23); s.118.1(23) Granting of an option; s118.1(24) Disposition of an option.

► 118.1(22) ◄

(22) Application of subsection (23). Subsection (23) applies if

(*a*) an option to acquire a property of an individual is granted to a qualified donee;

(*b*) the option is exercised so that the property is disposed of by the individual and acquired by the qualified donee at a particular time; and

(*c*) either

(i) the amount that is 80% of the fair market value of the property at the particular time is greater than or equal to the total of

(A) the consideration received by the individual from the qualified donee for the property, and

(B) the consideration received by the individual from the qualified donee for the option, or

(ii) the individual establishes to the satisfaction of the Minister that the granting of the option or the disposition of the property was made by the individual with the intention to make a gift to the qualified donee.

Editorial Note: See note to s. 118.1(21).

History: S. 118.1(22) was added by S.C. 2011, c. 24, s. 26(7), applicable in respect of options granted on or after March 22, 2011.

Related Sections: See related sections in s. 118.1(21).

► 118.1(23) ◄

(23) Granting of an option. If this subsection applies, notwithstanding subsection 49(3),

(*a*) the individual is deemed to have received proceeds of disposition of the property equal to the property's fair market value at the particular time; and

(*b*) there shall be included in the individual's total charitable gifts, for the taxation year that includes the particular time, the amount by which the property's fair market value exceeds the total described in subparagraph (22)(*c*)(i).

Editorial Note: See note to s. 118.1(21).

History: S. 118.1(23) was added by S.C. 2011, c. 24, s. 26(7), applicable in respect of options granted on or after March 22, 2011.

Related Sections: See related sections in s. 118.1(21).

► 118.1(24) ◄

(24) Disposition of an option. If an option to acquire a particular property of an individual is granted to a qualified donee and the option is disposed of by the qualified donee (otherwise than by the exercise of the option) at a particular time

(*a*) the individual is deemed to have disposed of a property at the particular time

(i) the adjusted cost base of which to the individual immediately before the particular time is equal to the consideration, if any, paid by the qualified donee for the option, and

(ii) the proceeds of disposition of which are equal to the lesser of the fair market value of the particular property at the particular time and the fair market value of any consideration (other than a non-qualifying security of any person) received by the qualified donee for the option; and

(*b*) there shall be included in the total charitable gifts of the individual for the individual's taxation year that includes the particular time the amount, if any, by which the proceeds of disposition as determined by paragraph (*a*) exceed the consideration, if any, paid by the donee for the option.

Editorial Note: See note to s. 118.1(21).

History: S. 118.1(24) was added by S.C. 2011, c. 24, s. 26(7), applicable in respect of options granted on or after March 22, 2011.

Related Sections: See related sections in s. 118.1(21).

► 118.1(25) ◄

(25) Returned property. Subsection (26) applies if a qualified donee has issued to an individual a receipt referred to in subsection (2) in respect of a transfer of a property (in this subsection and subsection (26) referred to as the "original property") and a particular property that is

(*a*) the original property is later transferred to the individual (unless that later transfer is reasonable consideration or remuneration for property acquired by or services rendered to a person); or

(*b*) any other property that may reasonably be considered compensation for or a substitute for, in whole or in part, the original property, is later transferred to the individual.

Editorial Note: Subsections 118.1(25) to (28) allow the Canada Revenue Agency to reassess a donor where property donated to a "qualified donee" (and in respect of which a receipt was issued to the donor) is subsequently returned to the donor. Superficially, if the donated property, an identical property, or another property that may be reasonably considered to be transferred in substitution for, or compensation for, the donated property is transferred by the qualified donee to the donor, the original gift is deemed not to have been made and the Minister of National Revenue has the authority to reassess any person whose income would reasonably be regarded as relating to the return of property. These rules do not apply, however, if the property is returned to the donor as reasonable consideration or remuneration for property or services. See CRA Charities Guidance Document CG-016.

If the returned property is not the original property, the donor is deemed to have disposed of the original property at the time it receives the returned property for proceeds of disposition equal to the greater of the fair market value of the returned property at that time and the fair market value of the original property at the time it was originally transferred by the donor to the donee. In such a case, if the fair market value of the original property at the time of the original donation exceeds the fair market value of the returned property at the time it is returned to the donor, the excess will be considered a gift made by the donor at the time of the gift of the original property.

If the value of the returned property is greater than $50, the transferor must file an information return containing prescribed information with the Minister not later than 90 days after the day on which the property was returned. A copy must be provided to the donor.

History: S. 118.1(25) was added by S.C. 2011, c. 24, s. 26(7), applicable to transfers of property made on or after March 22, 2011.

Related Sections: S. 118.1(26) Returned property; s. 118.1(27) Information return; s. 118.1(28) Reassessment.

► 118.1(26) ◄

(26) Returned property. If this subsection applies, then

(*a*) irrespective of whether the transfer of the original property by the individual to the qualified donee referred to in subsection (25) was a gift, the individual is deemed not to have disposed of the original property at the time of that transfer nor to have made a gift;

(*b*) if the particular property is identical to the original property, the particular property is deemed to be the original property; and

(*c*) if the particular property is not the original property, then

(i) the individual is deemed to have disposed of the original property at the time that the particular property is transferred to the individual for proceeds of disposition equal to the greater of the fair market value of the particular property at that time and the fair market value of the original property at the time that it was transferred by the individual to the donee, and

(ii) if the transfer of the original property by the individual would be a gift if this section were read without reference to paragraph (*a*), the individual is deemed to have, at the time of that transfer, transferred to the donee a property that is the subject of a gift having a fair market value equal to the amount, if any, by which the fair market value of the original property at the time of that transfer exceeds the fair market value of the particular property at the time that it is transferred to the individual.

Editorial Note: See note to s. 118.1(25).

History: S. 118.1(26) was added by S.C. 2011, c. 24, s. 26(7), applicable to transfers of property made on or after March 22, 2011.

Related Sections: See related sections to s. 118.1(25).

► 118.1(27) ◄

(27) Information return. If subsection (26) applies in respect of a transfer of property to an individual and that property has a fair market value greater than $50, the transferor must file an information return containing prescribed information with the Minister not later than 90 days after the day on which the property was transferred and provide a copy of the return to the individual.

Editorial Note: See note to s. 118.1(25).

History: S. 118.1(27) was added by S.C. 2011, c. 24, s. 26(7), applicable to transfers of property made on or after March 22, 2011, except that an information return that is filed before November 16, 2011 is deemed to have been filed on time.

Related Regulations: 3501.1.

Related Sections: See related sections to s. 118.1(25).

► 118.1(28) ◄

(28) Reassessment. If subsection (26) applies in respect of a transfer of property to an individual, the Minister may reassess a return of income of any person to the extent that the reassessment can reasonably be regarded as relating to the transfer.

Editorial Note: See note to s. 118.1(25).

History: S. 118.1(28) was added by S.C. 2011, c. 24, s. 26(7), applicable to transfers of property made on or after March 22, 2011.

Related Sections: See related sections to s. 118.1(25).

SECTION 118.2: Medical expense credit

► 118.2(1) ◄

(1) Medical expense credit. For the purpose of computing the tax payable under this Part by an individual for a taxation year, there may be deducted the amount determined by the formula

$$A \times [(B - C) + D]$$

where

A is the appropriate percentage for the taxation year;

B is the total of the individual's medical expenses in respect of the individual, the individual's spouse or common-law partner or a child of the individual who has not attained the age of 18 years before the end of the taxation year

(*a*) that are evidenced by receipts filed with the Minister,

(*b*) that were not included in determining an amount under this subsection, section 64 or subsection 122.51(2), for a preceding taxation year,

(*c*) that are not included in determining an amount under this subsection, section 64 or subsection 122.51(2), by any other taxpayer for any taxation year, and

(*d*) that were paid by the individual or the individual's legal representative within any period of 12 months that ends in the taxation year or, if those expenses were in respect of a person (including the individual) who died in the taxation year, within any period of 24 months that includes the day of the person's death;

C is the lesser of $1,813 and 3% of the individual's income for the taxation year; and

D is the total of all amounts each of which is, in respect of a dependant of the individual (within the meaning assigned by subsection 118(6), other than a child of the individual who has not attained the age of 18 years before the end of the taxation year), the amount determined by the formula

$$E - F$$

where

E is the total of the individual's medical expenses in respect of the dependant

(*a*) that are evidenced by receipts filed with the Minister,

(*b*) that were not included in determining an amount under this subsection, or subsection 122.51(2), in respect of the individual for a preceding taxation year,

(*c*) that are not included in determining an amount under this subsection, or subsection 122.51(2), by any other taxpayer for any taxation year, and

(*d*) that were paid by the individual or the individual's legal representative within the period referred to in paragraph (*d*) of the description of B; and

F is the lesser of $1,813 and 3% of the dependant's income for the taxation year.

CRA News Release

2.2% Indexation Factor for 2019

See the CRA Fact Sheet, dated November 16, 2018, that is reproduced following subsection117.1(1). This release announces a 2.2% indexation factor applicable for 2019 tax bracket thresholds, personal amounts and other amounts relating to non-refundable credits, as well as the refundable medical expense supplement, Old Age Security repayment threshold, certain board and lodging allowances, and the tradesperson's tools deduction. Increases to tax bracket thresholds, amounts relating to non-refundable credits, and most other amounts will take effect on January 1, 2019. However, increases in amounts for certain income-tested benefits (for example, the goods and services tax credit) will take effect on July 1, 2019.

History: S. 118.2(1), the portion of the description of B before paragraph (*a*) was replaced by S.C. 2013, c. 34, s. 249(1), applicable to taxation years that end after October 31, 2011, and formerly read:

B is the total of the individual's medical expenses in respect of the individual, the individual's spouse, the individual's common-law partner or a child of the individual who has not attained the age of 18 years before the end of the taxation year

S. 118.2(1), the portion of the description of D before the formula was replaced by S.C. 2011, c. 24, s. 27(1), applicable to the 2011 and subsequent taxation years. S. 118.2(1), the portion of the description of D before the formula formerly read:

D is the total of all amounts each of which is, in respect of a dependant of the individual (within the meaning assigned by subsection 118(6), other than a child of the individual who has not attained the age of 18 years before the end of the taxation year), the lesser of $10,000 and the amount determined by the formula

Related Regulations: 5700; 5701.

Related Sections: 118.041(4) Interaction with medical expense credit; S. 117.1(1) Annual adjustment (indexing); s. 118.2(2) Medical expenses; s. 118.2(3) Deemed medical expense; s. 118.3(2) Dependant having impairment; s. 118.4(1) Nature of impairment; s. 118.4(2) Reference to medical practitioners, etc.; s. 248(1), "individual".

Canadian Tax Foundation: Fuller and Muise, *Recent Court Decisions: Jordan v. R., 2012 TCC 394*, 2013 Prairie Provinces Tax Conference 1:10–12; Choran and Farina, *Medical Expenses Abroad*, 2013 Canadian Tax Highlights 21(4):8–9; Chu et al., *Curtailing Income Tax Relief for Cosmetic Medical Expenses*, 2010 Canadian Tax Journal 3:529–575; Rochwerg, *Tax and Estate Planning for Special Needs Individuals*, 2005 Conference Report 8:1–14; Katz, *Tax Assistance for the Disabled*, 1999 Canadian Tax Journal 3:663–691; Magee, *Tax Planning for the Disabled and Elderly and their Caregivers*, 1992 Canadian Tax Journal 6:1364–1383.

Income Tax Folios: *Primary* — S1-F1-C1 Medical Expense Tax Credit; *Secondary* — S1-F1-C2 Disablity Tax Credit; S1-F1-C3 Disability Supports Deduction.

Tax Window Files: METC & HATC for a dependant, *May 6, 2019*, CRA Document No. 2019-0791601E5.

Cases: The medical expense tax credit does not apply to surrogacy arrangements, as the person receiving the treatment is not the taxpayer. *Warnock v. The Queen*, 2014 DTC 1176 (T.C.C.)

Since the extraction of umbilical cord blood was not prescribed by a medical practitioner, the taxpayer's blood-storage expense was not eligible for the medical expense tax credit. *Shapiro v. The Queen*, 2014 DTC 1080 (T.C.C.)

The taxpayer was denied medical expense tax credits for his disabled son in relation to: a trip to certain wheelchair games in which his son participated; the purchase price of a van; and books, compact discs, videos, toys, computer equipment and entertainment. *Weeks v. The Queen*, 2001 DTC 5035 (F.C.A.), affirming 99 DTC 397 (T.C.C.)

The cost of special fixtures placed in a bathroom in order to accommodate a wheelchair was deductible as a medical expense. *Rankin v. M.N.R.*, 81 DTC 306 (T.R.B.)

► 118.2(2) ◄

(2) Medical expenses. For the purposes of subsection (1), a medical expense of an individual is an amount paid

(*a*) to a medical practitioner, dentist or nurse or a public or licensed private hospital in respect of medical or dental services provided to a person (in this subsection referred to as the "patient") who is the individual, the individual's spouse or common-law partner or a dependant of the individual (within the meaning assigned by subsection 118(6)) in the taxation year in which the expense was incurred;

(*b*) as remuneration for one full-time attendant (other than a person who, at the time the remuneration is paid, is the individual's spouse or common-law partner or is under 18 years of age) on, or for the full-time care in a nursing home of, the patient in respect of whom an amount would, but for paragraph 118.3(1)(*c*), be deductible under section 118.3 in computing a taxpayer's tax payable under this Part for the taxation year in which the expense was incurred;

(*b*.1) as remuneration for attendant care provided in Canada to the patient if

(i) the patient is a person in respect of whom an amount may be deducted under section 118.3 in computing a taxpayer's tax payable under this Part for the taxation year in which the expense was incurred,

(ii) no part of the remuneration is included in computing a deduction claimed in respect of the patient under section 63 or 64 or paragraph (*b*), (*b*.2), (*c*), (*d*) or (*e*) for any taxation year,

(iii) at the time the remuneration is paid, the attendant is neither the individual's spouse or common-law partner nor under 18 years of age, and

(iv) each receipt filed with the Minister to prove payment of the remuneration was issued by the payee and contains, where the payee is an individual, that individual's Social Insurance Number,

to the extent that the total of amounts so paid does not exceed $10,000 (or $20,000 if the individual dies in the year);

(*b*.2) as remuneration for the patient's care or supervision provided in a group home in Canada maintained and operated exclusively for the benefit of individuals who have a severe and prolonged impairment, if

(i) because of the patient's impairment, the patient is a person in respect of whom an amount may be deducted under section 118.3 in computing a taxpayer's tax payable under this Part for the taxation year in which the expense is incurred,

(ii) no part of the remuneration is included in computing a deduction claimed in respect of the patient under section 63 or 64 or paragraph (*b*), (*b*.1), (*c*), (*d*) or (*e*) for any taxation year, and

(iii) each receipt filed with the Minister to prove payment of the remuneration was issued by the payee and contains, where the payee is an individual, that individual's Social Insurance Number;

(*c*) as remuneration for one full-time attendant on the patient in a self-contained domestic establishment in which the patient lives, if

(i) the patient is, and has been certified in writing by a medical practitioner to be, a person who, by reason of mental or physical infirmity, is and is likely to be for a long-continued period of indefinite duration dependent on others for the patient's personal needs and care and who, as a result, requires a full-time attendant,

(ii) at the time the remuneration is paid, the attendant is neither the individual's spouse or common-law partner nor under 18 years of age, and

(iii) each receipt filed with the Minister to prove payment of the remuneration was issued by the payee and contains, where the payee is an individual, that individual's Social Insurance Number;

(*d*) for the full-time care in a nursing home of the patient, who has been certified in writing by a medical practitioner to be a person who, by reason of lack of normal mental capacity, is and in the foreseeable future will continue to be dependent on others for the patient's personal needs and care;

(*e*) for the care, or the care and training, at a school, an institution or another place of the patient, who has been certified in writing by an appropriately qualified person to be a person who, by reason of a physical or mental handicap, requires the equipment, facilities or personnel specially provided by that school, institution or other place for the care, or the care and training, of individuals suffering from the handicap suffered by the patient;

(*f*) for transportation by ambulance to or from a public or licensed private hospital for the patient;

(*g*) to a person engaged in the business of providing transportation services, to the extent that the payment is made for the transportation of

(i) the patient, and

(ii) one individual who accompanied the patient, where the patient was, and has been certified in writing by a medical practitioner to be, incapable of travelling without the assistance of an attendant

from the locality where the patient dwells to a place, not less than 40 kilometres from that locality, where medical services are normally provided, or from that place to that locality, if

(iii) substantially equivalent medical services are not available in that locality,

(iv) the route travelled by the patient is, having regard to the circumstances, a reasonably direct route, and

(v) the patient travels to that place to obtain medical services for himself or herself and it is reasonable, having regard to the circumstances, for the patient to travel to that place to obtain those services;

(*h*) for reasonable travel expenses (other than expenses described in paragraph (*g*)) incurred in respect of the patient and, where the patient was, and has been certified in writing by a medical practitioner to be, incapable of travelling without the assistance of an attendant, in respect of one individual who accompanied the patient, to obtain medical services in a place that is not less than 80 km from the locality where the patient dwells if the circumstances described in subparagraphs (g)(iii) to (v) apply;

(*i*) for, or in respect of, an artificial limb, an iron lung, a rocking bed for poliomyelitis victims, a wheel chair, crutches, a spinal brace, a brace for a limb, an ileostomy or colostomy pad, a truss for hernia, an artificial eye, a laryngeal speaking aid, an aid to hearing, an artificial kidney machine, phototherapy equipment for the treatment of psoriasis or other skin disorders, or an oxygen concentrator, for the patient;

(*i*.1) for or in respect of diapers, disposable briefs, catheters, catheter trays, tubing or other products required by the patient by reason of incontinence caused by illness, injury or affliction;

(*j*) for eye glasses or other devices for the treatment or correction of a defect of vision of the patient as prescribed by a medical practitioner or optometrist;

(*k*) for an oxygen tent or other equipment necessary to administer oxygen or for insulin, oxygen, liver extract injectible for pernicious anaemia or vitamin B12 for pernicious anaemia, for use by the patient as prescribed by a medical practitioner;

(*l*) on behalf of the patient who is blind or profoundly deaf or has severe autism, severe diabetes, severe epilepsy, severe mental impairment or a severe and prolonged impairment that markedly restricts the use of the patient's arms or legs,

(i) for an animal that is

(A) specially trained to

(I) in the case of severe mental impairment, perform specific tasks (excluding, for greater certainty, the provision of emotional support) that assist the patient in coping with the impairment, and

(II) in all other cases, assist the patient in coping with the impairment, and

(B) provided by a person or organization one of whose main purposes is such training of animals,

(ii) for the care and maintenance of such an animal, including food and veterinary care,

(iii) for reasonable travel expenses of the patient incurred for the purpose of attending a school, institution or other facility that trains, in the handling of such animals, individuals who are so impaired, and

(iv) for reasonable board and lodging expenses of the patient incurred for the purpose of the patient's full-time attendance at a school, institution or other facility referred to in subparagraph (iii);

(*l*.1) on behalf of the patient who requires a bone marrow or organ transplant,

(i) for reasonable expenses (other than expenses described in subparagraph (ii)), including legal fees and insurance premiums, to locate a compatible donor and to arrange for the transplant, and

(ii) for reasonable travel, board and lodging expenses (other than expenses described in paragraphs (*g*) and (*h*)) of the donor (and one other person who accompanies the donor) and the patient (and one other person who accompanies the patient) incurred in respect of the transplant;

(*l*.2) for reasonable expenses relating to renovations or alterations to a dwelling of the patient who lacks normal physical development or has a severe and prolonged mobility impairment, to enable the patient to gain access to, or to be mobile or functional within, the dwelling, provided that such expenses

(i) are not of a type that would typically be expected to increase the value of the dwelling, and

(ii) are of a type that would not normally be incurred by persons who have normal physical development or who do not have a severe and prolonged mobility impairment;

(*l*.21) for reasonable expenses relating to the construction of the principal place of residence of the patient who lacks normal physical development or has a severe and prolonged mobility impairment, that can reasonably be considered to be incremental costs incurred to enable the patient to gain access to, or to be mobile or functional within, the patient's principal place of residence, provided that such expenses

(i) are not of a type that would typically be expected to increase the value of the dwelling, and

(ii) are of a type that would not normally be incurred by persons who have normal physical development or who do not have a severe and prolonged mobility impairment;

(*l*.3) for reasonable expenses relating to rehabilitative therapy, including training in lip reading and sign language, incurred to adjust for the patient's hearing or speech loss;

(*l*.4) on behalf of the patient who has a speech or hearing impairment, for sign language interpretation services or real-time captioning services, to the extent that the payment is made to a person in the business of providing such services;

(*l*.41) on behalf of the patient who has a mental or physical impairment, for note-taking services, if

(i) the patient has been certified in writing by a medical practitioner to be a person who, because of that impairment, requires such services, and

(ii) the payment is made to a person in the business of providing such services;

(*l*.42) on behalf of the patient who has a physical impairment, for the cost of voice recognition software, if the patient has been certified in writing by a medical practitioner to be a person who, because of that impairment, requires that software;

(*l*.43) on behalf of the patient who is blind or has a severe learning disability, for reading services, if

(i) the patient has been certified in writing by a medical practitioner to be a person who, because of that impairment, requires such services, and

(ii) the payment is made to a person in the business of providing such services;

(*l*.44) on behalf of the patient who is blind and profoundly deaf, for deaf-blind intervening services, if the payment is made to a person in the business of providing those services;

(*l*.5) for reasonable moving expenses (within the meaning of subsection 62(3), but not including any expense deducted under section 62 for any taxation year) of the patient, who lacks normal physical development or has a severe and prolonged mobility impairment, incurred for the purpose of the patient's move to a dwelling that is more accessible by the patient or in which the patient is more mobile or functional, if the total of the expenses claimed under this paragraph by all persons in respect of the move does not exceed $2,000;

(*l*.6) for reasonable expenses relating to alterations to the driveway of the principal place of residence of the patient who has a severe and prolonged mobility impairment, to facilitate the patient's access to a bus;

(*l*.7) for a van that, at the time of its acquisition or within 6 months after that time, has been adapted for the transportation of the patient who requires the use of a wheelchair, to the extent of the lesser of $5,000 and 20% of the amount by which

(i) the amount paid for the acquisition of the van

exceeds

(ii) the portion, if any, of the amount referred to in subparagraph (i) that is included because of paragraph (*m*) in computing the individual's deduction under this section for any taxation year;

(*l*.8) for reasonable expenses (other than amounts paid to a person who was at the time of the payment the individual's spouse or common-law partner or a person under 18 years of age) to train the individual, or a person related to the individual, if the training relates to the mental or physical infirmity of a person who

(i) is related to the individual, and

(ii) is a member of the individual's household or is dependent on the individual for support;

(*l*.9) as remuneration for therapy provided to the patient because of the patient's severe and prolonged impairment, if

(i) because of the patient's impairment, an amount may be deducted under section 118.3 in computing a taxpayer's tax payable under this Part for the taxation year in which the remuneration is paid,

(ii) the therapy is prescribed by, and administered under the general supervision of,

(A) a medical doctor, a nurse practitioner or a psychologist, in the case of mental impairment, and

(B) a medical doctor, a nurse practitioner or an occupational therapist, in the case of a physical impairment,

(iii) at the time the remuneration is paid, the payee is neither the individual's spouse or common-law partner nor under 18 years of age, and

(iv) each receipt filed with the Minister to prove payment of the remuneration was issued by the payee and contains, where the payee is an individual, that individual's Social Insurance Number;

(*l*.91) as remuneration for tutoring services that are rendered to, and are supplementary to the primary education of, the patient who

(i) has a learning disability or a mental impairment, and

(ii) has been certified in writing by a medical practitioner to be a person who, because of that disability or impairment, requires those services,

if the payment is made to a person ordinarily engaged in the business of providing such services to individuals who are not related to the payee;

(*l*.92) as remuneration for the design of an individualized therapy plan for the patient because of the patient's severe and prolonged impairment, if

(i) because of the patient's impairment, an amount would be, if this Act were read without reference to paragraph 118.3(1)(*c*), deductible under section 118.3 in computing a taxpayer's tax payable under this Part for the taxation year in which the remuneration is paid,

(ii) the plan is required to access public funding for specialized therapy or is prescribed by

(A) a medical doctor, a nurse practitioner or a psychologist, in the case of mental impairment, or

(B) a medical doctor, a nurse practitioner or an occupational therapist, in the case of a physical impairment,

(iii) the therapy set out in the plan is prescribed by and, if undertaken, administered under the general supervision of

(A) a medical doctor, a nurse practitioner or a psychologist, in the case of mental impairment, or

(B) a medical doctor, a nurse practitioner or an occupational therapist, in the case of a physical impairment, and

(iv) the payment is made to a person ordinarily engaged in a business that includes the design of such plans for individuals who are not related to the payee;

(*m*) for any device or equipment for use by the patient that

(i) is of a prescribed kind,

(ii) is prescribed by a medical practitioner,

(iii) is not described in any other paragraph of this subsection, and

(iv) meets such conditions as are prescribed as to its use or the reason for its acquisition;

to the extent that the amount so paid does not exceed the amount, if any, prescribed in respect of the device or equipment;

(*n*) for

(i) drugs, medicaments or other preparations or substances (other than those described in paragraph (*k*))

(A) that are manufactured, sold or represented for use in the diagnosis, treatment or prevention of a disease, disorder or abnormal physical state, or its symptoms, or in restoring, correcting or modifying an organic function,

(B) that can lawfully be acquired for use by the patient only if prescribed by a medical practitioner or dentist, and

(C) the purchase of which is recorded by a pharmacist, or

(ii) drugs, medicaments or other preparations or substances that are prescribed by regulation;

(*o*) for laboratory, radiological or other diagnostic procedures or services together with necessary interpretations, for maintaining health, preventing disease or assisting in the diagnosis or treatment of any injury, illness or disability, for the patient as prescribed by a medical practitioner or dentist;

(*p*) to a person authorized under the laws of a province to carry on the business of a dental mechanic, for the making or repairing of an upper or lower denture, or for the taking of impressions, bite registrations and insertions in respect of the making, producing, constructing and furnishing of an upper or lower denture, for the patient;

(*q*) as a premium, contribution or other consideration under a private health services plan in respect of one or more of the individual, the individual's spouse or common-law partner and any member of the individual's household with whom the individual is connected by blood relationship, marriage, common-law partnership or adoption, except to the extent that the premium, contribution or consideration is deducted under subsection 20.01(1) in computing an individual's income from a business for any taxation year;

(*r*) on behalf of the patient who has celiac disease, the incremental cost of acquiring gluten-free food products as compared to the cost of comparable non-gluten-free food products, if the patient has been certified in writing by a medical practitioner to be a person who, because of that disease, requires a gluten-free diet;

(*s*) for drugs obtained under Health Canada's Special Access Programme in accordance with sections C.08.010 and C.08.011 of the *Food and Drug Regulations* and purchased for use by the patient;

(*t*) for medical devices obtained under Health Canada's Special Access Programme in accordance with Part 2 of the *Medical Devices Regulations* and purchased for use by the patient; or

(*u*) on behalf of the patient who is the holder of a *medical document* (as defined in subsection 264(1) of the *Cannabis Regulations*) to support their use of cannabis for medical purposes, for the cost of cannabis, cannabis oil, cannabis plant seeds or cannabis products purchased for medical purposes from a holder of a *licence for sale* (as defined in subsection 264(1) of the *Cannabis Regulations*).

(*v*) (Repealed by 2017, c. 33, s. 44(5).)

History: S. 118.2(2)(*u*) was replaced by S.C. 2019, c. 29, s. 17(1), deemed to have come into force on October 17, 2018. S. 118.2(2)(*u*) formerly read:

(*u*) on behalf of the patient who is authorized to possess marihuana, marihuana plants or seeds, cannabis or cannabis oil for their own medical use under the *Access to Cannabis for Medical Purposes Regulations* or section 56 of the *Controlled Drugs and Substances Act*, for the cost of marihuana, marihuana plants or seeds, cannabis or cannabis oil purchased in accordance with the *Access to Cannabis for Medical Purposes Regulations* or section 56 of the *Controlled Drugs and Substances Act*.

S. 118.2(2)(*l*), the portion before subparagraph (ii) was replaced by S.C. 2018, c. 12, s. 12(1), applicable in respect of expenses incurred after 2017, and formerly read:

(*l*) on behalf of the patient who is blind or profoundly deaf or has severe autism, severe diabetes, severe epilepsy or a severe and prolonged impairment that markedly restricts the use of the patient's arms or legs,

(i) for an animal specially trained to assist the patient in coping with the impairment and provided by a person or organization one of whose main purposes is such training of animals,

S. 118.2(2)(*l*.9)(ii)(A) and (B) were replaced by S.C. 2017, c. 33, s. 44(1), applicable in respect of expenses incurred after September 7, 2017, and formerly read:

(A) a medical doctor or a psychologist, in the case of mental impairment, and

(B) a medical doctor or an occupational therapist, in the case of a physical impairment,

S. 118.2(2)(*l*.92)(ii)(A) and (B) were replaced by S.C. 2017, c. 33, s. 44(2), applicable in respect of expenses incurred after September 7, 2017, and formerly read:

(A) a medical doctor or a psychologist, in the case of mental impairment, or

(B) a medical doctor or an occupational therapist, in the case of a physical impairment,

S. 118.2(2)(*l.92*)(iii)(A) and (B) were replaced by S.C. 2017, c. 33, s. 44(3), applicable in respect of expenses incurred after September 7, 2017, and formerly read:

(A) a medical doctor or a psychologist, in the case of mental impairment, or

(B) a medical doctor or an occupational therapist, in the case of a physical impairment, and

S. 118.2(2)(*u*) was replaced and (*v*) was repealed by S.C. 2017, c. 33, s. 44(5), deemed to have come into force on August 24, 2016, and formerly read:

(*u*) on behalf of the patient who is authorized to possess marihuana for medical purposes under the "Marihuana Medical Access Regulations" or section 56 of the "Controlled Drugs and Substances Act", for

(i) the cost of medical marihuana or marihuana seeds purchased from Health Canada, or

(ii) the cost of marihuana purchased from an individual who possesses, on behalf of that patient, a designated-person production license to produce marihuana under the "Marihuana Medical Access Regulations" or an exemption for cultivation or production under section 56 of the "Controlled Drugs and Substances Act"; or

(*v*) on behalf of the patient who is authorized to possess marihuana for medical purposes under the "Marihuana for Medical Purposes Regulations" or section 56 of the "Controlled Drugs and Substances Act", for the cost of marihuana purchased from

(i) a "licensed producer" (as defined in subsection 1 (1) of the "Marihuana for Medical Purposes Regulations"), in accordance with a "medical document" (as defined in subsection 1 (1) of the "Marihuana for Medical Purposes Regulations"),

(ii) a "health care practitioner" (as defined in subsection 1(1) of the "Marihuana for Medical Purposes Regulations") in the course of treatment for a medical condition,

(iii) a hospital, under subsection 65(2.1) of the "Narcotics Control Regulations", or

(iv) an individual who possesses an exemption for cultivation or production under section 56 of the "Controlled Drugs and Substances Act".

S. 118.2(2)(*v*) was added by S.C. 2017, c. 33, s. 44(4), deemed to have come into force on June 7, 2013.

S. 118.2(2)(*l*), the portion before subparagraph (i) was replaced by S.C. 2014, c. 20, s. 10(1), applicable in respect of expenses incurred after 2013, and formerly read:

(*l*) on behalf of the patient who is blind or profoundly deaf or has severe autism, severe epilepsy or a severe and prolonged impairment that markedly restricts the use of the patient's arms or legs,

S. 118.2(2)(*l.92*) was added by S.C. 2014, c. 20, s. 10(2), applicable in respect of expenses incurred after 2013.

S. 118.2(2)(*c*)(i) was replaced by S.C. 2013, c. 34, s. 249(2), applicable to certifications made after December 20, 2002, and formerly read:

(i) the patient is, and has been certified by a medical practitioner to be, a person who, by reason of mental or physical infirmity, is and is likely to be for a long-continued period of indefinite duration dependent on others for the patient's personal needs and care and who, as a result thereof, requires a full-time attendant,

S. 118.2(2)(*d*) and (*e*) were replaced by S.C. 2013, c. 34, s. 249(3), applicable to certifications made after December 20, 2002, and formerly read:

(*d*) for the full-time care in a nursing home of the patient, who has been certified by a medical practitioner to be a person who, by reason of lack of normal mental capacity, is and in the foreseeable future will continue to be dependent on others for the patient's personal needs and care;

(*e*) for the care, or the care and training, at a school, institution or other place of the patient, who has been certified by an appropriately qualified person to be a person who, by reason of a physical or mental handicap, requires the equipment, facilities or personnel specially provided by that school, institution or other place for the care, or the care and training, of individuals suffering from the handicap suffered by the patient;

S. 118.2(2)(*g*)(ii) was replaced by S.C. 2013, c. 34, s. 249(4), applicable to certifications made after December 20, 2002, and formerly read:

(ii) one individual who accompanied the patient, where the patient was, and has been certified by a medical practitioner to be, incapable of travelling without the assistance of an attendant

S. 118.2(2)(*h*) was replaced by S.C. 2013, c. 34, s. 249(5), applicable to certifications made after December 20, 2002, and formerly read:

(*h*) for reasonable travel expenses (other than expenses described in paragraph (*g*)) incurred in respect of the patient and, where the patient was, and has been certified by a medical practitioner to be, incapable of travelling without the assistance of an attendant, in respect of one individual who accompanied the patient, to obtain medical services in a place that is not less than 80 kilometres from the locality where the patient dwells if the circumstances described in subparagraphs (*g*)(iii), (iv) and (v) apply;

S. 118.2(2)(*l*) was replaced by S.C. 2013, c. 34, s. 249(6), in force on June 26, 2013, and formerly read:

(*l*) for, or in respect of, an artificial limb, an iron lung, a rocking bed for poliomyelitis victims, a wheel chair, crutches, a spinal brace, a brace for a limb, an iliostomy or colostomy pad, a truss for hernia, an artificial eye, a laryngeal speaking aid, an aid to hearing, an artificial kidney machine, phototherapy equipment for the treatment of psoriasis or other skin disorders, or an oxygen concentrator, for the patient;

S. 118.2(2)(*l.9*)(iii) was replaced by S.C. 2013, c. 34, s. 249(8), applicable to taxation years that end after October 31, 2011, and formerly read:

(iii) at the time the remuneration is paid, the payee is neither the individual's spouse nor an individual who is under 18 years of age, and

Related Regulations: 5700; 5701.

Related Sections: S. 6(1)(*a*) Value of benefits; s. 18(1)(*a*) General limitation; s. 20(1)(*qq*) Disability-related modifications to buildings; s. 20(1)(*rr*) Disability-related equipment; s. 20.01(1) PHSP premiums; s. 63(3), "child care expense"; s. 64 Disability supports deduction; s. 110.7(3) Restriction; s. 118.2(4) Deemed payment of medical expenses; s. 248(1), "private health services plan"; s. 251(6) Blood relationship, etc.

Canadian Tax Foundation: Champagne and Melville, *Credit Where It's Due: Tax Credits for Elder-Care Expenses and Other Tax Considerations,* 2018 Canadian Tax Journal 66(4):1013–1040; Golombeck et al., *Tuition Expenses and Tutoring Fees as Medical Expenses,* 2015 Canadian Tax Journal 2:543–564; Katz, *Tax Assistance for the Disabled,* 1999 Canadian Tax Journal 3:663–691.

Tax Topics: No. 2023-24, 2010 Canadian Tax Foundation CRA Roundtable: Pipelines, Privilege and Working Papers (Again!); No. 1714, Committee Report Concerning Tax Credits for Disabled Individuals; No. 1624, Attendant Care in a Retirement Home.

Forms: T929 — Attendant Care Expenses.

Income Tax Folios: *Primary* — S1-F1-C1 Medical Expense Tax Credit; *Secondary* — S1-F3-C1 Child Care Expense Deduction.

Information Circulars: IC 82-2R2 Social insurance number legislation that relates to the preparation of information slips.

Interpretation Bulletins: *Secondary* — IT-339R2 Meaning of "private health services plan".

Tax Window Files: Magnetotherapy devices & eligible medical expenses, *May 6, 2019,* CRA Document No. 2019-0798981E5; Cannabis for medical purposes, *May 7, 2019,* CRA Document No. 2019-0800911E5; Medical expenses, *February 7, 2019,* CRA Document No. 2017-0719651E5; Medical marihuana, *March 28, 2019,* CRA Document No. 2018-0777751E5; Summer camp fees - adults with disabilities, *February 12, 2019,* CRA Document No. 2018-0778121E5; METC consultation fees and pharmacogenomics test, *January 9, 2019,* CRA Document No. 2018-0760741E5; Medical expenses - sauna and hydrotherapy pool, *December 4, 2018,* CRA Document No. 2017-0683371E5; Medical expenses - whether they include HST or GST, *October 18, 2018,* CRA Document No. 2018-0767261M4; Medical marihuana, *October 18, 2018,* CRA Document No. 2017-0700781E5; Medical expenses - cost of doulas & birth centres, *January 26, 2018,* CRA Document No. 2017-0728281M4; medical expense tax credit, *April 11, 2018,* CRA Document No. 2017-0690361E5; Medical expense, *April 12, 2018,* CRA Document No. 2017-0724441E5; Medical expense tax credit, *February 21, 2018,* CRA Document No. 2017-0696851E5; 2017 CTF – Q16 – Medical assistance in dying, *November 21, 2017,* CRA Document No. 2017-0703891C6; Eligible Travel costs for the METC, *August 24, 2015,* CRA Document No. 2015-0584181E5; Attendant Care, *Technical Interpretation, Business and Partnership Division, September 25, 2003,* CRA Document No. 2003-0030965. A resident of a retirement home may be able to claim a portion of the amount paid to the retirement home as attendant care under paragraph 118.2(2)(*b.1*).

Cases: For tuition fees to qualify as medical expenses, they must be paid for the care and training of an individual with a mental handicap. A qualified person must certify that the individual requires the equipment, facilities, and personnel specially provided. The school did not provide special programs for students with learning disabilities. Any accommodations provided were ancillary to its purpose of providing a high school education. While the boy was diagnosed by a qualified person as suffering from a mental handicap, the clinical reports failed to establish a need for special equipment, facilities, or personnel. The taxpayer did not qualify for the credit. *Leibovich v. The Queen,* 2016 DTC 1016 (TCC)

The purpose of the travel component of the medical expense tax credit is to help Canadians forced to travel long distances to obtain medical services not available locally. The beneficial effects of a warm climate are not services provided to the taxpayer by a person or a hospital and do not qualify as medical services. *The Queen v. Tallon,* 2015 DTC 5082 (FCA)

The taxpayer suffers from severe chronic pain and, on medical advice, spends winters in warmer climates abroad. Her travel expenses were allowable METCs. In order to qualify, the medical treatment must not be available locally, the route taken must be direct, and it must be reasonable for the taxpayer to travel to obtain the treatment. Expenses can be claimed for an accompanying person if a medical certificate is obtained stating that the taxpayer cannot travel alone. *Tallon v. The Queen,* 2014 DTC 1148 (T.C.C.)

The taxpayer could claim a disability tax credit for the cost of installing laminate flooring since her husband had Parkinson's disease, which made walking on carpet unsafe. *Sotski v. The Queen,* 2013 DTC 1229 (T.C.C.).

The taxpayer was entitled to a medical expense tax credit for her son's tuition at a special education private school. *Karn v. The Queen,* 2013 DTC 1082 (T.C.C.)

The taxpayer claimed a medical expense tax credit ("METC") and a disability tax credit ("DTC") for accommodation at a home for the aged and nursing care expenses. The Minister allowed the METC but disallowed the DTC since the expenses qualified as attendant or nursing home expenses. The Court allowed her DTC claim since she claimed the METC under s. 118.2(2)(*e*), not s. 118.2(2)(*b*), and therefore the exclusion in s. 118.3(1)(*c*) did not apply. If an expense can qualify under different paragraphs of s. 118.2(2), the taxpayer may decide on the most favourable treatment. *Greenaway v. The Queen*, 2010 DTC 1065 (T.C.C.)

The taxpayer wasn't entitled to a medical expense credit for the cost of natural dietary supplements and vitamins that had been prescribed by a physician, but not "recorded by a pharmacist". *Wilson v. The Queen*, 2006 DTC 2157 (T.C.C.)

A credit for nursing home costs was denied because the certificates that were issued were too vague. They did not specify: that the patient lacked normal mental capacity; the mental or physical handicap from which the patient was suffering; or the equipment, facilities or personnel that the patient required. *The Queen v. The Estate of Harry Title*, 2001 DTC 5236 (F.C.A.), reversing 2000 DTC 1991 (T.C.C.)

An air conditioner had been "designed to assist a crippled individual in walking" within the meaning of regulation 5700(*i*), and its cost was therefore deductible as a medical expense when it had been developed in a medical context in order to lower body temperature and thereby assist in the restoration of mobility. *Brown v. The Queen*, 95 DTC 5126 (F.C.T.D.), reversing 89 DTC 1 (T.C.C.).

▶ 118.2(2.1) ◀

(2.1) Cosmetic purposes. The medical expenses referred to in subsection (2) do not include amounts paid for medical or dental services, nor any related expenses, provided purely for cosmetic purposes, unless necessary for medical or reconstructive purposes.

History: S. 118.2(2.1) was added by S.C. 2010, c. 12, s. 13(1), applicable to expenses incurred after March 4, 2010.

Income Tax Folios: *Primary* — S1-F1-C1 Medical Expense Tax Credit.

▶ 118.2(2.2) ◀

(2.2) Fertility expenses. An amount is deemed to be a medical expense of an individual for the purposes of this section if the amount

(*a*) is paid for the purpose of a patient (within the meaning of subsection (2)) conceiving a child; and

(*b*) would be a medical expense of the individual (within the meaning of subsection (2)) if the patient were incapable of conceiving a child because of a medical condition.

History: S. 118.2(2.2) was added by S.C. 2017, c. 20, s. 15(1), applicable to the 2017 and subsequent taxation years. However, if an individual makes a request for a refund in respect of a taxation year to the Minister of National Revenue within the time limit specified in paragraph 164(1.5)(*a*), s. 118.2(2.2) also applies in respect of that taxation year.

Tax Window Files: METC – list of fertility related procedures, *January 9, 2019*, CRA Document No. 2018-0753891E5; Embryo freezing costs, *November 5, 2018*, CRA Document No. 2018-0763791I7; METC – fertility expenses, *December 21, 2018*, CRA Document No. 2018-0751891I7.

▶ 118.2(3) ◀

(3) Deemed medical expense. For the purposes of subsection (1),

(*a*) any amount included in computing an individual's income for a taxation year from an office or employment in respect of a medical expense described in subsection (2) paid or provided by an employer at a particular time shall be deemed to be a medical expense paid by the individual at that time; and

(*b*) there shall not be included as a medical expense of an individual any expense to the extent that

(i) the individual,

(ii) the person referred to in subsection (2) as the patient,

(iii) any person related to a person referred to in subparagraph (i) or (ii), or

(iv) the legal representative of any person referred to in any of subparagraphs (i) to (iii)

is entitled to be reimbursed for the expense, except to the extent that the amount of the reimbursement is required to be included in computing income and is not deductible in computing taxable income.

Related Sections: S. 248(1), "amount", "individual".

Interpretation Bulletins: *Secondary* — IT-339R2 Meaning of "private health service plan".

▶ 118.2(4) ◀

(4) Deemed payment of medical expenses. Where, in circumstances in which a person engaged in the business of providing transportation services is not readily available, an individual makes use of a vehicle for a purpose described in paragraph (2)(*g*), the individual or the individual's legal representative shall be deemed to have paid to a person engaged in the business of providing transportation services, in respect of the operation of the vehicle, such amount as is reasonable in the circumstances.

SECTION 118.3: Credit for mental or physical impairment

▶ 118.3(1) ◀

(1) Credit for mental or physical impairment. Where

(*a*) an individual has one or more severe and prolonged impairments in physical or mental functions,

(*a*.1) the effects of the impairment or impairments are such that the individual's ability to perform more than one basic activity of daily living is significantly restricted where the cumulative effect of those restrictions is equivalent to having a marked restriction in the ability to perform a basic activity of daily living or are such that the individual's ability to perform a basic activity of daily living is markedly restricted or would be markedly restricted but for therapy that

(i) is essential to sustain a vital function of the individual,

(ii) is required to be administered at least three times each week for a total duration averaging not less than 14 hours a week, and

(iii) cannot reasonably be expected to be of significant benefit to persons who are not so impaired,

(*a*.2) in the case of an impairment in physical or mental functions the effects of which are such that the individual's ability to perform a single basic activity of daily living is markedly restricted or would be so restricted but for therapy referred to in paragraph (*a*.1), a medical practitioner has certified in prescribed form that the impairment is a severe and prolonged impairment in physical or mental functions the effects of which are such that the individual's ability to perform a basic activity of daily living is markedly restricted or would be markedly restricted, but for therapy referred to in paragraph (*a*.1), where the medical practitioner is a medical doctor, a nurse practitioner or, in the case of

(i) a sight impairment, an optometrist,

(ii) a speech impairment, a speech-language pathologist,

(iii) a hearing impairment, an audiologist,

(iv) an impairment with respect to an individual's ability in feeding or dressing themself, an occupational therapist,

(v) an impairment with respect to an individual's ability in walking, an occupational therapist, or after February 22, 2005, a physiotherapist, and

(vi) an impairment with respect to an individual's ability in mental functions necessary for everyday life, a psychologist,

(*a*.3) in the case of one or more impairments in physical or mental functions the effects of which are such that the individual's ability to perform more than one basic activity of daily living is significantly restricted, a medical practitioner has certified in prescribed form that the impairment or impairments are severe and prolonged impairments in physical or mental functions the effects of which are such that the individual's ability to perform more than one basic activity of daily living is significantly restricted and that the cumulative effect of those restrictions is equivalent to having a marked restriction in the ability to perform a single basic activity of daily living, where the medical practitioner is, in the case of

(i) an impairment with respect to the individual's ability in feeding or dressing themself, or in walking, a medical doctor, a nurse practitioner or an occupational therapist, and

(ii) in the case of any other impairment, a medical doctor or nurse practitioner,

has certified in prescribed form that the impairment is a severe and prolonged mental or physical impairment the effects of which are such that the individual's ability to perform a basic activity of daily living is markedly restricted or would be markedly restricted but for therapy referred to in paragraph (*a.1*),

(*b*) the individual has filed for a taxation year with the Minister the certificate described in paragraph (*a*.2) or (*a*.3), and

(*c*) no amount in respect of remuneration for an attendant or care in a nursing home, in respect of the individual, is included in calculating a deduction under section 118.2 (otherwise than because of paragraph 118.2(2)(*b*.1)) for the year by the individual or by any other person,

there may be deducted in computing the individual's tax payable under this Part for the year the amount determined by the formula

$$A \times (B + C)$$

where

A is the appropriate percentage for the year,

B is $6,000, and

C is

(*a*) where the individual has not attained the age of 18 years before the end of the year, the amount, if any, by which

(i) $3,500

exceeds

(ii) the amount, if any, by which

(A) the total of all amounts each of which is an amount paid in the year for the care or supervision of the individual and included in computing a deduction under section 63, 64 or 118.2 for a taxation year

exceeds

(B) $2,050, and

(*b*) in any other case, zero.

CRA News Release

2.2% Indexation Factor for 2019

See the CRA Fact Sheet, dated November 16, 2018, that is reproduced following subsection117.1(1). This release announces a 2.2% indexation factor applicable for 2019 tax bracket thresholds, personal amounts and other amounts relating to non-refundable credits, as well as the refundable medical expense supplement, Old Age Security repayment threshold, certain board and lodging allowances, and the tradesperson's tools deduction. Increases to tax bracket thresholds, amounts relating to non-refundable credits, and most other amounts will take effect on January 1, 2019. However, increases in amounts for certain income-tested benefits (for example, the goods and services tax credit) will take effect on July 1, 2019.

History: S. 118.3(1)(*a*.2), the portion before subparagraph (i) was replaced by S.C. 2017, c. 20, s. 16(1), applicable in respect of certifications made after March 21, 2017, and formerly read:

(*a*.2) in the case of an impairment in physical or mental functions the effects of which are such that the individual's ability to perform a single basic activity of daily living is markedly restricted or would be so restricted but for therapy referred to in paragraph (*a*.1), a medical practitioner has certified in prescribed form that the impairment is a severe and prolonged impairment in physical or mental functions the effects of which are such that the individual's ability to perform a basic activity of daily living is markedly restricted or would be markedly restricted, but for therapy referred to in paragraph (*a*.1), where the medical practitioner is a medical doctor or, in the case of

S. 118.3(1)(*a*.3)(i) and (ii) were replaced by S.C. 2017, c. 20, s. 16(2), applicable in respect of certifications made after March 21, 2017, and formerly read:

(i) an impairment with respect to the individual's ability in feeding or dressing themself, or in walking, a medical doctor or an occupational therapist, and

(ii) in the case of any other impairment, a medical doctor,

Related Sections: S. 6(16) Disability-related employment benefits; s. 108(1), "preferred beneficiary"; s. 117.1(1) Annual adjustment (indexing); s. 118.2(2)(*b*) Medical expenses; s. 118.2(2)(*b*.1) Medical expenses; s. 118.2(2)(*b*.2) Medical expenses; s. 118.2(2)(*l*.9)) Medical expenses; s. 118.3(2) Dependant having impairment; s. 118.4(1) Nature of impairment; s. 118.4(2) Reference to medical practitioners, etc.; s. 118.6(3) Students eligible for the disability tax credit; s. 118.8 Transfer of unused credits to spouse or common-law partner; s. 118.91 Part-year residents; s. 118.93 Credits in separate returns; s. 118.94 Tax payable by non-residents (credits restricted); s. 146.01(1), "specified disabled person"; s. 146.1(2)(*g*.1)(i)(B) Conditions for registration; s. 248(1), "individual".

Canadian Tax Foundation: Sprysak, *Personal Tax Planning — Income Tax Supports for Canadians with Disabilities*, 2018 Canadian Tax Journal 66(3):679–705; Rochwerg, *Tax and Estate Planning for Special Needs Individuals*, 2005 Conference Report 8:1–14; Gray, *Review of Tax Filings Required as a Result of the Death of a Taxpayer*, 2003 British Columbia Tax Conference 8:3–30; Katz, *Tax Assistance for the Disabled*, 1999 Canadian Tax Journal 3:663–691; Magee, *Tax Planning for the Disabled and Elderly and their Caregivers*, 1992 Canadian Tax Journal 6:1364–1383.

Tax Topics: No. 1714, Committee Report Concerning Tax Credits for Disabled Individuals; No. 1707, Claiming the Disability Tax Credit; No. 1610, The Continuing Saga of the Disability Tax Credit; No. 1594, Government's Response to Committee Report on the Disability Tax Credit; No. 1571, Continuing Discussions on the Disability Tax Credit.

Forms: T2201 — Disability Tax Credit Information.

Guides: RC4064 Information Concerning People with Disabilities.

Income Tax Folios: *Primary* — S1-F1-C2 Disability Tax Credit; *Secondary* — S1-F1-C1 Medical Expense Tax Credit; S1-F1-C3 Disability Supports Deduction; S1-F3-C1 Child Care Expense Deduction.

Information Circulars: IC 07-1 Taxpayer relief provisions.

Interpretation Bulletins: *Secondary* — IT-394R2 Preferred beneficiary election.

Tax Window Files: Disability tax credit - lab tests as therapy, *March 8, 2018*, CRA Document No. 2017-0724351I7; Form T2201 - meaning of medical doctor, *June 24, 2016*, CRA Document No. 2016-0632181E5.

Cases: The taxpayer's daughter was born with phenylketonuria, an impairment of the body's ability to metabolize the amino acid phenylalanine ("Phe"), which can cause permanent and severe brain damage. Treatment involves administration of a specific dosage of prescription medical formula, by ingestion of Phe through the consumption of specific medical foods, and ingestion of low-Phe food. To be eligible for the disability tax credit there must be a severe and prolonged impairment in physical or mental functions so that basic activities of daily life would be markedly restricted but for essential therapy. Therapy does not include time spent on activities related to dietary restrictions or regimes. However, the administration of daily precise amounts of Phe is therapy, which includes planning, preparing meals and snacks, supervising consumption, educating all those who provide food to the daughter, and calculating and recalculating daily Phe consumption. *Hughes v. The Queen*, 2019 DTC 2038 (TCC)

The taxpayer was denied a disability tax credit since her medical certificate indicted that she was not markedly restricted in her ability to dress herself. However, the judge noted that the form should state that dressing oneself includes the ability to perform basic personal hygiene and suggested that the doctor's response might have been different if she had understood this. *Wiley v. The Queen*, 2013 DTC 1198 (T.C.C.)

The taxpayer was blind in one eye, but was able to read and had an unrestricted driver's licence. He was denied a disability tax credit since his ability to perform a basic activity of daily living was not markedly restricted, and he produced no medical certificate showing a lack of ability. *Islam v. The Queen*, 2013 DTC 1143 (T.C.C.)

The taxpayer claimed a medical expense tax credit ("METC") and a disability tax credit ("DTC") for accommodation at a home for the aged and nursing care expenses. The Minister allowed the METC but disallowed the DTC since the expenses qualified as attendant or nursing home expenses. The Court allowed her DTC claim since she claimed the METC under s. 118.2(2)(*e*), not s. 118.2(2)(*b*), and therefore the exclusion in s. 118.3(1)(*c*) did not apply. If an expense can qualify under different paragraphs of s. 118.2(2), the taxpayer may decide on the most favourable treatment. *Greenaway v. The Queen*, 2010 DTC 1065 (T.C.C.)

When the taxpayer suffered from a brain dysfunction following exposure to toxic substances, the Tax Court was not obliged to accept her doctor's statement that she had no difficulties performing three of her basic activities. *Thomas v. The Queen*, 97 DTC 5024 (F.C.A.).

▶ 118.3(1.1) ◀

(1.1) Time spent on therapy. For the purpose of paragraph 118.3(1)(*a*.1), in determining whether therapy is required to be administered at least three times each week for a total duration averaging not less than an average of 14 hours a week, the time spent on administering therapy

(*a*) includes only time spent on activities that require the individual to take time away from normal everyday activities in order to receive the therapy;

(*b*) in the case of therapy that requires a regular dosage of medication that is required to be adjusted on a daily basis, includes (subject to paragraph (*d*)) time spent on activities that are directly related to the determination of the dosage of the medication;

(*c*) in the case of a child who is unable to perform the activities related to the administration of the therapy as a result of the child's age, includes the time, if any, spent by the child's primary caregivers performing or supervising those activities for the child; and

(*d*) does not include time spent on activities related to dietary or exercise restrictions or regimes (even if those restrictions or regimes are a factor in determining the daily dosage of medication), travel time, medical appointments, shopping for medication or recuperation after therapy.

Tax Window Files: DTC and caregivers, *September 28, 2018*, CRA Document No. 2018-0753261I7.

Cases: Disability tax credit legislation is to be interpreted in a humane and compassionate manner. The administration of daily precise amounts of phenylalanine for the treatment of phenylketonuria is therapy, which includes planning, preparing meals and snacks, supervising consumption, educating others, and calculating daily consumption. Without therapy, the taxpayer's daughter would suffer potentially devastating and irreversible adverse consequences. *Hughes v. The Queen*, 2018 DTC 1040 (TCC)

▶ 118.3(2) ◀

(2) Dependant having impairment. Where

(*a*) an individual has, in respect of a person (other than a person in respect of whom the person's spouse or common-law partner deducts for a taxation year an amount under section 118 or 118.8) who is resident in Canada at any time in the year and who is entitled to deduct an amount under subsection (1) for the year,

(i) claimed for the year a deduction under subsection 118(1) because of

(A) paragraph (*b*) of the description of B in that subsection, or

(B) paragraph (*d*) of that description where the person is a parent, grandparent, child, grandchild, brother, sister, aunt, uncle, nephew or niece of the individual, or of the individual's spouse or common-law partner, or

(ii) could have claimed for the year a deduction referred to in subparagraph (i) in respect of the person if

(A) the person had no income for the year and had attained the age of 18 years before the end of the year, and

(B) in the case of a deduction referred to in clause (i)(A), the individual were not married or not in a common-law partnership, and

(*b*) no amount in respect of remuneration for an attendant, or care in a nursing home, because of that person's mental or physical impairment, is included in calculating a deduction under section 118.2 (otherwise than under paragraph 118.2(2)(*b*.1)) for the year by the individual or by any other person,

there may be deducted, for the purpose of computing the tax payable under this Part by the individual for the year, the amount, if any, by which

(*c*) the amount deductible under subsection (1) in computing that person's tax payable under this Part for the year

exceeds

(*d*) the amount of that person's tax payable under this Part for the year computed before any deductions under this Division (other than under sections 118 to 118.07 and 118.7).

History: S. 118.3(2)(*a*)(i)(B) was replaced by S.C. 2017, c. 20, s. 16(3), applicable to the 2017 and subsequent taxation years, and formerly read:

(B) paragraph (*c*.1) or (*d*) of that description where the person is a parent, grandparent, child, grandchild, brother, sister, aunt, uncle, nephew or niece of the individual, or of the individual's spouse or common-law partner, or

S. 118.3(2)(*d*) was replaced by S.C. 2014, c. 20, s. 11(1), applicable to the 2014 and subsequent taxation years, and formerly read:

(*d*) the amount of that person's tax payable under this Part for the year computed before any deductions under this Division (other than under sections 118 to 118.06 and 118.7).

S. 118.3(2)(*d*) was replaced by S.C. 2011, c. 24, s. 28(1), applicable to the 2011 and subsequent taxation years. S. 118.3(2)(*d*) formerly read:

(*d*) the amount of that person's tax payable under this Part for the year computed before any deductions under this Division (other than under sections 118 to 118.05 and 118.7).

S. 118.3(2)(*d*) was replaced by S.C. 2009, c. 31, s. 5(2), applicable to the 2009 and subsequent taxation years. S. 118.3(2)(*d*) formerly read:

(*d*) the amount of that person's tax payable under this Part for the year computed before any deductions under this Division (other than sections 118 and 118.7).

▶ 118.3(3) ◀

(3) Partial dependency. Where more than one individual is entitled to deduct an amount under subsection (2) for a taxation year in respect of the same person, the total of all amounts so deductible for the year shall not exceed the maximum amount that would be deductible under that subsection for the year by an individual in respect of that person if that individual were the only individual entitled to deduct an amount under that subsection in respect of that person, and where the individuals cannot agree as to what portion of the amount each can deduct, the Minister may fix the portions.

Cases: A taxpayer deducted child support payments under s. 60. He also sought to deduct the "equivalent-to-married" amount for one child and the "dependant's disability deduction" for another. The children were deemed not to be children of the taxpayer since he had taken deductions under s. 60(*b*), (*c*) or (*c*.1) for the support payments made for them. *Gifford v. M.N.R.*, 91 DTC 953 (T.C.C.)

▶ 118.3(4) ◀

(4) Additional information. Where a claim under this section or under section 118.8 is made in respect of an individual's impairment

(*a*) if the Minister requests in writing information with respect to the individual's impairment, its effects on the individual and, where applicable, the therapy referred to in paragraph (1)(*a*.1) that is required to be administered, from any person referred to in subsection (1) or (2) or section 118.8 in connection with such a claim, that person shall provide the information so requested to the Minister in writing; and

(*b*) if the information referred to in paragraph (*a*) is provided by a person referred to in paragraph (1)(*a.2*) or (*a.3*), the information so provided is deemed to be included in a certificate in prescribed form.

History: S. 118.3(4)(*b*) was replaced by S.C. 2013, c. 34, s. 250(2), applicable to the 2005 and subsequent taxation years, and formerly read:

(*b*) if the information referred to in paragraph (*a*) is provided by a person referred to in paragraph (1)(*a*.2), the information so provided is deemed to be included in a certificate in prescribed form.

Related Sections: S. 162(7) Failure to comply.

SECTION 118.4: Nature of impairment

▶ 118.4(1) ◀

(1) Nature of impairment. For the purposes of subsection 6(16), sections 118.2 and 118.3 and this subsection,

(*a*) an impairment is prolonged where it has lasted, or can reasonably be expected to last, for a continuous period of at least 12 months;

(*b*) an individual's ability to perform a basic activity of daily living is markedly restricted only where all or substantially all of the time, even with therapy and the use of appropriate devices and medication, the individual is blind or is unable (or requires an inordinate amount of time) to perform a basic activity of daily living;

(*b*.1) an individual is considered to have the equivalent of a marked restriction in a basic activity of daily living only where all or substantially all of the time, even with therapy and the use of appropriate devices and medication, the individual's ability to perform more than one basic activity of daily living (including for this purpose, the ability to see) is significantly restricted, and the cumulative effect of those restrictions is tantamount to the individual's ability to perform a basic activity of daily living being markedly restricted;

(*c*) a basic activity of daily living in relation to an individual means

(i) mental functions necessary for everyday life,

(ii) feeding oneself or dressing oneself,

(iii) speaking so as to be understood, in a quiet setting, by another person familiar with the individual,

(iv) hearing so as to understand, in a quiet setting, another person familiar with the individual,

(v) eliminating (bowel or bladder functions), or

(vi) walking;

(*c*.1) mental functions necessary for everyday life include

(i) memory,

(ii) problem solving, goal-setting and judgement (taken together), and

(iii) adaptive functioning;

(*d*) for greater certainty, no other activity, including working, housekeeping or a social or recreational activity, shall be considered as a basic activity of daily living;

(*e*) feeding oneself does not include

(i) any of the activities of identifying, finding, shopping for or otherwise procuring food, or

(ii) the activity of preparing food to the extent that the time associated with the activity would not have been necessary in the absence of a dietary restriction or regime; and

(*f*) dressing oneself does not include any of the activities of identifying, finding, shopping for or otherwise procuring clothing.

Tax Topics: No. 1707, Claiming the Disability Tax Credit; No. 1571, Continuing Discussions on the Disability Tax Credit.

Forms: T2201 — Disability Tax Credit Information.

Guides: RC4064 Information Concerning People with Disabilities.

Income Tax Folios: *Primary* — S1-F1-C2 Disability Tax Credit; S1-F1-C1 Medical Expense Tax Credit.

Cases: The taxpayer's son's Attention Deficit Hyperactivity Disorder ("ADHD") and learning disability did not support a conclusion he had one or more severe and prolonged mental or physical impairments whose effects were such as to markedly restrict his ability to perform mental functions necessary for daily life, all or substantially all of the time. *Vrantsidis v. The Queen*, 2017 DTC 1122 (TCC)

To claim the disability tax credit, the taxpayer must have a severe and prolonged impairment in physical or mental function, the impairment must significantly restrict the basic activities of life, and a medical practitioner must provide a certificate to support the claim. It was evident the taxpayer suffered from a severe impairment — chronic fatigue syndrome — for which tax relief is provided. *Gibson v. The Queen*, 2014 DTC 1177 (T.C.C.)

A taxpayer's ability to walk, dress and feed himself was markedly restricted due to a congenital condition diagnosed as spinal epiphyseal dysplasia and a tax credit was allowed when he required canes, rail, wheelchairs and therapeutic exercise prior to dressing. *Johnston v. The Queen*, 98 DTC 6169 (F.C.A.), reversing 97 DTC 3272 (T.C.C.)

A taxpayer who required a half-hour or more to dress and, when walking, had to stop and take time every 100 metres because of chronic back pain was entitled to claim a physical impairment tax credit because he was taking an "inordinate amount of time" to perform a basic activity of daily living. *Conner v. The Queen*, 95 DTC 198 (T.C.C.).

▶ 118.4(2) ◀

(2) Reference to medical practitioners, etc. For the purposes of sections 63, 64, 118.2, 118.3 and 118.6, a reference to an audiologist, dentist, medical doctor, medical practitioner, nurse, nurse practitioner, occupational therapist, optometrist, pharmacist, physiotherapist, psychologist or speech-language pathologist is a reference to a person authorized to practise as such,

(*a*) where the reference is used in respect of a service rendered to a taxpayer, pursuant to the laws of the jurisdiction in which the service is rendered;

(*b*) where the reference is used in respect of a certificate issued by the person in respect of a taxpayer, pursuant to the laws of the jurisdiction in which the taxpayer resides or of a province; and

(*c*) where the reference is used in respect of a prescription issued by the person for property to be provided to or for the use of a taxpayer, pursuant to the laws of the jurisdiction in which the taxpayer resides, of a province or of the jurisdiction in which the property is provided.

History: S. 118.4(2), the portion before paragraph (*a*) was replaced by S.C. 2017, c. 20, s. 17(1), deemed to have come into force on March 22, 2017, and formerly read:

(2) *Reference to medical practitioners, etc.* For the purposes of sections 63, 64, 118.2, 118.3 and 118.6, a reference to an audiologist, dentist, medical doctor, medical practitioner, nurse, occupational therapist, optometrist,

pharmacist, physiotherapist, psychologist, or speech-language pathologist is a reference to a person authorized to practise as such,

Income Tax Folios: *Primary*— S1-F1-C1 Medical Expense Tax Credit.

SECTION 118.5: Tuition credit

► 118.5(1) ◄

(1) Tuition credit. Subject to subsection (1.2), for the purpose of computing the tax payable under this Part by an individual for a taxation year, there may be deducted,

(*a*) subject to subsection (1.1), where the individual was during the year a student enrolled at an educational institution in Canada that is

(i) a university, college or other educational institution providing courses at a post-secondary school level, or

(ii) certified by the Minister of Employment and Social Development to be an educational institution providing courses, other than courses designed for university credit, that furnish a person with skills for, or improve a person's skills in, an occupation,

an amount equal to the product obtained when the appropriate percentage for the year is multiplied by the amount of any fees for the individual's tuition paid in respect of the year to the educational institution, except to the extent that those fees

(ii.1) are paid to an educational institution described in subparagraph (i) in respect of courses that are not at the post-secondary school level, if

(A) the individual had not attained the age of 16 years before the end of the year, or

(B) the purpose of the individual's enrolment at the institution cannot reasonably be regarded as being to provide the individual with skills, or to improve the individual's skills, in an occupation,

(ii.2) are paid to an educational institution described in subparagraph (ii) if

(A) the individual had not attained the age of 16 years before the end of the year, or

(B) the purpose of the individual's enrolment at the institution cannot reasonably be regarded as being to provide the individual with skills, or to improve the individual's skills, in an occupation,

(iii) are paid on behalf of, or reimbursed to, the individual by the individual's employer and the amount paid or reimbursed is not included in the individual's income,

(iii.1) are fees in respect of which the individual is or was entitled to receive a reimbursement or any form of assistance under a program of Her Majesty in right of Canada or a province designed to facilitate the entry or re-entry of workers into the labour force, where the amount of the reimbursement or assistance is not included in computing the individual's income,

(iv) were included as part of an allowance received by the individual's parent on the individual's behalf from an employer and are not included in computing the income of the parent by reason of subparagraph 6(1)(*b*)(ix), or

(v) are paid on the individual's behalf, or are fees in respect of which the individual is or was entitled to receive a reimbursement, under a program of Her Majesty in right of Canada designed to assist athletes, where the payment or reimbursement is not included in computing the individual's income;

(*b*) where the individual was during the year a student in full-time attendance at a university outside Canada in a course leading to a degree, an amount equal to the product obtained when the appropriate percentage for the year is multiplied by the amount of any fees for the individual's tuition paid in respect of the year to the university, except any such fees

(i) paid in respect of a course of less than three consecutive weeks duration,

(ii) paid on the individual's behalf by the individual's employer to the extent that the amount of the fees is not included in computing the individual's income, or

(iii) paid on the individual's behalf by the employer of the individual's parent, to the extent that the amount of the fees is not included in computing the income of the parent by reason of subparagraph 6(1)(*b*)(ix);

(*c*) where the individual resided throughout the year in Canada near the boundary between Canada and the United States if the individual

(i) was at any time in the year a student enrolled at an educational institution in the United States that is a university, college or other educational institution providing courses at a post-secondary school level, and

(ii) commuted to that educational institution in the United States,

an amount equal to the product obtained when the appropriate percentage for the year is multiplied by the amount of any fees for the individual's tuition paid in respect of the year to the educational institution if those fees exceeds $100, except to the extent that those fees

(iii) are paid on the individual's behalf by the individual's employer and are not included in computing the individual's income, or

(iv) were included as part of an allowance received by the individual's parent on the individual's behalf from an employer and are not included in computing the income of the parent by reason of subparagraph 6(1)(*b*)(ix), and

(*d*) subject to subsection (1.1), if the individual has taken an examination (in this section referred to as an "occupational, trade or professional examination") in the year that is required to obtain a professional status recognized under a federal or provincial statute, or to be licensed or certified as a tradesperson, where that status, licence or certification allows the individual to practise the profession or trade in Canada, an amount equal to the product obtained when the appropriate percentage for the year is multiplied by the amount of any fees paid in respect of the occupational, trade or professional examination to an educational institution referred to in paragraph (*a*), a professional association, a provincial ministry or other similar institution, except to the extent that the occupational, trade or professional examination fees

(i) are paid on behalf of, or reimbursed to, the individual by the individual's employer and the amount paid or reimbursed is not included in the individual's income, or

(ii) are fees in respect of which the individual is or was entitled to receive a reimbursement or any form of assistance under a program of Her Majesty in right of Canada or a province designed to facilitate the entry or re-entry of workers into the labour force, where the amount of the reimbursement or assistance is not included in computing the individual's income.

History: S. 118.5(1), the portion before paragraph (*a*), was replaced by S.C. 2019, c. 29, s. 18(1), deemed to have come into force on January 1, 2019, and formerly read:

(1) *Tuition credit* For the purpose of computing the tax payable under this Part by an individual for a taxation year, there may be deducted,

S. 118.5(1)(*a*)(ii.1) was replaced by S.C. 2017, c. 20, s. 18(1), applicable to the 2017 and subsequent taxation years, and formerly read:

(ii.1) are paid to an educational institution described in subparagraph (i) in respect of courses that are not at the post-secondary school level,

S. 118.5(1)(*a*)(iii) was replaced by S.C. 2013, c. 34, s. 251, in force June 26, 2013, and formerly read:

(iii) are paid on the individual's behalf by the individual's employer and are not included in computing the individual's income,

S. 118.5(1)(*a*)(ii) was amended by S.C. 2013, c. 40, s. 238(1)(*i*), by replacing "*Minister of Human Resources and Skills Development*" with "*Minister of Employment and Social Development*", in force December 12, 2013.

S. 118.5(1)(*a*), the portion before subpagraph (ii.1) was replaced by S.C. 2011, c. 24, s. 29(1), applicable to the 2011 and subsequent taxation years. S. 118.5(1)(*a*), the portion before subpagraph (ii.1) formerly read:

(*a*) where the individual was during the year a student enrolled at an educational institution in Canada that is

(i) a university, college or other educational institution providing courses at a post-secondary school level, or

(ii) certified by the Minister of Human Resources and Skills Development to be an educational institution providing courses, other than courses designed for university credit, that furnish a person with skills for, or improve a person's skills in, an occupation,

an amount equal to the product obtained when the appropriate percentage for the year is multiplied by the amount of any fees for the individual's tuition paid in respect of the year to the educational institution if the total of those fees exceeds $100, except to the extent that those fees

S. 118.5(1)(*b*)(i) was replaced by S.C. 2011, c. 24, s. 29(2), applicable to tuition fees paid for the 2011 and subsequent taxation years. S. 118.5(1)(*b*)(i) formerly read:

(i) paid in respect of a course of less than 13 consecutive weeks duration,

S. 118.5(1)(*d*) was added by S.C. 2011, c. 24, s. 29(3), applicable to the 2011 and subsequent taxation years.

Related Sections: S. 118.5(2) Application to deemed residents; s. 118.8 Transfer of unused credits to spouse or common-law partner; s. 118.9 Transfer to parent or grandparent; s. 248(1), "amount", "individual".

Forms: TL11A — Tuition Fees Certificate — University Outside Canada; TL11B — Tuition Fees Certificate — Flying School or Club; T1 SCH 11 — Federal Tuition and Education Amounts; T2202A — Tuition and Education Amounts Certificate; TL11C — Tuition Fees Certificate — Commuter to the United States.

Guides: P105 Students and Income Tax.

Income Tax Folios: *Primary* — S1-F2-C2 Tuition Tax Credit.

Information Circulars: IC 75-23 Tuition fees and charitable donations paid to privately supported secular and religious schools.

Tax Window Files: Training assistance for adult basic education, *January 18, 2017*, CRA Document No. 2016-0644171E5; Fees paid to music coach ineligible for tuition tax credit, *February 20, 2012*, CRA Document No. 2016-0659941E5; Training assistance for ABE, *August 9, 2016*, CRA Document No. 2016-0644171E5.

Cases: The taxpayer was enrolled in a graduate studies program outside of Canada composed of three semesters, including the summer, fall, and spring sessions, each consisting of approximately 17 credits. The summer session comprised ten consecutive courses, each of which was of one or two weeks duration. The tuition credit for the summer credit was denied. However, based on the jurisprudence and a textual, contextual, and purposive analysis of the statute, the tuition fee paid for the summer semester met all the requirements. The taxpayer was in full-time attendance during the summer, attendance at all ten courses was mandatory, she registered for and paid a single fee in respect of the summer semester courses, and all the courses were taken consecutively over a ten-week semester. *Fortnum v. The Queen*, 2019 DTC 2088 (TCC)

The taxpayer completed an online MBA degree through a foreign university and claimed a tuition tax credit. The documentation issued by the university gave credits for the online course at a rate of 30% – 40% of the rate credits were accumulated for equivalent on-campus studies. The online program took three years to complete whereas the on-campus program took one year. The taxpayer was not enrolled on a full-time basis and the credit was denied. *Archibald v. The Queen*, 2018 DTC 5011 (FCA)

The taxpayer's 14-year old son was enrolled at a music school for piano and music theory classes. His music courses were at a post-secondary level, since he was beyond the level which was equivalent to a Grade 12 high school credit. The taxpayer was entitled to the tuition fee tax credit. The student's age is only relevant for courses described in s. 118.5(1)(*a*)(ii) and not for courses described in s. 118.5(1)(*a*)(i). *Tarkowski v. The Queen*, 2007 DTC 1555 (T.C.C.)

The taxpayer was enrolled in an online degree program at a U.S. university. Her online participation constituted full-time "attendance" within the meaning of s. 118.5(1)(*b*) and she was entitled to the tuition fee tax credit. *McGrath v. The Queen*, 2007 DTC 894 (T.C.C.)

► 118.5(1.1) ◄

(1.1) Minimum amount. No amount may be deducted for a taxation year by an individual under paragraph (1)(*a*) or (*d*) in respect of any fees paid to a particular institution unless the total of the fees described in those paragraphs and paid to the particular institution in the year by the individual exceeds $100.

History: S. 118.5(1.1) was added by S.C. 2011, c. 24, s. 29(4), applicable to the 2011 and subsequent taxation years.

► 118.5(1.2) ◄

(1.2) Canada training credit reduction. The amount that may be deducted for a taxation year by an individual under subsection (1) is to be reduced by the amount determined by the formula

$$A \times B$$

where

A is the appropriate percentage for the taxation year; and

B is the amount, if any, deemed to have been paid by the individual under subsection 122.91(1) in respect of the taxation year.

History: S. 118.5(1.2) was added by S.C. 2019, c. 29, s. 18(2), deemed to have come into force on January 1, 2019.

Related Sections: 122.91(1) Claimed amount.

► 118.5(2) ◄

(2) Application to deemed residents. Where an individual is deemed by section 250 to be resident in Canada throughout all or part of a taxation year, in applying subsection (1) in respect of the individual for the period when the individual is so deemed to be resident in Canada, paragraph (1)(*a*) shall be read without reference to the words "in Canada".

Forms: TL11D — Tuition Fees Certificate — Educational Institutions Outside Canada for a Deemed Resident of Canada.

Cases: Pierrefonds, Quebec lacked the element of proximity, contiguity or vicinity to the Canada–U.S. border zone contemplated by the word "near". *Van de Water v. M.N.R.*, 91 DTC 276 (T.C.C.)

► 118.5(3) ◄

(3) Inclusion of ancillary fees and charges. For the purpose of this section, "fees for an individual's tuition" includes ancillary fees and charges that are paid

(*a*) to an educational institution referred to in subparagraph (1)(*a*)(i), and

(*b*) in respect of the individual's enrolment at the institution in a program at a post-secondary school level,

but does not include

(*c*) any fee or charge to the extent that it is levied in respect of

(i) a student association,

(ii) property to be acquired by students,

(iii) services not ordinarily provided at educational institutions in Canada that offer courses at a post-secondary school level,

(iv) the provision of financial assistance to students, except to the extent that, if this Act were read without reference to subsection 56(3), the amount of the assistance would be required to be included in computing the income, and not be deductible in computing the taxable income, of the students to whom the assistance is provided, or

(v) the construction, renovation or maintenance of any building or facility, except to the extent that the building or facility is owned by the institution and used to provide

(A) courses at the post-secondary school level, or

(B) services for which, if fees or charges in respect of the services were required to be paid by all students of the institution, the fees or charges would be included because of this subsection in the fees for an individual's tuition, and

(*d*) any fee or charge for a taxation year that, but for this paragraph, would be included because of this subsection in the fees for the individual's tuition and that is not required to be paid by

(i) all of the institution's full-time students, where the individual is a full-time student at the institution, and

(ii) all of the institution's part-time students, where the individual is a part-time student at the institution,

to the extent that the total for the year of all such fees and charges paid in respect of the individual's enrolment at the institution exceeds $250.

History: S. 118.5(3)(*c*)(iv) was replaced by S.C. 2013, c. 40, s. 50(1), applicable to the 2012 and subsequent taxation years, and formerly read:

(iv) the provision of financial assistance to students, except to the extent that, if the reference in paragraph 56(1)(*n*) to "$500" were read as a reference to "nil", the amount of the assistance would be required to be included in computing the income, and not be deductible in computing the taxable income, of the students to whom the assistance is provided, or

► 118.5(4) ◄

(4) Ancillary fees and charges for examinations. For the purpose of this section, "fees paid in respect of the occupational, trade or professional examination" of an individual includes ancillary fees and charges, other than fees and charges included in subsection (3), that are paid to an educational institution referred to in subparagraph (1)(*a*)(i), a professional association, a provincial ministry or other similar institution, in respect of an occupation, trade or professional examination taken by the individual, but does not include any fee or charge to the extent that it is levied in respect of

(*a*) property to be acquired by an individual;

(*b*) the provision of financial assistance to an individual, except to the extent that, if this Act were read without reference to subsection 56(3), the financial assistance would be required to be included in computing the income, and would not be deductible in computing the taxable income, of the individual;

(*c*) the construction, renovation or maintenance of any building or facility; or

(*d*) any fee or charge for a taxation year that, but for this paragraph, would be included because of this subsection in the fees for the individual's occupational, trade or professional examination and that is not required to be paid by all the individuals taking the occupational, trade or professional examination to the extent that the total for the year of all such fees and charges paid in respect of the individual's fees for the occupational, trade or professional examination exceeds $250.

History: S. 118.5(4) was added by S.C. 2011, c. 24, s. 29(5), applicable to the 2011 and subsequent taxation years.

SECTION 118.6: [Education and textbook tax credits]

► 118.6(1) ◄

(1) Definitions. For the purposes of sections 63 and 64 and this subdivision,

Tax Window Files: Medical residents– situations similar to Kandasamy, *August 24, 2015*, CRA Document No. 2015-0592051I7; Education Tax Credit- Audit or Sampler courses, *March 1, 2012*, CRA Document No. 2011-0403811E5; Education Tax Credit and Scholarship Exemption, *March 19, 2012*, CRA Document No. 2011-0430791I7; Tuition education and textbook tax credit, *March 19, 2012*, CRA Document No. 2011-0402091E5; Remboursement - frais de scolarité, *December 16, 2011*, CRA Document No. 2011-0412502E5; Education Tax Credit for a practicum, *December 14, 2011*, CRA Document No. 2011-0398871E5; Post-doctoral Fellowship, *June 27, 2011*, CRA Document No. 2011-0404751M4; Education Tax Credit for internships, *September 29, 2010*, CRA Document No. 2010-0368431E5; Post-Doctoral Fellows--Scholarship Exemption, *July 13, 2010*, CRA Document No. 2009-0311901E5; Post-Doctoral Fellows--Scholarship Exemption, *June 22, 2010*, CRA Document No. 2008-0300441E5; Scholarship Exemption and PDFs, *June 1, 2010*, CRA Document No. 2008-0301601M4; Education Tax Credit — University Outside Canada, *Technical Interpretation, Financial Sector and Exempt Entities Division, August 28, 2008*, CRA Document No. 2008-0288251E5; Reporting — Scholarships and Bursaries, *Technical Interpretation, Business and Partnerships Division, January 14, 2007*, CRA Document No. 2006-0187471E5; Tuition and Education Deduction — Withholding of Form T2202A, *Technical Interpretation, Financial Industries Division, March 24, 2005*, CRA Document No. 2005-0119471E5; Non-resident — Transfer of Education and Tuition Credits, *Technical Interpretation, International and Trusts Division, January 15, 2004*, CRA Document No. 2003-0026827; Cumulative Eligible Capital — Acquisition from a Related Person, *Technical Interpretation, Business and Partnerships Division, December 16, 2003*, CRA Document No. 2003-0027245.

Cases: The legislation does not define "full-time students". It is possible to be both a full-time student and a full-time employee. At least 10 hours a week must be spent on courses or work. The medical residents worked at least 50 hours a week at the hospital and met all the eligibility criteria for the credit. *Kandasamy v. The Queen*, 2014 DTC 1075 (T.C.C.)

"designated educational institution" —"designated educational institution" means

(*a*) an educational institution in Canada that is

(i) a university, college or other educational institution designated by the lieutenant governor in council of a province as a specified educational institution under the *Canada Student Loans Act*, designated by an appropriate authority under the *Canada Student Financial Assistance Act*, or designated, for the purposes of *An Act respecting financial assistance for education expenses*, R.S.Q, c. A-13.3, by the Minister of the Province of Quebec responsible for the administration of that Act, or

(ii) certified by the Minister of Employment and Social Development to be an educational institution providing courses, other than courses designed for university credit, that furnish a person with skills for, or improve a person's skills in, an occupation,

(*b*) a university outside Canada at which the individual referred to in the definition "qualifying student" in this subsection was enrolled in a course, of not less than three consecutive weeks duration, leading to a degree, or

(*c*) if the individual referred to in the definition "qualifying student" in this subsection resided, throughout the year referred to in that definition, in Canada near the boundary between Canada and the United States, an educational institution in the United States to which the individual commuted that is a university, college or other educational institution providing courses at a post-secondary school level;

History: S. 118.6(1), paragraphs (*b*) and (*c*) of the definition "designated educational institution" were replaced by S.C. 2016, c. 7, s. 16(1), applicable to the 2017 and subsequent taxation years, and formerly read:

(*b*) a university outside Canada at which the individual referred to in subsection (2) was enrolled in a course, of not less than three consecutive weeks duration, leading to a degree, or

(*c*) if the individual referred to in subsection (2) resided, throughout the year referred to in that subsection, in Canada near the boundary between Canada and the United States, an educational institution in the United States to which the individual commuted that is a university, college or other educational institution providing courses at a post-secondary school level;

S. 118.6(1), subparagraph (*a*)(i) of the definition "designated educational institution" was replaced by S.C. 2013, c. 34, s. 252(1), applicable to the 1998 and subsequent taxation years, and formerly read:

(i) a university, college or other educational institution designated by the Lieutenant Governor in Council of a province as a specified educational institution under the *Canada Student Loans Act*, designated by an appropriate authority under the *Canada Student Financial Assistance Act*, or designated by the Minister of Higher Education and Science of the Province of Quebec for the purposes of *An Act respecting financial assistance for students* of the Province of Quebec, or

S. 118.6(1), paragraph (*b*) of the definition "designated educational institution" was replaced by S.C. 2011, c. 24, s. 30(1), applicable to tuition fees paid for the 2011 and subsequent taxation years. S. 118.6(1), paragraph (*b*) of the definition "designated educational institution" formerly read:

(*b*) a university outside Canada at which the individual referred to in subsection (2) was enrolled in a course, of not less than 13 consecutive weeks duration, leading to a degree, or

Related Regulations: 203 Requirement to file.

Related Sections: S. 146.02(1), "qualifying educational program"; s. 146.1(1), "post-secondary educational institution".

Income Tax Folios: *Primary* — S1-F2-C1 Education and Textbook Tax Credits.

Cases: The London School of Economics and Political Science is a "university outside Canada" since it forms part of the University of London and is permitted to grant degrees of the University of London. Schedule VIII of the Income Tax Regulations is not relevant since s. 118.6(1) does not require universities to be prescribed. *Shea v. The Queen*, 2008 DTC 3376 (T.C.C.).

"qualifying educational program" — "qualifying educational program" means a program of not less than three consecutive weeks duration that provides that each student taking the program spend not less than 10 hours per week on courses or work in the program and, in respect of a program at an institution described in the definition "designated educational institution" (other than an institution described in subparagraph (*a*)(ii) of that definition), that is a program that does not consist primarily of research (unless the program leads to a diploma from a college or a Collège d'enseignement général et professionnel, or a bachelor, masters, doctoral or equivalent degree) but, in relation to any particular student, does not include a program if the student receives, from a person with whom the student is dealing at arm's length, any allowance, benefit, grant or reimbursement for expenses in respect of the program other than

(*a*) an amount received by the student as or on account of a scholarship, fellowship or bursary, or a prize for achievement in a field of endeavour ordinarily carried on by the student,

(*b*) a benefit, if any, received by the student because of a loan made to the student in accordance with the requirements of the *Canada Student Loans Act*, the *Apprentice Loans Act* or *An Act respecting financial assistance for education expenses*, R.S.Q., c. A-13.3, or because of financial assistance given to the student in accordance with the requirements of the *Canada Student Financial Assistance Act*, or

(*c*) an amount that is received by the student in the year under a program referred to in subparagraph 56(1)(*r*)(ii) or (iii), a program established under the authority of the *Department of Employment and Social Development Act* or a prescribed program;

History: S. 118.6(1), the portion of the definition "qualifying educational program" before paragraph (*a*) was replaced by S.C. 2017, c. 20, s. 19(1), applicable to the 2017 and subsequent taxation years, and formerly read:

"qualifying educational program" — "qualifying educational program" means a program of not less than three consecutive weeks duration that provides that each student taking the program spend not less than ten hours per week on courses or work in the program and, in respect of a program at an institution described in the definition "designated educational institution" (other than an institution described in subparagraph (*a*)(ii) of that definition), that is a program at a post-secondary school level that does not consist primarily of research (unless the program leads to a diploma from a college or a Collège d'enseignement général et professionnel, or a bachelor, masters, doctoral or equivalent degree) but, in relation to any particular student, does not include a program if the student receives, from a person with whom the student is dealing at arm's length, any allowance, benefit, grant or reimbursement for expenses in respect of the program other than

S. 118.6(1), paragraph (*b*) of the definition "qualifying educational program" was replaced by S.C. 2016, c. 7, s. 16(2), deemed to have come into force on January 2, 2015, and formerly read:

(*b*) a benefit, if any, received by the student because of a loan made to the student in accordance with the requirements of the *Canada Student Loans Act* or *An Act respecting financial assistance for education expenses*, R.S.Q., c. A-13.3, or because of financial assistance given to the student in accordance with the requirements of the *Canada Student Financial Assistance Act*, or

S. 118.6(1), the portion of the definition "qualifying educational program" before paragraph (*a*) was replaced by S.C. 2011, c. 24, s. 30(2), applicable to the 2010 and subsequent taxation years. S. 118.6(1), the portion of the definition "qualifying educational program" before paragraph (*a*) formerly read:

"qualifying educational program" — "qualifying educational program" means a program of not less than three consecutive weeks duration that provides that each student taking the program spend not less than ten hours per week on courses or work in the program and, in respect of a program at an institution described in the definition "designated educational institution" (other than an institution described in subparagraph (*a*)(ii) of that definition), that is a program at a post-secondary school level but, in relation to any particular student, does not include a program if the student receives, from a person with whom the student is dealing at arm's length, any allowance, benefit, grant or reimbursement for expenses in respect of the program other than

S. 118.6(1), the definition "qualifying educational program", was amended by S.C. 2013, c. 40, s. 236(1)(*e*)(iii), by replacing "*Department of Human Resources and Skills Development Act*" with "*Department of Employment and Social Development Act*", in force December 12, 2013.

Related Sections: S. 146.02(1), "qualifying educational program"; s. 146.1(1), "qualifying educational program".

Income Tax Folios: *Primary* — S1-F2-C1 Education and Textbook Tax Credits.

"qualifying student" — "qualifying student", for a month in a taxation year, means an individual who,

(*a*) in the month,

(i) is enrolled in a qualifying educational program as a full-time student at a designated educational institution, or

(ii) is not described in subparagraph (i) and is enrolled at a designated educational institution in a specified educational program that provides that each student in the program spend not less than 12 hours in the month on courses in the program,

(*b*) if requested by the Minister, proves the enrolment by filing with the Minister a certificate in prescribed form issued by the designated educational institution and containing prescribed information,

(*c*) in the case of an individual who is enrolled in a program (other than a program at the post-secondary school level) at a designated educational institution described in subparagraph (*a*)(i) of the definition "designated educational institution" or who is enrolled in a program at a designated educational institution described in subparagraph (*a*)(ii) of that definition,

(i) has attained the age of 16 years before the end of the year, and

(ii) is enrolled in the program to obtain skills for, or improve the individual's skills in, an occupation, and

(*d*) in the case of an individual who is enrolled at a designated educational institution described in paragraph (*c*) of the definition "designated educational institution", is enrolled in a program that is at the post-secondary level;

History: S. 118.6(1), the portion of paragraph (*c*) before subparagraph (i) of the definition "qualifying student" was replaced by S.C. 2017, c. 20, s. 19(2), applicable to the 2017 and subsequent taxation years, and formerly read:

(*c*) in the case of an individual who is enrolled in a program at a designated educational institution described in subparagraph (*a*)(ii) of the definition "designated educational institution",

S. 118.6(1), paragraph (*d*) of the definition "qualifying student" was added by S.C. 2017, c. 20, s. 19(3), applicable to the 2017 and subsequent taxation years.

S. 118.6(1), the definition "qualifying student" was added by S.C. 2016, c. 7, s. 16(3), applicable to the 2017 and subsequent taxation years.

"specified educational program" —"specified educational program" means a program that would be a qualifying educational program if the definition "qualifying educational program" were read without reference to the words "that provides that each student taking the program spend not less than 10 hours per week on courses or work in the program".

► 118.6(2) ◄

(2) Education credit. (Repealed by S.C. 2016, c. 7, s. 16(4).)

History: S. 118.6(2) was repealed by S.C. 2016, c. 7, s. 16(4), applicable to the 2017 and subsequent taxation years, and formerly read:

(2) *Education credit.* There may be deducted in computing an individual's tax payable under this Part for a taxation year the amount determined by the formula

$$A \times B$$

where

A is the appropriate percentage for the year; and

B is the total of the products obtained when

(*a*) $400 is multiplied by the number of months in the year during which the individual is enrolled in a qualifying educational program as a full-time student at a designated educational institution, and

(*b*) $120 is multiplied by the number of months in the year (other than months described in paragraph (*a*)), each of which is a month during which the individual is enrolled at a designated educational institution in a specified educational program that provides that each student in the program spend not less than 12 hours in the month on courses in the program,

if the enrolment is proven by filing with the Minister a certificate in prescribed form issued by the designated educational institution and containing prescribed information and, in respect of a designated educational institution described in subparagraph (*a*)(ii) of the definition "designated educational institution" in subsection (1), the individual has attained the age of 16 years before the end of the year and is enrolled in the program to obtain skills for, or improve the individual's skills in, an occupation.

Related Sections: S. 63(2) Income exceeding income of supporting person; s. 118.8 Transfer of unused credits to spouse or common-law partner; s. 118.9 Transfer to parent or grandparent; s. 146.02(1), "repayment period".

Forms: T1 SCH 11 — Federal Tuition and Education Amounts; T2202 — Education Amount Certificate; T2202A — Tuition and Education Amounts Certificate.

Guides: P105 Students and Income Tax.

Income Tax Folios: *Primary*—S1-F2-C1 Education and Textbook Tax Credits; *Secondary*—S1-F2-C2 Tuition Tax Credit.

► 118.6(2.1) ◄

(2.1) Post-secondary textbook credit. (Repealed by S.C. 2016, c. 7, s. 16(4).)

History: S. 118.6(2.1) was repealed by S.C. 2016, c. 7, s. 16(4), applicable to the 2017 and subsequent taxation years, and formerly read:

(2.1) *Post-secondary textbook credit.* If an amount may be deducted under subsection (2) in computing the individual's tax payable for a taxation year, there may be deducted in computing the individual's tax payable under this Part for the year the amount determined by the formula

$$A \times B$$

where

A is the appropriate percentage for the year; and

B is the total of the products obtained when

(*a*) $65 is multiplied by the number of months referred to in paragraph (*a*) of the description of B in subsection (2), and

(*b*) $20 is multiplied by the number of months referred to in paragraph (*b*) of that description.

Income Tax Folios: *Primary*—S1-F2-C1 Education and Textbook Tax Credits.

► 118.6(3) ◄

(3) Students eligible for disability tax credit. For the purposes of subparagraph (*a*)(i) of the definition "qualifying student" in subsection (1), the reference to "full-time student" is to be read as "student" if

(*a*) an amount may be deducted under section 118.3 in respect of the individual for the year; or

(*b*) the individual has in the year a mental or physical impairment the effects of which on the individual have been certified in writing, to be such that the individual cannot reasonably be expected to be enrolled as a full-time student while so impaired, by a medical doctor, a nurse practitioner or, where the impairment is

(i) an impairment of sight, by a medical doctor, a nurse practitioner or an optometrist,

(i.1) a speech impairment, by a medical doctor, a nurse practitioner or a speech-language pathologist,

(ii) a hearing impairment, by a medical doctor, a nurse practitioner or an audiologist,

(iii) an impairment with respect to the individual's ability in feeding or dressing themself, by a medical doctor, a nurse practitioner or an occupational therapist,

(iii.1) an impairment with respect to the individual's ability in walking, by a medical doctor, a nurse practitioner, an occupational therapist or a physiotherapist, or

(iv) an impairment with respect to the individual's ability in mental functions necessary for everyday life (within the meaning assigned by paragraph 118.4(1)(*c*.1)), by a medical doctor, a nurse practitioner or a psychologist.

History: S. 118.6(3)(*b*) was replaced by S.C. 2017, c. 33, s. 45(1), applicable in respect of certifications made after September 7, 2017, and formerly read:

(*b*) the individual has in the year a mental or physical impairment the effects of which on the individual have been certified in writing, to be such that the individual cannot reasonably be expected to be enrolled as a full-time student while so impaired, by a medical doctor or, where the impairment is

(i) an impairment of sight, by a medical doctor or an optometrist,

(i.1) a speech impairment, by a medical doctor or a speech-language pathologist,

(ii) a hearing impairment, by a medical doctor or an audiologist,

(iii) an impairment with respect to the individual's ability in feeding or dressing themself, by a medical doctor or an occupational therapist,

(iii.1) an impairment with respect to the individual's ability in walking, by a medical doctor, an occupational therapist or a physiotherapist, or

(iv) an impairment with respect to the individual's ability in mental functions necessary for everyday life (within the meaning assigned by paragraph 118.4(1)(*c*.1)), by a medical doctor or a psychologist.

S. 118.6(3), the portion before paragraph (*a*) was replaced by S.C. 2016, c. 7, s. 16(5), applicable to the 2017 and subsequent taxation years, and formerly read:

(3) *Students eligible for the disability tax credit.* In calculating the amount deductible under subsection (2) or (2.1), the reference in subsection (2) to "full-time student" is to be read as "student" if

Related Sections: S. 146.02(1), "full-time student"; s. 248(1), "amount", "individual".

SECTION 118.61: Unused tuition, textbook and education tax credits

▶ 118.61(1) ◀

(1) Unused tuition, textbook and education tax credits. In this section, an individual's unused tuition, textbook and education tax credits at the end of a taxation year is the amount determined by the formula

$$A + (B - C) - (D + E)$$

where

A is the amount determined under this subsection in respect of the individual at the end of the preceding taxation year;

B is the total of all amounts each of which may be deducted under section 118.5 in computing the individual's tax payable under this Part for the year;

C is the lesser of the value of B and the amount that would be the individual's tax payable under this Part for the year if no amount were deductible under this Division (other than an amount deductible under this section and any of sections 118 to 118.07, 118.3 and 118.7);

D is the amount that the individual may deduct under subsection (2) for the year; and

E is the tuition tax credit transferred for the year by the individual to the individual's spouse, common-law partner, parent or grandparent.

History: S. 118.61(1), the description of B was replaced by S.C. 2016, c. 7, s. 17(1), applicable to the 2017 and subsequent taxation years, and formerly read:

B is the total of all amounts each of which may be deducted under section 118.5 or 118.6 in computing the individual's tax payable under this Part for the year;

S. 118.61(1), the description of E was replaced by S.C. 2016, c. 7, s. 17(2), applicable to the 2017 and subsequent taxation years, and formerly read:

E is the tuition, textbook and education tax credits transferred for the year by the individual to the individual's spouse, common-law partner, parent or grandparent.

S. 118.61(1), the description of C was replaced by S.C. 2014, c. 20, s. 12(1), applicable to the 2014 and subsequent taxation years, and formerly read:

C is the lesser of the value of B and the amount that would be the individual's tax payable under this Part for the year if no amount were deductible under this Division (other than an amount deductible under this section and any of sections 118 to 118.06, 118.3 and 118.7);

S. 118.61(1), the description of C was replaced by S.C. 2011, c. 24, s. 31(1), applicable to the 2011 and subsequent taxation years. S. 118.61(1), the description of C formerly read:

C is the lesser of the value of B and the amount that would be the individual's tax payable under this Part for the year if no amount were deductible under this Division (other than an amount deductible under this section and any of sections 118 to 118.05, 118.3 and 118.7);

S. 118.61(1), the description of C was replaced by S.C. 2009, c. 31, s. 6(1), applicable to the 2009 and subsequent taxation years. S. 118.61(1), the description of C formerly read:

C is the lesser of the value of B and the amount that would be the individual's tax payable under this Part for the year if no amount were deductible under this Division (other than an amount deductible under this section and any of sections 118, 118.01, 118.02, 118.03, 118.3 and 118.7);

Related Sections: S. 118.8 Transfer of unused credits to spouse or common-law partner; S. 118.81 Tuition, textbook and eduction tax credits transferred; S. 118.9 Transfer to parent or grandparent.

Income Tax Folios: *Secondary* — S1-F2-C1 Education and Textbook Tax Credits; S1-F2-C2 Tuition Tax Credit.

Tax Window Files: Tuition carry-forward pool, *March 11, 2019*, CRA Document No. 2018-0784491E5.

Cases: Where a taxpayer is permitted in a particular tax year to deduct an amount for tuition and education tax credits, any carryforward credits for future years are reduced by the annual amount regardless of whether the taxpayer actually claims such deduction or not. *Zhang v. The Queen*, 2018 DTC 1007 (TCC)

▶ 118.61(2) ◀

(2) Deduction of carryforward. For the purpose of computing an individual's tax payable under this Part for a taxation year, there may be deducted the lesser of

(*a*) the amount determined under subsection (1) in respect of the individual at the end of the preceding taxation year, and

(*b*) the amount that would be the individual's tax payable under this Part for the year if no amount were deductible under this Division (other than an amount deductible under this section and any of sections 118 to 118.07, 118.3 and 118.7).

History: S. 118.61(2)(*b*) was replaced by S.C. 2014, c. 20, s. 12(2), applicable to the 2014 and subsequent taxation years, and formerly read:

(*b*) the amount that would be the individual's tax payable under this Part for the year if no amount were deductible under this Division (other than an amount deductible under this section and any of sections 118 to 118.06, 118.3 and 118.7).

S. 118.61(2)(*b*) was replaced by S.C. 2011, c. 24, s. 31(2), applicable to the 2011 and subsequent taxation years. S. 118.61(2)(*b*) formerly read:

(*b*) the amount that would be the individual's tax payable under this Part for the year if no amount were deductible under this Division (other than an amount deductible under this section and any of sections 118 to 118.05, 118.3 and 118.7).

S. 118.61(2)(*b*) was replaced by S.C. 2009, c. 31, s. 6(2), applicable to the 2009 and subsequent taxation years. S. 118.61(2)(*b*) formerly read:

(*b*) the amount that would be the individual's tax payable under this Part for the year if no amount were deductible under this Division (other than an amount deductible under this section and any of sections 118, 118.01, 118.02, 118.03, 118.3 and 118.7).

▶ 118.61(3) ◀

(3) Unused tuition and education tax credits at the end of 2000 — (Repealed by S.C. 2007, c. 2, s. 24(3).)

▶ 118.61(4) ◀

(4) Change of appropriate percentage. For the purpose of determining the amount that may be deducted under subsection (2) in computing an individual's tax payable for a taxation year, in circumstances where the appropriate percentage for the taxation year is different from the appropriate percentage for the preceding taxation year, the individual's unused tuition, textbook and education tax credits at the end of the preceding taxation year is deemed to be the amount determined by the formula

$$A/B \times C$$

where

A is the appropriate percentage for the current taxation year;

B is the appropriate percentage for the preceding taxation year; and

C is the amount that would be the individual's unused tuition, textbook and education tax credits at the end of the preceding taxation year if this section were read without reference to this subsection.

History: S. 118.61(4) was replaced by S.C. 2016, c. 7, s. 17(3), applicable to the 2017 and subsequent taxation years, and formerly read:

(4) *Change of appropriate percentage.* For the purpose of determining the amount that may be deducted under subsection (2) or 118.6(2.1) in computing an individual's tax payable for a taxation year, in circumstances where the appropriate percentage for the taxation year is different from the appropriate percentage for the preceding taxation year, the individual's unused tuition, textbook and education tax credits at the end of the preceding taxation year is deemed to be the amount determined by the formula

SECTION 118.62: Credit for interest on student loan

For the purpose of computing an individual's tax payable under this Part for a taxation year, there may be deducted the amount determined by the formula

$$A \times B$$

where

A is the appropriate percentage for the year; and

B is the total of all amounts (other than any amount paid on account of or in satisfaction of a judgement) each of which is an amount of interest paid in the year (or in any of the five preceding taxation years that are after 1997, to the extent that it was not included in computing a deduction under this section for any other taxation year) by the individual or a person related to the individual on a loan made to, or other amount owing by, the individual under the *Canada Student Loans Act*, the *Canada Student Financial Assistance Act*, the *Apprentice Loans Act* or a law of a province governing the granting of financial assistance to students at the post-secondary school level.

History: S. 118.62, the description of B was replaced by S.C. 2014, c. 39, s. 35(1), in force January 2, 2015 [the day on which Division 30 of Part 6 of the *Economic Action Plan 2014 Act, No. 1* (2014, c. 20) came into force], and formerly read:

B is the total of all amounts (other than any amount paid on account of or in satisfaction of a judgement) each of which is an amount of interest paid in the year (or in any of the five preceding taxation years that are after 1997, to the extent that it was not included in computing a deduction under this section for any other taxation year) by the individual or a person related to the individual on a loan made to, or other amount owing by, the individual under the *Canada Student Loans Act*, the *Canada Student Financial Assistance Act* or a law of a province governing the granting of financial assistance to students at the post-secondary school level.

Related Sections: S. 118.91 Part-year residents; s. 118.92 Ordering of credits; s. 118.95 Credits in year of bankruptcy.

Guides: P105 Students and Income Tax.

Cases: Interest on a student line of credit does not qualify for the tax credit for student loan interest. *Mueller v. The Queen*, 2013 DTC 1044 (T.C.C.)

SECTION 118.7: Credit for EI and QPIP premiums and CPP contributions

For the purpose of computing the tax payable under this Part by an individual for a taxation year, there may be deducted the amount determined by the formula

$$A \times B$$

where

A is the appropriate percentage for the year; and

B is the total of

(*a*) the total of all amounts each of which is an amount payable by the individual as an employee's premium or a self-employment premium for the year under the *Employment Insurance Act*, not exceeding the maximum amount of such premiums payable by the individual for the year under that Act,

(*a*.1) the total of all amounts each of which is an amount payable by the individual as an employee's premium for the year under the *Act respecting parental insurance*, R.S.Q., c. A-29.011, not exceeding the maximum amount of such premiums payable by the individual for the year under that Act,

(a.2) the amount, if any, by which the total of all amounts each of which is an amount payable by the individual in respect of self-employed earnings for the year as a premium under the *Act respecting parental insurance*, R.S.Q., c. A-29.011, (not exceeding the maximum amount of such premiums payable by the individual for the year under that Act) exceeds the amount deductible under paragraph 60(*g*) in computing the individual's income for the year,

(*b*) the total of all amounts each of which is an amount payable by the individual for the year as an employee's contribution under subsection 8(1) of the *Canada Pension Plan* or as a like contribution under a *provincial pension plan*, as defined in section 3 of that Act, not exceeding the maximum amount of such contributions payable by the individual for the year under the plan, and

(*c*) the amount by which

(i) the total of all amounts each of which is an amount payable by the individual in respect of self-employed earnings for the year as a contribution under the *Canada Pension Plan* or under a provincial pension plan within the meaning assigned by section 3 of that Act (not exceeding the maximum amount of such contributions payable by the individual for the year under the plan)

exceeds

(ii) the amount deductible under paragraph 60(*e*) in computing the individual's income for the year.

History: S. 118.7, paragraph (b) of the description of B, was replaced by S.C. 2016, c. 14, s. 68(1), in force January 1, 2019, and formerly read:

(*b*) the total of all amounts each of which is an amount payable by the individual for the year as an employee's contribution under the *Canada Pension Plan* or under a provincial pension plan defined in section 3 of that Act, not exceeding the maximum amount of such contributions payable by the individual for the year under the plan, and

S. 118.7 was replaced by S.C. 2013, c. 34, s. 253(1), applicable to the 2006 and subsequent taxation years, except that for taxation years ending after 2005 and before 2010, paragraph (*a*) of the description of B in section 118.7 is to be read as follows:

"(*a*) the total of all amounts each of which is an amount payable by the individual as an employee's premium for the year under the *Employment Insurance Act*, not exceeding the maximum amount of such premiums payable by the individual for the year under that Act,"

S. 118.7 formerly read:

S. 118.7 *Credit for UI [EI] premium and CPP contribution.* For the purpose of computing the tax payable under this Part by an individual for a taxation year, there may be deducted an amount determined by the formula

$$A \times B$$

where

A is the appropriate percentage for the year; and

B is the total of

(*a*) the total of all amounts each of which is an amount payable by the individual as an employee's premium for the year under the *Employment Insurance Act*, not exceeding the maximum amount of such premiums payable by the individual for the year under that Act,

(*b*) the total of all amounts each of which is an amount payable by the individual for the year as an employee's contribution under the *Canada Pension Plan* or under a provincial pension plan defined in section 3 of that Act, not exceeding the maximum amount of such contributions payable by the individual for the year under the plan, and

(*c*) the amount by which

(i) the total of all amounts each of which is an amount payable by the individual in respect of self-employed earnings for the year as a contribution under the *Canada Pension Plan* or under a provincial pension plan within the meaning assigned by section 3 of that Act (not exceeding the maximum amount of such contributions payable by the individual for the year under the plan)

exceeds

(ii) the amount deductible under paragraph 60(*e*) in computing the individual's income for the year.

Related Sections: S. 8(1)(*l*.1) C.P.P. contributions and E.I. premiums.

Forms: T2204 — Employee Overpayment of 2012 Canada Pension Plan Contributions and 2012 Employment Insurance Premiums.

Information Circulars: IC 07-1 Taxpayer relief provisions.

SECTION 118.8: Transfer of unused credits to spouse or common-law partner

For the purpose of computing the tax payable under this Part for a taxation year by an individual who, at any time in the year, is a married person or a person who is in a common-law partnership (other than an individual who, by reason of a breakdown of their marriage or common-law partnership, is living separate and apart from the individual's spouse or common-law partner at the end of the year and for a period of 90 days commencing in the year), there may be deducted an amount determined by the formula

$$A + B - C$$

where

A is the tuition tax credit transferred for the year by the spouse or common-law partner to the individual;

B is the total of all amounts each of which is deductible under subsection 118(1), because of paragraph (*b*.1) of the description of B in that subsection, or subsection 118(2) or (3) or 118.3(1) in computing the spouse's or common-law partner's tax payable under this Part for the year; and

C is the amount, if any, by which

(*a*) the amount that would be the spouse's or common-law partner's tax payable under this Part for the year if no amount were deductible under this Division (other than an amount deductible under subsection 118(1) because of paragraph (*c*) of the description of B in that subsection, under subsection 118(10) or under any of sections 118.01 to 118.07, 118.3, 118.61 and 118.7)

exceeds

(*b*) the lesser of

(i) the total of all amounts that may be deducted under section 118.5 in computing the spouse's or common-law partner's tax payable under this Part for the year, and

(ii) the amount that would be the spouse's or common-law partner's tax payable under this Part for the year if no amount were deductible under this Division (other than an amount deductible under any of sections 118 to 118.07, 118.3, 118.61 and 118.7).

History: S. 118.8, the description of A was replaced by S.C. 2016, c. 7, s. 18(1), applicable to the 2017 and subsequent taxation years, and formerly read:

A is the tuition, textbook and education tax credits transferred for the year by the spouse or common-law partner to the individual;

S. 118.8, subparagraph (*b*)(i) of the description of C was replaced by S.C. 2016, c. 7, s. 18(2), applicable to the 2017 and subsequent taxation years, and formerly read:

(i) the total of all amounts that may be deducted under section 118.5 or 118.6 in computing the spouse's or common-law partner's tax payable under this Part for the year, and

S. 118.8, paragraph (*a*) of the description of C was replaced by S.C. 2014, c. 20, s. 13(1), applicable to the 2014 and subsequent taxation years, and formerly read:

(*a*) the amount that would be the spouse's or common-law partner's tax payable under this Part for the year if no amount were deductible under this Division (other than an amount deductible under subsection 118(1) because of paragraph (*c*) of the description of B in that subsection, under subsection 118(10) or under any of sections 118.01 to 118.06, 118.3, 118.61 and 118.7)

S. 118.8, subparagraph (*b*)(ii) of the description of C was replaced by S.C. 2014, c. 20, s. 13(2), applicable to the 2014 and subsequent taxation years, and formerly read:

(ii) the amount that would be the spouse's or common-law partner's tax payable under this Part for the year if no amount were deductible under this Division (other than an amount deductible under any of sections 118 to 118.06, 118.3, 118.61 and 118.7).

S. 118.8, paragraph (*a*) of the description of C was replaced by S.C. 2011, c. 24, s. 32(1), applicable to the 2011 and subsequent taxation years. S. 118.8, paragraph (*a*) of the description of C formerly read:

(*a*) the amount that would be the spouse's or common-law partner's tax payable under this Part for the year if no amount were deductible under this Division (other than an amount deductible under subsection 118(1) because of paragraph (*c*) of the description of B in that subsection, under subsection 118(10) or under any of sections 118.01 to 118.05, 118.3, 118.61 and 118.7).

S. 118.8, subparagraph (*b*)(ii) of the description of C was replaced by S.C. 2011, c. 24, s. 32(2), applicable to the 2011 and subsequent taxation years. S. 118.8, subparagraph (*b*)(ii) of the description of C formerly read:

(ii) the amount that would be the spouse's or common-law partner's tax payable under this Part for the year if no amount were deductible under this Division (other than an amount deductible under any of sections 118 to 118.05, 118.3, 118.61 and 118.7).

S. 118.8, paragraph (*a*) of the description of C was replaced by S.C. 2009, c. 31, s. 7(1), applicable to the 2009 and subsequent taxation years. S. 118.8, paragraph (*a*) of the description of C formerly read:

(*a*) the amount that would be the spouse's or common-law partner's tax payable under this Part for the year if no amount were deductible under this Division (other than an amount deductible under subsection 118(1) because of paragraph (*c*) of the description of B in that subsection or under section 118.61 or 118.7)

S. 118.8, subparagraph (*b*)(ii) of the description of C was replaced by S.C. 2009, c. 31, s. 7(2), applicable to the 2009 and subsequent taxation years. S. 118.8, subparagraph (*b*)(ii) of the description of C formerly read:

(ii) the amount that would be the spouse's or common-law partner's tax payable under this Part for the year if no amount were deductible under this Division (other than an amount deductible under section 118, 118.01, 118.02, 118.03, 118.3, 118.61 or 118.7).

Related Sections: S. 248(1), "amount", "common-law partner", "individual".

Income Tax Folios: *Secondary* — S1-F2-C2 Tuition Tax Credit; S1-F2-C1 Education and Textbook Tax Credits; S1-F1-C2 Disability Tax Credit; S1-F1-C1 Medical Expense Tax Credit.

SECTION 118.81: Tuition tax credit transferred

In this subdivision, the tuition tax credit transferred for a taxation year by a person to an individual is the lesser of

(*a*) the amount determined by the formula

$$A - B$$

where

A is the lesser of

(i) the total of all amounts that may be deducted under section 118.5 in computing the person's tax payable under this Part for the year, and

(ii) the amount determined by the formula

$$C \times D$$

where

C is the appropriate percentage for the taxation year, and

D is $5,000;

B is the amount that would be the person's tax payable under this Part for the year if no amount were deductible under this Division (other than an amount deductible under any of sections 118 to 118.07, 118.3, 118.61 and 118.7), and

(*b*) the amount for the year that the person designates in writing for the purpose of section 118.8 or 118.9.

History: S. 118.81, the portion before paragraph (*a*) was replaced by S.C. 2016, c. 7, s. 19(1), applicable to the 2017 and subsequent taxation years, and formerly read:

S. 118.81 *Tuition, textbook and education tax credits transferred.* In this subdivision, the tuition, textbook and education tax credits transferred for a taxation year by a person to an individual is the lesser of

S. 118.81(*a*), subparagraph (i) of the description of A was replaced by S.C. 2016, c. 7, s. 19(2), applicable to the 2017 and subsequent taxation years, and formerly read:

(i) the total of all amounts that may be deducted under section 118.5 or 118.6 in computing the person's tax payable under this Part for the year, and

S. 118.81(*a*), the description of B was replaced by S.C. 2014, c. 20, s. 14(1), applicable to the 2014 and subsequent taxation years, and formerly read:

B is the amount that would be the person's tax payable under this Part for the year if no amount were deductible under this Division (other than an amount deductible under any of sections 118 to 118.06, 118.3, 118.61 and 118.7), and

S. 118.81(*a*), the description of B was replaced by S.C. 2011, c. 24, s. 33(1), applicable to the 2011 and subsequent taxation years. S. 118.81(*a*), the description of B formerly read:

B is the amount that would be the person's tax payable under this Part for the year if no amount were deductible under this Division (other than an amount deductible under any of sections 118 to 118.05, 118.3, 118.61 and 118.7), and

S. 118.81, the description of B was replaced by S.C. 2009, c. 31, s. 8(1), applicable to the 2009 and subsequent taxation years. S. 118.81, the description of B formerly read:

B is the amount that would be the person's tax payable under this Part for the year if no amount were deductible under this Division (other than an amount deductible under any of sections 118, 118.01, 118.02, 118.03, 118.3, 118.61 and 118.7), and

SECTION 118.9: Transfer to parent or grandparent

If for a taxation year a parent or grandparent of an individual (other than an individual in respect of whom the individual's spouse or common-law partner deducts an amount under section 118 or 118.8 for the year) is the only person designated in writing by the individual for the year for the purpose of this section, there may be deducted in computing the tax payable under this Part for the year by the parent or grandparent, as the case may be, the tuition tax credit transferred for the year by the individual to the parent or grandparent, as the case may be.

History: S. 118.9 was replaced by S.C. 2016, c. 7, s. 20(1), applicable to the 2017 and subsequent taxation years, and formerly read:

S. 118.9 *Transfer to parent or grandparent.* If for a taxation year a parent or grandparent of an individual (other than an individual in respect of whom the individual's spouse or common-law partner deducts an amount under section 118 or 118.8 for the year) is the only person designated in writing by the individual for the year for the purpose of this section, there may be deducted in computing the tax payable under this Part for the year by the parent or grandparent, as the case may be, the tuition, textbook and education tax credits transferred for the year by the individual to the parent or grandparent, as the case may be.

Income Tax Folios: *Secondary*— S1-F2-C2 Tuition Tax Credit; S1-F2-C1 Education and Textbook Tax Credits.

SECTION 118.91: Part-year residents

Notwithstanding sections 118 to 118.9, where an individual is resident in Canada throughout part of a taxation year and throughout another part of the year is non-resident, for the purpose of computing the individual's tax payable under this Part for the year,

(*a*) the amount deductible for the year under each such provision in respect of the part of the year that is not included in the period or periods referred to in paragraph (*b*) shall be computed as though such part were the whole taxation year; and

(*b*) the individual shall be allowed only

(i) such of the deductions permitted under subsections 118(3) and (10) and sections 118.01 to 118.2, 118.5, 118.62 and 118.7 as can reasonably be considered wholly applicable to the period or periods in the year throughout which the individual is resident in Canada, computed as though that period or those periods were the whole taxation year, and

(ii) such part of the deductions permitted under sections 118 (other than subsections 118(3) and (10)), 118.3, 118.8 and 118.9 as can reasonably be considered applicable to the period or periods in the year throughout which the individual is resident in Canada, computed as though that period or those periods were the whole taxation year,

except that the amount deductible for the year by the individual under each such provision shall not exceed the amount that would have been deductible under that provision had the individual been resident in Canada throughout the year.

History: S. 118.91(*b*)(i) was replaced by S.C. 2016, c. 7, s. 21(1), applicable to the 2017 and subsequent taxation years, and formerly read:

(i) such of the deductions permitted under subsections 118(3) and (10) and 118.6(2.1) and sections 118.01 to 118.2, 118.5, 118.6, 118.62 and 118.7 as can reasonably be considered wholly applicable to the period or periods in the year throughout which the individual is resident in Canada, computed as though that period or those periods were the whole taxation year, and

S. 118.91(*b*) was replaced by S.C. 2009, c. 31, s. 9(1), applicable to the 2009 and subsequent taxation years. S. 118.91(*b*) formerly read:

(*b*) the individual shall be allowed only

(i) such of the deductions permitted under subsections 118(3), (10) and 118.6(2.1) and sections 118.01, 118.02, 118.03, 118.1, 118.2, 118.5, 118.6, 118.62 and 118.7 as can reasonably be considered wholly applicable, and

(ii) such part of the deductions permitted under sections 118 (other than subsection 118(3)), 118.3,118.8 and 118.9 as can reasonably be considered applicable

to the period or periods in the year throughout which the individual is resident in Canada, computed as though that period or those periods were the whole taxation year,

SECTION 118.92: Ordering of credits

In computing an individual's tax payable under this Part, the following provisions shall be applied in the following order: subsections 118(1) and (2), section 118.7, subsections 118(3) and (10) and sections 118.01, 118.04, 118.041, 118.05, 118.06, 118.07, 118.3, 118.61, 118.5, 118.9, 118.8, 118.2, 118.1, 118.62 and 121.

Amendment not yet in force

Budget Implementation Act, 2019, No. 1 [S.C. 2019, c. 29]

S. 118.92 was replaced by S.C. 2019, c. 29, s. 19(1), and will read as follows:

SECTION 118.92 Ordering of credits. In computing an individual's tax payable under this Part, the following provisions shall be applied in the following order: subsections 118(1) and (2), section 118.7, subsections 118(3) and (10) and sections 118.01, 118.02, 118.04, 118.041, 118.05, 118.06, 118.07, 118.3, 118.61, 118.5, 118.9, 118.8, 118.2, 118.1, 118.62 and 121.

Applicable: January 1, 2020.

History: S. 118.92 was replaced by S.C. 2017, c. 20, s. 20(1), applicable to the 2018 and subsequent taxation year, and formerly read:

S. 118.92 *Ordering of credits.* In computing an individual's tax payable under this Part, the following provisions shall be applied in the following order: subsections 118(1) and (2), section 118.7, subsections 118(3) and (10) and sections 118.01, 118.02, 118.031, 118.04, 118.041, 118.05, 118.06, 118.07, 118.3, 118.61, 118.5, 118.6, 118.9, 118.8, 118.2, 118.1, 118.62 and 121.

S. 118.92 was replaced by S.C. 2016, c. 7, s. 22(2), applicable to the 2017 and subsequent taxation years, and formerly read:

S. 118.92 *Ordering of credits.* In computing an individual's tax payable under this Part, the following provisions shall be applied in the following order: subsections 118(1) and (2), section 118.7, subsections 118(3) and (10) and sections 118.01, 118.02, 118.031, 118.04, 118.041, 118.05, 118.06, 118.07, 118.3, 118.61, 118.5, 118.6, 118.9, 118.8, 118.2, 118.1, 118.62 and 121.

S. 118.92 was replaced by S.C. 2016, c. 7, s. 22(1), applicable to the 2016 taxation year, and formerly read:

S. 118.92 *Ordering of credits.* In computing an individual's tax payable under this Part, the following provisions shall be applied in the following order: subsections 118(1) and (2), section 118.7, subsections 118(3) and (10) and sections 118.01, 118.02, 118.031, 118.04, 118.041, 118.05, 118.06, 118.07, 118.3, 118.61, 118.5, 118.6, 118.9, 118.8, 118.2, 118.1, 118.62, 119.1 and 121.

S. 118.92 was replaced by S.C. 2015, c. 36, s. 9(1), applicable to the 2016 and subsequent taxation years, and formerly read:

S. 118.92 *Ordering of credits.* In computing an individual's tax payable under this Part, the following provisions shall be applied in the following order: subsections 118(1) and (2), section 118.7, subsections 118(3) and (10) and sections 118.01, 118.02, 118.031, 118.04, 118.05, 118.06, 118.07, 118.3, 118.61, 118.5, 118.6, 118.9, 118.8, 118.2, 118.1, 118.62, 119.1 and 121.

S. 118.92 was replaced by S.C. 2015, c. 36, s. 31(2), applicable to the 2015 taxation year, and formerly read:

S. 118.92 **Ordering of credits.** In computing an individual's tax payable under this Part, the following provisions shall be applied in the following order: subsections 118(1) and (2), section 118.7, subsections 118(3) and (10) and sections 118.01, 118.02, 118.03, 118.031, 118.04, 118.05, 118.06, 118.07, 118.3, 118.61, 118.5, 118.6, 118.9, 118.8, 118.2, 118.1, 118.62, 119.1 and 121.

S. 118.92 was replaced by S.C. 2015, c. 36, s. 31(1), applicable to the 2014 taxation year, and formerly read:

S. 118.92 **Ordering of credits.** In computing an individual's tax payable under this Part, the following provisions shall be applied in the following order: subsections 118(1) and (2), section 118.7, subsections 118(3) and (10) and sections 118.01, 118.02, 118.031, 118.04, 118.05, 118.06, 118.07, 118.3, 118.61, 118.5, 118.6, 118.9, 118.8, 118.2, 118.1, 118.62 and 121.

S. 118.92 was replaced by S.C. 2014, c. 39, s. 36(1), applicable to the 2015 and subsequent taxation years, and formerly read:

S. 118.92 *Ordering of credits.* In computing an individual's tax payable under this Part, the following provisions shall be applied in the following order: subsections 118(1) and (2), section 118.7, subsections 118(3) and (10) and sections 118.01, 118.02, 118.03, 118.031, 118.04, 118.05, 118.06, 118.07, 118.3, 118.61, 118.5, 118.6, 118.9, 118.8, 118.2, 118.1, 118.62 and 121.

S. 118.92 was replaced by S.C. 2014, c. 20, s. 15(1), applicable to the 2014 and subsequent taxation years, and formerly read:

S. 118.92 *Ordering of credits.* In computing an individual's tax payable under this Part, the following provisions shall be applied in the following order: subsections 118(1) and (2), section 118.7, subsections 118(3) and (10) and sections 118.01, 118.02, 118.03, 118.031, 118.04, 118.05, 118.06, 118.3, 118.61, 118.5, 118.6, 118.9, 118.8, 118.2, 118.1, 118.62 and 121.

S. 118.92 was replaced by S.C. 2011, c. 24, s. 34(1), applicable to the 2011 and subsequent taxation years. S. 118.92 formerly read:

S. 118.92 *Ordering of credits.* In computing an individual's tax payable under this Part, the following provisions shall be applied in the following order: subsections 118(1) and (2), section 118.7, subsections 118(3) and (10) and sections 118.01, 118.02, 118.03, 118.04, 118.05, 118.3, 118.61, 118.5, 118.6, 118.9, 118.8, 118.2, 118.1, 118.62 and 121.

S. 118.92 was replaced by S.C. 2009, c. 31, s. 10(1), applicable to the 2009 and subsequent taxation years. S. 118.92 formerly read:

S. 118.92 *Ordering of credits.* In computing an individual's tax payable under this Part, the following provisions shall be applied in the following order: subsections 118(1) and (2), section 118.7, subsections 118(3) and (10) and sections 118.01, 118.02, 118.03, 118.3, 118.61, 118.5, 118.6, 118.9, 118.8, 118.2, 118.1, 118.62 and 121.

Interpretation Bulletins: *Primary* — IT-523 Order of provisions applicable in computing an individual's taxable income and tax payable.

SECTION 118.93: Credits in separate returns

If a separate return of income with respect to a taxpayer is filed under subsection 70(2), 104(23) or 150(4) for a particular period and another return of income under this Part with respect to the taxpayer is filed for a period ending in the calendar year in which the particular period ends, for the purpose of computing the tax payable under this Part by the taxpayer in those returns, the total of all deductions claimed in all those returns under any of subsections 118(3) and (10) and sections 118.01 to 118.7 and 118.9 shall not exceed the total that could be deducted under those provisions for the year with respect to the taxpayer if no separate returns were filed under any of subsections 70(2), 104(23) and 150(4).

Interpretation Bulletins: *Primary* — IT-326R3 Returns of deceased persons as "another person".

SECTION 118.94: Tax payable by non-residents (credits restricted)

Sections 118 to 118.07 and 118.2, subsections 118.3(2) and (3) and sections 118.8 and 118.9 do not apply for the purpose of computing the tax payable under this Part for a taxation year by an individual who at no time in the year is resident in Canada unless all or substantially all the individual's income for the year is included in computing the individual's taxable income earned in Canada for the year.

History: S. 118.94 was replaced by S.C. 2016, c. 7, s. 23(1), applicable to the 2017 and subsequent taxation years, and formerly read:

S. 118.94 *Tax payable by non-residents (credits restricted).* Sections 118 to 118.07 and 118.2, subsections 118.3(2) and (3) and sections 118.6, 118.8 and 118.9 do not apply for the purpose of computing the tax payable under this Part for a taxation year by an individual who at no time in the year is resident in Canada unless all or substantially all the individual's income for the year is included in computing the individual's taxable income earned in Canada for the year.

S. 118.94 was replaced by S.C. 2014, c. 20, s. 16(1), applicable to the 2014 and subsequent taxation years, and formerly read:

S. 118.94 *Tax payable by non-residents (credits restricted).* Sections 118 to 118.06 and 118.2, subsections 118.3(2) and (3) and sections 118.6, 118.8 and 118.9 do not apply for the purpose of computing the tax payable under this Part for a taxation year by an individual who at no time in the year is resident in Canada unless all or substantially all the individual's income for the year is included in computing the individual's taxable income earned in Canada for the year.

S. 118.94 was replaced by S.C. 2011, c. 24, s. 35(1), applicable to the 2011 and subsequent taxation years. S. 118.94 formerly read:

S. 118.94 *Tax payable by non-residents (credits restricted).* Sections 118 to 118.05 and 118.2, subsections 118.3(2) and (3) and sections 118.6, 118.8 and 118.9 do not apply for the purpose of computing the tax payable under this Part for a taxation year by an individual who at no time in the year is resident in Canada unless all or substantially all of the individual's income for the year is included in computing the individual's taxable income earned in Canada for the year.

S. 118.94 was replaced by S.C. 2009, c. 31, s. 11(1), applicable to the 2009 and subsequent taxation years. S. 118.94 formerly read:

S. 118.94 *Tax payable by non-residents (credits restricted).* Sections 118, 118.01, 118.02, 118.03 and 118.2, subsections 118.3(2) and (3) and sections 118.6, 118.8 and 118.9 do not apply for the purpose of computing the tax payable under this Part for a taxation year by an individual who at no time in the year is resident in Canada unless all or substantially all of the individual's income for the year is included in computing the individual's taxable income earned in Canada for the year.

Related Sections: S. 115(1) Non-resident's taxable income in Canada; s. 118.94 Tax payable by non-residents (credits restricted); s. 217 Alternative re Canadian benefits; s. 248, "amount", "individual", "non-resident", "taxable income earned in Canada"; s. 255 Canada.

SECTION 118.95: Credits in year of bankruptcy

Notwithstanding sections 118 to 118.9, for the purpose of computing an individual's tax payable under this Part for a taxation year that ends in a calendar year in which the individual becomes bankrupt, the individual shall be allowed only

(*a*) such of the deductions as the individual is entitled to under any of subsections 118(3) and (10) and sections 118.01 to 118.2, 118.5, 118.62 and 118.7, as can reasonably be considered wholly applicable to the taxation year, and

(*b*) such part of the deductions as the individual is entitled to under any of sections 118 (other than subsections 118(3) and (10)), 118.3, 118.8 and 118.9 as can reasonably be considered applicable to the taxation year,

except that the total of the amounts so deductible for all taxation years of the individual in the calendar year under any of those provisions shall not exceed the amount that would have been deductible under that provision in respect of the calendar year if the individual had not become bankrupt.

History: S. 118.95(*a*) was replaced by S.C. 2016, c. 7, s. 24(1), applicable to the 2017 and subsequent taxation years, and formerly read:

(*a*) such of the deductions as the individual is entitled to under any of subsections 118(3) and (10) and sections 118.01 to 118.2, 118.5, 118.6, 118.62 and 118.7, as can reasonably be considered wholly applicable to the taxation year, and

S. 118.95(*a*) and (*b*) were replaced by S.C. 2009, c. 31, s. 12(1), applicable to the 2009 and subsequent taxation years. S. 118.95(*a*) and (*b*) formerly read:

(*a*) such of the deductions as the individual is entitled to under subsections 118(3) and (10) and sections 118.01, 118.02, 118.03, 118.1, 118.2, 118.5, 118.6, 118.62 and 118.7 as can reasonably be considered wholly applicable to the taxation year, and

(*b*) such part of the deductions as the individual is entitled to under sections 118 (other than subsection 118(3)), 118.3, 118.8 and 118.9 as can reasonably be considered applicable to the taxation year,

Related Sections: S. 120.2(4) Where subsection (1) does not apply; s. 122.5(7) Effect of bankruptcy; s. 122.61(3.1) Effect of bankruptcy; s. 127.1(1) Refundable investment tax credit; s. 128(2) Where individual bankrupt; s. 248(1), "bankrupt".

SECTION 119: Former resident — credit for tax paid

If at any particular time an individual was deemed by subsection 128.1(4) to have disposed of a capital property that was a taxable Canadian property of the individual throughout the period that began at the particular time and that ends at the first time, after the particular time, at which the individual disposes of the property, there may be deducted in computing the individual's tax payable under this Part for the taxation year that includes the particular time the lesser of

(*a*) that proportion of the individual's tax for the year otherwise payable under this Part (within the meaning assigned by paragraph (*a*) of the definition "tax for the year otherwise payable under this Part" in subsection 126(7)) that

(i) the individual's taxable capital gain from the disposition of the property at the particular time

is of

(ii) the amount determined under paragraph 114(*a*) in respect of the individual for the year, and (*b*) that proportion of the individual's tax payable under Part XIII in respect of dividends received during the period by the individual in respect of the property and amounts deemed under Part XIII to have been paid during the period to the individual as dividends from corporations resident in Canada, to the extent that the amounts can reasonably be considered to relate to the property, that

(i) the amount by which the individual's loss from the disposition of the property at the end of the period is reduced by subsection 40(3.7)

is of

(ii) the total amount of those dividends.

Related Sections: S. 38 Taxable capital gain and allowable capital loss; s. 152(6.3) Reassessment for section 119 credit; s. 212(2) Tax on dividends; s. 248(1), "taxable Canadian property".

Canadian Tax Foundation: Shew, *Section 119: Flawed Relief from Departure Tax*, 2016 Canadian Tax Focus 6(2):9–10.

Tax Profile: December 2008 — Tax Planning for Emigration from Canada to the United States; November 2004 — Finance to Fix Technical Problem with Section 119.

SECTION 119.1: [Family Tax Cut Credit]

► 119.1(1) ◄

(1) Definitions — (Repealed by S.C. 2016, c. 7, s. 25(1).)

History: S. 119.1(1) was repealed by S.C. 2016, c. 7, s. 25(1), applicable to the 2016 and subsequent taxation years, and formerly read:

S. 119.1

(1) *Definitions.* The following definitions apply in this section.

adjusted base tax payable —"adjusted base tax payable", of an individual for a taxation year, means the amount that would be the individual's tax payable under this Part for the year, if

(*a*) the individual's taxable income for the year were the individual's split-adjusted income for the year; and

(*b*) no amount were deductible under this Division other than the individual's adjusted non-refundable tax credits amount for the year.

adjusted non-refundable tax credits amount —"adjusted non-refundable tax credits amount", of an individual for a taxation year, means the amount determined by the formula

$$A + B$$

where

A is the total of all amounts, each of which is an amount claimed by the individual — not exceeding the amount that may be deducted by the individual — in computing the individual's tax payable for the taxation year

(*a*) under any of subsections 118(2), (3) and (10) and sections 118.01 to 118.07, 118.1 to 118.3, 118.5 to 118.7 and 118.9, and

(*b*) under section 118.8, not exceeding the amount determined by the formula

$$A_1 - A_2$$

where

A_1 is the amount determined for the description of A in section 118.8 for the taxation year, and

A_2 is the amount, if any, by which the amount determined for the description of C in section 118.8 for the taxation year exceeds the amount determined for the description of B in that section for the taxation year; and

B is the amount that would be deductible by the individual under subsection 118(1) in computing the individual's tax payable for the taxation year if

(*a*) the dollar amount set out in the formula in subparagraph (*a*)(ii) of the description of B in that subsection were nil, and

(*b*) the amount determined for the description of C.1 in subparagraph (*a*)(ii) of the description of B in that subsection were determined by the formula

$$C - D$$

where

C is the income of the individual's spouse or common-law partner for the year, and

D is the dollar amount set out in subparagraph (*a*)(i) of the description of B in that subsection.

base tax payable —"base tax payable", of an individual for a taxation year, means the amount that would be the individual's tax payable under this Part for the year if no amount were deductible under this Division other than an amount deductible under any of sections 118 to 118.9.

combined adjusted base tax payable —"combined adjusted base tax payable", of a qualifying individual for a taxation year, means the total of the qualifying individual's adjusted base tax payable for the year and the adjusted base tax payable for the year of the qualifying individual's eligible relation.

combined base tax payable —"combined base tax payable", of a qualifying individual for a taxation year, means the total of the qualifying individual's base tax payable for the year and the base tax payable for the year of the qualifying individual's eligible relation.

eligible relation —"eligible relation", of a particular individual for a taxation year, means an individual who

(*a*) is resident in Canada,

(i) if the individual dies in the year, at the time that is immediately before the individual's death, and

(ii) in any other case, at the end of the year; and

(*b*) is at any time in the year, married to, or in a common-law partnership with, the particular individual and not, by reason of the breakdown of their marriage or common-law partnership, living separate and apart from the particular individual at the end of the year and for a period of at least 90 days commencing in the year.

qualifying individual —"qualifying individual", for a taxation year, means an individual who

(*a*) has an eligible relation for the year who has not deducted an amount under this section for the year;

(*b*) has a child who

(i) is under the age of 18 years at the end of the year, and

(ii) ordinarily resides throughout the year with the individual or the individual's eligible relation for the year;

(*c*) is resident in Canada,

(i) if the individual dies in the year, at the time that is immediately before the individual's death, and

(ii) in any other case, at the end of the year; and

(*d*) is not confined to a prison or similar institution for a period of at least 90 days during the year.

split-adjusted income —"split-adjusted income", of an individual for a taxation year, means

(*a*) if the individual's taxable income for the year is greater than the taxable income for the year of the individual's eligible relation, the amount that is the individual's taxable income less the individual's split adjustment for the year;

(*b*) if the individual's taxable income for the year is less than the taxable income for the year of the individual's eligible relation, the amount that is the individual's taxable income plus the individual's split adjustment for the year; and

(*c*) in any other case, the amount that is equal to the individual's taxable income for the year.

split adjustment —"split adjustment", of an individual for a taxation year, means the lesser of $50,000 and one half of the absolute value of the positive or negative amount determined by the formula

$$A - B$$

where

A is the individual's taxable income for the year; and

B is the taxable income for the year of the individual's eligible relation.

► 119.1(2) ◄

(2) Family tax cut credit — (Repealed by S.C. 2016, c. 7, s. 25(1).)

History: S. 119.1(2) was repealed by S.C. 2016, c. 7, s. 25(1), applicable to the 2016 and subsequent taxation years, and formerly read:

(2) *Family tax cut credit.* For the purpose of computing the tax payable under this Part by a qualifying individual for a taxation year, there may be deducted the lesser of $2,000 and the amount determined by the formula

$$A - B$$

where

A is the qualifying individual's combined base tax payable for the year; and

B is the qualifying individual's combined adjusted base tax payable for the year.

► 119.1(3) ◄

(3) Deduction not available — (Repealed by S.C. 2016, c. 7, s. 25(1).)

History: S. 119.1(3) was repealed by S.C. 2016, c. 7, s. 25(1), applicable to the 2016 and subsequent taxation years, and formerly read:

(3) *Deduction not available.* No amount is deductible under subsection (2) in computing an individual's tax payable under this Part for a taxation year if the individual or the individual's eligible relation

(*a*) does not file with the Minister a return of income in respect of the taxation year;

(*b*) becomes bankrupt in the calendar year in which the taxation year ends; or

(*c*) makes an election for the taxation year under section 60.03.

► 119.1(4) ◄

(4) Taxation year deeming rules — (Repealed by S.C. 2016, c. 7, s. 25(1).)

History: S. 119.1(4) was repealed by S.C. 2016, c. 7, s. 25(1), applicable to the 2016 and subsequent taxation years, and formerly read:

(4) *Taxation year deeming rules.* For the purpose of applying the definition "qualifying individual" in subsection (1), in determining whether a child ordinarily resides throughout a taxation year with an individual or the individual's eligible relation, the taxation year is deemed not to include

(*a*) in the case of a child who is born or is adopted in the year, the portion of the year before the child's birth or adoption;

(*b*) in the case of an individual who marries or becomes a common-law partner at any time in the year, the portion of the year before that time;

(*c*) in the case of an individual, an eligible relation of an individual or a child who dies in the year, the portion of the year after the death; and

(*d*) in the case of an individual or an eligible relation of an individual who becomes resident in Canada in the year, any portion of the year in which the person is non-resident.

History: S. 119.1 was added by S.C. 2015, c. 36, s. 32(1), applicable to the 2014 and subsequent taxation years.

SECTION 120: Income not earned in a province

▶ 120(1) ◀

(1) Income not earned in a province. There shall be added to the tax otherwise payable under this Part by an individual for a taxation year the amount that bears the same relation to 48% of the tax otherwise payable under this Part by the individual for the year that

(*a*) the individual's income for the year, other than the individual's income earned in the year in a province,

bears to

(*b*) the individual's income for the year.

Related Regulations: Part XXVI.

Related Sections: S. 120(3) Definition of "the individual's income for the year"; s. 120(4) Definitions; s. 127.5 Obligation to pay minimum tax.

Interpretation Bulletins: *Secondary* — IT-434R Rental of real property by individual.

▶ 120(2) ◀

(2) Amount deemed paid in prescribed manner. Each individual is deemed to have paid, in prescribed manner and on prescribed dates, on account of the individual's tax under this Part for a taxation year an amount that bears the same relation to 3% of the tax otherwise payable under this Part by the individual for the year that

(*a*) the individual's income earned in the year in a province that, on January 1, 1973, was a province providing schooling allowances within the meaning of the *Youth Allowances Act*, chapter Y-1 of the Revised Statutes of Canada, 1970,

bears to

(*b*) the individual's income for the year.

Related Regulations: 6401.

Related Sections: S. 120(2.1) Averaging for farmers and fishermen; s. 120(3) Definition of "the individual's income for the year".

Interpretation Bulletins: *Secondary* — IT-434R Rental of real property by individual.

Cases: Taxpayer's income from U.S. partnership constituted income from a business in respect of which the deduction as abatement for provincial taxes did not apply. The taxpayer met all the criteria of reg. 2601(2): she resided in Quebec on the last day of the taxation year and she received income from a business that had a permanent establishment outside the province. *Hollinger v. M.N.R.*, 74 DTC 6604 (F.C.A.), affirming 73 DTC 5003 (F.C.T.D.)

▶ 120(2.1) ◀

(2.1) Idem — (Repealed by S.C. 2001, c. 17, s. 103(2).)

▶ 120(2.2) ◀

(2.2) Amount deemed paid. An individual is deemed to have paid on the last day of a taxation year, on account of the individual's tax under this Part for the year, an amount equal to the individual's income tax payable for the year to an Aboriginal government pursuant to a law of that government made in accordance with a tax sharing agreement between that government and the Government of Canada.

▶ 120(3) ◀

(3) Definition of "the individual's income for the year". For the purpose of this section, "the individual's income for the year" means

(*a*) if section 114 applies to the individual in respect of the year, the amount determined under paragraph 114(*a*) in respect of the individual for the year;

(*b*) if the individual was non-resident throughout the year, the individual's taxable income earned in Canada for the year determined without reference to paragraphs 115(1)(*d*) to (*f*);

(*c*) in the case of an individual who is a specified individual in relation to the year, the individual's income for the year computed without reference to paragraph 20(1)(*ww*); and

(*d*) in the case of a SIFT trust, the amount, if any, by which its income for the year determined without reference to this paragraph exceeds its taxable SIFT trust distributions (as defined in subsection 122(3)) for the year.

Related Sections: S. 120.4(1), "specified individual"; s. 122.1(1), "SIFT trust".

▶ 120(3.1) ◀

(3.1) Additional deduction from tax — (Repealed by 1986, c. 6, s. 66(1).)

▶ 120(4) ◀

(4) Definitions. In this section,

"income earned in the year in a province" — "income earned in the year in a province" means amounts determined under rules prescribed for the purpose of regulations made on the recommendation of the Minister of Finance;

Related Regulations: 2600 Interpretation; 2601 Residents of Canada; 2602 Non-Residents; 2603 Income from Business; 2604 Bus and Truck Operators; 2605 More Than One Business; 2606 Limitations of Business Income; 2607 Dual Residence.

Interpretation Bulletins: *Secondary* — IT-434R Rental of real property by individual.

"province" — (Repealed by 1980-81-82-83, c. 48, s. 66(2).)

"tax otherwise payable under this Part" — "tax otherwise payable under this Part" by an individual for a taxation year means the total of

(*a*) the greater of

(i) the individual's minimum amount for the year determined under section 127.51, and

(ii) the amount that, but for this section, would be the individual's tax payable under this Part for the year if this Part were read without reference to

(A) subsection 117(2.1), section 119, subsection 120.4(2) and sections 126, 127, 127.4 and 127.41, and

(B) where the individual is a specified individual in relation to the year, section 121 in its application to dividends included in computing the individual's split income for the year, and

(*b*) where the individual is a specified individual in relation to the year, the amount, if any, by which

(i) the highest individual percentage for the year multiplied by the individual's split income for the year

exceeds

(ii) the total of all amounts each of which is an amount that may be deducted under section 121 and that can reasonably be considered to be in respect of a dividend included in computing the individual's split income for the year.

History: S. 120(4), subparagraph (*b*)(i) of the definition "tax otherwise payable under this Part" was replaced by S.C. 2016, c. 11, s. 3(1), applicable to the 2016 and subsequent taxation years, and formerly read:

(i) 29% of the individual's split income for the year

Related Sections: S. 2(2) Taxable income; s. 248(1), "amount", "individual", "prescribed", "province", "regulation"; ITAR s. 40(1) Payments out of pension funds, etc.; s. 40(2) Employee not resident in Canada; s. 40(3) Determination of amount of payment.

SECTION 120.1: Forward averaging credit

(Repealed by S.C. 2000, c. 19, s. 28(1).)

Related Sections: S. 110.4 Forward averaging; s. 127.5 Obligation to pay minimum tax.

SECTION 120.2: Minimum tax carry-over

► 120.2(1) ◄

(1) Minimum tax carry-over. There may be deducted from the amount that, but for this section, section 120 and subsection 120.4(2), would be an individual's tax payable under this Part for a particular taxation year such amount as the individual claims not exceeding the lesser of

(*a*) the portion of the total of the individual's additional taxes determined under subsection (3) for the 7 taxation years immediately preceding the particular year that was not deducted in computing the individual's tax payable under this Part for a taxation year preceding the particular year, and

(*b*) the amount, if any, by which

(i) the amount that, but for this section, section 120 and subsection 120.4(2), would be the individual's tax payable under this Part for the particular year if the individual were not entitled to any deduction under any of sections 126, 127 and 127.4

exceeds

(ii) the individual's minimum amount for the particular year determined under section 127.51.

► 120.2(2) ◄

(2) Death of individual — (Repealed by 1988, c. 55, s. 95(1).)

► 120.2(3) ◄

(3) Additional tax determined. For the purposes of subsection (1), additional tax of an individual for a taxation year is the amount, if any, by which

(*a*) the individual's minimum amount for the year determined under section 127.51

exceeds the total of

(*b*) the amount that, if this Act were read without reference to section 120, would be the individual's tax payable under this Part for the year if the individual were not entitled to any deduction under any of sections 126, 127 and 127.4, and

(*c*) that proportion of the amount, if any, by which

(i) the individual's special foreign tax credit for the year determined under section 127.54

exceeds

(ii) the total of all amounts deductible under section 126 from the individual's tax for the year

that

(iii) the amount of the individual's foreign taxes for the year within the meaning assigned by subsection 127.54(1)

is of

(iv) the amount that would be the individual's foreign taxes for the year within the meaning assigned by subsection 127.54(1) if the definition "foreign taxes" in that subsection were read without reference to "$^2/_3$ of".

History: S. 120.2(3)(*b*) was replaced by S.C. 2013, c. 34, s. 254(1), applicable to the 2000 and subsequent taxation years, and formerly read:

(*b*) the amount that, but for section 120 and subsection 120.4(2), would be the individual's tax payable under this Part for the year if the individual were not entitled to any deduction under any of sections 126, 127 and 127.4, and

► 120.2(4) ◄

(4) Where subsection (1) does not apply. Subsection (1) does not apply in respect of an individual's return of income filed under subsection 70(2), paragraph 104(23)(d) or 128(2)(f) or subsection 150(4).

SECTION 120.3: CPP/QPP disability benefits [and other CPP/QPP benefits] for previous years

There shall be added in computing an individual's tax payable under this Part for a particular taxation year the total of all amounts each of which is the amount, if any, by which

(*a*) the amount that would have been the tax payable under this Part by the individual for a preceding taxation year if that portion of any amount not included in computing the individual's income for the particular year because of subsection 56(8) and that relates to the preceding year had been included in computing the individual's income for the preceding year

exceeds

(*b*) the tax payable under this Part by the individual for the preceding year.

SECTION 120.31: Lump-sum Payments

► 120.31(1) ◄

(1) Definitions. The definitions in subsection 110.2(1) apply in this section.

► 120.31(2) ◄

(2) Addition to tax payable. There shall be added in computing an individual's tax payable under this Part for a particular taxation year the total of all amounts each of which is the amount, if any, by which

(*a*) the individual's notional tax payable for an eligible taxation year to which a specified portion of a qualifying amount received by the individual relates and in respect of which an amount is deducted under section 110.2 in computing the individual's taxable income for the particular year

exceeds

(*b*) the individual's tax payable under this Part for the eligible taxation year.

Canadian Tax Foundation: Frankovic, *The Taxation of Retroactive Lump-Sum Payments: The Practice and the Policy*, 2010 Canadian Tax Journal 1:1–23.

► 120.31(3) ◄

(3) Notional tax payable. For the purpose of subsection (2), an individual's notional tax payable for an eligible taxation year, calculated for the purpose of computing the individual's tax payable under this Part for a taxation year (in this subsection referred to as "the year of receipt") in which the individual received a qualifying amount, is the total of

(*a*) the amount, if any, by which

(i) the amount that would be the individual's tax payable under this Part for the eligible taxation year if the total of all amounts, each of which is the specified portion, in relation to the eligible taxation year, of a qualifying amount received by the individual before the end of the year of receipt, were added in computing the individual's taxable income for the eligible taxation year

exceeds

(ii) the total of all amounts each of which is an amount, in respect of a qualifying amount received by the individual before the year of receipt, that was included because of this paragraph in computing the individual's notional tax payable under this Part for the eligible taxation year, and

(*b*) if the eligible taxation year ended before the taxation year preceding the year of receipt, an amount equal to the amount that would be calculated as interest payable on the amount, if any, by which the amount determined under paragraph (*a*) in respect of the eligible taxation year exceeds the taxpayer's tax payable under this Part for that year, if the amount that would be calculated as interest payable on that excess were calculated

(i) for the period that began on May 1 of the year following the eligible taxation year and that ended immediately before the year of receipt, and

(ii) at the prescribed rate that is applicable for the purpose of subsection 164(3) with respect to the period.

History: S. 120.31(3)(*b*), the portion before subparagraph (i) was replaced by S.C. 2013, c. 34, s. 255(1), applicable to the 1995 and subsequent taxation years, and formerly read:

(*b*) where the eligible taxation year ended before the taxation year preceding the year of receipt, an amount equal to the amount that would be calculated as interest payable on the amount determined under paragraph (*a*) if it were so calculated

Tax Window Files: QRLSP through arbitration, *March 14, 2019*, CRA Document No. 2019-0796871E5.

Cases: The full amount of a lump sum settlement was included in income in the year of receipt since applying sections 110.2 and 120.31 would result in greater tax owing than the tax owing by bringing the full amount into income in the one year. *Milliken v. The Queen*, 2002 DTC 1510 (T.C.C.).

SECTION 120.4: Tax on split income [Kiddie tax]

► 120.4(1) ◄

(1) Definitions. The definitions in this subsection apply in this section.

Related Sections: S. 74.5(13) Exception from attribution rules.

Canadian Tax Foundation: Hoffstein and Lee, *Revisiting the Attribution Rules*, 2012 Ontario Tax Conference 9:1–40; Dulholke, *Kiddie Tax: The Income-Splitting Dance*, 2001 Tax for the Owner-Manager 1(2):5–6; Donnelly et al., *Income Splitting and the New Kiddie Tax: Major Changes for Minor Children*, 2000 Canadian Tax Journal 4:979–1018.

Tax Window Files: Revenu fractionné, *March 28, 2012*, CRA Document No. 2011-0422531E5.

arm's length capital —arm's length capital, of a specified individual, means property of the individual if the property, or property for which it is a substitute, was not

(*a*) acquired as income from, or a taxable capital gain or profit from the disposition of, another property that was derived directly or indirectly from a related business in respect of the specified individual;

(*b*) borrowed by the specified individual under a loan or other indebtedness; or

(*c*) transferred, directly or indirectly by any means whatever, to the specified individual from a person who was related to the specified individual (other than as a consequence of the death of a person).

History: S. 120.4(1), the definition "arm's length capital" was added by S.C. 2018, c. 12, s. 13(5), applicable to the 2018 and subsequent taxation years.

excluded amount —excluded amount, in respect of an individual for a taxation year, means an amount that is the individual's income for the year from, or the individual's taxable capital gain or profit for the year from the disposition of, a property to the extent that the amount

(*a*) if the individual has not attained the age of 24 years before the year, is from a property that was acquired by, or for the benefit of, the individual as a consequence of the death of a person who is

(i) a parent of the individual, or

(ii) any person, if the individual is

(A) enrolled as a full-time student during the year at a *post-secondary educational institution* (as defined in subsection 146.1(1)), or

(B) an individual in respect of whom an amount may be deducted under section 118.3 in computing a taxpayer's tax payable under this Part for the year;

(*b*) is from a property acquired by the individual under a transfer described in subsection 160(4);

(*c*) is a taxable capital gain that arises because of subsection 70(5);

(*d*) is a taxable capital gain for the year from the disposition by the individual of property that is, at the time of the disposition, *qualified farm or fishing property* or *qualified small business corporation shares* (as those terms are defined in subsection 110.6(1)), unless the amount would be deemed to be a dividend under subsection 120.4(4) or (5) if this definition were read without reference to this paragraph;

(*e*) if the individual has attained the age of 17 years before the year, is

(i) not derived directly or indirectly from a related business in respect of the individual for the year, or

(ii) derived directly or indirectly from an excluded business of the individual for the year;

(*f*) if the individual has attained the age of 17 years but not the age of 24 years before the year, is

(i) a safe harbour capital return of the individual, or

(ii) a reasonable return in respect of the individual, having regard only to the contributions of arm's length capital by the individual; or

(*g*) if the individual has attained the age of 24 years before the year, is

(i) income from, or a taxable capital gain from the disposition of, excluded shares of the individual, or

(ii) a reasonable return in respect of the individual.

Editorial Note: An excluded amount is not split income and therefore not subject to the tax on split income under section 120.4. Beginning in 2018, the following amounts are excluded amounts:

(a) If the specified individual had not attained 24 years of age before the year, income from a property or the taxable capital gain from the disposition of a property in a year, where the property was acquired by or for the benefit of the individual as a consequence of the death of the individual's parent. An excluded amount also includes income from property in a year if the property was inherited from anyone else, if the individual is eligible for the disability tax credit in the year, or if the individual is enrolled as a full-time student at a post-secondary educational institution during the year.

(b) Income from or a taxable capital gain from a property that was acquired by the specified individual's spouse or common-law partner under a court order or written agreement and upon the breakdown of the marriage or common-law relationship (property described in subsection 160(4)).

(c) A taxable capital gain that arises upon death under the deemed disposition rule in subsection 70(5).

(d) A taxable capital gain that qualifies for the capital gains exemption. However, a capital gain realized by an individual under the age of 18 on the disposition of shares in a private corporation to a non-arm's length person may be subject to the TOSI by virtue of subsection 120.4(4).

(e) Specified individuals 18 years of age or older: If the individual is aged 18 or more in the taxation year, an amount included in the individual's income is an excluded amount for the year if it is *not* derived directly or indirectly from a "related business" (subsection 120.4(1)) in respect of the individual, or if it *is* derived directly or indirectly from an "excluded business" (subsection 120.4(1)) in respect of the individual.

(f) Specified individuals aged 18 through 24: If the individual was over 17 years old but less than 25 years old at the end of the relevant taxation year, an excluded amount for the year includes a "safe harbour capital return", or a "reasonable return" in respect of the individual having regard only to the contributions of "arm's length capital" by the individual (all terms defined in subsection 120.4(1).

(g) Specified individuals over the age of 24: If the individual was 25 years of age or more at the end of the relevant year, an excluded amount for the year includes income of a taxable capital gain from "excluded shares" of the individual, or a "reasonable return" in respect of the individual (both defined in subsection 120.4(1)). This exclusion also applies to an individual who had not reached the age of 17 before the year but who acquired the shares or property from another individual who was 24 years of age or older before the year (subparagraph 120.4(1.1)(*b*)(iii)).

History: S. 120.4(1), the definition "excluded amount" was replaced by S.C. 2018, c. 12, s. 13(1), applicable to the 2018 and subsequent taxation years, and formerly read:

"excluded amount"—"excluded amount", in respect of an individual for a taxation year, means an amount that is the income from, or the taxable capital gain from the disposition of, a property acquired by or for the benefit of the individual as a consequence of the death of

(*a*) a parent of the individual; or

(*b*) any person, if the individual is

(i) enrolled as a full-time student during the year at a post-secondary educational institution (as defined in subsection 146.1(1)), or

(ii) an individual in respect of whom an amount may be deducted under section 118.3 in computing a taxpayer's tax payable under this Part for the year.

S. 120.4(1), the portion of the definition "excluded amount" before paragraph (*a*) was replaced by S.C. 2011, c. 24, s. 36(1), applicable to dispositions that occur on or after March 22, 2011. S. 120.4(1), the portion of the definition "excluded amount" before paragraph (*a*) formerly read:

"excluded amount"—"excluded amount", in respect of an individual for a taxation year, means an amount that is the income from a property acquired by or for the benefit of the individual as a consequence of the death of

Tax Topics: No. 2452, A Comprehensive Review of Every Interpretation of the Revised TOSI Rules.

Tax Window Files: 2018 CTF-Q9-TOSI–Excluded Amount - Non-Related Bus. Exception, *November 27, 2018*, CRA Document No. 2018-0779981C6.

excluded business —excluded business, of a specified individual for a taxation year, means a business if the specified individual is actively engaged on a regular, continuous and substantial basis in the activities of the business in either

(*a*) the taxation year, except in respect of an amount described in paragraph (*e*) of the definition *split income*; or

(*b*) any five prior taxation years of the specified individual.

Editorial Note: Generally, where an individual 18 years of age or older derives income from an excluded business, the income is an "excluded amount" (see paragraph (*e*) of that definition) and therefore not subject to the tax on split income. See also the editorial note to "excluded amount" and to subsection 120.4(2).

History: S. 120.4(1), the definition "excluded business" was added by S.C. 2018, c. 12, s. 13(5), applicable to the 2018 and subsequent taxation years.

Tax Window Files: TOSI and the meaning of "Excluded Business", *February 27, 2019*, CRA Document No. 2018-0783741E5.

excluded shares —excluded shares, of a specified individual at any time, means shares of the capital stock of a corporation owned by the specified individual if

(*a*) the following conditions are met:

(i) less than 90% of the business income of the corporation for the last taxation year of the corporation that ends at or before that time (or, if no such taxation year exists, for the taxation year of the corporation that includes that time) was from the provision of services, and

(ii) the corporation is not a professional corporation;

(*b*) immediately before that time, the specified individual owns shares of the capital stock of the corporation that

(i) give the holders thereof 10% or more of the votes that could be cast at an annual meeting of the shareholders of the corporation, and

(ii) have a fair market value of 10% or more of the fair market value of all of the issued and outstanding shares of the capital stock of the corporation; and

(*c*) all or substantially all of the income of the corporation for the relevant taxation year in subparagraph (*a*)(i) is income that is not derived, directly or indirectly, from one or more related businesses in respect of the specified individual other than a business of the corporation,

Editorial Note: Generally, for individuals 25 years of age or older, income or gain from the disposition of excluded shares is an "excluded amount" (see paragraph (*g*) of that definition) and therefore not subject to the tax on split income. See also the editorial note to "excluded amount" and to subsection 120.4(2).

History: S. 120.4(1), the definition "excluded shares" was added by S.C. 2018, c. 12, s. 13(5), applicable to the 2018 and subsequent taxation years. For the 2018 taxation year, the portion of paragraph (*b*) of the definition "excluded shares" in subsection 120.4(1) of the Act before subparagraph (i) is to be read as follows:

(*b*) immediately before that time or the end of 2018, the shares

Tax Topics: No. 2436, Tax on Split Income: Applicability for Investment and Holding Companies.

Tax Window Files: 2018 CTF - Q.10 – TOSI – Excluded Shares & Related Business, *November 27, 2018*, CRA Document No. 2018-0780081C6; 120.4 Excluded Shares, *August 21, 2018*, CRA Document No. 2018-0771811E5; Correspondence with XXXXXXXXXX re Tax on Split Income, *May 25, 2018*, CRA Document No. 2018-0761601E5; CALU Conference Question 6 - Tax on Split Income, *May 8, 2018*, CRA Document No. 2018-0745871C6; 2018 STEP Q6 – Excluded Shares – Holding Company, *May 29, 2018*, CRA Document No. 2018-0743971C6; STEP Question 5 - Tax on Split Income, *May 29, 2018*, CRA Document No. 2018-0743961C6.

reasonable return —reasonable return, in respect of a specified individual for a taxation year, means a particular amount derived directly or indirectly from a related business in respect of the specified individual that

(*a*) would, if this subsection were read without reference to subparagraph (*f*)(ii) or (*g*)(ii) of the definition *excluded amount*, be an amount described in the definition *split income* in respect of the specified individual for the year; and

(*b*) is reasonable having regard to the following factors relating to the relative contributions of the specified individual, and each source individual in respect of the specified individual, in respect of the related business:

(i) the work they performed in support of the related business,

(ii) the property they contributed, directly or indirectly, in support of the related business,

(iii) the risks they assumed in respect of the related business,

(iv) the total of all amounts that were paid or that became payable, directly or indirectly, by any person or partnership to, or for the benefit of, them in respect of the related business, and

(v) such other factors as may be relevant.

Editorial Note: See the note to the definition "excluded business".

History: S. 120.4(1), the definition "reasonable return" was added by S.C. 2018, c. 12, s. 13(5), applicable to the 2018 and subsequent taxation years.

related business —related business, in respect of a specified individual for a taxation year, means

(*a*) a business carried on by

(i) a source individual in respect of the specified individual at any time in the year, or

(ii) a partnership, corporation or trust if a source individual in respect of the specified individual at any time in the year is actively engaged on a regular basis in the activities of the partnership, corporation or trust related to earning income from the business;

(*b*) a business of a particular partnership, if a source individual in respect of the specified individual at any time in the year has an interest — including directly or indirectly — in the particular partnership; and

(*c*) a business of a corporation, if the following conditions are met at any time in the year:

(i) a source individual in respect of the specified individual owns

(A) shares of the capital stock of the corporation, or

(B) property that derives, directly or indirectly, all or part of its fair market value from shares of the capital stock of the corporation, and

(ii) it is the case that

$$0.1A \leq B + C$$

where

A is the total fair market value of all of the issued and outstanding shares of the capital stock of the corporation,

B is the total fair market value of property described in clause (i)(A), and

C is the portion of the total fair market value of property described in clause (i)(B) that is derived from shares of the capital stock of the corporation.

Editorial Note: See the note to subsection 120.4(2).

History: S. 120.4(1), the definition "related business" was added by S.C. 2018, c. 12, s. 13(5), applicable to the 2018 and subsequent taxation years.

safe harbour capital return —safe harbour capital return, of a specified individual for a taxation year, means an amount that does not exceed the amount determined by the formula

$$A \times B$$

where

A is the rate equal to the highest rate of interest prescribed under paragraph 4301(*c*) of the *Income Tax Regulations* in effect for a quarter in the year; and

B is the total of all amounts each of which is determined by the formula

$$C \times D/E$$

where

C is the fair market value of property contributed by the specified individual in support of a related business at the time it was contributed,

D is the number of days in the year that the property (or property substituted for it) is used in support of the related business and has not directly or indirectly, in any manner whatever, been returned to the specified individual, and

E is the number of days in the year.

Editorial Note: See the note to the definition "excluded business".

History: S. 120.4(1), the definition "safe harbour capital return" was added by S.C. 2018, c. 12, s. 13(5), applicable to the 2018 and subsequent taxation years.

source individual —source individual, in respect of a specified individual for a taxation year, means an individual (other than a trust) who, at any time in the year, is

(*a*) resident in Canada; and

(*b*) related to the specified individual.

History: S. 120.4(1), the definition "source individual" was added by S.C. 2018, c. 12, s. 13(5), applicable to the 2018 and subsequent taxation years.

specified individual —specified individual, for a taxation year, means an individual (other than a trust) who

(*a*) is resident in Canada

(i) in the case where the individual dies in the year, immediately before the death, and

(ii) in any other case, at the end of the year; and

(*b*) if the individual has not attained the age of 17 years before the year, has a parent resident in Canada at any time in the year.

History: S. 120.4(1), the definition "specified individual" was replaced by S.C. 2018, c. 12, s. 13(1), applicable to the 2018 and subsequent taxation years, and formerly read:

"*specified individual*"—"specified individual", in relation to a taxation year, means an individual who

(*a*) had not attained the age of 17 years before the year;

(*b*) at no time in the year was non-resident; and

(*c*) has a parent who is resident in Canada at any time in the year.

"split income" —"split income", of a specified individual for a taxation year, means the total of all amounts (other than excluded amounts) each of which is

(*a*) an amount required to be included in computing the individual's income for the year

(i) in respect of taxable dividends received by the individual in respect of shares of the capital stock of a corporation (other than shares of a class listed on a designated stock exchange or shares of the capital stock of a mutual fund corporation), or

(ii) because of the application of section 15 in respect of the ownership by any person of shares of the capital stock of a corporation (other than shares of a class listed on a designated stock exchange),

(*b*) a portion of an amount included because of the application of paragraph 96(1)(*f*) in computing the individual's income for the year, to the extent that the portion

(i) is not included in an amount described in paragraph (*a*), and

(ii) can reasonably be considered to be income derived directly or indirectly from

(A) one or more related businesses in respect of the individual for the year, or

(B) the rental of property by a particular partnership or trust, if a person who is related to the individual at any time in the year

(I) is actively engaged on a regular basis in the activities of the particular partnership or trust related to the rental of property, or

(II) in the case of a particular partnership, has an interest in the particular partnership directly or indirectly through one or more other partnerships,

(*c*) a portion of an amount included because of the application of subsection 104(13) or 105(2) in respect of a trust (other than a mutual fund trust or a trust that is deemed to be in existence by subsection 143(1)) in computing the individual's income for the year, to the extent that the portion

(i) is not included in an amount described in paragraph (*a*), and

(ii) can reasonably be considered

(A) to be in respect of taxable dividends received in respect of shares of the capital stock of a corporation (other than shares of a class listed on a designated stock exchange or shares of the capital stock of a mutual fund corporation),

(B) to arise because of the application of section 15 in respect of the ownership by any person of shares of the capital stock of a corporation (other than shares of a class listed on a designated stock exchange),

(C) to be income derived directly or indirectly from one or more related businesses in respect of the individual for the year, or

(D) to be income derived from the rental of property by a particular partnership or trust, if a person who is related to the individual at any time in the year is actively engaged on a regular basis in the activities of the particular partnership or trust related to the rental of property,

(*d*) an amount included in computing the individual's income for the year to the extent that the amount is in respect of a debt obligation that

(i) is of a corporation (other than a mutual fund corporation or a corporation shares of a class of the capital stock of which are listed on a designated stock exchange), partnership or trust (other than a mutual fund trust), and

(ii) is not

(A) described in paragraph (*a*) of the definition *fully exempt interest* in subsection 212(3),

(B) listed or traded on a public market, or

(C) a deposit, standing to the credit of the individual,

(I) within the meaning assigned by the *Canada Deposit Insurance Corporation Act*, or

(II) with a credit union or a branch in Canada of a bank, and

(*e*) an amount in respect of a property, to the extent that

(i) the amount

(A) is a taxable capital gain, or a profit, of the individual for the year from the disposition after 2017 of the property, or

(B) is included under subsection 104(13) or 105(2) in computing the individual's income for the year and can reasonably be considered to be attributable to a taxable capital gain, or a profit, of any person or partnership for the year from the disposition after 2017 of the property, and

(ii) the property is

(A) a share of the capital stock of a corporation (other than a share of a class listed on a designated stock exchange or a share of the capital stock of a mutual fund corporation), or

(B) a property in respect of which the following conditions are met:

(I) the property is

1 an interest in a partnership,

2 an interest as a beneficiary under a trust (other than a mutual fund trust or a trust that is deemed to be in existence by subsection 143(1)), or

3 a debt obligation (other than a debt obligation described in any of clauses (*d*)(ii)(A) to (C)), and

(II) either

1 in respect of the property an amount is included in the individual's split income for the year or an earlier taxation year, or

2 all or any part of the fair market value of the property, immediately before the disposition referred to in clause (i)(A) or (B), as the case may be, is derived, directly or indirectly, from a share described in clause (A).

History: S. 120.4(1), subparagraph (*b*)(ii) of the definition "split income" was replaced by S.C. 2018, c. 12, s. 13(2), applicable to the 2018 and subsequent taxation years, and formerly read:

(ii) can reasonably be considered to be income derived

(A) from the provision of property or services by a partnership or trust to, or in support of, a business carried on by

(I) a person who is related to the individual at any time in the year,

(II) a corporation of which a person who is related to the individual is a specified shareholder at any time in the year, or

(III) a professional corporation of which a person related to the individual is a shareholder at any time in the year, or

(B) from a business of, or the rental of property by, a particular partnership or trust, if a person who is related to the individual at any time in the year

(I) is actively engaged on a regular basis in the activities of the particular partnership or trust related to earning income from a business or the rental of property, or

(II) in the case of a particular partnership, has an interest in the particular partnership directly or indirectly through one or more other partnerships, or

S. 120.4(1), clauses (*c*)(ii)(C) and (D) of the definition "split income" was replaced by S.C. 2018, c. 12, s. 13(3), applicable to the 2018 and subsequent taxation years, and formerly read:

(C) to be income derived from the provision of property or services by a partnership or trust to, or in support of, a business carried on by

(I) a person who is related to the individual at any time in the year,

(II) a corporation of which a person who is related to the individual is a specified shareholder at any time in the year, or

(III) a professional corporation of which a person related to the individual is a shareholder at any time in the year, or

(D) to be income derived from a business of, or the rental of property by, a particular partnership or trust, if a person who is related to the individual at any time in the year is actively engaged on a regular basis in the activities of the particular partnership or trust related to earning income from a business or the rental of property.

S. 120.4(1), paragraphs (*d*) and (*e*) of the definition "split income" were added by S.C. 2018, c. 12, s. 13(4), applicable to the 2018 and subsequent taxation years.

S. 120.4(1), subparagraph (*b*)(ii) of the definition "split income" was replaced by S.C. 2014, c. 39, s. 37(1), applicable to the 2014 and subsequent taxation years, and formerly read:

(ii) can reasonably be considered to be income derived from the provision of property or services by a partnership or trust to, or in support of, a business carried on by

(A) a person who is related to the individual at any time in the year,

(B) a corporation of which a person who is related to the individual is a specified shareholder at any time in the year, or

(C) a professional corporation of which a person related to the individual is a shareholder at any time in the year, or

S. 120.4(1), the portion of paragraph (*c*) before subparagraph (i) of the definition "split income" was replaced by S.C. 2014, c. 39, s. 37(2), applicable to the 2014 and subsequent taxation years, and formerly read:

(*c*) a portion of an amount included because of the application of subsection 104(13) or 105(2) in respect of a trust (other than a mutual fund trust) in computing the individual's income for the year, to the extent that the portion

S. 120.4(1), clause (D) of the definition "split income" was added by S.C. 2014, c. 39, s. 37(3), applicable to the 2014 and subsequent taxation years.

S. 120.4(1), the portion of subparagraph (*b*)(ii) of the definition "split income" before clause (A) was replaced by S.C. 2013, c. 34, s. 256(1), applicable in computing split income of a specified individual for taxation years that begin after December 20, 2002, other than in computing an amount included in that income that is from a trust or partnership for a taxation year or fiscal period of the trust or partnership that began before December 21, 2002.

The portion of subparagraph (*b*)(ii) of the definition "split income" before clause (A) formerly read:

(ii) can reasonably be considered to be income derived from the provision of goods or services by a partnership or trust to or in support of a business carried on by

S. 120.4(1), the portion of clause (*c*)(ii)(C) of the definition "split income" before subclause (I) was replaced by S.C. 2013, c. 34, s. 256(2), applicable in computing split income of a specified individual for taxation years that begin after December 20, 2002, other than in computing an amount included in that income that is from a trust or partnership for a taxation year or fiscal period of the trust or partnership that began before December 21, 2002.

The portion of clause (*c*)(ii)(C) of the definition "split income" before subclause (I) formerly read:

(C) to be income derived from the provision of goods or services by a partnership or trust to or in support of a business carried on by

Related Sections: S. 20(1)(*ww*) Split income; s. 74.4(2)(*g*) Transfers and loans to corporations; s. 89(1), "taxable dividend".

Canadian Tax Foundation: Rio, *Prescribed-Rate Loan Planning with a Trust Under the New Rules*, 2018 Tax for the Owner Manager 18(2):3–5.

Tax Window Files: Kiddie Tax – Professional Income Split with Partnership with Trust for Minors as Member, *March 10, 2014*, CRA Document No. 2013-049397117; Tax on Split Income – Discretionary Family Trust, *October 11, 2013*, CRA Document No. 2013-0495651C6; Kiddie Tax, *March 26, 2013*, CRA Document No. 2012-0465001E5; Tax on Split Income — Taxable Capital Gain or Taxable Dividend, *External Technical Interpretation, Trusts and Financial Industries Division, October 22, 2012*, CRA Document No. 2012-0432241E5.

▶ 120.4(1.1) ◀

(1.1) Additional rules — specified individual. For the purpose of applying this section in respect of a specified individual in respect of a taxation year,

(*a*) an individual is deemed to be actively engaged on a regular, continuous and substantial basis in the activities of a business in a taxation year of the individual if the individual works in the business at least an average of 20 hours per week during the portion of the year in which the business operates;

(*b*) if an amount would — if this section were read without reference to this paragraph — be split income of a specified individual who has attained the age of 17 years before the year in respect of a property, and that property was acquired by, or for the benefit of, the specified individual as a consequence of the death of another person, then

(i) for the purpose of applying paragraph (*b*) of the definition *reasonable return* in subsection (1), to the extent that the particular amount referred to in that paragraph is in respect of the property, then the factors referred to in that paragraph in respect of the other person are to be included for the purpose of determining a reasonable return in respect of the individual,

(ii) for the purposes of this subparagraph and the definition *excluded business* in subsection (1), if the other person was actively engaged on a regular, substantial and continuous basis in the activities of a business throughout five previous taxation years, then the individual is deemed to have been actively engaged on a regular, substantial and continuous basis in the business throughout those five years, and

(iii) for the purpose of applying paragraph (*g*) of the definition *excluded amount* in subsection (1) in respect of that property, the individual is deemed to have attained the age of 24 years before the year if the other person had attained the age of 24 years before the year;

(*c*) an amount that is a specified individual's income for a taxation year from, or the specified individual's taxable capital gain or profit for the year from the disposition of, a property is deemed to be an excluded amount in respect of the specified individual for the taxation year if

(i) the following conditions are met:

(A) the amount would be an excluded amount in respect of the specified individual's spouse or common-law partner for the year, if the amount were included in computing the spouse or common-law partner's income for the year, and

(B) the spouse or common law partner has attained the age of 64 years before the year, or

(ii) the amount would have been an excluded amount in respect of an individual who was, immediately before their death, the specified individual's spouse or common-law partner, if the amount were included in computing the spouse or common-law partner's income for their last taxation year (determined as if this section applies in respect of that year);

(*d*) for greater certainty, an amount derived directly or indirectly from a business includes

(i) an amount that

(A) is derived from the provision of property or services to, or in support of, the business, or

(B) arises in connection with the ownership or disposition of an interest in the person or partnership carrying on the business, and

(ii) an amount derived from an amount described in this paragraph; and

(*e*) for the purposes of this section, an individual is deemed not to be related to their spouse or common-law partner at any time in a year if, at the end of the year, the individual is living separate and apart from their spouse or common-law partner because of a breakdown of their marriage or common-law partnership.

History: S. 120.4(1.1) was added by S.C. 2018, c. 12, s. 13(6), applicable to the 2018 and subsequent taxation years.

Tax Window Files: TOSI and dividend income, including from a trust, *November 7, 2018*, CRA Document No. 2018-0777361E5.

▶ 120.4(2) ◀

(2) Tax on split income. There shall be added to a specified individual's tax payable under this Part for a taxation year the highest individual percentage for the year multiplied by the individual's split income for the year.

Editorial Note: The tax on split income ("TOSI") is a tax that is applied at the highest marginal tax rate (which is currently 33%) on "split income" as defined in s. 120.4(1). Prior to 2018, the TOSI applied only to individuals under the age of 18. Beginning in 2018, the concept of TOSI is expanded and it can potentially apply to adult individuals. The pre-2018 rules and the rules beginning in 2018 are summarized below.

Split income before 2018: The TOSI applies only to a "specified individual" in a taxation year who has not reached the age of 17 in the preceding year. Before 2018, split income of a specified individual includes:

(1) An amount included in respect of a taxable dividend received on an unlisted share of a corporation (that is, a share that is not a share listed on a designated stock exchange or a share of a mutual fund corporation), whether received directly by the individual or through a partner-

ship of which the individual is a member or from a trust in which the individual is a beneficiary (other than a mutual fund trust).

(2) An amount included in the specified individual's income under the shareholder benefit or shareholder loan rules of section 15 of the Act in respect of unlisted shares, whether received directly or through a partnership of which the individual is a member or from a trust in which the individual is a beneficiary.

(3) Income from a trust or partnership that can reasonably be considered to be income derived from the provision of property or services by a trust or partnership to, or in support of, a business carried on by a person related to the specified individual, a corporation in which a person related to the specified individual is a "specified shareholder" (defined in subsection 248(1)), or a professional corporation in which a person related to the specified individual is a shareholder.

(4) Income from a partnership or trust (the "first" partnership or trust) that can reasonably be considered to be derived from a business of, or the rental of property by, a particular partnership or trust (whether it is the first partnership or trust or another partnership or trust). However, a person related to the individual must be actively engaged on a regular basis in the activities of the particular partnership or trust earning the business or rental income, or a related person must have an interest in the particular partnership whether through one or more partnerships.

Moreover, if a specified individual (directly or through a partnership or a trust) has a taxable capital gain for the year arising from the disposition of unlisted corporate shares to a non-arm's length person, twice the amount of the taxable capital gain is deemed to be received by the individual as a taxable dividend that is not an eligible dividend, such that the full amount of the capital gain will constitute split income under item (1) or (3) above.

Split income beginning in 2018:

(1) Item (1) as above remains unchanged.

(2) Item (2) as above remains unchanged.

(3) Item (3), which is slightly changed. It is income from a trust or partnership that can reasonably be considered to be income derived directly or indirectly from a "related business" in respect of the specified individual. A "related business" for a taxation year (subsection 120.4(1)) includes the following:

(a) A business carried on by a "source individual" (an individual who is resident at any time in the year and is related to the specified individual) in the year, or by a partnership, corporation, or trust if a source individual in the year is actively engaged on a regular basis in the business activities of the partnership, corporation, or trust;

(b) A business of a particular partnership if the source individual has a direct or indirect interest in the particular partnership in the year (e.g., as a member of the partnership or through a tiered partnership structure); and

(c) A business of a corporation if at any time in the year the source individual owns shares in the corporation, or owns property that derives all or part of its value from shares in the corporation (e.g., an interest in a partnership or trust that owns the shares), generally where the fair market value of the shares and the property that derives its value from the shares equals or exceeds 10% of the fair market value of all of the shares of the corporation.

(4) Item 4, which is essentially the same as item (4) above.

(5) An amount included in income in respect of a debt obligation (e.g., interest) of a corporation (other than a corporation on a designated stock exchange), partnership, or trust, with exceptions for publicly-traded debt, debt guaranteed by the Canadian government, and deposits to the credit of the specified individual with a bank or credit union (new paragraph (*d*) of the definition of "split income").

(6) A taxable capital gain or profit from a disposition of property by the individual, or included in the individual's income as a beneficiary under a trust because of a disposition of property (new paragraph (*e*) of the definition of "split income"). The property must be either an unlisted share in a corporation, or an interest in a partnership or trust or a debt obligation described in item (5) above, generally where income from the property was included in the individual's split income for the year or an earlier year, or where any of the value of such property was derived from a share in a corporation immediately before the disposition of the property.

As before, if a specified individual under the age of 18 has a taxable capital gain for the year arising from the disposition of unlisted corporate shares to a non-arm's length person, twice the amount of the taxable capital gain is deemed to be received by the individual as a taxable dividend that is not an eligible dividend, such that the full amount of the capital gain will constitute split income.

Excluded amount: An "excluded amount" is not split income. The concept is discussed in the editorial note to the definition in subsection 120.4(1).

History: S. 120.4(2) was replaced by S.C. 2016, c. 11, s. 4(1), applicable to the 2016 and subsequent taxation years, and formerly read:

(2) *Tax on split income.* There shall be added to a specified individual's tax payable under this Part for a taxation year 29% of the individual's split income for the year.

Related Sections: S. 20(1)(*ww*) Split income; s. 56(5) Exception for split income; s. 74.4(2)(*g*) Transfers and loans to corporations; s. 74.5(13) Exception from attribution rules; s. 89(1), "taxable dividend"; s. 104(1), "trust"; s. 108(5) Interpretation; s. 120.2(1) Minimum tax carry-over; s. 127.5 Obligation to pay minimum tax; s. 131(8), "mutual fund corporation"; s. 132(6), "mutual fund trust"; s. 132(7), "mutual fund trust"; s. 146.1(1), "post-secondary educational institution"; s. 160(1.2) Joint liability — tax on split income; s. 248(1), "mutual fund corporation", "mutual fund trust", "professional corporation", "specified shareholder", "trust"; s. 248(3), "trust"; s. 248(8), "consequence of the death"; s. 248(29), "prescribed stock exchange"; s. 252(2), "parent". (See also the "attribution rules", including sections 74.1 Transfers and loans to spouse; s. 74.2 Gain or loss deemed that of lender or transferor; s. 74.3 Transfers or loans to a trust; s. 74.4 Transfers and loans to corporations; s. 74.5 Transfers for fair market consideration; s. 75(2) Trusts).

Canadian Tax Foundation: Goetz et al., *TOSI and Alternative Remuneration Strategies*, 2018 British Columbia Tax Conference 3:1–37; Bollefer and Malach, *Tax on Split Income – A Detailed Analysis (Or How Not To Get Trapped In The TOSI Rabbit Hole)*, 2018 Ontario Tax Conference 3:1–84; London and Trahey, *Tax on Split Income (TOSI): How We Got Here and What It Means For the Owners of Private Businesses*, 2018 St. John's Tax Seminar 3:1–30; Gallant, *TOSI (Tax on Split Income) Rules - How They Now Work and Practical Applications*, 2018 Prairie Provinces Tax Conference 8:0; Gervais and Sideris, *Do the New Income Sprinkling Rules Affect My Family?*, 2017 Conference Report 14:1–24.

Tax Profile: February 2010 — Planning With Trusts; February 2008 — Income Splitting A–Z.

Tax Topics: No. 2393, A Roadmap of the Revised Income Sprinkling Proposals; No. 2389-90, Private Company Income-Splitting Proposal Part 3: The Government Responds.

Forms: T1206 — Tax on Split Income.

► 120.4(3) ◄

(3) Tax payable by a specified individual. Notwithstanding any other provision of this Act, if an individual is a specified individual for a taxation year, the individual's tax payable under this Part for the year shall not be less than the amount by which the amount added under subsection (2) to the individual's tax payable under this Part for the year exceeds the amount determined by the formula

$$A + B$$

where

A is the amount deducted under section 118.3 in computing the individual's tax payable under this Part for the year; and

B is the total of all amounts each of which is the amount that

(*a*) may be deducted under section 121 or 126 in computing the individual's tax payable under this Part for the year, and

(*b*) can reasonably be considered to be in respect of an amount included in computing the individual's split income for the year.

Editorial Note: Apart from the disability tax credit, the foreign tax credit and the dividend tax credit, there are generally no deductions or credits that reduce the tax on split income.

History: S. 120.4(3) was replaced by S.C. 2018, c. 12, s. 13(7), applicable to the 2018 and subsequent taxation years, and formerly read:

(3) *Tax payable by a specified individual.* Notwithstanding any other provision of this Act, where an individual is a specified individual in relation to a taxation year, the individual's tax payable under this Part for the year shall not be less than the amount by which

(*a*) the amount added under subsection (2) to the individual's tax payable under this Part for the year

exceeds

(*b*) the total of all amounts each of which is an amount that

(i) may be deducted under section 121 or 126 in computing the individual's tax payable under this Part for the year, and

(ii) can reasonably be considered to be in respect of an amount included in computing the individual's split income for the year.

Tax Window Files: Correspondence with XXXXXXXXXX re Tax on Split Income, *May 25, 2018*, CRA Document No. 2018-0761601E5; CALU Conference Question 6 - Tax on Split Income, *May 8, 2018*, CRA Document No. 2018-0745871C6; 2018 STEP Q6 – Excluded Shares – Holding Company, *May 29, 2018*, CRA Document No. 2018-0743971C6; STEP Question 5 - Tax on Split Income, *May 29, 2018*, CRA Document No. 2018-0743961C6; Tax on split income & preferred beneficiary, *July 6, 2018*, CRA Document No. 2018-0759521E5.

► 120.4(4) ◄

(4) Taxable capital gain. If a specified individual who has not attained the age of 17 years before a taxation year would have for the taxation year, if this Act were read without reference to this section, a taxable capital gain (other than an excluded amount) from a disposition of shares (other than shares of a class listed on a designated stock exchange or shares of a mutual fund corporation) that are transferred, either directly or indirectly, in any manner whatever, to a person with whom the specified individual does not deal at arm's length, then the amount of that taxable capital gain is deemed not to be a taxable capital gain and twice the amount is deemed to be received by the specified individual in the year as a taxable dividend that is not an eligible dividend.

Editorial Note: Since subsection 120.4(4) deems twice the taxable capital gain to be a dividend, it can constitute "split income" under paragraph (*a*) or (*c*) of that definition; see also the editorial note to subsection 120.4(2).

History: S. 120.4(4) was replaced by S.C. 2018, c. 12, s. 13(7), applicable to the 2018 and subsequent taxation years, and formerly read:

(4) *Taxable capital gain.* If a specified individual would have for a taxation year, if this Act were read without reference to this section, a taxable capital gain (other than an excluded amount) from a disposition of shares (other than shares of a class listed on a designated stock exchange or shares of a mutual fund corporation) that are transferred, either directly or indirectly, in any manner whatever, to a person with whom the specified individual does not deal at arm's length, then the amount of that taxable capital gain is deemed not to be a taxable capital gain and twice the amount is deemed to be received by the specified individual in the year as a taxable dividend that is not an eligible dividend.

S. 120.4(4) was added by S.C. 2011, c. 24, s. 36(2), applicable to dispositions that occur on or after March 22, 2011.

Canadian Tax Foundation: Thompson, *Revisiting the Attribution Rules*, 2013 British Columbia Tax Conference 12:1–24.

► 120.4(5) ◄

(5) Taxable capital gain of trust. If a specified individual who has not attained the age of 17 years before a the taxation year would be, if this Act were read without reference to this section, required under subsection 104(13) or 105(2) to include an amount in computing the specified individual's income for the taxation year, then to the extent that the amount can reasonably be considered to be attributable to a taxable capital gain (other than an excluded amount) of a trust from a disposition of shares (other than shares of a class listed on a designated stock exchange or shares of a mutual fund corporation) that are transferred, either directly or indirectly, in any manner whatever, to a person with whom the specified individual does not deal at arm's length, subsections 104(13) and 105(2) do not apply in respect of the amount and twice the amount is deemed to be received by the specified individual in the year as a taxable dividend that is not an eligible dividend.

Editorial Note: See the editorial note following s. 120.4(2).

History: S. 120.4(5) was replaced by S.C. 2018, c. 12, s. 13(7), applicable to the 2018 and subsequent taxation years, and formerly read:

(5) *Taxable capital gain of trust.* If a specified individual would be, if this Act were read without reference to this section, required under paragraph 104(13)(*a*) or subsection 105(2) to include an amount in computing the specified individual's income for a taxation year, then to the extent that the amount can reasonably be considered to be attributable to a taxable capital gain (other than an excluded amount) of a trust from a disposition of shares (other than shares of a class listed on a designated stock exchange or shares of a mutual fund corporation) that are transferred, either directly or indirectly, in any manner whatever, to a person with whom the specified individual does not deal at arm's length, paragraph 104(13)(*a*) and subsection 105(2) do not apply in respect of the amount and twice the amount is deemed to be received by the specified individual in the year as a taxable dividend that is not an eligible dividend.

S. 120.4(5) was added by S.C. 2011, c. 24, s. 36(2), applicable to dispositions that occur on or after March 22, 2011.

SECTION 121: Deduction for taxable dividends

There may be deducted from the tax otherwise payable under this Part by an individual for a taxation year the total of

(*a*) the product of the amount, if any, that is required by subparagraph 82(1)(*b*)(i) to be included in computing the individual's income for the year multiplied by

(i) for the 2018 taxation year, 8/11, and

(ii) for taxation years after 2018, 9/13, and

(*b*) the product of the amount, if any, that is required by subparagraph 82(1)(*b*)(ii) to be included in computing the individual's income for the year multiplied by

(i) for the 2009 taxation year, $^{11}/_{18}$,

(ii) for the 2010 taxation year, $^{10}/_{17}$,

(iii) for the 2011 taxation year, $^{13}/_{23}$, and

(iv) for taxation years after 2011, $^{6}/_{11}$.

Editorial Note: See the editorial note under s. 82(1).

History: S. 121(*a*) was replaced by S.C. 2018, c. 12, s. 14(1), applicable to the 2018 and subsequent taxation years, and formerly read:

(*a*) the product of the amount, if any, that is required by subparagraph 82(1)(*b*)(i) to be included in computing the individual's income for the year multiplied by 21/29, and

S. 121(*a*) was replaced by S.C. 2016, c. 7, s. 26(1), applicable to the 2016 and subsequent taxation years, and formerly read:

(*a*) the product of the amount, if any, that is required by subparagraph 82(1)(*b*)(i) to be included in computing the individual's income for the year multiplied by

(i) for the 2016 taxation year, 21/29,

(ii) for the 2017 and 2018 taxation years, 20/29, and

(iii) for taxation years after 2018, 9/13; and

S. 121(*a*) was replaced by S.C. 2015, c. 36, s. 10(1), applicable to the 2016 and subsequent taxation years, and formerly read:

(*a*) $^{13}/_{18}$ of the amount, if any, that is required by subparagraph 82(1)(*b*)(i) to be included in computing the individual's income for the year; and

S. 121(*a*) was replaced by S.C. 2013, c. 33, s. 11(1), applicable to dividends paid after 2013, and formerly read:

(*a*) $^{2}/_{3}$ of the amount, if any, that is required by subparagraph 82(1)(*b*)(i) to be included in computing the individual's income for the year; and

Related Sections: S. 56(8) CPP/QPP and UCCB benefits for previous years; s. 82(2) Certain dividends received by taxpayer; s. 89(1), "taxable dividends"; s. 126(7) Definitions; s. 248(1), "amount", "individual"; ITAR s. 40(1) Payments out of pension funds, etc.; 40(2) Employee not resident in Canada.

Tax Profile: October 2006 — New Rules for the Taxation of Dividends.

Tax Topics: No. 1809, New Tax on Income Trusts and Public Partnerships, Trick or treat — a taxing announcement.

Interpretation Bulletins: *Secondary* — IT-379R Employees profit sharing plan — Allocations to beneficiaries; IT-67R3 Taxable dividends from corporations resident in Canada; IT-295R4 Taxable dividends received after 1987 by a spouse; IT-524 Trusts — Flow-through of taxable dividends to a beneficiary — After 1987.

SECTION 122: Tax payable by trust

► 122(1) ◄

(1) Tax payable by trust. Notwithstanding section 117, the tax payable under this Part for a taxation year by a trust (other than a graduated rate estate or qualified disability trust) is the total of

(*a*) the highest individual percentage for the taxation year multiplied by the trust's amount taxable for the taxation year,

(*b*) if the trust is a SIFT trust for the taxation year, the positive or negative amount determined by the formula

$$A \times B$$

where

A is the positive or negative decimal fraction determined by the formula

$$C + D - E$$

where

C is the net corporate income tax rate in respect of the SIFT trust for the taxation year,

D is the provincial SIFT tax rate of the SIFT trust for the taxation year, and

E is the decimal fraction equivalent of the percentage rate of tax provided in paragraph (*a*) for the taxation year, and

B is the SIFT trust's taxable SIFT trust distributions for the taxation year, and

(c) if subsection (2) applies to the trust for the taxation year, the amount determined by the formula

$$A - (B - C)$$

where

A is the amount that would be determined for B for the year if

(i) the rate of tax payable under this Part by the trust for each taxation year referred to in the description of B were the highest individual percentage for the taxation year, and

(ii) the trust's taxable income for a particular taxation year referred to in the description of B were reduced by the total of

(A) the amount, if any, that was paid or distributed in satisfaction of all or part of an individual's interest as a beneficiary under the trust if

(I) the individual was an electing beneficiary of the trust for the particular year,

(II) the payment or distribution can reasonably be considered to be made out of that taxable income, and

(III) the payment or distribution was made in a taxation year referred to in the description of B,

(B) the amount that is the portion of the tax payable under this Part by the trust for the particular year that can reasonably be considered to relate to the amount determined under clause (A), and

(C) the amount that is the portion of the tax payable, under the law of the province in which the trust is resident for the particular year, that can reasonably be considered to relate to the amount determined under clause (A),

B is the total of all amounts each of which is the amount of tax payable under this Part by the trust for a taxation year that precedes the year if that preceding taxation year is

(i) the later of

(A) the first taxation year for which the trust was a qualified disability trust, and

(B) the last taxation year, if any, for which subsection (2) applied to the trust, or

(ii) a taxation year that ends after the taxation year described in subparagraph (i), and

C is the total of all amounts each of which is an amount determined for clause (ii)(B) of the description of A in determining the amount for A for the year.

Editorial Note: Subsection 122(1) applies flat top-rate taxation to *inter-vivos* trusts, and most testamentary trusts in the 2016 and subsequent taxation years. An exception is made for testamentary trusts that are "graduated rate estates" (generally, a deceased's estate for up to 36 months after death) and "qualified disability trusts" (see s. 122(3)).

By virtue of s. 122(1)(*b*), the tax rate for a SIFT trust in respect of its "taxable SIFT trust distributions" (s. 122(3)) will approximate the combined provincial and federal general corporate tax rate for the province of residence.

Paragraph 122(1)(*c*) provides a "recovery tax" that generally applies where a qualified disability trust no longer qualifies as such – more particularly, where subsection 122(2) applies to a taxation year. See the editorial note to s. 122(2).

History: S. 122(1)(*c*), the description of C was added by S.C. 2017, c. 33, s. 46(2), applicable to taxation years that end after September 15, 2016.

S. 122(1)(*c*), the formula was replaced by S.C. 2017, c. 33, s. 46(1), applicable to taxation years that end after September 15, 2016, and formerly read:

A - B

S. 122(1)(*c*), subparagraph (i) of the description of A was replaced by S.C. 2016, c. 7, s. 62(4), applicable to the 2016 and subsequent taxation years, and formerly read:

(i) the rate of tax payable under this Part by the trust for each taxation year referred to in the description of B were 29%, and

S. 122(1)(*a*) was replaced by S.C. 2016, c. 11, s. 5(1), applicable to the 2016 and subsequent taxation years, and formerly read:

(*a*) 29% of its amount taxable for the taxation year,

S. 122(1), the portion before paragraph (*a*) was replaced by S.C. 2014, c. 39, s. 38(1), applicable to the 2016 and subsequent taxation years and formerly read:

(1) *Tax payable by inter vivos trust.* Notwithstanding section 117, the tax payable under this Part for a taxation year by an *inter vivos* trust is the total of

S. 122(1)(*c*) was added by S.C. 2014, c. 39, s. 38(2), applicable to the 2016 and subsequent taxation years.

Related Sections: 122(3) qualified disability trust; 248(1) graduated rate estate; S. 104(1) Reference to trust or estate; s. 104(6) Deduction in computing income of trust; s. 104(16) SIFT deemed dividend; s. 108(1), "beneficiary", "inter vivos trust", "testamentary trust"; s. 122.1(1), "SIFT trust"; s. 132(6) Meaning of "mutual fund trust"; s. 248(1), "active business", "net corporate income tax rate", "property", "provincial tax factor", "provincial SIFT tax rate".

Canadian Tax Foundation: Watson, *The Future of Testamentary Trusts Under the Economic Action Plan 2016 and Beyond...*, 2014 Atlantic Provinces Tax Conference 8:1–24; McCue and Johnson, *Current Transactions: Cross-Border Income Trusts/Foreign Asset Investment Trusts*, 2012 Conference Report 8:1–33.

Tax Profile: September 2007 — U.S. and Canadian Tax Considerations in Acquiring Canadian Income Trusts; June 2007 — Canadian Income Trusts for Sale; January 2007 — Canadian Income Trusts — Guidance on Normal Growth Released; December 2006 — Major Changes to the Taxation of Income Trusts and Certain Flow-Through Entities.

Interpretation Bulletins: *Secondary* — IT-406R2 Tax payable by an *inter vivos* trust.

► 122(1.1) ◄

(1.1) Credits available to trusts. No deduction may be made under this subdivision (other than section 118.1, 120.2 or 121) in computing the tax payable by a trust for a taxation year.

History: S. 122(1.1) was replaced by S.C. 2014, c. 39, s. 38(3), applicable to the 2016 and subsequent taxation years, and formerly read:

(1.1) *Deductions not permitted.* No deduction may be made under section 118 in computing the tax payable by a trust for a taxation year.

► 122(2) ◄

(2) Qualified disability trust — application of (1)(c). This subsection applies to a trust for a particular taxation year if the trust was a qualified disability trust for a preceding taxation year and

(*a*) none of the beneficiaries under the trust at the end of the particular year was an electing beneficiary of the trust for a preceding year;

(*b*) the particular year ended immediately before the trust ceased to be resident in Canada; or

(*c*) an amount is paid or distributed in the particular year to a beneficiary under the trust in satisfaction of all or part of the beneficiary's interest in the trust unless

(i) the beneficiary is an electing beneficiary of the trust for the particular year or a preceding year,

(ii) the amount is deducted under paragraph 104(6)(*b*) in computing the trust's income for the particular year, or

(iii) the amount is paid or distributed in satisfaction of a right to enforce payment of an amount that was deducted under paragraph 104(6)(*b*) in computing the trust's income for a preceding year.

Editorial Note: Where one of the events in paragraphs (*a*) through (*c*) in s. 122(2) applies in a taxation year to a trust that was qualified disability trust in a previous year, the recovery tax in paragraph 122(1)(*c*) may apply to the trust in the year. The recovery tax, which is payable for the year but computed in respect of the previous years in which the trust was a qualified disability trust, generally equals the top marginal rate of tax applied to the previous year's taxable income (net of the part of such taxable income subsequently paid out as a distribution to an electing beneficiary and any tax already payable in respect of that part) minus the actual tax payable for the previous year. Basically, the intent of the recovery tax is to "top up" the tax payable in respect of those previous years where the after-tax income retained in the trust (after the prior application of graduated tax rates) was not distributed to an electing beneficiary.

History: S. 122(2) was replaced by S.C. 2014, c. 39, s. 38(3), applicable to the 2016 and subsequent taxation years, and formerly read:

(2) *Where subsection (1) does not apply.* Subsection (1) does not apply for a taxation year of an *inter vivos* trust that is not a mutual fund trust and that

(*a*) was established before June 18, 1971;

(*b*) was resident in Canada on June 18, 1971 and without interruption thereafter until the end of the year;

(*c*) did not carry on any active business in the year;

(*d*) has not received any property by way of gift since June 18, 1971;

(*d*.1) was not a trust to which a contribution (as defined by section 94 as it reads for taxation years that end after 2006) was made after June 22, 2000;

(*e*) has not, after June 18, 1971, incurred

(i) any debt, or

(ii) any other obligation to pay an amount,

to, or guaranteed by, any person with whom any beneficiary of the trust was not dealing at arm's length; and

(*f*) has not received any property after December 17, 1999, where

(i) the property was received as a result of a transfer from another trust,

(ii) subsection (1) applied to a taxation year of the other trust that began before the property was so received, and

(iii) no change in the beneficial ownership of the property resulted from the transfer.

S. 122(2)(*d*.1) was added by S.C. 2013, c. 34, s. 13(1), applicable to trust taxation years that begin after 2002.

S. 122(2), the portion before paragraph (*a*) was amended by S.C. 2013, c. 34, s. 257(1), applicable to trust taxation years that begin after 2002, and formerly read:

(2) *Where s. (1) does not apply.* Subsection (1) is not applicable for a taxation year of an *inter vivos* trust other than a mutual fund trust if the trust

Related Sections: 122(3) qualified disability trust; S. 104(1) Reference to trust or estate; s. 108(1), "inter vivos trust", "trust"; s. 132(6) Meaning of "mutual fund trust".

Interpretation Bulletins: *Primary* — IT-406R2 Tax payable by an *inter vivos* trust.

► 122(3) ◄

(3) Definitions. The following definitions apply in this section.

"beneficiary" —"beneficiary", under a trust, includes a person beneficially interested in the trust.

History: S. 122(3), the definition "beneficiary" was added by S.C. 2014, c. 39, s. 38(4), applicable to the 2016 and subsequent taxation years.

"electing beneficiary" —"electing beneficiary", for a taxation year of a qualified disability trust, means a beneficiary under the trust that for the year

(*a*) makes an election described in clause (*a*)(iii)(A) of the definition "qualified disability trust" in this subsection; and

(*b*) is described in paragraph (*b*) of that definition.

History: S. 122(3), the definition "electing beneficiary" was added by S.C. 2014, c. 39, s. 38(4), applicable to the 2016 and subsequent taxation years.

"non-deductible distributions amount" —"non-deductible distributions amount" for a taxation year has the meaning assigned by subsection 104(16).

Editorial Note: The "non-deductible distributions amount" of a SIFT trust is defined in s. 104(16) and generally reflects the trust's non-portfolio earnings that are payable to its beneficiaries, but are not deductible for the trust by virtue of the limitation in s. 104(6)(*b*)(iv). Such amount, when distributed to a beneficiary, is treated as an eligible dividend in the hands of the beneficiary.

"qualified disability trust" —"qualified disability trust", for a taxation year (in this definition referred to as the "trust year"), means a trust, if

(*a*) the trust

(i) is, at the end of the trust year, a testamentary trust that arose on and as a consequence of a particular individual's death,

(ii) is resident in Canada for the trust year, and

(iii) includes in its return of income under this Part for the trust year

(A) an election, made jointly with one or more beneficiaries under the trust in prescribed form, to be a qualified disability trust for the trust year, and

(B) the Social Insurance Number of each of those beneficiaries;

(*b*) each of those beneficiaries is an individual, named as a beneficiary by the particular individual in the instrument under which the trust was created,

(i) in respect of whom paragraphs 118.3(1)(*a*) to (*b*) apply for the individual's taxation year (in this definition referred to as the "beneficiary year") in which the trust year ends, and

(ii) who does not jointly elect with any other trust, for a taxation year of the other trust that ends in the beneficiary year, to be a qualified disability trust; and

(*c*) subsection (2) does not apply to the trust for the trust year.

History: S. 122(3), the definition "qualified disability trust" was added by S.C. 2014, c. 39, s. 38(4), applicable to the 2016 and subsequent taxation years.

Tax Window Files: 2016 STEP - Q4 - QDT & pref beneficiary election, *June 10, 2016*, CRA Document No. 2016-0645801C6.

"taxable SIFT trust distributions" —"taxable SIFT trust distributions", of a SIFT trust for a taxation year, means the lesser of

(*a*) its amount taxable for the taxation year, and

(*b*) the amount determined by the formula

$$A/(1 - (B + C))$$

where

A is its non-deductible distributions amount for the taxation year,

B is the net corporate income tax rate in respect of the SIFT trust for the taxation year, and

C is the provincial SIFT tax rate of the SIFT trust for the taxation year.

Editorial Note: The "taxable SIFT trust distributions" of a SIFT trust are effectively subject to the applicable combined provincial and federal general corporate tax rate by virtue of s. 122(1).

SECTION 122.1: [Specified investment flow-through ("SIFT") trust]

► 122.1(1) ◄

(1) Definitions. The following definitions apply in this section and in sections 104 and 122.

Canadian Petroleum Tax Journal: The Sift Rules: An Oil & Gas Perspective, Hegedus, 2007, Vol. 20, No. 1.

Tax Profile: May 2007 — Income Trusts and REIT Update.

"eligible resale property" —"eligible resale property", of an entity, means real or immovable property (other than capital property) of the entity

(*a*) that is contiguous to a particular real or immovable property that is capital property or eligible resale property, held by

(i) the entity, or

(ii) another entity affiliated with the entity; and

(*b*) the holding of which is ancillary to the holding of the particular property.

History: S. 122.1(1), the definition "eligible resale property" was added by S.C. 2013, c. 34, s. .258(11), applicable to (*a*) taxation years of a trust that end after 2006 and before 2011 if

(i) investments in the trust are, in one or more of those taxation years, listed or traded on a stock exchange or other public market, and

(ii) the trust elects, by notifying the Minister of National Revenue in writing on or before its filing due-date for its taxation year that includes June 26, 2013, to have those subsections so apply; and

(*b*) the 2011 and subsequent taxation years.

"entity" —"entity" means a corporation, trust or partnership.

"equity" —"equity", of an entity, means

(*a*) if the entity is a corporation, a share of the capital stock of the corporation;

(*b*) if the entity is a trust, an income or capital interest in the trust;

(*c*) if the entity is a partnership, an interest as a member of the partnership;

(*d*) a liability of the entity (and, for purposes of the definition "publicly-traded liability" in this section, a security of the entity that is a liability of another entity) if

(i) the liability is convertible into, or exchangeable for, equity of the entity or of another entity, or

(ii) any amount paid or payable in respect of the liability is contingent or dependent on the use of or production from property, or is computed by reference to revenue, profit, cash flow, commodity price or any other similar criterion or by reference to dividends paid or payable to shareholders of any class of shares of the capital stock of a corporation, or to income or capital paid or payable to any member of a partnership or beneficiary under a trust; and

(*e*) a right to, or to acquire, anything described in this paragraph and any of paragraphs (*a*) to (*d*).

History: S. 122.1(1), the definition "equity" was added by S.C. 2009, c. 2, s. 36(8), deemed to have come into force on October 31, 2006.

Related Sections: S. 104(1) Reference to trust or estate; s. 108(1), "capital interest".

"equity value" —"equity value", of an entity at any time, means the total fair market value at that time of

(*a*) if the entity is a corporation, all of the issued and outstanding shares of the capital stock of the corporation;

(*b*) if the entity is a trust, all of the income or capital interests in the trust; or

(*c*) if the entity is a partnership, all of the interests in the partnership.

"excluded subsidiary entity" —"excluded subsidiary entity", for a taxation year, means an entity none of the equity of which is at any time in the taxation year

(*a*) listed or traded on a stock exchange or other public market; nor

(*b*) held by any person or partnership other than

(i) a real estate investment trust,

(ii) a taxable Canadian corporation,

(iii) a SIFT trust (determined without reference to subsection (2)),

(iv) a SIFT partnership (determined without reference to subsection 197(8)),

(v) a person or partnership that does not have, in connection with the holding of a security of the entity, property the value of which is determined, all or in part, by reference to a security that is listed or traded on a stock exchange or other public market, or

(vi) an excluded subsidiary entity for the taxation year.

History: S. 122.1(1), paragraph (*b*) of the definition "excluded subsidiary entity" was amended by S.C. 2013, c. 40, s. 51(2) by replacing subparagraph (v) and adding subparagagph (vi), deemed to have come into force on October 31, 2006. However, it does not apply for the purpose of determining if an entity is an excluded subsidiary entity for taxation years of the entity that began before July 21, 2011 if the entity so elects in writing filed with the Minister of National Revenue by December 12, 2014 (within 365 days after the day on which this amendment receives royal assent).

S. 122.1(1), paragraph (*b*)(v) of the definition "excluded subsidiary entity" formerly read:

(v) an excluded subsidiary entity for the taxation year.

S. 122.1(1), the definition "excluded subsidiary entity" was added by S.C. 2009, c. 2, s. 36(8), deemed to have come into force on October 31, 2006.

"gross REIT revenue" —"gross REIT revenue", of an entity for a taxation year, means the amount, if any, by which the total of all amounts received or receivable in the year (depending on the method regularly followed by the entity in computing the entity's income) by the entity exceeds the total of all amounts each of which is the cost to the entity of a property disposed of in the year.

History: S. 122.1(1), the definition "gross REIT revenue" was added by S.C. 2013, c. 34, s. 258(11), applicable to

(*a*) taxation years of a trust that end after 2006 and before 2011 if

(i) investments in the trust are, in one or more of those taxation years, listed or traded on a stock exchange or other public market, and

(ii) the trust elects, by notifying the Minister of National Revenue in writing on or before its filing due-date for its taxation year that includes June 26, 2013, to have those subsections so apply; and

(*b*) the 2011 and subsequent taxation years.

"investment" —"investment", in a trust or partnership,

(*a*) means

(i) a property that is a security of the trust or partnership, or

(ii) a right which may reasonably be considered to replicate a return on, or the value of, a security of the trust or partnership; but

(*b*) does not include

(i) an unaffiliated publicly-traded liability of the trust or partnership, nor

(ii) regulated innovative capital.

History: S. 122.1(1), the definition "investment" was replaced by S.C. 2009, c. 2, s. 36(1), deemed to have come into force on October 31, 2006. S. 122.1(1), the definition "investment" formerly read:

"investment"—"investment", in a trust or partnership, means

(*a*) a property that is a security of the trust or partnership; or

(*b*) a right which may reasonably be considered to replicate a return on, or the value of, a security of the trust or partnership.

"non-portfolio earnings" —"non-portfolio earnings", of a SIFT trust for a taxation year, means the total of

(*a*) the amount, if any, by which

(i) the total of all amounts each of which is the SIFT trust's income for the taxation year from a business carried on by it in Canada or from a non-portfolio property, other than income that is a taxable dividend received by the SIFT trust,

exceeds

(ii) the total of all amounts each of which is the SIFT trust's loss for the taxation year from a business carried on by it in Canada or from a non-portfolio property, and

(*b*) the amount, if any, by which

(i) the total of

(A) all taxable capital gains of the SIFT trust from dispositions of non-portfolio properties during the taxation year, and

(B) one-half of the total of all amounts each of which is deemed under subsection 131(1) to be a capital gain of the SIFT trust for the taxation year in respect of a non-portfolio property of the SIFT trust for the taxation year

exceeds

(ii) the total of the allowable capital losses of the SIFT trust for the taxation year from dispositions of non-portfolio properties during the taxation year.

Editorial Note: Generally speaking, the "non-portfolio earnings" of a SIFT trust are not deductible by the trust if distributed to its beneficiaries (s. 104(6)(*b*)(iv)). The amounts so distributed but not deductible, referred to as the trust's "non-deductible distributions amount" for the taxation year (s. 104(16)), are treated as taxable eligible dividends in the hands of the recipient beneficiaries of the trust.

Related Sections: S. 104(6) Deduction in computing income of trust; s. 104(16) SIFT deemed dividend; s. 122(1) Tax payable by inter vivos trust; s. 122(3), "non-deductible distributions amount"; s. 197(1), "non-portfolio earnings".

Canadian Tax Foundation: McCue and Johnson, *Current Transactions: Cross-Border Income Trusts/Foreign Asset Investment Trusts*, 2012 Conference Report 8:1–33.

Income Tax Technical News: Issue No. 38, Definition of "Non-Portfolio Earnings" in Subsection 122.1(1).

"non-portfolio property" —"non-portfolio property", of a particular entity for a taxation year, means a property, held by the particular entity at any time in the taxation year, that is

(*a*) a security of a subject entity (other than a portfolio investment entity), if at that time the particular entity holds

(i) securities of the subject entity that have a total fair market value that is greater than 10% of the equity value of the subject entity, or

(ii) securities of the subject entity that, together with all the securities that the particular entity holds of entities affiliated with the subject entity, have a total fair market value that is greater than 50% of the equity value of the particular entity;

(*b*) a Canadian real, immovable or resource property, if at any time in the taxation year the total fair market value of all properties held by the particular entity that are Canadian real, immovable or resource properties is greater than 50% of the equity value of the particular entity; or

(*c*) a property that the particular entity, or a person or partnership with whom the particular entity does not deal at arm's length, uses at that time in the course of carrying on a business in Canada.

History: S. 122.1(1), the definition "non-portfolio property" was replaced by S.C. 2013, c. 40, s. 51(1), applicable to taxation years that end after July 20, 2011, and formerly read:

"non-portfolio property"—"non-portfolio property" of a trust or partnership for a taxation year means a property, held by the trust or partnership at any time in the taxation year, that is

(*a*) a security of a subject entity (other than a portfolio investment entity), if at that time the trust or partnership holds

(i) securities of the subject entity that have a total fair market value that is greater than 10% of the equity value of the subject entity, or

(ii) securities of the subject entity that, together with all of the securities that the trust or partnership holds of entities affiliated with the subject entity, have a total fair market value that is greater than 50% of the equity value of the trust or partnership;

(*b*) a Canadian real, immovable or resource property, if at any time in the taxation year the total fair market value of all properties held by the trust or partnership that are Canadian real, immovable or resource properties is greater than 50% of the equity value of the trust or partnership; or

(*c*) a property that the trust or partnership, or a person or partnership with whom the trust or partnership does not deal at arm's length, uses at that time in the course of carrying on a business in Canada.

S. 122.1(1), the portion of paragraph (*a*) before subparagraph (i) of the definition "non-portfolio property" was replaced by S.C. 2009, c. 2, s. 36(2), deemed to have come into force on October 31, 2006. S. 122.1(1), the portion of paragraph (*a*) before subparagraph (i) of the definition "non-portfolio property" formerly read:

(*a*) a security of a subject entity, if at that time the trust or partnership holds

Related Sections: S. 248(1), "Canadian real, immovable or resource property".

Tax Profile: August 2013 — Canadian Syndication of Foreign Income-Producing Real Estate.

"portfolio investment entity" —"portfolio investment entity" at any time means an entity that does not at that time hold any non-portfolio property.

History: S. 122.1(1), the definition "portfolio investment entity" was added by S.C. 2009, c. 2, s. 36(8), deemed to have come into force on October 31, 2006.

"publicly-traded liability" —"publicly-traded liability", of an entity, means a liability that is a security of the entity, that is not equity of the entity and that is listed or traded on a stock exchange or other public market.

History: S. 122.1(1), the definition "publicly-traded liability" was added by S.C. 2009, c. 2, s. 36(8), deemed to have come into force on October 31, 2006.

"public market" —"public market" includes any trading system or other organized facility on which securities that are qualified for public distribution are listed or traded, but does not include a facility that is operated solely to carry out the issuance of a security or its redemption, acquisition or cancellation by its issuer.

Canadian Tax Foundation: Sherman and Freeman, *The Gift of SIFT*, 2007 Conference Report 14:1–31.

"qualified REIT property" —"qualified REIT property", of a trust at any time, means a property that, at that time, is held by the trust and is

(*a*) a real or immovable property that is capital property, an eligible resale property, an indebtedness of a Canadian corporation represented by a bankers' acceptance, a property described by paragraph (*a*) or (*b*) of the definition "qualified investment" in section 204 or a deposit with a credit union;

(*b*) a security of a subject entity all or substantially all of the gross REIT revenue of which, for its taxation year that ends in the trust's taxation year that includes that time, is from maintaining, improving, leasing or managing real or immovable properties that are capital properties of the trust or of an entity of which the trust holds a share or an interest, including real or immovable properties that the trust, or an entity of which the trust holds a share or an interest, holds together with one or more other persons or partnerships;

(*c*) a security of a subject entity, if the entity holds no property other than

(i) legal title to real or immovable property of the trust or of another subject entity all of the securities of which are held by the trust (including real or immovable property that the trust or the other subject entity holds together with one or more other persons or partnerships), and

(ii) property described in paragraph (*d*); or

(*d*) ancillary to the earning by the trust of amounts described in subparagraphs (*b*)(i) and (iii) of the definition "real estate investment trust", other than

(i) an equity of an entity, or

(ii) a mortgage, hypothecary claim, mezzanine loan or similar obligation.

History: S. 122.1(1), the portion of the definition "qualified REIT property" before paragraph (*c*) was replaced by S.C. 2013, c. 34, s. 258(1), applicable to

(*a*) taxation years of a trust that end after 2006 and before 2011 if

(i) investments in the trust are, in one or more of those taxation years, listed or traded on a stock exchange or other public market, and

(ii) the trust elects, by notifying the Minister of National Revenue in writing on or before its filing due-date for its taxation year that includes June 26, 2013, to have those subsections so apply; and

(*b*) the 2011 and subsequent taxation years.

S. 122.1(1), the portion of the definition "qualified REIT property" before paragraph (*c*) formerly read:

"qualified REIT property"—"qualified REIT property" of a trust means a property, held by the trust, that is

(*a*) a real or immovable property;

(*b*) a security of a subject entity, if the entity derives all or substantially all of its revenues from maintaining, improving, leasing or managing real or immovable properties that are capital properties of the trust or of an entity of which the trust holds a share or an interest, including real or immovable properties that the trust, or an entity of which the trust holds a share or an interest, holds together with one or more other persons or partnerships;

S. 122.1(1), paragraph (*d*) of the definition "qualified REIT property" was replaced by S.C. 2013, c. 34, s. 258(2), applicable to

(*a*) taxation years of a trust that end after 2006 and before 2011 if

(i) investments in the trust are, in one or more of those taxation years, listed or traded on a stock exchange or other public market, and

(ii) the trust elects, by notifying the Minister of National Revenue in writing on or before its filing due-date for its taxation year that includes June 26, 2013, to have those subsections so apply; and

(*b*) the 2011 and subsequent taxation years.

S. 122.1(1), paragraph (*d*) of the definition "qualified REIT property" formerly read:

(*d*) ancillary to the earning by the trust of the amounts described in subparagraphs (*b*)(i) and (iii) of the definition "real estate investment trust".

S. 122.1(1), paragraph (*a*) of the definition "qualified REIT property" was replaced by S.C. 2009, c. 2, s. 36(3), deemed to have come into force on October 31, 2006. S. 122.1(1), paragraph (*a*) of the definition "qualified REIT property" formerly read:

(*a*) a real or immovable property situated in Canada;

S. 122.1(1), subparagraph (*c*)(i) of the definition "qualified REIT property" was replaced by S.C. 2009, c. 2, s. 36(4), deemed to have come into force on October 31, 2006. S. 122.1(1), paragraph (*a*) of the definition "qualified REIT property" formerly read:

(i) legal title to real or immovable property of the trust (including real or immovable property that the trust holds together with one or more other persons or partnerships), and

Tax Window Files: Qualified REIT Property— Roads and Sewers, *April 15, 2009*, CRA Document No. 2007-0255861E5.

Sec. 122.1(1) *"real estate investment trust"*

"real estate investment trust"—"real estate investment trust", for a taxation year, means a trust that is resident in Canada throughout the taxation year, if

(*a*) at each time in the taxation year the total fair market value at that time of all non-portfolio properties that are qualified REIT properties held by the trust is at least 90% of the total fair market value at that time of all non-portfolio properties held by the trust;

(*b*) not less than 90% of the trust's gross REIT revenue for the taxation year is from one or more of the following:

(i) rent from real or immovable properties,

(ii) interest,

(iii) dispositions of real or immovable properties that are capital properties,

(iv) dividends,

(v) royalties, and

(vi) dispositions of eligible resale properties;

(*c*) not less than 75% of the trust's gross REIT revenue for the taxation year is from one or more of the following:

(i) rent from real or immovable properties,

(ii) interest from mortgages, or hypothecs, on real or immovable properties, and

(iii) dispositions of real or immovable properties that are capital properties;

(*d*) at each time in the taxation year an amount, that is equal to 75% or more of the equity value of the trust at that time, is the amount that is the total fair market value of all properties held by the trust each of which is a real or immovable property that is capital property, an eligible resale property, an indebtedness of a Canadian corporation represented by a bankers' acceptance, a property described by paragraph (*a*) or (*b*) of the definition "qualified investment" in section 204 or a deposit with a credit union; and

(*e*) investments in the trust are, at any time in the taxation year, listed or traded on a stock exchange or other public market.

Editorial Note: A "real estate investment trust" is excluded from the definition of "SIFT trust" and therefore is not subject to the corporate tax-type regime that is imposed on SIFT trusts (i.e., under s. 122(1), s. 104(6)(*b*)(iv), and s. 104(16)). Thus, income distributed by the real estate investment trust is generally deductible by the trust and therefore not subject to tax at the trust level.

History: S. 122.1(1), paragraph (*a*) of the definition "real estate investment trust" was replaced by S.C. 2013, c. 34, s. 258(3), applicable to

(*a*) taxation years of a trust that end after 2006 and before 2011 if

(i) investments in the trust are, in one or more of those taxation years, listed or traded on a stock exchange or other public market, and

(ii) the trust elects, by notifying the Minister of National Revenue in writing on or before its filing due-date for its taxation year that includes June 26, 2013, to have those subsections so apply; and

(*b*) the 2011 and subsequent taxation years.

S. 122.1(1), paragraph (*a*) of the definition "real estate investment trust" formerly read:

(*a*) the trust at no time in the taxation year holds any non-portfolio property other than qualified REIT properties;

S. 122.1(1), the portion of paragraph (*b*) of the definition "real estate investment trust" before subparagraph (i) was replaced by S.C. 2013, c. 34, s. 258(4), applicable to

(*a*) taxation years of a trust that end after 2006 and before 2011 if

(i) investments in the trust are, in one or more of those taxation years, listed or traded on a stock exchange or other public market, and

(ii) the trust elects, by notifying the Minister of National Revenue in writing on or before its filing due-date for its taxation year that includes June 26, 2013, to have those subsections so apply; and

(*b*) the 2011 and subsequent taxation years.

S. 122.1(1), the portion of paragraph (*b*) of the definition "real estate investment trust" before subparagraph (i) formerly read:

(*b*) not less than 95% of the trust's revenues for the taxation year are derived from one or more of the following:

S. 122.1(1), subparagraph (*b*)(iii) of the definition "real estate investment trust" was replaced by S.C. 2013, c. 34, s. 258(5), applicable to

(*a*) taxation years of a trust that end after 2006 and before 2011 if

(i) investments in the trust are, in one or more of those taxation years, listed or traded on a stock exchange or other public market, and

(ii) the trust elects, by notifying the Minister of National Revenue in writing on or before its filing due-date for its taxation year that includes June 26, 2013, to have those subsections so apply; and

(*b*) the 2011 and subsequent taxation years.

S. 122.1(1), subparagraph (*b*)(iii) of the definition "real estate investment trust" formerly read:

(iii) capital gains from dispositions of real or immovable properties,

S. 122.1(1), subparagraph (*b*)(vi) of the definition "real estate investment trust" was added by S.C. 2013, c. 34, s. 258(6), applicable to

(*a*) taxation years of a trust that end after 2006 and before 2011 if

(i) investments in the trust are, in one or more of those taxation years, listed or traded on a stock exchange or other public market, and

(ii) the trust elects, by notifying the Minister of National Revenue in writing on or before its filing due-date for its taxation year that includes June 26, 2013, to have those subsections so apply; and

(*b*) the 2011 and subsequent taxation years.

S. 122.1(1), the portion of paragraph (*c*) of the definition "real estate investment trust" before subparagraph (i) was replaced by S.C. 2013, c. 34, s. 258(7), applicable to

(*a*) taxation years of a trust that end after 2006 and before 2011 if

(i) investments in the trust are, in one or more of those taxation years, listed or traded on a stock exchange or other public market, and

(ii) the trust elects, by notifying the Minister of National Revenue in writing on or before its filing due-date for its taxation year that includes June 26, 2013, to have those subsections so apply; and

(*b*) the 2011 and subsequent taxation years.

S. 122.1(1), the portion of paragraph (*c*) of the definition "real estate investment trust" before subparagraph (i) formerly read:

(*c*) not less than 75% of the trust's revenues for the taxation year are derived from one or more of the following:

S. 122.1(1), subparagraph (*c*)(iii) of the definition "real estate investment trust" was replaced by S.C. 2013, c. 34, s. 258(8), applicable to

(*a*) taxation years of a trust that end after 2006 and before 2011 if

(i) investments in the trust are, in one or more of those taxation years, listed or traded on a stock exchange or other public market, and

(ii) the trust elects, by notifying the Minister of National Revenue in writing on or before its filing due-date for its taxation year that includes June 26, 2013, to have those subsections so apply; and

(*b*) the 2011 and subsequent taxation years.

S. 122.1(1), subparagraph (*c*)(iii) of the definition "real estate investment trust" formerly read:

(iii) capital gains from dispositions of real or immovable properties; and

S. 122.1(1), paragraph (*d*) of the definition "real estate investment trust" was replaced and paragraph (*e*) was added by S.C. 2013, c. 34, s. 258(9), applicable to

(*a*) taxation years of a trust that end after 2006 and before 2011 if

(i) investments in the trust are, in one or more of those taxation years, listed or traded on a stock exchange or other public market, and

(ii) the trust elects, by notifying the Minister of National Revenue in writing on or before its filing due-date for its taxation year that includes June 26, 2013, to have those subsections so apply; and

(*b*) the 2011 and subsequent taxation years, except that s. 122.1(1), paragraph (*d*) of the definition "real estate investment trust" is to be read as follows for taxation years that end before 2013:

(*d*) at each time in the taxation year an amount, that is equal to 75% or more of the equity value of the trust at that time, is the amount that is the total fair market value of all properties held by the trust each of which is real or immovable property, indebtedness of a Canadian corporation represented by a bankers' acceptance, property described by either paragraph (*a*) or (*b*) of the definition "qualified investment" in section 204, or a deposit with a credit union; and

S. 122.1(1), paragraph (*d*) of the definition "real estate investment trust" formerly read:

(*d*) at each time in the taxation year an amount, that is equal to 75% or more of the equity value of the trust at that time, is the amount that is the total fair market value of all properties held by the trust each of which is real or immovable property, indebtedness of a Canadian corporation represented by a bankers' acceptance, property described by either paragraph (*a*) or (*b*) of the definition "qualified investment" in section 204, or a deposit with a credit union.

S. 122.1(1), paragraphs (*c*) and (*d*) of the definition "real estate investment trust" were replaced by S.C. 2009, c. 2, s. 36(5), deemed to have come into force on October 31, 2006. S. 122.1(1), paragraphs (*c*) and (*d*) of the definition "real estate investment trust" formerly read:

(*c*) not less than 75% of the trust's revenues for the taxation year are derived from one or more of the following:

(i) rent from real or immovable properties, to the extent that it is derived from real or immovable properties situated in Canada,

(ii) interest from mortgages, or hypothecs, on real or immovable properties situated in Canada, and

(iii) capital gains from dispositions of real or immovable properties situated in Canada; and

(*d*) at no time in the taxation year is the total fair market value of all properties held by the trust, each of which is a real or immovable property situated in Canada, cash, or a property described in paragraph (*a*) of the definition "fully exempt interest" in subsection 212(3), less than 75% of the equity value of the trust at that time.

Canadian Tax Foundation: Kraus et al., *Update on Real Estate Investment Trusts and Structuring Public Vehicles for Investment in Canadian and Foreign Real Estate*, 2013 Conference Report 15:1–64; Chagnon and Provost, *Cross-Border Canadian Real Estate Investment Trusts*, 2011 Conference Report 22:1–25; Berry and Freeman, *Righting REITs*, 2008 Conference Report 17:1–18.

Tax Profile: August 2013 — Canadian Syndication of Foreign Income-Producing Real Estate.

Tax Topics: No. 1867-68, 2007 Canadian Tax Foundation Annual Conference CRA Round Table.

Income Tax Technical News: Issue No. 38, SIFT Entities — Definition of "Real Estate Investment Trust" in Section 122.1.

"real or immovable property" —"real or immovable property", of a taxpayer,

(*a*) includes

(i) a security held by the taxpayer, if the security is a security of a trust that satisfies (or of any other entity that would, if it were a trust, satisfy) the conditions set out in paragraphs (*a*) to (*d*) of the definition "real estate investment trust", or

(ii) an interest in real property or a real right in immovables (other than a right to a rental or royalty described in paragraph (*d*) or (*e*) of the definition "Canadian resource property" in subsection 66(15)); but

(*b*) does not include any depreciable property, other than

(i) a property included, otherwise than by an election permitted by regulation, in Class 1, 3 or 31 of Schedule II to the *Income Tax Regulations*,

(ii) a property ancillary to the ownership or utilization of a property described in subparagraph (i), or

(iii) a lease in, or a leasehold interest in respect of, land or property described in subparagraph (i).

Canadian Tax Foundation: Kraus et al., *Update on Real Estate Investment Trusts and Structuring Public Vehicles for Investment in Canadian and Foreign Real Estate*, 2013 Conference Report 15:1–64.

"regulated innovative capital" —"regulated innovative capital" means equity of a trust, where

(*a*) since November 2006, the equity has been authorized, by the Superintendent of Financial Institutions or by a provincial regulatory authority having powers similar to those of the Superintendent, as Tier 1 or Tier 2 capital of a financial institution (as defined by subsection 181(1));

(*b*) the terms and conditions of the equity have not changed after August 1, 2008;

(*c*) the trust has not issued any equity after October 31, 2006; and

(*d*) the trust does not hold any non-portfolio property other than

(i) liabilities of the financial institution, and

(ii) shares of the capital stock of the financial institution that were acquired by the trust for the sole purpose of satisfying a right to require the trust to accept, as demanded by a holder of the equity, the surrender of the equity.

History: S. 122.1(1), the definition "regulated innovative capital" was added by S.C. 2009, c. 2, s. 36(8), deemed to have come into force on October 31, 2006.

"rent from real or immovable properties" —"rent from real or immovable properties"

(*a*) includes

(i) rent or similar payments for the use of, or right to use, real or immovable properties, and

(ii) payment for services ancillary to the rental of real or immovable properties and customarily supplied or rendered in connection with the rental of real or immovable properties, but

(iii) (Repealed by S.C. 2013, c. 34, s. 258(10).)

(*b*) does not include

(i) payment for services supplied or rendered, other than those described in subparagraph (*a*)(ii), to the tenants of such properties,

(ii) fees for managing or operating such properties,

(iii) payment for the occupation of, use of, or right to use a room in a hotel or other similar lodging facility, or

(iv) rent based on profits.

History: S. 122.1(1), paragraph (*a*)(iii) of the definition "rent from real or immovable properties" was repealed by S.C. 2013, c. 34, s. 258(10), applicable to

(*a*) taxation years of a trust that end after 2006 and before 2011 if

(i) investments in the trust are, in one or more of those taxation years, listed or traded on a stock exchange or other public market, and

(ii) the trust elects, by notifying the Minister of National Revenue in writing on or before its filing due-date for its taxation year that includes June 26, 2013, to have those subsections so apply; and

(*b*) the 2011 and subsequent taxation years.

S. 122.1(1), paragraph (*a*)(iii) of the definition "rent from real or immovable properties" formerly read:

(iii) a payment that is included under paragraph 104(13)(*a*) in computing the recipient's income and that was made from the part of a trust's income (determined without reference to subsection 104(6)) that was derived from rent from real or immovable properties; but

S. 122.1(1), subparagraph (*a*)(ii) of the definition "rent from real or immovable properties" was replaced, and subparagraph (iii) was added, by S.C. 2009, c. 2, s. 36(6), deemed to have come into force on October 31, 2006. S. 122.1(1), subparagraph (*a*)(ii) of the definition "rent from real or immovable properties" formerly read:

(ii) payment for services ancillary to the rental of real or immovable properties and customarily supplied or rendered in connection with the rental of real or immovable properties; but

"security" —"security" of a particular entity means any right, whether absolute or contingent, conferred by the particular entity or by an entity that is affiliated with the particular entity, to receive, either immediately or in the future, an amount that can reasonably be regarded as all or any part of the capital, of the revenue or of the income of the particular entity, or as interest paid or payable by the particular entity, and for greater certainty includes

(*a*) a liability of the particular entity;

(*b*) if the particular entity is a corporation,

(i) a share of the capital stock of the corporation, and

(ii) a right to control in any manner whatever the voting rights of a share of the capital stock of the corporation;

(*c*) if the particular entity is a trust, an income or a capital interest in the trust;

(*d*) if the particular entity is a partnership, an interest as a member of the partnership; and

(*e*) a right to, or to acquire, anything described in this paragraph and any of paragraphs (*a*) to (*d*).

"SIFT trust" —"SIFT trust", being a specified investment flow-through trust, for a taxation year means a trust (other than an excluded subsidiary entity, or a real estate investment trust, for the taxation year) that meets the following conditions at any time during the taxation year:

(*a*) the trust is resident in Canada;

(*b*) investments in the trust are listed or traded on a stock exchange or other public market; and

(*c*) the trust holds one or more non-portfolio properties.

Editorial Note: Generally speaking, a trust that is a "SIFT trust" for a taxation year, being a specified investment flow-through trust, is subject to tax under s. 122(1) on the before-tax amount of its non-portfolio earnings that are payable to its beneficiaries in the taxation year at a rate that approximates the general corporate tax rate of the province of residence. "Non-portfolio earnings" include the SIFT trust's net income from businesses it carries on in Canada, its net income from non-portfolio properties other than taxable dividends, and its taxable capital gains in excess of its allowable capital losses from dispositions of non-portfolio properties.

A SIFT trust is prohibited from deducting its non-portfolio earnings for a taxation year that are payable to its beneficiaries in the year (s. 104(6)(*b*)(iv)). The amounts so payable but not deductible, referred to in the aggregate as the trust's "non-deductible distributions amount" for the taxation year, are treated as taxable eligible dividends in the hands of the recipient beneficiaries of the trust (s. 104(16) and the definition of "eligible dividend" in s. 89(1)). Accordingly, the after-tax non-portfolio earnings of the trust that are distributed to its beneficiaries are treated similarly to the after-tax income of a public corporation that is distributed to its shareholders as taxable dividends.

A trust that otherwise would have been a SIFT trust on October 31, 2006 (the date the SIFT trust rules were first announced) is exempt from the SIFT trust taxation regime for taxation years that ended prior to 2011, assuming it did not exceed the normal growth guidelines referred to in s. 122.1(2).

History: S. 122.1(1), the portion of the definition "SIFT trust" before paragraph (*a*) was replaced by S.C. 2009, c. 2, s. 36(7), deemed to have come into force on October 31, 2006. S. 122.1(1), the portion of the definition "SIFT trust" before paragraph (*a*) formerly read:

"SIFT trust"—"SIFT trust", being a specified investment flow-through trust, for a taxation year means a trust (other than a trust that is a real estate investment trust for the taxation year) that meets the following conditions at any time during the taxation year:

Related Sections: S. 88.1(2) SIFT trust wind-up event; s. 107(3.1) SIFT trust wind-up event; s. 197(1), "SIFT partnership"; s. 248(1), "SIFT trust wind-up event", "SIFT wind-up entity".

Tax Window Files: SIFT Trusts, *February 9, 2010*, CRA Document No. 2008-0301681E5.

"subject entity" —"subject entity" means a person or partnership that is

(*a*) a corporation resident in Canada;

(*b*) a trust resident in Canada;

(*c*) a Canadian resident partnership; or

(*d*) a non-resident person, or a partnership that is not described in paragraph (*c*), the principal source of income of which is one or any combination of sources in Canada.

"unaffiliated publicly-traded liability" —"unaffiliated publicly-traded liability", of an entity at any time means a publicly-traded liability of the entity if, at that time the total fair market value of all publicly-traded liabilities of the entity that are held at that time by persons or partnerships that are not affiliated with the entity is at least 90% of the total fair market value of all publicly-traded liabilities of the entity.

History: S. 122.1(1), the definition "unaffiliated publicly-traded liability" was added by S.C. 2009, c. 2, s. 36(8), deemed to have come into force on October 31, 2006.

► 122.1(1.1) ◄

(1.1) Application of subsection (1.2). Subsection (1.2) applies to an entity for a taxation year in respect of an amount and another entity (referred to in this subsection and subsection (1.2) as the "parent entity", "specified amount" and "source entity", respectively), if

(*a*) at any time in the taxation year the parent entity

(i) is affiliated with the source entity, or

(ii) holds securities of the source entity that

(A) are described by any of paragraphs (*a*) to (*c*) of the definition "equity" in subsection (1), and

(B) have a total fair market value that is greater than 10% of the equity value of the source entity;

(*b*) the specified amount is included in computing the parent entity's gross REIT revenue for the taxation year in respect of a security of the source entity held by the parent entity; and

(*c*) in the case of a source entity that is a subject entity described in paragraph (*b*) of the definition "qualified REIT property" in subsection (1) in respect of the parent entity at each time during the taxation year at which the parent entity holds securities of the source entity, the specified amount cannot reasonably be considered to be derived from the source entity's gross REIT revenue from maintaining, improving, leasing or managing real or immovable properties that are capital properties of the parent entity or of an entity of which the parent entity holds a share or an interest, including real or immovable properties that the parent entity, or an entity of which the parent entity holds a share or an interest, holds together with one or more other persons or partnerships.

History: S. 122.1(1.1) was added by S.C. 2013, c. 34, s. 258(12), applicable to

(*a*) taxation years of a trust that end after 2006 and before 2011 if

(i) investments in the trust are, in one or more of those taxation years, listed or traded on a stock exchange or other public market, and

(ii) the trust elects, by notifying the Minister of National Revenue in writing on or before its filing due-date for its taxation year that includes June 26, 2013, to have those subsections so apply; and

(*b*) the 2011 and subsequent taxation years.

► 122.1(1.2) ◄

(1.2) Character preservation rule. If this subsection applies to a parent entity for a taxation year in respect of a specified amount and a source entity, then for the purposes of the definition "real estate investment trust" in subsection (1), to the extent that the specified amount can reasonably be considered to be derived from gross REIT revenue of the source entity having a particular character, the specified amount is deemed to be gross REIT revenue of the parent entity having the same character and not having any other character.

History: S. 122.1(1.2) was added by S.C. 2013, c. 34, s. 258(12), applicable to

(*a*) taxation years of a trust that end after 2006 and before 2011 if

(i) investments in the trust are, in one or more of those taxation years, listed or traded on a stock exchange or other public market, and

(ii) the trust elects, by notifying the Minister of National Revenue in writing on or before its filing due-date for its taxation year that includes June 26, 2013, to have those subsections so apply; and

(*b*) the 2011 and subsequent taxation years.

► 122.1(1.3) ◄

(1.3) Character of revenue — hedging arrangements. For the purposes of the definition "real estate investment trust" in subsection (1),

(*a*) if an amount is included in gross REIT revenue of a trust for a taxation year and it results from an agreement that can reasonably be considered to have been made by the trust to reduce its risk from fluctuations in interest rates in respect of debt incurred by the trust to acquire or refinance real or immovable property, the amount is deemed to have the same character as gross REIT revenue in respect of the real or immovable property and not any other character; and

(*b*) if a real or immovable property is situated in a country other than Canada and an amount included in gross REIT revenue of a trust for a taxation year

(i) is a gain from fluctuations in the value of the currency of that country relative to Canadian currency recognized on

(A) revenue in respect of the real or immovable property, or

(B) debt incurred by the trust for the purpose of earning revenue in respect of the real or immovable property, or

(ii) results from an agreement that

(A) provides for the purchase, sale or exchange of currency, and

(B) can reasonably be considered to have been made by the trust to reduce its risk from currency fluctuations described in subparagraph (i), the amount is deemed to have the same character as gross REIT revenue in respect of the real or immovable property and not any other character.

History: S. 122.1(1.3) was added by S.C. 2013, c. 34, s. 258(12), applicable to

(*a*) taxation years of a trust that end after 2006 and before 2011 if

(i) investments in the trust are, in one or more of those taxation years, listed or traded on a stock exchange or other public market, and

(ii) the trust elects, by notifying the Minister of National Revenue in writing on or before its filing due-date for its taxation year that includes June 26, 2013, to have those subsections so apply; and

(*b*) the 2011 and subsequent taxation years.

▶ 122.1(2) ◀

(2) Application of definition "SIFT trust". The definition "SIFT trust" applies to a trust for a taxation year of the trust that ends after 2006, except that if the trust would have been a SIFT trust on October 31, 2006 had that definition been in force and applied to the trust as of that date, that definition does not apply to the trust for a taxation year of the trust that ends before the earlier of

(*a*) 2011, and

(*b*) the first day after December 15, 2006 on which the trust exceeds normal growth as determined by reference to the normal growth guidelines issued by the Department of Finance on December 15, 2006, as amended from time to time, unless that excess arose as a result of a prescribed transaction.

Editorial Note: See the note following the definition of "SIFT trust" in s. 122.1(1).

Tax Topics: No. 1867-68, 2007 Canadian Tax Foundation Annual Conference CRA Round Table.

Income Tax Technical News: Issue No. 38, SIFT Rules — Transitional Normal Growth.

SECTION 122.2: Amount deemed paid in prescribed manner

▶ 122.2(1) ◀

(1) Amount deemed paid in prescribed manner — (Repealed by S.C. 1994, c. 7, Sched. VII, s. 10(2).)

Related Regulations: 6400.

Related Sections: S. 117.1(1) Annual adjustment (indexing).

▶ 122.2(2) ◀

(2) Definitions — (Repealed by S.C. 1994, c. 7, Sched. VII, s. 10(2).)

Cases: For the purposes of the child tax credit the grossed-up dividend is included in income. *Ford v. M.N.R.*, 86 DTC 1701 (T.C.C.)

"eligible child" — (Repealed by S.C. 1994, c. 7, Sched. VII, s. 10(2).)

Related Sections: S. 252(1) Extended meaning of "child".

"supporting person" — (Repealed by S.C. 1994, c. 7, Sched. VII, s. 10(2).)

SECTION 122.3: Overseas employment tax credit

▶ 122.3(1) ◀

(1) [Overseas employment tax credit]. If an individual is resident in Canada in a taxation year and, throughout any period of more than six consecutive months that began before the end of the year and included any part of the year (in this section referred to as the "qualifying period")

(*a*) was employed by a person who was a specified employer, other than for the performance of services under a prescribed international development assistance program of the Government of Canada, and

(*b*) performed all or substantially all the duties of the individual's employment outside Canada

(i) in connection with a contract under which the specified employer carried on business outside Canada with respect to

(A) the exploration for or exploitation of petroleum, natural gas, minerals or other similar resources,

(B) any construction, installation, agricultural or engineering activity, or

(C) any prescribed activity, or

(ii) for the purpose of obtaining, on behalf of the specified employer, a contract to undertake any of the activities referred to in clause (i)(A), (B) or (C),

there may be deducted, from the amount that would, but for this section, be the individual's tax payable under this Part for the year, an amount equal to that proportion of the tax otherwise payable under this Part for the year by the individual that the lesser of

(*c*) an amount equal to that proportion of the specified amount for the year that the number of days

(i) in that portion of the qualifying period that is in the year, and

(ii) on which the individual was resident in Canada

is of 365, and

(*d*) the specified percentage for the year of the individual's income for the year from that employment that is reasonably attributable to duties performed on the days referred to in paragraph (*c*)

is of

(*e*) the amount, if any, by which

(i) if the individual is resident in Canada throughout the year, the individual's income for the year, and

(ii) if the individual is non-resident at any time in the year, the amount determined under paragraph 114(*a*) in respect of the taxpayer for the year

exceeds

(iii) the total of all amounts each of which is an amount deducted under section 110.6 or paragraph 111(1)(*b*), or deductible under paragraph 110(1)(*d.2*), (*d.3*), (*f*) or (*g*), in computing the individual's taxable income for the year.

History: S. 122.3(1)(*e*)(iii) was replaced by S.C. 2017, c. 20, s. 21(1), in force January 1, 2018, and formerly read:

(iii) the total of all amounts each of which is an amount deducted under section 110.6 or paragraph 111(1)(*b*), or deductible under paragraph 110(1)(*d.2*), (*d.3*), (*f*), (*g*) or (*j*), in computing the individual's taxable income for the year.

S. 122.3(1), the portion before paragraph (*a*) was replaced by S.C. 2013, c. 34, s. 259(1), applicable to taxation years that begin after June 26, 2013, and formerly read:

S. 122.3 *[Overseas Employment Tax Credit].*

(1) *Deduction from tax payable where employment out of Canada.* Where an individual is resident in Canada in a taxation year and, throughout any period of more than 6 consecutive months that commenced before the

end of the year and included any part of the year (in this subsection referred to as the "qualifying period")

S. 122.3(1)(*c*), the portion before subparagraph (i) was replaced by S.C. 2012, c. 31, s. 26(1), applicable to the 2013 and subsequent taxation years. S. 122.3(1)(*c*), the portion before subparagraph (i) formerly read:

(*c*) an amount equal to that proportion of $80,000 that the number of days

S. 122.3(1)(*d*) was replaced by S.C. 2012, c. 31, s. 26(2), applicable to the 2013 and subsequent taxation years. S. 122.3(1)(*d*) formerly read:

(*d*) 80% of the individual's income for the year from that employment that is reasonably attributable to duties performed on the days referred to in paragraph (*c*)

Related Regulations: 3400; 6000.

Forms: T626 — Overseas Employment Tax Credit-Calendar Year.

Income Tax Folios: *Secondary* — S5-F2-C1 Foreign Tax Credit.

Information Circulars: IC 07-1 Taxpayer Relief Provisions.

Interpretation Bulletins: *Primary* — IT-497R4 Overseas employment tax credit.

Tax Window Files: overseas employment tax credit, *January 30, 2015*, CRA Document No. 2014-0521751E5.

Cases: The taxpayer was entitled to the overseas employment tax credit because throughout the qualifying period, which was the entire year, the taxpayer performed all or substantially all of his employment duties outside of Canada. It was not required that the taxpayer be employed outside of Canada for at least six continuous months in the year. *Rooke v. the Queen*, 2002 DTC 7442 (F.C.A.), reversing 2000 DTC 2206 (T.C.C.)

The taxpayer was denied an overseas employment tax credit because there was no evidence that his employer's activities outside of Canada amounted to carrying on a business as opposed to operating exclusively for charitable purposes. *Brown v. The Queen*, 2000 DTC 6410 (F.C.A.), affirming 99 DTC 3536 (T.C.C.)

When the taxpayer's employer entered into a contract with an international organization for the purpose of establishing dairy farms in Malawi, the taxpayer was entitled to deduct an overseas employment tax credit on the basis that his employer did carry on "business" in Malawi as required by s. 122.3(1). The definition of "business" in s. 248(1) contains no requirement for a predominant profit motive. *Timmins v. The Queen*, 99 DTC 5494 (F.C.A.), reversing 96 DTC 6378 (F.C.T.D.)

► 122.3(1.01) ◄

(1.01) Specified amount. For the purposes of paragraph (1)(*c*), the specified amount for a taxation year of an individual is

(*a*) for the 2013 to 2015 taxation years, the amount determined by the formula

$$[\$80{,}000 \times A/(A + B)] + [C \times B/(A + B)]$$

where

A is the individual's income described in paragraph (1)(*d*) for the taxation year that is earned in connection with a contract that was committed to in writing before March 29, 2012 by a specified employer of the individual,

B is the individual's income described in paragraph (1)(*d*) for the taxation year, other than income included in the description of A, and

C is

(i) for the 2013 taxation year, $60,000,

(ii) for the 2014 taxation year, $40,000, and

(iii) for the 2015 taxation year, $20,000; and

(*b*) for the 2016 and subsequent taxation years, nil.

History: S. 122.3(1.01) was added by S.C. 2012, c. 31, s. 26(3), applicable to the 2013 and subsequent taxation years.

► 122.3(1.02) ◄

(1.02) Specified percentage. For the purposes of paragraph (1)(*d*), the specified percentage for a taxation year of an individual is

(*a*) for the 2013 to 2015 taxation years, the amount determined by the formula

$$[80\% \times A/(A + B)] + [C \times B/(A + B)]$$

where

A is the value of A in subsection (1.01),

B is the value of B in subsection (1.01), and

C is

(i) for the 2013 taxation year, 60%,

(ii) for the 2014 taxation year, 40%, and

(iii) for the 2015 taxation year, 20%; and

(*b*) for the 2016 and subsequent taxation years, 0%.

History: S. 122.3(1.02) was added by S.C. 2012, c. 31, s. 26(3), applicable to the 2013 and subsequent taxation years.

► 122.3(1.1) ◄

(1.1) Excluded income. No amount may be included under paragraph (1)(*d*) in respect of an individual's income for a taxation year from the individual's employment by an employer

(*a*) if

(i) the employer carries on a business of providing services and does not employ in the business throughout the year more than five full-time employees,

(ii) the individual

(A) does not deal at arm's length with the employer, or is a specified shareholder of the employer, or

(B) where the employer is a partnership, does not deal at arm's length with a member of the partnership, or is a specified shareholder of a member of the partnership, and

(iii) but for the existence of the employer, the individual would reasonably be regarded as being an employee of a person or partnership that is not a specified employer; or

(*b*) if at any time in that portion of the qualifying period that is in the taxation year

(i) the employer provides the services of the individual to a corporation, partnership or trust with which the employer does not deal at arm's length, and

(ii) the fair market value of all the issued shares of the capital stock of the corporation or of all interests in the partnership or trust, as the case may be, that are held, directly or indirectly, by persons who are resident in Canada is less than 10% of the fair market value of all those shares or interests.

History: S. 122.3(1.1) was replaced by S.C. 2013, c. 34, s. 259(2), applicable to taxation years that begin after June 26, 2013, and formerly read:

(1.1) *Excluded income.* No amount may be included under paragraph (1)(*d*) in respect of an individual's income for a taxation year from the individual's employment by an employer where

(*a*) the employer carries on a business of providing services and does not employ in the business throughout the year more than 5 full-time employees;

(*b*) the individual

(i) does not deal at arm's length with the employer, or is a specified shareholder of the employer, or

(ii) where the employer is a partnership, does not deal at arm's length with a member of the partnership, or is a specified shareholder of a member of the partnership; and

(c) but for the existence of the employer, the individual would reasonably be regarded as an employee of a person or partnership that is not a specified employer.

► 122.3(2) ◄

(2) Definitions. In subsection (1),

"specified employer" —"specified employer" means

(*a*) a person resident in Canada,

(*b*) a partnership in which interests that exceed in total value 10% of the fair market value of all interests in the partnership are owned by persons resident in Canada or corporations controlled by persons resident in Canada, or

(*c*) a corporation that is a foreign affiliate of a person resident in Canada;

"tax otherwise payable under this Part for the year" —"tax otherwise payable under this Part for the year" means the amount that, but for this section, sections 120 and 120.2, subsection 120.4(2) and sections 121, 126, 127 and 127.4, would be the tax payable under this Part for the year.

SECTION 122.4: [Sales tax credit]

(Repealed by 1990, c. 45, s. 47(1).)

SECTION 122.5: [GST/HST credit]

► 122.5(1) ◄

(1) Definitions. The following definitions apply in this section.

"adjusted income" —"adjusted income", of an individual for a taxation year in relation to a month specified for the taxation year, means the total of the individual's income for the taxation year and the income for the taxation year of the individual's qualified relation, if any, in relation to the specified month, both calculated as if in computing that income no amount were

(*a*) included

(i) under paragraph 56(1)(*q.1*) or subsection 56(6),

(ii) in respect of any gain from a disposition of property to which section 79 applies, or

(iii) in respect of a gain described in subsection 40(3.21); or

(*b*) deductible under paragraph 20(1)(*ww*) or 60(*y*) or (*z*). *(revenu rajusté)*

History: S. 122.5(1), paragraph (*b*) of the definition "adjusted income" was replaced by S.C. 2018, c. 12, s. 15(1), applicable to the 2018 and subsequent taxation years, and formerly read:

(*b*) deductible under paragraph 60(*y*) or (*z*).

S. 122.5(1), the definition "adjusted income" was replaced by S.C. 2010, c. 25, s. 23(1), applicable to the 2000 and subsequent taxation years. S. 122.5(1), the definition "adjusted income" formerly read:

"adjusted income"—"adjusted income", of an individual for a taxation year in relation to a month specified for the taxation year, means the total of the individual's income for the taxation year and the income for the taxation year of the individual's qualified relation, if any, in relation to the specified month, both calculated as if no amount were included under paragraph 56(1)(*q.1*) or subsection 56(6) or in respect of any gain from a disposition of property to which section 79 applies in computing that income and as if no amount were deductible under paragraph 60(*y*) or (*z*) in computing that income.

Related Sections: S. 122.51(1), "Adjusted income"; s. 122.6, "adjusted income".

"cohabiting spouse or common-law partner" —"cohabiting spouse or common-law partner" of an individual at any time has the meaning assigned by section 122.6.

"eligible individual" —"eligible individual", in relation to a month specified for a taxation year, means an individual (other than a trust) who

(*a*) has, before the specified month, attained the age of 19 years; or

(*b*) was, at any time before the specified month,

(i) a parent who resided with their child, or

(ii) married or in a common-law partnership.

Related Sections: S. 122.51(1), "Eligible individual"; s. 122.6, "eligible individual".

"qualified dependant" —"qualified dependant" of an individual, in relation to a month specified for a taxation year, means a person who at the beginning of the specified month

(*a*) is the individual's child or is dependent for support on the individual or on the individual's cohabiting spouse or common-law partner;

(*b*) resides with the individual;

(*c*) is under the age of 19 years;

(*d*) is not an eligible individual in relation to the specified month; and

(*e*) is not a qualified relation of any individual in relation to the specified month.

"qualified relation" —"qualified relation" of an individual, in relation to a month specified for a taxation year, means the person, if any, who, at the beginning of the specified month, is the individual's cohabiting spouse or common-law partner.

Related Sections: S. 122.6, "cohabiting spouse or common-law partner"; s. 248(1), "individual".

"return of income" —"return of income", in respect of a person for a taxation year, means

(*a*) for a person who is resident in Canada at the end of the taxation year, the person's return of income (other than a return of income under subsection 70(2) or 104(23), paragraph 128(2)(*e*) or subsection 150(4)) that is required to be filed for the taxation year or that would be required to be filed if the person had tax payable under this Part for the taxation year; and

(*b*) in any other case, a prescribed form containing prescribed information that is filed for the taxation year with the Minister.

► 122.5(2) ◄

(2) Persons not eligible individuals, qualified relations or qualified dependants. Notwithstanding subsection (1), a person is not an eligible individual, is not a qualified relation and is not a qualified dependant, in relation to a month specified for a taxation year, if the person

(*a*) died before the specified month;

(*b*) is confined to a prison or similar institution for a period of at least 90 days that includes the first day of the specified month;

(*c*) is at the beginning of the specified month a non-resident person, other than a non-resident person who

(i) is at that time the cohabiting spouse or common-law partner of a person who is deemed under subsection 250(1) to be resident in Canada throughout the taxation year that includes the first day of the specified month, and

(ii) was resident in Canada at any time before the specified month;

(*d*) is at the beginning of the specified month a person described in paragraph 149(1)(*a*) or (*b*); or

(*e*) is a person in respect of whom a special allowance under the *Children's Special Allowances Act* is payable for the specified month.

► 122.5(3) ◄

(3) Deemed payment on account of tax. An eligible individual in relation to a month specified for a taxation year who files a return of income for the taxation year is deemed to have paid during the specified month on account of their tax payable under this Part for the taxation year an amount equal to 1/4 of the amount, if any, determined by the formula

$$A - B$$

where

A is the total of

(*a*) $213,

(*b*) $213 for the qualified relation, if any, of the individual in relation to the specified month,

(*c*) if the individual has no qualified relation in relation to the specified month and is entitled to deduct an amount for the taxation year under subsection 118(1) because of paragraph (*b*) of the description of B in that subsection in respect of a qualified dependant of the individual in relation to the specified month, $213,

(*d*) $112 times the number of qualified dependants of the individual in relation to the specified month, other than a qualified dependant in respect of whom an amount is included under paragraph (*c*) in computing the total for the specified month,

(*e*) if the individual has no qualified relation and has one or more qualified dependants, in relation to the specified month, $112, and

(*f*) if the individual has no qualified relation and no qualified dependant, in relation to the specified month, the lesser of $112 and 2% of the amount, if any, by which the individual's income for the taxation year exceeds $6,911; and

B is 5% of the amount, if any, by which the individual's adjusted income for the taxation year in relation to the specified month exceeds $27,749.

CRA News Release

2.2% Indexation Factor for 2019

See the CRA Fact Sheet, dated November 16, 2018, that is reproduced following subsection 117.1(1). This release announces a 2.2% indexation factor applicable for 2019 tax bracket thresholds, personal amounts and other amounts relating to non-refundable credits, as well as the refundable medical expense supplement, Old Age Security repayment threshold, certain board and lodging allowances, and the tradesperson's tools deduction. Increases to tax bracket thresholds, amounts relating to non-refundable credits, and most other amounts will take effect on January 1, 2019. However, increases in amounts for certain income-tested benefits (for example, the goods and services tax credit) will take effect on July 1, 2019.

History: S. 122.5(3), the portion before the formula was replaced by S.C. 2014, c. 20, s. 17(1), applicable to the 2014 and subsequent taxation years, and formerly read:

(3) *Deemed payment on account of tax.* An eligible individual in relation to a month specified for a taxation year who files a return of income for the taxation year and applies for an amount under this subsection is deemed to have paid during the specified month on account of their tax payable under this Part for the taxation year an amount equal to 1/4 of the amount, if any, determined by the formula

Related Sections: S. 117.1(1) Annual adjustment (indexing).

Information Circulars: IC 07-1 Taxpayer Relief Provisions.

► 122.5(3.01) ◄

(3.01) Shared-custody parent. Notwithstanding subsection (3), if an eligible individual is a shared-custody parent (within the meaning assigned by section 122.6, but with the words "qualified dependant" in that section having the meaning assigned by subsection (1)) in respect of one or more qualified dependants at the beginning of a month, the amount deemed by subsection (3) to have been paid during a specified month is equal to the amount determined by the following formula:

$$1/2 \times (A + B)$$

where

A is the amount determined by the formula in subsection (3), calculated without reference to this subsection, and

B is the amount determined by the formula in subsection (3), calculated without reference to this subsection and subparagraph (*b*)(ii) of the definition "eligible individual" in section 122.6.

History: S. 122.5(3.01) was added by S.C. 2010, c. 25, s. 23(2), applicable for amounts that are deemed to be paid during months after June 2011.

► 122.5(3.1) ◄

(3.1) When advance payment applies. Subsection (3.2) applies in respect of an eligible individual in relation to a particular month specified for a taxation year, and each subsequent month specified for the taxation year, if

(*a*) the amount deemed by that subsection to have been paid by the eligible individual during the particular month specified for the taxation year is less than $50; and

(*b*) it is reasonable to conclude that the amount deemed by that subsection to have been paid by the eligible individual during each subsequent month specified for the taxation year will be less than $50.

History: S. 122.5(3.1)(*a*) and (*b*) were replaced by S.C. 2011, c. 24, s. 37(1), applicable to amounts deemed to be paid during months specified for the 2010 and subsequent taxation years. S. 122.5(3.1)(*a*) and (*b*) formerly read:

(*a*) the amount deemed by that subsection to have been paid by the eligible individual during the particular month specified for the taxation year is less than $25; and (*b*) it is reasonable to conclude that the amount deemed by that subsection to have been paid by the eligible individual during each subsequent month specified for the taxation year will be less than $25.

► 122.5(3.2) ◄

(3.2) Advance payment. If this subsection applies, the total of the amounts that would otherwise be deemed by subsection (3) to have been paid on account of the eligible individual's tax payable under this Part for the taxation year during the particular month specified for the taxation year, and during each subsequent month specified for the taxation year, is deemed to have been paid by the eligible individual on account of their tax payable under this Part for the taxation year during the particular specified month for the taxation year, and the amount deemed by subsection (3) to have been paid by the eligible individual during those subsequent months specified for the taxation year is deemed, except for the purpose of this subsection, not to have been paid to the extent that it is included in an amount deemed to have been paid by this subsection.

► 122.5(4) ◄

(4) Months specified. For the purposes of this section, the months specified for a taxation year are July and October of the immediately following taxation year and January and April of the second immediately following taxation year.

► 122.5(5) ◄

(5) Only one eligible individual. If an individual is a qualified relation of another individual in relation to a month specified for a taxation year and both those individuals would be, but for this subsection, eligible individuals in relation to the specified month, only the individual that the Minister designates is the eligible individual in relation to the specified month.

History: S. 122.5(5) was replaced by S.C. 2014, c. 20, s. 17(2), applicable to the 2014 and subsequent taxation years, and formerly read:

(5) *Only one eligible individual.* If an individual is a qualified relation of another individual, in relation to a month specified for a taxation year, only one of them is an eligible individual in relation to that specified month, and if both of them claim to be eligible individuals, the individual that the Minister designates is the eligible individual in relation to that specified month.

Related Sections: S. 248(1), "amount", "individual"; s. 255 Canada.

► 122.5(5.1) ◄

(5.1) Exception — (Repealed by S.C. 2002, c. 9, s. 38(2).)

► 122.5(6) ◄

(6) Exception re qualified dependant. If a person would, if this Act were read without reference to this subsection, be the qualified dependant of two or more individuals, in relation to a month specified for a taxation year,

(*a*) the person is deemed to be a qualified dependant, in relation to that month, of the one of those individuals on whom those individuals agree;

(*b*) in the absence of an agreement referred to in paragraph (*a*), the person is deemed to be, in relation to that month, a qualified dependant of the individuals, if any, who are, at the beginning of that month, eligible individuals (within the meaning assigned by section 122.6, but with the words "qualified dependant" in that section having the meaning assigned by subsection (1)) in respect of that person; and

(*c*) in any other case, the person is deemed to be, in relation to that month, a qualified dependant only of the individual that the Minister designates.

History: S. 122.5(6)(*b*) was replaced by S.C. 2010, c. 25, s. 23(3), applicable for amounts that are deemed to be paid during months after June 2011. S. 122.5(6)(*b*) formerly read:

(*b*) in the absence of an agreement referred to in paragraph (*a*), the person is deemed to be, in relation to that month, a qualified dependant of the individual, if any, who is, at the beginning of that month, an eligible individual within the meaning assigned by section 122.6 in respect of the person; and

Related Sections: S. 248(1), "individual", "prescribed".

► 122.5(6.1) ◄

(6.1) Notification to Minister. An individual shall notify the Minister of the occurrence of any of the following events before the end of the month following the month in which the event occurs:

(*a*) the individual ceases to be an eligible individual;

(*b*) a person becomes or ceases to be the individual's qualified relation; and

(*c*) a person ceases to be a qualified dependant of the individual, otherwise than because of attaining the age of 19 years.

Forms: RC65 — Canada Child Tax Benefit — Election to Change Marital Status.

► 122.5(6.2) ◄

(6.2) Non-residents and part-year residents. For the purpose of this section, the income of a person who is non-resident at any time in a taxation year is deemed to be equal to the amount that would, if the person were resident in Canada throughout the year, be the person's income for the year.

► 122.5(7) ◄

(7) Effect of bankruptcy. For the purpose of this section, if in a taxation year an individual becomes bankrupt, the individual's income for the taxation year shall include the individual's income for the taxation year that begins on January 1 of the calendar year that includes the date of bankruptcy.

History: S. 122.5(7) was replaced by S.C. 2013, c. 34, s. 260, in force June 26, 2013, and formerly read:

(7) *Effect of bankruptcy.* For the purpose of this section, where in a taxation year an individual becomes bankrupt,

(*a*) the individual's income for the year shall include the individual's income for the taxation year that begins on January 1 of the calendar year that includes the date of bankruptcy; and

(*b*) the amount determined for the year under clause (3)(*e*)(ii)(B) shall include the amount determined for the purpose of paragraph (*c*) of the description of B in subsection 118(1) for the individual's taxation year that begins on January 1 of the calendar year that includes the date of bankruptcy.

Related Sections: S. 118.95 Credits in year of bankruptcy; s. 120.2(4) Where subsection (1) does not apply; s. 122.61(3.1) Effect of bankruptcy; s. 127.1(1) Refundable investment tax credit; s. 128(2) Where individual bankrupt; s. 248(1), "bankrupt".

SECTION 122.51: [Refundable medical expense supplement]

► 122.51(1) ◄

(1) Definitions. The definitions in this subsection apply in this section.

"adjusted income" — "adjusted income" of an individual for a taxation year has the meaning assigned by section 122.6.

"eligible individual" —"eligible individual" for a taxation year means an individual (other than a trust)

(*a*) who is resident in Canada throughout the year (or, if the individual dies in the year, throughout the portion of the year before the individual's death);

(*b*) who, before the end of the year, has attained the age of 18 years; and

(*c*) the total of whose incomes for the year from the following sources is at least $2,500:

(i) offices and employments (computed without reference to paragraph 6(1)(*f*)),

(ii) businesses each of which is a business carried on by the individual either alone or as a partner actively engaged in the business, and

(iii) the program established under the *Wage Earner Protection Program Act*.

History: S. 122.51(1), paragraph (*c*) of the definition "eligible individual" was replaced by S.C. 2009, c. 2, s. 37(1), applicable to the 2008 and subsequent taxation years. S. 122.51(1), paragraph (*c*) of the definition "eligible individual" formerly read:

(*c*) whose incomes for the year from all

(i) offices and employments (computed without reference to paragraph 6(1)(*f*)), and

(ii) businesses each of which is a business carried on by the individual either alone or as a partner actively engaged in the business

total $2,500 or more.

► 122.51(2) ◄

(2) Deemed payment on account of tax. Where a return of income (other than a return of income filed under subsection 70(2), paragraph 104(23)(*d*) or 128(2)(*e*) or subsection 150(4)) is filed in respect of an eligible individual for a particular taxation year that ends at the end of a calendar year, there is deemed to be paid at the end of the particular year on account of the individual's tax payable under this Part for the particular year the amount determined by the formula

$$A - B$$

where

A is the lesser of

(*a*) $1,000, and

(*b*) the total of

(i) the amount determined by the formula

$$(0.25/C) \times D$$

where

C is the appropriate percentage for the particular taxation year, and

D is the total of all amounts each of which is the amount determined by the formula in subsection 118.2(1) for the purpose of computing the individual's tax payable under this Part for a taxation year that ends in the calendar year, and

(ii) 25% of the total of all amounts each of which is the amount deductible under section 64 in computing the individual's income for a taxation year that ends in the calendar year; and

B is 5% of the amount, if any, by which

(*a*) the total of all amounts each of which is the individual's adjusted income for a taxation year that ends in the calendar year

exceeds

(*b*) $21,663.

CRA News Release

2.2% Indexation Factor for 2019

See the CRA Fact Sheet, dated November 16, 2018, that is reproduced following subsection117.1(1). This release announces a 2.2% indexation factor applicable for 2019 tax bracket thresholds, personal amounts and other amounts relating to non-refundable credits, as well as the refundable medical expense supplement, Old Age Security repayment threshold, certain board and lodging allowances, and the tradesperson's tools deduction. Increases to tax bracket thresholds, amounts relating to non-refundable credits, and most other amounts will take effect on January 1, 2019. However, increases in amounts for certain income-tested benefits (for example, the goods and services tax credit) will take effect on July 1, 2019.

History: S. 122.51(2), the formula in subparagraph (*b*)(i) of the description of A was replaced by S.C. 2017, c. 33, s. 47(1), applicable to the 2005 and subsequent taxation years, and formerly read:

$$(25/C) \times D$$

Related Sections: S. 117.1(1) Annual adjustment (indexing); s. 152(1)(*b*) Assessment; s. 152(4.2) Reassessment with taxpayer's consent.

Income Tax Folios: *Primary*— S1-F1-C1 Medical Expense Tax Credit.

Information Circulars: 07-1 Taxpayer relief provisions.

Subdivision a.1 — Canada Child Benefit

History: The heading of Subdivision a.1 of Division E was replaced by S.C. 2016, c. 7, s. 27(1), deemed to have come into force on July 1, 2016, and formerly read: "Canada Child Tax Benefit".

SECTION 122.6: Definitions

In this subdivision,

"adjusted earned income" — (Repealed by S.C. 1998, c. 21, s. 92(1).)

"adjusted income" —"adjusted income", of an individual for a taxation year, means the total of all amounts each of which would be the income for the year of the individual or of the person who was the individual's cohabiting spouse or common-law partner at the end of the year if in computing that income no amount were

(*a*) included

(i) under paragraph 56(1)(*q.1*) or subsection 56(6),

(ii) in respect of any gain from a disposition of property to which section 79 applies, or

(iii) in respect of a gain described in subsection 40(3.21), or

(*b*) deductible under paragraph 20(1)(*ww*) or 60(*y*) or (*z*);

History: S. 122.6, paragraph (*b*) of the definition "adjusted income" was replaced by S.C. 2018, c. 12, s. 16(1), applicable to the 2018 and subsequent taxation years, and formerly read:

(*b*) deductible under paragraph 60(*y*) or (*z*);

S. 122.6, the definition "adjusted income" was replaced by S.C. 2010, c. 25, s. 24(1), applicable to the 2000 and subsequent taxation years. S. 122.6, the definition "adjusted income" formerly read:

"adjusted income"—"adjusted income", of an individual for a taxation year, means the total of all amounts each of which would be the income for the year of the individual or of the person who was the individual's cohabiting spouse or common-law partner at the end of the year if no amount were included under paragraph 56(1)(*q.1*) or subsection 56(6) or in respect of any gain from a disposition of property to which section 79 applies in computing that income and if no amount were deductible under paragraph 60(*y*) or (*z*) in computing that income;

Related Sections: S. 122.5(1), "Adjusted income"; s. 122.51(1), "adjusted income"; s. 122.62(5) Death of cohabiting spouse; s. 122.62(6) Separation from cohabiting spouse.

"base taxation year" —"base taxation year" in relation to a month means

(*a*) where the month is any of the first 6 months of a calendar year, the taxation year that ended on December 31 of the second preceding calendar year, and

(*b*) where the month is any of the last 6 months of a calendar year, the taxation year that ended on December 31 of the preceding calendar year;

"cohabiting spouse or common-law partner" —"cohabiting spouse or common-law partner" of an individual at any time means the person who at that time is the individual's spouse or common-law partner and who is not at that time living separate and apart from the individual and, for the purpose of this definition, a person shall not be considered to be living separate and apart from an individual at any time unless they were living separate and apart at that time, because of a breakdown of their marriage or common-law partnership, for a period of at least 90 days that includes that time;

"earned income" — (Repealed by S.C. 1998, c. 21, s. 92(1).)

"eligible individual" —"eligible individual" in respect of a qualified dependant at any time means a person who at that time

(*a*) resides with the qualified dependant,

(*b*) is a parent of the qualified dependant who

(i) is the parent who primarily fulfils the responsibility for the care and upbringing of the qualified dependant and who is not a shared-custody parent in respect of the qualified dependant, or

(ii) is a shared-custody parent in respect of the qualified dependant,

(*c*) is resident in Canada or, where the person is the cohabiting spouse or common-law partner of a person who is deemed under subsection 250(1) to be resident in Canada throughout the taxation year that includes that time, was resident in Canada in any preceding taxation year,

(*d*) is not described in paragraph 149(1)(*a*) or (*b*), and

(*e*) is, or whose cohabiting spouse or common-law partner is, a Canadian citizen or a person who

(i) is a permanent resident within the meaning of subsection 2(1) of the *Immigration and Refugee Protection Act*,

(ii) is a temporary resident within the meaning of the *Immigration and Refugee Protection Act*, who was resident in Canada throughout the 18 month period preceding that time,

(iii) is a protected person within the meaning of the *Immigration and Refugee Protection Act*,

(iv) was determined before that time to be a member of a class defined in the *Humanitarian Designated Classes Regulations* made under the *Immigration Act*, or

(v) is an Indian within the meaning of the *Indian Act*,

and for the purposes of this definition,

(*f*) where a qualified dependant resides with the dependant's female parent, the parent who primarily fulfils the responsibility for the care and upbringing of the qualified dependant is presumed to be the female parent,

(*g*) the presumption referred to in paragraph (*f*) does not apply in prescribed circumstances,

(*h*) prescribed factors shall be considered in determining what constitutes care and upbringing; and

(i) an individual shall not fail to qualify as a parent (within the meaning assigned by section 252) of another individual solely because of the receipt of a social assistance amount that is payable under a program of the Government of Canada or the government of a province for the benefit of the other individual;

History: S. 122.6, subparagraph (*i*) of the definition "eligible individual" was added by S.C. 2018, c. 27, s. 11(1), deemed to have come into force on January 1, 2008.

S. 122.6, subparagraph (*e*)(v) of the definition "eligible individual" was added by S.C. 2016, c. 7, s. 28(1), deemed to have come into force on January 1, 2005. [The effective date was amended by S.C. 2018, c. 12, s. 38, in force on June 21, 2018, and formerly read: "July 1, 2016".]

S. 122.6, paragraph (*b*) of the definition "eligible individual" was replaced by S.C. 2010, c. 25, s. 24(2), applicable for overpayments that are deemed to arise after June 2011. S. 122.6, paragraph (*b*) of the definition "eligible individual" formerly read:

(*b*) is the parent of the qualified dependant who primarily fulfils the responsibility for the care and upbringing of the qualified dependant,

Related Regulations: 6301; 6302.

Related Sections: S. 122.5(1), "Eligible individual"; s. 122.51(1), "eligible individual"; s. 122.62(1) Eligible individuals.

Guides: T4114 Canada Child Benefits.

Tax Window Files: Status Indians eligible for Canada Child Benefit, *March 22, 2017*, CRA Document No. 2016-0675991E5.

Cases: S. 122.6 does not permit the proration of benefits between two persons who claim to be eligible parents. *The Queen v. Marshall et al.*, 96 DTC 6292 (F.C.A.).

"qualified dependant" —"qualified dependant" at any time means a person who at that time

(*a*) has not attained the age of 18 years,

(*b*) is not a person in respect of whom an amount was deducted under paragraph (*a*) of the description of B in subsection 118(1) in computing the tax payable under this Part by the person's spouse or common-law partner for the base taxation year in relation to the month that includes that time, and

(*c*) is not a person in respect of whom a special allowance under the *Children's Special Allowances Act* is payable for the month that includes that time;

"return of income" —"return of income" filed by an individual for a taxation year means

(*a*) where the individual was resident in Canada throughout the year, the individual's return of income (other than a return of income filed under subsection 70(2) or 104(23), paragraph 128(2)(*e*) or subsection 150(4)) that is filed or required to be filed under this Part for the year, and

(*b*) in any other case, a prescribed form containing prescribed information, that is filed with the Minister.

Related Sections: S. 164(2.3) Form deemed to be a return of income.

"shared-custody parent" —"shared-custody parent" in respect of a qualified dependant at a particular time means, where the presumption referred to in paragraph (*f*) of the definition "eligible individual" does not apply in respect of the qualified dependant, an individual who is one of the two parents of the qualified dependant who

(*a*) are not at that time cohabitating spouses or common-law partners of each other,

(*b*) reside with the qualified dependant on an equal or near equal basis, and

(*c*) primarily fulfil the responsibility for the care and upbringing of the qualified dependant when residing with the qualified dependant, as determined in consideration of prescribed factors.

History: S. 122.6, the definition "shared-custody parent" was added by S.C. 2010, c. 25, s. 24(3), applicable for overpayments that are deemed to arise after June 2011.

Cases: The definition of "shared-custody parent" requires that a child reside with each parent on an "equal or near equal basis". The taxpayer resided with her child between 57.14% and 59.38% of the time. Any percentage of time that cannot be rounded off to 50% would not qualify as "equal or near equal". The taxpayer was not a shared-custody parent and was entitled to receive the full amount of the benefit. *Morrissey v. The Queen*, 2019 DTC 5039 (FCA), reversing 2016 DTC 1152 (TCC)

Canadian Tax Foundation: Budd and Robinson, *The Canada Child Benefit and Child Custody*, 2016 Canadian Tax Focus 6(3):5–6.

Guides: T4114 Canada Child Benefits.

Tax Window Files: Taxability of Support Payments, *February 9, 2012*, CRA Document No. 2011-0406701E5; Shared Eligibility for the Canada Child Tax Benefit, *Technical Interpretation, Business and Partnerships Division, June 10, 2009*, CRA Document No. 2009-0308031E5; Lump-Sum Payments — Workers' Compensation, *Technical Interpretation, Business and Partnerships Division, May 12, 2006*, CRA Document No. 2006-0184781I7; Sharing of Canada Child Tax Benefit Between Parents, *Technical Interpretation, Business and Partnerships Division, July 13, 2005*, CRA Document No. 2005-0132631E5.

Cases: S. 122.6 does not permit the proration of benefits between two persons who claim to be eligible parents. *The Queen v. Marshall et al.*, 96 DTC 6292 (F.C.A.).

SECTION 122.61: Deemed overpayment

► 122.61(1) ◄

(1) Deemed overpayment. If a person and, if the Minister so demands, the person's cohabiting spouse or common-law partner at the end of a taxation year have filed a return of income for the year, an overpayment on account of the person's liability under this Part for the year is deemed to have arisen during a month in relation to which the year is the base taxation year, equal to the amount determined by the formula

$$(A + M)/12$$

where

A is the amount determined by the formula

$$E - Q$$

where

E is the total of

(*a*) the product obtained by multiplying $6,400 by the number of qualified dependants in respect of whom the person was an eligible individual at the beginning of the month who have not reached the age of six years at the beginning of the month, and

(*b*) the product obtained by multiplying $5,400 by the number of qualified dependants, other than those qualified dependants referred to in paragraph (*a*), in respect of whom the person was an eligible individual at the beginning of the month,

Q is

(*a*) if the person's adjusted income for the year is less than or equal to $30,000, nil,

(*b*) if the person's adjusted income for the year is greater than $30,000 but less than or equal to $65,000, and if the person is, at the beginning of the month, an eligible individual in respect of

(i) only one qualified dependant, 7% of the person's adjusted income for the year in excess of $30,000,

(ii) only two qualified dependants, 13.5% of the person's adjusted income for the year in excess of $30,000,

(iii) only three qualified dependants, 19% of the person's adjusted income for the year in excess of $30,000, or

(iv) more than three qualified dependants, 23% of the person's adjusted income for the year in excess of $30,000, and

(c) if the person's adjusted income for the year is greater than $65,000, and if the person is, at the beginning of the month, an eligible individual in respect of

(i) only one qualified dependant, the total of $2,450 and 3.2% of the person's adjusted income for the year in excess of $65,000,

(ii) only two qualified dependants, the total of $4,725 and 5.7% of the person's adjusted income for the year in excess of $65,000,

(iii) only three qualified dependants, the total of $6,650 and 8% of the person's adjusted income for the year in excess of $65,000, or

(iv) more than three qualified dependants, the total of $8,050 and 9.5% of the person's adjusted income for the year in excess of $65,000, and

R (Repealed by S.C. 2016, c. 7, s. 29(5).)

C (Repealed by S.C. 2016, c. 7, s. 29(4).)

M is the amount determined by the formula

N - O

where

N is the product obtained by multiplying $2,730 by the number of qualified dependants in respect of whom both

(a) an amount may be deducted under section 118.3 for the taxation year that includes the month, and

(b) the person is an eligible individual at the beginning of the month, and

O is

(a) if the person's adjusted income for the year is less than or equal to $65,000, nil, and

(b) if the person's adjusted income for the year is greater than $65,000,

(i) where the person is an eligible individual in respect of only one qualified dependant described in N, 3.2% of the person's adjusted income for the year in excess of $65,000, and

(ii) where the person is an eligible individual in respect of two or more qualified dependants described in N, 5.7% of the person's adjusted income for the year in excess of $65,000.

CRA News Release
2.2% Indexation Factor for 2019

See the CRA Fact Sheet, dated November 16, 2018, that is reproduced following subsection117.1(1). This release announces a 2.2% indexation factor applicable for 2019 tax bracket thresholds, personal amounts and other amounts relating to non-refundable credits, as well as the refundable medical expense supplement, Old Age Security repayment threshold, certain board and lodging allowances, and the tradesperson's tools deduction. Increases to tax bracket thresholds, amounts relating to non-refundable credits, and most other amounts will take effect on January 1, 2019. However, increases in amounts for certain income-tested benefits (for example, the goods and services tax credit) will take effect on July 1, 2019.

History: S. 122.61(1), the first formula was replaced by S.C. 2016, c. 7, s. 29(2), in force on July 1, 2018, and formerly read:

(A + C + M)/12

S. 122.61(1), the formula in the description of A was replaced by S.C. 2016, c. 7, s. 29(3), in force on July 1, 2018, and formerly read:

E - Q - R

S. 122.61(1), the description of C was repealed by S.C. 2016, c. 7, s. 29(4), in force on July 1, 2018, and formerly read:

C is the amount determined by the formula

F - (G x H)

where

F is, if the person is, at the beginning of the month, an eligible individual in respect of

(a) only one qualified dependant, $2,308, and

(b) two or more qualified dependants, the total of

(i) $2,308 for the first qualified dependant,

(ii) $2,042 for the second qualified dependant, and

(iii) $1,943 for each of the third and subsequent qualified dependants,

G is the amount determined by the formula

J - [K - (L/0.122)]

where

J is the person's adjusted income for the year,

K is $45,282, and

L is the amount referred to in paragraph (a) of the description of F, and

H is

(a) if the person is an eligible individual in respect of only one qualified dependant, 12.2%, and

(b) if the person is an eligible individual in respect of two or more qualified dependants, the fraction (expressed as a percentage rounded to the nearest one-tenth of one per cent) of which

(i) the numerator is the total that would be determined under the description of F in respect of the eligible individual if that description were applied without reference to the fourth and subsequent qualified dependants in respect of whom the person is an eligible individual, and

(ii) the denominator is the amount referred to in paragraph (a) of the description of F, divided by 0.122; and

S. 122.61(1), the description of R was repealed by S.C. 2016, c. 7, s. 29(5), in force on July 1, 2018, and formerly read:

R is the amount determined for C;

S. 122.61(1) was replaced by S.C. 2016, c. 7, s. 29(1), in force July 1, 2016, and formerly read:

(1) *Deemed overpayment.* Where a person and, where the Minister so demands, the person's cohabiting spouse or common-law partner at the end of a taxation year have filed a return of income for the year, an overpayment on account of the person's liability under this Part for the year is deemed to have arisen during a month in relation to which the year is the base taxation year, equal to the amount determined by the formula

1/12[(A - B) + C + M]

where

A is the total of

(a) the product obtained by multiplying $1,090 by the number of qualified dependants in respect of whom the person was an eligible individual at the beginning of the month, and

(b) the product obtained by multiplying $75 by the number of qualified dependants, in excess of 2, in respect of whom the person was an eligible individual at the beginning of the month;

(c) (Repealed.)

B is 4% (or where the person is an eligible individual in respect of only one qualified dependant at the beginning of the month, 2%) of the amount, if any, by which

(a) the person's adjusted income for the year exceeds

(b) the greater of $32,000 and the dollar amount, as adjusted annually and referred to in paragraph 117(2)(a), that is used for the calendar year following the base taxation year;

C is the amount determined by the formula

F - (G × H)

where

F is, where the person is, at the beginning of the month, an eligible individual in respect of

(a) only one qualified dependant, $1,463, and

(b) two or more qualified dependants, the total of

(i) $1,463 for the first qualified dependant,

(ii) $1,254 for the second qualified dependant, and

(iii) $1,176 for each of the third and subsequent qualified dependants,

G is the amount determined by the formula

$$J - [K - (L/0.122)]$$

where

J is the person's adjusted income for the year,

K is the amount referred to in paragraph (*b*) of the description of B, and

L is the amount referred to in paragraph (*a*) of the description of F, and

H is

(*a*) if the person is an eligible individual in respect of only one qualified dependant, 12.2%, and

(*b*) if the person is an eligible individual in respect of two or more qualified dependants, the fraction (expressed as a percentage rounded to the nearest one-tenth of one per cent) of which

(i) the numerator is the total that would be determined under the description of F in respect of the eligible individual if that description were applied without reference to the fourth and subsequent qualified dependants in respect of whom the person is an eligible individual, and

(ii) the denominator is the amount referred to in paragraph (*a*) of the description of F, divided by 0.122; and

M is the amount determined by the formula

$$N - (O \times P)$$

where

N is the product obtained by multiplying $2,300 by the number of qualified dependants in respect of whom both

(*a*) an amount may be deducted under section 118.3 for the taxation year that includes the month, and

(*b*) the person is an eligible individual at the beginning of the month,

O is the amount determined by the formula

$$J - [F/H + (K - L/0.122)]$$

where the descriptions of J, F, H, K, and L are described in the description of C, and

P is 4% (or where the person is an eligible individual in respect of only one qualified dependant included in the description of N at the beginning of the month, 2%) of the amount determined for the description of O,

Related Sections: S. 122.62 Eligible individuals; s. 122.63(1) Agreement.

Forms: RC65 — Canada Child Tax Benefit — Election to Change Marital Status; RC66 — Canada Child Tax Benefit Application; RC66 SCH — Status in Canada.

Guides: T4114 Canada Child Benefits.

► 122.61(1.1) ◄

(1.1) Shared-custody parent. Notwithstanding subsection (1), if an eligible individual is a shared-custody parent in respect of one or more qualified dependants at the beginning of a month, the overpayment deemed by subsection (1) to have arisen during the month is equal to the amount determined by the formula

$$1/2 \times (A + B)$$

where

A is the amount determined by the formula in subsection (1), calculated without reference to this subsection, and

B is the amount determined by the formula in subsection (1), calculated without reference to this subsection and subparagraph (*b*)(ii) of the definition "eligible individual" in section 122.6.

History: S. 122.61(1.1) was added by S.C. 2010, c. 25, s. 25(1), applicable for overpayments that are deemed to arise after June 2011.

► 122.61(2) ◄

(2) Exceptions. Notwithstanding subsection (1), if a particular month is the first month during which an overpayment that is less than $20 (or such other amount as is prescribed) is deemed under that subsection to have arisen on account of a person's liability under this Part for the base taxation year in relation to the particular month, any such overpayment that would, but for this subsection, reasonably be expected at the end of the particular month to arise during another month in relation to which the year is the base taxation year is deemed to arise under that subsection during the particular month and not during the other month.

History: S. 122.61(2) was replaced by S.C. 2011, c. 24, s. 38(1), applicable with respect to overpayments deemed to arise during months that are after June 2011. S. 122.61(2) formerly read:

(2) *Exceptions.* Notwithstanding subsection (1), where a particular month is the first month during which an overpayment that is less than $10 (or such other amount as is prescribed) is deemed under that subsection to have arisen on account of a person's liability under this Part for the base taxation year in relation to the particular month, any such overpayment that would, but for this subsection, reasonably be expected at the end of the particular month to arise during another month in relation to which the year is the base taxation year shall be deemed to arise under that subsection during the particular month and not during the other month.

► 122.61(3) ◄

(3) Non-residents and part-year residents. For the purposes of this section, if a person was non-resident at any time in a taxation year, the person's income for the year is, for greater certainty, deemed to be the amount that would have been the person's income for the year had the person been resident in Canada throughout the year.

History: S. 122.61(3) was replaced by S.C. 2013, c. 40, s. 52, in force December 12, 2013, and formerly read:

(3) *Non-residents and part-year residents.* For the purposes of this section, unless a person was resident in Canada throughout a taxation year,

(*a*) for greater certainty, the person's income for the year shall be deemed to be equal to the amount that would have been the person's income for the year had the person been resident in Canada throughout the year; and

(*b*) the person's earned income for the year shall not exceed that portion of the amount that would, but for this paragraph, be the person's earned income that is included because of section 114 or subsection 115(1) in computing the person's taxable income or taxable income earned in Canada, as the case may be, for the year.

► 122.61(3.1) ◄

(3.1) Effect of bankruptcy. For the purposes of this subdivision, where in a taxation year an individual becomes bankrupt,

(*a*) the individual's income for the year shall include the individual's income for the taxation year that begins on January 1 of the calendar year that includes the date of bankruptcy; and

(*b*) the total of all amounts deducted under section 63 in computing the individual's income for the year shall include the amount deducted under that section for the individual's taxation year that begins on January 1 of the calendar year that includes the date of bankruptcy.

(*c*) (Repealed by S.C. 1998, c. 21, s. 94.)

Related Sections: S. 118.95 Credits in year of bankruptcy; s. 120.2(4) Where subsection (1) does not apply; s. 122.5(7) Effect of bankruptcy; s. 127.1(1) Refundable investment tax credit; s. 128(2) Where individual bankrupt; s. 248(1), "bankrupt".

► 122.61(4) ◄

(4) Amount not to be charged, etc. A refund of an amount deemed by this section to be an overpayment on account of a person's liability under this Part for a taxation year

(*a*) shall not be subject to the operation of any law relating to bankruptcy or insolvency;

(*b*) cannot be assigned, charged, attached or given as security;

(*c*) does not qualify as a refund of tax for the purposes of the *Tax Rebate Discounting Act*;

(*d*) cannot be retained by way of deduction or set-off under the *Financial Administration Act*; and

(*e*) is not garnishable moneys for the purposes of the *Family Orders and Agreements Enforcement Assistance Act*.

Guides: T4114 Canada Child Benefits.

► 122.61(5) ◄

(5) Annual adjustment. Each amount expressed in dollars in subsection (1) shall be adjusted so that, where the base taxation year in relation to a particular month is after 2016, the amount to be used under that subsection for the month is the total of

(*a*) the amount that would, but for subsection (7), be the relevant amount used under subsection (1) for the month that is one year before the particular month, and

(*b*) the product obtained by multiplying

(i) the amount referred to in paragraph (*a*)

by

(ii) the amount, adjusted in such manner as is prescribed and rounded to the nearest one-thousandth or, where the result obtained is equidistant from 2 such consecutive one-thousandths, to the higher thereof, that is determined by the formula

$$(A/B) - 1$$

where

A is the "Consumer Price Index" (within the meaning assigned by subsection 117.1(4)) for the 12-month period that ended on September 30 of the base taxation year, and

B is the Consumer Price Index for the 12 month period preceding the period referred to in the description of A.

History: S. 122.61(5) before paragraph (*a*) was replaced by S.C. 2018, c. 12, s. 17, in force on June 21, 2018, and formerly read:

(5) *Annual adjustment.* Each amount expressed in dollars in subsection (1) shall be adjusted so that, where the base taxation year in relation to a particular month is after 2018, the amount to be used under that subsection for the month is the total of

S. 122.61(5) was added by S.C. 2016, c. 12, s. 43(1), in force December 15, 2015.

S. 122.61(5) was repealed by S.C. 2016, c. 7, s. 29(6), in force on July 1, 2016, and formerly read:

(5) *Annual adjustment.* Each amount expressed in dollars in subsection (1) shall be adjusted so that, where the base taxation year in relation to a particular month is after 1998, the amount to be used under that subsection for the month is the total of

(*a*) the amount that would, but for subsection (7), be the relevant amount used under subsection (1) for the month that is one year before the particular month, and

(*b*) the product obtained by multiplying

(i) the amount referred to in paragraph (*a*)

by

(ii) the amount, adjusted in such manner as is prescribed and rounded to the nearest one-thousandth or, where the result obtained is equidistant from 2 such consecutive one-thousandths, to the higher thereof, that is determined by the formula

$$(A/B) - 1$$

where

A is the Consumer Price Index (within the meaning assigned by subsection 117.1(4)) for the 12-month period that ended on September 30 of the base taxation year, and

B is the Consumer Price Index for the 12 month period preceding the period referred to in the description of A.

► 122.61(5.1) ◄

(5.1) Annual adjustment — (Repealed by S.C. 1998, c. 21, s. 93(3).)

► 122.61(6) ◄

(6) Additions to NCB supplement — July 2005 and 2006. Each amount referred to in the description of F in subsection (1) that is to be used for the purpose of determining the amount deemed to be an overpayment arising during months that are

(*a*) after June 2005 and before July 2006, is to be replaced with the amount that is the total of $185 and the amount otherwise determined under subsection (5) for those months; and

(*b*) after June 2006 and before July 2007, is to be replaced with the amount that is the total of $185 and the amount otherwise determined, for those months, by applying subsection (5) to the amount determined under paragraph (*a*).

► 122.61(6.1) ◄

(6.1) Agreement with a province. Notwithstanding subsection (5), for the purposes of any agreement referred to in section 122.63 with respect to overpayments deemed to arise during months that are after June 2001 and before July 2002, the amount determined under subparagraph (5)(*b*)(ii) for a month referred to in paragraph (6)(*b*) is deemed to be 0.012.

► 122.61(7) ◄

(7) Rounding. If an amount referred to in subsection (1), when adjusted as provided in subsection (5), is not a multiple of one dollar, it shall be rounded to the nearest multiple of one dollar or, where it is equidistant from 2 such consecutive multiples, to the higher thereof.

History: S. 122.61(7) was added by S.C. 2016, c. 12, s. 43(2), in force December 15, 2015.

S. 122.61(7) was repealed by S.C. 2016, c. 7, s. 29(7), in force on July 1, 2016, and formerly read:

(7) *Rounding.* Where an amount referred to in subsection (1), when adjusted as provided in subsection (5), is not a multiple of one dollar, it shall be rounded to the nearest multiple of one dollar or, where it is equidistant from 2 such consecutive multiples, to the higher thereof.

SECTION 122.62: Eligible individuals

► 122.62(1) ◄

(1) Eligible individuals. For the purposes of this subdivision, a person may be considered to be an eligible individual in respect of a particular qualified dependant at the beginning of a month only if the person has, no later than 11 months after the end of the month, filed with the Minister a notice in prescribed form containing prescribed information.

► 122.62(2) ◄

(2) Extension for notices. The Minister may, on or before the day that is 10 years after the beginning of the month referred to in subsection (1), extend the time for filing a notice under that subsection.

History: S. 122.62(2) was replaced by S.C. 2016, c. 7, s. 30(1), in force July 1, 2016, and formerly read:

(2) *Extension for notices.* The Minister may at any time extend the time for filing a notice under subsection (1).

► 122.62(3) ◄

(3) Exception. Where at the beginning of 1993 a person is an eligible individual in respect of a qualified dependant, subsection (1) does not apply to the person in respect of the qualified dependant if the qualified dependant was an eligible child (within the meaning assigned by subsection 122.2(2) because of subparagraph (*a*)(i) of the definition "eligible child" in that subsection) of the individual for the 1992 taxation year.

► 122.62(4) ◄

(4) Person ceasing to be an eligible individual. Where during a particular month a person ceases to be an eligible individual in respect of a particular qualified dependant (otherwise than because of the qualified dependant attaining the age of 18 years), the person shall notify the Minister of that fact before the end of the first month following the particular month.

► 122.62(5) ◄

(5) Death of cohabiting spouse. If the cohabiting spouse or common-law partner of an eligible individual in respect of a qualified dependant dies,

(*a*) the eligible individual shall notify the Minister in prescribed form of that event before the end of the first calendar month that begins after that event; and

(*b*) subject to subsection (8), for the purpose of determining the amount deemed under subsection 122.61(1) to be an overpayment arising in that first month and any subsequent month on account of the eligible individual's liability under this Part for the base taxation year in relation to that first month, the eligible individual's adjusted income for the year is deemed to be equal to the eligible individual's income for the year.

History: S. 122.62(5) was replaced by S.C. 2011, c. 24, s. 39(1), applicable in respect of events that occur after June 2011. S. 122.62(5) formerly read:

(5) *Death of cohabiting spouse.* Where

(*a*) before the end of a particular month the cohabiting spouse or common-law partner of an eligible individual in respect of a qualified dependant dies, and

(*b*) the individual so elects, before the end of the eleventh month after the particular month, in a form that is acceptable to the Minister,

for the purpose of determining the amount deemed under subsection 122.61(1) to be an overpayment arising in any month after the particular month on account of the individual's liability under this Part for the base taxation year in relation to the particular month, subject to any subsequent election under subsection (5) or (7), the individual's adjusted income for the year is deemed to be equal to the individual's income for the year.

(*c*) (Repealed by S.C. 1998, c. 21, s. 95.)

(*d*) (Repealed by S.C. 1998, c. 21, s. 95.)

Forms: RC65 — Canada Child Tax Benefit — Election to Change Marital Status.

► 122.62(6) ◄

(6) Separation from cohabiting spouse. If a person ceases to be an eligible individual's cohabiting spouse or common-law partner,

(*a*) the eligible individual shall notify the Minister in prescribed form of that event before the end of the first calendar month that begins after that event; and

(*b*) subject to subsection (8), for the purpose of determining the amount deemed under subsection 122.61(1) to be an overpayment arising in that first month and any subsequent month on account of the eligible individual's liability under this Part for the base taxation year in relation to that first month, the eligible individual's adjusted income for the year is deemed to be equal to the eligible individual's income for the year.

History: S. 122.62(6) was replaced by S.C. 2011, c. 24, s. 39(1), applicable in respect of events that occur after June 2011. S. 122.62(6) formerly read:

(6) *Separation from cohabiting spouse.* Where

(*a*) before the end of a particular month an eligible individual in respect of a qualified dependant begins to live separate and apart from the individual's cohabiting spouse or common-law partner, because of a breakdown of their marriage or common-law partnership, for a period of at least 90 days that includes a day in the particular month, and

(*b*) the individual so elects, before the end of the eleventh month after the particular month, in a form that is acceptable to the Minister,

for the purpose of determining the amount deemed under subsection 122.61(1) to be an overpayment arising in any month after the particular month on account of the individual's liability under this Part for the base taxation year in relation to the particular month, subject to any subsequent election under subsection (5) or (7), the individual's adjusted income for the year is deemed to be equal to the individual's income for the year.

(*c*) (Repealed by S.C. 1998, c. 21, s. 95.)

(*d*) (Repealed by S.C. 1998, c. 21, s. 95.)

Forms: RC65 — Canada Child Tax Benefit — Election to Change Marital Status.

► 122.62(7) ◄

(7) Person becoming a cohabiting spouse. If a taxpayer becomes the cohabiting spouse or common-law partner of an eligible individual,

(*a*) the eligible individual shall notify the Minister in prescribed form of that event before the end of the first calendar month that begins after that event; and

(*b*) subject to subsection (8), for the purpose of determining the amount deemed under subsection 122.61(1) to be an overpayment arising in that first month and any subsequent month on account of the eligible individual's liability under this Part for the base taxation year in relation to that first month, the taxpayer is deemed to have been the eligible individual's cohabiting spouse or common-law partner at the end of the base taxation year in relation to that month.

History: S. 122.62(7) was replaced by S.C. 2011, c. 24, s. 39(1), applicable in respect of events that occur after June 2011. S. 122.62(7) formerly read:

(7) *Person becoming a cohabiting spouse.* Where

(*a*) at any particular time before the end of a particular month a taxpayer has become the cohabiting spouse or common-law partner of an eligible individual, and

(*b*) the taxpayer and the eligible individual jointly so elect in prescribed form filed with the Minister before the end of the eleventh month after the particular month,

for the purpose of determining the amount deemed by subsection 122.61(1) to be an overpayment arising in any month after the particular month on account of the eligible individual's liability under this Part for the year, the taxpayer is deemed to have been the eligible individual's cohabiting spouse or common-law partner throughout the period that began immediately before the end of the base taxation year in relation to the particular month and ended at the particular time.

Forms: RC65 — Canada Child Tax Benefit — Election to Change Marital Status.

► 122.62(8) ◄

(8) Ordering of events. If more than one event referred to in subsections (5) to (7) occur in a calendar month, only the subsection relating to the last of those events to have occurred applies.

History: S. 122.62(8) was added by S.C. 2011, c. 24, s. 39(1), applicable in respect of events that occur after June 2011.

► 122.62(9) ◄

(9) Advice of Department of Human Resources Development — (Repealed by S.C. 1998, c. 19, s. 142(2).)

SECTION 122.63: Agreement

► 122.63(1) ◄

(1) Agreement. The Minister of Finance may enter into an agreement with the government of a province whereby the amounts determined under the description of E in subsection 122.61(1) with respect to persons resident in the province shall, for the purpose of calculating overpayments deemed to arise under that subsection, be replaced by amounts determined in accordance with the agreement.

History: S. 122.63(1) was added by S.C. 2016, c. 7, s. 31(2), in force July 1, 2017.

S. 122.63(1) was repealed by S.C 2016, c. 7, s. 31(1), in force July 1, 2016, and formerly read:

(1) *Agreement.* The Minister of Finance may enter into an agreement with the government of a province whereby the amounts determined under paragraph (*a*) of the description of A in subsection 122.61(1) with respect to persons resident in the province shall, for the purpose of calculating overpayments deemed to arise under that subsection, be replaced by amounts determined in accordance with the agreement.

Related Sections: S. 122.6, "Eligible individual".

► 122.63(2) ◄

(2) Agreement. The amounts determined under the description of E in subsection 122.61(1) for a base taxation year because of any agreement entered into with a province and referred to in subsection (1) shall be based on the age of qualified dependants of eligible individuals, or on the number of such qualified dependants, or both, and shall result in an amount in respect of a qualified dependant that is not less, in respect of that qualified dependant, than 85% of the amount that would otherwise be determined under that description in respect of that qualified dependant for that year.

History: S. 122.63(2) was added by S.C. 2016, c. 7, s. 31(2), in force July 1, 2017.

S. 122.63(2) was repealed by S.C 2016, c. 7, s. 31(1), in force July 1, 2016, and formerly read:

(2) *Idem.* The amounts determined under paragraph (*a*) of the description of A in subsection 122.61(1) for a base taxation year because of any agreement entered into with a province and referred to in subsection (1) shall be based on the age of qualified dependants of eligible individuals, or on the number of such qualified dependants, or both, and shall result in an amount in respect of a qualified dependant that is not less, in respect of that qualified dependant, than 85% of the amount that would otherwise be determined under that paragraph in respect of that qualified dependant for that year.

► 122.63(3) ◄

(3) Agreement. Any agreement entered into with a province and referred to in subsection (1) shall provide that, where the operation of the agreement results in a total of all amounts, each of which is an amount deemed under subsection 122.61(1) to be an overpayment on account of the liability under this Part for a taxation year of a person subject to the agreement, that exceeds 101% of the total of such overpayments that would have otherwise been deemed to have arisen under subsection 122.61(1), the excess shall be reimbursed by the government of the province to the Government of Canada.

History: S. 122.63(3) was added by S.C. 2016, c. 7, s. 31(2), in force July 1, 2017.

S. 122.63(3) was repealed by S.C 2016, c. 7, s. 31(1), in force July 1, 2016, and formerly read:

(3) *Idem.* Any agreement entered into with a province and referred to in subsection (1) shall provide that, where the operation of the agreement results in a total of all amounts, each of which is an amount deemed under subsection 122.61(1) to be an overpayment on account of the liability under this Part for a taxation year of a person subject to the agreement, that exceeds 101% of the total of such overpayments that would have otherwise been deemed to have arisen under subsection 122.61(1), the excess shall be reimbursed by the government of the province to the Government of Canada.

SECTION 122.64: Confidentiality of information

► 122.64(1) ◄

(1) Confidentiality of information. (Repealed by S.C. 2013, c. 40, s. 53.)

History: S. 122.64(1) was repealed by S.C. 2013, c. 40, s. 53, in force December 12, 2013, and formerly read:

(1) *Confidentiality of information.* Information obtained under this Act or the *Family Allowances Act* by or on behalf of the Minister of Human Resources and Skills Development is deemed to be obtained on behalf of the Minister of National Revenue for the purposes of this Act.

S. 122.64(1) was amended by S.C. 2012, c. 19, s. 694, by replacing "Minister of Social Development" with "Minister of Human Resources and Skills Development", in force March 1, 2013.

► 122.64(2) ◄

(2) Communication of information. (Repealed by S.C. 2013, c. 40, s. 53.)

History: S. 122.64(2) was repealed by S.C. 2013, c. 40, s. 53, in force December 12, 2013, and formerly read:

(2) *Communication of information.* Notwithstanding subsection 241(1), an official (as defined in subsection 241(10)) may provide information obtained under subsection 122.62(1), (4), (5), (6) or (7) or the *Family Allowances Act*

(*a*) to an official of the government of a province, solely for the purposes of the administration or enforcement of a prescribed law of the province; or

(*b*) to an official of the Department of Human Resources and Skills Development for the purposes of the administration of the *Family Allowances Act*, the *Canada Pension Plan* or the *Old Age Security Act*.

S. 122.64(2)(*b*) was amended by S.C. 2012, c. 19, s. 695(1), by replacing "Department of Social Development" with "Department of Human Resources and Skills Development", in force March 1, 2013.

Related Regulations: 3003.

► 122.64(3) ◄

(3) Taxpayer's address. (Repealed by S.C. 2013, c. 40, s. 53.)

History: S. 122.64(3) was repealed by S.C. 2013, c. 40, s. 53, in force December 12, 2013, and formerly read:

(3) *Taxpayer's address.* Notwithstanding subsection 241(1), an official or authorized person may provide a taxpayer's name and address that has been obtained by or on behalf of the Minister of National Revenue for the purposes of this subdivision, for the purposes of the administration or enforcement of Part I of the *Family Orders and Agreements Enforcement Assistance Act*.

► 122.64(4) ◄

(4) Offence. (Repealed by S.C. 2013, c. 40, s. 53.)

History: S. 122.64(4) was repealed by S.C. 2013, c. 40, s. 53, in force December 12, 2013, and formerly read:

(4) *Offence.* Every person to whom information has been provided under subsection (2) or (3) and who knowingly uses, communicates or allows to be communicated that information for any purpose other than that for which it was provided is guilty of an offence and is liable on summary conviction to a fine not exceeding $5,000 or to imprisonment for a term not exceeding 12 months or to both that fine and imprisonment.

► 122.64(5) ◄

(5) "Official" and "authorized person" — (Repealed by S.C. 1998, c. 19, s. 144(2).)

Subdivision a.2 — Canada Workers Benefit

History: The heading of Subdivision a.2 of Division E was replaced by S.C. 2018, c. 12, s. 18(1), in force January 1, 2019, and formerly read: "Working Income Tax Benefit".

SECTION 122.7: [Canada Workers Benefit]

► 122.7(1) ◄

(1) Definitions. The following definitions apply in this section.

Tax Window Files: Taxability of Support Payments, *February 9, 2012*, CRA Document No. 2011-0406701E5; Prestation fiscale pour le revenu de travail, *November 9, 2010*, CRA Document No. 2010-0357091E5.

"adjusted net income" —"adjusted net income" of an individual for a taxation year means the amount that would be the individual's income for the taxation year if

(*a*) (Repealed by S.C. 2018, c. 27, s. 12(2).)

(*b*) in computing that income, no amount were included under paragraph 56(1)(*q*.1) or subsection 56(6), in respect of any gain from a disposition of property to which section 79 applies or in respect of a gain described in subsection 40(3.21); and

(*c*) in computing that income, no amount were deductible under paragraph 20(1)(*ww*) or 60(*y*) or (*z*).

History: S. 122.7(1), paragraph (*a*) of the definition of "adjusted net income" was repealed by S.C. 2018, c. 27, s. 12(2), in force on January 1, 2019, and formerly read:

(*a*) this Act were read without reference to paragraph 81(1)(*a*) and subsection 81(4);

S. 122.7(1), paragraph (*c*) of the definition "adjusted net income" was replaced by S.C. 2018, c. 12, s. 19(1), applicable to the 2018 and subsequent taxation years, and formerly read:

(*c*) in computing that income, no amount were deductible under paragraph 60(*y*) or (*z*).

S. 122.7(1), paragraph (*b*) of the definition "adjusted net income" was replaced by S.C. 2010, c. 25, s. 26(1), applicable to the 2000 and subsequent taxation years. S. 122.7(1), paragraph (*b*) of the definition "adjusted net income" formerly read:

(*b*) in computing that income, no amount were included under paragraph 56(1)(*q.1*) or subsection 56(6), or in respect of any gain from a disposition of property to which section 79 applies; and

"cohabiting spouse or common-law partner" —"cohabiting spouse or common-law partner" of an individual at any time has the meaning assigned by section 122.6.

"designated educational institution" —"designated educational institution" has the meaning assigned by subsection 118.6(1).

"eligible dependant" —"eligible dependant" of an individual for a taxation year means a child of the individual who, at the end of the year,

(*a*) resided with the individual;

(*b*) was under the age of 19 years; and

(*c*) was not an eligible individual.

Related Sections: 122.7(1.2) Receipt of social assistance.

"eligible individual" —"eligible individual" for a taxation year means an individual (other than an ineligible individual) who was resident in Canada throughout the taxation year and who was, at the end of the taxation year,

(*a*) 19 years of age or older;

(*b*) the cohabiting spouse or common-law partner of another individual; or

(*c*) the parent of a child with whom the individual resides.

Related Sections: 122.7(1.2) Receipt of social assistance.

"eligible spouse" —"eligible spouse" of an eligible individual for a taxation year means an individual (other than an ineligible individual) who was resident in Canada throughout the taxation year and who was, at the end of the taxation year, the cohabiting spouse or common-law partner of the eligible individual.

"ineligible individual" —"ineligible individual" for a taxation year means an individual

(*a*) who is described in paragraph 149(1)(*a*) or (*b*) at any time in the taxation year;

(*b*) who, except where the individual has an eligible dependant for the taxation year, was enrolled as a full-time student at a designated educational institution for a total of more than 13 weeks in the taxation year; or

(*c*) who was confined to a prison or similar institution for a period of at least 90 days during the taxation year.

"return of income" —"return of income" filed by an individual for a taxation year means a return of income (other than a return of income filed under subsection 70(2) or 104(23), paragraph 128(2)(*e*) or subsection 150(4)) that is required to be filed for the taxation year or that would be required to be filed if the individual had tax payable under this Part for the taxation year.

"working income" —"working income", of an individual for a taxation year, means the total of

(*a*) the total of all amounts each of which would, if this Act were read without reference to section 8, be the individual's income for the taxation year from an office or employment,

(*b*) all amounts that are included because of paragraph 56(1)(*n*) or (*o*) or subparagraph 56(1)(*r*)(v) in computing the individual's income for a period in the taxation year, and

(*c*) the total of all amounts each of which is the individual's income for the taxation year from a business carried on by the individual otherwise than as a specified member of a partnership.

History: S. 122.7(1), the definition of "working income" was replaced by S.C. 2018, c. 27, s. 12(1), in force on January 1, 2019, and formerly read:

"working income"—"working income" of an individual for a taxation year means the total of

(*a*) the total of all amounts each of which would, if this Act were read without reference to section 8, paragraph 81(1)(*a*) and subsection 81(4), be the individual's income for the taxation year from an office or employment;

(*b*) all amounts that are included, or that would, but for paragraph 81(1)(*a*), be included, because of paragraph 56(1)(*n*) or (*o*) or subparagraph 56(1)(*r*)(v) in computing the individual's income for a period in the taxation year; and

(*c*) the total of all amounts each of which would, if this Act were read without reference to paragraph 81(1)(*a*), be the individual's income for the taxation year from a business carried on by the individual otherwise than as a specified member of a partnership.

S. 122.7(1), paragraph (*b*) of the definition "working income" was replaced by S.C. 2009, c. 2, s. 38(1), applicable to the 2008 and subsequent taxation years. S. 122.7(1), paragraph (*b*) of the definition "working income" formerly read:

(*b*) all amounts that are included, or that would, but for paragraph 81(1)(*a*), be included, because of paragraph 56(1)(*n*) or (*o*) in computing the individual's income for the taxation years; and

Related Sections: 122.91(2) Training amount limit.

► 122.7(1.1) ◄

(1.1) Optional amounts. An individual may determine the total amount for the definition "working income" for both the individual and the individual's eligible spouse, if applicable, for a taxation year as if the Act were read without reference to paragraph 81(1)(*a*) and subsection 81(4) and if so, the individual shall determine the total amount for the definition "adjusted net income" for both the individual and the individual's eligible spouse, if applicable, for the taxation year as if the Act were read without reference to paragraph 81(1)(*a*) and subsection 81(4).

History: S. 122.7(1.1) was added by S.C. 2018, c. 27, s. 12(3), in force on January 1, 2019.

► 122.7(1.2) ◄

(1.2) Receipt of social assistance. For the purposes of applying the definitions *eligible dependant* and *eligible individual* in subsection (1) for a taxation year, an individual shall not fail to qualify as a parent (within the meaning assigned by section 252) of another individual solely because of the receipt of a social assistance amount that is payable under a program of the Government of Canada or the government of a province for the benefit of the other individual, unless the amount is a special allowance under the *Children's Special Allowances Act* in respect of the other individual in the taxation year.

History: S. 122.7(1.2) was added by S.C. 2019, c. 29, s. 20(1), deemed to have come into force on January 1, 2009.

Related Sections: 122.7(1) "eligible dependant"; 122.7(1) "eligible individual"; 252(1) Extended meaning of "child".

► 122.7(2) ◄

(2) Deemed payment on account of tax. Subject to subsections (4) and (5), an eligible individual for a taxation year who files a return of income for the taxation year is deemed to have paid, at the end of the taxation year, on account of tax payable under this Part for the taxation year, an amount equal to the amount, if any, determined by the formula

$$A - B$$

where

A is

(*a*) if the individual had neither an eligible spouse nor an eligible dependant, for the taxation year, the lesser of $1,355 and 26% of the amount, if any, by which the individual's working income for the taxation year exceeds $ 3,000, or

(*b*) if the individual had an eligible spouse or an eligible dependant, for the taxation year, the lesser of $2,335 and 26% of the amount, if any, by which the total of the working incomes of the individual and, if applicable, of the eligible spouse, for the taxation year, exceeds $3,000; and

B is

(*a*) if the individual had neither an eligible spouse nor an eligible dependant, for the taxation year, 12% of the amount, if any, by which the adjusted net income of the individual for the taxation year exceeds $12,820, or

(*b*) if the individual had an eligible spouse or an eligible dependant, for the taxation year, 12% of the amount, if any, by which the total of the adjusted net incomes of the individual and, if applicable, of the eligible spouse, for the taxation year, exceeds $17,025.

CRA News Release

2.2% Indexation Factor for 2019

See the CRA Fact Sheet, dated November 16, 2018, that is reproduced following subsection117.1(1). This release announces a 2.2% indexation factor applicable for 2019 tax bracket thresholds, personal amounts and other amounts relating to non-refundable credits, as well as the refundable medical expense supplement, Old Age Security repayment threshold, certain board and lodging allowances, and the tradesperson's tools deduction. Increases to tax bracket thresholds, amounts relating to non-refundable credits, and most other amounts will take effect on January 1, 2019. However, increases in amounts for certain income-tested benefits (for example, the goods and services tax credit) will take effect on July 1, 2019. Although the Fact Sheet does not list the indexed amounts relating to the Working Income Tax Benefit specifically, indexing also applies to these amounts as set out in subsection117.1(1)in the Act.

History: S. 122.7(2), the portion before the formula was replaced by S.C. 2018, c. 27, s. 12(4), in force on January 1, 2019, and formerly read:

(2) *Deemed payment on account of tax.* Subject to subsections (4) and (5), an eligible individual for a taxation year who files a return of income for the taxation year and who makes a claim under this subsection, is deemed to have paid, at the end of the taxation year, on account of tax payable under this Part for the taxation year, an amount equal to the amount, if any, determined by the formula

S. 122.7(2), the descriptions of A and B were replaced by S.C. 2018, c. 12, s. 19(2), in force on January 1, 2019, and formerly read:

A is

(*a*) if the individual had neither an eligible spouse nor an eligible dependant, for the taxation year, the lesser of $925 and 25% of the amount, if any, by which the individual's working income for the taxation year exceeds $3,000, or

(*b*) if the individual had an eligible spouse or an eligible dependant, for the taxation year, the lesser of $1,680 and 25% of the amount, if any, by which the total of the working incomes of the individual and, if applicable, of the eligible spouse, for the taxation year, exceeds $3,000; and

B is

(*a*) if the individual had neither an eligible spouse nor an eligible dependant, for the taxation year, 15% of the amount, if any, by which the adjusted net income of the individual for the taxation year exceeds $10,500, or

(*b*) if the individual had an eligible spouse or an eligible dependant, for the taxation year, 15% of the amount, if any, by which the total of the adjusted net incomes of the individual and, if applicable, of the eligible spouse, for the taxation year, exceeds $14,500.

S. 122.7(2), the descriptions of A and B, were replaced by S.C. 2016, c. 14, s. 69(1), in force on January 1, 2019. However, this amendment was repealed by S.C. 2018, c. 12, s. 40. S. 122.7(2), the descriptions of A and B, as they were replaced by S.C. 2016, c. 14, s. 69(1), read as follows:

A is

(*a*) if the individual had neither an eligible spouse nor an eligible dependant, for the taxation year, the lesser of $1,192 and 26% of the amount, if any, by which the individual's working income for the taxation year exceeds $3,000, or

(*b*) if the individual had an eligible spouse or an eligible dependant, for the taxation year, the lesser of $2,165 and 26% of the amount, if any, by which the total of the working incomes of the individual and, if applicable, of the eligible spouse, for the taxation year, exceeds $3,000; and

B is

(a) if the individual had neither an eligible spouse nor an eligible dependant, for the taxation year, 14% of the amount, if any, by which the adjusted net income of the individual for the taxation year exceeds $10,500, or

(b) if the individual had an eligible spouse or an eligible dependant, for the taxation year, 14% of the amount, if any, by which the total of the adjusted net incomes of the individual and, if applicable, of the eligible spouse, for the taxation year, exceeds $14,500.

S. 122.7(3), the descriptions of C and D, were replaced by S.C. 2016, c. 14, s. 69(2), in force on January 1, 2019. However, this amendment was repealed by S.C. 2018, c. 12, s. 40. S. 122.7(2), the descriptions of A and B, as they were replaced by S.C. 2016, c. 14, s. 69(2), read as follows:

C is the lesser of $462.50 and 26% of the amount, if any, by which the individual's working income for the taxation year exceeds $1,150; and

D is

(a) if the individual had neither an eligible spouse nor an eligible dependant, for the taxation year, 14% of the amount, if any, by which the individual's adjusted net income for the taxation year exceeds $20,844,

(b) if the individual had an eligible spouse for the taxation year who was not entitled to deduct an amount under subsection 118.3(1) for the taxation year, or had an eligible dependant for the taxation year, 14% of the amount, if any, by which the total of the adjusted net incomes of the individual and, if applicable, of the eligible spouse, for the taxation year, exceeds $32,491, or

(c) if the individual had an eligible spouse for the taxation year who was entitled to deduct an amount under subsection 118.3(1) for the taxation year, 7% of the amount, if any, by which the total of the adjusted net incomes of the individual and of the eligible spouse, for the taxation year, exceeds $32,491.

S. 122.7(2), the descriptions of A and B were replaced by S.C. 2009, c. 31, s. 13(1), applicable to the 2009 and subsequent taxation years. S. 122.7(2), the descriptions of A and B formerly read:

A is

(a) if the individual had neither an eligible spouse nor an eligible dependant, for the taxation year, the lesser of $500 and 20% of the amount, if any, by which the individual's working income for the taxation year exceeds $3,000, or

(b) if the individual had an eligible spouse or an eligible dependant, for the taxation year, the lesser of $1,000 and 20% of the amount, if any, by which the total of the working incomes of the individual and, if applicable, of the eligible spouse of the individual, for the taxation year, exceeds $3,000; and

B is

(a) if the individual had neither an eligible spouse nor an eligible dependant, for the taxation year, 15% of the amount, if any, by which the individual's adjusted net income for the taxation year exceeds $9,500, or

(b) if the individual had an eligible spouse or an eligible dependant, for the taxation year, 15% of the amount, if any, by which the total of the adjusted net incomes of the individual and, if applicable, of the eligible spouse of the individual, for the taxation year, exceeds $14,500.

Related Sections: S. 117(2.1) Tax payable — WITB advance payment; s. 248(1), "common-law partner".

Forms: RC201 — Working Income Tax Benefit Advance Payments Application for 2008; T2 SCH 6 — Summary of Dispositions of Capital Property (2006 and later taxation years); T2201 — Disability Tax Credit Certificate.

Guides: RC4227 Working Income Tax Benefit.

▶ 122.7(3) ◀

(3) Deemed payment on account of tax — disability supplement. An eligible individual for a taxation year who files a return of income for the taxation year and who may deduct an amount under subsection 118.3(1) in computing tax payable under this Part for the taxation year is deemed to have paid, at the end of the taxation year, on account of tax payable under this Part for the taxation year, an amount equal to the amount, if any, determined by the formula

$$C - D$$

where

C is the lesser of $700 and 26% of the amount, if any, by which the individual's working income for the taxation year exceeds $1,150; and

D is

(a) if the individual had neither an eligible spouse nor an eligible dependant, for the taxation year, 12% of the amount, if any, by which the individual's adjusted net income for the taxation year exceeds $24,111,

(b) if the individual had an eligible spouse for the taxation year who was not entitled to deduct an amount under subsection 118.3(1) for the taxation year, or had an eligible dependant for the taxation year, 12% of the amount, if any, by which the total of the adjusted net incomes of the individual and, if applicable, of the eligible spouse, for the taxation year, exceeds $36,483, or

(c) if the individual had an eligible spouse for the taxation year who was entitled to deduct an amount under subsection 118.3(1) for the taxation year, 6% of the amount, if any, by which the total of the adjusted net incomes of the individual and of the eligible spouse, for the taxation year, exceeds $36,483.

CRA News Release

2.2% Indexation Factor for 2019

See the CRA Fact Sheet, dated November 16, 2018, that is reproduced following subsection117.1(1). This release announces a 2.2% indexation factor applicable for 2019 tax bracket thresholds, personal amounts and other amounts relating to non-refundable credits, as well as the refundable medical expense supplement, Old Age Security repayment threshold, certain board and lodging allowances, and the tradesperson's tools deduction. Increases to tax bracket thresholds, amounts relating to non-refundable credits, and most other amounts will take effect on January 1, 2019. However, increases in amounts for certain income-tested benefits (for example, the goods and services tax credit) will take effect on July 1, 2019. Although the Fact Sheet does not list the indexed amounts relating to the Working Income Tax Benefit specifically, indexing also applies to these amounts as set out in subsection117.1(1)in the Act.

History: S. 122.7(3), the descriptions of C and D were replaced by S.C. 2018, c. 12, s. 19(3), in force on January 1, 2019, and formerly read:

C is the lesser of $462.50 and 25% of the amount, if any, by which the individual's working income for the taxation year exceeds $1,150; and

D is

(a) if the individual had neither an eligible spouse nor an eligible dependant, for the taxation year, 15% of the amount, if any, by which the individual's adjusted net income for the taxation year exceeds $16,667,

(b) if the individual had an eligible spouse for the taxation year who was not entitled to deduct an amount under subsection 118.3(1) for the taxation year, or had an eligible dependant for the taxation year, 15% of the amount, if any, by which the total of the adjusted net incomes of the individual and, if applicable, of the eligible spouse, for the taxation year, exceeds $25,700, or

(c) if the individual had an eligible spouse for the taxation year who was entitled to deduct an amount under subsection 118.3(1) for the taxation year, 7.5% of the amount, if any, by which the total of the adjusted net incomes of the individual and of the eligible spouse, for the taxation year, exceeds $25,700.

S. 122.7(3), the descriptions of C and D were replaced by S.C. 2009, c. 31, s. 13(2), applicable to the 2009 and subsequent taxation years. S. 122.7(3), the descriptions of C and D formerly read:

C is the lesser of $250 and 20% of the amount, if any, by which the individual's working income for the taxation year exceeds $1,750, and

D is

(*a*) if the individual had neither an eligible spouse nor an eligible dependant, for the taxation year, 15% of the amount, if any, by which the individual's adjusted net income for the taxation year exceeds $12,833,

(*b*) if the individual had an eligible spouse for the taxation year who was not entitled to deduct an amount under subsection 118.3(1) for the taxation year, or had an eligible dependant for the taxation year, 15% of the amount, if any, by which the total of the adjusted net incomes of the individual and, if applicable, of the eligible spouse, for the taxation year, exceeds $21,167, or

(*c*) if the individual had an eligible spouse for the taxation year who was entitled to deduct an amount under subsection 118.3(1) for the taxation year, 7.5% of the amount, if any, by which the total of the adjusted net incomes of the individual and of the eligible spouse, for the taxation year, exceeds $21,167.

Forms: T2201 — Disability Tax Credit Certificate.

▶ 122.7(4) ◀

(4) Eligible spouse deemed not to be an eligible individual. An eligible spouse of an eligible individual for a taxation year is deemed, for the purpose of subsection (2), not to be an eligible individual for the taxation year if the eligible spouse made a joint application described in subsection (6) with the eligible individual and the eligible individual received an amount under subsection (7) in respect of the taxation year.

▶ 122.7(5) ◀

(5) Only one eligible individual. If an eligible individual has an eligible spouse for a taxation year and both those individuals would be, but for this subsection, eligible individuals for the purposes of subsection (2) in respect of the taxation year,

(*a*) if the individuals agree on which individual is the eligible individual for the taxation year, only that individual shall be an eligible individual for the purposes of subsection (2) in respect of the taxation year; and

(*b*) in any other case, only the individual that the Minister designates is the eligible individual for the purposes of subsection (2) in respect of the taxation year.

History: S. 122.7(5) was replaced by S.C. 2018, c. 27, s. 12(5), in force on January 1, 2019, and formerly read:

(5) *Amount deemed to be nil.* If an eligible individual had an eligible spouse for a taxation year and both the eligible individual and the eligible spouse make a claim for the taxation year under subsection (2), the amount deemed to have been paid under that subsection by each of them on account of tax payable under this Part for the taxation year, is nil.

▶ 122.7(6) ◀

(6) Application for advance payment. Subsection (7) applies to an individual for a taxation year if,

(*a*) at any time after January 1 and before September 1 of the taxation year, the individual makes an application (or in the case of an individual who has, at that time, a cohabiting spouse or common-law partner, the two of them make a joint application designating the individual for the purpose of subsection (7)), to the Minister in prescribed form, containing prescribed information; and

(*b*) where the individual and a cohabiting spouse or common-law partner have made a joint application referred to in paragraph (*a*)

(i) the individual's working income for the taxation year can reasonably be expected to be greater than the working income of the individual's cohabiting spouse or common-law partner for the taxation year, or

(ii) the individual can reasonably be expected to be deemed by subsection (3) to have paid an amount on account of tax payable under this Part for the taxation year.

Forms: RC201 — Working Income Tax Benefit Advance Payments Application for 2008.

▶ 122.7(7) ◀

(7) Advance payment. Subject to subsection (8), the Minister may pay to an individual before the end of January of the year following a taxation year, one or more amounts that, in total, do not exceed one-half of the total of the amounts that the Minister estimates will be deemed to be paid by the individual under subsection (2) or (3) at the end of the taxation year, and any amount paid by the Minister under this subsection is deemed to have been received by the individual in respect of the taxation year.

▶ 122.7(8) ◀

(8) Limitation — advance payment. No payment shall be made under subsection (7) to an individual in respect of a taxation year

(*a*) if the total amount that the Minister may pay under that subsection is less than $100; or

(*b*) before the day on which the individual has filed a return of income for a preceding taxation year in respect of which the individual received a payment under that subsection.

▶ 122.7(9) ◀

(9) Notification to Minister. If, in a taxation year, an individual makes an application described in subsection (6), the individual shall notify the Minister of the occurrence of any of the following events before the end of the month following the month in which the event occurs

(*a*) the individual ceases to be resident in Canada in the taxation year;

(*b*) the individual ceases, before the end of the taxation year, to be a cohabiting spouse or common-law partner of another person with whom the individual made the application;

(*c*) the individual enrols as a full-time student at a designated educational institution in the taxation year; or

(*d*) the individual is confined to a prison or similar institution in the taxation year.

▶ 122.7(10) ◀

(10) Special rules for eligible dependant. For the purpose of applying subsections (2) and (3), if an individual (referred to in this subsection as the "child") would be, but for this subsection, an eligible dependant of more than one eligible individual for a taxation year, the child is deemed only to be an eligible dependant of

(*a*) if the individuals agree, the agreed upon individual; and (*b*) in any other case, the individual designated by the Minister.

History: S. 122.7(10) was replaced by S.C. 2018, c. 27, s. 12(6), in force on January 1, 2019, and formerly read:

(10) *Special rule re eligible dependant.* For the purpose of applying subsections (2) and (3), an individual (referred to in this subsection as the "child") is deemed not to be an eligible dependant of an eligible individual for a taxation year if the child is an eligible dependant of another eligible individual for the taxation year and both eligible individuals identified the child as an eligible dependant for the purpose of claiming or computing an amount under this section for the taxation year.

▶ 122.7(11) ◀

(11) Effect of bankruptcy. For the purpose of this subdivision, if an individual becomes bankrupt in a particular calendar year

(*a*) notwithstanding subsection 128(2), any reference to the taxation year of the individual (other than in this subsection) is deemed to be a reference to the particular calendar year; and

(*b*) the individual's working income and adjusted net income for the taxation year ending on December 31 of the particular calendar year is deemed to include the individual's working income and adjusted net income for the taxation year that begins on January 1 of the particular calendar year.

Editorial Note: The bankrupt taxpayer must consider both his or her pre-bankruptcy and post-bankruptcy working income and adjusted net income to calculate his or her working income tax benefit.

▶ 122.7(12) ◀

(12) Special rules in the event of death. For the purpose of this subdivision, if an individual dies after June 30 of a calendar year

(*a*) the individual is deemed to be resident in Canada from the time of death until the end of the year and to reside at the same place in Canada as the place where the individual resided immediately before death;

(*b*) the individual is deemed to be the same age at the end of the year as the individual would have been if the individual were alive at the end of the year;

(*c*) the individual is deemed to be the cohabiting spouse or common-law partner of another individual (referred to in this paragraph as the "surviving spouse") at the end of the year if,

(i) immediately before death, the individual was the cohabiting spouse or common-law partner of the surviving spouse, and

(ii) the surviving spouse is not the cohabiting spouse or common-law partner of another individual at the end of the year; and

(*d*) any return of income filed by a legal representative of the individual is deemed to be a return of income filed by the individual.

Editorial Note: A taxpayer who dies after June 30 in a year will continue to meet the following status requirements for the rest of the year for the purpose of claiming the working income tax benefit: maintain Canadian residence until year-end; be the same age at year-end as that if he or she had been alive at year-end; be a cohabiting spouse or common-law partner at year-end if he or she was one immediately before his or her death and if the surviving spouse was not cohabiting with someone else at year-end; and be deemed to have filed a return of income for the year if one was filed by his or her legal representative.

SECTION 122.71: Modification for purposes of provincial program

The Minister of Finance may enter into an agreement with the government of a province whereby the amounts determined under subsections 122.7(2) and (3) with respect to an eligible individual resident in the province at the end of the taxation year shall, for the purpose of calculating amounts deemed to be paid on account of the tax payable of an individual under those subsections, be replaced by amounts determined in accordance with the agreement.

Subdivision a.3 — Climate Action Incentive

History: The heading of Subdivision a.3 of Division E was replaced by S.C. 2018, c. 27, s. 13(1), applicable to the 2018 and subsequent taxation years, and formerly read: "Child Fitness Tax Credit".

SECTION 122.8: Definitions

► 122.8(1) ◄

(1) Definitions. The following definitions apply in this section.

History: S. 122.8(1) was added by S.C. 2018, c. 27, s. 13(1), applicable to the 2018 and subsequent taxation years.

S. 122.8(1) was repealed by S.C. 2016, c. 7, s. 32(2), in force January 1, 2017, and formerly read:

(1) *Definitions.* The following definitions apply in this section.

"eligible fitness expense"—"eligible fitness expense" in respect of a qualifying child of an individual for a taxation year means the amount of a fee paid to a qualifying entity (other than an amount paid to a person that is, at the time the amount is paid, the individual's spouse or common-law partner or another individual who is under 18 years of age) to the extent that the fee is attributable to the cost of registration or membership of the qualifying child in a prescribed program of physical activity and, for the purposes of this section, that cost

(*a*) includes the cost to the qualifying entity of the program in respect of its administration, instruction, rental of required facilities, and uniforms and equipment that are not available to be acquired by a participant in the program for an amount less than their fair market value at the time, if any, they are so acquired; and

(*b*) does not include

(i) the cost of accommodation, travel, food or beverages, or

(ii) any amount deductible under section 63 in computing any person's income for any taxation year.

"qualifying child"—"qualifying child" of an individual for a taxation year means a child of the individual who is, at the beginning of the year,

(*a*) under 16 years of age; or

(*b*) in the case where an amount is deductible under section 118.3 in computing any person's tax payable under this Part for the year in respect of that child, under 18 years of age.

"qualifying entity"—"qualifying entity" means a person or partnership that offers one or more prescribed programs of physical activity.

"return of income"—"return of income" filed by an individual for a taxation year means a return of income (other than a return of income filed under subsection 70(2) or 104(23), paragraph 128(2)(*e*) or subsection 150(4)) that is required to be filed for the year or that would be required to be filed if the individual had tax payable under this Part for the year.

S. 122.8(1) was added by S.C. 2014, c. 39, s. 39(1), applicable to the 2015 and subsequent taxation years.

"cohabiting spouse or common-law partner" —"cohabiting spouse or common-law partner", of an individual at any time, has the same meaning as in section 122.6.

"eligible individual" —"eligible individual", for a taxation year, means an individual (other than a trust) who is, at the end of the taxation year,

(*a*) 18 years of age or older;

(*b*) a parent who resides with their child; or

(*c*) married or in a common-law partnership.

"qualified dependant" —"qualified dependant", of an individual for a taxation year, means a person who, at the end of the taxation year,

(*a*) is the individual's child or is dependent for support on the individual or on the individual's cohabiting spouse or common-law partner;

(*b*) resides with the individual;

(*c*) is under the age of 18 years;

(*d*) is not an eligible individual for the taxation year; and

(*e*) is not a qualified relation of any individual for the taxation year.

"qualified relation" —"qualified relation", of an individual for a taxation year, means the person, if any, who, at the end of the taxation year, is the individual's cohabiting spouse or common-law partner.

"return of income" —"return of income", in respect of a person for a taxation year, means the person's return of income (other than a return of income under subsection 70(2) or 104(23), paragraph 128(2)(*e*) or subsection 150(4)) that is required to be filed for the taxation year or that would be required to be filed if the person had tax payable under this Part for the taxation year.

► 122.8(2) ◄

(2) Persons not eligible individuals, qualified relations or qualified dependants. Notwithstanding subsection (1), a person is not an eligible individual, is not a qualified relation and is not a qualified dependant, for a taxation year, if the person

(*a*) died before April of the year following the taxation year;

(*b*) is confined to a prison or similar institution for a period of at least 90 days during the taxation year;

(*c*) is a non-resident person at any time in the taxation year;

(*d*) is a person described in paragraph 149(1)(*a*) or (*b*) at any time in the taxation year; or

(*e*) is a person in respect of whom a special allowance under the *Children's Special Allowances Act* is payable at any time in the taxation year.

History: S. 122.8(2) was added by S.C. 2018, c. 27, s. 13(1), applicable to the 2018 and subsequent taxation years.

S. 122.8(2) was repealed by S.C. 2016, c. 7, s. 32(2), in force January 1, 2017, and formerly read:

(2) *Deemed overpayment.* An individual who files a return of income for a taxation year and who makes a claim under this subsection is deemed to have paid, at the end of the year, on account of tax payable under this Part for the year, an amount equal to the amount determined by the formula

$$A \times B$$

where

A is the appropriate percentage for the year; and

B is the total of all amounts each of which is, in respect of a qualifying child of the individual for the year, the lesser of $500 and the amount determined by the formula

$$C - D$$

where

C is the total of all amounts each of which is an amount paid in the year by the individual, or by the individual's spouse or common law partner, that is an eligible fitness expense in respect of the qualifying child of the individual, and

D is the total of all amounts that any person is or was entitled to receive, each of which relates to an amount included in computing the value of C in respect of the qualifying child that is the amount of a reimbursement, allowance or any other form of assistance (other than an amount that is included in computing the income for any taxation year of that person and that is not deductible in computing the taxable income of that person).

S. 122.8(2), the portion of the description of B before the formula was replaced by 2016, c. 7, s. 32(1), applicable to the 2016 taxation year, and formerly read:

B is the total of all amounts each of which is, in respect of a qualifying child of the individual for the year, the lesser of $1,000 and the amount determined by the formula

S. 122.8(2) was added by S.C. 2014, c. 39, s. 39(1), applicable to the 2015 and subsequent taxation years.

► 122.8(3) ◄

(3) Residence. For the purposes of this section, an individual is considered to reside at any time only at their principal place of residence.

History: S. 122.8(3) was added by S.C. 2018, c. 27, s. 13(1), applicable to the 2018 and subsequent taxation years.

S. 122.8(3) was repealed by S.C. 2016, c. 7, s. 32(2), in force January 1, 2017, and formerly read:

(3) *Child with disability.* An individual who files a return of income for a taxation year and who makes a claim under this subsection is deemed to have paid, in respect of a qualifying child of the individual, at the end of the year, on account of tax payable under this Part for the year, an amount equal to $500 multiplied by the appropriate percentage for the year, if

(*a*) the amount referred to in the description of B in subsection (2) is $100 or more; and

(*b*) an amount is deductible in respect of the qualifying child under section 118.3 in computing any person's tax payable under this Part for the year.

S. 122.8(3) was added by S.C. 2014, c. 39, s. 39(1), applicable to the 2015 and subsequent taxation years.

► 122.8(4) ◄

(4) Deemed overpayment. An eligible individual who files a return of income for a taxation year and who makes a claim under this subsection is deemed to have paid, at the end of the taxation year, on account of tax payable under this Part for the taxation year, an amount equal to the amount determined by the formula

$$(A + B + C \times D) \times E$$

where

A is the amount specified by the Minister of Finance for an eligible individual for the taxation year for the province (in this subsection and subsection (6) referred to as the "relevant province") in which the eligible individual resides at the end of the taxation year;

B is

(*a*) the amount specified by the Minister of Finance for a qualified relation for the taxation year for the relevant province, if

(i) the eligible individual has a qualified relation at the end of the taxation year, or

(ii) subparagraph (i) does not apply and the eligible individual has a qualified dependant at the end of the taxation year, and

(*b*) in any other case, nil;

C is the amount specified by the Minister of Finance for a qualified dependant for the taxation year for the relevant province;

D is the number of qualified dependants of the eligible individual at the end of the taxation year, other than a qualified dependant in respect of whom an amount is included because of subparagraph (*a*)(ii) of the description of B for the taxation year; and

E is

(*a*) 1.1, if there is a census metropolitan area, as determined in the last census published by Statistics Canada before the taxation year, in the relevant province and the individual does not reside in a census metropolitan area at the end of the taxation year, and

(*b*) 1, in any other case.

History: S. 122.8(4) was added by S.C. 2018, c. 27, s. 13(1), applicable to the 2018 and subsequent taxation years.

S. 122.8(4) was repealed by S.C. 2016, c. 7, s. 32(2), in force January 1, 2017, and formerly read:

(4) *Apportionment of overpayment.* If more than one individual is entitled to make a claim under this section for a taxation year in respect of a qualifying child, the total of all amounts deemed to have been paid shall not exceed the maximum amount that could be deemed to have been paid for the year by any one of those individuals in respect of that qualifying child if that individual were the only individual entitled to claim an amount for the year under this section in respect of that qualifying child. If the individuals cannot agree as to what portion of the maximum amount each can so claim, the Minister may fix the portions.

S. 122.8(4) was added by S.C. 2014, c. 39, s. 39(1), applicable to the 2015 and subsequent taxation years.

► 122.8(5) ◄

(5) Authority to specify amounts. The Minister of Finance may specify amounts for a province for a taxation year for the purposes of this section. If the Minister of Finance does not specify a particular amount that is relevant for the purposes of this section, that particular amount is deemed to be nil for the purpose of applying this section.

History: S. 122.8(5) was added by S.C. 2018, c. 27, s. 13(1), applicable to the 2018 and subsequent taxation years.

S. 122.8(5) was repealed by S.C. 2016, c. 7, s. 32(2), in force January 1, 2017, and formerly read:

(5) *Effect of bankruptcy.* For the purposes of this subdivision, if an individual becomes bankrupt in a particular calendar year, notwithstanding subsection 128(2), any reference to the taxation year of the individual (other than in this subsection) is deemed to be a reference to the particular calendar year.

S. 122.8(5) was added by S.C. 2014, c. 39, s. 39(1), applicable to the 2015 and subsequent taxation years.

► 122.8(6) ◄

(6) Deemed rebate in respect of fuel charges. The amount deemed by this section to have been paid on account of tax payable for a taxation year is deemed to have been paid in the year following the taxation year as a rebate in respect of charges levied under Part 1 of the *Greenhouse Gas Pollution Pricing Act* in respect of the relevant province.

History: S. 122.8(6) was added by S.C. 2018, c. 27, s. 13(1), applicable to the 2018 and subsequent taxation years.

S. 122.8(6) was repealed by S.C. 2016, c. 7, s. 32(2), in force January 1, 2017, and formerly read:

(6) *Part-year residents.* If an individual is resident in Canada throughout part of a taxation year and is non-resident throughout another part of the year, the total of the amounts that are deemed to be paid by the individual under subsection (2) and (3) for the year cannot exceed the lesser of

(*a*) the total of

(i) the amounts deemed to be paid under those subsections that can reasonably be considered as wholly applicable to the period or periods in the year throughout which the individual is not resident in Canada, computed as though that period or those periods were the whole taxation year, and

(ii) the amounts deemed to be paid under those subsections that can reasonably be considered as wholly applicable to the period or periods in the year throughout which the individual is resident in Canada, computed as though that period or those periods were the whole taxation year, and

(*b*) the total of the amounts that would have been deemed to have been paid under those subsections for the year had the individual been resident in Canada throughout the year.

S. 122.8(6) was added by S.C. 2014, c. 39, s. 39(1), applicable to the 2015 and subsequent taxation years.

► 122.8(7) ◄

(7) Only one eligible individual. If an individual is a qualified relation of another individual for a taxation year and both those individuals would be, but for this subsection, eligible individuals for the taxation year, only the individual that the Minister designates is the eligible individual for the taxation year.

History: S. 122.8(7) was added by S.C. 2018, c. 27, s. 13(1), applicable to the 2018 and subsequent taxation years.

S. 122.8(7) was repealed by S.C. 2016, c. 7, s. 32(2), in force January 1, 2017, and formerly read:

(7) *Non-residents.* Subsections (2) and (3) do not apply in respect of a taxation year of an individual if the individual is, at no time in the year, resident in Canada, unless all or substantially all the individual's income for the year is included in computing the individual's taxable income earned in Canada for the year.

S. 122.8(7) was added by S.C. 2014, c. 39, s. 39(1), applicable to the 2015 and subsequent taxation years.

► 122.8(8) ◄

(8) Exception — qualified dependant. If a person would, if this Act were read without reference to this subsection, be the qualified dependant of two or more individuals, for a taxation year,

(*a*) the person is deemed to be a qualified dependant, for the taxation year, of the one of those individuals on whom those individuals agree; and

(*b*) in any other case, the person is deemed to be, for the taxation year, a qualified dependant only of the individual that the Minister designates.

History: S. 122.8(8) was added by S.C. 2018, c. 27, s. 13(1), applicable to the 2018 and subsequent taxation years.

► 122.8(9) ◄

(9) Effect of bankruptcy. For the purposes of this section, if an individual becomes bankrupt in a particular calendar year, notwithstanding subsection 128(2), any reference to the taxation year of the individual (other than in this subsection) is deemed to be a reference to the particular calendar year.

History: S. 122.8(9) was added by S.C. 2018, c. 27, s. 13(1), applicable to the 2018 and subsequent taxation years.

Subdivision a.4 — School Supplies Tax Credit

SECTION 122.9: [School Supplies Tax Credit]

► 122.9(1) ◄

(1) Definitions. The following definitions apply in this section.

History: S. 122.9(1) was added by S.C. 2016, c. 7, s. 33(1), applicable to the 2016 and subsequent taxation years.

"eligible educator" —"eligible educator", in respect of a taxation year, means an individual who, at any time during the taxation year,

(*a*) is employed in Canada as a teacher or an early childhood educator at

(i) an elementary or secondary school, or

(ii) a regulated child care facility; and

(*b*) holds a valid and recognized (in the province or territory in which the individual is employed)

(i) teaching certificate, licence, permit or diploma, or

(ii) certificate or diploma in early childhood education.

"eligible supplies expense" —"eligible supplies expense", of an eligible educator for a taxation year, means an amount (other than any amount deducted in computing any person's income for any taxation year or any amount otherwise included in computing a deduction from any person's tax payable under this Act for any taxation year) paid by the eligible educator in the taxation year for teaching supplies to the extent that

(*a*) the teaching supplies were

(i) purchased by the eligible educator for the purpose of teaching or facilitating students' learning, and

(ii) directly consumed or used in an elementary or secondary school or in a regulated child care facility in the performance of the duties of the eligible educator's employment; and

(*b*) the eligible educator is not entitled to receive a reimbursement, allowance or any other form of assistance (other than an amount that is included in computing the income for any taxation year of the eligible educator and that is not deductible in computing the taxable income of the eligible educator) in respect of the amount paid.

"return of income" —"return of income" filed by an eligible educator for a taxation year means a return of income (other than a return of income filed under subsection 70(2) or 104(23), paragraph 128(2)(*e*) or subsection 150(4)) that is required to be filed for the year or that would be required to be filed if the eligible educator had tax payable under this Part for the year.

"teaching supplies" —"teaching supplies" means

(*a*) consumable supplies; and

(*b*) prescribed durable goods.

Related Regulations: 9600.

► 122.9(2) ◄

(2) Deemed overpayment. An eligible educator who files a return of income for a taxation year and who makes a claim under this subsection is deemed to have paid, at the end of the year, on account of tax payable under this Part for the year, an amount equal to the amount determined by the formula

$$A \times B$$

where

A is the appropriate percentage for the year; and

B is the least of

(*a*) $1,000,

(*b*) the total of all amounts each of which is an eligible supplies expense of the eligible educator for the year, and

(*c*) if the eligible educator fails to provide the certificate referred to in subsection (3) in respect of the year, as and when requested by the Minister, nil.

History: S. 122.9(2) was added by S.C. 2016, c. 7, s. 33(1), applicable to the 2016 and subsequent taxation years.

► 122.9(3) ◄

(3) Certificate. If the Minister so demands, an eligible educator making a claim under this section in respect of a taxation year shall provide to the Minister a written certificate from their employer, or a delegated official of the employer, attesting to the eligible supplies expenses of the eligible educator for the year.

History: S. 122.9(3) was added by S.C. 2016, c. 7, s. 33(1), applicable to the 2016 and subsequent taxation years.

► 122.9(4) ◄

(4) Effect of bankruptcy. For the purposes of this subdivision, if an eligible educator becomes bankrupt in a particular calendar year, notwithstanding subsection 128(2), any reference to the taxation year of the eligible educator (other than in this subsection) is deemed to be a reference to the particular calendar year.

History: S. 122.9(4) was added by S.C. 2016, c. 7, s. 33(1), applicable to the 2016 and subsequent taxation years.

► 122.9(5) ◄

(5) Part-year residents. If an eligible educator is resident in Canada throughout part of a taxation year and is non-resident throughout another part of the year, the total of the amounts that are deemed to be paid by the eligible educator under subsection (2) for the year cannot exceed the lesser of

(*a*) the total of

(i) the amounts deemed to be paid under subsection (2) that can reasonably be considered as wholly applicable to the period or periods in the year throughout which the eligible educator is not resident in Canada, computed as though that period or those periods were the whole taxation year, and

(ii) the amounts deemed to be paid under subsection (2) that can reasonably be considered as wholly applicable to the period or periods in the year throughout which the eligible educator is resident in Canada, computed as though that period or those periods were the whole taxation year; and

(*b*) the total of the amounts that would have been deemed to have been paid under subsection (2) for the year had the eligible educator been resident in Canada throughout the year.

History: S. 122.9(5) was added by S.C. 2016, c. 7, s. 33(1), applicable to the 2016 and subsequent taxation years.

► 122.9(6) ◄

(6) Non-residents. Subsection (2) does not apply in respect of a taxation year of an eligible educator if the eligible educator is, at no time in the year, resident in Canada, unless all or substantially all the eligible educator's income for the year is included in computing the eligible educator's taxable income earned in Canada for the year.

History: S. 122.9(6) was added by S.C. 2016, c. 7, s. 33(1), applicable to the 2016 and subsequent taxation years.

Subdivision a.5 — Canada Training Credit

History: The heading of Subdivision a.5 of Division E was added by S.C. 2019, c. 29, s. 21(1), deemed to have come into force on January 1, 2019.

SECTION 122.91: Canada Training Credit

► 122.91(1) ◄

(1) Claimed amount. An individual who is resident in Canada throughout a taxation year, files a return of income for the taxation year and makes a claim under this subsection is deemed to have paid, at the end of the taxation year, on account of tax payable under this Part for the taxation year, an amount claimed by the individual that does not exceed the lesser of

(*a*) the training amount limit of the individual for the taxation year, and

(*b*) 50% of the amount that would be deductible under paragraph 118.5(1)(*a*) or (*d*) in computing the individual's tax payable under this Part for the taxation year if

(i) this Act were read without reference to subsections 118.5(1.2) and (2), and

(ii) the appropriate percentage for the taxation year were 100%.

Editorial Note: See the editorial note to subsection 122.91(2).

History: S. 122.91(1) was added by S.C. 2019, c. 29, s. 21(1), deemed to have come into force on January 1, 2019.

Related Sections: 118.5(1) Tuition credit; 118.5(1.2) Canada training credit reduction; 118.5(2) Application to deemed residents.

► 122.91(2) ◄

(2) Training amount limit. For the purposes of this section, the training amount limit of an individual for a taxation year is

(*a*) if the taxation year is after 2019 and the individual has attained the age of 26 years, and has not attained the age of 66 years, before the end of the taxation year, the lesser of

(i) the amount determined by the formula

A + B - C

where

A is the individual's training amount limit for the preceding taxation year,

B is

(A) $250, if

(I) the individual has filed a return of income for the preceding taxation year,

(II) the individual was resident in Canada throughout the preceding taxation year,

(III) the total of the following amounts is greater than or equal to $10,000:

1. the amount that would be the individual's "working income" (as defined in subsection 122.7(1)) for the preceding taxation year, if this Act were read without reference to paragraph 81(1)(*a*) and subsection 81(4),

2. the total of all amounts each of which is an amount payable to the individual under subsection 22(1), 23(1), 152.04(1) or 152.05(1) of the *Employment Insurance Act* in the preceding taxation year, and

3. the amount that would be included in the individual's income because of subparagraph 56(1)(*a*)(vii) in computing the individual's income for the preceding taxation year, if this Act were read without reference to paragraph 81(1)(*a*), and

(IV) the individual's income for the preceding taxation year under this Part does not exceed the higher dollar amount referred to in paragraph 117(2)(*c*), as adjusted under this Act for the preceding taxation year, and

(B) nil, in any other case, and

C is the amount deemed to have been paid by the individual under subsection (1) in respect of the preceding taxation year, and

(ii) the amount determined by the formula

$5,000 - D

where

D is the total of all amounts deemed to have been paid by the individual under subsection (1) in respect of a preceding taxation year; and

(*b*) nil, in any other case.

Editorial Note: Under subsection 122.91(1), an individual can accumulate and claim up to $250 per year in the individual's "training limit amount", to a lifetime maximum of $5,000. The $250 can accumulate in a year only if the individual meets the income thresholds and requirements in amount B of the formula. The training limit amount can be claimed in a year where the individual is 26 years of age or older but less than 66 at the end of the year. The credit claimable in a taxation year equals the lesser of the training limit amount and 50% of the eligible tuition fees paid in the year. Where the training credit is claimed, it reduces the amount of tuition that qualifies for the regular tuition credit under section 118.5.

History: S. 122.91(2) was added by S.C. 2019, c. 29, s. 21(1), deemed to have come into force on January 1, 2019.

Related Sections: 56(1)(a) Pension benefits, unemployment insurance benefits, etc.; 81(1)(a) Statutory exemptions; 81(4) Payments for volunteer services; 117(2) Rates for taxation years after 2015; 117.1(1) Annual adjustment; 122.7(1) Definitions.

► 122.91(3) ◄

(3) Effect of bankruptcy. For the purpose of this Subdivision, if an individual becomes bankrupt in a particular calendar year,

(*a*) notwithstanding subsection 128(2), any reference to the taxation year of the individual (other than in this subsection) is deemed to be a reference to the particular calendar year; and

(*b*) the individual's working income and income under this Part for the taxation year ending on December 31 of the particular calendar year is deemed to include the individual's working income and the income under this Part for the taxation year that begins on January 1 of the particular calendar year.

History: S. 122.91(3) was added by S.C. 2019, c. 29, s. 21(1), deemed to have come into force on January 1, 2019.

Related Sections: 128(2) Where individual bankrupt.

► 122.91(4) ◄

(4) Special rules in the event of death. For the purposes of this section, if an individual dies in a calendar year,

(*a*) the individual is deemed to be resident in Canada from the time of death until the end of the year;

(*b*) the individual is deemed to be the same age at the end of the year as the individual would have been if the individual were alive at the end of the year; and

(*c*) any return of income filed by a legal representative of the individual is deemed to be a return of income filed by the individual.

Editorial Note: Subsection 122.91(4) applies in the year of death of an individual and ensures that the training credit may be claimed in that year if the individual has a training amount limit (subsection 122.91(2)) for the year, assuming the individual was resident throughout the year up to the time of death and would have been at least 26 years old but under the age of 66 at the end of the year.

History: S. 122.91(4) was added by S.C. 2019, c. 29, s. 21(1), deemed to have come into force on January 1, 2019.

Subdivision b — Rules Applicable to Corporations

SECTION 123: Rate for corporations

▶ 123(1) ◀

(1) Rate for corporations. The tax payable under this Part for a taxation year by a corporation on its taxable income or taxable income earned in Canada, as the case may be, (in this section referred to as its "amount taxable") for the year is, except where otherwise provided,

(*a*) 38% of its amount taxable for the year.

(*b*) (Repealed by 1988, c. 28, s. 248(1).)

(*c*) (Repealed by 1988, c. 55, s. 100(2).)

(*d*) (Repealed by 1988, c. 55, s. 100(2).)

Related Sections: S. 133(3) Special tax rate; s. 143(3) Refusal to accept election; s. 149(1) Miscellaneous exemptions; s. 219(1) Branch tax; s. 248(1), "corporation", "taxable income", "taxable income earned in Canada"; s. 249 Definition of "taxation year"; s. 255 Canada.

Tax Topics: No. 1695, Corporate Tax Rates - How They (Now) Work; No. 1644, The Canadian Tax Advantage.

▶ 123(2) ◀

(2) Definitions — "Amount taxable earned by the corporation in the year in the Nova Scotia offshore area", "Nova Scotia offshore area" — (Repealed by 1988, c. 28, s. 248(2).)

Related Regulations: 414; 415.

SECTION 123.1: Corporation surtax

There shall be added to the tax otherwise payable under this Part for each taxation year by a corporation (other than a corporation that was throughout the year an investment corporation or a non-resident-owned investment corporation) an amount equal to that proportion of 5% of the amount, if any, by which

(*a*) the tax payable under this Part by the corporation for the year determined without reference to this section, sections 123.2 and 126 (except for the purposes of subsection 125(1) and section 125.1), subsections 127(3) and (5), 127.2(1) and 127.3(1) of this Act and paragraph 123(1)(*b*) and subsection 127(13) of the *Income Tax Act*, chapter 148 of the Revised Statutes of Canada, 1952, and as if subsection 124(1) of this Act were read without reference to the words "in a province" in that subsection

exceeds

(*b*) in the case of a Canadian-controlled private corporation to which subsection 125(1) applies, the amount, if any, by which

(i) 15% of the least of the amounts, if any, determined under paragraphs 125(1)(*a*) to (*c*) in respect of the corporation for the year

exceeds

(ii) the amount, if any, determined under paragraph 125.1(1)(*b*) in respect of the corporation for the year,

(*c*) in the case of a mutual fund corporation, the least of the amounts that would be determined under paragraphs (*a*) to (*c*) of the description of A in the definition "refundable capital gains tax on hand" in subsection 131(6) in respect of the corporation for the year if this Act were read without reference to this section, and

(*d*) in any other case, nil

that the number of days in that portion of the year that is after June 30, 1985 and before 1987 is of the number of days in the year.

Related Sections: S. 136(1) Cooperative not private corporation; s. 137(7) Credit union not private corporation.

SECTION 123.2: Corporation surtax

▶ 123.2(1) ◀

(1) Corporation surtax — (Repealed by S.C. 2006, c. 4, s. 72(2).)

Related Regulations: 8602.

▶ 123.2(2) ◀

(2) Specified percentage — (Repealed by S.C. 2006, c. 4, s. 72(2).)

▶ 123.2(3) ◀

(3) Taxable income — (Repealed by S.C. 2006, c. 4, s. 72(1).)

SECTION 123.3: Refundable tax on CCPC's investment income

There shall be added to the tax otherwise payable under this Part for each taxation year by a corporation that is throughout the year a Canadian-controlled private corporation an amount equal to 10 2/3% of the lesser of

(*a*) the corporation's aggregate investment income for the year (within the meaning assigned by subsection 129(4)), and

(*b*) the amount, if any, by which its taxable income for the year exceeds the least of the amounts determined in respect of it for the year under paragraphs 125(1)(*a*) to (*c*).

History: S. 123.3, the portion before paragraph (*a*) was replaced by S.C. 2016, c. 11, s. 6(1), applicable to taxation years that end after 2015 except that, for taxation years that end after 2015 and begin before 2016, the reference to "10 2/3%" in the portion of section 123.3 before paragraph (*a*) is to be read as a reference to the percentage determined by the formula

$$6\ 2/3\% + 4\%\ (A/B)$$

where

A is the number of days in the taxation year that are after 2015; and

B is the total number of days in the taxation year.

S. 123.3, the portion before paragraph (*a*) formerly read:

S. 123.3 *Refundable tax on CCPC's investment income.* There shall be added to the tax otherwise payable under this Part for each taxation year by a corporation that is throughout the year a Canadian-controlled private corporation an amount equal to 6 2/3% of the lesser of

Related Sections: S. 125(7), "Canadian-controlled private corporation"; s. 129(4), "aggregate investment income".

Tax Topics: No. 1695, Corporate Tax Rates - How They (Now) Work.

SECTION 123.4: Corporation tax reductions

▶ 123.4(1) ◀

(1) Definitions. The definitions in this subsection apply in this section.

Related Sections: S. 125(1) Small business deduction; s. 125(7), "Canadian-controlled private corporation"; s. 125.11(1), "taxable resource income"; s. 125.11(2) Resource deduction; s. 129(4) Definitions; s. 130(3) Meaning of expressions "investment corporation" and "taxed capital gains"; s. 130.1(6) Meaning of "mortgage investment corporation"; s. 131(8) Meaning of "mutual fund corporation"; s. 133(8), "non resident owned investment corporation".

Income Tax Folios: S4-F15-C1 Manufacturing and Processing.

"CCPC rate reduction percentage" — (Repealed by S.C. 2003, c. 15, s. 78(1).)

"full rate taxable income" —"full rate taxable income" of a corporation for a taxation year is

(*a*) if the corporation is not a corporation described in paragraph (*b*) or (*c*) for the year, the amount by which that portion of the corporation's taxable income for the year (or, for greater certainty, if the corporation is non-resident, that portion of its taxable income earned in Canada for the year) that is subject to tax under subsection 123(1) exceeds the total of

(i) if an amount is deducted under subsection 125.1(1) from the corporation's tax otherwise payable under this Part for the year, the amount obtained by dividing the amount so deducted by the corporation's general rate reduction percentage for the taxation year,

(ii) if an amount is deducted under subsection 125.1(2) from the corporation's tax otherwise payable under this Part for the year, the amount determined, in respect of the deduction, by the formula in that subsection,

(iii) the corporation's income for the year from a personal services business, and

(iv) if the corporation is a credit union throughout the year and the corporation deducted an amount for the year under subsection 125(1) (because of the application of subsections 137(3) and (4)), the amount, if any, that is the product of the amount, if any, determined for B in subsection 137(3) multiplied by the amount determined for C in subsection 137(3) in respect of the corporation for the year;

(*b*) if the corporation is a Canadian-controlled private corporation throughout the year, the amount by which that portion of the corporation's taxable income for the year that is subject to tax under subsection 123(1) exceeds the total of

(i) the amounts that would, if paragraph (*a*) applied to the corporation, be determined under subparagraphs (*a*)(i) to (iv) in respect of the corporation for the year,

(ii) the least of the amounts, if any, determined under paragraphs 125(1)(*a*) to (*c*) in respect of the corporation for the year, and

(iii) except for a corporation that is, throughout the year, a cooperative corporation (within the meaning assigned by subsection 136(2)) or a credit union, the corporation's aggregate investment income for the year, within the meaning assigned by subsection 129(4), and

(*c*) if the corporation is throughout the year an investment corporation, a mortgage investment corporation or a mutual fund corporation, nil.

Editorial Note: See editorial note under s. 123.4(2).

History: S. 123.4(1), subparagraph (*a*)(iv) of the definition "full rate taxable income" was replaced by S.C. 2013, c. 40, s. 54(1), applicable to taxation years that end after March 20, 2013, and formerly read:

(iv) if the corporation is a credit union throughout the year and the corporation deducted an amount for the year under subsection 125(1) (because of the application of subsections 137(3) and (4)), the amount, if any, determined for B in subsection 137(3) in respect of the corporation for the year;

S. 123.4(1), subparagraph (*a*)(iv) of the definition "full rate taxable income" was replaced by S.C. 2013, c. 33, s. 12(1), applicable to taxation years that end after March 20, 2013, and formerly read:

(iv) if the corporation is a credit union throughout the year and the corporation deducted an amount for the year under subsection 125(1) (because of the application of subsections 137(3) and (4)), the amount if any, by which, the lesser of the amounts described in paragraphs 137(3)(*a*) and (*b*) exceeds the amount described in paragraph 137(3)(*c*) in respect of the corporation for the year;

S. 123.4(1), subparagraph (*a*)(iii) of the definition "full rate taxable income" was added by S.C. 2013, c. 34, s. 261(1), applicable to taxation years that begin after October 31, 2011.

S. 123.4(1), the portion of paragraph (*b*) before subparagraph (i) of the definition "full rate taxable income" was added by S.C. 2013, c. 34, s. 261(2), applicable to taxation years that end after October 31, 2011, and formerly read:

(*b*) if the corporation is a Canadian-controlled private corporation throughout the year, the amount by which the corporation's taxable income for the year exceeds the total of

S. 123.4(1), subparagraph (*b*)(iii) of the definition "full rate taxable income" was replaced by S.C. 2013, c. 34, s. 261(3), applicable to the 2001 and subsequent taxation years, and formerly read:

(iii) the corporation's aggregate investment income for the year, within the meaning assigned by subsection 129(4);

Tax Topics: No. 2071, Should I Be Taking it Personally?.

"general rate reduction percentage" —"general rate reduction percentage" of a corporation for a taxation year is the total of

(*a*) that proportion of 7% that the number of days in the taxation year that are before 2008 is of the number of days in the taxation year,

(*b*) that proportion of 8.5% that the number of days in the taxation year that are in 2008 is of the number of days in the taxation year,

(*c*) that proportion of 9% that the number of days in the taxation year that are in 2009 is of the number of days in the taxation year,

(*d*) that proportion of 10% that the number of days in the taxation year that are in 2010 is of the number of days in the taxation year,

(*e*) that proportion of 11.5% that the number of days in the taxation year that are in 2011 is of the number of days in the taxation year, and

(*f*) that proportion of 13% that the number of days in the taxation year that are after 2011 is of the number of days in the taxation year.

Editorial Note: See editorial note under s. 123.4(2).

► 123.4(2) ◄

(2) General deduction from tax. There may be deducted from a corporation's tax otherwise payable under this Part for a taxation year the product obtained by multiplying the corporation's general rate reduction percentage for the year by the corporation's full-rate taxable income for the year.

Editorial Note: Section 123.4 of the Act contains rules that reduce a corporation's tax otherwise payable under Part I of the Act by a percentage of its "full rate taxable income" — i.e., 13% for calendar years after 2011 (the "general rate reduction percentage" defined by s. 123.4(1)). "Full rate taxable income" of a corporation for a taxation year is, in general terms, that part of the corporation's taxable income for the year that is not exempt from tax and has not benefited from any of the various tax rate reductions. "Full rate taxable income" excludes income earned by a corporation from a "personal services business", as defined in subsection 125(7), applicable to taxation years that begin after October 31, 2011 (so that dividends distributed from such income will also generally be subject to "under-integration").

Paragraph (*a*) of the definition of "full rate taxable income" applies to corporations other than CCPCs. Paragraph (*b*) applies to CCPCs. (Various "specialty corporations" are ineligible for the general rate reduction — see paragraph (*c*).) Per s. 123.4(1)(*a*)(i) of the definition, subtracted is income equivalent to benefits from M&P deductions — in other words, M&P benefits are netted out from s. 123.4 tax reductions. (Also subtracted are amounts re electricity generation and credit unions — see s. 123.4(1)(*a*)(ii) and (iv).) For CCPCs, in addition to the foregoing, income qualifying for the small business deduction (the least of the amounts in s. 125(1)(*a*)–(*c*)) and aggregate investment income (per s. 129(4)) are also subtracted. Thus, the general rate reduction does not generally apply to investment income, but such income is eligible for the refundable tax rules; however, there is a significant corporate-level deferral stemming from the general rate reduction (along with the non-application of the 6$^2/_3$% surtax in s. 123.3). S. 123.4 is also a factor in the "GRIP addition for 2006" in subsection 89(7) (see editorial note thereon) and the "relevant tax factor" under s. 95(1).

► 123.4(3) ◄

(3) CCPC deduction — (Repealed by S.C. 2003, c. 15, s. 78(5).)

SECTION 123.5: Tax on personal services business income

There shall be added to the tax otherwise payable under this Part for each taxation year by a corporation an amount equal to 5% of the corporation's taxable income for the year from a personal services business.

Editorial Note: Income of a Canadian-controlled private corporation (CCPC) from a personal services business (subsection 125(7)) is not eligible for the small business deduction or the general corporate tax rate deduction. As a result, starting in 2016, the income is subject to a tax rate of 28% plus the 5% additional tax under section 123.5, which coincides with the highest marginal tax rate of 33% applicable to individuals beginning in 2016.

History: S. 123.5 was added by S.C. 2016, c. 7, s. 62(5), applicable to taxation years that end after 2015 except that, for taxation years that end after 2015 and begin before 2016, the reference to 5% in section 123.5 is to be read as a reference to the percentage determined by the formula

$$5\% \ (A/B)$$

where

A is the number of days in the taxation year that are after 2015; and

B is the total number of days in the taxation year.

SECTION 124: Deduction from corporation tax

► 124(1) ◄

(1) Deduction from corporation tax. There may be deducted from the tax otherwise payable by a corporation under this Part for a taxation year an amount equal to 10% of the corporation's taxable income earned in the year in a province.

Related Regulations: Part IV.

Canadian Tax Foundation: Auger and Bélanger, *Interprovincial Allocation of Income*, 1999 Conference Report 10:1–43.

Tax Profile: May 2003 — The Interprovincial Transfer of Passive Corporate Income.

Cases: Taxpayer directed its real estate management and construction business from its main office in Canada. Although 90% of its income was generated in the U.S., it had no permanent establishment there, as on-site supervision lasted only until each project was completed. The taxpayer therefore qualified for the 10% tax reduction. *Hegeman-Harris Co. of Canada Ltd. v. M.N.R.*, (T.R.B.) 79 DTC 886.

► 124(2) ◄

(2) Idem — (Repealed by 1974-75-76, c. 71, s. 6(1).)

► 124(2.1) ◄

(2.1) Idem — (Repealed by 1974-75-76, c. 71, s. 6(1).)

► 124(2.2) ◄

(2.2) Calculation of percentage for particular taxation year — (Repealed by 1974-75-76, c. 71, s. 6(1).)

► 124(3) ◄

(3) Crown agents. Notwithstanding subsection (1), no deduction may be made under this section from the tax otherwise payable under this Part for a taxation year by a corporation in respect of any taxable income of the corporation for the year that is not, because of an Act of Parliament, subject to tax under this Part or by a prescribed federal Crown corporation that is an agent of Her Majesty.

Related Regulations: 7100.

► 124(4) ◄

(4) Definitions. In this section,

Proposed Amendment

Bill C-74, Canada–Quebec Gulf of St. Lawrence Petroleum Resources Accord Implementation Act (June 18, 2015)

The portion of subsection 124(4) of the English version of the *Income Tax Act* before the first definition is replaced by the following:

(4) Definitions. The following definitions apply in this section.

Applicable: On Royal Assent.

"province" —"province" includes the Newfoundland offshore area and the Nova Scotia offshore area;

Proposed Amendment

Bill C-74, Canada–Quebec Gulf of St. Lawrence Petroleum Resources Accord Implementation Act (June 18, 2015)

The definition "province" in subsection 124(4) of the Act is replaced by the following:

province —"province" includes the joint management area, the Nova Scotia offshore area and the Newfoundland offshore area.

Applicable: To taxation years that begin after the day on which an administration agreement in respect of tax imposed under section 235 of the *Canada–Quebec Gulf of St. Lawrence Petroleum Resources Accord Implementation Act* comes into effect.

Related Sections: S. 133(4) No deduction for foreign taxes; s. 248(1), "amount", "corporation", "Newfoundland offshore area", "prescribed", "taxable income"; s. 249 Definition of "taxation year".

Interpretation Bulletins: *Primary* — IT-177R2 (Consolid.) Permanent establishment of a corporation in a province.

"taxable income earned in the year in a province" —"taxable income earned in the year in a province" means the amount determined under rules prescribed for the purpose by regulations made on the recommendation of the Minister of Finance.

Related Regulations: 400 to 413.

SECTION 124.1: "Taxable production profits from a mineral resource in Canada" defined

(Repealed by 1974-75-76, c. 71, s. 7(1).)

SECTION 124.2: "Taxable production profits from oil or gas wells in Canada" defined

(Repealed by 1974-75-76, c. 71, s. 7(1).)

SECTION 125: Small business deduction

► 125(1) ◄

(1) Small business deduction. There may be deducted from the tax otherwise payable under this Part for a taxation year by a corporation that was, throughout the taxation year, a Canadian-controlled private corporation, an amount equal to the corporation's small business deduction rate for the taxation year multiplied by the least of

(*a*) the amount, if any, by which the total of

(i) the total of all amounts each of which is the amount of income of the corporation for the year from an active business carried on in Canada, other than an amount that is

(A) described in paragraph (*a*) of the description of A in the definition "specified partnership income" in subsection (7) for the year,

(B) described in subparagraph (*a*)(i) of the definition "specified corporate income" in subsection (7) for the year, or

(C) paid or payable to the corporation by another corporation with which it is associated, that is deemed by subsection 129(6) to be income for the year from an active business carried on by the corporation in circumstances where the associated corporation is not a Canadian-controlled private corporation or is a Canadian-controlled private corporation that has made an election under subsection 256(2) in respect of its taxation year in which the amount was paid or payable,

(ii) the specified partnership income of the corporation for the year, and

(ii.1) the specified corporate income of the corporation for the year

exceeds the total of

(iii) the total of all amounts each of which is a loss of the corporation for the year from an active business carried on in Canada (other than a loss of the corporation for the year from a business carried on by it as a member of a partnership), and

(iv) the specified partnership loss of the corporation for the year,

(*b*) the amount, if any, by which the corporation's taxable income for the year exceeds the total of

(i) 100/28 of the total of the amounts that would be deductible under subsection 126(1) from the tax for the year otherwise payable under this Part by it if those amounts were determined without reference to sections 123.3 and 123.4,

(ii) the amount determined by multiplying the total of the amounts that would be deductible under subsection 126(2) from the tax for the year otherwise payable under this Part by it, if those amounts were determined without reference to section 123.4, by the relevant factor for the year, and

(iii) the amount, if any, of the corporation's taxable income for the year that is not, because of an Act of Parliament, subject to tax under this Part, and

(*c*) the corporation's business limit for the year.

Editorial Note: The small business deduction is computed initially by multiplying the "small business deduction rate" (provided under s. 125(1.1)) by the least of the corporation's:

(1) under paragraph 125(1)(*a*), the total of its income from an active business carried on in Canada, its "specified partnership income", and its "specified corporate income", less non-partnership Canadian-active-business losses and "specified partnership losses" (see the definitions and editorial notes in s. 125(7));

(2) under paragraph 125(1)(*b*), a general limitation based on the corporation's taxable income, reduced by amounts designed to estimate the extent to which the corporation's taxable income is effectively sheltered by foreign tax credits, or is tax-exempt; and

(3) under paragraph 125(1)(*c*), its small business limit, which is normally $500,000, but may be reduced where the corporation is associated in the year with one or more corporations (see also s. 256(2)).

While a corporation must be a CCPC throughout the year to qualify for the small business deduction, s. 249(3.1) or (4) provides a deemed year end when CCPC status is lost. Special rules in s. 125(5) may apply for short taxation years, as well as where a corporation has two or more taxation years that end in the same calendar year. The small business deduction is phased out (s. 125(5.1)) based on taxable capital employed in Canada of between $10 million and $15 million. For taxation years beginning after 2018, the small business deduction is phased out on a 5:1 basis to the extent that the adjusted aggregate investment income (subsection 125(7)) of the CCPC exceeds $50,000 ($5 reduction in small business limit for every $1 of excess aggregate investment income). If both reductions potentially apply to a CCPC, the greater of the two reductions applies. See also the editorial note to subsection 125(5.1).

For taxation years beginning after March 21, 2016 (subject to transitional rules), the corporation's specified partnership income can include income earned by it as a "designated member" of a partnership (s. 125(7)) where it is not otherwise a partner at law, if the income is derived from goods or services provided to the partnership. However, the amount of income that can so qualify is deemed to be nil, unless an amount is assigned to the CCPC/designated member under s. 125(8). Furthermore, the amount of that income that can qualify for the small business deduction, as with other income earned by a corporation as a member of a partnership, is limited to a "specified partnership business limit" (s. 125(7)), which is basically a portion of the general $500,000 limit based on the corporation's pro-rata share of the partnership income. For a designated member to which an amount is assigned under s. 125(8), the amount is similarly subject to the assignor's specified partnership business limit (see s. 125(8) editorial note).

Also for taxation years beginning after March 21, 2016, clause 125(1)(*a*)(i)(C) adds a restriction in terms of the deeming rule in s. 129(6), which otherwise deems investment income of a particular corporation that is derived from an active business of an associated corporation to be active business income of the particular corporation. The restriction provides that such investment income received by a particular corporation from an associated corporation does not qualify for the small business deduction if the associated corporation is not a CCPC, or is a CCPC that has made an election under s. 256(2) not to be associated.

For taxation years that begin after March 21, 2016, the income of a corporation carrying on the business of farming or fishing ("selling corporation") from the sale of its farming or fishing products to an arm's length farming or fishing cooperative corporation ("purchasing corporation") is not eligible for the small business deduction.

History: S. 125(1)(*a*)(i) and (ii) were replaced and s. 125(1)(*a*)(ii.1) was added by S.C. 2016, c. 12, s. 44(1), applicable to

(a) taxation years that begin after March 21, 2016; and

(b) a person's taxation year that begins before March 22, 2016 and ends after March 21, 2016 if

(i) the person would be entitled to make an assignment to a corporation under subsection 125(3.2) (as enacted) or under subsection 125(8) (as enacted) if the amendments to section 125 applied to the person's taxation year that begins before March 22, 2016 and ends after March 21, 2016,

(ii) the taxation year of the corporation referred to in subparagraph (i) begins after March 21, 2016,

(iii) the person makes such an assignment for its taxation year that begins before March 22, 2016 and ends after March 21, 2016 and the assignment is to the corporation for its taxation year that begins after March 21, 2016, and

(iv) the person files with the Minister of National Revenue the prescribed form that is required to be filed under subsection 125(3.2) (as enacted) in its return of income for its taxation year that begins before March 22, 2016 and ends after March 21, 2016, on or before the day that is the later of the filing-due date of the person (as defined under subsection 248(1)) or 60 days after the *Budget Implementation Act, 2016, No. 2* (Bill C-29) receives royal assent [February 13, 2017].

S. 125(1)(*a*)(i) and (ii) formerly read:

(i) the total of all amounts each of which is the income of the corporation for the year from an active business carried on in Canada (other than the income of the corporation for the year from a business carried on by it as a member of a partnership), and

(ii) the specified partnership income of the corporation for the year

S. 125(1)(*b*)(i) was replaced by S.C. 2013, c. 34, s. 262(1), applicable to taxation years that end after October 31, 2011, except that, for a taxation year that includes that day, subparagraph (i) is to be read as follows:

"(i) the total of

(A) 10/3 of the total of the amounts that would be deductible under subsection 126(1) from the tax for the year otherwise payable under this Part by it if those amounts were determined without reference to sections 123.3 and 123.4, that the number of days in the taxation year that are on or before October 31, 2011 is of the total of days in the taxation year, and

(B) 100/28 of the total of the amounts that would be deductible under subsection 126(1) from the tax for the year otherwise payable under this Part by it if those amounts were determined without reference to sections 123.3 and 123.4, that the number of days in the taxation year that are after October 31, 2011 is of the total of days in the taxation year,"

S. 125(1)(*b*)(i) formerly read:

(i) 10/3 of the total of the amounts that would be deductible under subsection 126(1) from the tax for the year otherwise payable under this Part by it if those amounts were determined without reference to sections 123.3 and 123.4,

S. 125(1)(*b*)(ii) was replaced by S.C. 2013, c. 34, s. 262(1), applicable to the 2003 and subsequent taxation years, and formerly read:

(ii) 10/4 of the total of the amounts that would be deductible under subsection 126(2) from the tax for the year otherwise payable under this Part by it if those amounts were determined without reference to section 123.4, and

Related Sections: S. 89(1), "general rate income pool", "low rate income pool"; s. 89(11) Election: non-CCPC; s. 110.5 Additions for foreign tax deductions; s. 123.1 Corporation surtax; s. 123.3 Refundable tax on CCPC's investment income; s. 123.4(1), "full rate taxable income"; s. 125(1.1) Small business deduction rate; s. 125(2) Business limit; s. 125(6) Corporate partnerships; s. 125(6.1) Corporation deemed member of partnership; s. 125(6.2) Specified partnership income deemed nil; s. 125(6.3) Partnership deemed to be controlled; s. 125(7) definitions; s. 125.1 Manufacturing and processing profits deductions; s. 126(1) Foreign tax deduction — non-business income; s. 126(2) Employees of international organizations; s. 129(3) Definition of "refundable dividend tax on hand"; s. 129(4) Definitions; s. 129(6)(*b*) Investment income from associated corporation deemed to be active business income; s. 136(1) Cooperative not private corporation; s. 137(3) Additional deduction; s. 137(7) Credit union not private corporation.

Canadian Tax Foundation: Amirault and Baxter, *Professional Groups + Small Business Deduction Issues and Planning Opportunities*, 2017 Atlantic Provinces Tax Conference 2:1–25; Beswick and Young, *The Use of Holding Companies in the Private Business Context*, 2012 Canadian Tax Journal 1:169–191; Gosselin, *CCPC Status Despite Majority Non-Resident Ownership*, 2012 Tax for the Owner-Manager 12(3):3–5; McDougall and Lai, *Selected Aspects of Corporate Control: Groups of Persons and Control of Corporations by Trusts*, 2010 Conference Report 11:1–33; Dunn et al., *Unanimous Shareholder Agreements and the CCPC Definition (Canada Revenue Agency Round Table, Questions 13 and 14)*, 2009 Conference Report 3:13–14; Adams et al., *The More than Five Full-Time Employees Test (Canada Revenue Agency Round Table, Question 6)*, 2008 Conference Report 3:5–6; Kaplan, *Going Public: Tax Considerations for the Owner-Manager*, 2008 Canadian Tax Journal 4:990–1008; O'Brien, *Current Cases: Federal Court of Appeal — The Hypothetical (Or Mythical) Particular Shareholder Is at Last Revealed (Sedona Networks Corporation v. The Queen, 2007 FCA 169)*, 2008 Canadian Tax Journal 3:719–726; Brender, *Developments in the Concept of Corporate Control*, 2007 Conference Report 31:1–49; Jakolev and Turner, *Control Further Dissected*, 2006 Canadian Tax Highlights 14(4):8–9.

Tax Profile: July 2007 — Canadian Tax Traps; May 2006 — Professional Corporations for Physicians and Dentists in Ontario; June 2004 — Owner-Manager Remuneration: Bonuses Out of Non-Active Business Income; November 2003 — Revenue Canada Round Table.

Tax Topics: No. 2404, CCPC Passive Investment Income Saga Comes to an End; No. 1695, Corporate Tax Rates - How They (Now) Work; No. 1652, Owner-Manager Remuneration -- Is the CCRA Tightening the Screws?; No. 1579, Tax Rate Drops Change Business Tax Planning.

Forms: T2 SCH 7 — Calculation of Aggregate Investment Income and Active Business Income; T2 SCH 341 — Nova Scotia Corporate Tax Reduction for New Small Businesses.

Income Tax Technical News: Issue No. 30, Reasonableness of Shareholder/Manager Remuneration.

Information Circulars: IC 88-2 General anti-avoidance rule — Section 245 of the Income Tax Act (para. 11).

Interpretation Bulletins: *Primary* — IT-73R6 The small business deduction. *Secondary* — IT-189R2 Corporations used by practising members of professions; IT-232R3 Non-capital losses, net capital losses, restricted farm losses, farm losses and limited partnership losses — Their composition and deductibility in computing taxable income; IT-243R4 Dividend refund to private corporations; IT-362R Patronage dividends; IT-458R2 Canadian-controlled private corporation.

Tax Window Files: Campgrounds and the Small Business Deduction, *May 16, 2016*, CRA Document No. 2016-0647271E5.

Cases: The loss of an associated corporation did not reduce income for the purposes of the income threshold applicable to the small business deduction. *Airtel Communications Ltd. v. The Queen*, 91 DTC 5235 (N.B. Q.B.-T.D.)

A corporation was denied the small business deduction because its only activity was to provide a showroom for a related corporation. Its income was held to be derived from a "personal services business" and it was, therefore, not entitled to the deduction. *533702 Ontario Ltd. v. M.N.R.*, 91 DTC 982 (T.C.C.)

The holding of mortgages was not held to be active business since, even though they were linked with the sale of three commercial properties, the wholly-owned subsidiary of the taxpayer had made a decision to get out of the active business of owning and managing commercial properties. *Alexander Cole Ltd. v. M.N.R.*, 90 DTC 1894 (T.C.C.)

Capital gain can be added to business income for the purpose of calculating a patronage dividend deduction but not for the purpose of calculating the small business deduction.

► 125(1.1) ◄

(1.1) Small business deduction rate. For the purpose of subsection (1), a corporation's small business deduction rate for a taxation year is the total of

(*a*) that proportion of 17.5% that the number of days in the taxation year that are before 2018 is of the number of days in the taxation year,

(*b*) that proportion of 18% that the number of days in the taxation year that are in 2018 is of the number of days in the taxation year, and

(*c*) that proportion of 19% that the number of days in the taxation year that are after 2018 is of the number of days in the taxation year.

(*d*) (Repealed by S.C. 2016, c. 7, s. 34(1).)

(*e*) (Repealed by S.C. 2016, c. 7, s. 34(1).)

Editorial Note: Income eligible for the small business deduction is excluded from "full rate taxable income" per paragraph (*b*) of the definition in s. 123.4(1) and will therefore not qualify for the "general rate reduction" applicable to business income, per s. 123.4(1) and 123.4(2). Accordingly, for example, in 2017 the small business rate is 10.5% (28% – 17.5%), and the small business rate decreases to 10% in 2018 and to 9% in subsequent years.

History: S. 125(1.1)(*a*) and (*b*) were replaced, and (*c*) was added, by S.C. 2018, c. 12, s. 20(1), applicable to the 2018 and subsequent taxation years, and formerly read:

(*a*) that proportion of 17% that the number of days in the taxation year that are in 2015 is of the number of days in the taxation year, and

(*b*) that proportion of 17.5% that the number of days in the taxation year that are after 2015 is of the number of days in the taxation year.

S. 125(1.1)(*b*) was replaced by S.C. 2016, c. 7, s. 34(1), applicable to the 2016 and subsequent taxation years, and formerly read:

(*b*) that proportion of 17.5% that the number of days in the taxation year that are in 2016 is of the number of days in the taxation year,

S. 125(1.1)(*c*) to (*e*) were repealed by S.C. 2016, c. 7, s. 34(1), applicable to the 2016 and subsequent taxation years, and formerly read:

(*c*) that proportion of 18% that the number of days in the taxation year that are in 2017 is of the number of days in the taxation year,

(*d*) that proportion of 18.5% that the number of days in the taxation year that are in 2018 is of the number of days in the taxation year, and

(*e*) that proportion of 19% that the number of days in the taxation year that are after 2018 is of the number of days in the taxation year.

S. 125(1.1)(*a*) and (*b*) were replaced by S.C. 2015, c. 36, s. 11(1), applicable to the 2016 and subsequent taxation years, and formerly read:

(*a*) that proportion of 16% that the number of days in the taxation year that are before 2008 is of the number of days in the taxation year,

(*b*) that proportion of 17% that the number of days in the taxation year that are after 2007 is of the number of days in the taxation year.

Related Sections: S. 137(3) Additional deduction; s. 137.1(9) Special tax rate.

► 125(2) ◄

(2) Business limit. For the purpose of this section, a corporation's business limit for a taxation year is $500,000 unless the corporation is associated in the taxation year with one or more other Canadian-controlled private corporations, in which case, except as otherwise provided in this section, its business limit is nil.

Editorial Note: See the editorial note to s. 125(1). Provincial small business limits may vary from the limit specified in s. 125(2).

History: S. 125(2) was replaced by S.C. 2009, c. 2, s. 39(1), applicable to the 2009 and subsequent taxation years except that, for a 2009 or 2010 taxation year that began before 2009, the reference in subsection 125(2) to "$500,000" shall be read as a reference to the total of

(a) that proportion of $400,000 that the number of days in the taxation year that are before 2009 is of the number of days in the taxation year, and

(b) that proportion of $500,000 that the number of days in the taxation year that are after 2008 is of the number of days in the taxation year.

S. 125(2) formerly read:

(2) *Business limit.* For the purpose of this section, a corporation's business limit for a taxation year is $400,000 unless the corporation is associated in the taxation year with one or more other Canadian-controlled private corporations, in which case, except as otherwise provided in this section, its business limit is nil.

Related Sections: S. 87(2)(*oo.1*) Refundable investment tax credit and balance-due day; s. 88(1)(*e.9*) Winding-up; s. 125(3) Associated corporations; s. 125(4) Failure to file agreement; s. 125(5) Special rules for business limit; s. 125(5.1) Business limit reduction; s. 127.1(2), "qualifying corporation"; s. 182(2) Definitions; s. 248(1), "balance due day"; s. 256(2) Corporations associated through a third corporation.

► 125(3) ◄

(3) Associated corporations. Notwithstanding subsection (2), if all the Canadian-controlled private corporations that are associated with each other in a taxation year file with the Minister in prescribed form an agreement that assigns for the purpose of this section a percentage to one or more of them for the year, the business limit for the year of each of the corporations is

(*a*) if the total of the percentages assigned in the agreement does not exceed 100%, $500,000 multiplied by the percentage assigned to that corporation in the agreement; and

(*b*) in any other case, nil.

Editorial Note: Associated CCPCs have a business limit of nil unless they file an allocation agreement (Schedule 23). S. 125(4) requires the CRA to make an allocation if any associated corporation fails to file an agreement within 30 days after notice in writing that such an agreement is required.

History: S. 125(3)(*a*) was replaced by S.C. 2009, c. 2, s. 39(2), applicable to the 2009 and subsequent taxation years except that, for a 2009 or 2010 taxation year that began before 2009, the reference in paragraph 125(3)(*a*) to "$500,000" is to be read as a reference to "the amount that would, if the corporation were not associated in the year with any other corporation, be its business limit for the year determined without reference to subsections (5) and (5.1)".

S. 125(3)(*a*) formerly read:

(*a*) if the total of the percentages assigned in the agreement does not exceed 100%, $400,000 multiplied by the percentage assigned to that corporation in the agreement; and

Related Sections: S. 125(4) Failure to file agreement; s. 125(5) Special rules for business limit; s. 125(6) Corporate partnerships; s. 256 Associated corporations.

Forms: T2 SCH 23 — Agreement Among Associated Canadian-controlled Private Corporations to Allocate the Business Limit

Cases: Since a franchisor did not have *de facto* control over it's franchisees, the franchisees were not associated with each other for purposes of the small business deduction. *The Queen v. Lenester Sales Ltd. et al.*, 2004 DTC 6461 (F.C.A.), affirming 2003 DTC 997 (T.C.C.)

► 125(3.1) ◄

(3.1) Reduction — business limit. The business limit for the year of a corporation under subsection (2), (3) or (4) is reduced by the total of all amounts each of which is the portion, if any, of the business limit that the corporation assigns to another corporation under subsection (3.2).

Editorial Note: The amount assigned under subsection 125(3.2) reduces the CCPC assignor's small business limit; the assignment is discussed in the editorial note to s. 125(7) "specified corporation income".

History: S. 125(3.1) was added by S.C. 2016, c. 12, s. 44(2), applicable to

(a) taxation years that begin after March 21, 2016; and

(b) a person's taxation year that begins before March 22, 2016 and ends after March 21, 2016 if

(i) the person would be entitled to make an assignment to a corporation under subsection 125(3.2) (as enacted) or under subsection 125(8) (as enacted) if the amendments to section 125 applied to the person's taxation year that begins before March 22, 2016 and ends after March 21, 2016,

(ii) the taxation year of the corporation referred to in subparagraph (i) begins after March 21, 2016,

(iii) the person makes such an assignment for its taxation year that begins before March 22, 2016 and ends after March 21, 2016 and the assignment is to the corporation for its taxation year that begins after March 21, 2016, and

(iv) the person files with the Minister of National Revenue the prescribed form that is required to be filed under subsection 125(3.2) (as enacted) in its return of income for its taxation year that begins before March 22, 2016 and ends after March 21, 2016, on or before the day that is the later of the filing-due date of the person (as defined under subsection 248(1)) or 60 days after the *Budget Implementation Act, 2016, No. 2* (Bill C-29) receives royal assent [February 13, 2017].

► 125(3.2) ◄

(3.2) Assignment. For the purpose of this section, a Canadian-controlled private corporation (in this subsection referred to as the "first corporation") may assign all or any portion of its business limit under subsection (2), (3) or (4) for a taxation year of the first corporation to another Canadian-controlled private corporation (in this subsection referred to as the "second corporation") for a taxation year of the second corporation if

(*a*) the second corporation has an amount of income, for its taxation year, referred to in subparagraph (*a*)(i) of the definition "specified corporate income" in subsection (7) from the provision of services or property directly to the first corporation;

(*b*) the first corporation's taxation year ends in the second corporation's taxation year;

(*c*) the amount assigned does not exceed the amount determined by the formula

$$A - B$$

where

A is the amount of income referred to in paragraph (*a*), and

B is the portion of the amount described in A that is deductible by the first corporation in respect of the amount of income referred to in clause (1)(*a*)(i)(A) or (B) for the year; and

(*d*) a prescribed form is filed with the Minister by

(i) the first corporation in its return of income for its taxation year, and

(ii) the second corporation in its return of income for its taxation year.

Editorial Note: See the editorial note to s. 125(7), "specified corporate income".

History: S. 125(3.2) was added by S.C. 2016, c. 12, s. 44(2), applicable to

(a) taxation years that begin after March 21, 2016; and

(b) a person's taxation year that begins before March 22, 2016 and ends after March 21, 2016 if

(i) the person would be entitled to make an assignment to a corporation under subsection 125(3.2) (as enacted) or under subsection 125(8) (as enacted) if the amendments to section 125 applied to the person's taxation year that begins before March 22, 2016 and ends after March 21, 2016,

(ii) the taxation year of the corporation referred to in subparagraph (i) begins after March 21, 2016,

(iii) the person makes such an assignment for its taxation year that begins before March 22, 2016 and ends after March 21, 2016 and the assignment is to the corporation for its taxation year that begins after March 21, 2016, and

(iv) the person files with the Minister of National Revenue the prescribed form that is required to be filed under subsection 125(3.2) (as enacted) in its return of income for its taxation year that begins before March 22, 2016 and ends after March 21, 2016, on or before the day that is the later of the filing-due date of the person (as defined under subsection 248(1)) or 60 days after the *Budget Implementation Act, 2016, No. 2* (Bill C-29) receives royal assent [February 13, 2017].

Canadian Tax Foundation: Budd and Robinson, *Specified Corporate Income When Year-Ends Differ*, 2018 Canadian Tax Focus 8(1):2.

Tax Window Files: Ss 125(3.2) & 125(8) amending the business limit, *April 5, 2018*, CRA Document No. 2017-0728581I7; Subsections 125(3.2) & 125(5.1), *January 25, 2018*, CRA Document No. 2017-0709241E5; Business limit assignment, *January 29, 2018*, CRA Document No. 2017-0713051E5.

► 125(4) ◄

(4) Failure to file agreement. If any of the Canadian-controlled private corporations that are associated with each other in a taxation year has failed to file with the Minister an agreement as contemplated by subsection (3) within 30 days after notice in writing by the Minister has been forwarded to any of them that such an agreement is required for the purpose of any assessment of tax under this Part, the Minister shall, for the purpose of this section, allocate an amount to one or more of them for the taxation year. The total amount so allocated must equal the least of the amounts that would, if none of the corporations were associated with any other corporation during the year and if this Act were read without reference to subsections (5) and (5.1), be the business limits of the corporations for the year.

Editorial Note: See the editorial note to s. 125(3).

Related Sections: S. 125(3) Associated corporations; s. 125(6) Corporate partnerships; s. 256 Associated corporations.

► 125(5) ◄

(5) Special rules for business limit. Notwithstanding subsections (2), (3) and (4),

(*a*) where a Canadian-controlled private corporation (in this paragraph referred to as the "first corporation") has more than one taxation year ending in the same calendar year and it is associated in 2 or more of those taxation years with another Canadian-controlled private corporation that has a taxation year ending in that calendar year, the business limit of the first corporation for each taxation year ending in the calendar year in which it is associated with the other corporation that ends after the first such taxation year ending in that calendar year is, subject to the application of paragraph (*b*), an amount equal to the lesser of

(i) its business limit determined under subsection (3) or (4) for the first such taxation year ending in the calendar year, and

(ii) its business limit determined under subsection (3) or (4) for the particular taxation year ending in the calendar year; and

(*b*) where a Canadian-controlled private corporation has a taxation year that is less than 51 weeks, its business limit for the year is that proportion of its business limit for the year determined without reference to this paragraph that the number of days in the year is of 365.

Editorial Note: S. 125(5)(*b*) prorates the business limit for a taxation year of less than 51 weeks, based on the number of days in the taxation year, divided by 365.

S. 125(5)(*a*) is applicable where a corporation has two or more taxation years which end in the same calendar year, and is associated in at least two of those years with another CCPC that has a taxation year ending in the particular calendar year. The business limit of the corporation for the second and subsequent taxation years is the business limit allocated to the corporation for the first taxation year, or that of the particular year, if less. (Paragraph (*a*) is then subject to the application of paragraph (*b*); for an example of the interaction of paragraphs (*a*) and (*b*), see paragraph 28 of Interpretation Bulletin IT-73R6 (archived, as it doesn't meet current government web standards).) The provision could apply when there is a deemed year end, such as a change of status to/from a CCPC or an acquisition of control.

History: S. 125(5), the portion before paragraph (*a*) was replaced by S.C. 2016, c. 12, s. 44(3), applicable to

(a) taxation years that begin after March 21, 2016; and

(b) a person's taxation year that begins before March 22, 2016 and ends after March 21, 2016 if

(i) the person would be entitled to make an assignment to a corporation under subsection 125(3.2) (as enacted) or under subsection 125(8) (as enacted) if the amendments to section 125 applied to the person's taxation year that begins before March 22, 2016 and ends after March 21, 2016,

(ii) the taxation year of the corporation referred to in subparagraph (i) begins after March 21, 2016,

(iii) the person makes such an assignment for its taxation year that begins before March 22, 2016 and ends after March 21, 2016 and the assignment is to the corporation for its taxation year that begins after March 21, 2016, and

(iv) the person files with the Minister of National Revenue the prescribed form that is required to be filed under subsection 125(3.2) (as enacted) in its return of income for its taxation year that begins before March 22, 2016 and ends after March 21, 2016, on or before the day that is the later of the filing-due date of the person (as defined under subsection 248(1)) or 60 days after the *Budget Implementation Act, 2016, No. 2* (Bill C-29) receives royal assent [February 13, 2017].

S. 125(5), the portion before paragraph (*a*) formerly read:

S. (5) *Special rules for business limit.* Notwithstanding subsections (2) to (4),

A transitional rule for s. 125(5) was added by S.C. 2009, c. 2, s. 39(3), in force on Royal Assent, March 12, 2009. The transitional rule provides that in applying subsection 125(5) to a corporation for a 2009 or 2010 taxation year of the corporation that began before 2009, subparagraph 125(5)(*a*)(i) is to be read as follows:

"(i) the amount that would have been its business limit determined under subsection (3) or (4) for the first such taxation year ending in the calendar year if the reference to $400,000 in subsection (3), as it applied in respect of that first such taxation year, had been read in the same manner as it is read in respect of the particular taxation year ending in the calendar year, and"

Related Sections: S. 87(2)(*a*) Refundable dividend tax on hand; s. 127(10.2) Expenditure limit determined; s. 249(3.1) Year end on status change; s. 249(4) Loss restriction event – year end; s. 249.1 Definition of "fiscal period"; s. 256 Associated corporations.

► 125(5.1) ◄

(5.1) Business limit reduction. Notwithstanding subsections (2), (3), (4) and (5), a Canadian-controlled private corporation's business limit for a particular taxation year ending in a calendar year is the amount, if any, by which its business limit otherwise determined for the particular taxation year exceeds the greater of

(*a*) the amount determined by the formula

$$A \times B/\$11{,}250$$

where

A is the amount that would, but for this subsection, be the corporation's business limit for the particular taxation year, and

B is the amount determined by the formula

$$0.225\% \times (C - \$10 \text{ million})$$

where

C is

(i) if, in both the particular taxation year and the preceding taxation year, the corporation is not associated with any corporation, the taxable capital employed in Canada (within the meaning assigned by subsection 181.2(1) or 181.3(1) or section 181.4, as the case may be) of the corporation for the preceding taxation year,

(ii) if, in the particular taxation year, the corporation is not associated with any corporation but was associated with one or more corporations in the preceding taxation year, the taxable capital employed in Canada (within the meaning assigned by subsection 181.2(1) or 181.3(1) or section 181.4, as the case may be) of the corporation for the particular taxation year, or

(iii) if, in the particular taxation year, the corporation is associated with one or more particular corporations, the total of all amounts each of which is the taxable capital employed in Canada (within the meaning assigned by subsection 181.2(1) or 181.3(1) or section 181.4, as the case may be) of the corporation or of any of the particular corporations for its last taxation year that ended in the preceding calendar year, and

(*b*) the amount determined by the formula

$$D/\$500{,}000 \times 5(E - \$50{,}000)$$

where

D is the amount determined for A in paragraph (*a*), and

E is the total of all amounts each of which is the adjusted aggregate investment income of the corporation, or of any corporation with which it is associated at any time in the particular taxation year, for each taxation year of the corporation, or associated corporation, as the case may be, that ended in the preceding calendar year.

Editorial Note: The small business deduction (SBD) limit is phased out for a so-called "large corporation", generally meaning a corporation that would have been subject to the Part I.3 capital tax in its preceding taxation year had that tax not been repealed (it was repealed as of the 2006 taxation year). In general terms, the business limit — and, therefore, the SBD — is restricted on a straight-line basis for such corporations with taxable capital in excess of $10 million, with the deduction eliminated entirely where the taxable capital reaches $15 million. For taxation years beginning after 2018, the business limit and SBD are phased out if the "adjusted aggregate investment income" of the CCPC (s. 125(7)) exceeds $50,000 in the preceding taxation year. This latter phase-out occurs on a 5:1 basis, such that $5 of the limit is reduced for every $1 of the investment income exceeding $50,000. If both reductions potentially apply to a CCPC, the greater of the two reductions applies.

History: S. 125(5.1) was replaced by S.C. 2018, c. 12, s. 20(2), applicable to taxation years that begin after 2018, and also to a taxation year of a corporation that begins before 2019 and ends after 2018 if

(a) the corporation's preceding taxation year was, because of a transaction or event or a series of transactions or events, shorter than it would have been in the absence of that transaction, event or series; and

(b) one of the reasons for the transaction, event or series was to defer the application of subsections 20(2) and (3) or 22(1) to (5) [of the *Budget Implementation Act, 2018, No. 1*] to the corporation.

S. 125(5.1) formerly read:

(5.1) *Business limit reduction.* Notwithstanding subsections (2), (3), (4) and (5), a Canadian-controlled private corporation's business limit for a particular taxation year ending in a calendar year is the amount, if any, by which its business limit otherwise determined for the particular year exceeds the amount determined by the formula

$$A \times B/\$11{,}250$$

where

A is the amount that would, but for this subsection, be the corporation's business limit for the particular year; and

B is the amount determined by the formula

$$0.225\% \times (D - \$10 \text{ million})$$

where

D is

(*a*) if, in both the particular taxation year and the preceding taxation year, the corporation is not associated with any corporation, the taxable capital employed in Canada (within the meaning assigned by subsection 181.2(1) or 181.3(1) or section 181.4, as the case may be) of the corporation for the preceding taxation year,

(*b*) if, in the particular taxation year, the corporation is not associated with any corporation but was associated with one or more corporations in the preceding taxation year, the taxable capital employed in Canada (within the meaning assigned by subsection 181.2(1) or 181.3(1) or section 181.4, as the case may be) of the corporation for the particular taxation year, or

(*c*) if, in the particular taxation year, the corporation is associated with one or more particular corporations, the total of all amounts each of which is the taxable capital employed in Canada (within the meaning assigned by subsection 181.2(1) or 181.3(1) or section 181.4, as the case may be) of the corporation or of any of the particular corporations for its last taxation year that ended in the preceding calendar year.

S. 125(5.1), the portion before the formula was replaced by S.C. 2016, c. 12, s. 44(4), applicable to

(a) taxation years that begin after March 21, 2016; and

(b) a person's taxation year that begins before March 22, 2016 and ends after March 21, 2016 if

(i) the person would be entitled to make an assignment to a corporation under subsection 125(3.2) (as enacted) or under subsection 125(8) (as enacted) if the amendments to section 125 applied to the person's taxation year that begins before March 22, 2016 and ends after March 21, 2016,

(ii) the taxation year of the corporation referred to in subparagraph (i) begins after March 21, 2016,

(iii) the person makes such an assignment for its taxation year that begins before March 22, 2016 and ends after March 21, 2016 and the assignment is to the corporation for its taxation year that begins after March 21, 2016, and

(iv) the person files with the Minister of National Revenue the prescribed form that is required to be filed under subsection 125(3.2) (as enacted) in its return of income for its taxation year that begins before March 22, 2016 and ends after March 21, 2016, on or before the day that is the later of the filing-due date of the person (as defined under subsection 248(1)) or 60 days after the *Budget Implementation Act, 2016, No. 2* (Bill C-29) receives royal assent [February 13, 2017].

S. 125(5.1), the portion before the formula formerly read:

S. (5.1) *Business limit reduction.* Notwithstanding subsections (2) to (5), a Canadian-controlled private corporation's business limit for a particular taxation year ending in a calendar year is the amount, if any, by which its business limit otherwise determined for the particular year exceeds the amount determined by the formula

S. 125(5.1), the description of B was replaced by S.C. 2013, c. 34, s. 262(2), applicable to taxation years that begin after December 20, 2002, except that, in its application to a corporation described in s. 181.1(3) for taxation years of the corporation that began before June 26, 2013, the description of B in subsection 125(5.1) is to be read as follows:

"B is

(*a*) if, in both the particular taxation year and the preceding taxation year, the corporation is not associated with any corporation, the amount that would, but for subsections 181.1(2) and (4), be the corporation's tax payable under Part I.3 for the preceding taxation year,

(*b*) if, in the particular taxation year, the corporation is not associated with any corporation but was associated with one or more corporations in the preceding taxation year, the amount that would, but for subsections 181.1(2) and (4), be the corporation's tax payable under Part I.3 for the particular taxation year, and

(c) if, in the particular taxation year, the corporation is associated with one or more particular corporations, the amount determined by the formula

$$0.225\% \times (D - E)$$

where

D is the total of all amounts each of which is the taxable capital employed in Canada (within the meaning assigned by subsection 181.2(1) or 181.3(1) or section 181.4, as the case may be) of the corporation or of any of the particular corporations for its last taxation year that ended in the preceding calendar year, and

E is $10 million."

S. 125(5.1), the description of B formerly read:

B is

(a) where the corporation is not associated with any other corporation in the particular year, the amount that would, but for subsections 181.1(2) and (4), be the corporation's tax payable under Part I.3 for its preceding taxation year, and

(b) where the corporation is associated with one or more other corporations in the particular year, the total of all amounts each of which would, but for subsections 181.1(2) and (4), be the tax payable under Part I.3 by the corporation or any such other corporation for its last taxation year ending in the preceding calendar year.

Related Sections: S. 87(2)(*j.92*) Subsections 125(5.1) and 157.1(1); s. 125(4) Failure to file agreement; s. 125(7), "active asset"; s. 125(7), "adjusted aggregate investment income"; s. 181.1(1.2) Exceptions; s. 181.5(1.1) Lower capital deduction.; s. 181.5(4.1) Lower capital deduction allocation; s. 257 Negative amounts.

Canadian Tax Foundation: Walsh and Walsh, *Passive Investment Income – The Impacts on the Small Business Deduction and Refundable Dividend Tax on Hand*, 2018 St. John's Tax Seminar 4:1–25; Dolson and Taylor, *Passive Investment Income: Past and Future*, 2018 Prairie Provinces Tax Conference 11:0; Ghani et al., *The Passive Income Rules: New Ways To Grind the SBD*, 2018 Tax for the Owner Manager 18(4):2–3; Infanti, *2018 Budget Simplifies Passive Investment Rules*, 2018 Tax for the Owner Manager 18(2):1–2; Cepparo, *CRA Confirms Grind of Business Limit Before Its Assignment*, 2018 Canadian Tax Highlights 26(4):6–7; Pisesky, *Incentive Effects of the New SBD Clawback*, 2018 Canadian Tax Focus 8(2):1–2.

Tax Topics: No. 2426, The Passive Investment Rules and Their Associates. No. 2404, CCPC Passive Investment Income Saga Comes to an End.

Tax Window Files: 2018 CTF - Q16 - Passive Income Reduction Rules, *November 27, 2018*, CRA Document No. 2018-0780031C6; Subsections 125(3.2) & 125(5.1), *January 25, 2018*, CRA Document No. 2017-0709241E5.

► 125(5.2) ◄

(5.2) Anti-avoidance. A particular corporation and another corporation are deemed to be associated with each other at a particular time for the purposes of paragraph (5.1)(*b*) if

(*a*) the particular corporation lends or transfers property at any time, either directly or indirectly, by means of a trust or by any other means whatever, to the other corporation;

(*b*) the other corporation is, at the particular time, related to the particular corporation but is not associated with it; and

(*c*) it may reasonably be considered that one of the reasons the loan or transfer was made was to reduce the amount determined for E in paragraph (5.1)(*b*) in respect of the particular corporation, or of any corporation with which it is associated, for a taxation year.

History: S. 125(5.2) was added by S.C. 2018, c. 12, s. 20(2), applicable to taxation years that begin after 2018, and also to a taxation year of a corporation that begins before 2019 and ends after 2018 if

(a) the corporation's preceding taxation year was, because of a transaction or event or a series of transactions or events, shorter than it would have been in the absence of that transaction, event or series; and

(b) one of the reasons for the transaction, event or series was to defer the application of subsections 20(2) and (3) or 22(1) to (5) [of the *Budget Implementation Act, 2018, No. 1*] to the corporation.

► 125(6) ◄

(6) Corporate partnerships. Where in a taxation year a corporation is a member of a particular partnership and in the year the corporation or a corporation with which it is associated in the year is a member of one or more other partnerships and it may reasonably be considered that one of the main reasons for the separate existence of the partnerships is to increase the amount of a deduction of any corporation under subsection (1), the specified partnership income of the corporation for the year shall, for the purposes of this section, be computed in respect of those partnerships as if all amounts each of which is the income of one of the partnerships for a fiscal period ending in the year from an active business carried on in Canada were nil except for the greatest of those amounts.

Editorial Note: Ss. 125(6) to (6.3) are anti-avoidance rules directed against the use of partnerships to increase entitlement to the small business deduction. Per s. 125(6), where a corporation or associated corporation is a member of a number of partnerships and it may reasonably be considered that one of the main reasons for the separate existence of the partnerships is to increase the small business deduction, the specified partnership income is limited to the greatest income of one of the partnerships, with the remaining partnership income ignored.

Related Sections: S. 125(7), "specified partnership income".

Interpretation Bulletins: *Secondary* — IT-458R2 Canadian-controlled private corporation.

► 125(6.1) ◄

(6.1) Corporation deemed member of partnership. For the purposes of this section, a corporation that is a member, or is deemed by this subsection to be a member, of a partnership that is a member of another partnership shall be deemed to be a member of the other partnership and the corporation's share of the income of the other partnership for a fiscal period shall be deemed to be equal to the amount of that income to which the corporation was directly or indirectly entitled.

Editorial Note: S. 125(6.1), which is part of the anti-avoidance rules in ss. 125(6) to (6.3) pertaining to partnerships and the small business deduction, is a look-through rule for tiered partnerships, such that lower-tier income is considered to be that of the upper-tier partnership.

Related Sections: S. 125(7), "specified partnership income".

► 125(6.2) ◄

(6.2) Specified partnership income deemed nil. Notwithstanding any other provision of this section, where a corporation is a member of a partnership that was controlled, directly or indirectly in any manner whatever, by one or more non-resident persons, by one or more public corporations (other than a prescribed venture capital corporation) or by any combination thereof at any time in its fiscal period ending in a taxation year of the corporation, the income of the partnership for that fiscal period from an active business carried on in Canada shall, for the purposes of computing the specified partnership income of a corporation for the year, be deemed to be nil.

Editorial Note: Ss. 125(6.2) and (6.3) — part of the anti-avoidance rules in ss. 125(6) to (6.3) pertaining to partnerships and the small business deduction — are designed to impose a requirement at the partnership level which is similar to Canadian-controlled corporation status. Per s. 125(6.2), where a corporation is a member of a partnership that is controlled by non-residents and/or public corporations at any time in its fiscal period, Canadian active business income for the purpose of computing specified partnership income (i.e., income eligible for the small business deduction) is generally deemed to be nil. (It is not clear that the control test is necessarily based on 256(5.1) (*de facto* control).) S. 125(6.3) deems a partnership to be controlled by one or more persons if the total share of the partnership income from any source for the fiscal period exceeds 50% of the income from that source.

Related Sections: S. 125(7), "specified partnership income".

► 125(6.3) ◄

(6.3) Partnership deemed to be controlled. For the purposes of subsection (6.2), a partnership shall be deemed to be controlled by one or more persons at any time if the total of the shares of that person or those persons of the income of the partnership from any source for the fiscal period of the partnership that includes that time exceeds 1/2 of the income of the partnership from that source for that period.

Editorial Note: See the editorial note to s. 125(6.2).

Related Sections: S. 125(7), "specified partnership income".

► 125(7) ◄

(7) Definitions. In this section,

Tax Window Files: 2016 STEP–Q7 Deemed Resident Trust and CCPC Status, *June 10, 2016*, CRA Document No. 2016-0634911C6; Campgrounds and the Small Business Deduction, *May 16, 2016*, CRA Document No. 2016-0647271E5; Partnership contracting out to professional corps, *16XXXX*, CRA Document No. 2015-0612921R3.

Tax Window Files: Partnership contracting out to professional corps, *16XXXX*, CRA Document No. 2015-0612921R3.

"active asset" —"active asset", of a particular corporation at any time, means property that is

(*a*) used at that time principally in an active business carried on primarily in Canada by the particular corporation or by a Canadian-controlled private corporation that is related to the particular corporation,

(*b*) a share of the capital stock of another corporation if, at that time,

(i) the other corporation is connected with the particular corporation (within the meaning assigned by subsection 186(4) on the assumption that the other corporation is at that time a payer corporation within the meaning of that subsection), and

(ii) the share would be a "qualified small business corporation share" (as defined in subsection 110.6(1)) if

(A) the references in that definition to an "individual" were references to the particular corporation, and

(B) that definition were read without reference to "the individual's spouse or common law partner", or

(*c*) an interest in a partnership, if

(i) at that time, the fair market value of the particular corporation's interest in the partnership is equal to or greater than 10% of the total fair market value of all interests in the partnership,

(ii) throughout the 24-month period ending before that time, more than 50% of the fair market value of the property of the partnership was attributable to property described in this paragraph or in paragraph (*a*) or (*b*), and

(iii) at that time, all or substantially all of the fair market value of the property of the partnership was attributable to property described in this paragraph or in paragraph (*a*) or (*b*);

History: S. 125(7), the definition "active asset" was added by S.C. 2018, c. 12, s. 20(3), applicable to taxation years that begin after 2018, and also to a taxation year of a corporation that begins before 2019 and ends after 2018 if

(a) the corporation's preceding taxation year was, because of a transaction or event or a series of transactions or events, shorter than it would have been in the absence of that transaction, event or series; and

(b) one of the reasons for the transaction, event or series was to defer the application of subsections 20(2) and (3) or 22(1) to (5) [of the *Budget Implementation Act, 2018, No. 1*] to the corporation.

"active business carried on by a corporation" —"active business carried on by a corporation" means any business carried on by the corporation other than a specified investment business or a personal services business and includes an adventure or concern in the nature of trade;

Editorial Note: Active business income is defined negatively for the purposes of s. 125, as any business carried on by a corporation that includes an adventure or concern in the nature of trade, unless it is a specified investment business or a personal services business. Income from an active business is included in the amount on which a Canadian-controlled private corporation can claim the small business deduction.

The term "active business" is also defined more generally for the purposes of the Act as a whole in s. 248(1). That definition does not specifically include an adventure or concern in the nature of trade and applies to all taxpayers resident in Canada, not just corporations.

Business Income Presumption: There is a rebuttable presumption that income earned by a corporation is business income (see *Canadian Marconi Co.*, 86 DTC 6526 (S.C.C.)).

Cases: The principal activity of the taxpayer was the writing and recording of music. This was its primary source of revenue. The principal purpose of the taxpayer was to earn income from the writing and recording activities of its primary asset, Gagliese, its only employee. The vast majority of this income arose from the daily activities of Gagliese. It was not the principal purpose of the business to earn income from property. All the taxpayer's income, including residuals, was income from an active business. *Rocco Gagliese Productions Inc. v. The Queen*, 2018 DTC 1099 (TCC)

Income from short-term investments was income from an "active business" in a case where they had been held to satisfy the taxpayer's liquidity needs, i.e., as a "backup asset to be called on in support of" its business operations. *Cornwall Gravel Co. Ltd. v. The Queen*, 94 DTC 1709 (T.C.C.)

The taxpayer's income from the sale of building lots, renting a plaza and investing in mortgages and other securities was not active business income when its primary intention was to hold the plaza as an investment rather than sell it and derive business income from it. Its other investments were not required by its business, in the sense that their removal would not have put it at risk. *Lake Superior Investment Ltd. v. M.N.R.*, 93 DTC 898 (T.C.C.)

The taxpayer earned interest on U.S. dollar deposits in the Philippines, such funds being committed to the carrying on of the taxpayer's business there. It was held that the deposits were an integral part of the business and therefore the interest earned on them was active business income. *Ensite Limited v. The Queen*, 86 DTC 6521 (S.C.C.), affirming 83 DTC 5315 (F.C.A.), reversing 81 DTC 5326 (F.C.T.D.)

The taxpayer disposed of its broadcasting division when its broadcasting licence was not renewed. The sale proceeds were invested in short-term securities, and substantial effort was made to obtain a maximum return. The income from these investments was active business income rather than income from property. There is a rebuttable presumption that income earned by a company incorporated for the general purpose of earning income by doing business is business income, plus the commercial reality in this case was that the company had been compelled to enter into an investment business. *Canadian Marconi Co. v. The Queen*, 86 DTC 6526 (S.C.C.), reversing 84 DTC 6267 (F.C.A.) and 82 DTC 6236 (F.C.T.D.).

"adjusted aggregate investment income" —"adjusted aggregate investment income", of a corporation (other than a corporation that is deemed not to be a private corporation by subsection 136(1) or 137(7) or section 141.1) for a taxation year, means the amount that would be the "aggregate investment income" (as defined in subsection 129(4)) of the corporation for the year, if

(*a*) paragraph (*a*) of that definition read as follows:

(*a*) the amount, if any, by which

(i) the eligible portion of the corporation's taxable capital gains (other than taxable capital gains from the disposition of property that is, at the time of disposition, an active asset of the corporation) for the year

exceeds

(ii) the eligible portion of its allowable capital losses (other than allowable capital losses from the disposition of property that is, at the time of disposition, an active asset of the corporation) for the year, or

(*b*) subparagraph (*b*)(iii) of that definition read as follows:

(iii) a dividend from a corporation connected with it (within the meaning assigned by subsection 186(4) on the assumption that the corporation is at that time a payer corporation within the meaning of that subsection), and

(*c*) paragraph (*a*) of the definition *income* or *loss* in subsection 129(4) read as follows:

(*a*) includes

(i) the income or loss from a specified investment business carried on by it, and

(ii) amounts in respect of a life insurance policy that are included in computing the corporation's income for the year, to the extent that the amounts would not otherwise be included in the computation of the corporation's aggregate investment income, but

and

(*d*) no amount were deducted under subsection 91(4) by the corporation in computing its income for the year;

History: S. 125(7), the definition "adjusted aggregate investment income" was added by S.C. 2018, c. 12, s. 20(3), applicable to taxation years that begin after 2018, and also to a taxation year of a corporation that begins before 2019 and ends after 2018 if

(a) the corporation's preceding taxation year was, because of a transaction or event or a series of transactions or events, shorter than it would have been in the absence of that transaction, event or series; and

(b) one of the reasons for the transaction, event or series was to defer the application of subsections 20(2) and (3) or 22(1) to (5) [of the *Budget Implementation Act, 2018, No. 1*] to the corporation.

Related Sections: S. 129(4), adjusted aggregate investment income.

"Canadian-controlled private corporation"—"Canadian-controlled private corporation" means a private corporation that is a Canadian corporation other than

(*a*) a corporation controlled, directly or indirectly in any manner whatever, by one or more non-resident persons, by one or more public corporations (other than a prescribed venture capital corporation), by one or more corporations described in paragraph (*c*), or by any combination of them,

(*b*) a corporation that would, if each share of the capital stock of a corporation that is owned by a non-resident person, by a public corporation (other than a prescribed venture capital corporation), or by a corporation described in paragraph (*c*) were owned by a particular person, be controlled by the particular person,

(*c*) a corporation a class of the shares of the capital stock of which is listed on a designated stock exchange, or

(*d*) in applying subsection (1), paragraphs 87(2)(*vv*) and (*ww*) (including, for greater certainty, in applying those paragraphs as provided under paragraph 88(1)(*e.2*)), the definitions "excessive eligible dividend designation", "general rate income pool" and "low rate income pool" in subsection 89(1) and subsections 89(4) to (6), (8) to (10) and 249(3.1), a corporation that has made an election under subsection 89(11) and that has not revoked the election under subsection 89(12);

Editorial Note: Canadian-controlled private corporation ("CCPC") status is used, among other things, in determining eligibility for the small business deduction, payment of the refundable portion of Part I tax and the related addition to the applicable refundable dividend tax on hand account, and access to the enhanced refundable investment tax credit for scientific research and experimental development activities.

The definition is negative. A corporation that is both "Canadian" and "private", as both terms are defined in s. 89(1), will be a CCPC unless: a) it is controlled directly or indirectly in any manner whatever by one or more non-residents or public corporations, or any combination thereof (*de facto* control); b) all of its shares owned by non-residents or public corporations were owned by one person, in which case it would be controlled by that person (*de jure* control); or c) it is listed on a designated stock exchange. A corporation that has elected under s. 89(11), which deals with determining the corporation's general rate income pool, is not a CCPC only for the limited purposes set out in paragraph (d) of the definition.

S. 248(1) extends the definition in s. 125(7) to the Act as a whole.

De Facto *Control:* Despite the fact that two public corporations collectively owned 50% and a private corporation owned the other 50%, a corporation was found not to be a CCPC. It was indirectly controlled by the public corporations as they had the right to appoint four of five directors (see *International Mercantile Factors Ltd.*, 94 DTC 6365 (F.C.A.)).

De Jure *Control:* *De jure* control arises with the ability to elect the board of directors. The Canada Revenue Agency ("CRA") believes that a Unanimous Shareholders' Agreement is not to be considered in assessing de jure control (see Income Tax Technical News No. 44). However, this view may not be correct (see *Price Waterhouse Coopers Inc. Trustee in Bankruptcy of Bioartificial Gel Technologies (Bagtech) Inc.*, 2012 DTC 1142 (T.C.C.), affirmed by 2013 DTC 5155 (F.C.A.)). The de jure control test does not apply where all the shares of a corporation are already owned by a single person, but that person is in turn controlled directly by Canadian residents (see *Perfect Fry Company Ltd.*, 2007 DTC 588 (T.C.C.), affirmed by 2008 DTC 6472 (F.C.A.)).

Related Regulations: 6700.

Related Sections: S. 7(1.1) Employee stock options; s. 7(8) Deferral in respect of non-CCPC employee options; s. 39(1)(*c*) Meaning of capital gain and capital loss; s. 44.1(1), "eligible small business corporation"; s. 89(1), "Canadian corporation", "eligible dividend", "excessive eligible dividend designation", "general rate income pool", "low rate income pool", "private corporation", "public corporation"; s. 89(1.1) Capital dividend account where control acquired; 89(4) GRIP addition — becoming CCPC; 89(5) GRIP addition — post-amalgamation; 89(6) GRIP addition — post-winding-up; 89(7) GRIP addition for 2006; 89(8) LRIP addition — ceasing to be CCPC; 89(9) LRIP addition — amalgamation; 89(10) LRIP addition — winding-up; 89(11) Election: non-CCPC; 89(12) Revoking election; 89(13) Repeated elections — consent required; 89(14) Dividend designation; 89(14.1) Late designation; 89(15) Meaning of expression "deposit insurance corporation"; s. 110.6(1), "qualified small business corporation share"; s. 123.3 Refundable tax on CCPC's investment income; s. 123.4 Corporate tax reductions; s. 125(1) Small business deduction; s. 125(5) Special rules for business limit; s. 125.1(1) Manufacturing and processing profits deductions; s. 127 [Investment tax credit, etc.]; s. 127.1 Refundable investment tax credit; s. 129(3) Definition of "refundable dividend tax on hand"; s. 129(3.1) Application; s. 152(3.1) Definition of "normal reassessment period"; s. 157(1.1) Special case; s. 157(1.2) Small-CCPC; s. 181.5(7) Related corporations that are not associated; s. 185.2(3) Joint and several liability from excessive dividend designations; s. 248(1), "balance-due day", "small business corporation"; s. 249(3.1) Year end on status change; s. 251(5) Control by related groups, options, etc; s. 256(2) Corporations associated through a third corporation; s. 256(6.1) Simultaneous control.

Canadian Tax Foundation: Leroux, *MindReady: CCPCs, De Facto Control, and SR & ED*, 2015 Canadian Tax Focus 5(2):4; Friedlan, *The Unanimous Shareholders' Agreement and the Hypothetical Person Test: Duha in Dispute*, 2014 Tax for the Owner-Manager 14(1):4–5; Jung and McIntyre, *Current Issues: Canadian Controlled Private Corporation (CCPC) Status and the Meaning of Control*, 2013 Ontario Tax Conference 1:13–14.

Tax Profile: November 2011 — Corporate Control: An Evolving Canadian Concept; April 2006 — Concept of Control.

Tax Topics: No. 2461-2462, Part 3: Shareholders Agreements, the Act, and the Non-Specialist Advisor: The Impact of Control; No. 2460, Part 2: Shareholders Agreements, the Act, and the Non-Specialist Advisor: The Impact of Control; No. 2457, Part 1: Shareholders Agreements, the Act, and the Non-Specialist Advisor: The Impact of Control; No. 1971-72, 2009 Canadian Tax Foundation Conference: Wizards, Tiny Taxes and "Evil" Kirk; No. 1692, Income Tax Implications of Buy-Sell Provisions.

Income Tax Folios: S4-F8-C1 Business Investment Losses.

Income Tax Technical News: Issue No. 44, Unanimous Shareholder Agreements and the CCPC Definition; Issue No. 25, Silicon Graphics Ltd. v. The Queen.

Interpretation Bulletins: *Primary* — IT-458R2 Canadian-controlled private corporation. *Secondary* — IT-113R4 Benefits to employees — Stock options.

Cases: The taxpayer corporation argued that options to acquire shares in a corporation, if exercised, would have been contrary to the provisions of a certain provincial statute. The Court rejected the taxpayer's argument that, since paragraph 251(5)(*b*) deemed the options to be exercised, the options were void such that the corporation could qualify as a Canadian-controlled private corporation. *Line Durocher v. The Queen*, 2017 DTC 5050 (FCA)

The taxpayer was not a CCPC since a public corporation had *de facto* control over it, as the taxpayer could not have survived without the public corporation's financial support. *De facto* and *de jure* control can exist simultaneously for purposes of the Act without any specific provision to that effect. *Lyrtech RD Inc. v. The Queen*, 2013 DTC 1054 (T.C.C.)

Although the majority of its voting shares were held by non-residents, a corporation was a CCPC since a unanimous shareholder agreement prevented the non-resident shareholders from electing a majority of the board of directors, thereby giving *de jure* control to the Canadian shareholders. *Price Waterhouse Coopers Inc. v. The Queen*, 2013 DTC 1048 (T.C.C.)

The taxpayer was a CCPC although all of its shares were owned by a public corporation. The public corporation did not control the taxpayer because it was controlled by individual Canadian residents. Paragraph (*b*) of the CCPC definition does not require an attribution of share ownership to a single hypothetical shareholder, where all of the shares are already owned by a single shareholder. *Perfect Fry Company Ltd. v. The Queen*, 2008 DTC 6472 (F.C.A.), affirming 2007 DTC 588 (T.C.C.).

"designated member" —"designated member", of a particular partnership in a taxation year, means a Canadian-controlled private corporation that provides (directly or indirectly, in any manner whatever) services or property to the particular partnership at any time in the corporation's taxation year where, at any time in the year,

(*a*) the corporation is not a member of the particular partnership, and

(*b*) either

(i) one of its shareholders holds a direct or indirect interest in the particular partnership, or

(ii) if subparagraph (i) does not apply,

(A) the corporation does not deal at arm's length with a person that holds a direct or indirect interest in the particular partnership, and

(B) it is not the case that all or substantially all of the corporation's income for the year from an active business is from providing services or property to

(I) persons with which the corporation deals at arm's length, or

(II) partnerships (other than the particular partnership) with which the corporation deals at arm's length, other than a partnership in which a person that does not deal at arm's length with the corporation holds a direct or indirect interest;

Editorial Note: For taxation years beginning after March 21, 2016 (subject to transitional rules), the corporation's "specified partnership income" (see the definition below) can include income earned by it as a "designated member" of a partnership where it is not otherwise a partner at law, if the income is derived from goods or services provided to the partnership and it meets the criteria set out in paragraph (*b*) of the designated member definition. However, the amount of income that can so qualify is deemed to be nil, unless an amount is assigned to the CCPC/designated member under s. 125(8).

History: S. 125(7), the definition "designated member" was added by S.C. 2016, c. 12, s. 44(7), applicable to

(a) taxation years that begin after March 21, 2016; and

(b) a person's taxation year that begins before March 22, 2016 and ends after March 21, 2016 if

(i) the person would be entitled to make an assignment to a corporation under subsection 125(3.2) (as enacted) or under subsection 125(8) (as enacted) if the amendments to section 125 applied to the person's taxation year that begins before March 22, 2016 and ends after March 21, 2016,

(ii) the taxation year of the corporation referred to in subparagraph (i) begins after March 21, 2016,

(iii) the person makes such an assignment for its taxation year that begins before March 22, 2016 and ends after March 21, 2016 and the assignment is to the corporation for its taxation year that begins after March 21, 2016, and

(iv) the person files with the Minister of National Revenue the prescribed form that is required to be filed under subsection 125(3.2) (as enacted) in its return of income for its taxation year that begins before March 22, 2016 and ends after March 21, 2016, on or before the day that is the later of the filing-due date of the person (as defined under subsection 248(1)) or 60 days after the *Budget Implementation Act, 2016, No. 2* (Bill C-29) receives royal assent [February 13, 2017].

"income of the corporation for the year from an active business" —"income of the corporation for the year from an active business" means the total of

(*a*) the corporation's income for the year from an active business carried on by it including any income for the year pertaining to or incident to that business, other than income for the year from a source in Canada that is a property (within the meaning assigned by subsection 129(4)), and

(*b*) the amount, if any, included under subsection 12(10.2) in computing the corporation's income for the year;

Editorial Note: The income of a corporation for the year from an active business is eligible for the small business deduction. There are two components, the first of which is simply the corporation's income from an active business that the corporation carries on, including income that would not otherwise be income from an active business, but that is incidental thereto. The second component is the amount received from a NISA Fund No. 2, and is included in income under s. 12(10.2), which is otherwise income from property.

Section 129(6) deems income that would otherwise be income from a specified investment business to be income from an active business, where the income is earned from an associated corporation which deducts the amount in computing its income from an active business. This anti-avoidance rule is designed to stop corporate groups under common control from converting active business income into income from property in order to generate the refundable portion of Part I tax.

Incidental Income: It is a question of fact whether generating income from property is incidental to an active business or whether it constitutes income from a specified investment business. Income from short-term investments held to meet liquidity needs is income from an active business (see *Cornwall Gravel Co. Ltd.*, 94 DTC 1709 (T.C.C.)). However, investing cash surplus to working capital requirements is not an active business (see *Atlas Industries Ltd.*, 86 DTC 1756 (T.C.C.)). Where a cinema operator rented the entire cinema, it was engaged in an active business, but in renting a room in the basement and renting the parking lot to a Christmas tree vendor, it was not (see *Supreme Theatres Limited*, 81 DTC 5136 (F.C.T.D.)).

Canadian Tax Foundation: Cheng and Qubti, *Rental Income and ABI: Structuring Around the Five-Employee Test*, 2018 Canadian Tax Focus 8(2):2.

"personal services business" —"personal services business" carried on by a corporation in a taxation year means a business of providing services where

(*a*) an individual who performs services on behalf of the corporation (in this definition and paragraph 18(1)(*p*) referred to as an "incorporated employee"), or

(*b*) any person related to the incorporated employee

is a specified shareholder of the corporation and the incorporated employee would reasonably be regarded as an officer or employee of the person or partnership to whom or to which the services were provided but for the existence of the corporation, unless

(*c*) the corporation employs in the business throughout the year more than five full-time employees, or

(*d*) the amount paid or payable to the corporation in the year for the services is received or receivable by it from a corporation with which it was associated in the year;

Editorial Note: A personal services business is not an active business and the income arising therefrom does not qualify for the small business deduction. Personal services business income is also excluded from the definition of "full rate taxable income" and does not, therefore, qualify for the general rate reduction.

A personal services business arises where a corporation carries on a business of providing the personal services of an individual (the "incorporated employee") to another person who, absent the corporation, could reasonably be viewed as the individual's employer. A personal services business will not arise unless the incorporated employee, or a related person, owns at least 10% of the issued shares of any class of the corporation, nor will it arise if the corporation employs more than five full-time employees in the business. In addition, income that would otherwise be personal services business income, but which is paid by an associated corporation, is deemed not to be personal services business income. It becomes active business income by default.

Employment Relationship: To assess whether an individual is to be viewed as an employee, the tests set out in *Wiebe Door Services Ltd.* (87 DTC 5025 (F.C.A.)) are to be considered: the purported employer's control over the individual; who owns the tools that are used; whether the incorporated employee has a risk of loss or a chance for profit (see *G & J Muirhead Holdings*, 2014 DTC 1067 (T.C.C.), *Placements Marcel Lapointe Inc.*, 93 DTC 821 (T.C.C.), and *9016-9202 Quebec Inc.*, 2014 DTC 1201 (T.C.C.)).

More than five full-time employees: A business has more than five full-time employees if it has five full-time employees and at least one part-time employee (see *489599 B.C. Ltd*, 2008 DTC 4107 (T.C.C.)). Full-time employment is contrasted with part-time employment and an earlier judgment, which determined that working part of a day but five days a week was "full-time", was not the appropriate test (see *Baker et al*, 2005 DTC 5266 (F.C.A.), distinguished from *Ben Raedarc Holdings Limited*, 98 DTC 1218 (T.C.C.)).

Related Sections: S. 18(1)(*p*) Limitation re personal services business expenses; s. 125(1) Small business deduction; s. 248(1), "specified shareholder"; s. 251(2) Definition of "related persons"; s. 256(1) Associated corporations.

Canadian Tax Foundation: Magee, *Personal Services Businesses*, 2007 Canadian Tax Journal 1:160–183.

Tax Profile: August 2009 — Structuring a Services Business.

Tax Topics: No. 2071, Should I Be Taking it Personally?; No. 1784, One Step Too Far by the Court?.

Income Tax Technical News: Issue No. 41, The "More Than Five Full-Time Employees" Test.

Cases: EBI had garbage collection contracts with certain municipalities and engaged several corporations to perform collection tasks as "independent contractors". The taxpayer corporations used their own trucks and drivers, worked alone, were paid by the hour, and the drivers had formerly been EBI employees. Were it not for the separate corporate existence of the taxpayers, their truck-driver shareholders would have been EBI's employees. Accordingly, the taxpayers were operating personal services businesses and were not entitled to the small business deduction. *9016-9202 Québec Inc. v. The Queen*, 2014 DTC 1201 (T.C.C.)

G and his wife owned the taxpayer corporation, which was under contract to H Corp to provide oil well site and facilities services. G was the taxpayer's sole employee. To determine G's status, the factors of control, tools, chance of profit, and risk of loss were relevant. If one ignored that the taxpayer and G were to work directly for H Corp, he would be considered an employee and not as someone in business on his or her own. *G & J Muirhead Holdings v. The Queen*, 2014 DTC 1067 (T.C.C.)

The phrase "more than five full-time employees" does not mean "at least six full-time employees". It can mean five full-time employees plus one or more part-time employees. *489599 B.C. Ltd. v. The Queen*, 2008 DTC 4107 (T.C.C.)

A taxpayer was not carrying on a personal services business and she qualified for the small business deduction when she entered into two management agreements with two partnerships of which she was a partner. Given the lack of control, the presence of remuneration risk, the provision of her own work place and the fact that she was providing a total management service, she could not be considered as being under a contract of service with the partnerships and, as a partner, she could hardly be considered as an employee or officer. *Crestglen Investments Limited v. M.N.R.*, 93 DTC 462 (T.C.C.)

A corporation providing construction cost appraisal services which were in fact rendered by its president and principal shareholder, ML, was considered to operate a "personal services business" where the tests used to distinguish between an employee and a self-employed worker led to the conclusion that ML could reasonably be regarded as an officer or employee of the corporation. *Placements Marcel Lapointe Inc. v. M.N.R.*, 93 DTC 821 (T.C.C.)

"specified cooperative income" (Repealed by S.C. 2019, c. 29, s. 22(1).)

History: S. 125(7), the definition "specified cooperative income" was repealed by S.C. 2019, c. 29, s. 22(1), applicable to taxation years that begin after March 21, 2016. Any assessment of a taxpayer's tax, interest and penalties payable under the Act for any taxation year that ends before March 19, 2019 that would, in the absence of this subsection, be precluded because of subsections 152(4) to (5) of the Act is, if requested by the taxpayer, to be made to the extent necessary to take into account subsections (1) to (3) [of S.C. 2019, c. 29, s. 22]. S. 125(7), the definition "specified cooperative income" formerly read:

"specified cooperative income" — "specified cooperative income", of a corporation (in this definition referred to as the "selling corporation") for a taxation year, means income of the selling corporation (other than an amount included in the selling corporation's income under subsection 135(7)) from the sale of the farming products or fishing catches of the selling corporation's farming or fishing business to a corporation (in this definition referred to as the "purchasing corporation") if

(*a*) the purchasing corporation deals at arm's length with the selling corporation, and

(*b*) either

(i) the purchasing corporation would be a *cooperative corporation*, as defined in subsection 136(2), if the reference in paragraph (*c*) of that subsection to "business of farming" were read as "business of farming or fishing", or

(ii) the following conditions are met:

(A) the selling corporation (or one of its shareholders) or a person who does not deal at arm's length with the selling corporation (or one of its shareholders) holds a direct or indirect interest in a corporation that

(I) would be a *cooperative corporation*, as defined in subsection 136(2), if the reference in paragraph (*c*) of that subsection to "business of farming" were read as "business of farming or fishing", and

(II) holds a direct or indirect interest in the purchasing corporation, and

(B) the income from the sale of the farming products or fishing catches would not be an amount described in subparagraph (*a*)(i) of the definition *specified corporate income* if

(I) the condition in subclause (A)(I) were not met, and

(II) that subparagraph were read without reference to "(other than specified cooperative income)";

S. 125(7), the definition "specified cooperative income" was added by S.C. 2017, c. 33, s. 48(2), applicable to taxation years that begin after March 21, 2016.

Related Sections: 136(2) Definition of "cooperative corporation".

Tax Topics: No. 2362, Proposed Legislation To Insulate Cooperative Corporations From the New Small Business Deduction Rules.

"specified corporate income" — "specified corporate income", of a corporation for a taxation year, means the lesser of

(*a*) the lesser of

(i) the total of all amounts each of which is income (other than specified farming or fishing income of the corporation for the year) from an active business of the corporation for the year from the provision of services or property to a private corporation (directly or indirectly, in any manner whatever) if

(A) at any time in the year, the corporation (or one of its shareholders) or a person who does not deal at arm's length with the corporation (or one of its shareholders) holds a direct or indirect interest in the private corporation, and

(B) it is not the case that all or substantially all of the corporation's income for the year from an active business is from the provision of services or property to

(I) persons (other than the private corporation) with which the corporation deals at arm's length, or

(II) partnerships with which the corporation deals at arm's length, other than a partnership in which a person that does not deal at arm's length with the corporation holds a direct or indirect interest, and

(ii) the total of all amounts each of which is the portion, if any, of the business limit of a private corporation described in subparagraph (i) for a taxation year that the private corporation assigns to the corporation under subsection (3.2), and

(*b*) an amount that the Minister determines to be reasonable in the circumstances;

Editorial Note: The 2016 federal Budget introduced the concept of "specified corporate income" ("SCI") to prevent taxpayers from using corporations to multiply the small business deduction limit. Basically, the SCI of a CCPC is its active business income from providing property or services to a private corporation in which the CCPC, a shareholder of the CCPC, or a person who does not deal at arm's length with such shareholder, has a direct or indirect interest in the private corporation. An exception to the SCI rule can apply where the CCPC earns all or substantially all (90% or more) of its income from an active business for the year from the provision of services or goods to arm's length persons or partnerships. The CCPC cannot normally claim the small business deduction in respect of the SCI, although the private corporation may assign any or all of its business limit to the CCPC where certain conditions are met (s. 125(3.2)), in which case the CCPC can claim the small business deduction to the extent of the assigned limit. See also the limitation in s. 125(10).

For taxation years that begin after March 21, 2016, SCI does not include "specified farming or fishing income" (see definition below). Basically, this means that the income of a corporation carrying on the business of farming or fishing from the sale of its farming or fishing products to an arm's length corporation is not SCI and therefore eligible for the SBD.

History: S. 125(7), the portion of subparagraph (*a*)(i) before clause (A) of the definition "specified corporate income" was replaced by S.C. 2019, c. 29, s. 22(2), applicable to taxation years that begin after March 21, 2016. Any assessment of a taxpayer's tax, interest and penalties payable under the Act for any taxation year that ends before March 19, 2019 that would, in the absence of this subsection, be precluded because of subsections 152(4) to (5) of the Act is, if requested by the taxpayer, to be made to the extent necessary to take into account subsections (1) to (3) [of S.C. 2019, c. 29, s. 22]. S. 125(7), the portion of subparagraph (*a*)(i) before clause (A) of the definition "specified corporate income" formerly read:

(i) the total of all amounts each of which is income (other than specified cooperative income) from an active business of the corporation for the year from the provision of services or property to a private corporation (directly or indirectly, in any manner whatever) if

S. 125(7), the portion of subparagraph (*a*)(i) before clause (A) of the definition "specified corporate income" was replaced by S.C. 2017, c. 33, s. 48(1), applicable to taxation years that begin after March 21, 2016, and formerly read:

(i) the total of all amounts each of which is income from an active business of the corporation for the year from the provision of services or property to a private corporation (directly or indirectly, in any manner whatever) if

S. 125(7), the definition "specified corporate income" was added by S.C. 2016, c. 12, s. 44(7), applicable to

(a) taxation years that begin after March 21, 2016; and

(b) a person's taxation year that begins before March 22, 2016 and ends after March 21, 2016 if

(i) the person would be entitled to make an assignment to a corporation under subsection 125(3.2) (as enacted) or under subsection 125(8) (as enacted) if the amendments to section 125 applied to the person's taxation year that begins before March 22, 2016 and ends after March 21, 2016,

(ii) the taxation year of the corporation referred to in subparagraph (i) begins after March 21, 2016,

(iii) the person makes such an assignment for its taxation year that begins before March 22, 2016 and ends after March 21, 2016 and the assignment is to the corporation for its taxation year that begins after March 21, 2016, and

(iv) the person files with the Minister of National Revenue the prescribed form that is required to be filed under subsection 125(3.2) (as enacted) in its return of income for its taxation year that begins before March 22, 2016 and ends after March 21, 2016, on or before the day that is the later of the filing-due date of the person (as defined under subsection 248(1)) or 60 days after the *Budget Implementation Act, 2016, No. 2* (Bill C-29) receives royal assent [February 13, 2017].

Related Sections: 125(10) Computational rule — specified corporate income.

Canadian Tax Foundation: Purse and Hansen, *A Review of the Specified Corporate Income and Specified Partnership Income Rules and their Application*, 2018 Prairie Provinces Tax Conference 10:0; Thompson, *Small Business Deductions/Multiplication/Dealing with PCs*, 2016 British Columbia Tax Conference 8:1–28.

Tax Window Files: Specified corporate income, streaming of expenses, *February 7, 2018*, CRA Document No. 2017-0706401E5.

specified farming or fishing income —"specified farming or fishing income", of a particular corporation for a taxation year, means income of the particular corporation (other than an amount included in the particular corporation's income under subsection 135(7)), if

(*a*) the income is from the sale of the farming products or fishing catches of the particular corporation's farming or fishing business to another corporation, and

(*b*) the particular corporation deals at arm's length with the other corporation;

History: S. 125(7), the definition "specified farming or fishing income" was added by S.C. 2019, c. 29, s. 22(3), applicable to taxation years that begin after March 21, 2016. Any assessment of a taxpayer's tax, interest and penalties payable under the Act for any taxation year that ends before March 19, 2019 that would, in the absence of this subsection, be precluded because of subsections 152(4) to (5) of the Act is, if requested by the taxpayer, to be made to the extent necessary to take into account subsections (1) to (3) [of S.C. 2019, c. 29, s. 22].

Related Sections: 135(7) Payment to customer to be included in income.

"specified investment business" —"specified investment business", carried on by a corporation in a taxation year, means a business (other than a business carried on by a credit union or a business of leasing property other than real or immovable property) the principal purpose of which is to derive income (including interest, dividends, rents and royalties) from property but, except where the corporation was a prescribed labour-sponsored venture capital corporation at any time in the year, does not include a business carried on by the corporation in the year where

(*a*) the corporation employs in the business throughout the year more than 5 full-time employees, or

(*b*) any other corporation associated with the corporation provides, in the course of carrying on an active business, managerial, administrative, financial, maintenance or other similar services to the corporation in the year and the corporation could reasonably be expected to require more than 5 full-time employees if those services had not been provided;

Editorial Note: A specified investment business is not an active business, and the income arising therefrom does not qualify for the small business deduction. A specified investment business is one whose principal purpose is to earn income from property, including interest, dividends, rents, royalties, and leasing income from real property. A business of leasing property other than real property, such as equipment, is not a specified investment business. If the corporation employs more than five full-time employees in the business, or could reasonably be anticipated to require more than five full-time employees (but for managerial services provided by an associated corporation), the business in not a specified investment business.

More than five full-time employees: See references cited under "personal services business income".

History: S. 125(7), the portion of the definition of "specified investment business" before paragraph (*a*) was replaced by S.C. 2013, c. 34, s. 126, applicable June 26, 2013, and formerly read:

"specified investment business" —"specified investment business", carried on by a corporation in a taxation year means a business (other than a business carried on by a credit union or a business of leasing property other than real property) the principal purpose of which is to derive income (including interest, dividends, rents and royalties) from property but, except where the corporation was a prescribed labour-sponsored venture capital corporation at any time in the year, does not include a business carried on by the corporation in the year where

Related Regulations: 6701.

Related Sections: S. 95(1), "investment business"; s. 95(2.5), "specified deposit"; s. 125(7), "active business carried on by a corporation"; s. 129(4), "income or loss"; s. 248(1), "active business", "specified business".

Canadian Tax Foundation: Morrison, *Specified Investment Business Income Does Not Include Royalties*, 2018 Tax for the Owner Manager 18(4):5–6; Lanthier, *Business or Property Income*, 2015 Canadian Tax Highlights 23(4):5–6.

Tax Topics: No. 2293, *0742443 B.C. Ltd. v. The Queen*: The Tipping Point Between the Provision of Services and the Provision of Property.

Forms: T2 SCH 7 — Calculation of Aggregate Investment Income and Active Business Income; T2 SCH 70 — Active Business Income for the Purposes of the Accelerated Tax Reduction for Corporations with Specified Partnership Income.

Tax Window Files: Campgrounds and the Small Business Deduction, *May 16, 2016*, CRA Document No. 2016-0647271E5.

Cases: The principal business of the corporate taxpayer was to derive rental income from residential properties. The taxpayer argued its business qualified for the small business deduction under a statutory exemption from the definition of specified investment business. That exemption was provided for businesses that could, without the services of associated corporations, reasonably be expected to require more than five full-time employees. The evidence showed that, in the absence of services provided by its two associated corporations, the taxpayer would have required only one full-time employee.

The business was properly characterized as a specified investment business and did not qualify for the small business deduction. *Huntly Investments v. The Queen*, 2018 DTC 1010 (TCC)

The phrase "more than five full-time employees" does not mean "at least six full-time employees". It can mean five full-time employees plus one or more part-time employees. *489599 B.C. Ltd. v. The Queen*, 2008 DTC 4107 (T.C.C.)

Working 20 hours per week does not constitute full-time employment for the purpose of the definition of "specified investment business". The test set out in *Ben Raedarc Holdings Limited v. The Queen* (98 DTC 1218) (T.C.C.) is too narrow and subjective. *Baker et al. v. The Queen*, 2005 DTC 5266 (F.C.A), affirming 2004 DTC 2833 (T.C.C.)

A taxpayer who employed two full-time employees and shared the expenses of 15 others through co-ownership arrangements was considered a specified investment business and denied a small business deduction. *Lerric Investments Corp. v. The Queen*, 2001 DTC 5169 (F.C.A.), affirming 99 DTC 756 (T.C.C.).

"specified partnership business limit" —"specified partnership business limit", of a person for a taxation year, at any particular time, means the amount determined by the formula

$$(K/L) \times M - T$$

where

K is the total of all amounts each of which is the person's share of the income (determined in accordance with Subdivision J of Division B) of a partnership of which the person was a member for a fiscal period ending in the year from an active business carried on in Canada,

L is the total of all amounts each of which is the income of the partnership for a fiscal period referred to in paragraph (*a*) of the description of A in the definition "specified partnership income" in this subsection from an active business carried on in Canada,

M is the lesser of

(*a*) the amount of the business limit indicated in subsection (2) for a corporation that is not associated in a taxation year with one or more other Canadian-controlled private corporations, and

(*b*) the product obtained by the formula

$$(Q/R) \times S$$

where

Q is the amount referred to in paragraph (*a*),

R is 365, and

S is the total of all amounts each of which is the number of days in a fiscal period of the partnership that ends in the year, and

T is the total of all amounts each of which is an amount, if any, that the person assigns under subsection (8);

History: S. 125(7), the definition "specified partnership business limit" was added by S.C. 2016, c. 12, s. 44(7), applicable to

(a) taxation years that begin after March 21, 2016; and

(b) a person's taxation year that begins before March 22, 2016 and ends after March 21, 2016 if

(i) the person would be entitled to make an assignment to a corporation under subsection 125(3.2) (as enacted) or under subsection 125(8) (as enacted) if the amendments to section 125 applied to the person's taxation year that begins before March 22, 2016 and ends after March 21, 2016,

(ii) the taxation year of the corporation referred to in subparagraph (i) begins after March 21, 2016,

(iii) the person makes such an assignment for its taxation year that begins before March 22, 2016 and ends after March 21, 2016 and the assignment is to the corporation for its taxation year that begins after March 21, 2016, and

(iv) the person files with the Minister of National Revenue the prescribed form that is required to be filed under subsection 125(3.2) (as enacted) in its return of income for its taxation year that begins before March 22, 2016 and ends after March 21, 2016, on or before the day that is the later of the filing-due date of the person (as defined under subsection 248(1)) or 60 days after the *Budget Implementation Act, 2016, No. 2* (Bill C-29) receives royal assent [February 13, 2017].

"specified partnership income" —"specified partnership income" of a corporation for a taxation year means the amount determined by the formula

$$A + B$$

where

A is the total of all amounts each of which is an amount in respect of a partnership of which the corporation was a member, or a designated member, in the year equal to the least of

(*a*) the total of all amounts each of which is an amount in respect of an active business carried on in Canada by the corporation as a member, or a designated member, of the partnership determined by the formula

$$G - H$$

where

G is the total of all amounts each of which is

(i) the corporation's share of the income (determined in accordance with Subdivision J of Division B) of the partnership for a fiscal period of the business that ends in the year,

(ii) income of the corporation for the year from the provision (directly or indirectly, in any manner whatever) of services or property to the partnership, or

(iii) an amount included in the corporation's income for the year in respect of the business under any of subsections 34.2(2), (3) and (12), and

H is the total of all amounts deducted in computing the corporation's income for the year from the business (other than amounts that were deducted in computing the income of the partnership from the business or the income of the corporation described under subparagraph (ii) of the description of G) or in respect of the business under subsection 34.2(4) or (11),

(*b*) an amount equal to

(i) if the corporation was a member of the partnership, the corporation's specified partnership business limit for the year, and

(ii) if the corporation was a designated member of the partnership, the total of all amounts assigned to it under subsection (8) for the year and, where no such amounts have been assigned, nil, and

(*c*) nil, if

(i) the corporation is a member, or a designated member, of the partnership (including indirectly through one or more other partnerships) in the year, and

(ii) the partnership provides services or property to either

(A) a private corporation (directly or indirectly in any manner whatever) in the year, if

(I) the corporation (or one of its shareholders) or a person who does not deal at arm's length with the corporation (or one of its shareholders) holds a direct or indirect interest in the private corporation, and

(II) it is not the case that all or substantially all of the partnership's income for the year from an active business is from the provision of services or property to

1. persons (other than the private corporation) that deal at arm's length with the partnership and each person that holds a direct or indirect interest in the partnership, or

2. partnerships with which the partnership deals at arm's length, other than a partnership in which a person that does not deal at arm's length with the corporation holds a direct or indirect interest, or

(B) a particular partnership (directly or indirectly in any manner whatever) in the year, if

(I) the corporation (or one of its shareholders) does not deal at arm's length with the particular partnership or a person that holds a direct or indirect interest in the particular partnership, and

(II) it is not the case that all or substantially all of the partnership's income for the year from an active business is from the provision of services or property to

1. persons that deal at arm's length with the partnership and each person that holds a direct or indirect interest in the partnership, or

2. partnerships (other than the particular partnership) with which the partnership deals at arm's length, other than a partnership in which a person that does not deal at arm's length with the corporation holds a direct or indirect interest, and

B is the lesser of

(*a*) the total of the amounts determined in respect of the corporation for the year under subparagraphs (1)(*a*)(iii) and (iv), and

(*b*) the total of all amounts each of which is an amount in respect of a partnership of which the corporation was a member, or a designated member, in the year equal to the amount determined by the formula

$$N - O$$

where

N is the amount determined in respect of the partnership for the year under paragraph (*a*) of the description of A, and

O is the amount determined in respect of the partnership for the year

(i) if the corporation was a member of the partnership, under subparagraph (*b*)(i) of the description of A, and

(ii) if the corporation was a designated member of the partnership, under subparagraph (*b*)(ii) of the description of A;

Editorial Note: A corporation's partnership income is eligible for the small business deduction only to the extent that it is "specified partnership income". The meaning of the term "partnership", which is not defined in the *Income Tax Act*, is a matter of provincial jurisdiction. Every common law province/territory has a statute that defines the term partnership and a "contract of partnership" is defined in the Civil Code of Quebec. The most common definition of a partnership is: "the relation (or relationship) that subsists (or exists) between persons carrying on a business in common with a view to profit" (see paragraph 1.4 of Income Tax Folio S4-F16-C1).

Where the corporation is a member of a partnership, its specified partnership income for a taxation year is basically the lesser of: (a) the corporation's share of a partnership's income from active businesses carried on in Canada for the year, less amounts deducted by the corporation in respect of that income; and (b) its "specified partnership business limit" for the year, generally meaning that proportion of $500,000 that is the corporation's share of partnership income from an active business carried on in Canada relative to all partners' shares of the income.

For taxation years beginning after March 21, 2016 (subject to transitional rules), the corporation's specified partnership income can include income earned by it as a "designated member" of a partnership where it is not otherwise a partner at law, if the income is derived from goods or services provided to the partnership. However, the amount of income that can so qualify is deemed to be nil, unless an amount is assigned to the CCPC/designated member under subsection 125(8). Effectively, the latter rules ensure that business structures using designated members rather than actual partners cannot circumvent the specified partnership business limit.

Small Business Deduction: This an amount equal to the corporation's small business deduction rate multiplied by the least of three specified amounts that may be deducted from the tax otherwise payable under Part I for a taxation year by a corporation that was, throughout the taxation year, a Canadian-controlled private corporation (see s. 125(1)). Only a maximum aggregate amount of $500,000 of active business income earned by a partnership in a year is taken into account in determining the total small business deduction available to all of the partners in respect of the partnership income. Furthermore, if a corporation is a member of the partnership, and in the year, the corporation or an associated corporation is a member of one or more other partnerships (and it may be reasonable to conclude that one of the main reasons for the separate existence of the partnerships is to increase the corporation's specified partnership income beyond its share of the $500,000 limit per partnership), only the greatest amount of active business income from any single partnership is to be included, while the active business income of all the other partnerships is deemed to be nil (s. 127(6)).

Specified Partnership Loss: This is the corporation's share of losses of a partnership, of which it is a member, from active businesses carried on in Canada, plus the amount, if any, by which amounts deducted by a corporate partner in computing the corporation's specified partnership income exceed the corporation's share of income from that partnership (see s. 125(7) "specified partnership losses").

Offsetting Losses: In the event that the corporation has a loss in the year from an active business carried on in Canada by it or by a partnership of which it was a member, as well as income from the year from an active business carried on by it in Canada as a member of a partnership, the losses are to be offset first against the business income of the partnership that is not eligible for the small business deduction. This only applies if the corporation suffered losses from an active business and it had earned active business income through a partnership which would not otherwise qualify as "specified partnership income". If the partnership's fiscal period is less than 365 days, the $500,000 amount is prorated on a daily basis at $1,370 per day ($500,000 divided by 365).

Anti-Avoidance: Subsections 125(6)–(6.3) contain anti-avoidance rules pertaining to corporate partnerships, including the proliferation of partnerships to avoid the limitation amounts, as well as partnerships controlled by non-residents and/or public corporations.

History: S. 125(7), the description of A in the definition "specified partnership income" was replaced by S.C. 2016, c. 12, s. 44(5), applicable to

(a) taxation years that begin after March 21, 2016; and

(b) a person's taxation year that begins before March 22, 2016 and ends after March 21, 2016 if

(i) the person would be entitled to make an assignment to a corporation under subsection 125(3.2) (as enacted) or under subsection 125(8) (as enacted) if the amendments to section 125 applied to the person's taxation year that begins before March 22, 2016 and ends after March 21, 2016,

(ii) the taxation year of the corporation referred to in subparagraph (i) begins after March 21, 2016,

(iii) the person makes such an assignment for its taxation year that begins before March 22, 2016 and ends after March 21, 2016 and the assignment is to the corporation for its taxation year that begins after March 21, 2016, and

(iv) the person files with the Minister of National Revenue the prescribed form that is required to be filed under subsection 125(3.2) (as enacted) in its return of income for its taxation year that begins before March 22, 2016 and ends after March 21, 2016, on or before the day that is the later of the filing-due date of the person (as defined under subsection 248(1)) or 60 days after the *Budget Implementation Act, 2016, No. 2* (Bill C-29) receives royal assent [February 13, 2017].

S. 125(7), the description of A in the definition "specified partnership income" formerly read:

A is the total of all amounts each of which is an amount in respect of a partnership of which the corporation was a member in the year equal to the lesser of

(*a*) the total of all amounts each of which is an amount in respect of an active business carried on in Canada by the corporation as a member of the partnership determined by the formula

$$G - H$$

where

G is the total of all amounts each of which is the corporation's share of the income (determined in accordance with subdivision j of Division B) of the partnership for a fiscal period of the business that ends in the year, or an amount included in the corporation's income for the year in respect of the business under any of subsections 34.2(2), (3) and (12), and

H is the total of all amounts deducted in computing the corporation's income for the year from the business (other than amounts that were deducted in computing the income of the partnership from the business) or in respect of the business under subsection 34.2(4) or (11), and

(*b*) the amount determined by the formula

$$K/L \times M$$

where

K is the total of all amounts each of which is the corporation's share of the income (determined in accordance with subdivision j of Division B) of the partnership for a fiscal period ending in the year from an active business carried on in Canada

L is the total of all amounts each of which is the income of the partnership for a fiscal period referred to in paragraph (*a*) from an active business carried on in Canada, and

M is the lesser of

(i) $500,000, and

(ii) the product obtained when $1,370 is multiplied by the total of all amounts each of which is the number of days in a fiscal period of the partnership that ends in the year, and

S. 125(7), paragraph (*b*) of the description of B in the definition "specified partnership income" was replaced by S.C. 2016, c. 12, s. 44(6), applicable to

(a) taxation years that begin after March 21, 2016; and

(b) a person's taxation year that begins before March 22, 2016 and ends after March 21, 2016 if

(i) the person would be entitled to make an assignment to a corporation under subsection 125(3.2) (as enacted) or under subsection 125(8) (as enacted) if the amendments to section 125 applied to the person's taxation year that begins before March 22, 2016 and ends after March 21, 2016,

(ii) the taxation year of the corporation referred to in subparagraph (i) begins after March 21, 2016,

(iii) the person makes such an assignment for its taxation year that begins before March 22, 2016 and ends after March 21, 2016 and the assignment is to the corporation for its taxation year that begins after March 21, 2016, and

(iv) the person files with the Minister of National Revenue the prescribed form that is required to be filed under subsection 125(3.2) (as enacted) in its return of income for its taxation year that begins before March 22, 2016 and ends after March 21, 2016, on or before the day that is the later of the filing-due date of the person (as defined under subsection 248(1)) or 60 days after the *Budget Implementation Act, 2016, No. 2* (Bill C-29) receives royal assent [February 13, 2017].

S. 125(7), paragraph (*b*) of the description of B in the definition "specified partnership income" formerly read:

(*b*) the total of all amounts each of which is an amount in respect of a partnership of which the corporation was a member in the year equal to the amount determined by the formula

$$N - O$$

where

N is the amount determined in respect of the partnership for the year under paragraph (*a*) of the description of A, and

O is the amount determined in respect of the partnership for the year under paragraph (*b*) of the description of A;

S. 125(7), the descriptions of G and H in the definition "specified partnership income" were replaced by S.C. 2013, c. 40, s. 55(1), applicable to taxation years that end after March 22, 2011, and formerly read:

G is the total of all amounts each of which is the corporation's share of the income (determined in accordance with subdivision j of Division B) of the partnership for a fiscal period of the business that ends in the year or an amount included in the corporation's income for the year from the business because of subsection 34.2(5), and

H is the total of all amounts deducted in computing the corporation's income for the year from the business (other than amounts that were deducted in computing the income of the partnership from the business), and

S. 125(7), the description of M in the definition "specified partnership income" was replaced by S.C. 2009, c. 2, s. 39(4), applicable to fiscal periods of a partnership that end after 2008. S. 125(7), the description of M in the definition "specified partnership income" formerly read:

M is the lesser of

(*i*) $400,000, and

(*ii*) the product obtained when $1,096 is multiplied by the total of all amounts each of which is the number of days in a fiscal period of the partnership that ends in the year, and

Related Sections: S. 125(1) Small business deduction; s. 125(6) Corporate partnerships; s. 125(6.1) Corporation deemed member of partnership; s. 125(6.2) Specified partnership income deemed nil; s. 125(6.3) Partnership deemed to be controlled; s. 125(7), "specified partnership loss"; s. 257 Negative amounts.

Canadian Tax Foundation: Purse and Hansen, *A Review of the Specified Corporate Income and Specified Partnership Income Rules and their Application*, 2018 Prairie Provinces Tax Conference 10:0.

Tax Profile: August 2009 — Structuring a Services Business.

"specified partnership loss" — "specified partnership loss" of a corporation for a taxation year means the total of all amounts each of which is an amount in respect of a partnership of which the corporation was a member in the year determined by the formula

$$A + B$$

where

A is the total of all amounts each of which is the corporation's share of the loss (determined in accordance with subdivision j of Division B) of the partnership for a fiscal period ending in the year from an active business carried on in Canada by the corporation as a member of the partnership, and

B is the total of all amounts each of which is an amount determined by the formula

$$G - H$$

where

G is the amount determined for H in the definition "specified partnership income" in this subsection for the year in respect of the corporation's income from an active business carried on in Canada by the corporation as a member of the partnership, and

H is the amount determined for G in the definition "specified partnership income" in this subsection for the year in respect of the corporation's share of the income from the business.

Editorial Note: Just as a corporation includes its share of the active business income of a partnership in determining the amount on which it claims the small business deduction, partnership losses must also be taken into account. A specified partnership loss is the corporation's share of the loss of the partnership from an active business, increased by any related expenses incurred directly by the corporate partner. There is no limit on the amount of a specified partnership loss and no pro-ration if the partnership's fiscal period has fewer than 365 days.

Related Sections: S. 125(1) Small business deduction; s. 125(6) Corporate partnerships; s. 125(6.1) Corporation deemed member of partnership; s. 125(6.2) Specified partnership income deemed nil; s. 125(6.3) Partnership deemed to be controlled; s. 125(7), "specified partnership income"; s. 257 Negative amounts.

► 125(8) ◄

(8) Assignment — specified partnership business limit. For the purpose of the definition "specified partnership income" in subsection (7), a person that is a member of a partnership in a taxation year may assign to a designated member of the partnership — for a taxation year of the designated member — all or any portion of the person's specified partnership business limit (determined without reference to this assignment) in respect of the person's taxation year if (Repealed by 1984, c. 45, s. 40(1).)

(*a*) the person is described in paragraph (*b*) of the definition "designated member" in subsection (7) in respect of the designated member in the designated member's taxation year;

(*b*) the specified partnership business limit of the person is in respect of a fiscal period of the partnership that ends in the designated member's taxation year; and

(*c*) a prescribed form is filed with the Minister by

(i) the designated member in its return of income for the designated member's taxation year, and

(ii) the person in its return of income for the person's taxation year.

Editorial Note: See the editorial notes to subsection s. 125(7) "designated member" and "specified partnership income".

History: S. 125(8) was added by S.C. 2016, c. 12, s. 44(8), applicable to

(a) taxation years that begin after March 21, 2016; and

(b) a person's taxation year that begins before March 22, 2016 and ends after March 21, 2016 if

(i) the person would be entitled to make an assignment to a corporation under subsection 125(3.2) (as enacted) or under subsection 125(8) (as enacted) if the amendments to section 125 applied to the person's taxation year that begins before March 22, 2016 and ends after March 21, 2016,

(ii) the taxation year of the corporation referred to in subparagraph (i) begins after March 21, 2016,

(iii) the person makes such an assignment for its taxation year that begins before March 22, 2016 and ends after March 21, 2016 and the assignment is to the corporation for its taxation year that begins after March 21, 2016, and

(iv) the person files with the Minister of National Revenue the prescribed form that is required to be filed under subsection 125(3.2) (as enacted) in its return of income for its taxation year that begins before March 22, 2016 and ends after March 21, 2016, on or before the day that is the later of the filing-due date of the person (as defined under subsection 248(1)) or 60 days after the *Budget Implementation Act, 2016, No. 2* (Bill C-29) receives royal assent [February 13, 2017].

Tax Window Files: Ss 125(3.2) & 125(8) amending the business limit, *April 5, 2018*, CRA Document No. 2017-0728581I7.

► 125(9) ◄

(9) Anti-avoidance. If a corporation provides services or property to a person or partnership that holds a direct or indirect interest in a particular partnership or corporation and one of the reasons for the provision of the services or property to the person or partnership, instead of to the particular partnership or corporation, is to avoid the application of subparagraph (1)(*a*)(ii) or (ii.1) in respect of the income from the provision of the services or property, no amount in respect of the corporation's income from the provision of the services or property is to be included in the total amount determined under paragraph (1)(*a*). (Repealed by 1984, c. 45, s. 40(1).)

History: S. 125(9) was added by S.C. 2016, c. 12, s. 44(8), applicable to

(a) taxation years that begin after March 21, 2016; and

(b) a person's taxation year that begins before March 22, 2016 and ends after March 21, 2016 if

(i) the person would be entitled to make an assignment to a corporation under subsection 125(3.2) (as enacted) or under subsection 125(8) (as enacted) if the amendments to section 125 applied to the person's taxation year that begins before March 22, 2016 and ends after March 21, 2016,

(ii) the taxation year of the corporation referred to in subparagraph (i) begins after March 21, 2016,

(iii) the person makes such an assignment for its taxation year that begins before March 22, 2016 and ends after March 21, 2016 and the assignment is to the corporation for its taxation year that begins after March 21, 2016, and

(iv) the person files with the Minister of National Revenue the prescribed form that is required to be filed under subsection 125(3.2) (as enacted) in its return of income for its taxation year that begins before March 22, 2016 and ends after March 21, 2016, on or before the day that is the later of the filing-due date of the person (as defined under subsection 248(1)) or 60 days after the *Budget Implementation Act, 2016, No. 2* (Bill C-29) receives royal assent [February 13, 2017].

► 125(10) ◄

(10) Computational rule — specified corporate income. For the purpose of determining an amount for a taxation year in respect of a corporation under clause (1)(*a*)(i)(B) or subparagraph (1)(*a*)(ii.1), an amount of income is to be excluded if the amount is (Repealed by 1984, c. 45, s. 40(1).)

(*a*) income from an active business of the corporation for the year from the provision of services or property to another corporation with which the corporation is associated (in this subsection referred to as the "associated corporation"); and

(*b*) not deductible by the associated corporation for its taxation year in respect of an amount included in the income of the associated corporation that is

(i) referred to in any of clauses (1)(*a*)(i)(A) to (C), or

(ii) reasonable to consider as being attributable to or derived from an amount referred to in clause (1)(*a*)(i)(C).

History: S. 125(10) was added by S.C. 2016, c. 12, s. 44(8), applicable to

(a) taxation years that begin after March 21, 2016; and

(b) a person's taxation year that begins before March 22, 2016 and ends after March 21, 2016 if

(i) the person would be entitled to make an assignment to a corporation under subsection 125(3.2) (as enacted) or under subsection 125(8) (as enacted) if the amendments to section 125 applied to the person's taxation year that begins before March 22, 2016 and ends after March 21, 2016,

(ii) the taxation year of the corporation referred to in subparagraph (i) begins after March 21, 2016,

(iii) the person makes such an assignment for its taxation year that begins before March 22, 2016 and ends after March 21, 2016 and the assignment is to the corporation for its taxation year that begins after March 21, 2016, and

(iv) the person files with the Minister of National Revenue the prescribed form that is required to be filed under subsection 125(3.2) (as enacted) in its return of income for its taxation year that begins before March 22, 2016 and ends after March 21, 2016, on or before the day that is the later of the filing-due date of the person (as defined under subsection 248(1)) or 60 days after the *Budget Implementation Act, 2016, No. 2* (Bill C-29) receives royal assent [February 13, 2017].

► 125(11) ◄

(11) [Where corporation deemed to employ more than five full-time employees]. (Repealed by 1984, c. 45, s. 40(1).)

► 125(12) ◄

(12) [Definitions]. (Repealed by 1984, c. 45, s. 40(1).)

► 125(13) ◄

(13) [Connected partnerships]. (Repealed by 1984, c. 45, s. 40(1).)

► 125(14) ◄

(14) [Idem]. (Repealed by 1984, c. 45, s. 40(1).)

► 125(15) ◄

(15) [Appeal]. (Repealed by 1984, c. 45, s. 40(1).)

SECTION 125.1: Manufacturing and processing profits deductions

► 125.1(1) ◄

(1) Manufacturing and processing profits deductions. There may be deducted from the tax otherwise payable under this Part by a corporation for a taxation year an amount equal to the corporation's general rate reduction percentage for the taxation year (within the meaning assigned by subsection 123.4(1)) multiplied by the lesser of

(*a*) the amount, if any, by which the corporation's Canadian manufacturing and processing profits for the year exceed, where the corporation was a Canadian-controlled private corporation throughout the year, the least of the amounts determined under paragraphs 125(1)(*a*) to (*c*) in respect of the corporation for the year, and

(*b*) the amount, if any, by which the corporation's taxable income for the year exceeds the total of

(i) where the corporation was a Canadian-controlled private corporation throughout the year, the least of the amounts determined under paragraphs 125(1)(*a*) to (*c*) in respect of the corporation for the year,

(ii) the amount determined by multiplying the total of the amounts that would be deductible under subsection 126(2) from the tax for the year otherwise payable under this Part by it, if those amounts were determined without reference to section 123.4, by the relevant factor for the year, and

(iii) where the corporation was a Canadian-controlled private corporation throughout the year, its aggregate investment income for the year (within the meaning assigned by subsection 129(4)).

History: S. 125.1(1)(*b*)(ii) was replaced by S.C. 2013, c. 34, s. 263(1), applicable to the 2003 and subsequent taxation years, and formerly read:

(ii) 10/4 of the total of the amounts that would be deductible under subsection 126(2) from the tax for the year otherwise payable under this Part by the corporation if those amounts were determined without reference to section 123.4, and

Related Regulations: Part LII; 5200; 5201.

Related Sections: S. 110.5 Additions for foreign tax deductions; s. 125(7) Definitions.

Forms: T2 SCH 27 — Calculation of Canadian Manufacturing and Processing Profits Deduction; T2 SCH 426 — British Columbia Manufacturing and Processing Tax Credit; T2 SCH 404 — Saskatchewan Manufacturing and Processing Profits Tax Reduction; T2 SCH 440 — Yukon Manufacturing and Processing Tax Credit (1998 and later taxation years); T2 SCH 320 — Prince Edward Island Manufacturing and Processing Tax Credit (1998 and later taxation years); T2 SCH 300 — Newfoundland Manufacturing and Processing Profits Tax Credit (1998 and later taxation years).

Income Tax Folios: S4-F15-C1 Manufacturing and Processing.

Interpretation Bulletins: *Secondary* — IT-92R2 Income of contractors.

Cases: A taxpayer was not entitled to the M&P tax credit and ITCs it had claimed in respect of an asphalt plant which had been acquired primarily for the purpose of producing asphalt for use in its paving contracts, which were essentially contracts for work and materials. *Will-Kare Paving & Contracting Limited v. The Queen*, 2000 DTC 6467 (S.C.C.), affirming 98 DTC 6203 (F.C.A.) and 97 DTC 506 (T.C.C.)

The taxpayer's activities involving the replacement of parts of a customer's hydraulic systems with parts it itself manufactured did not constitute the manufacture of goods for sale since, in common law, "for sale" does not mean "for use in a repair process" and no commercial person would say that manufacture of parts to be used to repair a customer's defective equipment is a manufacture of those parts for sale. *The Queen v. Coopers & Lybrand Ltd.*, 94 DTC 6541 (F.C.A), reversing 92 DTC 6453 (F.C.T.D.), affirming unreported (T.C.C.)

When a corporation's business involved using data supplied by its customers to make images of sections of the earth on "seismic sections" from which it produced output tapes for them, it was in reality processing the raw information received from them and such processing could not be equated with the processing or manufacturing of goods. *The Queen v. Veritas Seismic (1987) Ltd.*, 94 DTC 6123 (F.C.A.)

A manufacturer of modular buildings was allowed to include in the "cost of manufacturing and processing labour" and "cost of labour" amounts paid to its subcontractors, other than plumbers and electricians. The unpredictable market demands for production experienced by the taxpayer required it to engage the subcontractors who performed the same services for the taxpayer as those performed by its own employees. *NRB Inc. v. M.N.R.*, 93 DTC 295 (T.C.C.)

The demolition activities carried on by a taxpayer with a view to selling a portion of the materials found at its demolition sites constituted "processing" where important transformation work was required with respect to the steel, wood, and bricks obtained at the demolition sites, in order to render them fit for sale. *Démolition A.M. de l'Est du Québec Inc. v. M.N.R.*, 93 DTC 889 (T.C.C.)

A corporate taxpayer engaged in providing diamond drilling services to its customers in the mining industry, primarily in the form of drilling core samples, was not manufacturing or processing goods for "sale or lease" but was providing drilling services when its customers never received possession of any of the products involved which were either consumed in the drilling process or returned to the taxpayer for future use or recycling. *Germac Enterprises Ltd. v. The Queen*, 93 DTC 1466 (T.C.C.)

Rebuilding aircraft engines that retained their identity through the process did not constitute "manufacturing or processing goods for sale". *Rolls-Royce (Canada) Ltd. v. The Queen*, 93 DTC 5031 (F.C.A.), affirming 91 DTC 5579 (F.C.T.D.)

A manufacturer of electronic equipment disposed of a broadcasting division when its licence was not renewed. The proceeds were invested in short-term securities, and effort was made to obtain a maximum return. The income from these investments was Canadian manufacturing and processing profits. There is a presumption that income earned by a company incorporated for the purpose of earning income by doing business is business income. The commercial reality in this case was that the company had been compelled to enter into an investment business. *Canadian Marconi Co. v. The Queen*, 86 DTC 6526 (S.C.C.), reversing 84 DTC 6267 (F.C.A.).

► 125.1(2) ◄

(2) Electrical energy and steam. A corporation that generates electrical energy for sale, or produces steam for sale, in a taxation year may deduct from its tax otherwise payable under this Part for the year an amount equal to the corporation's general rate reduction percentage for the taxation year (within the meaning assigned by subsection 123.4(1)) multiplied by the amount determined by the formula

$$A - B$$

where

A is the amount, if any, that would, if the definition "manufacturing or processing" in subsection (3), and in subsection 1104(9) of the Income Tax Regulations, were read without reference to paragraph (*h*) of those definitions (other than for the purpose of applying section 5201 of the *Income Tax Regulations*) and if subsection (5) applied for the purpose of subsection (1), be the lesser of

(*a*) the amount determined under paragraph (1)(*a*) in respect of the corporation for the year, and

(*b*) the amount determined under paragraph (1)(*b*) in respect of the corporation for the year; and

B is the amount, if any, that is the lesser of

(*a*) the amount determined under paragraph (1)(*a*) in respect of the corporation for the year, and

(*b*) the amount determined under paragraph (1)(*b*) in respect of the corporation for the year.

▶ 125.1(3) ◀

(3) Definitions. In this section,

"Canadian manufacturing and processing profits" — "Canadian manufacturing and processing profits" of a corporation for a taxation year means such portion of the total of all amounts each of which is the income of the corporation for the year from an active business carried on in Canada as is determined under rules prescribed for that purpose by regulation made on the recommendation of the Minister of Finance to be applicable to the manufacturing or processing in Canada of goods for sale or lease;

Related Regulations: Part LII.

Cases: Because the taxpayer made a tax overpayment out of profits earned in its business, when it received a tax refund, such refund represented a return of money that was intended for use in its business. Hence, the refund interest was active business income, and had to be included in its "adjusted business income" for MPP tax credit purposes. *The Queen v. Irving Oil Limited*, 2002 DTC 6716 (F.C.A.), affirming 2000 DTC 2164 (T.C.C.).

"manufacturing or processing" — "manufacturing or processing" does not include

(*a*) farming or fishing,

(*b*) logging,

(*c*) construction,

(*d*) operating an oil or gas well or extracting petroleum or natural gas from a natural accumulation of petroleum or natural gas,

(*e*) extracting minerals from a mineral resource,

(*f*) processing

(i) ore (other than iron ore or tar sands ore) from a mineral resource located in Canada to any stage that is not beyond the prime metal stage or its equivalent,

(ii) iron ore from a mineral resource located in Canada to any stage that is not beyond the pellet stage or its equivalent, or

(iii) tar sands ore from a mineral resource located in Canada to any stage that is not beyond the crude oil stage or its equivalent,

(*g*) producing industrial minerals,

(*h*) producing or processing electrical energy or steam, for sale,

(*i*) processing natural gas as part of the business of selling or distributing gas in the course of operating a public utility,

(*j*) processing heavy crude oil recovered from a natural reservoir in Canada to a stage that is not beyond the crude oil stage or its equivalent,

(*k*) Canadian field processing, or

(*l*) any manufacturing or processing of goods for sale or lease, if, for any taxation year of a corporation in respect of which the expression is being applied, less than 10% of its gross revenue from all active businesses carried on in Canada was from

(i) the selling or leasing of goods manufactured or processed in Canada by it, and

(ii) the manufacturing or processing in Canada of goods for sale or lease, other than goods for sale or lease by it.

Interpretation Bulletins: *Primary* — IT-411R Meaning of "construction".

Cases: The taxpayer's activities gathering, processing and providing information for wells drilled for oil and gas in Canada did not constitute manufacturing or processing, since information was not "goods" within the meaning of s. 125.1; the only "goods" involved (the tapes and microfiches) served simply as the medium on which the information was copied and their sale or lease was not the real source of the taxpayer's income. *The Queen v. International Petrodata Inc.*, 95 DTC 5335 (F.C.A.), reversing 93 DTC 110 (T.C.C.)

When a corporation's business involved using data supplied by its customers to make images of sections of the earth on "seismic sections" from which it produced output tapes for them, it was in reality processing the raw information received from them. Such processing could not be equated with the processing or manufacturing of goods. *The Queen v. Veritas Seismic (1987) Ltd.*, 94 DTC 6123 (F.C.A.)

▶ 125.1(4) ◀

(4) Determination of gross revenue. For the purposes of paragraph (*l*) of the definition "manufacturing or processing" in subsection (3), where a corporation was a member of a partnership at any time in a taxation year,

(*a*) there shall be included in the gross revenue of the corporation for the year from all active businesses carried on in Canada, that proportion of the gross revenue from each such business carried on in Canada by means of the partnership, for the fiscal period of the partnership coinciding with or ending in that year, that the corporation's share of the income of the partnership from that business for that fiscal period is of the income of the partnership from that business for that fiscal period; and

(*b*) there shall be included in the gross revenue of the corporation for the year from all activities described in subparagraphs (*l*)(i) and (ii) of the definition "manufacturing or processing" in subsection (3), that proportion of the gross revenue from each such activity engaged in in the course of a business carried on by means of the partnership, for the fiscal period of the partnership coinciding with or ending in that year, that the corporation's share of the income of the partnership from that business for that fiscal period is of the income of the partnership from that business for that fiscal period.

▶ 125.1(5) ◀

(5) Interpretation. For the purpose of the description of A in subsection (2) and for the purpose of applying the *Income Tax Regulations* (other than section 5201 of the Regulations) to that subsection other than the description of B,

(*a*) electrical energy and steam are deemed to be goods; and

(*b*) the generation of electrical energy for sale, and the production of steam for sale, are deemed to be, subject to paragraph (*l*) of the definition "manufacturing or processing" in subsection (3), manufacturing or processing.

SECTION 125.11: [Corporate rate reductions for resource income]

▶ 125.11(1) ◀

(1) Definitions — (Repealed by S.C. 2003, c. 28, s. 13(2).)

"resource rate reduction percentage" — (Repealed by S.C. 2003, c. 28, s. 13(2).)

"taxable resource income" — (Repealed by S.C. 2003, c. 28, s. 13(2).)

▶ 125.11(2) ◀

(2) Resource deduction — (Repealed by S.C. 2003, c. 28, s. 13(2).)

SECTION 125.2: Deduction of Part VI tax

▶ 125.2(1) ◀

(1) Deduction of Part VI tax — (Repealed by S.C. 2013, c. 34, s. 265(1).)

History: S. 125.2(1) was repealed by S.C. 2013, c. 34, s. 265(1), applicable to taxation years that begin after October 31, 2011, and formerly read:

S. 125.2

(1) *Deduction of Part VI tax.* There may be deducted in computing the tax payable under this Part for a taxation year by a corporation that was throughout the year a financial institution (within the meaning assigned by section 190) an amount equal to such part as the corporation claims of its unused Part VI tax credits for any of its 7 immediately preceding taxation years ending before 1992, to the extent that that amount does not exceed the amount, if any, by which

(*a*) its tax payable under this Part (determined without reference to this section) for the year

exceeds the total of

(*b*) the amount that would, but for subsection 190.1(3), be its tax payable under Part VI for the year, and

(*c*) the lesser of its Canadian surtax payable (within the meaning assigned by subsection 125.3(4)) for the year and the amount that would, but for subsection 181.1(4), be its tax payable under Part I.3 for the year.

Related Sections: S. 190 Tax on capital of financial institutions.

▶ 125.2(2) ◀

(2) Idem — (Repealed by S.C. 2013, c. 34, s. 265(1).)

History: S. 125.2(2) was repealed by S.C. 2013, c. 34, s. 265(1), applicable to taxation years that begin after October 31, 2011, and formerly read:

(2) *Idem.* For the purposes of this section,

(*a*) an amount may not be claimed under subsection (1) in computing a corporation's tax payable under this Part for a particular taxation year in respect of its unused Part VI tax credit for another taxation year until its unused Part VI tax credits for taxation years preceding the other year that may be claimed for the particular year have been claimed; and

(*b*) an amount in respect of a corporation's unused Part VI tax credit for a taxation year may be claimed under subsection (1) in computing its tax payable under this Part for another taxation year only to the extent that it exceeds the total of all amounts each of which is the amount claimed in respect of that unused Part VI tax credit in computing its tax payable under this Part for a taxation year preceding that other year.

▶ 125.2(3) ◀

(3) Definition of "unused Part VI tax credit" — (Repealed by S.C. 2013, c. 34, s. 265(1).)

History: S. 125.2(3) was repealed by S.C. 2013, c. 34, s. 265(1), applicable to taxation years that begin after October 31, 2011, and formerly read:

(3) *Definition of "unused Part VI tax credit".* For the purposes of this section, "unused Part VI tax credit" of a corporation for a taxation year is the lesser of

(*a*) its tax payable under Part VI (determined without reference to subsections 190.1(1.1) and (3)) for the year, and

(*b*) the amount determined by the formula

$$A - B$$

where

A is its tax payable under Part VI for the year (determined without reference to subsection 190.1(3)), and

B is the amount, if any, by which

(i) the amount that would, but for this section, be its tax payable under this Part for the year

exceeds

(ii) the lesser of its Canadian surtax payable (within the meaning assigned by subsection 125.3(4)) and the amount that would, but for subsection 181.1(4), be its tax payable under Part I.3 for the year.

SECTION 125.21: Part XIII tax — eligible bank affiliate

There may be deducted in computing the tax payable under this Part for a taxation year by a particular corporation that is throughout the year an eligible Canadian bank (as defined in subsection 95(2.43)) the total of all amounts, each of which is the amount, if any, by which

(*a*) an amount paid under paragraph 212(1)(*b*) in respect of interest paid or credited in the year by the particular corporation in respect of an upstream deposit (as defined in subsection 95(2.43)) owing to a non-resident corporation that is, throughout the year, an eligible bank affiliate (as defined in subsection 95(2.43)) of the particular corporation

exceeds

(*b*) the total of all amounts each of which is a portion of the amount described in paragraph (*a*) that is available to the non-resident corporation or any other person or partnership at any time as a credit or reduction of, or deduction from, any amount otherwise payable to the government of a country other than Canada, or a political subdivision of that country, having regard to all available provisions of the laws of that country, or political subdivision, as the case may be, any tax treaty with that country and any other agreements entered into by that country or political subdivision.

History: S. 125.21 was added by S.C. 2014, c. 39, s. 40(1), applicable in respect of taxation years that begin after October 2012.

SECTION 125.3: Deduction of Part I.3 tax

▶ 125.3(1) ◀

(1) Deduction of Part I.3 tax. There may be deducted in computing the tax payable under this Part for a taxation year by a corporation (other than a corporation that was throughout the year a financial institution, within the meaning assigned by section 190) an amount equal to such part as the corporation claims of its unused Part I.3 tax credits for any of its 7 immediately preceding taxation years ending before 1992, to the extent that that amount does not exceed the amount, if any, by which

(*a*) its Canadian surtax payable for the year

exceeds

(*b*) the amount that would, but for subsection 181.1(4), be its tax payable under Part I.3 for the year.

Related Sections: 181 Definitions; 181.1 Tax payable; 181.2 Taxable capital employed in Canada; 181.3 Taxable capital employed in Canada of financial institution; 181.4 Taxable capital employed in Canada of non-resident; 181.5 Capital deduction; 181.6 Return; 181.7 Provisions applicable to Part; 181.71 Provisions applicable — Crown corporations; 89(14.1) Late designation; 89(15) Meaning of expression "deposit insurance corporation".

Forms: T2 SCH 37 — Calculation of Unused Part I.3 Tax Credit.

▶ 125.3(1.1) ◀

(1.1) Idem. There may be deducted in computing the tax payable under this Part for a taxation year by a corporation that was a financial institution (within the meaning assigned by section 190) throughout the year an amount equal to such part as the corporation claims of its unused Part I.3 tax credits for any of its 7 immediately preceding taxation years ending before 1992, to the extent that that amount does not exceed the lesser of

(*a*) the amount, if any, by which its Canadian surtax payable for the year exceeds the amount that would, but for subsection 181.1(4), be its tax payable under Part I.3 for the year, and

(*b*) the amount, if any, by which its tax payable under this Part (determined without reference to this section) for the year exceeds the amount that would, but for subsections 181.1(4) and 190.1(3), be the total of its taxes payable under Parts I.3 and VI for the year.

History: S. 125.3(1.1)(*b*) was replaced by S.C. 2013, c. 34, s. 266(1), applicable to taxation years that begin after October 31, 2011, and formerly read:

(*b*) the amount, if any, by which its tax payable under this Part (determined without reference to this section and section 125.2) for the year exceeds the amount that would, but for subsections 181.1(4) and 190.1(3), be the total of its taxes payable under Parts I.3 and VI for the year.

► 125.3(2) ◄

(2) Special rules. For the purposes of this section,

(*a*) no amount may be claimed under subsection (1) in computing a corporation's tax payable under this Part for a particular taxation year in respect of its unused Part I.3 tax credit for another taxation year until its unused Part I.3 tax credits for taxation years preceding the other year that may be claimed for the particular year have been claimed; and

(*b*) an amount in respect of a corporation's unused Part I.3 tax credit for a taxation year may be claimed under subsection (1) in computing its tax payable under this Part for another taxation year only to the extent that it exceeds the total of all amounts each of which is the amount claimed in respect of that unused Part I.3 tax credit in computing its tax payable under this Part for a taxation year preceding that other year.

► 125.3(3) ◄

(3) Acquisition of control. Where, at any time, control of a corporation has been acquired by a person or group of persons, no amount in respect of its unused Part I.3 tax credit for a taxation year ending before that time is deductible by the corporation for a taxation year ending after that time and no amount in respect of its unused Part I.3 tax credit for a taxation year ending after that time is deductible by the corporation for a taxation year ending before that time, except that

(*a*) where a business was carried on by the corporation in a taxation year ending before that time, its unused Part I.3 tax credit for that year is deductible by the corporation for a particular taxation year ending after that time only if that business was carried on by the corporation for profit or with a reasonable expectation of profit throughout the particular year and only to the extent of that proportion of the corporation's Canadian surtax payable for the particular year that

(i) the amount, if any, by which

(A) the total of its income for the particular year from that business and, where properties were sold, leased, rented or developed or services rendered in the course of carrying on that business before that time, its income for the particular year from any other business substantially all the income of which was derived from the sale, leasing, rental or development, as the case may be, of similar properties or the rendering of similar services

exceeds

(B) the total of all amounts each of which is an amount deducted under paragraph 111(1)(*a*) or (*d*) for the particular year by the corporation in respect of a non-capital loss or a farm loss, as the case may be, for a taxation year in respect of that business or the other business,

is of the greater of

(ii) the amount determined under subparagraph (i), and

(iii) the corporation's taxable income for the particular year; and

(*b*) where a business was carried on by the corporation throughout a taxation year ending after that time, its unused Part I.3 tax credit for that year is deductible by the corporation for a particular taxation year ending before that time only if that business was carried on by the corporation for profit or with a reasonable expectation of profit in the particular year and only to the extent of that proportion of the corporation's Canadian surtax payable for the particular year that

(i) the amount, if any, by which

(A) the total of its income for the particular year from that business and, where properties were sold, leased, rented or developed or services rendered in the course of carrying on that business before that time, its income for the particular year from any other business substantially all the income of which was derived from the sale, leasing, rental or development, as the case may be, of similar properties or the rendering of similar services

exceeds

(B) the total of all amounts each of which is an amount deducted under paragraph 111(1)(*a*) or (*d*) for the particular year by the corporation in respect of a non-capital loss or a farm loss, as the case may be, for a taxation year in respect of that business or the other business,

is of the greater of

(ii) the amount determined under subparagraph (i), and

(iii) the corporation's taxable income for the particular year.

► 125.3(4) ◄

(4) Definitions. For the purposes of this section,

"Canadian surtax payable" — "Canadian surtax payable" of a corporation for a taxation year means

(*a*) in the case of a corporation that is non-resident throughout the year, the lesser of

(i) the amount determined under section 123.2 in respect of the corporation for the year, and

(ii) its tax payable under this Part for the year, and

(*b*) in any other case, the lesser of

(i) the prescribed proportion of the amount determined under section 123.2 in respect of the corporation for the year, and

(ii) its tax payable under this Part for the year;

Related Regulations: 8602.

"unused Part I.3 tax credit" — "unused Part I.3 tax credit" of a corporation for a taxation year means

(*a*) where the year ended before 1992, the amount, if any, by which its tax payable under Part I.3 for the year exceeds the amount deductible under subsection (1) in computing its tax payable under this Part for the year, and

(*b*) where the year ends after 1991, the amount, if any, by which the corporation's tax payable under

Part I.3 for the year (determined without reference to subsection 181.1(4)) exceeds its Canadian surtax payable under this Part for the year.

Canadian Film or Video Production Tax Credit

SECTION 125.4: [Film or video production tax credit]

► 125.4(1) ◄

(1) Definitions. The definitions in this subsection apply in this section.

Related Regulations: 8201.

Canadian Tax Foundation: Gill, *Financing Canadian Films Through Crowdfunding*, 2013 Canadian Tax Focus 3(1):4–5.

"assistance" —"assistance" means an amount, other than a prescribed amount or an amount deemed under subsection (3) to have been paid, that would be included under paragraph 12(1)(*x*) in computing a taxpayer's income for any taxation year if that paragraph were read without reference to

(*a*) subparagraphs 12(1)(*x*)(v) to (viii), if the amount were received

(i) from a person or partnership described in subparagraph 12(1)(*x*)(ii), or

(ii) in circumstances where clause 12(1)(*x*)(i)(C) applies; and

(*b*) subparagraphs 12(1)(*x*)(v) to (vii), in any other case.

History: S. 125.4(1), the definition "assistance" was replaced by S.C. 2014, c. 39, s. 41(2), applicable

(a) to film or video productions for which the production commencement time of the corporation (or, if there is more than one qualified corporation in respect of the production, of all such corporations) is on or after November 14, 2003; and

(b) to a corporation in respect of a film or video production for which the production commencement time of any corporation is before November 14, 2003

(i) if the earliest labour expenditure of the corporation (or, if there is more than one qualified corporation in respect of the production, of all those corporations) in respect of the production is made after 2003, or

(ii) if the corporation elects (or, if there is more than one qualified corporation in respect of the production, all those corporations jointly elect), in writing, and the election is filed with the Minister of National Revenue on or before the earliest filing-due date of any qualified corporation in respect of the production for that corporation's taxation year that includes the day on which the *Economic Action Plan 2014 Act, No. 2* [S.C. 2014, c. 39] receives royal assent [December 16, 2014], and the earliest labour expenditure of all such qualified corporations in respect of the production is made

(A) after the last taxation year of any such corporation that ended before November 14, 2003, or

(B) if the first taxation year of all such corporations includes November 14, 2003, in that taxation year.

The earliest labour expenditure referred to in the above application is to be determined under the provisions of subsections 125.4(1) and (2) of the Act that would apply if this amendment had not been enacted.

S. 125.4(1), the definition "assistance" formerly read:

"assistance"—"assistance" means an amount, other than a prescribed amount or an amount deemed under subsection (3) to have been paid, that would be included under paragraph 12(1)(*x*) in computing a taxpayer's income for any taxation year if that paragraph were read without reference to subparagraphs (v) to (vii).

Related Sections: S. 87(2)(*j*.94) Film or video productions.

"Canadian film or video production" —"Canadian film or video production" has the meaning assigned by regulation.

Related Regulations: 1106(4).

Related Sections: S. 87(2)(*j*.94) Film or video productions.

Cases: When assessing whether the production was an "excluded production", the Minister must determine on the facts whether it was "primarily" a "televised game", a "magazine", or a "documentary". *Zone3-XXXVI Inc. v. Canada (AG)*, 2016 DTC 5029 (FC)

"Canadian film or video production certificate" —"Canadian film or video production certificate" means a certificate issued in respect of a production by the Minister of Canadian Heritage certifying that the production is a Canadian film or video production in respect of which that Minister is satisfied that, except where the production is a treaty co-production (as defined in subsection 1106(3) of the *Income Tax Regulations*), an acceptable share of revenues from the exploitation of the production in non-Canadian markets is, under the terms of any agreement, retained by

(*a*) a qualified corporation that owns or owned an interest in, or for civil law a right in, the production;

(*b*) a prescribed taxable Canadian corporation related to the qualified corporation; or

(*c*) any combination of corporations described in paragraph (*a*) or (*b*).

History: S. 125.4(1), the definition "Canadian film or video production certificate" was replaced by S.C. 2014, c. 39, s. 41(3), applicable in respect of film or video productions in respect of which certificates are issued by the Minister of Canadian Heritage after December 20, 2002, except that, in respect of those film or video productions in respect of which certificates are issued by the Minister of Canadian Heritage before 2004, the definition "Canadian film or video production certificate" in subsection 125.4(1) of the Act is to be read as follows:

" 'Canadian film or video production certificate' means a certificate issued in respect of a production by the Minister of Canadian Heritage

(*a*) certifying that the production is a Canadian film or video production in respect of which that Minister is satisfied that, except where the production is a treaty co-production (as defined in subsection 1106(3) of the *Income Tax Regulations*), an acceptable share of revenues from the exploitation of the production in non-Canadian markets is, under the terms of any agreement, retained by

(i) a qualified corporation that owns or owned an interest in, or for civil law a right in, the production,

(ii) a prescribed taxable Canadian corporation related to the qualified corporation, or

(iii) any combination of corporations described in subparagraph (i) or (ii); and

(*b*) estimating amounts relevant for the purpose of determining the amount deemed under subsection (3) to have been paid in respect of the production."

S. 125.4(1), the definition "Canadian film or video production certificate" formerly read:

"Canadian film or video production certificate"—"Canadian film or video production certificate" means a certificate issued in respect of a production by the Minister of Canadian Heritage

(*a*) certifying that the production is a Canadian film or video production, and

(*b*) estimating amounts relevant for the purpose of determining the amount deemed under subsection 125.4(3) to have been paid in respect of the production.

Related Sections: S. 87(2)(*j*.94) Film or video productions.

"investor"(Repealed by S.C. 2014, c. 39, s. 41(1).)

History: S. 125.4(1), the definition "investor" was repealed by S.C. 2014, c. 39, s. 41(1), applicable

(a) to taxation years that end after November 14, 2003; and

(b) in respect of a film or video production in respect of which a corporation has, in a return of income filed before November 14, 2003, claimed an amount under subsection 125.4(3) in respect of a labour expenditure incurred after 1997.

S. 125.4(1), the definition "investor" formerly read:

"investor"—"investor" means a person, other than a prescribed person, who is not actively engaged on a regular, continuous and substantial basis in a business carried on through a permanent establishment (as defined by regulation) in Canada that is a Canadian film or video production business.

Related Regulations: 8201.

Related Sections: S. 87(2)(*j*.94) Film or video productions.

"labour expenditure" —"labour expenditure", of a corporation for a taxation year in respect of a Canadian film or video production, means, in the case of a corporation that is not a qualified corporation for the taxation year, nil, and in the case of a corporation that is a qualified corporation for the taxation year, subject to subsection (2), the total of the following amounts to the extent that they are reasonable in the circumstances and included in the cost to, or in the case of depreciable property the capital cost to, the corporation, or any other person or partnership, of the production:

(*a*) the salary or wages directly attributable to the production that are incurred after 1994 and in the taxation year, or the preceding taxation year, by the corporation for the stages of production of the property, from the production commencement time to the end of the post-production stage, and paid by it in the taxation year or within 60 days after the end of the taxation year (other than amounts incurred in that preceding taxation year that were paid within 60 days after the end of that preceding taxation year),

(*b*) that portion of the remuneration (other than salary or wages and other than remuneration that relates to services rendered in the preceding taxation year and that was paid within 60 days after the end of that preceding taxation year) that is directly attributable to the production of property, that relates to services rendered after 1994 and in the taxation year, or that preceding taxation year, to the corporation for the stages of production, from the production commencement time to the end of the post-production stage, and that is paid by it in the taxation year or within 60 days after the end of the taxation year to

(i) an individual who is not an employee of the corporation, to the extent that the amount paid

(A) is attributable to services personally rendered by the individual for the production of the property, or

(B) is attributable to and does not exceed the salary or wages of the individual's employees for personally rendering services for the production of the property,

(ii) another taxable Canadian corporation, to the extent that the amount paid is attributable to and does not exceed the salary or wages of the other corporation's employees for personally rendering services for the production of the property,

(iii) another taxable Canadian corporation all the issued and outstanding shares of the capital stock of which (except directors' qualifying shares) belong to an individual and the activities of which consist principally of the provision of the individual's services, to the extent that the amount paid is attributable to services rendered personally by the individual for the production of the property, or

(iv) a partnership that is carrying on business in Canada, to the extent that the amount paid

(A) is attributable to services personally rendered by an individual who is a member of the partnership for the production of the property, or

(B) is attributable to and does not exceed the salary or wages of the partnership's employees for personally rendering services for the production of the property, and

(*c*) where

(i) the corporation is a subsidiary wholly-owned corporation of another taxable Canadian corporation (in this section referred to as the "parent"), and

(ii) the corporation and the parent have agreed that this paragraph apply in respect of the production,

the reimbursement made by the corporation in the year, or within 60 days after the end of the year, of an expenditure that was incurred by the parent in a particular taxation year of the parent in respect of that production and that would be included in the labour expenditure of the corporation in respect of the property for the particular taxation year because of paragraph (*a*) or (*b*) if

(iii) the corporation had had such a particular taxation year, and

(iv) the expenditure were incurred by the corporation for the same purpose as it was by the parent and were paid at the same time and to the same person or partnership as it was by the parent.

History: S. 125.4(1), the portion of the definition "labour expenditure" before paragraph (*b*)(i) was replaced by S.C. 2014, c. 39, s. 41(4), applicable

(a) to film or video productions for which the production commencement time of the corporation (or, if there is more than one qualified corporation in respect of the production, of all such corporations) is on or after November 14, 2003; and

(b) to a corporation in respect of a film or video production for which the production commencement time of any corporation is before November 14, 2003

(i) if the earliest labour expenditure of the corporation (or, if there is more than one qualified corporation in respect of the production, of all those corporations) in respect of the production is made after 2003, or

(ii) if the corporation elects (or, if there is more than one qualified corporation in respect of the production, all those corporations jointly elect), in writing, and the election is filed with the Minister of National Revenue on or before the earliest filing-due date of any qualified corporation in respect of the production for that corporation's taxation year that includes the day on which the *Economic Action Plan 2014 Act, No. 2* [S.C. 2014, c. 39] receives royal assent [December 16, 2014], and the earliest labour expenditure of all such qualified corporations in respect of the production is made

(A) after the last taxation year of any such corporation that ended before November 14, 2003, or

(B) if the first taxation year of all such corporations includes November 14, 2003, in that taxation year.

The earliest labour expenditure referred to in the above application is to be determined under the provisions of subsections 125.4(1) and (2) of the Act that would apply if this amendment had not been enacted.

The portion of the definition "labour expenditure" before paragraph (*b*)(i) formerly read:

"labour expenditure"—"labour expenditure" of a corporation for a taxation year in respect of a property of the corporation that is a Canadian film or video production means, in the case of a corporation that is not a qualified corporation for the year, nil, and in the case of a corporation that is a qualified corporation for the year, subject to subsection (2), the total of the following amounts to the extent that they are reasonable in the circumstances and included in the cost or, in the case of depreciable property, the capital cost to the corporation of the property:

(*a*) the salary or wages directly attributable to the production that are incurred after 1994 and in the year, or the preceding taxation year, by the corporation for the stages of production of the property, from the final script stage to the end of the post-production stage, and paid by it in the year or within 60 days after the end of the year (other than amounts incurred in that preceding year that were paid within 60 days after the end of that preceding year),

(*b*) that portion of the remuneration (other than salary or wages and other than remuneration that relates to services rendered in the preceding taxation year and that was paid within 60 days after the end of that preceding year) that is directly attributable to the production of property, that relates to services rendered after 1994 and in the year, or that preceding year, to the corporation for the stages of production, from the final script stage to the end of the post-production stage, and that is paid by it in the year or within 60 days after the end of the year to

Related Regulations: 8201.

Related Sections: S. 87(2)(*j*.94) Film or video productions.

"production commencement time" —"production commencement time", in respect of a Canadian film or video production, means the earlier of

(*a*) the time at which principal photography of the production begins, and

(*b*) the latest of

(i) the time at which a qualified corporation that has an interest in, or for civil law a right in, the production, or the parent of the corporation, first makes an expenditure for salary or wages or other remuneration for activities, of scriptwriters, that are directly attributable to the development by the corporation of script material of the production,

(ii) the time at which the corporation or the parent of the corporation acquires a property, on which the production is based, that is a published literary work, screenplay, play, personal history or all or part of the script material of the production, and

(iii) two years before the date on which principal photography of the production begins.

History: S. 125.4(1), the definition "production commencement time" was added by S.C. 2014, c. 39, s. 41(7), applicable

(a) to film or video productions for which the production commencement time of the corporation (or, if there is more than one qualified corporation in respect of the production, of all such corporations) is on or after November 14, 2003; and

(b) to a corporation in respect of a film or video production for which the production commencement time of any corporation is before November 14, 2003

(i) if the earliest labour expenditure of the corporation (or, if there is more than one qualified corporation in respect of the production, of all those corporations) in respect of the production is made after 2003, or

(ii) if the corporation elects (or, if there is more than one qualified corporation in respect of the production, all those corporations jointly elect), in writing, and the election is filed with the Minister of National Revenue on or before the earliest filing-due date of any qualified corporation in respect of the production for that corporation's taxation year that includes the day on which the *Economic Action Plan 2014 Act, No. 2* [S.C. 2014, c. 39] receives royal assent [December 16, 2014], and the earliest labour expenditure of all such qualified corporations in respect of the production is made

(A) after the last taxation year of any such corporation that ended before November 14, 2003, or

(B) if the first taxation year of all such corporations includes November 14, 2003, in that taxation year.

The earliest labour expenditure referred to in the above application is to be determined under the provisions of subsections 125.4(1) and (2) of the Act that would apply if this amendment had not been enacted.

"qualified corporation" —"qualified corporation" for a taxation year means a corporation that is throughout the year a prescribed taxable Canadian corporation the activities of which in the year are primarily the carrying on through a permanent establishment (as defined by regulation) in Canada of a business that is a Canadian film or video production business.

Related Regulations: 8201.

Related Sections: S. 87(2)(*j*.94) Film or video productions.

"qualified labour expenditure" —"qualified labour expenditure", of a corporation for a taxation year in respect of a Canadian film or video production, means the lesser of

(*a*) the amount, if any, by which

(i) the total of

(A) the labour expenditure of the corporation for the year in respect of the production, and

(B) the amount by which the total of all amounts each of which is the labour expenditure of the corporation for a preceding taxation year in respect of the production exceeds the total of all amounts each of which is a qualified labour expenditure of the corporation in respect of the production for a preceding taxation year before the end of which the principal filming or taping of the production began

exceeds

(ii) where the corporation is a parent, the total of all amounts each of which is an amount that is the subject of an agreement in respect of the production referred to in paragraph (*c*) of the definition "labour expenditure" between the corporation and its wholly-owned corporation, and

(*b*) the amount determined by the formula

$$A - B$$

where

A is 60% of the amount by which

(i) the total of all amounts each of which is an expenditure by the corporation in respect of the production that is included in the cost to, or in the case of depreciable property the capital cost to, the corporation or any other person or partnership of the production at the end of the taxation year,

exceeds

(ii) the total of all amounts each of which is an amount of assistance in respect of that cost that, at the time of the filing of its return of income for the year, the corporation or any other person or partnership has received, is entitled to receive or can reasonably be expected to receive, that has not been repaid before that time pursuant to a legal obligation to do so (and that does not otherwise reduce that cost), and

B is the total of all amounts each of which is the qualified labour expenditure of the corporation in respect of the production for a preceding taxation year before the end of which the principal filming or taping of the production began.

History: S. 125.4(1), the portion of the definition "qualified labour expenditure" before paragraph (*a*) was replaced by S.C. 2014, c. 39, s. 41(5), applicable

(a) to film or video productions for which the production commencement time of the corporation (or, if there is more than one qualified corporation in respect of the production, of all such corporations) is on or after November 14, 2003; and

(b) to a corporation in respect of a film or video production for which the production commencement time of any corporation is before November 14, 2003

(i) if the earliest labour expenditure of the corporation (or, if there is more than one qualified corporation in respect of the production, of all those corporations) in respect of the production is made after 2003, or

(ii) if the corporation elects (or, if there is more than one qualified corporation in respect of the production, all those corporations jointly elect), in writing, and the election is filed with the Minister of National Revenue on or before the earliest filing-due date of any qualified corporation in respect of the production for that corporation's taxation year that includes the day on which the *Economic Action Plan 2014 Act, No. 2* [S.C. 2014, c. 39] receives royal assent [December 16, 2014], and the earliest labour expenditure of all such qualified corporations in respect of the production is made

(A) after the last taxation year of any such corporation that ended before November 14, 2003, or

(B) if the first taxation year of all such corporations includes November 14, 2003, in that taxation year.

The earliest labour expenditure referred to in the above application is to be determined under the provisions of subsections 125.4(1) and (2) of the Act that would apply if this amendment had not been enacted.

The portion of the definition "qualified labour expenditure" before paragraph (*a*) formerly read:

"qualified labour expenditure"—"qualified labour expenditure" of a corporation for a taxation year in respect of a property of the corporation that is a Canadian film or video production means the lesser of

S. 125.4(1), the portion of the description of A of the definition "qualified labour expenditure" in paragraph (*b*) before subparagraph (ii) was replaced by S.C. 2014, c. 39, s. 41(6), applicable

(a) to film or video productions for which the production commencement time of the corporation (or, if there is more than one qualified corporation in respect of the production, of all such corporations) is on or after November 14, 2003; and

(b) to a corporation in respect of a film or video production for which the production commencement time of any corporation is before November 14, 2003

(i) if the earliest labour expenditure of the corporation (or, if there is more than one qualified corporation in respect of the production, of all those corporations) in respect of the production is made after 2003, or

(ii) if the corporation elects (or, if there is more than one qualified corporation in respect of the production, all those corporations jointly elect), in writing, and the election is filed with the Minister of National Revenue on or before the earliest filing-due date of any qualified corporation in respect of the production for that corporation's taxation year that includes the day on which the *Economic Action Plan 2014 Act, No. 2* [S.C. 2014, c. 39] receives royal assent [December 16, 2014], and the earliest labour expenditure of all such qualified corporations in respect of the production is made

(A) after the last taxation year of any such corporation that ended before November 14, 2003, or

(B) if the first taxation year of all such corporations includes November 14, 2003, in that taxation year.

The earliest labour expenditure referred to in the above application is to be determined under the provisions of subsections 125.4(1) and (2) of the Act that would apply if this amendment had not been enacted.

The portion of the description of A of the definition "qualified labour expenditure" in paragraph (*b*) before subparagraph (ii) formerly read:

A is 48% of the amount by which

(i) the cost or, in the case of depreciable property, the capital cost to the corporation of the production at the end of the year,

exceeds

Related Sections: S. 125.4(2) Rules governing labour expenditure of a corporation.

"salary or wages"—"salary or wages" does not include an amount

(*a*) described in section 7;

(*b*) determined by reference to profits or revenues; or

(*c*) paid to a person in respect of services rendered by the person at a time when the person was non-resident, unless the person was at that time a Canadian citizen.

History: S. 125.4(1), the definition "salary or wages" was replaced by S.C. 2014, c. 39, s. 41(2), applicable

(a) to film or video productions for which the production commencement time of the corporation (or, if there is more than one qualified corporation in respect of the production, of all such corporations) is on or after November 14, 2003; and

(b) to a corporation in respect of a film or video production for which the production commencement time of any corporation is before November 14, 2003

(i) if the earliest labour expenditure of the corporation (or, if there is more than one qualified corporation in respect of the production, of all those corporations) in respect of the production is made after 2003, or

(ii) if the corporation elects (or, if there is more than one qualified corporation in respect of the production, all those corporations jointly elect), in writing, and the election is filed with the Minister of National Revenue on or before the earliest filing-due date of any qualified corporation in respect of the production for that corporation's taxation year that includes the day on which the *Economic Action Plan 2014 Act, No. 2* [S.C. 2014, c. 39] receives royal assent [December 16, 2014], and the earliest labour expenditure of all such qualified corporations in respect of the production is made

(A) after the last taxation year of any such corporation that ended before November 14, 2003, or

(B) if the first taxation year of all such corporations includes November 14, 2003, in that taxation year.

The earliest labour expenditure referred to in the above application is to be determined under the provisions of subsections 125.4(1) and (2) of the Act that would apply if this amendment had not been enacted.

S. 125.4(1), the definition "salary or wages" formerly read:

"salary or wages"—"salary or wages" does not include an amount described in section 7 or any amount determined by reference to profits or revenues.

"script material"—"script material", in respect of a production, means written material describing the story on which the production is based and, for greater certainty, includes a draft script, an original story, a screen story, a narration, a television production concept, an outline or a scene-by-scene schematic, synopsis or treatment.

History: S. 125.4(1), the definition "script material" was added by S.C. 2014, c. 39, s. 41(7), applicable

(a) to film or video productions for which the production commencement time of the corporation (or, if there is more than one qualified corporation in respect of the production, of all such corporations) is on or after November 14, 2003; and

(b) to a corporation in respect of a film or video production for which the production commencement time of any corporation is before November 14, 2003

(i) if the earliest labour expenditure of the corporation (or, if there is more than one qualified corporation in respect of the production, of all those corporations) in respect of the production is made after 2003, or

(ii) if the corporation elects (or, if there is more than one qualified corporation in respect of the production, all those corporations jointly elect), in writing, and the election is filed with the Minister of National Revenue on or before the earliest filing-due date of any qualified corporation in respect of the production for that corporation's taxation year that includes the day on which the *Economic Action Plan 2014 Act, No. 2* [S.C. 2014, c. 39] receives royal assent [December 16, 2014], and the earliest labour expenditure of all such qualified corporations in respect of the production is made

(A) after the last taxation year of any such corporation that ended before November 14, 2003, or

(B) if the first taxation year of all such corporations includes November 14, 2003, in that taxation year.

The earliest labour expenditure referred to in the above application is to be determined under the provisions of subsections 125.4(1) and (2) of the Act that would apply if this amendment had not been enacted.

► 125.4(2) ◄

(2) Rules governing labour expenditure of a corporation. For the purposes of the definitions "labour expenditure" and "qualified labour expenditure" in subsection (1),

(*a*) remuneration does not include remuneration

(i) determined by reference to profits or revenues, or

(ii) in respect of services rendered by a person at a time when the person was non-resident, unless the person was at that time a Canadian citizen;

(*b*) services referred to in paragraph (*b*) of that definition that relate to the post-production stage of the production include only the services that are rendered at that stage by a person who performs the duties of animation cameraman, assistant colourist, assistant mixer, assistant sound-effects technician, boom operator, colourist, computer graphics designer, cutter, developing technician, director of post production, dubbing technician, encoding technician, inspection technician — clean up, mixer, optical effects technician, picture editor, printing technician, projectionist, recording technician, senior editor, sound editor, sound-effects technician, special effects editor, subtitle technician, timer, video-film recorder operator, videotape operator or by a person who performs a prescribed duty;

(*c*) that definition does not apply to an amount to which section 37 applies; and

(*d*) an expenditure incurred in respect of a film or video production by a qualified corporation (in this paragraph referred to as the "co-producer") in respect of goods supplied or services rendered by another qualified corporation to the co-producer in respect of the production is not a labour expenditure to the co-producer or, for the purpose of applying this section to the co-producer, a cost or capital cost of the production.

History: S. 125.4(2), the portion before paragraph (*b*) was replaced by S.C. 2014, c. 39, s. 41(8), applicable

(a) to film or video productions for which the production commencement time of the corporation (or, if there is more than one qualified corporation in respect of the production, of all such corporations) is on or after November 14, 2003; and

(b) to a corporation in respect of a film or video production for which the production commencement time of any corporation is before November 14, 2003

(i) if the earliest labour expenditure of the corporation (or, if there is more than one qualified corporation in respect of the production, of all those corporations) in respect of the production is made after 2003, or

(ii) if the corporation elects (or, if there is more than one qualified corporation in respect of the production, all those corporations jointly elect), in writing, and the election is filed with the Minister of National Revenue on or before the earliest filing-due date of any qualified corporation in respect of the production for that corporation's taxation year that includes the day on which the *Economic Action Plan 2014 Act, No. 2* [S.C. 2014, c. 39] receives royal assent [December 16, 2014], and the earliest labour expenditure of all such qualified corporations in respect of the production is made

(A) after the last taxation year of any such corporation that ended before November 14, 2003, or

(B) if the first taxation year of all such corporations includes November 14, 2003, in that taxation year.

The earliest labour expenditure referred to in the above application is to be determined under the provisions of subsections 125.4(1) and (2) of the Act that would apply if this amendment had not been enacted.

S. 125.4(2), the portion before paragraph (*b*) formerly read:

(2) *Rules governing labour expenditure of a corporation.* For the purpose of the definition "labour expenditure" in subsection (1),

(*a*) remuneration does not include remuneration determined by reference to profits or revenues;

S. 125.4(2)(*d*) was added by S.C. 2014, c. 39, s. 41(9), applicable

(a) to film or video productions for which the production commencement time of the corporation (or, if there is more than one qualified corporation in respect of the production, of all such corporations) is on or after November 14, 2003; and

(b) to a corporation in respect of a film or video production for which the production commencement time of any corporation is before November 14, 2003

(i) if the earliest labour expenditure of the corporation (or, if there is more than one qualified corporation in respect of the production, of all those corporations) in respect of the production is made after 2003, or

(ii) if the corporation elects (or, if there is more than one qualified corporation in respect of the production, all those corporations jointly elect), in writing, and the election is filed with the Minister of National Revenue on or before the earliest filing-due date of any qualified corporation in respect of the production for that corporation's taxation year that includes the day on which the *Economic Action Plan 2014 Act, No. 2* [S.C. 2014, c. 39] receives royal assent [December 16, 2014], and the earliest labour expenditure of all such qualified corporations in respect of the production is made

(A) after the last taxation year of any such corporation that ended before November 14, 2003, or

(B) if the first taxation year of all such corporations includes November 14, 2003, in that taxation year.

The earliest labour expenditure referred to in the above application is to be determined under the provisions of subsections 125.4(1) and (2) of the Act that would apply if this amendment had not been enacted.

Related Regulations: 202(1.1); 1106.

► 125.4(3) ◄

(3) Tax credit. Where

(*a*) a qualified corporation for a taxation year files with its return of income for the year

(i) a Canadian film or video production certificate issued in respect of a Canadian film or video production of the corporation,

(ii) a prescribed form containing prescribed information, and

(iii) each other document prescribed in respect of the production, and

(*b*) the principal filming or taping of the production began before the end of the year,

the corporation is deemed to have paid on its balance-due day for the year an amount on account of its tax payable under this Part for the year equal to 25% of its qualified labour expenditure for the year in respect of the production.

Related Regulations: 1104(9); 1106.

Related Sections: S. 125.4(6) Revocation of a certificate; s. 248(1), "balance-due date".

Canadian Tax Foundation: Gill, *Financing Canadian Films Through Crowdfunding*, 2013 Canadian Tax Focus 3(1):4–5.

Forms: T2 SCH 302 — Additional Certificate Numbers for the Newfoundland Film and Video Industry Tax Credit; T2 SCH 345 — Additional Certificate Numbers for the Nova Scotia Film Industry Tax Credit; T2 SCH 365 — Additional Certificate Numbers for the New Brunswick Film Tax Credit; T2 SCH 382 — Additional Certificate Numbers for the Manitoba Film and Video Production Tax Credit; T2 SCH 410 — Additional Certificate Numbers for the Saskatchewan Film Employment Tax Credit; T1196 — BC Film and Television Tax Credit; T1131 — Claiming a Canadian Film or Video Production Tax Credit.

Guides: RC4164 Claiming a Canadian Film or Video Production Tax Credit-Guide to Form T1131.

► 125.4(4) ◄

(4) Exception. This section does not apply to a Canadian film or video production if the production — or an interest in a person or partnership that has, directly or indirectly, an interest in, or for civil law a right in, the production — is a tax shelter investment for the purpose of section 143.2.

History: S. 125.4(4) was replaced by S.C. 2014, c. 39, s. 41(10), applicable

(a) to taxation years that end after November 14, 2003; and

(b) in respect of a film or video production in respect of which a corporation has, in a return of income filed before November 14, 2003, claimed an amount under subsection 125.4(3) in respect of a labour expenditure incurred after 1997.

S. 125.4(4) formerly read:

(4) *Exception.* This section does not apply to a Canadian film or video production where an investor, or a partnership in which an investor has an interest, directly or indirectly, may deduct an amount in respect of the production in computing its income for any taxation year.

► 125.4(5) ◄

(5) When assistance received. For the purposes of this Act other than this section, and for greater certainty, the amount that a corporation is deemed under subsection (3) to have paid for a taxation year is assistance received by the corporation from a government immediately before the end of the year.

Related Sections: S. 12(1)(*x*) Inducement, reimbursement, etc.; s. 13(7.4) Deemed capital cost; s. 53(2)(*k*) Amounts to be deducted — Government assistance.

► 125.4(6) ◄

(6) Revocation of certificate. If an omission or incorrect statement was made for the purpose of obtaining a Canadian film or video production certificate in respect of a production, or if the production is not a Canadian film or video production,

(*a*) the Minister of Canadian Heritage may

(i) revoke the certificate, or

(ii) if the certificate was issued in respect of productions included in an episodic television series, revoke the certificate in respect of one or more episodes in the series;

(*b*) for greater certainty, for the purposes of this section, the expenditures and cost of production in respect of productions included in an episodic television series that relate to an episode in the series in respect of which a certificate has been revoked are not attributable to a Canadian film or video production; and

(*c*) for the purpose of subparagraph (3)(*a*)(i), a certificate that has been revoked is deemed never to have been issued.

History: S. 125.4(6) was replaced by S.C. 2014, c. 39, s. 41(11), deemed to have come into force on November 15, 2003, and formerly read:

(6) *Revocation of a certificate.* A Canadian film or video production certificate in respect of a production may be revoked by the Minister of Canadian Heritage where

(*a*) an omission or incorrect statement was made for the purpose of obtaining the certificate, or

(*b*) the production is not a Canadian film or video production,

and, for the purpose of subparagraph (3)(*a*)(i), a certificate that has been revoked is deemed never to have been issued.

► 125.4(7) ◄

(7) Guidelines. The Minister of Canadian Heritage shall issue guidelines respecting the circumstances under which the conditions in the definition "Canadian film or video production certificate" in subsection (1) are satisfied. For greater certainty, those guidelines are not statutory instruments as defined in the *Statutory Instruments Act*.

History: S. 125.4(7) was added by S.C. 2014, c. 39, s. 41(12), applicable iln respect of film or video productions in respect of which certificates are issued by the Minister of Canadian Heritage after December 20, 2002.

Film or Video Production Services Tax Credit

SECTION 125.5: [Film or video production services tax credit]

► 125.5(1) ◄

(1) Definitions. The definitions in this subsection apply in this section.

Related Regulations: 8201.

"accredited film or video production certificate" —"accredited film or video production certificate", in respect of a film or video production, means a certificate issued by the Minister of Canadian Heritage certifying that the production is an accredited production.

"accredited production" —"accredited production" has the meaning assigned by regulation.

Related Regulations: 9300.

"assistance" —"assistance" means an amount, other than an amount deemed under subsection (3) to have been paid, that would be included under paragraph 12(1)(*x*) in computing the income of a taxpayer for any taxation year if that paragraph were read without reference to subparagraphs (v) to (vii).

"Canadian labour expenditure" —"Canadian labour expenditure" of a corporation for a taxation year in respect of an accredited production means, in the case of a corporation that is not an eligible production corporation in respect of the production for the year, nil, and in any other case, subject to subsection (2), the total of the following amounts in respect of the production to the extent that they are reasonable in the circumstances:

(*a*) the salary or wages directly attributable to the production that are incurred by the corporation after October 1997, and in the year or the preceding taxation year, and that relate to services rendered in Canada for the stages of production of the production, from the final script stage to the end of the post-production stage, and paid by it in the year or within 60 days after the end of the year to employees of the corporation who were resident in Canada at the time the payments were made (other than amounts incurred in that preceding year that were paid within 60 days after the end of that preceding year),

(*b*) that portion of the remuneration (other than salary or wages and other than remuneration that relates to services rendered in the preceding taxation year and that was paid within 60 days after the end of that preceding year) that is directly attributable to the production, that relates to services rendered in Canada after October 1997 and in the year, or that preceding year, to the corporation for the stages of production of the production, from the final script stage to the end of the post-production stage, and that is paid by it in the year or within 60 days after the end of the year to a person or a partnership, that carries on a business in Canada through a permanent establishment (as defined by regulation), and that is

(i) an individual resident in Canada at the time the amount is paid and who is not an employee of the corporation, to the extent that the amount paid

(A) is attributable to services personally rendered by the individual in Canada in respect of the accredited production, or

(B) is attributable to and does not exceed the salary or wages paid by the individual to the individual's employees at a time when they were resident in Canada for personally rendering services in Canada in respect of the accredited production,

(ii) another corporation that is a taxable Canadian corporation, to the extent that the amount paid is attributable to and does not exceed the salary or wages paid to the other corporation's employees at a time when they were resident in Canada for personally rendering services in Canada in respect of the accredited production,

(iii) another corporation that is a taxable Canadian corporation, all the issued and outstanding shares of the capital stock of which (except directors' qualifying shares) belong to an individual who was resident in Canada and the activities of which consist principally of the provision of the individual's services, to the extent that the amount paid is attributable to services rendered personally in Canada by the individual in respect of the accredited production, or

(iv) a partnership, to the extent that the amount paid

(A) is attributable to services personally rendered in respect of the accredited production by an individual who is resident in Canada and who is a member of the partnership, or

(B) is attributable to and does not exceed the salary or wages paid by the partnership to its employees at a time when they were resident in Canada for personally rendering services in Canada in respect of the accredited production, and

(c) where

(i) the corporation is a subsidiary wholly-owned corporation of another corporation that is a taxable Canadian corporation (in this section referred to as the "parent"), and

(ii) the corporation and the parent have filed with the Minister an agreement that this paragraph apply in respect of the production,

the reimbursement made by the corporation in the year, or within 60 days after the end of the year, of an expenditure that was incurred by the parent in a particular taxation year of the parent in respect of the production and that would be included in the Canadian labour expenditure of the corporation in respect of the production for the particular taxation year because of paragraph (*a*) or (*b*) if

(iii) the corporation had had such a particular taxation year, and

(iv) the expenditure were incurred by the corporation for the same purpose as it was incurred by the parent and were paid at the same time and to the same person or partnership as it was paid by the parent.

Related Regulations: 9300.

"eligible production corporation"—"eligible production corporation", in respect of an accredited production for a taxation year, means a corporation, the activities of which in the year in Canada are primarily the carrying on through a permanent establishment (as defined by regulation) in Canada of a film or video production business or a film or video production services business and that

(*a*) owns the copyright in the accredited production throughout the period during which the production is produced in Canada, or

(*b*) has contracted directly with the owner of the copyright in the accredited production to provide production services in respect of the production, where the owner of the copyright is not an eligible production corporation in respect of the production,

except a corporation that is, at any time in the year,

(*c*) a person all or part of whose taxable income is exempt from tax under this Part,

(*d*) controlled directly or indirectly in any manner whatever by one or more persons all or part of whose taxable income is exempt from tax under this Part, or

(*e*) prescribed to be a labour-sponsored venture capital corporation for the purpose of section 127.4.

Related Regulations: 8201; 9300.

"qualified Canadian labour expenditure"—"qualified Canadian labour expenditure" of an eligible production corporation for a taxation year in respect of an accredited production means the amount, if any, by which

(*a*) the total of all amounts each of which is the corporation's Canadian labour expenditure for the year or a preceding taxation year

exceeds the aggregate of

(*b*) the total of all amounts, each of which is an amount of assistance that can reasonably be considered to be in respect of amounts included in the total determined under paragraph (*a*) in respect of the corporation for the year that, at the time of filing its return of income for the year, the corporation or any other person or partnership has received, is entitled to receive or can reasonably be expected to receive, that has not been repaid before that time pursuant to a legal obligation to do so (and that does not otherwise reduce that expenditure),

(*c*) the total of all amounts, each of which is the qualified Canadian labour expenditure of the corporation in respect of the accredited production for a preceding taxation year before the end of which the principal filming or taping of the production began, and

(*d*) where the corporation is a parent, the total of all amounts each of which is included in the total determined under paragraph (*a*) in respect of the corporation for the year and is the subject of an agreement in respect of the accredited production referred to in paragraph (*c*) of the definition "Canadian labour expenditure" between the corporation and its subsidiary wholly-owned corporation.

Related Regulations: 9300.

"salary or wages"—"salary or wages" does not include an amount described in section 7 or an amount determined by reference to profits or revenues.

► 125.5(2) ◄

(2) Rules governing Canadian labour expenditure of a corporation. For the purpose of the definition "Canadian labour expenditure" in subsection (1),

(*a*) remuneration does not include remuneration determined by reference to profits or revenues;

(*b*) services referred to in paragraph (*b*) of that definition that relate to the post-production stage of the accredited production include only the services that are rendered at that stage by a person who performs the duties of animation cameraman, assistant colourist, assistant mixer, assistant sound-effects technician, boom operator, colourist, computer graphics designer, cutter, developing technician, director of post production, dubbing technician, encoding technician, inspection technician — clean up, mixer, optical effects technician, picture editor, printing technician, projectionist, recording technician, senior editor, sound editor, sound-effects technician, special effects editor, subtitle technician, timer, video-film recorder operator, videotape operator or by a person who performs a prescribed duty;

(*c*) that definition does not apply to an amount to which section 37 applies; and (*d*) for greater certainty, that definition does not apply to an amount that is not a production cost including an amount in respect of advertising, marketing, promotion, market research or an amount related in any way to another film or video production.

Related Regulations: 202(1.1); 9300.

▶ 125.5(3) ◀

(3) Tax credit. An eligible production corporation in respect of an accredited production for a taxation year is deemed to have paid on its balance-due day for the year an amount on account of its tax payable under this Part for the year equal to 16% of its qualified Canadian labour expenditure for the year in respect of the production, if

(*a*) the corporation files with its return of income for the year

(i) a prescribed form containing prescribed information in respect of the production,

(ii) an accredited film or video production certificate in respect of the production, and

(iii) each other document prescribed in respect of the production; and

(*b*) the principal filming or taping of the production began before the end of the year.

Related Regulations: 9300.

Related Sections: S. 87(2)(*j*.94) Film or video productions; s. 152(1)(*b*) Assessment; s. 157(3)(*e*) Reduced instalments.

Tax Topics: No. 1688, Settlement in Film Tax Shelters.

Forms: T2 SCH 302 — Additional Certificate Numbers for the Newfoundland Film and Video Industry Tax Credit; T2 SCH 345 — Additional Certificate Numbers for the Nova Scotia Film Industry Tax Credit; T2 SCH 365 — Additional Certificate Numbers for the New Brunswick Film Tax Credit; T2 SCH 382 — Additional Certificate Numbers for the Manitoba Film and Video Production Tax Credit; T2 SCH 410 — Additional Certificate Numbers for the Saskatchewan Film Employment Tax Credit; T1197 — BC Production Services Tax Credit; T1177 — Claiming a Film or Video Production Services Tax Credit.

Guides: RC4385 Claiming a Film or Video Production Services Tax Credit.

▶ 125.5(4) ◀

(4) Canadian film or video production. Subsection (3) does not apply in respect of a production in respect of which an amount is deemed to have been paid under subsection 125.4(3).

▶ 125.5(5) ◀

(5) When assistance received. For the purposes of this Act other than this section, and for greater certainty, the amount that a corporation is deemed under subsection (3) to have paid for a taxation year is assistance received by the corporation from a government immediately before the end of the year.

▶ 125.5(6) ◀

(6) Revocation of certificate. An accredited film or video production certificate in respect of an accredited production may be revoked by the Minister of Canadian Heritage where

(*a*) an omission or incorrect statement was made for the purpose of obtaining the certificate, or

(*b*) the production is not an accredited production,

and, for the purpose of subparagraph (3)(*a*)(ii), a certificate that has been revoked is deemed never to have been issued.

SECTION 125.6: [Refundable labour tax credit for journalism organizations]

▶ 125.6(1) ◀

(1) Definitions. The following definitions apply in this section.

Related Sections: 87(2)(*j*.96) Journalism organizations.

assistance —"assistance" means an amount, other than an amount deemed under subsection (2) to have been paid, that would be included under paragraph 12(1)(*x*) in computing the income of a taxpayer for any taxation year if that paragraph were read without reference to

(*a*) subparagraphs 12(1)(*x*)(v) to (viii), if the amount were received

(i) from a person or partnership described in subparagraph 12(1)(*x*)(ii), or

(ii) in circumstances where clause 12(1)(*x*)(i)(C) applies; and

(*b*) subparagraphs 12(1)(*x*)(v) to (vii), in any other case.

History: S. 125.6(1), the definition of "assistance" was added by S.C. 2019, c. 29, s. 23(1), deemed to have come into force on January 1, 2019. For greater certainty, it does not apply in respect of salary or wages that are in respect of a period before January 1, 2019.

Related Sections: 12(1)(x) Inducement, reimbursement, etc.

eligible newsroom employee —"eligible newsroom employee", in respect of a qualifying journalism organization in a taxation year, means an individual who

(*a*) is employed by the organization in the taxation year;

(*b*) works, on average, a minimum of 26 hours per week throughout the portion of the taxation year in which the individual is employed by the organization;

(*c*) at any time in the taxation year, has been, or is reasonably expected to be, employed by the organization for a minimum period of 40 consecutive weeks that includes that time;

(*d*) spends at least 75% of their time engaged in the production of news content, including by researching, collecting information, verifying facts, photographing, writing, editing, designing and otherwise preparing content; and

(*e*) meets any prescribed conditions.

History: S. 125.6(1), the definition of "eligible newsroom employee" was added by S.C. 2019, c. 29, s. 23(1), deemed to have come into force on January 1, 2019. For greater certainty, it does not apply in respect of salary or wages that are in respect of a period before January 1, 2019.

qualifying journalism organization —"qualifying journalism organization", at any time, means a qualified Canadian journalism organization that meets the following conditions:

(*a*) it is primarily engaged in the production of original written news content;

(*b*) it does not carry on a "broadcasting undertaking" as defined in subsection 2(1) of the *Broadcasting Act;*

(*c*) it does not, in the taxation year in which the time occurs, receive an amount from the Aid to Publishers component of the Canada Periodical Fund; and (*d*) if it is a corporation having share capital, it meets the conditions in subparagraph (*e*)(iii) of the definition "Canadian newspaper" in subsection 19(5).

History: S. 125.6(1), the defintion of "qualifying journalism organization" was added by S.C. 2019, c. 29, s. 23(1), deemed to have come into force on January 1, 2019. For greater certainty, it does not apply in respect of salary or wages that are in respect of a period before January 1, 2019.

Related Sections: 19(5) "Canadian newspaper".

qualifying labour expenditure —"qualifying labour expenditure", of a taxpayer for a taxation year in respect of an eligible newsroom employee, means the lesser of

(*a*) the amount determined by the formula

$$\$55,000 \times A/365$$

where

A is the lesser of 365 and the number of days in the taxation year, and

(*b*) the amount determined by the formula

$$A - B$$

where

A is the salary or wages payable by the taxpayer to the eligible newsroom employee in respect of the portion of the taxation year throughout which the taxpayer is a qualifying journalism organization, and

B is the total of all amounts each of which is an amount of assistance that

(i) the taxpayer has received, is entitled to receive or can reasonably be expected to receive, in respect of amounts described in A, and

(ii) has not been repaid before the end of the year pursuant to a legal obligation to do so.

History: S. 125.6(1), the definition of "qualifying labour expenditure" was added by S.C. 2019, c. 29, s. 23(1), deemed to have come into force on January 1, 2019. For greater certainty, it does not apply in respect of salary or wages that are in respect of a period before January 1, 2019.

► 125.6(2) ◄

(2) Tax credit. A taxpayer that is a qualifying journalism organization at any time in a taxation year and that files a prescribed form containing prescribed information with its return of income for the year is deemed to have, on its balance-due day for the year, paid on account of its tax payable under this Part for the year an amount determined by the formula

$$0.25(A)$$

where

A is the total of all amounts each of which is a qualifying labour expenditure of the qualifying journalism organization for the year in respect of an eligible newsroom employee.

Editorial Note: The refundable credit in respect of each "eligible newsroom employee" of a "qualifying journalism organization" equals 25% of its "qualifying labour expenditures" payable to the employee in respect of a taxation year. The qualifying labour expenditures equal the salary and wages payable to the eligible newsroom employee in respect of the year less any government assistance that the organization receives or is reasonably expected to receive before the end of the year and that has not been repaid.

The qualifying labour expenditures are capped at $55,000 per year per eligible newsroom employee and is pro-rated for short taxation years. The credit applies to expenditures made on or after January 1, 2019.

History: S. 125.6(2) was added by S.C. 2019, c. 29, s. 23(1), deemed to have come into force on January 1, 2019. For greater certainty, it does not apply in respect of salary or wages that are in respect of a period before January 1, 2019.

Related Sections: 125.6(3) When assistance received.

► 125.6(3) ◄

(3) When assistance received. For the purposes of this Act other than this section, and for greater certainty, the amount that a qualifying journalism organization is deemed under subsection (2) to have paid for a taxation year is assistance received by it from a government immediately before the end of the year.

History: S. 125.6(3) was added by S.C. 2019, c. 29, s. 23(1), deemed to have come into force on January 1, 2019. For greater certainty, it does not apply in respect of salary or wages that are in respect of a period before January 1, 2019.

Related Sections: 125.6(2) Tax credit.

Subdivision c — Rules Applicable to All Taxpayers

SECTION 126: Foreign tax deduction

► 126(1) ◄

(1) Foreign tax deduction. A taxpayer who was resident in Canada at any time in a taxation year may deduct from the tax for the year otherwise payable under this Part by the taxpayer an amount equal to

(*a*) such part of any non-business-income tax paid by the taxpayer for the year to the government of a country other than Canada (except, where the taxpayer is a corporation, any such tax or part thereof that may reasonably be regarded as having been paid by the taxpayer in respect of income from a share of the capital stock of a foreign affiliate of the taxpayer) as the taxpayer may claim,

not exceeding, however,

(*b*) that proportion of the tax for the year otherwise payable under this Part by the taxpayer that

(i) the amount, if any, by which the total of the taxpayer's qualifying incomes exceeds the total of the taxpayer's qualifying losses

(A) for the year, if the taxpayer is resident in Canada throughout the year, and

(B) for the part of the year throughout which the taxpayer is resident in Canada, if the taxpayer is non-resident at any time in the year,

from sources in that country, on the assumption that

(C) no businesses were carried on by the taxpayer in that country,

(D) where the taxpayer is a corporation, it had no income from shares of the capital stock of a foreign affiliate of the taxpayer, and

(E) where the taxpayer is an individual,

(I) no amount was deducted under subsection 91(5) in computing the taxpayer's income for the year, and

(II) if the taxpayer deducted an amount under subsection 122.3(1) from the taxpayer's tax otherwise payable under this Part for the year, the taxpayer's income from employment in that country was not from a source in that country to the extent of the lesser of the amounts determined in respect thereof under paragraphs 122.3(1)(*c*) and (*d*) for the year,

is of

(ii) the total of

(A) the amount, if any, by which,

(I) if the taxpayer was resident in Canada throughout the year, the taxpayer's income for the year computed without reference to paragraph 20(1)(*ww*), and

(II) if the taxpayer was non-resident at any time in the year, the amount determined under paragraph 114(*a*) in respect of the taxpayer for the year

exceeds

(III) the total of all amounts each of which is an amount deducted under section 110.6 or paragraph 111(1)(*b*), or deductible under any of paragraphs 110(1)(*d*) to (*d*.3), (*f*) and (*g*) and sections 112 and 113, in computing the taxpayer's taxable income for the year, and

(B) the amount, if any, added under section 110.5 in computing the taxpayer's taxable income for the year.

History: S. 126(1)(*b*)(ii)(A)(III) was replaced by S.C. 2017, c. 20, s. 22(1), in force January 1, 2018, and formerly read:

(III) the total of all amounts each of which is an amount deducted under section 110.6 or paragraph 111(1)(*b*), or deductible under any of paragraphs 110(1)(*d*) to (*d*.3), (*f*), (*g*) and (*j*) and sections 112 and 113, in computing the taxpayer's taxable income for the year, and

Related Sections: S. 4(1) Income or loss from a source or from sources in a place; s. 4(3) Deductions applicable; s. 104(22) Designation of foreign source income by trust; s. 110.5 Additions for foreign tax deductions; s. 126(7) Definitions; s. 127.54 Foreign tax credit — Minimum tax; s. 129(3) Definition of "refundable dividend tax on hand"; s. 138(8) No deduction for foreign tax; s. 144(8.1) Foreign tax deduction.

Canadian Tax Foundation: Bernstein, *Canadian Foreign Tax Credit: US Inversions*, 2016 Canadian Tax Highlights 24(7):9–10; Doobay, *Foreign Tax Credit for Franchise Tax*, 2013 Canadian Tax Highlights 21(6):11–12; Snider, *Selecting the Foreign Business Entity: A Review of the Canadian Tax Treatment of U.S. Taxes Paid by a Member (Shareholder) of a U.S. Limited Liability Corporation*, 2002 Canadian Tax Journal 2:705–723; Snider, *The Foreign Tax Credit Rules*, 2001 Conference Report 14:1–36.

Tax Profile: December 2013 — Non-Resident Investment in Canadian Real Property — Case Studies; February 2013 — The Purchase of US Businesses by Canadians; November 2010 — Canadian Acquisition of U.S. Real Estate; February 2007 — U.S. Limited Liability Companies — The Good, the Bad and the Ugly; January 2006 — Foreign Source Income: Outbound Structures and Foreign Tax Credit Planning — Part I; February 2006 — Foreign Source Income: Outbound Structures and Foreign Tax Credit Planning — Part II; November 2003 — Revenue Canada Round Table.

Tax Topics: No. 1565, U.S. AMT Foreign Tax Credits.

Forms: T2036 — Provincial or Territorial Foreign Tax Credit; T2209 — Federal Foreign Tax Credits.

Income Tax Folios: *Primary* — S5-F2-C1 Foreign Tax Credit.

Income Tax Technical News: Issue No. 31R2, Social Security Taxes and the Foreign Tax Credit; Issue No. 30, Social Security Taxes and the Foreign Tax Credit.

Interpretation Bulletins: *Secondary* — IT-201R2 Foreign tax credit — Trust and beneficiaries; IT-273R2 Government assistance — General comments; IT-379R Employees Profit Sharing Plans — Allocations to Beneficiaries; IT-497R4 Overseas employment tax credit; IT-506 Foreign income taxes as a deduction from income.

Tax Window Files: 2017 STEP – Q4 - U.S. grantor trust, *June 13, 2017*, CRA Document No. 2017-0695141C6; 2017 STEP-Q8-Single-member disregarded U.S. LLC, *June 13, 2017*, CRA Document No. 2017-0693381C6; Foreign Tax Credit on Transfer of 401(k) to RRSP, *15XXXX*, CRA Document No. 2015-0572541R3; U.S. tax paid in respect of an LLC's income, *February 3, 2016*, CRA Document No. 2014-0548111E5.

Cases: The corporate resident taxpayer earned bond interest income arising in Brazil, and earned income from other sources that was taxable in Canada. Under the Act, interest income such as the bond interest in this case is taxed on a net basis after deducting the expenses incurred to earn that interest. The taxpayer's foreign tax credit was limited to the actual Canadian tax that it would otherwise pay on its Brazilian income according to the Act, and this amount had to be calculated on the taxpayer's net income derived from Brazil. The expenses relevant to income from a source in a particular place, moreover, are found in subsection 4(1) of the Act. *Société Générale Valeurs Mobilières Inc. v. The Queen*, 2017 DTC 5007 (FCA)

Contributions to the Maine State Retirement System were not a foreign tax for FTC purposes. *Nadeau v. The Queen*, 2004 DTC 2929 (T.C.C.).

► 126(1.1) ◄

(1.1) Authorized foreign bank. In applying subsections 20(12) and (12.1) and this section in respect of an authorized foreign bank,

(*a*) the bank is deemed, for the purposes of subsections (1), (4) to (5), (6) and (7), to be resident in Canada in respect of its Canadian banking business;

(*b*) the references in subsection 20(12) and paragraph (1)(*a*) to "country other than Canada" shall be read as a reference to "country that is neither Canada nor a country in which the taxpayer is resident at any time in the taxation year";

(*c*) the reference in subparagraph (1)(*b*)(i) to "from sources in that country" shall be read as a reference to "in respect of its Canadian banking business from sources in that country";

(*d*) subparagraph (1)(*b*)(ii) shall be read as follows:

"(ii) the lesser of

(A) the taxpayer's taxable income earned in Canada for the year, and

(B) the total of the taxpayer's income for the year from its Canadian banking business and the amount determined in respect of the taxpayer under subparagraph 115(1)(*a*)(vii) for the year;"

(*e*) in computing the non-business income tax paid by the bank for a taxation year to the government of a country other than Canada, there shall be included only taxes that relate to amounts that are included in computing the bank's taxable income earned in Canada from its Canadian banking business; and

(*f*) the definition "tax-exempt income" in subsection (7) shall be read as follows:

"'tax-exempt income' means income of a taxpayer from a source in a particular country in respect of which

(*a*) the taxpayer is, because of a comprehensive agreement or convention for the elimination of double taxation on income, which has the force of law in the particular country and to which a country in which the taxpayer is resident is a party, entitled to an exemption from all income or profits taxes, imposed in the particular country, to which the agreement or convention applies, and

(*b*) no income or profits tax to which the agreement or convention does not apply is imposed in the particular country;".

► 126(2) ◄

(2) Idem. Where a taxpayer who was resident in Canada at any time in a taxation year carried on business in the year in a country other than Canada, the taxpayer may deduct from the tax for the year otherwise payable under this Part by the taxpayer an amount not exceeding the least of

(*a*) such part of the total of the business-income tax paid by the taxpayer for the year in respect of businesses carried on by the taxpayer in that country and the taxpayer's unused foreign tax credits in respect of that country for the 10 taxation years immediately preceding and the 3 taxation years immediately following the year as the taxpayer may claim,

(*b*) the amount determined under subsection (2.1) for the year in respect of businesses carried on by the taxpayer in that country, and

(*c*) the amount by which

(i) the tax for the year otherwise payable under this Part by the taxpayer

exceeds

(ii) the amount or the total of amounts, as the case may be, deducted under subsection (1) by the taxpayer from the tax for the year otherwise payable under this Part.

Related Sections: S. 110.5 Additions for foreign tax deductions; s. 125(1) Small business deduction; s. 126(2.1) Amount determined for purposes of para. (2)(b); s. 126(6) Rules of construction; s. 126(7) Definitions; s. 129(3) Definition of "refundable dividend tax on hand"; s. 152(6) Reassessment where certain deductions claimed.

Canadian Petroleum Tax Journal: Selected Income Tax Considerations When Structuring Foreign Resource Ventures, William A. Brebber, 2002, Vol. 15, No. 1.

Tax Profile: February 2013 — The Purchase of US Businesses by Canadians; November 2010 — Canadian Acquisition of U.S. Real Estate; January 2006 — Foreign Source Income: Outbound Structures and Foreign Tax Credit Planning — Part I; February 2006 — Foreign Source Income: Outbound Structures and Foreign Tax Credit Planning — Part II.

Forms: T2036 — Provincial Foreign Tax Credit; T2209 — Federal Foreign Tax Credits.

Income Tax Folios: *Primary* — S5-F2-C1 Foreign Tax Credit.

Cases: Taxpayer became liable for U.K. tax at the end of a fiscal period, but the tax did not have to be paid for 14 months. The correct method of calculating the Canadian tax credit was to apply against the foreign tax the weighted average exchange rate which prevailed during the fiscal period in question rather than the rate which prevailed when the foreign tax was actually paid. *The Bank of Nova Scotia v. The Queen*, 81 DTC 5115 (F.C.A.). See also *Canadian Imperial Bank of Commerce v. The Queen*, 81 DTC 5119 (F.C.A.)

The U.S. social security tax was held to be an income tax; therefore it was eligible. *Seley v. M.N.R.*, 62 DTC 565 (T.A.B.). This decision was accepted by the Department of National Revenue in Interpretation Bulletin No. IT-122R.

► 126(2.1) ◄

(2.1) Amount determined for purposes of para. (2)(*b*). For the purposes of paragraph (2)(*b*), the amount determined under this subsection for a year in respect of businesses carried on by a taxpayer in a country other than Canada is the total of

(*a*) that proportion of the tax for the year otherwise payable under this Part by the taxpayer that

(i) the amount, if any, by which the total of the taxpayer's qualifying incomes exceeds the total of the taxpayer's qualifying losses

(A) for the year, if the taxpayer is resident in Canada throughout the year, and

(B) for the part of the year throughout which the taxpayer is resident in Canada, if the taxpayer is non-resident at any time in the year,

from businesses carried on by the taxpayer in that country

is of

(ii) the total of

(A) the amount, if any, by which

(I) if the taxpayer is resident in Canada throughout the year, the taxpayer's income for the year computed without reference to paragraph 20(1)(*ww*), and

(II) if the taxpayer is non-resident at any time in the year, the amount determined under paragraph 114(*a*) in respect of the taxpayer for the year

exceeds

(III) the total of all amounts each of which is an amount deducted under section 110.6 or paragraph 111(1)(*b*), or deductible under any of paragraphs 110(1)(*d*) to (*d*.3), (*f*) and (*g*) and sections 112 and 113, in computing the taxpayer's taxable income for the year, and

(B) the amount, if any, added under section 110.5 in computing the taxpayer's taxable income for the year, and

(*b*) that proportion of the amount, if any, added under subsection 120(1) to the tax for the year otherwise payable under this Part by the taxpayer that

(i) the amount determined under subparagraph (*a*)(i) in respect of the country

is of

(ii) the amount, if any, by which,

(A) where section 114 does not apply to the taxpayer in respect of the year, the taxpayer's income for the year, and

(B) where section 114 applies to the taxpayer in respect of the year, the total of the taxpayer's income for the period or periods referred to in paragraph 114(*a*) and the amount that would be determined under paragraph 114(*b*) in respect of the taxpayer for the year if subsection 115(1) were read without reference to paragraphs 115(1)(*d*) to (*f*)

exceeds

(C) the taxpayer's income earned in the year in a province (within the meaning assigned by subsection 120(4)).

History: S. 126(2.1)(*a*)(ii)(A)(III) was replaced by S.C. 2017, c. 20, s. 22(2), in force January 1, 2018, and formerly read:

(III) the total of all amounts each of which is an amount deducted under section 110.6 or paragraph 111(1)(*b*), or deductible under any of paragraphs 110(1)(*d*) to (*d.3*), (*f*), (*g*) and (*j*) and sections 112 and 113, in computing the taxpayer's taxable income for the year, and

Cases: The taxpayer's share of income from a U.S. limited partnership was $9 million but, since the partnership paid U.S. tax, the taxpayer only received $6 million as its share of after-tax income. The taxpayer had to include $9 million as income, but could claim a foreign tax credit for its $3 million share of the U.S. taxes. *4145356 Canada Limited v. The Queen*, 2011 DTC 1171 (T.C.C.).

► 126(2.2) ◄

(2.2) Non-resident's foreign tax deduction. If at any time in a taxation year a taxpayer who is not at that time resident in Canada disposes of a property that was deemed by subsection 48(2), as it read in its application before 1993, or by paragraph 128.1(4)(*e*), as it read in its application before October 2, 1996, to be taxable Canadian property of the taxpayer, the taxpayer may deduct from the tax for the year otherwise payable under this Part by the taxpayer an amount equal to the lesser of

(*a*) the amount of any non-business-income tax paid by the taxpayer for the year to the government of a country other than Canada that can reasonably be regarded as having been paid by the taxpayer in respect of any gain or profit from the disposition of the property, and

(*b*) that proportion of the tax for the year otherwise payable under this Part by the taxpayer that

(i) the taxable capital gain from the disposition of that property

is of

(ii) if the taxpayer is non-resident throughout the year, the taxpayer's taxable income earned in Canada for the year determined without reference to paragraphs 115(1)(*d*) to (*f*), and

(iii) if the taxpayer is resident in Canada at any time in the year, the amount that would have been the taxpayer's taxable income earned in Canada for the year if the part of the year throughout which the taxpayer was non-resident were the whole taxation year.

Interpretation Bulletins: *Secondary* — IT-451R Deemed disposition and acquisition on ceasing to be or becoming resident in Canada.

► 126(2.21) ◄

(2.21) Former resident — deduction. If at any particular time in a particular taxation year a non-resident individual disposes of a property that the individual last acquired because of the application, at any time (in this subsection referred to as the "acquisition time") after October 1, 1996, of paragraph 128.1(4)(*c*), there may be deducted from the individual's tax otherwise payable under this Part for the year (in this subsection referred to as the "emigration year") that includes the time immediately before the acquisition time an amount not exceeding the lesser of

(*a*) the total of all amounts each of which is the amount of any business-income tax or non-business-income tax paid by the individual for the particular year

(i) where the property is real or immovable property situated in a country other than Canada,

(A) to the government of that country, or

(B) to the government of a country with which Canada has a tax treaty at the particular time and in which the individual is resident at the particular time, or

(ii) where the property is not real or immovable property, to the government of a country with which Canada has a tax treaty at the particular time and in which the individual is resident at the particular time,

that can reasonably be regarded as having been paid in respect of that portion of any gain or profit from the disposition of the property that accrued while the individual was resident in Canada and before the time the individual last ceased to be resident in Canada, and

(*b*) the amount, if any, by which

(i) the amount of tax under this Part that was, after taking into account the application of this subsection in respect of dispositions that occurred before the particular time, otherwise payable by the individual for the emigration year

exceeds

(ii) the amount of such tax that would have been payable if the property had not been deemed by subsection 128.1(4) to have been disposed of in the emigration year.

History: S. 126(2.21)(*a*)(i), the portion before clause (A) was replaced by S.C. 2013, c. 34, s. 127(1), applicable June 26, 2013, and formerly read:

(i) where the property is real property situated in a country other than Canada,

S. 126(2.21)(*a*)(ii) was replaced by S.C. 2013, c. 34, s. 127(2), applicable June 26, 2013, and formerly read:

(ii) where the property is not real property, to the government of a country with which Canada has a tax treaty at the particular time and in which the individual is resident at the particular time,

Related Sections: S. 152(6) Reassessment where certain deductions claimed.

► 126(2.22) ◄

(2.22) Former resident — trust beneficiary. If at any particular time in a particular taxation year a non-resident individual disposes of a property that the individual last acquired at any time (in this subsection referred to as the "acquisition time") on a distribution after October 1, 1996 to which paragraphs 107(2)(*a*) to (*c*) do not apply only because of subsection 107(5), the trust may deduct from its tax otherwise payable under this Part for the year (in this subsection referred to as the "distribution year") that includes the acquisition time an amount not exceeding the lesser of

(*a*) the total of all amounts each of which is the amount of any business-income tax or non-business-income tax paid by the individual for the particular year

(i) where the property is real or immovable property situated in a country other than Canada,

(A) to the government of that country, or

(B) to the government of a country with which Canada has a tax treaty at the particular time and in which the individual is resident at the particular time, or

(ii) where the property is not real or immovable property, to the government of a country with which Canada has a tax treaty at the particular time and in which the individual is resident at the particular time,

that can reasonably be regarded as having been paid in respect of that portion of any gain or profit from the disposition of the property that accrued before the distribution and after the latest of the times, before the distribution, at which

(iii) the trust became resident in Canada,

(iv) the individual became a beneficiary under the trust, or

(v) the trust acquired the property, and

(*b*) the amount, if any, by which

(i) the amount of tax under this Part that was, after taking into account the application of this subsection in respect of dispositions that occurred before the particular time, otherwise payable by the trust for the distribution year

exceeds

(ii) the amount of such tax that would have been payable by the trust for the distribution year if the property had not been distributed to the individual.

History: S. 126(2.22)(*a*)(i), the portion before clause (A) was replaced by S.C. 2013, c. 34, s. 127(3), applicable June 26, 2013, and formerly read:

(i) where the property is real property situated in a country other than Canada,

S. 126(2.22)(*a*)(ii) was replaced by S.C. 2013, c. 34, s. 127(4), applicable June 26, 2013, and formerly read:

(ii) where the property is not real property, to the government of a country with which Canada has a tax treaty at the particular time and in which the individual is resident at the particular time,

Related Sections: S. 152(6) Reassessment where certain deductions claimed.

► 126(2.23) ◄

(2.23) Where foreign credit available. For the purposes of subsections (2.21) and (2.22), in computing, in respect of the disposition of a property by an individual in a taxation year, the total amount of taxes paid by the individual for the year to one or more governments of countries other than Canada, there shall be deducted any tax credit (or other reduction in the amount of a tax) to which the individual was entitled for the year, under the law of any of those countries or under a tax treaty between Canada and any of those countries, because of taxes paid or payable by the individual under this Act in respect of the disposition or a previous disposition of the property.

► 126(2.3) ◄

(2.3) Rules relating to unused foreign tax credit. For the purposes of this section,

(*a*) the amount claimed under paragraph (2)(*a*) by a taxpayer for a taxation year in respect of a country shall be deemed to be in respect of the business-income tax paid by the taxpayer for the year in respect of businesses carried on by the taxpayer in that country to the extent of the amount of that tax, and the remainder, if any, of the amount so claimed shall be deemed to be in respect of the taxpayer's unused foreign tax credits in respect of that country that may be claimed for the taxation year;

(*b*) no amount may be claimed under paragraph (2)(*a*) in computing a taxpayer's tax payable under this Part for a particular taxation year in respect of the taxpayer's unused foreign tax credit in respect of a country for a taxation year until the taxpayer's unused foreign tax credits in respect of that country for taxation years preceding the taxation year that may be claimed for the particular taxation year have been claimed; and

(*c*) an amount in respect of a taxpayer's unused foreign tax credit in respect of a country for a taxation year may be claimed under paragraph (2)(*a*) in computing the taxpayer's tax payable under this Part for a particular taxation year only to the extent that it exceeds the aggregate of all amounts each of which is the amount that may reasonably be considered to have been claimed in respect of that unused foreign tax credit in computing the taxpayer's tax payable under this Part for a taxation year preceding the particular taxation year.

Related Sections: S. 126(7) Definitions.

Income Tax Folios: *Primary* — S5-F2-C1 Foreign Tax Credit.

► 126(3) ◄

(3) Employees of international organizations. Where an individual is resident in Canada at any time in a taxation year, there may be deducted from the individual's tax for the year otherwise payable under this Part an amount equal to that proportion of the tax for the year otherwise payable under this Part by the individual that

(*a*) the individual's income

(i) for the year, if the individual is resident in Canada throughout the year, and

(ii) for the part of the year throughout which the individual was resident in Canada, if the individual is non-resident at any time in the year,

from employment with an international organization (other than a prescribed international organization), as defined for the purposes of section 2 of the *Foreign Missions and International Organizations Act*

is of

(*b*) the amount, if any, by which

(i) if the taxpayer is resident in Canada throughout the year, the taxpayer's income for the year computed without reference to paragraph 20(1)(ww), and

(ii) if the taxpayer is non-resident at any time in the year, the amount determined under paragraph 114(*a*) in respect of the taxpayer for the year

exceeds

(iii) the total of all amounts each of which is an amount deducted under section 110.6 or paragraph 111(1)(*b*), or deductible under any of paragraphs 110(1)(*d*) to (*d*.3), (*f*) and (*g*), in computing the taxpayer's taxable income for the year,

except that the amount deductible under this subsection in computing the individual's tax payable under this Part for the year may not exceed that proportion of the total of all amounts each of which is an amount paid by the individual to the organization as a levy (the proceeds of which are used to defray expenses of the organization), computed by reference to the remuneration received by the individual in the year from the organization in a manner similar to the manner in which income tax is computed, that

(*c*) the individual's income for the year from employment with the organization

is of

(*d*) the amount that would be the individual's income for the year from employment with the organization if this Act were read without reference to paragraph 81(1)(*a*).

History: S. 126(3)(*b*)(iii) was replaced by S.C. 2017, c. 20, s. 22(3), in force January 1, 2018, and formerly read:

(iii) the total of all amounts each of which is an amount deducted under section 110.6 or paragraph 111(1)(*b*), or deductible under any of paragraphs 110(1)(*d*) to (*d*.3), (*f*), (*g*) and (*j*), in computing the taxpayer's taxable income for the year,

Related Regulations: s. 8900.

Related Sections: S. 110(1)(*f*) Deductions for payments; s. 126(7) Definitions.

► 126(4) ◄

(4) Portion of foreign tax not included. For the purposes of this Act, an income or profits tax paid by a person resident in Canada to the government of a country other than Canada does not include a tax, or that portion of a tax, imposed by that government that would not be imposed if the person were not entitled under section 113 or this section to a deduction in respect of the tax or that portion of the tax.

► 126(4.1) ◄

(4.1) No economic profit. If a taxpayer acquires a property, other than a capital property, at any time after February 23, 1998 and it is reasonable to expect at that time that the taxpayer will not realize an economic profit in respect of the property for the period that begins at that time and ends when the taxpayer next disposes of the property, the total amount of all income or profits taxes (referred to as the "foreign tax" for the purpose of subsection 20(12.1)) in respect of the property for the period, and in respect of related transactions, paid by the taxpayer for any year to the government of any country other than Canada, is not included in computing the taxpayer's business-income tax or non-business-income tax for any taxation year.

Related Sections: S. 126(7), "Economic profit", "related transactions"; s. 248(28) Limitation respecting inclusions, deductions and tax credits.

Income Tax Folios: *Primary* — S5-F2-C1 Foreign Tax Credit.

► 126(4.11) ◄

(4.11) Denial of foreign tax credit. If a taxpayer is a member of a partnership, any income or profits tax paid to the government of a particular country other than Canada — in respect of the income of the partnership for a period during which the taxpayer's direct or indirect share of the income of the partnership under the income tax laws (referred to in subsection (4.12) as the "relevant foreign tax law") of any country other than Canada under the laws of which any income of the partnership is subject to income taxation, is less than the taxpayer's direct or indirect share of the income for the purposes of this Act — is not included in computing the taxpayer's business-income tax or non-business-income tax for any taxation year.

History: S. 126(4.11) was added by S.C. 2013, c. 34, s. 267(4), applicable to income or profits tax paid for taxation years of a taxpayer that end after March 4, 2010, except that, for taxation years of the taxpayer that end on or before August 27, 2010, subsection 126(4.11) is to be read as follows:

(4.11) If a taxpayer is a member of a partnership, any income or profits tax paid to the government of a particular country other than Canada — in respect of the income of the partnership for a period during which the taxpayer's share of the income of the partnership under the income tax laws (referred to in subsection (4.12) as the "relevant foreign tax law") of any country other than Canada under the laws of which the income of the partnership is subject to income taxation, is less than the taxpayer's share of the income for the purposes of this Act — is not included in computing the taxpayer's business-income tax or non-business-income tax for any taxation year.

► 126(4.12) ◄

(4.12) Exceptions. For the purposes of subsection (4.11), a taxpayer is not to be considered to have a lesser direct or indirect share of the income of a partnership under the relevant foreign tax law than for the purposes of this Act solely because of one or more of the following:

(*a*) a difference between the relevant foreign tax law and this Act in the manner of

(i) computing the income of the partnership, or

(ii) allocating the income of the partnership because of the admission to, or withdrawal from, the partnership of any of its members;

(*b*) the treatment of the partnership as a corporation under the relevant foreign tax law; or

(*c*) the fact that the taxpayer is not treated as a corporation under the relevant foreign tax law.

History: S. 126(4.12) was added by S.C. 2013, c. 34, s. 267(4), applicable to income or profits tax paid for taxation years of a taxpayer that end after March 4, 2010, except that, for taxation years of the taxpayer that end on or before August 27, 2010, the portion of subsection 126(4.12) before paragraph (*a*) is to be read as follows:

(4.12) For the purposes of subsection (4.11), a taxpayer is not to be considered to have a lesser share of the income of a partnership under the relevant foreign tax law than for the purposes of this Act solely because of one or more of the following:

► 126(4.13) ◄

(4.13) Tiered partnerships. For the purposes of subsections (4.11) and (4.12), if a taxpayer is (or is deemed by this subsection to be) a member of a particular partnership that is a member of another partnership, the taxpayer is deemed to be a member of the other partnership.

History: S. 126(4.13) was added by S.C. 2013, c. 34, s. 267(4), applicable to income or profits tax paid for taxation years of a taxpayer that end after March 4, 2010, except that, for taxation years of the taxpayer that end on or before August 27, 2010, section 126 is to be read without reference to its subsection (4.13).

► 126(4.2) ◄

(4.2) Short-term securities acquisitions. If at any particular time a taxpayer disposes of a property that is a share or debt obligation and the period that began at the time the taxpayer last acquired the property and ended at the particular time is one year or less, the amount included in business-income tax or non-business-income tax paid by the taxpayer for a particular taxation year on account of all taxes (referred to in this subsection and subsections (4.3) and 161(6.1) as the "foreign tax") that are

(*a*) paid by the taxpayer in respect of dividends or interest in respect of the period that are included in computing the taxpayer's income from the property for any taxation year,

(*b*) otherwise included in business-income tax or non-business-income tax for any taxation year, and

(*c*) similar to the tax levied under Part XIII

shall, subject to subsection (4.3), not exceed the amount determined by the formula

$$A \times (B - C) \times D/E$$

where

A is

(*a*) if the foreign tax would otherwise be included in business-income tax, the total of

(i) that proportion of 26.5% that the number of days in the taxation year that are in 2011 is of the number of days in the taxation year, and

(ii) that proportion of 25% that the number of days in the taxation year that are after 2011 is of the number of days in the taxation year, and

(*b*) if the foreign tax would otherwise be included in non-business-income tax, the total of

(i) if the taxpayer is a corporation that is a Canadian-controlled private corporation throughout the taxation year, that proportion of 28% that the number of days in the taxation year that are after 2010 is of the number of days in the taxation year, and

(ii) if the taxpayer is not a Canadian-controlled private corporation throughout the taxation year, the total of

(A) that proportion of 16.5% that the number of days in the taxation year that are in 2011 is of the number of days in the taxation year, and

(B) that proportion of 15% that the number of days in the taxation year that are after 2011 is of the number of days in the taxation year,

B is the total of the taxpayer's proceeds from the disposition of the property at the particular time and the amount of all dividends or interest from the property in respect of the period included in computing the taxpayer's income for any taxation year,

C is the total of the cost at which the taxpayer last acquired the property and any outlays or expenses made or incurred by the taxpayer for the purpose of disposing of the property at the particular time,

D is the amount of foreign tax that would otherwise be included in computing the taxpayer's business-income tax or non-business-income tax for the particular year, and

E is the total amount of foreign tax that would otherwise be included in computing the taxpayer's business-income tax or non-business-income tax for all taxation years.

History: S. 126(4.2), the description of A was replaced by S.C. 2013, c. 34, s. 267(5), applicable to taxation years that begin after October 31, 2011, and formerly read:

A is 40%, if the foreign tax would otherwise be included in business-income tax, and 30%, if the foreign tax would otherwise be included in non-business-income tax,

► 126(4.3) ◄

(4.3) Exceptions. Subsection (4.2) does not apply to a property of a taxpayer

(*a*) that is a capital property;

(*b*) that is a debt obligation issued to the taxpayer that has a term of one year or less and that is held by no one other than the taxpayer at any time;

(*c*) that was last acquired by the taxpayer before February 24, 1998; or

(*d*) in respect of which any foreign tax is, because of subsection (4.1), not included in computing the taxpayer's business-income tax or non-business-income tax.

► 126(4.4) ◄

(4.4) Dispositions ignored. For the purposes of subsections (4.1) and (4.2) and the definition "economic profit" in subsection (7),

(*a*) a disposition or acquisition of property deemed to be made by subsection 10(12) or (13) or 45(1), section 70, 128.1 or 132.2, subsections 138(11.3), 138.2(4) or 142.5(2), paragraph 142.6(1)(*b*) or subsections 142.6(1.1) or (1.2) or 149(10) is not a disposition or acquisition, as the case may be; and

(*b*) a disposition

(i) to which section 51.1 applies, of a convertible obligation in exchange for a new obligation,

(ii) to which subsection 86(1) applies, of old shares in exchange for new shares, or

(iii) to which subsections 87(4) and (8) apply, of old shares in exchange for new shares,

is not a disposition, and the convertible obligation and the new obligation, or the old shares and the new shares, as the case may be, are deemed to be the same property.

History: S. 126(4.4)(*a*) was replaced by S.C. 2017, c. 33, s. 49(1), applicable to taxation years that begin after 2017, and formerly read:

(*a*) a disposition or acquisition of property deemed to be made by subsection 10(12) or (13) or 45(1), section 70, 128.1 or 132.2, subsections 138(11.3) or 142.5(2), paragraph 142.6(1)(*b*) or subsections 142.6(1.1) or (1.2) or 149(10) is not a disposition or acquisition, as the case may be; and

S. 126(4.4)(*a*) was replaced by S.C. 2016, c. 12, s. 45(1), in force January 1, 2017, and formerly read:

(*a*) a disposition or acquisition of property deemed to be made by subsection 10(12) or (13), 14(14) or (15) or 45(1), section 70, 128.1 or 132.2, subsections 138(11.3) or 142.5(2), paragraph 142.6(1)(*b*) or subsections 142.6(1.1) or (1.2) or 149(10) is not a disposition or acquisition, as the case may be; and

S. 126(4.4)(*a*) was replaced by S.C. 2013, c. 34, s. 267(6), applicable to dispositions and acquisitions that occur after 1998, except that, in applying paragraph 126(4.4)(*a*) to dispositions and acquisitions that occur before June 28, 1999, that paragraph is to be read without reference to "10(12) or (13), 14(14) or (15), or". S. 126(4.4)(*a*) formerly read:

(*a*) a disposition or acquisition of property deemed to be made by subsection 10(12) or (13), 14(14) or (15) or 45(1), section 70 or 128.1, paragraph 132.2(1)(*f*), subsection 138(11.3), 142.5(2) or 142.6(1.1) or (1.2), paragraph 142.6(1)(*b*) or subsection 149(10) is not a disposition or acquisition, as the case may be; and

► 126(4.5) ◄

(4.5) Synthetic disposition — holding period. If a synthetic disposition arrangement is entered into in respect of a property owned by a taxpayer and the synthetic disposition period of the arrangement is 30 days or more,

(*a*) for the purpose of determining whether the period referred to in subsection (4.2) is one year or less, the period is deemed to begin at the earlier of

(i) the time that is immediately before the particular time referred to in subsection (4.2), and

(ii) the end, if any, of the synthetic disposition period; and

(*b*) for the purposes of subsection (4.6), the taxpayer is deemed not to own the property during the synthetic disposition period.

History: S. 126(4.5) was added by S.C. 2013, c. 40, s. 56(1), applicable to:

(*a*) an agreement or arrangement entered into after March 20, 2013; and

(*b*) an agreement or arrangement entered into before March 21, 2013, the term of which is extended after March 20, 2013, as if the agreement or arrangement were entered into at the time of the extension.

► 126(4.6) ◄

(4.6) Exception. Subsection (4.5) does not apply in respect of a property owned by a taxpayer in respect of a synthetic disposition arrangement if the taxpayer owned the property throughout the one-year period (determined without reference to this subsection) that ended immediately before the synthetic disposition period of the arrangement.

History: S. 126(4.6) was added by S.C. 2013, c. 40, s. 56(1), applicable, subject to the application below, to:

(*a*) an agreement or arrangement entered into after March 20, 2013; and

(*b*) an agreement or arrangement entered into before March 21, 2013, the term of which is extended after March 20, 2013, as if the agreement or arrangement were entered into at the time of the extension.

In respect of an agreement or arrangement referred to above that is entered into before September 13, 2013 and the term of which is not extended after September 12, 2013, subsection 126(4.6) is to be read as follows:

"(4.6) Subsection (4.5) does not apply in respect of a property owned by a taxpayer in respect of a synthetic disposition arrangement if the taxpayer owned the property throughout the one-year period that ended immediately before the synthetic disposition period of the arrangement."

► 126(5) ◄

(5) Foreign oil and gas levies. A taxpayer who is resident in Canada throughout a taxation year and carries on a foreign oil and gas business in a taxing country in the year is deemed for the purposes of this section to have paid in the year as an income or profits tax to the government of the taxing country an amount equal to the lesser of

(*a*) the amount, if any, by which

(i) the amount obtained by multiplying the taxpayer's income from the business in the taxing country for the year by the total of

(A) that proportion of 26.5% that the number of days in the taxation year that are in 2011 is of the number of days in the taxation year, and

(B) that proportion of 25% that the number of days in the taxation year that are after 2011 is of the number of days in the taxation year

exceeds

(ii) the total of all amounts that would, but for this subsection, be income or profits taxes paid in the year in respect of the business to the government of the taxing country, and

(*b*) the taxpayer's production tax amount for the business in the taxing country for the year.

History: S. 126(5)(*a*)(i) was replaced by S.C. 2013, c. 34, s. 267(7), applicable to taxation years that begin after October 31, 2011, and formerly read:

(i) 40% of the taxpayer's income from the business in the taxing country for the year

Canadian Petroleum Tax Journal: Selected Income Tax Considerations When Structuring Foreign Resource Ventures, William A. Brebber, 2002, Vol. 15, No. 1.

► 126(5.1) ◄

(5.1) Deductions for specified capital gains. Where in a taxation year an individual has claimed a deduction under section 110.6 in computing the individual's taxable income for the year, for the purposes of this section the individual shall be deemed to have claimed the deduction under section 110.6 in respect of such taxable capital gains or portion thereof as the individual may specify in the individual's return of income required to be filed pursuant to section 150 for the year or, where the individual has failed to so specify, in respect of such taxable capital gains as the Minister may specify in respect of the taxpayer for the year.

► 126(6) ◄

(6) Rules of construction. For the purposes of this section,

(*a*) the government of a country other than Canada includes the government of a state, province or other political subdivision of that country;

(*b*) where a taxpayer's income for a taxation year is in whole or in part from sources in more than one country other than Canada, subsections (1) and (2) shall be read as providing for separate deductions in respect of each of the countries other than Canada;

(*c*) if any income from a source in a particular country would be tax-exempt income but for the fact that a portion of the income is subject to an income or profits tax imposed by the government of a country other than Canada, the portion is deemed to be income from a separate source in the particular country; and

(*d*) if, in computing a taxpayer's income for a taxation year from a business carried on by the taxpayer in Canada, an amount is included in respect of interest paid or payable to the taxpayer by a person resident in a country other than Canada, and the taxpayer has paid to the government of that other country a non-business income tax for the year with respect to the amount, the amount is, in applying the definition "qualifying incomes" in subsection (7) for the purpose of subsection (1), deemed to be income from a source in that other country.

History: S. 126(6)(*d*) was added by S.C. 2013, c. 34, s. 267(8), applicable to amounts received after February 27, 2004.

► 126(7) ◄

(7) Definitions. In this section,

Income Tax Folios: *Primary*— S5-F2-C1 Foreign Tax Credit.

Interpretation Bulletins: *Secondary* — IT-506 Foreign income taxes as a deduction from income.

"business-income tax"—"business-income tax" paid by a taxpayer for a taxation year in respect of businesses carried on by the taxpayer in a country other than Canada (referred to in this definition as the "business country") means, subject to subsections (4.1) to (4.2), the portion of any income or profits tax paid by the taxpayer for the year to the government of a country other than Canada that can reasonably be regarded as tax in respect of the income of the taxpayer from a business carried on by the taxpayer in the business country, but does not include a tax, or the portion of a tax, that can reasonably be regarded as relating to an amount that

(*a*) any other person or partnership has received or is entitled to receive from that government, or

(*b*) was deductible under subparagraph 110(1)(*f*)(i) in computing the taxpayer's taxable income for the year;

History: S. 126(7), the portion of the definition "business-income tax" before paragraph (*a*) was replaced by S.C. 2013, c. 34, s. 267(9), applicable to income or profits tax paid for taxation years of a taxpayer that end after March 4, 2010, and formerly read:

"business-income tax"—"business-income tax" paid by a taxpayer for a taxation year in respect of businesses carried on by the taxpayer in a country other than Canada (in this definition referred to as the "business country") means, subject to subsections (4.1) and (4.2), the portion of any income or profits tax paid by the taxpayer for the year to the government of a country other than Canada that can reasonably be regarded as tax in respect of the income of the taxpayer from a business carried on by the taxpayer in the business country, but does not include a tax, or the portion of a tax, that can reasonably be regarded as relating to an amount that

Canadian Petroleum Tax Journal: Selected Income Tax Considerations When Structuring Foreign Resource Ventures, William A. Brebber, 2002, Vol. 15, No. 1.

Income Tax Folios: *Primary*— S5-F2-C1 Foreign Tax Credit.

"commercial obligation"—"commercial obligation" in respect of a taxpayer's foreign oil and gas business in a country means an obligation of the taxpayer to a particular person, undertaken in the course of carrying on the business or in contemplation of the business, if the law of the country would have allowed the taxpayer to undertake an obligation, on substantially the same terms, to a person other than the particular person;

"economic profit"—"economic profit" of a taxpayer in respect of a property for a period means the part of the taxpayer's profit, from the business in which the property is used, that is attributable to the property in respect of the period or to related transactions, determined as if the only amounts deducted in computing that part of the profit were

(*a*) interest and financing expenses incurred by the taxpayer and attributable to the acquisition or holding of the property in respect of the period or to a related transaction,

(*b*) income or profits taxes payable by the taxpayer for any year to the government of a country other than Canada, in respect of the property for the period or in respect of a related transaction, or

(*c*) other outlays and expenses that are directly attributable to the acquisition, holding or disposition of the property in respect of the period or to a related transaction;

Related Sections: S. 126(4.1) No economic profit; s. 126(7), "related transactions".

"foreign oil and gas business"—"foreign oil and gas business" of a taxpayer means a business, carried on by the taxpayer in a taxing country, the principal activity of which is the extraction from natural accumulations, or from oil or gas wells, of petroleum, natural gas or related hydrocarbons;

Canadian Petroleum Tax Journal: Selected Income Tax Considerations When Structuring Foreign Resource Ventures, William A. Brebber, 2002, Vol. 15, No. 1.

"Foreign-tax carryover"— (Repealed by 1984, c. 45, s. 42(5).)

"non-business-income tax"—"non-business-income tax" paid by a taxpayer for a taxation year to the government of a country other than Canada means, subject to subsections (4.1) to (4.2), the portion of any income or profits tax paid by the taxpayer for the year to the government of that country that

(*a*) was not included in computing the taxpayer's business-income tax for the year in respect of any business carried on by the taxpayer in any country other than Canada,

(*b*) was not deductible by virtue of subsection 20(11) in computing the taxpayer's income for the year, and

(*c*) was not deducted by virtue of subsection 20(12) in computing the taxpayer's income for the year,

but does not include a tax, or the portion of a tax,

(*c*.1) that is in respect of an amount deducted because of subsection 104(22.3) in computing the taxpayer's business-income tax,

(*d*) that would not have been payable had the taxpayer not been a citizen of that country and that cannot reasonably be regarded as attributable to income from a source outside Canada,

(*e*) that may reasonably be regarded as relating to an amount that any other person or partnership has received or is entitled to receive from that government,

(*f*) that, where the taxpayer deducted an amount under subsection 122.3(1) from the taxpayer's tax otherwise payable under this Part for the year, may reasonably be regarded as attributable to the taxpayer's income from employment to the extent of the lesser of the amounts determined in respect thereof under paragraphs 122.3(1)(*c*) and (*d*) for the year,

(*g*) that can reasonably be attributed to a taxable capital gain or a portion thereof in respect of which the taxpayer or a spouse or common-law partner of the taxpayer has claimed a deduction under section 110.6, or

(*h*) (Repealed by S.C. 2013, c. 33, s. 13(1).)

(*i*) that can reasonably be regarded as relating to an amount that was deductible under subparagraph 110(1)(*f*)(i) in computing the taxpayer's taxable income for the year;

History: S. 126(7), paragraph (*h*) of the definition "non-business-income tax" was repealed by S.C. 2013, c. 33, s. 13(1), applicable to taxation years that begin after March 20, 2013, and formerly read:

(*h*) that may reasonably be regarded as attributable to any amount received or receivable by the taxpayer in respect of a loan for the period in the year during which it was an eligible loan (within the meaning assigned by subsection 33.1(1)), or

S. 126(7), the portion of the definition "non-business-income tax" before paragraph (*a*) was replaced by S.C. 2013, c. 34, s. 267(10), applicable to income or profits tax paid for taxation years of a taxpayer that end after March 4, 2010, and formerly read:

"non-business-income tax"—"non-business-income tax" paid by a taxpayer for a taxation year to the government of a country other than Canada means, subject to subsections (4.1) and (4.2), the portion of any income or profits tax paid by the taxpayer for the year to the government of that country that

Related Sections: S. 80.1(2) Election re interest received or to be received on expropriation assets acquired by taxpayer.

Canadian Tax Foundation: Tollstam, *Foreign Tax Credit on 401(k) Transfer to RRSP*, 2016 Canadian Tax Highlights 24(1):6–7.

Income Tax Folios: *Primary*— S5-F2-C1 Foreign Tax Credit.

Income Tax Technical News: Issue No. 31R2, Social Security Taxes and the Foreign Tax Credit; Issue No. 30, Social Security Taxes and the Foreign Tax Credit.

Tax Window Files: Foreign tax deduction, *March 7, 2016*, CRA Document No. 2015-0572461I7.

Cases: The phrase "can reasonably be regarded" in s. 20(12) enables the Minister to evaluate the economic substance of a transaction regardless of legal form and "in respect of" just means connected with or related to. A US partnership owned a NSULC which owned shares in a US LLC. Since the NSULC and LLC were disregarded for US tax purposes, the partnership paid US tax on interest earned by the LLC. A Canadian corporate partner could not deduct any of this tax since it was, in substance, paid in respect of income from foreign affiliate shares. *FLSmidth Ltd. v. The Queen*, 2013 DTC 5118 (F.C.A.), affirming 2012 DTC 1052 (T.C.C.).

"production tax amount" —"production tax amount" of a taxpayer for a foreign oil and gas business carried on by the taxpayer in a taxing country for a taxation year means the total of all amounts each of which

(*a*) became receivable in the year by the government of the country because of an obligation (other than a commercial obligation) of the taxpayer, in respect of the business, to the government or an agent or instrumentality of the government,

(*b*) is computed by reference to the amount by which

(i) the amount or value of petroleum, natural gas or related hydrocarbons produced or extracted by the taxpayer in the course of carrying on the business in the year

exceeds

(ii) an allowance or other deduction that

(A) is deductible, under the agreement or law that creates the obligation described in paragraph (*a*), in computing the amount receivable by the government of the country, and

(B) is intended to take into account the taxpayer's operating and capital costs of that production or extraction, and can reasonably be considered to have that effect,

(*c*) would not, if this Act were read without reference to subsection (5), be an income or profits tax, and

(*d*) is not identified as a royalty under the agreement that creates the obligation or under any law of the country;

"qualifying incomes" —"qualifying incomes" of a taxpayer from sources in a country means incomes from sources in the country, determined in accordance with subsection (9);

Related Sections: S. 126(7), "Qualifying losses", "tax-exempt income".

"qualifying losses" —"qualifying losses" of a taxpayer from sources in a country means losses from sources in the country, determined in accordance with subsection (9);

Related Sections: S. 126(7), "Qualifying incomes", "tax-exempt income".

"related transactions" —"related transactions", in respect of a taxpayer's ownership of a property for a period, means transactions entered into by the taxpayer as part of the arrangement under which the property was owned;

Related Sections: S. 126(4.1) No economic profit; s. 126(7), "economic profit".

"tax for the year otherwise payable under this Part" —"tax for the year otherwise payable under this Part" by a taxpayer means

(*a*) in paragraph (1)(*b*) and subsection (3), the amount determined by the formula

$$A - B$$

where

A is the amount that would be the tax payable under this Part for the year by the taxpayer if that tax were determined without reference to section 120.3 and before making any deduction under any of sections 121, 122.3, 125 to 127.41 and, if the taxpayer is a Canadian-controlled private corporation throughout the year, section 123.4, and

B is the amounts deemed by subsections 120(2) and (2.2) to have been paid on account of tax payable under this Part by the taxpayer,

(*b*) in subparagraph (2)(*c*)(i) and paragraph (2.2)(*b*), the amount that would be the tax payable under this Part for the year by the taxpayer if that tax were determined without reference to sections 120.3 and 123.3 and before making any deduction under any of sections 121 and 122.3, subsection 123.4(3), and sections 124 to 127.41, and

(*c*) in subsection (2.1), the amount that would be the tax payable under this Part for the year by the taxpayer if that tax were determined without reference to subsection 120(1) and sections 120.3 and 123.3 and before making any deduction under any of sections 121 and 122.3, subsection 123.4(3) and sections 124 to 127.41;

"tax-exempt income" —"tax-exempt income" means income of a taxpayer from a source in a country in respect of which

(*a*) the taxpayer is, because of a tax treaty with that country, entitled to an exemption from all income or profits taxes, imposed in that country, to which the treaty applies, and

(*b*) no income or profits tax to which the treaty does not apply is imposed in any country other than Canada;

Related Sections: S. 126(7), "Qualifying incomes", "qualifying losses"; s. 126(8) Deemed dividend — partnership; s. 248(1), "tax treaty".

"taxing country" —"taxing country" means a country (other than Canada) the government of which regularly imposes, in respect of income from businesses carried on in the country, a levy or charge of general application that would, if this Act were read without reference to subsection (5), be an income or profits tax;

"unused foreign tax credit" —"unused foreign tax credit" of a taxpayer in respect of a country for a taxation year means the amount, if any, by which

(*a*) the business-income tax paid by the taxpayer for the year in respect of businesses carried on by the taxpayer in that country

exceeds

(*b*) the amount, if any, deductible under subsection (2) in respect of that country in computing the taxpayer's tax payable under this Part for the year.

► 126(8) ◄

(8) Deemed dividend — partnership. If an amount is deemed by subsection 96(1.11) to be a taxable dividend received by a person in a taxation year of the person in respect of a partnership, and it is reasonable to consider that all or part of the amount (in this subsection referred to as the "foreign-source portion") is attributable to income of the partnership from a source in a country other than Canada, the person is deemed for the purposes of this section to have an amount of income from that source for that taxation year equal to the amount determined by the formula

$$A \times B/C$$

where

A is the total amount included under subsection 82(1) in computing the income of the person in respect of the taxable dividend for that taxation year;

B is the foreign-source portion; and

C is the amount of the taxable dividend deemed to be received by the person.

Related Sections: S. 96(1.11) Deemed dividend of SIFT partnership; s. 126(7), "Tax-exempt income"; s. 197(2) Tax on partnership income.

► 126(9) ◄

(9) Computation of qualifying incomes and losses. The qualifying incomes and qualifying losses for a taxation year of a taxpayer from sources in a country shall be determined

(*a*) without reference to

(i) any portion of income that was deductible under subparagraph 110(1)(*f*)(i) in computing the taxpayer's taxable income,

(ii) for the purpose of subparagraph (1)(*b*)(i), any portion of income in respect of which an amount was deducted under section 110.6 in computing the taxpayer's income, or

(iii) any income or loss from a source in the country if any income of the taxpayer from the source would be tax-exempt income; and

(*b*) as if the total of all amounts each of which is that portion of an amount deducted under subsection 66(4), 66.21(4), 66.7(2) or 66.7(2.3) in computing those qualifying incomes and qualifying losses for the year that applies to those sources were the greater of

(i) the total of all amounts each of which is that portion of an amount deducted under subsection 66(4), 66.21(4), 66.7(2) or 66.7(2.3) in computing the taxpayer's income for the year that applies to those sources, and

(ii) the total of

(A) the portion of the maximum amount that would be deductible under subsection 66(4) in computing the taxpayer's income for the year that applies to those sources if the amount determined under subparagraph 66(4)(*b*)(ii) for the taxpayer in respect of the year were equal to the amount, if any, by which the total of

(I) the taxpayer's foreign resource income (within the meaning assigned by subsection 66.21(1)) for the year in respect of the country, determined as if the taxpayer had claimed the maximum amounts deductible for the year under subsections 66.7(2) and (2.3), and

(II) all amounts each of which would have been an amount included in computing the taxpayer's income for the year under subsection 59(1) in respect of a disposition of a foreign resource property in respect of the country, determined as if each amount determined under subparagraph 59(1)(*b*)(ii) were nil,

exceeds

(III) the total of all amounts each of which is a portion of an amount (other than a portion that results in a reduction of the amount otherwise determined under subclause (I)) that applies to those sources and that would be deducted under subsection 66.7(2) in computing the taxpayer's income for the year if the maximum amounts deductible for the year under that subsection were deducted,

(B) the maximum amount that would be deductible under subsection 66.21(4) in respect of those sources in computing the taxpayer's income for the year if

(I) the amount deducted under subsection 66(4) in respect of those sources in computing the taxpayer's income for the year were the amount determined under clause (A),

(II) the amounts deducted under subsections 66.7(2) and (2.3) in respect of those sources in computing the taxpayer's income for the year were the maximum amounts deductible under those subsections,

(III) for the purposes of the definition "cumulative foreign resource expense" in subsection 66.21(1), the total of the amounts designated under subparagraph 59(1)(*b*)(ii) for the year in respect of dispositions by the taxpayer of foreign resource properties in respect of the country in the year were the maximum total that could be so designated without any reduction in the maximum amount that would be determined under clause (A) in respect of the taxpayer for the year in respect of the country if no assumption had been made under subclause (A)(II) in respect of designations made under subparagraph 59(1)(*b*)(ii), and

(IV) the amount determined under paragraph 66.21(4)(*b*) were nil, and

(C) the total of all amounts each of which is the maximum amount, applicable to one of those sources, that is deductible under subsection 66.7(2) or (2.3) in computing the taxpayer's income for the year.

SECTION 126.1: [UI premium tax credit]

► 126.1(1) ◄

(1) Definitions — (Repealed by S.C. 2013, c. 34, s. 268(1).)

History: S. 126.1(1) was repealed by S.C. 2013, c. 34, s. 268(1), applicable in respect of forms filed after March 20, 2003, and formerly read:

S. 126.1 *[UI premium tax credit].*

(1) *Definitions.* In this section,

"1992 cumulative premium base"—"1992 cumulative premium base" of an employer on any particular day means the total of all qualifying employer premiums of the employer for the period beginning on January 1, 1992 and ending on the day that is 365 days earlier than the particular day that became payable on or before the last day of that period;

"1992 premium base"—"1992 premium base" of an employer means the total of all qualifying employer premiums for 1992 of the employer;

"1993 cumulative premium base"—"1993 cumulative premium base" of an employer on any particular day means the total of all qualifying employer premiums of the employer for the period beginning on January 1, 1993 and ending on the particular day that became payable on or before the last day of that period;

"1993 premium base"—"1993 premium base" of an employer means the total of all qualifying employer premiums for 1993 of the employer;

"employer"—"employer" at any time means any person or partnership (other than a person who at that time is exempt because of any of paragraphs 149(1)(*a*) to (*d*), (*h*.1), (*o*) to (*o*.2), (*o*.4) to (*s*) and (*u*) to (*y*) from tax under this Part on all or part of the person's taxable income) that has a qualifying employee in 1992 or 1993;

"qualifying employee"—"qualifying employee" of an employer means,

(*a*) where the employer is not exempt because of subsection 149(1) from tax under this Part on all or part of the employer's taxable income,

(i) any employee of the employer, other than any employee whose remuneration is not deductible in computing income from a business or property, and

(ii) any person in respect of whom the employer is deemed under any regulation under the *Unemployment Insurance Act* to be an employer for the purpose of determining an employer's UI premium, and

(*b*) in any other case, any employee of the employer;

"qualifying employer premium"—"qualifying employer premium" for a period of an employer means that portion of the employer's UI premium that can reasonably be attributed to the remuneration paid in the period to qualifying employees of the employer;

"remittance date"—"remittance date" for 1993 of an employer means the day prescribed under the *Unemployment Insurance Act* on or before which the employer is required to remit a UI premium in respect of remuneration paid in 1993;

"UI premium"—"UI premium" of an employer means a premium under subsection 51(2) of the *Unemployment Insurance Act* payable,

(*a*) where the employer is a partnership, by the members of the partnership in respect of remuneration paid by the partnership to employees of the partnership, and

(*b*) in any other case, by the employer.

Related Sections: S. 152(1.2) Provisions applicable; s. 160.1(2.2) Liability for excess refunds under section 126.1 to partners; s. 164(1.6) Refund of UI premium tax credit.

► 126.1(2) ◄

(2) Associated employers — (Repealed by S.C. 2013, c. 34, s. 268(1).)

History: S. 126.1(2) was repealed by S.C. 2013, c. 34, s. 268(1), applicable in respect of forms filed after March 20, 2003, and formerly read:

(2) *Associated employers.* For the purpose of this section,

(*a*) employers that are corporations that are associated with each other at any time shall be deemed to be employers that are associated with each other at that time; and

(*b*) where 2 employers

(i) would, but for this paragraph, not be associated with each other at any time, and

(ii) are associated, or are deemed by this subsection to be associated, with another corporation at that time,

they shall be deemed to be associated with each other at that time.

► 126.1(3) ◄

(3) Idem — (Repealed by S.C. 2013, c. 34, s. 268(1).)

History: S. 126.1(3) was repealed by S.C. 2013, c. 34, s. 268(1), applicable in respect of forms filed after March 20, 2003, and formerly read:

(3) *Idem.* In determining for the purpose of this section whether 2 or more employers are associated with each other at any time, and in determining whether an employer is at any time a specified employer in relation to another employer,

(*a*) where an employer at any time is an individual, the employer shall be deemed at that time to be a corporation all the issued shares of the capital stock of which, having full voting rights under all circumstances, are owned by the individual; and

(*b*) where an employer at any time is a partnership,

(i) the employer shall be deemed at that time to be a corporation having one class of issued shares, which shares have full voting rights under all circumstances, and

(ii) each member of the partnership shall be deemed to own at that time the greatest proportion of the number of issued shares of the capital stock of the corporation that

(A) the member's share of the income or loss of the partnership from any source for the fiscal period of the partnership that includes that time

is of

(B) the income or loss of the partnership from that source for that period

and for the purpose of this paragraph, where the income and loss of the partnership from any source for that period are nil, that proportion shall be computed as if the partnership had income from that source for that period in the amount of $1,000,000.

► 126.1(4) ◄

(4) Business carried on by another employer — (Repealed by S.C. 2013, c. 34, s. 268(1).)

History: S. 126.1(4) was repealed by S.C. 2013, c. 34, s. 268(1), applicable in respect of forms filed after March 20, 2003, and formerly read:

(4) *Business carried on by another employer.* Where at any time before 1994 an employer (referred to in this subsection and subsection (5) as the "successor") carries on, as a separate business or as part of another business, a business or part of a business that was carried on at any earlier time after 1991 by a specified employer in relation to the successor (which business or part of a business is referred to in this subsection as the "specified business"), in determining

(*a*) the UI premium tax credit of the specified employer and the successor, and

(*b*) each amount that is or would, but for subsection (13), be deemed by subsection (12) to be paid to the specified employer or the successor at any time after the successor began to carry on the specified business,

that portion of the qualifying employer premiums for any period of the specified employer that can reasonably be considered to relate to the specified business shall be deemed not to be qualifying employer premiums for the period of the specified employer and to be qualifying employer premiums for the period of the successor.

► 126.1(5) ◄

(5) Definition of "specified employer" — (Repealed by S.C. 2013, c. 34, s. 268(1).)

History: S. 126.1(5) was repealed by S.C. 2013, c. 34, s. 268(1), applicable in respect of forms filed after March 20, 2003, and formerly read:

(5) *Definition of "specified employer".* For the purposes of subsection (4), "specified employer" at any time in relation to a successor means any particular employer with whom the successor at that time is not or would not be dealing at arm's length if,

(*a*) where the particular employer ceased to exist before that time, the particular employer were in existence at that time, and (*b*) the particular employer were controlled at that time by each person or group of persons who at any time in 1992 or 1993 controlled the particular employer,

except that a particular employer is not a specified employer in relation to a successor where the successor is, for the purposes of this section, deemed by paragraph 87(2)(*mm*) or 88(1)(*e.2*) to be a continuation of, and the same corporation as, the particular employer.

▶ 126.1(6) ◀

(6) UI premium tax credit — (Repealed by S.C. 2013, c. 34, s. 268(1).)

History: S. 126.1(6) was repealed by S.C. 2013, c. 34, s. 268(1), applicable in respect of forms filed after March 20, 2003, and formerly read:

(6) *UI premium tax credit.* Where an employer (other than a partnership) files with the Minister a prescribed form containing prescribed information, an overpayment on account of the employer's liability under this Part for the employer's last taxation year beginning before 1994 equal to the employer's UI premium tax credit shall be deemed to have arisen on the later of March 1, 1994 and the day on which the form is so filed.

▶ 126.1(7) ◀

(7) Idem — (Repealed by S.C. 2013, c. 34, s. 268(1).)

History: S. 126.1(7) was repealed by S.C. 2013, c. 34, s. 268(1), applicable in respect of forms filed after March 20, 2003, and formerly read:

(7) *Idem.* Where a member of a partnership, acting on behalf of all of the members of the partnership, files with the Minister a prescribed form containing prescribed information, an overpayment on account of each taxpayer's liability under this Part for the taxpayer's last taxation year beginning before 1994 equal to that portion of the partnership's UI premium tax credit that can reasonably be considered to be the taxpayer's share thereof shall be deemed to have arisen on the later of March 1, 1994 and the day on which the form is so filed.

▶ 126.1(8) ◀

(8) Definition of "UI premium tax credit" — (Repealed by S.C. 2013, c. 34, s. 268(1).)

History: S. 126.1(8) was repealed by S.C. 2013, c. 34, s. 268(1), applicable in respect of forms filed after March 20, 2003, and formerly read:

(8) *Definition of "UI premium tax credit".* For the purposes of this section, an employer's "UI premium tax credit" is the lesser of

(*a*) the amount, if any, by which $30,000 exceeds the amount, if any, by which the employer's 1992 premium base exceeds $30,000, and

(*b*) the amount, if any, by which the employer's 1993 premium base exceeds the employer's 1992 premium base,

unless the employer is associated at the end of 1993 with any other employer, in which case, subject to subsection (11), the employer's UI premium tax credit is nil.

▶ 126.1(9) ◀

(9) Allocation by associated employers — (Repealed by S.C. 2013, c. 34, s. 268(1).)

History: S. 126.1(9) was repealed by S.C. 2013, c. 34, s. 268(1), applicable in respect of forms filed after March 20, 2003, and formerly read:

(9) *Allocation by associated employers.* An employer that is a member of a group of employers that are associated with each other at the end of 1993 (referred to in this subsection and in subsections (10) and (11) as "associated employers") may file with the Minister an agreement in prescribed form on behalf of the associated employers allocating among them an amount not exceeding the lesser of

(*a*) the amount, if any, by which $30,000 exceeds the amount, if any, by which the total of the 1992 premium bases of all of the associated employers exceeds $30,000, and

(*b*) the amount, if any, by which

(i) the total of the 1993 premium bases of all of the associated employers

exceeds

(ii) the total of the 1992 premium bases of all of the associated employers.

▶ 126.1(10) ◀

(10) Allocation by the Minister — (Repealed by S.C. 2013, c. 34, s. 268(1).)

History: S. 126.1(10) was repealed by S.C. 2013, c. 34, s. 268(1), applicable in respect of forms filed after March 20, 2003, and formerly read:

(10) *Allocation by the Minister.* The Minister may request any of the associated employers to file with the Minister an agreement referred to in subsection (9) and, where the employer does not file the agreement within 30 days after receiving the request, the Minister may allocate among them an amount not exceeding the lesser of the amounts determined under paragraphs (9)(*a*) and (*b*).

▶ 126.1(11) ◀

(11) UI premium tax credit — associated employers — (Repealed by S.C. 2013, c. 34, s. 268(1).)

History: S. 126.1(11) was repealed by S.C. 2013, c. 34, s. 268(1), applicable in respect of forms filed after March 20, 2003, and formerly read:

(11) *UI premium tax credit — associated employers.* For the purposes of this section, the least amount allocated to an associated employer under an agreement described in subsection (9) or the amount allocated to the employer by the Minister under subsection (10), as the case may be, is the UI premium tax credit of the employer.

▶ 126.1(12) ◀

(12) Prepayment of UI premium tax credit — (Repealed by S.C. 2013, c. 34, s. 268(1).)

History: S. 126.1(12) was repealed by S.C. 2013, c. 34, s. 268(1), applicable in respect of forms filed after March 20, 2003, and formerly read:

(12) *Prepayment of UI premium tax credit.* Where before March 1994 an employer or, where the employer is a partnership, any member of the partnership acting on behalf of all of the members of the partnership, files with the Minister a prescribed form containing prescribed information, the Minister shall, subject to subsection (13), be deemed to have paid to the employer on account of the overpayment determined under subsection (6) in respect of the employer, and the employer shall be deemed, for the purpose of paragraph 12(1)(*x*), to have received and, for the purposes of the *Unemployment Insurance Act* and regulations made under it, to have remitted to the Receiver General on account of the employer's UI premium, on each remittance date for 1993, an amount that is equal to,

(*a*) where the employer was not associated with any other employer on the remittance date, the lesser of

(i) the amount, if any, by which the lesser of

(A) the amount, if any, by which $30,000 exceeds the amount, if any, by which the 1992 premium base of the employer exceeds $30,000, and

(B) the amount, if any, by which

(I) the 1993 cumulative premium base of the employer on the remittance date

exceeds

(II) the 1992 cumulative premium base of the employer on the remittance date

exceeds the total of all amounts deemed or that would, but for subsection (13), be deemed by this subsection to have been paid to the employer before the remittance date, and

(ii) the amount determined by the formula

$$A - (B + C)$$

where

A is the total of all UI premiums of the employer payable on or before the remittance date that can reasonably be attributed to remuneration paid in the period beginning on January 1, 1993 and ending on the remittance date,

B is the total of all amounts (determined without reference to this subsection) remitted by the employer to the Receiver General on or before the remittance date on account of the UI premiums referred to in the description of A, and

C is the total of all amounts deemed or that would, but for subsection (13), be deemed by this subsection to have been paid to the employer before the remittance date; and

(*b*) where the employer (in this paragraph referred to as the "particular employer") was associated on the remittance date with any other employer (in this paragraph referred to as an "associated employer"), the lesser of

(i) the amount that would be determined under paragraph (*a*) in respect of the particular employer on the remittance date if the particular employer were not associated on the remittance date with any other employer, and

(ii) the amount, if any, by which the lesser of

(A) the amount, if any, by which $30,000 exceeds the amount, if any, by which the total of the 1992 premium bases of the particular employer and all associated employers exceeds $30,000, and

(B) the amount, if any, by which

(I) the total of all amounts each of which is the 1993 cumulative premium base of the particular employer or an associated employer on the remittance date

exceeds

(II) the total of all amounts each of which is the 1992 cumulative premium base of the particular employer or an associated employer on the remittance date

exceeds the total of

(C) all amounts each of which is an amount deemed or that would, but for subsection (13), be deemed by this subsection to have been paid to the particular employer or an associated employer before the remittance date, and

(D) all amounts each of which is an amount that would be determined under subparagraph (*a*)(ii) in respect of an associated employer on the remittance date if the associated employer were not associated on that date with any other employer.

► 126.1(13) ◄

(13) Idem — (Repealed by S.C. 2013, c. 34, s. 268(1).)

History: S. 126.1(13) was repealed by S.C. 2013, c. 34, s. 268(1), applicable in respect of forms filed after March 20, 2003, and formerly read:

(13) *Idem.* Where an amount would, but for this subsection, be deemed by subsection (12) to be paid at any time to a partnership, that portion of the amount that can reasonably be considered to be a taxpayer's share of it shall be deemed not to have been paid to the partnership and to have been paid at that time by the Minister to the taxpayer on account of the overpayment determined under subsection (7) in respect of the taxpayer.

► 126.1(14) ◄

(14) Excess prepayment — (Repealed by S.C. 2013, c. 34, s. 268(1).)

History: S. 126.1(14) was repealed by S.C. 2013, c. 34, s. 268(1), applicable in respect of forms filed after March 20, 2003, and formerly read:

(14) *Excess prepayment.* Where the total of all amounts paid under subsection (12) to a taxpayer exceeds the taxpayer's UI premium tax credit, the excess shall be deemed to have been refunded to the taxpayer, on the taxpayer's last remittance date for 1993, on account of the taxpayer's liability under this Part for the taxpayer's last taxation year beginning before 1994.

► 126.1(15) ◄

(15) Idem — (Repealed by S.C. 2013, c. 34, s. 268(1).)

History: S. 126.1(15) was repealed by S.C. 2013, c. 34, s. 268(1), applicable in respect of forms filed after March 20, 2003, and formerly read:

(15) *Idem.* Where the total of all amounts paid under subsection (13) to a taxpayer in respect of a partnership exceeds that portion of the partnership's UI premium tax credit that can reasonably be considered to be the taxpayer's share of it, the excess shall be deemed to have been refunded to the taxpayer, on the partnership's last remittance date for 1993, on account of the taxpayer's liability under this Part for the taxpayer's last taxation year beginning before 1994.

SECTION 127: [Investment tax credit, etc.]

► 127(1) ◄

(1) Logging tax deduction. There may be deducted from the tax otherwise payable by a taxpayer under this Part for a taxation year an amount equal to the lesser of

(*a*) 2/3 of any logging tax paid by the taxpayer to the government of a province in respect of income for the year from logging operations in the province, and

(*b*) 6 2/3% of the taxpayer's income for the year from logging operations in the province referred to in paragraph (*a*),

except that in no case shall the total of amounts in respect of all provinces that would otherwise be deductible under this subsection from the tax otherwise payable under this Part for the year by the taxpayer exceed 6 2/3% of the amount that would be the taxpayer's taxable income for the year or taxable income earned in Canada for the year, as the case may be, if this Part were read without reference to paragraphs 60(*b*), (*c*) to (*c*.2), (*i*) and (*v*) and sections 62, 63 and 64.

Related Regulations: Part VII.

Related Sections: S. 96(2.4) Limited partner; s. 110.5 Additions for foreign tax deductions.

Forms: T2 SCH 21 — Federal Foreign Income Tax Credits and Federal Logging Tax Credit.

► 127(2) ◄

(2) Definitions. In subsection (1),

"income for the year from logging operations in the province" — "income for the year from logging operations in the province" has the meaning assigned by regulation;

Related Regulations: 700(1), (2).

Cases: It was held that "income for the year from logging operations in a province" includes income from sources carried on or operated by the taxpayer and not from sources carried on by a third person. This decision indicates that interest income from a promissory note due to the taxpayer by a subsidiary that generates income from logging operations is not income from logging operations of the taxpayer for the purpose of the logging tax deduction. *MacMillan Bloedel (Alberni) Ltd. v. M.N.R.*, 73 DTC 5264 (F.C.T.D.). See also the discussion in *MacMillan Bloedel Limited v. the Queen*, 90 DTC 6219 (F.C.T.D.)

"logging tax" — "logging tax" means a tax imposed by the legislature of a province that is declared by regulation to be a tax of general application on income from logging operations.

Editorial Note: The relevant provinces are British Columbia and Quebec. (Province is defined in s. 35(1) of the *Interpretation Act* and includes the territories.)

Related Regulations: 700(3).

Cases: It was held that this definition must be used when calculating the logging tax credit even when the provincial statute imposing the tax computes income from logging operations in a different manner. *British Columbia Forest Products Ltd. v. M.N.R.*, 71 DTC 5178 (S.C.C.), affirming 69 DTC 5127 (Ex. Ct.)

► 127(3) ◄

(3) Contributions to registered parties and candidates. There may be deducted from the tax otherwise payable by a taxpayer under this Part for a taxation year in respect of the total of all amounts each of which is the eligible amount of a monetary contribution that is referred to in the *Canada Elections Act* and that is made by the taxpayer in the year to a registered party, a registered association or a candidate, as those terms are defined in that Act,

(*a*) when that total does not exceed $400, 75% of that total,

(*b*) when that total exceeds $400 and does not exceed $750, $300 plus 50% of the amount by which that total exceeds $400, and

(*c*) when that total exceeds $750, the lesser of

(i) $650, and

(ii) $475 plus 33 1/3% of the amount by which the total exceeds $750,

if payment of each monetary contribution that is included in that total is evidenced by filing with the Minister a receipt, signed by the agent authorized under that Act to accept that monetary contribution, that contains prescribed information.

Editorial Note: A tax credit may be claimed under s. 127(3) only in respect of contributions to a federal political party, candidate or association. The calculation of the credit encourages small contributions, with no credit for contributions over $1,275 per year. The maximum annual credit is $650. For the purposes of the credit, the "eligible amount" of contributions is defined in s. 248(30) to (41). Pursuant to amendments to the *Canada Elections Act* (s. 404), effective January 1, 2007, only an individual who is a citizen or permanent resident can contribute to a registered party, a registered association, a candidate, a leadership contestant, or a nomination contestant.

History: S. 127(3), the portion before paragraph (*a*) was replaced by S.C. 2013, c. 34, s. 269(5), applicable to monetary contributions made after December 20, 2002, except that, for monetary contributions made before 2004, the reference to "to a registered party, a registered association or a candidate" in subsection 127(3) is to be read as a reference to "to a registered party or a candidate".

S. 127(3), the portion before paragraph (*a*) formerly read:

(3) *Monetary contributions — Canada Elections Act.* There may be deducted from the tax otherwise payable by a taxpayer under this Part for a taxation year in respect of the total of all amounts each of which is a monetary contribution referred to in the *Canada Elections Act* made by the taxpayer in the year to a registered party, a provincial division of a registered party, a registered association or a candidate, as those terms are defined in that Act,

Related Regulations: Part XX.

Related Sections: S. 18(1)(*n*) Political contributions; s. 123.2(1)(*a*) Corporation surtax; s. 127(3.1) Issue of receipts; s. 127(3.2) Authorization required for receipts from registered associations; s. 127(3.3) Prohibition — issuance of receipts; s. 127(4.1) Monetary contributions — form and content; s. 230.1(1) Records re monetary contributions — Canada Elections Act; s. 248(31) Eligible amount of gift or monetary contribution.

Forms: T2092 — Contributions to a Registered Party Information Return; T2093 — Contributions to a Candidate at an Election — Information Return.

Information Circulars: IC 75-2R8 Contributions to a registered party a registered association or to a candidate at a federal election.

Interpretation Bulletins: *Secondary* — IT-143R3 Meaning of eligible capital expenditure.

▶ 127(3.1) ◀

(3.1) Issue of receipts. A receipt referred to in subsection (3) must be issued only in respect of the monetary contribution that it provides evidence for and only to the contributor who made it.

Related Sections: S. 238(1) Offences and punishment.

▶ 127(3.2) ◀

(3.2) Authorization required for receipts from registered associations. No agent of a registered association of a registered party shall issue a receipt referred to in subsection (3) unless the leader of the registered party has, in writing, notified the financial agent, as referred to in the *Canada Elections Act*, of the registered association that its agents are authorized to issue those receipts.

Information Circulars: IC 75-2R8 Contributions to a Registered Party a Registered Association or to a Candidate at a Federal Election.

▶ 127(3.3) ◀

(3.3) Prohibition — issuance of receipts. If the Commissioner of Canada Elections makes an application under subsection 521.1(2) of the *Canada Elections Act* in respect of a registered party, no registered agent of the party — including, for greater certainty, a registered agent appointed by a provincial division of the party — and no electoral district agent of a registered association of the party shall issue a receipt referred to in subsection (3) unless the Commissioner withdraws the application or the court makes an order under subsection 521.1(6) of that Act or dismisses the application.

▶ 127(4) ◀

(4) Definitions. (Repealed by S.C. 2003, c. 19, s. 73(1).)

▶ 127(4.1) ◀

(4.1) Monetary contributions — form and content. For the purpose of subsections (3) and (3.1), a monetary contribution made by a taxpayer may be in the form of cash or of a negotiable instrument issued by the taxpayer. However, it does not include

(*a*) a monetary contribution that a taxpayer who is an agent authorized under the *Canada Elections Act* to accept monetary contributions makes in that capacity; or

(*b*) a monetary contribution in respect of which a taxpayer has received or is entitled to receive a financial benefit of any kind (other than a prescribed financial benefit or a deduction under subsection (3)) from a government, municipality or other public authority, whether as a grant, subsidy, forgivable loan or deduction from tax or an allowance or otherwise.

Related Regulations: Part XX.

Related Sections: S. 230.1(1) Records re monetary contributions — Canada Elections Act; s. 237.1(1), "gifting arrangement", "tax shelter"; S. 230.1(1) Records re monetary contributions — Canada Elections Act; s. 248(31) Eligible amount of gift or monetary contribution.

▶ 127(4.2) ◀

(4.2) Allocation of amount contributed among partners. (Repealed by S.C. 2006, c. 9, s. 64(2).)

▶ 127(5) ◀

(5) Investment tax credit. There may be deducted from the tax otherwise payable by a taxpayer under this Part for a taxation year an amount not exceeding the lesser of

(*a*) the total of

(i) the taxpayer's investment tax credit at the end of the year in respect of property acquired before the end of the year, of the taxpayer's apprenticeship expenditure for the year or a preceding taxation year, of the taxpayer's flow-through mining expenditure for the year or a preceding taxation year, of the taxpayer's pre-production mining expenditure for the year or a preceding taxation year or of the taxpayer's SR&ED qualified expenditure pool at the end of the year or at the end of a preceding taxation year, and

(ii) the lesser of

(A) the taxpayer's investment tax credit at the end of the year in respect of property acquired in a subsequent taxation year, of the taxpayer's apprenticeship expenditure for a subsequent taxation year, of the taxpayer's flow-through mining expenditure for a subsequent taxation year, of the taxpayer's pre-production mining expenditure for a subsequent taxation year or of the taxpayer's SR&ED qualified expenditure pool at the end of the subsequent taxation year to the extent that an investment tax credit was not deductible under this subsection for the subsequent taxation year, and

(B) the amount, if any, by which the taxpayer's tax otherwise payable under this Part for the year exceeds the amount, if any, determined under subparagraph (i), and

(*b*) where Division E.1 applies to the taxpayer for the year, the amount, if any, by which

(i) the taxpayer's tax otherwise payable under this Part for the year

exceeds

(ii) the taxpayer's minimum amount for the year determined under section 127.51.

Editorial Note: The investment tax credit can be carried back three years or forward 20 years (for taxation years before 1998, the carryforward period was 10 years). See 127(9) "investment tax credit" and subsections 127(9.01) and 127(9.02).

History: S. 127(5)(*a*)(i) was replaced by S.C. 2017, c. 20, s. 23(1), applicable in respect of expenditures incurred after March 21, 2017, except that this amendment does not apply in respect of expenditures incurred before 2020 under a written agreement entered into before March 22, 2017. S. 127(5)(*a*)(i) formerly read:

(i) the taxpayer's investment tax credit at the end of the year in respect of property acquired before the end of the year, of the taxpayer's apprenticeship expenditure for the year or a preceding taxation year, of the taxpayer's child care space amount for the year or a preceding taxation year, of the taxpayer's flow-through mining expenditure for the year or a preceding taxation year, of the taxpayer's pre-production mining expenditure for the year or a preceding taxation year or of the taxpayer's SR&ED qualified expenditure pool at the end of the year or at the end of a preceding taxation year, and

S. 127(5)(*a*)(ii)(A) was replaced by S.C. 2017, c. 20, s. 23(2), applicable in respect of expenditures incurred after March 21, 2017, except that this amendment does not apply in respect of expenditures incurred before 2020 under a written agreement entered into before March 22, 2017. S. 127(5)(*a*)(ii)(A) formerly read:

(A) the taxpayer's investment tax credit at the end of the year in respect of property acquired in a subsequent taxation year, of the taxpayer's apprenticeship expenditure for a subsequent taxation year, of the taxpayer's child care space amount for a subsequent taxation year, of the taxpayer's flow-through mining expenditure for a subsequent taxation year, of the taxpayer's pre-production mining expenditure for a subsequent taxation year or of the taxpayer's SR&ED qualified expenditure pool at the end of the subsequent taxation year to the extent that an investment tax credit was not deductible under this subsection for the subsequent taxation year, and

Related Regulations: Part XLVI.

Related Sections: S. 12(1)(*t*) Investment tax credit; s. 13(7.1) Deemed capital cost of certain property; s. 13(21), "undepreciated capital cost"; s. 37(1)(*e*) Scientific research and experimental development; s. 37(13) Non-arm's length contract — linked work; s. 53(2)(*c*)(vi) Amounts to be deducted — Interest in a partnership; s. 53(2)(*h*)(ii) Amounts to be deducted — Capital interest in a trust; s. 53(2)(*k*)(ii) Amounts to be deducted — Government assistance; s. 66.1(6), "cumulative Canadian exploration expense"; s. 87(2)(*qq*) Continuation of corporation; s. 87(2.11) Vertical amalgamations; s. 88(2)(*c*) Winding-up of Canadian corporation; s. 123.2(1)(*a*) Corporation surtax; s. 127(9) Definitions; s. 127(11.2) Time of expenditure and acquisition; s. 127(12.2) Adjusted cost base deductions re partnership interest, trust capital interest and government assistance; s. 127(13) Agreement to transfer qualified expenditures; s. 127(17) Assessment; s. 127(26) Unpaid amounts; s. 127.1(1) Refundable investment tax credit; s. 127.1(2) Definitions; s. 127.1(3) Deemed deduction; s. 128(2)(*e*)(iii)(C) Where individual bankrupt; s. 149(10)(*c*) Exempt corporations; s. 152(6)(*d*) Reassessment where certain deductions claimed; s. 164(5)(*f*) Effect of carryback of loss, etc; s. 164(5.1) Interest — disputed amounts; s. 256.1 [Corporate tax-attribute trading].

Canadian Petroleum Tax Journal: R&D Recent Developments, Arthur, Chawla, and Kourtzoglou, 2007, Vol. 20, No. 1; Recent Cases of Interest — Capital Vs. Current Expense (Plus a Little SR&ED) — Pipeline Replacement and Repair, Gerald Grenon, 2000, Vol. 13, No. 1.

Canadian Tax Foundation: MacDonald and Robinson, *Supporting SR & ED Claims*, 2006 Tax for the Owner-Manager 6(4):8–9; Robinson, *Shop Floor SR & ED: Are You Missing Out?*, 2006 Tax for the Owner-Manager 6(2):6; Murray and De Luca, *SR & ED and Outsourcing*, 2006 Canadian Tax Highlights 14(4):6; Heselton, *Seizing the Opportunities: The New and Improved SR&ED Program/Pour Saisir l'Occasion: Le Programme de la RS & DE Nouveau et Ameliore*, 1999 Corporate Management Tax Conference 1:1–15.

Tax Profile: April 2006 — The SR&ED Deduction and Investment Tax Credits; March 2006 — Some Tax Considerations for Investing in Silicon Valley North.

Forms: T2SCH31 — Investment Tax Credit — Corporations; T2 SCH 301 — Newfoundland Research and Development Tax Credit; T2 SCH 321 — Prince Edward Island Corporate Investment Tax Credit; T2 SCH 340 — Nova Scotia Research and Development Tax Credit; T2 SCH 344 — Nova Scotia Manufacturing and Processing Investment Tax Credit; T2 SCH 360 — New Brunswick Research and Development Tax Credit; T2 SCH 380 — Manitoba Research and Development Tax Credit; T2 SCH 381 — Manitoba Manufacturing and Processing Tax Credit; T2 SCH 402 — Saskatchewan Manufacturing and Processing Investment Tax Credit; T2 SCH 403 — Saskatchewan Research and Development Tax Credit; T2 SCH 426 — British Columbia Manufacturing and Processing Tax Credit; T2 SCH 442 — Yukon Research and Development Tax Credit; T661 — Scientific Research and Experimental Development (SR&ED) Expenditures Claim; T666 — British Columbia Scientific Research and Experimental Development Tax Credit; T1129 — Newfoundland and Labrador Research and Development Tax Credit (Individuals); T1232 — Yukon Research and Development Tax Credit (Individuals); T1263 — Third-party payment for SR&ED; T2038(IND) — Investment Tax Credit (Individuals).

Guides: T4052 An Introduction to the Scientific Research and Experimental Development Program; T4088 Claiming Scientific Research and Experimental Development — Guide to Form T661; RC4290 Refunds for Small Business R&D.

Information Circulars: IC 78-4R3 Investment tax credit rates.

Interpretation Bulletins: *Secondary* — IT-92R2 Income of contractors; IT-411R Meaning of construction.

SR&ED Publications: SR&ED Investment Tax Credit Policy; Total Qualified SR&ED Expenditures for Investment Tax Credit Purposes Policy.

Tax Window Files: Scientific Research and Experimental Development — Tests and Studies Required to Meet Regulatory Requirements, *Technical Interpretation, Business and Partnerships Division, January 17, 2007*, CRA Document No. 2005-0152601E5; Investment Tax Credit, *Technical Interpretation, Business and Partnerships Division, July 29, 2005*, CRA Document No. 2005-0143681I7; Investment Tax Credit and Minimum Tax, *Technical Interpretation, Business and Partnerships Division, October 8, 2004*, CRA Document No. 2004-0093371I7; Investment Tax Credits — Carryback Denial After Wind-Up, *Technical Interpretation, Reorganizations and Resources Division, June 1, 2004*, CRA Document No. 2004-0078161I7.

Cases: "In respect of" is to be interpreted broadly. The sole purpose of the expenditures was to facilitate the projects by arranging for the cattle to be delivered to the feedlots, where the research (which was accepted as SR&ED) was carried out. The expenditures provided the subjects of the research and as such were in respect of the SR&ED. *Feedlot Health Management Services Ltd. v. Her Majesty the Queen*, 2015 DTC 1083 (T.C.C.)

► 127(6) ◄

(6) Investment tax credit of cooperative corporation. Where at any particular time in a taxation year a taxpayer that is a cooperative corporation within the meaning assigned by subsection 136(2) has, as required by subsection 135(3), deducted or withheld an amount from a payment made by it to any person pursuant to an allocation in proportion to patronage, the taxpayer may deduct from the amount otherwise required by that subsection to be remitted to the Receiver General, an amount, not exceeding the amount, if any, by which

(*a*) its investment tax credit at the end of the immediately preceding taxation year in respect of property acquired and expenditures made before the end of that preceding taxation year

exceeds the total of

(*b*) the amount deducted under subsection (5) from its tax otherwise payable under this Part for the immediately preceding taxation year in respect of property acquired and expenditures made before the end of that preceding taxation year, and

(*c*) the total of all amounts each of which is the amount deducted by virtue of this subsection from any amount otherwise required to be remitted by subsection 135(3) in respect of payments made by it before the particular time and in the taxation year,

and the amount, if any, so deducted from the amount otherwise required to be remitted by subsection 135(3)

(*d*) shall be deducted in computing the taxpayer's investment tax credit at the end of the taxation year, and

(*e*) shall be deemed to have been remitted by the taxpayer to the Receiver General on account of tax under this Part of the person to whom that payment was made.

Related Sections: S. 12(1)(*t*) Investment tax credit; s. 13(7.1) Deemed capital cost of certain property; s. 13(21), "undepreciated capital cost"; s. 53(2)(*k*)(ii) Amounts to be deducted — Government assistance; s. 66.1(6), "cumulative Canadian exploration expense".

Forms: T2 SCH 31 — Investment Tax Credit — Corporations; T661 — Scientific Research and Experimental Development (SR&ED) Expenditures Claim; T2038 — Investment Tax Credit (Individuals).

Interpretation Bulletins: *Secondary* — IT-362R Patronage dividends.

► 127(7) ◄

(7) Investment tax credit of certain trusts. If, in a particular taxation year of a taxpayer who is a beneficiary under a trust that is a graduated rate estate or that is deemed to be in existence by section 143, an amount is determined in respect of the trust under paragraph (*a*), (*a*.1), (*a*.4), (*b*) or (*e*.1) of the definition "investment tax credit" in subsection (9) for its taxation year that ends in that particular taxation year, the trust may, in its return of income for its taxation year that ends in that particular taxation year, designate the portion of that amount that can, having regard to all the circumstances including the terms and conditions of the trust, reasonably be considered to be attributable to the taxpayer and was not designated by the trust in respect of any other beneficiary of the trust, and that portion is to be added in computing the investment tax credit of the taxpayer at the end of that particular taxation year and is to be deducted in computing the investment tax credit of the trust at the end of its taxation year that ends in that particular taxation year.

Editorial Note: Effective for 2016 and subsequent taxation years, subsection 127(7) will apply to a graduated rates estate (defined in subsection 248(1)) but not to other testamentary trusts.

History: S. 127(7) was replaced by S.C. 2017, c. 20, s. 23(3), applicable in respect of expenditures incurred after March 21, 2017, except that this amendment does not apply in respect of expenditures incurred before 2020 under a written agreement entered into before March 22, 2017. S. 127(7) formerly read:

(7) *Investment tax credit of certain trusts.* If, in a particular taxation year of a taxpayer who is a beneficiary under a trust that is a graduated rate estate or that is deemed to be in existence by section 143, an amount is determined in respect of the trust under paragraph (*a*), (*a.1*), (*a.4*), (*a.5*), (*b*) or (*e.1*) of the definition "investment tax credit" in subsection (9) for its taxation year that ends in that particular taxation year, the trust may, in its return of income for its taxation year that ends in that particular taxation year, designate the portion of that amount that can, having regard to all the circumstances including the terms and conditions of the trust, reasonably be considered to be attributable to the taxpayer and was not designated by the trust in respect of any other beneficiary of the trust, and that portion is to be added in computing the investment tax credit of the taxpayer at the end of that particular taxation year and is to be deducted in computing the investment tax credit of the trust at the end of its taxation year that ends in that particular taxation year.

S. 127(7) was replaced by S.C. 2014, c. 39, s. 42(1), applicable to the 2016 and subsequent taxation years, and formerly read:

(7) *Investment tax credit of testamentary trust.* If, in a particular taxation year of a taxpayer who is a beneficiary under a testamentary trust or under an *inter vivos* trust that is deemed to be in existence by section 143, an amount is determined in respect of the trust under paragraph (*a*), (*a.1*), (*a.4*), (*a.5*), (*b*) or (*e.1*) of the definition "investment tax credit" in subsection (9) for its taxation year that ends in that particular taxation year, the trust may, in its return of income for its taxation year that ends in that particular taxation year, designate the portion of that amount that can, having regard to all the circumstances including the terms and conditions of the trust, reasonably be considered to be attributable to the taxpayer and was not designated by the trust in respect of any other beneficiary of the trust, and that portion shall be added in computing the investment tax credit of the taxpayer at the end of that particular taxation year and shall be deducted in computing the investment tax credit of the trust at the end of its taxation year that ends in that particular taxation year.

Related Sections: S. 53(2)(*h*)(ii) Amounts to be deducted — Capital interest in a trust; s. 127(5) Investment tax credit; s. 127(9) "investment tax credit"; s. 127(11.2) Time of expenditure and acquisition; 127(11.5) Adjustments to qualified expenditures; 127(11.6) Non-arm's length costs; 127(11.7) Definitions; 127(11.8) Interpretation for non-arm's length costs; s. 248(1) "graduated rate estate".

► 127(8) ◄

(8) Investment tax credit of partnership. Subject to subsection (28), where, in a particular taxation year of a taxpayer who is a member of a partnership, an amount would be determined in respect of the partnership, for its taxation year that ends in the particular taxation year, under paragraph (*a*), (*a*.1), (*a*.4), (*b*) or (*e*.1) of the definition "investment tax credit" in subsection (9), if

(*a*) except for the purpose of subsection (13), the partnership were a person and its fiscal period were its taxation year, and

(*b*) in the case of a taxpayer who is a specified member of the partnership in the taxation year of the partnership, that definition were read without reference to paragraph (*a*.1) thereof, and paragraph (*e*.1) of that definition were read without reference to subparagraphs (ii) to (iv) thereof,

the portion of that amount that can reasonably be considered to be the taxpayer's share thereof shall be added in computing the investment tax credit of the taxpayer at the end of the particular year.

History: S. 127(8), the portion before paragraph (*a*) was replaced by S.C. 2017, c. 20, s. 23(4), applicable in respect of expenditures incurred after March 21, 2017, except that this amendment does not apply in respect of expenditures incurred before 2020 under a written agreement entered into before March 22, 2017. S. 127(8) formerly read:

(8) *Investment tax credit of partnership.* Subject to subsections (28) and (28.1), where, in a particular taxation year of a taxpayer who is a member of a partnership, an amount would be determined in respect of the partnership, for its taxation year that ends in the particular taxation year, under paragraph (*a*), (*a.1*), (*a.4*), (*a.5*), (*b*) or (*e.1*) of the definition "investment tax credit" in subsection (9), if

Related Sections: S. 53(2)(*c*)(vi) Amounts to be deducted — Interest in a partnership; s. 96(2.1) Limited partnership losses; s. 127(8.1) Investment tax credit of limited partner; s. 127(8.3) Investment tax credit — allocation of unallocated partnership ITCs; s. 127(8.4) Renunciation to investment tax credit; s. 127(11.2) Time of expenditure and acquisition; s. 127(28) Recapture of investment tax credit of partnership.

SR&ED Publications: SR&ED Investment Tax Credit Policy; SR&ED Claims for Partnerships Policy; 2004-02R5, Filing Requirements for Claiming SR&ED.

► 127(8.1) ◄

(8.1) Investment tax credit of limited partner. Notwithstanding subsection (8), if a taxpayer is a limited partner of a partnership at the end of a fiscal period of the partnership, the amount, if any, determined under subsection (8) to be added in computing the taxpayer's investment tax credit at the end of the taxpayer's taxation year in which that fiscal period ends shall not exceed the lesser of

(*a*) the portion of the amount that would, if this section were read without reference to this subsection, be determined under subsection (8) to be the amount to be added in computing the taxpayer's investment tax credit at the end of the taxpayer's taxation year in which that fiscal period ends as is considered to have arisen because of the expenditure by the partnership of an amount equal to the taxpayer's expenditure base (as determined under subsection (8.2) in respect of the partnership) at the end of that fiscal period, and

(*b*) the taxpayer's at-risk amount in respect of the partnership at the end of that fiscal period.

Editorial Note: S. 127(8.1) limits the ITCs that a partnership can allocate to a limited partner, based on the limited partnership's expenditure base, as described in s. 127(8.2), and at-risk amount for the partnership, as described in s. 96(2.2).

Related Sections: S. 37(13) Non-arm's length contract — linked work; 96(2.1) Limited partnership losses; 96(2.11) Tiered partnerships — adjustments; 96(2.2) At-risk amount; 96(2.3) Idem; 96(2.4) Limited partner; s. 127(8.2) Expenditure base; s. 127(8.5) Definitions.

► 127(8.2) ◄

(8.2) Expenditure base. For the purposes of subsection (8.1), a taxpayer's expenditure base in respect of a partnership at the end of a taxation year of the partnership is the lesser of

(*a*) the amount, if any, by which the total of

(i) the taxpayer's at-risk amount in respect of the partnership at the time the taxpayer last became a limited partner of the partnership,

(ii) all amounts described in subparagraph 53(1)(*e*)(iv) contributed by the taxpayer after the time the taxpayer last became a limited partner of the partnership and before the end of the year that may reasonably be considered to have increased the taxpayer's at-risk amount in respect of the partnership at the end of the taxation year in which the contribution was made, and

(iii) the amount, if any, by which

(A) the total of all amounts each of which is the taxpayer's share of any income of the partnership as determined under paragraph 96(1)(*f*) for the year, or a preceding year ending after the time the taxpayer last became a limited partner of the partnership,

exceeds

(B) the total of all amounts each of which is the taxpayer's share of any loss of the partnership as determined under paragraph 96(1)(*g*) for one of those years

exceeds the total of

(iv) all amounts received by the taxpayer after the time the taxpayer last became a limited partner of the partnership and before the end of the year as, on account or in lieu of payment of, or in satisfaction of, a distribution of the taxpayer's share of partnership profits or partnership capital, and

(v) the total of all amounts each of which is the amount of an expenditure of the partnership referred to in paragraph (8.1)(*a*) in respect of the taxpayer for a preceding year, and

(*b*) that proportion of the lesser of

(i) the total of all amounts each of which is, if the partnership were a person and its fiscal period were its taxation year,

(A) an amount a specified percentage of which would be determined in respect of the partnership under paragraph (*a*), (*b*) or (*e*.1) of the definition "investment tax credit" in subsection (9) for the year,

(A.1) an amount that would be the apprenticeship expenditure of the partnership if the reference to "$2,000" in paragraph (*a*) of the definition "apprenticeship expenditure" in subsection (9) were read as a reference to "$20,000" and paragraph (*b*) of that definition were read without reference to "10% of", or

(A.2) (Repealed by S.C. 2017, c. 20, s. 23(5).)

(B) the amount that would be the SR&ED qualified expenditure pool of the partnership at the end of the year, and

(ii) the total of all amounts each of which is the amount determined under paragraph (*a*) in respect of each of the limited partners of the partnership at the end of the year

that

(iii) the amount determined in respect of the taxpayer under paragraph (*a*) for the year

is of

(iv) the amount determined under subparagraph (ii).

History: S. 127(8.2)(*b*)(i)(A.2) was repealed by S.C. 2017, c. 20, s. 23(5), applicable in respect of expenditures incurred after March 21, 2017, except that this amendment does not apply in respect of expenditures incurred before 2020 under a written agreement entered into before March 22, 2017. S. 127(8.2)(*b*)(i)(A.2) formerly read:

(A.2) an amount that would be the child care space amount in respect of a property of the partnership if the reference to "$10,000" in paragraph (*a*) of the definition "child care space amount" in subsection (9) were read as a reference to "$40,000" and paragraph (*b*) of that definition were read without reference to "25% of", or

Related Sections: S. 37(13) Non-arm's length contract — linked work.

► 127(8.3) ◄

(8.3) Investment tax credit — allocation of unallocated partnership ITCs. For the purpose of subsection (8), and subject to subsection (8.4), if a taxpayer is a member of a partnership (other than a specified member) throughout a fiscal period of the partnership, there shall be added to the amount that can reasonably be considered to be that member's share of the amount determined under subsection (8) the amount, if any, that is such portion of the amount determined under subsection (8.31) in respect of that fiscal period as is reasonable in the circumstances (having regard to the investment in the partnership, including debt obligations of the partnership, of each of those members of the partnership who was a member of the partnership throughout the fiscal period of the partnership and who was not a specified member of the partnership during the fiscal period of the partnership).

Related Sections: S. 37(13) Non-arm's length contract — linked work; 96(2.1) Limited partnership losses; 96(2.11) Tiered partnerships — adjustments; 96(2.2) At-risk amount; 96(2.3) Idem; 96(2.4) Limited partner; s. 127(8.5) Definitions.

► 127(8.31) ◄

(8.31) Amount of unallocated partnership ITC. For the purpose of subsection (8.3), the amount determined under this subsection in respect of a fiscal period of a partnership is the amount, if any, by which

(*a*) the total of all amounts each of which is an amount that would, if the partnership were a person and its fiscal period were its taxation year, be determined in respect of the partnership under paragraph (*a*), (*a*.1), (*a*.4), (*b*) or (*e*.1) of the definition "investment tax credit" in subsection (9) for a taxation year that is the fiscal period,

exceeds

(*b*) the total of

(i) the total of all amounts each of which is the amount determined under subsection (8) in respect of the fiscal period to be the share of the total determined under paragraph (*a*) of a partner of the partnership (other than a member of the partnership who was at any time in the fiscal period of the partnership a specified member of the partnership), and

(ii) the total of all amounts each of which is the amount determined under subsection (8), with reference to subsection (8.1), in respect of the fiscal period to be the share of the total determined under paragraph (*a*) of a partner of the partnership who was at any time in the fiscal period of the partnership a specified member of the partnership.

(iii) (Repealed by S.C. 2007, c. 35, s. 43(6).)

History: S. 127(8.31)(*a*) was replaced by S.C. 2017, c. 20, s. 23(6), applicable in respect of expenditures incurred after March 21, 2017, except that this amendment does not apply in respect of expenditures incurred before 2020 under a written agreement entered into before March 22, 2017. S. 127(8.31)(*a*) formerly read:

(*a*) the total of all amounts each of which is an amount that would, if the partnership were a person and its fiscal period were its taxation year, be determined in respect of the partnership under paragraph (*a*), (*a.1*), (*a.4*), (*a.5*), (*b*) or (*e.1*) of the definition "investment tax credit" in subsection (9) for a taxation year that is the fiscal period,

► 127(8.4) ◄

(8.4) Idem. Notwithstanding subsection (8), where, pursuant to subsections (8) and (8.3) an amount would, but for this subsection, be required to be added in computing the investment tax credit of a taxpayer for a taxation year, where the taxpayer so elects in prescribed form and manner in the taxpayer's return of income (other than a return of income filed under subsection 70(2) or 104(23), paragraph 128(2)(*e*) or subsection 150(4)) under this Part for the year, such portion of the amount as is elected by the taxpayer shall, for the purposes of this section, be deemed not to have been required by subsection (8) to have been added in computing the taxpayer's investment tax credit at the end of the year.

Forms: T932 — Election by a Member of a Partnership to Renounce Investment Tax Credits Pursuant to Subsection 127(8.4).

► 127(8.5) ◄

(8.5) Definitions. In subsections (8.1) to (8.4), the words "at-risk amount" of a taxpayer and "limited partner" of a partnership have the meanings assigned to those words by subsections 96(2.2) and (2.4), respectively.

► 127(9) ◄

(9) Idem. In this section,

Related Regulations: Part XXIX; Part XLVI; 2902.

Tax Window Files: Fishing vessels and Atlantic Investment Tax Credit, *April 28, 2015*, CRA Document No. 2015-0576511E5; *Investment Tax Credit and 16.1(1), October 6, 2011,* CRA Document No. 2011-0417811E5; *Specified employee for SRED credits, April 19, 2012,* CRA Document No. 2012-0439781E5; SR&ED — Exploit Results, *Income Tax Rulings Directorate, Business and Partnerships Division, November 10, 2008*, CRA Document No. 2008-0276121E5; SR&ED Government Assistance, *Technical Interpretation, Financial Sector and Exempt Entities Division, May 3, 2007*, CRA Document No. 2007-0224191E5; Lease of used equipment & non-arm's length party, *Technical Interpretation, Business and Partnerships Division, February 15, 2007*, CRA Document No. 2006-0206761I7; SR&ED Used Equipment, *Technical Interpretation, Business and Partnerships Division, January 30, 2007*, CRA Document No. 2006-0211041E5.

"annual investment tax credit limit" — (Repealed by S.C. 1994, c. 8, s. 15(2).)

"apprenticeship expenditure" — "apprenticeship expenditure" of a taxpayer for a taxation year in respect of an eligible apprentice is the lesser of

(*a*) $2,000, and

(*b*) 10% of the eligible salary and wages payable by the taxpayer in the taxation year to the eligible apprentice in respect of the eligible apprentice's employment, in the taxation year and on or after May 2, 2006, by the taxpayer in a business carried on in Canada by the taxpayer in the taxation year;

Related Sections: S. 127(9), "investment tax credit, paragraph (*a.4*); s. 127(11.1)(*c.4*) Investment tax credit.

"approved project" — "approved project" means a project with a total capital cost of depreciable property, determined without reference to subsection 13(7.1) or (7.4), of not less than $25,000 that has, on application in writing before July, 1988, been approved by such member of the Queen's Privy Council for Canada as is designated by the Governor in Council for the purposes of this definition in relation to projects in the appropriate province or region of a province;

"approved project property" — (Repealed by S.C. 1996, c. 21, s. 30(9).)

"Cape Breton" — "Cape Breton" means Cape Breton Island and that portion of the Province of Nova Scotia within the following described boundary:

beginning at a point on the southwesterly shore of Chedabucto Bay near Red Head, said point being S70 degrees E (Nova Scotia grid meridian) from Geodetic Station Sand, thence in a southwesterly direction to a point on the northwesterly boundary of highway 344, said point being southwesterly 240' from the intersection of King Brook with said highway boundary, thence northwesterly to Crown post 6678, thence continuing northwesterly to Crown post 6679, thence continuing northwesterly to Crown post 6680, thence continuing northwesterly to Crown post 6681, thence continuing northwesterly to Crown post 6632, thence continuing northwesterly to Crown post 6602, thence northerly to Crown post 8575; thence northerly to Crown post 6599, thence continuing northerly to Crown post 6600, thence northwesterly to the southwest angle of the Town of Mulgrave, thence along the westerly boundary of the Town of Mulgrave and a prolongation thereof northerly to the Antigonish-Guysborough county line, thence along said county line northeasterly to the southwesterly shore of the Strait of Canso, thence following the southwesterly shore of the Strait of Canso and the northwesterly shore of Chedabucto Bay southeasterly to the place of beginning;

"certified property" — "certified property" of a taxpayer means any property (other than an approved project property) described in paragraph (*a*) or (*b*) of the definition "qualified property" in this subsection

(*a*) that was acquired by the taxpayer

(i) after October 28, 1980 and

(A) before 1987, or

(B) before 1988 where the property is

(I) a building under construction before 1987, or

(II) machinery and equipment ordered in writing by the taxpayer before 1987,

(ii) after 1986 and before 1989, other than a property included in subparagraph (i),

(iii) after 1988 and before 1995,

(iv) after 1994 and before 1996 where

(A) the property is acquired by the taxpayer for use in a project that was substantially advanced by or on behalf of the taxpayer, as evidenced in writing, before February 22, 1994, and

(B) construction of the project by or on behalf of the taxpayer begins before 1995, or

(v) after 1994 where the property

(A) is acquired by the taxpayer under a written agreement of purchase and sale entered into by the taxpayer before February 22, 1994,

(B) was under construction by or on behalf of the taxpayer on February 22, 1994, or

(C) is machinery or equipment that will be a fixed and integral part of property under construction by or on behalf of the taxpayer on February 22, 1994,

and that has not been used, or acquired for use or lease, for any purpose whatever before it was acquired by the taxpayer, and

(*b*) that is part of a facility as defined for the purposes of the *Regional Development Incentives Act*, chapter R-3 of the Revised Statutes of Canada, 1970, and was acquired primarily for use by the taxpayer in a prescribed area;

Related Regulations: 4602.

"child care space amount" — (Repealed by S.C. 2017, c. 20, s. 23(7).)

History: S. 127(9), the definition "child care space amount" was repealed by S.C. 2017, c. 20, s. 23(7), applicable in respect of expenditures incurred after March 21, 2017, except that this amendment does not apply in respect of expenditures incurred before 2020 under a written agreement entered into before March 22, 2017. S. 127(9), the definition "child care space amount" formerly read:

"child care space amount"—"child care space amount" of a taxpayer for a taxation year is, if the provision of child care spaces is ancillary to one or more businesses of the taxpayer that are carried on in Canada in the taxation year and that do not otherwise include the provision of child care spaces, the lesser of

(*a*) the amount obtained when $10,000 is multiplied by the number of new child care spaces created by the taxpayer during the taxation year in a licensed child care facility for the benefit of children of the taxpayer's employees, or of a combination of children of the taxpayer's employees and other children; and

(*b*) 25% of the taxpayer's eligible child care space expenditure for the taxation year;

"contract payment" —"contract payment" means

(*a*) an amount paid or payable to a taxpayer, by a taxable supplier in respect of the amount, for scientific research and experimental development to the extent that it is performed

(i) for or on behalf of a person or partnership entitled to a deduction in respect of the amount because of subparagraph 37(1)(*a*)(i.01) or (i.1), and

(ii) at a time when the taxpayer is dealing at arm's length with the person or partnership, or

(*b*) an amount in respect of an expenditure of a current nature (within the meaning assigned by paragraph 37(8)(*d*)) of a taxpayer, other than a prescribed amount, payable by a Canadian government or municipality or other Canadian public authority or by a person exempt, because of section 149, from tax under this Part on all or part of the person's taxable income for scientific research and experimental development to be performed for it or on its behalf;

History: S. 127(9), subparagraph (*a*)(i) of the definition "contract payment" was replaced by S.C. 2012, c. 31, s. 27(1), applicable in respect of expenditures made after 2012. S. 127(9), subparagraph (*a*)(i) of the definition "contract payment" formerly read:

(i) for or on behalf of a person or partnership entitled to a deduction in respect of the amount because of subparagraph 37(1)(*a*)(i) or (i.1), and

S. 127(9), paragraph (*b*) of the definition "contract payment" was replaced by S.C. 2012, c. 31, s. 27(2), applicable in respect of expenditures made after 2013. S. 127(9), paragraph (*b*) of the definition "contract payment" formerly read:

(*b*) an amount, other than a prescribed amount, payable by a Canadian government or municipality or other Canadian public authority or by a person exempt, because of section 149, from tax under this Part on all or part of the person's taxable income for scientific research and experimental development to be performed for it or on its behalf;

Related Regulations: 4606.

Related Sections: S. 127(18) Reduction of qualified expenditures; s. 127(19) Reduction of qualified expenditures; s. 127(24) Exclusion from qualified expenditure; s. 127(25) Deemed contract payment.

Tax Topics: No. 1830, The CRA's Revised Position on SR&ED Contracts.

SR&ED Publications: Contract Expenditures for SR&ED Performed on Behalf of a Claimant Policy; Total Qualified SR&ED Expenditures for Investment Tax Credit Purposes Policy; 2005-02, General Rules Concerning the Treatment of Government and Non-Government Assistance; 2004-03, Prototypes, Pilot Plants/Commercial Plants, Custom Products and Commercial Assets; 2002-03, Taxable Supplier Rates; 94-04, Definition of "contract payment" in subsection 127(9).

Tax Window Files: Scientific Research and Experimental Development — Activities Performed on Behalf of Foreign Corporation, *2005 APFF Conference — Round Table on Federal Taxation, Question 7, October 7, 2005*, CRA Document No. 2005-0140991C6.

"designated region" — (Repealed by 1986, c. 6, s. 71(2).)

"eligible apprentice" —"eligible apprentice" means an individual who is employed in Canada in a trade prescribed in respect of a province or in respect of Canada, during the first twenty-four months of the individual's apprenticeship contract registered with the province or Canada, as the case may be, under an apprenticeship program designed to certify or license individuals in the trade;

Related Regulations: 7310.

"eligible child care space expenditure" — (Repealed by S.C. 2017, c. 20, s. 23(7).)

History: S. 127(9), the definition "eligible child care space expenditure" was repealed by S.C. 2017, c. 20, s. 23(7), applicable in respect of expenditures incurred after March 21, 2017, except that this amendment does not apply in respect of expenditures incurred before 2020 under a written agreement entered into before March 22, 2017. S. 127(9), the definition "eligible child care space expenditure" formerly read:

"eligible child care space expenditure"—"eligible child care space expenditure" of a taxpayer for a taxation year is the total of all amounts each of which is an amount

(*a*) that is incurred by the taxpayer in the taxation year for the sole purpose of the creation of one or more new child care spaces in a licensed child care facility operated for the benefit of children of the taxpayer's employees, or of a combination of children of the taxpayer's employees and other children, and

(*b*) that is

(i) incurred by the taxpayer to acquire depreciable property of a prescribed class (other than a specified property) for use in the child care facility, or

(ii) incurred by the taxpayer to make a specified child care start-up expenditure in respect of the child care facility;

"eligible salary and wages"—"eligible salary and wages" payable by a taxpayer to an eligible apprentice means the amount, if any, that is the salary and wages payable by the taxpayer to the eligible apprentice in respect of the first 24 months of the apprenticeship (other than a qualified expenditure incurred by the taxpayer in a taxation year, remuneration that is based on profits, bonuses, amounts described in section 6 or 7, and amounts deemed to be incurred by subsection 78(4));

History: S. 127(9), the definition "eligible salary and wages" was replaced by S.C. 2013, c. 34, s. 269(8), applicable to taxation years that end after November 5, 2010, and formerly read:

"eligible salary and wages"—"eligible salary and wages" payable by a taxpayer to an eligible apprentice means the amount, if any, that is the salary and wages payable by the taxpayer to the eligible apprentice in respect of the first 24 months of the apprenticeship (other than remuneration that is based on profits, bonuses, amounts described in section 6 or 7, and amounts deemed to be incurred by subsection 78(4));

Related Sections: S. 127(11.4) Special rule for eligible salary and wages — apprentices.

"eligible taxpayer"—"eligible taxpayer" means

(*a*) a corporation other than a non-qualifying corporation,

(*b*) an individual other than a trust,

(*c*) a trust all the beneficiaries of which are eligible taxpayers, and

(*d*) a partnership all the members of which are eligible taxpayers,

and, for the purpose of this definition, a beneficiary of a trust is a person or partnership that is beneficially interested in the trust;

Related Sections: S. 248(25) Beneficially interested.

"first term shared-use-equipment"—"first term shared-use-equipment", of a taxpayer, means depreciable property of the taxpayer (other than prescribed depreciable property of a taxpayer) acquired before 2014 that is used by the taxpayer, during its operating time in the period (in this subsection and subsection (11.1) referred to as the "first period") beginning at the time the property was acquired by the taxpayer and ending at the end of the taxpayer's first taxation year ending at least 12 months after that time, primarily for the prosecution of scientific research and experimental development in Canada, but does not include general purpose office equipment or furniture;

History: S. 127(9), the definition "first term shared-use-equipment" was replaced by S.C. 2012, c. 31, s. 27(3), deemed to have come into force on March 29, 2012. S. 127(9), the definition "first term shared-use-equipment" formerly read:

"first term shared-use-equipment"—"first term shared-use-equipment" of a taxpayer means depreciable property of the taxpayer (other than prescribed depreciable property of a taxpayer) that is used by the taxpayer, during its operating time in the period (in this subsection and subsection (11.1) referred to as the "first period") beginning at the time the property was acquired by the taxpayer and ending at the end of the taxpayer's first taxation year ending at least 12 months after that time, primarily for the prosecution of scientific research and experimental development in Canada, but does not include general purpose office equipment or furniture;

Related Regulations: 2900(11).

Related Sections: S. 88(1)(e.3) Winding-up; s. 127(11.5)(b).

SR&ED Publications: SR&ED Investment Tax Credit Policy; 2005-01, Shared-Use Equipment; 2003-01, Capital Property Intended to be Used All or Substantially All for SR&ED.

"flow-through mining expenditure"—"flow-through mining expenditure" of a taxpayer for a taxation year means an expense deemed by subsection 66(12.61) (or by subsection 66(18) as a consequence of the application of subsection 66(12.61) to the partnership, referred to in paragraph (*c*) of this definition, of which the taxpayer is a member) to be incurred by the taxpayer in the year

(*a*) that is a Canadian exploration expense incurred by a corporation after March 2019 and before 2025 (including, for greater certainty, an expense that is deemed by subsection 66(12.66) to be incurred before 2025) in conducting mining exploration activity from or above the surface of the earth for the purpose of determining the existence, location, extent or quality of a mineral resource described in paragraph (*a*) or (*d*) of the definition *mineral resource* in subsection 248(1),

(*b*) that

(i) is an expense described in paragraph (*f*) of the definition "Canadian exploration expense" in subsection 66.1(6), and

(ii) is not an expense in respect of

(A) trenching, if one of the purposes of the trenching is to carry out preliminary sampling (other than specified sampling),

(B) digging test pits (other than digging test pits for the purpose of carrying out specified sampling), and

(C) preliminary sampling (other than specified sampling),

(*c*) an amount in respect of which is renounced in accordance with subsection 66(12.6) by the corporation to the taxpayer (or a partnership of which the taxpayer is a member) under an agreement described in that subsection and made after March 2019 and before April 2024, and

(*d*) that is not an expense that was renounced under subsection 66(12.6) to the corporation (or a partnership of which the corporation is a member), unless that renunciation was under an agreement described in that subsection and made after March 2019 and before April 2024;

(*e*) (Repealed by S.C. 2003, c. 15, s. 81(2).)

History: S. 127(9), paragraph (*a*) of the definition "flow-through mining expenditure" was replaced by S.C. 2019, c. 29, s. 24(1), in respect of expenses renounced under a flow-through share agreement entered into after March 2019, and formerly read:

(*a*) that is a Canadian exploration expense incurred by a corporation after March 2018 and before 2020 (including, for greater certainty, an expense that is deemed by subsection 66(12.66) to be incurred before 2020) in conducting mining exploration activity from or above the surface of the earth for the purpose of determining the existence, location, extent or quality of a mineral resource described in paragraph (*a*) or (*d*) of the definition *mineral resource* in subsection 248(1),

S. 127(9), paragraphs (*c*) and (*d*) of the definition "flow-through mining expenditure" were replaced by S.C. 2019, c. 29, s. 24(2), in respect of expenses renounced under a flow-through share agreement entered into after March 2019, and formerly read:

(*c*) an amount in respect of which is renounced in accordance with subsection 66(12.6) by the corporation to the taxpayer (or a partnership of which the taxpayer is a member) under an agreement described in that subsection and made after March 2018 and before April 2019, and

(*d*) that is not an expense that was renounced under subsection 66(12.6) to the corporation (or a partnership of which the corporation is a member), unless that renunciation was under an agreement described in that subsection and made after March 2018 and before April 2019;

S. 127(9), paragraph (*a*) of the definition "flow-through mining expenditure" was replaced by S.C. 2018, c. 12, s. 21(1), applicable in respect of expenses renounced under a flow-through share agreement entered into after March 2018, and formerly read:

(*a*) that is a Canadian exploration expense incurred by a corporation after March 2017 and before 2019 (including, for greater certainty, an expense that is deemed by subsection 66(12.66) to be incurred before 2019) in conducting mining exploration activity from or above the surface of the earth for the purpose of determining the existence, location, extent or quality of a mineral resource described in paragraph (*a*) or (*d*) of the definition "mineral resource" in subsection 248(1),

S. 127(9), paragraphs (*c*) and (*d*) of the definition "flow-through mining expenditure" were replaced by S.C. 2018, c. 12, s. 21(2), applicable in respect of expenses renounced under a flow-through share agreement entered into after March 2018, and formerly read:

(*c*) an amount in respect of which is renounced in accordance with subsection 66(12.6) by the corporation to the taxpayer (or a partnership of which the taxpayer is a member) under an agreement described in that subsection and made after March 2017 and before April 2018, and

(*d*) that is not an expense that was renounced under subsection 66(12.6) to the corporation (or a partnership of which the corporation is a member), unless that renunciation was under an agreement described in that subsection and made after March 2017 and before April 2018;

S. 127(9), paragraph (*a*) of the definition "flow-through mining expenditure" was replaced by S.C. 2017, c. 20, s. 23(8), applicable to expenses renounced under a flow-through share agreement entered into after March 2017, and formerly read:

(*a*) that is a Canadian exploration expense incurred by a corporation after March 2016 and before 2018 (including, for greater certainty, an expense that is deemed by subsection 66(12.66) to be incurred before 2018) in conducting mining exploration activity from or above the surface of the earth for the purpose of determining the existence, location, extent or quality of a mineral resource described in paragraph (*a*) or (*d*) of the definition "mineral resource" in subsection 248(1),

S. 127(9), paragraphs (*c*) and (*d*) of the definition "flow-through mining expenditure" were replaced by S.C. 2017, c. 20, s. 23(9), applicable to expenses renounced under a flow-through share agreement entered into after March 2017, and formerly read:

(*c*) an amount in respect of which is renounced in accordance with subsection 66(12.6) by the corporation to the taxpayer (or a partnership of which the taxpayer is a member) under an agreement described in that subsection and made after March 2016 and before April 2017, and

(*d*) that is not an expense that was renounced under subsection 66(12.6) to the corporation (or a partnership of which the corporation is a member), unless that renunciation was under an agreement described in that subsection and made after March 2016 and before April 2017;

S. 127(9), paragraph (*a*) of the definition "flow-through mining expenditure" was replaced by S.C. 2016, c. 7, s. 35(1), applicable to expenses renounced under a flow-through share agreement entered into after March 2016, and formerly read:

(*a*) that is a Canadian exploration expense incurred by a corporation after March 2015 and before 2017 (including, for greater certainty, an expense that is deemed by subsection 66(12.66) to be incurred before 2017) in conducting mining exploration activity from or above the surface of the earth for the purpose of determining the existence, location, extent or quality of a mineral resource described in paragraph (*a*) or (*d*) of the definition "mineral resource" in subsection 248(1),

S. 127(9), paragraphs (*c*) and (*d*) of the definition "flow-through mining expenditure" were replaced by S.C. 2016, c. 7, s. 35(2), applicable to expenses renounced under a flow-through share agreement entered into after March 2016, and formerly read:

(*c*) an amount in respect of which is renounced in accordance with subsection 66(12.6) by the corporation to the taxpayer (or a partnership of which the taxpayer is a member) under an agreement described in that subsection and made after March 2015 and before April 2016, and

(*d*) that is not an expense that was renounced under subsection 66(12.6) to the corporation (or a partnership of which the corporation is a member), unless that renunciation was under an agreement described in that subsection and made after March 2015 and before April 2016;

S. 127(9), paragraph (*a*) of the definition "flow-through mining expenditure" was replaced by S.C. 2015, c. 36, s. 12(1), applicable to expenses renounced under a flow-through share agreement entered into after March 2015, and formerly read:

(*a*) that is a Canadian exploration expense incurred by a corporation after March 2014 and before 2016 (including, for greater certainty, an expense that is deemed by subsection 66(12.66) to be incurred before 2016) in conducting mining exploration activity from or above the surface of the earth for the purpose of determining the existence, location, extent or quality of a mineral resource described in paragraph (*a*) or (*d*) of the definition "mineral resource" in subsection 248(1),

S. 127(9), paragraphs (*c*) and (*d*) of the definition "flow-through mining expenditure" was replaced by S.C. 2015, c. 36, s. 12(2), applicable to expenses renounced under a flow-through share agreement entered into after March 2015, and formerly read:

(*c*) an amount in respect of which is renounced in accordance with subsection 66(12.6) by the corporation to the taxpayer (or a partnership of which the taxpayer is a member) under an agreement described in that subsection and made after March 2014 and before April 2015, and

(*d*) that is not an expense that was renounced under subsection 66(12.6) to the corporation (or a partnership of which the corporation is a member), unless that renunciation was under an agreement described in that subsection and made after March 2014 and before April 2015;

S. 127(9), paragraph (*a*) of the definition "flow-through mining expenditure" was replaced by S.C. 2014, c. 20, s. 18(1), applicable to expenses renounced under a flow-through share agreement entered into after March 2014, and formerly read:

(*a*) that is a Canadian exploration expense incurred by a corporation after March 2013 and before 2015 (including, for greater certainty, an expense that is deemed by subsection 66(12.66) to be incurred before 2015) in conducting mining exploration activity from or above the surface of the earth for the purpose of determining the existence, location, extent or quality of a mineral resource described in paragraph (*a*) or (*d*) of the definition "mineral resource" in subsection 248 (1),

S. 127(9), paragraphs (*c*) and (*d*) of the definition "flow-through mining expenditure" were replaced by S.C. 2014, c. 20, s. 18(2), applicable to expenses renounced under a flow-through share agreement entered into after March 2014, and formerly read:

(*c*) an amount in respect of which is renounced in accordance with subsection 66(12.6) by the corporation to the taxpayer (or a partnership of which the taxpayer is a member) under an agreement described in that subsection and made after March 2013 and before April 2014, and

(*d*) that is not an expense that was renounced under subsection 66(12.6) to the corporation (or a partnership of which the corporation is a member), unless that renunciation was under an agreement described in that subsection and made after March 2013 and before April 2014;

S. 127(9), paragraph (*a*) of the definition "flow-through mining expenditure" was replaced by S.C. 2013, c. 33, s. 14(1), applicable to expenses renounced under a flow-through share agreement entered into after March 2013, and formerly read:

(*a*) that is a Canadian exploration expense incurred by a corporation after March 2012 and before 2014 (including, for greater certainty, an expense that is deemed by subsection 66(12.66) to be incurred before 2014) in conducting mining exploration activity from or above the surface of the earth for the purpose of determining the existence, location, extent or quality of a mineral resource described in paragraph (*a*) or (*d*) of the definition "mineral resource" in subsection 248(1),

S. 127(9), paragraphs (*c*) and (*d*) of the definition "flow-through mining expenditure" were replaced by S.C. 2013, c. 33, s. 14(2), applicable to expenses renounced under a flow-through share agreement entered into after March 2013, and formerly read:

(*c*) an amount in respect of which is renounced in accordance with subsection 66(12.6) by the corporation to the taxpayer (or a partnership of which the taxpayer is a member) under an agreement described in that subsection and made after March 2012 and before April 2013, and

(*d*) that is not an expense that was renounced under subsection 66(12.6) to the corporation (or a partnership of which the corporation is a member), unless that renunciation was under an agreement described in that subsection and made after March 2012 and before April 2013;

S. 127(9), paragraph (*a*) of the definition "flow-through mining expenditure" was replaced by S.C. 2012, c. 19, s. 5(1), applicable to expenses renounced under a flow-through share agreement made after March 2012. S. 127(9), paragraph (*a*) of the definition "flow-through mining expenditure" formerly read:

(*a*) that is a Canadian exploration expense incurred by a corporation after March 2011 and before 2013 (including, for greater certainty, an expense that is deemed by subsection 66(12.66) to be incurred before 2013) in conducting mining exploration activity from or above the surface of the earth for the purpose of determining the existence, location, extent or quality of a mineral resource described in paragraph (*a*) or (*d*) of the definition "mineral resource" in subsection 248(1),

S. 127(9), paragraphs (*c*) and (*d*) of the definition "flow-through mining expenditure" were replaced by S.C. 2012, c. 19, s. 5(2), applicable to expenses renounced under a flow-through share agreement made after March 2012. S. 127(9), paragraphs (*c*) and (*d*) of the definition "flow-through mining expenditure" formerly read:

(*c*) an amount in respect of which is renounced in accordance with subsection 66(12.6) by the corporation to the taxpayer (or a partnership of which the taxpayer is a member) under an agreement described in that subsection and made after March 2011 and before April 2012, and

(*d*) that is not an expense that was renounced under subsection 66(12.6) to the corporation (or a partnership of which the corporation is a member), unless that renunciation was under an agreement described in that subsection and made after March 2011 and before April 2012;

S. 127(9), paragraph (*a*) of the definition "flow-through mining expenditure" was replaced by S.C. 2011, c. 24, s. 40(1), applicable to expenses renounced under a flow-through share agreement made after March 2011. S. 127(9), paragraph (*a*) of the definition "flow-through mining expenditure" formerly read:

(*a*) that is a Canadian exploration expense incurred by a corporation after March 2010 and before 2012 (including, for greater certainty, an expense that is deemed by subsection 66(12.66) to be incurred before 2012) in conducting mining exploration activity from or above the surface of the earth for the purpose of determining the existence, location, extent or quality of a mineral resource described in paragraph (*a*) or (*d*) of the definition "mineral resource" in subsection 248(1),

S. 127(9), paragraphs (*c*) and (*d*) of the definition "flow-through mining expenditure" were replaced by S.C. 2011, c. 24, s. 40(2), applicable to expenses renounced under a flow-through share agreement made after March 2011. S. 127(9), paragraphs (*c*) and (*d*) of the definition "flow-through mining expenditure" formerly read:

(*c*) an amount in respect of which is renounced in accordance with subsection 66(12.6) by the corporation to the taxpayer (or a partnership of which the taxpayer is a member) under an agreement described in that subsection and made after March 2010 and before April 2011, and

(*d*) that is not an expense that was renounced under subsection 66(12.6) to the corporation (or a partnership of which the corporation is a member), unless that renunciation was under an agreement described in that subsection and made after March 2010 and before April 2011;

S. 127(9), paragraph (*a*) of the definition "flow-through mining expenditure" was replaced by S.C. 2010, c. 12, s. 14(1), applicable to expenses renounced under a flow-through share agreement made after March 2010. S. 127(9), paragraph (*a*) of the definition "flow-through mining expenditure" formerly read:

(*a*) that is a Canadian exploration expense incurred by a corporation after March 2009 and before 2011 (including, for greater certainty, an expense that is deemed by subsection 66(12.66) to be incurred before 2011) in conducting mining exploration activity from or above the surface of the earth for the purpose of determining the existence, location, extent or quality of a mineral resource described in paragraph (*a*) or (*d*) of the definition "mineral resource" in subsection 248(1),

S. 127(9), paragraphs (*c*) and (*d*) of the definition "flow-through mining expenditure" were replaced by S.C. 2010, c. 12, s. 14(2), applicable to expenses renounced under a flow-through share agreement made after March 2010. S. 127(9), paragraphs (*c*) and (*d*) of the definition "flow-through mining expenditure" formerly read:

(*c*) an amount in respect of which is renounced in accordance with subsection 66(12.6) by the corporation to the taxpayer (or a partnership of which the taxpayer is a member) under an agreement described in that subsection and made after March 2009 and before April 2010, and

(*d*) that is not an expense that was renounced under subsection 66(12.6) to the corporation (or a partnership of which the corporation is a member), unless that renunciation was under an agreement described in that subsection and made after March 2009 and before April 2010;

S. 127(9), paragraph (*a*) of the definition "flow-through mining expenditure" was replaced by S.C. 2009, c. 2, s. 40(1), applicable to expenses renounced under a flow-through share agreement made after March 2009. S. 127(9), paragraph (*a*) of the definition "flow-through mining expenditure" formerly read:

(*a*) that is a Canadian exploration expense incurred by a corporation after March 2008 and before 2010 (including, for greater certainty, an expense that is deemed by subsection 66(12.66) to be incurred before 2010) in conducting mining exploration activity from or above the surface of the earth for the purpose of determining the existence, location, extent or quality of a mineral resource described in paragraph (*a*) or (*d*) of the definition "mineral resource" in subsection 248(1),

S. 127(9), paragraphs (*c*) and (*d*) of the definition "flow-through mining expenditure" were replaced by S.C. 2009, c. 2, s. 40(2), applicable to expenses renounced under a flow-through share agreement made after March 2009. S. 127(9), paragraphs (*c*) and (*d*) of the definition "flow-through mining expenditure" formerly read:

(*c*) an amount in respect of which is renounced in accordance with subsection 66(12.6) by the corporation to the taxpayer (or a partnership of which the taxpayer is a member) under an agreement described in that subsection and made after March 2008 and before April 2009, and

(*d*) that is not an expense that was renounced under subsection 66(12.6) to the corporation (or a partnership of which the corporation is a member), unless that renunciation was under an agreement described in that subsection and made after March 2008 and before April 2009;

Related Sections: S. 127(9), "investment tax credit"; s. 127(11.1)(*c.2*) Investment tax credit.

"Gaspé Peninsula" —"Gaspé Peninsula" means that portion of the Gaspé region of the Province of Quebec that extends to the western border of Kamouraska County and includes the Magdalen Islands;

Tax Window Files: Investment Tax Credits — Borders of Gaspe Peninsula, *Technical Interpretation, Business and Partnerships Division, April 20, 2005*, CRA Document No. 2004-0101461E5.

"government assistance" —"government assistance" means assistance from a government, municipality or other public authority whether as a grant, subsidy, forgivable loan, deduction from tax, investment allowance or as any other form of assistance other than as a deduction under subsection (5) or (6);

Related Sections: s. 12(1)(*x*) Inducement, reimbursement, etc.; s. 248(16) Goods and services tax — input tax credit and rebate; s. 248(16.1) Goods and services tax — input tax credit and rebate; s. 248(18) Goods and services tax — input tax credit and rebate; s. 248(18.1) Repayment of Quebec input tax refund.

SR&ED Publications: Assistance and Contract Payments Policy.

Tax Window Files: SR&ED Government Assistance, *Advance Income Tax Ruling, Financial Sector and Exempt Entities Division, May 3, 2007*, CRA Document No. 2007-0224191E5; Scientific Research and Experimental Development — Government Assistance, *Technical Interpretation, Reorganizations and Resources Division, December 23, 2004*, CRA Document No. 2004-0095621I7.

Cases: When the Coal Research Agreement between the taxpayer and the Province of Alberta required Alberta to sell its equity interest in the project to the taxpayer if it became commercially successful, the $725,000 payment made to the taxpayer constituted some form of government assistance considering that Alberta did not have an ordinary business interest in the project. *The Queen v. CCLC Technologies Inc.*, 96 DTC 6527 (F.C.A.), reversing 95 DTC 5685 (T.C.C.)

"investment tax credit" —"investment tax credit" of a taxpayer at the end of a taxation year means the amount, if any, by which the total of (*a*) the total of all amounts each of which is the specified percentage of the capital cost to the taxpayer of qualified property or qualified resource property acquired by the taxpayer in the year,

(*a*.1) 15% of the amount by which the taxpayer's SR&ED qualified expenditure pool at the end of the year exceeds the total of all amounts each of which is the super-allowance benefit amount for the year in respect of the taxpayer in respect of a province,

(*a*.2) where the taxpayer is an individual (other than a trust), 15% of the taxpayer's flow-through mining expenditures for the year,

(*a*.3) if the taxpayer is a taxable Canadian corporation, the total of

(i) the specified percentage of the portion of the taxpayer's pre-production mining expenditure described in subparagraph (*a*)(i) of the definition "pre-production mining expenditure", and

(ii) the specified percentage of the portion of the taxpayer's pre-production mining expenditure described in subparagraph (*a*)(ii) of the definition "pre-production mining expenditure",

(*a*.4) the total of all amounts each of which is an apprenticeship expenditure of the taxpayer for the taxation year in respect of an eligible apprentice,

(*a*.5) (Repealed by S.C. 2017, c. 20, s. 23(10).)

(*b*) the total of amounts required by subsection (7) or (8) to be added in computing the taxpayer's investment tax credit at the end of the year,

(*c*) the total of all amounts each of which is an amount determined under any of paragraphs (*a*) to (*b*) in respect of the taxpayer for any of the 10 taxation years immediately preceding or the 3 taxation years immediately following the year,

(*d*) (Repealed by S.C. 2006, c. 4, s. 75(1).)

(*e*) the total of all amounts each of which is an amount required by subsection (10.1) to be added in computing the taxpayer's investment tax credit at the end of the year or at the end of any of the 10 taxation years immediately preceding or the 3 taxation years immediately following the year,

(*e*.1) the total of all amounts each of which is the specified percentage of that part of a repayment made by the taxpayer in the year or in any of the 10 taxation years immediately preceding or the 3 taxation years immediately following the year that can reasonably be considered to be a repayment of government assistance, non-government assistance or a contract payment that reduced

(i) the capital cost to the taxpayer of a property under paragraph (11.1)(*b*),

(ii) the amount of a qualified expenditure incurred by the taxpayer under paragraph (11.1)(*c*) for taxation years that began before 1996,

(iii) the prescribed proxy amount of the taxpayer under paragraph (11.1)(*f*) for taxation years that began before 1996,

(iv) a qualified expenditure incurred by the taxpayer under any of subsections (18) to (20),

(v) the amount of a pre-production mining expenditure of the taxpayer under paragraph (11.1)(*c*.3), or

(vi) the amount of eligible salary and wages payable by the taxpayer to an eligible apprentice under paragraph (11.1)(*c*.4), to the extent that that reduction had the effect of reducing the amount of an apprenticeship expenditure of the taxpayer, and

(vii) (Repealed by S.C. 2017, c. 20, s. 23(11).)

(*e*.2) the total of all amounts each of which is the specified percentage of 1/4 of that part of a repayment made by the taxpayer in the year or in any of the 10 taxation years immediately preceding or the 3 taxation years immediately following the year that can reasonably be considered to be a repayment of government assistance, non-government assistance or a contract payment that reduced

(i) the amount of a qualified expenditure incurred by the taxpayer under paragraph (11.1)(*e*) for taxation years that began before 1996, or

(ii) a qualified expenditure incurred by the taxpayer under any of subsections (18) to (20),

in respect of first term shared-use-equipment or second term shared-use-equipment, and, for that purpose, a repayment made by the taxpayer in any taxation year preceding the first taxation year that ends coincidentally with the first period or the second period in respect of first term shared-use-equipment or second term shared-use-equipment, respectively, is deemed to have been incurred by the taxpayer in that first taxation year,

exceeds the total of

(*f*) the total of all amounts each of which is an amount deducted under subsection (5) from the tax otherwise payable under this Part by the taxpayer for a preceding taxation year in respect of property acquired, or an expenditure incurred, in the year or in any of the 10 taxation years immediately preceding or the 2 taxation years immediately following the year, or in respect of the taxpayer's SR&ED qualified expenditure pool at the end of such a year,

(*g*) the total of all amounts each of which is an amount required by subsection (6) to be deducted in computing the taxpayer's investment tax credit

(i) at the end of the year, or

(ii) (Repealed by S.C. 1996, c. 21, s. 30(15).)

(iii) at the end of any of the 9 taxation years immediately preceding or the 3 taxation years immediately following the year, (*h*) the total of all amounts each of which is an amount required by subsection (7) to be deducted in computing the taxpayer's investment tax credit

(i) at the end of the year, or

(ii) (Repealed by S.C. 1996, c. 21, s. 30(16).)

(iii) at the end of any of the 10 taxation years immediately preceding or the 3 taxation years immediately following the year,

(*i*) the total of all amounts each of which is an amount claimed under subparagraph 192(2)(*a*)(ii) by the taxpayer for the year or a preceding taxation year in respect of property acquired, or an expenditure made, in the year or the 10 taxation years immediately preceding the year,

(*j*) if the taxpayer is subject to a loss restriction event at any time before the end of the year, the amount determined under subsection (9.1) in respect of the taxpayer, and

(*k*) if the taxpayer is subject to a loss restriction event at any time after the end of the year, the amount determined under subsection (9.2) in respect of the taxpayer,

except that no amount shall be included in the total determined under any of paragraphs (*a*) to (*e*.2) in respect of an outlay, expense or expenditure that would, if this Act were read without reference to subsections (26) and 78(4), be made or incurred by the taxpayer in the course of earning income in a particular taxation year, and no amount shall be added under paragraph (*b*) in computing the taxpayer's investment tax credit at the end of a particular taxation year in respect of an outlay, expense or expenditure made or incurred by a trust or a partnership in the course of earning income, if

(*l*) any of the income is exempt income or is exempt from tax under this Part,

(*m*) the taxpayer does not file with the Minister a prescribed form containing prescribed information in respect of the amount on or before the day that is one year after the taxpayer's filing-due date for the particular year;

Editorial Note: The investment tax credit in respect of SR&ED (paragraph (a.1)) is 20% for taxation years ending before 2013, 15% thereafter, and prorated for taxation years that straddle the 2012 calendar year end. The credit rate in respect of qualified property (paragraph (*a*)) used in oil and gas and mining activities is reduced from 10% to 5% for property acquired in 2014 and 2015, and is eliminated for property acquired after 2015 (with some transitional relief; see paragraph (*a*.1) of the definition of "specified percentage" in subsection 127(9)). The credit rate for pre-production mining expenditures described in subparagraph (*a*.3)(i) is reduced from 10% to 5% for expenditures incurred in 2013, and is eliminated for expenditures after 2013. The credit rate for pre-production mining expenditures described in subparagraph (*a*.3)(ii) is reduced from 10% to 7% for expenditures incurred in 2014, 4% for expenditures incurred in 2015, and is eliminated for expenditures after 2015 (with some transitional relief; see paragraph (*k*) in the definition of "specified percentage").

History: S. 127(9), paragraph (*a*.5) of the definition "investment tax credit" was repealed by S.C. 2017, c. 20, s. 23(10), applicable in respect of expenditures incurred after March 21, 2017, except that this amendment does not apply in respect of expenditures incurred before 2020 under a written agreement entered into before March 22, 2017. S. 127(9), paragraph (*a*.5) of the definition "investment tax credit" formerly read:

(*a*.5) the child care space amount of the taxpayer for the taxation year,

S. 127(9), subparagraph (*e*.1)(vii) of the definition "investment tax credit" was repealed by S.C. 2017, c. 20, s. 23(11), applicable in respect of expenditures incurred after March 21, 2017, except that this amendment does not apply in respect of expenditures incurred before 2020 under a written agreement entered into before March 22, 2017. S. 127(9), subparagraph (*e*.1)(vii) of the definition "investment tax credit" formerly read:

(vii) the amount of an eligible child care space expenditure of the taxpayer under paragraph (11.1)(*c*.5), to the extent that that reduction had the effect of reducing the amount of a child care space amount of the taxpayer, and

S. 127(9), paragraphs (*j*) and (*k*) of the definition "investment tax credit" were replaced by S.C. 2013, c. 40, s. 57(2), deemed to have come into force on March 21, 2013, and formerly read:

(*j*) where the taxpayer is a corporation control of which has been acquired by a person or group of persons at any time before the end of the year, the amount determined under subsection (9.1) in respect of the taxpayer, and

(*k*) where the taxpayer is a corporation control of which has been acquired by a person or group of persons at any time after the end of the year, the amount determined under subsection (9.2) in respect of the taxpayer;

S. 127(9), paragraph (*a*) of the definition "investment tax credit" were replaced by S.C. 2012, c. 31, s. 27(4), applicable to taxation years ending after March 28, 2012. S. 127(9), paragraph (*a*) of the definition "investment tax credit" formerly read:

(*a*) the total of all amounts each of which is the specified percentage of the capital cost to the taxpayer of certified property or qualified property acquired by the taxpayer in the year,

S. 127(9), paragraph (*a*.1) of the definition "investment tax credit" was replaced by S.C. 2012, c. 31, s. 27(5), applicable to taxation years that end after 2013, except that for taxation years that include January 1, 2014, the reference to "15%" in paragraph (*a.1*) of the definition "investment tax credit" in subsection 127(9) is to be read as a reference to the percentage that is the total of

(i) 20% multiplied by the proportion that the number of days that are in the taxation year and before 2014 is of the number of days in the taxation year, and

(ii) 15% multiplied by the proportion that the number of days that are in the taxation year and after 2013 is of the number of days in the taxation year.

S. 127(9), paragraph (*a*.1) of the definition "investment tax credit" formerly read:

(*a*.1) 20% of the amount by which the taxpayer's SR&ED qualified expenditure pool at the end of the year exceeds the total of all amounts each of which is the super-allowance benefit amount for the year in respect of the taxpayer in respect of a province,

S. 127(9), paragraph (*a*.3) of the definition "investment tax credit" was replaced by S.C. 2012, c. 31, s. 27(6), applicable to taxation years ending after March 28, 2012. S. 127(9), paragraph (*a*.3) of the definition "investment tax credit" formerly read:

(*a*.3) where the taxpayer is a taxable Canadian corporation, the specified percentage of the taxpayer's pre-production mining expenditure for the year,

Related Sections: S. 37(10) Time for election; s. 87(2)(*qq*) Continuation of corporation; s. 87(2.11) Vertical amalgamations; s. 88(1)(*e*.3) Winding-up; s. 127(7) Investment tax credit of testamentary trust; s. 127(8) Investment tax credit of partnership; 127(9.01) Transitional application of investment tax credit definition; 127(9.02) Transitional application of investment tax credit definition; s. 127(9.1) Loss restriction event before end of year; s. 127(9.2) Loss restriction event after end of year; s. 127(10.1) Additions to investment tax credit; s. 127(10.8) Further additions to investment tax credit; s. 127(11.1) Investment tax credit; s. 127(11.2) Time of expenditure and acquisition; s. 127(26) Unpaid amounts; 127(27) Recapture of investment tax credit; 127(28) Recapture of investment tax credit of partnership; 127(29) Recapture of investment tax credit of allocating taxpayer; s. 127.1 Refundable investment tax credit; s. 220(2.2); s. 248(1), "investment tax credit".

Tax Topics: No. 1844, SR&ED Investment Tax Credit Claims: Making the CRA's Revised Procedures Work; No. 1824, Stamping of Hand-Delivered Mail at CRA Local Offices — SR&ED Implications.

Information Circulars: IC 78-4R3 Investment tax credit rates.

SR&ED Publications: SR&ED Filing Requirements Policy; Total Qualified SR&ED Expenditures for Investment Tax Credit Purposes Policy; SR&ED Investment Tax Credit Policy.

Tax Window Files: Scientific Research and Experimental Development — Activities Performed on Behalf of Foreign Corporation, *2005 APFF Confer-*

ence — Round Table on Federal Taxation, Question 7, October 7, 2005, CRA Document No. 2005-0140991C6; Investment Tax Credits — Borders of Gaspe Peninsula, *Technical Interpretation, Business and Partnerships Division, April 20, 2005,* CRA Document No. 2004-0101461E5; Investment Tax Credits — Carryback Denial After Wind-Up, *Technical Interpretation, Reorganizations and Resources Division, June 1, 2004,* CRA Document No. 2004-0078161I7.

Cases: The taxpayer, who operates a restaurant chain, was denied an ITC claim in respect of its buildings. Although the word "processing" does not exclude the preparation of food, the buildings were not being used "primarily" for processing. The most important factor was the portion of the building that was dedicated to processing, although other factors could be considered. *Burger King Restaurants of Canada Inc. v. The Queen,* 2000 DTC 6061 (F.C.A.), affirming 97 DTC 841 (T.C.C.)

The taxpayer's activities involving the replacement of parts of a customer's hydraulic systems with parts it itself manufactured did not constitute the manufacture of goods for sale since, in common law, "for sale" does not mean "for use in a repair process" and manufacture of parts to be used to repair a customer's defective equipment is not tantamount to manufacturing those parts for sale. *The Queen v. Coopers & Lybrand Ltd.,* 94 DTC 6541 (F.C.A), reversing 92 DTC 6453 (F.C.T.D.)

The taxpayer was involved in a SR&ED project but derived income from the sale of its experimental production of oysters. Considering the Minister's admission that 80% of the taxpayer's current expenditures qualified as SR&ED expenditures, he could not say that the "commercial production" stage had been reached. *Cultures Laflamme (1984) Inc. v. M.N.R.,* 93 DTC 603 (T.C.C.)

"non-government assistance" —"non-government assistance" means an amount that would be included in income under paragraph 12(1)(*x*) if that paragraph were read without reference to subparagraphs 12(1)(*x*)(v) to (vii);

History: S. 127(9), the definition of "non-government assistance", was replaced by S.C. 2013, c. 40, s. 57(1), deemed to have come into force on December 12, 2012, and formerly read:

"non-government assistance" —"non-government assistance" means an amount that would be included in income by virtue of paragraph 12(1)(*x*) if that paragraph were read without reference to subparagraphs 12(1)(*x*)(vi) and (vii);

SR&ED Publications: Assistance and Contract Payments Policy.

"non-qualifying corporation" —"non-qualifying corporation" at any time means

(*a*) a corporation that is, at that time, not a Canadian-controlled private corporation,

(*b*) a corporation that would be liable to pay tax under Part I.3 for the taxation year of the corporation that includes that time if that Part were read without reference to subsection 181.1(4) and if the amount determined under subsection 181.2(3) in respect of the corporation for the year were determined without reference to amounts described in any of paragraphs 181.2(3)(*a*), (*b*), (*d*) and (*f*) to the extent that the amounts so described were used to acquire property that would be qualified small-business property if the corporation were not a non-qualifying corporation, or

(*c*) a corporation that at that time is related for the purposes of section 181.5 to a corporation described in paragraph (*b*);

Related Sections: S. 181.5(7) Related corporations that are not associated.

"phase" —"phase", of a project, means a discrete expansion in the extraction, processing or production capacity of the project of a taxpayer beyond a capacity level that was attained before March 29, 2012 and which expansion in capacity was the taxpayer's demonstrated intention immediately before that date;

History: S. 127(9), the definition "phase" was added by S.C. 2012, c. 31, s. 27(18), deemed to have come into force on March 29, 2012.

"pre-production mining expenditure" —"pre-production mining expenditure", of a taxable Canadian corporation for a taxation year, means the total of all amounts each of which is an expenditure incurred after 2002 by the taxable Canadian corporation in the taxation year that

(*a*) is a Canadian exploration expense and would be

(i) described in paragraph (*f*) of the definition "Canadian exploration expense" in subsection 66.1(6) if the expression "mineral resource" in that paragraph were defined to mean a mineral deposit from which the principal mineral to be extracted is diamond, a base or precious metal deposit, or a mineral deposit from which the principal mineral to be extracted is an industrial mineral that, when refined, results in a base or precious metal, or

(ii) described in paragraph (*g*), (*g.3*) or (*g.4*) and not in paragraph (*f*), of the definition "Canadian exploration expense" in subsection 66.1(6) if the expression "mineral resource" in paragraph (*g*) of that definition were defined to mean a mineral deposit from which the principal mineral to be extracted is diamond, a base or precious metal deposit, or a mineral deposit from which the principal mineral to be extracted is an industrial mineral that, when refined, results in a base or precious metal, and

(*b*) is not an expense that

(i) was renounced under subsection 66(12.6) to the taxable Canadian corporation except if the corporation is, on the effective date of the renunciation,

(A) a corporation that would be a "principal business corporation", as defined in subsection 66(15), if that definition were read without reference to its paragraphs (*a*), (*a.1*), (*f*), (*h*) and (*i*), and

(B) the sole shareholder of the corporation that renounced the expenditure, or

(ii) is a member's share of an expense incurred by a partnership unless the expense was deemed by subsection 66(18) to have been made or incurred at the end of the fiscal period of the partnership by the member and throughout the fiscal period of the partnership in which the expense was incurred

(A) each member of the partnership would (otherwise than because of being a member of the partnership) be a "principal-business corporation" as defined in subsection 66(15) of the Act, if that definition were read without reference to its paragraphs (*a*), (*a.1*), (*f*), (*h*) and (*i*), and

(B) the corporation is a member of the partnership at the time the expenditure is incurred and would not be a specified member of the partnership if the definition "specified member" in subsection 248(1) were read without reference to its subparagraph (*b*)(ii),

History: S. 127(9), the definition "pre-production mining expenditure" was amended by S.C. 2017, c. 33, s. 50(1), by adding "or" at the end of subparagraph (*a*)(i), deemed in force on March 21, 2013.

S. 127(9), subparagraph (*a*)(ii) of the definition "pre-production mining expenditure" was replaced by S.C. 2013, c. 40, s. 57(3), deemed to have come into force on March 21, 2013, and formerly read:

(ii) described in paragraph (*g*), and not in paragraph (*f*), of the definition "Canadian exploration expense" in subsection 66.1(6) if the expression "mineral resource" in paragraph (*g*) were defined to mean a mineral deposit from which the principal mineral to be extracted is diamond, a base or precious metal deposit, or a mineral deposit from which the principal mineral to be extracted is an industrial mineral that, when refined, results in a base or precious metal, and

S. 127(9), paragraph (*b*) of the definition "pre-production mining expenditure" was replaced by S.C. 2013, c. 34, s. 269(9), applicable to the 2003 and subsequent taxation years, and formerly read:

(*b*) is not an expense that was renounced under subsection 66(12.6) to the taxable Canadian corporation;

S. 127(9), paragraph (*a*) of the definition "pre-production mining expenditure" was replaced by S.C. 2012, c. 31, s. 27(7), applicable in respect of expenditures incurred after March 28, 2012. S. 127(9), paragraph (*a*) of the definition "pre-production mining expenditure" formerly read:

(*a*) would be an expense described in paragraph (*f*) or (*g*) of the definition "Canadian exploration expense" in subsection 66.1(6) if the expression "mineral resource" in that paragraph were defined to mean a mineral deposit from which the principal mineral to be extracted is diamond, a base or precious metal deposit, or a mineral deposit from which the principal mineral to be extracted is an industrial mineral that, when refined, results in a base or precious metal, and

Related Sections: S. 127(9), "investment tax credit"; s. 127(11.1)(*c.3*) Investment tax credit.

"qualified Canadian exploration expenditure" — (Repealed by S.C. 1996, c. 21, s. 30(9).)

"qualified construction equipment" — (Repealed by S.C. 1996, c. 21, s. 30(9).)

"qualified expenditure" — "qualified expenditure" incurred by a taxpayer in a taxation year means

(*a*) an amount that is an expenditure incurred in the year by the taxpayer in respect of scientific research and experimental development and is

(i) an expenditure described in subparagraph 37(1)(*a*)(i), or

(ii) 80% of an expenditure described in any of subparagraphs 37(1)(*a*)(i.01) to (iii),

(iii) (Repealed by S.C. 2012, c. 31, s. 27(10).)

(iv) (Repealed by S.C. 2012, c. 31, s. 27(9).)

(*b*) a prescribed proxy amount of the taxpayer for the year,

but does not include

(*c*) a prescribed expenditure incurred in the year by the taxpayer,

(*d*) where the taxpayer is a corporation, an expenditure specified by the taxpayer for the year for the purpose of clause 194(2)(*a*)(ii)(A),

(*e*) (Repealed by S.C. 1998, c. 19, s. 33(2).)

(*f*) an expenditure (other than an expenditure that is salary or wages of an employee of the taxpayer) incurred by the taxpayer in respect of scientific research and experimental development to the extent that it is performed by another person or partnership at a time when the taxpayer and the person or partnership to which the expenditure is paid or payable do not deal with each other at arm's length,

(*g*) an expenditure described in paragraph 37(1)(*a*) that is paid or payable by the taxpayer to or for the benefit of a person or partnership that is not a taxable supplier in respect of the expenditure, other than an expenditure in respect of scientific research and experimental development directly undertaken by the taxpayer, and

(*h*) an amount that would otherwise be a qualified expenditure incurred by the taxpayer in the year to the extent of any reduction in respect of the amount that is required under any of subsections (18) to (20) to be applied;

Editorial Note: A taxpayer is entitled to a 15% or 35% investment tax credit in respect of qualified expenditures that are fully deductible under s. 37(1). If an expenditure is excluded under paragraph (*f*) of the definition "qualified expenditure" (i.e., because it was performed by a person not dealing at arm's length with the taxpayer), an election may be available under s. 127(13) to allow for the transfer of qualified expenditures between the non-arm's length taxpayers to qualify for a credit.

A qualified expenditure does not include a capital expenditure made after 2013 (see also the editorial note to subsection 37(1)). Effective for payments after 2012, only 80% of payments made to arm's length third parties to conduct SR&ED (described in subparagraphs 37(1)(*a*)(i.01) to 37(1)(*a*)(iii)) are qualified expenditures.

The prescribed proxy percentage (paragraph (*b*) and Regulation 2900(4)) is 55%, reduced from 60% for 2013 and 65% previously, with pro-rating for taxation years that straddle the end of the calendar 2012, 2013, and 2014 years.

History: S. 127(9), subparagraph (*a*)(iii) of the definition "qualified expenditure", was repealed by S.C. 2012, c. 31, s. 27(10), in force February 1, 2017, and formerly read:

(iii) an expenditure for first term shared-use-equipment or second term shared-use-equipment;

S. 127(9), paragraphs (*a*) and (*b*) of the definition "qualified expenditure" were replaced by S.C. 2012, c. 31, s. 27(8), applicable in respect of expenditures made after 2012. S. 127(9), paragraphs (*a*) and (*b*) of the definition "qualified expenditure" formerly read:

(*a*) an amount that is an expenditure incurred in the year by the taxpayer in respect of scientific research and experimental development that is an expenditure

(i) for first term shared-use-equipment or second term shared-use-equipment,

(ii) described in paragraph 37(1)(*a*), or

(iii) described in subparagraph 37(1)(*b*)(i), or

(*b*) a prescribed proxy amount of the taxpayer for the year (which, for the purpose of paragraph (*e*), is deemed to be an amount incurred in the year),

S. 127(9), subparagraph (*a*)(iv) of the definition "qualified expenditure", was repealed by S.C. 2012, c. 31, s. 27(9), applicable in respect of expenditures made after 2013. S. 127(9), subparagraph (*a*)(iv) of the definition "qualified expenditure" formerly read:

(iv) an expenditure described in subparagraph 37(1)(*b*)(i), or

Related Regulations: 2900(4) [Calculation of prescribed proxy amount]; 2900(5) [All or substantially all salaries or wages]; 2900(6) [Maximum prescribed proxy amount]; 2900(7) [Restrictions for specified employees]; 2900(8) [Specified employee employed by an associated corporation]; 2900(9) [Exclusions to salary base]; 2900(10) [Deemed associated corporation]; 2902.

Related Sections: S. 12(1)(*e*) Reserves for certain goods and services, etc.; s. 18(9)(*e*) Limitation respecting prepaid expenses; s. 37(1) Scientific research and experimental development; 127(11.5) Adjustments to qualified expenditures; 127(11.6) Non-arm's length costs; 127(13) Agreement to transfer qualified expenditures; 127(14) Identification of amounts transferred; 127(15) Invalid agreements; 127(16) Non-arm's length parties; 127(18)

Reduction of qualified expenditures; 127(19) Reduction of qualified expenditures; 127(20) Agreement to allocate; 127(21) Failure to allocate; 127(22) Invalid agreements; 127(23) Partnership's taxation year; 127(24) Exclusion from qualified expenditure; S. 143.3 Expenditures — Limitations.

Tax Profile: March 2006 — Some Tax Considerations for Investing in Silicon Valley North.

Tax Topics: No. 1830, The CRA's Revised Position on SR&ED Contracts; No. 1767, Draft Legislation Overrides Alcatel — Affects SR&ED ITCs and More.

Information Circulars: IC 78-4R3 Investment tax credit rates.

SR&ED Publications: SR&ED Filing Requirements Policy; Contract Expenditures for SR&ED Performed on Behalf of a Claimant Policy; SR&ED Capital Expenditures Policy; Total Qualified SR&ED Expenditures for Investment Tax Credit Purposes Policy; Assistance and Contract Payments Policy.

Tax Window Files: ITCs — Non-Arm's Length Lease of Used Equipment, *Technical Interpretation, Business and Partnerships Division, February 15, 2007*, CRA Document No. 2006-0206761I7; Scientific Research and Experimental Development — Employee Stock Options, *2005 APFF Conference — Round Table on Federal Taxation, Question 24, October 7, 2005*, CRA Document No. 2005-0141141C6.

Cases: SR&ED deductions for salaries paid to employees engaged in SR&ED extends to bonuses paid to them, unless they are "specified employees", which "C" was not. C's activities related entirely to the management of the taxpayer's SR&ED activities carried on at its research centre, and reassessment was ordered on the basis that 55% and 40% of his remuneration for 2010 and 2011, respectively, constituted deductible SR&ED expenses free of any "specified employee" restriction and qualified fully for the related investment tax credits. *Oldcastle v. The Queen*, 2016 DTC 1159 (CCI)

Stock option benefits provided by the taxpayer to its employees, who were engaged in SR&ED, were "salary or wages" and therefore qualified expenditures. *Alcatel Canada Inc. v. The Queen*, 2005 DTC 387 (T.C.C.)

"qualified property" — "qualified property", of a taxpayer, means property (other than a qualified resource property) that is

(*a*) a prescribed building to the extent that it is acquired by the taxpayer after June 23, 1975,

(*b*) prescribed machinery and equipment acquired by the taxpayer after June 23, 1975, or

(*b*.1) prescribed energy generation and conservation property acquired by the taxpayer after March 28, 2012,

that has not been used, or acquired for use or lease, for any purpose whatever before it was acquired by the taxpayer and that is

(*c*) to be used by the taxpayer in Canada primarily for the purpose of

(i) manufacturing or processing goods for sale or lease,

(ii) farming or fishing,

(iii) logging,

(iv) storing grain, or

(v) harvesting peat,

(vi) (Repealed by S.C. 2012, c. 31, s. 27(13).)

(vii) (Repealed by S.C. 2012, c. 31, s. 27(13).)

(viii) (Repealed by S.C. 2012, c. 31, s. 27(13).)

(ix) (Repealed by S.C. 2012, c. 31, s. 27(13).)

(x) (Repealed by S.C. 2012, c. 31, s. 27(13).)

(xi) (Repealed by S.C. 2012, c. 31, s. 27(13).)

(xii) (Repealed by S.C. 2012, c. 31, s. 27(13).)

(xiii) (Repealed by S.C. 2012, c. 31, s. 27(13).)

(*c*.1) property (other than property described in paragraph (*b*.1)) to be used by the taxpayer in Canada primarily for the purpose of producing or processing electrical energy or steam in a prescribed area, if

(i) all or substantially all of the energy or steam

(A) is used by the taxpayer for the purpose of gaining or producing income from a business (other than the business of selling the product of the particular property), or

(B) is sold directly (or indirectly by way of sale to a provincially regulated power utility operating in the prescribed area) to a person related to the taxpayer, and

(ii) the energy or steam is used by the taxpayer or the person related to the taxpayer primarily for the purpose of manufacturing or processing goods in the prescribed area for sale or lease, or

(*d*) to be leased by the taxpayer to a lessee (other than a person exempt from tax under this Part because of section 149) who can reasonably be expected to use the property in Canada primarily for any of the purposes referred to in paragraph (*c*), but this paragraph does not apply to property that is prescribed for the purposes of paragraph (*b*) or (*b.1*) unless

(i) the property is leased in the ordinary course of carrying on a business in Canada by a corporation whose principal business is leasing property, lending money, purchasing conditional sales contracts, accounts receivable, bills of sale, chattel mortgages or hypothecary claims on movables, bills of exchange or other obligations representing all or part of the sale price of merchandise or services, or any combination thereof,

(ii) the property is manufactured and leased in the ordinary course of carrying on business in Canada by a corporation whose principal business is manufacturing property that it sells or leases,

(iii) the property is leased in the ordinary course of carrying on business in Canada by a corporation whose principal business is selling or servicing property of that type, or

(iv) the property is a fishing vessel, including the furniture, fittings and equipment attached to it, leased by an individual (other than a trust) to a corporation, controlled by the individual, that carries on a fishing business in connection with one or more commercial fishing licences issued by the Government of Canada to the individual,

and, for the purpose of this definition, "Canada" includes the offshore region prescribed for the purpose of the definition "specified percentage";

History: S. 127(9), the portion of the definition "qualified property" before paragraph (*a*) was replaced by S.C. 2012, c. 31, s. 27(11), applicable in respect of property acquired after March 28, 2012. S. 127(9), the portion of the definition "qualified property" before paragraph (*a*) formerly read:

"qualified property"—"qualified property" of a taxpayer means property (other than an approved project property or a certified property) that is

S. 127(9), paragraph (*b*.1) of the definition "qualified property" was added by S.C. 2012, c. 31, s. 27(12), applicable in respect of property acquired after March 28, 2012.

S. 127(9), subparagraphs (*c*)(iv) to (xiii) of the definition "qualified property" were replaced by S.C. 2012, c. 31, s. 27(13), applicable in respect of property acquired after March 28, 2012. S. 127(9), subparagraphs (*c*)(iv) to (xiii) of the definition "qualified property" formerly read:

(iv) operating an oil or gas well or extracting petroleum or natural gas from a natural accumulation of petroleum or natural gas,

(v) extracting minerals from a mineral resource,

(vi) processing

(A) ore (other than iron ore or tar sands ore) from a mineral resource to any stage that is not beyond the prime metal stage or its equivalent,

(B) iron ore from a mineral resource to any stage that is not beyond the pellet stage or its equivalent, or

(C) tar sands ore from a mineral resource to any stage that is not beyond the crude oil stage or its equivalent,

(vii) producing industrial minerals,

(viii) processing heavy crude oil recovered from a natural reservoir in Canada to a stage that is not beyond the crude oil stage or its equivalent,

(ix) Canadian field processing,

(x) exploring or drilling for petroleum or natural gas,

(xi) prospecting or exploring for or developing a mineral resource,

(xii) storing grain, or

(xiii) harvesting peat,

S. 127(9), the portion of paragraph (*c*.1) of the definition "qualified property" before subparagraph (i) was replaced by S.C. 2012, c. 31, s. 27(14), applicable in respect of property acquired after March 28, 2012. S. 127(9), the portion of paragraph (*c*.1) of the definition "qualified property" before subparagraph (i) formerly read:

(*c*.1) to be used by the taxpayer in Canada primarily for the purpose of producing or processing electrical energy or steam in a prescribed area, where

S. 127(9), the portion of paragraph (*d*) of the definition "qualified property" before subparagraph (i) was replaced by S.C. 2012, c. 31, s. 27(15), applicable in respect of property acquired after March 28, 2012. S. 127(9), the portion of paragraph (*d*) of the definition "qualified property" before subparagraph (i) formerly read:

(*d*) to be leased by the taxpayer to a lessee (other than a person exempt from tax under this Part because of section 149) who can reasonably be expected to use the property in Canada primarily for any of the purposes referred to in subparagraphs (*c*)(i) to (xiii), but this paragraph does not apply to property that is prescribed for the purpose of paragraph (*b*) unless use of the property by the first person to whom it was leased began after June 23, 1975 and

Related Regulations: 4600(1); 4600(2); 4610.

Related Sections: S. 127(11) Interpretation; s. 248(1), "Canadian field processing.

Canadian Petroleum Tax Journal: Offshore Oil & Gas Interests: A Perspective on Exploration & Development of Offshore Petroleum and Natural Gas Resources in Eastern Canada, Michael R. Smith, CA and B. David Nielsen, CA, 2000, Vol. 13, No. 1.

Canadian Tax Foundation: Whalen, *When Is Fishing Considered To Be "in Canada"?*, 2017 Canadian Tax Focus 7(3):13.

Income Tax Folios: *Primary* — S3-F8-C2 Tax Incentives for Clean Energy Equipment. S4-F15-C1 Manufacturing and Processing.

Tax Window Files: Investment Tax Credit — Logging Truck, *Technical Interpretation, Reorganizations and Resources Division, November 29, 2005*, CRA Document No. 2005-0130101I7; Investment Tax Credit — Improvements to a Dry Kiln, *Technical Interpretation, Business and Partnerships Division, June 23, 2005*, CRA Document No. 2005-0118191I7.

Cases: A taxpayer was not entitled to the M&P tax credit and ITCs it had claimed in respect of an asphalt plant which had been acquired primarily for the purpose of producing asphalt for use in its paving contracts, which were essentially contracts for work and materials. *Will-Kare Paving & Contracting Limited v. The Queen*, 2000 DTC 6467 (S.C.C.), affirming 98 DTC 6203 (F.C.A.) and 97 DTC 506 (T.C.C.)

"qualified resource property" —"qualified resource property", of a taxpayer, means property that is a prescribed building or prescribed machinery and equipment, that is acquired by the taxpayer after March 28, 2012, that has not been used, or acquired for use or lease, for any purpose whatever before it was acquired by the taxpayer and that is

(*a*) to be used by the taxpayer in Canada primarily for the purpose of

(i) operating an oil or gas well or extracting petroleum or natural gas from a natural accumulation of petroleum or natural gas,

(ii) extracting minerals from a mineral resource,

(iii) processing

(A) ore (other than iron ore or tar sands ore) from a mineral resource to any stage that is not beyond the prime metal stage or its equivalent,

(B) iron ore from a mineral resource to any stage that is not beyond the pellet stage or its equivalent, or

(C) tar sands ore from a mineral resource to any stage that is not beyond the crude oil stage or its equivalent,

(iv) producing industrial minerals,

(v) processing heavy crude oil recovered from a natural reservoir in Canada to a stage that is not beyond the crude oil stage or its equivalent,

(vi) Canadian field processing,

(vii) exploring or drilling for petroleum or natural gas, or

(viii) prospecting or exploring for or developing a mineral resource, or

(*b*) to be leased by the taxpayer to a lessee (other than a person exempt from tax under this Part because of section 149) who can reasonably be expected to use the property in Canada primarily for any of the purposes referred to in paragraph (*a*), but this paragraph does not apply to prescribed machinery and equipment unless

(i) the property is leased in the ordinary course of carrying on a business in Canada by a corporation whose principal business is any of, or a combination of, leasing property, lending money, purchasing conditional sales contracts, accounts receivable, bills of sale, chattel mortgages or hypothecary claims on movables, bills of exchange or other obligations representing all or part of the sale price of merchandise or services,

(ii) the property is manufactured and leased in the ordinary course of carrying on business in Canada by a corporation whose principal business is manufacturing property that it sells or leases, or

(iii) the property is leased in the ordinary course of carrying on business in Canada by a corporation the principal business of which is selling or servicing property of that type,

and, for the purpose of this definition, "Canada" includes the offshore region prescribed for the purpose of the definition "specified percentage";

History: S. 127(9), the definition "qualified resource property" was added by S.C. 2012, c. 31, s. 27(18), deemed to have come into force on March 29, 2012.

"qualified small-business property" — (Repealed by S.C. 1996, c. 21, s. 30(9).)

"qualified transportation equipment" — (Repealed by S.C. 1996, c. 21, s. 30(9).)

"second term shared-use-equipment" —"second term shared-use-equipment" of a taxpayer means property of the taxpayer that was first term shared-use-equipment of the taxpayer and that is used by the taxpayer, during its operating time in the period (in this subsection and subsection (11.1) referred to as the "second period") beginning at the time the property was acquired by the taxpayer and ending at the end of the taxpayer's first taxation year ending at least 24 months after that time, primarily for the prosecution of scientific research and experimental development in Canada;

Related Sections: S. 88(1)(*e*.3) Winding-up; s. 127(11.5)(*b*) Adjustments to qualified expenditures.

SR&ED Publications: SR&ED Shared-Use-Equipment Policy; 2003-01, Capital Property Intended to be Used All or Substantially All for SR&ED.

"specified child care start-up expenditure" — (Repealed by S.C. 2017, c. 20, s. 23(7).)

History: S. 127(9), the definition "specified child care start-up expenditure" was repealed by S.C. 2017, c. 20, s. 23(7), applicable in respect of expenditures incurred after March 21, 2017, except that this amendment does not apply in respect of expenditures incurred before 2020 under a written agreement entered into before March 22, 2017. S. 127(9), the definition "specified child care start-up expenditure" formerly read:

"specified child care start-up expenditure" —"specified child care start-up expenditure" of a taxpayer in respect of a child care facility is an expenditure incurred by the taxpayer (other than to acquire a depreciable property) that is

(*a*) a landscaping cost incurred to create, at the child care facility, an outdoor play area for children,

(*b*) an architectural fee for designing the child care facility or a fee for advice on planning, designing and establishing the child care facility,

(*c*) a cost of construction permits in respect of the child care facility,

(*d*) an initial licensing or regulatory fee in respect of the child care facility, including fees for mandatory inspections,

(*e*) a cost of educational materials for children, or

(*f*) a similar amount incurred for the sole purpose of the initial establishment of the child care facility;

"specified percentage" —"specified percentage" means

(*a*) in respect of a qualified property

(i) acquired before April, 1977, 5%,

(ii) acquired after March 31, 1977 and before November 17, 1978 primarily for use in

(A) the Province of Nova Scotia, New Brunswick, Prince Edward Island or Newfoundland or the Gaspé Peninsula, 10%,

(B) a prescribed designated region, $7^1/_2$%, and

(C) any other area in Canada, 5%,

(iii) acquired primarily for use in the Province of Nova Scotia, New Brunswick, Prince Edward Island or Newfoundland or the Gaspé Peninsula,

(A) after November 16, 1978 and before 1989, 20%,

(B) after 1988 and before 1995, 15%,

(C) after 1994, 15% where the property

(I) is acquired by the taxpayer under a written agreement of purchase and sale entered into by the taxpayer before February 22, 1994,

(II) was under construction by or on behalf of the taxpayer on February 22, 1994, or

(III) is machinery or equipment that will be a fixed and integral part of property under construction by or on behalf of the taxpayer on February 22, 1994, and

(D) after 1994, 10% where the property is not property to which clause (C) applies,

(iv) acquired after November 16, 1978 and before February 26, 1986 primarily for use in a prescribed offshore region, 7%,

(v) acquired primarily for use in a prescribed offshore region and

(A) after February 25, 1986 and before 1989, 20%,

(B) after 1988 and before 1995, 15%,

(C) after 1994, 15% where the property

(I) is acquired by the taxpayer under a written agreement of purchase and sale entered into by the taxpayer before February 22, 1994,

(II) was under construction by or on behalf of the taxpayer on February 22, 1994, or

(III) is machinery or equipment that will be a fixed and integral part of property under construction by or on behalf of the taxpayer on February 22, 1994, and

(D) after 1994, 10% where the property is not property to which clause (C) applies,

(vi) acquired primarily for use in a prescribed designated region and

(A) after November 16, 1978 and before 1987, 10%,

(B) in 1987, 7%,

(C) in 1988, 3%, and

(D) after 1988, 0%, and

(vii) acquired primarily for use in Canada (other than a property described in subparagraph (iii), (iv), (v) or (vi)), and

(A) after November 16, 1978 and before 1987, 7%,

(B) in 1987, 5%,

(C) in 1988, 3%, and

(D) after 1988, 0%,

(*a*.1) in respect of a qualified resource property acquired by a taxpayer primarily for use in Nova Scotia, New Brunswick, Prince Edward Island, Newfoundland and Labrador, the Gaspé Peninsula or the prescribed offshore region, and that is acquired

(i) after March 28, 2012 and before 2014, 10%,

(ii) after 2013 and before 2017, 10% if the property

(A) is acquired by the taxpayer under a written agreement of purchase and sale entered into by the taxpayer before March 29, 2012, or

(B) is acquired as part of a phase of a project and

(I) the construction of the phase was started by, or on behalf of, the taxpayer before March 29, 2012 (and for this purpose construction does not include obtaining permits or regulatory approvals, conducting environmental assessments, community consultations or impact benefit studies, and similar activities), or

(II) the engineering and design work for the construction of the phase, as evidenced in writing, was started by, or on behalf of, the taxpayer before March 29, 2012 (and for this purpose engineering and design work does not include obtaining permits or regulatory approvals, conducting environmental assessments, community consultations or impact benefit studies, and similar activities), and

(iii) in any other case,

(A) in 2014 and 2015, 5%, and

(B) after 2015, 0%,

(*b*) in respect of qualified transportation equipment acquired

(i) before 1987, 7%,

(ii) in 1987, 5%, and

(iii) in 1988, 3%,

(*c*) in respect of qualified construction equipment acquired

(i) before 1987, 7%,

(ii) in 1987, 5%, and

(iii) in 1988, 3%,

(*d*) in respect of certified property

(i) included in subparagraph (*a*)(i) of the definition "certified property" in this subsection, 50%,

(ii) included in subparagraph (*a*)(ii) of that definition, 40%, and

(iii) in any other case, 30%,

(*e*) in respect of a qualified expenditure

(i) made after March 31, 1977 and before November 17, 1978 in respect of scientific research and experimental development to be carried out in

(A) the Province of Nova Scotia, New Brunswick, Prince Edward Island or Newfoundland or the Gaspé Peninsula, 10%,

(B) a prescribed designated region, $7^1/_2$%, and

(C) any other area in Canada, 5%,

(ii) made by a taxpayer after November 16, 1978 and before the taxpayer's taxation year that includes November 1, 1983 or made by the taxpayer in the taxpayer's taxation year that includes November 1, 1983 or a subsequent taxation year if the taxpayer deducted an amount under section 37.1 in computing the taxpayer's income for the year,

(A) where the expenditure was made by a Canadian-controlled private corporation in a taxation year of the corporation in which it is or would, if it had sufficient taxable income for the year, be entitled to a deduction under section 125 in computing its tax payable under this Part for the year, 25%, and

(B) where clause (A) is not applicable and the qualified expenditure was in respect of scientific research and experimental development to be carried out in

(I) the Province of Nova Scotia, New Brunswick, Prince Edward Island or Newfoundland or the Gaspé Peninsula, 20%, and

(II) any other area in Canada, 10%,

(iii) made by a taxpayer in the taxpayer's taxation year that ends after October 31, 1983 and before January 1, 1985, other than a qualified expenditure in respect of which subparagraph (ii) is applicable,

(A) where the expenditure was made by a Canadian-controlled private corporation in a taxation year of the corporation in which it is or would, if it had sufficient taxable income for the year, be entitled to a deduction under section 125 in computing its tax payable under this Part for the year, 35%, and

(B) where clause (A) is not applicable and the qualified expenditure was in respect of scientific research and experimental development to be carried out in

(I) the Province of Nova Scotia, New Brunswick, Prince Edward Island or Newfoundland or the Gaspé Peninsula, 30%, and

(II) any other area in Canada, 20%,

(iv) made by a taxpayer

(A) after the taxpayer's 1984 taxation year and before 1995, or

(B) after 1994 under a written agreement entered into by the taxpayer before February 22, 1994,

(other than a qualified expenditure in respect of which subparagraph (ii) applies) in respect of scientific research and experimental development to be carried out in

(C) the Province of Newfoundland, Prince Edward Island, Nova Scotia or New Brunswick or the Gaspé Peninsula, 30%, and

(D) in any other area in Canada, 20%, and

(v) made by a taxpayer after 1994, 20% where the amount is not an amount to which clause (iv)(B) applies,

(*f*) in respect of the repayment of government assistance, non-government assistance or a contract payment that reduced

(i) the capital cost to the taxpayer of a property under paragraph (11.1)(*b*),

(ii) the amount of a qualified expenditure incurred by the taxpayer under paragraph (11.1)(*c*) or (*e*) for taxation years that began before 1996, or

(iii) the prescribed proxy amount of the taxpayer under paragraph (11.1)(*f*) for taxation years that began before 1996,

the specified percentage that applied in respect of the property, the expenditure or the prescribed proxy amount, as the case may be,

(*f*.1) in respect of the repayment of government assistance, non-government assistance or a contract payment that reduced

(i) a qualified expenditure of a taxpayer under any of subsections (18) to (20), for the qualified expenditure incurred

(A) before 2015, 20%, and

(B) after 2014, 15%,

(ii) the amount of eligible salary and wages payable (by the taxpayer) to an eligible apprentice under paragraph (11.1)(*c.4*), 10%,

(iii) (Repealed by S.C. 2017, c. 20, s. 23(12).)

(*g*) in respect of an approved project property acquired

(i) before 1989, 60%, and

(ii) after 1988, 45%,

(*h*) in respect of the qualified Canadian exploration expenditure of a taxpayer for a taxation year, 25%,

(*i*) in respect of qualified small-business property, 10%,

(*j*) in respect of a pre-production mining expenditure of the taxpayer that is described in subparagraph (*a*)(i) of the definition "pre-production mining expenditure" and that is incurred

(i) before 2013, 10%,

(ii) in 2013, 5%, and

(iii) after 2013, 0%, and

(*k*) in respect of a pre-production mining expenditure of the taxpayer that is described in subparagraph (*a*)(ii) of the definition "pre-production mining expenditure" and that is incurred

(i) before 2014, 10%,

(ii) after 2013 and before 2016, 10% if the expenditure is incurred

(A) under a written agreement entered into by the taxpayer before March 29, 2012, or

(B) as part of the development of a new mine and

(I) the construction of the mine was started by, or on behalf of, the taxpayer before March 29, 2012 (and for this purpose construction does not include obtaining permits or regulatory approvals, conducting environmental assessments, community consultations or impact benefit studies, and similar activities), or

(II) the engineering and design work for the construction of the mine, as evidenced in writing, was started by, or on behalf of, the taxpayer before March 29, 2012 (and for this purpose engineering and design work does not include obtaining permits or regulatory approvals, conducting environmental assessments, community consultations or impact benefit studies, and similar activities), and

(iii) in any other case,

(A) in 2014, 7%,

(B) in 2015, 5% if the expense is described in paragraph (*a*)(ii) of the definition "pre-production mining expenditure" because of paragraph (*g.4*) of the definition "Canadian exploration expense" in subsection 66.1(6), and 4% otherwise, and

(C) after 2015, 0%;

History: S. 127(9), subparagraph (*f*.1)(i) of the definition "specified percentage" was replaced by S.C. 2017, c. 33, s. 50(2), applicable to repayments made after September 16, 2016, and formerly read:

(i) a qualified expenditure incurred by the taxpayer under any of subsections (18) to (20), 20%, or

S. 127(9), subparagraph (*f*.1)(iii) of the definition "specified percentage" was repealed by S.C. 2017, c. 20, s. 23(12), applicable in respect of expenditures incurred after March 21, 2017, except that this amendment does not apply in respect of expenditures incurred before 2020 under a written agreement entered into before March 22, 2017. S. 127(9), subparagraph (*f*.1)(iii) of the definition "specified percentage" formerly read:

(iii) the amount of the taxpayer's eligible child care space expenditure under paragraph (11.1)(*c.5*), 25%,

S. 127(9), clause (*k*)(iii)(B) of the definition "specified percentage" was replaced by S.C. 2013, c. 40, s. 57(4), deemed to have come into force on March 21, 2013, and formerly read:

(B) in 2015, 4%, and

S. 127(9), paragraph (*a*.1) of the definition "specified percentage" was added by S.C. 2012, c. 31, s. 27(16), applicable in respect of property acquired after March 28, 2012.

S. 127(9), paragraph (*j*) of the definition "specified percentage" was replaced, and paragraph (*k*) was added, by S.C. 2012, c. 31, s. 27(17), applicable in respect of expenditures incurred after March 28, 2012. S. 127(9), paragraph (*j*) of the definition "specified percentage" formerly read:

(*j*) in respect of a pre-production mining expenditure, if the expenditure was incurred

(i) in 2003, 5%,

(ii) in 2004, 7%, and

(iii) after 2004, 10%;

Related Regulations: 4607; 4609.

Related Sections: S. 127(10.1) Additions to investment tax credit; s. 127(10.7) Further additions to investment tax credit; s. 127(10.8) Further additions to investment tax credit.

Canadian Petroleum Tax Journal: Offshore Oil & Gas Interests: A Perspective on Exploration & Development of Offshore Petroleum and Natural Gas Resources in Eastern Canada, Michael R. Smith, CA and B. David Nielsen, CA, 2000, Vol. 13, No. 1.

Income Tax Folios: *Primary* — S3-F8-C2 Tax Incentives for Clean Energy Equipment.

Information Circulars: IC 78-4R3 Investment tax credit rates.

Tax Window Files: Investment Tax Credit — Logging Truck, *Technical Interpretation, Reorganizations and Resources Division, November 29, 2005,* CRA Document No. 2005-0130101I7; Investment Tax Credits — Borders of Gaspe Peninsula, *Technical Interpretation, Business and Partnerships Division, April 20, 2005,* CRA Document No. 2004-0101461E5.

"specified property" — (Repealed by S.C. 2017, c. 20, s. 23(7).)

History: S. 127(9), the definition "specified property" was repealed by S.C. 2017, c. 20, s. 23(7), applicable in respect of expenditures incurred after March 21, 2017, except that this amendment does not apply in respect of expenditures incurred before 2020 under a written agreement entered into before March 22, 2017. S. 127(9), the definition "specified property" formerly read:

"specified property"—"specified property" in respect of a taxpayer means any property that is

(*a*) a motor vehicle or any other motorized vehicle, or

(*b*) a property that is, or is located in, or attached to, a residence

(i) of the taxpayer,

(ii) an employee of the taxpayer,

(iii) a person who holds an interest in the taxpayer, or

(iv) a person related to a person referred to in any of subparagraphs (i) to (iii);

"specified sampling" —"specified sampling" means the collecting and testing of samples in respect of a mineral resource except that specified sampling does not include

(*a*) the collecting or testing of a sample that, at the time the sample is collected, weighs more than 15 tonnes, and

(*b*) the collecting or testing of a sample collected at any time in a calendar year in respect of any one mineral resource if the total weight of all such samples collected (by any person or partnership or any combination of persons and partnerships) in the period in the calendar year that is before that time (other than samples each of which weighs less than one tonne) exceeds 1,000 tonnes;

"SR&ED qualified expenditure pool" —"SR&ED qualified expenditure pool" of a taxpayer at the end of a taxation year means the amount determined by the formula

$$A + B - C$$

where

A is the total of all amounts each of which is a qualified expenditure incurred by the taxpayer in the year,

B is the total of all amounts each of which is an amount determined under paragraph (13)(*e*) for the year in respect of the taxpayer, and in respect of which the taxpayer files with the Minister a prescribed form containing prescribed information by the day that is 12 months after the taxpayer's filing-due date for the year, and

C is the total of all amounts each of which is an amount determined under paragraph (13)(*d*) for the year in respect of the taxpayer;

Related Sections: S. 127(5)(*a*) Investment tax credit; s. 127(9), "investment tax credit"; s. 127(10.1)(*b*) Additions to investment tax credit; s. 127(13) Agreement to transfer qualified expenditures; s. 127(14) Identification of amounts transferred; s. 257 Negative amounts.

Forms: T661 — Scientific Research and Experimental Development Expenditures Claim.

Guides: T4088 Claiming Scientific Research and Experimental Development Expenditures.

SR&ED Publications: Total Qualified SR&ED Expenditures for Investment Tax Credit Purposes Policy.

Tax Window Files: SR&ED Used Equipment, *Technical Interpretation, Business and Partnerships Division, January 30, 2007,* CRA Document No. 2006-0211041E5.

"super-allowance benefit amount" —"super-allowance benefit amount" for a particular taxation year in respect of a corporation in respect of a province means the amount determined by the formula

$$(A - B) \times C$$

where

A is the total of all amounts each of which is an amount that is or may become deductible by the corporation, in computing income or taxable income relevant in calculating an income tax payable by the corporation under a law of the province for any taxation year, in respect of an expenditure on scientific research and experimental development incurred in the particular year,

B is the amount by which the amount of the expenditure exceeds the total of all amounts that would be required by subsections (18) to (20) to reduce the corporation's qualified expenditures otherwise determined under this section if the definitions "government assistance" and "non-government assistance" did not apply to assistance provided under that law, and

C is,

(*a*) where the corporation's expenditure limit for the particular year is nil, the maximum rate of the province's income tax that applies for that year to active business income earned in the province by a corporation, and

(*b*) in any other case, the rate of the province's income tax for that year that would apply to the corporation if

(i) it were not associated with any other corporation in the year,

(ii) its taxable income for the year were less than $200,000, and

(iii) its taxable income for the year were earned in the province in respect of an active business carried on in the province;

Related Sections: S. 37(1)(*d*.1) Scientific research and experimental development; s. 127(9), "investment tax credit"; s. 127(10.1)(*b*) Additions to investment tax credit; s. 257 Negative amounts.

"taxable supplier" —"taxable supplier" in respect of an amount means

(*a*) a person resident in Canada or a Canadian partnership, or

(*b*) a non-resident person, or a partnership that is not a Canadian partnership,

(i) by which the amount was payable, or

(ii) by or for whom the amount was receivable

in the course of carrying on a business through a permanent establishment (as defined by regulation) in Canada.

Related Regulations: 8201.

SR&ED Publications: Total Qualified SR&ED Expenditures for Investment Tax Credit Purposes Policy.

Tax Window Files: Scientific Research and Experimental Development — Activities Performed on Behalf of Foreign Corporation, *2005 APFF Conference — Round Table on Federal Taxation, Question 7, October 7, 2005,* CRA Document No. 2005-0140991C6.

► 127(9.01) ◄

(9.01) Transitional application of investment tax credit definition. For the purpose of applying each of paragraphs (*c*) to (*f*), (*h*) and (*i*) of the definition "investment tax credit" in subsection (9) in respect of a taxpayer, the reference to "10" in that paragraph is to be read as a reference to the number that is the lesser of

(*a*) 20, and

(*b*) the number that is the total of 10 and the number of taxation years by which the number of taxation years of the taxpayer that have ended after 1997 exceeds 11.

History: S. 127(9.01)(*b*) was replaced by S.C. 2009, c. 2, s. 40(3), applicable in respect of the 2008 and subsequent taxation years. S. 127(9.01)(*b*) formerly read:

(*b*) the number that is the total of 10 and the number of taxation years by which the number of taxation years of the taxpayer that have ended after 2005 exceeds 11.

► 127(9.02) ◄

(9.02) Transitional application of investment tax credit definition. For the purpose of applying paragraph (*g*) of the definition "investment tax credit" in subsection (9) in respect of a taxpayer, the reference to "9" in that paragraph is to be read as a reference to the number that is the lesser of

(*a*) 19, and

(*b*) the number that is the total of 9 and the number of taxation years by which the number of taxation years of the taxpayer that have ended after 1997 exceeds 11.

History: S. 127(9.02)(*b*) was replaced by S.C. 2009, c. 2, s. 40(4), applicable in respect of the 2008 and subsequent taxation years. S. 127(9.02)(*b*) formerly read:

(*b*) the number that is the total of 9 and the number of taxation years by which the number of taxation years of the taxpayer that have ended after 2005 exceeds 11.

► 127(9.1) ◄

(9.1) Loss restriction event before end of year. If a taxpayer is subject to a loss restriction event at any time (in this subsection referred to as "that time") before the end of a taxation year of the taxpayer, the amount determined for the purposes of paragraph (*j*) of the definition "investment tax credit" in subsection (9) with respect to the taxpayer is the amount, if any, by which

(*a*) the amount, if any, by which

(i) the total of all amounts added in computing its investment tax credit at the end of the year in respect of a property acquired, or an expenditure made, before that time

exceeds

(ii) the total of all amounts each of which is an amount

(A) deducted in computing its investment tax credit at the end of the year under paragraph (*f*) or (*g*) of the definition "investment tax credit" in subsection (9), or

(B) deducted in computing its investment tax credit at the end of the taxation year immediately preceding the year under paragraph (*i*) of that definition,

to the extent that the amount may reasonably be considered to have been so deducted in respect of a property or expenditure in respect of which an amount is included in subparagraph (i)

exceeds the total of

(*b*) (Repealed by 1987, c. 46, s. 46(3).)

(*c*) the amount, if any, by which its refundable Part VII tax on hand at the end of the year exceeds the total of all amounts each of which is an amount designated under subsection 192(4) in respect of a share issued by it

(i) in the period commencing one month before that time and ending at that time, or

(ii) after that time,

and before the end of the year, and

(*d*) that proportion of the amount that, but for subsections (3) and (5) and sections 126, 127.2 and 127.3, would be its tax payable under this Part for the year that,

(i) if throughout the year the taxpayer carried on a particular business in the course of which a property was acquired, or an expenditure was made, before that time in respect of which an amount is included in computing its investment tax credit at the end of the year, the amount, if any, by which the total of all amounts each of which is

(A) its income for the year from the particular business, or

(B) its income for the year from any other business substantially all the income of which was derived from the sale, leasing, rental or development of properties or the rendering of services similar to the properties sold, leased, rented or developed, or the services rendered, as the case may be, by the taxpayer in carrying on the particular business before that time

exceeds

(C) the total of all amounts each of which is an amount deducted under paragraph 111(1)(*a*) or (*d*) for the year by the taxpayer in respect of a non-capital loss or a farm loss, as the case may be, for a taxation year in respect of the particular business or the other business,

is of the greater of

(ii) the amount determined under subparagraph (i), and

(iii) its taxable income for the year.

History: S. 127(9.1), the portion before paragraph (*a*) was replaced by S.C. 2013, c. 40, s. 57(5), deemed to have come into force on March 21, 2013, and formerly read:

(9.1) *Control acquired before the end of the year.* Where a taxpayer is a corporation the control of which has been acquired by a person or group of persons (each of whom is in this subsection referred to as the "purchaser") at any time (in this subsection referred to as "that time") before the end of a taxation year of the corporation, the amount determined for the purposes of paragraph (*j*) of the definition "investment tax credit" in subsection (9) is the amount, if any, by which

S. 127(9.1)(*d*)(i) was replaced by S.C. 2013, c. 40, s. 57(6), deemed to have come into force on March 21, 2013, and formerly read:

(i) where throughout the year the corporation carried on a particular business in the course of which a property was acquired, or an expenditure was made, before that time in respect of which an amount is included in computing its investment tax credit at the end of the year, the amount, if any, by which the total of all amounts each of which is

(A) its income for the year from the particular business, or

(B) its income for the year from any other business substantially all the income of which was derived from the sale, leasing, rental or development of properties or the rendering of services similar to the properties sold, leased, rented or developed, or the services rendered, as the case may be, by the corporation in carrying on the particular business before that time

exceeds

(C) the total of all amounts each of which is an amount deducted under paragraph 111(1)(*a*) or (*d*) for the year by the corporation in respect of a non-capital loss or a farm loss, as the case may be, for a taxation year in respect of the particular business or the other business,

Related Sections: S. 139.1(18) Acquisition of control; s. 249(4) Loss restriction event – year end; s. 251.2(2) Loss restriction event; s. 256(8) Deemed exercise of right.

SR&ED Publications: SR&ED Investment Tax Credit Policy.

► 127(9.2) ◄

(9.2) Loss restriction event after end of year. If a taxpayer is subject to a loss restriction event at any time (in this subsection referred to as "that time") after the end of a taxation year of the taxpayer, the amount determined for the purposes of paragraph (*k*) of the definition "investment tax credit" in subsection (9) is the amount, if any, by which

(*a*) the total of all amounts each of which is an amount included in computing its investment tax credit at the end of the year in respect of a property acquired, or an expenditure made, after that time

exceeds the total of

(*b*) (Repealed by 1987, c. 46, s. 46(6).)

(*c*) its refundable Part VII tax on hand at the end of the year, and

(*d*) that proportion of the amount that, but for subsections (3) and (5) and sections 126, 127.2 and 127.3, would be its tax payable under this Part for the year that,

(i) if the taxpayer acquired a property or made an expenditure, in the course of carrying on a particular business throughout the portion of a taxation year that is after that time, in respect of which an amount is included in computing its investment tax credit at the end of the year, the amount, if any, by which the total of all amounts each of which is

(A) its income for the year from the particular business, or

(B) if the taxpayer carried on a particular business in the year, its income for the year from any other business substantially all the income of which was derived from the sale, leasing, rental or development of properties or the rendering of services similar to the properties sold, leased, rented or developed, or the services rendered, as the case may be, by the taxpayer in carrying on the particular business before that time

exceeds

(C) the total of all amounts each of which is an amount deducted under paragraph 111(1)(*a*) or (*d*) for the year by the taxpayer in respect of a non-capital loss or a farm loss, as the case may be, for a taxation year in respect of the particular business or the other business

is of the greater of

(ii) the amount determined under subparagraph (i), and

(iii) its taxable income for the year.

History: S. 127(9.2), the portion before paragraph (*a*) was replaced by S.C. 2013, c. 40, s. 57(7), deemed to have come into force on March 21, 2013, and formerly read:

(9.2) *Control acquired after the end of the year.* Where a taxpayer is a corporation the control of which has been acquired by a person or group of persons at any time (in this subsection referred to as "that time") after the end of a taxation year of the corporation, the amount determined for the purposes of paragraph (*k*) of the definition "investment tax credit" in subsection (9) is the amount, if any, by which

S. 127(9.2)(*d*)(i) was replaced by S.C. 2013, c. 40, s. 57(8), deemed to have come into force on March 21, 2013, and formerly read:

(i) where the corporation acquired a property or made an expenditure, in the course of carrying on a particular business throughout the portion of a taxation year that is after that time, in respect of which an amount is included in computing its investment tax credit at the end of the year, the amount, if any, by which the total of all amounts each of which is

(A) its income for the year from the particular business, or

(B) where the corporation carried on a particular business in the year, its income for the year from any other business substantially all the income of which was derived from the sale, leasing, rental or development of properties or the rendering of services similar to the properties sold, leased, rented or developed, or the services rendered, as the case may be, by the corporation in carrying on the particular business before that time

exceeds

(C) the total of all amounts each of which is an amount deducted under paragraph 111(1)(*a*) or (*d*) for the year by the corporation in respect of a non-capital loss or a farm loss, as the case may be, for a taxation year in respect of the particular business or the other business

Related Sections: S. 139.1(18) Acquisition of control; s. 249(4) Loss restriction event – year end; s. 251.2(2) Loss restriction event; s. 256(8) Deemed exercise of right.

SR&ED Publications: SR&ED Investment Tax Credit Policy.

► 127(10) ◄

(10) Ascertainment of certain property. The Minister may

(*a*) obtain the advice of the appropriate minister for the purposes of the *Regional Development Incentives Act*, chapter R-3 of the Revised Statutes of Canada, 1970, as to whether any property is property as described in paragraph (*b*) of the definition "certified property" in subsection (9);

(*b*) obtain a certificate from the appropriate minister for the purposes of the *Regional Development Incentives Act* certifying that any property specified therein is property as described in paragraph (*b*) of that definition; or

(*c*) provide advice to the member of the Queen's Privy Council for Canada appointed to be the Minister for the purposes of the *Atlantic Canada Opportunities Agency Act* as to whether any property qualifies for certification under the definition "approved project property" in subsection (9).

► 127(10.1) ◄

(10.1) Additions to investment tax credit. For the purposes of paragraph (*e*) of the definition "investment tax credit" in subsection (9), if a corporation was throughout a taxation year a Canadian-controlled private corporation, there shall be added in computing the corporation's investment tax credit at the end of the year the amount that is 20% of the least of

(*a*) such amount as the corporation claims;

(*b*) the amount by which the corporation's SR&ED qualified expenditure pool at the end of the year exceeds the total of all amounts each of which is the super-allowance benefit amount for the year in respect of the corporation in respect of a province; and

(*c*) the corporation's expenditure limit for the year.

Editorial Note: S. 127(10.1) provides certain Canadian-controlled private corporations an additional 20% ITC for qualified SR&ED expenditures, bringing the total ITC to 35%. However, the additional ITC is not available to large corporations. S. 127(10.1)(*c*) ensures that the additional 20% is limited to the corporation's "expenditure limit" for the year, as defined in s. 127(10.2). The expenditure limit is $3 million, but is reduced where its taxable capital employed in Canada exceeds $10 million and is reduced to nil when such capital is $50 million or greater.

History: S. 127(10.1), the portion before paragraph (*a*) was replaced by S.C. 2012, c. 31, s. 27(19), applicable to taxation years that end after 2013, except that for taxation years that include January 1, 2014, the reference to "20%" in the portion of subsection 127(10.1) before paragraph (*a*) is to be read as a reference to the percentage that is the total of

(i) 15% multiplied by the proportion that the number of days that are in the taxation year and before 2014 is of the number of days in the taxation year, and

(ii) 20% multiplied by the proportion that the number of days that are in the taxation year and after 2013 is of the number of days in the taxation year.

S. 127(10.1), the portion before paragraph (*a*) formerly read:

(10.1) *Additions to investment tax credit.* For the purpose of paragraph (*e*) of the definition "investment tax credit" in subsection (9), where a corporation was throughout a taxation year a Canadian-controlled private corporation, there shall be added in computing the corporation's investment tax credit at the end of the year the amount that is 15% of the least of

Related Sections: S. 127(10.2) Expenditure limit determined; s. 127(10.7) Further additions to investment tax credit; s. 127.1(2), "refundable investment tax credit"; s. 127.1(2.01) Addition to refundable investment tax credit; s. 136(1) Cooperative not private corporation; s. 137(7) Credit union not private corporation.

Tax Profile: April 2006 — The SR&ED Deduction and Investment Tax Credits.

Forms: T2 SCH 31 — Investment Tax Credit — Corporations.

SR&ED Publications: SR&ED Investment Tax Credit Policy.

Tax Window Files: Investment Tax Credit — Expenditure Limit, *Technical Interpretation, Business Incentives and Capital Transactions Section, June 20, 2006*, CRA Document No. 2005-0165381E5.

► 127(10.2) ◄

(10.2) Expenditure limit. For the purpose of subsection (10.1), a particular corporation's expenditure limit for a particular taxation year is the amount determined by the formula

$$\$3 \text{ million} \times (\$40 \text{ million} - A)/\$40 \text{ million}$$

where

A is

(*a*) nil, if the following amount is less than or equal to $10 million:

(i) if the particular corporation is not associated with any other corporation in the particular taxation year, the amount that is its taxable capital employed in Canada (within the meaning assigned by section 181.2 or 181.3) for its immediately preceding taxation year, and

(ii) if the particular corporation is associated with one or more other corporations in the particular taxation year, the amount that is the total of all amounts, each of which is the taxable capital employed in Canada (within the meaning assigned by section 181.2 or 181.3) of the particular corporation for its, or of one of the other corporations for its, last taxation year that ended in the last calendar year that ended before the end of the particular taxation year, and

(*b*) in any other case, the lesser of $40 million and the amount by which the amount determined under subparagraph (*a*)(i) or (ii), as the case may be, exceeds $10 million.

Editorial Note: See the Editorial Note under s. 127(10.1).

History: S. 127(10.2) was replaced by S.C. 2019, c. 29, s. 24(3), applicable to taxation years that end after March 18, 2019, and formerly read:

(10.2) *Expenditure limit determined.* For the purpose of subsection (10.1), a particular corporation's expenditure limit for a particular taxation year is the amount determined by the formula

$$(\$8 \text{ million} - 10A) \times [(\$40 \text{ million} - B)/\$40 \text{ million}]$$

where

A is the greater of

(*a*) $500,000, and

(*b*) the amount that is

(i) if the particular corporation is not associated with any other corporation in the particular taxation year, the particular corporation's taxable income for its immediately preceding taxation year (determined before taking into consideration the specified future tax consequences for that preceding year), or

(ii) if the particular corporation is associated with one or more other corporations in the particular taxation year, the total of all amounts each of which is the taxable income of the particular corporation for its, or of one of the other corporations for its, last taxation year that ended in the last calendar year that ended before the end of the particular taxation year (determined before taking into consideration the specified future tax consequences for that last taxation year), and

B is

(*a*) nil, if the following amount is less than or equal to $10 million:

(i) if the particular corporation is not associated with any other corporation in the particular taxation year, the amount that is its taxable capital employed in Canada (within the meaning assigned by section 181.2 or 181.3) for its immediately preceding taxation year, or

(ii) if the particular corporation is associated with one or more other corporations in the particular taxation year, the amount that is the total of all amounts, each of which is the taxable capital employed in Canada (within the meaning assigned by section 181.2 or 181.3) of the particular corporation for its, or of one of the other corporations for its, last taxation year that ended in the last calendar year that ended before the end of the particular taxation year, or

(*b*) in any other case, the lesser of $40 million and the amount by which the amount determined under subparagraph (*a*)(i) or (ii), as the case may be, exceeds $10 million.

S. 127(10.2), the formula and paragraph (*a*) of the description of A were replaced by S.C. 2009, c. 2, s. 40(5) and 40(6) respectively, applicable to the 2010 and subsequent taxation years, except that the expenditure limit in subsection 127(10.2) in respect of a corporation for 2010 taxation years that begin before 2010, be determined by the formula

$$A + [(B - A) \times (C/D)]$$

where

A is the expenditure limit of the corporation for the taxation year determined in accordance with the formula in subsection 127(10.2) of the Act as that subsection read in its application to taxation years that end in 2009;

B is the expenditure limit of the corporation for the taxation year determined in accordance with the formula in subsection 127(10.2) of the Act, as that subsection would apply to the taxation year in the absence of this exception;

C is the number of days in the taxation year that are after 2009; and

D is the total number of days in the taxation year.

S. 127(10.2), the formula formerly read:

$$(\$7 \text{ million} - 10A) \times [(\$40 \text{ million} - B)/\$40 \text{ million}]$$

S. 127(10.2), paragraph (*a*) of the description of A formerly read:

(*a*) $400,000, and

S. 127(10.2), subparagraphs (*a*)(i) and (ii) of the description of B were replaced by S.C. 2009, c. 2, s. 40(7), applicable to taxation years that end on or after February 26, 2008. S. 127(10.2), subparagraphs (*a*)(i) and (ii) of the description of B formerly read:

(*i*) if the particular corporation is not associated with any other corporation in the particular taxation year, the amount that is its taxable capital employed in Canada (within the meaning assigned by section 181.2) for its immediately preceding taxation year, or

(*ii*) if the particular corporation is associated with one or more other corporations in the particular taxation year, the amount that is the total of all amounts, each of which is the taxable capital employed in Canada (within the meaning assigned by section 181.2) of the particular corporation for its, or of one of the other corporations for its, last taxation year that ended in the last calendar year that ended before the end of the particular taxation year, or

The wording for the descriptions of A and B was amended by S.C. 2009, c. 2, s. 82, to read as noted in the application above, in force on March 12, 2009.

S. 127(10.2) formerly read:

(10.2) *Expenditure limit determined.* For the purpose of subsection (10.1), a corporation's expenditure limit for a particular taxation year is the amount determined by the formula

$$(\$6{,}000{,}000 - 10A) \times B/C$$

where

A is the greater of $400,000 and either

(*a*) if the corporation is associated with one or more other corporations in the particular year and the particular year ends in a calendar year, the total of all amounts each of which is the taxable income of the corporation, or of such an associated corporation, for its last taxation year that ended in the preceding calendar year (determined before taking into consideration the specified future tax consequences for that last taxation year), or

(*b*) if paragraph (*a*) does not apply, the corporation's taxable income for its immediately preceding taxation year (determined before taking into consideration the specified future tax consequences for that preceding year),

B is the total of the business limits under section 125 for the particular year of the corporation and any such other corporations for the particular year, and

C is

(*a*) if the corporation is associated with one or more other corporations in the particular year, the total of all amounts each of which would be the business limit for the particular year of the corporation or of such an associated corporation, if this Act were read without reference to subsections 125(5) and (5.1), or

(*b*) if paragraph (*a*) does not apply, the amount that would, if this Act were read without reference to subsections 125(5) and (5.1), be the corporation's business limit for the particular year.

Related Sections: S. 87(2)(*j*.6) Continuing corporation; 127(10.1) Additions to investment tax credit; 127(10.21) Expenditure limits — associated CCPCs; 127(10.22) Deemed non-association of corporations; 127(10.23) Application of subsection (10.22); 127(10.3) Associated corporations; 127(10.4) Failure to file agreement; 127(10.6) Expenditure limit determination in certain cases; s. 248(1), "specified future tax consequences"; s. 257 Negative amounts.

SR&ED Publications: SR&ED Investment Tax Credit Policy.

Tax Window Files: Investment Tax Credit — Expenditure Limit, *Technical Interpretation, Business Incentives and Capital Transactions Section, June 20, 2006*, CRA Document No. 2005-0165381E5; Business Limit and Expenditure Limit — Associated Canadian- controlled Private Corporations with Multiple Taxation Years, *Technical Interpretation, Business and Partnerships Division, October 21, 2003*, CRA Document No. 2003-0031577.

► 127(10.21) ◄

(10.21) Expenditure limits — associated CCPCs. Notwithstanding subsection (10.2), the expenditure limit for a taxation year of a corporation that is associated in the taxation year with one or more other Canadian-controlled private corporations is, except as otherwise provided in this section, nil.

Related Sections: S. 127(10.3) Associated corporations.

Tax Window Files: Business Limit and Expenditure Limit — Associated Canadian-controlled Private Corporations with Multiple Taxation Years, *Technical Interpretation, Business and Partnerships Division, October 21, 2003*, CRA Document No. 2003-0031577.

► 127(10.22) ◄

(10.22) Deemed non-association of corporations. If a particular Canadian-controlled private corporation is associated with another corporation in circumstances where those corporations would not be associated if the Act were read without reference to paragraph 256(1.2)(*a*), the particular corporation has issued shares to one or more persons who have been issued shares by the other corporation and there is at least one shareholder of the particular corporation who is not a shareholder of the other corporation or one shareholder of the other corporation who is not a shareholder of the particular corporation, the particular corporation is deemed not to be associated with the other corporation for the purpose of determining the particular corporation's expenditure limit under subsection (10.2).

Editorial Note: S. 127(10.22) allows associated corporations to be considered not associated for purposes of SR&ED tax credits if they are associated through a third company and the conditions in s. 127(10.23) are met. However, s. 127(10.22) does not apply for purposes of claiming the small business deduction in s. 125. S. 127.1(2.2) provides a parallel rule for refundable investment tax credits.

History: S. 127(10.22) was replaced by S.C. 2009, c. 2, s. 40(8), applicable to taxation years that end on or after March 9, 2009. S. 127(10.22) formerly read:

(10.22) *Expenditure limits — associated CCPCs.* If a particular Canadian-controlled private corporation is associated with another corporation in circumstances where those corporations would not be associated if the Act were read without reference to paragraph 256(1.2)(*a*), the particular corporation has issued shares to one or more persons who have been issued shares by the other corporation and there is at least one shareholder of the particular corporation who is not a shareholder of the other corporation or one shareholder of the other corporation who is not a shareholder of the particular corporation, the particular corporation is not associated with the other corporation for the purpose of

(*a*) determining the particular corporation's expenditure limit under subsection (10.2); and

(*b*) determining the particular corporation's business limit under section 125, as applied for the purpose only of determining the particular corporation's expenditure limit under subsection (10.2).

Related Sections: S. 127(10.23) Application of subsection (10.22); s. 127.1(2.2) Refundable investment tax credit — associated CCPCs; s. 127.1(2.3) Application of subsection (2.2).

Tax Profile: March 2006 — Some Tax Considerations for Investing in Silicon Valley North.

Tax Window Files: Enhanced ITC for CCPCs, *Technical Interpretation, Business and Partnerships Division, May 18, 2005,* CRA Document No. 2005-0126891I7.

► 127(10.23) ◄

(10.23) Application of subsection (10.22). Subsection (10.22) applies to the particular corporation and the other corporation referred to in that subsection only if the Minister is satisfied that

(*a*) the particular corporation and the other corporation are not otherwise associated under this Act; and

(*b*) the existence of one or more shareholders of the particular corporation who is not a shareholder of the other corporation, or the existence of one or more shareholders of the other corporation who is not a shareholder of the particular corporation, is not for the purpose of satisfying the requirements of subsection (10.22) or 127.1(2.2).

Editorial Note: See the editorial note under s. 127(10.22).

Related Sections: S. 127.1(2.2) Refundable investment tax credit — associated CCPCs; s. 127.1(2.3) Application of subsection (2.2).

Tax Window Files: Enhanced ITC for CCPCs, *Technical Interpretation, Business and Partnerships Division, May 18, 2005,* CRA Document No. 2005-0126891I7.

► 127(10.3) ◄

(10.3) Associated corporations. If all of the Canadian-controlled private corporations that are associated with each other in a taxation year file with the Minister in prescribed form an agreement whereby, for the purpose of subsection (10.1), they allocate an amount to one or more of them for the year and the amount so allocated or the total of the amounts so allocated, as the case may be, does not exceed the amount determined for the year by the formula in subsection (10.2), the expenditure limit for the year of each of the corporations is the amount so allocated to it.

Related Sections: S. 127(10.4) Failure to file agreement.

Forms: T2 SCH 49 — Agreement Among Associated Canadian-controlled Private Corporations to Allocate the Expenditure Limit; T2 SCH 23 — T2SCH23 Agreement Among Associated Canadian-controlled Private Corporations to Allocate the Business Limit.

SR&ED Publications: SR&ED Filing Requirements Policy.

Tax Window Files: Business Limit and Expenditure Limit — Associated Canadian-controlled Private Corporations with Multiple Taxation Years, *Technical Interpretation, Business and Partnerships Division, October 21, 2003,* CRA Document No. 2003-0031577.

► 127(10.4) ◄

(10.4) Failure to file agreement. If any of the Canadian-controlled private corporations that are associated with each other in a taxation year fails to file with the Minister an agreement as contemplated by subsection (10.3) within 30 days after notice in writing by the Minister is forwarded to any of them that such an agreement is required for the purposes of this Part, the Minister shall, for the purpose of subsection (10.1), allocate an amount to one or more of them for the year, which amount or the total of which amounts, as the case may be, shall equal the amount determined for the year by the formula in subsection (10.2), and in any such case the expenditure limit for the year of each of the corporations is the amount so allocated to it.

► 127(10.5) ◄

(10.5) Failure to file agreement. (Repealed by 1985, c. 45, s. 72(6).)

► 127(10.6) ◄

(10.6) Expenditure limit determination in certain cases. Notwithstanding any other provision of this section,

(*a*) where a Canadian-controlled private corporation (in this paragraph referred to as the "first corporation") has more than one taxation year ending in the same calendar year and it is associated in two or more of those taxation years with another Canadian-controlled private corporation that has a taxation year ending in that calendar year, the expenditure limit of the first corporation for each taxation year in which it is associated with the other corporation ending in that calendar year is, subject to the application of paragraph (*b*), an amount equal to its expenditure limit for the first such taxation year determined without reference to paragraph (*b*); and

(*b*) where a Canadian-controlled private corporation has a taxation year that is less than 51 weeks, its expenditure limit for the year is that proportion of its expenditure limit for the year determined without reference to this paragraph that the number of days in the year is of 365.

(*c*) (Repealed by S.C. 2019, c. 29, s. 24(4).)

History: S. 127(10.6)(*c*) was repealed by S.C. 2019, c. 29, s. 24(4), applicable to taxation years that end after March 18, 2019, and formerly read:

(*c*) for the purpose of subsection (10.2), where a Canadian-controlled private corporation has a taxation year that is less than 51 weeks, the taxable income of the corporation for the year shall be determined by multiplying that amount by the ratio that 365 is of the number of days in that year.

S. 127(10.6)(*c*) was replaced by S.C. 2009, c. 2, s. 40(9), applicable to taxation years that end on or after March 9, 2009. S. 127(10.6)(*c*) formerly read:

(*c*) for the purpose of subsection (10.2), where a Canadian-controlled private corporation has a taxation year that is less than 51 weeks, the taxable income and business limit of the corporation for the year shall be determined by multiplying those amounts by the ratio that 365 is of the number of days in that year.

SR&ED Publications: SR&ED Investment Tax Credit Policy.

Tax Window Files: Business Limit and Expenditure Limit — Associated Canadian- controlled Private Corporations with Multiple Taxation Years, *Technical Interpretation, Business and Partnerships Division, October 21, 2003*, CRA Document No. 2003-0031577.

► 127(10.7) ◄

(10.7) Further additions to investment tax credit. Where a taxpayer has in a particular taxation year repaid an amount of government assistance, non-government assistance or a contract payment that was applied to reduce

(*a*) the amount of a qualified expenditure incurred by the taxpayer under paragraph (11.1)(*c*) for a preceding taxation year that began before 1996,

(*b*) the prescribed proxy amount of the taxpayer under paragraph (11.1)(*f*) for a preceding taxation year that began before 1996, or

(*c*) a qualified expenditure incurred by the taxpayer under any of subsections (18) to (20) for a preceding taxation year,

there shall be added to the amount otherwise determined under subsection (10.1) in respect of the taxpayer for the particular year the amount, if any, by which

(*d*) the amount that would have been determined under subsection (10.1) in respect of the taxpayer for that preceding year if subsections (11.1) and (18) to (20) had not applied in respect of the government assistance, non-government assistance or contract payment, as the case may be, to the extent of the amount so repaid,

exceeds

(*e*) the amount determined under subsection (10.1) in respect of the taxpayer for that preceding year.

Related Sections: S. 127(10.8) Further additions to investment tax credit.

SR&ED Publications: Assistance and Contract Payments Policy; 2005-02, General Rules Concerning the Treatment of Government and Non Government Assistance.

► 127(10.8) ◄

(10.8) Further additions to investment tax credit. For the purposes of paragraph (*e*.1) of the definition "investment tax credit" in subsection (9), subsection (10.7) and paragraph 37(1)(*c*), an amount of government assistance, non-government assistance or a contract payment that

(*a*) was applied to reduce

(i) the capital cost to a taxpayer of a property under paragraph (11.1)(*b*),

(ii) the amount of a qualified expenditure incurred by a taxpayer under paragraph (11.1)(*c*) for taxation years that began before 1996,

(iii) the prescribed proxy amount of a taxpayer under paragraph (11.1)(*f*) for taxation years that began before 1996, or

(iv) a qualified expenditure incurred by a taxpayer under any of subsections (18) to (20),

(*b*) was not received by the taxpayer, and

(*c*) ceased in a taxation year to be an amount that the taxpayer can reasonably be expected to receive,

is deemed to be the amount of a repayment by the taxpayer in the year of the government assistance, non-government assistance or contract payment, as the case may be.

Editorial Note: S. 127(10.8) allows a taxpayer to regenerate an investment tax credit when the assistance has not been received and entitlement to assistance expires.

Related Sections: S. 127(9), "contract payment", "government assistance", "non-government assistance", "qualified expenditure".

SR&ED Publications: Assistance and Contract Payments Policy.

► 127(11) ◄

(11) Interpretation. For the purposes of the definitions "qualified property" and "qualified resource property" in subsection (9),

(*a*) "manufacturing or processing" does not include any of the activities

(i) referred to in any of paragraphs (*a*) to (*e*) and (*g*) to (*i*) of the definition "manufacturing or processing" in subsection 125.1(3),

(ii) that would be referred to in paragraph (*f*) of that definition if that paragraph were read without reference to the expression "located in Canada",

(iii) that would be referred to in paragraph (*j*) of that definition if that paragraph were read without reference to the expression "in Canada", or

(iv) that would be referred to in paragraph (*k*) of that definition if the definition "Canadian field processing" in subsection 248(1) were read without reference to the expression "in Canada"; and

(*b*) for greater certainty, the purposes referred to in paragraph (*c*) of the definition "qualified property" and paragraph (*a*) of the definition "qualified resource property" in subsection (9) do not include

(i) storing (other than the storing of grain), shipping, selling or leasing finished goods,

(ii) purchasing raw materials,

(iii) administration, including clerical and personnel activities,

(iv) purchase and resale operations,

(v) data processing, or

(vi) providing facilities for employees, including cafeterias, clinics and recreational facilities.

History: S. 127(11), the portion before paragraph (*a*) was replaced by S.C. 2012, c. 31, s. 27(20), deemed to have come into force on March 29, 2012. S. 127(11), the portion before paragraph (*a*) formerly read:

(11) *Interpretation.* For the purposes of the definition "qualified property" in subsection (9),

S. 127(11)(*b*), the portion before subparagraph (i) was replaced by S.C. 2012, c. 31, s. 27(21), deemed to have come into force on March 29, 2012. S. 127(11)(*b*), the portion before subparagraph (i) formerly read:

(*b*) for greater certainty, the purposes referred to in paragraph (*c*) of the definition "qualified property" in subsection (9) do not include

Income Tax Folios: S4-F15-C1 Manufacturing and Processing.

Interpretation Bulletins: *Secondary* — IT-411R Meaning of "construction".

► 127(11.1) ◄

(11.1) Investment tax credit. For the purposes of the definition "investment tax credit" in subsection (9),

(*a*) the capital cost to a taxpayer of a property shall be computed as if no amount were added thereto by virtue of section 21;

(*b*) the capital cost to a taxpayer of a property shall be deemed to be the capital cost to the taxpayer of the property, determined without reference to subsections 13(7.1) and (7.4), less the amount of any government assistance or non-government assistance that can reasonably be considered to be in respect of, or for the acquisition of, the property and that, at the time of the filing of the taxpayer's return of income under this Part for the taxation year in which the property was acquired, the taxpayer has received, is entitled to receive or can reasonably be expected to receive;

(*c*) (Repealed by S.C. 1996, c. 21, s. 30(21).)

(*c*.1) the amount of a taxpayer's qualified Canadian exploration expenditure for a taxation year shall be deemed to be the amount of the taxpayer's qualified Canadian exploration expenditure for the year as otherwise determined less the amount of any government assistance, non-government assistance or contract payment (other than assistance under the *Petroleum Incentives Program Act* or the *Petroleum Incentives Program Act*, Chapter P-4.1 of the Statutes of Alberta, 1981) in respect of expenditures included in determining the taxpayer's qualified Canadian exploration expenditure for the year that, at the time of the filing of the taxpayer's return of income for the year, the taxpayer has received, is entitled to receive or can reasonably be expected to receive;

(*c*.2) the amount of a taxpayer's flow-through mining expenditure for a taxation year is deemed to be the amount of the taxpayer's flow-through mining expenditure for the year as otherwise determined less the amount of any government assistance or non-government assistance in respect of expenses included in determining the taxpayer's flow-through mining expenditure for the year that, at the time of the filing of the taxpayer's return of income for the year, the taxpayer has received, is entitled to receive or can reasonably be expected to receive;

(*c*.3) the amount of a taxpayer's pre-production mining expenditure for a taxation year is deemed to be the amount of the taxpayer's pre-production mining expenditure for the year as otherwise determined less the amount of any government assistance or non-government assistance in respect of expenses included in determining the taxpayer's pre-production mining expenditure for the year that, at the time of the filing of the taxpayer's return of income for the year, the taxpayer has received, is entitled to receive or can reasonably be expected to receive;

(*c*.4) the amount of a taxpayer's eligible salary and wages for a taxation year is deemed to be the amount of the taxpayer's eligible salary and wages for the year otherwise determined less the amount of any government assistance or non-government assistance in respect of the eligible salary and wages for the year that, at the time of the filing of the taxpayer's return of income for the year, the taxpayer has received, is entitled to receive or can reasonably be expected to receive; and

(*c*.5) (Repealed by S.C. 2017, c. 20, s. 23(13).)

(*d*) where at a particular time a taxpayer who is a beneficiary of a trust or a member of a partnership has received, is entitled to receive or can reasonably be expected to receive government assistance, non-government assistance or a contract payment, the amount thereof that may reasonably be considered to be in respect of, or for the acquisition of, depreciable property of the trust or partnership or in respect of an expenditure by the trust or partnership shall be deemed to have been received at that time by the trust or partnership, as the case may be, as government assistance, non-government assistance or as a contract payment in respect of the property or the expenditure, as the case may be.

(*e*) (Repealed by S.C. 1996, c. 21, s. 30(22).)

(*f*) (Repealed by S.C. 1996, c. 21, s. 30(22).)

History: S. 127(11.1)(*c*.5) was repealed by S.C. 2017, c. 20, s. 23(13), applicable in respect of expenditures incurred after March 21, 2017, except that this amendment does not apply in respect of expenditures incurred before 2020 under a written agreement entered into before March 22, 2017. S. 127(11.1)(*c*.5) formerly read:

(*c*.5) the amount of a taxpayer's eligible child care space expenditure for a taxation year is deemed to be the amount of the taxpayer's eligible child care space expenditure for the taxation year otherwise determined less the amount of any government assistance or non-government assistance in respect of the eligible child care space expenditure for the taxation year that, at the time of the filing of the taxpayer's return of income for the taxation year, the taxpayer has received, is entitled to receive or can reasonably be expected to receive; and

Tax Window Files: Quebec Capital Tax Credit, *Technical Interpretation, Business and Partnerships Division, January 22, 2007,* CRA Document No. 2006-0212641E5.

► 127(11.2) ◄

(11.2) Time of acquisition. In applying subsections (5), (7) and (8), paragraphs (*a*) and (*a*.1) of the definition "investment tax credit" in subsection (9) and section 127.1, qualified property and qualified resource property are deemed not to have been acquired by a taxpayer before the property is considered to have become available for use by the taxpayer, determined without reference to paragraphs 13(27)(*c*) and (28)(*d*).

History: S. 127(11.2) was replaced by S.C. 2017, c. 20, s. 23(14), applicable in respect of expenditures incurred after March 21, 2017, except that this amendment does not apply in respect of expenditures incurred before 2020 under a written agreement entered into before March 22, 2017. S. 127(11.2) formerly read:

(11.2) *Time of expenditure and acquisition.* In applying subsections (5), (7) and (8), paragraphs (*a*), (*a.1*) and (*a.5*) of the definition "investment tax credit" in subsection (9) and section 127.1,

(*a*) qualified property and qualified resource property are deemed not to have been acquired, and

(*b*) expenditures included in an eligible child care space expenditure are deemed not to have been incurred

by a taxpayer before the property is considered to have become available for use by the taxpayer, determined without reference to paragraphs 13(27)(*c*) and 13(28)(*d*), and subparagraph (27.12)(*b*)(i).

S. 127(11.2)(*a*) was replaced by S.C. 2012, c. 31, s. 27(23), in force February 1, 2017, and formerly read:

(*a*) qualified property, qualified resource property and first term shared-use-equipment are deemed not to have been acquired, and

S. 127(11.2)(*a*) was replaced by S.C. 2012, c. 31, s. 27(22), deemed to have come into force on March 29, 2012. S. 127(11.2)(*a*) formerly read:

(*a*) certified property, qualified property and first term shared-use-equipment are deemed not to have been acquired, and

S. 127(11.2)(*b*) was replaced by S.C. 2012, c. 31, s. 27(24), applicable in respect of expenditures made after 2013. S. 127(11.2)(*b*) formerly read:

(*b*) expenditures incurred to acquire property described in subparagraph 37(1)(*b*)(i) or included in an eligible child care expenditure are deemed not to have been incurred

Related Sections: 13(26) Restriction on deduction before available for use; 13(27) Interpretation — available for use; 13(28) Idem; 13(29) Idem; 13(30) Transfers of property; 13(31) Idem; s. 37(1.2) Deemed time of capital expenditure; s. 127(9), "certified property", "first term shared-use-equipment", "qualified property"; s. 248(19) When property available for use.

SR&ED Publications: SR&ED Capital Expenditures Policy.

► 127(11.3) ◄

(11.3) Decertification of approved project property. For the purposes of the definition "approved project property" in subsection (9), a property that has been certified by the Minister of Regional Industrial Expansion, the Minister of Industry, Science and Technology or the member of the Queen's Privy Council for Canada appointed to be the Minister for the purposes of the *Atlantic Canada Opportunities Agency Act* may have its certification revoked by the latter Minister where

(*a*) an incorrect statement was made in the furnishing of information for the purpose of obtaining the certificate, or

(*b*) the taxpayer does not conform to the plan described in that definition,

and a certificate that has been so revoked shall be void from the time of its issue.

► 127(11.4) ◄

(11.4) Special rule for eligible salary and wages — apprentices. For the purpose of the definition "eligible salary and wages" in subsection (9), the eligible salary and wages payable by a taxpayer in a taxation year to an eligible apprentice in respect of the eligible apprentice's employment in the taxation year is, if the eligible apprentice is employed by any other taxpayer who is related to the taxpayer (including a partnership that has a member that is related to the taxpayer) in the calendar year that includes the end of the taxpayer's taxation year, deemed to be nil unless the taxpayer is designated in prescribed form by all of those related taxpayers to be the only employer of the eligible apprentice for the purpose of the taxpayer applying that definition to the salary and wages payable by the taxpayer to the eligible apprentice in that taxation year, in which case

(*a*) the eligible salary and wages payable by the taxpayer in the taxation year to the eligible apprentice in respect of the eligible apprentice's employment in the taxation year shall be the amount determined without reference to this subsection; and

(*b*) the eligible salary and wages payable to the eligible apprentice by each of the other related taxpayers in their respective taxation years that end in the calendar year is deemed to be nil.

► 127(11.5) ◄

(11.5) Adjustments to qualified expenditures. For the purposes of the definition "qualified expenditure" in subsection (9), the amount of an expenditure (other than a prescribed proxy amount) incurred by a taxpayer in a taxation year is deemed to be the amount of the expenditure determined under subsection (11.6).

History: S. 127(11.5) was replaced by S.C. 2012, c. 31, s. 27(26), in force February 1, 2017, and formerly read:

(11.5) *Adjustments to qualified expenditures.* For the purpose of the definition "qualified expenditure" in subsection (9),

(*a*) the amount of an expenditure (other than a prescribed proxy amount or an amount described in paragraph (*b*)) incurred by a taxpayer in a taxation year is deemed to be the amount of the expenditure determined under subsection (11.6); and

(*b*) the amount of an expenditure incurred by a taxpayer in the taxation year that ends coincidentally with the end of the first period (within the meaning assigned in the definition "first term shared-use-equipment" in subsection (9)) or the second period (within the meaning assigned in the definition "second term shared-use-equipment" in subsection (9)) in respect of first term shared-use-equipment or second term shared-use-equipment, respectively, of the taxpayer is deemed to be 1/4 of the capital cost of the equipment determined after the application of subsection (11.6) in accordance with the following rules:

(i) the capital cost to the taxpayer shall be computed as if no amount were added thereto because of section 21, and

(ii) the capital cost to the taxpayer is determined without reference to subsections 13(7.1) and (7.4).

S. 127(11.5)(*a*) was replaced by S.C. 2012, c. 31, s. 27(25), applicable in respect of expenditures made after 2013. S. 127(11.5)(*a*) formerly read:

(*a*) the amount of an expenditure (other than a prescribed proxy amount or an amount described in paragraph (*b*)) incurred by a taxpayer in a taxation year is deemed to be the amount of the expenditure, determined without reference to subsections 13(7.1) and (7.4) and after the application of subsection (11.6); and

Related Sections: S. 12(1)(*x*)(vi) Inducement, reimbursement, etc.; s. 127(11.6) Non-arm's length costs; s. 127(18) Reduction of qualified expenditures.

► 127(11.6) ◄

(11.6) Non-arm's length costs. For the purpose of subsection (11.5), where

(*a*) a taxpayer would, if this Act were read without reference to subsection (26), incur at any time an expenditure as consideration for a person or partnership (referred to in this subsection as the "supplier") rendering a service (other than a service rendered by a person as an employee of the taxpayer) or providing a property to the taxpayer, and

(*b*) at that time the taxpayer does not deal at arm's length with the supplier, the amount of the expenditure incurred by the taxpayer for the service or property and the cost to the taxpayer of the property are deemed to be

(*c*) in the case of a service rendered to the taxpayer, the lesser of

(i) the amount of the expenditure otherwise incurred by the taxpayer for the service, and

(ii) the adjusted service cost to the supplier of rendering the service, and

(*d*) in the case of a property sold to the taxpayer, the lesser of

(i) the cost to the taxpayer of the property otherwise determined, and

(ii) the adjusted selling cost to the supplier of the property.

History: S. 127(11.6), the portion after paragraph (*b*) and before paragraph (*c*) was replaced by S.C. 2012, c. 31, in force February 1, 2017, and formerly read:

the amount of the expenditure incurred by the taxpayer for the service or property and the capital cost to the taxpayer of the property are deemed to be

S. 127(11.6)(*d*)(i) was replaced by S.C. 2012, c. 31, s. 27(28), in force February 1, 2017, and formerly read:

(i) the capital cost to the taxpayer of the property otherwise determined, and

Related Sections: S. 127(11.7) Definitions; s. 127(11.8) Interpretation for non-arm's length costs; s. 127(24) Exclusion from qualified expenditure.

SR&ED Publications: Total Qualified SR&ED Expenditures for Investment Tax Credit Purposes Policy.

► 127(11.7) ◄

(11.7) Definitions. The definitions in this subsection apply in this subsection and subsection (11.6).

Related Sections: S. 127(11.8) Interpretation for non-arm's length costs; s. 257 Negative amounts.

Tax Window Files: SR&ED Expenditures and Members in a Joint Venture, *Technical Interpretation, Business and Partnerships Division, October 15, 2008*, CRA Document No. 2008-0269721I7.

"adjusted selling cost" —"adjusted selling cost" to a person or partnership (referred to in this definition as the "supplier") of a property is the amount determined by the formula

$$A - B$$

where

A is

(*a*) where the property is purchased from another person or partnership with which the supplier does not deal at arm's length, the lesser of

(i) the cost to the supplier of the property, and

(ii) the adjusted selling cost to the other person or partnership of the property, and

(*b*) in any other case, the cost to the supplier of the property,

and for the purpose of paragraph (*b*),

(*c*) where part of the cost to a supplier of a particular property is attributable to another property acquired by the supplier from a person or partnership with which the supplier does not deal at arm's length, that part of the cost is deemed to be the lesser of

(i) the amount of that part of the cost otherwise determined, and

(ii) the adjusted selling cost to the person or the partnership of the other property,

(*d*) where part of the cost to a supplier of a property is attributable to a service (other than a service rendered by a person as an employee of the supplier) rendered to the supplier by a person or partnership with which the supplier does not deal at arm's length, that part of the cost is deemed to be the lesser of

(i) the amount of that part of the cost otherwise determined, and

(ii) the adjusted service cost to the person or partnership of rendering the service, and

(*e*) no part of the cost to a supplier of a property that is attributable to remuneration based on profits or a bonus paid or payable to an employee of the supplier shall be included, and

B is the total of all amounts each of which is the amount of government assistance or non-government assistance that can reasonably be considered to be in respect of the property and that the supplier has received, is entitled to receive or can reasonably be expected to receive.

"adjusted service cost" —"adjusted service cost" to a person or partnership (referred to in this definition as the "supplier") of rendering a particular service is the amount determined by the formula:

$$A - B - C - D - E$$

where

A is the cost to the supplier of rendering the particular service,

B is the total of all amounts each of which is the amount, if any, by which

(*a*) the cost to the supplier for a service (other than a service rendered by a person as an employee of the supplier) rendered by a person or partnership that does not deal at arm's length with the supplier to the extent that the cost is incurred for the purpose of rendering the particular service

exceeds

(*b*) the adjusted service cost to the person or partnership referred to in paragraph (*a*) of rendering the service referred to in that paragraph to the supplier,

C is the total of all amounts each of which is the amount, if any, by which

(*a*) the cost to the supplier of a property acquired by the supplier from a person or partnership that does not deal at arm's length with the supplier

exceeds

(*b*) the adjusted selling cost to the person or partnership referred to in paragraph (*a*) of the property,

to the extent that the excess relates to the cost of rendering the particular service,

D is the total of all amounts each of which is remuneration based on profits or a bonus paid or payable to an employee of the supplier to the extent that it is included in the cost to the supplier of rendering the particular service, and

E is the total of all amounts each of which is government assistance or non-government assistance that can reasonably be considered to be in respect of rendering the particular service and that the supplier has received, is entitled to receive or can reasonably be expected to receive.

▶ 127(11.8) ◀

(11.8) Interpretation for non-arm's length costs. For the purposes of this subsection and subsections (11.6) and (11.7),

(*a*) the cost to a person or partnership (referred to in this paragraph as the "supplier") of rendering a service or providing a property to another person or partnership (referred to in this paragraph as the "recipient") with which the supplier does not deal at arm's length does not include,

(i) where the cost to the recipient of the service rendered or property provided by the supplier would, but for this paragraph, be a cost to the recipient incurred in rendering a particular service or providing a particular property to a person or partnership with which the recipient does not deal at arm's length, any expenditure of the supplier to the extent that it would, if it were incurred by the recipient in rendering the particular service or providing the particular property, be excluded from a cost to the recipient because of this paragraph, and

(ii) in any other case, any expenditure of the supplier to the extent that it would, if it were incurred by the recipient, not be a qualified expenditure of the recipient; and

(*b*) paragraph 69(1)(*c*) does not apply in determining the cost of a property;

(*c*) (Repealed by S.C. 2012, c. 31, s. 27(29).)

History: S. 127(11.8)(*c*) was repealed by S.C. 2012, c. 31, s. 27(29), applicable in respect of expenditures made after 2013. S. 127(11.8)(*c*) formerly read:

(*c*) the leasing of a property is deemed to be the rendering of a service.

Tax Window Files: ITCs — Non-Arm's Length Lease of Used Equipment, *Technical Interpretation, Business and Partnerships Division, February 15, 2007,* CRA Document No. 2006-0206761I7.

▶ 127(12) ◀

(12) Interpretation. For the purposes of subsection 13(7.1), where, pursuant to a designation or an allocation from a trust or partnership, an amount is required by subsection (7) or (8) to be added in computing the investment tax credit of a taxpayer at the end of the taxpayer's taxation year, the portion thereof that can reasonably be considered to relate to depreciable property shall be deemed to have been received by the partnership or trust, as the case may be, at the end of its fiscal period in respect of which the designation or allocation was made as assistance from a government for the acquisition of depreciable property.

▶ 127(12.1) ◀

(12.1) Idem. For the purposes of section 37, where, pursuant to a designation or an allocation from a trust or partnership, an amount is required by subsection (7) or (8) to be added in computing the investment tax credit of a taxpayer at the end of the taxpayer's taxation year, the portion thereof that may reasonably be regarded as relating to expenditures of a current nature in respect of scientific research and experimental development that are qualified expenditures shall, at the end of the fiscal period of the trust or partnership, as the case may be, in respect of which the designation or allocation was made, reduce the total of such expenditures of a current nature as may be claimed by the trust or partnership in respect of scientific research and experimental development.

SR&ED Publications: SR&ED Claims for Partnerships Policy.

▶ 127(12.2) ◀

(12.2) Idem. For the purposes of paragraphs 53(2)(*c*), (*h*) and (*k*), where in a taxation year a taxpayer has deducted under subsection (5) an amount that may reasonably be regarded as attributable to amounts included in computing the investment tax credit of the taxpayer at the end of the year in respect of property acquired, or an expenditure made, in a subsequent taxation year, the taxpayer shall be deemed to have made the deduction under that subsection in that subsequent taxation year.

▶ 127(12.3) ◀

(12.3) Idem. For the purposes of the determination of J in the definition "cumulative Canadian exploration expense" in subsection 66.1(6), where, pursuant to a designation by a trust, an amount is required by subsection (7) to be added in computing the investment tax credit of a taxpayer at the end of the taxpayer's taxation year, the portion thereof that can reasonably be considered to relate to a qualified Canadian exploration expenditure of the trust for a taxation year shall be deemed to have been received by the trust at the end of its taxation year in respect of which the designation was made as assistance from a government in respect of that expenditure.

► 127(13) ◄

(13) Agreement to transfer qualified expenditures. Where a taxpayer (referred to in this subsection and subsections (15) and (16) as the "transferor") and another taxpayer (referred to in this subsection and subsection (15) as the "transferee") file with the Minister an agreement or an amended agreement in respect of a particular taxation year of the transferor, the least of

(*a*) the amount specified in the agreement for the purpose of this subsection,

(*b*) the amount that but for the agreement would be the transferor's SR&ED qualified expenditure pool at the end of the particular year, and

(*c*) the total of all amounts each of which is an amount that, if the transferor were dealing at arm's length with the transferee, would be a contract payment

(i) for the performance of scientific research and experimental development for, or on behalf of, the transferee,

(ii) that is paid by the transferee to the transferor on or before the day that is 180 days after the end of the particular year, and

(iii) that would be in respect of

(A) a qualified expenditure that

(I) would be incurred by the transferor in the particular year (if this Act were read without reference to subsections (26) and 78(4)) in respect of that portion of the scientific research and experimental development that was performed at a time when the transferor did not deal at arm's length with the transferee, and

(II) is paid by the transferor on or before the day that is 180 days after the end of the particular year, or

(B) an amount added because of this subsection to the transferor's SR&ED qualified expenditure pool at the end of the particular year where the amount is attributable to an expenditure in respect of the scientific research and experimental development

is deemed to be

(*d*) an amount determined in respect of the transferor for the particular year for the purpose of determining the value of C in the definition "SR&ED qualified expenditure pool" in subsection (9), and

(*e*) an amount determined in respect of the transferee for the transferee's first taxation year that ends at or after the end of the particular year for the purpose of determining the value of B in the definition "SR&ED qualified expenditure pool" in subsection (9),

and where the total of all amounts each of which is an amount specified in an agreement filed with the Minister under this subsection in respect of a particular taxation year of a transferor exceeds the amount that would be the transferor's SR&ED qualified expenditure pool at the end of the particular year if no agreement were filed with the Minister in respect of the particular year, the least of the amounts determined under paragraphs (*a*) to (*c*) in respect of each such agreement is deemed to be nil.

Related Sections: S. 37(1)(*e*)(iii) Scientific research and experimental development; s. 127(8)(*a*) Investment tax credit of partnership; s. 127(14) Identification of amounts transferred; s. 127(15) Invalid agreements; s. 127(16) Non-arm's length parties; s. 127(17) Assessment; s. 127(29)(*c*) Recapture of investment tax credit of allocating taxpayer.

Forms: T1146 — Agreement to Transfer Qualified Expenditures Incurred in Respect of Scientific Research and Experimental Development (SR&ED) Contracts.

SR&ED Publications: SR&ED Filing Requirements Policy; Total Qualified SR&ED Expenditures for Investment Tax Credit Purposes Policy.

► 127(14) ◄

(14) Identification of amounts transferred. Where

(*a*) a transferor and a transferee have filed an agreement under subsection (13) in respect of a taxation year of the transferor,

(*b*) the agreement includes a statement identifying the amount specified in the agreement for the purpose of subsection (13), or a part of that amount, as being related to

(i) a particular qualified expenditure included in the value of A in the formula in the definition "SR&ED qualified expenditure pool" in subsection (9) for the purpose of determining the transferor's SR&ED qualified expenditure pool at the end of the year, or

(ii) a particular amount included in the value of B in the formula in that definition for the purpose of determining the transferor's SR&ED qualified expenditure pool at the end of the year that is deemed by paragraph (*d*) to be a qualified expenditure, and

(*c*) the total of all amounts so identified in agreements filed by the transferor under subsection (13) as being related to the particular expenditure or the particular amount does not exceed the particular expenditure or the particular amount, as the case may be,

for the purposes of this section (other than the description of A in the definition "SR&ED qualified expenditure pool" in subsection (9)) and section 127.1,

(*d*) the amount so identified that is included in the value of B in the formula in that definition for the purpose of determining the transferee's SR&ED qualified expenditure pool at the end of the taxation year of the transferee is deemed to be a qualified expenditure either of a current nature or of a capital nature, incurred by the transferee in that year, where the particular expenditure or the particular amount was an expenditure of a current nature or of a capital nature, as the case may be, and

(*e*) except for the purpose of paragraph (*b*), the amount of the transferor's qualified expenditures of a current nature incurred in the taxation year of the transferor in respect of which the agreement is made is deemed not to exceed the amount by which the amount of such expenditures otherwise determined exceeds the total of all amounts identified under paragraph (*b*) by the transferor in agreements filed under subsection (13) in respect of the year as being related to expenditures of a current nature.

► 127(15) ◄

(15) Invalid agreements. An agreement or amended agreement referred to in subsection (13) between a transferor and a transferee is deemed not to have been filed with the Minister for the purpose of that subsection where

(*a*) it is not in prescribed form;

(*b*) it is not filed

(i) on or before the transferor's filing-due date for the particular taxation year to which the agreement relates,

(ii) in the period within which the transferor may serve a notice of objection to an assessment of tax payable under this Part for the particular year, or

(iii) in the period within which the transferee may serve a notice of objection to an assessment of tax payable under this Part for its first taxation year that ends at or after the end of the transferor's particular year;

(*c*) it is not accompanied by,

(i) where the transferor is a corporation and its directors are legally entitled to administer its affairs, a certified copy of their resolution authorizing the agreement to be made,

(ii) where the transferor is a corporation and its directors are not legally entitled to administer its affairs, a certified copy of the document by which the person legally entitled to administer its affairs authorized the agreement to be made,

(iii) where the transferee is a corporation and its directors are legally entitled to administer its affairs, a certified copy of their resolution authorizing the agreement to be made, and

(iv) where the transferee is a corporation and its directors are not legally entitled to administer its affairs, a certified copy of the document by which the person legally entitled to administer its affairs authorized the agreement to be made; or

(*d*) an agreement amending the agreement has been filed in accordance with subsection (13) and this subsection, except where subsection (16) applies to the original agreement.

► 127(16) ◄

(16) Non-arm's length parties. Where a taxpayer does not deal at arm's length with another taxpayer as a result of a transaction, event or arrangement, or a series of transactions or events, the principal purpose of which can reasonably be considered to have been to enable the taxpayers to enter into an agreement referred to in subsection (13), for the purpose of paragraph (13)(*e*) the least of the amounts determined under paragraphs (13)(*a*) to (*c*) in respect of the agreement is deemed to be nil.

Related Sections: S. 248(10) Series of transactions.

► 127(17) ◄

(17) Assessment. Notwithstanding subsections 152(4) and (5), such assessment of the tax, interest and penalties payable by any taxpayer in respect of any taxation year that began before the day an agreement or amended agreement is filed under subsection (13) or (20) shall be made as is necessary to take into account the agreement or the amended agreement.

► 127(18) ◄

(18) Reduction of qualified expenditures. Where on or before the filing-due date for a taxation year of a person or partnership (referred to in this subsection as the "taxpayer") the taxpayer has received, is entitled to receive or can reasonably be expected to receive a particular amount that is government assistance, non-government assistance or a contract payment that can reasonably be considered to be in respect of scientific research and experimental development, the amount by which the particular amount exceeds all amounts applied for preceding taxation years under this subsection or subsection (19) or (20) in respect of the particular amount shall be applied to reduce the taxpayer's qualified expenditures otherwise incurred in the year that can reasonably be considered to be in respect of the scientific research and experimental development.

Related Sections: S. 127(9), "contract payment", "government assistance", "investment tax credit", "non-government assistance", "qualified expenditure"; s. 127(10.7)(*c*), (*d*) Further additions to investment tax credit; s. 127(11.5) Adjustments to qualified expenditures; s. 127(21) Failure to allocate; s. 127(23) Partnership's taxation year; s. 248(1), "filing-due date".

SR&ED Publications: Assistance and Contract Payments Policy.

Tax Window Files: Reduction in qualified expenditures under 127(18), *Advance Income Tax Ruling, Business and Partnerships Division, June 18, 2007*, CRA Document No. 2007-0226411E5; SR&ED: Repayable Grants, *Round Table on Federal Taxation APFF — 2005 Conference, Question 23, October 7, 2005*, CRA Document No. 2005-0141131C6; Scientific Research and Experimental Development — Government Assistance, *Technical Interpretation, Reorganizations and Resources Division, December 23, 2004*, CRA Document No. 2004-0095621I7.

► 127(19) ◄

(19) Reduction of qualified expenditures. Where on or before the filing-due date for a taxation year of a person or partnership (referred to in this subsection as the "recipient") the recipient has received, is entitled to receive or can reasonably be expected to receive a particular amount that is government assistance, non-government assistance or a contract payment that can reasonably be considered to be in respect of scientific research and experimental development and the particular amount exceeds the total of

(*a*) all amounts applied for preceding taxation years under this subsection or subsection (18) or (20) in respect of the particular amount, (*b*) the total of all amounts each of which would be a qualified expenditure that is incurred in the year by the recipient and that can reasonably be considered to be in respect of the scientific research and experimental development if subsection (18) did not apply to the particular amount, and

(*c*) the total of all amounts each of which would, but for the application of this subsection to the particular amount, be a qualified expenditure

(i) that was incurred by a person or partnership in a taxation year of the person or partnership that ended in the recipient's taxation year, and

(ii) that can reasonably be considered to be in respect of the scientific research and experimental development to the extent that it was performed by the person or partnership at a time when the person or partnership was not dealing at arm's length with the recipient,

the particular amount shall be applied to reduce each qualified expenditure otherwise determined that is referred to in paragraph (*c*).

Related Sections: S. 127(9), "contract payment", "government assistance", "investment tax credit", "non-government assistance", "qualified expenditure"; s. 127(21) Failure to allocate; s. 127(23) Partnership's taxation year; s. 248(1), "filing-due date".

► 127(20) ◄

(20) Agreement to allocate. Where

(*a*) on or before the filing-due date for a taxation year of a person or partnership (referred to in this subsection and subsection (22) as the "taxpayer") the taxpayer has received, is entitled to receive or can reasonably be expected to receive a particular amount that is government assistance, non-government assistance or a contract payment that can reasonably be considered to be in respect of scientific research and experimental development,

(*b*) subsection (19) does not apply to the particular amount in respect of the year, and

(*c*) the taxpayer and a person or partnership (referred to in this subsection and subsection (22) as the "transferee") with which the taxpayer does not deal at arm's length file an agreement or amended agreement with the Minister,

the lesser of

(*d*) the amount specified in the agreement, and

(*e*) the total of all amounts each of which would, but for the agreement, be a qualified expenditure

(i) that was incurred by the transferee in a particular taxation year of the transferee that ended in the taxpayer's taxation year, and

(ii) that can reasonably be considered to be in respect of the scientific research and experimental development to the extent that it was performed by the transferee at a time when the transferee was not dealing at arm's length with the taxpayer

shall be applied to reduce the qualified expenditures otherwise determined that are described in paragraph (*e*).

Related Sections: S. 127(9), "contract payment", "government assistance", "investment tax credit", "non-government assistance", "qualified expenditure"; s. 127(17) Assessment; s. 127(21) Failure to allocate; s. 127(22) Invalid agreements; s. 127(23) Partnership's taxation year; s. 248(1), "filing-due date".

Forms: T1145 — Agreement to Allocate Assistance for Scientific Research & Experimental Development Expenditures (SR&ED) Between Persons Not Dealing at Arm's Length.

SR&ED Publications: SR&ED Filing Requirements Policy; Assistance and Contract Payments Policy.

► 127(21) ◄

(21) Failure to allocate. Where on or before the filing-due date for a taxation year of a person or partnership (referred to in this subsection as the "recipient") the recipient has received, is entitled to receive or can reasonably be expected to receive a particular amount that is government assistance, non-government assistance or a contract payment that can reasonably be considered to be in respect of scientific research and experimental development and subsection (19) does not apply to the particular amount in respect of the year, the lesser of

(*a*) the total of all amounts each of which is a qualified expenditure

(i) that was incurred by a particular person or partnership in a taxation year of the particular person or partnership that ended in the recipient's taxation year, and

(ii) that can reasonably be considered to be in respect of the scientific research and experimental development to the extent that it was performed by the particular person or partnership at a time when the particular person or partnership was not dealing at arm's length with the recipient, and

(*b*) the amount, if any, by which the particular amount exceeds the total of amounts applied for the year and preceding taxation years under subsection (18), (19) or (20) in respect of the particular amount

is deemed for the purposes of this section to be an amount of government assistance received at the end of the particular year by the particular person or partnership in respect of the scientific research and experimental development.

Related Sections: S. 127(9), "contract payment", "government assistance", "non-government assistance", "qualified expenditure"; s. 127(23) Partnership's taxation year; s. 248(1), "filing-due date".

► 127(22) ◄

(22) Invalid agreements. An agreement or amended agreement referred to in subsection (20) between a taxpayer and a transferee is deemed not to have been filed with the Minister where

(*a*) it is not in prescribed form;

(*b*) it is not filed

(i) on or before the taxpayer's filing-due date for the particular taxation year to which the agreement relates,

(ii) in the period within which the taxpayer may serve a notice of objection to an assessment of tax payable under this Part for the particular year, or

(iii) in the period within which the transferee may serve a notice of objection to an assessment of tax payable under this Part for its first taxation year that ends at or after the end of the taxpayer's particular year;

(*c*) it is not accompanied by,

(i) where the taxpayer is a corporation and its directors are legally entitled to administer its affairs, a certified copy of their resolution authorizing the agreement to be made,

(ii) where the taxpayer is a corporation and its directors are not legally entitled to administer its affairs, a certified copy of the document by which the person legally entitled to administer its affairs authorized the agreement to be made,

(iii) where the transferee is a corporation and its directors are legally entitled to administer its affairs, a certified copy of their resolution authorizing the agreement to be made, and

(iv) where the transferee is a corporation and its directors are not legally entitled to administer its affairs, a certified copy of the document by which the person legally entitled to administer its affairs authorized the agreement to be made; or

(*d*) an agreement amending the agreement has been filed in accordance with subsection (20) and this subsection.

Related Sections: S. 127(23) Partnership's taxation year; s. 248(1), "filing-due date".

► 127(23) ◄

(23) Partnership's taxation year. For the purposes of subsections (18) to (22), the taxation year of a partnership is deemed to be its fiscal period and its filing-due date for a taxation year is deemed to be the day that would be its filing-due date for the year if it were a corporation.

Related Sections: S. 248(1), "filing-due date".

► 127(24) ◄

(24) Exclusion from qualified expenditure. Where

(*a*) a person or partnership (referred to in this subsection as the "first person") does not deal at arm's length with another person or partnership (referred to in this subsection as the "second person"),

(*b*) there is an arrangement under which an amount is paid or payable by the first person to a person or partnership with which the first person deals at arm's length and an amount is received or receivable by the second person from a person or partnership with which the second person deals at arm's length, and

(*c*) one of the main purposes of the arrangement can reasonably be considered to be to cause the amount paid or payable by the first person to be a qualified expenditure,

the amount paid or payable by the first person is deemed not to be a qualified expenditure.

Related Sections: S. 127(9), "qualified expenditure"; s. 127(11.6) Non-arm's length costs.

SR&ED Publications: Contract Expenditures for SR&ED Performed on Behalf of a Claimant Policy.

► 127(25) ◄

(25) Deemed contract payment. Where

(*a*) a person or partnership (referred to in this subsection as the "first person") deals at arm's length with another person or partnership (referred to in this subsection as the "second person"),

(*b*) there is an arrangement under which an amount is paid or payable by the first person to a person or partnership (other than the second person) and a particular amount is received or receivable in respect of scientific research and experimental development by the second person from a person or partnership that is not a taxable supplier in respect of the particular amount, and

(*c*) one of the main purposes of the arrangement can reasonably be considered to be to cause the amount received or receivable by the second person not to be a contract payment,

the amount received or receivable by the second person is deemed to be a contract payment in respect of scientific research and experimental development.

► 127(26) ◄

(26) Unpaid amounts. For the purposes of subsections (5) to (25) and section 127.1, a taxpayer's expenditure described in paragraph 37(1)(*a*) that is unpaid on the day that is 180 days after the end of the taxation year in which the expenditure is otherwise incurred is deemed

(*a*) not to have been incurred in the year; and

(*b*) to be incurred at the time it is paid.

Related Sections: S. 127(11.6) Non-arm's length costs; s. 127(27) Recapture of investment tax credit.

► 127(27) ◄

(27) Recapture of investment tax credit. Where

(*a*) a taxpayer acquired a particular property from a person or partnership in a taxation year of the taxpayer or in any of the 10 preceding taxation years,

(*b*) the cost, or a portion of the cost, of the particular property was a qualified expenditure, or would if this Act were read without reference to subsection (26) be a qualified expenditure, to the taxpayer,

(*c*) the cost, or the portion of the cost, of the particular property is included, or would if this Act were read without reference to subsection (26) be included, in an amount, a percentage of which can reasonably be considered to be included in computing the taxpayer's investment tax credit at the end of the taxation year, and

(*d*) in the year and after February 23, 1998, the taxpayer converts to commercial use, or disposes of without having previously converted to commercial use, the particular property or another property that incorporates the particular property,

there shall be added to the taxpayer's tax otherwise payable under this Part for the year the lesser of

(*e*) the amount that can reasonably be considered to be included in the taxpayer's investment tax credit at the end of any taxation year, or that would be so included if this Act were read without reference to subsection (26), in respect of the particular property, and

(*f*) the amount that is the percentage — that is the sum of each percentage described in paragraph (c) that has been applied to compute the taxpayer's investment tax credit in respect of the particular property — of

(i) in the case where the particular property or the other property is disposed of to a person who deals at arm's length with the taxpayer,

(A) the proceeds of disposition of the property, if the property

(I) is the particular property and is neither first term shared-use equipment nor second term shared-use equipment, or

(II) is the other property,

(B) 25% of the proceeds of disposition of the property, if the property is the particular property, is first term shared-use equipment and is not second term shared-use equipment, and

(C) 50% of the proceeds of disposition of the property, if the property is the particular property and is second term shared-use equipment, and

(ii) in the case where the particular property or the other property is converted to commercial use or is disposed of to a person who does not deal at arm's length with the taxpayer,

(A) the fair market value of the property, if the property

(I) is the particular property and is neither first term shared-use equipment nor second term shared-use equipment, or

(II) is the other property,

(B) 25% of the fair market value of the property at the time of its conversion or disposition, if the particular property is first term shared-use equipment and is not second term shared-use equipment, and

(C) 50% of the fair market value of the property at the time of its conversion or disposition, if the particular property is second term shared-use equipment.

Editorial Note: S. 127(27) provides for a recapture of investment tax credit claims on the cost of property that is converted to commercial use or sold within 20 years (10 years prior to 2006 — see s. 127(36)). It overrides the Tax Court of Canada's decision in *Consoltex Inc. v. The Queen*, 97 DTC 724. S. 127(28) provides a parallel rule for partnerships.

History: S. 127(27)(*b*) and (*c*) were replaced by S.C. 2013, c. 34, s. 269(10), applicable to dispositions and conversions that occur after December 20, 2002, and formerly read:

(*b*) the cost of the particular property was a qualified expenditure to the taxpayer,

(*c*) the cost of the particular property is included in an amount, a percentage of which can reasonably be considered to be included in computing the taxpayer's investment tax credit at the end of the taxation year, and

S. 127(27), the portion after paragraph (*d*) was replaced by S.C. 2013, c. 34, s. 269(11), applicable to dispositions and conversions that occur after December 20, 2002, and formerly read:

there shall be added to the taxpayer's tax otherwise payable under this Part for the year the lesser of the amount that can reasonably be considered to be included in computing the taxpayer's investment tax credit in respect of the particular property and the amount that is the percentage (described in paragraph (*c*)) of

(*e*) if the particular property or the other property is disposed of to a person who deals at arm's length with the taxpayer, the proceeds of disposition of that property, and

(*f*) in any other case, the fair market value of the particular property or the other property at the time of the conversion or disposition.

Related Sections: S. 37(1)(*c.2*) Scientific research and experimental development; s. 127(28) Recapture of investment tax credit of partnership; s. 127(29) Recapture of investment tax credit of allocating taxpayer; s. 127(32) Meaning of cost; s. 127(33) Certain non-arm's length transfers; s. 127(36) Transitional application of investment tax credit recapture.

Canadian Tax Foundation: Braithwaite, *Setting Up Research Facilities and Contracts*, 1999 Corporate Management Tax Conference 13:1–32.

SR&ED Publications: Recapture of SR&ED Investment Tax Credit Policy.

► 127(27.1) ◄

(27.1) Recapture of investment tax credit — child care space amount. (Repealed by S.C. 2017, c. 20, s. 23(15).)

History: S. 127(27.1) was repealed by S.C. 2017, c. 20, s. 23(15), applicable in respect of expenditures incurred after March 21, 2017, except that this amendment does not apply in respect of expenditures incurred before 2020 under a written agreement entered into before March 22, 2017. S. 127(27.1) formerly read:

(27.1) *Recapture of investment tax credit — child care space amount.* There shall be added to a taxpayer's tax otherwise payable under this Part for a particular taxation year, the total of all amounts each of which is an amount determined under subsection (27.12) in respect of a disposition by the taxpayer in the particular taxation year of a property a percentage of the cost of which can reasonably be considered to have been included in the child care space amount of the taxpayer for a taxation year, if the property was acquired in respect of a child care space that was created at a time that is less than 60 months before the disposition.

► 127(27.11) ◄

(27.11) Disposition. (Repealed by S.C. 2017, c. 20, s. 23(15).)

History: S. 127(27.11) was repealed by S.C. 2017, c. 20, s. 23(15), applicable in respect of expenditures incurred after March 21, 2017, except that this amendment does not apply in respect of expenditures incurred before 2020 under a written agreement entered into before March 22, 2017. S. 127(27.11) formerly read:

(27.11) *Disposition.* For the purpose of subsection (27.1),

(*a*) if a particular child care space, in respect of which any amount is included in the child care space amount of a taxpayer or a partnership for a taxation year or a fiscal period, ceases at any particular time to be available, the child care space is, except where the child care space has been disposed of by the taxpayer or the partnership before the particular time, deemed to be a property

(i) disposed of by the taxpayer or the partnership, as the case may be, at the particular time,

(ii) a percentage of the cost of which can reasonably be considered to be included in the child care space amount of the taxpayer or the partnership, as the case may be, for a taxation year or a fiscal period, and

(iii) acquired in respect of a child care space that was created at the time the child care space was created, (*b*) child care spaces that cease to be available are deemed to so cease in reverse chronological order to their creation, and

(*c*) a property acquired by a taxpayer or a partnership in respect of a child care space is deemed to be disposed of by the taxpayer or the partnership, as the case may be, in a disposition described in clause (27.12)(*b*)(ii)(B) if the property is leased by the taxpayer or the partnership to a lessee for any purpose or is converted to a use by the taxpayer or the partnership other than to a use for the child care space.

► 127(27.12) ◄

(27.12) Amount of recapture. (Repealed by S.C. 2017, c. 20, s. 23(15).)

History: S. 127(27.12) was repealed by S.C. 2017, c. 20, s. 23(15), applicable in respect of expenditures incurred after March 21, 2017, except that this amendment does not apply in respect of expenditures incurred before 2020 under a written agreement entered into before March 22, 2017. S. 127(27.12) formerly read:

(27.12) *Amount of recapture.* For the purposes of subsection (27.1) and (27.11), the amount determined under this subsection in respect of a disposition of a property by a taxpayer or a partnership is,

(*a*) where the property disposed of is a child care space, the amount that can reasonably be considered to have been included under paragraph (*a.5*) of the definition "investment tax credit" in subsection (9) in respect of the taxpayer or partnership in respect of the child care space, and

(*b*) in any other case, the lesser of,

(i) the amount that can reasonably be considered to have been included under paragraph (*a.5*) of the definition "investment tax credit" in subsection (9) in respect of the taxpayer or partnership in respect of the cost of the property, and

(ii) 25% of

(A) if the property, or a part of the property, is disposed of to a person who deals at arm's length with the taxpayer or the partnership, the proceeds of disposition of the property, or of the part of the property, and

(B) in any other case, the fair market value of the property or of the part of the property, at the time of the disposition.

► 127(28) ◄

(28) Recapture of investment tax credit of partnership. For the purpose of computing the amount determined under subsection (8) in respect of a partnership at the end of a particular fiscal period, where

(*a*) a particular property, the cost of which is a qualified expenditure, is acquired by the partnership from a person or partnership in the particular fiscal period or in any of the 10 preceding fiscal periods of the partnership,

(*b*) the cost of the particular property is included in an amount, a percentage of which can reasonably be considered to have been included in computing the amount determined under subsection (8) in respect of the partnership at the end of a fiscal period, and

(*c*) in the particular fiscal period and after February 23, 1998, the partnership converts to commercial use, or disposes of without having previously converted to commercial use, the particular property or another property that incorporates the particular property,

there shall be deducted in computing the amount determined under subsection (8) in respect of the partnership at the end of the particular fiscal period the lesser of

(*d*) the amount that can reasonably be considered to have been included in respect of the particular property in computing the amount determined under subsection (8) in respect of the partnership, and

(*e*) the percentage (described in paragraph (*b*)) of

(i) where the particular property or the other property is disposed of to a person who deals at arm's length with the partnership, the proceeds of disposition of that property, and

(ii) in any other case, the fair market value of the particular property or the other property at the time of the conversion or disposition.

Editorial Note: See the editorial note under s. 127(27).

Related Sections: S. 127(30) Addition to tax; s. 127(32) Meaning of cost; s. 127(33) Certain non-arm's length transfers; s. 127(36) Transitional application of investment tax credit recapture.

SR&ED Publications: SR&ED Claims for Partnerships Policy.

► 127(28.1) ◄

(28.1) Recapture of partnership's investment tax credits — child care property. (Repealed by S.C. 2017, c. 20, s. 23(16).)

History: S. 127(28.1) was repealed by S.C. 2017, c. 20, s. 23(16), applicable in respect of expenditures incurred after March 21, 2017, except that this amendment does not apply in respect of expenditures incurred before 2020 under a written agreement entered into before March 22, 2017. S. 127(28.1) formerly read:

(28.1) *Recapture of partnership's investment tax credits — child care property.* For the purpose of computing the amount determined under subsection (8) in respect of a partnership at the end of a particular fiscal period of the partnership, there shall be deducted the total of all amounts, each of which is an amount determined under subsection (27.12) in respect of a disposition by the partnership in the particular fiscal period of a property a percentage of the cost of which can reasonably be considered to have been included in the child care space amount of the partnership for a fiscal period, if the property was acquired in respect of a child care space that was created at a time that is less than 60 months before the disposition.

► 127(29) ◄

(29) Recapture of investment tax credit of allocating taxpayer. Where

(*a*) a taxpayer acquired a particular property from a person or partnership in a taxation year or in any of the 10 preceding taxation years,

(*b*) the cost of the particular property was a qualified expenditure to the taxpayer,

(*c*) all or part of the qualified expenditure can reasonably be considered to have been the subject of an agreement made under subsection (13) by the taxpayer and another taxpayer (in this subsection referred to as the "transferee"), and

(*d*) in the year and after February 23, 1998, the taxpayer converts to commercial use, or disposes of without having previously converted to commercial use, the particular property or another property that incorporates the particular property,

there shall be added to the taxpayer's tax otherwise payable under this Part for the year the lesser of

(*e*) the amount that can reasonably be considered to have been included in computing the transferee's investment tax credit in respect of the qualified expenditure that was the subject of the agreement, and

(*f*) the amount determined by the formula

$$A \times B - C$$

where

A is the percentage applied by the transferee in determining its investment tax credit in respect of the qualified expenditure that was the subject of the agreement,

B is

(i) where the particular property or the other property is disposed of to a person who deals at arm's length with the taxpayer, the proceeds of disposition of that property, and

(ii) in any other case, the fair market value of the particular property or the other property at the time of the conversion or disposition, and

C is the amount, if any, added to the taxpayer's tax payable under subsection (27) in respect of the particular property.

Editorial Note: S. 127(29) implements the same rule as s. 127(27) when the original investment tax credit was transferred by agreement under s. 127(13).

Related Sections: S. 37(1)(*c*.2) Scientific research and experimental development; s. 127(32) Meaning of cost; s. 127(33) Certain non-arm's length transfers; s. 127(36) Transitional application of investment tax credit recapture; s. 257 Negative amounts.

► 127(30) ◄

(30) Addition to tax. Where a taxpayer is a member of a partnership at the end of a fiscal period of the partnership, there shall be added to the taxpayer's tax otherwise payable under this Part for the taxpayer's taxation year in which that fiscal period ends the amount that can reasonably be considered to be the taxpayer's share of the amount, if any, by which

(*a*) the total of

(i) the total of all amounts each of which is the lesser of the amounts described in paragraphs (28)(*d*) and (*e*) in respect of the partnership in respect of the fiscal period, and

(ii) the total of all amounts each of which is the lesser of the amounts described in paragraphs (35)(*c*) and (*d*) in respect of the partnership in respect of the fiscal period,

(iii) (Repealed by S.C. 2017, c. 20, s. 23(17).)

exceeds

(*b*) the amount that would be determined in respect of the partnership under subsection (8) if that subsection were read without reference to subsections (28) and (35).

History: S. 127(30)(*a*)(iii) was repealed by S.C. 2017, c. 20, s. 23(17), applicable in respect of expenditures incurred after March 21, 2017, except that this amendment does not apply in respect of expenditures incurred before 2020 under a written agreement entered into before March 22, 2017. S. 127(30)(*a*)(iii) formerly read:

(iii) the total of all amounts each of which is an amount required by subsection (28.1) to be deducted in computing the amount determined in respect of the partnership in respect of the fiscal period under subsection (8),

S. 127(30)(*b*) was replaced by S.C. 2017, c. 20, s. 23(18), applicable in respect of expenditures incurred after March 21, 2017, except that this amendment does not apply in respect of expenditures incurred before 2020 under a written agreement entered into before March 22, 2017. S. 127(30)(*b*) formerly read:

(*b*) the amount that would be determined in respect of the partnership under subsection (8) if that subsection were read without reference to subsections (28), (28.1), and (35).

Related Sections: S. 37(1)(*c*.3) Scientific research and experimental development; s. 53(1)(*c*)(xiii) Adjustments to cost base — Contributions of capital; s. 127(31) Tiered partnership.

► 127(31) ◄

(31) Tiered partnership. Where a taxpayer is a member of a particular partnership that is a member of another partnership and an amount would be added to the particular partnership's tax payable under this Part for the year pursuant to subsection (30) if the particular partnership were a person and its fiscal period were its taxation year, that amount is deemed to be an amount that is the lesser of the amounts described in paragraphs (28)(*d*) and (*e*), in respect of a property of the particular partnership, that is required by subsection (28) to be deducted in computing the amount under subsection (8) in respect of the particular partnership at the end of the fiscal period.

► 127(32) ◄

(32) Meaning of cost. For the purposes of subsections (27), (28) and (29), "cost of the particular property" to a taxpayer shall not exceed the amount paid by the taxpayer to acquire the particular property from a transferor of the particular property and, for greater certainty, does not include amounts paid by the taxpayer to maintain, modify or transform the particular property.

► 127(33) ◄

(33) Certain non-arm's length transfers. Subsections (27) to (29), (34) and (35) do not apply to a taxpayer or partnership (in this subsection referred to as the "transferor") that disposes of a property to a person or partnership (in this subsection and subsections (34) and (35) referred to as the "purchaser"), that does not deal at arm's length with the transferor, if the purchaser acquired the property in circumstances where the cost of the property to the purchaser would have been an expenditure of the purchaser described in subclause 37(8)(*a*)(ii)(A)(III) or (B)(III) (as those subclauses read on March 29, 2012) but for subparagraph 2902(*b*)(iii) of the *Income Tax Regulations*.

History: S. 127(33) was replaced by S.C. 2012, c. 31, s. 27(30), deemed to have come into force on March 29, 2012. S. 127(33) formerly read:

(33) *Certain non-arm's length transfers.* Subsections (27) to (29), (34) and (35) do not apply to a taxpayer or partnership (in this subsection referred to as the "transferor") that disposes of a property to a person or partnership (in this subsection and subsections (34) and (35) referred to as the "purchaser"), that does not deal at arm's length with the transferor, if the purchaser acquired the property in circumstances where the cost of the property to the purchaser would have been an expenditure of the purchaser described in subclause 37(8)(*a*)(ii)(A)(III) or (B)(III) but for subparagraph 2902(b)(iii) of the *Income Tax Regulations*.

► 127(34) ◄

(34) Recapture of investment tax credit. Where, at any particular time in a taxation year and after February 23, 1998, a purchaser (other than a partnership) converts to commercial use, or disposes of without having previously converted to commercial use, a property (*a*) that was acquired by the purchaser in circumstances described in subsection (33) or that is another property that incorporates a property acquired in such circumstances; and

(*b*) that was first acquired, or that incorporates a property that was first acquired, by a person or partnership (in this subsection referred to as the "original user") with which the purchaser did not deal at arm's length at the time at which the purchaser acquired the property, in the original user's taxation year or fiscal period that includes the particular time (on the assumption that the original user had such a taxation year or fiscal period) or in any of the original user's 10 preceding taxation years or fiscal periods,

there shall be added to the purchaser's tax otherwise payable under this Part for the year the lesser of

(*c*) the amount

(i) included, in respect of the property, in the investment tax credit of the original user, or

(ii) where the original user is a partnership, that can reasonably be considered to have been included in respect of the property in computing the amount determined under subsection (8) in respect of the original user, and

(*d*) the amount determined by applying the percentage that was applied by the original user in determining the amount referred to in paragraph (*c*) to

(i) if the property or the other property is disposed of to a person who deals at arm's length with the purchaser, the proceeds of disposition of that property, and

(ii) in any other case, the fair market value of the property or the other property at the time of the conversion or disposition.

Related Sections: S. 37(1)(*c.2*) Scientific research and experimental development; s. 127(30) Addition to tax; s. 127(33) Certain non-arm's length transfers; s. 127(36) Transitional application of investment tax credit recapture.

► 127(35) ◄

(35) Recapture of investment tax credit. Where, at any particular time in a fiscal period and after February 23, 1998, a purchaser is a partnership that converts to commercial use, or disposes of without having previously converted to commercial use, a property

(*a*) that was acquired by the purchaser in circumstances described in subsection (33) or that is another property that incorporates a property acquired in such circumstances, and

(*b*) that was first acquired, or that incorporates a property that was first acquired, by a person or partnership (in this subsection referred to as the "original user") with which the purchaser did not deal at arm's length at the time at which the purchaser acquired the property, in the original user's taxation year or fiscal period that includes the particular time (on the assumption that the original user had such a taxation year or fiscal period) or in any of the original user's 10 preceding taxation years or fiscal periods,

there shall be deducted in computing the amount determined under subsection (8) in respect of the purchaser at the end of the fiscal period the lesser of

(*c*) the amount

(i) included, in respect of the property, in the investment tax credit of the original user, or

(ii) where the original user is a partnership, that can reasonably be considered to have been included in respect of the property in computing the amount determined under subsection (8) in respect of the original user, and

(*d*) the amount determined by applying the percentage that was applied by the original user in determining the amount referred to in paragraph (*c*) to

(i) if the property or the other property is disposed of to a person who deals at arm's length with the purchaser, the proceeds of disposition of that property, and

(ii) in any other case, the fair market value of the property or the other property at the time of the conversion or disposition.

Related Sections: S. 127(30) Addition to tax; s. 127(33) Certain non-arm's length transfers; s. 127(36) Transitional application of investment tax credit recapture.

► 127(36) ◄

(36) Transitional application of investment tax credit recapture. For the purpose of applying each of subsection (27) or (29) in respect of a taxpayer, subsection (28) in respect of a partnership or subsection (34) or (35) in respect of a purchaser and an original user, as the case may be, (which taxpayer, partnership or original user is, in this subsection, referred to as the "taxpayer"), the reference to "10" in that subsection is to be read as a reference to the number that is the lesser of

(*a*) 20, and

(*b*) the number that is the total of 10 and the number of taxation years or fiscal periods, as the case may be, by which the number of taxation years or fiscal periods of the taxpayer that have ended after 1997 exceeds 11.

History: S. 127(36)(*b*) was replaced by S.C. 2009, c. 2, s. 40(10), applicable in respect of the 2008 and subsequent taxation years. S. 127(36)(*b*) formerly read:

(*b*) the number that is the total of 10 and the number of taxation years or fiscal periods, as the case may be, by which the number of taxation years or fiscal periods of the taxpayer that have ended after 2005 exceeds 11.

SECTION 127.1: Refundable investment tax credit

► 127.1(1) ◄

(1) Refundable investment tax credit. Where a taxpayer (other than a person exempt from tax under section 149) files

(*a*) with the taxpayer's return of income (other than a return of income filed under subsection 70(2) or 104(23), paragraph 128(2)(*f*) or subsection 150(4)) for a taxation year, or

(*b*) with a prescribed form amending a return referred to in paragraph (*a*)

a prescribed form containing prescribed information, the taxpayer is deemed to have paid on the taxpayer's balance-due day for the year an amount on account of the taxpayer's tax payable under this Part for the year equal to the lesser of

(*c*) the taxpayer's refundable investment tax credit for the year, and

(*d*) the amount designated by the taxpayer in the prescribed form.

Editorial Note: S. 127.1(1) allows a taxpayer to claim a refundable investment tax credit for a taxation year. The taxpayer is "deemed to have paid" the amount to its instalment account, the investment tax credit is fully refundable even if no tax is payable for the year. Generally, refundability of investment tax credits are available to Canadian-controlled private corporations, individuals and certain trusts.

Related Sections: S. 13(24) Loss restriction event; s. 127(14) Identification of amounts transferred; s. 127.1(3) Deemed deduction; s. 152(1) Assessment; s. 157(3)(*e*) Reduced instalments; s. 160.1(1) Where excess refunded; s. 164(1)(*a*) Refunds; s. 220(6) Assignment by corporation; s. 256(2.1) Anti-avoidance.

Canadian Tax Foundation: Robinson, *Shop Floor SR & ED: Are You Missing Out?*, 2006 Tax for the Owner-Manager 6(2):6.

Forms: T2 SCH 301 — Newfoundland and Labrador Research and Development Tax Credit; T2 SCH 340 — Nova Scotia Research and Development Tax Credit; T2 SCH 360 — New Brunswick Research and Development Tax Credit; T2 SCH 442 — Yukon Research and Development Tax Credit; T661 — Claim for Scientific Research and Experimental Development (SR&ED) Carried out in Canada; T666 — British Columbia Scientific Research and Experimental Development Tax Credit; T1129 — Newfoundland and Labrador Research and Development Tax Credit (Individuals); T1232 — Yukon Research and Development Tax Credit (Individuals); T2038(IND) — T2038(IND) Investment Tax Credit (Individuals); T2 SCH 31 — T2SCH31 Investment Tax Credit — Corporations.

Guides: T4088 Claiming Scientific Research and Experimental Development Expenditures — Guide to Form T661.

SR&ED Publications: SR&ED Investment Tax Credit Policy.

Tax Window Files: Scientific Research and Experimental Development — Activities Performed by Canadian Corporation on Behalf of Foreign Corporation, *2005 APFF Conference — Round Table on Federal Taxation, Question 7, October 7, 2005*, CRA Document No. 2005-0140991C6.

► 127.1(2) ◄

(2) Definitions. In this section,

"excluded corporation" —"excluded corporation" for a taxation year means a corporation that is, at any time in the year,

(*a*) controlled directly or indirectly, in any manner whatever, by

(i) one or more persons exempt from tax under this Part by virtue of section 149,

(ii) Her Majesty in right of a province, a Canadian municipality or any other public authority, or

(iii) any combination of persons each of whom is a person referred to in subparagraph (i) or (ii), or

(*b*) related to any person referred to in paragraph (*a*);

Related Sections: S. 256(5.1) Control in fact; s. 256(6.2) Application to control in fact.

"qualifying corporation" —"qualifying corporation", for a particular taxation year that ends in a calendar year, means a particular corporation that is a Canadian-controlled private corporation in the particular taxation year the taxable income of which for its immediately preceding taxation year — together with, if the particular corporation is associated in the particular taxation year with one or more other corporations (in this subsection referred to as "associated corporations"), the taxable income of each associated corporation for its last taxation year that ended in the preceding calendar year (determined before taking into consideration the specified future tax consequences for that last year) — does not exceed the qualifying income limit, if any, of the particular corporation for the particular taxation year;

History: S. 127.1(2), the definition "qualifying corporation" was replaced by S.C. 2013, c. 40, s. 58(1), applicable to taxation years that begin after December 21, 2012, and formerly read:

"qualifying corporation"—"qualifying corporation" for a particular taxation year that ends in a calendar year means a particular corporation that is a Canadian-controlled private corporation in the particular taxation year the taxable income of which for its immediately preceding taxation year — together with, if the particular corporation is associated in the particular taxation year with one or more other corporations (in this subsection referred to as "associated corporations"), the taxable income of each associated corporation for its last taxation year that ended in the preceding calendar year (determined before taking into consideration the specified future tax consequences for that last year) — does not exceed the qualifying income limit of the particular corporation for the particular taxation year;

S. 127.1(2), the definition "qualifying corporation" was replaced by S.C. 2009, c. 2, s. 41(1), applicable to taxation years that end on or after February 26, 2008. S. 127.1(2), the definition "qualifying corporation" formerly read:

"qualifying corporation"—"qualifying corporation" for a particular taxation year that ends in acalendar year means

(*a*) a corporation that is a Canadian-controlled privatecorporation throughout the particular year (other than acorporation associated with another corporation in the particularyear) the taxable income of which for its immediately precedingtaxation year (determined before taking into consideration thespecified future tax consequences for that preceding year) doesnot exceed its business limit for that preceding year, or

(*b*) a corporation that is a Canadian-controlled privatecorporation throughout the particular year and associated withanother corporation in the particular year, where the total of allamounts each of which is the taxable income of the corporationor such an associated corporation for its last taxation year thatended in the preceding calendar year (determined before takinginto consideration the specified future tax consequences for thatlast year) does not exceed the total of all amounts each of whichis the business limit of the corporation or such an associatedcorporation for that last year;

Related Sections: S. 87(2)(*oo*.1) Investment tax credit; s. 88(1)(*e*.9) Winding-up; s. 125(7), "Canadian-controlled private corporation"; s. 127.1(2.01) Addition to refundable investment tax credit; s. 127.1(2.2) Refundable investment tax credit — associated CCPCs; s. 127.1(2.3) Application of subsection (2.2); s. 248(1), "business limit", "specified future tax consequences".

Tax Window Files: Refundable Investment Tax Credit — Qualifying Corporation, *Technical Interpretation, Business Incentives and Capital Transactions Section, April 28, 2006*, CRA Document No. 2005-0161611I7; Refundable Investment Tax Credit — Qualifying Corporation, *Technical Interpretation, Business and Partnership Division, May 13, 2004*, CRA Document No. 2003-0047991I7.

"qualifying income limit" —"qualifying income limit" of a corporation for a particular taxation year is the amount determined by the formula

$500,000 × [($40 million - A)/$40 million]

where

A is

(*a*) nil, if $10 million is greater than or equal to the amount (in paragraph (*b*) referred to as the "taxable capital amount") that is the total of the corporation's taxable capital employed in Canada (within the meaning assigned by section 181.2 or 181.3) for its immediately preceding taxation year and the taxable capital employed in Canada (within the meaning assigned by section 181.2 or 181.3) of each associated corporation for the associated corporation's last taxation year that ended in the last calendar year that ended before the end of the particular taxation year, or

(*b*) in any other case, the lesser of $40 million and the amount by which the taxable capital amount exceeds $10 million;

History: S. 127.1(2), the definition "qualifying income limit" was added by S.C. 2009, c. 2, s. 41(2), applicable to taxation years that end on or after February 26, 2008, except that

(a) for taxation years that include February 26, 2008, the formula in the definition "qualifying income limit" in subsection 127.1(2) and the portion of that definition that follows that formula shall be read as follows:

"A + [($400,000 × [($40 million - B)/$40 million] - A) × (C/D)]

where

A is the business limit of the corporation for the particular taxation year determined in accordance with section 125 — together with, if the particular corporation is associated in the particular taxation year with one or more other corporations the business limit of each of those associated corporations for its last taxation year that ends in the particular taxation year (determined in accordance with section 125),

B is

(*a*) nil, if $10 million is greater than or equal to the amount (in paragraph (*b*) referred to as the "taxable capital amount") that is the total of the corporation's taxable capital employed in Canada (within the meaning assigned by section 181.2 or 181.3) for its immediately preceding taxation year and the taxable capital employed in Canada (within the meaning assigned by section 181.2 or 181.3) of each associated corporation for the associated corporation's last taxation year that ended in the last calendar year that ended before the end of the particular taxation year, or

(*b*) in any other case, the lesser of $40 million and the amount by which the taxable capital amount exceeds $10 million,

C is the number of days in the particular taxation year that are after February 25, 2008, and

D is the total number of days in the particular taxation year;"

(b) for taxation years that begin after February 26, 2008 and end before 2010, the reference to "$500,000" in the formula in the definition "qualifying income limit" in subsection 127.1(2) shall be read as a reference to "$400,000"; and

(c) for 2010 taxation years that begin before 2010, the reference to "$500,000" in the formula in the definition "qualifying income limit" in subsection 127.1(2) shall be read as a reference to an amount that is the total of $400,000 and that proportion of $100,000 that the number of days in the taxation year that are in 2010 is of the number of days in the taxation year.

"refundable investment tax credit" —"refundable investment tax credit" of a taxpayer for a taxation year means, in the case of a taxpayer who is

(*a*) a qualifying corporation for the year,

(*b*) an individual other than a trust, or

(*c*) a trust each beneficiary of which is a person referred to in paragraph (*a*) or (*b*),

an amount equal to 40% of the amount, if any, by which

(*d*) the total of all amounts included in computing the taxpayer's investment tax credit at the end of the year

(i) in respect of property (other than qualified small-business property) acquired, or a qualified expenditure (other than an expenditure in respect of which an amount is included under paragraph (*f*) in computing the taxpayer's refundable investment tax credit for the year) incurred, by the taxpayer in the year, or

(ii) because of paragraph (*b*) of the definition "investment tax credit" in subsection 127(9) in respect of a property (other than qualified small-business property) acquired or a qualified expenditure (other than an expenditure in respect of which an amount is included under paragraph (*f*) in computing the taxpayer's refundable investment tax credit for the year) incurred

exceeds

(*e*) the total of

(i) the portion of the total of all amounts deducted under subsection 127(5) for the year or a preceding taxation year (other than an amount deemed by subsection (3) to be so deducted for the year) that can reasonably be considered to be in respect of the total determined under paragraph (*d*), and

(ii) the portion of the total of all amounts required by subsection 127(6) or (7) to be deducted in computing the taxpayer's investment tax credit at the end of the year that can reasonably be considered to be in respect of the total determined under paragraph (*d*),

plus, where the taxpayer is a qualifying corporation (other than an excluded corporation) for the year, the amount, if any, by which

(*f*) the total of

(i) the portion of the amount required by subsection 127(10.1) to be added in computing the taxpayer's investment tax credit at the end of the year that is in respect of qualified expenditures incurred by the taxpayer in the year, and

(ii) all amounts determined under paragraph (*a*.1) of the definition "investment tax credit" in subsection 127(9) in respect of expenditures for which an amount is included in subparagraph (i)

exceeds

(*g*) the total of

(i) the portion of the total of all amounts deducted by the taxpayer under subsection 127(5) for the year or a preceding taxation year (other than an amount deemed by subsection (3) to be so deducted for the year) that can reasonably be considered to be in respect of the total determined under paragraph (*f*), and

(ii) the portion of the total of all amounts required by subsection 127(6) to be deducted in computing the taxpayer's investment tax credit at the end of the year that can reasonably be considered to be in respect of the total determined under paragraph (*f*).

History: S. 127.1(2), subparagraph (*h*)(i) of the definition of "refundable investment tax credit" was replaced by S.C. 2012, c. 31, s. 28(1), in force February 1, 2017, and formerly read:

(i) the portion of the amount required by subsection 127(10.1) to be added in computing the taxpayer's investment tax credit at the end of the year that is in respect of qualified expenditures (other than expenditures of a capital nature) incurred by the taxpayer in the year, and

Related Sections: S. 88(1)(*e*.9) Winding-up; s. 127(9) Definitions;, "investment tax credit"; s. 127(10.1) Additions to investment tax credit; s. 127(14) Identification of amounts transferred; s. 127.1(2.01) Addition to refundable investment tax credit; 127.1(2.2) Refundable investment tax credit — associated CCPCs; 127.1(2.3) Application of subsection (2.2); s. 136(1) Cooperative not private corporation; s. 137(7) Credit union not private corporation; s. 256(2.1) Anti-avoidance; s. 256(5.1) Control in fact; s. 256(6.2) Application to control in fact.

Tax Window Files: Refundable Investment Tax Credit — Qualifying Corporation, *Technical Interpretation, Business Incentives and Capital Transactions Section, April 28, 2006*, CRA Document No. 2005-0161611I7; Refundable Investment Tax Credit — Qualifying Corporation, *Technical Interpretation, Business and Partnership Division, May 13, 2004*, CRA Document No. 2003-0047991I7.

► 127.1(2.01) ◄

(2.01) Addition to refundable investment tax credit. In the case of a taxpayer that is a Canadian-controlled private corporation other than a qualifying corporation or an excluded corporation, the refundable investment tax credit of the taxpayer for a taxation year is the amount, if any, by which

(*a*) the total of

(i) the portion of the amount required by subsection 127(10.1) to be added in computing the taxpayer's investment tax credit at the end of the year that is in respect of qualified expenditures incurred by the taxpayer in the year, and

(ii) all amounts determined under paragraph (*a.1*) of the definition "investment tax credit" in subsection 127(9) in respect of expenditures for which an amount is included in subparagraph (i)

exceeds

(*b*) the total of

(i) the portion of the total of all amounts deducted by the taxpayer under subsection 127(5) for the year or a preceding taxation year (other than an amount deemed by subsection (3) to have been so deducted for the year) that can reasonably be considered to be in respect of the total determined under paragraph (*a*), and

(ii) the portion of the total of all amounts required by subsection 127(6) to be deducted in computing the taxpayer's investment tax credit at the end of the year that can reasonably be considered to be in respect of the total determined under paragraph (*a*).

Editorial Note: S. 127.1(2.01) permits a Canadian-controlled private corporation that is not a "qualifying corporation" under s. 127.1(2) (i.e., taxable income of associated group does not exceed the business limit) nor an "excluded corporation" under s. 127.1(2), to obtain partial refundability of the 35% investment tax credit for SR&ED expenditures, which is phased out as taxable income increases.

History: S. 127.1(2.01) was replaced by S.C. 2012, c. 31, s. 28(2), in force February 1, 2017, and formerly read:

(2.01) *Addition to refundable investment tax credit.* In the case of a taxpayer that is a Canadian-controlled private corporation other than a qualifying corporation or an excluded corporation, the refundable investment tax credit of the taxpayer for a taxation year is 40% of the amount, if any, by which

(*a*) the total of

(i) the portion of the amount required by subsection 127(10.1) to be added in computing the taxpayer's investment tax credit at the end of the year that is in respect of qualified expenditures (other than expenditures of a current nature) incurred by the taxpayer in the year, and

(ii) all amounts determined under paragraph (*a*.1) of the definition "investment tax credit" in subsection 127(9) in respect of expenditures for which an amount is included in subparagraph (i)

exceeds

(*b*) the total of

(i) the portion of the total of all amounts deducted by the taxpayer under subsection 127(5) for the year or a preceding taxation year (other than an amount deemed by subsection (3) to have been so deducted for the year) that can reasonably be considered to be in respect of the total determined under paragraph (*a*), and

(ii) the portion of the total of all amounts required by subsection 127(6) to be deducted in computing the taxpayer's investment tax credit at the end of the year that can reasonably be considered to be in respect of the total determined under paragraph (*a*)

plus the amount, if any, by which

(*c*) the total of

(i) the portion of the amount required by subsection 127(10.1) to be added in computing the taxpayer's investment tax credit at the end of the year that is in respect of qualified expenditures (other than expenditures of a capital nature) incurred by the taxpayer in the year, and

(ii) all amounts determined under paragraph (*a*.1) of the definition "investment tax credit" in subsection 127(9) in respect of expenditures for which an amount is included in subparagraph (i)

exceeds

(*d*) the total of

(i) the portion of the total of all amounts deducted by the taxpayer under subsection 127(5) for the year or a preceding taxation year (other than an amount deemed by subsection (3) to have been so deducted for the year) that can reasonably be considered to be in respect of the total determined under paragraph (*c*), and

(ii) the portion of the total of all amounts required by subsection 127(6) to be deducted in computing the taxpayer's investment tax credit at the end of the year that can reasonably be considered to be in respect of the total determined under paragraph (*c*).

Related Sections: S. 127(10.1) Additions to investment tax credit; s. 127(10.2) Expenditure limit determined.

► 127.1(2.1) ◄

(2.1) Application of s. 127(9). The definitions in subsection 127(9) apply to this section.

► 127.1(2.2) ◄

(2.2) Refundable investment tax credit — associated CCPCs. If a particular Canadian-controlled private corporation is associated with another corporation in circumstances where those corporations would not be associated if the Act were read without reference to paragraph 256(1.2)(*a*), the particular corporation has issued shares to one or more persons who have been issued shares by the other corporation and there is at least one shareholder of the particular corporation who is not a shareholder of the other corporation or one shareholder of the other corporation who is not a shareholder of the particular corporation, the particular corporation is not associated with the other corporation for the purpose of calculating that portion of the particular corporation's refundable investment tax credit that is in respect of qualified expenditures.

Editorial Note: S. 127.1(2.2) allows associated corporations to be considered not associated for purposes of SR&ED refundable tax credits if they are associated through a third company and the conditions in s. 127.1(2.3) are met. S. 127(10.22) provides a parallel rule for non-refundable investment tax credits.

Related Sections: S. 127(10.22) Deemed non-association of corporations; s. 127(10.23) Application of subsection (10.22); s. 127.1(2.3) Application of subsection (2.2); s. 256(1.2)(*a*) Control, etc.

Tax Profile: March 2006 — Some Tax Considerations for Investing in Silicon Valley North.

Tax Window Files: Enhanced ITC for CCPCs, *Technical Interpretation, Business and Partnerships Division, May 18, 2005,* CRA Document No. 2005-0126891I7.

► 127.1(2.3) ◄

(2.3) Application of subsection (2.2). Subsection (2.2) applies to the particular corporation and the other corporation referred to in that subsection only if the Minister is satisfied that

(*a*) the particular corporation and the other corporation are not otherwise associated under this Act; and

(*b*) the existence of one or more shareholders of the particular corporation who is not a shareholder of the other corporation, or the existence of one or more shareholders of the other corporation who is not a shareholder of the particular corporation, is not for the purpose of satisfying the requirements of subsection (2.2) or 127(10.22).

Editorial Note: See the editorial note under s. 127.1(2.2).

Related Sections: S. 127(10.22) Deemed non-association of corporations; s. 127(10.23) Application of subsection (10.22).

Tax Window Files: Enhanced ITC for CCPCs, *Technical Interpretation, Business and Partnerships Division, May 18, 2005,* CRA Document No. 2005-0126891I7.

► 127.1(3) ◄

(3) Deemed deduction. For the purposes of this Act, the amount deemed under subsection (1) to have been paid by a taxpayer for a taxation year shall be deemed to have been deducted by the taxpayer under subsection 127(5) for the year.

Editorial Note: S. 127.1(3) ensures that a taxpayer cannot claim more investment tax credits than the maximum allowed under s. 127(5).

Related Sections: S. 127(5) Investment tax credit.

Tax Window Files: Investment Tax Credit, *Technical Interpretation, Business and Partnerships Division, July 29, 2005,* CRA Document No. 2005-0143681I7.

► 127.1(4) ◄

(4) Qualifying income limit determined in certain cases. For the purpose of the definition of "qualifying corporation" in subsection (2), where a Canadian-controlled private corporation has a taxation year that is less than 51 weeks, the taxable income of the corporation for the year shall be determined by multiplying that amount by the ratio that 365 is of the number of days in that year.

History: S. 127.1(4) was added by S.C. 2009, c. 2, s. 41(3), applicable in respect of the 2008 and subsequent taxation years.

SECTION 127.2: Share-purchase tax credit

► 127.2(1) ◄

(1) Share-purchase tax credit. There may be deducted from the tax otherwise payable under this Part by a taxpayer for a taxation year an amount not exceeding the total of

(*a*) the taxpayer's share-purchase tax credit for the year, and

(*b*) the taxpayer's unused share-purchase tax credit for the taxation year immediately following the year.

Editorial Note: Section 127.2 applies generally only in respect of new share issues made in the period from June 30, 1983 to the end of 1986. See subsection 192(4) and the definition of "share-purchase tax credit" in subsection 127.2(6).

► 127.2(2) ◄

(2) Persons exempt from tax. Where a taxpayer who was throughout a taxation year a person described in any of paragraphs 149(1)(*e*) to (*y*) files with the taxpayer's return of income under this Part for the year a prescribed form containing prescribed information, the taxpayer shall be deemed to have paid, on the day on which the return is filed, an amount, on account of the taxpayer's tax under this Part for the year, equal to the taxpayer's share-purchase tax credit for the year.

► 127.2(3) ◄

(3) Trust. Where, in a particular taxation year of a taxpayer who is a beneficiary under a trust, an amount is included in computing the share-purchase tax credit of the trust for its taxation year ending in that particular taxation year, the trust may, in its return of income for its taxation year ending in that particular taxation year, designate as attributable to the taxpayer such portion of that amount

(*a*) as may, having regard to all the circumstances (including the terms and conditions of the trust arrangement), reasonably be considered to be attributable to the taxpayer, and

(*b*) as was not designated by the trust in respect of any other beneficiary of that trust,

and, where the trust so designates such a portion, an amount equal to that portion shall be

(*c*) added in computing the share-purchase tax credit of the taxpayer for the particular taxation year, and (*d*) deducted in computing the share-purchase tax credit of the trust for its taxation year ending in the particular taxation year.

► 127.2(3.1) ◄

(3.1) Exclusion of certain trusts. For the purposes of subsection (3), a trust does not include a trust that is

(*a*) governed by an employee benefit plan or a revoked deferred profit sharing plan; or

(*b*) exempt from tax under section 149.

► 127.2(4) ◄

(4) Partnership. Where, in a taxation year of a taxpayer who is a member of a partnership, an amount is included in computing the share-purchase tax credit of the partnership for its fiscal period ending in that year, such portion of that amount as may reasonably be considered to be the taxpayer's share thereof shall be

(*a*) added in computing the share-purchase tax credit of the taxpayer for that year; and

(*b*) deducted in computing the share-purchase tax credit of the partnership for that fiscal period.

► 127.2(5) ◄

(5) Cooperative corporation. Where at any particular time in a taxation year a taxpayer that is a cooperative corporation (within the meaning assigned by subsection 136(2)) has, as required by subsection 135(3), deducted or withheld an amount from a payment made by it to any person pursuant to an allocation in proportion to patronage, the taxpayer may deduct from the amount otherwise required by subsection 135(3) to be remitted to the Receiver General, an amount not exceeding the amount, if any, by which

(*a*) the amount that would, but for this subsection, be its share-purchase tax credit for the taxation year in which it made the payment if that year had ended immediately before the particular time

exceeds

(*b*) the total of all amounts each of which is the amount deducted by virtue of this subsection from any amount otherwise required to be remitted by subsection 135(3) in respect of payments made by it before the particular time and in the taxation year,

and the amount, if any, so deducted from the amount otherwise required to be remitted by subsection 135(3) shall be

(*c*) deducted in computing the share-purchase tax credit of the taxpayer for the taxation year, and

(*d*) deemed to have been remitted by the taxpayer to the Receiver General on account of tax under this Part of the person to whom that payment was made.

► 127.2(6) ◄

(6) Definitions. In this section,

"share-purchase tax credit" —"share-purchase tax credit" of a taxpayer for a taxation year means the amount determined by the formula

$$(A + B) - C$$

where

A is the total of all amounts each of which is an amount designated by a corporation under subsection 192(4) in respect of a share acquired by the taxpayer in the year where the taxpayer is the first person, other than a broker or dealer in securities, to be a registered holder,

B is the total of all amounts each of which is an amount required by subsection (3) or (4) to be added in computing the taxpayer's share-purchase tax credit for the year, and

C is the total of all amounts each of which is an amount required by subsection (3), (4) or (5) to be deducted in computing the taxpayer's share-purchase tax credit for the year;

"unused share-purchase tax credit" —"unused share-purchase tax credit" of a taxpayer for a taxation year means the amount determined by the formula

$$A - (B + C)$$

where

A is the taxpayer's share-purchase tax credit for the year,

B is the taxpayer's tax otherwise payable under this Part for the year, the amount deemed by subsection (2) to have been paid on account of the taxpayer's tax payable under this Part for the year or, where Division E.1 is applicable to the taxpayer for the year, the amount, if any, by which the taxpayer's tax otherwise payable under this Part for the year exceeds the taxpayer's minimum amount for the year determined under section 127.51, as the case may be, and

C is the taxpayer's refundable Part VII tax on hand at the end of the year.

Related Sections: S. 39(7) Unused share-purchase tax credit.

► 127.2(7) ◄

(7) Definition of "tax otherwise payable". In this section, "tax otherwise payable" under this Part by a taxpayer means the amount that would, but for this section and section 120.1, be the tax payable under this Part by the taxpayer.

► 127.2(8) ◄

(8) Deemed cost of acquisition. For the purposes of this Act, where, at any time in a taxation year, a taxpayer has acquired a share and is the first registered holder of the share, other than a broker or dealer in securities, and an amount is, at any time, designated by a corporation under subsection 192(4) in respect of the share, the following rules apply:

(*a*) the taxpayer shall be deemed to have acquired the share at a cost to the taxpayer equal to the amount by which

(i) its cost to the taxpayer as otherwise determined exceeds

(ii) the amount so designated in respect of the share; and

(*b*) where the amount determined under subparagraph (*a*)(ii) exceeds the amount determined under subparagraph (*a*)(i), the excess shall

(i) where the share is a capital property to the taxpayer, be deemed to be a capital gain of the taxpayer for the year from the disposition of that property, and

(ii) in any other case, be included in computing the income of the taxpayer for the year,

and the cost to the taxpayer of the share shall be deemed to be nil.

► 127.2(9) ◄

(9) Partnership. For the purposes of this section and subsection 193(5), a partnership shall be deemed to be a person and its taxation year shall be deemed to be its fiscal period.

► 127.2(10) ◄

(10) Election re first holder. Where a share of a public corporation has been lawfully distributed to the public in accordance with a prospectus, registration statement or similar document filed with a public authority in Canada pursuant to and in accordance with the law of Canada or of any province, and, where required by law, accepted for filing by such a public authority, the corporation, if it has designated an amount under subsection 192(4) in respect of the share, may, in the prescribed form required to be filed under that subsection, elect that, for the purposes of this section, the first person, other than a broker or dealer in securities, to have acquired the share (and no other person) shall be considered to be the first person to be a registered holder of the share.

► 127.2(11) ◄

(11) Calculation of consideration. For greater certainty,

(*a*) for the purposes of this section and Part VII, the amount of consideration for which a share is acquired and issued includes the amount of any consideration for the designation under subsection 192(4) in respect of the share; and

(*b*) the amount received by a corporation as consideration for a designation under subsection 192(4) in respect of a share issued by it shall not be included in computing its income.

SECTION 127.3: Scientific research and experimental development tax credit

► 127.3(1) ◄

(1) Scientific research and experimental development tax credit. There may be deducted from the tax otherwise payable under this Part by a taxpayer for a taxation year an amount not exceeding the total of the taxpayer's

(*a*) scientific research and experimental development tax credit for the year, and

(*b*) unused scientific research and experimental development tax credit for the taxation year immediately following the year.

Editorial Note: S. 127.3 generally ceased to apply in respect of shares issued after October 10, 1984, subject to transitional rules. See ss. 194(4) and (4.2).

Canadian Tax Foundation: De Luca et al., *The New SR & ED Regime: Evolution Rather Than Revolution*, 2012 Conference Report 16:1–25.

► 127.3(2) ◄

(2) Definitions. In this section,

"scientific research and experimental development tax credit" —"scientific research and experimental development tax credit" of a taxpayer for a taxation year means the amount determined by the formula

$$A - B$$

where

A is the total of all amounts each of which is an amount equal to

(*a*) where the taxpayer is a corporation, 50%, or

(*b*) where the taxpayer is an individual other than a trust, 34%

of an amount designated by a corporation under subsection 194(4) in respect of

(*c*) a share acquired by the taxpayer in the year where the taxpayer is the first person, other than a broker or dealer in securities, to be a registered holder thereof,

(*d*) a bond, debenture, bill, note, mortgage, hypothecary claim or similar obligation (in this section referred to as a "debt obligation") acquired by the taxpayer in the year where the taxpayer is the first person, other than a broker or dealer in securities, to be a registered holder of that debt obligation, or

(*e*) a right acquired by the taxpayer in the year where the taxpayer is the first person, other than a broker or dealer in securities, to have acquired that right, and

B is the total of all amounts required by subsection (5) to be deducted in computing the taxpayer's scientific research and experimental development tax credit for the year;

History: S. 127.3(2), paragraph (*d*) of the description of A in the definition "scientific research and experimental development tax credit" was replaced by S.C. 2013, c. 34, s. 128, in force June 26, 2013, and formerly read:

(*d*) a bond, debenture, bill, note, mortgage or similar obligation (in this section referred to as a "debt obligation") acquired by the taxpayer in the year where the taxpayer is the first person, other than a broker or dealer in securities, to be a registered holder of that debt obligation, or

Cases: Redemption of scientific research tax credit notes yielded capital since they were wholly artificial devices remote from trade, which were intended to procure a tax advantage. *Stanley Drug Products Ltd. v. M.N.R.*, 90 DTC 1664 (T.C.C.)

"unused scientific research and experimental development tax credit" —"unused scientific research and experimental development tax credit" of a taxpayer for a taxation year means the amount determined by the formula

$$A - (B + C)$$

where

A is the taxpayer's scientific research and experimental development tax credit for the year,

B is the taxpayer's tax otherwise payable under this Part for the year or, where Division E.1 is applicable to the taxpayer for the year, the amount, if any, by which the taxpayer's tax otherwise payable under this Part for the year exceeds the taxpayer's minimum amount for the year determined under section 127.51, as the case may be, and

C is the taxpayer's refundable Part VIII tax on hand at the end of the year.

▶ 127.3(3) ◀

(3) Trust. For the purposes of this section and section 53, where a taxpayer, other than a broker or dealer in securities, is a beneficiary under a trust and an amount is designated by a corporation under subsection 194(4) in respect of a share, debt obligation or right acquired by the trust in a taxation year of the trust where the trust is the first person, other than a broker or dealer in securities, to be a registered holder of the share or debt obligation or to have acquired the right, as the case may be,

(*a*) the trust may, in its return of income for that year, specify such portion of that amount as may, having regard to all the circumstances (including the terms and conditions of the trust arrangement), reasonably be considered to be attributable to the taxpayer and as was not specified by the trust in respect of any other beneficiary under that trust; and

(*b*) the portion specified pursuant to paragraph (*a*) shall be deemed to be an amount designated on the last day of that year by the corporation under subsection 194(4) in respect of a share, debt obligation or right, as the case may be, acquired by the taxpayer on that day where the taxpayer is the first person, other than a broker or dealer in securities, to be a registered holder of the share or debt obligation or to have acquired the right, as the case may be.

▶ 127.3(3.1) ◀

(3.1) Exclusion of certain trusts. For the purposes of subsection (3), a trust does not include a trust that is

(*a*) governed by an employee benefit plan or a revoked deferred profit sharing plan; or

(*b*) exempt from tax under section 149.

▶ 127.3(4) ◀

(4) Partnership. For the purposes of this section and section 53, where a taxpayer, other than a broker or dealer in securities, is a member of a partnership and an amount is designated by a corporation under subsection 194(4) in respect of a share, debt obligation or right acquired by the partnership in a taxation year of the partnership where the partnership is the first person, other than a broker or dealer in securities, to be a registered holder of the share or debt obligation or to have acquired the right, as the case may be, such portion of that amount as may reasonably be considered to be the taxpayer's share thereof shall be deemed to be an amount designated on the last day of that year by the corporation under subsection 194(4) in respect of a share, debt obligation or right, as the case may be, acquired by the taxpayer on that day where the taxpayer is the first person, other than a broker or dealer in securities, to be a registered holder of the share or debt obligation or to have acquired the right, as the case may be.

▶ 127.3(5) ◀

(5) Cooperative corporation. Where at any particular time in a taxation year a taxpayer that is a cooperative corporation (within the meaning assigned by subsection 136(2)) has, as required by subsection 135(3), deducted or withheld an amount from a payment made by it to any person pursuant to an allocation in proportion to patronage, the taxpayer may deduct from the amount otherwise required by subsection 135(3) to be remitted to the Receiver General, an amount not exceeding the amount, if any, by which

(*a*) the amount that would, but for this subsection, be its scientific research and experimental development tax credit for the taxation year in which it made the payment if that year had ended immediately before the particular time

exceeds

(*b*) the total of all amounts each of which is the amount deducted by virtue of this subsection from any amount otherwise required to be remitted by subsection 135(3) in respect of payments made by it before the particular time and in the taxation year,

and the amount, if any, so deducted from the amount otherwise required to be remitted by subsection 135(3) shall be

(*c*) deducted in computing the scientific research and experimental development tax credit of the taxpayer for the taxation year, and

(*d*) deemed to have been remitted by the taxpayer to the Receiver General on account of tax under this Part of the person to whom that payment was made.

▶ 127.3(6) ◀

(6) Deduction from cost. For the purposes of this Act, where at any time in a taxation year a taxpayer has acquired a share, debt obligation or right and is the first registered holder of the share or debt obligation or the first person to have acquired the right, as the case may be, other than a broker or dealer in securities, and an amount is, at any time, designated by a corporation under subsection 194(4), in respect of the share, debt obligation or right, the following rules apply:

(*a*) the taxpayer shall be deemed to have acquired the share, debt obligation or right at a cost to the taxpayer equal to the amount by which

(i) its cost to the taxpayer as otherwise determined

exceeds

(ii) 50% of the amount so designated in respect thereof; and

(*b*) where the amount determined under subparagraph (*a*)(ii) exceeds the amount determined under subparagraph (*a*)(i), the excess shall

(i) where the share, debt obligation or right, as the case may be, is a capital property to the taxpayer, be deemed to be a capital gain of the taxpayer for the year from the disposition of that property, and

(ii) in any other case, be included in computing the income of the taxpayer for the year,

and the cost to the taxpayer of the share, debt obligation or right, as the case may be, shall be deemed to be nil.

► 127.3(7) ◄

(7) Partnership. For the purposes of this section and Part VIII, a partnership shall be deemed to be a person and its taxation year shall be deemed to be its fiscal period.

► 127.3(8) ◄

(8) Definition of "tax otherwise payable". In this section, "tax otherwise payable" under this Part by a taxpayer means the amount that would, but for this section and section 120.1, be the tax payable under this Part by the taxpayer.

► 127.3(9) ◄

(9) Election re first holder. Where a share or debt obligation of a public corporation has been lawfully distributed to the public in accordance with a prospectus, registration statement or similar document filed with a public authority in Canada pursuant to and in accordance with the law of Canada or of any province, and, where required by law, accepted for filing by that public authority, the corporation, if it has designated an amount under subsection 194(4) in respect of the share or debt obligation, may, in the prescribed form required to be filed under that subsection, elect that, for the purposes of this section, the first person, other than a broker or dealer in securities, to have acquired the share or debt obligation, as the case may be, (and no other person) shall be considered to be the first person to be a registered holder thereof.

► 127.3(10) ◄

(10) Calculation of consideration. For greater certainty,

(*a*) for the purposes of this section and Part VIII, the amount of consideration for which a share, debt obligation or right was acquired and issued or granted includes the amount of any consideration for the designation under subsection 194(4) in respect of the share, debt obligation or right; and

(*b*) the amount received by a corporation as consideration for a designation under subsection 194(4) in respect of a share, debt obligation or right issued or granted by it shall not be included in computing its income.

SECTION 127.4: [Labour-sponsored funds tax credit]

► 127.4(1) ◄

(1) Definitions. In this section,

Tax Window Files: LSVCC, *June 15, 2010*, CRA Document No. 2010-0365461E5.

"approved share" —"approved share" means a share of the capital stock of a prescribed labour-sponsored venture capital corporation, but does not include

(*a*) a share issued by a registered labour-sponsored venture capital corporation the venture capital business of which was discontinued before the time of the issue, and

(*b*) a share issued by a prescribed labour-sponsored venture capital corporation that is not a registered labour-sponsored venture capital corporation if, at the time of the issue, no province under the laws (described in section 6701 of the *Income Tax Regulations*) of which the corporation is registered or established provides assistance in respect of the acquisition of the share;

History: S. 127.4(1), paragraph (*b*) of the definition "approved share" was replaced by S.C. 2013, c. 34, s. 270(1), applicable to acquisitions of shares that occur after 2003, and formerly read:

(*b*) a share issued by a prescribed labour-sponsored venture capital corporation (other than a registered labour-sponsored venture capital corporation) if, at the time of the issue, every province under the laws of which the corporation is a prescribed labour-sponsored venture capital corporation has suspended or terminated its assistance in respect of the acquisition of shares of the capital stock of the corporation;

Related Regulations: 6701; 6701.1.

Related Sections: S. 127.4(1.1) Amalgamations or mergers; s. 204.8(2) When venture capital business discontinued; s. 204.85(3) Amalgamations and mergers.

Forms: T5006 SUM — Summary of Registered Labour-Sponsored Venture Capital Corporation Class A Shares; T5006 — Statement of Registered Labor-Sponsored Venture Capital Corporation Class A Shares.

Tax Window Files: Labour-Sponsored Funds Tax Credit, *Technical Interpretation, Business and Partnerships Division, April 15, 2003*, CRA Document No. 2003-0006295.

"labour-sponsored funds tax credit" — (Repealed by S.C. 1997, c. 25, s. 38(2).)

Related Sections: S. 127.4(6) Labour-sponsored funds tax credit.

"net cost" —"net cost" to an individual of an approved share means the amount, if any, by which

(*a*) the amount of consideration paid by the individual to acquire or subscribe for the share

exceeds

(*b*) the amount of any assistance (other than an amount included in computing a tax credit of the individual in respect of that share) provided or to be provided by a government, municipality or any public authority in respect of, or for the acquisition of, the share;

"original acquisition" —"original acquisition" of a share means the first acquisition of the share, except that

(*a*) where the share is irrevocably subscribed and paid for before its first acquisition, subject to paragraphs (*b*) and (*c*), the original acquisition of the share is the first transaction whereby the share is irrevocably subscribed and paid for, (*b*) a share is deemed never to have been acquired and never to have been irrevocably subscribed and paid for unless the first registered holder of the share is, subject to paragraph (*c*), the first person to either acquire or irrevocably subscribe and pay for the share, and

(*c*) for the purpose of this definition, a broker or dealer in securities acting in that capacity is deemed never to acquire or subscribe and pay for the share and never to be the registered holder of the share;

Related Sections: S. 204.85(3) Amalgamations and mergers.

"qualifying trust" —"qualifying trust" for an individual in respect of a share means

(*a*) a trust governed by a registered retirement savings plan, under which the individual is the annuitant, that is not a spousal or common-law partner plan (in this definition having the meaning assigned by subsection 146(1)) in relation to another individual,

(*b*) a trust governed by a registered retirement savings plan, under which the individual or the individual's spouse or common-law partner is the annuitant, that is a spousal or common-law partner plan in relation to the individual or the individual's spouse or common-law partner, if the individual and no other person claims a deduction under subsection (2) in respect of the share, or

(*c*) a trust governed by a TFSA of which the individual is the holder;

History: S. 127.4(1), the definition "qualifying trust" was replaced by S.C. 2009, c. 2, s. 42(1), applicable to the 2001 and subsequent taxation years, except that the definition "qualifying trust" in subsection 127.4(1)

(a) shall, for taxation years before 2009, be read without reference to its paragraph (*c*); and

(b) if a taxpayer and a person have jointly elected under section 144 of the *Modernization of Benefits and Obligations Act* in respect of the 1998, 1999 or 2000 taxation year, applies to the taxpayer and the person in respect of that taxation year and subsequent taxation years.

S. 127.4(1), the definition "qualifying trust" formerly read:

"qualifying trust"—"qualifying trust" for an individual in respect of a share means

(*a*) a trust governed by a registered retirement savings plan, under which the individual is the annuitant, that is not a spousal plan (in this definition having the meaning assigned by subsection 146(1)) in relation to another individual, or

(*b*) a trust governed by a registered retirement savings plan, under which the individual or the individual's spouse or common-law partner is the annuitant, that is a spousal plan in relation to the individual or the individual's spouse or common-law partner, if the individual and no other person claims a deduction under subsection 127.4(2) in respect of the share;

Related Sections: S. 146(1), "annuitant", "registered retirement savings plan".

"tax otherwise payable" —"tax otherwise payable" by an individual means the amount that, but for this section, would be the individual's tax payable under this Part.

▶ 127.4(1.1) ◀

(1.1) Amalgamations or mergers. Subsections 204.8(2) and 204.85(3) apply for the purpose of this section.

Editorial Note: This subsection adopts the provisions in Part X.3 dealing with amalgamations and mergers where the amalgamated corporation is deemed to be registered, where the venture capital business of a corporation is discontinued, and where it is deemed to be a revoked corporation. See editorial notes under s. 127.4(2) regarding the phase-out of the federal LSVCC tax regime.

▶ 127.4(2) ◀

(2) Deduction of labour-sponsored funds tax credit. There may be deducted from the tax otherwise payable by an individual (other than a trust) for a taxation year such amount as the individual claims not exceeding the individual's labour-sponsored funds tax credit limit for the year.

Editorial Note: In 2013, the government enacted the phase-out of the federal LSVCC tax credit by 2017. The rules provided that, for investments up to $5,000 per year, individuals could claim a federal tax credit of 15% until the end of 2014 (10% for the 2015 taxation year, 5% for 2016, and eliminated for 2017 and future years) of the net cost of acquiring an "approved share" of a prescribed LSVCC, up to a maximum tax credit of $750 until the end of 2014 ($500 for the 2015 taxation year, $250 for 2016 and eliminated for 2017 and future years). In 2016, the government reversed its position and reinstated the 15% tax credit, but only for provincially-registered (not federally registered) LSVCC shares. The maximum tax credit limit is based on a hybrid 5%/15% formula for 2016 and is $750 after 2016. An "approved share" is generally a share of the capital stock of a prescribed LSVCC that is prescribed under s. 6701 of the Regulations; for provincially registered LSVCCs, a provincial income tax credit must be available for shares to be considered approved shares for the federal credit. In addition to phasing out the tax credit, transitional rules have been enacted in s. 204.81 for the deregistration of LSVCCs.

Related Sections: S. 127.4(5) Labour-sponsored funds tax credit limit; s. 204.8(2) When venture capital business discontinued; s. 204.85(3) Amalgamations and mergers.

Tax Window Files: Spousal RRSP LSF Tax Credit, *May 3, 2006*, CRA Document No. 2006-0178491E5; Labour-Sponsored Funds Tax Credit—Shares Acquired by Spousal RRSP, *Technical Interpretation, Financial Sector and Exempt Entities Division, March 16, 2006*, CRA Document No. 2005-0154871E5.

▶ 127.4(3) ◀

(3) 3-year cooling-off period — (Repealed by S.C. 1999, c. 22, s. 49(3).)

▶ 127.4(4) ◀

(4) Exceptions to cooling-off period — (Repealed by S.C. 1999, c. 22, s. 49(3).)

▶ 127.4(5) ◀

(5) Labour-sponsored funds tax credit limit. For the purpose of subsection (2), an individual's labour-sponsored funds tax credit limit for a taxation year is the lesser of

(*a*) $750, and,

(*b*) the amount, if any, by which

(i) the total of all amounts each of which is the individual's labour-sponsored funds tax credit in respect of an original acquisition in the year or in the first 60 days of the following taxation year of an approved share

exceeds

(ii) the portion of the total described in subparagraph (i) that was deducted under subsection (2) in computing the individual's tax payable under this Part for the preceding taxation year.

Editorial Note: See editorial notes under s. 127.4(2) regarding the partial phase-out of the federal LSVCC tax credit.

History: S. 127.4(5)(*a*) was replaced by S.C. 2016, c. 7, s. 36(2), applicable to the 2017 and subsequent taxation years, and formerly read:

(*a*) the amount determined by the formula

$$0.15 \times A + 0.05 \times B$$

where

A is the lesser of

(i) $5,000, and

(ii) the total of all amounts each of which is the net cost of the original acquisition of shares of a prescribed labour-sponsored venture capital corporation (other than a corporation that is a prescribed labour-sponsored venture capital corporation solely because it is a registered labour-sponsored venture capital corporation), and

B is the lesser of

(i) the amount if any by which $5,000 exceeds the amount determined under subparagraph (ii) of the description of A, and

(ii) the total of all amounts each of which is the net cost of the original acquisition of shares of a corporation that is a prescribed labour-sponsored venture capital corporation solely because it is a registered labour-sponsored venture capital corporation, and

S. 127.4(5)(*a*) was replaced by S.C. 2016, c. 7, s. 36(1), applicable to the 2016 taxation year, and formerly read:

(*a*) $250, and

S. 127.4(5)(*a*) was replaced by S.C. 2013, c. 40, s. 59(3), applicable to the 2016 taxation year, and formerly read:

(*a*) $500, and

S. 127.4(5)(*a*) was replaced by S.C. 2013, c. 40, s. 59(2), applicable to the 2015 taxation year, and formerly read:

(*a*) $750, and

Tax Window Files: Spousal RRSP LSF Tax Credit, *May 3, 2006*, CRA Document No. 2006-0178491E5; Labour-Sponsored Funds Tax Credit—Shares Acquired by Spousal RRSP, *Technical Interpretation, Financial Sector and Exempt Entities Division, March 16, 2006*, CRA Document No. 2005-0154871E5.

► 127.4(5.1) ◄

(5.1) Deemed original acquisition. If the Minister so directs, an original acquisition of an approved share that occurs in an individual's taxation year (other than in the first 60 days of the year) is deemed for the purpose of this section to have occurred at the beginning of the year and not at the time it actually occurred.

Editorial Note: The circumstances that will give rise to the exercise of the Minister's discretion are not set out in this provision but the explanatory notes accompanying similar provisions (such as s. 146(22)) indicate that the Minister may use this type of power to provide relief of hardship for a community or group of individuals. See editorial notes under s. 127.4(2) regarding the partial phase-out of the federal LSVCC tax credit.

► 127.4(6) ◄

(6) Labour-sponsored funds tax credit. For the purpose of subsection (5), an individual's labour-sponsored funds tax credit in respect of an original acquisition of an approved share is equal to the least of

(*a*) 15% of the net cost to the individual (or to a qualifying trust for the individual in respect of the share) for the original acquisition of the share by the individual or by the trust, if the share is a share of a prescribed labour-sponsored venture capital corporation (other than a corporation that is a prescribed labour-sponsored venture capital corporation solely because it is a registered labour-sponsored venture capital corporation),

(*a*.1) 5% of the net cost to the individual (or to a qualifying trust for the individual in respect of the share) for the original acquisition of the share by the individual or by the trust, if

(i) the taxation year for which a claim is made under subsection (2) in respect of the original acquisition is 2016, and

(ii) the share is a share of a corporation that is a prescribed labour-sponsored venture capital corporation solely because it is a registered labour-sponsored venture capital corporation,

(*a*.2) nil, if

(i) the taxation year for which a claim is made under subsection (2) in respect of the original acquisition is after 2016, and

(ii) the share is a share of a corporation that is a prescribed labour-sponsored venture capital corporation solely because it is a registered labour-sponsored venture capital corporation,

(*b*) nil, where the share was issued by a registered labour-sponsored venture capital corporation unless the information return described in paragraph 204.81(6)(*c*) is filed with the individual's return of income for the taxation year for which a claim is made under subsection (2) in respect of the original acquisition of the share (other than a return of income filed under subsection 70(2), paragraph 104(23)(*d*) or 128(2)(*e*) or subsection 150(4)),

(*c*) nil, where the individual dies after December 5, 1996 and before the original acquisition of the share,

(*d*) nil, where a payment in respect of the disposition of the share has been made under section 211.9, and

(*e*) nil, if the share is issued in exchange for another share of the corporation.

Editorial Note: The labour-sponsored funds tax credit is available only to individuals but may be claimed where the approved share is acquired by either the individual or by a "qualifying trust" for the individual, which includes the individual's RRSP, a spousal RRSP or, for 2009 and later taxation years, a TFSA. No credit is allowed where the required information return is not filed with the individual's tax return for the year. See editorial notes under s. 127.4(2) regarding the partial phase-out of the federal LSVCC tax credit.

History: S. 127.4(6)(*a*) and (*a.1*) were replaced by S.C. 2016, c. 7, s. 36(3), applicable to the 2016 and subsequent taxation years, and formerly read:

(*a*) 10% of the net cost to the individual (or to a qualifying trust for the individual in respect of the share) for the original acquisition of the share by the individual or by the trust, if the taxation year for which a claim is made under subsection (2) in respect of the original acquisition is 2015,

(*a*.1) 5% of the net cost to the individual (or to a qualifying trust for the individual in respect of the share) for the original acquisition of the share by the individual or by the trust, if the taxation year for which a claim is made under subsection (2) in respect of the original acquisition is 2016,

S. 127.4(6)(*a.2*) was added by S.C. 2016, c. 7, s. 36(3), applicable to the 2016 and subsequent taxation years.

S. 127.4(6)(*a*) was replaced and s. 127.4(6)(*a.1*) was added by S.C. 2013, c. 40, s. 59(5), applicable to the 2015 and 2016 taxation years. S. 127.4(6)(*a*) formerly read:

(*a*) 15% of the net cost to the individual (or to a qualifying trust for the individual in respect of the share) for the original acquisition of the share by the individual or by the trust,

S. 127.4(6)(*e*) was added by S.C. 2013, c. 34, s. 270(2), applicable to the 2004 and subsequent taxation years.

Tax Window Files: Spousal RRSP LSF Tax Credit, *May 3, 2006*, CRA Document No. 2006-0178491E5; Labour-Sponsored Funds Tax Credit—Shares Acquired by Spousal RRSP, *Technical Interpretation, Financial Sector and Exempt Entities Division, March 16, 2006*, CRA Document No. 2005-0154871E5; Labour-Sponsored Funds Tax Credit, *Technical Interpretation, Business and Partnerships Division, April 15, 2003*, CRA Document No. 2003-0006295.

SECTION 127.41: [Qualifying environmental trust tax credit]

► 127.41(1) ◄

(1) Part XII.4 tax credit. In this section, the Part XII.4 tax credit of a taxpayer for a particular taxation year means the total of (*a*) all amounts each of which is an amount determined by the formula

$$A \times B/C$$

where

A is the tax payable under Part XII.4 by a qualifying environmental trust for a taxation year (in this paragraph referred to as the "trust's year") that ends in the particular year,

B is the amount, if any, by which the total of all amounts in respect of the trust that were included (otherwise than because of being a member of a partnership) because of the application of subsection 107.3(1) in computing the taxpayer's income for the particular year exceeds the total of all amounts in respect of the trust that were deducted (otherwise than because of being a member of a partnership) because of the application of subsection 107.3(1) in computing that income, and

C is the trust's income for the trust's year, computed without reference to subsections 104(4) to (31) and sections 105 to 107, and

(*b*) in respect of each partnership of which the taxpayer was a member, the total of all amounts each of which is the amount that can reasonably be considered to be the taxpayer's share of the relevant credit in respect of the partnership and, for this purpose, the relevant credit in respect of a partnership is the amount that would, if a partnership were a person and its fiscal period were its taxation year, be the Part XII.4 tax credit of the partnership for its taxation year that ends in the particular year.

Related Sections: S. 248(1), "balance-due day".

Canadian Tax Foundation: Frankovic, *The Case for "Reverse Depreciation" of Reclamation Costs,* 2004 Canadian Tax Journal 1:1–58.

▶ 127.41(2) ◀

(2) Reduction of Part I tax. There may be deducted from a taxpayer's tax otherwise payable under this Part for a taxation year such amount as the taxpayer claims not exceeding the taxpayer's Part XII.4 tax credit for the year.

▶ 127.41(3) ◀

(3) Deemed payment of Part I tax. There is deemed to have been paid on account of the tax payable under this Part by a taxpayer (other than a taxpayer exempt from such tax) for a taxation year on the taxpayer's balance-due day for the year, such amount as the taxpayer claims not exceeding the amount, if any, by which

(*a*) the taxpayer's Part XII.4 tax credit for the year

exceeds

(*b*) the amount deducted under subsection (2) in computing the taxpayer's tax payable under this Part for the year.

Division E.1 — Minimum Tax

SECTION 127.5: Obligation to pay minimum tax

Notwithstanding any other provision of this Act but subject to subsection 120.4(3) and section 127.55, where the amount that, but for section 120, would be determined under Division E to be an individual's tax payable for a taxation year is less than the amount determined under paragraph (*a*) in respect of the individual for the year, the individual's tax payable under this Part for the year is the total of

(*a*) the amount, if any, by which

(i) the individual's minimum amount for the year determined under section 127.51

exceeds

(ii) the individual's special foreign tax credit determined under section 127.54 for the year, and

(*b*) the amount, if any, required by section 120 to be added to the individual's tax otherwise payable under this Part for the year.

Related Sections: S. 120.2(1) Minimum tax carry-over; s. 127.55 Application of s. 127.5.

Income Tax Folios: *Secondary* — S5-F2-C1 Foreign Tax Credit.

SECTION 127.51: Minimum amount determined

An individual's minimum amount for a taxation year is the amount determined by the formula

$$A(B - C) - D$$

where

A is the appropriate percentage for the year;

B is the individual's adjusted taxable income for the year determined under section 127.52;

C is

(*a*) $40,000, in the case of an individual (other than a trust) or a graduated rate estate; and

(*b*) nil, in any other case; and

D is the individual's basic minimum tax credit for the year determined under section 127.531.

History: S. 127.51, the description of C was replaced by S.C. 2014, c. 39, s. 43(1), applicable to the 2016 and subsequent taxation years, and formerly read:

C is the individual's basic exemption for the year determined under section 127.53; and

Related Sections: 248(1) graduated rate estate.

Forms: T3 SCH 12 — Minimum Tax; T691 — Alternative Minimum Tax.

SECTION 127.52: Adjusted taxable income determined

► 127.52(1) ◄

(1) Adjusted taxable income determined. Subject to subsection (2), an individual's adjusted taxable income for a taxation year is the amount that would be the individual's taxable income for the year or the individual's taxable income earned in Canada for the year, as the case may be, if it were computed on the assumption that

(*a*) (Repealed by S.C. 1999, c. 22, s. 50(2).)

(*b*) the total of all amounts each of which is an amount deductible under paragraph 20(1)(*a*) or any of paragraphs 20(1)(*c*) to (*f*) in computing the individual's income for the year in respect of a rental or leasing property (other than an amount included in the individual's share of a loss referred to in paragraph (*c*.1)) were the lesser of the total of all amounts otherwise so deductible and the amount, if any, by which the total of

(i) the total of all amounts each of which is the individual's income for the year from the renting or leasing of a rental or leasing property owned by the individual or by a partnership, computed without reference to paragraphs 20(1)(*a*) and (*c*) to (*f*), and

(ii) the amount, if any, by which

(A) the total of all amounts each of which is the individual's taxable capital gain for the year from the disposition of a rental or leasing property owned by the individual or by a partnership

exceeds

(B) the total of all amounts each of which is the individual's allowable capital loss for the year from the disposition of a rental or leasing property owned by the individual or by a partnership

exceeds the total of all amounts each of which is the individual's loss for the year from the renting or leasing of a rental or leasing property owned by the individual or by a partnership (other than an amount included in the individual's share of a loss referred to in paragraph (*c*.1)), computed without reference to paragraphs 20(1)(*a*) and (*c*) to (*f*);

(*c*) the total of all amounts each of which is an amount deductible under paragraph 20(1)(*a*) or any of paragraphs 20(1)(*c*) to (*f*) in computing the individual's income for the year in respect of a film property referred to in paragraph (*w*) of Class 10 of Schedule II to the *Income Tax Regulations* (other than an amount included in the individual's share of a loss referred to in paragraph (*c*.1)) were the lesser of the total of all amounts otherwise so deductible by the individual for the year and the amount, if any, by which the total of

(i) the total of all amounts each of which is the individual's income for the year from the renting or leasing of a film property owned by the individual or by a partnership, computed without reference to paragraphs 20(1)(*a*) and (*c*) to (*f*), and

(ii) the amount, if any, by which

(A) the total of all amounts each of which is the individual's taxable capital gain for the year from the disposition of such a film property owned by the individual or by a partnership

exceeds

(B) the total of all amounts each of which is the individual's allowable capital loss for the year from the disposition of such a film property owned by the individual or by a partnership

exceeds the total of all amounts each of which is the individual's loss for the year from such a film property owned by the individual or by a partnership (other than amounts included in the individual's share of a loss referred to in paragraph (*c*.1)), computed without reference to paragraphs 20(1)(*a*) and (*c*) to (*f*);

(*c*.1) if, during a partnership's fiscal period that ends in the year (other than a fiscal period that ends because of subsection 99(1)), the individual's interest in the partnership is an interest for which an identification number is required to be, or has been, obtained under section 237.1,

(i) the individual's share of allowable capital losses of the partnership for the fiscal period were the lesser of

(A) the total of all amounts each of which is the individual's

(I) share of a taxable capital gain for the fiscal period from the disposition of property (other than property acquired by the partnership in a transaction to which subsection 97(2) applied), or

(II) taxable capital gain for the year from the disposition of the individual's interest in the partnership if the individual, or a person who does not deal at arm's length with the individual, does not have an interest in the partnership (otherwise than because of the application of paragraph 98(1)(*a*) or 98.1(1)(*a*)) throughout the following taxation year, and

(B) the individual's share of allowable capital losses of the partnership for the fiscal period,

(ii) the individual's share of each loss from a business of the partnership for the fiscal period were the lesser of

(A) the individual's share of the loss, and

(B) the amount, if any, by which

(I) the total of all amounts each of which is the individual's

1. share of a taxable capital gain for the fiscal period from the disposition of property used by the partnership in the business (other than property acquired by the partnership in a transaction to which subsection 97(2) applied), or

2. taxable capital gain for the year from the disposition of the individual's interest in the partnership if the individual, or a person who does not deal at arm's length with the individual, does not have an interest in the partnership (otherwise than because of the application of paragraph 98(1)(*a*) or 98.1(1)(*a*)) throughout the following taxation year

exceeds

(II) the total of all amounts each of which is the individual's share of an allowable capital loss for the fiscal period, and

(iii) the individual's share of losses from property of the partnership for the fiscal period were the lesser of

(A) the total of

(I) the individual's share of incomes for the fiscal period from properties of the partnership, and

(II) the amount, if any, by which the total of all amounts each of which is the individual's

1. share of a taxable capital gain for the fiscal period from the disposition of property held by the partnership for the purpose of earning income from property (other than property acquired by the partnership in a transaction to which subsection 97(2) applied), or

2. taxable capital gain for the year from the disposition of the individual's interest in the partnership if the individual, or a person who does not deal at arm's length with the individual, does not have an interest in the partnership (otherwise than because of the application of paragraph 98(1)(*a*) or 98.1(1)(*a*)) throughout the following taxation year,

exceeds the total of all amounts each of which is the individual's share of an allowable capital loss for the fiscal period, and

(B) the individual's share of losses from property of the partnership for the fiscal period;

(*c*.2) where, during a fiscal period of a partnership that ends in the year (other than a fiscal period that ends because of the application of subsection 99(1)),

(i) the individual is a limited partner of the partnership, or is a member of the partnership who was a specified member of the partnership at all times since becoming a member of the partnership, or

(ii) the partnership owns a rental or leasing property or a film property and the individual is a member of the partnership,

the total of all amounts each of which is an amount deductible under any of paragraphs 20(1)(*c*) to (*f*) in computing the individual's income for the year in respect of the individual's acquisition of the partnership interest were the lesser of

(iii) the total of all amounts otherwise so deductible, and

(iv) the total of all amounts each of which is the individual's share of any income of the partnership for the fiscal period, determined in accordance with subsection 96(1);

(*c*.3) the total of all amounts each of which is an amount deductible in computing the individual's income for the year in respect of a property for which an identification number is required to be, or has been, obtained under section 237.1 (other than an amount to which any of paragraphs (*b*) to (*c*.2) applies) were nil;

(*d*) except in respect of dispositions of property occurring before 1986 or to which section 79 applies,

(i) the references to the fraction applicable to the individual for the year in each of paragraphs 38(*a*), (*b*) and (*c*) and section 41 were read as a reference to "4/5", other than in the case of a capital gain from a disposition that is the making of a gift of property to a qualified donee, and

(ii) each amount that is designated by a trust for a particular year of the trust in respect of the individual and deemed by subsection 104(21) to be a taxable capital gain for the year of the individual were equal to the amount obtained by the formula

$$4/5(A \times 1/B)$$

where

A is the amount so deemed to be a taxable capital gain for the year of the individual, and

B is the fraction in paragraph 38(*a*) applicable to the trust for the particular year of the trust for which the designation is made;

(iii) (Repealed by S.C. 2013, c. 34, s. 271(3).)

(*e*) the total of all amounts deductible under section 65, 66, 66.1, 66.2, 66.21 or 66.4 or under subsection 29(10) or (12) of the *Income Tax Application Rules* in computing the individual's income for the year were the lesser of the amounts otherwise so deductible by the individual for the year and the total of

(i) the individual's income for the year from royalties in respect of, and such part of the individual's income, other than royalties, for the year as may reasonably be considered as attributable to, the production of petroleum, natural gas and minerals, determined before deducting those amounts,

(i.1) the individual's income for the year from property, or from the business of selling the product of property, described in Class 43.1 or 43.2 in Schedule II to the *Income Tax Regulations*, determined before deducting those amounts, and

(ii) all amounts included in computing the individual's income for the year under section 59;

(*e*.1) the total of all amounts each of which is an amount deductible under any of paragraphs 20(1)(*c*) to (*f*) in computing the individual's income for the year in respect of a property that is a flow-through share (if the individual is the person to whom the share was issued under an agreement referred to in the definition "flow-through share" in subsection 66(15)), a Canadian resource property or a foreign resource property were the lesser of the total of the amounts otherwise so determined for the year and the amount, if any, by which

(i) the total of all amounts each of which is an amount described in subparagraph (*e*)(i) or (ii), determined without reference to paragraphs 20(1)(*c*) to (*f*),

exceeds

(ii) the total of all amounts each of which is an amount deductible under section 65, 66, 66.1, 66.2, 66.21 or 66.4 or under subsection 29(10) or (12) of the *Income Tax Application Rules* in computing the individual's income for the year;

(*f*) subsection 82(1) were read without reference to paragraph 82(1)(*b*);

(*g*) the total of all amounts deductible under section 104 in computing the income of a trust for the year were equal to the total of

(i) the total of all amounts otherwise deductible under that section, and

(ii) the total of all amounts each of which is 3/5 of

(A) an amount designated by the trust under subsection 104(21) for the year, or

(B) that portion of a net taxable capital gain of the trust that may reasonably be considered to

(I) be part of an amount included, by virtue of subsection 104(13) or section 105, in computing the income for the year of a non-resident beneficiary of the trust, or

(II) have been paid in the year by a trust governed by an employee benefit plan to a beneficiary thereunder;

(*h*) the only amounts deductible under sections 110 to 110.7 in computing the individual's taxable income for the year or taxable income earned in Canada for the year, as the case may be, were

(i) the amounts deducted under any of subsections 110(2), 110.6(2) and (2.1) and 110.7(1),

(ii) the amount deducted under paragraph 110(1)(*d*), not exceeding the total of

(A) the amount deducted under paragraph 110(1)(*d*.01), and

(B) 2/5 of the amount, if any, by which

(I) the amount deducted under paragraph 110(1)(*d*)

exceeds

(II) the amount determined under clause (A),

(iii) the amount deducted under paragraph 110(1)(*d*.01),

(iv) 2/5 of the amounts deducted under any of paragraphs 110(1)(*d*.1) to (*d*.3),

(v) the amount that would be deductible under paragraph 110(1)(*f*) if paragraph (*d*) were applicable in computing the individual's income for the year, and

(vi) the amount deducted under paragraph 110(1)(*g*);

(*h*.1) the formula in paragraph 110.6(21)(*a*) were read as

$$A - B$$

(*i*) in computing the individual's taxable income for the year or the individual's taxable income earned in Canada for the year, as the case may be, the only amounts deductible under

(i) paragraphs 111(1)(*a*), (*c*), (*d*) and (*e*) were the lesser of

(A) the amount deducted under those paragraphs for the year, and

(B) the total of all amounts that would be deductible under those paragraphs for the year if

(I) paragraphs (*b*), (*c*) and (*e*) of this subsection, as they read in respect of taxation years that began after 1985 and before 1995, applied in computing the individual's non-capital loss, restricted farm loss, farm loss and limited partnership loss for any of those years,

(II) paragraphs (*b*) to (*c.3*), (*e*) and (*e.1*) of this subsection, as they read in respect of taxation years that began after 1994 and ended before 2012, applied in computing the individual's non-capital loss, restricted farm loss, farm loss and limited partnership loss for any of those years, and

(III) paragraphs (*b*) to (*c.3*), (*e*) and (*e.1*) of this subsection applied in computing the individual's non-capital loss, restricted farm loss, farm loss and limited partnership loss for any taxation year that ends after 2011, and

(ii) paragraph 111(1)(*b*) were the lesser of

(A) the total of all amounts each of which is an amount that can reasonably be considered to be the amount that the individual would have deducted under paragraph 111(1)(*b*) had paragraph (*d*) of this subsection been applicable in computing the amount deductible under paragraph 111(1)(*b*), and

(B) the total of all amounts that would be deductible under that paragraph for the year if

(I) paragraph (*d*) of this subsection applied in computing the individual's net capital loss for any taxation year that began before 1995,

(II) paragraphs (*c.1*) and (*d*) of this subsection, as they read in respect of taxation years that began after 1994 and ended before 2012, applied in computing the individual's net capital loss for any of those years, and

(III) paragraphs (*c.1*) and (*d*) of this subsection applied in computing the individual's net capital loss for any taxation year that ends after 2011; and

(*j*) the *Income Tax Application Rules* were read without reference to section 40 of that Act.

History: S. 127.52(1)(*h*)(i) was replaced by S.C. 2014, c. 39, s. 44(2), applicable to amounts deducted in respect of the 2016 and subsequent taxation years, and formerly read:

(i) the amounts deducted under any of subsections 110(2), 110.6(2), (2.1), (2.2) and (12) and 110.7(1),

S. 127.52(1)(*h*)(i) was replaced by S.C. 2014, c. 39, s. 44(1), applicable to amounts deducted in respect of the 2014 and subsequent taxation years, and formerly read:

(i) the amounts deducted under any of subsections 110(2), 110.6(2), (2.1), (2.2) and (12) and 110.7(1),

S. 127.52(1)(*c.1*), the portion before subparagraph (i) was replaced by S.C. 2013, c. 40, s. 60(1), applicable to the 2012 and subsequent taxation years and, if an individual files an election in writing with the Minister of National Revenue before March 12, 2014 [the day that is 90 days after December 12, 2013, the day on which this Act received royal assent], for the individual, this amendment also applies to the 2003 to 2011 taxation years. [**Editorial Note**: Amended by S.C. 2017, c. 33, s. 82(*a*), in force December 14, 2017 (Royal Assent). It previously read "2006 to 2011 taxation years".]

Notwithstanding subsection 152(4) of the Act, the Minister of National Revenue may make such assessments, reassessments and determinations under Part I of the Act as are necessary to give effect to the election above.

S. 127.52(1)(*c.1*), the portion before subparagraph (i) formerly read:

(*c*.1) where, during a partnership's fiscal period that ends in the year (other than a fiscal period that ends because of the application of subsection 99(1)), the individual is a limited partner of the partnership or a member of the partnership who was a specified member of the partnership at all times since becoming a member of the partnership, or the individual's interest in the partnership is an interest for which an identification number is required to be, or has been, obtained under section 237.1,

S. 127.52(1)(*i*)(i)(B)(II) was replaced and s. 127.52(1)(*i*)(i)(B)(III) was added by S.C. 2013, c. 40, s. 60(2), applicable to the 2012 and subsequent taxation years and, if an individual files an election in writing with the Minister of National Revenue before March 12, 2014 [the day that is 90 days after December 12, 2013, the day on which this Act received royal assent], for the individual,

(*a*) the amendments also apply to the 2003 to 2011 taxation years; [**Editorial Note**: Amended by S.C. 2017, c. 33, s. 82(*a*), in force December 14, 2017 (Royal Assent). It previously read "2006 to 2011 taxation years".] and

(*b*) the references in clauses 127.52(1)(*i*)(i)(B) to "2011" and "2012" are to be read as "2002" and "2003", respectively. [**Editorial Note**: Amended by S.C. 2017, c. 33, s. 82(*b*), in force December 14, 2017 (Royal Assent). It previously read " '2005' and '2006', respectively".]

Notwithstanding subsection 152(4) of the Act, the Minister of National Revenue may make such assessments, reassessments and determinations under Part I of the Act as are necessary to give effect to the election above.

S. 127.52(1)(*i*)(i)(B)(II) formerly read:

(II) paragraphs (*b*) to (*c*.3), (*e*) and (*e*.1) of this subsection applied in computing the individual's non-capital loss, restricted farm loss, farm loss and limited partnership loss for any taxation year that begins after 1994, and

S. 127.52(1)(*i*)(ii)(B)(II) was replaced and s. 127.52(1)(*i*)(ii)(B)(III) was added by S.C. 2013, c. 40, s. 60(3), applicable to the 2012 and subsequent taxation years and, if an individual files an election in writing with the Minister of National Revenue before March 12, 2014 [the day that is 90 days after December 12, 2013, the day on which this Act received royal assent], for the individual,

(*a*) the amendments also apply to the 2003 to 2011 taxation years; [**Editorial Note**: Amended by S.C. 2017, c. 33, s. 82(*a*), in force December 14, 2017 (Royal Assent). It previously read "2006 to 2011 taxation years".] and

(*b*) the references in clauses 127.52(1)(*i*)(ii)(B) to "2011" and "2012" are to be read as "2002" and "2003", respectively. [**Editorial Note**: Amended by S.C. 2017, c. 33, s. 82(*b*), in force December 14, 2017 (Royal Assent). It previously read " '2005' and '2006', respectively".]

Notwithstanding subsection 152(4) of the Act, the Minister of National Revenue may make such assessments, reassessments and determinations under Part I of the Act as are necessary to give effect to the election above.

S. 127.52(1)(*i*)(ii)(B)(II) formerly read:

(II) paragraphs (*c*.1) and (*d*) of this subsection applied in computing the individual's net capital loss for any taxation year that begins after 1994; and

S. 127.52(1)(*d*)(ii), the portion before the formula was replaced by S.C. 2013, c. 34, s. 271(1), applicable to taxation years that begin after October 31, 2011, and formerly read:

(ii) each amount (other than an amount to which subsection 104(21.4) applies) that is designated by a trust for a particular year of the trust in respect of the individual and deemed by subsection 104(21) to be a taxable capital gain for the year of the individual were equal to the amount obtained by the formula

S. 127.52(1)(*d*)(iii) was repealed by S.C. 2013, c. 34, s. 271(3), applicable to taxation years that begin after October 31, 2011, and formerly read:

(iii) this Act were read without reference to subsection 104(21.6);

S. 127.52(1)(*d*)(iii) was added by S.C. 2013, c. 34, s. 271(2), applicable to the 2000 and subsequent taxation years.

S. 127.52(1)(*e*)(i.1) was added by S.C. 2013, c. 34, s. 271(4), applicable in respect of taxation years that end after 2008.

S. 127.52(1)(*h*)(i) was repealed by S.C. 2013, c. 34, s. 271(5), in force June 26, 2013, and formerly read:

(i) the amounts deducted under any of subsections 110(2), 110.6(2), (2.1), (2.2), (3) and (12) and 110.7(1),

Cases: Since the taxpayer never retained any power to recover the interests in two buildings he had transferred to his creditors, the untaxed portion of the capital gains realized from such a "disposition" was added to his adjusted taxable income for AMT purposes. *Hallbauer v. The Queen*, 98 DTC 6275 (F.C.A.), affirming 97 DTC 767 (T.C.C.).

▶ 127.52(2) ◀

(2) Partnerships. For the purposes of subsection (1) and this subsection, any amount deductible under a provision of this Act in computing the income or loss of a partnership for a fiscal period is, to the extent of a member's share of the partnership's income or loss, deemed to be deductible by the member under that provision in computing the member's income for the taxation year in which the fiscal period ends.

▶ 127.52(2.1) ◀

(2.1) Specified member of a partnership. Where it can reasonably be considered that one of the main reasons that a member of a partnership was not a specified member of the partnership at all times since becoming a member of the partnership is to avoid the application of this section to the member's interest in the partnership, the member is deemed for the purpose of this section to have been a specified member of the partnership at all times since becoming a member of the partnership.

Related Sections: S. 40(3.131) Specified member of a partnership.

▶ 127.52(3) ◀

(3) Definitions. For the purposes of this section,

"film property" — "film property" means a property described in paragraph (*n*) of Class 12, or paragraph (*w*) of Class 10, of Schedule II to the *Income Tax Regulations*;

"limited partner" — "limited partner" has the meaning that would be assigned by subsection 96(2.4) if that subsection were read without reference to "if the member's partnership interest is not an exempt interest (within the meaning assigned by subsection (2.5)) at that time and";

"rental or leasing property" — "rental or leasing property" means a property that is a rental property or a leasing property for the purpose of section 1100 of the *Income Tax Regulations*.

"residential property" — (Repealed by S.C. 1998, c. 19, s. 150(8).)

SECTION 127.53: Basic exemption

▶ 127.53(1) ◀

(1) Basic exemption — (Repealed by 2014, c. 39, s. 45(1).)

History: S. 127.53(1) was repealed by S.C. 2014, c. 39, s. 45(1), applicable to the 2016 and subsequent taxation years, and formerly read:

(1) *Basic exemption.* An individual's basic exemption for a taxation year is

(*a*) $40,000, in the case of an individual other than a trust;

(*b*) $40,000, in the case of a testamentary trust or an *inter vivos* trust described in subsection 122(2); and

(*c*) in any other case, nil.

▶ 127.53(2) ◀

(2) Multiple trusts — (Repealed by 2014, c. 39, s. 45(1).)

History: S. 127.53(2) was repealed by S.C. 2014, c. 39, s. 45(1), applicable to the 2016 and subsequent taxation years, and formerly read:

(2) *Multiple trusts.* Notwithstanding paragraph (1)(*b*), where more than one trust described in that paragraph arose as a consequence of contributions to the trusts by an individual and those trusts have filed with the Minister in prescribed form an agreement whereby, for the purpose of this Division, they allocate an amount to one or more of them for a taxation year and the total of the amounts so allocated does not exceed $40,000, the basic exemption for the year of each of the trusts is the amount so allocated to it.

▶ 127.53(3) ◀

(3) Failure to file agreement — (Repealed by 2014, c. 39, s. 45(1).)

History: S. 127.53(3) was repealed by S.C. 2014, c. 39, s. 45(1), applicable to the 2016 and subsequent taxation years, and formerly read:

(3) *Failure to file agreement.* Notwithstanding paragraph (1)(*b*), where more than one trust described in that paragraph arose as a consequence of contributions to the trusts by an individual and no agreement as contemplated by subsection (2) has been filed with the Minister before the expiration of 30 days after notice in writing has been forwarded by the Minister to any of the trusts that such an agreement is required for the purpose of an assessment of tax under this Part, the Minister may, for the purpose of this Division, allocate an amount to one or more of the trusts for a taxation year, the total of all of which amounts does not exceed $40,000, and the basic exemption for the year of each of the trusts is the amount so allocated to it.

SECTION 127.531: Basic minimum tax credit determined

An individual's basic minimum tax credit for a taxation year is the total of all amounts each of which is

(*a*) an amount deducted under any of subsections 118(1), (2) and (10), sections 118.01 to 118.07, subsection 118.3(1), sections 118.5 to 118.7 and 119 and subsection 127(1) in computing the individual's tax payable for the year under this Part; or

(*b*) the amount that was claimed under section 118.1 or 118.2 in computing the individual's tax payable for the year under this Part, determined without reference to this Division, to the extent that the amount claimed does not exceed the maximum amount deductible under that section in computing the individual's tax payable for the year under this Part, determined without reference to this Division.

History: S. 127.531(*a*) was replaced by S.C. 2014, c. 20, s. 19(1), applicable to the 2014 and subsequent taxation years, and formerly read:

(*a*) an amount deducted under any of subsections 118(1), (2) and (10), sections 118.01 to 118.06, subsection 118.3(1), sections 118.5 to 118.7 and 119 and subsection 127(1) in computing the individual's tax payable for the year under this Part; or

S. 127.531(*a*) was replaced by S.C. 2011, c. 24, s. 41(7), applicable to the 2011 and subsequent taxation years. S. 127.531(*a*) formerly read:

(*a*) an amount deducted under any of subsections 118(1), (2) and (10), sections 118.01 to 118.05, subsection 118.3(1), sections 118.5 to 118.7 and 119 and subsection 127(1) in computing the individual's tax payable for the year under this Part; or

S. 127.531(*a*) was replaced by S.C. 2011, c. 24, s. 41(6), applicable to the 2009 and subsequent taxation years. S. 127.531(*a*) formerly read:

(*a*) an amount deducted under any of subsections 118(1), (2) and (10), 118.01(2), 118.02(2), 118.03(2) and 118.3(1) and sections 118.5 to 118.7 and 119 in computing the individual's tax payable for the year under this Part; or

S. 127.531(*a*) was replaced by S.C. 2011, c. 24, s. 41(5), applicable to the 2007 and subsequent taxation years. S. 127.531(*a*) formerly read:

(*a*) an amount deducted under any of subsections 118(1), (2) and (10), 118.01(2), 118.02(2) and 118.3(1) and sections 118.5 to 118.7 and 119 in computing the individual's tax payable for the year under this Part; or

S. 127.531(*a*) was replaced by S.C. 2011, c. 24, s. 41(4), applicable to the 2006 and subsequent taxation years. S. 127.531(*a*) formerly read:

(*a*) an amount deducted under any of subsections 118(1) and (2), 118.01(2) and 118.3(1) and sections 118.5 to 118.7 and 119 in computing the individual's tax payable for the year under this Part; or

S. 127.531(*a*) was replaced by S.C. 2011, c. 24, s. 41(3), applicable to the 2005 and subsequent taxation years. S. 127.531(*a*) formerly read:

(*a*) an amount deducted under any of subsections 118(1) and (2) and 118.3(1) and sections 118.5 to 118.7 and 119 in computing the individual's tax payable for the year under this Part; or

S. 127.531 was replaced by S.C. 2011, c. 24, s. 41(2), applicable to the 2002 and subsequent taxation years. S. 127.531 formerly read:

S. 127.531 *Basic minimum tax credit determined.* An individual's basic minimum tax credit for a taxation year is the total of all amounts that may be deducted in computing the individual's tax payable for the year under this Part under any of subsections 118(1) and (2), sections 118.1 and 118.2, subsection 118.3(1) and sections 118.5 to 118.7 and 119.

S. 127.531 was replaced by S.C. 2011, c. 24, s. 41(1), applicable to dispositions after December 23, 1998 for individuals who ceased to be resident in Canada after October 1, 1996. S. 127.531 formerly read:

S. 127.531 *Basic minimum tax credit determined.* An individual's basic minimum tax credit for a taxation year is the total of all amounts each of which is

(*a*) an amount deducted under subsection 118(1), (2) or (10) or 118.3(1) or any of sections 118.01 to 118.05 and 118.5 to 118.7 in computing the individual's tax payable for the year under this Part; or

(*b*) the amount that was claimed under section 118.1 or 118.2 in computing the individual's tax payable for the year under this Part, determined without reference to this Division, to the extent that the amount claimed does not exceed the maximum amount deductible under that section in computing the individual's tax payable for the year under this Part, determined without reference to this Division.

S. 127.531(*a*) was replaced by S.C. 2009, c. 31, s. 14(1), applicable to the 2009 and subsequent taxation years. S. 127.531(*a*) formerly read:

(*a*) an amount deducted under subsection 118(1), (2) or (10), 118.01(2), 118.02(2), 118.03(2) or 118.3(1) or any of sections 118.5 to 118.7 in computing the individual's tax payable for the year under this Part; or

SECTION 127.54: [Foreign tax credit — Minimum tax]

► 127.54(1) ◄

(1) Definitions. In this section,

Income Tax Folios: *Secondary* — S5-F2-C1 Foreign Tax Credit.

"foreign income" — "foreign income" of an individual for a taxation year means the total of

(*a*) the individual's incomes for the year from businesses carried on by the individual in countries other than Canada, and

(*b*) the individual's incomes for the year from sources in countries other than Canada in respect of which the individual has paid non-business-income taxes, within the meaning assigned by subsection 126(7), to governments of countries other than Canada;

"foreign taxes" — "foreign taxes" of an individual for a taxation year means the total of the business-income taxes, within the meaning assigned by subsection 126(7), paid by the individual for the year in respect of businesses carried on by the individual in countries other than Canada and $^2/_3$ of the non-business-income taxes, within the meaning assigned by that subsection, paid by the individual for the year to the governments of countries other than Canada.

► 127.54(2) ◄

(2) Foreign tax credit. For the purposes of section 127.5, an individual's special foreign tax credit for a taxation year is the greater of

(*a*) the total of all amounts deductible under section 126 from the individual's tax for the year, and

(*b*) the lesser of

(i) the individual's foreign taxes for the year, and

(ii) the amount determined by the formula

$$A \times B$$

where

A is the appropriate percentage for the taxation year, and

B is the individual's foreign income for the year.

SECTION 127.55: Application of s. 127.5

Section 127.5 does not apply in respect of

(*a*) a return of income of an individual filed under subsection 70(2), paragraph 104(23)(*d*) or 128(2)(*e*) or subsection 150(4);

(*b*) (Repealed by S.C. 2001, c. 17, s. 121(1).)

(*c*) an individual for the taxation year in which the individual dies;

(*d*) an individual for the 1986 taxation year if the individual dies in 1987;

(*e*) a trust described in paragraph 104(4)(*a*) or (*a*.1) for its taxation year that includes the day determined in respect of the trust under that paragraph; and

(*f*) a taxation year of a trust throughout which the trust is

(i) a related segregated fund trust (within the meaning assigned by paragraph 138.1(1)(*a*)),

(ii) a mutual fund trust,

(iii) a trust prescribed to be a master trust, or

(iv) an employee life and health trust.

History: S. 127.55(*f*)(iv) was added by S.C. 2010, c. 25, s. 27(1), applicable after 2009.

Related Regulations: 4802(1.1).

Related Sections: S. 132(6) Meaning of "mutual fund trust"; s. 149(1)(*o*.4) Master trusts.

Interpretation Bulletins: *Primary* — IT-326R3 Returns of deceased persons as "another person".

Division F — Special Rules Applicable in Certain Circumstances

Bankruptcies

SECTION 128: [Bankruptcy]

► 128(1) ◄

(1) Where corporation bankrupt. Where a corporation has become a bankrupt, the following rules are applicable:

(*a*) the trustee in bankruptcy shall be deemed to be the agent of the bankrupt for all purposes of this Act;

(*b*) the estate of the bankrupt shall be deemed not to be a trust or an estate for the purposes of this Act;

(*c*) the income and the taxable income of the corporation for any taxation year of the corporation during which it was a bankrupt and for any subsequent year shall be calculated as if

(i) the property of the bankrupt did not pass to and vest in the trustee in bankruptcy on the bankruptcy order being made or the assignment filed but remained vested in the bankrupt, and

(ii) any dealing in the estate of the bankrupt or any act performed in the carrying on of the business of the bankrupt estate by the trustee was done as agent on behalf of the bankrupt and any income of the trustee from such dealing or carrying on is income of the bankrupt and not of the trustee;

(*d*) a taxation year of the corporation shall be deemed to have commenced on the day the corporation became a bankrupt and a taxation year of the corporation that would otherwise have ended after the corporation became a bankrupt shall be deemed to have ended on the day immediately before the day on which the corporation became a bankrupt;

(*e*) if, in the case of any taxation year of the corporation ending during the period the corporation is a bankrupt, the corporation fails to pay any tax payable by it under this Act for any such year, the corporation and the trustee in bankruptcy are jointly and severally, or solidarily, liable to pay the tax, except that

(i) the trustee is only liable to the extent of the property of the bankrupt in the trustee's possession, and

(ii) payment by either of them discharges the liability to the extent of the amount paid;

(*f*) in the case of any taxation year of the corporation ending during the period the corporation is a bankrupt, the corporation shall be deemed not to be associated with any other corporation in the year; and

(*g*) where an absolute order of discharge is granted in respect of the corporation, for the purposes of section 111 any loss of the corporation for any taxation year preceding the year in which the order of discharge was granted is not deductible by the corporation in computing its taxable income for the taxation year of the corporation in which the order was granted or any subsequent year.

History: S. 128(1)(*e*), the portion before subparagraph (i) was replaced by S.C. 2013, c. 34, s. 129(1), in force June 26, 2013, and formerly read:

(*e*) where, in the case of any taxation year of the corporation ending during the period the corporation is a bankrupt, the corporation fails to pay any tax payable by the corporation under this Act for any such year, the corporation and the trustee in bankruptcy are jointly and severally liable to pay the tax, except that

S. 128(1)(*e*)(ii) was replaced by S.C. 2013, c. 34, s. 129(2), in force June 26, 2013, and formerly read:

(ii) payment by either of them shall discharge the joint obligation;

Related Regulations: Part II.

Related Sections: S. 50(1) Debts established to be bad debts and shares of bankrupt corporation; s. 50(3) Disposal of R.H.O.S.P. properties; s. 248(1), "bankrupt", "estate of the bankrupt"; s. 256 Associated corporations.

Interpretation Bulletins: *Secondary* — IT-206R Separate businesses.

► 128(2) ◄

(2) Where individual bankrupt. Where an individual has become a bankrupt, the following rules are applicable:

(*a*) the trustee in bankruptcy shall be deemed to be the agent of the bankrupt for all purposes of this Act;

(*b*) the estate of the bankrupt shall be deemed not to be a trust or an estate for the purposes of this Act;

(*c*) the income and the taxable income of the individual for any taxation year during which the individual was a bankrupt and for any subsequent year shall be calculated as if

(i) the property of the bankrupt did not pass to and vest in the trustee in bankruptcy on the bankruptcy order being made or the assignment filed but remained vested in the bankrupt, and

(ii) any dealing in the estate of the bankrupt or any act performed in the carrying on of the business of the bankrupt estate by the trustee was done as agent on behalf of the bankrupt and any income of the trustee from such dealing or carrying on is income of the bankrupt and not of the trustee;

(*d*) except for the purposes of subsections 146(1), 146.01(4) and 146.02(4) and Part X.1,

(i) a taxation year of the individual is deemed to have begun at the beginning of the day on which the individual became a bankrupt, and

(ii) the individual's last taxation year that began before that day is deemed to have ended immediately before that day;

(*d*.1) where, by reason of paragraph (*d*), a taxation year of the individual is not a calendar year,

(i) paragraph 146(5)(*b*) shall, for the purpose of the application of subsection 146(5) to the taxation year, be read as follows:

"(*b*) the amount, if any, by which

(i) the amount, if any, by which the taxpayer's RRSP deduction limit for the particular calendar year in which the taxation year ends exceeds the total of all contributions made by an employer in the particular calendar year to a pooled registered pension plan in respect of the taxpayer

exceeds

(ii) the total of the amounts deducted under this subsection and subsection (5.1) in computing the taxpayer's income for any preceding taxation year that ends in the particular calendar year.",

and

(ii) paragraph 146(5.1)(*b*) shall, for the purpose of the application of subsection 146(5.1) to the taxation year, be read as follows:

"(*b*) the amount, if any, by which

(i) the amount, if any, by which the taxpayer's RRSP deduction limit for the particular calendar year in which the taxation year ends exceeds the total of all contributions made by an employer in the particular calendar year to a pooled registered pension plan in respect of the taxpayer

exceeds

(ii) the total of the amount deducted under subsection (5) in computing the taxpayer's income for the year and the amounts deducted under this subsection and subsection (5) in computing the taxpayer's income for any preceding taxation year that ends in the particular calendar year.";

(*d*.2) where, by reason of paragraph (*d*), the individual has two taxation years ending in a calendar year, each amount deducted in computing the individual's income for either of the taxation years shall be deemed, for the purposes of the definition "unused RRSP deduction room" in subsection 146(1) and Part X.1, to have been deducted in computing the individual's income for the calendar year;

(*e*) where the individual was a bankrupt at any time in a calendar year the trustee shall, within 90 days from the end of the year, file a return with the Minister, in prescribed form, on behalf of the individual of the individual's income for any taxation year occurring in the calendar year computed as if

(i) the only income of the individual for that taxation year was the income for the year, if any, arising from dealings in the estate of the bankrupt or acts performed in the carrying on of the business of the bankrupt by the trustee,

(ii) in computing the individual's taxable income for that taxation year, no deduction were permitted by Division C, other than

(A) an amount under any of paragraphs 110(1)(*d*) to (*d*.3) and section 110.6 to the extent that the amount is in respect of an amount included in income under subparagraph (i) for that taxation year, and

(B) an amount under section 111 to the extent that the amount was in respect of a loss of the individual for any taxation year that ended before the individual was discharged absolutely from bankruptcy, and

(iii) in computing the individual's tax payable under this Part for that taxation year, no deduction were allowed

(A) under any of sections 118 to 118.07, 118.2, 118.3, 118.5, 118.8 and 118.9,

(B) under section 118.1 with respect to a gift made by the individual on or after the day the individual became bankrupt,

(B.1) under section 118.62 with respect to interest paid on or after the day on which the individual became bankrupt, and

(C) under subsection 127(5) with respect to an expenditure incurred or property acquired by the individual in any taxation year that ends after the individual was discharged absolutely from bankruptcy,

and the trustee is liable to pay any tax so determined for that taxation year;

(*f*) notwithstanding paragraph (*e*), the individual shall file a separate return of the individual's income for any taxation year during which the individual was a bankrupt, computed as if

(i) the income required to be reported in respect of the year by the trustee under paragraph (*e*) was not the income of the individual,

(ii) in computing income, the individual was not entitled to deduct any loss sustained by the trustee in the year in dealing with the estate of the bankrupt or in carrying on the business of the bankrupt,

(iii) in computing the individual's taxable income for the year, no amount were deductible under any of paragraphs 110(1)(*d*) to (*d*.3) and section 110.6 in respect of an amount included in income under subparagraph (*e*)(i), and no amount were deductible under section 111, and

(iv) in computing the individual's tax payable under this Part for the year, no amount were deductible under

(A) section 118.1 in respect of a gift made before the day on which the individual became bankrupt,

(B) section 118.62 in respect of interest paid before the day on which the individual became bankrupt, or

(C) section 118.61 or 120.2 or subsection 127(5),

and the individual is liable to pay any tax so determined for that taxation year;

(*g*) notwithstanding subparagraphs (*e*)(ii) and (iii) and (*f*)(iii) and (iv), where at any time an individual was discharged absolutely from bankruptcy,

(i) in computing the individual's taxable income for any taxation year that ends after that time, no amount shall be deducted under section 111 in respect of losses for taxation years that ended before that time,

(ii) in computing the individual's tax payable under this Part for any taxation year that ends after that time,

(A) no amount shall be deducted under section 118.61 or 120.2 in respect of an amount for any taxation year that ended before that time,

(B) no amount shall be deducted under section 118.1 in respect of a gift made before the individual became bankrupt,

(B.1) no amount shall be deducted under section 118.62 in respect of interest paid before the day on which the individual became bankrupt, and

(C) no amount shall be deducted under subsection 127(5) in respect of an expenditure incurred or a property acquired by the individual in any taxation year that ended before that time, and

(iii) the individual's unused tuition, textbook and education tax credits (as determined under subsection 118.61(1)) at the end of the last taxation year that ended before that time is deemed to be nil;

(*h*) where, in a taxation year commencing after an order of discharge has been granted in respect of the individual, the trustee deals in the estate of the individual who was a bankrupt or performs any act in the carrying on of the business of the individual, paragraphs (*e*), (*f*) and (*g*) shall apply as if the individual were a bankrupt in the year; and (*i*) the portion of the individual's non-capital loss for a particular taxation year in which paragraph (*e*) applied in respect of the individual and any preceding taxation year that does not exceed the lesser of

(i) the amount of the individual's allowable business investment losses for the particular taxation year, and

(ii) any portion of the individual's non-capital loss for that particular year that was not deducted in computing the individual's taxable income for any taxation year in which paragraph (*e*) applied in respect of the individual or any preceding taxation year,

shall, for the purpose of determining the individual's cumulative gains limit under section 110.6 for taxation years following the taxation year in which paragraph (*e*) was last applicable in respect of the individual, be deemed not to have been an allowable business investment loss.

History: S. 128(2)(*e*)(iii)(A) was replaced by S.C. 2016, c. 7, s. 37(2), applicable to the 2017 and subsequent taxation years, and formerly read:

(A) under any of sections 118 to 118.07, 118.2, 118.3, 118.5, 118.6, 118.8 and 118.9,

S. 128(2)(*e*)(iii)(A) was replaced S.C. 2016, c. 7, s. 37(1), applicable to the 2016 taxation year, and formerly read:

(A) under any of sections 118 to 118.07, 118.2, 118.3, 118.5, 118.6, 118.8, 118.9 and 119.1,

S. 128(2)(*e*)(iii)(A) was replaced S.C. 2015, c. 36, s. 33(1), applicable to the 2014 and subsequent taxation years, and formerly read:

(A) under any of sections 118 to 118.07, 118.2, 118.3, 118.5, 118.6, 118.8 and 118.9,

S. 128(2)(*e*)(iii)(A) was replaced by S.C. 2014, c. 20, s. 20(1), applicable to the 2014 and subsequent taxation years, and formerly read:

(A) under any of sections 118 to 118.06, 118.2, 118.3, 118.5, 118.6, 118.8 and 118.9,

S. 128(2)(*g*)(iii) was replaced by S.C. 2013, c. 34, s. 272(1), applicable to the 2006 and subsequent taxation years, and formerly read:

(iii) the individual's unused tuition and education tax credits at the end of the last taxation year that ended before that time is deemed to be nil;

S. 128(2)(*d*.1) was replaced by S.C. 2012, c. 31, s. 29(1), in force December 14, 2012, and formerly read:

(*d*.1) where, by reason of paragraph (*d*), a taxation year of the individual is not a calendar year,

(i) paragraph 146(5)(*b*) shall, for the purpose of the application of subsection 146(5) to the taxation year, be read as follows:

"(*b*) the amount, if any, by which

(i) the taxpayer's RRSP deduction limit for the particular calendar year in which the taxation year ends

exceeds

(ii) the total of the amounts deducted under this subsection and subsection (5.1) in computing the taxpayer's income for any preceding taxation year that ends in the particular calendar year.",

and

(ii) paragraph 146(5.1)(*b*) shall, for the purpose of the application of subsection 146(5.1) to the taxation year, be read as follows:

"(*b*) the amount, if any, by which

(i) the taxpayer's RRSP deduction limit for the particular calendar year in which the taxation year ends

exceeds

(ii) the total of the amount deducted under subsection (5) in computing the taxpayer's income for the year and the amounts deducted under this subsection and subsection (5) in computing the taxpayer's income for any preceding taxation year that ends in the particular calendar year.";

S. 128(2)(*e*)(iii)(A) was replaced by S.C. 2011, c. 24, s. 42(1), applicable to the 2011 and subsequent taxation years. S. 128(2)(*e*)(iii)(A) formerly read:

(A) under any of sections 118 to 118.05, 118.2, 118.3, 118.5, 118.6, 118.8 and 118.9,

S. 128(2)(*e*)(iii)(A) was replaced by S.C. 2009, c. 31, s. 15(1), applicable to the 2009 and subsequent taxation years. S. 128(2)(*e*)(iii)(A) formerly read:

(A) under section 118, 118.01, 118.02, 118.03, 118.2, 118.3, 118.5, 118.6, 118.8 or 118.9,

Related Regulations: Part II.

Related Sections: S. 118.95 Credits in year of bankruptcy; s. 120.2(4) Where subsection (1) does not apply; s. 122.5(7) Effect of bankruptcy; s. 122.61(3.1) Effect of bankruptcy; s. 127.1(1) Refundable investment tax credit; s. 248(1), "bankrupt".

Interpretation Bulletins: *Secondary* — IT-124R6 Contributions to registered retirement savings plans.

Cases: A self-employed accountant entered into his second voluntary bankruptcy to avoid $400,000 in tax debt. He argued that filing returns was against his religion and that he was not a "person" bound by the *Income Tax Act*. His discharge was denied for three years under section 172.1 of the *Bankruptcy and Insolvency Act*. *Re Crischuk*, 2013 DTC 5139 (B.C.S.C.)

A taxpayer who became bankrupt was only liable for taxes on business income arising after the date of bankruptcy. Tax liability for the period prior to the bankruptcy was a claim provable in bankruptcy. *Stiliadis v. The Queen*, 99 DTC 341 (T.C.C.).

► 128(3) ◄

(3) Definitions of "bankrupt" and "estate of the bankrupt" — (Repealed by S.C. 1998, c. 19, s. 152(4).)

Changes in Residence

SECTION 128.1: [Immigration and emigration]

► 128.1(1) ◄

(1) Immigration. For the purposes of this Act, where at a particular time a taxpayer becomes resident in Canada,

Related Sections: S. 250 Person deemed resident.

Guides: T4055 Newcomers to Canada; T4056 Emigrants and Income Tax.

Income Tax Folios: *Secondary* — S5-F1-C1 Determining an Individual's Residence Status.

Interpretation Bulletins: *Secondary* — IT-259R4 Exchange of property.

► 128.1(1)(a) ◄

(a) Year-end, fiscal period — where the taxpayer is a corporation or a trust,

(i) the taxpayer's taxation year that would otherwise include the particular time shall be deemed to have ended immediately before the particular time and a new taxation year of the taxpayer shall be deemed to have begun at the particular time, and

(ii) for the purpose of determining the taxpayer's fiscal period after the particular time, the taxpayer shall be deemed not to have established a fiscal period before the particular time;

Related Sections: S. 249 Definition of "taxation year"; s. 249.1(1) Definition of "fiscal period".

Canadian Tax Foundation: Bernstein and Choudhury, *Immigration into Canada*, 2015 Canadian Tax Highlights 23(2):5–6; Rees et al., *Taxpayer Migration: Proposed Rules*, 1999 Conference Report 35:1–19.

► 128.1(1)(b) ◄

(b) Deemed disposition — the taxpayer is deemed to have disposed, at the time (in this subsection referred to as the "time of disposition") that is immediately before the time that is immediately before the particular time, of each property owned by the taxpayer, other than, if the taxpayer is an individual,

(i) property that is a taxable Canadian property,

(ii) property that is described in the inventory of a business carried on by the taxpayer in Canada at the time of disposition,

(iii) property included in Class 14.1 of Schedule II to the *Income Tax Regulations*, in respect of a business carried on by the taxpayer in Canada at the time of disposition, and

(iv) an excluded right or interest of the taxpayer, other than an interest described in paragraph (*k*) of the definition "excluded right or interest" in subsection (10),

(v) (Repealed by S.C. 2001, c. 17, S. 123(2).)

for proceeds equal to its fair market value at the time of disposition;

History: S. 128.1(1)(*b*)(iii) was replaced by S.C. 2016, c. 12, s. 46(1), in force January 1, 2017, and formerly read:

(iii) eligible capital property in respect of a business carried on by the taxpayer in Canada at the time of disposition, and

S. 128.1(1)(*b*)(iv) was replaced by S.C. 2014, c. 39, s. 46(1), applicable to the 2016 and subsequent taxation years, and formerly read:

(iv) an excluded right or interest of the taxpayer (other than an interest in a non-resident testamentary trust that was never acquired for consideration),

Related Regulations: 8201.

Related Sections: S. 128.1(10) Definitions; s. 248(1), "taxable Canadian property".

▶ 128.1(1)(c) ◀

(c) Deemed acquisition — the taxpayer shall be deemed to have acquired at the particular time each property deemed by paragraph (*b*) to have been disposed of by the taxpayer, at a cost equal to the proceeds of disposition of the property;

Related Sections: S. 248(1), "taxable Canadian property", "treaty-protected property".

Cases: The corporation became a resident of Canada for tax purposes as early as 1998 and the adjusted cost base of the farm partnership interest it disposed of in 2009 was correctly calculated from that date. *Landbouwbedrijf v. The Queen*, 2018 DTC 1104 (TCC)

▶ 128.1(1)(c.1) ◀

(c.1) Deemed dividend to immigrating corporation — if the taxpayer is a particular corporation that immediately before the time of disposition owned a share of the capital stock of another corporation resident in Canada, a dividend is deemed to have been paid by the other corporation, and received by the particular corporation, immediately before the time of disposition, equal to the amount, if any, by which the fair market value of the share immediately before the time of disposition exceeds the total of

(i) the paid-up capital in respect of the share immediately before the time of disposition, and

(ii) if the share immediately before the time of disposition was taxable Canadian property that is not treaty-protected property, the amount by which, at the time of disposition, the fair market value of the share exceeds its cost amount;

Related Sections: S. 215(1.1) Exception — corporate immigration; s. 248(1), "treaty-protected income".

▶ 128.1(1)(c.2) ◀

(c.2) Deemed dividend to shareholder of immigrating corporation — if the taxpayer is a corporation and an amount has been added to the paid-up capital in respect of a class of shares of the corporation's capital stock because of paragraph (2)(*b*),

(i) the corporation is deemed to have paid, immediately before the time of disposition, a dividend on the issued shares of the class equal to the amount of the paid-up capital adjustment in respect of the class, and

(ii) a dividend is deemed to have been received, immediately before the time of disposition, by each person (other than a person in respect of whom the corporation is a foreign affiliate) who held any of the issued shares of the class equal to that proportion of the dividend so deemed to have been paid that the number of shares of the class held by the person immediately before the time of disposition is of the number of issued shares of the class outstanding immediately before the time of disposition;

Related Sections: S. 53(1)(*b*.1) Adjustments to cost base — Deemed dividend from immigrating corporation.

▶ 128.1(1)(c.3) ◀

(c.3) Foreign affiliate dumping — immigrating corporation — if the taxpayer is a corporation that was, immediately before the particular time, controlled by a particular non-resident corporation and the taxpayer owned, immediately before the particular time, one or more shares of one or more non-resident corporations (each of which is in this paragraph referred to as a "subject affiliate") that, immediately after the particular time, were — or that became, as part of a transaction or event or series of transactions or events that includes the taxpayer having become resident in Canada — foreign affiliates of the taxpayer, then

> **Proposed Amendment**
> **2019 Federal Budget Resolutions**
>
> **The portion of paragraph 128.1(1)(*c*.3) of the Act before subparagraph (i) is replaced by the following:**
>
> (*c*.3) if the taxpayer is a corporation that was, immediately before the particular time, controlled by one non-resident person or, if no single non-resident person controlled the CRIC, a group of non-resident persons not dealing with each other at arm's length (in this section, that one non-resident person, or each member of the group of non-resident persons, as the case may be, is referred to as a "parent", and the group of non-resident persons, if any, is referred to as the "group of parents") and the taxpayer owned, immediately before the particular time, one or more shares of one or more non-resident corporations (each of which is in this paragraph referred to as a "subject affiliate") that, immediately after the particular time, were — or that became, as part of a transaction or event or series of transactions or events that includes the taxpayer having become resident in Canada — foreign affiliates of the taxpayer, then
>
> **Applicable:** In respect of transactions or events that occur on or after March 19, 2019.

(i) in computing the paid-up capital, at any time after the time that is immediately after the particular time, of any particular class of shares of the capital stock of the taxpayer there is to be deducted the amount determined by the formula

$$A \times B/C$$

where

A is the lesser of

(A) the paid-up capital in respect of all of the shares of the capital stock of the taxpayer at the time that is immediately after the particular time, and

(B) the total of all amounts each of which is the fair market value at the particular time of

(I) a share of the capital stock of a subject affiliate owned by the taxpayer at the particular time, or

(II) an amount owing by the subject affiliate to the taxpayer at the particular time,

B is the paid-up capital in respect of the particular class of shares of the capital stock of the taxpayer at the time that is immediately after the particular time, and

C is the paid-up capital in respect of all the shares of the capital stock of the taxpayer at the time that is immediately after the particular time, and

(ii) for the purposes of Part XIII, the taxpayer is deemed, immediately after the particular time, to have paid to the particular non-resident corporation, and the particular non-resident corporation is deemed, immediately after the particular time, to have received from the taxpayer, a dividend equal to the amount, if any, by which the amount determined under clause (B) of the description of A in subparagraph (i) exceeds the amount determined under clause (A) of the description of A in subparagraph (i); and

Proposed Amendment
2019 Federal Budget Resolutions

Subparagraph 128.1(1)(*c*.3)(ii) of the Act is replaced by the following:

(ii) for the purposes of Part XIII, the taxpayer is deemed, immediately after the particular time, to have paid to each parent, and each parent is deemed, immediately after the particular time, to have received from the taxpayer, a dividend in an amount determined by the formula

$$(A - B) \times C/D$$

where

A is the amount determined under clause (B) of the description of A in subparagraph (i),

B is the amount determined under clause (A) of the description of A in subparagraph (i),

C is the fair market value, immediately after the particular time, of the shares of the capital stock of the taxpayer that are held, directly or indirectly, by the parent, and

D is total of all amounts each of which is the fair market value, immediately after the particular time, of the shares of the capital stock of the taxpayer that are held, directly or indirectly, by a parent.

Applicable: In respect of transactions or events that occur on or after March 19, 2019.

History: S. 128.1(1)(*c*.3) was added by S.C. 2012, c. 31, s. 30(1), applicable in respect of corporations that become resident in Canada after March 28, 2012.

▶ 128.1(1)(d) ◀

(d) Foreign affiliate — where the taxpayer was, immediately before the particular time, a foreign affiliate of another taxpayer that is resident in Canada,

(i) the affiliate is deemed to have been a controlled foreign affiliate of the other taxpayer immediately before the particular time, and

(ii) the prescribed amount is to be included in the foreign accrual property income of the affiliate for its taxation year that ends immediately before the particular time.

History: S. 128.1(1)(*d*)(i) and (ii) were replaced by S.C. 2013, c. 34, s. 73(1), applicable to taxation years that begin after 2006.

Any assessment of a taxpayer's tax, interest and penalties payable under the Act for any taxation year that ends before June 26, 2013 that would, in the absence of this section, be precluded because of subsections 152(4) to (5) of the Act shall be made to the extent necessary to take into account the amendments by S.C. 2013, c. 34, s. 54 to 89.

S. 128.1(1)(*d*)(i) and (ii) formerly read:

(i) the affiliate shall be deemed to have been a controlled foreign affiliate (within the meaning assigned by subsection 95(1)) of the other taxpayer immediately before the particular time, and

(ii) such amount as is prescribed shall be included in the foreign accrual property income (within the meaning assigned by subsection 95(1)) of the affiliate for its taxation year ending immediately before the particular time.

▶ 128.1(1.1) ◀

(1.1) Trusts subject to subsection 94(3). Paragraph (1)(*b*) does not apply, at a time in a trust's particular taxation year, to the trust if the trust is resident in Canada for the particular taxation year for the purpose of computing its income.

History: S. 128.1(1.1) was added by S.C. 2013, c. 34, s. 14(1), applicable to taxation years that end after 2006. S. 128.1(1.1) also applies to each earlier taxation year of a trust to which subsection 94(1) applies [should be 94(3) — CCH].

▶ 128.1(1.2) ◀

(1.2) Trusts and partnerships look-through rule. For the purposes of this subsection and paragraph (1)(*c*.1), if at any time shares of the capital stock of a corporation resident in Canada are owned by a trust or a partnership (each referred to in this subsection as a "conduit"), each person or partnership with an interest as a beneficiary under the conduit or that is a member of the conduit (each referred to in this subsection as a "holder"), as the case may be, is deemed to own the shares of each class of the capital stock of the corporation that are owned by the conduit the number of which is determined by the formula

$$A \times B/C$$

where

A is the total number of shares of the class of the capital stock of the corporation that is owned by the conduit at that time;

B is the fair market value, at that time, of the holder's interest in the conduit; and

C is the total fair market value, at that time, of all interests in the conduit.

History: S. 128.1(1.2) was added by S.C. 2018, c. 27, s. 14(1), applicable in respect of transactions or events that occur after February 26, 2018.

▶ 128.1(2) ◀

(2) Paid-up capital adjustment. If a corporation becomes resident in Canada at a particular time,

(*a*) for the purposes of subsection (1) and this subsection, the "paid-up capital adjustment" in respect of a particular class of shares of the corporation's capital stock in respect of that acquisition of residence is the positive or negative amount determined by the formula

$$(A \times B/C) - D$$

where

A is the amount, if any, by which

(i) the total of all amounts each of which is an amount deemed by paragraph (1)(*c*) to be the cost to the corporation of property deemed under that paragraph to have been acquired by the corporation at the particular time exceeds

(ii) the total of all amounts each of which is the amount of a debt owing by the corporation, or any other obligation of the corporation to pay an amount, that is outstanding at the particular time,

B is the fair market value at the particular time of all of the shares of the particular class,

C is the total of all amounts each of which is the fair market value at the particular time of all of the shares of a class of shares of the corporation's capital stock, and

D is the paid-up capital at the particular time, determined without reference to this subsection, in respect of the particular class; and

(*b*) for the purposes of this Act, in computing the paid-up capital in respect of a class of shares of the corporation's capital stock at any time after the particular time and before the time, if any, at which the corporation next becomes resident in Canada, there shall be

(i) added the amount of the paid-up capital adjustment in respect of the particular class, if that amount is positive and the corporation so elects for all such classes in respect of that acquisition of residence by notifying the Minister in writing within 90 days after the particular time, and

(ii) deducted, if the amount of the paid-up capital adjustment in respect of the particular class is negative, the absolute value of that amount.

Related Sections: S. 52(8) Cost of shares of immigrant corporation.

▶ 128.1(3) ◀

(3) Paid-up capital adjustment. In computing the paid-up capital at any time in respect of a class of shares of the capital stock of a corporation

(*a*) there is to be deducted an amount equal to the lesser of A and B, and added an amount equal to the lesser of A and C, where

A is the absolute value of the difference between

(i) the total of all amounts deemed by subsection 84(3), (4) or (4.1) to be a dividend on shares of the class paid before that time by the corporation, and

(ii) the total that would be determined under subparagraph (i) if this Act were read without reference to subsection (2),

B is the total of all amounts required by subsection (2) to be added in computing the paid-up capital in respect of the class before that time, and

C is the total of all amounts required by subsection (2) to be deducted in computing the paid-up capital in respect of the class before that time; and

(*b*) there is to be added an amount equal to the lesser of

(i) the amount, if any, by which

(A) the total of all amounts deemed by subsection 84(3), (4) or (4.1) to be a dividend on shares of the class paid after March 28, 2012 and before that time by the corporation

exceeds

(B) the total that would be determined under clause (A) if this Act were read without reference to subparagraph (*c.3*)(i), and

(ii) the total of all amounts required by subparagraph (*c.3*)(i) to be deducted in computing the paid-up capital in respect of the class before that time.

History: S. 128.1(3) was replaced by S.C. 2012, c. 31, s. 30(2), deemed to have come into force on March 29, 2012. S. 128.1(3) formerly read:

(3) *Paid-up capital adjustment.* In computing the paid-up capital at any time in respect of a class of shares of the corporation's capital stock, there shall be deducted an amount equal to the lesser of A and B, and added an amount equal to the lesser of A and C, where

A is the absolute value of the difference between

(*a*) the total of all amounts deemed by subsection 84(3), (4) or (4.1) to be a dividend on shares of the class paid before that time by the corporation, and

(*b*) the total that would be determined under paragraph (*a*) if this Act were read without reference to subsection (2),

B is the total of all amounts required by subsection (2) to be added in computing the paid-up capital in respect of the class before that time, and

C is the total of all amounts required by subsection (2) to be subtracted in computing the paid-up capital in respect of the class before that time.

▶ 128.1(4) ◀

(4) Emigration. For the purposes of this Act, where at a particular time a taxpayer ceases to be resident in Canada,

Related Sections: S. 250 Person deemed resident.

Canadian Tax Foundation: Rajan, *Are You Sure You Want to Leave Canada? The New Taxpayer Migration Rules*, 1999 Canadian Tax Journal 5:1342–1366.

Tax Profile: December 2008 — Tax Planning for Emigration from Canada to the United States.

Forms: T2061A — Election by an Emigrant to Report Deemed Dispositions of Property and any Resulting Capital Gain or Loss.

Tax Window Files: 128.1(4) and Part XIII tax on future payments, *April 21, 2015*, CRA Document No. 2013-0494251E5.

▶ 128.1(4)(a) ◀

(a) Year-end, fiscal period — where the taxpayer is a corporation or a trust,

(i) the taxpayer's taxation year that would otherwise include the particular time shall be deemed to have ended immediately before the particular time and a new taxation year of the taxpayer shall be deemed to have begun at the particular time, and

(ii) for the purpose of determining the taxpayer's fiscal period after the particular time, the taxpayer shall be deemed not to have established a fiscal period before the particular time;

Related Sections: S. 249 Definition of "taxation year"; s. 249.1(1) Definition of "fiscal period".

Guides: T4056 Emigrants and Income Tax.

▶ 128.1(4)(a.1) ◀

(a.1) Fiscal period — if the taxpayer is an individual (other than a trust) and carries on a business at the particular time, otherwise than through a permanent establishment (as defined by regulation) in Canada,

(i) the fiscal period of the business is deemed to have ended immediately before the particular time and a new fiscal period of the business is deemed to have begun at the particular time, and

(ii) for the purpose of determining the fiscal period of the business after the particular time, the taxpayer is deemed not to have established a fiscal period of the business before the particular time;

▶ 128.1(4)(b) ◀

(b) Deemed disposition — the taxpayer is deemed to have disposed, at the time (in this paragraph and paragraph (*d*) referred to as the "time of disposition") that is immediately before the time that is immediately before the particular time, of each property owned by the taxpayer other than, if the taxpayer is an individual,

(i) real or immovable property situated in Canada, a Canadian resource property or a timber resource property,

(ii) capital property used in, property included in Class 14.1 of Schedule II to the *Income Tax Regulations* in respect of or property described in the inventory of, a business carried on by the taxpayer through a "permanent establishment" (as defined by regulation) in Canada at the particular time,

(iii) an excluded right or interest of the taxpayer,

(iv) if the taxpayer is not a trust and was not, during the 120-month period that ends at the particular time, resident in Canada for more than 60 months, property that was owned by the taxpayer at the time the taxpayer last became resident in Canada or that was acquired by the taxpayer by inheritance or bequest after the taxpayer last became resident in Canada, and

(v) any property in respect of which the taxpayer elects under paragraph (6)(*a*) for the taxation year that includes the first time, after the particular time, at which the taxpayer becomes resident in Canada,

for proceeds equal to its fair market value at the time of disposition, which proceeds are deemed to have become receivable and to have been received by the taxpayer at the time of disposition;

Editorial Note: Individuals ceasing to be resident in Canada can elect to post security with the CRA for the purpose of deferring the payment of tax that results from the deemed disposition of property under s. 128.1(4)(*b*). The payment of the tax can be deferred, without interest, until the property is actually sold. Security is not required for the first $100,000 of capital gains (actually, $50,000 of taxable income) resulting from the deemed disposition rules. See generally s. 220(4.5) through (4.71).

History: S. 128.1(4)(*b*)(ii) was replaced by S.C. 2016, c. 12, s. 46(2), in force January 1, 2017, and formerly read:

(ii) capital property used in, eligible capital property in respect of or property described in the inventory of, a business carried on by the taxpayer through a permanent establishment (as defined by regulation) in Canada at the particular time,

S. 128.1(4)(*b*)(i) was replaced by S.C. 2013, c. 34, s. 130(1), in force June 26, 2013, and formerly read:

(i) real property situated in Canada, a Canadian resource property or a timber resource property,

Related Regulations: 8201.

Related Sections: S. 126(2.21) Former resident — deduction; s. 220(3.2) Late, amended or revoked elections; s. 220(4.5) Security for departure tax.

Canadian Tax Foundation: Tollstam, *Planning for High Net Worth Individuals Leaving Canada*, 2007 Conference Report 38:1–14; Rajan, *Are You Sure You Want to Leave Canada? The New Taxpayer Migration Rules*, 1999 Canadian Tax Journal 5:1342–1366; Rees et al., *Taxpayer Migration: Proposed Rules*, 1999 Conference Report 35:1–19.

Tax Profile: September 2003 — Value of an Interest in a Discretionary Trust.

Forms: T1243 — Deemed Disposition of Property by an Emigrant of Canada.

Income Tax Folios: *Secondary* — S5-F2-C1 Foreign Tax Credit.

Information Circulars: IC 07-1 Taxpayer relief provisions.

► 128.1(4)(b.1) ◄

(b.1) Employee life and health trust — notwithstanding paragraph (*b*), if the taxpayer is or was at any time an employee life and health trust,

(i) the taxpayer is deemed

(A) to have disposed, at the time (in this paragraph referred to as the "time of disposition") that is immediately before the time that is immediately before the particular time, of each property owned by the taxpayer for proceeds equal to its fair market value at the time of disposition, which proceeds are deemed to have become receivable and to have been received by the taxpayer at the time of disposition, and

(B) to have carried on a business at the time of disposition, and

(ii) each property of the taxpayer is deemed

(A) to have been described in the inventory of the business referred to in clause (i)(B), and

(B) to have a cost of nil at the time of disposition;

History: S. 128.1(4)(*b.1*) was added by S.C. 2010, c. 25, s. 28(1), applicable after 2009.

► 128.1(4)(c) ◄

(c) Reacquisition — the taxpayer is deemed to have reacquired, at the particular time, each property deemed by paragraph (*b*) or (*b.1*) to have been disposed of by the taxpayer, at a cost equal to the proceeds of disposition of the property;

History: S. 128.1(4)(*c*) was replaced by S.C. 2010, c. 25, s. 28(1), applicable after 2009. S. 128.1(4)(*c*) formerly read:

(c) *Reacquisition* — the taxpayer shall be deemed to have reacquired, at the particular time, each property deemed by paragraph (*b*) to have been disposed of by the taxpayer, at a cost equal to the proceeds of disposition of the property;

► 128.1(4)(d) ◄

(d) Individual — elective disposition — notwithstanding paragraphs (*b*) to (*c*), if the taxpayer is an individual (other than a trust) and so elects in prescribed form and manner in respect of a property described in subparagraph (*b*)(i) or (ii),

(i) the taxpayer is deemed to have disposed of the property at the time of disposition for proceeds equal to its fair market value at that time and to have reacquired the property at the particular time at a cost equal to those proceeds,

(ii) the taxpayer's income for the taxation year that includes the particular time is deemed to be the greater of

(A) that income determined without reference to this subparagraph, and

(B) the lesser of

(I) that income determined without reference to this subsection, and

(II) that income determined without reference to subparagraph (i), and

(iii) each of the taxpayer's non-capital loss, net capital loss, restricted farm loss, farm loss and limited partnership loss for the taxation year that includes the particular time is deemed to be the lesser of

(A) that amount determined without reference to this subparagraph, and

(B) the greater of

(I) that amount determined without reference to this subsection, and

(II) that amount determined without reference to subparagraph (i); and

Related Regulations: 600(*c*).

Related Sections: S. 220(3.2) Late, amended or revoked elections.

Tax Topics: No. 1850, Elections Available Under the Emigration Rules.

Forms: T2061A — Election by an Emigrant to Report Deemed Dispositions of Property and any Resulting Capital Gain or Loss.

Guides: T4056 Emigrants and Income Tax.

Information Circulars: IC 07-1 Taxpayer relief provisions.

► 128.1(4)(d.1) ◄

(d.1) Employee CCPC stock option shares — if the taxpayer is deemed by paragraph (*b*) to have disposed of a share that was acquired before February 28, 2000 under circumstances to which subsection 7(1.1) applied, there shall be deducted from the taxpayer's proceeds of disposition the amount that would, if section 7 were read without reference to subsection 7(1.6), be added under paragraph 53(1)(*j*) in computing the adjusted cost base to the taxpayer of the share as a consequence of the deemed disposition.

Related Sections: S. 7(1.3) Order of disposition of securities; s. 7(7) Definitions.

► 128.1(4)(e) ◄

(e) Deemed property — (Repealed by S.C. 2001, c. 17, s. 123(4).)

► 128.1(4)(f) ◄

(f) Losses on election — (Repealed by S.C. 2001, c. 17, s. 123(4).)

► 128.1(5) ◄

(5) Instalment interest. If an individual is deemed by subsection (4) to have disposed of a property in a taxation year, in applying sections 155 and 156 and subsections 156.1(1) to (3) and 161(2), (4) and (4.01) and any regulations made for the purposes of those provisions, the individual's total tax payable under this Part for the year is deemed to be the lesser of

(*a*) the individual's total tax payable under this Part for the year, determined before taking into consideration the specified future tax consequences for the year, and

(*b*) the amount that would be determined under paragraph (*a*) if subsection (4) did not apply to the individual for the year.

History: S. 128.1(5), the portion before paragraph (*b*) was replaced by S.C. 2013, c. 34, s. 273(1), applicable to taxation years that begin after October 31, 2011, and formerly read:

(5) *Instalment interest.* If an individual is deemed by subsection (4) to have disposed of a property in a taxation year, in applying sections 155 and 156 and subsections 156.1(1) to (3) and 161(2), (4) and (4.01) and any regulations made for the purposes of those provisions, the individual's total taxes payable under this Part and Part I.1 for the year are deemed to be the lesser of

(*a*) the individual's total taxes payable under this Part and Part I.1 for the year, determined before taking into consideration the specified future tax consequences for the year, and

► 128.1(6) ◄

(6) Returning former resident. If an individual (other than a trust) becomes resident in Canada at a particular time in a taxation year and the last time (in this subsection referred to as the "emigration time"), before the particular time, at which the individual ceased to be resident in Canada was after October 1, 1996,

(*a*) subject to paragraph (*b*), if the individual so elects in writing and files the election with the Minister on or before the individual's filing-due date for the year, paragraphs (4)(*b*) and (*c*) do not apply to the individual's cessation of residence at the emigration time in respect of all properties that were taxable Canadian properties of the individual throughout the period that began at the emigration time and that ends at the particular time;

(*b*) where, if a property in respect of which an election under paragraph (*a*) is made had been acquired by the individual at the emigration time at a cost equal to its fair market value at the emigration time and had been disposed of by the individual immediately before the particular time for proceeds of disposition equal to its fair market value immediately before the particular time, the application of subsection 40(3.7) would reduce the amount that would, but for that subsection and this subsection, be the individual's loss from the disposition,

(i) the individual is deemed to have disposed of the property at the time of disposition (within the meaning assigned by paragraph (4)(*b*)) in respect of the emigration time for proceeds of disposition equal to the total of

(A) the adjusted cost base to the individual of the property immediately before the time of disposition, and

(B) the amount, if any, by which that reduction exceeds the lesser of

(I) the adjusted cost base to the individual of the property immediately before the time of disposition, and

(II) the amount, if any, that the individual specifies for the purposes of this paragraph in the election under paragraph (*a*) in respect of the property,

(ii) the individual is deemed to have reacquired the property at the emigration time at a cost equal to the amount, if any, by which the amount determined under clause (i)(A) exceeds the lesser of that reduction and the amount specified by the individual under subclause (i)(B)(II), and

(iii) for the purpose of section 119, the individual is deemed to have disposed of the property immediately before the particular time;

(*c*) if the individual so elects in writing and files the election with the Minister on or before the individual's filing-due date for the year, in respect of each property that the individual owned throughout the period that began at the emigration time and that ends at the particular time and that is deemed by paragraph (1)(*b*) to have been disposed of because the individual became resident in Canada, notwithstanding paragraphs (1)(*c*) and (4)(*b*) the individual's proceeds of disposition at the time of disposition (within the meaning assigned by paragraph (4)(*b*)), and the individual's cost of acquiring the property at the particular time, are deemed to be those proceeds and that cost, determined without reference to this paragraph, minus the least of

(i) the amount that would, but for this paragraph, have been the individual's gain from the disposition of the property deemed by paragraph (4)(*b*) to have occurred,

(ii) the fair market value of the property at the particular time, and

(iii) the amount that the individual specifies for the purposes of this paragraph in the election; and

(*d*) notwithstanding subsections 152(4) to (5), any assessment of tax that is payable under this Act by the individual for any taxation year that is before the year that includes the particular time and that is not before the year that includes the emigration time shall be made that is necessary to take an election under this subsection into account, except that no such assessment shall affect the computation of

(i) interest payable under this Act to or by a taxpayer in respect of any period that is before the day on which the taxpayer's return of income for the taxation year that includes the particular time is filed, or

(ii) any penalty payable under this Act.

Related Regulations: 600(*c*).

Related Sections: S. 40(3.7) Losses of non-resident; s. 220(3.2) Late, amended or revoked elections; s. 248(1), "taxable Canadian property, "filing-due date".

Canadian Tax Foundation: Tollstam, *Election to Unwind Departure Tax*, 2015 Canadian Tax Highlights 23(9):5.

Tax Profile: December 2008 — Tax Planning for Emigration from Canada to the United States.

Information Circulars: IC 07-1 Taxpayer relief provisions.

► 128.1(6.1) ◄

(6.1) Deemed taxable Canadian property. For the purposes of paragraph (6)(*a*), a property is deemed to be taxable Canadian property of the individual throughout the period that began at the emigration time and that ends at the particular time if

(*a*) the emigration time is before March 5, 2010; and

(*b*) the property was taxable Canadian property of the individual on March 4, 2010.

History: S. 128.1(6.1) was added by S.C. 2010, c. 12, s. 15(1), applicable in determining after March 4, 2010 whether a property is taxable Canadian property of a taxpayer.

► 128.1(7) ◄

(7) Returning trust beneficiary. If an individual (other than a trust)

(*a*) becomes resident in Canada at a particular time in a taxation year,

(*b*) owns at the particular time a property that the individual last acquired on a trust distribution to which subsection 107(2) would, but for subsection 107(5), have applied and at a time (in this subsection referred to as the "distribution time") that was after October 1, 1996 and before the particular time, and

(*c*) was a beneficiary of the trust at the last time, before the particular time, at which the individual ceased to be resident in Canada,

the following rules apply:

(*d*) subject to paragraphs (*e*) and (*f*), if the individual and the trust jointly so elect in writing and file the election with the Minister on or before the earlier of their filing-due dates for their taxation years that include the particular time, subsection 107(2.1) does not apply to the distribution in respect of all properties acquired by the individual on the distribution that were taxable Canadian properties of the individual throughout the period that began at the distribution time and that ends at the particular time,

(*e*) paragraph (*f*) applies in respect of the individual, the trust and a property in respect of which an election under paragraph (*d*) is made where, if the individual

(i) had been resident in Canada at the distribution time,

(ii) had acquired the property at the distribution time at a cost equal to its fair market value at that time,

(iii) had ceased to be resident in Canada immediately after the distribution time, and

(iv) had, immediately before the particular time, disposed of the property for proceeds of disposition equal to its fair market value immediately before the particular time,

the application of subsection 40(3.7) would reduce the amount that would, but for that subsection and this subsection, have been the individual's loss from the disposition,

(*f*) where this paragraph applies in respect of an individual, a trust and a property,

(i) notwithstanding paragraph 107(2.1)(*a*), the trust is deemed to have disposed of the property at the distribution time for proceeds of disposition equal to the total of

(A) the cost amount to the trust of the property immediately before the distribution time, and

(B) the amount, if any, by which the reduction under subsection 40(3.7) described in paragraph (*e*) exceeds the lesser of

(I) the cost amount to the trust of the property immediately before the distribution time, and

(II) the amount, if any, which the individual and the trust jointly specify for the purposes of this paragraph in the election under paragraph (*d*) in respect of the property, and

(ii) notwithstanding paragraph 107(2.1)(*b*), the individual is deemed to have acquired the property at the distribution time at a cost equal to the amount, if any, by which the amount otherwise determined under paragraph 107(2)(*b*) exceeds the lesser of the reduction under subsection 40(3.7) described in paragraph (*e*) and the amount specified under subclause (i)(B)(II),

(*g*) if the individual and the trust jointly so elect in writing and file the election with the Minister on or before the later of their filing-due dates for their taxation years that include the particular time, in respect of each property that the individual owned throughout the period that began at the distribution time and that ends at the particular time and that is deemed by paragraph (1)(*b*) to have been disposed of because the individual became resident in Canada, notwithstanding paragraphs 107(2.1)(*a*) and (*b*), the trust's proceeds of disposition under paragraph 107(2.1)(*a*) at the distribution time, and the individual's cost of acquiring the property at the particular time, are deemed to be those proceeds and that cost determined without reference to this paragraph, minus the least of

(i) the amount that would, but for this paragraph, have been the trust's gain from the disposition of the property deemed by paragraph 107(2.1)(*a*) to have occurred,

(ii) the fair market value of the property at the particular time, and

(iii) the amount that the individual and the trust jointly specify for the purposes of this paragraph in the election,

(*h*) if the trust ceases to exist before the individual's filing- due date for the individual's taxation year that includes the particular time,

(i) an election or specification described in this subsection may be made by the individual alone in writing if the election is filed with the Minister on or before that filing-due date, and

(ii) if the individual alone makes such an election or specification, the individual and the trust are jointly and severally, or solidarily, liable for any amount payable under this Act by the trust as a result of the election or specification, and

(*i*) notwithstanding subsections 152(4) to (5), such assessment of tax payable under the Act by the trust or the individual for any year that is before the year that includes the particular time and that is not before the year that includes the distribution time shall be made as is necessary to take an election under this subsection into account, except that no such assessment shall affect the computation of

(i) interest payable under this Act to or by the trust or the individual in respect of any period that is before the individual's filing-due date for the taxation year that includes the particular time, or

(ii) any penalty payable under this Act.

History: S. 128.1(7)(*h*)(ii) was replaced by S.C. 2013, c. 34, s. 130(2), in force June 26, 2013, and formerly read:

(ii) if the individual alone makes such an election or specification, the individual and the trust are jointly and severally liable for any amount payable under this Act by the trust as a result of the election or specification, and

Related Regulations: 600(*c*).

Related Sections: S. 220(3.2) Late, amended or revoked elections.

Tax Profile: April 2007 — Tax Planning for Emigration from Canada.

Information Circulars: IC 07-1 Taxpayer relief provisions.

► 128.1(8) ◄

(8) Post-emigration loss. If an individual (other than a trust)

(*a*) was deemed by paragraph (4)(*b*) to have disposed of a capital property at any particular time after October 1, 1996,

(*b*) has disposed of the property at a later time at which the property was a taxable Canadian property of the individual, and

(*c*) so elects in writing in the individual's return of income for the taxation year that includes the later time,

there shall, except for the purpose of paragraph (4)(*c*), be deducted from the individual's proceeds of disposition of the property at the particular time, and added to the individual's proceeds of disposition of the property at the later time, an amount equal to the least of

(*d*) the amount specified in respect of the property in the election,

(*e*) the amount that would, but for the election, be the individual's gain from the disposition of the property at the particular time, and

(*f*) the amount that would be the individual's loss from the disposition of the property at the later time, if the loss were determined having reference to every other provision of this Act including, for greater certainty, subsection 40(3.7) and section 112, but without reference to the election.

Related Regulations: 600(*c*).

Related Sections: S. 152(6) Reassessment where certain deductions claimed; s. 220(3.2) Late, amended or revoked elections.

Tax Topics: No. 1850, Elections Available Under the Emigration Rules.

► 128.1(9) ◄

(9) Information reporting. An individual who ceases at a particular time in a taxation year to be resident in Canada, and who owns immediately after the particular time one or more reportable properties the total fair market value of which at the particular time is greater than $25,000, shall file with the Minister in prescribed form, on or before the individual's filing-due date for the year, a list of all the reportable properties that the individual owned immediately after the particular time.

Forms: T1161 — List of Properties by an Emigrant of Canada.

► 128.1(10) ◄

(10) Definitions. The definitions in this subsection apply in this section.

"excluded right or interest" —"excluded right or interest" of a taxpayer who is an individual means

(*a*) a right of the individual under, or an interest of the individual in a trust governed by,

(i) a registered retirement savings plan or a plan referred to in subsection 146(12) as an "amended plan",

(ii) a registered retirement income fund,

(iii) a registered education savings plan,

(iii.1) a registered disability savings plan,

(iii.2) a TFSA,

(iv) a deferred profit sharing plan or a plan referred to in subsection 147(15) as a "revoked plan",

(v) an employees profit sharing plan,

(vi) an employee benefit plan (other than a plan described in subparagraph (*b*)(i) or (ii)),

(vi.1) an employee life and health trust,

(vii) a plan or arrangement (other than an employee benefit plan) under which the individual has a right to receive in a year remuneration in respect of services rendered by the individual in the year or a prior year,

(viii) a superannuation or pension fund or plan (other than an employee benefit plan),

(ix) a retirement compensation arrangement,

(x) a foreign retirement arrangement, or

(xi) a registered supplementary unemployment benefit plan;

(*b*) a right of the individual to a benefit under an employee benefit plan that is

(i) a plan or arrangement described in paragraph (*j*) of the definition "salary deferral arrangement" in subsection 248(1) that would, but for paragraphs (*j*) and (*k*) of that definition, be a salary deferral arrangement, or

(ii) a plan or arrangement that would, but for paragraph 6801(*c*) of the *Income Tax Regulations*, be a salary deferral arrangement,

to the extent that the benefit can reasonably be considered to be attributable to services rendered by the individual in Canada;

(*c*) a right of the individual under an agreement referred to in subsection 7(1);

(*d*) a right of the individual to a retiring allowance;

(*e*) a right of the individual under, or an interest of the individual in, a trust that is

(i) an employee trust,

(ii) an amateur athlete trust,

(iii) a cemetery care trust, or

(iv) a trust governed by an eligible funeral arrangement;

(*f*) a right of the individual to receive a payment under

(i) an annuity contract, or

(ii) an income-averaging annuity contract;

(*g*) a right of the individual to a benefit under

(i) the *Canada Pension Plan* or a provincial plan described in section 3 of that Act,

(ii) the *Old Age Security Act*, or

(iii) (Repealed by S.C. 2011, c. 24, s. 43(1))

(iv) a plan or arrangement instituted by the social security legislation of a country other than

Canada or of a state, province or other political subdivision of such a country;

(*h*) a right of the individual to a benefit described in any of subparagraphs 56(1)(*a*)(iii) to (vi);

(*i*) a right of the individual to a payment out of a NISA Fund No. 2;

(*j*) an interest of the individual in a personal trust resident in Canada if the interest was never acquired for consideration and did not arise as a consequence of a qualifying disposition by the individual (within the meaning that would be assigned by subsection 107.4(1) if that subsection were read without reference to paragraphs 107.4(1)(*h*) and (*i*));

(*k*) an interest of the individual in a non-resident testamentary trust that is an estate that arose on and as a consequence of a death if

(i) the interest was never acquired for consideration, and

(ii) the estate has been in existence for no more than 36 months; or

(*l*) an interest of the individual in a life insurance policy in Canada, except for that part of the policy in respect of which the individual is deemed by paragraph 138.1(1)(*e*) to have an interest in a related segregated fund trust.

Editorial Note: Subsection 128.1(10) defines the expression "excluded right or interest" for the purposes of the taxpayer migration rules in s. 128.1. This definition is primarily of relevance for s. 128.1(1)(*b*) and (4)(*b*), which treat individuals as having disposed of (and immediately reacquired) most of their property on immigrating to or emigrating from Canada. Generally, excluded rights or interests are exempted from these deemed disposition rules. Paragraph (a) of the definition refers to rights under, or an interest in a trust governed by, certain deferred income plans, including RRSPs and TFSAs.

For 2016 and subsequent years, subparagraph 128.1(1)(b)(iv) is amended to specifically refer to paragraph (*k*) of the definition of "excluded right or interest" in subsection 128.1(10), as the result of changes to that definition. For 2016 and subsequent years, paragraph (*k*) of the definition is amended to limit the relief to a beneficial interest, that was never acquired for consideration, in a non-resident testamentary trust that is an estate that has been in existence for no more than 36 months. This definitional change reflects the switch from the testamentary trust regime to the concept of a "graduated rate estate" for 2016 and subsequent years.

An "excluded right or interest" is exempt from the deemed disposition rule of s. 128.1(4)(*b*) upon a taxpayer's emigration from Canada and the deemed disposition rule of s. 128.1(1)(*b*) upon a taxpayer's immigration to Canada. Furthermore, excluded rights or interests (except those set out in paragraphs (*c*), (*j*) and (*l*) of the definition) are not "reportable properties" for the purposes of the reporting requirement for emigrating individuals found in s. 128.1(9).

History: S. 128.1(10), paragraph (*k*) of the definition "excluded right or interest" was replaced by S.C. 2014, c. 39, s. 46(2), applicable to the 2016 and subsequent taxation years, and formerly read:

(*k*) an interest of the individual in a non-resident testamentary trust if the interest was never acquired for consideration; or

S. 128.1(10), subparagraph (*g*)(iii) of the definition "excluded right or interest" was repealed by S.C. 2011, c. 24, s. 43(1), applicable to taxation years that begin after 2009. S. 128.1(10), subparagraph (*g*)(iii) of the definition "excluded right or interest" formerly read:

(iii) a provincial pension plan prescribed for the purpose of paragraph 60(*v*), or

S. 128.1(10), subparagraph (*a*)(vi.1) of the definition "excluded right or interest" was added by S.C. 2010, c. 25, s. 28(2), applicable after 2009.

Related Sections: S. 108(6) Variation of trusts; s. 108(7) Interests acquired for consideration.

"reportable property" — "reportable property" of an individual at a particular time means any property other than

(*a*) money that is legal tender in Canada and deposits of such money;

(*b*) property that would be an excluded right or interest of the individual if the definition "excluded right or interest" in this subsection were read without reference to paragraphs (*c*), (*j*) and (*l*) of that definition;

(*c*) if the individual is not a trust and was not, during the 120-month period that ends at the particular time, resident in Canada for more than 60 months, property described in subparagraph (4)(*b*)(iv) that is not taxable Canadian property; and

(*d*) any item of personal-use property the fair market value of which, at the particular time, is less than $10,000.

SECTION 128.2: Cross-border mergers

► 128.2(1) ◄

(1) Cross-border mergers. Where a corporation formed at a particular time by the amalgamation or merger of, or by a plan of arrangement or other corporate reorganization in respect of, 2 or more corporations (each of which is referred to in this section as a "predecessor") is at the particular time resident in Canada, a predecessor that was not immediately before the particular time resident in Canada shall be deemed to have become resident in Canada immediately before the particular time.

► 128.2(2) ◄

(2) Idem. Where a corporation formed at a particular time by the amalgamation or merger of, or by a plan of arrangement or other corporate reorganization in respect of, 2 or more corporations is at the particular time not resident in Canada, a predecessor that was immediately before the particular time resident in Canada shall be deemed to have ceased to be resident in Canada immediately before the particular time.

► 128.2(3) ◄

(3) Windings-up excluded. For greater certainty, subsections (1) and (2) do not apply to reorganizations occurring solely because of the acquisition of property of one corporation by another corporation, pursuant to the purchase of the property by the other corporation or because of the distribution of the property to the other corporation on the winding-up of the corporation.

SECTION 128.3: Former resident — replaced shares

If, in a transaction to which section 51, subparagraphs 85.1(1)(*a*)(i) and (ii), subsection 85.1(8) or section 86 or 87 applies, a person acquires a share (in this section referred to as the "new share") in exchange for another share or equity in a SIFT wind-up entity (in this section referred to as the "old share"), for the purposes of section 119, subsections 126(2.21) to (2.23), subparagraph 128.1(4)(*b*)(iv) and subsections 128.1(6) to (8), 180.1(1.4) and 220(4.5) and (4.6), the person is deemed not to have disposed of the old share, and the new share is deemed to be the same share as the old share.

History: S. 128.3 was replaced by S.C. 2013, c. 34, s. 274(1), applicable to taxation years that begin after 2001, except that, before December 20, 2007, section 128.3 is to be read as follows:

S. 128.3 **"Former resident — replaced shares.** If, in a transaction to which section 51, subparagraphs 85.1(1)(*a*)(i) and (ii) or section 86 or 87 applies, a person acquires a share (in this section referred to as the "new share") in exchange for another share (in this section referred to as the "old share"), for the purposes of section 119, subsections 126(2.21) to (2.23), subparagraph 128.1(4)(*b*)(iv) and subsections 128.1(6) to (8), 180.1(1.4) and 220(4.5) and (4.6), the person is deemed not to have disposed of the old share, and the new share is deemed to be the same share as the old share."

S. 128.3 formerly read:

S. 128.3 *Former resident — replaced shares.* If, in a transaction to which section 51, subparagraphs 85.1(1)(*a*)(i) and (ii), subsection 85.1(8) or section 86 or 87 applies, a person acquires a share (in this section referred to as the "new share") in exchange for another share or equity in a SIFT wind-up entity (in this section referred to as the "old share"), for the purposes of section 119, subsections 126(2.21) to (2.23), 128.1(6) to (8), 180.1(1.4) and 220(4.5) and (4.6), the person is deemed not to have disposed of the old share, and the new share is deemed to be the same share as the old share.

S. 128.3 was replaced by S.C. 2009, c. 2, s. 43(1), applicable after December 19, 2007. S. 128.3 formerly read:

S. 128.3 *Former resident — replaced shares.* If, in a transaction to which section 51, subparagraphs 85.1(1)(*a*)(i) and (ii) or section 86 or 87 apply, a person acquires a share (in this section referred to as the "new share") in exchange for another share (in this section referred to as the "old share"), for the purposes of section 119, subsections 126(2.21) to (2.23), 128.1(6) to (8), 180.1(1.4) and 220(4.5) and (4.6), the person is deemed not to have disposed of the old share, and the new share is deemed to be the same share as the old share.

Related Sections: S. 248(1), "person", "share", "SIFT wind-up entity", "SIFT wind-up entity equity".

Private Corporations

SECTION 129: Dividend refund to private corporation

► 129(1) ◄

(1) Dividend refund to private corporation. Where a return of a corporation's income under this Part for a taxation year is made within 3 years after the end of the year, the Minister

(*a*) may, on sending the notice of assessment for the year, refund without application an amount (in this Act referred to as its "dividend refund" for the year) in respect of taxable dividends paid by the corporation on shares of its capital stock in the year, and at a time when it was a private corporation, equal to the total of

(i) in respect of eligible dividends, an amount equal to the lesser of

(A) 38 1/3% of the total of all eligible dividends paid by it in the year, and

(B) its eligible refundable dividend tax on hand at the end of the year, and

(ii) in respect of taxable dividends (other than eligible dividends), an amount equal to the total of

(A) the lesser of

(I) 38 1/3% of the total of all taxable dividends (other than eligible dividends) paid by it in the year, and

(II) its non-eligible refundable dividend tax on hand at the end of the year, and

(B) either

(I) if the amount determined under subclause (A)(I) exceeds the amount determined under subclause (A)(II), the lesser of

1 the amount of the excess, and

2 the amount by which the corporation's eligible refundable dividend tax on hand at the end of the year exceeds the amount, if any, determined under subparagraph (i) for the year, and

(II) in any other case, nil; and

(*b*) shall, with all due dispatch, make the dividend refund after sending the notice of assessment if an application for it has been made in writing by the corporation within the period within which the Minister would be allowed under subsection 152(4) to assess tax payable under this Part by the corporation for the year if that subsection were read without reference to paragraph 152(4)(*a*).

Editorial Note: Private corporation status is required to obtain a dividend refund, which is limited to the lesser of 38 $^{1}/_{3}$% of taxable dividends paid by the corporation and the corporation's refundable dividend tax on hand ("RDTOH"). For taxation years beginning before 2019, both an eligible and ineligible dividend will generate a dividend refund, but a capital dividend will not. For taxation years prior to 2016 and years that straddle January 1, 2016, the increase in the dividend refund rate is prorated. See the historical note for this subsection for the applicable calculation of the rate.

For taxation years beginning after 2018, the RDTOH account is divided into two accounts: one account, the "non-eligible RDTOH", is similar to the pre-2019 RDTOH; and the second account, the "eligible RDTOH", includes Part IV tax payable in respect of eligible dividends received on portfolio shares. The two accounts are defined in subsection 129(4); see the editorial notes following those definitions. The payment of an eligible dividend, which qualifies for a more generous dividend tax credit for the recipient shareholder, can generate a refund under subsection 129(1) only to the extent of the corporation's eligible RDTOH. An eligible dividend cannot generate a refund out of the corporation's non-eligible RDTOH. If the corporation pays a non-eligible dividend, it is eligible for a refund to the extent of either its eligible or non-eligible RDTOH, although an ordering rule (clause 129(1)(*a*)(ii)(B)) provides that the non-eligible RDTOH is applied before the eligible RDTOH.

If a return is not filed within three years after the year of payment of the dividend, the CRA will deny the dividend refund. (see Document No. 2011-0421291I7). *Tawa Developments Inc. v. The Queen*, 2011 DTC 1324 (TCC), confirmed the three-year requirement. The taxpayer paid a dividend in the 2004 tax year and claimed a dividend refund. The Minister denied the refund on the basis that the taxpayer's 2004 tax return was filed more than three years after the end of the year, but also reduced the taxpayer's RDTOH by the amount that would have been the dividend refund. The Court upheld the denial of the dividend refund, but held that the denied dividend refund should not reduce the taxpayer's RDTOH.

Notwithstanding *Tawa*, the CRA maintained its position that a dividend refund that is denied due to a late-filed return should reduce the taxpayer's RDTOH. However, in *Presidential MSH Corporation v. The Queen*, 2015 DTC 1101 (TCC) and *1057513 Ontario Inc. v. The Queen*, 2015 DTC 5106 (FCA), the courts found that dividend refunds that are denied due to late-filed returns do not reduce the RDTOH balance. To be consistent with these decisions, the CRA changed its position (2015-0595591C6).

A denied dividend refund cannot be applied to another tax liability under s. 129(2) or re-appropriated for use against other tax debts under s. 221.2 (see Document No. 2011-0421291I7).

History: S. 129(1)(*a*) was replaced by S.C. 2018, c. 12, s. 22(1), applicable to taxation years that begin after 2018, and also to a taxation year of a corporation that begins before 2019 and ends after 2018 if

(a) the corporation's preceding taxation year was, because of a transaction or event or a series of transactions or events, shorter than it would have been in the absence of that transaction, event or series; and

(b) one of the reasons for the transaction, event or series was to defer the application of subsections 20(2) and (3) or 22(1) to (5) [of the *Budget Implementation Act, 2018, No. 1*] to the corporation.

S. 129(1)(*a*) formerly read:

(*a*) may, on sending the notice of assessment for the year, refund without application an amount (in this Act referred to as its "dividend refund" for the year) equal to the lesser of

(i) 38 $^{1}/_{3}$% of all taxable dividends paid by the corporation on shares of its capital stock in the year and at a time when it was a private corporation, and

(ii) its refundable dividend tax on hand at the end of the year; and

S. 129(1)(*a*)(i) was replaced by S.C. 2016, c. 11, s. 7(1), applicable to taxation years that end after 2015, except that, for taxation years that end after 2015 and begin before 2016, in computing the amount determined under subparagraph 129(1)(*a*)(i), the reference to "38 $^{1}/_{3}$%" is to be read as a reference to the percentage determined by the formula

$$33\ 1/3\% + 5\%\ (A/B)$$

where

A is the number of days in the taxation year that are after 2015; and

B is the total number of days in the taxation year.

S. 129(1)(*a*)(i) formerly read:

(i) $^{1}/_{3}$ of all taxable dividends paid by the corporation on shares of its capital stock in the year and at a time when it was a private corporation, and

S. 129(1)(*a*), the portion before subparagraph (i) was replaced by S.C. 2010, c. 25, s. 29(1), in force on Royal Assent, December 15, 2010. S. 129(1)(*a*), the portion before subparagraph (i) formerly read:

(*a*) may, on mailing the notice of assessment for the year, refund without application therefor an amount (in this Act referred to as its "dividend refund" for the year) equal to the lesser of

S. 129(1)(*b*) was replaced by S.C. 2010, c. 25, s. 29(2), in force on Royal Assent, December 15, 2010. S. 129(1)(*b*) formerly read:

(*b*) shall, with all due dispatch, make the dividend refund after mailing the notice of assessment if an application for it has been made in writing by the corporation within the period within which the Minister would be allowed under subsection 152(4) to assess tax payable under this Part by the corporation for the year if that subsection were read without reference to paragraph 152(4)(*a*).

Related Sections: S. 55(2) Deemed proceeds or capital gain; s. 87(2)(aa) Refundable dividend tax on hand; s. 89(1), "Canadian corporation", "private corporation", "taxable dividends"; s. 125(7), "Canadian-controlled private corporation"; s. 129(3) Definition of "refundable dividend tax on hand"; s. 131(5) Dividend refund to mutual fund corporation; s. 157(3) Reduced instalments; s. 157(3.1) Amount of payment — three-month period; s. 186 Tax on assessable dividends; s. 248(1), "dividend"; s. 260(7) Dividend refund; s. 261(5) Functional currency tax reporting; s. 261(9) Pre-transition debts.

Canadian Tax Foundation: Walsh and Walsh, *Passive Investment Income – The Impacts on the Small Business Deduction and Refundable Dividend Tax on Hand*, 2018 St. John's Tax Seminar 4:1–25; Dolson and Taylor, *Passive Investment Income: Past and Future*, 2018 Prairie Provinces Tax Conference 11:0; Infanti, *2018 Budget Simplifies Passive Investment*

Rules, 2018 Tax for the Owner Manager 19(2):1–2; Infanti, *FCA Agrees: Dividend Refund Timed Out and RDTOH Remains Intact*, 2016 Tax for the Owner-Manager 16(1):3–4; Wen, *Reduction of RDTOH When Dividend Refund Is Denied*, 2015 Canadian Tax Focus 2(3):2; Jung and McIntyre, *Current Issues: Part IV Tax/Denied Dividend Refund*, 2013 Ontario Tax Conference 1:31–32.

Tax Profile: April 2015 — Breaking the Link — Nature of a Forward Contract After a Section 85 Rollover.

Tax Topics: No. 2438, Minister Has Discretion To Provide Relief From the Tax-Return-Filing Requirement for Dividend Returns; No. 2404, CCPC Passive Investment Income Saga Comes to an End.

Interpretation Bulletins: *Primary* — IT-243R4 Dividend refund to private corporations.

Tax Window Files: 2016 CTF – Q4 – 55(2) and Part IV Tax, *November 29, 2016*, CRA Document No. 2016-0671491C6; Subsection 55(2) and Part IV tax, *October 11, 2016*, CRA Document No. 2016-0653451E5; T2 Late-Filing: Impact on Div. Refund and RDTOH, *November 24, 2015*, CRA Document No. 2015-0610691C6; Part IV Tax / Denied Dividend Refund, *October 18, 2012*, CRA Document No. 2012-0436181E5.

Cases: The taxpayer paid a dividend in the 2004 tax year and claimed a dividend refund. The Minister reduced the taxpayer's RDTOH, but denied the refund on the basis that the taxpayer's 2004 tax return was filed more than three years after the end of the year. The taxpayer's appeal was dismissed. Filing a return within three years of the end of the tax year is a condition to receiving a refund for that year under subsection 129(1). However, the taxpayer's RDTOH should not have been reduced since it did not receive a refund. *Tawa Developments Inc. v. The Queen*, (T.C.C.) 2011 DTC 1324

▶ 129(1.1) ◀

(1.1) Dividends paid to bankrupt controlling corporation. In determining the dividend refund for a taxation year ending after 1977 of a particular corporation, no amount may be included under clause (1)(*a*)(i)(A), subclause (1)(*a*)(ii)(A)(I) or sub-subclause (1)(*a*)(ii)(B)(I)1 in respect of a taxable dividend paid to a shareholder that

(*a*) was a corporation that controlled (within the meaning assigned by subsection 186(2)) the particular corporation at the time the dividend was paid; and

(*b*) was a bankrupt at any time during that taxation year of the particular corporation.

History: S. 129(1.1), the portion before paragraph (*a*) was replaced by S.C. 2018, c. 12, s. 22(2), applicable to taxation years that begin after 2018, and also to a taxation year of a corporation that begins before 2019 and ends after 2018 if

(a) the corporation's preceding taxation year was, because of a transaction or event or a series of transactions or events, shorter than it would have been in the absence of that transaction, event or series; and

(b) one of the reasons for the transaction, event or series was to defer the application of subsections 20(2) and (3) or 22(1) to (5) [of the *Budget Implementation Act, 2018, No. 1*] to the corporation.

S. 129(1.1), the portion before paragraph (*a*) formerly read:

(1.1) *Dividends paid to bankrupt controlling corporation.* In determining the dividend refund for a taxation year ending after 1977 of a particular corporation, no amount may be included by virtue of subparagraph (1)(*a*)(i) in respect of a taxable dividend paid to a shareholder that

S. 129(1.1)(*b*) was replaced by S.C. 2017, c. 33, s. 51(1), applicable in respect of bankruptcies that occur after April 26, 1995, and formerly read:

(*b*) was a bankrupt (within the meaning assigned by subsection 128(3)) at any time during that taxation year of the particular corporation.

▶ 129(1.2) ◀

(1.2) Dividends deemed not to be taxable dividends. Where a dividend is paid on a share of the capital stock of a corporation and the share (or another share for which the share was substituted) was acquired by its holder in a transaction or as part of a series of transactions one of the main purposes of which was to enable the corporation to obtain a dividend refund, the dividend shall, for the purpose of subsection (1), be deemed not to be a taxable dividend.

Editorial Note: Subsection 129(1.2) is an anti-avoidance rule designed to counter the abuse of the refundable tax provisions and operates by deeming a dividend not to be a taxable dividend, thus denying the dividend refund to the payer, if the share on which the dividend was paid was acquired in a transaction (or series of transactions) one of the main purposes of which was to obtain the dividend refund. Technically, there is no exception for related persons and the provision may apply even where tax is paid at the shareholder level (see Document No. 2013-0480361C6). A somewhat similar, but more complex, set of restrictions applies to "trading" in capital dividends (s. 83(2.1)–(2.4)).

Related Sections: S. 83(2.1) Capital dividend — anti-avoidance rule; s. 83(2.2) Capital dividend — exception to anti-avoidance rule; s. 83(2.3) Capital dividend — exception to anti-avoidance rule; s. 83(2.4) Capital dividend — exception to anti-avoidance rule; s. 87(2)(*aa*) Refundable dividend tax on hand.

Canadian Tax Foundation: Wen, *Dividend Refund Denied upon Redemption of Donated Private Company Shares*, 2018 Canadian Tax Focus 8(2):11–12; Strawson, *When Does Subsection 129(1.2) Apply To Deny a Dividend Refund?*, 2017 Tax for the Owner Manager 17(3):7–8; Hudson and McCamis, *Refresher on Specific Anti-Avoidance Provisions*, 2014 Prairie Provinces Tax Conference 12:1–41.

▶ 129(2) ◀

(2) Application to other liability. Instead of making a refund that might otherwise be made under subsection (1), the Minister may, where the corporation is liable or about to become liable to make any payment under this Act, apply the amount that would otherwise be refundable to that other liability and notify the corporation of that action.

▶ 129(2.1) ◀

(2.1) Interest on dividend refund. Where a dividend refund for a taxation year is paid to, or applied to a liability of, a corporation, the Minister shall pay or apply interest on the refund at the prescribed rate for the period beginning on the day that is the later of

(*a*) the day that is 120 days after the end of the year, and

(*b*) the day that is 30 days after the day on which the corporation's return of income under this Part for the year was filed under section 150, unless the return was filed on or before the day on or before which it was required to be filed,

and ending on the day on which the refund is paid or applied.

Related Regulations: 4301.

Related Sections: S. 161.1(1) Refund interest.

▶ 129(2.2) ◀

(2.2) Excess interest on dividend refund. Where, at any particular time, interest has been paid to, or applied to a liability of, a corporation under subsection (2.1) in respect of a dividend refund and it is determined at a subsequent time that the dividend refund was less than that in respect of which interest was so paid or applied,

(*a*) the amount by which the interest that was so paid or applied exceeds the interest, if any, computed in respect of the amount that is determined at the subsequent time to be the dividend refund shall be deemed to be an amount (in this subsection referred to as the "amount payable") that became payable under this Part by the corporation at the particular time;

(*b*) the corporation shall pay to the Receiver General interest at the prescribed rate on the amount payable, computed from the particular time to the day of payment; and

(*c*) the Minister may at any time assess the corporation in respect of the amount payable and, where the Minister makes such an assessment, the provisions of Divisions I and J apply, with such modifications as the circumstances require, in respect of the assessment as though it had been made under section 152.

Related Regulations: 4301.

Related Sections: S. 161.1(1) Refund interest.

▶ 129(3) ◀

(3) Definition of "refundable dividend tax on hand" — (Repealed by S.C. 2018, c. 12, s. 22(3).)

Editorial Note: Subsection 129(3) is repealed, effective for taxation years beginning after 2018. From that point on, the RDTOH account is split into two accounts — the eligible RDTOH and the non-eligible RDTOH accounts. These accounts are defined in subsection 129(4).

The calculation of a corporation's refundable dividend tax on hand ("RDTOH") is the total of (a) 30²/3% of aggregate investment income for the year (net of certain foreign tax adjustments) if the corporation is a Canadian-controlled private corporation ("CCPC"); (b) Part IV tax payable for the year; (c) the RDTOH balance at the end of the preceding year, if the corporation was a private corporation at the end of that year; less (d) the dividend refund for the preceding year.

With respect to (a), the corporation must be a CCPC throughout the year; however, s. 249(3.1) provides a deemed year end when that status is lost.

Subparagraph 129(3)(*a*)(i) adds 30²/3% of "aggregate investment income" (defined in s. 129(4)), net of an adjustment designed to reflect the reduction of Canadian tax due to foreign tax credits. Subparagraphs 129(3)(*a*)(ii) and (iii) are "limiting amounts"; s. 129(3)(*a*)(ii) is based on 30²/3% of taxable income, net of the small business deduction and adjustments for foreign tax credits; and s. 129(3)(*a*)(iii) is based on the corporation's Part I tax for the year. The 30²/3% rate takes into account the 10²/3% refundable tax on investment income, per s. 123.3.

Note that these tax and refund rates changed effective January 1, 2016. For the prior rates and transitional rules, see the historical note for this subsection.

History: S. 129(3) was repealed by S.C. 2018, c. 12, s. 22(3), applicable to taxation years that begin after 2018, and also to a taxation year of a corporation that begins before 2019 and ends after 2018 if

(a) the corporation's preceding taxation year was, because of a transaction or event or a series of transactions or events, shorter than it would have been in the absence of that transaction, event or series; and

(b) one of the reasons for the transaction, event or series was to defer the application of subsections 20(2) and (3) or 22(1) to (5) [of the *Budget Implementation Act, 2018, No. 1*] to the corporation.

S. 129(3) formerly read:

(3) *Definition of "refundable dividend tax on hand"*. In this section, "refundable dividend tax on hand" of a corporation at the end of a taxation year means the amount, if any, by which the total of

(*a*) where the corporation was a Canadian-controlled private corporation throughout the year, the least of

(i) the amount determined by the formula

A - B

where

A is 30 ²/3% of the corporation's aggregate investment income for the year, and

B is the amount, if any, by which

(I) the amount deducted under subsection 126(1) from the tax for the year otherwise payable by it under this Part

exceeds

(II) 8% of its foreign investment income for the year,

(ii) 30 ²/3% of the amount, if any, by which the corporation's taxable income for the year exceeds the total of

(A) the least of the amounts determined under paragraphs 125(1)(*a*) to (*c*) in respect of the corporation for the year,

(B) 100/(38 ²/3) of the total of amounts deducted under subsection 126(1) from its tax for the year otherwise payable under this Part, and

(C) the amount determined by multiplying the total of amounts deducted under subsection 126(2) from its tax for the year otherwise payable under this Part, by the relevant factor for the year, and

(iii) the corporation's tax for the year payable under this Part,

(*b*) the total of the taxes under Part IV payable by the corporation for the year, and

(*c*) where the corporation was a private corporation at the end of its preceding taxation year, the corporation's refundable dividend tax on hand at the end of that preceding year

exceeds

(*d*) the corporation's dividend refund for its preceding taxation year.

S. 129(3)(*a*)(i), the description of A was replaced by S.C. 2016, c. 11, s. 7(2), applicable to taxation years that end after 2015, except that, for taxation years that end after 2015 and begin before 2016, in computing the amount determined under subparagraph 129(3)(*a*)(i), the references to "30 ²/3%" is to be read as a reference to the percentage determined by the formula

26 2/3% + 4% (A/B)

where

A is the number of days in the taxation year that are after 2015; and

B is the total number of days in the taxation year.

S. 129(3)(*a*)(i), the description of A formerly read:

A is 26²/3% of the corporation's aggregate investment income for the year, and

S. 129(3)(*a*)(i), subclause (II) of the description of B was replaced by S.C. 2016, c. 11, s. 7(3), applicable to taxation years that end after 2015, except that, for taxation years that end after 2015 and begin before 2016, in computing the amount determined under subparagraph 129(3)(*a*)(i) the reference to "8%" in subclause (II) of the description of B is to be read as a reference to the percentage determined by the formula

9 1/3% – 1 1/3% (A/B)

where

A is the number of days in the taxation year that are after 2015; and

B is the total number of days in the taxation year.

S. 129(3)(*a*)(i), subclause (II) of the description of B formerly read:

(II) 9¹/3% of its foreign investment income for the year,

S. 129(3)(*a*)(ii), the portion before clause (A) was replaced by S.C. 2016, c. 11, s. 7(4), applicable to taxation years that end after 2015, except that, for taxation years that end after 2015 and begin before 2016, in computing the amount determined under subparagraph 129(3)(*a*)(ii), the references to "30 ²/3%" is to be read as a reference to the percentage determined by the formula

26 2/3% + 4% (A/B)

where

A is the number of days in the taxation year that are after 2015; and

B is the total number of days in the taxation year.

S. 129(3)(*a*)(ii), the portion before clause (A) formerly read:

(ii) 26²/3% of the amount, if any, by which the corporation's taxable income for the year exceeds the total of

S. 129(3)(*a*)(ii)(B) was replaced by S.C. 2016, c. 11, s. 7(5), applicable to taxation years that end after 2015, except that, for taxation years that end after 2015 and begin before 2016, the reference to "100/(38 ²/3)" in clause 129(3)(*a*)(ii)(B) is to be read as a reference to the amount determined by the formula

100/(35 + 3 2/3(A/B))

where

A is the number of days in the taxation year that are after 2015; and

B is the total number of days in the taxation year.

S. 129(3)(*a*)(ii)(B) formerly read:

(B) ¹⁰⁰/35 of the total of amounts deducted under subsection 126(1) from its tax for the year otherwise payable under this Part, and

S. 129(3)(*a*)(ii)(B) was replaced by S.C. 2013, c. 34, s. 275(1), applicable to taxation years that begin after October 31, 2011, and formerly read:

(B) ²⁵/9 of the total of amounts deducted under subsection 126(1) from its tax for the year otherwise payable under this Part, and

S. 129(3)(*a*)(ii)(C) was replaced by S.C. 2013, c. 34, s. 275(1), applicable to the 2003 and subsequent taxation years, and formerly read:

(C) ¹⁰/4 of the total of amounts deducted under subsection 126(2) from its tax for the year otherwise payable under this Part, and

S. 129(3)(*a*)(iii) was replaced by S.C. 2013, c. 34, s. 275(2), applicable to taxation years that begin after 2007, and formerly read:

(iii) the corporation's tax for the year payable under this Part determined without reference to section 123.2,

Related Sections: S. 87(2)(*aa*) Refundable dividend tax on hand; s. 89(1), "private corporation"; s. 123.3 Refundable tax on CCPC's investment income; s. 125(1) Small business deduction; s. 125(7), "Canadian-controlled private corporation"; s. 126(1) Foreign tax deduction — non-business income; s. 126(2) Foreign tax deduction — business income; s. 129(1) Dividend refund to private corporation; s. 129(3.1) Application; s. 129(4) Definitions; s. 131(5) Dividend refund to mutual fund corporation; s. 131(11) Rules respecting prescribed labour-sponsored venture capital corporations; s. 186(1) Tax on assessable dividends; s. 186(5) Deemed private corporation.

Tax Profile: April 2015 — Breaking the Link — Nature of a Forward Contract After a Section 85 Rollover.

► 129(3.1) ◄

(3.1) Application. Where, in a taxation year that begins after November 12, 1981, a corporation that last became a private corporation on or before that date and that was throughout the year a private corporation, other than a Canadian-controlled private corporation, has included in its income for the year an amount in respect of property that the corporation

(*a*) disposed of before November 13, 1981,

(*b*) was obligated to dispose of under the terms of an agreement in writing entered into before November 13, 1981, or

(*c*) is deemed by subsection 44(2) to have disposed of at any time after November 12, 1981 because of an event referred to in paragraph (*b*), (*c*) or (*d*) of the definition "proceeds of disposition" in section 54 in respect of the disposition that occurred before November 13, 1981,

paragraph 3(*a*) shall apply as if the corporation were a Canadian-controlled private corporation throughout the year, except that the total of the amounts determined under that paragraph in respect of the corporation for the year shall not exceed the amount that would be so determined if the only income of the corporation for the year were the amount included in respect of the disposition of such property.

► 129(3.2)-(3.5) ◄

(3.2)-(3.5) — (Repealed by S.C. 1996, c. 21, s. 32(2).)

► 129(4) ◄

(4) Definitions. The definitions in this subsection apply in this section.

Tax Window Files: Small Business Deduction, *February 14, 2012*, CRA Document No. 2011-0407051E5.

"aggregate investment income" — "aggregate investment income" of a corporation for a taxation year means the amount, if any, by which the total of all amounts, each of which is

(*a*) the amount, if any, by which

(i) the eligible portion of the corporation's taxable capital gains for the year

exceeds the total of

(ii) the eligible portion of its allowable capital losses for the year, and

(iii) the amount, if any, deducted under paragraph 111(1)(*b*) in computing its taxable income for the year, or

(*b*) the corporation's income for the year from a source that is a property, other than

(i) exempt income,

(ii) an amount included under subsection 12(10.2) in computing the corporation's income for the year,

(iii) the portion of any dividend that was deductible in computing the corporation's taxable income for the year, and

(iv) income that, but for paragraph 108(5)(*a*), would not be income from a property,

exceeds the total of all amounts, each of which is the corporation's loss for the year from a source that is a property.

Editorial Note: A corporation's aggregate investment income for a year is the total of: (a) the "eligible portion" of its taxable capital gains for the year (see the editorial note for the definition of "eligible portion") net of the eligible portion of its allowable capital losses for the year and its capital loss carry-overs deducted for the year; and (b) its income from property (with certain exceptions, including exempt income and deductible dividends), including "specified investment business" income, for the year net of its losses from property for the year.

Related Sections: S. 89(1), "general rate income pool", "low rate income pool; s. 123.3 Refundable tax on CCPC's investment income; s. 123.4(1), "full rate taxable income"; s. 125(7), "active business carried on by a corporation", "specified investment business"; s. 125.1 Manufacturing and processing profits deductions; s. 131(11) Rules respecting prescribed labour-sponsored venture capital corporations; s. 248(1), "aggregate investment income".

Forms: T2 SCH 7 — Calculation of Aggregate Investment Income and Active Business Income.

"Canadian investment income" — (Repealed by S.C. 1996, c. 21, s. 32(2).)

"eligible portion" — "eligible portion" of a corporation's taxable capital gains or allowable capital losses for a taxation year is the total of all amounts each of which is the portion of a taxable capital gain or an allowable capital loss, as the case may be, of the corporation for the year from a disposition of a property that, except where the property was a designated property (within the meaning assigned by subsection 89(1)), cannot reasonably be regarded as having accrued while the property, or a property for which it was substituted, was property of a corporation other than a Canadian-controlled private corporation, an investment corporation, a mortgage investment corporation or a mutual fund corporation.

Editorial Note: This definition limits additions to a corporation's refundable dividend tax on hand ("RDTOH") for taxable capital gains to those accrued while the corporation was a Canadian-controlled private corporation ("CCPC") (or certain other specialty corporations). However, certain "old" gains (in respect of "designated property") are grandfathered — basically, gains from qualifying capital property held before the ability to generate RDTOH (otherwise than where Part IV tax applies) became limited to CCPCs in 1981.

Related Sections: S. 89(1), "designated property"; s. 129(4), "aggregate investment income".

"eligible refundable dividend tax on hand" — "eligible refundable dividend tax on hand", of a particular corporation at the end of a taxation year, means the amount, if any, by which the total of

(*a*) the total of the taxes payable under Part IV by the particular corporation for the year in respect of

(i) eligible dividends received by the particular corporation in the year from corporations other than corporations with which the particular corporation is connected (in this paragraph, within the meaning assigned by subsection 186(4) on the assumption that the other corporation is at that time a payer corporation within the meaning of that subsection), and

(ii) taxable dividends received by the particular corporation in the year from corporations that are connected with the particular corporation to the extent that such dividends caused a dividend refund to those corporations from their eligible refundable dividend tax on hand, and

(*b*) where the particular corporation was a private corporation at the end of its preceding taxation year, the particular corporation's eligible refundable dividend tax on hand at the end of that preceding year

exceeds

(*c*) the total of all amounts each of which is the portion, if any, of the particular corporation's dividend refund from its eligible refundable dividend tax on hand determined, for its preceding taxation year, under

(i) subparagraph (1)(*a*)(i), and

(ii) clause (1)(*a*)(ii)(B).

History: S. 129(4), the definition "eligible refundable dividend tax on hand" was added by S.C. 2018, c. 12, s. 22(4), applicable to taxation years that begin after 2018, and also to a taxation year of a corporation that begins before 2019 and ends after 2018 if

(a) the corporation's preceding taxation year was, because of a transaction or event or a series of transactions or events, shorter than it would have been in the absence of that transaction, event or series; and

(b) one of the reasons for the transaction, event or series was to defer the application of subsections 20(2) and (3) or 22(1) to (5) [of the *Budget Implementation Act, 2018, No. 1*] to the corporation.

"foreign investment income" — "foreign investment income" of a corporation for a taxation year is the amount that would be its aggregate investment income for the year if

(*a*) every amount of its income, loss, capital gain or capital loss for the year that can reasonably be regarded as being from a source in Canada were nil,

(*b*) no amount were deducted under paragraph 111(1)(*b*) in computing its taxable income for the year, and

(*c*) this Act were read without reference to paragraph (*a*) of the definition "income" or "loss" in this subsection.

Related Sections: S. 129(4.1) Interpretation of "income" or "loss"; s. 129(4.2) Idem; s. 129(6) Investment income from associated corporation deemed to be active business income.

Income Tax Folios: S4-F8-C1 Business Investment Losses.

Cases: The taxpayer earned interest on U.S. dollar deposits in the Philippines, such funds being committed to the carrying on of the taxpayer's business there. It was held that the deposits were an integral part of the business and therefore the interest earned on them was not foreign investment income. *Ensite Limited v. The Queen*, 86 DTC 6521 (S.C.C.). See also *The Queen v. Irving Garber Sales Canada Limited*, 92 DTC 6498 (F.C.T.D.)

"income" or "loss" —"income" or "loss" of a corporation for a taxation year from a source that is a property

(*a*) includes the income or loss from a specified investment business carried on by it in Canada other than income or loss from a source outside Canada, but

(*b*) does not include the income or loss from any property

(i) that is incident to or pertains to an active business carried on by it, or

(ii) that is used or held principally for the purpose of gaining or producing income from an active business carried on by it.

Cases: Surface lease and royalty income from oil wells located on farming property were "active business" income qualifying for the small business deduction since it was incidental to the taxpayer's principal activity of farming and was used principally for that purpose. *Alamar Farms Ltd. v. The Queen*, 93 DTC 121 (T.C.C.)

"non-eligible refundable dividend tax on hand" —"non-eligible refundable dividend tax on hand", non-eligible refundable dividend tax on hand, of a corporation at the end of a taxation year, means the amount, if any, by which the total of

(*a*) if the corporation was a Canadian-controlled private corporation throughout the year, the least of

(i) the amount determined by the formula

$$A - B$$

where

A is 30 2/3% of the corporation's aggregate investment income for the year, and

B is the amount, if any, by which

(A) the amount deducted under subsection 126(1) from the tax for the year otherwise payable by it under this Part

exceeds

(B) 8% of its foreign investment income for the year,

(ii) 30 2/3% of the amount, if any, by which the corporation's taxable income for the year exceeds the total of

(A) the least of the amounts determined under paragraphs 125(1)(*a*) to (*c*) in respect of the corporation for the year,

(B) 100/(38 2/3) of the total of amounts deducted under subsection 126(1) from its tax for the year otherwise payable under this Part, and

(C) the amount determined by multiplying the total of amounts deducted under subsection 126(2) from its tax for the year otherwise payable under this Part, by the relevant factor for the year, and

(iii) the corporation's tax for the year payable under this Part,

(*b*) the total of the taxes payable under Part IV by the corporation for the year less the amount determined under paragraph (*a*) of the definition "eligible refundable dividend tax on hand" in respect of the corporation for the year, and

(*c*) if the corporation was a private corporation at the end of its preceding taxation year, the corporation's non-eligible refundable dividend tax on hand at the end of that preceding year

exceeds

(*d*) the portion, if any, of the corporation's dividend refund from its non-eligible refundable dividend tax on hand determined, for its preceding taxation year, under clause (1)(*a*)(ii)(A).

History: S. 129(4), the definition "non-eligible refundable dividend tax on hand" was added by S.C. 2018, c. 12, s. 22(4), applicable to taxation years that begin after 2018, and also to a taxation year of a corporation that begins before 2019 and ends after 2018 if

(a) the corporation's preceding taxation year was, because of a transaction or event or a series of transactions or events, shorter than it would have been in the absence of that transaction, event or series; and

(b) one of the reasons for the transaction, event or series was to defer the application of subsections 20(2) and (3) or 22(1) to (5) [of the *Budget Implementation Act, 2018, No. 1*] to the corporation.

► 129(4.1) ◄

(4.1) Conditions for subsection (4.2). Subsection (4.2) applies in respect of a particular taxation year of a particular corporation if the following conditions are met:

(*a*) the particular corporation has an amount of tax payable for the year under Part IV;

(*b*) the particular corporation has claimed amounts under paragraph 186(1)(*c*) or (*d*) in respect of the year; and

(*c*) the particular corporation would, in the absence of paragraphs 186(1)(*c*) and (*d*), have an amount determined, at the end of the year, under both paragraph (*a*) of the definition "eligible refundable dividend tax on hand" and paragraph (*b*) of the definition "non-eligible refundable dividend tax on hand" in subsection (4).

History: S. 129(4.1) was added by S.C. 2018, c. 27, s. 15(1), applicable to taxation years that begin after 2018.

► 129(4.2) ◄

(4.2) Part IV tax — allocation of losses. If this subsection applies in respect of a particular taxation year of a corporation, for the purpose of determining the amount under paragraph (*a*) of the definition "eligible refundable dividend tax on hand" in subsection (4), in respect of the corporation at the end of the year, the amount determined under subsection 186(1) in respect of the corporation for the year is deemed to be the amount determined by the formula

$$A + B - C$$

where

A is the amount determined under paragraph 186(1)(*a*) in respect of the corporation for the year in respect of eligible dividends;

B is the amount determined under paragraph 186(1)(*b*) in respect of the corporation for the year in respect of dividends that resulted in dividend refunds from the eligible refundable dividend tax on hand of other corporations; and

C is the amount determined by the formula

$$38\ 1/3\%\ (D + E) - (F + G)$$

where

D is the amount claimed by the corporation under paragraph 186(1)(*c*) for the year,

E is the amount claimed by the corporation under paragraph 186(1)(*d*) for the year,

F is the amount determined under paragraph 186(1)(*a*) in respect of the corporation for the year in respect of taxable dividends (other than eligible dividends), and

G is the amount determined under paragraph 186(1)(*b*) in respect of the corporation for the year in respect of dividends that resulted in dividend refunds from the non-eligible refundable dividend tax on hand of other corporations.

History: S. 129(4.2) was added by S.C. 2018, c. 27, s. 15(1), applicable to taxation years that begin after 2018.

▶ 129(4.3) ◀

(4.3) Definition of "designated property" — (Repealed by S.C. 1996, c. 21, s. 32(2).)

▶ 129(5) ◀

(5) 2019 transitional RDTOH. The following rules apply to a corporation's first taxation year in respect of which the definition "eligible refundable dividend tax on hand" in subsection (4) applies:

(*a*) if the corporation is a Canadian-controlled private corporation throughout the taxation year and its preceding taxation year and is not a corporation in respect of which an election under subsection 89(11) applies to the taxation year or the preceding taxation year,

(i) for the purpose of applying paragraph (*b*) of the definition "eligible refundable dividend tax on hand" in respect of the corporation at the end of the taxation year, the corporation's eligible refundable dividend tax on hand at the end of its preceding taxation year is deemed to be the amount, if any, that is the lesser of

(A) the amount determined by the formula

$$A - B$$

where

A is the corporation's refundable dividend tax on hand at the end of its preceding taxation year, and

B is the corporation's dividend refund for its preceding taxation year, and

(B) the amount determined by the formula

$$(C - D) \times E$$

where

C is the corporation's general rate income pool at the end of its preceding taxation year,

D is the amount, if any, by which

(I) the total of all amounts each of which is an eligible dividend paid by the corporation in its preceding taxation year

exceeds

(II) the total of all amounts each of which is an excessive eligible dividend designation made by the corporation in its preceding taxation year, and

E is 38 1/3%, and

(ii) for the purpose of applying paragraph (*c*) of the definition "non-eligible refundable dividend tax on hand" in respect of the corporation at the end of the taxation year, the corporation's non-eligible refundable dividend tax on hand at the end of its preceding taxation year is deemed to be the amount determined by the formula

$$A - B$$

where

A is the amount determined under clause (*a*)(i)(A) in respect of the corporation at the end of the preceding taxation year, and

B is the amount determined under clause (*a*)(i)(B) in respect of the corporation at the end of the preceding taxation year; and

(*b*) in any other case, for the purpose of applying paragraph (*b*) of the definition *eligible refundable dividend tax on hand* in respect of the corporation at the end of the taxation year, the corporation's eligible refundable dividend tax on hand at the end of its preceding taxation year is deemed to be the amount that would be determined for clause (*a*)(i)(A) if paragraph (*a*) applied to the corporation in respect of the taxation year.

Editorial Note: For taxation years beginning after 2018, the payment of an eligible dividend by a private corporation, which qualifies for a more generous dividend tax credit for the recipient shareholder, can generate a refund under subsection 129(1) only to the extent of the corporation's eligible RDTOH account. If the corporation pays a non-eligible dividend, it is eligible for a refund to the extent of either its eligible or non-eligible RDTOH account.

Subsection 129(5) provides a transitional rule for the two RDTOH accounts for the first taxation year of a Canadian-controlled private corporation ("CCPC") that begins after 2018, where the CCPC had an RDTOH account under the pre-2019 rules. Out of the CCPC's existing RDTOH at the end of the previous taxation year, an amount equal to 38 1/3 per cent of the CCPC's general rate income pool at the end of the previous year (basically, taxable income that was subject to the general corporate rate) will be allocated to its eligible RDTOH. The remainder of the existing RDTOH, if any, will be allocated to the CCPC's non-eligible RDTOH. For non-CCPC corporations, the existing RDTOH will be allocated in full to eligible RDTOH.

History: S. 129(5) was added by S.C. 2018, c. 12, s. 22(5), applicable to taxation years that begin after 2018, and also to a taxation year of a corporation that begins before 2019 and ends after 2018 if

(a) the corporation's preceding taxation year was, because of a transaction or event or a series of transactions or events, shorter than it would have been in the absence of that transaction, event or series; and

(b) one of the reasons for the transaction, event or series was to defer the application of subsections 20(2) and (3) or 22(1) to (5) [of the *Budget Implementation Act, 2018, No. 1*] to the corporation.

▶ 129(5.1) ◀

(5.1) 2019 transitional RDTOH — amalgamations. Subsection (5) applies with such modifications as are necessary for the purpose of applying paragraph 87(2)(*aa*) in respect of a corporation if

(*a*) the corporation is a predecessor corporation (within the meaning assigned by subsection 87(1)) in respect of an amalgamation (within the meaning assigned by subsection 87(1));

(*b*) the corporation has an amount of refundable dividend tax on hand at the end of its taxation year that ends because of paragraph 87(2)(*a*); and

(*c*) the first taxation year of the new corporation (within the meaning assigned by subsection 87(1)) in respect of the amalgamation is one to which the definition "eligible refundable dividend tax on hand" in subsection (4) applies.

History: S. 129(5.1) was added by S.C. 2018, c. 12, s. 22(5), applicable to taxation years that begin after 2018, and also to a taxation year of a corporation that begins before 2019 and ends after 2018 if

(a) the corporation's preceding taxation year was, because of a transaction or event or a series of transactions or events, shorter than it would have been in the absence of that transaction, event or series; and

(b) one of the reasons for the transaction, event or series was to defer the application of subsections 20(2) and (3) or 22(1) to (5) [of the *Budget Implementation Act, 2018, No. 1*] to the corporation.

▶ 129(6) ◀

(6) Investment income from associated corporation deemed to be active business income. Where any particular amount paid or payable to a corporation (in this subsection referred to as the "recipient corporation") by another corporation (in this subsection referred to as the "associated corporation") with which the recipient corporation was associated in any particular taxation year commencing after 1972, would otherwise be included in computing the income of the recipient corporation for the particular year from a source in Canada that is a property, the following rules apply:

(*a*) for the purposes of subsection (4), in computing the recipient corporation's income for the year from a source in Canada that is a property,

(i) there shall not be included any portion (in this subsection referred to as the "deductible portion") of the particular amount that was or may be deductible in computing the income of the associated corporation for any taxation year from an active business carried on by it in Canada, and

(ii) no deduction shall be made in respect of any outlay or expense, to the extent that that outlay or expense may reasonably be regarded as having been made or incurred by the recipient corporation for the purpose of gaining or producing the deductible portion; and

(*b*) for the purposes of this subsection and section 125,

(i) the deductible portion shall be deemed to be income of the recipient corporation for the particular year from an active business carried on by it in Canada, and

(ii) any outlay or expense, to the extent described in subparagraph (*a*)(ii), shall be deemed to have been made or incurred by the recipient corporation for the purpose of gaining or producing that income.

Editorial Note: Subsection 129(6) expands the concept of active business income to include Canadian-source payments from associated corporations which, when viewed in isolation, would not qualify as active business income (e.g., interest and rent), but which are deductible in computing the payer corporation's active business income. Where this provision applies, for the purpose of section 129(4), the recipient does not include the income as income from property such that it does not generate refundable tax on hand (RDTOH). Also, for the purpose of section 125 (and subsection 129(6) itself), the amount is deemed to be active business income which may qualify for the small business deduction. However, even if the recipient is not a Canadian-controlled private corporation ("CCPC"), the provision may be advantageous if the small business deduction is not available, since the income will attract the general corporate "business rate" rather than the "investment rate" and may generate eligible dividends. Subsection 129(6) is irrelevant for determining a company's status as a "small business corporation" per the definition in s. 248(1) (even though the income may be deemed under s. 129(6) to be income from an active business — see Document No. 2012-0435101E5).

For taxation years beginning after March 21, 2016, income of a CCPC that is deemed by subsection 129(6) to be active business income does not qualify for the subsection 125(1) small business deduction if the payor associated corporation is not a CCPC or is a CCPC that makes an election under subsection 256(2) not to be associated. See also the editorial notes to subsections 125(1) and 256(2).

Related Sections: S. 89(1), "general rate income pool"; s. 125 Small business deduction; s. 129(4) Definitions; s. 256(1) Associated corporations; s. 256(1.1) Definition of "specified class"; s. 256(1.2) Control, etc.; s. 256(1.3) Parent deemed to own shares; s. 256(1.4) Options and rights; s. 256(1.5) Person related to himself, herself or itself; s. 256(1.6) Exception; s. 256(2) Corporations associated through a third corporation; s. 256(2.1) Anti-avoidance; s. 256(3) Saving provision — associated corporations; s. 256(4) Saving provision — associated corporations; s. 256(5) Saving provision — associated corporations; s. 256(5.1) Control in fact; s. 256(6) Saving provision — controlled corporations; s. 256(6.1) Simultaneous control; s. 256(6.2) Application to control in fact.

Interpretation Bulletins: *Secondary* — IT-73R6 The small business deduction.

► 129(7) ◄

(7) Meaning of "taxable dividend". For the purposes of this section, "taxable dividend" does not include a capital gains dividend within the meaning assigned by subsection 131(1).

► 129(8) ◄

(8) Application of s. 125. Expressions used in this section and not otherwise defined for the purposes of this section have the same meanings as in section 125.

Related Sections: S. 125(7) Definitions.

Investment Corporations

SECTION 130: [Investment corporation]

► 130(1) ◄

(1) Deduction from tax. A corporation that was, throughout a taxation year, an investment corporation may deduct from the tax otherwise payable by it under this Part for the year an amount equal to 20% of the amount, if any, by which its taxable income for the year exceeds its taxed capital gains for the year.

Related Sections: S. 123(1) Rate for corporations.

Forms: T2 SCH 18 — Federal and Provincial or Territorial Capital Gains Refund.

► 130(2) ◄

(2) Application of subsections 131(1) to (3.2), (4.1) and (6). Where a corporation was an investment corporation throughout a taxation year (other than a corporation that was a mutual fund corporation throughout the year), subsections 131(1) to (3.2), (4.1) and (6) apply in respect of the corporation for the year

(*a*) as if the corporation had been a mutual fund corporation throughout that and all previous taxation years ending after 1971 throughout which it was an investment corporation; and

(*b*) as if its capital gains redemptions for that and all previous taxation years ending after 1971, throughout which it would, but for the assumption made by paragraph (*a*), not have been a mutual fund corporation, were nil.

Editorial Note: See the editorial note for subsection 131(4.1) regarding "switch funds".

History: S. 130(2), the portion before paragraph (*a*) was replaced by S.C. 2016, c. 12, s. 47(1), in force January 1, 2017, and formerly read:

(2) *Application of ss. 131(1) to (3.2) and (6).* Where a corporation was an investment corporation throughout a taxation year (other than a corporation that was a mutual fund corporation throughout the year), subsections 131(1) to (3.2) and (6) apply in respect of the corporation for the year

Forms: T5 Sum. — T5SUM Return of Investment Income; T5 — Statement of Investment Income.

► 130(3) ◄

(3) Meaning of expressions "investment corporation" and "taxed capital gains". For the purposes of this section,

(*a*) a corporation is an "investment corporation" throughout any taxation year in respect of which the expression is being applied if it complied with the following conditions:

(i) it was throughout the year a Canadian corporation that was a public corporation,

(ii) at least 80% of its property throughout the year consisted of shares, bonds, marketable securities or cash,

(iii) not less than 95% of its income (determined without reference to subsection 49(2)) for the year was derived from, or from dispositions of, investments described in subparagraph (ii),

(iv) not less than 85% of its gross revenue for the year was from sources in Canada,

(v) not more than 25% of its gross revenue for the year was from interest,

(vi) at no time in the year did more than 10% of its property consist of shares, bonds or securities of any one corporation or debtor other than Her

Majesty in right of Canada or of a province or a Canadian municipality,

(vii) no person would have been a specified shareholder of the corporation in the year if

(A) the portion of the definition "specified shareholder" in subsection 248(1) before paragraph (*a*) were read as follows:

" 'specified shareholder' of a corporation in a taxation year means a taxpayer who owns, directly or indirectly, at any time in the year, more than 25% of the issued shares of any class of the capital stock of the corporation and, for the purposes of this definition,"

(B) paragraph (*a*) of that definition were read as follows:

"(*a*) a taxpayer is deemed to own each share of the capital stock of a corporation owned at that time by a person related to the taxpayer,"

(B.1) (Repealed.)

(C) that definition were read without reference to paragraph (*d*) of that definition,

(C.1) (Repealed.)

and

(D) paragraph 251(2)(*a*) were read as follows:

"(*a*) an individual and

(i) the individual's child (as defined in subsection 70(10)) who is under 19 years of age, or

(ii) the individual's spouse or common-law partner;"

(viii) an amount not less than 85% of the total of

(A) $^2/_3$ of the amount, if any, by which its taxable income for the year exceeds its taxed capital gains for the year, and

(B) the amount, if any, by which all taxable dividends received by it in the year to the extent of the amount thereof deductible under section 112 or 113 from its income for the year exceeds the amount that the corporation's non-capital loss for the year would be if the amount determined in respect of the corporation for the year under paragraph 3(*b*) was nil,

(less any dividends or interest received by it in the form of shares, bonds or other securities that had not been sold before the end of the year) was distributed, otherwise than by way of capital gains dividends, to its shareholders before the end of the year; and

(*b*) the amount of the "taxed capital gains" of a taxpayer for a taxation year is the amount, if any, by which

(i) its taxable capital gains for the year from dispositions of property

exceeds

(ii) the total of its allowable capital losses for the year from dispositions of property and the amount, if any, deducted under paragraph 111(1)(*b*) for the purpose of computing its taxable income for the year.

History: S. 130(3)(*a*)(vii), as enacted by S.C. 1998, c. 19, s. 155(2) and S.C. 1999, c. 22, s. 92(1), was amended by S.C. 2013, c. 34, s. 371(1), by adding clause (B.1), deemed in force June 18, 1998. S. 130(3)(*a*)(vii)(B.1) was repealed by 2013, c. 34, s. 371(3), applicable to taxation years that begin after October 31, 2011. S. 130(3)(*a*)(vii)(B.1) formerly read:

(B.1) paragraph (*b*) of that definition were read as follows:

"(*b*) each beneficiary of a trust (except a beneficiary of a trust governed by a registered education savings plan who has not attained 19 years of age) is deemed to own that proportion of all such shares owned by the trust at that time that the fair market value at that time of the beneficial interest of the beneficiary in the trust is of the fair market value at that time of all beneficial interests in the trust,"

S. 130(3)(*a*)(vii), as enacted by S.C. 1998, c. 19, s. 155(2) and S.C. 1999, c. 22, s. 92(1), was amended by S.C. 2013, c. 34, s. 371(2), by adding clause (C.1), deemed in force June 18, 1998. S. 130(3)(*a*)(vii)(C.1) was repealed by 2013, c. 34, s. 371(4), applicable to taxation years that begin after October 31, 2011. S. 130(3)(*a*)(vii)(C.1) formerly read:

(C.1) paragraph (*e*) of that definition were read as follows:

"(*e*) notwithstanding paragraph (*b*), where a beneficiary's share of the income or capital of the trust depends on the exercise by any person of, or the failure by any person to exercise, any discretionary power, the beneficiary (except a beneficiary of a trust governed by a registered education savings plan who has not attained 19 years of age) is deemed to own each share of the capital stock of a corporation owned at that time by the trust;"

Related Sections: S. 4(1) Income or loss from a source or from sources in a place; s. 38 Taxable capital gain and allowable capital loss; s. 39, "capital gain"; s. 89(1), "Canadian corporation", "public corporation", "taxable dividends"; s. 131(1) Election re capital gains dividend; s. 131(3) Application to other liability; s. 131(4) Application of s. 84; s. 131(6) Definitions relating to mutual fund corporations; s. 131(8) Meaning of "mutual fund corporation"; s. 131(10) Restricted financial institution; s. 132(5) Definition of "taxed capital gains"; s. 184(2) Tax on excessive elections; s. 248(1), "gross revenue", "property", "province", "share"; s. 255 Canada.

▶ 130(4) ◀

(4) Wholly owned subsidiaries. Where a corporation so elects in its return of income under this Part for a taxation year, each of the corporation's properties that is a share or indebtedness of another Canadian corporation that is at any time in the year a subsidiary wholly owned corporation of the corporation shall, for the purposes of subparagraphs (3)(*a*)(ii) and (vi), be deemed not to be owned by the corporation at any such time in the year, and each property owned by the other corporation at that time shall, for the purposes of those subparagraphs, be deemed to be owned by the corporation at that time.

Mortgage Investment Corporations

SECTION 130.1: [Mortgage investment corporations]

▶ 130.1(1) ◀

(1) Deduction from tax. In computing the income for a taxation year of a corporation that was, throughout the year, a mortgage investment corporation,

(*a*) there may be deducted the total of

(i) all taxable dividends, other than capital gains dividends, paid by the corporation during the year or within 90 days after the end of the year to the extent that those dividends were not deductible by the corporation in computing its income for the preceding year, and

(ii) $^1/_2$ of all capital gains dividends paid by the corporation during the period commencing 91 days after the commencement of the year and ending 90 days after the end of the year; and

(*b*) no deduction may be made under section 112 in respect of taxable dividends received by it from other corporations.

▶ 130.1(2) ◀

(2) Dividend equated to bond interest. For the purposes of this Act, any amount received from a mortgage investment corporation by a shareholder of the corporation as or on account of a taxable dividend, other than a capital gains dividend, shall be deemed to have been received by the shareholder as interest payable on a bond issued by the corporation after 1971.

Related Sections: S. 214(3) Deemed payments.

▶ 130.1(3) ◀

(3) Application of s. (2). Subsection (2) applies where the taxable dividend (other than a capital gains dividend) described in that subsection was paid during a taxation year throughout which the paying corporation was a mortgage investment corporation or within 90 days thereafter.

► 130.1(4) ◄

(4) Election re capital gains dividend. Where at any particular time during the period that begins 91 days after the beginning of a taxation year of a corporation that was, throughout the year, a mortgage investment corporation and ends 90 days after the end of the year, a dividend is paid by the corporation to shareholders of the corporation, if the corporation so elects in respect of the full amount of the dividend in prescribed manner and at or before the earlier of the particular time and the first day on which any part of the dividend was paid,

(*a*) the dividend shall be deemed to be a capital gains dividend to the extent that it does not exceed the amount, if any, by which

(i) twice the taxed capital gains of the corporation for the year

exceeds

(ii) the total of all dividends, and parts of dividends, paid by the corporation during the period and before the particular time that are deemed by this paragraph to be capital gains dividends; and

(*b*) notwithstanding any other provision of this Act, if an amount is received by a taxpayer in a taxation year as, on account of, in lieu of payment of or in satisfaction of, the dividend, the amount

(i) shall not be included in computing the taxpayer's income for the year as income from a share of the capital stock of the corporation, and

(ii) is deemed to be a capital gain of the taxpayer from the disposition of capital property in the year.

History: S. 130.1(4)(*b*) was replaced by S.C. 2013, c. 34, s. 276(1), applicable to taxation years that begin after October 31, 2011, except that if any part of a dividend declared by a corporation is in respect of capital gains of the corporation from dispositions of property that occurred before October 18, 2000, then paragraph 130.1(4)(*b*) is to be read, in its application to that part of the dividend, as it read in its application to the corporation's last taxation year that began before November 1, 2011.

S. 130.1(4)(*b*) formerly read:

(*b*) notwithstanding any other provision of this Act, any amount received by a taxpayer in a taxation year as, on account of, in lieu of payment of or in satisfaction of, the dividend shall not be included in computing the taxpayer's income for the year as income from a share of the capital stock of the corporation, and

(i) where the dividend was in respect of capital gains of the corporation from dispositions of property that occurred before February 28, 2000 and the taxation year of the taxpayer began after February 27, 2000 and ended before October 18, 2000, 9/8 of the dividend is deemed to be a capital gain of the taxpayer from the disposition by the taxpayer of a capital property in the year,

(ii) where the dividend was in respect of capital gains of the corporation from dispositions of property that occurred before February 28, 2000, and the taxation year of the taxpayer includes February 27, 2000, the dividend is deemed to be a capital gain of the taxpayer from the disposition by the taxpayer of a capital property in the year and before February 28, 2000,

(iii) where the dividend was in respect of capital gains of the corporation from dispositions of property that occurred before February 28, 2000 and the taxation year of the taxpayer began after October 17, 2000, 3/2 of the dividend is deemed to be a capital gain of the taxpayer from the disposition by the taxpayer of a capital property in the year,

(iii.1) where the dividend was in respect of capital gains of the corporation from dispositions of property that occurred before February 28, 2000 and the taxation year of the taxpayer begins after February 27, 2000 and ends after October 17, 2000, 9/8 of the dividend is deemed to be a capital gain of the taxpayer from the disposition by the taxpayer of capital property in the year and before October 18, 2000,

(iv) where the dividend was in respect of capital gains of the corporation from dispositions of property that occurred after February 27, 2000 and before October 18, 2000, and the taxation year of the taxpayer began after October 17, 2000, 4/3 of the dividend is deemed to be a capital gain of the taxpayer from the disposition by the taxpayer of a capital property in the year,

(v) where the dividend was in respect of capital gains of the corporation from dispositions of property that occurred after February 27, 2000, and before October 18, 2000 and the taxation year of the taxpayer includes October 17, 2000, the dividend is deemed to be a capital gain of the taxpayer from the disposition by the taxpayer of a capital property in the year and in the period that began after February 27, 2000 and ended before October 18, 2000,

(vi) where the dividend was in respect of capital gains of the corporation from dispositions of property that occurred after February 27, 2000, and before October 17, 2000 and the taxation year of the taxpayer began after February 27, 2000 and ended before October 17, 2000, the dividend is deemed to be a capital gain of the taxpayer from the disposition by the taxpayer of a capital property in the year, and

(vii) in any other case, the dividend is deemed to be a capital gain of the taxpayer from the disposition of capital property after October 17, 2000 and in the year.

Related Regulations: 2104.1.

Related Sections: S. 184(2) Tax on excessive elections; s. 185(1) Assessment of tax; s. 212(2).

Forms: T5 Sum. — T5SUM Return of Investment Income; T5 — Statement of Investment Income; T2012 — Election in Respect of a Capital Gains Dividend Under Subsection 130.1(4).

► 130.1(4.1) ◄

(4.1) Application of ss. 131(1.1) to (1.4). Where at any particular time a mortgage investment corporation paid a dividend to its shareholders and subsection (4) would have applied to the dividend except that the corporation did not make an election under that subsection on or before the day on or before which it was required by that subsection to be made, subsections 131(1.1) to (1.4) apply with such modifications as the circumstances require.

► 130.1(4.2) ◄

(4.2) Reporting — (Repealed by S.C. 2013, c. 34, s. 276(2).)

History: S. 130.1(4.2) was repealed by S.C. 2013, c. 34, s. 276(2), applicable to taxation years that begin after October 31, 2011, and formerly read:

(4.2) *Reporting.* Where paragraph (4)(*b*) applies to a dividend paid by a mortgage investment corporation to a shareholder of any class of shares of its capital stock in the period that begins 91 days after the beginning of the corporation's taxation year that includes February 28, 2000 or October 17, 2000 and ends 90 days after the end of that year, the corporation shall disclose to the shareholder in prescribed form the amount of the dividend that is in respect of capital gains realized on dispositions of property that occurred

(*a*) before February 28, 2000,

(*b*) after February 27, 2000 and before October 18, 2000, and

(*c*) after October 17, 2000

and, if it does not do so, the dividend is deemed to be in respect of capital gains from dispositions of property that occurred before February 28, 2000.

► 130.1(4.3) ◄

(4.3) Allocation — (Repealed by S.C. 2013, c. 34, s. 276(2).)

History: S. 130.1(4.3) was repealed by S.C. 2013, c. 34, s. 276(2), applicable to taxation years that begin after October 31, 2011, and formerly read:

(4.3) *Allocation.* Where subsection (4) applies in respect of a dividend paid by a mortgage investment corporation at any time in the period that begins 91 days after the beginning of the corporation's taxation year that includes February 28, 2000 or October 17, 2000 and ends 90 days after the end of that year, and the corporation does not elect under subsection (4.4), the following rules apply:

(*a*) the portion of the dividend that is in respect of capital gains from dispositions of property that occurred in the year and in the particular period that began at the beginning of the year and ended at the end of February 27, 2000 is deemed to be that proportion of the dividend that the net capital gains of the corporation from the dispositions of property in the particular period is of the total of the corporation's net capital gains from the dispositions of property in each of the particular periods referred to in this subsection,

(*b*) the portion of the dividend that is in respect of capital gains from dispositions of property that occurred in the year and in the particular period that began at the beginning of February 28, 2000 and ended at the end of October 17, 2000 is deemed to be that proportion of the dividend that the net capital gains of the corporation from the dispositions of property in the particular period is of the total of the corporation's net capital gains from the dispositions of property in each of the particular periods referred to in this subsection,

(*c*) the portion of the dividend that is in respect of capital gains from dispositions of property that occurred in the year and in the particular period that begins at the beginning of October 18, 2000 and ends at the end of the year, is deemed to be that proportion of the dividend that the net capital gains of the corporation from the dispositions of property in the particular period is of the total of the corporation's net capital gains from the dispositions of property in each of the periods referred to in this subsection, and

in this subsection net capital gains from dispositions of property in a particular period means the amount, if any, by which the corporation's capital gains from dispositions of property in the particular period exceeds the corporation's capital losses from dispositions of property in the particular period.

► 130.1(4.4) ◄

(4.4) Allocation — (Repealed by S.C. 2013, c. 34, s. 276(2).)

History: S. 130.1(4.4) was repealed by S.C. 2013, c. 34, s. 276(2), applicable to taxation years that begin after October 31, 2011, and formerly read:

(4.4) *Allocation.* Where subsection (4) applies in respect of a dividend paid by a mortgage investment corporation in the period that begins 91 days after the beginning of the corporation's taxation year that includes February 28, 2000 or October 17, 2000 and ends 90 days after the end of that year, and the corporation so elects under this subsection in its return of income for the year, the following rules apply:

(*a*) the portion of the dividend that is in respect of capital gains from dispositions of property that occurred in the year and before February 28, 2000 is deemed to be that proportion of the dividend that the number of days that are in that year and before February 28, 2000 is of the number of days that are in that year;

(*b*) the portion of the dividend that is in respect of capital gains from dispositions of property that occurred in the year and in the period that began at the beginning of February 28, 2000 and ended at the end of October 17, 2000 is deemed to be that proportion of the dividend that the number of days that are in the year and in that period is of the number of days that are in the year; and

(*c*) the portion of the dividend that is in respect of capital gains from dispositions of property that occurred in the year and in the period that begins at the beginning of October 18, 2000 and ends at the end of the year, is deemed to be that proportion of the dividend that the number of days that are in the year and in that period is of the number of days that are in the year.

► 130.1(4.5) ◄

(4.5) Allocation — (Repealed by S.C. 2013, c. 34, s. 276(2).)

History: S. 130.1(4.5) was repealed by S.C. 2013, c. 34, s. 276(2), applicable to taxation years that begin after October 31, 2011, and formerly read:

(4.5) *Allocation.* Where no dividend to which subsection (4.4) applies is paid by a mortgage investment corporation in respect of its net taxable capital gains for its taxation year that includes February 28, 2000 or October 17, 2000, the corporation has net capital gains or net capital losses from dispositions of property in the year, and the corporation so elects under this subsection in its return of income for the year

(*a*) the portion of those net capital gains and net capital losses that is in respect of capital gains and losses from dispositions of property that occurred before February 28, 2000 is deemed to be that proportion of the net capital gains or net capital losses respectively that the number of days that are in the year and before February 28, 2000 is of the number of days that are in the year,

(*b*) the portion of those net capital gains and net capital losses that is in respect of capital gains and losses from dispositions of property that occurred in the year and in the period that began at the beginning of February 28, 2000 and ended at the end of October 17, 2000, is deemed to be that proportion of the net capital gains or net capital losses respectively that the number of days that are in the year and in that period is of the number of days that are in the year, and

(*c*) the portion of those net capital gains and net capital losses that is in respect of capital gains and losses from dispositions of property that occurred in the year and in the period that began at the beginning of October 18, 2000 and ended at the end of the year, is deemed to be that proportion of the net capital gains or net capital losses respectively that the number of days that are in the year and in that period is of the number of days that are in the year,

and, for the purpose of this subsection,

(*d*) the net capital gains of a mortgage investment corporation from dispositions of property in a year is the amount, if any, by which the corporation's capital gains from dispositions of property in a year exceeds the corporation's capital losses from dispositions of property in the year, and

(*e*) the net capital losses of a mortgage investment corporation from dispositions of property in a year is the amount, if any, by which the corporation's capital losses from dispositions of property in a year exceeds the corporation's capital gains from dispositions of property in the year.

► 130.1(5) ◄

(5) Public corporation. Notwithstanding any other provision of this Act, a mortgage investment corporation shall be deemed to be a public corporation.

► 130.1(6) ◄

(6) Meaning of "mortgage investment corporation". For the purposes of this section, a corporation is a "mortgage investment corporation" throughout a taxation year if, throughout the year,

(*a*) it was a Canadian corporation;

(*b*) its only undertaking was the investing of funds of the corporation and it did not manage or develop any real or immovable property;

(*c*) none of the property of the corporation consisted of

(i) debts owing to the corporation that were secured on real or immovable property situated outside Canada,

(ii) debts owing to the corporation by non-resident persons, except any such debts that were secured on real or immovable property situated in Canada,

(iii) shares of the capital stock of corporations not resident in Canada, or

(iv) real or immovable property situated outside Canada, or any leasehold interest in such property;

(*d*) there were 20 or more shareholders of the corporation and no person would have been a specified shareholder of the corporation at any time in the year if

(i) the portion of the definition "specified shareholder" in subsection 248(1) before paragraph (*a*) were read as follows:

"'specified shareholder' of a corporation at any time means a taxpayer who owns, directly or indirectly, at that time, more than 25% of the issued shares of any class of the capital stock of the corporation and, for the purposes of this definition,"

(ii) paragraph (*a*) of that definition were read as follows:

"(*a*) a taxpayer is deemed to own each share of the capital stock of a corporation owned at that time by a person related to the taxpayer,"

(iii) that definition were read without reference to paragraph (*d*) of that definition, and

(iv) paragraph 251(2)(*a*) were read as follows:

"(*a*) an individual and

(i) the individual's child (as defined in subsection 70(10)) who is under 18 years of age, or

(ii) the individual's spouse or common-law partner;"

(*e*) any holders of preferred shares of the corporation had a right, after payment to them of their preferred dividends, and payment of dividends in a like amount per share to the holders of the common shares of the corporation, to participate *pari passu* with the holders of the common shares in any further payment of dividends;

(*f*) the cost amount to the corporation of such of its property as consisted of

(i) debts owing to the corporation that were secured, whether by mortgages, hypothecs or in any other manner, on houses (as defined in section 2 of the *National Housing Act*) or on property included within a housing project (as defined in that section as it read on June 16, 1999), and

(ii) amounts of any deposits standing to the corporation's credit in the records of

(A) a bank or other corporation any of whose deposits are insured by the Canada Deposit Insurance Corporation or the *Régie de l'assurance-dépôts du Québec*, or

(B) a credit union,

plus the amount of any money of the corporation was at least 50% of the cost amount to it of all its property;

(*g*) the cost amount to the corporation of all real or immovable property of the corporation, including leasehold interests in such property (except real or immovable property acquired by the corporation by foreclosure or otherwise after default made on a mortgage, hypothec or agreement of sale of real or immovable property) did not exceed 25% of the cost amount to it of all its property;

(*h*) its liabilities did not exceed 3 times the amount by which the cost amount to it of all its property exceeded its liabilities, where at any time in the year the cost amount to it of such of its property as consisted of property described in subparagraphs (*f*)(i) and (ii) plus the amount of any money of the corporation was less than ⅔ of the cost amount to it of all of its property; and

(*i*) its liabilities did not exceed 5 times the amount by which the cost amount to it of all its property exceeded its liabilities, where paragraph (*h*) is not applicable.

History: S. 130.1(6)(*f*)(i) was replaced by S.C. 2013, c. 34, s. 276(3), applicable to property acquired by a corporation after October 31, 2011, unless

(*a*) the property is a particular debt

(i) that is owing to the corporation and secured on property (referred to in this paragraph as the "subject property"),

(ii) that replaces a debt (referred to in this paragraph as the "old debt") that was on October 31, 2011 owing to the corporation and secured on the subject property, and

(iii) that has a maximum term for repayment that does not exceed the maximum term for repayment, in effect on October 31, 2011, of the old debt; and

(*b*) the corporation would be a mortgage investment corporation for its taxation year that includes October 31, 2011 if that taxation year were determined as though it ended on October 31, 2011.

If property that is held by a corporation on October 31, 2011 consists of debt, the term for repayment of the debt is extended by agreement entered into on a particular date that is after October 31, 2011, and the extended term exceeds the maximum term for repayment of the debt in effect on October 31, 2011, then the property is deemed to have been acquired by the corporation on the particular date.

S. 130.1(6)(*f*)(i) formerly read:

(i) debts owing to the corporation that were secured, whether by mortgages, hypothecs or in any other manner, on houses (as defined in section 2 of the *National Housing Act*) or on property included within a housing project (as defined in that section), and

S. 130.1(6)(*b*) and (*c*) were replaced by S.C. 2013, c. 34, s. 131(1), in force June 26, 2013, and formerly read:

(*b*) its only undertaking was the investing of funds of the corporation and it did not manage or develop any real property;

(*c*) none of the property of the corporation consisted of

(i) debts owing to the corporation that were secured on real property situated outside Canada,

(ii) debts owing to the corporation by non-resident persons, except any such debts that were secured on real property situated in Canada,

(iii) shares of the capital stock of corporations not resident in Canada, or

(iv) real property situated outside Canada, or any leasehold interest in such property;

S. 130.1(6)(*g*) was replaced by S.C. 2013, c. 34, s. 131(2), in force June 26, 2013, and formerly read:

(*g*) the cost amount to the corporation of all real property of the corporation, including leasehold interests in such property, (except real property acquired by the corporation by foreclosure or otherwise after default made on a mortgage, hypothec or agreement of sale of real property) did not exceed 25% of the cost amount to it of all its property;

Related Sections: S. 253.1 Investments in limited partnerships.

Tax Window Files: Mortgage Investment Corporation Definition, *January 12, 2018*, CRA Document No. 2016-0669431E5; Establishment of a MIC, *October 26, 2015*, CRA Document No. 2015-0599021E5.

▶ 130.1(7) ◀

(7) How shareholders counted. In paragraph (6)(*d*), a trust governed by a registered pension plan or deferred profit sharing plan by which shares of the capital stock of a corporation are held shall be counted as four shareholders of the corporation for the purpose of determining the number of shareholders of the corporation, but as one shareholder for the purpose of determining whether any person is a specified shareholder (as defined for the purpose of that paragraph).

▶ 130.1(8) ◀

(8) First taxation year. For the purposes of subsection (6), a corporation that was incorporated after 1971 shall be deemed to have complied with paragraph (6)(*d*) throughout the first taxation year of the corporation in which it carried on business if it complied with that paragraph on the last day of that taxation year.

▶ 130.1(9) ◀

(9) Definitions. In this section,

"liabilities" —"liabilities" of a corporation at any particular time means the total of all debts owing by the corporation, and all other obligations of the corporation to pay an amount, that were outstanding at that time;

"non-qualifying real property" — (Repealed by S.C. 1995, c. 3, s. 40(2).)

"non-qualifying taxed capital gains" — (Repealed by S.C. 1995, c. 3, s. 40(2).)

"qualifying taxed capital gains" — (Repealed by S.C. 1995, c. 3, s. 40(2).)

"taxed capital gains" —"taxed capital gains" has the meaning assigned by paragraph 130(3)(*b*).

Mutual Fund Corporations

SECTION 131: [Mutual fund corporations]

▶ 131(1) ◀

(1) Election re capital gains dividend. Where at any particular time a dividend became payable by a corporation, that was throughout the taxation year in which the dividend became payable a mutual fund corporation, to shareholders of any class of its capital stock, if the corporation so elects in respect of the full amount of the dividend in prescribed manner and at or before the earlier of the particular time and the first day on which any part of the dividend was paid,

(*a*) the dividend shall be deemed to be a capital gains dividend payable out of the corporation's capital gains dividend account to the extent that it does not exceed the corporation's capital gains dividend account at the particular time; and

(*b*) notwithstanding any other provision of this Act (other than paragraph (5.1)(*b*)), if an amount is received by a taxpayer in a taxation year as, on account of, in lieu of payment of or in satisfaction of, the dividend, the amount

(i) shall not be included in computing the taxpayer's income for the year as income from a share of the capital stock of the corporation, and

(ii) is deemed to be a capital gain of the taxpayer from the disposition of capital property in the year.

History: S. 131(1)(*b*) was replaced by S.C. 2013, c. 34, s. 277(1), applicable to taxation years that begin after October 31, 2011, except that, if any part of a dividend declared by a corporation is in respect of capital gains of the corporation from dispositions of property that occurred before October 18, 2000, then paragraph 131(1)(*b*) is to be read, in its application to that part of the dividend, as it read in its application to the corporation's last taxation year that began before November 1, 2011.

S. 131(1)(*b*) formerly read:

(*b*) notwithstanding any other provision of this Act (other than paragraph (5.1)(*b*)), any amount received by a taxpayer in a taxation year as, on account of, in lieu of payment of or in satisfaction of, the dividend shall not be included in computing the taxpayer's income for the year as income from a share of the capital stock of the corporation, and

(i) where the dividend was in respect of capital gains of the corporation from dispositions of property that occurred before February 28, 2000, and the taxation year of the taxpayer began after February 27, 2000 and ended before October 18, 2000, $^{9}/_{8}$ of the dividend is deemed to be a capital gain of the taxpayer from the disposition by the taxpayer of a capital property in the year,

(ii) where the dividend was in respect of capital gains of the corporation from dispositions of property that occurred before February 28, 2000, and the taxation year of the taxpayer includes February 27, 2000, the dividend is deemed to be a capital gain of the taxpayer from the disposition by the taxpayer of a capital property in the year and before February 28, 2000,

(iii) where the dividend was in respect of capital gains of the corporation from dispositions of property that occurred before February 28, 2000, and the taxation year of the taxpayer began after October 17, 2000, $^{3}/_{2}$ of the dividend is deemed to be a capital gain of the taxpayer from the disposition by the taxpayer of a capital property in the year,

(iii.1) where the dividend was in respect of capital gains of the corporation from dispositions of property that occurred before February 28, 2000 and the taxation year of the taxpayer begins after February 27, 2000 and ends after October 17, 2000, $^{9}/_{8}$ of the dividend is deemed to be a capital gain of the taxpayer from the disposition by the taxpayer of capital property in the year and before October 18, 2000,

(iv) where the dividend was in respect of capital gains of the corporation from dispositions of property that occurred after February 27, 2000 and before October 18, 2000, and the taxation year of the taxpayer began after October 17, 2000, $^{4}/_{3}$ of the dividend is deemed to be a capital gain of the taxpayer from the disposition by the taxpayer of a capital property in the year,

(v) where the dividend was in respect of capital gains of the corporation from dispositions of property that occurred after February 27, 2000 and before October 18, 2000, and the taxation year of the taxpayer includes October 17, 2000, the dividend is deemed to be a capital gain of the taxpayer from the disposition by the taxpayer of a capital property in the year and in the period that began after February 27, 2000 and ended before October 18, 2000,

(vi) where the dividend was in respect of capital gains of the corporation from dispositions of property that occurred after February 27, 2000, and before October 17, 2000 and the taxation year of the taxpayer began after February 27, 2000 and ended before October 18, 2000, the dividend is deemed to be a capital gain of the taxpayer from the disposition by the taxpayer of a capital property in the year, and

(vii) in any other case, the dividend is deemed to be a capital gain of the taxpayer from the disposition of capital property after October 17, 2000 and in the year,

and, for the purpose of this paragraph,

(viii) dividends paid by a corporation are deemed to be paid in respect of the corporation's net capital gains in the order in which those net capital gains were realized by the corporation,

(viii.1) capital gains redemptions are deemed to be made in respect of net capital gains in the order in which those net capital gains were realized by the corporation to the extent that they are not reduced by dividends, and

(ix) for the purposes of applying subparagraphs (viii) and (viii.1)

(A) net capital gains of a corporation for a year is the amount by which the corporation's capital gains from dispositions of property in the year exceed the corporation's capital losses from dispositions of property in the year,

(B) net capital losses of a corporation for a year is the amount by which the corporation's capital losses from dispositions of property in the year exceed the corporation's capital gains from dispositions of property in the year,

(C) net capital gains of a corporation for a year are deemed to be realized evenly throughout the year, and

(D) net capital losses of a corporation for a year are deemed to be a capital loss of the corporation from the disposition of property in the following year.

Related Regulations: Part XXI; 2104.

Related Sections: S. 39, "capital gain", "capital loss"; s. 112(6) Meaning of certain expressions; s. 129(7) Meaning of "taxable dividend"; s. 130(2) Application of ss. 131(1) to (3.2) and (6); s. 130(3) Meaning of expressions "investment corporation" and "taxed capital gains"; s. 131(1.1) Deemed date of election; s. 131(4) Application of s. 84; s. 131(6) Definitions relating to mutual fund corporations; s. 184(2) Tax on excessive elections; s. 185(1) Assessment of tax; s. 185(2) Payment of tax and interest; s. 212(2) Tax on dividends; s. 248(1), "dividend", "prescribed".

Forms: T5 Sum. — T5SUM Return of Investment Income; T5 — Statement of Investment Income; T2055 — Election in Respect of a Capital Gains Dividend Under Subsection 131(1).

► 131(1.1) ◄

(1.1) Deemed date of election. Where at any particular time a dividend has become payable by a mutual fund corporation to shareholders of any class of shares of its capital stock and subsection (1) would have applied to the dividend except that the election referred to in that subsection was not made on or before the day on or before which the election was required by that subsection to be made, the election shall be deemed to have been made at the particular time or on the first day on which any part of the dividend was paid, whichever is the earlier, if

(*a*) the election is thereafter made in prescribed manner and prescribed form;

(*b*) an estimate of the penalty in respect of the election is paid by the corporation when the election is made; and

(*c*) the directors or other person or persons legally entitled to administer the affairs of the corporation have, before the time the election is made, authorized the election to be made.

Related Sections: 131(1.2) Request to make election; 131(1.3) Penalty; 131(1.4) Assessment and payment of penalty.

► 131(1.2) ◄

(1.2) Request to make election. The Minister may at any time, by written request served personally or by registered mail, request that an election referred to in paragraph (1.1)(*a*) be made by a mutual fund corporation and where the mutual fund corporation on which such a request is served does not comply therewith within 90 days after service of the request, subsection (1.1) does not apply to such an election made thereafter by it.

► 131(1.3) ◄

(1.3) Penalty. For the purposes of this section, the penalty in respect of an election referred to in paragraph (1.1)(*b*) is an amount equal to the lesser of

(*a*) 1% per annum of the amount of the dividend referred to in the election for each month or part of a month during the period commencing with the time that the dividend became payable, or the first day on which any part of the dividend was paid if that day is earlier, and ending with the day on which the election was made, and

(*b*) the product obtained when $500 is multiplied by the proportion that the number of months or parts of months during the period referred to in paragraph (*a*) bears to 12.

► 131(1.4) ◄

(1.4) Assessment and payment of penalty. The Minister shall, with all due dispatch, examine each election referred to in paragraph (1.1)(*a*), assess the penalty payable and send a notice of assessment to the mutual fund corporation and the corporation shall pay forthwith to the Receiver General, the amount, if any, by which the penalty so assessed exceeds the total of all amounts previously paid on account of that penalty.

► 131(1.5) ◄

(1.5) Reporting — (Repealed by S.C. 2013, c. 34, s. 277(2).)

History: S. 131(1.5) was repealed by S.C. 2013, c. 34, s. 277(2), applicable to taxation years that begin after October 31, 2011, and formerly read:

(1.5) *Reporting.* Where paragraph (1)(*b*) applies to a dividend paid by a mutual fund corporation to a shareholder of any class of shares of its capital stock, the corporation shall disclose to the shareholder in prescribed form the amount of the dividend that is in respect of capital gains realized on dispositions of property that occurred

(*a*) before February 28, 2000,

(*b*) after February 27, 2000 and before October 18, 2000, and

(*c*) after October 17, 2000,

and if it does not do so, the dividend is deemed to be in respect of capital gains from dispositions of property that occurred before February 28, 2000.

► 131(1.6) ◄

(1.6) Allocation — (Repealed by S.C. 2013, c. 34, s. 277(2).)

History: S. 131(1.6) was repealed by S.C. 2013, c. 34, s. 277(2), applicable to taxation years that begin after October 31, 2011, and formerly read:

(1.6) *Allocation.* Where subsection (1) applies in respect of a dividend paid by a mutual fund corporation in the period that begins 60 days after the beginning of the corporation's taxation year that includes February 28, 2000 or October 17, 2000 and ends 60 days after the end of that year, and the corporation does not elect under subsection (1.7), the following rules apply:

(*a*) the portion of the dividend that is in respect of capital gains of the mutual fund corporation from dispositions of property by the mutual fund corporation in the year and in the particular period that began at the beginning of the year and ended at the end of February 27, 2000 is deemed to be that proportion of the dividend that the corporation's net capital gains from dispositions of property in the particular period to which the dividend relates is of the total of the corporation's net capital gains from dispositions of property in each of the particular periods referred to in this subsection,

(*b*) the portion of the dividend that is in respect of capital gains of the mutual fund corporation from dispositions of property by the mutual fund corporation in the year and in the particular period that began at the beginning of February 28, 2000 and ended at the end of October 17, 2000 is deemed to be that proportion of the dividend that the corporation's net capital gains from dispositions of property in the particular period is of the total of the corporation's net capital gains from dispositions of property in each of the particular periods referred to in this subsection, and

(*c*) the portion of the dividend that is in respect of capital gains of the mutual fund corporation from dispositions of property by the mutual fund corporation in the year and in the particular period that begins at the beginning of October 18, 2000 and ends at the end of the year, is deemed to be that proportion of the dividend that the corporation's net capital gains from dispositions of property in the particular period is of the total of the corporation's net capital gains from dispositions of property in each of the particular periods referred to in this subsection,

and, in this subsection and in subsection (1.8), net capital gains from dispositions of property in a particular period means the amount, if any, by which the corporation's capital gains from dispositions of property in the particular period exceeds the corporation's capital losses from dispositions of property in the particular period.

► 131(1.7) ◄

(1.7) Allocation — (Repealed by S.C. 2013, c. 34, s. 277(2).)

History: S. 131(1.7) was repealed by S.C. 2013, c. 34, s. 277(2), applicable to taxation years that begin after October 31, 2011, and formerly read:

(1.7) *Allocation.* Where subsection (1) applies in respect of a dividend paid by a mutual fund corporation in the period that begins 60 days after the beginning of the corporation's taxation year that includes February 28, 2000 or October 17, 2000 and ends 60 days after the end of that year, and the corporation so elects under this paragraph in its return of income

(*a*) the portion of the dividend that is in respect of capital gains from dispositions of property that occurred in the year and before February 28, 2000 is deemed to be that proportion of the dividend that the number of days that are in that year and before February 28, 2000 is of the number of days that are in that year;

(*b*) the portion of the dividend that is in respect of capital gains from dispositions of property that occurred in the year and in the period that began at the beginning of February 28, 2000 and ended at the end of October 17, 2000 is deemed to be that proportion of the dividend that the number of days that are in the year and in that period is of the number of days that are in the year; and

(*c*) the portion of the dividend that is in respect of capital gains from dispositions of property that occurred in the year and in the period that begins at the beginning of October 18, 2000 and ends at the end of the year, is deemed to be that proportion of the dividend that the number of days that are in the year and in that period is of the number of days that are in the year.

► 131(1.8) ◄

(1.8) Allocation — (Repealed by S.C. 2013, c. 34, s. 277(2).)

History: S. 131(1.8) was repealed by S.C. 2013, c. 34, s. 277(2), applicable to taxation years that begin after October 31, 2011, and formerly read:

(1.8) *Allocation.* For the purposes of subsection (1.6) and (1.7), where the total amount of dividends paid by a mutual fund corporation in the period that begins 60 days after the beginning of the corporation's taxation year that includes February 28, 2000 or October 17, 2000 and ends 60 days after the end of that year and to which subsection (1) applies exceeds the total amount of the corporation's net capital gains from dispositions of property in that year

(*a*) the amount of those dividends to which subsections (1.6) and (1.7) apply is the amount of the corporation's net capital gains from dispositions of property in that year, and

(*b*) the amount, if any, by which total amount of the dividends paid by the corporation in the period exceeds the total amount of the corporation's net capital gains from dispositions of property in that year is deemed to be a dividend in respect of capital gains from dispositions of property in the first of the periods described in subsection (1.6) that ends in the year.

► 131(1.9) ◄

(1.9) Allocation — (Repealed by S.C. 2013, c. 34, s. 277(2).)

History: S. 131(1.9) was repealed by S.C. 2013, c. 34, s. 277(2), applicable to taxation years that begin after October 31, 2011, and formerly read:

(1.9) *Allocation.* Where no dividend to which subsection (1.7) applies is paid by a mutual fund corporation in respect of its net taxable capital gains for its taxation year that includes February 28, 2000 or October 17, 2000, the corporation has net capital gains or net capital losses from dispositions of property in the year, and the corporation so elects under this subsection in its return of income for the year

(*a*) the portion of those net capital gains and net capital losses that is in respect of capital gains and losses from dispositions of property that occurred before February 28, 2000 is deemed to be that proportion of the net capital gains or net capital losses respectively that the number of days that are in the year and before February 28, 2000 is of the number of days that are in the year,

(*b*) the portion of those net capital gains and net capital losses that is in respect of capital gains and losses from dispositions of property that occurred in the year and in the period that began at the beginning of February 28, 2000 and ended at the end of October 17, 2000, is deemed to be that proportion of the net capital gains or net capital losses respectively that the number of days that are in the year and in that period is of the number of days that are in the year, and

(*c*) the portion of those net capital gains and net capital losses that is in respect of capital gains and losses from dispositions of property that occurred in the year and in the period that began at the beginning of October 18, 2000 and ended at the end of the year, is deemed to be that proportion of the net capital gains or net capital losses respectively that the number of days that are in the year and in that period is of the number of days that are in the year,

and, for the purpose of this subsection,

(*d*) the net capital gains of a mutual fund corporation from dispositions of property in the year is the amount, if any, by which the corporation's capital gains from dispositions of property in a year exceeds the corporation's capital losses from dispositions of property in the year, and

(*e*) the net capital losses of a mutual fund corporation from dispositions of property in the year is the amount, if any, by which the corporation's capital losses from dispositions of property in a year exceeds the corporation's capital gains from dispositions of property in the year.

► 131(2) ◄

(2) Capital gains refund to mutual fund corporation. Where a corporation was, throughout a taxation year, a mutual fund corporation and a return of its income for the year has been made within 3 years from the end of the year, the Minister

(*a*) may, on sending the notice of assessment for the year, refund an amount (in this subsection referred to as its "capital gains refund" for the year) equal to the lesser of

(i) the total of

(A) 14% of the total of

(I) all capital gains dividends paid by the corporation in the period commencing 60 days after the beginning of the year and ending 60 days after the end of the year, and

(II) its capital gains redemptions for the year, and

(B) the amount, if any, that the Minister determines to be reasonable in the circumstances, after giving consideration to the percentages applicable in determining the corporation's capital gains refund for the year and preceding taxation years and the percentages applicable in determining the corporation's refundable capital gains tax on hand at the end of the year, and

(ii) the corporation's refundable capital gains tax on hand at the end of the year; and

(*b*) shall, with all due dispatch, make that capital gains refund after sending the notice of assessment if an application for it has been made in writing by the corporation within the period within which the Minister would be allowed under subsection 152(4) to assess tax payable under this Part by the corporation for the year if that subsection were read without reference to paragraph 152(4)(*a*).

History: S. 131(2)(*b*) was replaced by S.C. 2010, c. 25, s. 30, in force on Royal Assent, December 15, 2010. S. 131(2)(*b*) formerly read:

(*b*) shall, with all due dispatch, make that capital gains refund after mailing the notice of assessment if an application for it has been made in writing by the corporation within the period within which the Minister would be allowed under subsection 152(4) to assess tax payable under this Part by the corporation for the year if that subsection were read without reference to paragraph 152(4)(*a*).

Related Sections: S. 130(2) Application of ss. 131(1) to (3.2) and (6); s. 131(3) Application to other liability; s. 157(3) Reduced instalments.

Forms: T2 SCH 18 — Federal and Provincial or Territorial Capital Gains Refund.

► 131(3) ◄

(3) Application to other liability. Instead of making a refund that might otherwise be made under subsection (2), the Minister may, where the corporation is liable or about to become liable to make any payment under this Act, apply the amount that would otherwise be refunded to that other liability and notify the corporation of that action.

Related Sections: S. 130(2) Application of ss. 131(1) to (3.2) and (6).

► 131(3.1) ◄

(3.1) Interest on capital gains refund. Where a capital gains refund for a taxation year is paid to, or applied to a liability of, a corporation, the Minister shall pay or apply interest on the refund at the prescribed rate for the period beginning on the day that is the later of

(*a*) the day that is 120 days after the end of the year, and

(*b*) the day that is 30 days after the day on which the corporation's return of income under this Part for the year was filed under section 150, unless the return was filed on or before the day on or before which it was required to be filed,

and ending on the day the refund is paid or applied.

Related Sections: S. 161.1(1) Refund interest.

► 131(3.2) ◄

(3.2) Excess interest on capital gains refund. Where at any particular time interest has been paid to, or applied to a liability of, a corporation under subsection (3.1) in respect of a capital gains refund and it is determined at a subsequent time that the capital gains refund was less than that in respect of which interest was so paid or applied,

(*a*) the amount by which the interest that was so paid or applied exceeds the interest, if any, computed in respect of the amount that is determined at the subsequent time to be the capital gains refund shall be deemed to be an amount (in this subsection referred to as the "amount payable") that became payable under this Part by the corporation at the particular time;

(*b*) the corporation shall pay to the Receiver General interest at the prescribed rate on the amount payable, computed from the particular time to the day of payment; and

(*c*) the Minister may at any time assess the corporation in respect of the amount payable and, where the Minister makes such an assessment, the provisions of Divisions I and J apply, with such modifications as the circumstances require, in respect of the assessment as though it had been made under section 152.

Related Sections: S. 161.1(1) Refund interest.

► 131(4) ◄

(4) Application of s. 84. Section 84 does not apply to deem a dividend to have been paid by a corporation to any of its shareholders, or to deem any of the shareholders of a corporation to have received a dividend on any shares of the capital stock of the corporation, if at the time the dividend would, but for this subsection, be deemed by that section to have been so paid or received, as the case may be, the corporation was a mutual fund corporation.

Related Sections: S. 84 Deemed dividend.

► 131(4.1) ◄

(4.1) Sections not applicable. Sections 51, 85, 85.1, 86 and 87 do not apply to a taxpayer that holds a share (in this subsection referred to as the "old share") of a class of shares, that is recognized under securities legislation as or as part of an investment fund, of a mutual fund corporation if the taxpayer exchanges or otherwise disposes of the old share for another share (in this subsection referred to as the "new share") of a mutual fund corporation, unless

(*a*) if the exchange or disposition occurs in the course of a transaction, event or series of transactions or events described in subsections 86(1) or 87(1),

(i) all shares of the class (determined without reference to subsection 248(6)) that includes the old share at the time of the exchange or disposition are exchanged for shares of the class that includes the new share,

(ii) the old share and the new share derive their value in the same proportion from the same property or group of properties, and

(iii) the transaction, event or series was undertaken solely for *bona fide* purposes and not to cause this paragraph to apply; or

(*b*) if the old share and the new share are shares of the same class (determined without reference to subsection 248(6)) of shares of the same mutual fund corporation,

(i) the old share and the new share derive their value in the same proportion from the same property or group of properties held by the corporation that is allocated to that class, and

(ii) that class is recognized under securities legislation as or as part of a single investment fund.

Editorial Note: A mutual fund corporation as described in section 131 may be organized as having a number of "switch funds". This type of mutual fund corporation uses separate share classes in the same corporation to hold the assets for each fund. Before 2017, shareholders were able to exchange shares of one class of the mutual fund corporation for shares of another class and rely on rollover provisions such as section 51 and 85 so as not to trigger any tax on the exchange.

For transactions after 2016, subsection 131(4.1) changes the above situation. It provides that an exchange of shares of a mutual fund corporation (or investment corporation) that results in the investor switching between funds will be considered for tax purposes to be a disposition at fair market value. In particular, subsection 131(4.1) provides that the rollover provisions of sections 51, 85, 85.1, 86, and 87 do not apply to a taxpayer that holds a share (old share) of a class of shares, that is recognized under securities legislation as an investment fund, of a mutual fund corporation if the taxpayer exchanges or otherwise disposes of the old share for another share (new share) of a mutual fund corporation. There are two exceptions, described in paragraphs (*a*) and (*b*) of the provision.

History: S. 131(4.1) was added by S.C. 2016, c. 12, s. 48(1), applicable in respect of transactions and events that occur after 2016.

Related Sections: S. 130(2) Application of subsections 131(1) to (3.2), (4.1) and (6).

▶ 131(5) ◀

(5) Dividend refund to mutual fund corporation. A corporation that was a mutual fund corporation throughout a taxation year

(*a*) is deemed for the purposes of paragraph 87(2)(*aa*) and section 129 to have been a private corporation throughout the year, except that its "non-eligible refundable dividend tax on hand" (as defined in subsection 129(4)) at the end of the year shall be determined without reference to paragraph (*a*) of that definition; and

(*b*) where it was not an investment corporation throughout the year, is deemed for the purposes of Part IV to have been a private corporation throughout the year except that, in applying subsection 186(1) to the corporation in respect of the year, that subsection shall be read without reference to paragraph 186(1)(*b*).

History: S. 131(5)(*a*) was replaced by S.C. 2018, c. 12, s. 23(1), applicable to taxation years that begin after 2018, and also to a taxation year of a corporation that begins before 2019 and ends after 2018 if

(a) the corporation's preceding taxation year was, because of a transaction or event or a series of transactions or events, shorter than it would have been in the absence of that transaction, event or series; and

(b) one of the reasons for the transaction, event or series was to defer the application of subsections 20(2) and (3) or 22(1) to (5) [of the *Budget Implementation Act, 2018, No. 1*] to the corporation.

S. 131(5)(*a*) formerly read:

(*a*) is deemed for the purposes of paragraph 87(2)(*aa*) and section 129 to have been a private corporation throughout the year, except that its refundable dividend tax on hand at the end of the year (within the meaning assigned by subsection 129(3)) shall be determined without reference to paragraph 129(3)(*a*); and

Related Sections: S. 130(3) Meaning of expressions "investment corporation" and "taxed capital gains"; s. 131(8) Meaning of "mutual fund corporation"; s. 157(3) Reduced instalments.

▶ 131(5.1) ◀

(5.1) TCP gains distribution. If a mutual fund corporation elects under subsection (1) to treat a dividend as a capital gains dividend, for the purposes of this Part and Part XIII,

(*a*) each shareholder to whom the dividend is paid is deemed to receive from the corporation, at the time the dividend is paid, a TCP gains distribution equal to the lesser of the amount of the dividend and the shareholder's pro rata portion at that time of the mutual fund corporation's TCP gains balance; and

(*b*) where the dividend is paid to a shareholder who is a non-resident person or a partnership that is not a Canadian partnership,

(i) subparagraph (1)(*b*)(ii) does not apply in respect of the dividend, to the extent of the TCP gains distribution, and

(ii) the TCP gains distribution is a taxable dividend that, except for the purpose of the definition of "capital gains dividend account" in subsection (6), is not a capital gains dividend.

History: S. 131(5.1)(*b*)(i) was replaced by S.C. 2013, c. 34, s. 277(3), applicable to taxation years that begin after October 31, 2011, and formerly read:

(i) subparagraph (1)(*b*)(vii) does not apply to the dividend, to the extent of the TCP gains distribution, and

Related Sections: S. 102(1) Definition of "Canadian partnership"; s. 212(2) Tax on dividends; s. 218.3(2) Tax payable.

▶ 131(5.2) ◀

(5.2) Application of subsection (5.1). Subsection (5.1) applies to a dividend paid by a mutual fund corporation in a taxation year only if more than 5% of the dividend is received by or on behalf of shareholders each of whom is a non-resident person or is a partnership that is not a Canadian partnership.

▶ 131(6) ◀

(6) Definitions. In this section,

"capital gains dividend account" —"capital gains dividend account" of a mutual fund corporation at any time means the amount, if any, by which

(*a*) the total of

(i) its capital gains, for all taxation years that began more than 60 days before that time, from dispositions of property after 1971 and before that time while it was a mutual fund corporation, and

(ii) all amounts each of which is an amount in respect of a distribution made by a trust to the corporation, at a time that is after its 2004 taxation year and at which it is a mutual fund corporation, in respect of capital gains of the trust equal to twice the amount determined by the following formula:

$$A - B$$

where

A is the amount of the distribution, and

B is the amount designated under subsection 104(21) by the trust in respect of the net taxable capital gains of the trust attributable to those capital gains

exceeds

(*b*) the total of

(i) its capital losses, for all taxation years that began more than 60 days before that time, from dispositions of property after 1971 and before that time while it was a mutual fund corporation,

(ii) all capital gains dividends that became payable by the corporation before that time and more than 60 days after the end of the last taxation year that ended more than 60 days before that time, and

(iii) an amount equal to $^{100}/_{14}$ of its capital gains refund for any taxation year throughout which it was a mutual fund corporation where the year ended more than 60 days before that time;

History: S. 131(6), paragraph (*a*) of the definition "capital gains dividend account" was replaced by S.C. 2013, c. 34, s. 277(4), applicable to the 2005 and subsequent taxation years, and formerly read:

(*a*) its capital gains, for all taxation years that began more than 60 days before that time, from dispositions of property after 1971 and before that time while it was a mutual fund corporation

S. 131(6), subparagraph (*b*)(iii) of the definition "capital gains dividend account" was replaced by S.C. 2013, c. 34, s. 277(5), applicable to taxation years that begin after October 31, 2011, except that if a corporation had a capital gains refund for a taxation year that began before November 2011, then in computing the capital gains dividend account of the corporation at any time in a taxation year of the corporation that begins after October 31, 2011, subparagraph (*b*)(iii) of the definition "capital gains dividend account" in subsection 131(6) is to be read, in its application to the corporation, as it read in its application to the corporation's last taxation year that began before November 1, 2011.

S. 131(6), subparagraph (*b*)(iii) of the definition "capital gains dividend account" formerly read:

(iii) the total of all amounts each of which is

(A) an amount equal to $^{100}/_{21}$ of its capital gains refund for any taxation year throughout which it was a mutual fund corporation where the year ended

(I) more than 60 days before that time, and

(II) before February 28, 2000,

(B) an amount equal to 100/18.7 of its capital gains refund for any taxation year throughout which it was a mutual fund corporation where the year ended

(I) more than 60 days before that time, and

(II) after February 27, 2000 and before October 18, 2000, or

(C) an amount equal to 100/14 of its capital gain refund for any taxation year throughout which it was a mutual fund corporation where the year ended

(I) more than 60 days before that time, and

(II) after October 17, 2000;

Related Sections: S. 87(2)(*bb*) Mutual fund and investment corporations.

"capital gains redemptions" —"capital gains redemptions" of a mutual fund corporation for a taxation year means the amount determined by the formula

$$A/B \times (C + D)$$

where

A is the sum of

(*a*) the total of all amounts paid by the corporation in the year on the redemption of shares of its capital stock, and

(*b*) the total of all amounts each of which is an amount equal to the fair market value of the shares of the corporation's capital stock that were exchanged in the year for other shares of the corporation's capital stock if

(i) paragraph (4.1) applies to the exchange, and

(ii) the amount is not included in the amount determined for paragraph (*a*),

B is the total of the fair market value at the end of the year of all the issued shares of its capital stock and the amount determined for A in respect of the corporation for the year,

C is 100/14 of the corporation's refundable capital gains tax on hand at the end of the year, and

D is the amount determined by the formula

$$(K + L) - (M + N)$$

where

K is the amount of the fair market value at the end of the year of all the issued shares of the corporation's capital stock,

L is the total of all amounts each of which is the amount of any debt owing by the corporation, or of any other obligation of the corporation to pay an amount, that was outstanding at that time,

M is the total of the cost amounts to the corporation at that time of all its properties, and

N is the amount of any money of the corporation on hand at that time;

History: S. 131(6), the description of A in the definition "capital gains redemptions" was replaced by S.C. 2016, c. 12, s. 48(2), in force January 1, 2017, and formerly read:

A is the total of all amounts paid by the corporation in the year on the redemption of shares of its capital stock,

"non-qualifying real property" — (Repealed by S.C. 1995, c. 3, s. 41(2).)

"non-qualifying real property capital gains dividend account" — (Repealed by S.C. 1995, c. 3, s. 41(2).)

"pro rata portion" —"pro rata portion", of a shareholder at any time, of a mutual fund corporation's TCP gains balance, in respect of a dividend paid by the mutual fund corporation on a class of shares of its capital stock, means the amount determined by the formula

$$A \times B/C$$

where

A is the mutual fund corporation's TCP gains balance immediately before that time,

B is the amount received in respect of the dividend by the shareholder, and

C is the total amount of the dividend;

"refundable capital gains tax on hand" —"refundable capital gains tax on hand" of a mutual fund corporation at the end of a taxation year means the amount determined by the formula

$$A - B$$

where

A is the total of all amounts each of which is an amount in respect of that or any previous taxation year throughout which the corporation was a mutual fund corporation, equal to the least of

(*a*) 28% of its taxable income for the year,

(*b*) 28% of its taxed capital gains for the year, and

(*c*) the tax payable by it under this Part for the year determined without reference to section 123.2, and

B is the total of all amounts each of which is an amount in respect of any previous taxation year throughout which the corporation was a mutual fund corporation, equal to its capital gains refund for the year;

Related Sections: S. 87(2)(*bb*) Mutual fund and investment corporations; s. 123.2 Corporation surtax; s. 131(2) Capital gains refund to mutual fund corporation; s. 131(7) Definition of "taxed capital gains".

"TCP gains balance" —"TCP gains balance", of a mutual fund corporation at any time, means the amount, if any, by which

(*a*) the total of

(i) the mutual fund corporation's capital gains from dispositions, after March 22, 2004 and at or before that time, of taxable Canadian properties, and

(ii) the TCP gains distributions (including those defined in section 132) received by the mutual fund corporation at or before that time

exceeds

(*b*) the total of

(i) the mutual fund corporation's capital losses from dispositions, after March 22, 2004 and at or before that time, of taxable Canadian properties, and

(ii) the total of all amounts deemed, in respect of dividends paid by the mutual fund corporation before that time, to be TCP gains distributions received by shareholders from the mutual fund corporation;

Related Sections: S. 132(4), "TCP gains distribution"; s. 248(1), "taxable Canadian property".

"TCP gains distribution" —"TCP gains distribution" means a TCP gains distribution described in subsection (5.1).

▶ 131(7) ◀

(7) Definition of "taxed capital gains". In subsection (6), "taxed capital gains" of a taxpayer for a taxation year has the meaning assigned by subsection 130(3).

Related Sections: S. 111(1)(*b*) Net capital losses; s. 132(5) Definition of "taxed capital gains".

▶ 131(8) ◀

(8) Meaning of "mutual fund corporation". Subject to subsection (8.1), a corporation is, for the purposes of this section, a mutual fund corporation at any time in a taxation year if, at that time, it was a prescribed labour-sponsored venture capital corporation or

(*a*) it was a Canadian corporation that was a public corporation;

(*b*) its only undertaking was

(i) the investing of its funds in property (other than real property or an interest in real property or an immovable or a real right in an immovable),

(ii) the acquiring, holding, maintaining, improving, leasing or managing of any real property (or interest in real property) or of any immovable (or real right in immovables) that is capital property of the corporation, or

(iii) any combination of the activities described in subparagraphs (i) and (ii), and

(*c*) the issued shares of the capital stock of the corporation included shares

(i) having conditions attached thereto that included conditions requiring the corporation to accept, at the demand of the holder thereof and at prices determined and payable in accordance with the conditions, the surrender of the shares, or fractions or parts thereof, that are fully paid, or

(ii) qualified in accordance with prescribed conditions relating to the redemption of the shares,

and the fair market value of such of the issued shares of its capital stock as had conditions attached thereto that included such conditions or as were so qualified, as the case may be, was not less than 95% of the fair market value of all of the issued shares of the capital stock of the corporation (such fair market values being determined without regard to any voting rights attaching to shares of the capital stock of the corporation).

History: S. 131(8)(*b*)(i) and (ii) were replaced by S.C. 2013, c. 34, s. 132, in force June 26, 2013, and formerly read:

(i) the investing of its funds in property (other than real property or an interest in real property),

(ii) the acquiring, holding, maintaining, improving, leasing or managing of any real property (or interest in real property) that is capital property of the corporation, or

Related Regulations: 6701.

Related Sections: S. 89(1), "Canadian corporation", "public corporation"; s. 108(2) When trust is a unit trust; s. 132(6) Meaning of "mutual fund trust"; s. 248(4) Interest in real property; s. 253.1 Investments in limited partnerships.

▶ 131(8.01) ◀

(8.01) Election to be a mutual fund corporation. A corporation is deemed to be a mutual fund corporation, from the date it was incorporated until the earlier of the date the corporation meets the conditions to qualify as a mutual fund corporation under subsection (8) and December 31, 2017, if the corporation

(*a*) was incorporated after 2014 and before March 22, 2016;

(*b*) would have been a mutual fund corporation on March 22, 2016 if it could have elected on or before that date to be a public corporation under paragraph (*b*) of the definition "public corporation" in subsection 89(1), had the conditions prescribed in paragraph 4800(1)(*b*) of the *Income Tax Regulations* been satisfied;

(*c*) on March 22, 2016, had at least one class of shares that was recognized under securities legislation as an investment fund; and

(*d*) elects to have this subsection apply in the corporation's return of income for the corporation's first taxation year that ends after March 21, 2016.

History: S. 131(8.01) was added by S.C. 2016, c. 12, s. 48(3), in force January 1, 2017.

▶ 131(8.1) ◀

(8.1) Idem. Where, at any time, it can reasonably be considered that a corporation, having regard to all the circumstances, including the terms and conditions of the shares of its capital stock, was established or is maintained primarily for the benefit of non-resident persons, the corporation shall be deemed not to be a mutual fund corporation after that time unless

(*a*) throughout the period that begins on the later of February 21, 1990 and the day of its incorporation and ends at that time, all or substantially all of its property consisted of property other than property that would be taxable Canadian property if the definition "taxable Canadian property" in subsection 248(1) were read without reference to paragraph (*b*) of that definition; or

(*b*) it has not issued a share (other than a share issued as a stock dividend) of its capital stock after February 20, 1990 and before that time to a person who, after reasonable inquiry, it had reason to believe was non-resident, except where the share was issued to that person under an agreement in writing entered into before February 21, 1990.

▶ 131(9) ◀

(9) Reduction of refundable capital gains tax on hand. Notwithstanding any other provision of this section, the amount determined for A in the definition "refundable capital gains tax on hand" in subsection (6) in respect of the 1972 or 1973 taxation year of a corporation is,

(*a*) in respect of its 1972 taxation year, 91.25% of the amount so determined; and

(*b*) in respect of its 1973 taxation year, the total of

(i) 91.25% of that proportion of the amount so determined that the number of days in that portion of the year that is before 1973 is of the number of days in the whole year, and

(ii) 100% of that proportion of the amount so determined that the number of days in that portion of the year that is after 1972 is of the number of days in the whole year.

▶ 131(10) ◀

(10) Restricted financial institution. Notwithstanding any other provision of this Act, a mutual fund corporation or an investment corporation that at any time would, but for this subsection, be a restricted financial institution shall, if it has so elected in prescribed manner and prescribed form before that time, be deemed not to be a restricted financial institution at that time.

Related Sections: S. 112(2.1) Where no deduction permitted.

Forms: T2143 — Election Not To Be A Restricted Financial Institution.

▶ 131(11) ◀

(11) Rules respecting prescribed labour-sponsored venture capital corporations. Notwithstanding any other provision of this Act, in applying this Act to a corporation that was at any time a prescribed labour-sponsored venture capital corporation,

(*a*) for the purposes of subparagraphs (*a*)(i) and (ii) of the definition "non-eligible refundable dividend tax on hand" in subsection 129(4), the amount deducted under paragraph 111 (1)(*b*) from the corporation's income for each taxation year ending after that time shall be deemed to be nil;

(*b*) the definition "aggregate investment income" in subsection 129(4) shall be read without reference to paragraph (*a*) of that definition in its application to taxation years that end after that time;

(*c*) notwithstanding subsection (4), if it so elects in its return of income under this Part for a taxation year ending after that time, subsection 84(1) applies for that year and all subsequent taxation years;

(*d*) subsection (5) does not apply for taxation years ending after that time; and

(*e*) the amount of the corporation's capital dividend account at any time after that time shall be deemed to be nil.

History: S. 131(11)(*a*) was replaced by S.C. 2018, c. 12, s. 23(2), applicable to taxation years that begin after 2018, and also to a taxation year of a corporation that begins before 2019 and ends after 2018 if

(a) the corporation's preceding taxation year was, because of a transaction or event or a series of transactions or events, shorter than it would have been in the absence of that transaction, event or series; and

(b) one of the reasons for the transaction, event or series was to defer the application of subsections 20(2) and (3) or 22(1) to (5) [of the *Budget Implementation Act, 2018, No. 1*] to the corporation.

S. 131(11)(*a*) formerly read:

(*a*) for the purposes of subparagraphs 129(3)(*a*)(i) and (ii), the amount deducted under paragraph 111(1)(*b*) from the corporation's income for each taxation year ending after that time shall be deemed to be nil;

Related Regulations: 6701.

Mutual Fund Trusts

SECTION 132: Capital gains refund to mutual fund trust

► 132(1) ◄

(1) Capital gains refund to mutual fund trust. Where a trust was, throughout a taxation year, a mutual fund trust and a return of its income for the year has been made within 3 years from the end of the year, the Minister

(*a*) may, on sending the notice of assessment for the year, refund an amount (in this subsection referred to as its "capital gains refund" for the year) equal to the lesser of

(i) the total of

(A) 16.5% of the total of the trust's capital gains redemptions for the year, and

(B) the positive or negative amount, if any, that the Minister determines to be reasonable in the circumstances, after giving consideration to the percentages applicable in determining the trust's capital gains refunds for the year or any previous taxation year and the percentages applicable in determining the trust's refundable capital gains tax on hand at the end of the year, and

(ii) the trust's refundable capital gains tax on hand at the end of the year; and

(*b*) shall, with all due dispatch, make that capital gains refund after sending the notice of assessment if an application for it has been made in writing by the trust within the period within which the Minister would be allowed under subsection 152(4) to assess tax payable under this Part by the trust for the year if that subsection were read without reference to paragraph 152(4)(*a*).

History: S. 132(1)(*a*)(i)(A) and (B) were replaced by S.C. 2016, c. 7, s. 62(6), applicable to the 2016 and subsequent taxation years, and formerly read:

(A) 14.5% of the total of the trust's capital gains redemptions for the year, and

(B) the amount, if any, that the Minister determines to be reasonable in the circumstances, after giving consideration to the percentages applicable in determining the trust's capital gains refunds for the year and preceding taxation years and the percentages applicable in determining the trust's refundable capital gains tax on hand at the end of the year, and

S. 132(1)(*b*) was replaced by S.C. 2010, c. 25, s. 31, in force on Royal Assent, December 15, 2010. S. 132(1)(*b*) formerly read:

(*b*) shall, with all due dispatch, make that capital gains refund after mailing the notice of assessment if an application for it has been made in writing by the trust within the period within which the Minister would be allowed under subsection 152(4) to assess tax payable under this Part by the trust for the year if that subsection were read without reference to paragraph 152(4)(*a*).

Related Sections: S. 132(2) Application to other liability.

Canadian Tax Foundation: Kraus et al., *Update on Real Estate Investment Trusts and Structuring Public Vehicles for Investment in Canadian and Foreign Real Estate*, 2013 Conference Report 15:1–64; McCue and Johnson, *Current Transactions: Cross-Border Income Trusts/Foreign Asset Investment Trusts*, 2012 Conference Report 8:1–33.

Tax Profile: August 2004 — Canadian Tax Treatment of Index Participation Units and Exchange-Traded Index Derivatives.

Forms: T184 — Capital Gains Refund for a Mutual Fund Trust.

► 132(2) ◄

(2) Application to other liability. Instead of making a refund that might otherwise be made under subsection (1) the Minister may, where the trust is liable or about to become liable to make any payment under this Act, apply the amount that would otherwise be refunded to that other liability and notify the trust of that action.

Related Sections: S. 108(1) Definitions; s. 108(2) When trust is a unit trust; s. 132(1) Capital gains refund to mutual fund trust; s. 132(4), "capital gains redemptions", "refundable capital gains tax on hand"; s. 132(6) Meaning of "mutual fund trust".

► 132(2.1) ◄

(2.1) Interest on capital gains refund. If a capital gains refund for a taxation year is paid to, or applied to a liability of, a mutual fund trust, the Minister shall pay or apply interest on the refund at the prescribed rate for the period beginning on the day that is 30 days after the later of

(*a*) the day that is 90 days after the end of the year, and

(*b*) the day on which the trust's return of income under this Part for the year was filed under section 150

and ending on the day on which the refund is paid or applied.

Related Regulations: 4301.

Related Sections: S. 161.1 Offset of refund interest and arrears interest.

► 132(2.2) ◄

(2.2) Excess interest on capital gains refund. Where at any particular time interest has been paid to, or applied to a liability of, a trust under subsection (2.1) in respect of a capital gains refund and it is determined at a subsequent time that the capital gains refund was less than that in respect of which interest was so paid or applied,

(*a*) the amount by which the interest that was so paid or applied exceeds the interest, if any, computed in respect of the amount that is determined at the subsequent time to be the capital gains refund shall be deemed to be an amount (in this subsection referred to as the "amount payable") that became payable under this Part by the trust at the particular time;

(*b*) the trust shall pay to the Receiver General interest at the prescribed rate on the amount payable, computed from the particular time to the day of payment; and

(*c*) the Minister may at any time assess the trust in respect of the amount payable and, where the Minister makes such an assessment, the provisions of Divisions I and J apply, with such modifications as the circumstances require, in respect of the assessment as though it had been made under section 152.

Related Regulations: 4301.

Related Sections: S. 161.1 Offset of refund interest and arrears interest.

► 132(3) ◄

(3) Application of s. 104(20). In its application in respect of a mutual fund trust, subsection 104(20) shall be read as if the reference therein to "a dividend (other than a taxable dividend)" were read as a reference to "a capital dividend".

► 132(4) ◄

(4) Definitions. In this section,

"capital gains redemptions" — "capital gains redemptions" of a mutual fund trust for a taxation year means the amount determined by the formula

$$(A/B \times (C + D)) - E$$

where

A is the total of all amounts each of which is the portion of an amount paid by the trust in the year on the redemption of a unit in the trust that is included in the proceeds of disposition in respect of that redemption,

B is the total of the fair market value at the end of the year of all the issued units of the trust and the amount determined for A in respect of the trust for the year,

C is 100/16.5 of the trust's refundable capital gains tax on hand at the end of the year,

D is the amount determined by the formula

$$(K + L) - (M + N)$$

where

K is the amount of the fair market value at the end of the year of all the issued units of the trust,

L is the total of all amounts each of which is the amount of any debt owing by the trust, or of any other obligation of the trust to pay an amount, that was outstanding at that time,

M is the total of the cost amounts to the trust at that time of all its properties, and

N is the amount of any money of the trust on hand at that time, and

E is twice the total of all amounts each of which is an amount designated under subsection 104(21) for the year by the trust in respect of a unit of the trust redeemed by the trust at any time in the year and after December 21, 2000;

History: S. 132(4), the description of C in the definition "capital gains redemptions" was replaced by S.C. 2016, c. 7, s. 62(7), applicable to the 2016 and subsequent taxation years, and formerly read:

C is 100/14.5 of the trust's refundable capital gains tax on hand at the end of the year,

"pro rata portion" — "pro rata portion", of a beneficiary, of a mutual fund trust's TCP gains balance for a taxation year, in respect of an amount designated under subsection 104(21) by the mutual fund trust for the taxation year, means the amount determined by the formula

$$A \times B/C$$

where

A is the mutual fund trust's TCP gains balance for the taxation year,

B is the amount the mutual fund trust has designated under that subsection in respect of the beneficiary for the taxation year, and

C is the total of all amounts designated under that subsection by the mutual fund trust for the taxation year;

"refundable capital gains tax on hand" — "refundable capital gains tax on hand" of a mutual fund trust at the end of a taxation year means the amount determined by the formula

$$A - B$$

where

A is the total of all amounts each of which is an amount in respect of that or any previous taxation year throughout which the trust was a mutual fund trust, equal to the least of

(*a*) the highest individual percentage for the year multiplied by its taxable income for the year,

(*b*) the highest individual percentage for the year multiplied by its taxed capital gains for the year, and

(*c*) where the taxation year ended after May 6, 1974, the tax payable under this Part by it for the year, and

B is the total of all amounts each of which is an amount in respect of any previous taxation year throughout which the trust was a mutual fund trust, equal to its capital gains refund for the year.

History: S. 132(4), paragraphs (*a*) and (*b*) of the description of A in the definition "refundable capital gains tax on hand" were replaced by S.C. 2016, c. 7, s. 62(8), applicable to the 2016 and subsequent taxation years, and formerly read:

(*a*) 29% of its taxable income for the year,

(*b*) 29% of its taxed capital gains for the year, and

Related Sections: S. 132(5) Definition of "taxed capital gains".

Tax Window Files: Refundable Capital Gains Tax On Hand, *August 7, 2013*, CRA Document No. 2013-0497961I7.

"TCP gains balance" — "TCP gains balance", of a mutual fund trust for a particular taxation year, means the amount, if any, by which

(*a*) the total of

(i) the mutual fund trust's capital gains from dispositions, after March 22, 2004 and at or before the end of the particular taxation year, of taxable Canadian properties, and

(ii) the TCP gains distributions (including those defined in section 131) received by the mutual fund trust at or before the end of the particular taxation year

exceeds

(*b*) the total of

(i) the mutual fund trust's capital losses from dispositions, after March 22, 2004 and at or before the end of the particular taxation year, of taxable Canadian properties, and

(ii) the total of all amounts deemed, in respect of amounts designated by the mutual fund trust under subsection 104(21) for taxation years that preceded the particular taxation year, to be TCP gains distributions received by beneficiaries under the mutual fund trust;

Related Sections: S. 131(6), "TCP gains distribution"; s. 248(1), "taxable Canadian property".

"TCP gains distribution" — "TCP gains distribution" means a TCP gains distribution described in subsection (5.1);

► 132(5) ◄

(5) Definition of "taxed capital gains". In subsection (4), "taxed capital gains" of a taxpayer for a taxation year has the meaning assigned by subsection 130(3).

Related Sections: S. 111(1)(*b*) Net capital losses; s. 131(7) Definition of "taxed capital gains".

► 132(5.1) ◄

(5.1) TCP gains distribution. If a mutual fund trust designates an amount under subsection 104(21) for a taxation year of the trust in respect of a beneficiary under the trust, for the purposes of this Part and Part XIII,

(*a*) the beneficiary is deemed to have received from the mutual fund trust a TCP gains distribution equal to the lesser of

(i) twice the amount designated, and

(ii) the beneficiary's pro rata portion of the mutual fund trust's TCP gains balance for the taxation year; and

(*b*) where the beneficiary is a non-resident person or a partnership that is not a Canadian partnership,

(i) the amount designated is deemed by subsection 104(21) to be a taxable capital gain of the beneficiary only to the extent that it exceeds one half of the TCP gains distribution, and

(ii) one half of the TCP gains distribution is to be added to the amount otherwise included under subsection 104(13) in computing the income of the beneficiary, and is deemed to be an amount to which paragraph 212(1)(*c*) applies.

Related Sections: S. 102(1) Definition of "Canadian partnership"; s. 212(1)(*c*) Estate or trust income; s. 218.3(2) Tax payable.

Tax Profile: October 2011 — Hedge Funds and Private Equity Funds in Canada.

► 132(5.2) ◄

(5.2) Application of subsection (5.1). Subsection (5.1) applies to an amount designated under subsection 104(21) by a mutual fund trust for a taxation year only if more than 5% of the total of all amounts each of which is an amount designated under that subsection by the mutual fund trust for the taxation year was designated in respect of beneficiaries under the mutual fund trust each of whom is a non-resident person or is a partnership that is not a Canadian partnership.

Proposed Amendment
2019 Federal Budget Resolutions

Section 132 of the Act is amended by adding the following after subsection (5.2):

(5.3) Allocation to redeemers. If a trust that is a mutual fund trust throughout a taxation year paid or made payable, at any time in the taxation year, to a beneficiary an amount on a redemption by that beneficiary of a unit of the trust (in this subsection referred to as the "allocated amount"), and the beneficiary's proceeds from the disposition of that unit do not include the allocated amount, in computing its income for the taxation year no deduction may be made by the trust in respect of

(*a*) the portion of the allocated amount that would be, without reference to subsection 104(6), an amount paid out of the income (other than taxable capital gains) of the trust; and

(*b*) the portion of the allocated amount determined by the formula

$$A - 1/2 (B + C - D)$$

where

A is the portion of the allocated amount that would be, without reference to subsection 104(6), an amount paid out of the taxable capital gains of the trust,

B is the beneficiary's proceeds from the disposition of the unit on the redemption,

C is the allocated amount, and

D is the beneficiary's cost amount of that unit.

Applicable: To taxation years that begin on or after March 19, 2019.

► 132(6) ◄

(6) Meaning of "mutual fund trust". Subject to subsection (7), for the purposes of this section, a trust is a mutual fund trust at any time if at that time

(*a*) it was a unit trust resident in Canada,

(*b*) its only undertaking was

(i) the investing of its funds in property (other than real property or an interest in real property or an immovable or a real right in an immovable),

(ii) the acquiring, holding, maintaining, improving, leasing or managing of any real property (or interest in real property) or of any immovable (or real right in immovables) that is capital property of the trust, or

(iii) any combination of the activities described in subparagraphs (i) and (ii), and

(*c*) it complied with prescribed conditions.

History: S. 132(6)(*c*) was replaced by S.C. 2013, c. 34, s. 278(1), applicable to the 2000 and subsequent taxation years, and formerly read:

(*c*) it complied with prescribed conditions relating to the number of its unit holders, dispersal of ownership of its units and public trading of its units.

S. 132(6)(*b*)(i) and (ii) were replaced by S.C. 2013, c. 34, s. 133, in force June 26, 2013, and formerly read:

(i) the investing of its funds in property (other than real property or an interest in real property),

(ii) the acquiring, holding, maintaining, improving, leasing or managing of any real property (or interest in real property) that is capital property of the trust, or

Related Regulations: Part XLVIII; 4801.

Related Sections: S. 89(1), "taxable dividend"; s. 104(1) Reference to trust or estate; s. 108(1) Definitions; s. 108(2) When trust is a unit trust; s. 131(8) Meaning of "mutual fund corporation"; s. 156(2) Payment by mutual fund trusts; s. 248(4) Interest in real property; s. 253.1 Investments in limited partnerships; s. 255 Canada; ITAR s. 65(1) Part XI of amended Act — foreign property acquired after June 18, 1971 and before July 1, 1972.

Canadian Tax Foundation: Kraus et al., *Update on Real Estate Investment Trusts and Structuring Public Vehicles for Investment in Canadian and Foreign Real Estate*, 2013 Conference Report 15:1–64; McCue and Johnson, *Current Transactions: Cross-Border Income Trusts/Foreign Asset Investment Trusts*, 2012 Conference Report 8:1–33.

Tax Profile: October 2011 — Hedge Funds and Private Equity Funds in Canada; August 2004 — Canadian Tax Treatment of Index Participation Units and Exchange-Traded Index Derivatives.

Tax Topics: No. 1608, Business Income Trusts — Part II; No. 1606-07, Business Income Trusts — Part I.

Income Tax Technical News: Issue No. 34, Income Trusts and Subparagraph 132(6)(b)(i) — "its only undertaking was the investing of funds.".

► 132(6.1) ◄

(6.1) Election to be mutual fund. Where a trust becomes a mutual fund trust at any particular time before the 91st day after the end of its first taxation year, and the trust so elects in its return of income for that year, the trust is deemed to have been a mutual fund trust from the beginning of that year until the particular time.

Related Sections: 251.2(7) Filing and other deadlines; S. 142.6(1) Becoming or ceasing to be a financial institution.

► 132(6.2) ◄

(6.2) Retention of status as mutual fund trust. A trust is deemed to be a mutual fund trust throughout a calendar year where

(*a*) at any time in the year, the trust would, if this section were read without reference to this subsection, have ceased to be a mutual fund trust

(i) because the condition described in paragraph 108(2)(*a*) ceased to be satisfied,

(ii) because of the application of paragraph (6)(*c*), or

(iii) because the trust ceased to exist;

(*b*) the trust was a mutual fund trust at the beginning of the year; and (*c*) the trust would, throughout the portion of the year throughout which it was in existence, have been a mutual fund trust if

(i) in the case where the condition described in paragraph 108(2)(*a*) was satisfied at any time in the year, that condition were satisfied throughout the year,

(ii) subsection (6) were read without reference to paragraph (*c*) of that subsection, and

(iii) this section were read without reference to this subsection.

► 132(7) ◄

(7) Idem. Where, at any time, it can reasonably be considered that a trust, having regard to all the circumstances, including the terms and conditions of the units of the trust, was established or is maintained primarily for the benefit of non-resident persons, the trust shall be deemed not to be a mutual fund trust after that time unless

(*a*) at that time, all or substantially all of its property consisted of property other than property that would be taxable Canadian property if the definition "taxable Canadian property" in subsection 248(1) were read without reference to paragraph (*b*) of that definition; or

(*b*) it has not issued any unit (other than a unit issued to a person as a payment, or in satisfaction of the person's right to enforce payment, of an amount out of the trust's income determined before the application of subsection 104(6), or out of the trust's capital gains) of the trust after February 20, 1990 and before that time to a person who, after reasonable inquiry, it had reason to believe was non-resident, except where the unit was issued to that person under an agreement in writing entered into before February 21, 1990.

Editorial Note: Subsection 132(7) provides that a trust will be deemed not to be a mutual fund trust in certain circumstances where it can be reasonably considered that the trust was established or is maintained primarily for the benefit of non-residents.

Tax Profile: August 2004 — Canadian Tax Treatment of Index Participation Units and Exchange-Traded Index Derivatives.

Income Tax Technical News: Issue No. 34, Income Trusts and Non-Resident Ownership.

SECTION 132.1: Amounts designated by mutual fund trust

► 132.1(1) ◄

(1) Amounts designated by mutual fund trust. Where a trust in its return of income under this Part for a taxation year throughout which it was a mutual fund trust designates an amount in respect of a particular unit of the trust owned by a taxpayer at any time in the year equal to the total of

(*a*) such amount as the trust may determine in respect of the particular unit for the year not exceeding the amount, if any, by which

(i) the total of all amounts that were determined by the trust under subsection 104(16) of the *Income Tax Act*, chapter 148 of the Revised Statutes of Canada, 1952, for taxation years of the trust commencing before 1988

exceeds

(ii) the total of all amounts determined by the trust under this paragraph for the year or a preceding taxation year in respect of all units of the trust, other than amounts determined in respect of the particular unit for the year under this paragraph, and

(*b*) such amount as the trust may determine in respect of the particular unit for the year not exceeding the amount, if any, by which

(i) the total of all amounts described in subparagraph 53(2)(*h*)(i.1) that became payable by the trust after 1987 and before the year

exceeds

(ii) the total of all amounts determined by the trust under this paragraph for the year or a preceding taxation year in respect of all units of the trust, other than amounts determined in respect of the particular unit for the year under this paragraph,

the amount so designated shall

(*c*) subject to subsection (3), be deductible in computing the income of the trust for the year, and

(*d*) be included in computing the income of the taxpayer for the taxpayer's taxation year in which the year of the trust ends, except that where the particular unit was owned by two or more taxpayers during the year, such part of the amount so designated as the trust may determine shall be included in computing the income of each such taxpayer for the taxpayer's taxation year in which the year of the trust ends if the total of the parts so determined is equal to the amount so designated.

Related Sections: S. 54, "adjusted cost base"; s. 132(6) Meaning of "mutual fund trust"; s. 214(3) Deemed payments; s. 248(1), "amount".

► 132.1(2) ◄

(2) Adjusted cost base of unit where designation made. In computing, at any time in a taxation year of a taxpayer, the adjusted cost base to the taxpayer of a unit in a mutual fund trust, there shall be added that part of the amount included under subsection (1) in computing the taxpayer's income that is reasonably attributable to the amount determined under paragraph (1)(*b*) by the trust for its taxation year ending in the year in respect of the unit owned by the taxpayer.

► 132.1(3) ◄

(3) Limitation on current year deduction. The total of amounts deductible by reason of paragraph (1)(*c*) in computing the income of a trust for a taxation year shall not exceed the amount that would be the income of the trust for the year if no deductions were made under this section and subsection 104(6).

► 132.1(4) ◄

(4) Carryover of excess. The amount, if any, by which the total of all amounts each of which is an amount designated for the year under subsection (1) exceeds the amount deductible under this section in computing the income of the trust for the year, shall, for the purposes of paragraph (1)(*c*) and subsection (3), be deemed designated under subsection (1) by the trust for its immediately following taxation year.

► 132.1(5) ◄

(5) Where designation has no effect. Where it is reasonable to conclude that an amount determined by a mutual fund trust

(*a*) under paragraph (1)(*a*) or (*b*) for a taxation year of the trust in respect of a unit owned at any time in the year by a taxpayer who was a person exempt from tax under this Part by reason of subsection 149(1), or

(*b*) under paragraph (1)(*d*) for the year in respect of the amount designated under subsection (1) for the year in respect of the unit differs from the amount that would have been so determined for the year in respect of the taxpayer had the taxpayer not been a person exempt from tax under this Part by reason of subsection 149(1), the amount designated for the year in respect of the unit under subsection (1) shall have no effect for the purposes of paragraph (1)(*c*).

SECTION 132.11: Taxation year of mutual fund trust

► 132.11(1) ◄

(1) Taxation year of mutual fund trust. Notwithstanding any other provision of this Act, where a trust (other than a prescribed trust) that was a mutual fund trust on the 74th day after the end of a particular calendar year so elects in writing filed with the Minister with the trust's return of income for the trust's taxation year that includes December 15 of the particular year,

(*a*) the trust's taxation year that began before December 16 of the particular year and, but for this paragraph, would end at the end of the particular year (or, where the first taxation year of the trust began after December 15 of the preceding calendar year and no return of income was filed for a taxation year of the trust that ended at the end of the preceding calendar year, at the end of the preceding calendar year) is deemed to end at the end of December 15 of the particular year;

(*b*) if the trust's taxation year ends on December 15 because of paragraph (*a*), subject to subsection (1.1), each subsequent taxation year of the trust is deemed to be the period that begins at the beginning of December 16 of a calendar year and that ends at the end of December 15 of the following calendar year or at any earlier time that is determined under paragraph 128.1(4)(*a*), 132.2(3)(*b*), 142.6(1)(*a*) or 249(4)(*a*); and

(*c*) each fiscal period of the trust that begins in a taxation year of the trust that ends on December 15 because of paragraph (*a*) or that ends in a subsequent taxation year of the trust shall end no later than the end of the year or the subsequent year, as the case may be.

History: S. 132.11(1)(*b*) was replaced by S.C. 2016, c. 12, s. 49(1), deemed to have come into force on March 21, 2013, and formerly read:

(*b*) if the trust's taxation year ends on December 15 because of paragraph (*a*), subject to subsection (1.1), each subsequent taxation year of the trust is deemed to be the period that begins at the beginning of December 16 of a calendar year and ends at the end of December 15 of the following calendar year or at any earlier time that is determined under paragraph 132.2(3)(*b*) or subsection 142.6(1); and

S. 132.11(1)(*b*) was replaced by S.C. 2013, c. 34, s. 279(1), deemed to have come into force on January 1, 1999, except that, in applying paragraph 132.11(1)(*b*) to taxation years that end before 2000, that paragraph is to be read without reference to "subject to subsection (1.1)".

S. 132.11(1)(*b*) formerly read:

(*b*) where the trust's taxation year ends on December 15 because of paragraph (*a*), subject to subsection (1.1), each subsequent taxation year of the trust is deemed to be the period that begins at the beginning of December 16 of a calendar year and ends at the end of December 15 of the following calendar year or at such earlier time as is determined under paragraph 132.2(1)(*b*) or subsection 142.6(1); and

Related Regulations: 4801.01.

► 132.11(1.1) ◄

(1.1) Revocation of election. Where a particular taxation year of a trust ends on December 15 of a calendar year because of an election made under paragraph (1)(*a*), the trust applies to the Minister in writing before December 15 of that calendar year (or before a later time that is acceptable to the Minister) to have this subsection apply to the trust, with the concurrence of the Minister

(*a*) the trust's taxation year following the particular taxation year is deemed to begin immediately after the end of the particular taxation year and end at the end of that calendar year; and

(*b*) each subsequent taxation year of the trust is deemed to be determined as if that election had not been made.

► 132.11(2) ◄

(2) Electing trust's share of partnership income and losses. Where a trust is a member of a partnership a fiscal period of which ends in a calendar year after December 15 of the year and a particular taxation year of the trust ends on December 15 of the year because of subsection (1), each amount otherwise determined under paragraph 96(1)(*f*) or (*g*) to be the trust's income or loss for a subsequent taxation year of the trust is deemed to be the trust's income or loss determined under paragraph 96(1)(*f*) or (*g*) for the particular year and not for the subsequent year.

► 132.11(3) ◄

(3) Electing trust's income from other trusts. Where a particular trust is a beneficiary under another trust a taxation year of which (in this subsection referred to as the "other year") ends in a calendar year after December 15 of the year and a particular taxation year of the trust ends on December 15 of the year because of subsection (1), each amount determined or designated under subsection 104(13), (19), (21), (22) or (29) for the other year that would otherwise be included, or taken into account, in computing the income of the particular trust for a subsequent taxation year of the trust shall

(*a*) be included, or taken into account, in computing the particular trust's income for the particular year; and

(*b*) not be included, or taken into account, in computing the particular trust's income for the subsequent year.

► 132.11(4) ◄

(4) Amounts paid or payable to beneficiaries. Notwithstanding subsection 104(24), for the purposes of subsections (5) and (6) and 104(6) and (13) and paragraph (*i*) of the definition "disposition" in subsection 248(1) each amount that is paid, or that becomes payable, by a trust to a beneficiary after the end of a particular taxation year of the trust that ends on December 15 of a calendar year because of subsection (1) and before the end of that calendar year, is deemed to have been paid or to have become payable, as the case may be, to the beneficiary at the end of the particular year and not at any other time.

History: S. 132.11(4) was replaced by S.C. 2013, c. 34, s. 279(3), applicable to amounts that, after 1999, are paid or have become payable by a trust, and formerly read:

(4) *Amounts paid or payable to beneficiaries.* For the purposes of subsections (5) and (6) and 104(6) and (13) and notwithstanding subsection 104(24), each amount that is paid, or that becomes payable, by a trust to a beneficiary after the end of a particular taxation year of the trust that ends on December 15 of a calendar year because of subsection (1) and before the end of that calendar year, is deemed to have been paid or to have become payable, as the case may be, to the beneficiary at the end of the particular year and not at any other time.

► 132.11(5) ◄

(5) Special rules where change in status of beneficiary. Where an amount is deemed by subsection (4) to have been paid or to have become payable at the end of December 15 of a calendar year by a trust to a beneficiary who was not a beneficiary under the trust at that time,

(*a*) notwithstanding any other provision of this Act, where the beneficiary did not exist at that time, except for the purpose of this paragraph, the first taxation year of the beneficiary is deemed to include the period that begins at that time and ends immediately before the beginning of the first taxation year of the beneficiary;

(*b*) the beneficiary is deemed to exist throughout the period described in paragraph (*a*); and

(*c*) where the beneficiary was not a beneficiary under the trust at that time, the beneficiary is deemed to have been a beneficiary under the trust at that time.

► 132.11(6) ◄

(6) Additional income of electing trust. Where a particular amount is designated under this subsection by a trust in its return of income for a particular taxation year that ends on December 15 because of subsection (1) or throughout which the trust was a mutual fund trust and the trust does not designate an amount under subsection 104(13.1) or (13.2) for the particular year,

(*a*) the particular amount shall be added in computing its income for the particular year; and

(*b*) for the purposes of subsections 104(6) and (13), each portion of the particular amount that is allocated under this paragraph to a beneficiary under the trust in the trust's return of income for the particular year in respect of an amount paid or payable to the beneficiary in the particular year shall be considered to be additional income of the trust for the particular year (determined without reference to subsection 104(6)) that was paid or payable, as the case may be, to the beneficiary at the end of the particular year.

(*c*) (Repealed by S.C. 2001, c. 17, s. 130(4).)

► 132.11(7) ◄

(7) Deduction. Subject to subsection (8), the lesser of the amount designated under subsection (6) by a trust for a taxation year and the total of all amounts each of which is allocated by the trust under paragraph (6)(*b*) in respect of the year shall be deducted in computing the trust's income for the following taxation year.

► 132.11(8) ◄

(8) Anti-avoidance. Subsection (7) does not apply in computing the income of a trust for a taxation year where it is reasonable to consider that the designation under subsection (6) for the preceding taxation year was part of a series of transactions or events that includes a change in the composition of beneficiaries under the trust.

SECTION 132.2: [Mutual funds – Qualifying exchange]

► 132.2(1) ◄

(1) Definitions re qualifying exchange of mutual funds. The following definitions apply in this section.

Canadian Tax Foundation: Moch and Johnson, *Recent Developments and Transactions Affecting Income Funds and Royalty Trusts*, 2005 Conference Report 17:1–40; Jack et al., *Income Trust Reorganizations (Canada Revenue Agency Round Table)*, 2005 Conference Report 6A:5–6; Ruby, *Recent Transactions of Interest*, 2004 Conference Report 4:1–43.

"first post-exchange year" — "first post-exchange year", of a fund in respect of a qualifying exchange, means the taxation year of the fund that begins immediately after the acquisition time.

History: S. 132.2(1), the definition "first post-exchange year" was added by S.C. 2013, c. 34, s. 280(1), applicable to qualifying exchanges that occur after 1998.

"qualifying exchange" — "qualifying exchange" means a transfer at any time (in this section referred to as the "transfer time") if

(*a*) the transfer is a transfer of all or substantially all of the property (including an exchange of a unit of a mutual fund trust for another unit of that trust) of

(i) a mutual fund corporation (other than a SIFT wind-up corporation) to one or more mutual fund trusts, or

(ii) a mutual fund trust to a mutual fund trust;

(*b*) all or substantially all of the shares issued by the mutual fund corporation referred to in subparagraph (*a*)(i) or the first mutual fund trust referred to in subparagraph (*a*)(ii) (in this section referred to as the "transferor") and outstanding immediately before the transfer time are within 60 days after the transfer time disposed of to the transferor;

(*c*) no person disposing of shares of the transferor to the transferor within that 60-day period (otherwise than pursuant to the exercise of a statutory right of dissent) receives any consideration for the shares other than units of one or more mutual fund trusts referred to in subparagraph (*a*)(i) or the second mutual fund trust referred to in subparagraph (*a*)(ii) (in this section referred to as a "transferee" and, together with the transferor, as the "funds");

(*d*) if property of the transferor has been transferred to more than one transferee,

(i) all shares of each class of shares, that is recognized under securities legislation as or as part of an investment fund, of the transferor are disposed of to the transferor within 60 days after the transfer time, and

(ii) the units received in consideration for a particular share of a class of shares, that is recognized under securities legislation as or as part of an investment fund, of the transferor are units of the transferee to which all or substantially all of the assets that were allocated to that investment fund immediately before the transfer time were transferred; and

(*e*) the funds jointly so elect, by filing a prescribed form with the Minister on or before the election's due date.

History: S. 132.2(1), the definition "qualifying exchange" was replaced by S.C. 2017, c. 33, s. 52(1), applicable in respect of transfers that occur after March 21, 2017, and formerly read:

"qualifying exchange" — "qualifying exchange" means a transfer at any time (in this section referred to as the "transfer time") of all or substantially all of the property of a mutual fund corporation (other than a SIFT wind-up corporation) or a mutual fund trust to a mutual fund trust (in this section referred to as the "transferor" and "transferee", respectively, and as the "funds") if

(*a*) all or substantially all of the shares issued by the transferor and outstanding immediately before the transfer time are within 60 days after the transfer time disposed of to the transferor;

(*b*) no person disposing of shares of the transferor to the transferor within that 60-day period (otherwise than pursuant to the exercise of a statutory right of dissent) receives any consideration for the shares other than units of the transferee; and

(*c*) the funds jointly so elect, by filing a prescribed form with the Minister on or before the election's due date.

S. 132.2(1), the definition "qualifying exchange" was added by S.C. 2013, c. 34, s. 280(1), applicable to transfers that occur after June 1994, except that, before December 20, 2007, the portion of the definition "qualifying exchange" in subsection 132.2(1) before paragraph (*a*) is to be read as follows:

"*'qualifying exchange'* — "qualifying exchange" means a transfer at any time (in this section referred to as the "transfer time") of all or substantially all of the property of a mutual fund corporation or a mutual fund trust to a mutual fund trust (in this section referred to as the "transferor" and "transferee", respectively, and as the "funds") if"

If an election under paragraph (*c*) of the definition "qualifying exchange" [as it previously read] in subsection 132.2(2) was made, the election continues to have the effect of having section 132.2 of the Act, as modified from time to time, apply to the transfer.

See the history note following s. 132.2(2) for the former reading of the definition "qualifying exchange".

Related Sections: s. 248(1), "SIFT wind-up corporation".

Forms: T1169 — Election on Disposition of Property by a Mutual Fund Corporation (or a Mutual Fund Trust) to a Mutual Fund Trust.

"share" — "share" means a share of the capital stock of a mutual fund corporation and a unit of a mutual fund trust.

History: S. 132.2(1), the definition "share" was replaced by S.C. 2013, c. 34, s. 280(1), applicable to qualifying exchanges that occur after 1998. See the history note following s. 132.2(2) for the former reading of the definition "share".

For qualifying exchanges that occurred after June 1994 and before 1999,

- paragraph 132.2(1)(*j*) [as it formerly read] is to be read as follows:

"(*j*) where shares of the transferor have been disposed of by a taxpayer to the transferor in exchange for units of the transferee within 60 days after the transfer time,

(i) the taxpayer's proceeds of disposition of the shares and the cost to the taxpayer of the units are deemed to be equal to the cost amount to the taxpayer of the shares immediately before the transfer time,

(ii) if all of the taxpayer's shares of the transferor have been so disposed of, for the purposes of applying section 39.1 in respect of the taxpayer after that disposition, the transferee is deemed to be the same entity as the transferor, and

(iii) for the purpose of the definition "designated beneficiary" in section 210, the units are deemed not to have been held at any time by the transferor;"

- subsection 132.2(1) [as it formerly read] is to be read as if it contained a paragraph (*j.1*) that read as follows:

"(*j.1*) if shares of the transferor have been disposed of by a taxpayer to the transferor in exchange for units of the transferee within 60 days after the transfer time, for the purposes of applying section 116 in respect of the disposition, the shares are deemed to be excluded property of the taxpayer;"

If an election under subsection 159(4) of the *Income Tax Amendments Act, 1997*, S.C. 1998, c. 19, was made in respect of a transfer to read subsection 132.2(1) of the *Income Tax Act* without reference to paragraph 132.2(1)(*p*) of that Act, the election is, on the application of subsection (1), deemed to have the effect of reading subsection 132.2(3), in respect of the transfer without reference to its paragraph (i).

S. 132.2(1) formerly read:

(1) *Mutual funds — qualifying exchange.* Where a mutual fund corporation or a mutual fund trust has at any time disposed of a property to a mutual fund trust in a qualifying exchange,

(*a*) the transferee shall be deemed to have acquired the property at the time (in this subsection referred to as the "acquisition time") that is immediately after the time that is immediately after the transfer time, and not to have acquired the property at the transfer time;

(*b*) subject to paragraph (*o*), the last taxation years of the funds that began before the transfer time shall be deemed to have ended at the acquisition time, and their next taxation years shall be deemed to have begun immediately after those last taxation years ended;

(*c*) the transferor's proceeds of disposition of the property and the transferee's cost of the property shall be deemed to be the lesser of

(i) the fair market value of the property at the transfer time, and

(ii) the greatest of

(A) the cost amount to the transferor of the property at the transfer time or, where the property is depreciable property, the lesser of its capital cost and its cost amount to the transferor immediately before the transfer time,

(B) the amount that the funds have agreed upon in respect of the property in their election in respect of the qualifying exchange, and

(C) the fair market value at the transfer time of the consideration (other than units of the transferee) received by the transferor for the disposition of the property;

(*d*) where the property is depreciable property and its capital cost to the transferor exceeds the transferor's proceeds of disposition of the property under paragraph (*c*), for the purposes of sections 13 and 20 and any regulations made for the purposes of paragraph 20(1)(*a*),

(i) the property's capital cost to the transferee shall be deemed to be the amount that was its capital cost to the transferor, and

(ii) the excess shall be deemed to have been allowed to the transferee in respect of the property under regulations made for the purposes of paragraph 20(1)(*a*) in computing income for taxation years ending before the transfer time;

(*e*) where two or more depreciable properties of a prescribed class are disposed of by the transferor to the transferee in the same qualifying exchange, paragraph (*c*) applies as if each property so disposed of had been separately disposed of in the order designated by the transferor at the time of making the election in respect of the qualifying exchange or, if the transferor does not so designate any such order, in the order designated by the Minister;

(*f*) each property of a fund, other than

(i) depreciable property of a prescribed class to which paragraph (*g*) would, but for this paragraph, apply, and

(ii) property disposed of by the transferor to the transferee at the transfer time

shall be deemed to have been disposed of, and to have been reacquired by the fund, immediately before the acquisition time for an amount equal to the lesser of

(iii) the fair market value of the property at the transfer time, and

(iv) the greater of

(A) its cost amount or, where the property is depreciable property, the lesser of its capital cost and its cost amount to the disposing fund at the transfer time, and

(B) the amount that the fund designates in respect of the property in a notification to the Minister accompanying the election in respect of the qualifying exchange;

(*g*) where the undepreciated capital cost to a fund of depreciable property of a prescribed class immediately before the acquisition time exceeds the total of

(i) the fair market value of all the property of that class immediately before the acquisition time, and

(ii) the amount in respect of property of that class otherwise allowed under regulations made for the purposes of paragraph 20(1)(*a*) or deductible under subsection 20(16) in computing the fund's income for the taxation year that includes the transfer time,

the excess shall be deducted in computing the fund's income for the taxation year that includes the transfer time and shall be deemed to have been allowed in respect of property of that class under regulations made for the purposes of paragraph 20(1)(*a*);

(*h*) except as provided in paragraph (*p*), the transferor's cost of any particular property received by the transferor from the transferee as consideration for the disposition of the property is deemed to be

(i) nil, where the particular property is a unit of the transferee, and

(ii) the particular property's fair market value at the transfer time, in any other case;

(*i*) the transferor's proceeds of disposition of any units of the transferee received as consideration for the disposition of the property that were disposed of by the transferor within 60 days after the transfer time in exchange for shares of the transferor shall be deemed to be nil;

(*j*) where shares of the transferor have been disposed of by a taxpayer to the transferor in exchange for units of the transferee within 60 days after the transfer time,

(i) the taxpayer's proceeds of disposition of the shares and the cost to the taxpayer of the units shall be deemed to be equal to the cost amount to the taxpayer of the shares immediately before the transfer time, and

(ii) where all of the taxpayer's shares of the transferor have been so disposed of, for the purposes of applying section 39.1 in respect of the taxpayer after that disposition, the transferee shall be deemed to be the same entity as the transferor;

(*k*) if a share to which paragraph (*j*) applies would, but for this paragraph, cease to be a qualified investment (within the meaning assigned by subsection 146(1), 146.1(1) or 146.3(1), section 204 or subsection 205(1) or 207.01(1)) as a consequence of the qualifying exchange, the share is deemed to be a qualified investment until the earlier of the day that is 60 days after the transfer time and the time at which it is disposed of in accordance with paragraph (*j*);

(*l*) there shall be added to the amount determined under the description of A in the definition "refundable capital gains tax on hand" in subsection 132(4) in respect of the transferee for its taxation years that begin after the transfer time the amount, if any, by which

(i) the transferor's refundable capital gains tax on hand (within the meaning assigned by subsection 131(6) or 132(4), as the case may be) at the end of its taxation year that includes the transfer time

exceeds

(ii) the transferor's capital gains refund (within the meaning assigned by paragraph 131(2)(*a*) or 132(1)(*a*), as the case may be) for that year;

(*m*) no amount in respect of a non-capital loss, net capital loss, restricted farm loss, farm loss or limited partnership loss of a fund for a taxation year that began before the transfer time is deductible in computing its taxable income for a taxation year that begins after the transfer time;

(*n*) where the transferor is a mutual fund trust, for the purposes of subsections 132.1(1) and (3) to (5), the transferee shall be deemed after the transfer time to be the same mutual fund trust as, and a continuation of, the transferor;

(*o*) where the transferor is a mutual fund corporation,

(i) for the purposes of subsection 131(4), the transferor is deemed in respect of any share disposed of in accordance with paragraph (*j*) to be a mutual fund corporation at the time of the disposition, and

(ii) for the purposes of Part I.3, the transferor's taxation year that, but for this paragraph, would have included the transfer time is deemed to have ended immediately before the transfer time (except that, for greater certainty, nothing in this paragraph shall affect the computation of any amount determined under this Part);

(*p*) for the purpose of determining the funds' capital gains redemptions (as defined in subsection 131(6) or 132(4)), for their taxation years that include the transfer time,

(i) the total of the cost amounts to the transferor of all its properties at the end of the year is deemed to be the total of all amounts each of which is

(A) the transferor's proceeds of disposition of a property that was transferred to a transferee on the qualifying exchange, or

(B) the cost amount to the transferor at the end of the year of a property that was not transferred on the qualifying exchange, and

(ii) the transferee is deemed not to have acquired any property that was transferred to it on the qualifying exchange; and

(*q*) except as provided in subparagraph (*o*)(i), the transferor is, notwithstanding subsections 131(8) and 132(6), deemed to be neither a mutual fund corporation nor a mutual fund trust for taxation years that begin after the transfer time.

Related Sections: S. 7(1.4) Exchange of options; s. 7(1.5) Rules where securities exchanged; s. 84(3) Redemption, etc; s. 248(1), "cost amount".

Canadian Tax Foundation: Ruby and Shragie, *Policy Forum: Hidden Tax Traps in Section 132.2 Mergers — Trusts, REITs, and Other Businesses*, 2006 Canadian Tax Journal 2:450–456; Ewens, *Mergers of Income Funds*, 2001 Conference Report 3:1–8; Chasmar and Chua, *The Taxation of Corporate Reorganizations — Reorganizations of Investment Funds*, 2001 Canadian Tax Journal 2:482–497; Fyfe and Webster, *Current Mutual Fund Developments And Products*, 2000 Conference Report 21:1–60.

Tax Profile: December 2002 — Update on Current CCRA GAAR Activity.

Forms: T1169 — Election on Disposition of Property by a Mutual Fund Corporation (or a Mutual Fund Trust) to a Mutual Fund Trust.

Income Tax Technical News: Issue No. 34, Income Trust Reorganizations.

► 132.2(2) ◄

(2) Timing. In respect of a qualifying exchange, a time referred to in the following list immediately follows the time that precedes it in the list

(*a*) the transfer time;

(*b*) the first intervening time;

(*c*) the acquisition time;

(*d*) the beginning of the funds' first post-exchange years;

(*e*) the depreciables disposition time;

(*f*) the second intervening time; and

(*g*) the depreciables acquisition time.

History: S. 132.2(2) was replaced by S.C. 2013, c. 34, s. 280(1), applicable to qualifying exchanges that occur after 1998, and formerly read:

(2) *Definitions.* In this section,

"qualifying exchange" — "qualifying exchange" means a transfer at any time (in this section referred to as the "transfer time") of all or substantially all of the property of a mutual fund corporation (other than a SIFT wind-up corporation) or mutual fund trust to a mutual fund trust (in this section referred to as the "transferor" and "transferee", respectively, and as the "funds"), if

(*a*) all or substantially all of the shares issued by the transferor and outstanding immediately before the transfer time are within 60 days after the transfer time disposed of to the transferor,

(*b*) no person disposing of shares of the transferor to the transferor within that 60-day period (otherwise than pursuant to the exercise of a statutory right of dissent) receives any consideration for the shares other than units of the transferee, and

(*c*) the funds jointly elect, by filing a prescribed form with the Minister within 6 months after the transfer time, to have this section apply with respect to the transfer;

"share" — "share" means a share of the capital stock of a mutual fund corporation and a unit of a mutual fund trust.

S. 132.2(2), the portion of the definition "qualifying exchange" before paragraph (*a*) was replaced by S.C. 2009, c. 2, s. 44(1), applicable after December 19, 2007. S. 132.2(2), the portion of the definition "qualifying exchange" before paragraph (*a*) formerly read:

"qualifying exchange" — "qualifying exchange" means a transfer at any time (in this section referred to as the "transfer time") of all or substantially all of the property of a mutual fund corporation or mutual fund trust to a mutual fund trust (in this section referred to as the "transferor" and "transferee", respectively, and as the "funds") where

► 132.2(3) ◄

(3) General. In respect of a qualifying exchange,

(*a*) each property of a fund, other than property disposed of by the transferor to a transferee at the transfer time and depreciable property, is deemed to have been disposed of, and to have been reacquired by the fund, at the first intervening time, for an amount equal to the lesser of

(i) the fair market value of the property at the transfer time, and

(ii) the greater of

(A) its cost amount, and

(B) the amount that the fund designates in respect of the property in a notification to the Minister accompanying the election in respect of the qualifying exchange;

(*a*.1) in respect of each property transferred by the transferor to a transferee, including an exchange of a unit of a transferee for another unit of that transferee, the transferor is deemed to have disposed of the property to the transferee, and to have received units of the transferee as consideration for the disposition of the property, at the transfer time;

(*b*) subject to paragraph (*l*), the last taxation years of the funds that began before the transfer time are deemed to have ended at the acquisition time, and their first post-exchange years are deemed to have begun immediately after those last taxation years ended;

(*c*) each depreciable property of a fund (other than property to which subsection (5) applies and property to which paragraph (*d*) would, if this Act were read without reference to this paragraph, apply) is deemed to have been disposed of, and to have been reacquired, by the fund at the second intervening time for an amount equal to the lesser of

(i) the fair market value of the property at the depreciables disposition time, and

(ii) the greater of

(A) the lesser of its capital cost and its cost amount to the disposing fund at the depreciables disposition time, and

(B) the amount that the fund designates in respect of the property in a notification to the Minister accompanying the election in respect of the qualifying exchange;

(*d*) if at the second intervening time the undepreciated capital cost to a fund of depreciable property of a prescribed class exceeds the fair market value of all the property of that class, the excess is to be deducted in computing the fund's income for the taxation year that includes the transfer time and is deemed to have been allowed in respect of property of that class under regulations made for the purpose of paragraph 20(1)(*a*);

(*e*) except as provided in paragraph (*m*), the transferor's cost of any particular property received by the transferor from a transferee as consideration for the disposition of the property is deemed to be

(i) nil, if the particular property is a unit of the transferee, and

(ii) the particular property's fair market value at the transfer time, in any other case;

(*f*) the transferor's proceeds of disposition of any units of a transferee that were disposed of by the transferor at any particular time that is within 60 days after the transfer time in exchange for shares of the transferor, are deemed to be equal to the cost amount of the units to the transferor immediately before the particular time;

(*g*) if, at any particular time that is within 60 days after the transfer time, a taxpayer disposes of shares of the transferor to the transferor in exchange for units of a transferee

(i) the taxpayer's proceeds of disposition of the shares and the cost to the taxpayer of the units are deemed to be equal to the cost amount to the taxpayer of the shares immediately before the particular time,

(ii) for the purposes of applying section 116 in respect of the disposition, the shares are deemed to be excluded property of the taxpayer,

(iii) where the qualifying exchange occurs after 2004, for the purposes of applying section 218.3 in respect of that exchange, the payment or crediting of the units to the taxpayer by the transferor is deemed not to be an assessable distribution,

(iv) where all of the taxpayer's shares of the transferor have been so disposed of, for the purpose of applying section 39.1 in respect of the taxpayer after that disposition, the transferee is deemed to be the same entity as the transferor,

(v) for the purpose of the definition "designated beneficiary" in section 210, the units are deemed not to have been held at any time by the transferor, and

(vi) if the taxpayer is at the particular time affiliated with the transferor or the transferee,

(A) those units are deemed not to be identical to any other units of the transferee,

(B) if the taxpayer is the transferee, and the units cease to exist when the taxpayer acquires them (or, for greater certainty, when the taxpayer would but for that cessation have acquired them), the taxpayer is deemed

(I) to have acquired those units at the particular time, and

(II) to have disposed of those units immediately after the particular time for proceeds of disposition equal to the cost amount to the taxpayer of those units at the particular time, and

(C) in any other case, for the purpose of computing any gain or loss of the taxpayer from the taxpayer's first disposition, after the particular time, of each of those units,

(I) if that disposition is a renunciation or surrender of the unit by the taxpayer for no consideration, and is not in favour of any person other than the transferee, the taxpayer's proceeds of disposition of that unit are deemed to be equal to that unit's cost amount to the taxpayer immediately before that disposition, and

(II) if subclause (I) does not apply, the taxpayer's proceeds of disposition of that unit are deemed to be equal to the greater of that unit's fair market value and its cost amount to the taxpayer immediately before that disposition;

(*h*) where a share to which paragraph (*g*) applies would, if this Act were read without reference to this paragraph, cease to be a *qualified investment* (within the meaning assigned by subsection 146(1), 146.1(1), 146.3(1) or 146.4(1), section 204 or subsection 207.01(1)) as a consequence of the qualifying exchange, the share is deemed to be a qualified investment until the earlier of the day that is 60 days after the day that includes the transfer time and the time at which it is disposed of in accordance with paragraph (*g*);

(*i*) there shall be added to the amount determined under the description of A in the definition *refundable capital gains tax on hand* in subsection 132(4) in respect of a transferee for its taxation years that begin after the transfer time the amount determined by the formula

$$(A - B) \times C/D$$

where

A is the transferor's *refundable capital gains tax on hand* (within the meaning assigned by subsection 131(6) or 132(4), as the case may be) at the end of its taxation year that includes the transfer time,

B is the transferor's *capital gains refund* (within the meaning assigned by paragraph 131 (2)(*a*) or 132(1)(*a*), as the case may be) for that year,

C is the total fair market value of property of the transferor disposed of to, net of liabilities assumed by, the transferee on the qualifying exchange, and

D is the total fair market value of property of the transferor disposed of to, net of liabilities assumed by, all transferees on the qualifying exchange;

(*j*) no amount in respect of a non-capital loss, net capital loss, restricted farm loss, farm loss or limited partnership loss of a fund for a taxation year that began before the transfer time is deductible in computing the taxable income of any of the funds for a taxation year that begins after the transfer time;

(*k*) if the transferor is a mutual fund trust, for the purposes of subsections 132.1(1) and (3) to (5), the transferee is deemed after the transfer time to be the same mutual fund trust as, and a continuation of, the transferor;

(*l*) if the transferor is a mutual fund corporation

(i) for the purpose of subsection 131(4) but, for greater certainty, without having any effect on the computation of any amount determined under this Part, the transferor is deemed in respect of any share disposed of in accordance with paragraph (*g*) to be a mutual fund corporation at the time of the disposition,

(ii) for the purpose of Part I.3 but, for greater certainty, without having any effect on the computation of any amount determined under this Part, the transferor's taxation year that, if this Act were read without reference to this paragraph, would have included the transfer time is deemed to have ended immediately before the transfer time, and

(iii) for the purpose of subsection 131 (1), a dividend that is made payable at a particular time after the acquisition time but within the 60-day period commencing immediately after the transfer time, and paid before the end of that period, by the transferor to taxpayers that held shares of a class of shares of the transferor, that was recognized under securities legislation as or as part of an investment fund, immediately before the transfer time is deemed to have become payable at the first intervening time if the transferor so elects in respect of the full amount of the dividend in prescribed manner on or before the day on which any part of the dividend was paid;

(*m*) for the purpose of determining the funds' capital gains redemptions (as defined in subsection 131(6) or 132(4), as the case may be), for their taxation years that include the transfer time,

(i) the total of the cost amounts to the transferor of all its properties at the end of the year is deemed to be the total of all amounts each of which is

(A) the transferor's proceeds of disposition of a property that was transferred to a transferee on the qualifying exchange, or

(B) the cost amount to the transferor at the end of the year of a property that was not transferred on the qualifying exchange,

(ii) a transferee is deemed not to have acquired any property that was transferred to it on the qualifying exchange; and

(iii) the amounts determined under the descriptions of A and B in the definition *capital gains redemptions* shall be determined as if the year ended immediately before the transfer time; and

(*n*) except as provided in subparagraph (*l*)(i), the transferor is, notwithstanding subsections 131(8) and (8.01) and 132(6), deemed to be neither a mutual fund corporation nor a mutual fund trust for taxation years that begin after the transfer time.

History: S. 132.2(3)(*n*) was replaced by S.C. 2017, c. 33, s. 52(13), applicable in respect of transfers that occur after March 21, 2017, and formerly read:

(*n*) except as provided in subparagraph (*l*)(i), the transferor is, notwithstanding subsections 131(8) and 132(6), deemed to be neither a mutual fund corporation nor a mutual fund trust for taxation years that begin after the transfer time.

S. 132.2(3)(*m*)(iii) was added by S.C. 2017, c. 33, s. 52(12), applicable in respect of qualifying exchanges where an election in respect of the qualifying exchange is filed or amended after September 7, 2017.

S. 132.2(3)(*m*)(ii) was replaced by S.C. 2017, c. 33, s. 52(11), applicable in respect of transfers that occur after March 21, 2017, and formerly read:

(ii) the transferee is deemed not to have acquired any property that was transferred to it on the qualifying exchange; and

S. 132.2(3)(*l*)(iii) was added by S.C. 2017, c. 33, s. 52(10), applicable in respect of transfers that occur after March 21, 2017.

S. 132.2(3)(*i*) and (*j*) were replaced by S.C. 2017, c. 33, s. 52(9), applicable in respect of transfers that occur after March 21, 2017, and formerly read:

(*i*) there shall be added to the amount determined under the description of A in the definition "refundable capital gains tax on hand" in subsection 132(4) in respect of the transferee for its taxation years that begin after the transfer time the amount, if any, by which

(i) the transferor's refundable capital gains tax on hand (within the meaning assigned by subsection 131(6) or 132(4), as the case may be) at the end of its taxation year that includes the transfer time

exceeds

(ii) the transferor's capital gains refund (within the meaning assigned by paragraph 131(2)(*a*) or 132(1)(*a*), as the case may be) for that year;

(*j*) no amount in respect of a non-capital loss, net capital loss, restricted farm loss, farm loss or limited partnership loss of a fund for a taxation year that began before the transfer time is deductible in computing the taxable income of either of the funds for a taxation year that begins after the transfer time;

S. 132.2(3)(*h*) was replaced by S.C. 2017, c. 33, s. 52(8), deemed to have come into force on March 23, 2017, and formerly read:

(*h*) where a share to which paragraph (*g*) applies would, if this Act were read without reference to this paragraph, cease to be a qualified investment (within the meaning assigned by subsection 146(1), 146.1(1) or 146.3(1), section 204 or subsection 205(1) or 207.01(1)) as a consequence of the qualifying exchange, the share is deemed to be a qualified investment until the earlier of the day that is 60 days after the day that includes the transfer time and the time at which it is disposed of in accordance with paragraph (*g*);

S. 132.2(3)(*g*)(vi), the portion before clause (A) was replaced by S.C. 2017, c. 33, s. 52(7), applicable in respect of transfers that occur after March 21, 2017, and formerly read:

(vi) where the taxpayer is at the particular time affiliated with one or both of the funds,

S. 132.2(3)(*g*), the portion before subparagraph (i) was replaced by S.C. 2017, c. 33, s. 52(6), applicable in respect of transfers that occur after March 21, 2017, and formerly read:

(*g*) if, at any particular time that is within 60 days after the transfer time, a taxpayer disposes of shares of the transferor to the transferor in exchange for units of the transferee

S. 132.2(3)(*f*) was replaced by S.C. 2017, c. 33, s. 52(5), applicable in respect of transfers that occur after March 21, 2017, and formerly read:

(*f*) the transferor's proceeds of disposition of any units of the transferee that were disposed of by the transferor at any particular time that is within 60 days after the transfer time in exchange for shares of the transferor, are deemed to be equal to the cost amount of the units to the transferor immediately before the particular time;

S. 132.2(3)(*e*), the portion before subparagraph (i) was replaced by S.C. 2017, c. 33, s. 52(4), applicable in respect of transfers that occur after March 21, 2017, and formerly read:

(*e*) except as provided in paragraph (*m*), the transferor's cost of any particular property received by the transferor from the transferee as consideration for the disposition of the property is deemed to be

S. 132.2(3)(*a.1*) was added by S.C. 2017, c. 33, s. 52(3), applicable in respect of transfers that occur after March 21, 2017.

S. 132.2(3)(*a*), the portion before subparagraph (i) was replaced by S.C. 2017, c. 33, s. 52(2), applicable in respect of transfers that occur after March 21, 2017, and formerly read:

(*a*) each property of a fund, other than property disposed of by the transferor to the transferee at the transfer time and depreciable property, is deemed to have been disposed of, and to have been reacquired by the fund, at the first intervening time, for an amount equal to the lesser of

S. 132.2(3) was added by S.C. 2013, c. 34, s. 280(1), applicable to qualifying exchanges that occur after 1998, except that,

(*a*) if a qualifying exchange occurred before July 18, 2005 and the transferee has, before that day, filed a return of income, for any taxation year, that identified the realization of any loss that would not have been realized if paragraphs 132.2(3)(*f*) and (*g*) had applied in respect of the qualifying exchange, those paragraphs are to be read in their application to the qualifying exchange as follows:

"(*f*) the transferor's proceeds of disposition of any units of the transferee that were received by the transferor as consideration for the disposition of the property, and that were disposed of by the transferor within 60 days after the transfer time in exchange for shares of the transferor, are deemed to be nil;

(*g*) if, within 60 days after the transfer time, a taxpayer disposes of shares of the transferor to the transferor in exchange for units of the transferee

(i) the taxpayer's proceeds of disposition of the shares and the cost to the taxpayer of the units are deemed to be equal to the cost amount to the taxpayer of the shares immediately before the transfer time,

(ii) for the purposes of applying section 116 in respect of the disposition, the shares are deemed to be excluded property of the taxpayer,

(iii) where the qualifying exchange occurs after 2004, for the purposes of applying section 218.3 in respect of that exchange, the payment or crediting of the units to the taxpayer by the transferor is deemed not to be an assessable distribution,

(iv) where all of the taxpayer's shares of the transferor have been so disposed of, for the purpose of applying section 39.1 in respect of the taxpayer after that disposition, the transferee is deemed to be the same entity as the transferor, and

(v) for the purpose of the definition "designated beneficiary" in section 210, the units are deemed not to have been held at any time by the transferor;"

(*b*) before the 2008 taxation year, paragraph 132.2(3)(*h*) is to be read as follows:

"(*h*) where a share to which paragraph (*g*) applies would, if this Act were read without reference to this paragraph, cease to be a qualified investment (within the meaning assigned by subsection 146(1), 146.1(1) or 146.3(1) or section 204) as a consequence of the qualifying exchange, the share is deemed to be a qualified investment until the earlier of the day that is 60 days after the transfer time and the time at which it is disposed of in accordance with paragraph (*g*);"

and

(*c*) for the 2008 taxation year, paragraph 132.2(3)(*h*) is to be read as follows:

"(*h*) where a share to which paragraph (*g*) applies would, if this Act were read without reference to this paragraph, cease to be a qualified investment (within the meaning assigned by subsection 146(1), 146.1(1) or 146.3(1), section 204 or subsection 205(1)) as a consequence of the qualifying exchange, the share is deemed to be a qualified investment until the earlier of the day that is 60 days after the transfer time and the time at which it is disposed of in accordance with paragraph (*g*);"

If an election under subsection 159(4) of the *Income Tax Amendments Act, 1997*, S.C. 1998, c. 19, was made in respect of a transfer to read subsection 132.2(1) of the *Income Tax Act* without reference to paragraph 132.2(1)(*p*) of that Act, the election is, on the application of subsection (1), deemed to have the effect of reading subsection 132.2(3), in respect of the transfer without reference to its paragraph (i).

See also the history note for s. 132.2(1) for the provision as it formerly read.

► 132.2(4) ◄

(4) Qualifying exchange — non-depreciable property. If a transferor transfers a property, other than a depreciable property, to a transferee in a qualifying exchange,

(*a*) the transferee is deemed to have acquired the property at the acquisition time and not to have acquired the property at the transfer time;

(*b*) the transferor's proceeds of disposition of the property and the transferee's cost of the property are deemed to be the lesser of

(i) the fair market value of the property at the transfer time, and

(ii) the greatest of

(A) the cost amount to the transferor of the property at the transfer time,

(B) the amount that the transferor and the transferee agree on in respect of the property in their election, and

(C) the fair market value at the transfer time of the consideration (other than units of the transferee) received by the transferor for the disposition of the property; and

(*c*) if the property is a unit of the transferee and the unit ceases to exist when the transferee acquires it (or, for greater certainty, when the transferee would but for that cessation have acquired it), paragraphs (*a*) and (*b*) do not apply to the transferee.

History: S. 132.2(4)(*c*) was added by S.C. 2017, c. 33, s. 52(15), applicable in respect of transfers that occur after March 21, 2017.

S. 132.2(4)(*b*)(ii)(B) was replaced by S.C. 2017, c. 33, s. 52(14), applicable in respect of transfers that occur after March 21, 2017, and formerly read:

(B) the amount that the funds agree on in respect of the property in their election, and

S. 132.2(4) was added by S.C. 2013, c. 34, s. 280(1), applicable to qualifying exchanges that occur after 1998.

► 132.2(5) ◄

(5) Depreciable property. If a transferor transfers a depreciable property to a transferee in a qualifying exchange,

(*a*) the transferor is deemed to have disposed of the property at the depreciables disposition time, and not to have disposed of the property at the transfer time;

(*b*) the transferee is deemed to have acquired the property at the depreciables acquisition time, and not to have acquired the property at the transfer time;

(*c*) the transferor's proceeds of disposition of the property and the transferee's cost of the property are deemed to be the lesser of

(i) the fair market value of the property at the transfer time, and

(ii) the greatest of

(A) the lesser of its capital cost and its cost amount to the transferor immediately before the depreciables disposition time,

(B) the amount that the transferor and the transferee agree on in respect of the property in their election, and

(C) the fair market value at the transfer time of the consideration (other than units of the transferee) received by the transferor for the disposition of the property;

(*d*) where the capital cost of the property to the transferor exceeds the transferor's proceeds of disposition of the property under paragraph (*c*), for the purposes of sections 13 and 20 and any regulations made for the purpose of paragraph 20(1)(*a*),

(i) the property's capital cost to the transferee is deemed to be the amount that was its capital cost to the transferor, and

(ii) the excess is deemed to have been allowed to the transferee in respect of the property under regulations made for the purpose of paragraph 20(1)(*a*) in computing income for taxation years ending before the transfer time; and

(*e*) where two or more depreciable properties of a prescribed class are disposed of by the transferor to the transferee in the same qualifying exchange, paragraph (*c*) applies as if each property so disposed of had been separately disposed of in the order designated by the transferor at the time of making the election in respect of the qualifying exchange or, if the transferor does not so designate any such order, in the order designated by the Minister.

History: S. 132.2(5)(*c*)(ii)(B) was replaced by S.C. 2017, c. 33, s. 52(16), applicable in respect of transfers that occur after March 21, 2017, and formerly read:

(B) the amount that the funds agree on in respect of the property in their election, and

S. 132.2(5) was added by S.C. 2013, c. 34, s. 280(1), applicable to qualifying exchanges that occur after 1998.

► 132.2(6) ◄

(6) Due date. The due date of an election referred to in paragraph (*c*) of the definition "qualifying exchange" in subsection (1) is

(*a*) the day that is six months after the day that includes the transfer time; and

(*b*) on joint application by the funds, any later day that the Minister accepts.

History: S. 132.2(6) was added by S.C. 2013, c. 34, s. 280(1), applicable to transfers that occur after June 1994.

► 132.2(7) ◄

(7) Amendment or revocation of election. The Minister may, on joint application by the funds on or before the due date of an election referred to in paragraph (*e*) of the definition *qualifying exchange* in subsection (1), grant permission to amend or revoke the election.

History: S. 132.2(7) was replaced by S.C. 2017, c. 33, s. 52(17), applicable in respect of transfers that occur after March 21, 2017, and formerly read:

(7) *Amendment or Revocation of Election.* The Minister may, on joint application by the funds on or before the due date of an election referred to in paragraph (*c*) of the definition "qualifying exchange" in subsection (1), grant permission to amend or revoke the election.

S. 132.2(7) was added by S.C. 2013, c. 34, s. 280(1), applicable to transfers that occur after June 1994.

Non-Resident-Owned Investment Corporations

SECTION 133: [Non-resident-owned investment corporations]

► 133(1) ◄

(1) Computation of income. In computing the income of a non-resident-owned investment corporation for a taxation year,

(*a*) no deduction may be made in respect of interest on its bonds, debentures, securities or other indebtedness, and

(*b*) no deduction may be made under subsection 65(1),

and its income and taxable income shall be computed as if

(*c*) the only taxable capital gains and allowable capital losses referred to in paragraph 3(*b*) were from dispositions of taxable Canadian property,

(*d*) any taxable capital gain or allowable capital loss of the corporation were an amount equal to twice the amount thereof otherwise determined, and

(*e*) subsection 83(2) were read without reference to paragraph 83(2)(*b*).

Tax Topics: No. 1618, The End of the NRO.

► 133(2) ◄

(2) Non-resident-owned investment corporations. In computing the taxable income of a non-resident-owned investment corporation for a taxation year, no deduction may be made from its income for the year, except

(*a*) interest received in the year from other non-resident-owned investment corporations;

(*b*) taxes paid to the government of a country other than Canada in respect of any part of the income of the corporation for the year derived from sources therein; and

(*c*) net capital losses as provided for by section 111.

Related Sections: S. 133(9), "allowable refundable tax on hand", "cumulative taxable income".

► 133(3) ◄

(3) Special tax rate. The tax payable under this Part by a corporation for a taxation year when it was a non-resident-owned investment corporation is an amount equal to 25% of its taxable income for the year.

► 133(4) ◄

(4) No deduction for foreign taxes. No deduction from the tax payable under this Part by a non-resident-owned investment corporation may be made under section 124 or in respect of taxes paid to the government of a country other than Canada.

Related Sections: S. 113(3) Definitions; s. 133(1) Computation of income; s. 133(2) Non-resident-owned investment corporations; s. 133(8), "non-resident-owned investment corporation".

► 133(5) ◄

(5) 1971 undistributed income and capital surplus on hand — (Repealed by 1977-78, c. 1, s. 66(1), applicable after December 31, 1978.)

► 133(6) ◄

(6) Allowable refund to non-resident-owned investment corporations. If the return of a non-resident-owned investment corporation's income for a taxation year has been made within 3 years from the end of the year, the Minister

(*a*) may, on sending the notice of assessment for the year, refund without application its allowable refund for the year; and

(*b*) shall, with all due dispatch, make that allowable refund after sending the notice of assessment if an application for it has been made in writing by the corporation within the period within which the Minister would be allowed under subsection 152(4) to assess tax payable by the corporation for the year if that subsection were read without reference to paragraph 152(4)(*a*).

History: S. 133(6)(*a*) and (*b*) were replaced by S.C. 2010, c. 25, s. 32, in force on Royal Assent, December 15, 2010. S. 133(6)(*a*) and (*b*) formerly read:

(*a*) may, on mailing the notice of assessment for the year, refund without application therefor its allowable refund for the year; and

(*b*) shall, with all due dispatch, make that allowable refund after mailing the notice of assessment if an application for it has been made in writing by the corporation within the period within which the Minister would be allowed under subsection 152(4) to assess tax payable by the corporation for the year if that subsection were read without reference to paragraph 152(4)(*a*).

Related Sections: S. 133(7) Application to other liability.

► 133(7) ◄

(7) Application to other liability. Instead of making a refund that might otherwise be made under subsection (6), the Minister may, where the taxpayer is liable or about to become liable to make any payment under this Act, apply the amount that would otherwise be refunded to that other liability and notify the taxpayer of that action.

► 133(7.01) ◄

(7.01) Interest on allowable refund. Where an allowable refund for a taxation year is paid to, or applied to a liability of, a non-resident-owned investment corporation, the Minister shall pay or apply interest on the refund at the prescribed rate for the period beginning on the day that is the later of

(*a*) the day that is 120 days after the end of the year, and

(*b*) the day that is 30 days after the day on which the corporation's return of income under this Part for the year was filed under section 150, unless the return was filed on or before the day on or before which it was required to be filed,

and ending on the day the refund is paid or applied.

Related Regulations: 4301.

Related Sections: S. 161.1 Refund interest.

► 133(7.02) ◄

(7.02) Excess interest on allowable refund. Where at any particular time interest has been paid to, or applied to a liability of, a corporation under subsection (7.01) in respect of an allowable refund and it is determined at a subsequent time that the allowable refund was less than that in respect of which interest was so paid or applied,

(*a*) the amount by which the interest that was so paid or applied exceeds the interest, if any, computed in respect of the amount that is determined at the subsequent time to be the allowable refund shall be deemed to be an amount (in this subsection referred to as the "amount payable") that became payable under this Part by the corporation at the particular time;

(*b*) the corporation shall pay to the Receiver General interest at the prescribed rate on the amount payable, computed from the particular time to the day of payment; and

(*c*) the Minister may at any time assess the corporation in respect of the amount payable and, where the Minister makes such an assessment, the provisions of Divisions I and J apply, with such modifications as the circumstances require, in respect of the assessment as though it had been made under section 152.

Related Regulations: 4301.

Related Sections: S. 161.1 Refund interest.

► 133(7.1) ◄

(7.1) Election re capital gains dividend. Where at any particular time after 1971 a dividend has become payable by a non-resident-owned investment corporation to shareholders of any class of shares of its capital stock, if the corporation so elects in respect of the full amount of the dividend, in prescribed manner and prescribed form and at or before the particular time or the first day on which any part of the dividend was paid if that day is earlier than the particular time, the following rules apply:

(*a*) the dividend shall be deemed to be a capital gains dividend to the extent that it does not exceed the corporation's capital gains dividend account immediately before the particular time; and

(*b*) any amount received by another non-resident-owned investment corporation in a taxation year as, on account or in lieu of payment of, or in satisfaction of the capital gains dividend shall not be included in computing its income for the year.

Related Regulations: 2105.

Related Sections: S. 83(2) Capital dividend; s. 89(1) Capital dividend account; s. 115(1)(*b*) Non-resident's taxable income in Canada; s. 133(7.2) Simultaneous dividends; s. 133(7.3) Application of ss. 131(1.1) to (1.4); s. 133(8), "Canadian property", "capital gains dividend account", "taxable dividend"; s. 212(2) Tax on dividends.

Forms: T5 Sum. — Return of Investment Income; T5 — Statement of Investment Income; T2063 — Election in Respect of a Capital Gains Dividend Under Subsection 133(7.1).

Interpretation Bulletins: *Secondary* — IT-149R4 Winding-up dividend.

► 133(7.2) ◄

(7.2) Simultaneous dividends. Where a dividend becomes payable at the same time on more than one class of shares of the capital stock of a non-resident-owned investment corporation, for the purposes of subsection (7.1), the dividend on any such class of shares shall be deemed to become payable at a different time than the dividend on the other class or classes of shares and to become payable in the order designated

(*a*) by the corporation on or before the day on or before which the election described in subsection (7.1) is required to be filed; or

(*b*) in any other case, by the Minister.

► 133(7.3) ◄

(7.3) Application of ss. 131(1.1) to (1.4). Where at any particular time a non-resident-owned investment corporation paid a dividend to its shareholders and subsection (7.1) would have applied to the dividend except that the corporation did not make an election under that subsection on or before the day on or before which it was required by that subsection to be made, subsections 131(1.1) to (1.4) apply with such modifications as the circumstances require.

► 133(7.4) ◄

(7.4) Request to make election — (Repealed by 1985, c. 45, s. 77.)

► 133(7.5) ◄

(7.5) Penalty — (Repealed by 1985, c. 45, s. 77.)

► 133(7.6) ◄

(7.6) Assessment and payment of penalty — (Repealed by 1985, c. 45, s. 77.)

► 133(8) ◄

(8) Definitions. In this section,

"allowable refund" —"allowable refund" of a non-resident-owned investment corporation for a taxation year means the total of amounts each of which is an amount in respect of a taxable dividend paid by the corporation in the year on a share of its capital stock, determined by the formula

$$A/B \times C$$

where

A is the corporation's allowable refundable tax on hand immediately before the dividend was paid,

B is the greater of the amount of the dividend so paid and the corporation's cumulative taxable income immediately before the dividend was paid, and

C is the amount of the dividend so paid;

Canadian Tax Foundation: Fontaine and Kong, *The March 16, 2001 Draft Legislation: Thin Capitalization, Non-Resident-Owned Investment Corporations and Foreign Spinoff Relief,* 2001 Canadian Tax Journal 2:383–401.

"Canadian property" —"Canadian property" means

(*a*) taxable Canadian property, and

(*b*) any other property not being foreign property within the meaning assigned by section 206;

"capital gains dividend account" —"capital gains dividend account" of a non-resident-owned investment corporation at any particular time means the amount determined by the formula

$$A - B$$

where

A is the total of the following amounts in respect of the period commencing January 1, 1972 and ending immediately after the corporation's last taxation year ending before the particular time:

(*a*) the corporation's capital gains for taxation years ending in the period from dispositions in the period of Canadian property or shares of another non-resident-owned investment corporation, and

(*b*) amounts received by the corporation in the period as, on account or in lieu of payment of, or in satisfaction of capital gains dividends from other non-resident-owned investment corporations, and

B is the total of the following amounts in respect of the period referred to in the description of A:

(*a*) the corporation's capital losses for taxation years ending in the period from dispositions in the period of Canadian property or shares of another non-resident-owned investment corporation,

(*b*) all capital gains dividends that became payable by the corporation before the particular time, and

(*c*) the amount determined by the formula

$$0.25 \times (M - N)$$

where

M is the total of the corporation's capital gains for taxation years ending in the period from dispositions in the period of taxable Canadian property, and

N is the total of the corporation's capital losses for the taxation years ending in the period from dispositions in the period of property of the kinds referred to in the description of M;

"increase in capital" —"increase in capital" in respect of a corporation means a transaction (other than a transaction carried out pursuant to an agreement in writing made before February 28, 2000, referred to in this definition as a "specified transaction") in the course of which the corporation issues additional shares of its capital stock or incurs indebtedness, if the transaction has the effect of increasing the total of

(*a*) the corporation's liabilities, and

(*b*) the fair market value of all the shares of its capital stock

to an amount that is substantially greater than that total would have been on February 27, 2000 if all specified transactions had been carried out immediately before that day;

"non-resident-owned investment corporation" —"non-resident-owned investment corporation" means a corporation incorporated in Canada that, throughout the whole of the period commencing on the later of June 18, 1971 and the day on which it was incorporated and ending on the last day of the taxation year in respect of which the expression is being applied, complied with the following conditions:

(*a*) all of its issued shares and all of its bonds, debentures and other funded indebtedness were

(i) beneficially owned by non-resident persons (other than any foreign affiliate of a taxpayer resident in Canada),

(ii) owned by trustees for the benefit of non-resident persons or their unborn issue, or

(iii) owned by a non-resident-owned investment corporation, all of the issued shares of which and all of the bonds, debentures and other funded indebtedness of which were beneficially owned by non-resident persons or owned by trustees for the benefit of non-resident persons or their unborn issue, or by two or more such corporations,

(*b*) its income for each taxation year ending in the period was derived from

(i) ownership of, or trading or dealing in, bonds, shares, debentures, mortgages, hypothecary claims, bills, notes or other similar property or any interest, or for civil law any right, therein,

(ii) lending money with or without security,

(iii) rents, hire of chattels, charterparty fees or remunerations, annuities, royalties, interest or dividends,

(iv) estates or trusts, or

(v) disposition of capital property,

(*c*) not more than 10% of its gross revenue for each taxation year ending in the period was derived from rents, hire of chattels, charterparty fees or charterparty remunerations,

(*d*) its principal business in each taxation year ending in the period was not

(i) the making of loans, or

(ii) trading or dealing in bonds, shares, debentures, mortgages, hypothecary claims, bills, notes or other similar property or any interest therein,

(*e*) it has, on or before the earlier of February 27, 2000 and the day that is 90 days after the beginning of its first taxation year that begins after 1971, elected in prescribed manner to be taxed under this section, and

(*f*) it has not, before the end of the last taxation year in the period, revoked in prescribed manner its election,

except that

(*g*) a new corporation (within the meaning assigned by section 87) formed as a result of an amalgamation after June 18, 1971 of two or more predecessor corporations is not a non-resident-owned investment corporation unless each of the predecessor corporations was, immediately before the amalgamation, a non-resident-owned investment corporation,

(*h*) where a corporation is a new corporation described in paragraph (*g*), and each of the predecessor corporations elected in a timely manner under paragraph (*e*), paragraph (*e*) shall be read, in its application to the new corporation, without reference to the words "the earlier of February 27, 2000 and", and

(*i*) subject to section 134.1, a corporation is not a non-resident-owned investment corporation in any taxation year that ends after the earlier of,

(i) the first time, if any, after February 27, 2000 at which the corporation effects an increase in capital, and

(ii) the corporation's last taxation year that begins before 2003;

History: S. 133(8), subparagraph (*b*)(i) of the definition "non-resident owned investment corporation" was replaced by S.C. 2013, c. 34, s. 134(1), in force June 26, 2013, and formerly read:

(i) ownership of, or trading or dealing in, bonds, shares, debentures, mortgages, hypothecary claims, bills, notes or other similar property or any interest therein,

Related Regulations: 500; 501; 502.

Related Sections: ITAR s. 59(2) Non-resident-owned investment corporation.

Tax Topics: No. 1618, The End of the NRO.

Forms: T2Sch97 — Additional Information on Non-Resident Corporations in Canada.

Interpretation Bulletins: *Secondary* — IT-465R Non-resident beneficiaries of trusts.

"taxable dividend" —"taxable dividend" does not include a capital gains dividend.

► 133(9) ◄

(9) Definitions. In the definition "allowable refund" in subsection (8),

"allowable refundable tax on hand" —"allowable refundable tax on hand" of a corporation at any particular time means the amount determined by the formula

$$(A + B + C) - (D + E + F)$$

where

A is the total of all amounts each of which is an amount in respect of any taxation year commencing after 1971 and ending before the particular time, equal to the tax under this Part payable by the corporation for the year,

B is an amount equal to 15% of the amount determined for B in the definition "cumulative taxable income" in this subsection in respect of the corporation,

C where the corporation's 1972 taxation year commenced before 1972, is an amount equal to 10% of the amount that would be determined for C in the definition "cumulative taxable income" in this subsection if the reference in the description of C in that definition to "the 1972 taxation year or any taxation year commencing after 1971 and ending before the particular time" were read as a reference to "the 1972 taxation year",

D is the total of all amounts each of which is an amount, in respect of the 1972 taxation year or any taxation year commencing after 1971 and ending before the particular time, determined by the formula

$$0.25 \times [L - (M + N)]$$

where

L is the total of the corporation's taxable capital gains for the year from dispositions after 1971 of property described in paragraph (1)(*c*), computed in accordance with the assumption set out in paragraph (1)(*d*),

M is the total of the corporation's allowable capital losses for the year from dispositions after 1971 of property described in paragraph (1)(*c*), computed in accordance with the same assumption, and

N is the amount deductible from the corporation's income for the year by virtue of paragraph (2)(*c*),

E is the total of all amounts each of which is an amount equal to $^1/_3$ of any amount paid or credited by the corporation after the commencement of its 1972 taxation year and before the particular time, as, on account or in lieu of payment of, or in satisfaction of interest, and

F is the total of all amounts each of which is an amount in respect of any taxable dividend paid by the corporation on a share of its capital stock before the particular time and after the commencement of its first taxation year commencing after 1971, equal to the amount in respect of the dividend determined under the definition "allowable refund" in subsection (8);

Related Sections: S. 87(2)(*cc*) Non-resident-owned investment corporation.

"cumulative taxable income" —"cumulative taxable income" of a corporation at any particular time means the amount determined by the formula

$$(A + B) - (C + D + E)$$

where

A is the total of the corporation's taxable incomes for taxation years commencing after 1971 and ending before the particular time,

B where the corporation's 1972 taxation year commenced before 1972, is the amount determined by the formula

$$L - (M + N)$$

where

L is the corporation's taxable income for its 1972 taxation year,

M is the total of all amounts received by the corporation as described in paragraph 196(4)(*b*), and

N is the lesser of the amount determined under paragraph 196(4)(*e*) in respect of the corporation and the amount, if any, by which the total of amounts determined under paragraphs 196(4)(*d*) to (*f*) in respect of the corporation exceeds the total of amounts determined under paragraphs 196(4)(*a*) to (*c*) in respect of the corporation,

C is the total of all amounts each of which is an amount, in respect of the 1972 taxation year or any taxation year commencing after 1971 and ending before the particular time, determined by the formula

$$P - (Q + R)$$

where

P is the total of the corporation's taxable capital gains for the year from dispositions after 1971 of property described in paragraph (1)(*c*), computed in accordance with the assumption set out in paragraph (1)(*d*),

Q is the total of the corporation's allowable capital losses for the year from dispositions after 1971 of property described in paragraph (1)(*c*), computed in accordance with the same assumption, and

R is the amount deductible from the corporation's income for the year by virtue of paragraph (2)(*c*),

D is the total of all amounts each of which is an amount equal to $^4/_3$ of any amount paid or credited by the corporation, after the commencement of its 1972 taxation year and before the particular time, as, on account or in lieu of payment of, or in satisfaction of interest, and

E is the total of all amounts each of which is the amount of any taxable dividend paid by the corporation on a share of its capital stock before the particular time and after the commencement of its first taxation year commencing after 1971.

Related Sections: S. 2(2) Taxable income; s. 38 Taxable capital gain and allowable capital loss; s. 39, "capital gain", "capital loss"; s. 54, "capital property"; s. 89(1), "taxable dividend"; s. 95(1), "foreign affiliate"; s. 104(1) Reference to trust or estate; s. 111(8), "net capital loss"; s. 133(8), "non-resident-owned investment corporation"; s. 157(3) Reduced instalments; s. 248(1), "amount", "annuity", "assessment", "corporation", "dividend", "gross revenue", "non-resident", "prescribed", "property", "share", "taxable Canadian property"; s. 255 Canada.

SECTION 134: Non-resident-owned corporation not a Canadian corporation, etc

Notwithstanding any other provision of this Act, a non-resident-owned investment corporation that would, but for this section, be a Canadian corporation, taxable Canadian corporation or private corporation shall be deemed not to be a Canadian corporation, taxable Canadian corporation or private corporation, as the case may be, except for the purposes of section 87, subsection 88(2) and sections 212.1 and 219.

Related Sections: S. 83(1) Qualifying dividends; s. 87 Amalgamations; s. 89(1), "Canadian corporation", "private corporation"; s. 133(8), "non-resident-owned investment corporation"; s. 219 Branch tax.

SECTION 134.1: [Non-resident-owned investment corporations — transition]

► 134.1(1) ◄

(1) NRO — transition. This section applies to a corporation that

(*a*) was a non-resident-owned investment corporation in a taxation year;

(*b*) is not a non-resident-owned investment corporation in the following taxation year (in this section referred to as the corporation's "first non-NRO year"); and

(*c*) elects in writing filed with the Minister on or before the corporation's filing-due date for its first non-NRO year to have this section apply.

► 134.1(2) ◄

(2) Application. For the purposes of applying subsections 104(10) and (11) and 133(6) to (9) (other than the definition "non-resident-owned investment corporation" in subsection 133(8)), section 212 and any tax treaty, a corporation described in subsection (1) is deemed to be a non-resident-owned investment corporation in its first non-NRO year in respect of dividends paid in that year on shares of its capital stock to a non-resident person, to a trust for the benefit of non-resident persons or their unborn issue or to a non-resident-owned investment corporation.

History: S. 134.1(2) was replaced by S.C. 2013, c. 34, s. 281(1), applicable to a corporation that ceases to be a non-resident-owned investment corporation because of a transaction or an event that occurs, or a circumstance that arises, in a taxation year of the corporation that ends after February 27, 2000. S. 134.1(2) formerly read:

(2) *Application.* A corporation to which this section applies is deemed to be a non-resident-owned investment corporation in its first non-NRO year for the purposes of applying, in respect of dividends paid on shares of its capital stock in its first non-NRO year to a non-resident person or a non-resident-owned investment corporation, subsections 133(6) to (9) (other than the definition "non-resident-owned investment corporation" in subsection 133(8)) and section 212 and any tax treaty.

SECTION 134.2: Revocation

► 134.2(1) ◄

(1) Revocation. This section applies to a corporation that

(*a*) revokes at any time (in this section described as the "revocation time") its election to be taxed under section 133;

(*b*) elects to have this section apply, by filing an election in writing with the Minister on or before the corporation's filing-due date for the taxation year of the corporation (in this section referred to as the "revocation year") that would have included the revocation time if the corporation had not so elected; and

(*c*) specifies in the election a time (in this section referred to as the "elected time") that is in the revocation year and is not after the revocation time.

► 134.2(2) ◄

(2) Consequences. Where this section applies to a corporation,

(*a*) the corporation's taxation year that would have included the elected time, if the corporation had not elected to have this section apply, is deemed to end immediately before the elected time;

(*b*) a new taxation year of the corporation is deemed to begin at the elected time; and

(*c*) notwithstanding paragraph (*f*) of the definition "non-resident-owned investment corporation" in subsection 133(8), the corporation is deemed to be a non-resident-owned investment corporation for the period that begins at the beginning of the revocation year and ends immediately before the elected time.

Patronage Dividends

SECTION 135: Deduction in computing income

► 135(1) ◄

(1) Deduction in computing income. Notwithstanding anything in this Part, other than subsections (1.1) to (2.1) and 135.1(3), there may be deducted, in computing the income of a taxpayer for a taxation year, the total of the payments made, pursuant to allocations in proportion to patronage, by the taxpayer

(*a*) within the year or within 12 months thereafter to the taxpayer's customers of the year; and

(*b*) within the year or within 12 months thereafter to the taxpayer's customers of a previous year, the deduction of which from income of a previous taxation year was not permitted.

Related Regulations: 218.

Related Sections: S. 20(1)(*u*) Patronage dividends; S. 87(2)(*g.5*) Patronage dividends; s. 135(2) Limitation where non-member customer; s. 135(4), "allocation in proportion to patronage", "customer", "payment"; s. 212(1)(*g*) Patronage dividend.

Tax Profile: November 2004 — New Restrictions Repeal Patronage Deduction for Canadian Corporations.

Forms: T2 SCH 16 — Patronage Dividend Deduction.

Interpretation Bulletins: *Primary* — IT-362R Patronage dividends.

► 135(1.1) ◄

(1.1) Limitation where non-arm's length customer. Subsection (1) applies to a payment made by a taxpayer to a customer with whom the taxpayer does not deal at arm's length only if

(*a*) the taxpayer is a cooperative corporation described in subsection 136(2) or a credit union; or

(*b*) the payment is prescribed.

Related Regulations: 3200.

► 135(2) ◄

(2) Limitation where non-member customer. If a taxpayer has not made allocations in proportion to patronage in respect of all of the taxpayer's customers of the year, at the same rate, with appropriate differences for different types, classes, grades or qualities of goods, products or services, the amount that may be deducted by the taxpayer under subsection (1) is an amount equal to the lesser of

(*a*) the total of the payments mentioned in that subsection, and

(*b*) the total of

(i) the part of the income of the taxpayer for the year attributable to business done with members, and

(ii) the allocations in proportion to patronage made to non-member customers of the year.

Related Sections: S. 135(2.1) Deduction carried over; s. 135(4), "allocation in proportion to patronage", "customer", "income of the taxpayer attributable to business done with members", "member", "non-member customer".

► 135(2.1) ◄

(2.1) Deduction carried over. Where, in a taxation year ending after 1985, all or a portion of a payment made by a taxpayer pursuant to an allocation in proportion to patronage to the taxpayer's customers who are members is not deductible in computing the taxpayer's income for the year because of the application of subsection (2) (in this subsection referred to as the "undeducted amount"), there may be deducted in computing the taxpayer's income for a subsequent taxation year, an amount equal to the lesser of

(*a*) the undeducted amount, except to the extent that that amount was deducted in computing the taxpayer's income for any preceding taxation year, and

(*b*) the amount, if any, by which

(i) the taxpayer's income for the subsequent taxation year (computed without reference to this subsection) attributable to business done with the taxpayer's customers of that year who are members

exceeds

(ii) the amount deducted in computing the taxpayer's income for the subsequent taxation year by virtue of subsection (1) in respect of payments made by the taxpayer pursuant to allocations in proportion to patronage to the taxpayer's customers of that year who are members.

► 135(3) ◄

(3) Amount to be deducted or withheld from payment to customer. Subject to subsection 135.1(6), a taxpayer who makes at any particular time in a calendar year a payment pursuant to an allocation in proportion to patronage to a person who is resident in Canada and is not exempt from tax under section 149 shall, notwithstanding any agreement or any law to the contrary, deduct or withhold from the payment an amount equal to 15% of the lesser of the amount of the payment and the amount, if any, by which

(*a*) the total of the amount of the payment and the amounts of all other payments pursuant to allocations in proportion to patronage made by the taxpayer to that person in the calendar year and before the particular time

exceeds

(*b*) $100,

and forthwith remit that amount to the Receiver General on behalf of that person on account of that person's tax under this Part.

Related Sections: S. 135(2) Limitation where non-member customer; s. 135(6) Amount of payment to customer; s. 227.1(1) Liability of directors for failure to deduct.

▶ 135(4) ◀

(4) Definitions. For the purposes of this section and section 135.1,

"allocation in proportion to patronage" —"allocation in proportion to patronage" for a taxation year means an amount credited by a taxpayer to a customer of that year on terms that the customer is entitled to or will receive payment thereof, computed at a rate in relation to the quantity, quality or value of the goods or products acquired, marketed, handled, dealt in or sold, or services rendered by the taxpayer from, on behalf of or to the customer, whether as principal or as agent of the customer or otherwise, with appropriate differences in the rate for different classes, grades or qualities thereof, if

(*a*) the amount was credited

(i) within the year or within 12 months thereafter, and

(ii) at the same rate in relation to quantity, quality or value aforesaid as the rate at which amounts were similarly credited to all other customers of that year who were members or to all other customers of that year, as the case may be, with appropriate differences aforesaid for different classes, grades or qualities, and

(*b*) the prospect that amounts would be so credited was held out by the taxpayer to the taxpayer's customers of that year who were members or non-member customers of that year, as the case may be;

"consumer goods or services" —"consumer goods or services" means goods or services the cost of which was not deductible by the taxpayer in computing the income from a business or property;

"customer" —"customer" means a customer of a taxpayer and includes a person who sells or delivers goods or products to the taxpayer, or for whom the taxpayer renders services;

"income of the taxpayer attributable to business done with members" —"income of the taxpayer attributable to business done with members" of any taxation year means that proportion of the income of the taxpayer for the year (before making any deduction under this section) that the value of the goods or products acquired, marketed, handled, dealt in or sold or services rendered by the taxpayer from, on behalf of, or for members, is of the total value of goods or products acquired, marketed, handled, dealt in or sold or services rendered by the taxpayer from, on behalf of, or for all customers during the year;

"member" —"member" means a person who is entitled as a member or shareholder to full voting rights in the conduct of the affairs of the taxpayer (being a corporation) or of a corporation of which the taxpayer is a subsidiary wholly-owned corporation;

"non-member customer" —"non-member customer" means a customer who is not a member;

"payment" —"payment" includes

(*a*) the issue of a certificate of indebtedness or shares of the taxpayer or of a corporation of which the taxpayer is a subsidiary wholly-owned corporation if the taxpayer or that corporation has in the year or within 12 months thereafter disbursed an amount of money equal to the total face value of all certificates or shares so issued in the course of redeeming or purchasing certificates of indebtedness or shares of the taxpayer or that corporation previously issued,

(*b*) the application by the taxpayer of an amount to a member's liability to the taxpayer (including, without restricting the generality of the foregoing, an amount applied in fulfilment of an obligation of the member to make a loan to the taxpayer and an amount applied on account of payment for shares issued to a member) pursuant to a by-law of the taxpayer, pursuant to statutory authority or at the request of the member, or

(*c*) the amount of a payment or transfer by the taxpayer that, under subsection 56(2), is required to be included in computing the income of a member.

▶ 135(5) ◀

(5) Holding out prospect of allocations. For the purpose of this section a taxpayer shall be deemed to have held out the prospect that amounts would be credited to a customer of a taxation year by way of allocation in proportion to patronage, if

(*a*) throughout the year the statute under which the taxpayer was incorporated or registered, its charter, articles of association or by-laws or its contract with the customer held out the prospect that amounts would be so credited to customers who are members or non-member customers, as the case may be; or

(*b*) prior to the commencement of the year or prior to such other day as may be prescribed for the class of business in which the taxpayer is engaged, the taxpayer has published an advertisement in prescribed form in a newspaper or newspapers of general circulation throughout the greater part of the area in which the taxpayer carried on business holding out that prospect to customers who are members or non-member customers, as the case may be, and has filed copies of the newspapers with the Minister before the end of the 30th day of the taxation year or within 30 days from the prescribed day, as the case may be.

Related Sections: S. 135(4), "allocation in proportion to patronage".

▶ 135(6) ◀

(6) Amount of payment to customer. For greater certainty, the amount of any payment pursuant to an allocation in proportion to patronage is the amount thereof determined before deducting any amount required by subsection (3) to be deducted or withheld from that payment.

Related Sections: S. 135(3) Amount to be deducted or withheld from payment to customer.

▶ 135(7) ◀

(7) Payment to customer to be included in income. Where a payment pursuant to an allocation in proportion to patronage (other than an allocation in respect of consumer goods or services) has been received by a taxpayer, the amount of the payment shall, subject to subsection 135.1(2), be included in computing the recipient's income for the taxation year in which the payment was received and, without restricting the generality of the foregoing, where a certificate of indebtedness or a share was issued to a person pursuant to an allocation in proportion to patronage, the amount of the payment by virtue of that issuance shall be included in computing the recipient's income for the taxation year in which the certificate or share was received and not in computing the recipient's income for the year in which the indebtedness was subsequently discharged or the share was redeemed.

Related Regulations: Part II.

Related Sections: S. 212(1)(*g*) Patronage dividend.

► 135(8) ◄

(8) Patronage dividends. For the purposes of this section, where

(*a*) a person has sold or delivered a quantity of goods or products to a marketing board established by or pursuant to a law of Canada or a province,

(*b*) the marketing board has sold or delivered the same quantity of goods or products of the same class, grade or quality to a taxpayer of which the person is a member, and

(*c*) the taxpayer has credited that person with an amount based on the quantity of goods or products of that class, grade or quality sold or delivered to it by the marketing board,

the quantity of goods or products referred to in paragraph (*c*) shall be deemed to have been sold or delivered by that person to the taxpayer and to have been acquired by the taxpayer from that person.

Related Sections: S. 20(1)(*u*) Patronage dividends; s. 135(4), "consumer goods or services"; s. 212(1)(*g*) Patronage dividend; s. 248(1), "amount", "business", "corporation", "prescribed", "property", "share", "shareholder", "subsidiary wholly-owned corporation"; s. 255 Canada.

Agricultural Cooperatives — Tax-Deferred Patronage Dividends

SECTION 135.1: [Agricultural cooperatives — Tax-deferred patronage dividends]

► 135.1(1) ◄

(1) Definitions. The following definitions apply in this section and section 135.

"agricultural business" —"agricultural business" means a business, carried on in Canada, that consists of one or any combination of

(*a*) farming (including, if the person carrying on the business is a corporation described in paragraph (*a*) of the definition "agricultural cooperative corporation", the production, processing, storing and wholesale marketing of the products of its members' farming activities); or

(*b*) the provision of goods or services (other than financial services) that are required for farming.

"agricultural cooperative corporation" —"agricultural cooperative corporation" at any time means a corporation

(*a*) that was incorporated or continued by or under the provisions of a law, of Canada or of a province, that provide for the establishment of the corporation as a cooperative corporation or that provide for the establishment of cooperative corporations; and

(*b*) that has at that time

(i) as its principal business an agricultural business, or

(ii) members, making up at least 75% of all members of the corporation, each of whom

(A) is an agricultural cooperative corporation, or

(B) has as their principal business a farming business.

"allowable disposition" —"allowable disposition" means a disposition by a taxpayer of a tax deferred cooperative share less than five years after the day on which the share was issued if

(*a*) before the disposition,

(i) the agricultural cooperative corporation is notified in writing that the taxpayer has after the share was issued become disabled and permanently unfit for work, or terminally ill, or

(ii) the taxpayer ceases to be a member of the agricultural cooperative corporation; or

(*b*) the agricultural cooperative corporation is notified in writing that the share is held by a person on whom the share has devolved as a consequence of the death of the taxpayer.

"eligible member" —"eligible member" of an agricultural cooperative corporation means a member who carries on an agricultural business and who is

(*a*) an individual resident in Canada;

(*b*) an agricultural cooperative corporation;

(*c*) a corporation resident in Canada that carries on the business of farming in Canada; or

(*d*) a partnership that carries on the business of farming in Canada, all of the members of which are described in any of paragraphs (*a*) to (*c*) or this paragraph.

"tax deferred cooperative share" —"tax deferred cooperative share" at any time means a share

(*a*) issued, after 2005 and before 2021, by an agricultural cooperative corporation to a person or partnership that is at the time the share is issued an eligible member of the agricultural cooperative corporation, pursuant to an allocation in proportion to patronage;

(*b*) the holder of which is not entitled to receive on the redemption, cancellation or acquisition of the share by the agricultural cooperative corporation or by any person with whom the agricultural cooperative corporation does not deal at arm's length an amount that is greater than the amount that would, if this Act were read without reference to this section, be included under subsection 135(7) in computing the eligible member's income for their taxation year in which the share was issued;

(*c*) that has not before that time been deemed by subsection (4) to have been disposed of; and

(*d*) that is of a class

(i) the terms of which provide that the agricultural cooperative corporation shall not, otherwise than pursuant to an allowable disposition, redeem, acquire or cancel a share of the class before the day that is five years after the day on which the share was issued, and

(ii) that is identified by the agricultural cooperative corporation in prescribed form and manner as a class of tax deferred cooperative shares.

History: S. 135.1(1), paragraph (*a*) of the definition "tax deferred cooperative share" was replaced by S.C. 2015, c. 36, s. 13, applicable on Royal Assent, June 23, 2015, and formerly read:

> (*a*) issued, after 2005 and before 2016, by an agricultural cooperative corporation to a person or partnership that is at the time the share is issued an eligible member of the agricultural cooperative corporation, pursuant to an allocation in proportion to patronage;

"tax paid balance" —"tax paid balance" of a taxpayer at the end of a particular taxation year of the taxpayer means the amount, if any, by which

(*a*) the total of

(i) the taxpayer's tax paid balance at the end of the immediately preceding taxation year, and

(ii) the amount, if any, that is included in computing the taxpayer's income under this Part for the particular taxation year because of an election described in subparagraph (2)(*a*)(ii),

exceeds

(*b*) the total of all amounts each of which is the taxpayer's proceeds of disposition of a tax deferred cooperative share that the taxpayer disposed of in the particular taxation year.

► 135.1(2) ◄

(2) Income inclusion. In computing the income of a taxpayer for a particular taxation year, there shall be included under subsection 135(7), in respect of the taxpayer's receipt, as an eligible member, of tax deferred cooperative shares of an agricultural cooperative corporation in the particular taxation year, only the total of

(*a*) the lesser of

(i) the total of all amounts, in respect of the taxpayer's receipt in the particular taxation year of tax deferred cooperative shares, that would, if this Act were read without reference to this section, be included under subsection 135(7) in computing the taxpayer's income for the particular taxation year, and

(ii) the greater of nil and the amount, if any, specified by the taxpayer in an election in prescribed form that is filed with the taxpayer's return of income for the particular taxation year, and

(*b*) the amount, if any, by which

(i) the total of all amounts each of which is the taxpayer's proceeds of disposition of a tax deferred cooperative share disposed of by the taxpayer in the particular taxation year

exceeds

(ii) the total of

(A) the taxpayer's tax paid balance at the end of the immediately preceding taxation year, and

(B) the amount, if any, that is included in computing the taxpayer's income for the particular taxation year because of an election described in subparagraph (*a*)(ii).

Editorial Note: Where an agricultural co-op pays a patronage dividend in the form of tax deferred cooperative shares, the recipient is allowed to defer the recognition of some or all of the income until such time as the shares are sold or redeemed. A share must meet a number of conditions in order to qualify for the deferral and such shares must be issued prior to 2021.

► 135.1(3) ◄

(3) Deductibility limit. The amount that may be deducted under subsection 135(1) for a particular taxation year by an agricultural cooperative corporation in respect of payments, in the form of tax deferred cooperative shares, made pursuant to allocations in proportion to patronage shall not exceed 85% of the agricultural cooperative corporation's income of the taxation year attributable to business done with members.

► 135.1(4) ◄

(4) Deemed disposition. A taxpayer who holds a tax deferred cooperative share is deemed to have disposed of the share, for proceeds of disposition equal to the amount that would, if this Act were read without reference to this section, have been included under subsection 135(7), in respect of the share, in computing the taxpayer's income for the taxation year in which the share was issued, at the earliest time at which

(*a*) the paid-up capital of the share is reduced otherwise than by way of a redemption of the share; or

(*b*) the taxpayer pledges, or for civil law hypothecates, assigns or in any way alienates the share as security for indebtedness of any kind.

► 135.1(5) ◄

(5) Reacquisition. A taxpayer who is deemed by subsection (4) to have disposed at any time of a tax deferred cooperative share is deemed to have reacquired the share, immediately after that time, at a cost equal to the taxpayer's proceeds of disposition from that disposition.

► 135.1(6) ◄

(6) Exclusion from withholding obligation. Subsection 135(3) does not apply to a payment pursuant to an allocation in proportion to patronage that is paid by an agricultural cooperative corporation through the issuance of a tax deferred cooperative share.

► 135.1(7) ◄

(7) Withholding on redemption. A person or partnership (in this subsection referred to as the "redeeming entity") that redeems, acquires or cancels a shareholder's share shall withhold and forthwith remit to the Receiver General, on account of the shareholder's tax liability, 15% from the amount otherwise payable on the redemption, acquisition or cancellation, if

(*a*) the share was, at the time it was issued, a tax deferred cooperative share;

(*b*) the redeeming entity is the corporation that issued the share, or a person or partnership with whom the corporation does not deal at arm's length; and

(*c*) the shareholder is not a trust whose taxable income is exempt from tax under this Part because of paragraph 149(1)(*r*) or (*x*).

Editorial Note: There is a withholding tax requirement in respect of any share classified as a tax-deferred cooperative share of an agricultural cooperative corporation at the time of share issuance. If the share is redeemed, acquired, or cancelled by the agricultural cooperative or by a person or partnership with whom it does not deal at arm's length, that cooperative, partnership, or person must withhold 15% tax from the proceeds otherwise payable on the redemption, acquisition, or cancellation of the shares and remit it to the Receiver General on behalf of the shareholder's tax liability.

After 2007, there is an exemption from the withholding requirement if the amount payable is to a trust governed by an RRSP or RRIF exempt from tax under s. 149. Basically, the withholding exemption is only available in rare circumstances where an eligible member forgoes the share's deferred tax treatment by transferring it to a trust governed by an RRSP or RRIF. There is no withholding requirement on these transactions if the transaction is an exchange as defined in s. 87(2)(*s*) or a reorganization of share capital of the agricultural cooperative as envisioned in s. 135.1(9) and (10).

History: S. 135.1(7) was replaced by S.C. 2013, c. 34, s. 282(1), applicable to redemptions, acquisitions and cancellations that occur after 2007, and formerly read:

(7) *Withholding on redemption.* If a share that was, at the time it was issued, a tax deferred cooperative share of an agricultural cooperative corporation is redeemed, acquired or cancelled by the agricultural cooperative corporation, or by a person or partnership with whom the agricultural cooperative corporation does not deal at arm's length, the agricultural cooperative corporation or the person or partnership, as the case may be, shall withhold and forthwith remit to the Receiver General, on account of the shareholder's tax liability, 15% from the amount otherwise payable on the redemption, acquisition or cancellation.

► 135.1(8) ◄

(8) Application of subsections 84(2) and (3). Subsections 84(2) and (3) do not apply to a tax deferred cooperative share.

► 135.1(9) ◄

(9) Application of subsection (10). Subsection (10) applies in respect of the disposition, after September 28, 2009, by a taxpayer of a tax deferred cooperative share (in this subsection and subsection (10) referred to as the "old share") of an agricultural cooperative corporation if (*a*) the disposition results from the acquisition, cancellation or redemption of the old share in the course of a reorganization of the capital of the corporation;

(*b*) in exchange for the old share the corporation issues to the taxpayer a share (in this subsection and subsection (10) referred to as the "new share") that is described in all of paragraphs (*b*) to (*d*) of the definition "tax deferred cooperative share" in subsection (1); and

(*c*) the amount of paid-up capital, and the amount, if any, that the taxpayer is entitled to receive on a redemption, acquisition or cancellation, of the new share are equal to those amounts, respectively, in respect of the old share.

Editorial Note: A taxpayer will not have an income inclusion under s. 135.1(2) if the taxpayer disposes of a tax-deferred cooperative share (the "old share") and the following s. 135.1(9) criteria are met:

- the disposition is a result of a reorganization of the share capital of an agricultural cooperative;
- the only consideration received for the disposition of the old share by the taxpayer is a new share of the same agricultural cooperative that meets the criteria and definition of a "tax-deferred cooperative share"; and
- the amounts to be received on the redemption, cancellation, or acquisition are equal to the amounts received for the old share in a similar transaction.

Where these criteria are met, no amount is included in income, no withholding tax is payable on the disposition itself, and the new share will be treated as a tax-deferred cooperative share until its ultimate disposition by the taxpayer.

The new share must be issued pursuant to an allocation in proportion to patronage at the time the old share was issued, and the agricultural cooperative cannot claim a deduction on the issuance of the new share since it was previously claimed on the old share or the first share in a series of multiple reorganizations. If no other person or partnership receives any consideration for the old share other than the new share, the old share is deemed disposed of for nil proceeds when applying the income inclusion and withholding tax rules in s. 135.1.

These rules apply after September 28, 2009 with transitional rules in respect of new shares received on a s. 87(2)(*s*) exchange that occurs before October 31, 2011.

History: S. 135.1(9) was added by 2013, c. 34, s. 282(2), deemed to have come into force on September 29, 2009.

► 135.1(10) ◄

(10) Shares issued on corporate reorganizations. If this subsection applies in respect of an exchange of a taxpayer's old share for a new share, for the purposes of this section (other than subsection (9)),

(*a*) the new share issued in exchange for the old share is deemed to have been issued, pursuant to an allocation in proportion to patronage, at the time the old share was issued; and

(*b*) provided that no person or partnership receives at any time any consideration (other than the new share) in exchange for the old share, for the purposes of subsections (2) and (7) the taxpayer is deemed to have disposed of the old share for nil proceeds.

History: S. 135.1(10) was added by 2013, c. 34, s. 282(2), deemed to have come into force on September 29, 2009, except that in its application to an exchange of shares described by subparagraph 87(2)(s)(ii) of the Act, as enacted by subsection 223(8), that occurs before October 31, 2011,

(*a*) with respect to a new share received on the exchange that has been disposed of before October 31, 2011, paragraph 135.1(10)(*a*) is to be read as follows:

"(*a*) the new share issued in exchange for the old share is deemed to have been issued at the time the old share was issued; and"

and

(*b*) paragraph 135.1(10)(*b*) is to be read as follows:

"(*b*) for the purposes of subsections (2) and (7) the taxpayer is deemed to have disposed of the old share for nil proceeds."

Continuance of the Canadian Wheat Board

SECTION 135.2: Continuance of the Canadian Wheat Board

► 135.2(1) ◄

(1) Definitions. The following definitions apply in this section.

History: S. 135.2(1) was added by S.C. 2016, c. 7, s. 38(1), deemed to have come into force on July 1, 2015, except that, before December 31, 2015, each reference to "graduated rate estate" in section 135.2 is to be read as "estate".

"application for continuance" — "application for continuance" means the application for continuance referred to in paragraph (*a*) of the definition *Canadian Wheat Board continuance*.

"Canadian Wheat Board" — "Canadian Wheat Board" means the corporation referred to in subsection 4(1) of the *Canadian Wheat Board (Interim Operations)* Act, as it read before its repeal, that is continued under the *Canada Business Corporations Act* pursuant to the application for continuance.

"Canadian Wheat Board continuance" — "Canadian Wheat Board continuance" means the series of transactions or events that includes

(*a*) the application for continuance under the *Canada Business Corporations Act* that is

(i) made by the corporation referred to in subsection 4(1) of the *Canadian Wheat Board (Interim Operations) Act*, as it read before its repeal, and

(ii) approved by the Minister of Agriculture and Agri-Food under Part III of the *Marketing Freedom for Grain Farmers Act*;

(*b*) the issuance of a promissory note or other evidence of indebtedness by the Canadian Wheat Board to the eligible trust; and

(*c*) the disposition of the eligible debt by the eligible trust, in the same taxation year of the trust in which the eligible debt is issued to it, in exchange for consideration that includes the issuance of shares by the Canadian Wheat Board that have a total fair market value at the time of their issuance that is equal to the amount by which the principal amount of the eligible debt exceeds $10 million.

"eligible debt" — "eligible debt" means the promissory note or other evidence of indebtedness referred to in paragraph (*b*) of the definition *Canadian Wheat Board continuance*.

"eligible share" — "eligible share" means a common share of the capital stock of the Canadian Wheat Board that is issued in exchange for the eligible debt, as referred to in paragraph (*c*) of the definition *Canadian Wheat Board continuance*.

"eligible trust" — "eligible trust", at any time, means a trust that meets the following conditions:

(*a*) it was established in connection with the application for continuance;

(*b*) it is resident in Canada at that time;

(*c*) immediately before it acquired the eligible debt, it held only property of nominal value;

(*d*) it is not exempt because of subsection 149(1) from tax on its taxable income for any period in its taxation year that includes that time;

(*e*) all of the interests of beneficiaries under it at that time are described by reference to units that are eligible units in it;

(*f*) the only persons who have acquired an interest as a beneficiary under the trust from it before that time are persons who were participating farmers at the time they acquired the interest;

(*g*) all or substantially all of the fair market value of its property at that time is based on the value of property that is

(i) eligible debt,

(ii) shares of the capital stock of the Canadian Wheat Board, or

(iii) property described in paragraph (*a*) or (*b*) of the definition *qualified investment* if in section 204 or a deposit with a credit union;

(*h*) the property that it has paid or distributed at or before that time to a beneficiary under the trust in satisfaction of the beneficiary's eligible unit in the trust is

(i) money denominated in Canadian dollars, or

(ii) shares distributed as an eligible wind-up distribution of the trust; and

(*i*) at no time in its taxation year that includes that time is any other trust an eligible trust.

"eligible unit" —"eligible unit", in a trust at any time, means a unit that describes all or part of an interest as a beneficiary under the trust, if,

(*a*) the total of all amounts each of which is the value of a unit at the time it was issued by the trust to a participating farmer does not exceed the amount by which the principal amount of the eligible debt exceeds $10 million; and

(*b*) all of the interests as a beneficiary under the trust are *fixed interests* if (as defined in subsection 251.2(1)) in the trust.

"eligible wind-up distribution" —"eligible wind-up distribution", of a trust, means a distribution of property by the trust to a person if

(*a*) the distribution includes a share of the capital stock of the Canadian Wheat Board that is listed on a designated stock exchange;

(*b*) the only property (other than a share described in paragraph (*a*)) distributed by the trust on the distribution is money denominated in Canadian dollars;

(*c*) the distribution results in the disposition of all of the person's interest as a beneficiary under the trust; and

(*d*) the trust ceases to exist immediately after the distribution or immediately after the last of a series of eligible wind-up distributions (determined without reference to this paragraph) of the trust that includes the distribution.

"participating farmer" —"participating farmer", in respect of a trust at any time, means a person

(*a*) who is eligible to receive units of the trust pursuant to the plan under which the trust directs its trustees to grant units to persons who have delivered grain under a contract with the Canadian Wheat Board on or after August 1, 2013; and

(*b*) engaged in the production of grain or any person entitled, as landlord, vendor or mortgagee or hypothecary creditor, to grain produced by a person engaged in the production of grain or to any share of that grain.

"person" —"person" includes a partnership.

▶ 135.2(2) ◀

(2) Trust acquires an eligible debt. If, at any time, an eligible trust acquires eligible debt, the principal amount of the eligible debt is deemed not to be included in computing the income of the eligible trust for the taxation year of the eligible trust that includes that time.

History: S. 135.2(2) was added by S.C. 2016, c. 7, s. 38(1), deemed to have come into force on July 1, 2015, except that, before December 31, 2015, each reference to "graduated rate estate" in section 135.2 is to be read as "estate".

▶ 135.2(3) ◀

(3) Disposition of eligible debt. If, at any time, an eligible trust disposes of eligible debt in exchange for consideration that includes the issuance of eligible shares

(*a*) for the purpose of computing the income of the eligible trust for its taxation year that includes that time

(i) an amount, in respect of the disposition of the eligible debt, equal to the fair market value of all property (other than eligible shares) received on the exchange by the trust is included,

(ii) no amount in respect of the disposition of the eligible debt is included (other than the amount described in subparagraph (i)), and

(iii) no amount in respect of the receipt of the eligible shares is included;

(*b*) the cost to the eligible trust of each eligible share is deemed to be nil;

(*c*) in computing the paid-up capital in respect of the class of the capital stock of the Canadian Wheat Board that includes the eligible shares, at any time after the shares are issued, there shall be deducted an amount equal to the amount of the paid-up capital in respect of that class at the time the shares are issued;

(*d*) subsection 75(2) does not apply to property

(i) that is held by the trust in a taxation year that ends at or after that time, and

(ii) that is

(A) received by the trust on the exchange, or

(B) a substitute for property described in subparagraph (i); and

(*e*) subsections 84(2) and (3) and section 85 do not apply at any time to eligible shares.

History: S. 135.2(3) was added by S.C. 2016, c. 7, s. 38(1), deemed to have come into force on July 1, 2015, except that, before December 31, 2015, each reference to "graduated rate estate" in section 135.2 is to be read as "estate".

▶ 135.2(4) ◀

(4) Eligible trust. The following rules apply in respect of a trust that is an eligible trust at any time in a taxation year of the trust:

(*a*) in computing the trust's income for the year

(i) no deduction may be made by the trust under subsection 104(6), except to the extent of the income of the trust (determined without reference to subsection 104(6)) for the year that is paid in the year, and

(ii) no deduction may be made by the trust under subsection 104(6), if the trust ceased to be an eligible trust at the beginning of the following taxation year;

(*b*) for the purposes of applying Part XII.2 in respect of the year

(i) the trust's designated income for the year is deemed to be the trust's income for the year determined without reference to subsections 104(6) and (30), and

(ii) the designated beneficiaries under the trust at any time in the year are deemed to include any beneficiary under the trust that is at that time

(A) non-resident,

(B) a partnership (other than a partnership that is, throughout its fiscal period that includes that time, a Canadian partnership), or

(C) exempt because of subsection 149(1) from tax under this Part on the person's taxable income;

(*c*) each property held by the trust that is the eligible debt or an eligible share is deemed to have a cost amount to the trust of nil;

(*d*) if the trust disposes of a property,

(i) subject to subsection (14), the disposition is deemed to occur for proceeds equal to the fair market value of the property immediately before the disposition,

(ii) the gain, if any, of the trust from the disposition is

(A) deemed not to be a capital gain, and

(B) to be included in computing the trust's income for the trust's taxation year that includes the time of disposition, and

(iii) the loss, if any, of the trust from the disposition is

(A) deemed not to be a capital loss, and

(B) to be deducted in computing the trust's income for the trust's taxation year that includes the time of disposition;

(*e*) the trust is deemed not to be a

(i) personal trust,

(ii) unit trust,

(iii) trust prescribed for the purpose of subsection 107(2), or

(iv) trust any interest in which is an excluded right or interest in applying section 128.1;

(*f*) any *security* (in this paragraph and paragraph (*g*), as defined in subsection 122.1(1)) of the trust that is held by a trust governed by a deferred profit sharing plan, RDSP, RESP, RRIF, RRSP or TFSA (referred to in this paragraph and paragraph (*g*) as the *registered plan trust*) is deemed not to be a qualified investment for the registered plan trust;

(*g*) if a registered plan trust governed by a TFSA acquires at any time a security of the trust, Part XI.01 applies in respect of the security as though the acquisition is an advantage

(i) in relation to the TFSA that is extended at that time to the controlling individual of the TFSA, and

(ii) that is a benefit the fair market value of which is the fair market value of the security at that time; and

(*h*) paragraph (*h*) of the definition *disposition* in subsection 248(1) does not apply in respect of eligible units of the trust.

Editorial Note: The former Canadian Wheat Board ("CWB") was continued under the *Canadian Business Corporations Act* ("CBCA"). The majority of the shares of CWB are owned by a corporation while the remaining 49.9% of the shares are held in trust (the "eligible trust") for farmers participating with the CWB. Subsection 135.2(4) provides rules applicable to the eligible trust.

History: S. 135.2(4) was added by S.C. 2016, c. 7, s. 38(1), deemed to have come into force on July 1, 2015, except that, before December 31, 2015, each reference to "graduated rate estate" in section 135.2 is to be read as "estate".

► 135.2(5) ◄

(5) Participating farmer — acquisition of eligible unit. If, at any time, a participating farmer acquires an eligible unit in an eligible trust from the trust,

(*a*) no amount in respect of the acquisition of the eligible unit is included in computing the income of the participating farmer; and

(*b*) the cost amount to the participating farmer of the eligible unit is deemed to be nil.

History: S. 135.2(5) was added by S.C. 2016, c. 7, s. 38(1), deemed to have come into force on July 1, 2015, except that, before December 31, 2015, each reference to "graduated rate estate" in section 135.2 is to be read as "estate".

► 135.2(6) ◄

(6) Eligible unit issued to estate. If a participating farmer has, immediately before the participating farmer's death, not received an eligible unit of an eligible trust for which the participating farmer was eligible — pursuant to the plan under which the eligible trust directs its trustees to grant units to persons who have delivered grain under a contract with the Canadian Wheat Board on or after August 1, 2013 — and the eligible trust issues the unit to the estate that arose on and as a consequence of the death,

(*a*) the participating farmer is deemed to have acquired the unit at the time that is immediately before the time that is immediately before the death, as a participating farmer from the eligible trust, and to own the unit at the time that is immediately before the death;

(*b*) for the purpose of paragraph (*f*) of the definition *eligible trust* in subsection (1), the estate is deemed not to have acquired the unit from the trust; and

(*c*) for the purposes of paragraphs (8)(*b*) and (*c*), the estate is deemed to have acquired the eligible unit on and as a consequence of the death.

History: S. 135.2(6) was added by S.C. 2016, c. 7, s. 38(1), deemed to have come into force on July 1, 2015, except that, before December 31, 2015, each reference to "graduated rate estate" in section 135.2 is to be read as "estate".

► 135.2(7) ◄

(7) Eligible unit — gain (loss). If a person disposes of an eligible unit in a trust that is an eligible trust at the time of the disposition

(*a*) the gain, if any, of the person from the disposition is

(i) deemed not to be a capital gain, and

(ii) to be included in computing the person's income for the person's taxation year that includes that time; and

(*b*) the loss, if any, of the person from the disposition is

(i) deemed not to be a capital loss, and

(ii) to be deducted in computing the person's income for the person's taxation year that includes that time.

History: S. 135.2(7) was added by S.C. 2016, c. 7, s. 38(1), deemed to have come into force on July 1, 2015, except that, before December 31, 2015, each reference to "graduated rate estate" in section 135.2 is to be read as "estate".

► 135.2(8) ◄

(8) Death of a participating farmer. If, immediately before an individual's death, the individual owns an eligible unit that the individual acquired as a participating farmer from an eligible trust

(*a*) the individual is deemed to dispose (referred to in this subsection as the *particular disposition*) of the eligible unit immediately before death;

(*b*) if paragraph (*d*) does not apply,

(i) the individual's proceeds from the particular disposition are deemed to be equal to the unit's fair market value immediately before the particular disposition,

(ii) the gain from the particular disposition is deemed to be included, under subsection 70(1) and not under any other provision, in the individual's income for the individual's taxation year in which the individual dies,

(iii) subsection 159(5) applies in respect of the individual who has died (determined as though a reference in that subsection to subsection 70(5.2) includes a reference to subsection 70(1) in the application of subsection 159(5) to the gain from the particular disposition) in respect of the particular disposition, and

(iv) the person who acquires the eligible unit as a consequence of the individual's death is deemed to have acquired the eligible unit at the time of the death at a cost equal to the individual's proceeds, described in subparagraph (i), from the particular disposition;

(*c*) paragraph (*d*) applies if

(i) the individual is resident in Canada immediately before the individual's death,

(ii) the individual's graduated rate estate acquires the eligible unit on and as a consequence of the death,

(iii) the individual's legal representative elects in prescribed form in the course of administering the individual's graduated rate estate that paragraph (*b*) not apply to the individual in respect of the particular disposition,

(iv) the election is filed with the individual's return of income under this Part for the individual's taxation year in which the death occurred,

(v) the estate distributes the eligible unit to the individual's spouse or common-law partner at a time at which it is the individual's graduated rate estate,

(vi) the individual's spouse or common-law partner is resident in Canada at the time of the distribution, and

(vii) the estate does not dispose of the unit before the distribution; and

(*d*) if this paragraph applies,

(i) the individual's gain from the disposition is deemed to be nil,

(ii) the cost amount to the estate of the eligible unit is deemed to be nil,

(iii) any amount that is included in the estate's income (determined without reference to this subparagraph and subsections 104(6) and (12)) for a taxation year from a source that is the eligible unit is, notwithstanding subsection 104(24), deemed

(A) to have become payable in that taxation year by the estate to the spouse or common-law partner, and

(B) not be have become payable to any other beneficiary,

(iv) the distribution is deemed to be a disposition by the estate of the eligible unit for proceeds equal to the cost amount to the estate of the unit,

(v) the part of the spouse or common-law partner's interest as a beneficiary under the estate that is disposed of as a result of the distribution is deemed to be disposed of for proceeds of disposition equal to the cost amount to the spouse or common-law partner of that part immediately before the disposition,

(vi) the cost amount to the spouse or common-law partner of the eligible unit is deemed to be nil, and

(vii) the spouse or common-law partner is, except for the purposes of paragraph (*c*), deemed to have acquired the eligible unit as a participating farmer from an eligible trust.

History: S. 135.2(8) was added by S.C. 2016, c. 7, s. 38(1), deemed to have come into force on July 1, 2015, except that, before December 31, 2015, each reference to "graduated rate estate" in section 135.2 is to be read as "estate".

► 135.2(9) ◄

(9) Participating farmer — disposition of eligible unit. If, at any time, an eligible unit of an eligible trust that was acquired by a participating farmer from the eligible trust is disposed of by the participating farmer (other than a disposition described in paragraph (8)(*a*), (10)(*d*) or (11)(*b*)),

(*a*) the participating farmer's proceeds from the disposition are deemed to be equal to the fair market value of the unit immediately before its disposition;

(*b*) if the disposition results from a distribution of money denominated in Canadian dollars by the trust to the participating farmer in a taxation year of the trust, the money is proceeds from the disposition in that taxation year by the trust of other property and, at the time of the disposition, the participating farmer is not a person described in any of clauses (4)(*b*)(ii)(A) to (C), the trust's gain, if any, from the disposition of the other property is reduced to the extent that the proceeds so distributed would, in the absence of this paragraph, be included under subsection 104(13) in the participating farmer's income for the taxation year of the participating farmer in which the taxation year of the trust ends; and

(*c*) if the participating farmer is a Canadian-controlled private corporation, for the purposes of section 125, the gain from the disposition is deemed to be income from an active business carried on by the corporation.

History: S. 135.2(9) was added by S.C. 2016, c. 7, s. 38(1), deemed to have come into force on July 1, 2015, except that, before December 31, 2015, each reference to "graduated rate estate" in section 135.2 is to be read as "estate".

► 135.2(10) ◄

(10) Eligible wind-up distribution. If, at any time, an eligible trust distributes property as an eligible wind-up distribution of the trust to a person

(*a*) subsection 107(2.1) does not apply in respect of the distribution;

(*b*) the trust is deemed to have disposed of the property for proceeds equal to its fair market value at that time;

(*c*) the trust's gain from the disposition of the property is, notwithstanding subsection 104(24), deemed

(i) to have become payable at that time by the trust to the person, and

(ii) not to have become payable to any other beneficiary;

(*d*) the person is deemed to acquire the property at a cost equal to the trust's proceeds from the disposition;

(*e*) the person's proceeds from the disposition of the eligible unit, or part of it, that results from the distribution are deemed to be equal to the cost amount of the unit to the person immediately before that time; and

(*f*) for greater certainty, no part of the trust's gain from the disposition is to be included in the cost to the person of the property, other than as determined by paragraph (*d*).

History: S. 135.2(10) was added by S.C. 2016, c. 7, s. 38(1), deemed to have come into force on July 1, 2015, except that, before December 31, 2015, each reference to "graduated rate estate" in section 135.2 is to be read as "estate".

► 135.2(11) ◄

(11) Ceasing to be an eligible trust. If a trust ceases to be an eligible trust at a particular time

(*a*) subsection 149(10) applies to the trust as if

(i) it ceased at that particular time to be exempt from tax under this Part on its taxable income, and

(ii) the list of provisions in paragraph 149(10)(*c*) included a reference to this section; and

(*b*) each person who holds at the particular time an eligible unit in the trust is deemed to have

(i) disposed of, at the time that is immediately before the time that is immediately before the particular time, each of the eligible units for proceeds equal to the cost amount of the unit to the person, and

(ii) reacquired the eligible unit at the time that is immediately before the particular time at a cost equal to the fair market value of the unit at the time that is immediately before the particular time.

History: S. 135.2(11) was added by S.C. 2016, c. 7, s. 38(1), deemed to have come into force on July 1, 2015, except that, before December 31, 2015, each reference to "graduated rate estate" in section 135.2 is to be read as "estate".

► 135.2(12) ◄

(12) Stock dividends — Canadian Wheat Board shares. If, at any time, the eligible trust holds an eligible share (or another share of the Canadian Wheat Board acquired before that time as a stock dividend) and the Canadian Wheat Board issues, as a stock dividend paid in respect of such a share, a share of a class of its capital stock, the amount by which the paid-up capital is increased — in respect of the issuance of all shares paid by the Canadian Wheat Board to the eligible trust as the stock dividend or any other stock dividend paid to other shareholders in connection with that stock dividend — for all classes of shares of the Canadian Wheat Board is, for the purposes of this Act, deemed to be no more than $1.

History: S. 135.2(12) was added by S.C. 2016, c. 7, s. 38(1), deemed to have come into force on July 1, 2015, except that, before December 31, 2015, each reference to "graduated rate estate" in section 135.2 is to be read as "estate".

► 135.2(13) ◄

(13) Reorganization of capital — Canadian Wheat Board. Subsection (14) applies in respect of the disposition by an eligible trust of all of the shares (in this subsection and subsection (14) referred to collectively as the *old shares* and individually as an *old share*) of a class of the capital stock of the Canadian Wheat Board owned by the eligible trust if

(*a*) the disposition of the old shares results from the acquisition, cancellation or redemption in the course of a reorganization of the capital of the Canadian Wheat Board;

(*b*) the Canadian Wheat Board issues to the eligible trust, in exchange for the old shares, shares (in this subsection and subsection (14) referred to collectively as the *new shares* and individually as a *new share*) of a class of the capital stock of the Canadian Wheat Board the terms and conditions of which — including the entitlement to receive an amount on a redemption, acquisition or cancellation — are in all material respects the same as those of the old shares;

(*c*) the amount that is the total fair market value of all of the new shares acquired by the eligible trust on the exchange equals the total fair market value of all of the old shares disposed of by the eligible trust; and

(*d*) the amount that is the total paid-up capital in respect of all of the new shares acquired by the eligible trust on the exchange is equal to the amount that is the total paid-up capital in respect of all of the old shares disposed of on the exchange.

History: S. 135.2(13) was added by S.C. 2016, c. 7, s. 38(1), deemed to have come into force on July 1, 2015, except that, before December 31, 2015, each reference to "graduated rate estate" in section 135.2 is to be read as "estate".

► 135.2(14) ◄

(14) Rollover of shares on reorganization. If this subsection applies in respect of an exchange of an eligible trust's old share for a new share,

(*a*) the old share is deemed to be disposed of by the eligible trust for proceeds equal to its cost amount to the eligible trust;

(*b*) the new share acquired for the old share referred to in paragraph (*a*) is deemed to be acquired for a cost equal to the amount referred to in paragraph (*a*);

(*c*) if the old share was an eligible share, the new share is deemed to be an eligible share; and

(*d*) if new shares are deemed to be eligible shares because of paragraph (*c*) and those shares are included in a class of shares that also includes other shares that are not eligible shares, those eligible shares are deemed to have been issued in a separate series of the class and the other shares are deemed to have been issued in a separate series of the class.

History: S. 135.2(14) was added by S.C. 2016, c. 7, s. 38(1), deemed to have come into force on July 1, 2015, except that, before December 31, 2015, each reference to "graduated rate estate" in section 135.2 is to be read as "estate".

► 135.2(15) ◄

(15) Information filing requirement. A trust shall file with the Minister a prescribed form in prescribed manner in respect of each taxation year of the trust in which it is an eligible trust on or before the trust's filing-due date for the year.

History: S. 135.2(15) was added by S.C. 2016, c. 7, s. 38(1), deemed to have come into force on July 1, 2015, except that, before December 31, 2015, each reference to "graduated rate estate" in section 135.2 is to be read as "estate".

▶ 135.2(16) ◀

(16) Failure to file prescribed form. If a trust fails to file the form required by subsection (15) on or before the day that is the trust's filing-due date for a taxation year,

(*a*) in addition to any other penalty for which the trust may be liable under this Act in respect of the failure, the trust is liable to a penalty equal to the product obtained when $1,000 is multiplied by the number of days during which the failure continues; and

(*b*) if, within 30 days after the trust is served personally or by registered mail with a demand in writing from the Minister for the form to be filed, the trust has not filed the form with the Minister, the trust is deemed to cease to be an eligible trust at the end of the day on which the demand was served.

History: S. 135.2(16) was added by S.C. 2016, c. 7, s. 38(1), deemed to have come into force on July 1, 2015, except that, before December 31, 2015, each reference to "graduated rate estate" in section 135.2 is to be read as "estate".

Cooperative Corporations

SECTION 136: [Cooperative corporations]

▶ 136(1) ◀

(1) Cooperative not private corporation. Notwithstanding any other provision of this Act, a cooperative corporation that would, but for this section, be a private corporation is deemed not to be a private corporation except for the purposes of section 15.1, paragraphs 87(2)(*vv*) and (*ww*) (including, for greater certainty, in applying those paragraphs as provided under paragraph 88(1)(*e.2*)), the definitions "excessive eligible dividend designation", "general rate income pool" and "low rate income pool" in subsection 89(1), subsections 89(4) to (6) and (8) to (10), sections 123.4, 125, 125.1, 127 and 127.1, the definition "mark-to-market property" in subsection 142.2(1), sections 152 and 157, subsection 185.2(3), the definition "small business corporation" in subsection 248(1) (as it applies for the purposes of paragraph 39(1)(*c*)) and subsection 249(3.1).

History: S. 136(1) was replaced by S.C. 2013, c. 40, s. 61(1), applicable to taxation years that begin after December 21, 2012, and formerly read:

(1) *Cooperative not private corporation.* Notwithstanding any other provision of this Act, a cooperative corporation that would, if this Act were read without reference to this section, be a private corporation is deemed not to be a private corporation except for the purposes of sections 15.1, 123.4, 125, 125.1, 127, 127.1, 152 and 157, the definition "mark-to-market property" in subsection 142.2(1) and the definition "small business corporation" in subsection 248(1) as it applies for the purpose of paragraph 39(1)(*c*).

S. 136(1) was replaced by S.C. 2013, c. 34, s. 283(1), applicable to the 2001 and subsequent taxation years, and formerly read:

(1) *Cooperative not private corporation.* Notwithstanding any other provision of this Act, a cooperative corporation that would, but for this section, be a private corporation is deemed not to be a private corporation except for the purposes of sections 15.1, 125, 125.1, 127, 127.1, 152 and 157, the definition "mark-to-market property" in subsection 142.2(1) and the definition "small business corporation" in subsection 248(1) as it applies for the purpose of paragraph 39(1)(*c*).

Tax Window Files: *Cooperative Housing and 149(1)(l), July 28, 2011*, CRA Document No. 2011-0394981I7.

▶ 136(2) ◀

(2) Definition of "cooperative corporation". In this section, "cooperative corporation" means a corporation that was incorporated or continued by or under the provisions of a law, of Canada or of a province, that provide for the establishment of the corporation as a cooperative corporation or that provide for the establishment of cooperative corporations, for the purpose of marketing (including processing incident to or connected to the marketing) natural products belonging to or acquired from its members or customers, of purchasing supplies, equipment or household necessaries for or to be sold to its members or customers or of performing services for its members or customers, if

(*a*) the statute by or under which it was incorporated, its charter, articles of association or by-laws or its contracts with its members or its members and customers held out the prospect that payments would be made to them in proportion to patronage;

(*b*) none of its members (except other cooperative corporations) have more than one vote in the conduct of the affairs of the corporation;

(*c*) at least 90% of its members are individuals, other cooperative corporations, or corporations or partnerships that carry on the business of farming; and

(*d*) at least 90% of its shares, if any, are held by members described in paragraph (*c*) or by trusts governed by registered retirement savings plans, registered retirement income funds, TFSAs or registered education savings plans, the annuitants, holders or subscribers under which are members described in that paragraph.

History: S. 136(2)(*c*) was replaced by S.C. 2013, c. 34, s. 283(2), applicable to the 1998 and subsequent taxation years, and formerly read:

(*c*) at least 90% of its members are individuals, other cooperative corporations, or corporations or partnerships that carry on the business of farming, and at least 90% of its shares, if any, are held by those persons or partnerships.

S. 136(2)(*d*) was added by S.C. 2013, c. 34, s. 283(2), applicable to the 1998 and subsequent taxation years, except that, in its application to taxation years that end before 2009, paragraph 136(2)(*d*) is to be read as follows:

"(*d*) at least 90% of its shares, if any, are held by members described in paragraph (*c*) or by trusts governed by registered retirement savings plans, registered retirement income funds or registered education savings plans, the annuitants or subscribers under which are members described in that paragraph."

Related Sections: S. 89(1), "private corporation"; s. 135 Deduction in computing income; s. 248(1), "corporation", "individual", "province", "shares".

Credit Unions, Savings and Credit Unions and Deposit Insurance Corporations

SECTION 137: [Credit unions]

▶ 137(1) ◀

(1) Deductions in computing income — (Repealed by 1988, c. 55, s. 123(1).)

▶ 137(2) ◀

(2) Payments pursuant to allocations in proportion to borrowing. Notwithstanding anything in this Part, there may be deducted, in computing the income for a taxation year of a credit union, the total of bonus interest payments and payments pursuant to allocations in proportion to borrowing made by the credit union within the year or within 12 months thereafter to members of the credit union, to the extent that those payments were not deductible under this subsection in computing the income of the credit union for the immediately preceding taxation year.

Related Sections: S. 137(6), "maximum cumulative reserve".

Forms: T2 SCH 17 — Credit Union Deductions.

▶ 137(3) ◀

(3) Additional deduction. There may be deducted from the tax otherwise payable under this Part for a taxation year by a corporation that was, throughout the year, a credit union, an amount equal to the amount determined by the formula

$$A \times B \times C$$

where

A is the rate that would, if subsection 125(1.1) applied to the corporation for the year, be its small business deduction rate for the year within the meaning assigned by that subsection,

B is the amount, if any, determined by the formula

$$D - E$$

where

D is the lesser of

(*a*) the corporation's taxable income for the year, and

(*b*) the amount, if any, by which 4/3 of the corporation's maximum cumulative reserve at the end of the year exceeds the corporation's preferred-rate amount at the end of the immediately preceding taxation year, and

E is the least of the amounts determined under paragraphs 125 (1)(*a*) to (*c*) in respect of the corporation for the year, and

C is the percentage that is the total of

(*a*) the proportion of 100% that the number of days in the year that are before March 21, 2013 is of the number of days in the year,

(*b*) the proportion of 80% that the number of days in the year that are after March 20, 2013 and before 2014 is of the number of days in the year,

(*c*) the proportion of 60% that the number of days in the year that are in 2014 is of the number of days in the year,

(*d*) the proportion of 40% that the number of days in the year in 2015 is of the number of days in the year,

(*e*) the proportion of 20% that the number of days in the year in 2016 is of the number of days in the year, and

(*f*) if one or more days in the year are after 2016, 0%.

History: S. 137(3) was replaced by S.C. 2013, c. 33, s. 15(1), applicable to taxation years that end after March 20, 2013, and formerly read:

(3) *Additional deduction.* There may be deducted from the tax otherwise payable under this Part for a taxation year by a corporation that was, throughout the year, a credit union, an amount equal to the amount determined by multiplying the rate that would, if subsection 125(1.1) applied to the corporation for the year, be its small business deduction rate for the year within the meaning assigned by that subsection, by the amount, if any, by which the lesser of

(*a*) the corporation's taxable income for the year, and

(*b*) the amount, if any, by which 4/3 of the corporation's maximum cumulative reserve at the end of the year exceeds the corporation's preferred-rate amount at the end of the immediately preceding taxation year

exceeds

(*c*) the least of the amounts determined under paragraphs 125(1)(*a*) to (*c*) in respect of the corporation for the year.

Related Sections: S. 137(4) Amount deemed deductible under s. 125; s. 137(4.3) Determination of preferred-rate amount of a corporation.

Forms: T2 SCH 17 — Credit Union Deductions.

► 137(4) ◄

(4) Amount deemed deductible under s. 125. For the purposes of this Act, any amount deductible or any deduction under subsection (3) from the tax otherwise payable by a credit union under this Part for a taxation year shall be deemed to be an amount deductible or a deduction, as the case may be, under section 125 from that tax.

Related Sections: S. 125 Small business deduction; s. 137(6), "maximum cumulative reserve".

► 137(4.1) ◄

(4.1) Payments in respect of shares. Notwithstanding any other provision of this Act, an amount paid or payable by a credit union to a person is deemed to be paid or payable, as the case may be, by the credit union as interest and to be received or receivable, as the case may be, by the person as interest, if

(*a*) the amount is in respect of a share held by the person of the capital stock of the credit union, other than an amount paid or payable as or on account of a reduction of the paid-up capital, redemption, acquisition or cancellation of the share by the credit union to the extent of the paid-up capital of the share;

(*b*) the share is not listed on a stock exchange; and

(*c*) the person is

(i) a member of the credit union, or

(ii) a member of another credit union if the share is issued by the credit union after March 28, 2012 and the other credit union is a member of the credit union.

History: S. 137(4.1) was replaced by S.C. 2013, c. 40, s. 62(1), applicable to the 2012 and subsequent taxation years, and formerly read:

(4.1) *Payments in respect of shares.* Notwithstanding any other provision of this Act, an amount paid or payable by a credit union to a member thereof in respect of a share of a class of the capital stock of the credit union (other than any such amount paid or payable as or on account of a reduction of the paid-up capital, redemption, acquisition or cancellation of the share by the credit union to the extent of the paid-up capital of the share) shall, where the share is not listed on a designated stock exchange, be deemed to have been paid or payable, as the case may be, by the credit union as interest and to have been received or to have been receivable, as the case may be, by the member as interest.

Related Regulations: Part XXXII.

Related Sections: S. 12(1)(*c*) Interest.

► 137(4.2) ◄

(4.2) Deemed interest not a dividend. Notwithstanding any other provision of this Act, an amount that is deemed by subsection (4.1) to be interest shall be deemed not to be a dividend.

Related Sections: S. 84(2) Distribution on winding-up, etc; s. 84(3) Redemption, etc; s. 84(4) Reduction of paid-up capital.

► 137(4.3) ◄

(4.3) Determination of preferred-rate amount of a corporation. For the purposes of subsection (3),

(*a*) the preferred-rate amount of a corporation at the end of a taxation year is determined by the formula

$$A + B/C$$

where

A is its preferred-rate amount at the end of its immediately preceding taxation year,

B is the amount deductible under section 125 from the tax for the taxation year otherwise payable by it under this Part, and

C is its small business deduction rate for the taxation year within the meaning of subsection 125(1.1);

(*b*) where at any time a new corporation has been formed as a result of an amalgamation of two or more predecessor corporations, within the meaning of subsection 87(1), it shall be deemed to have had a taxation year ending immediately before that time and to have had, at the end of that year, a preferred-rate amount equal to the total of the preferred-rate amounts of each of the predecessor corporations at the end of their last taxation years; and

(*c*) where there has been a winding-up as described in subsection 88(1), the preferred-rate amount of the parent (referred to in that subsection) at the end of its taxation year immediately preceding its taxation year in which it received the assets of the subsidiary (referred to in that subsection) on the winding-up shall be deemed to be the total of the amount that would otherwise be its preferred-rate amount at the end of that year and the preferred-rate amount of the subsidiary at the end of its taxation year in which its assets were distributed to the parent on the winding-up.

History: S. 137(4.3)(*a*) was replaced by S.C. 2015, c. 36, s. 14(1), applicable to the 2016 and subsequent taxation years, and formerly read:

(*a*) the preferred-rate amount of a corporation at the end of a taxation year is an amount equal to the total of its preferred-rate amount at the end of its immediately preceding taxation year and $^{100}/_{17}$ of the amount deductible under section 125 from the tax for the year otherwise payable by it under this Part;

S. 137(4.3)(*a*) was replaced by S.C. 2013, c. 34, s. 284(1), applicable to the 2008 and subsequent taxation years, except that, in the application of paragraph 137(4.3) to a particular taxation year of a credit union that began in 2007 and ended in 2008, the preferred-rate amount of the credit union at the end of the particular taxation year is equal to the total of

(*a*) the preferred-rate amount of the credit union at the end of the taxation year that immediately preceded the particular taxation year; and

(*b*) the total of

(i) that proportion of the amount obtained by multiplying 25/4 by the amount deductible under section 125 for the particular taxation year, that the number of days in the particular taxation year that are in 2007 is of the number of days in the particular taxation year, and

(ii) that proportion of the amount obtained by multiplying 100/17 by the amount deductible under section 125 for the particular taxation year, that the number of days in the particular taxation year that are in 2008 is of the number of days in the particular taxation year.

S. 137(4.3)(*a*) formerly read:

(*a*) the preferred-rate amount of a corporation at the end of a taxation year is an amount equal to the total of its preferred-rate amount at the end of its immediately preceding taxation year and $^{25}/_{4}$ of the amount deductible under section 125 from the tax for the year otherwise payable by it under this Part;

▶ 137(5) ◀

(5) Member's income. Where a payment has been received by a taxpayer from a credit union in a taxation year in respect of an allocation in proportion to borrowing, the amount thereof shall, if the money so borrowed was used by the taxpayer for the purpose of earning income from a business or property (otherwise than to acquire property the income from which would be exempt or to acquire a life insurance policy), be included in computing the taxpayer's income for the year.

▶ 137(5.1) ◀

(5.1) Allocations of taxable dividends and capital gains. A credit union (referred to in this subsection and in subsection (5.2) as the "payer") may, at any time within 120 days after the end of its taxation year, elect in prescribed form to allocate in respect of the year to a member that is a credit union such portion of each of the following amounts as may reasonably be regarded as attributable to the member:

(*a*) the total of all amounts each of which is the amount of a taxable dividend received by the payer from a taxable Canadian corporation in the year;

(*b*) the amount, if any, by which

(i) the total of all amounts each of which is the amount by which the payer's capital gain from the disposition of a property in the year exceeds the payer's taxable capital gain from the disposition

exceeds

(ii) the total of all amounts each of which is the amount by which the payer's capital loss from the disposition of a property in the year exceeds the payer's allowable capital loss from the disposition; and

(*c*) each amount deductible under paragraph (5.2)(*c*) in computing the payer's taxable income for the year.

Forms: T2004 — Election by a Credit Union to Allocate Taxable Dividends and Net Non-Taxable Capital Gains to Member Credit Unions.

▶ 137(5.2) ◀

(5.2) Idem. Notwithstanding any other provision of this Act,

(*a*) there shall be deducted from the amount that would, but for this subsection, be deductible under section 112 in computing a payer's taxable income for a taxation year such portion of the total referred to in paragraph (5.1)(*a*) as the payer allocated to its members under subsection (5.1) in respect of the year;

(*b*) there shall be included in computing the income of a payer for a taxation year an amount equal to that portion of the amounts referred to in paragraphs (5.1)(*b*) and (*c*) that the payer allocated under subsection (5.1) in respect of the year to its members; and

(*c*) each amount allocated under subsection (5.1) to a member may be deducted by that member in computing the member's taxable income for its taxation year that includes the last day of the payer's taxation year in respect of which the amount was so allocated.

▶ 137(6) ◀

(6) Definitions. In this section,

"allocation in proportion to borrowing" —"allocation in proportion to borrowing" for a taxation year means an amount credited by a credit union to a person who was a member of the credit union in the year on terms that the member is entitled to or will receive payment thereof, computed at a rate in relation to

(*a*) the amount of interest payable by the member on money borrowed from the credit union, or

(*b*) the amount of money borrowed by the member from the credit union,

if the amount was credited at the same rate in relation to the amount of interest or money, as the case may be, as the rate at which amounts were similarly credited for the year to all other members of the credit union of the same class;

"bonus interest payment" —"bonus interest payment" for a taxation year means an amount credited by a credit union to a person who was a member of the credit union in the year on terms that the member is entitled to or will receive payment thereof, computed at a rate in relation to

(*a*) the amount of interest payable in respect of the year by the credit union to the member on money standing to the member's credit from time to time in the records or books of account of the credit union, or

(*b*) the amount of money standing to the member's credit from time to time in the year in the records or books of account of the credit union,

if the amount was credited at the same rate in relation to the amount of interest or money, as the case may be, as the rate at which amounts were similarly credited in the year to all other members of the credit union of the same class;

"credit union" —"credit union" means a corporation, association or federation incorporated or organized as a credit union or cooperative credit society if

(*a*) it derived all or substantially all of its revenues from

(i) loans made to, or cashing cheques for, members,

(ii) debt obligations or securities of, or guaranteed by, the Government of Canada or a province, a Canadian municipality, or an agency thereof, or debt obligations or securities of a municipal or public body performing a function of government in Canada or an agency thereof,

(iii) debt obligations of or deposits with, or guaranteed by, a corporation, commission or association not less than 90% of the shares or capital of which was owned by the Government of Canada or a province or by a municipality in Canada,

(iv) debt obligations of or deposits with, or guaranteed by, a bank, or debt obligations of or deposits with a corporation licensed or otherwise authorized under a law of Canada or a province to carry on in Canada the business of offering to the public its services as trustee,

(v) charges, fees and dues levied against members or members of members,

(vi) loans made to or deposits with a credit union or cooperative credit society of which it is a member, or

(vii) a prescribed revenue source,

(*b*) all or substantially all the members thereof having full voting rights therein were corporations, associations or federations

(i) incorporated as credit unions or cooperative credit societies, all of which derived all or substantially all of their revenues from the sources described in paragraph (*a*), or all or substantially all of the members of which were credit unions, cooperatives or a combination thereof,

(ii) incorporated, organized or registered under, or governed by a law of Canada or a province with respect to cooperatives, or

(iii) incorporated or organized for charitable purposes,

or were corporations, associations or federations no part of the income of which was payable to, or otherwise available for the personal benefit of, any shareholder or member thereof, or

(*c*) the corporation, association or federation would be a credit union by virtue of paragraph (*b*) if all the members (other than individuals) having full voting rights in each member thereof that is a credit union were members having full voting rights in the corporation, association or federation;

"maximum cumulative reserve" —"maximum cumulative reserve" of a credit union at the end of any particular taxation year means an amount determined by the formula

$$0.05 \times (A + B)$$

where

A is the total of all amounts each of which is the amount of any debt owing by the credit union to a member thereof or of any other obligation of the credit union to pay an amount to a member thereof, that was outstanding at the end of the year, including, for greater certainty, the amount of any deposit standing to the credit of a member of the credit union in the records of the credit union, but excluding, for greater certainty, any share in the credit union of any member thereof, and

B is the total of all amounts each of which is the amount, as of the end of the year, of any share in the credit union of any member thereof;

Related Sections: ITAR s. 58(3.2) Determination of maximum cumulative reserve at end of taxation year.

"member" —"member", of a credit union, means

(*a*) a person who is recorded as a member on the records of the credit union and is entitled to participate in and use the services of the credit union, and

(*b*) a registered retirement savings plan, a registered retirement income fund, a TFSA or a registered education savings plan, the annuitant, holder or subscriber under which is a person described in paragraph (*a*).

History: S. 137(6), the definition "member" was replaced by S.C. 2013, c. 34, s. 284(2), applicable to the 1996 and subsequent taxation years except that, in its application to taxation years that end before 2009, paragraph (*b*) of the definition "member" in subsection 137(6) is to be read as follows:

"(*b*) a registered retirement savings plan, a registered retirement income fund or a registered education savings plan, the annuitant or subscriber under which is a person described in paragraph (*a*)."

S. 137(6), the definition "member" formerly read:

"member"—"member" of a credit union means a person who is recorded as a member on the records of the credit union and is entitled to participate in and use the services of the credit union.

► 137(7) ◄

(7) Credit union not private corporation. Notwithstanding any other provision of this Act, a credit union that would, if this Act were read without reference to this section, be a private corporation is deemed not to be a private corporation except for the purposes of sections 123.1, 123.4, 125, 127, 127.1, 152 and 157 and the definition "small business corporation" in subsection 248(1) as it applies for the purpose of paragraph 39(1)(*c*).

History: S. 137(7) was replaced by S.C. 2013, c. 34, s. 284(3), applicable to the 2001 and subsequent taxation years, and formerly read:

(7) *Credit union not private corporation.* Notwithstanding any other provision of this Act, a credit union that would, but for this section, be a private corporation shall be deemed not to be a private corporation except for the purposes of sections 123.1, 125, 127, 127.1, 152 and 157 and the definition "small business corporation" in subsection 248(1) as it applies for the purposes of paragraph 39(1)(*c*).

Related Sections: S. 89(1), "private corporation"; s. 248(1), "business", "prescribed".

SECTION 137.1: [Deposit insurance corporations]

► 137.1(1) ◄

(1) Amounts included in income of deposit insurance corporation. For the purpose of computing the income for a taxation year of a taxpayer that is a deposit insurance corporation, the following rules apply:

(*a*) the corporation's income shall, except as otherwise provided in this section, be computed in accordance with the rules applicable in computing income for the purposes of this Part; and

(*b*) there shall be included in computing the corporation's income such of the following amounts as are applicable:

(i) the total of profits or gains made in the year by the corporation in respect of bonds, debentures, mortgages, hypothecary claims, notes or other similar obligations owned by it that were disposed of by it in the year, and

(ii) the total of each such portion of each amount, if any, by which the principal amount, at the time it was acquired by the corporation, of a bond, debenture, mortgage, hypothecary claim, note or other similar obligation owned by the corporation at the end of the year exceeds the cost to the corporation of acquiring it as was included by the corporation in computing its profit for the year.

Related Sections: S. 137.1(3) Amounts deductible in computing income of deposit insurance corporation; s. 137.1(5), "deposit insurance corporation".

► 137.1(2) ◄

(2) Amounts not included in income. The following amounts shall not be included in computing the income of a deposit insurance corporation for a taxation year:

(*a*) any premium or assessment received, or receivable, by the corporation in the year from a member institution; and

(*b*) any amount received by the corporation in the year from another deposit insurance corporation to the extent that that amount can reasonably be considered to have been paid out of amounts referred to in paragraph (*a*) received by that other deposit insurance corporation in any taxation year.

History: S. 137.1(2) was replaced by S.C. 2013, c. 34, s. 285(1), applicable to the 1998 and subsequent taxation years, and formerly read:

(2) *Amounts not included in income.* The amount of any premiums or assessments received or receivable by a taxpayer that is a deposit insurance corporation from its member institutions in a taxation year shall not be included in computing its income.

Related Sections: S. 137.1(4) Limitation on deduction; s. 137.1(11) Deduction by member institutions.

► 137.1(3) ◄

(3) Amounts deductible in computing income of deposit insurance corporation. There may be deducted in computing the income for a taxation year of a taxpayer that is a deposit insurance corporation such of the following amounts as are applicable:

(*a*) the total of losses sustained in the year by the corporation in respect of bonds, debentures, mortgages, hypothecary claims, notes or other similar obligations owned by it and issued by a person other than a member institution that were disposed of by it in the year;

(*b*) the total of each such portion of each amount, if any, by which the cost to the corporation of acquiring a bond, debenture, mortgage, hypothecary claim, note or other similar obligation owned by the corporation at the end of the year exceeds the principal amount of the bond, debenture, mortgage, hypothecary claim, note or other similar obligation, as the case may be, at the time it was so acquired as was deducted by the corporation in computing its profit for the year;

(*c*) (Repealed by 1988, c. 55, s. 124(2).)

(*d*) the total of all expenses incurred by the taxpayer in collecting premiums or assessments from member institutions;

(*e*) the total of all expenses incurred by the taxpayer

(i) in the performance of its duties as curator of a bank, or as liquidator or receiver of a member institution when duly appointed as such a curator, liquidator or receiver,

(ii) in the course of making or causing to be made such inspections as may reasonably be considered to be appropriate for the purposes of assessing the solvency or financial stability of a member institution, and

(iii) in supervising or administering a member institution in financial difficulty; and

(*f*) the total of all amounts each of which is an amount that is not otherwise deductible by the taxpayer for the year or any other taxation year and that is

(i) an amount paid by the taxpayer in the year pursuant to a legal obligation to pay interest on borrowed money used

(A) to lend money to, or otherwise provide assistance to, a member institution in financial difficulty,

(B) to assist in the payment of any losses suffered by members or depositors of a member institution in financial difficulty,

(C) to lend money to a subsidiary wholly-owned corporation of the taxpayer where the subsidiary is deemed by subsection (5.1) to be a deposit insurance corporation,

(D) to acquire property from a member institution in financial difficulty, or

(E) to acquire shares of the capital stock of a member institution in financial difficulty, or

(ii) an amount paid by the taxpayer in the year pursuant to a legal obligation to pay interest on an amount that would be deductible under subparagraph (i) if it were paid in the year.

Related Sections: S. 137.1(5) Definitions.

► 137.1(4) ◄

(4) Limitation on deduction. No deduction shall be made in computing the income for a taxation year of a taxpayer that is a deposit insurance corporation in respect of

(*a*) any grant, subsidy or other assistance to member institutions provided by it;

(*b*) an amount equal to the amount, if any, by which the amount paid or payable by it to acquire property exceeds the fair market value of the property at the time it was so acquired;

(*c*) any amounts paid to its member institutions as allocations in proportion to any amounts described in subsection (2);

(*d*) any amount paid by it to another deposit insurance corporation that is, because of paragraph (2)(*b*), not included in computing the income of that other deposit insurance corporation; or

(*e*) any amount that may otherwise be deductible under paragraph 20(1)(*p*) in respect of debts owing to it by any of its member institutions that has not been included in computing its income for the year or a preceding taxation year.

History: S. 137.1(4)(*d*) was added by S.C. 2013, c. 34, s. 285(2), applicable to the 1998 and subsequent taxation years.

Related Sections: S. 20(1)(*l*) Doubtful or impaired debts; s. 137.1(2) Amounts not included in income.

► 137.1(5) ◄

(5) Definitions. In this section,

"amortized cost" — (Repealed by 1988, c. 55, s. 124(5).)

"deposit insurance corporation" —"deposit insurance corporation" means

(*a*) a corporation that was incorporated by or under a law of Canada or a province respecting the establishment of a stabilization fund or board if

(i) it was incorporated primarily

(A) to provide or administer a stabilization, liquidity or mutual aid fund for credit unions, and

(B) to assist in the payment of any losses suffered by members of credit unions in liquidation, and

(ii) throughout any taxation year in respect of which the expression is being applied,

(A) it was a Canadian corporation, and

(B) the cost amount to the corporation of its investment property was at least 50% of the cost amount to it of all its property (other than a debt obligation of, or a share of the capital stock of, a member institution issued by the member institution at a time when it was in financial difficulty, or

(*b*) a corporation incorporated by the *Canada Deposit Insurance Corporation Act*;

Related Sections: S. 89(1), "Canadian corporation"; s. 137.1(5.1) Deeming provision; s. 137.1(8) Deemed compliance.

"investment property" —"investment property" means

(*a*) bonds, debentures, mortgages, hypothecary claims, notes or other similar obligations

(i) of or guaranteed by the Government of Canada,

(ii) of the government of a province or an agent thereof,

(iii) of a municipality in Canada or a municipal or public body performing a function of government in Canada,

(iv) of a corporation, commission or association not less than 90% of the shares or capital of which is owned by Her Majesty in right of a province or by a Canadian municipality, or of a subsidiary wholly-owned corporation that is subsidiary to such a corporation, commission or association, or

(v) of an educational institution or a hospital if repayment of the principal amount thereof and payment of the interest thereon is to be made, or is guaranteed, assured or otherwise specifically provided for or secured by the government of a province,

(*b*) any deposits, deposit certificates or guaranteed investment certificates with

(i) a bank,

(ii) a corporation licensed or otherwise authorized under the laws of Canada or a province to carry on in Canada the business of offering to the public its services as trustee, or

(iii) a credit union or central that is a member of the Canadian Payments Association or a credit union that is a shareholder or member of a central that is a member of the Canadian Payments Association,

(*c*) any money of the corporation, and

(*d*) in relation to a particular deposit insurance corporation, debt obligations of, and shares of the capital stock of, a subsidiary wholly-owned corporation of the particular corporation where the subsidiary is deemed by subsection (5.1) to be a deposit insurance corporation;

"member institution" —"member institution", in relation to a particular deposit insurance corporation, means

(*a*) a corporation whose liabilities in respect of deposits are insured by, or

(*b*) a credit union that is qualified for assistance from that deposit insurance corporation.

► 137.1(5.1) ◄

(5.1) Deeming provision. For the purposes of this section, other than subsection (2), paragraph (3)(*d*), subparagraph (3)(*e*)(i), subsection (9) and paragraph 11(*a*), a subsidiary wholly-owned corporation of a particular corporation described in the definition "deposit insurance corporation" in subsection (5) shall be deemed to be a deposit insurance corporation, and any member institution of the particular corporation shall be deemed to be a member institution of the subsidiary, where all or substantially all of the property of the subsidiary has at all times since the subsidiary was incorporated consisted of

(*a*) investment property;

(*b*) shares of the capital stock of a member institution of the particular corporation obtained by the subsidiary at a time when the member institution was in financial difficulty;

(*c*) debt obligations issued by a member institution of the particular corporation at a time when the member institution was in financial difficulty;

(*d*) property acquired from a member institution of the particular corporation at a time when the member institution was in financial difficulty; or

(*e*) any combination of property described in paragraphs (*a*) to (*d*).

► 137.1(6) ◄

(6) Deemed not to be a private corporation. Notwithstanding any other provision of this Act, a deposit insurance corporation that would, but for this subsection, be a private corporation shall be deemed not to be a private corporation.

Related Sections: S. 89(1), "private corporation".

► 137.1(7) ◄

(7) Deposit insurance corporation deemed not a credit union. Notwithstanding any other provision of this Act, a deposit insurance corporation that would, but for this subsection, be a credit union shall be deemed not to be a credit union.

Related Sections: S. 137 Deductions in computing income.

► 137.1(8) ◄

(8) Deemed compliance. For the purposes of subsection (5), a corporation shall be deemed to have complied with clause (*a*)(ii)(B) of the definition "deposit insurance corporation" in subsection (5) throughout the 1975 taxation year if it complied with that clause on the last day of that taxation year.

Related Sections: S. 137.1(5) Definitions.

► 137.1(9) ◄

(9) Special tax rate. The tax payable under this Part by a corporation for a taxation year throughout which it was a deposit insurance corporation (other than a corporation incorporated under the *Canada Deposit Insurance Corporation Act*) is the amount determined by the formula:

$$(38\% - A) \times B$$

where

A is the rate that would, if subsection 125(1.1) applied to the corporation for the taxation year, be the corporation's small business deduction rate for the taxation year within the meaning assigned by that subsection; and

B is the corporation's taxable income for the taxation year.

► 137.1(10) ◄

(10) Amounts paid by a deposit insurance corporation. Where in a taxation year a taxpayer is a member institution, there shall be included in computing its income for the year the total of all amounts each of which is

(*a*) an amount received by the taxpayer in the year from a deposit insurance corporation that is an amount described in any of paragraphs (4)(*a*) to (*c*), to the extent that the taxpayer has not repaid the amount to the deposit insurance corporation in the year,

(*b*) an amount received from a deposit insurance corporation in the year by a depositor or member of the taxpayer as, on account of, in lieu of payment of, or in satisfaction of, deposits with, or share capital of, the taxpayer, to the extent that the taxpayer has not repaid the amount to the deposit insurance corporation in the year, or

(*c*) the amount by which

(i) the principal amount of any obligation of the taxpayer to pay an amount to a deposit insurance corporation that is settled or extinguished in the year without any payment by the taxpayer or by the payment by the taxpayer of an amount less than the principal amount

exceeds

(ii) the amount, if any, paid by the taxpayer on the settlement or extinguishment of the obligation

to the extent that the excess is not otherwise required to be included in computing the taxpayer's income for the year or a preceding taxation year.

Related Sections: S. 137.1(10.1) Principal amount of an obligation to pay interest; s. 137.1(11) Deduction by member institutions.

Cases: For s. 137.1(10) to apply, any dividend paid by the Stabilization Central Credit Union of British Columbia ("STAB") to Spruce Credit Union ("Spruce") would have to have been paid in proportion to the regulatory assessments paid by Spruce. Such proportionality did not exist because STAB's dividends to Spruce were proportional to its shareholdings in STAB, and not proportional to the regulatory assessments Spruce paid to the Credit Union Deposit Insurance Corporation. *The Queen v. Spruce Credit Union*, 2014 DTC 5079 (F.C.A.)

► 137.1(10.1) ◄

(10.1) Principal amount of an obligation to pay interest. For the purposes of paragraph (10)(*c*), an amount of interest payable by a member institution to a deposit insurance corporation on an obligation shall be deemed to have a principal amount equal to that amount.

► 137.1(11) ◄

(11) Deduction by member institutions. There may be deducted in computing the income for a taxation year of a taxpayer that is a member institution such of the following amounts as are applicable:

(*a*) any amount paid or payable by the taxpayer in the year that is described in subsection (2) to the extent that it was not deducted in computing the taxpayer's income for a preceding taxation year; and

(*b*) any amount repaid by the taxpayer in the year to a deposit insurance corporation on account of an amount described in paragraph (10)(*a*) or (*b*) that was received in a preceding taxation year to the extent that it was not, by reason of subsection (12), excluded from the taxpayer's income for the preceding year.

► 137.1(12) ◄

(12) Repayment excluded. Where

(*a*) a member institution has in a taxation year repaid an amount to a deposit insurance corporation on account of an amount that was included by virtue of paragraph (10)(*a*) or (*b*) in computing its income for a preceding taxation year,

(*b*) the member institution has filed its return of income required by section 150 for the preceding year, and

(*c*) on or before the day on or before which the member institution is required by section 150 to file a return of income for the taxation year, it has filed an amended return for the preceding year excluding from its income for that year the amount repaid,

the amount repaid shall be excluded from the amount otherwise included by virtue of paragraph (10)(*a*) or (*b*) in computing the member institution's income for the preceding year and the Minister shall make such reassessment of the tax, interest and penalties payable by the member institution for preceding taxation years as is necessary to give effect to the exclusion.

SECTION 137.2: Computation of income for 1975 and subsequent years

For the purpose of computing the income of a deposit insurance corporation for the 1975 and subsequent taxation years,

(*a*) property of the corporation that is a bond, debenture, mortgage, hypothecary claim, note or other similar obligation owned by it at the commencement of the corporation's 1975 taxation year shall be valued at its cost to the corporation less the total of all amounts that, before that time, the corporation was entitled to receive as, on account or in lieu of payment of, or in satisfaction of, the principal amount of the bond, debenture, mortgage, hypothecary claim, note or other similar obligation,

(i) plus a reasonable amount in respect of the amortization of the amount by which the principal amount of the property at the time it was acquired by the corporation exceeded its actual cost to the corporation, or

(ii) minus a reasonable amount in respect of the amortization of the amount by which its actual cost to the corporation exceeded the principal amount of the property at the time it was acquired by the corporation;

(*b*) property of the corporation that is a debt owing to the corporation (other than property described in paragraph (*a*) or a debt that became a bad debt before its 1975 taxation year) acquired by it before the commencement of its 1975 taxation year shall be valued at any time at the amount thereof outstanding at that time;

(*c*) property of the corporation (other than property in respect of which any amount for the year has been included under paragraph (*a*)) that was acquired, by foreclosure or otherwise, after default made under a mortgage or hypothec shall be valued at its cost amount to the corporation; and

(*d*) any other property shall be valued at its cost amount to the corporation.

Insurance Corporations

SECTION 138: Insurance corporations

► 138(1) ◄

(1) Insurance corporations. It is hereby declared that a corporation, whether or not it is a mutual corporation, that has, in a taxation year, been a party to insurance contracts or other arrangements or relationships of a particular class whereby it can reasonably be regarded as undertaking

(*a*) to insure other persons against loss, damage or expense of any kind, or (*b*) to pay insurance moneys to other persons

(i) on the death of any person,

(ii) on the happening of an event or contingency dependent on human life,

(iii) for a term dependent on human life, or

(iv) at a fixed or determinable future time,

whether or not such persons are members or shareholders of the corporation, shall, regardless of the form or legal effect of those contracts, arrangements or relationships, be deemed, for the purposes of this Act, to have been carrying on an insurance business of that class in the year for profit, and in any such case, for the purpose of computing the income of the corporation, the following rules apply:

(*c*) every amount received by the corporation under, in consideration of, in respect of or on account of such a contract, arrangement or relationship shall be deemed to have been received by it in the course of that business,

(*d*) the income shall, except as otherwise provided in this section, be computed in accordance with the rules applicable in computing income for the purposes of this Part,

(*e*) all income from property vested in the corporation shall be deemed to be income of the corporation, and

(*f*) all taxable capital gains and allowable capital losses from dispositions of property vested in the corporation shall be deemed to be taxable capital gains or allowable capital losses, as the case may be, of the corporation.

Related Sections: S. 38 Taxable capital gain and allowable capital loss; s. 54, "capital property"; s. 89(1), "taxable dividend"; s. 138(6) Deduction for dividends from taxable corporations; s. 138(9) Computation of income; s. 141 Deeming rules for life insurance corporations; s. 141.1 Deemed not to be a private corporation; s. 146(1), "registered retirement savings plan"; s. 148(1) Amounts included in computing policyholder's income; s. 248(1), "annuity", "gross revenue", "group term life insurance policy", "insurance corporation", "insurer", "life insurance business", "life insurer", "taxable Canadian corporation".

Tax Window Files: Carrying on an Insurance Business, *Technical Interpretation, Financial Industries Division, May 26, 2005*, CRA Document No. 2005-0126031C6.

► 138(2) ◄

(2) Insurer's income or loss. Notwithstanding any other provision of this Act,

(*a*) if a life insurer resident in Canada carries on an insurance business in Canada and in a country other than Canada in a taxation year, its income or loss for the year from carrying on an insurance business is the amount of its income or loss for the taxation year from carrying on the insurance business in Canada;

(*b*) if a life insurer resident in Canada carries on an insurance business in Canada and in a country other than Canada in a taxation year, for greater certainty,

(i) in computing the insurer's income or loss for the taxation year from the insurance business carried on by it in Canada, no amount is to be included in respect of the insurer's gross investment revenue for the taxation year derived from property used or held by it in the course of carrying on an insurance business that is not designated insurance property for the taxation year of the insurer, and

(ii) in computing the insurer's taxable capital gains or allowable capital losses for the taxation year from dispositions of capital property (referred to in this subparagraph as "insurance business property") that, at the time of the disposition, was used or held by the insurer in the course of carrying on an insurance business,

(A) there is to be included each taxable capital gain or allowable capital loss of the insurer for the taxation year from a disposition in the taxation year of an insurance business property that was a designated insurance property for the taxation year of the insurer, and

(B) there is not to be included any taxable capital gain or allowable capital loss of the insurer for the taxation year from a disposition in the taxation year of an insurance business property that was not a designated insurance property for the taxation year of the insurer;

(*c*) if a non-resident insurer carries on an insurance business in Canada in a taxation year, its income or loss for the taxation year from carrying on an insurance business is the amount of its income or loss for the taxation year from carrying on the insurance business in Canada; and

(*d*) if a non-resident insurer carries on an insurance business in Canada in a taxation year,

(i) in computing the non-resident insurer's income or loss for the taxation year from the insurance business carried on by it in Canada, no amount is to be included in respect of the non-resident insurer's gross investment revenue for the taxation year derived from property used or held by it in the course of carrying on an insurance business that is not designated insurance property for the taxation year of the non-resident insurer, and

(ii) in computing the non-resident insurer's taxable capital gains or allowable capital losses for the taxation year from dispositions of capital property (referred to in this subparagraph as "insurance business property") that, at the time of the disposition, was used or held by the non-resident insurer in the course of carrying on an insurance business,

(A) there is to be included each taxable capital gain or allowable capital loss of the non-resident insurer for the taxation year from a disposition in the taxation year of an insurance business property that was a designated insurance property for the taxation year of the non-resident insurer, and

(B) there is not to be included any taxable capital gain or allowable capital loss of the non-resident insurer for the taxation year from a disposition in the taxation year of an insurance business property that was not a designated insurance property for the taxation year of the non-resident insurer.

History: S. 138(2) was replaced by S.C. 2013, c. 34, s. 286(1), applicable to taxation years that end after 1999, and formerly read:

(2) *Insurer's income or loss.* Notwithstanding any other provision of this Act, where a life insurer resident in Canada carries on an insurance business in Canada and in a country other than Canada in a taxation year

(*a*) its income or loss for the year from carrying on an insurance business is the amount of its income or loss for the year, computed in accordance with this Act, from the business in Canada; and

(*b*) no amount shall be included in computing its income for the year in respect of its taxable capital gains and allowable capital losses from dispositions of property (other than property disposed of in a taxation year in which it was designated insurance property) of the insurer used or held by it in the course of carrying on an insurance business.

Related Sections: S. 20(7) Where para. (1)(m) does not apply; s. 138(1) Insurance corporations; s. 138(6) Deduction for dividends from taxable corporations; s. 138(9) Computation of income; s. 138(12), "designated insurance property".

Tax Window Files: Demutualization Expenses, *November 17, 2003*, CRA Document No. 2003-0044367; Deductibility of Demutualization Expenses, *Technical Interpretation, Financial Industries Division, October 24, 2003*, CRA Document No. 2003-0183447.

Cases: The life insurer, a non-resident of Canada, was required to include interest received on the overpayment of taxes as income from its life insurance business in Canada. *Munich Reinsurance Company (Canadian Branch) v. The Queen*, 2002 DTC 6701 (F.C.A.), affirming 2000 DTC 2009 (T.C.C.). As a result of the decision, a technical amendment was proposed (re-released July 16, 2010)

► 138(2.1) ◄

(2.1) Income — designated foreign insurance business. If a life insurer resident in Canada has a designated foreign insurance business in a taxation year,

(*a*) for the purposes of computing the life insurer's income or loss from carrying on an insurance business in Canada for that taxation year, the life insurer's insurance business carried on in Canada is deemed to include the insurance of the specified Canadian risks that are insured as part of the designated foreign insurance business;

(*b*) if, in the immediately preceding taxation year, the designated foreign insurance business was not a designated foreign insurance business, for the purposes of paragraph (4)(*a*), subsection (9), the definition *designated insurance property* in subsection (12) and paragraphs 12(1)(*d*) to (*e*), the life insurer is deemed to have carried on the business in Canada in that immediately preceding year and to have claimed the maximum amounts to which it would have been entitled under paragraphs (3)(*a*) (other than under subparagraph (3)(*a*)(ii.1), (iii) or (v)), 20(1)(*l*) and (*l*.1) and 20(7)(*c*) in respect of those specified Canadian risks if that designated foreign insurance business had been a designated foreign insurance business in that immediately preceding year; and

(*c*) for the purposes of subparagraph (3)(*a*)(ii.1) and subsection 20(22),

(i) the life insurer is deemed to have carried on the business in Canada in that immediately preceding year, and

(ii) the amounts, if any, that would have been prescribed in respect of the insurer for the purposes of paragraphs (4)(*b*) and 12(1)(*e*.1) for that immediately preceding year in respect of the insurance policies in respect of those specified Canadian risks are deemed to have been included in computing its income for that year.

History: S. 138(2.1) was added by S.C. 2017, c. 33, s. 53(1), applicable to taxation years of a taxpayer that begin after March 21, 2017.

► 138(2.2) ◄

(2.2) Insurance swaps. For the purposes of this section, one or more risks insured by a life insurer resident in Canada, as part of an insurance business carried on in a country other than Canada, that would not be specified Canadian risks if this Act were read without reference to this subsection, are deemed to be specified Canadian risks if those risks would be deemed to be specified Canadian risks because of paragraph 95(2)(*a*.21) if the life insurer were a foreign affiliate of a taxpayer.

History: S. 138(2.2) was added by S.C. 2017, c. 33, s. 53(1), applicable to taxation years of a taxpayer that begin after March 21, 2017.

► 138(2.3) ◄

(2.3) Insurance swaps. Subsection (2.4) applies in respect of one or more agreements or arrangements if

(*a*) subsection (2.2) applies to deem one or more risks insured by a particular life insurer resident in Canada to be specified Canadian risks; and

(*b*) those agreements or arrangements are in respect of risks described in paragraph (*a*) and have been entered into by any of the following (in subsection (2.4), referred to as an "agreeing party"):

(i) the particular life insurer,

(ii) another life insurer resident in Canada that does not deal at arm's length with the particular life insurer,

(iii) a partnership of which a life insurer described in subparagraph (i) or (ii) is a member,

(iv) a foreign affiliate of either the particular life insurer or a person that does not deal at arm's length with the particular life insurer, and

(v) a partnership of which a foreign affiliate described in subparagraph (iv) is a member.

History: S. 138(2.3) was added by S.C. 2017, c. 33, s. 53(1), applicable to taxation years of a taxpayer that begin after March 21, 2017.

► 138(2.4) ◄

(2.4) Insurance swaps. If this subsection applies in respect of one or more agreements or arrangements,

(*a*) to the extent that activities performed in connection with those agreements or arrangements can reasonably be considered to be performed for the purpose of obtaining the result described in subparagraph 95(2)(*a*.21)(ii) (with any modifications that the circumstances require), those activities are deemed to be,

(i) if the agreeing party is a life insurer resident in Canada, or a partnership of which such a life insurer is a member, part of the life insurer's insurance business carried on in Canada, and

(ii) if the agreeing party is a foreign affiliate of a taxpayer, or a partnership of which such an affiliate is a member, a separate business, other than an active business, carried on by the affiliate; and

(*b*) any income from those activities (including income that pertains to or is incident to those activities) is deemed to be,

(i) if the agreeing party is a life insurer resident in Canada, income from the life insurer's insurance business carried on in Canada, and

(ii) if the agreeing party is a foreign affiliate of a taxpayer, income from the business, other than an active business.

History: S. 138(2.4) was added by S.C. 2017, c. 33, s. 53(1), applicable to taxation years of a taxpayer that begin after March 21, 2017.

► 138(2.5) ◄

(2.5) Ceding of Canadian risks. Any income of a life insurer resident in Canada for a taxation year, from its insurance business carried on in a country other than Canada, in respect of the ceding of specified Canadian risks that would, if the life insurer were a foreign affiliate of a taxpayer, be included in computing the life insurer's income from a business, other than an active business, for the taxation year because of subparagraph 95(2)(*a*.2)(iii), is to be included in computing the life insurer's income or loss for that taxation year from its insurance business carried on in Canada, except to the extent it is already included because of subsection (2.1), (2.2) or (2.4).

History: S. 138(2.5) was added by S.C. 2017, c. 33, s. 53(1), applicable to taxation years of a taxpayer that begin after March 21, 2017.

▶ 138(2.6) ◀

(2.6) Anti-avoidance. For the purposes of this section,

(*a*) a risk is deemed to be a specified Canadian risk that is insured as part of an insurance business carried on in Canada by a particular life insurer resident in Canada if

(i) the particular life insurer insured the risk as part of a transaction or series of transactions,

(ii) the risk would not be a specified Canadian risk if this Act were read without reference to this subsection, and

(iii) it can reasonably be concluded that one of the purposes of the transaction or series of transactions was to avoid

(A) having a designated foreign insurance business, or

(B) the application of any of subsections (2.1) to (2.5) to the risk; and

(*b*) if one or more agreements or arrangements in respect of the risk have been entered into by any of the persons or partnerships described in subparagraphs (2.3)(*b*)(i) to (v) (in this paragraph, referred to as an "agreeing party"),

(i) any activities performed in connection with those agreements or arrangements are deemed to be

(A) if the agreeing party is a life insurer resident in Canada, or a partnership of which such a life insurer is a member, part of the life insurer's insurance business carried on in Canada, and

(B) if the agreeing party is a foreign affiliate of a taxpayer, or a partnership of which such an affiliate is a member, a separate business, other than an active business, carried on by the affiliate, and

(ii) any income from those activities (including income that pertains to or is incident to those activities) is deemed to be,

(A) if the agreeing party is a life insurer resident in Canada, income from the life insurer's insurance business carried on in Canada, and

(B) if the agreeing party is a foreign affiliate of a taxpayer, income from the business, other than an active business.

History: S. 138(2.6) was added by S.C. 2017, c. 33, s. 53(1), applicable to taxation years of a taxpayer that begin after March 21, 2017.

▶ 138(3) ◀

(3) Deductions allowed in computing income. In computing a life insurer's income for a taxation year from carrying on its life insurance business in Canada, there may be deducted

(*a*) such of the following amounts as are applicable:

(i) any amount that the insurer claims as a policy reserve for the year in respect of its life insurance policies, not exceeding the total of amounts that the insurer is allowed by regulation to deduct in respect of the policies,

(ii) any amount that the insurer claims as a reserve in respect of claims that were received by the insurer before the end of the year under its life insurance policies and that are unpaid at the end of the year, not exceeding the total of amounts that the insurer is allowed by regulation to deduct in respect of the policies,

(ii.1) the amount included under paragraph (4)(*b*) in computing the insurer's income for the taxation year preceding the year,

(iii) the amount determined by the following formula:

$$A - B$$

where

A is the total of policy dividends (except the portion paid out of segregated funds) that became payable by the insurer after its 1968 taxation year and before the end of the year under its participating life insurance policies, and

B is the total of amounts deductible under this subparagraph (including as determined under subsection (3.1) as it read in its application to the insurer's last taxation year that began before November 2011) in computing its incomes for taxation years before the year, and

(iv) (Repealed by S.C. 2013, c. 34, s. 286(2).)

(v) each amount (other than an amount credited under a participating life insurance policy) that would be deductible under section 140 in computing the insurer's income for the year if the reference in that section to "an insurance business other than a life insurance business" were read as a reference to "a life insurance business in Canada";

(*b*) the total of amounts each of which is a policy loan made by the insurer in the year and after 1977; and

(*c*) the amount of tax under Part XII.3 payable by the insurer in respect of its taxable Canadian life investment income for the year.

(*d*) (Repealed by S.C. 1995, c. 21, s. 57(2).)

(*e*) (Repealed by S.C. 2013, c. 34, s. 286(3).)

(*f*) (Repealed by S.C. 2013, c. 34, s. 286(3).)

(*g*) (Repealed by S.C. 2013, c. 34, s. 286(3).)

History: S. 138(3)(*a*)(iii) was replaced by S.C. 2013, c. 34, s. 286(2), applicable to taxation years that begin after October 31, 2011, and formerly read:

(iii) an amount equal to the lesser of

(A) the amount, if any, by which the total of policy dividends (except the portion thereof paid out of segregated funds) that became payable by the insurer after its 1968 taxation year and before the end of the year under its participating life insurance policies exceeds the total of amounts deductible under this subparagraph in computing its incomes for taxation years before the year, and

(B) the amount, if any, by which the total of all amounts, each of which is the insurer's income, determined in accordance with prescribed rules, for the year or a preceding taxation year ending after 1968 from its participating life insurance business carried on in Canada exceeds the total of all amounts each of which is an amount deductible under this subparagraph or subparagraph (iv) in computing its incomes for taxation years ending before the year,

S. 138(3)(*a*)(iv) was repealed by S.C. 2013, c. 34, s. 286(2), applicable to taxation years that begin after October 31, 2011, and formerly read:

(iv) an amount as a reserve for policy dividends that will become payable by the insurer in the immediately following taxation year equal to the least of

(A) that portion of policy dividends that has accrued in the year or a preceding taxation year to or for the benefit of participating life insurance policyholders of the insurer, to the extent that an amount in respect thereof has not been included, either explicitly or implicitly, in the calculation of the amount deductible by the insurer for the year under subparagraph (i) and, for the purpose of this clause, a policy dividend in respect of a life insurance policy shall be deemed to accrue in equal daily amounts between anniversary dates of the policy,

(B) 110% of the amount paid or unconditionally credited in the taxation year immediately following the year in respect of the portion referred to in clause (A) of policy dividends that has accrued in the year or a preceding taxation year, and

(C) the amount, if any, by which the amount described in clause (iii)(B) for the year exceeds the amount described in clause (iii)(A) for the year, and

S. 138(3)(*b*) and (*c*) were added by S.C. 2013, c. 34, s. 286(3), applicable to taxation years that begin after October 31, 2011.

S. 138(3)(*e*), (*f*), and (*g*) were repealed by S.C. 2013, c. 34, s. 286(3), applicable to taxation years that begin after October 31, 2011, and formerly read:

(*e*) the total of amounts each of which is a policy loan made by the insurer in the year and after 1977;

(*f*) where the taxation year is the first taxation year of the insurer ending after November 12, 1981, the total of all amounts each of which is the amount, if any, in respect of interest on a policy loan that was included in computing the insurer's income for a taxation year ending before November 13, 1981

(i) to the extent that the interest had accrued to it before the commencement of its 1969 taxation year, or

(ii) to the extent that the interest had been included in computing its income for a preceding taxation year; and

(*g*) the amount of tax under Part XII.3 payable by the insurer in respect of its taxable Canadian life investment income for the year.

Related Regulations: 309.1 Income From Participating Life Insurance Businesses; 1401; 1402; 1403 to 1408.

Related Sections: S. 4(1) Income or loss from a source or from sources in a place; s. 18(1)(*e*.1) Unpaid claims under insurance policies; s. 20(7) Where para. (1)(m) does not apply; s. 138(4) Amounts included in computing income; s. 138(5.2) Idem; s. 138(9) Computation of income; s. 138(12), "designated insurance property", "life insurance policy in Canada", "maximum tax actuarial reserve"; s. 139.1(8) Policy dividends; s. 148(1) Amounts included in computing policyholder's income; s. 148(2) Deemed proceeds of disposition; 211 [Interpretation].

Forms: T2Sch150 — Net Income (Loss) for Income Tax Purposes for Life Insurance Companies.

Tax Window Files: Tax on Investment Income of Life Insurers — Universal Life Policies, *Technical Interpretation, Charitable and Financial Institution Sectors, March 28, 2006*, CRA Document No. 2005-0145821E5; Reinsurance Reserve, *Technical Interpretation, Financial Industries Division, January 8, 2004*, CRA Document No. 2003-0035797; Large Corporations Tax — Policy Loans, *Technical Interpretation, Financial Industries Division, January 15, 2003*, CRA Document No. 2002-0168217.

Cases: The taxpayer was successful in excluding certain components in the calculation of its reserves under the policy premiums method. *National Life Assurance Co. of Canada v. The Queen*, 2008 DTC 6141 (F.C.A.), affirming 2006 DTC 3633 (T.C.C.)

► 138(3.1) ◄

(3.1) Excess policy dividend deduction deemed deductible — (Repealed by S.C. 2013, c. 34, s. 286(4).)

History: S. 138(3.1) was repealed by S.C. 2013, c. 34, s. 286(4), applicable to taxation years that begin after October 31, 2011, and formerly read:

(3.1) *Excess policy dividend deduction deemed deductible.* For the purposes of clause (3)(*a*)(iii)(A),

(*a*) an insurer's 1975-76 excess policy dividend deduction shall be deemed to be an amount that was deductible under subparagraph (3)(*a*)(iii) in computing its incomes for taxation years before its 1977 taxation year; and

(*b*) the amount prescribed to be an insurer's 1977 excess policy dividend deduction shall be deemed to be an amount that was deductible under subparagraph (3)(*a*)(iii) in computing its incomes for taxation years before its 1978 taxation year.

Related Regulations: 2407.

► 138(4) ◄

(4) Amounts included in computing income. In computing a life insurer's income for a taxation year from carrying on its life insurance business in Canada, there shall be included

(*a*) each amount deducted under paragraph (3)(*a*), other than under subparagraph (3)(*a*)(ii.1), (iii) or (v), in computing the insurer's income for the preceding taxation year;

(*b*) the amount prescribed in respect of the insurer for the year in respect of its life insurance policies; and

(*c*) the total of all amounts received by the insurer in the year in respect of the repayment of policy loans or in respect of interest on policy loans.

History: S. 138(4)(*a*) was replaced by S.C. 2013, c. 34, s. 286(5), applicable to taxation years that begin after October 31, 2011, and formerly read:

(*a*) each amount deducted under subparagraph (3)(*a*)(i), (ii) or (iv) in computing the insurer's income for the preceding taxation year;

Related Sections: S. 138(1) Insurance corporations; s. 138(3) Deductions allowed in computing income; s. 138(9) Computation of income.

► 138(4.01) ◄

(4.01) Life insurance policy. For the purposes of subsections (3) and (4), a life insurance policy includes a benefit under a group life insurance policy or a group annuity contract.

► 138(4.1) ◄

(4.1) Idem — (Repealed by S.C. 2013, c. 34, s. 286(6).)

History: S. 138(4.1) was repealed by S.C. 2013, c. 34, s. 286(6), applicable to taxation years that begin after October 31, 2011, and formerly read:

(4.1) *Idem.* For the purposes of paragraph (4)(*a*), an insurer shall be deemed to have deducted in computing its income for its 1976 taxation year,

(*a*) under subparagraph (3)(*a*)(i), the total of

(i) the amount deducted under that subparagraph in computing its income from its life insurance business in Canada for its 1976 taxation year, and

(ii) the lesser of

(A) the amount, if any, of its 1975-76 excess policy reserves, and

(B) the amount, if any, by which its 1975 branch accounting election deficiency exceeds the total of

(I) the amount determined under subparagraph (*d*)(ii),

(II) the total of amounts each of which is an amount determined under paragraph 13(22)(*b*) with respect to depreciable property of a prescribed class of the insurer,

(III) the amount determined under subparagraph (*b*)(ii), and

(IV) the total of amounts each of which is a portion of a non-capital loss that is deemed by subsection 111(7.1) to have been deductible in computing the insurer's income for a taxation year ending before 1977;

(*b*) under subparagraph (3)(*a*)(ii), the total of

(i) the amount deducted under that subparagraph in computing its income from its life insurance business in Canada for its 1976 taxation year, and

(ii) the lesser of

(A) the amount, if any, of its 1975-76 excess additional group term reserves, and

(B) the amount, if any, by which its 1975 branch accounting election deficiency exceeds the total of

(I) the amount determined under subparagraph (*d*)(ii),

(II) the total of amounts each of which is an amount determined under paragraph 13(22)(*b*) with respect to depreciable property of a prescribed class of the insurer, and

(III) the total described in subclause (*a*)(ii)(B)(IV);

(*c*) under subparagraph (3)(*a*)(iv), the total of

(i) the amount deducted under that subparagraph in computing its income from its life insurance business in Canada for its 1976 taxation year, and

(ii) the amount, if any, of its 1975-76 excess policy dividend reserve; and

(*d*) under paragraph 138(3)(*c*) of the *Income Tax Act*, chapter 148 of the Revised Statutes of Canada, 1952, the total of

(i) the amount deducted under that paragraph in computing its income from its life insurance business in Canada for its 1976 taxation year, and

(ii) the lesser of

(A) the amount, if any, of its 1975-76 excess investment reserve, and

(B) the amount, if any, of its 1975 branch accounting election deficiency.

► 138(4.2) ◄

(4.2) Idem — (Repealed by S.C. 2013, c. 34, s. 286(6).)

History: S. 138(4.2) was repealed by S.C. 2013, c. 34, s. 286(6), applicable to taxation years that begin after October 31, 2011, and formerly read:

(4.2) *Idem.* For the purposes of paragraph (4)(*a*), a life insurer shall be deemed to have deducted the following amounts in computing its income for its 1977 taxation year

(*a*) under subparagraph (3)(*a*)(i), the amount if any, by which the total of

(i) the insurer's maximum tax actuarial reserve for its 1977 taxation year, if that reserve had been determined on the basis of the rules applicable to its 1978 taxation year,

(ii) where the insurer has deducted the amount of any policy loan made by it in the year in computing its income from its life insurance business in Canada for any taxation year before its 1978 taxation year or not included interest in respect of any such loan in computing its gross investment revenue for any taxation year before its 1978 taxation year, the total of amounts that were outstanding at the end of the insurer's 1977 taxation year each of which is an amount payable to it in respect of a policy loan, and

(iii) that portion of the amount deducted by the insurer under subparagraph (3)(*a*)(i) in computing its income for its 1977 taxation year that is in respect of segregated fund policies

exceeds

(iv) the amount prescribed to be its 1977 carryforward deduction;

(*b*) under subparagraph (3)(*a*)(iv), the total of

(i) the amount deducted under that subparagraph in computing its income from its life insurance business in Canada for its 1977 taxation year, and

(ii) the amount, if any, by which

(A) the amount that would have been deductible under that subparagraph for its 1977 taxation year if that subparagraph were read without reference to clause (3)(*a*)(iv)(C),

exceeds

(B) the amount determined under subparagraph (i) for that taxation year; and

(*c*) under paragraph 138(3)(*c*) of the *Income Tax Act*, chapter 148 of the Revised Statutes of Canada, 1952, the total of

(i) the amount deducted under that paragraph in computing its income from its life insurance business in Canada for its 1977 taxation year, and

(ii) the amount, if any, by which,

(A) where the insurer has made an election under subsection (9) in respect of its 1975 taxation year, the amount that would have been deductible under paragraph 138(3)(*c*) of that Act in computing its income for its 1977 taxation year if the insurer had claimed the maximum allowable amount in its 1977 taxation year, or

(B) where the insurer has not made an election under subsection (9) in respect of its 1975 taxation year, the amount that would have been deductible under paragraph 138(3)(*c*) of that Act in computing its income for its 1977 taxation year if the insurer had claimed the maximum allowable amount in each of its taxation years ending before 1978 and after 1974

exceeds

(C) the amount determined under subparagraph (i).

► 138(4.3) ◄

(4.3) Idem — (Repealed by S.C. 2013, c. 34, s. 286(6).)

History: S. 138(4.3) was repealed by S.C. 2013, c. 34, s. 286(6), applicable to taxation years that begin after October 31, 2011, and formerly read:

(4.3) *Idem.* For the purposes of paragraph (4)(*a*), in computing a life insurer's income from carrying on its life insurance business in Canada for its first taxation year ending after 1984, the amount, if any, by which

(*a*) the total of all amounts each of which is an amount deducted by the insurer in computing its income for a taxation year ending after 1968 and before 1985 in respect of a claim under a life insurance policy that was likely to arise after the end of the particular taxation year in respect of a death that occurred in the particular taxation year

exceeds

(*b*) the total of all amounts each of which is an amount paid by the insurer or included in computing its income before the commencement of its first taxation year ending after 1984 in respect of amounts described in paragraph (*a*)

shall be deemed to be an amount that was deducted by the insurer under subparagraph (3)(*a*)(i) in computing its income from that business for its last taxation year ending before 1985.

► 138(4.4) ◄

(4.4) Income inclusion. If, for a period of time in a taxation year, a life insurer

(*a*) owned land (other than land referred to in paragraph (*c*) or (*d*)) or an interest, or for civil law a right, therein that was not held primarily for the purpose of gaining or producing income from the land for the period,

(*b*) had an interest, or for civil law a right, in a building that was being constructed, renovated or altered,

(*c*) owned land subjacent to the building referred to in paragraph (*b*) or an interest, or for civil law a right, therein, or

(*d*) owned land immediately contiguous to the land referred to in paragraph (*c*) or an interest, or for civil law a right, therein that was used or was intended to be used for a parking area, driveway, yard, garden or other use necessary for the use or intended use of the building referred to in paragraph (*b*),

there shall be included in computing the insurer's income for the year, where the land, building, or interest or right, was designated insurance property of the insurer for the year, or property used or held by it in the year in the course of carrying on an insurance business in Canada, the total of all amounts each of which is the amount prescribed in respect of the insurer's cost or capital cost, as the case may be, of the land, building, or interest or right, for the period, and the amount prescribed shall, at the end of the period, be included in computing

(*e*) where the land, or interest or right therein, is property described in paragraph (*a*), the cost to the insurer of the land, or of the interest or right therein, and

(*f*) where the land, building, or interest or right therein, is property described in paragraphs (*b*) to (*d*), the capital cost to the insurer of the interest or right in the building described in paragraph (*b*).

History: S. 138(4.4) was replaced by S.C. 2013, c. 34, s. 135(1), in force June 26, 2013, and formerly read:

(4.4) *Idem.* Where, for a period of time in a taxation year, a life insurer

(*a*) owned land (other than land referred to in paragraph (*c*) or (*d*)) or an interest therein that was not held primarily for the purpose of gaining or producing income from the land for the period,

(*b*) had an interest in a building that was being constructed, renovated or altered,

(*c*) owned land subjacent to the building referred to in paragraph (*b*) or an interest therein, or

(*d*) owned land immediately contiguous to the land referred to in paragraph (*c*) or an interest therein that was used or was intended to be used for a parking area, driveway, yard, garden or other use necessary for the use or intended use of the building referred to in paragraph (*b*),

there shall be included in computing the insurer's income for the year, where the land, building or interest was designated insurance property of the insurer for the year, or property used or held by it in the year in the course of carrying on an insurance business in Canada, the total of all amounts each of which is the amount prescribed in respect of the insurer's cost or capital cost, as the case may be, of the land, building or interest for the period, and the amount prescribed shall, at the end of the period, be included in computing

(*e*) where the land or interest therein is property described in paragraph (*a*), the cost to the insurer of the land or the interest therein, and

(*f*) where the land, building or interest therein is property described in paragraphs (*b*) to (*d*), the capital cost to the insurer of the interest in the building described in paragraph (*b*).

Related Regulations: 2410.

Related Sections: S. 138(4.5) Application; s. 138(4.6) Completion; s. 138(12), "designated insurance property".

► 138(4.5) ◄

(4.5) Application. Where a life insurer transfers or lends property, directly or indirectly in any manner whatever, to a person or partnership (in this subsection referred to as the "transferee") that is affiliated with the insurer or a person or partnership that does not deal at arm's length with the insurer and

(*a*) that property,

(*b*) property substituted for that property, or

(*c*) property the acquisition of which was assisted by the transfer or loan of that property

was property described in paragraph (4.4)(*a*), (*b*), (*c*) or (*d*) of the transferee for a period of time in a taxation year of the insurer, the following rules apply:

(*d*) subsection (4.4) shall apply to include an amount in the insurer's income for the year on the assumption that the property was owned by the insurer for the period, was property described in paragraph (4.4)(*a*), (*b*), (*c*) or (*d*) of the insurer and was used or held by it in the year in the course of carrying on an insurance business in Canada, and

(*e*) an amount included in the insurer's income for the year under subsection (4.4) by reason of the application of this subsection shall

(i) where subparagraph (ii) does not apply, be added by the insurer in computing the cost to it of shares of the capital stock of or an interest in the transferee at the end of the year, or

(ii) where the insurer and the transferee have jointly elected in prescribed form on or before the day that is the earliest of the days on or before which any taxpayer making the election is required to file a return pursuant to section 150 for the taxation year that includes the period, be added in computing

(A) where the property is land or an interest, or for civil law a right, therein of the transferee described in paragraph (4.4)(*a*), the cost to the transferee of the land, or of the interest or right therein, and

(B) where the property is land or a building, or an interest therein or for civil law a right therein, described in paragraphs (4.4)(*b*) to (*d*), the capital cost to the transferee of the interest or of the right in the building described in paragraph (4.4)(*b*).

History: S. 138(4.5)(*e*)(ii)(A) and (B) were replaced by S.C. 2013, c. 34, s. 135(3), in force June 26, 2013, and formerly read:

(A) where the property is land or an interest therein of the transferee described in paragraph (4.4)(*a*), the cost to the transferee of the land or the interest therein, and

(B) where the property is land, a building or an interest therein described in paragraphs (4.4)(*b*) to (*d*), the capital cost to the transferee of the interest in the building described in paragraph (4.4)(*b*).

► 138(4.6) ◄

(4.6) Completion. For the purposes of subsection (4.4), the construction, renovation or alteration of a building is completed at the earlier of the day on which the construction, renovation or alteration is actually completed and the day on which all or substantially all of the building is used for the purpose for which it was constructed, renovated or altered.

► 138(5) ◄

(5) Deductions not allowed. Notwithstanding any other provision of this Act,

(*a*) in the case of an insurer, no deduction may be made under paragraph 20(1)(*l*) in computing its income for a taxation year from an insurance business in Canada in respect of a premium or other consideration for a life insurance policy in Canada or an interest therein; and

(*b*) in the case of a non-resident insurer or a life insurer resident in Canada that carries on any of its insurance business in a country other than Canada, no deduction may be made under paragraph 20(1)(*c*) or (*d*) in computing its income for a taxation year from carrying on an insurance business in Canada, except in respect of

(i) interest on borrowed money used to acquire designated insurance property for the year, or to acquire property for which designated insurance property for the year was substituted property, for the period in the year during which the designated insurance property was held by the insurer in respect of the business,

(ii) interest on amounts payable for designated insurance property for the year in respect of the business, or

(iii) interest on deposits received or other amounts held by the insurer that arose in connection with life insurance policies in Canada or with policies insuring Canadian risks.

(iv) (Repealed by S.C. 2001, c. 17, s. 133(2).)

Related Regulations: 2400.

Related Sections: S. 20(1)(*p*) Bad debts; s. 138(12), "designated insurance property"; s. 248(5) Substituted property.

Tax Window Files: Interest Expense — Insurer, *CLHIA Conference, Question 8, May 26, 2005*, CRA Document No. 2005-0126051C6.

► 138(5.1) ◄

(5.1) No deduction. No deduction shall be made under subsection 20(12) in computing the income of a life insurer resident in Canada in respect of foreign taxes attributable to its insurance business.

Interpretation Bulletins: *Secondary* — IT-506 Foreign income taxes as a deduction from income.

► 138(5.2) ◄

(5.2) Idem — (Repealed by S.C. 1995, c. 21, s. 57(5).)

► 138(6) ◄

(6) Deduction for dividends from taxable corporations. In computing the taxable income of a life insurer for a taxation year, no deduction from the income of the insurer for the year may be made under section 112 but, except as otherwise provided by that section, there may be deducted from that income the total of taxable dividends (other than dividends on term preferred shares that are acquired in the ordinary course of the business carried on by the life insurer) included in computing the insurer's income for the year and received by the insurer in the year from taxable Canadian corporations.

Related Sections: S. 55(2) Deemed proceeds or gain; s. 112(2.2) Guaranteed shares; s. 112(2.4) Where no deduction permitted; s. 112(3) Loss on share that is capital property; s. 112(5) Disposition of share by financial institution; s. 112(5.1) Share held for less than one year; s. 112(5.2) Adjustment re dividends; s. 112(5.3) Adjustment not applicable; s. 112(5.4) Deemed dispositions; s. 112(5.5) Stop-loss rules not applicable; s. 112(5.6) Stop-loss rules restricted; s. 112(6) Meaning of certain expressions; s. 112(7) Rules where shares exchanged; s. 248(14) Related corporations.

Interpretation Bulletins: *Secondary* — IT-232R3 Non-capital losses, net capital losses, restricted farm losses, farm losses and limited partnership losses — Their composition and deductibility in computing taxable income; IT-328R3 Losses on shares on which dividends have been received.

► 138(7) ◄

(7) Amounts paid to shareholders included in taxable income — (Repealed by S.C. 1997, c. 25, s. 39(8).)

► 138(8) ◄

(8) No deduction for foreign tax. No deduction shall be made under section 126 from the tax payable under this Part for a taxation year by a life insurer resident in Canada in respect of such part of an income or profits tax as can reasonably be attributable to income from its insurance business.

Related Sections: S. 126 Foreign tax deduction.

► 138(9) ◄

(9) Computation of income. Where in a taxation year an insurer (other than an insurer resident in Canada that does not carry on a life insurance business) carries on an insurance business in Canada and in a country other than Canada, there shall be included in computing its income for the year from carrying on its insurance businesses in Canada the total of

(*a*) its gross investment revenue for the year from its designated insurance property for the year, and

(*b*) the amount prescribed in respect of the insurer for the year.

Related Regulations: Part XXIV.

Related Sections: S. 138(3) Deductions allowed in computing income; s. 138(7) Amounts paid to shareholders included in taxable income; s. 138(10) Application of financial institution rules; s. 138(12), "designated insurance property", "property used by it in the year in, or held by it in the year in the course of"; s. 142 Taxable capital gains etc; s. 148(1) Amounts included in computing policyholder's income; s. 219(4) Non-resident insurers; s. 219(5) Additional tax on insurer.

Forms: T2016 — Part XIII Tax Return — Tax on Income from Canada of Approved Non-Resident Insurers.

Tax Window Files: Insurer's Canadian Reserve Liabilities — Reserves for Reinsurance Ceded to Unregistered Insurers, *Technical Interpretation, Charitable and Financial Institutions Sectors, November 24, 2005*, CRA Document

No. 2004-0082571I7; Computation of Insurer's CRL, *Technical Interpretation, November 24, 2005*, CRA Document No. 2004-0082571I7; Insurance Business — Value of Property, *CLHIA Conference — Question 7, May 26, 2005*, CRA Document No. 2005-0164701C6; Designation of Assets and the Canada–U.S. Tax Treaty, *Technical Interpretation, Financial Industries Division, March 8, 2005*, CRA Document No. 2003-0054281I7; Insurers — Designated Property, *Technical Interpretation, Financial Industries Division, May 8, 2003*, CRA Document No. 2002-0167477.

Cases: A Canadian resident multi-national life insurer was required to exclude certain investments as "investment property" of the taxpayer, for purposes of the "fill" to the "Canadian Investment Fund for the Year". *Great-West Life Assurance Company v. The Queen*, 98 DTC 2101 (T.C.C.)

A non-resident life insurer was required to include in its "Canadian reserve liabilities" its hail insurance reserve and its deferred acquisition expenses in excess of 30% unearned premiums as the definition in question was broad enough to include reserves and liabilities that were, directly or indirectly, connected to insurance policies in Canada. *Munich Reinsurance Company (Canada Branch) v. Minister of National Revenue*, 96 DTC 6185 (F.C.T.D.) affirming 91 DTC 1137 (T.C.C.)

In calculating the Canadian Investment Fund, the taxpayer was required to include in its "Canadian Revenue Liabilities" the reserve for reinsurance ceded to unlicensed reinsurers. *The Victory Reinsurance Company Limited v. Minister of National Revenue*, 92 DTC 1869 (T.C.C.)

An Canadian insurer, that had an agency agreement with a firm in Bermuda was carrying on business both in Canada and outside Canada and therefore was eligible to make the election under subsection 138(9) of the ITA. *London Life Insurance Company v. The Queen*, 90 DTC 6001 (F.C.A.) affirming 87 DTC 5312 (F.C.T.D.).

▶ 138(9.1) ◀

(9.1) Gross investment revenue — (Repealed by 1988, c. 55, s. 125(11).)

▶ 138(10) ◀

(10) Application of financial institution rules. Notwithstanding sections 142.3, 142.4, 142.5 and 142.51, where in a taxation year an insurer (other than an insurer resident in Canada that does not carry on a life insurance business) carries on an insurance business in Canada and in a country other than Canada, in computing its income for the year from carrying on an insurance business in Canada,

(*a*) sections 142.3, 142.5 and 142.51 apply only in respect of property that is designated insurance property for the year in respect of the business; and

(*b*) section 142.4 applies only in respect of the disposition of property that, for the taxation year in which the insurer disposed of it, was designated insurance property in respect of the business.

History: S. 138(10), the portion before paragraph (*b*) was replaced by S.C. 2009, c. 2, s. 45(1), applicable to taxation years that begin after September 2006. S. 138(10), the portion before paragraph (*b*) formerly read:

(10) *Application of financial institution rules.* Notwithstanding sections 142.3, 142.4 and 142.5, where in a taxation year an insurer (other than an insurer resident in Canada that does not carry on a life insurance business) carries on an insurance business in Canada and in a country other than Canada, in computing its income for the year from carrying on an insurance business in Canada,

(*a*) sections 142.3 and 142.5 apply only in respect of property that is designated insurance property for the year in respect of the business; and

▶ 138(11) ◀

(11) Profit or loss in respect of Canada security — (Repealed by S.C. 1995, c. 21, s. 57(7).)

▶ 138(11.1) ◀

(11.1) Identical properties. For the purpose of section 47, any property of a life insurance corporation that would, but for this subsection, be identical to any other property of the corporation is deemed not to be identical to the other property unless both properties are

(*a*) designated insurance property of the insurer in respect of a life insurance business carried on in Canada; or

(*b*) designated insurance property of the insurer in respect of an insurance business in Canada other than a life insurance business.

Related Sections: S. 47 Identical properties; s. 138(12), "designated insurance property".

Interpretation Bulletins: *Secondary* — IT-387R2 (Consolid.) Meaning of "identical properties".

▶ 138(11.2) ◀

(11.2) Computation of capital gain on pre-1969 depreciable property. For the purposes of computing the amount of a capital gain from the disposition of any depreciable property acquired by a life insurer before 1969, the capital cost of the property to the insurer shall be its capital cost determined without reference to paragraph 32(1)(*a*) of *An Act to amend the Income Tax Act*, chapter 44 of the Statutes of Canada, 1968-69, as it read in its application to the 1971 taxation year.

▶ 138(11.3) ◀

(11.3) Deemed disposition. Subject to subsection (11.31), where a property of a life insurer resident in Canada that carries on an insurance business in Canada and in a country other than Canada or of a non-resident insurer is

(*a*) designated insurance property of the insurer for a taxation year, was owned by the insurer at the end of the preceding taxation year and was not designated insurance property of the insurer for that preceding year, or

(*b*) not designated insurance property for a taxation year, was owned by the insurer at the end of the preceding taxation year and was designated insurance property of the insurer for that preceding year,

the following rules apply:

(*c*) the insurer is deemed to have disposed of the property at the beginning of the year for proceeds of disposition equal to its fair market value at that time and to have reacquired the property immediately after that time at a cost equal to that fair market value,

(*d*) where paragraph (*a*) applies, any gain or loss arising from the disposition is deemed not to be a gain or loss from designated insurance property of the insurer in the year, and

(*e*) where paragraph (*b*) applies, any gain or loss arising from the disposition is deemed to be a gain or loss from designated insurance property of the insurer in the year.

Related Sections: S. 54, "superficial loss"; s. 138(11.4) Deduction of loss; s. 138(11.41) Inclusion of gain; s. 138(12), "designated insurance property".

Cases: Subsection 138(11.3) does not apply in the first year that a Canadian resident life insurance company starts to carry on an insurance business in another country. Since 2006 was the first year the taxpayer carried on the insurance business in two jurisdictions, there was no application of subsection 138(11.3) for that year. The addition of property to the designated insurance property list would only commence in the second year the taxpayer was carrying on business in another country. *SCDA v. The Queen*, 2017 DTC 5108 (FCA)

▶ 138(11.31) ◀

(11.31) Exclusion from deemed disposition. Subsection (11.3) does not apply

(*a*) to deem a disposition in a taxation year of a property of an insurer where subsection 142.5(2) deemed the insurer to have disposed of the property in its preceding taxation year; nor

(*b*) for the purposes of paragraph 20(1)(*l*), the description of A and paragraph (*b*) of the description of F in the definition "undepreciated capital cost" in subsection 13(21) and the definition "designated insurance property" in subsection (12).

▶ 138(11.4) ◀

(11.4) Deduction of loss. Notwithstanding any other provision of this Act, where an insurer has a loss for a taxation year from the disposition, because of subsection (11.3), of a property other than a specified debt obligation (as defined in subsection 142.2(1)), and the loss would, but for this subsection, have been deductible in the year, the loss shall be deductible only in the taxation year in which the taxpayer disposes of the property otherwise than because of subsection (11.3).

▶ 138(11.41) ◀

(11.41) Inclusion of gain — (Repealed by 1995, c. 21, s. 57(12).)

▶ 138(11.5) ◀

(11.5) Transfer of insurance business by non-resident insurer. Where

(*a*) a non-resident insurer (in this subsection referred to as the "transferor") has, at any time in a taxation year, ceased to carry on all or substantially all of an insurance business carried on by it in Canada in that year,

(*b*) the transferor has, at that time or within 60 days after that time, transferred all or substantially all of the property (in this subsection referred to as the "transferred property") that is owned by it at that time and that was designated insurance property in respect of the business for the taxation year that, because of paragraph (*h*), ended immediately before that time

(i) to a corporation (in this subsection referred to as the "transferee") that is a qualified related corporation (within the meaning assigned by subsection 219(8)) of the transferor that began immediately after that time to carry on that insurance business in Canada, and

(ii) for consideration that includes shares of the capital stock of the transferee,

(*c*) the transferee has, at that time or within 60 days thereafter, assumed or reinsured all or substantially all of the obligations of the transferor that arose in the course of carrying on that insurance business in Canada, and

(*d*) the transferor and the transferee have jointly elected in prescribed form and in accordance with subsection (11.6),

the following rules apply:

(*e*) subject to paragraph (*k*.1), where the fair market value, at that time, of the consideration (other than shares of the capital stock of the transferee or a right to receive any such shares) received or receivable by the transferor for the transferred property does not exceed the total of the cost amounts to the transferor, at that time, of the transferred property, the proceeds of disposition of the transferor and the cost to the transferee of the transferred property shall be deemed to be the cost amount, at that time, to the transferor of the transferred property, and in any other case, the provisions of subsection 85(1) shall be applied in respect of the transfer,

(*f*) where the provisions of subsection 85(1) are not required to be applied in respect of the transfer, the cost to the transferor of any particular property (other than shares of the capital stock of the transferee or a right to receive any such shares) received or receivable by it as consideration for the transferred property shall be deemed to be the fair market value, at that time, of the particular property,

(*g*) where the provisions of subsection 85(1) are not required to be applied in respect of the transfer, the cost to the transferor of any shares of the capital stock of the transferee received or receivable by the transferor as consideration for the transferred property shall be deemed to be

(i) where the shares are preferred shares of any class of the capital stock of the transferee, the lesser of

(A) the fair market value of those shares immediately after the transfer of the transferred property, and

(B) the amount determined by the formula

$$A \times B/C$$

where

A is the amount, if any, by which the proceeds of disposition of the transferor of the transferred property determined under paragraph (*e*) exceed the fair market value, at that time, of the consideration (other than shares of the capital stock of the transferee or a right to receive any such shares) received or receivable by the transferor for the transferred property,

B is the fair market value, immediately after the transfer of the transferred property, of those preferred shares of that class, and

C is the fair market value, immediately after the transfer of the transferred property, of all preferred shares of the capital stock of the transferee receivable by the transferor as consideration for the transferred property, and

(ii) where the shares are common shares of any class of the capital stock of the transferee, the amount determined by the formula

$$A \times B/C$$

where

A is the amount, if any, by which the proceeds of disposition of the transferor of the transferred property determined under paragraph (*e*) exceed the total of the fair market value, at that time, of the consideration (other than shares of the capital stock of the transferee or a right to receive any such shares) received or receivable by the transferor for the transferred property and the cost to the transferor of all preferred shares of the capital stock of the transferee receivable by the transferor as consideration for the transferred property,

B is the fair market value, immediately after the transfer of the transferred property, of those shares of that class, and

C is the fair market value, immediately after the transfer of the transferred property, of all common shares of the capital stock of the transferee receivable by the transferor as consideration for the transferred property,

(*h*) for the purposes of this Act, the transferor and the transferee shall be deemed to have had taxation years ending immediately before that time and, for the purposes of determining the fiscal periods of the transferor and transferee after that time, they shall be deemed not to have established fiscal periods before that time, (*i*) for the purpose of determining the amount of gross investment revenue required by subsection (9) to be included in computing the transferor's income for the particular taxation year referred to in paragraph (*h*) and its gains and losses from its designated insurance property for its subsequent taxation years, the transferor is deemed to have transferred the business referred to in paragraph (*a*), the property referred to in paragraph (*b*) and the obligations referred to in paragraph (*c*) to the transferee on the last day of the particular year,

(*j*) for the purpose of determining the income of the transferor and the transferee for their taxation years following their taxation years referred to in paragraph (*h*), amounts deducted by the transferor as reserves under paragraph (3)(*a*) (other than under subparagraph (3)(*a*)(ii.1), (iii) or (v)), paragraphs 20(1)(*l*) and (*l.1*) and 20(7)(*c*) of this Act and section 33 and paragraph 138(3)(*c*) of the *Income Tax Act*, chapter 148 of the Revised Statutes of Canada, 1952, in its taxation year referred to in paragraph (*h*) in respect of the transferred property referred to in paragraph (*b*) or the obligations referred to in paragraph (*c*) are deemed to have been deducted by the transferee, and not the transferor, for its taxation year referred to in paragraph (*h*),

(*j*.1) for the purpose of determining the income of the transferor and the transferee for their taxation years following their taxation years referred to in paragraph (*h*), amounts included under paragraphs (4)(*b*) and 12(1)(*e*.1) in computing the transferor's income for its taxation year referred to in paragraph (*h*) in respect of the insurance policies of the business referred to in paragraph (*a*) are deemed to have been included in computing the income of the transferee, and not of the transferor, for their taxation years referred to in paragraph (*h*),

(*k*) for the purposes of this section, sections 12, 12.4, 20, 138.1, 140 and 142, paragraphs 142.4(4)(*c*) and (*d*), section 148 and Part XII.3, the transferee is, in its taxation years following its taxation year referred to in paragraph (*h*), deemed to be the same person as, and a continuation of, the transferor in respect of the business referred to in paragraph (*a*), the transferred property referred to in paragraph (*b*) and the obligations referred to in paragraph (*c*),

(*k*.1) except for the purpose of this subsection, where the provisions of subsection 85(1) are not required to be applied in respect of the transfer,

(i) the transferor shall be deemed not to have disposed of a transferred property that is a specified debt obligation (other than a mark-to-market property), and

(ii) the transferee shall be deemed, in respect of a transferred property that is a specified debt obligation (other than a mark-to-market property), to be the same person as, and a continuation of, the transferor,

and for the purpose of this paragraph, "mark-to-market property" and "specified debt obligation" have the meanings assigned by subsection 142.2(1),

(*k*.2) for the purposes of subsections 112(5) to (5.2) and (5.4) and the definition "mark-to-market property" in subsection 142.2(1), the transferee shall be deemed, in respect of the transferred property, to be the same person as, and a continuation of, the transferor,

(*l*) for the purposes of this subsection and subsections (11.7) and (11.9), the fair market value of consideration received by the transferor from the transferee in respect of the assumption or reinsurance of a particular obligation referred to in paragraph (*c*) is deemed to be the total of the amounts deducted by the transferor as a reserve under paragraph (3)(*a*) (other than under subparagraph (3)(*a*)(ii.1), (iii) or (v)) and paragraph 20(7)(*c*) in its taxation year referred to in paragraph (*h*) in respect of the particular obligation, and

(*m*) for the purpose of computing the income of the transferor or the transferee for their taxation years following their taxation years referred to in paragraph (*h*),

(i) an amount in respect of a reinsurance premium paid or payable by the transferor to the transferee in respect of the obligations referred to in paragraph (*c*), or

(ii) an amount in respect of a reinsurance commission paid or payable by the transferee to the transferor in respect of the amount referred to in subparagraph (i)

under a reinsurance arrangement undertaken to effect the transfer of the insurance business to which this subsection applied shall be included or deducted, as the case may be, only to the extent that may be reasonably regarded as necessary to determine the appropriate amount of income of both the transferor and the transferee.

History: S. 138(11.5)(*j*) was replaced by S.C. 2013, c. 34, s. 286(7), applicable to taxation years that begin after October 31, 2011, and formerly read:

(*j*) for the purpose of determining the income of the transferor and the transferee for their taxation years following their taxation years referred to in paragraph (*h*), amounts deducted by the transferor as reserves under subparagraphs (3)(*a*)(i), (ii) and (iv), paragraphs 20(1)(*l*) and (*l*.1) and 20(7)(*c*) of this Act and section 33 and paragraph 138(3)(*c*) of the *Income Tax Act*, chapter 148 of the Revised Statutes of Canada, 1952, in its taxation year referred to in paragraph (*h*) in respect of the transferred property referred to in paragraph (*b*) or the obligations referred to in paragraph (*c*) shall be deemed to have been deducted by the transferee, and not the transferor, for its taxation year referred to in paragraph (*h*),

S. 138(11.5)(*k*) was replaced by S.C. 2013, c. 34, s. 286(8), applicable to taxation years that begin after October 31, 2011, and formerly read:

(*k*) for the purposes of this section, sections 12, 12.3, 12.4, 20, 138.1, 140 and 142, subsections 142.5(5) and (7), paragraphs 142.4(4)(*c*) and (*d*), section 148 and Part XII.3, the transferee shall, in its taxation years following its taxation year referred to in paragraph (*h*), be deemed to be the same person as, and a continuation of, the transferor in respect of the business referred to in paragraph (*a*), the transferred property referred to in paragraph (*b*) and the obligations referred to in paragraph (*c*),

S. 138(11.5)(*l*) was replaced by S.C. 2013, c. 34, s. 286(9), applicable to taxation years that begin after October 31, 2011, and formerly read:

(*l*) for the purposes of this subsection and subsections (11.7) and (11.9), the fair market value of consideration received by the transferor from the transferee in respect of the assumption or reinsurance of a particular obligation referred to in paragraph (*c*) shall be deemed to be the total of the amounts deducted by the transferor as a reserve under subparagraphs (3)(*a*)(i), (ii) and (iv) and paragraph 20(7)(*c*) in its taxation year referred to in paragraph (*h*) in respect of the particular obligation, and

Related Regulations: 2401.

Related Sections: 138(11.6) Time of election; 138(11.7) Computation of paid-up capital; 138(11.8) Rules on transfers of depreciable property; 138(11.9) Computation of contributed surplus; s. 138(11.94) Transfer of insurance business by resident insurer; s. 138(12), "designated insurance property".

Canadian Tax Foundation: Welch, *Rare Rollovers: The Reorganization of a Life Insurance Business — Part 1*, 1998 Canadian Tax Journal 4:908–918.

Forms: T2100 — Joint Election in Respect of an Insurance Business Transferred by a Non-Resident Insurer.

► 138(11.6) ◄

(11.6) Time of election. Any election under subsection (11.5) shall be made on or before the day that is the earliest of the days on or before which any taxpayer making the election is required to file a return of income pursuant to section 150 for the taxation year in which the transactions to which the election relates occurred.

► 138(11.7) ◄

(11.7) Computation of paid-up capital. Where, after December 15, 1987, subsection (11.5) is applicable in respect of a transfer of property by a non-resident insurer to a qualified related corporation of the insurer and the provisions of subsection 85(1) were not required to be applied in respect of the transfer, the following rules apply:

(*a*) in computing the paid-up capital, at any time after the transfer, in respect of any particular class of shares of the capital stock of the qualified related corporation, there shall be deducted an amount determined by the formula

$$(A - B) \times C/A$$

where

A is the increase, if any, determined without reference to this subsection as it applies to the transfer, in the paid-up capital in respect of all the shares of the capital stock of the corporation as a result of the transfer,

B is the amount, if any, by which the cost of the transferred property to the corporation, immediately after the transfer, exceeds the fair market value, immediately after the transfer, of any consideration (other than shares of the capital stock of the corporation) received or receivable by the insurer from the corporation for the property, and

C is the increase, if any, determined without reference to this subsection as it applies to the transfer, in the paid-up capital in respect of the particular class of shares as a result of the acquisition by the corporation of the transferred property; and

(*b*) in computing the paid-up capital, at any time after December 15, 1987, in respect of any particular class of shares of the capital stock of the qualified related corporation, there shall be added an amount equal to the lesser of

(i) the amount, if any, by which

(A) the total of all amounts each of which is an amount deemed by subsection 84(3), (4) or (4.1) to be a dividend on shares of that class paid after December 15, 1987 and before that time by the corporation

exceeds

(B) the total of such dividends that would have been determined under clause (A) if this Act were read without reference to paragraph (*a*), and

(ii) the total of all amounts each of which is an amount required by paragraph (*a*) to be deducted in computing the paid-up capital in respect of that class of shares after December 15, 1987 and before that time.

Related Sections: S. 257 Negative amounts.

► 138(11.8) ◄

(11.8) Rules on transfers of depreciable property. Where

(*a*) subsection (11.5) is applicable in respect of a transfer of depreciable property by a non-resident insurer to a qualified related corporation,

(*b*) the provisions of subsection 85(1) were not required to be applied in respect of the transfer, and

(*c*) the capital cost to the insurer of the depreciable property exceeds its proceeds of disposition therefor,

for the purposes of sections 13 and 20 and any regulations made under paragraph 20(1)(*a*), the following rules apply:

(*d*) the capital cost of the depreciable property to the corporation shall be deemed to be the amount that was the capital cost thereof to the insurer, and

(*e*) the excess shall be deemed to have been allowed to the corporation in respect of the property under regulations made under paragraph 20(1)(*a*) in computing its income for taxation years ending before the transfer.

► 138(11.9) ◄

(11.9) Computation of contributed surplus. Where, after December 15, 1987, subsection (11.5) or 85(1) is applicable in respect of a transfer of property by a person or partnership to an insurance corporation resident in Canada and

(*a*) the total of

(i) the fair market value, immediately after the transfer, of any consideration (other than shares of the capital stock of the corporation) received or receivable by the person or partnership from the corporation for the transferred property,

(ii) the increase, if any, in the paid-up capital of all the shares of the capital stock of the corporation (determined without reference to subsection (11.7) or 85(2.1) as it applies in respect of the transfer) arising on the transfer, and

(iii) the increase, if any, in the contributed surplus of the corporation (determined without reference to this subsection as it applies in respect of the transfer) arising on the transfer

exceeds

(*b*) the total of

(i) the total of all amounts each of which is an amount required to be deducted in computing the paid-up capital of a class of shares of the capital stock of the corporation under subsection (11.7) or 85(2.1), as the case may be, as it applies in respect of the transfer, and

(ii) the cost to the corporation of the transferred property,

for the purposes of paragraph 84(1)(*c*.1) and subsections 219(5.2) and (5.3), the contributed surplus of the corporation arising on the transfer shall be deemed to be the amount, if any, by which the amount of the contributed surplus otherwise determined exceeds the amount, if any, by which the total determined under paragraph (*a*) exceeds the total determined under paragraph (*b*).

► 138(11.91) ◄

(11.91) Computation of income of non-resident insurer. Where, at any time in a particular taxation year,

(*a*) a non-resident insurer carries on an insurance business in Canada, and

(*b*) immediately before that time, the insurer was not carrying on an insurance business in Canada or ceased to be exempt from tax under this Part on any income from such business by reason of any Act of Parliament or anything approved, made or declared to have the force of law thereunder,

for the purpose of computing the income of the insurer for the particular taxation year, (*c*) the insurer shall be deemed to have had a taxation year ending immediately before the commencement of the particular taxation year,

(*d*) for the purposes of paragraph (4)(*a*), subsection (9), the definition *designated insurance property* in subsection (12) and paragraphs 12(1)(*d*), (*d*.1) and (*e*), the insurer is deemed to have carried on the business in Canada in that preceding year and to have claimed the maximum amounts to which it would have been entitled under paragraphs (3)(*a*) (other than under subparagraph (3)(*a*)(ii.1), (iii) or (v)), 20(1)(*l*) and (*l*.1) and 20(7)(*c*) for that year,

(*d*.1) for the purposes of subsection 20(22) and subparagraph (3)(*a*)(ii.1),

(i) the insurer is deemed to have carried on the business referred to in paragraph (*a*) in Canada in the preceding taxation year referred to in paragraph (*c*), and

(ii) the amounts, if any, that would have been prescribed in respect of the insurer for the purposes of paragraphs (4)(*b*) and 12(1)(*e*.1) for that preceding year in respect of the insurance policies of that business are deemed to have been included in computing its income for that year, and

(*e*) the insurer is deemed to have disposed, immediately before the beginning of the particular taxation year, of each property owned by it at that time that is designated insurance property in respect of the business referred to in paragraph (*a*) for the particular taxation year, for proceeds of disposition equal to the fair market value at that time and to have reacquired, at the beginning of the particular taxation year, the property at a cost equal to that fair market value.

(*f*) (Repealed by S.C. 2013, c. 34, s. 286(12).)

History: S. 138(11.91)(*d*) was replaced by S.C. 2017, c. 33, s. 53(2), applicable to taxation years of a taxpayer that begin after March 21, 2017, and formerly read:

(*d*) for the purposes of paragraph (4)(*a*), subsection (9), the definition "designated insurance property" in subsection (12) and paragraphs 12(1)(*d*) and (*e*), the insurer is deemed to have carried on the business in Canada in that preceding year and to have claimed the maximum amounts to which it would have been entitled under paragraphs (3)(*a*) (other than under subparagraph (3)(*a*)(ii.1), (iii) or (v)), 20(1)(*l*) and (*l*.1) and 20(7)(*c*) for that year,

S. 138(11.91)(*d*) was replaced by S.C. 2013, c. 34, s. 286(10), applicable to taxation years that begin after October 31, 2011, and formerly read:

(*d*) for the purposes of paragraphs 12(1)(*d*) and (*e*), paragraph (4)(*a*), subsection (9) and the definition "designated insurance property" in subsection (12), the insurer is deemed to have carried on the business in Canada in that preceding year and to have claimed the maximum amounts to which it would have been entitled under paragraphs 20(1)(*l*) and (*l*.1) and 20(7)(*c*) and subparagraphs (3)(*a*)(i), (ii) and (iv) for that year,

S. 138(11.91)(*f*) was repealed by S.C. 2013, c. 34, s. 286(12), applicable to taxation years that end after 1999, and formerly read:

(*f*) where paragraph (*e*) applies in respect of depreciable property of the insurer and the cost thereof to the insurer immediately before the commencement of the particular taxation year exceeds the fair market value thereof at that time, for the purposes of sections 13 and 20 and any regulations made under paragraph 20(1)(*a*),

(i) the capital cost of the property to the insurer at that time shall be deemed to be the cost thereof to the insurer at that time, and

(ii) the excess shall be deemed to have been allowed to the insurer in respect of the property under regulations made under paragraph 20(1)(*a*) in computing its income for taxation years ending before the commencement of the particular taxation year.

Related Sections: S. 138(12), "designated insurance property".

► 138(11.92) ◄

(11.92) Computation of income where insurance business is transferred. Where, at any time in a taxation year, an insurer (in this subsection referred to as the "vendor") has disposed of

(*a*) all or substantially all of an insurance business carried on by it in Canada, or

(*b*) all or substantially all of a line of business of an insurance business carried on by it in Canada

to a person (in this subsection referred to as the "purchaser") and obligations in respect of the business or line of business, as the case may be, in respect of which a reserve may be claimed under subparagraph (3)(*a*)(i) or (ii) or paragraph 20(7)(*c*) (in this subsection referred to as the "obligations") were assumed by the purchaser, the following rules apply:

(*c*) for the purpose of determining the amount of the gross investment revenue required to be included in computing the income of the vendor and the purchaser under subsection (9) and the amount of the gains and losses of the vendor and the purchaser from designated insurance property for the year

(i) the vendor and the purchaser shall, in addition to their normal taxation years, be deemed to have had a taxation year ending immediately before that time, and

(ii) for the taxation years of the vendor and the purchaser following that time, the business or line of business, as the case may be, disposed of to, and the obligations assumed by, the purchaser shall be deemed to have been disposed of or assumed, as the case may be, on the last day of the taxation year referred to in subparagraph (i),

(*d*) for the purpose of computing the income of the vendor and the purchaser for taxation years ending after that time,

(i) an amount paid or payable by the vendor to the purchaser in respect of the obligations, or

(ii) an amount in respect of a commission paid or payable by the purchaser to the vendor in respect of the amount referred to in subparagraph (i)

shall be deemed to have been paid or payable or received or receivable, as the case may be, by the vendor or the purchaser, as the case may be, in the course of carrying on the business or line of business, as the case may be, and

(*e*) where the vendor has disposed of all or substantially all of an insurance business referred to in paragraph (*a*), the vendor shall, for the purposes of section 219, be deemed to have ceased to carry on that business at that time.

Related Sections: S. 138(12), "designated insurance property".

► 138(11.93) ◄

(11.93) Property acquired on default in payment. Where, at any time in a taxation year of an insurer, the beneficial ownership of property is acquired or reacquired by the insurer in consequence of the failure to pay all or any part of an amount (in this subsection referred to as the "insurer's claim") owing to the insurer at that time in respect of a bond, debenture, mortgage, hypothecary claim, agreement of sale or any other form of indebtedness owned by the insurer, the following rules apply to the insurer:

(*a*) section 79.1 does not apply in respect of the acquisition or reacquisition;

(*b*) the insurer shall be deemed to have acquired or reacquired, as the case may be, the property at an amount equal to the fair market value of the property, immediately before that time;

(*c*) the insurer shall be deemed to have disposed at that time of the portion of the indebtedness represented by the insurer's claim for proceeds of disposition equal to that fair market value and, immediately after that time, to have reacquired that portion of the indebtedness at a cost of nil;

(*d*) the acquisition or reacquisition shall be deemed to have no effect on the form of the indebtedness; and

(*e*) in computing the insurer's income for the year or a subsequent taxation year, no amount is deductible under paragraph 20(1)(*l*) in respect of the insurer's claim.

▶ 138(11.94) ◀

(11.94) Transfer of insurance business by resident insurer. Where

(*a*) an insurer resident in Canada (in this subsection referred to as the "transferor") has, at any time in a taxation year, ceased to carry on all or substantially all of an insurance business carried on by it in Canada in that year,

(*b*) the transferor has, at that time or within 60 days after that time,

(i) in the case of a transferor that is a life insurer and that carries on an insurance business in Canada and in a country other than Canada in the year, transferred all or substantially all of the property (in subsection (11.5) referred to as the "transferred property") that is owned by it at that time and that was designated insurance property in respect of the business for the taxation year that, because of paragraph (11.5)(*h*), ended immediately before that time, or

(ii) in any other case, transferred all or substantially all of the property owned by it at that time and used by it in the year in, or held by it in the year in the course of, carrying on that insurance business in Canada in that year (in subsection (11.5) referred to as the "transferred property")

to a corporation resident in Canada (in this subsection referred to as the "transferee") that is a qualified related corporation (within the meaning assigned by subsection 219(8)) of the transferor that, immediately after that time, began to carry on that insurance business in Canada for consideration that includes shares of the capital stock of the transferee,

(*c*) the transferee has, at that time or within 60 days thereafter, assumed or reinsured all or substantially all of the obligations of the transferor that arose in the course of carrying on that insurance business in Canada, and

(*d*) the transferor and the transferee have jointly elected in prescribed form and in accordance with subsection (11.6),

paragraphs (11.5)(*e*) to (*m*) and subsections (11.7) to (11.9) apply in respect of the transfer.

History: S. 138(11.94)(*b*), the portion after subparagraph (ii) was replaced by S.C. 2013, c. 34, s. 286(13), applicable to transfers made after October 2004, and formerly read:

> to a corporation resident in Canada (in this subsection referred to as the "transferee") that is a subsidiary wholly-owned corporation of the transferor that, immediately after that time, began to carry on that insurance business in Canada for consideration that includes shares of the capital stock of the transferee,

Related Sections: S. 138(12), "designated insurance property".

Canadian Tax Foundation: Welch, *Rare Rollovers: The Reorganization of a Life Insurance Business — Part 1*, 1998 Canadian Tax Journal 4:908–918.

▶ 138(12) ◀

(12) Definitions. In this section,

Interpretation Bulletins: *Secondary* — IT-291R3 Transfer of property to a corporation under subsection 85(1).

"accumulated 1968 deficit" — (Repealed by S.C. 1997, c. 25, s. 39(16).)

"amortized cost" — (Repealed by 1988, c. 55, s. 125(17).)

"amount payable" — "amount payable", in respect of a policy loan at a particular time, means the amount of the policy loan and the interest thereon that is outstanding at that time;

Related Sections: S. 148(9), "Amount payable".

"base year" — "base year" of a life insurer means the life insurer's taxation year that immediately precedes its transition year;

History: S. 138(12), the definition "base year" was added by S.C. 2009, c. 2, s. 45(2), applicable to taxation years that begin after September 2006.

"Canada security" — (Repealed by S.C. 1995, c. 21, s. 57(15).)

"cost" — (Repealed by 1995, c. 21, s. 57(15).)

"deposit accounting insurance policy" — "deposit accounting insurance policy" in respect of a life insurer's taxation year means an insurance policy of the life insurer that, according to generally accepted accounting principles, is not an insurance contract for that taxation year;

History: S. 138(12), the definition "deposit accounting insurance policy" was added by S.C. 2010, c. 25, s. 33(2), applicable to taxation years that begin after 2010.

"designated foreign insurance business" — "designated foreign insurance business", of a life insurer resident in Canada in a taxation year, means an insurance business that is carried on by the life insurer in a country other than Canada in the year unless more than 90% of the gross premium revenue from the business for the year from the insurance of risks (net of reinsurance ceded) is in respect of the insurance of risks (other than specified Canadian risks) of persons with whom the life insurer deals at arm's length.

History: S. 138(12), the definition "designated foreign insurance business" was added by S.C. 2017, c. 33, s. 53(3), applicable to taxation years of a taxpayer that begin after March 21, 2017.

"designated insurance property" — "designated insurance property" for a taxation year of an insurer (other than an insurer resident in Canada that at no time in the year carried on a life insurance business) that, at any time in the year, carried on an insurance business in Canada and in a country other than Canada, means property determined in accordance with prescribed rules except that, in its application to any taxation year, "designated insurance property" for the 1998 or a preceding taxation year means property that was, under this subsection as it read in its application to taxation years that ended in 1996, property used by it in the year in, or held by it in the year in the course of, carrying on an insurance business in Canada;

Related Regulations: Part XXIV.

Interpretation Bulletins: *Secondary* — IT-291R3 Transfer of property to a corporation under subsection 85(1).

"excluded policy" — "excluded policy" in respect of a life insurer's base year means an insurance policy of the life insurer that would be a deposit accounting insurance policy for the life insurer's base year if the International Financial Reporting Standards adopted by the Accounting Standards Board and effective as of January 1, 2011 applied for that base year;

History: S. 138(12), the definition "excluded policy" was added by S.C. 2010, c. 25, s. 33(2), applicable to taxation years that begin after 2010.

"gross investment revenue" — "gross investment revenue" of an insurer for a taxation year means the amount determined by the formula

$$A + B + C + D + E + F - G$$

where

A is the total of the following amounts included in its gross revenue for the year:

(*a*) taxable dividends, and

(*b*) amounts received or receivable as, on account of, in lieu of or in satisfaction of, interest, rentals or royalties, other than amounts in respect of debt obligations to which subsection 142.3(1) applies for the year,

B is its income for the year from each trust of which it is a beneficiary,

C is its income for the year from each partnership of which it is a member,

D is the total of all amounts required by subsection 16(1) to be included in computing its income for the year,

E is the total of

(*a*) all amounts required by paragraph 142.3(1)(*a*) to be included in computing its income for the year, and

(*b*) all amounts required by subsection 12(3) or 20(14) to be included in computing its income for the year except to the extent that those amounts are included in the computation of A,

F is the amount determined by the formula

$$V - W$$

where

V is the total of all amounts included under paragraph 56(1)(*d*) in computing its income for the year, and

W is the total of all amounts deducted under paragraph 60(*a*) in computing its income for the year; and

G is the total of all amounts each of which is

(*a*) an amount deemed by subparagraph 16(6)(*a*)(ii) to be paid by it in respect of the year as interest, or

(*b*) an amount deductible under paragraph 142.3(1)(*b*) in computing its income for the year;

"insurance" —"insurance", of a risk, includes the reinsurance of the risk;

History: S. 138(12), the definition "insurance" was added by S.C. 2017, c. 33, s. 53(3), applicable to taxation years of a taxpayer that begin after March 21, 2017.

"interest" —"interest", in relation to a policy loan, means the amount in respect of the policy loan that is required to be paid under the terms and conditions of the policy in order to maintain the policyholder's interest in the policy;

Related Sections: S. 148(9), "Interest".

"life insurance policy" —"life insurance policy" includes an annuity contract and a contract all or any part of the insurer's reserves for which vary in amount depending on the fair market value of a specified group of assets;

Related Sections: S. 39(1) Meaning of capital gain and capital loss; s. 148(9), "relevant authority".

Interpretation Bulletins: *Secondary* — IT-87R2 Policyholders' income from life insurance policies.

"life insurance policy in Canada" —"life insurance policy in Canada" means a life insurance policy issued or effected by an insurer on the life of a person resident in Canada at the time the policy was issued or effected;

"maximum tax actuarial reserve" —"maximum tax actuarial reserve" for a particular class of life insurance policy for a taxation year of a life insurer means, except as otherwise expressly prescribed, the maximum amount allowable under subparagraph (3)(*a*)(i) as a policy reserve for the year in respect of policies of that class;

"net Canadian life investment income" — (Repealed by 1980-81, c. 48, s. 79(4).)

"non-segregated property" —"non-segregated property" of an insurer means its property other than property included in a segregated fund;

"participating life insurance policy" —"participating life insurance policy" means a life insurance policy under which the policyholder is entitled to share (other than by way of an experience rating refund) in the profits of the insurer other than profits in respect of property in a segregated fund;

"policy loan" —"policy loan" means an amount advanced at a particular time by an insurer to a policyholder in accordance with the terms and conditions of a life insurance policy in Canada;

"property used by it in the year in, or held by it in the year in the course of" — (Repealed by S.C. 1997, c. 25, s. 39(16).)

Related Regulations: 2400.

"qualified related corporation" —"qualified related corporation" of a non-resident insurer has the meaning assigned by subsection 219(8);

"relevant authority" — (Repealed by S.C. 1997, c. 25, s. 39(16).)

"reserve transition amount" —"reserve transition amount" of a life insurer, in respect of a life insurance business carried on by it in Canada in its transition year, is the positive or negative amount determined by the formula

$$A - B$$

where

A is the maximum amount that the life insurer would be permitted to claim under subparagraph 138(3)(*a*)(i) (and that would be prescribed by section 1404 of the Regulations for the purpose of subparagraph 138(3)(*a*)(i)) as a policy reserve for its base year in respect of its life insurance policies in Canada if

(*a*) the generally accepted accounting principles that applied to the life insurer in valuing its assets and liabilities for its transition year had applied to it for its base year, and

(*b*) section 1404 of the Regulations were read in respect of the life insurer's base year as it reads in respect of its transition year, and

B is the maximum amount that the life insurer is permitted to claim under subparagraph 138(3)(*a*)(i) as a policy reserve for its base year;

History: S. 138(12), the definition "reserve transition amount" was added by S.C. 2009, c. 2, s. 45(2), applicable to taxation years that begin after September 2006.

"segregated fund" —"segregated fund" has the meaning given that expression in subsection 138.1(1);

"specified Canadian risk" —"specified Canadian risk" has the same meaning as in paragraph 95(2)(*a*.23).

History: S. 138(12), the definition "specified Canadian risk" was added by S.C. 2017, c. 33, s. 53(3), applicable to taxation years of a taxpayer that begin after March 21, 2017.

"surplus funds derived from operations" —"surplus funds derived from operations" of an insurer as of the end of a particular taxation year means the amount determined by the formula

(A + B + C) - (D + E + F + G)

where

A is the total of the insurer's income for each taxation year in the period beginning with its 1969 taxation year and ending with the particular year from all insurance businesses carried on by it,

B is the total of all amounts each of which is a portion of a non-capital loss that was deemed by subsection 111(7.1) as it read in its application to the 1976 taxation year to have been deductible in computing the insurer's income for a taxation year that ended before 1977,

C is the total of all profits or gains made by the insurer in the period in respect of non-segregated property of the insurer disposed of by it that was used by it in, or held by it in the course of, carrying on an insurance business in Canada, except to the extent that those profits or gains have been or are included in computing the insurer's income or loss, if any, for any taxation year in the period from carrying on an insurance business,

D is the total of its loss, if any, for each taxation year in the period from all insurance businesses carried on by it,

E is the total of all losses sustained by the insurer in the period in respect of non-segregated property disposed of by it that was used by it in, or held by it in the course of, carrying on an insurance business in Canada, except to the extent that those losses have been or are included in computing the insurer's income or loss, if any, for any taxation year in the period from carrying on an insurance business,

F is the total of

(*a*) all taxes payable under this Part by the insurer, and all income taxes payable by it under the laws of each province, for each taxation year in the period, except such portion thereof as would not have been payable by it if subsection (7) had not been enacted, and

(*b*) all taxes payable under Parts I.3 and VI by the insurer for each taxation year in the period, and

G is the total of all gifts made in the period by the insurer to a qualified donee,

H (Repealed by S.C. 2013, c. 34, s. 286(15).)

History: S. 138(12), the formula in the definition "surplus funds derived from operations" was replaced by S.C. 2013, c. 34, s. 286(15), applicable to taxation years that begin after October 31, 2011, and formerly read:

(A + B + C) - (D + E + F + G + H)

S. 138(12), the description of B in the definition "surplus funds derived from operations" was replaced by S.C. 2013, c. 34, s. 286(16), applicable to taxation years that begin after October 31, 2011, and formerly read:

B is the total described in subclause (4.1)(*a*)(ii)(B)(IV), and

S. 138(12), the description of H in the definition "surplus funds derived from operations" was repealed by S.C. 2013, c. 34, s. 286(17), applicable to taxation years that begin after October 31, 2011, and formerly read:

H is the amount determined by the formula

M - N

where

M is the amount determined in respect of the insurer for the particular taxation year under clause (3)(*a*)(iii)(A), and

N is the amount so determined under clause (3)(*a*)(iii)(B);

S. 138(12), the description of G in the definition "surplus funds derived from operations" was replaced by S.C. 2011, c. 24, s. 44(1), in force January 1, 2012. S. 138(12), the description of G in the definition of "surplus funds derived from operations" formerly read:

G is the total of all gifts made in the period by the insurer to a person or organization described in paragraph 110.1(1)(*a*) or (*b*), and

Related Regulations: Part XXIV.

"transition year" —"transition year" of a life insurer means

(*a*) in respect of the accounting standards adopted by the Accounting Standards Board and effective as of October 1, 2006, the life insurer's first taxation year that begins after September 2006,

(*b*) in respect of the International Financial Reporting Standards adopted by the Accounting Standards Board and effective as of January 1, 2011, the life insurer's first taxation year that begins after 2010, and

(*c*) in respect of the amendment to paragraph 1406(*b*) of the *Income Tax Regulations* effective as of the life insurer's 2012 taxation year, the life insurer's 2012 taxation year.

History: S. 138(12), paragraph (*c*) of the definition "transition year" was added by S.C. 2013, c. 34, s. 286(18), applicable to the 2012 and subsequent taxation years.

S. 138(12), the definition "transition year" was replaced by S.C. 2010, c. 25, s. 33(1), applicable to taxation years that begin after 2010. S. 138(12), the definition "transition year" formerly read:

"transition year"—"transition year" of a life insurer means the life insurer's first taxation year that begins after September 2006;

S. 138(12), the definition "transition year" was added by S.C. 2009, c. 2, s. 45(2), applicable to taxation years that begin after September 2006.

"1975 branch accounting election deficiency" — (Repealed by S.C. 2013, c. 34, s. 286(14).)

History: S. 138(12), the definition "1975 branch accounting election deficiency" was repealed by S.C. 2013, c. 34, s. 286(14), applicable to taxation years that begin after October 31, 2011, and formerly read:

"1975 branch accounting election deficiency"—"1975 branch accounting election deficiency" of an insurer that has made an election under subsection 138(9) of the *Income Tax Act*, chapter 148 of the Revised Statutes of Canada, 1952, as it read in its application to the 1977 taxation year, in respect of its 1975 taxation year means the amount determined by the formula

(A + B) - (C + D + E + F + G)

where

A is such portion of the total of the insurer's gross investment revenue and all amounts determined under paragraphs (4)(*b*) and (*c*) as would have been required to be included in computing its income for its 1975 taxation year if

(*a*) it had not made the election under subsection 138(9) of that Act in respect of that year, and

(*b*) where it had made the election under subsection 138(9) of that Act in respect of its 1974 taxation year, it had adopted for its 1975 taxation year, with the concurrence of the Minister, the method required by subsection 138(9) of that Act if it had not elected under that subsection and the Minister had specified no terms and conditions under subsection 138(10) of that Act,

B is the total of the amounts deducted in computing the insurer's income for its 1975 taxation year under paragraphs (3)(*b*) and (*d*),

C is the total of the insurer's gross investment revenue included in computing its income for its 1975 taxation year and the amounts included in computing its income for that year under paragraphs (4)(*b*) and (*c*),

D is such portion of the total of all amounts determined under paragraphs (3)(*b*) and (*d*) as would have been deductible in computing the insurer's income for its 1975 taxation year if

(*a*) it had not made the election under subsection 138(9) of that Act in respect of that year, and

(*b*) where it had made the election under subsection 138(9) of that Act in respect of its 1974 taxation year, it had adopted for its 1975 taxation year, with the concurrence of the Minister, the method required by subsection 138(9) of that Act if it had not elected under that subsection and the Minister had specified no terms and conditions under subsection 138(10) of that Act,

E is the amount determined by the formula

P - Q

where

P is the total of the insurer's outlays or expenses that would have been deductible in computing its income from its insurance businesses for its 1975 taxation year (other than amounts deductible under subsection (3), section 140 and regulations made under paragraphs 20(1)(*a*) and 20(7)(*c*)), if

(*a*) it had not made the election under subsection 138(9) of that Act in respect of that year, and

(*b*) where it had made the election under subsection 138(9) of that Act in respect of its 1974 taxation year, it had adopted for its 1975 taxation year, with the concurrence of the Minister, the method required by subsection 138(9) of that Act if it had not elected under that subsection and the Minister had specified no terms and conditions under subsection 138(10) of that Act,

Q is the total of the insurer's outlays or expenses deducted in computing its income from its insurance businesses for its 1975 taxation year (other than amounts deducted under subsection (3), section 140 and regulations made under paragraphs 20(1)(*a*) and 20(7)(*c*)),

F is the amount of the insurer's 1975-76 excess policy dividend deduction, and

G is the amount of the insurer's 1975-76 excess policy dividend reserve;

"1975-76 excess additional group term reserve" — (Repealed by S.C. 2013, c. 34, s. 286(14).)

History: S. 138(12), the definition "1975-76 excess additional group term reserve" was repealed by S.C. 2013, c. 34, s. 286(14), applicable to taxation years that begin after October 31, 2011, and formerly read:

"1975-76 excess additional group term reserve" — "1975-76 excess additional group term reserve" of an insurer that has made an election under subsection 138(9) of the *Income Tax Act*, chapter 148 of the Revised Statutes of Canada, 1952, as it read in its application to the 1977 taxation year, in respect of its 1975 taxation year means the amount determined by the formula

A - B

where

A is the amount that would have been deductible under subparagraph (3)(*a*)(ii) in computing the insurer's income for its 1976 taxation year if it had claimed the maximum allowable amount under that subparagraph for that year, and

B is the amount deducted under that subparagraph in computing its income for its 1976 taxation year;

"1975-76 excess capital cost allowance" — (Repealed by S.C. 2013, c. 34, s. 286(14).)

History: S. 138(12), the definition "1975-76 excess capital cost allowance" was repealed by S.C. 2013, c. 34, s. 286(14), applicable to taxation years that begin after October 31, 2011, and formerly read:

"1975-76 excess capital cost allowance" — "1975-76 excess capital cost allowance" of depreciable property of a prescribed class of an insurer that has made an election under subsection 138(9) of the *Income Tax Act*, chapter 148 of the Revised Statutes of Canada, 1952, as it read in its application to the 1977 taxation year, in respect of its 1975 taxation year means the amount determined by the formula

(A + B) - C

where

A is the amount determined by the formula

P - Q

where

P is the amount that would have been deductible under paragraph 20(1)(*a*) by the insurer in computing its income for its 1975 taxation year with respect to that class, if it had claimed the maximum allowable amount under that paragraph in that year with respect to that class and if

(*a*) it had not made the election under subsection 138(9) of that Act in respect of its 1975 taxation year, and

(*b*) where it made the election under subsection 138(9) of that Act in respect of its 1974 taxation year, it had adopted for its 1975 taxation year, with the concurrence of the Minister, the method required by subsection 138(9) of that Act if it had not elected under that subsection and the Minister had specified no terms and conditions under subsection 138(10) of that Act, and

Q is the amount deducted under paragraph 20(1)(*a*) by the insurer in computing its income for its 1975 taxation year with respect to that class,

B is the amount determined by the formula

R - S

where

R is the amount that would have been deductible under paragraph 20(1)(*a*) by the insurer in computing its income for its 1976 taxation year with respect to that class if it had claimed the maximum allowable amount under that paragraph in that year and in its 1975 taxation year with respect to that class on the basis of the assumptions made in paragraphs (*a*) to (*d*) of the description of A in the definition "1975-76 excess policy dividend reserve" in this subsection, and

S is the amount deducted under paragraph 20(1)(*a*) by the insurer in computing its income for its 1976 taxation year with respect to that class, and

C is the amount determined by the formula

T - U

where

T is the amount determined for S, and

U is the amount determined for R;

"1975-76 excess investment reserve" — (Repealed by S.C. 2013, c. 34, s. 286(14).)

History: S. 138(12), the definition "1975-76 excess investment reserve" was repealed by S.C. 2013, c. 34, s. 286(14), applicable to taxation years that begin after October 31, 2011, and formerly read:

"1975-76 excess investment reserve" — "1975-76 excess investment reserve" of an insurer that has made an election under subsection 138(9) of the *Income Tax Act*, chapter 148 of the Revised Statutes of Canada, 1952, as it read in its application to the 1977 taxation year, in respect of its 1975 taxation year means the amount determined by the formula

A - B

where

A is the amount that would have been deductible under paragraph 138(3)(*c*) of the *Income Tax Act*, chapter 148 of the Revised Statutes of Canada, 1952, by the insurer in computing its income for its 1976 taxation year if it had claimed the maximum allowable amount under that paragraph in that year and that amount was determined without reference to subparagraph 138(3)(*c*)(ii) of that Act, and

B is the amount deducted by the insurer under paragraph 138(3)(*c*) of the *Income Tax Act*, chapter 148 of the Revised Statutes of Canada, 1952, in computing its income for its 1976 taxation year;

"1975-76 excess policy dividend deduction" — (Repealed by S.C. 2013, c. 34, s. 286(14).)

History: S. 138(12), the definition "1975-76 excess policy dividend deduction" was repealed by S.C. 2013, c. 34, s. 286(14), applicable to taxation years that begin after October 31, 2011, and formerly read:

"1975-76 excess policy dividend deduction" — "1975-76 excess policy dividend deduction" of an insurer that has made an election under subsection 138(9) of the *Income Tax Act*, chapter 148 of the Revised Statutes of Canada, 1952, as it read in its application to the 1977 taxation year, in respect of its 1975 taxation year means the amount determined by the formula

(A + B) - C

where

A is the amount determined by the formula

P - Q

where

P is the amount that would have been deductible under subparagraph (3)(*a*)(iii) by the insurer in computing its income for its 1975 taxation year if that amount had been determined on the assumptions made in paragraphs (*a*) to (*d*) of the description of A in the definition "1975-76 excess policy dividend reserve" in this subsection, and

Q is the amount deducted under subparagraph (3)(*a*)(iii) by the insurer in computing its income for its 1975 taxation year,

B is the amount determined by the formula

R - S

where

R is the amount that would have been deductible under subparagraph (3)(*a*)(iii) by the insurer in computing its income for its 1976 taxation year if that amount had been determined on the basis that the amount of its income for that year from its participating life insurance business carried on in Canada was computed in accordance with prescribed rules on the assumptions made in paragraph (*e*) of the description of A in the definition "1975-76 excess policy dividend reserve" in this subsection, and

S is the amount deducted by the insurer under subparagraph (3)(*a*)(iii) in computing its income for its 1976 taxation year, and

C is the amount determined by the formula

T - U

where

T is the amount determined for S, and

U is the amount determined for R;

"1975-76 excess policy dividend reserve" — (Repealed by S.C. 2013, c. 34, s. 286(14).)

History: S. 138(12), the definition "1975-76 excess policy dividend reserve" was repealed by S.C. 2013, c. 34, s. 286(14), applicable to taxation years that begin after October 31, 2011, and formerly read:

"1975-76 excess policy dividend reserve" — "1975-76 excess policy dividend reserve" of an insurer that has made an election under subsection 138(9) of the *Income Tax Act*, chapter 148 of the Revised Statutes of Canada, 1952, as it read in its application to the 1977 taxation year, in respect of its 1975 taxation year means the amount determined by the formula

A - B

where

A is the amount that would have been deductible under subparagraph (3)(*a*)(iv) by the insurer in computing its income for its 1976 taxation year if

(*a*) it had not made the election under subsection 138(9) of that Act in respect of its 1975 taxation year,

(*b*) where it made an election under subsection 138(9) of that Act in respect of its 1974 taxation year, it had adopted for its 1975 taxation year, with the concurrence of the Minister, the method required by subsection 138(9) of that Act if it had not elected under that subsection and the Minister had specified no terms and conditions under subsection 138(10) of that Act,

(*c*) it had claimed the maximum allowable amount under paragraph 138(3)(*c*) of the *Income Tax Act*, chapter 148 of the Revised Statutes of Canada, 1952, in computing its income for its 1975 taxation year,

(*d*) it had claimed the maximum allowable amount that would have been deductible under regulations made under paragraph 20(1)(*a*) in computing its income for its 1975 taxation year with respect to property of each of its prescribed classes, and

(*e*) the amount of its income for its 1976 taxation year from its participating life insurance business carried on in Canada was computed in accordance with prescribed rules and as if the amount deducted under subparagraph (3)(*a*)(iv) by it in computing its income for its 1975 taxation year was the amount that would have been deductible under that subparagraph on the basis of the assumptions made in paragraphs (*a*) to (*d*) of this description, and

B is the amount deducted by the insurer under subparagraph (3)(*a*)(iv) in computing its income for its 1976 taxation year;

"1975-76 excess policy reserves" — (Repealed by S.C. 2013, c. 34, s. 286(14).)

History: S. 138(12), the definition "1975-76 excess policy reserves" was repealed by S.C. 2013, c. 34, s. 286(14), applicable to taxation years that begin after October 31, 2011, and formerly read:

"1975-76 excess policy reserves"—"1975-76 excess policy reserves" of an insurer that has made an election under subsection 138(9) of the *Income Tax Act*, chapter 148 of the Revised Statutes of Canada, 1952, as it read in its application to the 1977 taxation year, in respect of its 1975 taxation year means the amount determined by the formula

$$A - B$$

where

A is the amount that would have been deductible under subparagraph (3)(*a*)(i) in computing the insurer's income for its 1976 taxation year if it had claimed the maximum allowable amount under that subparagraph for that year, and

B is the amount deducted under that subparagraph in computing its income for its 1976 taxation year.

► 138(13) ◄

(13) Variation in "tax basis" and "amortized cost". Where

(*a*) in a taxation year that ended after 1968 and before 1978 an insurer carried on a life insurance business in Canada and an insurance business in a country other than Canada,

(*b*) the insurer did not make an election in respect of the year under subsection 138(9) of the *Income Tax Act*, chapter 148 of the Revised Statutes of Canada, 1952, as it applied to that year, and

(*c*) the ratio of the value for the year of the insurer's specified Canadian assets to its Canadian investment fund for the year exceeded one,

each of the amounts included or deducted as follows in respect of the year shall be multiplied by the ratio referred to in paragraph (*c*):

(*d*) under paragraph (*c*), (*d*), (*k*) or (*l*) of the definition "tax basis" in subsection 142.4(1) in determining the tax basis of a debt obligation to the insurer, or

(*e*) under paragraph (*c*), (*d*), (*f*) or (*h*) of the definition "amortized cost" in subsection 248(1) in determining the amortized cost of a debt obligation to the insurer.

► 138(14) ◄

(14) Meaning of certain expressions. For the purposes of subsection (13), the expressions "Canadian investment fund for a taxation year", "specified Canadian assets" and "value for the taxation year" have the meanings prescribed therefor.

Related Regulations: Part XXIV.

► 138(15) ◄

(15) Definition not to apply. In this section, in construing the meaning of the expression "group term insurance policy", the definition "group term life insurance policy" in subsection 248(1) does not apply.

► 138(16) ◄

(16) Transition year income inclusion. There shall be included in computing a life insurer's income for its transition year from a life insurance business carried on by it in Canada in the transition year, the positive amount, if any, of the life insurer's reserve transition amount in respect of that life insurance business.

History: S. 138(16) was added by S.C. 2009, c. 2, s. 45(3), applicable to taxation years that begin after September 2006.

► 138(17) ◄

(17) Transition year income deduction. There shall be deducted in computing a life insurer's income for its transition year from a life insurance business carried on by it in Canada in the transition year, the absolute value of the negative amount, if any, of the life insurer's reserve transition amount in respect of that life insurance business.

History: S. 138(17) was added by S.C. 2009, c. 2, s. 45(3), applicable to taxation years that begin after September 2006.

► 138(17.1) ◄

(17.1) IFRS transition — reversals. In applying subsections (18) and (19) to a life insurer for a taxation year of the life insurer in respect of the International Financial Reporting Standards adopted by the Accounting Standards Board and effective as of January 1, 2011,

(*a*) the reference to "policy reserve" in B of the formula in the definition "reserve transition amount" in subsection (12) is to be read as a reference to "policy reserve determined without reference to the life insurer's excluded policies";

(*b*) the reference in those subsections to "that ends after the beginning of the transition year" is to be read as a reference to "that ends no sooner than two years after the beginning of the transition year"; and

(*c*) the reference in those subsections to "the first day of the transition year" is to be read as a reference to "the first day of the first year that ends no sooner than two years after the beginning of the transition year".

History: S. 138(17.1) was added by S.C. 2010, c. 25, s. 33(3), applicable to taxation years that begin after 2010.

► 138(18) ◄

(18) Transition year income inclusion reversal. If an amount has been included under subsection (16) in computing a life insurer's income for its transition year from a life insurance business carried on by it in Canada, there shall be deducted in computing the life insurer's income, for each particular taxation year of the life insurer that ends after the beginning of the transition year, from that life insurance business, the amount determined by the formula

$$A \times B/1825$$

where

A is the amount included under subsection (16) in computing the life insurer's income for the transition year from that life insurance business; and

B is the number of days in the particular taxation year that are before the day that is 1825 days after the first day of the transition year.

History: S. 138(18) was added by S.C. 2009, c. 2, s. 45(3), applicable to taxation years that begin after September 2006.

► 138(19) ◄

(19) Transition year income deduction reversal. If an amount has been deducted under subsection (17) in computing a life insurer's income for its transition year from a life insurance business carried on by it in Canada, there shall be included in computing the life insurer's income, for each particular taxation year of the life insurer that ends after the beginning of the transition year, from that life insurance business, the amount determined by the formula

$$A \times B/1825$$

where

A is the amount deducted under subsection (17) in computing the life insurer's income for the transition year from that life insurance business; and

B is the number of days in the particular taxation year that are before the day that is 1825 days after the first day of the transition year.

History: S. 138(19) was added by S.C. 2009, c. 2, s. 45(3), applicable to taxation years that begin after September 2006.

▶ 138(20) ◀

(20) Winding-up. If a life insurer has, in a winding-up to which subsection 88(1) has applied, been wound-up into another corporation (referred to in this subsection as the "parent"), and immediately after the winding-up the parent carries on a life insurance business, in applying subsections (18) and (19) in computing the income of the life insurer and of the parent for particular taxation years that end on or after the first day (referred to in this subsection as the "start day") on which assets of the life insurer were distributed to the parent on the winding-up,

(*a*) the parent is, on and after the start day, deemed to be the same corporation as and a continuation of the life insurer in respect of

(i) any amount included under subsection (16) or deducted under subsection (17) in computing the life insurer's income from a life insurance business for its transition year,

(ii) any amount deducted under subsection (18) or included under subsection (19) in computing the life insurer's income from a life insurance business for a taxation year of the life insurer that begins before the start day, and

(iii) any amount that would — in the absence of this subsection and if the life insurer existed and carried on a life insurance business on each day that is the start day or a subsequent day and on which the parent carries on a life insurance business — be required to be deducted or included, in respect of any of those days, under subsection (18) or (19) in computing the life insurer's income from a life insurance business; and

(*b*) the life insurer is, in respect of each of its particular taxation years, to determine the value for B in the formulas in subsections (18) and (19) without reference to the start day and days after the start day.

History: S. 138(20) was added by S.C. 2009, c. 2, s. 45(3), applicable to taxation years that begin after September 2006.

▶ 138(21) ◀

(21) Amalgamations. If there is an amalgamation (within the meaning assigned by subsection 87(1)) of a life insurer with one or more other corporations to form one corporation (referred to in this subsection as the "new corporation"), and immediately after the amalgamation the new corporation carries on a life insurance business, in applying subsections (18) and (19) in computing the income of the new corporation for particular taxation years of the new corporation that begin on or after the day on which the amalgamation occurred, the new corporation is, on and after that day, deemed to be the same corporation as and a continuation of the life insurer in respect of

(*a*) any amount included under subsection (16) or deducted under subsection (17) in computing the life insurer's income from a life insurance business for its transition year;

(*b*) any amount deducted under subsection (18) or included under subsection (19) in computing the life insurer's income from a life insurance business for a taxation year that begins before the day on which the amalgamation occurred; and

(*c*) any amount that would — in the absence of this subsection and if the life insurer existed and carried on a life insurance business on each day that is the day on which the amalgamation occurred or a subsequent day and on which the new corporation carries on a life insurance business — be required to be deducted or included, in respect of any of those days, under subsection (18) or (19) in computing the life insurer's income from a life insurance business.

History: S. 138(21) was added by S.C. 2009, c. 2, s. 45(3), applicable to taxation years that begin after September 2006.

▶ 138(22) ◀

(22) Application of subsection (23). Subsection (23) applies if, at any time, a life insurer (referred to in this subsection and subsection (23) as the "transferor") transfers, to a corporation (referred to in this subsection and subsection (23) as the "transferee") that is related to the transferor, property in respect of a life insurance business carried on by the transferor in Canada (referred to in this subsection and subsection (23) as the "transferred business") and

(*a*) subsection 138(11.5) or (11.94) applies to the transfer; or

(*b*) subsection 85(1) applies to the transfer, the transfer includes all or substantially all of the property and liabilities of the transferred business and, immediately after the transfer, the transferee carries on a life insurance business.

History: S. 138(22) was added by S.C. 2009, c. 2, s. 45(3), applicable to taxation years that begin after September 2006.

▶ 138(23) ◀

(23) Transfer of life insurance business. If this subsection applies in respect of the transfer, at any time, of property

(*a*) the transferee is, at and after that time, deemed to be the same corporation as and a continuation of the transferor in respect of

(i) any amount included under subsection (16) or deducted under subsection (17) in computing the transferor's income for its transition year that can reasonably be attributed to the transferred business,

(ii) any amount deducted under subsection (18) or included under subsection (19) in computing the transferor's income for a taxation year of the transferor that begins before that time that can reasonably be attributed to the transferred business, and

(iii) any amount that would — in the absence of this subsection and if the transferor existed and carried on a life insurance business on each day that includes that time or is a subsequent day and on which the transferee carries on a life insurance business — be required to be deducted or included, in respect of any of those days, under subsection (18) or (19) in computing the transferor's income that can reasonably be attributed to the transferred business; and

(*b*) in determining, in respect of the day that includes that time or any subsequent day, any amount that is required under subsection (18) or (19) to be deducted or included in computing the transferor's income for each particular taxation year from the transferred business, the description of A in the formulas in those subsections is deemed to be nil.

History: S. 138(23) was added by S.C. 2009, c. 2, s. 45(3), applicable to taxation years that begin after September 2006.

► 138(24) ◄

(24) Ceasing to carry on business. If at any time a life insurer ceases to carry on all or substantially all of a life insurance business (referred to in this subsection as the "discontinued business"), and none of subsections (20) to (22) apply,

(*a*) there shall be deducted, in computing the life insurer's income from the discontinued business for the life insurer's taxation year that includes the time that is immediately before that time, the amount determined by the formula

$$A - B$$

where

A is the amount included under subsection (16) in computing the life insurer's income from the discontinued business for its transition year, and

B is the total of all amounts each of which is an amount deducted under subsection (18) in computing the life insurer's income from the discontinued business for a taxation year that began before that time; and

(*b*) there shall be included, in computing the life insurer's income from the discontinued business for the life insurer's taxation year that includes the time that is immediately before that time, the amount determined by the formula

$$C - D$$

where

C is the amount deducted under subsection (17) in computing the life insurer's income from the discontinued business for its transition year, and

D is the total of all amounts each of which is an amount included under subsection (19) in computing the life insurer's income from the discontinued business for a taxation year that began before that time.

History: S. 138(24) was added by S.C. 2009, c. 2, s. 45(3), applicable to taxation years that begin after September 2006.

► 138(25) ◄

(25) Ceasing to exist. If at any time a life insurer that carried on a life insurance business ceases to exist (otherwise than as a result of a winding-up or amalgamation described in subsection (20) or (21)), for the purposes of subsection (24), the life insurer is deemed to have ceased to carry on the life insurance business at the earlier of

(*a*) the time (determined without reference to this subsection) at which the life insurer ceased to carry on the life insurance business, and

(*b*) the time that is immediately before the end of the last taxation year of the life insurer that ended at or before the time at which the life insurer ceased to exist.

History: S. 138(25) was added by S.C. 2009, c. 2, s. 45(3), applicable to taxation years that begin after September 2006.

► 138(26) ◄

(26) Policy reserve transition — application rules. In applying subsections (16), (17), (18) and (19) to a life insurer for a taxation year of the life insurer,

(*a*) if the application of one or more of those subsections is in respect of the amendment to paragraph 1406(*b*) of the *Income Tax Regulations* effective as of the life insurer's 2012 taxation year, the life insurer's reserve transition amount for its transition year in respect of that amendment is to be determined as though the description of A in the definition "reserve transition amount" in subsection (12) read as follows:

A is the maximum amount that the life insurer would be permitted to claim under subparagraph (3)(*a*)(i) (and that would be prescribed by section 1404 of the *Income Tax Regulations* for the purposes of subparagraph (3)(*a*)(i)) as a policy reserve for its base year in respect of its life insurance policies in Canada if paragraph 1406(*b*) of the *Income Tax Regulations* were read as it applies to the life insurer's 2012 taxation year, and;

(*b*) if one or more of those subsections applies in the same taxation year in respect of both the amendment to paragraph 1406(*b*) of the *Income Tax Regulations* effective as of the life insurer's 2012 taxation year, and the International Financial Reporting Standards adopted by the Accounting Standards Board and effective as of January 1, 2011, then, for the purposes of applying those subsections in respect of a transition year described by paragraph (*b*) of the definition "transition year" in subsection (12), the reference to "as it reads in respect of its transition year" in paragraph (*b*) of the description of A in the definition "reserve transition amount" in subsection (12) is to be read as a reference to "as it reads in respect of its transition year (determined without reference to the amendment to paragraph 1406(*b*) of the *Income Tax Regulations* effective as of the life insurer's 2012 taxation year); and

(*c*) if the life insurer has more than one transition year for the same taxation year of the life insurer

(i) for each transition year, the computation of the reserve transition amount for the transition year, and the requirements to include, or rights to deduct, under any of those subsections an amount in respect of that reserve transition amount, shall be determined as if that transition year were the only transition year of the life insurer for that taxation year, and

(ii) for greater certainty, the references in subsections (16), (17), (18) and (19) to a transition year include each of those transition years.

History: S. 138(26) was added by S.C. 2013, c. 34, s. 286(19), applicable to the 2012 and subsequent taxation years.

SECTION 138.1: Rules relating to segregated funds

► 138.1(1) ◄

(1) Rules relating to segregated funds. In respect of life insurance policies for which all or any part of an insurer's reserves vary in amount depending on the fair market value of a specified group of properties (in this section referred to as a "segregated fund"), for the purposes of this Part, the following rules apply:

(*a*) a trust (in this section and section 138.2 referred to as the "related segregated fund trust") is deemed to be created at the time that is the later of

(i) the day that the segregated fund is created, and

(ii) the day on which the insurer's 1978 taxation year commences,

and to continue in existence throughout the period during which the fund determines any portion of the benefits under those policies that vary in amount depending on the fair market value of the property in the segregated fund (in this section referred to as "segregated fund policies");

(*b*) property that has been allocated to and that remains a part of the segregated fund, and any income that has accrued on that property is deemed to be the property and income of the related segregated fund trust and not to be the property and income of the insurer;

(*c*) the insurer is deemed to be

(i) the trustee who has ownership or control of the related segregated fund trust property,

(ii) a resident of Canada in respect of the related segregated fund trust property used or held by it in the course of carrying on the insurer's life insurance business in Canada, and

(iii) a non-resident of Canada in respect of the related segregated fund trust property not used or held by it in the course of carrying on the insurer's life insurance business in Canada;

(*d*) where at a particular time there is property in the segregated fund that was not funded with premiums paid under a segregated fund policy,

(i) the insurer is deemed to have an interest in the related segregated fund trust that is not in respect of any particular property or source of income, and

(ii) the cost at any time of that interest to the insurer is deemed to be the total of

(A) for property of the trust at that time allocated by the insurer to the segregated fund prior to 1978, the amount that would be its adjusted cost base to the insurer if the interest had been a capital property at all relevant times prior to 1978 and if the rules in this section had been applicable for the taxation years after 1971 and before 1978, and

(B) for property of the trust at that time allocated by the insurer to the segregated fund after 1977, the fair market value of the property at the time it was last allocated to the segregated fund by the insurer;

(*e*) where at any particular time there is property in the segregated fund that was funded with a portion of the premiums paid before that time under a segregated fund policy,

(i) the respective segregated fund policyholder is deemed to have an interest in the related segregated fund trust that is not in respect of any particular property or source of income,

(ii) the cost of that interest is deemed to be the amount that is the total of

(A) the amount that would be its adjusted cost base to the insurer at December 31, 1977 if the interest had been a capital property at all relevant times prior to 1978 and if the rules in this section (if subsection (3) were read without reference to the expressions "or capital loss" and "or loss") had been applicable for taxation years after 1971 and before 1978, and

(B) the total of amounts each of which is that portion of a premium paid before that time and after the day referred to in subparagraph (*a*)(ii) under a segregated fund policy that was or is to be used by the insurer to fund property allocated to the segregated fund (other than the portion of the premium that is an acquisition fee), and

(iii) the portion of a premium included in a segregated fund is deemed not to be an amount paid in respect of a premium under the policy;

(*f*) the taxable income of the related segregated fund trust is deemed for the purposes of subsections 104(6), (13) and (24) to be an amount that has become payable in the year to the beneficiaries under the segregated fund trust and the amount therefor in respect of any particular beneficiary is equal to the amount determined by reference to the terms and conditions of the segregated fund policy;

(*g*) where at a particular time the fair market value of property transferred by the insurer to the segregated fund results in an increase at that time in the portion of the insurer's reserves for a segregated fund policy held by a policyholder that vary with the fair market value of the segregated fund and a decrease in the portion of its reserves for the policy that do not so vary, the amount of that increase shall,

(i) for the purpose of the determination of H in the definition "adjusted cost basis" in subsection 148(9), be deemed to be proceeds of disposition that the policyholder became entitled to receive at that time,

(ii) for the purpose of computing the adjusted cost base to the policyholder of the policyholder's interest in the related segregated fund trust, be added at that time to the cost to the policyholder of that interest, and

(iii) for the purpose of computing the insurer's income, be deemed to be a payment under the terms and conditions of the policy at that time;

(*h*) where at a particular time the fair market value of property transferred by the insurer from the segregated fund results in an increase at that time in the portion of the insurer's reserves for a segregated fund policy that do not vary with the fair market value of the segregated fund and a decrease in the portion of its reserves for the policy that so vary, the amount of that increase shall, for the purpose of calculating the insurer's income, be deemed to be a premium received by the insurer at that time;

(*i*) where at a particular time the policyholder of a segregated fund policy disposes of all or a portion of the policyholder's interest in the related segregated fund trust, that proportion of the amount, if any, by which the acquisition fee with respect to the particular policy exceeds the total of amounts each of which is an amount determined under this paragraph with respect to the particular policy before that time, that

(i) the fair market value of the interest disposed of at that time

is of

(ii) the fair market value of the policyholder's interest in the particular segregated fund trust immediately before that time,

is deemed to be a capital loss of the related segregated fund trust that reduces the policyholder's benefits under the particular policy by that amount for the purposes of subsection (3);

(*j*) the obligations of an insurer in respect of a benefit that is payable under a segregated fund policy, the amount of which benefit varies with the fair market value of the segregated fund at the time the benefit becomes payable, are deemed to be obligations of the trustee under the related segregated fund trust and not of the insurer and any amount received by the policyholder or that the policyholder became entitled to receive at any particular time in a year in respect of those obligations is deemed to be proceeds from the disposition of an interest in the related segregated fund trust;

(*k*) a reference to "the terms and conditions of the trust arrangement" in section 104 or subsection 127.2(3) is deemed to include a reference to the terms and conditions of the related segregated fund policy and the trustee is deemed to have designated the amounts referred to in that section in accordance with those terms and conditions; and

(*l*) where at any time an insurer acquires a share as a first registered holder thereof and allocates the share to a related segregated fund trust, the trust shall be deemed to have acquired the share at that time as the first registered holder thereof for the purpose of computing its share-purchase tax credit and the insurer shall be deemed not to have acquired the share for the purpose of computing its share-purchase tax credit.

Editorial Note: S. 138.1 outlines the rules applicable to segregated funds of life insurance companies and its segregated fund holders, for the purposes of Parts I and XII.3 of the Act. The segregated fund is treated essentially as a flow-through entity and the tax treatment of the entity and its holders is somewhat similar, but there are important differences to the rules applicable to mutual fund trusts and their holders in s. 132. These include the following:

- capital losses of segregated funds are treated as capital losses of the holders;
- the taxable income of a segregated fund is allocated automatically to the holders with the result that it is not a taxable entity, in its own right; and
- there is no refundable capital gains tax like there is for a mutual fund trust.

These rules do not apply to segregated fund holders where they are PRPPs, RPPs, RRSPs, RRIFs, or TFSAs.

History: S. 138.1(1)(*f*) was replaced by S.C. 2017, c. 33, s. 54(2), applicable to taxation years that begin after 2017, and formerly read:

(*f*) the income of the related segregated fund trust is deemed for the purposes of subsections 104(6), (13) and (24) to be an amount that has become payable in the year to the beneficiaries under the segregated fund trust and the amount therefor in respect of any particular beneficiary is equal to the amount determined by reference to the terms and conditions of the segregated fund policy;

S. 138.1(1)(*a*), the portion before subparagraph (i) was replaced by S.C. 2017, c. 33, s. 54(1), applicable to taxation years that begin after 2017, and formerly read:

(*a*) a trust (in this section referred to as the "related segregated fund trust") is deemed to be created at the time that is the later of

S. 138.1(1)(*a*), the portion before subparagraph (i) was replaced by S.C. 2014, c. 39, s. 47(1), applicable to the 2016 and subsequent taxation years, and formerly read:

(*a*) an *inter vivos* trust (in this section referred to as the "related segregated fund trust") is deemed to be created at the time that is the later of

Related Regulations: 302(1); 1401(2); 1406(6); 1408(1); 1900(1); 5101(1).

Related Sections: S. 38(*a*.1) Taxable capital gain and allowable capital loss; s. 39(1) Meaning of capital gain and capital loss; s. 39.1(1), "flow-through entity"; s. 53(1)(*l*) Adjustments to cost base — Interest in related segregated fund trust; s. 53(2)(*q*) Amounts to be deducted — Interest in related segregated fund trust; s. 75(3) Exceptions; s. 87(2.2) Amalgamation of insurers; s. 88(1)(*g*) Winding-up; s. 107.4(1)(*j*) Qualifying disposition; s. 107.4(3)(*g*) Tax consequences of qualifying dispositions; s. 108(1)(*b*) Definitions; s. 127.5 Obligation to pay minimum tax; s. 127.55 Application of s. 127.5; s. 128.1(10) Definitions; s. 138(11.5)(*k*) Transfer of insurance business by non-resident insurer; s. 138(12), "segregated fund"; s. 138.1(6), "acquisition fee"; s. 138.1(7) Where ss. (1) to (6) do not apply; s. 148(9) Definitions; s. 149(1.2) Income test; s. 211(1) Definitions; s. 218.1 Application of s. 138.1; s. 248(1), "disposition", "amount", "property".

Tax Window Files: Disposition of Segregated Fund Units, *Technical Interpretation, Financial Sector and Exempt Entities Division, October 24, 2006*, CRA Document No. 2006-0174091E5; Segregated Fund and Financial Institution, *Advance Income Tax Ruling, Financial Sector and Exempt Entities Division, October 4, 2006*, CRA Document No. 2006-0187361R3; Life Insurance Policy — Foreign-Issued Investment, *Technical Interpretation, Financial Sector and Exempt Entities Division, March 7, 2006*, CRA Document No. 2005-0152041E5; Segregated Fund Allocation Method, *Technical Interpretation, Financial Sector and Exempt Division, November 3, 2005*, CRA Document No. 2005-0156951E5; Deemed Trust Created for Segregated Fund — Master Trust, *Technical Interpretation, Financial Sector and Exempt Entities Division, July 14, 2005*, CRA Document No. 2005-0129441E5; Segregated Fund Annuity Court Settlement, *Technical Interpretation, Charitable and Financial Institution Sectors, May 30, 2005*, CRA Document No. 2005-0125261E5; Disposition of Related Segregated Fund Trust, *Technical Interpretation, Financial Industries Division, January 30, 2003*, CRA Document No. 2002-0163437.

► 138.1(2) ◄

(2) Rules relating to property in segregated funds at end of 1977 taxation year. Where an insurer holds property at the end of its 1977 taxation year in connection with a segregated fund, the following rules apply:

(*a*) the property is deemed to have been acquired by the related segregated fund trust on the day determined under paragraph (1)(*a*) at a cost equal to the adjusted cost base of the property to the insurer on that day and that transaction is deemed to be a transaction between persons not dealing at arm's length;

(*b*) the property is deemed to have been disposed of by the insurer on the day referred to in paragraph (*a*) for proceeds equal to the adjusted cost base of the property to the insurer on that day; and

(*c*) for the purpose of computing the insurer's income for its 1978 taxation year it shall be deemed to have made a payment to its policyholders in satisfaction of their rights under their segregated fund policies in that year equal to that portion of the amount deducted under subparagraph 138(3)(*a*)(i) in computing its income for its 1977 taxation year that is in respect of segregated fund policies.

► 138.1(2.1) ◄

(2.1) Transition — pre-2018 non-capital losses. For the purpose of determining the taxable income of a related segregated fund trust for a taxation year that begins after 2017, the non-capital losses of the related segregated fund trust that arise in a taxation year that begins before 2018 are deemed to be nil.

History: S. 138.1(2.1) was added by S.C. 2017, c. 33, s. 54(3), in force December 14, 2017 (Royal Assent).

► 138.1(3) ◄

(3) Capital gains and capital losses of related segregated fund trusts. A capital gain or capital loss of a related segregated fund trust from the disposition of any property shall, to the extent that a policyholder's benefits under a policy or the interest in the trust of any other beneficiary is affected by that gain or loss, be deemed to be a capital gain or capital loss, as the case may be, of the policyholder or other beneficiary and not that of the trust.

Related Sections: S. 53(2) Amounts to be deducted.

► 138.1(3.1) ◄

(3.1) Deemed gains and losses — (Repealed by S.C. 2013, c. 34, s. 287(1).)

History: S. 138.1(3.1) was repealed by S.C. 2013, c. 34, s. 287(1), applicable to taxation years that begin after October 31, 2011, and formerly read:

(3.1) *Deemed gains and losses.* Where an amount is deemed under subsection (3) to be a capital gain or capital loss of a policyholder or other beneficiary (in this subsection referred to as the "taxpayer") of a related segregated fund trust, in respect of capital gains or losses realized in a taxation year of the related segregated fund trust that includes February 28, 2000 or October 17, 2000, and the related segregated fund trust so elects under this subsection in its return of income for the year,

(*a*) the portion of the gains and losses that are in respect of capital gains or losses from dispositions of property that occurred before February 28, 2000 is deemed to be that proportion of the gains or losses that the number of days that are in the year and before February 28, 2000 is of the number of days that are in the year;

(*b*) the portion of the gains and losses that is in respect of capital gains or losses from dispositions of property that occurred in the year and in the period that begins at the beginning of February 28, 2000 and ends at the end of October 17, 2000, is deemed to be that proportion of the gains or losses that the number of days that are in the year and in that period is of the number of days that are in the year; and

(*c*) the portion of the gains and losses that is in respect of capital gains or losses from dispositions of property that occurred in the year and in the period that begins at the beginning of October 18, 2000 and ends at the end of the year, is deemed to be that proportion of the gains or losses that the number of days that are in the year and in that period is of the number of days that are in the year.

► 138.1(3.2) ◄

(3.2) Deemed gains and losses — taxpayer — (Repealed by S.C. 2013, c. 34, s. 287(1).)

History: S. 138.1(3.2) was repealed by S.C. 2013, c. 34, s. 287(1), applicable to taxation years that begin after October 31, 2011, and formerly read:

(3.2) *Deemed gains and losses — taxpayer.* Where a capital gain or a capital loss is deemed by subsection (3) to be a capital gain or a capital loss of a taxpayer and not that of a related segregated fund trust,

(*a*) if the capital gain or capital loss was in respect of capital gains or capital losses from dispositions of property by the related segregated fund trust that occurred before February 28, 2000 and that taxation year of the taxpayer includes February 27, 2000, the capital gain or the capital loss is deemed to be a capital gain or a capital loss, as the case may be, of the taxpayer from the disposition by the taxpayer of capital property in the taxpayer's taxation year and before February 28, 2000;

(*b*) if the capital gain or capital loss was in respect of capital gains or capital losses from dispositions of property by the related segregated fund trust that occurred before February 28, 2000 and the taxation year of the taxpayer began after February 27, 2000 and ended before October 18, 2000, $^{9}/_{8}$ of the capital gain or the capital loss is deemed to be a capital gain or a capital loss, as the case may be, of the taxpayer from the disposition by the taxpayer of capital property in the taxpayer's taxation year;

(*c*) if the capital gain or capital loss was in respect of capital gains or capital losses from dispositions of property by the related segregated fund trust that occurred before February 28, 2000 and the taxation year of the taxpayer began after February 27, 2000 and ended after October 17, 2000, $^{9}/_{8}$ of the capital gain or the capital loss is deemed to be a capital gain or a capital loss, as the case may be, of the taxpayer from the disposition by the taxpayer of capital property in the taxpayer's taxation year and before October 18, 2000;

(*d*) if the capital gain or capital loss was in respect of capital gains or capital losses from dispositions of property by the related segregated fund trust that occurred before February 28, 2000 and the taxation year of the taxpayer began after October 17, 2000, $^{3}/_{2}$ of the capital gain or the capital loss is deemed to be a capital gain or a capital loss, as the case may be, of the taxpayer from the disposition by the taxpayer of capital property in the taxpayer's taxation year;

(*e*) if the capital gain or capital loss was in respect of capital gains or capital losses from dispositions of property by the related segregated fund that occurred after February 27, 2000 and before October 18, 2000 and the taxation year of the taxpayer began after October 17, 2000, $^{4}/_{3}$ of the capital gain or capital loss is deemed to be a capital gain or a capital loss, as the case may be, of the taxpayer from the disposition by the taxpayer of capital property in the taxpayer's taxation year;

(*f*) if the capital gain or capital loss was in respect of capital gains or capital losses from dispositions of property by the related segregated fund trust that occurred after February 27, 2000 and before October 18, 2000 and the taxation year of the taxpayer includes February 28, 2000 and October 17, 2000, the capital gain or the capital loss is deemed to be a capital gain or a capital loss, as the case may be, of the taxpayer from the disposition by the taxpayer of capital property in the taxpayer's taxation year and in the period that began after February 27, 2000 and ended before October 18, 2000;

(*g*) if the capital gain or capital loss was in respect of capital gains or capital losses from dispositions of property by the related segregated fund trust that occurred after February 27, 2000 and before October 17, 2000 and the taxation year of the taxpayer began after February 27, 2000 and ended before October 17, 2000, the capital gain or the capital loss is deemed to be a capital gain or a capital loss, as the case may be, of the taxpayer from the disposition by the taxpayer of capital property in the taxpayer's taxation year; and

(*h*) in any other case, the capital gain or the capital loss is deemed to be a capital gain or a capital loss, as the case may be, of the taxpayer from the disposition of capital property by the taxpayer in the taxpayer's taxation year and after October 17, 2000.

► 138.1(4) ◄

(4) Election and allocation. Where at any particular time after 1977, a policyholder withdraws all or part of the policyholder's interest in a segregated fund policy, the trustee of a related segregated fund trust may elect in prescribed manner and prescribed form to treat any capital property of the trust as having been disposed of, whereupon the property shall be deemed to have been disposed of on any day designated by the trustee for proceeds of disposition equal to

(*a*) the fair market value of the property on that day,

(*b*) the adjusted cost base to the trust of the property on that day, or

(*c*) an amount that is neither greater than the greater of nor less than the lesser of the amounts determined under paragraphs (*a*) and (*b*),

whichever is designated by the trustee, and to have been reacquired by the trust immediately thereafter at a cost equal to those proceeds, and where the trustee of a related segregated fund trust has made such an election, the following rules apply:

(*d*) the amount of any capital gain or capital loss resulting from the deemed disposition shall be allocated by the trustee to any policyholder withdrawing all or part of the policyholder's interest in the policyholder's policy at that time to the extent that the amount of the policyholder's benefits under the policy at that time is affected by the capital gain or capital loss in respect of property held by the related segregated fund trust at that time,

(*e*) the allocation referred to in paragraph (*d*) is deemed to have been made immediately before the withdrawal,

(*f*) any capital gain not so allocated is deemed to be allocated in accordance with the terms and conditions of the policy, and

(*g*) any capital loss not so allocated is deemed to be a superficial loss of each policyholder to the extent that the policyholder's benefits under the policy would be affected by the loss.

Related Regulations: 6100.

Related Sections: S. 53(1) Adjustments to cost base; s. 53(2) Amounts to be deducted.

Forms: T3018 — Election Under Subsection 138.1(4) of the Deemed Disposition of Capital Property of a Life Insurance Segregated Fund.

► 138.1(5) ◄

(5) Adjusted cost base of property in related segregated fund trust. At any particular time, the adjusted cost base of each capital property of a related segregated fund trust shall be deemed to be the amount, if any, by which

(*a*) the adjusted cost base of the property to the trust immediately before that time

exceeds

(*b*) the total of amounts each of which is an amount in respect of the disposition by a policyholder of all or part of the policyholder's interest in the related segregated fund trust at that time equal to that proportion of the amount, if any, by which

(i) the adjusted cost base to the policyholder of that interest at that time

exceeds

(ii) the policyholder's proceeds of the disposition of that interest in the trust

that

(iii) the fair market value of the capital property at that time

is of

(iv) the total of amounts each of which is the fair market value of a capital property of the related segregated fund trust at that time.

▶ 138.1(6) ◀

(6) Definition of "acquisition fee". In this section, "acquisition fee" means the amount, if any, by which the total of amounts each of which is

(*a*) that portion of a premium charged by the insurer under a segregated fund policy that is not included in the related segregated fund or cannot reasonably be regarded as an amount required to fund a mortality or maturity benefit,

(*b*) a transfer from the segregated fund that cannot reasonably be regarded as an amount required to fund a mortality or maturity benefit other than an annual administration fee or charge, or

(*c*) any amount by which the proceeds payable to the policyholder under a particular segregated fund policy is reduced on the surrender or partial surrender of the policy that may reasonably be regarded as a surrender fee,

exceeds

(*d*) the total of amounts each of which is that portion of an amount described in paragraph (*a*), (*b*) or (*c*) that may reasonably be considered to be in respect of an interest in the segregated fund that was disposed of before 1978.

Related Sections: S. 248(1), "amount", "insurer".

▶ 138.1(7) ◀

(7) Non-application of subsections (1) to (6). Subsections (1) to (6) do not apply to the holder of a segregated fund policy with respect to such a policy that is issued or effected as or under a pooled registered pension plan, registered pension plan, registered retirement income fund, registered retirement savings plan or TFSA.

History: S. 138.1(7) was replaced by S.C. 2012, c. 31, s. 31(1), in force December 14, 2012, and formerly read:

(7) *Where ss. (1) to (6) do not apply.* Subsections (1) to (6) do not apply to the holder of a segregated fund policy with respect to such a policy that is issued or effected as a registered retirement savings plan, registered retirement income fund or TFSA or that is issued under a registered pension plan.

SECTION 138.2: Rules relating to segregated funds

▶ 138.2(1) ◀

(1) Qualifying transfer of funds. For the purposes of this section, a qualifying transfer occurs at a particular time (in this section referred to as the "transfer time") if

(*a*) all of the property that, immediately before the transfer time, was property of a related segregated fund trust has become, at the transfer time, the property of another related segregated fund trust (in this section referred to as the "transferor" and "transferee", respectively, and collectively as the "funds");

(*b*) every person that had an interest in the transferor immediately before the transfer time (in this section referred to as a "beneficiary") has ceased to be a beneficiary of the transferor at the transfer time and has received no consideration for the interest other than an interest in the transferee;

(*c*) the trustee of the funds is a resident of Canada; and

(*d*) the trustee of the funds so elects, by filing a prescribed form with the Minister on or before the election's due date.

History: S. 138.2(1) was added by S.C. 2017, c. 33, s. 55(1), deemed in force January 1, 2018.

Forms: T2185 Election on Disposition of Property by a Segregated Fund Trust to a Related Segregated Fund Trust.

▶ 138.2(2) ◀

(2) General. If there has been a qualifying transfer,

(*a*) the last taxation years of the funds that began before the transfer time are deemed to have ended at the transfer time and the next taxation year of the transferee is deemed to have begun immediately after the transfer time;

(*b*) no amount in respect of a non-capital loss, net capital loss, restricted farm loss, farm loss or limited partnership loss of a fund for a taxation year that began before the transfer time is deductible in computing the taxable income of the funds for a taxation year that begins after the transfer time;

(*c*) each beneficiary's interest in the transferor is deemed to have been disposed of at the transfer time for proceeds of disposition, and each beneficiary's interest in the transferee received in the qualifying transfer is deemed to have been acquired at a cost, equal to the cost amount to the beneficiary of the interest in the transferor immediately before the transfer time;

(*d*) any amount determined under subsection 138.1(6) in respect of a policyholder's interest in the transferor is deemed

(i) to have been charged, transferred or paid in respect of the policyholder's interest in the transferee that is acquired on the qualifying transfer, and

(ii) to not have been charged, transferred or paid in respect of the policyholder's interest in the transferor; and

(*e*) subsections 138.1(4) and (5) do not apply in respect of any disposition of an interest in the transferor arising on the qualifying transfer.

History: S. 138.2(2) was added by S.C. 2017, c. 33, s. 55(1), deemed in force January 1, 2018.

Forms: T2185 Election on Disposition of Property by a Segregated Fund Trust to a Related Segregated Fund Trust.

▶ 138.2(3) ◀

(3) Transferor - capital gains and losses. In respect of a qualifying transfer, each property of the transferor held immediately before the transfer time is deemed to have been disposed of by the transferor immediately before the transfer time for proceeds of disposition, and to have been acquired by the transferee at the transfer time for a cost, equal to the lesser of

(*a*) the fair market value of the property immediately before the transfer time, and

(*b*) the greater of

(i) the cost amount of the property to the transferor immediately before the transfer time, and

(ii) the amount that is designated in respect of the property in the election in respect of the qualifying transfer.

History: S. 138.2(3) was added by S.C. 2017, c. 33, s. 55(1), deemed in force January 1, 2018.

► 138.2(4) ◄

(4) Transferee - capital gains and losses. In respect of a qualifying transfer, each property of the transferee held immediately before the transfer time is deemed to have been disposed of by the transferee immediately before the transfer time for proceeds of disposition, and to have been reacquired by the transferee at the transfer time for a cost, equal to the lesser of

(*a*) the fair market value of the property immediately before the transfer time, and

(*b*) the greater of

(i) the cost amount of the property to the transferee immediately before the transfer time, and

(ii) the amount that is designated in respect of the property in the election in respect of the qualifying transfer.

History: S. 138.2(4) was added by S.C. 2017, c. 33, s. 55(1), deemed in force January 1, 2018.

► 138.2(5) ◄

(5) Loss limitation. Subsection 138.1(3) does not apply to capital losses of a fund from the disposition of property on a qualifying transfer under subsection (3) or (4) to the extent that the amount of such capital losses exceeds the amount of capital gains of the fund from the disposition of property on the qualifying transfer under subsection (3) or (4), as the case may be.

History: S. 138.2(5) was added by S.C. 2017, c. 33, s. 55(1), deemed in force January 1, 2018.

► 138.2(6) ◄

(6) Due date. The due date of an election referred to in paragraph (1)(*d*) is the later of

(*a*) the day that is six months after the day that includes the transfer time, and

(*b*) a day that the Minister may specify.

History: S. 138.2(6) was added by S.C. 2017, c. 33, s. 55(1), deemed in force January 1, 2018.

Forms: T2185 Election on Disposition of Property by a Segregated Fund Trust to a Related Segregated Fund Trust.

SECTION 139: Conversion of insurance corporations into mutual corporations

Where an insurance corporation that is a Canadian corporation applies an amount in payment for shares of the corporation purchased or otherwise acquired by it under a mutualization proposal under Division III of Part VI of the *Insurance Companies Act* or under a law of the province under the laws of which the corporation is incorporated that provides for the conversion of the corporation into a mutual corporation by the purchase of its shares in accordance with that law,

(*a*) section 15 does not apply to require the inclusion, in computing the income of a shareholder of the corporation, of any part of that amount; and

(*b*) no part of that amount shall be deemed, for the purpose of subsection 138(7), to have been paid to shareholders or, for the purpose of section 84, to have been received as a dividend.

Related Sections: S. 15 Benefit conferred on shareholder; s. 84 Deemed dividend; s. 138(7) Amounts paid to shareholders included in taxable income (Repealed.); s. 248(1), "life insurance corporation".

Demutualization of Insurance Corporations

SECTION 139.1: [Demutualization of insurance corporations]

► 139.1(1) ◄

(1) Definitions. The definitions in this subsection apply in this section and sections 139.2 and 147.4.

"conversion benefit" —"conversion benefit" means a benefit received in connection with the demutualization of an insurance corporation because of an interest, before the demutualization, of any person in an insurance policy to which the insurance corporation has been a party.

"deadline" —"deadline" for a payment in respect of a demutualization of an insurance corporation means the latest of

(*a*) the end of the day that is 13 months after the time of the demutualization,

(*b*) where the entire amount of the payment depends on the outcome of an initial public offering of shares of the corporation or a holding corporation in respect of the insurance corporation, the end of the day that is 60 days after the day on which the offering is completed,

(*c*) where the payment is made after the initial deadline for the payment and it is reasonable to conclude that the payment was postponed beyond that initial deadline because there was not sufficient information available 60 days before that initial deadline with regard to the location of a person, the end of the day that is six months after such information becomes available, and

(*d*) the end of any other day that is acceptable to the Minister.

"demutualization" —"demutualization" means the conversion of an insurance corporation from a mutual company into a corporation that is not a mutual company.

"holding corporation" —"holding corporation" means a corporation that

(*a*) in connection with the demutualization of an insurance corporation, has issued shares of its capital stock to stakeholders; and

(*b*) owns shares of the capital stock of the insurance corporation acquired in connection with the demutualization that entitle it to 90% or more of the votes that could be cast in respect of shares under all circumstances at an annual meeting of

(i) shareholders of the insurance corporation, or

(ii) shareholders of the insurance corporation and holders of insurance policies to which the insurance corporation is a party.

"initial deadline" —"initial deadline" for a payment is the time that would, if the definition "deadline" were read without reference to paragraph (*c*) of that definition, be the deadline for the payment.

"mutual holding corporation" —"mutual holding corporation" in respect of an insurance corporation, means a mutual company established to hold shares of the capital stock of the insurance corporation, where the only persons entitled to vote at an annual meeting of the mutual company are policyholders of the insurance corporation.

"ownership rights" —"ownership rights" means

(*a*) in a particular mutual holding corporation, the following rights and interests held by a person in respect of the particular corporation because of an interest or former interest of any person in an insurance policy to which an insurance corporation, in respect of which the particular corporation is the mutual holding corporation, has been a party:

(i) rights that are similar to rights attached to shares of the capital stock of a corporation, and

(ii) all other rights with respect to, and interests in, the particular corporation as a mutual company; and

(*b*) in a mutual insurance corporation, the following rights and interests held by a person in respect of the mutual insurance corporation because of an interest or former interest of any person in an insurance policy to which that corporation has been a party:

(i) rights that are similar to rights attached to shares of the capital stock of a corporation,

(ii) all other rights with respect to, and interests in, the mutual insurance corporation as a mutual company, and

(iii) any contingent or absolute right to receive a benefit in connection with the demutualization of the mutual insurance corporation.

"person" —"person" includes a partnership.

"share" —"share" of the capital stock of a corporation includes a right granted by the corporation to acquire a share of its capital stock.

"specified insurance benefit" —"specified insurance benefit" means a taxable conversion benefit that is

(*a*) an enhancement of benefits under an insurance policy;

(*b*) an issuance of an insurance policy;

(*c*) an undertaking by an insurance corporation of an obligation to pay a policy dividend; or

(*d*) a reduction in the amount of premiums that would otherwise be payable under an insurance policy.

"stakeholder" —"stakeholder" means a person who is entitled to receive or who has received a conversion benefit but, in respect of the demutualization of an insurance corporation, does not include a holding corporation in connection with the demutualization or a mutual holding corporation in respect of the insurance corporation.

"taxable conversion benefit" —"taxable conversion benefit" means a conversion benefit received by a stakeholder in connection with the demutualization of an insurance corporation, other than a conversion benefit that is

(*a*) a share of a class of the capital stock of the corporation;

(*b*) a share of a class of the capital stock of a corporation that is or becomes a holding corporation in connection with the demutualization; or

(*c*) an ownership right in a mutual holding corporation in respect of the insurance corporation.

► 139.1(2) ◄

(2) Rules of general application. For the purpose of this section,

(*a*) subject to paragraphs (*b*) to (*g*), if in providing a benefit in respect of a demutualization, a corporation becomes obligated, either absolutely or contingently, to make or arrange a payment, the person to whom the undertaking to make or arrange the payment was given is considered to have received a benefit

(i) as a consequence of the undertaking of the obligation, and

(ii) not as a consequence of the making of the payment;

(*b*) where, in providing a benefit in respect of a demutualization, a corporation makes a payment (other than a payment, made pursuant to the terms of an insurance policy, that is not a policy dividend) at any time on or before the deadline for the payment,

(i) subject to paragraphs (*f*) and (*g*), the recipient of the payment is considered to have received a benefit as a consequence of the making of the payment, and

(ii) no benefit is considered to have been received as a consequence of the undertaking of an obligation, that is either contingent or absolute, to make or arrange the payment;

(*c*) no benefit is considered to have been received as a consequence of the undertaking of an absolute or contingent obligation of a corporation to make or arrange a payment (other than a payment, made pursuant to the terms of an insurance policy, that is not a policy dividend) unless it is reasonable to conclude that there is sufficient information with regard to the location of a person to make or arrange the payment;

(*d*) where a corporation's obligation to make or arrange a payment in connection with a demutualization ceases on or before the initial deadline for the payment and without the payment being made in whole or in part, no benefit is considered to have been received as a consequence of the undertaking of the obligation unless the payment was to be a payment (other than a policy dividend) pursuant to the terms of an insurance policy;

(*e*) no benefit is considered to have been received as a consequence of the undertaking of an absolute or contingent obligation of a corporation to make or arrange a payment where

(i) paragraph (*a*) would, but for this paragraph, apply with respect to the obligation,

(ii) paragraph (*d*) would, if that paragraph were read without reference to the words "on or before the initial deadline for the payment", apply in respect of the obligation,

(iii) it is reasonable to conclude that there was not, before the initial deadline for the payment, sufficient information with regard to the location of a person to make or arrange the payment, and

(iv) such information becomes available on a particular day after the initial deadline and the obligation ceases not more than six months after the particular day;

(*f*) no benefit is considered to have been received as a consequence of

(i) an undertaking of an absolute or contingent obligation of a corporation to make or arrange an annuity payment through the issuance of an annuity contract, or

(ii) a receipt of an annuity payment under the contract so issued

where it is reasonable to conclude that the purpose of the undertaking or the making of the annuity payment is to supplement benefits provided under either an annuity contract to which subsection 147.4(1) or paragraph 254(*a*) applied or a group annuity contract that had been issued under, or pursuant to, a registered pension plan that has wound up;

(*g*) no benefit is considered to have been received as a consequence of

(i) an amendment to which subsection 147.4(2) would, but for subparagraph 147.4(2)(*a*)(ii), apply, or

(ii) a substitution to which paragraph 147.4(3)(*a*) applies;

(*h*) the time at which a stakeholder is considered to receive a benefit in connection with the demutualization of an insurance corporation is

(i) where the benefit is a payment made at or before the time of the demutualization or is a payment to which paragraph (*b*) applies, the time at which the payment is made, and

(ii) in any other case, the latest of

(A) the time of the demutualization,

(B) where the extent of the benefit or the stakeholder's entitlement to it depends on the outcome of an initial public offering of shares of the corporation or a holding corporation in respect of the insurance corporation and the offering is completed before the day that is 13 months after the time of the demutualization, the time at which the offering is completed,

(C) where the entire amount of the benefit depends on the outcome of an initial public offering of shares of the corporation or a holding corporation in respect of the insurance corporation, the time at which the offering is completed,

(D) where it is reasonable to conclude that the person conferring the benefit does not have sufficient information with regard to the location of the stakeholder before the later of the times determined under clauses (A) to (C), to advise the stakeholder of the benefit, the time at which sufficient information with regard to the location of the stakeholder to so advise the stakeholder was received by that person, and

(E) the end of any other day that is acceptable to the Minister;

(*i*) the time at which an insurance corporation is considered to demutualize is the time at which it first issues a share of its capital stock (other than shares of its capital stock issued by it when it was a mutual company if the corporation did not cease to be a mutual company because of the issuance of those shares); and

(*j*) subject to paragraph (3)(*b*), the value of a benefit received by a stakeholder is the fair market value of the benefit at the time the stakeholder receives the benefit.

Related Sections: S. 49.1 No disposition where obligation satisfied; s. 56(1)(*a*) Pension benefits, unemployment insurance benefits, etc.; s. 56(1)(*d*) Annuity payments.

► 139.1(3) ◄

(3) Special cases. For the purpose of this section,

(*a*) where benefits under an insurance policy are enhanced (otherwise than by way of an amendment to which subsection 147.4(2) would, but for subparagraph 147.4(2)(*a*)(ii), apply) in connection with a demutualization, the value of the enhancement is deemed to be a benefit received by the policyholder and not by any other person;

(*b*) where premiums payable under an insurance policy to an insurance corporation are reduced in connection with a demutualization, the policyholder is deemed, as a consequence of the undertaking to reduce the premiums, to have received a benefit equal to the present value at the time of the demutualization of the additional premiums that would have been payable if the premiums had not been reduced in connection with the demutualization;

(*c*) the payment of a policy dividend by an insurance corporation or an undertaking of an obligation by the corporation to pay a policy dividend is considered to be in connection with the demutualization of the corporation only to the extent that

(i) the policy dividend is referred to in the demutualization proposal sent by the corporation to stakeholders,

(ii) the obligation to make the payment is contingent on stakeholder approval for the demutualization, and

(iii) the payment or undertaking cannot reasonably be considered to have been made or given, as the case may be, to ensure that policy dividends are not adversely affected by the demutualization;

(*d*) except for the purposes of paragraphs (*c*), (*e*) and (*f*), where part of a policy dividend is a conversion benefit in respect of the demutualization of an insurance corporation and part of it is not, each part of the dividend is deemed to be a policy dividend that is separate from the other part;

(*e*) a policy dividend includes an amount that is in lieu of payment of, or in satisfaction of, a policy dividend;

(*f*) the payment of a policy dividend includes the application of the policy dividend to pay a premium under an insurance policy or to repay a policy loan;

(*g*) where the demutualization of an insurance corporation is effected by the merger of the corporation with one or more other corporations to form one corporate entity, that entity is deemed to be the same corporation as, and a continuation of, the insurance corporation;

(*h*) an insurance corporation shall be considered to have become a party to an insurance policy at the time that the insurance corporation becomes liable in respect of obligations of an insurer under the policy; and

(*i*) notwithstanding paragraph 248(7)(*a*), where a cheque or other means of payment sent to an address is returned to the sender without being received by the addressee, it is deemed not to have been sent.

Related Sections: S. 147.4(2) Amended contract; s. 147.4(3) New contract.

▶ 139.1(4) ◀

(4) Consequences of demutualization. Where a particular insurance corporation demutualizes,

(*a*) each of the income, loss, capital gain and capital loss of a taxpayer, from the disposition, alteration or dilution of the taxpayer's ownership rights in the particular corporation as a result of the demutualization, is deemed to be nil;

(*b*) no amount paid or payable to a stakeholder in connection with the disposition, alteration or dilution of the stakeholder's ownership rights in the particular corporation may be included in Class 14.1 of Schedule II to the *Income Tax Regulations*;

(*c*) no election may be made under subsection 85(1) or (2) in respect of ownership rights in the particular corporation;

(*d*) where the consideration given by a person for a share of the capital stock of the particular corporation or a holding corporation in connection with the demutualization (or for particular ownership rights in a mutual holding corporation in respect of the particular corporation) includes the transfer, surrender, alteration or dilution of ownership rights in the particular corporation, the cost of the share (or the particular ownership rights) to the person is deemed to be nil;

(*e*) where a holding corporation in connection with the demutualization acquires, in connection with the demutualization, a share of the capital stock of the particular corporation from the particular corporation and issues a share of its own capital stock to a stakeholder as consideration for the share of the capital stock of the particular corporation, the cost to the holding corporation of the share of the capital stock of the particular corporation is deemed to be nil;

(*f*) where at any time a stakeholder receives a taxable conversion benefit and subsection (14) does not apply to the benefit,

(i) the corporation that conferred the benefit is deemed to have paid a dividend at that time on shares of its capital stock equal to the value of the benefit, and

(ii) subject to subsection (16), the benefit received by the stakeholder is deemed to be a dividend received by the stakeholder at that time;

(*g*) for the purposes of this Part, where a dividend is deemed by paragraph (*f*) or by paragraph (16)(*i*) to have been paid by a non-resident corporation, that corporation is deemed in respect of the payment of the dividend to be a corporation resident in Canada that is a taxable Canadian corporation unless any amount is claimed under section 126 in respect of tax on the dividend;

(*h*) for the purposes of section 70, subsection 104(4) and section 128.1, the fair market value of rights to benefits that are to be received in connection with the demutualization is, before the time of the receipt, deemed to be nil; and

(*i*) where a person acquires an annuity contract in respect of which, because of the application of paragraph (2)(*f*), no benefit is considered to have been received for the purpose of this section,

(i) the cost of the annuity contract to the person is deemed to be nil, and

(ii) section 12.2 does not apply to the annuity contract.

History: S. 139.1(4)(*b*) was replaced by S.C. 2016, c. 12, s. 50(1), in force January 1, 2017, and formerly read:

(*b*) no amount paid or payable to a stakeholder in connection with the disposition, alteration or dilution of the stakeholder's ownership rights in the particular corporation is an eligible capital expenditure;

Related Sections: S. 14(5), "eligible capital expenditure".

▶ 139.1(5) ◀

(5) Fair market value of ownership rights. For the purposes of section 70, subsection 104(4) and section 128.1, where an insurance corporation makes, at any time, a public announcement that it intends to seek approval for its demutualization, the fair market value of ownership rights in the corporation is deemed to be nil throughout the period that

(*a*) begins at that time; and

(*b*) ends either at the time of the demutualization or, in the event that the corporation makes at any subsequent time a public announcement that it no longer intends to demutualize, at the subsequent time.

▶ 139.1(6) ◀

(6) Paid-up capital — insurance corporation. Where an insurance corporation resident in Canada has demutualized, in computing the paid-up capital at any particular time in respect of a class of shares of the capital stock of the corporation,

(*a*) there shall be deducted the total of all amounts each of which would, but for this subsection, have been deemed by subsection 84(1) to have been paid at or before the particular time by the corporation as a dividend on a share of that class because of an increase in paid-up capital (determined without reference to this subsection) in connection with the demutualization; and

(*b*) there shall be added the amount, if any, by which

(i) the total of all amounts each of which is deemed by subsection 84(3), (4) or (4.1) to be a dividend on shares of that class paid by the corporation before the particular time

exceeds

(ii) the total of all amounts each of which would be deemed by subsection 84(3), (4) or (4.1) to be a dividend on shares of that class paid by the corporation before the particular time, if this Act were read without reference to this subsection.

Related Sections: S. 89(1), "paid-up capital".

▶ 139.1(7) ◀

(7) Paid-up capital — holding corporation. Where a particular corporation resident in Canada was at any time a holding corporation in connection with the demutualization of an insurance corporation, in computing the paid-up capital at any particular time in respect of a class of shares of the capital stock of the particular corporation,

(*a*) there shall be deducted the total of all amounts each of which is an amount by which the paid-up capital would, but for this subsection, have increased at or before the particular time as a result of the acquisition of shares of a class of the capital stock of the insurance corporation from the corporation on its demutualization; and

(*b*) there shall be added the amount, if any, by which

(i) the total of all amounts each of which is deemed by subsection 84(3), (4) or (4.1) to be a dividend on shares of that class paid by the particular corporation before the particular time

exceeds

(ii) the total of all amounts each of which would be deemed by subsection 84(3), (4) or (4.1) to be a dividend on shares of that class paid by the particular corporation before the particular time, if this Act were read without reference to this subsection.

▶ 139.1(8) ◀

(8) Policy dividends. Where the payment of a policy dividend by an insurance corporation is a taxable conversion benefit,

(*a*) for the purposes of this Act other than this section, the policy dividend is deemed not to be a policy dividend; and

(*b*) no amount in respect of the policy dividend may be included, either explicitly or implicitly, in the calculation of an amount deductible by the insurer for any taxation year under paragraph 20(7)(*c*) or subsection 138(3).

▶ 139.1(9) ◀

(9) Payment and receipt of premium. Where, in connection with the demutualization of an insurance corporation, a person would, if subsection (2) were read without reference to paragraphs (*f*) and (*g*) and paragraph (3)(*a*) were read without reference to the application of subsection 147.4(2), receive a particular benefit that is a specified insurance benefit,

(*a*) the insurance corporation that is obligated to pay benefits under the policy to which the particular benefit relates is deemed to have received a premium at the time of the demutualization in respect of that policy equal to the value of the particular benefit;

(*b*) for the purpose of paragraph (*a*), to the extent that the obligations of a particular insurance corporation under the policy were assumed by another insurance corporation before the time of the demutualization, the particular corporation is deemed not to be obligated to pay benefits under the policy; and

(*c*) subject to paragraph (15)(*e*), where the person receives the particular benefit, the person is deemed to have paid, at the time of demutualization, a premium in respect of the policy to which the benefit relates equal to the value of the particular benefit.

▶ 139.1(10) ◀

(10) Cost of taxable conversion benefit. Where, in connection with the demutualization of an insurance corporation, a stakeholder receives a taxable conversion benefit (other than a specified insurance benefit), the stakeholder is deemed to have acquired the benefit at a cost equal to the value of the benefit.

▶ 139.1(11) ◀

(11) No shareholder benefit. Subsection 15(1) does not apply to a conversion benefit.

▶ 139.1(12) ◀

(12) Exclusion of benefit from RRSP and other rules. Subject to subsection (14), for the purposes of the provisions of this Act (other than paragraph (9)(*c*)) that relate to registered retirement savings plans, registered retirement income funds, retirement compensation arrangements, deferred profit sharing plans and superannuation or pension funds or plans, the receipt of a conversion benefit shall be considered to be neither a contribution to, nor a distribution from, such a plan, fund or arrangement.

▶ 139.1(13) ◀

(13) RRSP registration rules, etc. For the purposes of this Act, paragraphs 146(2)(*c*.4) and 146.3(2)(*g*) and subsection 198(6) shall be applied without reference to any conversion benefit.

▶ 139.1(14) ◀

(14) Retirement benefit. A conversion benefit received because of an interest in a life insurance policy held by a trust governed by a registered retirement savings plan, registered retirement income fund, deferred profit sharing plan or superannuation or pension fund or plan is deemed to be received under the plan or fund, as the case may be, if it is received by any person (other than the trust).

▶ 139.1(15) ◀

(15) Employee-paid insurance. Where

(*a*) a stakeholder receives a conversion benefit because of the stakeholder's interest in a group insurance policy under which individuals have been insured in the course of or because of their employment,

(*b*) at all times before the payment of a premium described in paragraph (*c*), the full cost of a particular insurance coverage under the policy was borne by the individuals who were insured under the particular coverage,

(*c*) the stakeholder pays a premium under the policy in respect of the particular coverage or under another group insurance policy in respect of coverage that has replaced the particular coverage, and

(*d*) either

(i) the premium is deemed by paragraph (9)(*c*) to have been paid, or

(ii) it is reasonable to conclude that the purpose of the premium is to apply, for the benefit of the individuals who are insured under the particular coverage or the replacement coverage, all or part of the value of the portion of the conversion benefit that can reasonably be considered to be in respect of the particular coverage,

the following rules apply:

(*e*) for the purposes of paragraph 6(1)(*f*) and regulations made for the purposes of subsection 6(4), the premium is deemed to be an amount paid by the individuals who are insured under the particular coverage or the replacement coverage, as the case may be, and not to be an amount paid by the stakeholder, and

(*f*) no amount may be deducted in respect of the premium in computing the stakeholder's income.

▶ 139.1(16) ◀

(16) Flow-through of conversion benefits to employees and others. Where

(*a*) a stakeholder receives a conversion benefit (in this subsection referred to as the "relevant conversion benefit") because of the interest of any person in an insurance policy,

(*b*) the stakeholder makes a payment of an amount (otherwise than by way of a transfer of a share that was received by the stakeholder as all or part of the relevant conversion benefit and that was not so received as a taxable conversion benefit) to a particular individual

(i) who has received benefits under the policy,

(ii) who has, or had at any time, an absolute or contingent right to receive benefits under the policy,

(iii) for whose benefit insurance coverage was provided under the policy, or

(iv) who received the amount because an individual satisfied the condition in subparagraph (i), (ii) or (iii),

(*c*) it is reasonable to conclude that the purpose of the payment is to distribute an amount in respect of the relevant conversion benefit to the particular individual,

(*d*) either

(i) the main purpose of the policy was to provide retirement benefits or insurance coverage to individuals in respect of their employment with an employer, or

(ii) all or part of the cost of insurance coverage under the policy had been borne by individuals (other than the stakeholder),

(*e*) subsection (14) does not apply to the relevant conversion benefit, and

(*f*) one of the following applies, namely,

(i) the particular individual is resident in Canada at the time of the payment, the stakeholder is a person the taxable income of which is exempt from tax under this Part and the payment would, if this section were read without reference to this subsection, be included in computing the income of the particular individual,

(ii) the payment is received before December 7, 1999, and the stakeholder elects in writing filed with the Minister, on a day that is not more than six months after the end of the taxation year in which the stakeholder receives the relevant conversion benefit (or a later day acceptable to the Minister), that this subsection applies in respect of the payment,

(iii) the payment is received after December 6, 1999, the payment would, if this section were read without reference to this subsection, be included in computing the income of the particular individual and the stakeholder elects in writing filed with the Minister, on a day that is not more than six months after the end of the taxation year in which the stakeholder receives the relevant conversion benefit (or a later day acceptable to the Minister), that this subsection applies in respect of the payment, or

(iv) the payment is received after December 6, 1999 and the payment would, if this section were read without reference to this subsection, not be included in computing the income of the particular individual,

the following rules apply:

(*g*) subject to paragraph (*l*), no amount is, because of the making of the payment, deductible in computing the stakeholder's income,

(*h*) except for the purpose of this subsection and without affecting the consequences to the particular individual of any transaction or event that occurs after the time that the payment was made, the payment is deemed not to have been received by, or made payable to, the particular individual,

(*i*) the corporation that conferred the relevant conversion benefit is deemed to have paid to the particular individual at the time the payment was made, and the particular individual is deemed to have received at that time, a dividend on shares of the capital stock of the corporation equal to the amount of the payment,

(*j*) all obligations that would, but for this subsection, be imposed by this Act or the Regulations on the corporation because of the payment of the dividend apply to the stakeholder as if the stakeholder were the corporation, and do not apply to the corporation,

(*k*) where the relevant conversion benefit is a taxable conversion benefit, except for the purpose of this subsection and the purposes of determining the obligations imposed by this Act or the Regulations on the corporation because of the conferral of the relevant conversion benefit, the stakeholder is deemed, to the extent of the fair market value of the payment, not to have received the relevant conversion benefit, and

(*l*) where the relevant conversion benefit was a share received by the stakeholder (otherwise than as a taxable conversion benefit),

(i) where the share is, at the time of the payment, capital property held by the stakeholder, the amount of the payment shall, after that time, be added in computing the adjusted cost base to the stakeholder of the share,

(ii) where subparagraph (i) does not apply and the share was capital property disposed of by the stakeholder before that time, the amount of the payment is deemed to be a capital loss of the stakeholder from the disposition of a property for the taxation year of the stakeholder in which the payment is made, and

(iii) in any other case, paragraph (*g*) shall not apply to the payment.

Related Sections: S. 53(1)(*d*.01) Adjustments to cost base — Share of demutualized insurer; s. 54, "adjusted cost base".

► 139.1(17) ◄

(17) Flow-through of share benefits to employees and others. Where

(*a*) because of the interest of any person in an insurance policy, a stakeholder receives a conversion benefit (other than a taxable conversion benefit) that consists of shares of the capital stock of a corporation,

(*b*) the stakeholder transfers some or all of the shares at any time to a particular individual

(i) who has received benefits under the policy,

(ii) who has, or had at any time, an absolute or contingent right to receive benefits under the policy,

(iii) for whose benefit insurance coverage was provided under the policy, or

(iv) who received the shares because an individual satisfied the condition in subparagraph (i), (ii) or (iii), (*c*) it is reasonable to conclude that the purpose of the transfer is to distribute all or any portion of the conversion benefit to the particular individual,

(*d*) either

(i) the main purpose of the policy was to provide retirement benefits or insurance coverage to individuals in respect of their employment with an employer, or

(ii) all or part of the cost of insurance coverage under the policy had been borne by individuals (other than the stakeholder),

(*e*) subsection (14) does not apply to the conversion benefit, and

(*f*) one of the following applies, namely,

(i) the particular individual is resident in Canada at the time of the transfer, the stakeholder is a person the taxable income of which is exempt from tax under this Part and the amount of the transfer would, if this section were read without reference to this subsection, be included in computing the income of the particular individual,

(ii) the transfer is made before December 7, 1999 and the stakeholder elects in writing filed with the Minister, on a day that is not more than six months after the end of the taxation year in which the stakeholder receives the conversion benefit (or a later day acceptable to the Minister), that this subsection applies in respect of the transfer,

(iii) the transfer is made after December 6, 1999, the amount of the transfer would, if this section were read without reference to this subsection, be included in computing the income of the particular individual and the stakeholder elects in writing filed with the Minister, on a day that is not more than six months after the end of the taxation year in which the stakeholder receives the conversion benefit (or a later day acceptable to the Minister), that this subsection applies in respect of the transfer, or

(iv) the transfer is made after December 6, 1999 and the amount of the transfer would, if this section were read without reference to this subsection, not be included in computing the income of the particular individual,

the following rules apply:

(*g*) no amount is, because of the transfer, deductible in computing the stakeholder's income,

(*h*) except for the purpose of this subsection and without affecting the consequences to the particular individual of any transaction or event that occurs after the time that the transfer was made, the transfer is deemed not to have been made to the particular individual nor to represent an amount payable to the particular individual, and

(*i*) the cost of the shares to the particular individual is deemed to be nil.

► 139.1(18) ◄

(18) Acquisition of control. For the purposes of subsections 10(10), 13(21.2) and (24) and 18(15), sections 18.1 and 37, subsection 40(3.4), the definition "superficial loss" in section 54, section 55, subsections 66(11), (11.4) and (11.5), 66.5(3) and 66.7(10) and (11), section 80, paragraph 80.04(4)(*h*), subsections 85(1.2) and 88(1.1) and (1.2), sections 111 and 127 and subsections 249(4) and 256(7), control of an insurance corporation (and each corporation controlled by it) is deemed not to be acquired solely because of the acquisition of shares of the capital stock of the insurance corporation, in connection with the demutualization of the insurance corporation, by a particular corporation that at a particular time becomes a holding corporation in connection with the demutualization where, immediately after the particular time,

(*a*) the particular corporation is not controlled by any person or group of persons; and

(*b*) 95% of the fair market value of all the assets of the particular corporation is less than the total of all amounts each of which is

(i) the amount of the particular corporation's money,

(ii) the amount of a deposit, with a financial institution, of such money standing to the credit of the particular corporation,

(iii) the fair market value of a bond, debenture, note or similar obligation that is owned by the particular corporation that had, at the time of its acquisition, a maturity date of not more than 24 months after that time, or

(iv) the fair market value of a share of the capital stock of the insurance corporation held by the particular corporation.

History: S. 139.1(18), the portion before paragraph (*a*) was replaced by S.C. 2016, c. 12, s. 50(2), in force January 1, 2017, and formerly read:

S. (18) *Acquisition of control.* For the purposes of subsections 10(10), 13(21.2) and (24), 14(12) and 18(15), sections 18.1 and 37, subsection 40(3.4), the definition "superficial loss" in section 54, section 55, subsections 66(11), (11.4) and (11.5), 66.5(3) and 66.7(10) and (11), section 80, paragraph 80.04(4)(*h*), subsections 85(1.2) and 88(1.1) and (1.2), sections 111 and 127 and subsections 249(4) and 256(7), control of an insurance corporation (and each corporation controlled by it) is deemed not to be acquired solely because of the acquisition of shares of the capital stock of the insurance corporation, in connection with the demutualization of the insurance corporation, by a particular corporation that at a particular time becomes a holding corporation in connection with the demutualization where, immediately after the particular time,

SECTION 139.2: Mutual holding corporations

Where at any time a mutual holding corporation (as defined in subsection 139.1(1)) in respect of an insurance corporation distributes property to a policyholder of the insurance corporation, the mutual holding corporation is deemed to have paid, and the policyholder is deemed to have received from the mutual holding corporation, at that time a dividend on shares of the capital stock of the mutual holding corporation, equal to the fair market value of the property.

Related Sections: S. 212.2 Deemed dividend.

SECTION 140: [Income deduction and inclusion]

► 140(1) ◄

(1) Deductions in computing income. In computing the income for a taxation year of an insurance corporation, whether a mutual corporation or a joint stock company, from carrying on an insurance business other than a life insurance business, there may be deducted every amount credited in respect of that business for the year or a preceding taxation year to a policyholder of the corporation by way of a policy dividend, refund of premiums or refund of premium deposits if the amount was, during the year or within 12 months thereafter,

(*a*) paid or unconditionally credited to the policyholder; or

(*b*) applied in discharge, in whole or in part, of a liability of the policyholder to pay premiums to the corporation.

Related Sections: S. 138(3) Deductions allowed in computing income; s. 248(1), "amount", "business", "corporation", "insurance corporation", "life insurance business", "policy dividend".

▶ 140(2) ◀

(2) Inclusion in computing income. There shall be included in computing the income of an insurance corporation, whether a mutual corporation or a joint stock company, from carrying on an insurance business for its first taxation year that commences after June 17, 1987 and ends after 1987 (in this subsection referred to as its "1988 taxation year") the amount, if any, by which

(*a*) the total of all amounts each of which is an amount deducted by the corporation in computing its income for a taxation year ending before its 1988 taxation year pursuant to paragraph 140(*c*) of the *Income Tax Act*, chapter 148 of the Revised Statutes of Canada, 1952, or pursuant to that paragraph by reason of subparagraph 138(3)(*a*)(v) of that Act as it read in respect of those taxation years in respect of amounts credited to the account of the policyholder on terms that the policyholder is entitled to payment thereof on or before the expiration or termination of the policy

exceeds

(*b*) the total of all amounts each of which is an amount paid or unconditionally credited to a policyholder or applied in discharge, in whole or in part, of a liability of the policyholder to pay premiums to the corporation before the corporation's 1988 taxation year in respect of the amounts credited to the account of the policyholder referred to in paragraph (*a*).

SECTION 141: [Deemed public corporation]

▶ 141(1) ◀

(1) Definitions. In this section, "demutualization" and "holding corporation" have the same meaning as in subsection 139.1(1).

Related Sections: S. 89(1), "public corporation"; s. 138(1) Insurance corporations; s. 142 Taxable capital gains etc; s. 248(1), "life insurance corporation"; s. 255 Canada.

▶ 141(2) ◀

(2) Life insurance corporation deemed to be public corporation. Notwithstanding any other provision of this Act, a life insurance corporation that is resident in Canada is deemed to be a public corporation.

Related Sections: S. 89(1), "public corporation"; s. 248(1), "life insurance corporation".

▶ 141(3) ◀

(3) Holding corporation deemed to be public corporation. A corporation resident in Canada that is a holding corporation because of its acquisition of shares in connection with the demutualization of a life insurance corporation resident in Canada is deemed to be a public corporation at each time in the specified period of the holding corporation at which the holding corporation would have satisfied conditions prescribed under subparagraph (*b*)(i) of the definition "public corporation" in subsection 89(1) if the words "shareholders, the dispersal of ownership of its shares and the public trading of its shares" in that subparagraph were read as "shareholders and the dispersal of ownership of its shares".

Related Sections: S. 141(4) Specified period; s. 248(1), "life insurance corporation".

▶ 141(4) ◀

(4) Specified period. For the purpose of subsection (3), the specified period of a corporation

(*a*) begins at the time the corporation becomes a holding corporation; and

(*b*) ends at the first time the corporation is a public corporation because of any provision of this Act other than subsection (3).

▶ 141(5) ◀

(5) Exclusion from taxable Canadian property. For the purpose of paragraph (*d*) of the definition "taxable Canadian property" in subsection 248(1), a share of the capital stock of a corporation is deemed to be listed at any time on a designated stock exchange if

(*a*) the corporation is

(i) a life insurance corporation resident in Canada that has demutualized and that, at that time, would have satisfied conditions prescribed under subparagraph (*b*)(i) of the definition "public corporation" in subsection 89(1) if the words "shareholders, the dispersal of ownership of its shares and the public trading of its shares" in that subparagraph were read as "shareholders and the dispersal of ownership of its shares", or

(ii) a holding corporation that is deemed by subsection (3) to be a public corporation at that time;

(*b*) no share of the capital stock of the corporation is listed on any stock exchange at that time; and

(*c*) that time is not later than six months after the time of the demutualization of

(i) the corporation, where the corporation is a life insurance corporation, and

(ii) in any other case, the life insurance corporation in respect of which the corporation is a holding corporation.

SECTION 141.1: Deemed not to be a private corporation

Notwithstanding any other provision of this Act, an insurance corporation (other than a life insurance corporation) that would, but for this section, be a private corporation is deemed not to be a private corporation for the purposes of subsection 55(5), the definition "capital dividend account" in subsection 89(1) and sections 123.3 and 129.

Related Sections: S. 89(1), "Private corporation"; s. 141(2) Life insurance corporation deemed to be public corporation; s. 248(1), "insurance company", "life insurance company".

SECTION 142: Taxable capital gains etc

(Repealed by S.C. 1997, c. 25, s. 40(1).)

SECTION 142.1: Application of s. 138(12)

(Repealed by S.C. 1997, c. 25, s. 40(1).)

Financial Institutions Interpretation

SECTION 142.2: [Interpretation]

▶ 142.2(1) ◀

(1) Definitions. In this section and sections 142.3 to 142.7,

"excluded property" —"excluded property" of a taxpayer for a taxation year means property, held at any time in the taxation year by the taxpayer, that is

(*a*) a share of the capital stock of a corporation if, at any time in the taxation year, the taxpayer has a significant interest in the corporation;

(*b*) a property that is, at all times in the taxation year at which the taxpayer held the property, a prescribed payment card corporation share of the taxpayer, (*c*) if the taxpayer is an investment dealer, a property that is, at all times in the taxation year at which the taxpayer held the property, a prescribed securities exchange investment of the taxpayer,

(*d*) a share of the capital stock of a corporation if

(i) control of the corporation is, at any time (referred to in this paragraph as the "acquisition of control time") that is in the 24-month period that begins immediately after the end of the year, acquired by

(A) the taxpayer,

(B) one or more persons related to the taxpayer (otherwise than by reason of a right referred to in paragraph 251(5)(*b*)), or

(C) the taxpayer and one or more persons described in clause (B), and

(ii) the taxpayer elects in writing to have subparagraph (i) apply and files the election with the Minister on or before the taxpayer's filing-due date for the taxpayer's taxation year that includes the acquisition of control time, or

(*e*) a prescribed property;

History: S. 142.2(1), the definition "excluded property" was added by S.C. 2009, c. 2, s. 46(4), applicable to taxation years that begin after September 2006 except that any election made under paragraph (*d*) of the definition "excluded property" is deemed to have been made on a timely basis if it is filed with the Minister of National Revenue on or before the taxpayer's filing-due date for the taxpayer's taxation year in which this Act is assented to [R.A. March 12, 2009].

Related Regulations: 9001(2); 9002; 9002.1.

Related Sections: 10.1(4) Application; S. 142.2(2), "significant interest"; s. 142.2(3) Rules re significant interest; s. 152(6.2) Extended reassessment period; s. 251(5)(*b*) Control by related groups, options, etc.

"fair value property" —"fair value property" of a taxpayer for a taxation year means property, held at any time in the taxation year by the taxpayer, that is — or it is reasonable to expect would, if the taxpayer held the property at the end of the taxation year, be — valued (otherwise than solely because its fair value was less than its cost to the taxpayer or, if the property is a specified debt obligation, because of a default of the debtor) in accordance with generally accepted accounting principles, at its fair value (determined in accordance with those principles) in the taxpayer's balance sheet as at the end of the taxation year;

History: S. 142.2(1), the definition "fair value property" was added by S.C. 2009, c. 2, s. 46(4), applicable to taxation years that begin after September 2006.

Related Sections: S. 142.2(1), "specified debt obligation".

"financial institution" —"financial institution" at any time means

(*a*) a corporation that is, at that time,

(i) a corporation referred to in any of paragraphs (*a*) to (*e*.1) of the definition "restricted financial institution" in subsection 248(1),

(ii) an investment dealer, or

(iii) a corporation controlled by one or more persons or partnerships each of which is a financial institution at that time, other than a corporation the control of which was acquired by reason of the default of a debtor where it is reasonable to consider that control is being retained solely for the purpose of minimizing any losses in respect of the debtor's default, and

(*b*) a trust or partnership more than 50% of the fair market value of all interests in which are held at that time by one or more financial institutions,

but does not include

(*c*) a corporation that is, at that time,

(i) an investment corporation,

(ii) a mortgage investment corporation,

(iii) a mutual fund corporation, or

(iv) a deposit insurance corporation (as defined in subsection 137.1(5)),

(*d*) a trust that is a mutual fund trust at that time, nor

(*e*) a prescribed person or partnership;

Department of Finance Comfort Letters (June 18, 2018) [XXXX and Mark-to-Market Rules]

Dear Mr. XXXX:

I am writing in respect of an issue raised in discussions between you and officials of the Department concerning the role of XXXX in promoting capital investments in the agricultural sector. As part of its mandate, XXXX supports venture capital funds (the Funds), structured as partnerships; that seek to ensure that higher risk venture capital is available to innovative agricultural firms.

The issue you raised concerns the potential tax implications of XXXX's involvement in the Funds for private sector investors in the Funds. Specifically, there is a concern that XXXX's participation in the Funds, as an investor, would engage several aspects of the mark-to-market rules in the *Income Tax Act* (the Act). In general terms, the mark-to-market rules provide certainty in respect of the character and timing of gain and loss recognition on certain investment property owned by financial institutions. Under these rules, the increase or decrease in the value of this investment property each taxation year must be recognized as income or as a loss for income tax purposes in the year.

You have noted that XXXX would be characterized as a "financial institution" as that term is defined in subsection 142.2(1) of the Act, and that it would therefore be subject to the mark-to-market rules. You have also indicated that XXXX is, at least in the early years of the Funds, expected to hold over 50 per cent of the fair market value of all interests in each of the Funds. Since paragraph (*b*) of the definition "financial institution" refers to a trust or partnership more than 50 per cent of the fair market value of all interests in which are held at any time by one or more financial institutions, you have concluded that the Funds (at least in their early years) would also be characterized as financial institutions under the mark- to-market rules because of XXXX's participation. As such, they would be required to recognize in each taxation year the increase or decrease in the value of their "mark-to-market property" (as defined in subsection 142.2(1) of the Act).

You are concerned that some private sector investors in the Funds, while not characterized as financial institutions under the mark-to-market rules, might still indirectly be impacted by the rules by virtue of the Funds being financial institutions. Specifically, since the Funds are structured as partnerships, all taxable investors in the Funds would be required to include in their income each year all accrued gains allocated to them for that year. You have noted that XXXX is a tax-exempt corporation under subsection 149(1) of the Act and that its tax position is therefore not impacted by the mark-to-market rules. As such, you question whether it is appropriate in tax policy terms for the status of a corporation that is itself exempt from tax to influence the tax position of other entities by virtue of the mark-to-market rules.

Based on the foregoing, we agree that XXXX's participation in the Funds should not give rise to the application of the mark-to-market rules to the Funds. Accordingly, we are prepared to recommend to the Minister of Finance an amendment that would prevent XXXX from being treated as a financial institution for the purposes of the mark-to-market rules.

We would recommend that this amendment apply to the 2016 and subsequent taxation years.

While I cannot offer any assurance that the Minister will agree with our recommendation, I hope that that [*sic*] this statement of our intention is helpful to you.

Yours sincerely,

Brian Ernewein

General Director — Legislation

Tax Policy Branch

Editorial Note: S. 142.2 to 142.6 apply only to financial institutions. The intention of these sections is to standardize the tax treatment of securities held by financial institutions, and to force financial institutions to realize annually gains and losses accrued on certain types of securities. The rules apply to two types of property held by financial institutions: (i) "specified debt obligations" and (ii) "mark-to-market property." Certain segregated funds maintained by life insurers are prescribed to be excluded from this definition by virtue of Regulation 9000 if created less than two years before the relevant time and where the cost of the insurer's interest is $5 million or less. This exclusion generally allows a period during which an insurer can start-up a segregated fund without the fund initially being subject to the rules in s. 142.2 to 142.6. Additional exclusions listed in Part XC of the Regulations exist in respect of "qualified small business corporation" shares, certain sovereign debt, lending assets and "term preferred shares".

Related Regulations: 9000.

Related Sections: 10.1(1) Mark-to-market election; S. 20(1)(*l*)(ii) Doubtful or impaired debts; s. 20(1)(*p*)(ii)(B) Bad debts; s. 85(1.4) Definitions; s. 87(1.5) Definitions; s. 87(2)(*e.3*) Financial institutions — specified debt obligation; s. 87(2)(*e.4*) Financial institutions — mark-to-market property; s. 112(5.6) Stop-loss rules restricted; s. 112(6)(*c*) Meaning of certain expressions; s. 142.6(1) Becoming or ceasing to be a financial institution; s. 248(1), "investment corporation", "mortgage investment corporation", "mutual fund corporation", "mutual fund trust".

"investment dealer" — "investment dealer" at any time means a corporation that is, at that time, a registered securities dealer;

Related Sections: S. 142.2(1), "financial institution", "mark-to-market property"; s. 248(1), "registered securities dealer".

"mark-to-market property" — "mark-to-market property" of a taxpayer for a taxation year means property (other than an excluded property) held at any time in the taxation year by the taxpayer that is

(*a*) a share,

(*b*) if the taxpayer is not an investment dealer, a specified debt obligation that is a fair value property of the taxpayer for the taxation year,

(*c*) if the taxpayer is an investment dealer, a specified debt obligation, or

(*d*) a tracking property of the taxpayer that is a fair value property of the taxpayer for the taxation year;

Editorial Note: Pursuant to the rules in s. 142.5, financial institutions are required to "mark-to-market" certain types of securities on an annual basis, thereby realizing annually any accrued gains or losses. Moreover, the mark-to-market rules deny capital gains treatment for dispositions of most types of debt and equity, and requires that gains or losses realized on actual dispositions be on income account. Previously, some financial institutions were entitled to treat some types of investments as inventory, and so reflected their value annually at the lower of cost and market. This enabled the institutions to realize accrued losses, but to defer the realization of accrued gains until actual dispositions. Under the mark-to-market rules, both accrued gains and losses are realized annually.

History: S. 142.2(1), the definition "mark-to-market property" was replaced by S.C. 2009, c. 2, s. 46(3), applicable to taxation years that begin after September 2006 except that for taxation years that begin before November 7, 2007, the definition "mark-to-market property" in subsection 142.2(1) is to be read without its paragraph (*d*). S. 142.2(1), the definition "mark-to-market property" formerly read:

"mark-to-market property" — "mark-to-market property" of a taxpayer for a taxation year means property held by the taxpayer in the year that is

(*a*) a share,

(*b*) where the taxpayer is not an investment dealer, a specified debt obligation that

(i) was carried at fair market value in the taxpayer's financial statements

(A) for the year, where the taxpayer held the obligation at the end of the year, and

(B) for each preceding taxation year that ended after the taxpayer acquired the obligation, or

(ii) was acquired and disposed of in the year, where it is reasonable to expect that the obligation would have been carried in the taxpayer's financial statements for the year at fair market value if the taxpayer had not disposed of the obligation,

other than a specified debt obligation of the taxpayer that was (or would have been) carried at fair market value

(iii) solely because its fair market value was less than its cost to the taxpayer, or

(iv) because of a default of the debtor, and

(*c*) where the taxpayer is an investment dealer, a specified debt obligation,

but does not include

(*d*) a share of a corporation in which the taxpayer has a significant interest at any time in the year,

(*d.1*) a property that is, at all times in the year at which the taxpayer holds the property, a prescribed payment card corporation share of the taxpayer,

(*d.2*) if the taxpayer is an investment dealer and the year begins after 1998, a property that is, at all times in the year at which the taxpayer holds the property, a prescribed securities exchange investment of the taxpayer,

(*d.3*) a share of a corporation held, at any time in the year, by the taxpayer if

(i) control of the corporation is, at any time (referred to in this paragraph as the "acquisition of control time") that is after 2001 and is in the 24-month period that begins immediately after the end of the year, acquired by

(A) the taxpayer,

(B) one or more persons related to the taxpayer (otherwise than by reason of a right referred to in paragraph 251(5)(*b*)), or

(C) the taxpayer and one or more persons described in clause (B), and

(ii) the taxpayer elects in writing to have subparagraph (i) apply and files the election with the Minister on or before the taxpayer's filing-due date for the taxpayer's taxation year that includes the acquisition of control time, or

(*e*) a prescribed property;

S. 142.2(1), paragraph (*d*) of the definition "mark-to-market property" was replaced, and paragraphs (*d.1*), (*d.2*) and (*d.3*) were added, by S.C. 2009, c. 2, s. 46(2), applicable to taxation years that end after February 22, 1994, except that any election made under paragraph (*d.3*) of the definition "mark-to-market property" in subsection 142.2(1) is deemed to have been made on a timely basis if it is filed with the Minister of National Revenue on or before the taxpayer's filing-due date for the taxpayer's taxation year in which this Act is assented to [R.A. March 12, 2009]. S. 142.2(1), paragraph (*d*) of the definition "mark-to-market property" formerly read:

(*d*) a share of a corporation in which the taxpayer has a significant interest at any time in the year, nor

Related Regulations: 9001; 9002.

Related Sections: 10.1(1) Mark-to-market election; S. 85(1.4) Definitions; s. 87(1.5) Definitions; s. 87(2)(*e.3*) Financial institutions — specified debt obligation; s. 87(2)(*e.4*) Financial institutions — mark-to-market property; s. 112(6)(*c*) Meaning of certain expressions; s. 136(1) Cooperative not private corporation; s. 138(11.5)(*k.2*) Transfer of insurance business by non-resident insurer; s. 142.5 Mark-to-Market Properties.

"specified debt obligation" — "specified debt obligation" of a taxpayer means the interest held by the taxpayer in

(*a*) a loan, bond, debenture, mortgage, hypothecary claim, note, agreement of sale or any other similar indebtedness, or

(*b*) a debt obligation, where the taxpayer purchased the interest,

other than an interest in

(*c*) an income bond, an income debenture, a small business development bond, a small business bond or a prescribed property, or

(*d*) an instrument issued by or made with a person to whom the taxpayer is related or with whom the taxpayer does not otherwise deal at arm's length, or in which the taxpayer has a significant interest.

Editorial Note: Specified debt obligations held by financial institutions are governed by the rules contained in s. 142.3 to 142.4. Generally, s. 142.3 requires that a financial institution's total economic return on a specified debt obligation be included in income on an accrual basis. S. 142.4 requires that on a disposition of a specified debt obligation, the resulting profit or loss is generally required to be recognized on income account.

It is significant that this definition refers to the "interest" of a taxpayer in the particular types of indebtedness. The Department of Finance has indicated that this definition is not intended to include an interest in derivative instruments, such as interest rate or currency swaps. Neither "indebtedness" nor "debt obligation" is defined in the Act. The definition of "specified debt obligation" thus lacks both clarity and certainty. Similarly, mortgages and notes are not indebtedness, but are security for, or evidence of, indebtedness.

Related Regulations: 9004.

Related Sections: S. 85(1.4) Definitions; s. 87(1.5) Definitions; s. 87(2)(*e.3*) Financial institutions — specified debt obligation; s. 138(11.5)(*k.1*) Transfer of insurance business by non-resident insurer; s. 142.3 Income from Specified Debt Obligations; s. 142.4 Disposition of specified debt obligations; s. 248(1), ""income bond" or "income debenture"", "small business bond", "small business development bond"; s. 251(5)(*b*) Control by related groups, options, etc.

"tracking property" — "tracking property" of a taxpayer means property of the taxpayer the fair market value of which is determined primarily by reference to one or more criteria in respect of property (referred to in this definition as "tracked property") that, if owned by the taxpayer, would be mark-to-market property of the taxpayer, which criteria are

(*a*) the fair market value of the tracked property,

(*b*) the profits or gains from the disposition of the tracked property,

(*c*) the revenue, income or cash flow from the tracked property, or

(*d*) any other similar criteria in respect of the tracked property;

Editorial Note: The "tracking property" concept was introduced to prevent a financial institution from avoiding the mark-to-market regime by investing through an intermediary or through other forms of financial instruments (i.e., derivatives) that are designed to mirror the economic effect of one of the other enumerated categories of mark-to-market properties. The CRA has indicated that the definition of "tracking property" includes, but is not limited to, the following: certain trust investments, including mutual fund trusts or unit trusts; equity derivatives, or similar derivative instruments; and, American Depository Receipts or similar instruments. (See CRA Document No. 2009-0316681C6). See CRA Document No. 2009-0328781E5 for additional discussion of the tracking property concept.

History: S. 142.2(1), the definition "tracking property" was added by S.C. 2009, c. 2, s. 46(4), applicable to taxation years that begin after September 2006.

Related Sections: 10.1(4) Application.

► 142.2(2) ◄

(2) Significant interest. For the purposes of the definitions "excluded property" and "specified debt obligation" in subsection (1) and subsection 142.6(1.6), a taxpayer has a significant interest in a corporation at any time if

(*a*) the taxpayer is related (otherwise than because of a right referred to in paragraph 251(5)(*b*)) to the corporation at that time; or

(*b*) the taxpayer holds, at that time,

(i) shares of the corporation that give the taxpayer 10% or more of the votes that could be cast under all circumstances at an annual meeting of shareholders of the corporation, and

(ii) shares of the corporation having a fair market value of 10% or more of the fair market value of all the issued shares of the corporation.

History: S. 142.2(2), the portion before paragraph (*a*), was replaced by S.C. 2013, c. 40, s. 63, in force December 12, 2013, and formerly read:

(2) *Significant interest.* For the purposes of the definitions "excluded property", "mark-to-market property" and "specified debt obligation" in subsection (1) and subsections (5) and 142.6(1.6), a taxpayer has a significant interest in a corporation at any time if

S. 142.2(2), the portion before paragraph (*a*) was replaced by S.C. 2009, c. 2, s. 46(5), applicable to taxation years that begin after September 2006. S. 142.2(2), the portion before paragraph (*a*) formerly read:

(2) *Significant interest.* For the purpose of subsection (5) and the definition "mark-to-market property" in subsection (1), a taxpayer has a significant interest in a corporation at any time if

Related Sections: S. 251(5)(*b*) Control by related groups, options, etc.

► 142.2(3) ◄

(3) Rules re significant interest. For the purpose of determining under subsection (2) whether a taxpayer has a significant interest in a corporation at any time,

(*a*) the taxpayer shall be deemed to hold each share that is held at that time by a person or partnership to whom the taxpayer is related (otherwise than because of a right referred to in paragraph 251(5)(*b*));

(*b*) a share of the corporation acquired by the taxpayer by reason of the default of a debtor shall be disregarded where it is reasonable to consider that the share is being retained for the purpose of minimizing any losses in respect of the debtor's default; and

(*c*) a share of the corporation that is prescribed in respect of the taxpayer shall be disregarded.

Related Regulations: 9003.

Related Sections: S. 251(5)(*b*) Control by related groups, options, etc.

► 142.2(4) ◄

(4) Extension of meaning of "related". For the purposes of this subsection and subsections (2) and (3), in determining if, at a particular time, a person or partnership is related to another person or partnership, the rules in section 251 are to be applied as if,

(*a*) a partnership (other than a partnership in respect of which any amount of the income or capital of the partnership that any entity may receive directly from the partnership at any time as a member of the partnership depends on the exercise by any entity of, or the failure by any entity to exercise, a discretionary power) were a corporation having capital stock of a single class divided into 100 issued shares and each member of the partnership owned, at the particular time, that proportion of the issued shares of that class that

(i) the fair market value of the member's interest in the partnership at the particular time

is of

(ii) the fair market value of all interests in the partnership at the particular time; and

(*b*) a trust (other than a trust in respect of which any amount of the income or capital of the trust that any entity may receive directly from the trust at any time as a beneficiary under the trust depends on the exercise by any entity of, or the failure by any entity to exercise, a discretionary power) were a corporation having capital stock of a single class divided into 100 issued shares and each beneficiary under the trust owned, at the particular time, that proportion of the issued shares of that class that

(i) the fair market value of the beneficiary's beneficial interest in the trust at the particular time

is of

(ii) the fair market value at that time of all beneficial interests in the trust.

History: S. 142.2(4) was replaced by S.C. 2009, c. 2, s. 46(6), applicable to taxation years that begin after September 2006. S. 142.2(4) formerly read:

(4) *Extension of meaning of "related".* For the purposes of this subsection and subsections (2) and (3), a person or partnership shall be deemed to be related to a person or partnership where they would be related if, for the purpose of section 251,

(*a*) every partnership and trust were considered to be a corporation;

(*b*) subject to paragraph (*c*), all decisions relating to the conduct of a trust were made by majority vote of the beneficiaries of the trust, with each beneficiary having, at any time, a number of votes equal to the number determined by the formula

$$100 \times A/B$$

where

A is the fair market value at that time of the beneficiary's beneficial interest in the trust, and

B is the total of all amounts each of which is the fair market value at that time of a beneficial interest in the trust; and

(*c*) where the amount that would be determined for B in paragraph (*b*) in respect of a trust is nil, the trust were considered not to be controlled by any person, partnership or group each member of which is a person or partnership.

Related Sections: S. 251 Arm's length.

► 142.2(5) ◄

(5) Significant interest — transition — (Repealed by S.C. 2009, c. 2, s. 46(6).)

History: S. 142.2(5) was repealed by S.C. 2009, c. 2, s. 46(6), applicable to taxation years that begin after September 2006. S. 142.2(5) formerly read:

(5) *Significant interest— transition.* For the purpose of the definition "mark-to-market property" in subsection (1), where

(*a*) on October 31, 1994, a taxpayer whose 1994 taxation year ends after October 30, 1994 held a share of a corporation in which the taxpayer did not have a significant interest at any time in the year, and

(*b*) at any time after the end of the year and before May 1995, the taxpayer has a significant interest in the corporation,

the taxpayer has a significant interest in the corporation in the year and in any subsequent taxation year ending before the earliest time referred to in paragraph (*b*).

Income from Specified Debt Obligations

SECTION 142.3: Amounts to be included and deducted

▶ 142.3(1) ◀

(1) Amounts to be included and deducted. Subject to subsections (3) and (4), where a taxpayer that is, in a taxation year, a financial institution holds a specified debt obligation at any time in the year,

(*a*) there shall be included in computing the income of the taxpayer for the year the amount, if any, prescribed in respect of the obligation;

(*b*) there shall be deducted in computing the income of the taxpayer for the year the amount, if any, prescribed in respect of the obligation; and

(*c*) except as provided by this section, paragraphs 12(1)(*d*) and (i) and 20(1)(*l*) and (*p*) and section 142.4, no amount shall be included or deducted in respect of payments under the obligation (other than fees and similar amounts) in computing the income of the taxpayer for the year.

Editorial Note: Specified debt obligations that are not mark-to-market properties are subject to the income computation rules contained in s. 142.3 and the disposition rules contained in s. 142.4. As a specified debt obligation owned by an investment dealer is always a mark-to-market property, these provisions will only apply to specified debt obligations that are owned by financial institutions other than investment dealers.

Related Regulations: 9101.

Related Sections: S. 87(2)(*e.3*) Financial institutions — specified debt obligation; s. 138(10) Application of financial institution rules; s. 138(12), "gross investment revenue"; s. 142.4(1), "tax basis"; s. 142.4(9) Disposition of part of obligation.

▶ 142.3(2) ◀

(2) Failure to report accrued amounts. Subject to subsection (3), where

(*a*) a taxpayer holds a specified debt obligation at any time in a particular taxation year in which the taxpayer is a financial institution, and

(*b*) all or part of an amount required by paragraph (1)(*a*) or subsection 12(3) to be included in respect of the obligation in computing the taxpayer's income for a preceding taxation year was not so included,

that part of the amount shall be included in computing the taxpayer's income for the particular year, to the extent that it was not included in computing the taxpayer's income for a preceding taxation year.

Related Sections: S. 142.4(1), "tax basis".

▶ 142.3(3) ◀

(3) Exception for certain obligations. Subsections (1) and (2) do not apply for a taxation year in respect of a taxpayer's specified debt obligation that is

(*a*) a mark-to-market property for the year; or

(*b*) an indexed debt obligation, other than a prescribed obligation.

▶ 142.3(4) ◀

(4) Impaired specified debt obligations. Subsection (1) does not apply to a taxpayer in respect of a specified debt obligation for the part of a taxation year throughout which the obligation is impaired where an amount in respect of the obligation is deductible because of subparagraph 20(1)(*l*)(ii) in computing the taxpayer's income for the year.

Related Sections: S. 12(4.1) Impaired debt obligations; s. 16(7) Impaired indexed debt obligations.

Disposition of Specified Debt Obligations

SECTION 142.4: [Disposition of specified debt obligations]

▶ 142.4(1) ◀

(1) Definitions. In this section,

"tax basis" — "tax basis" of a specified debt obligation at any time to a taxpayer means the amount, if any, by which the total of all amounts each of which is

(*a*) the cost of the obligation to the taxpayer,

(*b*) an amount included under subsection 12(3) or 16(2) or (3), paragraph 142.3(1)(*a*) or subsection 142.3(2) in respect of the obligation in computing the taxpayer's income for a taxation year that began before that time,

(*c*) subject to subsection 138(13), where the taxpayer acquired the obligation in a taxation year ending before February 23, 1994, the part of the amount, if any, by which

(i) the principal amount of the obligation at the time it was acquired

exceeds

(ii) the cost to the taxpayer of the obligation

that was included in computing the taxpayer's income for a taxation year ending before February 23, 1994,

(*d*) subject to subsection 138(13), where the taxpayer is a life insurer, an amount in respect of the obligation that was deemed by paragraph 142(3)(*a*) of the *Income Tax Act*, chapter 148 of the Revised Statutes of Canada, 1952, as it read in its application to the 1977 taxation year, to be a gain for a taxation year ending before 1978,

(*e*) where the obligation is an indexed debt obligation, an amount determined under subparagraph 16(6)(*a*)(i) in respect of the obligation and included in computing the income of the taxpayer for a taxation year beginning before that time,

(*f*) an amount in respect of the obligation that was included in computing the taxpayer's income for a taxation year ending at or before that time in respect of changes in the value of the obligation attributable to the fluctuation in the value of a currency of a country other than Canada relative to Canadian currency, other than an amount included under paragraph 142.3(1)(*a*),

(*g*) an amount in respect of the obligation that was included under paragraph 12(1)(*i*) in computing the taxpayer's income for a taxation year beginning before that time, or

(*h*) where the obligation was a capital property of the taxpayer on February 22, 1994, an amount required by paragraph 53(1)(*f*) or (*f*.1) to be added in computing the adjusted cost base of the obligation to the taxpayer on that day

exceeds the total of all amounts each of which is

(*i*) an amount deducted under paragraph 142.3(1)(*b*) in respect of the obligation in computing the taxpayer's income for a taxation year beginning before that time,

(*j*) the amount of a payment received by the taxpayer under the obligation at or before that time, other than

(i) a fee or similar payment, and

(ii) proceeds of disposition of the obligation,

(*k*) subject to subsection 138(13), where the taxpayer acquired the obligation in a taxation year ending before February 23, 1994, the part of the amount, if any, by which

(i) the cost to the taxpayer of the obligation

exceeds

(ii) the principal amount of the obligation at the time it was acquired

that was deducted in computing the taxpayer's income for a taxation year ending before February 23, 1994,

(*l*) subject to subsection 138(13), where the taxpayer is a life insurer, an amount in respect of the obligation that was deemed by paragraph 142(3)(*b*) of the *Income Tax Act*, chapter 148 of the Revised Statutes of Canada, 1952, as it read in its application to the 1977 taxation year, to be a loss for a taxation year ending before 1978,

(*m*) an amount that was deducted under subsection 20(14) in respect of the obligation in computing the taxpayer's income for a taxation year beginning before that time,

(*n*) where the obligation is an indexed debt obligation, an amount determined under subparagraph 16(6)(*a*)(ii) in respect of the obligation and deducted in computing the income of the taxpayer for a taxation year beginning before that time,

(*o*) an amount in respect of the obligation that was deducted in computing the taxpayer's income for a taxation year ending at or before that time in respect of changes in the value of the obligation attributable to the fluctuation in the value of a currency of a country other than Canada relative to Canadian currency, other than an amount deducted under paragraph 142.3(1)(*b*),

(*p*) an amount in respect of the obligation that was deducted under paragraph 20(1)(*p*) in computing the taxpayer's income for a taxation year ending at or before that time, or

(*q*) where the obligation was a capital property of the taxpayer on February 22, 1994, an amount required by paragraph 53(2)(*b*.2) or (*g*) to be deducted in computing the adjusted cost base of the obligation to the taxpayer on that day;

Editorial Note: S. 142.4 provides the rules for measuring and timing gains and losses to financial institutions from the disposition of specified debt obligations, other than mark-to-market property. The general purpose of these provisions is that any gain or loss on the disposition of a specified debt obligation (other than a mark-to-market property) be realized on income account, calculated in accordance with specific rules, and amortized over the remaining period to the maturity date of the obligation. See Editorial Note to s. 142.2(1), "specified debt obligation."

Related Sections: S. 138(13) Variation in "tax basis" and "amortized cost"; s. 261(5)(*f*) Functional currency tax reporting.

"transition amount" — "transition amount" of a taxpayer in respect of the disposition of a specified debt obligation has the meaning assigned by regulation.

Related Regulations: 9201 Transition Amount.

► 142.4(2) ◄

(2) Scope of section. This section applies to the disposition of a specified debt obligation by a taxpayer that is a financial institution, except that this section does not apply to the disposition of a specified debt obligation that is a mark-to-market property for the taxation year in which the disposition occurs.

Related Sections: S. 87(2)(*e.3*) Financial institutions — specified debt obligation; s. 138(10) Application of financial institution rules; s. 142.3(1) Amounts to be included and deducted.

► 142.4(3) ◄

(3) Rules applicable to disposition. Where a taxpayer has disposed of a specified debt obligation after February 22, 1994,

(*a*) except as provided by paragraph 79.1(7)(*d*) or this section, no amount shall be included or deducted in respect of the disposition in computing the taxpayer's income; and

(*b*) except where the obligation is an indexed debt obligation (other than a prescribed obligation), paragraph 20(14)(*a*) shall not apply in respect of the disposition.

► 142.4(4) ◄

(4) Inclusions and deductions re disposition. Subject to subsection (5), where after 1994 a taxpayer disposes of a specified debt obligation in a taxation year,

(*a*) where the transition amount in respect of the disposition of the obligation is positive, it shall be included in computing the income of the taxpayer for the year;

(*b*) where the transition amount in respect of the disposition of the obligation is negative, the absolute value of the transition amount shall be deducted in computing the income of the taxpayer for the year;

(*c*) where the taxpayer has a gain from the disposition of the obligation,

(i) the current amount of the gain shall be included in computing the income of the taxpayer for the year, and

(ii) there shall be included in computing the taxpayer's income for taxation years that end on or after the day of disposition the amount allocated, in accordance with prescribed rules, to the year in respect of the residual portion of the gain; and

(*d*) where the taxpayer has a loss from the disposition of the obligation,

(i) the current amount of the loss shall be deducted in computing the taxpayer's income for the year, and

(ii) there shall be deducted in computing the taxpayer's income for taxation years that end on or after the day of disposition the amount allocated, in accordance with prescribed rules, to the year in respect of the residual portion of the loss.

Related Regulations: 9204.

Related Sections: S. 39(1)(*a*)(ii.2) Meaning of capital gain and capital loss; s. 87(2)(*g.2*) Financial institution rules.

▶ 142.4(5) ◀

(5) Gain or loss not amortized. Where after February 22, 1994 a taxpayer disposes of a specified debt obligation in a taxation year, and

(*a*) the obligation is

(i) an indexed debt obligation (other than a prescribed obligation), or

(ii) a debt obligation prescribed in respect of the taxpayer,

(*b*) the disposition occurred

(i) before 1995,

(ii) after 1994 in connection with the transfer of all or part of a business of the taxpayer to a person or partnership, or

(iii) because of paragraph 142.6(1)(*c*), or

(*c*) in the case of a taxpayer other than a life insurance corporation,

(i) the disposition occurred before 1996, and

(ii) the taxpayer elects in writing, filed with the Minister before July 1997, to have this paragraph apply,

the following rules apply:

(*d*) subsection (4) does not apply to the disposition,

(*e*) there shall be included in computing the taxpayer's income for the year the amount, if any, by which the taxpayer's proceeds of disposition exceed the tax basis of the obligation to the taxpayer immediately before the disposition, and

(*f*) there shall be deducted in computing the taxpayer's income for the year the amount, if any, by which the tax basis of the obligation to the taxpayer immediately before the disposition exceeds the taxpayer's proceeds of disposition.

Related Regulations: 9202.

Related Sections: S. 39(1)(*a*)(ii.2) Meaning of capital gain and capital loss.

▶ 142.4(6) ◀

(6) Gain or loss from disposition of obligation. For the purposes of this section,

(*a*) where the amount determined under paragraph (*c*) in respect of the disposition of a specified debt obligation by a taxpayer is positive, that amount is the taxpayer's gain from the disposition of the obligation;

(*b*) where the amount determined under paragraph (*c*) in respect of the disposition of a specified debt obligation by a taxpayer is negative, the absolute value of that amount is the taxpayer's loss from the disposition of the obligation; and

(*c*) the amount determined under this paragraph in respect of the disposition of a specified debt obligation by a taxpayer is the positive or negative amount determined by the formula

$$A - (B + C)$$

where

A is the taxpayer's proceeds of disposition,

B is the tax basis of the obligation to the taxpayer immediately before the time of disposition, and

C is the taxpayer's transition amount in respect of the disposition.

▶ 142.4(7) ◀

(7) Current amount. For the purposes of subsections (4) and (8), the current amount of a taxpayer's gain or loss from the disposition of a specified debt obligation is

(*a*) where the taxpayer has a gain from the disposition of the obligation, the part, if any, of the gain that is reasonably attributable to a material increase in the probability, or perceived probability, that the debtor will make all payments as required by the obligation; and

(*b*) where the taxpayer has a loss from the disposition of the obligation, the amount that the taxpayer claims not exceeding the part, if any, of the loss that is reasonably attributable to a default by the debtor or a material decrease in the probability, or perceived probability, that the debtor will make all payments as required by the obligation.

Editorial Note: Essentially, the "current amount" of a gain or loss from the disposition of a specified debt obligation is the credit related portion (the part of the gain or loss attributable to a material increase or decrease in the probability that the debtor will make all payments) of the gain or loss from the disposition of the obligation. The current amount which is positive whether there is a gain or a loss, is included in computing income for the year of disposition where a gain is realized on disposition, and where a loss is realized on disposition the current amount is deducted in computing income for the year of disposition.

The Department has not provided any guidance as to the circumstances in which a gain or loss will be considered "reasonably attributable" to a "material" increase or decrease in the creditworthiness of the debtor. Furthermore, the Department of Finance has indicated that the inclusion of credit-related losses in the current amount is intended to enable a financial institution to claim an immediate deduction for the bad or doubtful portion of the debt obligation. Without this provision, a financial institution could have an immediate inclusion of a doubtful debt reserve while being required to amortize a loss on the disposition over the following years until the maturity date of the obligation.

▶ 142.4(8) ◀

(8) Residual portion of gain or loss. For the purpose of subsection (4), the residual portion of a taxpayer's gain or loss from the disposition of a specified debt obligation is the amount, if any, by which the gain or loss exceeds the current amount of the gain or loss.

▶ 142.4(9) ◀

(9) Disposition of part of obligation. Where a taxpayer disposes of part of a specified debt obligation, section 142.3 and this section apply as if the part disposed of and the part retained were separate specified debt obligations.

Related Sections: S. 248(27) Parts of debt obligations.

▶ 142.4(10) ◀

(10) Penalties and bonuses. Notwithstanding subsection 18(9.1), where a taxpayer that holds a specified debt obligation receives a penalty or bonus because of the repayment before maturity of all or part of the principal amount of the debt obligation, the payment is deemed to be received by the taxpayer as proceeds of disposition of the specified debt obligation.

▶ 142.4(11) ◀

(11) Payments received on or after disposition. For the purposes of this section, where at any time a taxpayer receives a payment (other than proceeds of disposition) under a specified debt obligation on or after the disposition of the obligation, the payment is deemed not to have been so received at that time but to have been so received immediately before the disposition.

Mark-to-Market Properties

SECTION 142.5: Income treatment for profits and losses

► 142.5(1) ◄

(1) Income treatment for profits and losses. Where, in a taxation year that begins after October 1994, a taxpayer that is a financial institution in the year disposes of a property that is a mark-to-market property for the year,

(*a*) there shall be included in computing the taxpayer's income for the year the profit, if any, from the disposition; and

(*b*) there shall be deducted in computing the taxpayer's income for the year the loss, if any, from the disposition.

Editorial Note: Whereas s. 142.3 and 142.4 relate to income and gain recognition respectively in relation to a "specified debt obligation" that is not a "mark-to-market property", s. 142.5 provides the rules that apply to "mark-to-market property." The general rule under s. 142.5 is that any gain or loss of a financial institution from the disposition of a mark-to-market property is to be included in computing the financial institution's income for the year. See Editorial Note to s. 142.2(1), "mark-to-market property."

Related Sections: S. 39(1)(*a*)(ii.2) Meaning of capital gain and capital loss; s. 138(10) Application of financial institution rules; s. 142.2(1), "financial institution", "mark-to-market property".

► 142.5(2) ◄

(2) Mark-to-market requirement. Where a taxpayer that is a financial institution in a taxation year holds, at the end of the year, a mark-to-market property for the year, the taxpayer shall be deemed

(*a*) to have disposed of the property immediately before the end of the year for proceeds equal to its fair market value at the time of disposition, and

(*b*) to have reacquired the property at the end of the year at a cost equal to those proceeds.

Related Sections: S. 54, "superficial loss"; s. 88(1)(*i*) Winding-up; s. 112(5.6) Stop-loss rules restricted; s. 138(10) Application of financial institution rules; s. 138(11.31) Exclusion from deemed disposition; s. 142.2(1), "financial institution", "mark-to-market property".

► 142.5(3) ◄

(3) Mark-to-market debt obligation. Where a taxpayer is a financial institution in a particular taxation year that begins after October 1994, the following rules apply with respect to a specified debt obligation that is a mark-to-market property of the taxpayer for the particular year:

(*a*) paragraph 12(1)(*c*) and subsections 12(3) and 20(14) and (21) do not apply to the obligation in computing the taxpayer's income for the particular year;

(*b*) there shall be included in computing the taxpayer's income for the particular year an amount received by the taxpayer in the particular year as, on account of, in lieu of payment of, or in satisfaction of, interest on the obligation, to the extent that the interest was not included in computing the taxpayer's income for a preceding taxation year; and

(*c*) for the purpose of paragraph (*b*), where the taxpayer was deemed by subsection (2) or paragraph 142.6(1)(*b*) to have disposed of the obligation in a preceding taxation year, no part of an amount included in computing the income of the taxpayer for that preceding year because of the disposition shall be considered to be in respect of interest on the obligation.

Related Sections: S. 138(10) Application of financial institution rules; s. 142.2(1), "financial institution", "mark-to-market property", "specified debt obligation".

► 142.5(4) ◄

(4) Proceeds — mark-to-market property. For greater certainty, if a taxpayer is a financial institution in a taxation year and disposes of a share that is mark-to-market property of the taxpayer for the year, the taxpayer's proceeds from the disposition do not include any amount that would otherwise be proceeds from the disposition to the extent that the amount is deemed by subsection 84(2) or (3) to be a dividend received except to the extent the dividend is deemed by subparagraph 88(2)(*b*)(ii) not to be a dividend.

History: S. 142.5(4) was added by S.C. 2018, c. 27, s. 16(1), applicable in respect of dispositions that occur after February 26, 2018.

S. 142.5(4) was repealed by S.C. 2013, c. 34, s. 288(1), applicable to taxation years that begin after October 31, 2011, and formerly read:

(4) *Transition — deduction re non-capital amounts.* There may be deducted in computing the income of a taxpayer for the taxpayer's taxation year that includes October 31, 1994 such amount as the taxpayer claims not exceeding a prescribed amount in respect of properties (other than capital properties) disposed of by the taxpayer because of subsection (2).

Related Regulations: 8102.

Related Sections: S. 138(11.5)(*k*) Transfer of insurance business by non-resident insurer.

► 142.5(5) ◄

(5) Transition — inclusion re non-capital amounts — (Repealed by S.C. 2013, c. 34, s. 288(1).)

History: S. 142.5(5) was repealed by S.C. 2013, c. 34, s. 288(1), applicable to taxation years that begin after October 31, 2011, and formerly read:

(5) *Transition — inclusion re non-capital amounts.* Where an amount is deducted under subsection (4) in computing a taxpayer's income, there shall be included, in computing the taxpayer's income for each taxation year that begins before 1999 and ends after October 30, 1994, the total of all amounts prescribed for the year.

► 142.5(6) ◄

(6) Transition — deduction re net capital gains — (Repealed by S.C. 2013, c. 34, s. 288(1).)

History: S. 142.5(6) was repealed by S.C. 2013, c. 34, s. 288(1), applicable to taxation years that begin after October 31, 2011, and formerly read:

(6) *Transition — deduction re net capital gains.* Such amount as a taxpayer elects, not exceeding a prescribed amount in respect of capital properties disposed of by the taxpayer because of subsection (2), is deemed to be an allowable capital loss of the taxpayer for its taxation year that includes October 31, 1994 from the disposition of property (or, where the taxpayer is non-resident throughout the year, from the disposition of taxable Canadian property).

► 142.5(7) ◄

(7) Transition — inclusion re net capital gains — (Repealed by S.C. 2013, c. 34, s. 288(1).)

History: S. 142.5(7) was repealed by S.C. 2013, c. 34, s. 288(1), applicable to taxation years that begin after October 31, 2011, and formerly read:

(7) *Transition — inclusion re net capital gains.* A taxpayer that elects an amount under subsection (6) is deemed, for each taxation year that begins before 1999 and ends after October 30, 1994, to have a taxable capital gain for the year from the disposition of property (or, where the taxpayer is non-resident throughout the year, from the disposition of taxable Canadian property) equal to the total of all amounts prescribed for the year.

► 142.5(8) ◄

(8) First deemed disposition of debt obligation. Where

(*a*) in a particular taxation year that ends after October 30, 1994, a taxpayer disposed of a specified debt obligation that is a mark-to-market property of the taxpayer for the following taxation year, and

(*b*) either

(i) the disposition occurred because of subsection (2) and the particular year includes October 31, 1994, or

(ii) the disposition occurred because of paragraph 142.6(1)(*b*),

the following rules apply:

(*c*) subsection 20(21) does not apply to the disposition, and

(*d*) where

(i) an amount has been deducted under paragraph 20(1)(*p*) in respect of the obligation in computing the taxpayer's income for the particular year or a preceding taxation year, and

(ii) section 12.4 does not apply to the disposition,

there shall be included in computing the taxpayer's income for the particular year the amount, if any, by which

(iii) the total of all amounts referred to in subparagraph (i)

exceeds

(iv) the total of all amounts included under paragraph 12(1)(*i*) in respect of the obligation in computing the taxpayer's income for the particular year or a preceding taxation year.

► 142.5(8.1) ◄

(8.1) Application of subsection (8.2). Subsection (8.2) applies to a taxpayer for its transition year if

(*a*) subsection (2) deems the taxpayer to have disposed of a particular specified debt obligation immediately before the end of its transition year (in subsection (8.2) referred to as "the particular disposition"); and

(*b*) the particular specified debt obligation was owned by the taxpayer at the end of its base year and was not a mark-to-market property of the taxpayer for its base year.

History: S. 142.5(8.1) was added by S.C. 2009, c. 2, s. 47(1), applicable to taxation years that begin after September 2006.

Related Sections: S. 142.2(1), "mark-to-market property", "specified debt obligation"; s. 142.51(1), "base year", "transition amount", "transition property", "transition year".

► 142.5(8.2) ◄

(8.2) Rules applicable to first deemed disposition of debt obligation. If this subsection applies to a taxpayer for its transition year, the following rules apply to the taxpayer in respect of the particular disposition:

(*a*) subsection 20(21) does not apply to the taxpayer in respect of the particular disposition; and

(*b*) if section 12.4 does not apply to the taxpayer in respect of the particular disposition, there shall be included in computing the taxpayer's income for its transition year the amount, if any, by which

(i) the total of all amounts each of which is

(A) an amount deducted under paragraph 20(1)(*l*) in respect of the particular specified debt obligation of the taxpayer in computing the taxpayer's income for its base year, or

(B) an amount deducted under paragraph 20(1)(*p*) in respect of the particular specified debt obligation of the taxpayer in computing the taxpayer's income for a taxation year that preceded its transition year,

exceeds

(ii) the total of all amounts each of which is

(A) an amount included under paragraph 12(1)(*d*) in respect of the particular specified debt obligation of the taxpayer in computing the taxpayer's income for its transition year, or

(B) an amount included under paragraph 12(1)(*i*) in respect of the particular specified debt obligation of the taxpayer in computing the taxpayer's income for its transition year or a preceding taxation year.

History: S. 142.5(8.2) was added by S.C. 2009, c. 2, s. 47(1), applicable to taxation years that begin after September 2006.

Related Sections: S. 142.2(1), "specified debt obligation"; s. 142.51(1), "base year", "transition amount", "transition property", "transition year".

► 142.5(9) ◄

(9) Transition — property acquired on rollover. Where

(*a*) a taxpayer acquired a property before October 31, 1994 at a cost less than the fair market value of the property at the time of acquisition,

(*b*) the property was transferred, directly or indirectly, to the taxpayer by a person that would never have been a financial institution before the transfer if the definition "financial institution" in subsection 142.2(1) had always applied,

(*c*) the cost is less than the fair market value because subsection 85(1) applied in respect of the disposition of the property by the person, and

(*d*) subsection (2) deemed the taxpayer to have disposed of the property in its particular taxation year that includes October 31, 1994,

the following rules apply:

(*e*) where the taxpayer would, but for this paragraph, have a taxable capital gain for the particular year from the disposition of the property, the part of the taxable capital gain that can reasonably be considered to have arisen while the property was held by a person described in paragraph (*b*) shall be deemed to be a taxable capital gain of the taxpayer from the disposition of the property for the taxation year in which the taxpayer disposes of the property otherwise than because of subsection (2), and not to be a taxable capital gain for the particular year, and

(*f*) where the taxpayer has a profit (other than a capital gain) from the disposition of the property, the part of the profit that can reasonably be considered to have arisen while the property was held by a person described in paragraph (*b*) shall be included in computing the taxpayer's income for the taxation year in which the taxpayer disposes of the property otherwise than because of subsection (2), and shall not be included in computing the taxpayer's income for the particular year.

SECTION 142.51: [Transitional rules for financial institutions]

► 142.51(1) ◄

(1) Definitions. The following definitions apply for the purposes of this section and subsections 142.5(8.1) and (8.2).

"base year" — "base year" of a taxpayer means the taxpayer's taxation year that immediately precedes its transition year.

History: S. 142.51(1), the definition "base year" was added by S.C. 2009, c. 2, s. 48(1), applicable to taxation years that begin after September 2006.

Related Sections: S. 142.51(1), "transition year".

"transition amount" — "transition amount" of a taxpayer for the taxpayer's transition year is the positive or negative amount determined by the formula

$$A - B$$

where

A is the total of all amounts each of which is the fair market value, at the end of the taxpayer's base year, of a transition property of the taxpayer; and

B is the total of all amounts each of which is the cost amount to the taxpayer, at the end of the taxpayer's base year, of a transition property of the taxpayer.

History: S. 142.51(1), the definition "transition amount" was added by S.C. 2009, c. 2, s. 48(1), applicable to taxation years that begin after September 2006.

Related Sections: S. 248(1), "cost amount".

"transition property" —"transition property" of a taxpayer means a property that

(*a*) was a specified debt obligation held by the taxpayer at the end of the taxpayer's base year;

(*b*) was not a mark-to-market property of the taxpayer for the taxpayer's base year, but would have been a mark-to-market property of the taxpayer for the taxpayer's base year if the property had been carried at the property's fair market value in the taxpayer's balance sheet as at the end of each taxation year of the taxpayer that ends after the taxpayer last acquired the property (otherwise than by reason of a reacquisition under subsection 142.5(2)) and before the commencement of the taxpayer's transition year; and

(*c*) was a mark-to-market property of the taxpayer for the transition year of the taxpayer.

History: S. 142.51(1), the definition "transition property" was added by S.C. 2009, c. 2, s. 48(1), applicable to taxation years that begin after September 2006.

Related Sections: S. 142.2(1), "mark-to-market property", "specified debt obligation"; s. 142.5(2) Mark-to-market requirement.

"transition year" —"transition year" of a taxpayer means the taxpayer's first taxation year that begins after September 2006.

History: S. 142.51(1), the definition "transition year" was added by S.C. 2009, c. 2, s. 48(1), applicable to taxation years that begin after September 2006.

► 142.51(2) ◄

(2) Transition year income inclusion. If a taxpayer is a financial institution in its transition year, there shall be included in computing the taxpayer's income for its transition year the absolute value of the negative amount, if any, of the taxpayer's transition amount.

History: S. 142.51(2) was added by S.C. 2009, c. 2, s. 48(1), applicable to taxation years that begin after September 2006.

Related Sections: S. 138(10) Application of financial institution rules; s. 142.2(1), "financial institution"; s. 142.51(1), "transition amount", "transition year".

► 142.51(3) ◄

(3) Transition year income deduction. If a taxpayer is a financial institution in its transition year, there shall be deducted in computing the taxpayer's income for its transition year the positive amount, if any, of the taxpayer's transition amount.

History: S. 142.51(3) was added by S.C. 2009, c. 2, s. 48(1), applicable to taxation years that begin after September 2006.

Related Sections: S. 138(10) Application of financial institution rules; s. 142.2(1), "financial institution".

► 142.51(4) ◄

(4) Transition year income inclusion reversal. If an amount has been included under subsection (2) in computing a taxpayer's income for its transition year there shall be deducted in computing the taxpayer's income for each particular taxation year of the taxpayer that ends after the beginning of the transition year, and in which particular taxation year the taxpayer is a financial institution, the amount determined by the formula

$$A \times B/1825$$

where

A is the amount included under subsection (2) in computing the taxpayer's income for the transition year; and

B is the number of days in the particular taxation year that are before the day that is 1825 days after the first day of the transition year.

History: S. 142.51(4) was added by S.C. 2009, c. 2, s. 48(1), applicable to taxation years that begin after September 2006.

Related Sections: S. 142.2(1), "financial institution"; s. 142.51(1), "transition year"; s. 142.51(2) Transition year income inclusion; s. 142.51(6) Winding-up; s. 142.51(7) Amalgamations; s. 142.51(9) Transfer of a business; s. 142.51(10) Continuation of a partnership; s. 142.51(11) Ceasing to carry on a business.

► 142.51(5) ◄

(5) Transition year income deduction reversal. If an amount has been deducted under subsection (3) in computing a taxpayer's income for its transition year, there shall be included in computing the taxpayer's income, for each particular taxation year of the taxpayer ending after the beginning of the transition year, and in which particular taxation year the taxpayer is a financial institution, the amount determined by the formula

$$A \times B/1825$$

where

A is the amount deducted under subsection (3) in computing the taxpayer's income for the transition year; and

B is the number of days in the particular taxation year that are before the day that is 1825 days after the first day of the transition year.

History: S. 142.51(5) was added by S.C. 2009, c. 2, s. 48(1), applicable to taxation years that begin after September 2006.

Related Sections: S. 142.2(1), "financial institution"; s. 142.51(1), "transition year"; s. 142.51(3) Transition year income deduction; s. 142.51(6) Winding-up; s. 142.51(7) Amalgamations; s. 142.51(9) Transfer of a business; s. 142.51(10) Continuation of a partnership; s. 142.51(11) Ceasing to carry on a business.

► 142.51(6) ◄

(6) Winding-up. If a taxpayer has, in a winding-up to which subsection 88(1) has applied, been wound-up into another corporation (referred to in this subsection as the "parent"), and immediately after the winding-up the parent is a financial institution, in applying subsections (4) and (5) in computing the income of the taxpayer and of the parent for particular taxation years that end on or after the first day (referred to in this subsection as the "start day") on which assets of the taxpayer were distributed to the parent on the winding-up,

(*a*) the parent is, on and after the start day, deemed to be the same corporation as and a continuation of the taxpayer in respect of

(i) any amount included under subsection (2) or deducted under subsection (3) by the taxpayer in computing the taxpayer's income for its transition year,

(ii) any amount deducted under subsection (4) or included under subsection (5) in computing the taxpayer's income for a taxation year of the taxpayer that begins before the start day, and

(iii) any amount that would — in the absence of this subsection and if the taxpayer existed and was a financial institution on each day that is the start day or a subsequent day and on which the parent is a financial institution — be required to be deducted or included, in respect of any of those days, under subsection (4) or (5) in computing the taxpayer's income for its transition year; and (*b*) the taxpayer is, in respect of each of its particular taxation years, to determine the value for B in the formulas in subsections (4) and (5) without reference to the start day and days after the start day.

History: S. 142.51(6) was added by S.C. 2009, c. 2, s. 48(1), applicable to taxation years that begin after September 2006.

Related Sections: S. 142.2(1), "financial institution"; s. 142.51(1), "transition year"; s. 142.51(2) Transition year income inclusion; s. 142.51(3) Transition year income deduction; s. 142.51(4) Transition year income inclusion reversal; s. 142.51(5) Transition year income deduction reversal.

► 142.51(7) ◄

(7) Amalgamations. If there is an amalgamation (within the meaning assigned by subsection 87(1)) of a taxpayer with one or more other corporations to form one corporation (referred to in this subsection as the "new corporation"), and immediately after the amalgamation the new corporation is a financial institution, in applying subsections (4) and (5) in computing the income of the new corporation for particular taxation years of the new corporation that begin on or after the day on which the amalgamation occurred, the new corporation is, on and after that day, deemed to be the same corporation as and a continuation of the taxpayer in respect of

(*a*) any amount included under subsection (2) or deducted under subsection (3) in computing the taxpayer's income for its transition year of the taxpayer;

(*b*) any amount deducted under subsection (4) or included under subsection (5) in computing the taxpayer's income for a taxation year of the taxpayer that begins before the day on which the amalgamation occurred; and

(*c*) any amount that would — in the absence of this subsection and if the taxpayer existed and was a financial institution on each day that is the day on which the amalgamation occurred or a subsequent day and on which the new corporation is a financial institution — be required to be deducted or included, in respect of any of those days, under subsection (4) or (5) in computing the taxpayer's income.

History: S. 142.51(7) was added by S.C. 2009, c. 2, s. 48(1), applicable to taxation years that begin after September 2006.

Related Sections: S. 142.2(1), "financial institution"; s. 142.51(2) Transition year income inclusion; s. 142.51(3) Transition year income deduction; s. 142.51(4) Transition year income inclusion reversal; s. 142.51(5) Transition year income deduction reversal.

► 142.51(8) ◄

(8) Application of subsection (9). Subsection (9) applies if, at any time, a taxpayer (referred to in this subsection and subsection (9) as the "transferor") transfers, to a corporation (referred to in this subsection and subsection (9) as the "transferee") that is related to the transferor, property in respect of a business carried on by the transferor in Canada (referred to in this subsection and subsection (9) as the "transferred business") and

(*a*) subsection 138(11.5) or (11.94) applies to the transfer; or

(*b*) subsection 85(1) applies to the transfer, the transfer includes all or substantially all of the property and liabilities of the transferred business and, immediately after the transfer, the transferee is a financial institution.

History: S. 142.51(8) was added by S.C. 2009, c. 2, s. 48(1), applicable to taxation years that begin after September 2006.

Related Sections: S. 142.2(1), "financial institution"; s. 142.51(9) Transfer of business; s. 251 Arm's length.

► 142.51(9) ◄

(9) Transfer of a business. If this subsection applies in respect of the transfer, at any time, of property

(*a*) the transferee is, at and after that time, deemed to be the same corporation as and a continuation of the transferor in respect of

(i) any amount included under subsection (2) or deducted under subsection (3) in computing the transferor's income for its transition year that can reasonably be attributed to the transferred business,

(ii) any amount deducted under subsection (4) or included under subsection (5) in computing the transferor's income for a taxation year of the transferor that begins before that time that can reasonably be attributed to the transferred business, and

(iii) any amount that would — in the absence of this subsection and if the transferor existed and was a financial institution on each day that includes that time or is a subsequent day and on which the transferee is a financial institution — be required to be deducted or included, in respect of any of those days, under subsection (4) or (5) in computing the transferor's income that can reasonably be attributed to the transferred business; and

(*b*) in determining, in respect of the day that includes that time or any subsequent day, any amount that is required under subsection (4) or (5) to be deducted or included in computing the transferor's income for each particular taxation year from the transferred business, the description of A in the formulas in those subsections is deemed to be nil.

History: S. 142.51(9) was added by S.C. 2009, c. 2, s. 48(1), applicable to taxation years that begin after September 2006.

Related Sections: S. 142.2(1), "financial institution; s. 142.51(1), "transition year; s. 142.51(2) Transition year income inclusion; s. 142.51(3) Transition year income deduction; s. 142.51(4) Transition year income inclusion reversal; s. 142.51(5) Transition year income deduction reversal; s. 142.51(8) Application of subsection (9).

► 142.51(10) ◄

(10) Continuation of a partnership. If subsection 98(6) deems a partnership (in this subsection referred to as the "new partnership") to be a continuation of another partnership (in this subsection referred to as the "predecessor partnership") and, at the time that is immediately after the predecessor partnership ceases to exist, the new partnership is a financial institution, in applying subsections (4) and (5) in computing the income of the new partnership for particular taxation years of the new partnership that begin on or after the day on which it comes into existence, the new partnership is, on and after that day, deemed to be the same partnership as and a continuation of the predecessor partnership in respect of

(*a*) any amount included under subsection (2) or deducted under subsection (3) in computing the predecessor partnership's income for its transition year;

(*b*) any amount deducted under subsection (4) or included under subsection (5) in computing the predecessor partnership's income for a taxation year of the predecessor partnership that begins before the day on which the new partnership comes into existence; and

(*c*) any amount that would — in the absence of this subsection and if the predecessor partnership existed and was a financial institution on each day that is the day on which the new partnership comes into existence or a subsequent day and on which the new partnership is a financial institution — be required to be deducted or included, in respect of any of those days, under subsection (4) or (5) in computing the predecessor partnership's income.

History: S. 142.51(10) was added by S.C. 2009, c. 2, s. 48(1), applicable to taxation years that begin after September 2006.

Related Sections: S. 142.2(1), "financial institution"; s. 142.51(1), "transition year"; s. 142.51(2) Transition year income inclusion; s. 142.51(3) Transition year income deduction; s. 142.51(4) Transition year income inclusion reversal; s. 142.51(5) Transition year income deduction reversal.

► 142.51(11) ◄

(11) Ceasing to carry on a business. If at any time, a taxpayer ceases to be a financial institution

(*a*) there shall be deducted, in computing the income of the taxpayer for the taxation year of the taxpayer that includes the time that is immediately before that time, the amount determined by the formula

$$A - B$$

where

A is the amount included under subsection (2) in computing the taxpayer's income for its transition year, and

B is the total of all amounts each of which is an amount deducted under subsection (4) in computing the income of the taxpayer for a taxation year that began before that time; and

(*b*) there shall be included, in computing the income of the taxpayer for the taxation year of the taxpayer that includes the time that is immediately before that time, the amount determined by the formula

$$C - D$$

where

C is the amount deducted under subsection (3) in computing the taxpayer's income for its transition year, and

D is the total of all amounts each of which is an amount included under subsection (5) in computing the taxpayer's income for a taxation year that began before that time.

History: S. 142.51(11) was added by S.C. 2009, c. 2, s. 48(1), applicable to taxation years that begin after September 2006.

Related Sections: S. 142.2(1), "financial institution"; s. 142.51(1), "transition year"; s. 142.51(2) Transition year income inclusion; s. 142.51(3) Transition year income deduction; s. 142.51(4) Transition year income inclusion reversal; s. 142.51(5) Transition year income deduction reversal.

► 142.51(12) ◄

(12) Ceasing to exist. If at any time a taxpayer ceases to exist (otherwise than as a result of a merger to which subsection 87(2) applies, a winding-up to which subsection 88(1) applies or a continuation to which subsection 98(6) applies), for the purposes of subsection (11), the taxpayer is deemed to have ceased to be a financial institution at the earlier of

(*a*) the time (determined without reference to this subsection) at which the taxpayer ceased to be a financial institution, and

(*b*) the time that is immediately before the end of the last taxation year of the taxpayer that ended at or before the time at which the taxpayer ceased to exist.

History: S. 142.51(12) was added by S.C. 2009, c. 2, s. 48(1), applicable to taxation years that begin after September 2006.

Related Sections: S. 142.2(1), "financial institution"; s. 142.51(11) Ceasing to carry on a business.

Additional Rules

SECTION 142.6: Becoming or ceasing to be a financial institution

► 142.6(1) ◄

(1) Becoming or ceasing to be a financial institution. Where, at a particular time after February 22, 1994, a taxpayer becomes or ceases to be a financial institution,

(*a*) where a taxation year of the taxpayer would not, but for this paragraph, end immediately before the particular time,

(i) except for the purpose of subsection 132(6.1), the taxpayer's taxation year that would otherwise have included the particular time is deemed to have ended immediately before that time and a new taxation year of the taxpayer is deemed to have begun at that time, and

(ii) for the purpose of determining the taxpayer's fiscal period after the particular time, the taxpayer shall be deemed not to have established a fiscal period before that time;

(*b*) if the taxpayer becomes a financial institution, the taxpayer is deemed to have disposed, immediately before the end of its particular taxation year that ends immediately before the particular time, of each of the following properties held by the taxpayer for proceeds equal to the property's fair market value at the time of that disposition:

(i) a specified debt obligation, or

(ii) a mark-to-market property of the taxpayer for the particular taxation year or for the taxpayer's taxation year that includes the particular time;

(*c*) where the taxpayer ceases to be a financial institution, the taxpayer shall be deemed to have disposed, immediately before the end of its taxation year that ends immediately before the particular time, of each property held by the taxpayer that is a specified debt obligation (other than a mark-to-market property of the taxpayer for the year), for proceeds equal to its fair market value at the time of disposition; and

(*d*) the taxpayer is deemed to have reacquired, at the end of its taxation year that ends immediately before the particular time, each property deemed by paragraph (*b*) or (*c*) to have been disposed of by the taxpayer, at a cost equal to the proceeds of disposition of the property.

History: S. 142.6(1)(*b*) was replaced by S.C. 2013, c. 34, s. 289(1), applicable to taxation years that end after 1998, and formerly read:

(*b*) where the taxpayer becomes a financial institution, the taxpayer shall be deemed to have disposed, immediately before the end of its taxation year that ends immediately before the particular time, of each property held by the taxpayer that is

(i) a specified debt obligation (other than a mark-to-market property for the year), or

(ii) where the year ends after October 30, 1994, a mark-to-market property for the year

for proceeds equal to its fair market value at the time of disposition;

S. 142.6(1)(*d*) was replaced by S.C. 2013, c. 34, s. 289(2), applicable to taxation years that end after 1998, and formerly read:

(*d*) the taxpayer shall be deemed to have reacquired, at the end of the taxation year referred to in paragraph (*b*) or (*c*), each property deemed by that paragraph to have been disposed of by the taxpayer, at a cost equal to the proceeds of disposition of the property.

Related Sections: S. 54, "superficial loss"; s. 87(2)(*g.2*) Financial institution rules; s. 112(5.6) Stop-loss rules restricted; s. 142.4(5)(*b*)(iii) Gain or loss not amortized s. 142.5(8)(*b*)(ii) First deemed disposition of debt obligation.

► 142.6(1.1) ◄

(1.1) Ceasing to use property in Canadian business. If at a particular time in a taxation year a taxpayer that is a non-resident financial institution (other than a life insurance corporation) ceases to use, in connection with a business or part of a business carried on by the taxpayer in Canada immediately before the particular time, a property that is a mark-to-market property of the taxpayer for the year or a specified debt obligation, but that is not a property that was disposed of by the taxpayer at the particular time,

(*a*) the taxpayer is deemed

(i) to have disposed of the property immediately before the time that was immediately before the particular time for proceeds equal to its fair market value at the time of disposition and to have received those proceeds at the time of disposition in the course of carrying on the business or the part of the business, as the case may be, and

(ii) to have reacquired the property at the particular time at a cost equal to those proceeds; and

(*b*) in determining the consequences of the disposition in subparagraph (*a*)(i), subsection 142.4(11) does not apply to any payment received by the taxpayer after the particular time.

Related Sections: S. 10(12) Removing property from inventory; s. 14(14) Ceasing to use property in Canadian business; s. 76.1 Non-resident moving debt from Canadian business.

► 142.6(1.2) ◄

(1.2) Beginning to use property in a Canadian business. If at a particular time a taxpayer that is a non-resident financial institution (other than a life insurance corporation) begins to use, in connection with a business or part of a business carried on by the taxpayer in Canada, a property that is a mark-to-market property of the taxpayer for the year that includes the particular time or a specified debt obligation, but that is not a property that was acquired by the taxpayer at the particular time, the taxpayer is deemed

(*a*) to have disposed of the property immediately before the time that was immediately before the particular time for proceeds equal to its fair market value at the time of disposition; and

(*b*) to have reacquired the property at the particular time at a cost equal to those proceeds.

Related Sections: S. 10(13) Adding property to inventory; s. 14(15) Beginning to use property in Canadian business; s. 76.1 Non-resident moving debt from Canadian business.

► 142.6(1.3) ◄

(1.3) Specified debt obligation marked to market. In applying subsection (1.1) to a taxpayer in respect of a property in a taxation year,

(*a*) the definition "mark-to-market property" in subsection 142.2(1) shall be applied as if the year ended immediately before the particular time referred to in subsection (1.1); and

(*b*) if the taxpayer does not have financial statements for the period ending immediately before the particular time referred to in subsection (1.1), references in the definition to financial statements for the year shall be read as references to the financial statements that it is reasonable to expect would have been prepared if the year had ended immediately before the particular time.

► 142.6(1.4) ◄

(1.4) Change in status — prescribed payment card corporation share. If, at any particular time in a taxation year of a taxpayer that is a financial institution for the taxation year, a property becomes a mark-to-market property of the taxpayer for the taxation year because it ceased, at the particular time, to be a prescribed payment card corporation share of the taxpayer,

(*a*) the taxpayer is deemed

(i) to have disposed of the property immediately before the particular time for proceeds of disposition equal to its fair market value immediately before the particular time, and

(ii) to have acquired the property, at the particular time, at a cost equal to those proceeds; and

(*b*) subsection 142.5(1) does not apply to the disposition under subparagraph (*a*)(i).

History: S. 142.6(1.4) was added by S.C. 2009, c. 2, s. 49(1), applicable to taxation years that end after February 22, 1994.

Related Regulations: 9002.1.

Related Sections: S. 142.2(1), "financial institution", "mark-to-market property"; s. 142.5(2) Mark-to-market requirement.

► 142.6(1.5) ◄

(1.5) Change in status — prescribed securities exchange investment. If, at any particular time in a taxation year of a taxpayer that is a financial institution for the taxation year, a property becomes a mark-to-market property of the taxpayer for the taxation year because it ceased, at the particular time, to be a prescribed securities exchange investment of the taxpayer,

(*a*) the taxpayer is deemed

(i) to have disposed of the property immediately before the particular time for proceeds of disposition equal to its fair market value immediately before the particular time, and

(ii) to have acquired the property, at the particular time, at a cost equal to those proceeds; and

(*b*) subsection 142.5(1) does not apply to the disposition under subparagraph (*a*)(i).

History: S. 142.6(1.5) was added by S.C. 2009, c. 2, s. 49(1), applicable to taxation years that begin after 1998.

Related Regulations: 9002.2.

Related Sections: S. 142.2(1), "financial institution", "mark-to-market property"; s. 142.5(2) Mark-to-market requirement.

► 142.6(1.6) ◄

(1.6) Change in status — significant interest. If, at the end of a particular taxation year of a taxpayer that is a financial institution for the taxation year, the taxpayer holds a share of the capital stock of a corporation, the taxpayer has a significant interest in that corporation at any time in the particular taxation year and the share is mark-to-market property of the taxpayer for the immediately following taxation year, the taxpayer is deemed to have,

(*a*) disposed of the share immediately before the end of the particular taxation year for proceeds of disposition equal to the fair market value, at that time, of the share; and

(*b*) acquired the share at the end of the particular taxation year at a cost equal to those proceeds.

History: S. 142.6(1.6) was added by S.C. 2009, c. 2, s. 49(1), applicable to taxation years that begin after September 2006.

Related Sections: S. 142.2(1), "financial institution", "mark-to-market property"; s. 142.2(2) Significant interest; s. 142.2(3) Rules re significant interest; s. 142.5(2) Mark-to-market requirement.

► 142.6(2) ◄

(2) Deemed disposition not applicable. For the purposes of this Act, the determination of when a taxpayer acquired a share shall be made without regard to a disposition or acquisition that occurred because of subsection 142.5(2) or subsection (1), (1.1), (1.2), (1.4), (1.5) or (1.6).

History: S. 142.6(2) was replaced by S.C. 2009, c. 2, s. 49(2), applicable to taxation years that begin after September 2006. S. 142.6(2) formerly read:

(2) *Deemed disposition not applicable.* For the purposes of this Act, the determination of when a taxpayer acquired a share shall be made without regard to a disposition or acquisition that occurred because of subsection 142.5(2) or subsection (1), (1.1) or (1.2).

► 142.6(3) ◄

(3) Property not inventory. Where a taxpayer is a financial institution in a taxation year, inventory of the taxpayer in the year does not include property that is

(*a*) a specified debt obligation (other than a mark-to-market property for the year); or

(*b*) where the year begins after October 1994, a mark-to-market property for the year.

Related Sections: S. 66.3(1)(*a*)(ii) Exploration and development shares.

► 142.6(4) ◄

(4) Property that ceases to be inventory. Where a taxpayer that was a financial institution in its particular taxation year that includes February 23, 1994 held, on that day, a specified debt obligation (other than a mark-to-market property for the year) that was inventory of the taxpayer at the end of its preceding taxation year,

(*a*) the taxpayer shall be deemed to have disposed of the property at the beginning of the particular year for proceeds equal to

(i) where subparagraph (ii) does not apply, the amount at which the property was valued at the end of the preceding taxation year for the purpose of computing the taxpayer's income for the year, and

(ii) where the taxpayer is a bank and the property is prescribed property for the particular year, the cost of the property to the taxpayer (determined without reference to paragraph (*b*));

(*b*) for the purpose of determining the taxpayer's profit or loss from the disposition, the cost of the property to the taxpayer shall be deemed to be the amount referred to in subparagraph (*a*)(i); and

(*c*) the taxpayer shall be deemed to have reacquired the property, immediately after the beginning of the particular year, at a cost equal to the proceeds of disposition of the property.

Related Regulations: 9002(1).

► 142.6(5) ◄

(5) Debt obligations acquired in rollover transactions. Where,

(*a*) on February 23, 1994, a financial institution that is a corporation held a specified debt obligation (other than a mark-to-market property for the taxation year that includes that day) that was at any particular time before that day held by another corporation, and

(*b*) between the particular time and February 23, 1994, the only transactions affecting the ownership of the property were rollover transactions,

the financial institution shall be deemed, in respect of that obligation, to be the same corporation as, and a continuation of, the other corporation.

Related Sections: S. 87(2)(*e*) Capital property; s. 87(2)(*e.2*) Security or debt obligation; s. 87(2)(*e.3*) Financial institutions — specified debt obligation; s. 138(11.5)(*k.1*) Transfer of insurance business by non-resident insurer.

► 142.6(6) ◄

(6) Definition of "rollover transaction". For the purpose of subsection (5), "rollover transaction" means a transaction to which subsection 87(2), 88(1) or 138(11.5) or (11.94) applies, other than a transaction to which paragraph 138(11.5)(*e*) requires the provisions of subsection 85(1) to be applied.

► 142.6(7) ◄

(7) Superficial loss rule not applicable. Subsection 18(13) does not apply to the disposition of a property by a taxpayer after October 30, 1994 where

(*a*) the taxpayer is a financial institution when the disposition occurs and the property is a specified debt obligation or a mark-to-market property for the taxation year in which the disposition occurs; or

(*b*) the disposition occurs because of paragraph (1)(*b*).

► 142.6(8) ◄

(8) Accrued capital gains and losses election. Where a taxpayer that is a financial institution in its first taxation year that ends after February 22, 1994 so elects by notifying the Minister in writing before July 1998 or within 90 days after the day on which a notice of assessment of tax payable under this Part for the year, notification that no tax is payable under this Part for the year or notification that an election made by the taxpayer under this subsection is deemed by subsection (9) or (10) not to have been made is mailed to the taxpayer,

(*a*) each property of the taxpayer

(i) that was a capital property (other than a depreciable property) of the taxpayer at the end of the taxpayer's last taxation year that ended before February 23, 1994,

(ii) that was a mark-to-market property for, or a specified debt obligation in, the taxpayer's first taxation year that begins after that time,

(iii) that had a fair market value at that time greater than its adjusted cost base to the taxpayer at that time, and

(iv) that is designated by the taxpayer in the election

is deemed to have been disposed of by the taxpayer at that time for proceeds of disposition equal to, and to have been reacquired by the taxpayer immediately after that time at a cost equal to, the lesser of

(v) the fair market value of the property at that time, and

(vi) the greater of the adjusted cost base to the taxpayer of the property immediately before that time and the amount designated by the taxpayer in the election in respect of the property;

(*b*) each property of the taxpayer

(i) that was a capital property (other than a depreciable property) of the taxpayer at the end of the taxpayer's last taxation year that ended before February 23, 1994,

(ii) that was not a mark-to-market property for, or a specified debt obligation in, the taxpayer's first taxation year that begins after that time,

(iii) that had an adjusted cost base to the taxpayer at that time greater than its fair market value at that time, and

(iv) that is designated by the taxpayer in the election

is deemed to have been disposed of by the taxpayer at that time for proceeds of disposition equal to, and to have been reacquired by the taxpayer immediately after that time at a cost equal to, the greater of

(v) the fair market value of the property at that time, and

(vi) the lesser of the adjusted cost base to the taxpayer of the property immediately before that time and the amount designated by the taxpayer in the election in respect of the property; and

(*c*) notwithstanding subsections 152(4) to (5), such assessment of the taxpayer's tax payable under this Act for the taxpayer's last taxation year that ended before February 23, 1994 shall be made as is necessary to take the election into account.

► 142.6(9) ◄

(9) Accrued capital gains election limit. Where a taxpayer has made an election under subsection (8) in which a property was designated under subparagraph (8)(*a*)(iv), the election is deemed not to have been made where

(*a*) the amount that would be the taxpayer's taxable capital gains from dispositions of property for the taxpayer's last taxation year that ended before February 23, 1994 if this subsection and subsection (10) did not apply

exceeds the total of

(*b*) the amount that would be the taxpayer's allowable capital losses for the year from dispositions of property if this subsection and subsection (10) did not apply,

(*c*) the maximum amount that would have been deductible in computing the taxpayer's taxable income for the year in respect of the taxpayer's net capital losses for preceding taxation years if there were sufficient taxable capital gains for the year from dispositions of property, and

(*d*) the amount, if any, by which

(i) the amount that would be the taxpayer's taxable capital gains for the taxpayer's last taxation year that ended before February 23, 1994 from dispositions of property if no election were made under subsection (8)

exceeds the total of

(ii) the amount that would be the taxpayer's allowable capital losses for the year from dispositions of property if no election were made under subsection (8), and

(iii) the maximum amount that would have been deductible in computing the taxpayer's taxable income for the year in respect of the taxpayer's net capital losses for preceding taxation years if no election were made under subsection (8).

► 142.6(10) ◄

(10) Accrued capital losses election limit. Where a taxpayer has made an election under subsection (8) in which a property was designated under subparagraph (8)(*b*)(iv), the election is deemed not to have been made where

(*a*) the total of the amounts determined under paragraphs (9)(*b*) and (*c*) in respect of the taxpayer exceeds the amount determined under paragraph (9)(*a*) in respect of the taxpayer; or

(*b*) the total of all amounts each of which would, if this subsection did not apply, be the taxpayer's allowable capital loss for the taxpayer's last taxation year that ended before February 23, 1994 from the disposition of a property deemed to have been disposed of under paragraph (8)(*b*) exceeds the total of all amounts each of which is the taxpayer's taxable capital gain for the year from the disposition of a property deemed to have been disposed of under paragraph (8)(*a*).

Conversion of Foreign Bank Affiliate to Branch

SECTION 142.7: [Conversion of foreign bank affiliate to branch]

► 142.7(1) ◄

(1) Definitions. The definitions in this subsection apply in this section.

Related Sections: S. 18(1)(*v*) Interest — authorized foreign bank; s. 20.2(5) Notional interest; s. 212(13.3) Application of Part XIII to authorized foreign bank; s. 218.2(2) Taxable interest expense; s. 248(1), "authorized foreign bank".

"Canadian affiliate" —"Canadian affiliate" of an entrant bank at any particular time means a Canadian corporation that was, immediately before the particular time, affiliated with the entrant bank and that was, at all times during the period that began on February 11, 1999 and ended immediately before the particular time,

(*a*) affiliated with either

(i) the entrant bank, or

(ii) a foreign bank (within the meaning assigned by section 2 of the *Bank Act*) that is affiliated with the entrant bank at the particular time; and

(*b*) either

(i) a bank,

(ii) a corporation authorized under the *Trust and Loan Companies Act* to carry on the business of offering to the public its services as trustee, or

(iii) a corporation of which the principal activity in Canada consists of any of the activities referred to in subparagraphs 518(3)(*a*)(i) to (v) of the *Bank Act* and in which the entrant bank or a non-resident person affiliated with the entrant bank holds shares under the authority, directly or indirectly, of an order issued by the Minister of Finance or the Governor in Council under subsection 521(1) of that Act.

"eligible property" —"eligible property" of a Canadian affiliate at any time means a property described in any of paragraphs 85(1.1)(*a*) to (*g.1*) that is, immediately before that time, used or held by it in carrying on its business in Canada.

"entrant bank" —"entrant bank" means a non-resident corporation that is, or has applied to the Superintendent of Financial Institutions to become, an authorized foreign bank.

"qualifying foreign merger" —"qualifying foreign merger" means a merger or combination of two or more corporations that would be a "foreign merger" within the meaning assigned by subsection 87(8.1) if that subsection were read without reference to the words "and otherwise than as a result of the distribution of property to one corporation on the winding-up of another corporation".

► 142.7(2) ◄

(2) Qualifying foreign merger. Where an entrant bank was formed as the result of a qualifying foreign merger, after February 11, 1999, of two or more corporations (referred to in this subsection as "predecessors"), and at the time immediately before the merger, there were one or more Canadian corporations (referred to in this subsection as "predecessor affiliates"), each of which at that time would have been a Canadian affiliate of a predecessor if the predecessor were an entrant bank at that time,

(*a*) for the purpose of the definition "Canadian affiliate" in subsection (1),

(i) each predecessor affiliate is deemed to have been affiliated with the entrant bank throughout the period that began on February 11, 1999 and ended at the time of the merger,

(ii) the expression "entrant bank" in subparagraph (*b*)(iii) of the definition is deemed to include a predecessor, and

(iii) if two or more of the predecessor affiliates are amalgamated or merged at any time after February 11, 1999 to form a new corporation, the new corporation is deemed to have been affiliated with the entrant bank throughout the period that began on February 11, 1999 and ended at the time of the amalgamation or merger of the predecessor affiliates; and

(*b*) if at least one of the predecessors complied with the terms of subsection (11)(*a*), the entrant bank is deemed to have complied with those terms.

► 142.7(3) ◄

(3) Branch-establishment rollover. If a Canadian affiliate of an entrant bank transfers an eligible property to the entrant bank, the entrant bank begins immediately after the transfer to use or hold the transferred property in its Canadian banking business and the Canadian affiliate and the entrant bank jointly elect, in accordance with subsection (11), to have this subsection apply in respect of the transfer, subsections 85(1) (other than paragraph (*e*.2)), (1.1), (1.4) and (5) apply, with any modifications that the circumstances require, in respect of the transfer, except that the portion of subsection 85(1) before paragraph (*a*) shall be read as follows:

"**85(1)** Where a taxpayer that is a Canadian affiliate of an entrant bank (within the meanings assigned by subsection 142.7(1)) has, in a taxation year, disposed of any of the taxpayer's property to the entrant bank (referred to in this subsection as the "corporation"), if the taxpayer and the corporation have jointly elected under subsection 142.7(3), the following rules apply:".

Editorial Note: S. 142.7 permits a bank to transfer the Canadian banking operation that it carries on through a Canadian subsidiary to an affiliate Canadian branch on a tax-deferred basis. The rules of s. 142.7(3) are based on the existing rules in s. 85(1), with some modifications, the most notable being that the Canadian affiliate need not take back any shares of the entrant bank as part of the consideration. Additionally, in contrast to other rollover provisions, such as s. 85, 93 and 104, there are no specific provisions that permit the CRA to accept a late filed or amended election under these rules.

Related Regulations: 5301(8).

Related Sections: S. 248(1), "Canadian banking business".

► 142.7(4) ◄

(4) Deemed fair market value. If a Canadian affiliate of an entrant bank and the entrant bank make an election under subsection (3) in respect of a transfer of property by the Canadian affiliate to the entrant bank, for the purposes of subsections 15(1), 52(2), 69(1), (4) and (5), 246(1) and 247(2) in respect of the transfer, the fair market value of the property is deemed to be the amount agreed by the Canadian affiliate and the entrant bank in their election.

► 142.7(5) ◄

(5) Specified debt obligations. If a Canadian affiliate of an entrant bank transfers a specified debt obligation to the entrant bank in a transaction in respect of which an election is made under subsection (3), the Canadian affiliate is a financial institution in its taxation year in which the transfer is made, and the amount that the Canadian affiliate and the entrant bank agree on in their election in respect of the obligation is equal to the tax basis of the obligation within the meaning assigned by subsection 142.4(1), the entrant bank is deemed, in respect of the obligation, for the purposes of sections 142.2 to 142.4 and 142.6, to be the same corporation as, and a continuation of, the Canadian affiliate.

► 142.7(6) ◄

(6) Mark-to-market property. If a Canadian affiliate of an entrant bank described in paragraph (11)(*a*) transfers at any time within the period described in paragraph (11)(*c*) to the entrant bank a property that is, for the Canadian affiliate's taxation year in which the property is transferred, a mark-to-market property of the Canadian affiliate,

(*a*) for the purposes of subsections 112(5) to (5.21) and (5.4), the definition "mark-to-market property" in subsection 142.2(1) and subsection 142.5(9), the entrant bank is deemed, in respect of the property, to be the same corporation as and a continuation of, the Canadian affiliate; and

(*b*) for the purpose of applying subsection 142.5(2) in respect of the property, the Canadian affiliate's taxation year in which the property is transferred is deemed to have ended immediately before the time the property was transferred.

► 142.7(7) ◄

(7) Reserves. If

(*a*) at a particular time,

(i) a Canadian affiliate of an entrant bank transfers to the entrant bank property that is a loan or lending asset, or a right to receive an unpaid amount in respect of a disposition before the particular time of property by the affiliate, or

(ii) the entrant bank assumes an obligation of the Canadian affiliate that is an instrument or commitment described in paragraph 20(1)(*l.1*) or an obligation in respect of goods, services, land, or chattels or movable property, described in subparagraph 20(1)(*m*)(i), (ii) or (iii),

(*b*) the property is transferred or the obligation is assumed for an amount equal to its fair market value at the particular time,

(*c*) the entrant bank begins immediately after the particular time to use or hold the property or owe the obligation in its Canadian banking business, and

(*d*) the Canadian affiliate and the entrant bank jointly elect in accordance with subsection (11) to have this subsection apply in respect of the transfer or assumption,

then

(*e*) in applying paragraphs 20(1)(*l*), (*l*.1), (*m*), (*n*) and (*p*) in respect of the obligation or property, the taxation year of the affiliate that would, but for this paragraph, include the particular time is deemed to end immediately before the particular time, and

(*f*) in computing the income of the Canadian affiliate and the entrant bank for taxation years that end on or after the particular time,

(i) any amount deducted under paragraph 20(1)(*l*), (*l*.1), (*m*) or (*n*) by the Canadian affiliate in respect of the property or obligation in computing its income for its taxation year that ended immediately before the particular time, or under paragraph 20(1)(*p*) in computing its income for that year or for a preceding taxation year (to the extent that the amount has not been included in the affiliate's income under paragraph 12(1)(*i*)), is deemed to have been so deducted by the entrant bank in computing its income for its last taxation year that ended before the particular time and not to have been deducted by the Canadian affiliate,

(ii) in applying paragraph 20(1)(*m*), an amount in respect of the goods, services, land, chattels or movable property, that was included under paragraph 12(1)(*a*) in computing the Canadian affiliate's income from a business is deemed to have been so included in computing the entrant bank's income from its Canadian banking business for a preceding taxation year,

(iii) in applying paragraph 20(1)(*n*) in respect of a property described in subparagraph (*a*)(i) and paragraphs (*b*), (*c*) and (*d*) sold by the Canadian affiliate in the course of a business, the property is deemed to have been disposed of by the entrant bank (and not by the Canadian affiliate) at the time it was disposed of by the Canadian affiliate, and the amount in respect of the sale that was included in computing the Canadian affiliate's income from a business is deemed to have been included in computing the entrant bank's income from its Canadian banking business for its taxation year that includes the time at which the property was so disposed of, and

(iv) in applying paragraph 40(1)(*a*) or 44(1)(*e*) in respect of a property described in subparagraph (*a*)(i) and paragraphs (*b*), (*c*) and (*d*) disposed of by the Canadian affiliate, the property is deemed to have been disposed of by the entrant bank (and not by the Canadian affiliate) at the time it was disposed of by the Canadian affiliate, the amount determined under subparagraph 40(1)(*a*)(i) or 44(1)(*e*)(i) in respect of the Canadian affiliate is deemed to be the amount determined under that subparagraph in respect of the entrant bank, and any amount claimed by the Canadian affiliate under subparagraph 40(1)(*a*)(iii) or 44(1)(*e*)(iii) in computing its gain from the disposition of the property for its last taxation year that ended before the particular time is deemed to have been so claimed by the entrant bank for its last taxation year that ended before the particular time.

History: S. 142.7(7)(*a*)(ii) was amended by S.C. 2013, c. 34, s. 136(1), in force June 26, 2013, and formerly read:

(ii) the entrant bank assumes an obligation of the Canadian affiliate that is an instrument or commitment described in paragraph 20(1)(*l*.1) or an obligation in respect of goods, services, lands or chattels described in subparagraph 20(1)(*m*)(i), (ii) or (iii),

S. 142.7(7)(*f*)(ii) was amended by S.C. 2013, c. 34, s. 136(2), in force June 26, 2013, and formerly read:

(ii) in applying paragraph 20(1)(*m*), an amount in respect of the goods, services, land or chattels that was included under paragraph 12(1)(*a*) in computing the Canadian affiliate's income from a business is deemed to have been so included in computing the entrant bank's income from its Canadian banking business for a preceding taxation year,

► 142.7(8) ◄

(8) Assumption of debt obligation. If a Canadian affiliate of an entrant bank described in paragraph (11)(*a*) transfers at any time within the period described in paragraph (11)(*c*) property to the entrant bank, and any part of the consideration for the transfer is the assumption by the entrant bank in respect of its Canadian banking business of a debt obligation of the Canadian affiliate,

(*a*) where the Canadian affiliate and the entrant bank jointly elect in accordance with subsection (11) to have this paragraph apply,

(i) both

(A) the value of that part of the consideration for the transfer of the property, and

(B) for the purpose of determining the consequences of the assumption of the obligation and any subsequent settlement or extinguishment of it, the value of the consideration given to the entrant bank for the assumption of the obligation,

are deemed to be an amount (in this paragraph referred to as the "assumption amount") equal to the amount outstanding on account of the principal amount of the obligation at that time, and

(ii) the assumption amount shall not be considered a term of the transaction that differs from that which would have been made between persons dealing at arm's length solely because it is not equal to the fair market value of the obligation at that time;

(*a*.1) (Repealed by S.C. 2013, c. 34, s. 290(2).)

(*b*) where the obligation is denominated in a foreign currency, and the Canadian affiliate and the entrant bank jointly elect in accordance with subsection (11) to have this paragraph apply,

(i) the amount of any income, loss, capital gain or capital loss in respect of the obligation due to the fluctuation in the value of the foreign currency relative to Canadian currency realized by

(A) the Canadian affiliate on the assumption of the obligation is deemed to be nil, and

(B) the entrant bank on the settlement or extinguishment of the obligation shall be determined based on the amount of the obligation in Canadian currency at the time it became an obligation of the Canadian affiliate, and

(ii) for the purpose of an election made in respect of the obligation under paragraph (*a*), the amount outstanding on account of the principal amount of the obligation at that time is the total of all amounts each of which is an amount that was advanced to the Canadian affiliate on account of principal, that remains outstanding at that time, and that is determined using the exchange rate that applied between the foreign currency and Canadian currency at the time of the advance; and

(*c*) for the purpose of applying paragraphs 20(1)(*e*) and (*f*) in respect of the debt obligation, the obligation is deemed not to have been settled or extinguished by virtue of its assumption by the entrant bank and the entrant bank is deemed to be the same corporation as, and a continuation of, the Canadian affiliate.

History: S. 142.7(8)(*a.1*) was repealed by S.C. 2013, c. 34, s. 290(2), deemed to have come into force on January 1, 2008, and formerly read:

(*a*.1) for the purpose of applying subparagraph 212(1)(*b*)(vii) in respect of the debt obligation, the obligation is deemed to have been issued by the entrant bank at the time that the obligation was issued by the Canadian affiliate;

S. 142.7(8)(*a.1*) was added by S.C. 2013, c. 34, s. 290(1), deemed to have come into force on June 28, 1999.

Related Sections: S. 261(2)(*b*) Canadian currency requirement; s. 261(5)(*c*) and s. 261(5)(*f*)(i) Functional currency tax reporting.

► 142.7(9) ◄

(9) Branch-establishment dividend. Notwithstanding any other provision of this Act, the rules in subsection (10) apply if

(*a*) a dividend is paid by a Canadian affiliate of an entrant bank to the entrant bank or to a person that is affiliated with the Canadian affiliate and that is resident in the country in which the entrant bank is resident, or

(*b*) a dividend is deemed to be paid for the purposes of this Part or Part XIII (other than by paragraph 214(3)(*a*)) as a result of a transfer of property from the Canadian affiliate to such a person,

and the Canadian affiliate and the entrant bank jointly elect in accordance with subsection (11) to have subsection (10) apply in respect of the dividend.

► 142.7(10) ◄

(10) Treatment of dividend. If the conditions in subsection (9) are met,

(*a*) the dividend is deemed (except for the purposes of subsections 112(3) to (7)) not to be a taxable dividend; and

(*b*) there is added to the amount otherwise determined under paragraph 219(1)(*g*) in respect of the entrant bank for its first taxation year that ends after the time at which the dividend is paid, the amount of the dividend less, where the dividend is paid by means of, or arises as a result of, a transfer of eligible property in respect of which the Canadian affiliate and the entrant bank have jointly elected under subsection (3), the amount by which the fair market value of the property transferred exceeds the amount the Canadian affiliate and the entrant bank have agreed on in their election.

► 142.7(11) ◄

(11) Elections. An election under subsection (3) or (7), paragraph (8)(*a*) or (*b*) or subsection (10), (12) or (14) is valid only if

(*a*) the entrant bank by which the election is made has, on or before the day that is 6 months after the day on which the *Income Tax Amendments Act, 2000* receives royal assent [S.C. 2001, c. 17, Royal Assent June 14, 2001], complied with paragraphs 1.1(*b*) and (*c*) of the "Guide to Foreign Bank Branching" in respect of the establishment and commencement of business of a foreign bank branch in Canada issued by the Office of the Superintendent of Financial Institutions, as it read on December 31, 2000;

(*b*) the election is made in prescribed form on or before the earlier of the filing-due date of the Canadian affiliate and the filing-due date of the entrant bank, for the taxation year that includes the time at which

(i) in the case of an election under subsection (3) or (7), paragraph (8)(*a*) or (*b*) or subsection (10), the dividend, transfer or assumption to which the election relates is paid, made or effected, or

(ii) in the case of an election under subsection (12), the dissolution order was granted or the winding up commenced; and

(*c*) in the case of an election under subsection (3) or (7), paragraph (8)(*a*) or (*b*) or subsection (10), the dividend, transfer or assumption to which the election relates is paid, made or effected within the period that

(i) begins on the day on which the Superintendent makes an order in respect of the entrant bank under subsection 534(1) of the *Bank Act*, and

(ii) ends on the later of

(A) the earlier of

(I) the day that is one year after the day referred to subparagraph (i), and

(II) the day that is three years after the day on which the *Income Tax Amendments Act, 2000* receives royal assent [S.C. 2001, c. 17, Royal Assent June 14, 2001], and

(B) the day that is one year after the day on which the *Income Tax Amendments Act, 2000* receives royal assent [S.C. 2001, c. 17, Royal Assent June 14, 2001].

► 142.7(12) ◄

(12) Winding-up of Canadian affiliate: losses. If

(*a*) within the period described in paragraph (11)(*c*) in respect of the entrant bank,

(i) the Minister of Finance has issued letters patent under section 342 of the *Bank Act* or section 347 of the *Trust and Loan Companies Act* dissolving the Canadian affiliate or an order under section 345 of the *Bank Act* or section 350 of the *Trust and Loan Companies Act* approving the Canadian affiliate's application for dissolution (such letters patent or order being referred to in this subsection as the "dissolution order"), or

(ii) the affiliate has been wound up under the terms of the corporate law that governs it,

(*b*) the entrant bank carries on all or part of the business in Canada that was formerly carried on by the Canadian affiliate, and

(*c*) the Canadian affiliate and the entrant bank jointly elect in accordance with subsection (11) to have this section apply

then in applying section 111 for the purpose of computing the taxable income earned in Canada of the entrant bank for any taxation year that begins after the date of the dissolution order or the commencement of the winding up, as the case may be,

(*d*) subject to paragraphs (*e*) and (*h*), the portion of a non-capital loss of the Canadian affiliate for a taxation year (in this paragraph referred to as the "Canadian affiliate's loss year") that can reasonably be regarded as being its loss from carrying on a business in Canada (in this paragraph referred to as the "loss business") or being in respect of a claim made under section 110.5, to the extent that it

(i) was not deducted in computing the taxable income of the Canadian affiliate or any other entrant bank for any taxation year, and

(ii) would have been deductible in computing the taxable income of the Canadian affiliate for any taxation year that begins after the date of the dissolution order or the commencement of the winding up, as the case may be, on the assumption that it had such a taxation year and that it had sufficient income for that year, is deemed, for the taxation year of the entrant bank in which the Canadian affiliate's loss year ended, to be a non-capital loss of the entrant bank from carrying on the loss business (or, in respect of a claim made under section 110.5, to be a non-capital loss of the entrant bank in respect of a claim under subparagraph 115(1)(*a*)(vii)) that was not deductible by the entrant bank in computing its taxable income earned in Canada for any taxation year that began before the date of the dissolution order or the commencement of the winding up, as the case may be,

(*e*) if at any time control of the Canadian affiliate or entrant bank has been acquired by a person or group of persons, no amount in respect of the Canadian affiliate's non-capital loss for a taxation year that ends before that time is deductible in computing the taxable income earned in Canada of the entrant bank for a particular taxation year that ends after that time, except that the portion of the loss that can reasonably be regarded as the Canadian affiliate's loss from carrying on a business in Canada and, where a business was carried on by the Canadian affiliate in Canada in the earlier year, the portion of the loss that can reasonably be regarded as being in respect of an amount deductible under paragraph 110(1)(*k*) in computing its taxable income for the year are deductible only

(i) if that business is carried on by the Canadian affiliate or the entrant bank for profit or with a reasonable expectation of profit throughout the particular year, and

(ii) to the extent of the total of the entrant bank's income for the particular year from that business, and where properties were sold, leased, rented or developed or services rendered in the course of carrying on that business before that time, from any other business substantially all of the income of which was derived from the sale, leasing, rental or development, as the case may be, of similar properties or the rendering of similar services,

and, for the purpose of this paragraph, where subsection 88(1.1) applied to the dissolution of another corporation in respect of which the Canadian affiliate was the parent and paragraph 88(1.1)(*e*) applied in respect of losses of that other corporation, the Canadian affiliate is deemed to be the same corporation as, and a continuation of, that other corporation with respect to those losses,

(*f*) subject to paragraphs (*g*) and (*h*), a net capital loss of the Canadian affiliate for a taxation year (in this paragraph referred to as the "Canadian affiliate's loss year") is deemed to be a net capital loss of the entrant bank for its taxation year in which the Canadian affiliate's loss year ended to the extent that the loss

(i) was not deducted in computing the taxable income of the Canadian affiliate or any other entrant bank for any taxation year, and

(ii) would have been deductible in computing the taxable income of the Canadian affiliate for any taxation year beginning after the date of the dissolution order or the commencement of the winding-up, as the case may be, on the assumption that the Canadian affiliate had such a taxation year and that it had sufficient income and taxable capital gains for that year,

(*g*) if at any time control of the Canadian affiliate or the entrant bank has been acquired by a person or group of persons, no amount in respect of the Canadian affiliate's net capital loss for a taxation year that ends before that time is deductible in computing the entrant bank's taxable income earned in Canada for a taxation year that ends after that time, and

(*h*) any loss of the Canadian affiliate that would otherwise be deemed by paragraph (*d*) or (*f*) to be a loss of the entrant bank for a particular taxation year that begins after the date of the dissolution order or the commencement of the winding-up, as the case may be, is deemed, for the purpose of computing the entrant bank's taxable income earned in Canada for taxation years that begin after that date, to be such a loss of the entrant bank for its immediately preceding taxation year and not for the particular year, if the entrant bank so elects in its return of income for the particular year.

► 142.7(13) ◄

(13) Winding-up of Canadian affiliate: stop loss. If a Canadian affiliate and its entrant bank have at any time made a joint election under either of subsection (3) or (12),

(*a*) in respect of any transfer of property, directly or indirectly, by the Canadian affiliate to the entrant bank or a person with whom the entrant bank does not deal at arm's length,

(i) subparagraph 13(21.2)(*e*)(iii) shall be read without reference to clause (E) of that subparagraph,

(ii) (Repealed by S.C. 2016, c. 12, s. 51(1).)

(iii) paragraph 18(15)(*b*) shall be read without reference to subparagraph (iv) of that paragraph, and

(iv) paragraph 40(3.4)(*b*) shall be read without reference to subparagraph (v) of that paragraph;

(*b*) in respect of any property of the Canadian affiliate appropriated to or for the benefit of the entrant bank or any person with whom the entrant bank does not deal at arm's length, section 69(5) shall be read without reference to paragraph (*d*); and

(*c*) for the purposes of applying subsection 13(21.2), 18(15) and 40(3.4) to any property that was disposed of by the affiliate, after the dissolution or winding-up of the affiliate, the entrant bank is deemed to be the same corporation as, and a continuation of, the affiliate.

History: S. 142.7(13)(*a*)(ii) was repealed by S.C. 2016, c. 12, s. 51(1), in force January 1, 2017, and formerly read:

(ii) subsection 14(12) shall be read without reference to paragraph (*g*) of that subsection,

S. 142.7(13)(*c*) was replaced by S.C. 2016, c. 12, s. 51(2), in force January 1, 2017, and formerly read:

(*c*) for the purposes of applying subsection 13(21.2), 14(12), 18(15) and 40(3.4) to any property that was disposed of by the affiliate, after the dissolution or winding-up of the affiliate, the entrant bank is deemed to be the same corporation as, and a continuation of, the affiliate.

► 142.7(14) ◄

(14) Winding-up of Canadian affiliate: SDOs. If a Canadian affiliate of an entrant bank and the entrant bank meet the conditions set out in paragraphs (12)(*a*) and (*b*) and jointly elect in accordance with subsection (11) to have this subsection apply, and the Canadian affiliate has not made an election under this subsection with any other entrant bank, the entrant bank is deemed to be the same corporation as, and a continuation of, the Canadian affiliate for the purposes of paragraphs 142.4(4)(*c*) and (*d*) in respect of any specified debt obligation disposed of by the Canadian affiliate.

Communal Organizations

SECTION 143: Communal organizations

► 143(1) ◄

(1) Communal organizations. Where a congregation, or one or more business agencies of the congregation, carries on one or more businesses for purposes that include supporting or sustaining the congregation's members or the members of any other congregation, the following rules apply:

(*a*) a trust is deemed to be created on the day that is the later of

(i) December 31, 1976, and

(ii) the day the congregation came into existence;

(*b*) the trust is deemed to have been continuously in existence from the day determined under paragraph (*a*);

(*c*) the property of the congregation is deemed to be the property of the trust;

(*d*) the property of each business agency of the congregation in a calendar year is deemed to be property of the trust throughout the portion of the year throughout which the trust exists;

(*e*) where the congregation is a corporation, the corporation is deemed to be the trustee having control of the trust property;

(*f*) where the congregation is not a corporation, its council, committee of leaders, executive committee, administrative committee, officers or other group charged with its management are deemed to be the trustees having control of the trust property;

(*g*) the congregation is deemed to act and to have always acted as agent for the trust in all matters relating to its businesses and other activities;

(*h*) each business agency of the congregation in a calendar year is deemed to have acted as agent for the trust in all matters in the year relating to its businesses and other activities;

(*i*) the members of the congregation are deemed to be the beneficiaries under the trust;

(*j*) tax under this Part is payable by the trust on its taxable income for each taxation year;

(*k*) in computing the income of the trust for any taxation year,

(i) subject to paragraph (*l*), no deduction may be made in respect of salaries, wages or benefits of any kind provided to the members of the congregation, and

(ii) no deduction may be made under subsection 104(6), except to the extent that any portion of the trust's income (determined without reference to that subsection) is allocated to the members of the congregation in accordance with subsection (2);

(*l*) for the purpose of applying section 20.01 to the trust,

(i) each member of the congregation is deemed to be a member of the trust's household, and

(ii) section 20.01 shall be read without reference to paragraphs 20.01(2)(*b*) and (*c*) and subsection 20.01(3); and

(*m*) where the congregation or one of the business agencies is a corporation, section 15.1 shall, except for the purposes of paragraphs 15.1(2)(*a*) and (*c*) (other than subparagraphs 15.1(2)(*c*)(i) and (ii)), apply as if this subsection were read without reference to paragraphs (*c*), (*d*), (*g*) and (*h*).

History: S. 143(1)(*a*), the portion before subparagraph (i) was replaced by S.C. 2014, c. 39, s. 48(1), applicable to the 2016 and subsequent taxation years, and formerly read:

(*a*) an *inter vivos* trust is deemed to be created on the day that is the later of

Related Regulations: 206.

Related Sections: S. 104(6) Deduction in computing income of trust; s. 104(13) Income of beneficiary; s. 108(1), "beneficiary", "*inter vivos* trust"; s. 143(2) Election in respect of income; s. 143(4) Definitions.

Information Circulars: IC 78-5R3 Communal organizations.

Cases: The community of Bountiful did not meet the definition of a "congregation" and could not allocate income to individual members. *Blackmore v. The Queen*, 2014 DTC 5123 (F.C.A.)

► 143(2) ◄

(2) Election in respect of income. If the trust referred to in subsection (1) in respect of a congregation so elects in respect of a taxation year in writing filed with the Minister on or before the trust's filing-due date for the year and all the congregation's participating members are specified in the election in accordance with subsection (5), the following rules apply:

(*a*) for the purposes of subsections 104(6) and (13), the amount payable in the year to a particular participating member of the congregation out of the income of the trust (determined without reference to subsection 104(6)) is the amount determined by the formula

$$0.8\ (A \times B/C) + D + (0.2A - E)/F$$

where

A is the taxable income of the trust for the year (determined without reference to subsection 104(6) and specified future tax consequences for the year),

B is

(i) where the particular member is identified in the election as a person to whom this subparagraph applies (in this subsection referred to as a "designated member"), 1, and

(ii) in any other case, 0.5,

C is the total of

(i) the number of designated members of the congregation, and

(ii) 1/2 of the number of other participating members of the congregation in respect of the year,

D is the amount, if any, that is specified in the election as an additional allocation under this subsection to the particular member,

E is the total of all amounts each of which is an amount specified in the election as an additional allocation under this subsection to a participating member of the congregation in respect of the year, and

F is the number of participating members of the congregation in respect of the year;

(*b*) the designated member of each family at the end of the year is deemed to have supported the other members of the family during the year and the other members of the family are deemed to have been wholly dependent on the designated member for support during the year;

(*c*) the taxable income for the year of each member of the congregation shall be computed without reference to subsection 110(2); and

(*d*) if the trust earns income from a business in the year, then the portion of the amount payable in the year to a particular participating member of the congregation out of the income of the trust under paragraph (*a*) that can reasonably be considered to relate to that income from a business is deemed to be income from a business carried on by the particular member.

History: S. 143(2)(*d*) was added by S.C. 2019, c. 29, s. 25(1), applicable to the 2014 and subsequent taxation years.

S. 143(2), the portion before paragraph (*a*) was replaced by S.C. 2014, c. 39, s. 48(2), applicable to the 2016 and subsequent taxation years, and formerly read:

(2) *Election in respect of income.* Where the *inter vivos* trust referred to in subsection (1) in respect of a congregation so elects in respect of a taxation year in writing filed with the Minister on or before the trust's filing-due date for the year and all the congregation's participating members are specified in the election in accordance with subsection (5), the following rules apply:

Related Regulations: 600(b).

Related Sections: S. 108(1), "*inter vivos* trust"; s. 220(3.2) Late, amended or revoked elections.

Information Circulars: IC 78-5R3 Communal organizations; IC 07-1 Taxpayer Relief Provisions.

► 143(3) ◄

(3) Refusal to accept election. An election under subsection (2) in respect of a congregation for a particular taxation year is not binding on the Minister unless all taxes, interest and penalties payable under this Part, as a consequence of the application of subsection (2) to the congregation for preceding taxation years, are paid at or before the end of the particular year.

► 143(3.1) ◄

(3.1) Election in respect of gifts. For the purposes of section 118.1, if the eligible amount of a gift made in a taxation year by a trust referred to in subsection (1) in respect of a congregation would, but for this subsection, be included in the total charitable gifts, total cultural gifts or total ecological gifts of the trust for the year and the trust so elects in its return of income under this Part for the year,

(*a*) the trust is deemed not to have made the gift; and

(*b*) each participating member of the congregation is deemed to have made, in the year, such a gift the eligible amount of which is the amount determined by the formula

$$A \times B/C$$

where

A is the eligible amount of the gift made by the trust,

B is the amount determined for the year in respect of the member under paragraph (2)(*a*) as a consequence of an election under subsection (2) by the trust, and

C is the total of all amounts each of which is an amount determined for the year in respect of a participating member of the congregation under paragraph (2)(*a*) as a consequence of an election under subsection (2) by the trust.

History: S. 143(3.1), the portion before paragraph (*a*) was replaced by S.C. 2014, c. 39, s. 48(3), applicable to the 2016 and subsequent taxation years, and formerly read:

(3.1) *Election in respect of gifts.* For the purposes of section 118.1, if the eligible amount of a gift made in a taxation year by an *inter vivos* trust referred to in subsection (1) in respect of a congregation would, but for this subsection, be included in the total charitable gifts, total Crown gifts, total cultural gifts or total ecological gifts of the trust for the year and the trust so elects in its return of income under this Part for the year,

S. 143(3.1), the portion before the description of B in paragraph (*b*) was replaced by S.C. 2013, c. 34, s. 291(1), applicable to gifts made after December 20, 2002, and formerly read:

(3.1) *Election in respect of gifts.* For the purposes of section 118.1, where the fair market value of a gift made in a taxation year by an *inter vivos* trust referred to in subsection (1) in respect of a congregation would, but for this subsection, be included in the total charitable gifts, total Crown gifts, total cultural gifts or total ecological gifts of the trust for the year and the trust so elects in its return of income under this Part for the year,

(*a*) the trust is deemed not to have made the gift; and

(*b*) each participating member of the congregation is deemed to have made, in the year, such a gift the fair market value of which is the amount determined by the formula

$$A \times B/C$$

where

A is the fair market value of the gift made by the trust,

Related Sections: S. 108(1), "*inter vivos* trust"; s. 248(31) Eligible amount of gift or monetary contribution.

► 143(4) ◄

(4) Definitions. For the purposes of this section,

"adult" — "adult" means an individual who, before the time at which the term is applied, has attained the age of eighteen years or is married or in a common-law partnership;

"business agency" — "business agency", of a congregation at any time in a particular calendar year, means a corporation, trust or other person, where the congregation owned all the shares of the capital stock of the corporation (except directors' qualifying shares) or every interest in the trust or other person, as the case may be, throughout the portion of the particular calendar year throughout which both the congregation and the corporation, trust or other person, as the case may be, were in existence;

"congregation" — "congregation" means a community, society or body of individuals, whether or not incorporated,

(*a*) the members of which live and work together,

(*b*) that adheres to the practices and beliefs of, and operates according to the principles of, the religious organization of which it is a constituent part,

(*c*) that does not permit any of its members to own any property in their own right, and

(*d*) that requires its members to devote their working lives to the activities of the congregation;

"family" — "family" means,

(*a*) in the case of an adult who is unmarried and who is not in a common-law partnership, that person and the person's children who are not adults, not married and not in a common-law partnership, and

(*b*) in the case of an adult who is married or in a common-law partnership, that person and the person's spouse or common-law partner and the children of either or both of them who are not adults, not married and not in a common-law partnership

but does not include an individual who is included in any other family or who is not a member of the congregation in which the family is included;

"member of a congregation" — "member of a congregation" means

(*a*) an adult, living with the members of the congregation, who conforms to the practices of the religious organization of which the congregation is a constituent part whether or not that person has been formally accepted into the organization, and (*b*) a child who is unmarried and not in a common-law partnership, other than an adult, of an adult referred to in paragraph (*a*), if the child lives with the members of the congregation;

"participating member" —"participating member", of a congregation in respect of a taxation year, means an individual who, at the end of the year, is an adult who is a member of the congregation;

"religious organization" —"religious organization" means an organization, other than a registered charity, of which a congregation is a constituent part, that adheres to beliefs, evidenced by the religious and philosophical tenets of the organization, that include a belief in the existence of a supreme being.

"total charitable gifts" —"total charitable gifts" has the meaning assigned by subsection 118.1(1);

"total Crown gifts" — (Repealed by 2014, c. 39, s. 48(4).)

History: S. 143(4), the definition "total Crown gifts" was repealed by S.C. 2014, c. 39, s. 48(4), applicable to the 2016 and subsequent taxation years, and formerly read:

"total Crown gifts" —"total Crown gifts" has the meaning assigned by subsection 118.1(1);

"total cultural gifts" —"total cultural gifts" has the meaning assigned by subsection 118.1(1);

"total ecological gifts" —"total ecological gifts" has the same meaning as in subsection 118.1(1).

► 143(5) ◄

(5) Specification of family members. For the purpose of applying subsection (2) to a particular election by the trust referred to in subsection (1) in respect of a congregation for a particular taxation year,

(*a*) subject to paragraph (*b*), a participating member of the congregation is considered to have been specified in the particular election in accordance with this subsection only if the member is identified in the particular election and

(i) where the member's family includes only one adult at the end of the particular year, the member is identified in the particular election as a person to whom subparagraph (i) of the description of B in subsection (2) (in this subsection referred to as the "relevant subparagraph") applies, and

(ii) in any other case, only one of the adults in the member's family is identified in the particular election as a person to whom the relevant subparagraph applies; and

(*b*) an individual is considered not to have been specified in the particular election in accordance with this subsection if

(i) the individual is one of two individuals who were married to each other, or in a common-law partnership, at the end of a preceding taxation year of the trust and at the end of the particular year,

(ii) one of those individuals was

(A) where the preceding year ended before 1998, specified in an election under subsection (2) by the trust for the preceding year, and

(B) in any other case, identified in an election under subsection (2) by the trust for the preceding year as a person to whom the relevant subparagraph applied, and

(iii) the other individual is identified in the particular election as a person to whom the relevant subparagraph applies.

History: S. 143(5), the portion before paragraph (*a*) was replaced by S.C. 2014, c. 39, s. 48(5), applicable to the 2016 and subsequent taxation years, and formerly read:

(5) *Specification of family members.* For the purpose of applying subsection (2) to a particular election by the *inter vivos* trust referred to in subsection (1) in respect of a congregation for a particular taxation year,

Related Sections: S. 2(2) Taxable income; s. 89(1), "Canadian corporation"; s. 104(1) Reference to trust or estate; s. 108(1), "inter vivos trust"; s. 248(1), "corporation", "dividend", "exempt income", "gross revenue"; s. 255 Canada.

SECTION 143.1: [Amateur athletes' reserve funds]

► 143.1(1) ◄

(1) Definitions. The definitions in this subsection apply in this section.

"amateur athlete" —"amateur athlete" at any time means an individual (other than a trust) who is, at that time,

(*a*) a member of a registered Canadian amateur athletic association;

(*b*) eligible to compete, in an international sporting event sanctioned by an international sports federation, as a Canadian national team member; and

(*c*) not a professional athlete.

History: S. 143.1(1), the definition "amateur athlete" was added by S.C. 2009, c. 2, s. 50(1), applicable to the 2008 and subsequent taxation years.

"professional athlete" —"professional athlete" means an individual who receives income that is compensation for, or is otherwise attributable to, the individual's activities as a player or athlete in a professional sport.

History: S. 143.1(1), the definition "professional athlete" was added by S.C. 2009, c. 2, s. 50(1), applicable to the 2008 and subsequent taxation years.

"qualifying performance income" —"qualifying performance income" of an individual means income that

(*a*) is received by the individual in a taxation year in which

(i) the individual was, at any time, an amateur athlete, and

(ii) the individual was not, at any time, a professional athlete;

(*b*) may reasonably be considered to be in connection with the individual's participation as an amateur athlete in one or more international sporting events referred to in the definition "amateur athlete"; and

(*c*) is endorsement income, prize money, or income from public appearances or speeches.

History: S. 143.1(1), the definition "qualifying performance income" was added by S.C. 2009, c. 2, s. 50(1), applicable to the 2008 and subsequent taxation years.

"third party" —"third party" in respect of an arrangement described in paragraph (1.1)(*b*) means a person who deals at arm's length with the amateur athlete in respect of the arrangement.

History: S. 143.1(1), the definition "third party" was added by S.C. 2009, c. 2, s. 50(1), applicable to the 2008 and subsequent taxation years.

S. 143.1(1) was replaced by S.C. 2009, c. 2, s. 50(1), applicable to the 2008 and subsequent taxation years. S. 143.1(1) formerly read:

(1) *Amateur athletes' reserve funds.* Where a national sport organization that is a registered Canadian amateur athletic association receives an amount for the benefit of an individual under an arrangement made under rules of an international sport federation that require amounts to be held, controlled and administered by the organization in order to preserve the eligibility of the individual to compete in a sporting event sanctioned by the federation,

(*a*) an *inter vivos* trust (in this section referred to as an "amateur athlete trust") shall be deemed to be created on the day that is the later of

(i) the day on which the first such amount is received by the organization, and

(ii) January 1, 1992,

and to exist continuously thereafter until subsection (3) or (4) applies in respect of the trust;

(*b*) all property required to be held after 1991 under the arrangement shall be deemed to be property of the trust and not property of any other person;

(*c*) any amount received at any time under the arrangement by the organization shall, to the extent that it would, but for this subsection, be included in computing the individual's income for the taxation year that includes that time, be deemed to be income of the trust for the taxation year and not to be income of the individual;

(*d*) all amounts paid at any time by the organization under the arrangement to or for the benefit of the individual shall be deemed to be amounts distributed at that time to the individual by the trust;

(*e*) the individual shall be deemed to be the beneficiary under the trust;

(*f*) the organization shall be deemed to be the trustee of the trust; and

(*g*) no tax is payable under this Part by the trust on its taxable income for any taxation year.

Related Sections: S. 212(1)(*u*) Amateur athlete trust payments.

Forms: T3ATH(IND) — Amateur Athlete Trust Income Tax Return; T1061 — Canadian Amateur Athletic Trust Group Information Return.

► 143.1(1.1) ◄

(1.1) Where subsection (1.2) applies. Subsection (1.2) applies where, at any time,

(*a*) a national sport organization that is a registered Canadian amateur athletic association receives an amount for the benefit of an individual under an arrangement made under rules of an international sport federation that require amounts to be held, controlled and administered by the organization in order to preserve the eligibility of the individual to compete in a sporting event sanctioned by the federation; or

(*b*) an individual enters into an arrangement that

(i) is an account with an issuer described in paragraph (*b*) of the definition "qualifying arrangement" in subsection 146.2(1), or that would be so described if that definition applied at that time,

(ii) provides that no amount may be deposited, credited or added to the account, other than an amount that is qualifying performance income of the individual or that is interest or other income in respect of the property deposited, credited or added to the account,

(iii) provides that a third party is a mandatory signatory on any payment from the account, and

(iv) is not a registered retirement savings plan or a TFSA.

History: S. 143.1(1.1) was added by S.C. 2009, c. 2, s. 50(1), applicable to the 2008 and subsequent taxation years.

► 143.1(1.2) ◄

(1.2) Amateur athletes' reserve funds. If this subsection applies in respect of an arrangement referred to in subsection (1.1),

(*a*) a trust (in this section referred to as the "amateur athlete trust") is deemed

(i) to be created on the day on which the first amount referred to in paragraph (1.1)(*a*) or (*b*) is received by the sport organization or by the issuer, as the case may be, in respect of the arrangement, and

(ii) to exist until subsection (3) or (4) applies in respect of the trust;

(*b*) all property held under the arrangement is deemed to be the property of the amateur athlete trust and not property of any other person;

(*c*) if, at any time, the sport organization or the issuer, as the case may be, receives an amount under the arrangement and the amount would, in the absence of this subsection, be included in computing the income of the individual in respect of the arrangement for the taxation year that includes that time, the amount is deemed to be income of the amateur athlete trust for that taxation year and not to be income of the individual;

(*d*) if, at any time, the sport organization or the issuer, as the case may be, pays or transfers an amount under the arrangement to or for the benefit of the individual, the amount is deemed to be an amount distributed at that time to the individual by the amateur athlete trust;

(*e*) the individual is deemed to be the beneficiary under the amateur athlete trust;

(*f*) the sport organization or the third party, as the case may be, in respect of the arrangement is deemed to be the trustee of the amateur athlete trust; and

(*g*) no tax is payable under this Part by the amateur athlete trust on its taxable income for any taxation year.

History: S. 143.1(1.2)(*a*), the portion before subparagraph (i) was replaced by S.C. 2014, c. 39, s. 49(1), applicable to the 2016 and subsequent taxation years, and formerly read:

(*a*) an *inter vivos* trust (in this section referred to as the "amateur athlete trust") is deemed

S. 143.1(1.2) was added by S.C. 2009, c. 2, s. 50(1), applicable to the 2008 and subsequent taxation years except that, if the individual in respect of an amateur athlete trust elects in writing filed with the Minister of National Revenue on or before the individual's filing-due date for the 2008 taxation year, in its application to the individual and the amateur athlete trust for the 2008 taxation year, paragraph 143.1(1.2)(*c*) is to be read as follows:

"(*c*) if, at any time before March 3, 2009, the sport organization or the issuer, as the case may be, receives an amount under the arrangement and the amount would, in the absence of this subsection, be included in computing the income of the individual in respect of the arrangement for the 2008 taxation year, the amount is deemed to be income of the amateur athlete trust for its 2009 taxation year and not to be income of the individual;"

► 143.1(2) ◄

(2) Amounts included in beneficiary's income. In computing the income for a taxation year of the beneficiary under an amateur athlete trust, there shall be included the total of all amounts distributed in the year to the beneficiary by the trust.

Related Sections: S. 214(3) Deemed payments.

► 143.1(3) ◄

(3) Termination of amateur athlete trust. Where an amateur athlete trust holds property on behalf of a beneficiary who has not competed in an international sporting event as a Canadian national team member for a period of 8 years that ends in a particular taxation year and that begins in the year that is the later of

(*a*) where the beneficiary has competed in such an event, the year in which the beneficiary last so competed, and

(*b*) the year in which the trust was created,

the trust shall be deemed to have distributed, at the end of the particular taxation year to the beneficiary, an amount equal to

(*c*) if the trust is liable to pay tax under Part XII.2 in respect of the particular year, 60% of the fair market value of all property held by it at that time, and

(*d*) in any other case, the fair market value of all property held by it at that time.

History: S. 143.1(3)(*c*) was replaced by S.C. 2016, c. 7, s. 62(9), applicable to the 2016 and subsequent taxation years, and formerly read:

(*c*) where the trust is liable to pay tax under Part XII.2 in respect of the particular year, 64% of the fair market value of all property held by it at that time, and

► 143.1(4) ◄

(4) Death of beneficiary. Where an amateur athlete trust holds property on behalf of a beneficiary who dies in a year, the trust shall be deemed to have distributed, immediately before the death, to the beneficiary, an amount equal to

(*a*) if the trust is liable to pay tax under Part XII.2 in respect of the year, 60% of the fair market value of all property held by it at that time; and

(*b*) in any other case, the fair market value of all property held by it at that time.

History: S. 143.1(4)(*a*) was replaced by S.C. 2016, c. 7, s. 62(10), applicable to the 2016 and subsequent taxation years, and formerly read:

(*a*) where the trust is liable to pay tax under Part XII.2 in respect of the year, 64% of the fair market value of all property held by it at that time; and

Cost of Tax Shelter Investments and Limited-recourse Debt in Respect of Gifting Arrangements

History: The heading before section 143.2 was replaced by S.C. 2013, c. 34, s. 292(1), deemed to have come into force on February 19, 2003. The heading before section 143.2 formerly read "Cost of Tax Shelter Investments".

SECTION 143.2: [Cost of tax shelter investments and limited-recourse debt in respect of gifting arrangements]

► 143.2(1) ◄

(1) Definitions. The definitions in this subsection apply in this section.

Tax Window Files: *Rente assurée, March 31, 2010,* CRA Document No. 2009-0340381R3; Tax Shelter, *Technical Interpretation, 2006 APFF Conference Round Table on the Federal Taxation Question 29, October 6, 2006,* CRA Document No. 2006-0196251C6.

"expenditure" —"expenditure" means an outlay or expense or the cost or capital cost of a property.

"limited partner" —"limited partner" has the meaning that would be assigned by subsection 96(2.4) if that subsection were read without reference to "if the member's partnership interest is not an exempt interest (within the meaning assigned by subsection (2.5)) at that time and".

"limited-recourse amount" —"limited-recourse amount" means the unpaid principal amount of any indebtedness for which recourse is limited, either immediately or in the future and either absolutely or contingently.

"taxpayer" —"taxpayer" includes a partnership.

"tax shelter investment" —"tax shelter investment" means

(*a*) a property that is a tax shelter for the purpose of subsection 237.1(1); or

(*b*) a taxpayer's interest in a partnership where

(i) an interest in the taxpayer

(A) is a tax shelter investment, and

(B) the taxpayer's partnership interest would be a tax shelter investment if

(I) this Act were read without reference to this paragraph and to the words "having regard to statements or representations made or proposed to be made in connection with the property" in the definition "tax shelter" in subsection 237.1(1),

(II) the references in that definition to "represented" were read as references to "that can reasonably be expected", and

(III) the reference in that definition to "is represented" were read as a reference to "can reasonably be expected",

(ii) another interest in the partnership is a tax shelter investment, or

(iii) the taxpayer's interest in the partnership entitles the taxpayer, directly or indirectly, to a share of the income or loss of a particular partnership where

(A) another taxpayer holding a partnership interest is entitled, directly or indirectly, to a share of the income or loss of the particular partnership, and

(B) that other taxpayer's partnership interest is a tax shelter investment.

Related Sections: S. 53(2)(*c*) Amounts to be deducted — Interest in a partnership; s. 150(1)(*d*) Individuals; s. 249.1(5) Alternative method not applicable to tax shelter investments.

Canadian Tax Foundation: Watkins, *The Tax-Shelter Rules: An Update,* 1998 Conference Report 5:1–32.

► 143.2(2) ◄

(2) At-risk adjustment. For the purpose of this section, an at-risk adjustment in respect of an expenditure of a particular taxpayer, other than the cost of a partnership interest to which subsection 96(2.2) applies, means any amount or benefit that the particular taxpayer, or another taxpayer not dealing at arm's length with the particular taxpayer, is entitled, either immediately or in the future and either absolutely or contingently, to receive or to obtain, whether by way of reimbursement, compensation, revenue guarantee, proceeds of disposition, loan or any other form of indebtedness, or in any other form or manner whatever, granted or to be granted for the purpose of reducing the impact, in whole or in part, of any loss that the particular taxpayer may sustain in respect of the expenditure or, where the expenditure is the cost or capital cost of a property, any loss from the holding or disposition of the property.

► 143.2(3) ◄

(3) Amount or benefit not included. For the purpose of subsection (2), an at-risk adjustment in respect of a taxpayer's expenditure does not include an amount or benefit

(*a*) to the extent that it is included in determining the value of J in the definition "cumulative Canadian exploration expense" in subsection 66.1(6), of M in the definition "cumulative Canadian development expense" in subsection 66.2(5) or of I in the definition "cumulative Canadian oil and gas property expense" in subsection 66.4(5) in respect of the taxpayer; or

(*b*) the entitlement to which arises

(i) because of a contract of insurance with an insurance corporation dealing at arm's length with the taxpayer (and, where the expenditure is the cost of an interest in a partnership, with each member of the partnership) under which the taxpayer is insured against any claim arising as a result of a liability incurred in the ordinary course of carrying on the business of the taxpayer or the partnership,

(ii) as a consequence of the death of the taxpayer,

(iii) in respect of an amount not included in the expenditure, determined without reference to subparagraph (6)(*b*)(ii), or

(iv) because of an excluded obligation (as defined in subsection 6202.1(5) of the *Income Tax Regulations*) in relation to a share issued to the taxpayer or, where the expenditure is the cost of an interest in a partnership, to the partnership.

► 143.2(4) ◄

(4) Amount or benefit. For the purposes of subsections (2) and (3), where the amount or benefit to which a taxpayer is entitled at any time is provided by way of an agreement or other arrangement under which the taxpayer has a right, either immediately or in the future and either absolutely or contingently (otherwise than as a consequence of the death of the taxpayer), to acquire property, for greater certainty the amount or benefit to which the taxpayer is entitled under the agreement or arrangement is considered to be not less than the fair market value of the property at that time.

► 143.2(5) ◄

(5) Amount or benefit. For the purposes of subsections (2) and (3), where the amount or benefit to which a taxpayer is entitled at any time is provided by way of a guarantee, security or similar indemnity or covenant in respect of any loan or other obligation of the taxpayer, for greater certainty the amount or benefit to which the taxpayer is entitled under the guarantee or indemnity at any particular time is considered to be not less than the total of the unpaid amount of the loan or obligation at that time and all other amounts outstanding in respect of the loan or obligation at that time.

► 143.2(6) ◄

(6) Amount of expenditure. Notwithstanding any other provision of this Act, the amount of any expenditure that is, or is the cost or capital cost of, a taxpayer's tax shelter investment, and the amount of any expenditure of a taxpayer an interest in which is a tax shelter investment, shall be reduced to the amount, if any, by which

(*a*) the amount of the taxpayer's expenditure otherwise determined

exceeds

(*b*) the total of

(i) the limited-recourse amounts of

(A) the taxpayer, and

(B) all other taxpayers not dealing at arm's length with the taxpayer

that can reasonably be considered to relate to the expenditure,

(ii) the taxpayer's at-risk adjustment in respect of the expenditure, and

(iii) each limited-recourse amount and at-risk adjustment, determined under this section when this section is applied to each other taxpayer who deals at arm's length with and holds, directly or indirectly, an interest in the taxpayer, that can reasonably be considered to relate to the expenditure.

Related Sections: S. 96(2.2)(*c*) At-risk amount.

Tax Profile: December 2011 — Partnership Taxation.

► 143.2(6.1) ◄

(6.1) Limited-recourse debt in respect of a gift or monetary contribution. The limited-recourse debt in respect of a gift or monetary contribution of a taxpayer, at the time the gift or monetary contribution is made, is the total of

(*a*) each limited-recourse amount at that time, of the taxpayer and of all other taxpayers not dealing at arm's length with the taxpayer, that can reasonably be considered to relate to the gift or monetary contribution,

(*b*) each limited-recourse amount at that time, determined under this section when this section is applied to each other taxpayer who deals at arm's length with and holds, directly or indirectly, an interest in the taxpayer, that can reasonably be considered to relate to the gift or monetary contribution, and

(*c*) each amount that is the unpaid amount at that time of any other indebtedness, of any taxpayer referred to in paragraph (*a*) or (*b*), that can reasonably be considered to relate to the gift or monetary contribution if there is a guarantee, security or similar indemnity or covenant in respect of that or any other indebtedness.

History: S. 143.2(6.1) was added by S.C. 2013, c. 34, s. 293(1), applicable in respect of expenditures, gifts and monetary contributions made after February 18, 2003.

Related Sections: S. 248(32) Amount of advantage.

► 143.2(7) ◄

(7) Repayment of indebtedness. For the purpose of this section, the unpaid principal of an indebtedness is deemed to be a limited-recourse amount unless

(*a*) *bona fide* arrangements, evidenced in writing, were made, at the time the indebtedness arose, for repayment by the debtor of the indebtedness and all interest on the indebtedness within a reasonable period not exceeding 10 years; and

(*b*) interest is payable at least annually, at a rate equal to or greater than the lesser of

(i) the prescribed rate of interest in effect at the time the indebtedness arose, and

(ii) the prescribed rate of interest applicable from time to time during the term of the indebtedness,

and is paid in respect of the indebtedness by the debtor no later than 60 days after the end of each taxation year of the debtor that ends in the period.

Related Regulations: 4301.

► 143.2(8) ◄

(8) Limited-recourse amount. For the purpose of this section, the unpaid principal of an indebtedness is deemed to be a limited-recourse amount of a taxpayer where the taxpayer is a partnership and recourse against any member of the partnership in respect of the indebtedness is limited, either immediately or in the future and either absolutely or contingently.

► 143.2(9) ◄

(9) Timing. Where at any time a taxpayer has paid an amount (in this subsection referred to as the "repaid amount") on account of the principal amount of an indebtedness that was, before that time, the unpaid principal amount of a loan or any other form of indebtedness to which subsection (2) applies (in this subsection referred to as the "former amount or benefit") relating to an expenditure of the taxpayer,

(*a*) the former amount or benefit is considered to have been an amount or benefit under subsection (2) in respect of the taxpayer at all times before that time; and

(*b*) the expenditure is, subject to subsection (6), deemed to have been made or incurred at that time to the extent of, and by the payment of, the repaid amount.

► 143.2(10) ◄

(10) Timing. Where at any time a taxpayer has paid an amount (in this subsection referred to as the "repaid amount") on account of the principal amount of an indebtedness which was, before that time, an unpaid principal amount that was a limited-recourse amount (in this subsection referred to as the "former limited-recourse indebtedness") relating to an expenditure of the taxpayer, (*a*) the former limited-recourse indebtedness is considered to have been a limited-recourse amount at all times before that time; and

(*b*) the expenditure is, subject to subsection (6), deemed to have been made or incurred at that time to the extent of, and by the amount of, the repaid amount.

▶ 143.2(11) ◀

(11) Short-term debt. Where a taxpayer pays all of the principal of an indebtedness no later than 60 days after that indebtedness arose and the indebtedness would otherwise be considered to be a limited- recourse amount solely because of the application of subsection (7) or (8), that subsection does not apply to the indebtedness unless

(*a*) any portion of the repayment is made with a limited-recourse amount; or

(*b*) the repayment can reasonably be considered to be part of a series of loans or other indebtedness and repayments that ends more than 60 days after the indebtedness arose.

▶ 143.2(12) ◀

(12) Series of loans or repayments. For the purpose of paragraph (7)(*a*), a debtor is considered not to have made arrangements to repay an indebtedness within 10 years where the debtor's arrangement to repay can reasonably be considered to be part of a series of loans or other indebtedness and repayments that ends more than 10 years after it begins.

▶ 143.2(13) ◀

(13) Information located outside Canada. For the purpose of this section, if it can reasonably be considered that information relating to indebtedness that relates to a taxpayer's expenditure, gift or monetary contribution is available outside Canada and the Minister is not satisfied that the unpaid principal of the indebtedness is not a limited-recourse amount, the unpaid principal of the indebtedness relating to the taxpayer's expenditure, gift or monetary contribution is deemed to be a limited-recourse amount relating to the expenditure, gift or monetary contribution unless

(*a*) the information is provided to the Minister; or

(*b*) the information is located in a country with which the Government of Canada has entered into a tax convention or agreement that has the force of law in Canada and includes a provision under which the Minister can obtain the information.

History: S. 143.2(13), the portion before paragraph (*a*) was replaced by S.C. 2013, c. 34, s. 293(2), applicable in respect of expenditures, gifts and monetary contributions made after February 18, 2003, and formerly read:

(13) *Information located outside Canada.* For the purpose of this section, where it can reasonably be considered that information relating to indebtedness that relates to a taxpayer's expenditure is available outside Canada and the Minister is not satisfied that the unpaid principal of the indebtedness is not a limited-recourse amount, the unpaid principal of the indebtedness relating to the taxpayer's expenditure is deemed to be a limited-recourse amount relating to the expenditure unless

▶ 143.2(14) ◀

(14) Information located outside Canada. For the purpose of this section, where it can reasonably be considered that information relating to whether a taxpayer is not dealing at arm's length with another taxpayer is available outside Canada and the Minister is not satisfied that the taxpayer is dealing at arm's length with the other taxpayer, the taxpayer and the other taxpayer are deemed not to be dealing with each other at arm's length unless

(*a*) the information is provided to the Minister; or

(*b*) the information is located in a country with which the Government of Canada has entered into a tax convention or agreement that has the force of law in Canada and includes a provision under which the Minister can obtain the information.

▶ 143.2(15) ◀

(15) Assessments. Notwithstanding subsections 152(4) to (5), such assessments, determinations and redeterminations may be made as are necessary to give effect to this section.

SECTION 143.3: Expenditure — Limitations

▶ 143.3(1) ◀

(1) Definitions. The following definitions apply in this section.

"expenditure" —"expenditure" of a taxpayer means an expense, expenditure or outlay made or incurred by the taxpayer, or a cost or capital cost of property acquired by the taxpayer.

History: S. 143.3(1), the definition "expenditure" was added by S.C. 2013, c. 34, s. 294(1), deemed to have come into force on November 17, 2005.

"option" —"option" means

(*a*) a security that is issued or sold by a taxpayer under an agreement referred to in subsection 7(1); or

(*b*) an option, warrant or similar right, issued or granted by a taxpayer, giving the holder the right to acquire an interest in the taxpayer or in another taxpayer with whom the taxpayer does not, at the time the option, warrant or similar right is issued or granted, deal at arm's length.

History: S. 143.3(1), the definition "option" was added by S.C. 2013, c. 34, s. 294(1), deemed to have come into force on November 17, 2005, except that for securities issued or sold before October 24, 2012, the definition "option" in subsection 143.3(1) is to be read without reference to its paragraph (*a*).

"taxpayer" —"taxpayer" includes a partnership.

History: S. 143.3(1), the definition "taxpayer" was added by S.C. 2013, c. 34, s. 294(1), deemed to have come into force on November 17, 2005.

▶ 143.3(2) ◀

(2) Options — limitation. In computing a taxpayer's income, taxable income or tax payable or an amount considered to have been paid on account of the taxpayer's tax payable, an expenditure of the taxpayer is deemed not to include any portion of the expenditure that would — if this Act were read without reference to this subsection — be included in determining the expenditure because of the taxpayer having granted or issued an option on or after November 17, 2005.

History: S. 143.3(2) was added by S.C. 2013, c. 34, s. 294(1), deemed to have come into force on November 17, 2005.

Canadian Tax Foundation: Lamarre, *Critical Issues in the Determination of Cost Under the Income Tax Act*, 2012 Conference Report 17:1–28.

▶ 143.3(3) ◀

(3) Corporate shares — limitation. In computing a corporation's income, taxable income or tax payable or an amount considered to have been paid on account of the corporation's tax payable, an expenditure of the corporation that would — if this Act were read without reference to this subsection — include an amount because of the corporation having issued a share of its capital stock at any particular time on or after November 17, 2005 is reduced by

(*a*) if the issuance of the share is not a consequence of the exercise of an option, the amount, if any, by which the fair market value of the share at the particular time exceeds

(i) if the transaction under which the share is issued is a transaction to which section 85, 85.1 or 138 applies, the amount determined under that section to be the cost to the issuing corporation of the property acquired in consideration for issuing the share, or

(ii) in any other case, the amount of the consideration that is the fair market value of the property transferred or issued to, or the services provided to, the issuing corporation for issuing the share; and

(*b*) if the issuance of the share is a consequence of the exercise of an option, the amount, if any, by which the fair market value of the share at the particular time exceeds the amount paid, pursuant to the terms of the option, by the holder to the issuing taxpayer for issuing the share.

History: S. 143.3(3) was added by S.C. 2013, c. 34, s. 294(1), deemed to have come into force on November 17, 2005.

Canadian Tax Foundation: Lamarre, *Critical Issues in the Determination of Cost Under the Income Tax Act*, 2012 Conference Report 17:1–28.

► 143.3(4) ◄

(4) Non-corporate interests — limitation. In computing a taxpayer's (other than a corporation's) income, taxable income or tax payable or an amount considered to have been paid on account of the taxpayer's tax payable, an expenditure of the taxpayer that would — if this Act were read without reference to this subsection — include an amount because of the taxpayer having issued an interest, or because of an interest being created, in itself at any particular time on or after November 17, 2005 is reduced by

(*a*) if the issuance or creation of the interest is not a consequence of the exercise of an option, the amount, if any, by which the fair market value of the interest at the particular time exceeds

(i) if the transaction under which the interest is issued is a transaction to which paragraph 70(6)(*b*) or 73(1.01)(*c*), subsection 97(2) or section 107.4 or 132.2 applies, the amount determined under that provision to be the cost to the taxpayer of the property acquired for the interest, or

(ii) in any other case, the amount of the consideration that is the fair market value of the property transferred or issued to, or the services provided to, the taxpayer for the interest; and

(*b*) if the issuance or creation of the interest is a consequence of the exercise of an option, the amount, if any, by which the fair market value of the interest at the particular time exceeds the amount paid, pursuant to the terms of the option, by the holder to the taxpayer for the interest.

History: S. 143.3(4) was added by S.C. 2013, c. 34, s. 294(1), deemed to have come into force on November 17, 2005.

► 143.3(5) ◄

(5) Clarification. For greater certainty,

(*a*) subsection (2) does not apply to reduce an expenditure that is a commission, fee or other amount for services rendered by a person as a salesperson, agent or dealer in securities in the course of the issuance of an option;

(*b*) subsections (3) and (4) do not apply to reduce an expenditure of a taxpayer to the extent that the expenditure does not include an amount determined to be an excess under those subsections;

(*c*) this section does not apply to determine the cost or capital cost of property determined under subsection 70(6), section 73, 85 or 85.1, subsection 97(2) or section 107.4, 132.2 or 138; and

(*d*) this section does not apply to determine the amount of a taxpayer's expenditure if the amount of the expenditure as determined under section 69 is less than the amount that would, if this subsection were read without reference to this paragraph, be the amount of the expenditure as determined under this section.

> **Proposed Amendment**
>
> **Notice of Ways and Means Motion to amend the Income Tax Act (June 17, 2019)**
>
> **Subsection 143.3(5) of the Act is amended by striking out "and" at the end of paragraph (*c*), by adding "and" at the end of paragraph (*d*) and by adding the following after paragraph (*d*):**
>
> (*e*) this section does not apply to prohibit the deduction of an amount under paragraph 110(1)(*e*).
>
> **Applicable:** On January 1, 2020.

History: S. 143.3(5) was added by S.C. 2013, c. 34, s. 294(1), deemed to have come into force on November 17, 2005.

SECTION 143.4: Expenditure — Limit for Contingent Amount

► 143.4(1) ◄

(1) Definitions. The following definitions apply in this section.

Related Sections: S. 87(2)(*l.5*) Contingent amount — section 143.4.

"contingent amount" —"contingent amount", of a taxpayer at any time (other than a time at which the taxpayer is a bankrupt), includes an amount to the extent that the taxpayer, or another taxpayer that does not deal at arm's length with the taxpayer, has a right to reduce the amount at that time.

History: S. 143.4(1), the definition "contingent amount" was added by S.C. 2013, c. 34, s. 295(1), applicable in respect of taxation years that end on or after March 16, 2011.

"expenditure" —"expenditure", of a taxpayer, means an expense, expenditure or outlay made or incurred by the taxpayer, or a cost or capital cost of property acquired by the taxpayer.

History: S. 143.4(1), the definition "expenditure" was added by S.C. 2013, c. 34, s. 295(1), applicable in respect of taxation years that end on or after March 16, 2011.

"right to reduce" —"right to reduce" means a right to reduce or eliminate an amount in respect of an expenditure at any time, including, for greater certainty, a right to reduce that is contingent upon the occurrence of an event, or in any other way contingent, if it is reasonable to conclude, having regard to all the circumstances, that the right will become exercisable.

History: S. 143.4(1), the definition "right to reduce" was added by S.C. 2013, c. 34, s. 295(1), applicable in respect of taxation years that end on or after March 16, 2011.

"taxpayer" —"taxpayer" includes a partnership.

History: S. 143.4(1), the definition "taxpayer" was added by S.C. 2013, c. 34, s. 295(1), applicable in respect of taxation years that end on or after March 16, 2011.

► 143.4(2) ◄

(2) Limitation of amount of expenditure. For the purposes of this Act, if in a taxation year of a taxpayer an expenditure of the taxpayer occurs, the amount of the expenditure at any time is the lesser of (*a*) the amount of the expenditure at the time calculated under this Act without reference to this section, and

(*b*) the least amount of the expenditure calculated by reducing the amount of the expenditure determined under paragraph (*a*) by the amount that is the amount, if any, by which

(i) the total of all amounts each of which is a contingent amount of the taxpayer in the year in respect of the expenditure

exceeds

(ii) the total of all amounts each of which is

(A) an amount paid by the taxpayer to obtain a right to reduce an amount in respect of the expenditure, or

(B) a limited-recourse amount for the purposes of paragraph 143.2(6)(*b*) that reduces the expenditure under subsection 143.2(6) to the extent that the amount is also a contingent amount described in subparagraph (i) in respect of the expenditure.

History: S. 143.4(2) was added by S.C. 2013, c. 34, s. 295(1), applicable in respect of taxation years that end on or after March 16, 2011.

Canadian Tax Foundation: Lamarre, *Critical Issues in the Determination of Cost Under the Income Tax Act*, 2012 Conference Report 17:1–28.

► 143.4(3) ◄

(3) Payment of contingent amount. For the purposes of this Act, if in a particular taxation year, a taxpayer pays all or a portion of a contingent amount referred to in paragraph (2)(*b*) that reduces the amount of the taxpayer's expenditure referred to in paragraph (2)(*a*), the portion of the contingent amount paid by the taxpayer in the particular year for the purpose of earning income, and to that extent only, is deemed

(*a*) to have been incurred by the taxpayer in the particular year;

(*b*) to have been incurred for the same purpose and to have the same character as the expenditure so reduced; and

(*c*) to have become payable by the taxpayer in respect of the particular year.

History: S. 143.4(3) was added by S.C. 2013, c. 34, s. 295(1), applicable in respect of taxation years that end on or after March 16, 2011.

► 143.4(4) ◄

(4) Subsequent years. Subject to subsection (6), if at any time in a taxation year that is after a taxation year in which an expenditure of the taxpayer occurred, the taxpayer, or another taxpayer not dealing at arm's length with the taxpayer, has a right to reduce an amount in respect of the expenditure (in this subsection and subsection (5) referred to as the "prior expenditure") that would, if the taxpayer or the other taxpayer had had the right to reduce in a particular taxation year that ended before the time, have resulted in subsection (2) applying in the particular taxation year to reduce or eliminate the amount of the prior expenditure, the taxpayer's subsequent contingent amount in respect of the prior expenditure, as determined under subsection (5), is deemed, to the extent subsection (2) and this subsection have not previously applied in respect of the expenditure,

(*a*) to be an amount received by the taxpayer at the time in the course of earning income from a business or property from a person described in subparagraph 12(1)(*x*)(i); and

(*b*) to be an amount referred to in subparagraph 12(1)(*x*)(iv).

History: S. 143.4(4) was added by S.C. 2013, c. 34, s. 295(1), applicable in respect of taxation years that end on or after March 16, 2011.

Tax Window Files: Whether s. 80 or s. 143.4 applies, *16XXXX*, CRA Document No. 2016-0661071R3.

► 143.4(5) ◄

(5) Subsequent contingent amount. For the purposes of subsection (4), a taxpayer's subsequent contingent amount in respect of a prior expenditure of the taxpayer is the amount, if any, by which

(*a*) the maximum amount by which the amount (in this subsection referred to as the "particular amount") in respect of the prior expenditure may be reduced pursuant to a right to reduce the particular amount

exceeds

(*b*) the amount, if any, paid to obtain the right to reduce the particular amount.

History: S. 143.4(5) was added by S.C. 2013, c. 34, s. 295(1), applicable in respect of taxation years that end on or after March 16, 2011.

► 143.4(6) ◄

(6) Anti-avoidance. If a taxpayer, or another taxpayer that does not deal at arm's length with the taxpayer, has a right to reduce an amount in respect of an expenditure of the taxpayer in a taxation year that is after the taxation year in which the expenditure otherwise occurred, determined without reference to subsection (3), the taxpayer is deemed to have the right to reduce in the taxation year in which that expenditure otherwise occurred if it is reasonable to conclude having regard to all the circumstances that one of the purposes for having the right to reduce after the end of the year in which the expenditure otherwise occurred was to avoid the application of subsection (2) to the amount of the expenditure.

History: S. 143.4(6) was added by S.C. 2013, c. 34, s. 295(1), applicable in respect of taxation years that end on or after March 16, 2011.

► 143.4(7) ◄

(7) Assessments. Notwithstanding subsections 152(4) to (5), such assessments, determinations and redeterminations may be made as are necessary to give effect to this section.

History: S. 143.4(7) was added by S.C. 2013, c. 34, s. 295(1), applicable in respect of taxation years that end on or after March 16, 2011.

Division G — Deferred and Other Special Income Arrangements

Employees Profit Sharing Plans

SECTION 144: [Employee profit sharing plans]

► 144(1) ◄

(1) Definitions. The definitions in this subsection apply in this section.

"employees profit sharing plan" —"employees profit sharing plan" at a particular time means an arrangement

(*a*) under which payments computed by reference to

(i) an employer's profits from the employer's business,

(ii) the profits from the business of a corporation with which the employer does not deal at arm's length, or

(iii) any combination of the amounts described in subparagraphs (i) and (ii)

are required to be made by the employer to a trustee under the arrangement for the benefit of employees of the employer or of a corporation with which the employer does not deal at arm's length; and

(*b*) in respect of which the trustee has, since the later of the beginning of the arrangement and the end of 1949, allocated, either contingently or absolutely, to those employees

(i) in each year that ended at or before the particular time, all amounts received in the year by the trustee from the employer or from a corporation with which the employer does not deal at arm's length,

(ii) in each year that ended at or before the particular time, all profits for the year from the property of the trust (determined without regard to any capital gain made by the trust or capital loss sustained by it at any time after 1955),

(iii) in each year that ended after 1971 and at or before the particular time, all capital gains and capital losses of the trust for the year,

(iv) in each year that ended after 1971, before 1993 and at or before the particular time, $^{100}/_{15}$ of the total of all amounts each of which is deemed by subsection (9) to be paid on account of tax under this Part in respect of an employee because the employee ceased to be a beneficiary under the plan in the year, and

(v) in each year that ended after 1991 and at or before the particular time, the total of all amounts each of which is an amount that may be deducted under subsection (9) in computing the employee's income because the employee ceased to be a beneficiary under the plan in the year.

Related Sections: S. 144(9) Deduction for forfeited amounts; s. 144(10) Payments out of profits; s. 251 Arm's length.

Tax Profile: May 2012 — Employee Profit-Sharing Plans.

Information Circulars: IC 77-1R5 Deferred profit sharing plan.

Interpretation Bulletins: *Primary* — IT-280R Employees profit sharing plans — Payments computed by reference to profits; IT-379R Employees profit sharing plans — Allocations to beneficiaries.

Tax Window Files: Employer contributions, *February 11, 2019*, CRA Document No. 2018-0738561E5; Employees Profit Sharing Plan, *June 10, 2010*, CRA Document No. 2009-0328661E5.

Cases: The taxpayer's employee profit sharing plan was not valid since payments were arbitrary and not computed by reference to profits. Setting a minimum annual payment per participating beneficiary did not meet the requirement. *Gary Jackson Professional Corporation v. MNR*, 2013 DTC 5108 (F.C.A.)

A taxpayer was entitled to deduct payments made in respect of an informal profit sharing plan despite the plan having been formed without any written agreement where the plan created an enforceable obligation against the taxpayer. *534325 Ontario Corporation v. M.N.R.*, 89 DTC 679 (T.C.C.)

Stock purchase plan under which a company made contributions equal to 50% of a member's monthly contributions plus an annual contribution based on profits if such profits exceeded a certain percentage of invested capital, was held not to be an employees profit sharing plan as defined in former s. 79(1) (now s. 144(1)). *Lade v. M.N.R.*, 65 DTC 5297 (S.C.C.)

"unused portion of a beneficiary's exempt capital gains balance" —"unused portion of a beneficiary's exempt capital gains balance" in respect of a trust governed by an employees profit sharing plan, at any particular time in a taxation year of the beneficiary, means

(*a*) where the year ends before 2005, the amount, if any, by which the beneficiary's exempt capital gains balance (in this paragraph having the same meaning as in subsection 39.1(1)) in respect of the trust for the year exceeds the total of all amounts each of which is an amount by which a capital gain is reduced under section 39.1 in the year because of the beneficiary's exempt capital gains balance in respect of the trust; or

(*b*) where the year ends after 2004, the amount, if any, by which

(i) the amount, if any, that would, if the definition "exempt capital gains balance" in subsection 39.1(1) were read without reference to "that ends before 2005", be the beneficiary's exempt capital gains balance in respect of the trust for the year

exceeds

(ii) where there has been a disposition of an interest or a part of an interest of the beneficiary in the trust after the beneficiary's 2004 taxation year (other than a disposition that is a part of a transaction described in paragraph (7.1)(*c*) in which property is received in satisfaction of all or a portion of the beneficiary's interests in the trust), the total of all amounts each of which is an amount by which the adjusted cost base of an interest or a part of an interest disposed of by the beneficiary (other than an interest or a part of an interest that is all or a portion of the beneficiary's interests referred to in paragraph (7.1)(*c*)) was increased because of paragraph 53(1)(*p*), and

(iii) in any other case, nil.

Related Sections: S. 110.6(19) Election for property owned on February 22, 1994.

► 144(2) ◄

(2) No tax while trust governed by plan. No tax is payable under this Part by a trust on the taxable income of the trust for a taxation year throughout which the trust is governed by an employees profit sharing plan.

Related Sections: S. 149(1)(*p*) Trusts under profit sharing plan.

▶ 144(3) ◀

(3) Allocation contingent or absolute taxable. There shall be included in computing the income for a taxation year of an employee who is a beneficiary under an employees profit sharing plan each amount that is allocated to the employee contingently or absolutely by the trustee under the plan at any time in the year otherwise than in respect of

(*a*) a payment made by the employee to the trustee;

(*b*) a capital gain made by the trust before 1972;

(*c*) a capital gain of the trust for a taxation year ending after 1971;

(*d*) a gain made by the trust after 1971 from the disposition of a capital property except to the extent that the gain is a capital gain described in paragraph (*c*); or

(*e*) a dividend received by the trust from a taxable Canadian corporation.

(*f*) (Repealed by S.C. 1994, c. 21, s. 68(2).)

Related Regulations: Part II.

Related Sections: S. 81(1)(*k*) Employees profit sharing plan; s. 144(8) Allocation of credit for dividends.

Canadian Petroleum Tax Journal: Current Trends in Executive Compensation Structures and Their Taxation, Rachel Colabella and Denise McMullen, 2000, Vol. 13, No. 1.

Forms: T4PS Sum. — Return of Allocations and Payments Under Employees Profit Sharing Plan; T4PS — Statement of Employee Profit Sharing Plan Allocations and Payments.

Interpretation Bulletins: *Primary* — IT-379R Employees profit sharing plans — Allocations to beneficiaries.

Cases: After the taxpayer terminated his employment, an amount previously allocated to him was included in his income. Although he lost the right to receive the amount, he was not entitled to deduct a corresponding amount from the previous year's income. *Aspinall v. M.N.R.*, 86 DTC 1281 (T.C.C.)

▶ 144(4) ◀

(4) Allocated capital gains and losses. Each capital gain and capital loss of a trust governed by an employees profit sharing plan from the disposition of any property shall, to the extent that it is allocated by the trust to an employee who is a beneficiary under the plan, be deemed to be a capital gain or capital loss, as the case may be, of the employee from the disposition of that property for the taxation year of the employee in which the allocation was made and, for the purposes of section 110.6, the property shall be deemed to have been disposed of by the employee on the day on which it was disposed of by the trust.

Related Sections: S. 6(1)(*d*) Allocations, etc., under profit sharing plan.

Interpretation Bulletins: *Secondary* — IT-379R Employees profit sharing plans — Allocations to beneficiaries.

▶ 144(4.1) ◀

(4.1) Idem. Notwithstanding subsection 26(6) of the *Income Tax Application Rules*, where at any time before 1976 the trustee of a trust governed by an employees profit sharing plan so elects in prescribed manner, the trust shall be deemed

(*a*) to have, on December 31, 1971, disposed of each property owned by the trust on that day for proceeds of disposition equal to the fair market value of the property on that day, and

(*b*) to have, on January 1, 1972, reacquired each property described in paragraph (*a*) for the amount referred to in that paragraph,

if the trustee under the plan has, before 1976, allocated the total of all capital gains and capital losses resulting from the deemed dispositions among the employees or other beneficiaries under the plan to the extent that the trustee under the plan has not previously so allocated them.

Related Regulations: Part XV; 1500(1).

Related Sections: S. 38 Taxable capital gain and allowable capital loss; s. 54, "proceeds of disposition"; ITAR s. 26(6) Reacquired property.

Interpretation Bulletins: *Secondary* — IT-379R Employees profit sharing plans — Allocations to beneficiaries.

▶ 144(4.2) ◀

(4.2) Idem. Where a trust governed by an employees profit sharing plan

(*a*) was governed by an employees profit sharing plan on December 31, 1971, and the trustee of the trust has made an election under subsection (4.1), or

(*b*) was not governed by an employees profit sharing plan on December 31, 1971,

the trustee of the trust may, in any taxation year after 1973, elect in prescribed manner and prescribed form to treat any capital property of the trust as having been disposed of, in which event the property shall be deemed to have been disposed of on any day designated by the trustee for proceeds of disposition equal to

(*c*) the fair market value of the property on that day,

(*d*) the adjusted cost base to the trust of the property on that day, or

(*e*) an amount that is neither greater than the greater of the amounts determined under paragraphs (*c*) and (*d*) nor less than the lesser of the amounts determined under those paragraphs

whichever is designated by the trustee and to have been reacquired by the trust immediately thereafter at a cost equal to those proceeds.

Related Regulations: Part XV; 1500(2).

Related Sections: S. 54, "Adjusted cost base", "proceeds of disposition"; s. 144(4.1) Election — deemed disposition of trust property on December 31, 1971 and reacquisition on January 1, 1972.

Forms: T3009 — Election from Deemed Disposition and Reacquisition of any Capital Property of an Employees Profit Sharing Plan under Subsection 144(4.2).

Interpretation Bulletins: *Secondary* — IT-379R Employees profit sharing plans — Allocations to beneficiaries.

▶ 144(5) ◀

(5) Employer's contribution to trust deductible. An amount paid by an employer to a trustee under an employees profit sharing plan during a taxation year or within 120 days thereafter may be deducted in computing the employer's income for the taxation year to the extent that it was not deductible in computing income for a previous taxation year.

Related Sections: S. 6(1)(*d*) Allocations, etc., under profit sharing plan; s. 12(1)(*m*) Benefits from trusts; s. 18(1)(*k*) Limitation re employer's contribution under profit sharing plan; s. 20(1)(*w*) Employer's contributions under profit sharing plan.

Canadian Petroleum Tax Journal: Current Trends in Executive Compensation Structures and Their Taxation, Rachel Colabella and Denise McMullen, 2000, Vol. 13, No. 1.

▶ 144(6) ◀

(6) Beneficiary's receipts deductible. An amount received in a taxation year by a beneficiary from a trustee under an employees profit sharing plan shall not be included in computing the beneficiary's income for the year.

▶ 144(7) ◀

(7) Beneficiary's receipts that are not deductible. Notwithstanding subsection (6), such portion of an amount received in a taxation year by a beneficiary from the trustee under an employees profit sharing plan as cannot be established to be attributable to

(*a*) payments made by the employee to the trustee,

(*b*) amounts required to be included in computing the income of the employee for that or a previous taxation year,

(*c*) a capital gain made by the trust before 1972,

(*d*) a capital gain made by the trust for a taxation year ending after 1971, to the extent allocated by the trust to the beneficiary,

(*e*) a gain made by the trust after 1971 from the disposition of a capital property, except to the extent that the gain is a capital gain made by the trust for a taxation year ending after 1971,

(*f*) the portion, if any, of the increase in the value of property transferred to the beneficiary by the trustee that would have been considered to be a capital gain made by the trust in 1971 if the trustee had sold the property on December 31, 1971 for its fair market value at that time, or

(*g*) a dividend received by the trust from a taxable Canadian corporation other than a dividend described in subsection 83(1), to the extent allocated by the trust to the beneficiary,

shall be included in computing the beneficiary's income for the year in which the amount was received, except that in determining the amount of any payments or other things described in any paragraph of this subsection, the amount thereof otherwise determined shall be reduced by such portion of the total of all capital losses of the trust for taxation years ending after 1971 as has been allocated by the trust to the beneficiary and has not been applied to reduce the amount of any payments or other things described in any other paragraph of this subsection.

Related Sections: S. 6(1)(*d*) Allocations, etc., under profit sharing plan; s. 212 Taxation of non-residents.

Forms: T4PS Sum. — Return of Allocations and Payments Under Employees Profit Sharing Plan; T4PS — Statement of Employee Profit Sharing Plan Allocations and Payments.

Interpretation Bulletins: *Secondary* — IT-379R Employees profit sharing plans — Allocations to beneficiaries.

▶ 144(7.1) ◀

(7.1) Where property other than money received by beneficiary. Where, at any particular time in a taxation year of a trust governed by an employees profit sharing plan, an amount was received by a beneficiary from the trustee under the plan and the amount so received was property other than money, the following rules apply in respect of each such property so received by the beneficiary at the particular time:

(*a*) the amount that was the cost amount to the trust of the property immediately before the particular time shall be deemed to be the trust's proceeds of disposition of the property;

(*b*) that proportion of

(i) such portion of the amount received by the beneficiary as can be established to be attributable to the payments or other things described in paragraphs (7)(*a*) to (*g*) (on the assumption that the amount of any payments or other things described in any such paragraph is the amount thereof determined as provided in subsection (7))

that

(ii) the cost amount to the trust of the property immediately before the particular time

is of

(iii) the cost amounts to the trust of all properties, other than money, so received by the beneficiary at the particular time,

is, subject to paragraph (*c*), deemed to be

(iv) the cost to the beneficiary of the property, and

(v) for the purposes of subsection (7) but not for the purposes of this subsection, the amount so received by the beneficiary by virtue of the receipt by the beneficiary of the property; and

(*c*) where a particular property received is all or a portion of property received in satisfaction of all or a portion of the beneficiary's interests in the trust and the beneficiary files with the Minister on or before the beneficiary's filing-due date for the taxation year that includes the particular time an election in respect of the particular property in prescribed form, there shall be included in the cost to the beneficiary of the particular property determined under paragraph (*b*) the least of

(i) the amount, if any, by which the unused portion of the beneficiary's exempt capital gains balance in respect of the trust at the particular time exceeds the total of all amounts each of which is an amount included because of this paragraph in the cost to the beneficiary of another property received by the beneficiary at or before the particular time in the year,

(ii) the amount, if any, by which the fair market value of the particular property at the particular time exceeds the amount deemed by subparagraph (*b*)(iv) to be the cost to the beneficiary of the particular property, and

(iii) the amount designated in the election in respect of the particular property.

Forms: T4PS Sum. — Return of Allocations and Payments Under Employees Profit Sharing Plan; T4PS — Statement of Employee Profit Sharing Plan Allocations and Payments.

Interpretation Bulletins: *Secondary* — IT-379R Employees profit sharing plans — Allocations to beneficiaries.

▶ 144(8) ◀

(8) Allocation of credit for dividends. Where there has been included in computing the income of a trust for a taxation year during which the trust was governed by an employees profit sharing plan taxable dividends from taxable Canadian corporations and there has been allocated by the trustee under the plan for the purposes of this subsection an amount for the year to one or more of the employees who are beneficiaries under the plan, which amount or the total of which amounts does not exceed the amount of the taxable dividends so included, each of the employees who are beneficiaries under the plan shall be deemed to have received a taxable dividend from a taxable Canadian corporation equal to the lesser of

(*a*) the amount, if any, that would be included in computing the employee's income for the year by virtue of this section, if this section were read without reference to paragraph (3)(*e*), and

(*b*) the amount, if any, so allocated for the purposes of this subsection to the employee.

Related Sections: S. 82(1) Taxable dividends received; s. 89(1), "taxable Canadian corporation", "taxable dividend".

Interpretation Bulletins: *Secondary* — IT-379R Employees profit sharing plans — Allocations to beneficiaries.

▶ 144(8.1) ◀

(8.1) Foreign tax deduction. For the purpose of subsection 126(1), the following rules apply:

(*a*) such portion of the income for a taxation year of a trust governed by an employees profit sharing plan from sources (other than businesses carried on by it) in a foreign country as

(i) may reasonably be considered (having regard to all the circumstances including the terms and conditions of the plan) to be part of

(A) the income that, by virtue of subsection (3), was included in computing the income for a taxation year of a particular employee who was a beneficiary under the plan, or

(B) the amount, if any, by which

(I) the total of amounts each of which is a capital gain of the trust that, by virtue of subsection (4), was deemed to be a capital gain of the particular employee for a taxation year

exceeds

(II) the total of amounts each of which is a capital loss of the trust that, by virtue of subsection (4), was deemed to be a capital loss of the particular employee for the taxation year, and

(ii) was not designated by the trust in respect of any other employee who was a beneficiary under the plan,

shall, if so designated by the trust in respect of the particular employee in its return of income for the year under this Part, be deemed to be income of the particular employee for the taxation year from sources in that country; and

(*b*) an employee who is a beneficiary under an employees profit sharing plan shall be deemed to have paid as non-business-income tax for a taxation year, on the income that the employee is deemed by paragraph (*a*) to have for the year from sources in a foreign country, to the government of that country an amount equal to that proportion of the non-business-income tax paid by the trust governed by the plan for the year to the government of that country, or to the government of a state, province or other political subdivision of that country (except such portion of that tax as was deductible under subsection 20(11) in computing its income for the year) that

(i) the income that the employee is deemed by paragraph (*a*) to have for the year from sources in that country

is of

(ii) the income of the trust for the year from sources (other than businesses carried on by it) in that country.

Related Sections: S. 126(1) Foreign tax deduction — non-business income.

Tax Window Files: Foreign tax credit on employees profit sharing, *January 31, 2018*, CRA Document No. 2016-0676431E5.

▶ 144(8.2) ◀

(8.2) Allocation of interest income deduction — (Repealed by S.C. 1994, c. 21, s. 68(3).)

▶ 144(9) ◀

(9) Deduction for forfeited amounts. Where a person ceases at any time in a taxation year to be a beneficiary under an employees profit sharing plan and does not become a beneficiary under the plan after that time and in the year, there may be deducted in computing the person's income for the year the amount determined by the formula

$$A - B - C/4 - D$$

where

A is the total of all amounts each of which is an amount included in computing the person's income for the year or a preceding taxation year (other than an amount received before that time under the plan or an amount under the plan that the person is entitled at that time to receive) because of an allocation (other than an allocation to which subsection (4) applies) to the person made contingently under the plan before that time;

B is the portion, if any, of the value of A that is included in the value of A because of paragraph 82(1)(*b*);

C is the total of all taxable dividends deemed to be received by the person because of allocations under subsection (8) in respect of the plan; and

D is the total of all amounts deductible under this subsection in computing the person's income for a preceding taxation year because the person ceased to be a beneficiary under the plan in a preceding taxation year.

Related Sections: S. 8(1)(*o*.1) Forfeited amounts re employee profit sharing plans; s. 144(3) Allocation contingent or absolute taxable; s. 144(10) Payments out of profits; s. 164 Refunds.

► 144(10) ◄

(10) Payments out of profits. Where the terms of an arrangement under which an employer makes payments to a trustee specifically provide that the payments shall be made "out of profits", the arrangement shall, if the employer so elects in prescribed manner, be deemed, for the purpose of subsection (1), to be an arrangement under which payments computed by reference to the employer's profits are required.

Related Regulations: Part XV; 1500(3).

Related Sections: S. 87(2)(*r*) Employees profit sharing plan.

Information Circulars: IC 77-1R5 Deferred profit sharing plan.

Interpretation Bulletins: *Secondary* — IT-280R Employees profit sharing plans — Payments computed by reference to profits.

► 144(11) ◄

(11) Taxation year of trust. Where an employees profit sharing plan is accepted for registration by the Minister as a deferred profit sharing plan, the taxation year of the trust governed by the employees profit sharing plan shall be deemed to have ended immediately before the plan is deemed to have become registered as a deferred profit sharing plan pursuant to subsection 147(5).

Related Sections: S. 2(2) Taxable income; s. 20(1)(*w*) Employer's contributions under profit sharing plan; s. 38 Taxable capital gain and allowable capital loss; s. 39, "capital gain", "capital loss"; s. 54, "capital property"; s. 81(1)(*k*) Employees profit sharing plan; s. 89(1), "Canadian corporation", "taxable dividend"; s. 104(1) Reference to trust or estate; s. 108(1), "beneficiary"; s. 144(3) Allocation contingent or absolute taxable; s. 147(11) Portion of receipts deductible; s. 248(1), "amount", "business", "corporation", "employee", "employer", "property", "province"; s. 249 Definition of "taxation year".

Employee Life and Health Trust

SECTION 144.1: [Employee life and health trust]

► 144.1(1) ◄

(1) Definitions. The following definitions apply in this section.

History: S. 144.1(1) was added by S.C. 2010, c. 25, s. 34(1), applicable to trusts established after 2009.

Tax Window Files: *ELHT - Bankrupt employer, February 13, 2012* CRA Document No. 2011-0419811E5; *Employee Life and Health Trust, July 14, 2011,* CRA Document No. 2010-0389651R3; *HWTs and Employee Life & Health Trusts, June 10, 2011,* CRA Document No. 2011-0398371C6.

"actuary" —"actuary" means a Fellow of the Canadian Institute of Actuaries.

History: S. 144.1(1), the definition "actuary" was added by S.C. 2010, c. 25, s. 34(1), applicable to trusts established after 2009.

"class of beneficiaries" —"class of beneficiaries" of a trust means a group of beneficiaries who have identical rights or interests under the trust.

History: S. 144.1(1), the definition "class of beneficiaries" was added by S.C. 2010, c. 25, s. 34(1), applicable to trusts established after 2009.

"designated employee benefit" —"designated employee benefit" means a benefit from a group sickness or accident insurance plan, a group term life insurance policy or a private health services plan.

Editorial Note: Generally, the tax treatment of the designated employee benefit to the employee is the same as it would be in the absence of the trust. Thus, benefits from an employer-funded group sickness or accident insurance plan or in respect of a group term life insurance policy will be included in income. A benefit under a private health services plan, such as where the employer pays premiums of a private health insurance plan, is generally not included in income.

History: S. 144.1(1), the definition "designated employee benefit" was added by S.C. 2010, c. 25, s. 34(1), applicable to trusts established after 2009.

"employee" —"employee" means a current or former employee of an employer and includes an individual in respect of whom the employer has assumed responsibility for the provision of designated employee benefits as a result of the acquisition by the employer of a business in which the individual was employed.

History: S. 144.1(1), the definition "employee" was added by S.C. 2010, c. 25, s. 34(1), applicable to trusts established after 2009.

"key employee" —"key employee", of an employer in respect of a taxation year, means an employee who

(*a*) was at any time in the taxation year or in a preceding taxation year, a specified employee of the employer; or

(*b*) was an employee whose employment income from the employer in any two of the five taxation years preceding the year exceeded five times the Year's Maximum Pensionable Earnings (as determined under section 18 of the *Canada Pension Plan*) for the calendar year in which the employment income was earned.

History: S. 144.1(1), the definition "key employee" was added by S.C. 2010, c. 25, s. 34(1), applicable to trusts established after 2009.

► 144.1(2) ◄

(2) Employee life and health trust. A trust that is established for employees of one or more employers (each referred to in this subsection as a "participating employer") is an employee life and health trust for a taxation year if, throughout the taxation year, under the terms that govern the trust,

(*a*) the only purpose of the trust is to provide designated employee benefits to, or for the benefit of, persons described in subparagraphs (*d*)(i) or (ii); and

(*b*) on wind-up or reorganization, the property of the trust may only be distributed to

(i) each remaining beneficiary of the trust who is described in subparagraph (*d*)(i) or (ii) (other than a key employee or an individual who is related to a key employee) on a *pro rata* basis,

(ii) another employee life and health trust, or

(iii) after the death of the last beneficiary described in subparagraph (*d*)(i) or (ii), Her Majesty in right of Canada or a province;

(*c*) the trust is required to be resident in Canada, determined without reference to section 94;

Proposed Amendment

Legislative Proposals Relating to the Income Tax Act, Employee Life and Health Trusts (May 27, 2019)

Paragraph 144.1(2)(*c*) of the *Income Tax Act* is replaced by the following:

(*c*) the trust meets one of the following two conditions:

(i) the trust is required to be resident in Canada determined without reference to section 94, and

(ii) if the condition in subparagraph (i) is not met, it is the case that

(A) employee benefits are provided to employees who are resident in Canada and to employees who are not resident in Canada,

(B) one or more participating employers are employers who are resident in a country other than Canada, and

(C) the trust is required to be resident in a country in which a participating employer resides;

Applicable: Deemed to have come into force on February 27, 2018. As of that date, section 144.1 of the Act, as amended, applies in respect of trusts regardless of the date that the trust was established.

(*d*) the trust may not have any beneficiaries other than persons each of whom is

(i) an employee of a participating employer,

(ii) an individual who, in respect of an employee of a participating employer, is (or, if the employee is deceased, was, at the time of the employee's death)

Proposed Amendment

Legislative Proposals Relating to the Income Tax Act, Employee Life and Health Trusts (May 27, 2019)

The portion of paragraph 144.1(2)(*d*) of the Act before clause (ii)(A) is replaced by the following:

(*d*) the trust may not have any beneficiaries other than persons each of whom is

(i) an employee of a participating employer or former participating employer,

(ii) an individual who, in respect of an employee of a participating employer or former participating employer, is (or, if the employee is deceased, was, at the time of the employee's death)

Applicable: Deemed to have come into force on February 27, 2018. As of that date, section 144.1 of the Act, as amended, applies in respect of trusts regardless of the date that the trust was established.

(A) the spouse or common law partner of the employee, or

(B) related to the employee and either a member of the employee's household or dependent on the employee for support,

(iii) another employee life and health trust, or

(iv) Her Majesty in right of Canada or a province;

(*e*) the trust contains at least one class of beneficiaries where

(i) the members of the class represent at least 25% of all of the beneficiaries of the trust who are employees of the participating employer, and

(ii) at least 75% of the members of the class are not key employees of the participating employer;

(*f*) the rights under the trust of each key employee of a participating employer are not more advantageous than the rights of a class of beneficiaries described in paragraph (*e*);

(*g*) no participating employer, nor any person who does not deal at arm's length with a participating employer, has any rights under the trust as a beneficiary or otherwise, except rights to

(i) designated employee benefits,

(ii) to enforce covenants, warranties or similar provisions regarding

(A) the maintenance of the trust as an employee life and health trust, or

(B) the operation of the trust in a manner that prevents subsection (3) from applying to prohibit the deduction of an amount by the trust under subsection 104(6), or

(iii) prescribed payments;

(*h*) the trust may not make a loan to, or an investment in, a participating employer or a person or partnership with whom the participating employer does not deal at arm's length;

Proposed Amendment

Legislative Proposals Relating to the Income Tax Act, Employee Life and Health Trusts (May 27, 2019)

Subsection 144.1(2) is amended by striking out "and" at the end of paragraph (*a*), by adding "and" at the end of paragraph (*g*) and by repealing paragraph (*h*).

Applicable: Deemed to have come into force on February 27, 2018. As of that date, section 144.1 of the Act, as amended, applies in respect of trusts regardless of the date that the trust was established.

(*i*) representatives of one or more participating employers do not constitute the majority of the trustees of the trust or otherwise control the trust.

Proposed Amendment

Legislative Proposals Relating to the Income Tax Act, Employee Life and Health Trusts (May 27, 2019)

Paragraph 144.1(2)(*i*) of the Act is replaced by the following:

(*i*) a majority of the trustees must deal at arm's length with each participating employer.

Applicable: Deemed to have come into force on February 27, 2018. As of that date, section 144.1 of the Act, as amended, applies in respect of trusts regardless of the date that the trust was established.

Department of Finance Comfort Letters

(December 19, 2012) [Amendment to s. 144.1(2)(*h*) Re: Employee Life and Health Trust Making Loan To a Investment In a Participating Employer]

Dear XXXX:

I am writing in respect of an issue that you have raised with departmental officials relating to the consequences to an employee life and health trust of the acquisition of an investment that may not comply with employee life and health trust terms required by paragraph 144.1(2)(*h*) of the *Income Tax Act* (the Act).

Paragraph 144.1(*h*) provides that the terms of an employee life and health trust must require it to avoid making a loan to, or an investment in, a participating employer (or a person or partnership that does not deal at arm's length with a participating employer). You have indicated that the trustees of the employee life and health trust established for retirees of General Motors of Canada Limited have expressed concern that it would be possible to inadvertently acquire an investment in an entity that did not deal at arm's length with a participating employer, particularly given the factual nature of the determination of arm's length dealing, the complexity of the organization and dealings of some participating employers, and the imperfect knowledge that trustees may have regarding these details.

If such an investment were acquired, the trust would be in breach of its terms and, under subsection 144.1(3) of the Act, would be precluded from the deduction of any amount by the trust under subsection 104(6) for any taxation year during which the breach of the required trust term continued. As discussed with departmental officials. the financial costs to the trust if this were to occur could be significantly larger than the dollar value of the investment that caused the breach of the required trust terms.

We agree that this result could be unfair in situations of inadvertence. particularly in cases of larger employee life and health trusts, where one investment may represent only a small fraction of the total trust capital. We will therefore recommend the following alternative regime, to apply to the 2014 and subsequent taxation years, with elective application before that time:

- Repeal paragraph 144.1(2)(*h*) and replace it with provisions that impose tax consequences (set out below) [not released with letter] specific to the acquisition of an investment in, or the making of a loan to, the participating employer (or a non-arm's length person or partnership in respect of the participating employer).
- Specifically, the acquisition of such a "prohibited investment" would be subject to a tax equal to 50% of its fair market value. As well, a 50% tax would apply on any income from the investment. In circumstances where the acquisition was unintentional, and the investment is disposed of promptly (by the end of the year following the year of acquisition) the tax on the investment's fair market value would be refundable.

While I cannot offer any assurance that the legislative amendments that we intend to recommend will be adopted, I trust that this statement of our position is helpful to you.

Yours sincerely,

Brian Ernewein
General Director - Legislation
Tax Policy Branch

Editorial Note: In its explanatory notes to the rules applicable to employee life and health trusts, the Department of Finance states that the rules "are based to a large extent on Canada Revenue Agency administrative positions regarding Health and Welfare Trusts. At this time, the government does not intend to make any changes to the tax rules applicable to Health and Welfare Trusts."

History: S. 144.1(2) was added by S.C. 2010, c. 25, s. 34(1), applicable to trusts established after 2009.

Related Regulations: 9500.

► 144.1(3) ◄

(3) Breach of terms etc. No amount may be deducted in a taxation year by an employee life and health trust pursuant to subsection 104(6) if in the taxation year the trust

(*a*) is not operated in accordance with the terms required by subsection (2) to govern the trust, or

Proposed Amendment

Legislative Proposals Relating to the Income Tax Act, Employee Life and Health Trusts (May 27, 2019)

Paragraph 144.1(3)(*a*) of the Act is replaced by the following:

(*a*) is not operated in accordance with the terms required by subsection (2) to govern the trust, unless it reasonable to conclude that its trustees neither knew nor ought to have known that designated employee benefits have been provided to, or contributions have been made in respect of, beneficiaries other than those described in subparagraph (2)(*d*)(i) or (ii); or

Applicable: Deemed to have come into force on February 27, 2018. As of that date, section 144.1 of the Act, as amended, applies in respect of trusts regardless of the date that the trust was established.

(*b*) is operated or maintained primarily for the benefit of one or more key employees or their family members described in subparagraph 2(*d*)(ii).

History: S. 144.1(3) was added by S.C. 2010, c. 25, s. 34(1), applicable to trusts established after 2009.

► 144.1(4) ◄

(4) Deductibility of employer contributions. In computing the income of an employer,

(*a*) the employer may deduct for a taxation year the portion of its contributions to an employee life and health trust made in the year that may reasonably be regarded as having been contributed to enable the trust to

(i) pay premiums to an insurance corporation that is licensed to provide insurance under the laws of Canada or a province for insurance coverage for the year or a prior year in respect of designated employee benefits for beneficiaries described in subparagraph (2)(*d*)(i) or (ii), or

(ii) otherwise provide

(A) group term life insurance as described in clause 18(9)(*a*)(iii)(B), or

(B) any designated employee benefits payable in the year or a prior year to, or for the benefit of, beneficiaries described in subparagraph (2)(*d*)(i) or (ii); and

(*b*) the portion of any contribution made to an employee life and health trust that exceeds the amount deductible under paragraph (*a*) and that may reasonably be regarded as enabling the trust to provide or pay benefits described in subparagraphs (*a*)(i) or (ii) in a subsequent taxation year is deductible for that year.

Editorial Note: Under s. 144.1(4)(*a*), an employer's deduction for contributions made in the year to an employee life and health trust (ELHT) is generally limited to the amount of those contribution that enable the ELHT to pay premiums to a private insurance company for insurance coverage for the year or a prior year in respect of an employee (or a spouse or common-law partner of an employee, or a person related to an employee who is a member of the employee's household or dependent on the employee for support), or to provide group term life insurance or designated employee benefits that are payable in the year or a prior year. Subsection 144.1(5) provides that an actuarial report in this regard is determinative, in the absence of evidence to the contrary. Under s. 144.1(4)(*b*), excess contributions in the year that enable the trust to provide or pay benefits described in (a) in a subsequent year are deductible in that subsequent year. Special rules apply to a multi-employer ELHT under s. 144.1(6), which are meant to be similar to those that apply to specified multi-employer pension plans under the regulations.

History: S. 144.1(4) was added by S.C. 2010, c. 25, s. 34(1), applicable to trusts established after 2009.

Related Sections: S. 6(1)(*a*) Value of benefits; s. 6(1)(*f*) Employment insurance benefits; s. 6(4) Group term life insurance; s. 18(9) Limitation respecting prepaid expenses; s. 20(1)(*s*) Employer's contributions under employee life and health trust.

► 144.1(5) ◄

(5) Actuarial determination. For the purposes of subsection (4), if, in respect of an employer's obligations to fund an employee life and health trust, a report has been prepared by an independent actuary, using accepted actuarial principles and practices, before the time of a contribution by the employer, the portion of the contribution that the report specifies to be the amount that the employee life and health trust is reasonably expected to pay or incur in a taxation year in order to provide designated employee benefits to beneficiaries described in subparagraph (2)(*d*)(i) or (ii) for a taxation year is, in the absence of evidence to the contrary, presumed to have been contributed to enable the trust to provide those benefits for the year.

History: S. 144.1(5) was added by S.C. 2010, c. 25, s. 34(1), applicable to trusts established after 2009.

► 144.1(6) ◄

(6) Multi-employer plans. Notwithstanding subsection (4) and paragraph 18(9)(*a*), an employer may deduct in computing its income for a taxation year the amount that it is required to contribute for the year to an employee life and health trust if the following conditions are met at the time that the contribution is made:

(*a*) it is reasonable to expect that

(i) at no time in the year will more than 95% of the employees who are beneficiaries of the trust be employed by a single employer or by a related group of employers, and

(ii) at least 15 employers will contribute to the trust in respect of the year or at least 10% of the employees who are beneficiaries of the trust will be employed in the year by more than one participating employer and, for the purpose of this condition, all employers who are related to each other are deemed to be a single employer;

(*b*) employers contribute to the trust under a collective bargaining agreement and in accordance with a negotiated contribution formula that does not provide for any variation in contributions determined by reference to the financial experience of the trust; and

(*c*) contributions that are to be made by each employer are determined, in whole or in part, by reference to the number of hours worked by individual employees of the employer or some other measure that is specific to each employee with respect to whom contributions are made to the trust.

Proposed Amendment

Legislative Proposals Relating to the Income Tax Act, Employee Life and Health Trusts (May 27, 2019)

Subsection 144.1(6) of the Act is replaced by the following:

(6) Deductibility — collective agreement. Notwithstanding subsection (4) and paragraph 18(9)(*a*), an employer may deduct in computing its income for a taxation year the amount that it is required to contribute for the year to an employee life and health trust if the following conditions are met at the time that the contribution is made:

(*a*) the employer contributes to the trust under a collective bargaining agreement, or a participation agreement in respect of the collective bargaining agreement, and in accordance with a negotiated contribution formula that does not provide for any variation in contributions determined by reference to the financial experience of the trust; and

(*b*) contributions that are to be made by each employer are determined, in whole or in part, by reference to the number of hours worked by individual employees of the employer or some other measure that is specific to each employee with respect to whom contributions are made to the trust.

Applicable: Deemed to have come into force on February 27, 2018. As of that date, section 144.1 of the Act, as amended, applies in respect of trusts regardless of the date that the trust was established.

History: S. 144.1(6) was added by S.C. 2010, c. 25, s. 34(1), applicable to trusts established after 2009.

► 144.1(7) ◄

(7) Maximum deductible. The amount deducted in a taxation year by an employer in computing its income in respect of contributions made to an employee life and health trust shall not exceed the amount determined by the formula

$$A - B$$

where

A is the total of all amounts contributed by the employer to the trust in the year or in a preceding taxation year; and

B is the total of all amounts deducted by the employer in a preceding taxation year in respect of amounts contributed by the employer to the trust.

History: S. 144.1(7) was added by S.C. 2010, c. 25, s. 34(1), applicable to trusts established after 2009.

► 144.1(8) ◄

(8) Employer promissory note. If an employer issues a promissory note or provides other evidence of its indebtedness to an employee life and health trust in respect of its obligation to the trust,

(*a*) the issuance of the note or the provision of the evidence of indebtedness to the trust is not a contribution to the trust; and

(*b*) a payment by the employer to the trust in full or partial satisfaction of its liability under the note or the evidence of indebtedness, whether stated to be of principal or interest or any other amount, is deemed to be an employer contribution to the trust that is subject to this section and not a payment of principal or interest on the note or indebtedness.

Editorial Note: An employer's issuance of a promissory note to an ELHT is not deductible as a contribution. Instead, the subsequent payment of principal or interest on the note is deemed to be a contribution, and potentially deductible under the provisions of subsection 144.1(4).

History: S. 144.1(8) was added by S.C. 2010, c. 25, s. 34(1), applicable to trusts established after 2009.

► 144.1(9) ◄

(9) Trust status — subsequent times. For the purposes of determining whether an amount is deductible by an employer under subsection (4), if a trust was an employee life and health trust at the time that a promissory note or other evidence of indebtedness referred to in subsection (8) was issued or provided, the trust is deemed to be an employee life and health trust at each time that an employer contribution is deemed to have been made under paragraph (8)(*b*) in respect of the note or other indebtedness.

History: S. 144.1(9) was added by S.C. 2010, c. 25, s. 34(1), applicable to trusts established after 2009.

► 144.1(10) ◄

(10) Employee contributions. For the purposes of paragraph 6(1)(*f*), subsection 6(4) and paragraph 118.2(2)(*q*), employee contributions to an employee life and health trust, to the extent that they are, and are identified by the trust at the time of contribution as, contributions in respect of a particular designated employee benefit, are deemed to be payments by the employee in respect of the particular designated employee benefit.

Editorial Note: Subsection 144.1(10) generally provides a flow through for the tax treatment of employee contributions to an employee life and health trust (ELHT) by deeming the contributions to be in respect of the relevant designated employee benefit. For example, employee contributions made to the ELHT for a group sickness or accident benefit plan will generally be deductible for the employee against future payments out of the plan that are included under s. 6(1)(*f*). Employee contributions that relate to premiums under a private health services plan will qualify for the medical tax credit.

History: S. 144.1(10) was added by S.C. 2010, c. 25, s. 34(1), applicable to trusts established after 2009.

► 144.1(11) ◄

(11) Income inclusion. If a trust that is, or was, at any time, an employee life and health trust pays an amount as a distribution from the trust to any person in a taxation year, the amount of the distribution shall be included in computing the person's income for the year, except to the extent that the amount is

(*a*) a payment of a designated employee benefit that is not included in the person's income because of section 6; or

(*b*) a distribution to another employee life and health trust that is a beneficiary of the employee life and health trust.

Editorial Note: Although a payment out of a group sickness or accident insurance plan will be included in the income of the recipient employee by virtue of this provision, the recipient employee will get a corresponding deduction for previous contributions by virtue of s. 144.1(10). If no employer contributions had been made to the group sickness or accident plan, the payment will be non-taxable by virtue of s. 144.1(11)(*a*). S. 144.1(11)(*b*) allows tax-free transfers from one employee life and health trust (ELHT) to another ELHT that is a beneficiary of the first.

History: S. 144.1(11) was added by S.C. 2010, c. 25, s. 34(1), applicable to trusts established after 2009.

► 144.1(12) ◄

(12) Deemed separate trusts. Where contributions have been received by an employee life and health trust from more than one employer, the trust is deemed to be a separate trust established in respect of the property held for the benefit of beneficiaries described in subparagraph (2)(*d*)(i) or (ii) in respect of a particular employer, if

(*a*) the trustee designates the property to be held in a separate trust for the benefit of those beneficiaries in an election made on or before the filing-due date of the first taxation year of the separate trust described in this subsection; and

(*b*) under the terms of the trust, contributions from the employer and the income derived from those contributions accrues solely for the benefit of those beneficiaries.

History: S. 144.1(12) was added by S.C. 2010, c. 25, s. 34(1), applicable to trusts established after 2009.

► 144.1(13) ◄

(13) Non-capital losses. No non-capital loss is deductible by an employee life and health trust in computing its taxable income for a taxation year, except as provided by subsections 111(7.3) to (7.5).

Proposed Amendment

Legislative Proposals Relating to the Income Tax Act, Employee Life and Health Trusts (May 27, 2019)

Section 144.1 of the Act is amended by adding the following after subsection (13):

(14) Conditions — deemed employee life and health trust. Subsection (15) applies in respect of a trust if

(*a*) the trust was established before February 28, 2018;

(*b*) the contributions to the trust are determined under a collective bargaining agreement;

(*c*) all or substantially all of the employee benefits provided by the trust are designated employee benefits; and

(*d*) the trust elects in prescribed form and manner that subsection (15) applies as of a particular date that is after 2018.

(15) Deemed employee life and health trust. If this subsection applies in respect of a trust,

(*a*) the trust is deemed for the purposes of this Act to be an employee life and health trust from the particular date referred to in paragraph (14)(*d*) until the earliest of

(i) the effective date of the next collective bargaining agreement, relating to benefits under the trust, that is entered into after Announcement Date,

(ii) the end of 2022,

(iii) the day that the trust satisfies the conditions in subsection (2), and

(iv) the day on which the condition in paragraph (14)(*c*) is no longer satisfied; and

(*b*) at any time that the trust is an employee life and health trust because of paragraph (*a*),

(i) subsection 111(7.5) applies to the trust as if the reference in that subsection to "subsection 144.1(3)" were read as a reference to "paragraph 144.1(3)(*b*)", and

(ii) subsection 144.1(3) applies to the trust without reference to its paragraph (*a*).

(16) Trust-to-trust transfer. If a property is transferred from a trust that provides employee benefits substantially all of which are designated employee benefits (referred to in this subsection as the "transferor trust") to an employee life and health trust (referred to in this subsection as the "receiving trust"), and if the Minister has been so notified in prescribed form, then

(*a*) the transferred property is deemed to have been disposed of by the transferor trust, and to have been acquired by the receiving trust, for an amount equal to the cost amount of the property to the transferor trust immediately before the disposition; and

(*b*) section 107.1 does not apply to the transfer.

(17) Deductibility of transferred property. If subsection (16) applies to a transfer of property to an employee life and health trust, the transfer shall not be considered to be a contribution to the employee life and health trust for the purposes of subsections (4) and (6).

Applicable: Deemed to have come into force on February 27, 2018. As of that date, section 144.1 of the Act, as amended, applies in respect of trusts regardless of the date that the trust was established.

Editorial Note: Under s. 111(7.4), non-capital losses of an employee life and health trust (ELHT) can be carried back three years or forward three years. Note that s. 104(6)(*a.4*) allows an ELHT to deduct amounts that became payable in a year as designated employee benefits, regardless of whether those amounts exceed the revenues of the trust.

History: S. 144.1(13) was added by S.C. 2010, c. 25, s. 34(1), applicable to trusts established after 2009.

Related Sections: S. 6(1)(*a*) Value of benefits; s. 6(1)(*f*) Employment insurance benefits; s. 56(1)(*z.2*) Employee life and health trust; s. 104(6)(*a.4*) Deduction in computing income of trust.

Registered Supplementary Unemployment Benefit Plans

SECTION 145: [Registered supplementary unemployment benefit plans]

► 145(1) ◄

(1) Definitions. In this section,

Information Circulars: IC 72-5R2 Registered Supplementary Unemployment Benefit Plans; IC 78-14R4 Guidelines for trust companies and other persons responsible for filing T3GR, T3D, T3P, T3S, T3RI, and T3F returns.

"registered supplementary unemployment benefit plan" — "registered supplementary unemployment benefit plan" means a supplementary unemployment benefit plan accepted by the Minister for registration for the purposes of this Act in respect of its constitution and operations for the taxation year under consideration;

Forms: T3S — Supplementary Unemployment Benefit Plan Information and Income Tax Return.

"supplementary unemployment benefit plan" —"supplementary unemployment benefit plan" means an arrangement, other than an arrangement in the nature of a superannuation or pension fund or plan or an employees profit sharing plan, under which payments are made by an employer to a trustee in trust exclusively for the payment of periodic amounts to employees or former employees of the employer who are or may be laid off for any temporary or indefinite period.

Forms: T3S — Supplementary Unemployment Benefit Plan Information and Income Tax Return.

Information Circulars: IC 72-5R2 Registration of supplementary unemployment benefit plans.

► 145(2) ◄

(2) No tax while trust governed by plan. No tax is payable under this Part by a trust on the taxable income of the trust for a period during which the trust was governed by a registered supplementary unemployment benefit plan.

► 145(3) ◄

(3) Amounts received taxable. There shall be included in computing the income of a taxpayer for a taxation year each amount received by the taxpayer under a supplementary unemployment benefit plan from the trustee under the plan at any time in the year.

Related Regulations: 202(2), (3).

Related Sections: S. 6(1)(*a*)(i) Value of benefits; s. 56(1)(*g*) Supplementary unemployment benefit plan.

► 145(4) ◄

(4) Amounts received on amendment or winding-up of plan. There shall be included in computing the income for a taxation year of a taxpayer who, as an employer, has made any payment to a trustee under a supplementary unemployment benefit plan, any amount received by the taxpayer in the year as a result of an amendment to or modification of the plan or as a result of the termination or winding-up of the plan.

► 145(5) ◄

(5) Payments by employer deductible. An amount paid by an employer to a trustee under a registered supplementary unemployment benefit plan during a taxation year or within 30 days thereafter may be deducted in computing the employer's income for the taxation year to the extent that it was not deductible in computing income for a previous taxation year.

Related Sections: S. 2(2) Taxable income; s. 18(1)(*i*) Limitation re employer's contribution under supplementary unemployment benefit plan; s. 20(1)(*x*) Employer's contributions under registered supplementary unemployment benefit plan; s. 56(1)(*g*) Supplementary unemployment benefit plan; s. 104(1) Reference to trust or estate; s. 144(1), "employees profit sharing plan"; s. 149(1)(*q*) Trusts under a registered supplementary unemployment benefit plan; s. 212 Taxation of non-residents; s. 248(1), "amount", "employee", "employer", "superannuation or pension benefits"; s. 249 Definition of "taxation year".

Registered Retirement Savings Plans

SECTION 146: [Registered retirement savings plans]

► 146(1) ◄

(1) Definitions. In this section,

Information Circulars: IC 72-22R9 Registered retirement savings plans; IC 78-14R4 Guidelines for trust companies and other persons responsible for filing T3GR, T3D, T3P, T3S, T3RI, and T3F returns.

Interpretation Bulletins: *Primary* — IT-500R Registered retirement savings plans — Death of annuitant. *Secondary* — IT-124R6 Contributions to registered retirement savings plans; IT-415R2 Deregistration of registered retirement savings plans.

"annuitant" —"annuitant" means

(*a*) until such time after maturity of the plan as an individual's spouse or common-law partner becomes entitled, as a consequence of the individual's death, to receive benefits to be paid out of or under the plan, the individual referred to in paragraph (*a*) or (*b*) of the definition "retirement savings plan" in this subsection for whom, under a retirement savings plan, a retirement income is to be provided, and

(*b*) thereafter, the spouse or common-law partner referred to in paragraph (*a*);

Related Regulations: 104(3); 104(3.01); 104(3.1); 104(4); 104.1.

"benefit" —"benefit" includes any amount received out of or under a retirement savings plan other than

(*a*) the portion thereof received by a person other than the annuitant that can reasonably be regarded as part of the amount included in computing the income of an annuitant by virtue of subsections (8.8) and (8.9),

(*b*) an amount received by the person with whom the annuitant has the contract or arrangement described in the definition "retirement savings plan" in this subsection as a premium under the plan,

(*b*.1) an amount in respect of which the annuitant pays a tax under Part XI.01, unless the tax is waived, cancelled or refunded,

(*c*) an amount, or part thereof, received in respect of the income of the trust under the plan for a taxation year for which the trust was not exempt from tax by virtue of paragraph (4)(*c*), and (*c*.1) a tax-paid amount described in paragraph (*b*) of the definition "tax-paid amount" in this subsection that relates to interest or another amount included in computing income otherwise than because of this section

and without restricting the generality of the foregoing includes any amount paid to an annuitant under the plan

(*d*) in accordance with the terms of the plan,

(*e*) resulting from an amendment to or modification of the plan, or

(*f*) resulting from the termination of the plan;

History: S. 146(1), paragraph (*b.1*) of the definition "benefit" was added by S.C. 2011, c. 24, s. 45(2), applicable to transactions occurring, income earned, capital gains accruing and investments acquired after March 22, 2011.

"earned income"—"earned income" of a taxpayer for a taxation year means the amount, if any, by which the total of all amounts each of which is

(*a*) the taxpayer's income (other than an amount described in paragraph 12(1)(*z*)) for a period in the year throughout which the taxpayer was resident in Canada from

(i) an office or employment, determined without reference to paragraphs 8(1)(*c*), (*m*) and (*m*.2),

(ii) a business carried on by the taxpayer either alone or as a partner actively engaged in the business, or

(iii) property, where the income is derived from the rental of real or immovable property or from royalties in respect of a work or invention of which the taxpayer was the author or inventor,

(*b*) an amount included under paragraph 56(1)(*b*), (*c*.2), (*g*) or (*o*) or subparagraph 56(1)(*r*)(v) in computing the taxpayer's income for a period in the year throughout which the taxpayer was resident in Canada,

(*b*.1) an amount received by the taxpayer in the year and at a time when the taxpayer is resident in Canada as, on account of, in lieu of payment of or in satisfaction of, a disability pension under the *Canada Pension Plan* or a provincial pension plan as defined in section 3 of that Act,

(*b*.2) the taxpayer's qualifying performance income (as defined in subsection 143.1(1)) that is deemed by paragraph 143.1(1.2)(*c*) to be income of an amateur athlete trust for the year,

(*c*) the taxpayer's income (other than an amount described in paragraph 12(1)(*z*)) for a period in the year throughout which the taxpayer was not resident in Canada from

(i) the duties of an office or employment performed by the taxpayer in Canada, determined without reference to paragraphs 8(1)(*c*), (*m*) and (*m*.2), or

(ii) a business carried on by the taxpayer in Canada, either alone or as a partner actively engaged in the business

except to the extent that the income is exempt from income tax in Canada by reason of a provision contained in a tax convention or agreement with another country that has the force of law in Canada, or

(*d*) in the case of a taxpayer described in subsection 115(2), the total that would be determined under paragraph 115(2)(*e*) in respect of the taxpayer for the year if

(i) that paragraph were read without reference to subparagraph 115(2)(*e*)(iv), and

(ii) subparagraph 115(2)(*e*)(ii) were read without any reference therein to paragraph 56(1)(*n*),

except any part thereof included in the total determined under this definition by reason of paragraph (*c*) or exempt from income tax in Canada by reason of a provision contained in a tax convention or agreement with another country that has the force of law in Canada,

exceeds the total of all amounts each of which is

(*e*) the taxpayer's loss for a period in the year throughout which the taxpayer was resident in Canada from

(i) a business carried on by the taxpayer, either alone or as a partner actively engaged in the business, or

(ii) property, where the loss is sustained from the rental of real or immovable property,

(*f*) an amount deductible under paragraph 60(*b*), or deducted under paragraph 60(*c*.2), in computing the taxpayer's income for the year, or

(*g*) the taxpayer's loss for a period in the year throughout which the taxpayer was not resident in Canada from a business carried on by the taxpayer in Canada, either alone or as a partner actively engaged in the business,

(*h*) (Repealed by S.C. 2016, c. 12, s. 52(1).)

and, for the purposes of this definition, the income or loss of a taxpayer for any period in a taxation year is the taxpayer's income or loss computed as though that period were the whole taxation year;

History: S. 146(1), paragraph (*h*) of the definition of "earned income" was repealed by S.C. 2016, c. 12, s. 52(1), in force January 1, 2017, and formerly read:

(*h*) the portion of an amount included under subparagraph (*a*)(ii) or (*c*)(ii) in determining the taxpayer's earned income for the year because of paragraph 14(1)(*b*)

S. 146(1), the portion of paragraph (*a*) of the definition "earned income" before subparagraph (i) was replaced by S.C. 2014, c. 39, s. 50(1), applicable to an individual's 2014 and subsequent taxation years, except that if an individual elects in writing under subsection 50(4) of the *Economic Action Plan 2014 Act, No. 2* [S.C. 2014, c. 39] in respect of the individual's 2011, 2012 or 2013 taxation year and the election is filed with the Minister of National Revenue before March 3, 2015, this amendment applies to the individual's taxation year in respect of which the election is filed and subsequent taxation years.

The portion of paragraph (*a*) of the definition "earned income" before subparagraph (i) formerly read:

(*a*) the taxpayer's income for a period in the year throughout which the taxpayer was resident in Canada from

S. 146(1), paragraph (*b.2*) of the definition "earned income" was added by S.C. 2014, c. 39, s. 50(2), applicable to an individual's 2014 and subsequent taxation years, except that if an individual elects in writing under subsection 50(4) of the *Economic Action Plan 2014 Act, No. 2* [S.C. 2014, c. 39] in respect of the individual's 2011, 2012 or 2013 taxation year and the election is filed with the Minister of National Revenue before March 3, 2015, this amendment applies to the individual's taxation year in respect of which the election is filed and subsequent taxation years.

S. 146(1), the portion of paragraph (*c*) of the definition "earned income" before subparagraph (i) was replaced by S.C. 2014, c. 39, s. 50(3), applicable to an individual's 2014 and subsequent taxation years, except that if an individual elects in writing under subsection 50(4) of the *Economic Action Plan 2014 Act, No. 2* [S.C. 2014, c. 39] in respect of the individual's 2011, 2012 or 2013 taxation year and the election is filed with the Minister of National Revenue before March 3, 2015, this amendment applies to the individual's taxation year in respect of which the election is filed and subsequent taxation years.

The portion of paragraph (*c*) of the definition "earned income" before subparagraph (i) formerly read:

(*c*) the taxpayer's income for a period in the year throughout which the taxpayer was not resident in Canada from

S. 146(1), subparagraph (*a*)(iii) of the definition "earned income" was replaced by S.C. 2013, c. 34, s. 137(1), in force June 26, 2013, and formerly read:

(iii) property, where the income is derived from the rental of real property or from royalties in respect of a work or invention of which the taxpayer was the author or inventor,

S. 146(1), subparagraph (*e*)(ii) of the definition "earned income" was replaced by S.C. 2013, c. 34, s. 137(2), in force June 26, 2013, and formerly read:

(ii) property, where the loss is sustained from the rental of real property,

S. 146(1), subparagraph (*d*)(i) of the definition "earned income" was replaced by S.C. 2013, c. 34, s. 296(2), applicable to the 1993 and subsequent taxation years, and formerly read:

(i) that paragraph were read without reference to subparagraphs 115(2)(*e*)(iii) and (iv), and

S. 146(1), paragraph (*f*) of the definition "earned income" was replaced by S.C. 2013, c. 34, s. 296(3), applicable to the 1997 and subsequent taxation years, and formerly read:

(*f*) an amount deductible under paragraph 60(*b*), (*c*) or (*c*.1), or deducted under paragraph 60(*c*.2), in computing the taxpayer's income for the year,

S. 146(1), paragraph (*h*) of the definition "earned income" was replaced by S.C. 2013, c. 34, s. 296(4), applicable to amounts included in computing income for taxation years in respect of business fiscal periods that end after February 27, 2000, and formerly read:

(*h*) the portion of an amount included under subparagraph (*a*)(ii) or (*c*)(ii) in determining the taxpayer's earned income for the year because of subparagraph 14(1)(*a*)(v)

S. 146(1), paragraph (*b*) of the definition "earned income" was replaced by S.C. 2009, c. 2, s. 51(1), applicable to the 1997 and subsequent taxation years, except that in its application to the 1997 to 2007 taxation years, paragraph (*b*) of the definition "earned income" is to be read without reference to "or subparagraph 56(1)(*r*)(v)". S. 146(1), paragraph (*b*) of the definition "earned income" formerly read:

(*b*) an amount included under paragraph 56(1)(*b*), (*c*), (*c*.1), (*c*.2), (*g*) or (*o*) in computing the taxpayer's income for a period in the year throughout which the taxpayer was resident in Canada,

Related Sections: s. 147.5(33) Exempt contributions not over-contributions.

Interpretation Bulletins: *Secondary* — IT-434R Rental of real property by individual.

"issuer" —"issuer" means the person referred to in the definition "retirement savings plan" in this subsection with whom an annuitant has a contract or arrangement that is a retirement savings plan;

"maturity" —"maturity" means the date fixed under a retirement savings plan for the commencement of any retirement income the payment of which is provided for by the plan;

Related Regulations: 215.

"net past service pension adjustment" —"net past service pension adjustment" of a taxpayer for a taxation year means the positive or negative amount determined by the formula

$$P + Q - G$$

where

P is the total of all amounts each of which is the taxpayer's past service pension adjustment for the year in respect of an employer,

Q is the total of all amounts each of which is a prescribed amount in respect of the taxpayer for the year, and

G is the amount of the taxpayer's PSPA withdrawals for the year, determined as of the end of the year in accordance with prescribed rules;

Related Regulations: 8307(5).

Related Sections: S. 248(1), "past service pension adjustment".

"non-qualified investment" —"non-qualified investment" has the same meaning as in subsection 207.01(1);

History: S. 146(1), the definition "non-qualified investment" was replaced by S.C. 2011, c. 24, s. 45(1), applicable in respect of investments acquired after March 22, 2011. S. 146(1), the definition "non-qualified investment" formerly read:

"non-qualified investment"—"non-qualified investment", in relation to a trust governed by a registered retirement savings plan, means property acquired by the trust after 1971 that is not a qualified investment for the trust;

Related Sections: S. 146(1), "qualified investment"; s. 207.01(1), "non-qualified investment".

Income Tax Folios: *Primary* — S3-F10-C1 Qualified Investments – RRSPs, RESPs, RRIFs, RDSPs and TFSAs; S3-F10-C2 Prohibited Investments - RRSPs, RRIFs and TFSAs.

Cases: Cross mortgages between the taxpayer and an acquaintance made with RRSP funds were "non-qualified" investments because the parties were not dealing at arm's length and they acted in concert to produce for themselves a favourable investment. *Sayers v. M.N.R.*, 81 DTC 790 (T.R.B.). See also *McCracken v. M.N.R.*, 81 DTC 793 (T.R.B.); *Giusti et al. v. M.N.R.*, 82 DTC 981 (T.R.B.); *Schuss v. M.N.R.*, 83 DTC 350 (T.R.B.); *Ciccone v. M.N.R.*, 83 DTC 353 (T.R.B.), 354

"premium" —"premium" means any periodic or other amount paid or payable under a retirement savings plan

(*a*) as consideration for any contract referred to in paragraph (*a*) of the definition "retirement savings plan" to pay a retirement income, or

(*b*) as a contribution or deposit referred to in paragraph (*b*) of that definition for the purpose stated in that paragraph

but except for the purposes of paragraph (*b*) of the definition "benefit" in this subsection, paragraph (2)(*b*.3), subsection (22) and the definition "excluded premium" in subsection 146.02(1), does not include a repayment to which paragraph (*b*) or (*d*) of the definition "excluded withdrawal" in subsection 146.01(1), or paragraph (*b*) of the definition "excluded withdrawal" in subsection 146.02(1), applies or an amount that is designated under subsection 146.01(3) or 146.02(3);

History: S. 146(1), the portion of the definition "premium" after paragraph (*b*) was replaced by S.C. 2019, c. 29, s. 26(1), applicable in respect of repayments made after 2019, and formerly read:

but, except for the purposes of paragraph (*b*) of the definition "benefit" in this subsection, paragraph (2)(*b*.3), subsection (22) and the definition "excluded premium" in subsection 146.02(1), does not include a repayment to which paragraph (*b*) of the definition "excluded withdrawal" in either subsection 146.01(1) or 146.02(1) applies or an amount that is designated under subsection 146.01(3) or 146.02(3);

Related Sections: 146.02(1), "excluded withdrawal".

Interpretation Bulletins: *Secondary* — IT-528 Transfers of funds between registered plans.

"qualified investment" —"qualified investment" for a trust governed by a registered retirement savings plan means

(*a*) an investment that would be described by any of paragraphs (*a*) to (*d*), (*f*) and (*g*) of the definition "qualified investment" in section 204 if the reference in that definition to "a trust governed by a deferred profit sharing plan or revoked plan" were read as a reference to "a trust governed by a registered retirement savings plan" and if that definition were read without reference to the words "with the exception of excluded property in relation to the trust",

(*b*) (Repealed.)

(*c*) an annuity described in the definition "retirement income" in respect of the annuitant under the plan, if purchased from a licensed annuities provider,

(*c*.1) a contract for an annuity issued by a licensed annuities provider where

(i) the trust is the only person who, disregarding any subsequent transfer of the contract by the trust, is or may become entitled to any annuity payments under the contract, and

(ii) the holder of the contract has a right to surrender the contract at any time for an amount that would, if reasonable sales and administration charges were ignored, approximate the value of funds that could otherwise be applied to fund future periodic payments under the contract,

(*c*.2) a contract for an annuity issued by a licensed annuities provider where

(i) annual or more frequent periodic payments are or may be made under the contract to the holder of the contract,

(ii) the trust is the only person who, disregarding any subsequent transfer of the contract by the trust, is or may become entitled to any annuity payments under the contract,

(iii) neither the time nor the amount of any payment under the contract may vary because of the length of any life, other than the life of the annuitant under the plan (in this definition referred to as the "RRSP annuitant"),

(iv) the day on which the periodic payments began or are to begin (in this paragraph referred to as the "start date") is not later than the end of the year in which the RRSP annuitant attains 72 years of age,

(v) either

(A) the periodic payments are payable for the life of the RRSP annuitant and either there is no guaranteed period under the contract or there is a guaranteed period that begins at the start date and does not exceed a term equal to 90 years minus the lesser of

(I) the age in whole years at the start date of the RRSP annuitant (determined on the assumption that the RRSP annuitant is alive at the start date), and

(II) the age in whole years at the start date of a spouse or common-law partner of the RRSP annuitant (determined on the assumption that a spouse or common-law partner of the RRSP annuitant at the time the contract was acquired is a spouse or common-law partner of the RRSP annuitant at the start date), or

(B) the periodic payments are payable for a term equal to

(I) 90 years minus the age described in subclause (A)(I), or

(II) 90 years minus the age described in subclause (A)(II), and

(vi) the periodic payments

(A) are equal, or

(B) are not equal solely because of one or more adjustments that would, if the contract were an annuity under a retirement savings plan, be in accordance with subparagraphs (3)(*b*)(iii) to (v) or that arise because of a uniform reduction in the entitlement to the periodic payments as a consequence of a partial surrender of rights to the periodic payments, and

(*d*) such other investments as may be prescribed by regulations of the Governor in Council made on the recommendation of the Minister of Finance;

Proposed Amendment

2019 Federal Budget Resolutions

The Act is modified to give effect to the proposals relating to permitting additional types of annuities under registered plans described in the budget documents tabled by the Minister of Finance in the House of Commons on Budget Day.

Explanatory Note:
Dentons Canada LLP Commentary

Budget 2019 proposes to provide "qualified investment" status to the following additional types of annuities for certain registered plans, effective for 2020 and subsequent taxation years:

- advanced life deferred annuities will be permitted under a registered retirement savings plan (RRSP), registered retirement income fund (RRIF), deferred profit sharing plan (DPSP), pooled registered pension plan (PRPP) and defined contribution registered pension plan (RPP); and
- variable payment life annuities will be permitted under a PRPP and defined contribution RPP.

Advanced Life Deferred Annuities (ALDA)

The tax rules generally require an annuity purchased with a registered plan to commence by the end of the year in which the annuitant attains 71 years of age. An ALDA will be a life annuity the commencement of which may be deferred until the end of the year in which the annuitant turns 85 and meets certain other prescribed conditions. A lifetime limit of 25% of the value of the plan (including payments for the ALDA) and $150,000 will apply.

Annuity payments to a surviving spouse or common-law partner will be taxable in the year of receipt. Lump-sum payments to a surviving spouse, common-law partner or dependent child or grandchild (provided that the child or grandchild is dependent by reason of physical or mental infirmity) will qualify for a tax-deferred transfer to an RRSP, RRIF or other eligible vehicle of the annuitant.

Variable Payment Life Annuity (VPLA)

Existing rules generally require retirement benefits from a PRPP or defined contribution RPP be provided to a member by means of a transfer of funds from the account to an RRSP or RRIF. Budget 2019 proposes that commencing in 2020 and subsequent years, PRPP and RPPs be able to provide a VPLA directly to members from the plan. A VPLA will provide payments that vary based on the investment performance of the underlying annuities fund and on the mortality experience of VPLA annuitants.

PRPP and defined contribution RPP administrators will be permitted to establish a separate annuities fund under the plan to receive transfers of amounts from members' accounts to provide for VPLAs. A minimum of 10 retired members will be required to participate in a VPLA. VPLAs will be required to comply with certain existing tax rules applicable to PRPPs and defined contribution RPPs, as well as additional requirements. On death, VPLAs will be subject to the existing tax treatment of annuities purchased with PRPP and defined contribution RPP savings.

Editorial Note: The definition of "qualified investment" for a trust governed by an RRSP incorporates by reference much of the similar definition in s. 204 that applies to deferred profit sharing plans. The definition also includes investments that are prescribed under Part XLIX (s. 4900) of the Regulations.

Related Regulations: 221; 4900(1), (2), (4), (6), (9), (14).

Related Sections: S. 87(10) Share deemed listed; s. 204 Definitions; s. 207.1(1) Tax payable by trust under registered retirement savings plan; s. 248(1), "licensed annuities provider".

Canadian Tax Foundation: Gosselin, *Reversing Prohibited Status of Small Business Shares in RRSPs*, 2015 Tax for the Owner-Manager 15(4):2–3; De Lisser and Krieger, *Registered Savings Plans: Investing Without Penalty*, 2013 Canadian Tax Journal 3:769–796.

Tax Profile: August 2004 — Canadian Tax Treatment of Index Participation Units and Exchange-Traded Index Derivatives.

Forms: T3F — Investments Prescribed to be Qualified Information Return.

Income Tax Folios: *Primary* — S3-F10-C1 Qualified Investments – RRSPs, RESPs, RRIFs, RDSPs and TFSAs. *Secondary* — S3-F10-C2 Prohibited Investments - RRSPs, RRIFs and TFSAs.

Cases: Since a taxpayer had no personal stake in a private corporation aside from his former employment with it, his investments in its shares were qualified investments for RRSP. *Bates v. The Queen*, 98 DTC 1516 (T.C.C.).

"RRSP deduction limit" —"RRSP deduction limit" of a taxpayer for a taxation year means the amount determined by the formula

$$A + B + R - C$$

where

A is the taxpayer's unused RRSP deduction room at the end of the preceding taxation year,

B is the amount, if any, by which

(*a*) the lesser of the RRSP dollar limit for the year and 18% of the taxpayer's earned income for the preceding taxation year

exceeds the total of all amounts each of which is

(*b*) the taxpayer's pension adjustment for the preceding taxation year in respect of an employer, or

(*c*) a prescribed amount in respect of the taxpayer for the year,

C is the taxpayer's net past service pension adjustment for the year, and

R is the taxpayer's total pension adjustment reversal for the year;

Related Regulations: 8301; 8308(2); 8308.2; 8308.4(2); 8309.

Related Sections: S. 146(1), "net past service adjustment", "RRSP dollar limit", "unused RRSP deduction room"; s. 146(5) Amount of RRSP premiums deductible; s. 146(5.1) Amount of spousal RRSP premiums deductible; S. 147.5(10) Employer contributions deductible; S. 147.5(11) Member contributions; s. 248(1), "pension adjustment", "total pension adjustment reversal".

"RRSP dollar limit" —"RRSP dollar limit" for a calendar year means

(*a*) for years other than 1996 and 2003, the money purchase limit for the preceding year,

(*b*) for 1996, $13,500, and

(*c*) for 2003, $14,500;

Editorial Note: The "RRSP dollar limit" is one factor that is used in determining the "RRSP deduction limit" that is described in s. 146(1). For years other than 1996 and 2003, the "RRSP dollar limit" is the amount of the "money purchase limit" for the preceding year. See the definition of "money purchase limit" in s. 147.1(1).

Related Sections: S. 146(1) Definitions; s. 147.1(1), "money purchase limit"; s. 204.2(1.1) Cumulative excess amount in respect of RRSPs.

"refund of premiums" —"refund of premiums" means any amount paid out of or under a registered retirement savings plan (other than a tax-paid amount in respect of the plan) as a consequence of the death of the annuitant under the plan,

(*a*) to an individual who was, immediately before the death, a spouse or common-law partner of the annuitant, where the annuitant died before the maturity of the plan, or

(*b*) to a child or grandchild of the annuitant who was, immediately before the death, financially dependent on the annuitant for support;

Editorial Note: See the editorial note for s. 146(8).

Related Sections: S. 60(*l*) Transfer of refund of premiums under RRSP; s. 146(1), "annuitant", "tax-paid amount"; s. 146(1.1) Restriction — financially dependent; s. 146(8.1) Deemed receipt of refund of premiums.

Canadian Tax Foundation: Doobay, *Consent Order Not Rectification*, 2015 Canadian Tax Highlights 23(2):6–8.

"registered retirement savings plan" —"registered retirement savings plan" means a retirement savings plan accepted by the Minister for registration for the purposes of this Act as complying with the requirements of this section;

Related Regulations: 215.

Related Sections: S. 146(1), "retirement savings plan".

Interpretation Bulletins: *Secondary* — IT-528 Transfers of funds between registered plans.

"retirement income" —"retirement income" means

(*a*) an annuity commencing at maturity, and with or without a guaranteed term commencing at maturity, not exceeding the term referred to in paragraph (*b*), or, in the case of a plan entered into before March 14, 1957, not exceeding 20 years, payable to

(i) the annuitant for the annuitant's life, or

(ii) the annuitant for the lives, jointly, of the annuitant and the annuitant's spouse or common-law partner and to the survivor of them for the survivor's life, or

(*b*) an annuity commencing at maturity, payable to the annuitant, or to the annuitant for the annuitant's life and to the spouse or common-law partner after the annuitant's death, for a term of years equal to 90 minus either

(i) the age in whole years of the annuitant at the maturity of the plan, or

(ii) where the annuitant's spouse or common-law partner is younger than the annuitant and the annuitant so elects, the age in whole years of the spouse or common-law partner at the maturity of the plan,

issued by a person described in the definition "retirement savings plan" in this subsection with whom an individual may have a contract or arrangement that is a retirement savings plan,

or any combination thereof;

Related Sections: S. 146(1), "annuitant", "tax-paid amount"; s. 146(1.1) Restriction — financially dependent.

Information Circulars: IC 72-22R9 Registered retirement savings plans.

"retirement savings plan" —"retirement savings plan" means

(*a*) a contract between an individual and a person licensed or otherwise authorized under the laws of Canada or a province to carry on in Canada an annuities business, under which, in consideration of payment by the individual or the individual's spouse or common-law partner of any periodic or other amount as consideration under the contract, a retirement income commencing at maturity is to be provided for the individual, or

(*b*) an arrangement under which payment is made by an individual or the individual's spouse or common-law partner

(i) in trust to a corporation licensed or otherwise authorized under the laws of Canada or a province to carry on in Canada the business of offering to the public its services as trustee, of any periodic or other amount as a contribution under the trust,

(ii) to a corporation approved by the Governor in Council for the purposes of this section that is licensed or otherwise authorized under the laws of Canada or a province to issue investment contracts providing for the payment to or to the credit of the holder thereof of a fixed or determinable amount at maturity, of any periodic or other amount as a contribution under such a contract between the individual and that corporation, or

(iii) as a deposit with a branch or office, in Canada, of

(A) a person who is, or is eligible to become, a member of the Canadian Payments Association, or

(B) a credit union that is a shareholder or member of a body corporate referred to as a "central" for the purposes of the *Canadian Payments Act*,

to be used, invested or otherwise applied by that corporation or that depositary, as the case may be, for the purpose of providing for the individual, commencing at maturity, a retirement income;

History: S. 146(1), clause (*b*)(iii)(B) of the definition "retirement savings plan" was replaced by S.C. 2017, c. 33, s. 56(1), deemed to have come into force on October 24, 2001, and formerly read:

(B) a credit union that is a shareholder or member of a body corporate referred to as a "central" for the purposes of the *Canadian Payments Association Act*, (in this section referred to as a "depositary")

Related Regulations: S. 214.1.

Related Sections: S. 146(1), "retirement income".

Forms: T3GR — Group Income Tax and Information Return for RRSP, RRIF, RESP or RDSP Trusts; T4RSP — Statement of RRSP Income; T4RSP SUM — Summary of Income from a Registered Retirement Savings Plan; T550 — Application for Registration of: RSP's, ESP's, or RIF's Under Section 146, 146.2 and 146.3 of the Income Tax Act.

"spousal or common-law partner plan" —"spousal or common-law partner plan", in relation to a taxpayer, means

(*a*) a registered retirement savings plan

(i) to which the taxpayer has, at a time when the taxpayer's spouse or common-law partner was the annuitant under the plan, paid a premium, or

(ii) that has received a payment out of or a transfer from a registered retirement savings plan or a registered retirement income fund that was a spousal or common-law partner plan in relation to the taxpayer, or

(*b*) a registered retirement income fund that has received a payment out of or a transfer from a spousal or common-law partner plan in relation to the taxpayer;

Related Sections: S. 248(1), "common-law partner".

"spousal plan" — (Repealed by S.C. 2001, c. 17, s. 246(1).)

"tax-paid amount" —"tax-paid amount" paid to a person in respect of a registered retirement saving plan means

(*a*) an amount paid to the person in respect of the amount that would, if this Act were read without reference to subsection 104(6), be income of a trust governed by the plan for a taxation year for which the trust was subject to tax because of paragraph (4)(*c*), or

(*b*) where

(i) the plan is a deposit with a depositary referred to in clause (*b*)(iii)(B) of the definition "retirement savings plan" in this subsection, and

(ii) an amount is received at any time out of or under the plan by the person,

the portion of the amount that can reasonably be considered to relate to interest or another amount in respect of the deposit that was required to be included in computing the income of any person (other than the annuitant) otherwise than because of this section;

Related Sections: S. 146(8.9) Deduction from deemed receipt before death by deceased annuitant.

"unused RRSP deduction room" —"unused RRSP deduction room" of a taxpayer at the end of a taxation year means,

(*a*) for taxation years ending before 1991, nil, and

(*b*) for taxation years that end after 1990, the amount, which can be positive or negative, determined by the formula

$$A + B + R - (C + D)$$

where

A is the taxpayer's unused RRSP deduction room at the end of the preceding taxation year,

B is the amount, if any, by which

(i) the lesser of the RRSP dollar limit for the year and 18% of the taxpayer's earned income for the preceding taxation year

exceeds the total of all amounts each of which is

(ii) the taxpayer's pension adjustment for the preceding taxation year in respect of an employer, or

(iii) a prescribed amount in respect of the taxpayer for the year,

C is the taxpayer's net past service pension adjustment for the year,

D is the total of all amounts each of which is

(i) an amount deducted by the taxpayer under any of subsections (5) to (5.2), in computing the taxpayer's income for the year,

(ii) an amount deducted by the taxpayer under paragraph 10 of Article XVIII of the *Canada-United States Tax Convention* signed at Washington on September 26, 1980 or a similar provision in another tax treaty, in computing the taxpayer's taxable income for the year,

(iii) a contribution made by an employer in the year to a pooled registered pension plan in respect of the taxpayer, or

(iv) the amount, if any, by which the taxpayer's exempt-income contribution amount (as defined in subsection 147.5(1)) for the year exceeds the taxpayer's unused non-deductible PRPP room (as defined in subsection 147.5(1)) at the end of the preceding taxation year, and

R is the taxpayer's total pension adjustment reversal for the year.

History: S. 146(1), the description of D in paragraph (*b*) of the definition "unused RRSP deduction room" was replaced by S.C. 2012, c. 31, s. 32(1), in force December 14, 2012. S. 146(1), the description of D in paragraph (*b*) of the definition "unused RRSP deduction room" formerly read:

D is the total of all amounts each of which is an amount deducted by the taxpayer,

(i) under subsection (5) or (5.1) or paragraph 60(*v*), in computing the taxpayer's income for the year, or

(ii) under paragraph 10 of Article XVIII of the *Canada–United States Tax Convention* signed at Washington on September 26, 1980 or a similar provision in another tax treaty, in computing the taxpayer's taxable income for the year, and

S. 146(1), the description of D in paragraph (*b*) of the definition "unused RRSP deduction room" was replaced by S.C. 2009, c. 2, s. 51(2), applicable to the 2009 and subsequent taxation years. S. 146(1), the description of D in paragraph (*b*) of the definition "unused RRSP deduction room" formerly read:

D is the total of the amounts deducted by the taxpayer under subsections (5) and (5.1) and paragraph 60(*v*) in computing the taxpayer's income for the year, and

Related Regulations: 8308(2); 8308.2; 8308.4(2); 8309.

Related Sections: S. 146(1), "net past service pension adjustment", "RRSP dollar limit"; S. 147.5(33) Exempt contributions not over-contributions; s. 204.2(1.1), "pension adjustment"; s. 248(1), "total pension adjustment reversal".

► 146(1.1) ◄

(1.1) Restriction — financially dependent. For the purposes of paragraph (*b*) of the definition "refund of premiums" in subsection (1), clause 60(*l*)(v)(B.01), the definition "eligible individual" in subsection 60.02(1), subparagraph 104(27)(*e*)(i) and section 147.5, it is assumed, unless the contrary is established, that an individual's child or grandchild was not financially dependent on the individual for support immediately before the individual's death if the income of the child or grandchild for the taxation year preceding the taxation year in which the individual died exceeded the amount determined by the formula

$$A + B$$

where

A is the amount used under paragraph (*c*) of the description of B in subsection 118(1) for that preceding taxation year; and

B is nil, unless the financial dependency was because of mental or physical infirmity, in which case it is $6,180 adjusted for each such preceding taxation year that is after 2002 in the manner set out in section 117.1.

Editorial Note: The amount used for Variable A is the same as the basic personal amount in s. 118(1)(*c*). The dollar figure in Variable B is the same as the disability amount (s. 118.3(1)). See the CRA Fact Sheet reproduced following s. 117.1(1) for the indexed amounts.

History: S. 146(1.1), the portion before the formula was replaced by S.C. 2012, c. 31, s. 32(2), and comes into force on December 14, 2012. S. 146(1.1), the portion before the formula formerly read:

(1.1) *Restriction — financially dependent.* For the purpose of paragraph (*b*) of the definition "refund of premiums" in subsection (1), clause 60(*l*)(v)(B.01), the definition "eligible individual" in subsection 60.02(1) and subparagraph 104(27)(*e*)(i), it is assumed, unless the contrary is established, that an individual's child or grandchild was not financially dependent on the individual for support immediately before the individual's death if the income of the child or grandchild for the taxation year preceding the taxation year in which the individual died exceeded the amount determined by the formula

S. 146(1.1), the portion before the formula was replaced by S.C. 2011, c. 24, s. 45(3), deemed to have come into force on March 4, 2010. S. 146(1.1), the portion before the formula formerly read:

(1.1) *Restriction — financially dependent.* For the purpose of paragraph (*b*) of the definition "refund of premiums" in subsection (1), clause 60(*l*)(v)(B.01) and subparagraph 104(27)(*e*)(i), it is assumed, unless the contrary is established, that an individual's child or grandchild was not financially dependent on the individual for support immediately before the individual's death if the income of the child or grandchild for the taxation year preceding the taxation year in which the individual died exceeded the amount determined by the formula

► 146(2) ◄

(2) Acceptance of plan for registration. The Minister shall not accept for registration for the purposes of this Act any retirement savings plan unless, in the Minister's opinion, it complies with the following conditions:

(*a*) the plan does not provide for the payment of any benefit before maturity except

(i) a refund of premiums, and

(ii) a payment to the annuitant;

(*b*) the plan does not provide for the payment of any benefit after maturity except

(i) by way of retirement income to the annuitant,

(ii) to the annuitant in full or partial commutation of retirement income under the plan, and

(iii) in respect of a commutation referred to in paragraph (*c*.2);

(*b*.1) the plan does not provide for a payment to the annuitant of a retirement income except by way of equal annual or more frequent periodic payments until such time as there is a payment in full or partial commutation of the retirement income and, where that commutation is partial, equal annual or more frequent periodic payments thereafter;

(*b*.2) the plan does not provide for periodic payments in a year under an annuity after the death of the first annuitant, the total of which exceeds the total of the payments under the annuity in a year before that death;

(*b*.3) the plan does not provide for the payment of any premium after maturity;

(*b*.4) the plan does not provide for maturity after the end of the year in which the annuitant attains 71 years of age;

(*c*) the plan provides that retirement income under the plan may not be assigned in whole or in part;

(*c*.1) notwithstanding paragraph (*a*), the plan permits the payment of an amount to a taxpayer where the amount is paid to reduce the amount of tax otherwise payable under Part X.1 by the taxpayer;

(*c*.2) the plan requires the commutation of each annuity payable thereunder that would otherwise become payable to a person other than an annuitant under the plan;

(*c*.3) the plan, where it involves a depositary, includes provisions stipulating that

(i) the depositary has no right of offset as regards the property held under the plan in connection with any debt or obligation owing to the depositary, and

(ii) the property held under the plan cannot be pledged, assigned or in any way alienated as security for a loan or for any purpose other than that of providing for the annuitant, commencing at maturity, a retirement income; and

(*c*.4) (Repealed.)

(*d*) the plan in all other respects complies with regulations of the Governor in Council made on the recommendation of the Minister of Finance.

Editorial Note: The maturity deadline for RRSPs (see s. 146(2)(*b*.4)) is the end of the year in which the annuitant turns 71 years of age. Previously, from 1997 through 2006, the deadline was the end of the year in which the annuitant turned 69 years of age.

History: S. 146(2)(*c*.4) was repealed by S.C. 2011, c. 24, s. 45(4), deemed to have come into force on March 23, 2011. S. 146(2)(*c*.4) formerly read:

(*c*.4) the plan requires that no advantage, other than

(i) a benefit,

(i.1) an amount described in paragraph (*a*) or (*c*) of the definition "benefit" in subsection (1),

(ii) the payment or allocation of any amount to the plan by the issuer,

(iii) an advantage from life insurance in effect on December 31, 1981, or

(iv) an advantage derived from the provision of administrative or investment services in respect of the plan,

that is conditional in any way on the existence of the plan may be extended to the annuitant or to a person with whom the annuitant was not dealing at arm's length; and

Related Sections: S. 56(1)(*h*) Registered retirement savings plan, etc.; s. 60(*l*) Transfer of refund of premiums under RRSP; s. 139.1(13) RRSP registration rules, etc; s. 146(1), "annuitant", "benefit", "earned income", "maturity", "premium", "qualified investment", "refund of premiums", "retirement income", "retirement savings plan", "registered retirement savings plan"; s. 149(1)(*r*) Trusts under registered retirement savings plan; s. 160.2(1) Joint and several liability in respect of amounts received out of or under RRSP; s. 212(1)(*l*) Registered retirement savings plan payments; s. 248(1), "annuity", "common-law partner", "death benefit"; ITAR s. 65(1) Part XI of amended Act — foreign property acquired after June 18, 1971 and before July 1, 1972; (3) Cost of acquisition of capital property owned on Dec. 31, 1971.

Tax Topics: No. 1665, RRSP Incentives.

Forms: T550 — Application for Registration of: RSP's, ESP's, or RIF's Under Section 146, 146.2 and 146.3 of the Income Tax Act.

Guides: T4040 RRSPs and Other Registered Plans for Retirement.

Information Circulars: IC 72-22R9 Registered retirement savings plans.

Interpretation Bulletins: *Secondary* — IT-124R6 Contributions to registered retirement savings plans.

Tax Window Files: RRSP — Beneficiary Designation/Settlement Annuity, *Technical Interpretation, Financial Sector and Exempt Entities Division, July 20, 2005*, CRA Document No. 2005-0120161E5; Registered Retirement Savings Plan — Prohibited Advantages, *Technical Interpretations, Financial Industries Division, March 22, 2004 and April 16, 2004*, CRA Document No. 2004-0056431E5; Registered Retirement Savings Plans — Donation Made for Contributions, *Technical Interpretation, Financial Industries Division, May 1, 2003*, CRA Document No. 2002-0178105.

Cases: The provisions of the Act which require a taxpayer to collapse an RRSP at age 71 did not infringe any of the taxpayer's Charter rights and, in any event, would be a reasonable limitation upon those rights. *Gerol v. Attorney General of Canada*, 85 DTC 5561 (O.H.C.J.).

► 146(3) ◄

(3) Idem. The Minister may accept for registration for the purposes of this Act any retirement savings plan notwithstanding that the plan

(*a*) provides for the payment of a benefit after maturity by way of dividend;

(*b*) provides for any annual or more frequent periodic amount payable

(i) to the annuitant referred to in subparagraph (*a*)(ii) of the definition "retirement income" in subsection (1) by way of an annuity described in paragraph (*a*) of that definition to be reduced, in the event of the death of the annuitant's spouse or common-law partner during the lifetime of the annuitant, in such manner as to provide for the payment of equal annual or more frequent periodic amounts throughout the lifetime of the annuitant thereafter,

(ii) to any person by way of an annuity, to be reduced if a pension becomes payable to that person under the *Old Age Security Act*, by an annual or other periodic amount not exceeding the amount payable to that person in that period under that Act,

(iii) to any person by way of an annuity, to be increased or reduced depending on the increase or reduction in the value of a specified group of assets constituting the assets of a separate and distinct account or fund maintained in respect of a variable annuities business by a person licensed or otherwise authorized under the laws of Canada or a province to carry on in Canada that business,

(iii.1) to any person by way of an annuity under a contract that provides for the increase or reduction of the annuity in accordance only with a change in the interest rate on which the annuity is based, if the interest rate, as increased or reduced, equals or approximates a generally available Canadian market interest rate,

(iv) that may be adjusted annually to reflect

(A) in whole or in part increases in the Consumer Price Index, as published by Statistics Canada under the authority of the *Statistics Act*, or

(B) increases at a rate specified in the annuity contract, not exceeding 4% per annum, or

(v) to the annuitant by way of an annuity to be increased annually to the extent the amount or rate of return that would have been earned on a pool of investment assets (available for purchase by the public and specified in the annuity contract) exceeds an amount or rate specified in the plan and provides that no other increase may be made in the amount payable;

(*c*) (Repealed by 1986, c. 55, s. 56(2).)

(*d*) provides for the payment of any amount after the death of an annuitant thereunder;

(*e*) is adjoined to a contract or other arrangement that is not a retirement savings plan; or

(*f*) contains such other terms and provisions, not inconsistent with this section, as are authorized or permitted by regulations of the Governor in Council made on the recommendation of the Minister of Finance.

Related Sections: S. 172(3) Appeal from refusal to register, revocation of registration, etc.

Interpretation Bulletins: *Secondary* — IT-124R6 Contributions to registered retirement savings plans.

▶ 146(4) ◀

(4) No tax while trust governed by plan. Except as provided in subsection (10.1), no tax is payable under this Part by a trust on the taxable income of the trust for a taxation year if, throughout the period in the year during which the trust was in existence, the trust was governed by a registered retirement savings plan, except that

(*a*) if the trust has borrowed money (other than money used in carrying on a business) in the year or has, after June 18, 1971, borrowed money (other than money used in carrying on a business) that it has not repaid before the commencement of the year, tax is payable under this Part by the trust on its taxable income for the year;

(*b*) in any case not described in paragraph (*a*), if the trust has carried on any business or businesses in the year, tax is payable under this Part by the trust on the amount, if any, by which

(i) the amount that its taxable income for the year would be if it had no incomes or losses from sources other than from that business or those businesses, as the case may be,

exceeds

(ii) such portion of the amount determined under subparagraph (i) in respect of the trust for the year as can reasonably be considered to be income from, or from the disposition of, qualified investments for the trust; and

(*c*) if the last annuitant under the plan has died, tax is payable under this Part by the trust on its taxable income for each year after the year following the year in which the last annuitant died.

Related Sections: S. 146(10) Where acquisition of non-qualified investment by trust; s. 146(20) Credited or added amount deemed not received; s. 149(1)(*r*) Trusts under registered retirement savings plan; s. 207.1(1) Tax payable by trust under registered retirement savings plan.

▶ 146(5) ◀

(5) Amount of RRSP premiums deductible. There may be deducted in computing a taxpayer's income for a taxation year such amount as the taxpayer claims not exceeding the lesser of

(*a*) the amount, if any, by which the total of all amounts each of which is a premium paid by the taxpayer after 1990 and on or before the day that is 60 days after the end of the year under a registered retirement savings plan under which the taxpayer was the annuitant at the time the premium was paid, other than the portion, if any, of the premium

(i) that was deducted in computing the taxpayer's income for a preceding taxation year,

(ii) that was designated for any taxation year for the purposes of paragraph 60(*j*), (*j*.1) or (*l*),

(iii) in respect of which the taxpayer received a payment that was deducted under subsection (8.2) in computing the taxpayer's income for a preceding taxation year,

(iii.1) that was an exempt-income contribution amount (as defined in subsection 147.5(1)) for any taxation year,

(iv) that was deductible under subsection (6.1) in computing the taxpayer's income for any taxation year or

(iv.1) that would be considered to be withdrawn by the taxpayer as an eligible amount (as defined in subsection 146.01(1) or 146.02(1)) less than 90 days after it was paid, if earnings in respect of a registered retirement savings plan were considered to be withdrawn before premiums paid under that plan and premiums were considered to be withdrawn in the order in which they were paid

exceeds

(v) the amount, if any, by which

(A) the total of all amounts deducted under subsection 147.3(13.1) in computing the taxpayer's income for the year or a preceding taxation year

exceeds

(B) the total of all amounts, in respect of transfers occurring before 1991 from registered pension plans, deemed by paragraph 147.3(10)(*b*) or (*c*) to be a premium paid by the taxpayer to a registered retirement savings plan, and

(*b*) the amount, if any, by which the taxpayer's RRSP deduction limit for the year exceeds the total of all contributions made by an employer in the year to a pooled registered pension plan in respect of the taxpayer.

Editorial Note: Contributions to an RRSP in excess of the RRSP deduction limit for the year are normally subject to a monthly penalty tax under Part X.1, although taxpayers are allowed a $2,000 overcontribution "cushion" for these purposes; see ss. 204.1(2) and 204.2(1.1). Deductions under s. 146(5) reduce the amount deductible for contributions to a spousal or common-law partner plan under s. 146(5.1). "RRSP deduction limit" is defined in s. 146(1).

History: S. 146(5)(*a*)(iii.1) was added by S.C. 2012, c. 31, s. 32(3), in force December 14, 2012.

S. 146(5)(*b*) was replaced by S.C. 2012, c. 31, s. 32(4), and comes into force on December 14, 2012. S. 146(5)(*b*) formerly read:

(*b*) the taxpayer's RRSP deduction limit for the year.

Related Regulations: 100(3)(c); 214.1.

Related Sections: S. 60(*i*) Premium or payment under RRSP or RRIF; s. 146(1), "premium", "RRSP deduction limit"; s. 146(5.1) Amount of spousal RRSP premiums deductible; s. 146(8.21) Premium deemed not paid; s. 146(16) Transfer of funds; s. 146(22) Deemed payment of RRSP premiums and provincial pension plan contributions; s. 147.3(13.1) Withdrawal of excessive transfers to RRSPs and RRIFs; S. 147.5(10) Employer contributions deductible; S. 147.5(11) Member contributions; s. 204.94(2) Charging provision; s. 249 Definition of "taxation year"; Part X.1 — Tax in Respect of Over-Contributions to Deferred Income Plans.

Information Circulars: IC 72-22R9 Registered retirement savings plans.

Interpretation Bulletins: *Primary* — IT-124R6 Contributions to registered retirement savings plans. *Secondary* — IT-307R4 Spousal or common-law partner registered retirement savings plans.

Tax Window Files: Foreign Tax Credit on Transfer of 401(k) to RRSP, *15XXXX*, CRA Document No. 2015-0572541R3.

Cases: A cheque post-dated more than 60 days after year-end is not paid within 60 days as required. *Vlasblom v. M.N.R.*, 87 DTC 215 (T.C.C.)

▶ 146(5.1) ◀

(5.1) Amount of spousal RRSP premiums deductible. There may be deducted in computing a taxpayer's income for a taxation year such amount as the taxpayer claims not exceeding the lesser of

(*a*) the total of all amounts each of which is a premium paid by the taxpayer after 1990 and on or before the day that is 60 days after the end of the year under a registered retirement savings plan under which the taxpayer's spouse or common-law partner (or, where the taxpayer died in the year or within 60 days after the end of the year, an individual who was the taxpayer's spouse or common-law partner immediately before the death) was the annuitant at the time the premium was paid, other than the portion, if any, of the premium

(i) that was deducted in computing the taxpayer's income for a preceding taxation year,

(ii) that was designated for any taxation year for the purposes of paragraph 60(*j*.2),

(iii) in respect of which the taxpayer or the taxpayer's spouse or common-law partner has received a payment that has been deducted under subsection (8.2) in computing the taxpayer's income for a preceding taxation year, or

(iv) that would be considered to be withdrawn by the taxpayer's spouse or common-law partner as an eligible amount (as defined in subsection 146.01(1) or 146.02(1)) less than 90 days after it was paid, if earnings in respect of a registered retirement savings plan were considered to be withdrawn before premiums paid under that plan and premiums were considered to be withdrawn in the order in which they were paid, and

(*b*) the amount, if any, by which the taxpayer's RRSP deduction limit for the year exceeds the total of all amounts each of which is

(i) the amount deducted under subsection (5) in computing the taxpayer's income for the year, or

(ii) a contribution made by an employer in the year to a pooled registered pension plan in respect of the taxpayer.

Editorial Note: Contributions to a spousal RRSP can be made after the contributor's own RRSP has matured. Contributions can also be made within 60 days after the end of the year in which the contributor dies.

S. 146(5.1) effectively allows income splitting between spouses (or common-law partners), as the contributor is permitted the deduction while the spouse includes any amount withdrawn from the spousal RRSP. But see the attribution rule in s. 146(8.3) where amounts are withdrawn from the spousal RRSP in the year of the contribution or either of the two following years.

History: S. 146(5.1)(*b*) was replaced by S.C. 2012, c. 31, s. 32(5), and comes into force on December 14, 2012. S. 146(5.1)(*b*) formerly read:

(*b*) the amount, if any, by which the taxpayer's RRSP deduction limit for the year exceeds the amount deducted under subsection (5) in computing the taxpayer's income for the year.

Related Regulations: 100(3)(c); 214.1.

Related Sections: S. 146(5) Amount of RRSP premiums deductible; s. 146(8.21) Premium deemed not paid; s. 146(8.3) Spousal or common-law partner payments; s. 146(22) Deemed payment of RRSP premiums and provincial pension plan contributions; s. 204.94(2) Charging provision; s. 248(1), "common-law partner".

Interpretation Bulletins: *Primary* — IT-124R6 Contributions to registered retirement savings plans; IT-307R4 Spousal or common-law partner registered retirement savings plans.

▶ 146(5.2) ◀

(5.2) RRSP premium. If a taxpayer's entitlement to benefits under a defined benefit provision of a registered pension plan is transferred in accordance with subsection 147.3(4) after February 2009 and before 2011, there may be deducted in computing the taxpayer's income for a taxation year that ends on or after the day on which the transfer was made, the amount claimed by the taxpayer in respect of premiums paid by the taxpayer in the year to a registered retirement savings plan under which the taxpayer is the annuitant, not exceeding the amount, if any, determined by the formula

$$A - B - C$$

where

A is the amount, if any, that is the lesser of

(*a*) the prescribed amount that would have been determined for the purpose of paragraph 147.3(4)(*c*) if subsection 8517(3.01) of the Regulations had applied in respect of the transfer, and

(*b*) the amount of the taxpayer's entitlement to benefits under the provision commuted in connection with the transfer;

B is the prescribed amount for the purpose of paragraph 147.3(4)(*c*) that applied in respect of the transfer; and

C is the total of all amounts deducted by the taxpayer under this subsection for a preceding taxation year.

History: S. 146(5.2) was added by S.C. 2011, c. 24, s. 45(5), applicable in respect of transfers made after February 2009.

Related Regulations: 8517(3) Underfunded Pension; 8517(3.001); 8517(3.01); 8517(3.02) Underfunded Pension.

▶ 146(5.201) ◀

(5.201) Transitional rule. For the purpose of subsection (5.2), a premium paid by a taxpayer before 2013 is deemed to have been paid in the taxation year in which the transfer referred to in that subsection was made and not in the year in which it was actually paid, if the taxpayer so elects in prescribed form.

History: S. 146(5.201) was added by S.C. 2011, c. 24, s. 45(5), applicable in respect of transfers made after February 2009.

► 146(5.21) ◄

(5.21) Anti-avoidance. Notwithstanding any other provision of this section, where

(*a*) a registered pension plan is amended or administered in such a manner as to terminate, suspend or delay

(i) the membership of an individual in the plan for the individual's 1990 taxation year,

(ii) contributions under the plan by or for the benefit of the individual in respect of the year, or

(iii) the accrual of retirement benefits under the plan for the individual in respect of the year, or

(*b*) a deferred profit sharing plan is amended or administered in such a manner as to terminate, suspend or delay contributions under the plan for the year in respect of an individual,

and one of the main reasons for the termination, suspension or delay may reasonably be considered to be to reduce the pension adjustment of the individual for the year in respect of an employer, the only amount that may be deducted in computing the income for the year of the individual, in respect of premiums paid to registered retirement savings plans, is the amount that would have been deductible had that termination, suspension or delay not occurred.

Related Sections: S. 248(1), "pension adjustment".

► 146(5.3)-(5.5) ◄

(5.3)-(5.5) — (Repealed by 1986, c. 6, s. 81(3).)

► 146(6) ◄

(6) Disposition of non-qualified investment — (Repealed by S.C. 2011, c. 24, s. 45(6).)

History: S. 146(6) was repealed by S.C. 2011, c. 24, s. 45(6), applicable in respect of investments acquired after March 22, 2011.

(6) *Disposition of non-qualified investment.* Where in a taxation year a trust governed by a registered retirement savings plan disposes of a property that, when acquired, was a non-qualified investment, there may be deducted, in computing the income for the taxation year of the taxpayer who is the annuitant under the plan, an amount equal to the lesser of

(*a*) the amount that, by virtue of subsection (10), was included in computing the income of that taxpayer in respect of the acquisition of that property, and

(*b*) the proceeds of disposition of the property.

► 146(6.1) ◄

(6.1) Recontribution of certain withdrawals. There may be deducted in computing a taxpayer's income for a particular taxation year the total of all amounts each of which is such portion of a prescribed premium for the particular year as was not designated for any taxation year for the purposes of paragraph 60(*j*), (*j*.1) or (*l*).

Related Regulations: 8307(7).

Related Sections: S. 146.01(1), "excluded premium"; S. 146.02(1), "excluded premium".

Interpretation Bulletins: *Secondary* — IT-124R6 Contributions to registered retirement savings plans.

► 146(7) ◄

(7) Recovery of property used as security. Where in a taxation year a loan, for which a trust governed by a registered retirement savings plan has used or permitted to be used trust property as security, ceases to be extant, and the fair market value of the property so used was included by virtue of subsection (10) in computing the income of the taxpayer who is the annuitant under the plan, there may be deducted, in computing the income of the taxpayer for the taxation year, an amount equal to the amount, if any, remaining when

(*a*) the net loss (exclusive of payments by the trust as or on account of interest) sustained by the trust in consequence of its using the property, or permitting it to be used, as security for the loan and not as a result of a change in the fair market value of the property

is deducted from

(*b*) the amount so included in computing the income of the taxpayer in consequence of the trust's using the property, or permitting it to be used, as security for the loan.

Related Regulations: 214(2).

Forms: T3GR — Group Income Tax and Information Return for RRSP, RRIF, RESP or RDSP Trusts; T4RSP — Statement of RRSP Income; T4RSP SUM — Summary of Income from a Registered Retirement Savings Plan.

► 146(8) ◄

(8) Benefits taxable. There shall be included in computing a taxpayer's income for a taxation year the total of all amounts received by the taxpayer in the year as benefits out of or under registered retirement savings plans, other than excluded withdrawals (as defined in subsection 146.01(1) or 146.02(1)) of the taxpayer and amounts that are included under paragraph (12)(*b*) in computing the taxpayer's income.

Editorial Note: If the taxpayer receives an amount from an RRSP as a consequence of the annuitant's death, a corresponding deduction is available if the taxpayer was the annuitant's spouse or common-law partner or financially dependent child or grandchild. In the case of a recipient spouse or common-law partner, or child or grandchild financially dependent by reason of mental or physical infirmity, the deduction is allowed to the extent the amount is contributed to the recipient's RRSP, RRIF or life annuity payable to age 90. In the case of any other financially dependent child or grandchild under the age of 18, the deduction is allowed to the extent the amount is used to acquire an annuity payable to age 18. See s. 146(1) "refund of premiums" and s. 60(*l*).

Related Regulations: 214(1)(*a*); 214(4).

Related Sections: S. 56(1)(*h*) Registered retirement savings plan, etc.; s. 60(*l*) Transfer of refund of premiums under RRSP; s. 61(2) Income-averaging annuity — eligible income; s. 146(1), "benefit"; s. 146(8) Benefits taxable; s. 146(8.3) Spousal or common-law partner payments; s. 146.01(4) Portion of eligible amount not repaid; s. 146.02(1), "eligible amount"; s. 146.02(4) If portion of eligible amount not repaid; s. 147.3(13.1) Withdrawal of excessive transfers to RRSPs and RRIFs; s. 153(1)(*j*) Withholding.

Canadian Tax Foundation: Van Cauwenberghe, *Estate Planning — Tips and Traps*, 2012 Ontario Tax Conference 8:1–40.

Forms: T4RSP — Statement of RRSP Income; T4RSP SUM — Summary of Income from a Registered Retirement Savings Plan.

Guides: T4079, T4RSP and T4RIF Guide.

Income Tax Technical News: Issue No. 39, Settlement of a Shareholder Class Action Suit — Compensation by Way of Cash and Shares.

Information Circulars: IC 72-22R9 Registered retirement savings plans.

Interpretation Bulletins: *Secondary* — IT-307R4 Spousal or common-law partner registered retirement savings plans.

Cases: When the Minister disallowed the taxpayer's contribution to an RRSP because he had no earned income for the year, the taxpayer, wishing to withdraw the contribution without terminating the plan, established a second RRSP to which he transferred the funds. Shortly thereafter he withdrew the contribution and deregistered the second plan. The Minister treated the amount withdrawn as income pursuant to s. 146(1)(*b*)(iii). The taxpayer successfully appealed stating that since he had to add the amount back into his income when the first plan was disallowed, he was being subjected to double taxation. *Grimson v. M.N.R.*, 77 DTC 101 (T.R.B.)

► 146(8.01) ◄

(8.01) Subsequent re-calculation. If a designated withdrawal (as defined in subsection 146.01(1)) or an amount referred to in paragraph (*a*) of the definition "eligible amount" in subsection 146.02(1) is received by a taxpayer in a taxation year and, at any time after that year, it is determined that the amount is not an excluded withdrawal (as defined in subsection 146.01(1) or 146.02(1)), notwithstanding subsections 152(4) to (5), such assessments of tax, interest and penalties shall be made as are necessary to give effect to the determination.

► 146(8.1) ◄

(8.1) Deemed receipt of refund of premiums. If a payment out of or under a registered retirement savings plan of a deceased annuitant to the annuitant's legal representative would have been a refund of premiums if it had been paid under the plan to an individual who is a beneficiary (as defined in subsection 108(1)) under the deceased's estate, the payment is, to the extent it is so designated jointly by the legal representative and the individual in prescribed form filed with the Minister, deemed to be received by the individual (and not by the legal representative) at the time it was so paid as a benefit that is a refund of premiums.

Editorial Note: See the editorial notes under ss. 146(8) and (8.8).

History: S. 146(8.1) was replaced by S.C. 2013, c. 34, s. 296(5), deemed to have come into force on January 1, 1989, except that, before 1999, subsection 146(8.1) is to be read as follows:

"(8.1) Such portion of an amount paid in a taxation year out of or under a registered retirement savings plan of a deceased annuitant to the annuitant's legal representative as, had that portion been paid under the plan to an individual who is a beneficiary (as defined in subsection 108(1)) under the deceased's estate, would have been a refund of premiums is, to the extent it is so designated jointly by the legal representative and the individual in prescribed form filed with the Minister, deemed to be received by the individual in the year as a benefit that is a refund of premiums."

S. 146(8.1) formerly read:

(8.1) *Deemed receipt of refund of premiums.* Where a portion of an amount paid out of or under a registered retirement savings plan of a deceased annuitant to the annuitant's legal representative would have been a refund of premiums if it had been paid under the plan to a beneficiary of the deceased's estate, it is, to the extent it is so designated jointly by the legal representative and the beneficiary in prescribed form filed with the Minister, deemed to be received by the beneficiary (and not by the legal representative) at the time it was so paid as a benefit that is a refund of premiums.

Related Sections: S. 146(1), "refund of premiums"; s. 146(8.9) Deduction from deemed receipt before death by deceased annuitant; s. 214(3)(*c*) Deemed payments.

Forms: T2019 — Death of an RRSP Annuitant–Refund of Premiums.

► 146(8.2) ◄

(8.2) Amount deductible. Where

(*a*) all or any portion of the premiums paid in a taxation year by a taxpayer to one or more registered retirement savings plans under which the taxpayer or the taxpayer's spouse or common-law partner was the annuitant was not deducted in computing the taxpayer's income for any taxation year,

(*b*) the taxpayer or the taxpayer's spouse or common-law partner can reasonably be regarded as having received a payment from a registered retirement savings plan or a registered retirement income fund in respect of such portion of the undeducted premiums as

(i) was not paid by way of a transfer of an amount from a registered pension plan to a registered retirement savings plan,

(ii) was not paid by way of a transfer of an amount from a deferred profit sharing plan to a registered retirement savings plan in accordance with subsection 147(19), and

(iii) was not paid by way of a transfer of an amount to a registered retirement savings plan from

(A) a pooled registered pension plan in circumstances to which subsection 147.5(21) applied, or

(B) a specified pension plan in circumstances to which subsection (21) applied,

(*c*) the payment is received by the taxpayer or the taxpayer's spouse or common-law partner in a particular taxation year that is

(i) the year in which the premiums were paid by the taxpayer,

(ii) the year in which a notice of assessment for the taxation year referred to in subparagraph (i) was sent to the taxpayer, or

(iii) the year immediately following the year referred to in subparagraph (i) or (ii), and

(*d*) the payment is included in computing the taxpayer's income for the particular year,

the payment (except to the extent that it is a prescribed withdrawal) may be deducted in computing the taxpayer's income for the particular year unless it is reasonable to consider that

(*e*) the taxpayer did not reasonably expect that the full amount of the premiums would be deductible in the taxation year in which the premiums were paid or in the immediately preceding taxation year, and

(*f*) the taxpayer paid all or any portion of the premiums with the intent of receiving a payment that, but for this paragraph and paragraph (*e*), would be deductible under this subsection.

History: S. 146(8.2)(*b*)(iii) was replaced by S.C. 2012, c. 31, s. 32(6), in force December 14, 2012. S. 146(8.2)(*b*)(iii) formerly read:

(iii) was not paid by way of a transfer of an amount from a specified pension plan to a registered retirement savings plan in circumstances to which subsection (21) applied,

S. 146(8.2)(*b*)(iii) was replaced by S.C. 2011, c. 24, s. 45(7), applicable to taxation years that begin after 2009. S. 146(8.2)(*b*)(iii) formerly read:

(iii) was not paid by way of a transfer of an amount from a provincial pension plan prescribed for the purpose of paragraph 60(*v*) to a registered retirement savings plan in circumstances to which subsection (21) applied,

Related Regulations: 8307(6).

Related Sections: S. 146(1), "premium"; s. 146(8.21) Premium deemed not paid; s. 146(16) Transfer of funds; s. 147.3(13.1) Withdrawal of excessive transfers to RRSPs and RRIFs; S. 147.5(11) Member contributions; S. 147.5(12) Member's account.

Forms: T3012A — Tax Deduction Waiver on the Refund of Your Undeducted RRSP Contributions Made in —; T746 — Calculating Your Deduction for Refund of Undeducted RRSP Contributions.

Interpretation Bulletins: *Secondary* — IT-124R6 Contributions to registered retirement savings plans; IT-307R4 Spousal or common-law partner registered retirement savings plans.

► 146(8.21) ◄

(8.21) Premium deemed not paid. Where a taxpayer or the taxpayer's spouse or common-law partner has, at any time in a taxation year, received a payment from a registered retirement savings plan or a registered retirement income fund in respect of all or any portion of a premium paid by the taxpayer to a registered retirement savings plan and the payment has been deducted under subsection (8.2) in computing the taxpayer's income for the year, the premium or portion thereof, as the case may be, shall,

(*a*) for the purposes of determining, after that time, the amount that may be deducted under subsection (5) or (5.1) in computing the taxpayer's income for the year or a preceding taxation year, and

(*b*) for the purposes of subsections (8.3) and 146.3(5.1) after that time, in the case of a payment received by the taxpayer,

be deemed not to have been a premium paid by the taxpayer to a registered retirement savings plan.

Interpretation Bulletins: *Secondary* — IT-124R6 Contributions to registered retirement savings plans.

► 146(8.3) ◄

(8.3) Spousal or common-law partner payments. Where at any time in a taxation year a particular amount in respect of a registered retirement savings plan that is a spousal or common-law partner plan in relation to a taxpayer is required by reason of subsection (8) or paragraph (12)(*b*) to be included in computing the income of the taxpayer's spouse or common-law partner before the plan matures or as a payment in full or partial commutation of a retirement income under the plan and the taxpayer is not living separate and apart from the taxpayer's spouse or common-law partner at that time by reason of the breakdown of their marriage or common-law partnership, there shall be included at that time in computing the taxpayer's income for the year an amount equal to the lesser of

(*a*) the total of all amounts each of which is a premium paid by the taxpayer in the year or in one of the two immediately preceding taxation years to a registered retirement savings plan under which the taxpayer's spouse or common-law partner was the annuitant at the time the premium was paid, and

(*b*) the particular amount.

Editorial Note: Although s. 146(8.3) is an anti-avoidance provision, it implicitly provides for an income splitting opportunity through a spousal or common-law partner RRSP — namely, by way of a deductible contribution to the RRSP (s. 146(5.1)) and a withdrawal of the amount by the spouse or common-law partner annuitant in the third or subsequent year after the year of contribution. The attributed amount under subsection 146(8.3), if any, is deducted in computing the recipient spouse's income under subsection 146(8.6).

Related Sections: S. 146(1), "premium", "spousal or common-law partner plan"; s. 146(8.21) Premium deemed not paid; s. 146(8.5) Ordering; s. 146(8.6) Spouse's income; s. 146(8.7) Where s. (8.3) does not apply; s. 146.3(5.4) Spouse's income; s. 147.3(13.1) Withdrawal of excessive transfers to RRSPs and RRIFs.

Forms: T2205 — Amounts from a Spousal or Common-Law Partner RRSP or RRIF to Include in Income for _____.

Interpretation Bulletins: *Secondary* — IT-124R6 Contributions to registered retirement savings plans; IT-307R4 Spousal or common-law partner registered retirement savings plans.

Cases: In February 1987, the taxpayer contributed $6,500 to an RRSP registered in his wife's name which he deducted in computing his income for 1986. When in 1989, his wife withdrew this sum, her withdrawal had to be included in the taxpayer's income for that year. *Gilbert v. The Queen*, 93 DTC 5124 (F.C.A.).

► 146(8.4) ◄

(8.4) Interpretation — (Repealed by 1990, c. 35, s. 13(14).)

► 146(8.5) ◄

(8.5) Ordering. Where a taxpayer has paid more than one premium described in subsection (8.3), such a premium or part thereof paid by the taxpayer at any time shall be deemed to have been included in computing the taxpayer's income by virtue of that subsection before premiums or parts thereof paid by the taxpayer after that time.

Interpretation Bulletins: *Secondary* — IT-307R4 Spousal or common-law partner registered retirement savings plans.

► 146(8.6) ◄

(8.6) Spouse's [or common-law partner's] income. Where, in respect of an amount required at any time in a taxation year to be included in computing the income of a taxpayer's spouse or common-law partner, all or part of a premium has by reason of subsection (8.3) been included in computing the taxpayer's income for the year, the following rules apply:

(*a*) the premium or part thereof, as the case may be, shall, for the purposes of subsections (8.3) and 146.3(5.1) after that time, be deemed not to have been a premium paid to a registered retirement savings plan under which the taxpayer's spouse or common-law partner was the annuitant; and

(*b*) an amount equal to the premium or part thereof, as the case may be, may be deducted in computing the income of the spouse or common-law partner for the year.

Interpretation Bulletins: *Secondary* — IT-307R4 Spousal or common-law partner registered retirement savings plans.

► 146(8.7) ◄

(8.7) Where s. (8.3) does not apply. Subsection (8.3) does not apply

(*a*) in respect of a taxpayer at any time during the year in which the taxpayer died;

(*b*) in respect of a taxpayer where either the taxpayer or the taxpayer's spouse or common-law partner is a non-resident at the particular time referred to in that subsection;

(*c*) in respect of amounts paid out of or under a plan referred to in subsection (12) as an "amended plan" to which paragraph (12)(*a*) applied before May 26, 1976;

(*d*) to any payment that is received in full or partial commutation of a registered retirement income fund or a registered retirement savings plan and in respect of which a deduction was made under paragraph 60(*l*) if, where the deduction was in respect of the acquisition of an annuity, the terms of the annuity provide that it cannot be commuted, and it is not commuted, in whole or in part within 3 years after the acquisition; or (*e*) in respect of an amount that is deemed by subsection (8.8) to have been received by an annuitant under a registered retirement savings plan immediately before the annuitant's death.

Interpretation Bulletins: *Secondary* — IT-307R4 Spousal or common-law partner registered retirement savings plans.

► 146(8.8) ◄

(8.8) Effect of death where person other than spouse becomes entitled. Where the annuitant under a registered retirement savings plan (other than a plan that had matured before June 30, 1978) dies after June 29, 1978, the annuitant shall be deemed to have received, immediately before the annuitant's death, an amount as a benefit out of or under a registered retirement savings plan equal to the amount, if any, by which

(*a*) the fair market value of all the property of the plan at the time of death

exceeds

(*b*) where the annuitant died after the maturity of the plan, the fair market value at the time of the death of the portion of the property described in paragraph (*a*) that, as a consequence of the death, becomes receivable by a person who was the annuitant's spouse or common-law partner immediately before the death, or would become so receivable should that person survive throughout all guaranteed terms contained in the plan.

Editorial Note: The deceased's income inclusion under s. 146(8.8) will be reduced generally to the extent that the RRSP is left to the deceased's spouse or common-law partner or financially dependent child or grandchild; see s. 146(1)"refund of premiums", s. 146(8.8)(*b*), s. 146(8.9), and the deeming rules in ss. 146(8.1) and (8.91). See also the editorial note under s. 146(8) regarding the recipient spouse's or child's inclusion and the potential deduction available under s. 60(*l*).

Related Regulations: 214(4).

Related Sections: S. 146(1), "annuitant"; s. 146(8.9) Deduction from deemed receipt before death by deceased annuitant; s. 160.2(1) Joint and several liability in respect of amounts received out of or under RRSP; s. 214(3)(*i*) Deemed payments.

Forms: T4RSP — Statement of RRSP Income; T4RSP SUM — Summary of Income from a Registered Retirement Savings Plan.

Guides: RC4177 Death of an RRSP Annuitant.

Interpretation Bulletins: *Secondary* — IT-307R4 Spousal or common-law partner registered retirement savings plans.

Cases: Subsection 146(8.8) requires the estate, and not the beneficiaries, to pay the taxes due in respect of an RRSP held by the deceased. Under the subsection, the RRSP funds are deemed to be payments to the deceased immediately before his death, and are liable to tax as such. *Curley et al. v. MacDonald et al.*, 2001 DTC 5141 (Ont.Sup.Ct.)

The annuitant did not change his RRSP beneficiary designation following his divorce. When he died, the proceeds of his RRSPs were paid directly to the designated beneficiary (his ex-wife). However, under s. 146(8.8), the annuitant's estate, and not the beneficiary, was liable for the tax in respect of the proceeds. *Slater v. Klassen Estate*, 2000 DTC 6336 (Man. Q.B.).

► 146(8.9) ◄

(8.9) Idem. There may be deducted from the amount deemed by subsection (8.8) to have been received by an annuitant as a benefit out of or under a registered retirement savings plan an amount not exceeding the amount determined by the formula

$$A \times [1 - ((B + C - D) / (B + C))]$$

where

A is the total of

(*a*) all refunds of premiums in respect of the plan,

(*b*) all tax-paid amounts in respect of the plan paid to individuals who, otherwise than because of subsection (8.1), received refunds of premiums in respect of the plan, and

(*c*) all amounts each of which is a tax-paid amount in respect of the plan paid to the legal representative of the annuitant under the plan, to the extent that the legal representative would have been entitled to designate that tax-paid amount under subsection (8.1) if tax-paid amounts were not excluded in determining refunds of premiums;

B is the fair market value of the property of the plan at the particular time that is the later of

(*a*) the end of the first calendar year that begins after the death of the annuitant, and

(*b*) the time immediately after the last time that any refund of premiums in respect of the plan is paid out of or under the plan;

C is the total of all amounts paid out of or under the plan after the death of the annuitant and before the particular time; and

D is the lesser of

(*a*) the fair market value of the property of the plan at the time of the annuitant's death, and

(*b*) the sum of the values of B and C in respect of the plan.

Related Sections: S. 146(1), "refund of premiums", "tax-paid amount"; s. 257 Negative amounts.

► 146(8.91) ◄

(8.91) Amounts deemed receivable by spouse or common-law partner. Where, as a consequence of the death of an annuitant after the maturity of the annuitant's registered retirement savings plan, the annuitant's legal representative has become entitled to receive amounts out of or under the plan for the benefit of the spouse or common-law partner of the deceased and the legal representative and the spouse or common-law partner file with the Minister a joint election in prescribed form,

(*a*) the spouse or common-law partner shall be deemed to have become the annuitant under the plan as a consequence of the annuitant's death; and

(*b*) those amounts shall be deemed to be receivable by the spouse or common-law partner and, when paid, to be received by the spouse or common-law partner as a benefit under the plan, and not to be received by any other person.

Editorial Note: See the editorial notes under ss. 146(8) and (8.8).

Related Sections: S. 146(1), "benefit"; s. 214(3)(*i*) Deemed payments; s. 248(1), "common-law partner".

► 146(8.92) ◄

(8.92) Deduction for post-death reduction in value. If the annuitant under a registered retirement savings plan dies before the maturity of the plan, there may be deducted in computing the annuitant's income for the taxation year in which the annuitant dies an amount not exceeding the amount determined, after all amounts payable out of or under the plan have been paid, by the formula

$$A - B$$

where

A is the total of all amounts each of which is

(*a*) the amount deemed by subsection (8.8) to have been received by the annuitant as a benefit out of or under the plan,

(*b*) an amount (other than an amount described in paragraph (*c*)) received, after the death of the annuitant, by a taxpayer as a benefit out of or under the plan and included, because of subsection (8), in computing the taxpayer's income, or

(*c*) a tax-paid amount in respect of the plan; and

B is the total of all amounts paid out of or under the plan after the death of the annuitant.

History: S. 146(8.92) was added by S.C. 2009, c. 2, s. 51(3), applicable in respect of a registered retirement savings plan in respect of which the last payment out of the plan is made after 2008.

Related Regulations: 214(6).

► 146(8.93) ◄

(8.93) Subsection (8.92) not applicable. Except where the Minister has waived in writing the application of this subsection with respect to all or any portion of the amount determined in subsection (8.92) in respect of a registered retirement savings plan, that subsection does not apply if

(*a*) at any time after the death of the annuitant, a trust governed by the plan held a non-qualified investment; or

(*b*) the last payment out of or under the plan was made after the end of the year following the year in which the annuitant died.

History: S. 146(8.93) was added by S.C. 2009, c. 2, s. 51(3), applicable in respect of a registered retirement savings plan in respect of which the last payment out of the plan is made after 2008.

► 146(9) ◄

(9) Where disposition of property by trust. Where in a taxation year a trust governed by a registered retirement savings plan

(*a*) disposes of property for a consideration less than the fair market value of the property at the time of the disposition, or for no consideration, or

(*b*) acquires property for a consideration greater than the fair market value of the property at the time of the acquisition,

the difference between the fair market value and the consideration, if any, shall be included in computing the income for the taxation year of the annuitant under the plan.

Related Regulations: 214(2).

Related Sections: S. 146(11) Life insurance policies; s. 214(3)(*l*) Deemed payments.

Forms: T3GR — Group Income Tax and Information Return for RRSP, RRIF, RESP or RDSP Trusts; T4RSP — Statement of RRSP Income; T4RSP SUM — Summary of Income from a Registered Retirement Savings Plan.

Guides: T4079, T4RSP and T4RIF Guide.

► 146(10) ◄

(10) Property used as security for loan. If at any time in a taxation year a trust governed by a registered retirement savings plan uses or permits to be used any property of the trust as security for a loan, the fair market value of the property at the time it commenced to be so used shall be included in computing the income for the year of the taxpayer who is the annuitant under the plan at that time.

Editorial Note: See s. 146(7), which permits deductions when the secured loan ceases to exist. See also s. 207.04(1)with respect to prohibited and non-qualified investments and s. 207.05(1) with respect to advantages.

History: S. 146(10) was replaced by S.C. 2011, c. 24, s. 45(8), applicable in respect of investments acquired after March 22, 2011. S. 146(10) formerly read:

(10) *Where acquisition of non-qualified investment by trust.* Where at any time in a taxation year a trust governed by a registered retirement savings plan

(*a*) acquires a non-qualified investment, or

(*b*) uses or permits to be used any property of the trust as security for a loan,

the fair market value of

(*c*) the non-qualified investment at the time it was acquired by the trust, or

(*d*) the property used as security at the time it commenced to be so used,

as the case may be, shall be included in computing the income for the year of the taxpayer who is the annuitant under the plan at that time.

Related Regulations: 214(2).

Related Sections: S. 146(7) Recovery of property used as security; s. 198(6) Life insurance policies — special rules; s. 214(3)(*l*) Deemed payments; s. 259(1) Proportional holdings in trust property.

Forms: T3GR — Group Income Tax and Information Return for RRSP, RRIF, RESP or RDSP Trusts; T4RSP — Statement of RRSP Income; T4RSP SUM — Summary of Income from a Registered Retirement Savings Plan.

► 146(10.1) ◄

(10.1) Where tax payable. Where in a taxation year a trust governed by a registered retirement savings plan holds a property that is a non-qualified investment,

(*a*) tax is payable under this Part by the trust on the amount that its taxable income for the year would be if it had no incomes or losses from sources other than non-qualified investments and no capital gains or losses other than from dispositions of non-qualified investments; and

(*b*) for the purposes of paragraph (*a*),

(i) "income" includes dividends described in section 83, and

(ii) paragraphs 38(*a*) and (*b*) are to be read as if the fraction set out in each of those paragraphs were replaced by the word "all".

History: S. 146(10.1)(*b*)(ii) was replaced by S.C. 2013, c. 34, s. 296(6), in force June 26, 2013, and formerly read:

(ii) paragraphs 38(*a*) and (*b*) shall be read without reference to the fractions set out in those paragraphs.

Related Sections: S. 122(1) Tax payable by inter vivos trust; s. 146(4) No tax while trust governed by plan; s. 207.1(1) Tax payable by trust under registered retirement savings plan; s. 259(1) Proportional holdings in trust property.

► 146(11) ◄

(11) Life insurance policies — (Repealed by S.C. 2011, c. 24, s. 45(9).)

History: S. 146(11) was repealed by S.C. 2011, c. 24, s. 45(9), applicable in respect of investments acquired after March 22, 2011. S. 146(11) formerly read:

(11) *Life insurance policies.* Subsections 198(6) and (8) are applicable, with such modifications as the circumstances require, to subsections (6), (9) and (10), except that in the application of subsection 198(8) to the latter subsections paragraph 198(8)(*a*) shall be read as follows:

"(*a*) the trust shall be deemed, for the purposes of subsection 146(6), to have disposed of each non-qualified investment that, by virtue of payments under the policy, it was deemed by subsection 146(10) to have acquired, and"

► 146(11.1) ◄

(11.1) Exception — (Repealed by S.C. 2011, c. 24, s. 45(9).)

History: S. 146(11.1) was repealed by S.C. 2011, c. 24, s. 45(9), applicable in respect of investments acquired after March 22, 2011. S. 146(11.1) formerly read:

(11.1) *Exception.* Subsection (11) does not apply to annuity contracts issued after 1997.

► 146(12) ◄

(12) Change in plan after registration. Where, on any day after a retirement savings plan has been accepted by the Minister for registration for the purposes of this Act, the plan is revised or amended or a new plan is substituted for it, and the plan as revised or amended or the new plan, as the case may be (in this subsection referred to as the "amended plan"), does not comply with the requirements of this section for its acceptance by the Minister for registration for the purposes of this Act, subject to subsection (13.1), the following rules apply:

(*a*) the amended plan shall be deemed, for the purposes of this Act, not to be a registered retirement savings plan; and

(*b*) the taxpayer who was the annuitant under the plan before it became an amended plan shall, in computing the taxpayer's income for the taxation year that includes that day, include as income received at that time an amount equal to the fair market value of all the property of the plan immediately before that time.

Related Regulations: 202(2),(3); 214(3).

Related Sections: S. 146(8.3) Spousal or common-law partner payments; s. 146(13) Deemed creation of new plan — changes to rights or obligations; s. 146(13.1) RRSP advantages; s. 146(13.3) Notice; s. 147.3(13.1) Withdrawal of excessive transfers to RRSPs and RRIFs; s. 153(1)(*j*) Withholding; s. 204.1(2) Amount deemed repaid; s. 204.2(1.4) Deemed receipt where RRSP or RRIF amended; s. 204.2(2) Where terminated plan deemed to continue to exist; s. 212(1)(*l*) Registered retirement savings plan payments; s. 214(3)(*i*) Deemed payments.

Forms: T2205 — Amounts from a Spousal or Common-Law Partner RRSP or RRIF to Include in Income for ____.

Information Circulars: IC 72-22R9 Registered retirement savings plans; IC 78-14R4 Guidelines for trust companies and other persons responsible for filing T3GR, T3D, T3P, T3S, T3RI, and T3F returns.

Interpretation Bulletins: *Secondary* — IT-307R4 Spousal or common-law partner registered retirement savings plans.

► 146(13) ◄

(13) Idem. For the purposes of subsection (12), an arrangement under which a right or obligation under a retirement savings plan is released or extinguished either wholly or in part and either in exchange or substitution for any right or obligation, or otherwise (other than an arrangement the sole object and legal effect of which is to revise or amend the plan) or under which payment of any amount by way of loan or otherwise is made on the security of a right under a retirement savings plan, shall be deemed to be a new plan substituted for that retirement savings plan.

Related Sections: S. 146(1), "retirement savings plan"; s. 146(2) Acceptance of plan for registration — prohibited conditions; s. 146(3) Acceptance of plan for registration — acceptable conditions.

► 146(13.1) ◄

(13.1) RRSP advantages — (Repealed by S.C. 2011, c. 24, s. 45(10).)

History: S. 146(13.1) was repealed by S.C. 2011, c. 24, s. 45(10), applicable to transactions occurring, income earned, capital gains accruing and investments acquired after March 22, 2011. S. 146(13.1) formerly read:

(13.1) *RRSP advantages.* Where an issuer of a registered retirement savings plan or any person not dealing at arm's length with the issuer has extended an advantage to the annuitant of the plan (or to a person not dealing at arm's length with the annuitant) and that advantage would have been prohibited if the plan had met the requirement for registration contained in paragraph (2)(*c*.4),

(*a*) paragraphs (12)(*a*) and (*b*) do not apply by reason only of the extension of that advantage; and

(*b*) the issuer is liable to a penalty equal to the greater of $100 and the amount or value of that advantage.

Tax Topics: No. 1665, RRSP Incentives.

Information Circulars: IC 72-22R9 Registered retirement savings plans.

► 146(13.2) ◄

(13.2) Maturity after age 69 — (Repealed by S.C. 2007, c. 29, s. 17(4).)

► 146(13.3) ◄

(13.3) Notice — (Repealed by S.C. 2007, c. 29, s. 17(4).)

► 146(14) ◄

(14) Premiums paid in taxation year. Where any amount has been paid in a taxation year as a premium under a retirement savings plan that was, at the end of that taxation year, a registered retirement savings plan, the amount so paid shall be deemed, for the purposes of this Act, to have been paid in that year as a premium under a registered retirement savings plan.

Related Regulations: 214.1.

Related Sections: S. 146(1), "premium", "registered retirement savings plan", "retirement savings plan"; s. 146(5) Amount of RRSP premiums deductible; s. 146(5.1) Amount of spousal RRSP premiums deductible.

► 146(15) ◄

(15) Plan not registered at end of year entered into. Notwithstanding anything in this section, where an amount is received in a taxation year as a benefit under a registered retirement savings plan that was not, at the end of the year in which the plan was entered into, a registered retirement savings plan, such part, if any, of the amount so received as may be prescribed shall be deemed, for the purposes of this Act, to have been received in the taxation year otherwise than as a benefit or other payment under a registered retirement savings plan.

Related Sections: S. 146(1), "benefit".

► 146(16) ◄

(16) Transfer of funds. Notwithstanding any other provision in this section, a registered retirement savings plan may at any time be revised or amended to provide for the payment or transfer before the maturity of the plan, on behalf of the annuitant under the plan (in this subsection referred to as the "transferor"), of any property thereunder by the issuer thereof

(*a*) to a registered pension plan for the benefit of the transferor or to a registered retirement savings plan or registered retirement income fund under which the transferor is the annuitant, or

(*b*) to a registered retirement savings plan or registered retirement income fund under which the spouse or common-law partner or former spouse or common-law partner of the transferor is the annuitant, where the transferor and the transferor's spouse or common-law partner or former spouse or common-law partner are living separate and apart and the payment or transfer is made under a decree, order or judgment of a competent tribunal, or under a written separation agreement, relating to a division of property between the transferor and the transferor's spouse or common-law partner or former spouse or common-law partner in settlement of rights arising out of, or on the breakdown of, their marriage or common-law partnership,

and, where there has been such a payment or transfer of such property on behalf of the transferor before the maturity of the plan,

(*c*) the amount of the payment or transfer shall not, solely because of the payment or transfer, be included in computing the income of the transferor or the transferor's spouse or common-law partner or former spouse or common-law partner,

(*d*) no deduction may be made under subsection (5), (5.1) or (8.2) or section 8 or 60 in respect of the payment or transfer in computing the income of any taxpayer, and

(*e*) where the payment or transfer was made to a registered retirement savings plan, for the purposes of subsection (8.2), the amount of the payment or transfer shall be deemed not to be a premium paid to that plan by the taxpayer.

Related Regulations: 214(5), (6); 214.1.

Related Sections: S. 146(1), "annuitant", "maturity"; s. 146.3(2)(*f*) Acceptance of fund for registration; S. 147.5(12) Member's account; s. 248(1), "common-law partner"; s. 252(3) Extended meaning of "spouse" and "former spouse".

Tax Topics: No. 1702, Income Tax Issues To Be Considered in Negotiating Marriage Contracts.

Forms: T2033 — Direct Transfer under subsection 146.3(14.1) or paragraph 146(16)(a) or 146.3(2)(e); T2220 — Transfer From an RRSP or a RRIF to Another RRSP or RRIF on Marriage Breakdown.

Information Circulars: IC 72-22R9 Registered retirement savings plans.

Interpretation Bulletins: *Primary* — IT-528 Transfers of funds between registered plans. *Secondary* — IT-307R4 Spousal or common-law partner registered retirement savings plans.

Registered Plans Directorate Newsletters: No. 91-4R, Registration rules for money purchase provisions.

► 146(17) ◄

(17) Interpretation — (Repealed by 1990, c. 35, s. 13(18).)

► 146(18) ◄

(18) Where plan matures before annuitant attains age of 60 — (Repealed by 1986, c. 55, s. 56(7).)

► 146(19) ◄

(19) Transitional — (Repealed by 1986, c. 55, s. 56(7).)

► 146(20) ◄

(20) Credited or added amount deemed not received. Where

(*a*) an amount is credited or added to a deposit with a depositary referred to in subparagraph (*b*)(iii) of the definition "retirement savings plan" in subsection (1) as interest or income in respect of the deposit,

(*b*) the deposit is a registered retirement savings plan at the time the amount is credited or added to the deposit, and

(*c*) during the calendar year in which the amount is credited or added or during the preceding calendar year, the annuitant under the plan was alive,

the amount shall be deemed not to be received by the annuitant or any other person solely because of the crediting or adding.

Related Sections: S. 146(1), "registered retirement savings plan"; s. 149(1)(*r*) Trusts under registered retirement savings plan; s. 255 Canada.

Information Circulars: IC 72-22R9 Registered retirement savings plans.

► 146(21) ◄

(21) Specified pension plan. Where

(*a*) an amount (other than an amount that is part of a series of periodic payments) is transferred directly from an individual's account under a specified pension plan

(i) to a registered retirement savings plan or registered retirement income fund under which the individual, or a spouse or common-law partner or former spouse or common-law partner of the individual, is the annuitant,

(ii) to acquire from a licensed annuities provider an annuity that would be described in subparagraph 60(*l*)(ii) if the individual, or a spouse or common-law partner or former spouse or common-law partner of the individual, were the taxpayer referred to in that subparagraph and if that subparagraph were read without reference to clause 60(*l*)(ii)(B), or

(iii) to an account under the plan of a spouse or common-law partner or former spouse or common-law partner of the individual, and

(*b*) if the transfer is in respect of a spouse or common-law partner or former spouse or common-law partner of the individual,

(i) the individual and the spouse or common-law partner or former spouse or common-law partner are living separate and apart and the transfer is made under a decree, order or judgment of a competent tribunal, or under a written separation agreement, relating to a division of property in settlement of rights arising out of, or on the breakdown of, their marriage or common-law partnership, or

(ii) the amount is transferred as a consequence of the individual's death,

the following rules apply:

(*c*) the amount shall not, solely because of the transfer, be included because of subparagraph 56(1)(*a*)(i) in computing the income of a taxpayer, and

(*d*) no deduction may be made under any provision of this Act in respect of the transfer in computing the income of a taxpayer.

History: S. 146(21), the portion before subparagraph (*a*)(i) was replaced by S.C. 2011, c. 24, s. 45(11), applicable to taxation years that begin after 2009. S. 146(21), the portion before subparagraph (*a*)(i) formerly read:

(21) *Prescribed provincial pension plans.* Where

(*a*) an amount (other than an amount that is part of a series of periodic payments) is transferred directly from an individual's account under a provincial pension plan prescribed for the purpose of paragraph 60(*v*)

S. 146(21), the portion before subparagraph (*a*)(i) was replaced by S.C. 2011, c. 24, s. 45(11), applicable to taxation years that begin after 2009. S. 146(21), the portion before subparagraph (*a*)(i) formerly read:

(21) *Prescribed provincial pension plans.* Where

(*a*) an amount (other than an amount that is part of a series of periodic payments) is transferred directly from an individual's account under a provincial pension plan prescribed for the purpose of paragraph 60(*v*)

Related Sections: S. 212(1)(*h*) Pension benefits; s. 248(1), "common-law partner", "specified pension plan".

Interpretation Bulletins: *Primary* — IT-528 Transfers of funds between registered plans.

► 146(21.1) ◄

(21.1) Specified pension plan — contribution. For the purposes of this section, paragraphs 18(11)(*b*), 60(*j*), (*j.1*) and (*l*), 74.5(12)(*a*), 146.01(3)(*a*) and 146.02(3)(*a*) and Parts X.1 and X.5, and for the purposes of section 214.1 of the *Income Tax Regulations*, a contribution made by an individual to an account of the individual, or of the individual's spouse or common-law partner, under a specified pension plan is deemed to be a premium paid by the individual to a registered retirement savings plan under which the individual, or the individual's spouse or common-law partner, as the case may be, is the annuitant.

History: S. 146(21.1) was added by S.C. 2011, c. 24, s. 45(12), applicable to taxation years that begin after 2009, except that, for taxation years that begin before 2011, subsection 146(21.1) is to be read without reference to ", and for the purposes of section 214.1 of the *Income Tax Regulations*,".

► 146(21.2) ◄

(21.2) Specified pension plan — account. For the purposes of paragraph (8.2)(*b*), subsection (8.21), paragraphs (16)(*a*) and (*b*) and 18(1)(*u*), subparagraph (*a*)(i) of the definition *excluded right or interest* in subsection 128.1(10), paragraph (*b*) of the definition *excluded premium* in subsection 146.01(1), paragraph (*c*) of the definition *excluded premium* in subsection 146.02(1), subsections 146.3(14) and 147(19), section 147.3 and paragraphs 147.5(21)(*c*) and 212(1)(*j*.1) and (*m*) and for the purposes of any regulations made under subsection 147.1 (18), an individual's account under a specified pension plan is deemed to be a registered retirement savings plan under which the individual is the annuitant.

History: S. 146(21.2) was replaced by S.C. 2017, c. 33, s. 56(2), deemed to have come into force on January 1, 2010, except that in its application before December 14, 2012, subsection 146(21.2) of the Act is to be read without reference to "147.5(21)(c) and". S. 146(21.2) formerly read:

(21.2) *Specified pension plan — account.* For the purposes of paragraph (8.2)(*b*), subsection (8.21), paragraphs (16)(*a*) and (*b*) and 18(1)(*u*), subparagraph (*a*)(i) of the definition "excluded right or interest" in subsection 128.1(10), paragraph (*b*) of the definition "excluded premium" in subsection 146.01(1), paragraph (*c*) of the definition "excluded premium" in subsection 146.02(1), subsections 146.3(14) and 147(19), section 147.3 and paragraph 147.5(21)(*c*), and for the purposes of any regulations made under subsection 147.1(18), an individual's account under a specified pension plan is deemed to be a registered retirement savings plan under which the individual is the annuitant.

S. 146(21.2) was replaced by S.C. 2012, c. 31, s. 32(7), in force December 14, 2012. S. 146(21.2) formerly read:

(21.2) *Specified pension plan — account.* For the purposes of paragraph (8.2)(*b*), subsection (8.21), paragraphs (16)(*a*) and (*b*) and 18(1)(*u*), subparagraph (*a*)(i) of the definition "excluded right or interest" in subsection 128.1(10), paragraph (*b*) of the definition "excluded premium" in subsection 146.01(1), paragraph (*c*) of the definition "excluded premium" in subsection 146.02(1), subsections 146.3(14) and 147(19) and section 147.3, and for the purposes of any regulations made under subsection 147.1(18), an individual's account under a specified pension plan is deemed to be a registered retirement savings plan under which the individual is the annuitant.

S. 146(21.2) was added by S.C. 2011, c. 24, s. 45(12), applicable to taxation years that begin after 2009.

Related Sections: 212(1)(j.1) Retiring allowances; 212(1)(m) Deferred profit sharing plan payments.

► 146(21.3) ◄

(21.3) Specified pension plan — payment. For the purposes of subsections (8.3) to (8.7), a payment received by an individual from a specified pension plan is deemed to be a payment received by the individual from a registered retirement savings plan.

History: S. 146(21.3) was added by S.C. 2011, c. 24, s. 45(12), applicable to taxation years that begin after 2010.

► 146(22) ◄

(22) Deemed payment of RRSP premiums. If the Minister so directs,

(*a*) except for the purposes of subparagraphs (5)(*a*)(iv.1) and (5.1)(*a*)(iv), an amount paid by an individual in a taxation year (other than an amount paid in the first 60 days of the year) as a premium is deemed to have been paid at the beginning of the year and not at the time it was actually paid;

(*b*) all or part of the amount may be designated in writing by the individual for the purpose of paragraph 60(*j*), (*j*.1) or (*l*) or subsection 146.01(3) or 146.02(3); and

(*c*) the designation is deemed to have been made in the individual's return of income for the preceding taxation year or in a prescribed form filed with that return, as the case may be.

History: S. 146(22), the portion before paragraph (*b*) was replaced by S.C. 2011, c. 24, s. 45(13), applicable to taxation years that begin after 2009. S. 146(22), the portion before paragraph (*b*) formerly read:

(22) *Deemed payment of RRSP premiums and provincial pension plan contributions.* If the Minister so directs,

(*a*) except for the purposes of subparagraphs (5)(*a*)(iv.1) and (5.1)(*a*)(iv), an amount paid by an individual in a taxation year (other than an amount paid in the first 60 days of the year) as a contribution to an account under a prescribed provincial pension plan or as a premium is deemed to have been paid at the beginning of the year and not at the time it was actually paid;

Related Sections: S. 146(1), "premium".

Home Buyers' Plan

SECTION 146.01: [Home buyers' plan]

► 146.01(1) ◄

(1) Definitions. In this section,

"annuitant" —"annuitant" has the meaning assigned by subsection 146(1);

"benefit" —"benefit" has the meaning assigned by subsection 146(1);

"completion date" —"completion date", in respect of an amount received by an individual, is

(*a*) where the amount was received before March 2, 1993, October 1, 1993,

(*b*) where the amount was received after March 1, 1993 and before March 2, 1994, October 1, 1994, and

(*c*) in any other case, October 1 of the calendar year following the calendar year in which the amount was received;

"designated withdrawal" —"designated withdrawal" of an individual is an amount received by the individual, as a benefit out of or under a registered retirement savings plan, pursuant to the individual's written request in the prescribed form referred to in paragraph (*a*) of the definition "eligible amount" (as that definition read in its application to amounts received before 1999), paragraph (*a*) of the definition "regular eligible amount" or paragraph (*a*) of the definition "supplemental eligible amount";

Related Sections: S. 146(8.01) Subsequent re-calculation.

"eligible amount" —"eligible amount" of an individual is a regular eligible amount or supplemental eligible amount of the individual;

Related Regulations: 214(1)(b).

Related Sections: S. 146(5)(*a*)(iv.1) Amount of RRSP premiums deductible; s. 146(5.1)(*a*)(iv) Amount of spousal RRSP premiums deductible; s. 146(8) Benefits taxable; s. 146.01(4) Portion of eligible amount not repaid.

Forms: T1036 — Home Buyers' Plan (HBP) Request to Withdraw Funds from an RRSP.

"excluded premium" —"excluded premium" in respect of an individual means a premium under a registered retirement savings plan where the premium

(*a*) was designated by the individual for the purposes of paragraph 60(*j*), (*j*.1), (*j*.2) or (*l*),

(*b*) was an amount transferred directly from a registered retirement savings plan, registered pension plan, registered retirement income fund or deferred profit sharing plan,

(*c*) was deductible under subsection 146(6.1) in computing the individual's income for any taxation year, or

(*d*) was deducted in computing the individual's income for the 1991 taxation year;

History: S. 146.01(1), paragraph (*b*) of the definition "excluded premium" was replaced by S.C. 2011, c. 24, s. 46(1), applicable to taxation years that begin after 2009. S. 146.01(1), paragraph (*b*) of the definition "excluded premium" formerly read:

(*b*) was an amount transferred directly from a registered retirement savings plan, registered pension plan, registered retirement income fund, deferred profit sharing plan or a provincial pension plan prescribed for the purpose of paragraph 60(*v*),

Related Sections: s. 147.5(12) Member's account.

"excluded withdrawal" —"excluded withdrawal" of an individual means

(*a*) an eligible amount received by the individual,

(*b*) a particular amount (other than an eligible amount) received while the individual was resident in Canada and in a calendar year if

(i) the particular amount would be an eligible amount of the individual if the definition "regular eligible amount" were read without reference to paragraphs (*c*) and (*g*) of that definition and the definition "supplemental eligible amount" were read without reference to paragraphs (*d*) and (*f*) of that definition,

(ii) a payment (other than an excluded premium) equal to the particular amount is made by the individual under a retirement saving plan that is, at the end of the taxation year of the payment, a registered retirement savings plan under which the individual is the annuitant,

(iii) the payment is made before the particular time that is

(A) if the individual was not resident in Canada at the time the individual filed a return of income for the taxation year in which the particular amount was received, the earlier of

(I) the end of the following calendar year, and

(II) the time at which the individual filed the return,

(B) where clause (A) does not apply and the particular amount would, but for subclause (2)(*c*)(ii)(A)(II), be an eligible amount, the end of the second following calendar year, and

(C) in any other case, the end of the following calendar year, and

(iv) either

(A) if the particular time is before 2000, the payment is made, as a repayment of the particular amount, to the issuer of the registered retirement savings plan from which the particular amount was received, no other payment is made as a repayment of the particular amount and that issuer is notified of the payment in prescribed form submitted to the issuer at the time the payment is made, or

(B) the payment is made after 1999 and before the particular time and the payment (and no other payment) is designated under this clause as a repayment of the particular amount in prescribed form filed with the Minister on or before the particular time (or before such later time as is acceptable to the Minister), or

(*c*) an amount (other than an eligible amount) that is received in a calendar year before 1999 and that would be an eligible amount of the individual if the definition "eligible amount", as it applied to amounts received before 1999, were read without reference to paragraphs (*c*) and (*e*) of that definition, where the individual

(i) died before the end of the following calendar year, and

(ii) was resident in Canada throughout the period that began immediately after the amount was received and ended at the time of the death;

Amendment not yet in force

Budget Implementation Act, 2019, No. 1 [S.C. 2019, c. 29]

S. 146.01(1), paragraph (*d*) of the definition of "excluded withdrawal" was added by S.C. 2019, c. 29, s. 27(1), and will read as follows:

(*d*) a particular amount (other than an eligible amount) received while the individual was resident in Canada and in a calendar year if

(i) the particular amount would be a regular eligible amount if subsection (2.1) were read without reference to its subparagraph (*a*)(iii),

(ii) a payment (other than an excluded premium) equal to the particular amount is made by the individual under a retirement saving plan that is, at the end of the taxation year of the payment, a registered retirement savings plan under which the individual is the annuitant, and

(iii) the payment is made before the end of the second calendar year after the calendar year that includes the particular time referred to in subsection (2.1);

Applicable: In respect of amounts received after 2019.

Editorial Note: Withdrawals from registered retirement savings plans are generally included in income under s. 146(8) and s. 56(1)(*h*). An exception applies to an excluded withdrawal under the home buyers' plan rules. If eligible, up to $35,000 can be withdrawn for the purchase of a qualifying home by October 1 of the year following the year of withdrawal (see definition of "regular eligible amount"). An individual can also withdraw up to $35,000 for the purchase of a home by a specified disabled person (see definition of "supplemental eligible amount"). Amounts withdrawn under the home buyers' rules must generally be repaid to the individual's RRSP within a 15-year period, beginning with the second year following the year of withdrawal. Where withdrawn amounts ultimately are not used to purchase a qualifying home (but they otherwise met the requirements under the home buyers' plan), they must generally be repaid by the end of the following year. If the withdrawn amounts are not repaid, they are included in income.

Effective after 2019, subsection 146.01(2.1) effectively allows a taxpayer to receive an eligible amount after the breakdown of a marriage or common-law partnership, for the purpose of buying a new home, or to buy out the taxpayer's spouse or partner's interest in their previous home. In the former case, if the taxpayer already owns an existing home, that home must be disposed by the end of the second year following the receipt of the amount. If such an amount does not qualify as a regular eligible amount, either because the existing home was not sold on time or the taxpayer did not buy out the spouse's or partner's interest in the previous home, the amount will be an "excluded withdrawal" as long as it is repaid to the taxpayer's RRSP before the end of the second year after the year in which the amount was received.

Related Sections: S. 146(1), "premium"; s. 146(8) Benefits taxable; s. 146(8.01) Subsequent re-calculation; s. 146.02(1), "excluded premium".

"HBP balance" —"HBP balance" of an individual at any time means the amount, if any, by which the total of all eligible amounts received by the individual at or before that time exceeds the total of

(*a*) all amounts designated under subsection (3) by the individual for taxation years that ended before that time, and

(*b*) all amounts each of which is included under subsection (4) or (5) in computing the individual's income for a taxation year that ended before that time;

Related Sections: S. 150(1.1) Exception.

"issuer" —"issuer" has the meaning assigned by subsection 146(1);

"participation period" —"participation period" of an individual means each period

(*a*) that begins at the beginning of a calendar year in which the individual receives an eligible amount, and

(*b*) that ends immediately before the beginning of the first subsequent calendar year at the beginning of which the individual's HBP balance is nil;

"premium" —"premium" has the meaning assigned by subsection 146(1);

"qualifying home" —"qualifying home" means

(*a*) a housing unit located in Canada, or

(*b*) a share of the capital stock of a cooperative housing corporation, the holder of which is entitled to possession of a housing unit located in Canada,

except that, where the context so requires, a reference to a qualifying home that is a share described in paragraph (*b*) means the housing unit to which the share described in that paragraph relates;

Tax Window Files: HBP purchase of portion of housing unit, *April 30, 2018*, CRA Document No. 2017-0730991E5.

"quarter" — (Repealed by S.C. 2013, c. 34, s. 297(1).)

History: S. 146.01(1), the definition of "quarter" was repealed by S.C. 2013, c. 34, s. 297(1), applicable in respect of the 2002 and subsequent taxation years, and formerly read:

"quarter"—"quarter" means any of the following periods in a calendar year:

(*a*) the period beginning on January 1 and ending on March 31,

(*b*) the period beginning on April 1 and ending on June 30,

(*c*) the period beginning on July 1 and ending on September 30, and

(*d*) the period beginning on October 1 and ending on December 31;

"regular eligible amount" —"regular eligible amount" of an individual means an amount received at a particular time by the individual as a benefit out of or under a registered retirement savings plan if

(*a*) the amount is received pursuant to the individual's written request in a prescribed form in which the individual sets out the location of a qualifying home that the individual has begun, or intends not later than one year after its acquisition by the individual to begin, using as a principal place of residence,

(*b*) the individual entered into an agreement in writing before the particular time for the acquisition of it or with respect to its construction,

(*c*) the individual

(i) acquires the qualifying home (or a replacement property for the qualifying home) before the completion date in respect of the amount, or

(ii) dies before the end of the calendar year that includes the completion date in respect of the amount,

(*d*) neither the individual nor the individual's spouse or common-law partner acquired the qualifying home more than 30 days before the particular time,

(*e*) the individual did not have an owner-occupied home in the period

(i) that began at the beginning of the fourth preceding calendar year that ended before the particular time, and

(ii) that ended on the 31st day before the particular time,

(*f*) the individual's spouse or common-law partner did not, in the period referred to in paragraph (*e*), have an owner-occupied home

(i) that was inhabited by the individual during the spouse's or common-law partner's marriage or common-law partnership to the individual, or

(ii) that was a share of the capital stock of a cooperative housing corporation that relates to a housing unit inhabited by the individual during the spouse's or common-law partner's marriage or common-law partnership to the individual,

(*g*) the individual

(i) acquired the qualifying home before the particular time and is resident in Canada at the particular time, or

(ii) is resident in Canada throughout the period that begins at the particular time and ends at the earlier of the time of the individual's death and the earliest time at which the individual acquires the qualifying home or a replacement property for it,

(*h*) the total of the amount and all other eligible amounts received by the individual in the calendar year that includes the particular time does not exceed $35,000, and

(*i*) the individual's HBP balance at the beginning of the calendar year that includes the particular time is nil;

History: S. 146.01(1), paragraph (*h*) of the definition "regular eligible amount" was replaced by S.C. 2019, c. 29, s. 27(2), applicable to the 2019 and subsequent taxation years in respect of amounts received after March 19, 2019, and formerly read:

(*h*) the total of the amount and all other eligible amounts received by the individual in the calendar year that includes the particular time does not exceed $25,000, and

S. 146.01(1), paragraph (*h*) of the definition "regular eligible amount" was replaced by S.C. 2009, c. 2, s. 52(1), applicable to the 2009 and subsequent taxation years in respect of withdrawals made after January 27, 2009. S. 146.01(1), paragraph (*h*) of the definition "regular eligible amount" formerly read:

(*h*) the total of the amount and all other eligible amounts received by the individual in the calendar year that includes the particular time does not exceed $20,000, and

Related Sections: S. 248(1), "common-law partner".

"replacement property" —"replacement property" for a particular qualifying home in respect of an individual, or of a specified disabled person in respect of the individual, means another qualifying home that

(*a*) the individual or the specified disabled person agrees to acquire, or begins the construction of, at a particular time that is after the latest time that the individual made a request described in the definition "designated withdrawal" in respect of the particular qualifying home,

(*b*) at the particular time, the individual intends to be used by the individual or the specified disabled person as a principal place of residence not later than one year after its acquisition, and

(*c*) none of the individual, the individual's spouse or common-law partner, the specified disabled person or that person's spouse or common-law partner had acquired before the particular time;

Related Sections: S. 248(1), "common-law partner".

"specified disabled person" —"specified disabled person", in respect of an individual at any time, means a person who

(*a*) is the individual or is related at that time to the individual, and

(*b*) would be entitled to a deduction under subsection 118.3(1) in computing tax payable under this Part for the person's taxation year that includes that time if that subsection were read without reference to paragraph (*c*) of that subsection;

"supplemental eligible amount" —"supplemental eligible amount" of an individual means an amount received at a particular time by the individual as a benefit out of or under a registered retirement savings plan if

(*a*) the amount is received pursuant to the individual's written request in a prescribed form identifying a specified disabled person in respect of the individual and setting out the location of a qualifying home

(i) that has begun to be used by that person as a principal place of residence, or

(ii) that the individual intends to be used by that person as a principal place of residence not later than one year after its first acquisition after the particular time,

(*b*) the purpose of receiving the amount is to enable the specified disabled person to live

(i) in a dwelling that is more accessible by that person or in which that person is more mobile or functional, or

(ii) in an environment better suited to the personal needs and care of that person,

(*c*) the individual or the specified disabled person entered into an agreement in writing before the particular time for the acquisition of the qualifying home or with respect to its construction,

(*d*) either

(i) the individual or the specified disabled person acquires the qualifying home (or a replacement property for it) after 1998 and before the completion date in respect of the amount, or

(ii) the individual dies before the end of the calendar year that includes the completion date in respect of the amount,

(*e*) none of the individual, the spouse or common-law partner of the individual, the specified disabled person or the spouse or common-law partner of that person acquired the qualifying home more than 30 days before the particular time,

(*f*) either

(i) the individual or the specified disabled person acquired the qualifying home before the particular time and the individual is resident in Canada at the particular time, or

(ii) the individual is resident in Canada throughout the period that begins at the particular time and ends at the earlier of the time of the individual's death and the earliest time at which

(A) the individual acquires the qualifying home or a replacement property for it, or

(B) the specified disabled person acquires the qualifying home or a replacement property for it,

(*g*) the total of the amount and all other eligible amounts received by the individual in the calendar year that includes the particular time does not exceed $35,000, and

(*h*) the individual's HBP balance at the beginning of the calendar year that includes the particular time is nil.

History: S. 146.01(1), paragraph (*g*) of the definition "supplemental eligible amount" was replaced by S.C. 2019, c. 29, s. 27(3), applicable to the 2019 and subsequent taxation years in respect of amounts received after March 19, 2019, and formerly read:

(*g*) the total of the amount and all other eligible amounts received by the individual in the calendar year that includes the particular time does not exceed $25,000, and

S. 146.01(1), paragraph (*g*) of the definition "supplemental eligible amount" was replaced by S.C. 2009, c. 2, s. 52(2), applicable to the 2009 and subsequent taxation years in respect of withdrawals made after January 27, 2009. S. 146.01(1), paragraph (*g*) of the definition "supplemental eligible amount" formerly read:

(*g*) the total of the amount and all other eligible amounts received by the individual in the calendar year that includes the particular time does not exceed $20,000, and

Related Sections: S. 248(1), "common-law partner".

► 146.01(2) ◄

(2) Special Rules. For the purposes of this section,

(*a*) an individual shall be considered to have acquired a qualifying home if the individual acquired it jointly with one or more other persons;

(*a*.1) an individual shall be considered to have an owner-occupied home at any time where, at that time, the individual owns, whether jointly with another person or otherwise, a housing unit or a share of the capital stock of a cooperative housing corporation and

(i) the housing unit is inhabited by the individual as the individual's principal place of residence at that time, or

(ii) the share was acquired for the purpose of acquiring a right to possess a housing unit owned by the corporation and that unit is inhabited by the individual as the individual's principal place of residence at that time;

(*b*) where an individual agrees to acquire a condominium unit, the individual shall be deemed to have acquired it on the day the individual is entitled to immediate vacant possession of it;

(*c*) except for the purposes of subparagraph (*g*)(ii) of the definition "regular eligible amount" and subparagraph (*f*)(ii) of the definition "supplemental eligible amount", an individual or a specified disabled person in respect of the individual is deemed to have acquired, before the completion date in respect of a designated withdrawal received by the individual, the qualifying home in respect of which the designated withdrawal was received if

(i) neither the qualifying home nor a replacement property for it was acquired by the individual or the specified disabled person before that completion date, and

(ii) either

(A) the individual or the specified disabled person

(I) is obliged under the terms of a written agreement in effect on that completion date to acquire the qualifying home (or a replacement property for it) on or after that date, and

(II) acquires the qualifying home or a replacement property for it before the day that is one year after that completion date, or

(B) the individual or the specified disabled person made payments, the total of which equalled or exceeded the total of all designated withdrawals that were received by the individual in respect of the qualifying home,

(I) to persons with whom the individual was dealing at arm's length,

(II) in respect of the construction of the qualifying home or a replacement property for it, and

(III) in the period that begins at the time the individual first received a designated withdrawal in respect of the qualifying home and that ends before that completion date; and

(*d*) an amount received by an individual in a particular calendar year is deemed to have been received by the individual at the end of the preceding calendar year and not at any other time if

(i) the amount is received in January of the particular year (or at such later time as is acceptable to the Minister),

(ii) the amount would not be an eligible amount if this section were read without reference to this paragraph, and

(iii) the amount would be an eligible amount if the definition "regular eligible amount" in subsection (1) were read without reference to paragraph (*i*) of that definition and the definition "supplemental eligible amount" were read without reference to paragraph (*h*) of that definition.

(*e*) (Repealed by S.C. 1999, c. 22, s. 60(5).)

(*f*) (Repealed by S.C. 1999, c. 22, s. 60(5).)

Amendment not yet in force

Budget Implementation Act, 2019, No. 1 [S.C. 2019, c. 29]

S. 146.01(2.1) was added by S.C. 2019, c. 29, s. 27(4), and will read as follows:

(2.1) Marriage or common-law partnership. Notwithstanding paragraph (2)(*a*.1), for the purposes of the definition "regular eligible amount",

(*a*) an individual, and a spouse or common-law partner of the individual, are deemed not to have an owner-occupied home in a period ending before a particular time referred to in that definition if

(i) at the particular time, the individual

(A) is living separate and apart from the individual's spouse or common-law partner because of a breakdown of their marriage or common-law partnership,

(B) has been living separate and apart from the individual's spouse or common-law partner for a period of at least 90 days, and

(C) began living separate and apart from the individual's spouse or common-law partner in the calendar year that includes the particular time or any time in the four preceding calendar years,

(ii) in the absence of this subsection, the individual would not be precluded from having a regular eligible amount because of the application of paragraph (*f*) of that definition in respect of a spouse or common-law partner (other than the spouse or common-law partner referred to in clauses (i)(A) to (C)), and

(iii) where the individual has an owner-occupied home at the particular time,

(A) the home is not the qualifying home referred to in that definition and the individual disposes of the home no later than the end of the second calendar year after the calendar year that includes the particular time, or

(B) the individual acquires the interest, or for civil law the right, of the spouse or common-law partner in the home; and

(*b*) if an individual to whom paragraph (*a*) applies has an owner-occupied home at the particular time referred to in that paragraph and the individual acquires the interest, or for civil law the right, of a spouse or common-law partner in the home, the individual is deemed for the purposes of paragraphs (*c*) and (*d*) of that definition to have acquired a qualifying home on the date that the individual acquired the interest or the right.

Applicable: In respect of amounts received after 2019.

Tax Topics: No. 2403, HBP Relieving Provision Unintentionally Creates Hardship.

► 146.01(3) ◄

(3) Repayment of eligible amount. An individual may designate a single amount for a taxation year in a prescribed form filed with the individual's return of income for the year if the amount does not exceed the lesser of

(*a*) the total of all amounts (other than excluded premiums, repayments to which paragraph (*b*) of the definition "excluded withdrawal" in subsection (1) applies and amounts paid by the individual in the first 60 days of the year that can reasonably be considered to have been deducted in computing the individual's income, or designated under this subsection, for the preceding taxation year) paid by the individual in the year or within 60 days after the end of the year under a retirement savings plan that is at the end of the year or the following taxation year a registered retirement savings plan under which the individual is the annuitant, and

Amendment not yet in force

Budget Implementation Act, 2019, No. 1 [S.C. 2019, c. 29]

S. 146.01(3)(*a*) was replaced by S.C. 2019, c. 29, s. 27(5), and will read as follows:

(*a*) the total of all amounts (other than excluded premiums, repayments to which paragraph (*b*) or (*d*) of the definition *excluded withdrawal* in subsection (1) applies and amounts paid by the individual in the first 60 days of the year that can reasonably be considered to have been deducted in computing the individual's income, or designated under this subsection, for the preceding taxation year) paid by the individual in the year or within 60 days after the end of the year under a retirement savings plan that is at the end of the year or the following taxation year a registered retirement savings plan under which the individual is the annuitant, and

Applicable: In respect of repayments made after 2019.

(*b*) the amount, if any, by which

(i) the total of all eligible amounts received by the individual before the end of the year

exceeds the total of

(ii) all amounts designated by the individual under this subsection for preceding taxation years, and

(iii) all amounts each of which is an amount included in computing the income of the individual under subsection (4) or (5) for a preceding taxation year.

Editorial Note: Eligible amounts withdrawn under the home buyers' plan must generally be repaid over a period of not longer than 15 years, starting with the second taxation year beginning after the receipt by the individual of an eligible amount. Under s. 146.01(3), an individual may designate a contribution to an RRSP, under which the individual is the annuitant, as a repayment of an "eligible amount". The repayment can be made in the year or in the first 60 days of the following taxation year. In the first year that repayment is required, the minimum repayment is 1/15th of the amount withdrawn less any repayments that have been made. In the second, the minimum repayment is 1/14th of the outstanding unpaid amount, and so on. If the minimum payments are not made, the portion that is not repaid is included in income under s. 146.01(4) and s. 56(1)(*h.1*). The amount included in income reduces future repayments. Effective for repayments made after 2019, subsection 146.01(3) also allows for repayments described under paragraph (d) of the definition "excluded withdrawal" under 146.01(1). This is essentially where a taxpayer makes an HBP withdrawal following a marriage breakdown but later fails to qualify, and therefore repays the HBP withdrawal before the end of the second year after the year in which the withdrawal was made.

Related Sections: S. 146(1), "premium"; s. 146(22) Deemed payment of RRSP premiums and provincial pension plan contributions; s. 146.02(1), "excluded premium"; s. 147.5(11) Member contributions; s. 150(1.1) Exception; s. 248(1), "filing-due date".

Forms: T1 SCH 7 — RRSP Unused Contributions, Transfers, and HBP or LLP Activities.

Guides: RC4135 Home Buyers' Plan (HBP).

► 146.01(4) ◄

(4) Portion of eligible amount not repaid. There shall be included in computing an individual's income for a particular taxation year included in a particular participation period of the individual the amount determined by the formula

$$[(A - B - C) / (15 - D)] - E$$

where

A is

(*a*) where

(i) the individual died or ceased to be resident in Canada in the particular year, or

(ii) the completion date in respect of an eligible amount received by the individual was in the particular year

nil, and

(*b*) in any other case, the total of all eligible amounts received by the individual in preceding taxation years included in the particular period,

B is

(*a*) nil, if the completion date in respect of an eligible amount received by the individual was in the preceding taxation year, and

(*b*) in any other case, the total of all amounts each of which is designated under subsection (3) by the individual for a preceding taxation year included in the particular period;

C is the total of all amounts each of which is included under this subsection or subsection (5) in computing the individual's income for a preceding taxation year included in the particular period;

D is the lesser of 14 and the number of taxation years of the individual ending in the period beginning (*a*) where the completion date in respect of an eligible amount received by the individual was before 1995, January 1, 1995, and

(*b*) in any other case, January 1 of the first calendar year beginning after the completion date in respect of an eligible amount received by the individual

and ending at the beginning of the particular year, and

E is

(*a*) if the completion date in respect of an eligible amount received by the individual was in the preceding taxation year, the total of all amounts each of which is designated under subsection (3) by the individual for the particular year or any preceding taxation year included in the particular period, and

(*b*) in any other case, the amount designated under subsection (3) by the individual for the particular year.

Related Sections: S. 56(1)(*h*.1) Home buyers' plan; s. 257 Negative amounts.

► 146.01(5) ◄

(5) Where individual becomes a non-resident. Where at any time in a taxation year an individual ceases to be resident in Canada, there shall be included in computing the income of the individual for the period in the year during which the individual was resident in Canada the amount, if any, by which

(*a*) the total of all amounts each of which is an eligible amount received by the individual in the year or a preceding taxation year

exceeds the total of

(*b*) all amounts designated under subsection (3) by the individual in respect of amounts paid not later than 60 days after that time and before the individual files a return of income for the year, and

(*c*) all amounts included under subsection (4) or this subsection in computing the individual's income for preceding taxation years.

Related Sections: S. 56(1)(*h*.1) Home buyers' plan.

► 146.01(6) ◄

(6) Death of individual. If an individual dies at any time in a taxation year, there shall be included in computing the individual's income for the year the amount, if any, by which

(*a*) the individual's HBP balance immediately before that time

exceeds

(*b*) the amount designated under subsection (3) by the individual for the year.

Related Sections: S. 56(1)(*h*.1) Home buyers' plan.

► 146.01(7) ◄

(7) Exception. If a spouse or common-law partner of an individual was resident in Canada immediately before the individual's death at a particular time in a taxation year and the spouse or common-law partner and the individual's legal representatives jointly so elect in writing in the individual's return of income for the year,

(*a*) subsection (6) does not apply to the individual;

(*b*) the spouse or common-law partner is deemed to have received a particular eligible amount at the particular time equal to the amount that, but for this subsection, would be determined under subsection (6) in respect of the individual;

(*c*) for the purposes of subsection (4) and paragraph (*d*), the completion date in respect of the particular amount is deemed to be

(i) if the spouse or common-law partner received an eligible amount before the death (other than an eligible amount received in a participation period of the spouse or common-law partner that ended before the beginning of the year), the completion date in respect of that amount, and

(ii) in any other case, the completion date in respect of the last eligible amount received by the individual; and

(*d*) for the purpose of subsection (4), the completion date in respect of each eligible amount received by the spouse or common-law partner, after the death and before the end of the spouse's or common-law partner's participation period that includes the time of the death, is deemed to be the completion date in respect of the particular amount.

Related Regulations: 600(b).

Related Sections: S. 220(3.2) Late, amended or revoked elections; s. 248(1), "common-law partner".

Information Circulars: IC 07-1 Taxpayer Relief Provisions.

► 146.01(8) ◄

(8) Filing of prescribed form — (Repealed by S.C. 2013, c. 34, s. 297(2).)

History: S. 146.01(8) was repealed by S.C. 2013, c. 34, s. 297(2), applicable in respect of the 2002 and subsequent taxation years, and formerly read:

(8) *Filing of prescribed form.* A prescribed form referred to in this section that is submitted to an issuer shall be filed with the Minister by the issuer not later than 15 days after the quarter in which it was submitted to the issuer.

► 146.01(9)-(13) ◄

(9)-(13) — (Repealed by S.C. 1995, c. 3, s. 44(13).)

Lifelong Learning Plan

SECTION 146.02: [Lifelong learning plan]

► 146.02(1) ◄

(1) Definitions. The definitions in this subsection apply in this section.

"annuitant" — "annuitant" has the meaning assigned by subsection 146(1).

"benefit" — "benefit" has the meaning assigned by subsection 146(1).

"eligible amount" — "eligible amount" of an individual means a particular amount received at a particular time in a calendar year by the individual as a benefit out of or under a registered retirement savings plan if

(*a*) the particular amount is received after 1998 pursuant to the individual's written request in a prescribed form;

(*b*) in respect of the particular amount, the individual designates in the form a person (in this definition referred to as the "designated person") who is the individual or the individual's spouse or common-law partner;

(*c*) the total of the particular amount and all other eligible amounts received by the individual at or before the particular time and in the year does not exceed $10,000;

(*d*) the total of the particular amount and all other eligible amounts received by the individual at or before the particular time (other than amounts received in participation periods of the individual that ended before the year) does not exceed $20,000;

(*e*) the individual did not receive an eligible amount at or before the particular time in respect of which someone other than the designated person was designated (other than an amount received in a participation period of the individual that ended before the year);

(*f*) the designated person

(i) is enrolled at the particular time as a full-time student in a qualifying educational program, or

(ii) has received written notification before the particular time that the designated person is absolutely or contingently entitled to enrol before March of the following year as a full-time student in a qualifying educational program;

(*g*) the individual is resident in Canada throughout the period that begins at the particular time and ends immediately before the earlier of

(i) the beginning of the following year, and

(ii) the time of the individual's death;

(*h*) except where the individual dies after the particular time and before April of the following year, the designated person is enrolled as a full-time student in a qualifying educational program after the particular time and before March of the following year and

(i) the designated person completes the program before April of the following year,

(ii) the designated person does not withdraw from the program before April of the following year, or

(iii) less than 75% of the tuition paid, after the beginning of the year and before April of the following year, in respect of the designated person and the program is refundable; and

(*i*) if an eligible amount was received by the individual before the year, the particular time is neither

(i) in the individual's repayment period for the individual's participation period that includes the particular time, nor

(ii) after January (or a later month where the Minister so permits) of the fifth calendar year of that participation period.

Related Regulations: 104.1(1); 214(1)(*c*).

Related Sections: S. 146(5)(*a*)(iv.1) Amount of RRSP premiums deductible; s. 146(5.1)(*a*)(iv) Amount of spousal RRSP premiums deductible; s. 146(8.01) Subsequent re-calculation; s. 248(1), "common-law partner".

Guides: RC4112 Lifelong Learning Plan (LLP).

Tax Window Files: Lifelong Learning Plan — Withdrawal of amounts for Taxpayer's and Spouse's Education not Permitted, *Technical Interpretation, Financial Industries Division, October 29, 2003*, CRA Document No. 2003-0036905 [Cannot withdraw amounts for taxpayer's and spouse's education].

"excluded premium" — "excluded premium" of an individual means a premium that

(*a*) was designated by the individual for the purpose of paragraph 60(*j*), (*j*.1) or (*l*) or subsection 146.01(3);

(*b*) was a repayment to which paragraph (*b*) of the definition "excluded withdrawal" in subsection 146.01(1) applies;

> **Amendment not yet in force**
>
> **Budget Implementation Act, 2019, No. 1 [S.C. 2019, c. 29]**
>
> **S. 146.02(1), paragraph (*b*) of the definition of "excluded premium" was replaced by S.C. 2019, c. 29, s. 28(1), and will read as follows:**
>
> (*b*) was a repayment to which paragraph (*b*) or (*d*) of the definition "excluded withdrawal" in subsection 146.01(1) applies;
>
> **Applicable:** In respect of repayments made after 2019.

(*c*) was an amount transferred directly from a registered retirement savings plan, registered pension plan, registered retirement income fund or deferred profit sharing plan; or

(*d*) was deductible under subsection 146(6.1) in computing the individual's income for any taxation year.

History: S. 146.02(1), paragraph (*c*) of the definition "excluded premium" was replaced by S.C. 2011, c. 24, s. 47(1), applicable to taxation years that begin after 2009. S. 146.02(1), paragraph (*c*) of the definition "excluded premium" formerly read:

(*c*) was an amount transferred directly from a registered retirement savings plan, registered pension plan, registered retirement income fund, deferred profit sharing plan or a provincial pension plan prescribed for the purpose of paragraph 60(*v*); or

Related Sections: S. 146(1), "premium"; S. 146.01(1), "excluded withdrawal".

"excluded withdrawal" — "excluded withdrawal" of an individual means

(*a*) an eligible amount received by the individual; or

(*b*) a particular amount (other than an eligible amount) received while the individual was resident in Canada and in a calendar year if

(i) the particular amount would be an eligible amount of the individual if the definition "eligible amount" were read without reference to paragraphs (*g*) and (*h*) of that definition,

(ii) a payment (other than an excluded premium) equal to the particular amount is paid by the individual under a retirement savings plan that is, at the end of the taxation year of payment, a registered retirement savings plan under which the individual is the annuitant,

(iii) the payment is made before the particular time that is,

(A) if the individual was not resident in Canada at the time the individual filed a return of income for the taxation year in which the particular amount was received, the earlier of

(I) the end of the following calendar year, and

(II) the time at which the individual filed the return, and

(B) in any other case, the end of the following calendar year, and

(iv) the payment (and no other payment) is designated under this subparagraph as a repayment of the particular amount in prescribed form filed with the Minister on or before the particular time (or before such later time as is acceptable to the Minister).

Editorial Note: Withdrawals from registered retirement savings plans are generally included in income under s. 146(8) and s. 56(1)(*h*). An exception applies to an excluded withdrawal under the lifelong learning plan. An excluded withdrawal is either an "eligible amount" or an amount that would have qualified as an eligible amount of the individual but for the fact that the student did not ultimately enroll in a qualifying educational program or the individual failed to meet the residency requirement. Generally, for an amount to qualify as an eligible amount, the individual must be enrolled in a qualifying educational program. The maximum eligible amount for a particular year is $10,000 and the total amount withdrawn cannot exceed $20,000. Eligible amounts withdrawn under the lifelong leaning plan must be repaid beginning in the second year after the individual is not entitled to claim the education credit under s. 118.6(2) for full-time study of at least three months or in the fifth year after the first amount was withdrawn.

Related Sections: S. 146(8) Benefits taxable; s. 146(1), "premium"; s. 146(8.01) Subsequent re-calculation.

"full-time student" —"full-time student" in a taxation year includes an individual to whom subsection 118.6(3) applies for the purpose of computing tax payable under this Part for the year or the following taxation year.

"LLP balance" —"LLP balance" of an individual at any time means the amount, if any, by which the total of all eligible amounts received by the individual at or before that time exceeds the total of

(*a*) all amounts designated under subsection (3) by the individual for taxation years that ended before that time, and

(*b*) all amounts each of which is included under subsection (4) or (5) in computing the individual's income for a taxation year that ended before that time.

"participation period" —"participation period" of an individual means each period

(*a*) that begins at the beginning of a calendar year

(i) in which the individual receives an eligible amount, and

(ii) at the beginning of which the individual's LLP balance is nil; and

(*b*) that ends immediately before the beginning of the first subsequent calendar year at the beginning of which the individual's LLP balance is nil.

"premium" —"premium" has the meaning assigned by subsection 146(1).

"qualifying educational program" —"qualifying educational program" means a program at a designated educational institution, as defined in subsection 118.6(1), of not less than three consecutive months duration that requires that each student taking the program spend not less than ten hours per week on courses or work in the program and that is

(*a*) of a technical or vocational nature designed to furnish a person with skills for, or improve a person's skills in, an occupation, if the program is at an institution described in subparagraph (*a*)(ii) of that definition; and

(*b*) at a post-secondary school level, in any other case.

Related Regulations: 104.1(2).

"repayment period" —"repayment period" of an individual for a participation period of the individual in respect of a person designated under paragraph (*b*) of the definition "eligible amount" means the period, if any, within the participation period

(*a*) that begins

(i) at the beginning of the third calendar year within the participation period if, in each of the second and third calendar years within the participation period,

(A) for calendar years before 2017, the person would not be entitled to claim an amount under subsection 118.6(2) (as it read in the year) in respect of at least three months in the year, if that subsection were read without reference to paragraph (*b*) of the description of B in that subsection, and

(B) for calendar years after 2016, the person would not be a *qualifying student* (as defined in subsection 118.6(1)) in respect of at least three months in the year, if that definition were read without reference to its subparagraph (*a*)(ii),

(ii) at the beginning of the fourth calendar year within the participation period if, in each of the third and fourth calendar years within the participation period,

(A) for calendar years before 2017, the person would not be entitled to claim an amount under subsection 118.6(2) (as it read in the year) in respect of at least three months in the year, if that subsection were read without reference to paragraph (*b*) of the description of B in that subsection, and

(B) for calendar years after 2016, the person would not be a *qualifying student* (as defined in subsection 118.6(1)) in respect of at least three months in the year, if that definition were read without reference to its subparagraph (*a*)(ii),

(iii) at the beginning of the fifth calendar year within the participation period if, in each of the fourth and fifth calendar years within the participation period,

(A) for calendar years before 2017, the person would not be entitled to claim an amount under subsection 118.6(2) (as it read in the year) in respect of at least three months in the year, if that subsection were read without reference to paragraph (*b*) of the description of B in that subsection, and

(B) for calendar years after 2016, the person would not be a *qualifying student* (as defined in subsection 118.6(1)) in respect of at least three months in the year, if that definition were read without reference to its subparagraph (*a*)(ii), and

(iv) in any other case, at the beginning of the sixth calendar year within the participation period; and

(*b*) that ends at the end of the participation period.

History: S.146.02(1), subparagraphs (*a*)(i) to (iii) of the definition "repayment period" were replaced by S.C. 2016, c. 7, s. 39, in force June 22, 2016, and formerly read:

(i) at the beginning of the third calendar year within the participation period, if the person would not be entitled to claim an amount under subsection 118.6(2) in respect of at least three months in each of the second and third calendar years within the participation period, if that subsection were read without reference to paragraph (*b*) of the description of B in that subsection,

(ii) at the beginning of the fourth calendar year within the participation period, if subparagraph (i) does not apply and the person would not be entitled to claim an amount under subsection 118.6(2) in respect of at least three months in each of the third and fourth calendar years within the participation period, if that subsection were read without reference to paragraph (*b*) of the description of B in that subsection,

(iii) at the beginning of the fifth calendar year within the participation period, if subparagraphs (i) and (ii) do not apply and the person would not be entitled to claim an amount under subsection 118.6(2) in respect of at least three months in each of the fourth and fifth calendar years within that period, if that subsection were read without reference to paragraph (*b*) of the description of B in that subsection, and

► 146.02(2) ◄

(2) Rule of application. For the purpose of the definition "eligible amount" in subsection (1), a particular person is deemed to be the only person in respect of whom a particular amount was designated under paragraph (*b*) of that definition if

(*a*) an individual received the particular amount;

(*b*) the individual files a prescribed form with the Minister in which the particular person is specified in connection with the receipt of the particular amount;

(*c*) the particular amount would be an eligible amount of the individual if

(i) that definition were read without reference to paragraphs (*b*) and (*e*) of that definition, and

(ii) each reference in the portion of that definition after paragraph (*d*) to "designated person" were read as "individual" or "individual's spouse or common-law partner"; and

(*d*) the Minister so permits.

Forms: RC96 — Lifelong Learning Plan (LLP), Request to Withdraw Funds from an RRSP.

► 146.02(3) ◄

(3) Repayment of eligible amount. An individual may designate a single amount for a taxation year in prescribed form filed with the individual's return of income for the year if the amount does not exceed the lesser of

(*a*) the total of all amounts (other than excluded premiums, repayments to which paragraph (*b*) of the definition "excluded withdrawal" in subsection (1) applies and amounts paid by the individual in the first 60 days of the year that can reasonably be considered to have been deducted in computing the individual's income, or designated under this subsection, for the preceding taxation year) paid by the individual in the year or within 60 days after the end of the year under a retirement savings plan that is at the end of the year or the following taxation year a registered retirement savings plan under which the individual is the annuitant, and

(*b*) the individual's LLP balance at the end of the year.

Editorial Note: Eligible amounts withdrawn under the lifelong learning plan must generally be repaid over a period of not longer than 10 years, beginning not later than five years after the first withdrawal under the plan. S. 146.02(3) provides that an individual may designate a contribution to an RRSP, under which the individual is the annuitant as a repayment of an "eligible amount". The repayment can be made in the year or in the first 60 days of the following taxation year. In the first year that repayment is required, the minimum repayment is 1/10th of the amount withdrawn less any repayments. In the second, the minimum repayment is 1/9th of the outstanding unpaid amount, and so on. If the minimum payments are not made, the portion that is not repaid is included in income and reduces the future repayments.

Related Sections: S. 146(1), "Premium"; s. 146(5) Amount of RRSP premiums deductible; s. 146(5.1) Amount of spousal RRSP premiums deductible; s. 146(22) Deemed payment of RRSP premiums and provincial pension plan contributions; S. 147.5(11), Member contributions.

Forms: T1 SCH 7 — RRSP Unused Contributions, Transfers, and HBP or LLP Activities.

► 146.02(4) ◄

(4) If portion of eligible amount not repaid. There shall be included in computing an individual's income for a particular taxation year that begins after 2000 the amount determined by the formula

$$[(A - B - C)/(10 - D)] - E$$

where

A is

(*a*) nil, if

(i) the individual died or ceased to be resident in Canada in the particular year, or

(ii) the beginning of the particular year is not included in a repayment period of the individual, and

(*b*) in any other case, the total of all eligible amounts received by the individual in preceding taxation years (other than taxation years in participation periods of the individual that ended before the particular year);

B is

(*a*) nil, if the particular year is the first taxation year in a repayment period of the individual, and

(*b*) in any other case, the total of all amounts designated under subsection (3) by the individual for preceding taxation years (other than taxation years in participation periods of the individual that ended before the particular year);

C is the total of all amounts each of which is included under this subsection or subsection (5) in computing the individual's income for a preceding taxation year (other than a taxation year included in a participation period of the individual that ended before the particular year);

D is the lesser of nine and the number of taxation years of the individual that end in the period that

(*a*) begins at the beginning of the individual's last repayment period that began at or before the beginning of the particular year, and

(*b*) ends at the beginning of the particular year; and

E is

(*a*) if the particular year is the first taxation year within a repayment period of the individual, the total of the amount designated under subsection (3) by the individual for the particular year and all amounts so designated for preceding taxation years (other than taxation years in participation periods of the individual that ended before the particular year), and

(*b*) in any other case, the amount designated under subsection (3) by the individual for the particular year.

Related Sections: S. 56(1)(*h*.2) Lifelong learning plan; s. 257 Negative amounts.

► 146.02(5) ◄

(5) Ceasing residence in Canada. If at any time in a taxation year an individual ceases to be resident in Canada, there shall be included in computing the individual's income for the period in the year during which the individual was resident in Canada the amount, if any, by which

(*a*) the total of all amounts each of which is an eligible amount received by the individual in the year or a preceding taxation year

exceeds the total of

(*b*) all amounts designated under subsection (3) by the individual in respect of amounts paid not later than 60 days after that time and before the individual files a return of income for the year, and

(*c*) all amounts included under subsection (4) or this subsection in computing the individual's income for preceding taxation years.

Related Sections: S. 56(1)(*h*.2) Lifelong learning plan.

► 146.02(6) ◄

(6) Death of individual. If an individual dies at any time in a taxation year, there shall be included in computing the individual's income for the year the amount, if any, by which

(*a*) the individual's LLP balance immediately before that time

exceeds

(*b*) the amount designated under subsection (3) by the individual for the year.

Related Sections: S. 56(1)(*h*.2) Lifelong learning plan.

► 146.02(7) ◄

(7) Exception. If a spouse or common-law partner of an individual was resident in Canada immediately before the individual's death at a particular time in a taxation year and the spouse or common-law partner and the individual's legal representatives jointly so elect in writing in the individual's return of income for the year,

(*a*) subsection (6) does not apply to the individual;

(*b*) the spouse or common-law partner is deemed to have received a particular eligible amount at the particular time equal to the amount that, but for this subsection, would be determined under subsection (6) in respect of the individual;

(*c*) subject to paragraph (*d*), for the purpose of applying this section after the particular time, the spouse or common-law partner is deemed to be the person designated under paragraph (*b*) of the definition "eligible amount" in subsection (1) in respect of the particular amount; and

(*d*) where the spouse or common-law partner received an eligible amount before the particular time in the spouse's or common-law partner's participation period that included the particular time and the particular individual designated under paragraph (*b*) of the definition "eligible amount" in subsection (1) in respect of that eligible amount was not the spouse or common-law partner, for the purpose of applying this section after the particular time the particular individual is deemed to be the person designated under that paragraph in respect of the particular amount.

Related Regulations: 600(*b*).

Related Sections: S. 220(3.2) Late, amended or revoked elections; s. 248(1), "common-law partner".

Registered Education Savings Plans

SECTION 146.1: [Registered education savings plans]

► 146.1(1) ◄

(1) Definitions. In this section,

"accumulated income payment"—"accumulated income payment" under an education savings plan means any amount paid out of the plan, other than a payment described in any of paragraphs (*a*) and (*c*) to (*e*) of the definition "trust", to the extent that the amount so paid exceeds the fair market value of any consideration given to the plan for the payment of the amount;

Related Sections: S. 56(1)(*q*) Education savings plan payments; s. 60(*x*) Repayment under Canada Education Savings Act; s. 146.1(2)(*d*.1) Conditions for registration; s. 146.1(2)(*i*.1)Conditions for registration; s. 146.1(2)(*i*.2) Conditions for registration; s. 146.1(2.2) Waiver of conditions for accumulated income payments; s. 146.1(7.1) Other income inclusions; s. 204.94(2) Charging provision.

"beneficiary"—"beneficiary", in respect of an education savings plan, means a person, designated by a subscriber, to whom or on whose behalf an educational assistance payment under the plan is agreed to be paid if the person qualifies under the plan;

"contribution"—"contribution" to an education savings plan does not include an amount paid into the plan under or because of

(*a*) the *Canada Education Savings Act* or a designated provincial program, or

(*b*) any other program that has a similar purpose to a designated provincial program and that is funded, directly or indirectly, by a province (other than an amount paid into the plan by a public primary caregiver in its capacity as subscriber under the plan);

History: S. 146.1(1), the definition "contribution" was replaced by S.C. 2010, c. 12, s. 16(1), applicable to the 2009 and subsequent taxation years. S. 146.1(1), the definition "contribution" formerly read:

"contribution"—"contribution", into an education savings plan, does not include an amount paid into the plan under the *Canada Education Savings Act* or under a designated provincial program;

Editorial Note: See the CRA's RESP Bulletin No. 1R1, updated January 14, 2015, and No. 2, dated May 24, 2011.

Related Sections: S. 18(11) Borrowed money used for contribution; Part X.4 — Tax in Respect of Overpayment to Registered Education Savings Plans.

"designated provincial program" —"designated provincial program" means

(*a*) a program administered pursuant to an agreement entered into under section 12 of the *Canada Education Savings Act*, or

(*b*) a program established under the laws of a province to encourage the financing of children's post-secondary education through savings in registered education savings plans;

History: S. 146.1(1), paragraph (*b*) of the definition "designated provincial program" was replaced by S.C. 2010, c. 12, s. 16(2), applicable to the 2007 and subsequent taxation years. S. 146.1(1), paragraph (*b*) of the definition "designated provincial program" formerly read:

(*b*) a prescribed program;

Editorial Note: See the CRA's RESP Bulletin No. 1R1, updated January 14, 2015, and No. 2, dated May 24, 2011.

Related Sections: S. 60(*x*) Repayment under Canada Education Savings Act.

"educational assistance payment" —"educational assistance payment" means any amount, other than a refund of payments, paid out of an education savings plan to or for an individual to assist the individual to further the individual's education at a post-secondary school level;

Editorial Note: See the CRA's RESP Bulletin No. 1R1, updated January 14, 2015, and No. 2, dated May 24, 2011.

"education savings plan" —"education savings plan" means an arrangement entered into between

(*a*) any of the following, namely,

(i) an individual (other than a trust),

(ii) an individual (other than a trust) and the spouse or common-law partner of the individual, and

(iii) a public primary caregiver of a beneficiary, and

(*b*) a person (in this definition referred to as the "promoter")

under which the promoter agrees to pay or to cause to be paid educational assistance payments to or for one or more beneficiaries;

Editorial Note: Pursuant to the definition of "education savings plan", an RESP may be structured as a trust arrangement or a contractual arrangement.

History: S. 146.1(1), paragraph (*b*) of the definition "education savings plan" was replaced by S.C. 2017, c. 33, s. 57(1), deemed to have come into force on March 23, 2017, and formerly read:

(*b*) a person or organization (in this section referred to as a "promoter")

Related Sections: S. 248(1), "common-law partner".

"post-secondary educational institution" —"post-secondary educational institution" means

(*a*) an educational institution in Canada that is described in paragraph (*a*) of the definition "designated educational institution" in subsection 118.6(1), or

(*b*) an educational institution outside Canada that provides courses at a post-secondary school level and that is

(i) a university, college or other educational institution at which a beneficiary was enrolled in a course of not less than 13 consecutive weeks, or

(ii) a university at which a beneficiary was enrolled on a full-time basis in a course of not less than three consecutive weeks;

History: S. 146.1(1), paragraph (*b*) of the definition "post-secondary educational institution" was replaced by S.C. 2011, c. 24, s. 48(1), applicable to educational assistance payments made after 2010. S. 146.1(1), paragraph (*b*) of the definition "post-secondary educational institution" formerly read:

(*b*) an educational institution outside Canada that is a university, college or other educational institution that provides courses at a post-secondary school level at which a beneficiary was enrolled in a course of not less than 13 consecutive weeks;

Related Sections: S. 120.4(1), "excluded amount".

"post-secondary school level" —"post-secondary school level" includes a program of courses, at an institution described in subparagraph (*a*)(ii) of the definition "designated educational institution" in subsection 118.6(1), of a technical or vocational nature designed to furnish a person with skills for, or improve a person's skills in, an occupation;

"pre-1972 income" — (Repealed by S.C. 1998, c. 19, s. 38(1).)

"promoter" —"promoter", of an arrangement, means the person described as the promoter in the definition *education savings plan*;

History: S. 146.1(1), the definition "promoter" was added by S.C. 2017, c. 33, s. 57(2), deemed to have come into force on March 23, 2017.

"public primary caregiver" —"public primary caregiver", of a beneficiary under an education savings plan in respect of whom a special allowance is payable under the *Children's Special Allowances Act*, means the department, agency or institution that maintains the beneficiary or the public trustee or public curator of the province in which the beneficiary resides;

"qualified investment" —"qualified investment" for a trust governed by a registered education savings plan means

(*a*) an investment that would be described by any of paragraphs (*a*) to (*d*), (*f*) and (*g*) of the definition "qualified investment" in section 204 if the reference in that definition to "a trust governed by a deferred profit sharing plan or revoked plan" were read as a reference to "a trust governed by a registered education savings plan" and if that definition were read without reference to the words "with the exception of excluded property in relation to the trust",

(*b*) (Repealed.)

(*c*) a contract for an annuity issued by a licensed annuities provider where

(i) the trust is the only person who, disregarding any subsequent transfer of the contract by the trust, is or may become entitled to any annuity payments under the contract, and

(ii) the holder of the contract has a right to surrender the contract at any time for an amount that would, if reasonable sales and administration charges were ignored, approximate the value of funds that could otherwise be applied to fund future periodic payments under the contract, (*d*) an investment that was acquired by the trust before October 28, 1998, and

(*e*) a prescribed investment;

Editorial Note: The definition of "qualified investment" for a trust governed by a RESP incorporates by reference much of the similar definition in s. 204 that applies to deferred profit sharing plans. The definition also includes investments that are prescribed under Part XLIX (s. 4900) of the Regulations.

Related Regulations: 4300; 4900(1); 4900(5); 4900(6); 4900(8); 4900(9); 4900(10); 4900(12); 4900(13).

Related Sections: S. 87(10) Share deemed listed; s. 132.2(1)(*k*) Mutual funds — qualifying exchange; s. 207.1(3) Tax payable by trust under registered education savings plan.

Canadian Tax Foundation: De Lisser and Krieger, *Registered Savings Plans: Investing Without Penalty*, 2013 Canadian Tax Journal 3:769–796.

Tax Profile: August 2004 — Canadian Tax Treatment of Index Participation Units and Exchange-Traded Index Derivatives.

Income Tax Folios: *Primary* — S3-F10-C1 Qualified Investments - RRSPs, RESPs, RRIFs, RDSPs and TFSAs. *Secondary* — S3-F10-C2 Prohibited Investments - RRSPs, RRIFs and TFSAs.

"qualifying educational program" —"qualifying educational program" means a program at a post-secondary school level of not less than three consecutive weeks duration that requires that each student taking the program spend not less than ten hours per week on courses or work in the program;

"refund of payments" —"refund of payments" at any time under a particular registered education savings plan means

(*a*) a refund at that time of a contribution that had been made at a previous time, if the contribution was made

(i) otherwise than by way of a transfer from another registered education savings plan, and

(ii) into the particular plan by or on behalf of a subscriber under the particular plan, or

(*b*) a refund at that time of an amount that was paid at a previous time into the particular plan by way of a transfer from another registered education savings plan, where the amount would have been a refund of payments under the other plan if it had been paid at the previous time directly to a subscriber under the other plan;

Related Sections: S. 146.1(1), "contribution".

"registered education savings plan" or "RESP" —"registered education savings plan" or "RESP" means

(*a*) an education savings plan registered for the purposes of this Act, or

(*b*) a registered education savings plan as it is amended from time to time

but, except for the purposes of subsections (7) and (7.1) and Part X.4, a plan ceases to be a registered education savings plan immediately after the day as of which its registration is revoked under subsection (13);

Editorial Note: Registered education savings plans allow subscribers to accumulate income, on a tax-deferred basis, to be used to pay the costs of post-secondary education. Pursuant to the definition in s. 204.9(1), the RESP lifetime limit for each beneficiary is $50,000 for 2007 and subsequent years. Contributions also earn a Canada Education Savings Grant which is paid to the plan. Paragraph 146.1(2)(i) provides that the plan must be wound up by the end of the 35th year following the year in which it is set up (40th year if a "specified plan").

History: S. 146.1(1), the portion of the definition "registered education savings plan" before paragraph (*a*) was replaced by S.C. 2012, c. 31, s. 33(1), in force on Royal Assent, December 14, 2012. S. 146.1(1), the portion of the definition "registered education savings plan" before paragraph (*a*) formerly read:

"registered education savings plan"—"registered education savings plan" means

Related Sections: S. 149(1)(*u*) Registered education savings plans.

Guides: RC4092 Registered Education Savings Plans (RESPs).

"RESP annual limit" — (Repealed by S.C. 2007, c. 29, s. 18(1).)

"specified educational program" —"specified educational program" means a program at a post-secondary school level of not less than three consecutive weeks duration that requires each student taking the program to spend not less than 12 hours per month on courses in the program;

"specified plan" —"specified plan" means an education savings plan

(*a*) that does not allow more than one beneficiary under the plan at any one time,

(*b*) under which the beneficiary is an individual in respect of whom paragraphs 118.3(1)(*a*) to (*b*) apply for the beneficiary's taxation year that ends in the 31st year following the year in which the plan was entered into, and

(*c*) that provides that, at all times after the end of the 35th year following the year in which the plan was entered into, no other individual may be designated as a beneficiary under the plan;

"subscriber" —"subscriber" under an education savings plan at any time means

(*a*) each individual or the public primary caregiver with whom the promoter of the plan enters into the plan,

(*a*.1) another individual or another public primary caregiver who has before that time, under a written agreement, acquired a public primary caregiver's rights as a subscriber under the plan,

(*b*) an individual who has before that time acquired a subscriber's rights under the plan pursuant to a decree, order or judgment of a competent tribunal, or under a written agreement, relating to a division of property between the individual and a subscriber under the plan in settlement of rights arising out of, or on the breakdown of, their marriage or common-law partnership, or

(*c*) after the death of an individual described in any of paragraphs (*a*) to (*b*), any other person (including the estate of the deceased individual) who acquires the individual's rights as a subscriber under the plan or who makes contributions into the plan in respect of a beneficiary

but does not include an individual or a public primary caregiver whose rights as a subscriber under the plan had, before that time, been acquired by an individual or public primary caregiver in the circumstances described in paragraph (*a*.1) or (*b*);

Related Sections: S. 146.1(1), "beneficiary", "contribution", "education savings plan", "public primary caregiver"; s. 248(1), "common-law partnership".

"tax-paid income" — (Repealed by S.C. 1998, c. 19, s. 38(1).)

"trust" —"trust", except in this definition and the definition "education savings plan", means any person who irrevocably holds property under an education savings plan for any of, or any combination of, the following purposes:

(*a*) the payment of educational assistance payments,

(*b*) the payment after 1997 of accumulated income payments,

(*c*) the refund of payments,

(*c*.1) the repayment of amounts (and the payment of amounts related to that repayment) under the *Canada Education Savings Act* or under a designated provincial program,

(*d*) the payment to, or to a trust in favour of, designated educational institutions in Canada referred to in subparagraph (*a*)(i) of the definition of that expression in subsection 118.6(1), or

(*e*) the payment to a trust that irrevocably holds property pursuant to a registered education savings plan for any of the purposes set out in paragraphs (*a*) to (*d*).

Editorial Note: See the CRA's RESP Bulletin No. 1R1, updated January 14, 2015, and No. 2, dated May 24, 2011.

Related Sections: S. 60(*x*) Repayment under Canada Education Savings Act; 146.1(1), "accumulated income payment", "designated provincial program", "educational assistance payment", "refund of payments"; s. 146.1(7) Educational assistance payments.

► 146.1(1.1) ◄

(1.1) Election. A subscriber under an RESP that allows accumulated income payments and a holder of an RDSP may jointly elect in prescribed form to have subsection (1.2) apply in respect of a beneficiary under the RESP if, at the time the election is made, the beneficiary is also the beneficiary under the RDSP and

(*a*) the beneficiary has a severe and prolonged mental impairment that prevents, or can reasonably be expected to prevent, the beneficiary from enrolling in a qualifying educational program at a post-secondary educational institution; or

(*b*) the RESP meets the conditions described in clause (2)(*d.1*)(iii)(A) or (B) to make an accumulated income payment.

Editorial Note: Effective January 1, 2014, accumulated income payments may be rolled over on a tax-free basis from an RESP to a registered disability savings plan (RDSP) if both plans have a common beneficiary. The rollover is found in subsections 146.1(1.1) and (1.2). The rollover is elective.

Generally, to qualify for the rollover, one of the following conditions must be fulfilled at the time the election is made:

- the beneficiary has a severe and prolonged mental impairment that can reasonably be expected to prevent the beneficiary from pursuing a post-secondary education;
- the RESP has existed for at least 10 years and the beneficiary is at least 21 years of age and is not pursuing a post-secondary education; or
- the RESP has existed for at least 35 years (or 40 years, if it is a "specified plan").

History: S. 146.1(1.1) was added by S.C. 2012, c. 31, s. 33(2), and comes into force on January 1, 2014.

Related Sections: s. 146.4(1), "contribution"; s. 147.5(1), "qualifying survivor".

► 146.1(1.2) ◄

(1.2) Effect of election. If an election is made under subsection (1.1) and is filed by the promoter of the RESP with the Minister without delay, then notwithstanding paragraph (2)(*d.1*) and any terms of the RESP required by that paragraph, an accumulated income payment under the RESP may be made to the RDSP.

History: S. 146.1(1.2) was added by S.C. 2012, c. 31, s. 33(2), and comes into force on January 1, 2014.

► 146.1(2) ◄

(2) Conditions for registration. The Minister shall not accept for registration for the purposes of this Act any education savings plan of a promoter unless, in the Minister's opinion, the following conditions are complied with:

(*a*) the plan provides that the property of any trust governed by the plan (after the payment of trustee and administration charges) is irrevocably held for any of the purposes described in the definition "trust" in subsection (1) by a corporation licensed or otherwise authorized under the laws of Canada or a province to carry on in Canada the business of offering to the public its services as a trustee;

(*b*) at the time of the application by the promoter for registration of the plan, there are not fewer than 150 plans entered into with the promoter each of which complied, at the time it was entered into, with all the other conditions set out in this subsection, as it read at that time;

(*b*.1) application for registration of the plan is made by the promoter in prescribed form containing prescribed information;

(*c*) the promoter and all trusts governed by the plan are resident in Canada;

(*d*) the plan does not allow for any payment before 1998 to a subscriber, other than a refund of payments, unless the subscriber is also the beneficiary under the plan;

(*d*.1) subject to subsection (2.2), if the plan allows accumulated income payments, the plan provides that an accumulated income payment is permitted to be made only if

(i) the payment is made to, or on behalf of, a subscriber under the plan who is resident in Canada when the payment is made,

(ii) the payment is not made jointly to, or on behalf of, more than one subscriber, and

(iii) any of

(A) the payment is made after the 9th year that follows the year in which the plan was entered into and each individual (other than a deceased individual) who is or was a beneficiary under the plan has attained 21 years of age before the payment is made and is not, when the payment is made, eligible under the plan to receive an educational assistance payment,

(B) the payment is made in the year in which the plan is required to be terminated in accordance with paragraph (*i*), or

(C) each individual who was a beneficiary under the plan is deceased when the payment is made;

(*e*) the plan is substantially similar to the type of plan described in or annexed to a prospectus filed by the promoter with a securities commission in Canada or a body performing a similar function in a province;

(*f*) in the event that a trust governed by the plan is terminated, the property held by the trust is required to be used for any of the purposes described in the definition "trust" in subsection (1);

(*g*) the plan does not allow for the payment of educational assistance payments before 1997 to an individual unless the individual is, at the time the payment is made, a student in full-time attendance at a post-secondary educational institution and enrolled in a qualifying educational program at the institution;

(*g*.1) the plan does not allow for the payment of an educational assistance payment to or for an individual at any time after 1996 unless

(i) either

(A) the individual is, at that time, enrolled as a student in a qualifying educational program at a post-secondary educational institution, or

(B) the individual has, before that time, attained the age of 16 years and is, at that time, enrolled as a student in a specified educational program at a post-secondary educational institution, and

(ii) either

(A) the individual satisfies, at that time, the condition set out in clause (i)(A), and

(I) has satisfied that condition throughout at least 13 consecutive weeks in the 12-month period that ends at that time, or

(II) the total of the payment and all other educational assistance payments made under a registered education savings plan of the promoter to or for the individual in the 12-month period that ends at that time does not exceed $5,000 or any greater amount that the Minister designated for the purpose of the *Canada Education Savings Act* approves in writing with respect to the individual, or

(B) the individual satisfies, at that time, the condition set out in clause (i)(B) and the total of the payment and all other educational assistance payments made under a registered education savings plan of the promoter to or for the individual in the 13-week period that ends at that time does not exceed $2,500 or any greater amount that the Minister designated for the purpose of the *Canada Education Savings Act* approves in writing with respect to the individual;

(*g*.2) the plan does not allow for any contribution into the plan, other than a contribution made by or on behalf of a subscriber under the plan in respect of a beneficiary under the plan or a contribution made by way of transfer from another registered education savings plan;

(*g*.3) the plan provides that an individual is permitted to be designated as a beneficiary under the plan, and that a contribution to the plan in respect of an individual who is a beneficiary under the plan is permitted to be made, only if

(i) in the case of a designation, the individual's Social Insurance Number is provided to the promoter before the designation is made and either

(A) the individual is resident in Canada when the designation is made, or

(B) the designation is made in conjunction with a transfer of property into the plan from another registered education savings plan under which the individual was a beneficiary immediately before the transfer, and

(ii) in the case of a contribution, either

(A) the individual's Social Insurance Number is provided to the promoter before the contribution is made and the individual is resident in Canada when the contribution is made, or

(B) the contribution is made by way of transfer from another registered education savings plan under which the individual was a beneficiary immediately before the transfer;

(*h*) the plan provides that no contribution (other than a contribution made by way of a transfer from another registered education savings plan) may be made into the plan after

(i) in the case of a specified plan, the 35th year following the year in which the plan was entered into, and

(ii) in any other case, the 31st year following the year in which the plan was entered into;

(*i*) the plan provides that it must be terminated on or before the last day of

(i) in the case of a specified plan, the 40th year following the year in which the plan was entered into, and

(ii) in any other case, the 35th year following the year in which the plan was entered into;

(*i*.1) if the plan allows accumulated income payments, the plan provides that it must be terminated before March of the year following the year in which the first such payment is made out of the plan;

(*i*.2) the plan does not allow for the receipt of property by way of direct transfer from another registered education savings plan after the other plan has made any accumulated income payment;

(*j*) if the plan allows more than one beneficiary under the plan at any one time, the plan provides

(i) that each of the beneficiaries under the plan is required to be connected to each living subscriber under the plan, or to have been connected to a deceased original subscriber under the plan, by blood relationship or adoption,

(ii) that a contribution into the plan in respect of a beneficiary is permitted to be made only if

(A) the beneficiary had not attained 31 years of age before the time of the contribution, or

(B) the contribution is made by way of transfer from another registered education savings plan that allows more than one beneficiary at any one time, and

(iii) that an individual is permitted to become a beneficiary under the plan at any particular time only if

(A) the individual had not attained 21 years of age before the particular time, or

(B) the individual was, immediately before the particular time, a beneficiary under another registered education savings plan that allows more than one beneficiary at any one time;

(*k*) (Repealed by S.C. 2007, c. 29, s. 18(5).)

(*l*) the plan provides that the promoter shall, within 90 days after an individual becomes a beneficiary under the plan, notify the individual (or, where the individual is under 19 years of age at that time and either ordinarily resides with a parent of the individual or is maintained by a public primary caregiver of the individual, that parent or public primary caregiver) in writing of the existence of the plan and the name and address of the subscriber in respect of the plan;

(*m*) the Minister has no reasonable basis to believe that the promoter will not take all reasonable measures to ensure that the plan will continue to comply with the conditions set out in paragraphs (*a*), (*c*) to (*d*.1) and (*f*) to (*l*) for its registration for the purposes of this Act; and

(*n*) the Minister has no reasonable basis to believe that the plan will become revocable.

History: S. 146.1(2)(*g.3*) was added by S.C. 2013, c. 34, s. 298(1), deemed to have come into force on January 1, 2004.

S. 146.1(2)(*i*.1) was replaced by S.C. 2012, c. 31, s. 33(3), and comes into force on January 1, 2014. S. 146.1(2)(*i*.1) formerly read:

(*i*.1) if the plan allows accumulated income payments in accordance with paragraph (*d*.1), the plan provides that it must be terminated before March of the year following the year in which the first such payment is made out of the plan;

Related Sections: S. 118.6(3) Students eligible for the disability tax credit; s. 146.1(1), "accumulated income payment", "beneficiary", "contribution", "educational assistance payment", "education savings plan", "post-secondary educational institution", "public primary caregiver", "qualifying educational program", "refund of payments", "registered education savings plan", "specified plan", "subscriber", "trust"; s. 146.1(2)(*d*.1) Conditions for registration; s. 146.1(4) Registration of plans without prospectus; s. 146.4(1), "contribution"; s. 147.5(1), "qualifying survivor"; 204.9 [Interpretation]; 204.91 Tax payable by subscribers; 204.92 Return and payment of tax; 204.93 Provisions applicable to Part; s. 204.94(2) Charging provision; s. 251(6) Blood relationship, etc.

Canadian Tax Foundation: Donnelly et al., *Registered Education Savings Plans: A Tax Incentive Response to Higher Education Access*, 1999 Canadian Tax Journal 1:81–109; Magee, *Tax Planning for Post-Secondary Education*, 1998 Canadian Tax Journal 5:1079–1115.

Forms: T3GR — Group Income Tax and Information Return for RRSP, RRIF, RESP or RDSP Trusts; T550 — Application for Registration of: RSP's, ESP's, or RIF's Under Section 146, 146.2 and 146.3 of the Income Tax Act; T1171 — Tax Withholding Waiver on Accumulated Income Payments from RESPs; T1172 — Additional Tax on Accumulated Income Payments from RESPs.

Guides: RC4092 Registered Education Savings Plans (RESPs).

Information Circulars: IC 78-14R4 Guidelines for trust companies and other persons responsible for filing T3GR, T3D, T3P, T3S, T3RI, and T3F returns; IC 93-3R1 Registered education savings plans.

► 146.1(2.1) ◄

(2.1) RESP is revocable. For the purposes of paragraphs (2)(*n*) and (12.1)(*d*), a registered education savings plan is revocable at any time after October 27, 1998 at which

(*a*) (Repealed by S.C. 2017, c. 33, s. 57(3).)

(*b*) (Repealed by S.C. 2017, c. 33, s. 57(3).)

(*c*) a trust governed by the plan begins carrying on a business; or

(*d*) a trustee that holds property in connection with the plan borrows money for the purposes of the plan, except where

(i) the money is borrowed for a term not exceeding 90 days,

(ii) the money is not borrowed as part of a series of loans or other transactions and repayments, and

(iii) none of the property of the trust is used as security for the borrowed money.

History: S. 146.1(2.1)(*a*) and (*b*) were repealed by S.C. 2017, c. 33, s. 57(3), applicable in respect of

(a) any investment acquired after March 22, 2017; and

(b) any investment acquired before March 23, 2017 that ceases to be a "qualified investment" (as defined in subsection 146.1(1) of the Act) after March 22, 2017.

S. 146.1(2.1)(*a*) and (*b*) formerly read:

(*a*) a trust governed by the plan acquires property that is not a qualified investment for the trust;

(*b*) property held by a trust governed by the plan ceases to be a qualified investment for the trust and the property is not disposed of by the trust within 60 days after that time;

Related Sections: S. 207.1(3) Tax payable by trust under registered education savings plan.

► 146.1(2.2) ◄

(2.2) Waiver of conditions for accumulated income payments. The Minister may, on written application of the promoter of a registered education savings plan, waive the application of the conditions in clause (2)(*d*.1)(iii)(A) in respect of the plan where a beneficiary under the plan suffers from a severe and prolonged mental impairment that prevents, or can reasonably be expected to prevent, the beneficiary from enrolling in a qualifying educational program at a post-secondary educational institution.

Related Sections: S. 146.1(1), "accumulated income payment", "beneficiary", "post-secondary educational institution", "qualifying educational program".

► 146.1(2.21) ◄

(2.21) Extension for making educational assistance payments. Notwithstanding paragraph (2)(*g.1*), an education savings plan may allow for the payment of an educational assistance payment to or for an individual at any time in the six-month period immediately following the particular time at which the individual ceases to be enrolled as a student in a qualifying educational program or a specified educational program, as the case may be, if the payment would have complied with the requirements of paragraph (2)(*g.1*) had the payment been made immediately before the particular time.

Related Sections: S. 146.1(1), "educational assistance payment", "qualifying educational program", "specified educational program".

Tax Window Files: Application of 146.1(2.21) to deceased beneficiary, *August 10, 2015*, CRA Document No. 2014-0527981I7.

► 146.1(2.22) ◄

(2.22) Timing of payment. An educational assistance payment that is made at any time in accordance with subsection (2.21) but not in accordance with paragraph (2)(*g.1*) is deemed, for the purposes of applying that paragraph at and after that time, to have been made immediately before the particular time referred to in subsection (2.21).

► 146.1(2.3) ◄

(2.3) Social Insurance Number not required. Notwithstanding paragraph (2)(*g.3*), an education savings plan may provide that an individual's Social Insurance Number need not be provided in respect of

(*a*) a contribution to the plan, if the plan was entered into before 1999; and

(*b*) a designation of a non-resident individual as a beneficiary under the plan, if the individual was not assigned a Social Insurance Number before the designation is made.

History: S. 146.1(2.3) was added by S.C. 2013, c. 34, s. 298(2), deemed to have come into force on January 1, 2004.

► 146.1(3) ◄

(3) Deemed registration. Where in any year an education savings plan cannot be accepted for registration solely because the condition set out in paragraph (2)(*b*) has not been complied with, if the plan is subsequently registered, it shall be deemed to have been registered on the first day of January of

(*a*) the year in which all of the conditions set out in subsection (2) (except in paragraph (2)(*b*)) were complied with, or

(*b*) the year preceding the year in which the plan was subsequently registered,

whichever is the later.

Related Sections: S. 146.1(12) Deemed date of registration.

► 146.1(4) ◄

(4) Registration of plans without prospectus. Notwithstanding paragraph (2)(*e*), where a promoter has not filed a prospectus in respect of an education savings plan referred to in that paragraph, the Minister may register the plan if the promoter is not otherwise required by the laws of Canada or a province to file such a prospectus with a securities commission in Canada or a body performing a similar function in a province and the plan complies with the other conditions set out in subsection (2).

► 146.1(4.1) ◄

(4.1) Obligation to file amendment. When a registered education savings plan is amended, the promoter shall file the text of the amendment with the Minister not later than 60 days after the day on which the plan is amended.

► 146.1(5) ◄

(5) Trust not taxable. No tax is payable under this Part by a trust that is governed by a RESP on its taxable income for a taxation year, except that, if at any time in the taxation year, it holds one or more properties that are not qualified investments for the trust, tax is payable under this Part by the trust on the amount that would be its taxable income for the taxation year if it had no income or losses from sources other than those properties, and no capital gains or capital losses other than from dispositions of those properties, and for that purpose,

(*a*) income includes dividends described in section 83;

(*b*) the trust's taxable capital gain or allowable capital loss from the disposition of a property is equal to its capital gain or capital loss, as the case may be, from the disposition; and

(*c*) the trust's income shall be computed without reference to subsection 104(6).

History: S. 146.1(5) was replaced by S.C. 2017, c. 33, s. 57(4), applicable in respect of

(a) any investment acquired after March 22, 2017; and

(b) any investment acquired before March 23, 2017 that ceases to be a "qualified investment" (as defined in subsection 146.1(1) of the Act) after March 22, 2017.

S. 146.1(5) formerly read:

(5) *Trust not taxable.* No tax is payable under this Part by a trust on the taxable income of the trust for a taxation year if, throughout the period in the year during which the trust was in existence, the trust was governed by a registered education savings plan.

Related Sections: S. 146.1(1), "registered education savings plan", "trust"; s. 149(1)(*u*) Registered education savings plans.

► 146.1(6) ◄

(6) Subscriber not taxable. No tax is payable by a subscriber on the income of a trust for a taxation year after 1971 throughout which the trust was governed by a registered education savings plan.

Related Sections: S. 146.1(1), "subscriber".

► 146.1(6.1) ◄

(6.1) Transfers between plans. Where property irrevocably held by a trust governed by a registered education savings plan (in this subsection referred to as the "transferor plan") is transferred to a trust governed by another registered education savings plan (in this subsection referred to as the "transferee plan"),

(*a*) (Repealed by S.C. 1998, c. 19, s. 38(13).)

(*b*) for the purposes of this paragraph, the definition "specified plan" in subsection (1) and paragraphs (2)(*d.1*), (*h*) and (*i*), the transferee plan is deemed to have been entered into on the day that is the earlier of

(i) the day on which the transferee plan was entered into, and

(ii) the day on which the transferor plan was entered into; and

(*c*) notwithstanding subsections (7) and (7.1), no amount shall be included in computing the income of any person because of the transfer.

Related Sections: 146.1(2)(i.2); S. 204.9(5) Transfers between plans.

► 146.1(7) ◄

(7) Educational assistance payments. There shall be included in computing an individual's income for a taxation year the total of all educational assistance payments paid out of registered education savings plans to or for the individual in the year that exceeds the total of all excluded amounts in respect of those plans and the individual for the year.

History: S. 146.1(7) was replaced by S.C. 2017, c. 33, s. 57(5), deemed to have come into force on March 23, 2017, and formerly read:

(7) *Educational assistance payments.* There shall be included in computing an individual's income for a taxation year the total of all educational assistance payments paid out of registered education savings plans to or for the individual in the year.

Related Sections: S. 56(1)(*q*) Education savings plan payments; s. 60(*x*) Repayment under Canada Education Savings Act; s. 146.1(1), "educational assistance payment", "registered education savings plan"; s. 146.1(6.1) Transfers between plans; s. 212(1)(*r*) Registered education savings plan.

► 146.1(7.1) ◄

(7.1) Other income inclusions. There shall be included in computing a taxpayer's income for a taxation year

(*a*) each accumulated income payment (other than an accumulated income payment made under subsection (1.2)) received in the year by the taxpayer under a registered education savings plan that exceeds the total of all excluded amounts in respect of those plans and the individual for the year; and

(*b*) each amount received in the year by the taxpayer in full or partial satisfaction of a subscriber's interest under a registered education savings plan (other than any excluded amount in respect of the plan).

History: S. 146.1(7.1)(*a*) was replaced by S.C. 2017, c. 33, s. 57(6), deemed to have come into force on March 23, 2017, and formerly read:

(*a*) each accumulated income payment (other than an accumulated income payment made under subsection (1.2)) received in the year by the taxpayer under a registered education savings plan; and

S. 146.1(7.1)(*a*) was replaced by S.C. 2012, c. 31, s. 33(4), and comes into force on January 1, 2014. S. 146.1(7.1)(*a*) formerly read:

(*a*) each accumulated income payment received in the year by the taxpayer under a registered education savings plan; and

Related Sections: S. 56(1)(*q*) Education savings plan payments; s. 146.1(1), "accumulated income payment", "registered education savings plan"; s. 146.1(6.1) Transfers between plans; s. 146.1(7.2) Excluded amount; s. 212(1)(*r*) Registered education savings plan.

Forms: T1171 — Tax Withholding Waiver on Accumulated Income Payments from RESPs; T1172 — Additional Tax on Accumulated Income Payments from RESPs.

► 146.1(7.2) ◄

(7.2) Excluded amount. An excluded amount in respect of a registered education savings plan is,

(*a*) for the purposes of subsection (7) and paragraph (7.1)(*a*), an amount in respect of which a subscriber pays a tax under section 207.05 in respect of the plan, or another plan for which the plan was substituted by the subscriber, that

(i) has not been waived, cancelled or refunded, and

(ii) has not reduced any other amount that would otherwise be included under subsections (7) or (7.1) in computing an individual's income for the year or a preceding year; and

(*b*) for the purposes of paragraph (7.1)(*b*),

(i) any amount received under the plan,

(ii) any amount received in satisfaction of a right to a refund of payments under the plan, or

(iii) any amount received by a taxpayer under a decree, order or judgment of a competent tribunal, or under a written agreement, relating to a division of property between the taxpayer and the taxpayer's spouse or common-law partner or former spouse or common-law partner in settlement of rights arising out of, or on the breakdown of, their marriage or common-law partnership.

History: S. 146.1(7.2) was replaced by S.C. 2017, c. 33, s. 57(7), deemed to have come into force on March 23, 2017, and formerly read:

(7.2) *Excluded amount.* For the purpose of paragraph (7.1)(*b*), an excluded amount in respect of a registered education savings plan is

(*a*) any amount received under the plan;

(*b*) any amount received in satisfaction of a right to a refund of payments under the plan; or

(*c*) any amount received by a taxpayer under a decree, order or judgment of a competent tribunal, or under a written agreement, relating to a division of property between the taxpayer and the taxpayer's spouse or common-law partner or former spouse or common-law partner in settlement of rights arising out of, or on the breakdown of, their marriage or common-law partnership.

Related Sections: S. 146.1(1), "refund of payments", "registered education savings plan;"; s. 248(1), "common-law partner".

► 146.1(8) ◄

(8) Definition of "beneficiary's portion of the tax-paid income" — (Repealed by S.C. 1998, c. 19, s. 38(15).)

► 146.1(9) ◄

(9) Limitation on allocation of tax-paid income — (Repealed by S.C. 1998, c. 19, s. 38(15).)

► 146.1(10) ◄

(10) Allocation of tax-paid income — (Repealed by S.C. 1998, c. 19, s. 38(15).)

► 146.1(11) ◄

(11) Trust deemed to be inter vivos trust — (Repealed by 2014, c. 39, s. 51(1).)

History: S. 146.1(11) was repealed by S.C. 2014, c. 39, s. 51(1), applicable to the 2016 and subsequent taxation years, and formerly read:

(11) *Trust deemed to be inter vivos trust.* For any taxation year during which an education savings plan is not registered, a trust governed by the plan shall be deemed, for the purposes of section 122, to be a trust referred to in subsection 122(1) established after June 17, 1971.

► 146.1(12) ◄

(12) Deemed date of registration. Subject to subsection (3), an education savings plan that is registered

(*a*) before 1976 shall be deemed to have been registered since the later of

(i) January 1, 1972, and

(ii) the first day of January of the year in which the plan was created; and

(*b*) after 1975 shall be deemed to have been registered on the first day of January in the year of registration.

► 146.1(12.1) ◄

(12.1) Notice of intent to revoke registration. When a particular day is

(*a*) a day on which a registered education savings plan ceases to comply with the conditions of subsection (2) for the plan's registration, (*b*) a day on which a registered education savings plan ceases to comply with any provision of the plan,

(*c*) the last day of a month in respect of which tax is payable under Part X.4 by an individual because of contributions made, or deemed for the purpose of Part X.4 to have been made, by or on behalf of the individual into a registered education savings plan,

(*d*) a day on which a registered education savings plan is revocable, or

(*e*) a day on which a person fails to comply with a condition or an obligation, imposed under the *Canada Education Savings Act* or under a program administered pursuant to an agreement entered into under section 12 of that Act, that applies with respect to a registered education savings plan,

the Minister may send written notice (referred to in this subsection and subsection (12.2) as a "notice of intent") to the promoter of the plan that the Minister proposes to revoke the registration of the plan as of the day specified in the notice of intent, which day shall not be earlier than the particular day.

Related Sections: S. 146.1(2.1) RESP is revocable; s. 146.1(2.2) Waiver of conditions for accumulated income payments; s. 172(3)(*e*.1) Appeal from refusal to register, revocation of registration, etc.; s. 172(4) Deemed refusal to register — no notification within 180 days; s. 180(1)(*c*.1) Appeals to Federal Court of Appeal.

► 146.1(12.2) ◄

(12.2) Notice of revocation. When the Minister sends a notice of intent to revoke the registration of a registered education savings plan to the promoter of the plan, the Minister may, after 30 days after the receipt by the promoter of the notice, send written notice (referred to in this subsection and subsection (13) as a "notice of revocation") to the promoter that the registration of the plan is revoked as of the day specified in the notice of revocation, which day shall not be earlier than the day specified in the notice of intent.

► 146.1(13) ◄

(13) Revocation of registration. When the Minister sends a notice of revocation of the registration of a registered education savings plan under subsection (12.2) to the promoter of the plan, the registration of the plan is revoked as of the day specified in the notice of revocation, unless the Federal Court of Appeal or a judge thereof, on application made at any time before the determination of an appeal under subsection 172(3), orders otherwise.

Related Sections: S. 146.1(1), "registered education savings plan".

► 146.1(13.1) ◄

(13.1) RESP information. Every trustee under a registered education savings plan shall, in prescribed form and manner, file with the Minister information returns in respect of the plan.

Forms: T3GR — Group Income Tax and Information Return for RRSP, RRIF, RESP or RDSP Trusts.

► 146.1(14) ◄

(14) Former Act. A reference

(*a*) in this section, in paragraph 60(*x*) or in subparagraph 241(4)(*d*)(vii.1) to the *Canada Education Savings Act*, to an amount paid, to the payment of an amount or to the repayment of an amount, or to a condition or an obligation imposed, under that Act includes a reference to Part III.1 of the *Department of Human Resources Development Act*, or to an amount paid, to the payment of an amount or to the repayment of an amount, or to a condition or an obligation imposed, as the case may be, under that Part as it read at the time the reference is relevant; and

(*b*) in clause (2)(*g*.1)(ii)(B) to an amount that the Minister designated for the purpose of the *Canada Education Savings Act* approves in writing with respect to an individual includes a reference to an amount that the Minister of Human Resources Development or the Minister of State to be styled Minister of Human Resources and Skills Development has approved in writing, before the day on which a Minister is designated for the purposes of that Act, with respect to the individual.

► 146.1(15) ◄

(15) Regulations. The Governor in Council may make regulations requiring promoters of education savings plans to file information returns in respect of the plans.

Tax-Free Savings Accounts

SECTION 146.2: [Tax-free savings accounts]

► 146.2(1) ◄

(1) Definitions. The following definitions apply in this section and in Part XI.01.

Canadian Tax Foundation: MacEachern and Clarke, *Taxing TFSAs That Carry On a Securities Trading Business*, 2015 Canadian Tax Focus 1(1).

"distribution" —"distribution" under an arrangement of which an individual is the holder means a payment out of or under the arrangement in satisfaction of all or part of the holder's interest in the arrangement.

"holder" —"holder" of an arrangement means

(*a*) until the death of the individual who entered into the arrangement with the issuer, the individual,

(*b*) at and after the death of the individual, the individual's survivor, if the survivor acquires

(i) all of the individual's rights as the holder of the arrangement, and

(ii) to the extent it is not included in the rights described in subparagraph (i), the unconditional right to revoke any beneficiary designation made, or similar direction imposed, by the individual under the arrangement or relating to property held in connection with the arrangement, and

(*c*) at and after the death of a holder described in paragraph (*b*) or in this paragraph, the holder's survivor, if the survivor acquires

(i) all of the holder's rights as the holder of the arrangement, and

(ii) to the extent it is not included in the rights described in subparagraph (i), the unconditional right to revoke any beneficiary designation made, or similar direction imposed, by the holder under the arrangement or relating to property held in connection with the arrangement.

History: S. 146.2(1), paragraph (*c*) of the definition "holder" was added by S.C. 2013, c. 34, s. 299(1), applicable to the 2009 and subsequent taxation years.

Related Sections: S. 146.2(9) Trust ceasing to be a TFSA on death of holder; s. 207.01(3) Survivor as successor holder; s. 207.04(1) Tax payable on prohibited or non-qualified investment; s. 207.04(6) Additional tax payable on prohibited investment.

Tax Topics: No. 1968, Death of a TFSA Holder: Quebec and the Rest of Canada.

"issuer" —"issuer" of an arrangement means the person described as the issuer in the definition "qualifying arrangement".

Related Regulations: 223.

"qualifying arrangement" —"qualifying arrangement", at a particular time, means an arrangement

(*a*) that is entered into after 2008 between a person (in this definition referred to as the "issuer") and an individual (other than a trust) who is at least 18 years of age;

(*b*) that is

(i) an arrangement in trust with an issuer that is a corporation licensed or otherwise authorized under the laws of Canada or a province to carry on in Canada the business of offering to the public its services as trustee,

(ii) an annuity contract with an issuer that is a licensed annuities provider, or

(iii) a deposit with an issuer that is

(A) a person who is, or is eligible to become, a member of the Canadian Payments Association, or

(B) a credit union that is a shareholder or member of a body corporate referred to as a "central" for the purposes of the *Canadian Payments Act*;

(*c*) that provides for contributions to be made under the arrangement to the issuer in consideration of, or to be used, invested or otherwise applied for the purpose of, the issuer making distributions under the arrangement to the holder;

(*d*) under which the issuer and the individual agree, at the time the arrangement is entered into, that the issuer will file with the Minister an election to register the arrangement as a TFSA; and

(*e*) that, at all times throughout the period that begins at the time the arrangement is entered into and that ends at the particular time, complies with the conditions in subsection (2).

History: S. 146.2(1), subparagraph (*b*)(ii) of the definition "qualifying arrangement" was replaced by S.C. 2009, c. 2, s. 53(1), applicable to the 2009 and subsequent taxation years. S. 146.2(1), subparagraph (*b*)(ii) of the definition "qualifying arrangement" formerly read:

(ii) an annuity contract with an issuer that is a licensed annuities provider, other than a contract that is adjoined to another contract or arrangement, or

Related Sections: S. 137(1), "licensed annuities provider"; s. 146.2(2) Qualifying arrangement conditions.

Tax Topics: No. 1914, Tax-free Savings Accounts.

"survivor" —"survivor" of an individual means another individual who is, immediately before the individual's death, a spouse or common-law partner of the individual.

Related Sections: S. 207.01(2) Exempt contribution to survivor TFSA s. 207.01(3) Survivor as successor holder.

Tax Topics: No. 1968, Death of a TFSA Holder: Quebec and the Rest of Canada.

► 146.2(2) ◄

(2) Qualifying arrangement conditions. The conditions referred to in paragraph (*e*) of the definition "qualifying arrangement" in subsection (1) are as follows:

(*a*) the arrangement requires that it be maintained for the exclusive benefit of the holder (determined without regard to any right of a person to receive a payment out of or under the arrangement only on or after the death of the holder);

(*b*) the arrangement prohibits, while there is a holder of the arrangement, anyone that is neither the holder nor the issuer of the arrangement from having rights under the arrangement relating to the amount and timing of distributions and the investing of funds;

(*c*) the arrangement prohibits anyone other than the holder from making contributions under the arrangement;

(*d*) the arrangement permits distributions to be made to reduce the amount of tax otherwise payable by the holder under section 207.02 or 207.03;

(*e*) the arrangement provides that, at the direction of the holder, the issuer shall transfer all or any part of the property held in connection with the arrangement (or an amount equal to its value) to another TFSA of the holder;

(*f*) if the arrangement is an arrangement in trust, it prohibits the trust from borrowing money or other property for the purposes of the arrangement; and

(*g*) the arrangement complies with prescribed conditions.

Editorial Note: The tax-free savings account ("TFSA") allows Canadian-resident individuals to earn investment income, including interest, dividends and capital gains, on a tax-free basis. Contributions to the TFSA are not deductible, but the income in the account is not subject to tax while in the account or upon withdrawal. However, the TFSA may be subject to tax if it acquires a non-qualified investment or carries on a business (s. 146.2(6)).

The annual contribution limit for a TFSA was initially increased annually for inflation, but rounded to the nearest $500. The limit each year for 2013 and 2014 is $5,500. For 2015, the annual limit was $10,000. For 2016 and subsequent taxation years, the limit is reduced back to $5,500 and again subject to indexation. Unused TFSA room can be carried forward indefinitely. Withdrawals from the account will free more TFSA room in the year following withdrawal. (See the definitions in s. 207.01(1).) Contributions or re-contributions to the TFSA in the year of withdrawal will be subject to the excess contributions tax if there was not sufficient contribution room. Excess contributions are subject to a 1% tax per month (s. 207.02). Other potential penalties apply if a non-resident contributes to the TFSA, if the TFSA acquires a prohibited or non-qualified investment, or if the TSFA confers an advantage on the holder or a person not at arm's length with the holder (s. 207.02 through 207.05).

Tax Window Files: TFSA contributions, *August 20, 2018*, CRA Document No. 2018-0739761E5; TFSA contributions, *August 20, 2018*, CRA Document No. 2017-0731541E5; Whether a TFSA account may be subject to setoff, *January 22, 2018*, CRA Document No. 2017-0727421I7; Overdrafts in a TFSA, *October 22, 2015*, CRA Document No. 2013-0486491I7; Group TFSA and Non-Employees, *November 25, 2008*, CRA Document No. 2008-0296231I7; Flexible Employee Benefit Program — TFSA, *November 18, 2008*, CRA Document No. 2008-0272891E5.

► 146.2(3) ◄

(3) Paragraphs (2)(*a*), (*b*) and (*e*) not applicable. The conditions in paragraphs (2)(*a*), (*b*) and (*e*) do not apply to the extent that they are inconsistent with subsection (4).

History: S. 146.2(3) was replaced by S.C. 2009, c. 2, s. 53(2), applicable to the 2009 and subsequent taxation years. S. 146.2(3) formerly read:

(3) *TFSA*. If the issuer of an arrangement that is, at the time it is entered into, a qualifying arrangement files with the Minister, on or before the day that is 60 days after the end of the calendar year in which the arrangement was entered into, an election in prescribed form and manner to register the arrangement as a TFSA under the Social Insurance Number of the individual with whom the arrangement was entered into, the arrangement becomes a TFSA at the time the arrangement was entered into and ceases to be a TFSA immediately before the earliest of the following events:

(*a*) the death of the last holder of the arrangement,

(*b*) the arrangement ceasing to be a qualifying arrangement, and

(*c*) the arrangement not being administered in accordance with the conditions in subsection (2).

► 146.2(4) ◄

(4) Using TFSA interest as security for a loan. A holder of a TFSA may use the holder's interest or, for civil law, right in the TFSA as security for a loan or other indebtedness if

(*a*) the terms and conditions of the indebtedness are terms and conditions that persons dealing at arm's length with each other would have entered into; and

(*b*) it can reasonably be concluded that none of the main purposes for that use is to enable a person (other than the holder) or a partnership to benefit from the exemption from tax under this Part of any amount in respect of the TFSA.

History: S. 146.2(4) was replaced by S.C. 2009, c. 2, s. 53(2), applicable to the 2009 and subsequent taxation years. S. 146.2(4) formerly read:

(4) *Trust not taxable*. No tax is payable under this Part by a trust that is governed by a TFSA on its taxable income for a taxation year, except that, if at any time in the taxation year, it carries on one or more businesses or holds one or more properties that are non-qualified investments (as defined in subsection 207.01(1)) for the trust, tax is payable under this Part by the trust on the amount that would be its taxable income for the taxation year if it had no incomes or losses from sources other than those businesses and properties, and no capital gains or capital losses other than from dispositions of those properties, and for that purpose,

(*a*) "income" includes dividends described in section 83; and

(*b*) the trust's taxable capital gain or allowable capital loss from the disposition of a property is equal to its capital gain or capital loss, as the case may be, from the disposition.

Tax Topics: No. 1914, Tax-free Savings Accounts.

► 146.2(5) ◄

(5) TFSA. If the issuer of an arrangement that is, at the time it is entered into, a qualifying arrangement files with the Minister, before March of the calendar year following the calendar year in which the arrangement was entered into, an election in prescribed form and manner to register the arrangement as a TFSA under the Social Insurance Number of the individual with whom the arrangement was entered into, the arrangement becomes a TFSA at the time the arrangement was entered into and ceases to be a TFSA at the earliest of the following times:

(*a*) the time at which the last holder of the arrangement dies;

(*b*) the time at which the arrangement ceases to be a qualifying arrangement; or

(*c*) the earliest time at which the arrangement is not administered in accordance with the conditions in subsection (2).

History: S. 146.2(5) was replaced by S.C. 2009, c. 2, s. 53(2), applicable to the 2009 and subsequent taxation years. S. 146.2(5) formerly read:

(5) *Amount credited to a deposit*. An amount that is credited or added to a deposit that is a TFSA as interest or other income in respect of the TFSA is deemed not to be received by the holder of the TFSA solely because of that crediting or adding.

Tax Topics: No. 1914, Tax-free Savings Accounts.

Forms: RC236 — Application for a Tax-Free Savings Account Identification Number.

Guides: RC4466 Tax-Free Savings Account (TFSA): Information Sheet.

► 146.2(6) ◄

(6) Trust not taxable. No tax is payable under this Part by a trust that is governed by a TFSA on its taxable income for a taxation year, except that, if at any time in the taxation year, it carries on one or more businesses or holds one or more properties that are non-qualified investments (as defined in subsection 207.01(1)) for the trust, tax is payable under this Part by the trust on the amount that would be its taxable income for the taxation year if it had no incomes or losses from sources other than those businesses and properties, and no capital gains or capital losses other than from dispositions of those properties, and for that purpose,

(*a*) "income" includes dividends described in section 83;

(*b*) the trust's taxable capital gain or allowable capital loss from the disposition of a property is equal to its capital gain or capital loss, as the case may be, from the disposition; and

(*c*) the trust's income shall be computed without reference to subsection 104(6).

Editorial Note: S. 146.2(6) provides that a TFSA is not subject to Part 1 tax unless it carries on a business or acquires a non-qualified investment. See also the potential penalty tax in s. 207.04(1) that can apply if the TFSA acquires a non-qualified investment (or a prohibited investment).

History: S. 146.2(6)(*c*) was added by S.C. 2010, c. 25, s. 35(1), applicable to the 2010 and subsequent taxation years.

S. 146.2(6) was replaced by S.C. 2009, c. 2, s. 53(2), applicable to the 2009 and subsequent taxation years. S. 146.2(6) formerly read:

(6) *Trust ceasing to be a TFSA*. If an arrangement that governs a trust ceases, at a particular time, to be a TFSA,

(*a*) the trust is deemed

(i) to have disposed, immediately before the particular time, of each property held by the trust for proceeds equal to the property's fair market value immediately before the particular time, and

(ii) to have acquired, at the particular time, each such property at a cost equal to that fair market value;

(*b*) the trust's last taxation year that began before the particular time is deemed to have ended immediately before the particular time; and

(*c*) a taxation year of the trust is deemed to begin at the particular time.

Related Sections: S. 146.2(6.1) Carrying on a business; s. 207.01(1), "non-qualified investment", "qualified investment"; s. 207.04(1) Tax payable on prohibited or non-qualified investment.

Canadian Tax Foundation: Davies and Demner, *Taxing TFSAs on Business Income*, 2015 Canadian Tax Highlights 23(7):8–9.

Tax Topics: No. 2146, The US Tax Implications Of A Tax-Free Savings Account.

► 146.2(6.1) ◄

(6.1) Carrying on a business. If tax is payable under this Part for a taxation year because of subsection (6) by a trust that is governed by a TFSA that carries on one or more businesses at any time in the taxation year,

(*a*) the holder of the TFSA is jointly and severally, or solidarily, liable with the trust to pay each amount payable under this Act by the trust that is attributable to that business or those businesses; and

(*b*) the issuer's liability at any time for amounts payable under this Act in respect of that business or those businesses shall not exceed the total of

(i) the amount of property of the trust that the issuer is in possession or control of at that time in its capacity as legal representative of the trust, and

(ii) the total amount of all distributions of property from the trust on or after the date that the notice of assessment was sent in respect of the taxation year and before that time.

History: S. 146.2(6.1) was added by S.C. 2019, c. 29, s. 29(1), applicable in respect of business activities in a TFSA for the 2019 and subsequent taxation years.

Related Sections: 146.2(6) Trust not taxable.

► 146.2(7) ◄

(7) Amount credited to a deposit. An amount that is credited or added to a deposit that is a TFSA as interest or other income in respect of the TFSA is deemed not to be received by the holder of the TFSA solely because of that crediting or adding.

History: S. 146.2(7) was replaced by S.C. 2009, c. 2, s. 53(2), applicable to the 2009 and subsequent taxation years. S. 146.2(7) formerly read:

(7) *Annuity contract ceasing to be a TFSA.* If an annuity contract ceases, at a particular time, to be a TFSA,

(*a*) the holder of the TFSA is deemed to have disposed of the contract immediately before the particular time for proceeds equal to its fair market value immediately before the particular time;

(*b*) the contract is deemed to be a separate annuity contract issued and effected at the particular time otherwise than pursuant to or as a TFSA; and

(*c*) each person who has an interest or, for civil law, a right in the separate annuity contract at the particular time is deemed to acquire the interest at the particular time at a cost equal to its fair market value at the particular time.

► 146.2(8) ◄

(8) Trust ceasing to be a TFSA. If an arrangement that governs a trust ceases, at a particular time, to be a TFSA,

(*a*) the trust is deemed

(i) to have disposed, immediately before the particular time, of each property held by the trust for proceeds equal to the property's fair market value immediately before the particular time, and

(ii) to have acquired, at the particular time, each such property at a cost equal to that fair market value;

(*b*) the trust's last taxation year that began before the particular time is deemed to have ended immediately before the particular time; and

(*c*) a taxation year of the trust is deemed to begin at the particular time.

History: S. 146.2(8) was replaced by S.C. 2009, c. 2, s. 53(2), applicable to the 2009 and subsequent taxation years. S. 146.2(8) formerly read:

(8) *Deposit ceasing to be a TFSA.* If a deposit ceases, at a particular time, to be a TFSA,

(*a*) the holder of the TFSA is deemed to have disposed of the deposit immediately before the particular time for proceeds equal to its fair market value immediately before the particular time; and

(*b*) each person who has an interest or, for civil law, a right in the deposit at the particular time is deemed to acquire the interest at the particular time at a cost equal to its fair market value at the particular time.

► 146.2(9) ◄

(9) Trust ceasing to be a TFSA on death of holder. If an arrangement that governs a trust ceases to be a TFSA because of the death of the holder of the TFSA,

(*a*) the arrangement is deemed, for the purposes of subsections (6) and (8), any regulations made under subsection (13), the definition "trust" in subsection 108(1), paragraph 149(1)(*u.2*) and the definitions "qualified investment" and "non-qualified investment" in subsection 207.01(1), to continue to be a TFSA until, and to cease to be a TFSA immediately after, the exemption-end time, being in this subsection the earlier of

(i) the time at which the trust ceases to exist, and

(ii) the end of the first calendar year that begins after the holder dies;

(*b*) there shall be included in computing a taxpayer's income for a taxation year the total of all amounts each of which is an amount determined by the formula

$$A - B$$

where

A is the amount of a payment made out of or under the trust, in satisfaction of all or part of the taxpayer's beneficial interest in the trust, in the taxation year, after the holder's death and at or before the exemption-end time, and

B is an amount designated by the trust not exceeding the lesser of

(i) the amount of the payment, and

(ii) the amount by which the fair market value of all of the property held by the trust immediately before the holder's death exceeds the total of all amounts each of which is the value of B in respect of any other payment made out of or under the trust; and

(*c*) there shall be included in computing the trust's income for its first taxation year, if any, that begins after the exemption-end time the amount determined by the formula

$$A - B$$

where

A is the fair market value of all of the property held by the trust at the exemption-end time, and

B is the amount by which the fair market value of all of the property held by the trust immediately before the holder's death exceeds the total of all amounts each of which is the value of B in paragraph (*b*) in respect of a payment made out of or under the trust.

History: S. 146.2(9) was replaced by S.C. 2009, c. 2, s. 53(2), applicable to the 2009 and subsequent taxation years. S. 146.2(9) formerly read:

(9) *Arrangement is TFSA only.* An arrangement that is a qualifying arrangement at the time it is entered into is deemed not to be a retirement savings plan, an education savings plan, a retirement income fund or a disability savings plan.

Related Regulations: 223(2).

Related Sections: S. 12(1)(z.5) TFSA amounts.

► 146.2(10) ◄

(10) Annuity contract ceasing to be a TFSA. If an annuity contract ceases, at a particular time, to be a TFSA,

(*a*) the holder of the TFSA is deemed to have disposed of the contract immediately before the particular time for proceeds equal to its fair market value immediately before the particular time;

(*b*) the contract is deemed to be a separate annuity contract issued and effected at the particular time otherwise than pursuant to or as a TFSA; and

(*c*) each person who has an interest or, for civil law, a right in the separate annuity contract at the particular time is deemed to acquire the interest at the particular time at a cost equal to its fair market value at the particular time.

History: S. 146.2(10) was added by S.C. 2009, c. 2, s. 53(2), applicable to the 2009 and subsequent taxation years.

► 146.2(11) ◄

(11) Deposit ceasing to be a TFSA. If a deposit ceases, at a particular time, to be a TFSA,

(*a*) the holder of the TFSA is deemed to have disposed of the deposit immediately before the particular time for proceeds equal to its fair market value immediately before the particular time; and

(*b*) each person who has an interest or, for civil law, a right in the deposit at the particular time is deemed to acquire the interest at the particular time at a cost equal to its fair market value at the particular time.

History: S. 146.2(11) was added by S.C. 2009, c. 2, s. 53(2), applicable to the 2009 and subsequent taxation years.

► 146.2(12) ◄

(12) Arrangement is TFSA only. An arrangement that is a qualifying arrangement at the time it is entered into is deemed not to be a retirement savings plan, an education savings plan, a retirement income fund or a disability savings plan.

History: S. 146.2(12) was added by S.C. 2009, c. 2, s. 53(2), applicable to the 2009 and subsequent taxation years.

► 146.2(13) ◄

(13) Regulations. The Governor in Council may make regulations requiring issuers of TFSAs to file information returns in respect of TFSAs.

History: S. 146.2(13) was added by S.C. 2009, c. 2, s. 53(2), applicable to the 2009 and subsequent taxation years.

Related Regulations: 223.

Registered Retirement Income Funds

SECTION 146.3: Registered retirement income funds

► 146.3(1) ◄

(1) Definitions. In this section,

Information Circulars: IC 78-14R4 Guidelines for trust companies and other persons responsible for filing T3GR, T3D, T3P, T3S, T3RI, and T3F returns; IC 78-18R6 Registered Retirement Income Funds.

"annuitant" —"annuitant" under a retirement income fund at any time means

(*a*) the first individual to whom the carrier has undertaken to make payments described in the definition "retirement income fund" out of or under the fund, where the first individual is alive at that time,

(*b*) after the death of the first individual, a spouse or common-law partner (in this definition referred to as the "survivor") of the first individual to whom the carrier has undertaken to make payments described in the definition "retirement income fund" out of or under the fund after the death of the first individual, if the survivor is alive at that time and the undertaking was made

(i) pursuant to an election that is described in that definition and that was made by the first individual, or

(ii) with the consent of the legal representative of the first individual, and

(*c*) after the death of the survivor, another spouse or common-law partner of the survivor to whom the carrier has undertaken, with the consent of the legal representative of the survivor, to make payments described in the definition "retirement income fund" out of or under the fund after the death of the survivor, where that other spouse or common-law partner is alive at that time;

History: S. 146.3(1), paragraph (*b*) of the definition "annuitant" was replaced by S.C. 2013, c. 34, s. 300(1), applicable to the 2001 and subsequent taxation years, except that, if a taxpayer and a person have jointly elected under section 144 of the *Modernization of Benefits and Obligations Act*, in respect of the 1998, 1999 or 2000 taxation years, paragraph (*b*) of the definition "annuitant" applies to the taxpayer and the person in respect of the applicable taxation year and subsequent taxation years. S. 146.3(1), paragraph (*b*) of the definition "annuitant" formerly read:

(*b*) after the death of the first individual, a spouse or common-law partner (in this definition referred to as the "survivor") of the first individual to whom the carrier has undertaken to make payments described in the definition "retirement income fund" out of or under the fund after the death of the first individual, where the survivor is alive at that time and the undertaking was made pursuant to an election described in that definition of the first individual with the consent of the legal representative of the first individual, and

Related Sections: S. 248(1), "common-law partner".

"carrier" —"carrier" of a retirement income fund means

(*a*) a person licensed or otherwise authorized under the laws of Canada or a province to carry on in Canada an annuities business,

(*b*) a corporation licensed or otherwise authorized under the laws of Canada or a province to carry on in Canada the business of offering to the public its services as trustee,

(*c*) a corporation approved by the Governor in Council for the purposes of section 146 that is licensed or otherwise authorized under the laws of Canada or a province to issue investment contracts, or

(*d*) a person referred to as a depositary in section 146,

that has agreed to make payments under a retirement income fund to the individual who is the annuitant under the fund;

Related Sections: S. 146.3(15) Credited or added amount deemed not received.

Forms: T3GR — Group Income Tax and Information Return for RRSP, RRIF, or RESP Trusts; T550 — Application for Registration of: RSP's, ESP's, or RIF's Under Section 146, 146.2 and 146.3 of the Income Tax Act.

"designated benefit" — "designated benefit" of an individual in respect of a registered retirement income fund means the total of

(*a*) such amounts paid out of or under the fund after the death of the last annuitant thereunder to the legal representative of that annuitant

(i) as would, had they been paid under the fund to the individual, have been refunds of premiums (in this paragraph having the meaning assigned by subsection 146(1)) if the fund were a registered retirement savings plan that had not matured before the death, and

(ii) as are designated jointly by the legal representative and the individual in prescribed form filed with the Minister, and

(*b*) amounts paid out of or under the fund after the death of the last annuitant thereunder to the individual that would be refunds of premiums had the fund been a registered retirement savings plan that had not matured before the death;

Related Sections: S. 60(*l*) Transfer of refund of premiums under RRSP; s. 146.3(6.11) Transfer of designated benefit; s. 146.3(6.1) Designated benefit deemed received; s. 146.3(6.2) Amount deductible.

Forms: T1090 — Death of an RRIF Annuitant — Designated Benefit.

"minimum amount" — "minimum amount" under a retirement income fund for a year means, for the year in which the fund was entered into, a nil amount, and, for any other year, the amount determined by the formula

$$(A \times B) + C$$

where

A is the total fair market value of all properties held in connection with the fund at the beginning of the year (other than annuity contracts held by a trust governed by the fund that, at the beginning of the year, are not described in paragraph (*b*.1) of the definition "qualified investment");

B is

(*a*) where the first annuitant under the fund elected in respect of the fund under paragraph (*b*) of the definition "minimum amount" in this subsection, as it read before 1992, or under subparagraph 146.3(1)(*f*)(i) of the *Income Tax Act*, chapter 148 of the Revised Statutes of Canada, 1952, to use the age of another individual, the prescribed factor for the year in respect of the other individual,

(*b*) where paragraph (*a*) does not apply and the first annuitant under the fund so elects before any payment has been made under the fund by the carrier, the prescribed factor for the year in respect of an individual who was the spouse or common-law partner of the first annuitant at the time of the election, and

(*c*) in any other case, the prescribed factor for the year in respect of the first annuitant under the fund, and

C is, where the fund governs a trust, the total of all amounts each of which is

(*a*) a periodic payment under an annuity contract held by the trust at the beginning of the year (other than an annuity contract described at the beginning of the year in paragraph (*b*.1) of the definition "qualified investment") that is paid to the trust in the year, or

(*b*) if the periodic payment under such an annuity contract is not made to the trust because the trust disposed of the right to that payment in the year, a reasonable estimate of that payment on the assumption that the annuity contract had been held throughout the year and no rights under the contract were disposed of in the year;

Editorial Note: The minimum amount that must be withdrawn from a RIF increases annually until reaching a withdrawal requirement of 20% of the assets in the fund at age 95 (and over). There are two schedules of minimum payments prescribed in the Regulations (7308); one for "qualifying" RIFs (RIFs entered into prior to 1993, where the carrier has not accepted any property for the fund after 1992 and other RIFs, where the only property accepted by the carrier has been transferred from another qualifying RIF) and the second for other RIFs. Payments may be made until the latest of the death of the first annuitant, the surviving spouse or common-law partner (the "survivor"), the spouse or common-law partner of the survivor or the fund's assets are depleted.

Related Regulations: 7308.

Related Sections: S. 56(1)(*h*) Registered retirement savings plan, etc.; s. 56(1)(*t*) Registered retirement income fund; s. 146.3(1), "annuitant"; s. 146.3(2)(*e*), (*e*.1) and (*e*.2); Acceptance of fund for registration; s. 146.3(5.1) Amount included in income; s. 248(1), "common-law partner".

Canadian Tax Foundation: Milevsky, *Rethinking RRIF Withdrawals: New Rates and Methodologies for New Realities*, 2014 Canadian Tax Journal 4:971-983.

Information Circulars: IC 78-18R6 Registered retirement income funds.

Interpretation Bulletins: *Secondary* — IT-528 Transfers of funds between registered plans.

Tax Window Files: T4RIFs and theoretical value for min amount, *February 21, 2017*, CRA Document No. 2016-0669361E5.

"property held" — "property held" in connection with a retirement income fund means property held by the carrier of the fund, whether held by the carrier as trustee or beneficial owner thereof, the value of which, or the income or loss from which, is relevant in determining the amount for a year payable to the annuitant under the fund;

Related Regulations: 7308.

Related Sections: S. 40(2)(*g*)(iv) Limitations.

"qualified investment" — "qualified investment" for a trust governed by a registered retirement income fund means

(*a*) an investment that would be described by any of paragraphs (*a*) to (*d*), (*f*) and (*g*) of the definition "qualified investment" in section 204 if the reference in that definition to "a trust governed by a deferred profit sharing plan or revoked plan" were read as a reference to "a trust governed by a registered retirement income fund" and if that definition were read without reference to the words "with the exception of excluded property in relation to the trust",

(*b*) (Repealed.)

(*b*.1) a contract for an annuity issued by a licensed annuities provider where

(i) the trust is the only person who, disregarding any subsequent transfer of the contract by the trust, is or may become entitled to any annuity payments under the contract, and

(ii) the holder of the contract has a right to surrender the contract at any time for an amount that would, if reasonable sales and administration charges were ignored, approximate the value of funds that could otherwise be applied to fund future periodic payments under the contract,

(*b*.2) a contract for an annuity issued by a licensed annuities provider where

(i) annual or more frequent periodic payments are or may be made under the contract to the holder of the contract,

(ii) the trust is the only person who, disregarding any subsequent transfer of the contract by the trust, is or may become entitled to any annuity payments under the contract,

(iii) neither the time nor the amount of any payment under the contract may vary because of the length of any life, other than

(A) if the annuitant under the fund (in this paragraph referred to as the "RRIF annuitant") has made the election referred to in the definition "retirement income fund" in respect of the fund and a spouse or common-law partner, the life of the RRIF annuitant or the life of the spouse or common-law partner, and

(B) in any other case, the life of the RRIF annuitant,

(iv) the day on which the periodic payments began or are to begin (in this paragraph referred to as the "start date") is not later than the end of the year following the year in which the contract was acquired by the trust,

(v) either

(A) the periodic payments are payable for the life of the RRIF annuitant or the joint lives of the RRIF annuitant and the RRIF annuitant's spouse or common-law partner and either there is no guaranteed period under the contract or there is a guaranteed period that begins at the start date and does not exceed a term equal to 90 years minus the lesser of

(I) the age in whole years at the start date of the RRIF annuitant (determined on the assumption that the RRIF annuitant is alive at the start date), and

(II) the age in whole years at the start date of a spouse or common-law partner of the RRIF annuitant (determined on the assumption that a spouse or common-law partner of the RRIF annuitant at the time the contract was acquired is a spouse or common-law partner of the RRIF annuitant at the start date), or

(B) the periodic payments are payable for a term equal to

(I) 90 years minus the age described in subclause (A)(I), or

(II) 90 years minus the age described in subclause (A)(II), and

(vi) the periodic payments

(A) are equal, or

(B) are not equal solely because of one or more adjustments that would, if the contract were an annuity under a retirement savings plan, be in accordance with subparagraphs 146(3)(*b*)(iii) to (v) or that arise because of a uniform reduction in the entitlement to the periodic payments as a consequence of a partial surrender of rights to the periodic payments, and

(*c*) such other investments as may be prescribed by regulations of the Governor in Council made on the recommendation of the Minister of Finance;

Proposed Amendment

2019 Federal Budget Resolutions

The Act is modified to give effect to the proposals relating to permitting additional types of annuities under registered plans described in the budget documents tabled by the Minister of Finance in the House of Commons on Budget Day.

Explanatory Note:
Dentons Canada LLP Commentary

Budget 2019 proposes to provide "qualified investment" status to the following additional types of annuities for certain registered plans, effective for 2020 and subsequent taxation years:

- advanced life deferred annuities will be permitted under a registered retirement savings plan (RRSP), registered retirement income fund (RRIF), deferred profit sharing plan (DPSP), pooled registered pension plan (PRPP) and defined contribution registered pension plan (RPP); and
- variable payment life annuities will be permitted under a PRPP and defined contribution RPP.

Advanced Life Deferred Annuities (ALDA)

The tax rules generally require an annuity purchased with a registered plan to commence by the end of the year in which the annuitant attains 71 years of age. An ALDA will be a life annuity the commencement of which may be deferred until the end of the year in which the annuitant turns 85 and meets certain other prescribed conditions. A lifetime limit of 25% of the value of the plan (including payments for the ALDA) and $150,000 will apply.

Annuity payments to a surviving spouse or common-law partner will be taxable in the year of receipt. Lump-sum payments to a surviving spouse, common-law partner or dependent child or grandchild (provided that the child or grandchild is dependent by reason of physical or mental infirmity) will qualify for a tax-deferred transfer to an RRSP, RRIF or other eligible vehicle of the annuitant.

Variable Payment Life Annuity (VPLA)

Existing rules generally require retirement benefits from a PRPP or defined contribution RPP be provided to a member by means of a transfer of funds from the account to an RRSP or RRIF. Budget 2019 proposes that commencing in 2020 and subsequent years, PRPP and RPPs be able to provide a VPLA directly to members from the plan. A VPLA will provide payments that vary based on the investment performance of the underlying annuities fund and on the mortality experience of VPLA annuitants.

PRPP and defined contribution RPP administrators will be permitted to establish a separate annuities fund under the plan to receive transfers of amounts from members' accounts to provide for VPLAs. A minimum of 10 retired members will be required to participate in a VPLA. VPLAs will be required to comply with certain existing tax rules applicable to PRPPs and defined contribution RPPs, as well as additional requirements. On death, VPLAs will be subject to the existing tax treatment of annuities purchased with PRPP and defined contribution RPP savings.

Editorial Note: The definition of "qualified investment" for a trust governed by a RRIF incorporates by reference much of the similar definition in s. 204 that applies to deferred profit sharing plans. The definition also includes investments that are prescribed under Part XLIX (s. 4900) of the Regulations.

Related Regulations: 221; 4900(1), (2), (4), (6), (9), (14).

Related Sections: S. 87(10) Share deemed listed; s. 146.3(1), "annuitant", "common-law partner", "minimum amount"; 146.3(9) Tax payable on income from non-qualified investment; s. 207.1(4) Tax payable by trust under registered retirement income fund. See also related matter for subsection 146.3(7), Acquisition of non-qualified investment by trust.

Canadian Tax Foundation: De Lisser and Krieger, *Registered Savings Plans: Investing Without Penalty*, 2013 Canadian Tax Journal 3:769–796.

Tax Profile: August 2004 — Canadian Tax Treatment of Index Participation Units and Exchange-Traded Index Derivatives.

Forms: T3F — Investments Prescribed to be Qualified or not to be Foreign Property Information Return.

Income Tax Folios: *Primary* — S3-F10-C1 Qualified Investments – RRSPs, RESPs, RRIFs, RDSPs and TFSAs. *Secondary* — S3-F10-C2 Prohibited Investments - RRSPs, RRIFs and TFSAs.

Information Circulars: IC 78-18R6 Registered retirement income funds.

"registered retirement income fund" —"registered retirement income fund" means a retirement income fund accepted by the Minister for registration for the purposes of this Act and registered under the Social Insurance Number of the first annuitant under the fund;

Editorial Note: A registered retirement income fund is one of the retirement options for funds accumulated in a registered retirement savings plan (s. 146) before it reaches maturity, or for funds transferred from certain other deferred income plans, including a registered pension plan (see s. 146.3(2)(*f*)). Payments from the plan are taxable when received (s. 146.3(5) — see also the definition of "minimum amount"). The annuitant will also be taxable if the plan uses its property as security for a loan (s. 146.3(7)), buys or sells property at other than fair market value (s. 146.3(4)), acquires a prohibited or non-qualified investment (s. 207.04(1)) or extends an advantage on the annuitant or a person not at arm's length with the annuitant (s. 207.05(1)).

Interpretation Bulletins: *Secondary* — IT-528 Transfers of funds between registered plans.

"retirement income fund" —"retirement income fund" means an arrangement between a carrier and an annuitant under which, in consideration for the transfer to the carrier of property, the carrier undertakes to pay amounts to the annuitant (and, where the annuitant so elects, to the annuitant's spouse or common-law partner after the annuitant's death), the total of which is, in each year in which the minimum amount under the arrangement for the year is greater than nil, not less than the minimum amount under the arrangement for that year, but the amount of any such payment does not exceed the value of the property held in connection with the arrangement immediately before the time of the payment.

Related Sections: S. 146.3(1), "annuitant", "carrier", "common-law partner", "minimum amount"; s. 146.3(2)(*a*) Acceptance of fund for registration.

Information Circulars: IC 78-18R6 Registered retirement income funds.

Tax Window Files: T4RIFs and theoretical value for min amount, *February 21, 2017*, CRA Document No. 2016-0669361E5.

► 146.3(1.1) ◄

(1.1) Adjusted minimum amount for 2008. The minimum amount under a retirement income fund for 2008 is 75 per cent of the amount that would, in the absence of this subsection, be the minimum amount under the fund for the year.

History: S. 146.3(1.1) was added by S.C. 2009, c. 2, s. 54(1), in force on Royal Assent, March 12, 2009.

Related Sections: S. 60.021.

► 146.3(1.2) ◄

(1.2) Exceptions. Subsection (1.1) does not apply to a retirement income fund

(*a*) for the purposes of subsections (5.1) and 153(1) and the definition "periodic pension payment" in section 5 of the *Income Tax Conventions Interpretation Act*; nor

(*b*) if the individual who was the annuitant under the fund on January 1, 2008 attained 70 years of age in 2007.

History: S. 146.3(1.2) was added by S.C. 2009, c. 2, s. 54(1), in force on Royal Assent, March 12, 2009.

► 146.3(1.3) ◄

(1.3) Exceptions. For the purposes of subsections (5.1) and 153(1) and the definition "periodic pension payment" in section 5 of the *Income Tax Conventions Interpretation Act*, the minimum amount under a retirement income fund for 2015 is the amount that would be the minimum amount under the fund for the year if it were determined using the prescribed factors under subsection 7308(3) or (4), as the case may be, of the *Income Tax Regulations* as they read on December 31, 2014.

History: S. 146.3(1.3) was added by S.C. 2015, c. 36, s. 15, in force on Royal Assent, June 23, 2015.

► 146.3(2) ◄

(2) Acceptance of fund for registration. The Minister shall not accept for registration for the purposes of this Act any retirement income fund of an individual unless, in the Minister's opinion, the following conditions are complied with:

(*a*) the fund provides that the carrier shall make only those payments described in any of paragraphs (*d*) and (*e*), the definition "retirement income fund" in subsection (1), and subsections (14) and (14.1);

(*b*) the fund provides that payments thereunder may not be assigned in whole or in part;

(*c*) if the carrier is a person referred to as a depositary in section 146, the fund provides that

(i) the carrier has no right of offset as regards the property held in connection with the fund in respect of any debt or obligation owing to the carrier, and

(ii) the property held in connection with the fund cannot be pledged, assigned or in any way alienated as security for a loan or for any purpose other than that of the making by the carrier to the annuitant those payments described in paragraph (*a*);

(*d*) the fund provides that, except where the annuitant's spouse or common-law partner becomes the annuitant under the fund, the carrier shall, as a consequence of the death of the annuitant, distribute the property held in connection with the fund at the time of the annuitant's death or an amount equal to the value of such property at that time;

(*e*) the fund provides that, at the direction of the annuitant, the carrier shall transfer all or part of the property held in connection with the fund, or an amount equal to its value at the time of the direction (other than property required to be retained in accordance with the provision described in paragraph (*e*.1) or (*e*.2)), together with all information necessary for the continuance of the fund, to a person who has agreed to be a carrier of another registered retirement income fund of the annuitant;

(*e*.1) where the fund does not govern a trust or the fund governs a trust created before 1998 that does not hold an annuity contract as a qualified investment for the trust, the fund provides that if an annuitant, at any time, directs that the carrier transfer all or part of the property held in connection with the fund, or an amount equal to its value at that time, to a person who has agreed to be a carrier of another registered retirement income fund of the annuitant or to a registered pension plan in accordance with subsection (14.1), the transferor shall retain an amount equal to the lesser of

(i) the fair market value of such portion of the property as would, if the fair market value thereof does not decline after the transfer, be sufficient to ensure that the minimum amount under the fund for the year in which the transfer is made may be paid to the annuitant in the year, and

(ii) the fair market value of all the property;

(*e*.2) where paragraph (*e*.1) does not apply, the fund provides that if an annuitant, at any time, directs that the carrier transfer all or part of the property held in connection with the fund, or an amount equal to its value at that time, to a person who has agreed to be a carrier of another registered retirement income fund of the annuitant or to a registered pension plan in accordance with subsection (14.1), the transferor shall retain property in the fund sufficient to ensure that the total of

(i) all amounts each of which is the fair market value, immediately after the transfer, of a property held in connection with the fund that is

(A) property other than an annuity contract, or

(B) an annuity contract described, immediately after the transfer, in paragraph (*b*.1) of the definition "qualified investment" in subsection (1), and

(ii) all amounts each of which is a reasonable estimate, as of the time of the transfer, of the amount of an annual or more frequent periodic payment under an annuity contract (other than an annuity contract described in clause (i)(B)) that the trust may receive after the transfer and in the year of the transfer

is not less than the amount, if any, by which the minimum amount under the fund for that year exceeds the total of all amounts received out of or under the fund before the transfer that are included in computing the income of the annuitant under the fund for that year;

(*f*) the fund provides that the carrier shall not accept property as consideration thereunder other than property transferred from

(i) a registered retirement savings plan under which the individual is the annuitant,

(ii) another registered retirement income fund under which the individual is the annuitant,

(iii) the individual to the extent only that the amount of the consideration was an amount described in subparagraph 60(*l*)(v),

(iv) a registered retirement income fund or registered retirement savings plan of the individual's spouse or common-law partner or former spouse or common-law partner under a decree, order or judgment of a competent tribunal, or under a written separation agreement, relating to a division of property between the individual and the individual's spouse or common-law partner or former spouse or common-law partner in settlement of rights arising out of, or on the breakdown of, their marriage or common-law partnership,

(iv.1) a deferred profit sharing plan in accordance with subsection 147(19),

(v) a registered pension plan of which the individual is a member (within the meaning assigned by subsection 147.1(1)),

(vi) a registered pension plan in accordance with subsection 147.3(5) or (7),

(vii) a specified pension plan in circumstances to which subsection 146(21) applies, or

(viii) a pooled registered pension plan in accordance with subsection 147.5(21);

(*g*) (Repealed.)

(*h*) the fund in all other respects complies with regulations of the Governor in Council made on the recommendation of the Minister of Finance.

History: S. 146.3(2)(*c*), the portion before subparagraph (i) was replaced by S.C. 2013, c. 34, s. 300(2), deemed to have come into force on January 1, 2002, and formerly read:

(*c*) where the carrier is a person referred to as a depository in section 146, the fund provides that

S. 146.3(2)(*f*)(iv.1) was added by S.C. 2013, c. 34, s. 300(3), deemed to have come into force on March 21, 2003.

S. 146.3(2)(*f*)(viii) was added by S.C. 2012, c. 31, s. 34(1), in force December 14, 2012.

S. 146.3(2)(*f*)(vii) was replaced by S.C. 2011, c. 24, s. 49(1), applicable to taxation years that begin after 2009. S. 146.3(2)(*f*)(vii) formerly read:

(vii) a provincial pension plan in circumstances to which subsection 146(21) applies;

S. 146.3(2)(*g*) was repealed by S.C. 2011, c. 24, s. 49(2), deemed to have come into force on March 23, 2011. S. 146.3(2)(*g*) formerly read:

(*g*) the fund requires that no benefit or loan, other than

(i) a benefit the amount of which is required to be included in computing the annuitant's income,

(ii) an amount referred to in paragraph (5)(*a*) or (*b*), or

(iii) the benefit derived from the provision of administrative or investment services in respect of the fund,

that is conditional in any way on the existence of the fund may be extended to the annuitant or to a person with whom the annuitant was not dealing at arm's length; and

Related Regulations: 4900(1), (2), (4), (6), (9), (10), (12), (13); 7308.

Related Sections: S. 139.1(13) RRSP registration rules, etc; s. 146.3(13) Deemed creation of new plan — prohibited loans or benefits; s. 146.3(14.2) Taxation of amount transferred; s. 146(16) Transfer of funds; s. 172(3) Appeal from refusal to register, revocation of registration, etc.; s. 172(4) Deemed refusal to register — no notification within 180 days; s. 248(1), "common-law partner"; s. 252(3) Extended meaning of "spouse" and "former spouse"; Part X.2 — Tax in Respect of Registered Investments; Part XI — Tax in Respect of Certain Property Acquired by Trusts, etc., Governed by Deferred Income Plans.

Canadian Tax Foundation: Kaplan, *Registered Retirement Income Funds: An Update*, 1999 Canadian Tax Journal 1:134–147.

Forms: T550 — Application for Registration of: RSP's, ESP's, or RIF's Under Section 146, 146.2 and 146.3 of the Income Tax Act; T2033 — Direct Transfer under subsection 46.3(14.1) or paragraph 146(16)(a) or 146.3(2)(e).

Guides: T4040 RRSPs and Other Registered Plans for Retirement.

Information Circulars: IC 78-18R6 Registered retirement income funds.

► 146.3(3) ◄

(3) No tax while trust governed by fund. Except as provided in subsection (9), no tax is payable under this Part by a trust on the taxable income of the trust for a taxation year if, throughout the period in the year during which the trust was in existence, the trust was governed by a registered retirement income fund of an individual, except that if the trust has

(*a*) borrowed money in the year or has borrowed money that it has not repaid before the commencement of the year,

(*b*) received a gift of property (other than a transfer from a registered retirement savings plan under which the individual is the annuitant (within the meaning of subsection 146(1)) or a transfer from a registered retirement income fund under which the individual is the annuitant)

(i) in the year, or

(ii) in a preceding year and has not divested itself of the property or any property substituted therefor before the commencement of the year, or

(*c*) carried on any business or businesses in the year,

tax is payable under this Part by the trust,

(*d*) where paragraph (*a*) or (*b*) applies, on its taxable income for the year, and

(*e*) where neither paragraph (*a*) nor (*b*) applies and where paragraph (*c*) applies, on the amount, if any, by which

(i) the amount that its taxable income for the year would be if it had no incomes or losses from sources other than from the business or businesses, as the case may be,

exceeds

(ii) such portion of the amount determined under subparagraph (i) in respect of the trust for the year as can reasonably be considered to be income from, or from the disposition of, qualified investments for the trust.

Related Sections: S. 107.4(2) Application of paragraph (1)(a); s. 138.1(7) Where ss. (1) to (6) do not apply; s. 146.3(3.1) Exception; s. 149(1)(*x*) Registered retirement income funds; s. 207.1(4) Tax payable by trust under registered retirement income fund; Part X.1 Tax in Respect of Over-Contributions to Deferred Income Plans; Part X.2 Tax in Respect of Registered Investments; Part X.3 Labour-Sponsored Venture Capital Corporations.

Information Circulars: IC 78-14R4 Guidelines for trust companies and other persons responsible for filing T3GR, T3D, T3P, T3S, T3RI, and T3F returns; IC 78-18R6 Registered retirement income funds.

► 146.3(3.1) ◄

(3.1) Exception. Notwithstanding subsection (3), if the last annuitant under a registered retirement income fund has died, tax is payable under this Part by the trust governed by the fund on its taxable income for each year after the year following the year in which the last annuitant under the fund died.

Related Sections: S. 104(6)(*a.2*) Deduction in computing income of trust; s. 146.3(5) Benefits taxable.

► 146.3(4) ◄

(4) Disposition or acquisition of property by trust. Where at any time in a taxation year a trust governed by a registered retirement income fund

(*a*) disposes of property for a consideration less than the fair market value of the property at the time of the disposition, or for no consideration, or

(*b*) acquires property for a consideration greater than the fair market value of the property at the time of the acquisition,

2 times the difference between that fair market value and the consideration, if any, shall be included in computing the income for the taxation year of the taxpayer who is the annuitant under the fund at that time.

Related Regulations: 215(3).

Related Sections: S. 107.4(2) Application of paragraph (1)(a); s. 214(3)(i) Deemed payments; s. 248(25.1) Trust-to-trust transfers.

Forms: T4RIF Summ. — Summary of Income from a Registered Retirement Income Fund; T4RIF — Statement of Income from a Registered Retirement Income Fund.

Guides: T4079 T4RSP and T4RIF Guide.

Information Circulars: IC 78-18R6 Registered retirement income funds.

► 146.3(5) ◄

(5) Benefits taxable. There shall be included in computing the income of a taxpayer for a taxation year all amounts received by the taxpayer in the year out of or under a registered retirement income fund other than the portion thereof that can reasonably be regarded as

(*a*) part of the amount included in computing the income of another taxpayer by virtue of subsections (6) and (6.2);

(*b*) an amount received in respect of the income of the trust under the fund for a taxation year for which the trust was not exempt from tax by virtue of subsection (3.1);

(*c*) an amount that relates to interest, or to another amount included in computing income otherwise than because of this section, and that would, if the fund were a registered retirement savings plan, be a tax-paid amount (within the meaning assigned by paragraph (*b*) of the definition "tax-paid amount" in subsection 146(1)); or

(*d*) an amount in respect of which the annuitant pays a tax under Part XI.01, unless the tax is waived, cancelled or refunded.

History: S. 146.3(5)(*d*) was added by S.C. 2011, c. 24, s. 49(3), applicable to transactions occurring, income earned, capital gains accruing and investments acquired after March 22, 2011.

Related Regulations: 202(2), (3); 215(2).

Related Sections: S. 56(1)(*t*) Registered retirement income fund; s. 75(3) Exceptions; s. 118(3) Pension credit; s. 118(7), "pension income"; s. 128.1(10) Definitions; s. 139.1(14) Retirement benefit; s. 146.3(2)(*g*) Acceptance of fund for registration; s. 146.3(6.11) Transfer of designated benefit; s. 153(1)(*l*) Withholding; s. 160.2(2) Joint and several liability in respect of amounts received out of or under RRIF; s. 212(1)(*q*) Registered retirement income fund payments.

Canadian Tax Foundation: Van Cauwenberghe, *Estate Planning — Tips and Traps*, 2012 Ontario Tax Conference 8:1–40.

Forms: T4RIF Summ. — Summary of Income from a Registered Retirement Income Fund; T4RIF — Statement of Income from a Registered Retirement Income Fund.

Guides: T4079 T4RSP and T4RIF Guide.

Income Tax Technical News: Issue No. 39, Settlement of a Shareholder Class Action Suit — Compensation by Way of Cash and Shares.

▶ 146.3(5.1) ◀

(5.1) Amount included in income. If at any time in a taxation year a particular amount in respect of a registered retirement income fund that is a spousal or common-law partner plan (within the meaning assigned by subsection 146(1)) in relation to a taxpayer is required to be included in the income of the taxpayer's spouse or common-law partner and the taxpayer is not living separate and apart from the taxpayer's spouse or common-law partner at that time by reason of the breakdown of their marriage or common-law partnership, there shall be included at that time in computing the taxpayer's income for the year an amount equal to the least of

(*a*) the total of all amounts each of which is a premium (within the meaning assigned by subsection 146(1)) paid by the taxpayer in the year or in one of the two immediately preceding taxation years to a registered retirement savings plan under which the taxpayer's spouse or common-law partner was the annuitant (within the meaning assigned by subsection 146(1)) at the time the premium was paid,

(*b*) the particular amount, and

(*c*) the amount, if any, by which

(i) the total of all amounts each of which is an amount in respect of the fund that is required, in the year and at or before that time, to be included in the income of the taxpayer's spouse or common-law partner

exceeds

(ii) the minimum amount under the fund for the year.

History: S. 146.3(5.1), the portion before paragraph (*a*) was replaced by S.C. 2013, c. 34, s. 300(4), applicable to the 2001 and subsequent taxation years, except that, if a taxpayer and a person have jointly elected under section 144 of the *Modernization of Benefits and Obligations Act*, in respect of the 1998, 1999 or 2000 taxation years, the portion of section 146.3(5.1) before paragraph (*a*) applies to the taxpayer and the person in respect of the applicable taxation year and subsequent taxation years. S. 146.3(5.1), the portion before paragraph (*a*) formerly read:

> (5.1) *Amount included in income.* Where at any time in a taxation year a particular amount in respect of a registered retirement income fund that is a spousal plan (within the meaning assigned by subsection 146(1)) in relation to a taxpayer is required to be included in the income of the taxpayer's spouse or common-law partner and the taxpayer is not living separate and apart from the taxpayer's spouse or common-law partner at that time by reason of the breakdown of their marriage or common-law partnership, there shall be included at that time in computing the taxpayer's income for the year an amount equal to the least of

Related Regulations: 7308.

Related Sections: S. 118.1(5.3) Direct designation — RRSPs, RRIFs and TFSAs; s. 128.1(10) Definitions; s. 146(1), "minimum amount"; s. 146(1.1) Restriction — financially dependent; s. 146.3(5.3) Ordering; s. 146.3(5.4) Spouse's income; s. 146.3(5.5) Where s. (5.1) does not apply; s. 146(8.21) Premium deemed not paid; s. 146(8.6) Spouse's income; s. 153(1)(*l*) Withholding; s. 212(1)(*q*) Registered retirement income fund payments s. 252(3) Extended meaning of "spouse" and "former spouse"; s. 248(1), "common-law partner".

Interpretation Bulletins: *Secondary* — IT-124R6 Contributions to registered retirement savings plans; IT-307R4 Spousal or common-law partner registered retirement savings plans.

▶ 146.3(5.2) ◀

(5.2) Interpretation — (Repealed by 1990, c. 35, s. 14(4).)

▶ 146.3(5.3) ◀

(5.3) Ordering. Where a taxpayer has paid more than one premium described in subsection (5.1), such a premium or part thereof paid by the taxpayer at any time shall be deemed to have been included in computing the taxpayer's income by virtue of that subsection before premiums or parts thereof paid by the taxpayer after that time.

▶ 146.3(5.4) ◀

(5.4) Spouse's [or common-law partner's] income. Where, in respect of an amount required at any time in a taxation year to be included in computing the income of a taxpayer's spouse or common-law partner, all or part of a premium has, by reason of subsection (5.1), been included in computing the taxpayer's income for the year, the following rules apply:

(*a*) the premium or part thereof, as the case may be, shall, for the purposes of subsections (5.1) and 146(8.3) after that time, be deemed not to have been a premium paid to a registered retirement savings plan under which the taxpayer's spouse or common-law partner was the annuitant (within the meaning assigned by subsection 146(1)); and

(*b*) an amount equal to the premium or part thereof, as the case may be, may be deducted in computing the income of the spouse or common-law partner for the year.

▶ 146.3(5.5) ◀

(5.5) Where s. (5.1) does not apply. Subsection (5.1) does not apply

(*a*) in respect of a taxpayer at any time during the year in which the taxpayer dies;

(*b*) in respect of a taxpayer where either the taxpayer or the annuitant is a non-resident at the particular time referred to in that subsection;

(*c*) to any payment that is received in full or partial commutation of a registered retirement savings plan or a registered retirement income fund and in respect of which a deduction was made under paragraph 60(*l*) if, where the deduction was in respect of the acquisition of an annuity, the terms of the annuity provide that it cannot be commuted, and it is not commuted, in whole or in part within 3 years after the acquisition; or

(*d*) in respect of an amount that is deemed by subsection (6) to have been received by an annuitant under a registered retirement income fund immediately before the annuitant's death.

▶ 146.3(6) ◀

(6) Where last annuitant dies. Where the last annuitant under a registered retirement income fund dies, that annuitant shall be deemed to have received, immediately before death, an amount out of or under a registered retirement income fund equal to the fair market value of the property of the fund at the time of the death.

Related Regulations: 215(4).

Related Sections: S. 118.1(5.3) Direct designation — RRSPs, RRIFs and TFSAs; s. 146.3(5)(*a*) Benefits taxable; s. 146.3(5.5) Where s. (5.1) does not apply; s. 146.3(6.2)Amount deductible; s. 160.2(2) Joint and several liability in respect of amounts received out of or under RRIF; s. 214(3)(*i*) Deemed payments.

Canadian Tax Foundation: Van Cauwenberghe, *Estate Planning — Tips and Traps*, 2012 Ontario Tax Conference 8:1–40.

Forms: T4RIF Summ. — Summary of Income from a Registered Retirement Income Fund; T4RIF — Statement of Income from a Registered Retirement Income Fund.

Guides: RC4178 Death of an RRIF Annuitant.

Information Circulars: IC 78-18R6 Registered retirement income funds.

► 146.3(6.1) ◄

(6.1) Designated benefit deemed received. A designated benefit of an individual in respect of a registered retirement income fund that is received by the legal representative of the last annuitant under the fund shall be deemed

(*a*) to be received by the individual out of or under the fund at the time it is received by the legal representative; and

(*b*) except for the purpose of the definition "designated benefit" in subsection (1), not to be received out of or under the fund by any other person.

Related Sections: S. 214(3)(*i*) Deemed payments.

► 146.3(6.11) ◄

(6.11) Transfer of designated benefit. For the purpose of subparagraph 60(*l*)(v), the eligible amount of a particular individual for a taxation year in respect of a registered retirement income fund is nil unless the particular individual was

(*a*) a spouse or common-law partner of the last annuitant under the fund, or

(*b*) a child or grandchild of that annuitant who was dependent because of physical or mental infirmity on that annuitant,

in which case the eligible amount shall be determined by the formula

$$A \times [1 - ((B - C) / D)]$$

where

A is the portion of the designated benefit of the particular individual in respect of the fund that is included because of subsection (5) in computing the particular individual's income for the year,

B is the minimum amount under the fund for the year,

C is the lesser of

(*a*) the total amounts included because of subsection (5) in computing the income of an annuitant under the fund for the year in respect of amounts received by the annuitant out of or under the fund, and

(*b*) the minimum amount under the fund for the year, and

D is the total of all amounts each of which is the portion of a designated benefit of an individual in respect of the fund that is included because of subsection (5) in computing the individual's income for the year.

Related Regulations: 7308.

Related Sections: S. 60(*l*) Transfer of refund of premiums under RRSP; s. 146(1.1) Restriction — financially dependent; s. 146.3(1), "annuitant", "designated benefit", "minimum amount"; s. 248(1), "common-law partner".

► 146.3(6.2) ◄

(6.2) Amount deductible. There may be deducted from the amount deemed by subsection (6) to be received by an annuitant out of or under a registered retirement income fund an amount not exceeding the amount determined by the formula

$$A \times [1 - ((B + C - D) / (B + C))]$$

where

A is the total of

(*a*) all designated benefits of individuals in respect of the fund,

(*b*) all amounts that would, if the fund were a registered retirement savings plan, be tax-paid amounts (in this subsection having the meaning assigned by subsection 146(1)) in respect of the fund received by individuals who received, otherwise than because of subsection (6.1), designated benefits in respect of the fund, and

(*c*) all amounts each of which is an amount that would, if the fund were a registered retirement savings plan, be a tax-paid amount in respect of the fund received by the legal representative of the last annuitant under the fund, to the extent that the legal representative would have been entitled to designate that tax-paid amount under paragraph (*a*) of the definition "designated benefit" in subsection (1) if tax-paid amounts were not excluded in determining refunds of premiums (as defined in subsection 146(1));

B is the fair market value of the property of the fund at the particular time that is the later of

(*a*) the end of the first calendar year that begins after the death of the annuitant, and

(*b*) the time immediately after the last time that any designated benefit in respect of the fund is received by an individual;

C is the total of all amounts paid out of or under the fund after the death of the last annuitant thereunder and before the particular time; and

D is the lesser of

(*a*) the fair market value of the property of the fund at the time of the death of the last annuitant thereunder, and

(*b*) the sum of the values of B and C in respect of the fund.

Related Sections: S. 146.3(5)(*a*) Benefits taxable; s. 146.3(6) Where last annuitant dies.

► 146.3(6.3) ◄

(6.3) Deduction for post-death reduction in value. If the last annuitant under a registered retirement income fund dies, there may be deducted in computing the annuitant's income for the taxation year in which the annuitant dies an amount not exceeding the amount determined, after all amounts payable out of or under the fund have been paid, by the formula

$$A - B$$

where

A is the total of all amounts each of which is

(*a*) the amount deemed by subsection (6) to have been received by the annuitant out of or under the fund,

(*b*) an amount (other than an amount described in paragraph (*c*)) received, after the death of the annuitant, by a taxpayer out of or under the fund and included, because of subsection (5), in computing the taxpayer's income, or

(*c*) an amount that would, if the fund were a registered retirement savings plan, be a tax-paid amount (within the meaning assigned by subsection 146(1)) in respect of the fund; and

B is the total of all amounts paid out of or under the fund after the death of the annuitant.

History: S. 146.3(6.3) was added by S.C. 2009, c. 2, s. 54(2), applicable in respect of a registered retirement income fund in respect of which the last payment out of the fund is made after 2008.

Related Regulations: 215(6).

Related Sections: S. 60(*l*) Premium or payment under RRSP or RRIF; s. 146(8.92) Deduction for post-death reduction in value.

► 146.3(6.4) ◄

(6.4) Subsection (6.3) not applicable. Except where the Minister has waived in writing the application of this subsection with respect to all or any portion of the amount determined in subsection (6.3) in respect of a registered retirement income fund, that subsection does not apply if

(*a*) at any time after the death of the annuitant, a trust governed by the fund held an investment that is not a qualified investment; or

(*b*) the last payment out of or under the fund was made after the end of the year following the year in which the annuitant died.

History: S. 146.3(6.4) was added by S.C. 2009, c. 2, s. 54(2), applicable in respect of a registered retirement income fund in respect of which the last payment out of the fund is made after 2008.

► 146.3(7) ◄

(7) Property used as security for loan. If at any time in a taxation year a trust governed by a registered retirement income fund uses or permits to be used any property of the trust as security for a loan, the fair market value of the property at the time it commenced to be so used shall be included in computing the income for the year of the taxpayer who is the annuitant under the fund at that time.

History: S. 146.3(7) was replaced by S.C. 2011, c. 24, s. 49(4), applicable in respect of investments acquired after March 22, 2011. S. 146.3(7) formerly read:

(7) *Acquisition of non-qualified investment by trust.* Where at any time in a taxation year a trust governed by a registered retirement income fund

(*a*) acquires an investment that is not a qualified investment, or

(*b*) uses or permits to be used a property of the trust as security for a loan,

the fair market value of

(*c*) the investment at the time it was acquired by the trust, or

(*d*) the property used as security at the time it commenced to be so used

as the case may be, shall be included in computing the income for the year of the taxpayer who is the annuitant under the fund at that time.

Related Regulations: 215(3); 4900(1), (2), (4), (6), (9), (10), (12), (13).

Related Sections: S. 146.3(8) Disposition of non-qualified investment; s. 146.3(10) Recovery of property used as security; s. 207.1(4) Tax payable by trust under registered retirement income fund; s. 214(3)(*l*) Deemed payments; s. 259(1) Proportional holdings in trust property. See also related matter for the definition of "qualified investment".

Forms: T4RIF Summ. — Summary of Income from a Registered Retirement Income Fund; T4RIF — Statement of Income from a Registered Retirement Income Fund.

► 146.3(8) ◄

(8) Disposition of non-qualified investment — (Repealed by S.C. 2011, c. 24, s. 48(4).)

History: S. 146.3(8) was repealed by S.C. 2011, c. 24, s. 49(4), applicable in respect of investments acquired after March 22, 2011. S. 146.3(8) formerly read:

(8) *Disposition of non-qualified investment.* Where at any time in a taxation year a trust governed by a registered retirement income fund disposes of a property that, when acquired, was not a qualified investment, there may be deducted in computing the income for the taxation year of the taxpayer who is the annuitant under the fund at that time, an amount equal to the lesser of

(*a*) the amount that, by virtue of subsection (7), was included in computing the income of a taxpayer in respect of the acquisition of that property, and

(*b*) the proceeds of disposition of the property.

► 146.3(9) ◄

(9) Tax payable on income from non-qualified investment. If a trust that is governed by a registered retirement income fund holds, at any time in a taxation year, a property that is not a qualified investment,

(*a*) tax is payable under this Part by the trust on the amount that its taxable income for the year would be if it had no incomes or losses from sources other than the property that is not a qualified investment or no capital gains or capital losses other than from the disposition of that property, as the case may be; and

(*b*) for the purposes of paragraph (*a*),

(i) "income" includes dividends described in section 83, and

(ii) paragraphs 38(*a*) and (*b*) are to be read as if the fraction set out in each of those paragraphs were replaced by the word "all".

History: S. 146.3(9), the portion before paragraph (*a*) was replaced by S.C. 2013, c. 34, s. 300(5), applicable to the 2003 and subsequent taxation years, and formerly read:

(9) *Tax payable where non-qualified investment acquired.* Where a trust governed by a registered retirement income fund has acquired a property that is not a qualified investment,

S. 146.3(9)(*b*)(ii) was replaced by S.C. 2013, c. 34, s. 300(6), in force June 26, 2013, and formerly read:

(ii) paragraphs 38(*a*) and (*b*) shall be read without reference to the fractions set out therein.

Related Regulations: 4900(1), (2), (4), (6), (9), (10), (12), (13).

Related Sections: S. 122(1) Tax payable by inter vivos trust; s. 146.3(3) No tax while trust governed by fund; s. 146.3(3.1) Exception; s. 206(2) Amount of tax payable; s. 207.1(4) Tax payable by trust under registered retirement income fund; s. 259(1) Proportional holdings in trust property.

Information Circulars: IC 78-18R6 Registered Retirement Income Funds.

► 146.3(10) ◄

(10) Recovery of property used as security. Where at any time in a taxation year a loan for which a trust governed by a registered retirement income fund has used or permitted to be used trust property as security ceases to be extant, and the fair market value of the property so used was included by virtue of subsection (7) in computing the income of a taxpayer who was the annuitant under the fund, there may be deducted in computing the income for a taxation year of the taxpayer who is at that time the annuitant, an amount equal to the amount, if any, remaining when

(*a*) the net loss (exclusive of payments by the trust as or on account of interest) sustained by the trust in consequence of its using or permitting to be used the property as security for the loan and not as a result of a change in the fair market value of the property

is deducted from

(*b*) the amount so included in computing the income of a taxpayer in consequence of the trust's using or permitting to be used the property as security for the loan.

Related Regulations: 215(3).

Forms: T4RIF Summ. — Summary of Income from a Registered Retirement Income Fund; T4RIF — Statement of Income from a Registered Retirement Income Fund.

► 146.3(11) ◄

(11) Change in fund after registration. Where, on any day after a retirement income fund has been accepted by the Minister for registration for the purposes of this Act, the fund is revised or amended or a new fund is substituted therefor, and the fund as revised or amended or the new fund substituted therefor, as the case may be, (in this subsection referred to as the "amended fund") does not comply with the requirements of this section for its acceptance by the Minister for registration for the purposes of this Act, the following rules apply:

(*a*) the amended fund shall be deemed, for the purposes of this Act, not to be a registered retirement income fund; and

(*b*) the taxpayer who was the annuitant under the fund before it became an amended fund shall, in computing the taxpayer's income for the taxation year that includes that day, include as income received out of the fund at that time an amount equal to the fair market value of all the property held in connection with the fund immediately before that time.

Related Sections: S. 146.3(12) Deemed creation of new plan — changes to rights or obligations; s. 146.3(13) Deemed creation of new plan — prohibited loans or benefits; s. 153(1)(*l*) Withholding; s. 204.2(1.4) Deemed receipt where RRSP or RRIF amended; s. 214(3)(*i*) Deemed payments.

Information Circulars: IC 78-14R4 Guidelines for trust companies and other persons responsible for filing T3GR, T3D, T3P, T3S, T3RI, and T3F returns; IC 78-18R6 Registered Retirement Income Funds.

► 146.3(11.1) ◄

(11.1) Idem — (Repealed by 1986, c. 55, s. 57(6).)

► 146.3(12) ◄

(12) Idem. For the purposes of subsection (11), an arrangement under which a right or obligation under a retirement income fund is released or extinguished either wholly or in part and either in exchange or substitution for any right or obligation, or otherwise (other than an arrangement the sole object and legal effect of which is to revise or amend the fund) or under which payment of any amount by way of loan or otherwise is made on the security of a right under a retirement income fund, shall be deemed to be a new fund substituted for the retirement income fund.

Related Regulations: 215(4).

► 146.3(13) ◄

(13) Idem — (Repealed by S.C. 2011, c. 24, s. 49(5).)

History: S. 146.3(13) was repealed by S.C. 2011, c. 24, s. 49(5), applicable to transactions occurring, income earned, capital gains accruing and investments acquired after March 22, 2011. S. 146.3(13) formerly read:

(13) *Idem.* Where at any time a benefit or loan is extended or continues to be extended as a consequence of the existence of a registered retirement income fund and that benefit or loan would be prohibited if the fund met the requirement for registration contained in paragraph (2)(*g*), for the purposes of subsection (11), the fund shall be deemed to have been revised or amended at that time so that it fails to meet the requirement for registration contained in paragraph (2)(*g*).

► 146.3(14) ◄

(14) Transfer on breakdown of marriage or common-law partnership. An amount is transferred from a registered retirement income fund of an annuitant in accordance with this subsection if the amount

(*a*) is transferred on behalf of an individual who is a spouse or common-law partner or former spouse or common-law partner of the annuitant and who is entitled to the amount under a decree, an order or a judgment of a competent tribunal, or under a written agreement, that relates to a division of property between the annuitant and the individual in settlement of rights that arise out of, or on a breakdown of, their marriage or common-law partnership; and

(*b*) is transferred directly to

(i) a registered retirement income fund under which the individual is the annuitant, or

(ii) a registered retirement savings plan under which the individual is the annuitant (within the meaning assigned by subsection 146(1)).

Related Regulations: 215(5).

Related Sections: S. 146.3(2)(*a*) Acceptance of fund for registration; s. 248(1), "common-law partner"; s. 252(3) Extended meaning of "spouse" and "former spouse".

Tax Topics: No. 1702, Income Tax Issues To Be Considered in Negotiating Marriage Contracts.

Information Circulars: IC 78-18R6 Registered retirement income funds.

Interpretation Bulletins: *Secondary* — IT-528 Transfers of funds between registered plans.

► 146.3(14.1) ◄

(14.1) Transfer to PRPP or RPP. An amount is transferred from a registered retirement income fund of an annuitant in accordance with this subsection if the amount

(*a*) is transferred at the direction of the annuitant directly to an account of the annuitant under a pooled registered pension plan; or

(*b*) is transferred at the direction of the annuitant directly to a registered pension plan of which, at any time before the transfer, the annuitant was a member (within the meaning assigned by subsection 147.1(1)) or to a prescribed registered pension plan and is allocated to the annuitant under a money purchase provision (within the meaning assigned by subsection 147.1(1)) of the plan.

History: S. 146.3(14.1) was replaced by S.C. 2012, c. 31, s. 34(2), in force December 14, 2012. S. 146.3(14.1) formerly read:

(14.1) *Transfer to money purchase RPP.* An amount is transferred from a registered retirement income fund of an annuitant in accordance with this subsection if the amount is transferred at the direction of the annuitant directly to a registered pension plan of which, at any time before the transfer, the annuitant was a member (within the meaning assigned by subsection 147.1(1)) or to a prescribed registered pension plan and allocated to the annuitant under a money purchase provision (within the meaning assigned by subsection 147.1(1)) of the plan.

Related Sections: S. 146.3(2)(*a*), (*e*.1) and (*e*.2) Acceptance of fund for registration.

Forms: T2033 — Direct Transfer under subsection 46.3(14.1) or paragraph 146(16)(*a*) or 146.3(2)(*e*).

► 146.3(14.2) ◄

(14.2) Taxation of amount transferred. An amount transferred on behalf of an individual in accordance with paragraph (2)(*e*) or subsection (14) or (14.1)

(*a*) is not, solely because of that transfer, to be included in computing the income of any taxpayer; and

(*b*) is not to be deducted in computing the income of any taxpayer.

► 146.3(15) ◄

(15) Credited or added amount deemed not received. Where

(*a*) an amount is credited or added to a deposit with a depositary referred to in paragraph (*d*) of the definition "carrier" in subsection (1) as interest or income in respect of the deposit,

(*b*) the deposit is a registered retirement income fund at the time the amount is credited or added to the deposit, and

(*c*) during the calendar year in which the amount is credited or added or during the preceding calendar year, the annuitant under the fund was alive,

the amount shall be deemed not to be received by the annuitant or any other person solely because of the crediting or adding.

Registered Disability Savings Plan

SECTION 146.4: [Registered disability savings plan]

► 146.4(1) ◄

(1) Definitions. The following definitions apply in this section.

History: The following application, regarding the extension of the deadline for the 2008 contribution year to March 2, 2009 from December 31, 2008 for opening an RDSP, making contributions, and applying for the matching grant and bond as announced in Department of Finance News Release 2008-110, dated December 23, 2008, was added by S.C. 2009, c. 2, s. 81(1), in force on Royal Assent, March 12, 2009, to read as follows:

"(1) For the purposes of the *Income Tax Act* and the *Canada Disability Savings Act*, specified RDSP events are deemed to have occurred, in the order that they actually occurred, on December 31, 2008 and not on the day or days that they actually occurred.

(2) For the purposes of subsection (1), "specified RDSP event" means an event occurring after 2008 and before March 3, 2009 that

(*a*) establishes a "disability savings plan" as defined in subsection 146.4(1) of the *Income Tax Act*;

(*b*) satisfies conditions in subsection 146.4(2) of the *Income Tax Act*;

(*c*) establishes a "registered disability savings plan" as defined in subsection 146.4(1) of the *Income Tax Act* for a beneficiary who is, in respect of the 2008 taxation year, a "DTC-eligible individual" as defined in subsection 146.4(1) of the *Income Tax Act* and who was resident in Canada at the end of that year;

(*d*) is the making of any contribution to the registered disability savings plan;

(*e*) satisfies the requirement in paragraph 3(*b*) of the *Canada Disability Savings Regulations*; or

(*f*) is the taking of any other action to ensure that the registered disability savings plan is validly established and contributions to the plan are validly made."

Information Circulars: IC 99-1R1 Registered Disability Savings Plans.

"assistance holdback amount" —"assistance holdback amount", in relation to a disability savings plan, has the meaning assigned under the *Canada Disability Savings Act*.

"contribution" —"contribution" to a disability savings plan does not include (other than for the purpose of paragraph (*b*) of the definition "disability savings plan")

(*a*) an amount paid into the plan under or because of the *Canada Disability Savings Act* or a designated provincial program;

(*b*) an amount paid into the plan under or because of any other program that has a similar purpose to a designated provincial program and that is funded, directly or indirectly, by a province (other than an amount paid into the plan by an entity described in subparagraph (*a*)(iii) of the definition "qualifying person" in its capacity as holder of the plan);

(*c*) an amount transferred to the plan in accordance with subsection (8); or

(*d*) other than for the purposes of paragraphs (4)(*f*) to (*h*) and (*n*),

(i) a specified RDSP payment as defined in subsection 60.02(1), or

(ii) an accumulated income payment made to the plan under subsection 146.1(1.2).

History: S. 146.4(1), the portion of paragraph (*d*) before subparagraph (i) of the definition "contribution" was replaced by S.C. 2017, c. 33, s. 58(1), deemed to have come into force on March 23, 2017, and formerly read:

(*d*) other than for the purposes of paragraphs (4)(*f*) to (*h*) and (*n*) and paragraph (*b*) of the definition "advantage" in subsection 205(1),

S. 146.4(1), paragraph (*d*) of the definition "contribution" was added by S.C. 2012, c. 31, s. 35(2), and comes into force on January 1, 2014. S. 146.4(1), paragraph (*d*) of the definition "contribution" formerly read:

(*d*) other than for the purposes of paragraphs (4)(*f*) to (*h*) and (*n*), a specified RDSP payment as defined in subsection 60.02(1).

S. 146.4(1), paragraph (*d*) of the definition "contribution" was added by S.C. 2010, c. 25, s. 36(1), applicable after June 2011.

S. 146.4(1), the definition "contribution" was replaced by S.C. 2010, c. 12, s. 17(1), applicable to the 2009 and subsequent taxation years. S. 146.4(1), the definition "contribution" formerly read:

"contribution" —"contribution" to a disability savings plan does not include (other than for the purpose of paragraph (*b*) of the definition "disability savings plan") an amount paid into the plan under the *Canada Disability Savings Act* or a prescribed payment.

Related Sections: S. 18(11) Borrowed money used for contribution.

"designated provincial program" —"designated provincial program" means a program that is established under the laws of a province and that supports savings in registered disability savings plans.

History: S. 146.4(1), the definition "designated provincial program" was added by S.C. 2010, c. 12, s. 17(2), applicable to the 2009 and subsequent taxation years.

"disability assistance payment" —"disability assistance payment", in relation to a disability savings plan of a beneficiary, means any payment made from the plan to the beneficiary or to the beneficiary's estate.

"disability savings plan" —"disability savings plan" of a beneficiary means an arrangement (*a*) between

(i) a corporation (in this definition referred to as the "issuer")

(A) that is licensed or otherwise authorized under the laws of Canada or a province to carry on in Canada the business of offering to the public its services as trustee, and

(B) with which the specified Minister has entered into an agreement that applies to the arrangement for the purposes of the *Canada Disability Savings Act*, and

(ii) one or more of the following:

(A) the beneficiary,

(B) an entity that, at the time the arrangement is entered into, is a qualifying person described in paragraph (*a*) or (*b*) of the definition "qualifying person" in relation to the beneficiary,

(B.1) if the arrangement is entered into before 2024, a qualifying family member in relation to the beneficiary who, at the time the arrangement is entered into, is a qualifying person in relation to the beneficiary,

(B.2) a qualifying family member in relation to the beneficiary who, at the time the arrangement is entered into, is not a qualifying person in relation to the beneficiary but is a holder of another arrangement that is a registered disability savings plan of the beneficiary, and

(C) a legal parent of the beneficiary who, at the time the arrangement is entered into, is not a qualifying person in relation to the beneficiary but is a holder of another arrangement that is a registered disability savings plan of the beneficiary;

(*b*) under which one or more contributions are to be made in trust to the issuer to be invested, used or otherwise applied by the issuer for the purpose of making payments from the arrangement to the beneficiary; and

(*c*) that is entered into in a taxation year in respect of which the beneficiary is a DTC-eligible individual.

History: S. 146.4(1), clause (*a*)(ii)(B.1) of the definition "disability savings plan" was replaced by S.C. 2018, c. 12, s. 24, in force on June 21, 2018, and formerly read:

(B.1) if the arrangement is entered into before 2019, a qualifying family member in relation to the beneficiary who, at the time the arrangement is entered into, is a qualifying person in relation to the beneficiary,

S. 146.4(1), the portion of subparagraph (*a*)(i) before clause (A) of the definition "disability savings plan" was replaced by S.C. 2017, c. 33, s. 58(2), deemed to have come into force on March 23, 2017, and formerly read:

(i) a corporation (in this section referred to as the "issuer")

S. 146.4(1), clause (*a*)(ii)(B.1), of the definition " disability savings plan" was replaced by S.C. 2015, c. 36, s. 16, in force on Royal Assent, June 23, 2015, and formerly read:

(B.1) if the arrangement is entered into before 2017, a qualifying family member in relation to the beneficiary who, at the time the arrangement is entered into, is a qualifying person in relation to the beneficiary,

S. 146.4(1), clause (*a*)(ii)(B) of the definition "disability savings plan" was replaced, and clauses (B.1) and (B.2) were added, by S.C. 2012, c. 19, s. 6(1), in force on Royal Assent, June 29, 2012. S. 146.4(1), clause (*a*)(ii)(B) of the definition "disability savings plan" formerly read:

(B) an entity that, at the time the arrangement is entered into, is a qualifying person in relation to the beneficiary, and

"DTC-eligible individual" —"DTC-eligible individual", in respect of a taxation year, means an individual in respect of whom an amount is deductible, or would if this Act were read without reference to paragraph 118.3(1)(*c*) be deductible, under section 118.3 in computing a taxpayer's tax payable under this Part for the taxation year.

Proposed Amendment

2019 Federal Budget Resolutions

The Act is modified to give effect to the proposals relating to the Registered Disability Savings Plan — cessation of eligibility for the disability tax credit measure described in the budget documents tabled by the Minister of Finance in the House of Commons on Budget Day.

Explanatory Note:
Dentons Canada LLP Commentary

Under the current regime, where a beneficiary of a registered disability savings plan ("RDSP") ceases to be eligible for the disability tax credit, the plan is required to close by the end of the year following the year throughout which the beneficiary was no longer eligible. Previous amendments provided an extension before closing the plan which required a medical practitioner's certification that states it is likely the beneficiary will become eligible again. Budget 2019 proposes to make amendments to the *Income Tax Act* to remove the time limitation on the period that an RDSP may remain open after a beneficiary becomes ineligible for the DTC. As well, a medical certification will no longer be required to attest to the annuitant's continuing disability in the future for the plan to remain open.

This measure will apply after 2020. An RDSP issuer will not, however, be required to close an RDSP on or after Budget Day and before 2021 solely because the RDSP beneficiary is no longer eligible for the DTC.

No specific amendments to the Income Tax Act were provided as part of Budget 2019.

Tax Topics: No. 2021, Appeal from Denial by CRA for a Disability Tax Credit.

"holder" —"holder" of a disability savings plan at any time means each of the following:

(*a*) an entity that has, at that time, rights as an entity with whom the issuer entered into the plan;

(*b*) an entity that has, at that time, rights as a successor or assignee of an entity described in paragraph (*a*) or in this paragraph; and

(*c*) the beneficiary if, at that time, the beneficiary is not an entity described in paragraph (*a*) or (*b*) and has rights under the plan to make decisions (either alone or with other holders of the plan) concerning the plan, except where the only such right is a right to direct that disability assistance payments be made as provided for in subparagraph (4)(*n*)(ii).

History: S. 146.4(1), paragraph (*c*) of the definition "holder" was replaced by S.C. 2012, c. 31, s. 35(3), and comes into force on January 1, 2014. S. 146.4(1), paragraph (*c*) of the definition "holder" formerly read:

(*c*) the beneficiary if, at that time, the beneficiary is not an entity described in paragraph (*a*) or (*b*) and has rights under the plan to make decisions (either alone or with other holders of the plan) concerning the plan, except where the only such right is a right to direct that disability assistance payments be made as provided for in subparagraph (4)(*n*)(iii)).

Related Sections: S. 206(3) Liability for tax; s. 206.1(3) Liability for tax; s. 206.2(3) Liability for tax.

"issuer" —"issuer", of an arrangement, means the person described as the "issuer" in the definition *disability savings plan*.

History: S. 146.4(1), the definition "issuer" was added by S.C. 2017, c. 33, s. 58(6), deemed to have come into force on March 23, 2017.

"lifetime disability assistance payments" —"lifetime disability assistance payments" under a disability savings plan of a beneficiary means disability assistance payments that are identified under the terms of the plan as lifetime disability assistance payments and that, after they begin to be paid, are payable at least annually until the earlier of the day on which the beneficiary dies and the day on which the plan is terminated.

"plan trust" —"plan trust", in relation to a disability savings plan, means the trust governed by the plan.

"qualified investment" —"qualified investment", for a trust governed by a RDSP, means

(*a*) an investment that would be described by any of paragraphs (*a*) to (*d*), (*f*) and (*g*) of the definition "qualified investment" in section 204 if the reference in that definition to "a trust governed by a deferred profit sharing plan or revoked plan" were read as a reference to "a trust governed by a RDSP" and if that definition were read without reference to the words "with the exception of excluded property in relation to the trust";

(*b*) a contract for an annuity issued by a licensed annuities provider where

(i) the trust is the only person who, disregarding any subsequent transfer of the contract by the trust, is or may become entitled to any annuity payments under the contract, and

(ii) the holder of the contract has a right to surrender the contract at any time for an amount that would, if reasonable sales and administration charges were ignored, approximate the value of funds that could otherwise be applied to fund future periodic payments under the contract;

(*c*) a contract for an annuity issued by a licensed annuities provider where

(i) annual or more frequent periodic payments are or may be made under the contract to the holder of the contract,

(ii) the trust is the only person who, disregarding any subsequent transfer of the contract by the trust, is or may become entitled to any annuity payments under the contract,

(iii) neither the time nor the amount of any payment under the contract may vary because of the length of any life, other than the life of the beneficiary under the plan,

(iv) the day on which the periodic payments began or are to begin is not later than the end of the later of

(A) the year in which the beneficiary under the plan attains the age of 60 years, and

(B) the year following the year in which the contract was acquired by the trust,

(v) the periodic payments are payable for the life of the beneficiary under the plan and either there is no guaranteed period under the contract or there is a guaranteed period that does not exceed 15 years,

(vi) the periodic payments

(A) are equal, or

(B) are not equal solely because of one or more adjustments that would, if the contract were an annuity under a retirement savings plan, be in accordance with subparagraphs 146(3)(*b*)(iii) to (v) or that arise because of a uniform reduction in the entitlement to the periodic payments as a consequence of a partial surrender of rights to the periodic payments, and

(vii) the contract requires that, in the event the plan must be terminated in accordance with paragraph (4)(*p*), any amounts that would otherwise be payable after the termination be commuted into a single payment; and

(*d*) a prescribed investment.

History: S. 146.4(1), the definition "qualified investment" was added by S.C. 2017, c. 33, s. 58(6), deemed to have come into force on March 23, 2017.

Related Regulations: 221(2); 4900(5).

"qualifying family member" —"qualifying family member", in relation to a beneficiary of a disability savings plan, at any time, means an individual who, at that time, is

(*a*) a legal parent of the beneficiary; or

(*b*) a spouse or common-law partner of the beneficiary who is not living separate and apart from the beneficiary by reason of a breakdown of their marriage or common-law partnership.

History: S. 146.4(1), the definition "qualifying family member" was added by S.C. 2012, c. 19, s. 6(3), in force on Royal Assent, June 29, 2012.

"qualifying person" —"qualifying person", in relation to a beneficiary of a disability savings plan, at any time, means

(*a*) if the beneficiary has not, at or before that time, attained the age of majority, an entity that is, at that time,

(i) a legal parent of the beneficiary,

(ii) a guardian, tutor, curator or other individual who is legally authorized to act on behalf of the beneficiary, or

(iii) a public department, agency or institution that is legally authorized to act on behalf of the beneficiary,

(*b*) if the beneficiary has, at or before that time, attained the age of majority and is not, at that time, contractually competent to enter into a disability savings plan, an entity that is, at that time, an entity described in subparagraph (*a*)(ii) or (iii), and

(*c*) other than for the purposes of subparagraph (4)(*b*)(iv), an individual who is a qualifying family member in relation to the beneficiary if

(i) at or before that time, the beneficiary has attained the age of majority and is not a beneficiary under a disability savings plan,

(ii) at that time, no entity described in subparagraph (*a*)(ii) or (iii) is legally authorized to act on behalf of the beneficiary, and

(iii) in the issuer's opinion after reasonable inquiry, the beneficiary's contractual competence to enter into a disability savings plan at that time is in doubt.

History: S. 146.4(1), paragraph (*c*) of the definition "qualifying person" was added by S.C. 2012, c. 19, s. 6(2), in force on Royal Assent, June 29, 2012.

"registered disability savings plan" or "RDSP" —"registered disability savings plan" or "RDSP" means a disability savings plan that satisfies the conditions in subsection (2), but does not include a plan to which subsection (3) or (10) applies.

History: S. 146.4(1), the definition "registered disability savings plan" was replaced by S.C. 2012, c. 31, s. 35(1), in force on Royal Assent, December 14, 2012. S. 146.4(1), the definition "registered disability savings plan" formerly read:

"registered disability savings plan"—"registered disability savings plan" means a disability savings plan that satisfies the conditions in subsection (2), but does not include a plan to which subsection (3) or (10) applies.

Related Sections: S. 107.4(1) Qualifying disposition; s. 108(1), " trust".

"specified maximum amount" —"specified maximum amount", for a calendar year in respect of a disability savings plan, means the amount that is the greater of

(*a*) the amount determined by the formula set out in paragraph (4)(*l*) in respect of the plan for the calendar year, and

(*b*) the amount determined by the formula

$$A + B$$

where

A is 10% of the fair market value of the property held by the plan trust at the beginning of the calendar year (other than annuity contracts held by the plan trust that, at the beginning of the calendar year, are not described in paragraph (*b*) of the definition *qualified investment*), and

B is the total of all amounts each of which is

(i) a periodic payment under an annuity contract held by the plan trust at the beginning of the calendar year (other than an annuity contract described at the beginning of the calendar year in paragraph (*b*) of the definition "qualified investment") that is paid to the plan trust in the calendar year, or

(ii) if the periodic payment under such an annuity contract is not made to the plan trust because the plan trust disposed of the right to that payment in the calendar year, a reasonable estimate of that payment on the assumption that the annuity contract had been held throughout the calendar year and no rights under the contract were disposed of in the calendar year.

History: S. 146.4(1), subparagraph (i) of the description of B in the definition "specified maximum amount" was replaced by S.C. 2017, c. 33, s. 58(4), deemed to have come into force on March 23, 2017, and formerly read:

(i) a periodic payment under an annuity contract held by the plan trust at the beginning of the calendar year (other than an annuity contract described at the beginning of the calendar year in paragraph (*b*) of the definition "qualified investment" in subsection 205(1)) that is paid to the plan trust in the calendar year, or

S. 146.4(1), the description of A in the definition "specified maximum amount" was replaced by S.C. 2017, c. 33, s. 58(3), deemed to have come into force on March 23, 2017, and formerly read:

A is 10% of the fair market value of the property held by the plan trust at the beginning of the calendar year (other than annuity contracts held by the plan trust that, at the beginning of the calendar year, are not described in paragraph (*b*) of the definition "qualified investment" in subsection 205(1)), and

S. 146.4(1), the definition "specified maximum amount" was added by S.C. 2012, c. 31, s. 35(4), and comes into force on January 1, 2014.

"specified Minister" —"specified Minister" means the minister designated under section 4 of the *Canada Disability Savings Act*.

"specified year" —"specified year", for a disability savings plan of a beneficiary means the particular calendar year in which a medical doctor or a nurse practitioner licensed to practise under the laws of a province (or of the place where the beneficiary resides) certifies in writing that the beneficiary's state of health is such that, in the professional opinion of the medical doctor or the nurse practitioner, the beneficiary is not likely to survive more than five years and

(*a*) if the plan is a specified disability savings plan, each subsequent calendar year, but does not include any calendar year prior to the calendar year in which the certification is provided to the issuer of the plan; or

(*b*) in any other case, each of the five calendar years following the particular calendar year, but does not include any calendar year prior to the calendar year in which the certification is provided to the issuer of the plan.

History: S. 146.4(1), the portion before paragraph (*a*) of the definition "specified year" was replaced by S.C. 2017, c. 33, s. 58(5), applicable in respect of certifications made after September 7, 2017, and formerly read:

"specified year"—"specified year" for a disability savings plan of a beneficiary means the particular calendar year in which a medical doctor licensed to practise under the laws of a province (or of the place where the beneficiary resides) certifies in writing that the beneficiary's state of health is such that, in the professional opinion of the medical doctor, the beneficiary is not likely to survive more than five years and

S. 146.4(1), the definition "specified year" was replaced by S.C. 2011, c. 15, s. 2(1), applicable to the 2011 and subsequent taxation years. S. 146.4(1), the definition "specified year" formerly read:

"specified year"—"specified year" for a disability savings plan of a beneficiary means the particular calendar year in which a medical doctor licensed to practice under the laws of a province (or of the place where the beneficiary resides) certifies in writing that the beneficiary's state of health is such that, in the professional opinion of the medical doctor, the beneficiary is not likely to survive more than five years, and each of the five calendar years following the particular calendar year, but does not include any calendar year prior to the calendar year in which the certification is provided to the issuer of the plan.

► 146.4(1.1) ◄

(1.1) Specified disability savings plan. If, in respect of a beneficiary under a registered disability savings plan, a medical doctor or a nurse practitioner licensed to practise under the laws of a province (or of the place where the beneficiary resides) certifies in writing that the beneficiary's state of health is such that, in the professional opinion of the medical doctor or the nurse practitioner, the beneficiary is not likely to survive more than five years, the holder of the plan elects in prescribed form and provides the election and the medical certification in respect of the beneficiary to the issuer of the plan, and the issuer notifies the specified Minister of the election in a manner and format acceptable to the specified Minister, then the plan becomes a specified disability savings plan at the time the notification is received by the specified Minister.

History: S. 146.4(1.1) was replaced by S.C. 2017, c. 33, s. 58(7), applicable in respect of certifications made after September 7, 2017, and formerly read:

(1.1) *Specified disability savings plan.* If, in respect of a beneficiary under a registered disability savings plan, a medical doctor licensed to practise under the laws of a province (or of the place where the beneficiary resides) certifies in writing that the beneficiary's state of health is such that, in the professional opinion of the medical doctor, the beneficiary is not likely to survive more than five years, the holder of the plan elects in prescribed form and provides the election and the medical certification in respect of the beneficiary to the issuer of the plan, and the issuer notifies the specified Minister of the election in a manner and format acceptable to the specified Minister, then the plan becomes a specified disability savings plan at the time the notification is received by the specified Minister.

S. 146.4(1.1) was added by S.C. 2011, c. 15, s. 2(2), applicable to the 2011 and subsequent taxation years, except that no election may be made under subsection 146.4(1.1) before June 26, 2011.

► 146.4(1.2) ◄

(1.2) Ceasing to be a specified disability savings plan. A plan ceases to be a specified disability savings plan at the earliest of the following times:

(*a*) the time that the specified Minister receives a notification, in a manner and format acceptable to the specified Minister, from the issuer of the plan that the holder elects that the plan is to cease to be a specified disability savings plan;

(*b*) the time that is immediately before the earliest time in a calendar year when the total disability assistance payments, other than non-taxable portions, made from the plan in the year and while it was a specified disability savings plan exceeds $10,000 (or such greater amount as is required to satisfy the condition in subparagraph (*d*)(i));

(*c*) the time that is immediately before the time that

(i) a contribution is made to the plan,

(ii) an amount described in any of paragraphs (*a*) and (*b*) and subparagraph (*d*)(ii) of the definition "contribution" in subsection (1) is paid into the plan,

(iii) the plan is terminated,

(iv) the plan ceases to be a registered disability savings plan as a result of the application of paragraph (10)(*a*), or

(v) is the beginning of the first calendar year throughout which the beneficiary under the plan has no severe and prolonged impairments with the effects described in paragraph 118.3(1)(*a.1*); and

(*d*) the time immediately following the end of a calendar year if

(i) in the year the total amount of disability assistance payments made from the plan to the beneficiary is less than the amount determined by the formula set out in paragraph (4)(*l*) in respect of the plan for the year (or such lesser amount as is supported by the property of the plan), and

(ii) the year is not the calendar year in which the plan became a specified disability savings plan.

(*e*) (Repealed by S.C. 2012, c. 31, s. 35(5).)

(*f*) (Repealed by S.C. 2012, c. 31, s. 35(5).)

History: S. 146.4(1.2)(*b*) to (*f*) were replaced by S.C. 2012, c. 31, s. 35(5), in force January 1, 2014. S. 146.4(1.2)(*b*) to (*f*) formerly read:

(*b*) the time that is immediately before the earliest time in a calendar year when the total disability assistance payments, other than non-taxable portions, made from the plan in the year and while it was a specified disability savings plan exceeds $10,000 (or, in the case of a plan to which paragraph (*f*) applies, such greater amount as is required to satisfy the condition in that paragraph);

(*c*) the time that is immediately before the time that

(i) a contribution is made to the plan, or

(ii) an amount described in paragraph (*a*) or (*b*) of the definition "contribution" in subsection (1) is paid into the plan;

(*d*) the time that is immediately before the time that

(i) the plan is terminated, or

(ii) the plan ceases to be a registered disability savings plan as a result of the application of paragraph (10)(*a*);

(*e*) if lifetime disability assistance payments have not begun to be paid before the end of the particular calendar year following the year in which the plan last became a specified disability savings plan, the time immediately following the end of that particular calendar year; and

(*f*) if in a calendar year the plan is a plan to which paragraph (4)(*n*) applies and the total amount of disability assistance payments made from the plan to the beneficiary in the calendar year is less than the amount determined by the formula set out in paragraph (4)(*l*) in respect of the plan for the calendar year (or such lesser amount as is supported by the property of the plan), the time immediately following the end of that calendar year.

S. 146.4(1.2) was added by S.C. 2011, c. 15, s. 2(2), applicable to the 2011 and subsequent taxation years, except that for a specified disability savings plan in respect of which the required medical certification is obtained before 2012, paragraph 146.4(1.2)(*b*), is, for 2012, to be read as follows:

"(*b*) the time that is immediately before the earliest time in a calendar year when the total disability assistance payments, other than non-taxable portions, made from the plan and while it was a specified disability savings plan exceeds $20,000 (or, in the case of a plan to which paragraph (*f*) applies, such greater amount as is required to satisfy the condition in that paragraph);"

► 146.4(1.3) ◄

(1.3) Waiting period. If at any time, a plan has ceased to be a specified disability savings plan because of subsection (1.2), then the holder of the plan may not make an election under subsection (1.1) until 24 months after that time.

History: S. 146.4(1.3) was added by S.C. 2011, c. 15, s. 2(2), applicable to the 2011 and subsequent taxation years.

► 146.4(1.4) ◄

(1.4) Waiver. The Minister may waive the application of subsections (1.2) or (1.3) if it is just and equitable to do so.

History: S. 146.4(1.4) was added by S.C. 2011, c. 15, s. 2(2), applicable to the 2011 and subsequent taxation years.

► 146.4(1.5) ◄

(1.5) Beneficiary replacing holder. Any holder of a disability savings plan who was a qualifying person in relation to the beneficiary under the plan at the time the plan (or another registered disability savings plan of the beneficiary) was entered into solely because of paragraph (*c*) of the definition "qualifying person" in subsection (1) ceases to be a holder of the plan and the beneficiary becomes the holder of the plan if

(*a*) the beneficiary is determined to be contractually competent by a competent tribunal or other authority under the laws of a province or, in the issuer's opinion after reasonable inquiry, the beneficiary's contractual competence to enter into a disability savings plan is no longer in doubt; and (*b*) the beneficiary notifies the issuer that the beneficiary chooses to become the holder of the plan.

History: S. 146.4(1.5), the portion before paragraph (*a*) was replaced by S.C. 2013, c. 33, s. 16(1), deemed to have come into force on June 29, 2012, and formerly read:

(1.5) *Beneficiary replacing holder.* Any holder of a disability savings plan who is a qualifying person in relation to the beneficiary under the plan solely because of paragraph (*c*) of the definition "qualifying person" in subsection (1) ceases to be a holder of the plan and the beneficiary becomes the holder of the plan if

S. 146.4(1.5) was added by S.C. 2012, c. 19, s. 6(4), in force on Royal Assent, June 29, 2012.

► 146.4(1.6) ◄

(1.6) Entity replacing holder. If an entity described in subparagraph (*a*)(ii) or (iii) of the definition "qualifying person" in subsection (1) is appointed in respect of a beneficiary of a disability savings plan and a holder of the plan was a qualifying person in relation to the beneficiary at the time the plan (or another registered disability savings plan of the beneficiary) was entered into solely because of paragraph (*c*) of that definition,

(*a*) the entity shall notify the issuer without delay of the entity's appointment;

(*b*) the holder of the plan ceases to be a holder of the plan; and

(*c*) the entity becomes the holder of the plan.

History: S. 146.4(1.6), the portion before paragraph (*a*) was replaced by S.C. 2013, c. 33, s. 16(2), deemed to have come into force on June 29, 2012, and formerly read:

(1.6) *Entity replacing holder.* If an entity described in subparagraph (*a*)(ii) or (iii) of the definition "qualifying person" in subsection (1) is appointed in respect of a beneficiary of a disability savings plan and a holder of the plan is a qualifying person solely because of paragraph (*c*) of that definition,

S. 146.4(1.6) was added by S.C. 2012, c. 19, s. 6(4), in force on Royal Assent, June 29, 2012.

► 146.4(1.7) ◄

(1.7) Rules applicable in case of dispute. If a dispute arises as a result of an issuer's acceptance of a qualifying family member who was a qualifying person in relation to the beneficiary at the time the plan (or another registered disability savings plan of the beneficiary) was entered into solely because of paragraph (*c*) of the definition "qualifying person" in subsection (1) as a holder of a disability savings plan, from the time the dispute arises until the time that the dispute is resolved or an entity becomes the holder of the plan under subsection (1.5) or (1.6), the holder of the plan shall use their best efforts to avoid any reduction in the fair market value of the property held by the plan trust, having regard to the reasonable needs of the beneficiary under the plan.

History: S. 146.4(1.7) was replaced by S.C. 2013, c. 33, s. 16(3), deemed to have come into force on June 29, 2012, and formerly read:

(1.7) *Rules applicable in case of dispute.* If a dispute arises as a result of an issuer's acceptance of a qualifying family member who is a qualifying person solely because of paragraph (*c*) of the definition "qualifying person" in subsection (1) as a holder of a disability savings plan, from the time the dispute arises until the time that the dispute is resolved or an entity becomes the holder of the plan under subsection (1.5) or (1.6), the holder of the plan shall use their best efforts to avoid any reduction in the fair market value of the property held by the plan trust, having regard to the reasonable needs of the beneficiary under the plan.

S. 146.4(1.7) was added by S.C. 2012, c. 19, s. 6(4), in force on Royal Assent, June 29, 2012.

► 146.4(2) ◄

(2) Registered status. The conditions that must be satisfied for a disability savings plan of a beneficiary to be a registered disability savings plan are as follows:

(*a*) before the plan is entered into, the issuer of the plan has received written notification from the Minister that, in the Minister's opinion, a plan whose terms are identical to the plan would, if entered into by entities eligible to enter into a disability savings plan, comply with the conditions in subsection (4);

(*b*) at or before the time the plan is entered into, the issuer of the plan has been provided with the Social Insurance Number of the beneficiary and the Social Insurance Number or business number, as the case may be, of each entity with which the issuer has entered into the plan; and

(*c*) at the time the plan is entered into, the beneficiary is resident in Canada, except that this condition does not apply if, at that time, the beneficiary is the beneficiary under another registered disability savings plan.

Editorial Note: In order to be registered as an RDSP, a disability savings plan must meet the conditions set out in s. 146.4(4). Subsection 146.4(1.1) sets out the conditions for a RDSP to become a specified disability savings plan, which provides greater flexibility to access funds for individuals with shortened life spans.

Information Circulars: IC 99-1 Registered disability savings plans.

► 146.4(3) ◄

(3) Registered status nullified. A disability savings plan is deemed never to have been a registered disability savings plan unless

(*a*) the issuer of the plan provides without delay notification of the plan's establishment in prescribed form containing prescribed information to the specified Minister; and

(*b*) if the beneficiary is the beneficiary under another registered disability savings plan at the time the plan is established, that other plan is terminated without delay.

History: S. 146.4(3) was replaced by S.C. 2012, c. 31, s. 35(6), in force on Royal Assent, December 14, 2012. S. 146.4(3) formerly read:

(3) *Registered status nullified.* A disability savings plan is deemed never to have been a registered disability savings plan if

(*a*) the issuer of the plan has not, on or before the day that is 60 days after the particular day on which the plan was entered into, provided notification of the plan's existence in prescribed form containing prescribed information to the specified Minister; or

(*b*) the beneficiary was, on the particular day, the beneficiary under another registered disability savings plan and that other plan has not been terminated on or before the day that is 120 days after the particular day or any later day that the specified Minister considers reasonable in the circumstances.

► 146.4(4) ◄

(4) Plan conditions. The conditions referred to in paragraph (2)(*a*) are as follows:

(*a*) the plan stipulates

(i) that it is to be operated exclusively for the benefit of the beneficiary under the plan,

(ii) that the designation of the beneficiary under the plan is irrevocable, and

(iii) that no right of the beneficiary to receive payments from the plan is capable, either in whole or in part, of surrender or assignment;

(*b*) the plan allows an entity to acquire rights as a successor or assignee of a holder of the plan only if the entity is

(i) the beneficiary,

(ii) the beneficiary's estate,

(iii) a holder of the plan at the time the rights are acquired,

(iv) a qualifying person in relation to the beneficiary at the time the rights are acquired, or

(v) an individual who is a legal parent of the beneficiary and was previously a holder of the plan;

(*c*) the plan provides that, where an entity (other than a qualifying family member in relation to the beneficiary) that is a holder of the plan ceases to be a qualifying person in relation to the beneficiary at any time, the entity ceases at that time to be a holder of the plan;

(*d*) the plan provides for there to be at least one holder of the plan at all times that the plan is in existence and may provide for the beneficiary (or the beneficiary's estate, as the case may be) to automatically acquire rights as a successor or assignee of a holder in order to ensure compliance with this requirement;

(*e*) the plan provides that, where an entity becomes a holder of the plan after the plan is entered into, the entity is prohibited (except to the extent otherwise permitted by the Minister or the specified Minister) from exercising their rights as a holder of the plan until the issuer has been advised of the entity having become a holder of the plan and been provided with the entity's Social Insurance Number or business number, as the case may be;

(*f*) the plan prohibits contributions from being made to the plan at any time if

(i) the beneficiary is not a DTC-eligible individual in respect of the taxation year that includes that time, unless the contribution is a specified RDSP payment in respect of the beneficiary and, at that time, there is a valid election referred to in subsection (4.1) in respect of the beneficiary, or

(ii) the beneficiary died before that time;

(*g*) the plan prohibits a contribution from being made to the plan at any time if

(i) the beneficiary attained the age of 59 years before the calendar year that includes that time,

(ii) the beneficiary is not resident in Canada at that time, or

(iii) the total of the contribution and all other contributions made at or before that time to the plan or to any other registered disability savings plan of the beneficiary would exceed $200,000;

(*h*) the plan prohibits contributions to the plan by any entity that is not a holder of the plan, except with the written consent of a holder of the plan;

(*i*) the plan provides that no payments may be made from the plan other than

(i) disability assistance payments,

(ii) a transfer in accordance with subsection (8), and

(iii) repayments under the *Canada Disability Savings Act* or a designated provincial program;

(*j*) the plan prohibits a disability assistance payment from being made if it would result in the fair market value of the property held by the plan trust immediately after the payment being less than the assistance holdback amount in relation to the plan;

(*k*) the plan provides for lifetime disability assistance payments to begin to be paid no later than the end of the particular calendar year in which the beneficiary attains the age of 60 years or, if the plan is established in or after the particular year, in the calendar year following the calendar year in which the plan is established;

(*l*) the plan provides that the total amount of lifetime disability assistance payments made in any calendar year (other than a specified year for the plan) shall not exceed the amount determined by the formula

$$A/(B + 3 - C) + D$$

where

A is the fair market value of the property held by the plan trust at the beginning of the calendar year (other than annuity contracts held by the plan trust that, at the beginning of the calendar year, are not described in paragraph (*b*) of the definition "qualified investment" in subsection (1)),

B is the greater of 80 and the age in whole years of the beneficiary at the beginning of the calendar year,

C is the age in whole years of the beneficiary at the beginning of the calendar year, and

D is the total of all amounts each of which is

(i) a periodic payment under an annuity contract held by the plan trust at the beginning of the calendar year (other than an annuity contract described at the beginning of the calendar year in paragraph (*b*) of the definition "qualified investment" in subsection (1)) that is paid to the plan trust in the calendar year, or

(ii) if the periodic payment under such an annuity contract is not made to the plan trust because the plan trust disposed of the right to that payment in the calendar year, a reasonable estimate of that payment on the assumption that the annuity contract had been held throughout the calendar year and no rights under the contract were disposed of in the calendar year;

(*m*) the plan stipulates whether or not disability assistance payments that are not lifetime disability assistance payments are to be permitted under the plan;

(*n*) the plan provides that when the total of all amounts paid under the *Canada Disability Savings Act* before the beginning of a calendar year to any registered disability savings plan of the beneficiary exceeds the total of all contributions made before the beginning of the calendar year to any registered disability savings plan of the beneficiary,

(i) if the calendar year is not a specified year for the plan, the total amount of disability assistance payments made from the plan to the beneficiary in the calendar year shall not exceed the specified maximum amount for the calendar year, except that, in calculating that total amount, any payment made following a transfer in the calendar year from another plan in accordance with subsection (8) is to be disregarded if it is made

(A) to satisfy an undertaking described in paragraph (8)(*d*), or

(B) in lieu of a payment that would otherwise have been permitted to be made from the other plan in the calendar year had the transfer not occurred, and

(ii) if the beneficiary attained the age of 27 years, but not the age of 59 years, before the calendar year, the beneficiary has the right to direct that, within the constraints imposed by subparagraph (i) and paragraph (*j*), one or more disability assistance payments be made from the plan to the beneficiary in the calendar year;

(iii) (Repealed by S.C. 2012, c. 31, s. 35(7).)

(*n*.1) the plan provides that, if the beneficiary attained the age of 59 years before a calendar year, the total amount of disability assistance payments made from the plan to the beneficiary in the calendar year shall not be less than the amount determined by the formula set out in paragraph (*l*) in respect of the plan for the calendar year (or such lesser amount as is supported by the property of the plan trust);

(*o*) the plan provides that, at the direction of the holders of the plan, the issuer shall transfer all of the property held by the plan trust (or an amount equal to its value) to another registered disability savings plan of the beneficiary, together with all information in its possession (other than information provided to the issuer of the other plan by the specified Minister) that may reasonably be considered necessary for compliance, in respect of the other plan, with the requirements of this Act and with any conditions and obligations imposed under the *Canada Disability Savings Act*; and

(*p*) the plan provides for any amounts remaining in the plan (after taking into consideration any repayments under the *Canada Disability Savings Act* or a designated provincial program) to be paid to the beneficiary or the beneficiary's estate, as the case may be, and for the plan to be terminated, by the end of the calendar year following the earlier of

(i) the calendar year in which the beneficiary dies, and

(ii) the first calendar year

(A) if an election is made under subsection (4.1), that includes the time that the election ceases because of paragraph (4.2)(*b*) to be valid, and

(B) in any other case, throughout which the beneficiary has no severe and prolonged impairments with the effects described in paragraph 118.3(1)(*a.1*).

History: S. 146.4(4)(*l*), subparagraph (i) of the description of D was replaced by S.C. 2017, c. 33, s. 58(10), deemed to have come into force on March 23, 2017, and formerly read:

(i) a periodic payment under an annuity contract held by the plan trust at the beginning of the calendar year (other than an annuity contract described at the beginning of the calendar year in paragraph (*b*) of the definition "qualified investment" in subsection 205(1)) that is paid to the plan trust in the calendar year, or

S. 146.4(4)(*l*), the description of A was replaced by S.C. 2017, c. 33, s. 58(9), deemed to have come into force on March 23, 2017, and formerly read:

A is the fair market value of the property held by the plan trust at the beginning of the calendar year (other than annuity contracts held by the plan trust that, at the beginning of the calendar year, are not described in paragraph (*b*) of the definition "qualified investment" in subsection 205(1)),

S. 146.4(4)(*f*)(i) was replaced by S.C. 2017, c. 33, s. 58(8), applicable to the 2014 and subsequent taxation years, and formerly read:

(i) the beneficiary is not a DTC-eligible individual in respect of the taxation year that includes that time, or

S. 146.4(4)(*c*) was replaced by S.C. 2013, c. 33, s. 16(4), deemed to have come into force on June 29, 2012, and formerly read:

(*c*) the plan provides that, where an entity (other than a legal parent of the beneficiary) that is a holder of the plan ceases to be a qualifying person in relation to the beneficiary at any time, the entity ceases at that time to be a holder of the plan;

S. 146.4(4)(*n*)(i) to (iii) were replaced by S.C. 2012, c. 31, s. 35(7), and comes into force on January 1, 2014. S. 146.4(4)(*n*)(i) to (iii) formerly read:

(i) if the calendar year is not a specified year for the plan, the total amount of disability assistance payments made from the plan to the beneficiary in the calendar year shall not exceed the amount determined by the formula set out in paragraph (*l*) in respect of the plan for the calendar year, except that, in calculating that total amount, any payment made following a transfer in the calendar year from another plan in accordance with subsection (8) is to be disregarded if it is made

(A) to satisfy an undertaking described in paragraph (8)(*d*), or

(B) in lieu of a payment that would otherwise have been permitted to be made from the other plan in the calendar year had the transfer not occurred,

(ii) if the beneficiary attained the age of 59 years before the calendar year, the total amount of disability assistance payments made from the plan to the beneficiary in the calendar year shall not be less than the amount determined by the formula set out in paragraph (*l*) in respect of the plan for the calendar year (or such lesser amount as is supported by the property of the plan trust), and

(iii) if the beneficiary attained the age of 27 years, but not the age of 59 years, before the calendar year, the beneficiary has the right to direct that, within the constraints imposed by subparagraph (i) and paragraph (*j*), one or more disability assistance payments be made from the plan to the beneficiary in the calendar year;

S. 146.4(4)(*n.1*) was added by S.C. 2012, c. 31, s. 35(8), and comes into force on January 1, 2014.

S. 146.4(4)(*o*) was replaced by S.C. 2012, c. 31, s. 35(9), in force on Royal Assent, December 14, 2012. S. 146.4(4)(*o*) formerly read:

(*o*) the plan provides that, at the direction of the holders of the plan, the issuer shall transfer all of the property held by the plan trust (or an amount equal to its value) to another registered disability savings plan of the beneficiary, together with all information in its possession that may reasonably be considered necessary for compliance, in respect of the other plan, with the requirements of this Act and with any conditions and obligations imposed under the *Canada Disability Savings Act*; and

S. 146.4(4)(*p*)(ii) was replaced by S.C. 2012, c. 31, s. 35(10), and comes into force on January 1, 2014. S. 146.4(4)(*p*)(ii) formerly read:

(ii) the first calendar year throughout which the beneficiary has no severe and prolonged impairments with the effects described in paragraph 118.3(1)(*a.1*).

S. 146.4(4)(*g*) was replaced by S.C. 2010, c. 12, s. 17(3), applicable to the 2009 and subsequent taxation years. S. 146.4(4)(*g*) formerly read:

(*g*) the plan prohibits a contribution from being made to the plan (other than as a transfer in accordance with subsection (8)) at any time if

(i) the beneficiary attained the age of 59 years before the calendar year that includes that time,

(ii) the beneficiary is not resident in Canada at that time, or

(iii) the total of the contribution and all other contributions made (other than as a transfer in accordance with subsection (8)) at or before that time to the plan or to any other registered disability savings plan of the beneficiary would exceed $200,000;

S. 146.4(4)(*l*)(iii) was replaced by S.C. 2010, c. 12, s. 17(4), applicable to the 2009 and subsequent taxation years. S. 146.4(4)(*l*)(iii) formerly read:

(iii) repayments under the *Canada Disability Savings Act*;

S. 146.4(4)(*n*), the portion before subparagraph (i) was replaced by S.C. 2010, c. 12, s. 17(5), applicable to the 2009 and subsequent taxation years. S. 146.4(4)(*n*), the portion before subparagraph (i) formerly read:

(*n*) the plan provides that when the total of all amounts paid under the *Canada Disability Savings Act* before the beginning of a calendar year to any registered disability savings plan of the beneficiary exceeds the total of all contributions made (other than as a transfer in accordance with subsection (8)) before the beginning of the calendar year to any registered disability savings plan of the beneficiary,

S. 146.4(4)(*p*), the portion before subparagraph (i) was replaced by S.C. 2010, c. 12, s. 17(6), applicable to the 2009 and subsequent taxation years. S. 146.4(4)(*p*), the portion before subparagraph (i) formerly read:

(*p*) the plan provides for any amounts remaining in the plan (after taking into consideration any repayments under the *Canada Disability Savings Act*) to be paid to the beneficiary or the beneficiary's estate, as the case may be, and for the plan to be terminated, by the end of the calendar year following the earlier of

Related Sections: S. 146.4(10) Non-compliance — cessation of registered status; s. 146.4(11) Non-compliance.

Guides: RC4460, Registered Disability Savings Plan.

Income Tax Folios: *Secondary* — S3-F10-C1 Qualified Investments – RRSPs, RESPs, RRIFs, RDSPs and TFSAs.

Information Circulars: IC 99-1R1 Registered Disability Savings Plans.

► 146.4(4.1) ◄

(4.1) Election on cessation of DTC-eligibility. A holder of a registered disability savings plan may elect in respect of a beneficiary under the plan who is not a DTC-eligible individual for a particular taxation year if

(*a*) a medical doctor or a nurse practitioner licensed to practise under the laws of a province certifies in writing that the nature of the beneficiary's condition is such that, in the professional opinion of the medical doctor or the nurse practitioner, the beneficiary is likely to become a DTC-eligible individual for a future taxation year;

(*b*) the beneficiary was a DTC-eligible individual for the year that immediately precedes the particular taxation year;

(*c*) the holder makes the election in a manner and format acceptable to the specified Minister before the end of the year immediately following the particular taxation year and provides the election and the medical certification in respect of the beneficiary to the issuer of the plan; and

(*d*) the issuer notifies the specified Minister of the election in a manner and format acceptable to the specified Minister.

History: S. 146.4(4.1)(*a*) was replaced by S.C. 2017, c. 33, s. 58(11), applicable in respect of certifications made after September 7, 2017, and formerly read:

(*a*) a medical doctor licensed to practise under the laws of a province certifies in writing that the nature of the beneficiary's condition is such that, in the professional opinion of the medical doctor, the beneficiary is likely to become a DTC-eligible individual for a future taxation year;

S. 146.4(4.1) was added by S.C. 2012, c. 31, s. 35(11), and comes into force on January 1, 2014.

► 146.4(4.2) ◄

(4.2) Election. An election under subsection (4.1) ceases to be valid at the time that is the earlier of

(*a*) the beginning of the first taxation year for which the beneficiary is again a DTC-eligible individual; and

(*b*) the end of the fourth taxation year following the particular taxation year referred to in subsection (4.1).

History: S. 146.4(4.2) was added by S.C. 2012, c. 31, s. 35(11), and comes into force on January 1, 2014.

► 146.4(4.3) ◄

(4.3) Transitional rule. Unless an election is made under subsection (4.1), if 2011 or 2012 is the first calendar year throughout which the beneficiary of a registered disability savings plan has no severe and prolonged impairments with the effects described in paragraph 118.3(1)(*a.1*) and the plan has not been terminated, then notwithstanding subparagraph (4)(*p*)(ii) as it read on March 28, 2012 and any terms of the plan required by that subparagraph, the plan must be terminated no later than December 31, 2014.

History: S. 146.4(4.3) was added by S.C. 2012, c. 31, s. 35(11), deemed to have come into force on March 29, 2012, except that before 2014 it is to be read as follows:

"(4.3) If 2011 or 2012 is the first calendar year throughout which the beneficiary of a registered disability savings plan has no severe and prolonged impairments with the effects described in paragraph 118.3(1)(*a.1*) and the plan has not been terminated, then notwithstanding subparagraph (4)(*p*)(ii) as it read on March 28, 2012 and any terms of the plan required by that subparagraph, the plan must be terminated no later than December 31, 2014."

► 146.4(5) ◄

(5) Trust not taxable. No tax is payable under this Part by a trust on the taxable income of the trust for a taxation year if, throughout the period in the year during which the trust was in existence, the trust was governed by a registered disability savings plan, except that

(*a*) tax is payable under this Part by the trust on its taxable income for the year if the trust has borrowed money

(i) in the year, or

(ii) in a preceding taxation year and has not repaid it before the beginning of the year; and

(*b*) if the trust is not otherwise taxable under paragraph (*a*) on its taxable income for the year and, at any time in the year, it carries on one or more businesses or holds one or more properties that are not qualified investments for the trust, tax is payable under this Part by the trust on the amount that its taxable income for the year would be if it had no incomes or losses from sources other than those businesses and properties, and no capital gains or losses other than from dispositions of those properties, and for this purpose,

(i) "income" includes dividends described in section 83, and

(ii) paragraphs 38(*a*) and (*b*) are to be read as if the fraction set out in each of those paragraphs were replaced by the word "all".

History: S. 146.4(5), the portion of (*b*) before subparagraph (i) was replaced by S.C. 2017, c. 33, s. 58(12), deemed to have come into force on March 23, 2017, and formerly read:

(*b*) if the trust is not otherwise taxable under paragraph (*a*) on its taxable income for the year and, at any time in the year, it carries on one or more businesses or holds one or more properties that are not qualified investments (as defined in subsection 205(1)) for the trust, tax is payable under this Part by the trust on the amount that its taxable income for the year would be if it had no incomes or losses from sources other than those businesses and properties, and no capital gains or losses other than from dispositions of those properties, and for this purpose,

Related Sections: S. 205(1), "qualified investment"; s. 206(3) Liability for tax; s. 206.1(3) Interpretation; s. 206.2(3) Liability for tax.

► 146.4(6) ◄

(6) Taxation of disability assistance payments. Where a disability assistance payment is made from a registered disability savings plan of a beneficiary, the amount, if any, by which the amount of the payment exceeds the non-taxable portion of the payment shall be included,

(*a*) if the beneficiary is alive at the time the payment is made, in computing the beneficiary's income for the beneficiary's taxation year in which the payment is made; and

(*b*) in any other case, in computing the income of the beneficiary's estate for the estate's taxation year in which the payment is made.

Related Sections: S. 56(1)(*q*.1) Registered disability savings plan payments; s. 60(*z*) Repayment under the Canada Disability Savings Act.

► 146.4(7) ◄

(7) Non-taxable portion of disability assistance payment. The non-taxable portion of a disability assistance payment made at a particular time from a registered disability savings plan of a beneficiary is the lesser of the amount of the disability assistance payment and the amount determined by the formula

$$A \times B/C + D$$

where

A is the amount of the disability assistance payment;

B is the amount, if any, by which

(*a*) the total of all amounts each of which is the amount of a contribution made before the particular time to any registered disability savings plan of the beneficiary

exceeds

(*b*) the total of all amounts each of which is the amount that would be the non-taxable portion of a disability assistance payment made before the particular time from any registered disability savings plan of the beneficiary, if the formula in this subsection were read without reference to the description of D;

C is the amount by which the fair market value of the property held by the plan trust immediately before the payment exceeds the assistance holdback amount in relation to the plan; and

D is the amount in respect of which a holder of the plan pays a tax under section 207.05 in respect of the plan, or another plan for which the plan was substituted by the holder, that

(*a*) has not been waived, cancelled or refunded; and

(*b*) has not otherwise been used in the year or a preceding year in computing the non-taxable portion of a disability assistance payment made from the plan or another plan for which the plan was substituted.

History: S. 146.4(7) was replaced by S.C. 2017, c. 33, s. 58(13), deemed to have come into force on March 23, 2017, and formerly read:

(7) *Non-taxable portion of disability assistance payment.* The non-taxable portion of a disability assistance payment made at a particular time from a registered disability savings plan of a beneficiary is the lesser of the amount of the disability assistance payment and the amount determined by the formula

$$A \times B/C$$

where

A is the amount of the disability assistance payment;

B is the amount, if any, by which

(*a*) the total of all amounts each of which is the amount of a contribution made before the particular time to any registered disability savings plan of the beneficiary

exceeds

(*b*) the total of all amounts each of which is the non-taxable portion of a disability assistance payment made before the particular time from any registered disability savings plan of the beneficiary; and

C is the amount by which the fair market value of the property held by the plan trust immediately before the payment exceeds the assistance holdback amount in relation to the plan.

S. 146.4(7), paragraph (*a*) of the description of B was replaced by S.C. 2010, c. 12, s. 17(7), applicable to the 2009 and subsequent taxation years. S. 146.4(7), paragraph (*a*) of the description of B formerly read:

(*a*) the total of all amounts each of which is the amount of a contribution made before the particular time to any registered disability savings plan of the beneficiary (other than as a transfer in accordance with subsection (8))

► 146.4(8) ◄

(8) Transfer of funds. An amount is transferred from a registered disability savings plan (in this subsection referred to as the "prior plan") of a beneficiary in accordance with this subsection if

(*a*) the amount is transferred directly to another registered disability savings plan (in this subsection referred to as the "new plan") of the beneficiary;

(*b*) the prior plan is terminated immediately after the transfer;

(*c*) the issuer of the prior plan provides the issuer of the new plan with all information in its possession concerning the prior plan (other than information provided to the issuer of the new plan by the specified Minister) as may reasonably be considered necessary for compliance, in respect of the new plan, with the requirements of this Act and with any conditions and obligations imposed under the *Canada Disability Savings Act*; and

(*d*) where the beneficiary attained the age of 59 years before the calendar year in which the transfer occurs, the issuer of the new plan undertakes to make (in addition to any other disability assistance payments that would otherwise have been made from the new plan in the year) one or more disability assistance payments from the plan in the year, the total of which is equal to the amount, if any, by which

(i) the total amount of disability assistance payments that would have been required to be made from the prior plan in the year if the transfer had not occurred

exceeds

(ii) the total amount of disability assistance payments made from the prior plan in the year.

History: S. 146.4(8)(*c*) was replaced by S.C. 2012, c. 31, s. 35(12), in force on Royal Assent, December 14, 2012. S. 146.4(8)(*c*) formerly read:

(*c*) the issuer of the prior plan provides the issuer of the new plan with all information in its possession concerning the prior plan as may reasonably be considered necessary for compliance, in respect of the new plan, with the requirements of this Act and with any conditions and obligations imposed under the *Canada Disability Savings Act*; and

▶ 146.4(9) ◀

(9) No income inclusion on transfer. An amount transferred in accordance with subsection (8) is not, solely because of that transfer, to be included in computing the income of any taxpayer.

▶ 146.4(10) ◀

(10) Non-compliance — cessation of registered status. Where, at any particular time, a registered disability savings plan is non-compliant as described in subsection (11),

(*a*) the plan ceases, as of the particular time, to be a registered disability savings plan (other than for the purposes of applying, as of the particular time, this subsection and subsection (11));

(*b*) a disability assistance payment is deemed to have been made from the plan at the time (in this subsection referred to as the "relevant time") immediately before the particular time to the beneficiary under the plan (or, if the beneficiary is deceased at the relevant time, to the beneficiary's estate), the amount of which payment is equal to the amount, if any, by which

(i) the fair market value of the property held by the plan trust at the relevant time

exceeds

(ii) the assistance holdback amount in relation to the plan; and

(*c*) if the plan is non-compliant because of a payment that is not in accordance with paragraph (4)(*j*), a disability assistance payment is deemed to have been made from the plan at the relevant time (in addition to the payment deemed by paragraph (*b*) to have been made) to the beneficiary under the plan (or, if the beneficiary is deceased at the relevant time, to the beneficiary's estate)

(i) the amount of which payment is equal to the amount by which the lesser of

(A) the assistance holdback amount in relation to the plan, and

(B) the fair market value of the property held by the plan trust at the relevant time

exceeds

(C) the fair market value of the property held by the plan trust immediately after the particular time, and

(ii) the non-taxable portion of which is deemed to be nil.

Related Sections: S. 56(1)(*q*.1) Registered disability savings plan payments; s. 146.4(6) Taxation of disability assistance payments; s. 206(1) Tax payable where inadequate consideration; s. 206.1(1) Tax payable on non-qualified investment; s. 206.2(1) Tax payable where advantage extended; s. 206.3(1) Tax payable on use of property as security.

▶ 146.4(11) ◀

(11) Non-compliance. A registered disability savings plan is non-compliant

(*a*) at any time that the plan fails to comply with a condition in subsection (4);

(*b*) at any time that there is a failure to administer the plan in accordance with its terms (other than those terms which the plan is required by subparagraph (4)(*a*)(i) to stipulate); and

(*c*) at any time that a person fails to comply with a condition or an obligation imposed, with respect to the plan, under the *Canada Disability Savings Act*, and the specified Minister has notified the Minister that, in the specified Minister's opinion, it is appropriate that the plan be considered to be non-compliant because of the failure.

▶ 146.4(12) ◀

(12) Non-application of subsection (11). Where a registered disability savings plan would otherwise be non-compliant at a particular time because of a failure described in paragraph (11)(*a*) or (*b*),

(*a*) the Minister may waive the application of the relevant paragraph with respect to the failure, if it is just and equitable to do so;

(*b*) the Minister may deem the failure to have occurred at a later time;

(*c*) if the failure consists of the making of a contribution that is prohibited under any of paragraphs (4)(*f*) to (*h*), an amount equal to the amount of the contribution has been withdrawn from the plan within such period as is specified by the Minister and the Minister has approved the application of this paragraph with respect to the failure,

(i) the contribution is deemed never to have been made, and

(ii) the withdrawal is deemed not to be a disability assistance payment and not to be in contravention of the condition in paragraph (4)(*i*); or

(*d*) if the failure consists of the plan not being terminated by the time set out in paragraph (4)(*p*) and the failure was due to the issuer being unaware of, or there being some uncertainty as to, the existence of circumstances requiring that the plan be terminated,

(i) the Minister may specify a later time by which the plan is to be terminated (but no later than is reasonably necessary for the plan to be terminated in an orderly manner), and

(ii) paragraph (4)(*p*) and the plan terms are, for the purposes of paragraphs (11)(*a*) and (*b*), to be read as though they required the plan to be terminated by the time so specified.

► 146.4(13) ◄

(13) Obligations of issuer. The issuer of a registered disability savings plan shall,

(*a*) where an entity becomes a holder of the plan after the plan is entered into, so notify the specified Minister in prescribed form containing prescribed information on or before the day that is 60 days after the later of

(i) the day on which the issuer is advised of the entity having become a holder of the plan, and

(ii) the day on which the issuer is provided with the new holder's Social Insurance Number or business number, as the case may be;

(*b*) not amend the plan before having received notification from the Minister that, in the Minister's opinion, a plan whose terms are identical to the amended plan would, if entered into by entities eligible to enter into a disability savings plan, comply with the conditions in subsection (4);

(*c*) where the issuer becomes aware that the plan is, or is likely to become, non-compliant (determined without reference to paragraph (11)(*c*) and subsection (12)), notify the Minister and the specified Minister of this fact on or before the day that is 30 days after the day on which the issuer becomes so aware; and

(*d*) (Repealed by S.C. 2017, c. 33, s. 58(14).)

(*e*) if the issuer enters into the plan with a qualifying family member who was a qualifying person in relation to the beneficiary at the time the plan (or another registered disability savings plan of the beneficiary) was entered into solely because of paragraph (*c*) of the definition "qualifying person" in subsection (1),

(i) so notify the beneficiary under the plan without delay in writing and include in the notification information setting out the circumstances in which the holder of the plan may be replaced under subsection (1.5) or (1.6), and

(ii) collect and use any information provided by the holder of the plan that is relevant to the administration and operation of the plan.

History: S. 146.4(13)(*d*) was repealed by S.C. 2017, c. 33, s. 58(14), deemed to have come into force on March 23, 2017, and formerly read:

(*d*) exercise the care, diligence and skill of a reasonably prudent person to minimize the possibility that a holder of the plan may become liable to pay tax under Part XI in connection with the plan; and

S. 146.4(13)(*e*), the portion before subparagraph (i) was replaced by S.C. 2013, c. 33, s. 16(5), deemed to have come into force on June 29, 2012, and formerly read:

(*e*) if the issuer enters into the plan with a qualifying family member who is a qualifying person solely because of paragraph (*c*) of the definition "qualifying person" in subsection (1),

S. 146.4(13)(*e*) was added by S.C. 2012, c. 19, s. 6(5), in force on Royal Assent, June 29, 2012.

Related Sections: S. 162(7) Failure to comply.

► 146.4(14) ◄

(14) Issuer's liability. If, after reasonable inquiry, an issuer of a disability savings plan is of the opinion that an individual's contractual competence to enter into a disability savings plan is in doubt, no action lies against the issuer for entering into a plan, under which the individual is the beneficiary, with a qualifying family member who was a qualifying person in relation to the beneficiary at the time the plan (or another registered disability savings plan of the beneficiary) was entered into solely because of paragraph (*c*) of the definition "qualifying person" in subsection (1).

History: S. 146.4(14) was replaced by S.C. 2013, c. 33, s. 16(6), deemed to have come into force on June 29, 2012, and formerly read:

(14) *Issuer's liability.* If, after reasonable inquiry, an issuer of a disability savings plan is of the opinion that an individual's contractual competence to enter into a disability savings plan is in doubt, no action lies against the issuer for entering into a plan, under which the individual is the beneficiary, with a qualifying family member who is a qualifying person in relation to the beneficiary solely because of paragraph (*c*) of the definition "qualifying person" in subsection (1).

S. 146.4(14) was added by S.C. 2012, c. 19, s. 6(6), in force on Royal Assent, June 29, 2012.

Deferred Profit Sharing Plans

SECTION 147: [Deferred profit sharing plans]

► 147(1) ◄

(1) Definitions. In this section,

Information Circulars: IC 77-1R5 Deferred profit sharing plan; IC 78-14R4 Guidelines for trust companies and other persons responsible for filing T3GR, T3D, T3P, T3S, T3RI, and T3F returns.

"deferred profit sharing plan" —"deferred profit sharing plan" means a profit sharing plan accepted by the Minister for registration for the purposes of this Act, on application therefor in prescribed manner by a trustee under the plan and an employer of employees who are beneficiaries under the plan, as complying with the requirements of this section;

Related Regulations: 1501.

Related Sections: S. 248(1), "employee trust".

Forms: T2214 — Application for Registration as a Deferred Profit Sharing Plan.

Information Circulars: IC 77-1R5 Deferred profit sharing plan.

Interpretation Bulletins: *Secondary* — IT-280R Employees profit sharing plans — Payments computed by reference to profits; IT-528 Transfers of funds between registered plans.

"forfeited amount" —"forfeited amount", under a deferred profit sharing plan or a plan the registration of which has been revoked pursuant to subsection (14) or (14.1), means an amount to which a beneficiary under the plan has ceased to have any rights, other than the portion thereof, if any, that is payable as a consequence of the death of the beneficiary to a person who is entitled thereto by virtue of the participation of the beneficiary in the plan;

"licensed annuities provider" —"licensed annuities provider" means a person licensed or otherwise authorized under the laws of Canada or a province to carry on in Canada an annuities business;

Related Sections: S. 146(1), "qualified investment"; s. 146.3(1), "qualified investment".

"profit sharing plan" —"profit sharing plan" means an arrangement under which payments computed by reference to an employer's profits from the employer's business, or by reference to those profits and the profits, if any, from the business of a corporation with which the employer does not deal at arm's length, are or have been made by the employer to a trustee in trust for the benefit of employees or former employees of that employer.

▶ 147(1.1) ◀

(1.1) Participating employer. An employer is considered to participate in a profit sharing plan where the employer makes or has made payments under the plan to a trustee in trust for the benefit of employees or former employees of the employer.

▶ 147(2) ◀

(2) Acceptance of plan for registration. The Minister shall not accept for registration for the purposes of this Act any profit sharing plan unless, in the Minister's opinion, it complies with the following conditions:

(*a*) the plan provides that each payment made under the plan to a trustee in trust for the benefit of beneficiaries thereunder is the total of amounts each of which is required to be allocated by the trustee in the year in which it is received by the trustee, to the individual beneficiary in respect of whom the amount was so paid;

(*a*.1) the plan includes a stipulation that no contribution may be made to the plan other than

(i) a contribution made in accordance with the terms of the plan by an employer for the benefit of the employer's employees who are beneficiaries under the plan, or

(ii) an amount transferred to the plan in accordance with subsection (19);

(*b*) the plan does not provide for the payment of any amount to an employee or other beneficiary thereunder by way of loan;

(*c*) the plan provides that no part of the funds of the trust governed by the plan may be invested in notes, bonds, debentures, bankers' acceptances or similar obligations of

(i) an employer by whom payments are made in trust to a trustee under the plan for the benefit of beneficiaries thereunder, or

(ii) a corporation with which that employer does not deal at arm's length;

(*d*) the plan provides that no part of the funds of the trust governed by the plan may be invested in shares of a corporation at least 50% of the property of which consists of notes, bonds, debentures, bankers' acceptances or similar obligations of an employer or a corporation described in paragraph (*c*);

(*e*) the plan includes a provision stipulating that no right of a person under the plan is capable of any surrender or assignment other than

(i) an assignment under a decree, an order or a judgment of a competent tribunal, or under a written agreement, that relates to a division of property between an individual and the individual's spouse or common-law partner, or former spouse or common-law partner, in settlement of rights that arise out of, or on a breakdown of, their marriage or common-law partnership,

(ii) an assignment by a deceased individual's legal representative on the distribution of the individual's estate, and

(iii) a surrender of benefits to avoid revocation of the plan's registration;

(*f*) the plan includes a provision stipulating that each of the trustees under the plan shall be resident in Canada;

(*g*) the plan provides that, if a corporation licensed or otherwise authorized under the laws of Canada or a province to carry on in Canada the business of offering to the public its services as trustee is not a trustee under the plan, there shall be at least 3 trustees under the plan who shall be individuals;

(*h*) the plan provides that all income received, capital gains made and capital losses sustained by the trust governed by the plan must be allocated to beneficiaries under the plan on or before a day 90 days after the end of the year in which they were received, made or sustained, as the case may be, to the extent that they have not been allocated in years preceding that year;

(*i*) the plan provides that each amount allocated or reallocated by a trustee under the plan to a beneficiary under the plan vests irrevocably in that beneficiary,

(i) in the case of an amount allocated or reallocated before 1991, at a time that is not later than 5 years after the end of the year in which it was allocated or reallocated, unless the beneficiary becomes, before that time, an individual who is not an employee of any employer who participates in the plan, and

(ii) in the case of any other amount, not later than the later of the time of allocation or reallocation and the day on which the beneficiary completes a period of 24 consecutive months as a beneficiary under the plan or under any other deferred profit sharing plan for which the plan can reasonably be considered to have been substituted;

(*i*.1) the plan requires that each forfeited amount under the plan and all earnings of the plan reasonably attributable thereto be paid to employers who participate in the plan, or be reallocated to beneficiaries under the plan, on or before the later of December 31, 1991 and December 31 of the year immediately following the calendar year in which the amount is forfeited, or such later time as is permitted in writing by the Minister under subsection (2.2);

(*j*) the plan provides that a trustee under the plan inform, in writing, all new beneficiaries under the plan of their rights under the plan;

(*k*) the plan provides that, in respect of each beneficiary under the plan who has been employed by an employer who participates in the plan, all amounts vested under the plan in the beneficiary become payable

(i) to the beneficiary, or

(ii) in the event of the beneficiary's death, to another person designated by the beneficiary or to the beneficiary's estate,

not later than the earlier of

(iii) the end of the year in which the beneficiary attains 71 years of age, and

(iv) 90 days after the earliest of

(A) the death of the beneficiary,

(B) the day on which the beneficiary ceases to be employed by an employer who participates in the plan where, at the time of ceasing to be so employed, the beneficiary is not employed by another employer who participates in the plan, and

(C) the termination or winding-up of the plan,

except that the plan may provide that, on election by the beneficiary, all or any part of the amounts payable to the beneficiary may be paid

(v) in equal instalments payable not less frequently than annually over a period not exceeding 10 years from the day on which the amount became payable, or

(vi) by a trustee under the plan to a licensed annuities provider to purchase for the beneficiary an annuity where

(A) payment of the annuity is to begin not later than the end of the year in which the beneficiary attains 71 years of age, and

(B) the guaranteed term, if any, of the annuity does not exceed 15 years;

(*k*.1) the plan requires that no benefit or loan, other than

(i) a benefit the amount of which is required to be included in computing the beneficiary's income,

(ii) an amount referred to in paragraph (10)(*b*),

(ii.1) an amount paid pursuant to or under the plan by a trustee under the plan to a licensed annuities provider to purchase for a beneficiary under the plan an annuity to which subparagraph (*k*)(vi) applies,

(iii) a benefit derived from an allocation or reallocation referred to in subsection (2), or

(iv) the benefit derived from the provision of administrative or investment services in respect of the plan,

that is conditional in any way on the existence of the plan may be extended to a beneficiary thereunder or to a person with whom the beneficiary was not dealing at arm's length;

(*k*.2) the plan provides that no individual who is

(i) a person related to the employer,

(ii) a person who is, or is related to, a specified shareholder of the employer or of a corporation related to the employer,

(iii) where the employer is a partnership, a person related to a member of the partnership, or

(iv) where the employer is a trust, a person who is, or is related to, a beneficiary under the trust

may become a beneficiary under the plan; and

(*l*) the plan, in all other respects, complies with regulations of the Governor in Council made on the recommendation of the Minister of Finance.

History: S. 147(2)(*e*) was replaced by S.C. 2013, c. 34, s. 301(1), deemed to have come into force on March 21, 2003, and formerly read:

(*e*) the plan includes a provision stipulating that no right or interest under the plan of an employee who is a beneficiary thereunder is capable, either in whole or in part, of surrender or assignment;

Related Regulations: Part II; Part XLIX.

Related Sections: S. 118(7), "pension income"; s. 144(11) Taxation year of trust; s. 172(3) Appeal from refusal to register, revocation of registration, etc.; 198 Tax on non-qualified investments and use of assets as security; 199 Tax on initial non-qualified investments not disposed of; 200 Distribution deemed disposition; 201 Tax where inadequate consideration on purchase or sale; 202 Returns and payment of estimated tax; 203 Application to other taxes; 204 Definitions.

Forms: T2214 — Application for Registration as a Deferred Profit Sharing Plan.

Information Circulars: IC 72-13R8 Employees' pension plans; IC 77-1R5 Deferred profit sharing plan; IC 78-14R4 Guidelines for trust companies and other persons responsible for filing T3GR, T3D, T3P, T3S, T3RI, and T3F returns.

► 147(2.1) ◄

(2.1) Terms limiting contributions. The Minister shall not accept for registration for the purposes of this Act a profit sharing plan unless it includes terms that are adequate to ensure that the requirements of subsection (5.1) in respect of the plan will be satisfied for each calendar year.

Information Circulars: IC 77-1R5 Deferred profit sharing plan.

► 147(2.2) ◄

(2.2) Reallocation of forfeitures. The Minister may, on written application, extend the time for satisfying the requirements of paragraph (2)(*i*.1) where

(*a*) the total of the forfeited amounts arising in a calendar year is greater than normal because of unusual circumstances; and

(*b*) the forfeited amounts are to be reallocated on a reasonable basis to a majority of beneficiaries under the plan.

► 147(3) ◄

(3) Acceptance of employees profit sharing plan for registration. The Minister shall not accept for registration for the purposes of this Act any employees profit sharing plan unless all the capital gains of or made by the trust governed by the plan before the date of application for registration of the plan and all the capital losses of or sustained by the trust before that date have been allocated by the trustee under the plan to employees and other beneficiaries thereunder.

► 147(4) ◄

(4) Capital gains determined. For the purposes of subsections (3) and (11), such amount as may be determined by the Minister, on request in prescribed manner by the trustee of a trust governed by an employees profit sharing plan, shall be deemed to be the amount of

(*a*) the capital gains of or made by the trust governed by the plan before the date of application for registration of the plan, or (*b*) the capital losses of or sustained by the trust before that date,

as the case may be.

► 147(5) ◄

(5) Registration date. Where a profit sharing plan is accepted by the Minister for registration as a deferred profit sharing plan, the plan shall be deemed to have become registered as a deferred profit sharing plan

(*a*) on the date the application for registration of the plan was made; or

(*b*) where in the application for registration a later date is specified as the date on which the plan is to commence as a deferred profit sharing plan, on that date.

Related Sections: S. 144(11) Taxation year of trust.

► 147(5.1) ◄

(5.1) Contribution limits. For the purposes of subsections (2.1) and (9) and paragraph (14)(*c*.4), the requirements of this subsection in respect of a deferred profit sharing plan are satisfied for a calendar year if, in the case of each beneficiary under the plan and each employer in respect of whom the beneficiary's pension credit (as prescribed by regulation) for the year under the plan is greater than nil,

(*a*) the total of all amounts each of which is the beneficiary's pension credit (as prescribed by regulation) for the year in respect of the employer under a deferred profit sharing plan does not exceed the lesser of

(i) ½ of the money purchase limit for the year, and

(ii) 18% of the amount that would be the beneficiary's compensation (within the meaning assigned by subsection 147.1(1)) from the employer for the year if the definition "compensation" in subsection 147.1(1) were read without reference to paragraph (*b*) of that definition;

(*b*) the total of all amounts each of which is the beneficiary's pension credit (as prescribed by regulation) for the year under a deferred profit sharing plan in respect of

(i) the employer, or

(ii) any other employer who, at any time in the year, does not deal at arm's length with the employer

does not exceed ½ of the money purchase limit for the year; and

(*c*) the total of

(i) the beneficiary's pension adjustment for the year in respect of the employer, and

(ii) the total of all amounts each of which is the beneficiary's pension adjustment for the year in respect of any other employer who, at any time in the year, does not deal at arm's length with the employer

does not exceed the lesser of

(iii) the money purchase limit for the year, and

(iv) 18% of the total of all amounts each of which is the beneficiary's compensation (within the meaning assigned by subsection 147.1(1)) for the year from the employer or any other employer referred to in subparagraph (ii).

Editorial Note: All deferred profit sharing plans must comply with the limits outlined under s. 147(5.1). If any of these limits are not met, the Minister may revoke the registration of the plan (see s. 147(14)(*c*.4)). The Minister may also refuse the registration of the plan where the terms are such that the limits under s. 147(5.1) may not be met (see s. 147(2.1)). S. 147(5.1) provides for three separate limits which must all be met for a particular year. The first limit is in s. 147(5.1)(*a*) and requires that the aggregate of the individual's "pension credit" for the year as a result of his or her membership in a deferred profit sharing plan of his or her employer not exceed one-half of the "money purchase limit" for the year and 18% of the individual's "compensation" for the year. See the definitions of "money purchase limit" and "compensation" (which is to be read without reference to paragraph (b)) in s. 147.1(1). The individual's "pension credit" for a calendar year in respect of a deferred profit sharing plan of his or her employer is defined in regulation 8301(2). The second limit in s. 147(5.1)(*b*) provides that the aggregate of all of the individual's pension credits under all deferred profit sharing plans of the employer and of those employers that do not deal at arm's length with the employer cannot exceed one-half of the "money purchase limit" for the year. The third overall limit is described under s. 147(5.1)(*c*) and provides that the aggregate of the individual's "pension adjustment" for the year under all registered plans of the employer and those employers that do not deal at arm's length with the employer cannot exceed the lesser of the "money purchase limit" for the year and 18% of the individual's "compensation" for the year from all such employers.

Related Regulations: 214.1; 8301(2); 8301(2.1); 8301(3); 8301(15); 8304(2).

Related Sections: S. 18(1)(*j*) Limitation re employer's contribution under deferred profit sharing plan; s. 18(1)(*k*) Limitation re employer's contribution under profit sharing plan; s. 147.1(1), "money purchase limit"; Part X.1 Tax in Respect of Over-Contributions to Deferred Income Plans.

Information Circulars: IC 77-1R5 Deferred profit sharing plan.

Interpretation Bulletins: *Secondary* — IT-528 Transfers of funds between registered plans.

Registered Plans Directorate Newsletters: No. 96-1, Changes to retirement savings limits; No. 94-2, Technical questions and answers.

► 147(5.11) ◄

(5.11) Compensation — (Repealed by S.C. 2013, c. 34, s. 301(2).)

History: S. 147(5.11) was repealed by S.C. 2013, c. 34, s. 301(2), applicable to cessations of employment that occur after 2002, and formerly read:

(5.11) *Compensation.* Where at any time in a calendar year an individual ceases to be employed by an employer,

(*a*) for the purposes of paragraph (5.1)(*a*), the amount that would be the individual's compensation (in this subsection having the meaning assigned by subsection 147.1(1)) from the employer for the year if the definition "compensation" in subsection 147.1(1) were read without reference to paragraph (*b*) of that definition shall be deemed to be the greater of

(i) that amount determined without reference to this paragraph, and

(ii) the amount that would be the individual's compensation from the employer for the immediately preceding year if the definition "compensation" in subsection 147.1(1) were read without reference to paragraph (*b*) of that definition; and

(*b*) for the purposes of paragraph (5.1)(*c*), the individual's compensation from the employer for the year shall be deemed to be the greater of

(i) that compensation determined without reference to this paragraph, and

(ii) the individual's compensation from the employer for the immediately preceding year.

► 147(6) ◄

(6) Deferred plan not employees profit sharing plan. For a period during which a plan is a deferred profit sharing plan, the plan shall be deemed, for the purposes of this Act, not to be an employees profit sharing plan.

Related Sections: S. 144(11) Taxation year of trust.

► 147(7) ◄

(7) No tax while trust governed by plan. No tax is payable under this Part by a trust on the taxable income of the trust for a period during which the trust was governed by a deferred profit sharing plan.

Related Sections: S. 128(10), "excluded right or interest"; s. 149(1)(*s*) Trusts under deferred profit sharing plan; 198 Tax on non-qualified investments and use of assets as security; 199 Tax on initial non-qualified investments not disposed of; 200 Distribution deemed disposition; 201 Tax where inadequate consideration on purchase or sale; 202 Returns and payment of estimated tax; 203 Application to other taxes; 204 Definitions.

Information Circulars: IC 77-1R5 Deferred profit sharing plan.

▶ 147(8) ◀

(8) Amount of employer's contribution deductible. Subject to subsection (9), there may be deducted in computing the income of an employer for a taxation year the total of all amounts each of which is an amount paid by the employer in the year or within 120 days after the end of the year to a trustee under a deferred profit sharing plan for the benefit of the employer's employees who are beneficiaries under the plan, to the extent that the amount was paid in accordance with the terms of the plan and was not deducted in computing the employer's income for a preceding taxation year.

Related Sections: S. 6(1)(*a*) Value of benefits; s. 18(1)(*j*) Limitation re employer's contribution under deferred profit sharing plan; s. 20(1)(*y*) Employer's contributions under deferred profit sharing plan.

▶ 147(9) ◀

(9) Limitation on deduction. Where the requirements of subsection (5.1) in respect of a deferred profit sharing plan are not satisfied for a calendar year by reason that the pension credits of a beneficiary under the plan in respect of a particular employer do not comply with paragraph (5.1)(*a*) or the beneficiary's pension credits or pension adjustments in respect of a particular employer and other employers who do not deal at arm's length with the particular employer do not comply with paragraph (5.1)(*b*) or (*c*), the particular employer is not entitled to a deduction under subsection (8) in computing the particular employer's income for any taxation year in respect of an amount paid to a trustee under the plan in the calendar year except to the extent expressly permitted in writing by the Minister, and, for the purposes of this subsection, an amount paid to a trustee of a deferred profit sharing plan in the first two months of a calendar year shall be deemed to have been paid in the immediately preceding year and not to have been paid in the year to the extent that the amount can reasonably be considered to be in respect of the immediately preceding year.

Related Sections: S. 18(1)(*j*) Limitation re employer's contribution under deferred profit sharing plan; s. 18(1)(*k*) Limitation re employer's contribution under profit sharing plan; s. 20(1)(*y*) Employer's contributions under deferred profit sharing plan.

Information Circulars: IC 77-1R5 Deferred profit sharing plan.

▶ 147(9.1) ◀

(9.1) No deduction. Notwithstanding subsection (8), no deduction shall be made in computing the income of an employer for a taxation year in respect of an amount paid by the employer for the year to a trustee under a deferred profit sharing plan in respect of a beneficiary who is described in paragraph (2)(*k.2*) in respect of the plan.

▶ 147(10) ◀

(10) Amounts received taxable. There shall be included in computing the income of a beneficiary under a deferred profit sharing plan for a taxation year the amount, if any, by which

(*a*) the total of all amounts received by the beneficiary in the year from a trustee under the plan (other than as a result of acquiring an annuity described in subparagraph (2)(*k*)(vi) under which the beneficiary is the annuitant)

exceeds

(*b*) the total of all amounts each of which is an amount determined for the year under subsection (10.1), (11) or (12) in relation to the plan and in respect of the beneficiary.

Related Sections: S. 6(1)(*a*)(i) Value of benefits; s. 56(1)(*i*) Deferred profit sharing plan; s. 60(*j*) Transfer of superannuation benefits; s. 60(*k*) Transfers to deferred profit sharing plans; s. 104(27) Pension benefits; s. 104(27.1) DPSP benefits; s. 118(7), "pension income"; s. 128(10), "excluded right or interest"; s. 146(1), "earned income"; s. 153(1) Withholding; s. 214(3) Deemed payments; s. 248(1), "benefit under a deferred profit sharing plan".

Information Circulars: IC 77-1R5 Deferred profit sharing plan; IC 78-14R4 Guidelines for trust companies and other persons responsible for filing T3GR, T3D, T3P, T3S, T3RI, and T3F returns.

Interpretation Bulletins: *Secondary* — IT-528 Transfers of funds between registered plans.

Cases: Under the terms of a DPSP the taxpayer directed the trustee to have his non-deductible contributions invested in shares. When the plan was later restructured he withdrew his shares, which had increased in value, and some cash. The increase in value of the shares was taxable as income. *The Queen v. Powell*, 80 DTC 6301 (F.C.T.D.)

▶ 147(10.1) ◀

(10.1) Single payment on retirement, etc. For the purposes of subsections (10) and (10.2), where a beneficiary under a deferred profit sharing plan has received, in a taxation year and when the beneficiary was resident in Canada, from a trustee under the plan a single payment that included shares of the capital stock of a corporation that was an employer who contributed to the plan or of a corporation with which the employer did not deal at arm's length on the beneficiary's withdrawal from the plan or retirement from employment or on the death of an employee or former employee and has made an election in respect thereof in prescribed manner and prescribed form, the amount determined for the year under this subsection in relation to the plan and in respect of the beneficiary is the amount, if any, by which the fair market value of those shares, immediately before the single payment was made, exceeds the cost amount to the plan of those shares at that time.

Related Regulations: 1503.

Related Sections: S. 7(1.3) Order of disposition of securities; s. 47(3) Securities acquired by employee.

Forms: T2078 — Election Under Subsection 147(10.1) in Respect of a Single Payment Received From a Deferred Profit Sharing Plan.

Information Circulars: IC 77-1R5 Deferred profit sharing plan.

Interpretation Bulletins: *Primary* — IT-528 Transfers of funds between registered plans.

▶ 147(10.2) ◀

(10.2) Idem. Where a trustee under a deferred profit sharing plan has at any time in a taxation year made under the plan a single payment that included shares referred to in subsection (10.1) to a beneficiary who was resident in Canada at the time and the beneficiary has made an election under that subsection in respect of that payment,

(*a*) the trustee shall be deemed to have disposed of those shares for proceeds of disposition equal to the cost amount to the trust of those shares immediately before the single payment was made;

(*b*) the cost to the beneficiary of those shares shall be deemed to be their cost amount to the trust immediately before the single payment was made;

(*c*) the cost to the beneficiary of each of those shares shall be deemed to be the amount determined by the formula

$$A \times B/C$$

where

A is the amount determined under paragraph (*a*) in respect of all of those shares,

B is the fair market value of that share at the time the single payment was made, and

C is the fair market value of all those shares at the time the single payment was made; and

(*d*) for the purposes of paragraph 60(*j*), the cost to the beneficiary of those shares is an eligible amount in respect of the beneficiary for the year.

Interpretation Bulletins: *Secondary* — IT-528 Transfers of funds between registered plans.

► 147(10.3) ◄

(10.3) Amount contributed to or forfeited under a plan. There shall be included in computing the income for a taxation year of a beneficiary described in paragraph (2)(*k*.2) the total of amounts allocated or reallocated to the beneficiary in the year in respect of

(*a*) any amount contributed after December 1, 1982 by an employer to, or

(*b*) any forfeited amount under

a deferred profit sharing plan or a plan the registration of which has been revoked pursuant to subsection (14) or (14.1).

Related Sections: S. 147(1) Definitions.

Information Circulars: IC 77-1R5 Deferred profit sharing plan.

► 147(10.4) ◄

(10.4) Income on disposal of shares. Where a taxpayer has a share in respect of which the taxpayer has made an election under subsection (10.1), there shall be included in computing the taxpayer's income for the taxation year in which the taxpayer disposed of or exchanged the share or ceased to be a resident of Canada, whichever is the earlier, the amount, if any, by which the fair market value of the share at the time the taxpayer acquired it exceeds the cost to the taxpayer, determined under paragraph (10.2)(*c*), of the share at the time the taxpayer acquired it.

Related Sections: S. 7(1.3) Order of disposition of securities; s. 52(1) Cost of certain property the value of which included in income; s. 110(1)(*d*.3) Employer's shares.

► 147(10.5) ◄

(10.5) Amended contract. Where an amendment is made to an annuity contract to which subparagraph (2)(*k*)(vi) applies, the sole effect of which is to defer annuity commencement to no later than the end of the calendar year in which the individual in respect of whom the contract was purchased attains 71 years of age, the annuity contract is deemed not to have been disposed of by the individual.

► 147(10.6) ◄

(10.6) Commencement of annuity after age 69 — (Repealed by S.C. 2007, c. 29, s. 20(6).)

► 147(11) ◄

(11) Portion of receipts deductible. For the purposes of subsections (10), (10.1) and (12), where an amount was received in a taxation year from a trustee under a deferred profit sharing plan by an employee or other beneficiary thereunder, and the employee was a beneficiary under the plan at a time when the plan was an employees profit sharing plan, the amount determined for the year under this subsection in relation to the plan and in respect of the beneficiary is such portion of the total of the amounts so received in the year as does not exceed

(*a*) the total of

(i) each amount included in respect of the plan in computing the income of the employee for the year or for a previous taxation year by virtue of section 144,

(ii) each amount paid by the employee to a trustee under the plan at a time when it was an employees profit sharing plan, and

(iii) each amount that was allocated to the employee or other beneficiary by a trustee under the plan, at a time when it was an employees profit sharing plan, in respect of a capital gain made by the trust before 1972,

minus

(*b*) the total of

(i) each amount received by the employee or other beneficiary in a previous taxation year from a trustee under the plan at a time when it was an employees profit sharing plan,

(ii) each amount received by the employee or other beneficiary in a previous taxation year from a trustee under the plan at a time when it was a deferred profit sharing plan, and

(iii) each amount allocated to the employee or other beneficiary by a trustee under the plan, at a time when it was an employees profit sharing plan, in respect of a capital loss sustained by the trust before 1972.

Information Circulars: IC 77-1R5 Deferred profit sharing plan.

► 147(12) ◄

(12) Idem. For the purposes of subsections (10) and (10.1), where an amount was received in a taxation year from a trustee under a deferred profit sharing plan by an employee or other beneficiary thereunder, and the employee has made a payment in the year or a previous year to a trustee under the plan at a time when the plan was a deferred profit sharing plan, the amount determined for the year under this subsection in relation to the plan and in respect of the beneficiary is such portion of the total of the amounts so received in the year (minus any amount determined for the year under subsection (11) in relation to the plan and in respect of the beneficiary) as does not exceed (*a*) the total of all amounts each of which was so paid by the employee in the year or a previous year to the extent that the payment was not deductible in computing the employee's income,

minus

(*b*) the total of all amounts each of which was received by the employee or other beneficiary from a trustee under the plan, at a time when it was a deferred profit sharing plan, to the extent that it was included in the computation of an amount determined for a previous year under this subsection in relation to the plan and in respect of the employee or other beneficiary.

Related Sections: S. 60(*j*) Transfer of superannuation benefits; s. 60(*k*) Transfers to deferred profit sharing plans; s. 212(1)(*m*) Deferred profit sharing plan payments.

Information Circulars: IC 77-1R5 Deferred profit sharing plan.

► 147(13) ◄

(13) Appropriation of trust property by employer. Where funds or property of a trust governed by a deferred profit sharing plan have been appropriated in any manner whatever to or for the benefit of a taxpayer who is

(*a*) an employer by whom payments are made in trust to a trustee under the plan, or

(*b*) a corporation with which that employer does not deal at arm's length,

otherwise than in payment of or on account of shares of the capital stock of the taxpayer purchased by the trust, the amount or value of the funds or property so appropriated shall be included in computing the income of the taxpayer for the taxation year of the taxpayer in which the funds or property were so appropriated, unless the funds or property or an amount in lieu thereof equal to the amount or value of the funds or property was repaid to the trust within one year from the end of the taxation year, and it is established by subsequent events or otherwise that the repayment was not made as part of a series of appropriations and repayments.

Related Sections: S. 212(1)(*m*) Deferred profit sharing plan payments; s. 214(3) Deemed payments.

► 147(14) ◄

(14) Revocation of registration. Where, at any time after a profit sharing plan has been accepted by the Minister for registration for the purposes of this Act,

(*a*) the plan has been revised or amended or a new plan has been substituted therefor, and the plan as revised or amended or the new plan substituted therefor, as the case may be, ceased to comply with the requirements of this section for its acceptance by the Minister for registration for the purposes of this Act,

(*b*) any provision of the plan has not been complied with,

(*c*) the plan is a plan that did not, as of January 1, 1968,

(i) comply with the requirements of paragraphs (2)(*a*), (*b*) to (*h*), (*j*) and (*k*), and paragraph 147(2)(*i*) of the *Income Tax Act*, chapter 148 of the Revised Statutes of Canada, 1952, as it read on January 1, 1972, and

(ii) provide that the amounts held by the trust for the benefit of beneficiaries thereunder that remained unallocated on December 31, 1967 must be allocated or reallocated, as the case may be, before 1969,

(*c*.1) the plan becomes a revocable plan pursuant to subsection (21),

(*c*.2) the plan does not comply with the requirements of paragraphs (2)(*a*) to (*k*) and (*l*),

(*c*.3) in the case of a plan that became registered after March, 1983, the plan does not comply with the requirements of paragraphs (2)(*k*.1) and (*k*.2),

(*c*.4) the requirements of subsection (5.1) in respect of the plan are not satisfied for a calendar year, or

(*c*.5) an employer who participates in the plan fails to file an information return reporting a pension adjustment of a beneficiary under the plan as and when required by regulation,

the Minister may revoke the registration of the plan,

(*d*) where paragraph (*a*) applies, as of the date that the plan ceased so to comply, or any subsequent date,

(*e*) where paragraph (*b*) applies, as of the date that any provision of the plan was not so complied with, or any subsequent date,

(*f*) where paragraph (*c*) applies, as of any date following January 1, 1968,

(*g*) where paragraph (*c*.1) applies, as of the date on which the plan became a revocable plan, or any subsequent date,

(*h*) where paragraph (*c*.2) or (*c*.3) applies, as of the date on which the plan did not so comply, or any subsequent date, but not before January 1, 1991,

(*i*) where paragraph (*c*.4) applies, as of the end of the year for which the requirements of subsection (5.1) in respect of the plan are not satisfied, or any subsequent date, and

(*j*) where paragraph (*c*.5) applies, as of any date after the date by which the information return was required to be filed,

and the Minister shall thereafter give notice of the revocation by registered mail to a trustee under the plan and to an employer of employees who are beneficiaries under the plan.

Information Circulars: IC 77-1R5 Deferred profit sharing plan.

► 147(14.1) ◄

(14.1) Idem. Where on any day after June 30, 1982 a benefit or loan is extended or continues to be extended as a consequence of the existence of a deferred profit sharing plan and that benefit or loan would be prohibited if the plan met the requirement for registration contained in paragraph (2)(*k*.1), the Minister may revoke the registration of the plan as of that or any subsequent day that is specified by the Minister in a notice given by registered mail to a trustee under the plan and to an employer of employees who are beneficiaries under the plan.

► 147(15) ◄

(15) Rules applicable to revoked plan. Where the Minister revokes the registration of a deferred profit sharing plan, the plan (in this section referred to as the "revoked plan") shall be deemed, for the purposes of this Act, not to be a deferred profit sharing plan, and notwithstanding any other provision of this Act, the following rules shall apply:

(*a*) the revoked plan shall not be accepted for registration for the purposes of this Act or be deemed to have become registered as a deferred profit sharing plan at any time within a period of one year commencing on the date the plan became a revoked plan;

(*b*) subsection (7) does not apply to exempt the trust governed by the plan from tax under this Part on the taxable income of the trust for a taxation year in which, at any time therein, the trust was governed by the revoked plan;

(*c*) no deduction shall be made by an employer in computing the employer's income for a taxation year in respect of an amount paid by the employer to a trustee under the plan at a time when it was a revoked plan;

(*d*) there shall be included in computing the income of a taxpayer for a taxation year

(i) all amounts received by the taxpayer in the year from a trustee under the revoked plan that, by virtue of subsection (10), would have been so included if the revoked plan had been a deferred profit sharing plan at the time the taxpayer received those amounts, and

(ii) the amount or value of any funds or property appropriated to or for the benefit of the taxpayer in the year that, by virtue of subsection (13), would have been so included if the revoked plan had been a deferred profit sharing plan at the time of the appropriation of the funds or property; and

(*e*) the revoked plan shall be deemed, for the purposes of this Act, not to be an employees profit sharing plan or a retirement compensation arrangement.

Related Regulations: 202(2), (3).

Related Sections: S. 110.6(1), "investment income"; s. 118(7), "pension income"; s. 128(10), "excluded right or interest"; s. 146(1), "earned income"; s. 214(3) Deemed payments; Part X Taxes on Deferred Profit Sharing Plans and Revoked Plans.

► 147(16) ◄

(16) Payments out of profits. Where the terms of an arrangement under which an employer makes payments to a trustee specifically provide that the payments shall be made "out of profits", the arrangement shall be deemed, for the purpose of subsection (1), to be an arrangement for payments "computed by reference to an employer's profits from the employer's business".

Related Sections: S. 147(1) Definitions.

► 147(17) ◄

(17) Interpretation of "other beneficiary". Where the expression "employee or other beneficiary" under a profit sharing plan occurs in this section, the words "other beneficiary" shall be construed as meaning any person, other than the employee, to whom any amount is or may become payable by a trustee under the plan as a result of payments made to the trustee under the plan in trust for the benefit of employees, including the employee.

Related Sections: S. 202(1) Returns and payment of estimated tax.

► 147(18) ◄

(18) Inadequate consideration on purchase from or sale to trust. Where a trust governed by a deferred profit sharing plan or revoked plan

(*a*) disposes of property to a taxpayer for a consideration less than the fair market value of the property at the time of the transaction, or for no consideration, or

(*b*) acquires property from a taxpayer for a consideration greater than the fair market value of the property at the time of the transaction,

the difference between that fair market value and the consideration, if any,

(*c*) shall, for the purposes of subsections (10) and (15), be deemed to be an amount received by the taxpayer at the time of the disposal or acquisition, as the case may be, from a trustee under the plan as if the taxpayer were a beneficiary under the plan, and

(*d*) is an amount taxable under section 201 for the calendar year in which the trust disposes of or acquires the property, as the case may be.

Related Sections: S. 201 Tax where inadequate consideration on purchase or sale.

Information Circulars: IC 77-1R5 Deferred profit sharing plan.

Cases: Two taxpayers did not receive a taxable benefit when they purchased shares from a profit sharing plan trust at allegedly less than their fair market value. *Johansen v. M.N.R.*, 72 DTC 1528 (T.R.B.)

► 147(19) ◄

(19) Transfer to RPP, RRSP or DPSP. An amount is transferred from a deferred profit sharing plan in accordance with this subsection if the amount

(*a*) is not part of a series of periodic payments;

(*b*) is transferred on behalf of an individual

(i) who is an employee or former employee of an employer who participated in the plan on the employee's behalf, or

(ii) who is a spouse or common-law partner, or former spouse or common-law partner, of an employee or former employee referred to in subparagraph (i) and who is entitled to the amount

(A) as a consequence of the death of the employee or former employee, or

(B) under a decree, an order or a judgment of a competent tribunal, or under a written agreement, that relates to a division of property between the employee or former employee and the individual in settlement of rights that arise out of, or on a breakdown of, their marriage or common-law partnership;

in full or partial satisfaction of the individual's entitlement to benefits under the plan;

(*c*) would, if it were paid directly to the individual, be included under subsection (10) in computing the individual's income for a taxation year; and (*d*) is transferred for the benefit of the individual directly to

(i) a registered pension plan,

(ii) a registered retirement savings plan under which the individual is the annuitant (within the meaning assigned by subsection 146(1)),

(iii) a deferred profit sharing plan that can reasonably be expected to have at least 5 beneficiaries at all times throughout the calendar year in which the transfer is made, or

(iv) a registered retirement income fund under which the individual is the annuitant (within the meaning assigned by subsection 146.3(1)).

History: S. 147(19)(*b*)(ii) was replaced by S.C. 2013, c. 34, s. 301(3), applicable to transfers that occur after March 20, 2003, and formerly read:

(ii) who is entitled to the amount as a consequence of the death of an employee or former employee referred to in subparagraph (i) and who was, at the date of the employee's death, a spouse or common-law partner of the employee,

S. 147(19)(*d*)(iv) was added by S.C. 2013, c. 34, s. 301(5), applicable to transfers that occur after March 20, 2003.

Related Sections: S. 60(*j*) Transfer of superannuation benefits; s. 146(8.2) Amount deductible; s. 204.2(1) Definition of "excess amount for a year in respect of registered retirement savings plans"; s. 204.2(1.2) Undeducted RRSP premiums; s. 204.2(4) Definition of "excess amount" for a DPSP; s. 212(1)(*m*) Deferred profit sharing plan payments; s. 248(1), "common-law partner"; s. 252(3) Extended meaning of "spouse" and "former spouse".

Forms: T2151 — Direct Transfer of a Single Amount Under Subsection 147(19) or Section 147.3.

Information Circulars: IC 77-1R5 Deferred profit sharing plan.

Interpretation Bulletins: *Primary* — IT-528 Transfers of funds between registered plans.

Registered Plans Directorate Newsletters: No. 91-4R, Registration rules for money purchase provisions.

► 147(20) ◄

(20) Taxation of amount transferred. Where an amount is transferred on behalf of an individual in accordance with subsection (19),

(*a*) the amount shall not, by reason only of that transfer, be included by virtue of this section in computing the income of any taxpayer; and

(*b*) no deduction may be made under any provision of this Act in respect of the amount in computing the income of any taxpayer.

Related Sections: S. 212(1)(*m*) Deferred profit sharing plan payments.

Interpretation Bulletins: *Primary* — IT-528 Transfers of funds between registered plans.

► 147(21) ◄

(21) Restriction re transfers. A deferred profit sharing plan becomes a revocable plan at any time that an amount is transferred from the plan to a registered pension plan, a registered retirement savings plan or another deferred profit sharing plan unless

(*a*) the transfer is in accordance with subsection (19); or

(*b*) the amount is deductible under paragraph 60(*j*) or (*j*.2) of this Act or paragraph 60(*k*) of the *Income Tax Act*, chapter 148 of the Revised Statutes of Canada, 1952, by the individual on whose behalf the transfer is made.

Interpretation Bulletins: *Primary* — IT-528 Transfers of funds between registered plans.

► 147(22) ◄

(22) Excess transfer. Where

(*a*) the transfer of an amount from a deferred profit sharing plan in a calendar year on behalf of a beneficiary under the plan would, but for this subsection, be in accordance with subsection (19), and

(*b*) the requirements of subsection (5.1) in respect of the plan are not satisfied for the year by reason that the beneficiary's pension credits or pension adjustments do not comply with any of paragraphs (5.1)(*a*) to (*c*),

such portion of the amount transferred as may reasonably be considered to derive from amounts allocated or reallocated to the beneficiary in the year or from earnings reasonably attributable to those amounts shall, except to the extent otherwise expressly provided in writing by the Minister, be deemed to be an amount that was not transferred in accordance with subsection (19).

Interpretation Bulletins: *Primary* — IT-528 Transfers of funds between registered plans.

Registered Pension Plans

SECTION 147.1: [Registered pension plans]

► 147.1(1) ◄

(1) Definitions. In this section and sections 147.2 and 147.3,

Related Regulations: 8501(1); 8507(1), (2).

Information Circulars: IC 72-13R8 Employees' pension plans; IC 98-2 Prescribed compensation for registered pension plans.

Interpretation Bulletins: *Secondary* — IT-124R6 Contributions to registered retirement savings plans.

Tax Window Files: General Info re IPPs, *July 23, 2015*, CRA Document No. 2014-0553991E5.

Canadian Tax Foundation: Downing, *Pension and Retirement Plans: An Update*, 1999 Conference Report 32:1–18.

"actuary" —"actuary" means a Fellow of the Canadian Institute of Actuaries;

"administrator" —"administrator" of a pension plan means the person or body of persons that has ultimate responsibility for the administration of the plan;

"average wage" —"average wage" for a calendar year means the amount that is obtained by dividing by 12 the total of all amounts each of which is the wage measure for a month in the 12 month period ending on June 30 of the immediately preceding calendar year;

"compensation" —"compensation" of an individual from an employer for a calendar year means the total of all amounts each of which is

(*a*) an amount in respect of

(i) the individual's employment with the employer, or

(ii) an office in respect of which the individual is remunerated by the employer

that is required (or that would be required but for paragraph 81(1)(*a*) as it applies with respect to the *Indian Act* or the *Foreign Missions and International Organizations Act*) by section 5 or 6 to be included in computing the individual's income for the year, except such portion of the amount as

(iii) may reasonably be considered to relate to a period throughout which the individual was not resident in Canada, and

(iv) is not attributable to the performance of the duties of the office or employment in Canada or is exempt from income tax in Canada by reason of a provision contained in a tax convention or agreement with another country that has the force of law in Canada,

(*b*) a prescribed amount, or

(*c*) an amount acceptable to the Minister in respect of remuneration received by the individual from any employer for a period in the year throughout which the individual was not resident in Canada, to the extent that the amount is not otherwise included in the total;

History: S. 147.1(1), the portion of paragraph (*a*) of the definition "compensation" that is after subparagraph (ii) and before subparagraph (iii) was replaced by S.C. 2013, c. 34, s. 302(1), deemed to have come into force on January 1, 1991, and formerly read:

that is required (or that would be required but for paragraph 81(1)(*a*) as it applies with respect to the *Indian Act*) by section 5 or 6 to be included in computing the individual's income for the year, except such portion of the amount as

Related Regulations: S. 8507.

Related Sections: S. 147(5.1) Contribution limits; s. 147(5.11) Compensation.

Information Circulars: IC 98-2 Prescribed compensation for registered pension plans.

Registered Plans Directorate Newsletters: No. 93-2, Foreign service newsletter.

"defined benefit provision" —"defined benefit provision" of a pension plan means terms of the plan under which benefits in respect of each member are determined in any way other than that described in the definition "money purchase provision" in this subsection;

Editorial Note: See the Editorial Note under the definition of "money purchase provision".

Interpretation Bulletins: *Secondary* — IT-528 Transfers of funds between registered plans.

"former limit" —"former limit" for each calendar year after 2005 and before 2010 means the greater of

(*a*) the product (rounded to the nearest multiple of $10, or, if that product is equidistant from two such consecutive multiples, to the higher multiple) of

(i) $18,000, and

(ii) the quotient obtained when the average wage for the year is divided by the average wage for 2005, and

(*b*) for 2006, $18,000, and for any other of those calendar years, the former limit for the preceding calendar year;

"member" —"member" of a pension plan means an individual who has a right, either immediate or in the future and either absolute or contingent, to receive benefits under the plan, other than an individual who has such a right only by reason of the participation of another individual in the plan;

Related Sections: S. 146.3(2) Acceptance of fund for registration; s. 146.3(14.1) Transfer to money purchase RPP.

"money purchase limit" —"money purchase limit" for a calendar year means

(*a*) for years before 1990, nil,

(*b*) for 1990, $11,500,

(*c*) for 1991 and 1992, $12,500,

(*d*) for 1993, $13,500,

(*e*) for 1994, $14,500,

(*f*) for 1995, $15,500,

(*g*) for years after 1995 and before 2003, $13,500,

(*h*) for 2003, $15,500,

(*i*) for 2004, $16,500,

(*j*) for 2005, $18,000,

(*k*) for 2006, the greater of $19,000 and the former limit for the year,

(*l*) for 2007, the greater of $20,000 and the former limit for the year,

(*m*) for 2008, the greater of $21,000 and the former limit for the year,

(*n*) for 2009, the greater of $22,000 and the former limit for the year, and

(*o*) for each year after 2009, the greater of

(i) the product (rounded to the nearest multiple of $10, or, if that product is equidistant from two such consecutive multiples, to the higher multiple) of

(A) the money purchase limit for 2009, and

(B) the quotient obtained when the average wage for the year is divided by the average wage for 2009, and

(ii) the money purchase limit for the preceding year;

Editorial Note: Indexing based on the increase in the average wage for the year applies after 2009. The money purchase limit also applies to RRSP contributions, see the definition of "RRSP dollar limit" in s. 146(1), and to the contribution limit applicable to deferred profit sharing plans, see s. 147(5.1).

Related Sections: S. 146(1), "RRSP dollar limit"; s. 147(5.1) Contribution limits.

Registered Plans Directorate Newsletters: No. 96-1, Changes to retirement savings limits.

"money purchase provision" —"money purchase provision" of a pension plan means terms of the plan

(*a*) which provide for a separate account to be maintained in respect of each member, to which are credited contributions made to the plan by, or in respect of, the member and any other amounts allocated to the member, and to which are charged payments made in respect of the member, and

(*b*) under which the only benefits in respect of a member are benefits determined solely with reference to, and provided by, the amount in the member's account;

Editorial Note: Pension plans are generally divided into two broad types; "defined benefit" plans and "money purchase" or "defined contribution" plans. Under a "money purchase" plan, employer and employee contributions are fixed and the amount of the pension provided depends on the amount of the contributions made by and on behalf of the member together with the earnings that have accumulated thereon. Under a "defined benefit" plan, the pension provided is predetermined by a formula based on the employee's earnings and his/her length of service.

Related Sections: S. 146.3(14.1) Transfer on breakdown of marriage or common-law partnership; s. 248(1), "additional voluntary contribution".

Interpretation Bulletins: *Secondary* — IT-528 Transfers of funds between registered plans.

Registered Plans Directorate Newsletters: No. 91-4R, Registration rules for money purchase provisions.

"multi-employer plan" —"multi-employer plan" in a calendar year has the meaning assigned by regulation;

Related Regulations: 8500(1); 8510(1); 8510(5).

Related Sections: S. 252.1 Union employer.

Information Circulars: IC 98-2 Prescribed compensation for registered pension plans.

"participating employer"—"participating employer", in relation to a pension plan, means an employer who has made, or is required to make, contributions to the plan in respect of the employer's employees or former employees, or payments under the plan to the employer's employees or former employees, and includes a prescribed employer;

Related Regulations: 8308(7).

"past service event"—"past service event" has the meaning assigned by regulation;

Related Regulations: 8300(1), (2).

"single amount"—"single amount" means an amount that is not part of a series of periodic payments;

Interpretation Bulletins: *Secondary* — IT-528 Transfers of funds between registered plans.

"specified multi-employer plan"—"specified multi-employer plan" in a calendar year has the meaning assigned by regulation;

Related Regulations: 8510(2) Definition of "Specified Multi-Employer Plan"; 8510(3) Qualification as a Specified Multi-Employer Plan; 8510(4) Minister's Notice; 8510(6) Special Rules — Specified Multi-Employer Plan; 8510(7) Additional Prescribed Conditions; 8510(8) Purchase of Additional Benefits.

"spouse"—(Repealed by S.C. 1994, c. 7, Sched. VIII, s. 85(2).)

"wage measure"—"wage measure" for a month means the average weekly wages and salaries of

(*a*) the Industrial Aggregate in Canada for the month as published by Statistics Canada under the *Statistics Act*, or

(*b*) in the event that the Industrial Aggregate ceases to be published, such other measure for the month as is prescribed by regulation under the *Canada Pension Plan* for the purposes of paragraph 18(5)(*b*) of that Act.

Related Sections: S. 248(1), "registered pension plan".

► 147.1(2) ◄

(2) Registration of plan. The following rules apply with respect to the registration of pension plans:

(*a*) the Minister shall not register a pension plan unless

(i) application for registration is made in prescribed manner by the plan administrator,

(ii) the plan complies with prescribed conditions for registration, and

(iii) where the plan is required to be registered under the *Pension Benefits Standards Act, 1985* or a similar law of a province, application for such registration has been made;

(*b*) where a pension plan that was submitted for registration before 1992 is registered by the Minister, the registration is effective from the day specified in writing by the Minister; and

(*c*) where a pension plan that is submitted for registration after 1991 is registered by the Minister, the registration is effective from the later of

(i) January 1 of the calendar year in which application for registration is made in prescribed manner by the plan administrator, and

(ii) the day the plan began.

Editorial Note: A superannuation or pension benefit, as defined in s. 248(1) is included in the recipient's income under s. 56(1)(*a*) regardless of whether it is paid out of a registered or unregistered pension plan.

Related Regulations: 8501(1); 8512(1).

Related Sections: S. 248(1), "registered pension plan".

Forms: T510 — Application for Registration of a Pension Plan.

Guides: T4040 RRSPs and Other Registered Plans for Retirement.

Information Circulars: IC 72-13R8 Employees' pension plans.

Registered Plans Directorate Newsletters: No. 04-2R, Registered Pension Plan Applications — Processing an Incomplete Application; No. 98-1, Simplified pension plans; 95-6R1 Specimen Pension Plans – Speeding up the Process; No. 95-2R1, Registered Plans Directorate Services; No. 95-1, New Approach to plan registration; No. 93-3, Service in Canada; No. 91-1, Transitional registration rules for pension plans; No. 91-4R, Registration rules for money purchase provisions; No. 91-5, Transitional rules and other administrative issues for pension plans.

► 147.1(3) ◄

(3) Deemed registration. Where application is made to the Minister for registration of a pension plan for the purposes of this Act and, where the manner for making the application has been prescribed, the application is made in that manner by the administrator,

(*a*) subject to paragraph (*b*), the plan is, for the purposes of this Act other than paragraphs 60(*j*) and (*j*.2) and sections 147.3 and 147.4, deemed to be a registered pension plan throughout the period that begins on the latest of

(i) January 1 of the calendar year in which the application is made,

(ii) the day of commencement of the plan, and

(iii) January 1, 1989

and ending on the day on which a final determination is made with respect to the application; and

(*b*) where the final determination made with respect to the application is a refusal to register the plan, this Act shall, after the day of the final determination, apply as if the plan had never been deemed, under paragraph (*a*), to be a registered pension plan, except that

(i) any information return otherwise required to be filed under subsection 207.7(3) before the particular day that is 90 days after the day of the final determination is not required to be filed until the particular day, and

(ii) subsections 227(8) and (8.2) are not applicable with respect to contributions made to the plan on or before the day of the final determination.

Related Regulations: 8303(7); 8512(1).

Related Sections: S. 147.3 Transfer — money purchase to money purchase, RRSP or RRIF; s. 147.4 RPP annuity contract.

Registered Plans Directorate Newsletters: No. 91-5, Transitional rules and other administrative issues for pension plans.

► 147.1(4) ◄

(4) Acceptance of amendments. The Minister shall not accept an amendment to a registered pension plan unless

(*a*) application for the acceptance is made in prescribed manner by the plan administrator;

(*b*) the plan as amended complies with prescribed conditions for registration; and

(*c*) the amendment complies with prescribed conditions.

Related Regulations: 8501(1); 8511; 8512(2); 8512(3).

Forms: T920 — Application for Acceptance of an Amendment to a Registered Pension Plan.

Registered Plans Directorate Newsletters: 95-6R1 Specimen Pension Plans – Speeding up the Process; No. 95-1, New Approach to plan registration.

▶ 147.1(5) ◀

(5) Additional conditions. The Minister may, at any time, impose reasonable conditions applicable with respect to registered pension plans, a class of such plans or a particular registered pension plan.

Registered Plans Directorate Newsletters: No. 04-1, Transfers from a Defined Benefit Provision to a Money Purchase Provision, an RRSP, or a RRIF and Transfers between Defined Benefit Provisions; No. 98-1, Simplified pension plans; No. 96-3, Flexible pension plans; No. 93-2, Foreign service newsletter.

▶ 147.1(6) ◀

(6) Administrator. There shall, for each registered pension plan, be a person or a body of persons that has ultimate responsibility for the administration of the plan and, except as otherwise permitted in writing by the Minister, the person or a majority of the persons who constitute the body shall be a person or persons resident in Canada.

▶ 147.1(7) ◀

(7) Obligations of administrator. The administrator of a registered pension plan shall

(*a*) administer the plan in accordance with the terms of the plan as registered except that, where the plan fails to comply with the prescribed conditions for registration or any other requirement of this Act or the regulations, the administrator may administer the plan as if it were amended to so comply;

(*b*) before July, 1990, in the case of a person or body that is the administrator on January 1, 1989 or becomes the administrator before June, 1990, and, in any other case, within 30 days after becoming the administrator, inform the Minister in writing

(i) of the name and address of the person who is the administrator, or

(ii) of the names and addresses of the persons who constitute the body that is the administrator; and

(*c*) where there is any change in the information provided to the Minister in accordance with this paragraph or paragraph (*b*), inform the Minister in writing, within 60 days after the change, of the new information.

Related Regulations: 8300(1); 8300(1.1); 8300(2); 8300(4); 8300(5); 8300(6); 8300(7).

Related Sections: S. 238(1) Offences and punishment.

Registered Plans Directorate Newsletters: No. 09-1, Administrative Relief Procedures for Retroactive Lump-Sum Catch-Up Payments; No. 98-1, Simplified pension plans; No. 91-5, Transitional rules and other administrative issues for pension plans.

▶ 147.1(8) ◀

(8) Pension adjustment limits. Except as otherwise provided by regulation, a registered pension plan (other than a multi-employer plan) becomes, at the end of a calendar year after 1990, a revocable plan where

(*a*) the pension adjustment for the year of a member of the plan in respect of a participating employer exceeds the lesser of

(i) the money purchase limit for the year, and

(ii) 18% of the member's compensation from the employer for the year; or

(*b*) the total of

(i) the pension adjustment for the year of a member of the plan in respect of a participating employer, and

(ii) the total of all amounts each of which is the member's pension adjustment for the year in respect of an employer who, at any time in the year, does not deal at arm's length with the employer referred to in subparagraph (i)

exceeds the money purchase limit for the year.

Related Regulations: 8301(1) Pension Adjustment with Respect to Employer; 8301(2) Pension Credit — Deferred Profit Sharing Plan; 8301(4) Pension Credit — Money Purchase Provision; 8301(4.1) Money Purchase Pension Credits Based on Amounts Allocated; 8301(5) Pension Credit — Defined Benefit Provision of a Specified Multi-Employer Plan; 8301(6) Pension Credit — Defined Benefit Provision; 8301(7) Pension Credit — Defined Benefit Provision of a Multi-Employer Plan; 8509(6), (12).

Related Sections: S. 147.3(13) Excess transfer.

Guides: T4084 Pension Adjustment Guide.

Information Circulars: IC 98-2 Prescribed compensation for registered pension plans.

Interpretation Bulletins: *Secondary* — IT-528 Transfers of funds between registered plans.

Registered Plans Directorate Newsletters: No. 96-1, Changes to retirement savings limits; No. 93-4, Exception to filing amendments for the Income Tax Act and Regulations.

▶ 147.1(9) ◀

(9) Idem — multi-employer plans. Except as otherwise provided by regulation, a registered pension plan that is a multi-employer plan (other than a specified multi-employer plan) in a calendar year after 1990 becomes, at the end of the year, a revocable plan where

(*a*) for a member and an employer, the total of all amounts each of which is the member's pension credit (as prescribed by regulation) for the year in respect of the employer under a defined benefit or money purchase provision of the plan exceeds the lesser of

(i) the money purchase limit for the year, and

(ii) 18% of the member's compensation from the employer for the year; or

(*b*) for a member, the total of all amounts each of which is the member's pension credit (as prescribed by regulation) for the year in respect of an employer under a defined benefit or money purchase provision of the plan exceeds the money purchase limit for the year.

Related Regulations: 8301(4) Pension Credit — Money Purchase Provision; 8301(4.1) Money Purchase Pension Credits Based on Amounts Allocated; 8301(5) Pension Credit — Defined Benefit Provision of a Specified Multi-Employer Plan; 8301(6) Pension Credit — Defined Benefit Provision; 8301(8) Non-Vested Termination from RPP; 8301(9) Multi-Employer Plans; 8302; 8304(2) Replacement of Money Purchase Benefits; 8509(6) PA Limits for Grandfathered Plan for 1991; 8509(8) Benefit Accrual Rate Greater Than 2 Per Cent; 8509(12) PA Limits — 1996 to 2002.

Related Sections: S. 147.3(13) Excess transfer.

Guides: T4084 Pension Adjustment Guide.

Information Circulars: IC 98-2 Prescribed compensation for registered pension plans.

Interpretation Bulletins: *Secondary* — IT-528 Transfers of funds between registered plans.

Registered Plans Directorate Newsletters: No. 96-1, Changes to retirement savings limits; No. 93-4, Exception to filing amendments for the Income Tax Act and Regulations.

▶ 147.1(10) ◀

(10) Past service benefits. With respect to each past service event that is relevant to the determination of benefits in respect of a member under a defined benefit provision of a registered pension plan, such benefits as are in respect of periods after 1989 and before the calendar year in which the event occurred shall be determined, for the purpose of a payment to be made from the plan or a contribution to be made to the plan at a particular time, with regard to the event only if

(*a*) where the member is alive at the particular time and except as otherwise provided by regulation, the Minister has certified in writing, before the particular time, that prescribed conditions are satisfied,

(*b*) where the member died before the particular time and the event occurred before the death of the member,

(i) this subsection did not require that the event be disregarded in determining benefits that were payable to the member immediately before the member's death (or that would have been so payable had the member been entitled to receive benefits under the provision immediately before the member's death), or

(ii) the event, as it affects the benefits provided to each individual who is entitled to benefits as a consequence of the death of the member, is acceptable to the Minister,

(*c*) where the member died before the particular time and the event occurred after the death of the member, the event, as it affects the benefits provided to each individual who is entitled to benefits as a consequence of the death of the member, is acceptable to the Minister, and

(*d*) no past service event that occurred before the event is required by reason of the application of this subsection to be disregarded at the particular time in determining benefits in respect of the member,

and, for the purposes of this subsection as it applies with respect to contributions that may be made to a registered pension plan, where application has been made for a certification referred to in paragraph (*a*) and the Minister has not refused to issue the certification, the Minister shall be deemed to have issued the certification.

Related Regulations: 8300(1), "certifiable past service event"; 8303(3), (5), (7); 8304(5); 8306; 8307(1) Application for Certification; 8307(2) Prescribed Condition; 8307(3) Qualifying Withdrawals; 8307(4) Eligibility of Withdrawn Amount for Designation; 8307(5) PSPA Withdrawals; 8308; 8404(3); 8519.

Related Sections: S. 241(4) Where taxpayer information may be disclosed.

Forms: T1006 — Designation of an RRSP Withdrawal as Qualifying Withdrawal; T1004 — Applying for the Certification of a Provisional PSPA.

Guides: T4104 Past Service Pension Adjustment Guide.

Information Circulars: IC 98-2 Prescribed compensation for registered pension plans.

► 147.1(11) ◄

(11) Revocation of registration — notice of intention. Where, at any time after a pension plan has been registered by the Minister,

(*a*) the plan does not comply with the prescribed conditions for registration,

(*b*) the plan is not administered in accordance with the terms of the plan as registered,

(*c*) the plan becomes a revocable plan,

(*d*) a condition imposed by the Minister in writing and applicable with respect to the plan (including a condition applicable generally to registered pension plans or a class of such plans and a condition first imposed before 1989) is not complied with,

(*e*) a requirement under subsection (6) or (7) is not complied with,

(*f*) a benefit is paid by the plan, or a contribution is made to the plan, contrary to subsection (10),

(*g*) the administrator of the plan fails to file an information return or actuarial report relating to the plan or to a member of the plan as and when required by regulation,

(*h*) a participating employer fails to file an information return relating to the plan or to a member of the plan as and when required by regulation, or

(*i*) registration of the plan under the *Pension Benefits Standards Act, 1985* or a similar law of a province is refused or revoked,

the Minister may give notice (in this subsection and subsection (12) referred to as a "notice of intent") by registered mail to the plan administrator that the Minister proposes to revoke the registration of the plan as of a date specified in the notice of intent, which date shall not be earlier than the date as of which,

(*j*) where paragraph (*a*) applies, the plan failed to so comply,

(*k*) where paragraph (*b*) applies, the plan was not administered in accordance with its terms as registered,

(*l*) where paragraph (*c*) applies, the plan became a revocable plan,

(*m*) where paragraph (*d*) or (*e*) applies, the condition or requirement was not complied with,

(*n*) where paragraph (*f*) applies, the benefit was paid or the contribution was made,

(*o*) where paragraph (*g*) or (*h*) applies, the information return or actuarial report was required to be filed, and

(*p*) where paragraph (*i*) applies, the registration referred to in that paragraph was refused or revoked.

Related Regulations: Part LXXXIV; 8501(1), (2); 8503(15); 8506(4); 8515(9).

Related Sections: S. 147.4(1) RPP annuity contract; s. 147.1(8) Pension adjustment limits; s. 147.1(9) Idem — multi-employer plans; s. 172(3) Appeal from refusal to register, revocation of registration, etc.

Information Circulars: IC 98-2 Prescribed compensation for registered pension plans.

► 147.1(12) ◄

(12) Notice of revocation. Where the Minister gives a notice of intent to the administrator of a registered pension plan, or the plan administrator applies to the Minister in writing for the revocation of the plan's registration, the Minister may,

(*a*) where the plan administrator has applied to the Minister in writing for the revocation of the plan's registration, at any time after receiving the administrator's application, and

(*b*) in any other case, after 30 days after the day of mailing of the notice of intent,

give notice (in this subsection and subsection (13) referred to as a "notice of revocation") by registered mail to the plan administrator that the registration of the plan is revoked as of the date specified in the notice of revocation, which date may not be earlier than the date specified in the notice of intent or the administrator's application, as the case may be.

► 147.1(13) ◄

(13) Revocation of registration. Where the Minister gives a notice of revocation to the administrator of a registered pension plan, the registration of the plan is revoked as of the date specified in the notice of revocation, unless the Federal Court of Appeal or a judge thereof, on application made at any time before the determination of an appeal pursuant to subsection 172(3), orders otherwise.

► 147.1(14) ◄

(14) Anti-avoidance — multi-employer plans. Where at any time the Minister gives written notice to the administrators of two or more registered pension plans, each of which is a multi-employer plan, that this subsection is applicable in relation to those plans with respect to a calendar year,

(*a*) each of those plans that is a specified multi-employer plan in the year shall, for the purposes of subsection (9) (other than for the purpose of determining the pension credits referred to in paragraphs (9)(*a*) and (*b*)), be deemed to be a multi-employer plan that is not a specified multi-employer plan; and

(*b*) the totals determined for the year under paragraphs (9)(*a*) and (*b*) shall be the amounts that would be determined if all the plans were a single plan.

Registered Plans Directorate Newsletters: No. 98-1, Simplified pension plans.

► 147.1(15) ◄

(15) Plan as registered. Any reference in this Act and the regulations to a pension plan as registered means the terms of the plan on the basis of which the Minister has registered the plan for the purposes of this Act and as amended by

(*a*) each amendment that has been accepted by the Minister, and

(*b*) each amendment that has been submitted to the Minister for acceptance and that the Minister has neither accepted nor refused to accept, if it is reasonable to expect the Minister to accept the amendment,

and includes all terms that are not contained in the documents constituting the plan but that are terms of the plan by reason of the *Pension Benefits Standards Act, 1985* or a similar law of a province.

Related Sections: S. 147.1(7)(*a*) Obligations of administrator.

► 147.1(16) ◄

(16) Separate liability for obligations. Every person who is a member of a body that is the administrator of a registered pension plan is subject to all obligations imposed on administrators by this Act or a regulation as if the person were the administrator of the plan.

► 147.1(17) ◄

(17) Superintendent of Financial Institutions. The Minister may, for the purposes of this Act, obtain the advice of the Superintendent of Financial Institutions with respect to any matter relating to pension plans.

► 147.1(18) ◄

(18) Regulations. The Governor in Council may make regulations

(*a*) prescribing conditions for the registration of pension plans and enabling the Minister to impose additional conditions or waive any conditions that are prescribed;

(*b*) prescribing circumstances under which a registered pension plan becomes a revocable plan;

(*c*) specifying the manner of determining, or enabling the Minister to determine, the portion of a member's benefits under a registered pension plan that is in respect of any period;

(*d*) requiring administrators of registered pension plans to make determinations in connection with the computation of pension adjustments, past service pension adjustments, total pension adjustment reversals or any other related amounts (all such amounts referred to in this subsection as "specified amounts");

(*e*) requiring that the method used to determine a specified amount be acceptable to the Minister, where more than one method would otherwise comply with the regulations;

(*f*) enabling the Minister to permit or require a specified amount to be determined in a manner different from that set out in the regulations;

(*g*) requiring that any person who has information required by another person in order to determine a specified amount provide the other person with that information;

(*h*) enabling the Minister to require any person to provide the Minister with information relating to the method used to determine a specified amount;

(*i*) enabling the Minister to require any person to provide the Minister with information relevant to a claim that paragraph (10)(*a*) is not applicable by reason of an exemption provided by regulation;

(*j*) respecting applications for certifications for the purposes of subsection (10);

(*k*) enabling the Minister to waive the requirement for a certification for the purposes of subsection (10);

(*l*) prescribing rules for the purposes of subsection (10), so that that subsection applies or does not apply with respect to benefits provided as a consequence of particular transactions, events or circumstances;

(*m*) requiring any person to provide the Minister or the administrator of a registered pension plan with information in connection with an application for certification for the purposes of subsection (10);

(*n*) requiring any person who obtains a certification for the purposes of subsection (10) to provide the individual in respect of whom the certification was obtained with an information return;

(*o*) requiring administrators of registered pension plans to file information with respect to amendments to such plans and to the arrangements for funding benefits thereunder;

(*p*) requiring administrators of registered pension plans to file information returns respecting such plans;

(*q*) enabling the Minister to require any person to provide the Minister with information for the purpose of determining whether the registration of a pension plan may be revoked;

(*r*) requiring administrators of registered pension plans to submit reports to the Minister, prescribing the class of persons by whom the reports shall be prepared and prescribing information to be contained in those reports;

(*s*) enabling the Minister to impose any requirement that may be imposed by regulation made under paragraph (*r*);

(*t*) defining, for the purposes of this Act, the expressions "multi-employer plan", "past service event", "past service pension adjustment", "pension adjustment", "specified multi-employer plan" and "total pension adjustment reversal"; and

(*u*) generally to carry out the purposes and provisions of this Act relating to registered pension plans and the determination and reporting of specified amounts.

Related Regulations: Part LXXXIII; Part LXXXIV; Part LXXXV.

Related Sections: S. 238(1) Offences and punishment.

► 147.1(19) ◄

(19) Reasonable error. The administrator of a registered pension plan may make a payment (other than a payment made to avoid the revocation of the registration of the plan) that is a return of all or a portion of a contribution made by a member of the plan, or an employer who participates in the plan, if

(*a*) the contribution was made to the plan as a consequence of a reasonable error;

(*b*) the payment is made to the member or employer, as the case may be, who made the contribution; and

(*c*) the payment is made no later than December 31 of the year following the year in which the contribution was made.

History: S. 147.1(19) was added by S.C. 2013, c. 40, s. 64(1), applicable to contributions made on or after January 1, 2014.

Related Sections: S. 56(1) Pension benefits.

SECTION 147.2: Pension contributions deductible — employer contributions

► 147.2(1) ◄

(1) Pension contributions deductible — employer contributions. For a taxation year ending after 1990, there may be deducted in computing the income of a taxpayer who is an employer the total of all amounts each of which is a contribution made by the employer after 1990 and either in the taxation year or within 120 days after the end of the taxation year to a registered pension plan in respect of the employer's employees or former employees, to the extent that

(*a*) in the case of a contribution in respect of a money purchase provision of a plan, the contribution was made in accordance with the plan as registered and in respect of periods before the end of the taxation year;

(*b*) in the case of a contribution in respect of the defined benefit provisions of a plan (other than a specified multi-employer plan), the contribution

(i) is an eligible contribution,

(ii) was made to fund benefits provided to employees and former employees of the employer in respect of periods before the end of the taxation year, and

(iii) complies with subsection 147.1(10);

(*c*) in the case of a contribution made to a plan that is a specified multi-employer plan, the contribution was made in accordance with the plan as registered and in respect of periods before the end of the taxation year; and

(*d*) the contribution was not deducted in computing the income of the employer for a preceding taxation year.

Editorial Note: S. 20(1)(*q*) provides for the deduction of employer contributions to a registered pension plan made in the taxation year or within 120 days after the end of the taxation year in accordance with s. 147.2(1). The contributions must be determined in a manner that is acceptable to the Minister in accordance with regulation 8506(2)(*a*). Contributions under a defined benefit provision must be made pursuant to a recommendation by an actuary and must meet the requirements of s. 147.2(2).

Related Regulations: 8515.

Related Sections: S. 20(1)(*q*) Employer's contributions to registered pension plan; s. 147.1(1) Definitions; s. 147.1(10) Past service benefits.

Registered Plans Directorate Newsletters: No. 91-4R, Registration rules for money purchase provisions.

Tax Window Files: General Info re IPPs, *July 23, 2015*, CRA Document No. 2014-0553991E5; Characterization of a Remedial Payment, *15XXXX*, CRA Document No. 2013-0506291R3.

► 147.2(2) ◄

(2) Employer contributions — defined benefit provisions. For the purposes of subsection (1), a contribution made by an employer to a registered pension plan in respect of the defined benefit provisions of the plan is an eligible contribution if it is a prescribed contribution or if it complies with prescribed conditions and is made pursuant to a recommendation by an actuary in whose opinion the contribution is required to be made so that the plan will have sufficient assets to pay benefits under the defined benefit provisions of the plan, as registered, in respect of the employees and former employees of the employer, where

(*a*) the recommendation is based on an actuarial valuation that complies with the following conditions, except the conditions in subparagraphs (iii) and (iv) to the extent that they are inconsistent with any other conditions that apply for the purpose of determining whether the contribution is an eligible contribution:

(i) the effective date of the valuation is not more than 4 years before the day on which the contribution is made,

(ii) actuarial liabilities and current service costs are determined in accordance with an actuarial funding method that produces a reasonable matching of contributions with accruing benefits,

(iii) all assumptions made for the purposes of the valuation are reasonable at the time the valuation is prepared and at the time the contribution is made,

(iv) the valuation is prepared in accordance with generally accepted actuarial principles,

(v) the valuation complies with prescribed conditions, which conditions may include conditions regarding the benefits that may be taken into account for the purposes of the valuation, and

(vi) where more than one employer participates in the plan, assets and actuarial liabilities are apportioned in a reasonable manner among participating employers in respect of their employees and former employees, and

(*b*) the recommendation is approved by the Minister in writing,

and, for the purposes of this subsection and except as otherwise provided by regulation,

(*c*) the benefits taken into account for the purposes of a recommendation may include anticipated cost-of-living and similar adjustments where the terms of a pension plan do not require that those adjustments be made but it is reasonable to expect that they will be made, and

(*d*) a recommendation with respect to the contributions required to be made by an employer in respect of the defined benefit provisions of a pension plan may be prepared without regard to such portion of the assets of the plan apportioned to the employer in respect of the employer's employees and former employees as does not exceed the lesser of

(i) the amount of actuarial surplus in respect of the employer, and

(ii) 25% of the amount of actuarial liabilities apportioned to the employer in respect of the employer's employees and former employees.

History: S. 147.2(2)(*d*) was replaced by S.C. 2010, c. 12, s. 18(1), applicable to contributions made after 2009 to fund benefits provided in respect of periods of pensionable service after 2009. S. 147.2(2)(*d*) formerly read:

(*d*) a recommendation with respect to the contributions required to be made by an employer in respect of the defined benefit provisions of a pension plan may be prepared without regard to such portion of the assets of the plan apportioned to the employer in respect of the employer's employees and former employees as does not exceed the least of

(i) the amount of actuarial surplus in respect of the employer,

(ii) 20% of the amount of actuarial liabilities apportioned to the employer in respect of the employer's employees and former employees, and

(iii) the greater of

(A) 2 times the estimated amount of current service contributions that would, if there were no actuarial surplus, be required to be made by the employer and the employer's employees for the 12 months immediately following the effective date of the actuarial valuation on which the recommendation is based, and

(B) the amount that would be determined under subparagraph (ii) if the reference therein to "20%" were read as a reference to "10%".

Related Regulations: 8502 "permissible contributions"; 8515; 8516.

Information Circulars: IC 72-13R8 Employees' pension plans.

Registered Plans Directorate Newsletters: No. 96-1, Changes to retirement savings limits; No. 95-3, Actuarial report content; No. 91-5, Transitional rules and other administrative issues for pension plans.

▶ 147.2(3) ◀

(3) Filing of actuarial report. Where, for the purposes of subsection (2), a person seeks the Minister's approval of a recommendation made by an actuary in connection with the contributions to be made by an employer to a registered pension plan in respect of the defined benefit provisions of the plan, the person shall file with the Minister a report prepared by the actuary that contains the recommendation and any other information required by the Minister.

Registered Plans Directorate Newsletters: No. 95-3, Actuarial report content.

▶ 147.2(4) ◀

(4) Amount of employee's pension contributions deductible. There may be deducted in computing the income of an individual for a taxation year ending after 1990 an amount equal to the total of

Editorial Note: Paragraph 8(1)(*m*) provides for the deduction of employee contributions to a registered pension plan as determined under s. 147.2(4).

▶ 147.2(4)(a) ◀

(a) Service after 1989 — the total of all amounts each of which is a contribution (other than a prescribed contribution) made by the individual in the year to a registered pension plan that is in respect of a period after 1989 or that is a prescribed eligible contribution, to the extent that the contribution was made in accordance with the plan as registered,

Related Regulations: 8501(6.1); 8501(6.2); 8503; 8504.

Related Sections: S. 8(1)(*m*) Employee's registered pension plan contributions; s. 147.1(8) Pension adjustment limits; s. 147.1(9) Idem — multi-employer plans; s. 152(6) Reassessment where certain deductions claimed; s. 161(7) Effect of carryback of loss, etc; s. 163(4) Effect of carryback of losses etc; s. 164(5) Effect of carryback of loss, etc.

Tax Profile: October 2007 — Important Changes Announced to the Canada–U.S. Income Tax Convention.

▶ 147.2(4)(b) ◀

(b) Service before 1990 while not a contributor — the least of

(i) the amount, if any, by which

(A) the total of all amounts each of which is a contribution (other than an additional voluntary contribution or a prescribed contribution) made by the individual in the year or a preceding taxation year and after 1945 to a registered pension plan in respect of a particular year before 1990, if all or any part of the particular year is included in the individual's eligible service under the plan and if

(I) in the case of a contribution that the individual made before March 28, 1988 or was obliged to make under the terms of an agreement in writing entered into before March 28, 1988, the individual was not a contributor to the plan in the particular year, or

(II) in any other case, the individual was not a contributor to any registered pension plan in the particular year

exceeds

(B) the total of all amounts each of which is an amount deducted, in computing the individual's income for a preceding taxation year, in respect of contributions included in the total determined in respect of the individual for the year under clause (A),

(ii) $3,500, and

(iii) the amount determined by the formula

$$(\$3{,}500 \times Y) - Z$$

where

Y is the number of calendar years before 1990 each of which is a year

(A) all or any part of which is included in the individual's eligible service under a registered pension plan to which the individual has made a contribution that is included in the total determined under clause (i)(A) and in which the individual was not a contributor to any registered pension plan, or

(B) all or any part of which is included in the individual's eligible service under a registered pension plan to which the individual has made a contribution

(I) that is included in the total determined under clause (i)(A), and

(II) that the individual made before March 28, 1988 or was obliged to make under the terms of an agreement in writing entered into before March 28, 1988, and in which the individual was not a contributor to the plan, and

Z is the total of all amounts each of which is an amount deducted, in computing the individual's income for a preceding taxation year,

(A) in respect of contributions included in the total determined in respect of the individual for the year under clause (i)(A), or

(B) where the preceding year was before 1987, under subparagraph 8(1)(*m*)(ii) (as it read in its application to that preceding year) in respect of additional voluntary contributions made in respect of a year that satisfies the conditions in the description of Y, and

► 147.2(4)(c) ◄

(c) Service before 1990 while a contributor — the lesser of

(i) the amount, if any, by which

(A) the total of all amounts each of which is a contribution (other than an additional voluntary contribution, a prescribed contribution or a contribution included in the total determined in respect of the individual for the year under clause (*b*)(i)(A)) made by the individual in the year or a preceding taxation year and after 1962 to a registered pension plan in respect of a particular year before 1990 that is included, in whole or in part, in the individual's eligible service under the plan

exceeds

(B) the total of all amounts each of which is an amount deducted, in computing the individual's income for a preceding taxation year, in respect of contributions included in the total determined in respect of the individual for the year under clause (A), and

(ii) the amount, if any, by which $3,500 exceeds the total of the amounts deducted by reason of paragraphs (*a*) and (*b*) in computing the individual's income for the year.

► 147.2(5) ◄

(5) Teachers. For the purpose of determining whether a teacher may deduct an amount contributed by the teacher to a registered pension plan in computing the teacher's income for a taxation year ending after 1990 and before 1995 during which the teacher was employed by Her Majesty or a person exempt from tax for the year under section 149,

(*a*) clause (4)(*b*)(i)(A) shall be read without reference to subclauses (4)(*b*)(i)(A)(I) and (II); and

(*b*) the description of Y in subparagraph (4)(*b*)(iii) shall be read as follows:

"Y is the number of calendar years before 1990 each of which is a year all or any part of which is included in the individual's eligible service under a registered pension plan to which the individual has made a contribution that is included in the total determined under clause (i)(A), and"

► 147.2(6) ◄

(6) Deductible contributions when taxpayer dies. Where a taxpayer dies in a taxation year, for the purpose of computing the taxpayer's income for the year and the preceding taxation year,

(*a*) paragraph (4)(*b*) shall be read without reference to subparagraph (ii) and as if the reference to "the least of" were a reference to "the lesser of"; and

(*b*) paragraph (4)(*c*) shall be read without reference to subparagraph (ii) and the words "the lesser of".

Related Sections: S. 161(7)(*a*)(viii.1) Effect of carryback of loss, etc; s. 163(4) Effect of carryback of losses etc; s. 164(5) Effect of carryback of loss, etc; s. 164(5.1) Interest — disputed amounts.

► 147.2(7) ◄

(7) Letter of credit. For the purposes of this section and any regulations made under subsection 147.1(18) in respect of eligible contributions, an amount paid to a registered pension plan by the issuer of a letter of credit issued in connection with an employer's funding obligations under a defined benefit provision of the plan is deemed to be an eligible contribution made to the plan in respect of the provision by the employer with respect to the employer's employees or former employees, if

(*a*) the amount is paid under the letter of credit;

(*b*) the use of the letter of credit is permitted under the *Pension Benefits Standards Act, 1985* or a similar law of a province; and

(*c*) the amount would have been an eligible contribution under subsection (2) if

(i) it had been paid to the plan by the employer, and

(ii) this section were read without reference to this subsection.

History: S. 147.2(7), the portion before paragraph (*a*) was replaced by S.C. 2013, c. 34, s. 303(1), deemed to have come into force on November 6, 2010, and formerly read:

(7) *Letter of credit.* For the purposes of this section and any regulations made under subsection (2) or under subsection 147.1(18), an amount paid to a registered pension plan by the issuer of a letter of credit issued in connection with an employer's funding obligations under a defined benefit provision of the plan is deemed to be an eligible contribution made to the plan in

respect of the provision by the employer with respect to the employer's employees or former employees, if

► 147.2(8) ◄

(8) Former employee of predecessor employer. For the purposes of this section and any regulations made under subsection 147.1(18) in respect of eligible contributions, a former employee of a predecessor employer (as defined by regulation) of a participating employer in relation to a pension plan is deemed to be a former employee of the participating employer in relation to the plan if

(*a*) the former employee would not otherwise be an employee or former employee of the participating employer; and

(*b*) benefits are provided to the former employee under a defined benefit provision of the plan in respect of periods of employment with the predecessor employer.

History: S. 147.2(8) was added by S.C. 2013, c. 34, s. 303(2), applicable to contributions made after 1990.

Related Regulations: 8500(1.2); 8504(2.1) Predecessor Employer.

SECTION 147.3: Transfer — money purchase to money purchase, RRSP or RRIF

► 147.3(1) ◄

(1) Transfer — money purchase to money purchase, RRSP or RRIF. An amount is transferred from a registered pension plan in accordance with this subsection if the amount

(*a*) is a single amount;

(*b*) is transferred on behalf of a member in full or partial satisfaction of the member's entitlement to benefits under a money purchase provision of the plan as registered; and

(*c*) is transferred directly to

(i) another registered pension plan to provide benefits in respect of the member under a money purchase provision of that plan,

(ii) a registered retirement savings plan under which the member is the annuitant (within the meaning assigned by subsection 146(1)), or

(iii) a registered retirement income fund under which the member is the annuitant (within the meaning assigned by subsection 146.3(1)).

Related Sections: S. 147.1(1) Definitions; s. 204.2(1) Definition of "excess amount for a year in respect of registered retirement savings plans"; s. 204.2(1.2) Undeducted RRSP premiums.

Forms: T2151 — Direct Transfer of a Single Amount Under Subsection 147(19) or Section 147.3.

Interpretation Bulletins: *Primary* — IT-528 Transfers of funds between registered plans.

Registered Plans Directorate Newsletters: No. 91-4R, Registration rules for money purchase provisions.

► 147.3(2) ◄

(2) Transfer — money purchase to defined benefit. An amount is transferred from a registered pension plan in accordance with this subsection if the amount

(*a*) is a single amount;

(*b*) is transferred on behalf of a member in full or partial satisfaction of the member's entitlement to benefits under a money purchase provision of the plan as registered; and

(*c*) is transferred directly to another registered pension plan to fund benefits provided in respect of the member under a defined benefit provision of that plan.

Forms: T2151 — Direct Transfer of a Single Amount Under Subsection 147(19) or Section 147.3.

Interpretation Bulletins: *Primary* — IT-528 Transfers of funds between registered plans.

Registered Plans Directorate Newsletters: No. 91-4R, Registration rules for money purchase provisions.

► 147.3(3) ◄

(3) Transfer — defined benefit to defined benefit. An amount is transferred from a registered pension plan (in this subsection referred to as the "transferor plan") in accordance with this subsection if the amount

(*a*) is a single amount;

(*b*) consists of all or any part of the property held in connection with a defined benefit provision of the transferor plan;

(*c*) is transferred directly to another registered pension plan to be held in connection with a defined benefit provision of the other plan; and

Proposed Amendment
2019 Federal Budget Resolutions

Paragraph 147.3(3)(c) of the Act is replaced by the following:

(*c*) is transferred directly to another registered pension plan to be held in connection with a defined benefit provision of the other plan, unless the transfer is to an *individual pension plan* (as defined by regulation) and is in respect of benefits that are attributable to employment with a former employer that is not a participating employer (or its predecessor employer); and

Applicable: Deemed to have come into force on March 19, 2019.

(*d*) is transferred as a consequence of benefits becoming provided under the defined benefit provision of the other plan to one or more individuals who were members of the transferor plan.

Forms: T2151 — Direct Transfer of a Single Amount Under Subsection 147(19) or Section 147.3.

Interpretation Bulletins: *Primary* — IT-528 Transfers of funds between registered plans.

Registered Plans Directorate Newsletters: No. 04-1, Transfers from a Defined Benefit Provision to a Money Purchase Provision, an RRSP, or a RRIF and Transfers between Defined Benefit Provisions.

► 147.3(4) ◄

(4) Transfer — defined benefit to money purchase, RRSP or RRIF. An amount is transferred from a registered pension plan in accordance with this subsection if the amount

(*a*) is a single amount no portion of which relates to an actuarial surplus;

(*b*) is transferred on behalf of a member in full or partial satisfaction of benefits to which the member is entitled, either absolutely or contingently, under a defined benefit provision of the plan as registered;

(*c*) does not exceed a prescribed amount; and

(*d*) is transferred directly to

(i) another registered pension plan and allocated to the member under a money purchase provision of that plan,

(ii) a registered retirement savings plan under which the member is the annuitant (within the meaning assigned by subsection 146(1)), or

(iii) a registered retirement income fund under which the member is the annuitant (within the meaning assigned by subsection 146.3(1)).

Related Regulations: 8517.

Related Sections: S. 60(*j*.01) Transfer of surplus; s. 204.2(1) Definition of "excess amount for a year in respect of registered retirement savings plans"; s. 204.2(1.2) Undeducted RRSP premiums.

Forms: T2151 — Direct Transfer of a Single Amount Under Subsection 147(19) or Section 147.3.

Interpretation Bulletins: *Primary* — IT-528 Transfers of funds between registered plans.

Registered Plans Directorate Newsletters: No. 04-1, Transfers from a Defined Benefit Provision to a Money Purchase Provision, an RRSP, or a RRIF and Transfers between Defined Benefit Provisions; No. 98-2, Treating excess member contributions under a registered pension plan; No. 95-5, Conversion of a defined benefit provision to a money purchase provision; No. 94-2, Technical questions and answers; No. 91-4R, Registration rules for money purchase provisions.

Cases: An amount can be transferred from an RPP to an RRSP on a tax-exempt basis if no portion of that amount relates to an actuarial surplus. The amount received by the taxpayer related to an actuarial surplus and was not exempt. *Mangal v. The Queen*, 2018 DTC 1018 (TCC)

► 147.3(4.1) ◄

(4.1) Transfer of surplus — defined benefit to money purchase. An amount is transferred from a registered pension plan in accordance with this subsection if the amount

(*a*) is transferred in respect of the actuarial surplus under a defined benefit provision of the plan; and

(*b*) is transferred directly to another registered pension plan and allocated under a money purchase provision of that plan to one or more members of that plan.

Related Sections: S. 204.2(1) Definition of "excess amount for a year in respect of registered retirement savings plans"; s. 204.2(1.2) Undeducted RRSP premiums.

Interpretation Bulletins: *Primary* — IT-528 Transfers of funds between registered plans.

Registered Plans Directorate Newsletters: No. 95-5, Conversion of a defined benefit provision to a money purchase provision; No. 91-4R, Registration rules for money purchase provisions.

► 147.3(5) ◄

(5) Transfer to RPP, RRSP or RRIF for spouse on marriage breakdown. An amount is transferred from a registered pension plan in accordance with this subsection if the amount

(*a*) is a single amount no portion of which relates to an actuarial surplus;

(*b*) is transferred on behalf of an individual who is a spouse or common-law partner or former spouse or common-law partner of a member of the plan and who is entitled to the amount under a decree, order or judgment of a competent tribunal, or under a written agreement, relating to a division of property between the member and the individual in settlement of rights arising out of, or on a breakdown of, their marriage or common-law partnership; and

(*c*) is transferred directly to

(i) another registered pension plan for the benefit of the individual,

(ii) a registered retirement savings plan under which the individual is the annuitant (within the meaning assigned by subsection 146(1)), or

(iii) a registered retirement income fund under which the individual is the annuitant (within the meaning assigned by subsection 146.3(1)).

Related Sections: S. 146.3(2) Acceptance of fund for registration; s. 204.2(1) Definition of "excess amount for a year in respect of registered retirement savings plans"; s. 204.2(1.2) Undeducted RRSP premiums; s. 248(1), "common-law partner"; s. 252(3) Extended meaning of "spouse" and "former spouse".

Interpretation Bulletins: *Primary* — IT-528 Transfers of funds between registered plans. *Secondary* — IT-440R2 Transfer of rights to income.

Registered Plans Directorate Newsletters: No. 91-4R, Registration rules for money purchase provisions.

► 147.3(6) ◄

(6) Transfer — pre-1991 contributions. An amount is transferred from a registered pension plan in accordance with this subsection if the amount

(*a*) is a single amount;

(*b*) is transferred on behalf of a member who is entitled to the amount as a return of contributions made (or deemed by regulation to have been made) by the member under a defined benefit provision of the plan before 1991, or as interest (computed at a rate not exceeding a reasonable rate) in respect of those contributions; and

(*c*) is transferred directly to

(i) another registered pension plan for the benefit of the member,

(ii) a registered retirement savings plan under which the member is the annuitant (within the meaning assigned by subsection 146(1)), or

(iii) a registered retirement income fund under which the member is the annuitant (within the meaning assigned by subsection 146.3(1)).

History: S. 147.3(6)(*b*) was replaced by S.C. 2013, c. 34, s. 304(1), applicable to transfers that occur after 1999, and formerly read:

(*b*) is transferred on behalf of a member who is entitled to the amount as a return of contributions made by the member under a defined benefit provision of the plan before 1991, or as interest (computed at a rate not exceeding a reasonable rate) in respect of those contributions; and

Related Regulations: 8500(9).

Related Sections: S. 204.2(1) Definition of "excess amount for a year in respect of registered retirement savings plans"; s. 204.2(1.2) Undeducted RRSP premiums.

Interpretation Bulletins: *Primary* — IT-528 Transfers of funds between registered plans.

Registered Plans Directorate Newsletters: No. 98-2, Treating excess member contributions under a registered pension plan; No. 91-4R, Registration rules for money purchase provisions.

► 147.3(7) ◄

(7) Transfer — lump sum benefits on death. An amount is transferred from a registered pension plan in accordance with this subsection if the amount

(*a*) is a single amount no portion of which relates to an actuarial surplus;

(*b*) is transferred on behalf of an individual who is entitled to the amount as a consequence of the death of a member of the plan and who was a spouse or common-law partner or former spouse or common-law partner of the member at the date of the member's death; and

(*c*) is transferred directly to

(i) another registered pension plan for the benefit of the individual,

(ii) a registered retirement savings plan under which the individual is the annuitant (within the meaning assigned by subsection 146(1)), or

(iii) a registered retirement income fund under which the individual is the annuitant (within the meaning assigned by subsection 146.3(1)).

Related Sections: S. 60(*j*) Transfer of superannuation benefits; s. 60(l) Transfer of refund of premiums under RRSP; s. 104(27) Pension benefits; s. 146(2) Acceptance of plan for registration — prohibited conditions; s. 204.2(1) Definition of "excess amount for a year in respect of registered retirement savings plans"; s. 204.2(1.2) Undeducted RRSP premiums; s. 252(3) Extended meaning of "spouse" and "former spouse".

Interpretation Bulletins: *Primary* — IT-528 Transfers of funds between registered plans.

Registered Plans Directorate Newsletters: No. 91-4R, Registration rules for money purchase provisions.

► 147.3(7.1) ◄

(7.1) Transfer where money purchase plan replaces money purchase plan. An amount is transferred from a registered pension plan (in this subsection referred to as the "transferor plan") in accordance with this subsection if

(*a*) the amount is a single amount;

(*b*) the amount is transferred in respect of the surplus (as defined by regulation) under a money purchase provision (in this subsection referred to as the "former provision") of the transferor plan;

(*c*) the amount is transferred directly to another registered pension plan to be held in connection with a money purchase provision (in this subsection referred to as the "current provision") of the other plan;

(*d*) the amount is transferred in conjunction with the transfer of amounts from the former provision to the current provision on behalf of all or a significant number of members of the transferor plan whose benefits under the former provision are replaced by benefits under the current provision; and

(*e*) the transfer is acceptable to the Minister and the Minister has so notified the administrator of the transferor plan in writing.

Related Regulations: 8300(8)(a)(iv); 8301(4)(b)(ii.2); 8500(1.1); 8500(7)(d); 8502(d)(ii); 8502(k).

► 147.3(8) ◄

(8) Transfer where money purchase plan replaces defined benefit plan. An amount is transferred from a registered pension plan (in this subsection referred to as the "transferor plan") in accordance with this subsection if

(*a*) the amount is a single amount;

(*b*) the amount is transferred in respect of the actuarial surplus under a defined benefit provision of the transferor plan;

(*c*) the amount is transferred directly to another registered pension plan to be held in connection with a money purchase provision of the other plan;

(*d*) the amount is transferred in conjunction with the transfer of amounts from the defined benefit provision to the money purchase provision on behalf of all or a significant number of members of the transferor plan whose benefits under the defined benefit provision are replaced by benefits under the money purchase provision; and

(*e*) the transfer is acceptable to the Minister and the Minister has so notified the administrator of the transferor plan in writing.

Interpretation Bulletins: *Primary* — IT-528 Transfers of funds between registered plans.

Registered Plans Directorate Newsletters: No. 95-5, Conversion of a defined benefit provision to a money purchase provision; No. 91-4R, Registration rules for money purchase provisions.

► 147.3(9) ◄

(9) Taxation of amount transferred. Where an amount is transferred in accordance with any of subsections (1) to (8),

(*a*) the amount shall not, by reason only of that transfer, be included by reason of subparagraph 56(1)(*a*)(i) in computing the income of any taxpayer; and

(*b*) no deduction may be made under any provision of this Act in respect of the amount in computing the income of any taxpayer.

Related Sections: S. 212(1)(*h*) Pension benefits.

Interpretation Bulletins: *Primary* — IT-528 Transfers of funds between registered plans.

► 147.3(10) ◄

(10) Idem. Where, on behalf of an individual, an amount is transferred from a registered pension plan (in this subsection referred to as the "transferor plan") to another plan or fund (in this subsection referred to as the "transferee plan") that is a registered pension plan, a registered retirement savings plan or a registered retirement income fund and the transfer is not in accordance with any of subsections (1) to (7),

(*a*) the amount is deemed to have been paid from the transferor plan to the individual;

(*b*) subject to paragraph (*c*), the individual shall be deemed to have paid the amount as a contribution or premium to the transferee plan; and

(*c*) where the transferee plan is a registered retirement income fund, for the purposes of subsection 146(5) and Part X.1, the individual shall be deemed to have paid the amount at the time of the transfer as a premium under a registered retirement savings plan under which the individual was the annuitant (within the meaning assigned by subsection 146(1)).

Related Sections: S. 146(5) Amount of RRSP premiums deductible.

Interpretation Bulletins: *Primary* — IT-528 Transfers of funds between registered plans.

► 147.3(11) ◄

(11) Division of transferred amount. Where an amount is transferred from a registered pension plan to another registered pension plan, to a registered retirement savings plan or to a registered retirement income fund and a portion, but not all, of the amount is transferred in accordance with any of subsections (1) to (8),

(*a*) subsection (9) applies with respect to the portion of the amount that is transferred in accordance with any of subsections (1) to (8); and

(*b*) subsection (10) applies with respect to the remainder of the amount.

► 147.3(12) ◄

(12) Restriction re transfers. A registered pension plan becomes a revocable plan at any time that an amount is transferred from the plan to another registered pension plan, to a registered retirement savings plan or to a registered retirement income fund unless

(*a*) the amount is transferred in accordance with any of subsections (1) to (8); or

(*b*) where the amount is transferred on behalf of an individual,

(i) the amount is deductible by the individual under paragraph 60(*j*) or (*j*.2), or

(ii) the *Pension Benefits Standards Act, 1985* or a similar law of a province prohibits the payment of the amount to the individual.

Related Sections: S. 147.1(11) Revocation of registration — notice of intention; s. 147.1(12) Notice of revocation; s. 147.1(13) Revocation of registration.

Interpretation Bulletins: *Primary* — IT-528 Transfers of funds between registered plans.

► 147.3(13) ◄

(13) Excess transfer. Where

(*a*) the transfer in a calendar year of an amount from a registered pension plan on behalf of a member of the plan would, but for this subsection, be in accordance with subsection (1) or (2), and

(*b*) the plan becomes, at the end of the year, a revocable plan as a consequence of an excess determined under any of paragraphs 147.1(8)(*a*) and (*b*) and (9)(*a*) and (*b*) with respect to the member (whether or not such an excess is also determined with respect to any other member),

such portion of the amount transferred as may reasonably be considered to derive from amounts allocated or reallocated to the member in the year or from earnings reasonably attributable to those amounts shall, except to the extent otherwise expressly provided in writing by the Minister, be deemed to be an amount that was not transferred in accordance with subsection (1) or (2), as the case may be.

Related Sections: S. 147.1(8) Pension adjustment limits; s. 147.1(9) Idem — multi-employer plans; Part X.

Interpretation Bulletins: *Primary* — IT-528 Transfers of funds between registered plans.

► 147.3(13.1) ◄

(13.1) Withdrawal of excessive transfers to RRSPs and RRIFs. There may be deducted in computing the income of an individual for a taxation year the lesser of

(*a*) the amount, if any, by which

(i) the total of all amounts each of which is an amount included under clause 56(1)(*a*)(i)(C), paragraph 56(1)(*z*.3), subsections 146(8), (8.3) or (12) or 146.3(5), (5.1) or (11) in computing the individual's income for the year, to the extent that the amount is not a prescribed withdrawal,

exceeds

(ii) the total of all amounts each of which is an amount deductible under paragraph 60(*l*) or subsection 146(8.2) in computing the income of the individual for the year, and

(*b*) the amount, if any, by which

(i) the total of all amounts each of which is an amount that was

(A) transferred to a registered retirement savings plan or registered retirement income fund under which the individual was the annuitant (within the meaning assigned by subsection 146(1) or 146.3(1), as the case may be),

(B) included in computing the income of the individual for the year or a preceding taxation year, and

(C) deemed by paragraph (10)(*b*) or (*c*) to have been paid by the individual as a premium to a registered retirement savings plan,

exceeds

(ii) the total of all amounts each of which is an amount

(A) deductible under this subsection in computing the individual's income for a preceding taxation year, or

(B) deducted under subsection 146(5) in computing the individual's income for a preceding taxation year, to the extent that the amount can reasonably be considered to be in respect of an amount referred to in subparagraph (i).

History: S. 147.3(13.1)(*a*)(i) was replaced by S.C. 2017, c. 33, s. 59(1), deemed to have come into force on January 1, 2010, except that in its application before December 14, 2012, subparagraph 147.3(13.1)(*a*)(i) is to be read without reference to "paragraph 56(1)(z3)". S. 147.3(13.1)(*a*)(i) formerly read:

> (i) the total of all amounts each of which is an amount included under subsection 146(8), (8.3) or (12) or 146.3(5), (5.1) or (11) in computing the individual's income for the year, to the extent that the amount is not a prescribed withdrawal,

Related Sections: 56(1)(a) Pension benefits, unemployment insurance benefits, etc.; 56(1)(z.3) Pooled registered pension plan; 60(*l*) Premium or payment under RRSP or RRIF; 146(5) Amount of RRSP premiums deductible.

Forms: T1043 — Calculating Your Deduction to Offset RRSP or RRIF Income if an Excess Amount from an RPP Has Been Transferred to an RRSP or a RRIF.

Interpretation Bulletins: *Primary* — IT-528 Transfers of funds between registered plans. *Secondary* — IT-124R6 Contributions to registered retirement savings plans.

► 147.3(14) ◄

(14) Deemed transfer. For the purposes of this section and the regulations, where property held in connection with a particular pension plan is made available to pay benefits under another pension plan, the property shall be deemed to have been transferred from the particular plan to the other plan.

► 147.3(14.1) ◄

(14.1) Transfer of property between provisions. Where property held in connection with a benefit provision of a registered pension plan is made available to pay benefits under another benefit provision of the plan, subsections (9) to (11) apply in respect of the transaction by which the property is made so available in the same manner as they would apply if the other benefit provision were in another registered pension plan.

► 147.3(15) ◄

(15) Annuity contract commencing after age 69 — (Repealed by S.C. 1998, c. 19, s. 175(2).)

SECTION 147.4: RPP annuity contract

► 147.4(1) ◄

(1) RPP annuity contract. Where

(*a*) at any time an individual acquires, in full or partial satisfaction of the individual's entitlement to benefits under a registered pension plan, an interest in an annuity contract purchased from a licensed annuities provider,

(*b*) the rights provided for under the contract are not materially different from those provided for under the plan as registered,

(*c*) the contract does not permit premiums to be paid at or after that time, other than a premium paid at that time out of or under the plan to purchase the contract,

(*d*) either the plan is not a plan in respect of which the Minister may, under subsection 147.1(11), give a notice of intent to revoke the registration of the plan or the Minister waives the application of this paragraph with respect to the contract and so notifies the administrator of the plan in writing, and

(*e*) the individual does not acquire the interest as a consequence of a transfer of property from the plan to a registered retirement savings plan or a registered retirement income fund,

the following rules apply for the purposes of this Act:

(*f*) the individual is deemed not to have received an amount out of or under the registered pension plan as a consequence of acquiring the interest, and

(*g*) other than for the purposes of sections 147.1 and 147.3, any amount received at or after that time by any individual under the contract is deemed to have been received under the registered pension plan.

Related Sections: S. 139.1(2) Rules of general application; s. 147.1(11) Revocation of registration — notice of intention; s. 254 Contract under pension plan.

► 147.4(2) ◄

(2) Amended contract. Where

(*a*) an amendment is made at any time to an annuity contract to which subsection (1) or paragraph 254(*a*) applies, other than an amendment the sole effect of which is to

(i) defer annuity commencement to no later than the end of the calendar year in which the individual in respect of whom the contract was purchased attains 71 years of age, or

(ii) enhance benefits under the annuity contract in connection with the demutualization (as defined by subsection 139.1(1)) of an insurance corporation that is considered for the purpose of section 139.1 to have been a party to the annuity contract, and

(*b*) the rights provided for under the contract are materially altered as a consequence of the amendment,

the following rules apply for the purposes of this Act:

(*c*) each individual who has an interest in the contract immediately before that time is deemed to have received at that time the payment of an amount under a pension plan equal to the fair market value of the interest immediately before that time,

(*d*) the contract as amended is deemed to be a separate annuity contract issued at that time otherwise than pursuant to or under a superannuation or pension fund or plan, and

(*e*) each individual who has an interest in the separate annuity contract immediately after that time is deemed to have acquired the interest at that time at a cost equal to the fair market value of the interest immediately after that time.

Related Sections: S. 139.1(2) Rules of general application; s. 139.1(3) Special cases.

► 147.4(3) ◄

(3) New contract. For the purposes of this Act, where an annuity contract (in this subsection referred to as the "original contract") to which subsection (1) or paragraph 254(*a*) applies is, at any time, substituted by another contract,

(*a*) if the rights provided for under the other contract

(i) are not materially different from those provided for under the original contract, or

(ii) are materially different from those provided for under the original contract only because of an enhancement of benefits that can reasonably be considered to have been provided solely in connection with the demutualization (as defined by subsection 139.1(1)) of an insurance corporation that is considered for the purposes of section 139.1 to have been a party to the original contract,

the other contract is deemed to be the same contract as, and a continuation of, the original contract; and

(*b*) in any other case, each individual who has an interest in the original contract immediately before that time is deemed to have received at that time the payment of an amount under a pension plan equal to the fair market value of the interest immediately before that time.

Related Sections: S. 139.1(2) Special cases.

► 147.4(4) ◄

(4) RPP annuity contract beginning after age 69 — (Repealed by S.C. 2007, c. 29, s. 21(2).)

Pooled Registered Pension Plans

SECTION 147.5: [Pooled registered pension plans]

► 147.5(1) ◄

(1) Definitions. The following definitions apply in this section.

History: S. 147.5(1) was added by S.C. 2012, c. 31, s. 36(1), in force December 14, 2012.

"administrator" — "administrator", of a pooled pension plan, means

(*a*) a corporation resident in Canada that is responsible for the administration of the plan and that is authorized under the *Pooled Registered Pension Plans Act* or a similar law of a province to act as an administrator for one or more pooled pension plans; or

(*b*) an entity designated in respect of the plan under section 21 of the *Pooled Registered Pension Plans Act* or any provision of a law of a province that is similar to that section.

"designated pooled pension plan" —"designated pooled pension plan", for a calendar year, means a pooled pension plan that, at any time in the year (other than the year in which the plan became registered as a PRPP), meets any of the following conditions:

(*a*) the plan has fewer than 10 participating employers;

(*b*) the fair market value of the property held in connection with the accounts of all members of the plan employed by a particular participating employer exceeds 50% of the fair market value of the property held in connection with the plan;

(*c*) more than 50% of the members of the plan are employed by a particular participating employer; or

(*d*) it is reasonable to conclude that the participation in the plan of one or more participating employers occurs primarily to avoid the application of any of paragraphs (*a*) to (*c*).

"exempt earned income" —"exempt earned income", of a taxpayer for a taxation year, means the total of all amounts each of which is an amount that is

(*a*) not included in the taxpayer's earned income (as defined in subsection 146(1)) for the year and that would be so included but for paragraph 81(1)(*a*) as it applies with respect to the *Indian Act*; and

(*b*) reported by the taxpayer in prescribed form filed with the Minister by the taxpayer's filing-due date for the year, or such later date as is acceptable to the Minister, provided that the later date is within three calendar years following the end of the year.

Related Sections: S. 146(1), "earned income"; s. 81(1) Amounts not included in income.

"exempt-income contribution amount" —"exempt-income contribution amount", of a taxpayer for a taxation year, means the total of

(*a*) all amounts each of which is a contribution to a PRPP made by the taxpayer for the year that is not deductible in computing the income of the taxpayer because of subsection (32), and

(*b*) the amount, if any, designated under subsection (34) by the taxpayer for the year in prescribed form filed with the Minister by the taxpayer's filing-due date for the year, or such later date as is acceptable to the Minister, provided that the later date is within three calendar years following the end of the year.

"member" —"member", of a pooled pension plan, means an individual (other than a trust) who holds an account under the plan.

"participating employer" —"participating employer", in relation to a pooled pension plan for a calendar year, means an employer that, in the year,

(*a*) makes contributions to the plan in respect of all or a class of its employees or former employees; or

(*b*) remits to the administrator of the plan contributions made by members of the plan under a contract with the administrator in respect of all or a class of its employees.

"pooled pension plan" —"pooled pension plan" means a plan that is registered under the *Pooled Registered Pension Plans Act* or a similar law of a province.

"pooled registered pension plan" or "PRPP" —"pooled registered pension plan" or "PRPP" means a pooled pension plan that has been accepted for registration by the Minister for the purposes of this Act, which registration has not been revoked.

"qualifying annuity" —"qualifying annuity", for an individual, means an annuity that

(*a*) is payable to

(i) the individual for the individual's life, or

(ii) the individual for the lives, jointly, of the individual and the individual's spouse or common-law partner and to the survivor of them for the survivor's life;

(*b*) is payable beginning no later than the later of

(i) the end of the calendar year in which the individual attains 71 years of age, and

(ii) the end of the calendar year in which the annuity is acquired;

(*c*) unless the annuity is subsequently commuted into a single payment, is payable

(i) at least annually, and

(ii) in equal amounts or is not so payable solely because of an adjustment that would, if the annuity were an annuity under a retirement savings plan, in accordance with any of subparagraphs 146(3)(*b*)(iii) to (v);

(*d*) if the annuity includes a guaranteed period, requires that

(i) the period not exceed 15 years, and

(ii) in the event of the later of the death of the individual and that of the individual's spouse or common-law partner during the period, any remaining amounts otherwise payable be commuted into a single payment as soon as practicable after the later death; and

(*e*) does not permit any premiums to be paid, other than the premium paid from the PRPP to acquire the annuity.

Proposed Amendment

2019 Federal Budget Resolutions

The Act is modified to give effect to the proposals relating to permitting additional types of annuities under registered plans described in the budget documents tabled by the Minister of Finance in the House of Commons on Budget Day.

Explanatory Note:
Dentons Canada LLP Commentary

Budget 2019 proposes to provide "qualified investment" status to the following additional types of annuities for certain registered plans, effective for 2020 and subsequent taxation years:

- advanced life deferred annuities will be permitted under a registered retirement savings plan (RRSP), registered retirement income fund (RRIF), deferred profit sharing plan (DPSP), pooled registered pension plan (PRPP) and defined contribution registered pension plan (RPP); and

- variable payment life annuities will be permitted under a PRPP and defined contribution RPP.

Advanced Life Deferred Annuities (ALDA)

The tax rules generally require an annuity purchased with a registered plan to commence by the end of the year in which the annuitant attains 71 years of age. An ALDA will be a life annuity the commencement of which may be deferred until the end of the year in which the annuitant turns 85 and meets certain other prescribed conditions. A lifetime limit of 25% of the value of the plan (including payments for the ALDA) and $150,000 will apply.

Annuity payments to a surviving spouse or common-law partner will be taxable in the year of receipt. Lump-sum payments to a surviving spouse, common-law partner or dependent child or grandchild (provided that the child or grandchild is dependent by reason of physical or mental infirmity) will qualify for a tax-deferred transfer to an RRSP, RRIF or other eligible vehicle of the annuitant.

Variable Payment Life Annuity (VPLA)

Existing rules generally require retirement benefits from a PRPP or defined contribution RPP be provided to a member by means of a transfer of funds from the account to an RRSP or RRIF. Budget 2019 proposes that commencing in 2020 and subsequent years, PRPP and RPPs be able to provide a VPLA directly to members from the plan. A VPLA will provide payments that vary based on the investment performance of the underlying annuities fund and on the mortality experience of VPLA annuitants.

PRPP and defined contribution RPP administrators will be permitted to establish a separate annuities fund under the plan to receive transfers of amounts from members' accounts to provide for VPLAs. A minimum of 10 retired members will be required to participate in a VPLA. VPLAs will be required to comply with certain existing tax rules applicable to PRPPs and defined contribution RPPs, as well as additional requirements. On death, VPLAs will be subject to the existing tax treatment of annuities purchased with PRPP and defined contribution RPP savings.

"qualifying survivor" —"qualifying survivor", in relation to a member of a PRPP, means an individual who, immediately before the death of the member

(*a*) was a spouse or common-law partner of the member, or

(*b*) was a child or grandchild of the member who was financially dependent on the member for support.

Related Sections: S. 146(1.1) Restriction — financially dependent; s. 147.5(16) Qualifying survivor.

"restricted investment" —"restricted investment", for a pooled pension plan, means

(*a*) a debt of a member of the plan;

(*b*) a share of, an interest in, or a debt of

(i) a corporation, partnership or trust in which a member of the plan has a significant interest, or

(ii) a person or partnership that does not deal at arm's length with the member of the plan or with a person or partnership described in subparagraph (i);

(*c*) an interest (or, for civil law, a right) in, or a right to acquire, a share, interest or debt described in paragraph (*a*) or (*b*); or

(*d*) prescribed property.

Related Sections: S. 147.5(30) Significant interest.

"single amount" —"single amount" means an amount that is not part of a series of periodic payments.

"successor member" —"successor member" means an individual who was the spouse or common-law partner of a member of a PRPP immediately before the death of the member and who acquires, as a consequence of the death, all of the member's rights in respect of the member's account under the PRPP.

Related Sections: S. 147.5(14) Treatment on death — no successor member; s. 147.5(15) Treatment on death — successor member.

"unused non-deductible PRPP room" —"unused non-deductible PRPP room", of a taxpayer at the end of a taxation year, means the amount determined by the formula

$$A - B$$

where

A is the amount of the taxpayer's unused RRSP deduction room at the end of the year, determined in accordance with subsection (33); and

B is the taxpayer's unused RRSP deduction room at the end of the year.

Editorial Note: The *Pooled Registered Pension Plans Act* and accompanying amendments to the *Income Tax Act* became effective on December 14, 2012. The tax rules relating to pooled registered pension plans (PRPPs) allow employers and their employees, or self-employed individuals, to make tax-deductible contributions to the plans similar to those made to money-purchase registered pension plans (RPPs). An employer's contributions to a PRPP in a taxation year or within 120 days after the year are deductible under subsection 147.5(10). The employer's contribution for a year will reduce the employee's RRSP deduction room for the same year. The employee's contribution in a year is deemed to be a premium paid to an RRSP and therefore deductible, and like other premiums also reduces the employee's RRSP deduction room for the year. Income earned in the PRPP is exempt from tax while in the plan. Distributions from the PRPP to the employee are normally included in the employee's income and can qualify for the pension credit under subsection 118(3).

► 147.5(2) ◄

(2) Registration conditions. The Minister may accept for registration a pooled pension plan for the purposes of this Act, but shall not accept for registration any plan unless application for registration is made in prescribed manner by the plan administrator and, in the Minister's opinion, the plan complies with the following conditions:

(*a*) the primary purpose of the plan is to accept and invest contributions in order to provide retirement income to plan members, subject to the limits and other requirements under this Act;

(*b*) a single and separate account is maintained for each member under the member's Social Insurance Number

(i) to which are credited all contributions made to the plan in respect of the member, and any earnings of the plan allocated to the member, and

(ii) to which are charged all payments and distributions made in respect of the member;

(*c*) the only benefits provided under the plan in respect of each member are benefits determined solely with reference to, and provided by, the amount in the member's account;

(*d*) all earnings of the plan are allocated to plan members on a reasonable basis and no less frequently than annually;

(*e*) the arrangement under which property is held in connection with the plan is acceptable to the Minister;

(*f*) no right of a person under the plan is capable of being assigned, charged, anticipated, given as security or surrendered, other than

(i) an assignment pursuant to a decree, order or judgment of a competent tribunal, or under a written agreement, relating to a division of property between the member and the member's spouse or common-law partner or former spouse or common-law partner, in settlement of rights arising out of, or on a breakdown of, their marriage or common-law partnership, or

(ii) an assignment by the legal representative of a deceased individual on the distribution of the individual's estate;

(*g*) the plan requires that all amounts contributed or allocated to a member's account vest immediately and indefeasibly for the benefit of the member;

(*h*) the plan permits the payment of an amount to a member if the amount is paid to reduce the amount of tax that would otherwise be payable under Part X.1 by the member;

(*i*) any amount payable from an account of a member after the death of the member is paid as soon as practicable after the death;

(*j*) there is no reason to expect that the plan may become a revocable plan; and

(*k*) any prescribed conditions.

History: S. 147.5(2) was added by S.C. 2012, c. 31, s. 36(1), in force December 14, 2012.

STEP Canada: Jillian Welch, "2013 Budget Proposal on LIAs & "Pensionable" Uses of Insurance," PowerPoint presentation to the 15th National Conference of STEP Canada, Toronto, June 10-11, 2013.

Information Circulars: IC 13-1R1 Pooled registered pension plans.

► 147.5(3) ◄

(3) Conditions applicable to PRPPs. A pooled registered pension plan becomes a revocable plan at any time that

(*a*) a contribution is made to the plan other than an amount

(i) paid by a member of the plan,

(ii) paid by an employer or former employer of a member of the plan in respect of the member, or

(iii) transferred to the plan in accordance with any of subsections (21), 146(16) and (21), 146.3(14) and (14.1), 147(19) and 147.3(1), (4) and (5) to (7);

(*b*) a contribution is made to the plan in respect of a member after the calendar year in which the member attains 71 years of age, other than an amount

(i) described in subparagraph (*a*)(iii), or

(ii) if subsection 60.022(1) applies, described in any of subclauses 60(*l*)(v)(B.2)(II) to (IV) as read in that subsection;

(*c*) a participating employer makes contributions to the plan in a calendar year in respect of a member of the plan in excess of the RRSP dollar limit for the year, except in accordance with a direction by the member;

(*d*) a distribution is made from the plan other than

(i) a payment of benefits in accordance with subsection (5), or

(ii) a return of contributions

(A) if a contribution to the plan has been made as a result of a reasonable error by a member of the plan or a participating employer in relation to the plan and the return of contributions is made to the person who made the contribution no later than December 31 of the year following the calendar year in which the contribution was made,

(B) to avoid the revocation of the registration of the plan,

(C) to reduce the amount of tax that would otherwise be payable under Part X.1 by a member, or

(D) to comply with any requirement under this Act;

(*e*) property is held in connection with the plan that

(i) the administrator knew or ought to have known was a restricted investment for the plan, or

(ii) in the case of a designated pooled pension plan, is a share or debt of, or an interest in, a participating employer of the plan or any person or partnership that does not deal at arm's length with a participating employer, or an interest (or, for civil law, a right) in, or a right to acquire, such a share, debt or interest;

(*f*) the value of a member's right under the plan depends on the value of, or income or capital gains in respect of, property that would be described in paragraph (*e*) if it were held in connection with the plan;

(*g*) the administrator borrows money or other property for the purposes of the plan; or

(*h*) the plan or the administrator does not comply with a prescribed condition.

History: S. 147.5(3)(*b*) was replaced by S.C. 2015, c. 36, s. 17, in force on Royal Assent, June 23, 2015, and formerly read:

> (*b*) a contribution is made to the plan in respect of a member after the calendar year in which the member attains 71 years of age, other than an amount described in subparagraph (*a*)(iii);

S. 147.5(3) was added by S.C. 2012, c. 31, s. 36(1), in force December 14, 2012.

Related Sections: 56(1)(z.3) Pooled registered pension plan; 60.022(1) Additions to clause 60(l)(v)(B.2) for 2015; S. 147.5(24) Notice of intent.

► 147.5(4) ◄

(4) Non-payment of minimum amount. A PRPP becomes a revocable plan at the beginning of a calendar year if the total amount distributed from a member's account under the PRPP in the calendar year is less than the amount that would be the minimum amount for the calendar year under subsection 8506(5) of the *Income Tax Regulations* if the member's account were an account under a money purchase provision of a registered pension plan.

History: S. 147.5(4) was added by S.C. 2012, c. 31, s. 36(1), in force December 14, 2012.

Related Sections: S. 147.5(24) Notice of intent.

► 147.5(5) ◄

(5) Permissible benefits. The following benefits may be provided under a pooled pension plan:

(*a*) the payment of benefits to a member that would be in accordance with paragraph 8506(1)(*e.1*) of the *Income Tax Regulations* if the benefits were provided under a money purchase provision of a registered pension plan; and

(*b*) the payment of a single amount from the member's account.

History: S. 147.5(5) was added by S.C. 2012, c. 31, s. 36(1), in force December 14, 2012.

▶ 147.5(6) ◀

(6) Additional conditions. The Minister may, at any time, impose reasonable conditions, in writing, applicable with respect to PRPPs, a class of PRPPs or a particular PRPP.

History: S. 147.5(6) was added by S.C. 2012, c. 31, s. 36(1), in force December 14, 2012.

▶ 147.5(7) ◀

(7) Acceptance of amendments. The Minister shall not accept an amendment to a PRPP unless

(*a*) application for the acceptance is made in prescribed manner by the administrator of the PRPP; and

(*b*) the amendment and the PRPP as amended comply with the registration conditions specified in subsection (2).

History: S. 147.5(7) was added by S.C. 2012, c. 31, s. 36(1), in force December 14, 2012.

▶ 147.5(8) ◀

(8) Trust not taxable. No tax is payable under this Part by a trust governed by a PRPP on its taxable income for a taxation year, except that, if at any time in the year, it carries on a business, tax is payable under this Part by the trust on the amount that would be its taxable income for the year if it had no income or losses from sources other than the business, and for this purpose,

(*a*) all capital gains and capital losses from the disposition of property held in connection with the business are deemed to be income or losses, as the case may be, from the business; and

(*b*) the trust's income is to be computed without reference to subsections 104(6), (19) and (21).

History: S. 147.5(8) was added by S.C. 2012, c. 31, s. 36(1), in force December 14, 2012.

▶ 147.5(9) ◀

(9) Obligations of administrator. The administrator of a PRPP shall exercise the care, diligence and skill of a reasonably prudent trustee to minimize the possibility that the registration of the PRPP may be revoked other than at the request of the administrator.

History: S. 147.5(9) was added by S.C. 2012, c. 31, s. 36(1), in force December 14, 2012.

Related Sections: S. 162(7) Failure to comply.

▶ 147.5(10) ◀

(10) Employer contributions deductible. There may be deducted in computing a taxpayer's income for a taxation year, the total of all amounts each of which is a contribution made by the taxpayer in the year or within 120 days after the end of the year to a PRPP in respect of the taxpayer's employees or former employees to the extent that the contribution

(*a*) was made in accordance with the PRPP as registered and in respect of periods before the end of the year; and

(*b*) was not deducted in computing the taxpayer's income for a preceding taxation year.

History: S. 147.5(10) was added by S.C. 2012, c. 31, s. 36(1), in force December 14, 2012.

Related Sections: S. 146(5) Amount of RRSP premiums deductible.

▶ 147.5(11) ◀

(11) Member contributions. For the purposes of paragraphs 60(*j*), (*j.1*) and (*l*), section 146 (other than subsections (8.3) to (8.7)), paragraphs 146.01(3)(*a*) and 146.02(3)(*a*) and Parts X.1 and X.5, a contribution made to a PRPP by a member of a PRPP is deemed to be a premium paid by the member to an RRSP under which the member is the annuitant.

History: S. 147.5(11) was added by S.C. 2012, c. 31, s. 36(1), in force December 14, 2012.

▶ 147.5(12) ◀

(12) Member's account. For the purposes of paragraph 18(1)(*u*), subparagraph (*a*)(i) of the definition "excluded right or interest" in subsection 128.1(10), paragraph 146(8.2)(*b*), subsection 146(8.21), paragraphs 146(16)(*a*) and (*b*), subparagraph 146(21)(*a*)(i), paragraph (*b*) of the definition "excluded premium" in subsection 146.01 (1), paragraph (*c*) of the definition "excluded premium" in subsection 146.02(1), subsections 146.3(14) and 147(19) to (21), section 147.3 and paragraphs 212(1)(*j.1*) and (*m*), and of regulations made under subsection 147.1(18), a member's account under a PRPP is deemed to be a registered retirement savings plan under which the member is the annuitant.

History: S. 147.5(12) was replaced by S.C. 2017, c. 33, s. 60(1), deemed to have come into force on December 14, 2012, and formerly read:

(12) *Member's account.* For the purposes of paragraph 18(1)(*u*), subparagraph (*a*)(i) of the definition "excluded right or interest" in subsection 128.1(10), paragraph 146(8.2)(*b*), subsection 146(8.21), paragraphs 146(16)(*a*) and (*b*), subparagraph 146(21)(*a*)(i), paragraph (*b*) of the definition "excluded premium" in subsection 146.01(1), paragraph (*c*) of the definition "excluded premium" in subsection 146.02(1), subsections 146.3(14) and 147(19) to (21), section 147.3 and paragraphs 212(1)(*j.1*) and (*m*), and of regulations made under 147.1(18), a member's account under a PRPP is deemed to be a registered retirement savings plan under which the member is the annuitant.

S. 147.5(12) was added by S.C. 2012, c. 31, s. 36(1), in force December 14, 2012.

▶ 147.5(13) ◀

(13) Taxable amounts. There shall be included in computing the income of a taxpayer for a taxation year

(*a*) if the taxpayer is a member of a PRPP, the total of all amounts each of which is a distribution made in the year from the member's account under the PRPP, other than an amount that is

(i) included in computing the income of another taxpayer for the year under paragraph (*b*),

(ii) described in subsection (22), or

(iii) distributed after the death of the member;

(*b*) if the taxpayer is a participating employer in relation to a PRPP, the total of all amounts each of which is a return of contributions that is described in clause (3)(*d*)(ii)(A) and that is made to the taxpayer in the year.

Editorial Note: S. 147.5(13) provides that where a member (employee) of a PRPP receives a distribution in a year from the member's account under the PRPP, it is included in the member's income. An exception is made for direct transfers made to the member's (or spouse's) PRPP or other deferred income plan under subsections 147.5(21) and (22), which allow certain tax-free transfers from the PRPP to the individual's other PRPP account, an RPP, an RRSP, or to acquire a qualifying annuity. There is also an exception for amounts distributed out of the PRPP after the member's death.

History: S. 147.5(13) was added by S.C. 2012, c. 31, s. 36(1), in force December 14, 2012.

► 147.5(14) ◄

(14) Treatment on death — no successor member. If a member of a PRPP dies and there is no successor member in respect of the deceased member's account under the PRPP, an amount, equal to the amount by which the fair market value of all property held in connection with the account immediately before the death exceeds the total of all amounts distributed from the account that are described in subsection (16), is deemed to have been distributed from the account immediately before the death.

Editorial Note: Upon the death of a member of a PRPP, the fair market value of the member's account is generally included in the member's income, unless the member's spouse or common-law partner or financially dependent child or grandchild receives distributions from the PRPP as a consequence of the death of the member. The fair market value inclusion rule similarly does not apply if the spouse or common-law partner acquires, as a consequence of the death, all of the member's rights in respect of the member's account under the PRPP.

History: S. 147.5(14) was added by S.C. 2012, c. 31, s. 36(1), in force December 14, 2012.

Related Sections: S. 147.5(1), "successor member".

► 147.5(15) ◄

(15) Treatment on death — successor member. If a member of a PRPP dies and there is a successor member in respect of the deceased member's account under the PRPP,

(*a*) the account ceases to be an account of the deceased member at the time of the death;

(*b*) the successor member is, after the time of the death, deemed to hold the account as a member of the PRPP; and

(*c*) the successor member is deemed to be a separate member in respect of any other account under the PRPP that the successor member holds.

History: S. 147.5(15) was added by S.C. 2012, c. 31, s. 36(1), in force December 14, 2012.

Related Sections: S. 147.5(1), "successor member".

► 147.5(16) ◄

(16) Qualifying survivor. If, as a consequence of the death of a member of a PRPP, an amount is distributed in a taxation year from the member's account under the PRPP to, or on behalf of, a qualifying survivor of the member, the amount shall be included in computing the survivor's income for the year, except to the extent that it is an amount described in subsection (22).

Editorial Note: Upon the death of a member of a pooled registered pension plan ("PRPP"), an amount that is transferred from that member's account to, or on behalf of, a qualifying survivor is considered to be income of the survivor except where: (i) it is a single amount, (ii) the survivor was the spouse or common-law partner immediately before death, and (iii) the transfer is directly to a PRPP, RPP, RRSP, RRIF, or qualifying annuity of the survivor. Where the transfer is not considered income to the survivor, there is no corresponding deduction to any other taxpayer.

History: S. 147.5(16) was added by S.C. 2012, c. 31, s. 36(1), in force December 14, 2012.

► 147.5(17) ◄

(17) Deemed distribution to qualifying survivor. If an amount is distributed at any time from a deceased member's account under a PRPP to the member's legal representative and a qualifying survivor of the member is entitled to all or a portion of the amount in full or partial satisfaction of the survivor's rights as a beneficiary (as defined in subsection 108(1)) under the deceased's estate, then, for the purposes of subsection (16), the amount or portion of the amount, as the case may be, is deemed to have been distributed at that time from the member's account to the qualifying survivor (and not to the legal representative) to the extent that it is so designated jointly by the legal representative and the qualifying survivor in prescribed form filed with the Minister.

History: S. 147.5(17) was added by S.C. 2012, c. 31, s. 36(1), in force December 14, 2012.

Related Sections: S. 147.5(1), "qualifying survivor".

► 147.5(18) ◄

(18) Post-death increase in value. There shall be included in computing the income for a taxation year of a taxpayer who is not a qualifying survivor in relation to a member of a PRPP, the total of all amounts each of which is an amount determined by the formula

$$A - B$$

where

A is the amount of a distribution made in the year from the member's account under the PRPP as a consequence of the member's death to, or on behalf of, the taxpayer, and

B is an amount designated by the administrator of the PRPP not exceeding the lesser of

(*a*) the amount of the distribution, and

(*b*) the amount by which the fair market value of all property held in connection with the account immediately before the death exceeds the total of all amounts each of which is

(i) the value of B in respect of any prior distribution made from the account, or

(ii) an amount included under subsection (16) in computing the income of a qualifying survivor in relation to the member.

Editorial Note: For any taxation year of a non-qualifying survivor of a pooled registered pension plan ("PRPP") member there shall be an income inclusion for the post-death increase in the fair value of PRPP assets. The inclusion is the excess of: (a) the current year distribution to or on behalf of the taxpayer as a result of the PRPP member's death; less (b) an amount designated by the PRPP administrator not to exceed the lesser of: (i) the distribution amount, and (ii) the amount by which the fair market value of the PRPP assets before death exceeds the total of the value described in (b) in respect of previous distributions and any amounts included in the income of a qualifying survivor under s. 147.5(16).

History: S. 147.5(18) was added by S.C. 2012, c. 31, s. 36(1), in force December 14, 2012.

Related Sections: S. 147.5(1), "qualifying survivor".

► 147.5(19) ◄

(19) Post-death decrease in value. There may be deducted in computing the income of a member of a PRPP for the taxation year in which the member dies, an amount not exceeding the amount determined, after all amounts payable from the member's account under the PRPP have been distributed, by the formula

$$A - B$$

where

A is the total of all amounts each of which is an amount in respect of the account

(*a*) included in the member's income under subsection (13) because of the application of subsection (14),

(*b*) included in the income of another taxpayer under subsection (16) or (18), or

(*c*) transferred in accordance with subsection (21) in circumstances described in subparagraph (21)(*b*)(iii); and

B is the total of all distributions made from the account after the member's death.

Editorial Note: In the taxation year that a pooled registered pension plan ("PRPP") member dies there may be a deduction from taxable income for the post-death decrease in fair value of the PRPP assets after distribution of all amounts payable. The deduction is the excess of the aggregate of amounts included in the deceased's income under s. 147.5(13), amounts included in other taxpayers' income under s. 147.5(16) or (18) and less amounts transferred to a spouse or common-law partner as a consequence of the death under 147.5(21), over all distributions made after the member's death.

History: S. 147.5(19) was added by S.C. 2012, c. 31, s. 36(1), in force December 14, 2012.

► 147.5(20) ◄

(20) Subsection (19) not applicable. Except where the Minister has waived in writing the application of this subsection with respect to all or any portion of the amount determined in subsection (19) in respect of a member's account under a PRPP, that subsection does not apply if the last distribution from the account was made after the end of the calendar year following the year in which the member died.

History: S. 147.5(20) was added by S.C. 2012, c. 31, s. 36(1), in force December 14, 2012.

► 147.5(21) ◄

(21) Transfer of amounts. An amount is transferred from a member's account under a PRPP in accordance with this subsection if the amount

(*a*) is a single amount;

(*b*) is transferred on behalf of an individual who

(i) is the member,

(ii) is a spouse or common-law partner or former spouse or common-law partner of the member and who is entitled to the amount under a decree, order or judgment of a competent tribunal, or under a written agreement, relating to a division of property between the member and the individual, in settlement of rights arising out of, or on a breakdown of, their marriage or common-law partnership, or

(iii) is entitled to the amount as a consequence of the death of the member and was a spouse or common-law partner of the member immediately before the death; and

(*c*) is transferred directly to

(i) the individual's account under the PRPP,

(ii) another PRPP in respect of the individual,

(iii) a registered pension plan for the benefit of the individual,

(iv) a registered retirement savings plan or registered retirement income fund under which the individual is the annuitant, or

(v) a licensed annuities provider to acquire a qualifying annuity for the individual.

History: S. 147.5(21) was added by S.C. 2012, c. 31, s. 36(1), in force December 14, 2012.

Related Sections: S. 60(*l*) Transfer of refund of premiums under RRSP.

► 147.5(22) ◄

(22) Taxation of transfers. If subsection (21) applies to an amount transferred from a member's account under a PRPP on behalf of an individual,

(*a*) the amount shall not, by reason only of that transfer, be included in computing the income of the individual; and

(*b*) no deduction may be made in respect of the amount in computing the income of any taxpayer.

History: S. 147.5(22) was added by S.C. 2012, c. 31, s. 36(1), in force December 14, 2012.

► 147.5(23) ◄

(23) Taxation of qualifying annuity. If an amount is transferred in accordance with subsection (21) to acquire a qualifying annuity, there shall be included — under this section and not under any other provision of this Act — in computing an individual's income for a taxation year any amount received by the individual during the year out of or under the annuity or as proceeds from a disposition in respect of the annuity.

History: S. 147.5(23) was added by S.C. 2012, c. 31, s. 36(1), in force December 14, 2012.

► 147.5(24) ◄

(24) Notice of intent. The Minister may give notice (in subsections (25) and (26) referred to as a "notice of intent") to an administrator of a PRPP in writing that the Minister intends to revoke the registration of the plan as a PRPP if

(*a*) the plan does not comply with the conditions for registration in subsection (2);

(*b*) the plan is not administered in accordance with the terms of the plan as registered;

(*c*) the plan becomes a revocable plan;

(*d*) a condition imposed under subsection (6) that applies with respect to the plan is not complied with; or

(*e*) registration of the plan under the *Pooled Registered Pension Plans Act* or a similar law of a province is refused or revoked.

History: S. 147.5(24) was added by S.C. 2012, c. 31, s. 36(1), in force December 14, 2012.

► 147.5(25) ◄

(25) Date of revocation. The notice of intent shall specify the date on which revocation of a PRPP is to be effective, which date shall not be earlier than the earliest date on which one of the events described in subsection (24) occurs.

History: S. 147.5(25) was added by S.C. 2012, c. 31, s. 36(1), in force December 14, 2012.

► 147.5(26) ◄

(26) Notice of revocation. At any time after 30 days after the day on which the notice of intent is mailed to an administrator of a PRPP, the Minister may give notice (in this subsection and in subsection (27) referred to as a "notice of revocation") in writing to the administrator that the registration of the PRPP is revoked as of the date specified in the notice of revocation and that date may not be earlier than the date specified in the notice of intent.

History: S. 147.5(26) was added by S.C. 2012, c. 31, s. 36(1), in force December 14, 2012.

► 147.5(27) ◄

(27) Revocation of registration. If the Minister gives a notice of revocation to the administrator of a PRPP, the registration of the PRPP is revoked as of the date specified in the notice of revocation, unless the Federal Court of Appeal or a judge of that Court, on application made at any time before the determination of an appeal pursuant to subsection 172(3), orders otherwise.

History: S. 147.5(27) was added by S.C. 2012, c. 31, s. 36(1), in force December 14, 2012.

► 147.5(28) ◄

(28) Voluntary revocation. If the administrator of a PRPP so requests in writing, the Minister may give notice in writing to the administrator that the registration of the PRPP is revoked as of a specified date and that date may not be earlier than the date specified in the administrator's request.

History: S. 147.5(28) was added by S.C. 2012, c. 31, s. 36(1), in force December 14, 2012.

► 147.5(29) ◄

(29) Single employer. For the purposes of the definition "designated pooled pension plan" in subsection (1), all employers that are related to each other are deemed to be a single employer and all the structural units of a trade union, including each local, branch, national and international unit, are deemed to be a single employer.

History: S. 147.5(29) was added by S.C. 2012, c. 31, s. 36(1), in force December 14, 2012.

► 147.5(30) ◄

(30) Significant interest. For the purposes of the definition "restricted investment" in subsection (1), a member of a pooled pension plan has a significant interest in a corporation, trust or partnership at any time if, at that time,

(*a*) in the case of a corporation, the member is a specified shareholder of the corporation; and

(*b*) in the case of a partnership or trust,

(i) the member is a specified unitholder of the partnership or the trust, as the case may be, or

(ii) the total fair market value of the member's interests in the partnership or the trust, as the case may be, together with all interests in the partnership or the trust held by persons or partnerships with whom the member does not deal at arm's length or is affiliated, is 10% or more of the fair market value of all interests in the partnership or the trust.

History: S. 147.5(30) was added by S.C. 2012, c. 31, s. 36(1), in force December 14, 2012.

Related Sections: S. 248(1), "specified unitholder"; s. 248(1), "specified shareholder".

► 147.5(31) ◄

(31) Contributions from exempt income. Contributions may be made to a PRPP in respect of a member of the PRPP as if the member's earned income (as defined in subsection 146(1)) for a taxation year included the member's exempt earned income for the year.

History: S. 147.5(31) was added by S.C. 2012, c. 31, s. 36(1), in force December 14, 2012.

Related Sections: S. 146(5) Amount of RRSP premiums deductible.

► 147.5(32) ◄

(32) Non-deductible contributions. A contribution made by a member of a PRPP to the member's account under the PRPP out of or from the member's exempt earned income may not be deducted in computing the income of the member for any taxation year.

History: S. 147.5(32) was added by S.C. 2012, c. 31, s. 36(1), in force December 14, 2012.

► 147.5(32.1) ◄

(32.1) Contribution deemed not paid. Where a member of a PRPP or a participating employer in relation to the PRPP has, at any time in a taxation year, received a distribution from the member's account under the PRPP that is a return of a contribution described in clause 147.5(3)(*d*)(ii)(A) or (B), the contribution is deemed not to have been a contribution made by the member or the participating employer, as the case may be, to the PRPP to the extent that the contribution is not deducted in computing the taxpayer's income for the year or a preceding taxation year.

History: S. 147.5(32.1) was added by S.C. 2017, c. 33, s. 60(2), deemed to have come into force on December 14, 2012.

► 147.5(33) ◄

(33) Exempt contributions not over-contributions. For the purposes of Part X.1 as it applies because of subsection (11) in respect of contributions made to a PRPP,

(*a*) an individual's earned income (as defined in subsection 146(1)) for any taxation year after 2012 includes the individual's exempt earned income for that year;

(*b*) an individual's exempt-income contribution amount for any taxation year is deemed to have been deducted by the individual under subsection 146(5) in computing the individual's income for that year; and

(*c*) the description of D in paragraph (*b*) of the definition "unused RRSP deduction room" in subsection 146(1) is to be read without reference to subparagraph (iv).

Editorial Note: Contributions to a PRPP are subject to the 18% "earned income" limitation applicable to contributions to RRSPs. For these purposes, subsection 147.5(31) expands the concept of earned income for PRPP purposes to include "exempt earned income", which is income that would be earned income but for the fact that it is earned on a reserve and therefore exempt from taxation under paragraph 81(1)(*a*) by virtue of the *Indian Act*. Although contributions out of exempt earned income to the PRPP are thus allowed, they are not deductible for the member by virtue of subsection 147.5(32). Subsection 147.5(33) generally ensures that the contributions of exempt earned income will not attract the Part X.1 penalty tax (to the extent they are within the RRSP deduction limit and the additional PRPP limit owing the expanded earned income concept).

History: S. 147.5(33) was added by S.C. 2012, c. 31, s. 36(1), in force December 14, 2012.

► 147.5(34) ◄

(34) Designation of exempt-income contribution amount. A taxpayer may designate an amount as the taxpayer's exempt-income contribution amount for a taxation year if the amount designated does not exceed the lesser of

(*a*) the taxpayer's unused non-deductible PRPP room at the end of the preceding taxation year, and

(*b*) the total of the taxpayer's contributions as a member to a PRPP for the year (other than contributions to which subsection (32) applies).

History: S. 147.5(34) was added by S.C. 2012, c. 31, s. 36(1), in force December 14, 2012.

► 147.5(35) ◄

(35) Regulations — other. The Governor in Council may make regulations

(*a*) prescribing conditions applicable to administrators;

(*b*) requiring administrators to file information returns respecting pooled pension plans;

(*c*) enabling the Minister to require any person to provide the Minister with information for the purposes and provisions of this Act relating to PRPPs; and

(*d*) generally to carry out the purposes and provisions of this Act relating to PRPPs.

History: S. 147.5(35) was added by S.C. 2012, c. 31, s. 36(1), in force December 14, 2012.

SECTION 148: Life Insurance Policies

► 148(1) ◄

(1) Amounts included in computing policyholder's income. There shall be included in computing the income for a taxation year of a policyholder in respect of the disposition of an interest in a life insurance policy, other than a policy that is or is issued pursuant to

(*a*) a registered pension fund or plan,

(*b*) a registered retirement savings plan,

(*b*.1) a registered retirement income fund,

(*b*.2) a TFSA,

(*b*.3) a pooled registered pension plan,

(*c*) an income-averaging annuity contract,

(*d*) a deferred profit sharing plan, or

(*e*) an annuity contract if

(i) the payment for the annuity contract was deductible under paragraph 60(*l*) in computing the policyholder's income,

(i.1) the annuity contract is a qualifying trust annuity with respect to a taxpayer and the amount paid to acquire it was deductible under paragraph 60(*l*) in computing the taxpayer's income, or

(ii) the policyholder acquired the annuity contract in circumstances to which subsection 146(21) applied,

the amount, if any, by which the proceeds of the disposition of the policyholder's interest in the policy that the policyholder, beneficiary or assignee, as the case may be, became entitled to receive in the year exceeds the adjusted cost basis to the policyholder of that interest immediately before the disposition.

Editorial Note: Proceeds from the disposition of a life insurance policy in excess of the adjusted cost basis of the policy are generally included in income under s. 56(1)(*j*). Specifically excluded, under s. 148(1), are amounts received with respect to policies held by registered deferred income plans, an income-averaging annuity contract, and an annuity the cost of which is deductible under s. 60(*l*) or was acquired pursuant to a prescribed provincial pension plan. Amounts with respect to qualifying trust annuities where the cost was deductible under s. 60(*l*) are also excluded. A disposition of a life insurance policy excludes a payment under a policy, other than an annuity contract, as a consequence of the death of an individual if the policy was last acquired before December 2, 1982 or is an exempt policy. See the definition of "disposition" in s. 148(9).

History: S. 148(1)(*e*) was replaced by S.C. 2013, c. 34, s. 305(2), deemed to have come into force on September 1, 1992, and formerly read:

(*e*) an annuity contract

(i) the payment for which was deductible in computing the policyholder's income by virtue of paragraph 60(*l*), or

(ii) that is a qualifying trust annuity with respect to a taxpayer, the payment for which was deductible under paragraph 60(*l*) in computing the taxpayer's income,

S. 148(1)(*e*) was replaced by S.C. 2013, c. 34, s. 305(1), deemed to have come into force on January 1, 1989, and formerly read:

(*e*) an annuity contract where

(i) the payment for the annuity contract was deductible under paragraph 60(*l*) in computing the policyholder's income, or

(ii) the policyholder acquired the annuity contract in circumstances to which subsection 146(21) applied,

S. 148(1)(*b.3*) was added by S.C. 2012, c. 31, s. 37(1), in force December 14, 2012.

Related Regulations: 217; 301; 307.

Related Sections: S. 56(1)(*j*) Life insurance policy proceeds; s. 60(*s*) Repayment of policy loan; s. 115(1) Non-resident's taxable income in Canada; s. 138(3) Deductions allowed in computing income; s. 148(2) Deemed proceeds of disposition; s. 148(9), "adjusted cost basis", "policy loan".

Canadian Tax Foundation: Wark, *Review of Proposed Changes to the Exempt Test Legislation*, 2013 Ontario Tax Conference 13A:1–16.

Tax Topics: No. 1682, Life Insurance: Exploring the Corporate Edge — Part II.

Interpretation Bulletins: *Secondary* — IT-87R2 Policyholders' income from life insurance policies; IT-244R3 Gifts by individuals of life insurance policies as charitable donations; IT-379R Employees profit sharing plans — Allocations to beneficiaries; IT-430R3 (Consolid.) — Life insurance proceeds received by a private corporation or a partnership as a consequence of death.

Cases: The lump sum received by a taxpayer was not proceeds from the disposition of an interest in his insurance policies but proceeds from the disposition of his proprietary interest since, as a policyholder, he had become entitled to a proprietary interest in the company's surplus, which he elected to take in the form of cash as opposed to shares of a new holding company. *Sirois v. M.N.R.*, 90 DTC 1840 (T.C.C.)

► 148(1.1) ◄

(1.1) Amount included in computing taxpayer's income. There shall be included in computing the income for a taxation year of a taxpayer in respect of a disposition of an interest in a life insurance policy described in paragraph (*e*) of the definition "disposition" in subsection (9) the amount, if any, by which the amount of a payment described in paragraph (*e*) of that definition that the taxpayer became entitled to receive in the year exceeds the amount that would be the taxpayer's adjusted cost basis of the taxpayer's interest in the policy immediately before the disposition if, for the purposes of the definition "adjusted cost basis" in subsection (9), the taxpayer were, in respect of that interest in the policy, the policyholder.

Related Regulations: 217(2).

Related Sections: S. 56(1)(*j*) Life insurance policy proceeds.

► 148(2) ◄

(2) Deemed proceeds of disposition. For the purposes of subsections (1) and 20(20) and the definition "adjusted cost basis" in subsection (9)

(*a*) where at any time a policyholder becomes entitled to receive under a life insurance policy a particular amount as, on account of, in lieu of payment of or in satisfaction of, a policy dividend, the policyholder shall be deemed

(i) to have disposed of an interest in the policy at that time, and

(ii) to have become entitled to receive proceeds of the disposition equal to the amount, if any, by which

(A) the particular amount

exceeds

(B) the part of the particular amount applied immediately after that time to pay a premium under the policy or to repay a policy loan under the policy, as provided for under the terms and conditions of the policy;

(*b*) where in a taxation year a holder of an interest in, or a person whose life is insured or who is the annuitant under, a life insurance policy (other than an annuity contract or an exempt policy) last acquired after December 1, 1982 or an annuity contract (other than a life annuity contract, as defined by regulation, entered into before November 13, 1981 or a prescribed annuity contract) dies, the policyholder shall be deemed to have disposed of the policyholder's interest in the policy or the contract, as the case may be, immediately before the death;

(*c*) where, as a consequence of a death, a disposition of an interest in a life insurance policy is deemed to have occurred under paragraph (*b*), the policyholder immediately after the death shall be deemed to have acquired the interest at a cost equal to the accumulating fund in respect thereof, as determined in prescribed manner, immediately after the death;

(*d*) where at any time a life insurance policy last acquired after December 1, 1982, or a life insurance policy to which subsection 12.2(9) of the *Income Tax Act*, chapter 148 of the Revised Statutes of Canada, 1952, applies by virtue of paragraph 12.2(9)(*b*) of that Act, ceases to be an exempt policy (otherwise than as a consequence of the death of an individual whose life is insured under the policy or at a time when that individual is totally and permanently disabled), the policyholder shall be deemed to have disposed of the policyholder's interest in the policy at that time for proceeds of disposition equal to the accumulating fund with respect to the interest, as determined in prescribed manner, at that time and to have reacquired the interest immediately after that time at a cost equal to those proceeds; and

(*e*) a policyholder with an interest in a life insurance policy, issued after 2016, that gives rise to an entitlement (of the policyholder, beneficiary or assignee, as the case may be) to receive all or a portion of an excess described in subparagraph (iv) is deemed, at a particular time, to dispose of a part of the interest and to be entitled to receive proceeds of the disposition equal to that excess or portion, as the case may be, if

(i) the policy is an exempt policy,

(ii) a *benefit on death* (as defined in subsection 1401(3) of the *Income Tax Regulations)* under a *coverage* (as defined in section 310 of the *Income Tax Regulations* for the purposes of section 306 of the *Income Tax Regulations)* under the policy is paid at the particular time,

(iii) the payment results in the termination of the coverage but not the policy, and

(iv) the amount of the *fund value benefit* (as defined in subsection 1401(3) of the *Income Tax Regulations)* paid at the particular time in respect of the coverage exceeds the amount

(A) in the case where there is no *policy anniversary* (as defined in section 310 of the *Income Tax Regulations)* before the date of death of the individual whose life is insured under the coverage, that would be determined — on the policy anniversary that is on or that first follows that date of death and as though the coverage were not terminated — in respect of the coverage under subclause (A)(I) of the description of B in subparagraph 306(4)(*a*)(iii) of the *Income Tax Regulations*, and

(B) in any other case, that is determined — on the last policy anniversary before the date of the death of the individual whose life is insured under the coverage — in respect of the coverage under subclause (A)(I) of the description of B in subparagraph 306(4)(*a*)(iii) of the *Income Tax Regulations* as it applies for the purpose of subparagraph 306(1)(*b*)(ii) of the *Income Tax Regulations*.

History: S. 148(2)(*e*) was replaced by S.C. 2017, c. 33, s. 61(1), in force December 14, 2017, and formerly read:

(*e*) if, in respect of a life insurance policy issued after 2016 that is an exempt policy, a benefit on death (as defined in subsection 1401(3) of the *Income Tax Regulations*) under a coverage (as defined in subsection 1401(3) of the *Income Tax Regulations*) under the policy is paid at any time, the payment results in the termination of the coverage but not the policy and the amount of the fund value benefit (as defined in subsection 1401(3) of the *Income Tax Regulations*) paid in respect of the coverage at that time exceeds the amount determined in respect of the coverage under subclause (A)(I) of the description of B in subparagraph 306(4)(*a*)(iii) of the *Income Tax Regulations* on the policy anniversary (as defined in section 310 of the *Income Tax Regulations*) that is on, or that first follows, the date of the death of an individual whose life is insured under the coverage, then a policyholder with an interest in the policy that gives rise to an entitlement (of the policyholder, beneficiary or assignee, as the case may be) to receive all or a portion of that excess, is deemed, at that time, to dispose of a part of the interest and to be entitled to receive proceeds of the disposition equal to that excess or portion, as the case may be.

S. 148(2)(*e*) was added by S.C. 2014, c. 39, s. 52(1), in force December 16, 2014.

Related Regulations: 301; 304.

Related Sections: S. 70(1) Death of a taxpayer; s. 87(2.2) Amalgamation of insurers; s. 88(1) Winding-up; s. 89(1), "taxable Canadian corporation"; s. 116(5.4) Presumption; s. 121 Deduction for taxable dividends; s. 138(3) Deductions allowed in computing income; s. 138(11.5) Transfer of insurance business by non-resident insurer.

Interpretation Bulletins: *Secondary* — IT-87R2 Policyholders' income from life insurance policies; IT-430R3 (Consolid.) — Life insurance proceeds received by a private corporation or a partnership as a consequence of death.

► 148(3) ◄

(3) Special rules for certain policies. For the purposes of this section, where all or any part of an insurer's reserves for a life insurance policy vary in amount depending on the fair market value of a specified group of properties (in this subsection referred to as a "segregated fund"),

(*a*) in computing the adjusted cost basis of the policy,

(i) an amount paid by the policyholder or on the policyholder's behalf as or on account of premiums under the policy or to acquire an interest in the policy shall, to the extent that the amount was used by the insurer to acquire property for the purposes of the segregated fund, be deemed not to have been so paid, and

(ii) any transfer of property by the insurer from the segregated fund that resulted in an increase in the portion of its reserves for the policy that do not vary with the fair market value of the segregated fund shall be deemed to have been a premium paid under the policy by the policyholder; and

(*b*) the proceeds of the disposition of an interest in the policy shall be deemed not to include the portion thereof, if any, payable out of the segregated fund.

(*c*) (Repealed by 1977-78, c. 1, s. 74(2).)

Editorial Note: Income from and gains and/or losses from the disposition of a segregated fund are allocated in accordance with the provisions of s. 138.1 and the trust rules in s. 104.

► 148(4) ◄

(4) Partial surrender — ACB prorated. If a taxpayer disposes (other than because of paragraph (2)(*a*) or as described in paragraph (*b*) of the definition "disposition" in subsection (9)) of a part of the taxpayer's interest in a life insurance policy (other than an annuity contract) last acquired after December 1, 1982 or an annuity contract, the adjusted cost basis to the taxpayer, immediately before the disposition, of the part is the amount determined by the formula

$$A \times B/C$$

where

A is the adjusted cost basis to the taxpayer of the taxpayer's interest immediately before the disposition,

B is the proceeds of the disposition, and

C is

(*a*) if the policy is a policy (other than an annuity contract) issued after 2016, the amount determined by the formula

$$D - E$$

where

D is the interest's cash surrender value immediately before the disposition, and

E is the total of all amounts each of which is an amount payable, immediately before the disposition, by the taxpayer in respect of a policy loan in respect of the policy, and

(*b*) in any other case, the accumulating fund with respect to the taxpayer's interest, as determined in prescribed manner, immediately before the disposition.

History: S. 148(4) was replaced by S.C. 2014, c. 39, s. 52(2), in force December 16, 2014, and formerly read:

(4) *Income from disposition.* For the purpose of computing a taxpayer's income from the disposition (other than a disposition deemed to have occurred under paragraph (2)(*a*) or a disposition described in paragraph (*b*) of the definition "disposition" in subsection (9)) of a part of the taxpayer's interest in a life insurance policy (other than an annuity contract) last acquired after December 1, 1982 or an annuity contract, the adjusted cost basis to the taxpayer, immediately before the disposition, of the part is the proportion of the adjusted cost basis to the taxpayer of the taxpayer's interest immediately before the disposition that

(*a*) the proceeds of the disposition

are of

(*b*) the accumulating fund with respect to the taxpayer's interest, as determined in prescribed manner, immediately before the disposition.

Related Regulations: 307.

► 148(4.01) ◄

(4.01) Repayment of policy loan on partial surrender. For the purposes of the definition "adjusted cost basis" in subsection (9) and paragraph 60(*s*), a particular amount is deemed to be a repayment made immediately before a particular time by a taxpayer in respect of a policy loan in respect of a life insurance policy if

(*a*) the policy is issued after 2016;

(*b*) the taxpayer disposes of a part of the taxpayer's interest in the policy at the particular time;

(*c*) paragraph (*a*) of the definition "proceeds of the disposition" in subsection (9) applies to determine the proceeds of the disposition of the interest;

(*d*) the particular amount is not

(i) otherwise a repayment by the taxpayer in respect of the policy loan, and

(ii) described in subparagraph (i) of the description of C in paragraph (*a*) of the definition *proceeds of the disposition* in subsection (9); and

(*e*) the amount payable by the taxpayer in respect of the policy loan is reduced by the particular amount as a consequence of the disposition.

History: S. 148(4.01)(*d*)(ii) was replaced by S.C. 2017, c. 33, s. 61(4), in force December 14, 2017, and formerly read:

(ii) described in subparagraph (i) of the description of C in the definition "adjusted cost basis" in subsection (9); and

S. 148(4.01)(*b*) was replaced by S.C. 2017, c. 33, s. 61(3), in force December 14, 2017, and formerly read:

(*b*) the taxpayer disposes of a part of the taxpayer's interest in the policy immediately after the particular time;

S. 148(4.01), the portion before paragraph (*a*) was replaced by S.C. 2017, c. 33, s. 61(2), in force December 14, 2017, and formerly read:

(4.01) *Repayment of policy loan on partial surrender.* For the purposes of the definition "adjusted cost basis" in subsection (9) and paragraph 60(*s*), a particular amount is deemed to be a repayment made at a particular time by a taxpayer in respect of a policy loan in respect of a life insurance policy if

S. 148(4.01) was added by S.C. 2014, c. 39, s. 52(2), in force December 16, 2014.

► 148(4.1) ◄

(4.1) Interest deduction from tax — (Repealed by 1977-78, c. 1, s. 74(2).)

► 148(5) ◄

(5) 10/8 policy surrender. If a policyholder has after March 20, 2013 and before April 2014 disposed of an interest in a 10/8 policy because of a partial or complete surrender of the policy, the policyholder may deduct in computing their income for the taxation year in which the disposition occurs an amount that does not exceed the least of

(*a*) the portion of an amount, included under subsection (1) in computing their income for the year in respect of the disposition, that is attributable to an investment account described in paragraph (*b*) of the definition "10/8 policy" in subsection 248(1) in respect of the policy,

(*b*) the total of all amounts each of which is an amount, to the extent that the amount has not otherwise been included in determining an amount under this paragraph, of a payment made after March 20, 2013 and before April 2014 that reduces the amount outstanding of a borrowing or policy loan, as the case may be, described in paragraph (*a*) of the definition "10/8 policy" in subsection 248(1) in respect of the policy, and

(*c*) the total of all amounts each of which is an amount, to the extent that the amount has not otherwise been included in determining an amount under this paragraph, that the policyholder is entitled to receive as a result of the disposition and that is paid after March 20, 2013 and before April 2014 out of an investment account described in paragraph (*b*) of the definition "10/8 policy" in subsection 248(1) in respect of the policy.

History: S. 148(5) was added by S.C. 2013, c. 40, s. 65(1), applicable to taxation years that end after March 20, 2013.

Canadian Tax Foundation: Everett, *Life Insurance Planning After the 2013 Budget*, 2013 Conference Report 32:1–23.

► 148(6) ◄

(6) Proceeds receivable as annuity. Where, under the terms of a life insurance policy (other than an annuity contract) last acquired before December 2, 1982, a policyholder became entitled to receive from the insurer at any time before the death of the person whose life was insured thereunder, all the proceeds (other than policy dividends) payable at that time under the policy in the form of an annuity contract or annuity payments,

(*a*) the payments shall be regarded as annuity payments made under an annuity contract;

(*b*) the purchase price of the annuity contract shall be deemed to be the adjusted cost basis of the policy to the policyholder immediately before the first payment under that contract became payable; and

(*c*) the annuity contract or annuity payments shall be deemed not to be proceeds of the disposition of an interest in the policy.

► 148(7) ◄

(7) Disposition at non-arm's length and similar cases. If an interest of a policyholder in a life insurance policy is, at any time (referred to in this subsection as the "disposition time"), disposed of (other than a disposition under paragraph (2)(*b*)) by way of a gift, by distribution from a corporation or by operation of law only to any person, or in any manner whatever to any person with whom the policyholder was not dealing at arm's length,

(*a*) the policyholder is deemed to become entitled to receive, at the disposition time, proceeds of the disposition equal to the greatest of

(i) the value of the interest at the disposition time,

(ii) an amount equal to

(A) if the disposition time is before March 22, 2016, nil, and

(B) if the disposition time is after March 21, 2016, the fair market value at the disposition time of the consideration, if any, given for the interest, and

(iii) an amount equal to

(A) if the disposition time is before March 22, 2016, nil, and

(B) if the disposition time is after March 21, 2016, the adjusted cost basis to the policyholder of the interest immediately before the disposition time;

(*b*) the person that acquires the interest because of the disposition is deemed to acquire it, at the disposition time, at a cost equal to the amount determined under paragraph (*a*) in respect of the disposition;

(*c*) in computing the paid-up capital in respect of each class of shares of the capital stock of a corporation at any time at or after the disposition time there shall be deducted the amount determined by the formula

$$(A - B \times C/D) \times E/A$$

where

A is the increase, if any, as a result of the disposition, in the paid-up capital in respect of all the shares of the capital stock of the corporation,

B is the amount determined under paragraph (*a*) in respect of the disposition,

C is

(i) if consideration is given for the interest, the fair market value at the disposition time of consideration that is shares of the capital stock of the corporation given for the interest, and

(ii) if no consideration is given for the interest, 1,

D is

(i) if consideration is given for the interest, the fair market value at the disposition time of the consideration given for the interest, and

(ii) if no consideration is given for the interest, 1, and

E is the increase, if any, as a result of the disposition, in the paid-up capital in respect of the class of shares, computed without reference to this paragraph as it applies to the disposition;

(*d*) any contribution of capital to a corporation or partnership in connection with the disposition is deemed, to the extent that it exceeds the amount determined under subparagraph (*a*)(i) in respect of the disposition, not to result in a contribution of capital for the purpose of applying paragraphs 53(1)(*c*) and (*e*) at or after the disposition time;

(*e*) any contributed surplus of a corporation that arose in connection with the disposition is deemed, to the extent that it exceeds the amount determined under subparagraph (*a*)(i) in respect of the disposition, not to be contributed surplus for the purpose of applying subsection 84(1) at or after the disposition time; and

(*f*) if the disposition time is before March 22, 2016,

(i) subparagraphs (ii) and (iii) and paragraphs (*c*) to (*e*) apply in respect of the disposition only if the disposition is after 1999 and at least one person whose life was insured under the policy before March 22, 2016 is alive on March 22, 2016,

(ii) in applying paragraphs (*c*) to (*e*) in respect of the disposition, a reference in those paragraphs to "the disposition time" is to be read as "the beginning of March 22, 2016",

(iii) if at any time (referred to in this subparagraph as the "conversion time") before March 22, 2016 the paid-up capital of a class of shares of the capital stock of a corporation was increased, the increase occurred as a result of any action by which the corporation converted any of its contributed surplus into paid-up capital in respect of the class of shares, the contributed surplus arose in connection with the disposition, and subsection 84(1) did not apply to deem the corporation to pay a dividend at the conversion time in respect of the increase, in computing the paid-up capital in respect of that class of shares after March 21, 2016, there shall be deducted the amount determined by the formula

$$(A - B \times A/D) \times C/A$$

where

A is the increase, if any, as a result of the conversion, in the paid-up capital in respect of all the shares of the capital stock of the corporation, computed without reference to this paragraph as it applies to the disposition,

B is the amount determined under subparagraph (*a*)(i) in respect of the disposition,

C is the increase, if any, as a result of the conversion, in the paid-up capital in respect of the class of shares, computed without reference to this paragraph as it applies to the disposition, and

D is the total amount of the corporation's contributed surplus that arose in connection with the disposition, and

(iv) if any consideration given for the interest includes a share of the capital stock of a corporation, the share (or a share substituted for the share) is disposed of (referred to in this subparagraph as the "share disposition") after March 21, 2016 by a taxpayer and subsection 84.1(1) applies in respect of the share disposition, then for the purposes of applying section 84.1, the adjusted cost base to the taxpayer of the share immediately before the share disposition is to be reduced by the amount determined by the formula

$$(A - B \times A/C)/D$$

where

A is the total of all amounts each of which is the fair market value at the disposition time of a share of that capital stock given as consideration for the interest,

B is the greater of the amount determined under subparagraph 148(7)(*a*)(i) in respect of the disposition and the adjusted cost basis to the policyholder of the interest immediately before the disposition,

C is the fair market value at the disposition time of the consideration, if any, given for the interest, and

D is the total number of shares of that capital stock given as consideration for the interest.

Editorial Note: Where a policyholder disposes of a life insurance policy by way of gift, whether *inter vivos*, testamentary, or in any other manner whatsoever in a non-arm's length transaction, for dispositions after March 21, 2016, the policyholder's deemed proceeds of disposition are the amount that is the greatest of (i) the fair market value of any consideration given for the interest, (ii) the interest's value, and (iii) the adjusted cost base of the interest to the disposing shareholder. For dispositions before March 22, 2016, the proceeds of disposition are the amount that is the value of the interest. The cost of the interest to the acquiring policyholder is an amount equal to the proceeds of the interest determined for the disposing policyholder in respect of the disposition.

Arm's length: The term "arm's length" is defined in section 251.

History: S. 148(7) was replaced by S.C. 2016, c. 12, s. 53, in force December 15, 2016, and formerly read:

(7) *Disposition at non-arm's length and similar cases.* Where, otherwise than by virtue of a deemed disposition under paragraph (2)(*b*), an interest of a policyholder in a life insurance policy is disposed of by way of a gift (whether during the policyholder's lifetime or by the policyholder's will), by distribution from a corporation or by operation of law only to any person, or in any manner whatever to any person with whom the policyholder was not dealing at arm's length, the policyholder shall be deemed thereupon to become entitled to receive proceeds of the disposition equal to the value of the interest at the time of the disposition, and the person who acquires the interest by virtue of the disposition shall be deemed to acquire it at a cost equal to that value.

Related Sections: S. 251 Arm's length.

Tax Topics: No. 1682, Life Insurance: Exploring the Corporate Edge — Part II.

► 148(8) ◄

(8) Idem. Notwithstanding any other provision in this section, where

(*a*) an interest of a policyholder in a life insurance policy (other than an annuity contract) has been transferred to the policyholder's child for no consideration, and

(*b*) a child of the policyholder or a child of the transferee is the person whose life is insured under the policy,

the interest shall be deemed to have been disposed of by the policyholder for proceeds of the disposition equal to the adjusted cost basis to the policyholder of the interest immediately before the transfer, and to have been acquired by the person who acquired the interest at a cost equal to those proceeds.

Related Regulations: 6500(1).

Interpretation Bulletins: *Secondary* — IT-87R2 Policyholders' income from life insurance policies.

Tax Window Files: CALU 2018 Q3 - Subsection 148(8) transfer, *May 8, 2018*, CRA Document No. 2018-0745831C6.

► 148(8.1) ◄

(8.1) Inter vivos transfer to spouse. Notwithstanding any other provision of this section, where

(*a*) an interest of a policyholder in a life insurance policy (other than a policy that is, or is issued under, a plan or contract referred to in any of paragraphs (1)(*a*) to (*e*)) is transferred to

(i) the policyholder's spouse or common-law partner, or

(ii) a former spouse or common-law partner of the policyholder in settlement of rights arising out of their marriage or common-law partnership, and

(iii) (Repealed.)

(*b*) both the policyholder and the transferee are resident in Canada at the time of the transfer,

unless an election is made in the policyholder's return of income under this Part for the taxation year in which the interest was transferred to have this subsection not apply, the interest shall be deemed to have been disposed of by the policyholder for proceeds of the disposition equal to the adjusted cost basis to the policyholder of the interest immediately before the transfer and to have been acquired by the transferee at a cost equal to those proceeds.

Related Sections: S. 252(3) Extended meaning of "spouse" and "former spouse".

► 148(8.2) ◄

(8.2) Transfer to spouse at death. Notwithstanding any other provision of this section, where, as a consequence of the death of a policyholder who was resident in Canada immediately before the policyholder's death, an interest of the policyholder in a life insurance policy (other than a policy that is or is issued under a plan or contract referred to in any of paragraphs (1)(*a*) to (*e*)) is transferred or distributed to the policyholder's spouse or common-law partner who was resident in Canada immediately before the death, unless an election is made in the policyholder's return of income under this Part for the taxation year in which the policyholder died to have this subsection not apply, the interest shall be deemed to have been disposed of by the policyholder immediately before the death for proceeds of the disposition equal to the adjusted cost basis to the policyholder of the interest immediately before the transfer and to have been acquired by the spouse or common-law partner at a cost equal to those proceeds.

Related Sections: S. 252(3) Extended meaning of "spouse" and "former spouse".

► 148(9) ◄

(9) Definitions. In this section and paragraph 56(1)(*d*.1) of the *Income Tax Act*, chapter 148 of the Revised Statutes of Canada, 1952,

Tax Window Files: *US Annuities, August 18, 2010,* CRA Document No. 2010-0371161E5; *Gift of an interest in a life insurance policy, June 8, 2010,* CRA Document No. 2010-0363091C6; *Cost of interest life insurance policy 248(35), May 4, 2010,* CRA Document No. 2010-0359391C6; *Police d'assurance-vie, July 9, 2012,* CRA Document No. 2012-0438751E5.

"adjusted cost basis" —"adjusted cost basis", at any time to a policyholder of the policyholder's interest in a life insurance policy, means the amount determined by the formula

$$(A + B + C + D + E + F + G + G.1) - (H + I + J + K + L + M + N + O)$$

where

A is the total of all amounts each of which is the cost of an interest in the policy acquired by the policyholder before that time but not including an amount referred to in the description of B or E,

B is the total of all amounts each of which is an amount paid before that time by or on behalf of the policyholder in respect of a premium under the policy, other than amounts referred to in clause (2)(*a*)(ii)(B), in subparagraph (iii) of the description of C in paragraph (*a*) of the definition "proceeds of the disposition" or in subparagraph (*b*)(i) of that definition,

C is the total of all amounts each of which is an amount in respect of the disposition of an interest in the policy before that time that was required to be included in computing the policyholder's income or taxable income earned in Canada for a taxation year,

D is the total of all amounts each of which is an amount in respect of the policyholder's interest in the policy that was included by virtue of subsection 12(3) or section 12.2 or of paragraph 56(1)(*d*.1) of the *Income Tax Act*, chapter 148 of the Revised Statutes of Canada, 1952, in computing the policyholder's income for any taxation year ending before that time or the portion of an amount paid to the policyholder in respect of the policyholder's interest in the policy on which tax was imposed by virtue of paragraph 212(1)(*o*) before that time,

E is the total of all amounts each of which is an amount that is in respect of the repayment, before that time and after March 31, 1978, of a policy loan and that does not exceed the amount determined by the formula,

$$E.1 - E.2$$

where

E.1 is the total of

(*a*) the proceeds of the disposition, if any, in respect of the loan,

(*b*) if the policy is issued after 2016 (and, in the case where the particular time at which the policy is issued is determined under subsection (11), the repayment is at or after the particular time), the portion of the loan applied, immediately after the loan, to pay a premium under the policy as provided for under the terms and conditions of the policy (except to the extent that the portion is described in subparagraph (i) of the description of C in paragraph (*a*) of the definition "proceeds of the disposition" in this subsection), and

(*c*) the amount, if any, described in the description of J in this definition (but not including any payment of interest) in respect of the loan, and

E.2 is the total all amounts each of which is an amount in respect of a repayment, of the loan, referred to in clause (2)(*a*)(ii)(B) or deductible under paragraph 60(*s*) of this Act or paragraph 20(1)(*hh*) of the *Income Tax Act*, chapter 148 of the *Revised Statutes of Canada*, 1952 (as it applied in taxation years before 1985),

F is the amount, if any, by which the cash surrender value of the policy as at its first anniversary date after March 31, 1977 exceeds the adjusted cost basis (determined under the *Income Tax Act*, chapter 148 of the Revised Statutes of Canada, 1952, as it would have read on that date if subsection 148(8) of that Act, as it read in its application to the period ending immediately before April 1, 1978, had not been applicable) of the policyholder's interest in the policy on that date,

G is, in the case of an interest in a life annuity contract, as defined by regulation, to which subsection 12.2(1) applies for the taxation year that includes that time (or would apply if the contract had an anniversary day in the year at a time when the taxpayer held the interest), the total of all amounts each of which is a mortality gain, as defined by regulation and determined by the issuer of the contract in accordance with the regulations, in respect of the interest immediately before the end of the calendar year ending in a taxation year commencing before that time,

G.1 is, in the case of an interest in a life insurance policy (other than an annuity contract) to which subsection (8.2) applied before that time, the total of all amounts each of which is a mortality gain, as defined by regulation and determined by the issuer of the policy in accordance with the regulations, in respect of the interest immediately before the end of the calendar year that ended in a taxation year that began before that time,

H is the total of all amounts each of which is the proceeds of the disposition of the policyholder's interest in the policy that the policyholder became entitled to receive before that time,

I is the total of all amounts each of which is an amount in respect of the policyholder's interest in the policy that was deducted by virtue of subsection 20(19) in computing the policyholder's income for any taxation year commencing before that time,

J is the amount payable on March 31, 1978 in respect of a policy loan in respect of the policy,

K is the total of all amounts each of which is an amount received before that time in respect of the policy that the policyholder was entitled to deduct under paragraph 60(*a*) in computing the policyholder's income for a taxation year,

L is

(*a*) in the case of an interest in a life insurance policy (other than an annuity contract) that was last acquired after December 1, 1982 by the policyholder, the total of all amounts each of which is the net cost of pure insurance, as defined by regulation and determined by the issuer of the policy in accordance with the regulations, in respect of the interest immediately before the end of the calendar year ending in a taxation year commencing after May 31, 1985 and before that time,

(*b*) in the case of an interest in an annuity contract to which subsection 12.2(1) applies for the taxation year that includes that time (or would apply if the contract had an anniversary day in the year and while the taxpayer held the interest), the total of all annuity payments paid in respect of the interest before that time and while the policyholder held the interest, or

(*c*) in the case of an interest in a contract referred to in the description of G, the total of all amounts each of which is a mortality loss, as defined by regulation and determined by the issuer of the contract in accordance with the regulations, in respect of the interest before that time,

M is, in the case of a policy that is issued after 2016 and is not an annuity contract, the total of all amounts each of which is a premium paid by or on behalf of the policyholder, or a cost of insurance charge incurred by the policyholder, before that time (and, in the case where the particular time at which the policy is issued is determined under subsection (11), at or after the particular time), to the extent that the premium or charge is in respect of a benefit under the policy other than a benefit on death (as defined in subsection 1401(3) of the *Income Tax Regulations*),

N is, in the case of a policy that is issued after 2016 and is not an annuity contract, the total of all amounts each of which is the policyholder's interest in an amount paid — to the extent that the cash surrender value of the policy, if any, or the fund value of the policy (as defined in subsection 1401(3) of the *Income Tax Regulations*), if any, is reduced by the amount paid — before that time (and, in the case where the particular time at which the policy is issued is determined under subsection (11), at or after the particular time) that

(*a*) is a benefit on death (as defined in subsection 1401(3) of the *Income Tax Regulations*), or a disability benefit, under the policy, and

(*b*) does not result in the termination of a coverage (as defined in subsection 1401(3) of the *Income Tax Regulations*) under the policy,

O is, in the case of a policy that is issued after 2016 and is not an annuity contract, the total of all amounts each of which is — if a *benefit on death* (as defined in subsection 1401(3) of the *Income Tax Regulations*) under a "coverage" (as defined in section 310 of the *Income Tax Regulations* for the purposes of section 306 of the *Income Tax Regulations*) under the policy is paid before that time as a consequence of the death of an individual whose life is insured under the coverage (and, in the case where the particular time at which the policy is issued is determined under subsection (11), at or after the particular time) and the payment results in the termination of the coverage — the amount, if any, determined with respect to the coverage by the formula

$$[P \times (Q + R + S)/T] - U$$

where

P is the adjusted cost basis of the policyholder's interest immediately before the termination,

Q is the amount of the "fund value benefit" (as defined in subsection 1401(3) of the *Income Tax Regulations)* under the policy paid in respect of the "coverage" (as defined in section 310 of the *Income Tax Regulations* for the purposes of section 306 of the *Income Tax Regulations)* on the termination,

R is the total of all amounts — each of which is in respect of a "coverage" (as defined in subsection 1401(3) of the *Income Tax Regulations)* in respect of a specific life or two or more specific lives jointly insured under the coverage referred to in the description of O — that would be the present value, determined for the purposes of section 307 of the *Income Tax Regulations*, on the last "policy anniversary" (as defined in section 310 of the *Income Tax Regulations)* on or before the termination, of the "fund value of the coverage" (as defined in subsection 1401(3) of the *Income Tax Regulations)* if the fund value of the coverage on that policy anniversary were equal to the fund value of the coverage on the termination,

S is the total of all amounts — each of which is in respect of a "coverage" (as defined in subsection 1401(3) of the *Income Tax Regulations* and referred to in this description as a "particular coverage") in respect of a specific life or two or more specific lives jointly insured under the coverage referred to in the description of O — that would be determined, on that policy anniversary, for paragraph (*a*) of the description of C in the definition "net premium reserve" in subsection 1401(3) of the *Income Tax Regula-*

tions in respect of the particular coverage, if the benefit on death under the particular coverage, and the "fund value of the coverage" (as defined in subsection 1401(3) of the *Income Tax Regulations*), on that policy anniversary were equal to the benefit on death under the particular coverage and the fund value of the coverage, as the case may be, on the termination,

T is the amount that would be, on that policy anniversary, the "net premium reserve" (as defined in subsection 1401(3) of the *Income Tax Regulations*) in respect of the policy for the purposes of section 307 of the *Income Tax Regulations*, if the "fund value benefit" (as defined in subsection 1401(3) of the *Income Tax Regulations*) under the policy, the benefit on death under each "coverage" (as defined in subsection 1401(3) of the *Income Tax Regulations*) and the fund value of each coverage (as defined in subsection 1401(3) of the *Income Tax Regulations*) on that policy anniversary were equal to the fund value benefit, the benefit on death under each coverage and the fund value of each coverage, as the case may be, under the policy on the termination, and

U is the amount, if any, determined under subsection (4) in respect of a disposition before that time of the interest because of paragraph (2)(*e*) in respect of the payment in respect of the fund value benefit under the policy paid in respect of the "coverage" (as defined in section 310 of the *Income Tax Regulations* for the purposes of section 306 of the *Income Tax Regulations*) on the termination;

History: S. 148(9), the portion of the definition "adjusted cost basis" after the description of P was replaced by S.C. 2017, c. 33, s. 61(7), in force December 14, 2017, and formerly read:

Q is the amount of the fund value benefit (as defined in subsection 1401(3) of the *Income Tax Regulations*) under the policy paid in respect of the coverage on the termination,

R is the amount that would be the present value, determined for the purposes of section 307 of the *Income Tax Regulations*, on the last policy anniversary (as defined in section 310 of the *Income Tax Regulations*) on or before the termination, of the fund value of the coverage (as defined in subsection 1401(3) of the *Income Tax Regulations*) if the fund value of the coverage on that policy anniversary were equal to the fund value of the coverage on the termination,

S is the amount that would be determined, on that policy anniversary, for paragraph (*a*) of the description of C in the definition "net premium reserve" in subsection 1401(3) of the *Income Tax Regulations* in respect of the coverage, if the benefit on death under the coverage, and the fund value of the coverage, on that policy anniversary were equal to the benefit on death under the coverage and the fund value of the coverage, as the case may be, on the termination,

T is the amount that would be, on that policy anniversary, the net premium reserve (as defined in subsection 1401(3) of the *Income Tax Regulations*) in respect of the policy for the purposes of section 307 of the *Income Tax Regulations*, if the fund value benefit under the policy, the benefit on death under each coverage and the fund value of each coverage on that policy anniversary were equal to the fund value benefit, the benefit on death under each coverage and the fund value of each coverage, as the case may be, under the policy on the termination, and

U is the amount, if any, determined under subsection (4) in respect of a disposition before that time of the interest because of paragraph (2)(*e*) in respect of the payment in respect of the fund value benefit under the policy paid in respect of the coverage on the termination;

S. 148(9), the portion of the description of O before the formula in the definition "adjusted cost basis" was replaced by S.C. 2017, c. 33, s. 61(6), in force December 14, 2017, and formerly read:

O is, in the case of a policy that is issued after 2016 and is not an annuity contract, the total of all amounts each of which is — if a benefit on death (as defined in subsection 1401(3) of the *Income Tax Regulations*) under a coverage (as defined in subsection 1401(3) of the *Income Tax Regulations*) under the policy is paid before that time (and, in the case where the particular time at which the policy is issued is determined under subsection (11), at or after the particular time) and the payment results in the termination of the coverage — the amount, if any, determined with respect to the coverage by the formula

S. 148(9), paragraph (*b*) of the description of E.1 in the definition "adjusted cost basis" was replaced by S.C. 2017, c. 33, s. 61(5), in force December 14, 2017, and formerly read:

(*b*) if the policy is issued after 2016 (and, in the case where the particular time at which the policy is issued is determined under subsection (11), the repayment is at or after the particular time), the portion of the loan applied, immediately after the loan, to pay a premium under the policy as provided for under the terms and conditions of the policy (except to the extent that the portion is described in subparagraph (i) of the description of C in the definition "proceeds of the disposition" in this subsection), and

S. 148(9), the portion of the definition "adjusted cost basis" before the description of A was replaced by S.C. 2014, c. 39, s. 52(3), in force December 16, 2014, and formerly read:

"adjusted cost basis" —"adjusted cost basis" to a policyholder as at a particular time of the policyholder's interest in a life insurance policy means the amount determined by the formula

$$(A + B + C + D + E + F + G + G.1) - (H + I + J + K + L)$$

where

S. 148(9), the description of E in the definition "adjusted cost basis" was replaced by S.C. 2014, c. 39, s. 52(4), in force December 16, 2014, and formerly read:

E is the total of all amounts each of which is an amount in respect of the repayment before that time and after March 31, 1978 of a policy loan not exceeding the total of the proceeds of the disposition, if any, in respect of that loan and the amount, if any, described in the description of J but not including any payment of interest thereon, any loan repayment that was deductible under paragraph 60(*s*) of this Act or paragraph 20(1)(*hh*) of the *Income Tax Act*, chapter 148 of the Revised Statutes of Canada, 1952 (as it applied in taxation years before 1985) or any loan repayment referred to in clause (2)(*a*)(ii)(B),

S. 148(9), the description of G.1 in the definition "adjusted cost basis" was replaced by S.C. 2014, c. 39, s. 52(5), in force December 16, 2014, and formerly read:

G.1 in the case of an interest in a life insurance policy (other than an annuity contract) to which subsection (8.2) applied before that time, the total of all amounts each of which is a mortality gain, as defined by regulation and determined by the issuer of the policy in accordance with the regulations, in respect of the interest immediately before the end of the calendar year ending in a taxation year beginning before that time,

S. 148(9), the descriptions of M to U in the definition "adjusted cost basis" were added by S.C. 2014, c. 39, s. 52(6), in force December 16, 2014.

Related Regulations: 301; 308.

Related Sections: S. 12.2(1) Amount to be included; s. 20(2.1) Limitation of expression "interest"; s. 20(20) Life insurance policy; s. 53(1)(*e*) Adjustments to cost base — Interest in a partnership; s. 87(2)(*j*.4) Accrual rules; s. 89(1), "capital dividend account"; s. 138.1(1) Rules relating to segregated funds; s. 148(2) Deemed proceeds of disposition; s. 148(8) Disposition to policyholder's child for no consideration.

Interpretation Bulletins: *Secondary* — IT-379R Employees profit sharing plans — Allocations to beneficiaries.

"amount payable" —"amount payable", in respect of a policy loan, has the meaning assigned by subsection 138(12);

"cash surrender value" —"cash surrender value" at a particular time of a life insurance policy means its cash surrender value at that time computed without regard to any policy loans made under the policy, any policy dividends (other than paid-up additions) payable under the policy or any interest payable on those dividends;

Related Sections: S. 70(5.3) Fair market value; s. 110.6(15) Value of assets of corporations.

"child" —"child" of a policyholder includes a child as defined in subsection 70(10);

"disposition" —"disposition", in relation to an interest in a life insurance policy, includes

(*a*) a surrender thereof,

(*b*) a policy loan made after March 31, 1978,

(*c*) the dissolution of that interest by virtue of the maturity of the policy,

(*d*) a disposition of that interest by operation of law only, and

(*e*) the payment by an insurer of an amount (other than an annuity payment, a policy loan or a policy dividend) in respect of a policy (other than a policy described in paragraph (1)(*a*), (*b*), (*c*), (*d*) or (*e*)) that is a life annuity contract, as defined by regulation, entered into after November 16, 1978, and before November 13, 1981,

but does not include

(*f*) an assignment of all or any part of an interest in the policy for the purpose of securing a debt or a loan other than a policy loan,

(*g*) a lapse of the policy in consequence of the premiums under the policy remaining unpaid, if the policy was reinstated not later than 60 days after the end of the calendar year in which the lapse occurred,

(*h*) a payment under a policy as a disability benefit or as an accidental death benefit,

(*i*) an annuity payment,

(*j*) a payment under a life insurance policy (other than an annuity contract) that

(i) was last acquired before December 2, 1982, or

(ii) is an exempt policy

in consequence of the death of any person whose life was insured under the policy, or

(*k*) any transaction or event by which an individual becomes entitled to receive, under the terms of an exempt policy, all of the proceeds (including or excluding policy dividends) payable under the policy in the form of an annuity contract or annuity payments, if, at the time of the transaction or event, the individual whose life is insured under the policy was totally and permanently disabled;

Related Regulations: 301.

Related Sections: S. 20(20) Life insurance policy; s. 60(*s*) Repayment of policy loan; s. 87(2.2) Amalgamation of insurers; s. 88(1) Winding-up; s. 116(5.4) Presumption; s. 138(11.5) Transfer of insurance business by non-resident insurer; s. 148(1.1) Amount included in computing taxpayer's income; s. 148(2) Deemed proceeds of disposition; s. 211(1), "specified transaction or event".

Tax Topics: No. 1858, Viatical Settlements ... What?.

Interpretation Bulletins: *Primary* — IT-430R3 (Consolid.) — Life insurance proceeds received by a private corporation or a partnership as a consequence of death. *Secondary* — IT-85R2 Health and welfare trusts for employees; IT-87R2 Policyholders' income from life insurance policies.

"interest" —"interest", in relation to a policy loan, has the meaning assigned by subsection 138(12);

"policy loan" —"policy loan" means an amount advanced by an insurer to a policyholder in accordance with the terms and conditions of the life insurance policy;

Related Sections: S. 60(*s*) Repayment of policy loan.

Tax Window Files: Policy loan interest, *May 31, 2017*, CRA Document No. 2016-0658641E5.

"premium" —"premium" under a policy includes

(*a*) interest paid after 1977 to a life insurer in respect of a policy loan, other than interest deductible in the 1978 or any subsequent taxation year pursuant to paragraph 20(1)(*c*) or (*d*), and

(*b*) a prepaid premium under the policy to the extent that it cannot be refunded otherwise than on termination or cancellation of the policy,

but does not include

(*c*) the portion of any amount paid under the policy with respect to an accidental death benefit, a disability benefit, an additional risk as a result of insuring a substandard life, an additional risk in respect of the conversion of a term policy into another policy after the end of the year, an additional risk under a settlement option, or an additional risk under a guaranteed insurability benefit, if

(i) in the case of an annuity contract, a policy issued before 2017 or in respect of which the particular time at which the policy is issued is determined under subsection (11), where the interest in the policy was last acquired after December 1, 1982, the payment is made after May 31, 1985 and, if the particular time at which the policy is issued is determined under subsection (11), before the particular time, or

(ii) in the case where the taxpayer's interest in the policy was last acquired before December 2, 1982,

(A) subsection 12.2(9) of the *Income Tax Act*, chapter 148 of the Revised Statutes of Canada, 1952, applies to the interest,

(B) the particular time at which the policy is issued is determined under subsection (11), and

(C) the payment is made in the period that starts at the later of May 31, 1985 and the first time at which that subsection 12.2(9) applies in respect of the interest and that ends at the particular time;

History: S. 148(9), paragraph (*c*) of the definition "premium" was replaced by S.C. 2014, c. 39, s. 52(7), in force December 16, 2014, and formerly read:

(*c*) where the interest in the policy was last acquired after December 1, 1982, that portion of any amount paid after May 31, 1985 under the policy with respect to

(i) an accidental death benefit,

(ii) a disability benefit,

(iii) an additional risk as a result of insuring a substandard life,

(iv) an additional risk in respect of the conversion of a term policy into another policy after the end of the year,

(v) an additional risk under a settlement option,

(vi) an additional risk under a guaranteed insurability benefit, or

(vii) any other prescribed benefit that is ancillary to the policy;

Related Sections: S. 211(1), "specified transaction or event".

"proceeds of the disposition" —"proceeds of the disposition" of an interest in a life insurance policy means the amount of the proceeds that the policyholder, beneficiary or assignee, as the case may be, is entitled to receive on a disposition of an interest in the policy and for greater certainty,

(*a*) in respect of a surrender or maturity thereof, means the amount determined by the formula

$$(A - B) - C$$

where

A is the cash surrender value of the interest in the policy at the time of surrender or maturity,

B is that portion of the cash surrender value represented by A that is applicable to the policyholder's interest in the related segregated fund trust as referred to in paragraph 138.1(1)(*e*), and

C is the total of amounts each of which is

(i) an amount by which the amount payable in respect of a policy loan in respect of the policy is reduced as a consequence of the disposition, except that if the policy is issued after 2016 and the disposition is of a part of the interest (and, in the case where the particular time at which the policy is issued is determined under subsection (11), the disposition occurs at or after the particular time), only to the extent that the amount represents the portion of the loan applied, immediately after the loan, to pay a premium under the policy, as provided for under the terms and conditions of the policy,

(ii) a premium under the policy that is due but unpaid at that time, or

(iii) an amount applied, immediately after the time of the surrender, to pay a premium under the policy, as provided for under the terms and conditions of the policy,

(*b*) in respect of a policy loan made after March 31, 1978 means the lesser of

(i) the amount of the loan, other than the part thereof applied, immediately after the loan, to pay a premium under the policy, as provided for under the terms and conditions of the policy, and

(ii) the amount, if any, by which the cash surrender value of the policy immediately before the loan was made exceeds the total of the balances outstanding at that time of any policy loans in respect of the policy,

(*c*) in respect of a payment described in paragraph (*e*) of the definition "disposition" in this subsection, means the amount of that payment, and

(*d*) in respect of a disposition deemed to have occurred under paragraph (2)(*b*), means the accumulating fund in respect of the interest, as determined in prescribed manner,

(i) immediately before the time of death in respect of a life insurance policy (other than an annuity contract) last acquired after December 1, 1982, or

(ii) immediately after the time of death in respect of an annuity contract;

History: S. 148(9), subparagraph (i) of the description of C in paragraph (*a*) of the definition "proceeds of the disposition" was replaced by S.C. 2014, c. 39, s. 52(8), in force December 16, 2014, and formerly read:

(i) an amount payable at that time by the policyholder in respect of a policy loan in respect of the policy,

Related Regulations: 307.

"relevant authority" — (Repealed by S.C. 1997, c. 25, s. 46.)

"tax anniversary date" — "tax anniversary date", in relation to a life insurance policy, means the second anniversary date of the policy to occur after October 22, 1968;

"value" — "value" at a particular time of an interest in a life insurance policy means

(*a*) where the interest includes an interest in the cash surrender value of the policy, the amount in respect thereof that the holder of the interest would be entitled to receive if the policy were surrendered at that time, and

(*b*) in any other case, nil.

▶ 148(9.1) ◀

(9.1) Application of s. 12.2(11). The definitions in subsection 12.2(11) apply to this section.

▶ 148(10) ◀

(10) Life annuity contracts. For the purposes of this section,

(*a*) a reference to "insurer" or "life insurer" shall be deemed to include a reference to a person who is licensed or otherwise authorized under a law of Canada or a province to issue contracts that are annuity contracts;

(*b*) a reference to a "person whose life was insured" shall be deemed to include a reference to an annuitant under a life annuity contract, as defined by regulation, entered into before November 17, 1978;

(*c*) where a policyholder is a person who has held an interest in a life insurance policy continuously since its issue date, the interest shall be deemed to have been acquired on the later of the date on which

(i) the policy came into force, and

(ii) the application in respect of the policy signed by the policyholder was filed with the insurer;

(*d*) except as otherwise provided, a policyholder shall be deemed not to have disposed of or acquired an interest in a life insurance policy (other than an annuity contract) as a result only of the exercise of any provision (other than a conversion into an annuity contract) of the policy; and

(*e*) where an interest in a life insurance policy (other than an annuity contract) last acquired before December 2, 1982 to which subsection 12.2(9) of the *Income Tax Act*, chapter 148 of the Revised Statutes of Canada, 1952, does not apply has been acquired by a taxpayer from a person with whom the taxpayer was not dealing at arm's length, the interest shall be deemed to have been last acquired by the taxpayer before December 2, 1982.

Related Regulations: 301.

Related Sections: S. 12.2(13) "Application of s. 148(10)"; s. 56(1)(*j*) Life insurance policy proceeds; s. 89(1), "taxable Canadian corporation", "taxable dividend"; s. 146(1), "registered retirement savings plan"; s. 248(1), "amount", "annuity", "dividend", "gross revenue", "insurance corporation", "insurer", "non-resident", "property", "share".

Tax Window Files: Splitting of a Multiple Life Insurance Policy, *February 17, 2016*, CRA Document No. 2015-0608261E5.

▶ 148(11) ◀

(11) Loss of grandfathering. For the purposes of determining at and after a particular time whether a life insurance policy (other than an annuity contract) issued before 2017 is treated as issued after 2016 under this section (other than this subsection) and sections 306 (other than subsections (9) and (10)), 307, 308, 310, 1401 and 1403 of the *Income Tax Regulations* (except as they apply for the purposes of subsection 211.1(3)), the policy is deemed to be a policy issued at the particular time if the particular time is the first time after 2016 at which life insurance — in respect of a life, or two or more lives jointly insured, and in respect of which a particular schedule of premium or cost of insurance rates applies — is

(*a*) if the insurance is term insurance, converted to permanent life insurance within the policy; or (*b*) if the insurance (other than insurance paid for with policy dividends or that is reinstated) is medically underwritten after 2016 (other than to obtain a reduction in the premium or cost of insurance rates under the policy), added to the policy.

History: S. 148(11), the portion before paragraph (*b*) was replaced by S.C. 2017, c. 33, s. 61(8), in force December 14, 2017, and formerly read:

(11) *Loss of grandfathering.* For the purposes of determining at and after a particular time whether a life insurance policy (other than an annuity contract) issued before 2017 is treated as issued after 2016 under this section (other than this subsection) and sections 306 (other than subsection (9)), 307, 308, 310, 1401 and 1403 of the *Income Tax Regulations* (except as they apply for the purposes of subsection 211.1(3)), the policy is deemed to be a policy issued at the particular time if the particular time is the first time after 2016 at which life insurance — in respect of a life, or two or more lives jointly insured, and in respect of which a particular schedule of premium or cost of insurance rates applies — is

(*a*) converted (other than only because of a change in premium or cost of insurance rates) into another type of life insurance; or

S. 148(11) was added by S.C. 2014, c. 39, s. 52(9), in force December 16, 2014.

Related Regulations: 306(1); 20(1)(xx) Derivative forward agreement.

Eligible Funeral Arrangements

SECTION 148.1: [Eligible funeral arrangements]

► 148.1(1) ◄

(1) Definitions. In this section,

"cemetery care trust" —"cemetery care trust" means a trust established pursuant to an Act of a province for the care and maintenance of a cemetery;

Related Sections: S. 108(1), "trust"; s. 149(1)(s.2) Cemetery care trust.

"cemetery services" —"cemetery services" with respect to an individual means property (including interment vaults, markers, flowers, liners, urns, shrubs and wreaths) and services that relate directly to cemetery arrangements in Canada in consequence of the death of the individual including, for greater certainty, property and services to be funded out of a cemetery care trust;

"custodian" —"custodian" of an arrangement means

(*a*) where a trust is governed by the arrangement, a trustee of the trust, and

(*b*) in any other case, a qualifying person who receives a contribution under the arrangement as a deposit for the provision by the person of funeral or cemetery services;

"eligible funeral arrangement" —"eligible funeral arrangement" at a particular time means an arrangement established and maintained by a qualifying person solely for the purpose of funding funeral or cemetery services with respect to one or more individuals and of which there is one or more custodians each of whom was resident in Canada at the time the arrangement was established, where

(*a*) each contribution made before the particular time under the arrangement was made for the purpose of funding funeral or cemetery services to be provided by the qualifying person with respect to an individual, and

(*b*) for each such individual, the total of all relevant contributions made before the particular time in respect of the individual does not exceed

(i) $15,000, where the arrangement solely covers funeral services with respect to the individual,

(ii) $20,000, where the arrangement solely covers cemetery services with respect to the individual, and

(iii) $35,000, in any other case,

and, for the purpose of this definition, any payment (other than the portion of the payment to be applied as a contribution to a cemetery care trust) that is made in consideration for the immediate acquisition of a right to burial in or on property that is set apart or used as a place for the burial of human remains or of any interest in a building or structure for the permanent placement of human remains, shall be considered to have been made pursuant to a separate arrangement that is not an eligible funeral arrangement;

"funeral or cemetery services" —"funeral or cemetery services" with respect to an individual means funeral services with respect to the individual, cemetery services with respect to the individual or any combination of such services;

"funeral services" —"funeral services" with respect to an individual means property and services (other than cemetery services with respect to the individual) that relate directly to funeral arrangements in Canada in consequence of the death of the individual;

"qualifying person" —"qualifying person" means a person licensed or otherwise authorized under the laws of a province to provide funeral or cemetery services with respect to individuals;

"relevant contribution" —"relevant contribution" in respect of an individual under a particular arrangement means

(*a*) a contribution under the particular arrangement (other than a contribution made by way of a transfer from an eligible funeral arrangement) for the purpose of funding funeral or cemetery services with respect to the individual, or

(*b*) such portion of a contribution to another arrangement that was an eligible funeral arrangement (other than any such contribution made by way of a transfer from any eligible funeral arrangement) as can reasonably be considered to have subsequently been used to make a contribution under the particular arrangement by way of a transfer from an eligible funeral arrangement for the purpose of funding funeral or cemetery services with respect to the individual.

► 148.1(2) ◄

(2) Exemption for eligible funeral arrangements. Notwithstanding any other provision of this Act,

(*a*) no amount that has accrued, is credited or is added to an eligible funeral arrangement shall be included in computing the income of any person solely because of such accrual, crediting or adding;

(*b*) subject to paragraph (*c*) and subsection (3), no amount shall be

(i) included in computing a person's income solely because of the provision by another person of funeral or cemetery services under an eligible funeral arrangement, or

(ii) included in computing a person's income because of the disposition of an interest under an eligible funeral arrangement or an interest in a trust governed by an eligible funeral arrangement; and

(*c*) subparagraph (*b*)(ii) shall not affect the consequences under this Act of the disposition of any right under an eligible funeral arrangement to payment for the provision of funeral or cemetery services.

Editorial Note: The rules for eligible funeral arrangements became effective for 1993 and subsequent taxation years. Contributions under an eligible funeral arrangement cannot exceed $35,000, $15,000 for funeral services and $20,000 for cemetery services (see definition in s. 148.1(1)). Contributions are not deductible; however, income earned under eligible funeral arrangements is accumulated tax free. The accumulated income is taxable to the provider of the funeral and/or cemetery services when received. If a distribution of accumulated income is made to someone other than to provide funeral or cemetery services, the distribution will be included in income under s. 148(3).

► 148.1(3) ◄

(3) Income inclusion on return of funds. Where at any particular time in a taxation year a particular amount is distributed (otherwise than as payment for the provision of funeral or cemetery services with respect to an individual) to a taxpayer from an arrangement that was, at the time it was established, an eligible funeral arrangement and the particular amount is paid from the balance in respect of the individual under the arrangement, there shall be added in computing the taxpayer's income for the year from property the lesser of the particular amount and the amount determined by the formula

$$A + B - C$$

where

A is the balance in respect of the individual under the arrangement immediately before the particular time (determined without regard to the value of property in a cemetery care trust);

B is the total of all payments made from the arrangement before the particular time for the provision of funeral or cemetery services with respect to the individual (other than cemetery services funded by property in a cemetery care trust); and

C is the amount determined by the formula

$$D - E$$

where

D is the total of all relevant contributions made before the particular time in respect of the individual under the arrangement (other than contributions in respect of the individual that were in a cemetery care trust), and

E is the total of all amounts each of which is the amount, if any, by which

(a) an amount relating to the balance in respect of the individual under the arrangement that is deemed by subsection (4) to have been distributed before the particular time from the arrangement

exceeds

(b) the portion of the amount referred to in paragraph (*a*) that is added, because of this subsection, in computing a taxpayer's income.

History: S. 148.1(3), the description of C was replaced by S.C. 2013, c. 34, s. 306(2), applicable to amounts that are transferred, credited or added after December 20, 2002, and formerly read:

C is the total of all relevant contributions made before the particular time in respect of the individual under the particular arrangement (other than contributions in respect of the individual that were in a cemetery care trust).

Related Sections: S. 12(1)(z4) Eligible funeral arrangements; s. 212(1)(v) Payments under an eligible funeral arrangement.

► 148.1(4) ◄

(4) Deemed distribution on transfer. If at a particular time an amount relating to the balance in respect of an individual (referred to in this subsection and in subsection (5) as the "transferor") under an eligible funeral arrangement (referred to in this subsection and in subsection (5) as the "transferor arrangement") is transferred, credited or added to the balance in respect of the same or another individual (referred to in this subsection and in subsection (5) as the "recipient") under the same or another eligible funeral arrangement (referred to in this subsection and in subsection (5) as the "recipient arrangement"),

(*a*) the amount is deemed to be distributed to the transferor (or, if the transferor is deceased at the particular time, to the recipient) at the particular time from the transferor arrangement and to be paid from the balance in respect of the transferor under the transferor arrangement; and

(*b*) the amount is deemed to be a contribution made (other than by way of a transfer from an eligible funeral arrangement) at the particular time under the recipient arrangement for the purpose of funding funeral or cemetery services with respect to the recipient.

History: S. 148.1(4) was added by S.C. 2013, c. 34, s. 306(3), applicable to amounts that are transferred, credited or added after December 20, 2002.

► 148.1(5) ◄

(5) Non-application of subsection (4). Subsection (4) does not apply if

(*a*) the transferor and the recipient are the same individual;

(*b*) the amount that is transferred, credited or added to the balance in respect of the individual under the recipient arrangement is equal to the balance in respect of the individual under the transferor arrangement immediately before the particular time; and

(*c*) the transferor arrangement is terminated immediately after the transfer.

History: S. 148.1(5) was added by S.C. 2013, c. 34, s. 306(3), applicable to amounts that are transferred, credited or added after December 20, 2002.

Division H — Exemptions

Miscellaneous Exemptions

SECTION 149: Miscellaneous exemptions

▶ 149(1) ◀

(1) Miscellaneous exemptions. No tax is payable under this Part on the taxable income of a person for a period when that person was

▶ 149(1)(a) ◀

(a) Employees of a country other than Canada — an officer or servant of the government of a country other than Canada whose duties require that person to reside in Canada

(i) if, immediately before assuming those duties, the person resided outside Canada,

(ii) if that country grants a similar privilege to an officer or servant of Canada of the same class,

(iii) if the person was not, at any time in the period, engaged in a business or performing the duties of an office or employment in Canada other than the person's position with that government, and

(iv) if the person was not during the period a Canadian citizen;

Tax Window Files: Foreign doctors working in Canada, *January 14, 2014*, CRA Document No. 2013-0510061E5.

▶ 149(1)(b) ◀

(b) Members of the family and servants of employees of a country other than Canada — a member of the family of a person described in paragraph (*a*) who resides with that person, or a servant employed by a person described in that paragraph,

(i) if the country of which the person described in paragraph (*a*) is an officer or servant grants a similar privilege to members of the family residing with and servants employed by an officer or servant of Canada of the same class,

(ii) in the case of a member of the family, if that member was not at any time lawfully admitted to Canada for permanent residence, or at any time in the period engaged in a business or performing the duties of an office or employment in Canada,

(iii) in the case of a servant, if, immediately before assuming his or her duties as a servant of a person described in paragraph (*a*), the servant resided outside Canada and, since first assuming those duties in Canada, has not at any time engaged in a business in Canada or been employed in Canada other than by a person described in that paragraph, and

(iv) if the member of the family or servant was not during the period a Canadian citizen;

Related Sections: S. 227(14) Application of other Parts.

▶ 149(1)(c) ◀

(c) Municipal authorities — a municipality in Canada, or a municipal or public body performing a function of government in Canada;

Canadian Petroleum Tax Journal: Understanding and Doing Business with Tax-Exempt Entities, Pashkowich, 2003, Vol. 16, No. 1.

Tax Window Files: School Boards - 149(1)(c), *August 6, 2014*, CRA Document No. 2013-0500321I7; 149(1)(c) — municipal corporation, *March 12, 2014*, CRA Document No. 2014-0518651E5; 149(1)(c) Ruling, *14XXXX*, CRA Document No. 2013-0484541R3; First Nation 149(1)(c) — partnership income, *2013*, CRA Document No. 2012-0447241R3.

▶ 149(1)(d) ◀

(d) Corporations owned by the Crown — a corporation, commission or association all of the shares (except directors' qualifying shares) or of the capital of which was owned by one or more persons each of which is Her Majesty in right of Canada or Her Majesty in right of a province;

Related Sections: S. 27(2) Presumption; s. 227(16) Municipal or provincial corporation excepted.

Canadian Petroleum Tax Journal: Understanding and Doing Business with Tax-Exempt Entities, Pashkowich, 2003, Vol. 16, No. 1.

Tax Topics: No. 1625, Provincial Crown Corporation Not Bound by the *Income Tax Act*.

▶ 149(1)(d.1) ◀

(d.1) Corporations 90% owned by the Crown — a corporation, commission or association not less than 90% of the shares (except directors' qualifying shares) or of the capital of which was owned by one or more persons each of which is Her Majesty in right of Canada or Her Majesty in right of a province;

▶ 149(1)(d.2) ◀

(d.2) Wholly-owned corporations — a corporation all of the shares (except directors' qualifying shares) or of the capital of which was owned by one or more persons each of which is a corporation, commission or association to which this paragraph or paragraph (*d*) applies for the period;

▶ 149(1)(d.3) ◀

(d.3) 90% owned corporations — a corporation, commission or association not less than 90% of the shares (except directors' qualifying shares) or of the capital of which was owned by

(i) one or more persons each of which is Her Majesty in right of Canada or a province or a person to which paragraph (*d*) or (*d*.2) applies for the period, or

(ii) one or more municipalities in Canada in combination with one or more persons each of which is Her Majesty in right of Canada or a province or a person to which paragraph (*d*) or (*d*.2) applies for the period;

▶ 149(1)(d.4) ◀

(d.4) Combined ownership — a corporation all of the shares (except directors' qualifying shares) or of the capital of which was owned by one or more persons each of which is a corporation, commission or association to which this paragraph or any of paragraphs (*d*) to (*d*.3) applies for the period;

▶ 149(1)(d.5) ◀

(d.5) Income within boundaries of entities — subject to subsections (1.2) and (1.3), a corporation, commission or association not less than 90% of the capital of which was owned by one or more entities each of which is a municipality in Canada, or a municipal or public body performing a function of government in Canada, if the income for the period of the corporation, commission or association from activities carried on outside the geographical boundaries of the entities does not exceed 10% of its income for the period;

History: S. 149(1)(*d.5*) was replaced by S.C. 2013, c. 34, s. 307(1), applicable to taxation years that begin after May 8, 2000, and formerly read:

(*d.5*) *Municipal corporations* — subject to subsections (1.2) and (1.3), a corporation, commission or association not less than 90% of the capital of which was owned by one or more municipalities in Canada, if the income for the period of the corporation, commission or association from activities carried on outside the geographical boundaries of the municipalities does not exceed 10% of its income for the period;

In addition, notwithstanding subsections 152(4) to (5), any assessment of a taxpayer's tax payable under the Act for any taxation year that began before October 24, 2012 is to be made that is necessary to give effect to the amendment to paragraph 149(1)(*d.5*).

Tax Window Files: Municipal Corporation, *June 4, 2015*, CRA Document No. 2014-0530241E5.

▶ 149(1)(d.6) ◀

(d.6) Subsidiaries of municipal corporations — subject to subsections (1.2) and (1.3), a particular corporation all of the shares (except directors' qualifying shares) or of the capital of which was owned by one or more entities (referred to in this paragraph as "qualifying owners") each of which is, for the period, a corporation, commission or association to which paragraph (*d.5*) applies, a corporation to which this paragraph applies, a municipality in Canada, or a municipal or public body performing a function of government in Canada, if no more than 10% of the particular corporation's income for the period is from activities carried on outside

(i) if a qualifying owner is a municipality in Canada, or a municipal or public body performing a function of government in Canada, the geographical boundaries of each such qualifying owner,

(ii) if paragraph (*d.5*) applies to a qualifying owner, the geographical boundaries of the municipality, or municipal or public body, referred to in that paragraph in its application to each such qualifying owner, and

(iii) if this paragraph applies to a qualifying owner, the geographical boundaries of the municipality, or municipal or public body, referred to in subparagraph (i) or paragraph (*d.5*), as the case may be, in their respective applications to each such qualifying owner;

History: S. 149(1)(*d.6*) was replaced by S.C. 2013, c. 34, s. 307(3), applicable in respect of taxation years that end after April 2004, and formerly read:

(*d.6*) *Subsidiaries of municipal corporations* — subject to subsections (1.2) and (1.3), a particular corporation all of the shares (except directors' qualifying shares) or of the capital of which was owned by one or more persons each of which is a corporation, commission or association to which paragraph (*d.5*) or this paragraph applies for the period if the income for the period of the particular corporation from activities carried on outside

(i) if paragraph (*d.5*) applies to the other corporation, commission or association, the geographical boundaries of the entities referred to in that paragraph in its application to that other corporation, commission or association, or

(ii) if this paragraph applies to the other corporation, commission or association, the geographical boundaries of the entities referred to in subparagraph (i) in its application to that other corporation, commission or association,

does not exceed 10% of its income for the period;

S. 149(1)(*d.6*)(i) and (ii) were replaced by S.C. 2013, c. 34, s. 307(2), applicable to taxation years that begin after May 8, 2000, and formerly read:

(i) if paragraph (*d.5*) applies to the other corporation, commission or association, the geographical boundaries of the municipalities referred to in that paragraph in its application to that other corporation, commission or association, or

(ii) if this paragraph applies to the other corporation, commission or association, the geographical boundaries of the municipalities referred to in subparagraph (i) in its application to that other corporation, commission or association,

In addition, notwithstanding subsections 152(4) to (5), any assessment of a taxpayer's tax payable under the Act for any taxation year that began before October 24, 2012 is to be made that is necessary to give effect to the amendments to subparagraphs 149(1)(*d.6*)(i) and (ii).

▶ 149(1)(e) ◀

(e) Certain organizations — an agricultural organization, a board of trade or a chamber of commerce, no part of the income of which was payable to, or was otherwise available for the personal benefit of, any proprietor, member or shareholder thereof;

Related Sections: S. 149(2) Determination of income.

Tax Window Files: Agricultural co-op patronage dividends, *March 5, 2015*, CRA Document No. 2014-0551921E5.

▶ 149(1)(f) ◀

(f) Registered charities — a registered charity;

Related Regulations: Part XXXV.

Related Sections: S. 149(2) Determination of income; s. 149.1 Charities.

▶ 149(1)(g) ◀

(g) Registered Canadian amateur athletic association — a registered Canadian amateur athletic association;

History: S. 149(1)(*g*) was added by S.C. 2011, c. 24, s. 50(1), in force January 1, 2012.

▶ 149(1)(h) ◀

(h) Charitable trusts — (Repealed by 1976-77, c. 4, s. 59(1).)

Amendment not yet in force

Budget Implementation Act, 2019, No. 1 [S.C. 2019, c. 29]

S. 149(1), paragraph (*h*) was added by S.C. 2019, c. 29, s. 30(1), and will read as follows:

(h) Registered journalism organizations — a registered journalism organization;

Applicable: In force January 1, 2020.

▶ 149(1)(h.1) ◀

(h.1) Association of Universities and Colleges of Canada — the Association of Universities and Colleges of Canada, incorporated by the *Act to incorporate Association of Universities and Colleges of*

Canada, chapter 75 of the Statutes of Canada, 1964-65;

► 149(1)(i) ◄

(i) Certain housing corporations — a corporation that was constituted exclusively for the purpose of providing low-cost housing accommodation for the aged, no part of the income of which was payable to, or was otherwise available for the personal benefit of, any proprietor, member or shareholder thereof;

Related Sections: S. 149(2) Determination of income.

► 149(1)(j) ◄

(j) Non-profit corporations for scientific research and experimental development — a corporation that was constituted exclusively for the purpose of carrying on or promoting scientific research and experimental development, no part of whose income was payable to, or was otherwise available for the personal benefit of, any proprietor, member or shareholder thereof, that has not acquired control of any other corporation and that, during the period,

(i) did not carry on any business, and

(ii) expended amounts in Canada each of which is

(A) an expenditure on scientific research and experimental development (within the meaning that would be assigned by paragraph 37(8)(*a*) if subsection 37(8) were read without reference to paragraph 37(8)(*d*)) directly undertaken by or on behalf of the corporation, or

(B) a payment to an association, university, college or research institute or other similar institution, described in clause 37(1)(*a*)(ii)(A) or (B) to be used for scientific research and experimental development, and

the total of which is not less than 90% of the amount, if any, by which the corporation's gross revenue for the period exceeds the total of all amounts paid in the period by the corporation because of subsection (7.1);

Related Sections: S. 149(2) Determination of income; s. 149(7.1) Penalty for failure to file on time; 149(8) Interpretation of para. (1)(j); 149(9) Rules for determining gross revenue.

Information Circulars: IC 86-4R3 Scientific Research and Experimental Development.

SR&ED Publications: SR&ED Filing Requirements Policy.

► 149(1)(k) ◄

(k) Labour organizations — a labour organization or society or a benevolent or fraternal benefit society or order;

Related Sections: S. 149(3) Application of s. (1) — income from life insurance business; s. 149(4) Application of s. (1) — income from life insurance business.

Tax Window Files: Return of Funds on Annulment of Labour Association, *Technical Interpretation, Business and Partnerships Division, June 17, 2005*, CRA Document No. 2005-0134441E5; Fund Established for the Benefit of Former Employees, *Technical Interpretation, Business and Partnerships Division, October 28, 2004*, CRA Document No. 2003-0048901E5; Benevolent or Fraternal Benefit Society, *Technical Interpretation, Business and Partnerships Division, October 31, 2003*, CRA Document No. 2003-0035615.

Cases: Profits from a newspaper business, channelled to members through a labour union, were not exempt from tax *Ferris et al. v. M.N.R.*, 77 DTC 17 (T.R.B.). See also *O'Brien v. The Queen*, 85 DTC 5202 (F.C.T.D.) and *L.I.U.N.A. Local 527 Members' Training Trust Fund v. The Queen*, 92 DTC 2365 (T.C.C.)

► 149(1)(l) ◄

(l) Non-profit organizations — a club, society or association that, in the opinion of the Minister, was not a charity within the meaning assigned by subsection 149.1(1) and that was organized and operated exclusively for social welfare, civic improvement, pleasure or recreation or for any other purpose except profit, no part of the income of which was payable to, or was otherwise available for the personal benefit of, any proprietor, member or shareholder thereof unless the proprietor, member or shareholder was a club, society or association the primary purpose and function of which was the promotion of amateur athletics in Canada;

Related Sections: S. 149(2) Determination of income; s. 149(5) Exception re investment income of certain clubs.

Tax Topics: No. 2023-24, 2010 Canadian Tax Foundation CRA Roundtable: Pipelines, Privilege and Working Papers (Again!); No. 2006, Hold the Cookies — The CRA Outlaws Bake Sales for Not-For-Profits.

Forms: T1044 — Non-Profit Organization (NPO) Information Return.

Guides: T4117 Income Tax Guide to the Non-Profit Organization (NPO) Information Return.

Interpretation Bulletins: *Primary* — IT-304R2 Condominiums; IT-496R Non-profit organizations. *Secondary* — IT-83R3 Non-profit organizations — Taxation of income from property.

Tax Window Files: Acceptable uses of accumulated surplus by an NPO, *August 31, 2015*, CRA Document No. 2015-0565601E5; NPO - rental income, *August 2, 2013*, CRA Document No. 2013-0475041E5; Status of 149(1)(l) Entity, *February 14, 2012*, CRA Document No. 2011-0392841E5; Meaning of "Operated"--149(1)(l), *November 19, 2010*, CRA Document No. 2010-0383001I7.

Cases: The taxpayer provided audience measurement data to its members in exchange for members' fees. The taxpayer was established and operated for a non-profit purpose and was therefore a non-profit organization. The taxpayer lacked a significant attribute of a commercial business; that is, there was no opportunity for its members to benefit financially by way of profits, distributions, or the like. *BBM Canada (formerly BBM Bureau of Measurement) v. The Queen*, 2008 DTC 4129 (T.C.C.).

The taxpayer's Letters Patent, general by-law and its profit and loss results supported its claim that it was a non-profit organization exempt from tax. The taxpayer's high level of commercial activity and large stabilization reserve did not prove that the taxpayer was being operated for profit. *The Canadian Bar Insurance Association v. The Queen*, 99 DTC 653 (T.C.C.)

► 149(1)(m) ◄

(m) Mutual insurance corporations — a mutual insurance corporation that received its premiums wholly from the insurance of churches, schools or other charitable organizations;

► 149(1)(n) ◄

(n) Housing companies — a limited-dividend housing company (within the meaning of that expression as defined in section 2 of the *National Housing Act*), all or substantially all of the business of which is the construction, holding or management of low-rental housing projects;

Tax Window Files: Capital Dividend Account and 149(1)(n), *August 17, 2016*, CRA Document No. 2016-0639251I7.

► 149(1)(o) ◄

(o) Pension trusts — a trust governed by a registered pension plan;

Related Sections: S. 138.1(7) Where ss. (1) to (6) do not apply; s. 144(2) No tax while trust governed by plan; s. 146 Registered retirement savings plans;

s. 147 Deferred profit sharing plans; s. 205(1) Definitions; s. 205(2) Definitions in subsection 146.4(1).

Forms: T3P — Employee's Pension Plan Information and Income Tax Return.

► 149(1)(o.1) ◄

(o.1) Pension corporations — a corporation

(i) incorporated and operated throughout the period either

(A) solely for the administration of a registered pension plan, or

(B) for the administration of a registered pension plan and for no other purpose other than acting as trustee of, or administering, a trust governed by a retirement compensation arrangement, where the terms of the arrangement provide for benefits only in respect of individuals who are provided with benefits under the registered pension plan, and

(ii) accepted by the Minister as a funding medium for the purpose of the registration of the pension plan;

Related Regulations: 8502(g).

► 149(1)(o.2) ◄

(o.2) Idem — a corporation

(i) incorporated before November 17, 1978 solely in connection with, or for the administration of, a registered pension plan,

(ii) that has at all times since the later of November 16, 1978 and the date on which it was incorporated

(A) limited its activities to

(I) acquiring, holding, maintaining, improving, leasing or managing capital property that is real property or an interest in real property — or immovables or a real right in immovables — owned by the corporation, another corporation described by this subparagraph and subparagraph (iv) or a registered pension plan, and

(II) investing its funds in a partnership that limits its activities to acquiring, holding, maintaining, improving, leasing or managing capital property that is real property or an interest in real property — or immovables or a real right in immovables — owned by the partnership,

(B) made no investments other than in real property or an interest in real property — or immovables or a real right in immovables — or investments that a pension plan is permitted to make under the *Pension Benefits Standards Act, 1985* or a similar law of a province, and

(C) borrowed money solely for the purpose of earning income from real property or an interest in real property or from immovables or a real right in immovables,

(ii.1) that throughout the period

(A) limited its activities to

(I) acquiring Canadian resource properties by purchase or by incurring Canadian exploration expense or Canadian development expense, or

(II) holding, exploring, developing, maintaining, improving, managing, operating or disposing of its Canadian resource properties,

(B) made no investments other than in

(I) Canadian resource properties,

(II) property to be used in connection with Canadian resource properties described in clause (A),

(III) loans secured by Canadian resource properties for the purpose of carrying out any activity described in clause (A) with respect to Canadian resource properties, or

(IV) investments that a pension fund or plan is permitted to make under the *Pension Benefits Standards Act, 1985* or a similar law of a province, and

(C) borrowed money solely for the purpose of earning income from Canadian resource properties, or

(iii) that made no investments other than investments that a pension fund or plan was permitted to make under the *Pension Benefits Standards Act, 1985* or a similar law of a province, and

(A) the assets of which were at least 98% cash and investments,

(B) that had not accepted deposits or issued bonds, notes, debentures or similar obligations, and

(C) that had derived at least 98% of its income for the period that is a taxation year of the corporation from, or from the disposition of, investments

if, at all times since the later of November 16, 1978 and the date on which it was incorporated,

(iv) all of the shares, and rights to acquire shares, of the capital stock of the corporation are owned by

(A) one or more registered pension plans,

(B) one or more trusts all the beneficiaries of which are registered pension plans,

(C) one or more related segregated fund trusts (within the meaning assigned by paragraph 138.1(1)(*a*)) all the beneficiaries of which are registered pension plans, or

(D) one or more prescribed persons, or

(v) in the case of a corporation without share capital, all the property of the corporation has been held exclusively for the benefit of one or more registered pension plans,

and for the purposes of subparagraph (iv), where a corporation has been formed as a result of the merger of two or more other corporations, it shall be deemed to be the same corporation as, and a continuation of, each such other corporation and the shares of the merged corporations shall be deemed to have been altered, in form only, by virtue of the merger and to have continued in existence in the form of shares of the corporation formed as a result of the merger;

History: S. 149(1)(*o.2*)(iii)(B) was replaced by S.C. 2013, c. 34, s. 307(4), applicable to taxation years that end after February 21, 1994, and formerly read:

(B) that had not issued debt obligations or accepted deposits, and

S. 149(1)(*o.2*)(ii)(A) to (C) were replaced by S.C. 2013, c. 34, s. 138, in force June 26, 2013, and formerly read:

(A) limited its activities to

(I) acquiring, holding, maintaining, improving, leasing or managing capital property that is real property or an interest in real property owned by the corporation, another corporation described by this subparagraph and subparagraph (iv) or a registered pension plan, and

(II) investing its funds in a partnership that limits its activities to acquiring, holding, maintaining, improving, leasing or managing capital property that is real property or an interest in real property owned by the partnership,

(B) made no investments other than in real property or an interest therein or investments that a pension plan is permitted to make under the *Pension Benefits Standards Act, 1985* or a similar law of a province, and

(C) borrowed money solely for the purpose of earning income from real property or an interest therein,

Related Regulations: 4802(1).

Related Sections: S. 253.1 Investments in limited partnerships.

Canadian Tax Foundation: MacNevin, *Comparative Tax Advantages of Canadian Pension Funds as Investors in Real Estate,* 2013 Canadian Tax Journal 1:41-78.

Tax Topics: No. 1867-68, 2007 Canadian Tax Foundation Annual Conference CRA Round Table.

Income Tax Technical News: Issue No. 38, Pension Fund Corporations.

Tax Window Files: Application of quantitative limit for pension corporations, May 3, 2017, CRA Document No2013-0508321I7.

► 149(1)(o.3) ◄

(o.3) Prescribed small business investment corporations — a corporation that is prescribed to be a small business investment corporation;

Related Regulations: Part LI.

► 149(1)(o.4) ◄

(o.4) Master trusts — a trust that is prescribed to be a master trust and that elects to be such a trust under this paragraph in its return of income for its first taxation year ending in the period;

Related Regulations: 4802(1.1).

Canadian Tax Foundation: Krasa, *Income Tax Implications of Joint Investment by Pension Plans Through a Private Pooled Fund Vehicle,* 1997 Canadian Tax Journal 1:1-24.

Interpretation Bulletins: *Secondary* — IT-286R2 Trusts — Amount payable.

► 149(1)(p) ◄

(p) Trusts under profit sharing plan — a trust under an employees profit sharing plan to the extent provided by section 144;

Related Sections: S. 144 Employee profit sharing plans; s. 149(1)(*j*) Non-profit corporations for scientific research and experimental development.

► 149(1)(q) ◄

(q) Trusts under a registered supplementary unemployment benefit plan — a trust under a registered supplementary unemployment benefit plan to the extent provided by section 145;

Related Sections: S. 145 Registered supplementary unemployment benefit plans.

Information Circulars: IC 72-5R2 Registered supplementary unemployment benefit plans.

► 149(1)(q.1) ◄

(q.1) RCA trusts — an RCA trust (within the meaning assigned by subsection 207.5(1));

► 149(1)(r) ◄

(r) Trusts under registered retirement savings plan — a trust under a registered retirement savings plan to the extent provided by section 146;

Related Sections: S. 138.1(7) Where ss. (1) to (6) do not apply; s. 146 Registered retirement savings plans.

Information Circulars: IC 72-22R9 Registered retirement savings plans.

► 149(1)(s) ◄

(s) Trusts under deferred profit sharing plan — a trust under a deferred profit sharing plan to the extent provided by section 147;

Related Sections: S. 147 Deferred profit sharing plans.

Information Circulars: IC 77-1R5 Deferred profit sharing plan.

► 149(1)(s.1) ◄

(s.1) Trust governed by eligible funeral arrangement — a trust governed by an eligible funeral arrangement;

Related Sections: 148.1 [Eligible funeral arrangements].

► 149(1)(s.2) ◄

(s.2) Cemetery care trust — a cemetery care trust;

Related Sections: S. 108(1), "trust"; s. 148.1(1), "cemetery care trust"; s. 248(1), "cemetery care trust".

► 149(1)(t) ◄

(t) Farmers' and fishermen's insurer — (Repealed by S.C. 2017, c. 20, s. 24(1).)

History: S.149(1)(*t*) was repealed by S.C. 2017, c. 20, s. 24(1), applicable to taxation years that begin after 2018, and formerly read:

(*t*) *Farmers' and fishermen's insurer* — an insurer that, throughout the period, is not engaged in any business other than insurance if, in the opinion of the Minister, on the advice of the Superintendent of Financial Institutions or of the superintendent of insurance of the province under the laws of which the insurer is incorporated, not less than 20% of the total of the gross premium income (net of reinsurance ceded) earned in the period by the insurer and, where the insurer is not a prescribed insurer, by all other insurers that

(i) are specified shareholders of the insurer,

(ii) are related to the insurer, or

(iii) where the insurer is a mutual corporation, are part of a group that controls, directly or indirectly in any manner whatever, or are controlled, directly or indirectly in any manner whatever by, the insurer,

is in respect of insurance of property used in farming or fishing or residences of farmers or fishermen;

Related Regulations: 4802(2).

Related Sections: S. 138 Insurance corporations; s. 149(3) Application of s. (1) — income from life insurance business; s. 149(4.1) Farmers' and fishermen's insurer; s. 149(4.2) Farmers' and fishermen's insurer; s. 149(10) Exempt corporations.

► 149(1)(u) ◄

(u) Registered education savings plans — a trust governed by a registered education savings plan to the extent provided by section 146.1;

Related Sections: S. 146.1 Registered education savings plans; s. 146.1(5) Trust not taxable.

▶ 149(1)(u.1) ◀

(u.1) Trusts under registered disability savings plans — a trust governed by a registered disability savings plan to the extent provided by section 146.4;

▶ 149(1)(u.2) ◀

(u.2) TFSA trust — a trust governed by a TFSA to the extent provided by section 146.2;

▶ 149(1)(u.3) ◀

(u.3) Pooled registered pension plan — a trust governed by a pooled registered pension plan to the extent provided under section 147.5;

Editorial Note: Pooled registered pension plans are exempt from Part 1 tax on taxable income earned in the plans. However, if the plan carries on a business, it will be subject to Part 1 tax on its income from the business. For these purposes, any capital gains or losses from the disposition of property held in connection with the business will be deemed to income or loss from the business. Furthermore, the trust will be precluded from deducting any amounts of such business allocated to its members (see s. 147.5(8)).

History: S. 149(1)(*u.3*) was added by S.C. 2012, c. 31, s. 38(1), in force December 14, 2012.

▶ 149(1)(v) ◀

(v) Amateur athlete trust — an amateur athlete trust;

▶ 149(1)(w) ◀

(w) Trusts to provide compensation — a trust established as required under a law of Canada or of a province in order to provide funds out of which to compensate persons for claims against an owner of a business identified in the relevant law where that owner is unwilling or unable to compensate a customer or client, if no part of the property of the trust, after payment of its proper trust expenses, is available to any person other than as a consequence of that person being a customer or client of a business so identified;

Tax Window Files: funds held in settlement account, *June 28, 2017*, CRA Document No. 2017-0705431E5.

▶ 149(1)(x) ◀

(x) Registered retirement income funds — a trust governed by a registered retirement income fund to the extent provided by section 146.3;

Information Circulars: IC 78-18R6 Registered retirement income funds.

▶ 149(1)(y) ◀

(y) Trusts to provide vacation pay — a trust established pursuant to the terms of a collective agreement between an employer or an association of employers and employees or their labour organization for the sole purpose of providing for the payment of vacation or holiday pay, if no part of the property of the trust, after payment of its reasonable expenses, is

(i) available at any time after 1980, or

(ii) paid after December 11, 1979

to any person (other than a person described in paragraph (*k*)) otherwise than as a consequence of that person being an employee or an heir or legal representative thereof;

▶ 149(1)(z) ◀

(z) Qualifying environmental trust — a qualifying environmental trust.

Related Sections: S. 12(1)(z.1) Qualifying environmental trusts; s. 12(1)(z.2) Dispositions of interests in qualifying environmental trusts; s. 20(1)(*ss*) Qualifying environmental trusts; s. 20(1)(*tt*) Acquisition of interests in qualifying environmental trusts; s. 75(3) Exceptions; s. 107.3 Treatment of beneficiaries under qualifying environmental trusts; s. 211.6 Tax on qualifying environmental trusts; s. 248(1), "qualifying environmental trust"; s. 250(7) Residence of a qualifying environmental trust.

▶ 149(1)(z.1) ◀

(z.1) *Environmental Quality Act* trust — a trust

(i) that was created because of a requirement imposed by section 56 of the *Environment Quality Act*, R.S.Q., c. Q-2,

(ii) that is resident in Canada, and

(iii) in which the only persons that are beneficially interested are

(A) Her Majesty in right of Canada,

(B) Her Majesty in right of a province, or

(C) a municipality (as defined in section 1 of that Act) that is exempt because of this subsection from tax under this Part on all of its taxable income; or

History: S. 149(1)(*z.1*) was added by S.C. 2011, c. 24, s. 50(2), applicable to the 1997 and subsequent taxation years.

▶ 149(1)(z.2) ◀

(z.2) *Nuclear Fuel Waste Act* trust — a trust

(i) that was created because of a requirement imposed by subsection 9(1) of the *Nuclear Fuel Waste Act*, S.C. 2002, c. 23,

(ii) that is resident in Canada, and

(iii) in which the only persons that are beneficially interested are

(A) Her Majesty in right of Canada,

(B) Her Majesty in right of a province,

(C) a nuclear energy corporation (as defined in section 2 of that Act) all the shares of the capital stock of which are owned by one or more persons described in clause (A) or (B),

(D) the waste management organization established under section 6 of that Act if all the shares of its capital stock are owned by one or more nuclear energy corporations described in clause (C), or

(E) Atomic Energy of Canada Limited, being the company incorporated or acquired in accordance with subsection 10(2) of the *Atomic Energy Control Act*, R.S.C. 1970, c. A-19.

History: S. 149(1)(*z.2*) was added by S.C. 2011, c. 24, s. 50(2), applicable to the 1997 and subsequent taxation years.

▶ 149(1.1) ◀

(1.1) Exception. Where at a particular time

(*a*) a corporation, commission or association (in this subsection referred to as "the entity") would, but for this subsection, be described in any of paragraphs (1)(*d*) to (*d*.6),

(*b*) one or more other persons (other than Her Majesty in right of Canada or a province, a municipality in Canada or a person which, at the particular time, is a person described in any of subparagraphs (1)(*d*) to (*d*.6)) have at the particular time one or more rights in equity or otherwise, either immediately or in the future and either absolutely or contingently to, or to acquire, shares or capital of the entity, and

(*c*) the exercise of the rights referred to in paragraph (*b*) would result in the entity not being a person described in any of paragraphs (1)(*d*.1) to (*d*.6) at the particular time,

the entity is deemed not to be, at the particular time, a person described in any of paragraphs (1)(*d*) to (*d*.6).

► 149(1.11) ◄

(1.11) Election. Subsection (1) does not apply in respect of a person's taxable income for a particular taxation year that begins after 1998 where

(*a*) paragraph (1)(*d*) did not apply in respect of the person's taxable income for the person's last taxation year that began before 1999;

(*b*) paragraph (1)(*d*.2), (*d*.3) or (*d*.4) would, but for this subsection, have applied in respect of the person's taxable income for the person's first taxation year that began after 1998;

(*c*) there has been no change in the direct or indirect control of the person during the period that

(i) began at the beginning of the person's first taxation year that began after 1998, and

(ii) ends at the end of the particular year;

(*d*) the person elects in writing before 2002 that this subsection apply; and

(*e*) the person has not notified the Minister in writing before the particular year that the election has been revoked.

► 149(1.12) ◄

(1.12) Deemed election. If at any time there is an amalgamation (within the meaning assigned by subsection 87(1)) of a corporation (in this subsection referred to as the "parent") and one or more other corporations (each of which in this subsection is referred to as the "subsidiary") each of which is a subsidiary wholly-owned corporation of the parent, and immediately before that time the parent is a person to which subsection (1) does not apply by reason of the application of subsection (1.11), the new corporation is deemed, for the purposes of subsection (1.11), to be the same corporation as, and a continuation of, the parent.

History: S. 149(1.12) was added by S.C. 2013, c. 34, s. 307(5), applicable to amalgamations that occur after October 4, 2004.

► 149(1.2) ◄

(1.2) Income test. For the purposes of paragraphs (1)(*d*.5) and (*d*.6), income of a corporation, a commission or an association from activities carried on outside the geographical boundaries of a municipality or of a municipal or public body does not include income from activities carried on

(*a*) under an agreement in writing between

(i) the corporation, commission or association, and

(ii) a person who is Her Majesty in right of Canada or of a province, a municipality, a municipal or public body or a corporation to which any of paragraphs (1)(*d*) to (*d*.6) applies and that is controlled by Her Majesty in right of Canada or of a province, by a municipality in Canada or by a municipal or public body in Canada

within the geographical boundaries of,

(iii) if the person is Her Majesty in right of Canada or a corporation controlled by Her Majesty in right of Canada, Canada,

(iv) if the person is Her Majesty in right of a province or a corporation controlled by Her Majesty in right of a province, the province,

(v) if the person is a municipality in Canada or a corporation controlled by a municipality in Canada, the municipality, and

(vi) if the person is a municipal or public body performing a function of government in Canada or a corporation controlled by such a body, the area described in subsection (11) in respect of the person; or

(*b*) in a province as

(i) a producer of electrical energy or natural gas, or

(ii) a distributor of electrical energy, heat, natural gas or water,

where the activities are regulated under the laws of the province.

History: S. 149(1.2), the portion before paragraph (*b*) was replaced by S.C. 2013, c. 34, s. 307(6), applicable to taxation years that begin after May 8, 2000, and formerly read:

(1.2) *Income test.* For the purposes of paragraphs (1)(*d*.5) and (*d*.6), income of a corporation, commission or association from activities carried on outside the geographical boundaries of a municipality does not include income from activities carried on

(*a*) under an agreement in writing between

(i) the corporation, commission or association, and

(ii) a person who is Her Majesty in right of Canada or a province or a municipality or corporation to which any of paragraphs (1)(*d*) to (*d*.6) applies and that is controlled by Her Majesty in right of Canada or a province or by a municipality in Canada

within the geographical boundaries of,

(iii) where the person is Her Majesty in right of Canada or a corporation controlled by Her Majesty in right of Canada, Canada,

(iv) where the person is Her Majesty in right of a province or a corporation controlled by Her Majesty in right of a province, the province, and

(v) where the person is a municipality in Canada or a corporation controlled by a municipality in Canada, the municipality; or

In addition, notwithstanding subsections 152(4) to (5), any assessment of a taxpayer's tax payable under the Act for any taxation year that began before October 24, 2012 is to be made that is necessary to give effect to the amendment to the portion of subsection 149(1.2) before paragraph (*b*).

Tax Window Files: Limited Partnership operating a XXXXXXXXXX, *15XXXX*, CRA Document No. 2015-0578671R3.

► 149(1.3) ◄

(1.3) Votes or de facto control. Paragraphs (1)(*d*) to (*d*.6) do not apply in respect of a person's taxable income for a period in a taxation year if at any time during the period

(*a*) the person is a corporation shares of the capital stock of which are owned by one or more other persons that, in total, give them more than 10% of the votes that could be cast at a meeting of shareholders of the corporation, other than shares that are owned by one or more persons each of which is

(i) Her Majesty in right of Canada or of a province,

(ii) a municipality in Canada,

(iii) a municipal or public body performing a function of government in Canada, or

(iv) a corporation, a commission or an association, to which any of paragraphs (1)(*d*) to (*d.6*) apply; or

(*b*) the person is, or would be if the person were a corporation, controlled, directly or indirectly in any manner whatever, by a person, or by a group of persons that includes a person, who is not

(i) Her Majesty in right of Canada or of a province,

(ii) a municipality in Canada,

(iii) a municipal or public body performing a function of government in Canada, or

(iv) a corporation, a commission or an association, to which any of paragraphs (1)(*d*) to (*d.6*) apply.

History: S. 149(1.3) was replaced by S.C. 2013, c. 34, s. 307(7), applicable to taxation years that begin after May 8, 2000, except that, for those taxation years that began before December 21, 2002, subsection 149(1.3) is to be read as follows:

"(1.3) For the purposes of paragraph (1)(*d.5*) and subsection (1.2), 90% of the capital of a corporation that has issued share capital is owned by one or more entities, each of which is a municipality or a municipal or public body, only if the entities own shares of the capital stock of the corporation that give the entities 90% or more of the votes that could be cast under all circumstances at an annual meeting of shareholders of the corporation."

In addition, notwithstanding subsections 152(4) to (5), any assessment of a taxpayer's tax payable under the Act for any taxation year that began before October 24, 2012 is to be made that is necessary to give effect to the amendment to subsection 149(1.3).

S. 149(1.3) formerly read:

(1.3) *Capital ownership.* For the purposes of paragraph (1)(*d.5*) and subsection (1.2), 90% of the capital of a corporation that has issued share capital is owned by one or more municipalities only when the municipalities own shares of the capital stock of the corporation that give the municipalities 90% or more of the votes that could be cast under all circumstances at an annual meeting of shareholders of the corporation.

Related Sections: S. 256(5.1) Control in fact.

► 149(2) ◄

(2) Determination of income. For the purposes of paragraphs (1)(*e*), (*i*), (*j*) and (*l*), in computing the part, if any, of any income that was payable to or otherwise available for the personal benefit of any person or the total of any amounts that is not less than a percentage specified in any of those paragraphs of any income for a period, the amount of such income shall be deemed to be the amount thereof determined on the assumption that the amount of any taxable capital gain or allowable capital loss is nil.

Related Sections: 149(1)(e) Certain organizations; 149(1)(i) Certain housing corporations; 149(1)(j) Non-profit corporations for scientific research and experimental development; 149(1)(l) Non-profit organizations; s. 149(5) Exception re investment income of certain clubs.

► 149(3) ◄

(3) Application of s. (1). Subsection (1) does not apply in respect of the taxable income of a benevolent or fraternal society or order from carrying on a life insurance business or, for greater certainty, from the sale of property used by it in the year in, or held by it in the year in the course of, carrying on a life insurance business.

Related Sections: S. 149(1)(*k*) Labour organizations; s. 149(4) Application of s. (1) — income from life insurance business.

Cases: A fraternal society, carrying on a life insurance business, had to include in its income only the investment income for the assets related to its life insurance business. *ACTRA Fraternal Benefit Society v. The Queen*, 97 DTC 5243 (F.C.A.), reversing 96 DTC 1723 (T.C.C.)

A fraternal society carrying on a life insurance business was required to compute its investment income in accordance with the specific rules in Part XXIV of ITR's and not by analogy to situations described in that Part. *Lutheran Life Insurance Society of Canada v. The Queen*, 91 DTC 5553 (T.C.C.).

► 149(4) ◄

(4) Idem. For the purposes of subsection (3), the taxable income of a benevolent or fraternal benefit society or order from carrying on a life insurance business shall be computed on the assumption that it had no income or loss from any other sources.

Editorial Note: The decision by the Federal Court of Appeal in *ACTRA Fraternal Benefit Society v. The Queen*, 97 DTC 5243 supported the position of the taxpayer that "the onus rested on the taxpayer to establish what proportion of investment income related to 'the life insurance business.'" This decision is important where the assets in the life fund presumably supporting the life business are far greater than is required.

Related Sections: S. 149(1)(*k*) Labour organizations; s. 149(3) Application of s. (1) — income from life insurance business.

► 149(4.1) ◄

(4.1) Income exempt under 149(1)(*t*). (Repealed by S.C. 2017, c. 20, s. 24(2).)

History: S.149(4.1) was repealed by S.C. 2017, c. 20, s. 24(2), applicable to taxation years that begin after 2018, and formerly read:

(4.1) *Income exempt under 149(1)(t).* Subject to subsection (4.2), subsection (1) applies to an insurer described in paragraph (1)(*t*) only in respect of the part of its taxable income for a taxation year determined by the formula

$$(A \times B \times C) / D$$

where

A is its taxable income for the year;

B is

(*a*) $^1/_2$, where less than 25% of the total of the gross premium income (net of reinsurance ceded) earned in the year by it and, where it is not a prescribed insurer for the purpose of paragraph (1)(*t*), by all other insurers that

(i) are specified shareholders of the insurer,

(ii) are related to the insurer, or

(iii) where the insurer is a mutual corporation, are part of a group that controls, directly or indirectly in any manner whatever, or are controlled, directly or indirectly in any manner whatever by, the insurer,

is in respect of insurance of property used in farming or fishing or residences of farmers or fishermen; and

(*b*) 1 in any other case;

C is the part of the gross premium income (net of reinsurance ceded) earned by it in the year that, in the opinion of the Minister, on the advice of the Superintendent of Financial Institutions or of the superintendent of insurance of the province under the laws of which it is incorporated, is in respect of insurance of property used in farming or fishing or residences of farmers or fishermen; and

D is the gross premium income (net of reinsurance ceded) earned by it in the year.

Related Sections: S. 149(4.2) Farmers' and fishermen's insurer; s. 149(4.3) Computation of taxable income of insurer; s. 168(1) Notice of intention to revoke registration.

► 149(4.2) ◄

(4.2) Idem. (Repealed by S.C. 2017, c. 20, s. 24(2).)

History: S.149(4.2) was repealed by S.C. 2017, c. 20, s. 24(2), applicable to taxation years that begin after 2018, and formerly read:

(4.2) *Idem.* Subsection (4.1) does not apply to an insurer described in paragraph (1)(*t*) in respect of the taxable income of the insurer for a taxation year where more than 90% of the total of the gross premium income (net of reinsurance ceded) earned in the year by the insurer and, where the insurer is not a prescribed insurer, by all other insurers that

(*a*) are specified shareholders of the insurer,

(*b*) are related to the insurer, or

(*c*) where the insurer is a mutual corporation, are part of a group that controls, directly or indirectly in any manner whatever, or are controlled, directly or indirectly in any manner whatever, by, the insurer,

is in respect of insurance of property used in farming or fishing or residences of farmers or fishermen.

Related Sections: S. 251 Arm's length.

▶ 149(4.3) ◀

(4.3) Computation of taxable income of insurer. (Repealed by S.C. 2017, c. 20, s. 24(2).)

History: S.149(4.3) was repealed by S.C. 2017, c. 20, s. 24(2), applicable to taxation years that begin after 2018, and formerly read:

(4.3) *Computation of taxable income of insurer.* For the purposes of this Part, in computing the taxable income of an insurer for a particular taxation year, the insurer shall be deemed to have deducted under paragraphs 20(1)(*a*), 20(7)(*c*) and 138(3)(*a*) and section 140 in each taxation year preceding the particular year and in respect of which paragraph (1)(*t*) applied to the insurer, the greater of

(*a*) the amount it claimed or deducted under those provisions for that preceding year, and

(*b*) the greatest amount that could have been claimed or deducted under those provisions to the extent that the total thereof does not exceed the amount that would be its taxable income for that preceding year if no amount had been claimed or deducted under those provisions.

▶ 149(5) ◀

(5) Exception — investment income of certain clubs. Notwithstanding subsections (1) and (2), where a club, society or association was for any period, a club, society or association described in paragraph (1)(*l*) the main purpose of which was to provide dining, recreational or sporting facilities for its members (in this subsection referred to as the "club"), a trust is deemed to have been created on the later of the commencement of the period and the end of 1971 and to have continued in existence throughout the period, and, throughout that period, the following rules apply:

(*a*) the property of the club shall be deemed to be the property of the trust;

(*b*) where the club is a corporation, the corporation shall be deemed to be the trustee having control of the trust property;

(*c*) where the club is not a corporation, the officers of the club shall be deemed to be the trustees having control of the trust property;

(*d*) tax under this Part is payable by the trust on its taxable income for each taxation year;

(*e*) the income and taxable income of the trust for each taxation year shall be computed on the assumption that it had no incomes or losses other than

(i) incomes and losses from property, and

(ii) taxable capital gains and allowable capital losses from dispositions of property, other than property used exclusively for and directly in the course of providing the dining, recreational or sporting facilities provided by it for its members;

(*f*) in computing the taxable income of the trust for each taxation year

(i) there may be deducted, in addition to any other deductions permitted by this Part, $2,000, and

(ii) no deduction shall be made under section 112 or 113; and

(*g*) the provisions of subdivision k of Division B (except subsections 104(1) and (2)) do not apply in respect of the trust.

(*h*) (Repealed by 1983-84, c. 1, s. 83(3).)

History: S. 149(5), the portion before paragraph (*a*) was replaced by S.C. 2014, c. 39, s. 53(1), applicable to the 2016 and subsequent taxation years, and formerly read:

(5) *Exception re investment income of certain clubs.* Notwithstanding subsections (1) and (2), where a club, society or association was for any period, a club, society or association described in paragraph (1)(*l*) the main purpose of which was to provide dining, recreational or sporting facilities for its members (in this subsection referred to as the "club"), an *inter vivos* trust shall be deemed to have been created on the later of the commencement of the period and the end of 1971 and to have continued in existence throughout the period, and, throughout that period, the following rules apply:

Related Sections: 104(1) Reference to trust or estate; 104(2) Taxed as individual; s. 122(1) Tax payable by inter vivos trust.

Interpretation Bulletins: *Primary* — IT-83R3 Non-profit organizations — Taxation of income from property. *Secondary* — IT-406R2 Tax payable by an inter vivos trust.

Tax Window Files: 2012 Ontario CTF Conference Question #16, October 30, 2012, 2012-0462861C6.

Cases: The taxpayer, a golf club, invested its revenues in excess of its operating expenses in short term deposits. The interest generated on the deposits were used to pay the taxpayer's operating expenses. The taxpayer was a non-profit organization and so its investment activities could only be passive and incidental to its principal activities. In order to be business income, the interest income would have to be incidental to activities aimed at earning business income, which cannot be the case. The interest was income from property and all such income is taxable where subsection 149(5) applies. *Elm Ridge Country Club Inc. v. The Queen*, 99 DTC 5127 (F.C.A.)

▶ 149(6) ◀

(6) Apportionment rule. Where it is necessary for the purpose of this section to ascertain the taxable income of a taxpayer for a period that is a part of a taxation year, the taxable income for the period shall be deemed to be the proportion of the taxable income for the taxation year that the number of days in the period is of the number of days in the taxation year.

Related Sections: S. 8(7) Cost of tool; s. 149(1) Miscellaneous exemptions.

▶ 149(7) ◀

(7) Time for filing. A corporation the taxable income of which for a taxation year is exempt from tax under this Part because of paragraph (1)(*j*) shall file with the Minister a prescribed form containing prescribed information on or before its filing-due date for the year.

Related Sections: S. 248(1), "filing-due date".

▶ 149(7.1) ◀

(7.1) Penalty for failure to file on time. Where a corporation fails to file the prescribed form as required by subsection (7) for a taxation year, it is liable to a penalty equal to the amount determined by the formula

$$A \times B$$

where

A is the greater of

(*a*) $500, and

(*b*) 2% of its taxable income for the year; and

B is the lesser of

(*a*) 12, and

(*b*) the number of months in whole or in part that are in the period that begins on the day on or before which the prescribed form is required to be filed and ends on the day it is filed.

▶ 149(8) ◀

(8) Interpretation of para. (1)(*j*). For the purpose of paragraph (1)(*j*),

(*a*) a corporation is controlled by another corporation if more than 50% of its issued share capital (having full voting rights under all circumstances) belongs to

(i) the other corporation, or

(ii) the other corporation and persons with whom the other corporation does not deal at arm's length,

but a corporation shall be deemed not to have acquired control of a corporation if it has not purchased (or otherwise acquired for a consideration) any of the shares in the capital stock of that corporation; and

(*b*) there shall be included in computing a corporation's income and in determining its gross revenue the amount of all gifts received by the corporation and all amounts contributed to the corporation to be used for scientific research and experimental development.

Related Sections: S. 251Arm's length.

▶ 149(9) ◀

(9) Rules for determining gross revenue. In determining the gross revenue of a corporation for the purpose of determining whether it is described by paragraph (1)(*j*) for a taxation year,

(*a*) there may be deducted an amount not exceeding its gross revenue for the year computed without including or deducting any amount under this subsection; and

(*b*) there shall be included any amount that has been deducted under this subsection for the preceding taxation year.

Income Tax Folios: S2-F1-C1 Health and Welfare Trusts.

▶ 149(10) ◀

(10) Becoming or ceasing to be exempt. (Repealed by S.C. 2017, c. 20, s. 24(3).)

History: S.149(10) was repealed by S.C. 2017, c. 20, s. 24(3), applicable to taxation years that begin after 2018, and formerly read:

(10) *Becoming or ceasing to be exempt.* If at any time (in this subsection referred to as "that time"), a person — that is a corporation or, if that time is after September 12, 2013, a trust — becomes or ceases to be exempt from tax under this Part on its taxable income otherwise than by reason of paragraph (1)(*t*), the following rules apply:

S. 149(10)(*d*) was repealed by S.C. 2016, c. 12, s. 54(1), in force January 1, 2017, and formerly read:

(*d*) there is to be deducted under paragraph 20(1)(*b*) in computing the person's income from a business for the taxation year that ended immediately before that time the amount, if any, by which the person's cumulative eligible capital immediately before the disposition time in respect of the business exceeds the total of

(i) 3/4 of the fair market value of the eligible capital property in respect of the business, and

(ii) the amount otherwise deducted under paragraph 20(1)(*b*) in computing the person's income from the business for the taxation year that ended immediately before that time.

S. 149(10) was replaced by S.C. 2013, c. 40, s. 66(1), deemed to have come into forced on March 21, 2013, and formerly read:

(10) *Exempt corporations.* Where, at any time (in this subsection referred to as "that time"), a corporation becomes or ceases to be exempt from tax under this Part on its taxable income otherwise than by reason of paragraph (1)(*t*), the following rules apply:

(*a*) the taxation year of the corporation that would otherwise have included that time is deemed to have ended immediately before that time, a new taxation year of the corporation is deemed to have begun at that time and, for the purpose of determining the taxpayer's fiscal period after that time, the taxpayer is deemed not to have established a fiscal period before that time;

(*a*.1) for the purpose of computing the corporation's income for its first taxation year ending after that time, the corporation shall be deemed to have deducted under sections 20, 138 and 140 in computing its income for its taxation year ending immediately before that time, the greatest amount that could have been claimed or deducted for that year as a reserve under those sections;

(*b*) the corporation is deemed to have disposed, at the time (in this subsection referred to as the "disposition time") that is immediately before the time that is immediately before that time, of each property that was owned by it immediately before that time for an amount equal to its fair market value at that time and to have reacquired the property at that time at a cost equal to that fair market value;

(*c*) for the purposes of applying sections 37, 65 to 66.4, 66.7, 111 and 126, subsections 127(5) to (36) and section 127.3 to the corporation, the corporation is deemed to be a new corporation the first taxation year of which began at that time; and

(*d*) where, immediately before the disposition time, the corporation's cumulative eligible capital in respect of a business exceeds the total of

(i) 3/4 of the fair market value of the eligible capital property in respect of the business, and

(ii) the amount otherwise deducted under paragraph 20(1)(*b*) in computing the corporation's income from the business for the taxation year that ended immediately before that time,

the excess shall be deducted under paragraph 20(1)(*b*) in computing the corporation's income from the business for the taxation year that ended immediately before that time.

S. 149(10)(*c*) was replaced by S.C. 2013, c. 34, s. 307(8), applicable to each corporation that after 2006 becomes or ceases to be exempt from tax on its taxable income under Part I of the Act, and formerly read:

(*c*) for the purposes of applying sections 37, 65 to 66.4, 66.7, 111 and 126, subsections 127(5) to (26) and section 127.3 to the corporation, the corporation is deemed to be a new corporation the first taxation year of which began at that time; and

Related Sections: S. 66.7(10)(*b*) Change of control; s. 87(2.1)(*b*) Non-capital losses, etc., of predecessor corporations; s. 249.1(1) Definition of "fiscal period".

Tax Window Files: Capital Dividend Account and 149(1)(n), *August 17, 2016*, CRA Document No. 2016-0639251I7.

▶ 149(11) ◀

(11) Geographical boundaries — body performing government functions. For the purpose of this section, the geographical boundaries of a municipal or public body performing a function of government are

(*a*) the geographical boundaries that encompass the area in respect of which an Act of Parliament or an agreement given effect by an Act of Parliament recognizes or grants to the body a power to impose taxes; or

(*b*) if paragraph (*a*) does not apply, the geographical boundaries within which that body has been authorized by the laws of Canada or of a province to exercise that function.

History: S. 149(11) was added by S.C. 2013, c. 34, s. 307(9), applicable to taxation years that begin after May 8, 2000. In addition, notwithstanding subsections 152(4) to (5), any assessment of a taxpayer's tax payable under the Act for any taxation year that began before October 24, 2012 is to be made that is necessary to give effect to the addition of subsection 149(11).

▶ 149(12) ◀

(12) Information returns. Every person who, because of paragraph (1)(*e*) or (*l*), is exempt from tax under this Part on all or part of the person's taxable income shall, within 6 months after the end of each fiscal period of the person and without notice or demand therefor, file with the Minister an information return for the period in prescribed form and containing prescribed information, if

(*a*) the total of all amounts each of which is a taxable dividend or an amount received or receivable by the person as, on account of, in lieu of or in satisfaction of, interest, rentals or royalties in the period exceeds $10,000;

(*b*) at the end of the person's preceding fiscal period the total assets of the person (determined in accordance with generally accepted accounting principles) exceeded $200,000; or

(*c*) an information return was required to be filed under this subsection by the person for a preceding fiscal period.

Forms: T1044 — Non-Profit Organization (NPO) Information Return; T2052 — Registered Canadian Amateur Athletic Association Return of Information.

Guides: T4117 Income tax guide to the Non-Profit Organization (NPO) Information Return.

SECTION 149.01: [Information return]

► 149.01(1) ◄

(1) Definitions — (Repealed by S.C. 2017, c. 12, s. 12.)

History: S. 149.01(1) was repealed by S.C. 2017, c. 12, s. 12, in force June 19, 2017, and formerly read:

(1) *Definitions.* The following definitions apply in section 149 and in this section.

"labour organization"—"labour organization" includes a labour society and any organization formed for purposes which include the regulation of relations between employers and employees, and includes a duly organized group or federation, congress, labour council, joint council, conference, general committee or joint board of such organizations.

"labour relations activities"—"labour relations activities" means activities associated with the preparation for, and participation in, the negotiation of collective bargaining agreements and the administration and enforcement of collective agreements to which the labour organization is a signatory.

"labour trust"—"labour trust" means a trust or fund in which a labour organization has a legal, beneficial or financial interest or that is established or maintained in whole or in part for the benefit of a labour organization, its members or the persons it represents.

S. 149.01(1) was added by S.C. 2015, c. 41, s. 1, applicable in respect of fiscal periods that begin after December 31, 2015.

► 149.01(2) ◄

(2) Information return. (Repealed.)

History: S. 149.01(2) was repealed by S.C. 2017, c. 12, s. 12, in force June 19, 2017, and formerly read:

(2) *Information return.* Every labour organization and every labour trust shall, by way of electronic filing (as defined in subsection 150.1(1)) and within six months from the end of each fiscal period, file with the Minister an information return for the year, in prescribed form and containing prescribed information.

S. 149.01(2) was added by S.C. 2015, c. 41, s. 1, applicable in respect of fiscal periods that begin after December 31, 2015.

Related Sections: 239(2.31) Offence: section 149.01.

► 149.01(3) ◄

(3) Content of return. (Repealed.)

History: S. 149.01(3) was repealed by S.C. 2017, c. 12, s. 12, in force June 19, 2017, and formerly read:

(3) *Content of return.* The information return referred to in subsection (2) shall include:

(*a*) a set of financial statements for the fiscal period, in such form and containing such particulars and other information as may be prescribed relating to the financial position of the labour organization or labour trust, including

(i) a balance sheet showing the assets and liabilities of the labour organization or labour trust made up as of the last day of the fiscal period, and

(ii) a statement of income and expenditures of the labour organization or labour trust for the fiscal period;

(*b*) a set of statements for the fiscal period setting out the aggregate amount of all transactions and all disbursements — or book value in the case of investments and assets — with all transactions and all disbursements, the cumulative value of which in respect of a particular payer or payee for the period is greater than $5,000, shown as separate entries along with the name of the payer and payee and setting out for each of those transactions and disbursements its purpose and description and the specific amount that has been paid or received, or that is to be paid or received, and including

(i) a statement of accounts receivable,

(ii) a statement of loans exceeding $250 receivable from officers, employees, members or businesses,

(iii) a statement showing the sale of investments and fixed assets including a description, cost, book value, and sale price,

(iv) a statement showing the purchase of investments and fixed assets including a description, cost, book value, and price paid,

(v) a statement of accounts payable,

(vi) a statement of loans payable,

(vii) a statement of disbursements to officers, directors and trustees, to employees with compensation over $100,000 and to persons in positions of authority who would reasonably be expected to have, in the ordinary course, access to material information about the business, operations, assets or revenue of the labour organization or labour trust, including gross salary, stipends, periodic payments, benefits (including pension obligations), vehicles, bonuses, gifts, service credits, lump sum payments, other forms of remuneration and, without limiting the generality of the foregoing, any other consideration provided,

(vii.1) a statement with a reasonable estimate of the percentage of time dedicated by persons referred to in subparagraph (vii) to each of political activities, lobbying activities and other non-labour relations activities,

(viii) a statement with the aggregate amount of disbursements to employees and contractors including gross salary, stipends, periodic payments, benefits (including pension obligations), vehicles, bonuses, gifts, service credits, lump sum payments, other forms of remuneration and, without limiting the generality of the foregoing, any other consideration provided,

(viii.1) a statement with a reasonable estimate of the percentage of time dedicated by persons referred to in subparagraph (viii) to each of political activities, lobbying activities and other non-labour relations activities,

(ix) a statement with the aggregate amount of disbursements on labour relations activities,

(x) a statement of disbursements on political activities,

(xi) a statement of disbursements on lobbying activities,

(xii) a statement of contributions, gifts, and grants,

(xiii) a statement with the aggregate amount of disbursements on administration,

(xiv) a statement with the aggregate amount of disbursements on general overhead,

(xv) a statement with the aggregate amount of disbursements on organizing activities,

(xvi) a statement with the aggregate amount of disbursements on collective bargaining activities,

(xvii) a statement of disbursements on conference and convention activities,

(xviii) a statement of disbursements on education and training activities,

(xix) a statement with the aggregate amount of disbursements on legal activities, excluding information protected by solicitor-client privilege,

(xix.1) a statement of disbursements (other than disbursements included in a statement referred to in any of subparagraphs (iv), (vii), (viii) and (ix) to (xix)) on all activities other than those that are primarily carried on for members of the labour organization or labour trust, excluding information protected by solicitor-client privilege, and

(xx) any other prescribed statements;

(*c*) a statement for the fiscal period listing the sales of investments and fixed assets to, and the purchases of investments and fixed assets from, non-arm's length parties, including for each property a description of the property and its cost, book value and sale price;

(*d*) a statement for the fiscal period listing all other transactions with non-arm's length parties; and

(*e*) in the case of a labour organization or labour trust having its headquarters situated outside Canada, a statement in the prescribed form and containing such particulars as may be prescribed showing

(i) amounts paid or credited to the labour organization or labour trust in the fiscal period by, on behalf of or in respect of taxpayers resident in Canada, and

(ii) expenditures made by the labour organization or labour trust in the fiscal period inside or outside Canada and recorded separately in the accounts of the labour organization or labour trust as being directly related to its operations in Canada.

S. 149.01(3) was added by S.C. 2015, c. 41, s. 1, applicable in respect of fiscal periods that begin after December 31, 2015.

► 149.01(4) ◄

(4) Communication of information. (Repealed.)

History: S. 149.01(4) was repealed by S.C. 2017, c. 12, s. 12, in force June 19, 2017, and formerly read:

(4) *Communication of information.* Despite section 241, the information contained in the information return referred to in subsection 149.01(2) shall be made available to the public by the Minister, including publication on the departmental Internet site in a searchable format.

S. 149.01(4) was added by S.C. 2015, c. 41, s. 1, applicable in respect of fiscal periods that begin after December 31, 2015.

► 149.01(5) ◄

(5) Disbursement. (Repealed.)

History: S. 149.01(5) was repealed by S.C. 2017, c. 12, s. 12, in force June 19, 2017, and formerly read:

(5) *Disbursement.* For greater certainty, a disbursement referred to in any of subparagraphs (3)(*b*)(viii) to (xx) includes a disbursement made through a third party or contractor.

S. 149.01(5) was added by S.C. 2015, c. 41, s. 1, applicable in respect of fiscal periods that begin after December 31, 2015.

► 149.01(6) ◄

(6) Subsection (2) does not apply. (Repealed.)

History: S. 149.01(6) was repealed by S.C. 2017, c. 12, s. 12, in force June 19, 2017, and formerly read:

(6) *Subsection (2) does not apply.* Subsection (2) does not apply to

(*a*) a labour-sponsored venture capital corporation; and

(*b*) a labour trust the activities and operations of which are limited exclusively to the administration, management or investments of a deferred profit sharing plan, an employee life and health trust, a group sickness or accident insurance plan, a group term life insurance policy, a private health services plan, a registered pension plan or a supplementary unemployment benefit plan.

S. 149.01(6) was added by S.C. 2015, c. 41, s. 1, applicable in respect of fiscal periods that begin after December 31, 2015.

► 149.01(7) ◄

(7) Reporting not required. (Repealed.)

History: S. 149.01(7) was repealed by S.C. 2017, c. 12, s. 12, in force June 19, 2017, and formerly read:

(7) *Reporting not required.* Subsection (3) does not require the reporting of

(*a*) information, regarding disbursements and transactions of, or the value of investments held by, a labour trust (other than a trust described in paragraph (6)(*b*)), that is limited exclusively to the direct expenditures or transactions by the labour trust in respect of a plan, trust or policy described in paragraph (6)(*b*);

(*b*) the address of a person in respect of whom paragraph (3)(*b*) applies; or

(*c*) the name of a payer or payee in respect of a statement referred to in any of subparagraphs (3)(*b*)(i), (v), (ix), (xiii) to (xvi) and (xix).

S. 149.01(7) was added by S.C. 2015, c. 41, s. 1, applicable in respect of fiscal periods that begin after December 31, 2015.

Qualified Donees

SECTION 149.1: [Charities and other organizations]

► 149.1(1) ◄

(1) Definitions. In this section and section 149.2,

History: The heading before s. 149.1 was replaced by S.C. 2011, c. 24, s. 51(1), in force January 1, 2012. The heading before s. 149.1 formerly read "Charities".

Related Regulations: 3500 Interpretation; 3501 Contents of Receipts; 3501.1 Contents of Information Returns; 3502 Employees' Charity Trusts.

Information Circulars: IC 77-6R Registered charities: Designation as associated charities.

Interpretation Bulletins: *Secondary* — IT-496R Non-profit organizations.

Other Publications: CG-024 Ineligible Individuals.

"Canadian amateur athletic association" —"Canadian amateur athletic association" means an association that

(*a*) was created under any law in force in Canada,

(*b*) is resident in Canada,

(*c*) has no part of its income payable to, or otherwise available for the personal benefit of, any proprietor, member or shareholder of the association unless the proprietor, member or shareholder was a club, society or association the primary purpose and primary function of which was the promotion of amateur athletics in Canada,

(*d*) has the promotion of amateur athletics in Canada on a nationwide basis as its exclusive purpose and exclusive function, and

(*e*) devotes all its resources to that purpose and function;

Editorial Note: Registered Canadian amateur athletic associations ("RCAAAs") are "qualified donees" under s. 149.1(1) and are thus able to issue charitable receipts to taxpayers who make gifts to them. This allows individuals making a gift to claim a charitable donations tax credit under s. 118.1 and corporations to deduct the amount of the gift from income pursuant to s. 110.1. Moreover, as of January 1, 2012, RCAAAs and registered charities are subject to many of the same restrictions, requirements and penalties under the Act. See the CRA's *Charities Connection Newsletter* No. 11, "Budget 2011 — Changes for Registered Canadian Amateur Athletic Associations".

History: S. 149.1(1), the definition "Canadian amateur athletic association" was added by S.C. 2011, c. 24, s. 52(2), in force January 1, 2012.

Related Sections: S. 149.1(4.2) Revocation of registration; s. 149.1(6.01) Devoting resources to purpose and function; s. 149.1(6.201) Political activities; s. 248(1), "registered Canadian amateur athletic association".

Canadian Tax Foundation: Hayhoe and Black, *Charities and Not-For-Profit Update*, 2011 Prairie Provinces Tax Conference 3:1–30; Hayhoe and Stacey, *Charities and Not-for-Profits Update*, 2010 Conference Report 33:1–22; Yuill, *Charities and Not-for-Profits: An Update*, 2010 Atlantic Provinces Tax Conference 8B:1–43; Mason and Burr, *Registered Charities, the Disbursement Quota and Federal Budget 2010*, 2010 British Columbia Tax Conference 15:1–20; Maerov, *Current Cases — Back to Bake Sales: Defining the Scope of Related Businesses Conducted by Charitable Organizations and Foundations, 2003 DTC 5016*, 2003 Canadian Tax Journal 4:1602–1607.

"capital gains pool" — (Repealed by S.C. 2010, c. 25, s. 37(1).)

Editorial Note: A charity's "capital gains pool" was a component of a charity's annual "disbursement quota", as defined in subsection 149.1(1). However, amendments to the disbursement quota requirements in 2010 eliminated the relevance of the capital gains pool.

History: S. 149.1(1), the definition "capital gains pool" was repealed by S.C. 2010, c. 25, s. 37(1), applicable to taxation years that end on or after March 4, 2010. S. 149.1(1), the definition "capital gains pool" formerly read:

"capital gains pool" —"capital gains pool", of a registered charity for a taxation year, means the amount by which

(*a*) the total of all amounts, each of which is the amount of a capital gain of the charity from the disposition of an enduring property after March 22, 2004 and before the end of the taxation year (other than a capital gain from a disposition of a bequest or an inheritance received by the charity in a taxation year that included any time before 1994) that is declared by the charity in an information return under subsection (14) for the taxation year during which the disposition occurred,

exceeds

(*b*) the total of all amounts, each of which is the amount, determined for a preceding taxation year of the charity that began after March 22, 2004, that is the lesser of the amount determined under paragraph (*a*) of the description of A.1 in the definition "disbursement quota" and the amount claimed by the charity under paragraph (*b*) of that description;

"charitable activities" —"charitable activities" includes public policy dialogue and development activities carried on in furtherance of a charitable purpose;

History: S. 149.1(1), the definition "charitable activities" was added by S.C. 2018, c. 27, s. 17(4), deemed to have come into force

(a) on January 1, 2008 in respect of organizations, corporations and trusts that are registered charities on September 14, 2018; and

(b) on September 14, 2018 in any other case.

"charitable foundation"—"charitable foundation" means a corporation or trust that is constituted and operated exclusively for charitable purposes, no part of the income of which is payable to, or is otherwise available for, the personal benefit of any proprietor, member, shareholder, trustee or settlor thereof, and that is not a charitable organization;

Editorial Note: There are two distinct types of charities: (i) charitable foundations; and (ii) charitable organizations. Charitable foundations may, in turn, be separated into two separate sub-categories: (i) public foundations; and (ii) private foundations. At its simplest, a charitable organization undertakes the actual charitable activities while the foundations provide funds to the charitable organization. A charitable foundation must be a corporation or a trust; however, a charitable organization may be a corporation, trust, or unincorporated entity. A charity that qualifies as a charitable organization, will not be a charitable foundation. Upon an entity's registration as a charity, the Minister determines whether the entity qualifies as a public or private charitable foundation or a charitable organization. Classification may be changed by the Minister if the charity subsequently meets the criteria for a different type of charity.

The charity is designated by the Minister via notice sent by registered mail (see s. 149.1(6.3)).

Related Regulations: Part XXXVII.

Related Sections: S. 149.1(6.1) Charitable purposes; s. 248(1), "registered charity".

"charitable organization"—"charitable organization", at any particular time, means an organization, whether or not incorporated,

(*a*) constituted and operated exclusively for charitable purposes,

(*a*.1) all the resources of which are devoted to charitable activities carried on by the organization itself,

(*b*) no part of the income of which is payable to, or is otherwise available for, the personal benefit of any proprietor, member, shareholder, trustee or settlor thereof,

(*c*) more than 50% of the directors, trustees, officers or like officials of which deal at arm's length with each other and with

(i) each of the other directors, trustees, officers and like officials of the organization,

(ii) each person described by subparagraph (*d*)(i) or (ii), and

(iii) each member of a group of persons (other than Her Majesty in right of Canada or of a province, a municipality, another registered charity that is not a private foundation, and any club, society or association described in paragraph 149(1)(*l*)) who do not deal with each other at arm's length, if the group would, if it were a person, be a person described by subparagraph (*d*)(i), and

(*d*) that is not, at the particular time, and would not at the particular time be, if the organization were a corporation, controlled directly or indirectly in any manner whatever

(i) by a person (other than Her Majesty in right of Canada or of a province, a municipality, another registered charity that is not a private foundation, and any club, society or association described in paragraph 149(1)(*l*)),

(A) who immediately after the particular time, has contributed to the organization amounts that are, in total, greater than 50% of the capital of the organization immediately after the particular time, and

(B) who immediately after the person's last contribution at or before the particular time, had contributed to the organization amounts that were, in total, greater than 50% of the capital of the organization immediately after the making of that last contribution, or

(ii) by a person, or by a group of persons that do not deal at arm's length with each other, if the person or any member of the group does not deal at arm's length with a person described in subparagraph (i);

Editorial Note: In general terms, a charitable organization is a trust, corporation, or unincorporated organization that is constituted and operated for charitable purposes wherein (i) all of the resources are devoted to charitable activities carried on by the organization (see below); (ii) no part of the income is payable to or available for the benefit of the proprietor, member, shareholder, trustee, or settlor; (iii) more than 50% of the directors, trustees, officers, and similar officials deal with each other and with certain other persons and groups of persons at arm's length; and (iv) that is not controlled by a person who has contributed more than 50% of the capital to the charity, or by a person or non-arm's length group of persons who does not deal at arm's length with such a person. See also the editorial note for s. 149.1 "charitable foundation".

Charitable activities are now expressly defined to include "public policy dialogue and development activities carried on in furtherance of a charitable purpose", which allows for some political activity as long as the charity does not use any of its resources to the direct or indirect support of, or opposition to, any political party or candidate for public office; see also s. 149.1(6.1) and (6.2).

History: S. 149.1(1), paragraph (*a*) of the definition "charitable organization" was replaced by S.C. 2018, c. 27, s. 17(3), deemed to have come into force

(a) on January 1, 2008 in respect of organizations, corporations and trusts that are registered charities on September 14, 2018; and

(b) on September 14, 2018 in any other case.

S. 149.1(1), paragraph (*a*) of the definition "charitable organization" formerly read:

(*a*) all the resources of which are devoted to charitable activities carried on by the organization itself,

S. 149.1(1), paragraph (*a.1*) of the definition "charitable organization" was added by S.C. 2018, c. 27, s. 17(3), deemed to have come into force

(a) on January 1, 2008 in respect of organizations, corporations and trusts that are registered charities on September 14, 2018; and

(b) on September 14, 2018 in any other case.

S. 149.1(1), the portion of the definition "charitable organization" before paragraph (*a*) was replaced by S.C. 2013, c. 34, s. 308(2), deemed to have come into force on January 1, 2000, and formerly read:

"charitable organization"—"charitable organization" means an organization, whether or not incorporated,

S. 149.1(1), paragraphs (*c*) and (*d*) of the definition "charitable organization" were replaced by S.C. 2013, c. 34, s. 308(3), deemed to have come into force on January 1, 2000, except that, in respect of a charitable organization that has not been designated before 2000 as a private foundation or a public foundation under subsection 149.1(6.3) or under subsection 110(8.1) or (8.2) of the *Income Tax Act*, chapter 148 of the Revised Statutes of Canada, 1952, and that has not applied after February 15, 1984 for registration under paragraph 110(8)(*c*) of that Act or under the definition "registered charity" in subsection 248(1), subparagraphs (*c*)(ii) and (iii) of the definition "charitable organization" in subsection 149.1(1), apply after the earlier of the day, if any, on which the organization is designated after 1999 as a private foundation or a public foundation under subsection 149.1(6.3) and December 31, 2004.

S. 149.1(1), paragraphs (*c*) and (*d*) of the definition "charitable organization" formerly read:

(*c*) more than 50% of the directors, trustees, officers or like officials of which deal with each other and with each of the other directors, trustees, officers or officials at arm's length, and

(*d*) where it has been designated as a private foundation or public foundation pursuant to subsection (6.3) of this section or subsection 110(8.1) or (8.2) of the *Income Tax Act*, chapter 148 of the Revised Statutes of Canada, 1952, or has applied after February 15, 1984 for registration under paragraph 110(8)(*c*) of that Act or under the definition "registered charity" in subsection 248(1), not more than 50% of the capital of which has been contributed or otherwise paid into the organization by one person or members of a group of persons who do not deal with each other at arm's length and, for the purpose of this paragraph, a reference to any person or to members of a group does not include a reference to

Her Majesty in right of Canada or a province, a municipality, another registered charity that is not a private foundation, or any club, society or association described in paragraph 149(1)(*l*);

Related Sections: S. 149.1(6.2) Charitable activities; s. 248(1), "registered charity"; s. 256(5.1) Control in fact; s. 256(6) Saving provision — controlled corporations.

Forms: T1235 — Directors/Trustees Worksheet; T1240 — Registered Charity Adjustment Request; T2050 — Application to Register Charity Under the Income Tax Act; T2095 — Registered Charities Application for Re-Designation; T3010 — Registered Charity Information Return.

Guides: T4033 Completing the Registered Charity Information Return; T4063 Registering a Charity for Income Tax Purposes.

Cases: A charitable organization must devote all of its resources to its charitable activities, maintain direction and control over its resources and activities, and keep adequate records. The activities may be conducted through an agent, but the onus is on the charity to establish that its status should not be revoked. The taxpayer failed to meet these requirements, and the Minister's proposal to revoke its charitable registration was upheld. *Public Television Association of Quebec v. MNR*, 2015 DTC 5085 (FCA)

An association, whose primary purpose was to promote amateur sport, did not qualify as a registered Canadian amateur athletic association since it only operated on a provincial level. It was not a charitable organization because its objective did not constitute a charitable purpose or activity. *A.Y.S.A. Amateur Youth Soccer Association v. C.R.A.*, 2007 DTC 5527 (S.C.C.), affirming 2006 DTC 6314 (F.C.A.)

The taxpayer's charitable registration was revoked because, despite the objects stated in its constituting document, its true mission was that of advocating its strongly held convictions on important social and moral issues in a one-sided manner. It had exceeded the permitted 10% limit on resources devoted to political activities set out in s. 149.1(6.2). *Alliance for Life v. The Queen*, 99 DTC 5228 (F.C.A.)

Since the principal activities of an immigrant women's society, such as networking, referral services, liaising for accreditation of credentials, and soliciting job opportunities for immigrant women were not charitable, its application for charitable tax status was denied. The operation of the charitable registration scheme does not violate the Charter equality rights of the Society's intended beneficiaries. *Vancouver Society of Immigrant and Visible Minority Women v. M.N.R.*, 99 DTC 5034 (S.C.C.), affirming 96 DTC 6232 (F.C.A.)

A non-profit organization offering free access to the "information highway", including the Internet, was granted charity status on the basis that free exchange of information among members of society has long been recognized as a public good. *Vancouver Regional FreeNet Association v. M.N.R.*, 96 DTC 6440 (F.C.A.)

A community legal clinic was not a "charity" because it engaged in political activity *Scarborough Community Legal Services v. The Queen*, 85 DTC 5102 (F.C.A.)

Other Publications: CG-027 Public Policy Dialogue and Development Activities by Charities.

"charitable purposes" —"charitable purposes" includes the disbursement of funds to a qualified donee;

Editorial Note: The making of a gift, including the disbursement of funds to a qualified donee, is considered a charitable purpose. Previously, a gift was not for charitable purposes if it was reasonably considered that a purpose of the gift was to support the political activities of the qualified donee. Under recent changes, the restriction on "political activities" of a charity has been replaced with a restriction that provides that a charity is not constituted or organized for charitable purposes if any of its resources are used to support, or oppose, any political party or candidate for public office; see s. 149.1(6.1) and (6.2). At the same time, a relieving rule provides that charitable activities include "public policy dialogue and development activities carried on in furtherance of a charitable purpose" (s. 149.1(1) "charitable activities"). The changes are effective as of June 29, 2012 in respect of charities that were registered on September 14, 2018, and as of September 14, 2018 in any other case.

History: S. 149.1(1), the definition "charitable purposes" was replaced by S.C. 2018, c. 27, s. 17(2), deemed to have come into force

(*a*) on June 29, 2012 in respect of organizations, corporations and trusts that are registered charities on September 14, 2018 and in respect of associations that are registered Canadian amateur athletic associations on that date; and

(*b*) on September 14, 2018 in any other case.

S. 149.1(1), the definition "charitable purposes" formerly read:

"charitable purposes"—"charitable purposes" includes the disbursement of funds to a qualified donee, other than a gift the making of which is a political activity;

S. 149.1(1), the definition "charitable purposes" was replaced by S.C. 2012, c. 19, s. 7(1), in force on Royal Assent, June 29, 2012. S. 149.1(1), the definition "charitable purposes" formerly read:

"charitable purposes"—"charitable purposes" includes the disbursement of funds to qualified donees;

Other Publications: CG-027 Public Policy Dialogue and Development Activities by Charities.

"charity" —"charity" means a charitable organization or charitable foundation;

Related Sections: S. 149(1)(*l*) Non-profit organizations.

"designated gift" —"designated gift" means that portion of a gift of property made in a taxation year by a particular registered charity, to another registered charity with which it does not deal at arm's length, that is designated by the particular registered charity in its information return for the taxation year;

Editorial Note: This definition replaced the former term "specified gift" after the amendments to the disbursement quota rules. To qualify, the gift must be between charities that are non-arm's length and must be designated by the donor charity. Pursuant to s. 149.1(1.1), a designated gift cannot be used to satisfy the donor charity's disbursement quota or to create a disbursement excess. This ensures that the amount of a designated gift can be applied toward the disbursement quota requirements of one charity only.

History: S. 149.1(1), the definition "designated gift" was added by S.C. 2010, c. 25, s. 37(3), applicable to taxation years that end on or after March 4, 2010.

Related Sections: S. 149.1(1.1) Exclusions; s. 149.1(4.1) Revocation of registration of charities; s. 149.1(12)(*b*)(i) Exclusion from charity's income; s. 188.1(12) Penalties.

"disbursement quota" —"disbursement quota", for a taxation year of a registered charity, means the amount determined by the formula

$$A \times B \times 0.035/365$$

where

A is the number of days in the taxation year, and

B is

(*a*) the prescribed amount for the year, in respect of all or a portion of a property owned by the charity at any time in the 24 months immediately preceding the taxation year that was not used directly in charitable activities or administration, if that amount is greater than

(i) if the registered charity is a charitable organization, $100,000, and

(ii) in any other case, $25,000, and

(*b*) in any other case, nil;

Editorial Note: The disbursement quota generally establishes the amount that a charity must expend annually on charitable activities. The disbursement quota was substantially amended for fiscal years of a charity that end on or after March 4, 2010, by eliminating the requirement to expend at least 80% of the previous year's tax-receipted donations and by modifying the rules relating to the requirement to disburse certain accumulations of capital. These amendments will allow most charities greater operational flexibility. In general terms, the rule now provides that the required disbursement is 3.5% of the average value of a charity's property (not otherwise utilized for charitable activities or administration) during the 24 months preceding the tax year, and will apply only if such property exceeds the valuation threshold of $100,000 for charitable organizations or $25,000 for charitable foundations. Failure to meet the disbursement quota can result in revocation of charitable status. It is important to note that charities must always use their capital for charitable purposes, even where assets are not required to be disbursed under the disbursement quota rules.

History: S. 149.1(1), the definition "disbursement quota" was replaced by S.C. 2010, c. 25, s. 37(2), applicable to taxation years that end on or after March 4, 2010. S. 149.1(1), the definition "disbursement quota" formerly read:

"disbursement quota"—"disbursement quota", for a taxation year of a registered charity, means the amount determined by the formula

$$A + A.1 + B + B.1$$

where

A is 80% of the total of all amounts each of which is the eligible amount of a gift for which the charity issued a receipt described in subsection 110.1(2) or 118.1(2) in its immediately preceding taxation year, other than a gift that is

(*a*) an enduring property, or

(*b*) received from another registered charity,

A.1 is the amount, if any, by which

(*a*) the sum of

(i) 80% of the total of all amounts, each of which is the amount of an enduring property of the charity (other than an enduring property described in subparagraph (ii), an enduring property that was received by the charity as a specified gift, or a bequest or an inheritance received by the charity in a taxation year that included any time before 1994) to the extent that it is expended in the year, and

(ii) the total of all amounts, each of which is the fair market value, when transferred, of an enduring property (other than an enduring property that was received by the charity as a specified gift) transferred by the charity in the taxation year by way of gift to a qualified donee

exceeds

(b) the amount, if any, claimed by the charity, that may not exceed the lesser of

(i) 3.5% of the amount determined for D, and

(ii) the capital gains pool of the charity for the taxation year,

B is

(a) in the case of a private foundation, the total of all amounts each of which is an amount received by it in its immediately preceding taxation year from a registered charity, other than an amount that is a specified gift or an enduring property, or

(b) in the case of a charitable organization or a public foundation, 80% of the total of all amounts each of which is an amount received by it in its immediately preceding taxation year from a registered charity, other than an amount that is a specified gift or an enduring property, and

B.1 is the amount determined by the formula

$$C \times 0.035\ [D - (E + F)]/365$$

where

C is the number of days in the taxation year,

D is

(a) the prescribed amount for the year, in respect of all or a portion of a property (other than a prescribed property) owned by the charity at any time in the 24 months immediately preceding the taxation year that was not used directly in charitable activities or administration, if that amount is greater than $25,000, and

(b) in any other case, nil,

E is the total of the amount determined for subparagraph (a)(ii) of the description of A.1, and $^5/_4$ of the total of the amounts determined for A and subparagraph (a)(i) of the description of A.1, for the year in respect of the charity, and

F is the amount equal to

(a) in the case of a private foundation, the amount determined for B for the year in respect of the charity in accordance with paragraph (a) of the description of B, or

(b) in the case of a charitable organization or a public foundation, $^5/_4$ of the amount determined for B for the year in respect of the charity in accordance with paragraph (b) of the description of B;

Related Regulations: 3701.

Related Sections: S. 110.1(2) Proof of gift; s. 118.1(2) Proof of gift; s. 149.1(1.2) Authority of Minister; s. 149.1(2)(b) Requirement of charitable organization; s. 149.1(3)(b) Requirement of public foundation; s. 149.1(4)(b) Requirement of private foundation; s. 149.1(5) Reduction; s. 149.1(8), "accumulation of property"; s. 149.1(20) and (21) Treatment of disbursement excess; s. 188.1(11) Delay of expenditure.

Forms: T2094 — Registered Charities Application to Reduce Disbursement Quota.

"divestment obligation percentage"—"divestment obligation percentage" of a private foundation for a particular taxation year, in respect of a class of shares of the capital stock of a corporation, is the percentage, if any, that is the lesser of

(a) the excess, if any, at the end of the taxation year, of the percentage of issued and outstanding shares of that class that are held by the private foundation over the exempt shares percentage of the private foundation, and

(b) the percentage determined by the formula

$$A + B - C$$

where

A is the percentage determined under this paragraph in respect of the private foundation in respect of the class for the preceding taxation year,

B is the total of all percentages, each of which is the portion of a net increase in the excess corporate holdings percentage of the private foundation in respect of the class for the particular taxation year or for a preceding taxation year that is allocated to the particular taxation year in accordance with subsection 149.2(5), and

C is the total of all percentages, each of which is the portion of a net decrease in the excess corporate holdings percentage of the private foundation in respect of the class for the particular taxation year or for a preceding taxation year that is allocated to the particular taxation year in accordance with subsection 149.2(7);

Editorial Note: Section 149.2 provides for an "excess corporate holdings" regime that limits the percentage of shares of each class of a corporation (both publicly listed and unlisted) that a private foundation may hold. The intention of these rules is generally to limit the opportunity for an individual to donate shares of certain companies to a private foundation and effectively maintain control over such shares through the donor's relationship with the foundation. A private foundation's "divestment obligation percentage" is relevant in determining its requirement to divest certain shares. Generally, where a private foundation and other relevant persons own more than 20% of the issued and outstanding shares of any class, the foundation must divest the excess shares in accordance with the specific rules set out in s. 149.2. Certain shares, referred to as "exempt shares", are not subject to the divestiture obligation. Moreover, holdings that constitute an "insignificant interest" (generally 2% or less of the issued and outstanding shares of any class of the capital stock of a corporation — even where the 20% threshold is otherwise met) are not subject to the divestment requirements (see s. 149.2(1)(b)). Failure to divest in accordance with these rules may lead to the application of the penalty provisions found in s. 188.1(3.1) or to the revocation of the foundation's charitable status.

History: S. 149.1(1), the definition "divestment obligation percentage" was replaced by S.C. 2009, c. 2, s. 55(2), applicable after March 18, 2007. S. 149.1(1), the definition "divestment obligation percentage" formerly read:

"divestment obligation percentage"—"divestment obligation percentage" of a private foundation for a particular taxation year, in respect of a class of shares of the capital stock of a corporation, is the percentage, if any, greater than 0%, determined by the formula

$$A + B - C$$

where

A is the percentage determined under this definition in respect of the private foundation in respect of the class for the preceding taxation year,

B is the total of all percentages, each of which is the portion of a net increase in the excess corporate holdings percentage of the private foundation in respect of the class for the particular taxation year or for a preceding taxation year that is allocated to the particular taxation year in accordance with subsection 149.2(5), and

C is the total of all percentages, each of which is the portion of a net decrease in the excess corporate holdings percentage of the private foundation in respect of the class for the particular taxation year or for a preceding taxation year that is allocated to the particular taxation year in accordance with subsection 149.2(7);

Related Sections: S. 149.1(1), "excess corporate holdings percentage", "exempt shares", "exempt shares percentage", "material transaction", "relevant person", "substituted shares", "total corporate holdings percentage"; s. 149.1(4) Revocation of registration of private foundation; 149.2 Material and insignificant interests; s. 188.1(3.1) Penalty for excess corporate holdings; 188.1(3.2) Avoidance of divestiture; 188.1(3.3) Where subsection (3.5) applies; 188.1(3.4) Rules applicable; 188.1(3.5) Avoidance of divestiture.

"enduring property" — (Repealed by S.C. 2010, c. 25, s. 37(1).)

History: S. 149.1(1), the definition "enduring property" was repealed by S.C. 2010, c. 25, s. 37(1), applicable to taxation years that end on or after March 4, 2010. S. 149.1(1), the definition "enduring property" formerly read:

"enduring property"—"enduring property" means property of a registered charity that is

(a) a gift received by the charity by way of bequest or inheritance, including a gift deemed by subsection 118.1(5.2) or (5.3),

(b) if the registered charity is a charitable organization, a gift from another registered charity (other than a gift described by paragraph (d) or received from another charity in respect of which more than 50% of the members of the board of directors or trustees do not deal at arm's length with each member of the board of directors or trustees of the charitable organization) that is subject to a trust or direction to the effect that the property given, or property substituted for the gift,

(i) is to be held by the charitable organization for a period of not more than five years from the date that the gift was received by the charitable organization, and

(ii) is to be expended in its entirety over the period referred to in the trust or direction

(A) to acquire a tangible capital property of the charitable organization to be used directly in charitable activities or administration,

(B) in the course of a program of charitable activities of the charitable organization that could not reasonably be completed before the end of the first taxation year of the charitable organization ending after the taxation year in which the gift was received, or

(C) any combination of the uses described in clauses (A) and (B),

(*c*) a gift received by the registered charity (referred to in this definition as the "original recipient charity"), other than a gift received from another registered charity, that is subject to a trust or direction to the effect that the property given, or property substituted for the gift, is to be held by the original recipient charity or by another registered charity (referred to in this definition as a "transferee") for a period of not less than 10 years from the date that the gift was received by the original recipient charity, except that the trust or direction may allow the original recipient charity or the transferee to expend the property before the end of that period to the extent of the amount determined for a taxation year (for the charity or the transferee, as the case may be) by B.1 in the formula in the definition "disbursement quota", or

(*d*) a gift received by the registered charity as a transferee from an original recipient charity or another transferee of a property that was, before that gift was so received, an enduring property of the original recipient charity or of the other transferee because of paragraph (*a*) or (*c*) or this paragraph, or property substituted for the gift, if, in the case of a property that was an enduring property of an original recipient charity because of paragraph (*c*), the gift is subject to the same terms and conditions under the trust or direction as applied to the original recipient charity;

S. 149.1(1), the definition "enduring property", paragraph (*d*), as it read above, immediately before it was repealed by S.C. 2010, c. 25, s. 37(1), was replaced by S.C. 2013, c. 34, s. 308(4), applicable to taxation years that begin after March 22, 2004 but that end before March 4, 2010. For greater certainty, paragraph (*d*) of the definition "enduring property" in subsection 149.1(1) is deemed to have been repealed in respect of taxation years that end on or after March 4, 2010.

S. 149.1(1), the definition "enduring property", paragraph (*d*) formerly read:

(*d*) a gift received by the registered charity as a transferee from an original recipient charity or another transferee of a property that was, before that gift was so received, an enduring property of the original recipient charity or of the other transferee because of paragraph (*a*) or (*b*) or this paragraph, or property substituted for the gift, if, in the case of a property that was an enduring property of an original recipient charity because of paragraph (*b*), the gift is subject to the same terms and conditions under the trust or direction as applied to the gift to the original recipient charity;

"entrusted shares percentage" — (Repealed by S.C. 2009, c. 2, s. 55(1).)

History: S. 149.1(1), the definition "entrusted shares percentage" was repealed by S.C. 2009, c. 2, s. 55(1), applicable after March 18, 2007. S. 149.1(1), the definition "entrusted shares percentage" formerly read:

"entrusted shares percentage"—"entrusted shares percentage" of a private foundation, in respect of a class of shares of the capital stock of a corporation, at any particular time means the percentage of the issued and outstanding shares of that class that are held at the particular time by the private foundation that are shares that were acquired by the private foundation by way of a gift that was subject to a trust or direction that the shares are to be held by the private foundation for a period ending not earlier than the particular time, if the gift was made

(*a*) before March 19, 2007,

(*b*) on or after March 19, 2007 and before March 19, 2012

(i) under the terms of a will that was executed by a taxpayer before March 19, 2007 and not amended, by codicil or otherwise, on or after March 19, 2007, and

(ii) in circumstances where no other will of the taxpayer was executed or amended on or after March 19, 2007, or

(*c*) on or after March 19, 2007, under the terms of a testamentary or *inter vivos* trust created before March 19, 2007, and not amended on or after March 19, 2007;

"equity percentage" —"equity percentage" of a person in a corporation has, subject to subsection 149.2(2.1), the same meaning as defined in subsection 95(4);

History: S. 149.1(1), the definition "equity percentage" was added by S.C. 2009, c. 2, s. 55(4), applicable after March 18, 2007.

"excess corporate holdings percentage" —"excess corporate holdings percentage" of a private foundation, in respect of a class of shares of the capital stock of a corporation, at any time means

(*a*) if the private foundation is not, at that time, a registered charity, 0%,

(*b*) if the private foundation holds, at that time, an insignificant interest in respect of the class, 0%, and

(*c*) in any other case, the number of percentage points, if any, by which the total corporate holdings percentage of the private foundation in respect of the class, at that time, exceeds the greater of 20% and the exempt shares percentage, at that time, of the private foundation in respect of the class;

Editorial Note: A private foundation's "excess corporate holdings percentage" is relevant in determining its "divestment obligation percentage", which is based on the percentage of shares of a class held by the foundation and all "relevant persons" in respect of the foundation that hold a "material interest" in the corporation. A "material interest" in a class of shares is defined in s. 149.2(1) to mean either ownership of more than 0.5% of all issued and outstanding shares of the class or of shares of the class having a fair market value in excess of $100,000. See also the editorial note for s. 149.1(1) "divestment obligation percentage".

History: S. 149.1(1), paragraph (*c*) of the definition "excess corporate holdings percentage" was replaced by S.C. 2009, c. 2, s. 55(3), applicable after March 18, 2007. S. 149.1(1), paragraph (*c*) of the definition "excess corporate holdings percentage" formerly read:

(c) in any other case, the number of percentage points, if any, by which the total corporate holdings percentage of the private foundation in respect of the class, at that time, exceeds the greater of 20% and the entrusted shares percentage, at that time, of the private foundation in respect of the class;

Related Sections: S. 149.1(1), "exempt shares percentage", "divestment obligation percentage", "total corporate holdings percentage"; s. 149.2(1) Material and insignificant interests; s. 149.2(8) Transitional rule.

Forms: T2081 — Excess Corporate Holdings Worksheet for Private Foundations.

Guides: T2082 Excess Corporate Holdings Regime for Private Foundations.

"exempt shares" —"exempt shares" held by a private foundation at any particular time means shares, of a class of the capital stock of a corporation,

(*a*) that were acquired by the private foundation by way of a gift that was subject to a trust or direction that the shares are to be held by the private foundation for a period ending not earlier than the particular time, if the gift was made

(i) before March 19, 2007,

(ii) on or after March 19, 2007 and before March 19, 2012

(A) under the terms of a will that was executed by a taxpayer before March 19, 2007 and not amended, by codicil or otherwise, on or after March 19, 2007, and

(B) in circumstances where no other will of the taxpayer was executed or amended on or after March 19, 2007, or

(iii) on or after March 19, 2007, under the terms of a trust created before March 19, 2007, and not amended on or after March 19, 2007,

(*b*) that were last acquired by the private foundation before March 19, 2007, other than shares that, at the particular time,

(i) are described in paragraph (*a*),

(ii) are listed on a designated stock exchange, or

(iii) are shares of the capital stock of a particular corporation, which particular corporation has an equity percentage greater than 0% in a public corporation, a class of the shares of the capital stock of which is listed on a designated stock exchange, if

(A) a corporation (in this subparagraph referred to as a "controlled corporation" and which may, for greater certainty, be the particular corporation)

(I) owns one or more shares of a class of the capital stock of the public corporation, and

(II) is controlled, directly or indirectly in any manner whatever, by one or more relevant persons in respect of the private foundation, or by the private foundation alone or together with one or more such relevant persons,

(B) the private foundation, if it held directly the shares described in subclause (A)(I), would have an excess corporate holdings percentage (determined without reference to subsection 149.2(8)) in respect of that class of shares that is greater than 0%, and

(C) the private foundation, alone or together with all controlled corporations, holds more than an insignificant interest in respect of the class of shares described in subclause (A)(I), or

(*c*) that are substituted shares held by the private foundation;

Editorial Note: Where a private foundation's "total corporate holdings percentage" of a class of share exceeds 20%, the foundation will have an "excess corporate holdings percentage" equal to that excess and will have a corresponding "divestment obligation percentage" for purposes of determining its requirement to divest shares under s. 149.2. However, shares that qualify as "exempt shares" are excluded from this calculation. "Exempt shares" generally include: (i) shares that were acquired by the foundation by way of a gift that was subject to a trust or direction that the shares are to be held for a period not ending before the particular time, if the gift was made prior to March 19, 2007 or under the terms of a will signed or trust settled before March 19, 2007, provided the document was not amended on or after that date (note that in the case of shares donated by a will, the gift must have been made before March 19, 2012 and the testator must not have executed or amended any other will on or after March 19, 2007); (ii) shares of a corporation that are not listed on a designated stock exchange and that were last acquired by the foundation before March 19, 2007 and that satisfy certain other conditions; and (iii) "substituted shares" acquired by the private foundation in exchange for exempt shares pursuant to either s. 51, 86, 87 or 85.1(1). See also the editorial notes for s. 149.1(1), "divestment obligation percentage" and "excess corporate holdings percentage".

History: S. 149.1(1), subparagraph (*a*)(iii) of the definition "exempt shares" was replaced by S.C. 2014, c. 39, s. 54(1), applicable to the 2016 and subsequent taxation years, and formerly read:

(iii) on or after March 19, 2007, under the terms of a testamentary or *inter vivos* trust created before March 19, 2007, and not amended on or after March 19, 2007,

S. 149.1(1), the definition "exempt shares" was added by S.C. 2009, c. 2, s. 55(4), applicable after March 18, 2007.

"exempt shares percentage"—"exempt shares percentage" of a private foundation at any time, in respect of a class of shares of the capital stock of a corporation, is the total of all amounts, each of which is the percentage of the issued and outstanding shares of that class that are exempt shares held by the private foundation at that time;

Editorial Note: See the editorial note for s. 149.1(1), "exempt shares".

History: S. 149.1(1), the definition "exempt shares percentage" was added by S.C. 2009, c. 2, s. 55(4), applicable after March 18, 2007.

Related Sections: S. 149.1(1), "exempt shares percentage", "substituted shares"; s. 149.2(1) Material and insignificant interests; s. 149.2(2.1) Ownership; s. 149.2(10) Shares held through a trust on March 18, 2007; s. 149.2(11) Discretionary trusts.

S. 149.1(1), "divestment obligation percentage", "exempt shares".

"ineligible individual"—"ineligible individual", at any time, means an individual who has been

(*a*) convicted of a relevant criminal offence unless it is a conviction for which

(i) a pardon has been granted and the pardon has not been revoked or ceased to have effect, or

(ii) a record suspension has been ordered under the *Criminal Records Act* and the record suspension has not been revoked or ceased to have effect,

(*b*) convicted of a relevant offence in the five-year period preceding that time,

(*c*) a director, trustee, officer or like official of a registered charity or a registered Canadian amateur athletic association during a period in which the charity or association engaged in conduct that can reasonably be considered to have constituted a serious breach of the requirements for registration under this Act and for which the registration of the charity or association was revoked in the five-year period preceding that time,

(*d*) an individual who controlled or managed, directly or indirectly, in any manner whatever, a registered charity or a registered Canadian amateur athletic association during a period in which the charity or association engaged in conduct that can reasonably be considered to have constituted a serious breach of the requirements for registration under this Act and for which its registration was revoked in the five-year period preceding that time, or

(*e*) a promoter in respect of a tax shelter that involved a registered charity or a registered Canadian amateur athletic association, the registration of which was revoked in the five-year period preceding that time for reasons that included or were related to participation in the tax shelter;

Editorial Note: Charities and registered Canadian amateur athletic associations ("RCAAAs") may incur significant sanctions, including deregistration, or may be refused registration, if an "ineligible individual" (i.e., a person with a history of certain enumerated types of misconduct) is a director, trustee, officer, or like official of the charity or controls or manages the charity directly or indirectly in any manner whatever. The steps to be undertaken to ensure a charity does not appoint an ineligible individual are unclear; however, the CRA has advised that the charity will not be expected to undertake background checks in order to demonstrate compliance with the provisions. The CRA can also refuse registration of a charity or RCAAA if the application for registration is made by an ineligible individual. See also s. 149.1(4.1) and 188.2.

History: S. 149.1(1), paragraph (*a*) of the definition "ineligible individual" was replaced by S.C. 2011, c. 24, s. 103, in force on March 13, 2012 [on R.A. of Bill C-10, S.C. 2012, c. 1 (*Safe Streets and Communities Act*)]. S. 149.1(1), paragraph (*a*) of the definition "ineligible individual" formerly read:

(*a*) convicted of a relevant criminal offence unless it is a conviction for which a pardon has been granted or issued and the pardon has not been revoked or ceased to have effect,

S. 149.1(1), the definition "ineligible individual" was added by S.C. 2011, c. 24, s. 52(2), in force January 1, 2012.

Related Sections: S. 149.1(4.1)(*e*) Revocation of charity's registration; s. 149.1(4.2)(*c*) Revocation of registered amateur athletic association's registration; s. 149.1(25) Refusal to register charity or registered amateur athletic association; s. 188.1 Penalties; s. 188.2 Suspension.

Other Publications: CG-024 Ineligible Individuals.

"material transaction"—"material transaction" of a private foundation, in respect of a class of shares of the capital stock of a corporation, means a transaction or a series of transactions or events in shares of the class, in respect of which the total fair market value of the shares of the class that are acquired or disposed of by the private foundation or any relevant person in respect of the private foundation as part of the transaction or series (determined at the time of the transaction, or at the end of the series, as the case may be) exceeds the lesser of (*a*) $100,000, and

(*b*) 0.5% of the total fair market value of all of the issued and outstanding shares of the class;

Editorial Note: A private foundation is required to report all material transactions in its information return. Penalties may be imposed under s. 188.1(3.1) for failure to do so. See also the editorial notes for s. 149.1(1), "divestment obligation percentage" and "excess corporate holdings percentage".

Related Sections: S. 149.2(2) Anti-avoidance.

"non-qualified investment" — "non-qualified investment" of a private foundation means

(*a*) a debt (other than a pledge or undertaking to make a gift) owing to the foundation by

(i) a person (other than an excluded corporation)

(A) who is a member, shareholder, trustee, settlor, officer, official or director of the foundation,

(B) who has, or is a member of a group of persons who do not deal with each other at arm's length who have, contributed more than 50% of the capital of the foundation, or

(C) who does not deal at arm's length with any person described in clause (A) or (B), or

(ii) a corporation (other than an excluded corporation) controlled by the foundation, by any person or group of persons referred to in subparagraph (i), by the foundation and any other private foundation with which it does not deal at arm's length or by any combination thereof,

(*b*) a share of a class of the capital stock of a corporation (other than an excluded corporation) referred to in paragraph (*a*) held by the foundation (other than a share listed on a designated stock exchange or a share that would be a qualifying share within the meaning assigned by subsection 192(6) if that subsection were read without reference to the expression "issued after May 22, 1985 and before 1987"), and

(*c*) a right held by the foundation to acquire a share referred to in paragraph (*b*),

and, for the purpose of this definition, an "excluded corporation" is

(*d*) a limited-dividend housing company to which paragraph 149(1)(*n*) applies,

(*e*) a corporation all of the property of which is used by a registered charity in its administration or in carrying on its charitable activities, or

(*f*) a corporation all of the issued shares of which are held by the foundation;

Editorial Note: Section 189 imposes a tax liability on certain taxpayers who have borrowed money from a private foundation or in whom the private foundation holds certain shares or rights to acquire such shares if such debt, rights or shares are "non-qualified investments". For more information, see CRA charities guidance document CG-006, "Non-Qualified Investment — Tax Liability".

Related Sections: S. 189 Tax regarding non-qualified investments; s. 262 Designated stock exchanges.

"original corporate holdings percentage" — "original corporate holdings percentage" of a private foundation, in respect of a class of shares of the capital stock of a corporation, means the total corporate holdings percentage of the private foundation, in respect of that class, held on March 18, 2007;

Editorial Note: The definition of "original corporate holdings percentage" is relevant to determining a private foundation's divestment obligation. Subsection 149.2(8) provides a transitional rule that applies where a private foundation has an original corporate holdings percentage (that is, the foundation's total corporate holdings percentage on March 18, 2007) in respect of a class of shares in excess of 20%. This provision allows the foundation to divest its excess holdings in respect of that class of shares over an extended time period of up to 20 years.

"political activity"(Repealed by S.C. 2018, c. 27, s. 17(1).)

History: S. 149.1(1), the definition "political activity" was repealed by S.C. 2018, c. 27, s. 17(1), deemed to have come into force

(a) on June 29, 2012 in respect of organizations, corporations and trusts that are registered charities on September 14, 2018 and in respect of associations that are registered Canadian amateur athletic associations on that date; and

(b) on September 14, 2018 in any other case.

S. 149.1(1), the definition "political activity" formerly read:

"political activity" — "political activity" includes the making of a gift to a qualified donee if it can reasonably be considered that a purpose of the gift is to support the political activities of the qualified donee;

S. 149.1(1), the definition "political activity" was added by S.C. 2012, c. 19, s. 7(3), in force on Royal Assent, June 29, 2012.

"private foundation" — "private foundation" means a charitable foundation that is not a public foundation;

Editorial Note: Where a charitable foundation is not a public foundation, by default it is a private foundation. See the editorial note to s. 149.1(1), "charitable foundation".

Related Sections: S. 149.1(6.3) Designation as public foundation, etc.; s. 149.1(13) Designation of private foundation as public.

Canadian Tax Foundation: Radu, *Public/Private Foundations — Issues and Planning Opportunities*, 2009 Canadian Tax Journal 1:119–142.

"promoter" — "promoter" has the meaning assigned by section 237.1;

History: S. 149.1(1), the definition "promoter" was added by S.C. 2011, c. 24, s. 52(2), in force January 1, 2012.

Related Sections: S. 149.1(1), "ineligible individual".

"public foundation" — "public foundation", at a particular time, means a charitable foundation

(*a*) more than 50% of the directors, trustees, officers or like officials of which deal at arm's length with each other and with

(i) each of the other directors, trustees, officers and like officials of the foundation,

(ii) each person described by subparagraph (*b*)(i) or (ii), and

(iii) each member of a group of persons (other than Her Majesty in right of Canada or of a province, a municipality, another registered charity that is not a private foundation, and any club, society or association described in paragraph 149(1)(*l*)) who do not deal with each other at arm's length, if the group would, if it were a person, be a person described by subparagraph (*b*)(i), and

(*b*) that is not, at the particular time, and would not at the particular time be, if the foundation were a corporation, controlled directly or indirectly in any manner whatever

(i) by a person (other than Her Majesty in right of Canada or of a province, a municipality, another registered charity that is not a private foundation, and any club, society or association described in paragraph 149(1)(*l*)),

(A) who immediately after the particular time, has contributed to the foundation amounts that are, in total, greater than 50% of the capital of the foundation immediately after the particular time, and

(B) who immediately after the person's last contribution at or before the particular time, had contributed to the foundation amounts that were, in total, greater than 50% of the capital of the foundation immediately after the making of that last contribution, or

(ii) by a person, or by a group of persons that do not deal at arm's length with each other, if the person or any member of the group does not deal at arm's length with a person described in subparagraph (i);

Editorial Note: A public foundation is, in general terms, a charitable foundation: (i) in which more than 50% of the directors, trustees, officers, and similar officials deal with each other and with certain other persons and groups of persons at arm's length; and (ii) which is not controlled, directly or indirectly in any manner whatever, by a person who has contributed more than 50% of the capital to the charity or by a person or non-arm's length group of persons who do not deal at arm's length with a person who has contributed more than 50% of the capital to the charity. Also see the editorial note to s. 149.1, "charitable foundation". Typically a public foundation will provide funds to charitable organizations, but public foundations can also undertake charitable activities.

History: S. 149.1(1), the definition "public foundation" was replaced by S.C. 2013, c. 34, s. 308(1), deemed to have come into force on January 1, 2000, except that, in respect of a foundation that has not been designated before 2000 as a private foundation or a charitable organization under subsection 149.1(6.3) or under subsection 110(8.1) or (8.2) of the *Income Tax Act*, chapter 148 of the Revised Statutes of Canada, 1952, and that has not applied after February 15, 1984 for registration under paragraph 110(8)(*c*) or under the definition "registered charity" in subsection 248(1), subparagraph (*a*)(iii) and paragraph (*b*) of the definition "public foundation" in subsection 149.1(1) are, in their application before the earlier of the day, if any, on which the foundation is designated after 1999 as a private foundation or a charitable organization under subsection 149.1(6.3) and January 1, 2005, to be read

"(*a*) without reference to "(other than Her Majesty in right of Canada or of a province, a municipality, another registered charity that is not a private foundation, and any club, society or association described in paragraph 149(1)(*l*)"; and

(*b*) as if the references to "50%" in paragraph (*b*) of that definition were references to '75%' ".

S. 149.1(1), the definition "public foundation" formerly read:

"*public foundation*"—"public foundation" means a charitable foundation of which,

(*a*) where the foundation has been registered after February 15, 1984 or designated as a charitable organization or private foundation pursuant to subsection (6.3) or to subsection 110(8.1) or (8.2) of the *Income Tax Act*, chapter 148 of the Revised Statutes of Canada, 1952,

(i) more than 50% of the directors, trustees, officers or like officials deal with each other and with each of the other directors, trustees, officers or officials at arm's length, and

(ii) not more than 50% of the capital contributed or otherwise paid in to the foundation has been so contributed or otherwise paid in by one person or members of a group of such persons who do not deal with each other at arm's length, or

(*b*) in any other case,

(i) more than 50% of the directors or trustees deal with each other and with each of the other directors or trustees at arm's length, and

(ii) not more than 75% of the capital contributed or otherwise paid in to the foundation has been so contributed or otherwise paid in by one person or by a group of persons who do not deal with each other at arm's length

and, for the purpose of subparagraph (*a*)(ii), a reference to any person or to members of a group does not include a reference to Her Majesty in right of Canada or a province, a municipality, another registered charity that is not a private foundation, or any club, society or association described in paragraph 149(1)(*l*);

Related Sections: S. 149.1(6.3) Designation as public foundation, etc; s. 149.1(13) Designation of private foundation as public.

Canadian Tax Foundation: Radu, *Public/Private Foundations — Issues and Planning Opportunities*, 2009 Canadian Tax Journal 1:119–142.

Cases: The definition of "public foundation" implies that it must have more than one trustee (or director, officer, or like official). The taxpayer was a private foundation since it had only one trustee. *The Sheldon Inwentash and Lynn Factor Charitable Foundation v. The Queen*, 2012 DTC 5090 (F.C.A.)

"qualified donee" —"qualified donee", at any time, means a person that is

(*a*) registered by the Minister and that is

(i) a housing corporation resident in Canada and exempt from tax under this Part because of paragraph 149(1)(*i*) that has applied for registration,

(ii) a municipality in Canada,

(iii) a municipal or public body performing a function of government in Canada that has applied for registration,

(iv) a university outside Canada, the student body of which ordinarily includes students from Canada, that has applied for registration, or

(v) a foreign charity that has applied to the Minister for registration under subsection (26),

(*b*) a registered charity,

Amendment not yet in force

Budget Implementation Act, 2019, No. 1 [S.C. 2019, c. 29]

S. 149.1(1), paragraph (*b*.1) of the definition of "qualified donee" was added by S.C. 2019, c. 29, s. 31(1), and will read as follows:

(*b*.1) a registered journalism organization,

Applicable: In force January 1, 2020.

(*c*) a registered Canadian amateur athletic association, or

(*d*) Her Majesty in right of Canada or a province, the United Nations or an agency of the United Nations;

Editorial Note: The primary benefit of "qualified donee" status, which includes not only registered charities but other enumerated categories of entities and associations, is the ability to issue charitable receipts. Individual taxpayers who make a gift to a qualified donee are entitled to claim a tax credit under s. 118.1, subject to certain limitations, and donations made by corporate taxpayers are deductible under s. 110.1, subject to certain limitations. Largely as a result of this ability to issue charitable receipts, most qualified donees are subject to strict governance and operational restrictions and must comply with numerous reporting and documentary requirements under the Act. Failure to do so may result in penalties or deregistration. See the CRA's *Charities Connection Newsletter* No. 11, "Budget 2011 — Changes for Qualified Donees Could Affect Your Charity".

History: S. 149.1(1), subparagraph (*a*)(iv) of the definition "qualified donee" was replaced by S.C. 2018, c. 12, s. 25(1), deemed to have come into force on February 27, 2018, except that

(a) if a university has applied for registration prior to February 27, 2018 and is registered by the Minister on or after that day, [the replacement to subparagraph (*a*)(iv)] applies in respect of the university as of the day it applied for registration; and

(b) any university named in Schedule VIII to the *Income Tax Regulations* at the end of February 26, 2018 is deemed to have applied for registration.

S. 149.1(1), subparagraph (*a*)(iv) of the definition "qualified donee" formerly read:

(iv) a university outside Canada that is prescribed to be a university the student body of which ordinarily includes students from Canada, or

S. 149.1(1), subparagraph (*a*)(v) of the definition "qualified donee" was replaced by S.C. 2015, c. 36, s. 18(1), applicable to applications made on or after the day on which this amendment receives royal assent, June 23, 2015, and formerly read:

(v) a foreign organization that has applied to the Minister for registration under subsection (26),

S. 149.1(1), subparagraph (*a*)(v) of the definition "qualified donee" was replaced by S.C. 2012, c. 19, s. 7(2), and comes into force on January 1, 2013, except that subparagraph (*a*)(v) of the definition "qualified donee" in subsection 149.1(1) does not apply in respect of registrations of charitable organizations outside Canada made before January 1, 2013. S. 149.1(1), subparagraph (*a*)(v) of the definition "qualified donee" formerly read:

(v) a charitable organization outside Canada to which Her Majesty in right of Canada has made a gift in the 36-month period that begins 24 months before that time,

S. 149.1(1), the definition "qualified donee" was replaced by S.C. 2011, c. 24, s. 52(1), in force January 1, 2012. S. 149.1(1), the definition "qualified donee" formerly read:

"*qualified donee*"—"qualified donee" means a donee described in any of paragraphs 110.1(1)(*a*) and (*b*) and the definitions "total charitable gifts" and "total Crown gifts" in subsection 118.1(1);

Related Regulations: 3503, Schedule VIII.

Related Sections: 149.1(26) Foreign charities; S. 110.1(1)(*a*) Charitable gifts; s. 118.1(1), "total charitable gifts".

Forms: T1236 — Qualified Donees Worksheet.

"qualified investment" — (Repealed by 1984, c. 45, s. 57(5).)

> **Amendment not yet in force**
>
> **Budget Implementation Act, 2019, No. 1 [S.C. 2019, c. 29]**
>
> **S. 149.1(1), the definition of "qualifying journalism organization" was added by S.C. 2019, c. 29, s. 31(2), and will read as follows:**
>
> ***qualifying journalism organization*** —"qualifying journalism organization" means a corporation or trust that meets the following conditions:
>
> (*a*) it is a qualified Canadian journalism organization,
>
> (*b*) it is constituted and operated for purposes exclusively related to journalism,
>
> (*c*) any business activities it carries on are related to its purposes,
>
> (*d*) it has trustees or a board of directors, each of whom deals at arm's length with each other,
>
> (*e*) it is not controlled, directly or indirectly in any manner whatever, by a person or by a group of persons that do not deal with each other at arm's length,
>
> (*f*) it may not, in a taxation year, receive gifts from any one source that represent more than 20% of its total revenues (including donations) for the taxation year, other than a gift
>
> (i) made by way of bequest,
>
> (ii) made within 12 months after the time the organization is first registered, or
>
> (iii) approved, on a case-by-case basis, by the Minister, and
>
> (*g*) no part of its income is payable to, or otherwise available for the personal benefit of, any proprietor, member, shareholder, director, trustee, settlor or like individual;
>
> **Applicable:** In force January 1, 2020.

"related business" —"related business", in relation to a charity or Canadian amateur athletic association, includes a business that is unrelated to the purposes of the charity or association if substantially all persons employed by the charity or association in the carrying on of that business are not remunerated for that employment;

Editorial Note: Generally, charitable organizations, public foundations, and registered Canadian amateur athletic associations may carry on businesses linked to their charitable purposes, provided such businesses are subordinate to such purposes. A private foundation may not carry on any business, whether or not the business is related to the foundation's charitable purpose. See also s. 149.1(6) and the CRA Policy Statement CPS-019, "What Is a Related Business?"

History: S. 149.1(1), the definition "related business" was replaced by S.C. 2011, c. 24, s. 52(1), in force January 1, 2012. S. 149.1(1), the definition "related business" formerly read:

"related business"—"related business", in relation to a charity, includes a business that is unrelated to the objects of the charity if substantially all persons employed by the charity in the carrying on of that business are not remunerated for that employment;

Related Sections: S. 149.1(2) Revocation of registration of charitable organization; s. 149.1(3) Revocation of registration of public foundation; s. 149.1(4) Revocation of registration of private foundation; s. 149.1(4.2) Revocation of registration of registered Canadian amateur athletic association; s. 149.1(6) Devoting resources to charitable activity; s. 149.1(6.01) Devoting resources to purpose and function.

"relevant criminal offence" —"relevant criminal offence" means a criminal offence under the laws of Canada, and an offence that would be a criminal offence if it were committed in Canada, that

(*a*) relates to financial dishonesty, including tax evasion, theft and fraud, or

(*b*) in respect of a charity or Canadian amateur athletic association, is relevant to the operation of the charity or association;

Editorial Note: See notes to 149.1(1), "ineligible individual".

History: S. 149.1(1), the definition "relevant criminal offence" was added by S.C. 2011, c. 24, s. 52(2), in force January 1, 2012.

Related Sections: S. 149.1(1), "ineligible individual".

"relevant offence" —"relevant offence" means an offence, other than a relevant criminal offence, under the laws of Canada or a province, and an offence that would be such an offence if it took place in Canada, that

(*a*) relates to financial dishonesty, including an offence under charitable fundraising legislation, consumer protection legislation and securities legislation, or

(*b*) in respect of a charity or Canadian amateur athletic association, is relevant to the operation of the charity or association;

Editorial Note: See notes to 149.1(1), "ineligible individual".

History: S. 149.1(1), the definition "relevant offence" was added by S.C. 2011, c. 24, s. 52(2), in force January 1, 2012.

Related Sections: S. 149.1(1), "ineligible individual".

"relevant person" —"relevant person" in respect of a private foundation means a person who, at any time in respect of which the expression is relevant, deals not at arm's length with the private foundation (determined as if subsection 251(2) were applied as if the private foundation were a corporation), but does not include

(*a*) a person who at that time is considered to deal not at arm's length with the private foundation solely because of a right referred to in paragraph 251(5)(*b*), or

(*b*) an individual

(i) who at that time has attained the age of 18 years and lives separate and apart from any other individual (referred to in this definition as a "controlling individual") who would, if the private foundation were a corporation, control, or be a member of a related group that controls, the private foundation, and

(ii) in respect of whom the Minister is satisfied, upon review of an application by the private foundation, that the individual would, if subsection 251(1) were read without reference to its paragraphs (*a*) and (*b*), at that time, deal at arm's length with all controlling individuals;

Editorial Note: The definition of "relevant person" is pertinent to the excess corporate holdings regime. If a private foundation holds more than 2% of the issued and outstanding shares of a class of a corporation, it must report the "material transactions" of relevant persons in respect of the foundation in respect of that class, as well as the shareholdings of relevant persons with a "material interest" in that class. Further, when determining a private foundation's "total corporate holdings percentage", and thus divestment obligation, in respect of a class of shares, the shares of that class held by relevant persons in respect of the foundation that have a "material interest" in that class are included. See also the editorial notes for s. 149.1(1), "divestment obligation percentage" and "excess corporate holdings percentage".

"specified gift" — (Repealed by S.C. 2010, c. 25, s. 37(1).)

History: S. 149.1(1), the definition "specified gift" was repealed by S.C. 2010, c. 25, s. 37(1), applicable to taxation years that end on or after March 4, 2010. S. 149.1(1), the definition "specified gift" formerly read:

"specified gift"—"specified gift" means that portion of a gift, made in a taxation year by a registered charity, that is designated as a specified gift in its information return for the year;

"substituted shares" —"substituted shares" held by a private foundation means shares acquired by the private foundation, in exchange for exempt shares held by the private foundation, in the course of a transaction to which section 51, subsection 85.1(1) or section 86 or 87 applies;

History: S. 149.1(1), the definition "substituted shares" was added by S.C. 2009, c. 2, s. 55(4), applicable after March 18, 2007.

"taxation year" —"taxation year" means, in the case of a registered charity or registered Canadian amateur athletic association, a fiscal period;

History: S. 149.1(1), the definition "taxation year" was replaced by S.C. 2011, c. 24, s. 52(1), in force January 1, 2012. S. 149.1(1), the definition "taxation year" formerly read:

"taxation year"—"taxation year" means, in the case of a registered charity, a fiscal period.

"total corporate holdings percentage" —"total corporate holdings percentage" of a private foundation, in respect of a class of shares of the capital stock of a corporation, at any particular time means the percentage of the issued and outstanding shares of that class that are held at that time by the private foundation, or by a relevant person in respect of the private foundation who holds a material interest in respect of that class;

Editorial Note: See Editorial Notes to s. 149.1(1), "divestment obligation percentage", "excess corporate holdings percentage" and "exempt shares".

Related Sections: S. 149.1(1), "divestment obligation percentage", "excess corporate holdings percentage", "total corporate holdings percentage"; s. 149.2(1) Material and insignificant interests; s. 149.2(10) Shares held through a trust on March 18, 2007; s. 149.2(11) Discretionary trusts.

▶ 149.1(1.01) ◀

(1.01) Deeming rule — Safe Streets and Communities Act. In this section, a reference to a record suspension is deemed also to be a reference to a pardon that is granted or issued under the *Criminal Records Act*.

History: S. 149.1(1.01) was added by S.C. 2011, c. 24, s. 103, in force March 13, 2012 [on R.A. of Bill C-10, S.C. 2012, c. 1 (*Safe Streets and Communities Act*)].

▶ 149.1(1.1) ◀

(1.1) Exclusions. For the purposes of paragraphs (2)(*b*), (3)(*b*) and (4)(*b*) and subsection (21), the following shall be deemed to be neither an amount expended in a taxation year on charitable activities nor a gift made to a qualified donee:

(*a*) a designated gift; and

(*b*) (Repealed by S.C. 2018, c. 27, s. 17(6).)

(*c*) a transfer that has, because of paragraph (*c*) of the description of B in subsection 188(1.1), paragraph 189(6.2)(*b*) or subsection 189(6.3), reduced the amount of a liability under Part V.

Editorial Note: Subsection 149.1(1.1) prevents designated gifts and certain transfers that reduce the transferor 's liability for tax under Part V from being used to satisfy a registered charity's disbursement quota or to create a disbursement excess. See also the editorial note for s. 149.1(1) "designated gifts".

History: S. 149.1(1.1), the portion before paragraph (*a*) was replaced by S.C. 2018, c. 27, s. 17(5), in force December 13, 2018, and formerly read:

(1.1) *Exclusions.* For the purposes of paragraphs (2)(*b*), (3)(*b*), (4)(*b*) and (21)(*a*), the following shall be deemed to be neither an amount expended in a taxation year on charitable activities nor a gift made to a qualified donee:

S. 149.1(1.1)(*b*) was repealed by S.C. 2018, c. 27, s. 17(6), deemed in force

(a) on January 1, 2008 in respect of organizations, corporations and trusts that are registered charities on September 14, 2018; and

(b) on September 14, 2018 in any other case.

S. 149.1(1.1)(*b*) formerly read:

(*b*) an expenditure on political activities made by a charitable organization or a charitable foundation; and

S. 149.1(1.1)(*a*) was replaced by S.C. 2010, c. 25, s. 37(4), applicable to taxation years that end on or after March 4, 2010. S. 149.1(1.1)(*a*) formerly read:

(*a*) a specified gift;

Related Sections: S. 149.1(6.1) Charitable purposes [political activities]; s. 149.1(6.2) Charitable activities [political activities].

▶ 149.1(1.2) ◀

(1.2) Authority of Minister. For the purposes of the determination of B in the definition "disbursement quota" in subsection 149.1(1), the Minister may

(*a*) authorize a change in the number of periods chosen by a registered charity in determining the prescribed amount; and

(*b*) accept any method for the determination of the fair market value of property or a portion thereof that may be required in determining the prescribed amount.

History: S. 149.1(1.2), the portion before paragraph (*b*) was replaced by S.C. 2010, c. 25, s. 37(5), applicable to taxation years that end on or after March 4, 2010. S. 149.1(1.2), the portion before paragraph (*b*) formerly read:

(1.2) *Authority of Minister.* For the purposes of the determination of D in the definition "disbursement quota" in subsection (1), the Minister may

(*a*) authorize a change in the number of periods chosen by a charitable foundation in determining the prescribed amount; and

▶ 149.1(2) ◀

(2) Revocation of registration of charitable organization. The Minister may, in the manner described in section 168, revoke the registration of a charitable organization for any reason described in subsection 168(1) or where the organization

(*a*) carries on a business that is not a related business of that charity;

(*b*) fails to expend in any taxation year, on charitable activities carried on by it and by way of gifts made by it to qualified donees, amounts the total of which is at least equal to the organization's disbursement quota for that year; or

(*c*) makes a disbursement by way of a gift, other than a gift made

(i) in the course of charitable activities carried on by it, or

(ii) to a donee that is a qualified donee at the time of the gift.

Editorial Note: In addition to the revocation provisions of s. 168, the Minister may revoke a charitable organization's registration where (i) the charity carries on a business that is not a related business; (ii) the charity does not meet its disbursement quota; or (iii) a gift is made by the charity otherwise than in the course of its charitable activities or to a qualified donee. This final rule seeks to prevent the gifting of assets or funds from a Canadian charity to a foreign charity that is not a qualified donee. Subsection 168(1) provides for revocation of the registration of a charitable organization if the organization (i) ceases to comply with the requirements for registration; (ii) issues a receipt for a gift otherwise than in accordance with the Act and Regulations or that contains false information; (iii) fails to file an information return; or (iv) breaches any of the ongoing duties to report or maintain proper records contained in s. 230–231.5. Where charitable registration is revoked, revocation tax may be applicable under s. 188(1). As an alternative to revocation, the Minister may impose penalties for certain failures or acts of non-compliance by a charity. See the editorial notes for s. 188.1 and 188.2.

History: S. 149.1(2)(*c*) was added by S.C. 2013, c. 34, s. 308(5), applicable to gifts made after December 20, 2002.

Related Sections: S. 149.1(1.1) Exclusions; s. 149.1(5) Reduction; s. 168(1) Notice of intention to revoke registration; s. 168(4) Objection to proposal or designation; s. 172(3) Appeal from refusal to register, revocation of registration, etc.; s. 188(1) Deemed year-end on notice of revocation; s. 188(1.1) Revocation tax.

Forms: T2046 — Tax Return Where Registration of a Charity is Revoked.

Guides: RC4424 Completing the Tax Return Where Registration of a Charity is Revoked.

Interpretation Bulletins: *Secondary* — IT-244R3 Gifts by individuals of life insurance policies as charitable donations.

► 149.1(3) ◄

(3) Revocation of registration of public foundation. The Minister may, in the manner described in section 168, revoke the registration of a public foundation for any reason described in subsection 168(1) or where the foundation

(*a*) carries on a business that is not a related business of that charity;

(*b*) fails to expend in any taxation year, on charitable activities carried on by it and by way of gifts made by it to qualified donees, amounts the total of which is at least equal to the foundation's disbursement quota for that year;

(*b*.1) makes a disbursement by way of a gift, other than a gift made

(i) in the course of charitable activities carried on by it, or

(ii) to a donee that is a qualified donee at the time of the gift;

(*c*) since June 1, 1950, acquired control of any corporation;

(*d*) since June 1, 1950, incurred debts, other than debts for current operating expenses, debts incurred in connection with the purchase and sale of investments and debts incurred in the course of administering charitable activities; or

(*e*) at any time within the 24 month period preceding the day on which notice is given to the foundation by the Minister pursuant to subsection 168(1) and at a time when the foundation was a private foundation, took any action or failed to expend amounts such that the Minister was entitled, pursuant to subsection (4), to revoke its registration as a private foundation.

Editorial Note: In addition to the reasons listed in the editorial note for s. 149.1(2) with respect to charitable organizations, the registration of a public foundation may also be revoked where the foundation (i) acquired control of a corporation after June 1, 1950; (ii) incurred debts after June 1, 1950, other than for current operating expenses, in connection with the purchase and sale of investments, or in the course of administering charitable activities; or (iii) was at any time in the previous 24-month period a private foundation and took an action or failed to expend amounts that could have led to its revocation as a private foundation under s. 149.1(4).

History: S. 149.1(3)(*b.1*) was added by S.C. 2013, c. 34, s. 308(6), applicable to gifts made after December 20, 2002.

Related Sections: S. 149.1(1.1) Exclusions; s. 149.1(5) Reduction; s. 168(1) Notice of intention to revoke registration; s. 168(4) Objection to proposal or designation; s. 172(3) Appeal from refusal to register, revocation of registration, etc.; s. 188(1) Deemed year-end on notice of revocation; s. 188(1.1) Revocation tax.

► 149.1(4) ◄

(4) Revocation of registration of private foundation. The Minister may, in the manner described in section 168, revoke the registration of a private foundation for any reason described in subsection 168(1) or where the foundation

(*a*) carries on any business;

(*b*) fails to expend in any taxation year, on charitable activities carried on by it and by way of gifts made by it to qualified donees, amounts the total of which is at least equal to the foundation's disbursement quota for that year;

(*b*.1) makes a disbursement by way of a gift, other than a gift made

(i) in the course of charitable activities carried on by it, or

(ii) to a donee that is a qualified donee at the time of the gift;

(*c*) has, in respect of a class of shares of the capital stock of a corporation, a divestment obligation percentage at the end of any taxation year;

(*d*) since June 1, 1950, incurred debts, other than debts for current operating expenses, debts incurred in connection with the purchase and sale of investments and debts incurred in the course of administering charitable activities.

Editorial Note: The registration of a private foundation may be revoked for the reasons set out in s. 168(1) or if it (i) carries on any business (including a related business); (ii) does not meet its disbursement quota; (iii) makes a gift other than in the course of its charitable activities or to a qualified donee; (iv) has a divestment obligation percentage at the end of any taxation year; or (v) has incurred debts since June 1, 1950, other than for current operating expenses, in connection with the purchase and sale of investments or in the course of administering charitable activities. See the editorial note for s. 149.1(2).

History: S. 149.1(4)(*b.1*) was added by S.C. 2013, c. 34, s. 308(7), applicable to gifts made after December 20, 2002.

Related Sections: S. 149.1(1.1) Exclusions; s. 149.1(5) Reduction; s. 168(1) Notice of intention to revoke registration; s. 168(4) Objection to proposal or designation; s. 172(3) Appeal from refusal to register, revocation of registration, etc.; s. 188(1) Deemed year-end on notice of revocation; s. 188(1.1) Revocation tax.

Interpretation Bulletins: *Secondary* — IT-244R3 Gifts by individuals of life insurance policies as charitable donations.

► 149.1(4.1) ◄

(4.1) Revocation of registration of registered charity. The Minister may, in the manner described in section 168, revoke the registration

(*a*) of a registered charity, if it has entered into a transaction (including a gift to another registered charity) and it may reasonably be considered that a purpose of the transaction was to avoid or unduly delay the expenditure of amounts on charitable activities;

(*b*) of a registered charity, if it may reasonably be considered that a purpose of entering into a transaction (including the acceptance of a gift) with another registered charity to which paragraph (*a*) applies was to assist the other registered charity in avoiding or unduly delaying the expenditure of amounts on charitable activities;

(*c*) of a registered charity, if a false statement, within the meaning assigned by subsection 163.2(1), was made in circumstances amounting to culpable conduct, within the meaning assigned by that subsection, in the furnishing of information for the purpose of obtaining registration of the charity;

(*d*) of a registered charity, if it has in a taxation year received a gift of property (other than a designated gift) from another registered charity with which it does not deal at arm's length and it has expended, before the end of the next taxation year, in addition to its disbursement quota for each of those taxation years, an amount that is less than the fair market value of the property, on charitable activities carried on by it or by way of gifts made to qualified donees with which it deals at arm's length;

(*e*) of a registered charity, if an ineligible individual is a director, trustee, officer or like official of the charity, or controls or manages the charity, directly or indirectly, in any manner whatever; and

(*f*) of a registered charity, if it accepts a gift from a foreign state, as defined in section 2 of the *State*

Immunity Act, that is set out on the list referred to in subsection 6.1(2) of that Act.

Editorial Note: This subsection permits the Minister to revoke a charity's registration in three general types of situations: (i) the charity avoids its annual disbursement quota requirements; (ii) the charity is managed or controlled by an "ineligible individual" or accepts a gift from a foreign state supporting terrorism; or (iii) the charity makes a false statement in the course of registration. Transactions described in (i) may also attract penalties of up to 110% of the amount of the avoided expenditure under s. 188.1(11) and (12). See also the editorial note for s. 149.1(2).

History: S. 149.1(4.1)(*f*) was added by S.C. 2014, c. 20, s. 21(1), applicable in respect of gifts accepted after February 10, 2014.

S. 149.1(4.1)(*e*) was added by S.C. 2011, c. 24, s. 52(3), in force January 1, 2012.

S. 149.1(4.1)(*a*) and (*b*) were replaced by S.C. 2010, c. 25, s. 37(6), applicable to taxation years that end on or after March 4, 2010. S. 149.1(4.1)(*a*) and (*b*) formerly read:

(*a*) of a registered charity, if the registered charity has made a gift to another registered charity and it can reasonably be considered that one of the main purposes of making the gift was to unduly delay the expenditure of amounts on charitable activities;

(*b*) of the other charity referred to in paragraph (*a*), if it can reasonably be considered that, by accepting the gift, it acted in concert with the registered charity to which paragraph (*a*) applies; and

S. 149.1(4.1)(*d*) was added by S.C. 2010, c. 25, s. 37(7), applicable to taxation years that end on or after March 4, 2010.

Related Sections: S. 149.1(1.1) Exclusions; s. 149.1(5) Reduction; s. 168(1) Notice of intention to revoke registration; s. 168(4) Objection to proposal or designation; s. 172(3) Appeal from refusal to register, revocation of registration, etc.; s. 188(1) Deemed year-end on notice of revocation; s. 188(1.1) Revocation tax.

► 149.1(4.2) ◄

(4.2) Revocation of registration of Canadian amateur athletic association. The Minister may, in the manner described in section 168, revoke the registration of a registered Canadian amateur athletic association

(*a*) for any reason described in subsection 168(1);

(*b*) if the association carries on a business that is not a related business of that association;

(*c*) if an ineligible individual is a director, trustee, officer or like official of the association, or controls or manages the association, directly or indirectly, in any manner whatever; or

(*d*) if the association accepts a gift from a foreign state, as defined in section 2 of the *State Immunity Act*, that is set out on the list referred to in subsection 6.1(2) of that Act.

Editorial Note: Similar to registered charities, a registered Canadian amateur athletic association ("RCAAA") can have its registered status (and therefore its ability to issue donation receipts) revoked in certain circumstances, including where the RCAAA carries on an unrelated business, accepts a gift from a foreign state supporting terrorism, or has an ineligible individual performing certain functions of management and control. An RCAAA's registration may also be revoked for the reasons set out in s. 168(1), including the acceptance of a gift, the granting of which was conditional on the RCAAA making a gift to another person, club, society, or association. See also the editorial note for s. 149.1(2). As an alternative to revocation, the Minister may impose penalties for certain failures or acts of non-compliance by an RCAAA. See the editorial notes for s. 188.1 and 188.2.

History: S. 149.1(4.2)(*d*) was added by S.C. 2014, c. 20, s. 21(2), applicable in respect of gifts accepted after February 10, 2014.

S. 149.1(4.2) was added by S.C. 2011, c. 24, s. 52(4), in force January 1, 2012.

Related Sections: S. 168(1) Notice of intention to revoke registration; s. 168(4) Objection to proposal or designation; s. 172(3) Appeal from refusal to register, revocation of registration, etc.

► 149.1(4.3) ◄

(4.3) Revocation of a qualified donee. The Minister may, in the manner described in section 168, revoke the registration of a qualified donee referred to in paragraph (*a*) of the definition "qualified donee" in subsection (1) for any reason described in subsection 168(1).

Amendment not yet in force
Budget Implementation Act, 2019, No. 1 [S.C. 2019, c. 29]

S. 149.1(4.3) was replaced by S.C. 2019, c. 29, s. 31(3), and will read as follows:

(4.3) Revocation of a qualified donee. The Minister may, in the manner described in section 168, revoke the registration of a qualified donee referred to in paragraph (*a*) or (*b.1*) of the definition "qualified donee" in subsection (1) for any reason described in subsection 168(1).

Applicable: In force January 1, 2020.

Editorial Note: Qualified donees can also have their registration revoked for the reasons described in s. 168. The qualified donees that are subject to this rule include:

(i) registered municipalities in Canada;

(ii) registered municipal and public bodies performing a function of government in Canada that have applied for registration;

(iii) registered housing corporations in Canada constituted exclusively to provide low-cost housing for the aged that have applied for registration;

(iv) a registered university outside of Canada, the student body of which ordinarily includes students from Canada, that has applied for registration (unless it was prescribed in the Regulations before February 27, 2018);

(v) registered foreign charities outside of Canada that have received a gift from Her Majesty in right of Canada and have applied for registration under subsection 149.1(26);

(vi) registered charities; and

(vii) effective January 1, 2020, registered journalism organizations.

The purpose of the rule in s. 149.1(4.3) is to ensure that these categories of qualified donees are subject to the same general governmental oversight and compliance requirements as other qualified donees, such as registered charities and registered Canadian amateur athletic associations.

History: S. 149.1(4.3) was added by S.C. 2011, c. 24, s. 52(4), in force January 1, 2012.

Related Sections: S. 168(1) Notice of intention to revoke registration; s. 168(4) Objection to proposal or designation; s. 172(3) Appeal from refusal to register, revocation of registration, etc.

► 149.1(5) ◄

(5) Reduction. The Minister may, on application made to the Minister in prescribed form by a registered charity, specify an amount in respect of the charity for a taxation year and, for the purpose of paragraph (2)(*b*), (3)(*b*) or (4)(*b*), as the case may be, that amount shall be deemed to be an amount expended by the charity in the year on charitable activities carried on by it.

Editorial Note: A charity may apply to have its disbursement quota reduced. The application must be in the prescribed form. The application is especially of use in low-interest investment environments.

Related Sections: S. 149.1(1), "specified gift".

Forms: T2094 — Registered Charities: Application to Reduce Quota.

► 149.1(6) ◄

(6) Devoting resources to charitable activity. A charitable organization shall be considered to be devoting its resources to charitable activities carried on by it to the extent that

(*a*) it carries on a related business;

(*b*) in any taxation year, it disburses not more than 50% of its income for that year to qualified donees; or

(*c*) it disburses income to a registered charity that the Minister has designated in writing as a charity associated with it.

Editorial Note: A charitable organization must devote all its resources to charitable activities. This test will be met where the charitable organization devotes resources to (i) a related business; (ii) making disbursements of up to 50% of its income for the year to qualified donees; or (iii) disbursing income to registered charities that are associated with it. A disbursement to a qualified donee or associated charity that is a gift, the making of which is a political activity, will not be considered a charitable activity. A gift will be considered a political activity where it can reasonably be considered that a purpose of the gift is to support the political activities of the recipient. See also the editorial note for s. 149.1(7) regarding associated charities.

History: S. 149.1(6)(*b*) and (*c*) were replaced by S.C. 2018, c. 27, s. 17(7), deemed to have come into force

(a) on June 29, 2012 in respect of organizations, corporations and trusts that are registered charities on September 14, 2018 and in respect of associations that are registered Canadian amateur athletic associations on that date; and

(b) on September 14, 2018 in any other case.

S. 149.1(6)(*b*) and (*c*) formerly read:

(*b*) it disburses income to qualified donees, other than income disbursed by way of a gift the making of which is a political activity, if the total amount of the charitable organization's income that is disbursed to qualified donees in a taxation year does not exceed 50% of its income for the year; or

(*c*) it disburses income to a registered charity that the Minister has designated in writing as a charity associated with it, other than income disbursed by way of a gift the making of which is a political activity.

S. 149.1(6)(*b*) and (*c*) were replaced by S.C. 2012, c. 19, s. 7(4), in force on Royal Assent, June 29, 2012. S. 149.1(6)(*b*) and (*c*) formerly read:

(*b*) in any taxation year, it disburses not more than 50% of its income for that year to qualified donees; or

(*c*) it disburses income to a registered charity that the Minister has designated in writing as a charity associated with it.

Information Circulars: IC 77-6R Registered charities: Designation as associated charities.

► 149.1(6.01) ◄

(6.01) Devoting resources to purpose and function. A Canadian amateur athletic association is considered to devote its resources to its exclusive purpose and exclusive function to the extent that it carries on

(*a*) a related business; or

(*b*) activities involving the participation of professional athletes, if those activities are ancillary and incidental to its exclusive purpose and exclusive function.

Editorial Note: A registered Canadian amateur athletic association ("RCAAA") must devote all of its resources to its exclusive purpose and function, namely, the promotion of amateur athletics in Canada on a nationwide basis. This test will be met where the RCAAA devotes resources to a related business or to activities involving the participation of professional athletes, provided such activities are ancillary and incidental to its exclusive purpose and function.

History: S. 149.1(6.01) was added by S.C. 2011, c. 24, s. 52(5), in force January 1, 2012.

Related Sections: S. 149.1(6.201) Political activities of Canadian amateur athletic association.

► 149.1(6.1) ◄

(6.1) Charitable purposes. For the purposes of the definition "charitable foundation" in subsection (1), a corporation or trust that devotes any part of its resources to the direct or indirect support of, or opposition to, any political party or candidate for public office shall not be considered to be constituted and operated exclusively for charitable purposes.

Editorial Note: Previously, s. 149.1(6.1) effectively allowed a charitable foundation to expend up to 10% of its resources on political activities that were incidental and ancillary to its charitable purposes and did not include the direct or indirect support of, or opposition to, a particular party or candidate for office (technically, as long as it devoted all or substantially all of its resources to charitable purposes). See also CRA Policy Statement CPS-022, "Political Activities".

The 10% restriction has been repealed, although the current restriction provides that if a foundation devotes *any part* of its resources to the direct or indirect support of, or opposition to, any political party or candidate for public office, it is not considered to be constituted and operated exclusively for charitable purposes. At the same time, the current rules allow the "charitable activities" of public policy dialogue and development activities carried on in furtherance of a charitable purpose (s. 149.1(1) "charitable activities"). The changes are effective as of June 29, 2012 in respect of charities that were registered on September 14, 2018, and as of September 14, 2018 in any other case. Essentially the same changes apply to rules governing charitable organizations (s. 149.1(6.2)) and Canadian amateur athletic associations (s. 149.1(6.201)).

History: S. 149.1(6.1) was replaced by S.C. 2018, c. 27, s. 17(8), deemed to have come into force

(a) on January 1, 2008 in respect of organizations, corporations and trusts that are registered charities on September 14, 2018; and

(b) on September 14, 2018 in any other case.

S. 149.1(6.1) formerly read:

(6.1) *Charitable purposes.* For the purposes of the definition "charitable foundation" in subsection (1), where a corporation or trust devotes substantially all of its resources to charitable purposes and

(*a*) it devotes part of its resources to political activities,

(*b*) those political activities are ancillary and incidental to its charitable purposes, and

(*c*) those political activities do not include the direct or indirect support of, or opposition to, any political party or candidate for public office,

the corporation or trust shall be considered to be constituted and operated for charitable purposes to the extent of that part of its resources so devoted.

Other Publications: CG-027 Public Policy Dialogue and Development Activities by Charities.

► 149.1(6.2) ◄

(6.2) Charitable purposes. For the purposes of the definition "charitable organization" in subsection (1), an organization that devotes any part of its resources to the direct or indirect support of, or opposition to, any political party or candidate for public office shall not be considered to be constituted and operated exclusively for charitable purposes.

Editorial Note: See editorial notes to 149.1(6.1).

History: S. 149.1(6.2) was replaced by S.C. 2018, c. 27, s. 17(8), deemed to have come into force

(a) on January 1, 2008 in respect of organizations, corporations and trusts that are registered charities on September 14, 2018; and

(b) on September 14, 2018 in any other case.

S. 149.1(6.2) formerly read:

(6.2) *Charitable activities.* For the purposes of the definition "charitable organization" in subsection (1), where an organization devotes substantially all of its resources to charitable activities carried on by it and

(*a*) it devotes part of its resources to political activities,

(*b*) those political activities are ancillary and incidental to its charitable activities, and

(*c*) those political activities do not include the direct or indirect support of, or opposition to, any political party or candidate for public office,

the organization shall be considered to be devoting that part of its resources to charitable activities carried on by it.

Canadian Tax Foundation: Cudmore, *Charities' Political Activity Limit*, 2018 Canadian Tax Focus 8(4):5–6.

Other Publications: CG-027 Public Policy Dialogue and Development Activities by Charities.

► 149.1(6.201) ◄

(6.201) Activities of Canadian amateur athletic associations. For the purposes of the definition "Canadian amateur athletic association" in subsection (1), an association that devotes any part of its resources to the direct or indirect support of, or opposition to, any political party or candidate for public office shall not be considered to devote that part of its resources to its exclusive purpose and exclusive function.

Editorial Note: See editorial notes to 149.1(6.1).

History: S. 149.1(6.201) was replaced by S.C. 2018, c. 27, s. 17(9), deemed to have come into force

(a) on January 1, 2012 in respect of associations that are registered Canadian amateur athletic associations on September 14, 2018; and

(b) on September 14, 2018 in any other case.

S. 149.1(6.201) formerly read:

(6.201) *Political activities of Canadian amateur athletic association.* For the purpose of the definition "Canadian amateur athletic association" in subsection (1), an association that devotes part of its resources to political activities is considered to devote those resources to its exclusive purpose and exclusive function if

(*a*) it devotes substantially all its resources to its purpose and function; and (*b*) those political activities

(i) are ancillary and incidental to its purpose and function, and

(ii) do not include the direct or indirect support of, or opposition to, any political party or candidate for public office.

S. 149.1(6.201) was added by S.C. 2011, c. 24, s. 52(6), in force January 1, 2012.

Related Sections: S. 149.1(6.01) Devoting resources to purpose and function.

▶ 149.1(6.21) ◀

(6.21) Marriage for civil purposes. For greater certainty, subject to subsections (6.1) and (6.2), a registered charity with stated purposes that include the advancement of religion shall not have its registration revoked or be subject to any other penalty under Part V solely because it or any of its members, officials, supporters or adherents exercises, in relation to marriage between persons of the same sex, the freedom of conscience and religion guaranteed under the *Canadian Charter of Rights and Freedoms*.

▶ 149.1(6.3) ◀

(6.3) Designation as public foundation, etc. The Minister may, by notice sent by registered mail to a registered charity, on the Minister's own initiative or on application made to the Minister in prescribed form, designate the charity to be a charitable organization, private foundation or public foundation and the charity shall be deemed to be registered as a charitable organization, private foundation or public foundation, as the case may be, for taxation years commencing after the day of mailing of the notice unless and until it is otherwise designated under this subsection or its registration is revoked under subsection (2), (3), (4), (4.1) or 168(2).

Editorial Note: See the editorial notes to the definition of "charitable foundation" in 149.1(1).

History: Under S.C. 2013, c. 34, s. 308(16), an application referred to in subsection 149.1(6.3), in respect of one or more taxation years after 1999, may be made after 1999 and before September 24, 2013 [the 90th day after royal assent]. If a designation referred to in subsection 149.1(6.3) for any of those taxation years is made in response to the application, the charity is deemed to be registered as a charitable organization, a public foundation or a private foundation, as the case may be, for the taxation years that the Minister of National Revenue specifies.

Forms: T2095 — Canadian Charities: Application for Re-Designation.

▶ 149.1(6.4) ◀

(6.4) National arts service organizations. Where an organization that

(*a*) has, on written application to the Minister of Canadian Heritage describing all of its objects and activities, been designated by that Minister on approval of those objects and activities to be a national arts service organization,

(*b*) has, as its exclusive purpose and its exclusive function, the promotion of arts in Canada on a nationwide basis,

(*c*) is resident in Canada and was formed or created in Canada, and

(*d*) complies with prescribed conditions

applies in prescribed form to the Minister of National Revenue for registration, that Minister may register the organization for the purposes of this Act and, where the organization so applies or is so registered, this section, paragraph 38(*a*.1), sections 110.1, 118.1, 168, 172, 180 and 230, subsection 241(3.2) and Part V apply, with such modifications as the circumstances require, to the organization as if it were an applicant for registration as a charitable organization or as if it were a registered charity that is designated as a charitable organization, as the case may be.

Editorial Note: Pursuant to s. 149.1(6.4), a national arts service organization can apply for registration to be treated as a charitable organization for the purposes of the enumerated provisions

Related Regulations: 8700.

▶ 149.1(6.5) ◀

(6.5) Revocation of designation. The Minister of Canadian Heritage may, at any time, revoke the designation of an organization made for the purpose of subsection (6.4) where

(*a*) an incorrect statement was made in the furnishing of information for the purpose of obtaining the designation, or

(*b*) the organization has amended its objects after its last designation was made,

and, where the designation is so revoked, the organization shall be deemed for the purpose of section 168 to have ceased to comply with the requirements of this Act for its registration under this Act.

▶ 149.1(7) ◀

(7) Designation of associated charities. On application made to the Minister in prescribed form, the Minister may, in writing, designate a registered charity as a charity associated with one or more specified registered charities where the Minister is satisfied that the charitable aim or activity of each of the registered charities is substantially the same, and on and after a date specified in such a designation, the charities to which it relates shall, until such time, if any, as the Minister revokes the designation, be deemed to be associated.

Editorial Note: Charitable organizations must devote all of their resources to charitable activities carried on by the organizations themselves. Charitable organizations are generally deemed to have put income disbursed to associated charities towards their own charitable activities. The process and requirements for applying for associated status are dealt with in s. 149.1(7). In general, the Minister will designate registered charities as associated charities if satisfied that the aim and activities of the charities are the same. Charities undertaking a joint project may also be associated. An application for associated status can be made using form T3011. See CRA Policy Commentary CPC-028, Associated Status for Unrelated Charities.

Forms: T3011 — Registered Charities Application for Designation as Associated Charities.

Information Circulars: IC 77-6R Registered charities: Designation as associated charities.

▶ 149.1(8) ◀

(8) Accumulation of property. A registered charity may, with the approval in writing of the Minister, accumulate property for a particular purpose, on terms and conditions and over any period of time that the Minister specifies in the approval. Any property accumulated after receipt of and in accordance with the approval, including any income earned in respect of the accumulated property, is not to be included in calculating the prescribed amount in paragraph (*a*) of the description of B in the definition "disbursement quota" in subsection (1) for the portion of any taxation year in the period, except to the extent that the registered charity is not in compliance with the terms and conditions of the approval.

Editorial Note: The CRA has a certain amount of discretion to permit a charity to accumulate property without violating the disbursement quota in certain circumstances. For example, the CRA has noted that such permission may be granted where temporary accumulation is necessary to make a major expenditure, such as buying a building or a costly piece of equipment which cannot be financed out of the charity's current revenue. A request to accumulate property must identify, among other things, (i) the specific purpose to which the funds will be used; (ii) the amount required; and (iii) the length of time needed to accumulate the funds (minimum of three years and maximum of 10 years). Any property accumulated by the charity after the receipt of, and in accordance with, such Ministerial approval (including any income earned in respect of the accumulated property) is generally excluded from the computation of the charity's capital accumulation requirement for the disbursement quota.

History: S. 149.1(8) was replaced by S.C. 2010, c. 25, s. 37(8), applicable to taxation years that end on or after March 4, 2010. S. 149.1(8) formerly read:

(8) *Accumulation of property.* A registered charity may, with the approval in writing of the Minister, accumulate property for a particular purpose, on terms and conditions, and over such period of time, as the Minister specifies in the approval, and any property accumulated after receipt of such an approval and in accordance therewith, including any income earned in respect of the property so accumulated, shall be deemed

(*a*) to have been expended on charitable activities carried on by the charity in the taxation year in which it was so accumulated; and

(*b*) not to have been expended in any other year.

► 149.1(9) ◄

(9) Idem — (Repealed by S.C. 2010, c. 25, s. 37(8).)

History: S. 149.1(9) was repealed by S.C. 2010, c. 25, s. 37(8), applicable to taxation years that end on or after March 4, 2010. S. 149.1(9) formerly read:

(9) *Idem.* Property accumulated by a registered charity as provided in subsection (8), including any income earned in respect of that property, that is not used for the particular purpose for which it was accumulated either

(*a*) before the expiration of any period of time specified by the Minister in the Minister's approval of the accumulation, or

(*b*) at an earlier time at which the registered charity decides not to use the property for that purpose

is, notwithstanding subsection (8), deemed to be income of the charity for, and the eligible amount of a gift for which it issued a receipt described in subsection 110.1(2) or 118.1(2) in, its taxation year in which the period referred to in paragraph (*a*) expires or the time referred to in paragraph (*b*) occurs, as the case may be.

S. 149.1(9), the portion after paragraph (*b*), as it read above, immediately before it was repealed by S.C. 2010, c. 25, s. 37(8), was replaced by S.C. 2013, c. 34, s. 308(8), deemed to have come into force on December 21, 2002 but applicable only to taxation years that end before March 4, 2010. For greater certainty, subsection 149.1(9) is deemed to have been repealed in respect of taxation years that end on or after March 4, 2010.

S. 149.1(9), the portion after paragraph (*b*) formerly read:

shall, notwithstanding subsection (8), be deemed to be income of the charity for, and the amount of a gift for which it issued a receipt described in subsection 110.1(2) or 118.1(2) in, its taxation year in which the period referred to in paragraph (*a*) expires or the time referred to in paragraph (*b*) occurs, as the case may be.

► 149.1(10) ◄

(10) Deemed charitable activity. An amount paid by a charitable organization to a qualified donee that is not paid out of the income of the charitable organization is deemed to be a devotion of a resource of the charitable organization to a charitable activity carried on by it.

Editorial Note: Where a charitable organization pays an amount other than income (e.g., out of gifts or capital) to a qualified donee, that amount is deemed to be a devotion of resources to its own charitable activities, unless the amount is a gift the making of which is a political activity. See also the editorial note for s. 149.1(6).

History: S. 149.1(10) was replaced by S.C. 2018, c. 27, s. 17(10), deemed to have come into force

(a) on June 29, 2012 in respect of organizations, corporations and trusts that are registered charities on September 14, 2018 and in respect of associations that are registered Canadian amateur athletic associations on that date; and

(b) on September 14, 2018 in any other case.

S. 149.1(10) formerly read:

(10) *Deemed charitable activity.* An amount paid by a charitable organization to a qualified donee that is not paid out of the income of the charitable organization is deemed to be a devotion of a resource of the charitable organization to a charitable activity carried on by it, unless the amount paid is a gift the making of which is a political activity.

S. 149.1(10) was replaced by S.C. 2012, c. 19, s. 7(5), in force on Royal Assent, June 29, 2012. S. 149.1(10) formerly read:

(10) *Deemed charitable activity.* An amount paid by a charitable organization to a qualified donee that is not paid out of the income of the charitable organization shall be deemed to be a devotion of a resource of the charitable organization to a charitable activity carried on by it.

► 149.1(10.1) ◄

(10.1) Public policy activities. Subject to subsections (6.1) and (6.2), public policy dialogue and development activities carried on by an organization, corporation or trust in support of its stated purposes shall be considered to be carried on in furtherance of those purposes and not for any other purpose.

History: S. 149.1(10.1) was added by S.C. 2018, c. 27, s. 17(11), deemed to have come into force

(a) on January 1, 2008 in respect of organizations, corporations and trusts that are registered charities on September 14, 2018; and

(b) on September 14, 2018 in any other case.

► 149.1(11) ◄

(11) Partnership look-through rule. For the purposes of this section and sections 149.2 and 188.1, each member of a partnership at any time is deemed at that time to own the portion of each property of the partnership equal to the proportion that the fair market value of the member's interest in the partnership at that time is of the fair market value of all interests in the partnership at that time.

History: S. 149.1(11) was added by S.C. 2016, c. 7, s. 40(1), deemed to have come into force on April 21, 2015.

Related Sections: 253.1(2) Investments in limited partnerships.

► 149.1(12) ◄

(12) Rules. For the purposes of this section,

(*a*) a corporation is controlled by a charitable foundation if more than 50% of the corporation's issued share capital, having full voting rights under all circumstances, belongs to

(i) the foundation, or

(ii) the foundation and persons with whom the foundation does not deal at arm's length,

but, for the purpose of paragraph (3)(*c*), a charitable foundation is deemed not to have acquired control of a corporation if it has not purchased or otherwise acquired for consideration more than 5% of the issued shares of any class of the capital stock of that corporation;

(*b*) there shall be included in computing the income of a charity for a taxation year all gifts received by it in the year including gifts from any other charity but not including

(i) a designated gift,

(ii) any gift or portion of a gift in respect of which it is established that the donor is not a charity and

(A) has not been allowed a deduction under paragraph 110.1(1)(*a*) in computing the donor's taxable income or under subsection 118.1(3) in computing the donor's tax payable under this Part, or

(B) was not taxable under section 2 for the taxation year in which the gift was made, or

(iii) any gift or portion of a gift in respect of which it is established that the donor is a charity and that the gift was not made out of the income of the donor; and

(*c*) subsections 104(6) and (12) are not applicable in computing the income of a charitable foundation that is a trust.

Editorial Note: Under s. 149.1(3)(*c*), the Minister may revoke the registration of a public foundation if it acquires control of a corporation. A corporation will be considered to be controlled by a charitable foundation if more than 50% of its issued share capital having full voting rights under all circumstances belongs to the foundation or to it and persons with whom it does not deal at arm's length.

These provisions do not prevent a charitable foundation from acquiring control of a corporation provided the corporation's shares have been gifted to the foundation. Paragraph 149.1(12)(*a*) provides that if the foundation has not purchased or otherwise acquired for consideration more than 5% of the issued shares of any class of shares of the corporation, it is deemed not to have acquired control of the corporation. For example, a donor could gift 51% of the voting shares of a corporation to a foundation, and the foundation could retain the shares without risk of its registration being revoked. However, where a foundation purchased a 10% share interest in a corporation as an investment and later a donor gifted a further 41% share interest to the foundation, the exempting provisions of s. 149.1(12)(*a*) would not have been satisfied because the foundation would have acquired more than 5% of its shares by purchase. In these circumstances the Minister could revoke the foundation's registration.

A charitable organization may disburse up to 50% of its income for a year to qualified donees or may disburse its income to an associated charity. "Income" for these purposes, which includes capital gains, is calculated according to several special rules. Firstly, under s. 149.1(12)(*b*), income of a charity generally includes gifts received in the year (including gifts received from another charity), unless the gift (*a*) is a "designated gift"; (*b*) is from a donor that is a charity but the gift was not made out of the donor charity's income; or (*c*) is from a donor who is not a charity and either the donor (i) has not been allowed a deduction for the gift under s. 110.1(1)(*a*) (in the case of a corporation) or a tax credit under s. 118.1, or (ii) is not subject to tax under Part I in the year the gift is made. In addition, where a charitable foundation is a trust, income is not reduced by distributions to the beneficiaries as it is for other trusts under s. 104(6) and 104(12). See s. 149.1(12)(*c*).

History: S. 149.1(12)(*b*)(i) was replaced by S.C. 2010, c. 25, s. 37(9), applicable to taxation years that end on or after March 4, 2010. S. 149.1(12)(*b*)(i) formerly read:

> (i) a specified gift or a gift referred to in paragraph (*a*) or (*b*) of the description of A in the definition "disbursement quota" in subsection (1),

Interpretation Bulletins: *Secondary* — IT-244R3 Gifts by individuals of life insurance policies as charitable donations.

► 149.1(13) ◄

(13) Designation of private foundation as public. On application made to the Minister by a private foundation, the Minister may, on such terms and conditions as the Minister considers appropriate, designate the foundation to be a public foundation, and on and after the date specified in such a designation, the foundation to which it relates shall, until such time, if any, as the Minister revokes the designation, be deemed to be a public foundation.

Editorial Note: Charitable foundations that do not qualify as public foundations are classified as private foundations. However, a private foundation may apply to the Minister to be designated as a public foundation.

Forms: T2095 — Canadian Charities: Application for Re-Designation.

► 149.1(14) ◄

(14) Information returns. Every registered charity and registered Canadian amateur athletic association shall, within six months from the end of each taxation year of the charity or association and without notice or demand, file with the Minister both an information return and a public information return for the year in prescribed form and containing prescribed information.

> **Amendment not yet in force**
>
> **Budget Implementation Act, 2019, No. 1 [S.C. 2019, c. 29]**
>
> **S. 149.1(14.1) was added by S.C. 2019, c. 29, s. 31(4), and will read as follows:**
>
> **(14.1) Information returns.** Every registered journalism organization shall, within six months from the end of each taxation year of the organization without notice or demand, file with the Minister both an information return and a public information return for the year in prescribed form and containing prescribed information including, for the public information return, for each donor whose total gifts to the organization in the year exceed $5,000, the name of the donor and the total amount donated.
>
> **Applicable:** In force January 1, 2020.

Editorial Note: Subsection 149.1(14) requires every registered charity and registered Canadian amateur athletic association to file an information return and a public information return within six months after the end of each taxation year. See the CRA's *Charities Connection Newsletter* No. 5, "The New Form T3010-1, Registered Charity Information Return", and No. 6, "Filing a Complete T3010, Registered Charity Information Return".

History: S. 149.1(14) was replaced by S.C. 2011, c. 24, s. 52(7), applicable to fiscal periods that begin on or after January 1, 2012. S. 149.1(14) formerly read:

> (14) *Information returns.* Every registered charity shall, within 6 months from the end of each taxation year of the charity, file with the Minister both an information return and a public information return for the year, each in prescribed form and containing prescribed information, without notice or demand therefor.

Related Sections: S. 149.1(15) Information may be communicated; s. 168(1) Notice of intention to revoke registration; s. 188.1(6) Failure to file information returns; s. 189(6.1) Revoked charity to file returns; s. 241(3.2) Registered charities and registered Canadian amateur athletic associations — public disclosure of information.

Forms: T1235 Directors/Trustees and Like Officials Worksheet; T1236 Qualified donees worksheet / Amounts provided to other organizations; T1240 Registered Charity Adjustment Request; T2052 Registered Canadian Amateur Athletic Association Return of Information; T3010 Registered Charity Information Return.

Guides: T4033 Completing the Registered Charity Information Return.

► 149.1(15) ◄

(15) Information may be communicated. Notwithstanding section 241,

(*a*) the information contained in a public information return referred to in subsection (14) shall be communicated or otherwise made available to the public by the Minister in such manner as the Minister deems appropriate;

(*b*) the Minister may make available to the public in any manner that the Minister considers appropriate, in respect of each registered, or previously registered, charity, Canadian amateur athletic association and qualified donee referred to in paragraph (*a*) of the definition "qualified donee" in subsection (1),

(i) its name, address and date of registration,

(ii) in the case of a registered, or previously registered, charity or Canadian amateur athletic association, its registration number, and

(iii) the effective date of any revocation, annulment or termination of registration; and

> **Amendment not yet in force**
>
> **Budget Implementation Act, 2019, No. 1 [S.C. 2019, c. 29]**
>
> **S. 149.1(15)(*a*) and (*b*) were replaced by S.C. 2019, c. 29, s. 31(5), and will read as follows:**
>
> (*a*) the information contained in a public information return referred to in subsection 149.1(14) or (14.1) shall be communicated or otherwise made available to the public by the Minister in such manner as the Minister deems appropriate;
>
> (*b*) the Minister may make available to the public in any manner that the Minister considers appropriate, in respect of each registered, or previously registered, charity, Canadian amateur athletic association, journalism organization and qualified donee referred to in paragraph (*a*) of the definition "qualified donee" in subsection (1),
>
> (i) its name, address and date of registration,
>
> (ii) in the case of a registered, or previously registered, charity, Canadian amateur athletic association or journalism organization, its registration number, and
>
> (iii) the effective date of any revocation, annulment or termination of registration; and
>
> **Applicable:** In force January 1, 2020.

(*c*) if, at any time during a taxation year of a private foundation that is a registered charity, the private foundation holds more than an insignificant interest in respect of a class of shares of the capital stock of a corporation, the Minister shall make available to the public in such manner as the Minister deems appropriate,

(i) the name of the corporation, and

(ii) in respect of each class of shares of the corporation, that portion of the total corporate holdings percentage of the private foundation in respect of the class that is attributable to

(A) holdings of shares of that class by the private foundation, and

(B) the total of all holdings of shares of that class by relevant persons in respect of the private foundation;

(*d*) (Repealed by S.C. 2017, c. 20, s. 25(1).)

Editorial Note: Notwithstanding the usual rule that returns are to be held by the CRA as confidential, the Minister *shall* disclose to the public anything contained in a public information return for a charity, registered Canadian amateur athletic association, and effective January 1, 2020, registered journalism organization, and information relating to certain shares held by private foundations. The Minister *may* also disclose to the public a list of registered and previously registered charities, Canadian amateur athletic associations, registered journalism organizations, and certain other "qualified donees", along with certain registration and related information. Prior to March 22, 2017, the Minister may have also disclosed a list of the registered charities in respect of which an opinion has been formed for the purpose of s. 110.1(8)(*e*), or revoked under s. 110.1(9) (both of which were repealed as of March 22, 2017).

History: S. 149.1(15)(*d*) was repealed by S.C. 2017, c. 20, s. 25(1), applicable in respect of gifts made after March 21, 2017, and formerly read:

(*d*) the Minister, or a Minister referred to in paragraph 110.1(8)(*e*), may make available to the public in any manner a listing of the registered charities in respect of which an opinion has been formed for the purpose of paragraph 110.1(8)(*e*) or revoked under subsection 110.1(9).

S. 149.1(15)(*b*) was replaced by S.C. 2011, c. 24, s. 52(8), in force January 1, 2012. S. 149.1(15)(*b*) formerly read:

(*b*) the Minister may make available to the public in such manner as the Minister deems appropriate an annual listing of all registered or previously registered charities indicating for each the name, location, registration number, date of registration and, in the case of a charity the registration of which has been revoked, annulled or terminated, the effective date of the revocation, annulment or termination;

S. 149.1(15)(*d*) was added by S.C. 2009, c. 2, s. 55(5), in force on Royal Assent, March 12, 2009.

Related Sections: 149.1(14) Information returns; 241(3.2) Registered charities and registered Canadian amateur athletic associations.

▶ 149.1(16) ◀

(16) Penalty tax — (Repealed by 1984, c. 45, s. 57(17).)

▶ 149.1(17) ◀

(17) Idem — (Repealed by 1984, c. 45, s. 57(17).)

▶ 149.1(18) ◀

(18) Rules relating to computation of income — (Repealed by 1984, c. 45, s. 57(17).)

▶ 149.1(19) ◀

(19) Election in respect of first taxation year — (Repealed by 1980-81, c. 48, s. 84.1(2).)

▶ 149.1(20) ◀

(20) Rule regarding disbursement excess. Where a registered charity has expended a disbursement excess for a taxation year, the charity may, for the purpose of determining whether it complies with the requirements of paragraph (2)(*b*), (3)(*b*) or (4)(*b*), as the case may be, for the immediately preceding taxation year of the charity and 5 or less of its immediately subsequent taxation years, include in the computation of the amounts expended on charitable activities carried on by it and by way of gifts made by it to qualified donees, such portion of that disbursement excess as was not so included under this subsection for any preceding taxation year.

Editorial Note: Under s. 149.1(20), a registered charity that expends a "disbursement excess" as defined in s. 149.1(21) in one year may apply such excess to satisfy its minimum disbursement quota as set out in s. 149.1(1) in its immediately preceding taxation year and its five immediately subsequent taxation years. "Disbursement excess" is defined in s. 149.1(21) to mean the amount, if any, by which the aggregate of amounts expended in the year by a registered charity on charitable activities carried on by it or by way of gifts to qualified donees exceeds the minimum disbursement quota of the registered charity as set out in s. 149.1(1). It should be noted that s. 149.1(1.1) provides that, for the purpose of determining a charity's disbursement excess, designated gifts and expenditures on political activities by charitable organizations or charitable foundations are deemed not to be amounts expended on charitable activities or gifts to qualified donees. Subsection 149.1(1.1) also provides that certain transfers to other registered charities that reduce the transferor charity's liability for tax under Part V are similarly deemed not to be amounts expended on charitable activities nor gifts made to qualified donees.

With the loosening of the disbursement quota rules, the importance of these sections has become questionable.

▶ 149.1(21) ◀

(21) Definition of "disbursement excess". For the purpose of subsection (20), "disbursement excess", for a taxation year of a charity, means the amount, if any, by which the total of amounts expended in the year by the charity on charitable activities carried on by it and by way of gifts made by it to qualified donees exceeds its disbursement quota for the year.

Editorial Note: See the editorial note for s. 149.1(20).

▶ 149.1(22) ◀

(22) Refusal to register. The Minister may, by registered mail, give notice to a person that the application of the person for registration, as a registered charity, registered Canadian amateur athletic association or qualified donee referred to in subparagraph (*a*)(i) or (iii) of the definition "qualified donee" in subsection (1), is refused.

Amendment not yet in force
Budget Implementation Act, 2019, No. 1 [S.C. 2019, c. 29]

S. 149.1(22) was replaced by S.C. 2019, c. 29, s. 31(6), and will read as follows:

(22) Refusal to register. The Minister may, by registered mail, give notice to a person that the application of the person for registration as a registered charity, registered Canadian amateur athletic association, registered journalism organization or qualified donee referred to in subparagraph (*a*)(i) or (iii) of the definition "qualified donee" in subsection (1) is refused.

Applicable: In force January 1, 2020.

Editorial Note: Subsection 149.1(22) permits the Minister to give notice to a person by registered mail that the application submitted by the person for registration as a registered charity, registered Canadian amateur athletic association, registered journalism organization (effective January 1, 2020), or certain types of "qualified donee" status has been refused. Similarly, s. 149.1(23) permits the Minister to give notice by registered mail to a registered charity that its registration has been annulled, in which case it is deemed not to have been registered. This can be done where the registration was issued in error or where the person, solely as a result of a change in the law, has ceased to be a charity. In the case of an annulment under s. 149.1(23), s. 149.1(24) provides that receipts issued before that time that would have been valid if the person were a registered charity are deemed to be valid for the purposes of Part I of the Act. These subsections are a codification of the CRA's previous administrative practice.

Since a charity whose registration is annulled is deemed never to have been registered, the s. 188 Part V revocation tax does not apply to such a charity.

History: S. 149.1(22) was replaced by S.C. 2011, c. 24, s. 52(9), in force January 1, 2012. S. 149.1(22) formerly read:

(22) *Refusal to register.* The Minister may, by registered mail, give notice to a person that the application of the person for registration as a registered charity is refused.

Related Sections: S. 149.1(25) Refusal to register — ineligible individual; s. 168(4) Objection to proposal or designation; s. 172(3) Appeal from refusal to register, revocation of registration, etc.

▶ 149.1(23) ◀

(23) Annulment of registration. The Minister may, by registered mail, give notice to a person that the registration of the person as a registered charity is annulled and deemed not to have been so registered, if the person was so registered by the Minister in error or the person has, solely as a result of a change in law, ceased to be a charity.

Editorial Note: See the editorial note for s. 149.1(22).

▶ 149.1(24) ◀

(24) Receipts issued before annulment. An official receipt referred to in Part XXXV of the *Income Tax Regulations* issued, by a person whose registration has been annulled under subsection (23), before that annulment is, if the receipt would have been valid were the person a registered charity at the time the receipt was issued, deemed to be a valid receipt under that Part.

Editorial Note: See the editorial note for s. 149.1(22).

▶ 149.1(25) ◀

(25) Refusal to register — ineligible individual. The Minister may refuse to register a charity or Canadian amateur athletic association that has applied for registration as a registered charity or registered Canadian amateur athletic association if

(*a*) the application for registration is made on its behalf by an ineligible individual;

(*b*) an ineligible individual is a director, trustee, officer or like official of the charity or association, or controls or manages the charity or association, directly or indirectly, in any manner whatever; or

(*c*) the charity or association has accepted a gift from a foreign state, as defined in section 2 of the *State Immunity Act*, that is set out on the list referred to in subsection 6.1(2) of that Act.

Editorial Note: Pursuant to subsection 149.1(25), the Minister can refuse to register a charity or Canadian amateur athletic association if the application for registration is made by an "ineligible individual" or if an "ineligible individual" is a director, trustee, officer, or like official of the charity or association, or controls or manages the charity or association. Registration may also be refused where the association has accepted a gift from a foreign state supporting terrorism. See also the editorial note for the definition of "ineligible individual" in s. 149.1(1).

History: S. 149.1(25)(*c*) was added by S.C. 2014, c. 20, s. 21(3), applicable in respect of gifts accepted after February 10, 2014.

S. 149.1(25) was added by S.C. 2011, c. 24, s. 52(10), in force January 1, 2012.

Related Sections: S. 149.1(1), "ineligible individual"; s. 149.1(22) Refusal to register; s. 168(4) Objection to proposal or designation; s. 172(3) Appeal from refusal to register, revocation of registration, etc.

▶ 149.1(26) ◀

(26) Foreign charities. For the purposes of subparagraph (*a*)(v) of the definition "qualified donee" in subsection (1), the Minister may register, in consultation with the Minister of Finance, a foreign charity for a 24-month period that includes the time at which Her Majesty in right of Canada has made a gift to the foreign charity, if

(*a*) the foreign charity is not resident in Canada; and

(*b*) the Minister is satisfied that the foreign charity is

(i) carrying on relief activities in response to a disaster,

(ii) providing urgent humanitarian aid, or

(iii) carrying on activities in the national interest of Canada.

History: S. 149.1(26), the portion before subparagraph (*b*)(i), was replaced by S.C. 2015, c. 36, s. 18(2), applicable to applications made on or after the day on which this amendment receives royal assent, June 23, 2015, and formerly read:

(26) **Foreign charitable organizations.** For the purposes of subparagraph (*a*)(v) of the definition "qualified donee" in subsection (1), the Minister may register, in consultation with the Minister of Finance, a foreign organization for a 24-month period that includes the time at which Her Majesty in right of Canada has made a gift to the foreign organization, if

(*a*) the foreign organization is a charitable organization that is not resident in Canada; and

(*b*) the Minister is satisfied that the foreign organization is

S. 149.1(26) was added by S.C. 2012, c. 19, s. 7(6), and comes into force on January 1, 2013, except that subsection 149.1(26) does not apply in respect of registrations of charitable organizations outside Canada made before January 1, 2013.

Related Sections: 149.1(1) qualified donee.

SECTION 149.2: Material and insignificant interests

▶ 149.2(1) ◀

(1) Material and insignificant interests. In this section and section 149.1,

(*a*) a person has, at any time, a material interest in respect of a class of shares of the capital stock of a corporation if, at that time,

(i) the percentage of the shares of that class held by the person exceeds 0.5% of all the issued and outstanding shares of that class, or

(ii) the fair market value of the shares so held exceeds $100,000; and

(*b*) a private foundation has, at any time, an insignificant interest in respect of a class of shares of the capital stock of a corporation if, at that time, the percentage of shares of that class held by the private foundation does not exceed 2% of all the issued and outstanding shares of that class.

Editorial Note: Section 149.2 sets out the rules which must be followed by a private foundation to divest itself of excess shares and draws on numerous definitions contained in s. 149.1(1).

A private foundation will be required to divest shares pursuant to s. 149.2 if it has a "divestment obligation percentage", which is determined with reference to the foundation's "excess corporate holdings percentage". A private foundation's excess corporate holdings percentage is based on the percentage of shares of a class held by the foundation and all "relevant persons" in respect of the foundation that hold a "material interest" in the corporation (i.e., the foundation's "total corporate holdings percentage"). A "material interest" is defined in s. 149.2(1) to mean either ownership at a particular time of more than 0.5% of all issued and outstanding shares of a class or ownership of shares of a class having a fair market value at that time in excess of $100,000.

Generally, if the foundation's total corporate holdings percentage of a class of shares exceeds 20%, the foundation will have an excess corporate holdings percentage equal to that excess and will have a corresponding divestment obligation. However, shares that qualify as "exempt shares" are generally excluded in determining whether the 20% threshold has been exceeded (see the definition in s. 149.1(1)). A private foundation's excess corporate holdings percentage also excludes holdings that constitute an "insignificant interest" in a class of shares of the capital stock of a corporation (i.e., 2% or less of the issued and outstanding shares of the class).

If the foundation has a divestment obligation percentage at the end of a taxation year that is greater than 0%, the foundation is subject to penalties under s. 188.1(3.1). As any divestment obligation percentage of a foundation at the end of the taxation year is added to its divestment obligation percentage for the next taxation year, it may be subject to penalty again in the next year unless the divestment obligation percentage has been reduced to zero in that year.

Guides: T2082 Excess Corporate Holdings Regime for Private Foundations.

▶ 149.2(2) ◀

(2) Material transaction — anti-avoidance. If a private foundation or a relevant person in respect of the private foundation has engaged in one or more transactions or series of transactions or events, a purpose of which may reasonably be considered to be to avoid the application of the definition "material transaction", each of those transactions or series of transactions or events is deemed to be a material transaction.

Editorial Note: See the editorial notes for s. 149.1(1) "material transaction" and s. 149.2(1).

▶ 149.2(2.1) ◀

(2.1) Ownership. For the purposes of the definition "equity percentage", and subparagraph (*b*)(iii) of the definition "exempt shares", in subsection 149.1(1), a person who, if paragraph 251(5)(*b*) applied would be deemed by that paragraph to have the same position in relation to the control of a corporation as if the person owned a share, is deemed to own the share.

History: S. 149.2(2.1) was added by S.C. 2009, c. 2, s. 56(1), applicable after March 18, 2007.

▶ 149.2(3) ◀

(3) Net increase in excess corporate holdings percentage. The net increase in the excess corporate holdings percentage of a private foundation for a taxation year, in respect of a class of shares of the capital stock of a corporation, is the number of percentage points, if any, determined by the formula

$$A - B$$

where

A is the excess corporate holdings percentage of the private foundation at the end of the taxation year, in respect of the class, and

B is

(*a*) 0%, if

(i) at the beginning of the taxation year the private foundation was not both a private foundation and a registered charity, or

(ii) the private foundation was both a registered charity and a private foundation on March 18, 2007 and the taxation year is the first taxation year of the private foundation that begins after that date; and

(*b*) in any other case, the excess corporate holdings percentage of the private foundation in respect of the class at the end of its preceding taxation year.

Editorial Note: The divestment obligation percentage of a private foundation for a particular year is determined by adding to the divestment obligation percentage from the preceding year the net increase in the excess corporate holdings percentage allocated to that year under s. 149.2(5) less the net decrease allocated to that year under s. 149.2(7). See also the editorial note for s. 149.2(1).

▶ 149.2(4) ◀

(4) Net decrease in excess corporate holdings percentage. The net decrease in the excess corporate holdings percentage of a private foundation for a taxation year, in respect of a class of shares of the capital stock of a corporation, is the number of percentage points, if any, by which the percentage determined for B in the formula in subsection (3) for the taxation year exceeds the percentage determined for A in that formula for the taxation year.

Editorial Note: See the editorial notes for s. 149.2(1) and (3).

▶ 149.2(5) ◀

(5) Allocation of net increase in excess corporate holdings percentage. For the purpose of the description of B in the definition "divestment obligation percentage" in subsection 149.1(1), the net increase in the excess corporate holdings percentage of a private foundation in respect of a class of shares of the capital stock of a corporation, for a taxation year (in this subsection referred to as the "current year") is to be allocated in the following order:

(*a*) first to the divestment obligation percentage of the private foundation in respect of that class for the current year, to the extent that the private foundation has in the current year acquired for consideration shares of that class;

(*b*) then to the divestment obligation percentage of the private foundation in respect of that class for its fifth subsequent taxation year, to the extent of the lesser of

(i) that portion of the net increase in the excess corporate holdings percentage of the private foundation in respect of that class for the current year that is not allocated under paragraph (*a*), and

(ii) the percentage of the issued and outstanding shares of that class that were acquired by the private foundation in the current year by way of bequest;

(*c*) then to the divestment obligation percentage of the private foundation in respect of that class for its second subsequent taxation year, to the extent of the lesser of

(i) that portion of the net increase in the excess corporate holdings percentage of the private foundation in respect of that class for the current year that is not allocated under paragraph (*a*) or (*b*), and

(ii) the total of

(A) the percentage of the issued and outstanding shares of that class that were acquired by the private foundation in the current year by way of gift, other than from a relevant person or by way of bequest, and

(B) the portion of the net increase in the excess corporate holdings percentage of the private foundation that is attributable to the redemption, acquisition or cancellation of any of the issued and outstanding shares of that class in the current year by the corporation; and

(*d*) then to the divestment obligation percentage of the private foundation in respect of that class for its subsequent taxation year, to the extent of that portion of the net increase in the excess corporate holdings percentage of the private foundation in respect of that class for the current year that is not allocated under paragraph (*a*), (*b*) or (*c*).

Editorial Note: Under the provisions of s. 149.2(5), the net increase in a private foundation's excess corporate holdings percentage determined under s. 149.2(3) is allocated to its divestment obligation percentage for a particular year based on how the excess arose: (a) if the net increase arose as a result of shares purchased for consideration, the net increase is added to the divestment obligation percentage for the current year; (b) if the net increase arose as a result of shares acquired by bequest (i.e., a gift by will), the net increase is added to the divestment obligation percentage for the fifth subsequent taxation year; (c) if the net increase arose as a result of shares acquired by gift, other than from a relevant person or by bequest, the net increase is added to the divestment obligation percentage for the second subsequent taxation year; (d) if the net increase arose as a result of the redemption, acquisition, or cancellation of shares, the net increase is added to the divestment obligation percentage for the second subsequent taxation year; and (e) if the net increase arose in any other manner, it is added to the divestment obligation percentage for the next subsequent taxation year. Pursuant to s. 149.2(6), the Minister has discretion, on application by the foundation, to defer the year to which a net increase will be allocated to any of the ten taxation years subsequent to that year if it would be just and equitable to do so. See also the editorial notes for s. 149.2(1) and (3).

History: The application for s. 149.2(5)(*b*) and (*c*) was amended by S.C. 2009, c. 2, s. 56(5), in force on Royal Assent, March 12, 2009, to read as follows:

"If a registered charity was on March 19, 2007 a private foundation, in applying paragraphs 149.2(5)(*b*) and (*c*) of the Act to the first taxation year of the registered charity that begins after that date, the reference in those paragraphs to 'in the current year' shall be read as a reference to 'in the period that begins on March 18, 2007 and ends at the end of the current year'."

Forms: T2081 — Excess Corporate Holdings Worksheet for Private Foundations.

Guides: T2082 Excess Corporate Holdings Regime for Private Foundations.

► 149.2(6) ◄

(6) Minister's discretion. Notwithstanding subsection (5), on application by a private foundation, the Minister may, if the Minister believes it would be just and equitable to do so, reallocate any portion of the net increase in the excess corporate holdings percentage of the private foundation in respect of a class of shares of the capital stock of a corporation for a taxation year, that would otherwise be allocated under subsection (5) to the private foundation's divestment obligation percentage in respect of that class for a particular taxation year, to the private foundation's divestment obligation percentage in respect of that class for any of the ten taxation years subsequent to the particular taxation year.

Editorial Note: See the editorial notes for s. 149.2(1) and (5).

► 149.2(7) ◄

(7) Allocation of net decrease in excess corporate holdings percentage. For the purpose of the description of C in the definition "divestment obligation percentage" in subsection 149.1(1), the net decrease in the excess corporate holdings percentage of a private foundation in respect of a class of shares of the capital stock of a corporation for a taxation year (in this subsection referred to as the "current year") is to be allocated in the following order:

(*a*) first, to the divestment obligation percentage of the private foundation in respect of that class for the current year, to the extent of that divestment obligation percentage; and

(*b*) then to the divestment obligation percentage of the private foundation in respect of that class for a subsequent taxation year of the private foundation (referred to in this paragraph as the "subject year"), to the extent of the lesser of

(i) that portion of the net decrease in the excess corporate holdings percentage of the private foundation in respect of that class for the current year that is not allocated under paragraph (*a*), or under this paragraph, to the divestment obligation percentage of the private foundation in respect of that class for a taxation year of the private foundation that precedes the subject year, and

(ii) the amount of the divestment obligation percentage of the private foundation in respect of that class for the subject year, calculated as at the end of the current year and without reference to this subsection.

Editorial Note: Under the provisions of s. 149.2(7), any net decrease in a year in the excess corporate holdings percentage of a private foundation is allocated: (a) first, to reduce the divestment obligation percentage for the current year; and (b) then, to reduce the divestment obligation percentage of each subsequent taxation year in chronological order. If at the end of the year in which the decrease arose the allocation of the decrease has resulted in the elimination of the divestment obligation percentage for the current and all subsequent taxation years, any remaining amount of the decrease will expire. It cannot later be used to reduce an increase that arises in a subsequent year. See also the editorial notes for s. 149.2(1) and (3).

► 149.2(8) ◄

(8) Transitional rule. If the original corporate holdings percentage of a private foundation in respect of a class of shares of the capital stock of a corporation exceeds 20%, for the purpose of applying the definition "excess corporate holdings percentage" in subsection 149.1(1) to

(*a*) the first taxation year of the private foundation that begins after March 18, 2007, the reference to 20% in that definition in respect of that class is to be read as the original corporate holdings percentage of the private foundation in respect of that class;

(*b*) taxation years of the private foundation that are after the taxation year referred to in paragraph (*a*) and that begin before March 19, 2012, the reference to 20% in that definition in respect of that class is to be read as the greater of

(i) 20%, and

(ii) the lesser of

(A) the total corporate holdings percentage of the private foundation in respect of the class at the end of the immediately preceding taxation year, and

(B) the original corporate holdings percentage in respect of that class;

(*c*) taxation years of the private foundation that begin after March 18, 2012 and before March 19, 2017, the reference to 20% in that definition in respect of that class is to be read as the greater of

(i) 20%, and

(ii) the lesser of

(A) the total corporate holdings percentage of the private foundation in respect of the class at the end of the preceding taxation year, and

(B) the number of percentage points, if any, by which the private foundation's original corporate holdings percentage in respect of that class exceeds 20%;

(*d*) taxation years of the private foundation that begin after March 18, 2017 and before March 19, 2022, the reference to 20% in that definition in respect of that class is to be read as the greater of

(i) 20%, and

(ii) the lesser of

(A) the total corporate holdings percentage of the private foundation in respect of the class at the end of the preceding taxation year, and

(B) the number of percentage points, if any, by which the private foundation's original corporate holdings percentage in respect of that class exceeds 40%; and

(*e*) taxation years of the private foundation that begin after March 18, 2022 and before March 19, 2027, the reference to 20% in that definition in respect of that class is to be read as the greater of

(i) 20%, and

(ii) the lesser of

(A) the total corporate holdings percentage of the private foundation in respect of the class at the end of the preceding taxation year, and

(B) the number of percentage points, if any, by which the private foundation's original corporate holdings percentage in respect of that class exceeds 60%.

Editorial Note: Subsection 149.2(8) provides a transitional rule for a private foundation with an "original corporate holdings percentage" (i.e., the "total corporate holdings percentage" on March 18, 2007) in respect of a class of shares in excess of 20%. This provision allows the private foundation to divest its excess holdings over a more extended time period of up to 20 years. See also the editorial note for s. 149.2(1).

► 149.2(9) ◄

(9) Where subsection (10) applies. Subsection (10) applies for the purposes of applying section 149.1 and subsections (8) and 188.1(3.1) to a private foundation at a particular time if, both on March 18, 2007 and at the particular time,

(*a*) the private foundation was the sole trustee of a trust, or was a majority interest beneficiary (within the meaning assigned by section 251.1) of a trust more than 50% of the trustees of which were the private foundation and one or more relevant persons in respect of the private foundation; and

(*b*) the trust held one or more shares of a class of the capital stock of a corporation.

Editorial Note: Subsections 149.2(9) to (11) attribute to a private foundation at a particular time shares that were held by a trust on March 18, 2007 and at the particular time if the foundation was either (a) the sole trustee of the trust; or (b) a majority interest beneficiary (within the meaning assigned by s. 251.1) of a trust, more than 50% of the trustees of which were the private foundation and one or more "relevant persons" in respect of the private foundation. If the conditions for applicability are satisfied, the foundation is deemed to hold at the particular time the shares held by the trust in proportion to the value of the foundation's proportionate interest in the trust. Pursuant to s. 149.2(11), the valuation of a foundation's proportionate interest in a discretionary trust is to be determined by deeming the person with discretionary power to have exercised (or to have failed to exercise) the relevant power, as the case may be. The normal rules apply in determining whether the foundation would be required to divest any shares held by a trust. See also the editorial note for s. 149.2(1).

History: S. 149.2(9) was added by S.C. 2009, c. 2, s. 56(2), applicable to taxation years, of private foundations, that begin on or after February 26, 2008.

► 149.2(10) ◄

(10) Shares held through a trust on March 18, 2007. If this subsection applies at a particular time to a private foundation in respect of shares of a class of the capital stock of a corporation held by a trust, the private foundation is deemed to hold at the particular time that number of those shares as is determined by the formula

$$A \times B/C$$

where

A is the lesser of the number of those shares held by the trust on March 18, 2007 and the number so held at the particular time;

B is the total fair market value of all interests held by the private foundation in the trust at the particular time; and

C is the total fair market value of all property held by the trust at the particular time.

Editorial Note: See the editorial notes for s. 149.2(1) and (9).

History: S. 149.2(10) was added by S.C. 2009, c. 2, s. 56(2), applicable to taxation years, of private foundations, that begin on or after February 26, 2008.

► 149.2(11) ◄

(11) Discretionary trusts. For the purpose of subsection (10), if the amount of income or capital of a trust that a person may receive as a beneficiary under the trust depends on the exercise by any person of, or the failure by any person to exercise, a discretionary power, that person is deemed to have fully exercised, or to have failed to exercise, the power, as the case may be.

Editorial Note: See the editorial notes for s. 149.2(1) and (9).

History: S. 149.2(11) was added by S.C. 2009, c. 2, s. 56(2), applicable to taxation years, of private foundations, that begin on or after February 26, 2008.

Division I — Returns, Assessments, Payment and Appeals

Returns

SECTION 150: [Filing returns of income]

► 150(1) ◄

(1) Filing returns of income — general rule. Subject to subsection (1.1), a return of income that is in prescribed form and that contains prescribed information shall be filed with the Minister, without notice or demand for the return, for each taxation year of a taxpayer,

Editorial Note: S. 150(1) sets out the time within which various taxpayers are required to file returns of their income. Generally, a corporation has six months from the end of its taxation year to file a return and a trust or estate must file within 90 days of the end of the year (i.e., usually by the end of March). For individuals other than trusts, there are three potential filing deadlines: (i) April 30 (the general rule), (ii) June 15, if the taxpayer or the taxpayer's spouse carried on a business in the year, or (iii) where the taxpayer died during the year, but after October 31, within six months of the date of death. S. 150(1.1) lists the instances where a taxpayer is not legally required to file a return. In some cases, the taxpayer may still wish to file so as to obtain certain government benefits or to ensure an assessment (or "nil assessment"), which begins the limitation period for the return under s. 152(3.1).

Related Regulations: Part II.

Related Sections: 11(1) Proprietor of business; 70 Death of a taxpayer; 104(23) Deceased beneficiary of graduated rate estate; 119 Former resident — credit for tax paid; 150(3) Trustees, etc; 150(4) Death of partner or proprietor; 152(6) Reassessment where certain deductions claimed; 152(7) Assessment not dependent on return or information; 162(1) Failure to file return of income; 162(2) Repeated failure to file; 162(2.1) Failure to file — non-resident corporation; 162(3) Failure to file by trustee; 220(3) Extensions for returns; 238(1) Offences and punishment; s. 249(1) Definition of "taxation year".

Information Circulars: IC 97-2R15 Customized Forms; IC 00-1R4 Voluntary Disclosures Program.

Interpretation Bulletins: *Secondary* — IT-232.

Cases: The filing of a "temporary return" before April 30th, where a taxpayer mentioned an income estimate figure was held not to be sufficient to constitute a return within the meaning of the Act. *Carlson et al. v. The Queen*, 73 DTC 5192 (F.C.T.D.), affirming 72 DTC 1428 (T.R.B.)

► 150(1)(a) ◄

(a) Corporations — in the case of a corporation, by or on behalf of the corporation within six months after the end of the year if

(i) at any time in the year the corporation

(A) is resident in Canada,

(B) carries on business in Canada, unless the corporation's only revenue from carrying on business in Canada in the year consists of amounts in respect of which tax was payable by the corporation under subsection 212(5.1),

(C) has a taxable capital gain (otherwise than from an excluded disposition), or

(D) disposes of a taxable Canadian property (otherwise than in an excluded disposition), or

(ii) tax under this Part

(A) is payable by the corporation for the year, or

(B) would be, but for a tax treaty, payable by the corporation for the year (otherwise than in respect of a disposition of taxable Canadian property that is treaty-protected property of the corporation);

Related Sections: S. 150(5) Excluded disposition.

Tax Profile: August 2007 — Professionals and Other Service Providers Beware — A Canadian Trap.

Forms: T2 — Corporation Income Tax Return; T2Sch97 — Additional Information on Non-Resident Corporations in Canada; T2Sch150 — Net Income (Loss) for Income Tax Purposes for Life Insurance Companies (1999 and later taxation years).

Guides: T4012 Information for Corporations -T2 Corporation Income Tax Guide.

Income Tax Technical News: Issue No. 38, Single Administration of Ontario Corporate Tax.

Interpretation Bulletins: *Primary* — IT-304R2 Condominiums.

Tax Window Files: Canadian tax treatment of US LLPs and LLLPs, *June 14, 2017*, CRA Document No. 2017-0691131C6; , *June 14, 2017*, CRA Document No. 2017-0691131C6.

► 150(1)(b) ◄

(b) Deceased individuals — in the case of an individual who dies after October of the year and on or before the day that would be the individual's filing due date for the year if the individual had not died, by the individual's legal representatives on or before the day that is the later of the day on or before which the return would otherwise be required to be filed and the day that is 6 months after the day of death;

Related Regulations: Part II.

Related Sections: S. 248(1), "filing-due date", "legal representative".

► 150(1)(c) ◄

(c) Trusts or estates — in the case of an estate or trust, within 90 days from the end of the year;

Related Regulations: Part II; Part X.

Related Sections: 251.2(7) Filing and other deadlines.

Forms: T3GR — Group Income Tax and Information Return for RRSP, RRIF, RESP or RDSP Trusts; T3 RET — Trust Income Tax and Information Return.

Information Circulars: IC 78-5R3 Communal organizations; IC 78-14R4 Guidelines for trust companies and other persons responsible for filing T3GR, T3D, T3P, T3S, T3RI, and T3F returns.

► 150(1)(d) ◄

(d) Individuals — in the case of any other person, on or before

(i) the following April 30 by that person or, if the person is unable for any reason to file the return, by the person's guardian, committee or other legal representative (in this paragraph referred to as the person's "guardian"),

(ii) the following June 15 by that person or, if the person is unable for any reason to file the return, by the person's guardian where the person is

(A) an individual who carried on a business in the year, unless the expenditures made in the course of carrying on the business were primarily the cost or capital cost of tax shelter investments (as defined in subsection 143.2(1)), or

(B) at any time in the year a cohabiting spouse or common-law partner (within the meaning assigned by section 122.6) of an individual to whom clause (A) applies, or

(iii) where at any time in the year the person is a cohabiting spouse or common-law partner (within the meaning assigned by section 122.6) of an individual to whom paragraph (*b*) applies for the year, on or before the day that is the later of the day on or before which the person's return would otherwise be required to be filed and the day that is 6 months after the day of the individual's death; or

Related Sections: S. 237(1) Social Insurance Number; s. 248(1), "legal representative".

Forms: T1 — General Income Tax and Benefit Return.

Guides: 5000-G General Income Tax and Benefit Guide; General Income Tax and Benefit Guide for Non-Residents and Deemed Residents of Canada.

► 150(1)(e) ◄

(e) Designated persons — in a case where no person described by paragraph (*a*), (*b*) or (*d*) has filed the return, by such person as is required by notice in writing from the Minister to file the return, within such reasonable time as the notice specifies.

Related Regulations: Part II.

► 150(1.1) ◄

(1.1) Exception. Subsection (1) does not apply to a taxation year of a taxpayer if

Proposed Amendment

Legislative Proposals Relating to Income Tax Act and Other Legislation (July 27, 2018)

The portion of subsection 150(1.1) of the Act before paragraph (*a*) is replaced by the following:

(1.1) Exception. Subject to subsection (1.2), subsection (1) does not apply to a taxation year of a taxpayer if

Applicable: To taxation years that end after December 30, 2021.

(*a*) the taxpayer is a corporation that was a registered charity throughout the year; or

(*b*) the taxpayer is an individual unless

(i) tax is payable under this Part by the individual for the year,

(ii) where the individual is resident in Canada at any time in the year, the individual has a taxable capital gain or disposes of capital property in the year,

(iii) where the individual is non-resident throughout the year, the individual has a taxable capital gain (otherwise than from an excluded disposition) or disposes of a taxable Canadian property (otherwise than in an excluded disposition) in the year, or

(iv) at the end of the year the individual's HBP balance or LLP balance (as defined in subsection 146.01(1) or 146.02(1)) is a positive amount.

Proposed Amendment

Legislative Proposals Relating to Income Tax Act and Other Legislation (July 27, 2018)

Section 150 of the Act is amended by adding the following after subsection (1.1):

(1.2) Exception trusts. Subsection (1.1) does not apply to a taxation year of a trust if the trust is resident in Canada and is an express trust, or for civil law purposes a trust other than a trust that is established by law or by judgement, unless the trust

(*a*) had been in existence for less than three months at the end of the year;

(*b*) holds assets with a total fair market value that does not exceed $50,000 throughout the year, if the only assets held by the trust throughout the year are one or more of

(i) cash,

(ii) a debt obligation described in paragraph (*a*) of the definition *fully exempt interest* in subsection 212(3),

(iii) a share, debt obligation or right listed on a designated stock exchange,

(iv) a share of the capital stock of a mutual fund corporation,

(v) a unit of a mutual fund trust, and

(vi) an interest in a related segregated fund (within the meaning assigned by paragraph 138.1(1)(*a*));

(*c*) is required under the relevant rules of professional conduct or the laws of Canada or a province to hold funds for the purposes of the activity that is regulated under those rules or laws, provided the trust is not maintained as a separate trust for a particular client or clients;

(*d*) is a registered charity;

(*e*) is a club, society or association described in paragraph 149(1)(*l*);

(*f*) is a mutual fund trust;

(*g*) is, for greater certainty, a related segregated fund trust, within the meaning assigned by paragraph 138.1(1)(*a*);

(*h*) is prescribed to be a master trust;

(*i*) is, for greater certainty, a graduated rate estate;

(*j*) is a *qualified disability trust*, as defined in subsection 122(3);

(*k*) is an employee life and health trust;

(*l*) is a trust described under paragraph 81(1)(*g*.3);

(*m*) is a trust under or governed by

(i) a deferred profit sharing plan,

(ii) a pooled registered pension plan,

(iii) a registered disability savings plan,

(iv) a registered education savings plan,

(v) a registered pension plan,

(vi) a registered retirement income fund,

(vii) a registered retirement savings plan, or

(viii) a tax-free savings account; or

(*n*) a cemetery care trust or a trust governed by an eligible funeral arrangement.

Applicable: To taxation years that end after December 30, 2021.

Tax Topics: No. 2040, CRA Roundtable at Association de planification fiscale et financière (APFF) 2010 Conference.

Forms: T1261 — Application for a Canada Revenue Agency Individual Tax Number (ITN) for Non-Residents.

Tax Window Files: 2016 STEP - Q13 -Filing Obligation for 75(2) trust, *June 10, 2016*, CRA Document No. 2016-0645811C6.

► 150(2) ◄

(2) Demands for returns. Every person, whether or not the person is liable to pay tax under this Part for a taxation year and whether or not a return has been filed under subsection (1) or (3), shall, on demand sent by the Minister, file, within such reasonable time stipulated in the demand, with the Minister in prescribed form and containing prescribed information a return of the income for the taxation year designated in the demand.

History: S. 150(2) was replaced by S.C. 2012, c. 19, s. 8, in force on Royal Assent, June 29, 2012. S. 150(2) formerly read:

(2) *Demands for returns.* Every person, whether or not the person is liable to pay tax under this Part for a taxation year and whether or not a return has been filed under subsection (1) or (3), shall, on demand from the Minister, served personally or by registered letter, file, within such reasonable time as may be stipulated in the demand, with the Minister in prescribed form and containing prescribed information a return of the income for the taxation year designated in the demand.

Related Sections: S. 162(2) Repeated failure to file; s. 202(3) Provisions applicable to Part; s. 207(3) Multiple holders; s. 207.2(3) Provisions applicable to Part; s. 238(1) Offences and punishment.

Cases: A failure to file a return on demand constitutes an offence and the person guilty of such an offence is liable to a penalty under section 238. *Regina v. O'Donnell*, 57 DTC 1287 (Ont. C.A.).

► 150(3) ◄

(3) Trustees, etc. Every trustee in bankruptcy, assignee, liquidator, curator, receiver, trustee or committee and every agent or other person administering, managing, winding up, controlling or otherwise dealing with the property, business, estate or income of a person who has not filed a return for a taxation year as required by this section shall file a return in prescribed form of that person's income for that year.

Related Regulations: 204.

Related Sections: S. 150(2) Demands for returns; s. 162(2) Repeated failure to file; s. 207(3) Multiple holders; s. 207.2(3) Provisions applicable to Part; s. 220(2.1) Waiver of filing of documents; s. 248(1), "bankrupt", "estate of the bankrupt".

► 150(4) ◄

(4) Death of partner or proprietor. Where

(*a*) subsection 34.1(9) or 34.2(8) applies in computing an individual's income for a taxation year from a business, or

(*b*) an individual who carries on a business in a taxation year dies in the year and after the end of a fiscal period of the business that ends in the year, another fiscal period of the business (in this subsection referred to as the "short period") ends in the year because of the individual's death, and the individual's legal representative elects that this subsection apply,

the individual's income from businesses for short periods, if any, shall not be included in computing the individual's income for the year and the individual's legal representative shall file an additional return of income for the year in respect of the individual as if the return were filed in respect of another person and shall pay the tax payable under this Part by that other person for the year computed as if

(*c*) the other person's only income for the year were the amount determined by the formula

$$A + B - C$$

where

A is the total of all amounts each of which is the individual's income from a business for a short fiscal period,

B is the total of all amounts each of which is an amount deducted under subsection 34.2(8) in computing the individual's income for the taxation year in which the individual dies, and

C is the total of all amounts each of which is an amount included under subsection 34.1(9) in computing the individual's income for the taxation year in which the individual dies, and

(*d*) subject to sections 114.2 and 118.93, that other person were entitled to the deductions to which the individual is entitled under sections 110, 118 to 118.7 and 118.9 for the year in computing the individual's taxable income or tax payable under this Part, as the case may be, for the year.

Related Regulations: Part II.

Related Sections: S. 11(1) Proprietor of business; s. 70 Death of a taxpayer; s. 104(23)(*d*) Testamentary trusts; s. 114.2 Deductions in separate returns; s. 159(1) Person acting for another; s. 162(3) Failure to file by trustee; s. 249 Definition of "taxation year"; s. 249.1(1) Definition of "fiscal period".

Interpretation Bulletins: *Secondary* — IT-278R2 Death of a partner or of a retired partner; IT-326R3 Returns of deceased persons as "another person".

► 150(5) ◄

(5) Excluded disposition. For the purposes of this section, a disposition of a property by a taxpayer at any time in a taxation year is an excluded disposition if

(*a*) the taxpayer is non-resident at that time;

(*b*) no tax is payable under this Part by the taxpayer for the taxation year;

(*c*) the taxpayer is, at that time, not liable to pay any amount under this Act in respect of any previous taxation year (other than an amount for which the Minister has accepted, and holds, adequate security under section 116 or 220); and

(*d*) each taxable Canadian property disposed of by the taxpayer in the taxation year is

(i) excluded property within the meaning assigned by subsection 116(6), or

(ii) a property in respect of the disposition of which the Minister has issued to the taxpayer a certificate under subsection 116(2), (4) or (5.2).

SECTION 150.1: [Electronic filing]

► 150.1(1) ◄

(1) Definition of "electronic filing". For the purposes of this section, "electronic filing" means using electronic media in a manner specified in writing by the Minister.

Canadian Tax Foundation: Baron, *Current Issues: Mandatory E-filing*, 2012 Ontario Tax Conference 1A:23–24.

► 150.1(2) ◄

(2) Filing of return by electronic transmission. A person who meets the criteria specified in writing by the Minister may file a return of income for a taxation year by way of electronic filing.

Related Sections: S. 244(21) Proof of return filed; s. 244(22) Filing of information returns.

Tax Topics: No. 2243, Saber & Sone Group v. MNR - Accounting Firm Loses Efile Privileges.

Forms: T183 — Information Return for Individuals Filing Electronically; T183 Corp — Information Return for Corporations Filing Electronically.

Guides: RC4018 Electronic Filers Manual; T4077 E-FILE On-line for Tax Professionals.

► 150.1(2.1) ◄

(2.1) Mandatory filing of return by electronic transmission. If a corporation is, in respect of a taxation year, a prescribed corporation, the corporation shall file its return of income for the taxation year by way of electronic filing.

History: S. 150.1(2.1) was added by S.C. 2009, c. 2, s. 57(1), applicable to taxation years that end after 2009.

Related Regulations: 205.1(2).

► 150.1(2.2) ◄

(2.2) Definition of "tax preparer". In this section and subsection 162(7.3), "tax preparer", for a calendar year, means a person or partnership who, in the year, accepts consideration to prepare more than 10 returns of income of corporations or more than 10 returns of income of individuals (other than trusts), but does not include an employee who prepares returns of income in the course of performing their duties of employment.

History: S. 150.1(2.2) was added by S.C. 2012, c. 19, s. 9(1), applicable in respect of returns of income for the 2012 and subsequent taxation years that are filed after 2012.

► 150.1(2.3) ◄

(2.3) Electronic filing — tax preparer. A tax preparer shall file any return of income prepared by the tax preparer for consideration by way of electronic filing, except that 10 of the returns of corporations and 10 of the returns of individuals may be filed other than by way of electronic filing.

History: S. 150.1(2.3) was added by S.C. 2012, c. 19, s. 9(1), applicable in respect of returns of income for the 2012 and subsequent taxation years that are filed after 2012.

Canadian Tax Foundation: Baron, *Current Issues: Mandatory E-filing*, 2012 Ontario Tax Conference 1A:23–24.

► 150.1(2.4) ◄

(2.4) Exceptions. Subsection (2.3) does not apply to a tax preparer for a calendar year in respect of a return of income

(*a*) of a type for which the tax preparer has applied to the Minister for authority to file by way of electronic filing for the year and for which that authority has not been granted because the tax preparer does not meet the criteria referred to in subsection (2);

(*b*) of a corporation described in any of paragraphs 205.1(2)(*a*) to (*c*) of the *Income Tax Regulations*; or

(*c*) of a type that the Minister does not accept by way of electronic filing.

History: S. 150.1(2.4) was added by S.C. 2012, c. 19, s. 9(1), applicable in respect of returns of income for the 2012 and subsequent taxation years that are filed after 2012.

► 150.1(3) ◄

(3) Deemed date of filing. For the purposes of section 150, where a return of income of a taxpayer for a taxation year is filed by way of electronic filing, it shall be deemed to be a return of income filed with the Minister in prescribed form on the day the Minister acknowledges acceptance of it.

► 150.1(4) ◄

(4) Declaration. Where a return of income of a taxpayer for a taxation year is filed by way of electronic filing by a particular person (in this subsection referred to as the "filer") other than the person who is required to file the return, the person who is required to file the return shall make an information return in prescribed form containing prescribed information, sign it, retain a copy of it and provide the filer with the information return, and that return and the copy shall be deemed to be a record referred to in section 230 in respect of the filer and the other person.

Forms: T183 CORP — Information Return for Corporations Filing Electronically; T183 — Information Return for Electronic Filing.

► 150.1(5) ◄

(5) Application to other Parts. This section also applies to Parts I.2 to XIII, with such modifications as the circumstances require.

Estimate of Tax

SECTION 151: Estimate of tax

Every person required by section 150 to file a return of income shall in the return estimate the amount of tax payable.

Related Sections: 104(23) Deceased beneficiary of graduated rate estate; 153(2) Deemed withholding; 156(1) Other individuals; 157(1) Payment by corporation; 157(2) Application to SIFT trusts; 162(3) Failure to file by trustee; 187(3) Provisions applicable to Part; 189(3) Share deemed to be debt; 193(3) Interest; 195(3) Interest; 219(3) Provisions applicable to Part; s. 248(1), definition of "amount".

Tax Topics: No. 2127, CRA Panel: Rulings Update and Other Department News.

Information Circulars: IC 70-6R9 Advance Income Tax Rulings and Technical Interpretations.

Assessment

SECTION 152: Assessment

► 152(1) ◄

(1) Assessment. The Minister shall, with all due dispatch, examine a taxpayer's return of income for a taxation year, assess the tax for the year, the interest and penalties, if any, payable and determine

(*a*) the amount of refund, if any, to which the taxpayer may be entitled by virtue of section 129, 131, 132 or 133 for the year; or

(*b*) the amount of tax, if any, deemed by subsection 120(2) or (2.2), 122.5(3), 122.51(2), 122.7(2) or (3), 122.8(4), 122.9(2), 122.91(1), 125.4(3), 125.5(3), 125.6(2), 127.1(1), 127.41(3) or 210.2(3) or (4) to be paid on account of the taxpayer's tax payable under this Part for the year.

Editorial Note: Under s. 152(1), the Minister is required, with all due dispatch, to examine a return for the taxation year and assess any tax, interest and penalties payable. The Minister is also required to determine the amount of refund, if any, that may be available to the taxpayer for the year in the following circumstances:

(1) The refund of refundable dividend tax on hand to a private corporation upon payment of a taxable dividend (s. 129);

(2) The refund of refundable capital gains tax on hand to a mutual fund corporation upon the paying of a capital gains dividend or the making of a capital gains redemption(s. 131);

(3) The refund of refundable capital gains tax on hand to a mutual fund trust upon the trust making a capital gains redemption (s. 132); and

(4) The refund of allowable refundable tax on hand to a non-resident-owned investment corporation upon payment of a taxable dividend (s. 133).

In addition, the Minister is required to determine the amount of tax deemed to have been paid by a taxpayer in respect of:

- the partial abatement of tax for income earned in Quebec under s. 120(2);
- the individual's income tax payable to an Aboriginal government under s. 120(2.2);
- the goods and services tax credit under s. 122.5(3);
- the medical expense supplement under s. 122.51(2);

- the working income tax benefit under s. 122.7(2) or (3);
- the climate action incentive credit under s. 122.8(4) (effective for 2018 and subsequent years);
- the school supplies tax credit under s. 122.9(2);
- the Canada Training Credit under s. 122.91(2) (effective January 1, 2019);
- the refundable Canadian film or video production service tax credit under ss. 125.4(3) and 125.5(3);
- the refundable labour tax credit for journalism under s. 125.6(2) (effective January 1, 2019);
- the refundable investment tax credit available to the taxpayer under s. 127.1(1);
- the tax credit that a beneficiary of a mining reclamation trust may claim under s. 127.41(3); or
- amounts included as designated income of trusts under s. 210.2(3) or (4).

History: S. 152(1)(*b*) was replaced by S.C. 2019, c. 29, s. 32(1), deemed to have come into force on January 1, 2019, and formerly read:

(*b*) the amount of tax, if any, deemed by subsection 120(2) or (2.2), 122.5(3), 122.51(2), 122.7(2) or (3), 122.8(4), 122.9(2), 125.4(3), 125.5(3), 127.1(1), 127.41(3) or 210.2(3) or (4) to be paid on account of the taxpayer's tax payable under this Part for the year.

S. 152(1)(*b*) was replaced by S.C. 2018, c. 27, s. 18(1), applicable to the 2018 and subsequent taxation years, and formerly read:

(*b*) the amount of tax, if any, deemed by subsection 120(2) or (2.2), 122.5(3), 122.51(2), 122.7(2) or (3), 122.9(2), 125.4(3), 125.5(3), 127.1(1), 127.41(3) or 210.2(3) or (4) to be paid on account of the taxpayer's tax payable under this Part for the year.

S. 152(1)(*b*) was replaced by S.C. 2016, c. 7, s. 41(2), applicable to the 2017 and subsequent taxation years, and formerly read:

(*b*) the amount of tax, if any, deemed by subsection 120(2) or (2.2), 122.5(3), 122.51(2), 122.7(2) or (3), 122.8(2) or (3), 122.9(2), 125.4(3), 125.5(3), 127.1(1), 127.41(3) or 210.2(3) or (4) to be paid on account of the taxpayer's tax payable under this Part for the year.

S. 152(1)(*b*) was replaced by S.C. 2016, c. 7, s. 41(1), applicable to the 2016 taxation year, and formerly read:

(*b*) the amount of tax, if any, deemed by subsection 120(2) or (2.2), 122.5(3), 122.51(2), 122.7(2) or (3), 122.8(2) or (3), 125.4(3), 125.5(3), 127.1(1), 127.41(3) or 210.2(3) or (4) to be paid on account of the taxpayer's tax payable under this Part for the year.

S. 152(1)(*b*) was replaced by S.C. 2014, c. 39, s. 55(1), applicable to the 2015 and subsequent taxation years, and formerly read:

(*b*) the amount of tax, if any, deemed by subsection 120(2) or (2.2), 122.5(3), 122.51(2), 122.7(2) or (3), 125.4(3), 125.5(3), 127.1(1), 127.41(3) or 210.2(3) or (4) to be paid on account of the taxpayer's tax payable under this Part for the year.

Related Sections: 122.91(1) Claimed amount; 125.6(2) Tax credit; 152(4) Assessment and reassessment; 152(5) Limitation on assessments.

Canadian Tax Foundation: Potter, *Assess with All Due Dispatch*, 2013 Canadian Tax Highlights 21(7):4–5; Couvrette, *Budget Dampens Ficek Relief for Tax Shelter Investors*, 2013 Canadian Tax Focus 3(3):3; Russell, *Assessments, Reassessments, and Waivers*, 2012 Tax Dispute Resolution, Compliance and Adminstration Conference 26:1–14.

Tax Topics: No. 2169, Minister Cannot Delay Assessing Return To Discourage Tax Shelter Participation.

Cases: The withholding of tax is not an assessment but a way for the government to ensure that the tax to which it is entitled will be received from non-residents. If withholding is not an assessment, a waiver authorizing a Canadian taxpayer to not withhold tax on the fees payable to a non-resident is also not an assessment. The Court did not have jurisdiction to grant the relief requested as no assessments had been issued. *Beggs et al. v. The Queen*, 2016 DTC 1044 (TCC)

The taxpayers were seeking rectification of an error in the corporate taxpayer's articles of incorporation. That error resulted in the taxpayer being reassessed under the shareholder benefit provisions. The CRA had been added as a party to the proceedings and this decision was upheld on appeal. Although the participation of the CRA was not essential, there was a connection between the tax assessment and the rectification. *Lau v. Canada (Attorney General)*, 2015 DTC 5020 (B.C.S.C.)

Where a charitable donation tax shelter was being audited, the Winnipeg Tax Center's policy was to defer donor's assessments pending the outcome of the audit. This breached the Minister's duty to assess with "all due dispatch" *Ficek v. Canada (AG)*, 2013 DTC 5104 (F.C.)

The non-resident taxpayer sold its shares of a Canadian corporation and the purchaser paid $5,350,603 to the Receiver General in escrow under s. 116. The taxpayer's assessment (and refund) was delayed by a GAAR audit. The taxpayer's application for an order of *mandamus* requiring such assessment together with the release of the $5,350,603 was dismissed because the GAAR audit constituted "special circumstances" justifying the Minister's delay in issuing the assessment. *Merlis Investments Limited v. The Queen*, 2000 DTC 6634 (F.C.T.D.)

Following a related Auditor General's report, the plaintiff was granted public interest standing to challenge the alleged preferential tax treatment given to certain family trusts. Standing was granted because: (a) no one apart from the plaintiff was likely to challenge what the Minister had done; (b) a serious issue was involved; (c) the plaintiff had a serious interest in the matter; and (d) there was no other way to bring the matter before the Court. *The Queen et al. v. Harris*, 2000 DTC 6373 (F.C.A.), affirming 99 DTC 5018 (F.C.T.D.)

Although the Minister's original assessment of the taxpayer's returns had not been made "with all due dispatch", the taxpayer's tax liability was not affected by the fact that no assessment had been made. *The Queen v. Ginsberg*, 96 DTC 6372 (F.C.A.), reversing 94 DTC 1430 (T.C.C.)

A return filed on March 2, 1977 and not assessed until July 5, 1983 was not assessed "with all due dispatch". If those words were not to be deprived of all meaning, the lapse of time in this case must be considered to be outside the period contemplated. *J. Stollar Construction Ltd. v. M.N.R.*, 89 DTC 134 (T.C.C.)

► 152(1.01) ◄

(1.01) Determination of disability tax credit eligibility. The Minister shall, if an individual requests by prescribed form, determine with all due dispatch whether an amount is deductible, or would if this Act were read without reference to paragraph 118.3(1)(*c*) be deductible, under section 118.3 in computing the individual's tax payable under this Part for a taxation year and send a notice of the determination to the individual.

History: S. 152(1.01) was added by S.C. 2011, c. 15, s. 3(1), applicable, subject to the application below, to taxation years that end after 2009 in respect of forms filed with the Minister of National Revenue after June 26, 2011.

If an individual, on or before June 26, 2011, has filed for a taxation year that ends after 2007 and before 2012 the certificate described in paragraph 118.3(1)(*a.2*) or (*a.3*) and, for that year, the Minister of National Revenue has issued a notice that no tax is payable, then

(a) in respect of the individual, the reference in the application above to "2009" is to be read as a reference to "2007";

(b) the Minister is deemed to have issued a notice of determination to the individual on the later of June 26, 2011 or the actual day the notice is issued; and

(c) subparagraph 165(1)(*a*)(ii) shall in respect of the determination be read as follows:

"(ii) the day that is 180 days after the day that the Minister is deemed to have issued a notice of determination; and"

► 152(1.1) ◄

(1.1) Determination of losses. Where the Minister ascertains the amount of a taxpayer's non-capital loss, net capital loss, restricted farm loss, farm loss or limited partnership loss for a taxation year and the taxpayer has not reported that amount as such a loss in the taxpayer's return of income for that year, the Minister shall, at the request of the taxpayer, determine, with all due dispatch, the amount of the loss and shall send a notice of determination to the person by whom the return was filed.

Related Sections: S. 152(1.2) Provisions applicable.

Information Circulars: IC 84-1 Revision of capital cost allowance claims and other permissive deductions.

► 152(1.11) ◄

(1.11) Determination pursuant to s. 245(2). Where at any time the Minister ascertains the tax consequences to a taxpayer by reason of subsection 245(2) with respect to a transaction, the Minister

(*a*) shall, in the case of a determination pursuant to subsection 245(8), or

(*b*) may, in any other case,

determine any amount that is relevant for the purposes of computing the income, taxable income or taxable income earned in Canada of, tax or other amount payable by, or amount refundable to, the taxpayer under this Act and, where such a determination is made, the Minister shall send to the taxpayer, with all due dispatch, a notice of determination stating the amount so determined.

Related Sections: S. 152(1.12) When determination not to be made; s. 152(1.2) Provisions applicable; s. 245(6) Request for adjustments; s. 245(7) Exception.

▶ 152(1.111) ◀

(1.111) Application of s. 245(1). The definitions in subsection 245(1) apply to subsection (1.11).

▶ 152(1.12) ◀

(1.12) When determination not to be made. A determination of an amount shall not be made with respect to a taxpayer under subsection (1.11) at a time where that amount is relevant only for the purposes of computing the income, taxable income or taxable income earned in Canada of, tax or other amount payable by, or amount refundable to, the taxpayer under this Act for a taxation year ending before that time.

▶ 152(1.2) ◀

(1.2) Provisions applicable. Paragraphs 56(1)(*l*) and 60(*o*), this Division and Division J, as they relate to an assessment or a reassessment and to assessing or reassessing tax, apply, with any modifications that the circumstances require, to a determination or redetermination under subsection (1.01) and to a determination or redetermination of an amount under this Division or an amount deemed under section 122.61 to be an overpayment on account of a taxpayer's liability under this Part, except that

(*a*) subsections (1) and (2) do not apply to determinations made under subsections (1.01), (1.1) and (1.11);

(*b*) an original determination of a taxpayer's non-capital loss, net capital loss, restricted farm loss, farm loss or limited partnership loss for a taxation year may be made by the Minister only at the request of the taxpayer;

(*c*) subsection 164(4.1) does not apply to a determination made under subsection (1.4); and

(*d*) if the Minister determines the amount deemed by subsection 122.5(3) to have been paid by an individual for a taxation year to be nil, subsection (2) does not apply to the determination unless the individual requests a notice of determination from the Minister.

History: S. 152(1.2)(*d*) was added by S.C. 2014, c. 20, s. 22(1), applicable to the 2014 and subsequent taxation years.

S. 152(1.2), the portion before paragraph (*b*) was replaced by S.C. 2011, c. 15, s. 3(2), applicable, subject to the application below, to taxation years that end after 2009 in respect of forms filed with the Minister of National Revenue after June 26, 2011.

If an individual, on or before June 26, 2011, has filed for a taxation year that ends after 2007 and before 2012 the certificate described in paragraph 118.3(1)(*a*.2) or (*a*.3) and, for that year, the Minister of National Revenue has issued a notice that no tax is payable, then

(a) in respect of the individual, the reference in the application above to "2009" is to be read as a reference to "2007";

(b) the Minister is deemed to have issued a notice of determination to the individual on the later of June 26, 2011 or the actual day the notice is issued; and

(c) subparagraph 165(1)(*a*)(ii) shall in respect of the determination be read as follows:

"(ii) the day that is 180 days after the day that the Minister is deemed to have issued a notice of determination; and"

S. 152(1.2), the portion before paragraph (*b*) formerly read:

(1.2) *Provisions applicable.* Paragraphs 56(1)(*l*) and 60(*o*), this Division and Division J, as they relate to an assessment or a reassessment and to assessing or reassessing tax, apply, with such modifications as the circumstances require, to a determination or redetermination of an amount under this Division or an amount deemed under section 122.61 or 126.1 to be an overpayment on account of a taxpayer's liability under this Part, except that

(*a*) subsections (1) and (2) do not apply to determinations made under subsections (1.1) and (1.11);

▶ 152(1.3) ◀

(1.3) Determination binding. For greater certainty, where the Minister makes a determination of the amount of a taxpayer's non-capital loss, net capital loss, restricted farm loss, farm loss or limited partnership loss for a taxation year or makes a determination under subsection (1.11) with respect to a taxpayer, the determination is (subject to the taxpayer's rights of objection and appeal in respect of the determination and to any redetermination by the Minister) binding on both the Minister and the taxpayer for the purpose of calculating the income, taxable income or taxable income earned in Canada of, tax or other amount payable by, or amount refundable to, the taxpayer, as the case may be, for any taxation year.

▶ 152(1.4) ◀

(1.4) Determination in respect of a partnership. The Minister may, within 3 years after the day that is the later of

(*a*) the day on or before which a member of a partnership is, or but for subsection 220(2.1) would be, required under section 229 of the *Income Tax Regulations* to make an information return for a fiscal period of the partnership, and

(*b*) the day the return is filed,

determine any income or loss of the partnership for the fiscal period and any deduction or other amount, or any other matter, in respect of the partnership for the fiscal period that is relevant in determining the income, taxable income or taxable income earned in Canada of, tax or other amount payable by, or any amount refundable to or deemed to have been paid or to have been an overpayment by, any member of the partnership for any taxation year under this Part.

Editorial Note: For 2011 and later years, the CRA has expanded the number of partnerships it will administratively require to file a return in accordance with Regulation 229. Under the revised administrative policy, where a partnership has at least one corporate member, it must file a return. Previously, a partnership with five or fewer partners that did not have a partnership as a partner did not have to file a return. An assets and income threshold test has been added to administratively determine if a return must be filed; this test replaces the old five or fewer partner test. For 2013 and 2014, family farm partnerships composed of only individuals are exempt from filing, but if one partner is a trust or a corporation, a T5013 is required. In addition, the partnership return, Form T5013, has become more detailed, requiring the partnership to compute, among other things, each partner's adjusted cost base in their partnership interest.

Related Sections: S. 165(1.15) Partnership.

Canadian Tax Foundation: Tollstam, *Amending Partnership Returns: Three-Year Limitation,* 2015 Canadian Tax Highlights 23(10):3–4.

Tax Topics: No. 1831, Should You File a Partnership Information Return?.

Tax Window Files: Amending a statute barred partnership return, *April 17, 2018*, CRA Document No. 2018-0739141I7; *Late determination for partnership*, March 8, 2017, CRA Document No. 2016-0648571I7.

▶ 152(1.5) ◀

(1.5) Notice of determination. Where a determination is made under subsection (1.4) in respect of a partnership for a fiscal period, the Minister shall send a notice of the determination to the partnership and to each person who was a member of the partnership during the fiscal period.

▶ 152(1.6) ◀

(1.6) Absence of notification. No determination made under subsection (1.4) in respect of a partnership for a fiscal period is invalid solely because one or more persons who were members of the partnership during the period did not receive a notice of the determination.

▶ 152(1.7) ◀

(1.7) Binding effect of determination. Where the Minister makes a determination under subsection (1.4) or a redetermination in respect of a partnership,

(*a*) subject to the rights of objection and appeal of the member of the partnership referred to in subsection 165(1.15) in respect of the determination or redetermination, the determination or redetermination is binding on the Minister and each member of the partnership for the purposes of calculating the income, taxable income or taxable income earned in Canada of, tax or other amount payable by, or any amount refundable to or deemed to have been paid or to have been an overpayment by, the members for any taxation year under this Part; and

(*b*) notwithstanding subsections (4), (4.01), (4.1) and (5), the Minister may, before the end of the day that is one year after the day on which all rights of objection and appeal expire or are determined in respect of the determination or redetermination, assess the tax, interest, penalties or other amounts payable and determine an amount deemed to have been paid or to have been an overpayment under this Part in respect of any member of the partnership and any other taxpayer for any taxation year as may be necessary to give effect to the determination or redetermination or a decision of the Tax Court of Canada, the Federal Court of Appeal or the Supreme Court of Canada.

Cases: The taxpayer owned units in Norfolk, a limited partnership tax shelter. For 2000, the taxpayer claimed his allocated proportionate share of Norfolk's losses as a deduction. On March 31, 2004, Norfolk and the CRA executed a settlement in the form of a letter wherein the CRA agreed to make a determination of Norfolk's losses. On November 26, 2004, the CRA confirmed the determination. On August 22, 2005, the Minister reassessed the taxpayer for 2000 to give effect to the determination as set out in the letter. On appeal, the taxpayer unsuccessfully argued the reassessment was statute-barred. The taxpayer was bound by the results of the determination, and Norfolk's rights of objection were determined when the Minister issued the confirmation. Those rights, whether or not they were exercised, further extended the period the Minister could reassess under s. 152(1.7)(*b*). *Cummings v. The Queen*, 2009 DTC 1178 (T.C.C.)

▶ 152(1.8) ◀

(1.8) Time to assess. Where, as a result of representations made to the Minister that a person was a member of a partnership in respect of a fiscal period, a determination is made under subsection (1.4) for the period and the Minister, the Tax Court of Canada, the Federal Court of Appeal or the Supreme Court of Canada concludes at a subsequent time that the partnership did not exist for the period or that, throughout the period, the person was not a member of the partnership, the Minister may, notwithstanding subsections (4), (4.1) and (5), within one year after that subsequent time, assess the tax, interest, penalties or other amounts payable, or determine an amount deemed to have been paid or to have been an overpayment under this Part, by any taxpayer for any taxation year, but only to the extent that the assessment or determination can reasonably be regarded

(*a*) as relating to any matter that was relevant in the making of the determination made under subsection (1.4);

(*b*) as resulting from the conclusion that the partnership did not exist for the period; or

(*c*) as resulting from the conclusion that the person was, throughout the period, not a member of the partnership.

Related Sections: S. 165(1.1) Limitation of right to object to assessments or determinations; s. 169(2) Limitation of right to appeal from assessments or determinations.

▶ 152(1.9) ◀

(1.9) Waiver of determination limitation period. A waiver in respect of the period during which the Minister may make a determination under subsection (1.4) in respect of a partnership for a fiscal period may be made by one member of the partnership if that member is

(*a*) designated for that purpose in the information return made under section 229 of the *Income Tax Regulations* for the fiscal period; or

(*b*) otherwise expressly authorized by the partnership to so act.

History: S. 152(1.9) was added by S.C. 2012, c. 19, s. 10, in force on Royal Assent, June 29, 2012.

▶ 152(2) ◀

(2) Notice of assessment. After examination of a return, the Minister shall send a notice of assessment to the person by whom the return was filed.

Related Sections: S. 152(4) Assessment and reassessment; s. 165 Objections to assessment; s. 166 Irregularities; s. 169 Appeal; s. 220(1) Minister's Duty.

Forms: T1132 — Alternative Address Authorization.

▶ 152(3) ◀

(3) Liability not dependent on assessment. Liability for the tax under this Part is not affected by an incorrect or incomplete assessment or by the fact that no assessment has been made.

Editorial Note: This provision should be read together with s. 152(4), which gives the Minister power to reassess within a certain period. It should be observed, however, that under s. 166, an assessment shall not be set aside because of any irregularity, informality, omission or error in the observation of any provision in the Act of a directory nature. Also, under s. 152(8), an assessment will be valid and binding notwithstanding any error unless it is appealed from in the manner prescribed by s. 165, 169 and 172, or is replaced by a reassessment voluntarily made by the Minister.

Related Sections: S. 152(4) Assessment and reassessment; s. 152(8) Assessment deemed valid and binding; s. 165 Objections to assessment; s. 166 Irregularities; s. 169 Appeal.

Tax Topics: No. 2015, When Can "Incorrect or Incomplete" Be Sufficient To Overcome Deemed Validity?.

Cases: Under former s. 46(3) (now s. 152(3)) liability for tax was not affected by an incorrect or incomplete assessment. Hence, if a transaction entered into by a taxpayer attracted tax, it did not escape tax because the Minister availed himself of one section of the Act rather than another. *Belle-Isle v. M.N.R.*, 66 DTC 5100 (S.C.C.), affirming 64 DTC 5041 (Ex. Ct.) and 63 DTC 347 (T.A.B.)

▶ 152(3.1) ◀

(3.1) Definition of "normal reassessment period". For the purposes of subsections (4), (4.01), (4.2), (4.3), (5) and (9), the normal reassessment period for a taxpayer in respect of a taxation year is

(*a*) if at the end of the year the taxpayer is a mutual fund trust or a corporation other than a Canadian-controlled private corporation, the period that ends four years after the earlier of the day of sending of a notice of an original assessment under this Part in respect of the taxpayer for the year and the day of sending of an original notification that no tax is payable by the taxpayer for the year; and

(*b*) in any other case, the period that ends three years after the earlier of the day of sending of a notice of an original assessment under this Part in respect of the taxpayer for the year and the day of sending of an original notification that no tax is payable by the taxpayer for the year.

History: S. 152(3.1)(*a*) and (*b*) were replaced by S.C. 2010, c. 25, s. 38(1), in force on Royal Assent, December 15, 2010. S. 152(3.1)(*a*) and (*b*) formerly read:

(*a*) where at the end of the year the taxpayer is a mutual fund trust or a corporation other than a Canadian-controlled private corporation, the period that ends 4 years after the earlier of the day of mailing of a notice of an original assessment under this Part in respect of the taxpayer for the year and the day of mailing of an original notification that no tax is payable by the taxpayer for the year; and

(*b*) in any other case, the period that ends 3 years after the earlier of the day of mailing of a notice of an original assessment under this Part in respect of the taxpayer for the year and the day of mailing of an original notification that no tax is payable by the taxpayer for the year.

Tax Window Files: T1135 - Normal Reassessment Period, *September 15, 2015*, CRA Document No. 2015-0572771I7.

▶ 152(3.2) ◀

(3.2) Determination of deemed overpayment. A taxpayer may, during any month, request in writing that the Minister determine the amount deemed by subsection 122.61(1) to be an overpayment on account of the taxpayer's liability under this Part for a taxation year that arose during the month or any of the 11 preceding months.

▶ 152(3.3) ◀

(3.3) Notice of determination. On receipt of the request referred to in subsection (3.2), the Minister shall, with all due dispatch, determine the amounts deemed by subsection 122.61(1) to be overpayments on account of the taxpayer's liability under this Part that arose during the months in respect of which the request was made or determine that there is no such amount, and shall send a notice of the determination to the taxpayer.

▶ 152(3.4) ◀

(3.4) Determination of UI premium tax credit — (Repealed by S.C. 2013, c. 34, s. 309(1).)

History: S. 152(3.4) was repealed by S.C. 2013, c. 34, s. 309(1), applicable in respect of forms filed after March 20, 2003, and formerly read:

(3.4) *Determination of UI premium tax credit.* A taxpayer may request in writing that the Minister determine the amount deemed by subsection 126.1(6) or (7) to be an overpayment on account of the taxpayer's liability under this Part for a taxation year.

▶ 152(3.5) ◀

(3.5) Notice of determination — (Repealed by S.C. 2013, c. 34, s. 309(1).)

History: S. 152(3.5) was repealed by S.C. 2013, c. 34, s. 309(1), applicable in respect of forms filed after March 20, 2003, and formerly read:

(3.5) *Notice of determination.* On receipt of the request referred to in subsection (3.4), the Minister shall, with all due dispatch, determine the amount deemed by subsection 126.1(6) or (7), as the case may be, to be an overpayment on account of the taxpayer's liability under this Part for a taxation year, or determine that there is no such amount, and shall send a notice of the determination to the taxpayer.

▶ 152(4) ◀

(4) Assessment and reassessment. The Minister may at any time make an assessment, reassessment or additional assessment of tax for a taxation year, interest or penalties, if any, payable under this Part by a taxpayer or notify in writing any person by whom a return of income for a taxation year has been filed that no tax is payable for the year, except that an assessment, reassessment or additional assessment may be made after the taxpayer's normal reassessment period in respect of the year only if

(*a*) the taxpayer or person filing the return

(i) has made any misrepresentation that is attributable to neglect, carelessness or wilful default or has committed any fraud in filing the return or in supplying any information under this Act, or

(ii) has filed with the Minister a waiver in prescribed form within the normal reassessment period for the taxpayer in respect of the year;

(*b*) the assessment, reassessment or additional assessment is made before the day that is 3 years after the end of the normal reassessment period for the taxpayer in respect of the year and

(i) is required under subsection (6) or (6.1), or would be so required if the taxpayer had claimed an amount by filing the prescribed form referred to in the subsection on or before the day referred to in the subsection,

(ii) is made as a consequence of the assessment or reassessment pursuant to this paragraph or subsection (6) of tax payable by another taxpayer,

(iii) is made

(A) as a consequence of a transaction involving the taxpayer and a non-resident person with whom the taxpayer was not dealing at arm's length, or

> **Proposed Amendment**
>
> **2019 Federal Budget Resolutions**
>
> **Clause 152(4)(*b*)(iii)(A) of the Act is replaced by the following:**
>
> (A) as a consequence of a *transaction* (as defined in subsection 247(1)) involving the taxpayer and a non-resident person with whom the taxpayer was not dealing at arm's length, or
>
> **Applicable:** To taxation years of a taxpayer in respect of which the normal reassessment period (as defined in subsection 152(3.1) of the Act) for the taxpayer ends on or after March 19, 2019.

(B) in respect of any income, loss or other amount in relation to a foreign affiliate of the taxpayer,

(iii.1) is made, if the taxpayer is non-resident and carries on a business in Canada, as a consequence of

(A) an allocation by the taxpayer of revenues or expenses as amounts in respect of the Canadian business (other than revenues and expenses that relate solely to the Canadian business, that are recorded in the books of account of the Canadian business, and the documentation in support of which is kept in Canada), or

(B) a notional transaction between the taxpayer and its Canadian business, where the transaction is recognized for the purposes of the computation of an amount under this Act or an applicable tax treaty,

(iv) is made as a consequence of a payment or reimbursement of any income or profits tax to or by the government of a country other than Canada or a government of a state, province or other political subdivision of any such country,

(v) is made as a consequence of a reduction under subsection 66(12.73) of an amount purported to be renounced under section 66,

(vi) is made in order to give effect to the application of subsection 118.1(15) or (16); or

(vii) is made to give effect to the application of any of sections 94, 94.1 and 94.2;

(*b*.1) an information return described in subsection 237.1(7) or 237.3(2) that is required to be filed in respect of a deduction or claim made by the taxpayer in relation to a tax shelter, or in respect of a tax benefit (as defined in subsection 245(1)) to the taxpayer from an avoidance transaction (as defined in subsection 245(3)), is not filed as and when required, and the assessment, reassessment or additional assessment is made before the day that is three years after the day on which the information return is filed;

(*b*.2) the assessment, reassessment or additional assessment is made before the day that is three years after the end of the normal reassessment period for the taxpayer in respect of the year and if

(i) the taxpayer, or a partnership of which the taxpayer is a member, has failed to file for the year a prescribed form as and when required under subsection 233.3(3) or to report on the prescribed form the information required in respect of a specified foreign property (as defined in subsection 233.3(1)) held by the taxpayer at any time during the year, and

(ii) the taxpayer has failed to report, in the return of income for the year, an amount in respect of a specified foreign property that is required to be included in computing the taxpayer's income for the year;

(*b*.3) the following conditions apply:

(i) the taxpayer, or a partnership of which the taxpayer is a member (directly or indirectly through one or more partnerships), disposes in the year of real or immovable property,

(ii) the taxpayer is not a *real estate investment trust* (as defined in subsection 122.1(1)) for the year,

(iii) if the disposition is by a corporation or partnership, the property is capital property of the corporation or partnership, as the case may be,

(iv) the disposition is not reported in

(A) if the disposition is by the taxpayer, the return of income of the taxpayer under this Part for the year, or

(B) if the disposition is by a partnership, the partnership's return required to be filed for the year under section 229 of the *Income Tax Regulations*, and

(v) in the case that the disposition is not reported in the return described in clause (iv)(A) or (B) and the taxpayer subsequently reports the disposition by filing a prescribed form amending the taxpayer's return of income under this Part for the year, the assessment, reassessment or additional assessment is made before the day that is three years after the day on which the prescribed form amending the return is filed;

(*b*.4) the assessment, reassessment or additional assessment is made before the day that is six years after the end of the normal reassessment period for the taxpayer in respect of the year if

(i) a reassessment of tax for the year was required under subsection (6), or would have been so required if the taxpayer had claimed an amount by filing the prescribed form referred to in that subsection on or before the day referred to in that subsection, in order to take into account a deduction claimed under section 111 in respect of a loss for a subsequent taxation year,

(ii) an assessment, reassessment, additional assessment of tax or notification that no tax is payable for the subsequent taxation year referred to in subparagraph (i) was made or issued after the normal reassessment period in respect of the subsequent taxation year as a consequence of a transaction involving the taxpayer and a non-resident person with whom the taxpayer was not dealing at arm's length, and

(iii) the assessment, reassessment, additional assessment or notification that no tax is payable referred to in subparagraph (ii) reduced the amount of the loss for the subsequent taxation year;

(*c*) the taxpayer or person filing the return of income has filed with the Minister a waiver in prescribed form within the additional three-year period referred to in paragraph (*b*) or (*b.1*);

(*c*.1) the taxpayer or person filing the return of income has filed with the Minister a waiver in prescribed form within the additional three-year period referred to in paragraph (*b.2*); or

(*d*) as a consequence of a change in the allocation of the taxpayer's taxable income earned in a province as determined under the law of a province that provides rules similar to those prescribed for the purposes of section 124, an assessment, reassessment or additional assessment of tax for a taxation year payable by a corporation under a law of a province that imposes on the corporation a tax similar to the tax imposed under this Part (in this paragraph referred to as a "provincial reassessment") is made, and as a consequence of the provincial reassessment, an assessment, reassessment or additional assessment is made on or before the day that is one year after the later of

(i) the day on which the Minister is advised of the provincial reassessment, and

(ii) the day that is 90 days after the day of sending of a notice of the provincial reassessment.

Editorial Note: Under s. 152(4), the Minister may make an original assessment, reassessment or additional assessment for taxes, interest or penalties. As a general rule, assessments or reassessments may only within the "normal reassessment period" (defined in s. 152(3.1)) for the taxpayer with respect to the year in question. For mutual fund trusts and corporations other than Canadian-controlled private corporations, this reassessment period is four years from the earlier of (i) the date of mailing of a notice of an original assessment, and (ii) the date of mailing of an original notification that no tax is payable for the taxation year. For all other taxpayers, the normal reassessment period is three years from the earlier of the two above-stated dates.

However, s. 152(4) also provides exceptions where the assessment or reassessment can be made beyond the normal reassessment period. For example, reassessments can also be issued outside the limitation period where there has been misrepresentation due to neglect, carelessness, wilful default, or fraud (s. 152(4)(*a*)). Where a reassessment of a taxpayer is required by s. 152(6) or (6.1) or as a result of a deduction claim in respect of losses, gifts, tax credits, or other deductions carried back from subsequent taxation years of the taxpayer or another taxpayer, the reassessment period is extended by three years to either six or seven years, for the purpose of taking into account the effects of the deduction claimed (s. 152(4)(*b*)(i) and (ii)). The normal reassessment period is extended by three years for an assessment of a taxpayer as a consequence of a transaction involving the taxpayer and a non-arm's length non-resident person, or in respect of income or loss or another amount of a foreign affiliate of the taxpayer (s. 152(4)(*b*)(i)). The normal reassessment period is also extended by three years in circumstances where the assessment is being The normal reassessment period is also extended by three years in circumstances where the assessment is being made to give effect to the rules governing non-resident trusts, offshore investment fund property, and specified foreign property income (s. 152(4)(*b*)(vii) and (*b.2*)). The normal reassessment period is also extended if a taxpayer failed to report the disposition of a real or immovable property (including a principal residence) on the taxpayer's return of income (s. 152(4)(*b.3*)). Where a taxpayer is required to file an information return in respect of a tax shelter or reportable transaction, the reassessment period may be extended to three years after the return is filed (s. 152(4)(*b.1*)). Taxpayers can waive the limitation period for a minimum of six months under s. 152(4)(*a*), (*c*), and (*c.1*), and 152(4.1). Certain other provisions within the Act, or in amending provisions to the Act, may also extend the reassessment period for particular provisions.

Applicable in respect of a loss for a subsequent taxation year that ends after February 26, 2018, the reassessment period is extended by six years in respect of a prior year if the reassessment relates to the adjustment of a loss being carried back from the subsequent year to the prior year under s. 152(6), and an assessment or reassessment is made for the subsequent year beyond its normal reassessment period as a consequence of a transaction involving a taxpayer and a non-resident person with whom the taxpayer does not deal at arm's length. (Previously, the reassessment period could only be extended by three years after the prior year's normal reassessment period.)

History: S. 152(4)(*b*)(iii) was replaced by S.C. 2018, c. 27, s. 18(3), applicable to taxation years of a taxpayer that begin after February 26, 2018, and formerly read:

(iii) is made as a consequence of a transaction involving the taxpayer and a non-resident person with whom the taxpayer was not dealing at arm's length,

S. 152(4)(*b.4*) was added by S.C. 2018, c. 27, s. 18(4), applicable in respect of a taxation year if a reassessment of tax for the year was required under subsection 152(6) of the Act, or would have been so required if the taxpayer had claimed an amount by filing the prescribed form referred to in that subsection on or before the day referred to in that subsection, in order to take into account a deduction claimed under section 111 of the Act in respect of a loss for a subsequent taxation year that ends after February 26, 2018.

S. 152(4)(*b.3*) was added by S.C. 2017, c. 33, s. 62(1), applicable to taxation years that end after October 2, 2016.

S. 152(4)(*c*) was replaced and s. 152(4)(*b.1*), (*b.2*), and (*c.1*) were added by S.C. 2013, c. 40, s. 67(1), applicable to the 2013 and subsequent taxation years, except that, in its application to taxation years that end before March 21, 2013, subsection 152(4) is to be read without reference to paragraph (*b.1*). S. 152(4)(*c*) formerly read:

(*c*) the taxpayer or person filing the return has filed with the Minister a waiver in prescribed form within the additional 3-year period referred to in paragraph (*b*); or

S. 152(4)(*b*)(vii) was added by S.C. 2013, c. 34, s. 15(1), applicable to taxation years that end after March 4, 2010.

S. 152(4)(*b*)(i) was replaced by S.C. 2013, c. 34, s. 34(1), applicable to taxation years that begin after November 1999.

Any assessment of a taxpayer's tax, interest and penalties payable under the Act for any taxation year that ends before June 26, 2013 that would, in the absence of this section, be precluded because of subsections 152(4) to (5) of the Act, shall be made to the extent necessary to take into account this amendment, if the taxpayer

(i) elects in writing in respect of all of its foreign affiliates that this section apply in respect of that provision, and

(ii) files that election with the Minister of National Revenue on or before December 26, 2013 [the day that is six months after royal assent].

S. 152(4)(*b*)(i) formerly read:

(i) is required pursuant to subsection (6) or would be so required if the taxpayer had claimed an amount by filing the prescribed form referred to in that subsection on or before the day referred to therein,

S. 152(4)(*d*)(ii) was replaced by S.C. 2010, c. 25, s. 38(2), in force on Royal Assent, December 15, 2010. S. 152(4)(*d*)(ii) formerly read:

(ii) the day that is 90 days after the day of mailing of a notice of the provincial reassessment.

S. 152(4)(*c*) and (*d*) were added by S.C. 2009, c. 2, s. 58(1), in force on Royal Assent, March 12, 2009.

Related Sections: S. 152(5) Limitation on assessments; s. 165(5) Validity of reassessment; s. 173(2) Time during consideration not to count; s. 174(5) Time during consideration of question not counted; s. 244(14) Mailing date; s. 244(15) Date when assessment made; ITAR s. 62(1) Assessments.

Canadian Tax Foundation: Friedlan and Friedlan, *Reassessing a Statute-Barred Year and the "Wise and Prudent Person" Test*, 2016 Tax for the Owner-Manager 16(1):6–7; Horrigan and Kreklewetz, *Misrepresentation and Statute-Barred Assessments*, 2015 Canadian Tax Highlights 23(9):3–4; Tollstam, *Deceased Return Assessed After Normal Period*, 2015 Canadian Tax Highlights 23(8):5; Rachert, *When Isn't Negligence Gross? Struggles With the Standard of Care*, 2014 British Columbia Tax Conference 11:1–38; Friedlan and Friedlan, *Reassessments When an Accountant Was Negligent*, 2014 Tax for the Owner-Manager 14(3):5–6; Hickey, *Canco Reassessment Period Extended*, 2013 Canadian Tax Highlights 21(10):6; Kopstein and Levi, *When Should the Courts Allow Reassessments Beyond the Limitation Period?*, 2010 Canadian Tax Journal 3:475–527; Kakkar, *Time Limits for Reassessing a Partnership and Its Partners*, 2005 Tax for the Owner-Manager 5(2):5–6; Innes and Bissell, *Basis for Assessment, Arguments, and Assumptions: An Examination of the Underlying Policy Considerations*, 2004 Canadian Tax Journal 1:59–105; Meghji and Grenon, *Current Cases: Federal Court of Appeal — New Life for the Limitation Period (Pedwell v. The Queen, 2000 DTC 6405)*, 2000 Canadian Tax Journal 5:1650–1654; Bendin, *Challenging and Defending Assessments Before the Tax Court of Canada and Appellate Courts: A Postscript to the Continental Bank Case*, 2000 Canadian Tax Journal 1:35–59; Meghji et al., *Does Procedure Matter?*, 1999 Conference Report 15:1–42.

Tax Profile: The Minister's Ability To Reassess Beyond the Normal Reassessment Period: What Constitutes a "Misrepresentation"?.

Tax Topics: No. 2019, Setting Sundog: Limitation Period on the Wane; No. 1919-20, 2008 Canadian Tax Foundation Annual Conference — Department of Finance Presentation and CRA Round Table; No. 1810, FAPI and Tax Treaty Interpretation: *Canwest Mediaworks Inc. v. Her Majesty the Queen*; No. 1797, To Waive or Not To Waive ... That is Not the Only Question!; No. 1577, Corporate Reassessments Outside the Normal Reassessment Period.

Forms: T2029 — Waiver in Respect of The Normal Reassessment Period.

Information Circulars: IC 71-17R5 Guidance on competent authority assistance under Canada's tax conventions; IC 75-7R3 Reassessment of a return of income; IC 77-11 Sales tax reassessments — Deductibility in computing income; IC 84-1 Revision of capital cost allowance claims and other permissive deductions; IC 07-1 Taxpayer Relief Provisions.

Interpretation Bulletins: *Secondary* — IT-384R Reassessment where option exercised in subsequent year.

Tax Window Files: T1135 - Normal Reassessment Period, *September 15, 2015*, CRA Document No. 2015-0572771I7; Change to loss application in a nil assessed year, *March 21, 2014*, CRA Document No. 2013-0504491I7; Application of 152(4)(b)(iv) and 110.5, *July 16, 2013*, CRA Document No. 2013-0481151I7.

Cases: The taxpayer was entitled to rely on the expiry of the normal reassessment period to finalize his tax payable for the 2009 taxation year and the Minister, in issuing the second revocation notice in 2017 and relying on it for purposes of reassessment, was seeking to do away with the limitation period, which had expired. *Mammone v. The Queen*, 2019 DTC 5033 (FCA), reversing 2018 DTC 1024 (TCC)

When filing the final return, the estate had made a misrepresentation. The person reviewing the return was in a position to be familiar with the estate's real estate holdings and should have noted the failure to properly report the recaptured CCA. The estate did not exercise the required degree of care, and the Minister was allowed to reassess outside the normal period. *Estate of Stanley Vine v. Her Majesty the Queen*, 2015 DTC 5063 (F.C.A.)

In analyzing reassessments beyond the normal reassessment period, the question is not whether the taxpayer was negligent, but whether the taxpayer was negligent at the time the misrepresentation was actually made. *Vachon v. The Queen*, 2014 DTC 5126 (F.C.A.)

The estate failed to include $288,164 in its date of death return. Had the executor exercised reasonable care, she would have reviewed the deceased's T4RIF, seen the $228,164, and looked for that amount in the return prior to signing. This was a misrepresentation attributable to neglect, and reassessment beyond the normal reassessment period was justified. *Krenbrink Estate v. The Queen*, 2014 DTC 5121 (F.C.A.), affirming 2014 DTC 1065 (T.C.C.)

Reassessments were made beyond the usual limitation period, but the taxpayer had signed a waiver. The waiver could not be set aside unless the taxpayer established on a balance of probabilities that he did not freely consent to the waiver. This question also includes the issue of whether the person had the capacity to consent. *Wiens v. The Queen*, 2011 DTC 1125 (T.C.C.)

The word "transaction" in s. 152(4)(*b*)(iii) does not include an arrangement or series of transactions. The definition of "transaction" in s. 247 does not apply to that word as it is used in s. 152. Accordingly, a reassessment based on a series of transactions was statute-barred since it did not fall within the excepting provisions of s. 152(4)(*b*)(iii). *Blackburn Radio Inc. v. The Queen*, 2009 DTC 1099 (T.C.C.)

The repayment to U.S. Bank of Fusion Co.'s loan was a transaction involving the taxpayer and Fusion Co. The Minister's reassessment beyond the normal reassessment period, therefore, was made as a consequence of a "transaction involving the taxpayer and a non-resident person ...", within the meaning of s. 152(4)(*b*)(iii) and was not statute-barred. *Shaw-Almex Industries Limited v. The Queen*, 2009 DTC 1377 (T.C.C.)

A taxpayer cannot argue that, for a reassessment to have been validly "made" under s. 152(4), a notice of it needs to have been communicated to that taxpayer. The Minister was able to prove that the reassessment was sent to the taxpayer, and was therefore "made" in accordance with s. 152(4). *Skalbania v. The Queen*, 2009 DTC 1373 (T.C.C.)

When a taxpayer who had been given shares by a venture capitalist had declared a cost of acquisition in excess of nil, this misrepresentation was considered sufficiently substantial to be attributable to neglect, carelessness or willful default. *Angus v. The Queen*, 98 DTC 6661 (F.C.A.), affirming 96 DTC 1823 (T.C.C.)

When the taxpayer's 1981 return, prepared by an accountant, reported the taxpayer's share of a capital gain as $71,392 rather than $711,392, the Minister could reassess in 1989 since the taxpayer's perfuntory perusal of the return did not amount to reasonable care. *Nesbitt v. The Queen*, 96 DTC 6588 (F.C.A.), affirming 96 DTC 6045 (F.C.T.D.)

A notice of assessment sent on December 28, 1981 was a determination by the Minister of the taxes payable by a corporation for the relevant fiscal period, even if that determination was erroneous as to the amount of tax payable. This notice of original assessment began the limitation period to assess or reassess so that the reassessment issued on October 26, 1987 was statute-barred. *Paramount Productions Inc. v. The Queen*, 93 DTC 5285 (F.C.T.D.).

► 152(4.01) ◄

(4.01) Extended period of assessment. Notwithstanding subsections (4) and (5), an assessment, reassessment or additional assessment to which paragraph (4)(*a*), (*b*), (*b.*1), (*b.*3), (*b.*4) or (*c*) applies in respect of a taxpayer for a taxation year may be made after the taxpayer's normal reassessment period in respect of the year to the extent that, but only to the extent that, it can reasonably be regarded as relating to,

(*a*) where paragraph (4)(*a*) applies to the assessment, reassessment or additional assessment,

(i) any misrepresentation made by the taxpayer or a person who filed the taxpayer's return of income for the year that is attributable to neglect, carelessness or wilful default or any fraud committed by the taxpayer or that person in filing the return or supplying any information under this Act, or

(ii) a matter specified in a waiver filed with the Minister in respect of the year;

(*b*) if paragraph 4(*b*), (*b.1*) or (*c*) applies to the assessment, reassessment or additional assessment,

(i) the assessment, reassessment or additional assessment to which subparagraph (4)(*b*)(i) applies,

(ii) the assessment or reassessment referred to in subparagraph (4)(*b*)(ii),

(iii) the transaction, income, loss or other amount referred to in subparagraph (4)(*b*)(iii),

(iv) the payment or reimbursement referred to in subparagraph (4)(*b*)(iv),

(v) the reduction referred to in subparagraph (4)(*b*)(v),

(vi) the application referred to in subparagraph (4)(*b*)(vi), or

(vii) the deduction, claim or tax benefit referred to in paragraph (4)(*b.1*);

(*c*) if paragraph (4)(*b*.3) applies to the assessment, reassessment or additional assessment, the disposition referred to in that paragraph; and

(*d*) if paragraph (4)(*b*.4) applies to the assessment, reassessment or additional assessment, the reduction under subparagraph (4)(*b*.4)(iii).

Editorial Note: In general, s. 152(4.01) limits the extent to which the Minister can reassess to specified matters, where a reassessment to which s. 152(4)(*a*), (*b*), (*b.1*), (*b.3*), (*b.4*), or (*c*) is made beyond the normal reassessment period for a taxpayer. For a description of those provisions where a reassessment can be made beyond the normal reassessment period, see the editorial note to s. 152(4).

History: S. 152(4.01), the portion before paragraph (*a*) was replaced by S.C. 2018, c. 27, s. 18(5), applicable in respect of a taxation year if a reassessment of tax for the year was required under subsection 152(6) of the Act, or would have been so required if the taxpayer had claimed an amount by filing the prescribed form referred to in that subsection on or before the day referred to in that subsection, in order to take into account a deduction claimed under section 111 of the Act in respect of a loss for a subsequent taxation year that ends after February 26, 2018.

S. 152(4.01), the portion before paragraph (*a*) formerly read:

(4.01) *Extended period assessment.* Notwithstanding subsections (4) and (5), an assessment, reassessment or additional assessment to which paragraph (4)(*a*), (*b*), (*b*.1), (*b*.3), or (*c*) applies in respect of a taxpayer for a taxation year may be made after the taxpayer's normal reassessment period in respect of the year to the extent that, but only to the extent that, it can reasonably be regarded as relating to,

S. 152(4.01)(*b*)(iii) was replaced by S.C. 2018, c. 27, s. 18(6), applicable to taxation years of a taxpayer that begin after February 26, 2018, and formerly read:

(iii) the transaction referred to in subparagraph (4)(*b*)(iii),

S. 152(4.01)(*d*) was added by S.C. 2018, c. 27, s. 18(7), applicable in respect of a taxation year if a reassessment of tax for the year was required under subsection 152(6) of the Act, or would have been so required if the taxpayer had claimed an amount by filing the prescribed form referred to in that subsection on or before the day referred to in that subsection, in order to take into account a deduction claimed under section 111 of the Act in respect of a loss for a subsequent taxation year that ends after February 26, 2018.

S. 152(4.01)(*c*) was added by S.C. 2017, c. 33, s. 62(3), applicable to taxation years that end after October 2, 2016.

S. 152(4.01), the portion before paragraph (*a*) was replaced by S.C. 2017, c. 33, s. 62(2), applicable to taxation years that end after October 2, 2016, and formerly read:

(4.01) *Extended period assessment.* Notwithstanding subsections (4) and (5), an assessment, reassessment or additional assessment to which paragraph (4)(*a*), (*b*), (*b.1*) or (*c*) applies in respect of a taxpayer for a taxation year may be made after the taxpayer's normal reassessment period in respect of the year to the extent that, but only to the extent that, it can reasonably be regarded as relating to,

S. 152(4.01), the portion before paragraph (*a*) was replaced by S.C. 2013, c. 40, s. 67(2), applicable to taxation years that end after March 20, 2013, and formerly read:

(4.01) *Assessment to which paragraph 152(4)(a), (b) or (c) applies.* Notwithstanding subsections (4) and (5), an assessment, reassessment or additional assessment to which paragraph (4)(*a*), (*b*) or (*c*) applies in respect of a taxpayer for a taxation year may be made after the taxpayer's normal reassessment period in respect of the year to the extent that, but only to the extent that, it can reasonably be regarded as relating to,

S. 152(4.01)(*b*), the portion before subparagraph (i) was replaced by S.C. 2013, c. 40, s. 67(3), applicable to taxation years that end after March 20, 2013, and formerly read:

(*b*) where paragraph 4(*b*) or (*c*) applies to the assessment, reassessment or additional assessment,

S. 152(4.01)(*b*)(vii) was added by S.C. 2013, c. 40, s. 67(4), applicable to taxation years that end after March 20, 2013.

S. 152(4.01), the portion before paragraph (*a*) was replaced by S.C. 2009, c. 2, s. 58(2), in force on Royal Assent, March 12, 2009. S. 152(4.01), the portion before paragraph (*a*) formerly read:

(4.01) *Assessment to which par. 152(4)(a) or (b) applies.* Notwithstanding subsections (4) and (5), an assessment, reassessment or additional assessment to which paragraph (4)(*a*) or (*b*) applies in respect of a taxpayer for a taxation year may be made after the taxpayer's normal reassessment period in respect of the year to the extent that, but only to the extent that, it can reasonably be regarded as relating to,

S. 152(4.01)(*b*), the portion before subparagraph (i) was replaced by S.C. 2009, c. 2, s. 58(3), in force on Royal Assent, March 12, 2009. S. 152(4.01)(*b*), the portion before subparagraph (i) formerly read:

(*b*) where paragraph (4)(*b*) applies to the assessment, reassessment or additional assessment,

Related Sections: S. 165(5) Validity of reassessment.

Cases: The taxpayer signed waivers allowing reassessment beyond the normal reassessment period on the basis of GAAR. The Minister could not amend the Reply to provide for an alternative justification for the reassessments under the FAPI rules. The new basis for reassessment could not be justified under s. 152(4.01) because it was not reasonably related to a matter specified in the waivers. *The Queen v. Honeywell Limited*, 2007 DTC 5073 (F.C.A.), affirming 2006 DTC 3124 (T.C.C.)

► 152(4.1) ◄

(4.1) If waiver revoked. If the Minister would, but for this subsection, be entitled to reassess, make an additional assessment or assess tax, interest or penalties by virtue only of the filing of a waiver under subparagraph (4)(*a*)(ii) or paragraph (4)(*c*) or (*c.1*), the Minister may not make such a reassessment, additional assessment or assessment after the day that is six months after the date on which a notice of revocation of the waiver in prescribed form is filed.

Editorial Note: Under s. 152(4.1), the Minister has six months to issue an assessment or reassessment after a taxpayer files a notice of revocation related to a waiver of the normal reassessment period.

History: S. 152(4.1) was replaced by S.C. 2013, c. 40, s. 67(5), applicable to the 2013 and subsequent taxation years, and formerly read:

(4.1) *If waiver revoked.* If the Minister would, but for this subsection, be entitled to reassess, make an additional assessment or assess tax, interest or penalties by virtue only of the filing of a waiver under subparagraph (4)(*a*)(ii) or paragraph (4)(*c*), the Minister may not make such a reassessment, additional assessment or assessment after the day that is six months after the date on which a notice of revocation of the waiver in prescribed form is filed.

S. 152(4.1) was replaced by S.C. 2013, c. 34, s. 309(2), in force June 26, 2013, and formerly read:

(4.1) *Where waiver revoked.* Where the Minister would, but for this subsection, be entitled to reassess, make an additional assessment or assess tax, interest or penalties by virtue only of the filing of a waiver under subparagraph (4)(*a*)(ii), the Minister may not make such a reassessment, additional assessment or assessment after the day that is six months after the date on which a notice of revocation of the waiver in prescribed form is filed.

Forms: T652 — Notice of Revocation of Waiver.

Tax Window Files: Request for Tax Refund for Pre-Bankruptcy Year, *Technical Interpretation, Business and Partnerships Division, May 14, 2008*, CRA Document No. 2007-0246481A11.

► 152(4.2) ◄

(4.2) Reassessment with taxpayer's consent. Notwithstanding subsections (4), (4.1) and (5), for the purpose of determining — at any time after the end of the normal reassessment period, of a taxpayer who is an individual (other than a trust) or a graduated rate estate, in respect of a taxation year — the amount of any refund to which the taxpayer is entitled at that time for the year, or a reduction of an amount payable under this Part by the taxpayer for the year, the Minister may, if the taxpayer makes an application for that determination on or before the day that is 10 calendar years after the end of that taxation year,

(*a*) reassess tax, interest or penalties payable under this Part by the taxpayer in respect of that year; and

(*b*) redetermine the amount, if any, deemed by subsection 120(2) or (2.2), 122.5(3), 122.51(2), 122.7(2) or (3), 122.8(4), 122.9(2), 122.91(1), 127.1(1), 127.41(3) or 210.2(3) or (4) to be paid on account of the taxpayer's tax payable under this Part for the year or deemed by subsection 122.61(1) to be an overpayment on account of the taxpayer's liability under this Part for the year.

Editorial Note: Subsection 152(4.2) permits the Minister to reassess or redetermine amounts outside the normal reassessment period at the request of the taxpayer, but only where the taxpayer makes an application on or before the day that is 10 calendar years after the end of that taxation year, and only for taxpayers that are individuals (other than trusts) or graduated rate estates.

History: S. 152(4.2)(*b*) was replaced by S.C. 2019, c. 29, s. 32(2), deemed to have come into force on January 1, 2019, and formerly read:

(*b*) redetermine the amount, if any, deemed by subsection 120(2) or (2.2), 122.5(3), 122.51(2), 122.7(2) or (3), 122.8(4), 122.9(2), 127.1(1), 127.41(3) or 210.2(3) or (4) to be paid on account of the taxpayer's tax payable under this Part for the year or deemed by subsection 122.61(1) to be an overpayment on account of the taxpayer's liability under this Part for the year.

S. 152(4.2)(*b*) was replaced by S.C. 2018, c. 27, s. 18(8), applicable to the 2018 and subsequent taxation years, and formerly read:

(*b*) redetermine the amount, if any, deemed by subsection 120(2) or (2.2), 122.5(3), 122.51(2), 122.7(2) or (3), 122.9(2), 127.1(1), 127.41(3) or 210.2(3) or (4) to be paid on account of the taxpayer's tax payable under this Part for the year or deemed by subsection 122.61(1) to be an overpayment on account of the taxpayer's liability under this Part for the year.

S. 152(4.2)(*b*) was replaced by S.C. 2016, c. 7, s. 41(4), applicable to the 2017 and subsequent taxation years, and formerly read:

(*b*) redetermine the amount, if any, deemed by subsection 120(2) or (2.2), 122.5(3), 122.51(2), 122.7(2) or (3), 122.8(2) or (3), 122.9(2), 127.1(1), 127.41(3) or 210.2(3) or (4) to be paid on account of the taxpayer's tax payable under this Part for the year or deemed by subsection 122.61(1) to be an overpayment on account of the taxpayer's liability under this Part for the year.

S. 152(4.2)(*b*) was replaced by S.C. 2016, c. 7, s. 41(3), applicable to the 2016 taxation year, and formerly read:

(*b*) redetermine the amount, if any, deemed by subsection 120(2) or (2.2), 122.5(3), 122.51(2), 122.7(2) or (3), 122.8(2) or (3), 127.1(1), 127.41(3) or 210.2(3) or (4) to be paid on account of the taxpayer's tax payable under this Part for the year or deemed by subsection 122.61(1) to be an overpayment on account of the taxpayer's liability under this Part for the year.

S. 152(4.2), the portion before paragraph (*a*) was replaced by S.C. 2014, c. 39, s. 55(2), applicable to the 2016 and subsequent taxation years, and formerly read:

(4.2) *Reassessment with taxpayer's consent.* Notwithstanding subsections (4), (4.1) and (5), for the purpose of determining, at any time after the end of the normal reassessment period of a taxpayer who is an individual (other than a trust) or a testamentary trust in respect of a taxation year, the amount of any refund to which the taxpayer is entitled at that time for the year, or a reduction of an amount payable under this Part by the taxpayer for the year, the Minister may, if the taxpayer makes an application for that determination on or before the day that is ten calendar years after the end of that taxation year,

S. 152(4.2)(*b*) was replaced by S.C. 2014, c. 39, s. 55(3), applicable to the 2015 and subsequent taxation years, and formerly read:

(*b*) redetermine the amount, if any, deemed by subsection 120(2) or (2.2), 122.5(3), 122.51(2), 122.7(2) or (3), 127.1(1), 127.41(3) or 210.2(3) or (4) to be paid on account of the taxpayer's tax payable under this Part for the year or deemed by subsection 122.61(1) to be an overpayment on account of the taxpayer's liability under this Part for the year.

[**Application Provision:**] If a provision in sections 169 to 412 of the *Technical Amendments Act, 2012* (S.C. 2013, c. 34) applies or comes into force before June 26, 2013, for the purpose of and to the extent necessary to take into account that provision, in applying subsection 152(4.2) to a taxation year that ends before that day, subsection 152(4.2) is to be read as follows:

"(4.2) Notwithstanding subsections (4), (4.1) and (5), for the purpose of determining, at any time after the end of the normal reassessment period of a taxpayer in respect of a taxation year, an amount payable under this Part by the taxpayer for the taxation year, the Minister may, if the taxpayer makes an application for that determination,

(*a*) reassess tax, interest or penalties payable under this Part by the taxpayer in respect of that taxation year; and

(*b*) redetermine the amount, if any, deemed by subsection 120(2) or (2.2), 122.5(3), 122.51(2), 122.7(2) or (3), 125.4(3), 125.5(3), 127.1(1), 127.41(3) or 210.2(3) or (4) to be paid on account of the taxpayer's tax payable under this Part for the year or deemed by subsection 122.61(1) to be an overpayment on account of the taxpayer's liability under this Part for the taxation year."

Related Sections: 122.91(1) Claimed amount.

Information Circulars: IC 75-7R3 Reassessment of a return of income.

Tax Window Files: Returns filed or amended by bankrupt taxpayer, *March 8, 2016*, CRA Document No. 2015-0614421I7; Application of 111(1)(a) and 152(4.2), *January 14, 2014*, CRA Document No. 2013-0514331I7.

Cases: The taxpayer was issued a reassessment denying a deduction for charitable donations and filed a notice of objection. Subsequently the taxpayer filed a request for reassessment to allow carrying charges, which the Minister granted. The taxpayer's request for reassessment was determined to have been made through a T1 adjustment, and not under subsection 152(4.2) which would have removed his appeal rights regarding the donations and precluded him from objecting. *DouangChanh v. The Queen*, 2013 DTC 1243 (T.C.C.)

The Courts have consistently held that there is no right of appeal from a s. 152(4.2) reassessment. *Mellish v. The Queen*, 2007 DTC 704 (T.C.C.)

▶ 152(4.3) ◀

(4.3) Consequential assessment. Notwithstanding subsections (4), (4.1) and (5), if the result of an assessment or a decision on an appeal is to change a particular balance of a taxpayer for a particular taxation year, the Minister may, or if the taxpayer so requests in writing, shall, before the later of the expiration of the normal reassessment period in respect of a subsequent taxation year and the end of the day that is one year after the day on which all rights of objection and appeal expire or are determined in respect of the particular year, reassess the tax, interest or penalties payable by the taxpayer, redetermine an amount deemed to have been paid or to have been an overpayment by the taxpayer or modify the amount of a refund or other amount payable to the taxpayer, under this Part in respect of the subsequent taxation year, but only to the extent that the reassessment, redetermination or modification can reasonably be considered to relate to the change in the particular balance of the taxpayer for the particular year.

History: S. 152(4.3) was replaced by S.C. 2013, c. 34, s. 309(3), applicable to reassessments, redeterminations and modifications in respect of taxation years that relate to changes in balances for other taxation years as a result of assessments made, or decisions on appeal rendered, after November 5, 2010. S. 152(4.3) formerly read:

(4.3) *Consequential assessment.* Notwithstanding subsections (4), (4.1) and (5), where the result of an assessment or a decision on an appeal is to change a particular balance of a taxpayer for a particular taxation year, the Minister may, or where the taxpayer so requests in writing, shall, before the later of the expiration of the normal reassessment period in respect of a subsequent taxation year and the end of the day that is one year after the day on which all rights of objection and appeal expire or are determined in respect of the particular year, reassess the tax, interest or penalties payable, or redetermine an amount deemed to have been paid or to have been an overpayment, under this Part by the taxpayer in respect of the subsequent taxation year, but only to the extent that the reassessment or redetermination can reasonably be considered to relate to the change in the particular balance of the taxpayer for the particular year.

▶ 152(4.4) ◀

(4.4) Definition of "balance". For the purpose of subsection (4.3), a "balance" of a taxpayer for a taxation year is the income, taxable income, taxable income earned in Canada or any loss of the taxpayer for the year, or the tax or other amount payable by, any amount refundable to, or any amount deemed to have been paid or to have been an overpayment by, the taxpayer for the year.

▶ 152(5) ◀

(5) Limitation on assessments. There shall not be included in computing the income of a taxpayer for a taxation year, for the purpose of an assessment, reassessment or additional assessment made under this Part after the taxpayer's normal reassessment period in respect of the year, any amount that was not included in computing the taxpayer's income for the purpose of an assessment, reassessment or additional assessment made under this Part before the end of the period.

Editorial Note: It should be noted that s. 152(5) only limits the ability of the Minister to include additional amounts in computing the "income" of a taxpayer. However, this provision does not appear to impose any limitations in respect of reassessments validly issued under s. 152(4) after the expiration of the normal limitation period where the reassessments merely vary the taxpayer's "taxable income" (Division C of Part I of the Act) or "tax" (Division E of Part I of the Act) without altering the taxpayer's "income" (Division B of Part I of the Act).

Related Sections: ITAR s. 62(1) Assessments.

Forms: T2029 — Waiver in Respect of The Normal Reassessment Period.

Cases: The Minister is still bound by s. 152(5) even in the case of an appeal disposed of on consent pursuant to s. 169(3). *Bolton Steel Tube Co. Ltd. v. The Queen*, 2014 DTC 1102 (T.C.C.)

▶ 152(6) ◀

(6) Reassessment where certain deductions claimed. Where a taxpayer has filed for a particular taxation year the return of income required by section 150 and an amount is subsequently claimed by the taxpayer or on the taxpayer's behalf for the year as

(*a*) a deduction under paragraph 3(*e*) of the *Income Tax Act*, chapter 148 of the Revised Statutes of Canada, 1952, by virtue of the taxpayer's death in a subsequent taxation year and the consequent application of section 71 of that Act in respect of an allowable capital loss for the year,

(*b*) a deduction under section 41 in respect of the taxpayer's listed-personal-property loss for a subsequent taxation year, (*b*.1) a deduction under paragraph 60(*i*) in respect of a premium (within the meaning assigned by subsection 146(1)) paid in a subsequent taxation year under a registered retirement savings plan where the premium is deductible by reason of subsection 146(6.1),

(*c*) a deduction under section 118.1 in respect of a gift made in a subsequent taxation year or under section 111 in respect of a loss for a subsequent taxation year,

(*c*.1) (Repealed by S.C. 2013, c. 34, s. 309(4).)

(*d*) a deduction under subsection 127(5) in respect of property acquired or an expenditure made in a subsequent taxation year,

(*e*) (Repealed by S.C. 2013, c. 34, s. 309(5).)

(*f*) a deduction under section 125.3 in respect of an unused Part I.3 tax credit (within the meaning assigned by subsection 125.3(3)) for a subsequent taxation year,

(*f*.1) a deduction under subsection 126(2) in respect of an unused foreign tax credit (within the meaning assigned by subsection 126(7)), or under subsection 126(2.21) or (2.22) in respect of foreign taxes paid, for a subsequent taxation year,

(*f*.2) a deduction under subsection 128.1(8) as a result of a disposition in a subsequent taxation year,

(*f*.3) a deduction (including for the purposes of this subsection a reduction of an amount otherwise required to be included in computing a taxpayer's income) under subsection 146(8.9) or (8.92), 146.3(6.2) or (6.3) or 147.5(14) or (19),

(*g*) a deduction under subsection 147.2(4) because of the application of subsection 147.2(6) as a result of the taxpayer's death in the subsequent taxation year, or

(*h*) a deduction by virtue of an election for a subsequent taxation year under paragraph 164(6)(*c*) or (*d*) by the taxpayer's legal representative,

by filing with the Minister, on or before the day on or before which the taxpayer is, or would be if a tax under this Part were payable by the taxpayer for that subsequent taxation year, required by section 150 to file a return of income for that subsequent taxation year, a prescribed form amending the return, the Minister shall reassess the taxpayer's tax for any relevant taxation year (other than a taxation year preceding the particular taxation year) in order to take into account the deduction claimed.

History: S. 152(6)(*c.1*) was repealed by S.C. 2013, c. 34, s. 309(4), applicable to taxation years that end after October 1, 1996, and formerly read:

(*c*.1) a deduction under section 119 in respect of a disposition in a subsequent taxation year,

S. 152(6)(*e*) was repealed by S.C. 2013, c. 34, s. 309(5), applicable to taxation years that begin after October 31, 2011, and formerly read:

(*e*) a deduction under section 125.2 in respect of an unused Part VI tax credit (within the meaning assigned by subsection 125.2(3)) for a subsequent taxation year,

S. 152(6)(*f.3*) was replaced by S.C. 2012, c. 31, s. 39(1), in force December 14, 2012, and formerly read:

(*f*.3) a deduction (including for the purposes of this subsection a reduction of an amount otherwise required to be included in computing a taxpayer's income) under subsection 146(8.9) or (8.92) or 146.3(6.2) or (6.3),

S. 152(6)(*f.3*) was added by S.C. 2009, c. 2, s. 58(4), applicable in respect of a registered retirement income fund or a registered retirement savings plan in respect of which the last payment out of the fund or plan is made after 2008.

Forms: T1-Adj — T1 Adjustment Request.

Income Tax Folios: *Secondary* — S5-F2-C1 Foreign Tax Credit.

Information Circulars: IC 75-7R3 Reassessment of a return of income.

Interpretation Bulletins: *Secondary* — IT-124R6 Contributions to registered retirement savings plans; IT-232R3 Non-capital losses, net capital losses, restricted farm losses, farm losses and limited partnership losses — Their composition and deductibility in computing taxable income.

▶ 152(6.1) ◀

(6.1) Reassessment if amount under subsection 91(1) is reduced. If

(*a*) a taxpayer has filed for a particular taxation year the return of income required by section 150,

(*b*) the amount included in computing the taxpayer's income for the particular year under subsection 91(1) is subsequently reduced because of a reduction in the foreign accrual property income of a foreign affiliate of the taxpayer for a taxation year (referred to in this paragraph as the "claim year") of the affiliate that ends in the particular year, if

(i) the reduction is

(A) attributable to a foreign accrual property loss (within the meaning assigned by subsection 5903(3) of the *Income Tax Regulations*) of the affiliate for a taxation year of the affiliate that ends in a subsequent taxation year of the taxpayer, and

(B) included in the description of F in the definition "foreign accrual property income" in subsection 95(1) in respect of the affiliate for the claim year, or

(ii) the reduction is

(A) attributable to a foreign accrual capital loss (within the meaning assigned by subsection 5903.1(3) of the *Income Tax Regulations*) of the affiliate for a taxation year of the affiliate that ends in a subsequent taxation year of the taxpayer, and

(B) included in the description of F.1 in the definition "foreign accrual property income" in subsection 95(1) in respect of the affiliate for the claim year, and

(*c*) the taxpayer has filed with the Minister, on or before the filing-due date for that subsequent taxation year, a prescribed form amending the return,

the Minister shall reassess the taxpayer's tax for any relevant taxation year (other than a taxation year preceding the particular year) in order to take into account the reduction in the amount included under subsection 91(1) in computing the income of the taxpayer for the particular year.

Editorial Note: S. 152(6.1), applicable to taxation years of a foreign affiliate that begin after November 1999, provides for the reassessment of all relevant taxation years (other than taxation years preceding the particular taxation year) where the taxpayer has filed a prescribed form carrying back a deductible loss from a subsequent taxation year that reduces the taxpayer's income for the particular year under s. 91(1). S. 152(6.1) was introduced as a consequence of the extension of the deductible loss carryover period for foreign accrued property losses in the description of F in the definition of "foreign accrual property income" in s. 95(1) and s. 5903 of the *Income Tax Regulations*. Further amendments were made for taxation years ending after

August 19, 2011, to reflect the introduction of "foreign accrual capital losses" in Regulation 5903.1.

History: S. 152(6.1)(*b*) was replaced by S.C. 2013, c. 34, s. 74(1), applicable to taxation years that end after August 19, 2011.

Any assessment of a taxpayer's tax, interest and penalties payable under the Act for any taxation year that ends before June 26, 2013 that would, in the absence of this section, be precluded because of subsections 152(4) to (5) of the Act shall be made to the extent necessary to take into account the amendments by S.C. 2013, c. 34, s. 54 to 89.

S. 152(6.1)(*b*) formerly read:

(*b*) the amount included in computing the taxpayer's income for the particular year under subsection 91(1) is subsequently reduced because of a reduction in the foreign accrual property income of a foreign affiliate of the taxpayer for a taxation year (referred to in this paragraph as the "claim year") of the affiliate that ends in the particular year, if the reduction in that foreign accrual property income is

(i) attributable to a foreign accrual property loss (within the meaning assigned by subsection 5903(3) of the *Income Tax Regulations*) of the affiliate for a taxation year of the affiliate that ends in a subsequent taxation year of the taxpayer, and

(ii) included in the description of F in the definition "foreign accrual property income" in subsection 95(1) in respect of the affiliate for the claim year, and

S. 152(6.1) was replaced by S.C. 2013, c. 34, s. 34(2), applicable to taxation years that begin after November 1999.

See the application following subsection 152(4) regarding the override of the statute-barring rules for assessments for taxation years that end before June 26, 2013.

S. 152(6.1) formerly read:

(6.1) *Reassessment where amount included in income under subsection 91(1) is reduced.* Where

(*a*) a taxpayer has filed for a particular taxation year the return of income required by section 150,

(*b*) the amount included in computing the taxpayer's income for the particular year under subsection 91(1) is subsequently reduced because of a reduction in the foreign accrual property income of a foreign affiliate of the taxpayer for a taxation year of the affiliate that ends in the particular year and is

(i) attributable to the amount prescribed to be the deductible loss of the affiliate for the year that arose in a subsequent year of the affiliate that ends in a subsequent taxation year of the taxpayer, and

(ii) included in the description of F of the definition "foreign accrual property income" in subsection 95(1) in respect of the affiliate for the year, and

(*c*) the taxpayer has filed with the Minister, on or before the filing-due-date for the taxpayer's subsequent taxation year, a prescribed form amending the return,

the Minister shall reassess the taxpayer's tax for any relevant taxation year (other than a taxation year preceding the particular taxation year) in order to take into account the reduction in the amount included under subsection 91(1) in computing the income of the taxpayer for the year.

Related Regulations: 5903(1).

Related Sections: S. 95(1), "foreign affiliate", "foreign accrual property income"; s. 150(1) Filing returns of income — general rule; s. 161(7) Effect of carryback of loss, etc.; s. 164(5) Effect of carryback of loss, etc.; s. 248(1), "filing-due date".

Forms: T1-Adj — T1 Adjustment Request.

► 152(6.2) ◄

(6.2) Extended reassessment period. The Minister shall reassess a taxpayer's tax for a particular taxation year, in order to take into account the application of paragraph (*d*) of the definition "excluded property" in subsection 142.2(1), or the application of subsection 142.6(1.6), in respect of property held by the taxpayer, if

(*a*) the taxpayer has filed for the particular taxation year the return of income required by section 150; and

(*b*) the taxpayer files with the Minister a prescribed form amending the return, on or before the filing-due date for the taxpayer's taxation year that

(i) if the filing is in respect of paragraph (*d*) of that definition "excluded property", includes the acquisition of control time referred to in that paragraph, and

(ii) if the filing is in respect of subsection 142.6(1.6), immediately follows the particular taxation year.

History: S. 152(6.2) was added by S.C. 2009, c. 2, s. 58(5), applicable to taxation years that begin after 2001, except that

(a) for taxation years that begin before October 1, 2006, each reference in subsection 152(6.2) to paragraph (*d*) of the definition "excluded property" shall be read as a reference to paragraph (*d.3*) of the definition "mark-to-market property"; and

(b) a prescribed form referred to in paragraph 152(6.2)(*b*) is deemed to have been filed by a taxpayer on a timely basis if it is filed by the taxpayer on or before the taxpayer's filing-due date for the taxpayer's taxation year that includes the day on which this Act is assented to [R.A. March 12, 2009].

► 152(6.3) ◄

(6.3) Reassessment for section 119 credit. If a taxpayer has filed for a particular taxation year the return of income required by section 150 and an amount is subsequently claimed by the taxpayer, or on the taxpayer's behalf, for the particular year as a deduction under section 119 in respect of a disposition in a subsequent taxation year, and the taxpayer files with the Minister a prescribed form amending the return on or before the filing-due date of the taxpayer for the subsequent taxation year, the Minister shall reassess the taxpayer's tax for any relevant taxation year (other than a taxation year preceding the particular taxation year) in order to take into account the deduction claimed.

History: S. 152(6.3) was added by S.C. 2013, c. 34, s. 309(6), applicable in respect of particular taxation years that end after October 1, 1996. However, if a prescribed form referred to in subsection 152(6.3) is filed with the Minister on or before the filing-due date of the taxpayer for the taxation year that includes June 26, 2013, the form is deemed to have been filed with the Minister on a timely basis.

► 152(7) ◄

(7) Assessment not dependent on return or information. The Minister is not bound by a return or information supplied by or on behalf of a taxpayer and, in making an assessment, may, notwithstanding a return or information so supplied or if no return has been filed, assess the tax payable under this Part.

Editorial Note: S. 152(7) is of importance mainly in cases where no return has been filed by a taxpayer, or where the Minister regards the return filed to be grossly inaccurate. In such cases, the Minister normally makes what is known as an arbitrary or net worth assessment.

Related Sections: S. 152(4) Assessment and reassessment.

► 152(8) ◄

(8) Assessment deemed valid and binding. An assessment shall, subject to being varied or vacated on an objection or appeal under this Part and subject to a reassessment, be deemed to be valid and binding notwithstanding any error, defect or omission in the assessment or in any proceeding under this Act relating thereto.

Related Sections: S. 166 Irregularities.

Tax Topics: No: 2015, When Can "Incorrect or Incomplete" Be Sufficient To Overcome Deemed Validity?.

► 152(9) ◄

(9) Alternative basis for assessment. At any time after the normal reassessment period, the Minister may advance an alternative basis or argument — including that all or any portion of the income to which an amount relates was from a different source — in support of all or any portion of the total amount determined on assessment to be payable or remittable by a taxpayer under this Act unless, on an appeal under this Act

(*a*) there is relevant evidence that the taxpayer is no longer able to adduce without the leave of the court; and

(*b*) it is not appropriate in the circumstances for the court to order that the evidence be adduced.

Editorial Note: Subsection 152(9) ensures that the Minister can advance alternative arguments in support of an assessment after the normal reassessment period has expired. "Normal assessment period" is defined in subsection 152(3.1). Attempts by the Minister to in effect reassess outside of the normal assessment period by introducing a new basis for liability are not allowed. In addition, pursuant to subsection 152(5), amounts which were not included in a taxpayer's income prior to the expiration of the taxpayer's normal reassessment period cannot be added to a taxpayer's income under subsection 152(9).

In light of a recent court decision, effective December 15, 2016, subsection 152(9) was amended to clarify that the Minister may advance alternative arguments in support of all or any portion of the total amount determined on assessment to be payable or remittable by a taxpayer at any time where the assessment is under objection or appeal. The alternative arguments may result in an increase or adjustment to an amount included in the assessment that is under objection or appeal in respect of a particular source of income, provided that the total amount determined on assessment to be payable or remittable does not increase.

Prejudice to taxpayer: Paragraphs 152(9)(*a*) and (*b*) prevent advancement of an alternative argument if it would prejudice the right of the taxpayer to introduce evidence to rebut the argument.

Minister's amended pleadings: The Minister was allowed to amend his pleadings prior to trial. The proposed amendment was characterized as a new argument in support of the assessment (as opposed to a new assessment) and thus allowed by subsection 152(9), notwithstanding that the new argument was raised well after the limitation period had expired. *Smithkline Beecham Animal Health Inc. v. The Queen*, 2000 DTC 1526 (T.C.C.), affirmed 2000 DTC 6141 (F.C.A.).

Alternative arguments: The Minister was entitled to plead and argue both carelessness and negligence because the taxpayer would not be prejudiced by the alternative argument. *Krenbrink Estate v. The Queen*, 2014 DTC 5121 (F.C.A.), affirming 2014 DTC 1065 (T.C.C.).

The Minister's alternative arguments were not about new transactions and did not result in prejudice to the taxpayer or abuse of process. *Gramiak v. The Queen*, 2015 DTC 5042 (F.C.A.), affirming 2014 DTC 1036 (T.C.C.).

History: S. 152(9), the portion before paragraph (*a*) was replaced by S.C. 2016, c. 12, s. 55(1), in force on December 15, 2016, except that it does not apply in respect of appeals instituted on or before that day, and formerly read:

S. (9) *Alternative basis for assessment.* The Minister may advance an alternative argument in support of an assessment at any time after the normal reassessment period unless, on an appeal under this Act

Canadian Tax Foundation: Hosanna, *Alternative Arguments on Appeal: Does Finance Get the Last Word?*, 2016 Tax for the Owner-Manager 16(4):3–5; McMechan, *Alternative Bases for Defending Assessments: "Blankets and Pillows" or "Fundamental Change"?*, 2004 Conference Report 32:1–18; Innes and Bissell, *Basis for Assessment, Arguments, and Assumptions: An Examination of the Underlying Policy Considerations*, 2004 Canadian Tax Journal 1:59–105; Malette, *Current Cases: Federal Court of Appeal — New Argument, New Basis — La même chose (The Queen v. Loewen, 2004 DTC 6321)*, 2004 Canadian Tax Journal 4:1173–1177; Thomas, *Current Cases: Federal Court of Appeal — New Basis or New Argument: No Difference (The Queen v. Anchor Pointe Energy Ltd., 2003 FCA 294)*, 2003 Canadian Tax Journal 4:1608–1613; Meghji and Grenon, *Current Cases: Federal Court of Appeal — New Life for the Limitation Period (Pedwell v. The Queen, 2000 DTC 6405)*, 2000 Canadian Tax Journal 5:1650–1654; Bendin, *Challenging and Defending Assessments Before the Tax Court of Canada and Appellate Courts: A Postscript to the Continental Bank Case*, 2000 Canadian Tax Journal 1:35–59; Meghji et al., *Does Procedure Matter?*, 1999 Conference Report 15:1–42.

Tax Topics: No. 1900, Taxpayers Elude Surprise Procedural Skirmish; No. 1679, Challenging Crown Pleadings in Tax Litigation.

Cases: The taxpayer was entitled to rely on the expiry of the normal reassessment period to finalize his tax payable for the 2009 taxation year and the Minister, in issuing the second revocation notice in 2017 and relying on it for purposes of reassessment, was seeking to do away with the limitation period, which had expired. *Mammone v. The Queen*, 2019 DTC 5033 (FCA), reversing 2018 DTC 1024 (TCC)

Even if section 152(9) was applicable, the Minister was entitled to plead and argue both carelessness and negligence because the taxpayer would not be prejudiced by the alternative argument. *Krenbrink Estate v. The Queen*, 2014 DTC 5121 (F.C.A.), affirming 2014 DTC 1065 (T.C.C.)

The Minister's alternative arguments, related to the assessment and waiver at issue, were not about new transactions and did not result in prejudice to the taxpayer or abuse of process. *Gramiak v. The Queen*, 2015 DTC 5042 (F.C.A.), affirming 2014 DTC 1036 (T.C.C.)

During closing arguments the Minister raised, for the first time, an allegation that the taxpayer had not filed a Form T2200 with his employer and was therefore prohibited from making the deductions claimed. The Minister breached the rules of procedural fairness and was precluded from relying on the alternative argument. However, the taxpayer's appeal was dismissed on other grounds. *Adler v. The Queen*, 2010 DTC 1020 (T.C.C.)

► 152(10) ◄

(10) Tax deemed not assessed. Notwithstanding any other provision of this section, an amount of tax is deemed, for the purpose of any agreement entered into by or on behalf of the Government of Canada under section 7 of the *Federal-Provincial Fiscal Arrangements Act*, not to have been assessed under this Act until

(*a*) the end of the period during which the security is accepted by the Minister, if adequate security for the tax is accepted by the Minister under subsection 220(4.5) or (4.6); or

(*b*) the amount is collected by the Minister, if information relevant to the assessment of the amount was provided to the Canada Revenue Agency under a contract entered into by a person under a program administered by the Canada Revenue Agency to obtain information relating to tax non-compliance.

History: S. 152(10) was replaced by S.C. 2014, c. 20, s. 22(2), in force June 19, 2014, and formerly read:

(10) *Where tax deemed not to be assessed.* Notwithstanding any other provision of this section, an amount of tax for which adequate security is accepted by the Minister under subsection 220(4.5) or (4.6) is, until the end of the period during which the security is accepted by the Minister, deemed for the purpose of any agreement entered into by or on behalf of the Government of Canada under section 7 of the *Federal–Provincial Fiscal Arrangements Act* not to have been assessed under this Act.

Payment of Tax

SECTION 153: Withholding

► 153(1) ◄

(1) Withholding. Every person paying at any time in a taxation year

(*a*) salary, wages or other remuneration, other than

(i) amounts described in subsection 212(5.1), and

(ii) amounts paid at any time by an employer to an employee if, at that time, the employer is a qualifying non-resident employer and the employee is a qualifying non-resident employee,

(*b*) a superannuation or pension benefit,

(*c*) a retiring allowance,

(*d*) a death benefit,

(*d*.1) an amount described in subparagraph 56(1)(*a*)(iv) or (vii),

(*d*.2) an amount described in paragraph 56(1)(*a.3*),

(*e*) an amount as a benefit under a supplementary unemployment benefit plan,

(*f*) an annuity payment or a payment in full or partial commutation of an annuity,

(*g*) fees, commissions or other amounts for services, other than amounts described in subsection 115(2.3) or 212(5.1), (*h*) a payment under a deferred profit sharing plan or a plan referred to in section 147 as a revoked plan,

(*i*) a payment from a registered disability savings plan,

(*j*) a payment out of or under a registered retirement savings plan or a plan referred to in subsection 146(12) as an "amended plan",

(*k*) an amount as, on account or in lieu of payment of, or in satisfaction of, proceeds of the surrender, cancellation or redemption of an income-averaging annuity contract,

(*l*) a payment out of or under a registered retirement income fund or a fund referred to in subsection 146.3(11) as an "amended fund",

(*m*) a prescribed benefit under a government assistance program,

(*m*.1) (Repealed by S.C. 1994, c. 21, s. 77(1).)

(*n*) one or more amounts to an individual who has elected for the year in prescribed form in respect of all such amounts,

(*o*) an amount described in paragraph 115(2)(*c*.1),

(*p*) a contribution under a retirement compensation arrangement,

(*q*) an amount as a distribution to one or more persons out of or under a retirement compensation arrangement,

(*r*) an amount on account of the purchase price of an interest in a retirement compensation arrangement,

(*s*) an amount described in paragraph 56(1)(*r*), (*z*.2) or (*z*.4), or

(*t*) a payment made under a plan that was a registered education savings plan

shall deduct or withhold from the payment the amount determined in accordance with prescribed rules and shall, at the prescribed time, remit that amount to the Receiver General on account of the payee's tax for the year under this Part or Part XI.3, as the case may be, and, where at that prescribed time the person is a prescribed person, the remittance shall be made to the account of the Receiver General at a designated financial institution.

Editorial Note: Subsection 153(1) establishes the statutory authority for numerous source withholding rules in the Regulations, most notably in respect of employee salary and wages (s. 153(1)(*a*)), payments out of an RRSP (s. 153(1)(*j*)) and payments out of an RRIF (s. 153(1)(*l*)). Paragraph 153(1)(*g*) is the basis for Regulation 105, which requires 15% withholding on payments to non-residents in respect of services rendered in Canada (the use of "in respect of" in the Regulations was found to be outside the scope of the authority granted by Parliament in *Weyerhaeuser Company Limited v. The Queen*, 2007 DTC 392) and that the withholding is limited to fees for services, a narrower base. While s. 153(1)(g) does not distinguish between residents and non-residents, there is currently no Regulation requiring withholding on payments made to a resident of Canada for services rendered where the recipient is an independent contractor and not an employee.

History: S. 153(1)(*a*) was replaced by S.C. 2016, c. 7, s. 42(1), applicable in respect of payments made after 2015, and formerly read:

(*a*) salary, wages or other remuneration, other than amounts described in subsection 115(2.3) or 212(5.1),

S. 153(1)(*s*) was replaced by S.C. 2014, c. 20, s. 23, in force June 19, 2014, and formerly read:

(*s*) an amount described in paragraph 56(1)(*r*) or (*z.2*), or

S. 153(1)(*d.1*) was replaced by S.C. 2013, c. 34, s. 310(1), applicable to the 2006 and subsequent taxation years, and formerly read:

(*d*.1) an amount described in subparagraph 56(1)(*a*)(iv),

S. 153(1)(*d.2*) was added by S.C. 2012, c. 27, s. 28(1), in force January 1, 2013.

S. 153(1)(*s*) was replaced by S.C. 2010, c. 25, s. 39(1), applicable after 2009. S. 153(1)(*s*) formerly read:

(*s*) an amount described in paragraph 56(1)(*r*), or

Related Regulations: 100; 101; 102; 103; 105; 105.1; 106(1); 108; 110; 200; 210; 5502; Schedule I.

Related Sections: S. 56(1)(*a*) Pension benefits, unemployment insurance benefits, etc.; s. 56(1)(*l*) Legal expenses; s. 60(*n*) Repayment of pension or benefits; s. 60(*o*) Legal expenses; s. 60(*v*.1) UI and EI benefit repayment; s. 78(1) Unpaid amounts — winding-up of a corporation; s. 146.4(1), "registered disability savings plan"; s. 153(1.1) Undue hardship; s. 153(1.2) Election to increase withholding; s. 153(1.3) Split-pension amount; s. 153(3) Deemed effect of deduction; s. 153(3.1) Amounts paid in error; s. 153(6) Definitions; s. 154 Agreements providing for tax transfer payments; s. 227(8) Penalty; s. 227(9) Penalty; s. 227(9.1) Penalty; s. 227.1(1) Liability of directors for failure to deduct; s. 238(2) Compliance orders; s. 241(1) Provision of information; s. 241(3) Communication where proceedings have been commenced; s. 241(4) Where taxpayer information may be disclosed; s. 241(10) Definitions.

Canadian Tax Foundation: Baker and Laher, *Regulation 102 Withholding Relief for Non-Resident Employers*, 2016 Canadian Tax Highlights 24(3):7–8; Tollstam, *USco Personnel: Employees of Canco?*, 2015 Canadian Tax Highlights 23(2):3–4; Arnold, *Policy Forum: Some Thoughts on the Supreme Court's Approach to the Determination of Abuse Under the General Anti-Avoidance Rule*, 2014 Canadian Tax Journal 1:113–127; Winters and Novotny, *The "Special Work Site" and "Remote Location" Exemptions*, 2014 Prairie Provinces Tax Conference 10:1–34; Di Maio and Hutchinson, *Cross-Border Potpourri Issues for Small and Mid-Sized Businesses (Canada-U.S. Tax Treaty Update)*, 2012 Ontario Tax Conference 3:1–49; Jadd et al., *Performing in Canada: Taxation of Non-Resident Artists, Athletes, and Other Service Providers*, 2008 Canadian Tax Journal 3:589–638; Boddez, *Regulation 105: Non-Resident Withholding in Light of Weyerhaeuser*, 2007 British Columbia Tax Conference 7:1–24; Moffat et al., *Certificate of Compliance and Waivers (Questions 7 to 10)*, 2005 British Columbia Tax Conference 19:5–9; Kellough, *Regulation 105 and Related Cross-Border Withholding Tax Issues*, 2005 Prairie Provinces Tax Conference 12:1–17; Fowlis, *Regulation 105 and Related Cross-Border Withholding Tax Issues*, 2005 Prairie Provinces Tax Conference 11:1–30; Hallam, *Regulation 105 and Other Cross-Border Withholding Issues*, 2004 British Columbia Tax Conference 21:1–28; Lerman, *Hot Issues in Tax Compliance: Regulation 105 — Payments to Non-Residents for Services Rendered in Canada*, 2002 Ontario Tax Conference 16:17–27; Kakkar, *Reg. 105: Who is the Non-Resident Person?*, 2002 Tax for the Owner-Manager 2(3):23–24; Clayden, *Corporate Tax Compliance Issues: Regulation 105 and Treaty-Based Returns*, 2000 British Columbia Tax Conference 12:3–31; Baker and Meister, *Non-Residents Rendering Services in Canada: Regulation 105 and Other Issues*, 1999 Canadian Tax Journal 5:1321–1341; Lowey, *Growing Businesses — Canada-US Cross-Border Business: Regulation 105, Permanent Establishment Revisited and Treaty Based Returns*, 1999 Prairie Provinces Tax Conference 11:1–47.

Tax Profile: October 2009 — New Rules under the Canada-U.S. Treaty and Canadian Withholding Taxes on Cross-Border Services; August 2005 — Canada Revenue Agency's Recent Attack on U.S. Companies; September 2002 — Canadian Withholding Taxes Update; August 2007 — Professionals and Other Service Providers Beware — A Canadian Trap.

Tax Topics: No. 2289, Update on the Exemption for Non-Residents from Payroll Withholding; No. 1819, The Implications of Withholding Requirements on Non-Residents Providing Services in Canada; No. 1719, Withholding Taxes — Purchase of Software from a Non-Resident; No. 1706, Retiring Allowances and E.I. Reimbursements: How Many Times Do You Have To Withhold?.

Forms: RC473 Application for Non-Resident Employer Certification; T737-RCA — Statement of Contributions Paid to a Custodian of a Retirement Compensation Arrangement (RCA); T737-RCA SUM — Return of Contributions Paid to a Custodian of a Retirement Compensation Arrangement; T4A-RCA — Statement of Amounts Paid from a Retirement Compensation Arrangement (RCA); T4A-RCA SUM — Return of Distributions from a Retirement Compensation Arrangement (RCA); T3D — Income Tax Return for Deferred Profit Sharing Plan (DPSP) or Revoked (DPSP); TD3F — Fishermen's Election for Tax Deductions at Source; T4 — Statement of Remuneration Paid; T4A — Statement of Pension, Retirement, Annuity, and Other Income; T4 Sum. — T4SUM Summary of Remuneration Paid; T4A Sum. — T4ASUM Summary of Pension, Retirement Annuity, and Other Income; T4 Seg. — T4SEG T4 Segment; T4F Sum. — T4FSUM Summary of Fishing Income; T4F — Summary of Fishing Income.

Guides: RC4120 Employers' Guide — Filing the T4 Slip and Summary Form; RC4157 Employers' Guide — Filing the T4A Slip and Summary Form; RC4200 Employers' Guide — Filing the T4F Slip and Summary Form; RC4163 Employers' Guide — Remitting Payroll Deductions; T4001 Employer's Guide to Payroll Deductions (Basic Information).

Income Tax Folios: *Primary* — S2-F1-C2 Retiring Allowances; S1-F2-C3 Scholarships, Research Grants and Other Education Assistance.

Information Circulars: IC 75-6R2 Required withholding from amounts paid to non-residents providing services in Canada; IC 98-1R4 Collections policies.

Interpretation Bulletins: *Secondary* — IT-109R2 Unpaid amounts; IT-379R Employees profit sharing plans — Allocations to beneficiaries.

Tax Window Files: Withholding on incentive payments to nonresidents, *September 24, 2015*, CRA Document No. 2013-0495611E5.

Cases: The s. 153(1)(*g*) withholding requirements do not apply to payments made to non-resident service providers for services rendered outside of Canada and reimbursement of out-of-pocket expenses. The phrase "fees, commissions or other amounts for services" must be limited to amounts having the character of income earned in Canada by non-resident recipients, since only those amounts are potentially subject to tax under s. 2(3). *Weyerhaeuser Company Limited v. The Queen*, 2007 DTC 392 (T.C.C.)

When the taxpayer was dismissed from his employment, he negotiated a settlement of $111,540 from which source deductions were to be withheld. He received the net amount of $72,500 but the employer never remitted the source deductions. The taxpayer was credited with $39,040 under s. 227(9.4). *Suermondt v. The Queen et al.*, 2001 DTC 5389 (F.C.A.), reversing 99 DTC 3513 (T.C.C.)

A U.S. resident produced a figure skating show which took place in facilities owned by the taxpayers. After each show, the taxpayers paid the net revenues to the producer. Because the payments were in respect of services provided in Canada, the taxpayers were liable for tax which they should have withheld under paragraph 153(1)(*g*). *Ogden Palladium Services (Canada) Inc. et al. v. The Queen*, 2001 DTC 345 (T.C.C.).

► 153(1.01) ◄

(1.01) Withholding — stock option benefits. An amount that is deemed to have been received by a taxpayer as a benefit under or because of any of paragraphs 7(1)(*a*) to (*d.1*) is remuneration paid as a bonus for the purposes of paragraph (1)(*a*), except the portion, if any, of the amount that is

(*a*) deductible by the taxpayer under paragraph 110(1)(*d*) in computing the taxpayer's taxable income for a taxation year;

(*b*) deemed to have been received in a taxation year as a benefit because of a disposition of securities to which subsection 7(1.1) applies; or

(*c*) determined under paragraph 110(2.1)(*b*) to be deductible by the taxpayer under paragraph 110(1)(*d.01*) in computing the taxpayer's taxable income for a taxation year.

History: S. 153(1.01) was added by S.C. 2010, c. 25, s. 39(2), applicable after 2010, except that s. 153(1.01) does not apply with respect to benefits arising from rights granted before 2011 to a taxpayer under an agreement to sell or issue securities that was entered into in writing before 4:00 p.m. Eastern Standard Time, March 4, 2010 and that included, at that time, a written condition prohibiting the taxpayer from disposing of the securities acquired under the agreement for a period of time after exercise.

Canadian Tax Foundation: Forgie et al., *Structuring Stock Options in Light of the 2010 Budget and Other Current Issues in Executive Compensation*, 2011 Conference Report 13:1–29.

► 153(1.1) ◄

(1.1) Undue hardship. Where the Minister is satisfied that the deducting or withholding of the amount otherwise required to be deducted or withheld under subsection (1) from a payment would cause undue hardship, the Minister may determine a lesser amount and that amount shall be deemed to be the amount determined under that subsection as the amount to be deducted or withheld from that payment.

Related Regulations: Part I.

Related Sections: S. 212(5.3) Reduction of withholding.

► 153(1.2) ◄

(1.2) Election to increase withholding. Where a taxpayer so elects in prescribed manner and prescribed form, the amount required to be deducted or withheld under subsection (1) from any payment to the taxpayer shall be deemed to be the total of

(*a*) the amount, if any, otherwise required to be deducted or withheld under that subsection from that payment, and

(*b*) the amount specified by the taxpayer in that election with respect to that payment or with respect to a class of payments that includes that payment.

Related Regulations: 109.

Forms: TD1 — Personal Tax Credits Return.

► 153(1.3) ◄

(1.3) Reduction not permitted. A joint election made or expected to be made under section 60.03 is not to be considered a basis on which the Minister may determine a lesser amount under subsection (1.1).

History: S. 153(1.3) was replaced by S.C. 2016, c. 7, s. 42(2), applicable to the 2016 and subsequent taxation years, and formerly read:

> (1.3) **Reduction not permitted.** The Minister shall not consider either of the following circumstances as a basis on which a lesser amount may be determined under subsection (1.1):
>
> (*a*) a joint election made or expected to be made under section 60.03; or
>
> (*b*) a deduction or an intention to claim a deduction under section 119.1.

S. 153(1.3) was replaced by S.C. 2015, c. 36, s. 34(1), applicable to the 2014 and subsequent taxation years, and formerly read:

> (1.3) **Split-pension amount.** A joint election made or expected to be made under section 60.03 is not to be considered a basis on which the Minister may determine a lesser amount under subsection (1.1).

Related Sections: S. 153(1.4) Exception — remittance to designated financial institution.

► 153(1.31) ◄

(1.31) Non-cash stock option benefit. An amount deemed to have been received as a benefit under or because of any of paragraphs 7(1)(*a*) to (*d.1*) shall not be considered a basis on which the Minister may determine a lesser amount under subsection (1.1) solely because it is received as a non-cash benefit.

Editorial Note: Effectively, withholding in respect of a stock option benefit enjoyed through the acquisition of non-CCPC securities (i.e., the non-cash benefit included because of s. 7(1)), which is required under s. 153(1.01), cannot be reduced under the "under hardship" provisions of s. 153(1.1).

History: S. 153(1.31) was added by S.C. 2010, c. 25, s. 39(3), applicable after 2010.

► 153(1.4) ◄

(1.4) Exception — remittance to designated financial institution. For the purpose of subsection (1), a prescribed person referred to in that subsection is deemed to have remitted an amount to the account of the Receiver General at a designated financial institution if the prescribed person has remitted the amount to the Receiver General at least one day before the day upon which the amount is due.

► 153(2) ◄

(2) Deemed withholding. If a pensioner and a pension transferee (as those terms are defined in section 60.03) make a joint election under section 60.03 in respect of a split-pension amount (as defined in that section) for a taxation year, the portion of the amount deducted or withheld under subsection (1) that may be reasonably considered to be in respect of the split-pension amount is deemed to have been deducted or withheld on account of the pension transferee's tax for the taxation year under this Part and not on account of the pensioner's tax for the taxation year under this Part.

Related Sections: S. 156.1 No instalment required; s. 227(2) Return filed with person withholding; s. 227(3) Failure to file return; s. 227(6) Excess withheld, returned or applied; s. 248(1), "balance due day".

► 153(3) ◄

(3) Deemed effect of deduction. When an amount has been deducted or withheld under subsection (1), it shall, for all the purposes of this Act, be deemed to have been received at that time by the person to whom the remuneration, benefit, payment, fees, commissions or other amounts were paid.

Related Sections: S. 227(1) Withholding taxes; s. 227(12) Agreement not to deduct void; s. 227(13) Minister's receipt discharges debtor.

Cases: Federal income tax must be calculated on the entire salary receivable and not the net amount received after deduction of provincial tax. *Morin v. The Queen*, 75 DTC 5061 (F.C.T.D.)

► 153(3.1) ◄

(3.1) Amounts paid in error. For the purposes of this Act, an amount (referred to in this subsection as the "excess amount") is deemed to not have been deducted or withheld under subsection (1) by a person if

(*a*) the excess amount was, absent the application of this subsection, deducted or withheld by the person under subsection (1);

(*b*) the excess amount is in respect of an excess payment (referred to in this subsection as the "total excess payment") of an individual's salary, wages or other remuneration by the person to the individual in a particular year, that was paid as a result of a clerical, administrative or system error;

(*c*) before the end of the third year after the calendar year in which the excess amount is deducted or withheld,

(i) the person elects in prescribed manner to have this subsection apply in respect of the excess amount, and

(ii) the individual has repaid, or made an arrangement to repay, the total excess payment less the excess amount;

(*d*) an information return correcting for the total excess payment has not been issued by the person to the individual prior to the making of the election in subparagraph (*c*)(i); and

(*e*) any additional criteria specified by the Minister have been met.

Editorial Note: Prior to the enactment of subsection 153(3.1), there was no specific rule that allowed the CRA to reimburse amounts withheld on excess remuneration paid in error. Effective for remuneration paid after 2015, the provision provides a mechanism under which the CRA can reimburse the withheld amounts on such excess remuneration to the employer. The provision applies where an "excess amount" was withheld under subsection 153(1) in respect of an excess payment of salary, wages or other remuneration ("total excess payment") made to an employee as a result of a clerical, administrative or system error. Additionally, by the end of the third calendar year following the withholding of the excess amount, the employer must make an election in prescribed form and the employee must repay the employer the total excess payment minus the excess amount (since the employee would not have received the excess amount that was withheld). Where subsection 153(3.1) applies, the excess amount is deemed not to have been deducted or withheld under subsection 153(1), which means that subsection 153(3) does not apply and the employee is not deemed to have received the excess amount. This in turn means that the CRA can reimburse the employer for the excess amount since the employee did not receive it and was not deemed to receive it.

History: S. 153(3.1) was added by S.C. 2019, c. 29, s. 33(1), in respect of excess payments of salary, wages, or other remuneration made after 2015.

Related Sections: 153(1) Withholding.

► 153(4) ◄

(4) Unclaimed dividends, interest and proceeds. Where at the end of a taxpayer's taxation year the person beneficially entitled to an amount received by the taxpayer after 1984 and before the year as or in respect of dividends, interest or proceeds of disposition of property is unknown to the taxpayer, the taxpayer shall remit to the Receiver General on or before the day that is 60 days after the end of the year on account of the tax payable under this Act by that person an amount equal to

(*a*) in the case of dividends, 33⅓% of the total amount of the dividends,

(*b*) in the case of interest, 50% of the total amount of the interest, and

(*c*) in the case of proceeds of disposition of property, 50% of the total of all amounts each of which is the amount, if any, by which the proceeds of disposition of a property exceed the total of any outlays and expenses made or incurred by the taxpayer for the purpose of disposing of the property (to the extent that those outlays and expenses were not deducted in computing the taxpayer's income for any taxation year or attributable to any other property),

except that no remittance under this subsection shall be required in respect of an amount that was included in computing the taxpayer's income for the year or a preceding taxation year or in respect of an amount on which the tax under this subsection was previously remitted.

Related Regulations: 108(3); 108(4); 210.

Related Sections: S. 153(5) Deemed effect of remittance.

Information Circulars: IC 71-9R Unclaimed dividends.

► 153(5) ◄

(5) Deemed effect of remittance. An amount remitted by a taxpayer under subsection (4) in respect of dividends, interest or proceeds of disposition of property shall be deemed

(*a*) to have been received by the person beneficially entitled thereto; and

(*b*) to have been deducted or withheld from the amount otherwise payable by the taxpayer to the person beneficially entitled thereto.

Related Sections: S. 78 Unpaid amounts — winding-up of a corporation; s. 145(1), "supplementary unemployment benefit plan"; s. 146(1), "registered retirement savings plan"; s. 147(1), "deferred profit sharing plan"; s. 227(6) Excess withheld, returned or applied; s. 227(9) Penalty; s. 227(10) Assessment — failure to deduct or withhold tax; s. 227(13) Minister's receipt discharges debtor; s. 248(1), "amount", "annuity", "dividend", "employees", "prescribed", "registered retirement income fund", "retirement compensation arrangement", "retiring allowance", "salary or wages", "share", "superannuation or pension benefit".

► 153(6) ◄

(6) Definitions. The following definitions apply in this section.

History: S. 153(6) was replaced by S.C. 2016, c. 7, s. 42(3), applicable in respect of payments made after 2015, and formerly read:

(6) *Meaning of "designated financial institution".* In this section, "designated financial institution" means a corporation that

(*a*) is a bank, other than an authorized foreign bank that is subject to the restrictions and requirements referred to in subsection 524(2) of the *Bank Act*;

(*b*) is authorized under the laws of Canada or a province to carry on the business of offering its services as a trustee to the public; or

(*c*) is authorized under the laws of Canada or a province to accept deposits from the public and carries on the business of lending money on the security of real property or immovables or investing in indebtedness on the security of mortgages on real property or of hypothecs on immovables.

S. 153(6)(*c*) was amended by S.C. 2013, c. 34, s. 139, in force June 26, 2013, and formerly read:

(*c*) is authorized under the laws of Canada or a province to accept deposits from the public and carries on the business of lending money on the security of real estate or investing in mortgages or hypothecs on real estate.

Related Regulations: 200(1.1).

Related Sections: 153(1) Withholding.

Canadian Tax Foundation: Baker and Laher, *Regulation 102 Withholding Relief for Non-Resident Employers*, 2016 Canadian Tax Highlights 24(3):7–8; Arnold, *Policy Forum: Some Thoughts on the Supreme Court's Approach to the Determination of Abuse Under the General Anti-Avoidance Rule*, 2014 Canadian Tax Journal 1:113–127.

"designated financial institution" —"designated financial institution" means a corporation that

(*a*) is a bank, other than an authorized foreign bank that is subject to the restrictions and requirements referred to in subsection 524(2) of the *Bank Act*;

(*b*) is authorized under the laws of Canada or a province to carry on the business of offering its services as a trustee to the public; or

(*c*) is authorized under the laws of Canada or a province to accept deposits from the public and carries on the business of lending money on the security of real property or immovables or investing in indebtedness on the security of mortgages on real property or of hypothecs on immovables.

"qualifying non-resident employee" —"qualifying non-resident employee", at any time in respect of a payment referred to in paragraph (1)(*a*), means an employee who

(*a*) is, at that time, resident in a country with which Canada has a tax treaty;

(*b*) is not liable to tax under this Part in respect of the payment because of that treaty; and

(*c*) works in Canada for less than 45 days in the calendar year that includes that time or is present in Canada for less than 90 days in any 12-month period that includes that time.

Forms: RC473 Application for Non-Resident Employer Certification.

"qualifying non-resident employer" —"qualifying non-resident employer", at any time, means an employer

(*a*) that at that time

(i) in the case of an employer that is not a partnership,

(A) is a resident of a country with which Canada has a tax treaty, or

(B) is a corporation that does not satisfy the condition in clause (A), but would be a resident of a country with which Canada has a tax treaty if the corporation were treated, for the purpose of income taxation in that country, as a body corporate, and

(ii) in the case of an employer that is a partnership, is a partnership in respect of which the total of all amounts, each of which is a share of the partnership's income or loss for the fiscal period that includes that time of a member that, at that time, is a resident of a country with which Canada has a tax treaty (or is a corporation that satisfies the condition in clause (i)(B)), is not less than 90% of the income or loss of the partnership for the period (for the purposes of this subparagraph, where the income and loss of the partnership are nil for the period, the income of the partnership for the period is deemed to be $1,000,000); and

(*b*) that is at that time certified by the Minister under subsection (7).

Forms: RC473 Application for Non-Resident Employer Certification.

▶ 153(7) ◀

(7) Certification by Minister. The Minister may

(*a*) certify an employer for a specified period of time if the employer has applied in prescribed form containing prescribed information and the Minister is satisfied that the employer

(i) meets the conditions in paragraph (*a*) of the definition *qualifying non-resident employer* in subsection (6), and

(ii) meets the conditions established by the Minister; and

(*b*) revoke an employer's certification if the Minister is no longer satisfied that the employer meets the conditions referred to in subparagraph (*a*)(i) or (ii).

History: S. 153(7) was added by S.C. 2016, c. 7, s. 42(3), applicable in respect of payments made after 2015.

SECTION 154: Agreements providing for tax transfer payments

▶ 154(1) ◀

(1) Agreements providing for tax transfer payments. The Minister may, with the approval of the Governor in Council, enter into an agreement with the government of a province to provide for tax transfer payments and the terms and conditions relating to such payments.

Related Sections: S. 154(2) Tax transfer payment; s. 154(3) Payment deemed received by individual; s. 154(4) Payment deemed received by Receiver General.

▶ 154(2) ◀

(2) Tax transfer payment. Where, on account of the tax for a taxation year payable by an individual under this Part, an amount has been deducted or withheld under subsection 153(1) on the assumption that the individual was resident in a place other than the province in which the individual resided on the last day of the year, and the individual

(*a*) has filed a return of income for the year with the Minister,

(*b*) is liable to pay tax under this Part for the year, and

(*c*) is resident on the last day of the year in a province with which an agreement described in subsection (1) has been entered into,

the Minister may make a tax transfer payment to the government of the province not exceeding an amount equal to the product obtained by multiplying the amount or the total of the amounts so deducted or withheld by a prescribed rate.

Related Regulations: 3300.

Related Sections: S. 153(1) Withholding.

▶ 154(3) ◀

(3) Payment deemed received by individual. Where, pursuant to an agreement entered into under subsection (1), an amount has been transferred by the Minister to the government of a province with respect to an individual, the amount shall, for all purposes of this Act, be deemed to have been received by the individual at the time the amount was transferred.

▶ 154(4) ◀

(4) Payment deemed received by Receiver General. Where, pursuant to an agreement entered into under subsection (1), an amount has been transferred by the government of a province to the Minister with respect to an individual, the amount shall, for all purposes of this Act, be deemed to have been received by the Receiver General on account of the individual's tax under this Part for the year in respect of which the amount was transferred.

▶ 154(5) ◀

(5) Amount not to include refund. In this section, an amount deducted or withheld does not include any refund made in respect of that amount.

Related Sections: S. 219(3) Provisions applicable to Part; s. 248(1), "amount", "individual", "prescribed".

SECTION 155: Farmers and fishermen

▶ 155(1) ◀

(1) Farmers and fishermen. Subject to section 156.1, every individual whose chief source of income for a taxation year is farming or fishing shall, on or before December 31 in the year, pay to the Receiver General in respect of the year, $^2/_3$ of

(*a*) the amount estimated by the individual to be the tax payable under this Part by the individual for the year, or

(*b*) the individual's instalment base for the preceding taxation year.

Related Sections: S. 248(1), "balance due day".

▶ 155(2) ◀

(2) Definition of "instalment base". In this section, "instalment base" of an individual for a taxation year means the amount determined in prescribed manner to be the individual's instalment base for the year.

Related Regulations: 5300(1).

Related Sections: S. 2(2) Taxable income; s. 119 Former resident — credit for tax paid; s. 151 Estimate of tax; s. 156(1) Other individuals; s. 161(2) Interest on instalments; s. 161(4) Limitation — farmers and fishermen; s. 248(1), "farming", "fishing", "individual"; s. 249 Definition of "taxation year".

SECTION 156: Other individuals

▶ 156(1) ◀

(1) Other individuals. Subject to section 156.1, in respect of each taxation year every individual (other than one to whom section 155 applies for the year) shall pay to the Receiver General

(*a*) on or before March 15, June 15, September 15 and December 15 in the year, an amount equal to $^1/_4$ of

(i) the amount estimated by the individual to be the tax payable under this Part by the individual for the year, or

(ii) the individual's instalment base for the preceding taxation year, or

(*b*) on or before

(i) March 15 and June 15 in the year, an amount equal to $^1/_4$ of the individual's instalment base for the second preceding taxation year, and

(ii) September 15 and December 15 in the year, an amount equal to $^1/_2$ of the amount, if any, by which

(A) the individual's instalment base for the preceding taxation year

exceeds

(B) $^1/_2$ of the individual's instalment base for the second preceding taxation year.

Editorial Note: The CRA uses the method of computing instalment payments under s. 156(1)(*b*) when it sends out instalment notices to individuals. However, individuals are allowed to use any of the three methods described in s. 156(1) without the imposition of interest charges. Generally speaking, instalment payments are required for individuals in a taxation year if their federal plus provincial tax payable minus amounts withheld at source is greater than $3,000 ($2,000 prior to 2008) in the year and in one of the two preceding years (see s. 156.1(2); the monetary threshold for Quebec residents is $1,800 ($1,200 prior to 2008) of federal tax).

Related Sections: S. 248(1), "balance-due day".

Forms: T1162A — Pre-Authorized Payment Plan (Personal Quarterly Instalment Payments).

Guides: P110 Paying Your Income Tax by Instalments.

Tax Window Files: 2016 STEP – Q6 – Trust Instalment Requirements, *June 10, 2016*, CRA Document No. 2016-0641461C6.

▶ 156(2) ◀

(2) Payment by mutual fund trusts. Notwithstanding subsection (1), the amount payable by a mutual fund trust to the Receiver General on or before any day referred to in paragraph (1)(*a*) in a taxation year shall be deemed to be the amount, if any, by which

(*a*) the amount so payable otherwise determined under that subsection,

exceeds

(*b*) $^1/_4$ of the trust's capital gains refund (within the meaning assigned by section 132) for the year.

▶ 156(3) ◀

(3) Definition of "instalment base". In this section, "instalment base" of an individual for a taxation year means the amount determined in prescribed manner to be the individual's instalment base for the year.

Related Regulations: 5300(1).

Related Sections: S. 155(2) Definition of "instalment base"; s. 161(9) Definitions of "instalment base", etc.

▶ 156(4) ◀

(4) Payments by SIFT trusts. Subsections (1) to (3) and section 156.1 do not apply to a SIFT trust.

History: S. 156(4) was added by S.C. 2013, c. 40, s. 68(1), applicable to taxation years that begin after July 20, 2011.

SECTION 156.1: [No instalment required]

▶ 156.1(1) ◀

(1) Definitions. For the purposes of this section,

"instalment threshold" — "instalment threshold" of an individual for a taxation year means

(*a*) in the case of an individual resident in the Province of Quebec at the end of the year, $1,800, and

(*b*) in any other case, $3,000;

Related Sections: S. 248(1), "Specified future tax consequences".

"net tax owing" — "net tax owing" by an individual for a taxation year means

(*a*) in the case of an individual resident in the Province of Quebec at the end of the year, the amount determined by the formula

$$A - C - D - F$$

and

(*b*) in any other case, the amount determined by the formula

$$A + B - C - E - F$$

where

A is the total of the taxes payable under this Part and Parts I.2, X.5 and XI.4 by the individual for the year,

B is the total of all income taxes payable by the individual for the year under any law of a province or of an Aboriginal government with which the Minister of Finance has entered into an agreement for the collection of income taxes payable by individuals to the province or Aboriginal government under that law,

C is the total of the taxes deducted or withheld under section 153 and Part I.2 on behalf of the individual for the year,

D is the amount determined under subsection 120(2) in respect of the individual for the year,

E is the total of all amounts deducted or withheld on behalf of the individual for the year under a law of a province or of an Aboriginal government with which the Minister of Finance has entered into an agreement for the collection of income taxes payable by individuals to the province or Aboriginal government under that law, and

F is the amount determined under subsection 120(2.2) in respect of the individual for the year.

History: S. 156.1(1), the description of A of the definition "net tax owing" was replaced by S.C. 2012, c. 31, s. 40(1), applicable to the 2012 and subsequent taxation years, and formerly read:

A is the total of the taxes payable under this Part and Parts I.2 and X.5 by the individual for the year,

Related Sections: S. 155(1) Farmers and fishermen; s. 156(1) Other individuals; s. 248(1), "balance-due day", "specified future tax consequences".

► 156.1(1.1) ◄

(1.1) Values of A and B in "net tax owing". For the purposes of determining the values of A and B in the definition "net tax owing" in subsection (1), income taxes payable by an individual for a taxation year are determined

(*a*) before taking into consideration the specified future tax consequences for the year; and

(*b*) after deducting all tax credits to which the individual is entitled for the year relating to those taxes (other than tax credits that become payable to the individual after the individual's balance-due day for the year, prescribed tax credits and amounts deemed to have been paid because of the application of either subsection 120(2) or (2.2)).

► 156.1(1.2) ◄

(1.2) Value of D in "net tax owing". For the purpose of determining the value of D in the definition "net tax owing" in subsection (1), the amount deemed by subsection 120(2) to have been paid on account of an individual's tax under this Part for a taxation year is determined before taking into consideration the specified future tax consequences for the year.

► 156.1(1.3) ◄

(1.3) Value of F in "net tax owing". For the purpose of determining the value of F in the definition "net tax owing" in subsection (1), the amount deemed by subsection 120(2.2) to have been paid on account of an individual's tax under this Part for a taxation year is determined before taking into consideration the specified future tax consequences for the year.

► 156.1(2) ◄

(2) No instalment required. Sections 155 and 156 do not apply to an individual for a particular taxation year where

(*a*) the individual's chief source of income for the particular year is farming or fishing and the individual's net tax owing for the particular year, or either of the 2 preceding taxation years, does not exceed the individual's instalment threshold for that year;

(*b*) the individual's net tax owing for the particular year, or for each of the 2 preceding taxation years, does not exceed the individual's instalment threshold for that year; or

(*c*) the individual is a graduated rate estate for the particular year.

History: S. 156.1(2)(*c*) was added by S.C. 2014, c. 39, s. 56(1), applicable to the 2016 and subsequent taxation years.

Related Sections: 248(1) graduated rate estate; S. 128.1(5) Instalment interest.

► 156.1(3) ◄

(3) Idem. Sections 155 and 156 do not require the payment of any amount in respect of an individual that would otherwise become due under either of those sections on or after the day on which the individual dies.

► 156.1(4) ◄

(4) Payment of remainder. Every individual shall, on or before the individual's balance-due day for each taxation year, pay to the Receiver General in respect of the year the amount, if any, by which the individual's tax payable under this Part for the year exceeds the total of

(*a*) all amounts deducted or withheld under section 153 from remuneration or other payments received by the individual in the year, and

(*b*) all other amounts paid to the Receiver General on or before that day on account of the individual's tax payable under this Part for the year.

Related Sections: S. 156 Instalments for individuals; s. 161 Interest; s. 227(2) Return filed with person withholding; s. 227(3) Failure to file return; s. 227(6) Excess withheld, returned or applied; s. 248(1), "balance-due day".

Information Circulars: IC 98-1R4 Collections policies.

SECTION 157: Payment by corporation

► 157(1) ◄

(1) Payment by corporation. Subject to subsections (1.1) and (1.5), every corporation shall, in respect of each of its taxation years, pay to the Receiver General

(*a*) either

(i) on or before the last day of each month in the year, an amount equal to 1/12 of the total of the amounts estimated by it to be the taxes payable by it under this Part and Parts VI, VI.1 and XIII.1 for the year,

(ii) on or before the last day of each month in the year, an amount equal to 1/12 of its first instalment base for the year, or

(iii) on or before the last day of each of the first two months in the year, an amount equal to 1/12 of its second instalment base for the year, and on or before the last day of each of the following months in the year, an amount equal to 1/10 of the amount remaining after deducting the amount computed pursuant to this subparagraph in respect of the first two months from its first instalment base for the year; and

(*b*) the remainder of the taxes payable by it under this Part and Parts VI, VI.1 and XIII.1 for the year on or before its balance-due day for the year.

Related Sections: S. 88(1) Winding-up; s. 137(7) Credit union not private corporation; s. 151 Estimate of tax; s. 161(2) Interest on instalments; s. 248(1), "specified future tax consequences"; s. 249 Definition of "taxation year".

Canadian Tax Foundation: Feltham and Macnaughton, *Optimal Payment Strategy for Corporate Income Tax Instalments*, 2000 Canadian Tax Journal 1:60–89.

Guides: T7B-CORP Corporation Installment Guide.

Cases: GAAR reassessments increased the taxpayer's Part I taxes for the year in issue. These increased taxes became payable by the taxpayer's balance-due date and interest accrued from that date and not the date of reassessment. *Quinco Financial Inc. v. The Queen*, 2018 DTC 5091 (FCA)

Where the previous year's income was reassessed by the Minister as being higher than originally computed by the corporation, interest was held to have been properly assessed on the deficient instalments which had been based on the incorrect lower figure of the previous year's income. *No. 384 v. M.N.R.*, 57 DTC 67 (T.A.B.)

► 157(1.1) ◄

(1.1) Special case. A small-CCPC may, in respect of each of its taxation years, pay to the Receiver General

(*a*) one of the following:

(i) on or before the last day of each three-month period in the taxation year (or if the period that remains in a taxation year after the end of the last such three-month period is less than three months, on or before the last day of that remaining period), an amount equal to 1/4 of the total of the amounts estimated by it to be the taxes payable by it under this Part and Part VI.1 for the taxation year,

(ii) on or before the last day of each three-month period in the taxation year (or if the period that remains in a taxation year after the end of the last such three-month period is less than three months, on or before the last day of that remaining period), an amount equal to 1/4 of its first instalment base for the taxation year, or

(iii) on or before the last day

(A) of the first period in the taxation year not exceeding three months, an amount equal to 1/4 of its second instalment base for the taxation year, and

(B) of each of the following three-month periods in the taxation year (or if the period that remains in a taxation year after the end of the last such three-month period is less than three months, on or before the last day of that remaining period), an amount equal to 1/3 of the amount remaining after deducting the amount computed pursuant to clause (A) from its first instalment base for the taxation year; and

(*b*) the remainder of the taxes payable by it under this Part and Part VI.1 for the taxation year on or before its balance-due day for the taxation year.

► 157(1.2) ◄

(1.2) Small-CCPC. For the purpose of subsection (1.1), a small-CCPC, at a particular time during a taxation year, is a Canadian-controlled private corporation

(*a*) for which the amount determined under subsection (1.3) for the taxation year, or for the preceding taxation year, does not exceed $500,000;

(*b*) for which the amount determined under subsection (1.4) for the taxation year, or for the preceding taxation year, does not exceed $10 million;

(*c*) in respect of which an amount is deducted under section 125 of the Act in computing the corporation's tax payable for the taxation year or for the preceding taxation year; and

(*d*) that has throughout the 12-month period that ends at the time its last remittance under this section is due,

(i) remitted, on or before the day on or before which the amounts were required to be remitted, all amounts that were required to be remitted under subsection 153(1), under Part IX of the *Excise Tax Act*, under subsection 82(1) of the *Employment Insurance Act* or under subsection 21(1) of the *Canada Pension Plan*; and

(ii) filed, on or before the day on or before which the returns were required to be filed, all returns that were required to be filed under this Act or under Part IX of the *Excise Tax Act*.

History: S. 157(1.2)(*a*) was replaced by S.C. 2009, c. 2, s. 59(1), applicable to taxation years ending after 2008, except that for taxation years that end in 2009, paragraph 157(1.2)(*a*) shall be read as follows:

"(*a*) for which

(i) the amount determined under subsection (1.3) for the taxation year does not exceed the amount that is the total of $400,000 and that proportion of $100,000 that the number of days in the taxation year that are in 2009 is of the number of days in the taxation year, or

(ii) the amount determined under subsection (1.3) for the preceding taxation year does not exceed $400,000;"

S. 157(1.2)(*a*) formerly read:

(*a*) for which the amount determined under subsection (1.3) for the taxation year, or for the preceding taxation year, does not exceed $400,000;

► 157(1.3) ◄

(1.3) Taxable income — small-CCPC. The amount determined under this subsection in respect of a corporation for a particular taxation year is

(*a*) if the corporation is not associated with another corporation in the particular taxation year, the amount that is the corporation's taxable income for the particular taxation year; or

(*b*) if the corporation is associated with another corporation in the particular taxation year, the amount that is the total of all amounts each of which is the taxable income of the corporation for the particular taxation year or the taxable income of a corporation with which it is associated in the particular taxation year for a taxation year of that other corporation that ends in the particular taxation year.

► 157(1.4) ◄

(1.4) Taxable capital — small-CCPC. The amount determined under this subsection in respect of a corporation for a particular taxation year is (*a*) if the corporation is not associated with another corporation in the particular taxation year, the amount that is the corporation's taxable capital employed in Canada (for the purpose of this subsection, within the meaning assigned by section 181.2 or 181.3, as the case may be) for the particular taxation year; or

(*b*) if the corporation is associated with another corporation in the particular taxation year, the amount that is the total of all amounts each of which is the taxable capital employed in Canada of the corporation for the particular taxation year or the taxable capital employed in Canada of a corporation with which it is associated in the particular taxation year for a taxation year of that other corporation that ends in the particular taxation year.

History: S. 157(1.4)(*a*) and (*b*) were replaced by S.C. 2013, c. 34, s. 311(1), applicable to taxation years that begin after 2007, and formerly read:

(*a*) if the corporation is not associated with another corporation in the particular taxation year, the amount that is the corporation's taxable capital employed in Canada (within the meaning assigned by section 181.2) for the particular taxation year; or

(*b*) if the corporation is associated with another corporation in the particular taxation year, the amount that is the total of all amounts each of which is the taxable capital employed in Canada (within the meaning assigned by section 181.2) of the corporation for the particular taxation year or the taxable capital employed in Canada (within the meaning assigned by section 181.2) of a corporation with which it is associated in the particular taxation year for a taxation year of that other corporation that ends in the particular taxation year.

► 157(1.5) ◄

(1.5) No longer a small-CCPC. Notwithstanding subsection (1), where a corporation, that has remitted amounts in accordance with subsection (1.1), ceases at any particular time in a taxation year to be eligible to remit in accordance with subsection (1.1), the corporation shall pay to the Receiver General, the following amounts for the taxation year,

(*a*) on or before the last day of each month, in the taxation year, that ends after the particular time, either

(i) the amount determined by the formula

$$(A - B)/C$$

where

A is the total of the amounts estimated by the corporation to be the taxes payable by it under this Part and Parts VI, VI.1 and XIII.1 for the taxation year,

B is the total of all payments payable by the corporation in the taxation year in accordance with subsection (1.1), and

C is the number of months that end in the taxation year and after the particular time, or

(ii) the total of

(A) the amount determined by the formula

$$(A - B)/C$$

where

A is the corporation's first instalment base for the taxation year,

B is the total of all payments payable by the corporation in the taxation year in accordance with subsection (1.1), and

C is the number of months that end in the taxation year and after the particular time; and

(B) the amount obtained when the estimated tax payable by the corporation, if any, under Parts VI and XIII.1 for the taxation year is divided by the number of months that end in the taxation year and after the particular time; and

(*b*) the remainder of the taxes payable by it under this Part and Parts VI, VI.1 and XIII.1 for the taxation year on or before its balance-due day for the year.

History: S. 157(1.5)(*a*)(ii)(B) was replaced by S.C. 2013, c. 40, s. 69(1), applicable to taxation years that begin after 2007, and formerly read:

(B) the amount obtained when the estimated tax payable by the corporation, if any, under Part VI and XIII.1 for the taxation year is divided by the number of months that end in the taxation year and after the particular time; and

S. 157(1.5)(*b*) was replaced by S.C. 2013, c. 40, s. 69(2), applicable to taxation years that begin after 2007, and formerly read:

(*b*) the remainder of the taxes payable by it under this Part and Parts VI, VI.1 and XIII.1 for the taxation year on or before its balance-due date for the taxation year.

► 157(2) ◄

(2) Application to SIFT trusts. Subsections (1), (2.1) and (4) apply to a SIFT trust with any modifications that the circumstances require.

History: S. 157(2) was added by S.C. 2013, c. 40, s. 69(3), applicable to taxation years that begin after July 20, 2011.

► 157(2.1) ◄

(2.1) $3,000 threshold. A corporation may, instead of paying the instalments required for a taxation year by paragraph (1)(*a*) or by subsection (1.1), pay to the Receiver General, under paragraph (1)(*b*), the total of the taxes payable by it under this Part and Parts VI, VI.1 and XIII.1 for the taxation year, if

(*a*) the total of the taxes payable under this Part and Parts VI, VI.1 and XIII.1 by the corporation for the taxation year (determined before taking into consideration the specified future tax consequences for the year) is equal to or less than $3,000; or

(*b*) the corporation's first instalment base for the year is equal to or less than $3,000.

Related Regulations: 5301.

► 157(3) ◄

(3) Reduced instalments. Notwithstanding subsection (1) and (1.5), the amount payable under subsection (1) or (1.5) for a taxation year by a corporation to the Receiver General on or before the last day of any month in the year is deemed to be the amount, if any, by which

(*a*) the amount so payable as determined under that subsection for the month

exceeds

(*b*) where the corporation is neither a mutual fund corporation nor a non-resident-owned investment corporation, $^{1}/_{12}$ of the corporation's dividend refund (within the meaning assigned by subsection 129(1)) for the year,

(*c*) if the corporation is a mutual fund corporation, $^{1}/_{12}$ of the total of

(i) the corporation's capital gains refund (within the meaning assigned by section 131) for the year, and

(ii) the amount that, because of subsection 131(5) or (11), is the corporation's dividend refund (within the meaning assigned by section 129) for the year,

(*d*) where the corporation is a non-resident-owned investment corporation, 1/12 of the corporation's allowable refund (within the meaning assigned by section 133) for the year, and

(*e*) 1/12 of the total of the amounts each of which is deemed by subsection 125.4(3), 125.5(3), 125.6(2), 127.1(1) or 127.41(3) to have been paid on account of the corporation's tax payable under this Part for the year.

History: S. 157(3)(*e*) was replaced by S.C. 2019, c. 29, s. 34(1), deemed to have come into force on January 1, 2019, and formerly read:

(*e*) 1/12 of the total of the amounts each of which is deemed by subsection 125.4(3), 125.5(3), 127.1(1) or 127.41(3) to have been paid on account of the corporation's tax payable under this Part for the year.

S. 157(3)(*c*) was replaced by S.C. 2013, c. 34, s. 311(2), applicable to the 1999 and subsequent taxation years, and formerly read:

(*c*) where the corporation is a mutual fund corporation, 1/12 of the total of

(i) the corporation's capital gains refund (within the meaning assigned by section 131) for the year, and

(ii) the amount that, by virtue of subsection 131(5), is the corporation's dividend refund (within the meaning assigned by section 129) for the year,

Related Sections: S. 131(8) Meaning of "mutual fund corporation"; s. 133(8), "non-resident owned investment corporation"; s. 125.6(2) Tax credit.

► 157(3.1) ◄

(3.1) Amount of payment — three-month period. Notwithstanding subsection (1.1), the amount payable under subsection (1.1) for a taxation year by a corporation to the Receiver General on or before the last day of any period in the year is deemed to be the amount, if any, by which

(*a*) the amount so payable as determined under that subsection for the period

exceeds the total of

(*b*) 1/4 of the corporation's dividend refund (within the meaning assigned by subsection 129(1)) for the taxation year, and

(*c*) 1/4 of the total of the amounts each of which is deemed by subsection 125.4(3), 125.5(3), 125.6(2), 127.1(1) or 127.41(3) to have been paid on account of the corporation's tax payable under this Part for the taxation year.

History: S. 157(3.1)(*c*) was replaced by S.C. 2019, c. 29, s. 34(2), deemed to have come into force on January 1, 2019, and formerly read:

(*c*) 1/4 of the total of the amounts each of which is deemed by subsection 125.4(3), 125.5(3), 127.1(1) or 127.41(3) to have been paid on account of the corporation's tax payable under this Part for the taxation year.

Related Sections: 125.6(2) Tax credit.

► 157(4) ◄

(4) Definitions. In this section, "first instalment base" and "second instalment base" of a corporation for a taxation year have the meanings prescribed by regulation.

Related Regulations: 5301.

SECTION 157.1: [Instalment deferral for January, February and March 2002]

► 157.1(1) ◄

(1) Instalment deferral for January, February and March 2002 — definitions. The following definitions apply in this section.

"eligible corporation" — "eligible corporation", for a particular taxation year, means a corporation

(*a*) that is resident in Canada throughout the particular taxation year; and

(*b*) of which the taxable capital employed in Canada, within the meaning assigned by Part I.3, for its preceding taxation year did not exceed,

(i) if the corporation is not associated with any other corporation in the particular taxation year, $15 million, and

(ii) if the corporation is associated with one or more other corporations in the particular taxation year, the amount by which $15 million exceeds the total of the taxable capital employed in Canada, within the meaning assigned by Part I.3, of those other corporations for their last taxation years that ended in the last calendar year that ended before the end of the particular taxation year.

"eligible instalment day" — "eligible instalment day" of an eligible corporation means a day in January, February or March, 2002, on which an instalment on account of the corporation's tax payable under this Part for the taxation year that includes that day would become payable

(*a*) if this Act were read without reference to this section; and

(*b*) if, in the case of a corporation that is not required by section 157 to make instalment payments on account of its tax payable under this Part for the taxation year, it were so required.

► 157.1(2) ◄

(2) Deferred balance-due day. An eligible corporation's balance-due day for a taxation year that ends after 2001 is deemed to be the later of

(*a*) the day that would otherwise be the corporation's balance-due day for the taxation year, and

(*b*) the day that is six months after the corporation's last eligible instalment day in the taxation year.

Related Sections: S. 157(1) Payment by corporations; s. 248(1), "balance-due day".

► 157.1(3) ◄

(3) Deferred instalment day. An amount that would, because of paragraph 157(1)(*a*), otherwise become payable in respect of a taxation year by an eligible corporation on an eligible instalment day of the corporation does not become payable on that day but becomes payable (*a*) if the particular day that is six months after the eligible instalment day is in the taxation year, on the particular day; and

(*b*) in any other case, on the day that is deemed by subsection (2) to be the corporation's balance-due day for the taxation year.

Related Sections: S. 157(1) Payment by corporations; s. 248(1), "balance-due day".

SECTION 158: Payment of remainder

Where the Minister mails a notice of assessment of any amount payable by a taxpayer, that part of the amount assessed then remaining unpaid is payable forthwith by the taxpayer to the Receiver General.

Related Sections: S. 164(4) Interest on interest repaid; s. 187(3) Provisions applicable to Part; s. 189(3) Share deemed to be debt; s. 202(3) Provisions applicable to Part; s. 207(3) Multiple holders; s. 207.2(3) Provisions applicable to Part; s. 219(3) Provisions applicable to Part; s. 220(4) Security; 223 [Certificates]; 223.1 Application of ss. 223(1) to (8) and (12); 224 Garnishment; 224.1 Recovery by deduction or set-off; 224.2 Acquisition of debtor's property; 224.3 Payment of moneys seized from tax debtor; 225 Seizure of goods, chattels or movable property; s. 248(1), "assessment".

Information Circulars: IC 98-1R4 Collections policies.

SECTION 159: Person acting for another

▶ 159(1) ◀

(1) Person acting for another. For the purposes of this Act, where a person is a legal representative of a taxpayer at any time,

(*a*) the legal representative is jointly and severally, or solidarily, liable with the taxpayer

(i) to pay each amount payable under this Act by the taxpayer at or before that time and that remains unpaid, to the extent that the legal representative is at that time in possession or control, in the capacity of legal representative, of property that belongs or belonged to, or that is or was held for the benefit of, the taxpayer or the taxpayer's estate, and

(ii) to perform any obligation or duty imposed under this Act on the taxpayer at or before that time and that remains outstanding, to the extent that the obligation or duty can reasonably be considered to relate to the responsibilities of the legal representative acting in that capacity; and

(*b*) any action or proceeding in respect of the taxpayer taken under this Act at or after that time by the Minister may be so taken in the name of the legal representative acting in that capacity and, when so taken, has the same effect as if it had been taken directly against the taxpayer and, if the taxpayer no longer exists, as if the taxpayer continued to exist.

Editorial Note: In general terms, s. 159(1) provides that the legal representative of a taxpayer is jointly and severally, or solidarily, liable with the taxpayer to pay amounts owing by the taxpayer under the Act, to the extent that the legal representative has possession or control of the taxpayer's property. If the representative distributes any such property without obtaining a certificate under s. 159(2) in respect of the taxpayer's amounts owing under the Act, the representative will be personally liable to pay such amounts under s. 159(3) to the extent of the value of the distributed property.

History: S. 159(1)(*a*), the portion before subparagraph (i) was replaced by S.C. 2013, c. 34, s. 140, in force June 26, 2013, and formerly read:

(*a*) the legal representative is jointly and severally liable with the taxpayer

Related Sections: S. 248(1), "legal representative".

Canadian Tax Foundation: Hosanna, *Groscki: Scope for Director's Liability Under Section 159*, 2018 Tax for the Owner Manager 18(2):9–10.

Cases: The application of section 159 turned on the definition of legal representative, which requires action as a fiduciary of a person legally authorized to administer, wind-up, prohibit, or permit the distribution or dealing with the taxpayer's property. This requires a factual determination, and the facts did not support a finding that the taxpayer was a legal representative. *Groscki v. The Queen*, 2018 DTC 1001 (TCC)

▶ 159(2) ◀

(2) Certificate before distribution. Every legal representative (other than a trustee in bankruptcy) of a taxpayer shall, before distributing to one or more persons any property in the possession or control of the legal representative acting in that capacity, obtain a certificate from the Minister, by applying for one in prescribed form, certifying that all amounts

(*a*) for which the taxpayer is or can reasonably be expected to become liable under this Act at or before the time the distribution is made, and

(*b*) for the payment of which the legal representative is or can reasonably be expected to become liable in that capacity

have been paid or that security for the payment thereof has been accepted by the Minister.

Editorial Note: See the editorial note under s. 159(1).

Related Sections: S. 248(1), "legal representative".

Forms: TX19 — Asking for a Clearance Certificate.

Information Circulars: IC 82-6R11 Clearance Certificate.

Cases: The issuance of a clearance certificate does not preclude the Minister from seeking to recover any unpaid tax from an estate or its beneficiaries. It merely relieves the personal representatives of the estate from personal liability for such tax. *Bougie et al. v. The Queen*, 90 DTC 6387 (F.C.T.D.)

▶ 159(3) ◀

(3) Personal liability. If a legal representative (other than a trustee in bankruptcy) of a taxpayer distributes to one or more persons property in the possession or control of the legal representative, acting in that capacity, without obtaining a certificate under subsection (2) in respect of the amounts referred to in that subsection,

(*a*) the legal representative is personally liable for the payment of those amounts to the extent of the value of the property distributed;

(*b*) the Minister may at any time assess the legal representative in respect of any amount payable because of this subsection; and

(*c*) the provisions of this Division (including, for greater certainty, the provisions in respect of interest payable) apply, with any modifications that the circumstances require, to an assessment made under this subsection as though it had been made under section 152 in respect of taxes payable under this Part.

Editorial Note: See the editorial note under s. 159(1).

History: S. 159(3) was replaced by S.C. 2013, c. 34, s. 312(1), applicable to assessments made after December 20, 2002, and formerly read:

(3) *Personal liability.* Where a legal representative (other than a trustee in bankruptcy) of a taxpayer distributes to one or more persons property in the possession or control of the legal representative, acting in that capacity, without obtaining a certificate under subsection (2) in respect of the amounts referred to in that subsection, the legal representative is personally liable for the payment of those amounts to the extent of the value of the property distributed, and the Minister may at any time assess the legal representative in respect of any amount payable because of this subsection, and the provisions of this Division apply, with any modifications that the circumstances require, to an assessment made under this subsection as though it had been made under section 152.

Related Sections: S. 248(1), "legal representative".

Information Circulars: IC 98-1R4 Collections policies.

▶ 159(3.1) ◀

(3.1) Appropriation of property. For the purposes of subsections (2) and (3), an appropriation by a legal representative of a taxpayer of property in the possession or control of the legal representative acting in that capacity is deemed to be a distribution of the property to a person.

Related Sections: S. 248(1), "legal representative".

▶ 159(4) ◀

(4) Election on emigration — (Repealed by S.C. 2001, c. 17, s. 154(1).)

▶ 159(4.1) ◀

(4.1) Idem — (Repealed by S.C. 2001, c. 17, s. 154(1).)

▶ 159(5) ◀

(5) Election where certain provisions applicable. Where subsection 70(2), (5) or (5.2) of this Act or subsection 70(9.4) of the *Income Tax Act*, chapter 148 of the Revised Statutes of Canada, 1952, is applicable in respect of a taxpayer who has died, and the taxpayer's legal representative so elects and furnishes the Minister with security acceptable to the Minister for payment of any tax the payment of which is deferred by the election, notwithstanding any provision of this Part or the *Income Tax Application Rules* respecting the time within which payment shall be made of the tax payable under this Part by the taxpayer for the taxation year in which the taxpayer died, all or any portion of such part of that tax as is equal to the amount, if any, by which that tax exceeds the amount that that tax would be, if this Act were read without reference to subsections 70(2), (5) and (5.2) and the *Income Tax Act*, chapter 148 of the Revised Statutes of Canada, 1952, were read without reference to subsections 70(2), (5), (5.2) and (9.4) of that Act, may be paid in such number (not exceeding 10) of equal consecutive annual instalments as is specified by the legal representative in the election, the first instalment of which shall be paid on or before the day on or before which payment of that tax would, but for the election, have been required to be made and each subsequent instalment of which shall be paid on or before the next following anniversary of that day.

Related Regulations: 1001.

Forms: T2075 — Election to Defer Payment of Income Tax, Under Subsection 159(5) of the Income Tax Act by a Deceased Taxpayer's Legal Representative or Trustee.

Interpretation Bulletins: *Secondary* — IT-125R4 Disposition of resource properties; IT-212R3 Income of deceased persons — Rights or things; IT-278R2 Death of a partner or of a retired partner.

▶ 159(5.1) ◀

(5.1) Idem. Where, in the taxation year in which a taxpayer dies, an amount is included in computing the taxpayer's income by virtue of paragraph 23(3)(*c*) of the *Income Tax Application Rules*, the provisions of subsection (5) apply, with such modifications as the circumstances require, as though the amount were an amount included in computing the taxpayer's income for the year by virtue of subsection 70(2) or an amount deemed to have been received by the taxpayer by virtue of subsection 70(5).

Related Sections: S. 70(2) Amounts receivable; s. 70(5) Capital property of a deceased taxpayer; s. 159(5) Election where certain provisions applicable; ITAR s. 23(3) Rules applicable.

Interpretation Bulletins: *Secondary* — IT-212R3 Income of deceased persons — Rights or things; IT-278R2 Death of a partner or of a retired partner.

▶ 159(6) ◀

(6) Idem. For the purposes of subsection (5), the "tax payable under this Part" by a taxpayer for the taxation year in which the taxpayer died includes any tax payable under this Part by virtue of an election in respect of the taxpayer's death made by the taxpayer's legal representative under subsection 70(2) or under the provisions of that subsection as they are required to be read by virtue of the *Income Tax Application Rules*.

▶ 159(6.1) ◀

(6.1) Election where subsection 104(4) applicable. Where a time determined under paragraph 104(4)(*a*), (*a*.1), (*a*.2), (*a*.3), (*a*.4), (*b*) or (*c*) in respect of a trust occurs in a taxation year of the trust and the trust so elects and furnishes to the Minister security acceptable to the Minister for payment of any tax the payment of which is deferred by the election, notwithstanding any other provision of this Part respecting the time within which payment shall be made of the tax payable under this Part by the trust for the year, all or any portion of the part of that tax that is equal to the amount, if any, by which that tax exceeds the amount that that tax would be if this Act were read without reference to paragraph 104(4)(*a*), (*a*.1), (*a*.2), (*a*.3), (*a*.4), (*b*) or (*c*), as the case may be, may be paid in the number (not exceeding 10) of equal consecutive annual instalments that is specified by the trust in the election, the first instalment of which shall be paid on or before the day on or before which payment of that tax would, but for the election, have been required to be made and each subsequent instalment of which shall be paid on or before the next following anniversary of that day.

Forms: T2223 — Election under Subsection 159(6.1) of the Income Tax Act by a Trust to Defer Payment of Income Tax.

▶ 159(7) ◀

(7) Form and manner of election and interest. Every election made by a taxpayer under subsection (4) or (6.1) or by the legal representative of a taxpayer under subsection (5) shall be made in prescribed form and on condition that, at the time of payment of any amount payment of which is deferred by the election, the taxpayer shall pay to the Receiver General interest on the amount at the prescribed rate in effect at the time the election was made, computed from the day on or before which the amount would, but for the election, have been required to be paid to the day of payment.

Related Regulations: 4301.

Related Sections: S. 104(1) Reference to trust or estate; s. 187(3) Provisions applicable to Part; s. 189(3) Share deemed to be debt; s. 219(3) Provisions applicable to Part; s. 248(1), "assessment", "property"; s. 248(11) Compound interest.

SECTION 160: Tax liability re property transferred not at arm's length

▶ 160(1) ◀

(1) Tax liability re property transferred not at arm's length. Where a person has, on or after May 1, 1951, transferred property, either directly or indirectly, by means of a trust or by any other means whatever, to

(*a*) the person's spouse or common-law partner or a person who has since become the person's spouse or common-law partner,

(*b*) a person who was under 18 years of age, or

(*c*) a person with whom the person was not dealing at arm's length,

the following rules apply:

(*d*) the transferee and transferor are jointly and severally, or solidarily, liable to pay a part of the transferor's tax under this Part for each taxation year equal to the amount by which the tax for the year is greater than it would have been if it were not for the operation of sections 74.1 to 75.1 of this Act and section 74 of the *Income Tax Act*, chapter 148 of the Revised Statutes of Canada, 1952, in respect of any income from, or gain from the disposition of, the property so transferred or property substituted for it, and

(*e*) the transferee and transferor are jointly and severally, or solidarily, liable to pay under this Act an amount equal to the lesser of

(i) the amount, if any, by which the fair market value of the property at the time it was transferred exceeds the fair market value at that time of the consideration given for the property, and

(ii) the total of all amounts each of which is an amount that the transferor is liable to pay under this Act (including, for greater certainty, an amount that the transferor is liable to pay under this section, regardless of whether the Minister has made an assessment under subsection (2) for that amount) in or in respect of the taxation year in which the property was transferred or any preceding taxation year,

but nothing in this subsection limits the liability of the transferor under any other provision of this Act or of the transferee for the interest that the transferee is liable to pay under this Act on an assessment in respect of the amount that the transferee is liable to pay because of this subsection.

Editorial Note: The transferee liability provisions in s. 160 apply where there has been a non-arm's length transfer, a transfer to a person who since became the transferor's spouse or common-law partner, or a transfer to a minor. The minor does not have to be related to the transfer in order for the provision to apply. There are two separate joint and several liability scenarios in s. 160(1). The first, found in s. (*d*), relates to the transferor's tax payable in respect of post-transfer income from the transferred property owing to the application of the income attribution rules. The second, found in s. (*e*), relates to any of the transferor's tax payable in the year of transfer and preceding years to the extent of the value of the transferred property in excess of the value of any consideration received therefor.

History: S. 160(1)(*d*) was replaced by S.C. 2013, c. 34, s. 141(1), in force June 26, 2013, and formerly read:

(*d*) the transferee and transferor are jointly and severally liable to pay a part of the transferor's tax under this Part for each taxation year equal to the amount by which the tax for the year is greater than it would have been if it were not for the operation of sections 74.1 to 75.1 of this Act and section 74 of the *Income Tax Act*, chapter 148 of the Revised Statutes of Canada, 1952, in respect of any income from, or gain from the disposition of, the property so transferred or property substituted therefor, and

S. 160(1)(*e*), the portion before subparagraph (i) was replaced by S.C. 2013, c. 34, s. 141(2), in force June 26, 2013, and formerly read:

(*e*) the transferee and transferor are jointly and severally liable to pay under this Act an amount equal to the lesser of

S. 160(1), the portion after subparagraph (*e*)(i) was replaced by S.C. 2013, c. 34, s. 313(1), applicable in respect of assessments made after December 20, 2002, and formerly read:

(ii) the total of all amounts each of which is an amount that the transferor is liable to pay under this Act in or in respect of the taxation year in which the property was transferred or any preceding taxation year,

but nothing in this subsection shall be deemed to limit the liability of the transferor under any other provision of this Act.

Canadian Tax Foundation: Herman and Wu, *TCC Pokes Holes in Section 160 for Provision of Services*, 2018 Canadian Tax Focus 8(4):7–8; Hennessey, *Friends Don't Let Friends Get Assessed Under Section 160*, 2018 Tax for the Owner Manager 18(1):8–9; Hennessey, *Another Reason To Avoid Shareholder Benefits*, 2016 Canadian Tax Focus 6(1):3–4; Doobay, *Designated Beneficiary and Creditors*, 2014 Canadian Tax Highlights 22(6):6–8; Kreklewetz and Bassindale, *Directors' Liability and Non-Arm's-Length Transfer*, 2014 Canadian Tax Highlights 22(1):4–5; Jiang, *Section 160: CRA's Collection Power Broadened?*, 2014 Canadian Tax Focus 4(3):4–5; Fabbro, *Proving the Existence of a Spousal Partnership*, 2014 Canadian Tax Focus 4(2):8; Grower, *Tax Collection: The Risk of Less Than Fair Market Value Property Transfers*, 2014 Canadian Tax Journal 2:501–521; Bassindale and Kreklewetz, *CRA May Unwind Debtor's Asset Sale*, 2013 Canadian Tax Highlights 21(11):3–4; Graham, *Section 160 Update*, 2009 British Columbia Tax Conference 11:1–32; Woodbury, *The Power to Tax Means Little Without the Power To Collect — Section 160 Assessments*, 2008 Atlantic Provinces Tax Conference 3A:1–22; Kreklewetz and Siu, *The Constructive Trust Defence in Section 160 and Section 325 Cases*, 2008 Tax for the Owner-Manager 8(4):2–3; Esmail, *Transfer of Legal Title Not Subject to Section 160*, 2008 Tax for the Owner-Manager 8(2):7–8; Wong, *CRA Delay and Section 160*, 2007 Canadian Tax Highlights 15(9):6–7; Lavitt, *Section 160: Undue CRA Delay*, 2007 Canadian Tax Highlights 15(5):1–2; Kreklewetz and Vipul, *Mortgage, Visa, and Cash Payments Subject to Derivative Assessment*, 2006 Tax for the Owner-Manager 6(4):4–5; McDonnell, *Practice Notes: Merchant v. The Queen*, 2005 Tax for the Owner-Manager 5(2):7–8; Truster, *Section 160 and Dividends*, 2004 Tax for the Owner-Manager 4(2):3–4; Friedlan, *Cascading Section 160 Assessments*, 2003 Tax for the Owner-Manager 3(4):3–4; Sibson, *Revenue Canada's Long Collection Arm: Jeopardy Orders, Section 160 Assessments, and Directors' Liability*, 1998 Conference Report 26:1–26.

Tax Profile: January 2012 — The Top 10 Cases of 2011; July 2007 — Canadian Tax Traps; July 2006 — Asset Protection Planning.

Tax Topics: No. 2328, October 20, 2016, The Case of the Kvas Brothers: The Application of Section 160 to "Transfers" from a Dissolved Corporation; No. 1880, The Effectiveness of Section 160: Darte v. Her Majesty the Queen, 2008 DTC 2567; No. 1702, Income Tax Issues To Be Considered in Negotiating Marriage Contracts.

Information Circulars: IC 07-1 Taxpayer Relief Provisions; IC 98-1R4 Collections policies.

Interpretation Bulletins: *Secondary* — IT-369R Attribution of trust income to settlor.

Cases: The father was either an unpaid employee or a volunteer and under either characterization he worked for the professional corporation for no consideration. What was involved was the provision of a service and not the transfer of property. *Aitchison Professional Corporation v. The Queen*, 2018 DTC 1101 (TCC)

The issue was whether the appellant and transferor were dealing at arm's length at the time of the transfer. Looking at the history of employment and the business relationship between the parties, they were not dealing at arm's length. At some point they developed a common-law relationship. The transferor was the controlling mind behind the transaction, and the goal was to provide the transferor with a vehicle without it being subject to collection. *McKay v. The Queen*, 2016 DTC 1185 (TCC)

The deposit constituted a non-arm's length transfer, despite a written agreement to the contrary, since the parties were acting in concert to avoid seizure proceedings. *The Queen v. 9101-2310 Québec Inc.*, 2013 DTC 5170 (F.C.A.)

The taxpayer was liable for tax her husband owed when he transferred their home to her for nominal consideration. She claimed there was market value consideration for the transfer since it was part of a series of transactions involving dissolution of their marriage, but the transactions were entirely separate and notarized documents refuted her claim. *Sokolowski Romar v. The Queen*, 2013 DTC 5032 (F.C.A.), affirming 2013 DTC 1003 (T.C.C.)

Judicial review is not available to challenge the length of the Minister's delay in issuing a s. 160 assessment since s. 160 provides that the Minister may assess "at any time". Furthermore, judicial review should not be used to circumvent the existing statutory appeal scheme. *The Queen et al. v. Addison & Leyen Ltd. et al.*, 2007 DTC 5368 (S.C.C.), reversing 2006 DTC 6248 (F.C.A.), reversing 2005 DTC 5212 (F.C.)

While he owed tax, the taxpayer's common-law partner made mortgage payments on the taxpayer's house. The taxpayer was not liable under s. 160(1) since the value of the consideration she provided (by allowing him to live in the house) exceeded the amount of the mortgage payments. *The Queen v. Ducharme*, 2005 DTC 5249 (F.C.A.), affirming 2004 DTC 2807 (T.C.C.)

The taxpayer received dividends from a corporation that owed tax at the time but the s. 160(1) assessment against the taxpayer was vacated because there was an arm's length relationship between the two corporations at the time of payment. *Gestion Yvan Drouin Inc. v. The Queen*, 2001 DTC 72 (T.C.C.)

The taxpayer was permitted to challenge her s. 160 assessment on the basis that the reassessments of C (the primary taxpayer) were statute-barred. Although C's underlying reassessments had been affirmed in another appeal, the taxpayer was not a party to those proceedings. *Gaucher v. The Queen*, 2000 DTC 6678 (F.C.A.), reversing 2000 DTC 2084 (T.C.C.)

The taxpayer's spouse deposited amounts from his RRSP into a joint bank account with her. The property in the deposits never vested in the taxpayer in her personal capacity, but only in her capacity as her spouse's agent. She never exercised the kind of personal control necessary to find that there had been a transfer of property within the meaning of s. 160(12). *Leblanc v. The Queen*, 99 DTC 410 (T.C.C.)

Taxpayer's husband made mortgage interest, property tax and other similar payments in respect of the matrimonial home directly to third parties through corporations of which he was a major shareholder. The payments did constitute a "transfer" of property by the husband to the taxpayer since the corporations were mere conduits. However, since these payments had been made in satisfaction of the husband's legal obligation to support his wife and children, they did not constitute a "transfer" within the meaning of s. 160. *Ferracuti v. The Queen*, 99 DTC 194 (T.C.C.)

Since her husband's mortgage payments resulted in a reduction of the taxpayer's own mortgage liability, an indirect transfer of property had been made while tax was owing by him and it fell within the purview of ss. 160(1). *Medland v. The Queen*, 98 DTC 6358 (F.C.A.), affirming 96 DTC 3302 (T.C.C.)

The taxpayer's liability for tax owing by her husband at the time at which he transferred his interest in their principal residence to her arose at the moment of the transfer so that the Minister could assess her even after her husband's discharge from bankruptcy. *The Queen v. Heavyside*, 97 DTC 5026 (F.C.A.)

When a taxpayer could not prove that her husband had never had a beneficial interest in the matrimonial home that he had transferred to a trustee to be transferred back to her alone for a nominal consideration and when she did not have sufficient funds of her own to pay for the home, she was personally liable for payment of the tax owed by her husband. *Cooke v. The Queen*, 97 DTC 5208 (F.C.A.), affirming 93 DTC 1561 (T.C.C.)

There was a "transfer of property" and joint liability for unpaid tax when a cash dividend was paid since property was taken from one patrimony and placed in another one. The same, however, could not be said for a stock dividend inasmuch as its payment does not involve a transfer of property, in the sense that the payor corporation does not divest itself of its assets. *Algoa Trust et al. v. The Queen*, 93 DTC 405 (T.C.C.)

The taxpayer's husband transferred land to her at a time when he owed tax. There was sufficient evidence of common intent to justify a finding that her husband was holding the properties in a resulting trust to the extent of one-half for the taxpayer and there was a sufficient element of unjust enrichment to warrant a finding that the properties were being held on a constructive trust with a 50% interest to the taxpayer. *Savoie v. the Queen*, 93 DTC 552 (T.C.C.)

The Minister could not assess transferees in respect of their transferor's provincial income tax liability. *Phillips v. the Queen*, 93 DTC 573(T.C.C.)

The taxpayer was not liable for the tax his parents owed when they purported to transfer him their house without his consent since their attempt did not divest them of their beneficial right to their house. *Mah v. the Queen*, 93 DTC 5267 (F.C.T.D.)

A taxpayer who had purchased land for $100,000 from her brother-in-law at a time when the fair market value of the land was $275,000 was jointly liable for the $16,198.14 of tax owed by her brother-in-law. *Ayoub v. The Queen*, 93 DTC 1118 (T.C.C.)

The taxpayer could not be held personally liable for the tax owed by her husband when she could prove the sums of cash he transferred to her were a combination of his contributions towards the charges of the house and family and the repayment of debts owing by him. *Dupuis v. the Queen*, 93 DTC 723 (T.C.C.)

The taxpayer received from her husband his pay cheques which she deposited in her own account or in a joint account to maintain the family home and the family. She was jointly liable for the payment of her husband's tax. *Fine v. M.N.R.*, 91 DTC 133 (T.C.C.)

However a taxpayer, whose father transferred property to her for subsequent transfer to her mother, as part of a separation agreement, was not jointly liable for the tax he owed at the time of the transfer, i.e. time of execution of the separation agreement on September 8, 1981. Prior to the amendments to s. 160(1)(*c*) on November 12, 1981, liability for tax was not imposed on transferees of property in the taxpayer's position who were not at arm's length with the transferors. *Kostiuk v. the Queen*, 93 DTC 5511 (F.C.T.D.), reversing 89 DTC 548 (T.C.C.)

► 160(1.1) ◄

(1.1) Joint and several, or solidary, liability — subsection 69(11). If a particular person or partnership is deemed by subsection 69(11) to have disposed of a property at any time, the person referred to in that subsection to whom a benefit described in that subsection was available in respect of a subsequent disposition of the property or property substituted for the property is jointly and severally, or solidarily, liable with each other taxpayer to pay a part of the other taxpayer's liabilities under this Act in respect of each taxation year equal to the amount determined by the formula

$$A - B$$

where

A is the total of amounts payable under this Act by the other taxpayer in respect of the year, and

B is the amount that would, if the particular person or partnership were not deemed by subsection 69(11) to have disposed of the property, be determined for A in respect of the other taxpayer in respect of the year,

but nothing in this subsection limits the liability of the other taxpayer under any other provision of this Act or of any person for the interest that the person is liable to pay under this Act on an assessment in respect of the amount that the person is liable to pay because of this subsection.

Editorial Note: See the editorial note to s. 69(11).

History: S. 160(1.1), the portion before the formula was replaced by S.C. 2013, c. 34, s. 141(3), in force June 26, 2013, and formerly read:

(1.1) *Joint liability where s. 69(11) applies.* Where a particular person or partnership is deemed by subsection 69(11) to have disposed of a property at any time, the person referred to in that subsection to whom a benefit described in that subsection was available in respect of a subsequent disposition of the property or property substituted for the property is jointly and severally liable with each other taxpayer to pay a part of the other taxpayer's liabilities under this Act in respect of each taxation year equal to the amount determined by the formula

S. 160(1.1), the portion after the description of B was replaced by S.C. 2013, c. 34, s. 313(2), applicable in respect of assessments made after December 20, 2002, and formerly read:

but nothing under this subsection is deemed to limit the liability of the other taxpayer under any other provision of this Act.

► 160(1.2) ◄

(1.2) Joint and several, or solidary, liability — tax on split income. If an amount is required to be added because of subsection 120.4(2) in computing a specified individual's tax payable under this Part for a taxation year and the specified individual has not attained the age of 24 years before the start of the year, the following rules apply:

(*a*) subject to paragraph (*b*), a particular individual is jointly and severally, or solidarily, liable with the specified individual for the amount if

(i) where the specified individual has not attained the age of 17 years before the year, the particular individual is a parent of the specified individual, and

(ii) where the specified individual has attained the age of 17 years before the year,

(A) the particular individual is a source individual in respect of the specified individual,

(B) the amount was derived directly or indirectly from a related business (within the meaning of paragraph 120.4(1.1)(*d*)) in respect of the specified individual, and

(C) the particular individual meets the conditions in any of paragraphs (*a*) to (*c*) in the definition *related business* in subsection 120.4(1) in respect of the related business;

(*b*) the particular individual's liability under paragraph (*a*) in respect of the specified individual for the year is to be determined as though the only amounts included in the specified individual's split income for the year are amounts derived from the related business referred to in subparagraph (*a*)(ii); and

(*c*) nothing in this subsection limits the liability of

(i) the specified individual under any other provision of this Act, or

(ii) the particular individual for the interest that the particular individual is liable to pay under this Act on an assessment in respect of the amount that the particular individual is liable to pay because of this subsection.

Editorial Note: If the specified individual did not turn 17 before the relevant taxation year, the joint and several liability extends to the parents of the individual. If the specified individual did turn 17 before the year, the joint and several liability extends to a "source individual" (subsection 120.4(1)), defined as an individual resident in Canada who is related to the specified individual. Owing to the limitation in paragraph 160(1.2), the joint and several liability extends only to income that is derived from a "related business" (subsection 120.4(1)) in respect of the specified individual.

History: S. 160(1.2) was replaced by S.C. 2018, c. 12, s. 26(1), applicable to the 2018 and subsequent taxation years, and formerly read:

(1.2) *Joint and several, or solidary, liability — tax on split income.* A parent of a specified individual is jointly and severally, or solidarily, liable with the individual for the amount required to be added because of subsection 120.4(2) in computing the specified individual's tax payable under this Part for a taxation year if, during the year, the parent

(*a*) carried on a business that was provided property or services by a partnership or trust all or a portion of the income of which partnership or trust is directly or indirectly included in computing the individual's split income for the year,

(*b*) was a specified shareholder of a corporation that was provided property or services by a partnership or trust all or a portion of the income of which partnership or trust is directly or indirectly included in computing the individual's split income for the year,

(*c*) was a specified shareholder of a corporation, dividends on the shares of the capital stock of which were directly or indirectly included in computing the individual's split income for the year;

(*d*) was a shareholder of a professional corporation that was provided property or services by a partnership or trust all or a portion of the income of which partnership or trust is directly or indirectly included in computing the individual's split income for the year, or

(*e*) was a shareholder of a professional corporation, dividends on the shares of the capital stock of which were directly or indirectly included in computing the individual's split income for the year,

but nothing in this subsection limits the liability of the specified individual under any other provision of this Act or of the parent for the interest that the parent is liable to pay under this Act on an assessment in respect of the amount that the parent is liable to pay because of this subsection.

S. 160(1.2), the portion before paragraph (*a*) was replaced by S.C. 2013, c. 34, s. 141(4), in force June 26, 2013, and formerly read:

(1.2) *Joint liability — tax on split income.* A parent of a specified individual is jointly and severally liable with the individual for the amount required to be added because of subsection 120.4(2) in computing the specified individual's tax payable under this Part for a taxation year if, during the year, the parent

S. 160(1.2)(*a*) and (*b*) were replaced by S.C. 2013, c. 34, s. 313(3), deemed to have come into force on December 21, 2002, and formerly read:

(*a*) carried on a business that purchased goods or services from a business the income of which is directly or indirectly included in computing the individual's split income for the year;

(*b*) was a specified shareholder of a corporation that purchased goods or services from a business the income of which is directly or indirectly included in computing the individual's split income for the year;

S. 160(1.2)(*d*) was replaced by S.C. 2013, c. 34, s. 313(4), deemed to have come into force on December 21, 2002, and formerly read:

(*d*) was a shareholder of a professional corporation that purchased goods or services from a business the income of which is directly or indirectly included in computing the individual's split income for the year; or

S. 160(1.2), the portion after paragraph (*e*) was added by S.C. 2013, c. 34, s. 313(5), applicable in respect of assessments made after December 20, 2002.

Related Sections: S. 120.4(1), "specified individual", "split income"; s. 248(1), "professional corporation", "specified shareholder".

► 160(1.3) ◄

(1.3) Joint liability — tax on split-pension income. Where a pensioner and a pension transferee (as those terms are defined in section 60.03) make a joint election under section 60.03 in respect of a split-pension amount (as defined in that section) for a taxation year, they are jointly and severally, or solidarily, liable for the tax payable by the pension transferee under this Part for the taxation year to the extent that that tax payable is greater than it would have been if no amount were required to be added because of paragraph 56(1)(*a*.2) in computing the income of the pension transferee under this Part for the taxation year.

► 160(1.4) ◄

(1.4) Joint liability — spousal and similar trusts. If subsection 104(13.4) deems an amount to have become payable in a taxation year of a trust to an individual, the individual and the trust are jointly and severally, or solidarily, liable for the tax payable by the individual under this Part for the individual's taxation year that includes the day on which the individual dies to the extent that that tax payable is greater than it would have been if the amount were not included in computing the individual's income under this Part for the taxation year.

History: S. 160(1.4) was added by S.C. 2014, c. 39, s. 57(1), applicable to the 2016 and subsequent taxation years.

Canadian Tax Foundation: Burr, *A Puzzling Extension of Vicarious Liability,* 2015 Canadian Tax Highlights 23(3):8–9.

► 160(2) ◄

(2) Assessment. The Minister may at any time assess a taxpayer in respect of any amount payable because of this section, and the provisions of this Division (including, for greater certainty, the provisions in respect of interest payable) apply, with any modifications that the circumstances require, in respect of an assessment made under this section as though it had been made under section 152 in respect of taxes payable under this Part.

History: S. 160(2) was replaced by S.C. 2013, c. 34, s. 313(6), applicable in respect of assessments made after December 20, 2002, and formerly read:

(2) *Assessment.* The Minister may at any time assess a taxpayer in respect of any amount payable because of this section and the provisions of this Division apply, with any modifications that the circumstances require, in respect of an assessment made under this section as though it had been made under section 152.

► 160(2.1) ◄

(2.1) Assessment. The Minister may at any time assess a taxpayer in respect of any amount payable because of paragraph 94(3)(*d*) or (*e*) or subsection 94(17) and the provisions of this Division (including, for greater certainty, the provisions in respect of interest payable) apply, with any modifications that the circumstances require, in respect of an assessment made under this section as though it had been made under section 152 in respect of taxes payable under this Part.

History: S. 160(2.1) was added by S.C. 2013, c. 34, s. 16(1), applicable to assessments made after 2006, except that

(*a*) subsection 160(2.1) is to be read without reference to "or subsection 94(17)" in its application to taxation years that end before March 5, 2010; and

(*b*) if subsection 94(1) applies to a taxation year of a taxpayer that ends before 2007, subsection 160(2.1) applies to assessments made on or after the first day of the first such taxation year of the taxpayer to which that subsection 94(1) applies [should be 94(3) – CCH].

► 160(3) ◄

(3) Discharge of liability. If a particular taxpayer has become jointly and severally, or solidarily, liable with another taxpayer under this section or because of paragraph 94(3)(*d*) or (*e*) or subsection 94(17) in respect of part or all of a liability under this Act of the other taxpayer,

(*a*) a payment by the particular taxpayer on account of that taxpayer's liability shall to the extent of the payment discharge their liability; but

(*b*) a payment by the other taxpayer on account of that taxpayer's liability discharges the particular taxpayer's liability only to the extent that the payment operates to reduce that other taxpayer's liability to an amount less than the amount in respect of which the particular taxpayer is, by this section, made jointly and severally, or solidarily, liable.

History: S. 160(3)(*b*) was replaced by S.C. 2013, c. 34, s. 141(6), in force June 26, 2013, and formerly read:

(*b*) a payment by the other taxpayer on account of that taxpayer's liability discharges the particular taxpayer's liability only to the extent that the payment operates to reduce that other taxpayer's liability to an amount less than the amount in respect of which the particular taxpayer is, by this section, made jointly and severally liable.

S. 160(3), the portion before paragraph (*b*) was replaced by S.C. 2013, c. 34, s. 16(2), applicable to assessments made after 2006, except that the portion of subsection 160(3) before paragraph (*a*) is to be read without reference to "or subsection 94(17)" in its application to taxation years that end before March 5, 2010.

S. 160(3), the portion before (*b*), formerly read:

(3) *Discharge of liability.* Where a particular taxpayer has become jointly and severally liable with another taxpayer under this section in respect of part or all of a liability under this Act of the other taxpayer,

(*a*) a payment by the particular taxpayer on account of that taxpayer's liability shall to the extent of the payment discharge the joint liability; but

S. 160(3), the portion before paragraph (*a*) was replaced by S.C. 2013, c. 34, s. 141(5), in force June 26, 2013, and formerly read:

(3) *Discharge of liability.* If a particular taxpayer has become jointly and severally liable with another taxpayer under this section or because of paragraph 94(3)(*d*) or (*e*) or subsection 94(17) in respect of part or all of a liability under this Act of the other taxpayer,

Related Sections: S. 104(1) Reference to trust or estate; s. 248(1), "amount", "assessment", "property".

▶ 160(3.1) ◀

(3.1) Fair market value of undivided interest or right. For the purposes of this section and section 160.4, the fair market value at any time of an undivided interest, or for civil law an undivided right, in a property, expressed as a proportionate interest or right in that property, is, subject to subsection (4), deemed to be equal to the same proportion of the fair market value of that property at that time.

History: S. 160(3.1) was replaced by S.C. 2013, c. 34, s. 141(7), in force June 26, 2013, and formerly read:

(3.1) *Fair market value of undivided interest.* For the purposes of this section and section 160.4, the fair market value at any time of an undivided interest in a property, expressed as a proportionate interest in that property, is, subject to subsection (4), deemed to be equal to the same proportion of the fair market value of that property at that time.

▶ 160(4) ◀

(4) Special rules re transfer of property to spouse or common-law partner. Notwithstanding subsection (1), where at any time a taxpayer has transferred property to the taxpayer's spouse or common-law partner pursuant to a decree, order or judgment of a competent tribunal or pursuant to a written separation agreement and, at that time, the taxpayer and the spouse or common-law partner were separated and living apart as a result of the breakdown of their marriage or common-law partnership, the following rules apply:

(*a*) in respect of property so transferred after February 15, 1984,

(i) the spouse or common-law partner shall not be liable under subsection (1) to pay any amount with respect to any income from, or gain from the disposition of, the property so transferred or property substituted therefor, and

(ii) for the purposes of paragraph (1)(*e*), the fair market value of the property at the time it was transferred shall be deemed to be nil, and

(*b*) in respect of property so transferred before February 16, 1984, where the spouse or common-law partner would, but for this paragraph, be liable to pay an amount under this Act by virtue of subsection (1), the spouse's or common-law partner's liability in respect of that amount shall be deemed to have been discharged on February 16, 1984,

but nothing in this subsection shall operate to reduce the taxpayer's liability under any other provision of this Act.

Tax Topics: No. 1702, Income Tax Issues To Be Considered in Negotiating Marriage Contracts.

Information Circulars: IC 98-1R4 Collections policies.

SECTION 160.1: Where excess refunded

▶ 160.1(1) ◀

(1) Where excess refunded. Where at any time the Minister determines that an amount has been refunded to a taxpayer for a taxation year in excess of the amount to which the taxpayer was entitled as a refund under this Act, the following rules apply:

(*a*) the excess shall be deemed to be an amount that became payable by the taxpayer on the day on which the amount was refunded; and

(*b*) the taxpayer shall pay to the Receiver General interest at the prescribed rate on the excess (other than any portion thereof that can reasonably be considered to arise as a consequence of the operation of section 122.5 or 122.61) from the day it became payable to the date of payment.

Related Regulations: 4301.

Related Sections: S. 161.1 Offset of refund interest and arrears interest; s. 248(11) Compound interest.

▶ 160.1(1.1) ◀

(1.1) Liability for refund by reason of s. 122.5. If a person is a qualified relation of an individual (within the meaning assigned by subsection 122.5(1)), in relation to one or more months specified for a taxation year, the person and the individual are jointly and severally, or solidarily, liable to pay the lesser of

(*a*) any excess described in subsection (1) that was refunded in respect of the taxation year to, or applied to a liability of, the individual as a consequence of the operation of section 122.5, and

(*b*) the total of the amounts deemed by subsection 122.5(3) to have been paid by the individual during those specified months.

Cases: The interest on an excess dividend refund ran from the date of the original payment. *A. J. Giles Investments Ltd. v. M.N.R.*, 91 DTC 606 (T.C.C.)

▶ 160.1(2) ◀

(2) Liability under other provisions. Subsection (1.1) does not limit a person's liability under any other provision of this Act.

▶ 160.1(2.1) ◀

(2.1) Liability for refunds by reason of section 122.61. If a person was a cohabiting spouse or common-law partner (within the meaning assigned by section 122.6) of an individual at the end of a taxation year, the person and the individual are jointly and severally, or solidarily, liable to pay any excess described in subsection (1) that was refunded in respect of the year to, or applied to a liability of, the individual as a consequence of the operation of section 122.61 if the person was the individual's cohabiting spouse or common-law partner at the time the excess was refunded, but nothing in this subsection is deemed to limit the liability of any person under any other provision of this Act.

History: S. 160.1(2.1) was amended by S.C. 2013, c. 34, s. 142, in force June 26, 2013, and formerly read:

(2.1) *Liability for refunds by reason of section 122.61.* Where a person was a cohabiting spouse or common-law partner (within the meaning assigned by section 122.6) of an individual at the end of a taxation year, the person and the individual are jointly and severally liable to pay any excess described in subsection (1) that was refunded in respect of the year to, or applied to a liability of, the individual as a consequence of the operation of section 122.61 if the person was the individual's cohabiting spouse or common-law partner at the time the excess was refunded, but nothing in this subsection shall be deemed to limit the liability of any person under any other provision of this Act.

► 160.1(2.2) ◄

(2.2) Liability for excess refunds under section 126.1 to partners. Every taxpayer who, on the day on which an amount has been refunded to, or applied to the liability of, a member of a partnership as a consequence of the operation of subsection 126.1(7) or (13) in excess of the amount to which the member was so entitled, is a member of that partnership is jointly and severally, or solidarily, liable with each other taxpayer who on that day is a member of the partnership to pay the excess and to pay interest on the excess, but nothing in this subsection is deemed to limit the liability of any person under any other provision of this Act.

History: S. 160.1(2.2) was amended by S.C. 2013, c. 34, s. 142, in force June 26, 2013, and formerly read:

(2.2) *Liability for excess refunds under section 126.1 to partners.* Every taxpayer who, on the day on which an amount has been refunded to, or applied to the liability of, a member of a partnership as a consequence of the operation of subsection 126.1(7) or (13) in excess of the amount to which the member was so entitled, is a member of that partnership is jointly and severally liable with each other taxpayer who on that day is a member of the partnership to pay the excess and to pay interest on the excess, but nothing in this subsection shall be deemed to limit the liability of any person under any other provision of this Act.

► 160.1(3) ◄

(3) Assessment. The Minister may at any time assess a taxpayer in respect of any amount payable by the taxpayer because of subsection (1) or (1.1) or for which the taxpayer is liable because of subsection (2.1) or (2.2), and the provisions of this Division (including, for greater certainty, the provisions in respect of interest payable) apply, with any modifications that the circumstances require, in respect of an assessment made under this section, as though it were made under section 152 in respect of taxes payable under this Part, except that no interest is payable on an amount assessed in respect of an excess referred to in subsection (1) that can reasonably be considered to arise as a consequence of the operation of section 122.5 or 122.61.

History: S. 160.1(3) was replaced by S.C. 2013, c. 34, s. 314(1), applicable to assessments made after December 20, 2002, and formerly read:

(3) *Assessment.* The Minister may at any time assess a taxpayer in respect of any amount payable by the taxpayer because of subsection (1) or (1.1) or for which the taxpayer is liable because of subsection (2.1) or (2.2), and this Division applies, with such modifications as the circumstances require, in respect of an assessment made under this section as though it were made under section 152.

► 160.1(4) ◄

(4) Where amount applied to liability. Where an amount is applied to a liability of a taxpayer to Her Majesty in right of Canada in excess of the amount to which the taxpayer is entitled as a refund under this Act, this section applies as though that amount had been refunded to the taxpayer on the day it was so applied.

SECTION 160.2: [Joint and several liability — RRSP, RRIF and annuity]

► 160.2(1) ◄

(1) Joint and several liability in respect of amounts received out of or under RRSP. Where

(*a*) an amount is received out of or under a registered retirement savings plan by a taxpayer other than an annuitant (within the meaning assigned by subsection 146(1)) under the plan, and

(*b*) that amount or part thereof would, but for paragraph (*a*) of the definition "benefit" in subsection 146(1), be received by the taxpayer as a benefit (within the meaning assigned by that definition),

the taxpayer and the last annuitant under the plan are jointly and severally, or solidarily, liable to pay a part of the annuitant's tax under this Part for the year of the annuitant's death equal to that proportion of the amount by which the annuitant's tax for the year is greater than it would have been if it were not for the operation of subsection 146(8.8) that the total of all amounts each of which is an amount determined under paragraph (*b*) in respect of the taxpayer is of the amount included in computing the annuitant's income because of that subsection, but nothing in this subsection limits the liability of the annuitant under any other provision of this Act or of the taxpayer for the interest that the taxpayer is liable to pay under this Act on an assessment in respect of the amount that the taxpayer is liable to pay because of this subsection.

History: S. 160.2(1), the portion after paragraph (*b*) was replaced by S.C. 2013, c. 34, s. 315(1), applicable to assessments made after December 20, 2002, and formerly read:

the taxpayer and the last annuitant under the plan are jointly and severally liable to pay a part of the annuitant's tax under this Part for the year of the annuitant's death equal to that proportion of the amount by which the annuitant's tax for the year is greater than it would have been if it were not for the operation of subsection 146(8.8) that the total of all amounts each of which is an amount determined under paragraph (*b*) in respect of the taxpayer is of the amount included in computing the annuitant's income by virtue of that subsection, but nothing in this subsection shall be deemed to limit the liability of the annuitant under any other provision of this Act.

Interpretation Bulletins: *Secondary* — IT-500R Registered retirement savings plans — Death of annuitant.

► 160.2(2) ◄

(2) Joint and several liability in respect of amounts received out of or under RRIF. Where

(*a*) an amount is received out of or under a registered retirement income fund by a taxpayer other than an annuitant (within the meaning assigned by subsection 146.3(1)) under the fund, and

(*b*) that amount or part thereof would, but for paragraph 146.3(5)(*a*), be included in computing the taxpayer's income for the year of receipt pursuant to subsection 146.3(5),

the taxpayer and the annuitant are jointly and severally, or solidarily, liable to pay a part of the annuitant's tax under this Part for the year of the annuitant's death equal to that proportion of the amount by which the annuitant's tax for the year is greater than it would have been if it were not for the operation of subsection 146.3(6) that the amount determined under paragraph (*b*) is of the amount included in computing the annuitant's income because of that subsection, but nothing in this subsection limits the liability of the annuitant under any other provision of this Act or of the taxpayer for the interest that the taxpayer is liable to pay under this Act on an assessment in respect of the amount that the taxpayer is liable to pay because of this subsection.

History: S. 160.2(2), the portion after paragraph (*b*) was replaced by S.C. 2013, c. 34, s. 315(2), applicable to assessments made after December 20, 2002, and formerly read:

the taxpayer and the annuitant are jointly and severally liable to pay a part of the annuitant's tax under this Part for the year of the annuitant's death equal to that proportion of the amount by which the annuitant's tax for the year is greater than it would have been if it were not for the operation of subsection 146.3(6) that the amount determined under paragraph (*b*) is of the amount included in computing the annuitant's income by virtue of that subsection, but nothing in this subsection shall be deemed to limit the liability of the annuitant under any other provision of this Act.

▶ 160.2(2.1) ◀

(2.1) Joint and several liability in respect of a qualifying trust annuity. If a taxpayer is deemed by section 75.2 to have received at any time an amount out of or under an annuity that is a qualifying trust annuity with respect to the taxpayer, the taxpayer, the annuitant under the annuity and the policyholder are jointly and severally, or solidarily, liable to pay the part of the taxpayer's tax under this Part for the taxation year of the taxpayer that includes that time that is equal to the amount, if any, determined by the formula

$$A - B$$

where

A is the amount of the taxpayer's tax under this Part for that taxation year; and

B is the amount that would be the taxpayer's tax under this Part for that taxation year if no amount were deemed by section 75.2 to have been received by the taxpayer out of or under the annuity in that taxation year.

History: S. 160.2(2.1) was added by S.C. 2013, c. 34, s. 315(3), applicable to assessments made after 2005.

Related Sections: S. 60.011(2) Meaning of "qualifying trust annuity".

▶ 160.2(2.2) ◀

(2.2) No limitation on liability. Subsection (2.1) limits neither

(*a*) the liability of the taxpayer referred to in that subsection under any other provision of this Act; nor

(*b*) the liability of an annuitant or policyholder referred to in that subsection for the interest that the annuitant or policyholder is liable to pay under this Act on an assessment in respect of the amount that the annuitant or policyholder is liable to pay because of that subsection.

History: S. 160.2(2.2) was added by S.C. 2013, c. 34, s. 315(3), applicable to assessments made after 2005.

▶ 160.2(3) ◀

(3) Assessment. The Minister may at any time assess a taxpayer in respect of any amount payable because of this section, and the provisions of this Division (including, for greater certainty, the provisions in respect of interest payable) apply, with any modifications that the circumstances require, in respect of an assessment made under this section as though it had been made under section 152 in respect of taxes payable under this Part.

History: S. 160.2(3) was replaced by S.C. 2013, c. 34, s. 315(4), applicable to assessments made after December 20, 2002, and formerly read:

(3) *Minister may assess recipient.* The Minister may at any time assess a taxpayer in respect of any amount payable by virtue of this section and the provisions of this Division are applicable, with such modifications as the circumstances require, in respect of an assessment made under this section as though it had been made under section 152.

▶ 160.2(4) ◀

(4) Rules applicable. If a taxpayer and an annuitant have, by virtue of subsection (1) or (2), become jointly and severally, or solidarily, liable in respect of part or all of a liability of the annuitant under this Act, the following rules apply:

(*a*) a payment by the taxpayer on account of the taxpayer's liability shall to the extent thereof discharge their liability; but

(*b*) a payment by the annuitant on account of the annuitant's liability discharges the taxpayer's liability only to the extent that the payment operates to reduce the annuitant's liability to an amount less than the amount in respect of which the taxpayer was, by subsection (1) or (2), as the case may be, made jointly and severally, or solidarily, liable.

History: S. 160.2(4), the portion before paragraph (*a*) was replaced by S.C. 2013, c. 34, s. 143(1), in force June 26, 2013, and formerly read:

(4) *Rules applicable.* Where a taxpayer and an annuitant have, by virtue of subsection (1) or (2), become jointly and severally liable in respect of part or all of a liability of the annuitant under this Act, the following rules apply:

S. 160.2(4)(*a*) was replaced by S.C. 2013, c. 34, s. 143(2), in force June 26, 2013, and formerly read:

(*a*) a payment by the taxpayer on account of the taxpayer's liability shall to the extent thereof discharge the joint liability; but

S. 160.2(4)(*b*) was replaced by S.C. 2013, c. 34, s. 143(3), in force June 26, 2013, and formerly read:

(*b*) a payment by the annuitant on account of the annuitant's liability only discharges the taxpayer's liability to the extent that the payment operates to reduce the annuitant's liability to an amount less than the amount in respect of which the taxpayer was, by subsection (1) or (2), as the case may be, made jointly and severally liable.

▶ 160.2(5) ◀

(5) Rules applicable — qualifying trust annuity. If an annuitant or policyholder has, because of subsection (2.1), become jointly and severally, or solidarily, liable with a taxpayer in respect of part or all of a liability of the taxpayer under this Act, the following rules apply:

(*a*) a payment by the annuitant on account of the annuitant's liability, or by the policyholder on account of the policyholder's liability, shall to the extent of the payment discharge their liability, but

(*b*) a payment by the taxpayer on account of the taxpayer's liability only discharges the annuitant's and the policyholder's liability to the extent that the payment operates to reduce the taxpayer's liability to an amount less than the amount in respect of which the annuitant and the policyholder were, by subsection (2.1), made liable.

History: S. 160.2(5) was added by S.C. 2013, c. 34, s. 315(5), applicable to assessments made after 2005.

SECTION 160.21: Joint and several liability — registered disability savings plan

▶ 160.21(1) ◀

(1) Joint and several liability — registered disability savings plan. Where, in computing income for a taxation year, a taxpayer is required to include an amount in respect of a disability assistance payment (as defined in subsection 146.4(1)) that is deemed by subsection 146.4(10) to have been made at any particular time from a registered disability savings plan, the taxpayer and each holder (as defined in subsection 146.4(1)) of the plan immediately after the particular time are jointly and severally, or solidarily, liable to pay the part of the taxpayer's tax under this Part for that taxation year that is equal to the amount, if any, determined by the formula

$$A - B$$

where

A is the amount of the taxpayer's tax under this Part for that taxation year; and

B is the amount that would be the taxpayer's tax under this Part for that taxation year if no disability assistance payment were deemed by subsection 146.4(10) to have been paid from the plan at the particular time.

► 160.21(2) ◄

(2) No limitation on liability. Subsection (1) limits neither

(*a*) the liability of the taxpayer referred to in that subsection under any other provision of this Act, nor

(*b*) the liability of any holder referred to in that subsection for the interest that the holder is liable to pay under this Act on an assessment in respect of the amount that the holder is liable to pay because of that subsection.

► 160.21(3) ◄

(3) Rules applicable — registered disability savings plans. Where a holder (as defined in subsection 146.4(1)) of a registered disability savings plan has, because of subsection (1), become jointly and severally, or solidarily, liable with a taxpayer in respect of part or all of a liability of the taxpayer under this Act, the following rules apply:

(*a*) a payment by the holder on account of the holder's liability shall to the extent of the payment discharge the holder's liability, but

(*b*) a payment by the taxpayer on account of the taxpayer's liability only discharges the holder's liability to the extent that the payment operates to reduce the taxpayer's liability to an amount less than the amount in respect of which the holder was, by subsection (1), made liable.

► 160.21(4) ◄

(4) Assessment. The Minister may at any time assess a taxpayer in respect of any amount payable because of this section, and the provisions of this Division (including, for greater certainty, the provisions in respect of interest payable) apply, with any modifications that the circumstances require, in respect of an assessment made under this section as though it had been made under section 152 in respect of taxes payable under this Part.

SECTION 160.3: Liability in respect of amounts received out of or under RCA trust

► 160.3(1) ◄

(1) Liability in respect of amounts received out of or under RCA trust. If an amount required to be included in the income of a taxpayer because of paragraph 56(1)(*x*) is received by a person with whom the taxpayer is not dealing at arm's length, that person is jointly and severally, or solidarily, liable with the taxpayer to pay a part of the taxpayer's tax under this Part for the taxation year in which the amount is received equal to the amount by which the taxpayer's tax for the year exceeds the amount that would be the taxpayer's tax for the year if the amount had not been received, but nothing in this subsection limits the liability of the taxpayer under any other provision of this Act or of the person for the interest that the person is liable to pay under this Act on an assessment in respect of the amount that the person is liable to pay because of this subsection.

History: S. 160.3(1) was replaced by S.C. 2013, c. 34, s. 316(1), applicable to assessments made after December 20, 2002, and formerly read:

(1) *Liability in respect of amounts received out of or under RCA trust.* Where an amount required to be included in the income of a taxpayer by virtue of paragraph 56(1)(*x*) is received by a person with whom the taxpayer is not dealing at arm's length, that person is jointly and severally liable with the taxpayer to pay a part of the taxpayer's tax under this Part for the taxation year in which the amount is received equal to the amount by which the taxpayer's tax for the year exceeds the amount that would be the taxpayer's tax for the year if the amount had not been received, but nothing in this subsection shall be deemed to limit the liability of the taxpayer under any other provision of this Act.

Related Sections: S. 160.3(2) Minister may assess recipient; s. 160.3(3) Rules applicable.

► 160.3(2) ◄

(2) Assessment. The Minister may at any time assess a person in respect of any amount payable because of this section, and the provisions of this Division (including, for greater certainty, the provisions in respect of interest payable) apply, with any modifications that the circumstances require, in respect of an assessment made under this section as though it had been made under section 152 in respect of taxes payable under this Part.

History: S. 160.3(2) was replaced by S.C. 2013, c. 34, s. 316(1), applicable to assessments made after December 20, 2002, and formerly read:

(2) *Minister may assess recipient.* The Minister may at any time assess a person in respect of any amount payable by the person by virtue of this section and the provisions of this Division are applicable, with such modifications as the circumstances require, in respect of an assessment made under this section as though it had been made under section 152.

► 160.3(3) ◄

(3) Rules applicable. If a taxpayer and another person have, by virtue of subsection (1), become jointly and severally, or solidarily, liable in respect of part or all of a liability of the taxpayer under this Act, the following rules apply:

(*a*) a payment by the other person on account of the other person's liability shall to the extent thereof discharge their liability; but

(*b*) a payment by the taxpayer on account of the taxpayer's liability discharges the other person's liability only to the extent that the payment operates to reduce the taxpayer's liability to an amount less than the amount in respect of which the other person was, by subsection (1), made jointly and severally, or solidarily, liable.

History: S. 160.3(3), the portion before paragraph (*a*) was replaced by S.C. 2013, c. 34, s. 144(1), in force June 26, 2013, and formerly read:

(3) *Rules applicable.* Where a taxpayer and another person have, by virtue of subsection (1), become jointly and severally liable in respect of part or all of a liability of the taxpayer under this Act, the following rules apply:

S. 160.3(3)(*a*) was replaced by S.C. 2013, c. 34, s. 144(2), in force June 26, 2013, and formerly read:

(*a*) a payment by the other person on account of the other person's liability shall to the extent thereof discharge the joint liability; but

S. 160.3(3)(*b*) was replaced by S.C. 2013, c. 34, s. 144(3), in force June 26, 2013, and formerly read:

(*b*) a payment by the taxpayer on account of the taxpayer's liability only discharges the other person's liability to the extent that the payment operates to reduce the taxpayer's liability to an amount less than the amount in respect of which the other person was, by subsection (1), made jointly and severally liable.

SECTION 160.4: Liability in respect of transfers by insolvent corporations

▶ 160.4(1) ◀

(1) Liability in respect of transfers by insolvent corporations. If property is transferred at any time by a corporation to a taxpayer with whom the corporation does not deal at arm's length at that time and the corporation is not entitled because of subsection 61.3(3) to deduct an amount under section 61.3 in computing its income for a taxation year because of the transfer or because of the transfer and one or more other transactions, the taxpayer is jointly and severally, or solidarily, liable with the corporation to pay the lesser of the corporation's tax payable under this Part for the year and the amount, if any, by which the fair market value of the property at that time exceeds the fair market value at that time of the consideration given for the property, but nothing in this subsection limits the liability of the corporation under any other provision of this Act or of the taxpayer for the interest that the taxpayer is liable to pay under this Act on an assessment in respect of the amount that the taxpayer is liable to pay because of this subsection.

History: S. 160.4(1) was replaced by S.C. 2013, c. 34, s. 317(1), applicable to assessments made after December 20, 2002, and formerly read:

(1) *Liability in respect of transfers by insolvent corporations.* Where property is transferred at any time by a corporation to a taxpayer with whom the corporation does not deal at arm's length at that time and the corporation is not entitled because of subsection 61.3(3) to deduct an amount under section 61.3 in computing its income for a taxation year because of the transfer or because of the transfer and one or more other transactions, the taxpayer is jointly and severally liable with the corporation to pay an amount of the corporation's tax under this Part for the year equal to the amount, if any, by which the fair market value of the property at that time exceeds the fair market value at that time of the consideration given for the property, but nothing in this subsection limits the liability of the corporation under any other provision of this Act.

▶ 160.4(2) ◀

(2) Indirect transfers. Where

(*a*) property is transferred at any time from a taxpayer (in this subsection referred to as the "transferor") to another taxpayer (in this subsection referred to as the "transferee") with whom the transferor does not deal at arm's length,

(*b*) the transferor is liable because of subsection (1) or this subsection to pay an amount of the tax of another person (in this subsection referred to as the "debtor") under this Part, and

(*c*) it can reasonably be considered that one of the reasons of the transfer would, but for this subsection, be to prevent the enforcement of this section,

the transferee is jointly and severally, or solidarily, liable with the transferor and the debtor to pay an amount of the debtor's tax under this Part equal to the lesser of the amount of that tax that the transferor was liable to pay at that time and the amount, if any, by which the fair market value of the property at that time exceeds the fair market value at that time of the consideration given for the property, but nothing in this subsection limits the liability of the debtor or the transferor under any provision of this Act or of the transferee for the interest that the transferee is liable to pay under this Act on an assessment in respect of the amount that the transferee is liable to pay because of this subsection.

History: S. 160.4(2), the portion after paragraph (*c*) was replaced by S.C. 2013, c. 34, s. 317(2), applicable to assessments made after December 20, 2002, and formerly read:

the transferee is jointly and severally liable with the transferor and the debtor to pay an amount of the debtor's tax under this Part equal to the lesser of the amount of such tax that the transferor was liable to pay at that time and the amount, if any, by which the fair market value of the property at that time exceeds the fair market value at that time of the consideration given for the property, but nothing in this subsection limits the liability of the debtor or the transferor under any provision of this Act.

▶ 160.4(3) ◀

(3) Assessment. The Minister may at any time assess a person in respect of any amount payable by the person because of this section, and the provisions of this Division (including, for greater certainty, the provisions in respect of interest payable) apply, with any modifications that the circumstances require, in respect of an assessment made under this section, as though it had been made under section 152 in respect of taxes payable under this Part.

History: S. 160.4(3) was replaced by S.C. 2013, c. 34, s. 317(3), applicable to assessments made after December 20, 2002, and formerly read:

(3) *Minister may assess recipient.* The Minister may at any time assess a person in respect of any amount payable by the person because of this section and the provisions of this Division apply, with such modifications as the circumstances require, in respect of an assessment made under this section, as though it had been made under section 152.

▶ 160.4(4) ◀

(4) Rules applicable. If a corporation and another person have, because of subsection (1) or (2), become jointly and severally, or solidarily, liable in respect of part or all of a liability of the corporation under this Act

(*a*) a payment by the other person on account of that person's liability shall to the extent thereof discharge their liability; and

(*b*) a payment by the corporation on account of the corporation's liability discharges the other person's liability only to the extent that the payment operates to reduce the corporation's liability to an amount less than the amount in respect of which the other person was, by subsection (1) or (2), as the case may be, made jointly and severally, or solidarily, liable.

History: S. 160.4(4), the portion before paragraph (*a*) was replaced by S.C. 2013, c. 34, s. 145(1), in force June 26, 2013, and formerly read:

(4) *Rules applicable.* Where a corporation and another person have, because of subsection (1) or (2), become jointly and severally liable in respect of part or all of a liability of the corporation under this Act

S. 160.4(4)(*a*) was replaced by S.C. 2013, c. 34, s. 145(2), in force June 26, 2013, and formerly read:

(*a*) a payment by the other person on account of that person's liability shall to the extent thereof discharge the joint liability; and

S. 160.4(4)(*b*) was replaced by S.C. 2013, c. 34, s. 145(3), in force June 26, 2013, and formerly read:

(*b*) a payment by the corporation on account of the corporation's liability discharges the other person's liability only to the extent that the payment operates to reduce the corporation's liability to an amount less than the amount in respect of which the other person was, by subsection (1) or (2), as the case may be, made liable.

Interest

SECTION 161: [Interest]

▶ 161(1) ◀

(1) General. Where at any time after a taxpayer's balance-due day for a taxation year

(*a*) the total of the taxpayer's taxes payable under this Part and Parts I.3, VI and VI.1 for the year

exceeds

(*b*) the total of all amounts each of which is an amount paid at or before that time on account of the taxpayer's tax payable and applied as at that time by the Minister against the taxpayer's liability for an amount payable under this Part or Part I.3, VI or VI.1 for the year,

the taxpayer shall pay to the Receiver General interest at the prescribed rate on the excess, computed for the period during which that excess is outstanding.

Editorial Note: The interest rate prescribed in Income Tax Regulation s. 4301(*a*) is the base rate of Government of Canada Treasury Bills described in s. 4301(*a*)(i) plus 4%, applicable to late or deficient income tax payments and unremitted withholdings; the interest rate prescribed in s. 4301(*b*) is the base rate described in s. 4301(*a*)(i) plus 2%, applicable to tax refunds on overpayments (other than to corporations as of July 1, 2010); and the interest rate prescribed in s. 4301(*c*), is the base rate described in s. 4301(*a*)(i), applicable to deemed interest on employee and shareholder loans and benefits and, effective July 1, 2010, to refunds of tax overpayments to corporations. The interest rate prescribed in s. 4301(*b.1*), in force on March 29, 2012, is the rate specified in s. 4301(*a*) rounded to two decimal points, applicable to subsection 17.1(1) of the Act.

Base rate of Government of Canada Treasury Bills described in s. 4301(*a*)(i):

	Quarter			
Year	**(1)**	**(2)**	**(3)**	**(4)**
2019	2%	2%		
2018	1%	2%	2%	2%
2017	1%	1%	1%	1%
2016	1%	1%	1%	1%
2015	1%	1%	1%	1%
2014	1%	1%	1%	1%
2013	1%	1%	1%	2%
2012	1%	1%	1%	1%
2011	1%	1%	1%	1%
2010	1%	1%	1%	1%
2009	2%	1%	1%	1%

Related Regulations: 4301.

Related Sections: S. 161.1 Offset of refund interest and arrears interest; s. 202(3) Provisions applicable to Part; s. 202(5) Interest; s. 207(3) Multiple holders; s. 207.2(3) Provisions applicable to Part; s. 248(1), "balance-due day"; s. 248(11) Compound interest; and ITAR s. 62(2) Interest.

Tax Topics: No. 2438, Arrears Interest Under a GAAR Reassessment (Still) Accrues From Balance-Due Date.

Information Circulars: IC 07-1 Taxpayer Relief Provisions; IC 98-1R4 Collections policies.

Cases: Where the Minister relies on GAAR to reassess a taxpayer, arrears interest accrues during the period from the taxpayer's balance-due day for the year up to the issuance of the reassessment. *Quinco Financial v. The Queen*, 2016 DTC 1175 (TCC)

▶ 161(2) ◀

(2) Interest on instalments. In addition to the interest payable under subsection (1), where a taxpayer who is required by this Part to pay a part or instalment of tax has failed to pay all or any part thereof on or before the day on or before which the tax or instalment, as the case may be, was required to be paid, the taxpayer shall pay to the Receiver General interest at the prescribed rate on the amount that the taxpayer failed to pay computed from the day on or before which the amount was required to be paid to the day of payment, or to the beginning of the period in respect of which the taxpayer is required to pay interest thereon under subsection (1), whichever is earlier.

Related Regulations: 4301.

Related Sections: S. 155(1) Farmers and fishermen; s. 156(1) Other individuals; s. 157(1) Payment by corporations; S. 161(2.2) Contra interest; s. 161(4) Limitation — farmers and fishermen; s. 161(4.1) Limitation — corporations; s. 161(7) Effect of carryback of loss, etc; s. 164(4) Interest on interest repaid; s. 248(11) Compound interest; and ITAR s. 62(2) Interest.

Information Circulars: IC 07-1 Taxpayer Relief Provisions.

Cases: Interest was not to be charged after the date on which the taxpayer instructed the Minister to apply his refund to his instalment liability. *Smith v. M.N.R.*, 91 DTC 526 (T.C.C.)

▶ 161(2.1) ◀

(2.1) Exception — (Repealed by S.C. 2003, c. 15, s. 116(1).)

▶ 161(2.2) ◀

(2.2) Contra interest. Notwithstanding subsections (1) and (2), the total amount of interest payable by a taxpayer (other than a graduated rate estate) under those subsections, for the period that begins on the first day of the taxation year for which a part or instalment of tax is payable and ends on the taxpayer's balance-due day for the year, in respect of the taxpayer's tax or instalments of tax payable for the year shall not exceed the amount, if any, by which

(*a*) the total amount of interest that would be payable for the period by the taxpayer under subsections (1) and (2) in respect of the taxpayer's tax and instalments of tax payable for the year if no amount were paid on account of the tax or instalments

exceeds

(*b*) the amount of interest that would be payable under subsection 164(3) to the taxpayer in respect of the period on the amount that would be refunded to the taxpayer in respect of the year or applied to another liability if

(i) no tax were payable by the taxpayer for the year,

(ii) no amount had been remitted under section 153 to the Receiver General on account of the taxpayer's tax for the year,

(iii) the rate of interest prescribed for the purpose of subsection (1) were prescribed for the purpose of subsection 164(3), and

(iv) the latest of the days described in paragraphs 164(3)(*a*), (*b*) and (*c*) were the first day of the year.

History: S. 161(2.2), the portion before paragraph (*a*) was replaced by S.C. 2014, c. 39, s. 58(1), applicable to the 2016 and subsequent taxation years, and formerly read:

(2.2) *Contra interest.* Notwithstanding subsections (1) and (2), the total amount of interest payable by a taxpayer (other than a testamentary trust) under those subsections, for the period that begins on the first day of the taxation year for which a part or instalment of tax is payable and ends on the taxpayer's balance-due day for the year, in respect of the taxpayer's tax or instalments of tax payable for the year shall not exceed the amount, if any, by which

Related Regulations: 4301.

Related Sections: S. 248(1), "balance-due day".

▶ 161(3) ◀

(3) Special case — (Repealed by S.C. 1994, c. 7, Sched. II, s. 133(3).)

▶ 161(4) ◀

(4) Limitation — farmers and fishermen. For the purposes of subsection (2) and section 163.1, where an individual is required to pay a part or instalment of tax for a taxation year computed by reference to a method described in subsection 155(1), the individual shall be deemed to have been liable to pay on or before the day referred to in subsection 155(1) a part or instalment computed by reference to

(*a*) the amount, if any, by which

(i) the tax payable under this Part by the individual for the year, determined before taking into consideration the specified future tax consequences for the year,

exceeds

(ii) the amounts deemed by subsections 120(2) and (2.2) to have been paid on account of the individual's tax under this Part for the year, determined before taking into consideration the specified future tax consequences for the year,

(*b*) the individual's instalment base for the preceding taxation year, or

(*c*) the amount stated to be the amount of the instalment payable by the individual for the year in the notice, if any, sent to the individual by the Minister,

whichever method gives rise to the least amount required to be paid by the individual on or before that day.

Related Sections: S. 155 Farmers and fishermen; s. 248(1), "specified future tax consequences".

▶ 161(4.01) ◀

(4.01) Limitation — other individuals. For the purposes of subsection (2) and section 163.1, where an individual is required to pay a part or instalment of tax for a taxation year computed by reference to a method described in subsection 156(1), the individual shall be deemed to have been liable to pay on or before each day referred to in subsection 156(1) a part or instalment computed by reference to

(*a*) the amount, if any, by which

(i) the tax payable under this Part by the individual for the year, determined before taking into consideration the specified future tax consequences for the year,

exceeds

(ii) the amounts deemed by subsections 120(2) and (2.2) to have been paid on account of the individual's tax under this Part for the year, determined before taking into consideration the specified future tax consequences for the year,

(*b*) the individual's instalment base for the preceding taxation year,

(*c*) the amounts determined under paragraph 156(1)(*b*) in respect of the individual for the year, or

(*d*) the amounts stated to be the amounts of instalments payable by the individual for the year in the notices, if any, sent to the individual by the Minister,

reduced by the amount, if any, determined under paragraph 156(2)(*b*) in respect of the individual for the year, whichever method gives rise to the least total amount of such parts or instalments required to be paid by the individual by that day.

Related Sections: S. 248(1), "specified future tax consequences".

▶ 161(4.1) ◀

(4.1) Limitation — corporations. For the purposes of subsection (2) and section 163.1, where a corporation is required to pay a part or instalment of tax for a taxation year computed by reference to a method described in subsection 157(1), (1.1) or (1.5), as the case may be, the corporation is deemed to have been liable to pay on or before each day on or before which subparagraph 157(1)(*a*)(i), (ii) or (iii), subparagraph 157(1.1)(*a*)(i), (ii) or (iii), or subparagraph 157(1.5)(*a*)(i) or (ii), as the case may be, requires a part or instalment to be made equal to the amount, if any, by which

(*a*) the part or instalment due on that day computed in accordance with whichever allowable method in the circumstances gives rise to the least total amount of such parts or instalments of tax for the year, computed by reference to

(i) the total of the taxes payable under this Part and Parts VI, VI.1 and XIII.1 by the corporation for the year, determined before taking into consideration the specified future tax consequences for the year,

(ii) its first instalment base for the year, or

(iii) its second instalment base and its first instalment base for the year,

exceeds

(*b*) the amount, if any, determined under any of paragraphs 157(3)(*b*) to (*e*) or under paragraph 157(3.1)(*b*) or (*c*), as the case may be, in respect of that instalment.

Related Sections: S. 248(1), "specified future tax consequences".

▶ 161(5) ◀

(5) Participation certificates — (Repealed by S.C. 2012, c. 19, s. 11.)

History: S. 161(5) was repealed by S.C. 2012, c. 19, s. 11, in force on Royal Assent, June 29, 2012. S. 161(5) formerly read:

(5) *Participation certificates.* Notwithstanding any other provision in this section, no interest is payable in respect of the amount by which the tax payable by a person is increased by a payment made by The Canadian Wheat Board on a participation certificate previously issued to the person until 30 days after the payment is made.

▶ 161(6) ◀

(6) Income of resident from a foreign country in blocked currency. Where the income of a taxpayer for a taxation year, or part thereof, is from sources in another country and the taxpayer by reason of monetary or exchange restrictions imposed by the law of that country is unable to transfer it to Canada, the Minister may, if the Minister is satisfied that payment as required by this Part of the whole of the additional tax under this Part for the year reasonably attributable to income from sources in that country would impose extreme hardship on the taxpayer, postpone the time for payment of the whole or a part of that additional tax for a period to be determined by the Minister, but no such postponement may be granted if any of the income for the year from sources in that country has been

(*a*) transferred to Canada,

(*b*) used by the taxpayer for any purpose whatever, other than payment of income tax to the government of that other country on income from sources in that country, or

(*c*) disposed of by the taxpayer,

and no interest is payable under this section in respect of that additional tax, or part thereof, during the period of postponement.

▶ 161(6.1) ◀

(6.1) Foreign tax credit adjustment. Notwithstanding any other provision in this section, where the tax payable under this Part by a taxpayer for a particular taxation year is increased because of

(*a*) an adjustment of an income or profits tax payable by the taxpayer to the government of a country other than Canada or to the government of a state, province or other political subdivision of such a country, or

(*b*) a reduction in the amount of foreign tax deductible under subsection 126(1) or (2) in computing the taxpayer's tax otherwise payable under this Part for the particular year, as a result of the application of subsection 126(4.2) in respect of a share or debt obligation disposed of by the taxpayer in the taxation year following the particular year,

no interest is payable, in respect of the increase in the taxpayer's tax payable, for the period

(*c*) that ends 90 days after the day on which the taxpayer is first notified of the amount of the adjustment, if paragraph (*a*) applies, and

(*d*) before the date of the disposition, if paragraph (*b*) applies.

► 161(6.2) ◄

(6.2) Flow-through share renunciations. Where the tax payable under this Part by a taxpayer for a taxation year is more than it otherwise would be because of a consequence for the year described in paragraph (*b*) of the definition "specified future tax consequence" in subsection 248(1) in respect of an amount purported to be renounced in a calendar year, for the purposes of the provisions of this Act (other than this subsection) relating to interest payable under this Act, an amount equal to the additional tax payable is deemed

(*a*) to have been paid on the taxpayer's balance-due day for the taxation year on account of the taxpayer's tax payable under this Part for the year; and

(*b*) to have been refunded on April 30 of the following calendar year to the taxpayer on account of the taxpayer's tax payable under this Part for the taxation year.

Related Sections: S. 66(12.6) Canadian exploration expenses to flow-through shareholder; s. 66(12.601) Flow-through share rules for first $1 million of Canadian development expenses; s. 66(12.66) Expenses in the first 60 days of year; s. 66(12.73) Reductions in renunciations; s. 248(1), "specified future tax consequences".

► 161(7) ◄

(7) Effect of carryback of loss, etc. For the purpose of computing interest under subsection (1) or (2) on tax or a part of an instalment of tax for a taxation year, and for the purpose of section 163.1,

(*a*) the tax payable under this Part and Parts I.3, VI and VI.1 by the taxpayer for the year is deemed to be the amount that it would be if the consequences of the deduction, reduction or exclusion of the following amounts were not taken into consideration:

(i) any amount deducted under section 119 in respect of a disposition in a subsequent taxation year,

(ii) any amount deducted under section 41 in respect of the taxpayer's listed-personal-property loss for a subsequent taxation year,

(iii) any amount excluded from the taxpayer's income for the year by virtue of section 49 in respect of the exercise of an option in a subsequent taxation year,

(iv) any amount deducted under section 118.1 in respect of a gift made in a subsequent taxation year or under section 111 in respect of a loss for a subsequent taxation year,

(iv.1) any amount deducted under subsection 126(2) in respect of an unused foreign tax credit (within the meaning assigned by subsection 126(7)), or under subsection 126(2.21) or (2.22) in respect of foreign taxes paid, for a subsequent taxation year,

(iv.2) any amount deducted in computing the taxpayer's income for the year by virtue of an election in a subsequent taxation year under paragraph 164(6)(*c*) or (*d*) by the taxpayer's legal representative,

(v) any amount deducted under subsection 127(5) in respect of property acquired or an expenditure made in a subsequent taxation year,

(vi) (Repealed by S.C. 2013, c. 34, s. 318(1).)

(vi.1) (Repealed.)

(vii) any amount deducted under section 125.3 in respect of an unused Part I.3 tax credit (within the meaning assigned by subsection 125.3(3)) for a subsequent taxation year,

(viii) any amount deducted, in respect of a repayment under subsection 68.4(7) of the *Excise Tax Act* made in a subsequent taxation year, in computing the amount determined under subparagraph 12(1)(*x*.1)(ii),

(viii.1) any amount deducted under subsection 147.2(4) in computing the taxpayer's income for the year because of the application of subsection 147.2(6) as a result of the taxpayer's death in the subsequent taxation year,

(ix) any amount deducted under subsection 181.1(4) in respect of any unused surtax credit (within the meaning assigned by subsection 181.1(6)) of the taxpayer for a subsequent taxation year,

(x) any amount deducted under subsection 190.1(3) in respect of any unused Part I tax credit (within the meaning assigned by subsection 190.1(5)) of the taxpayer for a subsequent taxation year,

(xi) any amount deducted under any of subsections 128.1(6) to (8) from the taxpayer's proceeds of disposition of a property because of an election made in a return of income for a subsequent taxation year, and

(xii) any amount by which the amount included under subsection 91(1) for the year is reduced because of a reduction referred to in paragraph 152(6.1)(*b*) in the foreign accrual property income of a foreign affiliate of the taxpayer for a taxation year of the affiliate that ends in the year; and

(*b*) the amount by which the tax payable under this Part and Parts I.3, VI and VI.1 by the taxpayer for the year is reduced as a consequence of the deduction or exclusion of amounts described in paragraph (*a*) is deemed to have been paid on account of the taxpayer's tax payable under this Part for the year on the day that is 30 days after the latest of

(i) the first day immediately following that subsequent taxation year,

(ii) the day on which the taxpayer's or the taxpayer's legal representative's return of income for that subsequent taxation year was filed,

(iii) if an amended return of the taxpayer's income for the year or a prescribed form amending the taxpayer's return of income for the year was filed under subsection 49(4) or 152(6) or (6.1) or paragraph 164(6)(e), the day on which the amended return or prescribed form was filed, and

(iv) where, as a consequence of a request in writing, the Minister reassessed the taxpayer's tax for the year to take into account the deduction or exclusion, the day on which the request was made.

History: S. 161(7)(*a*), the portion before subparagraph (i) was replaced by S.C. 2013, c. 34, s. 35(1), applicable to taxation years that begin after December 18, 2009.

Any assessment of a taxpayer's tax, interest and penalties payable under the Act for any taxation year that ends before June 26, 2013 that would, in the absence of this section, be precluded because of subsections 152(4) to (5) of the Act, shall be made to the extent necessary to take into account this amendment, if the taxpayer

(i) elects in writing in respect of all of its foreign affiliates that this section apply in respect of that provision, and

(ii) files that election with the Minister of National Revenue on or before December 26, 2013 [the day that is six months after royal assent].

S. 161(7)(*a*), the portion before subparagraph (i) formerly read:

(*a*) the tax payable under this Part and Parts I.3, VI and VI.1 by the taxpayer for the year is deemed to be the amount that it would be if the consequences of the deduction or exclusion of the following amounts were not taken into consideration:

S. 161(7)(*a*)(xii) was added by S.C. 2013, c. 34, s. 35(2), applicable to taxation years that begin after December 18, 2009.

See the application following the history note for s. 161(7)(*a*), the portion before subparagraph (i), above, regarding the override of the statute-barring rules for assessments for taxation years that end before June 26, 2013.

S. 161(7)(*b*)(iii) was replaced by S.C. 2013, c. 34, s. 35(3), applicable to taxation years that begin after December 18, 2009.

See the application following the history note for s. 161(7)(*a*), the portion before subparagraph (i), above, regarding the override of the statute-barring rules for assessments for taxation years that end before June 26, 2013.

S. 161(7)(*b*)(iii) formerly read:

(iii) where an amended return of the taxpayer's income for the year or a prescribed form amending the taxpayer's return of income for the year was filed in accordance with subsection 49(4) or 152(6) or paragraph 164(6)(*e*), the day on which the amended return or prescribed form was filed, and

S. 161(7)(*a*)(vi) was repealed by S.C. 2013, c. 34, s. 318(1), applicable to taxation years that begin after October 31, 2011, and formerly read:

(vi) any amount deducted under section 125.2 in respect of an unused Part VI tax credit (within the meaning assigned by subsection 125.2(3)) for a subsequent taxation year,

Canadian Tax Foundation: McDonnell, *Loss Carrybacks and Nil Assessments: Losing Interest*, 2014 Tax for the Owner-Manager 14(2):5–6.

Tax Window Files: Interest calculation - loss substitutions, *March 21, 2018*, CRA Document No. 2017-0736291E5.

Cases: Since s. 161(7) refers to "tax payable" on the basis of the particular way in which a taxpayer has chosen to compute its taxable income and not to the tax which might have been payable had another option been chosen, interest was owed by the taxpayer on an unreported taxable capital gain in 1981 which could have been offset by his capital losses in 1982. *Connaught Laboratories Limited v. The Queen*, 94 DTC 6697 (F.C.T.D.).

► 161(8) ◄

(8) Certain amounts deemed to be paid as instalments. For the purposes of subsection (2), where in a taxation year an amount has been paid by a non-resident person pursuant to subsection 116(2) or (4) or an amount has been paid on that person's behalf by another person in accordance with subsection 116(5), the amount shall be deemed to have been paid by that non-resident person in the year as an instalment of tax on the first day on which the non-resident person was required under this Act to pay an instalment of tax for that year.

Related Sections: S. 116(2) Certificate in respect of proposed disposition; s. 116(4) Certificate in respect of property disposed of; s. 116(5) Liability of purchaser; s. 161(2) Interest on instalments.

► 161(9) ◄

(9) Definitions of "instalment base", etc. In this section,

(*a*) "instalment base" of an individual for a taxation year means the amount determined in prescribed manner to be the individual's instalment base for the year; and

(*b*) "first instalment base" and "second instalment base" of a corporation for a taxation year have the meanings prescribed by regulation.

Related Regulations: 5300; 5301.

► 161(10) ◄

(10) When amount deemed paid. For the purposes of subsection (2), where an amount has been deducted by virtue of paragraph 127.2(1)(*a*) or 127.3(1)(*a*) in computing the tax payable under this Part by a taxpayer for a taxation year, the amount so deducted shall be deemed to have been paid by the taxpayer

(*a*) in the case of a taxpayer who has filed a return of income under this Part for the year as required by section 150, on the last day of the year; and

(*b*) in any other case, on the day on which the taxpayer filed the taxpayer's return of income under this Part for the year.

► 161(11) ◄

(11) Interest on penalties. Where a taxpayer is required to pay a penalty, the taxpayer shall pay the penalty to the Receiver General together with interest thereon at the prescribed rate computed,

(*a*) in the case of a penalty payable under section 162, 163 or 235, from the day on or before which

(i) the taxpayer's return of income for a taxation year in respect of which the penalty is payable was required to be filed, or would have been required to be filed if tax under this Part were payable by the taxpayer for the year, or

(ii) the information return, return, ownership certificate or other document in respect of which the penalty is payable was required to be made,

as the case may be, to the day of payment;

(*b*) in the case of a penalty payable for a taxation year because of section 163.1, from the taxpayer's balance-due day for the year to the day of payment of the penalty;

(*b*.1) in the case of a penalty under subsection 237.1(7.4) or 237.3(8), from the day on which the taxpayer became liable to the penalty to the day of payment; and

(*c*) in the case of a penalty payable by reason of any other provision of this Act, from the day of sending of the notice of original assessment of the penalty to the day of payment.

History: S. 161(11)(*b.1*) was replaced by S.C. 2013, c. 34, s. 318(2), applicable in respect of avoidance transactions that are entered into after 2010 or that are part of a series of transactions that began before 2011 and is completed after 2010.

S. 161(11)(*b.1*) formerly read:

(*b*.1) in the case of a penalty under subsection 237.1(7.4), from the day on which the taxpayer became liable to the penalty to the day of payment; and

S. 161(11)(*c*) was replaced by S.C. 2010, c. 25, s. 40, in force on Royal Assent, December 15, 2010. S. 161(11)(*c*) formerly read:

(*c*) in the case of a penalty payable by reason of any other provision of this Act, from the day of mailing of the notice of original assessment of the penalty to the day of payment.

Related Regulations: 4301.

Related Sections: S. 235 Penalty for failing to file corporate returns; s. 248(1), "balance-due day"; s. 248(11) Compound interest.

Information Circulars: IC 07-1 Taxpayer Relief Provisions.

► 161(12) ◄

(12) Partnership liable to interest — (Repealed by S.C. 2000, c. 19, s. 47(3).)

Offset of Refund Interest and Arrears Interest

SECTION 161.1: [Interest offset and arrears]

► 161.1(1) ◄

(1) Definitions. The definitions in this subsection apply in this section.

"accumulated overpayment amount" —"accumulated overpayment amount", of a corporation for a period, means the overpayment amount of the corporation for the period together with refund interest (including, for greater certainty, compound interest) that accrued with respect to the overpayment amount before the date specified under paragraph (3)(*b*) by the corporation in its application for the period.

"accumulated underpayment amount" —"accumulated underpayment amount", of a corporation for a period, means the underpayment amount of the corporation for the period together with arrears interest (including, for greater certainty, compound interest) that accrued with respect to the underpayment amount before the date specified under paragraph (3)(*b*) by the corporation in its application for the period.

"arrears interest" —"arrears interest" means interest computed under paragraph (5)(*b*), 129(2.2)(*b*), 131(3.2)(*b*), 132(2.2)(*b*), 133(7.02)(*b*) or 160.1(1)(*b*), subsection 161(1) or (11), paragraph 164(3.1)(*b*) or (4)(*b*) or subsection 187(2).

"overpayment amount" —"overpayment amount", of a corporation for a period, means the amount referred to in subparagraph (2)(*a*)(i) that is refunded to the corporation, or the amount referred to in subparagraph (2)(*a*)(ii) to which the corporation is entitled.

"refund interest" —"refund interest" means interest computed under subsection 129(2.1), 131(3.1), 132(2.1), 133(7.01) or 164(3) or (3.2).

"underpayment amount" —"underpayment amount", of a corporation for a period, means the amount referred to in paragraph (2)(*b*) payable by the corporation on which arrears interest is computed.

► 161.1(2) ◄

(2) Concurrent refund interest and arrears interest. A corporation may apply in writing to the Minister for the reallocation of an accumulated overpayment amount for a period that begins after 1999 on account of an accumulated underpayment amount for the period if, in respect of tax paid or payable by the corporation under this Part or Part I.3, II, IV, IV.1, VI, VI.1 or XIV,

(*a*) refund interest for the period

(i) is computed on an amount refunded to the corporation, or

(ii) would be computed on an amount to which the corporation is entitled, if that amount were refunded to the corporation; and

(*b*) arrears interest for the period is computed on an amount payable by the corporation.

► 161.1(3) ◄

(3) Contents of application. A corporation's application referred to in subsection (2) for a period is deemed not to have been made unless

(*a*) it specifies the amount to be reallocated, which shall not exceed the lesser of the corporation's accumulated overpayment amount for the period and its accumulated underpayment amount for the period;

(*b*) it specifies the effective date for the reallocation, which shall not be earlier than the latest of

(i) the date from which refund interest is computed on the corporation's overpayment amount for the period, or would be so computed if the overpayment amount were refunded to the corporation,

(ii) the date from which arrears interest is computed on the corporation's underpayment amount for the period, and

(iii) January 1, 2000; and

(*c*) it is made on or before the day that is 90 days after the latest of

(i) the day of sending of the first notice of assessment giving rise to any portion of the corporation's overpayment amount to which the application relates,

(ii) the day of sending of the first notice of assessment giving rise to any portion of the corporation's underpayment amount to which the application relates,

(iii) if the corporation has served a notice of objection to an assessment referred to in subparagraph (i) or (ii), the day of sending of the notification under subsection 165(3) by the Minister in respect of the notice of objection,

(iv) if the corporation has appealed, or applied for leave to appeal, from an assessment referred to in subparagraph (i) or (ii) to a court of competent jurisdiction, the day on which the court dismisses the application, the application or appeal is discontinued or final judgment is pronounced in the appeal, and

(v) the day of sending of the first notice to the corporation indicating that the Minister has determined any portion of the corporation's overpayment amount to which the application relates, if the overpayment amount has not been determined as a result of a notice of assessment sent before that day.

History: S. 161.1(3)(*c*)(i) to (v) were replaced by S.C. 2010, c. 25, s. 41, in force on Royal Assent, December 15, 2010. S. 161.1(3)(*c*)(i) to (v) formerly read:

(i) the day of mailing of the first notice of assessment giving rise to any portion of the corporation's overpayment amount to which the application relates,

(ii) the day of mailing of the first notice of assessment giving rise to any portion of the corporation's underpayment amount to which the application relates,

(iii) if the corporation has served a notice of objection to an assessment referred to in subparagraph (i) or (ii), the day of mailing of the notification under subsection 165(3) by the Minister in respect of the notice of objection,

(iv) if the corporation has appealed, or applied for leave to appeal, from an assessment referred to in subparagraph (i) or (ii) to a court of competent jurisdiction, the day on which the court dismisses the application, the application or appeal is discontinued or final judgment is pronounced in the appeal, and

(v) the day of mailing of the first notice to the corporation indicating that the Minister has determined any portion of the corporation's overpayment amount to which the application relates, if the overpayment amount has not been determined as a result of a notice of assessment mailed before that day.

► 161.1(4) ◄

(4) Reallocation. The amount to be reallocated that is specified under paragraph (3)(*a*) by a corporation is deemed to have been refunded to the corporation and paid on account of the accumulated underpayment amount on the date specified under paragraph (3)(*b*) by the corporation.

► 161.1(5) ◄

(5) Repayment of refund. If an application in respect of a period is made under subsection (2) by a corporation and a portion of the amount to be reallocated has been refunded to the corporation, the following rules apply:

(*a*) a particular amount equal to the total of

(i) the portion of the amount to be reallocated that was refunded to the corporation, and

(ii) refund interest paid or credited to the corporation in respect of that portion

is deemed to have become payable by the corporation on the day on which the portion was refunded; and

(*b*) the corporation shall pay to the Receiver General interest at the prescribed rate on the particular amount from the day referred to in paragraph (*a*) to the date of payment.

Related Sections: S. 248(11) Compound interest.

► 161.1(6) ◄

(6) Consequential reallocations. If a particular reallocation of an accumulated overpayment amount under subsection (4) results in a new accumulated overpayment amount of the corporation for a period, the new accumulated overpayment amount shall not be reallocated under this section unless the corporation so applies in its application for the particular reallocation.

► 161.1(7) ◄

(7) Assessments. Notwithstanding subsections 152(4), (4.01) and (5), the Minister shall assess or reassess interest and penalties payable by a corporation in respect of any taxation year as necessary in order to take into account a reallocation of amounts under this section.

SECTION 161.2: Period where interest not payable

Notwithstanding any other provision of this Act, if the Minister notifies a taxpayer that the taxpayer is required to pay a specified amount under this Act and the taxpayer pays the specified amount in full before the end of the period that the Minister specifies with the notice, interest is not payable on the specified amount for the period.

Related Sections: S. 161(1) Interest; s. 161(2) Interest on instalments.

Small Amounts Owing

SECTION 161.3: Interest and penalty amounts of $25 or less

If, at any time, a person pays an amount not less than the total of all amounts, other than interest and penalty, owing at that time to Her Majesty in right of Canada under this Act for a taxation year of the person and the total amount of interest and penalty payable by the person under this Act for that year is not more than $25.00, the Minister may cancel the interest and penalty.

SECTION 161.4: Taxpayer

► 161.4(1) ◄

(1) Taxpayer. If the Minister determines, at any time, that the total of all amounts owing by a person to Her Majesty in right of Canada under this Act does not exceed two dollars, those amounts are deemed to be nil.

► 161.4(2) ◄

(2) Minister. If, at any time, the total of all amounts payable by the Minister to a person under this Act does not exceed two dollars, the Minister may apply those amounts against any amount owing, at that time, by the person to Her Majesty in right of Canada. However, if the person, at that time, does not owe any amount to Her Majesty in right of Canada, those amounts payable are deemed to be nil.

Penalties

SECTION 162: Failure to file return of income

► 162(1) ◄

(1) Failure to file return of income. Every person who fails to file a return of income for a taxation year as and when required by subsection 150(1) is liable to a penalty equal to the total of

(*a*) an amount equal to 5% of the person's tax payable under this Part for the year that was unpaid when the return was required to be filed, and

(*b*) the product obtained when 1% of the person's tax payable under this Part for the year that was unpaid when the return was required to be filed is multiplied by the number of complete months, not exceeding 12, from the date on which the return was required to be filed to the date on which the return was filed.

Related Sections: S. 150(1) Filing returns of income — general rule; s. 161(11) Interest on penalties; s. 162(11) Effect of subsequent events; s. 239(3) Penalty on conviction; s. 248(1), "amount", "individual", "prescribed".

Canadian Tax Foundation: Sorensen et al., *Non-Criminal Penalties Under the Income Tax Act*, 2013 Ontario Tax Conference 12:1–50; Burbank et al, *Comprehensive Discussion on Penalties*, 2013 Prairie Provinces Tax Conference 9:1–40.

Tax Profile: August 2005 — Canada Revenue Agency's Recent Attack on U.S. Companies.

Information Circulars: IC 07-1 Taxpayer Relief Provisions; IC 00-1R4 Voluntary disclosures program.

Cases: Although the penalty is a strict one with no due diligence defence, even strict penalties should not be imposed if the taxpayer took all reasonable steps to comply. *Douglas v. The Queen*, 2012 DTC 1114 (T.C.C.)

A late filing penalty still applied although the tax owing had been subsequently reduced to nil through the application of a non-capital loss carry-back. All late filing penalties are to be computed as a percentage of the tax actually owing when the return was required to be filed. *Reemark Chelsea Terraces Project Ltd. v. the Queen*, 93 DTC 469 (T.C.C.)

Due to his wife's illness followed by her death on April 29, 1986, the taxpayer's 1985 tax return was not filed until May 16, 1986. Despite the obvious sympathy for the taxpayer, the penalty provisions of s. 162(1) left the Court with no alternative but to affirm the penalty of $1,314 which the Minister had imposed. *Biello v. M.N.R.*, 93 DTC 1169 (T.C.C.).

► 162(2) ◄

(2) Repeated failure to file. Every person

(*a*) who fails to file a return of income for a taxation year as and when required by subsection 150(1),

(*b*) to whom a demand for a return for the year has been sent under subsection 150(2), and

(*c*) by whom, before the time of failure, a penalty was payable under this subsection or subsection (1) in respect of a return of income for any of the 3 preceding taxation years

is liable to a penalty equal to the total of

(*d*) an amount equal to 10% of the person's tax payable under this Part for the year that was unpaid when the return was required to be filed, and

(*e*) the product obtained when 2% of the person's tax payable under this Part for the year that was unpaid when the return was required to be filed is multiplied by the number of complete months, not exceeding 20, from the date on which the return was required to be filed to the date on which the return was filed.

History: S. 162(2)(*b*) was replaced by S.C. 2012, c. 19, s. 12(1), in force on Royal Assent, June 29, 2012. S. 162(2)(*b*) formerly read:

(*b*) on whom a demand for a return for the year has been served under subsection 150(2), and

Related Sections: S. 150(3) Trustees, etc; s. 161(11) Interest on penalties; s. 162(11) Effect of subsequent events; s. 239(3) Penalty on conviction.

Information Circulars: IC 07-1 Taxpayer Relief Provisions; IC 00-1R4 Voluntary disclosures program.

► 162(2.1) ◄

(2.1) Failure to file — non-resident corporation. Notwithstanding subsections (1) and (2), if a non-resident corporation is liable to a penalty under subsection (1) or (2) for failure to file a return of income for a taxation year, the amount of the penalty is the greater of

(*a*) the amount computed under subsection (1) or (2), as the case may be, and

(*b*) an amount equal to the greater of

(i) $100, and

(ii) $25 times the number of days, not exceeding 100, from the day on which the return was required to be filed to the day on which the return is filed.

Related Sections: S. 239(3) Penalty on conviction.

Tax Profile: March 2011 — Canada 2010 — Year in Review; September 2010 — Recent Tax Developments Affecting Non-Residents; August 2010 — FCA Endorses Penalty for Late-Filed Tax Return Even When Taxes Are Not Owing.

Cases: The taxpayer asked if it was entitled to relief for the years prior to 2010 because there were two conflicting Tax Court decisions as to whether s. 162(2.1) should apply. The Minister failed to answer this question, so the taxpayer's application for judicial review was granted. *Cogesco Services Limited v. Canada (AG)*, 2014 DTC 5019 (F.C.C.)

► 162(3) ◄

(3) Failure to file by trustee. Every person who fails to file a return as required by subsection 150(3) is liable to a penalty of $10 for each day of default but not exceeding $50.

Related Sections: S. 239(3) Penalty on conviction.

Information Circulars: IC 07-1 Taxpayer relief provisions; IC 00-1R4 Voluntary disclosures program.

► 162(4) ◄

(4) Ownership certificate. Every person who

(*a*) fails to complete an ownership certificate as required by section 234,

(*b*) fails to deliver an ownership certificate in the manner prescribed at the time prescribed and at the place prescribed by regulations made under that section, or

(*c*) cashes a coupon or warrant for which an ownership certificate has not been completed pursuant to that section,

is liable to a penalty of $50.

Related Sections: S. 239(3) Penalty on conviction.

Information Circulars: IC 07-1 Taxpayer relief provisions; IC 00-1R4 Voluntary disclosures program.

► 162(5) ◄

(5) Failure to provide information on form. Every person who fails to provide any information required on a prescribed form made under this Act or a regulation is liable to a penalty of $100 for each such failure, unless

(*a*) in the case of information required in respect of another person or partnership, a reasonable effort was made by the person to obtain the information from the other person or partnership; or

(*b*) in the case of a failure to provide a Social Insurance Number on a return of income, the person had applied for the assignment of the Number and had not received it at the time the return was filed.

Related Sections: S. 237(2) Number required in information returns; s. 239(3) Penalty on conviction.

Information Circulars: IC 82-2R2 Social insurance number legislation that relates to the preparation of information slips; IC 07-1 Taxpayer relief provisions; IC 00-1R4 Voluntary disclosures program.

► 162(5.1) ◄

(5.1) Failure to provide claim preparer information. Every person or partnership who makes, or participates in, assents to or acquiesces in the making of, a false statement or omission in respect of claim preparer information required to be included in an SR&ED form is jointly and severally, or solidarily, liable, together with any claim preparer of the form, to a penalty equal to $1,000.

History: S. 162(5.1) was added by S.C. 2013, c. 40, s. 70(1), in force January 1, 2014.

Related Sections: S. 37(11) Filing requirement.

► 162(5.2) ◄

(5.2) Due diligence. A claim preparer of an SR&ED form is not liable for a penalty under subsection (5.1) in respect of a false statement or omission if the claim preparer has exercised the degree of care, diligence and skill to prevent the making of the false statement or omission that a reasonably prudent person would have exercised in comparable circumstances.

History: S. 162(5.2) was added by S.C. 2013, c. 40, s. 70(1), in force January 1, 2014.

► 162(5.3) ◄

(5.3) Definitions. The following definitions apply in this subsection and subsections (5.1) and (5.2).

History: S. 162(5.3) was added by S.C. 2013, c. 40, s. 70(1), in force January 1, 2014.

"claim preparer" —"claim preparer", of an SR&ED form, means a person or partnership who agrees to accept consideration to prepare, or assist in the preparation of, the form but does not include an employee who prepares, or assists in the preparation of, the form in the course of performing their duties of employment.

"claim preparer information" —"claim preparer information" means prescribed information regarding

(*a*) the identity of the claim preparer, if any, of an SR&ED form, and

(*b*) the arrangement under which the claim preparer agrees to accept consideration in respect of the preparation of the form.

"SR&ED form" —"SR&ED form" means a prescribed form required to be filed under subsection 37(11).

► 162(6) ◄

(6) Failure to provide identification number. Every person or partnership who fails to provide on request their business number, their Social Insurance Number, their trust account number or their U.S. federal taxpayer identifying number to a person required under this Act or the Regulations to make an information return requiring the number is liable to a penalty of $100 for each such failure, unless

(*a*) an application for the assignment of the number is made within 15 days (or, in the case of a U.S. federal taxpayer identifying number, 90 days) after the request was received; and

(*b*) the number is provided to the person who requested the number within 15 days after the person or partnership received it.

History: S. 162(6), the portion before paragraph (*a*) was replaced by S.C. 2018, c. 12, s. 27(1), applicable to the 2018 and subsequent taxation years, and formerly read:

(6) *Failure to provide identification number.* Every person or partnership who fails to provide on request their Social Insurance Number, their business number or their U.S. federal taxpayer identifying number to a person required under this Act or a regulation to make an information return requiring the number is liable to a penalty of $100 for each such failure, unless

S. 162(6), the portion before paragraph (*b*) was replaced by S.C. 2014, c. 20, s. 100(1), in force July 1, 2014, and formerly read:

(6) *Failure to provide identification number.* Every person or partnership who fails to provide on request their Social Insurance Number or their business number to a person required under this Act or a regulation to make an information return requiring the number is liable to a penalty of $100 for each such failure, unless

(*a*) an application for the assignment of the number is made within 15 days after the request was received; and

Related Sections: S. 237 Social Insurance Number; s. 239(2.3) Offence with respect to an identification number; s. 239(3) Penalty on conviction; s. 248(1), "business number".

Canadian Tax Foundation: Moriartey, *Repeated Failure-To-File Penalty: Scope Narrowed*, 2017 Canadian Tax Focus 7(3):2–3.

Information Circulars: IC 82-2R2 Social insurance number legislation that relates to the preparation of information slips; IC 07-1 Taxpayer relief provisions; IC 00-1R4 Voluntary disclosures program.

► 162(7) ◄

(7) Failure to comply. Every person (other than a registered charity) or partnership who fails

(*a*) to file an information return as and when required by this Act or the regulations, or

(*b*) to comply with a duty or obligation imposed by this Act or the regulations

is liable in respect of each such failure, except where another provision of this Act (other than subsection (10) or (10.1) or 163(2.22)) sets out a penalty for the failure, to a penalty equal to the greater of $100 and the product obtained when $25 is multiplied by the number of days, not exceeding 100, during which the failure continues.

Related Sections: S. 147.5(9) Obligations of administrator; s. 239(3) Penalty on conviction.

Canadian Tax Foundation: Wen, *Late-Filing Penalties Without Unpaid Tax*, 2015 Canadian Tax Focus 2(4):6–7; Gibson Saab, *Late Not-for-Profit Returns (Form T1044)*, 2014 Canadian Tax Focus 4(2):6.

Tax Profile: March 2011 — Canada 2010 — Year in Review; September 2010 — Recent Tax Developments Affecting Non-Residents; August 2010 — FCA Endorses Penalty for Late-Filed Tax Return Even When Taxes Are Not Owing; August 2005 — Canada Revenue Agency's Recent Attack on U.S. Companies.

Tax Topics: No. 2023-24, 2010 Canadian Tax Foundation CRA Roundtable: Pipelines, Privilege and Working Papers (Again!).

Information Circulars: IC 89-4 Tax shelter reporting; IC 07-1 Taxpayer relief provisions; IC 00-1R4 Voluntary disclosures program.

► 162(7.01) ◄

(7.01) Late filing penalty — prescribed information returns. Every person (other than a registered charity) or partnership who fails to file, when required by this Act or the regulations, one or more information returns of a type prescribed for the purpose of this subsection is liable to a penalty equal to the greater of $100 and

(*a*) where the number of those information returns is less than 51, $10 multiplied by the number of days, not exceeding 100, during which the failure continues;

(*b*) where the number of those information returns is greater than 50 and less than 501, $15 multiplied by the number of days, not exceeding 100, during which the failure continues;

(*c*) where the number of those information returns is greater than 500 and less than 2,501, $25 multiplied by the number of days, not exceeding 100, during which the failure continues;

(*d*) where the number of those information returns is greater than 2,500 and less than 10,001, $50 multiplied by the number of days, not exceeding 100, during which the failure continues; and

(*e*) where the number of those information returns is greater than 10,000, $75 multiplied by the number of days, not exceeding 100, during which the failure continues.

History: S. 162(7.01) was added by S.C. 2009, c. 2, s. 60(1), applicable to returns required to be filed after 2009.

Related Regulations: 205(3).

Tax Window Files: Subsection 162(7.01) penalty calculation, *August 15, 2018*, CRA Document No. 2018-0748441I7.

► 162(7.02) ◄

(7.02) Failure to file in appropriate manner — prescribed information returns. Every person (other than a registered charity) or partnership who fails to file, in the manner required by the regulations, one or more information returns of a type prescribed for the purpose of this subsection is liable to a penalty equal to

(*a*) where the number of those information returns is greater than 50 and less than 251, $250;

(*b*) where the number of those information returns is greater than 250 and less than 501, $500;

(*c*) where the number of those information returns is greater than 500 and less than 2,501, $1,500;

(*d*) where the number of those information returns is greater than 2,500, $2,500; and

(*e*) in any other case, nil.

History: S. 162(7.02) was added by S.C. 2009, c. 2, s. 60(1), applicable to returns required to be filed after 2009.

Related Regulations: S. 205.1.

► 162(7.1) ◄

(7.1) Failure to make partnership information return. Where a member of a partnership fails to file an information return as a member of the partnership for a fiscal period of the partnership as and when required by this Act or the regulations and subsection (10) does not set out a penalty for the failure, the partnership is liable to a penalty equal to the greater of $100 and the product obtained when $25 is multiplied by the number of days, not exceeding 100, during which the failure continues.

Related Sections: S. 239(3) Penalty on conviction.

Information Circulars: IC 00-1R4 Voluntary disclosures program.

► 162(7.2) ◄

(7.2) Failure to file in appropriate manner — return of income. Every person who fails to file a return of income for a taxation year as required by subsection 150.1(2.1) is liable to a penalty equal to $1,000.

History: S. 162(7.2) was added by S.C. 2009, c. 2, s. 60(2), applicable to taxation years that end after 2010 except that, in its application to the 2011 and 2012 taxation years, the reference to $1,000 in subsection 162(7.2) is to be read as

(a) $250, for the 2011 taxation year; and

(b) $500, for the 2012 taxation year.

► 162(7.3) ◄

(7.3) Failure to file in appropriate manner — tax preparer. Every tax preparer who fails to file a return of income as required by subsection 150.1(2.3) is liable to a penalty equal to

(*a*) $25 for each such failure in respect of a return of an individual; and

(*b*) $100 for each such failure in respect of a return of a corporation.

History: S. 162(7.3) was added by S.C. 2012, c. 19, s. 12(2), in force January 1, 2013.

► 162(8) ◄

(8) Repeated failure to file. Where

(*a*) a penalty was payable under subsection (7.1) in respect of a failure by a member of a partnership to file an information return as a member of the partnership for a fiscal period of the partnership,

(*b*) a demand for the return or for information required to be contained in the return has been served under section 233 on the member, and

(*c*) a penalty was payable under subsection (7.1) in respect of the failure by a member of a partnership to file an information return as a member of the partnership for any of the 3 preceding fiscal periods,

the partnership is liable, in addition to the penalty under subsection (7.1), to a penalty of $100 for each member of the partnership for each month or part of a month, not exceeding 24 months, during which the failure referred to in paragraph (*a*) continues.

Related Sections: S. 239(3) Penalty on conviction.

► 162(8.1) ◄

(8.1) Rules — partnership liable to a penalty. If a partnership is liable to a penalty under any of subsections (5) to (7.1), (7.3), (8) and (10), then sections 152, 158 to 160.1, 161 and 164 to 167 and Division J apply, with any modifications that the circumstances require, to the penalty as if the partnership were a corporation.

History: S. 162(8.1) was replaced by S.C. 2012, c. 19, s. 12(3), in force January 1, 2013. S. 162(8.1) formerly read:

(8.1) *Rules where partnership liable to a penalty.* Where a partnership is liable to a penalty under subsection (5), (6), (7), (7.1), (8) or (10), sections 152, 158 to 160.1, 161 and 164 to 167 and Division J apply, with any modifications that the circumstances require, to the penalty as if the partnership were a corporation.

► 162(9) ◄

(9) Tax shelter identification number — (Repealed by S.C. 1998, c. 19, s. 188(4).)

Related Sections: S. 237.1(4) Sales prohibited; s. 237.1(7.4) Penalty.

► 162(10) ◄

(10) Failure to furnish foreign-based information. Every person or partnership who,

(*a*) knowingly or under circumstances amounting to gross negligence, fails to file an information return as and when required by any of sections 233.1 to 233.4 and 233.8, or

(*b*) where paragraph (*a*) does not apply, knowingly or under circumstances amounting to gross negligence, fails to comply with a demand under section 233 to file a return

is liable to a penalty equal to the amount determined by the formula

$$(\$500 \times A \times B) - C$$

where

A is

(*c*) where paragraph (*a*) applies, the lesser of 24 and the number of months, beginning with the month in which the return was required to be filed, during any part of which the return has not been filed, and

(*d*) where paragraph (*b*) applies, the lesser of 24 and the number of months, beginning with the month in which the demand was served, during any part of which the return has not been filed,

B is

(*e*) where the person or partnership has failed to comply with a demand under section 233 to file a return, 2, and

(*f*) in any other case, 1, and

C is the penalty to which the person or partnership is liable under subsection (7) in respect of the return.

History: S. 162(10)(*a*) was replaced by S.C. 2016, c. 12, s. 56, in force December 15, 2016, and formerly read:

(*a*) knowingly or under circumstances amounting to gross negligence, fails to file an information return as and when required by any of sections 233.1 to 233.4, or

Related Sections: S. 239(3) Penalty on conviction.

Information Circulars: IC 00-1R4 Voluntary disclosures program.

► 162(10.1) ◄

(10.1) Additional penalty. Where

(*a*) a person or partnership is liable to a penalty under subsection (10) for the failure to file a return (other than an information return required to be filed under section 233.1),

(*b*) if paragraph (10)(*a*) applies, the number of months, beginning with the month in which the return was required to be filed, during any part of which the return has not been filed exceeds 24, and

(*c*) if paragraph (10)(*b*) applies, the number of months, beginning with the month in which the demand referred to in that paragraph was served, during any part of which the return has not been filed exceeds 24,

the person or partnership is liable, in addition to the penalty determined under subsection (10), to a penalty equal to the amount determined by the formula

$$A - B$$

where

A is

(*d*) if the return is required to be filed under section 233.2 in respect of a trust, 5% of the total of all amounts each of which is the fair market value, at the time it was made, of a contribution of the person or partnership made to the trust before the end of the last taxation year of the trust in respect of which the return is required,

(*e*) where the return is required to be filed under section 233.3 for a taxation year or fiscal period, 5% of the greatest of all amounts each of which is the total of the cost amounts to the person or partnership at any time in the year or period of a specified foreign property (as defined by subsection 233.3(1)) of the person or partnership, and

(*f*) where the return is required to be filed under section 233.4 for a taxation year or fiscal period in respect of a foreign affiliate of the person or partnership, 5% of the greatest of all amounts each of which is the total of the cost amounts to the person or partnership at any time in the year or period of a property of the person or partnership that is a share of the capital stock or indebtedness of the affiliate, and

B is the total of the penalties to which the person or partnership is liable under subsections (7) and (10) in respect of the return.

History: S. 162(10.1), paragraph (*d*) of the description of A, was amended by S.C. 2013, c. 34, s. 17(2), applicable to returns in respect of taxation years that end after 2006. Paragraph (*d*) of the description of A in subsection 162(10.1) also applies to returns in respect of an earlier taxation year of a taxpayer if subsection 94(1) applies to that earlier taxation year of the taxpayer [should be 94(3) – CCH].

S. 162(10.1), paragraph (*d*) of the description of A formerly read:

(*d*) where the return is required to be filed under section 233.2, 5% of the total of all amounts each of which is the fair market value of property transferred or loaned (determined as of the time of the transfer or loan) because of which there would, if no other transfer or loan were taken into account, be an obligation to file the return,

► 162(10.11) ◄

(10.11) Application to trust contributions. In paragraph (*d*) of the description of A in subsection (10.1), subsections 94(1), (2) and (9) apply.

History: S. 162(10.11) was added by S.C. 2013, c. 34, s. 17(3), applicable to returns in respect of taxation years that end after 2006. Subsection 162(10.11) also applies to returns in respect of an earlier taxation year of a taxpayer if subsection 94(1) applies to that earlier taxation year of the taxpayer [should be 94(3) – CCH].

► 162(10.2) ◄

(10.2) Shares or debt owned by controlled foreign affiliate. For the purpose of paragraph (*f*) of the description of A in subsection (10.1),

(*a*) shares or indebtedness owned by a controlled foreign affiliate of a person or partnership are deemed to be owned by the person or partnership; and

(*b*) the cost amount at any time of such shares or indebtedness to the person or partnership is deemed to be equal to 20% of the cost amount at that time to the controlled foreign affiliate of the shares or indebtedness.

► 162(10.3) ◄

(10.3) Application to partnerships. For the purposes of paragraph (*f*) of the description of A in subsection (10.1) and subsection (10.2), in determining whether a non-resident corporation or trust is a foreign affiliate or a controlled foreign affiliate of a partnership,

(*a*) the definitions "direct equity percentage" and "equity percentage" in subsection 95(4) shall be read as if a partnership were a person; and

(*b*) the definitions "controlled foreign affiliate" and "foreign affiliate" in subsection 95(1) shall be read as if a partnership were a taxpayer resident in Canada.

► 162(10.4) ◄

(10.4) Application to non-resident trusts. For the purposes of this subsection, paragraph (*f*) of the description of A in subsection (10.1) and subsection (10.2),

(*a*) a non-resident trust is deemed to be a controlled foreign affiliate of each beneficiary of which the trust is a controlled foreign affiliate for the purpose of section 233.4;

(*b*) the trust is deemed to be a non-resident corporation having a capital stock of a single class divided into 100 issued shares;

(*c*) each beneficiary under the trust is deemed to own at any time the number of the issued shares of the corporation that is equal to the proportion of 100 that

(i) the fair market value at that time of the beneficiary's beneficial interest in the trust

is of

(ii) the fair market value at that time of all beneficial interests in the trust; and

(*d*) the cost amount to a beneficiary at any time of a share of the corporation is deemed to be equal to the amount determined by the formula

$$A/B$$

where

A is the fair market value at that time of the beneficiary's beneficial interest in the trust, and

B is the number of shares deemed under paragraph (*c*) to be owned at that time by the beneficiary in respect of the corporation.

► 162(11) ◄

(11) Effect of subsequent events. For the purpose of computing a penalty under subsection (1) or (2) in respect of a person's return of income for a taxation year, the person's tax payable under this Part for the year shall be determined before taking into consideration the specified future tax consequences for the year.

Information Circulars: IC 00-1R4 Voluntary disclosures program.

SECTION 163: [Repeated failures, false statements and omissions]

▶ 163(1) ◀

(1) Repeated failure to report income. Every person is liable to a penalty who

(*a*) fails to report an amount, equal to or greater than $500, required to be included in computing the person's income in a return filed under section 150 for a taxation year (in this subsection and subsection (1.1) referred to as the *unreported amount*);

(*b*) had failed to report an amount, equal to or greater than $500, required to be included in computing the person's income in any return filed under section 150 for any of the three preceding taxation years; and

(*c*) is not liable to a penalty under subsection (2) in respect of the unreported amount.

History: S. 163(1) was replaced by S.C. 2016, c. 7, s. 43(1), applicable to taxation years that begin after 2014, and formerly read:

(1) *Repeated failures.* Every person who

(*a*) fails to report an amount required to be included in computing the person's income in a return filed under section 150 for a taxation year, and

(*b*) had failed to report an amount required to be so included in any return filed under section 150 for any of the three preceding taxation years

is liable to a penalty equal to 10% of the amount described in paragraph (*a*), except where the person is liable to a penalty under subsection (2) in respect of that amount.

Related Sections: S. 161(11) Interest on penalties.

Canadian Tax Foundation: Moriartey, *Repeated Failure-To-File Penalty: Scope Narrowed*, 2017 Canadian Tax Focus 7(3):2–3; Sorensen et al., *Non-Criminal Penalties Under the Income Tax Act*, 2013 Ontario Tax Conference 12:1–50; Burbank et al, *Comprehensive Discussion on Penalties*, 2013 Prairie Provinces Tax Conference 9:1–40; Campbell, *Application of the Charter to Civil Penalties in the Income Tax Act*, 2002 Canadian Tax Journal 1:1–22.

Information Circulars: IC 73-10R3 Tax evasion; IC 00-1R4 Voluntary disclosures program.

Cases: Given the harsh and potentially disproportionate results of the penalty and absent an express limitation, the taxpayer had a due diligence defence available. In the absence of evidence the taxpayer did not file his tax returns after receiving a notice of reassessment, the Minister did not meet its burden. *Galachiuk v. The Queen*, 2014 DTC 1153 (T.C.C.)

▶ 163(1.1) ◀

(1.1) Amount of penalty. The amount of the penalty to which the person is liable under subsection (1) is equal to the lesser of

(*a*) 10% of the unreported amount, and

(*b*) the amount determined by the formula

$$0.5 \times (A - B)$$

where

A is the total of the amounts that would be determined under paragraphs (2)(*a*) to (*g*) if subsection (2) applied in respect of the unreported amount, and

B is any amount deducted or withheld under subsection 153(1) that may reasonably be considered to be in respect of the unreported amount.

History: S. 163(1.1) was added by S.C. 2016, c. 7, s. 43(1), applicable to taxation years that begin after 2014.

▶ 163(2) ◀

(2) False statements or omissions. Every person who, knowingly, or under circumstances amounting to gross negligence, has made or has participated in, assented to or acquiesced in the making of, a false statement or omission in a return, form, certificate, statement or answer (in this section referred to as a "return") filed or made in respect of a taxation year for the purposes of this Act, is liable to a penalty of the greater of $100 and 50% of the total of

(*a*) the amount, if any, by which

(i) the amount, if any, by which

(A) the tax for the year that would be payable by the person under this Act

exceeds

(B) the amounts that would be deemed by subsections 120(2) and (2.2) to have been paid on account of the person's tax for the year

if the person's taxable income for the year were computed by adding to the taxable income reported by the person in the person's return for the year that portion of the person's understatement of income for the year that is reasonably attributable to the false statement or omission and if the person's tax payable for the year were computed by subtracting from the deductions from the tax otherwise payable by the person for the year such portion of any such deduction as may reasonably be attributable to the false statement or omission

exceeds

(ii) the amount, if any, by which

(A) the tax for the year that would have been payable by the person under this Act

exceeds

(B) the amounts that would be deemed by subsections 120(2) and (2.2) to have been paid on account of the person's tax for the year

had the person's tax payable for the year been assessed on the basis of the information provided in the person's return for the year,

(*b*) (Repealed by S.C. 1994, c. 7, Sched. VII, s. 17(1).)

(*c*) the total of all amounts each of which is the amount, if any, by which

(i) the amount that would be deemed by subsection 122.61(1) to be an overpayment on account of the person's liability under this Part for the year that arose during a particular month or, where that person is a cohabiting spouse or common-law partner (within the meaning assigned by section 122.6) of an individual at the end of the year and at the beginning of the particular month, of that individual's liability under this Part for the year that arose during the particular month, as the case may be, if that total were calculated by reference to the information provided

exceeds

(ii) the amount that is deemed by subsection 122.61(1) to be an overpayment on account of the liability of that person or that individual, as the case may be, under this Part for the year that arose during the particular month,

(*c*.1) the amount, if any, by which

(i) the total of all amounts each of which is an amount that would be deemed by section 122.5 to be paid by that person during a month specified for the year or, where that person is the qualified relation of an individual in relation to that specified month (within the meaning assigned by subsection 122.5(1)), by that individual, if that total were calculated by reference to the information provided in the person's return of income (within the meaning assigned by subsection 122.5(1)) for the year

exceeds

(ii) the total of all amounts each of which is an amount that is deemed by section 122.5 to be paid by that person or by an individual of whom the person is the qualified relation in relation to a month specified for the year (within the meaning assigned to subsection 122.5(1)),

(*c*.2) the amount, if any, by which

(i) the amount that would be deemed under subsection 122.51(2) to be paid on account of the person's tax payable under this Part for the year if the amount were calculated by reference to the information provided in the return

exceeds

(ii) the amount that is deemed under subsection 122.51(2) to be paid on account of the person's tax payable under this Part for the year,

(*c*.3) the amount, if any, by which

(i) the total of all amounts each of which is an amount that would be deemed by subsection 122.7(2) or (3) to be a payment on account of the person's tax payable under this Part or another person's tax payable under this Part for the year if those amounts were calculated by reference to the information provided in the return

exceeds

(ii) the total of all amounts each of which is an amount that is deemed by subsection 122.7(2) or (3) to be a payment on account of the person's tax payable under this Part and, where applicable, the other person's tax payable under this Part for the year,

(*c*.4) the amount, if any, by which

(i) the total of all amounts each of which is an amount that would be deemed by section 122.8 to be paid by that person for the year or, where that person is the "qualified relation" of an individual for that year (within the meaning assigned by subsection 122.8(1)), by that individual, if that total were calculated by reference to the information provided in the person's "return of income" (within the meaning assigned by subsection 122.8(1)) for the year

exceeds

(ii) the total of all amounts each of which is an amount that is deemed by section 122.8 to be paid by that person or by an individual of whom the person is the "qualified relation" for the year (within the meaning assigned by subsection 122.8(1)),

(*c*.5) the amount, if any, by which

(i) the total of all amounts each of which is an amount that would be deemed by subsection 122.9(2) to have been paid on account of the person's tax payable under this Part for the year if that amount were calculated by reference to the person's claim for the year under the subsection

exceeds

(ii) the total of all amounts each of which is the amount that the person is entitled to claim for the year under subsection 122.9(2),

(*c*.6) the amount, if any, by which

(i) the total of all amounts each of which is an amount that would be deemed by subsection 122.91(1) to have been paid on account of the person's tax payable under this Part for the year if those amounts were calculated by reference to the information provided in the return

exceeds

(ii) the total of all amounts each of which is an amount that is deemed by subsection 122.91(1) to be a payment on account of the person's tax payable under this Part for the taxation year,

(*d*) the amount, if any, by which

(i) the amount that would be deemed by subsection 127.1(1) to be paid for the year by the person if that amount were calculated by reference to the information provided in the return or form filed for the year pursuant to that subsection

exceeds

(ii) the amount that is deemed by that subsection to be paid for the year by the person,

(*e*) the amount, if any, by which

(i) the amount that would be deemed by subsection 127.41(3) to have been paid for the year by the person if that amount were calculated by reference to the person's claim for the year under that subsection

exceeds

(ii) the maximum amount that the person is entitled to claim for the year under subsection 127.41(3),

(*f*) the amount, if any, by which

(i) the amount that would be deemed by subsection 125.4(3) to have been paid for the year by the person if that amount were calculated by reference to the information provided in the return filed for the year pursuant to that subsection

exceeds

(ii) the amount that is deemed by that subsection to be paid for the year by the person,

(*g*) the amount, if any, by which

(i) the amount that would be deemed by subsection 125.5(3) to have been paid for the year by the person if that amount were calculated by reference to the information provided in the return filed for the year pursuant to that subsection

exceeds

(ii) the amount that is deemed by that subsection to be paid for the year by the person, and

(*h*) the amount, if any, by which

(i) the amount that would be deemed by subsection 125.6(2) to have been paid for the year by the person if that amount were calculated by reference to the information provided in the return filed for the year pursuant to that subsection

exceeds

(ii) the amount that is deemed by that subsection to be paid for the year by the person.

History: S. 163(2)(*c.6*) was added by S.C. 2019, c. 29, s. 35(1), deemed to have come into force on January 1, 2019.

S. 163(2)(*h*) was added by S.C. 2019, c. 29, s. 35(2), deemed to have come into force on January 1, 2019.

S. 163(2)(*c.4*) was added by S.C. 2018, c. 27, s. 19(1), applicable to the 2018 and subsequent taxation years.

S. 163(2)(*c.4*) was repealed by S.C. 2016, c. 7, s. 43(2), in force January 1, 2017, and formerly read:

(*c.4*) the amount, if any, by which

(i) the total of all amounts each of which is an amount that would be deemed by subsections 122.8(2) or (3) to have been paid on account of the person's tax payable under this Part for the year if that amount were calculated by reference to the person's claim for the year under those subsections

exceeds

(ii) the total of all amounts each of which is the amount that the person is entitled to claim for the year under subsections 122.8(2) or (3),

S. 163(2)(*c.5*) was added by S.C. 2016, c. 7, s. 43(3), applicable to the 2016 and subsequent taxation years.

S. 163(2)(*c.4*) was added by S.C. 2014, c. 39, s. 59(1), applicable to the 2015 and subsequent taxation years.

S. 163(2)(*c.1*) was replaced by S.C. 2013, c. 34, s. 320(1), applicable to amounts deemed to be paid during months specified for the 2001 and subsequent taxation years. S. 163(2)(*c.1*) formerly read:

(*c.1*) the amount, if any, by which

(i) the total of all amounts each of which is an amount that would be deemed by section 122.5 to be paid by that person during a month specified for the year or, where that person is a qualified relation of an individual for the year (within the meaning assigned by subsection 122.5(1)), by that individual, as the case may be, if that total were calculated by reference to the information provided in the prescribed form filed for the year under section 122.5

exceeds

(ii) the total of all amounts each of which is an amount that is deemed under section 122.5 to be paid by that person or that qualified relation during a month specified for the year,

Related Sections: S. 122.91(1) Claimed amount; s. 125.6(2) Tax credit; s. 161(11) Interest on penalties; s. 163(2.1) Interpretation; s. 163.2 Misrepresentation of a tax matter by a third party; s. 239(1) Other offences and punishment; s. 239(3) Penalty on conviction.

Canadian Tax Foundation: Sorensen et al., *Non-Criminal Penalties Under the Income Tax Act*, 2013 Ontario Tax Conference 12:1–50; Burbank et al., *Comprehensive Discussion on Penalties*, 2013 Prairie Provinces Tax Conference 9:1–40; Campbell, *Application of the Charter to Civil Penalties in the Income Tax Act*, 2002 Canadian Tax Journal 1:1–22.

Tax Topics: No. 2394, Wilful Blindness in the Context of the Act: Penalties Levied Under S. 163(2) Do Not Require an Intention To Cheat, Merely a Failure to Inquire.

Income Tax Folios: *Secondary* — S3-F9-C1 Lottery Winnings, Miscellaneous Receipts, and Income (and Losses) from Crime.

Information Circulars: IC 73-10R3 Tax evasion; IC 00-1R4 Voluntary disclosures program.

SR&ED Publications: 96-05, Penalties Under Subsection 163(2).

Cases: The taxpayers, who retained representatives to prepare their tax returns, signed off on returns claiming significant losses which were denied. There was no question that false statements were made, and there were ample warning signs, making them wilfully blind and subject to penalties for gross negligence. *Torres v. The Queen*, 2014 DTC 1028 (T.C.C.), appeal dismissed 2015 FCA 60 (F.C.A.)

Unreported proceeds of fraud were added to the taxpayer's income for 2004 and 2005. Her criminal conviction was *prima facie* proof of the underlying facts. However, gross negligence penalties for 2004 were deleted since the indictment only referred to 2005 and the Minister did not provide other evidence to meet the onus of proving gross negligence for 2004. *Raposo v. The Queen*, 2013 DTC 1216 (T.C.C.).

While the taxpayer failed to report an obviously large profit, the taxpayer used a tax preparer who was very competent, despite the fact she was his spouse. Gross negligence penalties were not justified in the circumstances. *Hine v. The Queen*, 2012 DTC 1244 (T.C.C.)

The taxpayer transferred assets to a corporation under a section 85 rollover but failed to report the resulting capital gain. Penalties were not justified because the gross negligence of the taxpayer's outside experts was not attributable to him. The Minister had failed to show that the taxpayer had knowledge of the omission. *Findlay v. The Queen*, 2000 DTC 6345 (F.C.A.), reversing 97 DTC 1150 (T.C.C.)

A penalty imposed under s. 163(2) is a civil penalty and is not imposed pursuant to a criminal proceeding. Therefore, where tax evasion charges are also brought, the issue of whether the two proceedings constitute double punishment contrary to the Charter, does not arise. *The Queen v. Sharma*, 87 DTC 5424 (S.C. Ont.). See also *Sommers v. M.N.R.*, 91 DTC 656 (T.C.C.)

► 163(2.1) ◄

(2.1) Interpretation. For the purposes of subsection (2), the taxable income reported by a person in the person's return for a taxation year shall be deemed not to be less than nil and the "understatement of income" for a year of a person means the total of

(*a*) the amount, if any, by which

(i) the total of all amounts that were not reported by the person in the person's return and that were required to be included in computing the person's income for the year

exceeds

(ii) the total of such of the amounts deductible by the person in computing the person's income for the year under the provisions of this Act as were wholly applicable to the amounts referred to in subparagraph (i) and were not deducted by the person in computing the person's income for the year reported by the person in the person's return,

(*b*) the amount, if any, by which

(i) the total of all amounts deducted by the person in computing the person's income for the year reported by the person in the person's return

exceeds

(ii) the total of such of the amounts referred to in subparagraph (i) as were deductible by the person in computing the person's income for the year in accordance with the provisions of this Act, and

(*c*) the amount, if any, by which

(i) the total of all amounts deducted by the person (otherwise than by virtue of section 111) from the person's income for the purpose of computing the person's taxable income for the year reported by the person in the person's return

exceeds

(ii) the total of all amounts deductible by the person (otherwise than by virtue of section 111) from the person's income for the purpose of computing the person's taxable income for the year in accordance with the provisions of this Act.

SR&ED Publications: 96-05, Penalties Under Subsection 163(2).

▶ 163(2.2) ◀

(2.2) False statement or omission. Every person who, knowingly or under circumstances amounting to gross negligence, has made or has participated in, assented to or acquiesced in the making of, a false statement or omission in a renunciation that was to have been effective as of a particular date and that is purported to have been made under any of subsections 66(10) to (10.3), (12.6), (12.601) and (12.62), otherwise than because of the application of subsection 66(12.66), is liable to a penalty of 25% of the amount, if any, by which

(*a*) the amount set out in the renunciation in respect of Canadian exploration expenses, Canadian development expenses or Canadian oil and gas property expenses

exceeds

(*b*) the amount in respect of Canadian exploration expenses, Canadian development expenses or Canadian oil and gas property expenses, as the case may be, that the corporation was entitled under the applicable subsection to renounce as of that particular date.

Related Sections: S. 66.1(6), "Canadian exploration expense"; s. 66.2(5), "Canadian development expense"; s. 66.4(5), "Canadian oil and gas property expense"; s. 163(4) Effect of carryback of losses etc; s. 163.2 Misrepresentation of a tax matter by a third party; s. 239(3) Penalty on conviction.

▶ 163(2.21) ◀

(2.21) False statement or omissions with respect to look-back rule. A person is liable to the penalty determined under subsection (2.22) where the person,

(*a*) knowingly or under circumstances amounting to gross negligence has made or has participated in, assented to or acquiesced in the making of, a false statement or omission in a document required to be filed under subsection 66(12.73) in respect of a renunciation purported to have been made because of the application of subsection 66(12.66); or

(*b*) fails to file the document on or before the day that is 24 months after the day on or before which it was required to be filed.

▶ 163(2.22) ◀

(2.22) Penalty. For the purpose of subsection (2.21), the penalty to which a person is liable in respect of a document required to be filed under subsection 66(12.73) is equal to 25% of the amount, if any, by which

(*a*) the portion of the excess referred to in subsection 66(12.73) in respect of the document that was known or that ought to have been known by the person

exceeds

(*b*) where paragraph (2.21)(*b*) does not apply, the portion of the excess identified in the document, and

(*c*) in any other case, nil.

Related Sections: S. 163.2 Misrepresentation of a tax matter by a third party; s. 239(3) Penalty on conviction.

▶ 163(2.3) ◀

(2.3) Idem. Every person who, knowingly or under circumstances amounting to gross negligence, makes or participates in, assents to or acquiesces in the making of, a false statement or omission in a prescribed form required to be filed under subsection 66(12.691) or (12.701) is liable to a penalty of 25% of the amount, if any, by which

(*a*) the assistance required to be reported in respect of a person or partnership in the prescribed form

exceeds

(*b*) the assistance reported in the prescribed form in respect of the person or partnership.

Related Sections: S. 66(12.691) Filing re assistance; s. 66(12.701) Filing re assistance; s. 163.2 Misrepresentation of a tax matter by a third party; s. 239(3) Penalty on conviction.

▶ 163(2.4) ◀

(2.4) False statement or omission. Every person or partnership who, knowingly or under circumstances amounting to gross negligence, makes or participates in, assents to or acquiesces in, the making of a false statement or omission in a return is liable to a penalty of

(*a*) where the return is required to be filed under section 233.1, $24,000;

(*b*) if the return is required to be filed under section 233.2 in respect of a trust, the greater of

(i) $24,000, and

(ii) 5% of the total of all amounts each of which is the fair market value, at the time it was made, of a contribution of the person or partnership made to the trust before the end of the last taxation year of the trust in respect of which the return is required;

(*c*) where the return is required to be filed under section 233.3 for a taxation year or fiscal period, the greater of

(i) $24,000, and

(ii) 5% of the greatest of all amounts each of which is the total of the cost amounts to the person or partnership at any time in the year or period of a specified foreign property (as defined by subsection 233.3(1)(*a*) of the person or partnership in respect of which the false statement or omission is made;

(*d*) where the return is required to be filed under section 233.4 for a taxation year or fiscal period, the greater of

(i) $24,000, and

(ii) 5% of the greatest of all amounts each of which is the total of the cost amounts to the person or partnership at any time in the year or period of a property of the person or partnership that is a share of the capital stock or indebtedness of the foreign affiliate in respect of which the return is being filed; and

(*e*) where the return is required to be filed under section 233.6 for a taxation year or fiscal period, the greater of

(i) $2,500, and

(ii) 5% of the total of

(A) all amounts each of which is the fair market value of a property that is distributed to the person or partnership in the year or period by the trust and in respect of which the false statement or omission is made, and

(B) all amounts each of which is the greatest unpaid principal amount of a debt that is owing to the trust by the person or partnership in the year or period and in respect of which the false statement or omission is made.

History: S. 163(2.4)(*b*) was replaced by S.C. 2013, c. 34, s. 18(1), applicable to taxation years that end after 2006. Paragraph 163(2.4)(*b*) also applies to returns in respect of an earlier taxation year of a taxpayer if subsection 94(1) applies to that earlier taxation year of the taxpayer [should be 94(3) – CCH]. S. 163(2.4)(*b*) formerly read:

(*b*) where the return is required to be filed under section 233.2, the greater of

(i) $24,000, and

(ii) 5% of the total of all amounts each of which is the fair market value of property transferred or loaned (determined as of the time of the transfer or loan) because of which there would, if no other transfer or loan were taken into account, be an obligation to file the return;

Related Sections: S. 163.2 Misrepresentation of a tax matter by a third party; s. 239(3) Penalty on conviction.

Information Circulars: IC 00-1R4 Voluntary disclosures program.

► 163(2.41) ◄

(2.41) Application to trust contributions. In subparagraph (2.4)(*b*)(ii), subsections 94(1), (2) and (9) apply.

History: S. 163(2.41) was added by S.C. 2013, c. 34, s. 18(2), applicable to taxation years that end after 2006. Subsection 163(2.41) also applies to returns in respect of an earlier taxation year of a taxpayer if subsection 94(1) applies to that earlier taxation year of the taxpayer [should be 94(3) – CCH].

► 163(2.5) ◄

(2.5) Shares or debt owned by controlled foreign affiliate. For the purpose of paragraph (2.4)(*d*),

(*a*) shares or indebtedness owned by a controlled foreign affiliate of a person or partnership are deemed to be owned by the person or partnership; and

(*b*) the cost amount at any time of such shares or indebtedness to the person or partnership is deemed to be equal to 20% of the cost amount at that time to the controlled foreign affiliate of the shares or indebtedness.

► 163(2.6) ◄

(2.6) Application to partnerships. For the purposes of paragraph (2.4)(*d*) and subsection (2.5), in determining whether a non-resident corporation or trust is a foreign affiliate or a controlled foreign affiliate of a partnership

(*a*) the definitions "direct equity percentage" and "equity percentage" in subsection 95(4) shall be read as if a partnership were a person; and

(*b*) the definitions "controlled foreign affiliate" and "foreign affiliate" in subsection 95(1) shall be read as if a partnership were a taxpayer resident in Canada.

► 163(2.7) ◄

(2.7) Application to partnerships. For the purpose of subsection (2.4), each act or omission of a member of a partnership in respect of an information return required to be filed by the partnership under section 233.3, 233.4 or 233.6 is deemed to be an act or omission of the partnership in respect of the return.

► 163(2.8) ◄

(2.8) Application to members of partnerships. For the purposes of this subsection and subsection (2.7), a person who is a member of a partnership that is a member of another partnership is deemed to be a member of the other partnership.

► 163(2.9) ◄

(2.9) Partnership liable to penalty. If a partnership is liable to a penalty under subsection (2.4) or section 163.2, 237.1 or 237.3, sections 152, 158 to 160.1, 161 and 164 to 167 and Division J apply, with any changes that the circumstances require, in respect of the penalty as if the partnership were a corporation.

History: S. 163(2.9) was replaced by S.C. 2013, c. 34, s. 320(2), applicable in respect of avoidance transactions that are entered into after 2010 or that are part of a series of transactions that began before 2011 and is completed after 2010. S. 163(2.9) formerly read:

(2.9) *Where partnership liable to penalty.* Where a partnership is liable to a penalty under subsection (2.4) or section 163.2 or 237.1, sections 152, 158 to 160.1, 161 and 164 to 167 and Division J apply, with any changes that the circumstances require, in respect of the penalty as if the partnership were a corporation.

► 163(2.91) ◄

(2.91) Application to non-resident trusts. For the purposes of this subsection, paragraph (2.4)(*d*) and subsection (2.5),

(*a*) a non-resident trust is deemed to be a controlled foreign affiliate of each beneficiary of which the trust is a controlled foreign affiliate for the purpose of section 233.4;

(*b*) the trust is deemed to be a non-resident corporation having a capital stock of a single class divided into 100 issued shares;

(*c*) each beneficiary under the trust is deemed to own at any time the number of the issued shares of the corporation that is equal to the proportion of 100 that

(i) the fair market value at that time of the beneficiary's beneficial interest in the trust

is of

(ii) the fair market value at that time of all beneficial interests in the trust; and

(*d*) the cost amount to a beneficiary at any time of a share of the corporation is deemed to be equal to the amount determined by the formula

$$A/B$$

where

A is the fair market value at that time of the beneficiary's beneficial interest in the trust, and

B is the number of shares deemed under paragraph (*c*) to be owned at that time by the beneficiary in respect of the corporation.

► 163(3) ◄

(3) Burden of proof in respect of penalties. Where, in an appeal under this Act, a penalty assessed by the Minister under this section or section 163.2 is in issue, the burden of establishing the facts justifying the assessment of the penalty is on the Minister.

Related Sections: S. 248(1), "amount", "assessment"; ITAR s. 62(3) Penalties.

Cases: While the burden of proof of willful or gross negligence with respect to penalties assessed under s. 163(3) clearly lies with the Minister, this does not alter the usual burden on the taxpayer to show that the Minister's assessment is wrong. *Can-Am Realty Ltd. v. the Queen*, 94 DTC 6069 (F.C.T.D.).

► 163(4) ◄

(4) Effect of carryback of losses etc. In determining under subsection (2.1) the understatement of income for a taxation year of a person, the following amounts shall be deemed not to be deductible or excludable in computing the person's income for the year:

(*a*) any amount that may be deducted under section 41 in respect of the person's listed-personal-property loss for a subsequent taxation year;

(*b*) any amount that may be excluded from the person's income because of section 49 in respect of the exercise of any option in a subsequent taxation year;

(*b*.1) any amount that may be deducted under subsection 147.2(4) in computing the person's income for the year because of the application of subsection 147.2(6) as a result of the person's death in the subsequent taxation year; and

(*c*) any amount that may be deducted in computing the person's income for the year because of an election made under paragraph 164(6)(*c*) or (*d*) in a subsequent taxation year by the person's legal representative.

Proposed Amendment

Legislative Proposals Relating to Income Tax Act and Other Legislation (July 27, 2018)

Section 163 of the Act is amended by adding the following after subsection (4):

(5) False statement or omission — trust return. A person or partnership is liable to a penalty if the person or partnership

(*a*) knowingly or under circumstances amounting to gross negligence

(i) makes — or participates in, assents to or acquiesces in, the making of — a false statement or omission in a return of income of a trust that is not subject to one of the exceptions listed in paragraphs 150(1.2)(*a*) to (*n*) for a taxation year, or

(ii) fails to file a return described in subparagraph (i); or

(*b*) fails to comply with a demand under subsection 150(2) or 231.2(1) to file a return described in subparagraph (*a*)(i).

(6) False statement or omission — trust return. The amount of the penalty to which the person or partnership is liable under subsection (5) is equal to the greater of

(*a*) $2,500; and

(*b*) 5% of the highest amount at any time in the year that is equal to the total fair market value of all the property held by the trust referred to in subsection (5) at that time.

Applicable: To taxation years that end after December 30, 2021.

SECTION 163.1: Penalty for late or deficient instalments

Every person who fails to pay all or any part of an instalment of tax for a taxation year on or before the day on or before which the instalment is required by this Part to be paid is liable to a penalty equal to 50% of the amount, if any, by which

(*a*) the interest payable by the person under section 161 in respect of all instalments for the year

exceeds the greater of

(*b*) $1,000, and

(*c*) 25% of the interest that would have been payable by the person under section 161 in respect of all instalments for the year if no instalment had been made for that year.

Related Sections: S. 239.1 [Electronic suppression of sales — Offences].

Information Circulars: IC 07-1 Taxpayer Relief Provisions; IC 00-1R4 Voluntary disclosures program.

Misrepresentation of a Tax Matter by a Third Party

SECTION 163.2: [Misrepresentation of a tax matter by a third party]

► 163.2(1) ◄

(1) Definitions. The definitions in this subsection apply in this section.

Canadian Tax Foundation: Rickards, *Civil Penalties — Evolving CCRA Administrative Positions*, 2001 British Columbia Tax Conference 16:1–24; Pustogorodsky, *So Now What? Contesting the Imposition of Civil Penalties*, 2001 Prairie Provinces Tax Conference 8:A1-B87; Gibson, *Strategies for Reducing the Risk of a Civil Penalty Assessment*, 2001 Prairie Provinces Tax Conference 7:1–21; Watkins et al., *Civil Penalties: Case Studies*, 2000 Conference Report 19:2–28; Mathew, *Civil Penalties — How Pervasive?*, 2000 British Columbia Tax Conference 15:1–28; Nichols, *Third Party Penalties*, 2000 Ontario Tax Conference 3:1–59; Nichols and Szyc, *Civil Penalties: Round Table Panel — Case Studies*, 2000 Ontario Tax Conference 2:1–17; McNary, *The New Civil Penalty Provisions — Professional Liability for Culpable Conduct*, 2000 Prairie Provinces Tax Conference 4:1–42; Nichols, *Civil Penalties for Third Parties*, 1999 Ontario Tax Conference 1:1–80; Heinrich, *The Tax Advisor at Risk: Civil Penalties and Criminal Sanctions*, 1999 British Columbia Tax Conference 11:1–48.

"culpable conduct" — "culpable conduct" means conduct, whether an act or a failure to act, that

(*a*) is tantamount to intentional conduct;

(*b*) shows an indifference as to whether this Act is complied with; or

(*c*) shows a wilful, reckless or wanton disregard of the law.

"entity" — "entity" includes an association, a corporation, a fund, a joint venture, an organization, a partnership, a syndicate and a trust.

"excluded activity" — "excluded activity", in respect of a false statement, means the activity of

(*a*) promoting or selling (whether as principal or agent or directly or indirectly) an arrangement, an entity, a plan, a property or a scheme (in this definition referred to as the "arrangement") where it can reasonably be considered that

(i) subsection 66(12.68) applies to the arrangement,

(ii) the definition "tax shelter" in subsection 237.1(1) applies to a person's interest in the arrangement, or

(iii) one of the main purposes for a person's participation in the arrangement is to obtain a tax benefit; or

(*b*) accepting (whether as principal or agent or directly or indirectly) consideration in respect of the promotion or sale of an arrangement.

"false statement" — "false statement" includes a statement that is misleading because of an omission from the statement.

"gross compensation" — "gross compensation" of a particular person at any time, in respect of a false statement that could be used by or on behalf of another person, means all amounts to which the particular person, or any person not dealing at arm's length with the particular person, is entitled, either before or after that time and either absolutely or contingently, to receive or obtain in respect of the statement.

"gross entitlements" —"gross entitlements" of a person at any time, in respect of a planning activity or a valuation activity of the person, means all amounts to which the person, or another person not dealing at arm's length with the person, is entitled, either before or after that time and either absolutely or contingently, to receive or obtain in respect of the activity.

"participate" —"participate" includes

(*a*) to cause a subordinate to act or to omit information; and

(*b*) to know of, and to not make a reasonable attempt to prevent, the participation by a subordinate in an act or an omission of information.

"person" —"person" includes a partnership.

"planning activity" —"planning activity" includes

(*a*) organizing or creating, or assisting in the organization or creation of, an arrangement, an entity, a plan or a scheme; and

(*b*) participating, directly or indirectly, in the selling of an interest in, or the promotion of, an arrangement, an entity, a plan, a property or a scheme.

"subordinate" —"subordinate", in respect of a particular person, includes any other person over whose activities the particular person has direction, supervision or control whether or not the other person is an employee of the particular person or of another person, except that, if the particular person is a member of a partnership, the other person is not a subordinate of the particular person solely because the particular person is a member of the partnership.

"tax benefit" —"tax benefit" means a reduction, avoidance or deferral of tax or other amount payable under this Act or an increase in a refund of tax or other amount under this Act.

"valuation activity" —"valuation activity" of a person means anything done by the person in determining the value of a property or a service.

► 163.2(2) ◄

(2) Penalty for misrepresentations in tax planning arrangements. Every person who makes or furnishes, participates in the making of or causes another person to make or furnish a statement that the person knows, or would reasonably be expected to know but for circumstances amounting to culpable conduct, is a false statement that could be used by another person (in subsections (6) and (15) referred to as the "other person") for a purpose of this Act is liable to a penalty in respect of the false statement.

Editorial Note: This controversial provision imposes harsh penalties on advisers who participate in the making or furnishing of false statements in circumstances amounting to "culpable conduct", the definition of which is based on court cases involving the meaning of gross negligence under the (50%-of-tax) penalty in s. 163(2). Subsections 163.2(2) and (4) are intended to apply to planning and valuation, and compliance activities, respectively. The penalties for the former can be based on the person's "gross entitlement", whereas the latter can be based on the s. 163(2) penalty of the taxpayer, to a ceiling of $100,000 plus the person's "gross compensation" in respect of the false statement.

Exceptions may apply to good faith reliance on information (s. 163.2(6)), secretarial or clerical services other than bookkeeping (s. 163.2(9)) and certain employees (s. 163.2(15)). However, the good faith reliance exception does not apply to an "excluded activity", which includes certain sales and promotion activities.

While the provisions have been referred to by the Department of Finance as "civil penalties", commentators have indicated that the penalties may be criminal in nature, so that Charter of Rights and Freedoms protections may apply, and so on. This was the finding of the Tax Court of Canada in *Guindon v. The Queen*, 2012 DTC 1283, which has been overturned by the Federal Court of Appeal (2013 DTC 5113); affirmed 2015 DTC 5086 (S.C.C.). The Federal Court of Appeal held that the Tax Court did not have jurisdiction to find that s. 163.2 created an offence triggering Charter rights because no notice of constitutional question had been served. Federal Court of Appeal (and the Supreme Court) also found that the assessment of a penalty under s. 163.2 is not the equivalent of being charged with a criminal offence.

Per s. 163.2(10) and (11), there would be a "reverse onus rule" whereby valuations in the course of an "excluded activity" are deemed to be "culpable conduct", if outside certain prescribed limits, unless otherwise established (this would not necessarily mean that there is no "culpable conduct" if the valuation is within the limits). However, as no regulations have been proposed for this provision, it is currently not in force, and it is not clear whether these provisions will ever become operative.

See s. 163.2(1) for definitions of "culpable conduct", "excluded activity", "gross compensation", and "gross entitlements".

These penalties are separate to those imposed in section 237.3, which imposes mandatory reporting requirements in respect of transactions with certain "hallmarks" which are common in aggressive tax-related transactions.

Related Sections: S. 18(1)(*t*) Payments under Act; s. 163(2) False statements or omissions; s. 163(2.9) Where partnership liable to penalty; s. 163(3) Burden of proof in respect of penalties; s. 188.1(9) False information; s. 188.1(10) Maximum amount; s. 239(3) Penalty on conviction.

Canadian Tax Foundation: Campbell, *Current Cases: Tax Court of Canada — Moving the Goalposts: The Distinction Between Civil and Criminal Penalties (Guindon v. The Queen, 2012 TCC 287)*, 2013 Canadian Tax Journal 1:193–198; Sorensen et al., *Non-Criminal Penalties Under the Income Tax Act*, 2013 Ontario Tax Conference 12:1–50; Burbank et al., *Comprehensive Discussion on Penalties*, 2013 Prairie Provinces Tax Conference 9:1–40; Doobay and MacPherson, *Guindon Penalty Upheld*, 2013 Canadian Tax Highlights 21(7):8–9; MacKnight, *Adviser Penalties Under Section 163.2*, 2013 Tax for the Owner-Manager 13(4):2–3; Doucette, *Advisor Penalties Revived by FCA*, 2013 Canadian Tax Focus 3(3):4–5; Hurowitz and Jung, *Due Diligence in the Tax Practice — What You Need to Do to Protect Yourself and Your Client*, 2012 Ontario Tax Conference 13:1–30; Clarke, *Civil Penalties*, 2012 Tax Dispute Resolution, Compliance and Adminstration Conference 20:1–28; Campbell, *Application of the Charter to Civil Penalties in the Income Tax Act*, 2002 Canadian Tax Journal 1:1–22; Innes and Burke, *Adviser Penalties: How Will the Courts Construe Section 163.2?*, 2001 Conference Report 37:1–38; Mitchell, *Civil Penalties: A Wolf in Sheep's Clothing?*, 2000 Conference Report 16:1–8; Innes and Williams, *Penalizing Tax Planners: Section 163.2 and the Role of the Courts*, 2001 Ontario Tax Conference 7:1–33.

Tax Profile: November 2004 — Application of Penalties.

Tax Topics: No. 1700, 2004 Canadian Tax Foundation Conference - CRA Round Table; No. 1531, Civil Penalties Roundtable.

Income Tax Technical News: Issue No. 34, Third Party Penalties.

Information Circulars: IC 01-1 Third Party Civil Penalties.

► 163.2(3) ◄

(3) Amount of penalty. The penalty to which a person is liable under subsection (2) in respect of a false statement is

(*a*) where the statement is made in the course of a planning activity or a valuation activity, the greater of $1,000 and the total of the person's gross entitlements, at the time at which the notice of assessment of the penalty is sent to the person, in respect of the planning activity and the valuation activity; and

(*b*) in any other case, $1,000.

► 163.2(4) ◄

(4) Penalty for participating in a misrepresentation. Every person who makes, or participates in, assents to or acquiesces in the making of, a statement to, or by or on behalf of, another person (in this subsection, subsections (5) and (6), paragraph (12)(*c*) and subsection (15) referred to as the "other person") that the person knows, or would reasonably be expected to know but for circumstances amounting to culpable conduct, is a false statement that could be used by or on behalf of the other person for a purpose of this Act is liable to a penalty in respect of the false statement.

Editorial Note: See the editorial note to s. 163.2(2).

Related Sections: S. 18(1)(*t*) Payments under Act; s. 163(2) False statements or omissions; s. 163(2.9) Where partnership liable to penalty; s. 163(3) Burden of proof in respect of penalties; s. 188.1(9) False information; s. 188.1(10) Maximum amount; s. 239(3) Penalty on conviction.

Canadian Tax Foundation: Doobay, *SCC Upholds Guindon Penalty*, 2015 Canadian Tax Highlights 23(8):4; Sorensen, *Current Cases: Federal Court of Appeal — Third-Party Penalties Revisited (Canada v. Guindon, 2013 FCA 153)*, 2013 Canadian Tax Journal 4:1131–1139; Friedlan, *Civil Penalties: Section 163.2 is a Criminal Provision*, 2013 Tax for the Owner-Manager 13(1):1–2; Hurowitz and Jung, *Due Diligence in the Tax Practice — What You Need to Do to Protect Yourself and Your Client*, 2012 Ontario Tax Conference 13:1–30; MacKnight, *Recent Cases*, 2012 Ontario Tax Conference 2A:1–21.

Tax Profile: November 2004 — Application of Penalties.

Tax Topics: No. 2119, Crime and (No) Punishment: *Julie Guindon v. Her Majesty The Queen*; No. 1566, Third Party Civil Penalties: Caution Needed When Filing T2 and T106 Returns; No. 1531, Civil Penalties Roundtable.

Income Tax Technical News: Issue No. 34, Third Party Penalties; Issue No. 32, Application of Penalties.

Information Circulars: IC 00-1R4 Voluntary disclosures program.

► 163.2(5) ◄

(5) Amount of penalty. The penalty to which a person is liable under subsection (4) in respect of a false statement is the greater of

(*a*) $1,000, and

(*b*) the lesser of

(i) the penalty to which the other person would be liable under subsection 163(2) if the other person made the statement in a return filed for the purposes of this Act and knew that the statement was false, and

(ii) the total of $100,000 and the person's gross compensation, at the time at which the notice of assessment of the penalty is sent to the person, in respect of the false statement that could be used by or on behalf of the other person.

► 163.2(6) ◄

(6) Reliance in good faith. For the purposes of subsections (2) and (4), a person (in this subsection and in subsection (7) referred to as the "advisor") who acts on behalf of the other person is not considered to have acted in circumstances amounting to culpable conduct in respect of the false statement referred to in subsection (2) or (4) solely because the advisor relied, in good faith, on information provided to the advisor by or on behalf of the other person or, because of such reliance, failed to verify, investigate or correct the information.

Editorial Note: An adviser will not be considered to act in circumstances amounting to "culpable conduct" solely because the person relies "in good faith" on information provided to the adviser or, because of such reliance, fails to verify, investigate or correct the information. However, per s. 163.2(7), this exclusion does not apply in the course of an "excluded activity" which (per s. 163.2(1)) pertains to:

(a) promoting or selling arrangements/plans (etc.) where it can reasonably considered that:

(i) s. 66(12.68) applies in respect of "flow-through shares";

(ii) the definition of "tax shelter" in s. 237.1(1) applies;

(iii) one of the main purposes for a person's participation in the arrangement is to obtain a "tax benefit", the definition of which is similar to GAAR in s. 245(1), or

(b) accepting consideration in respect of the promotion or sale of an arrangement/plan (etc.).

Related Sections: S. 66(12.68) Filing selling instruments; s. 237.1 Tax shelters; s. 245 General anti-avoidance rule.

Tax Topics: No. 1531, Civil Penalties Roundtable.

► 163.2(7) ◄

(7) Non-application of subsection (6). Subsection (6) does not apply in respect of a statement that an advisor makes (or participates in, assents to or acquiesces in the making of) in the course of an excluded activity.

► 163.2(8) ◄

(8) False statements in respect of a particular arrangement. For the purpose of applying this section (other than subsections (4) and (5)),

(*a*) where a person makes or furnishes, participates in the making of or causes another person to make or furnish two or more false statements, the false statements are deemed to be one false statement if the statements are made or furnished in the course of

(i) one or more planning activities that are in respect of a particular arrangement, entity, plan, property or scheme, or

(ii) a valuation activity that is in respect of a particular property or service; and

(*b*) for greater certainty, a particular arrangement, entity, plan, property or scheme includes an arrangement, an entity, a plan, a property or a scheme in respect of which

(i) an interest is required to have, or has, an identification number issued under section 237.1 that is the same number as the number that applies to each other interest in the property,

(ii) a selling instrument in respect of flow-through shares is required to be filed with the Minister because of subsection 66(12.68), or

(iii) one of the main purposes for a person's participation in the arrangement, entity, plan or scheme, or a person's acquisition of the property, is to obtain a tax benefit.

Editorial Note: Two or more false statements are deemed to be one false statement if made in the course of either one or more planning activities that are in respect of a particular arrangement/plan (etc.) or a valuation activity in respect of a particular property or service. Apparently, it was not intended that this relieving provision would apply to those who counsel tax return filing positions, who would therefore be liable for each false statement in a tax return.

Tax Topics: No. 1531, Civil Penalties Roundtable.

► 163.2(9) ◄

(9) Clerical services. For the purposes of this section, a person is not considered to have made or furnished, or participated in, assented to or acquiesced in the making of, a false statement solely because the person provided clerical services (other than bookkeeping services) or secretarial services with respect to the statement.

► 163.2(10) ◄

(10) Valuations. Notwithstanding subsections (6) and 163(3), a statement as to the value of a property or a service (which value is in this subsection referred to as the "stated value"), made by the person who opined on the stated value or by a person in the course of an excluded activity is deemed to be a statement that the person would reasonably be expected to know, but for circumstances amounting to culpable conduct, is a false statement if the stated value is

(*a*) less than the product obtained when the prescribed percentage for the property or service is multiplied by the fair market value of the property or service; or (*b*) greater than the product obtained when the prescribed percentage for the property or service is multiplied by the fair market value of the property or service.

Editorial Note: See the editorial note to s. 163.2(2).

Tax Topics: No. 1531, Civil Penalties Roundtable.

► 163.2(11) ◄

(11) Exception. Subsection (10) does not apply to a person in respect of a statement as to the value of a property or a service if the person establishes that the stated value was reasonable in the circumstances and that the statement was made in good faith and, where applicable, was not based on one or more assumptions that the person knew or would reasonably be expected to know, but for circumstances amounting to culpable conduct, were unreasonable or misleading in the circumstances.

► 163.2(12) ◄

(12) Special rules. For the purpose of applying this section,

(*a*) where a person is assessed a penalty that is referred to in subsection (2) the amount of which is based on the person's gross entitlements at any time in respect of a planning activity or a valuation activity and another assessment of the penalty is made at a later time,

(i) if the person's gross entitlements in respect of the activity are greater at that later time, the assessment of the penalty made at that later time is deemed to be an assessment of a separate penalty, and

(ii) in any other case, the notice of assessment of the penalty sent before that later time is deemed not to have been sent;

(*b*) a person's gross entitlements at any time in respect of a planning activity or a valuation activity, in the course of which the person makes or furnishes, participates in the making of or causes another person to make or furnish a false statement, shall exclude the total of all amounts each of which is the amount of a penalty (other than a penalty the assessment of which is void because of subsection (13)) determined under paragraph (3)(*a*) in respect of the false statement for which notice of the assessment was sent to the person before that time; and

(*c*) where a person is assessed a penalty that is referred to in subsection (4), the person's gross compensation at any time in respect of the false statement that could be used by or on behalf of the other person shall exclude the total of all amounts each of which is the amount of a penalty (other than a penalty the assessment of which is void because of subsection (13)) determined under subsection (5) to the extent that the false statement was used by or on behalf of that other person and for which notice of the assessment was sent to the person before that time.

► 163.2(13) ◄

(13) Assessment void. For the purposes of this Act, if an assessment of a penalty that is referred to in subsection (2) or (4) is vacated, the assessment is deemed to be void.

► 163.2(14) ◄

(14) Maximum penalty. A person who is liable at any time to a penalty under both subsections (2) and (4) in respect of the same false statement is liable to pay a penalty that is not more than the greater of

(*a*) the total amount of the penalties to which the person is liable at that time under subsection (2) in respect of the statement, and

(*b*) the total amount of the penalties to which the person is liable at that time under subsection (4) in respect of the statement.

► 163.2(15) ◄

(15) Employees. Where an employee (other than a specified employee or an employee engaged in an excluded activity) is employed by the other person referred to in subsections (2) and (4),

(*a*) subsections (2) to (5) do not apply to the employee to the extent that the false statement could be used by or on behalf of the other person for a purpose of this Act; and

(*b*) the conduct of the employee is deemed to be that of the other person for the purposes of applying subsection 163(2) to the other person.

Canadian Tax Foundation: Carr et al., *The New Civil Penalty Proposals*, 1999 Conference Report 18:1–22.

SECTION 163.3: [Electronic suppression of sales]

► 163.3(1) ◄

(1) Definitions. The following definitions apply in this section.

History: S. 163.3(1) was added by S.C. 2013, c. 40, s. 71(1), in force January 1, 2014.

"electronic cash register" — "electronic cash register" means a device that keeps a register or supporting documents through the means of an electronic device or computer system designed to record transaction data or any other electronic point-of-sale system.

"electronic suppression of sales device" — "electronic suppression of sales device" means

(*a*) a software program that falsifies the records of electronic cash registers, including transaction data and transaction reports; or

(*b*) a hidden programming option, whether preinstalled or installed at a later time, embedded in the operating system of an electronic cash register or hardwired into the electronic cash register that

(i) may be used to create a virtual second till, or

(ii) may eliminate or manipulate transaction records, which may or may not be preserved in digital formats, in order to represent the actual or manipulated record of transactions in the electronic cash register.

"service" — "service" has the same meaning as in subsection 123(1) of the *Excise Tax Act*.

► 163.3(2) ◄

(2) Penalty — use. Every person that uses, or that knowingly, or under circumstances attributable to neglect, carelessness or wilful default, participates in, assents to or acquiesces in the use of, an electronic suppression of sales device or a similar device or software in relation to records that are required to be kept by any person under section 230 is liable to a penalty of

(*a*) unless paragraph (*b*) applies, $5,000; or

(*b*) $50,000 if the action of the person occurs after the Minister has assessed a penalty payable by the person under this section or section 285.01 of the *Excise Tax Act*.

Editorial Note: Section 163.3 sets out administrative penalties related to the use, possession, manufacture, or sale of electronic suppression of sales software or devices, designed to falsify or manipulate transactional records. Penalties may be imposed on any person who uses such devices or who acquiesces in the use of such devices by reason of carelessness or wilful default. A defense of due diligence is available only with respect to penalties assessed for the possession, manufacture, or sale of subject devices. These penalties may be assessed at any time. Similar additional penalties may also be assessed under the *Excise Tax Act.*

History: S. 163.3(2) was added by S.C. 2013, c. 40, s. 71(1), in force January 1, 2014.

▶ 163.3(3) ◀

(3) Penalty — possession. Every person that acquires or possesses an electronic suppression of sales device or a right in respect of an electronic suppression of sales device that is, or is intended to be, capable of being used in relation to records that are required to be kept by any person under section 230 is liable to a penalty of

(*a*) unless paragraph (*b*) applies, $5,000; or

(*b*) $50,000 if the action of the person occurs after the Minister has assessed a penalty payable by the person under this section or section 285.01 of the *Excise Tax Act*.

History: S. 163.3(3) was added by S.C. 2013, c. 40, s. 71(1), in force January 1, 2014.

▶ 163.3(4) ◀

(4) Penalty — manufacturing or making available. Every person that designs, develops, manufactures, possesses for sale, offers for sale, sells, transfers or otherwise makes available to another person, or that supplies installation, upgrade or maintenance services for, an electronic suppression of sales device that is, or is intended to be, capable of being used in relation to records that are required to be kept by any person under section 230 is liable to a penalty of

(*a*) unless paragraph (*b*) or (*c*) applies, $10,000;

(*b*) unless paragraph (*c*) applies, $50,000 if the action of the person occurs after the Minister has assessed a penalty payable by the person under subsection (2) or (3) or subsection 285.01(2) or (3) of the *Excise Tax Act*; or

(*c*) $100,000 if the action of the person occurs after the Minister has assessed a penalty payable by the person under this subsection or subsection 285.01(4) of the *Excise Tax Act*.

History: S. 163.3(4) was added by S.C. 2013, c. 40, s. 71(1), in force January 1, 2014.

▶ 163.3(5) ◀

(5) Assessment. The Minister may at any time assess a taxpayer in respect of any penalty payable by a person under subsections (2) to (4), and the provisions of this Division apply, with any modifications that the circumstances require, in respect of an assessment made under subsections (2) to (4) as though it had been made under section 152.

History: S. 163.3(5) was added by S.C. 2013, c. 40, s. 71(1), in force January 1, 2014.

▶ 163.3(6) ◀

(6) Limitation. Despite section 152, if at any time the Minister assesses a penalty payable by a person under subsections (2) to (4), the Minister is not to assess, at or after that time, another penalty payable by the person under subsections (2) to (4) that is in respect of an action of the person that occurred before that time.

History: S. 163.3(6) was added by S.C. 2013, c. 40, s. 71(1), in force January 1, 2014.

▶ 163.3(7) ◀

(7) Certain defences not available. Except as otherwise provided in subsection (8), a person does not have a defence in relation to a penalty assessed under subsections (2) to (4) by reason that the person exercised due diligence to prevent the action from occurring.

History: S. 163.3(7) was added by S.C. 2013, c. 40, s. 71(1), in force January 1, 2014.

▶ 163.3(8) ◀

(8) Due diligence. A person is not liable for a penalty under subsection (3) or (4) in respect of an action of the person if the person exercised the degree of care, diligence and skill that a reasonably prudent person would have exercised in comparable circumstances to prevent the action from occurring.

History: S. 163.3(8) was added by S.C. 2013, c. 40, s. 71(1), in force January 1, 2014.

▶ 163.3(9) ◀

(9) Assessment vacated. For the purposes of subsections (2) to (8), if an assessment of a penalty under subsections (2) to (4) is vacated, the penalty is deemed to have never been assessed.

History: S. 163.3(9) was added by S.C. 2013, c. 40, s. 71(1), in force January 1, 2014.

Refunds

SECTION 164: Refunds

▶ 164(1) ◀

(1) Refunds. If the return of a taxpayer's income for a taxation year has been made within 3 years from the end of the year, the Minister

(*a*) may,

(i) before sending the notice of assessment for the year, where the taxpayer is, for any purpose of the definition "refundable investment tax credit" (as defined in subsection 127.1(2)), a qualifying corporation (as defined in that subsection) and claims in its return of income for the year to have paid an amount on account of its tax payable under this Part for the year because of subsection 127.1(1) in respect of its refundable investment tax credit (as defined in subsection 127.1(2)), refund all or part of any amount claimed in the return as an overpayment for the year, not exceeding the amount by which the total determined under paragraph (*f*) of the definition "refundable investment tax credit" in subsection 127.1(2) in respect of the taxpayer for the year exceeds the total determined under paragraph (*g*) of that definition in respect of the taxpayer for the year,

(ii) before sending the notice of assessment for the year, where the taxpayer is a "qualified corporation" (as defined in subsection 125.4(1)), an "eligible production corporation" (as defined in subsection 125.5(1)) or a "qualifying journalism organization" (as defined in subsection 125.6(1)) and an amount is deemed under subsection 125.4(3), 125.5(3) or 125.6(2) to have been paid on account of its tax payable under this Part for the year, refund all or part of any amount claimed in the return as an overpayment for the year, not exceeding the total of those amounts so deemed to have been paid, and

(iii) on or after sending the notice of assessment for the year, refund any overpayment for the year, to the extent that the overpayment was not refunded pursuant to subparagraph (i) or (ii); and

(*b*) shall, with all due dispatch, make the refund referred to in subparagraph (*a*)(iii) after sending the notice of assessment if application for it is made in writing by the taxpayer within the period within which the Minister would be allowed under subsection 152(4) to assess tax payable under this Part by the taxpayer for the year if that subsection were read without reference to paragraph 152(4)(*a*).

History: S. 164(1)(*a*)(ii) was replaced by S.C. 2019, c. 29, s. 36(1), deemed to have come into force on January 1, 2019, and formerly read:

(ii) before sending the notice of assessment for the year, where the taxpayer is a qualified corporation (as defined in subsection 125.4(1)) or an eligible production corporation (as defined in subsection 125.5(1)) and an amount is deemed under subsection 125.4(3) or 125.5(3) to have been paid on account of its tax payable under this Part for the year, refund all or part of any amount claimed in the return as an overpayment for the year, not exceeding the total of those amounts so deemed to have been paid, and

S. 164(1)(*a*) and (*b*) were replaced by S.C. 2010, c. 25, s. 42(1), in force on Royal Assent, December 15, 2010. S. 164(1)(*a*) and (*b*) formerly read:

(*a*) may,

(i) before mailing the notice of assessment for the year, where the taxpayer is, for any purpose of the definition "refundable investment tax credit" (as defined in subsection 127.1(2)), a qualifying corporation (as defined in that subsection) and claims in its return of income for the year to have paid an amount on account of its tax payable under this Part for the year because of subsection 127.1(1) in respect of its refundable investment tax credit (as defined in subsection 127.1(2)), refund all or part of any amount claimed in the return as an overpayment for the year, not exceeding the amount by which the total determined under paragraph (*f*) of the definition "refundable investment tax credit" in subsection 127.1(2) in respect of the taxpayer for the year exceeds the total determined under paragraph (*g*) of that definition in respect of the taxpayer for the year,

(ii) before mailing the notice of assessment for the year, where the taxpayer is a qualified corporation (as defined in subsection 125.4(1)) or an eligible production corporation (as defined in subsection 125.5(1)) and an amount is deemed under subsection 125.4(3) or 125.5(3) to have been paid on account of its tax payable under this Part for the year, refund all or part of any amount claimed in the return as an overpayment for the year, not exceeding the total of those amounts so deemed to have been paid, and

(iii) on or after mailing the notice of assessment for the year, refund any overpayment for the year, to the extent that the overpayment was not refunded pursuant to subparagraph (i) or (ii); and

(*b*) shall, with all due dispatch, make the refund referred to in subparagraph (*a*)(iii) after mailing the notice of assessment if application for it is made in writing by the taxpayer within the period within which the Minister would be allowed under subsection 152(4) to assess tax payable under this Part by the taxpayer for the year if that subsection were read without reference to paragraph 152(4)(*a*).

Related Sections: 125.6(1) "qualifying journalism organization"; 125.6(2) Tax credit; 144(9) Deduction for forfeited amounts; 164(7) Definition of "overpayment".

Tax Topics: No. 1902, Regulation 105 Withholding for Services Rendered By a Canadian Subcontractor.

Information Circulars: IC 75-7R3 Reassessment of a return of income; IC 07-1 Taxpayer relief provisions; IC 01-1 Third-party civil penalties.

Cases: The Tax Court of Canada lacked jurisdiction to hear an appeal for refund since the taxpayer was not seeking relief from an assessment, but rather the recovery of a debt allegedly owing. *Toner v. M.N.R.*, 90 DTC 1675 (T.C.C.)

The taxpayer failed to qualify for the refunds being sought where she had not filed returns for the taxation years in question within the requisite times. *Hughes v. The Queen*, 91 DTC 5290 (T.C.C.)

► 164(1.1) ◄

(1.1) Repayment on objections and appeals. Subject to subsection (1.2), where a taxpayer

(*a*) has under section 165 served a notice of objection to an assessment and the Minister has not within 120 days after the day of service confirmed or varied the assessment or made a reassessment in respect thereof, or

(*b*) has appealed from an assessment to the Tax Court of Canada,

and has applied in writing to the Minister for a payment or surrender of security, the Minister shall, where no authorization has been granted under subsection 225.2(2) in respect of the amount assessed, with all due dispatch repay all amounts paid on account of that amount or surrender security accepted therefor to the extent that

(*c*) the lesser of

(i) the total of the amounts so paid and the value of the security, and

(ii) the amount so assessed

exceeds

(*d*) the total of

(i) the amount, if any, so assessed that is not in controversy, and

(ii) 1/2 of the amount so assessed that is in controversy if

(A) the taxpayer is a large corporation (within the meaning assigned by subsection 225.1(8)), or

(B) the amount is in respect of a particular amount claimed under section 110.1 or 118.1 and the particular amount was claimed in respect of a tax shelter.

History: S. 164(1.1)(*d*)(ii) was replaced by S.C. 2013, c. 33, s. 17(1), applicable in respect of amounts assessed for taxation years that end after 2012, and formerly read:

(ii) where the taxpayer is a large corporation (within the meaning assigned by subsection 225.1(8)), 1/2 of the amount so assessed that is in controversy.

Related Sections: S. 164(1.2) Collection in jeopardy; s. 164(1.7) Limitation of repayment on objections and appeals; s. 164(5.1) Interest — disputed amounts.

Tax Topics: No. 1901, Narrowing of the Collection Restrictions — Set-Off Can Occur!.

Information Circulars: IC 07-1 Taxpayer relief provisions.

Cases: The setting aside of the jeopardy order meant that subsection 164(1.1) should be read as if that jeopardy order had never been issued, and the Minister was required to pay interest on the amount refunded. *Grenon v. The Queen*, 2017 DTC 5101 (FCA)

► 164(1.2) ◄

(1.2) Collection in jeopardy. Notwithstanding subsection (1.1), where, on application by the Minister made within 45 days after the receipt by the Minister of a written request by a taxpayer for repayment of an amount or surrender of a security, a judge is satisfied that there are reasonable grounds to believe that the collection of all or any part of an amount assessed in respect of the taxpayer would be jeopardized by the repayment of the amount or the surrender of the security to the taxpayer under that subsection, the judge shall order that the repayment of the amount or a part thereof not be made or that the security or part thereof not be surrendered or make such other order as the judge considers reasonable in the circumstances.

Related Sections: S. 164(1.3) Notice of application; s. 164(1.31) Application of ss. 225.2(4), (10), (12) and (13).

Information Circulars: IC 07-1 Taxpayer relief provisions; IC 98-1R4 Collections policies.

▶ 164(1.3) ◀

(1.3) Notice of application. The Minister shall give 6 clear days notice of an application under subsection (1.2) to the taxpayer in respect of whom the application is made.

▶ 164(1.31) ◀

(1.31) Application of ss. 225.2(4), (10), (12) and (13). Where an application under subsection (1.2) is made by the Minister, subsections 225.2(4), (10), (12) and (13) are applicable in respect of the application with such modifications as the circumstances require.

▶ 164(1.4) ◀

(1.4) Provincial refund. Where, at any time, a taxpayer is entitled to a refund or repayment on account of taxes imposed by a province or as a result of a deduction in computing the taxes imposed by a province and the Government of Canada has agreed to make the refund or repayment on behalf of the province, the amount thereof shall be a liability of the Minister of National Revenue to the taxpayer.

▶ 164(1.5) ◀

(1.5) Exception. Notwithstanding subsection (1), the Minister may, on or after sending a notice of assessment for a taxation year, refund all or any portion of any overpayment of a taxpayer for the year

(*a*) if the taxpayer is an individual (other than a trust) or a graduated rate estate for the year and the taxpayer's return of income under this Part for the year was filed on or before the day that is 10 calendar years after the end of the year;

(*b*) where an assessment or a redetermination was made under subsection 152(4.2) or 220(3.1) or (3.4) in respect of the taxpayer; or

(*c*) to the extent that the overpayment relates to an assessment of another taxpayer under subsection 227(10) or (10.1) (in this paragraph referred to as the "other assessment"), if the taxpayer's return of income under this Part for the taxation year is filed on or before the day that is two years after the date of the other assessment and if the other assessment relates to

(i) in the case of an amount assessed under subsection 227(10), a payment to the taxpayer of a fee, commission or other amount in respect of services rendered in Canada by a non-resident person or partnership, and

(ii) in the case of an amount assessed under subsection 227(10.1), an amount payable under subsection 116(5) or (5.3) in respect of a disposition of property by the taxpayer.

History: S. 164(1.5)(*a*) was replaced by S.C. 2014, c. 39, s. 60(1), applicable to the 2016 and subsequent taxation years, and formerly read:

(*a*) if the taxpayer is an individual (other than a trust) or is a testamentary trust and the taxpayer's return of income under this Part for the year was filed on or before the day that is ten calendar years after the end of the taxation year;

S. 164(1.5), the portion before paragraph (*a*) was replaced by S.C. 2010, c. 25, s. 42(2), in force on Royal Assent, December 15, 2010. S. 164(1.5), the portion before paragraph (*a*) formerly read:

(1.5) *Idem.* Notwithstanding subsection (1), the Minister may, on or after mailing a notice of assessment for a taxation year, refund all or any portion of any overpayment of a taxpayer for the year

S. 164(1.5)(*c*) was added by S.C. 2010, c. 12, s. 19(1), applicable to overpayments in respect of which applications for refunds are made after March 4, 2010.

Related Sections: S. 152(4.2) Reassessment with taxpayer's consent; s. 220(3.4) Assessments.

Tax Profile: September 2010 — Recent Tax Developments Affecting Non-Residents.

Information Circulars: IC 75-7R3 Reassessment of a return of income; IC 07-1 Taxpayer relief provisions.

▶ 164(1.51) ◀

(1.51) When subsection (1.52) applies. Subsection (1.52) applies to a taxpayer for a taxation year if, at any time after the beginning of the year

(*a*) the taxpayer has, in respect of the tax payable by the taxpayer under this Part (and, if the taxpayer is a corporation, Parts I.3, VI, VI.1 and XIII.1) for the year, paid under any of sections 155 to 157 one or more instalments of tax;

(*b*) it is reasonable to conclude that the total amount of those instalments exceeds the total amount of taxes that will be payable by the taxpayer under those Parts for the year; and

(*c*) the Minister is satisfied that the payment of the instalments has caused or will cause undue hardship to the taxpayer.

History: S. 164(1.51) was added by S.C. 2013, c. 34, s. 321(1), in force June 26, 2013.

▶ 164(1.52) ◀

(1.52) Instalment refund. If this subsection applies to a taxpayer for a taxation year, the Minister may refund to the taxpayer all or any part of the excess referred to in paragraph (1.51)(*b*).

History: S. 164(1.52) was added by S.C. 2013, c. 34, s. 321(1), in force June 26, 2013.

▶ 164(1.53) ◀

(1.53) Penalties, interest not affected. For the purpose of the calculation of any penalty or interest under this Act, an instalment is deemed not to have been paid to the extent that all or any part of the instalment can reasonably be considered to have been refunded under subsection (1.52).

History: S. 164(1.53) was added by S.C. 2013, c. 34, s. 321(1), in force June 26, 2013.

▶ 164(1.6) ◀

(1.6) Refund of UI premium tax credit — (Repealed by S.C. 2013, c. 34, s. 321(2).)

History: S. 164(1.6) was repealed by S.C. 2013, c. 34, s. 321(2), deemed to have come into force on March 21, 2003, and formerly read:

(1.6) *Refund of UI premium tax credit.* Notwithstanding subsection (1), where an overpayment on account of a taxpayer's liability under this Part is deemed to have arisen under subsection 126.1(6) or (7), the Minister shall, with all due dispatch, refund the amount of the overpayment without application for it.

▶ 164(1.7) ◀

(1.7) Limitation of repayment on objections and appeals. Subsection (1.1) does not apply in respect of an amount paid or security furnished under section 116 by a non-resident person.

► 164(1.8) ◄

(1.8) Request to pay refund to province. An individual (other than a trust) may, in the individual's return of income for a taxation year, request the Minister to pay to Her Majesty in right of a prescribed province all or any part of a refund for the year claimed by the individual in the return and, where the individual makes such a request,

(*a*) the Minister may make the payment to Her Majesty in right of the province in accordance with the request; and

(*b*) the amount of the payment is deemed to have been refunded under this section to the individual at the time a notice of an original assessment of tax payable under this Part by the individual for the year, or a notification that no tax is payable under this Part by the individual for the year, is sent to the individual.

► 164(2) ◄

(2) Application to other debts. Instead of making a refund or repayment that might otherwise be made under this section, the Minister may, where the taxpayer is, or is about to become, liable to make any payment to Her Majesty in right of Canada or in right of a province, apply the amount of the refund or repayment to that other liability and notify the taxpayer of that action.

Related Sections: S. 164(7) Definition of "overpayment"; s. 227(6) Excess withheld, returned or applied.

Information Circulars: IC 07-1 Taxpayer Relief Provisions.

► 164(2.01) ◄

(2.01) Withholding of refunds. The Minister shall not, in respect of a taxpayer, refund, repay, apply to other debts or set-off amounts under this Act at any time unless all returns of which the Minister has knowledge and that are required to be filed by the taxpayer at or before that time under this Act, the *Air Travellers Security Charge Act*, the *Excise Act, 2001* and the *Excise Tax Act* have been filed with the Minister.

Editorial Note: The Canada Revenue Agency announced in April 2012 that it would extend indefinitely its administrative position implemented in 2008 not to apply the requirements in subsection 164(2.01) to tax-exempt corporations. As a result, it will not withhold tax refunds or rebates from tax-exempt corporations that have not filed T2 returns for previous years. The entities affected include incorporated municipalities, universities, schools, hospitals, non-profit organizations, federal crown corporations, and Indian band councils. The CRA noted that this administrative position does not remove the legislative responsibility of these corporations for filing corporate tax returns under s. 150.

► 164(2.1) ◄

(2.1) Application respecting refunds under s. 122.5. Where an amount deemed under section 122.5 to be paid by an individual during a month specified for a taxation year is applied under subsection (2) to a liability of the individual and the individual's return of income for the year is filed on or before the individual's balance-due day for the year, the amount is deemed to have been so applied on the day on which the amount would have been refunded if the individual were not liable to make a payment to Her Majesty in right of Canada.

► 164(2.2) ◄

(2.2) Application respecting refunds re section 122.61. Subsection (2) does not apply to a refund to be made to a taxpayer and arising because of section 122.61 except to the extent that the taxpayer's liability referred to in that subsection arose from the operation of paragraph 160.1(1)(*a*) with respect to an amount refunded to the taxpayer in excess of the amount to which the taxpayer was entitled because of section 122.61.

► 164(2.3) ◄

(2.3) Form deemed to be return of income. For the purpose of subsection (1), where a taxpayer files the form referred to in paragraph (*b*) of the definition "return of income" in section 122.6 for a taxation year, the form is deemed to be a return of the taxpayer's income for that year and a notice of assessment in respect of that return is deemed to have been sent by the Minister.

History: S. 164(2.3) was replaced by S.C. 2010, c. 25, s. 42(3), in force on Royal Assent, December 15, 2010. S. 164(2.3) formerly read:

(2.3) *Form deemed to be a return of income.* For the purpose of subsection (1), where a taxpayer files the form referred to in paragraph (*b*) of the definition "return of income" in section 122.6 for a taxation year, the form shall be deemed to be a return of the taxpayer's income for that year and a notice of assessment thereof shall be deemed to have been mailed by the Minister.

► 164(3) ◄

(3) Interest on refunds and repayments. If, under this section, an amount in respect of a taxation year (other than an amount, or a portion of the amount, that can reasonably be considered to arise from the operation of section 122.5 or 122.61) is refunded or repaid to a taxpayer or applied to another liability of the taxpayer, the Minister shall pay or apply interest on it at the prescribed rate for the period that begins on the day that is the latest of the days referred to in the following paragraphs and that ends on the day on which the amount is refunded, repaid or applied:

(*a*) if the taxpayer is an individual, the day that is 30 days after the individual's balance-due day for the year;

(*b*) if the taxpayer is a corporation, the day that is 120 days after the end of the year;

(*c*) if the taxpayer is

(i) a corporation, the day that is 30 days after the day on which its return of income for the year was filed under section 150, unless the return was filed on or before the corporation's filing-due date for the year, and

(ii) an individual, the day that is 30 days after the day on which the individual's return of income for the year was filed under section 150;

(*d*) in the case of a refund of an overpayment, the day on which the overpayment arose; and

(*e*) in the case of a repayment of an amount in controversy, the day on which an overpayment equal to the amount of the repayment would have arisen if the total of all amounts payable on account of the taxpayer's liability under this Part for the year were the amount by which

(i) the lesser of the total of all amounts paid on account of the taxpayer's liability under this Part for the year and the total of all amounts assessed by the Minister as payable under this Part by the taxpayer for the year

exceeds

(ii) the amount repaid.

Editorial Note: Effective July 1, 2010, the prescribed interest rate for refunds of tax overpayments by corporations was changed to be the average yield of three-month Government of Canada treasury bills sold in the first month of the preceding quarter, rounded up to the nearest percentage point. Prior to July 1, 2010, the rate on refunds for all taxpayers was that rate plus 2% and it remains as that for taxpayers other than corporations. This change for refunds to corporations was implemented by an amendment to Regulation 4301 as a result of concern that the government was paying interest at a rate significantly higher than its cost of capital and that corporations were intentionally overpaying tax in order to obtain a higher rate of interest than otherwise available in similarly low-risk investments.

History: S. 164(3), the portion before paragraph (*a*) was replaced by S.C. 2013, c. 34, s. 321(3), applicable in respect of forms filed after March 20, 2003, and formerly read:

(3) *Interest on refunds and repayments.* Where under this section an amount in respect of a taxation year (other than an amount or portion of it that can reasonably be considered to arise from the operation of section 122.5, 122.61 or 126.1) is refunded or repaid to a taxpayer or applied to another liability of the taxpayer, the Minister shall pay or apply interest on it at the prescribed rate for the period beginning on the day that is the latest of the days referred to in the following paragraphs and ending on the day on which the amount is refunded, repaid or applied:

Related Regulations: 4301.

Related Sections: S. 164(4) Interest on interest repaid; s. 164(5) Effect of carryback of loss, etc; s. 164(5.1) Interest — disputed amounts; s. 161.1 Offset of refund interest and arrears interest; s. 248(1), "balance-due date", "filing-due date"; s. 248(11) Compound interest; and ITAR s. 62(2) Interest.

Cases: The taxpayer filed its tax returns for 1993 and 1995. The Part IV tax payable for the 1995 taxation year was paid on June 10, 1995. As the result of subsequent reassessments the taxpayer's Part IV liability for 1993 was increased significantly, while its Part IV liability for 1995 was reduced. On February 3, 2000, the Minister applied the resulting overpayment for 1995 to the outstanding amount for 1993. The date of payment for purposes of calculating interest in relation to amounts owed for 1993 was February 3, 2000, and not, as the taxpayer argued, June 10, 1995. *Bakorp Management v. MNR*, 2016 DTC 5037 (FCA)

A remission of tax is not the same as a refund of tax overpayment (which accrues interest on outstanding amounts). Accordingly, the taxpayers were not entitled to interest on the remission amounts received. *Imperial Oil Resources Ltd. v. Canada (AG)*, 2016 DTC 5057 (F.C.A.)

Because the taxpayer made a tax overpayment out of profits earned in its business, when it received a tax refund, such refund represented a return of money that was intended for use in its business. Hence, the refund interest was active business income, and had to be included in its "adjusted business income" for MPP tax credit purposes. *The Queen v. Irving Oil Limited*, 2002 DTC 6716 (F.C.A.), affirming 2000 DTC 2164 (T.C.C.).

► 164(3.1) ◄

(3.1) Idem. Where at a particular time interest has been paid to, or applied to a liability of, a taxpayer under subsection (3) or (3.2) in respect of an overpayment and it is determined at a subsequent time that the actual overpayment was less than the overpayment in respect of which interest was paid or applied,

(*a*) the amount by which the interest that has been paid or applied exceeds the interest, if any, computed in respect of the amount that is determined at the subsequent time to be the actual overpayment shall be deemed to be an amount (in this subsection referred to as "the amount payable") that became payable under this Part by the taxpayer at the particular time;

(*b*) the taxpayer shall pay to the Receiver General interest at the prescribed rate on the amount payable computed from that particular time to the day of payment; and

(*c*) the Minister may at any time assess the taxpayer in respect of the amount payable and, where the Minister makes such an assessment, the provisions of this Division are applicable, with such modifications as the circumstances require, in respect of the assessment as though it had been made under section 152.

Related Regulations: 4301.

Related Sections: S. 248(11) Compound interest.

► 164(3.2) ◄

(3.2) Interest where amounts cancelled. Notwithstanding subsection (3), if an overpayment of a taxpayer for a taxation year is determined because of an assessment made under subsection 152(4.2) or 220(3.1) or (3.4) and an amount in respect of the overpayment is refunded to, or applied to another liability of, the taxpayer under subsection (1.5) or (2), the Minister shall pay or apply interest on the overpayment at the prescribed rate for the period beginning on the day that is 30 days after the day on which the Minister received a request in a manner satisfactory to the Minister to apply those subsections and ending on the day on which the amount is refunded or applied.

► 164(4) ◄

(4) Interest on interest repaid. Where at any particular time interest has been paid to, or applied to a liability of, a taxpayer pursuant to subsection (3) in respect of the repayment of an amount in controversy made to, or applied to a liability of, the taxpayer and it is determined at a subsequent time that the repayment or a part thereof is payable by the taxpayer under this Part, the following rules apply:

(*a*) the interest so paid or applied on that part of the repayment that is determined at the subsequent time to be payable by the taxpayer under this Part shall be deemed to be an amount (in this subsection referred to as the "interest excess") that became payable under this Part by the taxpayer at the particular time;

(*b*) the taxpayer shall pay to the Receiver General interest at the prescribed rate on the interest excess computed from the particular time to the day of payment; and

(*c*) the Minister may at any time assess the taxpayer in respect of the interest excess and, where the Minister makes such an assessment, the provisions of this Division and Division J are applicable, with such modifications as the circumstances require, in respect of the assessment as though it had been made under section 152.

Related Regulations: 4301.

Related Sections: S. 161.1 Offset of refund interest and arrears interest; s. 248(11) Compound interest; ITAR s. 62(2) Interest.

Canadian Tax Foundation: Cuperfain, *Got Me Those "Low Capital Gain, High Dividend Tax, Stop-loss Rules, Estate Planning" Blues*, 2001 Canadian Tax Journal 3:764–794.

► 164(4.1) ◄

(4.1) Duty of Minister. Where the Tax Court of Canada, the Federal Court of Appeal or the Supreme Court of Canada has, on the disposition of an appeal in respect of taxes, interest or a penalty payable under this Act by a taxpayer resident in Canada,

(*a*) referred an assessment back to the Minister for reconsideration and reassessment, or

(*b*) varied or vacated an assessment,

the Minister shall with all due dispatch, whether or not an appeal from the decision of the Court has been or may be instituted,

(*c*) where the assessment has been referred back to the Minister, reconsider the assessment and make a reassessment in accordance with the decision of the Court, unless otherwise directed in writing by the taxpayer, and

(*d*) refund any overpayment resulting from the variation, vacation or reassessment,

and the Minister may repay any tax, interest or penalties or surrender any security accepted therefor by the Minister to that taxpayer or any other taxpayer who has filed another objection or instituted another appeal if, having regard to the reasons given on the disposition of the appeal, the Minister is satisfied that it would be just and equitable to do so, but for greater certainty, the Minister may, in accordance with the provisions of this Act, the *Tax Court of Canada Act*, the *Federal Courts Act* or the *Supreme Court Act* as they relate to appeals from decisions of the Tax Court of Canada or the Federal Court of Appeal, appeal from the decision of the Court notwithstanding any variation or vacation of any assessment by the Court or any reassessment made by the Minister under paragraph (*c*).

Editorial Note: Subsection 164(4.1) requires the Minister — unless directed otherwise in writing by the taxpayer — to with all due dispatch make any reassessment required by a court decision and make any consequential refund or repayment, notwithstanding the fact that the Minister may further appeal a decision that was made in the taxpayer's favour. The Minister may apply the refund or repayment to another liability of a taxpayer under s. 164(2).

Related Sections: S. 164(5.1) Interest — disputed amounts.

► 164(5) ◄

(5) Effect of carryback of loss, etc. For the purpose of subsection (3), the portion of any overpayment of the tax payable by a taxpayer for a taxation year that arose as a consequence of

(*a*) the deduction of an amount, in respect of a repayment under subsection 68.4(7) of the *Excise Tax Act* made in a subsequent taxation year, in computing the amount determined under subparagraph 12(1)(*x*.1)(ii),

(*a*.1) any amount deducted under section 119 in respect of the disposition of a taxable Canadian property in a subsequent taxation year,

(*b*) the deduction of an amount under section 41 in respect of the taxpayer's listed-personal property loss for a subsequent taxation year,

(*c*) the exclusion of an amount from the taxpayer's income for the year by virtue of section 49 in respect of the exercise of an option in a subsequent taxation year,

(*d*) the deduction of an amount under section 118.1 in respect of a gift made in a subsequent taxation year or under section 111 in respect of a loss for a subsequent taxation year,

(*e*) the deduction of an amount under subsection 126(2) in respect of an unused foreign tax credit (within the meaning assigned by subsection 126(7)), or under subsection 126(2.21) or (2.22) in respect of foreign taxes paid, for a subsequent taxation year,

(*f*) the deduction of an amount under subsection 127(5) in respect of property acquired or an expenditure made in a subsequent taxation year,

(*g*) (Repealed by S.C. 2013, c. 34, s. 321(4).)

(*h*) the deduction of an amount under section 125.3 in respect of an unused Part I.3 tax credit (within the meaning assigned by subsection 125.3(3)) for a subsequent taxation year,

(*h*.01) the deduction of an amount under subsection 147.2(4) in computing the taxpayer's income for the year because of the application of subsection 147.2(6) as a result of the taxpayer's death in the following taxation year,

(*h*.02) the deduction under any of subsections 128.1(6) to (8) of an amount from the taxpayer's proceeds of disposition of a property, because of an election made in a return of income for a subsequent taxation year,

(*h*.1) the deduction of an amount in computing the taxpayer's income for the year by virtue of an election for a subsequent taxation year under paragraph (6)(*c*) or (*d*) by the taxpayer's legal representative,

(*h*.2) the deduction of an amount under subsection 181.1(4) in respect of an unused surtax credit (within the meaning assigned by subsection 181.1(6)) of the taxpayer for a subsequent taxation year,

(*h*.3) the deduction of an amount under subsection 190.1(3) in respect of an unused Part I tax credit (within the meaning assigned by subsection 190.1(5)) of the taxpayer for a subsequent taxation year, or

(*h*.4) the reduction of the amount included under subsection 91(1) for the year because of a reduction referred to in paragraph 152(6.1)(*b*) in the foreign accrual property income of a foreign affiliate of the taxpayer for a taxation year of the affiliate that ends in the year,

is deemed to have arisen on the day that is 30 days after the latest of

(*i*) the first day immediately following that subsequent taxation year,

(*j*) the day on which the taxpayer's or the taxpayer's legal representative's return of income for that subsequent taxation year was filed,

(*k*) if an amended return of a taxpayer's income for the year or a prescribed form amending the taxpayer's return of income for the year was filed under paragraph (6)(*e*) or subsection 49(4) or 152(6) or (6.1), the day on which the amended return or prescribed form was filed, and

(*l*) where, as a consequence of a request in writing, the Minister reassessed the taxpayer's tax for the year to take into account the deduction or exclusion, the day on which the request was made.

Editorial Note: Subsection 164(5) provides that any portion of an overpayment of tax for a particular taxation year that arose as a result of the carryback of certain losses from a subsequent taxation year — or that resulted from certain other deductions or credits listed therein in respect of a subsequent year — will be deemed to have arisen on the latest of the four possible dates in s. 164(5)(*i*)-(*l*). The effect of this provision is that the taxpayer will not be entitled to interest under s. 164(3) on the refund of this portion of the overpayment until the day on which it is deemed to have arisen under s. 164(5). Even if an individual did not file a return of income for the particular taxation year because of one of the filing exceptions set out in s. 150, s. 164(5)(*j*) effectively requires the filing of a return of income for the subsequent year in order to be entitled to interest on any overpayment or repayment in respect of the particular year.

History: S. 164(5)(*h.4*) was added by S.C. 2013, c. 34, s. 36(1), applicable to taxation years that begin after December 18, 2009.

Any assessment of a taxpayer's tax, interest and penalties payable under the Act for any taxation year that ends before June 26, 2013 that would, in the absence of this section, be precluded because of subsections 152(4) to (5) of the Act, shall be made to the extent necessary to take into account this amendment, if the taxpayer

(i) elects in writing in respect of all of its foreign affiliates that this section apply in respect of that provision, and

(ii) files that election with the Minister of National Revenue on or before December 26, 2013 [the day that is six months after royal assent].

S. 164(5)(*k*) was replaced by S.C. 2013, c. 34, s. 36(2), applicable to taxation years that begin after December 18, 2009.

See the application following the history note for S. 164(5)(*h.4*) above, regarding the override of the statute-barring rules for assessments for taxation years that end before June 26, 2013.

S. 164(5)(*k*) formerly read:

(*k*) where an amended return of the taxpayer's income for the year or a prescribed form amending the taxpayer's return of income for the year was filed under paragraph (6)(*e*) or subsection 49(4) or 152(6), the day on which the amended return or prescribed form was filed, and

S. 164(5)(*g*) was repealed by S.C. 2013, c. 34, s. 321(4), applicable to taxation years that begin after October 31, 2011, and formerly read:

(*g*) the deduction of an amount under section 125.2 in respect of an unused Part VI tax credit (within the meaning assigned by subsection 125.2(3)) for a subsequent taxation year,

Related Sections: S. 161(7) Effect of carryback of loss, etc.

► 164(5.1) ◄

(5.1) Interest — disputed amounts. Where a portion of a repayment made under subsection (1.1) or (4.1), or an amount applied under subsection (2) in respect of a repayment, can reasonably be regarded as being in respect of a claim made by the taxpayer in an objection to or appeal from an assessment of tax for a taxation year for a deduction or exclusion described in subsection (5) in respect of a subsequent taxation year, interest shall not be paid or applied on the portion for any part of a period that is before the latest of the dates described in paragraphs (5)(*i*) to (*l*).

Editorial Note: Subsection 164(5.1) parallels s. 164(5) and effectively provides that where a repayment of tax in respect of a particular taxation year is made by the Minister under s. 164(1.1) or (4.1), or is applied by the Minister under s. 164(2) to offset a liability of the taxpayer, interest shall not be paid on the repayment until the beginning of the period starting with the latest of four possible dates.

► 164(6) ◄

(6) Disposition by legal representative of deceased. If in the course of administering the graduated rate estate of a taxpayer, the taxpayer's legal representative has, within the first taxation year of the estate,

(*a*) disposed of capital property of the estate so that the total of all amounts each of which is a capital loss from the disposition of a property exceeds the total of all amounts each of which is a capital gain from the disposition of a property, or

(*b*) disposed of all of the depreciable property of a prescribed class of the estate so that the undepreciated capital cost to the estate of property of that class at the end of the first taxation year of the estate is, by virtue of subsection 20(16) or any regulation made under paragraph 20(1)(*a*), deductible in computing the income of the estate for that year,

notwithstanding any other provision of this Act, the following rules apply:

(*c*) such parts of one or more capital losses of the estate from the disposition of properties in the year (the total of which is not to exceed the excess referred to in paragraph (*a*)) as the legal representative so elects, in prescribed manner and within a prescribed time, are deemed (except for the purpose of subsection 112(3) and this paragraph) to be capital losses of the deceased taxpayer from the disposition of the properties by the taxpayer in the taxpayer's last taxation year and not to be capital losses of the estate from the disposition of those properties,

(*d*) such part of the amount of any deduction described in paragraph (*b*) (not exceeding the amount that, but for this subsection, would be the total of the non-capital loss and the farm loss of the estate for its first taxation year) as the legal representative so elects, in prescribed manner and within a prescribed time, shall be deductible in computing the income of the taxpayer for the taxpayer's taxation year in which the taxpayer died and shall not be an amount deductible in computing any loss of the estate for its first taxation year,

(*e*) the legal representative shall, at or before the time prescribed for filing the election referred to in paragraphs (*c*) and (*d*), file an amended return of income for the deceased taxpayer for the taxpayer's taxation year in which the taxpayer died to give effect to the rules in those paragraphs, and

(*f*) in computing the taxable income of the deceased taxpayer for a taxation year preceding the year in which the taxpayer died, no amount may be deducted in respect of an amount referred to in paragraph (*c*) or (*d*).

Editorial Note: Subsection 164(6) allows an estate's capital losses net of its capital gains, or its terminal loss (not exceeding its non-capital loss, if any), for its first taxation year to be carried back and deducted in the deceased's terminal taxation year. The amount cannot reduce the deceased's taxable income for any previous years (i.e. the losses cannot be carried back from the terminal year). This provision is often used in post-mortem planning.

History: S. 164(6), the portion before paragraph (*a*) was replaced by S.C. 2014, c. 39, s. 60(2), applicable to the 2016 and subsequent taxation years, and formerly read:

(6) *Where disposition of property by legal representative of deceased taxpayer.* Where in the course of administering the estate of a deceased taxpayer, the taxpayer's legal representative has, within the first taxation year of the estate,

Related Regulations: 600(b); 1000.

Related Sections: 248(1) graduated rate estate; S. 70(5) Capital property of a deceased taxpayer; s. 220(3.2) Late, amended or revoked elections.

Canadian Tax Foundation: Minicucci, *Trusts and Post-Mortem Tax Planning — A 2014 Update*, 2014 Ontario Tax Conference 5B:1–29; Falk and Morand, *Current Issues Forum: Pipeline Planning; Subsection 164(6) Circularity Issue; Eligible Dividend Designations*, 2012 Ontario Tax Conference 1B:1–26; MacLeod, *Current Taxation Issues Related to Estate Planning*, 2009 Atlantic Provinces Tax Conference 5a:1–16; Valli, *Post-Mortem and Shareholder Agreement Considerations in Light of the Eligible Dividend Regime*, 2009 Prairie Provinces Tax Conference 7:1–22; Christian, *Post-Mortem Tax Planning*, 2007 Conference Report 37:1–27; Riggin, *Post-Mortem Planning Under the New Dividend Regime*, 2007 Ontario Tax Conference 10:1–24; Faccone and Gehlen, *Post-Mortem Estate Planning: Selected Canadian and US Tax Issues Relating to the Implementation of Post-Mortem Strategies*, 2006 British Columbia Tax Conference 12:1–34; Ireland, *Selected Developments in Post-Mortem Planning*, 2005 Conference Report 13:1–34; Barnett et al., *Post Mortem Planning for Private Company Shares: The New Regime*, 2002 Conference Report 32:1–86; Barnett et al., *Post Mortem Planning for Private Company Shares — The New Regime: Alternatives For Minimizing The Tax Exposure Arising On The Death Of The Owner Of Private Company Shares*, 2002 British Columbia Tax Conference 19:1–91; Sibson, *Private Companies:*

The Most Significant Tax Issue of the Last 12 Months, 2001 Conference Report 5:1–8; Cuperfain, *Got Me Those "Low Capital Gain, High Dividend Tax, Stop-loss Rules, Estate Planning" Blues*, 2001 Canadian Tax Journal 3:764–794; Marquette, *Selected Income Tax Issues of Particular Relevance to Shareholders Agreements: Part 2*, 2001 Canadian Tax Journal 2:407–437; Rees, *Testamentary Planning to Avoid Double Taxation*, 2000 Canadian Tax Journal 1:155–173.

Tax Profile: February 2012 — Post-Mortem Planning — Double Taxation on Death; June 2011 — Summary of Canada Revenue Agency Round Table Held at the 13th National STEP Canada Conference; January 2010 — Shareholders' Agreements — A Survey of Income Tax Issues; September 2004 — Review of Tax Implications of Corporate-Owned Life Insurance Buy-Sell Arrangements; June 2004 — Planning For Aging Parents.

Tax Topics: No. 1690, Estate Planning In The 21st Century; No. 1681, Life Insurance: Exploring the Corporate Edge — Part I; No. 1635, Estate Planning in the Twenty-First Century; No. 1595, Estate Planning in the 21st Century; No. 1582, Estate Planning in the 21st Century; No. 1570, Estate Planning in the 21st Century.

Income Tax Folios: S4-F8-C1 Business Investment Losses.

Information Circulars: IC 07-1 Taxpayer Relief Provisions.

Interpretation Bulletins: *Secondary* — IT-140R3 Buy-sell agreements.

► 164(6.1) ◄

(6.1) Realization of deceased employees' options. Notwithstanding any other provision of this Act, if a right to acquire securities (as defined in subsection 7(7)) under an agreement in respect of which a benefit was deemed by paragraph 7(1)(*e*) to have been received by a taxpayer (in this subsection referred to as "the right") is exercised or disposed of by the taxpayer's legal representative within the first taxation year of the graduated rate estate of the taxpayer and the representative so elects in prescribed manner and on or before a prescribed day,

(*a*) the amount, if any, by which

(i) the amount of the benefit deemed by paragraph 7(1)(*e*) to have been received by the taxpayer in respect of the right

exceeds the total of

(ii) the amount, if any, by which the value of the right immediately before the time it was exercised or disposed of exceeds the amount, if any, paid by the taxpayer to acquire the right, and

(iii) where in computing the taxpayer's taxable income for the taxation year in which the taxpayer died an amount was deducted under paragraph 110(1)(*d*) in respect of the benefit deemed by paragraph 7(1)(*e*) to have been received by the taxpayer in that year by reason of paragraph 7(1)(*e*) in respect of that right, 1/2 of the amount, if any, by which the amount determined under subparagraph (i) exceeds the amount determined under subparagraph (ii),

shall be deemed to be a loss of the taxpayer from employment for the year in which the taxpayer died;

(*b*) there shall be deducted in computing the adjusted cost base to the estate of the right at any time the amount of the loss that would be determined under paragraph (*a*) if that paragraph were read without reference to subparagraph (*a*)(iii); and

(*c*) the legal representative shall, at or before the time prescribed for filing the election under this subsection, file an amended return of income for the taxpayer for the taxation year in which the taxpayer died to give effect to paragraph (*a*).

History: S. 164(6.1), the portion before paragraph (*a*) was replaced by S.C. 2014, c. 39, s. 60(3), applicable to the 2016 and subsequent taxation years, and formerly read:

(6.1) *Realization of deceased employees' options.* Notwithstanding any other provision of this Act, if a right to acquire securities (as defined in subsection 7(7)) under an agreement in respect of which a benefit was deemed by paragraph 7(1)(*e*) to have been received by a taxpayer (in this subsection referred to as "the right") is exercised or disposed of by the taxpayer's legal representative within the first taxation year of the estate of the taxpayer and the representative so elects in prescribed manner and on or before a prescribed day,

Editorial Note: An employee who dies with unexercised options to acquire securities in an employer entity (e.g., stock options) is deemed in the year of death to receive an employment income benefit equal to the amount by which the value of the right immediately after the employee's death exceeds the amount the employee paid to acquire the right (i.e., the "stock option benefit"). Where the value of the option decreases after the date of death, a loss under s. 164(6.1) may be carried back against the deceased's final return, equal to the (stock option) benefit less the amount by which the value of the option immediately before it was exercised or disposed of exceeds the amount paid by the deceased for the option. A s. 164(6.1) election can be filed to apply this loss where the unexercised option either expires or is exercised or disposed of by the deceased's legal representative within the first taxation year of the deceased's estate. As well, only half the loss can be carried back if a deduction under s. 110(1)(*d*) was already claimed in the deceased's final tax return.

Related Regulations: 600(*b*); 1000.1.

Related Sections: S. 7(1) Agreement to issue securities to employees; s. 53(2)(*t*) Amounts to be deducted — Right to acquire shares or units; s. 110(1)(*d*) Employee options; s. 220(3.2) Late, amended or revoked elections.

Canadian Tax Foundation: Tollstam, *Unexercised Employee Stock Options on Death*, 2013 Canadian Tax Highlights 21(5):13–14.

► 164(7) ◄

(7) Definition of "overpayment". In this section, "overpayment" of a taxpayer for a taxation year means

(*a*) where the taxpayer is not a corporation, the total of all amounts paid on account of the taxpayer's liability under this Part for the year minus all amounts payable in respect thereof; and

(*b*) where the taxpayer is a corporation, the total of all amounts paid on account of the corporation's liability under this Part or Parts I.3, VI or VI.1 for the year minus all amounts payable in respect thereof.

Cases: A dividend refund is not an "overpayment of tax" entitling the taxpayer to interest. *McMillen Holdings Ltd. v. M.N.R.*, 87 DTC 585 (T.C.C.)

SECTION 164.1: Prepayment of child tax credit

(Repealed by S.C. 1994, c. 7, Sched. VII, s. 19(2).)

Objections to Assessments

SECTION 165: Objections to assessment

► 165(1) ◄

(1) Objections to assessment. A taxpayer who objects to an assessment under this Part may serve on the Minister a notice of objection, in writing, setting out the reasons for the objection and all relevant facts,

(*a*) if the assessment is in respect of the taxpayer for a taxation year and the taxpayer is an individual (other than a trust) or a graduated rate estate for the year, on or before the later of

(i) the day that is one year after the taxpayer's filing-due date for the year, and

(ii) the day that is 90 days after the day of sending of the notice of assessment; and

(*b*) in any other case, on or before the day that is 90 days after the day of sending of the notice of assessment.

History: S. 165(1)(*a*), the portion before subparagraph (i) was replaced by S.C. 2014, c. 39, s. 61(1), applicable to the 2016 and subsequent taxation years, and formerly read:

(*a*) where the assessment is in respect of the taxpayer for a taxation year and the taxpayer is an individual (other than a trust) or a testamentary trust, on or before the later of

S. 165(1)(*a*)(ii) was replaced by S.C. 2010, c. 25, s. 43(1), in force on Royal Assent, December 15, 2010. S. 165(1)(*a*)(ii) formerly read:

(ii) the day that is 90 days after the day of mailing of the notice of assessment; and

S. 165(1)(*b*) was replaced by S.C. 2010, c. 25, s. 43(2), in force on Royal Assent, December 15, 2010. S. 165(1)(*b*) formerly read:

(*b*) in any other case, on or before the day that is 90 days after the day of mailing of the notice of assessment.

Related Sections: 248(1) graduated rate estate; S. 165(6) Validity of notice of objection; s. 167(1) Extension of time to appeal; s. 207.2(3) Provisions applicable to Part; s. 248(1), "filing-due date".

Canadian Tax Foundation: Junkin, *Current Cases: Limitation Periods and Other Time Sensitive Matters*, 2003 British Columbia Tax Conference 5:12–16; Meghji et al., *Does Procedure Matter?*, 1999 Conference Report 15:1–42; Rand, *Objections by Large Corporations*, 1995 Ontario Tax Conference 3:1–7; Kroft, *Selected Issues in Administration, Appeals and Enforcement*, 1995 British Columbia Tax Conference 14:1–46; Beith, *Draft Legislation on Income Tax Objections and Appeals*, 1994 Conference Report 34ae:1–5; Hickey, *Objections Overruled*, 1994 Canadian Tax Highlights 2(10):73–74.

Tax Profile: September 2009 — Fixing Tax Mistakes; October 2006 — Tax Controversies in Canada: A Variety of Issues.

Tax Topics: No. 2459, Taxpayers May Validly Serve a Notice of Objection on the Minister After Receiving an Audit Proposal Letter Despite Not Yet Having Received a Notice of Assessment.

Forms: T400A — Objection–Income Tax Act.

Guides: P148 Your Appeal Rights Under the Income Tax Act.

Information Circulars: IC 07-1 Taxpayer relief provisions; IC 98-1R4 Collections policies.

Cases: Once a taxpayer asserts a Notice of Assessment was not mailed, the Minister must introduce sufficient evidence to prove on a balance of probabilities that it was mailed to the address on file. If the Minister does so, the mailing is deemed to have occurred on the date set out in that Notice, subject to contrary evidence provided by the taxpayer. The taxpayer's credibility is determined after the Minister provides evidence to show the Notice was mailed. The Minister provided sufficient evidence to meet the burden, but the taxpayer did not provide credible evidence regarding a change of address. As a result, there was no evidence that the Notices were mailed to the wrong address, and the taxpayer's appeal was dismissed. *Mpamugo v. The Queen*, 2016 DTC 1176 (TCC), affirmed 2017 DTC 5083 (FCA)

The Notices of Assessment were sent to the wrong address and the Court concluded that they had therefore not been sent to the taxpayer. Since the applicable limitation period had not begun to run, the taxpayer's Notices of Objection had been timely served. The issue of the timing of the taxpayer's application for an extension of time was moot. *Pilgrim v. The Queen*, 2015 DTC 1236 (TCC)

The Crown was unable to prove that it was more likely than not that the reassessment was mailed, so the taxpayer was granted an extension of time to file his objection. *Hamer v. The Queen*, 2014 DTC 1168 (T.C.C.)

A nil assessment refers to either the notice issued by the Minister that no taxes are payable or in case law to an assessment that cannot be appealed because no taxes are claimed. The Court does not have jurisdiction to hear an appeal on a nil assessment. *Nottawasaga Inn Ltd. v. The Queen*, 2014 DTC 1021 (T.C.C.)

Although s. 165(1) requires a notice of objection to be served within 90 days after the day of "mailing" a notice of assessment, personal service of notices of assessment was held to be sufficient to begin the limitation periods for filing objections and applications for time extensions. *Grunwald v. The Queen*, 2006 DTC 6016 (F.C.A.), affirming 2006 DTC 2075 (T.C.C.)

The appeal provisions in the Act may not be circumvented by direct appeal to the Federal Court. A notice of objection must be filed. *M.N.R. v. Parsons et al.*, 84 DTC 6345 (F.C.A.), reversing in part 83 DTC 5329 (F.C.T.D.)

► 165(1.1) ◄

(1.1) Limitation of right to object to assessments or determinations. Notwithstanding subsection (1), where at any time the Minister assesses tax, interest, penalties or other amounts payable under this Part by, or makes a determination in respect of, a taxpayer

(*a*) under subsection 67.5(2) or 152(1.8), subparagraph 152(4)(*b*)(i) or subsection 152(4.3) or (6), 161.1(7), 164(4.1), 220(3.4) or 245(8) or in accordance with an order of a court vacating, varying or restoring an assessment or referring the assessment back to the Minister for reconsideration and reassessment,

(*b*) under subsection (3) where the underlying objection relates to an assessment or a determination made under any of the provisions or circumstances referred to in paragraph (*a*), or

(*c*) under a provision of an Act of Parliament requiring an assessment to be made that, but for that provision, would not be made because of subsections 152(4) to (5),

the taxpayer may object to the assessment or determination within 90 days after the day of sending of the notice of assessment or determination, but only to the extent that the reasons for the objection can reasonably be regarded

(*d*) where the assessment or determination was made under subsection 152(1.8), as relating to any matter or conclusion specified in paragraph 152(1.8)(*a*), (*b*) or (*c*), and

(*e*) in any other case, as relating to any matter that gave rise to the assessment or determination

and that was not conclusively determined by the court, and this subsection shall not be read or construed as limiting the right of the taxpayer to object to an assessment or a determination issued or made before that time.

History: S. 165(1.1), the portion after paragraph (*c*) and before paragraph (*d*) was replaced by S.C. 2010, c. 25, s. 43(3), in force on Royal Assent, December 15, 2010. S. 165(1.1), the portion after paragraph (*c*) and before paragraph (*d*) formerly read:

the taxpayer may object to the assessment or determination within 90 days after the day of mailing of the notice of assessment or determination, but only to the extent that the reasons for the objection can reasonably be regarded

Related Sections: S. 169(2) Limitation of right to appeal from assessments or determinations.

Income Tax Technical News: Issue No. 32, Notice of Objection of Large Corporation: Impact of the Potash Corporation Case.

► 165(1.11) ◄

(1.11) Objections by large corporations. Where a corporation that was a large corporation in a taxation year (within the meaning assigned by subsection 225.1(8)) objects to an assessment under this Part for the year, the notice of objection shall

(*a*) reasonably describe each issue to be decided;

(*b*) specify in respect of each issue, the relief sought, expressed as the amount of a change in a balance (within the meaning assigned by subsection 152(4.4)) or a balance of undeducted outlays, expenses or other amounts of the corporation; and

(*c*) provide facts and reasons relied on by the corporation in respect of each issue.

Canadian Petroleum Tax Journal: Canada Customs and Revenue Agency 1999 Roundtable Questions and Answers, Question 7, 2000, Vol. 13, No. 1.

Canadian Tax Foundation: Kreklewetz and Horrigan, *Notice of Objection: Specified Person*, 2015 Canadian Tax Highlights 23(5):2–3; Bassindale and Kreklewetz, *A Reasonable Description of the Issue*, 2013 Canadian Tax Highlights 21(6):3–5.

Tax Profile: November 2004 — Notice of Objection for Large Corporations — Impact of Potash Corporation.

Tax Topics: No. 1700, 2004 Canadian Tax Foundation Conference - CRA Round Table.

Income Tax Technical News: Issue No. 32, Notice of Objection of Large Corporation: Impact of the Potash Corporation Case.

Cases: There is no provision in the Act specifically allowing a large corporation to amend its Notice of Objection. If, however, the Minister allows a large corporation to raise additional issues before the objection stage is completed, it is difficult to accept that the Minister would be prejudiced if the large corporation were then allowed to continue to pursue these additional issues at the Tax Court level. *Devon Canada Corporation v. The Queen*, 2015 DTC 5108 (FCA)

The taxpayer failed to adequately set out the issues on objection and to describe the nature and quantum of the dispute. It did not provide all the relevant provisions that it would have needed to rely on in its appeal. *Bakorp Management Ltd. v. The Queen*, 2014 DTC 5063 (F.C.A.)

▶ 165(1.12) ◀

(1.12) Late compliance. Notwithstanding subsection (1.11), where a notice of objection served by a corporation to which that subsection applies does not include the information required by paragraph (1.11)(*b*) or (*c*) in respect of an issue to be decided that is described in the notice, the Minister may in writing request the corporation to provide the information, and those paragraphs shall be deemed to be complied with in respect of the issue if, within 60 days after the request is made, the corporation submits the information in writing to a Chief of Appeals referred to in subsection (2).

▶ 165(1.13) ◀

(1.13) Limitation on objections by large corporations. Notwithstanding subsections (1) and (1.1), where under subsection (3) a particular assessment was made for a taxation year pursuant to a notice of objection served by a corporation that was a large corporation in the year (within the meaning assigned by subsection 225.1(8)), except where the objection was made to an earlier assessment made under any of the provisions or circumstances referred to in paragraph (1.1)(*a*), the corporation may object to the particular assessment in respect of an issue

(*a*) only if the corporation complied with subsection (1.11) in the notice with respect to that issue; and

(*b*) only with respect to the relief sought in respect of that issue as specified by the corporation in the notice.

▶ 165(1.14) ◀

(1.14) Application of subsection (1.13). Where a particular assessment is made under subsection (3) pursuant to an objection made by a taxpayer to an earlier assessment, subsection (1.13) does not limit the right of the taxpayer to object to the particular assessment in respect of an issue that was part of the particular assessment and not part of the earlier assessment.

▶ 165(1.15) ◀

(1.15) Partnership. Notwithstanding subsection (1), where the Minister makes a determination under subsection 152(1.4) in respect of a fiscal period of a partnership, an objection in respect of the determination may be made only by one member of the partnership, and that member must be either

(*a*) designated for that purpose in the information return made under section 229 of the *Income Tax Regulations* for the fiscal period; or

(*b*) otherwise expressly authorized by the partnership to so act.

▶ 165(1.2) ◀

(1.2) Limitation on objections. Notwithstanding subsections (1) and (1.1), no objection may be made by a taxpayer to an assessment made under subsection 118.1(11), 152(4.2), 169(3) or 220(3.1) nor, for greater certainty, in respect of an issue for which the right of objection has been waived in writing by the taxpayer.

Related Sections: S. 152(4.2) Reassessment with taxpayer's consent.

Other Publications: AD-19-01 Audit agreement and waiver of objection rights guidelines.

▶ 165(2) ◀

(2) Service. A notice of objection under this section shall be served by being addressed to the Chief of Appeals in a District Office or a Taxation Centre of the Canada Revenue Agency and delivered or mailed to that Office or Centre.

Related Sections: S. 165(6) Validity of notice of objection.

▶ 165(2.1) ◀

(2.1) Application. Notwithstanding any other provision of this Act, paragraph (1)(*a*) shall apply only in respect of assessments, determinations and redeterminations under this Part and Part I.2.

▶ 165(3) ◀

(3) Duties of Minister. On receipt of a notice of objection under this section, the Minister shall, with all due dispatch, reconsider the assessment and vacate, confirm or vary the assessment or reassess, and shall thereupon notify the taxpayer in writing of the Minister's action.

Related Sections: S. 164(1.1) Repayment on objections and appeals; s. 165(4) Effect of filing of notice of objection; s. 165(5) Validity of reassessment; s. 169 Appeal; s. 172(2) Appeal to Federal Court of Canada.

Canadian Tax Foundation: Kreklewetz and Siu, *TCC Is the Proper Forum for Determining Whether Notice of Assessment Was Mailed*, 2015 Tax for the Owner-Manager 15(2):6–7; Solhi, *CRA Reneges on Longstanding Assessment Agreement*, 2015 Tax for the Owner-Manager 15(2):5–6; Siu, *Incomplete Address: Notice of Assessment Not "Mailed"*, 2015 Canadian Tax Focus 1(1):12–13.

Information Circulars: IC 98-1R4 Collections Policies.

Cases: Although a taxpayer had filed a notice of objection on May 12, 1992 and the Minister had not dealt with it until March 31, 1993, it could not be said that he had failed to act "with all due dispatch" considering that the taxpayer had refused to speak on the phone to Revenue Canada and his files were complex. *Godsell v. The Queen*, 2001 DTC 5384 (F.C.A.), affirming 96 DTC 1292 (T.C.C.)

If the Minister does not act "with all due dispatch" upon receipt of a Notice of Objection by the taxpayer, his failure does not have the effect of vacating his assessment and the taxpayer's only recourse is to appeal under s. 169. *Bolton v. The Queen*, 96 DTC 6413 (F.C.A.). See also *James v. The Queen*, 96 DTC 6416 (F.C.T.D.)

Nothing in s. 165(3) requires that the confirmation of an assessment be served personally by the Minister on the taxpayer or that it be received by the taxpayer. *Kilroy v. The Queen*, 95 DTC 344 (T.C.C.).

▶ 165(3.1) ◀

(3.1) Decision by Minister of Human Resources Development — (Repealed by S.C. 1998, c. 19, s. 192(4).)

▶ 165(3.2) ◀

(3.2) Reconsideration of determination — (Repealed by S.C. 1998, c. 19, s. 192(4).)

▶ 165(4) ◀

(4) Effect of filing of notice of objection — (Repealed by S.C. 1994, c. 7, Sched. VIII, s. 98(3).)

▶ 165(5) ◀

(5) Validity of reassessment. The limitations imposed under subsections 152(4) and (4.01) do not apply to a reassessment made under subsection (3).

Related Sections: S. 152(4) Assessment and reassessment.

▶ 165(6) ◀

(6) Validity of notice of objection. The Minister may accept a notice of objection served under this section that was not served in the manner required by subsection (2).

Related Sections: S. 165(2) Service.

▶ 165(7) ◀

(7) Notice of objection not required. Where a taxpayer has served in accordance with this section a notice of objection to an assessment and thereafter the Minister reassesses the tax, interest, penalties or other amount in respect of which the notice of objection was served or makes an additional assessment in respect thereof and sends to the taxpayer a notice of the reassessment or of the additional assessment, as the case may be, the taxpayer may, without serving a notice of objection to the reassessment or additional assessment,

(*a*) appeal therefrom to the Tax Court of Canada in accordance with section 169; or

(*b*) amend any appeal to the Tax Court of Canada that has been instituted with respect to the assessment by joining thereto an appeal in respect of the reassessment or the additional assessment in such manner and on such terms, if any, as the Tax Court of Canada directs.

Related Sections: S. 167(1) Extension of time to appeal; s. 169 Appeal; s. 173(2) Time during consideration not to count; s. 174(5) Time during consideration of question not counted; s. 248(1), "assessment", "prescribed".

Cases: While an appeal from an assessment was before the court, a taxpayer filed directly with the court a Notice of Appeal dealing with a second, unrelated, matter. The Notice of Appeal was held to be invalid, because it had not been preceded by a Notice of Objection. Subsection 165(7) did not apply because the two assessments concerned different transactions, issues and taxpayers. *Graham v. The Queen*, 92 DTC 1012 (T.C.C.)

General

SECTION 166: Irregularities

An assessment shall not be vacated or varied on appeal by reason only of any irregularity, informality, omission or error on the part of any person in the observation of any directory provision of this Act.

Related Sections: S. 152(8) Assessment deemed valid and binding; s. 165(3) Duties of Minister; s. 248(1), "assessment".

SECTION 166.1: Extension of time by Minister

▶ 166.1(1) ◀

(1) Extension of time by Minister. Where no notice of objection to an assessment has been served under section 165, nor any request under subsection 245(6) made, within the time limited by those provisions for doing so, the taxpayer may apply to the Minister to extend the time for serving the notice of objection or making the request.

Related Sections: S. 245(6) Request for adjustments.

Tax Profile: September 2009 — Fixing Tax Mistakes.

▶ 166.1(2) ◀

(2) Contents of application. An application made under subsection (1) shall set out the reasons why the notice of objection or the request was not served or made, as the case may be, within the time otherwise limited by this Act for doing so.

▶ 166.1(3) ◀

(3) How application made. An application under subsection (1) shall be made by being addressed to the Chief of Appeals in a District Office or a Taxation Centre of the Canada Revenue Agency and delivered or mailed to that Office or Centre, accompanied by a copy of the notice of objection or a copy of the request, as the case may be.

▶ 166.1(4) ◀

(4) Idem. The Minister may accept an application under this section that was not made in the manner required by subsection (3).

▶ 166.1(5) ◀

(5) Duties of Minister. On receipt of an application made under subsection (1), the Minister shall, with all due dispatch, consider the application and grant or refuse it, and shall thereupon notify the taxpayer in writing of the Minister's decision.

▶ 166.1(6) ◀

(6) Date of objection or request if application granted. If an application made under subsection (1) is granted, the notice of objection or the request, as the case may be, is deemed to have been served or made on the day on which the decision of the Minister is sent to the taxpayer.

History: S. 166.1(6) was replaced by S.C. 2010, c. 25, s. 44, in force on Royal Assent, December 15, 2010. S. 166.1(6) formerly read:

(6) *Date of objection or request if application granted.* Where an application made under subsection (1) is granted, the notice of objection or the request, as the case may be, shall be deemed to have been served or made on the day the decision of the Minister is mailed to the taxpayer.

▶ 166.1(7) ◀

(7) When order to be made. No application shall be granted under this section unless

(*a*) the application is made within one year after the expiration of the time otherwise limited by this Act for serving a notice of objection or making a request, as the case may be; and

(*b*) the taxpayer demonstrates that

(i) within the time otherwise limited by this Act for serving such a notice or making such a request, as the case may be, the taxpayer

(A) was unable to act or to instruct another to act in the taxpayer's name, or

(B) had a *bona fide* intention to object to the assessment or make the request,

(ii) given the reasons set out in the application and the circumstances of the case, it would be just and equitable to grant the application, and

(iii) the application was made as soon as circumstances permitted.

Cases: The taxpayer filed amended returns for 2002-2005, but the CRA disallowed the amendments in a 2012 letter. An extension of time to object was denied since it was not filed within one year. The 2012 letter was not a reassessment and even if it was, the Court could not grant an extension since those years were statute-barred. Also, the Court could not enforce a CRA policy of treating amended returns as *de facto* waivers. *Newfoundland Transshipment Ltd. v. The Queen*, 2013 DTC 1208 (T.C.C.)

SECTION 166.2: Extension of time by Tax Court

▶ 166.2(1) ◀

(1) Extension of time by Tax Court. A taxpayer who has made an application under subsection 166.1 may apply to the Tax Court of Canada to have the application granted after either

(*a*) the Minister has refused the application, or

(*b*) 90 days have elapsed after service of the application under subsection 166.1(1) and the Minister has not notified the taxpayer of the Minister's decision, but no application under this section may be made after the expiration of 90 days after the day on which notification of the decision was mailed to the taxpayer.

► 166.2(2) ◄

(2) How application made. An application under subsection (1) shall be made by filing in the Registry of the Tax Court of Canada, in accordance with the provisions of the *Tax Court of Canada Act*, three copies of the documents referred to in subsection 166.1(3) and three copies of the notification, if any, referred to in subsection 166.1(5).

Cases: Applications for extensions of time to file Notices of Objection must either be filed in person or by registered mail, and service by courier was simply not authorized by s. 166.2(2). *Bordieri et al. v. The Queen*, 95 DTC 5243 (F.C.A.).

► 166.2(3) ◄

(3) Copy to Commissioner of Revenue. The Tax Court of Canada shall send a copy of each application made under this section to the office of the Commissioner of Revenue.

► 166.2(4) ◄

(4) Powers of Court. The Tax Court of Canada may grant or dismiss an application made under subsection (1) and, in granting an application, may impose such terms as it deems just or order that the notice of objection be deemed to have been served on the date of its order.

► 166.2(5) ◄

(5) When application to be granted. No application shall be granted under this section unless

(*a*) the application was made under subsection 166.1(1) within one year after the expiration of the time otherwise limited by this Act for serving a notice of objection or making a request, as the case may be; and

(*b*) the taxpayer demonstrates that

(i) within the time otherwise limited by this Act for serving such a notice or making such a request, as the case may be, the taxpayer

(A) was unable to act or to instruct another to act in the taxpayer's name, or

(B) had a *bona fide* intention to object to the assessment or make the request,

(ii) given the reasons set out in the application and the circumstances of the case, it would be just and equitable to grant the application, and

(iii) the application was made under subsection 166.1(1) as soon as circumstances permitted.

Cases: An application for extension was granted where the taxpayer provided credible testimony that he personally prepared and mailed a notice of objection on time, even though the Minister argued that it was not received until a year and a half later. *Poulin v. The Queen*, 2013 DTC 1102 (T.C.C.)

SECTION 167: Extension of time to appeal

► 167(1) ◄

(1) Extension of time to appeal. Where an appeal to the Tax Court of Canada has not been instituted by a taxpayer under section 169 within the time limited by that section for doing so, the taxpayer may make an application to the Court for an order extending the time within which the appeal may be instituted and the Court may make an order extending the time for appealing and may impose such terms as it deems just.

Related Sections: S. 167(2) Contents of application; s. 167(3) How application made; s. 167(5) When order to be made.

Cases: The taxpayers filed their application for an extension within the requisite one-year period and there were reasonable grounds for the appeal. The taxpayers had not exercised the required diligence in filing their applications, which must be filed as soon as circumstances permitted. They had ample time to file within the 90 days, but had not adequately explained their failure to do so. The extension was denied. *Amrite et al v. The Queen*, 2018 DTC 1026 (TCC)

The taxpayer's motion for extension for time to appeal was allowed where the Minister did not provide sufficient evidence that a notice of confirmation of the assessment was sent, especially since it was allegedly sent by registered mail. *Pyatuke v. The Queen*, 2014 DTC 1019 (T.C.C.)

An extension to file a notice of objection was granted where the taxpayer, a student with a limited knowledge of income tax, did not mention the assessment to her tax lawyer. *Stanwood v. M.N.R.*, 91 DTC 636 (T.C.C.)

An application for extension of time to appeal was dismissed when the taxpayer had not filed his returns within the three-year limitation period. *Michael v. M.N.R.*, 91 DTC 836 (T.C.C.)

► 167(2) ◄

(2) Contents of application. An application made under subsection (1) shall set out the reasons why the appeal was not instituted within the time limited by section 169 for doing so.

► 167(3) ◄

(3) How application made. An application made under subsection (1) shall be made by filing in the Registry of the Tax Court of Canada, in accordance with the provisions of the *Tax Court of Canada Act*, three copies of the application accompanied by three copies of the notice of appeal.

Related Sections: S. 165(2) Service.

► 167(4) ◄

(4) Copy to Deputy Attorney General. The Tax Court of Canada shall send a copy of each application made under this section to the office of the Deputy Attorney General of Canada.

► 167(5) ◄

(5) When order to be made. No order shall be made under this section unless

(*a*) the application is made within one year after the expiration of the time limited by section 169 for appealing; and

(*b*) the taxpayer demonstrates that

(i) within the time otherwise limited by section 169 for appealing the taxpayer

(A) was unable to act or to instruct another to act in the taxpayer's name, or

(B) had a *bona fide* intention to appeal,

(ii) given the reasons set out in the application and the circumstances of the case, it would be just and equitable to grant the application,

(iii) the application was made as soon as circumstances permitted, and

(iv) there are reasonable grounds for the appeal.

Related Sections: S. 169 Appeal; s. 248(1), "assessment".

Tax Topics: No. 2078, Fighting for an Extension of Time.

Cases: Although the taxpayer's case was part of a large group of related Indian exemption cases, she was granted an extension of time to appeal since the potential existence of untried facts and related arguments regarding disputed reserve lands warranted a hearing before a trial judge. *Turcotte v. The Queen*, 2013 DTC 1180 (T.C.C.)

Extension of time for filing an objection was allowed where the application was mailed in time but received late; and where an RCMP officer had been constrained from exercising a choice by an RCMP directive. See, respectively, *Batey v. M.N.R.*, 86 DTC 1294 (T.C.C.); and *Charpentier v. M.N.R.*, 86 DTC 1768 (T.C.C.). However, where the Minister had sent a letter advising the taxpayer to apply "no later than one-year from the 90-day limit" and efforts were being made to settle, no extension was allowed. *Pennington v. M.N.R.*, 87 DTC 5107 (F.C.A.), reversing 86 DTC 1371 (T.C.C.)

Revocation of Registration of Certain Organizations and Associations

SECTION 168: Notice of intention to revoke registration

► 168(1) ◄

(1) Notice of intention to revoke registration. The Minister may, by registered mail, give notice to a person described in any of paragraphs (*a*) to (*c*) of the definition "qualified donee" in subsection 149.1(1) that the Minister proposes to revoke its registration if the person

(*a*) applies to the Minister in writing for revocation of its registration;

(*b*) ceases to comply with the requirements of this Act for its registration;

(*c*) in the case of a registered charity or registered Canadian amateur athletic association, fails to file an information return as and when required under this Act or a regulation;

> **Amendment not yet in force**
>
> **Budget Implementation Act, 2019, No. 1 [S.C. 2019, c. 29]**
>
> **S. 168(1)(*c*) was replaced by S.C. 2019, c. 29, s. 37(1), and will read as follows:**
>
> (*c*) in the case of a registered charity, registered Canadian amateur athletic association or registered journalism organization, fails to file an information return as and when required under this Act or a regulation;
>
> **Applicable:** In force January 1, 2020.

(*d*) issues a receipt for a gift otherwise than in accordance with this Act and the regulations or that contains false information;

(*e*) fails to comply with or contravenes any of sections 230 to 231.5; or

(*f*) in the case of a registered Canadian amateur athletic association, accepts a gift the granting of which was expressly or implicitly conditional on the association making a gift to another person, club, society or association.

> **Amendment not yet in force**
>
> **Budget Implementation Act, 2019, No. 1 [S.C. 2019, c. 29]**
>
> **S. 168(1)(*f*) was replaced by S.C. 2019, c. 29, s. 37(2), and will read as follows:**
>
> (*f*) in the case of a registered Canadian amateur athletic association or registered journalism organization, accepts a gift the granting of which was expressly or implicitly conditional on the association or organization making a gift to another person, club, society, association or organization.
>
> **Applicable:** In force January 1, 2020.

Editorial Note: Section 168 provides that the Minister may give notice to certain "qualified donees", by registered mail, that he proposes to revoke their registration. The qualified donees that are subject to the rules in section 168 are:

(i) registered charities;

(ii) registered journalism organizations (effective January 1, 2020);

(iii) registered Canadian amateur athletic associations;

(iv) registered municipalities in Canada;

(v) registered municipal and public bodies performing a function of government in Canada that have applied for registration;

(vi) registered housing corporations in Canada constituted exclusively to provide low-cost housing for the aged that have applied for registration;

(vii) a registered university outside of Canada, the student body of which ordinarily includes students from Canada, that has applied for registration (unless it was prescribed in the Regulations before February 27, 2018); and

(viii) foreign charities outside of Canada that have received a gift from Her Majesty in right of Canada and have applied for registration under subsection 149.1(26).

The Minister is also given certain powers to refuse to register an applicant charity, Canadian amateur athletic association, or, effective January 1, 2020, registered journalism organization, or to revoke the registration of a registered charity in section 149.1. As an alternative to revoking registered status, the Minister has the ability to issue penalties for certain actions under s. 188.1. See the CRA's Charities Connection Newsletter No. 3, Service Clubs and Fraternal Societies.

History: S. 168(1) was replaced by S.C. 2011, c. 24, s. 53(1), in force January 1, 2012. S. 168(1) formerly read:

(1) *Notice of intention to revoke registration.* Where a registered charity or a registered Canadian amateur athletic association

(*a*) applies to the Minister in writing for revocation of its registration,

(*b*) ceases to comply with the requirements of this Act for its registration as such,

(*c*) fails to file an information return as and when required under this Act or a regulation,

(*d*) issues a receipt for a gift or donation otherwise than in accordance with this Act and the regulations or that contains false information,

(*e*) fails to comply with or contravenes any of sections 230 to 231.5, or

(*f*) in the case of a registered Canadian amateur athletic association, accepts a gift or donation the granting of which was expressly or impliedly conditional on the association making a gift or donation to another person, club, society or association,

the Minister may, by registered mail, give notice to the registered charity or registered Canadian amateur athletic association that the Minister proposes to revoke its registration.

Related Sections: S. 149.1(2) Revocation of registration of charitable organization; s. 149.1(3) Revocation of registration of public foundation; s. 149.1(4) Revocation of registration of private foundation; s. 149.1(4.1) Revocation of registration of registered charity; s. 149.1(4.2) Revocation of registration of registered Canadian amateur athletic association; s. 149.1(4.3) Revocation of a qualified donee; s. 149.1(6.5) Revocation of designation; s. 149.1(23) Annulment of registration; s. 168(4) Objection to proposal or designation; s. 172(3) Appeal from refusal to register, revocation of registration, etc.; s. 180(1) Appeals to Federal Court of Appeal; s. 188(1) Deemed year-end on notice of revocation; s. 188(1.1) Revocation tax; s. 230(2) Records and books; s. 248(1), "registered charity", "registered Canadian amateur athletic association".

Forms: T3010 — Registered Charity Information Return.

Guides: T4033 Completing the Registered Charity Information Return; RC4108 Registered Charities and the Income Tax Act.

Interpretation Bulletins: *Secondary* — IT-496 Non-profit organizations.

Cases: The taxpayer's registration as a charity was revoked on the ground that the magazine it published did not fall within the category of the advancement of education nor were its articles restricted to matters of direct relevance to Canada's poor. *Briarpatch Inc. v. The Queen*, 96 DTC 6294 (F.C.A.)

No member of a charitable society was to apply for an order requiring the Minister to revoke the society's status as registered charity. *Reed v. The Queen*, 89 DTC 5230 (F.C.T.D.)

► 168(2) ◄

(2) Revocation of registration. Where the Minister gives notice under subsection (1) to a registered charity or to a registered Canadian amateur athletic association,

(*a*) if the charity or association has applied to the Minister in writing for the revocation of its registration, the Minister shall, forthwith after the mailing of the notice, publish a copy of the notice in the *Canada Gazette*, and

> **Amendment not yet in force**
> **Budget Implementation Act, 2019, No. 1 [S.C. 2019, c. 29]**
> **S. 168(2), the portion before paragraph (b) was replaced by S.C. 2019, c. 29, s. 37(3), and will read as follows:**
> **(2) Revocation of registration.** If the Minister gives notice under subsection (1) to a registered charity, to a registered Canadian amateur athletic association or to a registered journalism organization,
> (*a*) if it has applied to the Minister in writing for the revocation of its registration, the Minister shall, forthwith after the mailing of the notice, publish a copy of the notice in the *Canada Gazette*, and on that publication of a copy of the notice, the registration is revoked; and
> **Applicable:** In force January 1, 2020.

(*b*) in any other case, the Minister may, after the expiration of 30 days from the day of mailing of the notice, or after the expiration of such extended period from the day of mailing of the notice as the Federal Court of Appeal or a judge of that Court, on application made at any time before the determination of any appeal pursuant to subsection 172(3) from the giving of the notice, may fix or allow, publish a copy of the notice in the *Canada Gazette*,

and on that publication of a copy of the notice, the registration of the charity or association is revoked.

> **Amendment not yet in force**
> **Budget Implementation Act, 2019, No. 1 [S.C. 2019, c. 29]**
> **S. 168(2), the portion after paragraph (a) was replaced by S.C. 2019, c. 29, s. 37(4), and will read as follows:**
> (*b*) in any other case, the Minister may, after the expiration of 30 days from the day of mailing of the notice, or after the expiration of such extended period from the day of mailing of the notice as the Federal Court of Appeal or a judge of that Court, on application made at any time before the determination of any appeal pursuant to subsection 172(3) from the giving of the notice, may fix or allow, publish a copy of the notice in the *Canada Gazette*, and on that publication of a copy of the notice, the registration is revoked.
> **Applicable:** In force January 1, 2020.

Related Sections: S. 168(1) Notice of intention to revoke registration; s. 172(3) Appeal from refusal to register, revocation of registration, etc.; s. 180(1) Appeals to Federal Court of Appeal; s. 248(1), "registered Canadian amateur athletic association", "registered charity", "regulation".

Cases: The de-registration of a charitable organization did not violate the Bill of Rights. The onus is on the charity to prove that its status should not be revoked. The Minister did not err in concluding that the charity failed to comply with the requirements of the Act and was not in control or direction of its international agent. *The Canadian Committee for the Tel Aviv Foundation v. The Queen*, 2002 DTC 6843 (F.C.A.).

► 168(3) ◄

(3) *Charities Registration (Security Information) Act*. Notwithstanding subsections (1), (2) and (4), if a registered charity is the subject of a certificate that is determined to be reasonable under subsection 7(1) of the *Charities Registration (Security Information) Act*, the registration of the charity is revoked as of the making of that determination.

► 168(4) ◄

(4) Objection to proposal or designation. A person may, on or before the day that is 90 days after the day on which the notice was mailed, serve on the Minister a written notice of objection in the manner authorized by the Minister, setting out the reasons for the objection and all the relevant facts, and the provisions of subsections 165(1), (1.1) and (3) to (7) and sections 166, 166.1 and 166.2 apply, with any modifications that the circumstances require, as if the notice were a notice of assessment made under section 152, if

(*a*) in the case of a person that is or was registered as a registered charity or is an applicant for such registration, it objects to a notice under any of subsections (1) and 149.1(2) to (4.1), (6.3), (22) and (23);

(*b*) in the case of a person that is or was registered as a registered Canadian amateur athletic association or is an applicant for such registration, it objects to a notice under any of subsections (1) and 149.1(4.2) and (22); or

(*c*) in the case of a person described in any of subparagraphs (*a*)(i) to (v) of the definition "qualified donee" in subsection 149.1(1), that is or was registered by the Minister as a qualified donee or is an applicant for such registration, it objects to a notice under any of subsections (1) and 149.1(4.3) and (22).

> **Amendment not yet in force**
> **Budget Implementation Act, 2019, No. 1 [S.C. 2019, c. 29]**
> **S. 168(4)(c) was replaced by S.C. 2019, c. 29, s. 37(5), and will read as follows:**
> (*c*) in the case of a person described in any of subparagraphs (*a*)(i) to (v) and paragraph (*b*.1) of the definition "qualified donee" in subsection 149.1(1), that is or was registered by the Minister as a qualified donee or is an applicant for such registration, it objects to a notice under any of subsections (1) and 149.1(4.3) and (22).
> **Applicable:** In force January 1, 2020.

Editorial Note: The Minister's notice proposing to revoke the registration of a "qualified donee" described in subsection 168(1) may be objected to by the affected qualified donee within 90 days following the mailing of such notice in accordance with the provisions of the Act relating to objections to assessments. If the objection is not allowed, it may be appealed to the Federal Court of Appeal pursuant to the provisions of subsection 172(3).

History: S. 168(4) was replaced by S.C. 2011, c. 24, s. 53(2), in force January 1, 2012. S. 168(4) formerly read:

(4) *Objection to proposal or designation.* A person that is or was registered as a registered charity or is an applicant for registration as a registered charity that objects to a notice under subsection (1) or any of subsections 149.1(2) to (4.1), (6.3), (22) and (23) may, on or before the day that is 90 days after the day on which the notice was mailed, serve on the Minister a written notice of objection in the manner authorized by the Minister, setting out the reasons for the objection and all the relevant facts, and the provisions of subsections 165(1), (1.1) and (3) to (7) and sections 166, 166.1 and 166.2 apply, with any modifications that the circumstances require, as if the notice were a notice of assessment made under section 152.

Related Sections: S. 149.1(1) "qualified donee"; s. 172(3) Appeal from refusal to register, revocation of registration, etc.; s. 180(1) Appeals to Federal Court of Appeal.

Tax Topics: No. 1743, Objections to Decisions Regarding Charities.

Division J — Appeals to the Tax Court of Canada and the Federal Court of Appeal

SECTION 169: Appeal

▶ 169(1) ◀

(1) Appeal. Where a taxpayer has served notice of objection to an assessment under section 165, the taxpayer may appeal to the Tax Court of Canada to have the assessment vacated or varied after either

(*a*) the Minister has confirmed the assessment or reassessed, or

(*b*) 90 days have elapsed after service of the notice of objection and the Minister has not notified the taxpayer that the Minister has vacated or confirmed the assessment or reassessed,

but no appeal under this section may be instituted after the expiration of 90 days from the day notice has been sent to the taxpayer under section 165 that the Minister has confirmed the assessment or reassessed.

History: S. 169(1), the portion after paragraph (*b*) was replaced by S.C. 2010, c. 25, s. 45, in force on Royal Assent, December 15, 2010. S. 169(1), the portion after paragraph (*b*) formerly read:

but no appeal under this section may be instituted after the expiration of 90 days from the day notice has been mailed to the taxpayer under section 165 that the Minister has confirmed the assessment or reassessed.

Related Sections: S. 165 Objections to assessment; s. 167 Extension of time to appeal; s. 172(2) Appeal to Federal Court of Canada; s. 173(2) Time during consideration not to count; s. 174(5) Time during consideration of question not counted; s. 196(4) Provisions applicable to Part; s. 248(1), "assessment"; ITAR s. 62(5) Appeals.

Canadian Tax Foundation: Bellefontaine, *No Relief for CRA Misfeasance*, 2013 Canadian Tax Highlights 21(3):3–4; Bendin, *Challenging and Defending Assessments before the Tax Court of Canada and Appellate Courts: A Postscript to the Continental Bank Case*, 2000 Canadian Tax Journal 1:35–59.

Tax Profile: October 2006 — Tax Controversies in Canada: A Variety of Issues.

Tax Topics: No. 2279, "Demolishing" the Crown: A Brief Review; No. 2269, *1455257 Ontario Inc. v. The Queen*: Must a Dissolved Corporation Be Revived Before It Can Pursue a Tax Appeal?; No. 2141, You Can't Always Get What You Want (But If You Try Sometimes, You Might Get What You Need); No. 2002, *Northland Properties:* An Interesting Perspective on Onus of Proof; No. 1923, A "New" Way To Challenge Decisions of the Minister of National Revenue?; No. 1908, Wait! Don't Strike Those Assumptions; No. 1906, Principles of *Res Judicata* Upheld; No. 1871, The Burden of Proof in Tax Cases: Anchor Pointe v. The Queen.

Guides: P148 Objection and Appeal Rights Under the Income Tax Act.

Cases: A dissolved corporation does not have the legal capacity to initiate and continue an appeal in the Tax Court of Canada. *1455257 Ontario Inc. v. The Queen*, 2016 DTC 5046 (FCA)

▶ 169(1.1) ◀

(1.1) Ecological gifts. Where at any particular time a taxpayer has disposed of a property, the fair market value of which has been confirmed or redetermined by the Minister of the Environment under subsection 118.1(10.4), the taxpayer may, within 90 days after the day on which that Minister has issued a certificate under subsection 118.1(10.5), appeal the confirmation or redetermination to the Tax Court of Canada.

Canadian Tax Foundation: Bassindale and Kreklewetz, *Change in "Issue" Costs Taxpayer Its Right of Appeal*, 2014 Tax for the Owner-Manager 14(3):9–11; Bassindale and Kreklewetz, *A Reasonable Description of the Issue*, 2013 Canadian Tax Highlights 21(6):3–5.

▶ 169(2) ◀

(2) Limitation of right to appeal from assessments or determinations. Notwithstanding subsection (1), where at any time the Minister assesses tax, interest, penalties or other amounts payable under this Part by, or makes a determination in respect of, a taxpayer

(*a*) under subsection 67.5(2) or 152(1.8), subparagraph 152(4)(*b*)(i) or subsection 152(4.3) or (6), 164(4.1), 220(3.4) or 245(8) or in accordance with an order of a court vacating, varying or restoring the assessment or referring the assessment back to the Minister for reconsideration and reassessment,

(*b*) under subsection 165(3) where the underlying objection relates to an assessment or a determination made under any of the provisions or circumstances referred to in paragraph (*a*), or

(*c*) under a provision of an Act of Parliament requiring an assessment to be made that, but for that provision, would not be made because of subsections 152(4) to (5),

the taxpayer may appeal to the Tax Court of Canada within the time limit specified in subsection (1), but only to the extent that the reasons for the appeal can reasonably be regarded

(*d*) where the assessment or determination was made under subsection 152(1.8), as relating to any matter specified in paragraph 152(1.8)(*a*), (*b*) or (*c*), and

(*e*) in any other case, as relating to any matter that gave rise to the assessment or determination

and that was not conclusively determined by the Court, and this subsection shall not be read or construed as limiting the right of the taxpayer to appeal from an assessment or a determination issued or made before that time.

Related Sections: S. 165(1.1) Limitation of right to object to assessments or determinations.

▶ 169(2.1) ◀

(2.1) Limitation on appeals by large corporations. Notwithstanding subsections (1) and (2), where a corporation that was a large corporation in a taxation year (within the meaning assigned by subsection 225.1(8)) served a notice of objection to an assessment under this Part for the year, the corporation may appeal to the Tax Court of Canada to have the assessment vacated or varied only with respect to

(*a*) an issue in respect of which the corporation has complied with subsection 165(1.11) in the notice, or

(*b*) an issue described in subsection 165(1.14) where the corporation did not, because of subsection 165(7), serve a notice of objection to the assessment that gave rise to the issue and, in the case of an issue described in paragraph (*a*), the corporation may so appeal only with respect to the relief sought in respect of the issue as specified by the corporation in the notice.

Canadian Tax Foundation: Bassindale and Kreklewetz, *Change in "Issue" Costs Taxpayer Its Right of Appeal*, 2014 Tax for the Owner-Manager 14(3):9–11; Bassindale and Kreklewetz, *A Reasonable Description of the Issue*, 2013 Canadian Tax Highlights 21(6):3–5.

Tax Topics: No. 1680, Large Corporation Tax Objections: Assert It Or Lose It.

Income Tax Technical News: Issue No. 32, Notice of Objection of Large Corporation: Impact of the Potash Corporation Case.

Cases: There is no provision in the Act specifically allowing a large corporation to amend its Notice of Objection. If, however, the Minister allows a large corporation to raise additional issues before the objection stage is completed, it is difficult to accept that the Minister would be prejudiced if the large corporation were then allowed to continue to pursue these additional issues at the Tax Court level. *Devon Canada Corporation v. The Queen*, 2015 DTC 5108 (FCA)

The taxpayer failed to adequately set out the issues on objection and to describe the nature and quantum of the dispute. It did not provide all the relevant provisions that it would have needed to rely on in its appeal. *Bakorp Management Ltd. v. The Queen*, 2014 DTC 5063 (F.C.A.).

The taxpayer was not entitled to amend its Notice of Appeal to include five new items in its computation of resource profits that were not described in the Notice of Objection. The taxpayer did not comply with s. 165(1.11) by simply specifying the issue to be tried as the computation of "resource allowance" or "resource profits", without specifying the particular elements of that computation that required a determination. *The Queen v. Potash Corporation of Saskatchewan Inc.*, 2004 DTC 6002 (F.C.A.), reversing 2003 DTC 509 (T.C.C.).

► 169(2.2) ◄

(2.2) Waived issues. Notwithstanding subsections (1) and (2), for greater certainty a taxpayer may not appeal to the Tax Court of Canada to have an assessment under this Part vacated or varied in respect of an issue for which the right of objection or appeal has been waived in writing by the taxpayer.

Other Publications: AD-19-01 Audit agreement and waiver of objection rights guidelines.

► 169(3) ◄

(3) Disposition of appeal on consent. Notwithstanding section 152, for the purpose of disposing of an appeal made under a provision of this Act, the Minister may at any time, with the consent in writing of the taxpayer, reassess tax, interest, penalties or other amounts payable under this Act by the taxpayer.

Cases: The issues were whether the taxpayer's former counsel had a mandate to settle the appeal and whether consent in writing signed by counsel constituted a valid consent. The taxpayer was asked to confirm both that he was in agreement with the settlement and that his counsel could sign the settlement. He agreed to both by e-mail. The former counsel had been counsel of record within the meaning of the Tax Court rules and could consent in writing on behalf of the taxpayer to settle an appeal. Subsection 169(3) does not require an out-of-court settlement to be signed by both parties, only the taxpayer's consent in writing is required. Such consent was provided in the e-mail to counsel. The argument that the agreement was invalid because it was not personally signed was dismissed. *Granofsky v. The Queen*, 2017 DTC 5072 (FCA)

The reassessment was void because the taxpayer never consented, either expressly or implicitly, to the Minister adding $1,006,217 to its reported income. *Bolton Steel Tube Co. Ltd. v. The Queen*, 2014 DTC 1102 (T.C.C.)

► 169(4) ◄

(4) Provisions applicable. Division I applies, with such modifications as the circumstances require, in respect of a reassessment made under subsection (3) as though it had been made under section 152.

SECTION 170: Notice to Commissioner

► 170(1) ◄

(1) Notice to Commissioner. Where an appeal is made to the Tax Court of Canada under section 18 of the *Tax Court of Canada Act*, the Court shall forthwith send a copy of the notice of the appeal to the office of the Commissioner of Revenue.

► 170(2) ◄

(2) Notice, etc., to be forwarded to Tax Court of Canada — (Repealed by S.C. 2013, c. 34, s. 322.)

History: S. 170(2) was repealed by S.C. 2013, c. 34, s. 322, in force June 26, 2013, and formerly read:

(2) *Notice, etc., to be forwarded to Tax Court of Canada.* Forthwith after receiving notice under subsection (1) of an appeal, the Commissioner of Revenue shall forward to the Tax Court of Canada copies of all returns, notices of assessment, notices of objection and notification, if any, that are relevant to the appeal.

SECTION 171: Disposal of Appeal

► 171(1) ◄

(1) Disposal of Appeal. The Tax Court of Canada may dispose of an appeal by

(*a*) dismissing it; or

(*b*) allowing it and

(i) vacating the assessment,

(ii) varying the assessment, or

(iii) referring the assessment back to the Minister for reconsideration and reassessment.

Related Sections: S. 169 Appeal.

► 171(1.1) ◄

(1.1) Ecological gifts. On an appeal under subsection 169(1.1), the Tax Court of Canada may confirm or vary the amount determined to be the fair market value of a property and the value determined by the Court is deemed to be the fair market value of the property determined by the Minister of the Environment.

► 171(2) ◄

(2) Partial disposition of appeal. If an appeal raises more than one issue, the Tax Court of Canada may, with the consent in writing of the parties to the appeal, dispose of a particular issue by

(*a*) dismissing the appeal with respect to the particular issue; or

(*b*) allowing the appeal with respect to the particular issue and

(i) varying the assessment, or

(ii) referring the assessment back to the Minister for reconsideration and reassessment.

History: S. 171(2) was added by S.C. 2013, c. 33, s. 18(1), applicable with respect to issues disposed of by the Tax Court of Canada after June 26, 2013.

► 171(3) ◄

(3) Disposal of remaining issues. If a particular issue has been disposed of under subsection (2), the appeal with respect to the remaining issues may continue.

History: S. 171(3) was added by S.C. 2013, c. 33, s. 18(1), applicable with respect to issues disposed of by the Tax Court of Canada after June 26, 2013.

► 171(4) ◄

(4) Appeal to Federal Court of Appeal. If the Tax Court of Canada has disposed of a particular issue under subsection (2), the parties to the appeal may, in accordance with the provisions of the *Tax Court of Canada Act* or the *Federal Courts Act*, as they relate to appeals from decisions of the Tax Court of Canada, appeal the disposition to the Federal Court of Appeal as if it were a final judgment of the Tax Court of Canada.

History: S. 171(4) was added by S.C. 2013, c. 33, s. 18(1), applicable with respect to issues disposed of by the Tax Court of Canada after June 26, 2013.

Related Sections: S. 248(1), "assessment"; ITAR s. 62(5) Appeals.

SECTION 172: Appeal from refusal to register, revocation of registration, etc

► 172(1) ◄

(1) Appeal from refusal to register, revocation of registration, etc — (Repealed by 1988, c. 61, s. 18(1).)

► 172(2) ◄

(2) Appeal to Federal Court of Canada — (Repealed by 1988, c. 61, s. 18(1).)

► 172(3) ◄

(3) Appeal from refusal to register, revocation of registration, etc. Where the Minister

(*a*) confirms a proposal or decision in respect of which a notice was issued under any of subsections 149.1(4.2) and (22) and 168(1) by the Minister, to a person that is or was registered as a registered Canadian amateur athletic association or is an applicant for registration as a registered Canadian amateur athletic association, or does not confirm or vacate that proposal or decision within 90 days after service of a notice of objection by the person under subsection 168(4) in respect of that proposal or decision,

(*a*.1) confirms a proposal, decision or designation in respect of which a notice was issued by the Minister to a person that is or was registered as a registered charity, or is an applicant for registration as a registered charity, under any of subsections 149.1(2) to (4.1), (6.3), (22) and (23) and 168(1), or does not confirm or vacate that proposal, decision or designation within 90 days after service of a notice of objection by the person under subsection 168(4) in respect of that proposal, decision or designation,

(*a*.2) confirms a proposal or decision in respect of which a notice was issued under any of subsections 149.1(4.3), (22) and 168(1) by the Minister, to a person that is a person described in any of subparagraphs (*a*)(i) to (v) of the definition "qualified donee" in subsection 149.1(1) that is or was registered by the Minister as a qualified donee or is an applicant for such registration, or does not confirm or vacate that proposal or decision within 90 days after service of a notice of objection by the person under subsection 168(4) in respect of that proposal or decision,

Amendment not yet in force

Budget Implementation Act, 2019, No. 1 [S.C. 2019, c. 29]

S. 172(3)(*a*.2) was replaced by S.C. 2019, c. 29, s. 38(1), and will read as follows:

(*a*.2) confirms a proposal or decision in respect of which a notice was issued under any of subsections 149.1(4.3) and (22) and 168(1) by the Minister, to a person that is a person described in any of subparagraphs (*a*)(i) to (v) and paragraph (*b*.1) of the definition "qualified donee" in subsection 149.1(1) that is or was registered by the Minister as a qualified donee or is an applicant for such registration, or does not confirm or vacate that proposal or decision within 90 days after service of a notice of objection by the person under subsection 168(4) in respect of that proposal or decision,

Applicable: In force January 1, 2020.

(*b*) refuses to accept for registration for the purposes of this Act any retirement savings plan,

(*c*) refuses to accept for registration for the purposes of this Act any profit sharing plan or revokes the registration of such a plan,

(*d*) (Repealed.)

(*e*) refuses to accept for registration for the purposes of this Act an education savings plan,

(*e*.1) sends notice under subsection 146.1(12.1) to a promoter that the Minister proposes to revoke the registration of an education savings plan,

(*f*) refuses to register for the purposes of this Act any pension plan or gives notice under subsection 147.1(11) to the administrator of a registered pension plan that the Minister proposes to revoke its registration,

(*f*.1) refuses to accept an amendment to a registered pension plan,

(*g*) refuses to accept for registration for the purposes of this Act any retirement income fund,

(*h*) refuses to accept for registration for the purposes of this Act any pooled pension plan or gives notice under subsection 147.5(24) to the administrator of a pooled registered pension plan that the Minister proposes to revoke its registration, or

(*i*) refuses to accept an amendment to a pooled registered pension plan,

the person described in paragraph (*a*), (*a.1*) or (*a.2*), the applicant in a case described in paragraph (*b*), (*e*) or (*g*), a trustee under the plan or an employer of employees who are beneficiaries under the plan, in a case described in paragraph (*c*), the promoter in a case described in paragraph (*e.1*), the administrator of the plan or an employer who participates in the plan, in a case described in paragraph (*f*) or (*f.1*), or the administrator of the plan in a case described in paragraph (*h*) or (*i*), may appeal from the Minister's decision, or from the giving of the notice by the Minister, to the Federal Court of Appeal.

History: S. 172(3)(*h*) and (*i*) were added by S.C. 2012, c. 31, s. 41(1), in force December 14, 2012.

S. 172(3), the portion after paragraph (*i*) was replaced by S.C. 2012, c. 31, s. 41(2), in force December 14, 2012, and formerly read:

the person in a case described in paragraph (*a*), (*a.1*) or (*a.2*), the applicant in a case described in paragraph (*b*), (*e*) or (*g*), a trustee under the plan or an employer of employees who are beneficiaries under the plan, in a case described in paragraph (*c*), the promoter in a case described in paragraph (*e.1*), or the administrator of the plan or an employer who participates in the plan, in a case described in paragraph (*f*) or (*f.1*), may appeal from the Minister's decision, or from the giving of the notice by the Minister, to the Federal Court of Appeal.

S. 172(3)(*a*) was replaced by S.C. 2011, c. 24, s. 54(1), in force January 1, 2012. S. 172(3)(*a*) formerly read:

(*a*) refuses to register an applicant for registration as a Canadian amateur athletic association,

S. 172(3)(*a.2*) was added by S.C. 2011, c. 24, s. 54(2), in force January 1, 2012.

S. 172(3)(*d*) was repealed by S.C. 2011, c. 24, s. 54(3), in force January 1, 2012. S. 172(3)(*d*) formerly read:

(*d*) refuses to issue a certificate of exemption under subsection 212(14),

S. 172(3), the portion following paragraph (*g*) was replaced by S.C. 2011, c. 24, s. 54(4), in force January 1, 2012. S. 172(3), the portion following paragraph (*g*) formerly read:

the applicant or the organization, foundation, association or registered charity, as the case may be, in a case described in paragraph (*a*) or (*a*.1), the applicant in a case described in paragraph (*b*), (*d*), (*e*) or (*g*), a trustee under the plan or an employer of employees who are beneficiaries under the plan, in a case described in paragraph (*c*), the promoter in a case described in paragraph (*e*.1), or the administrator of the plan or an employer who participates in the plan, in a case described in paragraph (*f*) or (*f*.1), may appeal from the Minister's decision, or from the giving of the notice by the Minister, to the Federal Court of Appeal.

Related Sections: S. 146(2) Acceptance of plan for registration — prohibited conditions; s. 146(3) Acceptance of plan for registration — acceptable conditions; s. 146.1 Registered education savings plans; s. 146.3(2) Acceptance of fund for registration; s. 147(2) Acceptance of plan for registration; s. 147(3) Acceptance of employees profit sharing plan for registration; s. 146.1(13) Revocation of registration; S. 149.1(1) "qualified donee"; s. 180(1) Appeals to Federal Court of Appeal.

Forms: T285 — Appeal from Minister's Refusal to Register as a Charity or Canadian Amateur Athletic Association.

Cases: A community legal clinic's appeal from the Minister's refusal to register it as a charitable organization was denied as the decision was purely administrative and in compliance with procedural fairness. The clinic's political activities also precluded charitable status. *Scarborough Community Legal Services v. The Queen*, 85 DTC 5102 (F.C.A.)

► 172(3.1) ◄

(3.1) Exception — *Charities Registration (Security Information) Act*. Paragraphs (3)(*a*) and (*a*.1) do not apply to an applicant or a registered charity that is the subject of a certificate that has been determined to be reasonable under subsection 7(1) of the *Charities Registration (Security Information) Act*.

► 172(4) ◄

(4) Deemed refusal to register. For the purposes of subsection (3), the Minister shall be deemed to have refused

(*a*) to register an applicant for registration as a Canadian amateur athletic association,

(*a*.1) (Repealed.)

(*b*) to accept for registration for the purposes of this Act any retirement savings plan or profit sharing plan,

(*c*) (Repealed.)

(*d*) to accept for registration for the purposes of this Act any education savings plan, or

(*e*) (Repealed by 1986, c. 6, s. 92(3).)

(*f*) to accept for registration for the purposes of this Act any retirement income fund,

where the Minister has not notified the applicant of the disposition of the application within 180 days after the filing of the application with the Minister, and, in any such case, subject to subsection (3.1), an appeal from the refusal to the Federal Court of Appeal pursuant to subsection (3) may, notwithstanding subsection 180(1), be instituted under section 180 at any time by filing a notice of appeal in the Court.

History: S. 172(4)(*c*) was repealed by S.C. 2011, c. 24, s. 54(5), in force January 1, 2012. S. 172(4)(*c*) formerly read:

(*c*) to issue a certificate of exemption under subsection 212(14),

Related Sections: S. 146(1), "retirement savings plan"; s. 146.1(1), "registered education savings plan"; s. 146.3(1), "registered retirement income fund"; s. 147(1), "profit sharing plan"; s. 248(1), "assessment"; ITAR s. 62(5) Appeals.

► 172(4.1) ◄

(4.1) Exception — *Charities Registration (Security Information) Act*. An appeal referred to in subsection (3) or (4) is suspended when an applicant or a registered charity is, under subsection 5(1) of the *Charities Registration (Security Information) Act*, served with a copy of a certificate that has been signed under that Act, whether the appeal was instituted before or after the certificate was so signed, and the appeal is

(*a*) discontinued on the determination, under subsection 7(1) of that Act, that the certificate is reasonable; or

(*b*) reinstated as of the date the certificate is, under subsection 7(2) of that Act, quashed.

► 172(5) ◄

(5) Idem. For the purposes of subsection (3), the Minister shall be deemed to have refused

(*a*) to register for the purposes of this Act any pension plan or pooled pension plan, or

(*b*) to accept an amendment to a registered pension plan or a pooled registered pension plan

where the Minister has not notified the applicant of the Minister's disposition of the application within 1 year after the filing of the application with the Minister, and, in any such case, an appeal from the refusal to the Federal Court of Appeal pursuant to subsection (3) may, notwithstanding anything in subsection 180(1), be instituted under section 180 at any time by filing a notice of appeal in the Court.

History: S. 172(5)(*a*) and (*b*) were replaced by S.C. 2012, c. 31, s. 41(3), in force December 14, 2012, and formerly read:

(*a*) to register for the purposes of this Act any pension plan, or

(*b*) to accept an amendment to a registered pension plan

► 172(6) ◄

(6) Application of s. 149.1(1). The definitions in subsection 149.1(1) apply to this section.

SECTION 173: References to Tax Court of Canada

► 173(1) ◄

(1) References to Tax Court of Canada. Where the Minister and a taxpayer agree in writing that a question of law, fact or mixed law and fact arising under this Act, in respect of any assessment, proposed assessment, determination or proposed determination, should be determined by the Tax Court of Canada, that question shall be determined by that Court.

Related Sections: S. 225.1(4) Collection restrictions — reference to Tax Court of Canada.

Cases: Application dismissed where no agreement as to facts. *Wright v. The Queen*, 87 DTC 5138 (F.C.T.D.).

► 173(2) ◄

(2) Time during consideration not to count. The time between the day on which proceedings are instituted in the Tax Court of Canada to have a question determined pursuant to subsection (1) and the day on which the question is finally determined shall not be counted in the computation of

(*a*) the periods determined under subsection 152(4),

(*b*) the time for service of a notice of objection to an assessment under section 165, or

(*c*) the time within which an appeal may be instituted under section 169,

for the purpose of making an assessment of the tax payable by the taxpayer who agreed in writing to the determination of the question, for the purpose of serving a notice of objection thereto or for the purpose of instituting an appeal therefrom, as the case may be.

Related Sections: S. 248(1), "assessment".

SECTION 174: Common questions

► 174(1) ◄

(1) Common questions. The Minister may apply to the Tax Court of Canada for a determination of a question if the Minister is of the opinion that the question is common to assessments or proposed assessments in respect of two or more taxpayers and is a question of law, fact or mixed law and fact arising out of

(*a*) one and the same transaction or occurrence or series of transactions or occurrences; or

(*b*) substantially similar transactions or occurrences or series of transactions or occurrences.

History: S. 174(1) was replaced by S.C. 2013, c. 33, s. 19(1), applicable in respect of applications made after June 26, 2013, and formerly read:

(1) *Reference of common questions to Tax Court of Canada.* Where the Minister is of the opinion that a question of law, fact or mixed law and fact arising out of one and the same transaction or occurrence or series of transactions or occurrences is common to assessments or proposed assessments in respect of two or more taxpayers, the Minister may apply to the Tax Court of Canada for a determination of the question.

Related Sections: S. 225.1(4) Collection restrictions — reference to Tax Court of Canada.

Cases: There is no condition precedent that there must be a pending assessment for a s. 174 request to succeed. This application was in respect of two taxpayers and the determination of the issue would be expeditious, less costly, and provide a consistent result. *The Queen v. ACI Properties Ltd.*, 2014 DTC 5036 (F.C.A.).

► 174(2) ◄

(2) Application to Court. An application under subsection (1)

(*a*) shall set out

(i) the question in respect of which the Minister requests a determination,

(ii) the names of the taxpayers that the Minister seeks to have bound by the determination of the question, and

(iii) the facts and reasons on which the Minister relies and on which the Minister based or intends to base assessments of tax payable by each of the taxpayers named in the application; and

(*b*) shall be served by the Minister on each of the taxpayers named in the application and on any other persons who, in the opinion of the Tax Court of Canada, are likely to be affected by the determination of the question,

(i) by sending a copy to each taxpayer so named and each other person so likely to be affected, or

(ii) on *ex parte* application by the Minister, in accordance with the directions of the Court.

History: S. 174(2) was replaced by S.C. 2013, c. 33, s. 19(1), applicable in respect of applications made after June 26, 2013, and formerly read:

(2) *Application to Court.* An application under subsection (1) shall set out

(*a*) the question in respect of which the Minister requests a determination,

(*b*) the names of the taxpayers that the Minister seeks to have bound by the determination of the question, and

(*c*) the facts and reasons on which the Minister relies and on which the Minister based or intends to base assessments of tax payable by each of the taxpayers named in the application,

and a copy of the application shall be served by the Minister on each of the taxpayers named in the application and on any other persons who, in the opinion of the Tax Court of Canada, are likely to be affected by the determination of the question.

Related Sections: S. 174(5) Time during consideration of question not counted.

► 174(3) ◄

(3) Determination of question by Tax Court. If the Tax Court of Canada is satisfied that a question set out in an application under this section is common to assessments or proposed assessments in respect of two or more taxpayers who have been served with a copy of the application, the Tax Court of Canada may

(*a*) make an order naming the taxpayers in respect of whom the question will be determined;

(*b*) if one or more of the taxpayers so served has or have appealed an assessment to the Tax Court of Canada in respect of which the question is relevant, make an order joining a party or parties to that or those appeals as it considers appropriate; and (*c*) proceed to determine the question in such manner as it considers appropriate.

History: S. 174(3) was replaced by S.C. 2013, c. 33, s. 19(1), applicable in respect of applications made after June 26, 2013, and formerly read:

(3) *Where Tax Court of Canada may determine question.* Where the Tax Court of Canada is satisfied that a determination of the question set out in an application under this section will affect assessments or proposed assessments in respect of two or more taxpayers who have been served with a copy of the application and who are named in an order of the Tax Court of Canada pursuant to this subsection, it may

(*a*) if none of the taxpayers so named has appealed from such an assessment, proceed to determine the question in such manner as it considers appropriate; or

(*b*) if one or more of the taxpayers so named has or have appealed, make such order joining a party or parties to that or those appeals as it considers appropriate and proceed to determine the question.

Related Sections: S. 174(4) Determination final and conclusive; s. 174(5) Time during consideration of question not counted.

Cases: Where the Minister's allocation of purchase price between land and buildings was challenged, the purchaser and vendor were joined as parties in the appeal. *Crown Trust Co. (Suburban Realty Co.) v. The Queen*, 77 DTC 5173 (F.C.T.D.).

► 174(4) ◄

(4) Determination final and conclusive. Subject to subsection (4.1), if a question set out in an application under this section is determined by the Tax Court of Canada, the determination is final and conclusive for the purposes of any assessments of tax payable by the taxpayers named in the order made under paragraph (3)(*a*).

History: S. 174(4) was replaced by S.C. 2013, c. 33, s. 19(1), applicable in respect of applications made after June 26, 2013, and formerly read:

(4) *Determination final and conclusive.* Subject to subsection (4.1), where a question set out in an application under this section is determined by the Tax Court of Canada, the determination thereof is final and conclusive for the purposes of any assessments of tax payable by the taxpayers named by it pursuant to subsection (3).

► 174(4.1) ◄

(4.1) Appeal. If a question set out in an application under this section is determined by the Tax Court of Canada, an appeal from the determination may, in accordance with the provisions of the *Tax Court of Canada Act* or the *Federal Courts Act*, as they relate to appeals from decisions of the Tax Court of Canada to the Federal Court of Appeal, be made by

(*a*) the Minister; or

(*b*) any taxpayer named in an order of the Court made under paragraph (3)(*a*) if

(i) the question arises out of one and the same transaction or occurrence or series of transactions or occurrences,

(ii) the taxpayer has appealed an assessment to the Tax Court of Canada in respect of which the question is relevant, or

(iii) the taxpayer has been granted leave by a judge of the Federal Court of Appeal.

History: S. 174(4.1) was replaced by S.C. 2013, c. 33, s. 19(1), applicable in respect of applications made after June 26, 2013, and formerly read:

(4.1) *Appeal.* Where a question set out in an application under this section is determined by the Tax Court of Canada, the Minister or any of the taxpayers who have been served with a copy of the application and who are named in an order of the Court pursuant to subsection (3) may, in accordance with the provisions of this Act, the *Tax Court of Canada Act* or the *Federal Courts Act*, as they relate to appeals from decisions of the Tax Court of Canada, appeal from the determination.

► 174(4.2) ◄

(4.2) Binding to appeal. Any taxpayer named in an order made under paragraph (3)(*a*) in respect of a question is bound by any determination in respect of the question under an appeal made to the Federal Court of Appeal or the Supreme Court of Canada.

History: S. 174(4.2) was added by S.C. 2013, c. 33, s. 19(1), applicable in respect of applications made after June 26, 2013.

► 174(5) ◄

(5) Time during consideration of question not counted. The time between the day on which an application under this section is served on a taxpayer pursuant to subsection (2) and

(*a*) in the case of a taxpayer named in an order of the Tax Court of Canada pursuant to subsection (3), the day on which the determination becomes final and conclusive and not subject to any appeal, or

(*b*) in the case of any other taxpayer, the day on which the taxpayer is served with notice that the taxpayer has not been named in an order of the Tax Court of Canada pursuant to subsection (3),

shall not be counted in the computation of

(*c*) the periods determined under subsection 152(4),

(*d*) the time for service of a notice of objection to an assessment under section 165, or

(*e*) the time within which an appeal may be instituted under section 169,

for the purpose of making an assessment of the tax, interest or penalties payable by the taxpayer, serving a notice of objection thereto or instituting an appeal therefrom, as the case may be.

Related Sections: S. 152(4) Assessment and reassessment; s. 172(2) Appeal to Federal Court of Canada; s. 248(1), "assessment".

SECTION 175: Institution of appeals

An appeal to the Tax Court of Canada under this Act, other than one referred to in section 18 of the *Tax Court of Canada Act*, shall be instituted in the manner set out in that Act or in any rules made under that Act.

SECTION 176: Notice, etc., to be forwarded to Tax Court of Canada

► 176(1) ◄

(1) Notice, etc., to be forwarded to Tax Court of Canada — (Repealed by 2013, c. 34, s. 323.)

History: S. 176(1) was repealed by S.C. 2013, c. 34, s. 323, in force June 26, 2013, and formerly read:

(1) *Notice, etc., to be forwarded to Tax Court of Canada.* As soon as is reasonably practicable after receiving notice of an appeal to the Tax Court of Canada, other than one referred to in section 18 of the *Tax Court of Canada Act*, the Minister shall cause to be transmitted to the Tax Court of Canada and to the appellant, copies of all returns, notices of assessment, notices of objection and notifications, if any, that are relevant to the appeal.

Cases: Subsection 176(1) is to be struck down in its entirety since it constitutes a significant intrusion on the privacy interests of an individual, and thus constitutes an unreasonable seizure, contrary to s. 8 of the Charter, since it creates the potential for any person to view a taxpayer's return. It is not saved by s. 1 of the Charter since its objective is not sufficiently important to warrant overriding a Charter right. *Gernhart v. The Queen*, 99 DTC 5749 (F.C.A.), reversing 97 DTC 5038 (F.C.T.D.).

► 176(2) ◄

(2) Documents to be transferred to Federal Court of Appeal — (Repealed by 2013, c. 34, s. 323.)

History: S. 176(2) was repealed by S.C. 2013, c. 34, s. 323, in force June 26, 2013, and formerly read:

(2) *Documents to be transferred to Federal Court of Appeal.* As soon as is reasonably practicable after receiving notice of an appeal to the Federal Court of Appeal in respect of which section 180 applies, the Minister shall cause to be transmitted to the registry of that Court copies of all documents that are relevant to the decision of the Minister appealed from.

SECTION 177: Disposal of appeal

(Repealed by 1988, c. 61, s. 21.)

SECTION 178: Court may order payment of tax, etc

► 178(1) ◄

(1) Court may order payment of tax, etc — (Repealed by 1988, c. 61, s. 21.)

► 178(2) ◄

(2) Costs payable by Minister in certain cases — (Repealed by 1988, c. 61, s. 21.)

SECTION 179: Hearings *in camera*

Proceedings in the Federal Court of Appeal under this Division may, on the application of the taxpayer, be held *in camera* if the taxpayer establishes to the satisfaction of the Court that the circumstances of the case justify *in camera* proceedings.

Related Sections: S. 248(1) Definitions.

SECTION 179.1: No reasonable grounds for appeal

Where the Tax Court of Canada disposes of an appeal by a taxpayer in respect of an amount payable under this Part or where such an appeal has been discontinued or dismissed without trial, the Court may, on the application of the Minister and whether or not it awards costs, order the taxpayer to pay to the Receiver General an amount not exceeding 10% of any part of the amount that was in controversy in respect of which the Court determines that there were no reasonable grounds for the appeal, if in the opinion of the Court one of the main purposes for instituting or maintaining any part of the appeal was to defer the payment of any amount payable under this Part.

Editorial Note: If in the opinion of the Tax Court one of the main purposes for an appeal was to defer the payment of tax then the Court may, on the application of the Minister, regardless of whether costs are assessed, order the taxpayer to pay to the Receiver General an amount not exceeding 10% of the controversial amount if there were no reasonable grounds for an appeal.

Cases: The fact that the taxpayer's statements of claim were poorly drawn by lawyers' standards, and had not, in any event, been properly prosecuted by the taxpayer, justified the dismissal thereof for want of prosecution. *Raynier v. M.N.R.*, 90 DTC 1387 (T.C.C.)

SECTION 180: Appeals to Federal Court of Appeal

► 180(1) ◄

(1) Appeals to Federal Court of Appeal. An appeal to the Federal Court of Appeal pursuant to subsection 172(3) may be instituted by filing a notice of appeal in the Court within 30 days from

(*a*) the day on which the Minister notifies a person under subsection 165(3) of the Minister's action in respect of a notice of objection filed under subsection 168(4),

(*b*) (Repealed.)

(*c*) the mailing of notice to the administrator of the registered pension plan under subsection 147.1(11),

(*c*.1) the sending of a notice to a promoter of a registered education savings plan under subsection 146.1(12.1),

(*c*.2) the mailing of notice to the administrator of the pooled registered pension plan under subsection 147.5(24), or

(*d*) the time the decision of the Minister to refuse the application for acceptance of the amendment to the registered pension plan or pooled registered pension plan was mailed, or otherwise communicated in writing, by the Minister to any person,

as the case may be, or within such further time as the Court of Appeal or a judge thereof may, either before or after the expiration of those 30 days, fix or allow.

History: S. 180(1)(*c.2*) was added by S.C. 2012, c. 31, s. 42(1), in force December 14, 2012.

S. 180(1)(*d*) was replaced by S.C. 2012, c. 31, s. 42(1), in force December 14, 2012, and formerly read:

(*d*) the time the decision of the Minister to refuse the application for acceptance of the amendment to the registered pension plan was mailed, or otherwise communicated in writing, by the Minister to any person,

S. 180(1)(*b*) was repealed by S.C. 2011, c. 24, s. 55(1), in force January 1, 2012. S. 180(1)(*b*) formerly read:

(*b*) the mailing of notice to a registered Canadian amateur athletic association under subsection 168(1),

Related Sections: S. 168(1) Notice of intention to revoke registration; s. 172(3) Appeal from refusal to register, revocation of registration, etc.; s. 172(4) Deemed refusal to register — no notification within 180 days; s. 212(14) Certificate of exemption.

Cases: "We think that in all appeals from judgments of the Exchequer Court in proceedings by way of appeal from the Income Tax Appeal Board the reasons for judgment given by members of the Board should be included in the Appeal Case filed in this Court" (i.e., the Supreme Court of Canada). *Beament v. M.N.R.*, 52 DTC 1183 [1952] 2 S.C.R. 486; (S.C.C.) at 1186

► 180(2) ◄

(2) No jurisdiction in a Tax Court of Canada or Federal Court. Neither the Tax Court of Canada nor the Federal Court has jurisdiction to entertain any proceeding in respect of a decision of the Minister from which an appeal may be instituted under this section.

► 180(3) ◄

(3) Summary disposition of appeal. An appeal to the Federal Court of Appeal instituted under this section shall be heard and determined in a summary way.

Part I.01
Tax in Respect of Stock Option Benefit Deferral

SECTION 180.01: Election — special tax and relief for deferral of stock option benefits

► 180.01(1) ◄

(1) Election — special tax and relief for deferral of stock option benefits. A taxpayer may make an election in prescribed form to have subsection (2) apply for a taxation year in respect of particular securities if

(*a*) the taxpayer elected to have subsection 7(8) apply, as that subsection applied before 4:00 p.m. Eastern Standard Time, March 4, 2010, in respect of the particular securities; and

(*b*) the taxpayer has, in the year and before 2015, disposed of the particular securities; and

(*c*) the election under this subsection is filed

(i) if the taxpayer has disposed of the particular securities before 2010, on or before the taxpayer's filing-due date for 2010, and

(ii) in any other case, on or before the taxpayer's filing-due date for the year of disposition of the particular securities.

Editorial Note: In the 2010 Federal Budget, the government announced that it eliminated the deferral for the recognition of the benefit for options in respect of shares listed on a designated stock exchange and units in mutual fund trusts under s. 7(8). For such options, the regular timing rule now applies such that the benefit will be included in income in the year in which the securities are acquired.

However, if the taxpayer elected that the deferral apply before that time, and the taxpayer disposed of the securities before 2015, an election under s. 180.01(1) was available that, under s. 180.01(2), had the effect of eliminating the taxable benefit from taxable income entirely, and replacing it with a capital gain equal to the lesser of that benefit and the capital loss otherwise incurred on the disposition of the securities. The allowable capital loss could have been used to offset the resulting taxable capital gain. However, the taxpayer was liable to pay a federal tax for the year of the disposition, equal to the taxpayer's proceeds of disposition (2/3 of the amount for Quebec residents).

History: S. 180.01(1) was added by S.C. 2010, c. 25, s. 46(1), deemed to have come into force on March 4, 2010.

Related Sections: S. 40(3.21) Deemed capital gain under section 180.01.

► 180.01(2) ◄

(2) Effect of election. If a taxpayer makes an election under subsection (1) for a taxation year in respect of particular securities, the following rules apply:

(*a*) paragraph 110(1)(*d*) shall be read without reference to the phrase "1/2 of" in respect of the amount of the benefit deemed by subsection 7(1) to have been received by the taxpayer in the year in respect of the particular securities;

(*b*) the taxpayer is deemed to have realized a capital gain for the year equal to the lesser of

(i) the amount that is deductible by the taxpayer under paragraph 110(1)(*d*), as modified by paragraph (*a*), and

(ii) the taxpayer's capital loss in respect of the disposition of the particular securities;

(*c*) the taxpayer is liable to pay a tax for the year equal to

(i) in the case of a taxpayer resident in the Province of Quebec at the end of the year, 2/3 of the taxpayer's proceeds of disposition (as defined in section 54, but determined without reference to subsection 73(1)) of the particular securities, and

(ii) in any other case, the taxpayer's proceeds of disposition (as defined in section 54, but determined without reference to subsection 73(1)) of the particular securities;

(*d*) to the extent that the taxation year is outside the normal reassessment period (as defined in subsection 152(3.1)), the election is deemed to be an application for reassessment under subsection 152(4.2);

(*e*) notwithstanding subsection 152(4) and as the circumstances require, the Minister shall re-determine the taxpayer's "net capital loss" (as defined in subsection 111(8)) for the taxation year and reassess any taxation year in which an amount has been deducted under paragraph 111(1)(*b*);

(*f*) subparagraph 127.52(1)(*h*)(ii) is to be read as "the amount deducted under paragraph 110(1)(*d*)" for the year in respect of the particular securities; and

(*g*) notwithstanding subsection 152(4) and as the circumstances require, the Minister shall re-determine the taxpayer's additional tax under subsection 120.2(3) for the taxation year and reassess any taxation year in which an amount has been deducted under subsection 120.2(1).

History: S. 180.01(2)(*f*) and (*g*) were added by S.C. 2011, c. 24, s. 56(1), deemed to have come into force on March 4, 2010.

S. 180.01(2) was added by S.C. 2010, c. 25, s. 46(1), deemed to have come into force on March 4, 2010.

► 180.01(3) ◄

(3) Non-application for employment insurance purposes. An amount included under subsection (2)(*b*) in computing a person's income under Part I of this Act for a taxation year shall not be included in determining the income of the person for the year under Part VII of the *Employment Insurance Act*.

History: S. 180.01(3) was added by S.C. 2010, c. 25, s. 46(1), deemed to have come into force on March 4, 2010.

► 180.01(4) ◄

(4) Provisions applicable to this Part. Subsection 150(3), sections 150.1 to 152, 155 to 156.1 and 158 to 167 and Division J of Part I apply to this Part with any modifications that the circumstances require.

History: S. 180.01(4) was added by S.C. 2010, c. 25, s. 46(1), deemed to have come into force on March 4, 2010.

Part I.1
Individual Surtax

SECTION 180.1: Individual surtax

(Repealed by S.C. 2001, c. 17, s. 161(1).)

Part I.2
Tax on Old Age Security Benefits

SECTION 180.2: Tax on Old Age Security Benefits

► 180.2(1) ◄

(1) Definitions. The definitions in this subsection apply in this Part.

"adjusted income"—"adjusted income" of an individual for a taxation year means the amount that would be the individual's income under Part I for the year if in computing that income no amount were

(*a*) included

(i) under paragraph 56(1)(*q.1*) or subsection 56(6),

(ii) in respect of a gain from a disposition of property to which section 79 applies, or

(iii) in respect of a gain described in subsection 40(3.21), or

(*b*) deductible under paragraph 20(1)(*ww*) or 60(*w*), (*y*) or (*z*);

History: S. 180.2(1), paragraph (*b*) of the definition "adjusted income" was replaced by S.C. 2018, c. 12, s. 28(1), applicable to the 2018 and subsequent taxation years, and formerly read:

(*b*) deductible under paragraph 60(*w*), (*y*) or (*z*);

S. 180.2(1), the definition "adjusted income" was replaced by S.C. 2010, c. 25, s. 47(1), applicable to the 2000 and subsequent taxation years. S. 180.2(1), the definition "adjusted income" formerly read:

"adjusted income"—"adjusted income" of an individual for a taxation year means the amount that would be the individual's income under Part I for the year if no amount were included under paragraph 56(1)(*q.1*) or subsection 56(6) or in respect of a gain from a disposition of property to which section 79 applies in computing that income and if no amount were deductible under paragraph 60(*w*), (*y*) or (*z*) in computing that income;

Tax Window Files: Impact of WSIB benefits on OAS clawback, *July 23, 2018*, CRA Document No. 2018-0762381M4.

"base taxation year"—"base taxation year" in relation to a month, means

(*a*) where the month is any of the first 6 months of a calendar year, the taxation year that ended on December 31 of the second preceding calendar year, and

(*b*) where the month is any of the last 6 months of a calendar year, the taxation year that ended on December 31 of the preceding calendar year;

"return of income"—"return of income" in respect of an individual for a taxation year means

(*a*) where the individual was resident in Canada throughout the year, the individual's return of income (other than a return of income filed under subsection 70(2) or 104(23), paragraph 128(2)(*e*) or subsection 150(4)) that is filed or required to be filed under Part I for the year, and

(*b*) in any other case, a prescribed form containing prescribed information.

Related Sections: S. 60(*w*) Tax under Part I.2; s. 180.2(4) Determination of amount to be withheld.

Cases: The inclusion of foreign pension income in the calculation of the "clawback" does not have the effect of imposing a tax on such income. *Swantje v. The Queen*, 96 DTC 6310 (S.C.C.), affirming 94 DTC 6633 (F.C.A.), reversing 94 DTC 1359 (T.C.C.)

Considering that the *Old Age Security Act* does not provide a contributory pension plan and the criterion on which the OAS clawback tax is levied is income level, not age, s. 180.2(1) did not contravene s. 15(1) of the Charter. *Lancey v. the Queen*, 94 DTC 6075 (F.C.A.).

► 180.2(2) ◄

(2) Tax payable. Every individual shall pay a tax under this Part for each taxation year equal to the amount determined by the formula

$$A(1 - B)$$

where

A is the lesser of

(*a*) the amount, if any, by which

(i) the total of all amounts each of which is the amount of any pension, supplement or spouse's or common-law partner's allowance under the *Old Age Security Act* included in computing the individual's income under Part I for the year

exceeds

(ii) the amount of any deduction allowed under subparagraph 60(*n*)(i) in computing the individual's income under Part I for the year, and

(*b*) 15% of the amount, if any, by which the individual's adjusted income for the year exceeds $50,000; and

B is the rate of tax payable by the individual under Part XIII on amounts described in paragraph (*a*) of the description of A.

CRA News Release

2.2% Indexation Factor for 2019

See the CRA Fact Sheet, dated November 16, 2018, that is reproduced following subsection117.1(1). This release announces a 2.2% indexation factor applicable for 2019 tax bracket thresholds, personal amounts and other amounts relating to non-refundable credits, as well as the refundable medical expense supplement, Old Age Security repayment threshold, certain board and lodging allowances, and the tradesperson's tools deduction. Increases to tax bracket thresholds, amounts relating to non-refundable credits, and most other amounts will take effect on January 1, 2019. However, increases in amounts for certain income-tested benefits (for example, the goods and services tax credit) will take effect on July 1, 2019.

Related Sections: S. 117.1 Annual adjustment.

Canadian Tax Foundation: Macnaughton, *Defer OAS To Avoid Clawback*, 2013 Canadian Tax Highlights 21(7).

► 180.2(3) ◄

(3) Withholding. Where at any time Her Majesty pays an amount described in paragraph (*a*) of the description of A in subsection (2) in respect of a month to an individual, there shall be deducted or withheld from that amount on account of the individual's tax payable under this Part for the year the amount determined under subsection (4) in respect of that amount.

► 180.2(4) ◄

(4) Determination of amount to be withheld. The amount determined in respect of a particular amount described in subsection (3) is

(*a*) where the individual has filed a return of income for the base taxation year in relation to the month in which the particular amount is paid, the lesser of

(i) the amount by which the particular amount exceeds the amount of tax payable under Part XIII by the individual on the particular amount, and

(ii) the amount determined by the formula

$$(0.0125A - \$665)(1 - B)$$

where

A is the individual's adjusted income for the base taxation year, and

B is the rate of tax payable under Part XIII by the individual on the particular amount;

(*b*) where the individual has not filed a return of income for the base taxation year in relation to the month and

(i) the Minister has demanded under subsection 150(2) that the individual file the return, or

(ii) the individual was non-resident at any time in the base taxation year,

the amount by which the particular amount exceeds the amount of tax payable under Part XIII by the individual on the particular amount; and

(*c*) in any other case, nil.

Editorial Note: The $665 amount is indexed annually as described in s. 117.1(1). The indexed amount can be calculated as 1/12 of 15% of the OAS repayment threshold figure set out in the CRA's annual press release for indexed amounts. See s. 117.1(1).

Forms: NR4-OAS — Statement of Old Age Security Pension Paid or Credited to Non-Residents of Canada.

Guides: T4155 Old Age Security Return of Income Guide for Non-Residents.

► 180.2(5) ◄

(5) Return. Every individual liable to pay tax under this Part for a taxation year shall

(*a*) file with the Minister, without notice or demand therefor,

(i) where the individual is resident in Canada throughout the taxation year, a return for the year under this Part in prescribed form and containing prescribed information on or before the individual's filing-due date for the year, and

(ii) in any other case, a return of income for the year on or before the individual's balance-due day for the year; and

(*b*) pay the individual's tax payable under this Part for the year on or before the individual's balance-due day for the year.

Forms: T1136 — Old Age Security Return of Income.

► 180.2(6) ◄

(6) Provisions applicable to this Part. Subsection 150(3), sections 150.1, 151 and 152, subsections 153(1.1), (1.2) and (3), sections 155 to 156.1 and 158 to 167 and Division J of Part I apply to this Part with any modifications that the circumstances require.

Part I.3
Tax on Large Corporations

SECTION 181: Definitions

► 181(1) ◄

(1) Definitions. For the purposes of this Part,

Interpretation Bulletins: *Primary* — IT-532 Part I.3 — Tax on Large Corporations.

"financial institution" —"financial institution", in respect of a taxation year, means a corporation that at any time in the year is

(*a*) a bank or credit union,

(*b*) an insurance corporation that carries on business in Canada,

(*c*) authorized under the laws of Canada or a province to carry on the business of offering its services as a trustee to the public,

(*d*) authorized under the laws of Canada or a province to accept deposits from the public and carries on the business of lending money on the security of real property or immovables or investing in indebtedness on the security of mortgages on real property or of hypothecs on immovables,

(*e*) a registered securities dealer,

(*f*) a mortgage investment corporation, or

(*g*) a corporation

(i) listed in the schedule, or

(ii) all or substantially all of the assets of which are shares or indebtedness of financial institutions to which the corporation is related;

History: S. 181(1), paragraph (*d*) of the definition "financial institution" was replaced by S.C. 2013, c. 34, s. 147, in force June 26, 2013, and formerly read:

(*d*) authorized under the laws of Canada or a province to accept deposits from the public and carries on the business of lending money on the security of real estate or investing in mortgages or hypothecary claims on real estate,

S. 181(1), paragraph (*g*) of the definition "financial institution" was replaced by S.C. 2013, c. 34, s. 324(1), deemed to have come into force on December 23, 1997, but in applying paragraph (*g*) of the definition "financial institution" in subsection 181(1) in respect of taxation years that end before December 20, 2002, that paragraph is to be read as follows:

"(*g*) prescribed, or listed in the schedule;"

S. 181(1), paragraph (*g*) of the definition "financial institution" formerly read:

(*g*) a prescribed corporation;

Forms: T2 SCH 33 — Part I.3 Tax on Large Corporations; T2 SCH 34 — Part I.3 Tax on Financial Institutions; T2 SCH 35 — Part I.3 Tax on Large Insurance Corporations; T2 SCH 36 — Agreement Among Related Corporations — Part I.3 Tax.

"long-term debt" —"long-term debt" means

(*a*) in the case of a bank, its subordinated indebtedness (within the meaning assigned by section 2 of the *Bank Act*) evidenced by obligations issued for a term of not less than 5 years,

(*b*) in the case of an insurance corporation, its subordinated indebtedness (within the meaning assigned by section 2 of the *Insurance Companies Act*) evidenced by obligations issued for a term of not less than 5 years, and

(*c*) in the case of any other corporation, its subordinated indebtedness (within the meaning that would be assigned by section 2 of the *Bank Act* if the definition of that expression in that section were applied with such modifications as the circumstances require) evidenced by obligations issued for a term of not less than 5 years,

but does not include, where the corporation is a prescribed federal Crown corporation for the purpose of section 27, any indebtedness evidenced by obligations issued to and held by Her Majesty in right of Canada;

Related Regulations: 7100.

Related Sections: S. 130.1(6) Meaning of "mortgage investment corporation"; s. 248(1), "mortgage investment corporation".

Forms: T2 SCH 33 — Part I.3 Tax on Large Corporations; T2 SCH 34 — Part I.3 Tax on Financial Institutions; T2 SCH 35 — Part I.3 Tax on Large Insurance Corporations; T2 SCH 36 — Agreement Among Related Corporations — Part I.3 Tax.

Income Tax Technical News: Issue No. 28, Large Corporations Tax — Long-Term Debt.

"reserves" —"reserves", in respect of a corporation for a taxation year, means the amount at the end of the year of all of the corporation's reserves, provisions and allowances (other than allowances in respect of depreciation or depletion) and, for greater certainty, includes any provision in respect of deferred taxes.

Related Sections: S. 130.1(6) Meaning of "mortgage investment corporation"; s. 248(1), "mortgage investment corporation".

Tax Topics: No. 1741, Large Corporation Tax Update.

Forms: T2 SCH 33 — Part I.3 Tax on Large Corporations; T2 SCH 34 — Part I.3 Tax on Financial Institutions; T2 SCH 35 — Part I.3 Tax on Large Insurance Corporations; T2 SCH 36 — Agreement Among Related Corporations — Part I.3 Tax.

► 181(2) ◄

(2) Prescribed expressions. For the purposes of this Part, the expressions "attributed surplus", "Canadian assets", "Canadian premiums", "Canadian reserve liabilities", "permanent establishment", "total assets", "total premiums" and "total reserve liabilities" have such meanings as may be prescribed.

Related Regulations: 8600.

► 181(3) ◄

(3) Determining values and amounts. For the purposes of determining the carrying value of a corporation's assets or any other amount under this Part in respect of a corporation's capital, investment allowance, taxable capital or taxable capital employed in Canada for a taxation year or in respect of a partnership in which a corporation has an interest,

(*a*) the equity and consolidation methods of accounting shall not be used; and (*b*) subject to paragraph (*a*) and except as otherwise provided in this Part, the amounts reflected in the balance sheet

(i) presented to the shareholders of the corporation (in the case of a corporation that is neither an insurance corporation to which subparagraph (ii) applies nor a bank) or the members of the partnership, as the case may be, or, where such a balance sheet was not prepared in accordance with generally accepted accounting principles or no such balance sheet was prepared, the amounts that would be reflected if such a balance sheet had been prepared in accordance with generally accepted accounting principles, or

(ii) accepted by the Superintendent of Financial Institutions, in the case of a bank or an insurance corporation that is required by law to report to the Superintendent, or the superintendent of insurance or other similar officer or authority of the province under whose laws the corporation is incorporated, in the case of an insurance corporation that is required by law to report to that officer or authority,

shall be used.

Tax Topics: No. 1741, Large Corporation Tax Update.

► 181(4) ◄

(4) Limitations respecting inclusions and deductions. Unless a contrary intention is evident, no provision of this Part shall be read or construed to require the inclusion or to permit the deduction, in computing the amount of a corporation's capital, investment allowance, taxable capital or taxable capital employed in Canada for a taxation year, of any amount to the extent that that amount has been included or deducted, as the case may be, in computing the first-mentioned amount under, in accordance with or by reason of any other provision of this Part.

Tax Window Files: Surplus Appropriations - Part VI Capital Tax, *December 4, 2015*, CRA Document No. 2015-0606291I7.

SECTION 181.1: Tax payable

► 181.1(1) ◄

(1) Tax payable. Every corporation shall pay a tax under this Part for each taxation year equal to the amount obtained by multiplying the corporation's specified percentage for the taxation year by the amount, if any, by which

(*a*) its taxable capital employed in Canada for the year exceeds

(*b*) its capital deduction for the year.

Related Sections: S. 125.3 Deduction of Part I.3 tax — general corporations.

Tax Topics: No. 1741, Large Corporation Tax Update.

Forms: T2 SCH 33 — Part I.3 Tax on Large Corporations; T2 SCH 34 — Part I.3 Tax on Financial Institutions; T2 SCH 35 — Part I.3 Tax on Large Insurance Corporations; T2 SCH 342 — Nova Scotia Tax on Large Corporations; T2 SCH 343 — Nova Scotia Tax on Large Corporations — Agreement Among Related Corporations; T2 SCH 361 — New Brunswick Tax on Large Corporations; T2 SCH 362 — New Brunswick Tax on Large Corporations — Agreement Among Related Corporations; T2 SCH 34 — Part I.3 Tax on Financial Institutions.

Interpretation Bulletins: *Primary* — IT-532 Part I.3 — Tax on large corporations.

► 181.1(1.1) ◄

(1.1) Specified percentage. For the purpose of subsection (1), the specified percentage of a corporation for a taxation year that ends after 2003 is the total of

(*a*) that proportion of 0.225% that the number of days in the taxation year that are before 2004 is of the number of days in the taxation year,

(*b*) that proportion of 0.200% that the number of days in the taxation year that are in 2004 is of the number of days in the taxation year, and

(*c*) that proportion of 0.175% that the number of days in the taxation year that are in 2005 is of the number of days in the taxation year.

(*d*) [Repealed.]

(*e*) [Repealed.]

► 181.1(1.2) ◄

(1.2) Exceptions. Notwithstanding subsection (1.1), for the purposes of applying subsection 125(5.1) and the definitions "unused surtax credit" in subsections (6) and 190.1(5), the amount of tax in respect of a corporation under subsection (1) for a taxation year is to be determined as if the specified percentage of the corporation for the taxation year were 0.225%.

► 181.1(2) ◄

(2) Short taxation years. Where a taxation year of a corporation is less than 51 weeks, the amount determined under subsection (1) for the year in respect of the corporation shall be reduced to that proportion of that amount that the number of days in the year is of 365.

Related Sections: S. 248(11) Compound interest.

► 181.1(3) ◄

(3) Where tax not payable. No tax is payable under this Part for a taxation year by a corporation

(*a*) that was a non-resident-owned investment corporation throughout the year;

(*b*) that was a bankrupt at the end of the year;

(*c*) that was throughout the year exempt from tax under section 149 on all of its taxable income;

(*d*) that neither was resident in Canada nor carried on business through a permanent establishment in Canada at any time in the year;

(*e*) that was throughout the year a deposit insurance corporation (within the meaning assigned by subsection 137.1(5)) or a corporation deemed by subsection 137.1(5.1) to be a deposit insurance corporation; or

(*f*) that was throughout the year a corporation described in subsection 136(2) the principal business of which was marketing (including processing incidental to or connected therewith) natural products belonging to or acquired from its members or customers.

History: S. 181.1(3)(*b*) was replaced by S.C. 2017, c. 33, s. 63(1), applicable in respect of bankruptcies that occur after April 26, 1995, and formerly read:

(*b*) that was a bankrupt (within the meaning assigned by subsection 128(3)) at the end of the year;

Related Regulations: 8600.

Related Sections: s. 133(8), "non-resident-owned investment corporation"; s. 136(2) Definition of "cooperative corporation"; s. 137.1(5), "deposit insurance corporation"; s. 137.1(5.1) Deeming provision; s. 149(1) Miscellaneous exemptions; s. 181(2) Prescribed expressions; 248(1) bankrupt; s. 248(1), "non-resident-owned investment corporation".

▶ 181.1(4) ◀

(4) Deduction. There may be deducted from a corporation's tax otherwise payable under this Part for a taxation year an amount equal to the total of

(*a*) its Canadian surtax payable for the year, and

(*b*) such part as the corporation claims of its unused surtax credits for its 7 immediately preceding and 3 immediately following taxation years,

to the extent that that total does not exceed the amount by which

(*c*) the amount that would, but for this subsection, be its tax payable under this Part for the year

exceeds

(*d*) the total of all amounts each of which is the amount deducted under subsection 125.3(1) in computing the corporation's tax payable under Part I for a taxation year ending before 1992 in respect of its unused Part I.3 tax credit (within the meaning assigned by section 125.3) for the year.

Related Sections: S. 125.3(1) Deduction of Part I.3 tax — general corporations.

Forms: T2 SCH 37 — Calculation of Unused Part I.3 Tax Credit.

▶ 181.1(5) ◀

(5) Idem. For the purposes of this subsection and subsections (4), (6) and (7),

(*a*) an amount may not be claimed under subsection (4) in computing a corporation's tax payable under this Part for a particular taxation year in respect of its unused surtax credit for another taxation year until its unused surtax credits, if any, for taxation years preceding the other year that may be claimed under this Part for the particular year have been claimed; and

(*b*) an amount in respect of a corporation's unused surtax credit for a taxation year may be claimed under subsection (4) in computing its tax payable under this Part for another taxation year only to the extent that it exceeds the total of all amounts each of which is an amount claimed in respect of that unused surtax credit in computing its tax payable under this Part or Part VI for a taxation year preceding that other year.

▶ 181.1(6) ◀

(6) Definitions. For the purposes of this subsection and subsections (4), (5) and (7),

"Canadian surtax payable" —"Canadian surtax payable" of a corporation for a taxation year has the meaning assigned by subsection 125.3(4);

Related Sections: S. 125.3(1) Deduction of Part I.3 tax — general corporations; s. 125.3(4), "Canadian surtax payable", "unused Part I.3 tax credit"; s. 190(1), "financial institution"; s. 190.1(3) Deduction; Part VI.

"unused surtax credit" —"unused surtax credit" for a taxation year ending after 1991

(*a*) of a corporation (other than a corporation that was throughout the year a financial institution, within the meaning assigned by section 190) means the amount, if any, by which

(i) its Canadian surtax payable for the year

exceeds the total of

(ii) the amount that would, but for subsection (4), be its tax payable under this Part for the year, and

(iii) the amount, if any, deducted under section 125.3 in computing the corporation's tax payable under Part I for the year, and

(*b*) of a corporation that was throughout the year a financial institution (within the meaning assigned by section 190) means the lesser of

(i) the amount, if any, by which

(A) its Canadian surtax payable for the year

exceeds the total of

(B) the amount that would, but for subsection (4), be its tax payable under this Part for the year, and

(C) the amount, if any, deducted under section 125.3 in computing the corporation's tax payable under Part I for the year, and

(ii) the amount, if any, by which its tax payable under Part I for the year exceeds the amount that would, but for subsection (4) and subsection 190.1(3), be the total of its taxes payable under Parts I.3 and VI for the year.

Related Sections: S. 125.3(1) Deduction of Part I.3 tax — general corporations; s. 125.3(4), "Canadian surtax payable";, "unused Part I.3 tax credit"; s. 190(1), "financial institution"; s. 190.1(3) Deduction; Part VI.

▶ 181.1(7) ◀

(7) Acquisition of control. Where at any time control of a corporation has been acquired by a person or group of persons, no amount in respect of its unused surtax credit for a taxation year ending before that time is deductible by the corporation for a taxation year ending after that time and no amount in respect of its unused surtax credit for a taxation year ending after that time is deductible by the corporation for a taxation year ending before that time, except that

(*a*) the corporation's unused surtax credit for a particular taxation year that ended before that time is deductible by the corporation for a taxation year that ends after that time (in this paragraph referred to as the "subsequent year") to the extent of that proportion of the corporation's Canadian surtax payable for the particular year that

(i) the amount, if any, by which

(A) the total of all amounts each of which is

(I) its income under Part I for the particular year from a business that was carried on by the corporation throughout the subsequent year for profit or with a reasonable expectation of profit, or

(II) where properties were sold, leased, rented or developed or services were rendered in the course of carrying on that business before that time, its income under Part I for the particular year from any other business all or substantially all of the income of which was derived from the sale, leasing, rental or development, as the case may be, of similar properties or the rendering of similar services

exceeds

(B) the total of all amounts each of which is an amount deducted under paragraph 111(1)(*a*) or (*d*) in computing its taxable income for the particular year in respect of a non-capital loss or a farm loss, as the case may be, for taxation year in respect of any business referred to in clause (A)

is of the greater of

(ii) the amount determined under subparagraph (i), and

(iii) the corporation's taxable income for the particular year; and

(*b*) the corporation's unused surtax credit for a particular taxation year that ends after that time is deductible by the corporation for a taxation year that ended before that time (in this paragraph referred to as the "preceding year") to the extent of that proportion of the corporation's Canadian surtax payable for the particular year that

(i) the amount, if any, by which

(A) the total of all amounts each of which is

(I) its income under Part I for the particular year from a business that was carried on by the corporation in the preceding year and throughout the particular year for profit or with a reasonable expectation of profit, or

(II) where properties were sold, leased, rented or developed or services were rendered in the course of carrying on that business before that time, the corporation's income under Part I for the particular year from any other business all or substantially all of the income of which was derived from the sale, leasing, rental or development, as the case may be, of similar properties or the rendering of similar services

exceeds

(B) the total of all amounts each of which is an amount deducted under paragraph 111(1)(*a*) or (*d*) in computing the corporation's taxable income for the particular year in respect of a non-capital loss or a farm loss, as the case may be, for a taxation year in respect of any business referred to in clause (A)

is of the greater of

(ii) the amount determined under subparagraph (i), and

(iii) the corporation's taxable income for the particular year.

Related Sections: S. 111(1) Losses deductible; s. 111(4) Loss restriction event — capital losses; s. 256.1 [Corporate tax-attribute trading].

SECTION 181.2: Taxable capital employed in Canada

► 181.2(1) ◄

(1) Taxable capital employed in Canada. The taxable capital employed in Canada of a corporation for a taxation year (other than a financial institution or a corporation that was throughout the year not resident in Canada) is the prescribed proportion of the corporation's taxable capital for the year.

Related Regulations: 8601.

Related Sections: S. 181(1), "financial institution".

Interpretation Bulletins: *Primary* — IT-532 Part I.3 — Tax on large corporations.

► 181.2(2) ◄

(2) Taxable capital. The taxable capital of a corporation (other than a financial institution) for a taxation year is the amount, if any, by which its capital for the year exceeds its investment allowance for the year.

Related Sections: S. 181(1), "financial institution"; s. 181.2(4) Investment allowance.

► 181.2(3) ◄

(3) Capital. The capital of a corporation (other than a financial institution) for a taxation year is the amount, if any, by which the total of

(*a*) the amount of its capital stock (or, in the case of a corporation incorporated without share capital, the amount of its members' contributions), retained earnings, contributed surplus and any other surpluses at the end of the year,

(*b*) the amount of its reserves for the year, except to the extent that they were deducted in computing its income for the year under Part I,

(*b*.1) the amount of its deferred unrealized foreign exchange gains at the end of the year,

(*c*) the amount of all loans and advances to the corporation at the end of the year,

(*d*) the amount of all indebtedness of the corporation at the end of the year represented by bonds, debentures, notes, mortgages, hypothecary claims, banker's acceptances or similar obligations,

(*e*) the amount of any dividends declared but not paid by the corporation before the end of the year,

(*f*) the amount of all other indebtedness (other than any indebtedness in respect of a lease) of the corporation at the end of the year that has been outstanding for more than 365 days before the end of the year, and (*g*) the total of all amounts, each of which is the amount, if any, in respect of a partnership in which the corporation held a membership interest at the end of the year, either directly or indirectly through another partnership, determined by the formula

$$(A - B) \times C/D$$

where

A is the total of all amounts that would be determined under paragraphs (*b*) to (*d*) and (*f*) in respect of the partnership for its last fiscal period that ends at or before the end of the year if

(a) those paragraphs applied to partnerships in the same manner that they apply to corporations, and

(b) those amounts were computed without reference to amounts owing by the partnership

(i) to any corporation that held a membership interest in the partnership either directly or indirectly through another partnership, or

(ii) to any partnership in which a corporation described in subparagraph (i) held a membership interest either directly or indirectly through another partnership,

B is the partnership's deferred unrealized foreign exchange losses at the end of the period,

C is the share of the partnership's income or loss for the period to which the corporation is entitled either directly or indirectly through another partnership, and

D is the partnership's income or loss for the period

exceeds the total of

(*h*) the amount of its deferred tax debit balance at the end of the year,

(*i*) the amount of any deficit deducted in computing its shareholders' equity (including, for this purpose, the amount of any provision for the redemption of preferred shares) at the end of the year,

(*j*) any amount deducted under subsection 135(1) in computing its income under Part I for the year, to the extent that the amount can reasonably be regarded as being included in the amount determined under any of paragraphs (*a*) to (*g*) in respect of the corporation for the year, and

(*k*) the amount of its deferred unrealized foreign exchange losses at the end of the year.

History: S. 181.2(3)(*g*) was replaced by S.C. 2013, c. 34, s. 325(2), applicable to the 2012 and subsequent taxation years, and formerly read:

(*g*) where the corporation was a member of a partnership at the end of the year, that proportion of the amount, if any, by which

(i) the total of all amounts (other than amounts owing to the member or to other corporations that are members of the partnership) that would, if this paragraph and paragraphs (*b*) to (*d*) and (*f*) applied to partnerships in the same way that they apply to corporations, be determined under those paragraphs in respect of the partnership at the end of its last fiscal period that ends at or before the end of the year

exceeds

(ii) the amount of the partnership's deferred unrealized foreign exchange losses at the end of that period

that the member's share of the partnership's income or loss for that period is of the partnership's income or loss for that period

S. 181.2(3)(*g*)(i) was replaced by S.C. 2013, c. 34, s. 325(1), applicable to taxation years that begin after December 20, 2002, and formerly read:

(i) the total of all amounts (other than amounts owing to the member or to other corporations that are members of the partnership) that would be determined under this paragraph and paragraphs (*b*) to (*d*) and (*f*) in respect of the partnership at the end of its last fiscal period that ends at or before the end of the year (if paragraphs (*b*) to (*d*) and (*f*) applied to partnerships in the same way that they apply to corporations)

S. 181.2(3)(*i*) was replaced by S.C. 2013, c. 34, s. 325(3), applicable to taxation years that begin after 1995, and formerly read:

(*i*) the amount of any deficit deducted in computing its shareholders' equity at the end of the year,

Related Sections: S. 135(1) Deduction in computing income; s. 181(1), "financial institution"; s. 248(1), "dividend".

Tax Topics: No. 1741, Large Corporation Tax Update.

Income Tax Technical News: Issue No. 29, Large Corporation Tax.

Cases: The taxpayer acquired buses financed by way of sales contracts with manufacturers, under which title did not pass until all payments were made. The manufacturer assigned these contracts to a bank. Amounts owing by the taxpayer to the bank under the contracts had to be included in the computation of the taxpayer's capital, since the relationship was one of lender-borrower and not vendor-purchaser. *Autobus Thomas Inc. v. The Queen*, 2001 DTC 5665 (S.C.C.), affirming 2000 DTC 6165 (F.C.A.), which affirmed 99 DTC 259 (T.C.C.)

Amounts owing by the corporate taxpayer to its customers must be included in the computation of its "capital" as "advances" for Part I.3 tax purposes. *Oerlikon Aérospatiale Inc. v. The Queen*, 99 DTC 5318 (F.C.A.), affirming 97 DTC 962 (T.C.C.).

► 181.2(4) ◄

(4) Investment allowance. The investment allowance of a corporation (other than a financial institution) for a taxation year is the total of all amounts each of which is the carrying value at the end of the year of an asset of the corporation that is

(*a*) a share of another corporation,

(*b*) a loan or advance to another corporation (other than a financial institution),

(*c*) a bond, debenture, note, mortgage, hypothecary claim or similar obligation of another corporation (other than a financial institution),

(*d*) long-term debt of a financial institution,

(*d*.1) a loan or advance to, or a bond, debenture, note, mortgage, hypothecary claim or similar obligation of, a partnership each member of which was, throughout the year,

(i) another corporation (other than a financial institution) that was not exempt from tax under this Part (otherwise than because of paragraph 181.1(3)(*d*)), or

(ii) another partnership described in this paragraph,

(*e*) an interest in a partnership, or

(*f*) a dividend payable to the corporation at the end of the year on a share of the capital stock of another corporation,

other than a share of the capital stock of, a dividend payable by, or indebtedness of, a corporation that is exempt from tax under this Part (otherwise than because of paragraph 181.1(3)(*d*)).

History: S. 181.2(4)(*d.1*) was replaced by S.C. 2013, c. 34, s. 325(4), applicable to the 2004 and subsequent taxation years, and formerly read:

(*d*.1) a loan or advance to, or a bond, debenture, note, mortgage, hypothecary claim or similar obligation of, a partnership all of the members of which, throughout the year, were other corporations (other than financial institutions) that were not exempt from tax under this Part (otherwise than because of paragraph 181.1(3)(*d*)),

In addition, in applying paragraphs 181.2(4)(*b*), (*c*) and (*d.1*) to a particular corporation in respect of an asset that is a loan or an advance to, or an obligation of, another corporation or partnership that the particular corporation holds at the end of a taxation year of the particular corporation that began before December 20, 2002, those paragraphs are to be read without reference to "(other than a financial institution)" and to "(other than financial institutions)" if, at the end of the taxation year,

(*a*) the particular corporation deals at arm's length with the other corporation or the partnership, as the case may be; and

(*b*) the other corporation is a financial institution, or the partnership is not a partnership described in paragraph 181.2(4)(*d.1*), as the case may be, solely because of amendments to paragraph (*g*) of the definition of "financial institution" in subsection 181(1) of the Act made by 2013, c. 34, s. 324 and the Schedule of Listed Corporations [reproduced after section 262] as added by 2013, c. 34, s. 366.

Related Sections: S. 181(1), "financial institution", "long-term debt"; s. 181.1(3) Where tax not payable.

Cases: The taxpayer was not entitled to deduct its bankers' acceptances from its investment allowance when computing its capital for Part I.3 tax purposes. *Federated Co-Operatives Limited v. The Queen*, 2001 DTC 5414 (F.C.A.), affirming 2000 DTC 1946 (T.C.C.)

► 181.2(5) ◄

(5) Value of interest in partnership. For the purposes of subsection (4) and this subsection, the carrying value at the end of a taxation year of an interest of a corporation or of a partnership (each of which is referred to in this subsection as the "member") in a particular partnership is deemed to be the member's specified proportion, for the particular partnership's last fiscal period that ends at or before the end of the taxation year, of the amount that would, if the particular partnership were a corporation, be the particular partnership's investment allowance at the end of that fiscal period.

History: S. 181.2(5) was replaced by S.C. 2013, c. 34, s. 325(5), applicable to taxation years that begin after December 20, 2002, and formerly read:

(5) *Value of interest in partnership.* For the purposes of subsection (4), the carrying value, at the end of a taxation year, of an interest of a corporation in a partnership shall be deemed to be an amount equal to that proportion of

(*a*) the total of all amounts each of which is the carrying value of an asset of the partnership, at the end of its last fiscal period ending at or before the end of the year, described in any of paragraphs (4)(*a*) to (*d*) and (*f*), other than an asset that is a share of the capital stock of, a dividend payable by, or indebtedness of, a corporation that is exempt from tax under this Part (otherwise than because of paragraph 181.1(3)(*d*)),

that

(*b*) the corporation's share of the partnership's income or loss for that period

is of

(*c*) the partnership's income or loss for that period.

Related Sections: S. 181.1(3) Where tax not payable.

► 181.2(6) ◄

(6) Loan. For the purpose of subsection (4), where a corporation made a particular loan to a trust that neither

(*a*) made any loans or advances to nor received any loans or advances from, nor

(*b*) acquired any bond, debenture, note, mortgage, hypothecary claim or similar obligation of nor issued any bond, debenture, note, mortgage, hypothecary claim or similar obligation to

a person not related to the corporation, as part of a series of transactions in which the trust made a loan to another corporation (other than a financial institution) to which the corporation is related, the least of

(*c*) the amount of the particular loan,

(*d*) the amount of the loan from the trust to the other corporation, and

(*e*) the amount, if any, by which

(i) the total of all amounts each of which is the amount of a loan from the trust to any corporation

exceeds

(ii) the total of all amounts each of which is the amount of a loan (other than the particular loan) from any corporation to the trust

at any time shall be deemed to be the amount of a loan from the corporation to the other corporation at that time.

Related Sections: S. 181(1), "financial institution"; s. 248(10) Series of transactions.

SECTION 181.3: Taxable capital employed in Canada of financial institution

► 181.3(1) ◄

(1) Taxable capital employed in Canada of financial institution. The taxable capital employed in Canada of a financial institution for a taxation year is the total of

(*a*) the total of all amounts each of which is the carrying value at the end of the year of an asset of the financial institution (other than property held by the institution primarily for the purpose of resale that was acquired by the financial institution, in the year or the preceding taxation year, as a consequence of another person's default, or anticipated default, in respect of a debt owed to the institution) that is tangible, or for civil law corporeal, property used in Canada and, in the case of a financial institution that is an insurance corporation, that is non-segregated property, within the meaning assigned by subsection 138(12),

(*b*) the total of all amounts each of which is an amount in respect of a partnership in which the financial institution has an interest at the end of the year equal to that proportion of

(i) the total of all amounts each of which is the carrying value of an asset of the partnership, at the end of its last fiscal period ending at or before the end of the year, that is tangible, or for civil law corporeal, property used in Canada

that

(ii) the financial institution's share of the partnership's income or loss for that period

is of

(iii) the partnership's income or loss for that period, and

(c) an amount that is equal to

(i) in the case of a financial institution other than an insurance corporation, that proportion of its taxable capital for the year that its Canadian assets at the end of the year is of its total assets at the end of the year,

(ii) in the case of an insurance corporation that was resident in Canada at any time during the year and carried on a life insurance business at any time in the year, the total of

(A) that proportion of the amount, if any, by which the total of

(I) its taxable capital for the year, and

(II) the amount prescribed for the year in respect of the corporation

exceeds

(III) the amount prescribed for the year in respect of the corporation

that its Canadian reserve liabilities as at the end of the year is of the total of

(IV) its total reserve liabilities as at the end of the year, and

(V) the amount prescribed for the year in respect of the corporation, and

(B) (Repealed.)

(iii) in the case of an insurance corporation that was resident in Canada at any time in the year and throughout the year did not carry on a life insurance business, that proportion of its taxable capital for the year that the total amount of its Canadian premiums for the year is of its total premiums for the year, and

(iv) in the case of an insurance corporation that was throughout the year not resident in Canada and carried on an insurance business in Canada at any time in the year, its taxable capital for the year.

History: S. 181.3(1)(*a*) was replaced by S.C. 2013, c. 34, s. 148(1), in force June 26, 2013, and formerly read:

(*a*) the total of all amounts each of which is the carrying value at the end of the year of an asset of the financial institution (other than property held by the institution primarily for the purpose of resale that was acquired by the financial institution, in the year or the preceding taxation year, as a consequence of another person's default, or anticipated default, in respect of a debt owed to the institution) that is tangible property used in Canada and, in the case of a financial institution that is an insurance corporation, that is non-segregated property, within the meaning assigned by subsection 138(12),

S. 181.3(1)(*b*)(i) was replaced by S.C. 2013, c. 34, s. 148(2), in force June 26, 2013, and formerly read:

(i) the total of all amounts each of which is the carrying value of an asset of the partnership, at the end of its last fiscal period ending at or before the end of the year, that is tangible property used in Canada

S. 181.3(1)(*c*)(ii)(B) was repealed by S.C. 2009, c. 2, s. 61(1), applicable to taxation years that begin after September 2006. S. 181.3(1)(*c*)(ii)(B) formerly read:

(B) the amount, if any, by which

(I) the amount of its reserves for the year (other than its reserves in respect of amounts payable out of segregated funds) that may reasonably be regarded as having been established in respect of its insurance businesses carried on in Canada

exceeds the total of

(II) the total of all amounts each of which is the amount of a reserve (other than a reserve described in subparagraph 138(3)(*a*)(i) to the extent that it was included in the amount determined under subclause (I) and was deducted in computing its income under Part I for the year,

(III) the total of all amounts each of which is the amount of a reserve described in subparagraph 138(3)(*a*)(i) to the extent that it was included in the amount determined under subclause (I) and was deductible under subparagraph 138(3)(*a*)(i) in computing its income under Part I for the year, and

(IV) the total of all amounts each of which is the amount outstanding (including any interest accrued thereon) as at the end of the year in respect of a policy loan (within the meaning assigned by subsection 138(12)) made by the corporation, to the extent that it was deducted in computing the total determined under subclause (III),

Related Regulations: 8600; 8601; 8605.

Related Sections: S. 138(3) Deductions allowed in computing income; s. 138(12), "non-segregated property", "policy loan"; s. 181(1), "financial institution"; s. 181(2), "Canadian assets", "Canadian premiums", "Canadian reserve liabilities", "total assets", "total premiums", "total reserve liabilities".

Forms: T2 SCH 34 — Part I.3 Tax on Financial Institutions.

Interpretation Bulletins: *Secondary* — IT-532 Part I.3 — Tax on large corporations.

► 181.3(2) ◄

(2) Taxable capital of financial institution. The taxable capital of a financial institution for a taxation year is the amount, if any, by which its capital for the year exceeds its investment allowance for the year.

Related Sections: S. 181(1), "financial institution"; s. 181.2(4) Investment allowance.

► 181.3(3) ◄

(3) Capital of financial institution. The capital of a financial institution for a taxation year is

(*a*) in the case of a financial institution, other than an authorized foreign bank or an insurance corporation, the amount, if any, by which the total at the end of the year of

(i) the amount of its long-term debt,

(ii) the amount of its capital stock (or, in the case of an institution incorporated without share capital, the amount of its members' contributions), retained earnings, contributed surplus and any other surpluses, and

(iii) the amount of its reserves for the year, except to the extent that they were deducted in computing its income under Part I for the year,

exceeds the total of

(iv) the amount of its deferred tax debit balance at the end of the year,

(v) the amount of any deficit deducted in computing its shareholders' equity (including, for this purpose, the amount of any provision for the redemption of preferred shares) at the end of the year, and

(vi) any amount deducted under subsection 130.1(1) or 137(2) in computing its income under Part I for the year, to the extent that the amount can reasonably be regarded as being included in the amount determined under subparagraph (i), (ii) or (iii) in respect of the institution for the year;

(*b*) in the case of an insurance corporation that was resident in Canada at any time in the year and carried on a life insurance business at any time in the year, the amount, if any, by which the total at the end of the year of

(i) the amount of its long-term debt, and

(ii) the amount of its capital stock (or, in the case of an insurance corporation incorporated without share capital, the amount of its members' contributions), retained earnings, contributed surplus and any other surpluses

exceeds the total of

(iii) the amount of its deferred tax debit balance at the end of the year, and

(iv) the amount of any deficit deducted in computing its shareholders' equity (including, for this purpose, the amount of any provision for the redemption of preferred shares) at the end of the year;

(*c*) in the case of an insurance corporation that was resident in Canada at any time in the year and throughout the year did not carry on a life insurance business, the amount, if any, by which the total at the end of the year of

(i) the amount of its long-term debt,

(ii) the amount of its capital stock (or, in the case of an insurance corporation incorporated without share capital, the amount of its members' contributions), retained earnings, contributed surplus and any other surpluses, and

(iii) the amount of its reserves for the year, except to the extent that they were deducted in computing its income under Part I for the year,

exceeds the total of

(iv) the amount of its deferred tax debit balance at the end of the year,

(v) the amount of any deficit deducted in computing its shareholders' equity (including, for this purpose, the amount of any provision for the redemption of preferred shares) at the end of the year,

(vi) the total amount of its deferred acquisition expenses in respect of its property and casualty insurance business in Canada, to the extent that it can reasonably be attributed to an amount included in the amount determined under subparagraph (iii), and

(vii) any amount recoverable through reinsurance, to the extent that it can reasonably be regarded as being included in the amount determined under subparagraph (iii) in respect of a claims reserve;

(*d*) in the case of an insurance corporation that was throughout the year not resident in Canada and carried on an insurance business in Canada at any time in the year, the total at the end of the year of

(i) the amount that is the greater of

(A) the amount, if any, by which

(I) the corporation's surplus funds derived from operations (as defined in subsection 138(12)) as of the end of the year, computed as if no tax were payable under this Part or Part VI for the year

exceeds the total of all amounts each of which is

(II) an amount on which the corporation was required to pay, or would but for subsection 219(5.2) have been required to pay, tax under Part XIV for a preceding taxation year, except the portion, if any, of the amount on which tax was payable, or would have been payable, because of subparagraph 219(4)(*a*)(i.1), and

(III) an amount on which the corporation was required to pay, or would but for subsection 219(5.2) have been required to pay, tax under subsection 219(5.1) for the year because of the transfer of an insurance business to which subsection 138(11.5) or (11.92) has applied, and

(B) the corporation's attributed surplus for the year,

(ii) any other surpluses relating to its insurance businesses carried on in Canada,

(iii) the amount of its long-term debt that may reasonably be regarded as relating to its insurance businesses carried on in Canada, and

(iv) the amount, if any, by which

(A) the amount of its reserves for the year (other than its reserves in respect of amounts payable out of segregated funds) that may reasonably be regarded as having been established in respect of its insurance businesses carried on in Canada

exceeds the total of

(B) the total of all amounts each of which is the amount of a reserve (other than a reserve described in subparagraph 138(3)(*a*)(i)) to the extent that it was included in the amount determined under clause (A) and was deducted in computing its income under Part I for the year,

(C) the total of all amounts each of which is the amount of a reserve described in subparagraph 138(3)(*a*)(i) to the extent that it was included in the amount determined under clause (A) and was deductible under subparagraph 138(3)(*a*)(i) in computing its income under Part I for the year,

(D) the total of all amounts each of which is the amount outstanding (including any interest accrued thereon) as at the end of the year in respect of a policy loan (within the meaning assigned by subsection 138(12)) made by the corporation, to the extent that it was deducted in computing the amount determined under clause (C),

(E) the total amount of its deferred acquisition expenses in respect of its property and casualty insurance business in Canada, to the extent that it can reasonably be attributed to an amount included in the amount determined under clause (A), and

(F) the total of all amounts each of which is an amount recoverable through reinsurance, to the extent that it can reasonably be regarded as being included in the amount determined under clause (A) in respect of a claims reserve; and

(*e*) in the case of an authorized foreign bank, the total of

(i) 10% of the total of all amounts, each of which is the risk-weighted amount at the end of the year of an on-balance sheet asset or an off-balance sheet exposure of the bank in respect of its Canadian banking business that the bank would be required to report under the OSFI risk-weighting guidelines if those guidelines applied and required a report at that time, and

(ii) the total of all amounts, each of which is an amount at the end of the year in respect of the bank's Canadian banking business that

(A) if the bank were a bank listed in Schedule II to the *Bank Act*, would be required under the risk-based capital adequacy guidelines issued by the Superintendent of Financial Institutions and applicable at that time to be deducted from the bank's capital in determining the amount of capital available to satisfy the Superintendent's requirement that capital equal a particular proportion of risk-weighted assets and exposures, and

(B) is not an amount in respect of a loss protection facility required to be deducted from capital under the Superintendent's guidelines respecting asset securitization applicable at that time.

History: S. 181.3(3)(*a*)(v) was replaced by S.C. 2013, c. 34, s. 326(1), applicable to taxation years that begin after 1995, and formerly read:

(v) the amount of any deficit deducted in computing its shareholders' equity at the end of the year; and

S. 181.3(3)(*b*)(iv) was replaced by S.C. 2013, c. 34, s. 326(2), applicable to taxation years that begin after 1995, and formerly read:

(iv) the amount of any deficit deducted in computing its shareholders' equity at the end of the year;

S. 181.3(3)(*c*)(v) was replaced by S.C. 2013, c. 34, s. 326(3), applicable to taxation years that begin after 1995, and formerly read:

(v) the amount of any deficit deducted in computing its shareholders' equity at the end of the year; and

S. 181.3(3)(*c*)(vii) was added by S.C. 2013, c. 34, s. 326(4), applicable to taxation years that begin after 1995.

S. 181.3(3)(*d*)(iv)(F) was added by S.C. 2013, c. 34, s. 326(5), applicable to taxation years that begin after 1995.

Related Regulations: "attributed surplus", Part LXXXVI.

Related Sections: S. 130.1(1) Deduction from tax; s. 137(2) Payments pursuant to allocations in proportion to borrowing; s. 138(3) Deductions allowed in computing income; s. 138(12), "policy loan", "surplus funds derived from operations"; s. 181(1), "long-term debt"; s. 181(2), "attributed surplus"; s. 248(1), "Canadian banking business", "OSFI risk-weighting guidelines".

Cases: Under accounting rules, the unamortized portion of realized gains were treated as an adjustment to the total carrying value of the relevant class of assets, rather than being shown as reserves or surpluses on the taxpayer's balance sheet. There was no scope for the Minister to change the amounts, or their characterizations, from those that have been accepted by the Superintendent of Financial Institutions. *The Queen v. The Manufacturers Life Insurance Company*, 2001 DTC 5396 (F.C.A.), affirming 2000 DTC 1600 (T.C.C.).

► 181.3(4) ◄

(4) Investment allowance of financial institution. The investment allowance for a taxation year of a corporation that is a financial institution is

(*a*) in the case of a corporation that was resident in Canada at any time in the year, the total of all amounts each of which is the carrying value at the end of the year of an eligible investment of the corporation;

(*b*) in the case of an insurance corporation that was throughout the year not resident in Canada, the total of all amounts each of which is the carrying value at the end of the year of an eligible investment of the corporation that was used or held by it in the year in the course of carrying on an insurance business in Canada;

(*c*) in the case of an authorized foreign bank, the total of all amounts each of which is the amount at the end of the year, before the application of risk weights, that the bank would be required to report under the OSFI risk-weighting guidelines if those guidelines applied and required a report at that time, of an eligible investment used or held by the bank in the year in the course of carrying on its Canadian banking business; and

(*d*) in any other case, nil.

Related Sections: S. 138(12), "non-segregated property"; s. 181(1), "financial institution", "long-term debt"; s. 181.5(6) Government-controlled corporation; s. 181.5(7) Related corporations that are not associated; s. 248(1), "Canadian banking business", "OSFI risk-weighting guidelines".

► 181.3(5) ◄

(5) Interpretation. For the purpose of subsection (4),

(*a*) an eligible investment of a corporation is a share of the capital stock or long-term debt (and, where the corporation is an insurance corporation, is non-segregated property within the meaning assigned by subsection 138(12)) of a financial institution that at the end of the year

(i) is related to the corporation,

(ii) is not exempt from tax under this Part, and

(iii) is resident in Canada or can reasonably be regarded as using the proceeds of the share or debt in a business carried on by the institution through a permanent establishment (as defined by regulation) in Canada; and

(*b*) a credit union and another credit union of which the credit union is a shareholder or member are deemed to be related to each other.

Related Regulations: 8201.

Related Sections: S. 138(12), "non-segregated property"; s. 181(1), "financial institution", "long-term debt"; s. 248(1), "authorized foreign bank".

SECTION 181.4: Taxable capital employed in Canada of non-resident

The taxable capital employed in Canada for a taxation year of a corporation (other than a financial institution) that was throughout the year not resident in Canada is the amount, if any, by which

(*a*) the total of all amounts each of which is the carrying value at the end of the year of an asset of the corporation used by it in the year in, or held by it in the year in the course of, carrying on any business carried on by it during the year through a permanent establishment in Canada

exceeds the total of

(*b*) the amount of the corporation's indebtedness at the end of the year (other than indebtedness described in any of paragraphs 181.2(3)(*c*) to (*f*)) that may reasonably be regarded as relating to a business carried on by it during the year through a permanent establishment in Canada,

(*c*) the total of all amounts each of which is the carrying value at the end of the year of an asset described in subsection 181.2(4) of the corporation that was used by it in the year in, or held by it in the year in the course of, carrying on any business carried on by it during the year through a permanent establishment in Canada; and

(*d*) the total of all amounts each of which is the carrying value at the end of the year of an asset of the corporation that

(i) is a ship or aircraft operated by the corporation in international traffic or is personal or movable property used in its business of transporting passengers or goods by ship or aircraft in international traffic, and

(ii) was used by the corporation in the year in, or held by it in the year in the course of, carrying on any business during the year through a permanent establishment in Canada,

if the country in which the corporation is resident imposed neither a capital tax for the year on similar assets nor a tax for the year on the income from the operation of a ship or aircraft in international traffic, of any corporation resident in Canada during the year.

History: S. 181.4(*d*)(i) was replaced by S.C. 2013, c. 34, s. 149, in force June 26, 2013, and formerly read:

(i) is a ship or aircraft operated by the corporation in international traffic or is personal property used in its business of transporting passengers or goods by ship or aircraft in international traffic, and

Related Regulations: 8600.

Related Sections: S. 181(1), "financial institution"; s. 181(2), "permanent establishment".

Interpretation Bulletins: *Secondary* — IT-532 Part I.3 — Tax on large corporations.

SECTION 181.5: Capital deduction

► 181.5(1) ◄

(1) Capital deduction. Subject to subsection (1.1), the capital deduction of a corporation for a taxation year is $50 million unless the corporation is related to another corporation at any time in the taxation year, in which case, subject to subsection (4), its capital deduction for the year is nil.

Interpretation Bulletins: *Primary* — IT-532 Part I.3 — Tax on large corporations.

► 181.5(1.1) ◄

(1.1) Exceptions. For the purposes of applying subsection 125(5.1), the definitions "unused surtax credit" in subsections 181.1(6) and 190.1(5), and subsection 225.1(8), the amount of tax in respect of a corporation under subsection 181.1(1) for a taxation year is to be determined as if the reference to "$50 million" in subsection (1) were a reference to "$10 million".

► 181.5(2) ◄

(2) Related corporations. Subject to subsection (4.1), a corporation that is related to any other corporation at any time in a taxation year of the corporation that ends in a calendar year may file with the Minister in prescribed form an agreement on behalf of the related group of which the corporation is a member under which an amount that does not exceed $50 million is allocated among all corporations that are members of the related group for each taxation year of each such corporation ending in the calendar year and at a time when it was a member of the related group.

Related Sections: S. 251(2) Definition of "related persons"; s. 251(5) Control by related groups, options, etc.

► 181.5(3) ◄

(3) Allocation by Minister. Subject to subsection (4.1), the Minister may request a corporation that is related to any other corporation at the end of a taxation year to file with the Minister an agreement referred to in subsection (2) and, if the corporation does not file such an agreement within 30 days after receiving the request, the Minister may allocate an amount among the members of the related group of which the corporation is a member for the taxation year not exceeding $50 million.

► 181.5(4) ◄

(4) Idem. The least amount allocated for a taxation year to a member of a related group under an agreement described in subsection (2) or by the Minister pursuant to subsection (3) is the capital deduction of that member for that taxation year.

▶ 181.5(4.1) ◀

(4.1) Exceptions. For the purposes of applying subsection 125(5.1), the definitions "unused surtax credit" in subsections 181.1(6) and 190.1(5), and subsection 225.1(8), subsections (2) to (4) are to be read as if the amount determined under subsection (2) or (3), as the case may be, in respect of the corporation for the taxation year were that proportion of $10 million that the amount otherwise determined in respect of the corporation for the taxation year under that subsection is of $50 million.

▶ 181.5(5) ◀

(5) Idem. Where a corporation (in this subsection referred to as the "first corporation") has more than one taxation year ending in the same calendar year and is related in 2 or more of those taxation years to another corporation that has a taxation year ending in that calendar year, the capital deduction of the first corporation for each such taxation year at the end of which it is related to the other corporation is an amount equal to its capital deduction for the first such taxation year.

▶ 181.5(6) ◀

(6) Idem. Two corporations that would, but for this subsection, be related to each other by reason only of

(*a*) the control of any corporation by Her Majesty in right of Canada or a province, or

(*b*) a right referred to in paragraph 251(5)(*b*),

are, for the purposes of this section and subsection 181.3(4), deemed not to be related to each other except that, where at any time a taxpayer has a right referred to in paragraph 251(5)(*b*) with respect to shares and it can reasonably be considered that one of the main purposes for the acquisition of the right was to avoid any limitation on the amount of a corporation's capital deduction for a taxation year, for the purpose of determining whether a corporation is related to any other corporation, the corporations are, for the purposes of this section, deemed to be in the same position in relation to each other as if the right were immediate and absolute and as if the taxpayer had exercised the right at that time.

Related Sections: S. 190.15(6) Government-controlled corporation; s. 256(8) Deemed exercise of right.

▶ 181.5(7) ◀

(7) Related corporations that are not associated. For the purposes of subsection 181.3(4) and this section, a Canadian-controlled private corporation and another corporation to which it would, but for this subsection, be related at any time shall be deemed not to be related to each other at that time where the corporations are not associated with each other at that time.

Related Sections: S. 125(7), "Canadian-controlled private corporation".

SECTION 181.6: Return

Every corporation that is or would, but for subsection 181.1(4), be liable to pay tax under this Part for a taxation year shall file with the Minister, not later than the day on or before which the corporation is required by section 150 to file its return of income for the year under Part I, a return of capital for the year in prescribed form containing an estimate of the tax payable under this Part by it for the year.

Related Sections: S. 181.1(4) Deduction.

Forms: T2 SCH 33 — Part I.3 Tax on Large Corporations; T2 SCH 34 — Part I.3 Tax on Financial Institutions; T2 SCH 35 — Tax on Large Insurance Corporations; T2 SCH 37 — Calculation of Unused Part I.3 Tax Credit.

SECTION 181.7: Provisions applicable to Part

Sections 152, 158 and 159, subsection 161(11), sections 162 to 167 and Division J of Part I apply to this Part with such modifications as the circumstances require and, for the purpose of this section, paragraph 152(6)(*a*) shall be read as follows:

"(*a*) a deduction under section 181.1(4) in respect of any unused surtax credit (within the meaning assigned by subsection 181.1(6)) for a subsequent taxation year,"

Interpretation Bulletins: *Primary* — IT-532 Part I.3 — Tax on large corporations.

SECTION 181.71: Provisions applicable — Crown corporations

Section 27 applies to this Part with any modifications that the circumstances require.

Related Sections: S. 187.61 Provisions applicable — Crown corporations; s. 190.211 Provisions applicable — Crown corporations; s. 191.4(3) Provisions applicable — Crown corporations.

Interpretation Bulletins: *Primary* — IT-532 Part I.3 — Tax on large corporations.

SECTION 181.8: Interest

(Repealed by S.C. 1994, c. 7, Sched. VIII, s. 109(1).)

SECTION 181.9: Provisions applicable to Part

(Repealed by S.C. 1994, c. 7, Sched. VIII, s. 109(1).)

Part II
Tobacco Manufacturers' Surtax (Repealed.)

History: Part II (sections 182 and 183) was repealed by S.C. 2017, c. 20, s. 27(1), applicable to taxation years that begin after March 22, 2017.

SECTION 182: Surtax

► 182(1) ◄

(1) [Surtax] — (Repealed by S.C. 2017, c. 20, s. 27(1).)

History: S. 182(1) was repealed by S.C. 2017, c. 20, s. 27(1), applicable to taxation years that begin after March 22, 2017, and formerly read:

(1) *Surtax.* Every corporation shall pay a tax under this Part for the corporation's taxation year equal to the amount determined by the formula

$$0.5A(B/C)$$

where

A is the corporation's Part I tax on tobacco manufacturing profits for the year;

B is the number of days in the year that are before March 23, 2017; and

C is the number of days in the year.

S. 182(1) was replaced by S.C. 2017, c. 20, s. 26(1), applicable to taxation years that include March 22, 2017, and formerly read:

(1) *Surtax.* Every corporation shall pay a tax under this Part for each taxation year equal to 50% of the corporation's Part I tax on tobacco manufacturing profits for the year.

► 182(2) ◄

(2) Definitions — (Repealed by S.C. 2017, c. 20, s. 27(1).)

History: S. 182(2) was repealed by S.C. 2017, c. 20, s. 27(1), applicable to taxation years that begin after March 22, 2017, and formerly read:

(2) *Definitions.* In this Part,

"exempt activity"—"exempt activity", of a particular corporation, means

(*a*) farming; or

(*b*) processing leaf tobacco, if

(i) that processing is done by, and is the principal business of, the particular corporation,

(ii) the particular corporation does not manufacture any tobacco product, and

(iii) the particular corporation is not related to any other corporation that carries on tobacco manufacturing (determined, in respect of the other corporation, as if the particular corporation did not exist and the definition "tobacco manufacturing" were read without reference to the words "in Canada");

"Part I tax on tobacco manufacturing profits"—"Part I tax on tobacco manufacturing profits" of a corporation for a taxation year means 21% of the amount determined by the formula

$$(A \times B/C) - D$$

where

A is the amount that would be the corporation's Canadian manufacturing and processing profits for the year, within the meaning assigned by subsection 125.1(3), if the total of all amounts, each of which is the corporation's loss for the year from an active business, other than tobacco manufacturing, carried on by it in Canada, were equal to the lesser of

(*a*) that total otherwise determined, and

(*b*) the total of all amounts, each of which is the amount of the corporation's income for the year from an active business, other than tobacco manufacturing, carried on by it in Canada,

B is the corporation's tobacco manufacturing capital and labour cost for the year,

C is the total of the corporation's cost of manufacturing and processing capital for the year and its cost of manufacturing and processing labour for the year, within the meanings assigned by regulations made for the purposes of section 125.1, and

D is

(*a*) where the corporation is a Canadian-controlled private corporation throughout the year, the corporation's business limit for the year as determined for the purpose of section 125, and

(*b*) in any other case, nil;

"tobacco manufacturing"—"tobacco manufacturing" means any activity, other than an exempt activity, relating to the manufacture or processing in Canada of tobacco or tobacco products in or into any form that is, or would after any further activity become, suitable for smoking;

"tobacco manufacturing capital and labour cost"—"tobacco manufacturing capital and labour cost" of a corporation for a taxation year means the total of the amounts that would be the corporation's cost of manufacturing and processing capital for the year and its cost of manufacturing and processing labour for the year, within the meanings assigned by regulations made for the purpose of section 125.1, if the manufacturing or processing referred to in the definition "qualified activities" in those regulations were tobacco manufacturing.

SECTION 183: Return

► 183(1) ◄

(1) Return — (Repealed by S.C. 2017, c. 20, s. 27(1).)

History: S. 183(1) was repealed by S.C. 2017, c. 20, s. 27(1), applicable to taxation years that begin after March 22, 2017, and formerly read:

(1) *Return.* Every corporation that is liable to pay tax under this Part for a taxation year shall file with the Minister a return for the year in prescribed form not later than the day on or before which the corporation is required by section 150 to file its return of income for the year under Part I.

► 183(2) ◄

(2) Payment — (Repealed by S.C. 2017, c. 20, s. 27(1).)

History: S. 183(2) was repealed by S.C. 2017, c. 20, s. 27(1), applicable to taxation years that begin after March 22, 2017, and formerly read:

(2) *Payment.* Every corporation shall pay to the Receiver General on or before its balance-due day for each taxation year its tax payable under this Part for the year.

► 183(3) ◄

(3) Provisions applicable — (Repealed by S.C. 2017, c. 20, s. 27(1).)

History: S. 183(3) was repealed by S.C. 2017, c. 20, s. 27(1), applicable to taxation years that begin after March 22, 2017, and formerly read:

(3) *Provisions applicable.* Subsections 150(2) and (3), sections 151, 152, 158 and 159, subsections 161(1) and (11), sections 162 to 167 and Division J of Part I apply to this Part with such modifications as the circumstances require.

Part II.1
Tax on Corporate Distributions

SECTION 183.1: [Tax payable]

▶ 183.1(1) ◀

(1) Application of Part. This Part applies to a corporation (other than a mutual fund corporation) for a taxation year in which the corporation, at any time in the year,

(*a*) was a public corporation; or

(*b*) was resident in Canada and had a class of shares outstanding that were purchased and sold in the manner in which such shares normally are purchased and sold by any member of the public in the open market.

Related Sections: S. 54, "proceeds of disposition"; s. 89(1)(*g*), "public corporation"; s. 248(1), "corporation", "dividend", "property", "share", "stock dividend".

Forms: T2141 — Part II.1 Tax Return — Tax on Corporate Distributions.

▶ 183.1(2) ◀

(2) Tax payable. Where, as a part of a transaction or series of transactions or events,

(*a*) a corporation, or any person with whom the corporation was not dealing at arm's length, has, at any time, paid an amount, directly or indirectly, to any person as proceeds of disposition of any property, and

(*b*) all or any portion of the amount may reasonably be considered, having regard to all the circumstances, to have been paid as a substitute for dividends that would otherwise have been paid in the normal course by the corporation,

the corporation shall, on or before its balance-due day for its taxation year that includes that time, pay tax of 45% of that amount or portion of it, as the case may be.

Related Sections: S. 150(1)(*a*) Corporations; 183.1(3) Stock dividend; 183.1(4) Purchase of shares; 183.1(5) Indirect payment; 183.1(6) Where s. (2) does not apply; s. 248(10) Series of transactions.

Information Circulars: IC 88-2 General anti-avoidance rule — Section 245 of the Income Tax Act.

▶ 183.1(3) ◀

(3) Stock dividend. Where, as a part of a transaction or series of transactions or events,

(*a*) a share was issued by a corporation as a stock dividend and the amount of the stock dividend was less than the fair market value of the share at the time that it was issued, and

(*b*) the share or any other share of the capital stock of the corporation was purchased, directly or indirectly, by the corporation, or by a person with whom the corporation was not dealing at arm's length, for an amount in excess of its paid-up capital,

that excess shall, for the purposes of subsection (2), be deemed to have been paid as a substitute for dividends that would otherwise have been paid in the normal course by the corporation.

Related Sections: S. 248(10) Series of transactions.

▶ 183.1(4) ◀

(4) Purchase of shares. Where, as a part of a transaction or series of transactions or events,

(*a*) a share of the capital stock of a corporation was purchased, directly or indirectly, by the corporation, or by any person with whom the corporation was not dealing at arm's length, and

(*b*) any portion of the amount paid for the share may reasonably be considered, having regard to all the circumstances, as consideration for a dividend that had been declared, but not yet paid, on the share,

that portion of the amount shall, for the purposes of subsection (2), be deemed to have been paid as a substitute for dividends that would otherwise have been paid in the normal course by the corporation notwithstanding that the dividend was actually paid thereafter.

Related Regulations: 6207.

Related Sections: S. 150(1)(*a*) Corporations; s. 248(10) Series of transactions.

▶ 183.1(5) ◀

(5) Indirect payment. Where, as a part of a transaction or series of transactions or events, a person received a payment from a corporation, or from any person with whom the corporation was not dealing at arm's length, in consideration, in whole or in part, for paying an amount to any other person as proceeds of disposition of any property, the corporation shall, for the purposes of subsection (2), be deemed to have paid the amount indirectly to the other person.

Related Sections: S. 248(10) Series of transactions.

▶ 183.1(6) ◀

(6) Where s. (2) does not apply. Subsection (2) does not apply if none of the purposes of the transaction or series of transactions or events referred to therein may reasonably be considered, having regard to all the circumstances, to have been to enable shareholders of a corporation who are individuals or non-resident persons to receive an amount, directly or indirectly, as proceeds of disposition of property rather than as a dividend on a share that was of a class that was listed on a stock exchange or that was purchased and sold in the manner in which shares are normally purchased and sold by any member of the public in the open market.

Related Sections: S. 248(10) Series of transactions.

▶ 183.1(7) ◀

(7) Where s. 110.6(8) does not apply. Where this section has been applied in respect of an amount, subsection 110.6(8) does not apply to the capital gain in respect of which the amount formed all or a part of the proceeds of disposition.

SECTION 183.2: Return

▶ 183.2(1) ◀

(1) Return. Every corporation liable to pay tax under this Part for a taxation year shall, on or before the day on or before which it is required to file its return of income under Part I for the year, file with the Minister a return for the year under this Part in prescribed form.

Forms: T2141 — Part II.1 Tax Return — Tax on Corporate Distributions.

▶ 183.2(2) ◀

(2) Provisions applicable to Part. Subsections 150(2) and (3), sections 152, 158 and 159, subsections 160.1(1) and 161(1) and (11), sections 162 to 167 and Division J of Part I are applicable to this Part with such modifications as the circumstances require.

Part III
Additional Tax on Excessive Elections

SECTION 184: [Tax on Excessive Elections]

► 184(1) ◄

(1) Tax on excess of dividend paid over portion payable out of tax-paid undistributed surplus or 1971 capital surplus — (Repealed by 1977-78, c. 1, s. 83(1).)

► 184(2) ◄

(2) Tax on excessive elections. If a corporation has elected in accordance with subsection 83(2), 130.1(4) or 131(1) in respect of the full amount of any dividend payable by it on shares of any class of its capital stock (in this section referred to as the "original dividend") and the full amount of the original dividend exceeds the portion of the original dividend deemed by that subsection to be a capital dividend or capital gains dividend, as the case may be, the corporation shall, at the time of the election, pay a tax under this Part equal to 3/5 of the excess.

Editorial Note: The penalty tax will apply if the full amount of an elected dividend under s. 83(2) (or s. 130.1(4) or 131(1)) exceeds the corporation's "capital dividend account" (s. 89(1)) such that the excess is not a capital dividend. As an alternative to the penalty tax, the corporation may elect under s. 184(3) to have the excess treated as a separate taxable dividend.

History: S. 184(2) was replaced by S.C. 2013, c. 34, s. 327(1), applicable to original dividends paid by a corporation after its 1999 taxation year, and formerly read:

(2) *Tax on excessive elections.* Where a corporation has elected in accordance with s. 83(2), 130.1(4) or 131(1) in respect of the full amount of any dividend payable by it on shares of any class of its capital stock and the full amount of the dividend exceeds the portion thereof deemed by that subsection to be a capital dividend or capital gains dividend, as the case may be, the corporation shall, at the time of the election, pay a tax under this Part equal to 3/4 of the excess.

Related Sections: s. 184(3) Election to treat excess as separate dividend; s. 185(1) Assessment of tax.

Income Tax Folios: *Primary* — S3-F2-C1 Capital Dividends.

► 184(2.1) ◄

(2.1) Reduction of excess — (Repealed by S.C. 2013, c. 34, s. 327(1).)

History: S. 184(2.1) was repealed by S.C. 2013, c. 34, s. 327(1), applicable to original dividends paid by a corporation after its 1999 taxation year, and formerly read:

(2.1) *Reduction of excess.* Notwithstanding subsection (2), where a corporation has elected in accordance with subsection 83(2) in respect of the full amount of a dividend that became payable by it at a particular time in its 1988 taxation year and before June 18, 1987, the amount of the excess referred to in subsection (2) in respect of the dividend shall be deemed, for the purposes of subsection (2), to be the amount of the excess that would have been determined under subsection (2) in respect of the dividend if the corporation's taxation year had ended on December 31, 1987.

► 184(3) ◄

(3) Election to treat excess as separate dividend. If, in respect of an original dividend payable at a particular time, a corporation would, but for this subsection, be required to pay a tax under this Part in respect of an excess referred to in subsection (2), and the corporation elects in prescribed manner on or before the day that is 90 days after the day of sending of the notice of assessment in respect of the tax that would otherwise be payable under this Part, the following rules apply:

(*a*) the portion of the original dividend deemed by subsection 83(2), 130.1(4) or 131(1) to be a capital dividend or capital gains dividend, as the case may be, is deemed for the purposes of this Act to be the amount of a separate dividend that became payable at the particular time;

(*b*) if the corporation identifies in its election any part of the excess, that part is, for the purposes of any election under subsection 83(2), 130.1(4) or 131(1) in respect of that part, and, where the corporation has so elected, for all purposes of this Act, deemed to be the amount of a separate dividend that became payable immediately after the particular time;

(*c*) the amount by which the excess exceeds any portion deemed by paragraph (*b*) to be a separate dividend for all purposes of this Act is deemed to be a separate taxable dividend that became payable at the particular time; and

(*d*) each person who held any of the issued shares of the class of shares of the capital stock of the corporation in respect of which the original dividend was paid is deemed

(i) not to have received any portion of the original dividend, and

(ii) to have received, at the time that any separate dividend determined under any of paragraphs (*a*) to (*c*) became payable, the proportion of that dividend that the number of shares of that class held by the person at the particular time is of the number of shares of that class outstanding at the particular time except that, for the purpose of Part XIII, the separate dividend is deemed to be paid on the day that the election in respect of this subsection is made.

Editorial Note: See the editorial note under s. 184(2).

History: S. 184(3) was replaced by S.C. 2013, c. 34, s. 327(1), applicable to original dividends paid by a corporation after its 1999 taxation year, except that the reference to "sending" is to be read as a reference to "mailing" for notices of assessments sent before December 15, 2010.

S. 184(3) formerly read:

(3) *Election to treat excess as separate dividend.* If, in respect of a dividend payable at a particular time after 1971, a corporation would, but for this subsection, be required to pay a tax under this Part equal to all or a portion of an excess referred to in subsection (2) of this section or subsection 184(1) of the *Income Tax Act*, chapter 148 of the Revised Statutes of Canada, 1952, it may elect in prescribed manner on or before a day that is not later than 90 days after the day of sending of the notice of assessment in respect of the tax that would otherwise be payable under this Part, and on such an election being made, subject to subsection (4), the following rules apply:

(*a*) the amount by which the full amount of the dividend exceeds the amount of the excess shall be deemed for the purposes of the election that the corporation made in respect of the dividend under subsection 83(2), 130.1(4) or 131(1) of this Act or subsection 83(1) of the *Income Tax Act*, chapter 148 of the Revised Statutes of Canada, 1952, and for all other purposes of this Act to be the full amount of a separate dividend that became payable at the particular time;

(*b*) such part of the excess as the corporation may claim shall, for the purposes of any election in respect thereof under subsection 83(2), 130.1(4) or 131(1) of this Act or subsection 83(1) of the *Income Tax Act*, chapter 148 of the Revised Statutes of Canada, 1952, and, where the corporation has so elected, for all purposes of this Act, be deemed to be the full amount of a separate dividend that became payable immediately after the particular time;

(*c*) the amount by which the excess exceeds any portion deemed by paragraph (*b*) to be a separate dividend for all purposes of this Act shall be deemed to be a separate dividend that is a taxable dividend that became payable at the particular time; and

(*d*) each person who held any of the issued shares of the class of shares of the capital stock of the corporation in respect of which the full amount of the dividend was paid shall be deemed

(i) not to have received any portion of the dividend, and

(ii) to have received at the time the dividend was paid the proportion of any separate dividend, determined under paragraph (*a*), (*b*) or (*c*), that the number of shares of that class held by the person at the time the dividend was paid is of the number of shares of that class outstanding at that time except that, for the purpose of Part XIII, a separate dividend that is a taxable dividend, a capital dividend or a life insurance capital dividend shall be deemed to have been paid on the day that the election in respect of this subsection is made.

S. 184(3), the portion before paragraph (*a*) was replaced by S.C. 2010, c. 25, s. 48, in force on Royal Assent, December 15, 2010. S. 184(3), the portion before paragraph (*a*) formerly read:

(3) *Election to treat excess as separate dividend.* Where, in respect of a dividend payable at a particular time after 1971, a corporation would, but for this subsection, be required to pay a tax under this Part equal to all or a portion of an excess referred to in subsection (2) of this section or subsection 184(1) of the *Income Tax Act*, chapter 148 of the Revised Statutes of Canada, 1952, it may elect in prescribed manner on or before a day that is not later than 90 days after the day that is the later of December 15, 1977 and the day of mailing of the notice of assessment in respect of the tax that would otherwise be payable under this Part, and on such an election being made, subject to subsection (4), the following rules apply:

Related Regulations: 600(b); 2106.

Related Sections: S. 184(3.1) Election to treat dividend as loan — qualifying dividend; s. 220(3.2) Late, amended or revoked elections.

Tax Profile: September 2009 — Fixing Tax Mistakes; October 2004 — Taxation of Dividends: A Survey in the Context of Private Corporations and Their Shareholders.

Tax Topics: No. 2040, CRA Roundtable at Association de planification fiscale et financière (APFF) 2010 Conference.

Income Tax Folios: *Primary* — S3-F2-C1 Capital Dividends.

Information Circulars: IC 07-1 Taxpayer relief provisions.

Tax Window Files: Objection Part III Tax -184(3) Election, *December 4, 2013*, CRA Document No. 2013-0504951E5.

► 184(3.1) ◄

(3.1) Election to treat dividend as loan — (Repealed by S.C. 2013, c. 34, s. 327(1).)

History: S. 184(3.1) was repealed by S.C. 2013, c. 34, s. 327(1), applicable to original dividends paid by a corporation after its 1999 taxation year, and formerly read:

(3.1) *Election to treat dividend as loan.* Where a corporation has elected in accordance with subsection 83(1) of the *Income Tax Act*, chapter 148 of the Revised Statutes of Canada, 1952, in respect of the full amount of any dividend that became payable by it at a particular time after March 31, 1977 and before 1979 and the corporation made a reasonable attempt to correctly determine its tax-paid undistributed surplus on hand immediately before the particular time and its 1971 capital surplus on hand immediately before the particular time and all or any portion of the dividend

(*a*) has given rise to a gain from the disposition of a share of the corporation by virtue of subsection 40(3), or

(*b*) is an excess referred to in subsection 184(1) of the *Income Tax Act*, chapter 148 of the Revised Statutes of Canada, 1952,

if the corporation so elects under this subsection,

(*c*) in any case referred to in paragraph (*a*), not later than December 31, 1982 or such earlier day as is 90 days after the latest of

(i) February 26, 1981,

(ii) the day on which a notice of assessment or reassessment is mailed to a shareholder of the corporation in respect of a gain referred to in paragraph (*a*), and

(iii) such day as is agreed to by the Minister in writing, or

(*d*) in any other case, not later than 90 days after the later of

(i) February 26, 1981, and

(ii) the day on which the Minister notifies the corporation by registered letter that it has an excess referred to in subsection 184(1) of the *Income Tax Act*, chapter 148 of the Revised Statutes of Canada, 1952, in respect of the dividend,

and the penalty referred to in subsection (5) in respect of the election is paid by the corporation at the time the election is made, the following rules apply:

(*e*) the whole dividend or such portion of it as the corporation may claim shall, for the purposes of this Act, be deemed not to be a dividend but to be a loan made at the particular time by the corporation to the persons who received all or any portion of the dividend if the full amount of the loan is repaid to the corporation before such date as is stipulated by the Minister and the corporation satisfies such terms and conditions as are specified by the Minister, and

(*f*) sections 15 and 80.4 do not apply to such a loan.

► 184(3.2) ◄

(3.2) Idem — (Repealed by S.C. 2013, c. 34, s. 327(1).)

History: S. 184(3.2) was repealed by S.C. 2013, c. 34, s. 327(1), applicable to original dividends paid by a corporation after its 1999 taxation year, and formerly read:

(3.2) *Idem.* Where a corporation has elected in accordance with subsection 83(2) in respect of the full amount of any dividend that became payable by it at a particular time after December 3, 1985 and before 1986 and the corporation made a reasonable attempt to correctly determine its capital dividend account immediately before the particular time and all or any portion of the dividend is an excess referred to in subsection (2), if

(*a*) the corporation so elects under this subsection not later than 90 days after the later of

(i) December 19, 1986, and

(ii) the day on which the Minister notifies the corporation by registered letter that it has an excess referred to in subsection (2) in respect of the dividend, and

(*b*) the penalty referred to in subsection (5) in respect of the election is paid by the corporation at the time the election under this subsection is made,

the following rules apply:

(*c*) the whole dividend or such portion of it as the corporation may claim shall, for the purposes of this Act, be deemed not to be a dividend but to be a loan made at the particular time by the corporation to the persons who received all or any portion of the dividend if the full amount of the loan is repaid to the corporation before such date as is stipulated by the Minister and the corporation satisfies such terms and conditions as are specified by the Minister, and

(*d*) sections 15 and 80.4 do not apply to such a loan.

► 184(4) ◄

(4) Concurrence with election. An election under subsection (3) is valid only if

(*a*) it is made with the concurrence of the corporation and all its shareholders

(i) who received or were entitled to receive all or any portion of the original dividend, and

(ii) whose addresses were known to the corporation; and

(*b*) either

(i) it is made on or before the day that is 30 months after the day on which the original dividend became payable, or

(ii) each shareholder described in subparagraph (*a*)(i) concurs with the election, in which case, notwithstanding subsections 152(4) to (5), any assessment of the tax, interest and penalties payable by each of those shareholders for any taxation year shall be made that is necessary to take the corporation's election into account.

History: S. 184(4) was replaced by S.C. 2013, c. 34, s. 327(1), applicable to original dividends paid by a corporation after its 1999 taxation year, and formerly read:

(4) *Concurrence with election.* An election under subsection (3) is not valid unless

(*a*) it is made with the concurrence of the corporation and all its shareholders

(i) who received or were entitled to receive all or any portion of the dividend in respect of which a tax would, but for subsection (3), be payable under this Part, and

(ii) whose addresses were known to the corporation; and

(*b*) either

(i) it is made on or before the day that is 30 months after the day on which the dividend became payable, or

(ii) each shareholder described in subparagraph (*a*)(i) concurs with the election, in which case, notwithstanding subsections 152(4) to (5), such assessment of the tax, interest and penalties payable by each such shareholder for any taxation year may be made as is necessary to take the corporation's election into account.

Income Tax Folios: *Primary* — S3-F2-C1 Capital Dividends.

► 184(5) ◄

(5) Exception for non-taxable shareholders. If each person who, in respect of an election made under subsection (3), is deemed by subsection (3) to have received a dividend at a particular time is also, at the particular time, a person all of whose taxable income is exempt from tax under Part I, (*a*) subsection (4) does not apply to the election; and

(*b*) the election is valid only if it is made on or before the day that is 30 months after the day on which the original dividend became payable.

History: S. 184(5) was replaced by S.C. 2013, c. 34, s. 327(1), applicable to original dividends paid by a corporation after its 1999 taxation year, except that an election made before September 24, 2013 [the 90th day after royal assent] is deemed to have been made in a timely manner.

S. 184(5) formerly read:

(5) *Penalty.* The penalty in respect of an election under subsection (3.1) or (3.2) in relation to a particular dividend is an amount equal to the product obtained when $500 is multiplied by the proportion that the number of months or parts of months during the period commencing on the day the dividend became payable and ending on the day on which that election was made is of 12.

Related Sections: S. 39, "capital gain"; s. 83(2), "capital dividend"; s. 248(1), "corporation", "dividend", "share".

SECTION 185: Assessment of tax

► 185(1) ◄

(1) Assessment of tax. The Minister shall, with all due dispatch, examine each election made by a corporation in accordance with subsection 83(2), 130.1(4) or 131(1), assess the tax, if any, payable under this Part in respect of the election and send a notice of assessment to the corporation.

Related Sections: S. 83(1) Qualifying dividends.

► 185(2) ◄

(2) Payment of tax and interest. Where an election has been made by a corporation in accordance with subsection 83(2), 130.1(4) or 131(1) and the Minister mails a notice of assessment under this Part in respect of the election, that part of the amount assessed then remaining unpaid and interest thereon at the prescribed rate computed from the day of the election to the day of payment is payable forthwith by the corporation to the Receiver General.

Related Regulations: 4301.

Related Sections: S. 248(11) Compound interest.

► 185(3) ◄

(3) Provisions applicable to Part. Subsections 152(3), (4), (5), (7) and (8) and 161(11), sections 163 to 167 and Division J of Part I are applicable to this Part with such modifications as the circumstances require.

Related Sections: S. 248(1), "assessment", "corporation", "prescribed".

► 185(4) ◄

(4) Joint and several, or solidary, liability from excessive elections. Each person who has received a dividend from a corporation in respect of which the corporation elected under subsection 83(2), 130.1(4) or 131(1) is jointly and severally, or solidarily, liable with the corporation to pay that proportion of the corporation's tax payable under this Part because of the election that

(*a*) the amount of the dividend received by the person is of

(*b*) the full amount of the dividend in respect of which the election was made,

but nothing in this subsection limits the liability of any person under any other provision of this Act.

History: S. 185(4), the portion before paragraph (*a*) was replaced by S.C. 2013, c. 34, s. 150(1), in force June 26, 2013, and formerly read:

(4) *Joint and several liability from excessive elections.* Each person who has received a dividend from a corporation in respect of which the corporation elected under subsection 83(2), 130.1(4) or 131(1) is jointly and severally liable with the corporation to pay that proportion of the corporation's tax payable under this Part because of the election that

► 185(5) ◄

(5) Assessment. The Minister may, at any time after the last day on which a corporation may make an election under subsection 184(3) in respect of a dividend, assess a person in respect of any amount payable under subsection (4) in respect of the dividend, and the provisions of Division I of Part I apply, with such modifications as the circumstances require, to an assessment made under this subsection as though it were made under section 152.

► 185(6) ◄

(6) Rules applicable. If under subsection (4) a corporation and another person have become jointly and severally, or solidarily, liable to pay part or all of the corporation's tax payable under this Part in respect of a dividend described in that subsection,

(*a*) a payment at any time by the other person on account of the liability shall, to the extent of the payment, discharge their liability after that time; and

(*b*) a payment at any time by the corporation on account of its liability shall discharge the other person's liability only to the extent of the amount determined by the formula

$$(A - B) \times C/D$$

where

A is the total of

(i) the amount of the corporation's liability, immediately before that time, under this Part in respect of the full amount of the dividend, and

(ii) the amount of the payment,

B is the amount of the corporation's liability, immediately before that time, under this Act,

C is the amount of the dividend received by the other person, and

D is the full amount of the dividend.

History: S. 185(6), the portion before paragraph (*a*) was replaced by S.C. 2013, c. 34, s. 150(2), in force June 26, 2013, and formerly read:

(6) *Rules applicable.* Where under subsection (4) a corporation and another person have become jointly and severally liable to pay part or all of the corporation's tax payable under this Part in respect of a dividend described in subsection (4),

S. 185(6)(*a*) was replaced by S.C. 2013, c. 34, s. 150(3), in force June 26, 2013, and formerly read:

(*a*) a payment at any time by the other person on account of the liability shall, to the extent of the payment, discharge the joint liability after that time; and

Part III.1
Additional Tax on Excessive Eligible Dividend Designations

SECTION 185.1: Tax on excessive eligible dividend designations

► 185.1(1) ◄

(1) Tax on excessive eligible dividend designations. A corporation that has made an excessive eligible dividend designation in respect of an eligible dividend paid by it at any time in a taxation year shall, on or before the corporation's balance-due day for the taxation year, pay a tax under this Part for the taxation year equal to the total of

(*a*) 20% of the excessive eligible dividend designation, and

(*b*) if the excessive eligible dividend designation arises because of the application of paragraph (*c*) of the definition "excessive eligible dividend designation" in subsection 89(1), 10% of the excessive eligible dividend designation.

Editorial Note: Part III.1 of the Act normally imposes a 20% tax on "excessive eligible dividend designations" (see the definition in s. 89(1)). Reminiscent of Part III tax on excessive capital dividends, a corporation subject to this tax can elect to treat a part of the excess eligible dividend designation as a separate ineligible dividend to which Part III.1 tax will not apply, provided that the election is made within 90 days after the notice of assessment in respect of the Part III.1 tax. Where the anti-avoidance rule in paragraph (*c*) of the "excessive eligible dividend designation" applies, the penalty tax is 30% of the eligible dividend; there is no ability to elect to have a portion of the dividend treated as an ineligible dividend.

Related Sections: S. 87(2)(*z.2*) Application of Parts III and III.1; s. 88(1)(*e.2*) Winding-up; s. 89(1), "eligible dividend", "excessive eligible dividend designation"; s. 185.2 Return; s. 248(1), "eligible dividend", "excessive eligible dividend designation".

Tax Profile: January 2007 — Update on New Rules for the Taxation of Dividends.

Forms: T2 Schedule 55 — Part III.1 Tax on Excessive Eligible Dividend Designations.

► 185.1(2) ◄

(2) Election to treat excessive eligible dividend designation as an ordinary dividend. If, in respect of an excessive eligible dividend designation that is not described in paragraph (1)(*b*) and that is made by a corporation in respect of an eligible dividend (in this subsection and subsection (3) referred to as the "original dividend") paid by it at a particular time, the corporation would, if this Act were read without reference to this subsection, be required to pay a tax under subsection (1), and it elects in prescribed manner on or before the day that is 90 days after the day of sending the notice of assessment in respect of that tax that would otherwise be payable under subsection (1), the following rules apply:

(*a*) notwithstanding the definition "eligible dividend" in subsection 89(1), the amount of the original dividend paid by the corporation is deemed to be the amount, if any, by which

(i) the amount of the original dividend, determined without reference to this subsection

exceeds

(ii) the amount claimed by the corporation in the election not exceeding the excessive eligible dividend designation, determined without reference to this subsection;

(*b*) an amount equal to the amount claimed by the corporation in the election is deemed to be a separate taxable dividend (other than an eligible dividend) that was paid by the corporation immediately before the particular time;

(*c*) each shareholder of the corporation who at the particular time held any of the issued shares of the class of shares in respect of which the original dividend was paid is deemed

(i) not to have received the original dividend, and

(ii) to have received at the particular time

(A) as an eligible dividend, the shareholder's *pro rata* portion of the amount of any dividend determined under paragraph (*a*), and

(B) as a taxable dividend (other than an eligible dividend) the shareholder's *pro rata* portion of the amount of any dividend determined under paragraph (*b*); and

(*d*) a shareholder's *pro rata* portion of a dividend paid at any time on a class of the shares of the capital stock of a corporation is that proportion of the dividend that the number of shares of that class held by the shareholder at that time is of the number of shares of that class outstanding at that time.

Editorial Note: See the editorial note to s. 185.1(1).

History: S. 185.1(2), the portion before paragraph (*a*) was replaced by S.C. 2010, c. 25, s. 49, in force on Royal Assent, December 15, 2010. S. 185.1(2), the portion before paragraph (*a*) formerly read:

(2) *Election to treat excessive eligible dividend designation as an ordinary dividend.* If, in respect of an excessive eligible dividend designation that is not described in paragraph (1)(*b*) and that is made by a corporation in respect of an eligible dividend (in this subsection and subsection (3) referred to as the "original dividend") paid by it at a particular time, the corporation would, if this Act were read without reference to this subsection, be required to pay a tax under subsection (1), and it elects in prescribed manner on or before the day that is 90 days after the day of mailing the notice of assessment in respect of that tax that would otherwise be payable under subsection (1), the following rules apply:

Related Sections: S. 82(1) Taxable dividends received; s. 82(3) Dividends received by spouse or common-law partner; s. 87(2)(*z.2*) Application of Parts III and III.1; s. 88(1)(*e.2*) Winding-up; s. 89(1), "eligible dividend", "excessive eligible dividend designation"; s. 185.2 Return; s. 248(1), "eligible dividend", "excessive eligible dividend designation".

Tax Profile: January 2007 — Update on New Rules for the Taxation of Dividends.

► 185.1(3) ◄

(3) Concurrence with election. An election under subsection (2) in respect of an original dividend is valid only if

(*a*) it is made with the concurrence of the corporation and all its shareholders

(i) who received or were entitled to receive all or any portion of the original dividend, and

(ii) whose addresses were known to the corporation; and

(*b*) either

(i) it is made on or before the day that is 30 months after the day on which the original dividend was paid, or

(ii) each shareholder described in subparagraph (*a*)(i) concurs with the election, in which case, notwithstanding subsections 152(4) to (5), any assessment of the tax, interest and penalties payable by each of those shareholders for any taxation year shall be made that is necessary to take the corporation's election into account.

Editorial Note: Elections to treat a part of the excess eligible dividend designation as a separate non-eligible dividend must generally be made either: (a) within 30 months of the original payment with the consent of all shareholders entitled to receive any portion of the dividend whose names and addresses are known to the corporation; or (b) if later, with the consent of all shareholders so entitled.

► 185.1(4) ◄

(4) Exception for non-taxable shareholders. If each shareholder who, in respect of an election made under subsection (2), is deemed by subsection (2) to have received a dividend at a particular time is also, at the particular time, a person all of whose taxable income is exempt from tax under Part I,

(*a*) subsection (3) does not apply to the election; and

(*b*) the election is valid only if it is made on or before the day that is 30 months after the day on which the original dividend was paid.

SECTION 185.2: Return

► 185.2(1) ◄

(1) Return. Every corporation resident in Canada that pays a taxable dividend (other than a capital gains dividend within the meaning assigned by subsection 130.1(4) or 131(1)) in a taxation year shall file with the Minister, not later than the corporation's filing-due date for the taxation year, a return for the year under this Part in prescribed form containing an estimate of the taxes payable by it under this Part for the taxation year.

► 185.2(2) ◄

(2) Provisions applicable to Part. Subsections 150(2) and (3), sections 151, 152, 158 and 159, subsections 161(1) and (11), sections 162 to 167 and Division J of Part I are applicable to this Part with such modifications as the circumstances require.

► 185.2(3) ◄

(3) Joint and several liability from excessive eligible dividend designations. Without limiting the liability of any person under any other provision of this Act, if a Canadian-controlled private corporation or a deposit insurance corporation pays an eligible dividend in respect of which it has made an excessive eligible dividend designation to a shareholder with whom it does not deal at arm's length, the shareholder is jointly and severally, or solidarily, liable with the corporation to pay that proportion of the corporation's tax payable under this Part because of the designation that the amount of the eligible dividend received by the shareholder is of the total of all amounts each of which is a dividend in respect of which the designation was made.

► 185.2(4) ◄

(4) Assessment. The Minister may, at any time after the last day on which a corporation may make an election under subsection 185.1(2) in respect of an excessive eligible dividend designation, assess a person in respect of any amount payable under subsection (3) in respect of the designation, and the provisions of Division I of Part I (including, for greater certainty, the provisions in respect of interest payable) apply, with any modifications that the circumstances require, to an assessment made under this subsection as though it were made under section 152.

► 185.2(5) ◄

(5) Rules applicable. If under subsection (3) a corporation and a shareholder have become jointly and severally, or solidarily, liable to pay part or all of the corporation's tax payable under this Part in respect of an excessive eligible dividend designation described in subsection (3),

(*a*) a payment at any time by the shareholder on account of the liability shall, to the extent of the payment, discharge their liability after that time; and

(*b*) a payment at any time by the corporation on account of its liability shall discharge the shareholder's liability only to the extent of the amount determined by the formula

$$(A - B) \times C/D$$

where

A is the total of

(i) the amount of the corporation's liability, immediately before that time, under this Part in respect of the designation, and

(ii) the amount of the payment,

B is the amount of the corporation's liability, immediately before that time, under this Act,

C is the amount of the eligible dividend received by the shareholder, and

D the total of all amounts each of which is a dividend in respect of which the designation was made.

Part IV
Tax on Taxable Dividends Received by Private Corporations

SECTION 186: Tax on assessable dividends

► 186(1) ◄

(1) Tax on assessable dividends. Every corporation (in this section referred to as the "particular corporation") that is at any time in a taxation year a private corporation or a subject corporation shall, on or before its balance-due day for the year, pay a tax under this Part for the year equal to the amount, if any, by which the total of

(*a*) 38 1/3% of all assessable dividends received by the particular corporation in the year from corporations other than payer corporations connected with it, and

(*b*) all amounts, each of which is an amount in respect of an assessable dividend received by the particular corporation in the year from a private corporation or a subject corporation that was a payer corporation connected with the particular corporation, equal to that proportion of the payer corporation's dividend refund (within the meaning assigned by paragraph 129(1)(*a*)) for its taxation year in which it paid the dividend that

(i) the amount of the dividend received by the particular corporation

is of

(ii) the total of all taxable dividends paid by the payer corporation in its taxation year in which it paid the dividend and at a time when it was a private corporation or a subject corporation

exceeds 38 1/3% of the total of

(*c*) such part of the particular corporation's non-capital loss and farm loss for the year as it claims, and

(*d*) such part of the particular corporation's

(i) non-capital loss for any of its 20 taxation years immediately preceding or 3 taxation years immediately following the year, and

(ii) farm loss for any of its 20 taxation years immediately preceding or 3 taxation years immediately following the year

as it claims, not exceeding the portion thereof that would have been deductible under section 111 in computing its taxable income for the year if subparagraph 111(3)(*a*)(ii) were read without reference to the words "the particular taxation year and" and if the corporation had sufficient income for the year.

Editorial Note: Part IV of the Act prevents the deferral of tax on dividends when received by a corporation rather than an individual, by effectively imposing a 38 1/3% refundable tax on dividends which would otherwise be tax free under Part I ("assessable dividends"). There is no special Part IV rate for "eligible dividends" (defined in s. 89(1)). Part IV tax is applicable to taxable dividends received by "private corporations" (see s. 89(1)) and "subject corporations" (non-private corporations controlled for the benefits of an individual or related group of individuals, other than trusts — see s. 186(3)).

Part IV tax is based on: (a) 38 1/3% of assessable dividends from non-connected corporations; and (b) an amount equivalent to the recipient's portion of the dividend refund in respect to assessable dividends from connected (private or subject) corporations, less 38 1/3% of the corporation's non-capital loss and farm loss (including carry forward and carry back balances) claimed by the corporation to reduce its Part IV tax liability. Note that such losses used to reduce Part IV tax may not be deducted again for Part I tax purposes; see s. 111(3)(*a*)(iii). Note that the percentages described were amended effective January 1, 2016. For the prior rates and transitional rules see the historical note for this subsection.

The CRA's position is that a dividend recipient's Part IV tax liability will be determined according to the dividend refund actually received by the connected corporation. Therefore, the recipient is not liable for Part IV tax with respect to dividends of which the dividend refund was denied due to the connected corporation not filing a tax return within the required three-year period (2015-0610691C6).

The meaning of "connected" is found in s. 186(4) and related provisions.

History: S. 186(1)(*a*) was replaced by S.C. 2016, c. 11, s. 8(1), applicable to taxation years of a corporation that end after 2015, except that, for taxation years that end after 2015 and begin before 2016

(*a*) in the application of subsection 186(1) to amounts described in paragraphs 186(1)(*a*) and (*b*) that were received by the corporation in the year and before 2016, the references to "38 1/3%" are to be read as "1/3"; and

(*b*) amounts deducted by the corporation for the year under paragraphs 186(1)(*c*) and (*d*)

(i) are deemed to have been deducted in respect of amounts described in paragraph 186(1)(*a*) and paragraph 186(1)(*b*) that were received by the corporation in the year and after 2015, and

(ii) to the extent that the amounts so deducted exceed the amounts referred to in subparagraph (i) are deemed to have been deducted in respect of amounts described in paragraph 186(1)(*a*) and paragraph 186(1)(*b*) that were received by the corporation in the year and before 2016.

S. 186(1)(*a*) formerly read:

(*a*) 1/3 of all assessable dividends received by the particular corporation in the year from corporations other than payer corporations connected with it, and

S. 186(1), the portion after paragraph (*b*) and before paragraph (*c*) was replaced by S.C. 2016, c. 11, s. 8(2), applicable to taxation years of a corporation that end after 2015, except that, for taxation years that end after 2015 and begin before 2016

(*a*) in the application of subsection 186(1) to amounts described in paragraphs 186(1)(*a*) and (*b*) that were received by the corporation in the year and before 2016, the references to "38 1/3%" are to be read as "1/3"; and

(*b*) amounts deducted by the corporation for the year under paragraphs 186(1)(*c*) and (*d*)

(i) are deemed to have been deducted in respect of amounts described in paragraph 186(1)(*a*) and paragraph 186(1)(*b*) that were received by the corporation in the year and after 2015, and

(ii) to the extent that the amounts so deducted exceed the amounts referred to in subparagraph (i) are deemed to have been deducted in respect of amounts described in paragraph 186(1)(*a*) and paragraph 186(1)(*b*) that were received by the corporation in the year and before 2016.

S. 186(1), the portion after paragraph (*b*) and before paragraph (*c*) formerly read:

exceeds 1/3 of the total of

Related Sections: S. 15.1(1) Interest on small business development bonds; s. 15.2(1) Interest on small business bond; s. 55(2) Deemed proceeds or capital gain; s. 88(1.1) Non-capital losses, etc., of subsidiary; s. 88(1.3) Computation of income and tax of parent; s. 89(1)(*f*), "private corporation";

s. 89(1)(*j*), "taxable dividend"; s. 104(1) Reference to trust or estate; s. 111(3) Limitation on deductibility; s. 111(8), "non-capital loss", "farm loss"; s. 112(1) Deduction of taxable dividends received by corporation resident in Canada; s. 113(1) Deduction in respect of dividend received from foreign affiliate; s. 113(2) Additional deduction; s. 129(1) Dividend refund to private corporation; s. 129(3) Definition of "refundable dividend tax on hand"; s. 131(5) Dividend refund to mutual fund corporation; s. 186(3) Definitions; s. 186.1 Exempt corporations; s. 186.2 Exempt dividends; s. 227(14) Application of other Parts; s. 227(16) Municipal or provincial corporation excepted; s. 248(1), "corporation", "dividend", "individual", "private corporation", "taxable dividend", "trust"; s. 248(25) Beneficially interested; s. 249(1) Definition of "taxation year".

Canadian Tax Foundation: Bleiwas and Ball, *Current Issues for Private Companies, Including Dividend Tax Credit Changes and Integration*, 2013 Conference Report 6:1–32; Perry and Truster, *Corporate Beneficiaries of Discretionary Family Trusts: The Part IV Tax Trap*, 2012 Tax for the Owner-Manager 12(2):4.

Tax Profile: October 2004 — Taxation of Dividends: A Survey in the Context of Private Corporations and Their Shareholders.

Forms: T2 SCH 3 — Dividends Received, Taxable Dividends Paid, and Part IV Tax Calculation.

Information Circulars: IC 88-2 General anti-avoidance rule — Section 245 of the Income Tax Act.

Interpretation Bulletins: *Primary* — IT-269R4 Part IV tax on taxable dividends received by a private corporation or a subject corporation. *Secondary* — IT-232R3 Non-capital losses, net capital losses, restricted farm losses, farm losses and limited partnership losses — Their composition and deductibility in computing taxable income; IT-302R3 Losses of a corporation — The effect on their deductibility of changes in control, amalgamation and winding-up; IT-328R3 Losses on shares on which dividends have been received.

► 186(1.1) ◄

(1.1) Reduction where Part IV.1 tax payable. Notwithstanding subsection (1), where an assessable dividend was received by a corporation in a taxation year and was included in an amount in respect of which tax under Part IV.1 was payable by the corporation for the year, the tax otherwise payable under this Part by the corporation for the year shall be reduced

(*a*) where the assessable dividend is described in paragraph (1)(*a*), by 10% of the assessable dividend, and

(*b*) where the assessable dividend is described in paragraph (1)(*b*), by 30% of the amount determined under that paragraph in respect of the assessable dividend.

► 186(2) ◄

(2) When corporation controlled. For the purposes of this Part, other than for the purpose of determining whether a corporation is a subject corporation, one corporation is controlled by another corporation if more than 50% of its issued share capital (having full voting rights under all circumstances) belongs to the other corporation, to persons with whom the other corporation does not deal at arm's length, or to the other corporation and persons with whom the other corporation does not deal at arm's length.

Editorial Note: See the editorial note to s. 186(4).

Related Sections: S. 111(1)(*a*) Non-capital losses; s. 112(1) Deduction of taxable dividends received by corporation resident in Canada.

Cases: The reference in s. 84.1 of the Act to s. 186(4) incorporates the definition of the word "control" as found in s. 186(2). *The Queen v. Olsen*, 2002 DTC 6770 (F.C.A.), reversing 2000 DTC 2121 (T.C.C.).

► 186(3) ◄

(3) Definitions. The definitions in this subsection apply in this Part.

"assessable dividend" — "assessable dividend" means an amount received by a corporation at a time when it is a private corporation or a subject corporation as, on account of, in lieu of payment of or in satisfaction of, a taxable dividend from a corporation, to the extent of the amount in respect of the dividend that is deductible under section 112, paragraph 113(1)(*a*), (*a.1*), (*b*) or (*d*) or subsection 113(2) in computing the recipient corporation's taxable income for the year.

History: S. 186(3), the definition "assessable dividend" was replaced by S.C. 2013, c. 34, s. 75(4), deemed to have come into force on August 20, 2011.

Any assessment of a taxpayer's tax, interest and penalties payable under the Act for any taxation year that ends before June 26, 2013 that would, in the absence of this section, be precluded because of subsections 152(4) to (5) of the Act shall be made to the extent necessary to take into account the amendments by S.C. 2013, c. 34, s. 54 to 89.

S. 186(3), the definition "assessable dividend" formerly read:

"assessable dividend" — "assessable dividend" means an amount received by a corporation at a time when it is a private corporation or a subject corporation as, on account of, in lieu of payment of or in satisfaction of, a taxable dividend from a corporation, to the extent of the amount in respect of the dividend that is deductible under section 112, paragraph 113(1)(*a*), (*b*) or (*d*) or subsection 113(2) in computing the recipient corporation's taxable income for the year.

"subject corporation" — "subject corporation" means a corporation (other than a private corporation) resident in Canada and controlled, whether because of a beneficial interest in one or more trusts or otherwise, by or for the benefit of an individual (other than a trust) or a related group of individuals (other than trusts).

► 186(4) ◄

(4) Corporations connected with particular corporation. For the purposes of this Part, a payer corporation is connected with a particular corporation at any time in a taxation year (in this subsection referred to as the "particular year") of the particular corporation if

(*a*) the payer corporation is controlled (otherwise than by virtue of a right referred to in paragraph 251(5)(*b*)) by the particular corporation at that time; or

(*b*) the particular corporation owned, at that time,

(i) more than 10% of the issued share capital (having full voting rights under all circumstances) of the payer corporation, and

(ii) shares of the capital stock of the payer corporation having a fair market value of more than 10% of the fair market value of all of the issued shares of the capital stock of the payer corporation.

Editorial Note: Under s. 186(4)(*a*), a corporation will be connected to another if it is "controlled" by the particular corporation (otherwise than by virtue of a right referred to in s. 251(5)(*b*) — see also the editorial note for s. 251(5)). Per s. 186(2), a corporation is controlled if more than 50% of the issued shares having full voting rights under all circumstances belong either to the other corporation or to a non-arm's length person. (Per s. 186(7), s. 186(2) applies for the entire *Income Tax Act*)

Part IV tax will apply to a dividend paid to a trust and allocated to a corporate beneficiary (e.g., in a "purification structure") unless the corporations are connected (Document No. 2005-0121931E5); this connectedness may be established pursuant to s. 186(4)(*a*) (see "Deferred Income Plans for the Owner Manager", Bank, 2009 British Columbia Tax Conference p.13:34/35/36; "Family Trusts and the Connected Status Rules", Léger and Neilson, *Tax for the Owner-Manager, Vol. 11, No. 2*). A recipient corporation should similarly consider those shares of the payer corporation that it holds through a partnership when determining connectedness and Part IV tax liability for the dividends it receives (Document No. 2013-0485691E5).

Under s. 186(4)(*b*), a corporation will be connected to a particular corporation if it owns more than 10% of the issued capital, in terms of both the fair market value and voting rights — i.e., full voting rights under all circumstances. In the former respect, the impact of minority discounts should be considered. "Ownership" means direct legal ownership (see Document No. 2002-0141295; see also *Army and Navy v. MNR*, 53 DTC 1185 (SCC)). Shares described in s. 186(4)(*b*)(i) (votes) need not be the same shares described in s. 186(4)(*b*)(ii) (value) (Document No. 2011-0426081E5). See also Document No. 2009-0330061C6, regarding where the fair market value of the shares is nil because of the corporation's financial difficulty; Document No. 1999-0010955, where the ability to elect board members is split between two classes of shares; Document No. 2006-0204901E5, regarding the full voting rights requirement where there is a veto right protecting a class of shares; and Document Nos. 9M19020 (1997 APFF q. 5.1) and 2014-0538081C6, where share classes have multiple voting rights). See also Document No. 2004-0099071E5 — Part IV Tax Circularity.

Related Sections: s. 84(11) Computation of contributed surplus; s. 84.1(1) Non-arm's length sale of shares; s. 89(1), "private corporation", "taxable dividends"; s. 110.6(1), "qualified small business corporation share"; s. 110.6(15)(a) Value of assets of corporations; s. 111(8), "farm loss", "non-capital loss"; s. 186(1) Tax on assessable dividends; s. 186(2) When corporation controlled; s. 186(7) Interpretation; s. 212.1(1) Non-arm's length sales of shares by non-residents; s. 248(1), "amount", "corporation", "dividend", "share"; "small business corporation"; s. 249 Definition of "taxation year".

▶ 186(5) ◀

(5) Deemed private corporation. A corporation that is at any time in a taxation year a subject corporation shall, for the purposes of paragraph 87(2)(*aa*) and section 129, be deemed to be a private corporation at that time, except that its "non-eligible refundable dividend tax on hand" (as defined in subsection 129(4)) at the end of the year shall be determined without reference to paragraph (*a*) of that definition.

History: S. 186(5) was replaced by S.C. 2018, c. 12, s. 29(1), applicable to taxation years that begin after 2018, and also to a taxation year of a corporation that begins before 2019 and ends after 2018 if

(a) the corporation's preceding taxation year was, because of a transaction or event or a series of transactions or events, shorter than it would have been in the absence of that transaction, event or series; and

(b) one of the reasons for the transaction, event or series was to defer the application of subsections 20(2) and (3) or 22(1) to (5) [of the *Budget Implementation Act, 2018, No. 1*] to the corporation.

S. 186(5) formerly read:

(5) *Deemed private corporation.* A corporation that is at any time in a taxation year a subject corporation shall, for the purposes of paragraph 87(2)(*aa*) and section 129, be deemed to be a private corporation at that time, except that its refundable dividend tax on hand (within the meaning assigned by subsection 129(3)) at the end of the year shall be determined without reference to paragraph 129(3)(*a*).

Related Sections: S. 87(2)(*aa*) Refundable dividend tax on hand; s. 88(1)(*e.5*) Winding-up; s. 89(1)(*f*), "private corporation"; s. 129(1) Dividend refund to private corporation; s. 129(3.5) Definition of "reduction at December 31, 1987 of refundable dividend tax on hand"; s. 186(1) Tax on assessable dividends; s. 248(1), "private corporation"; s. 249(1) Definition of "taxation year".

▶ 186(6) ◀

(6) Partnerships. For the purposes of this Part,

(*a*) all amounts received in a fiscal period by a partnership as, on account or in lieu of payment of, or in satisfaction of, taxable dividends shall be deemed to have been received by each member of the partnership in the member's fiscal period or taxation year in which the partnership's fiscal period ends, to the extent of that member's share thereof; and

(*b*) each member of a partnership shall be deemed to own at any time that proportion of the number of the shares of each class of the capital stock of a corporation that are property of the partnership at that time that the member's share of all dividends received on those shares by the partnership in its fiscal period that includes that time is of the total of all those dividends.

▶ 186(7) ◀

(7) Interpretation. For greater certainty, where a provision of this Act or the regulations indicates that the term "connected" has the meaning assigned by subsection 186(4), that meaning shall be determined by taking into account the application of subsection 186(2) unless the provision expressly provides otherwise.

Related Sections: S. 84.1(1) Non-arm's length sale of shares; s. 212.1(1) Non-arm's length sales of shares by non-residents.

SECTION 186.1: Exempt corporations

No tax is payable under this Part for a taxation year by a corporation

(*a*) that was, at any time in the year, a bankrupt; or

(*b*) that was, throughout the year,

(i) a bank,

(ii) a corporation licensed or otherwise authorized under the laws of Canada or a province to carry on in Canada the business of offering to the public its services as a trustee,

(iii) an insurance corporation,

(iv) a prescribed labour-sponsored venture capital corporation,

(v) a prescribed investment contract corporation,

(vi) a non-resident-owned investment corporation, or

(vii) a registered securities dealer that was throughout the year a member, or a participating organization, of a designated stock exchange in Canada.

History: S. 186.1(*a*) was replaced by S.C. 2017, c. 33, s. 64(1), applicable in respect of bankruptcies that occur after April 26, 1995, and formerly read:

(*a*) that was, at any time in the year, a bankrupt (within the meaning assigned by subsection 128(3)); or

Related Regulations: 6701; 6703.

Related Sections: S. 133(8) Definitions; 248(1) bankrupt; 248(1), "insurance corporation".

Interpretation Bulletins: *Primary* — IT-269R4 Part IV tax on taxable dividends received by a private corporation or a subject corporation. *Secondary* — IT-302R3 Losses of a corporation — The effect on their deductibility of changes in control, amalgamation and winding-up.

SECTION 186.2: Exempt dividends

For the purposes of subsection 186(1), dividends received in a taxation year by a corporation that was, throughout the year, a prescribed venture capital corporation from a corporation that was a prescribed qualifying corporation with respect to those dividends shall be deemed not to be taxable dividends.

Related Regulations: 6700; 6704.

Interpretation Bulletins: *Primary* — IT-269R4 Part IV tax on taxable dividends received by a private corporation or a subject corporation.

SECTION 187: Information return

▶ 187(1) ◀

(1) Information return. Every corporation that is liable to pay tax under this Part for a taxation year in respect of a dividend received by it in the year shall, on or before the day on or before which it is required to file its return of income under Part I for the year, file a return for the year under this Part in prescribed form.

Related Sections: S. 150(1)(*a*) Corporations; s. 186(1) Tax on assessable dividends.

Interpretation Bulletins: *Secondary* — IT-269R4 Part IV tax on taxable dividends received by a private corporation or a subject corporation; IT-302R3 Losses of a corporation — The effect on their deductibility of changes in control, amalgamation and winding-up.

▶ 187(2) ◀

(2) Interest. Where a corporation is liable to pay tax under this Part and has failed to pay all or any part thereof on or before the day on or before which the tax was required to be paid, it shall pay to the Receiver General interest at the prescribed rate on the amount that it failed to pay computed from the day on or before which the tax was required to be paid to the day of payment.

Related Regulations: 4301.

Related Sections: S. 161.1 Offset of refund interest and arrears interest; s. 248(11) Compound interest.

Tax Topics: No. 2247, Technically Inequitable — The Computation of Arrears Interest Under Subsection 187(2).

Interpretation Bulletins: *Secondary* — IT-302R3 Losses of a corporation — The effect on their deductibility of changes in control, amalgamation and winding-up.

Cases: The taxpayer filed its tax returns for 1993 and 1995. The Part IV tax payable for the 1995 taxation year was paid on June 10, 1995. As the result of subsequent reassessments the taxpayer's Part IV liability for 1993 was increased significantly, while its Part IV liability for 1995 was reduced. On February 3, 2000, the Minister applied the resulting overpayment for 1995 to the outstanding amount for 1993. The date of payment for purposes of calculating interest in relation to amounts owed for 1993 was February 3, 2000, and not, as the taxpayer argued, June 10, 1995. *Bakorp Management v. MNR*, 2016 DTC 5037 (FCA)

▶ 187(3) ◀

(3) Provisions applicable to Part. Sections 151, 152, 158 and 159, subsections 161(7) and (11), sections 162 to 167 and Division J of Part I are applicable to this Part with such modifications as the circumstances require.

Related Sections: S. 248(1), "amount", "corporation", "dividend", "share", "taxable dividend".

Interpretation Bulletins: *Secondary* — IT-302R3 Losses of a corporation — The effect on their deductibility of changes in control, amalgamation and winding-up.

Part IV.1
Taxes on Dividends on Certain Preferred Shares Received by Corporations

SECTION 187.1: Definition of "excepted dividend"

In this Part, "excepted dividend" means a dividend

(*a*) received by a corporation on a share of the capital stock of a foreign affiliate of the corporation, other than a dividend received by a specified financial institution on a share acquired in the ordinary course of the business carried on by the institution;

(*b*) received by a corporation from another corporation (other than a corporation described in any of paragraphs (*a*) to (*f*) of the definition "financial intermediary corporation" in subsection 191(1)) in which it has or would have, if the other corporation were a taxable Canadian corporation, a substantial interest (as determined under section 191) at the time the dividend was paid;

(*c*) received by a corporation that was, at the time the dividend was received, a private corporation or a financial intermediary corporation (within the meaning assigned by subsection 191(1));

(*d*) received by a corporation on a short-term preferred share of the capital stock of a taxable Canadian corporation other than a dividend described in paragraph (*b*) or (*c*) of the definition "excluded dividend" in subsection 191(1); or

(*e*) received by a corporation on a share (other than a taxable RFI share or a share that would be a taxable preferred share if the definition "taxable preferred share" in subsection 248(1) were read without reference to paragraph (*a*) of that definition) of the capital stock of a mutual fund corporation.

Related Sections: S. 89(1), "taxable Canadian corporation"; s. 95(1), "foreign affiliate"; s. 248(1), "corporation", "dividend", "share", "short-term preferred share", "taxable preferred share", "taxable RFI share".

SECTION 187.2: Tax on dividends on taxable preferred shares

Every corporation shall, on or before its balance-due day for a taxation year, pay a tax under this Part for the year equal to 10% of the total of all amounts each of which is a dividend, other than an excepted dividend, received by the corporation in the year on a taxable preferred share (other than a share of a class in respect of which an election under subsection 191.2(1) has been made) to the extent that an amount in respect of the dividend was deductible under section 112 or 113 or subsection 138(6) in computing its taxable income for the year or under subsection 115(1) in computing its taxable income earned in Canada for the year.

Related Sections: S. 227(14) Application of other Parts; s. 248(1), "amount", "corporation", "dividend", "taxable income", "taxable income earned in Canada", "taxable preferred share".

Canadian Tax Foundation: Moskowitz, *The Preferred Share Rules: Yes They Can Apply to You!*, 1997 Conference Report 9:1–47.

Forms: T2 SCH 43 — Calculation of Parts IV.1 and VI.1 Taxes.

SECTION 187.3: Tax on dividends on taxable RFI shares

► 187.3(1) ◄

(1) Tax on dividends on taxable RFI shares. Every restricted financial institution shall, on or before its balance-due day for a taxation year, pay a tax under this Part for the year equal to 10% of the total of all amounts each of which is a dividend, other than an excepted dividend, received by the institution at any time in the year on a share acquired by any person before that time and after 8:00 p.m. Eastern Daylight Saving Time, June 18, 1987 that was, at the time the dividend was paid, a taxable RFI share to the extent that an amount in respect of the dividend was deductible under section 112 or 113 or subsection 138(6) in computing its taxable income for the year or under subsection 115(1) in computing its taxable income earned in Canada for the year.

Related Sections: S. 248(1), "amount", "corporation", "dividend", "restricted financial institution", "share", "taxable income", "taxable income earned in Canada", "taxable RFI share".

► 187.3(2) ◄

(2) Time of acquisition of share. For the purposes of subsection (1),

(*a*) a share of the capital stock of a corporation acquired by a person after 8:00 p.m. Eastern Daylight Saving Time, June 18, 1987 pursuant to an agreement in writing entered into before that time shall be deemed to have been acquired by that person before that time;

(*b*) a share of the capital stock of a corporation acquired by a person after 8:00 p.m. Eastern Daylight Saving Time, June 18, 1987 and before 1988 as part of a distribution to the public made in accordance with the terms of a prospectus, preliminary prospectus, registration statement, offering memorandum or notice filed before 8:00 p.m. Eastern Daylight Saving Time, June 18, 1987 with a public authority pursuant to and in accordance with the securities legislation of the jurisdiction in which the shares are distributed shall be deemed to have been acquired by that person before that time;

(*c*) a share (in this paragraph referred to as the "new share") of the capital stock of a corporation that is acquired by a person after 8:00 p.m. Eastern Daylight Saving Time, June 18, 1987 in exchange for

(i) a share of a corporation that was issued before 8:00 p.m. Eastern Daylight Saving Time, June 18, 1987 or is a grandfathered share, or

(ii) a debt obligation of a corporation that was issued before 8:00 p.m. Eastern Daylight Saving Time, June 18, 1987, or issued after that time pursuant to an agreement in writing entered into before that time,

where the right to the exchange for the new share and all or substantially all the terms and conditions of the new share were established in writing before that time shall be deemed to have been acquired by that person before that time;

(*d*) a share of a class of the capital stock of a Canadian corporation listed on a designated stock exchange in Canada that is acquired by a person after 8:00 p.m. Eastern Daylight Saving Time, June 18, 1987 on the exercise of a right

(i) that was issued before that time and listed on a prescribed stock exchange in Canada, and

(ii) the terms of which at that time included the right to acquire the share,

where all or substantially all the terms and conditions of the share were established in writing before that time shall be deemed to have been acquired by that person before that time;

(*e*) where a share that was owned by a particular restricted financial institution at 8:00 p.m. Eastern Daylight Saving Time, June 18, 1987 has, by one or more transactions between related restricted financial institutions, been transferred to another restricted financial institution, the share shall be deemed to have been acquired by the other restricted financial institution before that time unless at any particular time after 8:00 p.m. Eastern Daylight Saving Time, June 18, 1987 and before the share was transferred to the other restricted financial institution the share was owned by a shareholder who, at that particular time, was a person other than a restricted financial institution related to the other restricted financial institution; and

(*f*) where, at any particular time, there has been an amalgamation within the meaning assigned by section 87, and

(i) each of the predecessor corporations was a restricted financial institution throughout the period from 8:00 p.m. Eastern Daylight Saving Time, June 18, 1987 to the particular time and the predecessor corporations were related to each other throughout that period, or

(ii) each of the predecessor corporations and the new corporation is a corporation described in any of paragraphs (*a*) to (*d*) of the definition "restricted financial institution" in subsection 248(1),

a taxable RFI share acquired by the new corporation from a predecessor corporation on the amalgamation shall be deemed to have been acquired by the new corporation at the time it was acquired by the predecessor corporation.

Related Sections: S. 262 Designated stock exchanges.

SECTION 187.4: Partnerships

For the purposes of this Part,

(*a*) all amounts received in a fiscal period by a partnership as, on account or in lieu of payment of, or in satisfaction of, dividends shall be deemed to have been received by each member of the partnership in the member's fiscal period or taxation year in which the partnership's fiscal period ends, to the extent of that member's share thereof;

(*b*) each member of a partnership shall be deemed to own at any time that proportion of the number of the shares of each class of the capital stock of a corporation that are property of the partnership at that time that the member's share of all dividends received on those shares by the partnership in its fiscal period that includes that time is of the total of all those dividends; and

(*c*) a reference to a person includes a partnership.

SECTION 187.5: Information return

Every corporation liable to pay tax under this Part for a taxation year shall file with the Minister, not later than the day on or before which it is required by section 150 to file its return of income for the year under Part I, a return for the year under this Part in prescribed form containing an estimate of the taxes payable by it under sections 187.2 and 187.3 for the year.

Forms: T2 SCH 43 — Calculation of Parts IV.1 and VI.1 Taxes.

SECTION 187.6: Provisions applicable to Part

Sections 152, 158 and 159, subsections 161(1), (2) and (11), sections 162 to 167 and Division J of Part I are applicable to this Part with such modifications as the circumstances require.

SECTION 187.61: Provisions applicable — Crown corporations

Section 27 applies to this Part with any modifications that the circumstances require.

Part V
Tax and Penalties in Respect of Qualified Donees

SECTION 187.7: Application of s. 149.1(1)

The definitions in subsection 149.1(1) apply to this Part.

Editorial Note: For the purposes of s. 188–189, the definitions of s. 149.1 apply.

History: The heading of Part V was replaced by S.C. 2011, c. 24, s. 57(1), in force January 1, 2012. The heading of Part V formerly read: "Tax and Penalties in Respect of Registered Charities".

SECTION 188: [Revocation tax and transfer of property tax]

► 188(1) ◄

(1) Deemed year-end on notice of revocation. If on a particular day the Minister issues a notice of intention to revoke the registration of a taxpayer as a registered charity under any of subsections 149.1(2) to (4.1) and 168(1) or it is determined, under subsection 7(1) of the *Charities Registration (Security Information) Act*, that a certificate served in respect of the charity under subsection 5(1) of that Act is reasonable on the basis of information and evidence available,

(*a*) the taxation year of the charity that would otherwise have included that day is deemed to end at the end of that day;

(*b*) a new taxation year of the charity is deemed to begin immediately after that day; and

(*c*) for the purpose of determining the charity's fiscal period after that day, the charity is deemed not to have established a fiscal period before that day.

Editorial Note: Section 188 provides for a revocation tax which may be exigible upon the revocation of the registration of a charity and a transfer of property tax.

Where the Minister of Revenue issues a notice of intention to revoke the registration of a charity in accordance with s. 149.1 or 168 or a determination is made that the charity's funds may be used for terrorism, then (i) the taxation year of the charity that would otherwise have included that day is deemed to end at the end of that day; (ii) a new taxation year of the charity is deemed to begin immediately after that day; and (iii) for the purpose of determining the charity's fiscal period after that day, the charity is deemed not to have established a fiscal period before that day.

Related Sections: S. 110.1(2) Proof of gift; s. 118.1(2) Proof of gift.

Cases: The taxpayer whose registration as a registered Canadian charitable organization had been revoked, had to be represented by counsel, although it was impecunious. *Institute of Applied Methodology v. The Queen*, 91 DTC 5237 (F.C.T.D.)

► 188(1.1) ◄

(1.1) Revocation tax. A charity referred to in subsection (1) is liable to a tax, for its taxation year that is deemed to have ended, equal to the amount determined by the formula

$$A - B$$

where

A is the total of all amounts, each of which is

(*a*) the fair market value of a property of the charity at the end of that taxation year,

(*b*) the amount of an appropriation (within the meaning assigned by subsection (2)) in respect of a property transferred to another person in the 120-day period that ended at the end of that taxation year, or

(*c*) the income of the charity for its winding-up period, including gifts received by the charity in that period from any source and any income that would be computed under section 3 as if that period were a taxation year; and

B is the total of all amounts (other than the amount of an expenditure in respect of which a deduction has been made in computing income for the winding-up period under paragraph (*c*) of the description of A), each of which is

(*a*) a debt of the charity that is outstanding at the end of that taxation year,

(*b*) an expenditure made by the charity during the winding-up period on charitable activities carried on by it, or

(*c*) an amount in respect of a property transferred by the charity during the winding-up period and not later than the latter [(*sic*) later — CCH] of one year from the end of the taxation year and the day, if any, referred to in paragraph (1.2)(*c*), to a person that was at the time of the transfer an eligible donee in respect of the charity, equal to the amount, if any, by which the fair market value of the property, when transferred, exceeds the consideration given by the person for the transfer.

Editorial Note: A revocation tax becomes payable with respect to the fiscal year deemed to have ended by s. 188(1). The tax consists of the sum of (i) the fair market value of the property of the charity at the end of that taxation year; (ii) the amount of any appropriation (within the meaning of s. 188(2), discussed below) in respect of a property transferred to another person in the 120-day period ending at the end of that taxation year; and (iii) the income of the charity for its winding-up period (as discussed below), including any gifts received by the charity in that period from any source and any income that would be computed under s. 3 of the Act as if that period were a taxation year. The amount of revocation tax payable is reduced by (i) debts of the charity at the end of that taxation year; (ii) expenditures made by the charity during the winding-up period on charitable activities carried on by it; and (iii) amounts in respect of property transferred by the charity during a specified time period to an eligible donee (as defined in s. 188(1.3)) equal to the amount by which the fair market value of the property transferred exceeds the consideration given by the person for the transfer.

Related Sections: S. 189(6.1) Revoked charity to file returns; s. 189(6.2) Reduction of revocation tax liability; s. 189(7) Minister may assess; s. 225.1(1.1) Collection-commencement day.

► 188(1.2) ◄

(1.2) Winding-up period. In this Part, the winding-up period of a charity is the period that begins immediately after the day on which the Minister issues a notice of intention to revoke the registration of a taxpayer as a registered charity under any of subsections 149.1(2) to (4.1) and 168(1) (or, if earlier, immediately after the day on which it is determined, under subsection 7(1) of the *Charities Registration (Security Information) Act*, that a certificate served in respect of the charity under subsection 5(1) of that Act is reasonable on the basis of information and evidence available), and that ends on the day that is the latest of

(*a*) the day, if any, on which the charity files a return under subsection 189(6.1) for the taxation year deemed by subsection (1) to have ended, but not later than the day on which the charity is required to file that return,

(b) the day on which the Minister last issues a notice of assessment of tax payable under subsection (1.1) for that taxation year by the charity, and

(c) if the charity has filed a notice of objection or appeal in respect of that assessment, the day on which the Minister may take a collection action under section 225.1 in respect of that tax payable.

► 188(1.3) ◄

(1.3) Eligible donee. In this Part, an eligible donee in respect of a particular charity is

(a) a registered charity

(i) of which more than 50% of the members of the board of directors or trustees of the registered charity deal at arm's length with each member of the board of directors or trustees of the particular charity,

(ii) that is not the subject of a suspension under subsection 188.2(1),

(iii) that has no unpaid liabilities under this Act or under the *Excise Tax Act*,

(iv) that has filed all information returns required by subsection 149.1(14), and

(v) that is not the subject of a certificate under subsection 5(1) of the *Charities Registration (Security Information) Act* or, if it is the subject of such a certificate, the certificate has been determined under subsection 7(1) of that Act not to be reasonable; or

(b) a municipality in Canada that is approved by the Minister in respect of a transfer of property from the particular charity.

History: S. 188(1.3) was replaced by S.C. 2018, c. 12, s. 30(1), applicable in respect of transfers of property made after February 26, 2018, and formerly read:

(1.3) *Eligible donee.* In this Part, an eligible donee in respect of a particular charity is a registered charity

(a) of which more than 50% of the members of the board of directors or trustees of the registered charity deal at arm's length with each member of the board of directors or trustees of the particular charity;

(b) that is not the subject of a suspension under subsection 188.2(1);

(c) that has no unpaid liabilities under this Act or under the *Excise Tax Act*;

(d) that has filed all information returns required by subsection 149.1(14); and

(e) that is not the subject of a certificate under subsection 5(1) of the *Charities Registration (Security Information) Act* or, if it is the subject of such a certificate, the certificate has been determined under subsection 7(1) of that Act not to be reasonable.

► 188(1.4) ◄

(1.4) Eligible donee. In this Part, an eligible donee in respect of a particular Canadian amateur athletic association is a registered Canadian amateur athletic association

(a) of which more than 50% of the members of the board of directors or trustees of the registered Canadian amateur athletic association deal at arm's length with each member of the board of directors or trustees of the particular Canadian amateur athletic association;

(b) that is not the subject of a suspension under subsection 188.2(1);

(c) that has no unpaid liabilities under this Act or under the *Excise Tax Act*; and

(d) that has filed all information returns required by subsection 149.1(14).

History: S. 188(1.4) was added by S.C. 2011, c. 24, s. 58(1), in force January 1, 2012.

► 188(2) ◄

(2) Shared liability — revocation tax. A person who, after the time that is 120 days before the end of the taxation year of a charity that is deemed by subsection (1) to have ended, receives property from the charity, is jointly and severally, or solidarily, liable with the charity for the tax payable under subsection (1.1) by the charity for that taxation year for an amount not exceeding the total of all appropriations, each of which is the amount by which the fair market value of such a property at the time it was so received by the person exceeds the consideration given by the person in respect of the property.

Editorial Note: Where a person received (appropriated) property from a registered charity within a period that is 120 days before the taxation year of that charity that is deemed to have ended by virtue of s. 188(1), that person is jointly and severally liable with that charity for the tax payable under s. 188(1.1) by that charity for that taxation year for an amount not exceeding the total of all such appropriations to the extent that the fair market value of such property exceeds the consideration given by such person for such property.

► 188(2.1) ◄

(2.1) Non-application of revocation tax. Subsections (1) and (1.1) do not apply to a charity in respect of a notice of intention to revoke given under any of subsections 149.1(2) to (4.1) and 168(1) if the Minister abandons the intention and so notifies the charity or if

(a) within the one-year period that begins immediately after the taxation year of the charity otherwise deemed by subsection (1) to have ended, the Minister has registered the charity as a charitable organization, private foundation or public foundation; and

(b) the charity has, before the time that the Minister has so registered the charity,

(i) paid all amounts, each of which is an amount for which the charity is liable under this Act (other than subsection (1.1)) or the *Excise Tax Act* in respect of taxes, penalties and interest, and

(ii) filed all information returns required by or under this Act to be filed on or before that time.

► 188(3) ◄

(3) Transfer of property tax. Where, as a result of a transaction or series of transactions, property owned by a registered charity that is a charitable foundation and having a net value greater than 50% of the net asset amount of the charitable foundation immediately before the transaction or series of transactions, as the case may be, is transferred before the end of a taxation year, directly or indirectly, to one or more charitable organizations and it may reasonably be considered that the main purpose of the transfer is to effect a reduction in the disbursement quota of the foundation, the foundation shall pay a tax under this Part for the year equal to the amount by which 25% of the net value of that property determined as of the day of its transfer exceeds the total of all amounts each of which is its tax payable under this subsection for a preceding taxation year in respect of the transaction or series of transactions.

Editorial Note: Subsection 188(3) imposes a transfer of property tax. The amount of tax payable by the foundation is equal to 25% of the net value of such property transferred determined as of the date of its transfer less any tax payable under the subsection for a preceding taxation year in respect of the transaction or series of transactions surrounding the transfer. This special tax was introduced to penalize charities that engaged in circular donation programs in order to lessen and delay their disbursement requirements under s. 149.1.

Related Sections: S. 248(10) Series of transactions.

▶ 188(3.1) ◀

(3.1) Non-application of subsection (3). Subsection (3) does not apply to a transfer that is a gift to which subsection 188.1(11) or (12) applies.

Editorial Note: The tax under s. 188(3) does not apply to a transfer that is a gift to which the penalty taxes under either s. 188.1(11) or (12) apply. These provisions generally relate to transactions entered into by a registered charity for the purpose of unduly delaying the expenditure of amounts on charitable activities (see the commentary under s. 188.1(11) and (12)). Accordingly, s. 188(3.1) eliminates the possibility of a double penalty tax arising in circumstances where a penalty under either s. 188.1(11) or (12) has already been imposed.

History: S. 188(3.1) was replaced by S.C. 2010, c. 25, s. 50(1), applicable to taxation years that end on or after March 4, 2010. S. 188(3.1) formerly read:

(3.1) *Non-application of subsection (3).* Subsection (3) does not apply to a transfer that is a gift to which subsection 188.1(11) applies.

▶ 188(4) ◀

(4) Joint and several, or solidary, liability — tax transfer. If property has been transferred to a charitable organization in circumstances described in subsection (3) and it may reasonably be considered that the organization acted in concert with a charitable foundation for the purpose of reducing the disbursement quota of the foundation, the organization is jointly and severally, or solidarily, liable with the foundation for the tax imposed on the foundation by that subsection in an amount not exceeding the net value of the property.

Editorial Note: Where property has been transferred to a charitable organization in circumstances described in s. 188(3) and it may be reasonably considered that the organization acted in concert with a charitable foundation for the purpose of reducing the disbursement quota of the foundation, the organization is jointly and severally liable with the foundation for the tax imposed on the foundation by s. 188(3) in an amount not exceeding the net value of the property.

History: S. 188(4) was replaced by S.C. 2013, c. 34, s. 151, in force June 26, 2013, and formerly read:

(4) *Idem.* Where property has been transferred to a charitable organization in circumstances described in subsection (3) and it may reasonably be considered that the organization acted in concert with a charitable foundation for the purpose of reducing the disbursement quota of the foundation, the organization is jointly and severally liable with the foundation for the tax imposed on the foundation by that subsection in an amount not exceeding the net value of the property.

▶ 188(5) ◀

(5) Definitions. In this section,

"net asset amount" — "net asset amount" of a charitable foundation at any time means the amount determined by the formula

$$A - B$$

where

A is the fair market value at that time of all the property owned by the foundation at that time, and

B is the total of all amounts each of which is the amount of a debt owing by or any other obligation of the foundation at that time;

"net value" — "net value" of property owned by a charitable foundation, as of the day of its transfer, means the amount determined by the formula

$$A - B$$

where

A is the fair market value of the property on that day, and

B is the amount of any consideration given to the foundation for the transfer.

SECTION 188.1: [Penalties]

▶ 188.1(1) ◀

(1) Penalty — carrying on business. Subject to subsection (2), a person is liable to a penalty under this Part equal to 5% of its gross revenue for a taxation year from any business that it carries on in the taxation year, if

(*a*) the person is a registered charity that is a private foundation;

(*b*) the person is a registered charity that is not a private foundation and the business is not a related business in relation to the charity; or

(*c*) the person is a registered Canadian amateur athletic association and the business is not a related business in relation to the association.

Editorial Note: S. 188.1 is applicable to taxation years of registered charities that begin after March 22, 2004 and to taxation years of Canadian amateur athletic associations (RCAAAs) that begin after December 31, 2011. The provision was designed to avoid the perceived harshness of the former rule where the only remedy available to the Minister where a registered charity infringed any of the various operating requirements set out in s. 149.1 was to revoke the charity's registration. S. 188.1 now gives the Minister a number of remedies targeted at specific infractions. These provisions do not, however, eliminate the Minister's discretionary power to revoke the registration of a charity or RCAAA in an appropriate case (although one would anticipate that this would be an infrequent occurrence confined to extreme cases or serial offenders). S. 189(8) provides that these intermediate penalties are subject to the normal notice of objection procedure and provides for an appeal to the Tax Court of Canada where there is no satisfactory resolution of these penalties at the notice of objection level.

S. 149.1(2)(*a*) and (3)(*a*) provide for the revocation of the registration of a charitable organization or public foundation, respectively, that carry on "a business that is not a related business"; s. 149.1(4)(*a*) provides for the revocation of the registration of a private foundation that carries on "any business"; s. 149.1(4.2)(*b*) provides for the revocation of the registration of an RCAAA that carries on a business that is not a related business of the association. S. 188.1(1) provides an alternative sanction being 5% of the "gross revenue" of the offending charity/RCAAA from the business in question. The severity of the penalty will obviously depend on the profitability of the business.

S. 188.1(2) provides a more severe penalty where a registered charity or RCAAA has been penalized for carrying on an impermissible business activity in the past five years. The penalty in such a case amounts to all of the gross revenue in the year from the same or another impermissible business activity.

History: S. 188.1(1) was replaced by S.C. 2011, c. 24, s. 59(1), applicable to taxation years that begin on or after January 1, 2012. S. 188.1(1) formerly read:

(1) *Penalties for charities — carrying on business.* Subject to subsection (2), a registered charity is liable to a penalty under this Part equal to 5% of its gross revenue for a taxation year from any business that it carries on in the taxation year, if the registered charity

(*a*) is a private foundation; or

(*b*) is not a private foundation and the business is not a related business in relation to the charity.

Related Sections: S. 149.1(2) Revocation of registration of charitable organization; s. 149.1(3) Revocation of registration of public foundation; s. 149.1(4) Revocation of registration of private foundation; s. 149.1(4.1) Revocation of registration of registered charity; s. 149.1(4.2) Revocation of registration of registered Canadian amateur athletic association; s. 188.1(2) Increased penalty for subsequent assessment; s. 189(6.3) Reduction for liabilities for penalties.

Canadian Tax Foundation: Hayhoe and Owens, *The New Tax Sanctions for Canadian Charities: Learning from the US Experience*, 2006 Canadian Tax Journal 1:57–86.

▶ 188.1(2) ◀

(2) Increased penalty for subsequent assessment. A person that, less than five years before a particular time, was assessed a liability under subsection (1) or this subsection, for a taxation year, is liable to a penalty under this Part equal to its gross revenue for a subsequent taxation year from any business that, after that assessment and in the subsequent taxation year, it carries on at the particular time if

(*a*) the person is a registered charity that is a private foundation;

(*b*) the person is a registered charity that is not a private foundation and the business is not a related business in relation to the charity; or

(*c*) the person is a registered Canadian amateur athletic association and the business is not a related business in relation to the association.

Editorial Note: See notes to s. 188.1(1).

History: S. 188.1(2) was replaced by S.C. 2011, c. 24, s. 59(1), applicable to taxation years that begin on or after January 1, 2012. S. 188.1(2) formerly read:

(2) *Increased penalty for subsequent assessment.* A registered charity that, less than five years before a particular time, was assessed a liability under subsection (1) or this subsection, for a taxation year, is liable to a penalty under this Part equal to its gross revenue for a subsequent taxation year from any business that, after that assessment and in the subsequent taxation year, it carries on at the particular time if the registered charity

(*a*) is a private foundation; or

(*b*) is not a private foundation and the business is not a related business in relation to the charity.

Related Sections: See related sections under s. 188.1(1), s. 149.1(2)(*a*), s. 149.1(3)(*a*), s. 149.1(4)(*a*)), s. 149.1(4.1) and s. 149.1(4.2)(*b*).

► 188.1(3) ◄

(3) Control of corporation by a charitable foundation. If at a particular time a charitable foundation has acquired control (within the meaning of subsection 149.1(12)) of a particular corporation, the foundation is liable to a penalty under this Part for a taxation year equal to

(*a*) 5% of the total of all amounts, each of which is a dividend received by the foundation from the particular corporation in the taxation year and at a time when the foundation so controlled the particular corporation, except if the foundation is liable under paragraph (*b*) for a penalty in respect of the dividend; or

(*b*) if the Minister has, less than five years before the particular time, assessed a liability under paragraph (*a*) or this paragraph for a preceding taxation year of the foundation in respect of a dividend received from any corporation, the total of all amounts, each of which is a dividend received, after the particular time, by the foundation, from the particular corporation, in the taxation year and at a time when the foundation so controlled the particular corporation.

Editorial Note: Paragraph 149.1(3)(*c*) provides for the revocation of the registration of a public foundation that has acquired control of a corporation since June 1, 1950. Control is defined for these purposes by s. 149.1(12)(*a*) and excludes control acquired in situations where the charity has not purchased or otherwise acquired for valuable consideration more than 5% of the issued shares of any class of the capital stock of that corporation. The initial penalty is set at 5% of dividends received in the taxation year at a time when the charity controlled the payer corporation, but, in the case of a second penalty within a five year period, the penalty is increased to 100% of dividends received in the taxation year at a time when the charity controlled the payer corporation.

Related Sections: See related sections under s. 188.1(1) and s. 149.1(3)(*c*) and s. 149.1(4)(*c*) and s. 149.1(12)(*a*).

► 188.1(3.1) ◄

(3.1) Penalty for excess corporate holdings. A private foundation is liable to a penalty under this Part for a taxation year, in respect of a class of shares of the capital stock of a corporation, equal to

(*a*) 5% of the amount, if any, determined by multiplying the divestment obligation percentage of the private foundation for the taxation year in respect of the class by the total fair market value of all of the issued and outstanding shares of the class, except if the private foundation is liable for the taxation year under paragraph (*b*) for a penalty in respect of the class; or

(*b*) 10% of the amount, if any, determined by multiplying the divestment obligation percentage of the private foundation for the taxation year in respect of the class by the total fair market value of all of the issued and outstanding shares of the class, if

(i) the private foundation has failed to disclose, in its return required under subsection 149.1(14) for the taxation year,

(A) a material transaction, in the taxation year, of the private foundation in respect of the class,

(B) a material interest held at the end of the taxation year by a relevant person in respect of the private foundation, or

(C) the total corporate holdings percentage of the private foundation in respect of the class at the end of the taxation year, unless at no time in the taxation year the private foundation held greater than an insignificant interest in respect of the class, or

(ii) the Minister has, less than five years before the end of the taxation year, assessed a liability under paragraph (*a*) or this paragraph for a preceding taxation year of the private foundation in respect of any divestment obligation percentage.

Editorial Note: Where a private foundation has a "divestment obligation percentage" at the end of the taxation year (defined in s. 149.1(1) that is greater than 0%, the foundation is subject to penalties under s. 188.1(3.1). As any divestment obligation percentage of a foundation at the end of the taxation year is added to the divestment obligation percentage of the next taxation year, it may be subject to penalty again in the next year unless the divestment obligation percentage has been reduced to zero in that year. Increased penalties apply where the foundation has failed to comply with certain reporting requirements or in the case of a second penalty within a five year period

Related Sections: S. 149.1(1), "divestment obligation percentage"; s. 149.1(4) Revocation of registration of private foundation; s. 149.2 Material and insignificant interests; 188.1(3.3) Where subsection (3.5) applies; 188.1(3.4) Rules applicable; 188.1(3.5) Avoidance of divestiture.

► 188.1(3.2) ◄

(3.2) Avoidance of divestiture. If, at the end of a taxation year, a private foundation would — but for a transaction or series of transactions entered into by the private foundation or a relevant person in respect of the private foundation (in this subsection referred to as the "holder") a result of which is that the holder holds, directly or indirectly, an interest (or for civil law, a right), in a corporation other than shares — have a divestment obligation percentage for that taxation year in respect of the private foundation's holdings of a class of shares of the capital stock of the corporation, and it can reasonably be considered that a purpose of the transaction or series is to avoid that divestment obligation percentage by substituting shares of the class for that interest or right, for the purposes of applying this section, subsection 149.1(1) and section 149.2,

(*a*) each of those interests or rights is deemed to have been converted, immediately after the time it was first held, directly or indirectly by the holder, into that number of shares of that class that would, if those shares were shares of the class that were issued by the corporation, have a fair market value equal to the fair market value of the interest or right at that time;

(*b*) each such share is deemed to be a share that is issued by the corporation and outstanding and to continue to be held by the holder until such time as the holder no longer holds the interest or right; and

(*c*) each of those shares is deemed to have a fair market value, at the particular time, equal to the fair market value, at the particular time, of a share of the class issued by the corporation, determined without reference to this subsection.

Editorial Note: Subsection 188.1(3.2) is intended to discourage a private foundation from converting shares into other interests in a corporation to avoid the penalties under s. 188.1(3.1).

History: S. 188.1(3.2)(*c*) was replaced by S.C. 2009, c. 2, s. 62(1), applicable to taxation years, of private foundations, that begin on or after February 26, 2008. S. 188.1(3.2)(*c*) formerly read:

(c) each such share is deemed to have a fair market value, at any particular time, equal to the fair market value, at the particular time, of a share of the class issued by the corporation.

▶ 188.1(3.3) ◀

(3.3) Where subsection (3.5) applies. Subsection (3.5) applies to a private foundation at a particular time in a taxation year if

(*a*) at the particular time, a person (in this subsection and subsection (3.5) referred to as an "insider" of the private foundation) that is the private foundation, or is a relevant person in respect of the private foundation, is a beneficiary under a trust;

(*b*) at or before the particular time

(i) the insider acquired an interest in or under the trust, or

(ii) the trust acquired a property;

(*c*) it may reasonably be considered that a purpose of the acquisition described in paragraph (*b*) was to hold, directly or indirectly, shares of a class of the capital stock of a corporation (referred to in subsection (3.5) as the "subject corporation");

(*d*) the shares described in paragraph (*c*) would, if they were held by the insider, cause the private foundation to have a divestment obligation percentage for the taxation year; and

(*e*) at the particular time, the insider holds the interest described in subparagraph (*b*)(i), or the trust holds the property described in subparagraph (*b*)(ii), as the case may be.

History: S. 188.1(3.3) was added by S.C. 2009, c. 2, s. 62(2), applicable to taxation years, of private foundations, that begin on or after February 26, 2008.

▶ 188.1(3.4) ◀

(3.4) Rules applicable. For the purpose of subsections (3.3) and (3.5),

(*a*) interests (or, for civil law, rights), other than shares, of a trust in a corporation that entitle the trust to a right described in paragraph 251(5)(*b*) in respect of a class of the capital stock of the corporation, are deemed to be converted into shares of that class in the manner described by paragraph (3.2)(*a*); and

(*b*) if the amount of income or capital of the trust that a person may receive as a beneficiary under the trust depends on the exercise by any person of, or the failure by any person to exercise, a discretionary power, that person is deemed to have fully exercised, or to have failed to exercise, the power, as the case may be.

History: S. 188.1(3.4) was added by S.C. 2009, c. 2, s. 62(2), applicable to taxation years, of private foundations, that begin on or after February 26, 2008.

▶ 188.1(3.5) ◀

(3.5) Avoidance of divestiture. If this subsection applies to a private foundation at a particular time in respect of an interest of an insider of the private foundation in a trust, for the purposes of applying this section, subsection 149.1(1) and section 149.2,

(*a*) the insider is deemed to hold at the particular time, in addition to any shares of the capital stock of the subject corporation that it holds otherwise than because of this subsection, the number of shares, of the class of shares referred to in paragraph (3.3)(*c*), determined by the formula

$$A \times B/C$$

where

A is the number of shares of that class that are held, directly or indirectly, by the trust at the particular time,

B is the total fair market value of all interests held by the insider in the trust at the particular time, and

C is the total fair market value of all property held by the trust at the particular time;

(*b*) each of those shares is deemed to be a share that is issued by the subject corporation and outstanding and to continue to be held by the holder until such time as the holder no longer holds the interest or right; and

(*c*) each of those shares is deemed to have a fair market value, at the particular time, equal to the fair market value, at the particular time, of a share of the class issued by the subject corporation, determined without reference to this subsection.

History: S. 188.1(3.5) was added by S.C. 2009, c. 2, s. 62(2), applicable to taxation years, of private foundations, that begin on or after February 26, 2008.

Related Sections: S. 149.1(1), "divestment obligation percentage", "relevant person"; s. 149.1(4) Revocation of registration of private foundation; s. 149.2(1) Material and insignificant interests; s. 188.1(3.1) Penalty for excess corporate holdings.

▶ 188.1(4) ◀

(4) Undue benefits. A registered charity or registered Canadian amateur athletic association that, at a particular time in a taxation year, confers on a person an undue benefit is liable to a penalty under this Part for the taxation year equal to (*a*) 105% of the amount of the benefit, except if the charity or association is liable under paragraph (*b*) for a penalty in respect of the benefit; or

(*b*) if the Minister has, less than five years before the particular time, assessed a liability under paragraph (*a*) or this paragraph for a preceding taxation year of the charity or association and the undue benefit was conferred after that assessment, 110% of the amount of the benefit.

Editorial Note: The concept of "undue benefit" found in s. 188.1(4) and 188.1(5) is generally derived from the prohibitions contained in the definitions of "charitable foundation" and "charitable organization" in s. 149.1(1), which provide that "no part of the income of which [charity] is payable to, or is otherwise available for, the personal benefit of any proprietor, member, shareholder, trustee or settler thereof, [and that is not a charitable organization]". The last parenthetical expression is only found in the definition of "charitable foundation". The original penalty is 105% of the benefit in question, increasing to 110% in the case of a second penalty within a five year period.

An "undue benefit" is defined in s. 188.1(5) and, in general terms, includes any income, rights, property or resources of a charity or registered Canadian amateur athletic association (RCAAA) that is paid, payable, assigned or otherwise made available for the personal benefit ("Benefits") of any proprietor, member, shareholder, trustee or settlor of the charity/RCAAA who has contributed or otherwise paid into the charity/RCAAA more than 50% of its capital. It also includes Benefits to a person who does not deal at arm's length with such a donor. It also includes Benefits to a person who does not deal at arm's length with the charity/RCAAA itself. It also includes any Benefits conferred upon a beneficiary by another person, at the direction or with the consent of the charity/RCAAA, that would otherwise be an amount to which the charity/RCAAA would have a right. Excluded from the concept of "undue benefit" are reasonable payments for property or services, gifts made by a charity/RCAAA in the ordinary course of its charitable/athletic promotion activities (except where the eligibility for the gift relates solely to the relationship of the beneficiary to the charity/RCAAA) and gifts to qualified donees.

History: S. 188.1(4) was replaced by S.C. 2011, c. 24, s. 59(2), applicable to taxation years that begin on or after January 1, 2012. S. 188.1(4) formerly read:

(4) *Undue benefits.* A registered charity that, at a particular time in a taxation year, confers on a person an undue benefit is liable to a penalty under this Part for the taxation year equal to

(*a*) 105% of the amount of the benefit, except if the charity is liable under paragraph (*b*) for a penalty in respect of the benefit; or

(*b*) if the Minister has, less than five years before the particular time, assessed a liability under paragraph (*a*) or this paragraph for a preceding taxation year of the charity and the undue benefit was conferred after that assessment, 110% of the amount of the benefit.

Related Sections: S. 189(6.3) Reduction for liabilities for penalties.

► 188.1(5) ◄

(5) Meaning of undue benefits. For the purposes of this Part, an undue benefit conferred on a person (referred to in this Part as the "beneficiary") by a registered charity or registered Canadian amateur athletic association includes a disbursement by way of a gift or the amount of any part of the income, rights, property or resources of the charity or association that is paid, payable, assigned or otherwise made available for the personal benefit of any person who is a proprietor, member, shareholder, trustee or settlor of the charity or association, who has contributed or otherwise paid into the charity or association more than 50% of the capital of the charity or association, or who deals not at arm's length with such a person or with the charity or association, as well as any benefit conferred on a beneficiary by another person, at the direction or with the consent of the charity or association, that would, if it were not conferred on the beneficiary, be an amount in respect of which the charity or association would have a right, but does not include a disbursement or benefit to the extent that it is

(*a*) an amount that is reasonable consideration or remuneration for property acquired by or services rendered to the charity or association;

(*b*) a gift made, or a benefit conferred,

(i) in the case of a registered charity, in the course of a charitable act in the ordinary course of the charitable activities carried on by the charity, unless it can reasonably be considered that the eligibility of the beneficiary for the benefit relates solely to the relationship of the beneficiary to the charity, and

(ii) in the case of a registered Canadian amateur athletic association, in the ordinary course of promoting amateur athletics in Canada on a nationwide basis; or

(*c*) a gift to a qualified donee.

Editorial Note: See editorial note for s. 188.1(4).

History: S. 188.1(5) was replaced by S.C. 2011, c. 24, s. 59(2), applicable to taxation years that begin on or after January 1, 2012. S. 188.1(5) formerly read:

(5) *Meaning of undue benefits.* For the purposes of this Part, an undue benefit conferred on a person (referred to in this Part as the "beneficiary") by a registered charity includes a disbursement by way of a gift or the amount of any part of the income, rights, property or resources of the charity that is paid, payable, assigned or otherwise made available for the personal benefit of any person who is a proprietor, member, shareholder, trustee or settlor of the charity, who has contributed or otherwise paid into the charity more than 50% of the capital of the charity, or who deals not at arm's length with such a person or with the charity, as well as any benefit conferred on a beneficiary by another person, at the direction or with the consent of the charity, that would, if it were not conferred on the beneficiary, be an amount in respect of which the charity would have a right, but does not include a disbursement or benefit to the extent that it is

(*a*) an amount that is reasonable consideration or remuneration for property acquired by or services rendered to the charity;

(*b*) a gift made, or a benefit conferred, in the course of a charitable act in the ordinary course of the charitable activities carried on by the charity, unless it can reasonably be considered that the eligibility of the beneficiary for the benefit relates solely to the relationship of the beneficiary to the charity; or

(*c*) a gift to a qualified donee.

Related Sections: S. 188.1(4) Undue benefits.

► 188.1(6) ◄

(6) Failure to file information returns. Every registered charity and registered Canadian amateur athletic association that fails to file a return for a taxation year as and when required by subsection 149.1(14) is liable to a penalty equal to $500.

Amendment not yet in force

Budget Implementation Act, 2019, No. 1 [S.C. 2019, c. 29]

S. 188.1(6) was replaced by S.C. 2019, c. 29, s. 39(1), and will read as follows:

(6) Failure to file information returns. Every registered charity, registered Canadian amateur athletic association and registered journalism organization that fails to file a return for a taxation year as and when required by subsection 149.1(14) or (14.1) is liable to a penalty equal to $500.

Applicable: In force January 1, 2020.

Editorial Note: Subsection 188.1(6) provides a flat penalty of $500 for every registered charity, registered Canadian amateur athletic association, or, effective January 1, 2020, registered journalism organization that fails to file a return for a taxation year as and when required by s. 149.1(14) or s. 149.1(14.1).

History: S. 188.1(6) was replaced by S.C. 2011, c. 24, s. 59(2), applicable to taxation years that begin on or after January 1, 2012. S. 188.1(6) formerly read:

(6) *Failure to file information returns.* Every registered charity that fails to file a return for a taxation year as and when required by subsection 149.1(14) is liable to a penalty equal to $500.

Related Sections: S. 149.1(14) Information returns; s. 189(6.3) Reduction for liabilities for penalties.

▶ 188.1(7) ◀

(7) Incorrect information. Except where subsection (8) or (9) applies, every registered charity and registered Canadian amateur athletic association that issues, in a taxation year, a receipt for a gift otherwise than in accordance with this Act and the regulations is liable for the taxation year to a penalty equal to 5% of the amount reported on the receipt as representing the amount in respect of which a taxpayer may claim a deduction under subsection 110.1(1) or a credit under subsection 118.1(3).

> **Amendment not yet in force**
>
> **Budget Implementation Act, 2019, No. 1 [S.C. 2019, c. 29]**
>
> **S. 188.1(7) was replaced by S.C. 2019, c. 29, s. 39(1), and will read as follows:**
>
> **(7) Incorrect information.** Except where subsection (8) or (9) applies, every registered charity, registered Canadian amateur athletic association and registered journalism organization that issues, in a taxation year, a receipt for a gift otherwise than in accordance with this Act and the regulations is liable for the taxation year to a penalty equal to 5% of the amount reported on the receipt as representing the amount in respect of which a taxpayer may claim a deduction under subsection 110.1(1) or a credit under subsection 118.1(3).
>
> **Applicable:** In force January 1, 2020.

Editorial Note: Subsections 188.1(7) through (10) deal with penalties for the issuance of receipts by a registered charity, registered Canadian amateur athletic association (RCAAA), or, effective January 1, 2020, registered journalism organization "otherwise than in accordance with [the] Act and the regulations". The penalty imposed under s. 188.1(7) is 5% of "the amount reported on a receipt as representing the amount in respect of which a taxpayer may claim a deduction under subsection 110.1(1) or a credit under subsection 118.1(3)", increasing under s. 188.1(8) to 10% of such amount reported on a receipt in a subsequent taxation year where the registered charity, RCAAA, or registered journalism organization has been assessed a penalty under s. 188.1(7) or (8) within the previous five years.

Subsection 188.1(9) provides for a third variety of "receipt" penalty of 125% of the amount in respect of which a taxpayer may claim a deduction under s. 110.1(1) or a credit under s. 118.1(3). This penalty is in lieu of the penalties under s. 188.1(7) and (8) and applies to any person (i.e., the penalty is not confined to registered charities, RCAAAs, or registered journalism organizations) who makes or furnishes, participates in the making of or causes another person to make or furnish a statement that the person knows, or would reasonably be expected to know but for circumstances amounting to culpable conduct (within the meaning assigned by s. 163.2(1)) is a false statement (within the meaning assigned by s. 163.2(1)). The penalty under s. 188.1(9) is a form of specific extension of the advisor penalties under s. 163.2 to the charitable sector. It is designed to impose a severe penalty (i.e., 125% of the amount of the receipt) where a person makes a false statement (or furnishes, participates in the making of or causes another person to make or furnish a false statement) on a charitable receipt. Such a false statement would normally be related to the amount of the gift or, in the case of a gift in kind, the value of the donated property. A person may be liable for a penalty under both s. 163.2 and s. 188.1(9) in which case s. 188.1(10) provides that the person shall only pay the greater of the two penalties.

History: S. 188.1(7) was replaced by S.C. 2011, c. 24, s. 59(2), applicable to taxation years that begin on or after January 1, 2012. S. 188.1(7) formerly read:

(7) *Incorrect information.* Except where subsection (8) or (9) applies, every registered charity that issues, in a taxation year, a receipt for a gift otherwise than in accordance with this Act and the regulations is liable for the taxation year to a penalty equal to 5% of the amount reported on the receipt as representing the amount in respect of which a taxpayer may claim a deduction under subsection 110.1(1) or a credit under subsection 118.1(3).

Related Sections: S. 188.1(8) Increased penalty for subsequent assessment; s. 188.1(9) False information; s. 188.1(10) Maximum amount; s. 189(6.3) Reduction for liabilities for penalties.

▶ 188.1(8) ◀

(8) Increased penalty for subsequent assessment. Except where subsection (9) applies, if the Minister has, less than five years before a particular time, assessed a penalty under subsection (7) or this subsection for a taxation year of a registered charity or registered Canadian amateur athletic association and, after that assessment and in a subsequent taxation year, the charity or association issues, at the particular time, a receipt for a gift otherwise than in accordance with this Act and the regulations, the charity or association is liable for the subsequent taxation year to a penalty equal to 10% of the amount reported on the receipt as representing the amount in respect of which a taxpayer may claim a deduction under subsection 110.1(1) or a credit under subsection 118.1(3).

> **Amendment not yet in force**
>
> **Budget Implementation Act, 2019, No. 1 [S.C. 2019, c. 29]**
>
> **S. 188.1(8) was replaced by S.C. 2019, c. 29, s. 39(1), and will read as follows:**
>
> **(8) Increased penalty for subsequent assessment.** Except where subsection (9) applies, if the Minister has, less than five years before a particular time, assessed a penalty under subsection (7) or this subsection for a taxation year of a registered charity, registered Canadian amateur athletic association or registered journalism organization and, after that assessment and in a subsequent taxation year, it issues, at the particular time, a receipt for a gift otherwise than in accordance with this Act and the regulations, it is liable for the subsequent taxation year to a penalty equal to 10% of the amount reported on the receipt as representing the amount in respect of which a taxpayer may claim a deduction under subsection 110.1(1) or a credit under subsection 118.1(3).
>
> **Applicable:** In force January 1, 2020.

Editorial Note: See the editorial note for s. 188.1(7).

History: S. 188.1(8) was replaced by S.C. 2011, c. 24, s. 59(2), applicable to taxation years that begin on or after January 1, 2012. S. 188.1(8) formerly read:

(8) *Increased penalty for subsequent assessment.* Except where subsection (9) applies, if the Minister has, less than five years before a particular time, assessed a penalty under subsection (7) or this subsection for a taxation year of a registered charity and, after that assessment and in a subsequent taxation year, the charity issues, at the particular time, a receipt for a gift otherwise than in accordance with this Act and the regulations, the charity is liable for the subsequent taxation year to a penalty equal to 10% of the amount reported on the receipt as representing the amount in respect of which a taxpayer may claim a deduction under subsection 110.1(1) or a credit under subsection 118.1(3).

▶ 188.1(9) ◀

(9) False information. If at any time a person makes or furnishes, participates in the making of or causes another person to make or furnish a statement that the person knows, or would reasonably be expected to know but for circumstances amounting to culpable conduct (within the meaning assigned by subsection 163.2(1)), is a false statement (within the meaning assigned by subsection 163.2(1)) on a receipt issued by, on behalf of or in the name of another person for the purposes of subsection 110.1(2) or 118.1(2), the person (or, where the person is an officer, employee, official or agent of a registered charity or registered Canadian amateur athletic association, the charity or association) is liable for their taxation year that includes that time to a penalty equal to 125% of the amount reported on the receipt as representing the amount in respect of which a taxpayer may claim a deduction under subsection 110.1(1) or a credit under subsection 118.1(3).

Amendment not yet in force

Budget Implementation Act, 2019, No. 1 [S.C. 2019, c. 29]

S. 188.1(9) was replaced by S.C. 2019, c. 29, s. 39(1), and will read as follows:

(9) False information. If at any time a person makes or furnishes, participates in the making of or causes another person to make or furnish a statement that the person knows, or would reasonably be expected to know but for circumstances amounting to "culpable conduct" (as defined in subsection 163.2(1)), is a "false statement" (as defined in subsection 163.2(1)) on a receipt issued by, on behalf of or in the name of another person for the purposes of subsection 110.1(2) or 118.1(2), the person (or, where the person is an officer, employee, official or agent of a registered charity, registered Canadian amateur athletic association or registered journalism organization, the charity, association or organization) is liable for their taxation year that includes that time to a penalty equal to 125% of the amount reported on the receipt as representing the amount in respect of which a taxpayer may claim a deduction under subsection 110.1(1) or a credit under subsection 118.1(3).

Applicable: In force January 1, 2020.

Editorial Note: See the editorial note for s. 188.1(7).

History: S. 188.1(9) was replaced by S.C. 2011, c. 24, s. 59(2), applicable to taxation years that begin on or after January 1, 2012. S. 188.1(9) formerly read:

(9) *False information.* If at any time a person makes or furnishes, participates in the making of or causes another person to make or furnish a statement that the person knows, or would reasonably be expected to know but for circumstances amounting to culpable conduct (within the meaning assigned by subsection 163.2(1)), is a false statement (within the meaning assigned by subsection 163.2(1)) on a receipt issued by, on behalf of or in the name of another person for the purposes of subsection 110.1(2) or 118.1(2), the person (or, where the person is an officer, employee, official or agent of a registered charity, the registered charity) is liable for their taxation year that includes that time to a penalty equal to 125% of the amount reported on the receipt as representing the amount in respect of which a taxpayer may claim a deduction under subsection 110.1(1) or a credit under subsection 118.1(3).

Related Sections: S. 163.2(1), "culpable conduct", "false statement".

► 188.1(10) ◄

(10) Maximum amount. A person who is liable at any time to penalties under both section 163.2 and subsection (9) in respect of the same false statement is liable to pay only the greater of those penalties.

Editorial Note: See the editorial note for s. 188.1(7).

► 188.1(11) ◄

(11) Delay of expenditure. If, in a taxation year, a registered charity has entered into a transaction (including a gift to another registered charity) and it may reasonably be considered that a purpose of the transaction was to avoid or unduly delay the expenditure of amounts on charitable activities, the registered charity is liable to a penalty under this Act for its taxation year equal to 110% of the amount of expenditure avoided or delayed, and in the case of a gift to another registered charity, both charities are jointly and severally, or solidarily, liable to the penalty.

Editorial Note: S. 149.1(2)(*b*), 149.1(3)(*b*) and 149.1(4)(*b*) require that charitable organizations, public foundations and private foundations, respectively, expend amounts at least equal to their disbursement quotas (defined in s. 149.1(1)) in each year on charitable activities and gifts to "qualified donees". S. 188.1(11) provides that where property is transferred by one registered charity to another under circumstances where it may reasonably be considered that one of the main purposes for the making of the gift was to unduly delay such expenditure each of the charities is jointly and severally, or solidarily, liable for a penalty for that taxation year equal to 110% of the fair market value of the property.

History: S. 188.1(11) was replaced by S.C. 2010, c. 25, s. 51(1), applicable to taxation years that end on or after March 4, 2010. S. 188.1(11) formerly read:

(11) *Delay of expenditure.* If, in a taxation year, a registered charity has made a gift of property to another registered charity and it may reasonably be considered that one of the main purposes for the making of the gift was to unduly delay the expenditure of amounts on charitable activities, each of those charities is jointly and severally, or solidarily, liable to a penalty under this Act for its respective taxation year equal to 110% of the fair market value of the property.

Related Sections: S. 149.1(1), "disbursement quota"; s. 149.1(2)(*b*) Revocation of registration of charitable organization; s. 149.1(3)(*b*) Revocation of registration of public foundation s. 149.1(4)(*b*) Revocation of registration of private foundation.

► 188.1(12) ◄

(12) Gifts not at arm's length. If a registered charity has in a taxation year received a gift of property (other than a designated gift) from another registered charity with which it does not deal at arm's length and it has expended, before the end of the next taxation year, in addition to its disbursement quota for each of those taxation years, an amount that is less than the fair market value of the property, on charitable activities carried on by it or by way of gifts made to qualified donees with which it deals at arm's length, the registered charity is liable to a penalty under this Act for that subsequent taxation year equal to 110% of the difference between the fair market value of the property and the additional amount expended.

Editorial Note: Subsection 188.1(12) provides a penalty where a registered charity (i) has in a taxation year received a gift of property (other than a "designated gift", as defined in s. 149.1(1)) from another registered charity with which it does not deal at arm's length; and (ii) has expended before the end of the next taxation year, in addition to its disbursement quota for each of those taxation years, an amount that is less than the fair market value of such property on charitable activities carried on by it or by way of gifts made to qualified donees with which it deals at arm's length. This rule essentially provides that when a registered charity receives a gift of property from a non-arm's length charity, it will need to spend an amount equal to the fair market value of the property on its own charitable activities or transfer the amount by way of gift to arm's length qualified donees within the current or subsequent taxation year. If the donor charity designates all or a portion of the gift of property as a "designated gift" (in the manner prescribed in the definition of that term in s. 149.1(1)), the designated portion will not be subject to the immediate disbursement requirement in the hands of the recipient charity. However, pursuant to s. 149.1(1.1), the donor charity will be prohibited from using the designated gift for purposes of satisfying its own disbursement quota for the year. Accordingly, s. 188.1(12) ensures that amounts transferred between non-arm's length charities can only be used to satisfy the disbursement quota requirements of one charity.

History: S. 188.1(12) was added by S.C. 2010, c. 25, s. 51(1), applicable to taxation years that end on or after March 4, 2010.

SECTION 188.2: [Notice of suspension]

► 188.2(1) ◄

(1) Notice of suspension with assessment. The Minister shall, with an assessment referred to in this subsection, give notice by registered mail to a registered charity or registered Canadian amateur athletic association that the authority of the charity or association to issue an official receipt referred to in Part XXXV of the *Income Tax Regulations* is suspended for one year from the day that is seven days after the day on which the notice is mailed, if the Minister has assessed the charity or association for a taxation year for

> **Amendment not yet in force**
> **Budget Implementation Act, 2019, No. 1 [S.C. 2019, c. 29]**
>
> **S. 188.2(1), the portion before paragraph (a) was replaced by S.C. 2019, c. 29, s. 40(1), and will read as follows:**
>
> **SECTION 188.2 Notice of suspension with assessment.**
>
> **(1)** The Minister shall, with an assessment referred to in this subsection, give notice by registered mail to a registered charity, registered Canadian amateur athletic association or registered journalism organization that its authority to issue an official receipt referred to in Part XXXV of the *Income Tax Regulations* is suspended for one year from the day that is seven days after the day on which the notice is mailed, if the Minister has assessed the charity, association or organization for a taxation year for
>
> **Applicable:** In force January 1, 2020.

(*a*) a penalty under subsection 188.1(2);

(*b*) a penalty under paragraph 188.1(4)(*b*) in respect of an undue benefit, other than an undue benefit conferred by the charity or association by way of a gift; or

(*c*) a penalty under subsection 188.1(9) if the total of all such penalties for the taxation year exceeds $25,000.

History: S. 188.2(1) was replaced by S.C. 2011, c. 24, s. 60(1), applicable to taxation years that begin on or after January 1, 2012. S. 188.2(1) formerly read:

(1) *Notice of suspension with assessment.* The Minister shall, with an assessment referred to in this subsection, give notice by registered mail to a registered charity that the authority of the charity to issue an official receipt referred to in Part XXXV of the *Income Tax Regulations* is suspended for one year from the day that is seven days after the notice is mailed, if the Minister has assessed the charity for a taxation year for

(*a*) a penalty under subsection 188.1(2);

(*b*) a penalty under paragraph 188.1(4)(*b*) in respect of an undue benefit, other than an undue benefit conferred by the charity by way of a gift; or

(*c*) a penalty under subsection 188.1(9) if the total of all such penalties for the taxation year exceeds $25,000.

► 188.2(2) ◄

(2) Notice of suspension — general. The Minister may give notice by registered mail to a person referred to in any of paragraphs (*a*) to (*c*) of the definition "qualified donee" in subsection 149.1(1) that the authority of the person to issue an official receipt referred to in Part XXXV of the *Income Tax Regulations* is suspended for one year from the day that is seven days after the day on which the notice is mailed

(*a*) if the person contravenes any of sections 230 to 231.5;

(*b*) if it may reasonably be considered that the person has acted, in concert with another person that is the subject of a suspension under this section, to accept a gift or transfer of property on behalf of that other person;

(*c*) in the case of a person referred to in paragraph (*a*) of the definition "qualified donee" in subsection 149.1(1), if the person has issued a receipt for a gift otherwise than in accordance with this Act and the regulations;

(*d*) in the case of a person that is a registered charity or registered Canadian amateur athletic association, if an ineligible individual is a director, trustee, officer or like official of the person, or controls or manages the person, directly or indirectly, in any manner whatever; or

(*e*) in the case of a person that is a registered charity or registered Canadian amateur athletic association, if the person devotes any part of its resources to the direct or indirect support of, or opposition to, any political party or candidate for public office.

(*f*) (Repealed by S.C. 2018, c. 27, s. 20(1).)

(*g*) (Repealed by S.C. 2018, c. 27, s. 20(1).)

History: S. 188.2(2)(*e*) was replaced by S.C. 2018, c. 27, s. 20(1), deemed to have come into force

(a) on June 29, 2012 in respect of organizations, corporations and trusts that are registered charities on September 14, 2018 and in respect of associations that are registered Canadian amateur athletic associations on that date; and

(b) on September 14, 2018 in any other case.

S. 188.2(2)(*e*) formerly read:

(*e*) in the case of a registered charity that is a charitable foundation, if the foundation devotes resources to political activities that are not considered under subsection 149.1(6.1) to be devoted to charitable purposes;

S. 188.2(2)(*f*) and (*g*) were repealed by S.C. 2018, c. 27, s. 20(1), deemed to have come into force

(a) on June 29, 2012 in respect of organizations, corporations and trusts that are registered charities on September 14, 2018 and in respect of associations that are registered Canadian amateur athletic associations on that date; and

(b) on September 14, 2018 in any other case.

S. 188.2(2)(*f*) and (*g*) formerly read:

(*f*) in the case of a registered charity that is a charitable organization, if the organization devotes resources to political activities that are not considered under subsection 149.1(6.2) to be devoted to charitable activities; or

(*g*) in the case of a registered Canadian amateur athletic association, if the association devotes resources to political activities that are not considered under subsection 149.1(6.201) to be devoted to its exclusive purpose and exclusive function.

S. 188.2(2)(*e*), (*f*) and (*g*) were added by S.C. 2012, c. 19, s. 13(1), in force on Royal Assent, June 29, 2012.

S. 188.2(2) was replaced by S.C. 2011, c. 24, s. 60(1), applicable to taxation years that begin on or after January 1, 2012. S. 188.2(2) formerly read:

(2) *Notice of suspension — general.* The Minister may give notice by registered mail to a registered charity that the authority of the charity to issue an official receipt referred to in Part XXXV of the *Income Tax Regulations* is suspended for one year from the day that is seven days after the notice is mailed

(*a*) if the charity contravenes any of sections 230 to 231.5; or

(*b*) if it may reasonably be considered that the charity has acted, in concert with another charity that is the subject of a suspension under this section, to accept a gift or transfer of property on behalf of that other charity.

► 188.2(2.1) ◄

(2.1) Suspension — failure to report. If a registered charity or a registered Canadian amateur athletic association fails to report information that is required to be included in a return filed under subsection 149.1(14), the Minister may give notice by registered mail to the charity or association that its authority to issue an official receipt referred to in Part XXXV of the *Income Tax Regulations* is suspended from the day that is seven days after the day on which the notice is mailed until such time as the Minister notifies the charity or association that the Minister has received the required information in prescribed form.

> **Amendment not yet in force**
> **Budget Implementation Act, 2019, No. 1 [S.C. 2019, c. 29]**
>
> **S. 188.2(2.1) was replaced by S.C. 2019, c. 29, s. 40(2), and will read as follows:**

(2.1) Suspension - failure to report. If a registered charity, a registered Canadian amateur athletic association or a registered journalism organization fails to report information that is required to be included in a return filed under subsection 149.1(14) or (14.1), the Minister may give notice by registered mail to the charity, association or organization that its authority to issue an official receipt referred to in Part XXXV of the *Income Tax Regulations* is suspended from the day that is seven days after the day on which the notice is mailed until such time as the Minister notifies the charity, association or organization that the Minister has received the required information in prescribed form.

Applicable: In force January 1, 2020.

History: S. 188.2(2.1) was added by S.C. 2012, c. 19, s. 13(2), in force on Royal Assent, June 29, 2012.

▶ 188.2(3) ◀

(3) Effect of suspension. If the Minister has issued a notice to a qualified donee under any of subsections (1) to (2.1), subject to subsection (4),

(*a*) the qualified donee is deemed, in respect of gifts made and property transferred to the qualified donee within the one-year period that begins on the day that is seven days after the day on which the notice is mailed, not to be a qualified donee for the purposes of subsections 110.1(1) and 118.1(1) and Part XXXV of the *Income Tax Regulations*; and

(*b*) if the qualified donee is, during that period, offered a gift from any person, the qualified donee shall, before accepting the gift, inform that person that

(i) it has received the notice,

(ii) no deduction under subsection 110.1(1) or credit under subsection 118.1(3) may be claimed in respect of a gift made to it in the period, and

(iii) a gift made to it in the period is not a gift to a qualified donee.

History: S. 188.2(3), the portion before paragraph (*a*) was replaced by S.C. 2012, c. 19, s. 13(3), in force on Royal Assent, June 29, 2012. S. 188.2(3), the portion before paragraph (*a*) formerly read:

(3) *Effect of suspension.* If the Minister has issued a notice to a qualified donee under subsection (1) or (2), subject to subsection (4),

S. 188.2(3) was replaced by S.C. 2011, c. 24, s. 60(1), applicable to taxation years that begin on or after January 1, 2012. S. 188.2(3) formerly read:

(3) *Effect of suspension.* If the Minister has issued a notice to a registered charity under subsection (1) or (2), subject to subsection (4),

(*a*) the charity is deemed, in respect of gifts made and property transferred to the charity within the one-year period that begins on the day that is seven days after the notice is mailed, not to be a donee, described in paragraph 110.1(1)(*a*) or in the definition "total charitable gifts" in subsection 118.1(1), for the purposes of

(i) subsections 110.1(1) and 118.1(1),

(ii) the definitions "qualified donee" and "registered charity" in subsection 248(1), and

(iii) Part XXXV of the *Income Tax Regulations*; and

(*b*) if the charity is, during that period, offered a gift from any person, the charity shall, before accepting the gift, inform that person that

(i) it has received the notice,

(ii) no deduction under subsection 110.1(1) or credit under subsection 118.1(3) may be claimed in respect of a gift made to it in the period, and

(iii) a gift made in the period is not a gift to a qualified donee.

▶ 188.2(4) ◀

(4) Application for postponement. If a notice of objection to a suspension under any of subsections (1) to (2.1) has been filed by a qualified donee, the qualified donee may file an application to the Tax Court of Canada for a postponement of that portion of the period of suspension that has not elapsed until the time determined by the Court.

History: S. 188.2(4) was replaced by S.C. 2012, c. 19, s. 13(4), in force on Royal Assent, June 29, 2012. S. 188.2(4) formerly read:

(4) *Application for postponement.* If a notice of objection to a suspension under subsection (1) or (2) has been filed by a qualified donee, the qualified donee may file an application to the Tax Court of Canada for a postponement of that portion of the period of suspension that has not elapsed until the time determined by the Court.

S. 188.2(4) was replaced by S.C. 2011, c. 24, s. 60(1), applicable to taxation years that begin on or after January 1, 2012. S. 188.2(4) formerly read:

(4) *Application for postponement.* If a notice of objection to a suspension under subsection (1) or (2) has been filed by a registered charity, the charity may file an application to the Tax Court of Canada for a postponement of that portion of the period of suspension that has not elapsed until the time determined by the Court.

▶ 188.2(5) ◀

(5) Grounds for postponement. The Tax Court of Canada may grant an application for postponement only if it would be just and equitable to do so.

SECTION 189: Tax regarding non-qualified investment

▶ 189(1) ◀

(1) Tax regarding non-qualified investment. Where at any particular time in a taxation year a debt (other than a debt in respect of which subsection 80.4(1) applies or would apply but for subsection 80.4(3)) is owing by a taxpayer to a registered charity that is a private foundation and at that time the debt was a non-qualified investment of the foundation, the taxpayer shall pay a tax under this Part for the year equal to the amount, if any, by which

(*a*) the amount that would be payable as interest on that debt for the period in the year during which it was outstanding and was a non-qualified investment of the foundation if the interest were payable at such prescribed rates as are in effect from time to time during the period

exceeds

(*b*) the amount of interest for the year paid on that debt by the taxpayer not later than 30 days after the end of the year.

Related Regulations: Part XLIII.

Related Sections: S. 149.1(1) Definitions; s. 248, "registered charity".

Forms: T2140 — Part V Tax Return — Tax on Non-Qualified Investments of a Registered Charity.

▶ 189(2) ◀

(2) Computation of interest on debt. For the purpose of paragraph (1)(*a*), where a debt in respect of which subsection (1) applies (other than a share or right that is deemed by subsection (3) to be a debt) is owing by a taxpayer to a private foundation, interest on that debt for the period referred to in that paragraph shall be computed at the least of

(*a*) such prescribed rates as are in effect from time to time during the period,

(*b*) the rate per annum of interest on that debt that, having regard to all the circumstances (including the terms and conditions of the debt), would have been agreed on, at the time the debt was incurred, had the taxpayer and the foundation been dealing with each other at arm's length and had the ordinary business of the foundation been the lending of money, and

(*c*) where that debt was incurred before April 22, 1982, a rate per annum equal to 6% plus 2% for each calendar year after 1982 and before the taxation year referred to in subsection (1).

Related Regulations: Part XLIII.

▶ 189(3) ◀

(3) Share deemed to be debt. For the purpose of subsection (1), where a share, or a right to acquire a share, of the capital stock of a corporation held by a private foundation at any particular time during the corporation's taxation year was at that time a non-qualified investment of the foundation, the share or right shall be deemed to be a debt owing at that time by the corporation to the foundation

(*a*) the amount of which was equal to,

(i) in the case of a share or right last acquired before April 22, 1982, the greater of its fair market value on April 21, 1982 and its cost amount to the foundation at the particular time, or

(ii) in any other case, its cost amount to the foundation at the particular time,

(*b*) that was outstanding throughout the period for which the share or right was held by the foundation during the year, and

(*c*) in respect of which the amount of interest paid in the year is equal to the total of all amounts each of which is the amount of a dividend received on the share by the foundation in the year,

and the reference in paragraph (1)(*a*) to "such prescribed rates as are in effect from time to time during the period" shall be read as a reference to "2/3 of such prescribed rates as are in effect from time to time during the period".

▶ 189(4) ◀

(4) Computation of interest with respect to a share. For the purposes of subsection (3), where a share or right in respect of which that subsection applies was last acquired before April 22, 1982, the reference therein to "2/3 of such prescribed rates as are in effect from time to time during the period" shall be read as a reference to "the lesser of

(*a*) a rate per annum equal to 4% plus 1% for each 5 calendar years contained in the period commencing after 1982 and ending before the particular time, and

(*b*) a rate per annum equal to 2/3 of such prescribed rates as are in effect from time to time during the year".

▶ 189(5) ◀

(5) Share substitution. For the purpose of subsection (3), where a share or right is acquired by a charity in exchange for another share or right in a transaction after April 21, 1982 to which section 51, 85, 85.1, 86 or 87 applies, it shall be deemed to be the same share or right as the one for which it was substituted.

▶ 189(6) ◀

(6) Taxpayer to file return and pay tax. Every taxpayer who is liable to pay tax under this Part (except a charity that is liable to pay tax under section 188(1)) for a taxation year shall, on or before the day on or before which the taxpayer is, or would be if tax were payable by the taxpayer under Part I for the year, required to file a return of income or an information return under Part I for the year,

(*a*) file with the Minister a return for the year in prescribed form and containing prescribed information, without notice or demand therefor;

(*b*) estimate in the return the amount of tax payable by the taxpayer under this Part for the year; and

(*c*) pay to the Receiver General the amount of tax payable by the taxpayer under this Part for the year.

Forms: T2140 — Part V Tax Return — Tax on Non-Qualified Investments of a Registered Charity; T2046 — Return of Tax Payable Where Registration of a Registered Charity is Revoked.

▶ 189(6.1) ◀

(6.1) Revoked charity to file returns. Every taxpayer who is liable to pay tax under subsection 188(1.1) for a taxation year shall, on or before the day that is one year from the end of the taxation year, and without notice or demand,

(*a*) file with the Minister

(i) a return for the taxation year, in prescribed form and containing prescribed information, and

(ii) both an information return and a public information return for the taxation year, each in the form prescribed for the purpose of subsection 149.1(14); and

(*b*) estimate in the return referred to in subparagraph (*a*)(i) the amount of tax payable by the taxpayer under subsection 188(1.1) for the taxation year; and

(*c*) pay to the Receiver General the amount of tax payable by the taxpayer under subsection 188(1.1) for the taxation year.

▶ 189(6.2) ◀

(6.2) Reduction of revocation tax liability. If the Minister has, during the one-year period beginning immediately after the end of a taxation year of a person, assessed the person in respect of the person's liability for tax under subsection 188(1.1) for that taxation year, has not after that period reassessed the tax liability of the person, and that liability exceeds $1,000, that liability is, at any particular time, reduced by the total of

(*a*) the amount, if any, by which

(i) the total of all amounts, each of which is an expenditure made by the charity, on charitable activities carried on by it, before the particular time and during the period (referred to in this subsection as the "post-assessment period") that begins immediately after a notice of the latest such assessment was sent and ends at the end of the one-year period

exceeds

(ii) the income of the charity for the post-assessment period, including gifts received by the charity in that period from any source and any income that would be computed under section 3 if that period were a taxation year, and (*b*) all amounts, each of which is an amount, in respect of a property transferred by the charity before the particular time and during the post-assessment period to a person that was at the time of the transfer an eligible donee in respect of the charity, equal to the amount, if any, by which the fair market value of the property, when transferred, exceeds the consideration given by the person for the transfer.

History: S. 189(6.2)(*a*)(i) was replaced by S.C. 2010, c. 25, s. 52, in force on Royal Assent, December 15, 2010. S. 189(6.2)(*a*)(i) formerly read:

(i) the total of all amounts, each of which is an expenditure made by the charity, on charitable activities carried on by it, before the particular time and during the period (referred to in this subsection as the "post-assessment period") that begins immediately after a notice of the latest such assessment was mailed and ends at the end of the one-year period

► 189(6.3) ◄

(6.3) Reduction of liability for penalties. If the Minister has assessed a particular person in respect of the particular person's liability for penalties under section 188.1 for a taxation year, and that liability exceeds $ 1,000, that liability is, at any particular time, reduced by the total of all amounts, each of which is an amount, in respect of a property transferred by the particular person after the day on which the Minister first assessed that liability and before the particular time to another person that was at the time of the transfer an eligible donee described in paragraph 188(1.3)(*a*) in respect of the particular person, equal to the amount, if any, by which the fair market value of the property, when transferred, exceeds the total of

(*a*) the consideration given by the other person for the transfer, and

(*b*) the part of the amount in respect of the transfer that has resulted in a reduction of an amount otherwise payable under subsection 188(1.1).

History: S. 189(6.3), the portion before paragraph (*a*) was replaced by S.C. 2018, c. 12, s. 31(1), in respect of transfers of property made on or after February 27, 2018, and formerly read:

(6.3) *Reduction of liability for penalties.* If the Minister has assessed a particular person in respect of the particular person's liability for penalties under section 188.1 for a taxation year, and that liability exceeds $1,000, that liability is, at any particular time, reduced by the total of all amounts, each of which is an amount, in respect of a property transferred by the particular person after the day on which the Minister first assessed that liability and before the particular time to another person that was at the time of the transfer an eligible donee in respect of the particular person, equal to the amount, if any, by which the fair market value of the property, when transferred, exceeds the total of

S. 189(6.3), the portion before paragraph (*b*) was replaced by S.C. 2011, c. 24, s. 61(1), applicable to taxation years that begin on or after January 1, 2012. S. 189(6.3), the portion before paragraph (*b*) formerly read:

(6.3) *Reduction of liability for penalties.* If the Minister has assessed a registered charity in respect of the charity's liability for penalties under section 188.1 for a taxation year, and that liability exceeds $1,000, that liability is, at any particular time, reduced by the total of all amounts, each of which is an amount, in respect of a property transferred by the charity after the day on which the Minister first assessed that liability and before the particular time to a person that was at the time of the transfer an eligible donee in respect of the charity, equal to the amount, if any, by which the fair market value of the property, when transferred, exceeds the total of

(*a*) the consideration given by the person for the transfer, and

Related Sections: S. 188.1 Penalties.

► 189(7) ◄

(7) Minister may assess. Without limiting the authority of the Minister to revoke the registration of a registered charity or registered Canadian amateur athletic association, the Minister may also at any time assess a taxpayer in respect of any amount that a taxpayer is liable to pay under this Part.

History: S. 189(7) was replaced by S.C. 2011, c. 24, s. 61(2), applicable to taxation years that begin on or after January 1, 2012. S. 189(7) formerly read:

(7) *Minister may assess.* Without limiting the authority of the Minister to revoke the registration of a registered charity, the Minister may also at any time assess a taxpayer in respect of any amount that a taxpayer is liable to pay under this Part.

Related Sections: S. 248(11) Compound interest.

► 189(8) ◄

(8) Provisions applicable to Part. Subsections 150(2) and (3), sections 152 and 158, subsection 161(11), sections 162 to 167 and Division J of Part I apply in respect of an amount assessed under this Part and of a notice of suspension under subsection 188.2(1) or (2) as if the notice were a notice of assessment made under section 152, with any modifications that the circumstances require including, for greater certainty, that a notice of suspension that is reconsidered or reassessed may be confirmed or vacated, but not varied, except that

(*a*) section 162 does not apply in respect of a return required to be filed under paragraph (6.1)(*a*); and

(*b*) the reference in each of subsections 165(2) and 166.1(3) to the expression "Chief of Appeals in a District Office or a Taxation Centre" is to be read as a reference to the expression "Assistant Commissioner, Appeals Branch".

► 189(8.1) ◄

(8.1) Clarification re objections under subsection 168(4). For greater certainty, in applying the provisions referred to in subsection (8), with any modifications that the circumstances require,

(*a*) a notice of objection referred to in subsection 168(4) does not constitute a notice of objection to a tax assessed under subsection 188(1.1); and

(*b*) an issue that could have been the subject of a notice of objection referred to in subsection 168(4) may not be appealed to the Tax Court of Canada under subsection 169(1).

► 189(9) ◄

(9) Interest. Subsection 161(11) does not apply to a liability of a taxpayer for a taxation year

(*a*) under subsection 188(1.1) to the extent that the liability is reduced by subsection (6.2), or paid, before the end of the one-year period that begins immediately after the end of the taxation year deemed to have ended by paragraph 188(1)(*a*); or

(*b*) under section 188.1 to the extent that the liability is reduced by subsection (6.3), or paid, before the end of the one-year period that begins immediately after the liability was first assessed.

Part VI
Tax on Capital of Financial Institutions

SECTION 190: [Interpretation]

► 190(1) ◄

(1) Definitions. For the purposes of this Part,

"financial institution"—"financial institution" means a corporation that

(*a*) is a bank,

(*b*) is authorized under the laws of Canada or a province to carry on the business of offering its services as a trustee to the public,

(*c*) is authorized under the laws of Canada or a province to accept deposits from the public and carries on the business of lending money on the security of real property or immovables or investing in indebtedness on the security of mortgages on real property or of hypothecs on immovables,

(*d*) is a life insurance corporation that carries on business in Canada, or

(*e*) is a corporation all or substantially all of the assets of which are shares or indebtedness of corporations described in any of paragraphs (*a*) to (*d*) or this paragraph to which the corporation is related;

History: S. 190(1), paragraph (*c*) of the definition "financial institution" was replaced by S.C. 2013, c. 34, s. 152, in force June 26, 2013, and formerly read:

(*c*) is authorized under the laws of Canada or a province to accept deposits from the public and carries on the business of lending money on the security of real estate or investing in mortgages or hypothecary claims on real estate;

"long-term debt"—"long-term debt" means

(*a*) in the case of a bank, its subordinated indebtedness (within the meaning assigned by section 2 of the *Bank Act*) evidenced by obligations issued for a term of not less than 5 years,

(*b*) in the case of an insurance corporation, its subordinated indebtedness (within the meaning assigned by section 2 of the *Insurance Companies Act*) evidenced by obligations issued for a term of not less than 5 years, and

(*c*) in the case of any other corporation, its subordinated indebtedness (within the meaning that would be assigned by section 2 of the *Bank Act* if the definition of that expression in that section were applied with such modifications as the circumstances require) evidenced by obligations issued for a term of not less than 5 years;

"reserves"—"reserves", in respect of a financial institution for a taxation year, means the amount at the end of the year of all of the institution's reserves, provisions and allowances (other than allowances in respect of depreciation or depletion) and, for greater certainty, includes any provision in respect of deferred taxes.

Related Regulations: 8603.

► 190(1.1) ◄

(1.1) Prescribed meanings. For the purposes of this Part, the expressions "attributed surplus", "Canadian assets", "Canadian reserve liabilities", "total assets" and "total reserve liabilities" have the meanings that are prescribed.

Related Regulations: 8603.

► 190(2) ◄

(2) Application of ss. 181(3) and (4). Subsections 181(3) and (4) apply to this Part with such modifications as the circumstances require.

Calculation of Capital Tax

SECTION 190.1: Tax payable

► 190.1(1) ◄

(1) Tax payable. Every corporation that is a financial institution at any time during a taxation year shall pay a tax under this Part for the year equal to 1.25% of the amount, if any, by which its taxable capital employed in Canada for the year exceeds its capital deduction for the year.

Related Regulations: 5301(10)(b).

Related Sections: s. 190.11 Taxable capital employed in Canada; s. 190.15 Capital deduction; s. 227(14) Application of other Parts.

Forms: T2 SCH 38 — T2SCH38 Part VI Tax on Capital of Financial Institutions.

► 190.1(1.1) ◄

(1.1) Additional tax payable by life insurance corporations—(Repealed by S.C. 2007, c. 2, s. 40(1).)

► 190.1(1.2) ◄

(1.2) Additional tax payable by deposit-taking institutions—(Repealed by S.C. 2007, c. 2, s. 40(1).)

► 190.1(2) ◄

(2) Short taxation years. Where a taxation year of a corporation is less than 51 weeks, the amount determined under subsection (1) for the year in respect of the corporation shall be reduced to that proportion of that amount that the number of days in the year is of 365.

Related Sections: S. 248(1), "amount", "corporation"; s. 249(1) Definition of "taxation year".

► 190.1(3) ◄

(3) Deduction. There may be deducted in computing a corporation's tax payable under this Part for a taxation year an amount equal to the total of

(*a*) the corporation's tax payable under Part I for the year; and

(*b*) such part as the corporation claims of its unused Part I tax credits and unused surtax credits for its 7 taxation years immediately before and its 3 taxation years immediately after the year.

(*c*) (Repealed.)

(*d*) (Repealed.)

History: S. 190.1(3)(*a*) was replaced by S.C. 2013, c. 34, s. 329(1), applicable to taxation years that begin after 2007, and formerly read:

(*a*) the amount, if any, by which

(i) the corporation's tax payable under Part I for the year exceeds the lesser of

(ii) the corporation's Canadian surtax payable (within the meaning assigned by section 125.3) for the year, and

(iii) the amount that would, but for subsection 181.1(4), be its tax payable under Part I.3 for the year, and

Related Sections: S. 3 Income for taxation year; s. 125.2(1) Deduction of Part VI tax; s. 125.3(4), "Canadian surtax payable"; s. 181.1(4) Deduction; s. 190.1(1.2) Additional tax payable by deposit-taking institutions; s. 190.1(5), "unused Part I tax credit", "unused surtax credit".

Forms: T2 SCH 42 — Calculation of Unused Part VI Tax Credit and Unused Part I Tax Credit.

► 190.1(4) ◄

(4) Idem. For the purposes of this subsection and subsections (3), (5) and (6),

(*a*) an amount may not be claimed under subsection (3) in computing a corporation's tax payable under this Part for a particular taxation year

(i) in respect of its unused Part I tax credit for another taxation year, until its unused Part I tax credits for taxation years preceding the other year that may be claimed under this Part for the particular year have been claimed, and

(ii) in respect of its unused surtax credit for another taxation year, until its unused surtax credits for taxation years preceding the other year that may be claimed under Part I.3 or this Part for the particular year have been claimed;

(*b*) an amount may be claimed under subsection (3) in computing a corporation's tax payable under this Part for a particular taxation year

(i) in respect of its unused Part I tax credit for another taxation year, only to the extent that it exceeds the total of all amounts each of which is the amount claimed in respect of that unused Part I tax credit in computing its tax payable under this Part for a taxation year preceding the particular year, and

(ii) in respect of its unused surtax credit for another taxation year, only to the extent that it exceeds the total of all amounts each of which is the amount claimed in respect of the unused surtax credit

(A) in computing its tax payable under this Part for a taxation year preceding the particular year, or

(B) in computing its tax payable under Part I.3 for the particular year or a taxation year preceding the particular year; and

(*c*) an amount may be claimed under paragraph (3)(*b*) in computing a corporation's tax payable under this Part for a taxation year that ends before July 1, 2006 in respect of its unused Part I tax credit for a taxation year that ends after July 1, 2006 (referred to in this paragraph as the "credit taxation year") only to the extent that the unused Part I tax credit exceeds the amount, if any, by which

(i) the amount that would, if this Part were read as it applied to the 2005 taxation year, be the corporation's tax payable under this Part for the credit taxation year

exceeds

(ii) the corporation's tax payable under this Part for the credit taxation year.

Related Sections: S. 3 Income for taxation year; s. 190.1(5), "unused Part I tax credit", "unused surtax credit"; s. 249(1) Definition of "taxation year"; Part I.

► 190.1(5) ◄

(5) Definitions. For the purposes of subsections (3), (4) and (6),

Related Sections: S. 181.1(1.2) Exceptions; s. 181.5(1.1) Lower capital deduction; s. 181.5(4.1) Lower capital deduction allocation.

"unused Part I tax credit" —"unused Part I tax credit", of a corporation for a taxation year, means the amount, if any, by which

(*a*) the corporation's tax payable under Part I for the year

exceeds

(*b*) the amount that would, but for subsection (3), be its tax payable under this Part for the year;

History: S. 190.1(5), the definition "unused Part I tax credit" was replaced by S.C. 2013, c. 34, s. 329(2), applicable to taxation years that begin after 2007, and formerly read:

"unused Part I tax credit"—"unused Part I tax credit" of a corporation for a taxation year ending after 1991 means the amount, if any, by which

(*a*) the corporation's tax payable under Part I for the year

exceeds the total of

(*b*) the amount that would, but for subsection (3), be its tax payable under this Part for the year, and

(*c*) the corporation's Canadian surtax payable (within the meaning assigned by section 125.3) for the year;

"unused surtax credit" —"unused surtax credit" of a corporation for a taxation year has the meaning assigned by subsection 181.1(6).

Related Sections: S. 125.3(4), "Canadian surtax payable"; s. 181.1(6), "unused surtax credit"; s. 248(1), "amount", "corporation".

► 190.1(6) ◄

(6) Acquisition of control. Where at any time control of a corporation was acquired by a person or group of persons, no amount in respect of its unused Part I tax credit or unused surtax credit for a taxation year ending before that time is deductible by the corporation for a taxation year ending after the time and no amount in respect of its unused Part I tax credit or unused surtax credit for a taxation year ending after that time is deductible by the corporation for a taxation year ending before that time, except that

(*a*) the corporation's unused Part I tax credit and unused surtax credit for a particular taxation year that ended before that time is deductible by the corporation for a taxation year that ends after that time (in this paragraph referred to as the "subsequent year") to the extent of that proportion of the corporation's tax payable under Part I for the particular year that

(i) the amount, if any, by which

(A) the total of all amounts each of which is

(I) its income under Part I for the particular year from a business that was carried on by the corporation for profit or with a reasonable expectation of profit throughout the subsequent year, or

(II) where properties were sold, leased, rented or developed or services were rendered in the course of carrying on that business before that time, its income under Part I for the particular year from any other business all or substantially all of the income of which was derived from the sale, leasing, rental or development, as the case may be, of similar properties or the rendering of similar services

exceeds

(B) the total of all amounts each of which is an amount deducted under paragraph 111(1)(*a*) or (*d*) in computing its taxable income for the particular year in respect of a non-capital loss or a farm loss, as the case may be, for a taxation year in respect of any business referred to in clause (A)

is of the greater of

(ii) the amount determined under subparagraph (i), and

(iii) the corporation's taxable income for the particular year; and

(*b*) the corporation's unused Part I tax credit and unused surtax credit for a particular taxation year that ends after that time is deductible by the corporation for a taxation year (in this paragraph referred to as the "preceding year") that ended before that time to the extent of that proportion of the corporation's tax payable under Part I for the particular year that

(i) the amount, if any, by which

(A) the total of all amounts each of which is

(I) its income under Part I for the particular year from a business that was carried on by the corporation in the preceding year and throughout the particular year for profit or with a reasonable expectation of profit, or

(II) where properties were sold, leased, rented or developed or services were rendered in the course of carrying on that business before that time, its income under Part I for the particular year from any other business all or substantially all of the income of which was derived from the sale, leasing, rental or development, as the case may be, of similar properties or the rendering of similar services

exceeds

(B) the total of all amounts each of which is an amount deducted under paragraph 111(1)(*a*) or (*d*) in computing its taxable income for the particular year in respect of a non-capital loss or a farm loss, as the case may be, for a taxation year in respect of any business referred to in clause (A)

is of the greater of

(ii) the amount determined under subparagraph (i), and

(iii) the corporation's taxable income for the particular year.

Related Sections: S. 111(1)(*a*) Non-capital losses; s. 111(1)(*d*) Farm losses; s. 111(8), "non-capital loss", "farm loss"; s. 190.1(5), "unused Part I tax credit", "unused surtax credit"; s. 248(1), "amount", "business", "corporation", "property", "taxation year"; s. 256(7) Acquiring control; s. 256.1 [Corporate tax-attribute trading].

SECTION 190.11: Taxable capital employed in Canada

For the purposes of this Part, the taxable capital employed in Canada of a financial institution for a taxation year is,

(*a*) in the case of a financial institution other than a life insurance corporation, that proportion of its taxable capital for the year that its Canadian assets at the end of the year is of its total assets at the end of the year;

(*b*) in the case of a life insurance corporation that was resident in Canada at any time in the year, the total of

(i) that proportion of the amount, if any, by which the total of

(A) its taxable capital for the year, and

(B) the amount prescribed for the year in respect of the corporation

exceeds

(C) the amount prescribed for the year in respect of the corporation

that its Canadian reserve liabilities as at the end of the year is of the total of

(D) its total reserve liabilities as at the end of the year, and

(E) the amount prescribed for the year in respect of the corporation, and

(ii) (Repealed.)

(*c*) in the case of a life insurance corporation that was non-resident throughout the year, its taxable capital for the year.

History: S. 190.11(*b*)(ii) was repealed by S.C. 2009, c. 2, s. 63(1), applicable to taxation years that begin after September 2006. S. 190.11(*b*)(ii) formerly read:

(ii) the amount, if any, by which

(A) the amount of its reserves for the year (other than its reserves in respect of amounts payable out of segregated funds) that can reasonably be regarded as having been established in respect of its insurance businesses carried on in Canada

exceeds the total of

(B) all amounts each of which is the amount of a reserve (other than a reserve described in subparagraph 138(3)(*a*)(i)), to the extent that it is included in the amount determined under clause (A) and is deducted in computing its income under Part I for the year,

(C) all amounts each of which is the amount of a reserve described in subparagraph 138(3)(*a*)(i), to the extent that it is included in the amount determined under clause (A) and is deductible under subparagraph 138(3)(*a*)(i) in computing its income under Part I for the year, and

(D) all amounts each of which is the amount outstanding (including any interest accrued thereon) at the end of the year in respect of a policy loan (within the meaning assigned by subsection 138(12)) made by the corporation, to the extent that it is deducted in computing the total determined under clause (C); and

Related Regulations: 8603; 8605.

Tax Window Files: Surplus Appropriations - Part VI Capital Tax, *December 4, 2015*, CRA Document No. 2015-0606291I7.

SECTION 190.12: Taxable capital

For the purposes of this Part, the taxable capital of a corporation for a taxation year is the amount, if any, by which its capital for the year exceeds the total determined under section 190.14 in respect of its investments for the year in financial institutions related to it.

Related Sections: S. 251(2) Definition of "related persons".

Cases: For the purposes of calculating capital under Part VI, where a particular tax reserve exceeds its matching book reserve, a negative amount should not be included in the calculation. Rather, the value of the book reserve should be reduced to zero. *National Trust Co. v. The Queen*, 96 DTC 6234 (F.C.T.D.).

SECTION 190.13: Capital

For the purposes of this Part, the capital of a financial institution for a taxation year is,

(*a*) in the case of a financial institution, other than an authorized foreign bank or a life insurance corporation, the amount, if any, by which the total at the end of the year of

(i) the amount of its long-term debt,

(ii) the amount of its capital stock (or, in the case of an institution incorporated without share capital, the amount of its members' contributions), retained earnings, contributed surplus and any other surpluses, and

(iii) the amount of its reserves, except to the extent that they were deducted in computing its income under Part I for the year,

exceeds the total at the end of the year of

(iv) the amount of its deferred tax debit balance, and

(v) the amount of any deficit deducted in computing its shareholders' equity (including, for this purpose, the amount of any provision for the redemption of preferred shares);

(*b*) in the case of a life insurance corporation that was resident in Canada at any time in the year, the amount, if any, by which the total at the end of the year of

(i) the amount of its long-term debt, and

(ii) the amount of its capital stock (or, in the case of an insurance corporation incorporated without share capital, the amount of its members' contributions), retained earnings, contributed surplus and any other surpluses

exceeds the total at the end of the year of

(iii) the amount of its deferred tax debit balance, and

(iv) the amount of any deficit deducted in computing its shareholders' equity (including, for this purpose, the amount of any provision for the redemption of preferred shares);

(*c*) in the case of a life insurance corporation that was non-resident throughout the year, the total at the end of the year of

(i) the amount that is the greater of

(A) the amount, if any, by which

(I) its surplus funds derived from operations (as defined in subsection 138(12)) as of the end of the year, computed as if no tax were payable under Part I.3 or this Part for the year

exceeds the total of all amounts each of which is

(II) an amount on which it was required to pay, or would but for subsection 219(5.2) have been required to pay, tax under Part XIV for a preceding taxation year, except the portion, if any, of the amount on which tax was payable, or would have been payable, because of subparagraph 219(4)(*a*)(i.1), and

(III) an amount on which it was required to pay, or would but for subsection 219(5.2) have been required to pay, tax under subsection 219(5.1) for the year because of the transfer of an insurance business to which subsection 138(11.5) or (11.92) has applied, and

(B) its attributed surplus for the year,

(ii) any other surpluses relating to its insurance businesses carried on in Canada,

(iii) the amount of its long-term debt that can reasonably be regarded as relating to its insurance businesses carried on in Canada, and

(iv) (Repealed.)

(*d*) in the case of an authorized foreign bank, the total of

(i) 10% of the total of all amounts, each of which is the risk-weighted amount at the end of the year of an on-balance sheet asset or an off-balance sheet exposure of the bank in respect of its Canadian banking business that the bank would be required to report under the OSFI risk-weighting guidelines if those guidelines applied and required a report at that time, and

(ii) the total of all amounts, each of which is an amount at the end of the year in respect of the bank's Canadian banking business that

(A) if the bank were a bank listed in Schedule II to the *Bank Act*, would be required under the risk-based capital adequacy guidelines issued by the Superintendent of Financial Institutions and applicable at that time to be deducted from the bank's capital in determining the amount of capital available to satisfy the Superintendent's requirement that capital equal a particular proportion of risk-weighted assets and exposures, and

(B) is not an amount in respect of a loss protection facility required to be deducted from capital under the Superintendent's guidelines respecting asset securitization applicable at that time.

History: S. 190.13(*a*)(v) was replaced by S.C. 2013, c. 34, s. 330(1), applicable to taxation years that begin after 1995, and formerly read:

(v) the amount of any deficit deducted in computing its shareholders' equity;

S. 190.13(*b*)(iv) was replaced by S.C. 2013, c. 34, s. 330(2), applicable to taxation years that begin after 1995, and formerly read:

(iv) the amount of any deficit deducted in computing its shareholders' equity;

S. 190.13(*c*)(iv) was repealed by S.C. 2009, c. 2, s. 64(1), applicable to taxation years that begin after September 2006. S. 190.13(*c*)(iv) formerly read:

(iv) the amount, if any, by which

(A) the amount of its reserves for the year (other than its reserves in respect of amounts payable out of segregated funds) that can reasonably be regarded as having been established in respect of its insurance businesses carried on in Canada

exceeds the total of

(B) all amounts each of which is the amount of a reserve (other than a reserve described in subparagraph 138(3)(*a*)(i)), to the extent that it is included in the amount determined under clause (A) and is deducted in computing its income under Part I for the year,

(C) all amounts each of which is the amount of a reserve described in subparagraph 138(3)(*a*)(i), to the extent that it is included in the amount determined under clause (A) and is deductible under subparagraph 138(3)(*a*)(i) in computing its income under Part I for the year, and

(D) all amounts each of which is the amount outstanding (including any interest accrued thereon) at the end of the year in respect of a policy loan (within the meaning assigned by subsection 138(12)) made by the corporation, to the extent that it is deducted in computing the amount determined under clause (C); and

Related Sections: S. 181.3(3) Capital of financial institution; s. 248(1), "authorized foreign bank", "Canadian banking business", "OSFI risk-weighting guidelines".

SECTION 190.14: Investment in related institutions

▶ 190.14(1) ◀

(1) Investment in related institutions. A corporation's investment for a taxation year in a financial institution related to it is

(*a*) in the case of a corporation that was resident in Canada at any time in the year, the total of all amounts each of which is the carrying value (or in the case of contributed surplus, the amount) at the end of the year of an eligible investment of the corporation in the financial institution;

(*b*) in the case of a life insurance corporation that was non-resident throughout the year, the total of all amounts each of which is the carrying value (or is, in the case of contributed surplus, the amount) at the end of the year of an eligible investment of the corporation in the financial institution that was used or held by the corporation in the year in the course of carrying on an insurance business in Canada (or that, in the case of contributed surplus, was contributed by the corporation in the course of carrying on that business); and

(*c*) in the case of a corporation that is an authorized foreign bank, the total of all amounts each of which is the amount at the end of the year, before the application of risk weights, that would be required to be reported under the OSFI risk- weighting guidelines if those guidelines applied and required a report at that time, of an eligible investment of the corporation in the financial institution that was used or held by the corporation in the year in the course of carrying on its Canadian banking business or, in the case of an eligible investment that is contributed surplus of the financial institution at the end of the year, the amount of the surplus contributed by the corporation in the course of carrying on that business.

Related Sections: S. 248(1), "authorized foreign bank", "Canadian banking business", "OSFI risk-weighting guidelines".

▶ 190.14(2) ◀

(2) Interpretation. For the purpose of subsection (1), an eligible investment of a corporation in a financial institution is a share of the capital stock or long-term debt (and, where the corporation is an insurance corporation, is non-segregated property within the meaning assigned by subsection 138(12)) of the financial institution or any surplus of the financial institution contributed by the corporation (other than an amount otherwise included as a share or debt) if the financial institution at the end of the year is

(*a*) related to the corporation; and

(*b*) resident in Canada or can reasonably be regarded as using the surplus or the proceeds of the share or debt in a business carried on by the financial institution through a permanent establishment (as defined by regulation) in Canada.

Related Regulations: 8201.

SECTION 190.15: Capital deduction

▶ 190.15(1) ◀

(1) Capital deduction. For the purposes of this Part, the capital deduction of a corporation for a taxation year during which it was at any time a financial institution is $1 billion unless the corporation was related to another financial institution at the end of the year, in which case, subject to subsection (4), its capital deduction for the year is nil.

▶ 190.15(2) ◀

(2) Related financial institution. A corporation that is a financial institution at any time during a taxation year and that was related to another financial institution at the end of the year may file with the Minister an agreement in prescribed form on behalf of the related group of which the corporation is a member under which an amount that does not exceed $1 billion is allocated among the members of the related group for the taxation year.

Forms: T2 SCH 39 — Agreement Among Related Financial Institutions — Part VI Tax.

▶ 190.15(3) ◀

(3) Allocation by Minister. The Minister may request a corporation that is a financial institution at any time during a taxation year and that was related to any other financial institution at the end of the year to file with the Minister an agreement referred to in subsection (2) and, if the corporation does not file such an agreement within 30 days after receiving the request, the Minister may allocate an amount among the members of the related group of which the corporation is a member for the year not exceeding $1 billion.

▶ 190.15(4) ◀

(4) Idem. For the purposes of this Part, the least amount allocated for a taxation year to each member of a related group under an agreement described in subsection (2) or by the Minister pursuant to subsection (3) is the capital deduction for the taxation year of that member, but, if no such allocation is made, the capital deduction of each member of the related group for that year is nil.

▶ 190.15(5) ◀

(5) Idem. Where a corporation (in this subsection referred to as the "first corporation") has more than one taxation year ending in the same calendar year and is related in 2 or more of those taxation years to another corporation that has a taxation year ending in that calendar year, the capital deduction of the first corporation for each such taxation year at the end of which it is related to the other corporation is, for the purposes of this Part, an amount equal to its capital deduction for the first such taxation year.

▶ 190.15(6) ◀

(6) Idem. Two corporations that would, but for this subsection, be related to each other solely because of (*a*) the control of any corporation by Her Majesty in right of Canada or a province, or

(*b*) a right referred to in paragraph 251(5)(*b*),

are, for the purposes of this section and section 190.14, deemed not to be related to each other except that, where at any time a taxpayer has a right referred to in paragraph 251(5)(*b*) with respect to shares and it can reasonably be considered that one of the main purposes for the acquisition of the right was to avoid any limitation on the amount of a corporation's capital deduction for a taxation year, for the purpose of determining whether a corporation is related to any other corporation, the corporations are, for the purpose of this section, deemed to be in the same position in relation to each other as if the right were immediate and absolute and as if the taxpayer had exercised the right at that time.

Related Sections: S. 181.5(6) Government-controlled corporation; s. 190.14 Investment in related institutions; s. 190.17(5) Provisions applicable to Part; s. 248(1), "corporation", "share"; s. 249(1) Definition of "taxation year"; s. 251(2) Definition of "related persons"; s. 256(8) Deemed exercise of right.

Transitional Provisions

SECTION 190.16: Application to taxation year including July 1, 2006

▶ 190.16(1) ◀

(1) Application to taxation year including July 1, 2006 — (Repealed by S.C. 2013, c. 34, s. 331(1).)

History: S. 190.16(1) and the heading before it were repealed by S.C. 2013, c. 34, s. 331(1), applicable to taxation years that begin after October 31, 2011, and formerly read:

S. 190.16

(1) *Application to taxation year including July 1, 2006.* If a taxation year of a corporation begins before and ends on or after July 1, 2006, notwithstanding any other provision of this Part, the tax payable under this Part by the corporation for the taxation year is equal to the total of

(*a*) that proportion of the amount that would be the tax payable by the corporation under this Part for the taxation year, if this Part were read as it applied to the 2005 taxation year, that the number of days in the taxation year that are before that day is of the number of days in the taxation year, and

(*b*) that proportion of the amount that would, if this Part were read without reference to this section, be the tax payable by the corporation under this Part for the taxation year that the number of days in the taxation year that are on or after that day is of the number of days in the taxation year.

▶ 190.16(2) ◀

(2) Proportionate allocation — (Repealed by S.C. 2013, c. 34, s. 331(1).)

History: S. 190.16(2) was repealed by S.C. 2013, c. 34, s. 331(1), applicable to taxation years that begin after October 31, 2011, and formerly read:

(2) *Proportionate allocation.* Any allocation made for the purpose of paragraph (1)(*a*) under subsection 190.15(2) or (3) shall be in the same proportion as the allocation, if any, made for the purpose of paragraph (1)(*b*) under subsection 190.15(2) or (3).

▶ 190.16(3) ◀

(3) Capital deduction deemed — (Repealed by S.C. 2013, c. 34, s. 331(1).)

History: S. 190.16(3) was repealed by S.C. 2013, c. 34, s. 331(1), applicable to taxation years that begin after October 31, 2011, and formerly read:

(3) *Capital deduction deemed.* For the purpose of applying subsection 190.15(5) to a corporation for a taxation year that is described in that subsection in circumstances where the "first such taxation year" referred to in that subsection is a taxation year to which subsection (1) applies, the capital deduction of the corporation for that "first such taxation year" is deemed to be the total of

(*a*) that proportion of the capital deduction amount allocated to the corporation for the purposes of paragraph (1)(*a*) that the number of days in the taxation year that are before July 1, 2006 is of the number of days in the taxation year, and

(*b*) that proportion of the capital deduction amount allocated to the corporation for the purposes of paragraph (1)(*b*) that the number of days in the taxation year that are after June 30, 2006 is of the number of days in the taxation year.

▶ 190.16(4) ◀

(4) Idem — (Repealed by S.C. 2007, c. 2, s. 42(1).)

▶ 190.16(5) ◀

(5) Provisions applicable to Part — (Repealed by S.C. 2007, c. 2, s. 42(1).)

SECTION 190.17: Enhanced capital deduction

(Repealed by S.C. 2007, c. 2, s. 42(1).)

SECTION 190.18: Special Rules

(Repealed by 1990, c. 39, s. 50(1).)

SECTION 190.19: Artificial reduction of capital tax

(Repealed by 1988, c. 55, s. 157(1).)

Administrative Provisions

SECTION 190.2: Return

A corporation that is or would, but for subsection 190.1(3), be liable to pay tax under this Part for a taxation year shall file with the Minister, not later than the day on or before which the corporation is required by section 150 to file its return of income for the year under Part I, a return of capital for the year in prescribed form containing an estimate of the tax payable under this Part by it for the year.

Related Sections: S. 150(1) Filing returns of income — general rule; s. 150.1(5) Application to other Parts; s. 248(1), "corporation"; s. 249(1) Definition of "taxation year".

Forms: T2 SCH 42 — Calculation of Unused Part VI Tax Credit and Unused Part I Tax Credit; T2 SCH 38 — Part VI Tax on Capital of Financial Institutions (1999 and later taxation years).

SECTION 190.21: Provisions applicable to Part

Sections 152, 158 and 159, subsection 161(11), sections 162 to 167 and Division J of Part I apply to this Part with such modifications as the circumstances require and, for the purpose of this section, paragraph 152(6)(*a*) shall be read as follows:

"(*a*) a deduction under subsection 190.1(3) in respect of any unused surtax credit or unused Part I tax credit (within the meanings assigned by subsection 190.1(5)) for a subsequent taxation year,".

Related Sections: S. 152(1) Assessment; s. 152(6) Reassessment where certain deductions claimed; s. 158 Payment of remainder; s. 159(1) Person acting for another; s. 161(11) Interest on penalties; s. 190(1) Tax on capital of financial institutions; s. 190.1(3) Deduction; s. 190.1(5), "unused Part I tax credit"; s. 249(1) Definition of "taxation year"; Division J.

SECTION 190.211: Provisions applicable — Crown corporations

Section 27 applies to this Part with any modifications that the circumstances require.

Related Sections: S. 181.71 Provisions applicable — Crown corporations; s. 187.61 Provisions applicable — Crown corporations; s. 191.4(3) Provisions applicable — Crown corporations.

SECTION 190.22: Instalment bases

(Repealed by S.C. 1994, c. 7, Sched. VIII, s. 114(1).)

SECTION 190.23: Interest

(Repealed by S.C. 1994, c. 7, Sched. VIII, s. 114(1).)

Related Sections: S. 248(11) Compound interest.

SECTION 190.24: Provisions applicable to Part

(Repealed by S.C. 1994, c. 7, Sched. VIII, s. 114(1).)

Part VI.1
Tax on Corporations Paying Dividends on Taxable Preferred Shares

SECTION 191: [Excluded dividends]

► 191(1) ◄

(1) Definitions. In this Part,

"excluded dividend" —"excluded dividend" means a dividend

(*a*) paid by a corporation to a shareholder that had a substantial interest in the corporation at the time the dividend was paid,

(*b*) paid by a corporation that was a financial intermediary corporation or a private holding corporation at the time the dividend was paid,

(*c*) paid by a particular corporation that would, but for paragraphs (*h*) and (*i*) of the definition "financial intermediary corporation" in this subsection, have been a financial intermediary corporation at the time the dividend was paid, except where the dividend was paid to a controlling corporation in respect of the particular corporation or to a specified person (within the meaning assigned by paragraph (*h*) of the definition "taxable preferred share" in subsection 248(1)) in relation to such a controlling corporation,

(*d*) paid by a mortgage investment corporation, or

(*e*) that is a capital gains dividend within the meaning assigned by subsection 131(1);

"financial intermediary corporation" —"financial intermediary corporation" means a corporation that is

(*a*) a corporation described in subparagraph (*b*)(ii) of the definition "retirement savings plan" in subsection 146(1),

(*b*) an investment corporation,

(*c*) a mortgage investment corporation,

(*d*) a mutual fund corporation,

(*e*) a prescribed venture capital corporation, or

(*f*) a prescribed labour-sponsored venture capital corporation,

but does not include

(*g*) a prescribed corporation,

(*h*) a corporation that is controlled by or for the benefit of one or more corporations (each of which is referred to in this subsection as a "controlling corporation") other than financial intermediary corporations or private holding corporations unless the controlling corporations and specified persons (within the meaning assigned by paragraph (*h*) of the definition "taxable preferred share" in subsection 248(1)) in relation to the controlling corporations do not own in the aggregate shares of the capital stock of the corporation having a fair market value of more than 10% of the fair market value of all of the issued and outstanding shares of the capital stock of the corporation (those fair market values being determined without regard to any voting rights attaching to those shares), or

(*i*) any particular corporation in which another corporation (other than a financial intermediary corporation or a private holding corporation) has a substantial interest unless the other corporation and specified persons (within the meaning assigned by paragraph (*h*) of the definition "taxable preferred share" in subsection 248(1)) in relation to the other corporation do not own in the aggregate shares of the capital stock of the particular corporation having a fair market value of more than 10% of the fair market value of all of the issued and outstanding shares of the capital stock of the particular corporation (those fair market values being determined without regard to any voting rights attaching to those shares);

Related Regulations: 6700, 6701.

"private holding corporation" —"private holding corporation" means a private corporation the only undertaking of which is the investing of its funds, but does not include

(*a*) a specified financial institution,

(*b*) any particular corporation that owns shares of another corporation in which it has a substantial interest, except where the other corporation would, but for that substantial interest, be a financial intermediary corporation or a private holding corporation, or

(*c*) any particular corporation in which another corporation owns shares and has a substantial interest, except where the other corporation would, but for that substantial interest, be a private holding corporation.

Related Regulations: 6700, 6701.

Related Sections: S. 248(1), "specified financial institution"; s. 253.1 Investments in limited partnerships.

► 191(2) ◄

(2) Substantial interest. For the purposes of this Part, a shareholder has a substantial interest in a corporation at any time if the corporation is a taxable Canadian corporation and

(*a*) the shareholder is related (otherwise than by reason of a right referred to in paragraph 251(5)(*b*)) to the corporation at that time; or

(*b*) the shareholder owned, at that time,

(i) shares of the capital stock of the corporation that would give the shareholder 25% or more of the votes that could be cast under all circumstances at an annual meeting of shareholders of the corporation,

(ii) shares of the capital stock of the corporation having a fair market value of 25% or more of the fair market value of all the issued shares of the capital stock of the corporation,

and either

(iii) shares (other than shares that would be taxable preferred shares if the definition "taxable preferred share" in subsection 248(1) were read without reference to subparagraph (*b*)(iv) thereof and if they were issued after June 18, 1987 and were not grandfathered shares) of the capital stock of the corporation having a fair market value of 25% or more of the fair market value of all those shares of the capital stock of the corporation, or

(iv) in respect of each class of shares of the capital stock of the corporation, shares of that class having a fair market value of 25% or more of the fair market value of all the issued shares of that class,

and for the purposes of this paragraph, a shareholder shall be deemed to own at any time each share of the capital stock of a corporation that is owned, otherwise than by reason of this paragraph, at that time by a person to whom the shareholder is related (otherwise than by reason of a right referred to in paragraph 251(5)(*b*)).

Editorial Note: A dividend paid by a corporation to a shareholder having a "substantial interest" in the corporation is exempt from Part VI.1 tax as an "excluded dividend". A shareholder can have a substantial interest in a corporation based on either of the following: (a) the shareholder is related to the corporation at the particular time (otherwise than by reason of a right to acquire shares etc. (i.e., referred to in s. 251(5)(*b*)); or (b) the shareholder owns shares that represent 25% or more of both the "votes and value" and either: (i) 25% or more (on a fair market value basis) of the shares of the corporation that are not taxable preferred shares; or (ii) 25% or more (on a fair market value basis) of each class of shares of the corporation.

A shareholder is usually considered to own any shares owned by a related person. See also the additional requirements in s. 191(3). Notably, there are more stringent requirements in the case of a shareholder which is a partnership or trust.

Related Sections: S. 191(3) Substantial interest — anti-avoidance rule; s. 248(11) Compound interest; s. 251(2) Definition of "related persons".

Canadian Tax Foundation: Diep, *Preferred Share Rules: The Expected, Unexpected and Unintended*, 2017 Prairie Provinces Tax Conference 13:1–29.

► 191(3) ◄

(3) Idem. Notwithstanding subsection (2),

(*a*) where it can reasonably be considered that the principal purpose for a person acquiring an interest that would, but for this subsection, be a substantial interest in a corporation is to avoid or limit the application of Part I or IV.1 or this Part, the person shall be deemed not to have a substantial interest in the corporation;

(*b*) where it can reasonably be considered that the principal purpose for an acquisition of a share of the capital stock of a corporation (in this paragraph referred to as the "issuer") by any person (in this paragraph referred to as the "acquirer") who had, immediately after the time of the acquisition, a substantial interest in the issuer from another person who did not, immediately before that time, have a substantial interest in the issuer, was to avoid or limit the application of Part I or IV.1 or this Part with respect to a dividend on the share, the acquirer and specified persons (within the meaning assigned by paragraph (*h*) of the definition "taxable preferred share" in subsection 248(1)) in relation to the acquirer shall be deemed not to have a substantial interest in the issuer with respect to any dividend paid on the share;

(*c*) a corporation described in paragraphs (*a*) to (*f*) of the definition "financial intermediary corporation" in subsection (1) shall be deemed not to have a substantial interest in another corporation unless it is related (otherwise than by reason of a right referred to in paragraph 251(5)(*b*)) to the other corporation;

(*d*) any partnership or trust, other than

(i) a partnership all the members of which are related to each other otherwise than by reason of a right referred to in paragraph 251(5)(*b*),

(ii) a trust in which each person who is beneficially interested is

(A) related (otherwise than because of a right referred to in paragraph 251(5)(*b*)) to each other person who is beneficially interested in the trust and who is not a registered charity, or

(B) a registered charity

and, for the purpose of this subparagraph, where a particular person who is beneficially interested in the trust is an aunt, uncle, niece or nephew of another person, the particular person and any person who is a child or descendant of the particular person shall be deemed to be related to the other person and to any person who is the child or descendant of the other person, or

(iii) a trust in which only one person (other than a registered charity) is beneficially interested,

shall be deemed not to have a substantial interest in a corporation; and

(*e*) where at any time a shareholder holds a share of the capital stock of a corporation to which paragraph (*g*) of the definition "taxable preferred share" in subsection 248(1) or paragraph (*e*) of the definition "taxable RFI share" in that subsection applies to deem the share to be a taxable preferred share or a taxable RFI share, the shareholder shall be deemed not to have a substantial interest in the corporation at that time.

Related Sections: S. 104(1) Reference to trust or estate; s. 191(1), "financial intermediary corporation"; s. 191(2) Substantial interest; s. 248(1), "corporation", "dividend", "registered charity", "share", "shareholder", "taxable preferred share", "taxable RFI share", "trust"; s. 248(25) Beneficially interested; s. 252(1) Extended meaning of "child"; Part IV.

► 191(4) ◄

(4) Deemed dividends. Where at any particular time

(*a*) a share of the capital stock of a corporation is issued,

(*b*) the terms or conditions of a share of the capital stock of a corporation are changed, or

(*c*) an agreement in respect of a share of the capital stock of a corporation is changed or entered into,

and the terms or conditions of the share or the agreement in respect of the share specify an amount in respect of the share, including an amount for which the share is to be redeemed, acquired or cancelled (together with, where so provided, any accrued and unpaid dividends thereon) and where paragraph (*a*) applies, the specified amount does not exceed the fair market value of the consideration for which the share was issued, and where paragraph (*b*) or (*c*) applies, the specified amount does not exceed the fair market value of the share immediately before the particular time, the amount of any dividend deemed to have been paid on a redemption, acquisition or cancellation of the share to which subsection 84(2) or (3) applies shall

(*d*) for the purposes of this Part and section 187.2, be deemed to be an excluded dividend and an excepted dividend, respectively, unless

(i) where paragraph (*a*) applies, the share was issued for consideration that included a taxable preferred share, or

(ii) where paragraph (*b*) or (*c*) applies, the share was, immediately before the particular time, a taxable preferred share, and

(*e*) be deemed not to be a dividend to which subsection 112(2.1) or 138(6) applies to deny a deduction with respect to the dividend in computing the taxable income of a corporation under subsection 112(1) or (2) or 138(6), unless

(i) where paragraph (*a*) applies, the share was issued for consideration that included a term preferred share or for the purpose of raising capital or as part of a series of transactions or events the purpose of which was to raise capital, and

(ii) where paragraph (*b*) or (*c*) applies, the share was, immediately before the particular time, a term preferred share, or the terms or conditions of the share were changed, or the agreement in respect of the share was changed or entered into for the purpose of raising capital or as part of a series of transactions or events the purpose of which was to raise capital.

Editorial Note: S. 191(4) and (5) provide exemptions from Part VI.1 tax in respect of deemed dividends arising under ss. 84(2) and (3) (relating to redemptions, acquisitions, etc.) which will apply in respect of many reorganizations, etc. The provisions may apply to exempt such a dividend where the terms or conditions of the share or an agreement in respect of the share specify an amount for which the share is to be redeemed, acquired or cancelled, which amount does not exceed the fair market value of the consideration for which the share was issued. Where either the terms or conditions of the share are changed or an agreement in respect of the share is changed or entered into, the specified amount cannot exceed the fair market value of the share immediately before the particular time (the shares must not have been "exchanged" for other taxable preferred shares — see s. 191(4)(*d*)). The CRA's administrative position is that a specified amount must be a fixed dollar amount, not subject to adjustment nor fixed by formula.

Related Sections: S. 248(10) Series of transactions; s. 256(1) Associated corporations.

Tax Profile: December 2004 — Taxation of Dividends: A Survey in the Context of Private Corporations and Their Shareholders — Part 2.

Tax Window Files: S. 191(4) and PAC, *May 4, 2016*, CRA Document No. 2016-0634551E5; Partie VI.1: Dividende Réputé Exclu, *October 5, 2007*, CRA Document No. 2007-0243101C6.

► 191(5) ◄

(5) Where subsection (4) does not apply. Subsection (4) does not apply to the extent that the total of

(*a*) the amount paid on the redemption, acquisition or cancellation of the share, and

(*b*) all amounts each of which is an amount (other than an amount deemed by subsection 84(4) to be a dividend) paid, after the particular time and before the redemption, acquisition or cancellation of the share, on a reduction of the paid-up capital of the corporation in respect of the share

exceeds the specified amount referred to in subsection (4).

Editorial Note: S. 191(5) limits the application of the s. 191(4) exemption to the extent that the total of the amount paid on the redemption, acquisition or cancellation of the share and all amounts paid upon a reduction in the paid-up capital of the share (other than an amount deemed to be a dividend under s. 84(4)) exceeds the specified amount referred to in subsection (4).

► 191(6) ◄

(6) Excluded dividend — partner. If at any time a corporation pays a dividend to a partnership, the corporation is, for the purposes of this subsection and paragraph (*a*) of the definition "excluded dividend" in subsection (1), deemed to have paid at that time to each member of the partnership a dividend equal to the amount determined by the formula

$$A \times B$$

where

A is the amount of the dividend paid to the partnership; and

B is the member's specified proportion for the last fiscal period of the partnership that ended before that time (or, if the partnership's first fiscal period includes that time, for that first fiscal period).

History: S. 191(6) was added by S.C. 2013, c. 34, s. 332(1), applicable to dividends paid after December 20, 2002.

SECTION 191.1: Tax on taxable dividends

► 191.1(1) ◄

(1) Tax on taxable dividends. Every taxable Canadian corporation shall pay a tax under this Part for each taxation year equal to the amount, if any, by which

(*a*) the total of

(i) the amount determined by multiplying the amount by which the total of all taxable dividends (other than excluded dividends) paid by the corporation in the year and after 1987 on short-term preferred shares exceeds the corporation's dividend allowance for the year, by

(A) 50% for dividends paid in a taxation year that ends before 2010,

(B) 45% for dividends paid in a taxation year that ends after 2009 and before 2012,

(C) 40% for dividends paid in a taxation year that ends after 2011,

(ii) 40% of the amount, if any, by which the total of all taxable dividends (other than excluded dividends) paid by the corporation in the year and after 1987 on taxable preferred shares (other than short-term preferred shares) of all classes in respect of which an election under subsection 191.2(1) has been made exceeds the amount, if any, by which the corporation's dividend allowance for the year exceeds the total of the dividends referred to in subparagraph (i),

(iii) 25% of the amount, if any, by which the total of all taxable dividends (other than excluded dividends) paid by the corporation in the year and after 1987 on taxable preferred shares (other than short-term preferred shares) of all classes in respect of which an election under subsection 191.2(1) has not been made exceeds the amount, if any, by which the corporation's dividend allowance for the year exceeds the total of the dividends referred to in subparagraphs (i) and (ii), and

(iv) the total of all amounts each of which is an amount determined for the year in respect of the corporation under paragraph 191.3(1)(*d*)

exceeds

(*b*) the total of all amounts each of which is an amount determined for the year in respect of the corporation under paragraph 191.3(1)(*c*).

Editorial Note: Parts IV.1 and VI.1 may be applicable in respect of many situations involving private corporations, where larger actual or deemed dividends (e.g., on a redemption of shares) are involved. The definition of "taxable preferred share" in s. 248(1) is very broad and includes most shares (including "freeze shares") with special arrangements relating to dividends, repayment (e.g., on liquidation, redemption, or reduction of paid-up capital), protection from losses, or returns. Such an arrangement may be in a shareholder's or other agreement, rather than the actual share terms. Tax under s. 191.1(1) is deductible from taxable income under s. 110(1)(*k*) (3.5 times the tax, for taxation years that end after 2011).

Important exceptions may include the annual dividend allowance in s. 191.1(2) ($500,000 per associated group of corporations), dividends received by shareholders with a "substantial interest" in the payer, and s. 191(4), which may exempt a specified amount for which the share is to be redeemed, acquired, or cancelled.

History: S. 191.1(1)(*a*)(i) was replaced by S.C. 2013, c. 34, s. 333(1), applicable to the 2003 and subsequent taxation years, and formerly read:

(i) $66^2/_3$% of the amount, if any, by which the total of all taxable dividends (other than excluded dividends) paid by the corporation in the year and after 1987 on short-term preferred shares exceeds the corporation's dividend allowance for the year,

Related Sections: S. 87(4.2) Exchanged shares — amalgamations after November 27, 1986; 89(1), "taxable Canadian corporation", "taxable dividend"; s. 110(1)(*k*) Part VI.1 tax; s. 157(1) Payment by corporations; s. 186(1.1) Reduction where Part IV.1 tax payable; s. 190.11 Taxable capital employed in Canada; s. 191 Tax on corporations paying dividends on taxable preferred shares; s. 191.2(1) Election; s. 191.3(1) Agreement respecting liability for tax; s. 227(14) Application of other Parts; s. 248(1), "amount", "short-term preferred share", "taxable preferred share"; Part IV.1.

Canadian Tax Foundation: Jung, *The Taxable Preferred Share Rules and the Private Corporation*, 2017 Ontario Tax Conference 12:1–20; Diep, *Preferred Share Rules: The Expected, Unexpected and Unintended*, 2017 Prairie Provinces Tax Conference 13:1–29; Moskowitz, *The Preferred Share Rules: Yes They Can Apply to You!*, 1997 Conference Report 9:1–47.

Tax Profile: October 2012 — Exchangeable Shares in Canada; February 2012 — Post-Mortem Planning — Double Taxation on Death; December 2004 — Taxation of Dividends: A Survey in the Context of Private Corporations and Their Shareholders — Part 2.

Forms: T2 SCH 43 — Calculation of Parts IV.1 and VI.1 Taxes.

▶ 191.1(2) ◀

(2) Dividend allowance. For the purposes of this section, a taxable Canadian corporation's "dividend allowance" for a taxation year is the amount, if any, by which

(*a*) $500,000

exceeds

(*b*) the amount, if any, by which the total of taxable dividends (other than excluded dividends) paid by it on taxable preferred shares, or shares that would be taxable preferred shares if they were issued after June 18, 1987 and were not grandfathered shares, in the calendar year immediately preceding the calendar year in which the taxation year ended exceeds $1,000,000,

unless the corporation is associated in the taxation year with one or more other taxable Canadian corporations, in which case, except as otherwise provided in this section, its dividend allowance for the year is nil.

▶ 191.1(3) ◀

(3) Associated corporations. If all of the taxable Canadian corporations that are associated with each other in a taxation year and that have paid taxable dividends (other than excluded dividends) on taxable preferred shares in the year have filed with the Minister in prescribed form an agreement whereby, for the purposes of this section, they allocate an amount to one or more of them for the taxation year, and the amount so allocated or the total of the amounts so allocated, as the case may be, is equal to the total dividend allowance for the year of those corporations and all other taxable Canadian corporations with which each such corporation is associated in the year, the dividend allowance for the year for each of the corporations is the amount so allocated to it.

Related Sections: S. 89(1), "taxable Canadian corporation", "taxable dividend"; s. 248(1), "short-term preferred share", "taxable preferred shares"; s. 249 Definition of "taxation year".

Forms: T2 SCH 45 — Agreement Respecting Liability for Part VI.1 Tax.

▶ 191.1(4) ◀

(4) Total dividend allowance. For the purposes of this section, the "total dividend allowance" of a group of taxable Canadian corporations that are associated with each other in a taxation year is the amount, if any, by which

(*a*) $500,000

exceeds

(*b*) the amount, if any, by which the total of taxable dividends (other than excluded dividends) paid by those corporations on taxable preferred shares, or shares that would be taxable preferred shares if they were issued after June 18, 1987 and were not grandfathered shares, in the calendar year immediately preceding the calendar year in which the taxation year ended exceeds $1,000,000.

▶ 191.1(5) ◀

(5) Failure to file agreement. If any of the taxable Canadian corporations that are associated with each other in a taxation year and that have paid taxable dividends (other than excluded dividends) on taxable preferred shares in the year has failed to file with the Minister an agreement as contemplated by subsection (3) within 30 days after notice in writing by the Minister has been forwarded to any of them that such an agreement is required for the purpose of any assessment of tax under this Part, the Minister shall, for the purpose of this section, allocate an amount to one or more of them for the taxation year, which amount or the total of which amounts, as the case may be, shall equal the total dividend allowance for the year for those corporations and all other taxable Canadian corporations with which each such corporation is associated in the year, and the dividend allowance for the year of each of the corporations is the amount so allocated to it.

▶ 191.1(6) ◀

(6) Dividend allowance in short years. Notwithstanding any other provision of this section,

(*a*) where a corporation has a taxation year that is less than 51 weeks, its dividend allowance for the year is that proportion of its dividend allowance for the year determined without reference to this paragraph that the number of days in the year is of 365; and

(*b*) where a taxable Canadian corporation (in this paragraph referred to as the "first corporation") has more than one taxation year ending in a calendar year and is associated in two or more of those taxation years with another taxable Canadian corporation that has a taxation year ending in that calendar year, the dividend allowance of the first corporation for each taxation year in which it is associated with the other corporation ending in that calendar year is, subject to the application of paragraph (*a*), an amount equal to the amount that would be its dividend allowance for the first such taxation year if the allowance were determined without reference to paragraph (*a*).

SECTION 191.2: Election

▶ 191.2(1) ◀

(1) Election. For the purposes of determining the tax payable by reason of subparagraphs 191.1(1)(*a*)(ii) and (iii), a taxable Canadian corporation (other than a financial intermediary corporation or a private holding corporation) may make an election with respect to a class of its taxable preferred shares the terms and conditions of which require an election to be made under this subsection by filing a prescribed form with the Minister

(*a*) not later than the day on or before which its return of income under Part I is required by section 150 to be filed for the taxation year in which shares of that class are first issued or first become taxable preferred shares; or

(*b*) within the 6 month period commencing on any of the following days, namely,

(i) the day of sending of any notice of assessment of tax payable under this Part or Part I by the corporation for that year,

(ii) where the corporation has served a notice of objection to an assessment described in subparagraph (i), the day of sending of a notice that the Minister has confirmed or varied the assessment,

(iii) where the corporation has instituted an appeal in respect of an assessment described in subparagraph (i) to the Tax Court of Canada, the day of mailing of a copy of the decision of the Court to the taxpayer, and

(iv) where the corporation has instituted an appeal in respect of an assessment described in subparagraph (i) to the Federal Court of Appeal or the Supreme Court of Canada, the day on which the judgment of the Court is pronounced or delivered or the day on which the corporation discontinues the appeal.

History: S. 191.2(1)(*b*)(i) and (ii) were replaced by S.C. 2010, c. 25, s. 53, in force on Royal Assent, December 15, 2010. S. 191.2(1)(*b*)(i) and (ii) formerly read:

(i) the day of mailing of any notice of assessment of tax payable under this Part or Part I by the corporation for that year,

(ii) where the corporation has served a notice of objection to an assessment described in subparagraph (i), the day of mailing of a notice that the Minister has confirmed or varied the assessment,

Related Sections: S. 89(1), "taxable Canadian corporation"; s. 248(1), "taxable preferred shares".

▶ 191.2(2) ◀

(2) Time of election. An election with respect to a class of taxable preferred shares filed in accordance with subsection (1) shall be deemed to have been filed before any dividend on a share of that class is paid.

▶ 191.2(3) ◀

(3) Assessment. Where an election has been filed under subsection (1), the Minister shall, notwithstanding subsections 152(4) and (5), assess or reassess the tax, interest or penalties payable under this Act by any corporation for any relevant taxation year in order to take into account the election.

SECTION 191.3: Agreement respecting liability for tax

▶ 191.3(1) ◀

(1) Agreement respecting liability for tax. Where a corporation (in this section referred to as the "transferor corporation") and a taxable Canadian corporation (in this section referred to as the "transferee corporation") that was related (otherwise than because of a right referred to in paragraph 251(5)(*b*) or because of the control of any corporation by Her Majesty in right of Canada or a province) to the transferor corporation

(*a*) throughout a particular taxation year of the transferor corporation (or, where the transferee corporation came into existence in that year, throughout the part of that year in which the transferee corporation was in existence), and

(*b*) throughout the last taxation year of the transferee corporation ending at or before the end of the particular taxation year (or, where the transferor corporation came into existence in that last taxation year of the transferee corporation, throughout that part of that last year in which the transferor corporation was in existence)

file as provided in subsection (2) an agreement or amended agreement with the Minister under which the transferee corporation agrees to pay all or any portion, as is specified in the agreement, of the tax for that taxation year of the transferor corporation that would, but for the agreement, be payable under this Part by the transferor corporation (other than any tax payable by the transferor corporation by reason of another agreement made under this section), the following rules apply, namely,

(*c*) the amount of tax specified in the agreement is an amount determined for that taxation year of the transferor corporation in respect of the transferor corporation for the purpose of paragraph 191.1(1)(*b*),

(*d*) the amount of tax specified in the agreement is an amount determined in respect of the transferee corporation for its last taxation year ending at or before the end of that taxation year of the transferor corporation for the purpose of subparagraph 191.1(1)(*a*)(iv), and

(*e*) the transferor corporation and the transferee corporation are jointly and severally, or solidarily, liable to pay the amount of tax specified in the agreement and any interest or penalty in respect thereof.

History: S. 191.3(1)(*e*) was replaced by S.C. 2013, c. 34, s. 153(1), in force June 26, 2013, and formerly read:

(*e*) the transferor corporation and the transferee corporation are jointly and severally liable to pay the amount of tax specified in the agreement and any interest or penalty in respect thereof.

Related Sections: S. 89(1), "taxable Canadian corporation".

Forms: T2 SCH 45 — T2SCH45 Agreement Respecting Liability for Part VI.1 Tax.

► 191.3(1.1) ◄

(1.1) Consideration for agreement. For the purposes of Part I of this Act, where property is acquired at any time by a transferee corporation as consideration for entering into an agreement with a transferor corporation that is filed under this section,

(*a*) where the property was owned by the transferor corporation immediately before that time,

(i) the transferor corporation shall be deemed to have disposed of the property at that time for proceeds equal to the fair market value of the property at that time, and

(ii) the transferor corporation shall not be entitled to deduct any amount in computing its income as a consequence of the transfer of the property, except any amount arising as a consequence of subparagraph (i);

(*b*) the cost at which the property was acquired by the transferee corporation at that time shall be deemed to be equal to the fair market value of the property at that time;

(*c*) the transferee corporation shall not be required to add an amount in computing its income solely because of the acquisition at that time of the property; and

(*d*) no benefit shall be deemed to have been conferred on the transferor corporation as a consequence of the transferor corporation entering into an agreement filed under this section.

► 191.3(2) ◄

(2) Manner of filing agreement. An agreement or amended agreement referred to in subsection (1) between a transferor corporation and a transferee corporation shall be deemed not to have been filed with the Minister unless

(*a*) it is in prescribed form;

(*b*) it is filed on or before the day on or before which the transferor corporation's return for the year in respect of which the agreement is filed is required to be filed under this Part or within the 90-day period beginning on the day of sending of a notice of assessment of tax payable under this Part or Part I by the transferor corporation for the year or by the transferee corporation for its taxation year ending in the calendar year in which the taxation year of the transferor corporation ends or the sending of a notification that no tax is payable under this Part or Part I for that taxation year;

(*c*) it is accompanied by,

(i) where the directors of the transferor corporation are legally entitled to administer its affairs, a certified copy of their resolution authorizing the agreement to be made,

(ii) where the directors of the transferor corporation are not legally entitled to administer its affairs, a certified copy of the document by which the person legally entitled to administer the corporation's affairs authorized the agreement to be made,

(iii) where the directors of the transferee corporation are legally entitled to administer its affairs, a certified copy of their resolution authorizing the agreement to be made, and

(iv) where the directors of the transferee corporation are not legally entitled to administer its affairs, a certified copy of the document by which the person legally entitled to administer the corporation's affairs authorized the agreement to be made; and

(*d*) where the agreement is not an agreement to which subsection (4) applies, an agreement amending the agreement has not been filed in accordance with this section.

(*e*) (Repealed by S.C. 1994, c. 7, Sched. II, s. 163(1).)

History: S. 191.3(2)(*b*) was replaced by S.C. 2010, c. 25, s. 54, in force on Royal Assent, December 15, 2010. S. 191.3(2)(*b*) formerly read:

(*b*) it is filed on or before the day on or before which the transferor corporation's return for the year in respect of which the agreement is filed is required to be filed under this Part or within the 90 day period commencing on the day of mailing of a notice of assessment of tax payable under this Part or Part I by the transferor corporation for the year or by the transferee corporation for its taxation year ending in the calendar year in which the taxation year of the transferor corporation ends or the mailing of a notification that no tax is payable under this Part or Part I for that taxation year;

► 191.3(3) ◄

(3) Assessment. Where an agreement or amended agreement between a transferor corporation and a transferee corporation has been filed under this section with the Minister, the Minister shall, notwithstanding subsections 152(4) and (5), assess or reassess the tax, interest and penalties payable under this Act by the transferor corporation and the transferee corporation for any relevant taxation year in order to take into account the agreement or amended agreement.

► 191.3(4) ◄

(4) Related corporations. Where, at any time, a corporation has become related to another corporation and it may reasonably be considered, having regard to all the circumstances, that the main purpose of the corporation becoming related to the other corporation was to transfer, by filing an agreement or an amended agreement under this section, the benefit of a deduction under paragraph 110(1)(*k*) to a transferee corporation, the amount of the tax specified in the agreement shall, for the purposes of paragraph (1)(*c*), be deemed to be nil.

► 191.3(5) ◄

(5) Assessment of transferor corporation. The Minister may at any time assess a transferor corporation in respect of any amount for which it is jointly and severally, or solidarily, liable by reason of paragraph (1)(*e*) and the provisions of Division I of Part I are applicable in respect of the assessment as though it had been made under section 152.

History: S. 191.3(5) was replaced by S.C. 2013, c. 34, s. 153(2), in force June 26, 2013, and formerly read:

(5) *Assessment of transferor corporation.* The Minister may at any time assess a transferor corporation in respect of any amount for which it is jointly and severally liable by reason of paragraph (1)(*e*) and the provisions of Division I of Part I are applicable in respect of the assessment as though it had been made under section 152.

► 191.3(6) ◄

(6) Payment by transferor corporation. If a transferor corporation and a transferee corporation are by reason of paragraph (1)(*e*) jointly and severally, or solidarily, liable in respect of tax payable by the transferee corporation under subparagraph 191.1(1)(*a*)(iv) and any interest or penalty in respect thereof, the following rules apply:

(*a*) a payment by the transferor corporation on account of the liability shall, to the extent thereof, discharge their liability; and

(*b*) a payment by the transferee corporation on account of its liability discharges the transferor corporation's liability only to the extent that the payment operates to reduce the transferee corporation's liability under this Act to an amount less than the amount in respect of which the transferor corporation was, by paragraph (1)(*e*), made jointly and severally, or solidarily, liable.

History: S. 191.3(6), the portion before paragraph (*a*) was replaced by S.C. 2013, c. 34, s. 153(3), in force June 26, 2013, and formerly read:

(6) *Payment by transferor corporation.* Where a transferor corporation and a transferee corporation are by reason of paragraph (1)(*e*) jointly and severally liable in respect of tax payable by the transferee corporation under subparagraph 191.1(1)(*a*)(iv) and any interest or penalty in respect thereof, the following rules apply:

S. 191.3(6)(*a*) was replaced by S.C. 2013, c. 34, s. 153(4), in force June 26, 2013, and formerly read:

(*a*) a payment by the transferor corporation on account of the liability shall, to the extent thereof, discharge the joint liability; and

S. 191.3(6)(*b*) was replaced by S.C. 2013, c. 34, s. 153(5), in force June 26, 2013, and formerly read:

(*b*) a payment by the transferee corporation on account of its liability discharges the transferor corporation's liability only to the extent that the payment operates to reduce the transferee corporation's liability under this Act to an amount less than the amount in respect of which the transferor corporation was, by paragraph (1)(*e*), made jointly and severally liable.

SECTION 191.4: Information return

► 191.4(1) ◄

(1) Information return. Every corporation that is or would, but for section 191.3, be liable to pay tax under this Part for a taxation year shall, not later than the day on or before which it is required by section 150 to file its return of income for the year under Part I, file with the Minister a return for the year under this Part in prescribed form containing an estimate of the tax payable by it under this Part for the year.

Forms: T2 SCH 43 — Calculation of Parts IV.1 and VI.1 Taxes.

► 191.4(2) ◄

(2) Provisions applicable to Part. Sections 152, 158 and 159, subsection 161(11), sections 162 to 167 and Division J of Part I apply to this Part with such modifications as the circumstances require.

► 191.4(3) ◄

(3) Provisions applicable — Crown corporations. Section 27 applies to this Part with any modifications that the circumstances require.

Related Sections: S. 181.71 Provisions applicable — Crown corporations; s. 187.61 Provisions applicable — Crown corporations; s. 190.211 Provisions applicable — Crown corporations.

Part VII
Refundable Tax on Corporations Issuing Qualifying Shares

SECTION 192: Corporation to pay tax

► 192(1) ◄

(1) Corporation to pay tax. Every corporation shall pay a tax under this Part for a taxation year equal to the total of all amounts each of which is an amount designated under subsection (4) in respect of a share issued by it in the year.

Interpretation Bulletins: *Secondary* — IT-328R3 Losses on shares on which dividends have been received.

► 192(2) ◄

(2) Definition of "Part VII refund". In this Part, the "Part VII refund" of a corporation for a taxation year means an amount equal to the lesser of

(*a*) the total of

(i) the amount, if any, by which the share-purchase tax credit of the corporation for the year exceeds the amount, if any, deducted in respect thereof by it for the year under subsection 127.2(1) from its tax otherwise payable under Part I for the year or the amount deemed by subsection 127.2(2) to have been paid on account of its tax payable under Part I for the year, as the case may be, and

(ii) such amount as the corporation may claim, not exceeding the amount that would, if paragraph (*i*) of the definition "investment tax credit" in subsection 127(9) were read without reference to the words "the year or", be its investment tax credit at the end of the year in respect of property acquired, or an expenditure made, after April 19, 1983 and on or before the last day of the year, and

(*b*) the refundable Part VII tax on hand of the corporation at the end of the year.

► 192(3) ◄

(3) Definition of "refundable Part VII tax on hand". In this Part, "refundable Part VII tax on hand" of a corporation at the end of a taxation year means the amount, if any, by which

(*a*) the total of the taxes payable by it under this Part for the year and all preceding taxation years

exceeds the total of

(*b*) the total of its Part VII refunds for all preceding taxation years, and

(*c*) the total of all amounts each of which is an amount of tax included in the total described in paragraph (*a*) in respect of a share that was issued by the corporation and that, at the time it was issued, was not a qualifying share.

► 192(4) ◄

(4) Corporation may designate amount. Every taxable Canadian corporation may, by filing a prescribed form with the Minister at any time on or before the last day of the month immediately following the month in which it issued a qualifying share of its capital stock (other than a share issued before July, 1983 or after 1986, or a share in respect of which the corporation has, on or before that day, designated an amount under subsection 194(4)), designate, for the purposes of this Part and Part I, an amount in respect of that share not exceeding 25% of the amount by which

(*a*) the amount of the consideration for which the share was issued

exceeds

(*b*) the amount of any assistance (other than an amount included in computing the share-purchase tax credit of a taxpayer in respect of that share) provided or to be provided by a government, municipality or any other public authority in respect of, or for the acquisition of, the share.

Related Regulations: 227; 5101 [Small business investment corporation]; 5102 [Small business investment limited partnership]; 5103 [Small business investment trust].

Related Sections: S. 89(1)(*l*), "taxable Canadian corporation"; s. 127.2 Share-purchase tax credit; s. 192(4.1) Computing paid-up capital after designation; s. 192(6) Definition of "qualifying share".

► 192(4.1) ◄

(4.1) Computing paid-up capital after designation. Where a corporation has designated an amount under subsection (4) in respect of shares issued at any time after May 23, 1985, in computing, at any particular time after that time, the paid-up capital in respect of the class of shares of the capital stock of the corporation that includes those shares

(*a*) there shall be deducted the amount, if any, by which

(i) the increase as a result of the issue of those shares in the paid-up capital in respect of all shares of that class, determined without reference to this subsection as it applies to those shares,

exceeds

(ii) the amount, if any, by which the total amount of consideration for which those shares were issued exceeds the total amount designated by the corporation under subsection (4) in respect of those shares; and

(*b*) there shall be added an amount equal to the lesser of

(i) the amount, if any, by which

(A) the total of all amounts each of which is an amount deemed by subsection 84(3), (4) or (4.1) to be a dividend on shares of that class paid by the corporation after May 23, 1985 and before the particular time

exceeds

(B) the total that would be determined under clause (A) if this Act were read without reference to paragraph (*a*), and

(ii) the total of all amounts each of which is an amount required by paragraph (*a*) to be deducted in computing the paid-up capital in respect of that class of shares after May 23, 1985 and before the particular time.

Cases: The filing by the issuer of Form T-2110 designating the shares as "qualified shares" is fundamental to the investors' entitlement to an SPTC in respect of those shares and is not a mere administrative requirement but a statutory pre-condition. *598606 Ontario Ltd. v. the Queen*, 93 DTC 142 (T.C.C.)

▶ 192(5) ◀

(5) Presumption. For the purposes of this Act, the Part VII refund of a corporation for a taxation year shall be deemed to be an amount paid on account of its tax under this Part for the year on the last day of the second month following the end of the year.

▶ 192(6) ◀

(6) Definition of "qualifying share". In this Part, "qualifying share", at any time, means a prescribed share of the capital stock of a taxable Canadian corporation issued after May 22, 1985 and before 1987.

Related Regulations: 6203.

Interpretation Bulletins: *Secondary* — IT-113R4 Benefits to employees — Stock options.

▶ 192(7) ◀

(7) Effect of obligation to acquire shares. When determining under section 251 whether a corporation and any other person do not deal with each other at arm's length for the purposes of any regulations made for the purposes of subsection (6), a person who has an obligation in equity, under a contract or otherwise, either immediately or in the future and either absolutely or contingently, to acquire shares in a corporation, shall be deemed to be in the same position in relation to the control of the corporation as if that person owned the shares.

▶ 192(8) ◀

(8) Late designation. Where a taxable Canadian corporation that issued a share does not designate an amount under subsection (4) in respect of the share on or before the day on or before which the designation was required by that subsection, the corporation shall be deemed to have made the designation on that day if

(*a*) the corporation has filed with the Minister a prescribed information return relating to the share-purchase tax credit in respect of the share within the time that it would have been so required to file the return had the designation been made on that day, and

(*b*) within 3 years after that day, the corporation has

(i) designated an amount in respect of the share by filing a prescribed form with the Minister, and

(ii) paid to the Receiver General, at the time the prescribed form referred to in subparagraph (i) is filed, an amount that is a reasonable estimate of the penalty payable by the corporation for the late designation in respect of the share,

except that, where the Minister has mailed a notice to the corporation that a designation has not been made in respect of the share under subsection (4), the designation and payment described in paragraph (*b*) must be made by the corporation on or before the day that is 90 days after the day of the mailing.

▶ 192(9) ◀

(9) Penalty for late designation. Where, pursuant to subsection (8), a corporation made a late designation in respect of a share issued in a month, the corporation shall pay, for each month or part of a month that elapsed during the period beginning on the last day on or before which an amount could have been designated by the corporation under subsection (4) in respect of the share and ending on the day that the late designation is made, a penalty for the late designation in respect of the share in an amount equal to 1% of the amount designated in respect of the share, except that the maximum penalty payable under this subsection by the corporation for a month shall not exceed $500.

▶ 192(10) ◀

(10) Deemed deduction. For the purposes of this Act, other than the definition "investment tax credit" in subsection 127(9), the amount, if any, claimed under subparagraph (2)(*a*)(ii) by a taxpayer for a taxation year shall be deemed to have been deducted by the taxpayer under subsection 127(5) for the year.

▶ 192(11) ◀

(11) Restriction. Where at any time a corporation has designated an amount under subsection (4) in respect of a share, no amount may be designated by the corporation at any subsequent time in respect of that share.

SECTION 193: Corporation to file return

▶ 193(1) ◀

(1) Corporation to file return. Every corporation that is liable to pay tax under this Part for a taxation year shall, on or before the day on or before which it is required to file its return of income under Part I for the year, file with the Minister a return for the year under this Part in prescribed form.

▶ 193(2) ◀

(2) Corporation to make payment on account of tax. Where, in a particular month in a taxation year, a corporation issues a share in respect of which it designates an amount under section 192, the corporation shall, on or before the last day of the month following the particular month, pay to the Receiver General on account of its tax payable under this Part for the year an amount equal to the total of all amounts so designated.

Related Regulations: Part XLIII.

▶ 193(3) ◀

(3) Interest. Where a corporation is liable to pay tax under this Part and has failed to pay all or any part or instalment thereof on or before the day on or before which the tax or instalment, as the case may be, was required to be paid, it shall pay to the Receiver General interest at the prescribed rate on the amount that it failed to pay computed from the day on or before which the amount was required to be paid to the day of payment.

Related Regulations: 4301.

Related Sections: S. 248(11) Compound interest.

► 193(4) ◄

(4) Idem. For the purposes of computing interest payable by a corporation under subsection (3) for any month or months in the period commencing on the first day of a taxation year and ending two months after the last day of the year in which period the corporation has designated an amount under section 192 in respect of a share issued by it in a particular month in the year, the corporation shall be deemed to have been liable to pay, on or before the last day of the month immediately following the particular month, a part or an instalment of tax for the year equal to that proportion of the amount, if any, by which its tax payable under this Part for the year exceeds its Part VII refund for the year that

(*a*) the total of all amounts so designated by it under section 192 in respect of shares issued by it in the particular month

is of

(*b*) the total of all amounts so designated by it under section 192 in respect of shares issued by it in the year.

► 193(5) ◄

(5) Evasion of tax. Where a corporation that is liable to pay tax under this Part in respect of a share issued by it wilfully, in any manner whatever, evades or attempts to evade payment of the tax and a purchaser of the share or, where the purchaser is a partnership, a member of the partnership knew or ought to have known, at the time the share was acquired, that the corporation would wilfully evade or attempt to evade the tax, for the purposes of section 127.2, the share shall be deemed not to have been acquired.

► 193(6) ◄

(6) Undue deferral. Where, in a transaction or as part of a series of transactions, a taxpayer acquires a share of a corporation that the taxpayer controls (within the meaning assigned by subsection 186(2)) and it may reasonably be considered that one of the main purposes of the acquisition was to reduce for a period interest on the taxpayer's liability for tax under this Part, the share shall, for the purposes of section 127.2 and this Part (other than this subsection), be deemed not to have been acquired by the taxpayer and not to have been issued by the corporation until the end of that period.

Related Sections: S. 248(10) Series of transactions.

► 193(7) ◄

(7) Avoidance of tax. Where, as part of a series of transactions or events one of the main purposes of which may reasonably be considered to be the avoidance of tax that might otherwise have been or become payable under Part II by any corporation, a particular corporation has issued a share in a taxation year in respect of which it has designated an amount under subsection 192(4), the particular corporation shall, on or before the last day of the second month after the end of the year, pay a tax under this Part for the year equal to 125% of the amount of tax under Part II that is or may be avoided by reason of the series of transactions or events.

Related Sections: S. 248(10) Series of transactions.

► 193(7.1) ◄

(7.1) Tax on excess. Where a corporation has in a taxation year made an election under subsection 127.2(10) in respect of any share that was part of a distribution of shares referred to in that subsection and, at the end of that year or any subsequent taxation year,

(*a*) the total of the amounts designated under subsection 192(4) in respect of those shares as evidenced by the prescribed information returns required by regulation to be filed with the Minister by a taxpayer other than the corporation

exceeds

(*b*) the total of the amounts designated under subsection 192(4) in respect of those shares acquired by the taxpayer and in respect of which another taxpayer was required by regulation to provide the taxpayer with a prescribed information return relating to the designation under that subsection,

the taxpayer is liable to pay a tax under this Part for the taxation year at the end of which there is such an excess equal to the amount of the excess, which tax is to be paid to the Receiver General within 60 days after the end of the taxation year, and the excess shall be included in determining the total under paragraph (*b*) for any taxation year of the taxpayer subsequent to that year.

► 193(8) ◄

(8) Provisions applicable to Part. Sections 151, 152, 158 and 159, subsection 161(11), sections 162 to 167 and Division J of Part I are applicable to this Part with such modifications as the circumstances require.

Part VIII
Refundable Tax on Corporations in Respect of Scientific Research and Experimental Development Tax Credit

SECTION 194: Corporation to pay tax

► 194(1) ◄

(1) Corporation to pay tax. Every corporation shall pay a tax under this Part for a taxation year equal to 50% of the total of all amounts each of which is an amount designated under subsection (4) in respect of a share or debt obligation issued by it in the year or a right granted by it in the year.

► 194(2) ◄

(2) Definition of "Part VIII refund". In this Part, the "Part VIII refund" of a corporation for a taxation year means an amount equal to the lesser of

(*a*) the total of

(i) the amount, if any, by which the scientific research and experimental development tax credit of the corporation for the year exceeds the amount, if any, deducted by it under subsection 127.3(1) from its tax otherwise payable under Part I for the year, and

(ii) such amount as the corporation may claim, not exceeding 50% of the amount, if any, by which

(A) the total of all expenditures made by it after April 19, 1983 and in the year or the immediately preceding taxation year each of which is an expenditure (other than an expenditure prescribed for the purposes of the definition "qualified expenditure" in subsection 127(9)) claimed under paragraph 37(1)(*a*) or (*b*) to the extent that the expenditure is specified by the corporation in its return of income under Part I for the year

exceeds the total of

(B) the total of all expenditures each of which is an expenditure made by it in the immediately preceding taxation year, to the extent that the expenditure was included in determining the total under clause (A) and resulted in

(I) a refund to it under this Part for the immediately preceding taxation year,

(II) a deduction by it under subsection 37(1) for the immediately preceding taxation year, or

(III) a deduction by it under subsection 127(5) for any taxation year, and

(C) twice the portion of the total of amounts each of which is an amount deducted by it in computing its income for the year or the immediately preceding taxation year under section 37.1 that can reasonably be considered to relate to expenditures that were included in determining the total under clause (A), and

(*b*) the refundable Part VIII tax on hand of the corporation at the end of the year.

Related Regulations: 2902.

► 194(3) ◄

(3) Definitions. In this Part,

"debt obligation" —"debt obligation" has the meaning assigned by paragraph (*d*) of the description of A in the formula found in the definition "scientific research and experimental development tax credit" in subsection 127.3(2);

"refundable Part VIII tax on hand" —"refundable Part VIII tax on hand" of a corporation at the end of a taxation year means the amount, if any, by which

(*a*) the total of the taxes payable by it under this Part for the year and all preceding taxation years

exceeds

(*b*) the total of its Part VIII refunds for all preceding taxation years.

► 194(4) ◄

(4) Corporation may designate amount. Every taxable Canadian corporation may, by filing a prescribed form with the Minister at any time on or before the last day of the month immediately following a month in which it issued a share or debt obligation or granted a right under a scientific research and experimental development financing contract (other than a share or debt obligation issued or a right granted before October, 1983, or a share in respect of which the corporation has, on or before that day, designated an amount under subsection 192(4)) designate, for the purposes of this Part and Part I, an amount in respect of that share, debt obligation or right not exceeding the amount by which

(*a*) the amount of the consideration for which it was issued or granted, as the case may be,

exceeds

(*b*) in the case of a share, the amount of any assistance (other than an amount included in computing the scientific research and experimental development tax credit of a taxpayer in respect of that share) provided, or to be provided by a government, municipality or any other public authority in respect of, or for the acquisition of, that share.

Related Regulations: 226.

Related Sections: S. 89(1)(*i*), "taxable Canadian corporation"; s. 127.3(2) Definitions; s. 194(4.1) Computing paid-up capital after designation; s. 194(4.2) Where amount may not be designated; s. 194(6) Definition of "scientific research and experimental development financing contract"; s. 194(7) Late designation.

▶ 194(4.1) ◀

(4.1) Computing paid-up capital after designation. Where a corporation has designated an amount under subsection (4) in respect of shares issued at any time after May 23, 1985, in computing, at any particular time after that time, the paid-up capital in respect of the class of shares of the capital stock of the corporation that includes those shares

(*a*) there shall be deducted the amount, if any, by which

(i) the increase as a result of the issue of those shares in the paid-up capital in respect of all shares of that class, determined without reference to this subsection as it applies to those shares,

exceeds

(ii) the amount, if any, by which the total amount of consideration for which those shares were issued exceeds 50% of the amount designated by the corporation under subsection (4) in respect of those shares; and

(*b*) there shall be added an amount equal to the lesser of

(i) the amount, if any, by which

(A) the total of all amounts each of which is an amount deemed by subsection 84(3), (4) or (4.1) to be a dividend on shares of that class paid by the corporation after May 23, 1985 and before the particular time

exceeds

(B) the total that would be determined under clause (A) if this Act were read without reference to paragraph (*a*), and

(ii) the total of all amounts each of which is an amount required by paragraph (*a*) to be deducted in computing the paid-up capital in respect of that class of shares after May 23, 1985 and before the particular time.

▶ 194(4.2) ◀

(4.2) Where amount may not be designated. Notwithstanding subsection (4), no amount may be designated by a corporation in respect of

(*a*) a share issued by the corporation after October 10, 1984, other than

(i) a qualifying share issued before May 23, 1985, or

(ii) a qualifying share issued after May 22, 1985 and before 1986

(A) under the terms of an agreement in writing entered into by the corporation before May 23, 1985, other than pursuant to an option to acquire the share if the option was not exercised before May 23, 1985, or

(B) as part of a lawful distribution to the public in accordance with a prospectus, preliminary prospectus or registration statement filed before May 24, 1985 with a public authority in Canada pursuant to and in accordance with the securities legislation of Canada or of any province and, where required by law, accepted for filing by that public authority;

(*b*) a share or debt obligation issued or a right granted by the corporation after October 10, 1984, other than a share or debt obligation issued or a right granted before 1986

(i) under the terms of an agreement in writing entered into by the corporation before October 11, 1984, other than pursuant to an option to acquire the share, debt obligation or right if the option was not exercised before October 11, 1984, or

(ii) where arrangements, evidenced in writing, for the issue of the share or debt obligation or the granting of the right were substantially advanced before October 10, 1984; or

(*c*) a share or debt obligation issued, or a right granted, at any time after June 15, 1984, by a corporation that was an excluded corporation (within the meaning assigned by subsection 127.1(2)) at that time.

Cases: The fact that the filing of a formal prospectus had been dispensed with by the Securities Commission did not make the document filed by the taxpayer fall outside the provisions of clause 194(4.2)(*a*)(ii)(B). *Gupta et al. v. M.N.R.*, 92 DTC 1542 (T.C.C.)

The designation made by a company did not comply with s. 194(4.2)(*b*)(ii) since the debt obligation was perfected after October 10, 1984 and had not been incurred pursuant to "arrangements evidenced in writing". *First Fund Genesis Corp. v. The Queen*, 90 DTC 6337 (F.C.T.D.)

▶ 194(5) ◀

(5) Presumption. For the purposes of this Act, the Part VIII refund of a corporation for a taxation year shall be deemed to be an amount paid on account of its tax under this Part for the year on the last day of the second month following the end of the year.

Cases: Five taxpayers purchased shares in a numbered company which had been designated under s. 194(4) pursuant to an agreement made effective May 21, 1985. On May 22, 1985, they sold them to OA Ltd. and on July 31, 1985, they caused the numbered company to be dissolved. Since the taxpayers were dealing at arm's length and they could not have expected the winding-up of the numbered company to occur within the 2-year period contemplated in clause 192(6)(*c*)(iii)(A), the numbered company's shares were "qualifying shares" under s. 192(6). *Penner et al. v. The Queen*, 94 DTC 6567 (F.C.T.D.)

▶ 194(6) ◀

(6) Definition of "scientific research and experimental development financing contract". In this Part, "scientific research and experimental development financing contract" means a contract in writing pursuant to which an amount is paid by a person to a corporation as consideration for the granting by the corporation to that person of any right, either absolute or contingent, to receive income, other than interest or dividends.

▶ 194(7) ◀

(7) Late designation. Where a taxable Canadian corporation that issued a share or debt obligation or granted a right under a scientific research and experimental development financing contract does not designate an amount under subsection (4) in respect of the share, debt obligation or right on or before the day on or before which the designation was required by that subsection, the corporation shall be deemed to have made the designation on that day if

(*a*) the corporation has filed with the Minister a prescribed information return relating to the scientific research and experimental development tax credit in respect of the share, debt obligation or right within the time that it would have been so required to file the return had the designation been filed on that day, and

(*b*) within 3 years after that day, the corporation has

(i) designated an amount in respect of the share, debt obligation or right by filing a prescribed form with the Minister, and

(ii) paid to the Receiver General, at the time the prescribed form referred to in subparagraph (i) is filed, an amount that is a reasonable estimate of the penalty payable by the corporation for the late designation in respect of the share, debt obligation or right,

except that, where the Minister has mailed a notice to the corporation that a designation has not been made in respect of the share, debt obligation or right under subsection (4), the designation and payment described in paragraph (*b*) must be made by the corporation on or before the day that is 90 days after the day of the mailing.

Cases: The Minister returned the taxpayer's late-filed SRTC designation, indicating in an accompanying letter that it could be resubmitted with penalty within 30 days. The letter did not constitute a notice of the type contemplated in s. 194(7). Accordingly, the taxpayer's failure to file the prescribed information returns on time was fatal to its claim that the late designation had been validly filed. *The Queen v. United Equities Limited*, 95 DTC 5042 (F.C.A.), reversing 92 DTC 6572 (F.C.T.D.), affirming 89 DTC 391 (T.C.C.).

► 194(8) ◄

(8) Penalty for late designation. Where, pursuant to subsection (7), a corporation made a late designation in respect of a share or debt obligation issued, or a right granted, in a month, the corporation shall pay, for each month or part of a month that elapsed during the period beginning on the last day on or before which an amount could have been designated by the corporation under subsection (4) in respect of the share, debt obligation or right and ending on the day that the late designation is made, a penalty for the late designation in respect of the share, debt obligation or right in an amount equal to 1% of the amount designated in respect of the share, debt obligation or right, except that the maximum penalty payable under this subsection by the corporation for a month shall not exceed $500.

Cases: The Minister returned the taxpayer's late-filed SRTC designation, indicating in an accompanying letter that it could be resubmitted with penalty within 30 days. The letter did not constitute a notice of the type contemplated in s. 194(7). Accordingly, the taxpayer's failure to file the prescribed information returns on time was fatal to its claim that the late designation had been validly filed. *The Queen v. United Equities Limited*, 95 DTC 5042 (F.C.A.), reversing 92 DTC 6572 (F.C.T.D.), affirming 89 DTC 391 (T.C.C.).

► 194(9) ◄

(9) Restriction. Where at any time a corporation has designated an amount under subsection (4) in respect of a share, debt obligation or right, no amount may be designated by the corporation at any subsequent time in respect of that share, debt obligation or right.

SECTION 195: Corporation to file return

► 195(1) ◄

(1) Corporation to file return. Every corporation that is liable to pay tax under this Part for a taxation year shall, on or before the day on or before which it is required to file its return of income under Part I for the year, file with the Minister a return for the year under this Part in prescribed form.

Related Regulations: Part XLIII.

Cases: A promissory note had been issued to the taxpayer in the amount of $120,000 which was designated in 1984 under s. 194(4) so that, in computing its 1984 income, the taxpayer claimed a SR&ED tax credit of $60,000. It would be contrary to the intent of the *Income Tax Act* to deprive the taxpayer of its $60,000 SR&ED tax credit, by unduly narrowly construing the words "consideration for which it (i.e. the note) was issued" in s. 194(4). *Groupmark Canada Ltd. v. The Queen*, 93 DTC 5179 (F.C.T.D.)

► 195(2) ◄

(2) Corporation to make payment on account of tax. Where, in a particular month in a taxation year, a corporation issues a share or debt obligation, or grants a right, in respect of which it designates an amount under section 194, the corporation shall, on or before the last day of the month following the particular month, pay to the Receiver General on account of its tax payable under this Part for the year an amount equal to 50% of the total of all amounts so designated.

► 195(3) ◄

(3) Interest. Where a corporation is liable to pay tax under this Part and has failed to pay all or any part or instalment thereof on or before the day on or before which the tax or instalment, as the case may be, was required to be paid, it shall pay to the Receiver General interest at the prescribed rate on the amount that it failed to pay computed from the day on or before which the amount was required to be paid to the day of payment.

Related Regulations: Part XLIII.

Related Sections: S. 248(11) Compound interest.

► 195(4) ◄

(4) Idem. For the purposes of computing interest payable by a corporation under subsection (3) for any month or months in the period commencing on the first day of a taxation year and ending two months after the last day of the year in which period the corporation has designated an amount under section 194 in respect of a share or debt obligation issued, or right granted, by it in a particular month in the year, the corporation shall be deemed to have been liable to pay, on or before the last day of the month immediately following the particular month, a part or an instalment of tax for the year equal to that proportion of the amount, if any, by which its tax payable under this Part for the year exceeds its Part VIII refund for the year that

(*a*) the total of all amounts so designated by it under section 194 in respect of shares or debt obligations issued, or rights granted, by it in the particular month

is of

(*b*) the total of all amounts so designated by it under section 194 in respect of shares or debt obligations issued, or rights granted, by it in the year.

► 195(5) ◄

(5) Evasion of tax. Where a corporation that is liable to pay tax under this Part in respect of a share or debt obligation issued or a right granted by it wilfully, in any manner whatever, evades or attempts to evade payment of the tax and a purchaser of the share, debt obligation or right or, where the purchaser is a partnership, a member of the partnership knew or ought to have known, at the time the share, debt obligation or right was acquired, that the corporation would wilfully evade or attempt to evade the tax, for the purposes of section 127.3, the share, debt obligation or right shall be deemed not to have been acquired.

► 195(6) ◄

(6) Undue deferral. Where, in a transaction or as part of a series of transactions, a taxpayer acquires a share or debt obligation of a corporation or a right granted by a corporation and the corporation is controlled (within the meaning assigned by subsection 186(2)) by the taxpayer and it may reasonably be considered that one of the main purposes of the acquisition was to reduce for a period interest on the taxpayer's liability for tax under this Part, the share, debt obligation or right shall, for the purposes of this Part (other than this subsection) and section 127.3, be deemed not to have been acquired by the taxpayer and not to have been issued or granted, as the case may be, by the corporation until the end of that period.

Related Sections: S. 248(10) Series of transactions.

► 195(7) ◄

(7) Avoidance of tax. Where, as part of a series of transactions or events one of the main purposes of which may reasonably be considered to be the avoidance of tax that might otherwise have been or become payable under Part II of the *Income Tax Act*, chapter 148 of the Revised Statutes of Canada, 1952, by any corporation, a particular corporation has issued a share or debt obligation or granted a right in a taxation year in respect of which it has designated an amount under subsection 194(4), the particular corporation shall, on or before the last day of the second month after the end of the year, pay a tax under this Part for the year equal to 125% of the amount of tax under Part II of the *Income Tax Act*, chapter 148 of the Revised Statutes of Canada, 1952, that is or may be avoided by reason of the series of transactions or events.

Related Sections: S. 248(10) Series of transactions.

► 195(7.1) ◄

(7.1) Tax on excess. Where a corporation has in a taxation year made an election under subsection 127.3(9) in respect of any share or debt obligation that was part of a distribution of shares or debt obligations referred to in that subsection and, at the end of that year or any subsequent taxation year,

(*a*) the total of the amounts designated under subsection 194(4) in respect of those shares or debt obligations as evidenced by the prescribed information returns required by regulation to be filed with the Minister by a taxpayer other than the corporation

exceeds

(*b*) the total of the amounts designated under subsection 194(4) in respect of those shares or debt obligations acquired by the taxpayer and in respect of which another taxpayer was required by regulation to provide the taxpayer with a prescribed information return relating to the designation under that subsection,

the taxpayer is liable to pay a tax under this Part, for the taxation year at the end of which there is such an excess, equal to 50% of the excess, which tax is to be paid to the Receiver General within 60 days after the end of the taxation year, and the excess shall be included in determining the total under paragraph (*b*) for any taxation year of the taxpayer subsequent to that year.

► 195(8) ◄

(8) Provisions applicable to Part. Sections 151, 152, 158 and 159, subsection 161(11), sections 162 to 167 (except subsections 164(1.1) to (1.3)) and Division J of Part I are applicable to this Part with such modifications as the circumstances require and, for greater certainty, the Minister may assess, before the end of a taxation year, an amount payable under this Part for the year.

Part IX
Tax on Deduction Under Section 66.5

SECTION 196: Tax in respect of cumulative offset account

▶ 196(1) ◀

(1) Tax in respect of cumulative offset account. Every corporation shall pay a tax under this Part for each taxation year equal to 30% of the amount deducted under subsection 66.5(1) in computing its income for the year.

▶ 196(2) ◀

(2) Return. Every corporation that is liable to pay tax under this Part for a taxation year shall file with the Minister, not later than the day on or before which it is required under section 150 to file a return of its income for the year under Part I, a return for the year under this Part in prescribed form containing an estimate of the amount of tax payable by it under this Part for the year.

▶ 196(3) ◀

(3) Instalments. Where a corporation is liable to pay tax for a taxation year under this Part, the corporation shall pay in respect of the year, to the Receiver General

(*a*) on or before the last day of each month in the year, an amount equal to 1/12 of the amount of tax payable by it under this Part for the year; and

(*b*) the remainder, if any, of the tax payable by it under this Part for the year, on or before its balance-due day for the year.

▶ 196(4) ◀

(4) Provisions applicable to Part. Sections 152, 158 and 159, subsections 161(1) and (2), sections 162 to 167 and Division J of Part I are applicable to this Part, with such modifications as the circumstances require.

Related Regulations: Part XXI; Part XLIII.

Part IX.1
Tax on SIFT Partnerships

SECTION 197: [Tax on SIFT partnership income]

► 197(1) ◄

(1) Definitions. The following definitions apply in this Part and in section 96.

Canadian Petroleum Tax Journal: The Sift Rules: An Oil & Gas Perspective, Hegedus, 2007, Vol. 20, No. 1.

"non-portfolio earnings" —"non-portfolio earnings", of a SIFT partnership for a taxation year, means the total of

(*a*) the amount, if any, by which

(i) the total of all amounts each of which is the SIFT partnership's income for the taxation year from a business carried on by it in Canada or from a non-portfolio property, other than income that is a taxable dividend received by the SIFT partnership,

exceeds

(ii) the total of all amounts each of which is the SIFT partnership's loss for the taxation year from a business carried on by it in Canada or from a non-portfolio property, and

(*b*) the amount, if any, by which all taxable capital gains of the SIFT partnership from dispositions of non-portfolio properties during the taxation year exceeds the total of the allowable capital losses of the SIFT partnership for the taxation year from dispositions of non-portfolio properties during the taxation year.

Related Sections: S. 89(1), "taxable dividend"; s. 248(1), "non-portfolio property".

"SIFT partnership" —"SIFT partnership", being a specified investment flow-through partnership, for any taxation year, means a partnership other than an excluded subsidiary entity (as defined in subsection 122.1(1)) for the taxation year that meets the following conditions at any time during the taxation year:

(*a*) the partnership is a Canadian resident partnership;

(*b*) investments (as defined in subsection 122.1(1)) in the partnership are listed or traded on a stock exchange or other public market; and

(*c*) the partnership holds one or more non-portfolio properties.

History: S. 197(1), the portion of the definition "SIFT partnership" before paragraph (*a*) was replaced by S.C. 2009, c. 2, s. 65(1), deemed to have come into force on October 31, 2006. S. 197(1), the portion of the definition "SIFT partnership" before paragraph (*a*) formerly read:

"SIFT partnership"—"SIFT partnership", being a specified investment flow-through partnership, for any taxation year, means a partnership that meets the following conditions at any time during the taxation year:

Related Sections: S. 122.1(1), "SIFT trust"; s. 248(1), "Canadian resident partnership", "non-portfolio property".

"taxable non-portfolio earnings" —"taxable non-portfolio earnings" of a SIFT partnership, for a taxation year, means the lesser of

(*a*) the amount that would, if the SIFT partnership were a taxpayer for the purposes of Part I and if subsection 96(1) were read without reference to its paragraph (*d*), be its income for the taxation year as determined under section 3; and

(*b*) its non-portfolio earnings for the taxation year.

► 197(2) ◄

(2) Tax on partnership income. Every partnership that is a SIFT partnership for a taxation year is liable to a tax under this Part equal to the amount determined by the formula

$$A \times (B + C)$$

where

A is the taxable non-portfolio earnings of the SIFT partnership for the taxation year;

B is the net corporate income tax rate in respect of the SIFT partnership for the taxation year; and

C is the provincial SIFT tax rate of the SIFT partnership for the taxation year.

Editorial Note: If Part IX.1 tax is payable by a SIFT partnership in a taxation year, s. 96(1.11) provides that the partnership is deemed to have received a taxable dividend in the year from a taxable Canadian corporation equal to the amount by which the partnership's taxable non-portfolio earnings for the year exceeds the partnership's Part IX.1 tax payable for the year. In other words, the partnership's taxable non-portfolio earnings, net of the Part IX.1 tax, are treated as a deemed taxable dividend and an eligible dividend (see definition in s. 89(1)), which is included in the Part 1 income of the partners pursuant to the general rules of s. 96(1).

Related Regulations: 414.

Related Sections: S. 248(1), "net corporate income tax rate", "provincial tax factor", "provincial SIFT tax rate".

► 197(3) ◄

(3) Ordering. This Part and section 122.1 are to be applied as if this Act were read without reference to subsection 96(1.11).

► 197(4) ◄

(4) Partnership to file return. Every member of a partnership that is liable to pay tax under this Part for a taxation year shall — on or before the day on or before which the partnership return is required to be filed for the year under section 229 of the *Income Tax Regulations* — file with the Minister a return for the taxation year under this Part in prescribed form containing an estimate of the tax payable by the partnership under this Part for the taxation year.

► 197(5) ◄

(5) Authority to file return. For the purposes of subsection (4), if, in respect of a taxation year of a partnership, a particular member of the partnership has authority to act for the partnership,

(*a*) if the particular member has filed a return as required by this Part for a taxation year, each other person who was a member of the partnership during the taxation year is deemed to have filed the return; and

(*b*) a return that has been filed by any other member of the partnership for the taxation year is not valid and is deemed not to have been filed by any member of the partnership.

► 197(6) ◄

(6) Provisions applicable to Part. Subsection 150(2), section 152, subsections 157(1), (2.1) and (4), sections 158, 159 and 161 to 167 and Division J of Part I apply to this Part, with any modifications that the circumstances require, and for greater certainty,

(*a*) a notice of assessment referred to in subsection 152(2) in respect of tax payable under this Part is valid notwithstanding that a partnership is not a person; and

(*b*) notwithstanding subsection 152(4), the Minister may at any time make an assessment or reassessment of tax payable under this Part or Part I to give effect to a determination made by the Minister under subsection 152(1.4), including the assessment or reassessment of Part I tax payable in respect of the disposition of an interest in a SIFT partnership by a member of the partnership.

History: S. 197(6), the portion before paragraph (*a*) was replaced by S.C. 2013, c. 40, s. 72(1), applicable to taxation years that begin after July 20, 2011, and formerly read:

(6) *Provisions applicable to Part.* Subsection 150(2), sections 152, 156, 156.1, 158, 159 and 161 to 167 and Division J of Part I apply to this Part, with any modifications that the circumstances require, and for greater certainty,

► 197(7) ◄

(7) Payment. Every SIFT partnership shall pay to the Receiver General, on or before its SIFT partnership balance-due day for each taxation year, its tax payable under this Part for the taxation year.

Related Sections: S. 248(1), "SIFT partnership balance-due day".

► 197(8) ◄

(8) Application of definition "SIFT partnership". The definition "SIFT partnership" applies to a partnership for a taxation year of the partnership that ends after 2006, except that if the partnership would have been a SIFT partnership on October 31, 2006 had that definition been in force and applied to the partnership as of that date, that definition does not apply to the partnership for a taxation year of the partnership that ends before the earlier of

(*a*) 2011, and

(*b*) the first day after December 15, 2006 on which the partnership exceeds normal growth as determined by reference to the normal growth guidelines issued by the Department of Finance on December 15, 2006, as amended from time to time, unless that excess arose as a result of a prescribed transaction.

Part X
Taxes on Deferred Profit Sharing Plans and Revoked Plans

SECTION 198: Tax on non-qualified investments and use of assets as security

► 198(1) ◄

(1) Tax on non-qualified investments and use of assets as security. Every trust governed by a deferred profit sharing plan or revoked plan that

(*a*) acquires a non-qualified investment, or

(*b*) uses or permits to be used any property of the trust as security for a loan,

shall pay a tax equal to the fair market value of

(*c*) the non-qualified investment at the time it was acquired by the trust, or

(*d*) the property used as security at the time it commenced to be so used.

Related Sections: S. 130(3) Meaning of expressions "investment corporation" and "taxed capital gains"; s. 146(1), "retirement savings plan"; s. 147(1)(*a*) Definitions; s. 147(14) Revocation of registration; s. 198(3) Trustee liable for tax; s. 198(6) Life insurance policies — special rules; s. 198(7) Life insurance policies — 25% of annual DPSP contributions; s. 198(8) Life insurance policies — surrender, cancellation, assignment etc.; 199 Tax on initial non-qualified investments not disposed of; 200 Distribution deemed disposition; 201 Tax where inadequate consideration on purchase or sale; 202 Returns and payment of estimated tax; 203 Application to other taxes; 204 Definitions; s. 207.1(2) Tax payable by trust under deferred profit sharing plan; s. 259(1) Proportional holdings in trust property.

Information Circulars: IC 77-1R5 Deferred profit sharing plan.

► 198(2) ◄

(2) Payment of tax. A trustee of a trust liable to pay tax under subsection (1) shall remit the amount of the tax to the Receiver General within 10 days of the day on which the non-qualified investment is acquired or the property is used as security for a loan, as the case may be.

► 198(3) ◄

(3) Trustee liable for tax. Where a trustee of a trust liable to pay tax under subsection (1) does not remit to the Receiver General the amount of the tax within the time specified in subsection (2), the trustee is personally liable to pay on behalf of the trust the full amount of the tax and is entitled to recover from the trust any amount paid by the trustee as tax under this section.

► 198(4) ◄

(4) Refund of tax on disposition of non-qualified investment. Where a trust disposes of a property that, when acquired, was a non-qualified investment, the trust is, on application in accordance with section 202, entitled to a refund of an amount equal to the lesser of

(*a*) the amount of the tax imposed under this section as a result of the acquisition of the property, and

(*b*) the proceeds of disposition of the property.

Related Sections: S. 198(6) Life insurance policies — special rules; s. 198(8) Life insurance policies — surrender, cancellation, assignment etc.; s. 200 Distribution deemed disposition; s. 202(4) Provisions applicable to refunds; s. 203 Application to other taxes.

► 198(5) ◄

(5) Refund of tax on recovery of property given as security. Where a loan, for which a trust has used or permitted to be used trust property as security, ceases to be extant, the trust is, on application in accordance with section 202, entitled to a refund of an amount equal to the amount remaining, if any, when

(*a*) the net loss (exclusive of payments by the trust as or on account of interest) sustained by the trust in consequence of its using or permitting to be used the property as security for the loan and not as a result of a change in the fair market value of the property

is deducted from

(*b*) the tax imposed under this section in consequence of the trust's using or permitting to be used the property as security for the loan.

Related Sections: S. 198(1) Tax on non-qualified investments and use of assets as security; 198(6) Special rules relating to life insurance policies; 198(6.1) Idem; 198(7) Idem; 198(8) Idem; s. 203 Application to other taxes.

► 198(6) ◄

(6) Special rules relating to life insurance policies. For the purposes of this section,

(*a*) the acquisition of an interest in or the payment of an amount under a life insurance policy shall be deemed not to be the acquisition of a non-qualified investment, and

(*b*) the disposition of an interest in a life insurance policy shall be deemed not to be the disposition of a non-qualified investment,

except that where a trust governed by a deferred profit sharing plan or revoked plan makes a payment under or to acquire an interest in a life insurance policy, other than a life insurance policy under which

(*c*) the trust is, or by virtue of the payment about to become, the only person entitled to any rights or benefits under the policy (other than the rights or benefits of the insurer),

(*d*) the cash surrender value of the policy (exclusive of accumulated dividends) is or will be, at or before the end of the year in which the insured person attains 71 years of age, if all premiums under the policy are paid, not less than the maximum total amount (exclusive of accumulated dividends) payable by the insurer under the policy, and

(*e*) the total of the premiums payable in any year under the policy is not greater than the total of the amounts that, if the annual premiums had been payable in monthly instalments, would have been payable as such instalments in the 12 months commencing with the date the policy was issued,

the making of the payment shall be deemed to be the acquisition of a non-qualified investment at a cost equal to the amount of the payment.

Related Sections: S. 139.1(13) RRSP registration rules, etc; s. 146(11) Life insurance policies; s. 198(7) Life insurance policies — 25% of annual DPSP contributions; s. 198(8) Life insurance policies — surrender, cancellation, assignment etc.

Information Circulars: IC 77-1R5 Deferred profit sharing plan.

► 198(6.1) ◄

(6.1) Idem. A life insurance policy giving an option to the policyholder to receive annuity payments that otherwise complies with paragraph (6)(*d*) shall be deemed,

(*a*) where the option has not been exercised, to comply with that paragraph; and

(*b*) where at a particular time the option is exercised, to have been disposed of at that time for an amount equal to the cash surrender value of the policy immediately before that time, and an annuity contract shall be deemed to have been acquired at that time at a cost equal to that amount.

Related Sections: S. 198(6) Life insurance policies — special rules.

► 198(7) ◄

(7) Idem. Notwithstanding subsection (6), where the total of all payments made in a year by a trust governed by a deferred profit sharing plan or revoked plan under or to acquire interests in life insurance policies in respect of which the trust is the only person entitled to any rights or benefits (other than the rights or benefits of the insurer) does not exceed an amount equal to 25% of the total of all amounts paid by employers to the trust in the year under the plan for the benefit of beneficiaries thereunder, the making of the payments under or to acquire interests in such policies shall be deemed, for the purposes of this section, not to be the acquisition of non-qualified investments.

► 198(8) ◄

(8) Idem. Where a trust surrenders, cancels, assigns or otherwise disposes of its interest in a life insurance policy,

(*a*) the trust shall be deemed, for the purposes of subsection (4), to have disposed of each non-qualified investment that, by virtue of payments under the policy, it was deemed by subsection (6) to have acquired; and

(*b*) the proceeds of the disposition shall be deemed to be the amount, if any, by which

(i) the amount received by the trust in consequence of the surrender, cancellation, assignment or other disposition of its interest in the policy

exceeds the total of

(ii) each amount paid by the trust under or to acquire an interest in the policy, the payment of which is deemed by this section not to be the acquisition of a non-qualified investment, and

(iii) the cash surrender value on December 21, 1966 of the interest of the trust in the policy on that date.

Related Sections: S. 104(1) Reference to trust or estate; s. 108(1), "beneficiary"; s. 146(11) Life insurance policies; s. 147(1), "deferred profit sharing plan"; s. 202(5) Interest; s. 204, "non-qualified investment", "qualified investment"; s. 248(1), "amount", "dividend", "employer", "insurer", "property".

SECTION 199: Tax on initial non-qualified investments not disposed of

► 199(1) ◄

(1) Tax on initial non-qualified investments not disposed of. Every trust governed by a deferred profit sharing plan or revoked plan shall pay a tax

(*a*) for 1967, equal to the amount, if any, by which 20% of the initial base of the trust exceeds the proceeds of disposition of its initial non-qualified investments disposed of after December 21, 1966 and before 1968;

(*b*) for 1968, equal to the amount, if any, by which 40% of the initial base of the trust exceeds the total of

(i) the proceeds of disposition of its initial non-qualified investments disposed of after December 21, 1966 and before 1969, and

(ii) the tax payable by the trust determined under paragraph (*a*);

(*c*) for 1969, equal to the amount, if any, by which 60% of the initial base of the trust exceeds the total of

(i) the proceeds of disposition of its initial non-qualified investments disposed of after December 21, 1966 and before 1970, and

(ii) the tax payable by the trust determined under paragraphs (*a*) and (*b*); and

(*d*) for 1970, equal to the amount, if any, by which 100% of the initial base of the trust exceeds the total of

(i) the proceeds of disposition of its initial non-qualified investments disposed of after December 21, 1966 and before 1971, and

(ii) the tax payable by the trust determined under paragraphs (*a*), (*b*) and (*c*).

Related Sections: S. 201 Tax where inadequate consideration on purchase or sale.

Information Circulars: IC 77-1R5 Deferred profit sharing plan.

► 199(2) ◄

(2) Refund. Where at the end of a year,

(*a*) the total of all taxes paid by a trust under subsection (1)

exceeds

(*b*) the total of

(i) all refunds made to the trust under this subsection, and

(ii) the amount, if any, by which the initial base of the trust exceeds the proceeds of disposition of its initial non-qualified investments disposed of after December 21, 1966 and before the end of the year, the trust is, on application in accordance with section 202, entitled to a refund equal to the amount by which the total described in paragraph (*a*) exceeds the total described in paragraph (*b*).

Related Sections: S. 104(1) Reference to trust or estate; s. 147(1), "deferred profit sharing plan"; s 201 Tax where inadequate consideration on purchase or sale; s. 204, "non-qualified investment"; s. 203 Application to other taxes; s. 248(1), "amount".

SECTION 200: Distribution deemed disposition

For the purposes of this Part, a distribution by a trust of a non-qualified investment to a beneficiary of the trust shall be deemed to be a disposition of that non-qualified investment and the proceeds of disposition of that non-qualified investment shall be deemed to be its fair market value at the time of the distribution.

Related Sections: S. 104(1) Reference to trust or estate; s. 108(1), "beneficiary"; s. 198(6) Life insurance policies — special rules; s. 198(7) Life insurance policies — 25% of annual DPSP contributions; s. 204, "non-qualified investment".

Information Circulars: IC 77-1R5 Deferred profit sharing plan.

SECTION 201: Tax where inadequate consideration on purchase or sale

Every trust governed by a deferred profit sharing plan or a revoked plan shall, for each calendar year after 1990, pay a tax equal to 50% of the total of all amounts each of which is, by reason of subsection 147(18), an amount taxable under this section for the year.

Related Sections: S. 104(1) Reference to trust or estate; s. 108(1), "beneficiary"; s. 147(1), "deferred profit sharing plan"; s. 147(7) No tax while trust governed by plan; s. 147(12) Exemption of employee contributions to the plan; s. 147(13) Appropriation of trust property by employer; s. 147(18) Inadequate consideration on purchase from or sale to trust; s. 248(1), "amount", "employee", "employer", "property".

Information Circulars: IC 77-1R5 Deferred profit sharing plan.

Interpretation Bulletins: *Secondary* — IT-396R Interest income.

SECTION 202: Returns and payment of estimated tax

▶ 202(1) ◀

(1) Returns and payment of estimated tax. Within 90 days from the end of each year after 1965, a trustee of every trust governed by a deferred profit sharing plan or revoked plan shall

(*a*) file with the Minister a return for the year under this Part in prescribed form and containing prescribed information, without notice or demand therefor;

(*b*) estimate in the return the amount of tax payable by the trust under this Part for the year;

(*c*) estimate in the return the amount of any refund to which the trust is entitled under this Part for the year; and

(*d*) pay to the Receiver General the unpaid balance of the trust's tax for the year minus any refund to which it is entitled under this Part, or apply in the return for any amount owing to it.

Related Sections: S. 202(2) Consideration of application for refund.

Forms: T3D — Income Tax Return for Deferred Profit Sharing Plan (DPSP) or Revoked (DPSP).

Information Circulars: IC 77-1R5 Deferred Profit Sharing Plan; IC 78-14R4 Guidelines for trust companies and other persons responsible for filing T3GR, T3D, T3P, T3S, T3RI, and T3F returns.

▶ 202(2) ◀

(2) Consideration of application for refund. Where a trustee of a trust has made application for an amount owing to it pursuant to subsection (1), the Minister shall

(*a*) consider the application;

(*b*) determine the amount of any refund; and

(*c*) send to the trustee a notice of refund and any amount owing to the trust, or a notice that no refund is payable.

Related Sections: S. 198(4) Refund of tax on disposition of non-qualified investment; s. 198(5) Refund of tax on recovery of property given as security.

▶ 202(3) ◀

(3) Provisions applicable to Part. Subsection 150(2), sections 152 and 158, subsections 161(1) and (11), sections 162 to 167 and Division J of Part I are applicable to this Part with such modifications as the circumstances require and, for the purposes of the application of those provisions to this Part, a notice of refund under this section shall be deemed to be a notice of assessment.

▶ 202(4) ◀

(4) Provisions applicable to refunds. Subsections 164(3) to (4) are applicable, with such modifications as the circumstances require, to refunds of tax under subsection 198(4) or (5) or 199(2).

Related Sections: S. 150(2) Demands for returns; 161(3) Special case; 161(3.1); 161(3.2); 161(4) Limitation — farmers and fishermen.

▶ 202(5) ◀

(5) Interest. In addition to the interest payable under subsection 161(1), where a taxpayer is required by section 198 to pay a tax and has failed to pay all or any part thereof on or before the day on or before which the tax was required to be paid, the taxpayer shall pay to the Receiver General interest at the prescribed rate on the amount that the taxpayer failed to pay computed from the day on or before which the amount was required to be paid to the day of payment or to the beginning of the period in respect of which the taxpayer is required by subsection 161(1) to pay interest thereon, whichever is earlier.

Related Regulations: 4301.

Related Sections: S. 248(11) Compound interest.

▶ 202(6) ◀

(6) Deemed payment of tax. For the purposes of subsections 161(1) and 202(5), where a trust is liable to pay tax under this Part on the acquisition by it of a non-qualified investment or on the use of its property as security for a loan, it shall, except to the extent that the tax has previously been paid, be deemed to have paid tax on the date on which the property is disposed of or on which the loan ceases to be extant, as the case may be, in an amount equal to the refund referred to in subsection 198(4) in respect of that property or subsection 198(5) in respect of the loan, as the case may be.

Related Sections: S. 104(1) Reference to trust or estate; s. 147(1), "deferred profit sharing plan"; s. 161(1) Interest s. 248(1), "amount", "assessment", "prescribed"; s. 198(4) Refund of tax on disposition of non-qualified investment; s. 198(5) Refund of tax on recovery of property given as security; s. 199(2) Refund; ITAR s. 62(2) Interest.

SECTION 203: Application to other taxes

Instead of making a refund to which a trust is entitled under subsection 198(4) or (5) or 199(2), the Minister may, where the trust is liable or about to become liable to make another payment under this Act, apply the amount of the refund or any part thereof to that other liability and notify a trustee of the trust of that action.

Related Sections: S. 104(1) Reference to trust or estate; s. 248(1), "amount".

SECTION 204: Definitions

In this Part,

Tax Window Files: *Due date for subparagraph 88.1(1)(d)(ii) election, February 9, 2011,* CRA Document No. 2011-0394271I7; *Option, February 8, 2011,* CRA Document No. 2010-0364811E5; *TFSA - Foreign Exchange Trading, January 5, 2011,* CRA Document No. 2009-0328861E5; *TFSA - Foreign Exchange Trading, January 5, 2011,* CRA Document No. 2009-0318671E5.

"debt obligation" —"debt obligation" means a bond, debenture, note or similar obligation;

"equity share" —"equity share" means

(*a*) a share, other than an excluded share or a non-participating share, the owner of which has, as owner thereof, a right

(i) to a dividend, and

(ii) to a part of the surplus of the corporation after repayment of capital and payment of dividend arrears on the redemption of the share, a reduction of the capital of the corporation or the winding-up of the corporation,

at least as great, in any event, as the right of the owner of any other share, other than a non-participating share, of the corporation, when the magnitude of the right in each case is expressed as a rate based on the paid-up capital value of the share to which the right relates, or

(*b*) a share, other than an excluded share or a non-participating share, the owner of which has, as owner thereof, a right

(i) to a dividend, after a dividend at a rate not in excess of 12% per annum of the paid-up capital value of each share has been paid to the owners of shares of a class other than the class to which that share belongs, and

(ii) to a part of the surplus of the corporation after repayment of capital and payment of dividend arrears on the redemption of the share, a reduction of the capital of the corporation or the winding-up of the corporation, after a payment of a part of the surplus at a rate not in excess of 10% of the paid-up capital value of each share has been made to the owners of shares of a class other than the class to which that share belongs,

at least as great, in any event, as the right of the owner of any other share, other than a non-participating share, of the corporation, when the magnitude of the right in each case is expressed as a rate based on the paid-up capital value of the share to which the right relates;

"excluded property" —"excluded property", in relation to a trust governed by a deferred profit sharing plan or revoked plan, means a debt obligation or bankers' acceptance issued by

(*a*) an employer by whom payments are made in trust to a trustee under the plan for the benefit of beneficiaries under the plan, or

(*b*) a corporation with whom that employer does not deal at arm's length;

"excluded share" —"excluded share" means each share of the capital stock of a private corporation where

(*a*) the paid-up capital of the corporation that is represented by all its issued and outstanding shares that would, but for this definition, be equity shares is less than 50% of the paid-up capital of the corporation that is represented by all its issued and outstanding shares other than non-participating shares, or

(*b*) a non-participating share of the corporation is issued and outstanding and the owner of which has, as owner thereof, a right to a dividend

(i) at a fixed annual rate in excess of 12%, or

(ii) at an annual rate not in excess of a fixed maximum annual rate, if the fixed maximum annual rate is in excess of 12%,

when the right to the dividend is expressed as a rate based on the paid-up capital value of the share to which the right relates;

"initial base" —"initial base" of a trust means the total of the values of all initial non-qualified investments held by the trust on December 21, 1966 when each such investment is valued at the lower of

(*a*) its cost to the trust, and

(*b*) its fair market value on December 21, 1966;

"initial non-qualified investment" —"initial non-qualified investment" of a trust means an investment held by the trust on December 21, 1966 that was, on that date, a non-qualified investment but does not include

(*a*) any interest in a life insurance policy, or

(*b*) an equity share that would be a qualified investment if the date of acquisition of the share were December 21, 1966;

"non-participating share" —"non-participating share" means

(*a*) in the case of a private corporation, a share the owner of which is not entitled to receive, as owner thereof, any dividend, other than a dividend, whether cumulative or not,

(i) at a fixed annual rate or amount, or

(ii) at an annual rate or amount not in excess of a fixed annual rate or amount, and

(*b*) in the case of a corporation other than a private corporation, any share other than a common share;

"non-qualified investment" —"non-qualified investment" means property that is not a qualified investment for a trust governed by a deferred profit sharing plan or revoked plan within the meaning of the definition "qualified investment" in this subsection;

"paid-up capital value" —"paid-up capital value" of a share means the amount determined by the formula

A/B

where

A is the paid-up capital of the corporation that is represented by the shares of the class to which that share belongs, and

B is the number of shares of that class that are in fact issued and outstanding;

"qualified investment" —"qualified investment" for a trust governed by a deferred profit sharing plan or revoked plan means, with the exception of excluded property in relation to the trust,

(*a*) money (other than money the fair market value of which exceeds its stated value as legal tender in the country of issuance or money that is held for its numismatic value) and deposits (within the meaning assigned by the *Canada Deposit Insurance Corporation Act* or with a branch in Canada of a bank) of such money standing to the credit of the trust,

(*b*) debt obligations described in paragraph (*a*) of the definition "fully exempt interest" in subsection 212(3),

(*c*) debt obligations issued by

(i) a corporation, mutual fund trust or limited partnership the shares or units of which are listed on a designated stock exchange in Canada,

(ii) a corporation the shares of which are listed on a designated stock exchange outside Canada, or

(iii) an authorized foreign bank and payable at a branch in Canada of the bank,

(*c*.1) debt obligations that meet the following criteria, namely,

(i) any of

(A) the debt obligations had, at the time of acquisition by the trust, an investment grade rating with a prescribed credit rating agency,

(B) the debt obligations have an investment grade rating with a prescribed credit rating agency, or

(C) the debt obligations were acquired by the trust in exchange for debt obligations that satisfied the condition in clause (A) and as part of a proposal to, or an arrangement with, the creditors of the issuer of the debt obligations that has been approved by a court under the *Bankruptcy and Insolvency Act* or the *Companies' Creditors Arrangement Act*, and

(ii) either

(A) the debt obligations were issued as part of a single issue of debt of at least $25 million, or

(B) in the case of debt obligations that are issued on a continuous basis under a debt issuance program, the issuer of the debt obligations had issued and outstanding debt under the program of at least $25 million,

(*d*) securities (other than futures contracts or other derivative instruments in respect of which the holder's risk of loss may exceed the holder's cost) that are listed on a designated stock exchange,

(*e*) equity shares of a corporation by which, before the date of acquisition by the trust of the shares, payments have been made in trust to a trustee under the plan for the benefit of beneficiaries thereunder, if the shares are of a class in respect of which

(i) there is no restriction on their transferability, and

(ii) in each of 4 taxation years of the corporation in the period of the corporation's 5 consecutive taxation years that ended less than 12 months before the date of acquisition of the shares by the trust, and in the corporation's last taxation year in that period, the corporation

(A) paid a dividend on each share of the class of an amount not less than 4% of the cost per share of the shares to the trust, or

(B) had earnings attributable to the shares of the class of an amount not less than the amount obtained when 4% of the cost per share to the trust of the shares is multiplied by the total number of shares of the class that were outstanding immediately after the acquisition,

(*f*) guaranteed investment certificates issued by a trust company incorporated under the laws of Canada or of a province,

(*g*) investment contracts described in subparagraph (*b*)(ii) of the definition "retirement savings plan" in subsection 146(1) and issued by a corporation approved by the Governor in Council for the purposes of that subparagraph, and

(*h*) prescribed investments.

(*i*) (Repealed by S.C. 2007, c. 29, s. 26.)

History: S. 204, paragraph (*c.1*) of the definition "qualified investment" was replaced by S.C. 2009, c. 2, s. 66(1), applicable in determining whether a property is, at any time after March 18, 2007, a qualified investment. S. 204, paragraph (*c.1*) of the definition "qualified investment" formerly read:

(*c*.1) debt obligations that, at the time of acquisition by the trust, met the following criteria, namely,

(i) the debt obligations had an investment grade rating with a prescribed credit rating agency, and

(ii) either

(A) the debt obligations were issued as part of a single issue of debt of at least $25 million, or

(B) in the case of debt obligations that are issued on a continuous basis, the issuer of the debt obligations had issued and outstanding debt of that type of at least $25 million,

Proposed Amendment

2019 Federal Budget Resolutions

The Act is modified to give effect to the proposals relating to permitting additional types of annuities under registered plans

described in the budget documents tabled by the Minister of Finance in the House of Commons on Budget Day.

Explanatory Note:
Dentons Canada LLP Commentary

Budget 2019 proposes to provide "qualified investment" status to the following additional types of annuities for certain registered plans, effective for 2020 and subsequent taxation years:

- advanced life deferred annuities will be permitted under a registered retirement savings plan (RRSP), registered retirement income fund (RRIF), deferred profit sharing plan (DPSP), pooled registered pension plan (PRPP) and defined contribution registered pension plan (RPP); and
- variable payment life annuities will be permitted under a PRPP and defined contribution RPP.

Advanced Life Deferred Annuities (ALDA)

The tax rules generally require an annuity purchased with a registered plan to commence by the end of the year in which the annuitant attains 71 years of age. An ALDA will be a life annuity the commencement of which may be deferred until the end of the year in which the annuitant turns 85 and meets certain other prescribed conditions. A lifetime limit of 25% of the value of the plan (including payments for the ALDA) and $150,000 will apply.

Annuity payments to a surviving spouse or common-law partner will be taxable in the year of receipt. Lump-sum payments to a surviving spouse, common-law partner or dependent child or grandchild (provided that the child or grandchild is dependent by reason of physical or mental infirmity) will qualify for a tax-deferred transfer to an RRSP, RRIF or other eligible vehicle of the annuitant.

Variable Payment Life Annuity (VPLA)

Existing rules generally require retirement benefits from a PRPP or defined contribution RPP be provided to a member by means of a transfer of funds from the account to an RRSP or RRIF. Budget 2019 proposes that commencing in 2020 and subsequent years, PRPP and RPPs be able to provide a VPLA directly to members from the plan. A VPLA will provide payments that vary based on the investment performance of the underlying annuities fund and on the mortality experience of VPLA annuitants.

PRPP and defined contribution RPP administrators will be permitted to establish a separate annuities fund under the plan to receive transfers of amounts from members' accounts to provide for VPLAs. A minimum of 10 retired members will be required to participate in a VPLA. VPLAs will be required to comply with certain existing tax rules applicable to PRPPs and defined contribution RPPs, as well as additional requirements. On death, VPLAs will be subject to the existing tax treatment of annuities purchased with PRPP and defined contribution RPP savings.

Related Regulations: 221; 4900 [Prescribed qualified investments].

Related Sections: S. 146(1), "qualified investment"; s. 146.1(1), "qualified investment"; s. 146.3(1), "qualified investment"; s. 207.1(2) Tax payable by trust under deferred profit sharing plan; s. 262 Designated stock exchange.

Forms: T3F — Investments Prescribed to be Qualified Information Return.

Income Tax Folios: *Primary* — S3-F10-C1 Qualified Investments – RRSPs, RESPs, RRIFs, RDSPs and TFSAs. *Secondary* — S3-F10-C2 Prohibited Investments - RRSPs, RRIFs and TFSAs.

"revoked plan" —"revoked plan" means a deferred profit sharing plan the registration of which has been revoked by the Minister pursuant to subsection 147(14) or (14.1).

Related Regulations: Part XV.

Related Sections: S. 89(1), "public corporation"; s. 104(1) Reference to trust or estate; s. 108(1), "beneficiary"; s. 130(3) Meaning of expressions "investment corporation" and "taxed capital gains"; s. 131(8) Meaning of "mutual fund corporation"; s. 132(6) Meaning of "mutual fund trust"; s. 146(1), "qualified investment"; s. 147(1), "deferred profit sharing plan"; s. 248(1), "amount", "business", "corporation", "dividend", "prescribed", "property", "regulation", "share"; s. 255 Canada.

Information Circulars: IC 77-1R5 Deferred Profit Sharing Plan.

Part X.1
Tax in Respect of Over-Contributions to Deferred Income Plans

SECTION 204.1: [Tax payable]

► 204.1(1) ◄

(1) Tax payable by individuals. Where, at the end of any month after May, 1976, an individual has an excess amount for a year in respect of registered retirement savings plans, the individual shall, in respect of that month, pay a tax under this Part equal to 1% of that portion of the total of all those excess amounts that has not been paid by those plans to the individual before the end of that month.

Forms: T1-OVP-S — Simplified Individual Income Tax Return for RRSP Excess Contributions.

Information Circulars: IC 77-1R5 Deferred Profit Sharing Plan.

Interpretation Bulletins: *Secondary* — IT-124R6 Contributions to registered retirement savings plans.

► 204.1(2) ◄

(2) Amount deemed repaid. For the purposes of subsection (1), where an amount in respect of a plan has been included in computing an individual's income pursuant to paragraph 146(12)(*b*), that amount shall be deemed to have been paid to the individual by the plan at the time referred to in that paragraph.

► 204.1(2.1) ◄

(2.1) Tax payable by individuals — contributions after 1990. Where, at the end of any month after December, 1990, an individual has a cumulative excess amount in respect of registered retirement savings plans, the individual shall, in respect of that month, pay a tax under this Part equal to 1% of that cumulative excess amount.

Editorial Note: Effective December 14, 2012, the cumulative excess amount can include contributions made to the taxpayer's pooled registered pension plan (PRPP) in the year (see s. 147.5(11), which deems contributions made by a member to a PRPP to be a premium paid by the member to an RRSP for the purposes of certain provisions in the Act including Part X.1)).

Cases: There is no legislative provision that specifically prevents a taxpayer from claiming RRSP deductions with respect to excess contributions, provided they are within the RRSP deduction limit, nor is there any provision that allows the Minister to eliminate unused RRSP contributions on the basis they represented excess contributions that cannot be withdrawn. The Minister's remedy for over-contributions is limited to the 1% over-contributions tax and any penalty imposed for the failure to file an over-contributions form. The Minister previously accepted the taxpayer's relief application and concluded that the excessive contributions were resolved. This was conclusive and binding, and it was not open to the Minister to later arbitrarily eliminate unused RRSP contributions. The taxpayer had the necessary contribution room for contributions made during 2013–2015. *Roy v. The Queen*, 2019 DTC 1045 (TCC)

► 204.1(3) ◄

(3) Tax payable by deferred profit sharing plan. Where, at the end of any month after May, 1976, a trust governed by a deferred profit sharing plan has an excess amount, the trust shall, in respect of that month, pay a tax under this Part equal to 1% of the excess amount.

► 204.1(4) ◄

(4) Waiver of tax. Where an individual would, but for this subsection, be required to pay a tax under subsection (1) or (2.1) in respect of a month and the individual establishes to the satisfaction of the Minister that

(*a*) the excess amount or cumulative excess amount on which the tax is based arose as a consequence of reasonable error, and

(*b*) reasonable steps are being taken to eliminate the excess,

the Minister may waive the tax.

SECTION 204.2: Definition of "excess amount for a year in respect of registered retirement savings plans"

► 204.2(1) ◄

(1) Definition of "excess amount for a year in respect of registered retirement savings plans". "Excess amount for a year in respect of registered retirement savings plans" of an individual at a particular time means,

(*a*) where the excess amount is for a year after 1990, nil; and

(*b*) where the excess amount is for a year before 1991, the amount, if any, by which the total of

(i) all amounts paid by the individual to such plans under which the individual or the individual's spouse or common-law partner is the annuitant, other than amounts

(A) to which paragraph 60(*j*), (*j*.01), (*j*.1), (*j*.2) or (*l*) applies or would, if the individual were resident in Canada throughout the year, apply, or

(B) transferred to the plan in accordance with any of subsections 146(16), 147(19) and 147.3(1) and (4) to (7), and

(ii) all gifts made to such a plan under which the individual is the annuitant, other than gifts made thereto by the individual's spouse or common-law partner,

in the year and before the particular time, exceeds the total of

(iii) all amounts that may be deducted in computing the individual's income for the immediately preceding year in respect of those payments, and

(iv) the greater of $5,500 and the amount that may be deducted in computing the individual's income for the year in respect of those payments.

Related Sections: S. 248(1), "common-law partner".

Interpretation Bulletins: *Secondary* — IT-124R6 Contributions to registered retirement savings plans; IT-500R Registered retirement savings plans — Death of an annuitant.

► 204.2(1.1) ◄

(1.1) Cumulative excess amount in respect of RRSPs. The cumulative excess amount of an individual in respect of registered retirement savings plans at any time in a taxation year is the amount, if any, by which

(*a*) the amount of the individual's undeducted RRSP premiums at that time

exceeds

(*b*) the amount determined by the formula

$$A + B + R + C + D + E$$

where

A is the individual's unused RRSP deduction room at the end of the preceding taxation year,

B is the amount, if any, by which

(i) the lesser of the RRSP dollar limit for the year and 18% of the individual's earned income (as defined in subsection 146(1)) for the preceding taxation year

exceeds the total of all amounts each of which is

(ii) the individual's pension adjustment for the preceding taxation year in respect of an employer, or

(iii) a prescribed amount in respect of the individual for the year,

C is, where the individual attained 18 years of age in a preceding taxation year, $2,000, and in any other case, nil,

D is the group plan amount in respect of the individual at that time,

E is, where the individual attained 18 years of age before 1995, the individual's transitional amount at that time, and in any other case, nil, and

R is the individual's total pension adjustment reversal for the year.

History: S. 204.2(1.1)(*b*), the description of D was replaced by S.C. 2012, c. 31, s. 43(1), in force December 14, 2012, and formerly read:

D is the group RRSP amount in respect of the individual at that time,

Related Regulations: 8308(2); 8308.2; 8308.4; 8309.

Related Sections: S. 204.2(1.3) Group RRSP amount; s. 204.2(1.5) Transitional amount.

Interpretation Bulletins: *Secondary* — IT-307R4 Spousal registered retirement savings plans.

► 204.2(1.2) ◄

(1.2) Undeducted RRSP premiums. For the purposes of subsection (1.1) and the description of K in paragraph (1.3)(*a*), the amount of undeducted RRSP premiums of an individual at any time in a taxation year is the amount determined by the formula

$$H + I - J$$

where

H is, for taxation years ending before 1992, nil, and for taxation years ending after 1991, the amount, if any, by which

(*a*) the amount of the individual's undeducted RRSP premiums at the end of the immediately preceding taxation year

exceeds

(*b*) the total of the amounts deducted under subsections 146(5) and (5.1) in computing the individual's income for the immediately preceding taxation year, to the extent that each amount was deducted in respect of premiums paid under registered retirement savings plans in or before that preceding year,

I is the total of all amounts each of which is

(*a*) a premium (within the meaning assigned by subsection 146(1)) paid by the individual in the year and before that time under a registered retirement savings plan under which the individual or the individual's spouse or common-law partner was the annuitant (within the meaning assigned by subsection 146(1)) at the time the premium was paid, other than

(i) an amount paid to the plan in the first 60 days of the year and deducted in computing the individual's income for the immediately preceding taxation year,

(ii) an amount paid to the plan in the year and deducted under paragraph 60(*j*), (*j*.1), (*j*.2) or (*l*) in computing the individual's income for the year or the immediately preceding taxation year,

(iii) an amount transferred to the plan on behalf of the individual in accordance with any of subsections 146(16), 147(19), 147.3(1) and (4) to (7) and 147.5(21) or in circumstances to which subsection 146(21) applies,

(iv) an amount deductible under subsection 146(6.1) in computing the individual's income for the year or a preceding taxation year,

(v) where the individual is a non-resident person, an amount that would, if the individual were resident in Canada throughout the year and the immediately preceding taxation year, be deductible under paragraph 60(*j*), (*j*.1), (*j*.2) or (*l*) in computing the individual's income for the year or the immediately preceding taxation year, or

(vi) an amount paid to the plan in the year that is not deductible in computing the individual's income for the year because of subparagraph 146(5)(*a*)(iv.1) or (5.1)(*a*)(iv),

(*b*) a gift made in the year and before that time to a registered retirement savings plan under which the individual is the annuitant (within the meaning assigned by subsection 146(1)), other than a gift made thereto by the individual's spouse or common-law partner, or

(*c*) an amount contributed in the year and before that time by an employer or former employer of the individual to an account of the individual under a pooled registered pension plan, and

J is the amount, if any, by which

(*a*) the total of all amounts each of which is an amount (other than the portion of it that reduces the amount on which tax is payable by the individual under subsection 204.1(1)) received by the individual in the year and before that time out of or under a pooled registered pension plan, a registered retirement savings plan, a registered retirement income fund or a specified pension plan and included in computing the individual's income for the year

exceeds

(*b*) the amount deducted under paragraph 60(*l*) in computing the individual's income for the year.

History: S. 204.2(1.2), paragraph (*a*) of the description of J was replaced by S.C. 2017, c. 33, s. 65(1), deemed to have come into force on January 1, 2010, except that in its application before December 14, 2012, paragraph (*a*) of the description of J in subsection 204.2(1.2) is to be read without reference to "a pooled registered pension plan". S. 204.2(1.2), paragraph (*a*) of the description of J formerly read:

(*a*) the total of all amounts each of which is an amount (other than the portion of it that reduces the amount on which tax is payable by the individual under subsection 204.1(1)) received by the individual in the year and before that time out of or under a pooled registered pension plan, a registered retirement savings plan or a registered retirement income fund and included in computing the individual's income for the year

S. 204.2(1.2), subparagraph (*a*)(iii) of the description of I was replaced by S.C. 2012, c. 31, s. 43(2), in force December 14, 2012, and formerly read:

(iii) an amount transferred to the plan on behalf of the individual in accordance with any of subsections 146(16), 147(19) and 147.3(1) and (4) to (7) or in circumstances to which subsection 146(21) applies,

S. 204.2(1.2), paragraph (*c*) of the description of I was added by S.C. 2012, c. 31, s. 43(3), in force December 14, 2012.

S. 204.2(1.2), paragraph (*a*) of the description of J was replaced by S.C. 2012, c. 31, s. 43(4), in force December 14, 2012, and formerly read:

(*a*) the total of all amounts each of which is an amount (other than the portion thereof that reduces the amount on which tax is payable by the individual under subsection 204.1(1)) received by the individual in the year and before that time out of or under a registered retirement savings plan or a registered retirement income fund and included in computing the individual's income for the year

► 204.2(1.3) ◄

(1.3) Group plan amount. For the purposes of this section, the group plan amount in respect of an individual at any time in a taxation year is the lesser of

(*a*) the lesser of the value of F and the amount determined by the formula

$$F - (G - K)$$

where

F is the lesser of

(i) the total of all amounts each of which is a qualifying group plan amount in respect of the individual, to the extent that the amount is included in determining the value of I in subsection (1.2) in respect of the individual at that time, and

(ii) the RRSP dollar limit for the following taxation year,

G is the amount that would be determined under paragraph (1.1)(*b*) in respect of the individual at that time if the values of C, D and E in that paragraph were nil, and

K is

(i) where the year is the 1996 taxation year, the amount, if any, by which the amount of the individual's undeducted RRSP premiums at the beginning of the year exceeds the individual's cumulative excess amount in respect of registered retirement savings plans at the end of the 1995 taxation year, and

(ii) in any other case, the group plan amount in respect of the individual at the end of the preceding taxation year, and

(*b*) the amount that would be the individual's cumulative excess amount in respect of registered retirement savings plans at that time if the value of D in paragraph (1.1)(*b*) were nil.

History: S. 204.2(1.3), the portion before paragraph (*a*) was replaced by S.C. 2012, c. 31, s. 43(5), in force December 14, 2012, and formerly read:

(1.3) *Group RRSP amount.* For the purposes of this section, the group RRSP amount in respect of an individual at any time in a taxation year is the lesser of

S. 204.2(1.3)(*a*), subparagraph (i) of the description F was replaced by S.C. 2012, c. 31, s. 43(6), in force December 14, 2012, and formerly read:

(i) the total of all amounts each of which is a qualifying group RRSP premium paid by the individual, to the extent that the premium is included in determining the value of I in subsection (1.2) in respect of the individual at that time, and

S. 204.2(1.3)(*a*), subparagraph (ii) of the description K was replaced by S.C. 2012, c. 31, s. 43(7), in force December 14, 2012, and formerly read:

(ii) in any other case, the group RRSP amount in respect of the individual at the end of the preceding taxation year, and

Related Regulations: "past service pension adjustment", 8303(1); 8303(2); 8307(5).

Related Sections: S. 248(1), "individual", "past service pension adjustment"; s. 249(1) Definition of "taxation year".

► 204.2(1.31) ◄

(1.31) Qualifying group plan amount. For the purposes of the description of F in paragraph (1.3)(*a*), a qualifying group plan amount in respect of an individual is a premium paid under a registered retirement savings plan or an amount contributed by an employer or former employer of the individual to an account of the individual under a pooled registered pension plan if

(*a*) the plan is part of a qualifying arrangement or is a pooled registered pension plan,

(*b*) the premium or contribution is an amount to which the individual is entitled for services rendered by the individual (whether or not as an employee), and

(*c*) the premium or contribution was remitted to the plan on behalf of the individual by the person or body of persons that is required to remunerate the individual for the services, or by an agent for that person or body,

but does not include the part, if any, of a premium or contribution that, by making (or failing to make) an election or exercising (or failing to exercise) any other right under the plan after beginning to participate in the plan and within 12 months before the time the premium was paid or the contribution was made, the individual could have prevented the premium or contribution and that would not as a consequence have been required to be remitted on behalf of the individual to another registered retirement savings plan or pooled registered pension plan or to a money purchase provision of a registered pension plan.

History: S. 204.2(1.31) was replaced by S.C. 2012, c. 31, s. 43(8), in force December 14, 2012, and formerly read:

(1.31) *Qualifying group RRSP premium.* For the purpose of the description of F in paragraph (1.3)(*a*), a qualifying group RRSP premium paid by an individual is a premium paid under a registered retirement savings plan where

(*a*) the plan is part of a qualifying arrangement,

(*b*) the premium is an amount to which the individual is entitled for services rendered by the individual (whether or not as an employee), and

(*c*) the premium was remitted to the plan on behalf of the individual by the person or body of persons that is required to remunerate the individual for the services, or by an agent for that person or body,

but does not include the part, if any, of a premium that, by making (or failing to make) an election or exercising (or failing to exercise) any other right under the arrangement after beginning to participate in the arrangement and within 12 months before the time the premium was paid, the individual could have prevented from being paid under the plan and that would not as a consequence have been required to be remitted on behalf of the individual to another registered retirement savings plan or to a registered pension plan in respect of a money purchase provision of the plan.

▶ 204.2(1.32) ◀

(1.32) Qualifying arrangement. For the purpose of paragraph (1.31)(*a*), a qualifying arrangement is an arrangement under which premiums that satisfy the conditions in paragraphs (1.31)(*b*) and (*c*) are remitted to registered retirement savings plans on behalf of two or more individuals, but does not include an arrangement where it is reasonable to consider that one of the main purposes of the arrangement is to reduce tax payable under this Part.

▶ 204.2(1.4) ◀

(1.4) Deemed receipt where RRSP or RRIF amended. For the purposes of subsection (1.2),

(*a*) where an amount in respect of a registered retirement savings plan has been included in computing an individual's income pursuant to paragraph 146(12)(*b*), that amount shall be deemed to have been received by the individual out of the plan at the time referred to in that paragraph; and

(*b*) where an amount in respect of a registered retirement income fund has been included in computing an individual's income pursuant to paragraph 146.3(11)(*b*), that amount shall be deemed to have been received by the individual out of the fund at the time referred to in that paragraph.

▶ 204.2(1.5) ◀

(1.5) Transitional amount. For the purpose of the description of E in paragraph (1.1)(*b*), an individual's transitional amount at any time in a taxation year is the lesser of

(*a*) $6,000, and

(*b*) where the value of L is nil, nil, and in any other case, the amount determined by the formula

$$L - M$$

where

L is the amount, if any, by which

(i) the amount that would be determined under subsection (1.2) to be the amount of the individual's undeducted RRSP premiums at that time if

(A) the value of I in that subsection were determined for the 1995 taxation year without including premiums paid after February 26, 1995,

(B) the value of I in that subsection were nil for the 1996 and subsequent taxation years, and

(C) the value of J in that subsection were determined for the 1995 and subsequent taxation years without including the part, if any, of an amount received by the individual out of or under a registered retirement savings plan or registered retirement income fund that can reasonably be considered to be in respect of premiums paid after February 26, 1995 by the individual under a registered retirement savings plan

exceeds

(ii) the total of all amounts each of which is an amount deducted under subsection 146(5) or (5.1) in computing the individual's income for a preceding taxation year, to the extent that the amount was deducted in respect of premiums paid after that year (other than premiums paid before February 27, 1995), and

M is the amount that would be determined by the formula in paragraph (1.1)(*b*) in respect of the individual at that time if the values of D and E in that paragraph were nil and section 257 did not apply to that formula.

▶ 204.2(2) ◀

(2) Where terminated plan deemed to continue to exist. Notwithstanding paragraph 146(12)(*a*), for the purposes of this Part, where a registered retirement savings plan ceases to exist and a payment or transfer of funds out of that plan has been made to which subsection 146(16) applied, if an individual's excess amount for a year in respect of registered retirement savings plans would have been greater had that plan not ceased to exist, for the purpose of computing the excess amount for a year in respect of registered retirement savings plans for so long as the individual or the individual's spouse or common-law partner is the annuitant under any registered retirement savings plan under which an annuity has not commenced to be paid to the annuitant, the plan that ceased to exist shall be deemed to remain in existence and the individual or the individual's spouse or common-law partner, as the case may be, shall be deemed to continue to be the annuitant thereunder.

Related Sections: S. 248(1), "common-law partner".

► 204.2(3) ◄

(3) When retirement savings plan deemed to be a registered plan. Where a retirement savings plan under which an individual or the individual's spouse or common-law partner is the annuitant (within the meaning assigned by subsection 146(1)) is accepted by the Minister for registration, for the purpose of determining

(*a*) the amount of undeducted RRSP premiums of the individual at any time, and

(*b*) the excess amount for a year in respect of registered retirement savings plans of the individual at any time,

the retirement savings plan shall be deemed to have become a registered retirement savings plan on the later of the day on which the plan came into existence and May 25, 1976.

Related Sections: S. 248(1), "common-law partner".

► 204.2(4) ◄

(4) Definition of "excess amount" for a DPSP. "Excess amount" at any time for a trust governed by a deferred profit sharing plan means the total of all amounts each of which is

(*a*) such portion of the total of all contributions made to the trust before that time and after May 25, 1976 by a beneficiary under the plan, other than

(i) contributions that have been deducted by the beneficiary under paragraph 60(*k*) of the *Income Tax Act*, chapter 148 of the Revised Statutes of Canada, 1952,

(ii) amounts transferred to the plan on behalf of the beneficiary in accordance with subsection 147(19), or

(iii) the portion of the contributions (other than contributions referred to in subparagraphs (i) and (ii)) made by the beneficiary in each calendar year before 1991 not in excess of $5,500,

as has not been returned to the beneficiary before that time; or

(*b*) a gift received by the trust before that time and after May 25, 1976.

► 204.2(5) ◄

(5) PRPP withdrawals. Notwithstanding the *Pooled Registered Pension Plans Act* or any similar law of a province, a member of a PRPP may withdraw an amount from the member's account under the PRPP to reduce the amount of tax that would otherwise be payable by the member under this Part, to the extent that the reduction cannot be achieved by withdrawals from plans other than PRPPs.

History: S. 204.2(5) was added by S.C. 2012, c. 31, s. 43(9), in force December 14, 2012.

SECTION 204.3: Return and payment of tax

► 204.3(1) ◄

(1) Return and payment of tax. Within 90 days after the end of each year after 1975, a taxpayer to whom this Part applies shall

(*a*) file with the Minister a return for the year under this Part in prescribed form and containing prescribed information, without notice or demand therefor;

(*b*) estimate in the return the amount of tax, if any, payable by the taxpayer under this Part in respect of each month in the year; and

(*c*) pay to the Receiver General the amount of tax, if any, payable by the taxpayer under this Part in respect of each month in the year.

Forms: T1-OVP — 1998 Individual Income Tax Return for RRSP Excess Contributions.

Information Circulars: IC 78-14R4 Guidelines for trust companies and other persons responsible for filing T3GR, T3D, T3P, T3S, T3RI, and T3F returns.

Interpretation Bulletins: *Secondary* — IT-124R6 Contributions to registered retirement savings plans.

► 204.3(2) ◄

(2) Provisions applicable to Part. Subsections 150(2) and (3), sections 152 and 158, subsections 161(1) and (11), sections 162 to 167 and Division J of Part I are applicable to this Part with such modifications as the circumstances require.

Part X.2
Tax in Respect of Registered Investments

SECTION 204.4: [Registration of plan or fund]

► 204.4(1) ◄

(1) Definition of "registered investment". In this Part, "registered investment" means a trust or a corporation that has applied in prescribed form as of a particular date in the year of application and has been accepted by the Minister as of that date as a registered investment for one or more of the following:

(*a*) registered retirement savings plans,

(*b*) (Repealed by 1986, c. 6, s. 107(1).)

(*c*) registered retirement income funds, and

(*d*) deferred profit sharing plans

and that has not been notified by the Minister that it is no longer registered under this Part.

Related Sections: S. 146.3(1), "qualified investment"; s. 204, "qualified investment"; s. 259(1) Proportional holdings in trust property.

Tax Topics: No. 1697, Registered Investments.

Information Circulars: IC 78-14R4 Guidelines for trust companies and other persons responsible for filing T3GR, T3D, T3P, T3S, T3RI, and T3F returns.

Interpretation Bulletins: *Secondary* — IT-320R3 RRSPs — Qualified investments.

► 204.4(2) ◄

(2) Acceptance of applicant for registration. The Minister may accept for registration for the purposes of this Part any applicant that is

(*a*) a trust that has as its sole trustee a corporation licensed or otherwise authorized under the laws of Canada or a province to carry on in Canada the business of offering to the public its services as trustee if, on the particular date referred to in subsection (1),

(i) all the property of the applicant is held in trust for the benefit of not fewer than 20 beneficiaries and

(A) not fewer than 20 beneficiaries are taxpayers described in any of paragraphs 149(1)(*o*) to (*o*.2), (*o*.4) or (*s*), or

(B) not fewer than 100 beneficiaries are taxpayers described in paragraph 149(1)(*r*) or (*x*),

(ii) the total of

(A) the fair market value at the time of acquisition of its

(I) shares, marketable securities and cash, and

(II) bonds, debentures, mortgages, hypothecary claims, notes and other similar obligations, and

(B) the amount by which the fair market value at the time of acquisition of its real or immovable property that may reasonably be regarded as being held for the purpose of producing income from property exceeds the total of all amounts each of which is owing by it on account of its acquisition of the real or immovable property

is not less than 80% of the amount by which the fair market value at the time of acquisition of all its property exceeds the total of all amounts each of which is owing by it on account of its acquisition of real or immovable property,

(iii) the fair market value at the time of acquisition of its shares, bonds, mortgages, hypothecary claims and other securities of any one corporation or debtor (other than bonds, mortgages, hypothecary claims and other securities of or guaranteed by Her Majesty in right of Canada or a province or Canadian municipality) is not more than 10% of the amount by which the fair market value at the time of acquisition of all its property exceeds the total of all amounts each of which is an amount owing by it on account of its acquisition of real or immovable property,

(iv) the amount by which

(A) the fair market value at the time of acquisition of any one of its real or immovable properties

exceeds

(B) the total of all amounts each of which is owing by it on account of its acquisition of the real or immovable property

is not more than 10% of the amount by which the fair market value at the time of acquisition of all its property exceeds the total of all amounts each of which is owing by it on account of its acquisition of real or immovable property,

(v) not less than 95% of the income of the applicant for its most recently completed fiscal period, or where no such period exists, that part of its current fiscal period before the particular date, was derived from investments described in subparagraph (ii),

(vi) the total value of all interests in the applicant owned by all trusts or corporations described in any of paragraphs 149(1)(*o*) to (*o*.2), (*o*.4) or (*s*) to which any one employer, either alone or together with persons with whom the employer was not dealing at arm's length, has made contributions does not exceed 25% of the value of all its property,

(vii) the total value of all interests in the applicant owned by all trusts described in paragraph 149(1)(*r*) or (*x*) to which any one taxpayer, either alone or together with persons with whom the taxpayer was not dealing at arm's length, has made contributions does not exceed 25% of the value of all its property, and

(viii) the applicant does not hold property acquired by it after May 26, 1975 that is

(A) a mortgage or hypothecary claim (other than a mortgage or hypothecary claim insured under the *National Housing Act* or by a corporation that offers its services to the public in Canada as an insurer of mortgages or hypothecary claims and that is approved as a private insurer of mortgages or hypothecary claims by the Superintendent of Financial Institutions pursuant to the powers assigned to the Superintendent under subsection 6(1) of the *Office of the Superintendent of Financial Institutions Act*), or an interest therein, or for civil law a right therein, in respect of which the mortgagor or hypothecary debtor is the annuitant under a registered retirement savings plan or registered retirement income fund, or a person with whom the annuitant is not dealing at arm's length, if any of the funds of a trust governed by such a plan or fund have been used to acquire an interest in the applicant, or

(B) a bond, debenture, note or similar obligation issued by a cooperative corporation (within the meaning assigned by subsection 136(2)) or a credit union that has granted any benefit or privilege to any annuitant or beneficiary under a plan or fund referred to in subsection (1) that is dependent on or related to

(I) ownership by a trust governed by any such plan or fund of shares, bonds, debentures, notes or similar obligations of the cooperative corporation or credit union, or

(II) ownership by the applicant of shares, bonds, debentures, notes or similar obligations of the cooperative corporation or credit union if the trust governed by any such plan or fund has used any of its funds to acquire an interest in the applicant;

(*b*) a trust that

(i) would be a trust described in paragraph (*a*) if that paragraph were read without reference to subparagraphs (*a*)(i), (vi) and (vii), and

(ii) holds only prescribed investments for the type of plan or fund in respect of which it has applied for registration;

(*c*) a mutual fund trust;

(*d*) a trust that

(i) would be a mutual fund trust if paragraph 132(6)(*c*) were not applicable, and

(ii) holds only prescribed investments for the type of plan or fund in respect of which it has applied for registration;

(*e*) a mutual fund corporation or investment corporation; or

(*f*) a corporation that

(i) would be a mutual fund corporation or investment corporation if it could have elected to be a public corporation under paragraph (*b*) of the definition "public corporation" in subsection 89(1) had the conditions prescribed therefor required only that a class of shares of its capital stock be qualified for distribution to the public, and

(ii) holds only prescribed investments for the type of plan or fund in respect of which it has applied for registration.

History: S. 204.4(2)(*a*)(ii), the portion after clause (A) was replaced by S.C. 2013, c. 34, s. 154(1), in force June 26, 2013, and formerly read:

(B) the amount by which the fair market value at the time of acquisition of its real property that may reasonably be regarded as being held for the purpose of producing income from property exceeds the total of all amounts each of which is owing by it on account of its acquisition of the real property

is not less than 80% of the amount by which the fair market value at the time of acquisition of all its property exceeds the total of all amounts each of which is owing by it on account of its acquisition of real property,

S. 204.4(2)(*a*)(iii) and (iv) were replaced by S.C. 2013, c. 34, s. 154(2), in force June 26, 2013, and formerly read:

(iii) the fair market value at the time of acquisition of its shares, bonds, mortgages, hypothecary claims and other securities of any one corporation or debtor (other than bonds, mortgages, hypothecary claims and other securities of or guaranteed by Her Majesty in right of Canada or a province or Canadian municipality) is not more than 10% of the amount by which the fair market value at the time of acquisition of all its property exceeds the total of all amounts each of which is an amount owing by it on account of its acquisition of real property,

(iv) the amount by which

(A) the fair market value at the time of acquisition of any one of its real properties

exceeds

(B) the total of all amounts each of which is owing by it on account of its acquisition of the real property

is not more than 10% of the amount by which the fair market value at the time of acquisition of all its property exceeds the total of all amounts each of which is owing by it on account of its acquisition of real property,

S. 204.4(2)(*a*)(viii)(A) was replaced by S.C. 2013, c. 34, s. 154(3), in force June 26, 2013, and formerly read:

(A) a mortgage or hypothecary claim (other than a mortgage or hypothecary claim insured under the *National Housing Act* or by a corporation that offers its services to the public in Canada as an insurer of mortgages and that is approved as a private insurer of mortgages by the Superintendent of Financial Institutions pursuant to the powers assigned to the Superintendent under subsection 6(1) of the *Office of the Superintendent of Financial Institutions Act*), or an interest therein, in respect of which the mortgagor or hypothecary debtor is the annuitant under a registered retirement savings plan or a registered retirement income fund, or a person with whom the annuitant is not dealing at arm's length, if any of the funds of a trust governed by such a plan or fund have been used to acquire an interest in the applicant, or

Related Regulations: 4901(1).

Related Sections: S. 204.4(6) Successor trust; s. 204.4(7) Deemed registration of registered investment; s. 204.6(1) Tax payable — non-prescribed investment; s. 204.6(2) Tax payable — share, bond, mortgage, hypothecary claim etc.; s. 204.6(3) Tax payable — real property.

Forms: T3RI — Registered Investment Income Tax Return; T2217 — Application for Registration as a Registered Investment.

Information Circulars: IC 78-14R4 Guidelines for trust companies and other persons responsible for filing T3GR, T3D, T3P, T3S, T3RI, and T3F returns.

► 204.4(3) ◄

(3) Revocation of registration. The Minister shall notify a registered investment that it is no longer registered

(*a*) on being satisfied that, at a date subsequent to its registration date, it no longer satisfies one or more of the conditions necessary for it to be acceptable for registration under this Part, other than a condition the failure of which to satisfy would make it liable for tax under section 204.6; or

(*b*) within 30 days after receipt of a request in prescribed form from the registered investment for termination of its registration.

Related Sections: S. 204.4(4) Suspension of revocation; s. 204.4(5) Cancellation of revocation.

► 204.4(4) ◄

(4) Suspension of revocation. Notwithstanding a notification to a taxpayer under subsection (3), for the purposes of sections 204.6 and 204.7, the taxpayer is deemed to be a registered investment for each month or part of a month after the notification during which an interest in, or a share of the capital stock of, the taxpayer continues, by virtue of having been a registered investment, to be a qualified investment for a plan or fund referred to in subsection (1).

► 204.4(5) ◄

(5) Cancellation of revocation. Where a registered investment has been notified pursuant to paragraph (3)(*a*) and within 3 months from the date of notification it satisfies the Minister that it is acceptable for registration under this Part, the Minister may declare the notification to be a nullity.

► 204.4(6) ◄

(6) Successor trust. Where at any time in a year a particular trust described in paragraph (2)(*a*) or (*b*) has substantially the same beneficiaries and can reasonably be regarded as being a continuation of another trust that was a registered investment in the year or the immediately preceding year, for the purposes of this Part, the particular trust shall be deemed to be the same trust as the other trust.

► 204.4(7) ◄

(7) Deemed registration of registered investment. Where at the end of any month a registered investment could qualify for acceptance at that time under subsection (2), it shall be deemed for the purposes of section 204.6 to have been registered under the first of the following paragraphs under which it is registrable regardless of the paragraph under which it was accepted for registration by the Minister:

(*a*) paragraph (2)(*c*) or (*e*), as the case may be;

(*b*) paragraph (2)(*a*);

(*c*) paragraph (2)(*d*) or (*f*), as the case may be; and

(*d*) paragraph (2)(*b*).

SECTION 204.5: Publication of list in *Canada Gazette*

Each year the Minister shall cause to be published in the *Canada Gazette* a list of all registered investments as of December 31 of the preceding year.

Tax Topics: No. 1697, Registered Investments.

SECTION 204.6: Tax payable

► 204.6(1) ◄

(1) Tax payable. Where at the end of any month a taxpayer that is a registered investment described in paragraph 204.4(2)(*b*), (*d*) or (*f*) holds property that is not a prescribed investment for that taxpayer, it shall, in respect of that month, pay a tax under this Part equal to 1% of the fair market value at the time of its acquisition of each such property.

Related Regulations: 4901(1).

Related Sections: S. 204.4(3) Revocation of registration; s. 204.4(4) Suspension of revocation.

Information Circulars: IC 78-14R4 Guidelines for trust companies and other persons responsible for filing T3GR, T3D, T3P, T3S, T3RI, and T3F returns.

► 204.6(2) ◄

(2) Tax payable. Where at the end of any month a taxpayer that is a registered investment described in paragraph 204.4(2)(*a*) or (*b*) holds property that is a share, bond, mortgage, hypothecary claim or other security of a corporation or debtor (other than bonds, mortgages, hypothecary claims and other securities of or guaranteed by Her Majesty in right of Canada or a province or Canadian municipality), it shall, in respect of that month, pay a tax under this Part equal to 1% of the amount, if any, by which

(*a*) the total of all amounts each of which is the fair market value of such a property at the time of its acquisition

exceeds

(*b*) 10% of the amount by which

(i) the total of all amounts each of which is the fair market value, at the time of acquisition, of one of its properties

exceeds

(ii) the total of all amounts each of which is an amount owing by the trust at the end of the month in respect of the acquisition of real property or immovables.

History: S. 204.6(2)(*b*)(ii) was replaced by S.C. 2013, c. 34, s. 155(1), in force June 26, 2013, and formerly read:

(ii) the total of all amounts each of which is an amount owing by the trust at the end of the month in respect of the acquisition of real property.

Information Circulars: IC 78-14R4 Guidelines for trust companies and other persons responsible for filing T3GR, T3D, T3P, T3S, T3RI, and T3F returns.

▶ 204.6(3) ◀

(3) Tax payable — real property or immovables. If at the end of any month a taxpayer that is a registered investment described in paragraph 204.4(2)(*a*) holds real or immovable property, it shall, in respect of that month, pay a tax under this Part equal to 1% of the total of all amounts each of which is the amount by which the excess of

(*a*) the fair market value at the time of its acquisition of any one real or immovable property of the taxpayer

over

(*b*) the total of all amounts each of which was an amount owing by it at the end of the month on account of its acquisition of the real or immovable property

was greater than 10% of the amount by which the total of all amounts each of which is the fair market value at the time of its acquisition of a property held by it at the end of the month exceeds the total of all amounts each of which was an amount owing by it at the end of the month on account of its acquisition of real or immovable property.

History: S. 204.6(3) was replaced by S.C. 2013, c. 34, s. 155(2), in force June 26, 2013, and formerly read:

(3) *Idem.* Where at the end of any month a taxpayer that is a registered investment described in paragraph 204.4(2)(*a*) holds real property, it shall, in respect of that month, pay a tax under this Part equal to 1% of the total of all amounts each of which is the amount by which the excess of

(*a*) the fair market value at the time of its acquisition of any one real property of the taxpayer

over

(*b*) the total of all amounts each of which was an amount owing by it at the end of the month on account of its acquisition of the real property

was greater than 10% of the amount by which the total of all amounts each of which is the fair market value at the time of its acquisition of a property held by it at the end of the month exceeds the total of all amounts each of which was an amount owing by it at the end of the month on account of its acquisition of real property.

SECTION 204.7: Return and payment of tax

▶ 204.7(1) ◀

(1) Return and payment of tax. Within 90 days from the end of each taxation year commencing after 1980, a registered investment shall

(*a*) file with the Minister a return for the year under this Part in prescribed form and containing prescribed information, without notice or demand therefor;

(*b*) estimate in the return the amount of tax, if any, payable by it under this Part for the year; and

(*c*) pay to the Receiver General the amount of tax, if any, payable by it under this Part for the year.

Related Sections: S. 204.4(4) Suspension of revocation; s. 204.7(2) Liability of trustee.

Forms: T3RI — Registered Investment Income Tax Return.

▶ 204.7(2) ◀

(2) Liability of trustee. Where the trustee of a registered investment that is liable to pay tax under this Part does not remit to the Receiver General the amount of the tax within the time specified in subsection (1), the trustee is personally liable to pay on behalf of the registered investment the full amount of the tax and is entitled to recover from the registered investment any amount paid by the trustee as tax under this section.

▶ 204.7(3) ◀

(3) Provisions applicable to Part. Subsections 150(2) and (3), sections 152 and 158, subsections 161(1) and (11), sections 162 to 167 and Division J of Part I are applicable to this Part with such modifications as the circumstances require.

Part X.3
Labour-Sponsored Venture Capital Corporations

SECTION 204.8: [Interpretation]

► 204.8(1) ◄

(1) Definitions. In this Part,

"annuitant" —"annuitant" has the meaning assigned by subsection 146(1);

"eligible business entity" —"eligible business entity", at any time, means a particular entity that is

(*a*) a prescribed corporation, or

(*b*) a Canadian partnership or a taxable Canadian corporation, all or substantially all of the fair market value of the property of which is, at that time, attributable to

(i) property used in a specified active business carried on by the particular entity or by a corporation controlled by the particular entity,

(ii) shares of the capital stock or debt obligations of one or more entities that, at that time, are eligible business entities related to the particular entity, or

(iii) any combination of properties described in subparagraph (i) or (ii);

Editorial Note: For these purposes, the CRA's long-held position is that "all or substantially all" means 90%. See also editorial notes under s. 127.4(2) and 204.81 regarding the phase-out of the federal LSVCC tax regime.

Related Regulations: 4801.02.

Related Sections: S. 248(1), "Canadian partnership", "taxable Canadian corporation"; s. 251 Arm's length; s. 256(6) Saving provision — controlled corporations; s. 256(6.1) Simultaneous control.

"eligible investment" —"eligible investment" of a particular corporation means

(*a*) a share that was issued to the particular corporation and that is a share of the capital stock of a corporation that was an eligible business entity at the time the share was issued,

(*b*) a particular debt obligation that was issued to the particular corporation by an entity that was an eligible business entity at the time the particular debt obligation was issued where

(i) the entity is not restricted by the terms of the particular debt obligation or by the terms of any agreement related to that obligation from incurring other debts,

(ii) the particular debt obligation, if secured, is secured solely by a floating charge on the assets of the entity or by a guarantee referred to in paragraph (*c*), and

(iii) the particular debt obligation, by its terms or any agreement relating to that obligation, is subordinate to all other debt obligations of the entity, except that, where the entity is a corporation, the particular debt obligation need not be subordinate to

(A) a debt obligation, issued by the entity, that is prescribed to be a small business security, or

(B) a debt obligation owing to a shareholder of the entity or to a person related to any such shareholder,

(*c*) a guarantee provided by the particular corporation in respect of a debt obligation that would, if the debt obligation had been issued to the particular corporation at the time the guarantee was provided, have been at that time an eligible investment because of paragraph (*b*), or

(*d*) an option or a right granted by an eligible business entity that is a corporation, in conjunction with the issue of a share or debt obligation that is an eligible investment, to acquire a share of the capital stock of the eligible business entity that would be an eligible investment if that share were issued at the time that the option or right was granted,

if the following conditions are satisfied:

(*e*) immediately after the time the share or debt obligation was issued, the guarantee was provided or the option or right was granted, as the case may be, the total of the costs to the particular corporation of all shares, options, rights and debt obligations of the eligible business entity and all corporations related to it and 25% of the amount of all guarantees provided by the particular corporation in respect of debt obligations of the eligible business entity and the related corporations does not exceed the lesser of $15,000,000 and 10% of the shareholders' equity in the particular corporation, determined in accordance with generally accepted accounting principles, on a cost basis and without taking into account any unrealized gains or losses on the investments of the particular corporation, and

(*f*) immediately before the time the share or debt obligation was issued, the guarantee was provided or the option or right was granted, as the case may be,

(i) the carrying value of the total assets of the eligible business entity and all corporations (other than prescribed labour-sponsored venture capital corporations) related to it (determined in accordance with generally accepted accounting principles on a consolidated or combined basis, where applicable) did not exceed $50,000,000, and

(ii) the total of

(A) the number of employees of the eligible business entity and all corporations related to it who normally work at least 20 hours per week for the entity and the related corporations, and

(B) 1/2 of the number of other employees of the entity and the related corporations,

did not exceed 500;

(*g*) (Repealed by 1998, c. 19, s. 51(1).)

Related Regulations: 5100(2); 6701; 6701.1.

"eligible labour body" —"eligible labour body" means a trade union, as defined in the *Canada Labour Code*, that represents employees in more than one province, or an organization that is composed of 2 or more such unions;

"labour-sponsored funds tax credit" — (Repealed by S.C. 1997, c. 25, s. 55(1).)

"national central labour body" — (Repealed by S.C. 1994, c. 7, Sched. VIII, s. 118(2).)

"original acquisition" —"original acquisition" of a share has the meaning assigned by subsection 127.4(1);

"original purchaser" — (Repealed by S.C. 1997, c. 25, s. 55(2).)

"registered labour-sponsored venture capital corporation" — (Repealed by S.C. 1997, c. 25, s. 55(1).)

"reserve" —"reserve" means

(*a*) property described in any of paragraphs (*a*), (*b*), (*c*), (*f*) and (*g*) of the definition "qualified investment" in section 204, and

(*b*) deposits with a credit union that is a "member institution" in relation to a deposit insurance corporation (within the meaning assigned by subsection 137.1(5));

History: S. 204.8(1), the definition "reserve" was replaced by S.C. 2013, c. 34, s. 335(1), applicable to taxation years that end after 2006, and formerly read:

"reserve"—"reserve" means property described in any of paragraphs (*a*), (*b*), (*c*), (*f*) and (*g*) of the definition "qualified investment" in section 204;

"revoked corporation" —"revoked corporation" means a corporation the registration of which has been revoked under subsection 204.81(6);

"specified active business" —"specified active business", at any time, means an active business that is carried on in Canada where

(*a*) at least 50% of the full-time employees employed at that time in respect of the business are employed in Canada, and

(*b*) at least 50% of the salaries and wages paid to employees employed at that time in respect of the business are reasonably attributable to services rendered in Canada by the employees;

"specified individual" —"specified individual", in respect of a share, means an individual (other than a trust) whose labour-sponsored funds tax credit (as defined by subsection 127.4(6)) in respect of the original acquisition of the share is not nil or would not be nil if this Act were read without reference to paragraphs 127.4(6)(*b*) and (*d*).

"start-up period" —"start-up period" of a corporation means

(*a*) subject to paragraph (*c*), in the case of a corporation that first issued Class A shares before February 17, 1999, the corporation's taxation year in which it first issued those shares and the four following taxation years,

(*b*) subject to paragraph (*c*), in the case of a corporation that first issues Class A shares after February 16, 1999, the corporation's taxation year in which it first issues those shares and the following taxation year, or

(*c*) where a corporation files an election with its return under this Part for a particular taxation year of the corporation that ends after 1998 and that is referred to in paragraph (*a*) or (*b*), the period, if any, consisting of the taxation years referred to in paragraph (*a*) or (*b*), as the case may be, other than the particular year and all taxation years following the particular year.

Related Sections: S. 204.82(1) Recovery of credit; s. 204.82(2) Liability for tax.

"terminating corporation" —"terminating corporation" in respect of a particular corporation means a predecessor corporation in circumstances where

(*a*) subsection 204.85(3) applies to a merger of the particular corporation and the predecessor corporation,

(*b*) Class A shares of the particular corporation have been issued to the predecessor corporation in exchange for property of the predecessor corporation, and

(*c*) within a reasonable period of time after the exchange, Class A shareholders of the predecessor corporation receive all of the Class A shares of the particular corporation issued to the predecessor corporation in the course of a wind-up of the predecessor corporation.

History: S. 204.8(1), the definition "terminating corporation" was added by S.C. 2013, c. 34, s. 335(2), deemed to have come into force on January 1, 2005.

► 204.8(2) ◄

(2) When venture capital business discontinued. For the purposes of section 127.4, this Part and Part XII.5, a corporation discontinues its venture capital business

(*a*) at the time its articles cease to comply with paragraph 204.81(1)(*c*) and would so cease to comply if it had been incorporated after December 5, 1996;

(*b*) at the time it begins to wind-up, and for the purpose of this paragraph a corporation is not to be considered to have begun to wind up solely because it discontinues its venture capital business under prescribed wind-up rules;

(*c*) immediately before the time it amalgamates or merges with one or more other corporations to form one corporate entity (other than an entity deemed by paragraph 204.85(3)(*d*) to have been registered under this Part);

(*d*) at the time it becomes a revoked corporation, if one of the grounds on which the Minister could revoke its registration for the purposes of this Part is set out in paragraph 204.81(6)(*a*.1); or

(*e*) at the first time after the revocation of its registration for the purposes of this Part that it fails to comply with any of the provisions of its articles governing its authorized capital, the management of its business and affairs, the reduction of paid-up capital or the redemption or transfer of its Class A shares.

History: S. 204.8(2)(*b*) was replaced by S.C. 2013, c. 34, s. 335(3), deemed to have come into force on October 24, 2012, and formerly read:

(*b*) at the time it begins to wind-up;

Related Sections: S. 204.841 Penalty tax where venture capital business discontinued.

► 204.8(3) ◄

(3) Date of issue of Class A shares. For the purposes of this Part and subsection 211.8(1), in determining the time of the issue or the original acquisition of Class A shares, identical Class A shares held by a person are deemed to be disposed of by the person in the order in which the shares were issued.

SECTION 204.81: Conditions for registration

► 204.81(1) ◄

(1) Conditions for registration. The Minister may register a corporation for the purposes of this Part if the corporation's application for registration was received before March 21, 2013 and if, in the opinion of the Minister, it complies with the following conditions:

(*a*) the corporation has applied in prescribed form to the Minister for registration;

(*b*) the corporation was caused to be incorporated under the *Canada Business Corporations Act* by an eligible labour body; and

(*c*) the articles of the corporation provide that

(i) the business of the corporation is restricted to assisting the development of eligible business entities and to creating, maintaining and protecting jobs by providing financial and managerial advice to such entities and by investing funds of the corporation in eligible investments and reserves,

(ii) the authorized capital of the corporation shall consist only of

(A) Class A shares that are issuable only to individuals (other than trusts), terminating corporations in respect of the corporation and trusts governed by registered retirement savings plans or by TFSAs and that entitle their holders

(I) to receive notice of and, subject to the *Canada Business Corporations Act*, to attend and vote at all meetings of the shareholders of the corporation,

(II) to receive dividends at the discretion of the board of directors of the corporation, and

(III) to receive, on dissolution of the corporation, all the assets of the corporation that remain after payment of all amounts payable to the holders of all other classes of shares of the corporation,

(B) Class B shares that are issuable only to and may be held only by eligible labour bodies, that entitle each of those shareholders

(I) to receive notice of and, subject to the *Canada Business Corporations Act*, to attend and vote at all meetings of the shareholders of the corporation, and

(II) to receive, on dissolution of the corporation, an amount equal to the amount of the consideration received by the corporation on the issue of the Class B shares,

but that do not entitle them to receive dividends, and

(C) any additional classes of shares that are authorized, if the rights, privileges, restrictions and conditions attached to the shares are approved by the Minister of Finance,

(iii) the business and affairs of the corporation shall be managed by a board of directors, at least 1/2 of whom are appointed by the Class B shareholders,

(iv) the corporation shall not reduce its paid-up capital in respect of a class of shares (other than Class B shares) otherwise than by way of

(A) a redemption of shares of the corporation, or

(B) a reduction in its paid-up capital attributable to a class of shares for which no shares have been issued in the eight-year period ending at the time of the reduction,

(v) the corporation shall not redeem a Class A share in respect of which an information return described in paragraph (6)(*c*) has been issued unless

(A) if the share is held by the specified individual in respect of the share, a spouse or common-law partner or former spouse or common-law partner of that individual or a trust governed by a registered retirement savings plan, TFSA or registered retirement income fund under which that individual, spouse or common-law partner is the annuitant,

(I) a request in writing to redeem the share is made by the holder to the corporation and the information return referred to in paragraph (6)(*c*) has been returned to the corporation, or

(II) (Repealed.)

(III) the corporation is notified in writing that the specified individual in respect of the share became disabled and permanently unfit for work or terminally ill after the share was issued,

(B) there is no specified individual in respect of the share,

(C) (Repealed.)

(D) the corporation is notified in writing that the share is held by a person on whom the share has devolved as a consequence of the death of

(I) a holder of the share, or

(II) an annuitant under a trust governed by a registered retirement savings plan, TFSA or registered retirement income fund that was a holder of the share,

(E) the redemption occurs

(I) more than eight years after the day on which the share was issued, or

(II) if the day that is eight years after that issuance is in February or March of a calendar year, in February or on March 1st of that calendar year but not more than 31 days before that day, or

(F) the holder of the share has satisfied such other conditions as are prescribed,

(vi) (Repealed.)

(vii) the corporation shall not register a transfer of a Class A share by the specified individual in respect of the share, a spouse or common-law partner of the specified individual or a trust governed by a registered retirement savings plan, TFSA or registered retirement income fund under which the specified individual or spouse or common-law partner is the annuitant, unless

(A) no information return has been issued under paragraph (6)(*c*) in respect of the share,

(B) the transfer occurs more than eight years after the day on which the share was issued,

(C) the transfer is to the specified individual, a spouse or common-law partner or former spouse or common-law partner of the specified individual or a trust governed by a registered retirement savings plan, TFSA or registered retirement income fund under which the specified individual or the spouse or common-law partner or former spouse or common-law partner of the specified individual is the annuitant,

(D) the corporation is notified in writing that the transfer occurs as a consequence of the death of the specified individual or a spouse or common-law partner of the specified individual,

(E) the corporation is notified in writing that the transfer occurs after the specified individual dies,

(F) (Repealed.)

(G) the corporation is notified in writing that the specified individual became disabled and permanently unfit for work or terminally ill after the share was issued and before the transfer, or

(H) such other conditions as are prescribed are satisfied.

(viii) the corporation shall not pay any fee or remuneration to a shareholder, director or officer of the corporation unless the payment was approved by a resolution of the directors of the corporation, and

(ix) the corporation shall not make any investment in an eligible business entity with which the corporation or any of the directors of the corporation does not deal at arm's length unless

(A) the corporation would deal at arm's length with the eligible business entity but for the corporation's interest as the holder of eligible investments in such entity, or

(B) the investment was approved by special resolution of the shareholders of the corporation before the investment was made.

Editorial Note: Section 204.81 sets out the conditions for federal registration of a labour-sponsored venture capital corporation ("LSVCC"). LSVCCs may also register provincially (see Regulation 6701). Since the LSVCC tax credit under s. 127.4 will be phased out by 2017, no new LSVCCs may be registered federally after March 20, 2013. Transitional rules have been enacted for revocation of federal registrations as a result of this phase-out (see subsection (8.3)).

History: S. 204.81(1), the portion before paragraph (*a*) was replaced by S.C. 2013, c. 40, s. 73(1), deemed to have come into force on March 21, 2013, and formerly read:

(1) *Conditions for registration.* The Minister may register a corporation for the purposes of this Part if, in the opinion of the Minister, it complies with the following conditions:

S. 204.81(1)(*c*)(ii)(A), the portion before subclause (I) was replaced by S.C. 2013, c. 34, s. 336(1), deemed to have come into force on January 1, 2005, and formerly read:

Class A shares that are issuable only to individuals (other than trusts), trusts governed by registered retirement savings plans and trusts governed by TFSAs and that entitle their holders

S. 204.81(1)(*c*)(iv) was replaced by S.C. 2013, c. 34, s. 336(2), deemed to have come into force on October 24, 2012, and formerly read:

(iv) the corporation shall not reduce its paid-up capital in respect of a class of shares (other than Class B shares) otherwise than by way of a redemption of shares of the corporation or in such other manner as is prescribed,

S. 204.81(1)(*c*)(v)(E) was replaced by S.C. 2013, c. 34, s. 336(3), applicable after February 6, 2000 to corporations incorporated at any time, and formerly read:

(E) the redemption occurs more than 8 years after the day on which the share was issued, or

S. 204.81(1)(*c*)(vii)(B) was added by S.C. 2013, c. 34, s. 336(4), applicable as of October 24, 2012 to corporations incorporated after March 5, 1996.

S. 204.81(1)(*c*)(v)(A), the portion before subclause (I) was replaced by S.C. 2010, c. 25, s. 55(1), applicable to the 2009 and subsequent taxation years. S. 204.81(1)(*c*)(v)(A), the portion before subclause (I) formerly read:

(A) where the share is held by the specified individual in respect of the share, a spouse or common-law partner or former spouse or common-law partner of that individual or a trust governed by a registered retirement savings plan or registered retirement income fund under which that individual, spouse or common-law partner is the annuitant,

S. 204.81(1)(*c*)(v)(D)(II) was replaced by S.C. 2010, c. 25, s. 55(2), applicable to the 2009 and subsequent taxation years. S. 204.81(1)(*c*)(v)(D)(II) formerly read:

(II) an annuitant under a trust governed by a registered retirement savings plan or registered retirement income fund that was a holder of the share,

S. 204.81(1)(c)(vii), the portion before clause (A) was replaced by S.C. 2010, c. 25, s. 55(3), applicable to the 2009 and subsequent taxation years. S. 204.81(1)(c)(vii), the portion before clause (A) formerly read:

(vii) the corporation shall not register a transfer of a Class A share by the specified individual in respect of the share, a spouse or common-law partner of the specified individual or a trust governed by a registered retirement savings plan or registered retirement income fund under which the specified individual or spouse or common-law partner is the annuitant, unless

S. 204.81(1)(c)(vii)(C) was replaced by S.C. 2010, c. 25, s. 55(4), applicable to the 2009 and subsequent taxation years. S. 204.81(1)(c)(vii)(C) formerly read:

(C) the transfer is to the specified individual, a spouse or common-law partner or former spouse or common-law partner of the specified individual or a trust governed by a registered retirement savings plan or registered retirement income fund under which the specified individual or the spouse or common-law partner or former spouse or common-law partner of the specified individual is the annuitant,

S. 204.81(1)(c)(ii)(A), the portion before subclause (I) was replaced by S.C. 2009, c. 2, s. 67(1), applicable to the 2009 and subsequent taxation years. S. 204.81(1)(c)(ii)(A), the portion before subclause (I) formerly read:

(A) Class A shares that are issuable only to individuals (other than trusts) and trusts governed by registered retirement savings plans, that entitle their holders

Related Regulations: 6706.

Related Sections: S. 127.4(1) Definitions.

Forms: T5005 — Application to Register a Labor-Sponsored Venture Capital Corporation.

► 204.81(1.1) ◄

(1.1) Corporations incorporated before March 6, 1996. In applying clause (1)(*c*)(v)(E) in relation to any time before 2004 in respect of a corporation incorporated before March 6, 1996, the references in that clause to "eight" are replaced with references to "five" if, at that time, the relevant statements in the corporation's articles refer to "five".

History: S. 204.81(1.1) was added by S.C. 2013, c. 34, s. 336(5), deemed to have come into force on February 7, 2000.

► 204.81(1.2) ◄

(1.2) Deemed provisions in articles. In applying subsection (1) in relation to any time before 2004, to a corporation incorporated before February 7, 2000, if the articles of the corporation comply with subclause (1)(*c*)(v)(E)(I) (as modified, where relevant, by subsection (1.1)), those articles are deemed to provide the statement required by subclause (1)(*c*)(v)(E)(II).

History: S. 204.81(1.2) was added by S.C. 2013, c. 34, s. 336(5), deemed to have come into force on February 7, 2000.

► 204.81(2) ◄

(2) Registration number. On registering a corporation under subsection (1), the Minister shall assign to it a registration number.

Related Regulations: 6708.

Related Sections: S. 127.4(1) Definitions.

► 204.81(3) ◄

(3) Successive registrations. Where an eligible labour body causes more than one corporation to be registered under this Part, for the purposes of paragraph (6)(*h*) and section 204.82, each of those corporations shall be deemed

(*a*) to have issued a Class A share at the earliest time any such corporation issued a Class A share,

and, where the corporation did not exist at the time referred to in paragraph (*a*),

(*b*) to have been in existence during the particular period beginning immediately before that time and ending immediately after the corporation was incorporated, and

(*c*) to have had, throughout the particular period, fiscal periods ending on the same calendar day in each year in the particular period as the calendar day on which its first fiscal period after it was incorporated ended.

Related Sections: S. 127.4(1) Definitions.

Forms: T5006 SUM — Summary of Registered Labour-Sponsored Venture Capital Corporation Class A Shares; T5006 — Statement of Registered Labor-Sponsored Venture Capital Corporation Class A Shares.

► 204.81(4) ◄

(4) Determination of cost. For the purposes of this Part, the cost at any time to a corporation of an eligible investment that is a guarantee shall be deemed to be 25% of the amount of the debt obligation subject to the guarantee at that time.

Related Sections: S. 127.4(1) Definitions.

► 204.81(5) ◄

(5) Registration date. Where the Minister registers a corporation for the purposes of this Part, the corporation shall be deemed to have become so registered on the later of

(*a*) the day the application for registration of the plan is received by the Minister, and

(*b*) where in the application for registration a day is specified as the day on which the registration is to take effect, that day.

Related Sections: S. 127.4(1) Definitions.

► 204.81(6) ◄

(6) Revocation of registration. The Minister may revoke the registration of a corporation for the purposes of this Part where

(*a*) the articles of the corporation do not comply with paragraph (1)(*c*) and would not comply with that paragraph if the corporation had been incorporated after December 5, 1996;

(*a*.1) the corporation does not comply with any of the provisions of its articles described in paragraph (1)(*c*), except where there would be no failure to comply if the provisions of its articles were consistent with the articles of a corporation that would be permitted to be registered under this Part if it had been incorporated after December 5, 1996;

(*b*) an individual acquires or irrevocably subscribes and pays for a Class A share of the capital stock of the corporation in the period beginning on the 61st day of a calendar year and ending on the 60th day of the following calendar year and the corporation fails to file with the Minister an information return in prescribed form containing prescribed information before April of that following calendar year;

(*c*) an individual acquires or irrevocably subscribes and pays for a Class A share of the capital stock of the corporation in the period beginning on the 61st day of a calendar year and ending on the 60th day of the following calendar year and the corporation fails to issue to the individual before April of that following calendar year an information return in prescribed form stating the amount of the consideration paid for the share in that period;

(*d*) the corporation issues more than one information return described in paragraph (*c*) in respect of the same acquisition of or subscription for a Class A share;

(*e*) the financial statements of the corporation presented to its shareholders are not prepared in accordance with generally accepted accounting principles;

(*f*) the corporation fails within 6 months after the end of any taxation year to have an independent valuation of its shares made as of the end of that year;

(*g*) (Repealed by 2000, c. 19, s. 55(1).)

(*h*) the corporation does not pay the tax or penalty payable under section 204.82 by it on or before the day on or before which that tax or penalty is required to be paid;

(*i*) tax was payable under subsection 204.82(3) by the corporation for 3 or more taxation years;

(*j*) the corporation provides a guarantee that is an eligible investment and fails to maintain, at any time during the term of the guarantee, a reserve equal to the cost to the corporation of the guarantee at that time;

(*k*) the corporation pays a fee or commission in excess of a reasonable amount in respect of the offering for sale, or the sale, of its shares; or

(*l*) the corporation has a monthly deficiency in 18 or more months in any 36-month period.

Related Sections: S. 127.4(1) Definitions; s. 204.8(2) When venture capital business discontinued; s. 204.81(4) Determination of cost; s. 204.81(7) Notice of intent to revoke registration; s. 204.81(8) Publication in Canada Gazette; s. 204.84 Penalty.

Forms: T2152 — Part X.3 Tax Return for a Labour-Sponsored Venture Capital Corporation; T5006 SUM — Summary of Registered Labour-Sponsored Venture Capital Corporation Class A Shares; T5006 — Statement of Registered Labor-Sponsored Venture Capital Corporation Class A Shares.

► 204.81(7) ◄

(7) Notice of intent to revoke registration. Where the Minister proposes to revoke the registration of a corporation under subsection (6), the Minister shall, by registered mail, give notice to the corporation of the proposal.

Related Sections: S. 127.4(1) Definitions.

► 204.81(8) ◄

(8) Idem. Where the Minister gives notice under subsection (7) to a registered labour-sponsored venture capital corporation, the Minister may, after the expiration of 30 days after the day of mailing of the notice, or after the expiration of such extended period after the day of mailing as the Federal Court of Appeal or a judge thereof, on application made at any time before the determination of any appeal under subsection (9) from the giving of the notice, may fix or allow, publish a copy of the notice in the *Canada Gazette* and, on the publication of a copy of the notice, the registration of the corporation is revoked.

Related Sections: S. 127.4(1) Definitions.

► 204.81(8.1) ◄

(8.1) Voluntary de-registration. Where at any time the Minister receives a certified copy of a resolution of the directors of a corporation seeking the revocation of the corporation's registration under this Part,

(*a*) the registration is revoked at that time; and

(*b*) the Minister shall, with all due dispatch, give notice in the *Canada Gazette* of the revocation.

Related Sections: S. 204.81(8.2) Application of subsection 248(7).

► 204.81(8.2) ◄

(8.2) Application of subsection 248(7). Subsection 248(7) does not apply for the purpose of subsection (8.1).

► 204.81(8.3) ◄

(8.3) Transitional rules. If a registered labour-sponsored venture capital corporation notifies the Minister in writing of its intent to revoke its registration under this Part, the following rules apply:

(*a*) the corporation shall not, on or after the day the notice is provided to the Minister (referred to in this subsection and subsection (8.4) as the "notification date"), issue any tax credit certificates, other than duplicate certificates to replace certificates issued before that day;

(*b*) section 204.841 does not apply on the discontinuance of its venture capital business;

(*c*) subsections 204.82(1) to (4) do not apply to taxation years of the corporation that begin on or after the notification date; and

(*d*) subsection 204.83(1) does not apply in respect of a period, referred to in that subsection as the "second period", that ends after the notification date.

History: S. 204.81(8.3), the portion before paragraph (*a*) was replaced by S.C. 2014, c. 20, s. 24(1), deemed to have come into force on November 27, 2013, and formerly read:

(8.3) *Discontinuance of provincial program.* If a corporation is a prescribed labour-sponsored venture capital corporation because of the laws of a province, which province has discontinued its labour-sponsored venture capital corporation credit program, notifies the Minister in writing of its intent to revoke its registration under this Part, and meets the requirements under prescribed wind-up rules, then the following rules apply:

S. 204.81(8.3) was added by S.C. 2013, c. 34, s. 336(6), deemed to have come into force on October 24, 2012.

Related Regulations: 6701; 6708.

► 204.81(8.4) ◄

(8.4) Discontinuance of provincial program. Subsection (8.3) applies to a corporation only if,

(*a*) on the notification date, the percentage determined in respect of the corporation by the following formula is less than 20 per cent:

$$A/(B - C) \times 100$$

where

A is the amount of equity capital received by the corporation on the issue of Class A shares that were issued in the 24 months immediately preceding the notification date and are still outstanding on that date,

B is the total amount of equity capital received by the corporation on the issue of Class A shares that are still outstanding on the notification date, and

C is the amount of equity capital received by the corporation on the issue of Class A shares that, as of the notification date, have been outstanding for at least eight years.

(*b*) the corporation has revoked its registration before the third anniversary of the notification date.

History: S. 204.81(8.4) was added by S.C. 2013, c. 34, s. 336(6), deemed to have come into force on October 24, 2012.

► 204.81(9) ◄

(9) Right of appeal. Where the Minister refuses to accept a corporation for registration under subsection (1) or gives notice of a proposal to revoke the registration of a corporation under subsection (7), the corporation may appeal to the Federal Court of Appeal from the decision or from the giving of the notice.

Related Sections: S. 127.4(1) Definitions.

SECTION 204.82: Recovery of credit

► 204.82(1) ◄

(1) Recovery of credit. Where, at any time that is both in a taxation year included in the start-up period of a corporation that was registered under this Part and before its venture capital business is first discontinued,

(*a*) 80% of the amount, if any, by which the total consideration received by it for Class A shares issued by it before that time exceeds the total of all amounts paid by it before that time to its shareholders as a return of capital on such shares

exceeds

(*b*) the total of all amounts each of which is the cost to the corporation of an eligible investment or reserve of the corporation at that time,

the corporation shall pay a tax under this Part for the year equal to the amount determined by the formula

$$(A \times 20\%) - B$$

where

A is the greatest amount by which the amount determined under paragraph (*a*) exceeds the amount determined under paragraph (*b*) for the year, and

B is the total of all taxes payable under this subsection by the corporation for preceding taxation years.

Editorial Note: This provision imposes a tax on a federally registered labour-sponsored venture capital corporation ("LSVCC") that is intended to recover the tax credits claimed by the individual shareholders where the corporation has failed to meet certain threshold investment levels during its start-up period. See also transitional rules for the revocation of LSVCC registrations under s. 204.81(8.3) and (8.4) and editorial notes under s. 204.81(1) and 127.4(2) regarding the phase-out of the LSVCC tax credit regime.

Related Sections: S. 204.8(1), "start-up period"; s. 204.8(2) When venture capital business discontinued; s. 204.81(4) Determination of cost.

► 204.82(2) ◄

(2) Liability for tax. Each corporation that has been registered under this Part shall, in respect of each month that ends before its venture capital business is first discontinued and in a particular taxation year of the corporation that begins after the end of the corporation's start-up period (or, where the corporation has no start-up period, that begins after the time the corporation first issues a Class A share), pay a tax under this Part equal to the amount obtained when the greatest investment shortfall at any time that is in the month and in the particular year (in this section and sections 204.81 and 204.83 referred to as the "monthly deficiency") is multiplied by $1/60$ of the prescribed rate of interest in effect during the month.

Editorial Note: Subsection 204.82(2) applies a tax on federally registered labour-sponsored venture capital corporations ("LSVCC") that fail to maintain certain investment levels after the applicable start-up period. Where these shortfalls persist for 12 consecutive months, there may be additional taxes imposed under s. 204.82(3) and penalties imposed under s. 204.82(4). However, there is a mechanism provided for in s. 204.83(1) to claim a refund of the taxes and a portion of the penalties imposed under ss. 204.82(3) and (4). See also transitional rules for the revocation of LSVCC registrations under s. 204.81(8.3) and (8.4) and editorial notes under s. 127.4(2) regarding the phase-out of the federal LSVCC tax credit regime.

Related Regulations: 4301.

Related Sections: S. 204.8(1), "start-up period"; s. 204.8(2) When venture capital business discontinued; s. 204.82(2.1) Determination of investment shortfall; s. 204.82(2.2) Investment shortfall; s. 204.82(3) Recovery of credit; s. 204.82(4) Penalty; s. 204.83(1) Refunds for federally registered LSVCCs.

► 204.82(2.1) ◄

(2.1) Determination of investment shortfall. Subject to subsection (2.2), a corporation's investment shortfall at any time in a particular taxation year is the amount determined by the formula

$$A - B - C$$

where

A is 60% of the lesser of

(*a*) the amount, if any, by which the amount of the shareholders' equity in the corporation at the end of the preceding taxation year exceeds the specified adjustment in respect of the shareholders' equity in the corporation at the end of that year, and

(*b*) the amount, if any, by which the amount of the shareholders' equity in the corporation at the end of the particular taxation year exceeds the specified adjustment in respect of the shareholders' equity in the corporation at the end of the particular year;

B is the greater of

(*a*) the total of all amounts each of which is the adjusted cost to the corporation of an eligible investment of the corporation at that time, and

(*b*) 50% of the total of all amounts each of which is

(i) the adjusted cost to the corporation of an eligible investment of the corporation at the beginning of the particular year, or

(ii) the adjusted cost to the corporation of an eligible investment of the corporation at the end of the particular year, and

C is 60% of the amount, if any, by which

(*a*) the total of all amounts each of which is a tax or penalty under subsection (3) or (4), or a prescribed tax or penalty, paid before that time by the corporation (other than the portion, if any, of that tax or penalty the liability for which resulted in a reduction in the amount of the shareholders' equity at the end of any preceding taxation year)

exceeds

(*b*) the total of all amounts each of which is a refund before that time of any portion of the total described in paragraph (*a*).

► 204.82(2.2) ◄

(2.2) Investment shortfall. For the purpose of this subsection and for the purpose of computing a corporation's investment shortfall under subsection (2.1) at any time in a taxation year (in this subsection referred to as the "relevant year"),

(*a*) unrealized gains and losses in respect of its eligible investments shall not be taken into account in computing the amount of the shareholders' equity in the corporation;

(*b*) where

(i) the relevant year ends after 1998, and

(ii) it is expected that a redemption of its Class A shares will occur after the end of a particular taxation year and, as a consequence, the amount of the shareholders' equity in the corporation at the end of the particular year would otherwise be reduced to take into account the expected redemption,

subject to paragraph (*c*), the amount (or, where the relevant year ends in 1999, 2000, 2001 or 2002, 20%, 40%, 60% or 80%, respectively of the amount) expected to be redeemed shall not be taken into account in determining the amount of the shareholders' equity in the corporation at the end of the particular year;

(*c*) paragraph (*b*) does not apply to a redemption expected to be made after the end of a taxation year where

(i) the redemption is made within 60 days after the end of the year, and

(ii) either

(A) tax under Part XII.5 became payable as a consequence of the redemption, or

(B) tax under Part XII.5 would not have become payable as a consequence of the redemption if the redemption had occurred at the end of the year;

(*c*.1) the specified adjustment in respect of shareholders' equity in the corporation at the end of a taxation year is the amount determined by the formula

$$(A \times (B/C)) - D$$

where

A is the shareholders' equity at the end of the year,

B is the total of

(i) the fair market value at the end of the year of all Class A shares issued by it before March 6, 1996 and more than five years before the end of the year,

(ii) the fair market value at the end of the year of all Class A shares issued by it after March 5, 1996 and more than eight years before the end of the year,

(iii) the fair market value at the end of the year of all Class A shares issued by it in the last 60 days of the year, and

(iv) if the corporation so elects in writing filed with the Minister not more than six months after the end of the year and is not a revoked corporation at the end of the year, the fair market value at the end of the year of all shares of classes, of the capital stock of the corporation, to which clause 204.81(1)(*c*)(ii)(C) applies,

C is the fair market value at the end of the year of all shares issued by it, and

D is the amount by which the shareholders' equity in the corporation at the end of the year has been reduced to take into account the expected subsequent redemption of shares of the capital stock of the corporation; and

(*d*) the adjusted cost to the corporation of an eligible investment of the corporation at any time is

(i) 150% of the cost to the corporation of the eligible investment at that time where the eligible investment is

(A) a property acquired by the corporation after February 18, 1997 (other than a property to which subparagraph (i.1) applies) that would be an eligible investment of the corporation if the reference to "$50,000,000" in paragraph (*f*) of the definition "eligible investment" in subsection 204.8(1) were read as "$10,000,000", or

(B) a share of the capital stock of a prescribed corporation,

(i.1) 200% of the cost to the corporation of the eligible investment at that time where the eligible investment is a property acquired by the corporation after February 16, 1999 (other than a property described in clause (i)(B)) that would be an eligible investment of the corporation if the reference to "$50,000,000" in paragraph (*f*) of the definition "eligible investment" in subsection 204.8(1) were read as "$2,500,000", and

(ii) in any other case, the cost to the corporation of the eligible investment of the corporation at that time.

Related Regulations: 4801.02.

► 204.82(3) ◄

(3) Recovery of credit. Where a corporation is liable under subsection (2) to pay a tax in respect of 12 consecutive months (in this subsection referred to as the "particular period"), the corporation shall pay a tax under this Part for a taxation year in respect of each particular period that ends in the year equal to the total of the amounts determined by the formula

$$(A/12 \times 20\%) - (B - C)$$

where

A is the total of the monthly deficiencies for each month in the particular period;

B is the total of all taxes payable by the corporation under subsection (1) for preceding taxation years and taxes payable by it under this subsection in respect of a period ending before the end of the particular period; and

C is the total of all amounts refunded under section 204.83 in respect of the tax paid under this subsection by the corporation for preceding taxation years.

Related Sections: S. 204.82(4) Penalty; s. 204.83(1) Refunds for federally registered LSVCCs.

► 204.82(4) ◄

(4) Penalty. Where a corporation is liable under subsection (3) to pay a tax for a taxation year, the corporation shall pay, in addition to the tax payable under that subsection, a penalty for the year equal to that tax.

Related Sections: S. 204.82(3) Recovery of credit; s. 204.83(1) Refunds for federally registered LSVCCs.

► 204.82(5) ◄

(5) Provincially registered LSVCCs. Where

(*a*) an amount (other than interest on an amount to which this subsection applies or an amount payable under or as a consequence of a prescribed provision of a law of a province) is payable to the government of a province by a corporation,

(*b*) the amount is payable as a consequence of a failure to acquire sufficient properties of a character described in the law of the province,

(*c*) the corporation has been prescribed for the purpose of the definition "approved share" in subsection 127.4(1), and

(*d*) the corporation is not a registered labour-sponsored venture capital corporation or a revoked corporation,

the corporation shall pay a tax under this Part for the taxation year in which the amount became payable equal to that amount.

Editorial Note: Payments (other than interest) to provincial tax authorities by certain LSVCCs that are only registered provincially and that are made as a consequence of the corporation's failure to meet certain investment thresholds established by provincial law will trigger taxes payable by the corporation under this provision of the Act for an equal amount. The provisions of s. 204.83(2) may apply to refund such amounts. See also editorial notes under s. 204.81(1) and 127.4(2) regarding the phase-out of the federal LSVCC tax credit regime.

Related Regulations: 6707.

Related Sections: S. 204.83(2) Refunds of amounts payable to provinces.

Forms: T2152A — Part X.3 Tax Return and Request for a Refund for a Labour-Sponsored Venture Capital Corporation.

► 204.82(6) ◄

(6) Further matching of amounts payable to a province. Where

(*a*) a particular amount is payable (other than interest on an amount to which this subsection applies) by a registered labour-sponsored venture capital corporation or a revoked corporation to the government of a province as a consequence of a failure of a prescribed corporation to acquire sufficient properties of a character described in a law of the province, and

(*b*) the particular amount became payable before the corporation first discontinued its venture capital business,

the corporation shall pay a tax under this Part for the taxation year in which the particular amount became payable equal to that amount.

Editorial Note: A federally registered LSVCC that is liable to pay amounts to a provincial tax authority prior to discontinuing its business as a consequence of the corporation's failure to meet certain investment thresholds established by provincial law will trigger taxes for an equal amount payable by the corporation under this provision of the Act. The provisions of s. 204.83(2) may apply to refund such amounts. See also transitional rules for the revocation of LSVCC registrations under s. 204.81(8.3) and (8.4) and editorial notes under s. 127.4(2) regarding the phase-out of the federal LSVCC tax credit regime.

Related Regulations: 4801.02.

Related Sections: S. 204.8(2) When venture capital business discontinued; s. 204.83(2) Refunds of amounts payable to provinces.

SECTION 204.83: Refunds for federally registered LSVCCs

► 204.83(1) ◄

(1) Refunds for federally registered LSVCCs. If a corporation is required, under subsections 204.82(3) and (4), to pay a tax and a penalty under this Part for a taxation year, it has no monthly deficiency throughout any period of 12 consecutive months (in this section referred to as the "second period") that begins after the 12-month period in respect of which the tax became payable (in this section referred to as the "first period") and it so requests in an application filed with the Minister in prescribed form, the Minister shall refund to it an amount equal to the total of the amount that was paid under subsection 204.82(3) and 80% of the amount that was paid under subsection 204.82(4) in respect of the first period on or before the later of

(*a*) the 30th day after receiving the application, and

(*b*) the 60th day after the end of the second period.

Forms: T2152A — Part X.3 Tax Return and Request for a Refund for a Labour-Sponsored Venture Capital Corporation.

► 204.83(2) ◄

(2) Refunds of amounts payable to provinces. Where

(*a*) the government of a province refunds, at any time, an amount to a corporation,

(*b*) the refund is of an amount that had been paid in satisfaction of a particular amount payable in a taxation year of the corporation, and

(*c*) tax was payable under subsection 204.82(5) or (6) by the corporation for a taxation year because the particular amount became payable,

the corporation is deemed to have paid at that time an amount equal to the refund on account of its tax payable under this Part for the year.

SECTION 204.84: Penalty

Every corporation that for a taxation year issues an information return described in paragraph 204.81(6)(*c*) in respect of

(*a*) the issuance of a share when the corporation was a revoked corporation, or

(*b*) a subscription in respect of a share if the share is not issued on or before the day that is 180 days after the day the information return was issued,

is liable to a penalty for the year equal to the amount of the consideration for which the share was or was to be issued.

SECTION 204.841: Penalty tax where venture capital business discontinued

Where, at a particular time in a taxation year, a particular corporation that is a registered labour-sponsored venture capital corporation or a revoked corporation first discontinues its venture capital business, the particular corporation shall pay a tax under this Part for the year equal to the total of all amounts each of which is the amount in respect of a Class A share of the capital stock of the particular corporation outstanding immediately before the particular time that is determined by the formula

$$A \times B$$

where

A is

(*a*) if the original acquisition of the share was before March 6, 1996 and less than five years before the particular time, 4% of the consideration received by the particular corporation for the issue of the share,

(*b*) if the original acquisition of the share was after March 5, 1996 and less than eight years before the particular time, 1.875% of the consideration received by the particular corporation for the issue of the share, and

(*c*) in any other case, nil; and

B is

(*a*) if the original acquisition of the share was before March 6, 1996, the number obtained when the number of whole years throughout which the share was outstanding before the particular time is subtracted from five, and

(*b*) in any other case, the number obtained when the number of whole years throughout which the share was outstanding is subtracted from eight.

Related Sections: S. 204.8(2) When venture capital business discontinued.

SECTION 204.85: Dissolution of federally registered LSVCCs

► 204.85(1) ◄

(1) Dissolution of federally registered LSVCCs. A registered labour-sponsored venture capital corporation or a revoked corporation that has issued any Class A shares shall send written notification of any proposed amalgamation, merger, liquidation or dissolution of the corporation to the Minister at least 30 days before the amalgamation, merger, liquidation or dissolution, as the case may be.

► 204.85(2) ◄

(2) Dissolution of other LSVCCs. Where

(*a*) an amount (other than interest on an amount to which this subsection applies or an amount payable under or as a consequence of a prescribed provision of a law of a province) is payable to the government of a province by a corporation,

(*b*) the amount is payable as a consequence of the amalgamation or merger of the corporation with another corporation, the winding-up or dissolution of the corporation or the corporation ceasing to be registered under a law of the province,

(*c*) the corporation has been prescribed for the purpose of the definition "approved share" in subsection 127.4(1), and

(*d*) the corporation is not a registered labour-sponsored venture capital corporation or a revoked corporation,

the corporation shall pay a tax under this Part for the taxation year in which the amount became payable equal to that amount.

Editorial Note: Payments (other than interest) to provincial tax authorities by certain LSVCCs that are only registered provincially and that are made as a consequence of the amalgamation or winding up of the corporation or upon the ceasing of the corporation to be registered under provincial law will trigger taxes for an equal amount payable by the corporation under this provision of the Act. See also editorial notes under s. 127.4(2) and 204.81(1) regarding the phase-out of the federal LSVCC tax credit regime.

Forms: T2152A — Part X.3 Tax Return and Request for a Refund for a Labour-Sponsored Venture Capital Corporation.

► 204.85(3) ◄

(3) Amalgamations and mergers. For the purposes of section 127.4, this Part and Part XII.5, where two or more corporations (each of which is referred to in this subsection as a "predecessor corporation") amalgamate or merge to form one corporate entity (in this subsection referred to as the "new corporation") and at least one of the predecessor corporations was, immediately before the amalgamation or merger, a registered labour-sponsored venture capital corporation or a revoked corporation,

(*a*) subject to paragraphs (*d*) and (*e*), the new corporation is deemed to be the same corporation as, and a continuation of, each predecessor corporation;

(*b*) where a predecessor corporation was authorized to issue a class of shares to which clause 204.81(1)(*c*)(ii)(C) applies, the new corporation is deemed to have received approval from the Minister of Finance to issue substantially similar shares at the time of the amalgamation or merger;

(*c*) where a share of a predecessor corporation (in this paragraph referred to as the "predecessor share") is replaced on the amalgamation or merger by a new share of the new corporation,

(i) the new share

(A) is deemed not to have been issued on the amalgamation or merger, and

(B) is deemed to have been issued by the new corporation at the time the predecessor corporation issued the predecessor share, and

(ii) if the new share was issued to a person who acquired the predecessor share as a consequence of a transfer the registration of which by the predecessor corporation was permitted under paragraph 204.81(1)(*c*), the issuance of the new share is deemed to be in compliance with the conditions described in paragraph 204.81(1)(*c*);

(*d*) the Minister is deemed to have registered the new corporation for the purposes of this Part unless

(i) the new corporation is not governed by the *Canada Business Corporations Act*,

(ii) one or more of the predecessor corporations was a registered labour-sponsored venture capital corporation the venture capital business of which was discontinued before the amalgamation or merger,

(iii) one or more of the predecessor corporations was, immediately before the amalgamation or merger, a revoked corporation,

(iv) immediately after the amalgamation or merger, the articles of the new corporation do not comply with paragraph 204.81(1)(*c*),

(v) shares other than Class A shares of the capital stock of the new corporation were issued to any shareholder of the new corporation in satisfaction of any share (other than a share to which clause 204.81(1)(*c*)(ii)(B) or (C) applied) of a predecessor corporation, or

(vi) immediately before the amalgamation or merger, one or more of the predecessor corporations is a corporation that has given notification under subsection 204.81(8.3) and one or more of the predecessor corporations is a registered labour-sponsored venture capital corporation that has not given notification under that subsection;

(*e*) where paragraph (*d*) does not apply, the new corporation is deemed to be a revoked corporation;

(*f*) subsection 204.82(1) does not apply to the new corporation; and

(*g*) subsection 204.82(2) shall, in its application to the new corporation, be read without reference to the words "that begins after the end of the corporation's start-up period (or, where the corporation has no start-up period, that begins after the time the corporation first issues a Class A share)".

History: S. 204.85(3)(*d*)(vi) was added by S.C. 2014, c. 20, s. 25(1), deemed to have come into force on November 27, 2013.

Related Sections: S. 87 Amalgamations; s. 211.7(2) Amalgamations and mergers.

Tax Window Files: Merger LSVCC, *August 30, 2006*, CRA Document No. 2006-0184981R3; Labour Sponsored Venture Capital Corporation, *May 17, 2006*, CRA Document No. 2006-0171471R3; Labour Sponsored Venture Capital Corporation, *November 2, 2005*, CRA Document No. 2005-0130171R3.

SECTION 204.86: Return and payment of tax for federally-registered LSVCCs

► 204.86(1) ◄

(1) Return and payment of tax for federally-registered LSVCCs. Every registered labour-sponsored venture capital corporation and every revoked corporation shall

(*a*) on or before its filing-due date for a taxation year, file with the Minister a return for the year under this Part in prescribed form and containing prescribed information, without notice or demand therefor;

(*b*) estimate in the return the amount of tax and penalties, if any, payable under this Part by it for the year; and

(*c*) on or before its balance-due day for the year, pay to the Receiver General the amount of tax and penalties, if any, payable under this Part by it for the year.

Forms: T2152 — Part X.3 Tax Return for a Labour-Sponsored Venture Capital Corporation.

► 204.86(2) ◄

(2) Return and payment of tax for other LSVCCs. Where tax is payable under this Part for a taxation year by a corporation because of subsection 204.82(5) or 204.85(2), the corporation shall

(*a*) on or before its filing-due date for the year, file with the Minister a return for the year under this Part in prescribed form and containing prescribed information, without notice or demand therefor;

(*b*) estimate in the return the amount of tax payable under this Part by it for the year; and

(*c*) on or before its balance-due day for the year, pay to the Receiver General the amount of tax payable under this Part by it for the year.

Forms: T2152A — Part X.3 Tax Return and Request for a Refund for a Labour-Sponsored Venture Capital Corporation.

SECTION 204.87: Provisions applicable to Part

Subsection 150(3), sections 152 and 158, subsections 161(1) and (11), sections 162 to 164 and 165 to 167, Division J of Part I and section 227.1 apply to this Part, with such modifications as the circumstances require.

Part X.4
Tax in Respect of Overpayment to Registered Education Savings Plans

SECTION 204.9: [Interpretation]

► 204.9(1) ◄

(1) Definitions. The definitions in this subsection apply in this Part.

Information Circulars: IC 93-3R1 Registered education savings plans.

"excess amount" —"excess amount" for a year at any time in respect of an individual means

(*a*) for years before 2007, the amount, if any, by which the total of all contributions made after February 20, 1990 in the year and before that time into all registered education savings plans by or on behalf of all subscribers in respect of the individual exceeds the lesser of

(i) the RESP annual limit for the year, and

(ii) the amount, if any, by which the RESP lifetime limit for the year exceeds the total of all contributions made into registered education savings plans by or on behalf of all subscribers in respect of the individual in all preceding years; and

(*b*) for years after 2006, the amount, if any, by which the total of all contributions made in the year and before that time into all registered education savings plans by or on behalf of all subscribers in respect of the individual exceeds the amount, if any, by which

(i) the RESP lifetime limit for the year

exceeds

(ii) the total of all contributions made into registered education savings plans by or on behalf of all subscribers in respect of the individual in all preceding years.

"RESP lifetime limit" —"RESP lifetime limit" for a year means

(*a*) for 1990 to 1995, $31,500;

(*b*) for 1996 to 2006, $42,000; and

(*c*) for 2007 and subsequent years, $50,000.

"subscriber's gross cumulative excess" —"subscriber's gross cumulative excess" at any time in respect of an individual means the total of all amounts each of which is the subscriber's share of the excess amount for a relevant year at that time in respect of the individual and, for the purpose of this definition, a relevant year at any time is a year that began before that time.

"subscriber's share of the excess amount" —"subscriber's share of the excess amount" for a year at any time in respect of an individual means the amount determined by the formula

$$(A/B) \times C$$

where

A is the total of all contributions made after February 20, 1990, in the year and before that time into all registered education savings plans by or on behalf of the subscriber in respect of the individual;

B is the total of all contributions made after February 20, 1990, in the year and before that time into all registered education savings plans by or on behalf of all subscribers in respect of the individual; and

C is the excess amount for the year at that time in respect of the individual.

► 204.9(1.1) ◄

(1.1) Application of s. 146.1(1). The definitions in subsection 146.1(1) apply to this Part.

► 204.9(2) ◄

(2) Agreements before February 21, 1990. Where a subscriber is required, pursuant to an agreement in writing entered into before February 21, 1990, to make payments of specified amounts on a periodic basis into a registered education savings plan in respect of a beneficiary, and the subscriber makes at least one payment under the agreement before that day,

(*a*) the excess amount for a year in respect of the beneficiary shall be deemed not to exceed the excess amount for the year that would be determined under subsection (1) if the total of all such payments made in the year and, where the agreement so provides, amounts paid in the year in satisfaction of the requirement to make such payments under all such agreements by all such subscribers in respect of the beneficiary were equal to the lesser of the amounts described in paragraphs (*a*) and (*b*) of the definition "excess amount" in subsection (1); and

(*b*) in determining a subscriber's share of an excess amount for a year, any payment included in the total described in paragraph (*a*) in respect of the year shall be excluded in determining the values for A and B in the definition "subscriber's share of the excess amount" in subsection (1).

► 204.9(3) ◄

(3) Refunds from unregistered plans. For the purposes of subsection (1) and section 146.1, where an individual entered into an education savings plan before February 21, 1990, pursuant to a preliminary prospectus issued by a promoter, and the promoter refunds all payments made into the plan and all income accrued thereon to the individual, each payment made by the individual into a registered education savings plan before December 31, 1990 shall be deemed to be a payment made before February 21, 1990, to the extent that the total of all such payments does not exceed the amount so refunded to the individual.

▶ 204.9(4) ◀

(4) New beneficiary. For the purposes of this Part, if at any particular time an individual (in this subsection referred to as the "new beneficiary") becomes a beneficiary under a registered education savings plan in place of another individual (in this subsection referred to as the "former beneficiary") who ceased at or before the particular time to be a beneficiary under the plan,

(*a*) except as provided by paragraph (*b*), each contribution made at an earlier time by or on behalf of a subscriber into the plan in respect of the former beneficiary is deemed also to have been made at that earlier time in respect of the new beneficiary;

(*b*) except for the purpose of applying this subsection to a replacement of a beneficiary after the particular time, applying subsection (5) to a distribution after the particular time and applying subsection 204.91(3) to events after the particular time, paragraph (*a*) does not apply as a consequence of the replacement at the particular time of the former beneficiary if

(i) the new beneficiary had not attained 21 years of age before the particular time and a parent of the new beneficiary was a parent of the former beneficiary, or

(ii) both beneficiaries were connected by blood relationship or adoption to an original subscriber under the plan and neither had attained 21 years of age before the particular time; and

(*c*) except where paragraph (*b*) applies, each contribution made by or on behalf of a subscriber under the plan in respect of the former beneficiary under the plan is, without affecting the determination of the amount withdrawn from the plan in respect of the new beneficiary, deemed to have been withdrawn at the particular time from the plan to the extent that it was not withdrawn before the particular time.

Related Sections: S. 251(6) Blood relationship, etc.

▶ 204.9(5) ◀

(5) Transfers between plans. For the purposes of this Part, if property held by a trust governed by a registered education savings plan (in this subsection referred to as the "transferor plan") is distributed at a particular time to a trust governed by another registered education savings plan (in this subsection referred to as the "transferee plan"),

(*a*) except as provided by paragraphs (*b*) and (*c*), the amount of the distribution is deemed not to have been contributed into the transferee plan;

(*b*) subject to paragraph (*c*), each contribution made at any earlier time by or on behalf of a subscriber into the transferor plan in respect of a beneficiary under the transferor plan is deemed also to have been made at that earlier time by the subscriber in respect of each beneficiary under the transferee plan;

(*c*) except for the purpose of applying this subsection to a distribution after the particular time, applying subsection (4) to a replacement of a beneficiary after the particular time and applying subsection 204.91(3) to events after the particular time, paragraph (*b*) does not apply as a consequence of the distribution where

(i) any beneficiary under the transferee plan was, immediately before the particular time, a beneficiary under the transferor plan, or

(ii) a parent of a beneficiary under the transferee plan was a parent of an individual who was, immediately before the particular time, a beneficiary under the transferor plan and

(A) the transferee plan is a plan that allows more than one beneficiary under the plan at any one time, or

(B) in any other case, the beneficiary under the transferee plan had not attained 21 years of age at the time the transferee plan was entered into;

(*d*) where subparagraph (c)(i) or (ii) applies in respect of the distribution, the amount of the distribution is deemed not to have been withdrawn from the transferor plan; and

(*e*) each subscriber under the transferor plan is deemed to be a subscriber under the transferee plan.

History: S. 204.9(5)(*c*)(ii) was replaced by S.C. 2011, c. 24, s. 62(1), applicable in respect of property transferred after 2010. S. 204.9(5)(*c*)(ii) formerly read:

> (ii) a beneficiary under the transferee plan had not attained 21 years of age at the particular time and a parent of the beneficiary was a parent of an individual who was, immediately before the particular time, a beneficiary under the transferor plan;

SECTION 204.91: Tax payable by subscribers

▶ 204.91(1) ◀

(1) Tax payable by subscribers. Every subscriber under a registered education savings plan shall pay a tax under this Part in respect of each month equal to 1% of the amount, if any, by which

(*a*) the total of all amounts each of which is the subscriber's gross cumulative excess at the end of the month in respect of an individual

exceeds

(*b*) the total of all amounts each of which is the portion of such an excess that has been withdrawn from a registered education savings plan before the end of the month.

Editorial Note: After 2006, the "excess amount" and therefore a "subscriber's gross cumulative excess" reflects the amount by which the total of all contributions made in the year to an RESP in respect of the beneficiary, plus contributions made before the year, exceeds the lifetime limit of $50,000. In other words, after 2006, there no longer is an annual contribution limit, although there remains a lifetime contribution limit per beneficiary. Contributions that go over the $50,000 lifetime limit will be subject to the Part X.4 tax. If there is more than one subscriber, each may be subject to the tax based on their pro rata shares of the excess amount (see s. 204.9(1) "subscriber's share of the excess amount").

Information Circulars: IC 93-3R1 Registered education savings plans.

► 204.91(2) ◄

(2) Waiver of tax. If a subscriber under a registered education savings plan would, but for this subsection, be required to pay a tax in respect of a month under subsection (1) in respect of an individual, the Minister may waive or cancel all or part of the tax where it is just and equitable to do so having regard to all the circumstances, including

(*a*) whether the tax arose as a consequence of reasonable error;

(*b*) whether, as a consequence of one or more transactions or events to which subsection 204.9(4) or (5) applies, the tax is excessive; and

(*c*) the extent to which further contributions could be made into registered education savings plans in respect of the individual before the end of the month without causing additional tax to be payable under this Part if this Part were read without reference to this subsection.

► 204.91(3) ◄

(3) Marriage or common-law partnership breakdown. If at any time an individual (in this subsection referred to as the "former subscriber") ceases to be a subscriber under a registered education savings plan as a consequence of the settlement of rights arising out of, or on the breakdown of, the marriage or common-law partnership of the former subscriber and another individual (in this subsection referred to as the "current subscriber") who is a subscriber under the plan immediately after that time, for the purpose of determining tax payable under this Part in respect of a month that ends after that time, each contribution made before that time into the plan by or on behalf of the former subscriber is deemed to have been made into the plan by the current subscriber and not by or on behalf of the former subscriber.

► 204.91(4) ◄

(4) Deceased subscribers. For the purpose of applying this section where a subscriber has died, the subscriber's estate is deemed to be the same person as, and a continuation of, the subscriber for each month that ends after the death.

SECTION 204.92: Return and payment of tax

Every person who is liable to pay tax under this Part in respect of a month in a year shall, within 90 days after the end of the year,

(*a*) file with the Minister a return for the year under this Part in prescribed form and containing prescribed information, without notice or demand therefor;

(*b*) estimate in the return the amount of tax, if any, payable under this Part by the person in respect of each month in the year; and

(*c*) pay to the Receiver General the amount of tax, if any, payable by the person under this Part in respect of each month in the year.

Forms: T1E-OVP — Individual Income Tax Return for RESP Overcontributions for 1996 and Future Years.

SECTION 204.93: Provisions applicable to Part

Subsections 150(2) and (3), sections 152, 158 and 159, subsections 161(1) and (11), sections 162 to 167 and Division J of Part I are applicable to this Part, with such modifications as the circumstances require.

Part X.5
Payments Under Registered Education Savings Plans

SECTION 204.94: [Tax on accumulated income payments]

► 204.94(1) ◄

(1) Definitions. The definitions in subsection 146.1(1) apply for the purposes of this Part, except that the definition "subscriber" in that subsection shall be read without reference to paragraph (*c*).

► 204.94(2) ◄

(2) Charging provision. Every person (other than a public primary caregiver that is exempt from tax under Part I) shall pay a tax under this Part for each taxation year equal to the amount determined by the formula

$$(A + B - C) \times D$$

where

A is the total of all amounts each of which is an accumulated income payment made at any time that is

(*a*) either

(i) under a registered education savings plan under which the person is a subscriber at that time, or

(ii) under a registered education savings plan under which there is no subscriber at that time, where the person has been a spouse or common-law partner of an individual who was a subscriber under the plan, and

(*b*) included in computing the person's income under Part I for the year;

B is the total of all amounts each of which is an accumulated income payment that is

(*a*) not included in the value of A in respect of the person for the year, and

(*b*) included in computing the person's income under Part I for the year;

C is the lesser of

(*a*) the lesser of the value of A in respect of the person for the year and the total of all amounts each of which is an amount deducted under subsection 146(5) or (5.1) in computing the person's income under Part I for the year, and

(*b*) the amount, if any, by which $50,000 exceeds the total of all amounts each of which is an amount determined under paragraph (*a*) in respect of the person for a preceding taxation year; and

D is

(*a*) where a tax, similar to the tax provided under this Part, is payable by the person for the year under a law of the province of Quebec, 12%, and

(*b*) in any other case, 20%.

History: S. 204.94(2), the portion before the formula was replaced by S.C. 2013, c. 34, s. 338(1), applicable to the 2007 and subsequent taxation years, and formerly read:

(2) *Charging provision.* Every person shall pay a tax under this Part for each taxation year equal to the amount determined by the formula

Related Sections: S. 248(1), "common-law partner".

Information Circulars: IC 93-3R1 Registered education savings plans.

► 204.94(3) ◄

(3) Return and payment of tax. Every person who is liable to pay tax under this Part for a taxation year shall, on or before the person's filing-due date for the year,

(*a*) file with the Minister a return for the year under this Part in prescribed form and containing prescribed information, without notice or demand therefor;

(*b*) estimate in the return the amount of tax payable under this Part by the person for the year; and

(*c*) pay to the Receiver General the amount of tax payable under this Part by the person for the year.

Forms: T1171 — Tax Withholding Waiver on Accumulated Income Payments from RESPs; T1172 — Additional Tax on Accumulated Income Payments from RESPs.

► 204.94(4) ◄

(4) Administrative rules. Subsections 150(2) and (3), sections 152, 155 to 156.1 and 158 to 167 and Division J of Part I apply with any modifications that the circumstances require.

Part XI
Taxes in Respect of Registered Disability Savings Plans [Repealed]

History: Part XI (sections 205 to 207) was repealed by S.C. 2017, c. 33, s. 66(1), applicable to transactions and events occurring, income earned, capital gains accruing and investments acquired after March 22, 2017.

History: Part XIX (sections 270 to 281) was added by S.C. 2016, c. 12, s. 71(1), in force July 1, 2017.

SECTION 205: [Interpretation]

► 205(1) ◄

(1) Definitions. The following definitions apply in this Part. (Repealed by S.C. 2017, c. 33, s. 66(1).)

History: S. 205(1) was repealed by S.C. 2017, c. 33, s. 66(1), applicable to transactions and events occurring, income earned, capital gains accruing and investments acquired after March 22, 2017, and formerly read:

S. 205. *[Interpretation].*

(1) *Definitions.* The following definitions apply in this Part.

"advantage" — (Repealed by S.C. 2017, c. 33, s. 66(1).)

History: S. 205(1), the definition "advantage" was repealed by S.C. 2017, c. 33, s. 66(1), applicable to transactions and events occurring, income earned, capital gains accruing and investments acquired after March 22, 2017, and formerly read:

"advantage"—"advantage", in relation to a registered disability savings plan, means any benefit or loan that is conditional in any way on the existence of the plan other than

(*a*) a disability assistance payment;

(*b*) a contribution made by, or with the written consent of, a holder of the plan;

(*c*) a transfer in accordance with subsection 146.4(8);

(*d*) an amount paid under or because of the *Canada Disability Savings Act* or a designated provincial program as defined in subsection 146.4(1);

(*e*) a benefit derived from the provision of administrative or investment services in respect of the plan; or

(*f*) a loan

(i) made in the ordinary course of the lender's ordinary business of lending money if, at the time the loan was made, *bona fide* arrangements were made for repayment of the loan within a reasonable time, and

(ii) whose sole purpose was to enable a person to make a contribution to the plan.

S. 205(1), paragraph (*d*) of the definition "advantage" was replaced by S.C. 2010, c. 12, s. 20(1), applicable to the 2009 and subsequent taxation years. S. 205(1), paragraph (*d*) of the definition "advantage" formerly read:

(*d*) an amount paid under the *Canada Disability Savings Act*;

"allowable refund" — (Repealed by S.C. 2017, c. 33, s. 66(1).)

History: S. 205(1), the definition "allowable refund" was repealed by S.C. 2017, c. 33, s. 66(1), applicable to transactions and events occurring, income earned, capital gains accruing and investments acquired after March 22, 2017, and formerly read:

"allowable refund"—"allowable refund" of a person for a calendar year means the total of all amounts each of which is a refund to which the person is entitled under subsection 206.1(4) for the year.

"benefit" — (Repealed by S.C. 2017, c. 33, s. 66(1).)

History: S. 205(1), the definition "benefit" was repealed by S.C. 2017, c. 33, s. 66(1), applicable to transactions and events occurring, income earned, capital gains accruing and investments acquired after March 22, 2017, and formerly read:

"benefit"—"benefit", in relation to a registered disability savings plan, includes any payment or allocation of an amount to the plan that is represented to be a return on investment in respect of property held by the plan trust, but which cannot reasonably be considered, having regard to all the circumstances, to be on terms and conditions that would apply to a similar transaction in an open market between parties dealing with each other at arm's length and acting prudently, knowledgeably and willingly.

"qualified investment" — (Repealed by S.C. 2017, c. 33, s. 66(1).)

History: S. 205(1), the definition "qualified investment" was repealed by S.C. 2017, c. 33, s. 66(1), applicable to transactions and events occurring, income earned, capital gains accruing and investments acquired after March 22, 2017, and formerly read:

"qualified investment"—"qualified investment" for a trust governed by a registered disability savings plan means

(*a*) an investment that would be described by any of paragraphs (*a*) to (*d*), (*f*) and (*g*) of the definition "qualified investment" in section 204 if the reference in that definition to "a trust governed by a deferred profit sharing plan or revoked plan" were read as a reference to "a trust governed by a registered disability savings plan" and if that definition were read without reference to the words "with the exception of excluded property in relation to the trust";

(*b*) a contract for an annuity issued by a licensed annuities provider where

(i) the trust is the only person who, disregarding any subsequent transfer of the contract by the trust, is or may become entitled to any annuity payments under the contract, and

(ii) the holder of the contract has a right to surrender the contract at any time for an amount that would, if reasonable sales and administration charges were ignored, approximate the value of funds that could otherwise be applied to fund future periodic payments under the contract;

(*c*) a contract for an annuity issued by a licensed annuities provider where

(i) annual or more frequent periodic payments are or may be made under the contract to the holder of the contract,

(ii) the trust is the only person who, disregarding any subsequent transfer of the contract by the trust, is or may become entitled to any annuity payments under the contract,

(iii) neither the time nor the amount of any payment under the contract may vary because of the length of any life, other than the life of the beneficiary under the plan,

(iv) the day on which the periodic payments began or are to begin is not later than the end of the later of

(A) the year in which the beneficiary under the plan attains the age of 60 years, and

(B) the year following the year in which the contract was acquired by the trust,

(v) the periodic payments are payable for the life of the beneficiary under the plan and either there is no guaranteed period under the contract or there is a guaranteed period that does not exceed 15 years,

(vi) the periodic payments

(A) are equal, or

(B) are not equal solely because of one or more adjustments that would, if the contract were an annuity under a retirement savings plan, be in accordance with subparagraphs 146(3)(*b*)(iii) to (v) or that arise because of a uniform reduction in the entitlement to the periodic payments as a consequence of a partial surrender of rights to the periodic payments, and

(vii) the contract requires that, in the event the plan must be terminated in accordance with paragraph 146.4(4)(*p*), any amounts that would otherwise be payable after the termination be commuted into a single payment; and

(*d*) a prescribed investment.

Canadian Tax Foundation: De Lisser and Krieger, *Registered Savings Plans: Investing Without Penalty*, 2013 Canadian Tax Journal 3:769–796.

► 205(2) ◄

(2) Definitions in subsection 146.4(1) — (Repealed by S.C. 2017, c. 33, s. 66(1).)

History: S. 205(2) was repealed by S.C. 2017, c. 33, s. 66(1), applicable to transactions and events occurring, income earned, capital gains accruing and investments acquired after March 22, 2017, and formerly read:

(2) *Definitions in subsection 146.4(1).* The definitions in subsection 146.4(1) apply in this Part.

SECTION 206: Tax payable where inadequate consideration

▶ 206(1) ◀

(1) Tax payable where inadequate consideration — (Repealed by S.C. 2017, c. 33, s. 66(1).)

History: S. 206(1) was repealed by S.C. 2017, c. 33, s. 66(1), applicable to transactions and events occurring, income earned, capital gains accruing and investments acquired after March 22, 2017, and formerly read:

S. 206. *Tax payable where inadequate consideration.*

(1) *Tax payable where inadequate consideration.* A tax is payable under this Part for a calendar year in connection with a registered disability savings plan if, in the year, a trust governed by the plan

(*a*) disposes of property for consideration less than the fair market value of the property at the time of the disposition, or for no consideration; or

(*b*) acquires property for consideration greater than the fair market value of the property at the time of the acquisition.

Canadian Tax Foundation: De Lisser and Krieger, *Registered Savings Plans: Investing Without Penalty*, 2013 Canadian Tax Journal 3:769–796.

▶ 206(2) ◀

(2) Amount of tax payable — (Repealed by S.C. 2017, c. 33, s. 66(1).)

History: S. 206(2) was repealed by S.C. 2017, c. 33, s. 66(1), applicable to transactions and events occurring, income earned, capital gains accruing and investments acquired after March 22, 2017, and formerly read:

(2) *Amount of tax payable.* The amount of tax payable in respect of each disposition or acquisition described in subsection (1) is

(*a*) the amount by which the fair market value differs from the consideration; or

(*b*) if there is no consideration, the amount of the fair market value.

▶ 206(3) ◀

(3) Liability for tax — (Repealed by S.C. 2017, c. 33, s. 66(1).)

History: S. 206(3) was repealed by S.C. 2017, c. 33, s. 66(1), applicable to transactions and events occurring, income earned, capital gains accruing and investments acquired after March 22, 2017, and formerly read:

(3) *Liability for tax.* Each person who is a holder of a registered disability savings plan at the time that a tax is imposed under subsection (1) in connection with the plan is jointly and severally, or solidarily, liable to pay the tax.

▶ 206(4) ◀

(4) Payment of amount collected to RDSP — (Repealed by S.C. 2017, c. 33, s. 66(1).)

History: S. 206(4) was repealed by S.C. 2017, c. 33, s. 66(1), applicable to transactions and events occurring, income earned, capital gains accruing and investments acquired after March 22, 2017, and formerly read:

(4) *Payment of amount collected to RDSP.* Where a tax has been imposed under subsection (1) in connection with a registered disability savings plan of a beneficiary, the Minister may pay all or part of any amount collected in respect of the tax to a trust governed by a registered disability savings plan of the beneficiary (referred to in this subsection as the "current plan") if

(*a*) it is just and equitable to do so having regard to all circumstances; and

(*b*) the Minister is satisfied that neither the beneficiary nor any existing holder of the current plan was involved in the transaction that gave rise to the tax.

▶ 206(5) ◀

(5) Deemed not to be a contribution — (Repealed by S.C. 2017, c. 33, s. 66(1).)

History: S. 206(5) was repealed by S.C. 2017, c. 33, s. 66(1), applicable to transactions and events occurring, income earned, capital gains accruing and investments acquired after March 22, 2017, and formerly read:

(5) *Deemed not to be a contribution.* A payment under subsection (4) is deemed not to be a contribution to a registered disability savings plan for the purposes of section 146.4.

SECTION 206.1: Tax payable on non-qualified investment

▶ 206.1(1) ◀

(1) Tax payable on non-qualified investment — (Repealed by S.C. 2017, c. 33, s. 66(1).)

History: S. 206.1(1) was repealed by S.C. 2017, c. 33, s. 66(1), applicable to transactions and events occurring, income earned, capital gains accruing and investments acquired after March 22, 2017, and formerly read:

S. 206.1 *Tax payable on non-qualified investment.*

(1) *Tax payable on non-qualified investment.* A tax is payable under this Part for a calendar year in connection with a registered disability savings plan if, in the year,

(*a*) the trust governed by the plan acquires property that is not a qualified investment for the trust; or

(*b*) property held by the trust governed by the plan ceases to be a qualified investment for the trust.

▶ 206.1(2) ◀

(2) Amount of tax payable — (Repealed by S.C. 2017, c. 33, s. 66(1).)

History: S. 206.1(2) was repealed by S.C. 2017, c. 33, s. 66(1), applicable to transactions and events occurring, income earned, capital gains accruing and investments acquired after March 22, 2017, and formerly read:

(2) *Amount of tax payable.* The amount of tax payable,

(*a*) in respect of each property described in paragraph (1)(*a*), is 50% of the fair market value of the property at the time it was acquired by the trust; and

(*b*) in respect of each property described in paragraph (1)(*b*), is 50% of the fair market value of the property at the time immediately before the time it ceased to be a qualified investment for the trust.

▶ 206.1(3) ◀

(3) Liability for tax — (Repealed by S.C. 2017, c. 33, s. 66(1).)

History: S. 206.1(3) was repealed by S.C. 2017, c. 33, s. 66(1), applicable to transactions and events occurring, income earned, capital gains accruing and investments acquired after March 22, 2017, and formerly read:

(3) *Liability for tax.* Each person who is a holder of a registered disability savings plan at the time that a tax is imposed under subsection (1) in connection with the plan is jointly and severally, or solidarily, liable to pay the tax.

▶ 206.1(4) ◀

(4) Refund of tax on disposition of non-qualified investment — (Repealed by S.C. 2017, c. 33, s. 66(1).)

History: S. 206.1(4) was repealed by S.C. 2017, c. 33, s. 66(1), applicable to transactions and events occurring, income earned, capital gains accruing and investments acquired after March 22, 2017, and formerly read:

(4) *Refund of tax on disposition of non-qualified investment.* Where in a calendar year a trust governed by a registered disability savings plan disposes of a property in respect of which a tax is imposed under subsection (1), the person or persons who are liable to pay the tax are entitled to a refund for the year of an amount equal to

(*a*) except where paragraph (*b*) applies, the lesser of

(i) the amount of the tax so imposed, and

(ii) the proceeds of disposition of the property; and

(*b*) nil,

(i) if it is reasonable to expect that any of those persons knew or ought to have known at the time the property was acquired by the trust that it was not, or would cease to be, a qualified investment for the trust, or

(ii) if the property is not disposed of by the trust before the end of the calendar year following the calendar year in which the tax arose, or any later time that the Minister considers reasonable in the circumstances.

▶ 206.1(5) ◀

(5) Apportionment of refund — (Repealed by S.C. 2017, c. 33, s. 66(1).)

History: S. 206.1(5) was repealed by S.C. 2017, c. 33, s. 66(1), applicable to transactions and events occurring, income earned, capital gains accruing and investments acquired after March 22, 2017, and formerly read:

(5) *Apportionment of refund.* Where more than one person is entitled to a refund under subsection (4) for a calendar year in respect of the disposition of a property, the total of all amounts so refundable shall not exceed the amount that would be so refundable for the year to any one of those persons in respect of that disposition if that person were the only person entitled to a refund for the year under that subsection in respect of the disposition. If the persons cannot agree as to what portion of the refund each can so claim, the Minister may fix the portions.

▶ 206.1(6) ◀

(6) Deemed disposition and reacquisition — (Repealed by S.C. 2017, c. 33, s. 66(1).)

History: S. 206.1(6) was repealed by S.C. 2017, c. 33, s. 66(1), applicable to transactions and events occurring, income earned, capital gains accruing and investments acquired after March 22, 2017, and formerly read:

(6) *Deemed disposition and reacquisition.* For the purposes of this Act, where at any time property held by a plan trust in respect of which a tax was imposed under subsection (1) subsequently becomes a qualified investment for the trust, the trust is deemed to have disposed of the property at that time for proceeds of disposition equal to its fair market value at that time and to have reacquired it immediately after that time at a cost equal to that fair market value.

SECTION 206.2: Tax payable where advantage extended

▶ 206.2(1) ◀

(1) Tax payable where advantage extended — (Repealed by S.C. 2017, c. 33, s. 66(1).)

History: S. 206.2(1) was repealed by S.C. 2017, c. 33, s. 66(1), applicable to transactions and events occurring, income earned, capital gains accruing and investments acquired after March 22, 2017, and formerly read:

S. 206.2 *Tax payable where advantage extended.*

(1) *Tax payable where advantage extended.* A tax is payable under this Part for a calendar year in connection with a registered disability savings plan if, in the year, an advantage in relation to the plan is extended to a person who is, or who does not deal at arm's length with, a beneficiary under, or a holder of, the plan.

▶ 206.2(2) ◀

(2) Amount of tax payable — (Repealed by S.C. 2017, c. 33, s. 66(1).)

History: S. 206.2(2) was repealed by S.C. 2017, c. 33, s. 66(1), applicable to transactions and events occurring, income earned, capital gains accruing and investments acquired after March 22, 2017, and formerly read:

(2) *Amount of tax payable.* The amount of tax payable in respect of an advantage described in subsection (1) is

(*a*) in the case of a benefit, the fair market value of the benefit; and

(*b*) in the case of a loan, the amount of the loan.

▶ 206.2(3) ◀

(3) Liability for tax — (Repealed by S.C. 2017, c. 33, s. 66(1).)

History: S. 206.2(3) was repealed by S.C. 2017, c. 33, s. 66(1), applicable to transactions and events occurring, income earned, capital gains accruing and investments acquired after March 22, 2017, and formerly read:

(3) *Liability for tax.* Each person who is a holder of a registered disability savings plan at the time that a tax is imposed under subsection (1) in connection with the plan is jointly and severally, or solidarily, liable to pay the tax. If, however, the advantage is extended by the issuer of the plan or by a person not dealing at arm's length with the issuer, the issuer is liable to pay the tax and not the holders.

SECTION 206.3: Tax payable on use of property as security

▶ 206.3(1) ◀

(1) Tax payable on use of property as security — (Repealed by S.C. 2017, c. 33, s. 66(1).)

History: S. 206.3(1) was repealed by S.C. 2017, c. 33, s. 66(1), applicable to transactions and events occurring, income earned, capital gains accruing and investments acquired after March 22, 2017, and formerly read:

S. 206.3 *Tax payable on use of property as security.*

(1) *Tax payable on use of property as security.* Every issuer of a registered disability savings plan shall pay a tax under this Part for a calendar year if, in the year, with the consent or knowledge of the issuer, a trust governed by the plan uses or permits to be used any property held by the trust as security for indebtedness of any kind.

▶ 206.3(2) ◀

(2) Amount of tax payable — (Repealed by S.C. 2017, c. 33, s. 66(1).)

History: S. 206.3(2) was repealed by S.C. 2017, c. 33, s. 66(1), applicable to transactions and events occurring, income earned, capital gains accruing and investments acquired after March 22, 2017, and formerly read:

(2) *Amount of tax payable.* The amount of tax payable in respect of each property described in subsection (1) is equal to the fair market value of the property at the time the property commenced to be used as security.

SECTION 206.4: Waiver of liability

(Repealed by S.C. 2017, c. 33, s. 66(1).)

History: S. 206.4 was repealed by S.C. 2017, c. 33, s. 66(1), applicable to transactions and events occurring, income earned, capital gains accruing and investments acquired after March 22, 2017, and formerly read:

S. 206.4 *Waiver of liability.* If a person would otherwise be liable to pay a tax under this Part for a calendar year, the Minister may waive or cancel all or part of the liability where it is just and equitable to do so having regard to all the circumstances, including

(*a*) whether the tax arose as a consequence of reasonable error; and

(*b*) the extent to which the transaction which gave rise to the tax also gave rise to another tax under this Part.

SECTION 207: Return and payment of tax

▶ 207(1) ◀

(1) Return and payment of tax — (Repealed by S.C. 2017, c. 33, s. 66(1).)

History: S. 207(1) was repealed by S.C. 2017, c. 33, s. 66(1), applicable to transactions and events occurring, income earned, capital gains accruing and investments acquired after March 22, 2017, and formerly read:

S. 207. *Return and payment of tax.*

(1) *Return and payment of tax.* Every person who is liable to pay tax under this Part for a calendar year shall within 90 days after the end of the year

(*a*) file with the Minister a return for the year under this Part in prescribed form and containing prescribed information including

(i) an estimate of the amount of tax payable under this Part by the person for the year, and

(ii) an estimate of the amount of any refund to which the person is entitled under this Part for the year; and

(*b*) pay to the Receiver General the amount, if any, by which the amount of the person's tax payable under this Part for the year exceeds the person's allowable refund for the year.

▶ 207(2) ◀

(2) Refund — (Repealed by S.C. 2017, c. 33, s. 66(1).)

History: S. 207(2) was repealed by S.C. 2017, c. 33, s. 66(1), applicable to transactions and events occurring, income earned, capital gains accruing and investments acquired after March 22, 2017, and formerly read:

(2) *Refund.* Where a person has filed a return under this Part for a calendar year within three years after the end of the year, the Minister

(*a*) may, on sending the notice of assessment for the year, refund without application any allowable refund of the person for the year, to the extent that it was not applied against the person's tax payable under paragraph (1)(*b*); and

(*b*) shall, with all due dispatch, make the refund referred to in paragraph (*a*) after sending the notice of assessment if an application for it has been made in writing by the person within three years after the sending of an original notice of assessment for the year.

S. 207(2)(*a*) and (*b*) were replaced by S.C. 2010, c. 25, s. 56, in force on Royal Assent, December 15, 2010. S. 207(2)(*a*) and (*b*) formerly read:

(*a*) may, on mailing the notice of assessment for the year, refund without application any allowable refund of the person for the year, to the extent that it was not applied against the person's tax payable under paragraph (1)(*b*); and

(*b*) shall, with all due dispatch, make the refund referred to in paragraph (*a*) after mailing the notice of assessment if an application for it has been made in writing by the person within three years after the mailing of an original notice of assessment for the year.

▶ 207(3) ◀

(3) Multiple holders — (Repealed by S.C. 2017, c. 33, s. 66(1).)

History: S. 207(3) was repealed by S.C. 2017, c. 33, s. 66(1), applicable to transactions and events occurring, income earned, capital gains accruing and investments acquired after March 22, 2017, and formerly read:

(3) *Multiple holders.* Where two or more holders of a registered disability savings plan are jointly and severally, or solidarily, liable with each other to pay a tax under this Part for a calendar year in connection with the plan,

(*a*) a payment by any of the holders on account of that tax liability shall to the extent of the payment discharge the joint liability; and

(*b*) a return filed by one of the holders as required by this Part for the year is deemed to have been filed by each other holder in respect of the joint liability to which the return relates.

▶ 207(4) ◀

(4) Provisions applicable to Part — (Repealed by S.C. 2017, c. 33, s. 66(1).)

History: S. 207(4) was repealed by S.C. 2017, c. 33, s. 66(1), applicable to transactions and events occurring, income earned, capital gains accruing and investments acquired after March 22, 2017, and formerly read:

(4) *Provisions applicable to Part.* Subsections 150(2) and (3), sections 152 and 158 to 167 and Division J of Part I apply to this Part with any modifications that the circumstances require.

Part XI.01
Taxes in Respect of Registered Plans

History: The heading of Part XI.01 was replaced by S.C. 2017, c. 33, s. 67(1), deemed to have come into force on March 23, 2017, and formerly read "Taxes in Respect of RRIFs, RRSPs and TFSAs".

SECTION 207.01: [Interpretation]

► 207.01(1) ◄

(1) Definitions. The following definitions and the definitions in subsections 146(1) (other than the definition *benefit*), 146.1(1), 146.2(1), 146.3(1) and 146.4(1) apply in this Part and Part XLIX of the *Income Tax Regulations*.

History: S. 207.01(1), the portion before the first definition was replaced by S.C. 2017, c. 33, s. 68(1), applicable to transactions and events occurring, income earned, capital gains accruing and investments acquired after March 22, 2017, and formerly read:

S. 207.01 *[Interpretation]*.

(1) The following definitions and the definitions in subsections 146(1) (other than the definition "benefit"), 146.2(1) and 146.3(1) apply in this Part and Part XLIX of the *Income Tax Regulations*.

S. 207.01(1), the portion before the definitions was replaced by S.C. 2013, c. 40, s. 74(1), deemed to have come into force on March 23, 2011, and formerly read:

(1) *Definitions.* The following definitions and the definitions in subsections 146(1) (other than the definition "benefit"), 146.2(1) and 146.3(1) apply in this Part and in Parts XLIX and L of the *Income Tax Regulations*.

The heading of Part XI.01 was replaced by S.C. 2011, c. 24, s. 63(1), deemed to have come into force on March 23, 2011. The heading of Part XI.01 formerly read "Taxes in Respect of TFSAs".

S. 207.01(1), the portion before the definition "advantage" was replaced by S.C. 2011, c. 24, s. 64(1), applicable to transactions occurring, income earned, capital gains accruing and investments acquired, after March 22, 2011. S. 207.01(1), the portion before the definition "advantage" formerly read:

(1) *Definitions.* The definitions in subsection 146.2(1) and the following definitions apply in this Part.

Canadian Tax Foundation: Forgie et al., *Tax-Free Savings Accounts*, 2008 Conference Report 31:1–11.

Tax Window Files: *Swap Transactions in RRSPs and RRIFs, January 16, 2012* CRA Document No. 2012-0432611E5; *Swap transactions in RRSPs and RRIFs, January 6, 2012*, CRA Document No. 2011-0429561M4; *TFSA - Swap Transaction, August 24, 2010*, CRA Document No. 2010-0359001E5; *TFSAs - Asset Transfer Transactions (Swaps), November 25, 2009*, CRA Document No. 2009-0345161E5.

"advantage" —"advantage", in relation to a registered plan, means

(*a*) any benefit, loan or indebtedness that is conditional in any way on the existence of the registered plan, other than

(i) a benefit derived from the provision of administrative or investment services in respect of the registered plan,

(ii) a loan or an indebtedness (including, in the case of a TFSA, the use of the TFSA as security for a loan or an indebtedness) the terms and conditions of which are terms and conditions that persons dealing at arm's length with each other would have entered into,

(iii) a payment out of or under the registered plan in satisfaction of all or part of a beneficiary's or controlling individual's interest in the registered plan,

(iv) the payment or allocation of any amount to the registered plan by the issuer, carrier or promoter,

(iv.1) an amount paid under or because of the *Canada Disability Savings Act*, the *Canada Education Savings Act* or under a designated provincial program, and

(v) a benefit provided under an incentive program that is — in a normal commercial or investment context in which parties deal with each other at arm's length and act prudently, knowledgeably and willingly — offered to a broad class of persons, if it is reasonable to conclude that none of the main purposes of the program is to enable a person or partnership to benefit from the exemption from tax under Part I of any amount in respect of the plan;

(*b*) a benefit that is an increase in the total fair market value of the property held in connection with the registered plan if it is reasonable to consider, having regard to all the circumstances, that the increase is attributable, directly or indirectly, to

(i) a transaction or event or a series of transactions or events that

(A) would not have occurred in a normal commercial or investment context in which parties deal with each other at arm's length and act prudently, knowledgeably and willingly, and

(B) had as one of its main purposes to enable a person or a partnership to benefit from the exemption from tax under Part I of any amount in respect of the registered plan,

(ii) a payment received as, on account or in lieu of, or in satisfaction of, a payment

(A) for services provided by a person who is, or who does not deal at arm's length with, the controlling individual of the registered plan, or

(B) of interest, of a dividend, of rent, of a royalty or of any other return on investment, or of proceeds of disposition, in respect of property (other than property held in connection with the registered plan) held by a person who is, or who does not deal at arm's length with, the controlling individual of the registered plan,

(iii) a swap transaction, or

(iv) specified non-qualified investment income that has not been paid from the registered plan to its controlling individual within 90 days of receipt by the controlling individual of a notice issued by the Minister under subsection 207.06(4);

(*c*) a benefit that is income (determined without reference to paragraph 82(1)(*b*)), or a capital gain, that is reasonably attributable, directly or indirectly, to

(i) a prohibited investment in respect of the registered plan or any other registered plan of the controlling individual,

(ii) in the case of a registered plan that is not a TFSA, an amount received by the controlling individual of the registered plan, or by a person who does not deal at arm's length with the controlling individual (if it is reasonable to consider, having regard to all the circumstances, that the amount was paid in relation to, or would not have been paid but for, property held in connection with the registered plan) and the amount was paid as, on account or in lieu of, or in satisfaction of, a payment

(A) for services provided by a person who is, or who does not deal at arm's length with, the controlling individual of the registered plan, or

(B) of interest, of a dividend, of rent, of a royalty or of any other return on investment, or of proceeds of disposition, or

(iii) a deliberate over-contribution;

(*d*) a registered plan strip in respect of the registered plan; and

(*e*) a prescribed benefit.

History: S. 207.01(1), paragraph (*d*) of the definition "advantage" was replaced by S.C. 2017, c. 33, s. 68(6), applicable to transactions and events occurring, income earned, capital gains accruing and investments acquired after March 22, 2017, and formerly read:

(*d*) an RRSP strip in respect of the registered plan; and

S. 207.01(1), the portion of subparagraph (*c*)(ii) before clause (A) of the definition "advantage" was replaced by S.C. 2017, c. 33, s. 68(5), applicable to transactions and events occurring, income earned, capital gains accruing and investments acquired after March 22, 2017, and formerly read:

(ii) in the case of a RRIF or RRSP, an amount received by the controlling individual of the registered plan, or by a person who does not deal at arm's length with the controlling individual (if it is reasonable to consider, having regard to all the circumstances, that the amount was paid in relation to, or would not have been paid but for, property held in connection with the registered plan) and the amount was paid as, on account or in lieu of, or in satisfaction of, a payment

S. 207.01(1), subparagraphs (*a*)(iii) and (iv) of the definition "advantage" were replaced and subparagraph (*a*)(iv.1) was added by S.C. 2017, c. 33, s. 68(4), applicable to transactions and events occurring, income earned, capital gains accruing and investments acquired after March 22, 2017. Subparagraphs (*a*)(iii) and (iv) of the definition "advantage" formerly read:

(iii) a payment out of or under the registered plan in satisfaction of all or part of the controlling individual's interest in the registered plan,

(iv) the payment or allocation of any amount to the registered plan by the issuer or carrier, and

S. 207.01(1), subparagraph (*a*)(v) of the definition "advantage" was added by S.C. 2013, c. 40, s. 74(3), deemed to have come into force on March 23, 2011.

S. 207.01(1), clause (*b*)(i)(A) of the definition "advantage" was replaced by S.C. 2013, c. 40, s. 74(4), deemed to have come into force on March 23, 2011, and formerly read:

(A) would not have occurred in an open market in which parties deal with each other at arm's length and act prudently, knowledgeably and willingly, and

S. 207.01(1), the portion of paragraph (*c*) before subparagraph (i) of the definition "advantage" was replaced by S.C. 2013, c. 40, s. 74(5), deemed to have come into force on March 23, 2011, and formerly read:

(*c*) a benefit that is income (including a capital gain) that is reasonably attributable, directly or indirectly, to

S. 207.01(1), the definition "advantage" was replaced by S.C. 2011, c. 24, s. 64(2), applicable to transactions occurring, income earned, capital gains accruing and investments acquired, after March 22, 2011. S. 207.01(1), the definition "advantage" formerly read:

"advantage"—"advantage", in relation to a TFSA, means

(*a*) any benefit, loan or indebtedness that is conditional in any way on the existence of the TFSA, other than

(i) a benefit derived from the provision of administrative or investment services in respect of the TFSA,

(ii) a loan or an indebtedness (including the use of the TFSA as security for a loan or an indebtedness) the terms and conditions of which are terms and conditions that persons dealing at arm's length with each other would have entered into,

(iii) a distribution under the TFSA, and

(iv) the payment or allocation of any amount to the TFSA by the issuer; and

(*b*) a benefit that is an increase in the total fair market value of the property held in connection with the TFSA if it is reasonable to consider, having regard to all the circumstances, that the increase is attributable, directly or indirectly, to

(i) a transaction or event or a series of transactions or events that

(A) would not have occurred in an open market in which parties deal with each other at arm's length and act prudently, knowledgeably and willingly, and

(B) had as one of its main purposes to enable a person or a partnership to benefit from the exemption from tax under Part I of any amount in respect of the TFSA,

(ii) a payment received as, on account or in lieu of, or in satisfaction of, a payment

(A) for services provided by a person who is, or who does not deal at arm's length with, the holder of the TFSA, or

(B) of interest, of a dividend, of rent, of a royalty or of any other return on investment, or of proceeds of disposition, in respect of property (other than property held in connection with the TFSA) held by a person who is, or who does not deal at arm's length with, the holder of the TFSA,

(iii) a swap transaction, or

(iv) specified non-qualified investment income that has not been distributed under the TFSA within 90 days of receipt by the holder of the TFSA of a notice issued by the Minister under subsection 207.06(4); and

(*c*) a benefit that is income (including a capital gain) that is reasonably attributable, directly or indirectly, to

(i) a deliberate over-contribution, or

(ii) a prohibited investment in respect of the TFSA or any other TFSA of the holder; and

(*d*) a prescribed benefit.

S. 207.01(1), subparagraphs (*b*)(iii) and (iv) of the definition "advantage" were added by S.C. 2010, c. 25, s. 57(1), applicable after October 16, 2009.

S. 207.01(1), paragraph (*c*) of the definition "advantage" was replaced, and paragraph (*d*) was added, by S.C. 2010, c. 25, s. 57(2), applicable after October 16, 2009, except that subparagraph (*c*)(ii) of the definition "advantage" does not apply in respect of income (including a capital gain) earned before October 17, 2009.

S. 207.01(1), paragraph (*c*) of the definition "advantage" formerly read:

(*c*) a prescribed benefit.

S. 207.01(1), subparagraphs (*a*)(iii) and (iv) of the definition "advantage" were added by S.C. 2009, c. 2, s. 68(2), applicable to the 2009 and subsequent taxation years.

S. 207.01(1), paragraph (*b*) of the definition "advantage" was replaced, and paragraph (*c*) was added, by S.C. 2009, c. 2, s. 68(3), applicable to the 2009 and subsequent taxation years. S. 207.01(1), paragraph (*b*) of the definition "advantage" formerly read:

(*b*) a prescribed benefit.

Tax Topics: No. 1971-72, 2009 Canadian Tax Foundation Conference: Wizards, Tiny Taxes and "Evil" Kirk.

Forms: RC298 — Advantage Tax Return for TFSA Issuers.

Income Tax Folios: S3-F10-C3 Advantages – RRSPs, RESPs, RRIFs, RDSPs and TFSAs.

Income Tax Technical News: Issue No. 44, Key Employee Tax-Free Savings Account.

Cases: Based on the definition of "advantage", the Court was required to determine whether it was reasonable to consider, having regard for all of the circumstances, whether the increase in the total fair market value of the taxpayer's TFSA was attributable directly or indirectly to a transaction or series of transactions that would not have occurred in an open market in which parties dealt with one another at arm's length and acted prudently, knowledgeably, and willingly. The taxpayer received an advantage in relation to her TFSA in 2009 since the parties in charge of the RRSP and CDN did not act "prudently, knowledgeably and willingly", as all of the swap transactions were carried out in a way to favour the TFSA to the detriment of the RRSP and CDN. *Louie v. The Queen*, 2018 DTC 1166 (TCC)

"allowable refund"—"allowable refund" of a person for a calendar year means the total of all amounts each of which is a refund, for the year, to which the person is entitled under subsection 207.04(4).

"controlling individual" —"controlling individual", of a registered plan, means

(*a*) the holder of a TFSA;

(*b*) a holder of a RDSP;

(*c*) a subscriber of a RESP; or

(*d*) the annuitant of a RRIF or RRSP.

History: S. 207.01(1), the definition "controlling individual" was replaced by S.C. 2017, c. 33, s. 68(3), applicable to transactions and events occurring, income earned, capital gains accruing and investments acquired after March 22, 2017, and formerly read:

"controlling individual"—"controlling individual" of a registered plan, means the holder of a TFSA or the annuitant of a RRIF or RRSP, as the case may be.

S. 207.01(1), the definition "controlling individual" was added by S.C. 2011, c. 24, s. 64(4), deemed to have come into force on March 23, 2011.

"deliberate over-contribution" —"deliberate over-contribution" of an individual means a contribution made under a TFSA by the individual that results in, or increases, an excess TFSA amount, unless it is reasonable to conclude that the individual neither knew nor ought to have known that the contribution could result in liability for a penalty, tax or similar consequence under this Act.

History: S. 207.01(1), the definition "deliberate over-contribution" was added by S.C. 2010, c. 25, s. 57(7), applicable to contributions made after October 16, 2009.

"equity" —"equity", of a corporation, trust or partnership, means

(*a*) in the case of a corporation, a share of the capital stock of the corporation;

(*b*) in the case of a trust, an income or capital interest in the trust; and

(*c*) in the case of a partnership, an interest as a member of the partnership.

History: S. 207.01(1), the definition "equity" was added by S.C. 2013, c. 40, s. 74(14), deemed to have come into force March 23, 2011.

"excess TFSA amount" —"excess TFSA amount" of an individual at a particular time in a calendar year means the amount, if any, determined by the formula

$$A - B - C - D - E$$

where

A is the total of all amounts each of which is a contribution made under a TFSA by the individual in the calendar year and at or before the particular time, other than a contribution that is

(*a*) a qualifying transfer, or

(*b*) an exempt contribution;

B is the individual's unused TFSA contribution room at the end of the preceding calendar year;

C is the total of all amounts each of which was a distribution made in the preceding calendar year under a TFSA of which the individual was the holder at the time of the distribution, other than a distribution that is

(*a*) a qualifying transfer, or

(*b*) a specified distribution;

D is

(*a*) the TFSA dollar limit for the calendar year if, at any time in the calendar year, the individual is resident in Canada, and

(*b*) nil, in any other case; and

E is the total of all amounts each of which is the qualifying portion of a distribution made in the calendar year and at or before the particular time under a TFSA of which the individual was the holder at the time of the distribution and, for this purpose, the qualifying portion of a distribution is

(*a*) nil, if the distribution is a qualifying transfer or a specified distribution, and

(*b*) in any other case, the lesser of

(i) the amount of the distribution, and

(ii) the amount that would be the individual's excess TFSA amount at the time of the distribution if the amount of the distribution were nil.

History: S. 207.01(1), paragraph (*b*) of the description of C in the definition "excess TFSA amount" was replaced by S.C. 2010, c. 25, s. 57(3), applicable after October 16, 2009. S. 207.01(1), paragraph (*b*) of the description of C in the definition "excess TFSA amount" formerly read:

(*b*) a prescribed distribution;

S. 207.01(1), paragraph (*a*) of the description of E in the definition "excess TFSA amount" was replaced by S.C. 2010, c. 25, s. 57(4), applicable after October 16, 2009. S. 207.01(1), paragraph (*a*) of the description of E in the definition "excess TFSA amount" formerly read:

(*a*) nil, if the distribution is a qualifying transfer or a prescribed distribution, and

S. 207.01(1), the description of E in the definition "excess TFSA amount" was replaced by S.C. 2009, c. 2, s. 68(4), applicable to the 2009 and subsequent taxation years. S. 207.01(1), the description of E in the definition "excess TFSA amount" formerly read:

E is the total of all amounts each of which is a distribution made in the calendar year and at or before the particular time under a TFSA of which the individual was the holder at the time of the distribution, other than a distribution that is

(*a*) a qualifying transfer, or

(*b*) a prescribed distribution.

Related Sections: S. 146.2(1), "distribution"; S. 207.02 Tax payable on excess TFSA amount; S. 207.05(1) Tax payable in respect of advantage.

"excluded property" —"excluded property", at any time for a trust governed by a registered plan, means

(*a*) property described in paragraph 4900(1)(*j.1*) of the *Income Tax Regulations;*

(*b*) an equity of a mutual fund corporation, mutual fund trust or registered investment if

(i) either

(A) the equity is equity of a mutual fund corporation or mutual fund trust that derives all or substantially all its value from one or more mutual funds that are subject to, and substantially comply with, the requirements of *National Instrument 81–102 Mutual Funds*, as amended from time to time, of the Canadian Securities Administrators, or

(B) the corporation, trust or registered investment follows a reasonable policy of investment diversification,

(ii) the time is

(A) during the 24-month period that begins on the day on which the first taxation year of the corporation, trust or registered investment begins,

(B) during the 24-month period that ends on the day on which the last taxation year of the corporation, trust or registered investment ends, or

(C) where the equity is a share of the capital stock of a mutual fund corporation and the share derives all or substantially all its value from a particular mutual fund,

(I) during the 24-month period that begins on the day on which the particular mutual fund is established, or

(II) during the 24-month period that ends on the day on which the particular mutual fund is terminated,

(iii) it is reasonable to conclude that none of the main purposes of the structure of the corporation, trust or registered investment, or of the terms and conditions of the equity, is to accommodate transactions or events that could affect the fair market value of the property held by the trust governed by the registered plan in a manner that would not occur in a normal commercial or investment context in which parties deal with each other at arm's length and act prudently, knowledgeably and willingly, and

(iv) it is reasonable to conclude that none of the main purposes of the incorporation, establishment or operation of the corporation, trust or registered investment, or of the particular mutual fund, is to benefit from this paragraph; or

(*c*) equity of a corporation, partnership or trust (in this paragraph referred to as the "investment entity") if at that time

(i) the fair market value of the equity (in this paragraph referred to as the "arm's length equity") of the investment entity that is owned by persons who deal at arm's length with the controlling individual of the registered plan is at least 90% of the fair market value of all the equity of the investment entity,

(ii) the total fair market value of the arm's length equity and the debt of the investment entity that is owned by persons who deal at arm's length with the controlling individual is at least 90% of the total fair market value of all the equity and debt of the investment entity,

(iii) the controlling individual, either alone or together with persons with whom the controlling individual does not deal at arm's length, does not have the right to cast at least 10% of the votes, if any, that could be cast regarding the governance of the investment entity,

(iv) the specific terms and conditions of each share or unit of equity of the investment entity held by the trust governed by the registered plan are the same as, or substantially similar to, the terms and conditions of particular equity that is included in the arm's length equity,

(v) the fair market value of the particular equity referred to in subparagraph (iv) is equal to at least 10% of the total fair market value of all equity of the investment entity having the specific terms and conditions referred to in subparagraph (iv) or terms and conditions that are substantially similar to those terms and conditions,

(vi) the controlling individual deals at arm's length with the investment entity, and

(vii) it is reasonable to conclude that none of the main purposes of the structure of the investment entity, or of the terms and conditions of the equity, is to accommodate transactions or events that could affect the fair market value of the property held by the trust governed by the registered plan in a manner that would not occur in a normal commercial or investment context in which parties deal with each other at arm's length and act prudently, knowledgeably and willingly.

History: S. 207.01(1), the definition "excluded property" was added by S.C. 2013, c. 40, s. 74(14), deemed to have come into force March 23, 2011.

"exempt contribution" —"exempt contribution" means a contribution made in a calendar year under a TFSA by the survivor of an individual if

(*a*) the contribution is made during the period (in this definition referred to as the "rollover period") that begins when the individual dies and that ends at the end of the first calendar year that begins after the individual dies (or at any later time that is acceptable to the Minister);

(*b*) a payment (in this definition referred to as the "survivor payment") was made to the survivor during the rollover period, as a consequence of the individual's death, directly or indirectly out of or under an arrangement that ceased, because of the individual's death, to be a TFSA;

(*c*) the survivor designates, in prescribed form filed in prescribed manner within 30 days after the day on which the contribution is made (or at any later time that is acceptable to the Minister), the contribution in relation to the survivor payment; and

(*d*) the amount of the contribution does not exceed the least of

(i) the amount, if any, by which

(A) the amount of the survivor payment

exceeds

(B) the total of all other contributions designated by the survivor in relation to the survivor payment,

(ii) the amount, if any, by which

(A) the total proceeds of disposition that would, if section 146.2 were read without reference to subsection 146.2(9), be determined in respect of the arrangement under paragraph 146.2(8)(*a*), (10)(*a*) or (11)(*a*), as the case may be,

exceeds

(B) the total of all other exempt contributions in respect of the arrangement made by the survivor at or before the time of the contribution, and

(iii) if the individual had, immediately before the individual's death, an excess TFSA amount or if payments described in paragraph (*b*) are made to more than one survivor of the individual, nil or the greater amount, if any, allowed by the Minister in respect of the contribution.

History: S. 207.01(1), paragraph (*c*) of the definition "exempt contribution" was replaced by S.C. 2013, c. 40, s. 74(6), deemed to have come into force on March 23, 2011, and formerly read:

(*c*) the survivor designates, in prescribed form filed in prescribed manner within 30 days after the day on which the contribution is made, the contribution in relation to the survivor payment; and

S. 207.01(1), the definition "exempt contribution" was added by S.C. 2009, c. 2, s. 68(7), applicable to the 2009 and subsequent taxation years.

Tax Window Files: *TFSA — Survivor payments to more than one survivor, October 5, 2012,* CRA Document No. 2012-0453171C6.

"non-qualified investment" —"non-qualified investment" for a trust governed by a registered plan means property that is not a qualified investment for the trust.

History: S. 207.01(1), the definition "non-qualified investment" was replaced by S.C. 2011, c. 24, s. 64(2), applicable to transactions occurring, income earned, capital gains accruing and investments acquired, after March 22, 2011. S. 207.01(1), the definition "non-qualified investment" formerly read:

"non-qualified investment"—"non-qualified investment" for a trust governed by a TFSA means property that is not a qualified investment for the trust.

Related Regulations: 222.

Related Sections: S. 146.2(6) Trust not taxable.

Income Tax Folios: *Secondary* — S3-F10-C1 Qualified Investments – RRSPs, RESPs, RRIFs, RDSPs and TFSAs. *Primary* — S3-F10-C2 Prohibited Investments - RRSPs, RRIFs and TFSAs.

"prohibited investment" —"prohibited investment", at any time for a trust governed by a registered plan, means property (other than excluded property for the trust) that is at that time

(*a*) a debt of the controlling individual of the registered plan;

(*b*) a share of the capital stock of, an interest in, or a debt of

(i) a corporation, partnership or trust in which the controlling individual has a significant interest, or

(ii) a person or partnership that does not deal at arm's length with the controlling individual;

(*c*) an interest (or, for civil law, a right) in, or a right to acquire, a share, interest or debt described in paragraph (*a*) or (*b*); or

(*d*) prescribed property.

History: S. 207.01(1), the portion of the definition "prohibited investment" before paragraph (*a*) was replaced by S.C. 2013, c. 40, s. 74(7), applicable after March 22, 2011 in respect of investments acquired at any time, and formerly read:

"prohibited investment"—"prohibited investment", at any time, for a trust governed by a registered plan, means property (other than prescribed excluded property) that is at that time

S. 207.01(1), subparagraph (*b*)(ii) of the definition "prohibited investment" was replaced by S.C. 2013, c. 40, s. 74(8), applicable after March 22, 2011 in respect of investments acquired at any time, and formerly read:

(ii) a person or partnership that does not deal at arm's length with the controlling individual or with a person or partnership described in subparagraph (i);

S. 207.01(1), the portion of the definition "prohibited investment" before paragraph (*c*) was replaced by S.C. 2011, c. 24, s. 64(3), applicable after March 22, 2011 in respect of investments acquired at any time. S. 207.01(1), the portion of the definition "prohibited investment" before paragraph (*c*) formerly read:

"prohibited investment"—"prohibited investment", at any time, for a trust governed by a TFSA means property (other than prescribed property) that is at that time

(*a*) a debt of the holder of the TFSA;

(*b*) a share of the capital stock of, an interest in, or a debt of

(i) a corporation, partnership or trust in which the holder has a significant interest, or

(ii) a person or partnership that does not deal at arm's length with the holder or with a person or partnership described in subparagraph (i);

S. 207.01(1), the portion of the definition "prohibited investment" before paragraph (*a*) was replaced by S.C. 2009, c. 2, s. 68(5), applicable to the 2009 and subsequent taxation years. S. 207.01(1), the portion of the definition "prohibited investment" before paragraph (*a*) formerly read:

"prohibited investment"—"prohibited investment", at any time, for a trust governed by a TFSA means property (other than prescribed property in relation to the trust) that is at that time

S. 207.01(1), paragraph (*d*) of the definition "prohibited investment" was replaced by S.C. 2009, c. 2, s. 68(6), applicable to the 2009 and subsequent taxation years. S. 207.01(1), paragraph (*d*) of the definition "prohibited investment" formerly read:

(*d*) restricted property.

Related Regulations: 4900(15).

Income Tax Folios: *Secondary* — S3-F10-C1 Qualified Investments – RRSPs, RESPs, RRIFs, RDSPs and TFSAs. *Primary* — S3-F10-C2 Prohibited Investments - RRSPs, RRIFs and TFSAs.

"qualified investment" —"qualified investment" for a trust governed by a TFSA means

(*a*) an investment that would be described by any of paragraphs (*a*) to (*d*), (*f*) and (*g*) of the definition "qualified investment" in section 204 if the reference in that definition to "a trust governed by a deferred profit sharing plan or revoked plan" were read as a reference to "a trust governed by a TFSA" and if that definition were read without reference to the words "with the exception of excluded property in relation to the trust";

(*b*) a contract for an annuity issued by a licensed annuities provider if

(i) the trust is the only person who, disregarding any subsequent transfer of the contract by the trust, is or may become entitled to any annuity payments under the contract, and

(ii) the holder of the contract has a right to surrender the contract at any time for an amount that would, if reasonable sales and administration charges were ignored, approximate the value of funds that could otherwise be applied to fund future periodic payments under the contract; and

(*c*) a prescribed investment.

Related Regulations: 221(2); 222; 4900; 4900(1).

Related Sections: S. 207.04(1) Tax payable on prohibited or non-qualified investment.

Canadian Tax Foundation: De Lisser and Krieger, *Registered Savings Plans: Investing Without Penalty,* 2013 Canadian Tax Journal 3:769–796.

Income Tax Folios: *Primary* — S3-F10-C1 Qualified Investments – RRSPs, RESPs, RRIFs, RDSPs and TFSAs. *Secondary* — S3-F10-C2 Prohibited Investments - RRSPs, RRIFs and TFSAs.

"qualifying transfer" —"qualifying transfer" means the transfer of an amount from a TFSA of which a particular individual is the holder if

(*a*) the amount is transferred directly to another TFSA, the holder of which is the particular individual; or

(*b*) the amount is transferred directly to another TFSA, the holder of which is a spouse or common-law partner or former spouse or common-law partner of the particular individual, and the following conditions are satisfied:

(i) the individuals are living separate and apart at the time of the transfer, and

(ii) the transfer is made under a decree, order or judgment of a competent tribunal, or under a written separation agreement, relating to a division of property between the individuals in settlement of rights arising out of, or on the breakdown of, their marriage or common-law partnership.

"registered plan" —"registered plan" means a RDSP, RESP, RRIF, RRSP or TFSA.

History: S. 207.01(1), the definition "registered plan" was replaced by S.C. 2017, c. 33, s. 68(3), applicable to transactions and events occurring, income earned, capital gains accruing and investments acquired after March 22, 2017, and formerly read:

"registered plan"—"registered plan" means a RRIF, RRSP or TFSA.

S. 207.01(1), the definition "registered plan" was added by S.C. 2011, c. 24, s. 64(4), deemed to have come into force on March 23, 2011.

"registered plan strip" —"registered plan strip", in respect of a registered plan that is not a TFSA, means the amount of a reduction in the fair market value of property held in connection with the registered plan, if the value is reduced as part of a transaction or event or a series of transactions or events one of the main purposes of which is to enable the controlling individual of the registered plan, or a person who does not deal at arm's length with the controlling individual, to obtain a benefit in respect of property held in connection with the registered plan or to obtain a benefit as a result of the reduction, but does not include an amount that is

(*a*) included in the income of a person under section 146, 146.1, 146.3 or 146.4;

(*b*) an excluded withdrawal under section 146.01 or 146.02;

(*c*) described in subsection 146(16), 146.3(14.2) or 146.4(8);

(*d*) a distribution to a trust governed by a RESP under circumstances to which subparagraph 204.9(5)(*c*)(i) or (ii) applies;

(*e*) an accumulated income payment made to a RDSP under circumstances to which subsection 146.1(1.2) applies;

(*f*) a refund of payments under a RESP; or

(*g*) the non-taxable portion of a disability assistance payment made from a RDSP.

History: S. 207.01(1), the definition "registered plan strip" was added by S.C. 2017, c. 33, s. 68(9), applicable to transactions and events occurring, income earned, capital gains accruing and investments acquired after March 22, 2017.

Income Tax Folios: S3-F10-C3 Advantages – RRSPs, RESPs, RRIFs, RDSPs and TFSAs.

"restricted property" — (Repealed by S.C. 2009, c. 2, s. 68(1).)

History: S. 207.01(1), the definition "restricted property" was repealed by S.C. 2009, c. 2, s. 68(1), applicable to the 2009 and subsequent taxation years. S. 207.01(1), the definition "restricted property" formerly read:

"restricted property"—"restricted property" has the meaning assigned by regulation.

"RRSP strip" — (Repealed by S.C. 2017, c. 33, s. 68(2).)

History: S. 207.01(1), the definition "RRSP Strip" was repealed by S.C. 2017, c. 33, s. 68(2), applicable to transactions and events occurring, income earned, capital gains accruing and investments acquired after March 22, 2017, and formerly read:

"RRSP strip"—"RRSP strip", in respect of a RRIF or RRSP, means the amount of a reduction in the fair market value of property held in connection with the RRIF or RRSP, if the value is reduced as part of a transaction or event or a series of transactions or events one of the main purposes of which is to enable the controlling individual of the RRIF or RRSP, or a person who does not deal at arm's length with the controlling individual, to obtain a benefit in respect of property held in connection with the RRIF or RRSP or to obtain a benefit as a result of the reduction, but does not include an amount that is

(*a*) included in the income of the controlling individual or their spouse or common-law partner under section 146 or 146.3;

(*b*) an excluded withdrawal under section 146.01 or 146.02; or

(*c*) described in subsection 146(16) or 146.3(14.2).

(*d*) (Repealed.)

S. 207.01(1), the portion of the definition "RRSP strip" before paragraph (*a*) was replaced by S.C. 2013, c. 40, s. 74(9), deemed to have come into force on March 23, 2011, and formerly read:

"RRSP strip"—"RRSP strip", in respect of a RRIF or RRSP, means an amount used or obtained by the controlling individual of the RRIF or RRSP, or a person who does not deal at arm's length with the controlling individual, as part of a transaction or event or a series of transactions or events one of the main purposes of which is to enable the controlling individual, or a person who does not deal at arm's length with the controlling individual, to use or obtain the benefit of property held in connection with the RRIF or RRSP, but does not include an amount that is

S. 207.01(1), paragraph (*d*) of the definition "RRSP strip" was repealed by S.C. 2013, c. 40, s. 74(10), deemed to have come into force on March 23, 2011, and formerly read:

(*d*) the principal amount of a debt obligation that is a prescribed excluded property.

S. 207.01(1), the definition "RRSP strip" was added by S.C. 2011, c. 24, s. 64(4), deemed to have come into force on March 23, 2011.

"specified distribution" —"specified distribution" means

(*a*) a distribution made under a TFSA to the extent that it is, or is reasonably attributable to, an amount that is

(i) an advantage in respect of the TFSA or any other TFSA of the holder,

(ii) specified non-qualified investment income,

(iii) an amount in respect of which tax was payable under Part I by a trust governed by the TFSA or any other TFSA of the holder, or

(iv) an amount described in subparagraph 207.06(1)(*b*)(ii); or

(*b*) a prescribed distribution.

History: S. 207.01(1), the definition "specified distribution" was added by S.C. 2010, c. 25, s. 57(7), applicable to distributions that occur after October 16, 2009, other than the portion of a distribution that is, or is reasonably attributable to, an advantage that was extended, or income earned, before October 17, 2009.

"specified non-qualified investment income" —"specified non-qualified investment income", in respect of a registered plan and its controlling individual, means income (determined without reference to paragraph 82(1)(*b*)), or a capital gain, that is reasonably attributable, directly or indirectly, to an amount in respect of which tax was payable under Part I by a trust governed by the registered plan or by any other registered plan of the controlling individual.

History: S. 207.01(1), the definition "specified non-qualified investment income" was replaced by S.C. 2013, c. 40, s. 74(2), deemed to have come into force on March 23, 2011, and formerly read:

"specified non-qualified investment income"—"specified non-qualified investment income", in respect of a registered plan and its controlling individual, means income (including a capital gain) that is reasonably attributable, directly or indirectly, to an amount in respect of which tax was payable under Part I by a trust governed by the registered plan or by any other registered plan of the controlling individual.

S. 207.01(1), the definition "specified non-qualified investment income" was replaced by S.C. 2011, c. 24, s. 64(2), applicable to transactions occurring, income earned, capital gains accruing and investments acquired, after March 22, 2011. S. 207.01(1), the definition "specified non-qualified investment income" formerly read:

"specified non-qualified investment income"—"specified non-qualified investment income", in respect of a TFSA and its holder, means income (including a capital gain) that is reasonably attributable, directly or indirectly, to an

amount in respect of which tax was payable under Part I by a trust governed by the TFSA or any other TFSA of the holder.

S. 207.01(1), the definition "specified non-qualified investment income" was added by S.C. 2010, c. 25, s. 57(7), applicable to the 2010 and subsequent taxation years.

"swap transaction" —"swap transaction", in respect of a registered plan, means a transfer of property between the registered plan and its controlling individual or a person with whom the controlling individual does not deal at arm's length, but does not include

(*a*) a payment out of or under the registered plan in satisfaction of all or part of the controlling individual's interest in the registered plan;

(*b*) a payment into the registered plan that is

(i) a contribution, a premium or an amount transferred in accordance with paragraph 146.3(2)(*f*),

(ii) described in paragraph (*a*) or (*b*) of the definition "contribution" in subsection 146.1(1), or

(iii) described in any of paragraphs (*a*) to (*d*) of the definition "contribution" in subsection 146.4(1);

(*c*) a transfer of a prohibited investment or a non-qualified investment from the registered plan for consideration, in circumstances where the controlling individual is entitled to a refund under subsection 207.04(4) on the transfer;

(*d*) a transfer of property from one registered plan of a controlling individual to another registered plan of the controlling individual if

(i) both registered plans are RRIFs or RRSPs,

(ii) both registered plans are TFSAs;

(iii) both registered plans are RDSPs, or

(iv) both registered plans are RESPs;

(*e*) a transfer of a prohibited investment from the registered plan for consideration, if subsection (13) applies in respect of all or part of the consideration received by the registered plan;

(*f*) a transfer of property from the registered plan in consideration for the issuance of a debt obligation that is an excluded property for the trust governed by the registered plan; or

(*g*) a payment into the registered plan that is a payment of, or in satisfaction of, the principal amount of, or interest on, a debt obligation that is an excluded property for the trust governed by the registered plan.

History: S. 207.01(1), subparagraphs (*d*)(iii) and (iv) of the definition "swap transaction" were added by S.C. 2017, c. 33, s. 68(8), applicable

(a) after 2021 in relation to transactions undertaken to remove a property from a RDSP or RESP if it is reasonable to conclude that tax would be payable under Part XI.01 of the Act if the property were retained in the RDSP or RESP;

(b) after 2027 in relation to transactions undertaken to remove a transitional prohibited property (as defined in subsection 207.01(1) of the Act, as amended by subsection (3)), from a RDSP or RESP if it is reasonable to conclude that tax would be payable under Part XI.01 of the Act if the property were retained in the RDSP or RESP; and

(c) in any other case, after June 2017.

S. 207.01(1), paragraph (*b*) of the definition "swap transaction" was replaced by S.C. 2017, c. 33, s. 68(7), applicable

(a) after 2021 in relation to transactions undertaken to remove a property from a RDSP or RESP if it is reasonable to conclude that tax would be payable under Part XI.01 of the Act if the property were retained in the RDSP or RESP;

(b) after 2027 in relation to transactions undertaken to remove a transitional prohibited property (as defined in subsection 207.01(1) of the Act, as amended by subsection (3)), from a RDSP or RESP if it is reasonable to conclude that tax would be payable under Part XI.01 of the Act if the property were retained in the RDSP or RESP; and

(c) in any other case, after June 2017.

S. 207.01(1), paragraph (*b*) of the definition "swap transaction" formerly read:

(*b*) a payment into the registered plan that is a contribution, a premium, or an amount transferred in accordance with paragraph 146.3(2)(*f*);

S. 207.01(1), paragraph (*c*) of the definition "swap transaction" was replaced by S.C. 2013, c. 40, s. 74(11), deemed to have come into force on July 1, 2011, except that they do not apply in relation to a swap transaction undertaken before 2022 to remove a property from a RRIF or RRSP if it is reasonable to conclude that tax would be payable under Part XI.01 of the Act if

(*a*) that Part were read without reference to subsection 207.05(4) of the Act; and

(*b*) the property were retained in the RRIF or RRSP.

S. 207.01(1), paragraph (*c*) of the definition "swap transaction" formerly read:

(*c*) a transfer of a prohibited investment or a non-qualified investment from the registered plan, in circumstances where the controlling individual is entitled to a refund under subsection 207.04(4) on the transfer; or

S. 207.01(1), paragraphs (*e*), (*f*), and (*g*) of the definition "swap transaction" were added by S.C. 2013, c. 40, s. 74(12), deemed to have come into force on July 1, 2011, except that they do not apply in relation to a swap transaction undertaken before 2022 to remove a property from a RRIF or RRSP if it is reasonable to conclude that tax would be payable under Part XI.01 of the Act if

(*a*) that Part were read without reference to subsection 207.05(4) of the Act; and

(*b*) the property were retained in the RRIF or RRSP.

S. 207.01(1), the definition "swap transaction" was replaced by S.C. 2011, c. 24, s. 64(2), applicable, as amended by S.C. 2013, c. 40, s. 95, after 2021 in relation to a swap transaction undertaken to remove a property from a RRIF or RRSP if it is reasonable to conclude that the retention of the property in the RRIF or RRSP would result in a tax being payable under Part XI.01 of the Act, if that Part were read without reference to subsection 207.05(4) and the property were retained in the RRIF or RRSP, and in any other case, after June 2011. S. 207.01(1), the definition "swap transaction" formerly read:

"swap transaction" —"swap transaction", in respect of a trust governed by a TFSA, means a transfer of property (other than a transfer that is a distribution or a contribution) occurring between the trust and the holder of the TFSA or a person with whom the holder does not deal at arm's length.

S. 207.01(1), the definition "swap transaction" was added by S.C. 2010, c. 25, s. 57(7), applicable to transfers of property that occur after October 16, 2009.

Income Tax Folios: S3-F10-C3 Advantages – RRSPs, RESPs, RRIFs, RDSPs and TFSAs.

"TFSA dollar limit" —"TFSA dollar limit" for a calendar year means,

(*a*) for 2009 to 2012, $5,000;

(*b*) for 2013 and 2014, $5,500; and

(*c*) for 2015, $10,000; and

(*d*) for each year after 2015, the amount (rounded to the nearest multiple of $500, or if that amount is equidistant from two such consecutive multiples, to the higher multiple) that is equal to $5,000 adjusted for each year after 2009 in the manner set out in section 117.1.

CRA News Release

2.2% Indexation Factor for 2019

See the CRA Fact Sheet, dated November 16, 2018, that is reproduced following subsection117.1(1). This release announces a 2.2% indexation factor applicable for 2019 tax bracket thresholds, personal amounts and other amounts relating to non-refundable credits, as well as the refundable medical expense supplement, Old Age Security repayment threshold, certain board and lodging allowances, and the

tradesperson's tools deduction. Increases to tax bracket thresholds, amounts relating to non-refundable credits, and most other amounts will take effect on January 1, 2019. However, increases in amounts for certain income-tested benefits (for example, the goods and services tax credit) will take effect on July 1, 2019.

Editorial Note: The annual TFSA contribution limit was $5,000 for 2009 to 2013, $5,500 for 2013 and 2014, $10,000 for 2015, and $5,500 for 2016. The original $5,000 limit for 2009 is indexed to inflation after 2009 and rounded to the nearest $500.

History: S. 207.01(1), paragraph (*c*) of the definition "TFSA dollar limit" was replaced by S.C. 2016, c. 11, s. 9(1), deemed to have come into force January 1, 2016, and formerly read:

(*c*) for each year after 2014, $10,000.

S. 207.01(1), paragraph (*d*) of the definition "TFSA dollar limit" was added by S.C. 2016, c. 11, s. 9(1), deemed to have come into force January 1, 2016.

S. 207.01(1), the definition "TFSA dollar limit" was replaced by S.C. 2015, c. 36, s. 19, in force on Royal Assent, June 23, 2015, and formerly read:

"TFSA dollar limit"—"TFSA dollar limit" for a calendar year means,

(*a*) for 2009, $5,000; and

(*b*) for each year after 2009, the amount (rounded to the nearest multiple of $500, or if that amount is equidistant from two such consecutive multiples, to the higher multiple) that is equal to $5,000 adjusted for each year after 2009 in the manner set out in section 117.1.

"transitional prohibited investment benefit" —"transitional prohibited investment benefit", of a controlling individual for a taxation year, means the amount determined by the formula

$$A - B$$

where

A is the total of all amounts each of which is income (determined without reference to paragraph 82(1)(*b*)) earned, or a capital gain realized, in the taxation year by a trust governed by a RRIF or RRSP of the controlling individual that

(*a*) is reasonably attributable, directly or indirectly, to a property that is a prohibited investment, and a transitional prohibited property, for the trust, and

(*b*) in the case of income, is earned after March 22, 2011 and, in the case of a capital gain, accrues after March 22, 2011; and

B is the total of all amounts each of which is a capital loss (determined without reference to subparagraph 40(2)(*g*)(i) and subsection 40(3.4)) realized in the taxation year by a trust governed by a RRIF or RRSP of the controlling individual that

(*a*) is reasonably attributable, directly or indirectly, to a property that is a prohibited investment, and a transitional prohibited property, for the trust, and

(*b*) accrues after March 22, 2011.

History: S. 207.01(1), the descriptions of A and B in the definition "transitional prohibited investment benefit" were replaced by S.C. 2013, c. 40, s. 74(13), deemed to have come into force on March 23, 2011, and formerly read:

A is the total of all amounts each of which is income earned, or a capital gain realized, in the taxation year by a trust governed by a RRIF or RRSP of the controlling individual that

(*a*) is attributable to a property that was, on March 23, 2011, a prohibited investment for a trust governed by a RRIF or RRSP of the controlling individual, and

(*b*) in the case of income, is earned after March 22, 2011 and before 2022 and, in the case of a capital gain, accrues after March 22, 2011 and is realized before 2022; and

B is the total of all amounts each of which is a capital loss, determined without reference to subparagraph 40(2)(*g*)(i) and subsection 40(3.4), realized in the taxation year by a trust governed by a RRIF or RRSP of the controlling individual that

(*a*) is attributable to a property that was, on March 23, 2011, a prohibited investment for a trust governed by a RRIF or RRSP of the controlling individual, and

(*b*) accrues after March 22, 2011 and is realized before 2022.

S. 207.01(1), the definition "transitional prohibited investment benefit" was added by S.C. 2011, c. 24, s. 64(4), deemed to have come into force on March 23, 2011.

"transitional prohibited property" —"transitional prohibited property", at any time for a particular trust governed by a registered plan (other than a TFSA) of a controlling individual, means a property that is held by the particular trust at that time, that was held

(*a*) on March 22, 2011 by a trust governed by a RRIF or RRSP of the controlling individual and that was a prohibited investment for that trust on March 23, 2011; or

(*b*) on March 22, 2017 by a trust governed by a RDSP or RESP of the controlling individual and that was a prohibited investment for that trust on March 23, 2017.

History: S. 207.01(1), the definition "transitional prohibited property" was replaced by S.C. 2017, c. 33, s. 68(3), applicable to transactions and events occurring, income earned, capital gains accruing and investments acquired after March 22, 2017, and formerly read:

"transitional prohibited property"—"transitional prohibited property", at any time, for a particular trust governed by a RRIF or RRSP of a controlling individual, means a property that is held by the particular trust at that time, that was held on March 22, 2011 by a trust governed by a RRIF or RRSP of the controlling individual and that was a prohibited investment for that trust on March 23, 2011.

S. 207.01(1), the definition "transitional prohibited property" was added by S.C. 2013, c. 40, s. 74(14), deemed to have come into force March 23, 2011.

"unused TFSA contribution room" —"unused TFSA contribution room" of an individual at the end of a calendar year means,

(*a*) if the year is before 2009, nil;

(*a*.1) in circumstances where the Minister has, in accordance with section 207.06, waived or cancelled all or part of the liability imposed on the individual, the amount determined by the Minister; and

(*b*) in any other case, the positive or negative amount determined by the formula

$$A + B + C - D$$

where

A is the individual's unused TFSA contribution room at the end of the preceding calendar year,

B is the total of all amounts each of which was a distribution made in the preceding calendar year under a TFSA of which the individual was the holder at the time of the distribution, other than a distribution that is

(i) a qualifying transfer, or

(ii) a specified distribution,

C is

(i) the TFSA dollar limit for the calendar year, if at any time in the calendar year the individual is 18 years of age or older and resident in Canada, and

(ii) nil, in any other case, and

D is the total of all amounts each of which is a contribution made under a TFSA by the individual in the calendar year, other than a contribution that is

(i) a qualifying transfer, or

(ii) an exempt contribution.

History: S. 207.01(1), paragraph (*a.1*) in the definition "unused TFSA contribution room" was added by S.C. 2010, c. 25, s. 57(5), applicable after October 16, 2009.

S. 207.01(1), subparagraph (ii) of the description of B in the definition "unused TFSA contribution room" was replaced by S.C. 2010, c. 25, s. 57(6), applicable after October 16, 2009. S. 207.01(1), subparagraph (ii) of the description of B in the definition "unused TFSA contribution room" formerly read:

(ii) a prescribed distribution,

Related Sections: S. 146.2(1), "distribution".

► 207.01(2) ◄

(2) Exempt contribution to survivor TFSA — (Repealed by S.C. 2009, c. 2, s. 68(8).)

History: S. 207.01(2) was repealed by S.C. 2009, c. 2, s. 68(8), applicable to the 2009 and subsequent taxation years. S. 207.01(2) formerly read:

(2) *Exempt contribution to survivor TFSA.* A contribution made in a taxation year under a TFSA by the survivor of an individual is an exempt contribution if

(*a*) the contribution is made during the period (in this subsection referred to as the "rollover period") that begins when the individual dies and that ends on the second anniversary of the individual's death (or on any later day that is acceptable to the Minister);

(*b*) a payment (in this subsection referred to as the "survivor payment") was made to the survivor during the rollover period, as a consequence of the individual's death, directly or indirectly out of or under an arrangement that ceased, because of the individual's death, to be a TFSA;

(*c*) the survivor designates, in prescribed form filed with the survivor's return of income for the taxation year, the contribution in relation to the survivor payment; and

(*d*) the amount of the contribution does not exceed the least of

(i) the amount, if any, by which

(A) the amount of the survivor payment

exceeds

(B) the total of all other contributions designated by the survivor in relation to the survivor payment,

(ii) the amount, if any, by which

(A) the total proceeds of disposition determined in respect of the arrangement under paragraph 146.2(6)(*a*), (7)(*a*) or (8)(*a*), as the case may be,

exceeds

(B) the total of all other exempt contributions in respect of the arrangement made by the survivor at or before the time of the contribution, and

(iii) if the individual had, immediately before the individual's death, an excess TFSA amount or if payments described in paragraph (*b*) are made to more than one survivor of the individual, nil or the greater amount, if any, allowed by the Minister in respect of the contribution.

► 207.01(3) ◄

(3) Survivor as successor holder. If an individual's survivor becomes the holder of a TFSA as a consequence of the individual's death and, immediately before the individual's death, the individual had an excess TFSA amount, the survivor is deemed (other than for the purposes of the definition "exempt contribution") to have made, at the beginning of the month following the individual's death, a contribution under a TFSA equal to the amount, if any, by which

(*a*) that excess TFSA amount

exceeds

(*b*) the total fair market value immediately before the individual's death of all property held in connection with arrangements that ceased, because of the individual's death, to be TFSAs.

History: S. 207.01(3), the portion before paragraph (*a*) was replaced by S.C. 2009, c. 2, s. 68(9), applicable to the 2009 and subsequent taxation years. S. 207.01(3), the portion before paragraph (*a*) formerly read:

(3) *Survivor as successor holder.* If an individual's survivor becomes the holder of a TFSA as a consequence of the individual's death and, immediately before the individual's death, the individual had an excess TFSA amount, the survivor is deemed (other than for the purposes of subsection (2)) to have made, at the beginning of the month following the individual's death, a contribution under a TFSA equal to the amount, if any, by which

Related Sections: S. 146.2(1), "holder", "survivor; s. 207.01(1), "excess TFSA amount".

Tax Topics: No. 1968, Death of a TFSA Holder: Quebec and the Rest of Canada.

► 207.01(4) ◄

(4) Significant interest. An individual has a significant interest in a corporation, partnership or trust at any time if

(*a*) in the case of a corporation, the individual would, at that time, be a specified shareholder of the corporation if the references in the portion of the definition "specified shareholder" in subsection 248(1) before paragraph (*a*) to "in a taxation year" and "at any time in the year" were read as "at any time" and "at that time", respectively;

(*b*) in the case of a partnership, the individual, or the individual together with persons and partnerships with which the individual does not deal at arm's length, holds at that time interests as a member of the partnership that have a fair market value of 10% or more of the fair market value of the interests of all members in the partnership; and

(*c*) in the case of a trust, the individual, or the individual together with persons and partnerships with which the individual does not deal at arm's length, holds at that time interests as a beneficiary (in this paragraph, as defined in subsection 108(1)) under the trust that have a fair market value of 10% or more of the fair market value of the interests of all beneficiaries under the trust.

History: S. 207.01(4)(*a*) was replaced by S.C. 2013, c. 40, s. 74(15), deemed to have come into force on January 1, 2009, and formerly read:

(*a*) in the case of a corporation, the individual is a specified shareholder of the corporation at that time;

► 207.01(5) ◄

(5) Obligation of issuer. The issuer, carrier or promoter of a registered plan shall exercise the care, diligence and skill of a reasonably prudent person to minimize the possibility that a trust governed by the registered plan holds a non-qualified investment.

History: S. 207.01(5) was replaced by S.C. 2017, c. 33, s. 68(10), deemed to have come into force on March 23, 2017, and formerly read:

(5) *Obligation of issuer.* The issuer or carrier of a registered plan shall exercise the care, diligence and skill of a reasonably prudent person to minimize the possibility that a trust governed by the registered plan holds a non-qualified investment.

S. 207.01(5) was replaced by S.C. 2011, c. 24, s. 64(5), deemed to have come into force on March 23, 2011. S. 207.01(5) formerly read:

(5) *Obligation of issuer.* The issuer of a TFSA shall exercise the care, diligence and skill of a reasonably prudent person to minimize the possibility that a trust governed by the TFSA holds a non-qualified investment.

► 207.01(6) ◄

(6) Deemed disposition and reacquisition of investments. If, at any time, a property held by a trust governed by a registered plan becomes, or ceases to be, a prohibited investment or non-qualified investment for the trust, the trust is deemed to have disposed of the property immediately before that time for proceeds of disposition equal to the fair market value of the property at that time and to have reacquired the property at that time at a cost equal to that fair market value.

History: S. 207.01(6) was added by S.C. 2013, c. 40, s. 74(16), deemed to have come into force on March 23, 2011.

► 207.01(7) ◄

(7) Adjusted cost base. For the purpose of computing the adjusted cost base to a trust governed by a registered plan (other than a TFSA) of a property that is a transitional prohibited property for the trust, the cost to the trust of the property until the property is disposed of by the trust is deemed to be equal to the fair market value of the property,

(*a*) in the case of a RRIF or RRSP, at the end of March 22, 2011; and

(*b*) in the case of a RDSP or RESP, at the end of March 22, 2017.

History: S. 207.01(7) was replaced by S.C. 2017, c. 33, s. 68(11), deemed to have come into force on March 23, 2017, and formerly read:

(7) *Adjusted cost base.* For the purpose of computing the adjusted cost base to a trust governed by a RRIF or RRSP of a property that is a transitional prohibited property for the trust, the cost to the trust of the property until the property is disposed of by the trust is deemed to be equal to the fair market value of the property at the end of March 22, 2011.

S. 207.01(7) was added by S.C. 2013, c. 40, s. 74(16), deemed to have come into force on March 23, 2011.

► 207.01(8) ◄

(8) Prohibited investment status. Subsection (9) applies in respect of a property if

(*a*) the property would, in the absence of subsection (9), have ceased at any time (in this subsection and subsection (9) referred to as the "relevant time") to be a prohibited investment for a trust governed by a registered plan (other than a TFSA) of a controlling individual;

(*b*) the property is a transitional prohibited property for the trust immediately before the relevant time;

(*c*) in the case of a property held under a RRIF or RRSP, the controlling individual elected under subsection 207.05(4); and

(*d*) the controlling individual elects in prescribed form that subsection (9) apply in respect of the property and the election is filed with the Minister on or before the day that is 90 days after the end of the taxation year of the controlling individual that includes the relevant time.

History: S. 207.01(8)(*c*) was replaced by S.C. 2017, c. 33, s. 68(13), deemed to have come into force on March 23, 2017, and formerly read:

(*c*) the controlling individual elected under subsection 207.05(4); and

S. 207.01(8)(*a*) was replaced by S.C. 2017, c. 33, s. 68(12), deemed to have come into force on March 23, 2017, and formerly read:

(*a*) the property would, in the absence of subsection (9), have ceased at any time (in this subsection and subsection (9) referred to as the "relevant time") to be a prohibited investment for a trust governed by a RRIF or RRSP of a controlling individual;

S. 207.01(8) was added by S.C. 2013, c. 40, s. 74(16), deemed to have come into force on March 23, 2011, except that an election referred to in paragraph 207.01(8)(*d*) is deemed to have been filed with the Minister of National Revenue on a timely basis if it is filed with the Minister on or before March 12, 2014 [the day that is 90 days after December 12, 2013 (the day on which this Act receives royal assent)].

► 207.01(9) ◄

(9) Prohibited investment status. If this subsection applies in respect of a property, the property is deemed to be a prohibited investment at and after the relevant time for every trust governed by a registered plan (other than a TFSA) of the controlling individual referred to in paragraph (8)(*a*).

History: S. 207.01(9) was replaced by S.C. 2017, c. 33, s. 68(14), deemed to have come into force on March 23, 2017, and formerly read:

(9) *Prohibited investment status.* If this subsection applies in respect of a property, the property is deemed to be a prohibited investment at and after the relevant time for every trust governed by a RRIF or RRSP of the controlling individual referred to in paragraph (8)(*a*).

S. 207.01(9) was added by S.C. 2013, c. 40, s. 74(16), deemed to have come into force on March 23, 2011.

► 207.01(10) ◄

(10) Breakdown of marriage or common-law partnership. Subsection (11) applies in respect of a property if

(*a*) the property is transferred at any time (in this subsection and subsection (11) referred to as the "transfer time") by a trust (in this subsection and subsection (11) referred to as the "transferor trust") governed by a RRIF or RRSP of a controlling individual (in this subsection and subsection (11) referred to as the "transferor") under paragraph 146(16)(*b*) or subsection 146.3(14) to a trust (in subsection (11) referred to as the "recipient trust") governed by a RRIF or RRSP of which the spouse or common-law partner or former spouse or common-law partner (in this subsection and subsection (11) referred to as the "recipient") of the transferor is the controlling individual;

(*b*) the property is a prohibited investment, and a transitional prohibited property, for the transferor trust immediately before the transfer time;

(*c*) the transferor elected under subsection 207.05(4); and

(*d*) the transferor and the recipient jointly elect in prescribed form that subsection (11) apply in respect of the property and the election

(i) is filed with the Minister on or before the day that is 90 days after the end of the taxation year of the transferor that includes the transfer time; and

(ii) designates an amount (in subsection (11) referred to as the "designated amount") in respect of the property that

(A) is not less than the adjusted cost base to the transferor trust of the property immediately before the transfer time, and

(B) does not exceed the greater of the amount determined under clause (A) and the fair market value of the property at the transfer time.

History: S. 207.01(10) was added by S.C. 2013, c. 40, s. 74(16), deemed to have come into force on March 23, 2011, except that an election referred to in paragraph 207.01(10)(*d*) is deemed to have been filed with the Minister of National Revenue on a timely basis if it is filed with the Minister on or before March 12, 2014 [the day that is 90 days after December 12, 2013 (the day on which this Act receives royal assent)].

► 207.01(11) ◄

(11) Breakdown of marriage or common-law partnership. If this subsection applies in respect of a property,

(*a*) the property is deemed to be, at and after the transfer time, a property that was held on March 22, 2011 by a trust governed by a RRIF or RRSP of the recipient and that was a prohibited investment for the trust on March 23, 2011;

(*b*) where the property would, in the absence of this paragraph, not be a prohibited investment for the recipient trust immediately after the transfer time, the property is deemed to be a prohibited investment at and after the transfer time for every trust governed by a RRIF or RRSP of the recipient;

(*c*) the recipient is deemed to have elected under subsection 207.05(4); and

(*d*) notwithstanding any other provision of this Act, the designated amount is deemed to be

(i) the proceeds of disposition to the transferor trust from the transfer described in paragraph (10)(*a*), and

(ii) the cost of the property to a trust governed by a RRIF or RRSP of the recipient until the property is disposed of by the trust.

History: S. 207.01(11) was added by S.C. 2013, c. 40, s. 74(16), deemed to have come into force on March 23, 2011.

► 207.01(12) ◄

(12) Exchange of property. Subsection (13) applies in respect of a property other than money if

(*a*) the property is acquired at any time (in this subsection and subsection (13) referred to as the "exchange time") by a trust (in this section and subsection (13) referred to as the "exchanging trust") governed by a registered plan (other than a TFSA) of a controlling individual in exchange for another property (in this subsection referred to as the "exchanged property") in a transaction to which any of section 51, subsection 85(1) and sections 85.1, 86 and 87 apply;

(*b*) the exchanged property is a prohibited investment, and a transitional prohibited property, for the exchanging trust immediately before the exchange time;

(*c*) the property is, or would be, if subsection 4900(14) of the *Income Tax Regulations* were read without reference to its paragraph (*b*), a qualified investment for the exchanging trust immediately after the exchange time; and

(*d*) in the case of a property held under a RRIF or RRSP, the controlling individual elected under subsection 207.05(4).

History: S. 207.01(12)(*d*) was replaced by S.C. 2017, c. 33, s. 68(16), deemed to have come into force on March 23, 2017, and formerly read:

(*d*) the controlling individual elected under subsection 207.05(4).

S. 207.01(12)(*a*) was replaced by S.C. 2017, c. 33, s. 68(15), deemed to have come into force on March 23, 2017, and formerly read:

(*a*) the property is acquired at any time (in this subsection and subsection (13) referred to as the "exchange time") by a trust (in this section and subsection (13) referred to as the "exchanging trust") governed by a RRIF or RRSP of a controlling individual in exchange for another property (in this subsection referred to as the "exchanged property") in a transaction to which any of section 51, subsection 85(1) and sections 85.1, 86 and 87 apply;

S. 207.01(12) was added by S.C. 2013, c. 40, s. 74(16), deemed to have come into force on March 23, 2011.

► 207.01(13) ◄

(13) Exchange of property. If this subsection applies in respect of a property,

(*a*) other than for the purposes of subsection (7), the property is deemed to be, at and after the exchange time, a property,

(i) in the case of a trust governed by a RRIF or RRSP, that was

(A) held on March 22, 2011 by a trust governed by a RRIF or RRSP of the controlling individual referred to in subsection (12), and

(B) a prohibited investment for the trust on March 23, 2011, and

(ii) in the case of a trust governed by a RDSP or RESP, that was

(A) held on March 22, 2017 by a trust governed by a RDSP or RESP of the controlling individual referred to in subsection (12), and

(B) a prohibited investment for the trust on March 23, 2017; and

(*b*) if the property would, in the absence of this paragraph, not be a prohibited investment for the exchanging trust immediately after the exchange time, the property is deemed to be a prohibited investment at and after the exchange time for every trust governed by a registered plan (other than a TFSA) of the controlling individual.

History: S. 207.01(13)(*a*) and (*b*) were replaced by S.C. 2017, c. 33, s. 68(17), deemed to have come into force on March 23, 2017, and formerly read:

(*a*) other than for the purposes of subsection (7), the property is deemed to be, at and after the exchange time, a property that was held on March 22, 2011 by a trust governed by a RRIF or RRSP of the controlling individual referred to in subsection (12) and that was a prohibited investment for the trust on March 23, 2011; and

(*b*) where the property would, in the absence of this paragraph, not be a prohibited investment for the exchanging trust immediately after the exchange time, the property is deemed to be a prohibited investment at and after the exchange time for every trust governed by a RRIF or RRSP of the controlling individual.

S. 207.01(13) was added by S.C. 2013, c. 40, s. 74(16), deemed to have come into force on March 23, 2011.

SECTION 207.02: Tax payable on excess TFSA amount

If, at any time in a calendar month, an individual has an excess TFSA amount, the individual shall, in respect of that month, pay a tax under this Part equal to 1% of the highest such amount in that month.

Editorial Note: The TFSA allows Canadian resident individuals to earn investment income, including interest, dividends, and capital gains, on a tax-free basis. Contributions to the TFSA are not deductible, but the income in the account is not subject to tax either while in the account or upon withdrawal. However, the TFSA may be subject to tax if it acquires a non-qualified investment or carries on a business. The requirements relating to the TFSA are found largely in s. 146.2.

Part XI.01 imposes penalties on a TFSA holder or certain other individuals in certain circumstances. Excess contributions to the TFSA are subject to a 1% tax per month (s. 207.02). For these purposes, in general terms, the annual TFSA contribution limit for 2019 is $6,000 (for 2013, 2014, 2016, 2017, and 2018 it was $5,500; for 2015 only, the annual TFSA dollar limit increased to $10,000), indexed and rounded to the closest $500. Unused TFSA room can be carried forward indefinitely. Furthermore, distributions from the account add to the TFSA contribution room in the year after the distribution. See the definitions of "excess TFSA amount" and "unused TFSA contribution room" in s. 207.01(1). Other potential penalties apply if a non-resident contributes to the TFSA (s. 207.03), if the TFSA acquires a prohibited or non-qualified investment (s. 207.04), or if the TSFA confers an advantage on the holder or a person not at arm's length with the holder (s. 207.05). Sections 207.04 and 207.05 also apply to annuitants of registered retirement savings plans and registered retirement income funds.

Related Sections: S. 207.01(1), "excess TFSA amount"; S. 207.06(1) Waiver of tax payable.

Canadian Tax Foundation: Tollstam, *CRA Relief for Short-Term TFSA Overdrafts*, 2016 Canadian Tax Highlights 24(2):6–7.

Forms: RC243 — Tax-Free Savings Account (TFSA) Return.

SECTION 207.03: Tax payable on non-resident contributions

If, at a particular time, a non-resident individual makes a contribution under a TFSA (other than a contribution that is a qualifying transfer or an exempt contribution), the individual shall pay a tax under this Part equal to 1% of the amount of the contribution in respect of each month that ends after the particular time and before the earlier of

(*a*) the first time after the particular time at which the amount of the contribution is equalled or exceeded by the total of all amounts each of which is a distribution

(i) that is made after the particular time under a TFSA of which the individual is the holder, and

(ii) that the individual designates in prescribed manner to be a distribution in connection with the contribution and not in connection with any other contribution, and

(*b*) the time at which the individual becomes resident in Canada.

Editorial Note: Section 207.03 imposes a penalty tax if an individual makes a contribution to a TFSA at a time that the individual is a non-resident. Subsection 207.06(1) allows the Minister to waive the tax if the individual establishes that the contribution was the result of a reasonable error and distributions are made out of the TFSA "without delay", equal to at least the non-resident contribution amount plus any income that is reasonably attributable to that amount (i.e., the income earned on the non-resident contribution, including capital gains). The income so distributed, if any, is included in the holder's Part 1 income (section 207.061).

History: S. 207.03, the portion before paragraph (*a*) was replaced by S.C. 2009, c. 2, s. 69(1), applicable to the 2009 and subsequent taxation years. S. 207.03, the portion before paragraph (*a*) formerly read:

S. 207.03 *Tax payable on non-resident contributions.* If, at a particular time, a non-resident individual makes a contribution under a TFSA, the individual shall pay a tax under this Part equal to 1% of the amount of the contribution in respect of each month that ends after the particular time and before the earlier of

Related Sections: S. 207.06(1) Waiver of tax payable.

Forms: RC243 — Tax-Free Savings Account (TFSA) Return.

SECTION 207.04: Tax payable on prohibited or non-qualified investment

► 207.04(1) ◄

(1) Tax payable on prohibited or non-qualified investment. The controlling individual of a registered plan that governs a trust shall pay a tax under this Part for a calendar year if, at any time in the year, the trust acquires property that is a prohibited investment, or a non-qualified investment, for the trust.

Editorial Note: Section 207.04 imposes a tax on the holder of a registered plan (TFSA, RRSP or RRIF) if the plan acquires a non-qualified investment or prohibited investment. The tax is equal to 50% of the fair market value of the property at the time it was acquired. Subsection 207.01(6) provides for a deemed disposition and reacquisition at fair market value if property held by a registered plan becomes or ceases to be a prohibited or non-qualified investment. As a result, s. 207.04(1) will be triggered where property held by a registered plan becomes a prohibited or non-qualified investment.

The 2017 Federal Budget amended section 207.04 so that it now applies to RESPs and RDSPs.

History: S. 207.04(1) was replaced by S.C. 2013, c. 40, s. 75(1), deemed to have come into force on March 23, 2011, and formerly read:

(1) *Tax payable on prohibited or non-qualified investment.* The controlling individual of a registered plan that governs a trust shall pay a tax under this Part for a calendar year if, at any time in the year,

(*a*) the trust acquires property that is a prohibited investment, or a non-qualified investment, for the trust; or

(*b*) property held by the trust becomes a prohibited investment, or a non-qualified investment, for the trust.

S. 207.04(1), the portion before paragraph (*a*) was replaced by S.C. 2011, c. 24, s. 65(1), applicable

(a) in respect of any investment acquired after March 22, 2011, except that it does not apply in the case of a prohibited investment acquired after that date by a RRIF or RRSP of an annuitant if the investment was a prohibited investment for another RRIF or RRSP of the same annuitant on March 23, 2011; and

(b) in respect of any investment acquired before March 23, 2011 that first becomes

(i) a prohibited investment after October 4, 2011, or

(ii) a non-qualified investment after March 22, 2011.

S. 207.04(1), the portion before paragraph (*a*) formerly read:

(1) *Tax payable on prohibited or non-qualified investment.* The holder of a TFSA that governs a trust shall pay a tax under this Part for a calendar year if, at any time in the year,

Related Regulations: 214(2) and 215(3).

Related Sections: S. 146.2(4) Using TFSA interest as security for a loan; s. 207.01(1), "non-qualified investment", "prohibited investment", "qualified investment"; S. 207.06(2) Waiver of tax payable.

Canadian Tax Foundation: White, *Income Tax Developments Relevant to the Mutual Fund Industry*, 2011 Conference Report 39:1–33.

Forms: RC243 — Tax-Free Savings Account (TFSA) Return.

Income Tax Folios: *Secondary* — S3-F10-C1 Qualified Investments – RRSPs, RESPs, RRIFs, RDSPs and TFSAs. *Primary* — S3-F10-C2 Prohibited Investments - RRSPs, RRIFs and TFSAs.

► 207.04(2) ◄

(2) Amount of tax payable. The amount of tax payable in respect of each property described in subsection (1) is 50% of the fair market value of the property at the time referred to in that subsection.

► 207.04(3) ◄

(3) Both prohibited and non-qualified investment. For the purposes of this section and subsections 146(10.1), 146.1(5), 146.2(6), 146.3(9), 146.4(5) and 207.01(6), if a trust governed by a registered plan holds property at any time that is, for the trust, both a prohibited investment and a non-qualified investment, the property is deemed at that time not to be a non-qualified investment, but remains a prohibited investment, for the trust.

Editorial Note: Subsection 207.04(3) provides that, for the purposes of the provisions specified therein, property that would otherwise be both a non-qualified investment and a prohibited investment is deemed to not be a non-qualified investment but to remain a prohibited investment. Effectively, the rule provides that income from the property will be considered an "advantage" and subject to the 100% tax of subsection 207.05(2), rather than the regular Part I tax that can apply to income earned from a non-qualified investment (e.g. subsection 146(10.1) for RRSPs).

History: S. 207.04(3) was replaced by S.C. 2017, c. 33, s. 69(1), deemed to have come into force on March 23, 2017, and formerly read:

(3) *Both prohibited and non-qualified investment.* For the purposes of this section and subsections 146(10.1), 146.2(6), 146.3(9) and 207.01(6), if a trust governed by a registered plan holds property at any time that is, for the trust, both a prohibited investment and a non-qualified investment, the property is deemed at that time not to be a non-qualified investment, but remains a prohibited investment, for the trust.

S. 207.04(3) was replaced by S.C. 2013, c. 40, s. 75(2), deemed to have come into force on March 23, 2011, and formerly read:

(3) *Both prohibited and non-qualified investment.* For the purposes of this section and subsections 146(10.1), 146.2(6) and 146.3(9), if a trust governed by a registered plan holds property at any time that is, for the trust, both a prohibited investment and a non-qualified investment, the property is deemed at that time not to be a non-qualified investment, but remains a prohibited investment, for the trust.

S. 207.04(3) was replaced by S.C. 2011, c. 24, s. 65(2), applicable

(a) in respect of any investment acquired after March 22, 2011, except that it does not apply in the case of a prohibited investment acquired after that date by a RRIF or RRSP of an annuitant if the investment was a prohibited investment for another RRIF or RRSP of the same annuitant on March 23, 2011; and

(b) in respect of any investment acquired before March 23, 2011 that first becomes

(i) a prohibited investment after October 4, 2011, or

(ii) a non-qualified investment after March 22, 2011.

S. 207.04(3) formerly read:

(3) *Where both prohibited and non-qualified investment.* For the purposes of this section and subsection 146.2(6), if a trust governed by a TFSA holds property at any time that is, for the trust, both a prohibited investment and a non-qualified investment, the property is deemed at that time not to be a non-qualified investment, but remains a prohibited investment, for the trust.

S. 207.04(3) was replaced by S.C. 2009, c. 2, s. 70(1), applicable to the 2009 and subsequent taxation years. S. 207.04(3) formerly read:

(3) *Where both prohibited and non-qualified investment.* For the purposes of subsection 146.2(4) and this section, if a trust governed by a TFSA holds property at any time that is, for the trust, both a prohibited investment and a non-qualified investment, the property is deemed at that time not to be a non-qualified investment, but remains a prohibited investment, for the trust.

Income Tax Folios: *Secondary* — S3-F10-C1 Qualified Investments – RRSPs, RESPs, RRIFs, RDSPs and TFSAs. *Primary* — S3-F10-C2 Prohibited Investments - RRSPs, RRIFs and TFSAs.

► 207.04(4) ◄

(4) Refund of tax on disposition of investment. If in a calendar year a trust governed by a registered plan disposes of a property in respect of which a tax is imposed under subsection (1) on the controlling individual of the registered plan, the controlling individual is entitled to a refund for the year of an amount equal to

(*a*) except where paragraph (*b*) applies, the amount of the tax so imposed; or

(*b*) nil,

(i) if it is reasonable to consider that the controlling individual knew, or ought to have known, at the time the property was acquired by the trust, that it was, or would become, a property described in subsection (1), or

(ii) if the property is not disposed of by the trust before the end of the calendar year following the calendar year in which the tax arose, or any later time that the Minister considers reasonable in the circumstances.

History: S. 207.04(4), the portion before paragraph (*a*) was replaced by S.C. 2011, c. 24, s. 65(3), applicable

(a) in respect of any investment acquired after March 22, 2011, except that it does not apply in the case of a prohibited investment acquired after that date by a RRIF or RRSP of an annuitant if the investment was a prohibited investment for another RRIF or RRSP of the same annuitant on March 23, 2011; and

(b) in respect of any investment acquired before March 23, 2011 that first becomes

(i) a prohibited investment after October 4, 2011, or

(ii) a non-qualified investment after March 22, 2011.

S. 207.04(4), the portion before paragraph (a) formerly read:

(4) *Refund of tax on disposition of investment.* If in a calendar year a trust governed by a TFSA disposes of a property in respect of which a tax is imposed under subsection (1) on the holder of the TFSA, the holder is entitled to a refund for the year of an amount equal to

S. 207.04(4)(*b*)(i) was replaced by S.C. 2011, c. 24, s. 65(4), applicable

(a) in respect of any investment acquired after March 22, 2011, except that it does not apply in the case of a prohibited investment acquired after that date by a RRIF or RRSP of an annuitant if the investment was a prohibited investment for another RRIF or RRSP of the same annuitant on March 23, 2011; and

(b) in respect of any investment acquired before March 23, 2011 that first becomes

(i) a prohibited investment after October 4, 2011, or

(ii) a non-qualified investment after March 22, 2011.

S. 207.04(4)(*b*)(i) formerly read:

(i) if it is reasonable to consider that the holder knew, or ought to have known, at the time the property was acquired by the trust, that it was, or would become, a property described in subsection (1), or

Related Regulations: 214(2) and 215(3).

► 207.04(5) ◄

(5) Apportionment of refund. If more than one person is entitled to a refund under subsection (4) for a calendar year in respect of the disposition of a property, the total of all amounts so refundable shall not exceed the amount that would be so refundable for the year to any one of those persons in respect of that disposition if that person were the only person entitled to a refund for the year under that subsection in respect of the disposition. If the persons cannot agree as to what portion of the refund each can so claim, the Minister may fix the portions.

History: S. 207.04(5) was added by S.C. 2017, c. 33, s. 69(2), deemed to have come into force on March 23, 2017.

S. 207.04(5) was repealed by S.C. 2013, c. 40, s. 75(3), deemed to have come into force on March 23, 2011, and formerly read:

(5) *Deemed disposition and reacquisition.* For the purposes of this Act, if property held by a trust in respect of which a tax was imposed under subsection (1) ceases, at any particular time after the tax is imposed, to be a prohibited investment, or a non-qualified investment, for the trust, the trust is deemed to have disposed of the property immediately before the particular time for proceeds of disposition equal to its fair market value at the particular time and to have reacquired it immediately after the particular time at a cost equal to that fair market value.

► 207.04(6) ◄

(6) Liability for tax. Each person who is a holder of a RDSP or a subscriber of a RESP at the time that a tax is imposed under subsection (1) in connection with the plan is jointly and severally, or solidarily, liable to pay the tax.

History: S. 207.04(6) was added by S.C. 2017, c. 33, s. 69(2), deemed to have come into force on March 23, 2017.

S. 207.04(6) was repealed by S.C. 2010, c. 25, s. 58(1), applicable after October 16, 2009. S. 207.04(6) formerly read:

(6) *Additional tax payable on prohibited investment.* The holder of a TFSA that governs a trust shall pay a tax under this Part for a calendar year, in addition to any tax imposed under subsection (1) for the year, if at any time in the year the trust holds one or more properties that are prohibited investments for the trust.

► 207.04(7) ◄

(7) Amount of additional tax payable — (Repealed by S.C. 2010, c. 25, s. 58(1).)

History: S. 207.04(7) was repealed by S.C. 2010, c. 25, s. 58(1), applicable after October 16, 2009. S. 207.04(7) formerly read:

(7) *Amount of additional tax payable.* The amount of tax payable under subsection (6) for a calendar year is 150% of the amount of tax that would be payable under Part I by the trust for the taxation year that ends in the calendar year if

(*a*) the Act were read without reference to paragraph 82(1)(*b*), section 121 and subsection 146.2(6); and

(*b*) the trust had no incomes or losses from sources other than the properties referred to in subsection (6), and no capital gains or capital losses other than from dispositions of those properties, and for that purpose,

(i) "income" includes dividends described in section 83, and

(ii) the trust's taxable capital gain or allowable capital loss from the disposition of a property is equal to its capital gain or capital loss, as the case may be, from the disposition.

S. 207.04(7), the portion before paragraph (*b*) was replaced by S.C. 2009, c. 2, s. 70(2), applicable to the 2009 and subsequent taxation years. S. 207.04(7), the portion before paragraph (*b*) formerly read:

(7) *Amount of additional tax payable.* The amount of tax payable under subsection (6) for a calendar year is the amount of tax that would be payable under Part I by the trust for the taxation year that ends in the calendar year if

(*a*) the Act were read without reference to paragraph 82(1)(*b*), section 121 and subsection 146.2(4); and

SECTION 207.05: Tax payable in respect of advantage

▶ 207.05(1) ◀

(1) Tax payable in respect of advantage. A tax is payable under this Part for a calendar year if, in the year, an advantage in relation to a registered plan is extended to, or is received or receivable by, the controlling individual of the registered plan, a trust governed by the registered plan, or any other person who does not deal at arm's length with the controlling individual.

Editorial Note: Section 207.05 imposes a penalty tax if a registered plan (TFSA, RRSP or RRIF) extends an "advantage" on the holder or annuitant, a trust governed by the registered plan, or a person not dealing at arm's length with the holder or annuitant. The tax equals the fair market value of the benefit, or, in the case of a loan or indebtedness or RRSP strip, the amount of the loan or indebtedness or RRSP strip, as applicable (subsection 207.05(2)). In other words, the tax is 100% of the advantage.

The 2017 Federal Budget amended section 207.05 so that it now applies to RESPs and RDSPs.

History: S. 207.05(1) was replaced by S.C. 2011, c. 24, s. 66(1), deemed to have come into force on March 23, 2011. S. 207.05(1) formerly read:

(1) *Tax payable in respect of advantage.* A tax is payable under this Part for a calendar year if, in the year, an advantage in relation to a TFSA is extended to, or is received or receivable by, a holder of the TFSA, a trust governed by the TFSA, or any other person who does not deal at arm's length with the holder of the TFSA.

S. 207.05(1) was replaced by S.C. 2010, c. 25, s. 59(1), applicable after October 16, 2009. S. 207.05(1) formerly read:

(1) *Tax payable where advantage extended.* A tax is payable under this Part for a calendar year in connection with a TFSA if, in the year, an advantage in relation to the TFSA is extended to a person who is, or who does not deal at arm's length with, the holder of the TFSA.

Related Sections: S. 207.01(1), "advantage".

Canadian Tax Foundation: Tollstam, *RRSP Anti-Avoidance Grandfathering Extended*, 2013 Canadian Tax Highlights 21(6):6; Demner, *TFSA Project Audit*, 2013 Canadian Tax Highlights 21(1):2–3; White, *Income Tax Developments Relevant to the Mutual Fund Industry*, 2011 Conference Report 39:1–33.

Tax Topics: No. 2090, Deadlines Approaching For RRSPs With "Prohibited Investments"; No. 1971-72, 2009 Canadian Tax Foundation Conference: Wizards, Tiny Taxes and "Evil" Kirk.

Forms: RC298 — Advantage Tax Return for TFSA Issuers.

Income Tax Folios: S3-F10-C3 Advantages – RRSPs, RESPs, RRIFs, RDSPs and TFSAs.

Income Tax Technical News: Issue No. 44, Key Employee Tax-Free Savings Account.

▶ 207.05(2) ◀

(2) Amount of tax payable. The amount of tax payable in respect of an advantage described in subsection (1) is

(*a*) in the case of a benefit, the fair market value of the benefit;

(*b*) in the case of a loan or an indebtedness, the amount of the loan or indebtedness; and

(*c*) in the case of a registered plan strip, the amount of the registered plan strip.

History: S. 207.05(2)(*c*) was replaced by S.C. 2017, c. 33, s. 70(1), deemed to have come into force on March 23, 2017, and formerly read:

c)in the case of an RRSP strip, the amount of the RRSP strip.

S. 207.05(2)(*c*) was added by S.C. 2011, c. 24, s. 66(2), deemed to have come into force on March 23, 2011.

▶ 207.05(3) ◀

(3) Liability for tax. Each controlling individual of a registered plan in connection with which a tax is imposed under subsection (1) is jointly and severally, or solidarily, liable to pay the tax except that, if the advantage is extended by the issuer, carrier or promoter of the registered plan or by a person with whom the issuer, carrier or promoter is not dealing at arm's length, the issuer, carrier or promoter, and not the controlling individual, is liable to pay the tax.

History: S. 207.05(3) was replaced by S.C. 2017, c. 33, s. 70(2), deemed to have come into force on March 23, 2017, and formerly read:

(3) *Liability for tax.* The controlling individual of a registered plan in connection with which a tax is imposed under subsection (1) is liable to pay the tax except that, if the advantage is extended by the issuer or carrier of the registered plan or by a person with whom the issuer or carrier is not dealing at arm's length, the issuer or carrier, and not the controlling individual, is liable to pay the tax.

S. 207.05(3) was replaced by S.C. 2011, c. 24, s. 66(3), deemed to have come into force on March 23, 2011. S. 207.05(3) formerly read:

(3) *Liability for tax.* The holder of a TFSA in connection with which a tax is imposed under subsection (1) is liable to pay the tax except that, if the advantage is extended by the issuer of the TFSA or by a person with whom the issuer is not dealing at arm's length, the issuer, and not the holder, is liable to pay the tax.

▶ 207.05(4) ◀

(4) Transitional rule. If an individual so elects before March 2, 2013 in prescribed form, subsection (1) does not apply in respect of any advantage that is an amount included in the calculation of the transitional prohibited investment benefit of the individual for a taxation year provided that the transitional prohibited investment benefit

(*a*) is paid to the individual, from a RRIF or RRSP of the individual, on or before the later of April 2, 2013 and the day that is 90 days after the end of the taxation year; and

(*b*) is not paid by way of transfer to another RRIF or RRSP of the individual.

History: S. 207.05(4), the portion before paragraph (*b*) was replaced by S.C. 2011, c. 40, s. 76(1), deemed to have come into force on March 23, 2011, and formerly read:

(4) *Transitional rule.* If an individual so elects before July 2012 in prescribed form, subsection (1) does not apply in respect of any advantage that is an amount included in the calculation of the transitional prohibited investment benefit of the individual for a taxation year provided that the transitional prohibited investment benefit

(*a*) is paid to the individual, from a RRIF or RRSP of the individual, within 90 days after the end of the taxation year; and

S. 207.05(4) was added by S.C. 2011, c. 24, s. 66(3), deemed to have come into force on March 23, 2011.

SECTION 207.06: Waiver of tax payable

▶ 207.06(1) ◀

(1) Waiver of tax payable. If an individual would otherwise be liable to pay a tax under this Part because of section 207.02 or 207.03, the Minister may waive or cancel all or part of the liability if

(*a*) the individual establishes to the satisfaction of the Minister that the liability arose as a consequence of a reasonable error; and

(*b*) one or more distributions are made without delay under a TFSA of which the individual is the holder, the total amount of which is not less than the total of

(i) the amount in respect of which the individual would otherwise be liable to pay the tax, and

(ii) income (including a capital gain) that is reasonably attributable, directly or indirectly, to the amount described in subparagraph (i).

History: S. 207.06(1)(*b*) was replaced by S.C. 2010, c. 25, s. 60(1), applicable after October 16, 2009. S. 207.06(1)(*b*) formerly read:

(*b*) the individual acts without delay to cause one or more distributions to be made, under one or more TFSAs, the total amount of which is not less than the amount in respect of which the individual would otherwise be liable to pay the tax.

Canadian Tax Foundation: Monaco et al., *Application for Waiver or Cancellation of Taxes Payable under Part XI.01 (CRA Roundtable, Question 16)*, 2012 Ontario Tax Conference 14:25–26.

Income Tax Folios: S3-F10-C3 Advantages – RRSPs, RESPs, RRIFs, RDSPs and TFSAs.

► 207.06(2) ◄

(2) Waiver of tax payable. If a person would otherwise be liable to pay a tax under this Part because of subsection 207.04(1) or section 207.05, the Minister may waive or cancel all or part of the liability where the Minister considers it just and equitable to do so having regard to all the circumstances, including

(*a*) whether the tax arose as a consequence of reasonable error;

(*b*) the extent to which the transaction or series of transactions that gave rise to the tax also gave rise to another tax under this Act; and

(*c*) the extent to which payments have been made from the person's registered plan.

History: S. 207.06(2)(*c*) was added by S.C. 2013, c. 40, s. 77(1), deemed to have come into force on March 23, 2011.

S. 207.06(2)(*b*) was replaced by S.C. 2011, c. 24, s. 67(1), deemed to have come into force on March 23, 2011. S. 207.06(2)(*b*) formerly read:

(*b*) the extent to which the transaction that gave rise to the tax also gave rise to another tax under this Part.

S. 207.06(2), the portion before paragraph (*a*) was replaced by S.C. 2009, c. 2, s. 71(1), applicable to the 2009 and subsequent taxation years. S. 207.06(2), the portion before paragraph (*a*) formerly read:

(2) *Waiver of tax payable.* If a person would otherwise be liable to pay a tax under this Part because of section 207.04 or 207.05, the Minister may waive or cancel all or part of the liability where the Minister considers it just and equitable to do so having regard to all the circumstances, including

► 207.06(3) ◄

(3) Waiver of tax payable — advantage. (Repealed by S.C. 2013, c. 40, s. 77(2).)

History: S. 207.06(3) was repealed by S.C. 2013, c. 40, s. 77(2), deemed to have come into force on March 23, 2011, and formerly read:

(3) *Waiver of tax payable — advantage.* The Minister shall not waive or cancel a liability imposed under subsection 207.05(3) on an individual in respect of a registered plan unless one or more payments are made without delay from the registered plan to the individual, the total amount of which is not less than the amount of the liability waived or cancelled.

S. 207.06(3) was replaced by S.C. 2011, c. 24, s. 67(2), deemed to have come into force on March 23, 2011. S. 207.06(3) formerly read:

(3) *Waiver of tax payable — advantage.* The Minister shall not waive or cancel a liability imposed under subsection 207.05(3) on an individual unless one or more distributions are made without delay under a TFSA of which the individual is the holder, the total amount of which is not less than the amount of the liability waived or cancelled.

S. 207.06(3) was added by S.C. 2010, c. 25, s. 60(2), applicable after October 16, 2009.

► 207.06(4) ◄

(4) Other powers of Minister. The Minister may notify the controlling individual of a registered plan that the controlling individual must cause a payment to be made from the registered plan to the controlling individual within 90 days of receipt of the notice, the amount of which is not less than the amount of specified non-qualified investment income in respect of the registered plan.

Editorial Note: "Specified non-qualified investment income" in respect of a registered plan means income (determined without reference to the dividend gross-up in s. 82(1)(*b*)) and capital gains reasonably attributable to an amount in respect of which tax was payable under Part I by the plan or any other registered plan of the holder or annuitant (e.g., income and capital gains earned on non-qualified investment income or income from a business). Pursuant to s. 207.06(4), the CRA may notify the controlling individual of the registered plan to remove specified non-qualified investment income from the registered plan within 90 days of the notice. If it is not removed within 90 days of receipt of the notice, it will be considered an "advantage" in respect of the registered plan and subject to the tax on advantages under s. 207.05. If it is removed from a TFSA, it is included in the holder's Part 1 income, notwithstanding that TFSA withdrawals are normally tax free (s. 207.061).

History: S. 207.06(4) was replaced by S.C. 2011, c. 24, s. 67(2), deemed to have come into force on March 23, 2011. S. 207.06(4) formerly read:

(4) *Other powers of Minister.* The Minister may notify the holder of a TFSA that the holder must cause a distribution to be made under the TFSA within 90 days of receipt of the notice, the amount of which is not less than the amount of the specified non-qualified investment income.

S. 207.06(4) was added by S.C. 2010, c. 25, s. 60(2), applicable after October 16, 2009.

Related Sections: S. 207.01(1), "advantage", "specified non-qualified investment income".

SECTION 207.061: Income inclusion

A holder of a TFSA shall include in computing the holder's income for a taxation year under Part I any portion of a distribution made in the year that is described in subparagraph (*a*)(ii) of the definition "specified distribution" in subsection 207.01(1) or subparagraph 207.06(1)(*b*)(ii) or that is specified by the Minister as part of an agreement to waive or cancel a liability for tax under this Part.

History: S. 207.061 was replaced by S.C. 2013, c. 40, s. 78(1), deemed to have come into force on March 23, 2011, and formerly read:

S. 207.061 *Income inclusion.* A holder of a TFSA shall include in computing the holder's income for a taxation year under Part I the total of all amounts each of which is the portion of a distribution made in the year that is described in

(*a*) subparagraph 207.06(1)(*b*)(ii);

(*b*) subsection 207.06(3); or

(*c*) subparagraph (*a*)(ii) of the definition "specified distribution".

S. 207.061 was added by S.C. 2010, c. 25, s. 61(1), applicable after October 16, 2009.

SECTION 207.062: Special limit on tax payable

If an individual is liable to pay an amount of tax under section 207.05 and under sections 207.02 or 207.03 in respect of the same contribution for the same calendar year, the tax payable under section 207.05 for the year shall be reduced by the amount of the tax payable under section 207.02 or 207.03, as the case may be, for the year.

History: S. 207.062 was added by S.C. 2010, c. 25, s. 61(1), applicable after October 16, 2009.

SECTION 207.07: Return and payment of tax

► 207.07(1) ◄

(1) Return and payment of tax. A person who is liable to pay tax under this Part for all or any part of a calendar year shall before July of the following calendar year

(*a*) file with the Minister a return for the year under this subsection in prescribed form and containing prescribed information including

(i) an estimate of the amount of tax payable under this Part by the person in respect of the year, and

(ii) an estimate of the amount of the person's allowable refund, if any, for the year; and

(*b*) pay to the Receiver General the amount, if any, by which the amount of the person's tax payable under this Part in respect of the year exceeds the person's allowable refund, if any, for the year.

History: S. 207.07(1), the portion before paragraph (*a*) was replaced by S.C. 2013, c. 40, s. 79, in force December 12, 2013, and formerly read:

(1) *Return and payment of tax.* A person who is liable to pay tax under this Part for all or any part of a calendar year shall within 90 days after the end of the year

Forms: RC243 — Tax-Free Savings Account (TFSA) Return.

► 207.07(1.1) ◄

(1.1) Multiple holders or subscribers. If two or more holders of a RDSP, or two or more subscribers of a RESP, are jointly and severally, or solidarily, liable with each other to pay a tax under this Part for a calendar year in connection with the plan,

(*a*) a payment by any of the holders, or any of the subscribers, on account of that tax liability shall to the extent of the payment discharge the joint liability; and

(*b*) a return filed by one of the holders, or one of the subscribers, as required by this Part for the year is deemed to have been filed by each other holder, or each other subscriber, in respect of the joint liability to which the return relates.

History: S. 207.07(1.1) was added by S.C. 2017, c. 33, s. 71(1), deemed to have come into force on March 23, 2017.

► 207.07(2) ◄

(2) Refund. If a person has filed a return under this Part for a calendar year within three years after the end of the year, the Minister

(*a*) may, on sending the notice of assessment for the year, refund without application any allowable refund of the person for the year, to the extent that it was not applied against the person's tax payable under paragraph (1)(*b*); and

(*b*) shall, with all due dispatch, make the refund referred to in paragraph (*a*) after sending the notice of assessment if an application for it has been made in writing by the person within three years after the sending of an original notice of assessment for the year.

History: S. 207.07(2)(*a*) and (*b*) were replaced by S.C. 2010, c. 25, s. 62, in force on Royal Assent, December 15, 2010. S. 207.07(2)(*a*) and (*b*) formerly read:

(*a*) may, on mailing the notice of assessment for the year, refund without application any allowable refund of the person for the year, to the extent that it was not applied against the person's tax payable under paragraph (1)(*b*); and

(*b*) shall, with all due dispatch, make the refund referred to in paragraph (*a*) after mailing the notice of assessment if an application for it has been made in writing by the person within three years after the mailing of an original notice of assessment for the year.

► 207.07(3) ◄

(3) Provisions applicable to Part. Subsections 150(2) and (3), sections 152 and 158 to 167 and Division J of Part I apply to this Part with any modifications that the circumstances require.

Part XI.1

Tax in Respect of Deferred Income Plans and Other Tax Exempt Persons

SECTION 207.1: [Tax payable]

► 207.1(1) ◄

(1) Tax payable by trust under registered retirement savings plan — (Repealed by S.C. 2011, c. 24, s. 68(1).)

History: S. 207.1(1) was repealed by S.C. 2011, c. 24, s. 68(1), applicable in respect of

(a) any investment acquired after March 22, 2011; and

(b) any investment acquired before March 23, 2011 that first becomes a non-qualified investment after March 22, 2011.

S. 207.1(1) formerly read:

(1) *Tax payable by trust under registered retirement savings plan.* Where, at the end of any month, a trust governed by a registered retirement savings plan holds property that is neither a qualified investment (within the meaning assigned by subsection 146(1)) nor a life insurance policy in respect of which, but for subsection 146(11), subsection 146(10) would have applied as a consequence of its acquisition, the trust shall, in respect of that month, pay a tax under this Part equal to 1% of the fair market value of the property at the time it was acquired by the trust of all such property held by it at the end of the month, other than

(*a*) property, the fair market value of which was included, by virtue of subsection 146(10), in computing the income, for any year, of an annuitant (within the meaning assigned by subsection 146(1)) under the plan; and

(*b*) property acquired by the trust before August 25, 1972.

► 207.1(2) ◄

(2) Tax payable by trust under deferred profit sharing plan. Where, at the end of any month, a trust governed by a deferred profit sharing plan holds property that is neither a qualified investment (within the meaning assigned by section 204) nor a life insurance policy (referred to in paragraphs 198(6)(*c*) to (*e*) or subsection 198(6.1)), the trust shall, in respect of that month, pay a tax under this Part equal to 1% of the fair market value of the property at the time it was acquired by the trust of all such property held by it at the end of the month, other than

(*a*) property in respect of the acquisition of which the trust has paid or is liable to pay a tax under subsection 198(1); and

(*b*) property acquired by the trust before August 25, 1972.

Related Sections: S. 147(1), "deferred profit sharing plan"; s. 204 Definitions; s. 206 Tax payable where inadequate consideration.

► 207.1(3) ◄

(3) Tax payable by trust under registered education savings plan — (Repealed by S.C. 2017, c. 33, s. 72(1).)

History: S. 207.1(3) was repealed by S.C. 2017, c. 33, s. 72(1), applicable in respect of (a) any investment acquired after March 22, 2017; and (b) any investment acquired before March 23, 2017 that ceases to be a *qualified investment* (as defined in subsection 146.1(1) of the Act) after March 22, 2017. S. 207.1(3) formerly read:

(3) *Tax payable by trust under registered education savings plan.* Every trust governed by a registered education savings plan shall, in respect of any month, pay a tax under this Part equal to 1% of the total of all amounts each of which is the fair market value of a property, at the time it was acquired by the trust, that

(*a*) is not a qualified investment (as defined in subsection 146.1(1)) for the trust; and

(*b*) is held by the trust at the end of the month.

Related Sections: S. 146.1(2.1) RESP is revocable; s. 146.1(12.1) Notice of intent to revoke registration.

► 207.1(4) ◄

(4) Tax payable by trust under registered retirement income fund — (Repealed by S.C. 2011, c. 24, s. 68(2).)

History: S. 207.1(4) was repealed by S.C. 2011, c. 24, s. 68(2), applicable in respect of

(a) any investment acquired after March 22, 2011; and

(b) any investment acquired before March 23, 2011 that first becomes a non-qualified investment after March 22, 2011.

S. 207.1(4) formerly read:

(4) *Tax payable by trust under registered retirement income fund.* Where, at the end of any month after 1978, a trust governed by a registered retirement income fund holds property that is not a qualified investment (within the meaning assigned by subsection 146.3(1)), the trust shall, in respect of that month, pay a tax under this Part equal to 1% of the fair market value of the property at the time it was acquired by the trust of all such property held by it at the end of the month other than property, the fair market value of which was included by virtue of subsection 146.3(7) in computing the income for any year of an annuitant (within the meaning assigned by subsection 146.3(1)) under the fund.

► 207.1(5) ◄

(5) Tax payable in respect of agreement to acquire shares. Where at any time a taxpayer whose taxable income is exempt from tax under Part I makes an agreement (otherwise than as a consequence of the acquisition or writing by it of an option listed on a designated stock exchange) to acquire a share of the capital stock of a corporation (otherwise than from the corporation) at a price that may differ from the fair market value of the share at the time the share may be acquired, the taxpayer shall, in respect of each month during which the taxpayer is a party to the agreement, pay a tax under this Part equal to the total of all amounts each of which is the amount, if any, by which the amount of a dividend paid on the share at a time in the month at which the taxpayer is a party to the agreement exceeds the amount, if any, of the dividend that is received by the taxpayer.

Related Regulations: Part XLIX; 4901(1.1).

Forms: T2000 — Calculation of Tax on Agreements to Acquire Shares (Section 207.1(5) of the Income Tax Act).

SECTION 207.2: Return and payment of tax

▶ 207.2(1) ◀

(1) Return and payment of tax. Within 90 days after the end of each year, a taxpayer to whom this Part applies shall

(*a*) file with the Minister a return for the year under this Part in prescribed form and containing prescribed information, without notice or demand therefor;

(*b*) estimate in the return the amount of tax, if any, payable by it under this Part in respect of each month in the year; and

(*c*) pay to the Receiver General the amount of tax, if any, payable by it under this Part in respect of each month in the year.

Forms: T3GR — Group Income Tax and Information Return for RRSP, RRIF, or RESP Trusts; T3D — Income Tax Return for Deferred Profit Sharing Plan (DPSP)or Revoked (DPSP).

Information Circulars: IC 78-14R4 Guidelines for trust companies and other persons responsible for filing T3GR, T3D, T3P, T3S, T3RI, and T3F returns.

▶ 207.2(2) ◀

(2) Liability of trustee. Where the trustee of a trust that is liable to pay tax under this Part does not remit to the Receiver General the amount of the tax within the time specified in subsection (1), the trustee is personally liable to pay on behalf of the trust the full amount of the tax and is entitled to recover from the trust any amount paid by the trustee as tax under this section.

▶ 207.2(3) ◀

(3) Provisions applicable to Part. Subsections 150(2) and (3), sections 152 and 158, subsections 161(1) and (11), sections 162 to 167 and Division J of Part I are applicable to this Part with such modifications as the circumstances require.

Part XI.2
Tax in Respect of Dispositions of Certain Properties

SECTION 207.3: Tax payable by institution or public authority

Every institution or public authority that, at any time in a year, disposes of an object within 10 years after the object became an object described in subparagraph 39(1)(*a*)(i.1) shall pay a tax under this Part, in respect of the year, equal to 30% of the object's fair market value at that time, unless the disposition was made to another institution or public authority that was, at that time, designated under subsection 32(2) of the *Cultural Property Export and Import Act* either generally or for a specified purpose related to that object.

Forms: T913 — Part XI.2 Tax Return — Tax in Respect of the Disposition of Certain Properties.

Interpretation Bulletins: *Secondary* — IT-407R4 (Consolid.) Disposition after 1987 of Canadian cultural property.

SECTION 207.31: [Ecological gift — tax payable]

► 207.31(1) ◄

(1) Ecological gift — tax payable. A charity, municipality in Canada or municipal or public body performing a function of government in Canada (each of which is referred to in this section as the "recipient") shall, in respect of a property, pay a tax under this Part in respect of a taxation year if

(*a*) at any time in the year, the recipient

(i) disposes of the property, or

(ii) in the opinion of the Minister of the Environment, or a person designated by that Minister, changes the use of the property;

(*b*) the property is described in paragraph 110.1(1)(*d*) or in the definition *total ecological gifts* in subsection 118.1 (1); and

(*c*) the disposition or change is made without the authorization of the Minister of the Environment or a person designated by that Minister.

History: S. 207.31 was replaced with s. 207.31(1) by S.C. 2017, c. 33, s. 73(1), applicable in respect of dispositions made, and changes of use that occur, after March 21, 2017. S. 207.31 formerly read

S. 207.31 *Tax payable by recipient of an ecological gift.* Any charity, municipality in Canada or municipal or public body performing a function of government in Canada (referred to in this section as the "recipient") that at any time in a taxation year, without the authorization of the Minister of the Environment or a person designated by that Minister, disposes of or changes the use of a property described in paragraph 110.1(1)(*d*) or in the definition "total ecological gifts" in subsection 118.1(1) and given to the recipient shall, in respect of the year, pay a tax under this Part equal to 50% of the amount that would be determined for the purposes of section 110.1 or 118.1, if this Act were read without reference to subsections 110.1(3) and 118.1(6), to be the fair market value of the property if the property were given to the recipient immediately before the disposition or change.

S. 207.31 was replaced by S.C. 2013, c. 34, s. 340(1), applicable in respect of dispositions of or changes of use of property after July 18, 2005, and formerly read:

S. 207.31 *Tax payable by recipient of an ecological gift.* Any charity or municipality that at any time in a taxation year, without the authorization of the Minister of the Environment or a person designated by that Minister, disposes of or changes the use of a property described in paragraph 110.1(1)(*d*) or in the definition "total ecological gifts" in subsection 118.1(1) and given to the charity or municipality after February 27, 1995 shall, in respect of the year, pay a tax under this Part equal to 50% of the amount that would be determined for the purposes of section 110.1 or 118.1, if this Act were read without reference to subsections 110.1(3) and 118.1(6), to be the fair market value of the property if the property were given to the charity or municipality immediately before the disposition or change.

► 207.31(2) ◄

(2) Ecological gift — amount of tax. The amount of tax to be paid under subsection (1) is equal to 50% of the amount that would be determined for the purposes of section 110.1 or 118.1, if this Act were read without reference to subsections 110.1 (3) and 118.1(6), to be the fair market value of the property referred to in subsection (1) if the property were given to the recipient immediately before the disposition or change referred to in paragraph (1)(*a*).

History: S. 207.31(2) was added by S.C. 2017, c. 33, s. 73(1), applicable in respect of dispositions made, and changes of use that occur, after March 21, 2017. S. 207.31 formerly read

S. 207.31 *Tax payable by recipient of an ecological gift.* Any charity, municipality in Canada or municipal or public body performing a function of government in Canada (referred to in this section as the "recipient") that at any time in a taxation year, without the authorization of the Minister of the Environment or a person designated by that Minister, disposes of or changes the use of a property described in paragraph 110.1(1)(*d*) or in the definition "total ecological gifts" in subsection 118.1(1) and given to the recipient shall, in respect of the year, pay a tax under this Part equal to 50% of the amount that would be determined for the purposes of section 110.1 or 118.1, if this Act were read without reference to subsections 110.1(3) and 118.1(6), to be the fair market value of the property if the property were given to the recipient immediately before the disposition or change.

Related Sections: S. 110.1 Deduction for gifts; s. 110.1(1)(*d*) Ecological gifts; s. 118.1 Charitable gifts; s. 118.1(1), "total ecological gifts".

SECTION 207.4: Return and payment of tax

► 207.4(1) ◄

(1) Return and payment of tax. Any institution, public authority, charity or municipality that is liable to pay a tax under subsection 207.3 or 207.31 in respect of a year shall, within 90 days after the end of the year,

(*a*) file with the Minister a return for the year under this Part in prescribed form and containing prescribed information without notice or demand therefor;

(*b*) estimate in the return the amount of tax payable by it under this Part in respect of the year; and

(*c*) pay to the Receiver General the amount of tax payable by it under this Part in respect of the year.

► 207.4(2) ◄

(2) Provisions applicable to Part. Subsections 150(2) and (3), sections 152 and 158, subsections 161(1) and (11), sections 162 to 167 and Division J of Part I are applicable to this Part with such modifications as the circumstances require.

Part XI.3
Tax in Respect of Retirement Compensation Arrangements

SECTION 207.5: [Interpretation]

► 207.5(1) ◄

(1) Definitions. In this Part,

Canadian Tax Foundation: Kahane et al., *A Fresh Look at Retirement Compensation Arrangements: A Flexible Vehicle for Retirement Planning*, 2013 Canadian Tax Journal 2:479–502; Gibeault, *Unexpected Application of Part XII.2 Tax to a Canadian Personal Trust*, 2013 Canadian Tax Focus 13(2):10–11; Strain, *Life Insurance — RCAs and Back-to-Back Arrangements*, 2000 Prairie Provinces Tax Conference 16:1–31.

"advantage" —"advantage", in relation to a retirement compensation arrangement, means

(*a*) any benefit, loan or indebtedness that is conditional in any way on the existence of the arrangement, other than

(i) a benefit derived from the provision of administrative or investment services in respect of the arrangement,

(ii) a loan or an indebtedness the terms and conditions of which are terms and conditions that persons dealing at arm's length with each other would have entered into, and

(iii) a payment out of or under the arrangement that is included in computing a taxpayer's income under Part I, and

(*b*) a benefit that is an increase in the total fair market value of the subject property of the arrangement if it is reasonable to consider, having regard to all the circumstances, that the increase is attributable, directly or indirectly, to a transaction or event or a series of transactions or events one of the main purposes of which was to enable a person or a partnership to benefit from a provision of this Part, or from the exemption from tax under paragraph 149(1)(*q.1*), if the transaction, event or series

(i) would not have occurred in a normal commercial or investment context in which parties deal with each other at arm's length and act prudently, knowledgeably and willingly, or

(ii) included a payment received as, on account or in lieu of, or in satisfaction of, a payment

(A) for services provided by a person who is, or does not deal at arm's length with, a specified beneficiary of the arrangement, or

(B) of interest, of a dividend, of rent, of a royalty or of any other return on investment, or of proceeds of disposition, in respect of property (other than subject property of the arrangement) held by a person who is, or does not deal at arm's length with, a specified beneficiary of the arrangement,

(*c*) a benefit that is income or a capital gain that is reasonably attributable, directly or indirectly, to

(i) a prohibited investment in respect of the arrangement,

(ii) an amount received by a specified beneficiary of the arrangement, or by a person who does not deal at arm's length with the specified beneficiary, if it is reasonable to consider, having regard to all the circumstances, that the amount was paid in relation to, or would not have been paid but for, subject property of the arrangement and the amount was paid as, on account or in lieu of, or in satisfaction of, a payment

(A) for services provided by a person who is, or who does not deal at arm's length with, the specified beneficiary, or

(B) of interest, of a dividend, of rent, of a royalty or of any other return on investment, or of proceeds of disposition,

(*d*) an RCA strip in respect of the arrangement, and

(*e*) a prescribed benefit;

History: S. 207.5(1), the definition "advantage" was added by S.C. 2012, c. 31, s. 44(1), applicable after March 28, 2012, except that the definition "advantage" does not apply in respect of transactions or events that relate to subject property of a retirement compensation arrangement acquired before March 29, 2012

(*a*) if the amount of what would otherwise be an advantage is included in computing the income of a beneficiary of the arrangement, or an employer in respect of the arrangement, for the taxation year in which the amount arose or the immediately following taxation year; or

(*b*) if the subject property is a promissory note or similar debt obligation, commercially reasonable payments of principal and interest are made at least annually after 2012 in respect of the note or obligation and no RCA strip arises after March 28, 2012 in respect of the arrangement. For the purposes of this paragraph, an amendment to the terms of the note or obligation to provide for such payments is deemed not to be a disposition or an acquisition of the note or obligation.

Tax Window Files: RCA advs - Life insurance policy held by an RCA, *December 14, 2015*, CRA Document No. 2014-0544211E5; RCA advantages-Life insurance policy held by an RCA, *December 14, 2015*, CRA Document No. 2013-0499501E5; RCA advantage tax rules, *September 16, 2016*, CRA Document No. 2013-0500581I7.

"prohibited investment" —"prohibited investment", for a retirement compensation arrangement at any time, means property (other than prescribed excluded property) that is at that time

(*a*) a debt of a specified beneficiary of the arrangement,

(*b*) a share of the capital stock of, an interest in, or a debt of

(i) a corporation, partnership or trust in which the specified beneficiary has a significant interest, or

(ii) a person or partnership that does not deal at arm's length with, or is affiliated with, the specified beneficiary,

(*c*) an interest (or, for civil law, a right) in, or a right to acquire, a share, interest or debt described in paragraph (*a*) or (*b*), or (*d*) prescribed property;

History: S. 207.5(1), the definition "prohibited investment" was added by S.C. 2012, c. 31, s. 44(1), applicable after March 28, 2012.

"RCA strip" —"RCA strip", in respect of a retirement compensation arrangement, means the amount of a reduction in the fair market value of subject property of the arrangement, if the value is reduced as part of a transaction or event or a series of transactions or events one of the main purposes of which is to enable a specified beneficiary of the arrangement, or a person or a partnership who does not deal at arm's length with the specified beneficiary, to benefit from a provision of this Part or to obtain a benefit in respect of subject property of the arrangement or as a result of the reduction, but does not include an amount that is included in computing the income of the specified beneficiary or of an employer or former employer of the specified beneficiary;

History: S. 207.5(1), the definition "RCA strip" was added by S.C. 2012, c. 31, s. 44(1), applicable after March 28, 2012.

"RCA trust" —"RCA trust" under a retirement compensation arrangement means

(*a*) any trust deemed by subsection 207.6(1) to be created in respect of subject property of the arrangement, and

(*b*) any trust governed by the arrangement;

Related Sections: S. 248(1), "retirement compensation arrangement".

"refundable tax" —"refundable tax" of a retirement compensation arrangement at the end of a taxation year of an RCA trust under the arrangement means the amount, if any, by which the total of

(*a*) 50% of all contributions made under the arrangement while it was a retirement compensation arrangement and before the end of the year, and

(*b*) 50% of the amount, if any, by which

(i) the total of all amounts each of which is the income (determined as if this Act were read without reference to paragraph 82(1)(*b*)) of an RCA trust under the arrangement from a business or property for the year or a preceding taxation year or a capital gain of the trust for the year or a preceding taxation year,

exceeds

(ii) the total of all amounts each of which is a loss of an RCA trust under the arrangement from a business or property for the year or a preceding taxation year or a capital loss of the trust for the year or a preceding taxation year,

exceeds

(*c*) 50% of all amounts paid as distributions to one or more persons (including amounts that are required by paragraph 12(1)(*n.3*) to be included in computing the recipient's income) under the arrangement while it was a retirement compensation arrangement and before the end of the year, other than a distribution paid where it is established, by subsequent events or otherwise, that the distribution was paid as part of a series of payments and refunds of contributions under the arrangement;

Related Sections: S. 248(1), "retirement compensation arrangement".

"significant interest" —"significant interest" has the same meaning as in subsection 207.01(4);

History: S. 207.5(1), the definition "significant interest" was added by S.C. 2012, c. 31, s. 44(1), applicable after March 28, 2012.

"specified beneficiary" —"specified beneficiary", of a retirement compensation arrangement, means an individual who has an interest or a right in respect of the arrangement and who has or had a significant interest in an employer or former employer in respect of the arrangement;

History: S. 207.5(1), the definition "specified beneficiary" was added by S.C. 2012, c. 31, s. 44(1), applicable after March 28, 2012.

"subject property of a retirement compensation arrangement" —"subject property of a retirement compensation arrangement" means property that is held in connection with the arrangement.

Related Sections: S. 248(1), "retirement compensation arrangement".

► 207.5(2) ◄

(2) Election. Notwithstanding the definition "refundable tax" in subsection (1), where the custodian of a retirement compensation arrangement so elects in the return under this Part for a taxation year of an RCA trust under the arrangement and all the subject property, if any, of the arrangement (other than a right to claim a refund under subsection 164(1) or 207.7(2)) at the end of the year consists only of cash, debt obligations, shares listed on a designated stock exchange, or any combination thereof, an amount equal to the total of

(*a*) the amount of that cash at the end of the year,

(*b*) the total of all amounts each of which is the greater of the principal amount of such a debt obligation outstanding at the end of the year and the fair market value of the obligation at the end of the year, and

(*c*) the fair market value of those shares at the end of the year

shall be deemed for the purposes of this Part to be the refundable tax of the arrangement at the end of the year.

Related Sections: S. 207.7(3) Payment of tax; s. 262 Designated stock exchanges.

Forms: T3-RCA — Part X1.3 Tax Returns — Retirement Compensation Arrangement (RCA).

Guides: T4041 Retirement Compensation Arrangements Guide.

► 207.5(3) ◄

(3) Limitation on election. Subsection (2) does not apply in respect of an RCA trust if any part of a decline in the fair market value of subject property of the retirement compensation arrangement is reasonably attributable to a prohibited investment for, or an advantage in relation to, the RCA trust unless the Minister is satisfied that it is just and equitable to allow the election to be made, having regard to all the circumstances, in which case, the Minister may adjust the amount deemed by subsection (2) to be the refundable tax of the arrangement to take into account all or part of the decline in the fair market value of the subject property.

History: S. 207.5(3) was added by S.C. 2012, c. 31, s. 44(2), applicable to elections in respect of tax paid under subsection 207.7(1) in respect of contributions made to a retirement compensation arrangement after March 28,

2012 and income earned, capital gains realized and losses incurred, in respect of such contributions.

SECTION 207.6: Creation of trust

► 207.6(1) ◄

(1) Creation of trust. In respect of the subject property of a retirement compensation arrangement, other than subject property of the arrangement held by a trust governed by a retirement compensation arrangement, for the purposes of this Part and Part I, the following rules apply:

(*a*) a trust is deemed to be created on the day that the arrangement is established;

(*b*) the subject property of the arrangement is deemed to be property of the trust and not to be property of any other person; and

(*c*) the custodian of the arrangement is deemed to be the trustee having ownership or control of the trust property.

History: S. 207.6(1)(*a*) was replaced by S.C. 2014, c. 39, s. 62(1), applicable to the 2016 and subsequent taxation years, and formerly read:

(*a*) an *inter vivos* trust is deemed to be created on the day that the arrangement is established;

Related Regulations: 6804; 8308.1.

Related Sections: S. 108(1), "inter vivos trust", "trust"; s. 138(12), "life insurance policy"; s. 248(1), "employee benefit plan", "retirement compensation arrangement".

Forms: T733 — Application for a Retirement Compensation Arrangement (RCA) Account Number; T735 — Application for a Remittance Number for Tax Withheld from a Retirement Compensation Arrangement (RCA).

Guides: T4041 Retirement Compensation Arrangements Guide.

► 207.6(2) ◄

(2) Life insurance policies. For the purposes of this Part and Part I, where by virtue of a plan or arrangement an employer is obliged to provide benefits that are to be received or enjoyed by any person on, after or in contemplation of any substantial change in the services rendered by a taxpayer, the retirement of a taxpayer or the loss of an office or employment of a taxpayer, and where the employer, former employer or a person or partnership with whom or which the employer or former employer does not deal at arm's length acquires an interest in a life insurance policy that may reasonably be considered to be acquired to fund, in whole or in part, those benefits, the following rules apply in respect of the plan or arrangement if it is not otherwise a retirement compensation arrangement and is not excluded from the definition "retirement compensation arrangement", in subsection 248(1), by any of paragraphs (*a*) to (*l*) and (*n*) thereof:

(*a*) the person or partnership that acquired the interest is deemed to be the custodian of a retirement compensation arrangement;

(*b*) the interest is deemed to be subject property of the retirement compensation arrangement;

(*c*) an amount equal to twice the amount of any premium paid in respect of the interest or any repayment of a policy loan thereunder is deemed to be a contribution under the retirement compensation arrangement; and

(*d*) any payment received in respect of the interest, including a policy loan, and any amount received as a refund of refundable tax is deemed to be an amount received out of or under the retirement compensation arrangement by the recipient and not to be a payment of any other amount.

► 207.6(3) ◄

(3) Incorporated employee. For the purpose of the provisions of this Act relating to retirement compensation arrangements, where

(*a*) a corporation that at any time carried on a personal services business, or an employee of the corporation, enters into a plan or arrangement with a person or partnership (referred to in this subsection as the "employer") to whom or which the corporation renders services, and

(*b*) the plan or arrangement provides for benefits to be received or enjoyed by any person on, after or in contemplation of the cessation of, or any substantial change in, the services rendered by the corporation, or an employee of the corporation, to the employer,

the following rules apply:

(*c*) the employer and the corporation are deemed to be an employer and employee, respectively, in relation to each other, and

(*d*) any benefits to be received or enjoyed by any person under the plan or arrangement are deemed to be benefits to be received or enjoyed by the person on, after or in contemplation of a substantial change in the services rendered by the corporation.

► 207.6(4) ◄

(4) Deemed contribution. Where at any time an employee benefit plan becomes a retirement compensation arrangement as a consequence of a change of the custodian of the plan or as a consequence of the custodian ceasing either to carry on business through a fixed place of business in Canada or to be licensed or otherwise authorized under the laws of Canada or a province to carry on in Canada the business of offering to the public its services as trustee,

(*a*) for the purposes of this Part and Part I, the custodian of the plan is deemed to have made a contribution to the arrangement immediately after that time, in an amount equal to the fair market value at that time of all the properties of the plan; and

(*b*) for the purposes of section 32.1, that amount is deemed to be a payment made at that time out of or under the plan to or for the benefit of employees or former employees of the employers who contributed to the plan.

► 207.6(5) ◄

(5) Residents' arrangement. For the purposes of this Act, where a resident's contribution has been made under a plan or arrangement (in this subsection referred to as the "plan"),

(*a*) the plan is deemed, in respect of its application to all resident's contributions made under the plan and all property that can reasonably be considered to be derived from those contributions, to be a separate arrangement (in this subsection referred to as the "residents' arrangement") independent of the plan in respect of its application to all other contributions and property that can reasonably be considered to derive from those other contributions;

(*b*) the residents' arrangement is deemed to be a retirement compensation arrangement; and

(*c*) each person and partnership to whom a contribution is made under the residents' arrangement is deemed to be a custodian of the residents' arrangement.

► 207.6(5.1) ◄

(5.1) Resident's contribution. For the purpose of subsection (5), "resident's contribution" means such part of a contribution made under a plan or arrangement (in this subsection referred to as the "plan") at a time when the plan would, but for paragraph (*l*) of the definition "retirement compensation arrangement" in subsection 248(1), be a retirement compensation arrangement as

(*a*) is not a prescribed contribution; and

(*b*) can reasonably be considered to have been made in respect of services rendered by an individual to an employer in a period

(i) throughout which the individual was resident in Canada and rendered services to the employer that were primarily services rendered in Canada or services rendered in connection with a business carried on by the employer in Canada (or a combination of such services), and

(ii) at the beginning of which the individual had been resident in Canada throughout at least 60 of the 72 preceding calendar months, where the individual was non-resident at any time before the period and became a member of the plan before the end of the month after the month in which the individual became resident in Canada,

and, for the purpose of this paragraph, where benefits provided to an individual under a particular plan or arrangement are replaced by benefits under another plan or arrangement, the other plan or arrangement shall be deemed, in respect of the individual, to be the same plan or arrangement as the particular plan or arrangement.

Related Regulations: 6804(4) Contributions Made Before 1992; 6804(5) Contributions Made in 1992, 1993 or 1994; 6804(6) Contributions Made after 1994; 6804(7) Replacement Plan.

► 207.6(6) ◄

(6) Prescribed plan or arrangement. For the purposes of the provisions of this Act relating to retirement compensation arrangements, the following rules apply in respect of a prescribed plan or arrangement:

(*a*) the plan or arrangement shall be deemed to be a retirement compensation arrangement;

(*b*) an amount credited at any time to the account established in the accounts of Canada or a province in connection with the plan or arrangement shall be, except to the extent that it is in respect of a refund determined under subsection 207.7(2), deemed to be a contribution under the plan or arrangement at that time;

(*c*) the custodian of the plan or arrangement shall be deemed to be

(i) where the account is established in the accounts of Canada, Her Majesty in right of Canada, and

(ii) where the account is established in the accounts of a province, Her Majesty in right of that province; and

(*d*) the subject property of the plan or arrangement, at any time, shall be deemed to include an amount of cash equal to the balance at that time in the account.

Related Regulations: 6801.1(2).

Related Sections: S. 8(1)(*m.2*) Employee RCA contributions; s. 207.5(1), "subject property of a retirement compensation arrangement"; s. 207.7(2) Refund; s. 248(1), "retirement compensation arrangement".

► 207.6(7) ◄

(7) Transfers. Where an amount (other than an amount that is part of a series of periodic payments) is transferred directly to a retirement compensation arrangement (other than an arrangement the custodian of which is non-resident or which is deemed by subsection (5) to be a retirement compensation arrangement) from another retirement compensation arrangement,

(*a*) the amount shall not, solely because of the transfer, be included in computing a taxpayer's income under Part I;

(*b*) no deduction may be made in respect of the amount in computing a taxpayer's income under Part I; and

(*c*) the amount is considered, for the purpose of the definition "refundable tax" in subsection 207.5(1), to be paid as a distribution to one or more persons under the arrangement from which the amount is transferred and to be a contribution made under the arrangement to which the amount is transferred.

Related Sections: S. 8(1)(*m.2*) Employee RCA contributions; s. 12(1)(*n.3*) Retirement compensation arrangement; s. 20(1)(*r*) Employer's contributions under retirement compensation arrangement; s. 56(1)(*x*) Retirement compensation arrangement — employee recipient; s. 56(1)(*z*) Retirement compensation arrangement — non-employee recipient; s. 60(*t*) RCA distributions; s. 60(*u*) RCA dispositions; s. 212(1)(*j*) Benefits.

SECTION 207.61: Tax payable on prohibited investment

► 207.61(1) ◄

(1) Tax payable on prohibited investment. A custodian of a retirement compensation arrangement shall pay a tax under this Part for a calendar year if, at any time in the year,

(*a*) the arrangement acquires property that is a prohibited investment for the arrangement; or

(*b*) subject property of the arrangement becomes a prohibited investment for the arrangement after March 29, 2012.

Editorial Note: Subsection 207.61(1) imposes a tax on any "prohibited investment" held by an RCA. The amount of the tax is 50% of the fair market value of the property at the time it is acquired or becomes a prohibited investment. The tax is payable by the custodian of the RCA (also see s. 207.63 regarding when a specified beneficiary will be jointly liable). The tax generally applies to acquisitions of prohibited investments by the RCA after March 28, 2012 (with some grandfathering provisions), and to property of the RCA that becomes a prohibited investment after March 29, 2012. The tax is refundable if the RCA disposes of the prohibited investment by the end of the calendar year following the calendar year in which the tax arose (or any such later time as the Minister considers reasonable), unless the custodian of the RCA or a specified beneficiary knew or ought to have known at the time of acquisition of the property that it was, or would become, a prohibited investment.

History: S. 207.61(1) was added by S.C. 2012, c. 31, s. 45(1), applicable after March 28, 2012. However, an amendment to the terms of a promissory note, or similar debt obligation, that is subject property of a retirement compensation arrangement acquired before March 29, 2012 to provide for commercially reasonable payments of principal and interest is deemed not to be a disposition or an acquisition of the note or obligation.

Related Sections: S. 207.5(1), "prohibited investment".

► 207.61(2) ◄

(2) Amount of tax payable. The amount of tax payable in respect of each property described in subsection (1) is 50% of the fair market value of the property at the time referred to in that subsection.

History: S. 207.61(2) was added by S.C. 2012, c. 31, s. 45(1), applicable after March 28, 2012. However, an amendment to the terms of a promissory note, or similar debt obligation, that is subject property of a retirement compensation arrangement acquired before March 29, 2012 to provide for commercially reasonable payments of principal and interest is deemed not to be a disposition or an acquisition of the note or obligation.

► 207.61(3) ◄

(3) Refund. If in a calendar year an RCA trust disposes of a property in respect of which a tax is imposed under subsection (1) on the custodian of the retirement compensation arrangement, the custodian is entitled to a refund for the year of an amount equal to

(*a*) the amount of the tax so imposed, unless paragraph (*b*) applies; or

(*b*) nil,

(i) if it is reasonable to consider that the custodian, or a specified beneficiary of the arrangement, knew, or ought to have known, at the time the property was acquired by the arrangement, that it was, or would become, a property described in subsection (1), or

(ii) if the property is not disposed of by the arrangement before the end of the calendar year following the calendar year in which the tax arose, or any later time that the Minister considers reasonable in the circumstances.

History: S. 207.61(3) was added by S.C. 2012, c. 31, s. 45(1), applicable after March 28, 2012. However, an amendment to the terms of a promissory note, or similar debt obligation, that is subject property of a retirement compensation arrangement acquired before March 29, 2012 to provide for commercially reasonable payments of principal and interest is deemed not to be a disposition or an acquisition of the note or obligation.

► 207.61(4) ◄

(4) Deemed disposition and reacquisition. If, at any time, a property held by an RCA trust ceases to be, or becomes, a prohibited investment for the RCA trust, the RCA trust is deemed to have disposed of the property immediately before that time for proceeds of disposition equal to the fair market value of the property at that time and to have reacquired the property at that time at a cost equal to that fair market value.

History: S. 207.61(4) was added by S.C. 2012, c. 31, s. 45(1), applicable after March 28, 2012. However, an amendment to the terms of a promissory note, or similar debt obligation, that is subject property of a retirement compensation arrangement acquired before March 29, 2012 to provide for commercially reasonable payments of principal and interest is deemed not to be a disposition or an acquisition of the note or obligation.

SECTION 207.62: Tax payable in respect of advantage

► 207.62(1) ◄

(1) Tax payable in respect of advantage. A custodian of a retirement compensation arrangement shall pay a tax under this Part for a calendar year if, in the year, an advantage in relation to the arrangement is extended to, or is received or receivable by, an RCA trust under the arrangement, a specified beneficiary of the arrangement or any person who does not deal at arm's length with the specified beneficiary.

Editorial Note: Section 207.62 subjects an RCA to an additional tax equal to the fair market value of or amount of any "advantage" extended to or received or receivable by the RCA trust, a "specified beneficiary" of the RCA or a person who does not deal at arm's length with a specified beneficiary. In other words, the penalty tax is a 100% tax in respect of the value or amount of the advantage. A specified beneficiary is an individual who has an interest or a right in respect of the RCA and who has or had a "significant interest" (see s. 207.01(4)) in an employer or former employer in respect of the RCA. If the employer is a corporation, this means an individual with an interest in the RCA who, together with persons with whom the individual does not deal at arm's length, owns 10% or more of the shares of any class in the capital stock of the corporation or a related corporation. The specified beneficiary is jointly and severally, or solidarily, liable with the RCA to pay the penalty tax "to the extent that the specified beneficiary participated in, assented to or acquiesced in the making of, the transaction or event or series of transactions or events that resulted in the liability" (s. 207.63).

History: S. 207.62(1) was added by S.C. 2012, c. 31, s. 45(1), applicable after March 28, 2012.

Related Sections: S. 207.5(1), "advantage".

► 207.62(2) ◄

(2) Amount of tax payable. The amount of tax payable in respect of an advantage described in subsection (1) is

(*a*) in the case of a benefit, the fair market value of the benefit;

(*b*) in the case of a loan or an indebtedness, the amount of the loan or indebtedness; and

(*c*) in the case of an RCA strip, the amount of the RCA strip.

History: S. 207.62(2) was added by S.C. 2012, c. 31, s. 45(1), applicable after March 28, 2012.

SECTION 207.63: Joint liability

If a custodian of a retirement compensation arrangement is liable to pay a tax under section 207.61 or 207.62, a specified beneficiary of the arrangement is jointly and severally, or solidarily, liable for that tax to the extent that the specified beneficiary participated in, assented to or acquiesced in the making of, the transaction or event or series of transactions or events that resulted in the liability.

History: S. 207.63 was added by S.C. 2012, c. 31, s. 45(1), applicable after March 28, 2012.

Related Sections: S. 207.5(1), "specified beneficiary".

SECTION 207.64: Waiver of tax payable

If a person would otherwise be liable to pay a tax under this Part because of any of sections 207.61 to 207.63, the Minister may waive or cancel all or part of the liability if the Minister considers it just and equitable to do so having regard to all the circumstances, including

(a) whether the tax arose as a consequence of reasonable error; and

(b) the extent to which the transaction or event or series of transactions or events that gave rise to the tax also gave rise to another tax under this Act.

History: S. 207.64 was added by S.C. 2012, c. 31, s. 45(1), applicable after March 28, 2012.

SECTION 207.65: Deemed distribution

For the purposes of the definition "refundable tax" in subsection 207.5(1), tax paid under section 207.61 or 207.62 by a custodian of a retirement compensation arrangement out of property held in connection with the arrangement is deemed to be a distribution under the arrangement for the taxation year in which the tax is paid to the extent that the tax has not been refunded, waived or cancelled.

History: S. 207.65 was added by S.C. 2012, c. 31, s. 45(1), applicable after March 28, 2012.

SECTION 207.7: Tax payable

► 207.7(1) ◄

(1) Tax payable. Every custodian of a retirement compensation arrangement shall pay a tax under this Part for each taxation year of an RCA trust under the arrangement equal to the amount, if any, by which the refundable tax of the arrangement at the end of the year exceeds the refundable tax of the arrangement at the end of the immediately preceding taxation year, if any.

Canadian Tax Foundation: Kahane et al., *A Fresh Look at Retirement Compensation Arrangements: A Flexible Vehicle for Retirement Planning*, 2013 Canadian Tax Journal 2:479–502.

Tax Profile: May 2012 — Retirement Compensation Arrangements; September 2010 — RCAs Under Attack.

Forms: T3-RCA — Part X1.3 Tax Returns — Retirement Compensation Arrangement (RCA).

► 207.7(2) ◄

(2) Refund. Where the custodian of a retirement compensation arrangement has filed a return under this Part for a taxation year within three years after the end of the year, the Minister

(a) may, on sending the notice of assessment for the year or a notification that no tax is payable for the year, refund without application an amount equal to the amount, if any, by which the refundable tax of the arrangement at the end of the immediately preceding year exceeds the refundable tax of the arrangement at the end of the year; and

(b) shall, with all due dispatch, make such a refund after sending the notice of assessment if application for it has been made in writing by the custodian within three years after the day of sending of a notice of an original assessment for the year or of a notification that no tax is payable for the year.

History: S. 207.7(2)(a) and (b) were replaced by S.C. 2010, c. 25, s. 63, in force on Royal Assent, December 15, 2010. S. 207.7(2)(a) and (b) formerly read:

(a) may, on mailing the notice of assessment for the year or a notification that no tax is payable for the year, refund without application therefor an amount equal to the amount, if any, by which the refundable tax of the arrangement at the end of the immediately preceding year exceeds the refundable tax of the arrangement at the end of the year; and

(b) shall, with all due dispatch, make such a refund after mailing the notice of assessment if application therefor has been made in writing by the custodian within three years after the day of mailing of a notice of an original assessment for the year or of a notification that no tax is payable for the year.

Forms: T3-RCA — Part X1.3 Tax Returns — Retirement Compensation Arrangement (RCA).

► 207.7(3) ◄

(3) Payment of tax. Every custodian of a retirement compensation arrangement shall, within 90 days after the end of each taxation year of an RCA trust under the arrangement,

(a) file with the Minister a return for the year under this Part in prescribed form and containing prescribed information, without notice or demand therefor;

(b) estimate in the return the amount of tax, if any, payable by the custodian under this Part for the year; and

(c) pay to the Receiver General the amount of tax, if any, payable by the custodian under this Part for the year.

Forms: T3-RCA — Part X1.3 Tax Returns — Retirement Compensation Arrangement (RCA).

Guides: T4041 Retirement Compensation Arrangements Guide.

► 207.7(4) ◄

(4) Provisions applicable to Part. Subsections 150(2) and (3), sections 152 and 158, subsections 161(1) and (11), sections 162 to 167 and Division J of Part I are applicable to this Part with such modifications as the circumstances require.

Forms: T3-RCA — Part X1.3 Tax Returns — Retirement Compensation Arrangement (RCA).

Guides: T4041 Retirement Compensation Arrangements Guide.

Part XI.4
Tax on Excess EPSP Amounts

SECTION 207.8: Excess EPSP amount

► 207.8(1) ◄

(1) Excess EPSP amount. In this Part, "excess EPSP amount", of a specified employee for a taxation year in respect of an employer, means the amount determined by the formula

$$A - (20\% \times B)$$

where

A is the portion of the total of all amounts paid by the employer of the specified employee (or by a corporation with which the employer does not deal at arm's length) to a trust governed by an employees profit sharing plan that is allocated for the year to the specified employee; and

B is the specified employee's total income for the year from an office or employment with the employer computed without reference to paragraph 6(1)(*d*) and sections 7 and 8.

Related Sections: S. 144(3) Allocation contingent or absolute taxable; S. 248(1), "specified employee".

► 207.8(2) ◄

(2) Tax payable. If a specified employee has an excess EPSP amount for a taxation year, the specified employee shall pay a tax for the year equal to the amount determined by the formula

$$(A + B) \times C$$

where

A is the highest individual percentage for the year;

B is

(*a*) if the specified employee is resident in Quebec at the end of the year, 0%,

(*b*) if the specified employee is resident in a province other than Quebec at the end of the year, the highest percentage rate of tax, including surtaxes but not taxes that are limited to a maximum amount, imposed by the province for the year on the income of an individual who is a resident of the province, or

(*c*) in any other case, 14%; and

C is the total of all excess EPSP amounts of the specified employee for the year.

History: S. 207.8(2), the description of A was replaced by S.C. 2016, c. 7, s. 62(11), applicable to the 2016 and subsequent taxation years, and formerly read:

A is 29%;

Related Sections: S. 6(1)(*d*) Allocations, etc., under profit sharing plan; s. 8(1)(*o.2*) Excess EPSP amounts; s. 144(3) Allocation contingent or absolute taxable.

► 207.8(3) ◄

(3) Waiver or cancellation. If a specified employee would otherwise be liable to pay a tax under subsection (2), the Minister may waive or cancel all or part of the liability if the Minister considers it just and equitable to do so having regard to all the circumstances.

► 207.8(4) ◄

(4) Return and payment of tax. Every person who is liable to pay tax under this Part for a taxation year shall

(*a*) on or before the person's filing-due date for the year, file with the Minister a return for the year under this Part in prescribed form and containing prescribed information; and

(*b*) on or before the person's balance-due day for the year, pay to the Receiver General the amount of tax payable under this Part by the person for the year.

► 207.8(5) ◄

(5) Provisions applicable to this Part. Subsections 150(2) and (3), sections 152, 155 to 156.1, 158 to 160.1, 161 and 161.2 to 167 and Division J of Part I apply to this Part with any modifications that the circumstances require.

Proposed Amendment

Legislative Proposals Relating to the Income Tax Act, Employee Life and Health Trusts (May 27, 2019)

The Act is amended by adding the following after Part XI.4:

Part XI.5 Tax in Respect of Employee Life and Health Trust

SECTION 207.9 (1) Definitions. The following definitions apply in this Part.

participating employer —*participating employer* of an employee life and health trust means an employer who is required to make contributions to the employee life and health trust in respect of the employer's employees.

prohibited investment —*prohibited investment*, at any time for an employee life and health trust, means property that is at that time

(*a*) a share of the capital stock of, an interest in or a debt of

(i) a participating employer of the employee life and health trust, or

(ii) a person or partnership that does not deal at arm's length with a participating employer of the employee life and health trust; or

(*b*) an interest (or, for civil law, a right) in, or a right to acquire, a share, interest or debt described in paragraph (*a*).

(2) Tax payable on prohibited investment. A trust shall pay a tax under this Part for a calendar year if, at a time in the year while the trust is an employee life and health trust,

(*a*) the trust acquires property that is a prohibited investment for the trust; or

(*b*) income is received or becomes receivable by the trust from, or the trust has a taxable capital gain from the disposition of, a prohibited investment for the trust.

(3) Amount of tax payable. The amount of tax payable in respect of each property described in subsection (2) is

(*a*) if paragraph (2)(*a*) applies, 50% of the fair market value of the property at the time it is acquired; and (*b*) if paragraph (2)(*b*) applies, 50% of the income or the taxable capital gain.

(4) Refund. If in a calendar year a trust disposes of a property in respect of which a tax is imposed on the trust under subsection (2), the trust is entitled to a refund for the year of an amount equal to

(*a*) the amount of the tax so imposed, unless paragraph (*b*) applies; or

(*b*) nil, if

(i) it is reasonable to consider that the trust knew, or ought to have known, at the time the property was acquired that it was, or would become, a property described in subsection (2), or

(ii) the property is not disposed of by the trust before the end of the calendar year following the calendar year in which the tax arose, or any later time that the Minister considers reasonable in the circumstances.

(5) Deemed disposition and reacquisition. If, at any time, a property held by an employee life and health trust ceases to be, or becomes, a prohibited investment for the trust, it is deemed to have disposed of the property immediately before that time for proceeds of disposition equal to the fair market value of the property at that time and to have reacquired the property at that time at a cost equal to that fair market value.

Applicable: To the 2014 and subsequent taxation years.

History: S. 207.8 was added by S.C. 2012, c. 31, s. 46(1), applicable to the 2012 and subsequent taxation years, except that it does not apply in respect of payments made to a trust governed by an employees profit sharing plan

(*a*) before March 29, 2012; or

(*b*) before 2013 pursuant to an obligation arising under a written agreement or arrangement entered into before March 29, 2012.

Part XII
Tax in Respect of Certain Royalties, Taxes, Lease Rentals, etc., Paid to a Government by a Tax Exempt Person [Repealed]

SECTION 208: Tax payable by exempt person

► 208(1) ◄

(1) Tax payable by exempt person — (Repealed by S.C. 2003, c. 28, s. 15(1).)

► 208(1.1) ◄

(1.1) Definition of "specified stage" — (Repealed by S.C. 2003, c. 28, s. 15(1).)

► 208(2) ◄

(2) Return and payment of tax — (Repealed by S.C. 2003, c. 28, s. 15(1).)

► 208(3) ◄

(3) Liability of trustee — (Repealed by S.C. 2003, c. 28, s. 15(1).)

► 208(4) ◄

(4) Provisions applicable to Part — (Repealed by S.C. 2003, c. 28, s. 15(1).)

Part XII.1
Tax on Carved-Out Income

SECTION 209: [Tax payable]

► 209(1) ◄

(1) Definitions. For the purposes of this Part,

"carved-out income"—"carved-out income" of a person for a taxation year from a carved-out property means the amount, if any, by which

(*a*) the person's income for the year attributable to the property computed under Part I on the assumption that in computing income no deduction was allowed under section 20, subdivision e of Division B of Part I or section 104,

exceeds the total of

(*b*) the amount deducted under subsection 66.4(2) in computing the person's income for the year to the extent that it may reasonably be considered to be attributable to the property, and

(*c*) to the extent that the property is an interest in a bituminous sands deposit or oil shale deposit, the amount deducted under subsection 66.2(2) in computing the person's income for the year to the extent that it can reasonably be considered to be attributable to the cost of that interest;

Related Sections: S. 66(14.6) Deduction of carved-out income.

"carved-out property"—"carved-out property" of a person means

(*a*) a Canadian resource property where

(i) all or substantially all of the amount that the person is or may become entitled to receive in respect of the property may reasonably be considered to be limited to a maximum amount or to an amount determinable by reference to a stated quantity of production from a mineral resource or an accumulation of petroleum, natural gas or related hydrocarbons,

(ii) the period of time during which the person's interest in the income attributable to the property may reasonably be expected to continue is

(A) where the property is a head lease or may reasonably be considered to derive from a head lease, less than the lesser of 10 years and the remainder of the term of the head lease, and

(B) in any other case, less than 10 years,

(iii) the person's interest in the income attributable to the property, expressed as a percentage of production for any period, may reasonably be expected to be reduced substantially,

(A) where the property is a head lease or may reasonably be considered to derive from a head lease, at any time before

(I) the expiration of a period of 10 years commencing when the property was acquired, or

(II) the expiration of the term of the head lease,

whichever occurs first, and

(B) in any other case, at any time before the expiration of a period of 10 years commencing when the property was acquired, or

(iv) another person has a right under an arrangement to acquire, at any time, the property or a portion thereof or a similar property from the person and it is reasonable to consider that one of the main reasons for the arrangement, or any series of transactions or events that includes the arrangement, was to reduce or postpone tax that would, but for this subparagraph, be payable under this Part, or

(*b*) an interest in a partnership or trust that holds a Canadian resource property where it is reasonable to consider that one of the main reasons for the existence of the interest is to reduce or postpone the tax that would, but for this paragraph, be payable under this Part,

but does not include

(*c*) an interest, or for civil law a right, in respect of a property that was acquired by the person solely in consideration of the person's undertaking under an agreement to incur Canadian exploration expense or Canadian development expense in respect of the property and, where the agreement so provides, to acquire gas or oil well equipment (as defined in subsection 1104(2) of the *Income Tax Regulations*) in respect of the property,

(*c*.1) an interest, or for civil law a right, in respect of a property that was retained by the person under an agreement under which another person obtained an absolute or conditional right to acquire another interest, or for civil law another right, in respect of the property, if the other interest or right is not carved-out property of the other person because of paragraph (*c*),

(*d*) a particular property acquired by the person under an arrangement solely as consideration for the sale of a Canadian resource property (other than a property that, immediately before the sale was a carved-out property of the person) that relates to the particular property except where it is reasonable to consider that one of the main reasons for the arrangement, or any series of transactions or events that includes the arrangement, was to reduce or postpone tax that would, but for this paragraph, be payable under this Act,

(*e*) a property retained or reserved by the person out of a Canadian resource property (other than a property that, immediately before the transaction by which the retention or reservation is made, was a carved-out property of the person) that was disposed of by the person except where it is reasonable to consider that one of the main reasons for the retention or reservation, or any series of transactions or events in which the property or interest was retained or reserved, was to reduce or postpone tax that would, but for this paragraph, be payable under this Act,

(*f*) a property acquired by the person from a taxpayer with whom the person did not deal at arm's length at the time of the acquisition and the property was acquired by the taxpayer or a person with whom the taxpayer did not deal at arm's length

(i) pursuant to an agreement in writing to do so entered into before July 20, 1985, or

(ii) under the circumstances described in this paragraph or paragraph (*d*) or (*e*),

except where it is reasonable to consider that one of the main reasons for the acquisition of the property, or any series of transactions or events in which the property was acquired, was to reduce or postpone tax that would, but for this paragraph, be payable under this Act,

(*f*.1) where the taxable income of the person is exempt from tax under Part I, a property of the person that

(i) does not relate to property of a person whose taxable income is not exempt from tax under Part I, and

(ii) is not, and does not relate to, property that was at any time a carved-out property of any other person, or

(*g*) a prescribed property;

History: S. 209(1)(*c*) and (*c*.1) of the definition "carved-out property" were replaced by S.C. 2013, c. 34, s. 156, in force June 26, 2013, and formerly read:

(*c*) an interest in respect of a property that was acquired by the person solely in consideration of the person's undertaking under an agreement to incur Canadian exploration expense or Canadian development expense in respect of the property and, where the agreement so provides, to acquire gas or oil well equipment (as defined in subsection 1104(2) of the *Income Tax Regulations*) in respect of the property,

(*c*.1) an interest in respect of a property that was retained by the person under an agreement under which another person obtained an absolute or conditional right to acquire another interest in respect of the property, if the other interest is not carved-out property of the other person because of paragraph (*c*),

Related Regulations: 7600.

Related Sections: S. 66(15), "Canadian resource property"; s. 248(10) Series of transactions.

"head lease" —"head lease" means a contract under which

(*a*) Her Majesty in right of Canada or a province grants, or

(*b*) an owner in fee simple, other than Her Majesty in right of Canada or a province, grants for a period of not less than 10 years

any right, licence or privilege to explore for, drill for or take petroleum, natural gas or related hydrocarbons in Canada or to prospect, explore, drill or mine for minerals in a mineral resource in Canada;

"term" —"term" of a head lease includes all renewal periods in respect of the head lease.

▶ 209(2) ◀

(2) Tax. Every person shall pay a tax under this Part for each taxation year equal to 45% of the total of the person's carved-out incomes for the year from carved-out properties.

Related Sections: S. 66(14.6) Deduction of carved-out income.

▶ 209(3) ◀

(3) Return. Every person liable to pay tax under this Part for a taxation year shall file with the Minister, not later than the day on or before which the person is or would be, if the person were liable to pay tax under Part I for the year, required under section 150 to file a return of the person's income for the year under Part I, a return for the year under this Part in prescribed form containing an estimate of the amount of tax payable by the person under this Part for the year.

Forms: T2096 — Part XII.1 Return — Tax On Carved-Out Income.

▶ 209(4) ◀

(4) Payment of tax. Where a person is liable to pay tax for a taxation year under this Part, the person shall pay in respect of the year, to the Receiver General

(*a*) on or before the last day of each month in the year, an amount equal to 1/12 of the amount of tax payable by the person under this Part for the year; and

(*b*) the remainder, if any, of the tax payable by the person under this Part for the year, on or before the person's balance-due day for the year.

▶ 209(5) ◀

(5) Provisions applicable to Part. Subsections 150(2) and (3) and sections 152, 158 and 159, subsections 161(1), (2) and (11), sections 162 to 167 and Division J of Part I are applicable to this Part with such modifications as the circumstances require.

▶ 209(6) ◀

(6) Partnerships. For the purposes of subsection (1), a partnership shall be deemed to be a person and its taxation year shall be deemed to be its fiscal period.

Part XII.2
Tax on Designated Income of Certain Trusts

SECTION 210: [Interpretation]

► 210(1) ◄

(1) Definitions. The following definitions apply in this Part.

"designated beneficiary" —"designated beneficiary", under a particular trust at any time, means a beneficiary, under the particular trust, who is at that time

(*a*) a non-resident person;

(*b*) (Repealed by S.C. 2014, c. 39, s. 63(1).)

(*c*) a person who is, because of subsection 149(1), exempt from tax under Part I on all or part of their taxable income and who acquired an interest as a beneficiary under the particular trust after October 1, 1987 directly or indirectly from a beneficiary under the particular trust except if

(i) the interest was, at all times after the later of October 1, 1987 and the day on which the interest was created, held by persons who were exempt from tax under Part I on all of their taxable income because of subsection 149(1), or

(ii) the person is a trust, governed by a registered retirement savings plan or a registered retirement income fund, who acquired the interest, directly or indirectly, from an individual or the spouse or common-law partner, or former spouse or common-law partner, of the individual who was, immediately after the interest was acquired, a beneficiary under the trust governed by the fund or plan;

(*d*) another trust (in this paragraph referred to as the "other trust") that is not a graduated rate estate, a mutual fund trust or a trust that is exempt because of subsection 149(1) from tax under Part I on all or part of its taxable income, if any beneficiary under the other trust is at that time

(i) a non-resident person,

(ii) (Repealed by S.C. 2014, c. 39, s. 63(3).)

(iii) a trust that is not

(A) a graduated rate estate,

(B) a mutual fund trust,

(C) a trust that is exempt because of subsection 149(1) from tax under Part I on all or part of its taxable income, or

(D) a trust

(I) whose interest, at that time, in the other trust was held, at all times after the day on which the interest was created, either by it or by persons who were exempt because of subsection 149(1) from tax under Part I on all of their taxable income, and

(II) none of the beneficiaries under which is, at that time, a designated beneficiary under it, or

(iv) a person or partnership that

(A) is a designated beneficiary under the other trust because of paragraph (*c*) or (*e*), or

(B) would be a designated beneficiary under the particular trust because of paragraph (*c*) or (*e*) if, instead of being a beneficiary under the other trust, the person or partnership were at that time a beneficiary, under the particular trust, whose interest as a beneficiary under the particular trust were

(I) identical to its interest (referred to in this clause as the "particular interest") as a beneficiary under the other trust,

(II) acquired from each person or partnership from whom it acquired the particular interest, and

(III) held, at all times after the later of October 1, 1987 and the day on which the particular interest was created, by the same persons or partnerships that held the particular interest at those times; or

(*e*) a particular partnership any of the members of which is at that time

(i) another partnership, except if

(A) each such other partnership is a Canadian partnership,

(B) the interest of each such other partnership in the particular partnership is held, at all times after the day on which the interest was created, by the other partnership or by persons who were exempt because of subsection 149(1) from tax under Part I on all of their taxable income,

(C) the interest of each member, of each such other partnership, that is a person exempt because of subsection 149(1) from tax under Part I on all or part of its taxable income was held, at all times after the day on which the interest was created, by that member or by persons who were exempt because of subsection 149(1) from tax under Part I on all of their taxable income, and

(D) the interest of the particular partnership in the particular trust was held, at all times after the day on which the interest was created, by the particular partnership or by persons who were exempt because of subsection 149(1) from tax under Part I on all of their taxable income,

(ii) a non-resident person,

(iii) (Repealed by S.C. 2014, c. 39, s. 63(5).)

(iv) another trust that is, under paragraph (*d*), a designated beneficiary of the particular trust or that would, under paragraph (*d*), be a designated beneficiary of the particular trust if the other trust were at that time a beneficiary under the particular trust whose interest as a beneficiary under the particular trust were

(A) acquired from each person or partnership from whom the particular partnership acquired its interest as a beneficiary under the particular trust, and

(B) held, at all times after the later of October 1, 1987 and the day on which the particular partnership's interest as a beneficiary under the particular trust was created, by the same persons or partnerships that held that interest of the particular partnership at those times, or

(v) a person exempt because of subsection 149(1) from tax under Part I on all or part of its taxable income except if the interest of the particular partnership in the particular trust was held, at all times after the day on which the interest was created, by the particular partnership or by persons who were exempt because of subsection 149(1) from tax under Part I on all of their taxable income.

History: S. 210(1), the portion of paragraph (*d*) of the definition "designated beneficiary" before subparagraph (i) was replaced by S.C. 2014, c. 39, s. 63(2), applicable to the 2016 and subsequent taxation years, and formerly read:

(*d*) another trust (referred to in this paragraph as the "other trust") that is not a testamentary trust, a mutual fund trust or a trust that is exempt because of subsection 149(1) from tax under Part I on all or part of its taxable income, if any beneficiary under the other trust is at that time

S. 210(1), clause (*d*)(iii)(A) of the definition "designated beneficiary" was replaced by S.C. 2014, c. 39, s. 63(4), applicable to the 2016 and subsequent taxation years, and formerly read:

(A) a testamentary trust,

S. 210(1), paragraph (*b*) of the definition "designated beneficiary" was repealed by S.C. 2014, c. 39, s. 63(1), in force December 16, 2014, and formerly read:

(*b*) a non-resident-owned investment corporation;

S. 210(1), subparagraph (*d*)(ii) of the definition "designated beneficiary" was repealed by S.C. 2014, c. 39, s. 63(3), in force December 16, 2014, and formerly read:

(ii) a non-resident-owned investment corporation,

S. 210(1), subparagraph (*e*)(iii) of the definition "designated beneficiary" was repealed by S.C. 2014, c. 39, s. 63(5), in force December 16, 2014, and formerly read:

(iii) a non-resident-owned investment corporation,

"designated income" —"designated income", of a trust for a taxation year, means the amount that would be the income of the trust for the year determined under section 3 if

(*a*) this Act were read without reference to subsections 104(6), (12) and (30);

(*b*) the trust had no income other than taxable capital gains from dispositions described in paragraph (*c*) and incomes from

(i) real or immovable properties in Canada (other than Canadian resource properties),

(ii) timber resource properties,

(iii) Canadian resource properties (other than properties acquired by the trust before 1972), and

(iv) businesses carried on in Canada;

(*c*) the only taxable capital gains and allowable capital losses referred to in paragraph 3(*b*) were from

(i) dispositions of taxable Canadian property, and

(ii) dispositions of particular property (other than property described in any of subparagraphs 128.1(4)(*b*)(i) to (iii)), or property for which the particular property is substituted, that was transferred at any particular time to a particular trust in circumstances in which subsection 73(1) or 107.4(3) applied, if

(A) it is reasonable to conclude that the property was so transferred in anticipation that a person beneficially interested at the particular time in the particular trust would subsequently cease to reside in Canada, and a person beneficially interested at the particular time in the particular trust did subsequently cease to reside in Canada, or

(B) when the property was so transferred, the terms of the particular trust satisfied the conditions in subparagraph 73(1.01)(*c*)(i) or (iii), and it is reasonable to conclude that the transfer was made in connection with the cessation of residence, on or before the transfer, of a person who was, at the time of the transfer, beneficially interested in the particular trust and a spouse or common-law partner, as the case may be, of the transferor of the property to the particular trust; and

(*d*) the only losses referred to in paragraph 3(*d*) were losses from sources described in any of subparagraphs (*b*)(i) to (iv).

History: S. 210 was replaced, and renumbered as s. 210(1), by S.C. 2013, c. 34, s. 341(1), applicable to the 1996 and subsequent taxation years, except that paragraph (*c*) of the definition "designated income" in subsection 210(1) is to be read

(*a*) in respect of dispositions that occur after October 1, 1996 and before December 21, 2002, as follows:

"(*c*) the only taxable capital gains and allowable capital losses referred to in paragraph 3(*b*) were from dispositions of taxable Canadian property; and"

(*b*) in respect of dispositions that occur in a 1996 taxation year and before October 2, 1996, as follows:

"(*c*) the only taxable capital gains and allowable capital losses referred to in paragraph 3(*b*) were from dispositions of property that would have been taxable Canadian property if, at no time in the year, the trust had been resident in Canada; and"

S. 210 formerly read:

S. 210. *Designated beneficiary.* In this Part, a "designated beneficiary" under a trust at any time means a beneficiary under the trust that was, at that time,

(*a*) a non-resident person;

(*b*) a non-resident-owned investment corporation;

(*c*) a person exempt from tax under Part I by reason of subsection 149(1), where that person acquired an interest in the trust after October 1, 1987 directly or indirectly from a beneficiary under the trust except

(i) where the interest was owned continuously since October 1, 1987 or the date on which the interest was created, whichever is later, by persons exempt from tax under Part I by reason of subsection 149(1), or

(ii) where the person was a trust governed by

(A) a registered retirement savings plan, or

(B) a registered retirement income fund,

and acquired the interest, directly or indirectly, from an individual or the spouse or common-law partner or former spouse or common-law partner of the individual who was, immediately after the interest was acquired, a beneficiary under the trust governed by the fund or plan;

(*d*) a trust resident in Canada (other than a testamentary trust, a mutual fund trust or a trust exempt, because of subsection 149(1), from tax under Part I on all or part of its taxable income), if

(i) a person described in paragraph (*a*), (*b*) or (*c*),

(ii) a partnership described in paragraph (*e*), or

(iii) a trust (other than a trust resident in Canada that is a testamentary trust)

is, at that time, a beneficiary thereunder; or

(*e*) a partnership, if a person described in paragraph (*a*), (*b*) or (*d*), a partnership or a person exempt from tax under Part I by reason of subsection 149(1) is, at that time, a member thereof.

Related Sections: S. 104(1) Reference to trust or estate; s. 108(1), "inter vivos trust", "testamentary trust"; s. 132(6) Meaning of "mutual fund trust"; s. 133(8), "non-resident-owned investment corporation"; s. 146(1), "registered retirement savings plan"; s. 146.3(1), "registered retirement income fund".

▶ 210(2) ◀

(2) Tax not payable. No tax is payable under this Part for a taxation year by a trust that was throughout the year

(*a*) a graduated rate estate;

(*b*) a mutual fund trust;

(*c*) exempt from tax under Part I because of subsection 149(1);

(*d*) a trust to which paragraph (*a*), (*a.1*) or (*c*) of the definition "trust" in subsection 108(1) applies; or

(*e*) non-resident.

Editorial Note: Beginning in 2016, the exception in paragraph (*a*) applies only to graduated rate estates (defined in subsection 248(1)) and not to other testamentary trusts.

History: S. 210(2)(*a*) was replaced by S.C. 2014, c. 39, s. 63(6), applicable to the 2016 and subsequent taxation years, and formerly read:

(*a*) a testamentary trust;

S. 210(2) was added by S.C. 2013, c. 34, s. 341(1), applicable to the 1996 and subsequent taxation years.

Related Sections: 248(1) graduated rate estate.

SECTION 210.1: Application of Part

(Repealed by S.C. 2013, c. 34, s. 341(1).)

SECTION 210.2: Tax on income of trust

► 210.2(1) ◄

(1) Tax on income of trust. Subject to section 210.3, if a trust deducts an amount under paragraph 104(6)(*b*) in computing its income under Part I for a taxation year, the trust shall pay a tax under this Part in respect of the year equal to 40% of the least of

(*a*) the designated income of the trust for the year,

(*b*) the amount that, but for subsections 104(6) and (30), would be the income of the trust for the year, and

(*c*) 100/60 of the amount deducted.

Editorial Note: In the absence of the Part XII.2 tax under subsection 210.2(1), a Canadian resident trust could earn business income or rental income earned in Canada, or taxable capital gains from the disposition of taxable Canadian property, and distribute the income to a non-resident beneficiary without the payment of the appropriate amount of tax. That is, the distributed income would be deductible in computing the trust's Part I tax, and thus would be subject to withholding tax only, at the rate of 25%, and often 15% as reduced by the income tax treaty. The Part XII.2 tax is meant to preserve the Canadian tax base in these situations, by imposing an additional tax on the trust in respect of such "designated income". A credit is available for beneficiaries who are not designated beneficiaries, generally to the extent of the trust Part XII.2 payable in respect of trust income included in their income.

Starting in 2016, the tax rate under subsection 210.2(1) is increased from 36% to 40%, owing to the four percentage point increase in the top marginal individual tax rate in that year, and the fraction in paragraph (*c*) is accordingly changed from 100/64 to 100/60.

History: S. 210.2(1), the portion before paragraph (*a*) was replaced by S.C. 2016, c. 7, s. 62(12), applicable to the 2016 and subsequent taxation years, and formerly read:

(1) *Tax on income of trust.* Subject to section 210.3, where an amount in respect of the income of a trust for a taxation year is or would, if all beneficiaries under the trust were persons resident in Canada to whom Part I was applicable, be included in computing the income under Part I of a person by reason of subsection 104(13) or 105(2), the trust shall pay a tax under this Part in respect of the year equal to 36% of the least of

S. 210.2(1)(*c*) was replaced by S.C. 2016, c. 7, s. 62(13), applicable to the 2016 and subsequent taxation years, and formerly read:

(*c*) 100/64 of the amount deducted under paragraph 104(6)(*b*) in computing the trust's income under Part I for the year.

Canadian Tax Foundation: Gibeault, *Unexpected Application of Part XII.2 Tax to a Canadian Personal Trust*, 2013 Canadian Tax Focus 13(2):10–11.

Tax Profile: March 2013 — Non-resident Investment in Canadian Real Estate.

Information Circulars: IC 77-1R5 Deferred profit sharing plan.

► 210.2(1.1) ◄

(1.1) Amateur athlete trusts — (Repealed by S.C. 2013, c. 34, s. 342(1).)

History: S. 210.2(1.1) was repealed by S.C. 2013, c. 34, s. 342(1), applicable to the 1996 and subsequent taxation years, and formerly read:

(1.1) *Amateur athlete trusts.* Notwithstanding section 210.1, where an amount described in subsection 143.1(2) in respect of an amateur athlete trust would, if Part I were applicable, be required to be included in computing the income for a taxation year of a designated beneficiary under the trust, the trust shall pay a tax under this Part in respect of the year equal to 36% of 100/64 of that amount.

► 210.2(2) ◄

(2) Amateur athlete trusts. Notwithstanding subsection 210(2), a trust shall pay a tax under this Part in respect of a particular taxation year of the trust equal to 2/3 of the amount that is required by subsection 143.1(2) to be included in computing the income under Part I for a taxation year of a beneficiary under the trust, if

(*a*) the beneficiary is at any time in the particular taxation year a designated beneficiary under the trust; and

(*b*) the particular taxation year ends in that taxation year of the beneficiary.

History: S. 210.2(2), the portion before paragraph (*a*) was replaced by S.C. 2016, c. 7, s. 62(14), applicable to the 2016 and subsequent taxation years, and formerly read:

(2) *Amateur athlete trusts.* Notwithstanding subsection 210(2), a trust shall pay a tax under this Part in respect of a particular taxation year of the trust equal to 56.25% of the amount that is required by subsection 143.1(2) to be included in computing the income under Part I for a taxation year of a beneficiary under the trust, if

S. 210.2(2) was replaced by S.C. 2013, c. 34, s. 342(1), applicable to the 1996 and subsequent taxation years, and formerly read:

(2) *Designated income.* For the purposes of subsection (1), the designated income of a trust for a taxation year means the amount that, but for subsections 104(6), (12) and (30), would be the income of the trust for the year determined under section 3 if

(*a*) it had no income other than taxable capital gains from dispositions described in paragraph (*b*) and incomes from

(i) real properties in Canada (other than Canadian resource properties),

(ii) timber resource properties,

(iii) Canadian resource properties (other than properties acquired by the trust before 1972), and

(iv) businesses carried on in Canada;

(*b*) the only taxable capital gains and allowable capital losses referred to in paragraph 3(*b*) were from dispositions of taxable Canadian property; and

(*c*) the only losses referred to in paragraph 3(*d*) were losses from sources described in subparagraphs (*a*)(i) to (iv).

► 210.2(3) ◄

(3) Tax deemed paid by beneficiary. Where an amount (in this subsection and subsection 210.3(2) referred to as the "income amount") in respect of the income of a trust for a taxation year is, by reason of subsection 104(13) or 105(2), included in computing

(*a*) the income under Part I of a person who was not at any time in the year a designated beneficiary under the trust, or

(*b*) the income of a non-resident person (other than a person who, at any time in the year, would be a designated beneficiary under the trust if section 210 were read without reference to paragraph (a) of the definition "designated beneficiary" in that section) that is subject to tax under Part I by reason of subsection 2(3) and is not exempt from tax under Part I by reason of a provision contained in a tax treaty,

an amount determined by the formula

$$A \times B/C$$

where

A is the tax paid under this Part by the trust for the year,

B is the income amount in respect of the person, and

C is the total of all amounts each of which is an amount that is or would be, if all beneficiaries under the trust were persons resident in Canada to whom Part I was applicable, included in computing the income under Part I of a beneficiary under the trust by reason of subsection 104(13) or 105(2) in respect of the year, shall, if designated by the trust in respect of the person in its return for the year under this Part, be deemed to be an amount paid on account of the person's tax payable under Part I for the person's taxation year in which the taxation year of the trust ends, on the day that is 90 days after the end of the taxation year of the trust.

History: S. 210.2(3)(*b*) was replaced by S.C. 2013, c. 34, s. 342(3), applicable to the 1996 and subsequent taxation years, except that, in applying paragraph 210.2(3)(*b*) for the 1996 and 1997 taxation years the reference to "treaty" is to be read as a reference to "convention or agreement with another country that has the force of law in Canada".

S. 210.2(3)(*b*) formerly read:

(*b*) the income of a non-resident person (other than a person who, at any time in the year, would be a designated beneficiary under the trust if section 210 were read without reference to paragraph 210(*a*)) that is subject to tax under Part I by reason of subsection 2(3) and is not exempt from tax under Part I by reason of a provision contained in a tax convention or agreement with another country that has the force of law in Canada,

Interpretation Bulletins: *Secondary* — IT-342R Trusts — Income payable to beneficiaries.

► 210.2(4) ◄

(4) Designations in respect of partnerships. Where a taxpayer is a member of a partnership in respect of which an amount is designated by a trust for a taxation year of the trust (in this subsection referred to as the "particular year") under subsection (3),

(*a*) no amount shall be deemed to be paid on account of the partnership's tax payable under Part I by reason of subsection (3) except in the application of that subsection for the purposes of subsection 104(31), and

(*b*) an amount determined by the formula

$$A \times B/C$$

where

A is the amount so designated,

B is the amount that may reasonably be regarded as the share of the taxpayer in the designated income of the trust received by the partnership in the fiscal period of the partnership in which the particular year ends (that fiscal period being referred to in this subsection as the "partnership's period"), and

C is the designated income received by the partnership from the trust in the partnership's period,

shall be deemed to be an amount paid on account of the taxpayer's tax payable under Part I for the person's taxation year in which the partnership's period ends, on the last day of that year.

► 210.2(5) ◄

(5) Returns. A trust shall, within 90 days after the end of each taxation year,

(*a*) file with the Minister a return for the year under this Part in prescribed form and containing prescribed information, without notice or demand therefor;

(*b*) estimate in the return the amount of tax, if any, payable by it under this Part for the year; and

(*c*) pay to the Receiver General the tax, if any, payable by it under this Part for the year.

Forms: T3 SCH 10 — Part XII.2 Tax and Part XIII Non-Resident Withholding Tax.

► 210.2(6) ◄

(6) Liability of trustee. A trustee of a trust is personally liable to pay to the Receiver General on behalf of the trust the full amount of any tax payable by the trust under this Part to the extent that the amount is not paid to the Receiver General within the time specified in subsection (5), and the trustee is entitled to recover from the trust any such amount paid by the trustee.

► 210.2(7) ◄

(7) Provisions applicable to Part. Subsections 150(2) and (3), sections 152 and 158, subsections 161(1) and (11), sections 162 to 167 and Division J of Part I are applicable to this Part with such modifications as the circumstances require.

SECTION 210.3: Where no designated beneficiaries

► 210.3(1) ◄

(1) Where no designated beneficiaries. No tax is payable under this Part by a trust for a taxation year in respect of which the trustee has certified in the trust's return under this Part for the year that no beneficiary under the trust was a designated beneficiary in the year.

► 210.3(2) ◄

(2) Where beneficiary deemed not designated. Where a trust would, if the trust paid tax under this Part for a taxation year, be entitled to designate an amount under subsection 210.2(3) in respect of a non-resident beneficiary and the income amount in respect of the beneficiary is included in computing the income of the beneficiary which is subject to tax under Part I by reason of subsection 2(3) and is not exempt from tax under Part I by reason of a provision contained in a tax convention or agreement with another country that has the force of law in Canada, for the purposes of subsection (1), the beneficiary shall be deemed not to be a designated beneficiary of the trust at any time in the year.

Part XII.3
Tax on Investment Income of Life Insurers

SECTION 211: [Interpretation]

► 211(1) ◄

(1) Definitions. For the purposes of this Part,

"existing guaranteed life insurance policy" —"existing guaranteed life insurance policy", at any time, means a non-participating life insurance policy in Canada in respect of which

(*a*) the amount of every premium that became payable before that time and after December 31, 1989,

(*b*) the number of premium payments under the policy, and

(*c*) the amount of each benefit under the policy at that time

were fixed and determined on or before December 31, 1989;

Related Regulations: 1900.

"life insurance policy" —"life insurance policy" includes a benefit under

(*a*) a group life insurance policy, and

(*b*) a group annuity contract

but does not include

(*c*) that part of a policy in respect of which the policyholder is deemed by paragraph 138.1(1)(*e*) to have an interest in a related segregated fund trust, or

(*d*) a reinsurance arrangement;

Related Regulations: 1900.

"life insurance policy in Canada" —"life insurance policy in Canada" means a life insurance policy issued or effected by an insurer on the life of a person resident in Canada at the time the policy was issued or effected;

Related Regulations: 1900.

"net interest rate" —"net interest rate", in respect of a liability, benefit, risk or guarantee under a life insurance policy of an insurer for a taxation year, is the positive amount, if any, determined by the formula

$$(A - B) \times C$$

where

A is the simple arithmetic average determined as of the first day of the year of the average yield (expressed as a percentage per year rounded to 2 decimal points) in each of the 60 immediately preceding months prevailing on all domestic Canadian-dollar Government of Canada bonds outstanding on the last Wednesday of that month that have a remaining term to maturity of more than 10 years,

B is

(*a*) in the case of a guaranteed benefit provided under the terms and conditions of the policy as they existed on March 2, 1988, other than a policy where, at any time after March 2, 1988, its terms and conditions relating to premiums and benefits were changed (otherwise than to give effect to the terms and conditions that were determined before March 3, 1988), the greater of

(i) the rate of interest (expressed as a percentage per year) used by the insurer in determining the amount of the guaranteed benefit, and

(ii) 4%, and

(*b*) in any other case, nil, and

C is

(*a*) in the case of a guaranteed benefit to which paragraph (*a*) of the description of B applies, 65%, and

(*b*) in any other case, 55%;

Related Regulations: 1900.

"non-participating life insurance policy" —"non-participating life insurance policy" means a life insurance policy that is not a participating life insurance policy;

Related Regulations: 1900.

"participating life insurance policy" —"participating life insurance policy" has the meaning assigned by subsection 138(12);

Related Regulations: 1900.

"policy loan" —"policy loan" has the meaning assigned by subsection 138(12);

Related Regulations: 1900.

"registered life insurance policy" —"registered life insurance policy" means a life insurance policy issued or effected as or under a pooled registered pension plan, a registered retirement savings plan, a deferred profit sharing plan or a registered pension plan;

History: S. 211(1), the definition "registered life insurance policy" was replaced by S.C. 2012, c. 31, s. 47(1), in force December 14, 2012. S. 211(1), the definition "registered life insurance policy" formerly read:

"registered life insurance policy"—"registered life insurance policy" means a life insurance policy issued or effected

(*a*) as a registered retirement savings plan, or

(*b*) pursuant to a registered retirement savings plan, a deferred profit sharing plan or a registered pension plan;

S. 211(1), paragraph (*a*) of the definition "registered life insurance policy" was replaced by S.C. 2009, c. 2, s. 72(1), applicable to the 2009 and subsequent taxation years. S. 211(1), paragraph (*a*) of the definition "registered life insurance policy" formerly read:

(*a*) as a registered retirement savings plan or TFSA, or

Related Regulations: 1900.

"reinsurance arrangement" —"reinsurance arrangement" does not include an arrangement under which an insurer has assumed the obligations of the issuer of a life insurance policy to the policyholder;

Related Regulations: 1900.

"segregated fund" —"segregated fund" has the meaning given that expression in subsection 138.1(1);

Related Regulations: 1900.

"specified transaction or event" —"specified transaction or event", in respect of a life insurance policy, means

(*a*) a change in underwriting class,

(*b*) a change in premium because of a change in frequency of premium payments within a year that does not alter the present value, at the beginning of the year, of the total premiums to be paid under the policy in the year,

(*c*) an addition under the terms of the policy as they existed on

(i) in the case of an existing guaranteed life insurance policy, December 31, 1989,

(ii) in any other case, March 2, 1988,

of accidental death, dismemberment, disability or guaranteed purchase option benefits,

(*d*) the deletion of a rider,

(*e*) redating lapsed policies within the reinstatement period referred to in paragraph (*g*) of the definition "disposition" in subsection 148(9) or redating for policy loan indebtedness, (*f*) a change in premium because of a correction of erroneous information,

(*g*) the payment of a premium after its due date, or no more than 30 days before its due date, as established on or before

(i) in the case of an existing guaranteed life insurance policy, December 31, 1989, and

(ii) in any other case, March 2, 1988, and

(*h*) the payment of an amount described in paragraph (*a*) of the definition "premium" in subsection 148(9);

Related Regulations: 1900.

"taxable life insurance policy" —"taxable life insurance policy" of an insurer at any time means a life insurance policy in Canada issued by the insurer (or in respect of which the insurer has assumed the obligations of the issuer of the policy to the policyholder), other than a policy that is at that time

(*a*) an existing guaranteed life insurance policy,

(*b*) an annuity contract (including a settlement annuity),

(*c*) a registered life insurance policy,

(*d*) a registered pension plan, or

(*e*) a retirement compensation arrangement.

Related Regulations: 1900.

► 211(2) ◄

(2) Riders and changes in terms. For the purposes of this Part,

(*a*) any rider added at any time after March 2, 1988 to a life insurance policy shall be deemed to be a separate life insurance policy issued and effected at that time; and

(*b*) a change in the terms or conditions of a life insurance policy resulting from a specified transaction or event shall be deemed not to have occurred and not to be a change.

Related Regulations: 1900.

SECTION 211.1: Tax payable

► 211.1(1) ◄

(1) Tax payable. Every life insurer shall pay a tax under this Part for each taxation year equal to 15% of its taxable Canadian life investment income for the year.

Tax Window Files: Tax on Investment Income of Life Insurers — Universal Life Policies, *Technical Interpretation, Charitable and Financial Institution Sectors, March 28, 2006,* CRA Document No. 2005-0145821E5.

► 211.1(2) ◄

(2) Taxable Canadian life investment income. For the purposes of this Part, the taxable Canadian life investment income of a life insurer for a taxation year is the amount, if any, by which its Canadian life investment income for the year exceeds the total of its Canadian life investment losses for the 20 taxation years immediately preceding the year, to the extent that those losses were not deducted in computing its taxable Canadian life investment income for any preceding taxation year.

► 211.1(3) ◄

(3) Canadian life investment income. For the purposes of this Part, the Canadian life investment income or loss of a life insurer for a taxation year is the positive or negative amount determined by the formula

A + B - C

where

A is, subject to subsection (4), the total of all amounts, each of which is in respect of a liability, benefit, risk or guarantee under a life insurance policy that was at any time in the year a taxable life insurance policy of the insurer, determined by multiplying the net interest rate in respect of the liability, benefit, risk or guarantee for the year by $1/2$ of the total of

(*a*) the maximum amount that would be determined under paragraph 1401(1)(*a*), (*c*) or (*d*) of the *Income Tax Regulations* (other than an amount that would be determined under subparagraph 1401(1)(*d*)(ii) of those Regulations in respect of a disabled life) in respect of the insurer for the year in respect of the liability, benefit, risk or guarantee if subsection 1401(1) of those Regulations applied to all life insurance policies and if that amount were determined without reference to any policy loan or reinsurance arrangement, and

(*b*) the maximum amount that would be determined under paragraph 1401(1)(*a*), (*c*) or (*d*) of the *Income Tax Regulations* (other than an amount that would be determined under subparagraph 1401(1)(*d*)(ii) of those Regulations in respect of a disabled life) in respect of the insurer for the preceding taxation year in respect of the liability, benefit, risk or guarantee if subsection 1401(1) of those Regulations applied to all life insurance policies and if that amount were determined without reference to any policy loan or reinsurance arrangement;

B is the total of all amounts, each of which is the positive or negative amount in respect of a life insurance policy that was at any time in the year a taxable life insurance policy of the insurer, determined by the formula

D - E

where

D is, subject to subsection (4), the amount determined by multiplying the percentage determined in the description of A in the definition "net interest rate" in subsection 211(1) in respect of the year by $1/2$ of the total of

(*a*) the maximum amount that would be determined under paragraph 1401(1)(c.1) of the *Income Tax Regulations* in respect of the insurer for the year in respect of the policy if subsection 1401(1) of those Regulations applied to all life insurance policies and if that amount were determined without reference to any policy loan or reinsurance arrangement, and

(*b*) the maximum amount that would be determined under paragraph 1401(1)(c.1) of the *Income Tax Regulations* in respect of the insurer for the preceding taxation year in respect of the policy if subsection 1401(1) of those Regulations applied to all life insurance policies and if that amount were determined without reference to any policy loan or reinsurance arrangement, and

E is the amount, if any, by which

(*a*) the total of all amounts determined in respect of the insurer under the description of D in respect of the policy for the year and any preceding taxation years ending after 1989

exceeds the total of

(*b*) all amounts determined in respect of the insurer under the description of E in respect of the policy for taxation years ending before the year, and

(*c*) the amount, if any, by which

(i) the maximum amount that would be determined under paragraph 1401(1)(c.1) of the *Income Tax Regulations* in respect of the insurer for the year in respect of the policy if subsection 1401(1) of those Regulations applied to all life insurance policies and if that amount were determined without reference to any policy loan or reinsurance arrangement

exceeds

(ii) the maximum amount that would be determined under paragraph 1401(1)(c.1) of the *Income Tax Regulations* in respect of the insurer for its last 1989 taxation year in respect of the policy if subsection 1401(1) of those Regulations applied to all life insurance policies and if that amount were determined without reference to any policy loan or reinsurance arrangement; and

C is the total of all amounts each of which is 100% of the amount required to be included in computing the income of a policyholder under section 12.2 or paragraph 56(1)(*j*) for which the insurer is required by regulation to prepare an information return in respect of the calendar year ending in the taxation year, in respect of a taxable life insurance policy of the insurer, except that the reference in this description to 100% shall be read as a reference to,

(*a*) where paragraph (*a*) of the description of B in the definition "net interest rate" in subsection 211(1) applies for any taxation year in respect of a guaranteed benefit under the policy,

0 %	for calendar years before 1991,
5 %	for 1991,
10 %	for 1992,
15 %	for 1993,
20 %	for 1994,
25 %	for 1995,
30 %	for 1996,
35 %	for 1997,
40 %	for 1998,
45 %	for 1999, and
50 %	for calendar years after 1999, and

(*b*) where the policy was at any time after 1989 an existing guaranteed life insurance policy,

0 %	for the calendar year in which it became a taxable life insurance policy of the insurer,
0 %	for the first following calendar year,
0 %	for the second following calendar year,
5 %	for the third following calendar year,
10 %	for the fourth following calendar year,
15 %	for the fifth following calendar year,
20 %	for the sixth following calendar year,
25 %	for the seventh following calendar year,
30 %	for the eighth following calendar year,
35 %	for the ninth following calendar year,
40 %	for the tenth following calendar year,
45 %	for the eleventh following calendar year, and
50 %	for the twelfth following and subsequent calendar years.

Related Regulations: 1401(1); 1900.

Tax Window Files: Insurer's Investment Income Tax, *Technical Interpretation, March 28, 2006,* CRA Document No. 2005-0145821E5.

► 211.1(4) ◄

(4) Short taxation year. Where a taxation year of a life insurer is less than 51 weeks, the values of A and D in subsection (3) for the year are that proportion of those values otherwise so determined that the number of days in the year (other than February 29) is of 365.

SECTION 211.2: Return

Every life insurer shall file with the Minister, not later than the day on or before which it is required by section 150 to file its return of income for a taxation year under Part I, a return of taxable Canadian life investment income for that year in prescribed form containing an estimate of the tax payable by it under this Part for the year.

Forms: T2142 — Part XII.3 Tax Return — Tax on Investment Income of Life Insurers.

SECTION 211.3: Instalments

► 211.3(1) ◄

(1) Instalments. Every life insurer shall, in respect of each of its taxation years, pay to the Receiver General on or before the last day of each month in the year, an amount equal to 1/12 of the lesser of

(*a*) the amount estimated by the insurer to be the annualized tax payable under this Part by it for the year, and

(*b*) the annualized tax payable under this Part by the insurer for the immediately preceding taxation year.

► 211.3(2) ◄

(2) Annualized tax payable. For the purposes of subsections (1) and 211.5(2), the annualized tax payable under this Part by a life insurer for a taxation year is the amount determined by the formula

$$(365/A) \times B$$

where

A is

(*a*) if the year is less than 357 days, the number of days in the year (other than February 29), and

(*b*) otherwise, 365; and

B is the tax payable under this Part by the insurer for the year.

SECTION 211.4: Payment of remainder of tax

Every life insurer shall pay, on or before its balance-due day for a taxation year, the remainder, if any, of the tax payable under this Part by the insurer for the year.

SECTION 211.5: Provisions applicable to Part

► 211.5(1) ◄

(1) Provisions applicable to Part. Section 152, subsection 157(2.1), sections 158 and 159, subsections 161(1), (2), (2.1), (2.2) and (11), sections 162 to 167 and Division J of Part I apply to this Part, with such modifications as the circumstances require.

► 211.5(2) ◄

(2) Interest on instalments. For the purposes of subsection 161(2) and section 163.1 as they apply to this Part, a life insurer is, in respect of a taxation year, deemed to have been liable to pay, on or before the last day of each month in the year, an instalment equal to 1/12 of the lesser of

(*a*) the annualized tax payable under this Part by the insurer for the year, and

(*b*) the annualized tax payable under this Part by the insurer for the immediately preceding taxation year.

Related Regulations: Part XLIII.

Part XII.4
Tax on Qualifying Environmental Trusts

SECTION 211.6: [Tax payable]

► 211.6(1) ◄

(1) Definitions. The definitions in this section apply for the purposes of this Part.

"excluded trust" —"excluded trust", at any time, means a trust that

(*a*) relates at that time to the reclamation of a well;

(*b*) is not maintained at that time to secure the reclamation obligations of one or more persons or partnerships that are beneficiaries under the trust;

(*c*) borrows money at that time;

(*d*) if the trust is not a trust to which paragraph (*e*) applies, acquires at that time any property that is not described by any of paragraphs (*a*), (*b*) and (*f*) of the definition "qualified investment" in section 204;

(*e*) if the trust is created after 2011 (or if the trust was created before 2012, it elects in writing filed with the Minister on or before its filing-due date for a particular taxation year to have subparagraphs (i) and (ii) apply to it for the particular taxation year and all subsequent taxation years, and that election is made jointly with Her Majesty in right of Canada or a particular province, depending upon the qualifying law or qualifying contract in respect of the trust),

(i) acquires at that time any property that is not described by any of paragraphs (*a*), (*b*), (*c*), (*c.1*), (*d*) and (*f*) of the definition "qualified investment" in section 204, or

(ii) holds at that time a prohibited investment;

(*f*) elected in writing filed with the Minister, before 1998 or before April of the year following the year in which the first contribution to the trust was made, never to have been a qualifying environmental trust; or

(*g*) was at any previous time during its existence not a qualifying environmental trust (as determined under the definition "qualifying environmental trust" in subsection 248(1) as it applied at that previous time).

"prohibited investment" —"prohibited investment", of a trust at any time, means a property that

(*a*) at the time it was acquired by the trust, was described by any of paragraphs (*c*), (*c.1*) or (*d*) of the definition "qualified investment" in section 204; and

(*b*) was issued by

(i) a person or partnership that has contributed property to, or that is a beneficiary under, the trust,

(ii) a person that is related to, or a partnership that is affiliated with, a person or partnership that has contributed property to, or that is a beneficiary under, the trust, or

(iii) a particular person or partnership if

(A) another person or partnership holds a significant interest (within the meaning assigned by subsection 207.01(4) with any modifications that the circumstances require) in the particular person or partnership, and

(B) the holder of that significant interest has contributed property to, or is a beneficiary under, the trust.

"QET income tax rate" —"QET income tax rate", for a trust's taxation year, means the amount, expressed as a decimal fraction, by which

(*a*) the percentage rate of tax provided under paragraph 123(1)(*a*) for the taxation year

exceeds

(*b*) the total of

(i) the percentage that would, if the trust were a corporation, be its general rate reduction percentage, within the meaning assigned by subsection 123.4(1), for the taxation year, and

(ii) the percentage deduction from tax provided under subsection 124(1) for the taxation year.

"qualifying contract" —"qualifying contract", in respect of a trust, means a contract entered into with Her Majesty in right of Canada or a province on or before the later of January 1, 1996 and the day that is one year after the day on which the trust was created.

"qualifying environmental trust" —"qualifying environmental trust" means a trust

(*a*) each trustee of which is

(i) Her Majesty in right of Canada or a province, or

(ii) a corporation resident in Canada that is licensed or otherwise authorized under the laws of Canada or a province to carry on in Canada the business of offering to the public its services as trustee;

(*b*) that is maintained for the sole purpose of funding the reclamation of a qualifying site;

(*c*) that is, or may become, required to be maintained under

(i) the terms of a qualifying contract, or

(ii) a qualifying law; and

(*d*) that is not an excluded trust.

"qualifying law" —"qualifying law", in respect of a trust, means (*a*) a law of Canada or a province that was enacted on or before the later of January 1, 1996 and the day that is one year after the day on which the trust was created; and

(*b*) if the trust was created after 2011, an order made

(i) by a tribunal constituted under a law described by paragraph (*a*), and

(ii) on or before the day that is one year after the day on which the trust was created.

"qualifying site" —"qualifying site", in respect of a trust, means a site in Canada that is or has been used primarily for, or for any combination of,

(*a*) the operation of a mine,

(*b*) the extraction of clay, peat, sand, shale or aggregates (including dimension stone and gravel),

(*c*) the deposit of waste, or

(*d*) if the trust was created after 2011, the operation of a pipeline.

History: S. 211.6(1) was replaced by S.C. 2011, c. 24, s. 69(2), applicable to the 2012 and subsequent taxation years. S. 211.6(1) formerly read:

(1) *Charging provision.* Every trust that is a qualifying environmental trust at the end of a taxation year (other than a trust that is at that time described in paragraph 149(1)(*z.1*) or (*z.2*)) shall pay a tax under this Part for the year equal to 28% of its income under Part I for the year.

S. 211.6(1) was replaced by S.C. 2011, c. 24, s. 69(1), applicable to the 1997 to 2011 taxation years. S. 211.6(1) formerly read:

(1) *Charging provision.* Every trust that is a qualifying environmental trust at the end of a taxation year shall pay a tax under this Part for the year equal to 28% of its income under Part I for the year.

Related Sections: S. 107.3(1) Treatment of beneficiaries under qualifying environmental trusts; s. 127.41 Part XII.4 tax credit; s. 149(1)(*z*) Qualifying environmental trust; s. 248(1), "qualifying environmental trust"; s. 250(7) Residence of a qualifying environmental trust.

Canadian Tax Foundation: Frankovic, *The Case for "Reverse Depreciation" of Reclamation Costs*, 2004 Canadian Tax Journal 1:1–58.

► 211.6(2) ◄

(2) Charging provision. Every trust that is a qualifying environmental trust at the end of a taxation year (other than a trust that is at that time described by paragraph 149(1)(*z.1*) or (*z.2*)) shall pay a tax under this Part for the year equal to the amount determined by the formula

$$A \times B$$

where

A is the trust's income (computed as if this Act were read without reference to subsections 104(4) to (31) and sections 105 to 107) under Part I for the year; and

B is the QET income tax rate for the year.

History: S. 211.6(2) was replaced by S.C. 2011, c. 24, s. 69(3), applicable to the 2012 and subsequent taxation years. S. 211.6(2) formerly read:

(2) *Computation of income.* For the purpose of subsection (1), the income under Part I of a qualifying environmental trust shall be computed as if this Act were read without reference to subsections 104(4) to (31) and sections 105 to 107.

► 211.6(3) ◄

(3) Return. Every trust that is a qualifying environmental trust at the end of a taxation year shall file with the Minister on or before its filing-due date for the year a return for the year under this Part in prescribed form containing an estimate of the amount of its tax payable under this Part for the year.

Forms: T3M — Environmental Trust Income Tax Return.

► 211.6(4) ◄

(4) Payment of tax. Every trust shall pay to the Receiver General its tax payable under this Part for each taxation year on or before its balance-due day for the year.

► 211.6(5) ◄

(5) Provisions applicable to Part. Subsections 150(2) and (3), sections 152, 158 and 159, subsections 161(1) and (11), sections 162 to 167 and Division J of Part I apply to this Part, with such modifications as the circumstances require.

Part XII.5
Recovery of Labour-Sponsored Funds Tax Credit

SECTION 211.7: [Interpretation]

▶ 211.7(1) ◀

(1) Definitions. The definitions in this section apply for the purposes of this Part.

"approved share" —"approved share" has the meaning assigned by subsection 127.4(1).

"labour-sponsored funds tax credit" —"labour-sponsored funds tax credit" in respect of a share is

(*a*) where the original acquisition of the share occurred before 1996, 20% of the net cost of the share on that acquisition;

(*b*) in any other case, the amount that would be determined under subsection 127.4(6) in respect of the share if this Act were read without reference to its paragraphs (*b*) and (*d*).

(*c*) (Repealed by S.C. 2016, c. 7, s. 44(1).)

History: S. 211.7(1), paragraph (*b*) of the definition "labour-sponsored funds tax credit" was replaced by S.C. 2016, c. 7, s. 44(1), applicable to the 2016 and subsequent taxation years, and formerly read:

(*b*) if the original acquisition of the share occurred after 1995 and before March 2, 2017, the amount that would be determined under subsection 127.4(6) — as that subsection would apply in respect of a claim made by the taxpayer under subsection 127.4(2) in respect of the original acquisition if subsection 127.4(6) were read without reference to paragraphs 127.4(6)(*b*) and (*d*) — in respect of the share; and

S. 211.7(1), paragraph (*c*) of the definition "labour-sponsored funds tax credit" was repealed by S.C. 2016, c. 7, s. 44(1), applicable to the 2016 and subsequent taxation years, and formerly read:

(*c*) in any other case, nil.

S. 211.7(1), the definition "labour-sponsored funds tax credit", was amended by S.C. 2013, c. 40, s. 80(1), by replacing paragraph (*b*) and adding paragraph (*c*), deemed to have come into force on March 21, 2013.
S. 211.7(1), paragraph (*b*) of the definition "labour-sponsored funds tax credit" formerly read:

(*b*) in any other case, the amount that would be determined under subsection 127.4(6) in respect of the share if this Act were read without reference to paragraphs 127.4(6)(*b*) and (*d*).

"net cost" —"net cost" has the meaning assigned by subsection 127.4(1).

"original acquisition" —"original acquisition" has the meaning assigned by subsection 127.4(1).

"qualifying exchange" —"qualifying exchange" means an exchange by a taxpayer of an approved share, that is part of a series of Class A shares of the capital stock of a corporation, for another approved share, that is part of another series of Class A shares of the capital stock of the corporation, if

(*a*) the only consideration received by the taxpayer on the exchange is the other share; and

(*b*) the rights in respect of the series are identical except for the portion of the reserve (within the meaning assigned by subsection 204.8(1)) of the corporation that is attributable to each series.

History: S. 211.7(1), the definition of "qualifying exchange" was added by S.C. 2013, c. 34, s. 343(1), deemed to have come into force on January 1, 2004.

"qualifying trust" —"qualifying trust" has the meaning assigned by subsection 127.4(1).

"revoked corporation" —"revoked corporation" means a corporation the registration of which has been revoked under subsection 204.81(6).

▶ 211.7(2) ◀

(2) Amalgamations and mergers. For the purposes of this Part, where two or more corporations (each of which is referred to in this subsection as a "predecessor corporation") amalgamate or merge to form a corporate entity deemed by paragraph 204.85(3)(*d*) to have been registered under Part X.3, the shares of each predecessor corporation are deemed not to be redeemed, acquired or cancelled by the predecessor corporation on the amalgamation or merger.

▶ 211.7(3) ◀

(3) Exchangeable shares. For the purposes of this Part and Part X.3, if an approved share of the capital stock of a corporation (referred to in this subsection as the "new share") has been issued in exchange for another approved share (referred to in this subsection as the "original share") in a qualifying exchange, the new share is deemed not to have been issued on the exchange and is deemed to have been issued at the time the corporation issued the original share.

History: S. 211.7(3) was added by S.C. 2013, c. 34, s. 343(2), deemed to have come into force on January 1, 2004.

SECTION 211.8: Disposition of approved share

▶ 211.8(1) ◀

(1) Disposition of approved share. If an approved share of the capital stock of a registered labour-sponsored venture capital corporation or a revoked corporation is, before the first discontinuation of its venture capital business, redeemed, acquired or cancelled by the corporation less than eight years after the day on which the share was issued (other than in circumstances described in subclause 204.81(1)(*c*)(v)(A)(I) or (III) or clause 204.81(1)(*c*)(v)(B) or (D) or other than if the share is a Class A share of the capital stock of the corporation that is exchanged for another Class A share of the capital stock of the corporation as part of a qualifying exchange) or any other share that was issued by any other labour-sponsored venture capital corporation is disposed of, the person who was the shareholder immediately before the redemption, acquisition, cancellation or disposition shall pay a tax under this Part equal to the lesser of (*a*) the amount determined by the formula

A x B

where

A is

(i) where the share was issued by a registered labour-sponsored venture capital corporation or a revoked corporation, the labour-sponsored funds tax credit in respect of the share, and

(ii) where the share was issued by any other labour-sponsored venture capital corporation and was at any time an approved share, the amount, if any, required to be remitted to the government of a province as a consequence of the redemption, acquisition, cancellation or disposition (otherwise than as a consequence of an increase in the corporation's liability for a penalty under a law of the province), and

B is

(i) nil, where the share was issued by a registered labour-sponsored venture capital corporation or a revoked corporation, the original acquisition of the share was before March 6, 1996 and the redemption, acquisition, cancellation or disposition is

(A) more than 2 years after the day on which it was issued, where the redemption, acquisition, cancellation or disposition is permitted under the articles of the corporation because an individual attains 65 years of age, retires from the workforce or ceases to be resident in Canada,

(B) more than five years after its issuance, or

(C) if the day that is five years after its issuance is in February or March of a calendar year, in February or on March 1st of that calendar year but not more than 31 days before that day,

(i.1) nil, where the share was issued by a registered labour-sponsored venture capital corporation or a revoked corporation, the original acquisition of the share was after March 5, 1996 and the redemption, acquisition or cancellation is in February or on March 1st of a calendar year but is not more than 31 days before the day that is eight years after the day on which the share was issued,

(ii) one, in any other case where the share was issued by a registered labour-sponsored venture capital corporation or a revoked corporation, and

(iii) in any other case, the quotient obtained when the labour-sponsored fund tax credit in respect of the share is divided by the tax credit provided under a law of a province in respect of any previous acquisition of the share, and

(*b*) the amount that would, but for subsection (2), be payable to the shareholder because of the redemption, acquisition, cancellation or disposition (determined after taking into account the amount determined under subparagraph (ii) of the description of A in paragraph (*a*)).

History: S. 211.8(1), the portion before paragraph (*a*) was replaced by S.C. 2013, c. 34, s. 344(1), applicable in respect of shares redeemed, acquired or cancelled after 2003, and formerly read:

(1) *Disposition of approved share.* Where an approved share of the capital stock of a registered labour-sponsored venture capital corporation or a revoked corporation is, before the first discontinuation of its venture capital business, redeemed, acquired or cancelled by the corporation less than eight years after the day on which the share was issued (other than in circumstances described in subclause 204.81(1)(*c*)(v)(A)(I) or (III) or clause 204.81(1)(*c*)(v)(B) or (D)) or any other share that was issued by any other labour-sponsored venture capital corporation is disposed of, the person who was the shareholder immediately before the redemption, acquisition, cancellation or disposition shall pay a tax under this Part equal to the lesser of

S. 211.8(1)(*a*), clause (i)(B) of the description of B was replaced by S.C. 2013, c. 34, s. 344(2), applicable to redemptions, acquisitions, cancellations and dispositions that occur after November 15, 1995, and formerly read:

(B) more than 5 years after the day on which it was issued,

S. 211.8(1)(*a*), clause (i)(C) of the description of B was added by S.C. 2013, c. 34, s. 344(2), applicable to redemptions, acquisitions, cancellations and dispositions that occur after November 15, 1995.

S. 211.8(1)(*a*), subparagraph (i.1) of the description of B was added by S.C. 2013, c. 34, s. 344(3), applicable to redemptions, acquisitions, cancellations and dispositions that occur after November 15, 1995.

► 211.8(1.1) ◄

(1.1) Rules of application. Subsections 204.8(2) and (3) and 204.85(3) apply for the purpose of subsection (1).

► 211.8(2) ◄

(2) Withholding and remittance of tax. Where a person or partnership (in this section referred to as the "transferee") redeems, acquires or cancels a share and, as a consequence, tax is payable under this Part by the person who was the shareholder immediately before the redemption, acquisition or cancellation, the transferee shall

(*a*) withhold from the amount otherwise payable on the redemption, acquisition or cancellation to the shareholder the amount of the tax;

(*b*) within 30 days after the redemption, acquisition or cancellation, remit the amount of the tax to the Receiver General on behalf of the shareholder; and

(*c*) submit with the remitted amount a statement in prescribed form.

Forms: T1149 — Remittance Form for Labour-Sponsored Funds Tax Credits Withheld on Redeemed Shares.

▶ 211.8(3) ◀

(3) Liability for tax. Where a transferee has failed to withhold any amount as required by subsection (2) from an amount paid or credited to a shareholder, the transferee is liable to pay as tax under this Part on behalf of the shareholder the amount the transferee failed to withhold, and is entitled to recover that amount from the shareholder.

SECTION 211.81: Tax for failure to reacquire certain shares

If a particular amount is payable under a prescribed provision of a provincial law for a taxation year of an individual as determined for the purposes of that provincial law (referred to in this section as the "relevant provincial year"), and an amount has been included in the computation of the labour-sponsored funds tax credit of the individual under subsection 127.4(6) in respect of an approved share that has been disposed of by a qualifying trust in respect of the individual, the individual shall pay a tax for the taxation year in which the relevant provincial year ends equal to the amount deducted by the individual under subsection 127.4(2) in respect of the share.

History: S. 211.81 was replaced by S.C. 2013, c. 40, s. 81(1), deemed to have come into force on October 24, 2012, and formerly read:

S. 211.81 *Tax for failure to re-acquire certain shares.* If a particular amount is payable under a prescribed provision of a provincial law for a taxation year of an individual as determined for the purposes of that provincial law (referred to in this section as the "relevant provincial year"), and an amount has been included in the computation of the labour-sponsored funds tax credit of the individual under subsection 127.4(6) in respect of an approved share that has been disposed of by a qualifying trust in respect of the individual, the individual shall pay a tax for the taxation year in which the relevant provincial year ends equal to the particular amount.

S. 211.81 was added by S.C. 2013, c. 34, s. 345(1), deemed to have come into force on October 24, 2012.

Related Regulations: 6709.

SECTION 211.82: Return

▶ 211.82(1) ◀

(1) Return. Every person that is liable to pay tax under this Part for a taxation year shall, not later than the day on or before which the person is required by section 150 to file a return of income for the year under Part I, file with the Minister a return for the year under this Part in prescribed form containing an estimate of the tax payable by the person for the year.

History: S. 211.82(1) was added by S.C. 2013, c. 34, s. 345(1), applicable to taxation years that end after October 24, 2012.

▶ 211.82(2) ◀

(2) Provisions applicable to this Part. Subsections 150(2) and (3), sections 152, 158 and 159, subsections 161(1) and (11), sections 162 to 167 and Division J of Part I apply to this Part, with any modifications that the circumstances require.

History: S. 211.82(2) was added by S.C. 2013, c. 34, s. 345(1), applicable to taxation years that end after October 24, 2012.

SECTION 211.9: Refund

(Repealed by S.C. 2013, c. 34, s. 346(1).)

History: S. 211.9 was repealed by S.C. 2013, c. 34, s. 346(1), applicable to taxation years that end after October 24, 2012, and formerly read:

S. 211.9 *Refund.* The Minister may pay to an individual (other than a trust) in respect of the disposition of a share, if application for the payment has been made in writing by the individual and filed with the Minister no later than two years after the end of the calendar year in which the disposition occurred, an amount not exceeding the lesser of

(*a*) the tax paid under this Part in respect of a disposition of the share, and

(*b*) 15% of the net cost of the share on the original acquisition by the individual (or by a qualifying trust for the individual in respect of the share).

Part XII.6
Tax on Flow-Through Shares

SECTION 211.91: Tax imposed

► 211.91(1) ◄

(1) Tax imposed. Every corporation shall pay a tax under this Part in respect of each month (other than January) in a calendar year equal to the amount determined by the formula

$$(A + B/2 - C - D/2) \times (E/12 + F/10)$$

where

A is the total of all amounts each of which is an amount that the corporation purported to renounce in the year under subsection 66(12.6) or (12.601) because of the application of subsection 66(12.66) (other than an amount purported to be renounced in respect of expenses incurred or to be incurred in connection with production or potential production in a province where a tax, similar to the tax provided under this Part, is payable by the corporation under the laws of the province as a consequence of the failure to incur the expenses that were purported to be renounced);

B is the total of all amounts each of which is an amount that the corporation purported to renounce in the year under subsection 66(12.6) or (12.601) because of the application of subsection 66(12.66) and that is not included in the value of A;

C is the total of all expenses described in paragraph 66(12.66)(*b*) that are

(*a*) made or incurred by the end of the month by the corporation, and

(*b*) in respect of the purported renunciations in respect of which an amount is included in the value of A;

D is the total of all expenses described in paragraph 66(12.66)(*b*) that are

(*a*) made or incurred by the end of the month by the corporation, and

(*b*) in respect of the purported renunciations in respect of which an amount is included in the value of B;

E is the rate of interest prescribed for the purpose of subsection 164(3) for the month; and

F is

(*a*) one, where the month is December, and

(*b*) nil, in any other case.

Related Regulations: 4301.

Canadian Petroleum Tax Journal: Flow-Through Shares: An Update, Angelo F. Toselli, 1997, Vol. 10, No. 1.

► 211.91(2) ◄

(2) Return and payment of tax. A corporation liable to tax under this Part in respect of one or more months in a calendar year shall, before March of the following calendar year,

(*a*) file with the Minister a return for the year under this Part in prescribed form containing an estimate of the tax payable under this Part by it in respect of each month in the year; and

(*b*) pay to the Receiver General the amount of tax payable under this Part by it in respect of each month in the year.

Forms: T100 — Flow-Through Share Information; T101C — Part XII.6 Tax Return.

► 211.91(3) ◄

(3) Provisions applicable to Part. Subsections 150(2) and (3), sections 152, 158 and 159, subsections 161(1) and (11), sections 162 to 167 and Division J of Part I apply to this Part, with any modifications that the circumstances require.

Part XIII
Tax on Income from Canada of Non-Resident Persons

SECTION 212: Tax

► 212(1) ◄

(1) Tax. Every non-resident person shall pay an income tax of 25% on every amount that a person resident in Canada pays or credits, or is deemed by Part I to pay or credit, to the non-resident person as, on account or in lieu of payment of, or in satisfaction of,

Editorial Note: The 25% withholding tax generally applies to passive investment income received by non-residents from Canadian sources (as more particularly set out in s. (1); see also s. (2), which deals with dividends, and s. (5), which deals with amounts paid for the use of motion picture film or television video). The tax is often reduced by treaty. Although the non-resident is liable for the tax, the Canadian resident payer of the income is obligated to withhold the tax and remit it to the Receiver General on behalf of the non-resident (s. 215(1)). See also ss. 212(13) through (13.2) regarding non-resident payers, and payers or payees who are partnerships. The rest of s. 212 provides various interpretive and application rules for the purposes of the withholding tax.

Related Regulations: Part II; Part VIII.

Related Sections: S. 2(3) Tax payable by non-resident persons; s. 134.1(2) Application; s. 142.7(8)(*d*) Assumption of debt obligation; 212(13) Rent and other payments; 212(13.1) Application of Part XIII tax where payer or payee is a partnership; 212(13.2) Application of Part XIII tax — non-resident operates in Canada; 212(13.3) Application of Part XIII to authorized foreign bank; s. 214 Special rules applicable to non-residents; s. 215 Withholding and remittance of tax; s. 216 Alternatives re rents and timber royalties; s. 216.1 Alternative re: acting services; s. 217 Alternative re Canadian benefits; s. 227 Withholding taxes; ITAR s. 10(6) Limitation on non-resident's tax rate.

Canadian Tax Foundation: Oakey, *Non-Residents Owning Canadian Real Property*, 2013 Atlantic Provinces Tax Conference 2B:1–20; Ormrod and Bain, *Taxation Aspects of Cloud Computing*, 2012 Conference Report 18:1–25; Baron, *Current Issues: Updated Guidance on Non-Resident Withholding Forms*, 2012 Ontario Tax Conference 1A:13–18; Chiu, *Taxation of Non-Resident Investors in Canadian Investment Funds*, 2010 Canadian Tax Journal 1:117–143; Ward et al., *A Resident of a Contracting State for Tax Treaty Purposes: A Case Comment on Crown Forest Industries*, 1996 Canadian Tax Journal 2:408–424.

Tax Profile: May 2013 — Current International Tax Issues In Cross-Border Corporate Finance and Capital Markets;; April 2012 — Fiscally Transparent Entities — Canada-U.S. Treaty; June 2011 — Part XIII Tax and Treaty Protection: Canada Revenue Agency's New Administrative Policy; December 2006 — "Beneficial Ownership" under Canadian Tax Treaties — Canadian Revenue Authorities Take Aim; September 2002 — Canadian Withholding Taxes Update; July 2002 — Doing Business in Canada.

Tax Topics: No. 2111, IFA 2012 Tax Seminar Roundtables; No. 1812, Beneficial Ownership: Indofood Run Wild.

Forms: NR4 Sum. — Return of Amounts Paid or Credited to Non-Residents of Canada; NR301 — Declaration of Eligibility for Benefits under a Tax Treaty for a Non-Resident Taxpayer; NR302 — Declaration of Eligibility for Benefits under a Tax Treaty for a Partnership with Non-Resident Partner; NR303 — Declaration of Eligibility for Benefits under a Tax Treaty for a Hybrid Entity; NRTA1 — Authorization for Non-Resident Tax Exemption.

Guides: T4061 Non-Resident Withholding Tax Guide.

Income Tax Folios: *Secondary* — S5-F1-C1 Determining an Individual's Residence Status.

Income Tax Technical News: Issue No. 35, Treaty Residence — Resident of Convenience.

Information Circulars: IC 76-12R6 Applicable rate of Part XIII tax on amounts paid or credited to persons in countries with which Canada has a Tax Convention; IC 77-16R4 Non-resident income tax (para. 15); IC 87-2R International Transfer Pricing.

Interpretation Bulletins: *Secondary* — IT-119R4 Debts of shareholders, certain persons connected with shareholders, etc; IT-168R3 Athletes and players employed by football, hockey and similar clubs; IT-500R Registered retirement savings plans (maturing after June 29, 1978) — Death of annuitant after June 29, 1978.

Cases: The word "credit" in s. 212(1) should be interpreted as "making available to" rather than defined in terms of the accounting entries that had been made in respect of capitalized interest. *La Compagnie Minière Quebec Cartier*, 84 DTC 1348 (T.C.C.)

Treaties often contain definitions of their own for certain purposes; where these conflict with definitions under the *Income Tax Act*, the treaty will prevail. *The Queen v. Saint John Shipbuilding and Dry Dock Co. Ltd.*, 80 DTC 6272 (F.C.A.). See also *The Queen v. Melford Developments Inc.*, 82 DTC 6281 (S.C.C.)

► 212(1)(a) ◄

(a) **Management fee** — a management or administration fee or charge;

Related Regulations: Part II.

Related Sections: S. 212(4) Interpretation of "management or administration fee or charge".

Canadian Tax Foundation: Purdy and Zanchelli, *Calculating and Supporting Management Fees (A Departure from the "Back of the Envelope" Approach)*, 1996 Canadian Tax Journal 1:157–187.

Tax Profile: September 2011 — Acquisition of Canadian Business by Non-Residents.

Tax Topics: No. 2409, Payment of Management or Administration Fees to a Non-Resident: Withholding, Reporting, and Remitting.

Forms: NR4 Sum. — Return of Amounts Paid or Credited to Non-Residents of Canada; NR4 — Statement of Amounts Paid or Credited to Non-Residents of Canada.

Information Circulars: IC 77-16R4 Non-resident income tax (paras. 15 and 16).

Interpretation Bulletins: *Primary* — IT-468R Management or administration fees paid to non-residents.

Cases: A non-resident portfolio investment fund manager made all the taxpayer's investment planning decisions and the taxpayer's profitability depended directly upon such decisions, which could be characterized as management tasks. *Peter Cundill & Associates Limited*, 91 DTC 5543 (F.C.A.), affirming 91 DTC 5085 (F.C.T.D.).

► 212(1)(b) ◄

(b) **Interest** — interest that

(i) is not fully exempt interest and is paid or payable

(A) to a person with whom the payer is not dealing at arm's length, or

(B) in respect of a debt or other obligation to pay an amount to a person with whom the payer is not dealing at arm's length, or

(ii) is participating debt interest;

Editorial Note: Paragraph 212(1)(*b*) imposes withholding tax on certain interest payments paid to a non-resident. Generally, withholding tax is imposed if the interest is not "fully exempt interest" and is payable to a person who is not dealing at arm's length with the payer. "Fully exempt interest" is defined in s. 212(3) and generally includes interest paid or payable by a federal, provincial or municipal government entity and mortgage interest in respect of non-Canadian real estate. "Arm's length" is defined as in s. 251(1). In addition, withholding tax is generally payable if the interest is "participating debt interest", which is defined in s. 212(3) to include most forms of interest that is contingent or dependent on the use of or production from Canadian property or is computed by reference to revenue, profit or another similar criterion or by reference to dividends paid to any shareholder of the payer.

In addition, if interest is not fully exempt interest and is paid in respect of a debt owed to a person who is not dealing at arm's length with the payer, such interest is subject to withholding tax even if the interest is payable to a person dealing at arm's length and is not participating interest. This provision deals with the situation where interest is payable to a person who is different from the owner of the principal of the debt and is a direct result of the Federal Court of Appeal decision in *Lehigh Cement* (2010 DTC 5081).

History: S. 212(1)(*b*)(i) was replaced by S.C. 2013, c. 34, s. 347(5), applicable to interest that is paid or payable by a person or partnership (referred to below as the "payer") to a person or partnership (referred to below as the "recipient") on or after March 16, 2011, unless:

(a) the interest is paid in respect of a debt or obligation incurred by the payer before March 16, 2011; and

(b) the recipient acquired the entitlement to the interest as a consequence of an agreement or other arrangement entered into by the recipient, and evidenced in writing, before March 16, 2011.

S. 212(1)(*b*)(i) formerly read:

(i) is not fully exempt interest, and is paid or payable to a person with whom the payer is not dealing at arm's length, or

S. 212(1)(*b*) was replaced by S.C. 2013, c. 34, s. 347(4), deemed to have come into force on January 1, 2008, and formerly read:

(*b*) *Interest* — interest that

(i) is not fully exempt interest, and is paid or payable to a person with whom the payer is not dealing at arm's length, or

(ii) is participating debt interest;

Related Regulations: 806; 806.1; 806.2; 6208; 7900.

Related Sections: s. 204, "qualified investment"; s. 212(3) Interest — definitions; 212(6) Interest on provincial bonds from wholly-owned subsidiaries; 212(7) Where s. (6) does not apply; s. 212(8) Bonds issued after December 20, 1960 in exchange for earlier bonds; s. 212(14) Certificate of exemption; s. 212(15) Certain obligations; s. 212(18) Return by financial institutions and registered securities dealers; s. 212(19) Tax on registered securities dealers; s. 214(2) Income and capital combined; s. 214(3)(*e*) Deemed payments; s. 214(6) Deemed interest; 214(7) Sale of obligation; 214(7.1) Idem; s. 214(8)(a) Meaning of "excluded obligation"; s. 214(11) Application of para. 212(1)(b); s. 214(15) Standby charges and guarantee fees; s. 218 Loan to wholly-owned subsidiary — direct borrowing by wholly-owned subsidiary whose principal business is money-lending; s. 240 Definition of "taxable obligation" and "non-taxable obligation"; s. 248(10) Series of transactions; s. 248(12) Identical properties; s. 251(1) Arm's length; s. 260(1), "securities lending arrangement"; s. 260(8) Non-resident withholding tax; ITAR s. 10(5) Certificates of exemption.

Canadian Petroleum Tax Journal: Café Annie's Tasty Inbound Financing, Jim McKee, 2002, Vol. 15, No. 1.

Canadian Tax Foundation: Lang, *Make-Whole Amounts After Withholding*, 2015 Canadian Tax Highlights 23(4):6; Kopstein and Pantry, *Subparagraph 212(1)(b)(vii) Withholding Tax Exemption*, 2005 Conference Report 15:1–44; Lobsinger, *Current Cases: Federal Court of Appeal — Subparagraph 212(1)(b)(vii) and Amendments to Loan Agreements (General Electric Capital Equipment Finance Inc. v. The Queen, 2002 DTC 6735)*, 2002 Canadian Tax Journal 2:696–698.

International Tax: No. 101, One and Done: CRA Ruling Holds That a Payment of Contingent Interest Will Subject All Future Interest Payments to Withholding Tax.

Tax Profile: March 2013 — Non-Resident Investment in Canadian Real Estate; February 2013 — The Purchase of US Businesses by Canadians; September 2011 — Acquisition of Canadian Business by Non-Residents; July 2011 — OECD Discussion Paper on Beneficial Ownership; April 2011 — Proposed Changes to Canada's Tax Laws — The Canadian Government Reacts To Close Perceived Abuses; September 2010 — Recent Tax Developments Affecting Non-Residents; November 2008 — 2008 Cross-Border Developments in Canada; October 2008 — Tax Consequences of Debt Restructuring and Workouts in Canada; August 2008 — Fifth Protocol to the Canada–U.S. Tax Convention: A Canadian Perspective; October 2007 — Important Changes Announced to the Canada — U.S. Income Tax Convention; October 2007 — Will Canadian Unlimited Liability Companies Survive?; May 2007 — Impact of 2007 Federal Budget on Cross-Border Transactions; May 2007 — Why Canada Should End Roadblock to Foreign Private Equity; March 2007 — Beneficial Ownership: An International Perspective; July 2005 — Alberta Introduces Alberta Unlimited Liability Corporations; November 2003 — Revenue Canada Round Table.

Tax Topics: No. 2075, 2011 Canadian Tax Foundation Roundtable; No. 1971-72, 2009 Canadian Tax Foundation Conference: Wizards, Tiny Taxes and "Evil" Kirk; No. 1929, Canada — U.S. Tax Treaty Protocol — Coming into Force Update; No. 1916, Withholding Tax Implications of Participating Interest and Convertible Debt; No. 1863, Amendments Affecting Non-Resident Withholding Tax; No. 1821, Recent CRA Rulings Relating to Subparagraph 212(1)(*b*)(vii); No. 1812, Beneficial Ownership: Indofood Run Wild.

Forms: NR4 Sum. — Return of Amounts Paid or Credited to Non-Residents of Canada; NR4 — Statement of Amounts Paid or Credited to Non-Residents of Canada.

Income Tax Technical News: Issue No. 44, Payments by ULC; Issue No. 44, Payments by a ULC to an LLC in 2009; Issue No. 38, Application of Subparagraph 212(1)(b)(VII); Issue No. 30, Withholding Tax on Interest.

Information Circulars: IC 76-12R6 Applicable rate of Part XIII tax on amounts paid or credited to persons in countries with which Canada has a Tax Convention; IC 77-16R4 Non-resident income tax (paras. 17 to 33).

Interpretation Bulletins: *Primary* — IT-155R3 Exemption from non-resident tax on interest payable on certain bonds, debentures, notes, hypothecs or similar obligations; IT-361R3 Exemption from tax on interest payments to non-residents.

Cases: Construction interest capitalized under s. 18(3.1) lost its character as "interest" and was therefore not subject to Part XIII tax when paid out to a non-resident lender. *Eastern Success Co. Ltd. v. The Queen*, 2004 DTC 3521 (T.C.C.)

The taxpayers owned fishing trawlers. A non-resident corporation, U, provided financing for the ships and marketed and sold all of the taxpayers' products in Denmark in return for a commission. Interest paid to U was subject to withholding tax but since the taxpayers were carrying on a business in Denmark, through U as their agent, s. 212(1)(*b*)(iii)(E) decreased their withholding tax liability. *Kinguk Trawl Inc. et al. v. The Queen*, 2003 DTC 5168 (F.C.A.), reversing 2002 DTC 1399 (T.C.C.)

The taxpayer's predecessor issued subordinated promissory notes to non-resident corporations. The terms of the notes were subsequently altered to such an extent as to result in the creation of completely new obligations, which were outside the exempting provisions of s. 212(1)(b)(vii). *General Electric Capital Equipment Finance Inc. v. The Queen*, 2002 DTC 6734 (F.C.A.), affirming 2000 DTC 6513 (F.C.T.D.)

A U.S. real estate company selling U.S. land to Canadians in Washington was not carrying on business in Canada, and was therefore subject to withholding tax on the interest portion of payments made by purchasers. *Sudden Valley Inc. v. The Queen*, 76 DTC 6448 (F.C.A.).

► 212(1)(c) ◄

(c) Estate or trust income — income of or from an estate or a trust to the extent that the amount

(i) is included in computing the income of the non-resident person under subsection 104(13), except to the extent that the amount is deemed by subsection 104(21) to be a taxable capital gain of the non-resident person, or

(ii) can reasonably be considered (having regard to all the circumstances including the terms and conditions of the estate or trust arrangement) to be a distribution of, or derived from, an amount received by the estate or trust as, on account of, in lieu of payment of or in satisfaction of, a dividend on a share of the capital stock of a corporation resident in Canada, other than a taxable dividend;

Related Regulations: Part II.

Related Sections: S. 53(2)(*h*) Amounts to be deducted — Capital interest in a trust; 132(5.1) TCP gains distribution; 132(5.2) Application of subsection (5.1); 210 [Interpretation]; 210.2 Tax on income of trust; 210.3 Where no designated beneficiaries; 212(9) Exemptions; 212(10) Trust beneficiaries residing outside of Canada; 212(11) Payment to beneficiary as income of trust; s. 212(17) Exception; s. 214(3) Deemed payments; Part XIII.2 (s. 218.3) Non-Resident investors in Canadian mutual funds; s. 250.1 Non-resident person's taxation year and income.

Canadian Tax Foundation: Shew and Cho, *Withholding Tax on Capital Distributions to Non-Residents*, 2017 Canadian Tax Focus 7(3):11.

Tax Profile: September 2011 — Acquisition of Canadian Business by Non-Residents; April 2004 — Mutual Funds and the 2004 Budget.

Forms: NR4 Sum. — Return of Amounts Paid or Credited to Non-Residents of Canada; NR4 — Statement of Amounts Paid or Credited to Non-Residents of Canada.

Information Circulars: IC 76-12R6 Applicable rate of Part XIII tax on amounts paid or credited to persons in countries with which Canada has a Tax Convention; IC 77-16R4 Non-resident income tax (paras. 34 to 37).

Interpretation Bulletins: *Primary* — IT-465R Non-resident beneficiaries of trusts. *Secondary* — IT-342R Trusts — Income payable to beneficiaries.

Cases: Estate income credited but not paid to a non-resident co-executor was held to be part of the non-resident's income. *Berry v. M.N.R.*, 81 DTC 224 (T.R.B.)

Income paid by a trust to a non-resident who was not a beneficiary of the trust under Quebec law was nonetheless held to be subject to withholding tax. *Doriga Trust v. M.N.R.*, 81 DTC 85 (T.R.B.)

► 212(1)(d) ◄

(d) Rents, royalties, etc. — rent, royalty or similar payment, including, but not so as to restrict the generality of the foregoing, any payment

(i) for the use of or for the right to use in Canada any property, invention, trade-name, patent, trade-mark, design or model, plan, secret formula, process or other thing whatever,

(ii) for information concerning industrial, commercial or scientific experience where the total amount payable as consideration for that information is dependent in whole or in part on

(A) the use to be made of, or the benefit to be derived from, that information,

(B) production or sales of goods or services, or

(C) profits,

(iii) for services of an industrial, commercial or scientific character performed by a non-resident person where the total amount payable as consideration for those services is dependent in whole or in part on

(A) the use to be made of, or the benefit to be derived from, those services,

(B) production or sales of goods or services, or

(C) profits,

but not including a payment made for services performed in connection with the sale of property or the negotiation of a contract,

(iv) unless paragraph (*i*) applies to the amount, made pursuant to an agreement between a person resident in Canada and a non-resident person under which the non-resident person agrees not to use or not to permit any other person to use any thing referred to in subparagraph (i) or any information referred to in subparagraph (ii), or

(v) that was dependent on the use of or production from property in Canada whether or not it was an instalment on the sale price of the property, but not including an instalment on the sale price of agricultural land,

but not including

(vi) a royalty or similar payment on or in respect of a copyright in respect of the production or reproduction of any literary, dramatic, musical or artistic work,

(vii) a payment in respect of the use by a railway company or by a person whose principal business is that of a common carrier of property that is railway rolling stock as defined in the definition "rolling stock" in section 2 of the *Railway Act*

(A) if the payment is made for the use of that property for a period or periods not expected to exceed in the aggregate 90 days in any 12 month period, or

(B) in any other case, if the payment is made pursuant to an agreement in writing entered into before November 19, 1974;

(viii) a payment made under a *bona fide* cost-sharing arrangement under which the person making the payment shares on a reasonable basis with one or more non-resident persons research and development expenses in exchange for an interest, or for civil law a right, in any or all property or other things of value that may result therefrom,

(ix) a rental payment for the use of or the right to use outside Canada any tangible, or for civil law corporeal, property,

(x) any payment made to a person with whom the payer is dealing at arm's length, to the extent that the amount thereof is deductible in computing the income of the payer under Part I from a business carried on by the payer in a country other than Canada,

(xi) a payment made to a person with whom the payer is dealing at arm's length for the use of or the right to use property that is

(A) an aircraft,

(B) furniture, fittings or equipment attached to an aircraft,

(C) a spare part for property described in clause (A) or (B),

(D) air navigation equipment utilized in the provision of services under the *Civil Air Navigation Services Commercialization Act* or computer software the use of which is necessary for the operation of that equipment that is used by the payer for no other purpose; or

(xii) an amount to which subsection (5) would apply if that subsection were read without reference to "to the extent that the amount relates to that use or reproduction";

History: S. 212(1)(*d*)(viii) and (ix) were replaced by S.C. 2013, c. 34, s. 157(1), in force June 26, 2013, and formerly read:

(viii) a payment made under a *bona fide* cost-sharing arrangement under which the person making the payment shares on a reasonable basis with one or more non-resident persons research and development expenses in exchange for an interest in any or all property or other things of value that may result therefrom,

(ix) a rental payment for the use of or the right to use outside Canada any corporeal property,

S. 212(1)(*d*)(iv) was replaced by S.C. 2013, c. 34, s. 347(7), applicable to amounts paid or credited after October 7, 2003, and formerly read:

(iv) made pursuant to an agreement between a person resident in Canada and a non-resident person under which the non-resident person agrees not to use or not to permit any other person to use any thing referred to in subparagraph (i) or any information referred to in subparagraph (ii), or

S. 212(1)(*d*)(xi)(D) was added by S.C. 2013, c. 34, s. 347(8), applicable to payments made after July 2003.

S. 212(1)(*d*)(xii) was added by S.C. 2013, c. 34, s. 347(9), applicable to the 2000 and subsequent taxation years.

Related Regulations: 202(1), (3).

Related Sections: S. 212(5) Motion picture films; s. 212(9) Exemptions; s. 212(16) Payments for temporary use of rolling stock; s. 216 Alternatives re rents and timber royalties; s. 251(1) Arm's length.

Canadian Tax Foundation: Wang and Cocco, *Exclusive Distribution Rights: Not Royalties*, 2018 Canadian Tax Highlights 26(5):2–3; Ormrod and Bain, *Taxation Aspects of Cloud Computing*, 2012 Conference Report 18:1–25; Brady and Marcovitz, *Property Leasing into Canada: How to Open a Closed Market*, 2009 Canadian Tax Journal 3:586–606; Bienvenue, *Payments in Lieu of Rent: "Taxable Intentions"?*, 2004 Tax for the Owner-Manager 4(4):4–5; Gonthier, *Les déclinaisons de la notion de redevance selon l'impôt de la partie XIII : Restrictions au concept élargi de redevance*, 2003 Canadian Tax Journal 6:2119–2190; Gonthier, *Les déclinaisons de la notion de redevance selon l'impôt de la partie XIII : Redevance et concept élargi de redevance*, 2003 Canadian Tax Journal 5:1825–1907; Osborne, *Revisiting Royalties in the Age of Electronic Commerce*, 1999 Canadian Tax Journal 2:410–455.

Tax Profile: January 2013 — Canadian Taxation of E-Commerce — An Overview; March 2012 — Beneficial Ownership: Another Canadian Victory for Taxpayers; September 2011 — Acquisition of Canadian Business by Non-Residents; July 2011 — OECD Discussion Paper on Beneficial Ownership; August 2008 — Fifth Protocol to the Canada–U.S. Tax Convention: A Canadian Perspective; May 2007 — Impact of 2007 Federal Budget on Cross-Border Transactions; May 2007 — Why Canada Should End Roadblock to Foreign Private Equity; March 2007 — Beneficial Ownership: An International Perspective; December 2006 — "Beneficial Ownership" under Canadian Tax Treaties — Canadian Revenue Authorities Take Aim; March 2006 — Some Tax Considerations for Investing in Silicon Valley North.

Tax Topics: No. 2009, The Federal Court of Appeal Decision in *GlaxoSmithKline Inc. v. The Queen*; No. 1965, Potential Double Taxation of Rental Income to Non-Residents?; No. 1812, Beneficial Ownership: Indofood Run Wild; No. 1719, Withholding Taxes — Purchase of Software from a Non-Resident; No. 1524, Income Taxation and Electronic Commerce.

Forms: NR4 Sum. — Return of Amounts Paid or Credited to Non-Residents of Canada; NR4 — Statement of Amounts Paid or Credited to Non-Residents of Canada; NR6 — Undertaking to File an Income Tax Return by a Non-Resident Receiving Rent from Real Property or Receiving a Timber Royalty for Tax Year ____.

Income Tax Technical News: Issue No. 25, E-Commerce; Issue No. 23, Computer Software.

Information Circulars: IC 76-12R6 Applicable rate of Part XIII tax on amounts paid or credited to persons in countries with which Canada has a Tax Convention; IC 77-16R4 Non-resident income tax (paras. 38 to 44).

Interpretation Bulletins: *Primary* — IT-303 Know-how and similar payments to non-residents; IT-494 Hire of ships and aircraft from non-residents. *Secondary* — IT-393R2 Election re tax on rents and timber royalties — Non-residents; IT-438R2 Crown charges — Resource properties in Canada.

Tax Window Files: Paragraph 212(1)(d)(vi), *January 5, 2018*, CRA Document No. 2017-0697811E5; Compensation for loss of rental income paid to non-resident, *March 22, 2017*, CRA Document No. 2015-0570011E5; Withholding on incentive payments to nonresidents, *September 24, 2015*, CRA Document No. 2013-0495611E5.

Cases: When the taxpayer paid royalties to a Netherlands company, the 10% withholding rate in the Netherlands treaty applied. Although the recipient paid 90% of the royalties to its parent company (located in a country which did not have a Canadian treaty) the parent was not the beneficial owner of the royalties since it had no right to control them. *Velcro Canada Inc. v. The Queen*, 2012 DTC 1100 (T.C.C.)

The phrase "in lieu of rent" in s. 212(1)(*d*) includes compensation for the anticipatory breach of a rental agreement. *Transocean Offshore Limited v. The Queen*, 2005 DTC 5201 (F.C.A.), affirming 2004 DTC 2915 (T.C.C.)

A "one-time license fee" accompanying an application for a franchise was not a rent or a royalty, but an application fee, and was not subject to Part XIII tax. *Zainul et al. v. The Queen*, 2004 DTC 3015 (T.C.C.)

The taxpayer had a license to reproduce and distribute software and paid royalties in respect of each software license agreement entered into. The royalties were exempt under s. 212(1)(*d*)(vi). *Syspro Software Ltd. v. The Queen*, 2003 DTC 931 (T.C.C.)

A payment for the use of a computer source code was made "on or in respect of a copyright in respect of the production or reproduction of any literary . . . work", and, hence, was exempt from Part XIII non-resident withholding tax under s. 212(1)(d)(vi). *Angoss International Limited v. The Queen*, 99 DTC 567 (T.C.C.)

As they were made for services performed "in connection with the sale of property", the commissions paid by the taxpayer to its non-resident purchasing agents on the basis of a percentage of the amount invoiced as the price of the toys purchased by them were not subject to withholding tax. *Hasbro Canada Inc. v. The Queen*, 98 DTC 2129 (T.C.C.)

When a taxpayer rented barges from a non-resident Bahamian corporation carrying on business in the U.S., the 25% withholding rate applied rather than the 10% rate under the Canada–U.S. Convention since the corporation's liability for U.S. tax was source income based whereas the grounds for taxation under the Convention were world-wide income based. *The Queen v. Crown Forest Industries Limited et al.*, 95 DTC 5389 (S.C.C.), reversing 94 DTC 6107 (F.C.A.) and 92 DTC 6305 (F.C.T.D.)

The taxpayer agreed to sell moulds under an agreement entitling it to lease them back for 3 years and buy them back afterward for $1. Despite its form, this agreement was a deferred purchase pursuant to which the taxpayer was paying for capital property by way of instalments and the non-resident withholding tax was not exigible. *Viceroy Rubber and Plastics Limited v. M.N.R.*, 93 DTC 347 (T.C.C.)

Treaties often contain definitions of their own for certain purposes; where these conflict with definitions under the *Income Tax Act*, the treaty will prevail. *The Queen v. Saint John Shipbuilding and Dry Dock Co. Ltd.*, 80 DTC 6272 (F.C.A.). See also *The Queen v. Melford Developments Inc.*, 82 DTC 6281 (S.C.C.)

Payments described in subparagraphs 212(1)(*d*)(i) to 212(1)(*d*)(v) are subject to withholding whether or not they are payments of a type that might traditionally be considered royalty payments. *The Queen v. Farmparts Distributing Ltd.*, 80 DTC 6157 (F.C.A.).

► 212(1)(e) ◄

(e) **Timber royalties** — a timber royalty in respect of a timber resource property or a timber limit in Canada (which, for the purposes of this Part, includes any consideration for a right under or pursuant to which a right to cut or take timber from a timber resource property or a timber limit in Canada is obtained or derived, to the extent that the consideration is dependent on, or computed by reference to, the amount of timber cut or taken);

Related Regulations: Part II.

Related Sections: S. 13(21), "timber resource property"; s. 212(13)(*b*) Rent and other payments; s. 216 Alternatives re rents and timber royalties.

Forms: NR4 Sum. — Return of Amounts Paid or Credited to Non-Residents of Canada; NR4 — Statement of Amounts Paid or Credited to Non-Residents of Canada.

Information Circulars: IC 77-16R4 Non-resident income tax (para. 6).

Interpretation Bulletins: *Secondary* — IT-393R2 Election re tax on rents and timber royalties — Non-residents.

► 212(1)(f) ◄

(f) **Alimony** — (Repealed by S.C. 1997, c. 25, s. 63(1).)

► 212(1)(g) ◄

(g) **Patronage dividend** — a patronage dividend, that is, a payment made pursuant to an allocation in proportion to patronage as defined by section 135 or an amount that would, under subsection 135(7), be included in computing the non-resident person's income if that person were resident in Canada;

Related Regulations: Part II.

Forms: NR4 Sum. — Return of Amounts Paid or Credited to Non-Residents of Canada; NR4 — Statement of Amounts Paid or Credited to Non-Residents of Canada.

Information Circulars: IC 77-16R4 Non-resident income tax (para. 6).

Interpretation Bulletins: *Secondary* — IT-362R Patronage dividends.

► 212(1)(h) ◄

(h) **Pension benefits** — a payment of a superannuation or pension benefit, other than

(i) (Repealed by 1996, c. 21, s. 55(1).)

(ii) an amount distributed from a pooled registered pension plan that has been designated by the administrator of the plan in accordance with subsection 147.5(18),

(iii) an amount or payment referred to in subsection 81(1) to the extent that that amount or payment would not, if the non-resident person had been resident in Canada throughout the taxation year in which the payment was made, be included in computing that person's income,

(iii.1) the portion of the payment that is transferred by the payer on behalf of the non-resident person, pursuant to an authorization in prescribed form, to a pooled registered pension plan, registered pension plan, registered retirement savings plan, registered retirement income fund or specified pension plan and that

(A) because of any of subsections 146(21), 147.3(9) and 147.5(22) would not, if the non-resident person had been resident in Canada throughout the taxation year in which the payment was made, be included in computing the non-resident person's income, or

(B) by reason of paragraph 60(*j*) or (*j*.2) would, if the non-resident person had been resident in Canada throughout the year, be deductible in computing the non-resident person's income for the year,

(iii.2) an amount referred to in paragraph 110(1)(*f*) to the extent that the amount would, if the non-resident person had been resident in Canada throughout the taxation year in which the amount was paid, be deductible in computing that person's taxable income or that of the spouse or common-law partner of that person,

(iv) in the case of a payment described in section 57, that portion of the payment that would, by virtue of that section, not be included in the recipient's income for the taxation year in which it was received, if the recipient were resident in Canada throughout that year, or

(iv.1) the portion of the payment that is transferred by the payer on behalf of the non-resident person, pursuant to an authorization in prescribed form, to acquire an annuity contract in circumstances to which subsection 146(21) applies,

except such portion, if any, of the payment as may reasonably be regarded as attributable to services rendered by the person, to or in respect of whom the payment is made, in taxation years

(v) during which the person at no time was resident in Canada, and

(vi) throughout which the person was not employed, or was only occasionally employed, in Canada;

History: S. 212(1)(*h*)(iii.1), the portion before clause (A) was replaced by S.C. 2017, c. 33, s. 74(1), deemed in force January 1, 2010, except that in its application before December 14, 2012, the portion of subparagraph 212(1)(*h*)(iii.1) of the Act before clause (A), as enacted, is to be read without reference to "pooled registered pension plan". S. 212(1)(*h*)(iii.1), the portion before clause (A) formerly read:

(iii.1) the portion of the payment that is transferred by the payer on behalf of the non-resident person, pursuant to an authorization in prescribed form, to a pooled registered pension plan, registered pension plan, registered retirement savings plan or registered retirement income fund and that

S. 212(1)(*h*)(ii) was added by S.C. 2012, c. 31, s. 48(1), in force December 14, 2012.

S. 212(1)(*h*)(iii.1), the portion before clause (B) was replaced by S.C. 2012, c. 31, s. 48(2), in force December 14, 2012. S. 212(1)(*h*)(iii.1), the portion before clause (B) formerly read:

(iii.1) the portion of the payment that is transferred by the payer on behalf of the non-resident person, pursuant to an authorization in prescribed form, to a registered pension plan, registered retirement savings plan or registered retirement income fund and that

(A) because of subsection 146(21) or 147.3(9) would not, if the non-resident person had been resident in Canada throughout the taxation year in which the payment was made, be included in computing the non-resident person's income, or

Related Regulations: Part II; Part VIII.

Related Sections: S. 56(1)(*a*)(i) Pension benefits, unemployment insurance benefits, etc.; s. 128.1(10)(*a*)(viii) and (*g*) Definitions; s. 180.2(2) Tax payable; s. 180.2(4) Determination of amount to be withheld; s. 212(13)(*c*) Rent and other payments; s. 215(5) Regulations reducing deduction or withholding; s. 217 Alternative re Canadian benefits; s. 248(1), "common-law partner", "superannuation or pension benefit".

Forms: NR4 Sum. — Return of Amounts Paid or Credited to Non-Residents of Canada; NR4 — Statement of Amounts Paid or Credited to Non-Residents of Canada; NRTA1 — Authorization for Non-Resident Tax Exemption.

Information Circulars: IC 76-12R6 Applicable rate of Part XIII tax on amounts paid or credited to persons in countries with which Canada has a Tax Convention; IC 77-16R4 Non-resident income tax (para. 6).

Interpretation Bulletins: *Primary* — IT-76R2 Exempt portion of pension when employee has been a non-resident. *Secondary* — IT-397R Amounts excluded from income — Statutory exemptions and certain service or RCMP pensions, allowances and compensation; IT-451R Deemed disposition and acquisition on ceasing to be or becoming resident in Canada.

Cases: CCP payments received by a Swiss resident were subject to 25% withholding tax rather than the 15% rate provided in the Canada-Swiss Tax Convention since payments made pursuant to social security legislation do not constitute a "pension" under article 18 of the Convention. *Dumoulin v. The Queen*, 2001 DTC 999 (T.C.C.)

The taxpayers were NHL hockey players who were not resident in Canada, and were employed and paid by U.S. corporations. They played only a small number of their total games in Canada. The taxpayers were "only occasionally employed in Canada" within the meaning of s. 212(1)(*h*) and therefore, no Part XIII withholding tax was exigible in respect of their pension payments. *Nanne et al. v. The Queen*, 2000 DTC 1653 (T.C.C.)

Benefits accrued under a pension fund to the benefit of former employees who were non-residents were paid at their direction to a Canadian RRSP. No withholding tax was payable as there was no payment to a non-resident in satisfaction of a pension benefit. *Forest et al., Trustees of the Academic Pension Plan of the University of Alberta v. The Queen*, 80 DTC 6149 (F.C.T.D.).

▶ 212(1)(i) ◀

(i) Restrictive covenant amount — an amount that would, if the non-resident person had been resident in Canada throughout the taxation year in which the amount was received or receivable, be required by paragraph 56(1)(*m*) or subsection 56.4(2) to be included in computing the non-resident person's income for the taxation year;

History: S. 212(1)(*i*) was added by S.C. 2013, c. 34, s. 347(10), applicable to amounts paid or credited after October 7, 2003.

International Tax: No. 99, Cross-Border Restrictive Covenants.

Cases: The transaction was a share sale by the taxpayer and other shareholders to a third party, including a Letter Agreement wherein the taxpayer agreed to waive its veto right under a Unanimous Shareholders Agreement. The consideration paid under the Letter Agreement to the taxpayer was $3,000,000 and the taxes in dispute were withheld from that amount. While the Letter Agreement was not a necessary precondition to the share sale transaction, it "affected" or was "intended to affect" the proposed disposition of shares, as set out in the definition of "restrictive covenant" in subsection 56.4(1), and was not eligible for treaty relief of withholding taxes. *Pangaea One Acquisition Holdings XII S.À.R.L v. The Queen*, 2018 DTC 1113 (TCC) (under appeal)

▶ 212(1)(j) ◀

(j) Benefits — any benefit described in any of subparagraphs 56(1)(*a*)(iii) to (vi), any amount described in paragraph 56(1)(*x*) or (*z*) (other than an amount transferred under circumstances in which subsection 207.6(7) applies) or the purchase price of an interest in a retirement compensation arrangement;

Related Regulations: 202(2), (3); Part VIII.

Related Sections: S. 128.1(10)(*a*)(ix) and (*h*); s. 214(3)(*b*.1) Deemed payments; s. 215(5) Regulations reducing deduction or withholding; s. 217 Alternative re Canadian benefits.

Forms: NR4 Sum. — Return of Amounts Paid or Credited to Non-Residents of Canada; NR4 — Statement of Amounts Paid or Credited to Non-Residents of Canada.

Information Circulars: IC 77-16R4 Non-resident income tax (para. 6).

Interpretation Bulletins: *Secondary* — IT-451R Deemed disposition and acquisition on ceasing to be or becoming resident in Canada.

▶ 212(1)(j.1) ◀

(j.1) Retiring allowances — a payment of any allowance described in subparagraph 56(1)(*a*)(ii), except

(i) such portion, if any, of the payment as may reasonably be regarded as attributable to services rendered by the person, to or in respect of whom the payment is made, in taxation years

(A) during which the person at no time was resident in Canada, and

(B) throughout which the person was not employed, or was only occasionally employed, in Canada, and

(ii) the portion of the payment transferred by the payer on behalf of the non-resident person pursuant to an authorization in prescribed form to a registered pension plan or to a registered retirement savings plan under which the non-resident person is the annuitant (within the meaning assigned by subsection 146(1)) that would, if the non-resident person had been resident in Canada throughout the year, be deductible in computing the income of the non-resident person by virtue of paragraph 60(*j*.1);

Related Sections: S. 128.1(10)(*d*) Definitions; 146(21.2) Specified pension plan — account; s. 215(5) Regulations reducing deduction or withholding; s. 248(1), "retiring allowance".

Income Tax Folios: *Primary* — S2-F1-C2 Retiring Allowances.

Information Circulars: IC 77-16R4 Non-resident income tax (para. 6).

Interpretation Bulletins: *Secondary* — IT-451R Deemed disposition and acquisition on ceasing to be or becoming resident in Canada.

► 212(1)(k) ◄

(k) Supplementary unemployment benefit plan payments — a payment by a trustee under a registered supplementary unemployment benefit plan;

Related Regulations: Part II.

Related Sections: S. 56(1)(*g*) Supplementary unemployment benefit plan; s. 128.1(10)(*a*)(xi) Definitions; s. 145(1), "registered supplementary unemployment benefit plan"; s. 212(13)(*e*) Rent and other payments; s. 215(5) Regulations reducing deduction or withholding; s. 217 Alternative re Canadian benefits.

Forms: NR4 Sum. — Return of Amounts Paid or Credited to Non-Residents of Canada; NR4 — Statement of Amounts Paid or Credited to Non-Residents of Canada.

► 212(1)(l) ◄

(l) Registered retirement savings plan payments — a payment out of or under a registered retirement savings plan or a plan referred to in subsection 146(12) as an "amended plan" that would, if the non-resident person had been resident in Canada throughout the taxation year in which the payment was made, be required by section 146 to be included in computing the income of the non-resident person for the year, other than the portion thereof that

(i) has been transferred by the payer on behalf of the non-resident person pursuant to an authorization in prescribed form

(A) to a registered retirement savings plan under which the non-resident person is the annuitant (within the meaning assigned by subsection 146(1)),

(B) to acquire an annuity described in subparagraph 60(*l*)(ii) under which the non-resident person is the annuitant, or

(C) to a carrier (within the meaning assigned by subsection 146.3(1)) as consideration for a registered retirement income fund under which the non-resident person is the annuitant (within the meaning assigned by subsection 146.3(1)), and

(ii) would, if the non-resident person had been resident in Canada throughout the year, be deductible in computing the income of the non-resident person for the year by virtue of paragraph 60(*l*);

Related Regulations: Part II; Part VIII.

Related Sections: S. 56(1)(*h*) Registered retirement savings plan, etc.; s. 128.1(10)(*a*)(i) Definitions; s. 146(1), "registered retirement savings plan", "retirement savings plan"; s. 146(8) Benefits taxable; s. 146(9) Where disposition of property by trust; s. 146(16) Transfer of funds; s. 212(13)(*e*) Rent and other payments; s. 214(3)(*c*) Deemed payments; s. 215(5) Regulations reducing deduction or withholding; s. 217 Alternative re Canadian benefits.

Forms: NR4 Sum. — Return of Amounts Paid or Credited to Non-Residents of Canada; NR4 — Statement of Amounts Paid or Credited to Non-Residents of Canada.

Information Circulars: IC 76-12R6 Applicable rate of Part XIII tax on amounts paid or credited to persons in countries with which Canada has a Tax Convention; IC 77-16R4 Non-resident income tax (para. 6).

Interpretation Bulletins: *Secondary* — IT-451R Deemed disposition and acquisition on ceasing to be or becoming resident in Canada.

► 212(1)(m) ◄

(m) Deferred profit sharing plan payments — a payment under a deferred profit sharing plan or a plan referred to in subsection 147(15) as a "revoked plan" that would, if the non-resident person had been resident in Canada throughout the taxation year in which the payment was made, be required by section 147, if it were read without reference to subsections 147(10.1) and (20), to be included in computing the non-resident person's income for the year, other than the portion thereof that is transferred by the payer on behalf of the non-resident person, pursuant to an authorization in prescribed form, to a registered pension plan or registered retirement savings plan and that

(i) by reason of subsection 147(20) would not, if the non-resident person had been resident in Canada throughout the year, be included in computing the non-resident person's income, or

(ii) by reason of paragraph 60(*j*.2) would, if the non-resident person had been resident in Canada throughout the year, be deductible in computing the non-resident person's income for the year;

Related Regulations: Part II; Part VIII.

Related Sections: S. 56(1)(*i*) Deferred profit sharing plan; s. 128.1(10)(*a*)(iv) Definitions; 146(21.2) Specified pension plan — account; s. 147(1), "deferred profit sharing plan"; s. 147(10) Amounts received taxable; s. 147(10.1) Single payment on retirement, etc; s. 147(12) Exemption of employee contributions to the plan; s. 147(15) Rules applicable to revoked plan; s. 147(19) Transfer to RPP, RRSP or DPSP; s. 212(13)(*e*) Rent and other payments; s. 214(3)(*d*) Deemed payments; s. 215(5) Regulations reducing deduction or withholding; s. 217 Alternative re Canadian benefits.

Forms: NR4 Sum. — Return of Amounts Paid or Credited to Non-Residents of Canada; NR4 — Statement of Amounts Paid or Credited to Non-Residents of Canada.

Information Circulars: IC 77-16R4 Non-resident income tax (para. 6).

Interpretation Bulletins: *Secondary* — IT-451R Deemed disposition and acquisition on ceasing to be or becoming resident in Canada.

► 212(1)(n) ◄

(n) Income-averaging annuity contract payments — a payment under an income-averaging annuity contract, any proceeds of the surrender, cancellation, redemption, sale or other disposition of an income-averaging annuity contract, or any amount deemed by subsection 61.1(1) to have been received by the non-resident person as proceeds of the disposition of an income-averaging annuity contract;

Related Regulations: Part II.

Related Sections: S. 56(1)(*d*) Annuity payments; s. 128.1(10)(*f*)(ii) Definitions; s. 212(13)(*e*) Rent and other payments; s. 214(3)(*b*) Deemed payments; s. 248(1), "income-averaging annuity contract".

Forms: NR4 Sum. — Return of Amounts Paid or Credited to Non-Residents of Canada; NR4 — Statement of Amounts Paid or Credited to Non-Residents of Canada.

Information Circulars: IC 76-12R6 Applicable rate of Part XIII tax on amounts paid or credited to persons in countries with which Canada has a Tax Convention; IC 77-16R4 Non-resident income tax (para. 6).

Interpretation Bulletins: *Secondary* — IT-451R Deemed disposition and acquisition on ceasing to be or becoming resident in Canada.

Cases: The commuted value of an income-averaging annuity contract paid to a U.S. resident is subject to Part XIII tax because such amounts do not fall under the exemption for "life-annuities" set out in the Protocol to the Canada–U.S. Tax Treaty. *Scott Estate v. The Queen*, 88 DTC 6012 (F.C.T.D.).

▶ 212(1)(o) ◀

(o) Other annuity payments — a payment under an annuity contract (other than a payment in respect of an annuity issued in the course of carrying on a life insurance business in a country other than Canada) to the extent of the amount in respect of the interest of the non-resident person in the contract that, if the non-resident person had been resident in Canada throughout the taxation year in which the payment was made,

(i) would be required to be included in computing the income of the non-resident person for the year, and

(ii) would not be deductible in computing that income;

Related Regulations: Part II.

Related Sections: S. 56(1)(*d*) Annuity payments; s. 60(*a*) Capital element of annuity payments; s. 128.1(10)(*f*)(i) Definitions; s. 148(9) Definitions; ITAR s. 10(4) Application of Part XIII of Amended Act.

Forms: NR4 Sum. — Return of Amounts Paid or Credited to Non-Residents of Canada; NR4 — Statement of Amounts Paid or Credited to Non-Residents of Canada.

Information Circulars: IC 76-12R6 Applicable rate of Part XIII tax on amounts paid or credited to persons in countries with which Canada has a Tax Convention; IC 77-16R4 Non-resident income tax (para. 6).

Interpretation Bulletins: *Secondary* — IT-451R Deemed disposition and acquisition on ceasing to be or becoming resident in Canada.

Cases: A taxpayer was liable for Part XIII tax that was not withheld from income annuities purchased prior to his departure from Canada. A letter to the insurance company holding the annuities informing them that the taxpayer was non-resident did not exonerate him from liability for the tax. *Tremblay v. M.N.R.*, 90 DTC 1120 (T.C.C.), 1124.

▶ 212(1)(p) ◀

(p) Former TFSA — an amount that would, if the non-resident person had been resident in Canada at the time at which the amount was paid, be required by paragraph 12(1)(*z.5*) to be included in computing the non-resident person's income for the taxation year that includes that time;

History: S. 212(1)(*p*) was replaced by S.C. 2009, c. 2, s. 73(1), applicable to the 2009 and subsequent taxation years. S. 212(1)(*p*) formerly read:

(*p*) *Payments from R.H.O.S.P.* — a payment out of or under a fund, plan or trust that was at the end of 1985 a registered home ownership savings plan (within the meaning assigned by paragraph 146.2(1)(*h*) of the *Income Tax Act*, chapter 148 of the Revised Statutes of Canada, 1952, as it read in its application to the 1985 taxation year), other than

(i) the portion of the payment that is a refund of an excess described in paragraph 146.2(7)(*a*) of that Act (as it read in its application to the 1985 taxation year) made on or before April 30, 1986, and

(ii) the portion of the payment that can reasonably be considered to be income of the fund, plan or trust after 1985;

Related Regulations: 202(2), (3).

Related Sections: S. 214(3)(*g*) Deemed payments.

Forms: NR4 Sum. — Return of Amounts Paid or Credited to Non-Residents of Canada; NR4 — Statement of Amounts Paid or Credited to Non-Residents of Canada.

Information Circulars: IC 77-16R4 Non-resident income tax (para. 6).

Interpretation Bulletins: *Secondary* — IT-451R Deemed disposition and acquisition on ceasing to be or becoming resident in Canada.

▶ 212(1)(q) ◀

(q) Registered retirement income fund payments — a payment out of or under a registered retirement income fund that would, if the non-resident person had been resident in Canada throughout the taxation year in which the payment was made, be required by section 146.3 to be included in computing the non-resident person's income for the year, other than the portion thereof that

(i) has been transferred by the payer on behalf of the non-resident person pursuant to an authorization in prescribed form

(A) to a registered retirement savings plan under which the non-resident person is the annuitant (within the meaning assigned by subsection 146(1)),

(B) to acquire an annuity described in subparagraph 60(*l*)(ii) under which the non-resident person is the annuitant, or

(C) to a carrier (within the meaning assigned by subsection 146.3(1)) as consideration for a registered retirement income fund under which the non-resident person is the annuitant (within the meaning assigned by subsection 146.3(1)), and

(ii) would, if the non-resident person had been resident in Canada throughout the year, be deductible in computing the non-resident person's income for the year by reason of paragraph 60(*l*);

Related Regulations: Part II.

Related Sections: S. 56(1)(*t*) Registered retirement income fund; s. 128.1(10)(*a*)(ii) Definitions; s. 146.3(1), "registered retirement income fund", "retirement income fund"; s. 146.3(5) Benefits taxable; s. 146.3(5.1) Amount included in income; s. 212(13)(*e*) Rent and other payments; s. 214(3)(*i*) Deemed payments; s. 215(5) Regulations reducing deduction or withholding; s. 217 Alternative re Canadian benefits.

Forms: NR4 Sum. — Return of Amounts Paid or Credited to Non-Residents of Canada; NR4 — Statement of Amounts Paid or Credited to Non-Residents of Canada.

Information Circulars: IC 76-12R6 Applicable rate of Part XIII tax on amounts paid or credited to persons in countries with which Canada has a Tax Convention; IC 77-16R4 Non-resident income tax (para. 6).

Interpretation Bulletins: *Secondary* — IT-451R Deemed disposition and acquisition on ceasing to be or becoming resident in Canada.

▶ 212(1)(r) ◀

(r) Registered education savings plan — a payment that is

(i) required by paragraph 56(1)(*q*) to be included in computing the non-resident person's income under Part I for a taxation year, and

(ii) not required to be included in computing the non-resident person's taxable income or taxable income earned in Canada for the year;

Related Regulations: 202(2), (3).

Related Sections: S. 128.1(10)(*a*)(iii) Definitions; 146.1 [Registered education savings plans].

Forms: NR4 Sum. — Return of Amounts Paid or Credited to Non-Residents of Canada; NR4 — Statement of Amounts Paid or Credited to Non-Residents of Canada.

Information Circulars: IC 77-16R4 Non-resident income tax (para. 6).

► 212(1)(r.1) ◄

(r.1) Registered disability savings plan — an amount that would, if the non-resident person had been resident in Canada throughout the taxation year in which the amount was paid, be required by paragraph 56(1)(*q.1*) to be included in computing the non-resident person's income for the taxation year;

Related Sections: S. 146.4(6) Taxation of disability assistance payments; s. 146.4(10) Non-compliance — cessation of registered status.

► 212(1)(s) ◄

(s) Home insulation or energy conversion grants — a grant under a prescribed program of the Government of Canada relating to home insulation or energy conversion;

Related Regulations: 202(2), (3); 224; 5500; 5501.

Related Sections: S. 12(1)(*u*) Home insulation or energy conversion grants; s. 56(1)(*s*) Grants under prescribed programs.

Forms: NR4 Sum. — Return of Amounts Paid or Credited to Non-Residents of Canada; NR4 — Statement of Amounts Paid or Credited to Non-Residents of Canada.

Information Circulars: IC 77-16R4 Non-resident income tax (para. 6).

► 212(1)(t) ◄

(t) NISA Fund No. 2 payments — a payment out of a NISA Fund No. 2 to the extent that that amount would, if Part I applied, be required by subsection 12(10.2) to be included in computing the person's income for a taxation year;

Related Sections: S. 12(10.2) NISA receipts; s. 128.1(10)(*l*) Definitions; s. 214(3)(*l*) Deemed payments; s. 248(1), "NISA Fund No. 2"; s. 249(1) Definition of "taxation year".

Information Circulars: IC 77-16R4 Non-resident income tax.

► 212(1)(u) ◄

(u) Amateur athlete trust payments — a payment in respect of an amateur athlete trust that would, if Part I applied, be required by section 143.1 to be included in computing the person's income for a taxation year;

Related Sections: S. 128.1(10)(*e*)(ii) Definitions; s. 143.1(1), "amateur athlete trust"; s. 143.1(2) Amounts included in beneficiary's income; s. 214(3)(*k*) Deemed payments; s. 248(1), "amateur athlete trust"; s. 249(1) Definition of "taxation year".

Information Circulars: IC 77-16R4 Non-resident income tax.

► 212(1)(v) ◄

(v) Payments under an eligible funeral arrangement — a payment made by a custodian (within the meaning assigned by subsection 148.1(1)) of an arrangement that was, at the time it was established, an eligible funeral arrangement, to the extent that such amount would, if the non-resident person were resident in Canada, be included because of subsection 148.1(3) in computing the person's income;

Related Sections: S. 128.1(10)(*e*)(iv) Definitions; s. 212(13)(*e*) Rent and other payments.

Information Circulars: IC 77-16R4 Non-resident income tax.

► 212(1)(w) ◄

(w) [Employee life and health trust payments] — a payment out of a trust that is, or was, at any time, an employee life and health trust, except to the extent that it is a payment of a designated employee benefit (as defined by subsection 144.1(1)); or

History: S. 212(1)(*w*) was added by S.C. 2010, c. 25, s. 64(1), applicable after 2009.

► 212(1)(x) ◄

(x) Tax informant program — a payment of an amount described in paragraph 56(1)(*z.4*).

History: S. 212(1)(*x*) was added by S.C. 2014, c. 20, s. 26, in force June 19, 2014.

► 212(2) ◄

(2) Tax on dividends. Every non-resident person shall pay an income tax of 25% on every amount that a corporation resident in Canada pays or credits, or is deemed by Part I or Part XIV to pay or credit, to the non-resident person as, on account or in lieu of payment of, or in satisfaction of,

(*a*) a taxable dividend (other than a capital gains dividend within the meaning assigned by subsection 130.1(4), 131(1) or 133(7.1)); or

(*b*) a capital dividend.

(*b*.1) (Repealed by 1986, c. 6, s. 116(6).)

(*c*) (Repealed by 1986, c. 6, s. 116(6).)

Related Regulations: Part II.

Related Sections: 40(3.7) Losses of non-resident; 83(2) Capital dividend; 84(1) Deemed dividend; 89(1) taxable dividend; 128.1(1)(c.1) Deemed dividend to immigrating corporation; 128.1(1)(c.2) Deemed dividend to shareholder of immigrating corporation; 131(5.1) TCP gains distribution; 131(5.2) Application of subsection (5.1); 212(1)(b)(xiii); 212(1)(c)(ii); 212(11) Payment to beneficiary as income of trust; 212(13.3)(a); 212.1 Non-arm's length sales of shares by non-residents; 212.2 [Deemed dividend]; 213(1) Tax non-payable by non-resident person; 214(3)(a); 215(1.1) Exception — corporate immigration; 218.3 [Tax payable]; 219 Additional tax; 250(5) Deemed non-resident.

Tax Profile: May 2013 — Current International Tax Issues In Cross-Border Corporate Finance and Capital Markets; April 2013 — Canadian Estate Freezes in Favour of U.S. Citizens; March 2013 — Non-Resident Investment in Canadian Real Estate; October 2012 — Exchangeable Shares in Canada; September 2012 — Canadian Refundable Withholding Taxes — Traps; August 2012 — U.S. Purchases and Sales of Canadian Businesses: Tax and Corporate Issues.

September 2011 — Acquisition of Canadian Business by Non-Residents; July 2011 — OECD Discussion Paper on Beneficial Ownership; June 2011 — Part XIII Tax and Treaty Protection: Canada Revenue Agency's New Administrative Policy; December 2010 — Holding Companies Under Attack; October 2010 — Non-Resident Investment in Canadian Real Estate; September 2010 — Recent Tax Developments Affecting Non-Residents; March 2009 — Beneficial Ownership Under Canadian Treaties — Canadian Court Respects Dutch Holding Company; November 2008 — 2008 Cross-Border Developments in Canada; August 2008 — Fifth Protocol to the Canada–U.S. Tax Convention: A Canadian Perspective; May 2008 — Beneficial Ownership by Holding Company Respected; October 2007 — Important Changes Announced to the Canada — U.S. Income Tax Convention; October 2007 — Will Canadian Unlimited Liability Companies Survive?; May 2007 — Impact of 2007 Federal Budget on Cross-Border Transactions; May 2007 — Why Canada Should End Roadblock to Foreign Private Equity; March 2007 — Beneficial Ownership: An International Perspective; December 2006 — "Beneficial Ownership" under Canadian Tax Treaties — Canadian Revenue Authorities Take Aim; April 2004 — Mutual Funds and the 2004 Budget.

Tax Topics: No. 2111, IFA 2012 Tax Seminar Roundtables.

No. 1963, The CRA Interprets the Fifth: An Update; No. 1931, Prévost Car Inc. (FCA): Holdco Confirmed as Beneficial Owner of Dividends; No. 1887,

Prévost Car and Beneficial Ownership: The Triumph of Reason; No. 1812, Beneficial Ownership: Indofood Run Wild.

Forms: NR4 Sum. — Return of Amounts Paid or Credited to Non-Residents of Canada; NR4 — Statement of Amounts Paid or Credited to Non-Residents of Canada.

Income Tax Folios: *Primary* — S3-F2-C1 Capital Dividends.

Income Tax Technical News: Issue No. 44, Paid-Up Capital Increase by an Unlimited Liability Company; Issue No. 44, Luxembourg Intermediary; Issue No. 44, Payments by a ULC to an LLC in 2009; Issue No. 41, 5th Protocol to the Canada-US Tax Convention — Hybrid Entities; Issue No. 41, 5th Protocol to the Canada-US Tax Convention — Limitation on Benefits; Issue No. 38, Limited Liability Company Under the Protocol.

Information Circulars: IC 77-16R4 Non-resident income tax (paras. 45 to 49); IC 88-2 General anti-avoidance rule — Section 245 of the Income Tax Act.

Interpretation Bulletins: *Secondary* — IT-465R Non-resident beneficiaries of trusts; IT-468R Management or administration fees paid to non-residents.

Cases: A Canadian corporation paid dividends to a Dutch holding company and withheld 5% tax under the Canada–Netherlands Treaty. The Dutch company then paid similar dividends to its Swedish and U.K. shareholders. The Canadian dividends were not beneficially owned by the Dutch company's shareholders, which would require higher Canadian withholding tax, since the Dutch company enjoyed all the attributes of ownership and was not a conduit for its shareholders. *The Queen v. Prévost Car Inc.*, 2009 DTC 5053 (F.C.A.), affirming 2008 DTC 3080 (T.C.C.)

The taxpayer purchased common shares of two Canadian corporations from non-residents. The payment to the non-residents was deemed to be a dividend from which withholding tax should have been deducted. *Placements Serco Ltée v. The Queen*, 87 DTC 5425 (F.C.A.)

▶ 212(2.1) ◀

(2.1) Exempt dividends. Subsection (2) does not apply to an amount paid or credited, by a borrower, under a securities lending arrangement if

(*a*) the amount is deemed by subparagraph 260(8)(*c*)(i) to be a dividend;

(*b*) the securities lending arrangement was entered into by the borrower in the course of carrying on a business outside Canada; and

(*c*) the security that is transferred or lent to the borrower under the securities lending arrangement is a share of a class of the capital stock of a non-resident corporation.

Proposed Amendment
2019 Federal Budget Resolutions
Subsection 212(2.1) of the Act is replaced by the following:

(2.1) Exempt dividends. Subsection (2) does not apply to an amount paid or credited, by a borrower, under a securities lending arrangement or a specified securities lending arrangement if

(*a*) the amount is deemed by subparagraph 260(8)(*a*)(ii) to be a dividend;

(*b*) the arrangement is a fully collateralized arrangement; and

(*c*) the security that is transferred or lent to the borrower under the securities lending arrangement is a share of a class of the capital stock of a non-resident corporation.

Applicable: In respect of amounts paid or payable or credited on or after March 19, 2019.

History: S. 212(2.1) was added by S.C. 2013, c. 34, s. 347(11), applicable to securities lending arrangements entered into after May 1995, except that, in its application to arrangements made before 2002, each reference to "subparagraph 260(8)(*c*)(i)" in paragraph 212(2.1)(*a*) is to be read as a reference to "subparagraph 260(8)(*a*)(i)".

▶ 212(3) ◀

(3) Interest — definitions. The following definitions apply for the purpose of paragraph (1)(*b*).

History: S. 212(3) was replaced by S.C. 2013, c. 34, s. 347(13), deemed to have come into force on January 1, 2008, and formerly read:

(3) *Interest — definitions.* The following definitions apply for the purpose of paragraph (1)(*b*).

"fully exempt interest" — "fully exempt interest" means

(*a*) interest that is paid or payable on a bond, debenture, note, mortgage, hypothecary claim or similar debt obligation

(i) of, or guaranteed (otherwise than by being insured by the Canada Deposit Insurance Corporation) by, the Government of Canada,

(ii) of the government of a province,

(iii) of an agent of a province,

(iv) of a municipality in Canada or a municipal or public body performing a function of government in Canada,

(v) of a corporation, commission or association to which any of paragraphs 149(1)(*d*) to (*d.6*) applies, or

(vi) of an educational institution or a hospital if repayment of the principal amount of the obligation and payment of the interest is to be made, or is guaranteed, assured or otherwise specifically provided for or secured by the government of a province;

(*b*) interest that is paid or payable on a mortgage, hypothecary claim or similar debt obligation secured by, or on an agreement for sale or similar obligation with respect to, real property situated outside Canada or an interest in any such real property, or to immovables situated outside Canada or a real right in any such immovable, except to the extent that the interest payable on the obligation is deductible in computing the income of the payer under Part I from a business carried on by the payer in Canada or from property other than real or immovable property situated outside Canada;

(*c*) interest that is paid or payable to a prescribed international organization or agency; or

(*d*) an amount paid or payable or credited under a securities lending arrangement that is deemed by subparagraph 260(8)(*a*)(i) to be a payment made by a borrower to a lender of interest, if

(i) the securities lending arrangement was entered into by the borrower in the course of carrying on a business outside Canada, and

(ii) the security that is transferred or lent to the borrower under the securities lending arrangement is described in paragraph (*b*) or (*c*) of the definition "qualified security" in subsection 260(1) and issued by a non-resident issuer.

"participating debt interest" — "participating debt interest" means interest (other than interest described in any of paragraphs (*b*) to (*d*) of the definition "fully exempt interest") that is paid or payable on an obligation, other than a prescribed obligation, all or any portion of which interest is contingent or dependent on the use of or production from property in Canada or is computed by reference to revenue, profit, cash flow, commodity price or any other similar criterion or by reference to dividends paid or payable to shareholders of any class of shares of the capital stock of a corporation.

International Tax: No. 101, One and Done: CRA Ruling Holds That a Payment of Contingent Interest Will Subject All Future Interest Payments to Withholding Tax.

Tax Profile: November 2008 — 2008 Cross-Border Developments in Canada.

Tax Topics: No. 1916, Withholding Tax Implications of Participating Interest and Convertible Debt.

Income Tax Technical News: Issue No. 44, Convertible Debentures and Part XIII.

"fully exempt interest" — "fully exempt interest" means

(*a*) interest that is paid or payable on a bond, debenture, note, mortgage, hypothecary claim or similar debt obligation

(i) of, or guaranteed (otherwise than by being insured by the Canada Deposit Insurance Corporation) by, the Government of Canada,

(ii) of the government of a province,

(iii) of an agent of a province,

(iv) of a municipality in Canada or a municipal or public body performing a function of government in Canada,

(v) of a corporation, commission or association to which any of paragraphs 149(1)(*d*) to (*d.6*) applies, or

(vi) of an educational institution or a hospital if repayment of the principal amount of the obligation and payment of the interest is to be made, or is guaranteed, assured or otherwise specifically provided for or secured by the government of a province;

(*b*) interest that is paid or payable on a mortgage, hypothecary claim or similar debt obligation secured by, or on an agreement for sale or similar obligation with respect to, real property situated outside Canada or an interest in any such real property, or to immovables situated outside Canada or a real right in any such immovable, except to the extent that the interest payable on the obligation is deductible in computing the income of the payer under Part I from a business carried on by the payer in Canada or from property other than real or immovable property situated outside Canada;

(*c*) interest that is paid or payable to a prescribed international organization or agency; or

(*d*) an amount paid or payable or credited under a securities lending arrangement that is deemed by subparagraph 260(8)(*c*)(i) to be a payment made by a borrower to a lender of interest, if

(i) the securities lending arrangement was entered into by the borrower in the course of carrying on a business outside Canada, and

(ii) the security that is transferred or lent to the borrower under the securities lending arrangement is described in paragraph (*b*) or (*c*) of the definition "qualified security" in subsection 260(1) and issued by a non-resident issuer.

Proposed Amendment

2019 Federal Budget Resolutions

Paragraph (*d*) of the definition *fully exempt interest* in subsection 212(3) of the Act is replaced by the following:

(*d*) an amount paid or payable or credited under a securities lending arrangement, or a specified securities lending arrangement, that is deemed by subparagraph 260(8)(*a*)(i) to be a payment made by a borrower to a lender of interest, if the arrangement is a fully collateralized arrangement, and

(i) the following conditions are met:

(A) the arrangement was entered into by the borrower in the course of carrying on a business outside Canada, and

(B) the security that is transferred or lent to the borrower under the arrangement is described in paragraph (*b*) of the definition qualified security in subsection 260(1) and issued by a non-resident issuer,

(ii) the security that is transferred or lent to the borrower under the arrangement is described in paragraph (*c*) of the definition *qualified security in* subsection 260(1), or

(iii) the security that is transferred or lent to the borrower under the arrangement is described in paragraph (*a*) or (*b*).

Applicable: In respect of amounts paid or payable or credited on or after March 19, 2019.

"participating debt interest" —"participating debt interest" means interest (other than interest described in any of paragraphs (*b*) to (*d*) of the definition "fully exempt interest") that is paid or payable on an obligation, other than a prescribed obligation, all or any portion of which interest is contingent or dependent on the use of or production from property in Canada or is computed by reference to revenue, profit, cash flow, commodity price or any other similar criterion or by reference to dividends paid or payable to shareholders of any class of shares of the capital stock of a corporation.

► 212(3.1) ◄

(3.1) Back-to-back loan arrangement. Subsection (3.2) applies at any time in respect of a taxpayer if

(*a*) the taxpayer pays or credits a particular amount at that time as, on account or in lieu of payment of, or in satisfaction of, interest (determined without reference to paragraph 18(6.1)(*b*) and subsection 214(16)) in respect of a particular debt or other obligation to pay an amount to a person or partnership (in this subsection and subsection (3.2) referred to as the "immediate funder");

(*b*) the immediate funder is not

(i) a person resident in Canada that does not deal at arm's length with the taxpayer, or

(ii) a partnership each member of which is a person described in subparagraph (i);

(*c*) at any time in the period during which the interest accrued (in this subsection and subsections (3.2) and (3.3) referred to as the "relevant period"), a relevant funder, in respect of a particular relevant funding arrangement,

(i) has an amount outstanding as or on account of a debt or other obligation to pay an amount to a person or partnership that meets any of the following conditions:

(A) recourse in respect of the debt or other obligation is limited in whole or in part, either immediately or in the future and either absolutely or contingently, to a relevant funding arrangement, or

(B) it can reasonably be concluded that all or a portion of the particular relevant funding arrangement was entered into, or was permitted to remain in effect, because

(I) all or a portion of the debt or other obligation was entered into or was permitted to remain outstanding, or

(II) the relevant funder anticipated that all or a portion of the debt or other obligation would become owing or remain outstanding, or

(ii) has a specified right in respect of a particular property that was granted directly or indirectly by a person or partnership and

(A) the existence of the specified right is required under the terms and conditions of the particular relevant funding arrangement, or

(B) it can reasonably be concluded that all or a portion of the particular relevant funding arrangement was entered into, or was permitted to remain in effect, because

(I) the specified right was granted, or

(II) the relevant funder anticipated that the specified right would be granted;

(*d*) the tax that would be payable under this Part in respect of the particular amount, if the particular amount were paid or credited to any ultimate funder rather than the immediate funder, is greater than the tax payable under this Part (determined without reference to this subsection and subsection (3.2)) in respect of the particular amount; and

(*e*) at any time during the relevant period, the total of all amounts — each of which is an amount outstanding as or on account of a debt or other obligation owed by the immediate funder that is a relevant funding arrangement or the fair market value of a particular property in respect of which the immediate funder is granted a specified right that is a relevant funding arrangement — is equal to at least 25% of the total of

(i) the amount outstanding as or on account of the particular debt or other obligation, and

(ii) the total of all amounts each of which is an amount (other than the amount described in subparagraph (i)) that the taxpayer, or a person or partnership that does not deal at arm's length with the taxpayer, has outstanding as or on account of a debt or other obligation to pay an amount to the immediate funder under the agreement, or an agreement that is connected to the agreement, under which the particular debt or other obligation was entered into where

(A) the immediate funder is granted a "security interest" (as defined in subsection 18(5)) in respect of a property that is the debt or other obligation owed by the immediate funder or the particular property, as the case may be, and the security interest secures the payment of two or more debts or other obligations that include the debt or other obligation and the particular debt or other obligation, and

(B) each security interest that secures the payment of a debt or other obligation referred to in clause (A) secures the payment of every debt or other obligation referred to in that clause.

History: S. 212(3.1) was replaced by S.C. 2016, c. 12, s. 57(1), applicable in respect of amounts paid or credited after 2016, and formerly read:

(3.1) *Back-to-back loan arrangement.* Subsections (3.2) and (3.3) apply at any time in respect of a taxpayer if

(*a*) the taxpayer pays or credits a particular amount at that time on account or in lieu of payment of, or in satisfaction of, interest (determined without reference to paragraph 18(6.1)(*b*) and subsection 214(16)) in respect of a particular debt or other obligation to pay an amount to a person or partnership (in this subsection referred to as the "intermediary");

(*b*) the intermediary is not

(i) a person resident in Canada that does not deal at arm's length with the taxpayer, or

(ii) a partnership each member of which is a person described in subparagraph (i);

(*c*) at any time in the period during which the interest accrued (in subsections (3.2) and (3.3) referred to as the "relevant period"), the intermediary, or a person or partnership that does not deal at arm's length with the intermediary,

(i) has an amount outstanding as or on account of a debt or other obligation to pay an amount to a non-resident person that meets any of the following conditions (in this subsection and subsection (3.2) referred to as the "intermediary debt"):

(A) recourse in respect of the debt or other obligation is limited in whole or in part, either immediately or in the future and either absolutely or contingently, to the particular debt or other obligation, or

(B) it can reasonably be concluded that all or a portion of the particular debt or other obligation became owing, or was permitted to remain owing, because

(I) all or a portion of the debt or other obligation was entered into or was permitted to remain outstanding, or

(II) the intermediary anticipated that all or a portion of the debt or other obligation would become owing or remain outstanding, or

(ii) has a specified right (as defined in subsection 18(5)) in respect of a particular property that was granted directly or indirectly by a non-resident person and

(A) the existence of the specified right is required under the terms and conditions of the particular debt or other obligation, or

(B) it can reasonably be concluded that all or a portion of the particular debt or other obligation became owing, or was permitted to remain owing, because

(I) the specified right was granted, or

(II) the intermediary anticipated that the specified right would be granted;

(*d*) the tax that would be payable under this Part in respect of the particular amount, if the particular amount were paid or credited to the non-resident person rather than the intermediary, is greater than the tax payable under this Part (determined without reference to this subsection and subsection (3.2)) in respect of the particular amount; and

(*e*) the total of all amounts — each of which is, in respect of the particular debt or other obligation, an amount outstanding as or on account of an intermediary debt or the fair market value of a particular property described in subparagraph (*c*)(ii) — is equal to at least 25% of the total of

(i) the amount outstanding as or on account of the particular debt or other obligation, and

(ii) the total of all amounts each of which is an amount (other than the amount described in subparagraph (i)) that the taxpayer, or a person or partnership that does not deal at arm's length with the taxpayer, has outstanding as or on account of a debt or other obligation to pay an amount to the intermediary under the agreement, or an agreement that is connected to the agreement, under which the particular debt or other obligation was entered into where

(A) the intermediary is granted a security interest (as defined in subsection 18(5)) in respect of a property that is the intermediary debt or the particular property, as the case may be, and the security interest secures the payment of two or more debts or other obligations that include the debt or other obligation and the particular debt or other obligation, and

(B) each security interest that secures the payment of a debt or other obligation referred to in clause (A) secures the payment of every debt or other obligation referred to in that clause.

S. 212(3.1) was added by S.C. 2014, c. 39, s. 64(1), applicable to amounts paid or credited after 2014.

Related Sections: 212(1)(b) Interest; 212(3.2) Back-to-back loan arrangement.

Tax Window Files: 2015 TEI Liaison Meeting Q.6 - Specified Right, *November 17, 2015*, CRA Document No. 2015-0614241C6.

► 212(3.2) ◄

(3.2) Back-to-back loan arrangement. If this subsection applies at any time in respect of a taxpayer, then for the purposes of paragraph (1)(*b*), the taxpayer is deemed, at that time, to pay interest to each ultimate funder, the amount of which is determined for each particular ultimate funder by the formula

$$(A - B) \times C/D \times (E - F)/E$$

where

A is the particular amount referred to in paragraph (3.1)(*a*);

B is the portion, if any, of the particular amount deemed by subsection 214(16) to have been paid by the taxpayer as a dividend;

C is the average of all amounts each of which is, at a particular time in the relevant period, the amount determined by the formula

$$G - H$$

where

G is the lesser of the following amounts:

(*a*) the amount of the particular debt or other obligation referred to in paragraph (3.1)(*a*) outstanding at the particular time, and

(*b*) the total of all amounts each of which is at that particular time

(i) an amount outstanding as or on account of a debt or other obligation that is owed to the particular ultimate funder under a relevant funding arrangement,

(ii) the fair market value of a particular property referred to in subparagraph (3.1)(*c*)(ii) in respect of which the particular ultimate funder has granted a specified right under a relevant funding arrangement, or

(iii) if neither subparagraph (i) nor (ii) applies at that particular time, nil, and

H is the total of all amounts each of which is, at the particular time, the amount that is

(*a*) an amount outstanding as or on account of a debt or other obligation that is owed by the particular ultimate funder under a relevant funding arrangement,

(*b*) the fair market value of a particular property referred to in subparagraph (3.1)(*c*)(ii) in respect of which the particular ultimate funder has a specified right under a relevant funding arrangement, or

(*c*) if neither paragraph (*a*) nor (*b*) applies at that particular time, nil;

D is the average of all amounts each of which is the amount of the particular debt or other obligation outstanding at a time in the relevant period;

E is the rate of tax (determined without reference to subsection 214(16)) that would be imposed under this Part on the particular amount if the particular amount were paid by the taxpayer to the particular ultimate funder at that time; and

F is the rate of tax (determined without reference to subsection 214(16)) imposed under this Part on the immediate funder in respect of all or the portion of the particular amount paid or credited to the immediate funder.

History: S. 212(3.2) was replaced by S.C. 2016, c. 12, s. 57(1), applicable in respect of amounts paid or credited after 2016, and formerly read:

(3.2) *Back-to-back loan arrangement*. If this subsection applies at any time in respect of a taxpayer, then for the purposes of paragraph (1)(*b*), the taxpayer is deemed, at that time, to pay interest to a non-resident person referred to in subparagraph (3.1)(*c*)(i) or (ii), the amount of which is determined by the formula

$$[(A \times B/C) - D] \times (E - F)/E$$

where

A is the particular amount referred to in paragraph (3.1)(*a*);

B is the average of all amounts each of which is the lesser of

(i) the amount of the particular debt or other obligation referred to in paragraph (3.1)(*a*) outstanding at a particular time in the relevant period; and

(ii) the total of all amounts each of which is at that particular time

(A) an amount outstanding as or on account of an intermediary debt, in respect of the particular debt or other obligation, that is owed to the non-resident person,

(B) the fair market value of a particular property referred to in subparagraph (3.1)(*c*)(ii) in respect of the particular debt or other obligation, or

(C) if neither clause (A) nor (B) applies at that particular time, nil;

C is the average of all amounts each of which is the amount of the particular debt or other obligation outstanding at a time in the relevant period;

D is the portion, if any, of the particular amount deemed by subsection 214(16) to have been paid by the taxpayer as a dividend;

E is the rate of tax (determined without reference to subsection 214(16)) that would be imposed under this Part on the particular amount if the particular amount were paid by the taxpayer to the non-resident person at that time; and

F is the rate of tax (determined without reference to subsection 214(16)) imposed under this Part on the intermediary in respect of all or the portion of the particular amount paid or credited to the intermediary.

S. 212(3.2) was added by S.C. 2014, c. 39, s. 64(1), applicable to amounts paid or credited after 2014.

Related Sections: 212(1)(b) Interest; 212(3.1) Back-to-back loan arrangement; 212(3.3) Excess funding.

► 212(3.21) ◄

(3.21) Back-to-back arrangement — election. Subsection (3.22) applies in respect of a taxpayer and two or more ultimate funders (referred to in this subsection and subsection (3.22) as the "electing ultimate funders") at any time if

(*a*) at that time, subsection (3.2) applies in respect of the taxpayer;

(*b*) prior to that time, the taxpayer and the electing ultimate funders have jointly filed an election under this subsection;

(*c*) the election designates one of the electing ultimate funders to be the recipient of interest payments that are deemed to be made by the taxpayer under subsection (3.22);

(*d*) at that time, the tax that would be payable under this Part in respect of an interest payment by the taxpayer to the designated ultimate funder is not less than the tax that would be payable under this Part if the interest payment were made by the taxpayer to any of the other electing ultimate funders; and

(*e*) the election has not been revoked prior to that time.

History: S. 212(3.21) was added by S.C. 2016, c. 12, s. 57(1), applicable in respect of amounts paid or credited after 2016.

► 212(3.22) ◄

(3.22) Back-to-back arrangement — election. If this subsection applies at any time in respect of a taxpayer and two or more electing ultimate funders, then each interest payment that would, in the absence of this subsection, have been deemed under subsection (3.2) to have been made at that time by the taxpayer to an electing ultimate funder, and received by the electing ultimate funder from the taxpayer, is deemed to have instead been

(*a*) made by the taxpayer to the designated ultimate funder; and

(*b*) received by the designated ultimate funder from the taxpayer.

History: S. 212(3.22) was added by S.C. 2016, c. 12, s. 57(1), applicable in respect of amounts paid or credited after 2016.

► 212(3.3) ◄

(3.3) Excess funding. Subsection (3.4) applies in respect of a particular relevant funder if the amount determined by the following formula is greater than nil:

$$A - B$$

where

A is the total of all amounts each of which is the amount owing by the particular relevant funder, or is the fair market value of a property in respect of which the particular relevant funder has a specified right, under a relevant funding arrangement; and

B is the total of all amounts each of which is the amount owed to the particular relevant funder, or is the fair market value of a property in respect of which the particular relevant funder has granted a specified right, under a relevant funding arrangement.

History: S. 212(3.3) was replaced by S.C. 2016, c. 12, s. 57(1), applicable in respect of amounts paid or credited after 2016, and formerly read:

(3.3) *Back-to-back loan arrangement.* If subsection (3.2) applies at any time to deem a taxpayer to pay interest at that time to more than one non-resident person referred to in subparagraph (3.1)(*c*)(i) or (ii) in respect of a particular debt or other obligation and the total of all amounts determined (without reference to this subsection) for B in subsection (3.2) in respect of the particular debt or other obligation exceeds the average of all amounts each of which is the amount of the particular debt or other obligation outstanding at a time in the relevant period, then the taxpayer may reduce the amount determined for B in respect of one or more of the non-resident persons by one or more amounts designated by the taxpayer, as is reasonable in the circumstances, the total of which designated amounts shall not be greater than that excess.

S. 212(3.3) was added by S.C. 2014, c. 39, s. 64(1), applicable to amounts paid or credited after 2014.

Related Sections: 212(3.2) Back-to-back loan arrangement.

► 212(3.4) ◄

(3.4) Excess funding — deemed funding allocation. If this subsection applies in respect of a particular relevant funder, for the purposes of subsections (3.2) to (3.4) (other than for the purpose of applying subsections (3.3) and (3.4) in respect of the particular relevant funder), each amount that is owed by the particular relevant funder, or that is the fair market value of a property in respect of which the particular relevant funder has been granted a specified right, under a relevant funding arrangement, is deemed to be the amount determined by the formula

$$C/D \times E$$

where

C is the amount owing or the fair market value of the property, as the case may be;

D is the amount determined for A in subsection (3.3); and

E is the amount determined for B in subsection (3.3).

History: S. 212(3.4) was added by S.C. 2016, c. 12, s. 57(1), applicable in respect of amounts paid or credited after 2016.

► 212(3.5) ◄

(3.5) Multiple funding arrangements. If an amount owing by a relevant funder or a specified right held by the relevant funder is a relevant funding arrangement in respect of more than one particular debt or other obligation referred to in paragraph (3.1)(*a*), for the purposes of applying subsections (3.2) to (3.4) in respect of each of the particular debts or other obligations, the amount owing, or the fair market value of the property in respect of which the specified right was granted, as the case may be, is deemed, in respect of each particular debt or other obligation, to be the amount determined by the formula

$$A/B \times C$$

where

A is the total of all amounts each of which is an amount owing to the relevant funder, or the fair market value of a property in respect of which the relevant funder has granted a specified right, under a relevant funding arrangement, in respect of the particular debt or other obligation;

B is the total of all amounts each of which is an amount owing to the relevant funder, or the fair market value of a property in respect of which the relevant funder has granted a specified right, under a relevant funding arrangement, in respect of all of the particular debts or other obligations; and

C is the amount owing by the relevant funder or the fair market value of the property in respect of which the relevant funder holds the specified right.

History: S. 212(3.5) was added by S.C. 2016, c. 12, s. 57(1), applicable in respect of amounts paid or credited after 2016.

► 212(3.6) ◄

(3.6) Back-to-back loan arrangement — character substitution. Subsection (3.7) applies in respect of

(*a*) shares (other than specified shares) of the capital stock of a particular relevant funder, in respect of a particular relevant funding arrangement, if — at any time at or after the time when the particular debt or other obligation referred to in paragraph (3.1)(*a*) was entered into — the particular relevant funder has an obligation to pay or credit an amount as, on account or in lieu of payment of, or in satisfaction of, a dividend on the shares, either immediately or in the future and either absolutely or contingently, to a person or partnership, and any of the following conditions is met:

(i) the amount of the dividend is determined, in whole or in part, by reference to an amount of interest paid or credited, or an obligation to pay or credit interest, under a relevant funding arrangement, or

(ii) it can reasonably be concluded that the particular relevant funding arrangement was entered into or was permitted to remain in effect, because

(A) the shares were issued or were permitted to remain issued and outstanding, or

(B) it was anticipated that the shares would be issued or would be permitted to remain issued and outstanding; or

(*b*) a specified royalty arrangement, if — at any time at or after the time when the particular debt or other obligation referred to in paragraph (3.1)(*a*) was entered into — a particular relevant funder, in respect of a particular relevant funding arrangement, is a specified licensee that has an obligation to pay or credit an amount under the specified royalty arrangement, either immediately or in the future and either absolutely or contingently, to a person or partnership, and any of the following conditions is met:

(i) the amount is determined, in whole or in part, by reference to an amount of interest paid or credited, or an obligation to pay or credit interest, under a relevant funding arrangement, or

(ii) it can reasonably be concluded that the particular relevant funding arrangement was entered into or was permitted to remain in effect, because

(A) the specified royalty arrangement was entered into or was permitted to remain in effect, or

(B) it was anticipated that the specified royalty arrangement would be entered into or remain in effect.

History: S. 212(3.6) was added by S.C. 2016, c. 12, s. 57(1), applicable in respect of amounts paid or credited after 2016.

► 212(3.7) ◄

(3.7) Back-to-back loan arrangement — character substitution. If this subsection applies in respect of a specified royalty arrangement (under which a particular relevant funder is a specified licensee) or shares of the capital stock of a particular relevant funder, then, for the purposes of subsections (3.1) to (3.8),

(*a*) the specified royalty arrangement or the holding of the shares, as the case may be, is deemed to be a relevant funding arrangement;

(*b*) the specified licensor or shareholder, as the case may be, in respect of the relevant funding arrangement, is deemed to be a relevant funder, in respect of the relevant funding arrangement;

(*c*) the conditions in paragraph (3.1)(*c*) are deemed to be met in respect of the relevant funding arrangement; and

(*d*) the relevant funder is deemed to be owed, under the relevant funding arrangement and by the particular relevant funder, an amount as or on account of a debt, the outstanding amount of which is determined by the formula

$$(A - B) \times C/D$$

where

A is the total of all amounts each of which is at the particular time,

(i) an amount outstanding as or on account of a debt or other obligation that is owed to the particular relevant funder under a relevant funding arrangement,

(ii) the fair market value of a particular property referred to in subparagraph (3.1)(*c*)(ii) in respect of which the particular relevant funder has granted a specified right under a relevant funding arrangement, or

(iii) if neither subparagraph (i) nor (ii) applies at that particular time, nil,

B is the total of all amounts each of which is, at the particular time, in respect of a relevant funding arrangement (other than a relevant funding arrangement deemed under paragraph (*a*)) and is

(i) an amount outstanding as or on account of a debt or other obligation that is owed by the particular relevant funder under the relevant funding arrangement,

(ii) the fair market value of a particular property referred to in subparagraph (3.1)(*c*)(ii) in respect of which the particular relevant funder has been granted a specified right under a relevant funding arrangement, or

(iii) if neither subparagraph (i) nor (ii) applies at that particular time, nil,

C is the fair market value, at the particular time, of

(i) if the relevant funding arrangement is described in paragraph (3.6)(*a*), the shares, or

(ii) if the relevant funding arrangement is described in paragraph (3.6)(*b*), the specified royalty arrangement, and

D is the total of all amounts each of which is, in respect of a relevant funding arrangement referred to in the description of C, the amount determined for C at the particular time.

History: S. 212(3.7) was added by S.C. 2016, c. 12, s. 57(1), applicable in respect of amounts paid or credited after 2016.

► 212(3.8) ◄

(3.8) Back-to-back loan arrangement — definitions. The following definitions apply in this subsection and subsections (3.1) to (3.7) and (3.81).

"relevant funder" — "relevant funder", in respect of a relevant funding arrangement, means

(*a*) if the relevant funding arrangement is described in paragraph (*a*) of the definition "relevant funding arrangement", the immediate funder referred to in paragraph (3.1)(*a*);

(*b*) if the relevant funding arrangement is described in paragraph (*b*) of the definition "relevant funding arrangement", the creditor in respect of the debt or other obligation or the grantor of the specified right, as the case may be; or

(*c*) a person or partnership that does not deal at arm's length with a person or partnership that is referred to in paragraph (*a*) or (*b*) and that deals at arm's length with the taxpayer.

"relevant funding arrangement" — "relevant funding arrangement" means

(*a*) the particular debt or other obligation referred to in paragraph (3.1)(*a*); and

(*b*) each debt or other obligation or specified right, owing by or granted to a relevant funder, in respect of a particular relevant funding arrangement, if the debt or other obligation or specified right meets the conditions in subparagraph (3.1)(*c*)(i) or (ii) in respect of a relevant funding arrangement.

"specified licensee" — "specified licensee" means

(*a*) a lessee, licensee or grantee of a right similar to a right granted under a lease or licence, under a specified royalty arrangement;

(*b*) an assignee under a specified royalty arrangement; or

(*c*) a purchaser under a specified royalty arrangement.

"specified licensor" —"specified licensor" means

(*a*) a lessor, licensor or grantor of a right similar to a right granted under a lease or licence, under a specified royalty arrangement;

(*b*) an assignor under a specified royalty arrangement; or

(*c*) a seller under a specified royalty arrangement.

"specified right" —"specified right" has the same meaning as in subsection 18(5).

"specified royalty arrangement" —"specified royalty arrangement" has the same meaning as in subsection (3.94).

"specified share" —"specified share" means a share of the capital stock of a corporation if, under the terms or conditions of the share, or any agreement or arrangement relating to the share,

(*a*) the holder of the share may cause the share to be redeemed, acquired or cancelled;

(*b*) the issuing corporation is, or may be, required to redeem, acquire or cancel the share at a specific time; or

(*c*) the share is convertible or exchangeable into a share that meets the conditions in paragraph (*a*) or (*b*).

"ultimate funder" —"ultimate funder" means a relevant funder, in respect of a relevant funding arrangement (other than the immediate funder) that either

(*a*) is not a debtor, or a holder of a specified right, under a relevant funding arrangement; or

(*b*) is a debtor, or a holder of a specified right, under a relevant funding arrangement, if the amount that would — if the relevant funder were an ultimate funder — be determined for C in the formula in subsection (3.2) is greater than nil.

History: S. 212(3.8) was added by S.C. 2016, c. 12, s. 57(1), applicable in respect of amounts paid or credited after 2016.

► 212(3.81) ◄

(3.81) Specified shares. For the purposes of subsections (3.1) to (3.8),

(*a*) specified shares of a relevant funder, in respect of a relevant funding arrangement, held at any time by a person or partnership are deemed to be a debt of the relevant funder owing to the person or partnership; and

(*b*) the amount outstanding at that time as or on account of the debt is deemed to be equal to the fair market value of the specified shares at that time.

History: S. 212(3.81) was added by S.C. 2016, c. 12, s. 57(1), applicable in respect of amounts paid or credited after 2016.

► 212(3.9) ◄

(3.9) Back-to-back arrangement — rents, royalties, similar payments. Subsection (3.91) applies at any time in respect of a taxpayer if

(*a*) the taxpayer pays or credits a particular amount at that time as, on account or in lieu of payment of, or in satisfaction of, rent, royalty or similar payment, in respect of a particular lease, licence or similar agreement, to a non-resident person or a partnership any member of which is a non-resident person (in this subsection and subsections (3.91) to (3.94) referred to as the "immediate licensor");

(*b*) at any time at or after the time when the particular lease, licence or similar agreement was entered into,

(i) a relevant licensor in respect of a particular relevant royalty arrangement has an obligation to pay or credit an amount, either immediately or in the future and either absolutely or contingently, to a person or partnership, in respect of a specified royalty arrangement, and either of the following additional conditions is met:

(A) the amount is determined, in whole or in part, by reference to

(I) an amount paid or credited, or an obligation to pay or credit an amount, in respect of a relevant royalty arrangement, or

(II) one or more of the fair market value of, any revenue, profits, income, or cash flow from, or any other similar criteria in respect of, a particular property, if a right in respect of the property is granted under the particular lease, licence or similar agreement, or

(B) it can reasonably be concluded that the particular relevant royalty arrangement was entered into, or was permitted to remain in effect, because

(I) the specified royalty arrangement was entered into or was permitted to remain in effect, or

(II) it was anticipated that the specified royalty arrangement would be entered into or remain in effect, and

(ii) either the person or partnership

(A) does not deal at arm's length with the taxpayer, or

(B) deals at arm's length with the taxpayer, if it can reasonably be concluded that one of the main purposes of the specified royalty arrangement was

(I) to reduce or avoid the tax payable under this Part in respect of the particular amount, or

(II) to avoid the application of subsection (3.91); and

(*c*) the tax that would be payable under this Part in respect of the particular amount, if the particular amount were paid or credited to an ultimate licensor rather than the immediate licensor, is greater than the tax payable under this Part (determined without reference to this subsection and subsection (3.91)) in respect of the particular amount.

History: S. 212(3.9) was added by S.C. 2016, c. 12, s. 57(1), applicable in respect of amounts paid or credited after 2016.

Canadian Tax Foundation: Gheorghiu, *Back-to-Back Royalty and Character Substitution Rules*, 2016 Canadian Tax Focus 6(4):14–15.

► 212(3.91) ◄

(3.91) Back-to-back arrangement — rents, royalties, similar payments. If this subsection applies at any time in respect of a taxpayer, then, for the purposes of paragraph (1)(*d*), the taxpayer is deemed, at that time, to pay to each ultimate licensor an amount — of the same character as the particular amount referred to in paragraph (3.9)(*a*) — determined for each particular ultimate licensor by the formula

$$(A \times B/C) \times (D - E)/D$$

where

A is the particular amount referred to in paragraph (3.9)(*a*);

B is

(*a*) the portion of the amount referred to in paragraph (3.9)(*a*) that is demonstrated, to the satisfaction of the Minister, to be reasonably allocable to the particular ultimate licensor, and

(*b*) if an amount is not demonstrated, to the satisfaction of the Minister, to be reasonably allocable to each particular ultimate licensor, one;

C is

(*a*) the total of all amounts, each of which is the portion of the amount referred to in paragraph (3.9)(*a*) that is demonstrated, to the satisfaction of the Minister, to be reasonably allocable to each ultimate licensor, and

(*b*) if an amount is not demonstrated, to the satisfaction of the Minister, to be reasonably allocable to each particular ultimate licensor, the number of ultimate licensors;

D is

(*a*) if an amount is not demonstrated, to the satisfaction of the Minister, to be reasonably allocable to each particular ultimate licensor, the highest rate of tax that would be imposed under this Part on the particular amount referred to in paragraph (3.9)(*a*) if the particular amount were paid by the taxpayer to any of the ultimate licensors at that time, and

(*b*) in any other case, the rate of tax that would be imposed under this Part on the particular amount referred to in paragraph (3.9)(*a*) if the particular amount were paid by the taxpayer to the particular ultimate licensor at that time; and

E is the rate of tax imposed under this Part at that time on the immediate licensor in respect of the particular amount, referred to in paragraph (3.9)(*a*), paid or credited to the immediate licensor.

History: S. 212(3.91) was added by S.C. 2016, c. 12, s. 57(1), applicable in respect of amounts paid or credited after 2016.

► 212(3.92) ◄

(3.92) Back-to-back arrangement — character substitution. Subsection (3.93) applies in respect of

(*a*) shares of the capital stock of a particular relevant licensor, in respect of a particular relevant royalty arrangement, if — at any time at or after the time when a particular lease, license or similar agreement referred to in paragraph (3.9)(*a*) was entered into — the particular relevant licensor has an obligation to pay or credit an amount as, on account or in lieu of payment of, or in satisfaction of, a dividend on the shares, either immediately or in the future and either absolutely or contingently, to a person or partnership, and

(i) either of the following conditions is met:

(A) the amount of the dividend is determined, in whole or in part, by reference to

(I) an amount of rent, royalty or similar payment paid or credited, or an obligation to pay or credit rent, royalty or similar payment, under a relevant royalty arrangement, or

(II) one or more of the fair market value of, any revenue profits, income or cash flow from, or any other similar criteria in respect of a particular property, if a right in respect of the property is granted under the particular lease, licence or similar agreement, or

(B) it can reasonably be concluded that the particular relevant royalty arrangement was entered into or was permitted to remain in effect, because

(I) the shares were issued or were permitted to remain issued and outstanding, or

(II) it was anticipated that the shares would be issued or would be permitted to remain issued and outstanding, and

(ii) either the person or partnership

(A) does not deal at arm's length with the taxpayer referred to in paragraph (3.9)(*a*), or

(B) deals at arm's length with that taxpayer, if it can reasonably be concluded that one of the main purposes of the issuance of the shares was

(I) to reduce or avoid the tax payable under this Part in respect of the particular amount referred to in paragraph (3.9)(*a*), or

(II) to avoid the application of subsection (3.91); and

(*b*) an amount outstanding as or on account of a debt or other obligation to pay an amount, if — at any time at or after the time when a particular lease, license or similar agreement referred to in paragraph (3.9)(*a*) was entered into — a particular relevant licensor, in respect of a particular relevant royalty arrangement, has an obligation to pay or credit an amount as, on account or in lieu of payment of, or in satisfaction of, interest under the debt or other obligation, either immediately or in the future and either absolutely or contingently, to a person or partnership, and

(i) either of the following conditions is met:

(A) the amount of the interest is determined, in whole or in part, by reference to

(I) an amount of rent, royalty or similar payment paid or credited, or an obligation to pay or credit rent, royalty or similar payment, under a relevant royalty arrangement, or

(II) one or more of the fair market value of, any revenue profits, income or cash flow from, or any other similar criteria in respect of a particular property, if a right in respect of the property is granted under the particular lease, licence or similar agreement, or

(B) it can reasonably be concluded that the particular relevant royalty arrangement was entered into or was permitted to remain in effect, because

(I) the debt or other obligation was entered into or was permitted to remain in effect, or

(II) it was anticipated that the debt or other obligation would be entered into or remain in effect, and

(ii) either the person or partnership

(A) does not deal at arm's length with the taxpayer referred to in paragraph (3.9)(*a*), or

(B) deals at arm's length with that taxpayer, if it can reasonably be concluded that one of the main purposes of entering into the debt or other obligation was

(I) to reduce or avoid the tax payable under this Part in respect of the particular amount referred to in paragraph (3.9)(*a*), or

(II) to avoid the application of subsection (3.91).

History: S. 212(3.92) was added by S.C. 2016, c. 12, s. 57(1), applicable in respect of amounts paid or credited after 2016.

Canadian Tax Foundation: Gheorghiu, *Back-to-Back Royalty and Character Substitution Rules*, 2016 Canadian Tax Focus 6(4):14–15.

▶ 212(3.93) ◀

(3.93) Back-to-back arrangement — character substitution. If this subsection applies in respect of a debt or other obligation to pay an amount (under which a particular relevant licensor is a borrower) or shares of the capital stock of a particular relevant licensor, then, for the purposes of subsections (3.9) to (3.94),

(*a*) the debt or other obligation or the holding of the shares, as the case may be, is deemed to be a relevant royalty arrangement;

(*b*) the creditor or shareholder, as the case may be, in respect of the relevant royalty arrangement, is deemed to be a relevant licensor, in respect of the relevant royalty arrangement; and

(*c*) the relevant royalty arrangement is deemed to be a specified royalty arrangement in respect of which the conditions in paragraph (3.9)(*b*) are met.

History: S. 212(3.93) was added by S.C. 2016, c. 12, s. 57(1), applicable in respect of amounts paid or credited after 2016.

▶ 212(3.94) ◀

(3.94) Back-to-back arrangement — definitions. The following definitions apply in this subsection and subsections (3.9) to (3.93).

"lease, licence or similar agreement" — "lease, licence or similar agreement" means an agreement under which a rent, royalty or similar payment is or could be made.

"relevant licensor" — "relevant licensor", in respect of a relevant royalty arrangement, means

(*a*) if the relevant royalty arrangement is described in paragraph (*a*) of the definition "relevant royalty arrangement", the immediate licensor referred to in paragraph (3.9)(*a*);

(*b*) if the relevant royalty arrangement is described in paragraph (*b*) of the definition "relevant royalty arrangement", a person or partnership that is the lessor, the licensor or the grantor of a right similar to a right granted under a lease or licence, the assignor or the seller, as the case may be; or

(*c*) a person or partnership that does not deal at arm's length with a relevant licensor referred to in paragraph (*a*) or (*b*).

"relevant royalty arrangement" — "relevant royalty arrangement" means

(*a*) the particular lease, licence or similar agreement referred to in paragraph (3.9)(*a*); and

(*b*) each specified royalty arrangement that

(i) meets, in respect of a relevant royalty arrangement, the conditions in clause (3.9)(*b*)(i)(A) or (B), and

(ii) is an arrangement in respect of which the person or partnership referred to in subparagraph (3.9)(*b*)(ii) meets the conditions in clause (3.9)(*b*)(ii)(A) or (B).

"rent, royalty or similar payment" — "rent, royalty or similar payment" means a rent, royalty or similar payment described in paragraph (1)(*d*) and, for greater certainty, includes any payment described in subparagraphs (1)(*d*)(i) to (v) but does not include any payment described in subparagraphs (1)(*d*)(vi) to (xii).

"specified royalty arrangement" — "specified royalty arrangement" means a lease, license or similar agreement, an assignment or an instalment sale.

"ultimate licensor" — "ultimate licensor" means a relevant licensor (other than the immediate licensor), in respect of a relevant royalty arrangement, that is not, under a relevant royalty arrangement,

(*a*) a lessee, a licensee or a grantee of a right similar to a right granted under a lease or licence;

(*b*) an assignee; or

(*c*) a purchaser.

History: S. 212(3.94) was added by S.C. 2016, c. 12, s. 57(1), applicable in respect of amounts paid or credited after 2016.

▶ 212(4) ◀

(4) Interpretation of "management or administration fee or charge". For the purpose of paragraph (1)(*a*), "management or administration fee or charge" does not include any amount paid or credited or deemed by Part I to have been paid or credited to a non-resident person as, on account or in lieu of payment of, or in satisfaction of,

(*a*) a service performed by the non-resident person if, at the time the non-resident person performed the service

(i) the service was performed in the ordinary course of a business carried on by the non-resident person that included the performance of such a service for a fee, and

(ii) the non-resident person and the payer were dealing with each other at arm's length, or

(*b*) a specific expense incurred by the non-resident person for the performance of a service that was for the benefit of the payer,

to the extent that the amount so paid or credited was reasonable in the circumstances.

Related Regulations: Part II.

Related Sections: S. 67 General limitation re expenses; s. 251(1) Arm's length.

Information Circulars: IC 76-12R6 Applicable rate of Part XIII tax on amounts paid or credited to persons in countries with which Canada has a Tax Convention; IC 77-16R4 Non-resident income tax (para. 15).

Interpretation Bulletins: *Secondary* — IT-468R Management or administration fees paid to non-residents.

Cases: A non-resident portfolio investment fund manager made all the taxpayer's investment planning decisions and the taxpayer's profitability depended directly upon such decisions, which could be characterized as management tasks*Peter Cundill & Associates Limited*, 91 DTC 5543 (F.C.A.), affirming 91 DTC 5085 (F.C.T.D.)

► 212(5) ◄

(5) Motion picture films. Every non-resident person shall pay an income tax of 25% on every amount that a person resident in Canada pays or credits, or is deemed by Part I to pay or credit, to the non-resident person as, on account or in lieu of payment of, or in satisfaction of, payment for a right in or to the use of

(*a*) a motion picture film, or

(*b*) a film, video tape or other means of reproduction for use in connection with television (other than solely in connection with and as part of a news program produced in Canada),

that has been, or is to be, used or reproduced in Canada to the extent that the amount relates to that use or reproduction.

History: S. 212(5), the portion after paragraph (*b*) was replaced by S.C. 2013, c. 34, s. 347(15), applicable to the 2000 and subsequent taxation years, and formerly read:

that has been or is to be used or reproduced in Canada.

Related Regulations: 202.

Related Sections: S. 212(1)(*d*) Rents, royalties, etc.

Forms: NR4 Sum. — Return of Amounts Paid or Credited to Non-Residents of Canada; NR4 — Statement of Amounts Paid or Credited to Non-Residents of Canada.

Information Circulars: IC 77-16R4 Non-resident income tax.

Interpretation Bulletins: *Secondary* — IT-303 Know-how and similar payments to non-residents.

Cases: Since the term "motion picture films" was used in relation to materials produced only for theatrical exhibition, but not for television, the royalties paid for exhibition of television films and video tapes were exempt from non-resident withholding tax under Art. XIIIC of the Canada-U.S. Income Tax Convention. Furthermore, the payments had been made on the own account of the wholly owned Canadian subsidiaries of the American taxpayer (rather than as its agent). *The Queen v. MCA Television Ltd.*, 96 DTC 411 (F.C.A.), affirming 94 DTC 6375. (F.C.T.D.)

A film distributing company, Head Office in Paris, made agreements with CBC whereby CBC obtained the possession and the exclusive right to broadcast certain films, for a fixed sum of money for each film and for a limited time. The film distributing company was taxable under s. 106(2) (now s. 212(5)). The agreement between the parties contained all the elements of a lease; the fact that payment was made in a lump sum did not alter the situation. *Vauban Productions Ltd. v. M.N.R.*, 79 DTC 5186 (F.C.A.)

► 212(5.1) ◄

(5.1) Acting services. Notwithstanding any regulation made under paragraph 214(13)(*c*), every person who is either a non-resident individual who is an actor or that is a corporation related to such an individual shall pay an income tax of 23% on every amount paid or credited, or provided as a benefit, to or on behalf of the person for the provision in Canada of the acting services of the actor in a film or video production.

Editorial Note: Subsection 212(5.1) imposes a tax of 23% on an amount paid, credited or provided as a benefit to a non-resident individual who is an actor or to a corporation related to such individual, for film and video acting services provided by the non-resident actor in Canada. Under s. 215(1), the payer is required to withhold and remit the 23% tax. Unless the recipient elects to file a Part I return of income under s. 216.1, the recipient's federal tax liability is the 23% amount and no return is required to be filed in respect of that amount. If the payment is made to a corporation, and such corporation does not elect under s. 216.1, the corporation is liable to pay the 23% tax on the payment, and when the corporation pays the actor for the acting services, such payment is not subject to the 23% tax except to the extent that the payment exceeds the payment made to the corporation. Therefore, there should not be any double taxation. Under s. 212(5.3), the Minister has the authority to reduce the amount of withholding required if the Minister determines that undue hardship would occur.

Related Regulations: 201(1.1).

Related Sections: S. 115(2.1) Non-resident actors; s. 115(2.2) Deferred payment by actor's corporation; s. 150(1)(*a*)(i)(B) Filing returns of income — general rule; s. 153(1)(*a*) and (*g*) Withholding; s. 212(13.1)(*a*.1) Application of Part XIII tax where payer or payee is a partnership; s. 216.1(1) Alternative re: acting services; s. 216.1(2) Deemed Part I payment; s. 251 Arm's length.

Tax Profile: September 2002 — Canadian Withholding Taxes Update.

Tax Topics: No. 1521, Withholding Tax in "Hollywood North".

Forms: NR603 — Remittance of Non-Resident Tax on Income from Film or Video Acting Services.

► 212(5.2) ◄

(5.2) Relief from double taxation. Where a corporation is liable to tax under subsection (5.1) in respect of an amount for acting services of an actor (in this subsection referred to as the "corporation payment") and the corporation pays, credits or provides as a benefit to the actor an amount for those acting services (in this subsection referred to as the "actor payment"), no tax is payable under subsection (5.1) with respect to the actor payment except to the extent that it exceeds the corporation payment.

Related Sections: S. 115(2.1) Non-resident actors; s. 115(2.2) Deferred payment by actor's corporation; s. 216.1(3) Deemed election and restriction.

► 212(5.3) ◄

(5.3) Reduction of withholding. If the Minister is satisfied that the deduction or withholding otherwise required by section 215 from an amount described in subsection (5.1), would cause undue hardship, the Minister may determine a lesser amount to be deducted or withheld and that lesser amount is deemed to be the amount so required to be deducted or withheld.

Related Sections: S. 153(1.1) Undue hardship.

► 212(6) ◄

(6) Interest on provincial bonds from wholly-owned subsidiaries. Where an amount described by subsection (1) relates to interest on bonds or other obligations of or guaranteed by Her Majesty in right of a province or interest on bonds or other obligations provision for the payment of which was made by a statute of a provincial legislature, the tax payable under subsection (1) is 5% of that amount.

Related Sections: S. 212(7) Where s. (6) does not apply; s. 240(1) Definition of "taxable obligation" and "non-taxable obligation".

Information Circulars: IC 77-16R4 Non-resident income tax (para. 19).

► 212(7) ◄

(7) Where s. (6) does not apply. Subsection (6) does not apply to interest on any bond or other obligation described therein that was issued after December 20, 1960, except any such bond or other obligation for the issue of which arrangements were made on or before that day with a dealer in securities, if the existence of the arrangements for the issue of the bond or other obligation can be established by evidence in writing given or made on or before that day.

Information Circulars: IC 77-16R4 Non-resident income tax (para. 19).

► 212(8) ◄

(8) Bonds issued after December 20, 1960 in exchange for earlier bonds. For the purposes of this Part, where any bond, except a bond to which clause (1)(*b*)(ii)(C) applies, was issued after December 20, 1960 in exchange for a bond issued on or before that day, it shall, if the terms on which the bond for which it was exchanged was issued conferred on the holder thereof the right to make the exchange, be deemed to have been issued on or before December 20, 1960.

Information Circulars: IC 77-16R4 Non-resident income tax (para. 19).

► 212(9) ◄

(9) Exemptions. Where

(*a*) a dividend or interest is received by a trust from a non-resident-owned investment corporation,

(*b*) an amount (in this subsection referred to as the "royalty payment") is received by a trust as, on account of, in lieu of payment of or in satisfaction of, a royalty on or in respect of a copyright in respect of the production or reproduction of any literary, dramatic, musical or artistic work,

(*c*) interest is received by a mutual fund trust maintained primarily for the benefit of non-resident persons, or

(*d*) a dividend or interest is received by a trust that is created under a reinsurance trust agreement

(i) to which a regulatory authority — being the Superintendent of Financial Institutions or a provincial regulatory authority having powers similar to those of the Superintendent — is a party, and

(ii) that accords with guidelines issued by the regulatory authority relating to reinsurance arrangements with unregistered insurers

and a particular amount is paid or credited to a non-resident person as income of or from the trust and can reasonably be regarded as having been derived from the dividend, interest or royalty payment, as the case may be, no tax is payable because of paragraph (1)(*c*) as a consequence of the payment or crediting of the particular amount if no tax would have been payable under this Part in respect of the dividend, interest or royalty payment, as the case may be, if it had been paid directly to the non-resident person instead of to the trust.

History: S. 212(9)(*d*) was added by S.C. 2013, c. 34, s. 347(16), applicable to amounts paid or credited after 2000. In addition, a written application made under subsection 227(6) in respect of a particular amount that has been paid to the Receiver General is deemed to be filed on time if

(*a*) the application is filed with the Minister of National Revenue by December 23, 2013 [within 180 days after royal assent]; and

(*b*) the particular amount is an amount on which tax would not be payable because of the application of subsection 212(9) if that subsection 212(9) were read without reference to its paragraphs (*a*) to (*c*).

See also the application provision under 227(6).

Related Sections: S. 104(1) Reference to trust or estate; s. 132(6) Meaning of "mutual fund trust"; s. 133(8), "non-resident owned investment corporation"; s. 134.1(1) NRO — transition.

Information Circulars: IC 77-16R4 Non-resident income tax.

Interpretation Bulletins: *Secondary* — IT-465R Non-resident beneficiaries of trusts.

► 212(10) ◄

(10) Trust beneficiaries residing outside of Canada. Where all the beneficiaries of a trust established before 1949 reside, during a taxation year, in one country other than Canada and all amounts included in computing the income of the trust for the taxation year were received from persons resident in that country, no tax is payable under paragraph (1)(*c*) on an amount paid or credited in the taxation year to a beneficiary as income of or from the trust.

Interpretation Bulletins: *Secondary* — IT-465R Non-resident beneficiaries of trusts.

► 212(11) ◄

(11) Payment to beneficiary as income of trust. An amount paid or credited by a trust or an estate to a beneficiary or other person beneficially interested therein shall be deemed, for the purpose of paragraph (1)(*c*) and without limiting the generality thereof, to have been paid or credited as income of the trust or estate, regardless of the source from which the trust or estate derived it.

Related Sections: s. 107(5) Distribution to non-resident; 210 [Interpretation]; 210.2 Tax on income of trust; 210.3 Where no designated beneficiaries; s. 248(25) Beneficially interested.

Interpretation Bulletins: *Secondary* — IT-465R Non-resident beneficiaries of trusts.

► 212(11.1) ◄

(11.1) Idem — (Repealed by 1988, c. 55, s. 161(6).)

► 212(11.2) ◄

(11.2) Idem — (Repealed by 1988, c. 55, s. 161(6).)

► 212(12) ◄

(12) Deemed payments to spouse, etc. Where by reason of subsection 56(4) or (4.1) or any of sections 74.1 to 75 of this Act or section 74 of the *Income Tax Act*, chapter 148 of the Revised Statutes of Canada, 1952, there is included in computing a taxpayer's income under Part I for a taxation year an amount paid or credited to a non-resident person in the year, no tax is payable under this section on that amount.

Interpretation Bulletins: *Secondary* — IT-369R Attribution of trust income to settlor; IT-440R2 Transfer of rights to income.

► 212(13) ◄

(13) Rent and other payments. For the purposes of this section, where a non-resident person pays or credits an amount as, on account or in lieu of payment of, or in satisfaction of,

(*a*) rent for the use in Canada of property (other than property that is rolling stock as defined in section 2 of the *Railway Act*),

(*b*) a timber royalty in respect of a timber resource property or a timber limit in Canada,

(*c*) a payment of a superannuation or pension benefit under a registered pension plan or of a distribution to one or more persons out of or under a retirement compensation arrangement,

(*d*) a payment of a retiring allowance or a death benefit to the extent that the payment is deductible in computing the payer's taxable income earned in Canada,

(*e*) a payment described in any of paragraphs (1)(*k*) to (*n*), (*q*) and (*v*),

(*f*) interest on any mortgage, hypothecary claim or other indebtedness entered into or issued or modified after March 31, 1977 and secured by real property situated in Canada or an interest therein, or by immovables situated in Canada or real rights therein, to the extent that the amount so paid or credited is deductible in computing the non-resident person's taxable income earned in Canada or the amount on which the non-resident person is liable to pay tax under Part I, or

(*g*) an amount to which paragraph (1)(*i*) would apply if the amount paid or credited were paid or credited by a person resident in Canada, and that amount affects, or is intended to affect, in any way whatever,

(i) the acquisition or provision of property or services in Canada,

(ii) the acquisition or provision of property or services outside Canada by a person resident in Canada, or

(iii) the acquisition or provision outside Canada of a taxable Canadian property,

the non-resident person shall be deemed in respect of that payment to be a person resident in Canada.

History: S. 212(13)(*f*) was replaced by S.C. 2013, c. 34, s. 157(2), in force June 26, 2013, and formerly read:

(*f*) interest on any mortgage, hypothecary claim or other indebtedness entered into or issued or modified after March 31, 1977 and secured by real property situated in Canada or an interest therein to the extent that the amount so paid or credited is deductible in computing the non-resident person's taxable income earned in Canada or the amount on which the non-resident person is liable to pay tax under Part I,

S. 212(13)(*g*) was added by S.C. 2013, c. 34, s. 347(17), applicable to amounts paid or credited after October 7, 2003, except that the portion of paragraph 212(13)(*g*) before subparagraph (i) is to be read as follows before July 16, 2010:

"(*g*) an amount to which paragraph (1)(*i*) applies if that amount affects, or is intended to affect, in any way whatever,"

Related Regulations: 202(4); 211.

Related Sections: S. 13(21),"timber resource property"; s. 212(1)(*d*) Rents, royalties, etc., (*e*) Timber royalties, (*h*) Pension benefits, (*j*) Benefits and (*j*.1) Retiring allowances; s. 248(1), "retiring allowance", "death benefit", "superannuation or pension benefit"; s. 248(4.1) Real right in immovables.

Tax Profile: March 2013 — Non-Resident Investment in Canadian Real Estate.

Information Circulars: IC 77-16R4 Non-resident income tax.

Interpretation Bulletins: *Secondary* — IT-303 Know-how and similar payments to non-residents.

► 212(13.1) ◄

(13.1) Application of Part XIII tax where payer or payee is a partnership. For the purposes of this Part, other than section 216,

(*a*) where a partnership pays or credits an amount to a non-resident person, the partnership shall, in respect of the portion of that amount that is deductible, or that would but for section 21 be deductible in computing the amount of the income or loss, as the case may be, referred to in paragraph 96(1)(*f*) or (*g*) if the references therein to "a particular place" and "that particular place" were read as references to "Canada", be deemed to be a person resident in Canada;

(*a*.1) where a partnership pays, credits or provides to a non-resident person an amount described in subsection (5.1), the partnership is deemed in respect of the amount to be a person; and

(*b*) where a person resident in Canada pays or credits an amount to a partnership (other than a Canadian partnership within the meaning assigned by section 102), the partnership shall be deemed, in respect of that payment, to be a non-resident person.

Related Regulations: 202(5).

Related Sections: S. 212(13.3)(b) Application of Part XIII to authorized foreign bank; s. 227(15) Partnership included in "person".

Canadian Petroleum Tax Journal: Update on Cross-Border Tax Issues, Stan R. Ebel and Edward C. Osterberg, Jr., 1997, Vol. 10, No. 1.

Canadian Tax Foundation: Brodlieb, *Payments to a Partnership with a Non-Resident Member*, 2015 Canadian Tax Focus 5(2):3–4.

Tax Profile: March 2013 — Non-Resident Investment in Canadian Real Estate; June 2012 — Use of Canadian Partnerships by Non-Residents; October 2010 — Non-Resident Investment in Canadian Real Estate.

Tax Topics: No. 1802, Non-Resident Partners and Canadian Real Estate.

Information Circulars: IC 77-16R4 Non-resident income tax.

Interpretation Bulletins: *Secondary* — IT-81R Partnerships — Income of non-resident partners; IT-303 Know-how and similar payments to non-residents.

Cases: The taxpayer held a note from a non-resident partnership which it converted into another form of indebtedness. The conversion did not constitute a payment or credit within the meaning of s. 212(13.1)(*b*) since the original note did not give rise to a credit, payment or loan and one instrument was simply substituted for another. *The Queen v. Gillette Canada Inc.*, 2003 DTC 5078 (F.C.A.), affirming 2001 DTC 895 (T.C.C.).

► 212(13.2) ◄

(13.2) Application of Part XIII tax — non-resident operates in Canada. For the purposes of this Part, a particular non-resident person, who in a taxation year pays or credits to another non-resident person an amount other than an amount to which subsection (13) applies, is deemed to be a person resident in Canada in respect of the portion of the amount that is deductible in computing the particular non-resident person's taxable income earned in Canada for any taxation year from a source that is neither a treaty-protected business nor a treaty-protected property.

History: S. 212(13.2) was replaced by S.C. 2013, c. 34, s. 347(18), applicable to amounts paid or credited under obligations entered into after December 20, 2002, and formerly read:

(13.2) *Application of Part XIII tax where non-resident operates in Canada.* For the purposes of this Part, where in a taxation year

(*a*) a non-resident person whose business was carried on principally in Canada, or

(*b*) a non-resident person who

(i) manufactures or processes goods in Canada,

(ii) operates an oil or gas well in Canada or extracts petroleum or natural gas from a natural accumulation thereof in Canada, or

(iii) extracts minerals from a mineral resource in Canada

Related Regulations: 202(6).

Canadian Tax Foundation: Wertschek, *Current Issues on Withholding Tax: Interest Paid by Non-Residents*, 2004 British Columbia Tax Conference 1:1–14.

Tax Profile: March 2013 — Non-Resident Investment in Canadian Real Estate.

Information Circulars: IC 77-16R4 Non-resident income tax.

Interpretation Bulletins: *Secondary* — IT-303 Know-how and similar payments to non-residents.

Cases: Construction interest capitalized under s. 18(3.1) was not "deductible in computing" the taxpayer's "taxable income earned in Canada for any taxation year" within the meaning of s. 212(13.2). *Eastern Success Co. Ltd. v. The Queen*, 2004 DTC 3521 (T.C.C.).

▶ 212(13.3) ◀

(13.3) Application of Part XIII to authorized foreign bank. An authorized foreign bank is deemed to be resident in Canada for the purposes of

(*a*) this Part, in respect of any amount paid or credited to or by the bank in respect of its Canadian banking business; and

(*b*) the application in paragraph (13.1)(*b*) of the definition "Canadian partnership" in respect of a partnership interest held by the bank in the course of its Canadian banking business.

Related Sections: S. 94.1(2)(*t*) Authorized foreign bank deemed Canadian resident; s. 102(1) Definition of "Canadian partnership"; s. 218.2 Branch interest tax; s. 248(1), "authorized foreign bank", "Canadian banking business".

▶ 212(14) ◀

(14) Certificate of exemption — (Repealed by S.C. 2007, c. 35, s. 59(4).)

Related Sections: S. 172(3)(*d*) Appeal from refusal to register, revocation of registration, etc.; s. 172(4)(*c*) Deemed refusal to register — no notification within 180 days; s. 212(1)(*b*)(iv) Interest.

Forms: NR6A — Application for Certificate of Exemption; NR7-R — Application for Refund of Non-Resident Tax Withheld.

Information Circulars: IC 77-16R4 Non-resident income tax (paras. 79 to 82).

▶ 212(15) ◀

(15) Certain obligations. For the purposes of subparagraph (1)(*b*)(ii), after November 18, 1974 interest on a bond, debenture, note, mortgage, hypothecary claim or similar obligation that is insured by the Canada Deposit Insurance Corporation is deemed not to be interest with respect to an obligation guaranteed by the Government of Canada.

Interpretation Bulletins: *Secondary* — IT-155R3 Exemption from non-resident tax on interest payable on certain bonds, debentures, notes, hypothecs or similar obligations.

▶ 212(16) ◀

(16) Payments for temporary use of rolling stock. Clause (1)(*d*)(vii)(A) does not apply to a payment in a year for the temporary use of railway rolling stock by a railway company to a person resident in a country other than Canada unless that country grants substantially similar relief for the year to the company in respect of payments received by it for the temporary use by a person resident in that country of railway rolling stock.

Information Circulars: IC 77-16R4 Non-resident income tax.

▶ 212(17) ◀

(17) Exception. This section is not applicable to payments out of or under an employee benefit plan or employee trust.

Related Sections: S. 2(3) Tax payable by non-resident persons; s. 248(1), "employee benefit plan", "employee trust".

Interpretation Bulletins: *Secondary* — IT-502 Employee benefit plans and employee trusts.

▶ 212(17.1) ◀

(17.1) Payments to the International Olympic Committee and the International Paralympic Committee. Notwithstanding subsections (1) and (2),

(*a*) the International Olympic Committee is not taxable under this Part on any amount paid or credited to it, after 2005 and before 2011, in respect of the 2010 Olympic Winter Games, and

(*b*) the International Paralympic Committee is not taxable under this Part on any amount paid or credited to it, after 2005 and before 2011, in respect of the 2010 Paralympic Winter Games.

▶ 212(18) ◀

(18) Undertaking. Every person who in a taxation year is a prescribed financial institution or a person resident in Canada who is a registered securities dealer shall on demand from the Minister, served personally or by registered letter, file within such reasonable time as may be stipulated in the demand, an undertaking in prescribed form relating to the avoidance of payment of tax under this Part.

Related Regulations: 806.

Related Sections: S. 248(1), "registered securities dealer".

Forms: NR4 Sum. — Return of Amounts Paid or Credited to Non-Residents of Canada; NR4 — Statement of Amounts Paid or Credited to Non-Residents of Canada.

▶ 212(19) ◀

(19) Tax on registered securities dealers. Every taxpayer who is a registered securities dealer resident in Canada shall pay a tax under this Part equal to the amount determined by the formula

$$1/365 \times .25 \times (A - B) \times C$$

where

A is the total of all amounts each of which is the amount of money provided before the end of a day to the taxpayer (and not returned or repaid before the end of the day) by or on behalf of a non-resident person as collateral or as consideration for a security that was lent or transferred under a designated securities lending arrangement,

B is the total of

(*a*) all amounts each of which is the amount of money provided before the end of the day by or on behalf of the taxpayer (and not returned or repaid before the end of the day) to a non-resident person as collateral or as consideration for a security that is described in paragraph (*a*) of the definition "fully exempt interest" in subsection (3), or that is an obligation of the government of any country, province, state, municipality or other political subdivision, and that was lent or transferred under a securities lending arrangement, and

(*b*) the greater of

(i) 10 times the greatest amount determined, under the laws of the province or provinces in which the taxpayer is a registered securities dealer, to be the capital employed by the taxpayer at the end of the day, and

(ii) 20 times the greatest amount of capital required, under the laws of the province or provinces in which the taxpayer is a registered securities dealer, to be maintained by the taxpayer as a margin in respect of securities described in paragraph (*a*) of the definition "fully exempt interest" in subsection (3), or that is an obligation of the government of any country, province, state, municipality or other political subdivision, at the end of the day, and

C is the prescribed rate of interest in effect for the day,

and shall remit that amount to the Receiver General on or before the 15th day of the month after the month in which the day occurs.

Related Regulations: 4301.

Related Sections: S. 260(1), "securities lending arrangement".

▶ 212(20) ◀

(20) Designated SLA. For the purpose of subsection (19), a designated securities lending arrangement is a securities lending arrangement

(*a*) under which

(i) the lender is a prescribed financial institution or a registered securities dealer resident in Canada,

(ii) the particular security lent or transferred is an obligation described in paragraph (*a*) of the definition "fully exempt interest" in subsection (3) or an obligation of the government of any country, province, state, municipality or other political subdivision,

(iii) the amount of money provided to the lender at any time during the term of the arrangement either as collateral or as consideration for the particular security does not exceed 110% of the fair market value at that time of the particular security; and

(*b*) that was neither intended, nor made as a part of a series of securities lending arrangements, loans or other transactions that was intended, to be in effect for more than 270 days.

SECTION 212.1: Non-arm's length sales of shares by non-residents

▶ 212.1(1) ◀

(1) [Non-arm's length sales of shares by non-residents]. Subsection (1.1) applies if a non-resident person disposes of shares (in this section referred to as the "subject shares") of any class of the capital stock of a corporation resident in Canada (in this section referred to as the "subject corporation") to another corporation resident in Canada (in this section referred to as the "purchaser corporation") with which the non-resident person does not (otherwise than because of a right referred to in paragraph 251(5)(*b*)) deal at arm's length and, immediately after the disposition, the subject corporation is connected (within the meaning that would be assigned by subsection 186(4) if the references in that subsection to "payer corporation" and "particular corporation" were read as "subject corporation" and "purchaser corporation", respectively, and if section 186 were read without reference to its subsection (6)) with the purchaser corporation.

Editorial Note: Section 212.1 applies when certain non-resident persons (which can include certain partnerships) dispose of shares (the subject shares) of a Canadian-resident corporation (the subject corporation) to another Canadian-resident corporation (the purchaser corporation), the non-resident person does not (other than because of s. 251(5)(*b*)) deal at arm's length with the purchaser corporation, and, immediately after the disposition, the subject corporation is connected with the purchaser corporation under s. 186(4). Subsection 212.1(3) expands the circumstances under which a non-resident will be considered not to deal at arm's length with the purchaser. In general terms, when a transfer is covered by this provision, the purchaser corporation is deemed to have paid a dividend equal to the amount by which the fair market value of the consideration (other than shares of the purchaser) received by the non-resident exceeds the paid-up capital of the transferred shares of the subject corporation. Such a deemed dividend will be subject to non-resident withholding tax under s. 212(2). In addition, the PUC of the shares of the purchaser corporation is reduced by the amount by which the increase in the PUC, if any, as a result of the disposition exceeds the PUC of the subject shares less the fair market value of any non-share consideration. Where there is an increase in the PUC of more than one class of shares, the amount of the reduction is applied proportionately. Subsection 212.1(4) provides a relieving exception to permit a Canadian-resident purchaser corporation that acquires shares of a non-resident corporation that itself owns shares of a Canadian corporation to simplify its corporate structure in the limited circumstances noted in paragraphs 212.1(4)(*a*) and (*b*).

In cases of a resident trust or a partnership ("conduit"), look-through rules in 212.1(7) apply where the conduit disposes of shares of a subject corporation to a purchaser corporation, or where a beneficiary or member of the conduit disposes of its interest in the conduit shares to a purchaser corporation and the fair market value of the interest is attributable to shares of a subject corporation. (Deeming rules also apply to determine whether one corporation is the subject corporation and the other is the purchaser corporation, and whether they are connected.) For a partnership that disposes of subject shares, the rules can apply if in respect of any non-resident member, if the non-resident member does not deal at arm's length with the purchaser corporation; for dispositions before February 27, 2018, the rules applied generally only if a majority-interest member or group of members of the partnership were non-resident. Further look-through rules under s. 212.1(6) apply where a trust or partnership is a beneficiary or member of another trust or partnership.

Section 212.1 provides the equivalent of s. 84.1 in respect of non-resident corporations and stops the artificial increase in paid-up capital by a non-resident corporation.

History: S. 212.1(1) was replaced by S.C. 2018, c. 27, s. 21(1), applicable in respect of dispositions that occur after February 26, 2018, and formerly read:

(1) *Non-arm's length sales of shares by non-residents.* Subsection (1.1) applies if a non-resident person or designated partnership (in this subsection and subsections (1.1) and (1.2) referred to as the "non-resident person") disposes of shares (in this section referred to as the "subject shares") of any class of the capital stock of a corporation resident in Canada (in this section referred to as the "subject corporation") to another corporation resident in Canada (in this section referred to as the "purchaser corporation") with which the non-resident person does not (otherwise than because of a right referred to in paragraph 251(5)(*b*)) deal at arm's length and, immediately after the disposition, the subject corporation is connected (within the meaning that would be assigned by subsection 186(4) if the references in that subsection to "payer corporation" and "particular corporation" were read as "subject corporation" and "purchaser corporation", respectively) with the purchaser corporation.

S. 212.1(1) was replaced by S.C. 2016, c. 12, s. 58(1), applicable in respect of dispositions that occur after March 21, 2016, and formerly read:

(1) *Non-arm's length sales of shares by non-residents.* If a non-resident person, a designated partnership or a non-resident-owned investment corporation (in this section referred to as the "non-resident person") disposes of shares (in this section referred to as the "subject shares") of any class of the capital stock of a corporation resident in Canada (in this section referred to as the "subject corporation") to another corporation resident in Canada (in this section referred to as the "purchaser corporation") with which the non-resident person does not (otherwise than because of a right referred to in paragraph 251(5)(*b*)) deal at arm's length and, immediately after the disposition, the subject corporation is connected (within the meaning that would be assigned by subsection 186(4) if the references in that subsection to "payer corporation" and "particular corporation" were read as "subject corporation" and "purchaser corporation", respectively) with the purchaser corporation,

(*a*) the amount, if any, by which the fair market value of any consideration (other than any share of the capital stock of the purchaser corporation) received by the non-resident person from the purchaser corporation for the subject shares exceeds the paid-up capital in respect of the subject shares immediately before the disposition shall, for the purposes of this Act, be deemed to be a dividend paid at the time of the disposition by the purchaser corporation to the non-resident person and received at that time by the non-resident person from the purchaser corporation; and

(*b*) in computing the paid-up capital at any particular time after March 31, 1977 of any particular class of shares of the capital stock of the purchaser corporation, there shall be deducted that proportion of the amount, if any, by which the increase, if any, by virtue of the disposition, in the paid-up capital, computed without reference to this section as it applies to the disposition, in respect of all of the shares of the capital stock of the purchaser corporation exceeds the amount, if any, by which

(i) the paid-up capital in respect of the subject shares immediately before the disposition

exceeds

(ii) the fair market value of the consideration described in paragraph (*a*),

that the increase, if any, by virtue of the disposition, in the paid-up capital, computed without reference to this section as it applies to the disposition, in respect of the particular class of shares is of the increase, if any, by virtue of the disposition, in the paid-up capital, computed without reference to this section as it applies to the disposition, in respect of all of the issued shares of the capital stock of the purchaser corporation.

Related Sections: S. 54, "proceeds of disposition"; s. 84(7) When dividend payable; s. 84.1(1) Non-arm's length sale of shares; s. 89(1), "Canadian corporation", "paid-up capital"; s. 133(8), "non-resident-owned investment corporation"; s. 134 Non-resident-owned corporation not a Canadian corporation, etc; s. 186(7) Interpretation; s. 212(2) Tax on dividends; s. 212.1(3)(*e*) Meaning of "designated partnership"; s. 212.1(4) Where section does not apply. s. 215(6) Liability for tax; s. 227(8) Penalty; s. 212.2(1)(*b*) Application.

Canadian Tax Foundation: Baxter et al., *Surplus Stripping — What's Acceptable, What's Not, and What Should Be?*, 2014 British Columbia Tax Conference 12:1–A5; Meredith and Fehr, *Surplus Stripping: In the Eye of the Beholder*, 2013 British Columbia Tax Conference 14:1–29; Biringer, *Surplus Stripping After Copthorne: Non-Resident Corporations*, 2012 Conference Report 14:1–21.

International Tax: No. 96, Univar — Abusive Surplus Stripping or Legitimate Arm's Length Acquisition Planning?.

Tax Profile: December 2004 — Taxation of Dividends: A Survey in the Context of Private Corporations and Their Shareholders — Part 2.

Forms: NR4 Sum. — Return of Amounts Paid or Credited to Non-Residents of Canada; NR4 — Statement of Amounts Paid or Credited to Non-Residents of Canada.

Information Circulars: IC 77-16R4 Non-resident income tax.

Interpretation Bulletins: *Primary* — IT-489R Non-arm's length sale of shares to a corporation. *Secondary* — IT-463R2 Paid-up capital.

Cases: The taxpayer purchased common shares of two Canadian corporations from non-residents. The payment to the non-residents was deemed to be a dividend from which withholding tax should have been deducted. *Placements Serco Ltée v. The Queen*, 87 DTC 5425 (F.C.A.)

► 212.1(1.1) ◄

(1.1) Non-arm's length sales of shares by non-residents. If this subsection applies,

(*a*) the amount, if any, by which the fair market value of any consideration (other than any share of the capital stock of the purchaser corporation) received by the non-resident person referred to in subsection (1) from the purchaser corporation for the subject shares exceeds the paid-up capital in respect of the subject shares immediately before the disposition shall, for the purposes of this Act, be deemed to be a dividend

(i) in the case that, immediately before the disposition, the purchaser corporation controlled the non-resident person,

(A) paid at the time of the disposition by the subject corporation to the non-resident person, and

(B) received at that time by the non-resident person from the subject corporation, and

(ii) in any other case,

(A) paid at the time of the disposition by the purchaser corporation to the non-resident person, and

(B) received at that time by the non-resident person from the purchaser corporation; and

(*b*) in computing the paid-up capital at any particular time after March 31, 1977 of any particular class of shares of the capital stock of the purchaser corporation, there shall be deducted that proportion of the amount, if any, by which the increase, if any, by virtue of the disposition, in the paid-up capital, computed without reference to this section as it applies to the disposition, in respect of all of the shares of the capital stock of the purchaser corporation exceeds the amount, if any, by which

(i) the paid-up capital in respect of the subject shares immediately before the disposition

exceeds

(ii) the fair market value of the consideration described in paragraph (*a*),

that the increase, if any, by virtue of the disposition, in the paid-up capital, computed without reference to this section as it applies to the disposition, in respect of the particular class of shares is of the increase, if any, by virtue of the disposition, in the paid-up capital, computed without reference to this section as it applies to the disposition, in respect of all of the issued shares of the capital stock of the purchaser corporation.

History: S. 212.1(1.1)(*a*), the portion before subparagraph (i) was replaced by S.C. 2018, c. 27, s. 21(2), applicable in respect of dispositions that occur after February 26, 2018, and formerly read:

> (*a*) the amount, if any, by which the fair market value of any consideration (other than any share of the capital stock of the purchaser corporation) received by the non-resident person from the purchaser corporation for the subject shares exceeds the paid-up capital in respect of the subject shares immediately before the disposition shall, for the purposes of this Act, be deemed to be a dividend

S. 212.1(1.1) was added by S.C. 2016, c. 12, s. 58(1), applicable in respect of dispositions that occur after March 21, 2016.

► 212.1(1.2) ◄

(1.2) Deemed consideration. For the purposes of subsections (1) and (1.1), if, in the absence of this subsection, no consideration would be received by the non-resident person referred to in subsection (1) from the purchaser corporation for the subject shares, the non-resident person is deemed to receive consideration other than shares of the capital stock of the purchaser corporation from the purchaser corporation for the subject shares, the fair market value of which is equal to the amount, if any, by which the fair market value of the subject shares disposed of by the non-resident person exceeds the amount of any increase because of the disposition in the fair market value of the shares of the capital stock of the purchaser corporation.

History: S. 212.1(1.2) was replaced by S.C. 2018, c. 27, s. 21(3), applicable in respect of dispositions that occur after February 26, 2018, and formerly read:

> (1.2) *Deemed consideration.* For the purposes of subsections (1) and (1.1), if, in the absence of this subsection, no consideration would be received by the non-resident person from the purchaser corporation for the subject shares, the non-resident person is deemed to receive consideration other than shares of the capital stock of the purchaser corporation from the purchaser corporation for the subject shares, the fair market value of which is equal to the amount, if any, by which the fair market value of the subject shares disposed of by the non-resident person exceeds the amount of any increase because of the disposition in the fair market value of the shares of the capital stock of the purchaser corporation.

S. 212.1(1.2) was added by S.C. 2016, c. 12, s. 58(1), applicable in respect of dispositions that occur after March 21, 2016.

► 212.1(2) ◄

(2) Idem. In computing the paid-up capital at any particular time after March 31, 1977 of any particular class of shares of the capital stock of a corporation, there shall be added an amount equal to the lesser of

(*a*) the amount, if any, by which

(i) the total of all amounts each of which is an amount deemed by subsection 84(3), (4) or (4.1) to be a dividend on shares of the particular class paid after March 31, 1977 and before the particular time by the corporation and received by a non-resident-owned investment corporation or by a person who is not a corporation resident in Canada

exceeds

(ii) the total that would be determined under subparagraph (i) if this Act were read without reference to paragraph (1.1)(*b*), and

(*b*) the total of all amounts each of which is an amount required by paragraph (1.1)(*b*) to be deducted in computing the paid-up capital in respect of the particular class of shares after March 31, 1977 and before the particular time.

History: S. 212.1(2)(*a*)(ii) was replaced by S.C. 2016, c. 12, s. 58(2), applicable in respect of dispositions that occur after March 21, 2016, and formerly read:

(ii) the total that would be determined under subparagraph (i) if this Act were read without reference to paragraph (1)(*b*), and

S. 212.1(2)(*b*) was replaced by S.C. 2016, c. 12, s. 58(3), applicable in respect of dispositions that occur after March 21, 2016, and formerly read:

(*b*) the total of all amounts each of which is an amount required by paragraph (1)(*b*) to be deducted in computing the paid-up capital in respect of the particular class of shares after March 31, 1977 and before the particular time.

Related Sections: S. 84.1(3) Addition to paid-up capital.

► 212.1(3) ◄

(3) Idem. For the purposes of this section,

(*a*) a non-resident person shall, for greater certainty, be deemed not to deal at arm's length with a purchaser corporation at the time of a disposition described in subsection (1) if the non-resident person was,

(i) immediately before the disposition, one of a group of less than 6 persons that controlled the subject corporation, and

(ii) immediately after the disposition, one of a group of less than 6 persons that controlled the purchaser corporation, each member of which was a member of the group referred to in subparagraph (i);

(*b*) for the purposes of determining whether or not a non-resident person referred to in paragraph (*a*) was a member of a group of less than six persons that controlled a corporation at any time, any shares of the capital stock of that corporation owned at that time by any of the following persons shall be deemed to be owned at that time by the non-resident person and not by the person who actually owned the shares at that time:

(i) the non-resident person's *child* (within the meaning assigned by subsection 70(10)), who is under 18 years of age, or the non-resident person's spouse or common-law partner,

(ii) a trust of which the non-resident person, a person described in subparagraph (i) or a corporation described in subparagraph (iii) is a beneficiary,

(iii) a corporation controlled by the non-resident person, a person described in subparagraph (i), a trust described in subparagraph (ii) or any combination thereof, and

(iv) a partnership of which the non-resident person or a person described in one of subparagraphs (i) to (iii) is a majority-interest partner or a member of a "majority-interest group of partners" (as defined in subsection 251.1(3));

(*c*) a trust and a beneficiary of the trust or a person related to a beneficiary of the trust shall be deemed not to deal with each other at arm's length;

(*d*) for the purpose of paragraph (*a*),

(i) a group of persons in respect of a corporation means any 2 or more persons each of whom owns shares of the capital stock of the corporation,

(ii) a corporation that is controlled by one or more members of a particular group of persons in respect of that corporation shall be considered to be controlled by that group of persons, and

(iii) a corporation may be controlled by a person or a particular group of persons notwithstanding that the corporation is also controlled or deemed to be controlled by another person or group of persons; and

(*e*) (Repealed by S.C. 2018, c. 27, s. 21(6).)

(*f*) in this subsection, a person includes a partnership.

History: S. 212.1(3)(*a*), the portion before subparagraph (i) was replaced by S.C. 2018, c. 27, s. 21(4), applicable in respect of dispositions that occur after February 26, 2018, and formerly read:

(*a*) a non-resident person or designated partnership shall, for greater certainty, be deemed not to deal at arm's length with a purchaser corporation at the time of a disposition described in subsection (1) if the non-resident person or designated partnership was,

S. 212.1(3)(*b*) was replaced by S.C. 2018, c. 27, s. 21(5), applicable in respect of dispositions that occur after February 26, 2018, and formerly read:

(*b*) for the purposes of determining whether or not a particular non-resident person or designated partnership (in this paragraph referred to as the "taxpayer") referred to in paragraph (*a*) was a member of a group of less than 6 persons that controlled a corporation at any time, any shares of the capital stock of that corporation owned at that time by

(i) the taxpayer's child (within the meaning assigned by subsection 70(10)), who is under 18 years of age, or the taxpayer's spouse or common-law partner,

(ii) a trust of which the taxpayer, a person described in subparagraph (i) or a corporation described in subparagraph (iii) is a beneficiary,

(iii) a corporation controlled by the taxpayer, a person described in subparagraph (i), a trust described in subparagraph (ii) or any combination thereof, or

(iv) a partnership of which the taxpayer or a person described in one of subparagraphs (i) to (iii) is a majority-interest partner or a member of a majority-interest group of partners (as defined in subsection 251.1(3))

shall be deemed to be owned at that time by the taxpayer and not by the person who actually owned the shares at that time;

S. 212.1(3)(*e*), was repealed by S.C. 2018, c. 27, s. 21(6), applicable in respect of dispositions that occur after February 26, 2018, and formerly read:

(*e*) a "designated partnership" means a partnership of which either a majority-interest partner or every member of a majority-interest group of partners (as defined in subsection 251.1(3)) is a non-resident person; and

S. 212.1(3)(*a*), the portion before subparagraph (i) was replaced by S.C. 2016, c. 12, s. 58(4), applicable in respect of dispositions that occur after March 21, 2016, and formerly read:

(*a*) in respect of any disposition described in subsection (1) by a non-resident person of shares of the capital stock of a subject corporation to a purchaser corporation, the non-resident person shall, for greater certainty, be deemed not to deal at arm's length with the purchaser corporation if the non-resident person was,

S. 212.1(3)(*b*), the portion before subparagraph (i) was replaced by S.C. 2016, c. 12, s. 58(5), applicable in respect of dispositions that occur after March 21, 2016, and formerly read:

(*b*) for the purposes of determining whether or not a particular non-resident person (in this paragraph referred to as the "taxpayer") referred to in paragraph (a) was a member of a group of less than 6 persons that controlled a corporation at any time, any shares of the capital stock of that corporation owned at that time by

S. 212.1(3)(b)(iv) was replaced by S.C. 2013, c. 40, s. 82(1), in force December 12, 2013, and formerly read:

(iv) a partnership of which the taxpayer or a person described in one of [sub]paragraphs (i) to (iii) is a majority interest partner or a member of a majority interest group of partners (as defined in subsection 251.1(3))

S. 212.1(3)(e) was replaced by S.C. 2013, c. 40, s. 82(2), in force December 12, 2013, and formerly read:

(e) a "designated partnership" means a partnership of which either a majority interest partner or every member of a majority interest group of partners (as defined in subsection 251.1(3)) is a non-resident person or a non-resident-owned investment corporation; and

Related Sections: S. 248(1), "common-law partner"; s. 251(1) Arm's length; s. 256(6) Exception to control; s. 256(6.1) Simultaneous control; s. 256(6.2) Application to control in fact.

► 212.1(4) ◄

(4) Where section does not apply. Notwithstanding subsection (1), subsection (1.1) does not apply in respect of a disposition by a non-resident corporation of shares of a subject corporation to a purchaser corporation if

(a) immediately before the disposition, the purchaser corporation controlled the non-resident corporation; and

(b) it is not the case that, at the time of the disposition, or as part of a transaction or event or series of transactions or events that includes the disposition, a non-resident person

(i) holds, directly or indirectly, shares of the capital stock of the purchaser corporation, and

(ii) does not deal at arm's length with the purchaser corporation.

History: S. 212.1(4)(b), the portion before before subparagraph (ii) was replaced by S.C. 2018, c. 27, s. 21(7), applicable in respect of dispositions that occur after February 26, 2018, and formerly read:

(b) it is not the case that, at the time of the disposition, or as part of a transaction or event or series of transactions or events that includes the disposition, a non-resident person or designated partnership

(i) owns, directly or indirectly, shares of the capital stock of the purchaser corporation, and

S. 212.1(4) was replaced by S.C. 2016, c. 12, s. 58(6), applicable in respect of dispositions that occur after March 21, 2016, and formerly read:

(4) *Where section does not apply.* Notwithstanding subsection (1), this section does not apply in respect of a disposition by a non-resident corporation of shares of a subject corporation to a purchaser corporation that immediately before the disposition controlled the non-resident corporation.

Related Sections: S. 256(6) Exception to control; s. 256(6.1) Simultaneous control; s. 256(6.2) Application to control in fact.

Canadian Tax Foundation: Pandher and Johnston, *Univar: Arm's-Length Surplus Strip Not Abusive*, 2018 Canadian Tax Focus 8(1):8–9.

Cases: The purpose of section 212.1 is not to prevent the removal from Canada by an arm's length purchaser of a Canadian corporation of any surplus such corporation accumulated prior to the acquisition of control. The transactions did not clearly frustrate the object, spirit, and purpose of section 212.1 as it was written in 2007, and 2016 amendments could not be used to make a finding that the avoidance transaction was abusive. *Univar v. The Queen*, 2017 DTC 5119 (FCA)

► 212.1(5) ◄

(5) Tiered trusts and partnerships. For the purposes of this section and paragraph (k) of the definition *proceeds of disposition* in section 54, a person or partnership that is, at any time, a beneficiary under a trust (other than a trust that is the non-resident person referred to in subsection (1)), or a member of a partnership (such trust or partnership referred to in this subsection as the "particular conduit"), that is a beneficiary under a trust or member of a partnership (such trust or partnership referred to in this subsection as the "other conduit") is deemed

(a) to be a beneficiary under or member of, as the case may be, the other conduit; and

(b) to hold the interest in the other conduit that is held by the particular conduit in the proportion expressed by the formula

$$A/B$$

where

A is the portion of the fair market value, at that time, of the person or partnership's interest in the particular conduit that is attributable to the interest in the other conduit held by the particular conduit, and

B is the total fair market value, at that time, of all direct interests (determined without reference to this subsection) in the other conduit.

History: S. 212.1(5) was added by S.C. 2018, c. 27, s. 21(8), applicable in respect of dispositions that occur after February 26, 2018.

► 212.1(6) ◄

(6) Trusts and partnerships look-through rule. The following rules apply for the following purposes:

(a) for the purposes of this subsection and subsections (1) and (1.1), if at any time an interest (in this paragraph referred to as the "pertinent interest") in a trust or a partnership (each referred to in this subsection as a "conduit") is disposed of by a person or partnership with an interest as a beneficiary under the conduit or that is a member of the conduit (each referred to in this subsection as a "holder"), as the case may be, to a purchaser and any portion of the fair market value of the pertinent interest is attributable to shares of the capital stock of a corporation resident in Canada held, directly or indirectly (unless all of the shares are held indirectly through one or more non-resident corporations), by the conduit (in this paragraph referred to as the "shares held by the conduit"), then

(i) the holder is deemed, on a class-by-class basis, to have disposed, at that time, of the shares held by the conduit to the purchaser, and the purchaser is deemed to have acquired the shares, in the proportion expressed by the formula

$$A/B$$

where

A is the portion of the fair market value, at that time, of the pertinent interest that is attributable to the shares held by the conduit, and

B is the total fair market value, at that time, of the shares held by the conduit, and

(ii) the holder is deemed to have received from the purchaser and the purchaser is deemed to have paid to the holder, as consideration for the shares deemed to have been disposed of in subparagraph (i), consideration (other than any share of the capital stock of the purchaser corporation) in an amount determined by the formula

$$A \times B/C$$

where

A is the fair market value of the consideration (other than any share of the capital stock of the purchaser corporation) that is received by the holder from the purchaser for the pertinent interest,

B is the amount determined for A in subparagraph (i), and

C is the total fair market value of the pertinent interest;

(*b*) for the purposes of subsections (1) and (1.1) and paragraph (*c*), if at any time a conduit (other than a non-resident trust) disposes of shares of the capital stock of a corporation resident in Canada to a purchaser, then

(i) each holder of an interest in the conduit is deemed, on a class-by-class basis, to have disposed, at that time, of the shares to the purchaser in the proportion expressed by the formula

$$A/B$$

where

A is the fair market value, at that time, of the holder's interest in the conduit, and

B is the total fair market value, at that time, of all direct interests (determined without reference to subsection (5)) in the conduit, and

(ii) each holder of an interest in the conduit is deemed to have received from the purchaser and the purchaser is deemed to have paid to each such holder, as consideration for the shares deemed to have been disposed of in subparagraph (i), consideration (other than any share of the capital stock of the purchaser corporation) in an amount determined by the formula

$$A \times B/C$$

where

A is the fair market value of the consideration (other than any share of the capital stock of the purchaser corporation) that is received by the conduit from the purchaser for the shares,

B is the amount determined for A in subparagraph (i), and

C is the amount determined for B in subparagraph (i);

(*c*) for the purposes of subsections (1) and (1.1), if at any time a conduit acquires shares of the capital stock of a corporation resident in Canada from a vendor, then

(i) each holder of an interest in the conduit is deemed to have acquired, at that time, the shares from the vendor, on a class-by-class basis, in the proportion expressed by the formula

$$A/B$$

where

A is the fair market value, at that time, of the holder's interest in the conduit, and

B is the total fair market value, at that time, of all direct interests (determined without reference to subsection (5)) in the conduit, and

(ii) each holder of an interest in the conduit is deemed to have paid to the vendor and the vendor is deemed to have received from each such holder, as consideration for the shares deemed to have been acquired in subparagraph (i), consideration (other than any share of the capital stock of the purchaser corporation) in an amount determined by the formula

$$A \times B/C$$

where

A is the fair market value of the consideration (other than any share of the capital stock of the purchaser corporation) that is paid by the conduit to the vendor for the shares,

B is the amount determined for A in subparagraph (i), and

C is the amount determined for B in subparagraph (i); and

(*d*) for the purpose of determining whether the subject corporation is connected with the purchaser corporation for the purposes of subsection (1) at any time, if at that time a conduit owns shares of the capital stock of the subject corporation, each holder of an interest in the conduit is deemed to own, at that time, the shares of each class of the capital stock of the subject corporation that are owned by the conduit the number of which is determined by the formula

$$A \times B/C$$

where

A is the total number of shares of the class of the capital stock of the subject corporation that are owned by the conduit at that time,

B is the fair market value, at that time, of the holder's interest in the conduit, and

C is the total fair market value, at that time, of all direct interests (determined without reference to subsection (5)) in the conduit.

History: S. 212.1(6) was added by S.C. 2018, c. 27, s. 21(8), applicable in respect of dispositions that occur after February 26, 2018.

► 212.1(7) ◄

(7) Avoidance of subsections (5) and (6). The amounts determined for A and B in paragraph (5)(*b*), for A and B in subparagraph (6)(*c*)(i) and for B and C in paragraph (6)(*d*) are, in respect of an interest as a beneficiary under a trust held by a person or partnership, deemed to be equal to one if

(*a*) the person or partnership's share of the accumulating income or capital of the trust depends on the exercise by any person of, or the failure by any person to exercise, any discretionary power; and

(*b*) it can reasonably be considered that one of the reasons for the discretionary power is to avoid or limit the application of subsection (1.1).

History: S. 212.1(7) was added by S.C. 2018, c. 27, s. 21(8), applicable in respect of dispositions that occur after February 26, 2018.

SECTION 212.2: [Deemed dividend]

► 212.2(1) ◄

(1) Application. This section applies where

(*a*) a taxpayer disposes at a particular time of a share of the capital stock of a corporation resident in Canada (or any property more than 10% of the fair market value of which can be attributed to shares of the capital stock of corporations resident in Canada) to

(i) a person resident in Canada,

(ii) a partnership in which any person resident in Canada has, directly or indirectly, an interest, or

(iii) a person or partnership that acquires the share or the property in the course of carrying on a business through a permanent establishment in Canada, as defined in the *Income Tax Regulations*;

(*b*) subsection 212.1(1.1) does not apply in respect of the disposition;

(*c*) the taxpayer is non-resident at the particular time;

(*d*) it is reasonable to conclude that the disposition is part of an expected series of transactions or events that includes the issue after December 15, 1998 of a particular share of the capital stock of a particular insurance corporation resident in Canada on the demutualization (within the meaning assigned by subsection 139.1(1)) of the particular corporation and

(i) after the particular time, the redemption, acquisition or cancellation of the particular share, or a share substituted for the particular share, by the particular corporation or the issuer of the substituted share, as the case may be,

(ii) after the particular time, an increase in the level of dividends declared or paid on the particular share or a share substituted for the particular share, or

(iii) the acquisition, at or after the particular time, of the particular share or a share substituted for the particular share by

(A) a person not dealing at arm's length with the particular corporation or with the issuer of the substituted share, as the case may be, or

(B) a partnership any direct or indirect interest in which is held by a person not dealing at arm's length with the particular corporation or with the issuer of the substituted share, as the case may be; and

(*e*) at the particular time, the person described in subparagraph (*a*)(i) or (iii) or any person who has, directly or indirectly, an interest in the partnership described in subparagraph (*a*)(ii) or (iii) knew, or ought reasonably to have known, of the expected series of transactions or events described in paragraph (*d*).

History: S. 212.2(1)(*b*) was replaced by S.C. 2016, c. 12, s. 59(1), applicable in respect of dispositions that occur after March 21, 2016, and formerly read:

(*b*) subsection 212.1(1) does not apply to the disposition;

Related Sections: S. 248(10) Series of transactions; s. 251(1) Arm's length.

► 212.2(2) ◄

(2) Deemed dividend. For the purposes of this Part, where property is disposed of at any time by a taxpayer to a person or partnership in circumstances in which this section applies,

(*a*) a taxable dividend is deemed to be paid at that time by the person or partnership to the taxpayer and received at the time by the taxpayer;

(*b*) the amount of the dividend is deemed to be equal to the amount determined by the formula

$$A - ((A/B) \times C)$$

where

A is the portion of the proceeds of disposition of the property that can reasonably be attributed to the fair market value of shares of a class of the capital stock of a corporation resident in Canada,

B is the fair market value immediately before that time of shares of that class, and

C is the paid-up capital immediately before that time of that class of shares; and

(*c*) in respect of the dividend, the person or partnership is deemed to be a corporation resident in Canada.

Editorial Note: Section 212.2 is an anti-avoidance rule dealing specifically with the demutualization of insurance corporations and prohibits transactions which would result in Canadian corporations distributing corporate surplus to non-residents free of withholding tax. The rules relating to the demutualization of insurance companies are set out in s. 139.1.

Related Sections: S. 54, "proceeds of disposition"; s. 89(1), "paid-up capital", "taxable dividend"; s. 139.1 Demutualization of insurance corporations; s. 139.2 Mutual holding corporations; s. 248(1), "insurance corporation".

SECTION 212.3: [Foreign affiliate dumping]

► 212.3(1) ◄

(1) Foreign affiliate dumping — conditions for application. Subsection (2) applies to an investment in a non-resident corporation (in this section referred to as the "subject corporation") made at any time (in this section referred to as the "investment time") by a corporation resident in Canada (in this section referred to as the "CRIC") if

(*a*) the subject corporation is immediately after the investment time, or becomes as part of a transaction or event or series of transactions or events that includes the making of the investment, a foreign affiliate of

(i) the CRIC, or

(ii) a corporation that does not deal at arm's length with the CRIC (if the condition in this paragraph is satisfied because of this subparagraph and not because of subparagraph (i), such a corporation is referred to in paragraph (*b*) as an "other Canadian corporation");

(*b*) the CRIC or an other Canadian corporation is immediately after the investment time, or becomes after the investment time and as part of a transaction or event or series of transactions or events that includes the making of the investment, controlled by a non-resident corporation (in this section referred to as the "parent"), and any of the following conditions is satisfied:

(i) if, at the investment time, the parent owned all shares of the capital stock of the CRIC and the other Canadian corporation, if applicable, that are owned — determined without reference to paragraph (25)(*b*) in the case of partnerships referred to in this subparagraph and as if all rights referred to in paragraph 251(5)(*b*), of the parent, each person that does not deal at arm's length with the parent and all of those partnerships, were immediate and absolute and the parent and each of the other persons and partnerships had exercised those rights at the investment time — by the parent, persons that are not dealing at arm's length with the parent and partnerships of which the parent or a non-resident person that is not dealing at arm's length with the parent is a member (other than a limited partner within the meaning assigned by subsection 96(2.4)), the parent would own shares of the capital stock of the CRIC or the other Canadian corporation that

Proposed Amendment

2019 Federal Budget Resolutions

The portion of paragraph 212.3(1)(*b*) of the Act before clause (i)(A) is replaced by the following:

(*b*) the CRIC or an other Canadian corporation is immediately after the investment time, or becomes after the investment time and as part of a transaction or event or series of transactions or events that includes the making of the investment, controlled by one non-resident person or, if no single non-resident person controls the CRIC, by a group of non-resident persons not dealing with each other at arm's length (in this section, that one non-resident person, or each member of the group of non-resident persons, as the case may be, is referred to as a "parent", and the group of non-resident persons, if any, is referred to as the "group of parents"), and any of the following conditions is satisfied:

(i) if, at the investment time, a parent owned all shares of the capital stock of the CRIC and the other Canadian corporation, if applicable, that are owned — determined without reference to paragraph (25)(*b*) in the case of partnerships referred to in this subparagraph and as if all rights referred to in paragraph 251(5)(*b*), of the parent, each person that does not deal at arm's length with the parent and all of those partnerships, were immediate and absolute and the parent and each of the other persons and partnerships had exercised those rights at the investment time — by the parent, persons that are not dealing at arm's length with the parent and partnerships of which the parent or a non-resident person that is not dealing at arm's length with the parent is a member (other than a limited partner within the meaning assigned by subsection 96(2.4)), the parent would own shares of the capital stock of the CRIC or the other Canadian corporation that

Applicable: In respect of transactions or events that occur on or after March 19, 2019.

(A) give the holders of those shares 25% or more of all of the votes that could be cast at any annual meeting of the shareholders in respect of all shares of the capital stock of the CRIC or the other Canadian corporation, as the case may be, or

(B) have a fair market value of 25% or more of the fair market value of all of the issued and outstanding shares of the capital stock of the CRIC or the other Canadian corporation, as the case may be,

(ii) the investment is an acquisition of shares of the capital stock of a subject corporation by a CRIC to which this subparagraph applies because of subsection (19), or

(iii) under an arrangement entered into in connection with the investment, a person or partnership, other than the CRIC or a person related to the CRIC, has in any material respect the risk of loss or opportunity for gain or profit in respect of a property that can reasonably be considered to relate to the investment; and

(*c*) neither subsection (16) nor (18) applies in respect of the investment.

Editorial Note: The "foreign affiliate dumping" rules were announced in the 2012 federal Budget and apply whenever a corporation resident in Canada (a "CRIC") (or, effective September 16, 2016, a corporation that does not deal at arm's length with the CRIC) that is controlled by a non-resident corporation makes an "investment" (as defined in s. 212.3(10)) in a non-resident corporation that is or becomes as part of the series of transactions that includes the investment a foreign affiliate of the CRIC (or, effective September 16, 2016, a foreign affiliate of a corporation that does not deal at arm's length with the CRIC). The rules are complicated and have been the subject of significant criticism as being unduly broad.

History: S. 212.3(1)(*a*) was replaced by S.C. 2017, c. 33, s. 75(1), applicable in respect of transactions or events that occur after September 15, 2016. For this purpose, a portion of a particular amount owing by, or debt obligation of, a subject corporation is deemed to be a separate amount owing or debt obligation that became owing or was acquired, as the case may be, on January 1, 2017 in the same manner and on the same terms as the particular amount owing or debt obligation, if.

(*a*) subsection 212.3(2) of the Act would not apply in respect of the separate amount owing or debt obligation absent the application of subsections (1) and (2);

(*b*) the particular amount owing or debt obligation became owing to, or was acquired by, a CRIC

(i) after March 28, 2012 and before September 16, 2016, or

(ii) before March 29, 2012, if its maturity date was extended after March 28, 2012 and before September 16, 2016; and

(*c*) the portion is the amount outstanding in respect of the particular amount owing or debt obligation on January 1, 2017.

S. 212.3(1)(*a*) formerly read:

(*a*) the subject corporation is immediately after the investment time, or becomes as part of a transaction or event or series of transactions or events that includes the making of the investment, a foreign affiliate of the CRIC;

S. 212.3(1)(*b*) was replaced by S.C. 2017, c. 33, s. 75(2), applicable in respect of transactions or events that occur after September 15, 2016. For this purpose, a portion of a particular amount owing by, or debt obligation of, a subject corporation is deemed to be a separate amount owing or debt obligation that became owing or was acquired, as the case may be, on January 1, 2017 in the same manner and on the same terms as the particular amount owing or debt obligation, if.

(*a*) subsection 212.3(2) of the Act would not apply in respect of the separate amount owing or debt obligation absent the application of subsections (1) and (2);

(*b*) the particular amount owing or debt obligation became owing to, or was acquired by, a CRIC

(i) after March 28, 2012 and before September 16, 2016, or

(ii) before March 29, 2012, if its maturity date was extended after March 28, 2012 and before September 16, 2016; and

(*c*) the portion is the amount outstanding in respect of the particular amount owing or debt obligation on January 1, 2017.

S. 212.3(1)(*b*) formerly read:

(*b*) the CRIC is immediately after the investment time, or becomes after the investment time and as part of a transaction or event or series of transactions or events that includes the making of the investment, controlled by a non-resident corporation (in this section referred to as the "parent"), and any of the following conditions is satisfied:

(i) if, at the investment time, the parent owned all shares of the capital stock of the CRIC that are owned — determined without reference to paragraph 212.3(25)(*b*) in the case of partnerships referred to in this subparagraph and as if all rights referred to in paragraph 251(5)(*b*), of the parent, each person that does not deal at arm's length with the parent and all of those partnerships, were immediate and absolute and the parent and each of the other persons and partnerships had exercised those rights at the investment time — by the parent, persons that are not dealing at arm's length with the parent and partnerships of which the parent or a non-resident person that is not dealing at arm's length with the parent is a member (other than a limited partner within the meaning assigned by subsection 96(2.4)), the parent would own shares of the capital stock of the CRIC that

(A) give the holders of those shares 25% or more of all of the votes that could be cast at any annual meeting of the shareholders in respect of all shares of the capital stock of the CRIC, or

(B) have a fair market value of 25% or more of the fair market value of all of the issued and outstanding shares of the capital stock of the CRIC,

S. 212.3(1)(*b*) was replaced by S.C. 2014, c. 39, s. 65(1), applicable in respect of transactions and events that occur after March 28, 2012.

If an election is made under subsection 49(3) of the *Jobs and Growth Act, 2012* [S.C. 2012, c. 31], section 212.3 of the *Income Tax Act* applies in the manner set out in that subsection in respect of transactions and events that occur after March 28, 2012 and before August 14, 2012.

S. 212.3(1)(*b*) formerly read:

(*b*) the CRIC is at the investment time, or becomes as part of a transaction or event or series of transactions or events that includes the making of the investment, controlled by a non-resident corporation (in this section referred to as the "parent"); and

S. 212.3(1) was added by S.C. 2012, c. 31, s. 49(1), applicable, subject to the election described below, in respect of transactions and events that occur after March 28, 2012. However, s. 212.3 does not apply to transactions that occur before 2013 between parties that deal at arm's length with each other if

(i) either

(A) in the case of an indirect acquisition referred to in paragraph 212.3(10)(*f*), the CRIC referred to in that paragraph is obligated to complete the direct acquisition referred to in that paragraph under the terms of an agreement in writing entered into before March 29, 2012 between the CRIC and a public corporation that is the other corporation resident in Canada referred to in that paragraph, or

(B) the parties are obligated to complete the transaction under the terms of an agreement in writing entered into between the parties before March 29, 2012, and

(ii) no party to the agreement may be excused from the obligation as a result of amendments to the Act.

If a corporation resident in Canada (in this subsection referred to as the "CRIC") and a non-resident corporation that controls the CRIC jointly elect in writing under this subsection in respect of all transactions and events to which subsection 212.3(2) would, in the absence of this subsection, apply and file the election with the Minister of National Revenue on or before the day that is the later of the CRIC's filing-due date for the CRIC's taxation year that includes the day on which this Act receives royal assent [December 14, 2012] and the day that is one year after the day on which this Act receives royal assent [R.A. December 14, 2012], then, in respect of transactions and events that occur before August 14, 2012, section 212.3 is to be read without reference to its subsections (3) to (7), (9), (11) to (14), (17) to (22) and (24) and the following rules apply:

(*a*) subsections 212.3(1) and (2) are to be read as follows:

"(1) Subsection (2) applies to an investment in a non-resident corporation (referred to in this section as the "subject corporation") that is made, at any time, by a corporation resident in Canada (referred to in this section as the "CRIC") if

(*a*) the subject corporation is, immediately after that time, or becomes, as part of a transaction or event or series of transactions or events that includes the investment, a foreign affiliate of the CRIC;

(*b*) the CRIC is at that time controlled by another non-resident corporation (referred to in this section as the "parent"); and

(*c*) the investment may not reasonably be considered to have been made by the CRIC, instead of being made or retained by the parent or another non-resident person that does not deal at arm's length with the parent, primarily for *bona fide* purposes other than to obtain a tax benefit (as defined in subsection 245(1)).

(2) If this subsection applies to an investment in a subject corporation,

(*a*) for the purposes of this Part, the CRIC is deemed to have paid to the parent at the time the investment was made, and the parent is deemed to have received from the CRIC at that time, a dividend equal to the total of all amounts each of which is the fair market value, at that time, of any property (not including shares of the capital stock of the CRIC) transferred, or obligation assumed or incurred, by the CRIC in respect of the investment; and

(*b*) in computing the paid-up capital at any time after March 28, 2012 of any class of shares of the capital stock of the CRIC, there is to be deducted the amount of any increase, because of the investment, in the paid-up capital in respect of the shares of the class, computed without reference to this section."

(*b*) subsection 212.3(8) is to be read as follows:

"(8) In computing the paid-up capital at any time after March 28, 2012 in respect of a class of shares of the capital stock of a corporation, there is to be added an amount equal to the lesser of

(*a*) the amount, if any, by which

(i) the total of all amounts deemed by subsection 84(3), (4) or (4.1) to be a dividend on shares of the class paid after March 28, 2012 and before that time by the corporation,

exceeds

(ii) the total that would be determined under subparagraph (i) if this Act were read without reference to paragraph (2)(*b*); and

(*b*) the total of all amounts required by paragraph (2)(*b*) to be deducted in computing the paid-up capital in respect of the class before that time."

(*c*) subsection 212.3(10) is to be read as follows:

"(10) For the purposes of this section, an investment made in a subject corporation by a CRIC means any of

(*a*) an acquisition of shares of the capital stock of the subject corporation by the CRIC;

(*b*) a contribution of capital to the subject corporation by the CRIC;

(*c*) a transaction under which an amount became owing by the subject corporation to the CRIC, other than an amount owing that arises in the ordinary course of the business of the CRIC and that is repaid within a commercially reasonable period;

(*d*) an acquisition of a debt obligation of the subject corporation by the CRIC from another person, other than, if the acquisition was made in the ordinary course of the business of the CRIC, an acquisition from a person with which the CRIC dealt, at the time of the acquisition, at arm's length;

(*e*) an acquisition by the CRIC of an option in respect of, or an interest in, or for civil law a right in, shares of the capital stock, or a debt obligation, of the subject corporation; and

(*f*) any transaction or event that is similar in effect to any of the transactions described in paragraphs (*a*) to (*e*)."

(*d*) subsections 212.3(15) and (16) are to be read as follows:

"(15) For the purposes of this section and paragraph 128.1(1)(*c.3*), a CRIC that is controlled by more than one non-resident corporation is deemed not to be controlled by any such non-resident that controls another non-resident corporation that controls the CRIC, unless the application of this subsection would otherwise result in no non-resident corporation controlling the CRIC.

(16) In determining whether paragraph (1)(*c*) applies, the following factors are to be given primary consideration:

(*a*) whether the business activities carried on by the subject corporation and any other corporation in which the subject corporation has, at the time referred to in subsection (1), an equity percentage (as defined in subsection 95(4)) are at that time, and are expected to remain, more closely connected to the business activities carried on by the CRIC (or by a corporation resident in Canada that is a subsidiary wholly-owned corporation of the CRIC or that is a corporation of which the CRIC is a subsidiary wholly-owned corporation) than to the business activities carried on by any non-resident corporation (other than the subject corporation or any corporation in which the subject corporation has such an equity percentage) with which the CRIC, at that time, does not deal at arm's length;

(*b*) whether the terms or conditions of any shares of the subject corporation that are owned by the CRIC at that time, or any agreement in respect of the shares or their issue, are such that the CRIC does not fully participate in the profits of the subject corporation or any appreciation in the value of the subject corporation (for greater certainty, the fact that the shares owned by the CRIC do fully participate in the profits of the subject corporation and any appreciation in the value of the subject corporation is not a relevant factor);

(*c*) whether the investment was made at the direction or request of a non-resident corporation with which the CRIC was not, at that time, dealing at arm's length;

(*d*) whether, in the case of an investment described in paragraph (10)(*a*), (*d*), (*e*) or (*f*), negotiations with the vendor in respect of the investment were initiated by senior officers of the CRIC who were resident in, and worked principally in, Canada or, if the vendor initiated the transaction, the vendor's principal point of contact was an officer of the CRIC who was resident in, and worked principally in, Canada;

(*e*) whether senior officers of the CRIC who were resident in, and worked principally in, Canada had and exercised the principal decision-making authority in respect of the making of the investment, and have and exercise the principal decision making authority in respect of the investment;

(*f*) whether the performance evaluation or compensation of senior officers of the CRIC who are resident in, and work principally in, Canada is connected to the results of operations of the subject corporation to a greater extent than the performance evaluation or compensation of any senior officers of a non-resident corporation (other than the subject corporation or a corporation controlled by the subject corporation) that does not deal at arm's length with the CRIC is so connected; and

(*g*) whether senior officers of the subject corporation report to, and are functionally accountable to, senior officers of the CRIC who are resident in, and work principally in, Canada to a greater extent than to any senior officers of any non-resident corporation (other than the subject corporation) that does not deal at arm's length with the CRIC."

(*e*) subsection 212.3(23) is to be read as follows:

"(23) A particular investment by a CRIC in a subject corporation that would, in the absence of this subsection, be excluded from the application of subsection (2) because of paragraph (1)(*c*) is not to be so excluded to the extent that one or more properties, if any, received by the subject corporation from the CRIC as a result of the particular investment, or property substituted for any such property, may reasonably be considered to have been used by the subject corporation, directly or indirectly as part of a transaction or event or series of transactions or events that includes the particular investment, to make another investment in a non-resident corporation that would, if the other investment had been made by the CRIC, have been subject to subsection (2)."

(*f*) subsection 212.3(25) is to be read as follows:

"(25) For the purposes of this section, paragraph 128.1(1)(*c.3*) and subsection 219.1(2),

(*a*) any transaction entered into by a partnership is deemed to have been entered into by each member of the partnership in proportion to the fair market value of the member's direct or indirect interest in the partnership;

(*b*) property that would, in the absence of this paragraph, be owned by a partnership is deemed to be owned by each member of the partnership in proportion to the fair market value of the member's direct or indirect interest in the partnership; and

(*c*) amounts that would, in the absence of this paragraph, be owing by a partnership are deemed to be owed by each member of the partnership in proportion to the fair market value of the member's direct or indirect interest in the partnership."

Related Sections: 212.3(2) Foreign affiliate dumping — consequences.

Canadian Tax Foundation: Bradley, *Living with the Foreign Affiliate Dumping Rules*, 2013 Canadian Tax Journal 4:1147–1166; Chong, *Section 212.3: Missing PUC Adjustments*, 2013 Canadian Tax Highlights 21(5):12–13; Chong, *Section 212.3: Missing PUC Adjustments, Part 2*, 2013 Canadian Tax Highlights 21(7):10–11; Nikolakakis and Woolford, *Foreign Affiliate Dumping*, 2012 Conference Report 26:1–58.

► 212.3(2) ◄

(2) Foreign affiliate dumping — consequences. If this subsection applies to an investment in a subject corporation made by a CRIC,

(*a*) for the purposes of this Part and subject to subsections (3) and (7), the CRIC is deemed to have paid to the parent, and the parent is deemed to have received from the CRIC, at the dividend time, a dividend equal to the total of all amounts each of which is the portion of the fair market value at the investment time of any property (not including shares of the capital stock of the CRIC) transferred, any obligation assumed or incurred, or any benefit otherwise conferred, by the CRIC, or of any property transferred to the CRIC which transfer results in the reduction of an amount owing to the CRIC, that can reasonably be considered to relate to the investment; and

Proposed Amendment

2019 Federal Budget Resolutions

Paragraph 212.3(2)(*a*) of the Act is replaced by the following:

(*a*) for the purposes of this Part and subject to subsections (3) and (7), the CRIC is deemed to have paid to each parent, and each parent is deemed to have received from the CRIC, at the dividend time, a dividend in an amount determined by the formula

$$A \times B/C$$

where

A is the total of all amounts each of which is the portion of the fair market value at the investment time of any property (not including shares of the capital stock of the CRIC) transferred, any obligation assumed or incurred, or any benefit otherwise conferred, by the CRIC, or of any property transferred to the CRIC which transfer results in the reduction of an amount owing to the CRIC, that can reasonably be considered to relate to the investment,

B is

(i) if there is one parent, one, and

(ii) if there is a group of parents, the fair market value at the dividend time of the shares of the capital stock of the CRIC that are held, directly or indirectly, by the parent, and

C is

(i) if there is one parent, one, and

(ii) if there is a group of parents, the total of all amounts each of which is the fair market value at the dividend time of the shares of the capital stock of the CRIC that are held, directly or indirectly, by a parent; and

Applicable: In respect of transactions or events that occur on or after March 19, 2019.

(*b*) in computing the paid-up capital in respect of any class of shares of the capital stock of the CRIC at any time that is at or after the investment time, there is to be deducted the amount of any increase in the paid-up capital in respect of the class, determined without reference to this section, that can reasonably be considered to relate to the investment.

Editorial Note: If s. 212.3(2) applies, the CRIC is deemed to have paid to the parent (and the parent is deemed to have received) a dividend that is generally equal to the amount of the investment. In addition, any paid-up capital in respect of shares of the CRIC that would otherwise have increased as a result of the investment is ground to nil.

In certain cases, it is possible to "reinstate" the paid-up capital reduced under s. 212.3(2)(*b*) in accordance with the provisions of s. 212.3(9). The paid-up capital reinstatement is available in circumstances including where the investment by the CRIC is:

(a) defined in s. 212.3(10)(*a*) (acquisition of shares of the subject corporation by the CRIC),

(b) defined in s. 212.3(10)(*b*) (a contribution of capital by the CRIC, which includes a benefit conferred by the CRIC on the subject corporation), or

(c) defined in s. 212.3(10)(*f*) (the "indirect investment" rule).

Where the investment is one of the enumerated types, and a paid-up capital grind is required under either of paragraphs 212.3(2)(*b*) or 212.3(7)(*b*), the paid-up capital is automatically increased immediately before the subsequent paid-up capital reduction by the least of three amounts:

(a) the amount of the initial paid-up capital reduction;

(b) the amount of the initial paid-up capital reduction less all amounts previously reinstated under s. 212.3(9), and

(c) the amount that is equal to either:

(i) if the property distributed on the reduction of paid-up capital is subject corporation shares, the fair market value of those shares (a tracing rule applies for shares substituted for subject corporation shares);

(ii) an amount the CRIC demonstrates was received, within a specified time period, as proceeds from the disposition of the subject corporation shares (a tracing rule applies for shares substituted for subject corporation shares), or as a dividend or qualifying return of capital (see s. 90(3)) on the subject corporation shares (a tracing rule applies for shares substituted for subject corporation shares); or

(iii) nil, where neither s. 212.3(9)(*c*)(i) nor (ii) applies.

History: S. 212.3(2)(*a*) was replaced by S.C. 2014, c. 39, s. 65(2), applicable in respect of transactions and events that occur after March 28, 2012.

If an election is made under subsection 49(3) of the *Jobs and Growth Act, 2012* [S.C. 2012, c. 31], section 212.3 of the *Income Tax Act* applies in the manner set out in that subsection in respect of transactions and events that occur after March 28, 2012 and before August 14, 2012.

S. 212.3(2) formerly read:

(*a*) for the purposes of this Part and subject to subsections (3) and (7), the CRIC is deemed to have paid to the parent, and the parent is deemed to have received from the CRIC, at the investment time, a dividend equal to the total of all amounts each of which is the portion of the fair market value at the investment time of any property (not including shares of the capital stock of the CRIC) transferred, any obligation assumed or incurred, or any benefit otherwise conferred, by the CRIC, or of any property transferred to the CRIC which transfer results in the reduction of an amount owing to the CRIC, that can reasonably be considered to relate to the investment; and

S. 212.3(2) was added by S.C. 2012, c. 31, s. 49(1), applicable generally in respect of transactions and events that occur after March 28, 2012. However, see the history note following s. 212.3(1) for the application where certain transactions occur before 2013 and for an election that can be made for transactions that occur before August 14, 2012.

Canadian Tax Foundation: Bradley, *Living with the Foreign Affiliate Dumping Rules*, 2013 Canadian Tax Journal 4:1147–1166; Chong, *Section 212.3: Missing PUC Adjustments*, 2013 Canadian Tax Highlights 21(5):12–13; Chong, *Section 212.3: Missing PUC Adjustments, Part 2*, 2013 Canadian Tax Highlights 21(7):10–11; Nikolakakis and Woolford, *Foreign Affiliate Dumping*, 2012 Conference Report 26:1–58.

► 212.3(3) ◄

(3) Dividend substitution election. If a CRIC (or a CRIC and a corporation that is a qualifying substitute corporation in respect of the CRIC at the dividend time) and the parent (or the parent and another non-resident corporation that at the dividend time does not deal at arm's length with the parent) jointly elect in writing under this subsection in respect of an investment, and the election is filed with the Minister on or before the filing-due date of the CRIC for its taxation year that includes the dividend time, then the dividend that would, in the absence of this subsection, be deemed under paragraph (2)(*a*) to have been paid by the CRIC to the parent and received by the parent from the CRIC is deemed to have instead been

(*a*) paid by the CRIC or the qualifying substitute corporation, as agreed on in the election; and

(*b*) paid to, and received by, the parent or the other non-resident corporation, as agreed on in the election.

Proposed Amendment
2019 Federal Budget Resolutions
Subsection 212.3(3) of the Act is replaced by the following:

(3) Dividend substitution election. If a CRIC (or a CRIC and a corporation that is a qualifying substitute corporation in respect of the CRIC at the dividend time) and a parent (or a parent and another non-resident person that at the dividend time is related to the parent) jointly elect in writing under this subsection in respect of an investment, and the election is filed with the Minister on or before the filing-due date of the CRIC for its taxation year that includes the dividend time, then the dividend that would, in the absence of this subsection, be deemed under paragraph (2)(*a*) to have been paid by the CRIC to the parent and received by the parent from the CRIC is deemed to have instead been

(*a*) paid by the CRIC or the qualifying substitute corporation, as agreed on in the election; and

(*b*) paid to, and received by, the parent or the other non-resident person, as agreed on in the election.

Applicable: In respect of transactions or events that occur on or after March 19, 2019.

Editorial Note: Where a deemed dividend arises under s. 212.3(2)(a), the "dividend substitution election" under s. 212.3(3) may be valuable. The dividend substitution election requires that the CRIC, all "qualifying substitute corporations" in respect of the CRIC and the parent (or the parent and another non-resident corporation that is controlled by the parent at the investment time) make a joint, irrevocable written election. (Pending amendments propose to relax this filing requirement so that only the qualifying substitute corporation that the CRIC elects to be the payer of the deemed dividend will be required to be party to the election.) The result of the election is that both the payer and recipient of the dividend can be corporations other than the CRIC and its controlling parent, possibly resulting in the availability of reduced withholding tax on the deemed dividend under a treaty.

History: S. 212.3(3) was replaced by S.C. 2014, c. 39, s. 65(3), applicable in respect of transactions and events that occur after March 28, 2012, except that an election referred to in subsection 212.3(3) is deemed to have been filed on a timely basis if the election is filed on or before the filing-due date of the electing CRIC for its taxation year that includes December 16, 2014.

If an election is made under subsection 49(3) of the *Jobs and Growth Act, 2012* [S.C. 2012, c. 31], section 212.3 of the *Income Tax Act* applies in the manner set out in that subsection in respect of transactions and events that occur after March 28, 2012 and before August 14, 2012.

S. 212.3(3) formerly read:

(3) *Dividend substitution election.* If a CRIC, all corporations that are, at the investment time, qualifying substitute corporations in respect of the CRIC, and the parent (or the parent and another non-resident corporation that is at the investment time controlled by the parent) jointly elect in writing under this subsection in respect of an investment, amounts are agreed on in respect of classes of shares of the capital stock of any of the CRIC and one or more of the qualifying substitute corporations, the total of the amounts agreed on equals the amount of the dividend that would, in the absence of this subsection, be deemed under paragraph (2)(*a*) to be paid and received, and the election is filed with the Minister on or before the earliest of the filing-due dates of the CRIC and the qualifying substitute corporations for their respective taxation years that include the investment time, then

(*a*) the dividend that would, in the absence of this subsection, be deemed under paragraph (2)(*a*) to have been paid by the CRIC to the parent and received by the parent from the CRIC

(i) is reduced by the total of all amounts each of which is an amount agreed on in the election in respect of a class of shares of the capital stock of a qualifying substitute corporation, and

(ii) is, as reduced by the application of subparagraph (i), deemed to be paid to, and received by, the parent or the other non-resident corporation (if the other non-resident corporation has elected under this subsection), as one or more dividends in the amounts, and in respect of the classes of shares of the capital stock of the CRIC, agreed on in the election; and

(*b*) a dividend is deemed, at the investment time, to be paid to either the parent or the other non-resident corporation, as the case may be, by each qualifying substitute corporation in respect of which an amount has been agreed on in the election, and received by the parent, or the other non-resident corporation, from that qualifying substitute corporation, in the amount, and in respect of each class referred to in subparagraph (*a*)(i), agreed on in the election.

S. 212.3(3) was added by S.C. 2012, c. 31, s. 49(1), applicable generally in respect of transactions and events that occur after March 28, 2012. However, any election referred to in subsection 212.3(3) that would otherwise be required to be filed with the Minister of National Revenue on or before the day that is 120 days after the day on which this Act receives royal assent [December 14, 2012] is deemed to have been filed with the Minister on a timely basis if it is filed with the Minister on or before the day that is 365 days after the day on which this Act receives royal assent [December 14, 2012].

See the history note following s. 212.3(1) for the application where certain transactions occur before 2013 and for an election that can be made for transactions that occur before August 14, 2012.

► 212.3(4) ◄

(4) Definitions. The following definitions apply in this section.

History: S. 212.3(4) was replaced by S.C. 2014, c. 39, s. 65(3), applicable in respect of transactions and events that occur after March 28, 2012, except that in respect of transactions and events that occur before August 29, 2014, subsection 212.3(4) is to be read without reference to paragraph (*b*) of the definition "cross-border class".

If an election is made under subsection 49(3) of the *Jobs and Growth Act, 2012* [S.C. 2012, c. 31], section 212.3 of the *Income Tax Act* applies in the manner set out in that subsection in respect of transactions and events that occur after March 28, 2012 and before August 14, 2012.

S. 212.3(4) formerly read:

(4) *Qualifying substitute corporation.* For the purposes of this section, "qualifying substitute corporation", at any time in respect of a CRIC, means a corporation resident in Canada

(*a*) that is, at that time, controlled by the parent;

(*b*) that has, at that time, an equity percentage (as defined in subsection 95(4)) in the CRIC; and

(*c*) shares of the capital stock of which are, at that time, owned by the parent or another non-resident corporation with which the parent does not, at that time, deal at arm's length.

S. 212.3(4) was added by S.C. 2012, c. 31, s. 49(1), applicable generally in respect of transactions and events that occur after March 28, 2012. However, see the history note following s. 212.3(1) for the application where certain transactions occur before 2013 and for an election that can be made for transactions that occur before August 14, 2012.

"cross-border class" —"cross-border class", in respect of an investment, means a class of shares of the capital stock of a CRIC or qualifying substitute corporation if, immediately after the dividend time in respect of the investment,

(*a*) the parent, or a non-resident corporation that does not deal at arm's length with the parent, owns at least one share of the class; and

(*b*) no more than 30% of the issued and outstanding shares of the class are owned by one or more persons resident in Canada that do not deal at arm's length with the parent.

"dividend time" —"dividend time", in respect of an investment, means

(*a*) if the CRIC is controlled by the parent at the investment time, the investment time; or

(*b*) in any other case, the earlier of

(i) the first time, after the investment time, at which the CRIC is controlled by the parent, and

(ii) the day that is one year after the day that includes the investment time.

"qualifying substitute corporation" —"qualifying substitute corporation", at any time in respect of a CRIC, means a corporation resident in Canada

(*a*) that is, at that time, controlled by the parent or by a non-resident corporation that does not deal at arm's length with the parent;

(*b*) that has, at that time, an equity percentage (as defined in subsection 95(4)) in the CRIC; and

(*c*) shares of the capital stock of which are, at that time, owned by the parent or another non-resident corporation with which the parent does not, at that time, deal at arm's length.

Proposed Amendment
2019 Federal Budget Resolutions
Subsection 212.3(4) of the Act is replaced by the following:

(4) Definitions. The following definitions apply in this section.

cross-border class —*cross-border class*, in respect of an investment, means a class of shares of the capital stock of a CRIC or qualifying substitute corporation if, immediately after the dividend time in respect of the investment,

(*a*) a parent, or a non-resident person that does not deal at arm's length with a parent, owns at least one share of the class; and

(*b*) no more than 30% of the issued and outstanding shares of the class are owned by one or more persons resident in Canada that do not deal at arm's length with a parent.

dividend time —*dividend time*, in respect of an investment, means

(*a*) if the CRIC is controlled by a parent or group of parents at the investment time, the investment time; and

(*b*) in any other case, the earlier of

(i) the first time, after the investment time, at which the CRIC is controlled by a parent or group of parents, as the case may be, and

(ii) the day that is one year after the day that includes the investment time.

qualifying substitute corporation —*qualifying substitute corporation*, at any time in respect of a CRIC, means a corporation resident in Canada

(*a*) that is, at that time, controlled by

(i) a parent,

(ii) a group of parents, or

(iii) a non-resident person that does not deal at arm's length with a parent;

(*b*) that has, at that time, an equity percentage (as defined in subsection 95(4)) in the CRIC; and

(*c*) shares of the capital stock of which are, at that time, owned by a parent or another non-resident person with which the parent does not, at that time, deal at arm's length.

Applicable: In respect of transactions or events that occur on or after March 19, 2019.

► 212.3(5) ◄

(5) Modification of terms — paragraph (10)(*e*). In the case of an investment described in paragraph (10)(*e*), the CRIC is deemed for the purposes of paragraph (2)(*a*) to transfer to the subject corporation property that relates to the investment, the fair market value of which property is

(*a*) if the investment is described in subparagraph (10)(*e*)(i), the amount owing in respect of the debt obligation referred to in that subparagraph immediately after the investment time, or

(*b*) if the investment is described in subparagraph (10)(*e*)(ii), the fair market value of the shares referred to in that subparagraph immediately after the investment time.

History: S. 212.3(5) was added by S.C. 2012, c. 31, s. 49(1), applicable generally in respect of transactions and events that occur after March 28, 2012. However, see the history note following s. 212.3(1) for the application where certain transactions occur before 2013 and for an election that can be made for transactions that occur before August 14, 2012.

► 212.3(5.1) ◄

(5.1) Sequential investments — paragraph (10)(*f*). In the case of an investment (in this subsection referred to as the "second investment") in a subject corporation by a CRIC described in paragraph (10)(*f*), the total referred to in paragraph (2)(*a*) in respect of the second investment is to be reduced by the total referred to in paragraph (2)(*a*) in respect of a prior investment (in this subsection referred to as the "first investment") in the subject corporation by another corporation resident in Canada if (*a*) the first investment is an investment that is described in paragraph (10)(*a*) or (*b*) and to which paragraph (2)(*a*) applies;

(*b*) immediately after the investment time in respect of the first investment, the other corporation is not controlled by the parent; and

(*c*) the other corporation becomes, after the time that is immediately after the investment time in respect of the first investment and as part of a transaction or event or series of transactions or events that includes the making of the first investment, controlled by the parent because of the second investment.

Proposed Amendment
2019 Federal Budget Resolutions
Subsection 212.3(5.1) of the Act is replaced by the following:

(5.1) Sequential investments — paragraph (10)(*f*). In the case of an investment (in this subsection referred to as the "second investment") in a subject corporation by a CRIC described in paragraph (10)(*f*), the amount determined for A in paragraph (2)(*a*) in respect of the second investment is to be reduced by the amount determined for A in paragraph (2)(*a*) in respect of a prior investment (in this subsection referred to as the "first investment") in the subject corporation by another corporation resident in Canada if

(*a*) the first investment is an investment that is described in paragraph (10)(*a*) or (*b*) and to which paragraph (2)(*a*) applies;

(*b*) immediately after the investment time in respect of the first investment, the other corporation is not controlled by,

(i) if there is one parent in respect of the CRIC, the parent, and

(ii) if there is a group of parents in respect of the CRIC, the group of parents; and

(*c*) the other corporation becomes, after the time that is immediately after the investment time in respect of the first investment and as part of a transaction or event or series of transactions or events that includes the making of the first investment, controlled by the parent or group of parents, as the case may be, because of the second investment.

Applicable: In respect of transactions or events that occur on or after March 19, 2019.

History: S. 212.3(5.1) was added by S.C. 2014, c. 39, s. 65(4), applicable in respect of transactions and events that occur after March 28, 2012.

If an election is made under subsection 49(3) of the *Jobs and Growth Act, 2012* [S.C. 2012, c. 31], section 212.3 of the *Income Tax Act* applies in the manner set out in that subsection in respect of transactions and events that occur after March 28, 2012 and before August 14, 2012.

► 212.3(6) ◄

(6) Anti-avoidance rule — cross-border class. A particular class of shares of the capital stock of a CRIC or a qualifying substitute corporation that, in the absence of this subsection, would be a cross-border class in respect of an investment is deemed not to be a cross-border class in respect of the investment if

(*a*) a particular corporation resident in Canada that does not deal at arm's length with the parent

Proposed Amendment
2019 Federal Budget Resolutions
The portion of paragraph 212.3(6)(*a*) of the Act before subparagraph (i) is replaced by the following:

(*a*) a particular corporation resident in Canada that does not deal at arm's length with a parent

Applicable: In respect of transactions or events that occur on or after March 19, 2019.

(i) acquires shares of the particular class (or shares that are substituted for those shares) as part of a transaction or event or series of transactions or events that includes the investment, or

(ii) owns shares of the particular class (or shares that are substituted for those shares) and, as part of a transaction or event or series of transactions or events that includes the investment,

(A) the paid-up capital in respect of the particular class is increased otherwise than as a result of an acquisition described in subparagraph (i), and

(B) the increase in paid-up capital in respect of the particular class can reasonably be considered to be connected to funding provided to the particular corporation or another corporation resident in Canada (other than the corporation that issued the particular class) by the parent or a non-resident person that does not deal at arm's length with the parent, unless

Proposed Amendment
2019 Federal Budget Resolutions
The portion of clause 212.3(6)(*a*)(ii)(B) of the act before subclause (I) is replaced by the following:

(B) the increase in paid-up capital in respect of the particular class can reasonably be considered to be connected to funding provided to the particular corporation or another corporation resident in Canada (other than the corporation that issued the particular class) by a parent or a non-resident person that does not deal at arm's length with a parent, unless

Applicable: In respect of transactions or events that occur on or after March 19, 2019.

(I) the funding results in an increase, equal to the amount funded, in the paid-up capital of shares of a class of the capital stock of the particular corporation, or the other corporation, that is a cross-border class in respect of the investment, and

(II) the increase referred to in subclause (I) occurred at or before the time of the increase to the paid-up capital in respect of the particular class; and

(*b*) it can reasonably be considered that one of the main reasons for the acquisition or for the funding, as the case may be, was to increase the amount of a deduction required under paragraph (7)(*b*) or (*c*) in computing the paid-up capital in respect of shares of the particular class held by the particular corporation.

History: S. 212.3(6) was added by S.C. 2014, c. 39, s. 65(6), applicable in respect of transactions and events that occur after August 28, 2014.

S. 212.3(6) was repealed by S.C. 2014, c. 39, s. 65(5), applicable in respect of transactions and events that occur after March 28, 2012.

If an election is made under subsection 49(3) of the *Jobs and Growth Act, 2012* [S.C. 2012, c. 31], section 212.3 of the *Income Tax Act* applies in the manner set out in that subsection in respect of transactions and events that occur after March 28, 2012 and before August 14, 2012.

S. 212.3(6) formerly read:

(6) *Application of subsection (7).* Subsection (7) applies if paragraph (2)(*a*) or (3)(*b*) applies to an investment in a subject corporation made by a CRIC and

(*a*) if an election is made under subsection (3) in respect of the investment,

(i) each class of shares of the capital stock of the CRIC or of a qualifying substitute corporation, in respect of which an amount has been agreed on in the election, is a class of which the parent, or another non-resident corporation with which the parent does not, at the investment time, deal at arm's length, owns shares, and

(ii) the election results in the greatest possible amount that is the total of all amounts each of which would, if subparagraph (7)(*b*)(i) applied in respect of the investment, be a reduction of paid-up capital in respect of a share of the capital stock of the CRIC, or a qualifying substitute corporation, that is owned by the parent or another non-resident corporation with which the parent does not, at the investment time, deal at arm's length; or

(*b*) in any other case, the following conditions are met:

(i) either

(A) there was only one class of issued and outstanding shares of the capital stock of the CRIC at the investment time, or

(B) the CRIC demonstrates that an amount of paid-up capital in respect of one or more classes of shares of the capital stock of the CRIC arose from one or more transfers of property to the CRIC and that

(I) in the case of an investment described in paragraph (10)(*f*), all the property transferred was used by the CRIC to make, in whole or in part, the direct acquisition referred to in that paragraph, and

(II) in any other case, all the property transferred was used by the CRIC to make, in whole or in part, the investment; and

(ii) at the investment time, each share of the capital stock of the CRIC that was not owned by the parent was owned by

(A) a person who was dealing at arm's length with the CRIC, or

(B) a non-resident person who was not dealing at arm's length with the CRIC.

S. 212.3(6) was added by S.C. 2012, c. 31, s. 49(1), applicable generally in respect of transactions and events that occur after March 28, 2012. However, see the history note following s. 212.3(1) for the application where certain transactions occur before 2013 and for an election that can be made for transactions that occur before August 14, 2012.

▶ 212.3(7) ◀

(7) Reduction of deemed dividend. If paragraph (2)(*a*) applies to an investment in a subject corporation made by a CRIC,

(*a*) where the CRIC demonstrates — in respect of one or more classes of shares of the capital stock of the CRIC, or of a qualifying substitute corporation, all the issued and outstanding shares of which are owned, immediately after the dividend time in respect of the investment, by persons that deal at arm's length with the CRIC — that an amount of paid-up capital in respect of each of the classes arose as a consequence of one or more transfers of property, directly or indirectly, to the CRIC and that all of the property transferred was used by the CRIC to make, in whole or in part, the investment (or, in the case of an investment described in paragraph (10)(*f*), the direct acquisition referred to in that paragraph), then

(i) the amount, determined without reference to this subsection, of the dividend deemed under paragraph (2)(*a*) to have been paid and received, is reduced by the lesser of

Proposed Amendment

2019 Federal Budget Resolutions

The portion of subparagraph 212.3(7)(*a*)(i) of the Act before clause (A) is replaced by the following:

(i) the amount determined, without reference to this subsection, for A in paragraph (2)(*a*), is reduced by the lesser of

Applicable: In respect of transactions or events that occur on or after March 19, 2019.

(A) that amount, and

(B) the total of all amounts of paid-up capital so demonstrated by the CRIC, and

(ii) in computing the paid-up capital in respect of each class described in this paragraph, at any time after the dividend time, there is to be deducted an amount equal to the portion of the amount determined under subparagraph (i) that can reasonably be considered to relate to that class;

(*b*) where the amount, determined without reference to this paragraph, of the dividend deemed under paragraph (2)(*a*) to have been paid and received is equal to or greater than the total of all amounts each of which is an amount of paid-up capital immediately after the dividend time, determined without reference to this paragraph, of a cross-border class in respect of the investment, then

Proposed Amendment

2019 Federal Budget Resolutions

The portion of paragraph 212.3(7)(*b*) of the Act before subparagraph (i) is replaced by the following:

(*b*) where the amount determined, without reference to this paragraph, for A in paragraph (2)(*a*) is equal to or greater than the total of all amounts each of which is an amount of paid-up capital immediately after the dividend time, determined without reference to this paragraph, of a cross-border class in respect of the investment, then

Applicable: In respect of transactions or events that occur on or after March 19, 2019.

(i) the amount of the dividend is reduced by the total referred to in this paragraph, and

(ii) in computing, at any time after the dividend time, the paid-up capital in respect of each cross-border class in respect of the investment, there is to be deducted an amount equal to the paid-up capital in respect of that class immediately after the dividend time, determined without reference to this paragraph;

(*c*) where paragraph (*b*) does not apply and there is at least one cross-border class in respect of the investment,

(i) the amount, determined without reference to this paragraph, of the dividend is reduced to nil,

(ii) in computing, at any time after the dividend time, the paid-up capital in respect of a particular cross-border class in respect of the investment, there is to be deducted the amount, if any, that when added to the total of all amounts that are deducted under this paragraph in computing the paid-up capital of other cross-border classes, results in the greatest total reduction because of this paragraph, immediately after the dividend time, of the paid-up capital in respect of shares of cross-border classes that are owned by the parent or another non-resident corporation with which the parent does not, at the dividend time, deal at arm's length,

(iii) if the proportion of the shares of a particular class owned, in aggregate, by the parent and non-resident corporations that do not deal at arm's length with the parent is equal to the proportion so owned of one or more other cross-border classes (in this subparagraph all those classes, together with the particular class, referred to as the "relevant classes"), then the proportion that the reduction under subparagraph (ii) to the paid-up capital in respect of the particular class is of the paid-up capital, determined immediately after the dividend time and without reference to this paragraph, in respect of that class is to be equal to the proportion that the total reduction under subparagraph (ii) to the paid-up capital in respect of all the relevant classes is of the total paid-up capital, determined immediately after the dividend time and without reference to this paragraph, of all the relevant classes, and

(iv) the total of all amounts each of which is an amount to be deducted under subparagraph (ii) in computing the paid-up capital of a cross-border class is to be equal to the amount by which the dividend is reduced under subparagraph (i); and

(*d*) if the amount of the dividend is reduced because of any of subparagraphs (*a*)(i), (*b*)(i) and (*c*)(i),

(i) the CRIC shall file with the Minister in prescribed manner a form containing prescribed information and the amounts of the paid-up capital, determined immediately after the dividend time and without reference to this subsection, of each class of shares that is described in paragraph (*a*) or that is a cross-border class in respect of the investment, the paid-up capital of the shares of each of those classes that are owned by the parent or another non-resident corporation that does not, at the dividend time, deal at arm's length with the parent, and the reduction under any of subparagraphs (*a*)(ii), (*b*)(ii) and (*c*)(ii) in respect of each of those classes, and

(ii) if the form is not filed on or before the CRIC's filing-due date for its taxation year that includes the dividend time, the CRIC is deemed to have paid to the parent, and the parent is deemed to have received from the CRIC, on the filing-due date, a dividend equal to the total of all amounts each of which is the amount of a reduction because of any of subparagraphs (*a*)(i), (*b*)(i) and (*c*)(i).

Proposed Amendment

2019 Federal Budget Resolutions

Paragraphs 212.3(7)(*c*) and (*d*) of the Act are replaced by the following:

(*c*) where paragraph (*b*) does not apply and there is at least one cross-border class in respect of the investment,

(i) the amount determined, without reference to this paragraph, for A in paragraph (2)(*a*) is reduced to nil,

(ii) in computing, at any time after the dividend time, the paid-up capital in respect of a particular cross-border class in respect of the investment, there is to be deducted the amount, if any, that when added to the total of all amounts that are deducted under this paragraph in computing the paid-up capital of other cross-border classes, results in the greatest total reduction because of this paragraph, immediately after the dividend time, of the paid-up capital in respect of shares of cross-border classes that are owned by a parent or another non-resident person with which a parent does not, at the dividend time, deal at arm's length,

(iii) if the proportion of the shares of a particular class owned, in aggregate, by parents and non-resident persons that do not deal at arm's length with parents is equal to the proportion so owned of one or more other cross-border classes (in this subparagraph all those classes, together with the particular class, referred to as the "relevant classes"), then the proportion that the reduction under subparagraph (ii) to the paid-up capital in respect of the particular class is of the paid-up capital, determined immediately after the dividend time and without reference to this paragraph, in respect of that class is to be equal to the proportion that the total reduction under subparagraph (ii) to the paid-up capital in respect of all the relevant classes is of the total paid-up capital, determined immediately after the dividend time and without reference to this paragraph, of all the relevant classes, and

(iv) the total of all amounts each of which is an amount to be deducted under subparagraph (ii) in computing the paid-up capital of a cross-border class is to be equal to the amount by which the amount determined for A in paragraph (2)(*a*) is reduced under subparagraph (i); and

(*d*) if the amount determined for A in paragraph (2)(*a*) is reduced because of any of subparagraphs (*a*)(i), (*b*)(i) and (*c*)(i),

(i) the CRIC shall file with the Minister in prescribed manner a form containing prescribed information and the amounts of the paid-up capital, determined immediately after the dividend time and without reference to this subsection, of each class of shares that is described in paragraph (*a*) or that is a cross-border class in respect of the investment, the paid-up capital of the shares of each of those classes that are owned by a parent or another nonresident person that does not, at the dividend time, deal at arm's length with a parent, and the reduction under any of subparagraphs (*a*)(ii), (*b*)(ii) and (*c*)(ii) in respect of each of those classes, and

(ii) if the form is not filed on or before the CRIC's filing-due date for its taxation year that includes the dividend time, the CRIC is deemed to have paid to each parent, and each parent is deemed to have received from the CRIC, on the filing-due date, a dividend equal to the total of all amounts each of which is the amount of a reduction because of any of subparagraphs (*a*)(i), (*b*)(i) and (*c*)(i) in the amount the CRIC is deemed under paragraph (2)(*a*) to have paid to the parent.

Applicable: In respect of transactions or events that occur on or after March 19, 2019.

Editorial Note: Subsection 212.3(7) provides a rule whereby the dividend that would ordinarily be deemed to arise as a result of an investment by a CRIC in a subject corporation is instead reduced or in some cases eliminated. The dividends are instead effectively "offset" against paid-up capital of the shares of the CRIC or qualifying substitute corporation, as the case may be. For this relief to be available, the requirements currently set out in s. 212.3(6) must be met.

History: S. 212.3(7) was replaced by S.C. 2014, c. 39, s. 65(7), applicable in respect of transactions and events that occur after March 28, 2012, except that

(c) a form referred to in paragraph 212.3(7)(*d*) is deemed to have been filed by the CRIC referred to in that paragraph on a timely basis if the form is filed on or before the day that is the later of the CRIC's filing-due date for its taxation year that includes the day on which the *Economic Action Plan 2014 Act, No. 2* [S.C. 2014, c. 39] receives royal assent [December 16, 2014] and one year after the day on which the *Economic Action Plan 2014 Act, No. 2* [S.C. 2014, c. 39] receives royal assent [December 16, 2015];

(d) in respect of transactions and events that occur before August 29, 2014, the reference to "on the filing-due date" in subparagraph 212.3(7)(*d*)(ii) is to be read as a reference to the time that is the later of the filing-due date for the CRIC's taxation year that includes the day on which the *Economic Action Plan 2014 Act, No. 2* [S.C. 2014, c. 39] receives royal assent [December 16, 2014] and one year after the day on which the *Economic Action Plan 2014 Act, No. 2* [S.C. 2014, c. 39] receives royal assent [December 16, 2015] ;

If an election is made under subsection 49(3) of the *Jobs and Growth Act, 2012* [S.C. 2012, c. 31], section 212.3 of the *Income Tax Act* applies in the manner set out in that subsection in respect of transactions and events that occur after March 28, 2012 and before August 14, 2012.

S. 212.3(7) formerly read:

(7) *Reduction of deemed dividend.* If this subsection applies, the following rules apply:

(*a*) the amount of any dividend deemed under this section to have been paid by the CRIC or a qualifying substitute corporation and to have been received by a non-resident corporation in respect of the investment is to be reduced by the lesser of

(i) the amount that would, in the absence of this subsection, be deemed to be paid and received as a dividend under this section, and

(ii) one of

(A) if paragraph (6)(*a*) applies, the amount of paid-up capital in respect of the class of shares in respect of which the dividend is deemed to be paid,

(B) if clause (6)(*b*)(i)(A) applies, the amount of paid-up capital in respect of the class referred to in that clause immediately before the investment time, or

(C) if clause (6)(*b*)(i)(B) applies, the total of all amounts of paid-up capital, determined under that clause, in respect of a class of shares of the capital stock of the CRIC; and

(*b*) in computing the paid-up capital in respect of a class of shares of the capital stock of the CRIC or a qualifying substitute corporation, as the case may be, at any time that is at or after the investment time, there is to be deducted

(i) if clause (*a*)(ii)(A) applies, the amount determined under paragraph (*a*) in respect of the class, and

(ii) if clause (*a*)(ii)(B) or (C) applies, the amount determined under paragraph (*a*) that can reasonably be considered to relate to the class.

S. 212.3(7) was added by S.C. 2012, c. 31, s. 49(1), applicable generally in respect of transactions and events that occur after March 28, 2012. However, see the history note following s. 212.3(1) for the application where certain transactions occur before 2013 and for an election that can be made for transactions that occur before August 14, 2012.

Related Sections: 227(6.2) Foreign affiliate dumping — late-filed form; 227(8.5) No penalty — certain deemed payments.

Tax Window Files: 212.3(7)(d) - Prescribed information, *June 12, 2015*, CRA Document No. 2015-0583821E5.

▶ 212.3(7.1) ◀

(7.1) Election to not reduce deemed dividend. Subsection (7) does not apply in respect of an investment made by a CRIC if

(*a*) the investment was made after March 28, 2012 and before August 16, 2013;

(*b*) at the investment time, each share of the capital stock of the CRIC, and each qualifying substitute corporation in respect of the CRIC, that was not owned by the parent was owned by persons or partnerships with which the parent did not deal at arm's length; and

(*c*) the CRIC files an election with the Minister before 2017 to have this subsection apply in respect of the investment.

History: S. 212.3(7.1) was added by S.C. 2017, c. 33, s. 75(3), deemed in force March 29, 2012.

Related Sections: 212.3(2) Foreign affiliate dumping — consequences.

▶ 212.3(8) ◀

(8) Paid-up capital adjustment. In computing the paid-up capital at any time after March 28, 2012 in respect of a class of shares of the capital stock of a corporation, there is to be added an amount equal to the lesser of

(*a*) the amount, if any, by which

(i) the total of all amounts deemed by subsection 84(3), (4) or (4.1) to be a dividend on shares of the class paid after March 28, 2012 and before that time by the corporation

exceeds

(ii) the total that would be determined under subparagraph (i) if this Act were read without reference to paragraph (2)(*b*) and subsections (7) and (9), and

(*b*) the amount, if any, by which

(i) the total of all amounts required by paragraph (2)(*b*) or subsection (7) to be deducted in computing the paid-up capital in respect of the class before that time

exceeds

(ii) the total of all amounts required by subsection (9) to be added in computing the paid-up capital in respect of the class before that time.

History: S. 212.3(8)(*a*)(ii) was replaced by S.C. 2014, c. 39, s. 65(8), applicable in respect of transactions and events that occur after March 28, 2012.

If an election is made under subsection 49(3) of the *Jobs and Growth Act, 2012* [S.C. 2012, c. 31], section 212.3 of the *Income Tax Act* applies in the manner set out in that subsection in respect of transactions and events that occur after March 28, 2012 and before August 14, 2012.

S. 212.3(8)(*a*)(ii) formerly read:

(ii) the total that would be determined under subparagraph (i) if this Act were read without reference to paragraphs (2)(*b*) and (7)(*b*) and subsection (9), and

S. 212.3(8)(*b*)(i) was replaced by S.C. 2014, c. 39, s. 65(9), applicable in respect of transactions and events that occur after March 28, 2012.

If an election is made under subsection 49(3) of the *Jobs and Growth Act, 2012* [S.C. 2012, c. 31], section 212.3 of the *Income Tax Act* applies in the manner set out in that subsection in respect of transactions and events that occur after March 28, 2012 and before August 14, 2012.

S. 212.3(8)(*b*)(i) formerly read:

(i) the total of all amounts required by paragraph (2)(*b*) or (7)(*b*) to be deducted in computing the paid-up capital in respect of the class before that time

S. 212.3(8) was added by S.C. 2012, c. 31, s. 49(1), applicable generally in respect of transactions and events that occur after March 28, 2012. However, see the history note following s. 212.3(1) for the application where certain transactions occur before 2013 and for an election that can be made for transactions that occur before August 14, 2012.

▶ 212.3(9) ◀

(9) Paid-up capital reinstatement. If, in respect of an investment in a subject corporation made by a CRIC that is described in any of paragraphs (10)(*a*) to (*f*), an amount is deducted under paragraph (2)(*b*) or subsection (7) in computing the paid-up capital in respect of a class of shares of the capital stock of a particular corporation and, at a time subsequent to the investment time, there is a reduction of paid-up capital referred to in subparagraph (*b*)(i) or a receipt of property referred to in the description of A in subparagraph (*b*)(ii), then the paid-up capital in respect of the class is to be increased, immediately before the subsequent time, by the lesser of

(*a*) the amount, if any, by which

(i) the total of all amounts deducted, before the subsequent time, under paragraph (2)(*b*) or subsection (7), in respect of the investment, in computing the paid-up capital in respect of the class

exceeds

(ii) the total of all amounts added under this subsection, in respect of the investment, to the paid-up capital in respect of the class before the time that is immediately before the subsequent time, and

(*b*) an amount that

(i) if the investment is described in paragraph (10)(*a*), (*b*) or (*f*), the paid-up capital in respect of the class is reduced at the subsequent time as part of or because of a distribution of property by the particular corporation and the property (in this paragraph referred to as the "distributed shares") is shares of the capital stock of the subject corporation or shares of the capital stock of a foreign affiliate of the particular corporation that were substituted for shares of the capital stock of the subject corporation, is equal to the amount determined by the formula

$$A/B$$

where

A is

(A) if the investment is described in paragraph (10)(*b*), the portion of the fair market value, immediately before the subsequent time, of the distributed shares that can reasonably be considered to relate to the contribution of capital that is the investment, and

(B) if the investment is described in paragraph (10)(*a*) or (*f*), the lesser of

(I) the portion of the fair market value, immediately before the subsequent time, of the distributed shares that can reasonably be considered to relate to the shares (in this paragraph referred to as the "acquired shares") of the capital stock of the subject corporation that were acquired on the investment (other than any portion described in clause (A)), and

(II) the proportion of the amount determined under subparagraph (*a*)(i) that the amount determined under subclause (I) is of the fair market value, immediately before the subsequent time, of the acquired shares, or the portion of the fair market value of shares that were substituted for the acquired shares that can reasonably be considered to relate to the acquired shares, and

B is

(A) if the particular corporation is, immediately after the dividend time, a qualifying substitute corporation in respect of the CRIC, the particular corporation's equity percentage (as defined in subsection 95(4)) in the CRIC immediately after the dividend time, and

(B) in any other case, 100%, and

(ii) in any other case, is equal to the amount determined by the formula

$$A \times B/C$$

where

A is the amount that is equal to the fair market value of property that the particular corporation demonstrates has been received at the subsequent time by it or by a corporation resident in Canada that was not dealing at arm's length with the particular corporation at that time (in this subparagraph referred to as the "recipient corporation")

(A) as proceeds from the disposition of the acquired shares, or other shares to the extent that the proceeds from the disposition of those other shares can reasonably be considered to relate to the acquired shares or to shares of the capital stock of the subject corporation in respect of which an investment described in paragraph (10)(*b*) was made, other than

(I) the fair market value of shares of the capital stock of another foreign affiliate of the taxpayer acquired by the recipient corporation as consideration for the disposition and as an investment to which subsection (16) or (18) applies, and

(II) proceeds from a disposition of shares to a corporation resident in Canada for which the acquisition of the shares is an investment to which subsection (16) or (18) applies,

(B) as a reduction of paid-up capital or dividend in respect of a class of shares of the capital stock of the subject corporation or the portion, of a reduction of paid-up capital or dividend in respect of a class of shares of the capital stock of a foreign affiliate of the particular corporation that were substituted for shares of the capital stock of the subject corporation, that can reasonably be considered to relate to the subject shares, or

(C) if the investment is described in paragraph (10)(*c*) or (*d*) or subparagraph (10)(*e*)(i),

(I) as a repayment of or as proceeds from the disposition of the debt obligation or amount owing, other than

1. if the debt obligation or amount owing was acquired by another foreign affiliate of the taxpayer, the portion of the fair market value of property received by the particular corporation as a result of an investment by the particular corporation that is described in paragraphs (10)(*a*) to (*f*) to which subsection (16) or (18) applies, or

2. as proceeds from a disposition to a corporation resident in Canada and that is affiliated with the particular corporation, and where subsection (16) or (18) applies to the other corporation in respect of its acquisition, or

(II) as interest on the debt obligation or amount owing,

B is the amount determined under paragraph (*a*) in respect of the class, and

C is the total of all amounts each of which is an amount determined under paragraph (*a*) in respect of all classes of shares of the capital stock of the particular corporation or of any corporation that does not deal at arm's length with the particular corporation.

Editorial Note: See the editorial note to s. 212.3(2).

History: S. 212.3(9) was replaced by S.C. 2014, c. 39, s. 65(10), applicable in respect of transactions and events that occur after March 28, 2012, except that in respect of transactions and events that occur before August 16, 2013, subparagraph 212.3(9)(*b*)(ii) is to be read without reference to subclause (A)(I) in the description of A.

If an election is made under subsection 49(3) of the *Jobs and Growth Act, 2012* [S.C. 2012, c. 31], section 212.3 of the *Income Tax Act* applies in the manner set out in that subsection in respect of transactions and events that occur after March 28, 2012 and before August 14, 2012.

If a taxpayer elects in writing under subsection 65(27) of the *Economic Action Plan 2014 Act, No. 2* [S.C. 2014, c. 39] and files the election with the Minister of National Revenue on or before the day that is the later of the taxpayer's filing-due date for its taxation year that includes the day on which the *Economic Action Plan 2014 Act, No. 2* [S.C. 2014, c. 39] receives royal assent [December 16, 2014] and the day that is one year after the day on which this Act receives royal assent [December 16, 2015], then, in respect of transactions and events that occur before August 16, 2013, subsection 212.3(9) is to be read as follows:

"(9) If, in respect of an investment in a subject corporation made by a CRIC that is described in any of paragraphs (10)(*a*) to (*f*), an amount is required by paragraph (2)(*b*) or subsection (7) to be deducted in computing the paid-up capital in respect of a class of shares of the capital stock of a particular corporation, and the paid-up capital in respect of the class is reduced at a time subsequent to the investment time, then the paid-up capital in respect of the class is to be increased, immediately before the subsequent time, by the least of

(*a*) the amount by which the paid-up capital of the class is reduced at the subsequent time,

(*b*) the amount, if any, by which

(i) the total of all amounts each of which is required, before the subsequent time, by paragraph (2)(*b*) or subsection (7) to be deducted, in respect of the investment, in computing the paid-up capital in respect of the class

exceeds

(ii) the total of all amounts required under this subsection to be added, in respect of the investment, to the paid-up capital of the class before the subsequent time, and

(*c*) an amount that

(i) if the paid-up capital of the class is reduced at the subsequent time as part of or because of a distribution of property by the particular corporation and the property is shares of the capital stock of the subject corporation (in this paragraph referred to as the "subject shares") or shares of the capital stock of a foreign affiliate of the particular corporation that were substituted for the subject shares, is equal to the fair market value of the subject shares, or the portion of the fair market value of the substituted shares that may reasonably be considered to relate to the subject shares, as the case may be, at the subsequent time,

(ii) is equal to the fair market value of property that the particular corporation demonstrates it has received directly or indirectly after the investment time and no more than 180 days before the subsequent time

(A) as proceeds from the disposition of the subject shares, or as the portion of the proceeds from the disposition of the substituted shares that may reasonably be considered to relate to the subject shares,

(B) as a dividend or qualifying return of capital, within the meaning assigned by subsection 90(3), in respect of a class of subject shares, or the portion of a dividend or reduction of paid-up capital in respect of a class of substituted shares that may reasonably be considered to relate to the subject shares, or

(C) if the investment is described in paragraph (10)(*c*) or (*d*) or subparagraph (10)(*e*)(i),

(I) as a repayment of or as proceeds from the disposition of the debt obligation, or amount owing, in connection with the investment, or

(II) as interest on the debt obligation or amount owing, or

(iii) if neither subparagraph (i) nor (ii) applies, is equal to nil."

S. 212.3(9) formerly read:

(9) *Paid-up capital reinstatement.* If, in respect of an investment in a subject corporation made by a CRIC that is described in paragraph (10)(*a*), (*b*) or (*f*), an amount is required by paragraph (2)(*b*) or (7)(*b*) to be deducted in computing the paid-up capital in respect of a class of shares of the capital stock of a particular corporation, and the particular corporation reduces, at a time subsequent to the investment time, the paid-up capital in respect of the class, then the paid-up capital in respect of the class is to be increased, immediately before the subsequent time, by the least of

(*a*) the amount of the reduction of the paid-up capital at the subsequent time,

(*b*) the amount, if any, by which

(i) the amount required by paragraph (2)(*b*) or (7)(*b*), as the case may be, to be deducted, in respect of the investment, in computing the paid-up capital in respect of the class

exceeds

(ii) the total of all amounts required under this subsection to be added, in respect of the investment, to the paid-up capital of the class in respect of a reduction of paid-up capital made before the subsequent time, and

(*c*) an amount that

(i) if the property distributed on the reduction of paid-up capital is shares of the capital stock of the subject corporation (in this paragraph referred to as the "subject shares") or shares of the capital stock of a foreign affiliate of the particular corporation that were substituted for the subject shares, is equal to the fair market value of the subject shares, or the portion of the fair market value of the substituted shares that may reasonably be considered to relate to the subject shares, as the case may be, at the subsequent time,

(ii) the particular corporation demonstrates that it has received directly or indirectly after the investment time and no more than 180 days before the subsequent time

(A) as proceeds from the disposition of the subject shares, or as the portion of the proceeds from the disposition of the substituted shares that may reasonably be considered to relate to the subject shares, other than as proceeds from a disposition in respect of which the related acquisition is one to which subsection (18) applies, or

(B) as a dividend or qualifying return of capital, within the meaning assigned by subsection 90(3), in respect of a class of subject shares, or the portion of a dividend or qualifying return of capital in respect of a class of substituted shares that may reasonably be considered to relate to the subject shares, or

(iii) if neither subparagraph (i) nor (ii) applies, is equal to nil.

S. 212.3(9)(*c*)(ii)(B) was replaced by S.C. 2013, c. 34, s. 427(2)(*d*), applicable in respect of transactions and events that occur after March 28, 2012, other than transactions and events to which subsections 212.3(9), (18) and (20) do not apply. See the history note following s. 212.3(1) for the application where certain transactions occur before 2013 and for an election that can be made for transactions that occur before August 14, 2012.

S. 212.3(9)(*c*)(ii)(B) formerly read:

(B) as a dividend or reduction of paid-up capital in respect of a class of subject shares, or the portion of a dividend or reduction of paid-up capital in respect of a class of substituted shares that may reasonably be considered to relate to the subject shares, or

S. 212.3(9) was added by S.C. 2012, c. 31, s. 49(1), applicable generally in respect of transactions and events that occur after March 28, 2012. However, see the history note following s. 212.3(1) for the application where certain transactions occur before 2013 and for an election that can be made for transactions that occur before August 14, 2012.

Tax Window Files: PUC reinstatement under 212.3(9), *16XXXX*, CRA Document No. 2016-0629011R3.

► 212.3(9.1) ◄

(9.1) Exchange of debt obligation for shares. For the purposes of subsection (9), if at any time a debt obligation that relates to a particular investment described in paragraph (10)(*c*) or (*d*) or subparagraph (10)(*e*)(i) is exchanged for shares of a subject corporation and as part of the exchange there is an acquisition of shares described in subparagraph (18)(*b*)(i) or paragraph 18(*d*), then all amounts, in respect of the particular investment, deducted under paragraph (2)(*b*) or subsection (7) from, or added under subsection (9) to, the paid-up capital in respect of a class of shares before that time are deemed to have been deducted or added, as the case may be, in respect of the acquisition of the shares and not the particular investment.

History: S. 212.3(9.1) was added by S.C. 2014, c. 39, s. 65(10), applicable in respect of transactions and events that occur after March 28, 2012

If an election is made under subsection 49(3) of the *Jobs and Growth Act, 2012* [S.C. 2012, c. 31], section 212.3 of the *Income Tax Act* applies in the manner set out in that subsection in respect of transactions and events that occur after March 28, 2012 and before August 14, 2012.

► 212.3(9.2) ◄

(9.2) Continuity for paid-up capital reinstatement. If at any particular time shares (in this subsection referred to as the "new shares") of a class of the capital stock of a corporation resident in Canada are acquired, in a transaction to which any of sections 51, 85, 85.1, 86 and 87 apply, in exchange for a share (in this subsection referred to as the "old share") of a class of the capital stock of a particular corporation that is either the corporation or another corporation resident in Canada, then for the purposes of subsections (8) and (9),

(*a*) if the corporation that issues the new shares is not the particular corporation, it is deemed to be the same corporation as, and a continuation of, the particular corporation;

(*b*) the new shares are deemed to be the same share, and of the same class of the capital stock of the particular corporation, as the old share; and

(*c*) if the old share remains outstanding after the exchange, it is deemed to be a share of a different class of the capital stock of the particular corporation.

History: S. 212.3(9.2) was added by S.C. 2014, c. 39, s. 65(10), applicable in respect of transactions and events that occur after March 28, 2012

If an election is made under subsection 49(3) of the *Jobs and Growth Act, 2012* [S.C. 2012, c. 31], section 212.3 of the *Income Tax Act* applies in the manner set out in that subsection in respect of transactions and events that occur after March 28, 2012 and before August 14, 2012.

► 212.3(10) ◄

(10) Investment in subject corporation. In this section, "investment", in a subject corporation made by a CRIC, means any of

(*a*) an acquisition of shares of the capital stock of the subject corporation by the CRIC;

(*b*) a contribution of capital to the subject corporation by the CRIC, which is deemed to include any transaction or event under which a benefit is conferred on the subject corporation by the CRIC;

(*c*) a transaction under which an amount becomes owing by the subject corporation to the CRIC, other than an amount owing

(i) that arises in the ordinary course of the business of the CRIC and that is repaid, other than as part of a series of loans or other transactions and repayments, within 180 days after the day on which the amount becomes owing,

(ii) that is a pertinent loan or indebtedness immediately after the time of the transaction, or

(iii) because a dividend has been declared, but not yet paid, by the subject corporation;

(*d*) an acquisition of a debt obligation of the subject corporation by the CRIC from a person, other than

(i) if the acquisition is made in the ordinary course of the business of the CRIC, a debt obligation acquired from a person with which the CRIC deals at arm's length at the time of the acquisition, or

(ii) a debt obligation that is a pertinent loan or indebtedness immediately after the time of the acquisition;

(*e*) an extension of

(i) the maturity date of a debt obligation (other than a debt obligation that is a pertinent loan or indebtedness immediately after the time of the extension) owing by the subject corporation to the CRIC, or

(ii) the redemption, acquisition or cancellation date of shares of the capital stock of the subject corporation owned by the CRIC;

(*f*) an indirect acquisition by the CRIC of shares of the capital stock of the subject corporation that results from a direct acquisition by the CRIC of shares of the capital stock of another corporation resident in Canada, of which the subject corporation is a foreign affiliate, if the total fair market value of all the shares that are held directly or indirectly by the other corporation and are shares of foreign affiliates of the other corporation exceeds 75% of the total fair market value (determined without reference to debt obligations of any corporation resident in Canada in which the other corporation has a direct or indirect interest) of all of the properties owned by the other corporation; and

(*g*) an acquisition by the CRIC of an option in respect of, or an interest in, or for civil law a right in, shares of the capital stock of, an amount owing by (other than an amount owing described in subparagraph (*c*)(i) or (ii)), or a debt obligation of (other than a debt obligation described in subparagraph (*d*)(i) or (ii)), the subject corporation.

Editorial Note: The "investments" that attract the application of the foreign affiliate dumping rules are enumerated in s. 212.3(10). While many of these would seem self-evident, s. 212.3(10)(*f*) is more controversial, providing that an indirect acquisition of subject corporation shares by the CRIC through the direct acquisition by the CRIC of shares of the capital stock of another Canadian-resident corporation of which the subject corporation is a foreign affiliate, where the total fair market value of all the shares of foreign affiliates held by the other corporation (directly or indirectly) exceeds 75% of the other corporation's total fair market value, is an investment. This rule can be engaged where a foreign corporation incorporates an acquisition company to acquire shares of a Canadian target, where the target holds shares of foreign affiliates. The 75% threshold was raised from 50% in an earlier draft of the legislation as a result of criticism of the potentially inappropriate application of this rule. Additional interpretive provisions are found in s. 212.3(14).

History: S. 212.3(10)(*c*)(iii) was added by S.C. 2014, c. 39, s. 65(11), applicable in respect of transactions and events that occur after March 28, 2012

If an election is made under subsection 49(3) of the *Jobs and Growth Act, 2012* [S.C. 2012, c. 31], section 212.3 of the *Income Tax Act* applies in the manner set out in that subsection in respect of transactions and events that occur after March 28, 2012 and before August 14, 2012.

S. 212.3(10) was added by S.C. 2012, c. 31, s. 49(1), applicable generally in respect of transactions and events that occur after March 28, 2012. However, see the history note following s. 212.3(1) for the application where certain transactions occur before 2013 and for an election that can be made for transactions that occur before August 14, 2012.

► 212.3(11) ◄

(11) Pertinent loan or indebtedness. For the purposes of subsection (10) and subject to subsection 17.1(3), "pertinent loan or indebtedness", at any time, means an amount owing at that time by the subject corporation to the CRIC in respect of which all of the following apply:

(*a*) either

(i) the amount became owing after March 28, 2012, or

(ii) the amount became owing before March 29, 2012 and is a debt obligation for which the maturity date was extended after March 28, 2012 and at or before that time;

(*b*) the amount owing is not an amount owing described in subparagraph (10)(*c*)(i) or a debt obligation described in subparagraph (10)(*d*)(i); and

(*c*) the CRIC and the parent jointly elect in writing under this paragraph in respect of the amount owing and file the election with the Minister on or before the filing-due date of the CRIC

> **Proposed Amendment**
> **2019 Federal Budget Resolutions**
>
> **The portion of paragraph 212.3(11)(c) of the Act before subparagraph (i) is replaced by the following:**
>
> (*c*) the CRIC and each parent jointly elect in writing under this paragraph in respect of the amount owing and file the election with the Minister on or before the filing-due date of the CRIC
>
> **Applicable:** In respect of transactions or events that occur on or after March 19, 2019.

(i) in the case of an amount owing described in subparagraph (*a*)(i), for the year in which the amount became owing, or

(ii) in the case of an amount owing described in subparagraph (*a*)(ii), for the year in which the extension was made.

Editorial Note: The "pertinent loan or indebtedness" ("PLOI") rules are an exclusion from the foreign affiliate dumping rules. Under subsection 212.3(11), a PLOI is an amount owing by a subject to a corporation to a CRIC where all of the following conditions are met:

- either the amount became owing after March 28, 2012 or the maturity date of the debt obligation was extended after March 28, 2012,
- the amount owing is not an amount excluded from the investment definition under the short-term loan or ordinary course of business exemptions, and
- a joint election is filed by the CRIC and the parent on or before the filing-due date of the CRIC for the year in which the amount became owing or the maturity date was extended, as the case may be.

See the editorial note to s. 17.1(1).

History: S. 212.3(3) was added by S.C. 2012, c. 31, s. 49(1), applicable generally in respect of transactions and events that occur after March 28, 2012. However, any election referred to in paragraph 212.3(11)(*c*) that would otherwise be required to be filed with the Minister of National Revenue on or before the day that is 120 days after the day on which this Act receives royal assent [December 14, 2012] is deemed to have been filed with the Minister on a timely basis if it is filed with the Minister on or before the day that is 365 days after the day on which this Act receives royal assent [December 14, 2012].

See the history note following s. 212.3(1) for the application where certain transactions occur before 2013 and for an election that can be made for transactions that occur before August 14, 2012.

► 212.3(12) ◄

(12) Late-filed elections. Where an election referred to in subsection (3) or paragraph (11)(*c*) was not made on or before the day on or before which the election was required by that paragraph to be made, the election is deemed to have been made on that day if the election is made on or before the day that is three years after that day and the penalty in respect of the election is paid by the CRIC when the election is made.

History: S. 212.3(12) was added by S.C. 2012, c. 31, s. 49(1), applicable generally in respect of transactions and events that occur after March 28, 2012. However, see the history note following s. 212.3(1) for the application where certain transactions occur before 2013 and for an election that can be made for transactions that occur before August 14, 2012.

► 212.3(13) ◄

(13) Penalty for late-filed election. For the purposes of subsection (12), the penalty in respect of an election referred to in that subsection is the amount equal to the product obtained by multiplying $100 by the number of months each of which is a month all or part of which is during the period commencing with the day on or before which the election is required by subsection (3) or paragraph (11)(*c*), as the case may be, to be made and ending on the day on which the election is made.

History: S. 212.3(13) was added by S.C. 2012, c. 31, s. 49(1), applicable generally in respect of transactions and events that occur after March 28, 2012. However, see the history note following s. 212.3(1) for the application where certain transactions occur before 2013 and for an election that can be made for transactions that occur before August 14, 2012.

► 212.3(14) ◄

(14) Rules for paragraph (10)(*f*). For the purposes of paragraph (10)(*f*),

(*a*) the condition in that paragraph is deemed to be satisfied at the time of the acquisition if

(i) any property (other than shares of foreign affiliates of the other corporation that is referred to in that paragraph) held directly or indirectly by that other corporation is disposed of, after the time of the acquisition, directly or indirectly by that corporation as part of a series of transactions or events that includes the acquisition, and

(ii) at any time that is subsequent to the time of the acquisition and that is in the period during which the series occurs, the condition in that paragraph would have been satisfied had the acquisition occurred at the subsequent time; and

(*b*) the fair market value of properties held directly or indirectly by the other corporation is not to be taken into account more than once in determining whether the condition in that paragraph is satisfied.

History: S. 212.3(14) was added by S.C. 2012, c. 31, s. 49(1), applicable generally in respect of transactions and events that occur after March 28, 2012. However, see the history note following s. 212.3(1) for the application where certain transactions occur before 2013 and for an election that can be made for transactions that occur before August 14, 2012.

▶ 212.3(15) ◀

(15) Control. For the purposes of this section and paragraph 128.1(1)(*c.3*),

(*a*) a CRIC or a taxpayer to which paragraph 128.1(1)(*c.3*) applies (in this paragraph referred to as the "specific corporation"), that would, in the absence of this subsection, be controlled at any time

(i) by more than one non-resident corporation is deemed not to be controlled at that time by any such non-resident that controls at that time another non-resident corporation that controls at that time the specific corporation, unless the application of this paragraph would otherwise result in no non-resident corporation controlling the specific corporation, and

(ii) by a particular non-resident corporation is deemed not to be controlled at that time by the particular corporation if the particular corporation is controlled at that time by another corporation that is at that time

(A) resident in Canada, and

(B) not controlled by any non-resident person; and

(*b*) if at any time a corporation would not, in the absence of this subsection, be controlled by any non-resident corporation, and a related group (determined without reference to paragraph 251(5)(*b*)), each member of which is a non-resident corporation, is in a position to control the corporation, the corporation is deemed to be controlled at that time by

(i) the member of the group that has the greatest direct equity percentage (within the meaning assigned by subsection 95(4)) in the corporation at that time, or

(ii) where no member of the group has a direct equity percentage in the corporation that is greater than that of every other member, the member determined by the corporation or, if the corporation does not make a determination, by the Minister.

Proposed Amendment
2019 Federal Budget Resolutions

Paragraphs 212.3(15)(*a*) and (*b*) of the Act are replaced by the following:

(*a*) a CRIC or a taxpayer to which paragraph 128.1(1)(*c.3*) applies (in this subsection referred to as the "specific corporation"), that would, in the absence of this subsection, be controlled at any time

(i) by more than one non-resident person, is deemed not to be controlled at that time by any such non-resident that controls at that time another non-resident person that controls at that time the specific corporation, unless the application of this paragraph would otherwise result in no non-resident person controlling the specific corporation, and

(ii) by a particular non-resident corporation is deemed not to be controlled at that time by the particular corporation if the particular corporation is controlled at that time by another corporation that is at that time

(A) resident in Canada, and

(B) not controlled by any non-resident person or group of non-resident persons not dealing with each other at arm's length; and

(*b*) a non-resident person is deemed not to be a member of a particular group of non-resident persons not dealing with each other at arm's length that controls the specific corporation if

(i) the non-resident person would, absent the application of this paragraph, be a member of the particular group, and

(ii) the non-resident person is a member of the particular group solely because it controls, or is a member of a group that controls, another member of the particular group.

Applicable: In respect of transactions or events that occur on or after March 19, 2019.

History: S. 212.3(15) was replaced by S.C. 2014, c. 39, s. 65(12), applicable in respect of transactions and events that occur after March 28, 2012, except that in respect of transactions and events that occur before August 16, 2013, subsection 212.3(15) is to be read without reference to paragraph (*b*).

If an election is made under subsection 49(3) of the *Jobs and Growth Act, 2012* [S.C. 2012, c. 31], section 212.3 of the *Income Tax Act* applies in the manner set out in that subsection in respect of transactions and events that occur after March 28, 2012 and before August 14, 2012.

S. 212.3(15) formerly read:

(15) *Control.* For the purposes of this section and paragraph 128.1(1)(*c.3*), a CRIC that would, in the absence of this subsection, be controlled at any time

(*a*) by more than one non-resident corporation is deemed not to be controlled at that time by any such non-resident that controls at that time another non-resident corporation that controls at that time the CRIC, unless the application of this subsection would otherwise result in no non-resident corporation controlling the CRIC; and

(*b*) by a particular non-resident corporation is deemed not to be controlled at that time by the particular corporation if the particular corporation is controlled at that time by another corporation that is at that time

(i) resident in Canada, and

(ii) not controlled by any non-resident person.

S. 212.3(15) was added by S.C. 2012, c. 31, s. 49(1), applicable generally in respect of transactions and events that occur after March 28, 2012. However, see the history note following s. 212.3(1) for the application where certain transactions occur before 2013 and for an election that can be made for transactions that occur before August 14, 2012.

▶ 212.3(16) ◀

(16) Exception — more closely connected business activities. Subject to subsection (19), subsection (2) does not apply to an investment in a subject corporation made by a CRIC if the CRIC demonstrates that all of the following conditions are met:

(*a*) the business activities carried on by the subject corporation and all other corporations (those other corporations in this subsection and subsection (17) referred to as the "subject subsidiary corporations") in which the subject corporation has, at the investment time, an equity percentage (as defined in subsection 95(4)) are at the investment time, and are expected to remain, on a collective basis, more closely connected to the business activities carried on in Canada by the CRIC, or by any corporation resident in Canada with which the CRIC does not, at the investment time, deal at arm's length, than to the business activities carried on by any non-resident corporation with which the CRIC, at the investment time, does not deal at arm's length, other than

Proposed Amendment
2019 Federal Budget Resolutions

The portion of paragraph 212.3(16)(*a*) before subparagraph (i) is replaced by the following:

(*a*) the business activities carried on by the subject corporation and all other corporations (those other corporations in this subsection and subsection (17) referred to as the "subject subsidiary corporations") in which the subject corporation has, at the investment time, an equity percentage (as defined in subsection 95(4)) are at the investment time, and are expected to remain, on a collective basis, more closely connected to the business activities carried on in Canada by the CRIC, or by any corporation resident in Canada with which the CRIC does not, at the investment time, deal at arm's length, than to the business activities carried on by any non-resident person with which the CRIC, at the investment time, does not deal at arm's length, other than

Applicable: In respect of transactions or events that occur on or after March 19, 2019.

(i) the subject corporation,

(ii) the subject subsidiary corporations, and

(iii) any corporation that is, immediately before the investment time, a controlled foreign affiliate of the CRIC for the purposes of section 17,

(*b*) officers of the CRIC, or of a corporation resident in Canada that did not, at the investment time, deal at arm's length with the CRIC, had and exercised the principal decision-making authority in respect of the making of the investment and a majority of those officers were, at the investment time, persons each of whom was resident, and working principally,

(i) in Canada, or

(ii) in a country in which a particular corporation is resident if the particular corporation (in this subsection and subsection (17) referred to as a "connected affiliate") is a controlled foreign affiliate of the CRIC for the purposes of section 17 and carries on business activities that are, at the investment time, and are expected to remain, at least as closely connected to those of the subject corporation and the subject subsidiary corporations, on a collective basis, as the business activities carried on in Canada by the CRIC, or any corporation resident in Canada with which the CRIC does not, at the investment time, deal at arm's length, as the case may be, are to those of the subject corporation and the subject subsidiary corporations, on a collective basis; and

(*c*) at the investment time, it is reasonably expected that

(i) officers of the CRIC, or of a corporation resident in Canada that does not deal at arm's length with the CRIC, will have and exercise the ongoing principal decision-making authority in respect of the investment,

(ii) a majority of those officers will be persons each of whom will be resident, and working principally, in Canada or in a country in which a connected affiliate is resident, and

(iii) the performance evaluation and compensation of the officers of the CRIC, or of the corporation resident in Canada that does not deal at arm's length with the CRIC, who are resident, and work principally, in Canada, or in a country in which a connected affiliate is resident, will be based on the results of operations of the subject corporation to a greater extent than will be the performance evaluation and compensation of any officer of a non-resident corporation (other than the subject corporation, a corporation controlled by the subject corporation or a connected affiliate) that does not deal at arm's length with the CRIC.

Editorial Note: Subsections 212.3(16) and (18) provide complete exceptions to the application of the foreign affiliate dumping rules. Both provisions are subject to the potential application of s. 212.3(19), which applies in respect of certain preferred share transactions. Subsection 212.3(16) is the "more closely connected" ("MCC") rule, and generally applies where the CRIC's decision-makers are Canadians, although it is understood that this exemption is unlikely to be available in most cases.

History: S. 212.3(16)(*b*), the portion before subparagraph (i) was replaced by S.C. 2014, c. 39, s. 65(13), applicable in respect of transactions and events that occur after March 28, 2012.

If an election is made under subsection 49(3) of the *Jobs and Growth Act, 2012* [S.C. 2012, c. 31], section 212.3 of the *Income Tax Act* applies in the manner set out in that subsection in respect of transactions and events that occur after March 28, 2012 and before August 14, 2012.

S. 212.3(16)(*b*), the portion before subparagraph (i) formerly read:

(*b*) officers of the CRIC had and exercised the principal decision-making authority in respect of the making of the investment and a majority of those officers were, at the investment time, persons each of whom was resident, and working principally,

S. 212.3(16)(*c*) was replaced by S.C. 2014, c. 39, s. 65(14), applicable in respect of transactions and events that occur after March 28, 2012.

If an election is made under subsection 49(3) of the *Jobs and Growth Act, 2012* [S.C. 2012, c. 31], section 212.3 of the *Income Tax Act* applies in the manner set out in that subsection in respect of transactions and events that occur after March 28, 2012 and before August 14, 2012.

S. 212.3(16)(*c*) formerly read:

(*c*) at the investment time, it is reasonably expected that

(i) officers of the CRIC will have and exercise the ongoing principal decision-making authority in respect of the investment,

(ii) a majority of those officers will be persons each of whom will be resident, and working principally, in Canada or in a country in which a connected affiliate is resident, and

(iii) the performance evaluation and compensation of the officers of the CRIC who are resident, and work principally, in Canada, or in a country in which a connected affiliate is resident, will be based on the results of operations of the subject corporation to a greater extent than will be the performance evaluation and compensation of any officer of a non-resident corporation (other than the subject corporation, a corporation controlled by the subject corporation or a connected affiliate) that does not deal at arm's length with the CRIC.

S. 212.3(16) was added by S.C. 2012, c. 31, s. 49(1), applicable generally in respect of transactions and events that occur after March 28, 2012. However, see the history note following s. 212.3(1) for the application where certain transactions occur before 2013 and for an election that can be made for transactions that occur before August 14, 2012.

Tax Window Files: "more closely connected business activities", *September 6, 2013*, CRA Document No. 2013-0474671E5.

► 212.3(17) ◄

(17) Dual officers. For the purposes of paragraphs (16)(*b*) and (*c*), any person who is an officer of the CRIC, or of a corporation resident in Canada that does not deal at arm's length with the CRIC, and of a non-resident corporation that does not, at the investment time, deal at arm's length with the CRIC (other than the subject corporation, a subject subsidiary corporation or a connected affiliate) is deemed to not be resident, and to not work principally, in a country in which a connected affiliate is resident.

History: S. 212.3(17) was replaced by S.C. 2014, c. 39, s. 65(15), applicable in respect of transactions and events that occur after March 28, 2012.

If an election is made under subsection 49(3) of the *Jobs and Growth Act, 2012* [S.C. 2012, c. 31], section 212.3 of the *Income Tax Act* applies in the manner set out in that subsection in respect of transactions and events that occur after March 28, 2012 and before August 14, 2012.

S. 212.3(17) formerly read:

(17) *Dual officers.* For the purposes of paragraphs (16)(*b*) and (*c*), any person who is an officer of the CRIC and of a non-resident corporation with which the CRIC, at the investment time, does not deal at arm's length (other than the subject corporation, a subject subsidiary corporation or a connected affiliate) is deemed to not be resident, and to not work principally, in a country in which a connected affiliate is resident.

S. 212.3(17) was added by S.C. 2012, c. 31, s. 49(1), applicable generally in respect of transactions and events that occur after March 28, 2012. However, see the history note following s. 212.3(1) for the application where certain transactions occur before 2013 and for an election that can be made for transactions that occur before August 14, 2012.

► 212.3(18) ◄

(18) Exception — corporate reorganizations. Subject to subsections (18.1) to (20), subsection (2) does not apply to an investment in a subject corporation made by a CRIC if

(*a*) the investment is described in paragraph (10)(*a*) or (*d*) and is an acquisition of shares of the capital stock, or a debt obligation, of the subject corporation

(i) from a corporation resident in Canada (in this paragraph referred to as the "disposing corporation") to which the CRIC is, immediately before the investment time, related (determined without reference to paragraph 251(5)(*b*)), and

(A) each shareholder of the disposing corporation immediately before the investment time is

(I) either the CRIC or a corporation resident in Canada that is, immediately before the investment time, related to the parent, and

(II) at no time that is in the period during which the series of transactions or events that includes the making of the investment occurs and that is before the investment time, dealing at arm's length (determined without reference to paragraph 251(5)(*b*)) with the parent or a non-resident corporation that participates in the series and is, at any time that is in the period and that is before the investment time, related to the parent, or

(B) the disposing corporation is, at no time that is in the period and that is before the investment time, dealing at arm's length (determined without reference to paragraph 251(5)(*b*)) with the parent or a non-resident corporation that participates in the series and is, at any time that is in the period and that is before the investment time, related to the parent, or

(ii) on an amalgamation described in subsection 87(1) of two or more corporations (each of which is in this subparagraph referred to as a "predecessor corporation") to form the CRIC if

(A) all of the predecessor corporations are, immediately before the amalgamation, related to each other (determined without reference to paragraph 251(5)(*b*)), and

(B) either

(I) none of the predecessor corporations are, at any time that is in the period during which the series of transactions or events that includes the making of the investment occurs and that is before the investment time, dealing at arm's length (determined without reference to paragraph 251(5)(*b*)) with the parent or a non-resident corporation that participates in the series and is, at any time that is in the period and that is before the investment time, related to the parent, or

(II) if the condition in subclause (I) is not satisfied in respect of a predecessor corporation, each shareholder of that predecessor immediately before the investment time is

1. either the CRIC or a corporation resident in Canada that is, immediately before the investment time, related to the parent, and

2. at no time that is in the period and that is before the investment time, dealing at arm's length (determined without reference to paragraph 251(5)(*b*)) with the parent or a non-resident corporation that participates in the series and is, at any time that is in the period and that is before the investment time, related to the parent;

Proposed Amendment

2019 Federal Budget Resolutions

Paragraph 212.3(18)(*a*) of the Act is replaced by the following:

(*a*) the investment is described in paragraph (10)(*a*) or (*d*) and is an acquisition of shares of the capital stock, or a debt obligation, of the subject corporation

(i) from a corporation resident in Canada (in this paragraph referred to as the "disposing corporation") to which the CRIC is, immediately before the investment time, related (determined without reference to paragraph 251(5)(*b*)), and

(A) each shareholder of the disposing corporation immediately before the investment time is,

(I) if there is only one parent in respect of the CRIC,

1 either the CRIC or a corporation resident in Canada that is, immediately before the investment time, related to the parent, and

2 at no time that is in the period during which the series of transactions or events that includes the making of the investment occurs and that is before the investment time, dealing at arm's length (determined without reference to paragraph 251(5)(*b*)) with the parent or a non-resident person that participates in the series and is, at any time that is in the period and that is before the investment time, related to the parent, and

(II) if there is a group of parents in respect of the CRIC,

1 either the CRIC or a corporation resident in Canada that is, immediately before the investment time, controlled by the group of parents, and

2 at all times that are in the period during which the series of transactions or events that includes the making of the investment occurs and that are

before the investment time, controlled by the group of parents, or

(B) the disposing corporation is,

(I) if there is only one parent in respect of the CRIC, at no time that is in the period and that is before the investment time, dealing at arm's length (determined without reference to paragraph 251(5)(*b*)) with the parent or a non-resident person that participates in the series and is, at any time that is in the period and that is before the investment time, related to the parent, and

(II) if there is a group of parents in respect of the CRIC, at all times that are in the period during which the series of transactions or events that includes the making of the investment occurs and that are before the investment time, controlled by the group of parents, or

(ii) on an amalgamation described in subsection 87(1) of two or more corporations (each of which is in this subparagraph referred to as a "predecessor corporation") to form the CRIC if all of the predecessor corporations are, immediately before the amalgamation, related to each other (determined without reference to paragraph 251(5)(*b*))and

(A) either

(I) if there is only one parent in respect of the CRIC, none of the predecessor corporations are, at any time that is in the period during which the series of transactions or events that includes the making of the investment occurs and that is before the investment time, dealing at arm's length (determined without reference to paragraph 251(5)(*b*)) with the parent or a non-resident person that participates in the series and is, at any time that is in the period and that is before the investment time, related to the parent, or

(II) if there is a group of parents in respect of the CRIC, all of the predecessor corporations are, at all times that are in the period during which the series of transactions or events that includes the making of the investment occurs and that are before the investment time, controlled by the group of parents, or

(B) if the condition in clause (A) is not satisfied in respect of a predecessor corporation, each shareholder of that predecessor immediately before the investment time is,

(I) if there is only one parent in respect of the CRIC,

1 either the CRIC or a corporation resident in Canada that is, immediately before the investment time, related to the parent, and

2 at no time that is in the period and that is before the investment time, dealing at arm's length (determined without reference to paragraph 251(5)(*b*)) with the parent or a non-resident person that participates in the series and is, at any time that is in the period and that is before the investment time, related to the parent, and

(II) if there is a group of parents in respect of the CRIC,

1 either the CRIC or a corporation resident in Canada that is, immediately before the investment time, controlled by the group of parents, and

2 at all times that are in the period during which the series of transactions or events that includes the making of the investment occurs and that are before the investment time, controlled by the group of parents;

Applicable: In respect of transactions or events that occur on or after March 19, 2019.

(*b*) the investment is described in paragraph (10)(*a*) and is an acquisition of shares of the capital stock of the subject corporation in which the shares are acquired by the CRIC

(i) in an exchange to which subsection 51(1) applies,

(ii) as consideration for a disposition of shares to which subsection 85.1(3) applies (determined without reference to subsection 85.1(4)),

(iii) in the course of a reorganization of the capital of the subject corporation to which subsection 86(1) applies,

(iv) as a result of a foreign merger (as defined in subsection 87(8.1)) under which the subject corporation was formed,

(v) on a liquidation and dissolution to which subsection 88(3) applies,

(vi) on a redemption of shares of another non-resident corporation that is, immediately before the investment time, a foreign affiliate of the CRIC,

(vii) as a dividend or a qualifying return of capital, within the meaning assigned by subsection 90(3), in respect of the shares of another non-resident corporation that is, immediately before the investment time, a foreign affiliate of the CRIC, or

(viii) as a result of a disposition of the shares by the CRIC to a partnership and to which subsection 97(2) applies;

(*c*) the investment is an indirect acquisition referred to in paragraph (10)(*f*) that results from a direct acquisition of shares of the capital stock of another corporation resident in Canada

(i) from a corporation (in this paragraph referred to as the "disposing corporation") to which the CRIC is, immediately before the investment time, related (determined without reference to paragraph 251(5)(*b*)), and

(A) each shareholder of the disposing corporation immediately before the investment time is

(I) either the CRIC or a corporation resident in Canada that, immediately before the investment time, is related to the parent, and

(II) at no time that is in the period during which the series of transactions or events that includes the making of the investment occurs and that is before the investment time, dealing at arm's length (determined without reference to paragraph 251(5)(*b*)) with the parent or a non-resident corporation that participates in the series and is, at any time that is in the period and that is before the investment time, related to the parent, or

(B) the disposing corporation is, at no time that is in the period and that is before the investment time, dealing at arm's length (determined without reference to paragraph 251(5)(*b*)) with the parent or a non-resident corporation that participates in the series and is, at any time that is in the period and that is before the investment time, related to the parent,

(ii) on an amalgamation described in subsection 87(1) of two or more corporations (each of which is in this subparagraph referred to as a "predecessor corporation") to form the CRIC, or a corporation of which the CRIC is a shareholder, if

(A) all of the predecessor corporations are, immediately before the amalgamation, related to each other (determined without reference to paragraph 251(5)(*b*)), and

(B) either

(I) none of the predecessor corporations are, at any time that is in the period during which the series of transactions or events that includes the making of the investment occurs and that is before the investment time, dealing at arm's length (determined without reference to paragraph 251(5)(*b*)) with the parent or a non-resident corporation that participates in the series and is, at any time that is in the period and that is before the investment time, related to the parent, or

(II) if the condition in subclause (I) is not satisfied in respect of a predecessor corporation, each shareholder of that predecessor immediately before the investment time is

1. either the CRIC or a corporation resident in Canada that, immediately before the investment time, is related to the parent, and

2. at no time that is in the period and that is before the investment time, dealing at arm's length (determined without reference to paragraph 251(5)(*b*)) with the parent or a non-resident corporation that participates in the series and is, at any time that is in the period and that is before the investment time, related to the parent,

Proposed Amendment
2019 Federal Budget Resolutions

The portion of paragraph 212.3(18)(*c*) of the Act before subparagraph (iii) is replaced by the following:

(*c*) the investment is an indirect acquisition referred to in paragraph (10)(*f*) that results from a direct acquisition of shares of the capital stock of another corporation resident in Canada

(i) from a corporation (in this paragraph referred to as the "disposing corporation") to which the CRIC is, immediately before the investment time, related (determined without reference to paragraph 251(5)(*b*)) and

(A) each shareholder of the disposing corporation immediately before the investment time is

(I) if there is only one parent in respect of the CRIC,

1 either the CRIC or a corporation resident in Canada that, immediately before the investment time, is related to the parent, and

2 at no time that is in the period during which the series of transactions or events that includes the making of the investment occurs and that is before the investment time, dealing at arm's length (determined without reference to paragraph 251(5)(*b*)) with the parent or a non-resident person that participates in the series and is, at any time that is in the period and that is before the investment time, related to the parent, and

(II) if there is a group of parents in respect of the CRIC,

1 either the CRIC or a corporation resident in Canada that is, immediately before the investment time, controlled by the group of parents, and

2 at all times that are in the period during which the series of transactions or events that includes the making of the investment occurs and that are before the investment time, controlled by the group of parents, or

(B) the disposing corporation is,

(I) if there is only one parent in respect of the CRIC, at no time that is in the period and that is before the investment time, dealing at arm's length (determined without reference to paragraph 251(5)(*b*)) with the parent or a non-resident person that participates in the series and is, at any time that is in the period and that is before the investment time, related to the parent, and

(II) if there is a group of parents in respect of the CRIC, at all times that are in the period during which the series of transactions or events that includes the making of the investment occurs and that are before the investment time, controlled by the group of parents, or

(ii) on an amalgamation described in subsection 87(1) of two or more corporations (each of which is in this subparagraph referred to as a "predecessor corporation") to form the CRIC, or a corporation of which the CRIC is a shareholder, if all of the predecessor corporations are, immediately before the amalgamation, related to each other (determined without reference to paragraph 251(5)(*b*)) and

(A) either

(I) if there is only one parent in respect of the CRIC, none of the predecessor corporations are, at any time that is in the period during which the series of transactions or events that includes the making of the investment occurs and that is before the investment time, dealing at arm's length (determined without reference to paragraph 251(5)(*b*)) with the parent or a non-resident person that participates in the series and is, at any time that is in the period and that is before the investment time, related to the parent, or

(II) if there is a group of parents in respect of the CRIC, all of the predecessor corporations are, at all times that are in the period during which the series of transactions or events that includes the making of the investment occurs and that are before the investment time, controlled by the group of parents, or

(B) if the condition in clause (A) is not satisfied in respect of a predecessor corporation, each shareholder of that predecessor immediately before the investment time is

(I) if there is only one parent in respect of the CRIC,

1 either the CRIC or a corporation resident in Canada that is, immediately before the investment time, related to the parent, and

2 at no time that is in the period and that is before the investment time, dealing at arm's length (determined without reference to paragraph 251(5)(*b*)) with the parent or a non-resident person that participates in the series and is, at any time that is in the period and that is before the investment time, related to the parent, and

(II) if there is a group of parents in respect of the CRIC,

1 either the CRIC or a corporation resident in Canada that is, immediately before the investment time, controlled by the group of parents, and

2 at all times that are in the period during which the series of transactions or events that includes the making of the investment occurs and that are before the investment time, controlled by the group of parents;

Applicable: In respect of transactions or events that occur on or after March 19, 2019.

(iii) in an exchange to which subsection 51(1) applies,

(iv) in the course of a reorganization of the capital of the other corporation to which subsection 86(1) applies,

(v) to the extent that an investment (other than one described in paragraph (10)(*f*)) is made in the subject corporation by the other corporation, or by a particular corporation resident in Canada to which the CRIC and the other corporation are related at the investment time, using property transferred, directly or indirectly, by the CRIC to the other corporation or the particular corporation, as the case may be, if the two investments

(A) occur within 90 days of each other, and

(B) are part of the same series of transactions or events, or

(vi) as a result of a disposition of the shares by the CRIC to a partnership and to which subsection 97(2) applies; or

(*d*) the investment is an acquisition of shares of the capital stock of the subject corporation that is described in paragraph (10)(*a*), or an indirect acquisition referred to in paragraph (10)(*f*) that results from a direct acquisition of shares of the capital stock of another corporation resident in Canada, if

(i) the shares are acquired by the CRIC in exchange for a bond, debenture or note, and

(ii) subsection 51(1) would apply to the exchange if the terms of the bond, debenture or note conferred on the holder the right to make the exchange.

Editorial Note: Under s. 212.3(18)(*a*), the foreign affiliate dumping rules will not apply if the investment is an acquisition by the CRIC of subject corporation shares from another corporation resident in Canada that is related to the CRIC immediately before the investment time (without considering the operation of s. 251(5)(*b*)) and that does not deal at arm's length with the CRIC at any time during the series of transactions that includes the investment time.

Paragraph 212.3(18)(*b*) provides relief where the CRIC acquired shares of a subject corporation under a number of tax-deferred transactions.

Paragraph 212.3(18)(*c*) provides relief where the indirect acquisition rule would apply from the direct acquisition of shares of another Canadian-resident corporation that is related to the CRIC immediately before the investment time (without considering the operation of s. 251(5)(*b*)) and that does not deal at arm's length with the CRIC at any time during the series of transactions that includes the investment time, or on an amalgamation of related Canadian corporations.

Paragraph 212.3(18)(*d*) applies where the CRIC has acquired shares of the subject corporation (either directly or by way of indirect investment), under which the subject corporation shares are acquired by the CRIC as the sole consideration for an exchange of a debt obligation owing to the CRIC (other than an exchange under s. 51).

History: S. 212.3(18), the portion before paragraph (*b*) was replaced by S.C. 2014, c. 39, s. 65(16), applicable in respect of transactions and events that occur after March 28, 2012, except that

(*e*) in respect of transactions and events that occur before August 16, 2013, the portion of subsection 212.3(18) before paragraph (*a*) is to be read as follows:

"(18) Subject to subsections (19) and (20), subsection (2) does not apply to an investment in a subject corporation made by a CRIC if"

(*f*) in respect of transactions and events that occur before August 29, 2014

(i) clause 212.3(18)(*a*)(i)(B) is to be read as follows:

"(B) the disposing corporation is, at no time that is in the period and that is before the investment time, dealing at arm's length (determined without reference to paragraph 251(5)(*b*)) with the CRIC, or"

(ii) subclause 212.3(18)(*a*)(ii)(B)(I) is to be read as follows:

"(I) none of the predecessor corporations deal at arm's length (determined without reference to paragraph 251(5)(*b*)) with another predecessor corporation at any time that is in the period during which the series of transactions or events that includes the making of the investment occurs and that is before the investment time, or"

If an election is made under subsection 49(3) of the *Jobs and Growth Act, 2012* [S.C. 2012, c. 31], section 212.3 of the *Income Tax Act* applies in the manner set out in that subsection in respect of transactions and events that occur after March 28, 2012 and before August 14, 2012.

S. 212.3(18), the portion before paragraph (*b*) formerly read:

(18) *Exception — corporate reorganizations.* Subject to subsections (19) and (20), subsection (2) does not apply to an investment in a subject corporation made by a CRIC if

(*a*) the investment is described in paragraph (10)(*a*) and is an acquisition of shares of the capital stock of the subject corporation

(i) from a corporation resident in Canada

(A) to which the CRIC is, immediately before the investment time, related (determined without reference to paragraph 251(5)(*b*)), and

(B) that is, at no time that is in the period during which the series of transactions or events that includes the making of the investment occurs and that is before the investment time, dealing at arm's length (determined without reference to paragraph 251(5)(*b*)) with the CRIC, or

(ii) on an amalgamation described in subsection 87(1) of two or more corporations (each of which is in this subparagraph referred to as a "predecessor corporation") to form the CRIC if

(A) all of the predecessor corporations are, immediately before the amalgamation, related to each other (determined without reference to paragraph 251(5)(*b*)), and

(B) none of the predecessor corporations deal at arm's length (determined without reference to paragraph 251(5)(*b*)) with another predecessor corporation at any time that is in the period during which the series of transactions or events that includes the making of the investment occurs and that is before the investment time;

S. 212.3(18)(*b*)(viii) was added by S.C. 2014, c. 39, s. 65(17), applicable in respect of transactions and events that occur after March 28, 2012.

If an election is made under subsection 49(3) of the *Jobs and Growth Act, 2012* [S.C. 2012, c. 31], section 212.3 of the *Income Tax Act* applies in the manner set out in that subsection in respect of transactions and events that occur after March 28, 2012 and before August 14, 2012.

S. 212.3(18)(*c*) was replaced by S.C. 2014, c. 39, s. 65(18), applicable in respect of transactions and events that occur after March 28, 2012, except that

(f) in respect of transactions and events that occur before August 29, 2014

(iii) clause 212.3(18)(*c*)(i)(B) is to be read as follows:

"(B) the disposing corporation is, at no time that is in the period and that is before the investment time, dealing at arm's length (determined without reference to paragraph 251(5)(*b*)) with the CRIC,"

(iv) subclause 212.3(18)(*c*)(ii)(B)(I) of the Act is to be read as follows:

"(I) none of the predecessor corporations deal at arm's length (determined without reference to paragraph 251(5)(*b*)) with another predecessor corporation at any time that is in the period during which the series of transactions or events that includes the making of the investment occurs and that is before the investment time, or"

If an election is made under subsection 49(3) of the *Jobs and Growth Act, 2012* [S.C. 2012, c. 31], section 212.3 of the *Income Tax Act* applies in the manner set out in that subsection in respect of transactions and events that occur after March 28, 2012 and before August 14, 2012.

S. 212.3(18)(*c*) formerly read:

(c) the investment is an indirect acquisition referred to in paragraph (10)(*f*) that results from a direct acquisition of shares of the capital stock of another corporation resident in Canada

(i) from a corporation

(A) to which the CRIC is, immediately before the investment time, related (determined without reference to paragraph 251(5)(*b*)), and

(B) that is, at no time that is in the period during which the series of transactions or events that includes the making of the investment occurs and that is before the investment time, dealing at arm's length (determined without reference to paragraph 251(5)(*b*)) with the CRIC,

(ii) on an amalgamation described in subsection 87(1) of two or more corporations (each of which is in this subparagraph referred to as a "predecessor corporation") to form the CRIC if

(A) all of the predecessor corporations are, immediately before the amalgamation, related to each other (determined without reference to paragraph 251(5)(*b*)), and

(B) none of the predecessor corporations deal at arm's length (determined without reference to paragraph 251(5)(*b*)) with another predecessor corporation at any time that is in the period during which the series of transactions or events that includes the making of the investment occurs and that is before the investment time,

(iii) in an exchange to which subsection 51(1) applies,

(iv) in the course of a reorganization of the capital of the other corporation to which subsection 86(1) applies, or

(v) to the extent that an investment (other than one described in paragraph (10)(*f*)) is made in the subject corporation by the other corporation, or by a particular corporation resident in Canada to which the CRIC and the other corporation are related at the investment time, using property transferred, directly or indirectly, by the CRIC to the other corporation or the particular corporation, as the case may be, if the two investments

(A) occur within 30 days of each other, and

(B) are part of the same series of transactions or events; or

S. 212.3(18)(*d*) was replaced by S.C. 2014, c. 39, s. 65(19), applicable in respect of transactions and events that occur after August 15, 2013, and formerly read:

(*d*) the investment is an acquisition of shares of the capital stock of the subject corporation that is described in paragraph (10)(*a*), or an indirect acquisition referred to in paragraph (10)(*f*) that results from a direct acquisition of shares of the capital stock of another corporation resident in Canada, under which the shares of the subject corporation or the other corporation, as the case may be, are received by the CRIC as the sole consideration for an exchange of a debt obligation owing to the CRIC, other than an exchange to which subsection 51(1) applies.

S. 212.3(18)(*b*)(vii) was replaced by S.C. 2013, c. 34, s. 427(2)(*e*), applicable in respect of transactions and events that occur after March 28, 2012, other than transactions and events to which subsections 212.3(9), (18) and (20) do not apply. See the history note following s. 212.3(1) for the application where certain transactions occur before 2013 and for an election that can be made for transactions that occur before August 14, 2012.

S. 212.3(18)(*b*)(vii) formerly read:

(vii) as a dividend or a reduction of paid-up capital in respect of the shares of another non-resident corporation that is, immediately before the investment time, a foreign affiliate of the CRIC;

S. 212.3(18) was added by S.C. 2012, c. 31, s. 49(1), applicable generally in respect of transactions and events that occur after March 28, 2012. However, see the history note following s. 212.3(1) for the application where certain transactions occur before 2013 and for an election that can be made for transactions that occur before August 14, 2012.

► 212.3(18.1) ◄

(18.1) Exchange — pertinent loan or indebtedness. Subsection (18) does not apply to an investment that is an acquisition of property if the property can reasonably be considered to have been received by the CRIC as repayment in whole or in part, or in settlement, of a pertinent loan or indebtedness.

History: S. 212.3(18.1) was added by S.C. 2014, c. 39, s. 65(20), applicable in respect of transactions and events that occur after August 15, 2013.

► 212.3(19) ◄

(19) Preferred shares. Subparagraph (1)(*b*)(ii) applies, and subsection (16) and paragraphs (18)(*b*) and (*d*) do not apply, to an acquisition of shares of the capital stock of a subject corporation by a CRIC if, having regard to all the terms and conditions of the shares and any agreement in respect of the shares, the shares cannot reasonably be considered to fully participate in the profits of the subject corporation and any appreciation in the value of the subject corporation, unless the subject corporation would be a subsidiary wholly-owned corporation of the CRIC throughout the period during which the series of transactions or events that includes the acquisition occurs if the CRIC owned all of the shares of the capital stock of the subject corporation that are owned by any of

(*a*) the CRIC;

(*b*) a corporation resident in Canada that is a subsidiary wholly-owned corporation of the CRIC; and

(*c*) a corporation resident in Canada of which the CRIC is a subsidiary wholly-owned corporation.

History: S. 212.3(19), the portion before paragraph (*a*) was replaced by S.C. 2014, c. 39, s. 65(21), applicable in respect of transactions and events that occur after March 28, 2012.

If an election is made under subsection 49(3) of the *Jobs and Growth Act, 2012* [S.C. 2012, c. 31], section 212.3 of the *Income Tax Act* applies in the manner set out in that subsection in respect of transactions and events that occur after March 28, 2012 and before August 14, 2012.

S. 212.3(19), the portion before paragraph (*a*) formerly read:

(19) *Preferred shares.* Subsection (16) and paragraphs (18)(*b*) and (*d*) do not apply to an acquisition of shares of the capital stock of a subject corporation by a CRIC if, having regard to all the terms and conditions of the shares and any agreement in respect of the shares, the shares may not reasonably be considered to fully participate in the profits of the subject corporation and any appreciation in the value of the subject corporation, unless the subject corporation would be a subsidiary wholly-owned corporation of the CRIC throughout the period during which the series of transactions or events that includes the acquisition occurs if the CRIC owned all of the shares of the capital stock of the subject corporation that are owned by any of

S. 212.3(19) was added by S.C. 2012, c. 31, s. 49(1), applicable generally in respect of transactions and events that occur after March 28, 2012. However, see the history note following s. 212.3(1) for the application where certain transactions occur before 2013 and for an election that can be made for transactions that occur before August 14, 2012.

► 212.3(20) ◄

(20) Assumption of debt on liquidation or distribution. Subsection (2) applies to an investment in a subject corporation made by a CRIC that is an acquisition of shares of the capital stock of the subject corporation described in any of subparagraphs (18)(*b*)(v) to (vii) to the extent of the lesser of

(*a*) the total of all amounts each of which is the amount of a debt obligation assumed by the CRIC in respect of the liquidation and dissolution, redemption, dividend or qualifying return of capital, as the case may be, and

(*b*) the fair market value of the shares at the investment time.

History: S. 212.3(20)(*a*) was replaced by S.C. 2013, c. 34, s. 427(2)(*f*), applicable in respect of transactions and events that occur after March 28, 2012, other than transactions and events to which subsections 212.3(9), (18) and (20) do not apply. See the history note following s. 212.3(1) for the application where certain transactions occur before 2013 and for an election that can be made for transactions that occur before August 14, 2012.

S. 212.3(20)(*a*) formerly read:

(*a*) the total of all amounts each of which is the amount of a debt obligation assumed by the CRIC in respect of the liquidation and dissolution, redemption, dividend or reduction of paid-up capital, as the case may be, and

S. 212.3(20) was added by S.C. 2012, c. 31, s. 49(1), applicable generally in respect of transactions and events that occur after March 28, 2012. However, see the history note following s. 212.3(1) for the application where certain transactions occur before 2013 and for an election that can be made for transactions that occur before August 14, 2012.

► 212.3(21) ◄

(21) Persons deemed not to be related. If it can reasonably be considered that one of the main purposes of one or more transactions or events is to cause two or more persons to be related to each other so that, in the absence of this subsection, subsection (2) would not apply because of subsection (18) to an investment in a subject corporation made by a CRIC, those persons are deemed not to be related to each other for the purposes of subsection (18).

Proposed Amendment
2019 Federal Budget Resolutions
Susection 212.3(21) is replaced by the following:

(21) Persons deemed not to be related. If it can reasonably be considered that one of the main purposes of one or more transactions or events is to cause two or more persons to be related to each other, or a person or group of persons to control another person, so that, in the absence of this subsection, subsection (2) would not apply because of subsection (18) to an investment in a subject corporation made by a CRIC, those persons are deemed not to be related to each other, or that person or group of persons is deemed not to control that other person, as the case may be, for the purposes of subsection (18).

Applicable: In respect of transactions or events that occur on or after March 19, 2019.

History: S. 212.3(21) was added by S.C. 2012, c. 31, s. 49(1), applicable generally in respect of transactions and events that occur after March 28, 2012. However, see the history note following s. 212.3(1) for the application where certain transactions occur before 2013 and for an election that can be made for transactions that occur before August 14, 2012.

► 212.3(22) ◄

(22) Mergers. For the purposes of this section and subsections 219.1(3) and (4),

(*a*) if there has been an amalgamation to which subsection 87(11) applies,

(i) the new corporation referred to in that subsection is deemed to be the same corporation as, and a continuation of, the parent and each subsidiary referred to in that subsection,

(ii) the new corporation is deemed not to acquire any property of the parent, or of any subsidiary, as a result of the amalgamation, and

(iii) each shareholder of the new corporation is deemed not to acquire indirectly any shares as a result of the amalgamation; and

(*b*) if there has been a winding-up to which subsection 88(1) applies,

(i) the parent referred to in that subsection is deemed to be the same corporation as, and a continuation of, the subsidiary referred to in that subsection, and

(ii) the parent is deemed not to acquire any property of the subsidiary as a result of the winding-up.

History: S 212.3(22)(*a*)(iii) was added by S.C. 2014, c. 39, s. 65(22), applicable in respect of transactions and events that occur after March 28, 2012.

If an election is made under subsection 49(3) of the *Jobs and Growth Act, 2012* [S.C. 2012, c. 31], section 212.3 of the *Income Tax Act* applies in the manner set out in that subsection in respect of transactions and events that occur after March 28, 2012 and before August 14, 2012.

S. 212.3(22) was added by S.C. 2012, c. 31, s. 49(1), applicable generally in respect of transactions and events that occur after March 28, 2012. However, see the history note following s. 212.3(1) for the application where certain transactions occur before 2013 and for an election that can be made for transactions that occur before August 14, 2012.

► 212.3(23) ◄

(23) Indirect investment. Subsection (2) applies to an investment in a subject corporation made by a CRIC to which, in the absence of this subsection, subsection (2) would not apply because of subsection (16) or (24), to the extent that one or more properties received by the subject corporation from the CRIC as a result of the investment, or property substituted for any such property, may reasonably be considered to have been used by the subject corporation, directly or indirectly as part of a series of transactions or events that includes the making of the investment, in a transaction or event to which subsection (2) would have applied if the CRIC had entered into the transaction, or participated in the event, as the case may be, instead of the subject corporation.

History: S. 212.3(23) was replaced by S.C. 2014, c. 39, s. 65(23), applicable in respect of transactions and events that occur after March 28, 2012.

If an election is made under subsection 49(3) of the *Jobs and Growth Act, 2012* [S.C. 2012, c. 31], section 212.3 of the *Income Tax Act* applies in the manner set out in that subsection in respect of transactions and events that occur after March 28, 2012 and before August 14, 2012.

S. 212.3(23) formerly read:

(23) *Indirect investment.* Subsection (2) applies to an investment in a subject corporation made by a CRIC to which, in the absence of this subsection, subsection (2) would not apply because of subsection (16), to the extent that one or more properties received by the subject corporation from the CRIC as a result of the investment, or property substituted for any such property, may reasonably be considered to have been used by the subject corporation, directly or indirectly as part of a series of transactions or events that includes the making of the investment, in a transaction or event to which subsection (2) would have applied if the CRIC had entered into the transaction, or participated in the event, as the case may be, instead of the subject corporation.

S. 212.3(23) was added by S.C. 2012, c. 31, s. 49(1), applicable generally in respect of transactions and events that occur after March 28, 2012. However, see the history note following s. 212.3(1) for the application where certain transactions occur before 2013 and for an election that can be made for transactions that occur before August 14, 2012.

► 212.3(24) ◄

(24) Indirect funding. Subsection (2) does not apply to an investment in a subject corporation made by a CRIC to which, in the absence of this subsection, subsection (2) would apply, if the CRIC demonstrates that

(*a*) all the properties received by the subject corporation from the CRIC as a result of the investment were used, at a particular time that is within 30 days after the investment time and at all times after the particular time, by the subject corporation

(i) to derive income from activities that can reasonably be considered to be directly related to active business activities carried on by a particular corporation and all of the income is income from an active business because of subparagraph 95(2)(*a*)(i), or

(ii) to make a loan or acquire a property, all or substantially all of the income from which is, or would be, if there were income from the loan or property, derived from amounts paid or payable, directly or indirectly, to the subject corporation by a particular corporation and is, or would be, income from an active business because of subparagraph 95(2)(*a*)(ii);

(*b*) the particular corporation was, at the particular time, a controlled foreign affiliate of the CRIC for the purposes of section 17; and

(*c*) the particular corporation is, throughout the period that begins at the investment time and during which the series of transactions or events that includes the activities of, or the making of the loan or acquisition of property by, the subject corporation occurs, a corporation in which an investment made by the CRIC would not be subject to subsection (2) because of subsection (16).

History: S. 212.3(24), paragraphs (*a*) to (*c*) were replaced by S.C. 2014, c. 39, s. 65(24), applicable in respect of transactions and events that occur after March 28, 2012.

If an election is made under subsection 49(3) of the *Jobs and Growth Act, 2012* [S.C. 2012, c. 31], section 212.3 of the *Income Tax Act* applies in the manner set out in that subsection in respect of transactions and events that occur after March 28, 2012 and before August 14, 2012.

S. 212.3(24), paragraphs (*a*) to (*c*) formerly read:

(*a*) all the properties received by the subject corporation from the CRIC as a result of the investment were used, at a particular time that is within 30 days after the investment time and at all times after the particular time, by the subject corporation to make a loan to a particular corporation that was, at the time of the loan, a controlled foreign affiliate of the CRIC for the purposes of section 17;

(*b*) the particular corporation is, throughout the period that begins at the investment time and during which the series of transactions or events that includes the making of the loan occurs, a corporation in which an investment made by the CRIC would not be subject to subsection (2) because of subsection (16); and

(*c*) the particular corporation uses, throughout the period during which the loan is outstanding, the proceeds of the loan in an active business (as defined in subsection 95(1)) carried on by it in the country in which it is resident.

S. 212.3(24) was added by S.C. 2012, c. 31, s. 49(1), applicable generally in respect of transactions and events that occur after March 28, 2012. However, see the history note following s. 212.3(1) for the application where certain transactions occur before 2013 and for an election that can be made for transactions that occur before August 14, 2012.

▶ 212.3(25) ◀

(25) Partnerships. For the purposes of this section, subsection 17.1(1) (as it applies in respect of a pertinent loan or indebtedness as defined in subsection (11)), paragraph 128.1(1)(*c.3*) and subsection 219.1(2),

(*a*) any transaction entered into, or event participated in, by a partnership is deemed to have been entered into, or participated in, as the case may be, by each member of the partnership in the proportion that the fair market value, at the time of the transaction or event, of the member's interest — held directly or indirectly through one or more other partnerships — in the partnership is of the fair market value, at that time, of all direct interests in the partnership;

(*b*) if at any time, based on the assumptions contained in paragraph 96(1)(*c*), property would be owned by a partnership, that property is deemed to be owned at that time by each member of the partnership in the proportion that the fair market value, at that time, of the member's interest — held directly or indirectly through one or more other partnerships — in the partnership is of the fair market value, at that time, of all direct interests in the partnership;

(*c*) if at any time there is an increase (including, for greater certainty, as a result of a particular acquisition of an interest in a partnership in which, immediately prior to the particular acquisition, the member did not have an interest) in the portion of a property that is deemed under paragraph (*b*) to be owned by a member of a partnership, the member is deemed at that time

(i) to acquire the additional portion of the property, and

(ii) to transfer property that relates to the acquisition of the additional portion and that has a fair market value equal to the fair market value at that time of the additional portion;

(*d*) if at any time, based on the assumptions contained in paragraph 96(1)(*c*), an amount would be owing by a partnership, that amount is deemed to be owed by each member of the partnership in the proportion that the fair market value, at that time, of the member's interest — held directly or indirectly through one or more other partnerships — in the partnership is of the fair market value, at that time, of all direct interests in the partnership;

(*e*) if a member of a partnership enters into a transaction, or participates in an event, with the partnership, paragraph (*a*) does not apply to the transaction or event to the extent that the transaction or event would, in the absence of this paragraph, be deemed by paragraph (*a*) to have been entered into, or participated in, as the case may be, by the member; and

(*f*) a person or partnership that is (or is deemed by this paragraph to be) a member of a particular partnership that is a member of another partnership is deemed to be a member of the other partnership.

Proposed Amendment

2019 Federal Budget Resolutions

Section 212.3 of the Act is amended by adding the following after subsection (25):

(26) For the purposes of this section, subsection 17.1(1) (as it applies in respect of a *pertinent loan or indebtedness* as defined in subsection (11)), paragraph 128.1(1)(*c*.3) and subsection 219.1(2) — and for the purpose of paragraph 251(1)(*a*) as it applies for the purposes of those provisions — in determining, at any time, whether two persons are related to each other or whether any person is controlled by any other person or group of persons, it shall be assumed that

(*a*) each trust is a corporation having a capital stock of a single class of voting shares divided into 100 issued shares;

(*b*) each beneficiary under a trust owned at that time the number of issued shares of that class determined by the formula

$$A/B \times 100$$

where

A is the fair market value at that time of the beneficiary's interest in the trust, and

B is the total fair market value at that time of all beneficiaries' interests under the trust; and

(*c*) if a beneficiary's share of the income or capital of a trust depends on the exercise by any person of, or the failure by any person to exercise, any discretionary power, the fair market value at any time of the beneficiary's interest under the trust is equal to the total fair market value at that time of all beneficiaries' interests under the trust.

Applicable: In respect of transactions or events that occur on or after March 19, 2019.

Editorial Note: Subsection 212.3(25) is a look-through rule for partnerships that applies for purposes of the foreign affiliate dumping rules in s. 212.3 and the related provisions in s. 17.1(1), s. 128.1(1)(*c.3*), and s. 219.1(2). Paragraph 212.3(25)(*a*) provides that each partner or a partnership is deemed to enter into the transaction relevant in determining the application of the foreign affiliate dumping rules entered into by the partnership on a pro rata basis according to the fair market value of that partner's partnership interest.

History: S. 212.3(25) was added by S.C. 2012, c. 31, s. 49(1), applicable generally in respect of transactions and events that occur after March 28, 2012. However, see the history note following s. 212.3(1) for the application where certain transactions occur before 2013 and for an election that can be made for transactions that occur before August 14, 2012.

SECTION 213: Tax non-payable by non-resident person

▶ 213(1) ◀

(1) Tax non-payable by non-resident person. Tax is not payable by a non-resident person under subsection 212(2) on a dividend in respect of a share of the capital stock of a foreign business corporation if not less than 90% of the total of the amounts received or receivable by it that are required to be included in computing its income for the taxation year in which the dividend was paid was received or receivable in respect of the operation by it of public utilities or from mining, transporting and processing of ore in a country in which

(*a*) if the non-resident person is an individual, the non-resident person resides; or

(*b*) if the non-resident person is a corporation, individuals who own more than 50% of its share capital (having full voting rights under all circumstances) reside.

▶ 213(2) ◀

(2) Idem. For the purposes of this section, if 90% of the total of the amounts received or receivable by a corporation that are required to be included in computing its income for a taxation year was received or receivable in respect of the operation by it of public utilities or from the mining, transporting and processing of ore, an amount received or receivable in that year from that corporation by another corporation shall, if it is required to be included in computing the receiving corporation's income for the year, be deemed to have been received by the receiving corporation in respect of the operation by it of public utilities or from the mining, transporting and processing of ore by it in the country in which the public utilities were operated or the mining, transporting and processing of ore was carried out by the payer corporation.

▶ 213(3) ◀

(3) Corporation deemed to be foreign business corporation. For the purposes of this section, a corporation shall be deemed to be a foreign business corporation at a particular time if it would have been a foreign business corporation within the meaning of section 71 of the *Income Tax Act*, chapter 148 of the Revised Statutes of Canada, 1952 (as that section read in its application to the 1971 taxation year), for the taxation year of the corporation in which the particular time occurred, if that section had been applicable to that taxation year.

Related Sections: S. 248(1), "amount", "dividend", "individual", "non-resident", "share"; s. 249 Definition of "taxation year".

SECTION 214: [Special rules applicable to non-residents]

▶ 214(1) ◀

(1) No deductions. The tax payable under section 212 is payable on the amounts described therein without any deduction from those amounts whatever.

Related Sections: S. 216 Taxation of non-residents on a net basis.

Information Circulars: IC 77-16R4 Non-resident income tax.

Interpretation Bulletins: *Secondary* — IT-438R2 Crown charges — Resource properties in Canada; IT-465R Non-resident beneficiaries of trusts.

Cases: Deduction of interest expenses was not permitted in computing the amount of interest subject to non-resident withholding tax. *Barki v. M.N.R.*, 75 DTC 228 (T.R.B.).

▶ 214(2) ◀

(2) Income and capital combined. Where paragraph 16(1)(*b*) would, if Part I were applicable, result in a part of an amount being included in computing the income of a non-resident person, that part of the amount shall, for the purposes of this Part, be deemed to have been paid or credited to the non-resident person in respect of property, services or otherwise, depending on the nature of that part of the amount.

Editorial Note: Subsection 214(2) deals with blended payments which involve a combination of income and capital. The subsection imposes withholding tax on amounts to which s. 16(1)(*b*) would apply if the recipient was subject to tax under Part I, namely, the portion of a blended payment which can reasonably be regarded as interest.

Related Sections: S. 214(12) Where s. (2) does not apply.

Information Circulars: IC 77-16R4 Non-resident income tax.

▶ 214(3) ◀

(3) Deemed payments. For the purposes of this Part,

(*a*) where section 15 or subsection 56(2) would, if Part I were applicable, require an amount to be included in computing a taxpayer's income, that amount shall be deemed to have been paid to the taxpayer as a dividend from a corporation resident in Canada;

(*b*) where paragraph 56(1)(*f*) would, if Part I were applicable, require an amount to be included in computing an individual's income, that amount shall be deemed to have been paid to the individual under an income-averaging annuity contract;

(*b*.1) where paragraph 56(1)(*y*) would, if Part I were applicable, require an amount to be included in computing a taxpayer's income, that amount shall be deemed to have been paid to the taxpayer to acquire an interest in a retirement compensation arrangement;

(*c*) where, because of subsection 146(8.1), (8.8), (8.91), (9), (10) or (12), an amount would, if Part I applied, be required to be included in computing a taxpayer's income, that amount shall be deemed to have been paid to the taxpayer as a payment under a registered retirement savings plan or an amended plan (within the meaning assigned by subsection 146(12)), as the case may be;

(*d*) where, by virtue of subsection 147(10), (13) or (15), an amount would, if Part I were applicable, be required to be included in computing a taxpayer's income, that amount shall be deemed to have been paid to the taxpayer as a payment under a deferred profit sharing plan or a plan referred to in subsection 147(15) as a "revoked plan", as the case may be;

(*e*) where subsection 130.1(2) would, if Part I were applicable, deem an amount received by a shareholder of a mortgage investment corporation to have been received by the shareholder as interest, that amount shall be deemed to have been paid to the shareholder as interest on a bond issued after 1971;

(*f*) where subsection 104(13) would, if Part I were applicable, require any part of an amount payable by a trust in its taxation year to a beneficiary to be included in computing the income of the non-resident person who is a beneficiary of the trust, that part is deemed to be an amount paid or credited to that person as income of or from the trust

(i) on, or at, the earliest of

(A) the day on which the amount was paid or credited,

(B) the day that is 90 days after the end of the taxation year, and

(C) if the taxation year is deemed by subparagraph 128.1(4)(*a*)(i) to end after July 25, 2012, the time that is immediately before the end of the taxation year, and

(ii) not at any later time;

(*f*.1) where paragraph 132.1(1)(*d*) would, if Part I were applicable, require an amount to be included in computing a taxpayer's income for a taxation year by reason of a designation by a mutual fund trust under subsection 132.1(1), that amount shall be deemed to be an amount paid or credited to that person as income of or from the trust on the day of the designation;

(*g*) where an individual who is a beneficiary under a fund, plan or trust that was a registered home ownership savings plan (within the meanings assigned by subparagraphs 146.2(1)(*a*) and (*h*) of the *Income Tax Act*, chapter 148 of the Revised Statutes of Canada, 1952, as they read in their application to the 1985 taxation year) on December 31, 1985 dies, an amount equal to the fair market value of the property in the fund, plan or trust at the time of death shall be deemed, for the purposes of section 212, to have been paid to the individual at the time of death as a payment out of or under a fund, plan or trust that was at the end of 1985 a registered home ownership savings plan;

(*h*) (Repealed by 1988, c. 55, s. 163(3).)

(*i*) where, because of subsection 146.3(4), (6), (6.1), (7) or (11), an amount would, if Part I applied, be required to be included in computing a taxpayer's income, that amount shall be deemed to have been paid to the taxpayer as a payment under a registered retirement income fund;

(*j*) (Repealed by 1998, c. 19, s. 63(1).)

(*k*) where, because of subsection 143.1(2), an amount distributed at any time by an amateur athlete trust would, if Part I were applicable, be required to be included in computing an individual's income, that amount shall be deemed to have been paid at that time to the individual as a payment in respect of an amateur athlete trust; and

(*l*) where, because of subsection 12(10.2), an amount would at any particular time, if Part I were applicable, be required to be included in computing a taxpayer's income, that amount shall be deemed to have been paid by Her Majesty in right of Canada at that time to the taxpayer out of the taxpayer's NISA Fund No. 2.

Editorial Note: Subsection 214(3) imposes withholding tax on various amounts which would be subject to tax if the recipient were a resident of Canada by deeming certain payments to be dividends or deeming such amounts to be paid to a non-resident. These include (1) the deemed income or deemed dividend under s. 15 arising on loans to shareholders or corporate benefits of a shareholder; (2) the deemed income under s. 56(2) on payments of income made with the concurrence of a taxpayer; (3) the deemed proceeds under s. 61.1(1) where an income-averaging annuity contract ceases to qualify; (4) amounts receivable in respect of disposing of an interest in a retirement compensation arrangement; (5) the amount paid to the estate of the deceased out of an RRSP under s. 146(8.1), as well as several other deemed payments out of an RRSP; (6) payments out of a deferred profit sharing plan; (7) taxable dividends paid by a mortgage investment corporation which are treated as interest under s. 130.1(2); and (8) the income of a trust payable in the year to a beneficiary which would be included in a resident beneficiary's income under s. 104(13).

History: S. 214(3)(*f*) was replaced by S.C. 2013, c. 40, s. 83(1), deemed to have come into force on July 25, 2012, and formerly read:

(*f*) where subsection 104(13) would, if Part I were applicable, require any part of an amount payable by a trust in its taxation year to a beneficiary to be included in computing the income of the non-resident person who is a beneficiary of the trust, that part shall be deemed to be an amount paid or credited to that person as income of or from the trust on the earlier of

(i) the day on which the amount was paid or credited, and

(ii) the day that is 90 days after the end of the taxation year

and not at any subsequent time when the amount was actually paid or credited;

Related Regulations: Part VIII.

Related Sections: S. 214(3.1) Time of deemed payment. s. 218.3(10) Provisions applicable; s. 227(6.1) Repayment of non-resident shareholder loan; s. 245 General anti-avoidance rule; s. 248(1), "dividend", "shareholder".

Information Circulars: IC 72-22R9 Registered Retirement Savings Plans; IC 77-16R4 Non-resident income tax.

Interpretation Bulletins: *Secondary* — IT-96R6 Options granted by corporations to acquire shares, bonds or debentures; IT-119R4 Debts of shareholders, certain persons connected with shareholders, etc; IT-335R2 Indirect payments; IT-432R2 Benefits conferred on shareholders; IT-465R Non-resident beneficiaries of trusts; IT-468R Management or administration fees paid to non-residents; IT-500R Registered retirement savings plans — Death of an annuitant.

► 214(3.1) ◄

(3.1) Time of deemed payment. Except as otherwise expressly provided, each amount deemed by subsection (3) to have been paid shall be deemed to have been paid at the time of the event or transaction as a consequence of which the amount would, if Part I were applicable, be required to be included in computing a taxpayer's income.

Cases: To pay for the corporate taxpayer's stock, an American corporation borrowed various sums interest-free from it without any arrangements for repayment. Such loans constituted deemed dividends subject to the withholding tax. *Industries P.W.I. Inc. v. M.N.R.*, 93 DTC 852 (T.C.C.)

A payment to a non-resident shareholder by way of a shareholder loan was deemed to be a dividend subject to withholding tax. *Euramca International Co. Ltd. v. M.N.R.*, 85 DTC 57 (T.C.C.)

▶ 214(4) ◀

(4) Securities. Where, if section 76 were applicable in computing a non-resident person's income, that section would require an amount to be included in computing the income, that amount shall, for the purpose of this Part, be deemed to have been, at the time the non-resident person received the security, right, certificate or other evidence of indebtedness, paid to the non-resident person on account of the debt in respect of which the non-resident person received it.

Related Sections: S. 214(5) Interpretation.

Information Circulars: IC 77-16R4 Non-resident income tax (paras. 23 to 31).

▶ 214(5) ◀

(5) Interpretation. Subsection (4) is enacted for greater certainty and shall not be construed as limiting the generality of the other provisions of this Part defining amounts on which tax is payable.

Cases: Where a non-resident parent company guaranteed repayment of money borrowed by its Canadian subsidiary, the fees paid for such guarantee were not subject to withholding tax. In the face of a tax treaty, the fees could not be deemed to constitute interest, and were therefore exempt from Canadian tax. *The Queen v. Associates Corporation of North America*, 80 DTC 6140 (F.C.A.)

▶ 214(6) ◀

(6) Deemed interest. Where, in respect of interest stipulated to be payable, on a bond, debenture, bill, note, mortgage, hypothecary claim or similar obligation that has been assigned or otherwise transferred by a non-resident person to a person resident in Canada, subsection 20(14) would, if Part I were applicable, require an amount to be included in computing the transferor's income, that amount is, for the purposes of this Part, deemed to be a payment of interest on that obligation made by the transferee to the transferor at the time of the assignment or other transfer of the obligation, if

(*a*) the obligation was issued by a person resident in Canada;

(*b*) the obligation was not an obligation described in paragraph (8)(*a*) or (*b*); and

(*c*) the assignment or other transfer is not an assignment or other transfer referred to in paragraph (7.1)(*b*).

Related Sections: 214(9) Deemed resident; 214(10) Reduction of tax; 214(13) Regulations respecting residents; 214(14) Assignment of obligation.

Canadian Tax Foundation: Kandev and Lennard, *Interpreting and Applying Deeming Provisions of the ITA*, 2012 Canadian Tax Journal 2:275–303; Fréchette and Rabinovitch, *Recent Issues Relating to Interest Deductability and Non-Traditional Forms of Indebtedness*, 2011 Conference Report 27:1–36.

▶ 214(7) ◀

(7) Sale of obligation. Where

(*a*) a non-resident person has at any time assigned or otherwise transferred to a person resident in Canada a bond, debenture, bill, note, mortgage, hypothecary claim or similar obligation issued by a person resident in Canada,

(*b*) the obligation was not an excluded obligation, and

(*c*) the assignment or other transfer is not an assignment or other transfer referred to in paragraph (7.1)(*b*),

the amount, if any, by which

(*d*) the price for which the obligation was assigned or otherwise transferred at that time,

exceeds

(*e*) the price for which the obligation was issued,

shall, for the purposes of this Part, be deemed to be a payment of interest on that obligation made by the person resident in Canada to the non-resident person at that time.

Related Sections: 214(8) Meaning of "excluded obligation"; 214(9) Deemed resident; 214(10) Reduction of tax; 214(12) Where s. (2) does not apply; 214(13) Regulations respecting residents; 214(14) Assignment of obligation.

Canadian Tax Foundation: Kandev and Lennard, *Interpreting and Applying Deeming Provisions of the ITA*, 2012 Canadian Tax Journal 2:275–303; Fréchette and Rabinovitch, *Recent Issues Relating to Interest Deductability and Non-Traditional Forms of Indebtedness*, 2011 Conference Report 27:1–36.

Tax Profile: November 2008 — 2008 Cross-Border Developments in Canada.

Tax Topics: No. 1919-20, 2008 Canadian Tax Foundation Annual Conference — Department of Finance Presentation and CRA Round Table; No. 1916, Withholding Tax Implications of Participating Interest and Convertible Debt.

Income Tax Technical News: Issue No. 41, Convertible Debt.

Information Circulars: IC 77-16R4 Non-resident income tax (paras. 23 to 31).

▶ 214(7.1) ◀

(7.1) Idem. Where

(*a*) a person resident in Canada has at a particular time assigned or otherwise transferred an obligation to a non-resident person,

(*b*) the non-resident person has at a subsequent time assigned or otherwise transferred the obligation back to the person resident in Canada, and

(*c*) subsection (6) or (7) would apply with respect to the assignment or other transfer referred to in paragraph (*b*), if those subsections were read without reference to paragraphs (6)(*c*) and (7)(*c*),

the amount, if any, by which

(*d*) the price for which the obligation was assigned or otherwise transferred at the subsequent time,

exceeds

(*e*) the price for which the obligation was assigned or otherwise transferred at the particular time,

shall, for the purposes of this Part, be deemed to be a payment of interest on that obligation made by the person resident in Canada to the non-resident person at the subsequent time.

Related Sections: 214(12) Where s. (2) does not apply; 214(13) Regulations respecting residents; 214(14) Assignment of obligation.

▶ 214(8) ◀

(8) Meaning of "excluded obligation". For the purposes of subsection (7), "excluded obligation" means any bond, debenture, bill, note, mortgage, hypothecary claim or similar obligation

(*a*) that is described in paragraph (*a*) of the definition "fully exempt interest" in subsection 212(3), or on which the interest would have been exempt under subparagraph 212(1)(*b*)(iii) or (vii) as they applied to the 2007 taxation year;

(*b*) that is prescribed to be a public issue security; or

(*c*) that is not an indexed debt obligation and that was issued for an amount not less than 97% of the principal amount thereof, and the yield from which, expressed in terms of an annual rate on the amount for which the obligation was issued (which annual rate shall, if the terms of the obligation or any agreement relating thereto conferred on the holder thereof a right to demand payment of the principal amount of the obligation or the amount outstanding as or on account of the principal amount thereof, as the case may be, before the maturity of the obligation, be calculated on the basis of the yield that produces the highest annual rate obtainable either on the maturity of the obligation or conditional on the exercise of any such right) does not exceed $4/3$ of the interest stipulated to be payable on the obligation, expressed in terms of an annual rate on

(i) the principal amount thereof, if no amount is payable on account of the principal amount before the maturity of the obligation, and

(ii) the amount outstanding from time to time as or on account of the principal amount thereof, in any other case.

Related Sections: S. 16(6) Indexed debt obligations; s. 214(6) Deemed interest; s. 248(1), "indexed debt obligation", "principal amount".

Tax Profile: November 2008 — 2008 Cross-Border Developments in Canada.

Tax Topics: No. 1919-20, 2008 Canadian Tax Foundation Annual Conference — Department of Finance Presentation and CRA Round Table; No. 1916, Withholding Tax Implications of Participating Interest and Convertible Debt.

Income Tax Technical News: Issue No. 44, Convertible Debentures and Part XIII; Issue No. 41, Convertible Debt.

▶ 214(9) ◀

(9) Deemed resident. Where

(*a*) the assignment or other transfer of an obligation to a non-resident person carrying on business in Canada would be described in subsection (6) or (7) if those subsections were read without reference to paragraphs (6)(*c*) and (7)(*c*) and if that non-resident person were a person resident in Canada, and

(*b*) that non-resident person

(i) may deduct, under subsection 20(14), in computing the non-resident person's taxable income earned in Canada for a taxation year an amount in respect of interest on the obligation, or

(ii) may deduct, under Part I, in computing the non-resident person's taxable income earned in Canada for a taxation year an amount in respect of any amount paid on account of the principal amount of the obligation,

the non-resident person shall, with respect to the assignment or other transfer of the obligation, be deemed, for the purposes of this Part, to be a person resident in Canada.

Related Sections: 214(13) Regulations respecting residents; 214(14) Assignment of obligation; s. 248(1), "business", "principal amount"; s. 249(1) Definition of "taxation year".

▶ 214(10) ◀

(10) Reduction of tax. Where a non-resident person has assigned or otherwise transferred to a person resident in Canada an obligation

(*a*) on which an amount of interest was deemed by subsection (6) or (7) to have been paid, and

(*b*) that the non-resident person had previously acquired from a person resident in Canada,

the amount of the tax under this Part that the non-resident person is liable to pay in respect thereof shall be deemed, for the purpose of subsection 227(6), to be that proportion of the tax the non-resident person would otherwise have been liable to pay in respect thereof that

(*c*) the number of days in the period commencing with the day the obligation was last acquired by the non-resident person from a person resident in Canada and ending with the day the obligation was last assigned or otherwise transferred by the non-resident person to a person resident in Canada

is of

(*d*) the number of days in the period commencing with the day the obligation was issued and ending with the day the obligation was last assigned or otherwise transferred by the non-resident person to a person resident in Canada.

Related Sections: 214(13) Regulations respecting residents; 214(14) Assignment of obligation.

▶ 214(11) ◀

(11) Application of para. 212(1)(*b*) — (Repealed by S.C. 2007, c. 35, s. 60(2).)

Related Sections: S. 133(8), "non-resident-owned investment corporation"; s. 214(14) Assignment of obligation.

▶ 214(12) ◀

(12) Where s. (2) does not apply. Subsection (2) does not apply in respect of a payment to a non-resident person under any obligation in respect of which that person is liable to pay tax under this Part by reason of subsection (7) or (7.1).

▶ 214(13) ◀

(13) Regulations respecting residents. The Governor in Council may make general or special regulations, for the purposes of this Part, prescribing

(*a*) who is or has been at any time resident in Canada;

(*b*) where a person was resident in Canada as well as in some other place, what amounts are taxable under this Part; and

(*c*) where a non-resident person carried on business in Canada, what amounts are taxable under this Part or what portion of the tax under this Part is payable by that person.

Related Regulations: 802; 805.

Related Sections: S. 212(5.1) Acting services; s. 248(1), "prescribed", "regulation"; s. 255 Canada.

▶ 214(14) ◀

(14) Assignment of obligation. For the purposes of this section, any transaction or event by which an obligation held by a non-resident person is redeemed in whole or in part or is cancelled shall be deemed to be an assignment of the obligation by the non-resident person.

▶ 214(15) ◀

(15) Standby charges and guarantee fees. For the purposes of this Part,

(*a*) where a non-resident person has entered into an agreement under the terms of which the non-resident person agrees to guarantee the repayment, in whole or in part, of the principal amount of a bond, debenture, bill, note, mortgage, hypothecary claim or similar obligation of a person resident in Canada, any amount paid or credited as consideration for the guarantee is deemed to be a payment of interest on that obligation; and

(*b*) where a non-resident person has entered into an agreement under the terms of which the non-resident person agrees to lend money, or to make money available, to a person resident in Canada, any amount paid or credited as consideration for so agreeing to lend money or to make money available shall, if the non-resident person would be liable to tax under this Part in respect of interest payable on any obligation issued under the terms of the agreement on the date it was entered into, be deemed to be a payment of interest.

Related Sections: S. 12(1)(*c*) Interest; s. 133(8), "non-resident-owned investment corporation"; s. 212(1)(*b*) Interest; s. 214(13) Regulations respecting residents; s. 248(1), "amount", "non-resident", "principal amount".

Tax Profile: March 2011 — Canada 2010 — Year in Review; September 2010 — Recent Tax Developments Affecting Non-Residents; August 2008 — Fifth Protocol to the Canada–U.S. Tax Convention: A Canadian Perspective.

Information Circulars: IC 77-16R4 Non-resident income tax (para. 21).

▶ 214(16) ◀

(16) Deemed dividends. For the purposes of this Part,

(*a*) an amount paid or credited as interest by a corporation resident in Canada, or by a partnership, in a taxation year of the corporation to a non-resident person is deemed to have been paid by the corporation as a dividend, and not to have been paid or credited by the corporation or the partnership as interest, to the extent that an amount in respect of the interest

(i) is not deductible in computing the income of the corporation for the year because of subsection 18(4), or

(ii) is included in computing the income of the corporation for the year under paragraph 12(1)(*l.1*); and

(*b*) to the extent that amounts paid or credited to a non-resident person in the year are deemed by paragraph (*a*) to have been paid by a corporation as dividends, the corporation may designate in its return of income under Part I for the year which amounts paid or credited as interest to the non-resident person in the year are deemed to have been paid as dividends and not as interest.

Editorial Note: S. 214(16) provides that where an amount of interest expense is denied for a corporation under the thin capitalization rules, either directly under subsection 18(4) or indirectly (in the case of a corporate partner) under the inclusion rule in paragraph 12(1)(*l.1*), the amount is deemed to be a dividend paid by the corporation rather than interest paid. The result of the provision is significant, in that interest paid to arm's length non-resident debtors is generally exempt from withholding tax (except for participating interest), while dividends paid to non-residents will be subject to withholding tax (but may be reduced by treaty). The issue is discussed in the lead article in Tax Topics No. 2114, "Thin Capitalization Amendments — Denied Interest May Be Subject to Withholding Tax".

History: S. 214(16) was added by S.C. 2012, c. 31, s. 50(1), applicable to taxation years that end after March 28, 2012, except that for taxation years that include March 29, 2012, the amount of each dividend deemed by paragraph 214(16)(*a*) to have been paid in the taxation year is the proportion of the amount of the dividend otherwise determined under the paragraph that the number of days in the taxation year that are after March 28, 2012 is of the number of days in the taxation year.

Tax Topics: No. 2114, Thin Capitalization Amendments — Denied Interest May Be Subject to Withholding Tax.

▶ 214(17) ◀

(17) Deemed interest payments. For the purposes of subsection (16),

(*a*) interest payable (other than interest payable pursuant to a legal obligation to pay interest on an amount of interest) by a corporation resident in Canada, or by a partnership, in respect of a taxation year of the corporation, but that has not been paid or credited in the year, is deemed to have been paid immediately before the end of the year and not to have been paid or credited at any other time; and

(*b*) if subsection (6) or (7) deems a payment of interest to have been made to a non-resident person in respect of a debt or other obligation of a corporation, interest that, at the time of the transfer or assignment, is payable by the corporation in respect of the debt or other obligation and has not been paid or credited is deemed to have been paid by the corporation immediately before that time to the non-resident person.

History: S. 214(17) was added by S.C. 2012, c. 31, s. 50(1), applicable to taxation years that end after March 28, 2012, except that before August 14, 2012, subsection 214(17) is to be read as follows:

"(17) For the purposes of subsection (16), interest payable (other than interest payable pursuant to a legal obligation to pay interest on an amount of interest) by a corporation resident in Canada, or by a partnership, in respect of a taxation year of the corporation, but that has not been paid or credited in the year, is deemed to have been paid immediately before the end of the year and not at any other time."

SECTION 215: Withholding and remittance of tax

▶ 215(1) ◀

(1) Withholding and remittance of tax. When a person pays, credits or provides, or is deemed to have paid, credited or provided, an amount on which an income tax is payable under this Part, or would be so payable if this Act were read without reference to subparagraph 94(3)(*a*)(viii) and to subsection 216.1(1), the person shall, notwithstanding any agreement or law to the contrary, deduct or withhold from it the amount of the tax and forthwith remit that amount to the Receiver General on behalf of the non-resident person on account of the tax and shall submit with the remittance a statement in prescribed form.

Editorial Note: Subsection 215(1) imposes an obligation on the payer of amounts which are subject to withholding tax to deduct or withhold the amount of tax and remit the amount to the CRA. It is important to understand that the tax imposed under Part XIII of the Act is imposed on the non-resident recipient of an amount. However, s. 215(1) imposes the withholding obligation on the payer and s. 215(6) makes the payer jointly and severally liable for the withholding tax with the non-resident. In addition to the liability for the withholding tax, a failure to withhold will render the payer subject to a penalty of 10% of the tax under s. 227(8)(*a*).

History: S. 215(1) was replaced by S.C. 2013, c. 34, s. 19(1), applicable to trust taxation years that end after 2006. Subsection 215(1) also applies to each earlier taxation year of a trust to which subsection 94(1) of the Act applies [should be 94(3) — CCH].

S. 215(1) formerly read:

(1) *Withholding and remittance of tax.* When a person pays, credits or provides, or is deemed to have paid, credited or provided, an amount on which an income tax is payable under this Part, or would be so payable if this Part were read without reference to subsection 216.1(1), the person shall, notwithstanding any agreement or law to the contrary, deduct or withhold from it the amount of the tax and forthwith remit that amount to the Receiver General on behalf of the non-resident person on account of the tax and shall submit with the remittance a statement in prescribed form.

Related Sections: S. 212(5.3) Reduction of withholding; s. 227; s. 227.1 Directors' liability; s. 248(1), "amount", "non-resident", "prescribed", "regulation"; s. 248(7)(*b*)(i) Receipt of things mailed; s. 255 Canada.

Canadian Tax Foundation: Chiu, *Taxation of Non-Resident Investors in Canadian Investment Funds,* 2010 Canadian Tax Journal 1:117–143.

Tax Profile: May 2013 — Current International Tax Issues In Cross-Border Corporate Finance and Capital Markets; March 2012 — Beneficial Ownership: Another Canadian Victory for Taxpayers.

Forms: T3 SCH 10 — Part XII.2 Tax and Part XIII Non-Resident Withholding Tax; NR4 — Statement of Amounts Paid or Credited to Non-Residents of Canada; NR4 Sum. — Return of Amounts Paid or Credited to Non-Residents of Canada; NR4 Seg. — NR4 Segment; NR603 — Remittance of Non-Resident Tax on Income from Film or Video Acting Services.

Information Circulars: IC 76-12R6 Applicable rate of Part XIII tax on amounts paid or credited to persons in countries with which Canada has a Tax Convention; IC 77-16R4 Non-resident income tax.

Interpretation Bulletins: *Secondary* — IT-362R Patronage dividends; IT-465R Non-resident beneficiaries of trusts; IT-494 Hire of ships and aircraft from non-residents.

Cases: When the taxpayer paid royalties to a Netherlands company, the 10% withholding rate in the Netherlands treaty applied. Although the recipient paid 90% of the royalties to its parent company (located in a country which did not have a Canadian treaty) the parent was not the beneficial owner of the royalties since it had no right to control them. *Velcro Canada Inc. v. The Queen,* 2012 DTC 1100 (T.C.C.)

▶ 215(1.1) ◀

(1.1) Exception — corporate immigration. Subsection (1) does not apply in respect of a dividend deemed to be paid under paragraph 128.1(1)(*c*.1) by a corporation to a non-resident corporation with which the corporation was dealing at arm's length.

Related Sections: S. 251(1) Arm's length.

▶ 215(2) ◀

(2) Idem. Where an amount on which an income tax is payable under this Part is paid or credited by an agent or other person on behalf of the debtor either by way of redemption of bearer coupons or warrants or otherwise, the agent or other person by whom the amount was paid or credited shall, notwithstanding any agreement or law to the contrary, deduct or withhold and remit the amount of the tax and shall submit therewith a statement in prescribed form as required by subsection (1) and shall thereupon, for purposes of accounting to or obtaining reimbursement from the debtor, be deemed to have paid or credited the full amount to the person otherwise entitled to payment.

Related Sections: S. 218.3(10) Provisions applicable; s. 227; s. 227.1 Directors' liability.

Information Circulars: IC 76-12R6 Applicable rate of Part XIII tax on amounts paid or credited to persons in countries with which Canada has a Tax Convention.

Interpretation Bulletins: *Secondary* — IT-362R Patronage dividends.

▶ 215(3) ◀

(3) Idem. Where an amount on which an income tax is payable under this Part was paid or credited to an agent or other person for or on behalf of the person entitled to payment without the tax having been deducted or withheld under subsection (1), the agent or other person shall, notwithstanding any agreement or law to the contrary, deduct or withhold therefrom the amount of the tax and forthwith remit that amount to the Receiver General on behalf of the person entitled to payment in payment of the tax and shall submit therewith a statement in prescribed form, and the agent or other person shall thereupon, for purposes of accounting to the person entitled to payment, be deemed to have paid or credited that amount to that person.

Related Sections: S. 216(4) Optional method of payment; s. 218.3(10) Provisions applicable; s. 227; s. 227.1 Directors' liability.

Information Circulars: IC 76-12R6 Applicable rate of Part XIII tax on amounts paid or credited to persons in countries with which Canada has a Tax Convention.

Interpretation Bulletins: *Secondary* — IT-362R Patronage dividends.

▶ 215(4) ◀

(4) Regulations creating exceptions. The Governor in Council may make regulations with reference to any non-resident person or class of non-resident persons who carries or carry on business in Canada, providing that subsections (1) to (3) are not applicable to amounts paid to or credited to that person or those persons and requiring the person or persons to file an annual return on a prescribed form and to pay the tax imposed by this Part within a time limited in the regulations.

Related Regulations: 800 Registered Non-Resident Insurers; 801 Filing of Returns by Registered Non-Resident Insurers; 802 Amounts Taxable; 803 Payment of Tax by Registered Non-Resident Insurers; 805.

Related Sections: S. 162(7) Failure to comply; s. 225.1(6) Where ss. (1) to (4) do not apply; s. 227(9) Penalty; s. 227(9.3) Interest on certain tax not paid; s. 235 Penalty for failing to file corporate returns.

Interpretation Bulletins: *Secondary* — IT-362R Patronage dividends.

▶ 215(5) ◀

(5) Regulations reducing deduction or withholding. The Governor in Council may make regulations in respect of any non-resident person or class of non-resident persons to whom any amount is paid or credited as, on account of, in lieu of payment of or in satisfaction of, any amount described in any of paragraphs 212(1)(*h*), (*j*) to (*m*) and (*q*) reducing the amount otherwise required by any of subsections (1) to (3) to be deducted or withheld from the amount so paid or credited.

Related Regulations: 809.

Related Sections: S. 115(1) Non-resident's taxable income in Canada; s. 162(7) Failure to comply; s. 217(1) Alternative re Canadian benefits.

Forms: NR5 — Application by a Non-Resident of Canada for a Reduction in the Amount of Non-Resident Tax Required to be Withheld.

Interpretation Bulletins: *Secondary* — IT-362R Patronage dividends.

▶ 215(6) ◀

(6) Liability for tax. Where a person has failed to deduct or withhold any amount as required by this section from an amount paid or credited or deemed to have been paid or credited to a non-resident person, that person is liable to pay as tax under this Part on behalf of the non-resident person the whole of the amount that should have been deducted or withheld, and is entitled to deduct or withhold from any amount paid or credited by that person to the non-resident person or otherwise recover from the non-resident person any amount paid by that person as tax under this Part on behalf thereof.

Related Regulations: 105.

Related Sections: S. 218.3(10) Provisions applicable; s. 227(1) Withholding taxes; s. 227(6) Excess withheld, returned or applied; 227(8) Penalty; 227(8.1) Joint and several, or solidary, liability; s. 227(8.3) Interest on amounts not deducted or withheld, s. (8.4) Liability to pay amount not deducted or withheld.

Information Circulars: IC 77-16R4 Non-resident income tax.

Interpretation Bulletins: *Secondary* — IT-362R Patronage dividends.

SECTION 216: Alternatives re rents and timber royalties

► 216(1) ◄

(1) Alternatives re rents and timber royalties. If an amount has been paid during a taxation year to a non-resident person or to a partnership of which that person was a member as, on account of, in lieu of payment of or in satisfaction of, rent on real or immovable property in Canada or a timber royalty, that person may, within two years (or, if that person has filed an undertaking described in subsection (4) in respect of the year, within six months) after the end of the year, file a return of income under Part I for that year in prescribed form. On so filing and without affecting the liability of the non-resident person for tax otherwise payable under Part I, the non-resident person is, in lieu of paying tax under this Part on that amount, liable to pay tax under Part I for the year as though

(*a*) the non-resident person were a person resident in Canada and not exempt from tax under section 149;

(*b*) the non-resident person's income from the non-resident person's interest in real property, or real right in immovables, in Canada and interest in, or for civil law right in, timber resource properties and timber limits in Canada, and the non-resident person's share of the income of a partnership of which the non-resident person was a member from its interest in real property, or real right in immovables, in Canada and interest in, or for civil law right in, timber resource properties and timber limits in Canada, were the non-resident person's only income;

(*c*) the non-resident person were entitled to no deductions from income for the purpose of computing the non-resident person's taxable income; and

(*d*) the non-resident person were entitled to no deductions under sections 118 to 118.9 in computing the non-resident person's tax payable under Part I for the year.

Editorial Note: S. 216(1) allows a non-resident person to report rental or timber royalty income as Part I net income (instead of Part XIII gross income) on Form T1159 within six months from year-end if he/she filed a Form NR6, and within two years from year-end if he/she did not file that form. Any filing after those two deadliness will be allowed unless the CRA has already advised the non-resident of his/her Part XIII tax responsibility in respect of such income, has already initiated action because of the non-resident's failure to comply with Part XIII tax, or has already approved a Form NR6 filed by the non-resident. For late filing, the CRA waives penalties but not interest chargeable on unremitted withholding tax or outstanding regular tax. Note that regular tax calculated on rental or timber royalty net income earned by a non-resident is usually lesser than non-resident tax withheld from rental or timber royalty gross income.

History: S. 216(1)(*b*) was replaced by S.C. 2013, c. 34, s. 158(1), in force June 26, 2013, and formerly read:

(*b*) the non-resident person's income from the non-resident person's interest in real property in Canada, timber resource properties and timber limits in Canada and the non-resident person's share of the income of a partnership of which the non-resident person was a member from its interest in real property in Canada, timber resource properties and timber limits in Canada were the non-resident person's only income;

S. 216(1), the portion before paragraph (*a*) was replaced by S.C. 2013, c. 34, s. 349(1), applicable to taxation years that end after December 20, 2002, and formerly read:

(1) *Alternatives re rents and timber royalties.* Where an amount has been paid during a taxation year to a non-resident person or to a partnership of which that person was a member as, on account of, in lieu of payment of or in satisfaction of, rent on real property in Canada or a timber royalty, that person may, within 2 years (or, where that person has filed an undertaking described in subsection (4) in respect of the year, within 6 months) after the end of the year, file a return of income under Part I in the form prescribed for a person resident in Canada for that year and the non-resident person shall, without affecting the liability of the non-resident person for tax otherwise payable under Part I, thereupon be liable, in lieu of paying tax under this Part on that amount, to pay tax under Part I for the year as though

Related Sections: S. 2(3); s. 13(21), "timber resource property"; s. 115(1) Non-resident's taxable income in Canada; s. 120(1) Income not earned in a province; s. 150 Manual filing of income return; s. 150.1 Electronic filing of income return; 212(1)(d) Rents, royalties, etc.; 212(1)(e) Timber royalties; s. 220(3) Extensions for returns; s. 248(1), "amount", "non-resident", "prescribed", "property"; s. 248(4) Interest in real property; s. 249 Definition of "taxation year"; s. 250.1 Non-resident person's taxation year and income; s. 255 Canada.

Tax Profile: March 2013 — Non-Resident Investment in Canadian Real Estate; March 2002 — Selected Tax Issues for Commercial Landlords and Tenants.

Tax Topics: No. 2023-24, 2010 Canadian Tax Foundation CRA Roundtable: Pipelines, Privilege and Working Papers (Again!); No. 1965, Potential Double Taxation of Rental Income to Non-Residents?; No. 1904, Section 216 Shortfall; No. 1802, Non-Resident Partners and Canadian Real Estate; No. 1560, CCRA Softens Stance on Late-Filed Subsection 216(1) Returns.

Forms: T2Sch97 — Additional Information on Non-Resident Corporations in Canada; NR6 — Undertaking to File an Income Tax Return by a Non-Resident Receiving Rent from Real Property or Receiving a Timber Royalty for Tax Year ____; T1159 — Income Tax Return for Electing Under Section 216.

Guides: T4144 Income Tax Guide for Non-Residents Electing Under Section 216.

Information Circulars: IC 77-16R4 Non-resident income tax (paras. 42 to 44).

Interpretation Bulletins: *Primary* — IT-393R2 Election re tax on rents and timber royalties — Non-residents. *Secondary* — IT-81R Partnerships — Income of non-resident partners; IT-434R Rental of real property by individual.

Cases: A resident is required to withhold and remit taxes on payments made to a non-resident, even if the non-resident pays Part I tax by virtue of a s. 216(1) election. Interest on unremitted withholding taxes is assessed against the payor under s. 227(8.3), while s. 227(8.1) renders the non-resident recipient jointly and severally liable for the interest. *Pechet v. The Queen*, 2009 DTC 5189 (F.C.A.), affirming 2008 DTC 3381 (T.C.C.)

Rent from an aircraft does not qualify under section 110 [216] since an aircraft is not real property. *Lea-Don Canada Ltd. v. M.N.R.*, 70 DTC 6271 (S.C.C.)

► 216(2) ◄

(2) Idem. Where a non-resident person has filed a return of income under Part I as permitted by this section, the amount deducted under this Part from

(*a*) rent on real or immovable property or from timber royalties paid to the person, and

(*b*) the person's share of the rent on real or immovable property or from timber royalties paid to a partnership of which the person is a member

and remitted to the Receiver General shall be deemed to have been paid on account of tax under this section and any portion of the amount so remitted to the Receiver General in a taxation year on the person's behalf in excess of the person's liability for tax under this Act for the year shall be refunded to the person.

History: S. 216(2)(*a*) and (*b*) were replaced by S.C. 2013, c. 34, s. 158(2), in force June 26, 2013, and formerly read:

(*a*) rent on real property or from timber royalties paid to the person, and

(*b*) the person's share of the rent on real property or from timber royalties paid to a partnership of which the person is a member

Related Sections: 212(1)(d) Rents, royalties, etc.; 212(1)(e) Timber royalties.

▶ 216(3) ◀

(3) Idem. Part I is applicable, with such modifications as the circumstances require, to payment of tax under this section.

Cases: Rent from an aircraft does not qualify under section 110 [216] since an aircraft is not real property. *Lea-Don Canada Ltd. v. M.N.R.*, 70 DTC 6271 (S.C.C.)

▶ 216(4) ◀

(4) Optional method of payment. If a non-resident person or, in the case of a partnership, each non-resident person who is a member of the partnership files with the Minister an undertaking in prescribed form to file within six months after the end of a taxation year a return of income under Part I for the year as permitted by this section, a person who is otherwise required by subsection 215(3) to remit in the year, in respect of the non-resident person or the partnership, an amount to the Receiver General in payment of tax on rent on real or immovable property or on a timber royalty may elect under this section not to remit under that subsection, and if that election is made, the elector shall,

(*a*) when any amount is available out of the rent or royalty received for remittance to the non-resident person or the partnership, as the case may be, deduct 25% of the amount available and remit the amount deducted to the Receiver General on behalf of the non-resident person or the partnership on account of the tax under this Part; and

(*b*) if the non-resident person or, in the case of a partnership, a non-resident person who is a member of the partnership

(i) does not file a return for the year in accordance with the undertaking, or

(ii) does not pay under this section the tax the non-resident person or member is liable to pay for the year within the time provided for payment,

pay to the Receiver General, on account of the non-resident person's or the partnership's tax under this Part, on the expiration of the time for filing or payment, as the case may be, the full amount that the elector would otherwise have been required to remit in the year in respect of the rent or royalty minus the amounts that the elector has remitted in the year under paragraph (*a*) in respect of the rent or royalty.

History: S. 216(4), the portion before paragraph (*a*) was replaced by S.C. 2013, c. 34, s. 158(3), in force June 26, 2013, and formerly read:

(4) *Optional method of payment.* Where a non-resident person or, in the case of a partnership, each non-resident person who is a member of the partnership files with the Minister an undertaking in prescribed form to file within 6 months after the end of a taxation year a return of income under Part I for the year as permitted by this section, a person who is otherwise required by subsection 215(3) to remit in the year, in respect of the non-resident person or the partnership, an amount to the Receiver General in payment of tax on rent on real property or on a timber royalty may elect under this section not to remit under that subsection, and if that election is made, the elector shall,

Related Sections: 212(1)(d) Rents, royalties, etc.; 212(1)(e) Timber royalties.

Canadian Tax Foundation: Tollstam, *Section 216: Net Rental Income*, 2014 Canadian Tax Highlights 22(10):11–12.

Tax Topics: No. 1904, Section 216 Shortfall.

Forms: NR6 — Undertaking to File an Income Tax Return by a Non-Resident Receiving Rent from Real Property or Receiving a Timber Royalty for Tax Year ____.

Information Circulars: IC 77-16R4 Non-resident income tax (paras. 42 to 44).

Cases: Rent from an aircraft does not qualify under section 110 [216] since an aircraft is not real property. *Lea-Don Canada Ltd. v. M.N.R.*, 70 DTC 6271 (S.C.C.)

▶ 216(4.1) ◀

(4.1) Optional method of payment. If a trust is deemed by subsection 94(3) to be resident in Canada for a taxation year for the purpose of computing the trust's income for the year, a person who is otherwise required by subsection 215(3) to remit in the year, in respect of the trust, an amount to the Receiver General in payment of tax on rent on real or immovable property or on a timber royalty may elect in prescribed form filed with the Minister under this subsection not to remit under subsection 215(3) in respect of amounts received after the election is made, and if that election is made, the elector shall,

(*a*) when any amount is available out of the rent or royalty received for remittance to the trust, deduct 25% of the amount available and remit the amount deducted to the Receiver General on behalf of the trust on account of the trust's tax under Part I; and

(*b*) if the trust does not file a return for the year as required by section 150, or does not pay the tax that the trust is liable to pay under Part I for the year within the time required by that Part, on the expiration of the time for filing or payment, as the case may be, pay to the Receiver General, on account of the trust's tax under Part I, the amount by which the full amount that the elector would otherwise have been required to remit in the year in respect of the rent or royalty exceeds the amounts that the elector has remitted in the year under paragraph (*a*) in respect of the rent or royalty.

History: S. 216(4.1) was added by S.C. 2013, c. 34, s. 20(1), applicable to trust taxation years that end after 2006, except that

(*a*) it also applies to each earlier taxation year of a trust to which subsection 94(1) applies [should be 94(3) — CCH]; and

(*b*) an election referred to in subsection 216(4.1) is deemed to have been filed with the Minister of National Revenue on a timely basis if it is filed with the Minister of National Revenue on or before the trust's filing-due date for the trust's taxation year that includes June 26, 2013.

▶ 216(5) ◀

(5) Disposition by non-resident. If a person or a trust under which a person is a beneficiary has filed a return of income under Part I for a taxation year as permitted by this section or as required by section 150 and, in computing the amount of the person's income under Part I an amount has been deducted under paragraph 20(1)(*a*), or is deemed by subsection 107(2) to have been allowed under that paragraph, in respect of property that is real property in Canada — or an interest therein — or an immovable in Canada — or a real right therein —, a timber resource property or a timber limit in Canada, the person shall file a return of income under Part I in prescribed form on or before the person's filing-due date for any subsequent taxation year in which the person is non-resident and in which the person, or a partnership of which the person is a member, disposes of that property or any interest, or for civil law any right, in it. On so filing and without affecting the person's liability for tax otherwise payable under Part I, the person is, in lieu of paying tax under this Part on any amount paid, or deemed by this Part to have been paid, in that subsequent taxation year in respect of any interest in, or for civil law any right in, that property to the person or to a partnership of which the person is a member, liable to pay tax under Part I for that subsequent taxation year as though

(*a*) the person were a person resident in Canada and not exempt from tax under section 149;

(*b*) the person's income from the person's interest in real property, or real right in immovables, in Canada or interest in, or for civil law right in, timber resource properties and timber limits in Canada, and the person's share of the income of a partnership of which the person was a member from its interest in real property, or real right in immovables, in Canada or interest in, or for civil law right in, timber resource properties and timber limits in Canada, were the person's only income;

(*c*) the person were entitled to no deductions from income for the purpose of computing the person's taxable income; and

(*d*) the person were entitled to no deductions under sections 118 to 118.9 in computing the person's tax payable under Part I for the year.

History: S. 216(5)(*b*) was replaced by S.C. 2013, c. 34, s. 158(4), in force June 26, 2013, and formerly read:

(*b*) the person's income from the person's interest in real property, timber resource property or timber limits in Canada and the person's share of the income of a partnership of which the person was a member from its interest in real property, timber resource property or timber limits in Canada were the person's only income;

S. 216(5), the portion before paragraph (*a*) was replaced by S.C. 2013, c. 34, s. 349(2), applicable to taxation years that end after December 20, 2002, and formerly read:

(5) *Disposition by non-resident of interest in real property, timber resource property or timber limit.* Where a person or a trust of which that person is a beneficiary has filed a return of income under Part I for a taxation year as permitted by this section or as required by section 150 and, in computing the amount of the person's income under Part I an amount has been deducted under paragraph 20(1)(*a*), or is deemed by subsection 107(2) to have been allowed under that paragraph, in respect of real property in Canada, a timber resource property or a timber limit in Canada, the person shall, within the time prescribed by section 150 for filing a return of income under Part I, file a return of income under Part I, in the form prescribed for a person resident in Canada, for any subsequent taxation year in which the person was a non-resident person and in which that real property, timber resource property or timber limit or any interest therein is disposed of, within the meaning of section 13, by the person or by a partnership of which the person is a member, and the person shall, without affecting the person's liability for tax otherwise payable under Part I, thereupon be liable, in lieu of paying tax under this Part on any amount paid, or deemed by this Part to have been paid to the person or to a partnership of which the person is a member in that subsequent taxation year in respect of any interest in real property, timber resource property or timber limit in Canada, to pay tax under Part I for that subsequent taxation year as though

Related Sections: S. 13(21), "timber resource property"; s. 110.1(3) Gifts of capital property; s. 118.1(6)(*b*) Gift of capital property; s. 248(4) Interest in real property.

Cases: Where a non-resident had never elected to be taxed as a Canadian resident, he was not subject to tax on recaptured capital cost allowance. *The Queen v. Arnos et al.*, 82 DTC 6165 (F.C.A.) affirming 81 DTC 5126 (F.C.T.D.)

Rent from an aircraft does not qualify under section 110 [216] since an aircraft is not real property. *Lea-Don Canada Ltd. v. M.N.R.*, 70 DTC 6271 (S.C.C.)

► 216(6) ◄

(6) Saving provision. Subsection (5) does not apply to require a non-resident person

(*a*) to file a return of income under Part I for a taxation year unless, by filing that return, there would be included in computing the non-resident person's income under Part I for that year an amount by virtue of section 13; or

(*b*) to include in computing the non-resident person's income for a taxation year any amount to the extent that that amount has been included in computing the non-resident person's taxable income earned in Canada for that taxation year by virtue of any provision of this Act other than subsection (5).

Related Sections: S. 115 Non-resident's taxable income in Canada; s. 217 Non-resident's Canadian benefits.

Cases: Rent from an aircraft does not qualify under section 110 [216] since an aircraft is not real property. *Lea-Don Canada Ltd. v. M.N.R.*, 70 DTC 6271 (S.C.C.)

► 216(7) ◄

(7) Election — (Repealed by S.C. 2013, c. 34, s. 349(3).)

History: S. 216(7) was repealed by S.C. 2013, c. 34, s. 349(3), in force June 26, 2013, and formerly read:

(7) *Election.* Where, by virtue of subsection (5), a non-resident person is liable to pay tax under Part I for a taxation year, for greater certainty section 61 is not applicable in computing the non-resident person's income for the year.

Forms: T1159 — Income Tax Return for Electing Under Section 216.

Cases: Rent from an aircraft does not qualify under section 110 [216] since an aircraft is not real property. *Lea-Don Canada Ltd. v. M.N.R.*, 70 DTC 6271 (S.C.C.)

► 216(8) ◄

(8) Restriction on deduction. For greater certainty, in determining the amount of tax payable by a non-resident person under Part I for a taxation year by reason of subsection (1) or (5), no deduction in computing the non-resident person's income or tax payable under Part I for the year shall be made to the extent that such a deduction by non-resident persons is not permitted under Part I.

Related Sections: S. 104(7) Non-resident beneficiary.

Cases: Rent from an aircraft does not qualify under section 110 [216] since an aircraft is not real property. *Lea-Don Canada Ltd. v. M.N.R.*, 70 DTC 6271 (S.C.C.)

SECTION 216.1: Alternative re: acting services

► 216.1(1) ◄

(1) Alternative re: acting services. No tax is payable under this Part on any amount described in subsection 212(5.1) that is paid, credited or provided to a non-resident person in a taxation year if the person

(*a*) files with the Minister, on or before the person's filing-due date for the year, a return of income under Part I for the year; and

(*b*) elects in the return to have this section apply for the year.

Editorial Note: Subsection 212(5.1) imposes a 23% tax on an amount paid, credited or provided as a benefit to a non-resident individual who is an actor or to a non-resident corporation related to such actor from film and video acting services provided by the non-resident actor in Canada. The payer is required to withhold the tax under s. 215(1). Under s. 216.1, the recipient, which could be either the actor or the corporation, can elect to have Part I applied to all the acting services payments made to the recipient. If the election is made, the 23% withholding tax does not apply, although the payer is still obliged to withhold 23% under s. 215(1) and the 23% amount withheld and remitted is treated as having been paid on account of the Part I tax liability.

Related Sections: 115(2.1) Non-resident actors; 115(2.2) Deferred payment by actor's corporation; s. 150 Filing returns of income — general rule; s. 150.1 Definition of "electronic filing"; s. 215(1) Withholding and remittance of tax; s. 249 Definition of "taxation year"; s. 250.1 Non-resident person's taxation year and income.

Forms: T1287 — Application by a Non-Resident of Canada (Individual) for a Reduction in the Amount of Non-Resident Tax Required to be Withheld on Income Earned From Acting in a Film or Video Production; T1288 — Application by a Non-Resident of Canada (Corporation) for a Reduction in the Amount of Non-Resident Tax Required to be Withheld on Income Earned From Acting in a Film or Video Production.

Tax Window Files: Subsection 216.1(1) and permanent establishment, *July 27, 2016*, CRA Document No. 2015-0603271E5.

► 216.1(2) ◄

(2) Deemed Part I payment. If in respect of a particular amount paid, credited or provided in a taxation year, a non-resident person has complied with paragraphs (1)(*a*) and (*b*), any amount deducted or withheld and remitted to the Receiver General on behalf of the person on account of tax under subsection 212(5.1) in respect of the particular amount is deemed to have been paid on account of the person's tax under Part I.

Related Sections: S. 115 Non-resident's taxable income in Canada.

► 216.1(3) ◄

(3) Deemed election and restriction. Where a corporation payment (within the meaning assigned by subsection 212(5.2)) has been made to a non-resident corporation in respect of an actor and at any time the corporation makes an actor payment (within the meaning assigned by subsection 212(5.2)) to or for the benefit of the actor, if the corporation makes an election under subsection (1) for the taxation year in which the corporation payment is made, the actor is deemed to make an election under subsection (1) for the taxation year of the actor in which the corporation makes the actor payment.

SECTION 217: Alternative re Canadian benefits

► 217(1) ◄

(1) Alternative re Canadian benefits. In this section, a non-resident person's "Canadian benefits" for a taxation year is the total of all amounts each of which is an amount paid or credited in the year and in respect of which tax under this Part would, but for this section, be payable by the person because of any of paragraphs 212(1)(*h*), (*j*) to (*m*) and (*q*).

Editorial Note: S. 217 provides that a non-resident may elect to pay tax under Part I rather than Part XIII withholding tax on certain Canadian-source pension payments and similar amounts, including payments out of RRSPs, RRIFs and DPSPs (the various amounts are described in s. 212(1)(*h*), (*j*) to (*m*) and (*q*)). In general terms, s. 217 ensures that the non-resident who receives such payments is not put in a less favourable position than if he or she were resident in Canada in regards to such payments, and could take certain deductions or tax credits that would reduce the tax payable under Part I; see ss. 217(4) and (5) regarding the application of the tax credits.

Related Regulations: Part VIII.

Related Sections: S. 2(2) Taxable income; s. 114 Individual resident in Canada for only part of year; s. 115 Non-resident's taxable income in Canada; s. 120(1) Income not earned in a province; s. 150 Manual filing of income return; s. 150.1 Electronic filing of income return. s. 248(1), "amount", "non-resident"; s. 249 Definition of "taxation year"; s. 255 Canada.

Forms: T1261 — Application for a Canada Revenue Agency Individual Tax Number (ITN) for Non-Residents; NR5 — Application by a Non-Resident of Canada for a Reduction in the Amount of Non-Resident Tax Required to be Withheld.

Guides: T4145 Electing Under Section 217 of the Income Tax Act.

► 217(2) ◄

(2) Part I return. No tax is payable under this Part in respect of a non-resident person's Canadian benefits for a taxation year if the person

(*a*) files with the Minister, within 6 months after the end of the year, a return of income under Part I for the year; and

(*b*) elects in the return to have this section apply for the year.

Related Regulations: Part VIII.

Forms: NR5 — Application by a Non-Resident of Canada for a Reduction in the Amount of Non-Resident Tax Required to be Withheld.

Guides: T4145 Electing Under Section 217 of the Income Tax Act.

► 217(3) ◄

(3) Taxable income earned in Canada. Where a non-resident person elects under paragraph (2)(*b*) for a taxation year, for the purposes of Part I

(*a*) the person is deemed to have been employed in Canada in the year; and

(*b*) the person's taxable income earned in Canada for the year is deemed to be the greater of

(i) the amount that would, but for subparagraph (ii), be the person's taxable income earned in Canada for the year if

(A) paragraph 115(1)(*a*) included the following subparagraph after subparagraph (i):

"(i.1) the non-resident person's Canadian benefits for the year, within the meaning assigned by subsection 217(1)," and

(B) paragraph 115(1)(*f*) were read as follows:

"(*f*) such of the other deductions permitted for the purpose of computing taxable income as can reasonably be considered wholly applicable to the amounts described in subparagraphs (*a*)(i) to (vi).", and

(ii) the person's income (computed without reference to subsection 56(8)) for the year minus the total of such of the deductions permitted for the purpose of computing taxable income as can reasonably be considered wholly applicable to the amounts described in subparagraphs 115(1)(*a*)(i) to (vi).

Related Regulations: Part VIII.

Related Sections: S. 2(3) Tax payable by non-resident persons; s. 250.1 Non-resident person's taxation year and income.

Forms: NR5 — Application by a Non-Resident of Canada for a Reduction in the Amount of Non-Resident Tax Required to be Withheld.

► 217(4) ◄

(4) Tax credits — limitation. Sections 118 to 118.91 and 118.94 do not apply in computing the tax payable under Part I for a taxation year by a non-resident person who elects under paragraph (2)(*b*) for the year, unless

(*a*) where section 114 applies to the person for the year, all or substantially all of the person's income for the year is included in computing the person's taxable income for the year; or

(*b*) in any other case, all or substantially all of the person's income for the year is included in computing the amount determined under subparagraph (3)(*b*)(i) in respect of the person for the year.

Related Regulations: Part VIII.

Forms: T1234 — Allowable Amount of Non-Refundable Tax Credits; NR5 — Application by a Non-Resident of Canada for a Reduction in the Amount of Non-Resident Tax Required to be Withheld.

► 217(5) ◄

(5) Tax credits allowed. In computing the tax payable under Part I for a taxation year by a non-resident person to whom neither paragraph (4)(*a*) nor paragraph (4)(*b*) applies for the year there may, notwithstanding section 118.94 and subsection (4), be deducted the lesser of

(*a*) the total of

(i) such of the amounts that would have been deductible under any of section 118.2, subsections 118.3(2) and (3) and sections 118.8 and 118.9 in computing the person's tax payable under Part I for the year if the person had been resident in Canada throughout the year, as can reasonably be considered wholly applicable, and

(ii) the amounts that would have been deductible under any of sections 118 and 118.1, subsection 118.3(1) and sections 118.5 and 118.7 in computing the person's tax payable under Part I for the year if the person had been resident in Canada throughout the year, and

(*b*) the appropriate percentage for the year of the person's Canadian benefits for the year.

History: S. 217(5)(*a*)(i) was replaced by S.C. 2016, c. 7, s. 45(1), applicable to the 2017 and subsequent taxation years, and formerly read:

(i) such of the amounts that would have been deductible under any of section 118.2, subsections 118.3(2) and (3) and sections 118.6, 118.8 and 118.9 in computing the person's tax payable under Part I for the year if the person had been resident in Canada throughout the year, as can reasonably be considered wholly applicable, and

Related Regulations: Part VIII.

Forms: T1234 — Allowable Amount of Non-Refundable Tax Credits; NR5 — Application by a Non-Resident of Canada for a Reduction in the Amount of Non-Resident Tax Required to be Withheld.

► 217(6) ◄

(6) Special credit. In computing the tax payable under Part I for a taxation year by a non-resident who elects under paragraph (2)(*b*) for the year, there may be deducted the amount determined by the formula

$$A \times [(B - C) / B]$$

where

A is the amount of tax under Part I that would, but for this subsection, be payable by the person for the year;

B is the amount determined under subparagraph (3)(*b*)(ii) in respect of the person for the year; and

C is the amount determined under subparagraph (3)(*b*)(i) in respect of the person for the year.

Related Regulations: Part VIII.

Related Sections: S. 2(2) Taxable income; s. 248(1), "amount", "non-resident"; s. 255 Canada; s. 257 Negative amounts.

Forms: NR5 — Application by a Non-Resident of Canada for a Reduction in the Amount of Non-Resident Tax Required to be Withheld.

SECTION 218: Loan to wholly-owned subsidiary

► 218(1) ◄

(1) Loan to wholly-owned subsidiary. For the purposes of this Act, where

(*a*) a non-resident corporation (in this section referred to as the "parent corporation") is indebted to

(i) a person resident in Canada, or

(ii) a non-resident insurance corporation carrying on business in Canada,

(in this section referred to as the "creditor") under an arrangement whereby the parent corporation is required to pay interest in Canadian currency, and

(*b*) the parent corporation has lent the money in respect of which it is so indebted, or a part thereof, to a subsidiary wholly-owned corporation resident in Canada whose principal business is the making of loans (in this section referred to as the "subsidiary corporation") under an arrangement whereby the subsidiary corporation is required to repay the loan to the parent corporation with interest at the same rate as is payable by the parent corporation to the creditor,

the amount so lent by the parent corporation to the subsidiary corporation shall be deemed to have been borrowed by the parent corporation as agent of the subsidiary corporation and interest paid by the subsidiary corporation to the parent corporation that has been paid by the parent corporation to the creditor shall be deemed to have been paid by the subsidiary corporation to the creditor and not by the subsidiary corporation to the parent corporation or by the parent corporation to the creditor.

Related Sections: S. 248(1), "corporation", "insurance corporation", "non-resident", "prescribed", "subsidiary wholly-owned corporation".

► 218(2) ◄

(2) Idem. Where a parent corporation has lent money to a subsidiary wholly-owned corporation resident in Canada whose principal business is not the making of loans and the money has been lent by that corporation to a subsidiary corporation wholly-owned by it and resident in Canada whose principal business is the making of loans, the loan by the parent corporation shall be deemed, for the purpose of subsection (1), to have been a loan to a subsidiary wholly-owned corporation whose principal business is the making of loans.

► 218(3) ◄

(3) Election. This section does not apply in respect of any payment of interest unless the parent corporation and the creditor have executed, and filed with the Minister, an election in prescribed form.

Forms: T2023 — Election in Respect of Loans from Non-Residents.

► 218(4) ◄

(4) Application of election. An election filed under subsection (3) does not apply in respect of any payment of interest made more than 12 months before the date on which the election was filed with the Minister.

Editorial Note: Section 218 exempts withholding tax on interest paid by a loan company resident in Canada to its non-resident parent company. The exemption from withholding tax only applies if the conditions set out in the section apply and requires an election to be made in prescribed form (form T2023).

SECTION 218.1: Application of s. 138.1

In respect of life insurance policies for which all or any part of an insurer's reserves vary in amount depending on the fair market value of a specified group of properties, the rules contained in section 138.1 apply for the purposes of this Part.

Related Sections: S. 138.1 Rules relating to segregated funds; s. 248(1), "insurer", "life insurance policy".

Part XIII.1
Additional Tax on Authorized Foreign Banks

SECTION 218.2: Branch interest tax

▶ 218.2(1) ◀

(1) Branch interest tax. Every authorized foreign bank shall pay a tax under this Part for each taxation year equal to 25% of its taxable interest expense for the year.

Related Sections: S. 18(1)(*v*) Interest — authorized foreign bank; s. 20.2(5) Notional interest; s. 157(1) Payment by corporations; s. 218.2(2) Taxable interest expense; s. 212(13.3) Application of Part XIII to authorized foreign bank; s. 219 Branch tax; s. 248(1), "authorized foreign bank".

Forms: T2Sch97 — Additional Information on Non-Resident Corporations in Canada.

▶ 218.2(2) ◀

(2) Taxable interest expense. The taxable interest expense of an authorized foreign bank for a taxation year is 15% of the amount, if any, by which

(*a*) the total of all amounts on account of interest that are deducted under section 20.2 in computing the bank's income for the year from its Canadian banking business

exceeds

(*b*) the total of all amounts that are included in paragraph (*a*) and that are in respect of a liability of the bank to another person or partnership.

▶ 218.2(3) ◀

(3) Where tax not payable. No tax is payable under this Part for a taxation year by an authorized foreign bank if

(*a*) the bank is resident in a country with which Canada has a tax treaty at the end of the year; and

(*b*) no tax similar to the tax under this Part would be payable in that country for the year by a bank resident in Canada carrying on business in that country during the year.

▶ 218.2(4) ◀

(4) Rate limitation. Notwithstanding any other provision of this Act, the reference in subsection (1) to 25% shall, in respect of a taxation year of an authorized foreign bank that is resident in a country with which Canada has a tax treaty on the last day of the year, be read as a reference to,

(*a*) if the treaty specifies the maximum rate of tax that Canada may impose under this Part for the year on residents of that country, that rate;

(*b*) if the treaty does not specify a maximum rate as described in paragraph (*a*) but does specify the maximum rate of tax that Canada may impose on a payment of interest in the year by a person resident in Canada to a related person resident in that country, that rate; and

(*c*) in any other case, 25%.

▶ 218.2(5) ◀

(5) Provisions applicable to Part. Sections 150 to 152, 158, 159, 160.1 and 161 to 167 and Division J of Part I apply to this Part with any modifications that the circumstances require.

Part XIII.2
Non-Resident Investors in Canadian Mutual Funds

SECTION 218.3: [Tax payable]

► 218.3(1) ◄

(1) Definitions. The following definitions apply in this Part.

"assessable distribution" — "assessable distribution", in respect of a Canadian property mutual fund investment, means the portion of any amount that is paid or credited (otherwise than as a SIFT trust wind-up event), by the mutual fund that issued the investment, to a non-resident investor who holds the investment, and that is not otherwise subject to tax under Part I or Part XIII.

History: S. 218.3(1), the definition "assessable distribution" was replaced by S.C. 2009, c. 2, s. 74(1), applicable after July 14, 2008. S. 218.3(1), the definition "assessable distribution" formerly read:

"assessable distribution" — "assessable distribution", in respect of a Canadian property mutual fund investment, means the portion of any amount that is paid or credited, by the mutual fund that issued the investment, to a non-resident investor who holds the investment, and that is not otherwise subject to tax under Part I or Part XIII.

Related Sections: S. 53(2)(*h*) Amounts to be deducted — Capital interest in a trust.

"Canadian property mutual fund investment" — "Canadian property mutual fund investment" means a share of the capital stock of a mutual fund corporation, or a unit of a mutual fund trust, if

(*a*) the share or unit is listed on a designated stock exchange; and

(*b*) more than 50% of the fair market value of the share or unit is attributable to one or more properties each of which is real property in Canada, a Canadian resource property or a timber resource property.

Related Sections: S. 131(8) Meaning of "mutual fund corporation"; s. 132(6) Meaning of "mutual fund trust".

"Canadian property mutual fund loss" — "Canadian property mutual fund loss" — of a non-resident investor for a taxation year for which the non-resident investor has filed, on or before their filing-due date for the taxation year, a return of income under this Part in prescribed form, in respect of a Canadian property mutual fund investment — means the lesser of

(*a*) the non-resident investor's loss (for greater certainty as determined under section 40) for the taxation year from the disposition of the Canadian property mutual fund investment, and

(*b*) the total of all assessable distributions that were paid or credited on the Canadian property mutual fund investment after the non-resident investor last acquired the investment and at or before the time of the disposition.

"non-resident investor" — "non-resident investor" means a non-resident person or a partnership other than a Canadian partnership.

Related Sections: S. 102(1) Definition of "Canadian partnership".

"unused Canadian property mutual fund loss" — "unused Canadian property mutual fund loss", of a non-resident investor for a taxation year, means the portion of the total of the non-resident investor's Canadian mutual fund property losses for preceding taxation years that has neither reduced under subsection (3) the amount of tax payable, nor increased under subsection (5) the amount of a refund, of tax paid, under this Part for any preceding taxation year.

► 218.3(2) ◄

(2) Tax payable. If at any time a person (referred to in this section as the "payer") pays or credits, to a non-resident investor who holds a Canadian property mutual fund investment, an amount as, on account of, in lieu of payment of or in satisfaction of, an assessable distribution,

(*a*) the non-resident investor is deemed for the purposes of this Act, other than section 150, to have disposed at that time, for proceeds equal to the amount of the assessable distribution, of a property

(i) that is a taxable Canadian property the adjusted cost base of which to the non-resident investor immediately before that time is nil, and

(ii) that is in all other respects identical to the Canadian property mutual fund investment;

(*b*) the non-resident investor is liable to pay an income tax of 15% on the amount of any gain (for greater certainty as determined under section 40) from the disposition; and

(*c*) the payer shall, notwithstanding any agreement or law to the contrary,

(i) deduct or withhold 15% from the amount paid or credited,

(ii) immediately remit that amount to the Receiver General on behalf of the non-resident investor on account of the tax, and

(iii) submit with the remittance a statement in prescribed form.

Related Regulations: 202(1); 210.

Related Sections: S. 115(1)(b) Non-resident's taxable income in Canada; s. 131(5.1) TCP gains distribution; s. 132(5.1) TCP gains distribution.

Forms: T1262 — Part XIII.2 Tax Return for Non-Resident's Investments in Canadian Mutual Funds.

► 218.3(3) ◄

(3) Use of losses. If a non-resident investor files, on or before their filing-due date for a taxation year, a return of income under this Part in prescribed form for the taxation year, the non-resident investor is liable, instead of paying tax under paragraph (2)(*b*) in respect of any amount paid or credited in the taxation year, to pay an income tax of 15% for the taxation year on the amount, if any, by which (*a*) the total of the non-resident investor's gains under subsection (2) for the taxation year

exceeds

(*b*) the total of the non-resident investor's Canadian property mutual fund losses for the year and the non-resident investor's unused Canadian property mutual fund loss for the taxation year.

Related Sections: S. 150(1) Filing returns of income — general rule; s. 248(1), "filing-due date".

► 218.3(4) ◄

(4) Deemed tax paid. If a non-resident investor files, on or before their filing-due date for a taxation year, a return of income under this Part in prescribed form for the taxation year, any amount that is remitted to the Receiver General in respect of an assessable distribution paid or credited to the non-resident investor in the taxation year is deemed to have been paid on account of the non-resident investor's tax under subsection (3) for the taxation year.

Related Sections: S. 150(1) Filing returns of income — general rule; s. 248(1), "filing-due date".

► 218.3(5) ◄

(5) Refund. The amount, if any, by which the total of all amounts paid on account of a non-resident investor's tax under subsection (3) for a taxation year exceeds the non-resident investor's liability for tax under this Part for the taxation year shall be refunded to the non-resident investor.

► 218.3(6) ◄

(6) Excess loss — carryback. If a non-resident investor files, on or before their filing-due date for a taxation year, a return of income under this Part in prescribed form for the taxation year, the Minister shall refund to the non-resident investor an amount equal to the lesser of

(*a*) the total amount of tax under this Part paid by the non-resident investor in each of the three preceding taxation years, to the extent that the Minister has not previously refunded that tax, and

(*b*) 15% of the amount, if any, by which

(i) the total of the non-resident investor's Canadian property mutual fund losses for the taxation year and the non-resident investor's unused Canadian property mutual fund loss for the taxation year

exceeds

(ii) the total of all assessable distributions paid or credited to the non-resident investor in the taxation year.

Related Sections: S. 150(1) Filing returns of income — general rule; s. 248(1), "filing-due date".

► 218.3(7) ◄

(7) Ordering. In applying subsection (6), amounts of tax are to be considered to be refunded in the order in which they were paid.

► 218.3(8) ◄

(8) Partnership filing-due date. For the purposes of this Part, the taxation year of a partnership is its fiscal period and the filing-due date for the taxation year is to be determined as if the partnership were a corporation.

Related Sections: S. 150(1) Filing returns of income — general rule; s. 248(1), "filing-due date".

► 218.3(9) ◄

(9) Partnership — member resident in Canada. If a non-resident investor is a partnership a member of which is resident in Canada, the portion of the tax paid by the partnership under this Part in respect of an assessable distribution paid or credited to the partnership in a particular taxation year of the partnership (or, if the partnership files a return of income for the particular taxation year in accordance with subsection (3), the portion of the tax paid by the partnership under that subsection for the taxation year) that can reasonably be considered to be the member's share is deemed

(*a*) to be an amount paid on account of that member's liability for tax under Part I for that member's taxation year in which the particular taxation year of the partnership ends; and

(*b*) except for the purposes of this subsection, to be neither a tax paid on account of the partnership's tax under this Part nor a tax paid by the partnership.

► 218.3(10) ◄

(10) Provisions applicable. Section 150.1, subsections 161(1), (7) and (11), sections 162 to 167, Division J of Part I, paragraph 214(3)(*f*), subsections 215(2), (3) and (6) and sections 227 and 227.1 apply to this Part with any modifications that the circumstances require.

Part XIV
Additional Tax on Non-Resident Corporations

SECTION 219: Additional tax

► 219(1) ◄

(1) Additional tax. Every corporation that is non-resident in a taxation year shall, on or before its balance-due day for the year, pay a tax under this Part for the year equal to 25% of the amount, if any, by which the total of

(*a*) the corporation's taxable income earned in Canada for the year (in this subsection referred to as the corporation's "base amount"),

(*b*) the amount deducted because of section 112 and paragraph 115(1)(*e*) in computing the corporation's base amount,

(*c*) (Repealed by S.C. 2003, c. 28, s. 17(1).)

(*d*) the amount, if any, by which the total of all amounts each of which is a taxable capital gain of the corporation for the year from a disposition of a taxable Canadian property exceeds the total of all amounts each of which is

(i) an allowable capital loss of the corporation for the year from a disposition of a taxable Canadian property, or

(ii) an amount deductible because of paragraphs 111(1)(*b*) and 115(1)(*d*) in computing the corporation's base amount,

(*e*) the total of all amounts each of which is an amount in respect of a grant or credit that

(i) can reasonably be considered to have been received by the corporation in the year as a reimbursement or repayment of, or as indemnification or compensation for, an amount deducted because of paragraph (*j*), as it read in its application to the 1995 taxation year, in computing the amount determined under this subsection for a preceding taxation year that began before 1996, and

(ii) was not included in computing the corporation's base amount for any taxation year,

(*f*) where, at any time in the year, the corporation has made one or more dispositions described in paragraph (*l*) of qualified property, the total of all amounts each of which is an amount in respect of one of those dispositions equal to the amount, if any, by which the fair market value of the qualified property at the time of the disposition exceeds the corporation's proceeds of disposition of the property, and

(*g*) the amount, if any, claimed for the immediately preceding taxation year under paragraph (*j*) by the corporation,

exceeds the total of

(*h*) that proportion of the total of

(i) the total of the taxes payable under Parts I, I.3 and VI for the year by the corporation, determined without reference to subsection (1.1), and

(ii) the total of the income taxes payable to the government of a province for the year by the corporation, determined without reference to subsection (1.1),

that the corporation's base amount is of the amount that would, if this Act were read without reference to subsection (1.1), be the corporation's base amount,

(*i*) the total of all amounts each of which is the amount of interest or a penalty paid by the corporation in the year

(i) under this Act, or

(ii) on or in respect of an income tax payable by it to the government of a province under a law of the province relating to income tax,

to the extent that the interest or penalty was not deductible in computing its base amount for any taxation year,

(*j*) where the corporation was carrying on business in Canada at the end of the year, the amount claimed by the corporation for the year, not exceeding the amount prescribed to be its allowance for the year in respect of its investment in property in Canada, and

Tax Window Files: Regulation 808, *September 22, 2017*, CRA Document No. 2016-0632881E5.

(*k*) (Repealed by S.C. 2003, c. 28, s. 17(3).)

(*l*) where the corporation has at any time in the year disposed of property (in this paragraph and paragraph (*f*) referred to as "qualified property") used by it immediately before that time for the purpose of gaining or producing income from a business carried on by it in Canada to a Canadian corporation (in this paragraph referred to as the "purchaser corporation") that was, immediately after the disposition, a qualified related corporation of the corporation for consideration that includes a share of the capital stock of the purchaser corporation, the total of all amounts each of which is an amount in respect of a disposition in the year of a qualified property equal to the amount, if any, by which

(i) the fair market value of the qualified property at the time of the disposition

exceeds the total of

(ii) the amount, if any, by which the paid-up capital in respect of the issued and outstanding shares of the capital stock of the purchaser corporation increased because of the disposition, and

(iii) the fair market value, at the time of receipt, of the consideration (other than shares) given by the purchaser corporation for the qualified property.

History: S. 219(1)(*d*)(ii) was replaced by S.C. 2013, c. 40, s. 84(1), applicable to the 1998 and subsequent taxation years, and formerly read:

(ii) an amount deductible because of paragraphs 111(1)(*b*) and 115(1)(*e*) in computing the corporation's base amount,

Related Regulations: 808.

Related Sections: s. 52(7) Cost of shares of subsidiary; s. 134 Non-resident-owned corporation not a Canadian corporation, etc; 142.7(9) Branch-establishment dividend; 142.7(10) Treatment of dividend; s. 212(2) Tax on dividends; s. 218.2 Deemed dividend; s. 219(4) Non-resident insurers; s. 219.1 Corporate emigration; s. 219.2 Limitation on rate of branch tax; s. 248(1), "taxable Canadian property"; s. 255 Canada.

Tax Profile: March 2013 — Non-Resident Investment in Canadian Real Estate; March 2011 — Canada 2010 — Year in Review; September 2010 — Recent Tax Developments Affecting Non-Residents; October 2007 — Will Canadian Unlimited Liability Companies Survive?; July 2002 — Doing Business in Canada.

Tax Topics: No. 2111, IFA 2012 Tax Seminar Roundtables; No. 2010, The Narrowing Scope of the CRA.

Forms: T2SCH20 — Part XIV Tax — Branch Tax; T2Sch97 — Additional Information on Non-Resident Corporations in Canada.

Income Tax Technical News: Issue No. 44, US LLC with a Canadian Branch.

Interpretation Bulletins: *Primary* — IT-137R3 Additional tax on certain corporations carrying on business in Canada.

Tax Window Files: Article X(6) Canada-US Treaty, *October 23, 2012*, CRA Document No. 2012-0440101E5; Branch Tax, *November 30, 2010*, CRA Document No. 2010-0386391C6.

Cases: A U.S. limited liability company was held to be resident in the United States for purposes of the Canada-U.S. Tax Treaty and was therefore entitled to the 5% reduced rate of Canadian branch tax. *TD Securities (USA) LLC v. The Queen*, 2010 DTC 1137 (TCC)

► 219(1.1) ◄

(1.1) Excluded gains. For the purposes of subsection (1), the definition "taxable Canadian property" in subsection 248(1) shall be read without reference to paragraphs (*a*) and (*c*) to (*e*) of that definition and as if the only options, interests or rights referred to in paragraph (*f*) of that definition were those in respect of property described in paragraph (*b*) of that definition.

History: S. 219(1.1) was replaced by S.C. 2013, c. 40, s. 84(2), deemed to have come into force on March 5, 2010, and formerly read:

(1.1) *Excluded gains.* For the purpose of subsection (1), the definition "taxable Canadian property" in subsection 248(1) shall be read without reference to paragraphs (*a*) and (*c*) to (*k*) of that definition and as if the only options, interests or rights referred to in paragraph (*l*) of that definition were those in respect of property described in paragraph (*b*) of that definition.

S. 219(1.1) was replaced by S.C. 2013, c. 34, s. 159, in force June 26, 2013, and formerly read:

(1.1) *Excluded gains.* For the purpose of subsection (1), the definition "taxable Canadian property" in subsection 248(1) shall be read without reference to paragraphs (*a*) and (*c*) to (*k*) of that definition and as if the only interests or options referred to in paragraph (*l*) of that definition were those in respect of property described in paragraph (*b*) of that definition.

► 219(2) ◄

(2) Exempt corporations. No tax is payable under this Part for a taxation year by a corporation that was, throughout the year,

(*a*) (Repealed by S.C. 2001, c. 17, s. 177(4).)

(*b*) a corporation whose principal business was

(i) the transportation of persons or goods,

(ii) communications, or

(iii) mining iron ore in Canada; or

(*c*) a corporation exempt from tax under section 149.

► 219(3) ◄

(3) Provisions applicable to Part. Sections 150 to 152, 154, 158, 159 and 161 to 167 and Division J of Part I are applicable to this Part with such modifications as the circumstances require.

► 219(4) ◄

(4) Non-resident insurers. No tax is payable under subsection (1) for a taxation year by a non-resident insurer, but where it elects, in prescribed manner and within the prescribed time, to deduct, in computing its Canadian investment fund as of the end of the immediately following taxation year, an amount not greater than the amount, if any, by which

(*a*) the amount, if any, by which the total of

(i) the insurer's surplus funds derived from operations as of the end of the year, and

(i.1) where, in any particular taxation year that began before the end of the year, the insurer transferred to a taxable Canadian corporation with which it did not deal at arm's length any designated insurance property of the insurer for the particular year, and

(A) the property was transferred before December 16, 1987 and subsection 138(11.5) of the *Income Tax Act*, chapter 148 of the Revised Statutes of Canada, 1952, applied in respect of the transfer, or

(B) the property was transferred before November 22, 1985 and subsection 85(1) of that Act applied in respect of the transfer,

the amount, if any, by which

(C) the total of the fair market value, at the time of the transfer, of all such property

exceeds

(D) the total of the insurer's proceeds of disposition of all such property,

exceeds the total of

(ii) each amount on which the insurer has paid tax under this Part for a previous taxation year,

(iii) the amount, if any, by which the insurer's accumulated 1968 deficit exceeds the amount of the insurer's maximum tax actuarial reserves for its 1968 taxation year for its life insurance policies in Canada,

(iv) the insurer's loss, if any, for each of its 5 consecutive taxation years ending with its 1968 taxation year, from all insurance businesses (other than its life insurance business) carried on by it in Canada (computed without reference to section 30 of the *Income Tax Act*, chapter 148 of the Revised Statutes of Canada, 1952, as it read in its application to those years), except to the extent that any such loss was deductible in computing its taxable income for any of its taxation years ending before 1969, and

(v) the total of all amounts in respect of which the insurer has filed an election under subsection (5.2) for a previous taxation year in accordance with that subsection,

exceeds

(*b*) the amount of the insurer's attributed surplus for the year,

the insurer shall, on or before the day on or before which it is required to file a return under Part I for the year, pay a tax for the year equal to 25% of the amount, if any, by which the amount it has so elected to deduct exceeds the amount in respect of which it filed an election under subsection (5.2) for the year in accordance with that subsection.

Related Regulations: 2403(1).

Related Sections: S. 54, "proceeds of disposition"; s. 138(9) Computation of income; s. 181.3(3)(*d*)(i)(A) Capital of financial institution; s. 190.13(*c*)(i)(A) Capital; s. 248(1), "insurer", "insurance corporation", "taxable Canadian corporation"; s. 249(1) Definition of "taxation year"; s. 251(1) Arm's length.

► 219(5) ◄

(5) Additional tax on insurer — (Repealed by 1977-78, c. 32, s. 52(1).)

► 219(5.1) ◄

(5.1) Additional tax on insurer. Where a non-resident insurer ceases in a taxation year to carry on all or substantially all of an insurance business in Canada, it shall, on or before its filing-due date for the year, pay a tax for the year equal to 25% of the amount, if any, by which

(*a*) that portion of the amount determined under paragraph (4)(*a*) for the year in respect of the insurer that can reasonably be attributed to the business, including the disposition by it of property that was its designated insurance property in respect of the business for the year in which the disposition occurred,

exceeds

(*b*) the amount the insurer and a qualified related corporation of the insurer jointly elect in accordance with subsection (5.2) for the year in respect of the business.

Related Sections: S. 18(1)(*t*) Payments under Act.

► 219(5.2) ◄

(5.2) Election by non-resident insurer. Where

(*a*) a non-resident insurer has ceased to carry on all or substantially all of an insurance business in Canada in a taxation year, and

(*b*) the insurer has transferred the business to a qualified related corporation of the insurer and the insurer and the corporation have elected to have subsection 138(11.5) apply in respect of the transfer,

the insurer and the corporation may elect, in prescribed manner and within prescribed time, to reduce the amount in respect of which the insurer would otherwise be liable to pay tax under subsection (5.1) by an amount not exceeding the lesser of

(*c*) the amount determined under paragraph (5.1)(*a*) in respect of the insurer in respect of the business, and

(*d*) the total of the paid-up capital of the shares of the capital stock of the corporation received by the insurer as consideration for the transfer of the business and any contributed surplus arising on the issue of those shares.

Related Regulations: 2403(2).

Related Sections: S. 85(2.1) Computing paid-up capital; s. 138(11.7) Computation of paid-up capital; s. 138(11.9) Computation of contributed surplus.

► 219(5.3) ◄

(5.3) Deemed payment of dividend. Where, at any time in a taxation year,

(*a*) a qualified related corporation of a non-resident insurer ceases to be a qualified related corporation of that insurer, or

(*b*) the tax deferred account of a qualified related corporation of a non-resident insurer exceeds the total of the paid-up capital in respect of all the shares of the capital stock of the corporation and its contributed surplus,

the corporation shall be deemed to have paid, immediately before that time, a dividend to the insurer in an amount equal to

(*c*) where paragraph (*a*) is applicable, the balance of the tax deferred account of the corporation at that time, or

(*d*) where paragraph (*b*) is applicable, the amount of the excess referred to in that paragraph at that time.

► 219(6) ◄

(6) Where election under ss. 138(9) — (Repealed by 1977-78, c. 32, s. 52(1).)

► 219(7) ◄

(7) Definitions. In this Part,

"accumulated 1968 deficit" — "accumulated 1968 deficit" of a life insurer means such amount as can be established by the insurer to be its deficit as of the end of its 1968 taxation year from carrying on its life insurance business in Canada on the assumption that the amounts of its assets and liabilities (including reserves of any kind)

(*a*) as of the end of any taxation year before its 1968 taxation year, were the amounts thereof determined for the purposes of the Superintendent of Insurance for Canada or other similar officer, and

(*b*) as of the end of its 1968 taxation year, were

(i) in respect of depreciable property, the capital cost thereof as of the first day of its 1969 taxation year,

(ii) in respect of policy reserves, the insurer's maximum tax actuarial reserves for its 1968 taxation year for life insurance policies issued by it in the course of carrying on its life insurance business in Canada, and

(iii) in respect of other assets and liabilities, the amounts thereof determined as of the end of that year for the purpose of computing its income for its 1969 taxation year;

Related Sections: S. 248(1), "depreciable property", "life insurer", "life insurance business", "life insurance corporation".

"attributed surplus"—"attributed surplus" of an insurer for a taxation year has the meaning assigned by regulation;

Related Regulations: 2400(1).

"Canadian investment fund"—"Canadian investment fund" has the meaning prescribed for that expression;

Related Regulations: 2400(1); 2405(3).

"maximum tax actuarial reserves"—"maximum tax actuarial reserves" has the meaning assigned by subsection 138(12);

"surplus funds derived from operations"—"surplus funds derived from operations" has the meaning assigned by subsection 138(12);

"tax deferred account"—"tax deferred account" of a qualified related corporation at any time means the amount determined by the formula

$$A - B$$

where

A is the total of all amounts each of which is an amount in respect of which the qualified related corporation and a non-resident insurer have elected jointly before that time in accordance with subsection (5.2), and

B is the total of all amounts each of which is the amount of a dividend deemed by subsection (5.3) to have been paid by the qualified related corporation before that time.

► 219(8) ◄

(8) Meaning of "qualified related corporation". For the purposes of this Part, a corporation is a "qualified related corporation" of a particular corporation if it is resident in Canada and all of the issued and outstanding shares (other than directors' qualifying shares) of its capital stock (having full voting rights under all circumstances) are owned by

(*a*) the particular corporation,

(*b*) a subsidiary wholly-owned corporation of the particular corporation,

(*c*) a corporation of which the particular corporation is a subsidiary wholly-owned corporation,

(*d*) a subsidiary wholly-owned corporation of a corporation of which the particular corporation is also a subsidiary wholly-owned corporation, or

(*e*) any combination of corporations each of which is a corporation described in paragraph (*a*), (*b*), (*c*) or (*d*),

and, for the purpose of this subsection, a subsidiary wholly-owned corporation of a particular corporation includes any subsidiary wholly-owned corporation of a corporation that is a subsidiary wholly-owned corporation of the particular corporation.

Related Sections: S. 134 Non-resident-owned corporation not a Canadian corporation, etc; s. 138(12), "qualified related corporation"; s. 248(1), "subsidiary wholly-owned corporation".

SECTION 219.1: Corporate emigration

► 219.1(1) ◄

(1) Corporate emigration. If a taxation year of a corporation (in this subsection and subsection (2) referred to as the "emigrating corporation") is deemed by paragraph 128.1(4)(*a*) to have ended at any time, the emigrating corporation shall, on or before its filing-due date for the year, pay a tax under this Part for the year equal to the amount determined by the formula

$$25\% \times (A - B)$$

where

A is the fair market value of all the property owned by the emigrating corporation immediately before that time; and

B is the total of

(*a*) the paid-up capital in respect of all the shares of the capital stock of the emigrating corporation immediately before that time,

(*b*) all amounts (other than amounts payable by the emigrating corporation in respect of dividends and amounts payable under this section) each of which is a debt owing by the emigrating corporation, or an obligation of the emigrating corporation to pay an amount, that is outstanding at that time, and

(*c*) if a tax was payable by the emigrating corporation under subsection 219(1) or this section for a preceding taxation year that began before 1996 and after the emigrating corporation last became resident in Canada, four times the total of all amounts that would, but for sections 219.2 and 219.3 and any tax treaty, have been so payable.

History: S. 219.1 was amended and renumbered as s. 219.1(1), applicable to corporations that cease to be resident in Canada after March 28, 2012. S. 219.1 formerly read:

S. 219.1 *Corporate emigration.* Where a taxation year of a corporation is deemed by paragraph 128.1(4)(*a*) to have ended at any time, the corporation shall, on or before its filing-due date for the year, pay a tax under this Part for the year equal to 25% of the amount, if any, by which

(*a*) the fair market value of all the property owned by the corporation immediately before that time

exceeds the total of

(*b*) the paid-up capital in respect of all the issued and outstanding shares of the capital stock of the corporation immediately before that time,

(*c*) all amounts (other than amounts payable by the corporation in respect of dividends and amounts payable under this section) each of which is a debt owing by the corporation, or an obligation of the corporation to pay an amount, that is outstanding at that time, and

(*d*) where a tax was payable by the corporation under subsection 219(1) or this section for a preceding taxation year that began before 1996 and after the corporation last became resident in Canada, 4 times the total of all amounts that would, but for sections 219.2 and 219.3 and any agreement or convention between the Government of Canada and the government of any other country that has the force of law in Canada, have been so payable.

Related Sections: S. 89(1), "paid-up capital"; s. 248(1), "dividend", "filing-due date"; s. 249(1) Definition of "taxation year"; s. 250(5.1) Continued corporation.

International Tax: No. 100, Buy, Bump, and Run With a Twist.

Forms: T2Sch97 — Additional Information on Non-Resident Corporations in Canada.

Interpretation Bulletins: *Primary* — IT-451R Deemed disposition and acquisition on ceasing to be or becoming resident in Canada. *Secondary* — IT-137R3 Additional tax on certain corporations carrying on business in Canada.

▶ 219.1(2) ◀

(2) Foreign affiliate dumping — emigrating corporation. The paid-up capital referred to in paragraph (*a*) of the description of B in subsection (1) is deemed to be nil if

(*a*) one or more shares of the emigrating corporation are, at the time the emigrating corporation ceases to be resident in Canada, owned by another corporation resident in Canada;

(*b*) the other corporation is controlled, at that time, by a non-resident corporation; and

> **Proposed Amendment**
> **2019 Federal Budget Resolutions**
> **Paragraph 219.1(2)(*b*) of the Act is replaced by the following:**
> (*b*) the other corporation is controlled, at that time, by a non-resident person or a group of non-resident persons not dealing with each other at arm's length; and
>
> **Applicable:** In respect of transactions or events that occur on or after March 19, 2019.

(*c*) the emigrating corporation is, immediately after that time — or becomes, as part of a transaction or event or series of transactions or events that includes the emigrating corporation ceasing to be resident in Canada — a foreign affiliate of the other corporation.

History: S. 219.1(2) was added by S.C. 2012, c. 31, s. 51(1), applicable to corporations that cease to be resident in Canada after March 28, 2012.

▶ 219.1(3) ◀

(3) Application of subsection (4). Subsection (4) applies if

(*a*) a corporation ceases to be resident in Canada at any time (referred to in subsection (4) as the "emigration time");

(*b*) an amount is required by paragraph 212.3(2)(*b*) or subsection 212.3(7) to be deducted in computing the paid-up capital in respect of a class of shares of the capital stock of the corporation because of an investment in a subject corporation made by a CRIC that is described in any of paragraphs 212.3(10)(*a*) to (*f*);

(*c*) subsection 212.3(9) has not applied in respect of any reduction of the paid-up capital in respect of a class of shares of the capital stock of the corporation or a specified predecessor corporation (as defined in subsection 95(1)) of the corporation; and

(*d*) subsection (2) does not apply in respect of the cessation of residence.

Editorial Note: Subsections 219.1(3) to (5) are part of the foreign affiliate dumping rules that are primarily contained in section 212.3. Subsections 219.1(3) and (4) contain rules, similar to subsection 212.3(9), that allow a corporation's PUC to be "reinstated" immediately before the corporation emigrates, where it has had a prior reduction of its PUC under paragraph 212.3(2)(*b*) or (7)(*b*). The result of such a PUC reinstatement is a reduction of the "departure tax" otherwise payable by an emigrating corporation under subsection 219.1(1).

Subsection 219.1(3) provides the conditions for the application of subsection 219.1(4). The first condition, in paragraph 219.1(3)(*a*) is, simply, that the corporation must cease to be resident in Canada. The second condition, in paragraph 219.1(3)(*b*), is that, prior to the corporation's emigration, its PUC must have been reduced under paragraph 212.3(2)(*b*) or (7)(*b*) as a result of an investment made by a CRIC in a subject corporation that is one of the types of investments described in paragraph 212.3(10)(*a*) (an acquisition of subject corporation shares), 212.3(10)(*b*) (a capital contribution to a subject corporation), or 212.3(10)(*f*) (an indirect acquisition of shares of a subject corporation resulting from a direct acquisition of shares of a Canadian-resident corporation). The third condition, in paragraph 219.1(3)(*c*), is that no PUC in respect of any class of shares of the emigrating corporation or a specified predecessor corporation (as defined in subsection 95(1)) of the emigrating corporation has been previously reinstated under subsection 212.3(9). Finally, paragraph 219.1(3)(*d*) requires that subsection 219.1(2) not be applicable in respect of the emigration.

If subsection 219.1(4) applies, the PUC in respect of the shares of the emigrating corporation is increased – two instants before the emigration time – for purposes of paragraph (*a*) of variable B in the formula in subsection 219.1(1), by the lesser of two amounts. The first amount is the total of all prior PUC reductions under paragraph 212.3(2)(*b*) or (7)(*b*) in respect of a class of shares of the emigrating corporation in connection with an investment described in paragraph 212.3(10)(*a*), (*b*) or (*f*). The second amount is the aggregate fair market value of shares of subject corporations that are owned by the emigrating corporation immediately before the emigration, or the portion of the fair market value of any foreign affiliate shares that are owned by the emigrating corporation and that were substituted for shares of a subject corporation.

Subsection 219.1(5) is a definitional provision that imports into subsections 219.1(3) and (4) the meaning of the terms "CRIC," "subject corporation," and "investment" from the foreign affiliate dumping rules in section 212.3.

The amendments to section 219.1 apply to corporate emigrations that occur after March 28, 2012.

History: S. 219.1(3)(*b*) was replaced by S.C. 2014, c. 39, s. 66(1), applicable to corporations that cease to be resident in Canada after March 28, 2012, and formerly read:

> (*b*) an amount is required by paragraph 212.3(2)(*b*) or (7)(*b*) to be deducted in computing the paid-up capital in respect of a class of shares of the capital stock of the corporation because of an investment in a subject corporation made by a CRIC that is described in paragraph 212.3(10)(*a*), (*b*) or (*f*);

S. 219.1(3) was added by S.C. 2012, c. 31, s. 51(1), applicable to corporations that cease to be resident in Canada after March 28, 2012.

Canadian Tax Highlights Newsletter – May 2013, Volume 21, Number 5.

▶ 219.1(4) ◀

(4) Paid-up capital reinstatement. If this subsection applies, the paid-up capital referred to in paragraph (*a*) of the description of B in subsection (1) is to be increased, immediately before the time that is immediately before the emigration time, by the lesser of

(*a*) the total of all amounts each of which is an amount by which the paid-up capital of a class of shares of the capital stock of the corporation was required by paragraph 212.3(2)(*b*) or subsection 212.3(7) to be reduced in respect of an investment in a subject corporation made by the CRIC that is described in any of paragraphs 212.3(10)(*a*) to (*f*), and

(*b*) the total of all amounts each of which is

(i) the fair market value of a share of the capital stock of a subject corporation that is owned by the corporation immediately before the emigration time,

(ii) the portion of the fair market value of a particular share of the capital stock of a foreign affiliate of the corporation owned by the corporation immediately before the emigration time that may reasonably be considered to relate to a share of the capital stock of a subject corporation that was previously owned by the corporation and for which the particular share was substituted, or

(iii) the fair market value of a debt obligation, other than a pertinent loan or indebtedness (as defined in subsection 212.3(11)), of a subject corporation that is owned by the corporation immediately before the emigration time.

Editorial Note: Subsections 219.1(3) to (5) are part of the foreign affiliate dumping rules that are primarily contained in section 212.3. Subsections 219.1(3) and (4) contain rules, similar to subsection 212.3(9), that allow a corporation's PUC to be "reinstated" immediately before the corporation emigrates, where it has had a prior reduction of its PUC under paragraph 212.3(2)(*b*) or (7)(*b*). The result of such a PUC reinstatement is a reduction of the "departure tax" otherwise payable by an emigrating corporation under subsection 219.1(1).

Subsection 219.1(3) provides the conditions for the application of subsection 219.1(4). The first condition, in paragraph 219.1(3)(*a*) is, simply, that the corporation must cease to be resident in Canada. The second condition, in paragraph 219.1(3)(*b*), is that, prior to the corporation's emigration, its PUC must have been reduced under paragraph 212.3(2)(*b*) or (7)(*b*) as a result of an investment made by a CRIC in a subject corporation that is one of the types of investments described in paragraph 212.3(10)(*a*) (an acquisition of subject corporation shares), 212.3(10)(*b*) (a capital contribution to a subject corporation), or 212.3(10)(*f*) (an indirect acquisition of shares of a subject corporation resulting from a direct acquisition of shares of a Canadian-resident corporation). The third condition, in paragraph 219.1(3)(*c*), is that no PUC in respect of any class of shares of the emigrating corporation or a specified predecessor corporation (as defined in subsection 95(1)) of the emigrating corporation has been previously reinstated under subsection 212.3(9). Finally, paragraph 219.1(3)(*d*) requires that subsection 219.1(2) not be applicable in respect of the emigration.

If subsection 219.1(4) applies, the PUC in respect of the shares of the emigrating corporation is increased – two instants before the emigration time – for purposes of paragraph (*a*) of variable B in the formula in subsection 219.1(1), by the lesser of two amounts. The first amount is the total of all prior PUC reductions under paragraph 212.3(2)(*b*) or (7)(*b*) in respect of a class of shares of the emigrating corporation in connection with an investment described in paragraph 212.3(10)(*a*), (*b*) or (*f*). The second amount is the aggregate fair market value of shares of subject corporations that are owned by the emigrating corporation immediately before the emigration, or the portion of the fair market value of any foreign affiliate shares that are owned by the emigrating corporation and that were substituted for shares of a subject corporation.

Subsection 219.1(5) is a definitional provision that imports into subsections 219.1(3) and (4) the meaning of the terms "CRIC," "subject corporation," and "investment" from the foreign affiliate dumping rules in section 212.3.

The amendments to section 219.1 apply to corporate emigrations that occur after March 28, 2012.

History: S. 219.1(4)(*a*) was replaced by S.C. 2014, c. 39, s. 66(2), applicable to corporations that cease to be resident in Canada after March 28, 2012, and formerly read:

(*a*) the total of all amounts each of which is an amount by which the paid-up capital of a class of shares of the capital stock of the corporation was required by paragraph 212.3(2)(*b*) or (7)(*b*) to be reduced in respect of an investment in a subject corporation made by the CRIC that is described in paragraph 212.3(10)(*a*), (*b*) or (*f*), and

S. 219.1(4)(*b*)(iii) was added by S.C. 2014, c. 39, s. 66(3), applicable to corporations that cease to be resident in Canada after March 28, 2012.

S. 219.1(4) was added by S.C. 2012, c. 31, s. 51(1), applicable to corporations that cease to be resident in Canada after March 28, 2012.

Canadian Tax Highlights Newsletter – May 2013, Volume 21, Number 5.

► 219.1(5) ◄

(5) Assigned meanings from section 212.3. For the purposes of subsections (3) and (4), "CRIC" and "subject corporation" have the meaning assigned to those terms by subsection 212.3(1) and "investment" has the same meaning as in subsection 212.3(10).

History: S. 219.1(5) was added by S.C. 2012, c. 31, s. 51(1), applicable to corporations that cease to be resident in Canada after March 28, 2012.

SECTION 219.2: Limitation on rate of branch tax

Notwithstanding any other provision of this Act, where an agreement or convention between the Government of Canada and the government of another country that has the force of law in Canada

(*a*) does not limit the rate of tax under this Part on corporations resident in that other country, and

(*b*) provides that, where a dividend is paid by a corporation resident in Canada to a corporation resident in that other country that owns all of the shares of the capital stock of the corporation resident in Canada, the rate of tax imposed on the dividend shall not exceed a specified rate,

any reference in section 219 to a rate of tax shall, in respect of a taxation year of a corporation to which that agreement or convention applies on the last day of that year, be read as a reference to the specified rate.

Related Sections: S. 219.1 Corporate emigration; s. 248(1), "corporation", "dividend"; s. 249(1) Definition of "taxation year".

Tax Profile: September 2010 — Recent Tax Developments Affecting Non-Residents.

Tax Topics: No. 2010, The Narrowing Scope of the CRA.

Interpretation Bulletins: *Secondary* — IT-137R3 Additional tax on certain corporations carrying on business in Canada.

SECTION 219.3: Effect of tax treaty

For the purpose of section 219.1, where an agreement or convention between the Government of Canada and the government of another country that has the force of law in Canada provides that the rate of tax imposed on a dividend paid by a corporation resident in Canada to a corporation resident in the other country that owns all of the shares of the capital stock of the corporation resident in Canada shall not exceed a specified rate, the reference in section 219.1 to "25%" shall, in respect of a corporation that ceased to be resident in Canada and to which the agreement or convention applies at the beginning of its first taxation year after its taxation year that is deemed by paragraph 128.1(4)(*a*) to have ended, be read as a reference to the specified rate unless it can reasonably be concluded that one of the main reasons that the corporation became resident in the other country was to reduce the amount of tax payable under this Part or Part XIII.

Related Sections: S. 248(1), "corporation", "dividend".

Part XV
Administration and Enforcement

Administration

SECTION 220: Minister's Duty

► 220(1) ◄

(1) Minister's Duty. The Minister shall administer and enforce this Act and the Commissioner of Revenue may exercise all the powers and perform the duties of the Minister under this Act.

► 220(2) ◄

(2) Officers, clerks and employees. Such officers, clerks and employees as are necessary to administer and enforce this Act shall be appointed or employed in the manner authorized by law.

► 220(2.01) ◄

(2.01) Delegation. The Minister may authorize an officer or a class of officers to exercise powers or perform duties of the Minister under this Act.

Cases: The standard of review for a CRA officer's decision is that of reasonableness. *R & S Industries Inc. v. Minister of National Revenue*, 2016 DTC 5040 (FC)

► 220(2.1) ◄

(2.1) Waiver of filing of documents. Where any provision of this Act or a regulation requires a person to file a prescribed form, receipt or other document, or to provide prescribed information, the Minister may waive the requirement, but the person shall provide the document or information at the Minister's request.

Canadian Tax Foundation: Gilbert and Potter, *Judicial Review Allowed: FCA Extends Application of Subsection 220(2.1)*, 2018 Tax for the Owner Manager 18(4):3–4.

Tax Topics: No. 2438, Minister Has Discretion To Provide Relief From the Tax-Return-Filing Requirement for Dividend Returns; No. 2422, If the Minister Is Too Busy, Can the FCA Help Out? A Comment on *Bonnybrook Park v. MNR*; No. 2398, Minister Cannot Waive Statutory Requirement To Serve a Notice of Objection; No. 1831, Should You File a Partnership Information Return?; No. 1770, Reversal of a Taxpayer Concession: The Bul River Decision.

Forms: RC342 — Request by an Insolvency Practitioner for a Waiver of the Requirement to file a T2 Corporation Income Tax Return.

Income Tax Folios: *Secondary* — S1-F3-C1 Child Care Expense Deduction.

SR&ED Publications: 2000-02R, Guidelines for resolving claimants' SR&ED concerns; 96-01, Reclassification of SR&ED expenditures per subsection 127(11.4).

Cases: Revenue Canada refused the taxpayer's request for a Ministerial waiver of filing requirements based on a departmental policy. The taxpayer's request for judicial review was granted because the refusal had elevated the departmental policy to the equivalent of a statutory requirement, and thus had unduly narrowly construed s. 220(2.1). *Alex Parallel Computers Research Inc. v. The Queen*, 99 DTC 5283 (F.C.T.D.)

► 220(2.2) ◄

(2.2) Exception. Subsection (2.1) does not apply in respect of a prescribed form, receipt or document, or prescribed information, that is filed with the Minister on or after the day specified, in respect of the form, receipt, document or information, in subsection 37(11) or paragraph (*m*) of the definition "investment tax credit" in subsection 127(9).

History: S. 220(2.2) was added by S.C. 2013, c. 34, s. 350(1), applicable in respect of a prescribed form, receipt and document, and prescribed information, filed with the Minister of National Revenue on or after November 17, 2005 other than a prescribed form, receipt or document, or prescribed information, in respect of which the Minister of National Revenue has received, before November 17, 2005, a request made in writing with the Minister that the Minister waive the filing requirements in subsection 37(11) and paragraph (*m*) of the definition "investment tax credit" in subsection 127(9) that apply, but for any waiver, to the expenditures to which the prescribed form, receipt or document, or prescribed information, relates.

► 220(3) ◄

(3) Extensions for returns. The Minister may at any time extend the time for making a return under this Act.

Tax Topics: No. 2438, Minister Has Discretion To Provide Relief From the Tax-Return-Filing Requirement for Dividend Returns; No. 2422, If the Minister Is Too Busy, Can the FCA Help Out? A Comment on *Bonnybrook Park v. MNR*.

► 220(3.1) ◄

(3.1) Waiver of penalty or interest. The Minister may, on or before the day that is ten calendar years after the end of a taxation year of a taxpayer (or in the case of a partnership, a fiscal period of the partnership) or on application by the taxpayer or partnership on or before that day, waive or cancel all or any portion of any penalty or interest otherwise payable under this Act by the taxpayer or partnership in respect of that taxation year or fiscal period, and notwithstanding subsections 152(4) to (5), any assessment of the interest and penalties payable by the taxpayer or partnership shall be made that is necessary to take into account the cancellation of the penalty or interest.

Related Sections: S. 152(4) Assessment and reassessment; s. 165(1.2) Determination of fair market value; s. 248(1) Definitions.

Canadian Tax Foundation: Friedman and Stirling, *Voluntary Disclosures Continue To Increase*, 2016 Canadian Tax Highlights 24(3):1–2; Ryan, *The Voluntary Disclosures Program from the Taxpayer's Perspective*, 2012 Tax Dispute Resolution, Compliance and Administration Conference 1:1–21; West and McMechan, *Fairness Request 10-Year Limitation*, 2011 Canadian Tax Highlights 19(6):8–9; Morris, *Current Cases: Federal Court — An Interesting Interpretation (Bozzer v. The Queen et al., 2010 DTC 5025)*, 2010 Canadian Tax Journal 2:340–346; Stilwell and Russell, *A Brief Review of Canada Revenue Agency's Voluntary Disclosures Program*, 2010 Atlantic Provinces Tax Conference 10B:1–21; Watson, *Taxpayer Relief*, 2010 Atlantic Provinces Tax Conference 10A:1–17; Bharwani, *Voluntary Disclosures Program in Canada — Representing the Client Through the Process*, 2010 Prairie Provinces Tax Conference 5:1–43; Campbell, *Taxpayer Relief Provisions — Voluntary Disclosure and Request for Cancellation or Waiver of Penalties and Interest*, 2009 British Columbia Tax Conference 14:1–27; Kepes and Winters, *Dealing with the CRA: An Update to the Voluntary Disclosure Program, Taxpayer Relief (Fairness) Provisions, and Matters Related to Dispute Resolution*, 2007 Ontario Tax Conference 5A:2–46; Friedlan, *Limitation on the Waiver of Penalty and Interest*, 2007 Tax for the Owner-Manager 7(2):4–5; Hirsch, *Fairness Package Update*, 1998 Conference Report 24:1–32.

Tax Profile: February 2018 — New Voluntary Disclosure Program Discloses No Intention To Attract Volunteers; January 2012 — Highlights from the 2011 Ontario Tax Conference: Q&A with the Tax Administration Panel; September 2009 — Fixing Tax Mistakes; December 2008 — Canadian Voluntary Disclosure Program; October 2006 — Tax Controversies in Canada: A Variety of Issues; December 2005 — Voluntary Disclosures: Holding the CRA to Account.

Tax Topics: No. 2384, Canada's New Voluntary Disclosure Program; No. 2110, When is Voluntary Disclosure Voluntary?; No. 2058, Bozzer: An Interest-ing Victory For All Canadian Taxpayers; No. 2031, Conjecture and The Voluntary Disclosure Program; No. 1645, Federal Court Allows Fairness Application; No. 1572, Auditor General's Report; No. 1581, Fairness Provisions; No. 1540, Seeking Absolution — Remission Orders; No. 1537, Can Applications for Judicial Review Succeed?.

Forms: RC199 — Taxpayer Agreement — Voluntary Disclosures Program.

Guides: T4060 Canada Customs and Revenue Agency's Collections Policies Individual Income Tax (T1).

Information Circulars: IC 98-1R4 Collections Policies; IC 00-1R4 Voluntary disclosures program; IC 07-1 Taxpayer Relief Provisions.

Cases: The standard of review of the decision was reasonableness. The questions for determining voluntariness were whether the CRA was engaged in enforcement action, and if so, whether enforcement action was likely to uncover the unfiled returns. *Matthew Boadi Professional Corp. v. Canada (AG),* 2018 DTC 5013 (FC)

The taxpayer had ample opportunity to make submissions concerning his relief application and the Minister was not obligated to discuss these with the taxpayer prior to reaching his first- and second-level decisions. Despite his arguments to the contrary, the taxpayer was not denied procedural fairness, the Minister's second-level decision was reasonable, and the Minister did not err in the way he exercised his discretionary power. *Larouche v. Canada,* 2015 DTC 5035 (F.C.)

The Minister's refusal to cancel interest and penalties was fair and reasonable. While the Court was sympathetic to the taxpayer's circumstances, he prioritized more than basic necessities, including repaying other loans to third parties, over tax debts. *Bird v. Canada (CRA),* 2014 DTC 5117 (F.C.)

The Minister rejected the taxpayer's allegation of financial hardship, and granted only partial relief from interest and penalties. The taxpayer had a record of tax non-compliance and evasion, and provided no evidence of financial hardship. There was no denial of procedural fairness, and the Minister's decision was transparent, intelligible, and reasonable *Higgins v. Canada (AG),* 2014 DTC 5025 (F.C.C.)

The Minister's decision not to grant relief was reasonable, though the resulting penalty was made harsh by applying to each family member owning a small percentage of property, whereas it would have applied only once if there had been only one owner. *Suissa v. Canada (AG),* 2013 DTC 5158 (F.C.)

A corporation treated its sole shareholder as an independent contractor despite CRA statements that he was an employee. Interest and penalties were imposed for its failure to withhold and remit tax and CPP on his income. It requested relief on the basis that he had personally remitted tax and CPP on that income and therefore the CRA had the benefit of that money while corporate interest was accruing, but relief was denied. *1148902 Ontario Limited v. CRA,* 2013 DTC 5120 (F.C.)

The Minister refused to waive interest on grounds that the request was made beyond the 10-year limitation period. However, s. 220(3.1) does not refer to the year of assessment. While the tax debt arose in 1989-1990, interest accrued in each subsequent year. The Minister could provide relief for any interest accrued within 10 years of the relief application. *Bozzer v. The Queen et al.,* 2011 DTC 5106 (F.C.A.), reversing 2010 DTC 5025 (F.C.)

There was a 31-month delay between the filing of Notices of Objection and the commencement of a review. This delay must be considered by the Minister in assessing a fairness request for the waiver of interest. *Hillier v. A.G. Canada,* 2001 DTC 5399 (F.C.A.), reversing 2000 DTC 6627 (F.C.T.D.)

Since the taxpayers' illnesses had not prevented them from complying with the Act, they could not be heard to argue that the Minister had disregarded relevant facts, in the exercise of his discretion not to waive the interest owing by them. *Young et al. v. The Queen,* 98 DTC 6028 (F.C.T.D.)

The Minister's refusal to waive interest was upheld when the evidence confirmed that the taxpayer's situation was not entirely a result of extraneous circumstances (the operative criterion in the guidelines set out in IC 92-2) and there was nothing to suggest that the Minister had not fulfilled his duty to act fairly or that he had ignored relevant evidence. *Towers v. The Queen,* 94 DTC 6118 (F.C.T.D.)

▶ 220(3.2) ◀

(3.2) Late, amended or revoked elections. The Minister may extend the time for making an election or grant permission to amend or revoke an election if

(*a*) the election was otherwise required to be made by a taxpayer or by a partnership, under a prescribed provision, on or before a day in a taxation year of the taxpayer (or in the case of a partnership, a fiscal period of the partnership); and

(*b*) the taxpayer or the partnership applies, on or before the day that is ten calendar years after the end of the taxation year or the fiscal period, to the Minister for that extension or permission.

Related Regulations: 600.

Related Sections: S. 13(4) Exchanges of property; s. 14(6) Exchange of property; s. 44(1) Exchanges of property; s. 66.7(7)(*c*) Acquisition of Canadian resource property; s. 66.7(7)(*d*) Acquisition of Canadian resource property; s. 66.7(7)(*e*) Acquisition of Canadian resource property; s. 66.7(8)(*c*) Acquisition of foreign resource property; s. 66.7(8)(*d*) Acquisition of foreign resource property; s. 66.7(8)(*e*) Acquisition of foreign resource property; s. 70(6.2) Election; s. 70(9) When subsection (9.01) applies; s. 70(9.1) When subsection (9.11) applies; s. 70(9.3) When subsection (9.31) applies; s. 72(2) Election by legal representative and transferee re reserves; s. 73(1) Inter vivos transfers by individuals; s. 104(14) Election by trust and preferred beneficiary; 220(3.3) Date of late election, amended election or revocation; 220(3.4) Assessments; 220(3.5) Penalty for late filed, amended or revoked elections; 220(3.6) Unpaid balance of penalty; 220(3.7) Idem; Part VI.

Canadian Tax Foundation: Cepparo, *No Shift to Cost-Recovery Method for Capital Gains,* 2015 Canadian Tax Highlights 23(1):10–11; Hirsch, *Fairness Package Update,* 1998 Conference Report 24:1–32.

Tax Profile: September 2009 — Fixing Tax Mistakes; June 2007 — Tax Impact of Modifying or Unwinding Transactions — Canada.

Income Tax Folios: *Secondary* — S1-F3-C2 Principal Residence.

Information Circulars: IC 07-1 Taxpayer Relief Provisions.

Cases: In response to the taxpayer trust's Fairness legislation application, the Minister's representatives decided that the trust was not entitled to relief from the late filing of certain preferred beneficiary elections. This decision not to allow the Fairness applications was reasonable and was not based on any error in law. *The Johnston Family 1991 Trust v. M.N.R.,* 99 DTC 5508 (F.C.T.D.).

▶ 220(3.201) ◀

(3.201) Joint election — pension income split. On application by a taxpayer, the Minister may extend the time for making an election, or grant permission to amend or revoke an election, under section 60.03 if

(*a*) the application is made on or before the day that is three calendar years after the taxpayer's filing-due date for the taxation year to which the election applies; and

(*b*) the taxpayer is resident in Canada

(i) if the taxpayer is deceased at the time of the application, at the time that is immediately before the taxpayer's death, or

(ii) in any other case, at the time of the application.

▶ 220(3.21) ◀

(3.21) Designations and allocations. For the purpose of subsection (3.2),

(*a*) a designation in any form prescribed for the purpose of paragraph 80(2)(*i*) or any of subsections 80(5) to (11) or 80.03(7) is deemed to be an election under a prescribed provision of this Act;

(*a*.1) a designation is deemed to be an election under a prescribed provision of this Act if the designation is made under the definition *principal residence* in section 54; and

(*b*) a designation or allocation under subsection 132.11(6) is deemed to be an election under a prescribed provision of this Act.

History: S. 220(3.21)(*a*.1) was added by S.C. 2017, c. 33, s. 76(1), applicable to taxation years that end after October 2, 2016.

▶ 220(3.3) ◀

(3.3) Date of late election, amended election or revocation. Where, under subsection (3.2), the Minister has extended the time for making an election or granted permission to amend or revoke an election,

(*a*) the election or the amended election, as the case may be, shall be deemed to have been made on the day on or before which the election was otherwise required to be made and in the manner in which the election was otherwise required to be made, and, in the case of an amendment to an election, that election shall be deemed, otherwise than for the purposes of this section, never to have been made; and

(*b*) the election that was revoked shall be deemed, otherwise than for the purposes of this section, never to have been made.

▶ 220(3.4) ◀

(3.4) Assessments. Notwithstanding subsections 152(4), (4.01), (4.1) and (5), such assessment of the tax, interest and penalties payable by each taxpayer in respect of any taxation year that began before the day an application is made under subsection (3.2) to the Minister shall be made as is necessary to take into account the election, the amended election or the revocation, as the case may be, referred to in subsection (3.3).

▶ 220(3.5) ◀

(3.5) Penalty for late filed, amended or revoked elections. Where, on application by a taxpayer or a partnership, the Minister extends the time for making an election or grants permission to amend or revoke an election (other than an extension or permission under subsection (3.201)), the taxpayer or the partnership, as the case may be, is liable to a penalty equal to the lesser of

(*a*) $8,000, and

(*b*) the product obtained when $100 is multiplied by the number of complete months from the day on or before which the election was required to be made to the day the application was made in a form satisfactory to the Minister.

Tax Window Files: Filing Due Date for Elections, *September 18, 2013*, CRA Document No. 2013-0487871I7.

▶ 220(3.6) ◀

(3.6) Unpaid balance of penalty. The Minister shall, with all due dispatch, examine each election, amended election and revoked election referred to in subsection (3.3), assess any penalty payable and send a notice of assessment to the taxpayer or the partnership, as the case may be, and the taxpayer or the partnership, as the case may be, shall pay forthwith to the Receiver General the amount, if any, by which the penalty so assessed exceeds the total of all amounts previously paid on account of that penalty.

▶ 220(3.7) ◀

(3.7) Idem. The provisions of Divisions I and J of Part I apply, with such modifications as the circumstances require, to an assessment made under this section as though it had been made under section 152.

▶ 220(3.8) ◀

(3.8) Dishonoured instruments. For the purposes of this Act and section 155.1 of the *Financial Administration Act*

(*a*) any charge that becomes payable at any time by a person under the *Financial Administration Act* in respect of an instrument tendered in payment or settlement of an amount that is payable or remittable under this Act is deemed to be an amount that becomes payable or remittable by the person at that time under this Act;

(*b*) sections 152, 158 and 159, subsections 161(1), (2) and (11), sections 162 to 167 and Division J of this Part are applicable to the amount deemed to become payable or remittable by this subsection with any modifications that the circumstances require;

(*c*) Part II of the *Interest and Administrative Charges Regulations* does not apply to the charge; and

(*d*) any debt under subsection 155.1(3) of the *Financial Administration Act* in respect of the charge is deemed to be extinguished at the time the total of the amount and any applicable interest under this Act is paid.

▶ 220(4) ◀

(4) Security. The Minister may, if the Minister considers it advisable in a particular case, accept security for payment of any amount that is or may become payable under this Act.

Related Regulations: 2200.

Related Sections: S. 159(2) Certificate before distribution.

Information Circulars: IC 98-1R4 Collections Policies.

▶ 220(4.1) ◀

(4.1) Idem. Where a taxpayer has objected to or appealed from an assessment under this Act, the Minister shall, while the objection or appeal is outstanding, accept adequate security furnished by or on behalf of the taxpayer for payment of the amount in controversy except to the extent that the Minister may collect the amount because of subsection 225.1(7).

Related Sections: S. 225.1(7) Where ss. (1) to (4) do not apply — large corporations; s. 248(1) Definitions.

▶ 220(4.2) ◀

(4.2) Surrender of excess security. Where at any time a taxpayer requests in writing that the Minister surrender any security accepted by the Minister under subsection (4) or (4.1), the Minister shall surrender the security to the extent that the value of the security exceeds the total of amounts payable under this Act by the taxpayer at that time.

▶ 220(4.3) ◀

(4.3) Security furnished by a member institution of a deposit insurance corporation. The Minister shall accept adequate security furnished by or on behalf of a taxpayer that is a member institution in relation to a deposit insurance corporation (within the meaning assigned by subsection 137.1(5)) for payment of

(*a*) the tax payable under this Act by the taxpayer for a taxation year, to the extent that the amount of that tax exceeds the amount that that tax would be if no amount that the taxpayer is obliged to repay to the corporation were included under paragraph 137.1(10)(*a*) or (*b*) in computing the taxpayer's income for the year or a preceding taxation year, and

(*b*) interest payable under this Act by the taxpayer on the amount determined under paragraph (*a*),

until the earlier of

(*c*) the day on which the taxpayer's obligation referred to in paragraph (*a*) to repay the amount to the corporation is settled or extinguished, and

(*d*) the day that is 10 years after the end of the year.

▶ 220(4.4) ◀

(4.4) Additional security. The adequacy of security furnished by or on behalf of a taxpayer under subsection (4.3) shall be determined by the Minister and the Minister may require additional security to be furnished from time to time by or on behalf of the taxpayer where the Minister determines that the security that has been furnished is no longer adequate.

► 220(4.5) ◄

(4.5) Security for departure tax. If an individual who is deemed by subsection 128.1(4) to have disposed of a property (other than a right to a benefit under, or an interest in a trust governed by, an employee benefit plan) at any particular time in a taxation year (in this section referred to as the individual's "emigration year") elects, in prescribed manner on or before the individual's balance-due day for the emigration year, that this subsection and subsections (4.51) to (4.54) apply in respect of the emigration year,

(*a*) the Minister shall, until the individual's balance-due day for a particular taxation year that begins after the particular time, accept adequate security furnished by or on behalf of the individual on or before the individual's balance-due day for the emigration year for the lesser of

(i) the amount determined by the formula

$$A - B - [((A - B)/A) \times C]$$

where

A is the total amount of taxes under Parts I and I.1 that would be payable by the individual for the emigration year if the exclusion or deduction of each amount referred to in paragraph 161(7)(*a*) were not taken into account,

B is the total amount of taxes under those Parts that would have been so payable if each property (other than a right to a benefit under, or an interest in a trust governed by, an employee benefit plan) deemed by subsection 128.1(4) to have been disposed of at the particular time, and that has not been subsequently disposed of before the beginning of the particular year, were not deemed by subsection 128.1(4) to have been disposed of by the individual at the particular time, and

C is the total of all amounts deemed under this or any other Act to have been paid on account of the individual's tax under this Part for the emigration year, and

(ii) if the particular year immediately follows the emigration year, the amount determined under subparagraph (i), and in any other case, the amount determined under this paragraph in respect of the individual for the taxation year that immediately precedes the particular year, and

(*b*) except for the purposes of subsections 161(2), (4) and (4.01),

(i) interest under this Act for any period that ends on the individual's balance-due day for the particular year and throughout which security is accepted by the Minister, and

(ii) any penalty under this Act computed with reference to an individual's tax payable for the year that was, without reference to this paragraph, unpaid

shall be computed as if the particular amount for which adequate security has been accepted under this subsection were an amount paid by the individual on account of the particular amount.

Tax Profile: December 2008 — Tax Planning for Emigration from Canada to the United States; September 2008 — Mission Impossible: The Provision of Private Company Shares as Security for Canadian Departure Tax; August 2003 — Taxpayer Emigration: The Provision of Security for Departure Tax.

Tax Topics: No. 1850, Elections Available Under the Emigration Rules.

Forms: T1244 — Election, Under Subsection 220(4.5) of The Income Tax Act, To Defer The Payment of Tax on Income Relating to the Deemed Disposition of Property.

► 220(4.51) ◄

(4.51) Deemed security. If an individual (other than a trust) elects under subsection (4.5) that that subsection apply in respect of a taxation year, for the purposes of this subsection and subsections (4.5) and (4.52) to (4.54), the Minister is deemed to have accepted at any time after the election is made adequate security for a total amount of taxes payable under Parts I and I.1 by the individual for the emigration year equal to the lesser of

(*a*) the total amount of those taxes that would be payable for the year by a trust resident in Canada (other than a graduated rate estate or a qualified disability trust as defined in subsection 122(3)) the taxable income of which for the year is $50,000, and

(*b*) the greatest amount for which the Minister is required to accept security furnished by or on behalf of the individual under subsection (4.5) at that time in respect of the emigration year,

and that security is deemed to have been furnished by the individual before the individual's balance-due day for the emigration year.

History: S. 220(4.51)(*a*) was replaced by S.C. 2014, c. 39, s. 67(1), applicable to the 2016 and subsequent taxation years, and formerly read:

(*a*) the total amount of those taxes that would be payable for the year by an *inter vivos* trust resident in Canada (other than a trust described in subsection 122(2)) the taxable income of which for the year is $50,000, and

► 220(4.52) ◄

(4.52) Limit. Notwithstanding subsections (4.5) and (4.51), the Minister is deemed at any time not to have accepted security under subsection (4.5) in respect of an individual's emigration year for any amount greater than the amount, if any, by which

(*a*) the total amount of taxes that would be payable by the individual under Parts I and I.1 for the year if the exclusion or deduction of each amount referred to in paragraph 161(7)(*a*), in respect of which the day determined under paragraph 161(7)(*b*) is after that time, were not taken into account

exceeds

(*b*) the total amount of taxes that would be determined under paragraph (*a*) if this Act were read without reference to subsection 128.1(4).

► 220(4.53) ◄

(4.53) Inadequate security. Subject to subsection (4.7), if it is determined at any particular time that security accepted by the Minister under subsection (4.5) is not adequate to secure the particular amount for which it was furnished by or on behalf of an individual,

(*a*) subject to a subsequent application of this subsection, the security shall be considered after the particular time to secure only the amount for which it is adequate security at the particular time;

(*b*) the Minister shall notify the individual in writing of the determination and shall accept adequate security, for all or any part of the particular amount, furnished by or on behalf of the individual within 90 days after the day of notification; and

(*c*) any security accepted in accordance with paragraph (*b*) is deemed to have been accepted by the Minister under subsection (4.5) on account of the particular amount at the particular time.

► 220(4.54) ◄

(4.54) Extension of time. If in the opinion of the Minister it would be just and equitable to do so, the Minister may at any time extend

(*a*) the time for making an election under subsection (4.5);

(*b*) the time for furnishing and accepting security under subsection (4.5); or

(*c*) the 90-day period for the acceptance of security under paragraph (4.53)(*b*).

► 220(4.6) ◄

(4.6) Security for tax on distributions of taxable Canadian property to non-resident beneficiaries. Where

(*a*) solely because of the application of subsection 107(5), paragraphs 107(2)(*a*) to (*c*) do not apply to a distribution by a trust in a particular taxation year (in this section referred to as the trust's "distribution year") of taxable Canadian property, and

(*b*) the trust elects, in prescribed manner on or before the trust's balance-due day for the distribution year, that this subsection and subsections (4.61) to (4.63) apply in respect of the distribution year,

the following rules apply:

(*c*) the Minister shall, until the trust's balance-due day for a subsequent taxation year, accept adequate security furnished by or on behalf of the trust on or before the trust's balance-due day for the distribution year for the lesser of

(i) the amount determined by the formula

$$A - B - [((A - B)/A) \times C]$$

where

A is the total amount of taxes under Parts I and I.1 that would be payable by the trust for the distribution year if the exclusion or deduction of each amount referred to in paragraph 161(7)(*a*) were not taken into account,

B is the total amount of taxes under those Parts that would have been so payable if the rules in subsection 107(2) (other than the election referred to in that subsection) had applied to each disposition by the trust in the distribution year of property (other than property subsequently disposed of before the beginning of the subsequent year) to which paragraph (*a*) applies, and

C is the total of all amounts deemed under this or any other Act to have been paid on account of the trust's tax under this Part for the distribution year, and

(ii) where the subsequent year immediately follows the distribution year, the amount determined under subparagraph (i), and in any other case, the amount determined under this paragraph in respect of the trust for the taxation year that immediately precedes the subsequent year, and

(*d*) except for the purposes of subsections 161(2), (4) and (4.01),

(i) interest under this Act for any period that ends on the trust's balance-due day for the subsequent year and throughout which security is accepted by the Minister, and

(ii) any penalty under this Act computed with reference to the trust's tax payable for the year that was, without reference to this paragraph, unpaid

shall be computed as if the particular amount for which adequate security has been accepted under this subsection were an amount paid by the trust on account of the particular amount.

► 220(4.61) ◄

(4.61) Limit. Notwithstanding subsection (4.6), the Minister is deemed at any time not to have accepted security under that subsection in respect of a trust's distribution year for any amount greater than the amount, if any, by which

(*a*) the total amount of taxes that would be payable by the trust under Parts I and I.1 for the year if the exclusion or deduction of each amount referred to in paragraph 161(7)(*a*), in respect of which the day determined under paragraph 161(7)(*b*) is after that time, were not taken into account

exceeds

(*b*) the total amount of taxes that would be determined under paragraph (*a*) if paragraphs 107(2)(*a*) to (*c*) had applied to each distribution by the trust in the year of property to which paragraph (1)(*a*) applies.

► 220(4.62) ◄

(4.62) Inadequate security. Subject to subsection (4.7), where it is determined at any particular time that security accepted by the Minister under subsection (4.6) is not adequate to secure the particular amount for which it was furnished by or on behalf of a trust,

(*a*) subject to a subsequent application of this subsection, the security shall be considered after the particular time to secure only the amount for which it is adequate security at the particular time;

(*b*) the Minister shall notify the trust in writing of the determination and shall accept adequate security, for all or any part of the particular amount, furnished by or on behalf of the trust within 90 days after the notification; and

(*c*) any security accepted in accordance with paragraph (*b*) is deemed to have been accepted by the Minister under subsection (4.6) on account of the particular amount at the particular time.

► 220(4.63) ◄

(4.63) Extension of time. Where in the opinion of the Minister it would be just and equitable to do so, the Minister may at any time extend

(*a*) the time for making an election under subsection (4.6);

(*b*) the time for furnishing and accepting security under subsection (4.6); or

(*c*) the 90-day period for the acceptance of the security under paragraph (4.62)(*b*).

► 220(4.7) ◄

(4.7) Undue hardship. If, in respect of any period of time, the Minister determines that an individual who has made an election under either subsection (4.5) or (4.6)

(*a*) cannot, without undue hardship, pay or reasonably arrange to have paid on the individual's behalf, an amount of taxes to which security under that subsection would relate, and

(*b*) cannot, without undue hardship, provide or reasonably arrange to have provided on the individual's behalf, adequate security under that subsection,

the Minister may, in respect of the election, accept for the period security different from, or of lesser value than, that which the Minister would otherwise accept under that subsection.

► 220(4.71) ◄

(4.71) Limit. In making a determination under subsection (4.7), the Minister shall ignore any transaction that is a disposition, lease, encumbrance, mortgage, hypothec, or other voluntary restriction by a person or partnership of the person's or partnership's rights in respect of a property, if the transaction can reasonably be considered to have been entered into for the purpose of influencing the determination.

► 220(5) ◄

(5) Administration of oaths. Any officer or servant employed in connection with the administration or enforcement of this Act, if designated by the Minister for the purpose, may, in the course of that employment, administer oaths and take and receive affidavits, declarations and affirmations for the purposes of or incidental to the administration or enforcement of this Act or regulations made thereunder, and every officer or servant so designated has for those purposes all the powers of a commissioner for administering oaths or taking affidavits.

Related Sections: S. 248(1), "employee", "employment", "property"; ITAR s. 65.1 Part XV of amended Act

► 220(6) ◄

(6) Assignment by corporation. Notwithstanding section 67 of the *Financial Administration Act* and any other provision of a law of Canada or a province, a corporation may assign any amount payable to it under this Act.

► 220(7) ◄

(7) Effect of assignment. An assignment referred to in subsection (6) is not binding on Her Majesty in right of Canada and, without limiting the generality of the foregoing,

(*a*) the Minister is not required to pay to the assignee the assigned amount;

(*b*) the assignment does not create any liability of Her Majesty in right of Canada to the assignee; and

(*c*) the rights of the assignee are subject to all equitable and statutory rights of set-off in favour of Her Majesty in right of Canada.

SECTION 221: Regulations

► 221(1) ◄

(1) Regulations. The Governor in Council may make regulations

(*a*) prescribing anything that, by this Act, is to be prescribed or is to be determined or regulated by regulation;

Related Regulations: Part II; Part IX.

Related Sections: S. 248(1), "common-law partner".

Tax Window Files: Construction Activities Reporting, *Technical Interpretation, Business and Partnerships Division, March 25, 2008,* CRA Document No. 2007-0226971E5; Information Return — Reimbursement of Expenses, *Technical Interpretation, Business and Partnerships Division, November 2, 2007,* CRA Document No. 2007-0229201E5; Returns for Deceased Persons, *Minister's Correspondence, June 20, 2007,* CRA Document No. 2007-0237141M4; Information Return — Real Estate Developer, *Technical Interpretation, Business and Partnerships Division, November 15, 2006,* CRA Document No. 2006-0202971I7; Limitation Period for Tax Debt Collection, *Technical Interpretation, Reorganizations and Resources Division, March 22, 2006,* CRA Document No. 2005-0133061E5; Construction Activities — Payments to Subcontractors, *Technical Interpretation, Business and Partnerships Division, April 14, 2005,* CRA Document No. 2004-0081371I7; Education Assistance Paid to Status Indians, *Technical Interpretation, Financial Industries Division, May 14, 2003,* CRA Document No. 2003-0015707.

Cases: Allegations that an income tax regulation is *ultra vires* have been made in several cases, but have never succeeded. See for instance *Attorney General of Canada v. Compagnie de Publication La Presse Limitée,* 66 DTC 5492 (S.C.C.) and *Regina v. Kerns Motor Town Sales Ltd.,* 68 DTC 5141 (B.C.C.A.).

(*b*) prescribing the evidence required to establish facts relevant to assessments under this Act;

(*c*) to facilitate the assessment of tax where deductions or exemptions of a taxpayer have changed in a taxation year;

(*d*) requiring any class of persons to make information returns respecting any class of information required in connection with assessments under this Act;

(*d*.1) requiring any person or partnership to provide any information — including their name, address, business number, Social Insurance Number or trust account number — to any class of persons required to make an information return containing that information;

(*d*.2) requiring any class of persons to make information available to the public for the purpose of making information returns respecting any class of information required in connection with assessments under this Act;

(*e*) requiring a person who is, by a regulation made under paragraph (*d*), required to make an information return to supply a copy of the information return or of a prescribed part thereof to the person to whom the information return or part thereof relates;

(*f*) (Repealed by 1998, c. 19, s. 222(2).)

(*g*) providing for the retention by way of deduction or set-off of the amount of a taxpayer's income tax or other indebtedness under this Act out of any amount or amounts that may be or become payable by Her Majesty to the taxpayer in respect of salary or wages;

(*h*) defining the classes of persons who may be regarded as dependent for the purposes of this Act;

(*i*) defining the classes of non-resident persons who may be regarded for the purposes of this Act

(i) as a spouse or common-law partner supported by a taxpayer, or

(ii) as a person dependent or wholly dependent on a taxpayer for support,

and specifying the evidence required to establish that a person belongs to any such class; and

(*j*) generally to carry out the purposes and provisions of this Act.

History: S. 221(1)(*d*.1) was replaced by S.C. 2018, c. 12, s. 32(1), applicable to the 2018 and subsequent taxation years, and formerly read:

(*d*.1) requiring any person or partnership to provide any information including their name, address, Social Insurance Number or business number to any class of persons required to make an information return containing that information;

► 221(2) ◄

(2) Effect. A regulation made under this Act shall have effect from the date it is published in the *Canada Gazette* or at such time thereafter as may be specified in the regulation unless the regulation provides otherwise and it

(*a*) has a relieving effect only;

(*b*) corrects an ambiguous or deficient enactment that was not in accordance with the objects of this Act or the *Income Tax Regulations*;

(*c*) is consequential on an amendment to this Act that is applicable before the date the regulation is published in the *Canada Gazette*; or

(*d*) gives effect to a budgetary or other public announcement, in which case the regulation shall not, except where paragraph (*a*), (*b*) or (*c*) applies, have effect

(i) before the date on which the announcement was made, in the case of a deduction or withholding from an amount paid or credited, and

(ii) before the taxation year in which the announcement is made, in any other case.

Related Sections: S. 248(1), "amount", "assessment", "employee", "non-resident", "prescribed", "regulation", "salary or wages".

► 221(3) ◄

(3) Regulations binding Crown. Regulations made under paragraph (1)(*d*) or (*e*) are binding on Her Majesty in right of Canada or a province.

► 221(4) ◄

(4) Incorporation by reference. A regulation made under this Act may incorporate by reference material as amended from time to time.

SECTION 221.01: Providing information returns in electronic format

A person may provide an information return electronically under subsection 209(5) of the *Income Tax Regulations* if the criteria specified by the Minister are met.

History: S. 221.01 was added by S.C. 2017, c. 20, s. 28(1), in force January 1, 2018.

Related Regulations: 209(5).

SECTION 221.1: Application of interest

For greater certainty, where an amendment to this Act or an amendment or enactment that relates to this Act applies to or in respect of any transaction, event or time, or any taxation year, fiscal period or other period of time or part thereof (in this section referred to as the "application time") occurring, or that is, before the day on which the amendment or enactment is assented to or promulgated, for the purposes of the provisions of this Act that provide for payment of, or liability to, any interest, the amendment or enactment shall, unless a contrary intention is evident, be deemed to have come into force at the beginning of the last taxation year beginning before the application time.

SECTION 221.2: Re-appropriation of amounts

► 221.2(1) ◄

(1) Re-appropriation of amounts. Where a particular amount was appropriated to an amount (in this section referred to as the "debt") that is or may become payable by a person under any enactment referred to in paragraphs 223(1)(*a*) to (*d*), the Minister may, on application by the person, appropriate the particular amount, or a part thereof, to another amount that is or may become payable under any such enactment and, for the purposes of any such enactment,

(*a*) the later appropriation shall be deemed to have been made at the time of the earlier appropriation;

(*b*) the earlier appropriation shall be deemed not to have been made to the extent of the later appropriation; and

(*c*) the particular amount shall be deemed not to have been paid on account of the debt to the extent of the later appropriation.

► 221.2(2) ◄

(2) Re-appropriation of amounts. Where a particular amount was appropriated to an amount (in this section referred to as the "debt") that is or may become payable by a person under this Act, the *Excise Tax Act*, the *Air Travellers Security Charge Act* or the *Excise Act, 2001*, the Minister may, on application by the person, appropriate the particular amount, or a part of it, to another amount that is or may become payable under any of those Acts and, for the purposes of any of those Acts,

(*a*) the later appropriation is deemed to have been made at the time of the earlier appropriation;

(*b*) the earlier appropriation is deemed not to have been made to the extent of the later appropriation; and

(*c*) the particular amount is deemed not to have been paid on account of the debt to the extent of the later appropriation.

SECTION 222: [Limitation period for collection of tax debts]

► 222(1) ◄

(1) Definitions. The following definitions apply in this section.

"action" —"action" means an action to collect a tax debt of a taxpayer and includes a proceeding in a court and anything done by the Minister under subsection 129(2), 131(3), 132(2) or 164(2), section 203 or any provision of this Part.

"tax debt" —"tax debt" means any amount payable by a taxpayer under this Act.

► 222(2) ◄

(2) Debts to Her Majesty. A tax debt is a debt due to Her Majesty and is recoverable as such in the Federal Court or any other court of competent jurisdiction or in any other manner provided by this Act.

Information Circulars: IC 98-1R4 Collections Policies.

► 222(3) ◄

(3) No actions after limitation period. The Minister may not commence an action to collect a tax debt after the end of the limitation period for the collection of the tax debt.

► 222(4) ◄

(4) Limitation period. The limitation period for the collection of a tax debt of a taxpayer

(*a*) begins

(i) if a notice of assessment, or a notice referred to in subsection 226(1), in respect of the tax debt is sent to or served on the taxpayer, after March 3, 2004, on the day that is 90 days after the day on which the last one of those notices is sent or served, and

(ii) if subparagraph (i) does not apply and the tax debt was payable on March 4, 2004, or would have been payable on that date but for a limitation period that otherwise applied to the collection of the tax debt, on March 4, 2004; and

(*b*) ends, subject to subsection (8), on the day that is 10 years after the day on which it begins.

History: S. 222(4)(*a*)(i) was replaced by S.C. 2010, c. 25, s. 65, in force on Royal Assent, December 15, 2010. S. 222(4)(*a*)(i) formerly read:

(i) if a notice of assessment, or a notice referred to in subsection 226(1), in respect of the tax debt is mailed to or served on the taxpayer, after March 3, 2004, on the day that is 90 days after the day on which the last one of those notices is mailed or served, and

► 222(5) ◄

(5) Limitation period restarted. The limitation period described in subsection (4) for the collection of a tax debt of a taxpayer restarts (and ends, subject to subsection (8), on the day that is 10 years after the day on which it restarts) on any day, before it would otherwise end, on which

(*a*) the taxpayer acknowledges the tax debt in accordance with subsection (6);

(*b*) the Minister commences an action to collect the tax debt; or

(*c*) the Minister, under subsection 159(3) or 160(2) or paragraph 227(10)(*a*), assesses any person in respect of the tax debt.

► 222(6) ◄

(6) Acknowledgement of tax debts. A taxpayer acknowledges a tax debt if the taxpayer

(*a*) promises, in writing, to pay the tax debt;

(*b*) makes a written acknowledgement of the tax debt, whether or not a promise to pay can be inferred from the acknowledgement and whether or not it contains a refusal to pay; or

(*c*) makes a payment, including a purported payment by way of a negotiable instrument that is dishonoured, on account of the tax debt.

► 222(7) ◄

(7) Agent or legal representative. For the purposes of this section, an acknowledgement made by a taxpayer's agent or legal representative has the same effect as if it were made by the taxpayer.

► 222(8) ◄

(8) Extension of limitation period. In computing the day on which a limitation period ends, there shall be added the number of days on which one or more of the following is the case:

(*a*) the Minister may not, because of any of subsections 225.1(2) to (5), take any of the actions described in subsection 225.1(1) in respect of the tax debt;

(*b*) the Minister has accepted and holds security in lieu of payment of the tax debt;

(*c*) if the taxpayer was resident in Canada on the applicable date described in paragraph (4)(*a*) in respect of the tax debt, the taxpayer is non-resident; or

(*d*) an action that the Minister may otherwise take in respect of the tax debt is restricted or not permitted under any provision of the *Bankruptcy and Insolvency Act*, of the *Companies' Creditors Arrangement Act* or of the *Farm Debt Mediation Act*.

► 222(9) ◄

(9) Bar to claims. Notwithstanding any law of Canada or a province, Her Majesty is not liable for any claim that arises because the Minister collected a tax debt after the end of any limitation period that applied to the collection of the tax debt and before March 4, 2004.

► 222(10) ◄

(10) Orders after March 3, 2004 and before effect. Notwithstanding any order or judgment made after March 3, 2004 that declares a tax debt not to be payable by a taxpayer, or that orders the Minister to reimburse to a taxpayer a tax debt collected by the Minister, because a limitation period that applied to the collection of the tax debt ended before royal assent to any measure giving effect to this section, the tax debt is deemed to have become payable on March 4, 2004.

Information Circulars: IC 98-1R4 Collections Policies.

Cases: Federal income tax collection proceedings are subject to the limitation period in s. 32 of the *Crown Liability and Proceedings Act.* In addition, s. 3(5) of the *B.C. Limitation Act* barred the Crown from collecting the taxpayer's provincial tax debt*The Queen v. Markevich et al.,* 2003 DTC 5185 (S.C.C.), affirming 2001 DTC 5305 (F.C.A.), reversing 99 DTC 5136 (F.C.T.D.).

SECTION 222.1: Court costs

Where an amount is payable by a person to Her Majesty because of an order, judgment or award of a court in respect of the costs of litigation relating to a matter to which this Act applies, subsections 220(4) and (4.2) and sections 223, 224 to 225 and 226 apply to the amount as if the amount were a debt owing by the person to Her Majesty on account of tax payable by the person under this Act.

History: S. 222.1 was added by S.C 1998, c. 19, s. 223(1), applicable to amounts that are payable after this Act is assented to, including amounts that became payable before this Act is assented to, June 18, 1998.

SECTION 223: [Certificates]

► 223(1) ◄

(1) Definition of "amount payable". For the purposes of subsection (2), an "amount payable" by a person means any or all of

(*a*) an amount payable under this Act by the person;

(*b*) an amount payable under the *Employment Insurance Act* by the person;

(*b*.1) an amount payable under the *Unemployment Insurance Act* by the person;

(*c*) an amount payable under the *Canada Pension Plan* by the person; and

(*d*) an amount payable by the person under an Act of a province with which the Minister of Finance has entered into an agreement for the collection of taxes payable to the province under that Act.

Related Sections: S. 225.1 Collection restrictions; s. 248(1), "amount".

Canadian Tax Foundation: Kreklewetz and Siu, *Equitable Interest Takes Priority Over CRA Liens,* 2013 Tax for the Owner-Manager 13(3):6–7.

Information Circulars: IC 98-1R4 Collections Policies.

► 223(2) ◄

(2) Certificates. An amount payable by a person (in this section referred to as a "debtor") that has not been paid or any part of an amount payable by the debtor that has not been paid may be certified by the Minister as an amount payable by the debtor.

Related Sections: S. 223(3) Registration in court; s. 223(4) Costs; s. 223(9) Sale, etc; s. 223(12) Details in certificates and memorials.

Canadian Tax Foundation: Kreklewetz and Siu, *Equitable Interest Takes Priority Over CRA Liens,* 2013 Tax for the Owner-Manager 13(3):6–7.

Cases: The Federal Court did not have jurisdiction to amend a certificate since the certificate, when registered, did not become a judgment or order of the Court but remained a certificate of the Minister who was the proper person to amend it. *The Queen v. Star Treck Holdings Ltd. et al.,* 77 DTC 5311 (F.C.T.D.).

► 223(3) ◄

(3) Registration in court. On production to the Federal Court, a certificate made under subsection (2) in respect of a debtor shall be registered in the Court and when so registered has the same effect, and all proceedings may be taken thereon, as if the certificate were a judgment obtained in the Court against the debtor for a debt in the amount certified plus interest thereon to the day of payment as provided by the statute or statutes referred to in subsection (1) under which the amount is payable and, for the purpose of any such proceedings, the certificate shall be deemed to be a judgment of the Court against the debtor for a debt due to Her Majesty, enforceable in the amount certified plus interest thereon to the day of payment as provided by that statute or statutes.

Related Sections: 223(5) Charge on property; 223(6) Creation of charge; 223(7) Proceedings in respect of memorial; 223(8) Presentation of documents.

Cases: The registration of a certificate within six years of the commencement of the limitation period was capable of supporting a writ of execution. Because the effect of filing a certificate was to make the taxpayer liable to execution, he continued to be liable to make a payment under the Act and his debt was not extinguished under the *B.C. Limitation Act. Ross v. The Queen,* 2002 DTC 6884 (F.C.T.D.)

A taxpayer's RRSP could be seized in the hands of a trust company in Manitoba since writs of execution for the enforcement of judgments of the Federal Court are to be executed in the same manner as similar writs issued out of the Superior Court of the province in which the property to be seized is situated. *M.N.R. v. Sinclair,* 93 DTC 5239 (F.C.T.D.)

An opposition by a taxpayer to the seizure of his RRSP on the grounds that an RRSP constitutes an annuity for a fixed term and, as such, is exempt from seizure under Quebec law was dismissed. The fact that the taxpayer could withdraw the proceeds of his RRSP at any time prior to its maturity meant that it could not be shown that the method of distribution of the revenues accumulated therein was in the nature of a fixed term annuity. *In re Jean Crevier and the Royal Bank of Canada,* 93 DTC 5510 (F.C.T.D.)

Such damages, however, had to be limited to half the sale price and municipal school taxes, so that the co-owner was not entitled to additional damages for the additional land value of which he had allegedly been deprived by being required to reconvey his undivided share. *The Queen v. Lovell et al.,* 93 DTC 5432 (F.C.A.), reversing in part 90 DTC 6116 (F.C.T.D.)

► 223(4) ◄

(4) Costs. All reasonable costs and charges incurred or paid in respect of the registration in the Court of a certificate made under subsection (2) or in respect of any proceedings taken to collect the amount certified are recoverable in like manner as if they had been included in the amount certified in the certificate when it was registered.

► 223(5) ◄

(5) Charge on property. A document issued by the Federal Court evidencing a certificate in respect of a debtor registered under subsection (3), a writ of that Court issued pursuant to the certificate or any notification of the document or writ (such document, writ or notification in this section referred to as a "memorial") may be filed, registered or otherwise recorded for the purpose of creating a charge, lien or priority on, or a binding interest in, property in a province, or any interest in, or for civil law any right in, such property, held by the debtor in the same manner as a document evidencing

(*a*) a judgment of the superior court of the province against a person for a debt owing by the person, or (*b*) an amount payable or required to be remitted by a person in the province in respect of a debt owing to Her Majesty in right of the province

may be filed, registered or otherwise recorded in accordance with or pursuant to the law of the province to create a charge, lien or priority on, or a binding interest in, the property or interest.

History: S. 223(5), the portion before paragraph (*a*) was replaced by S.C. 2013, c. 34, s. 160(1), in force June 26, 2013, and formerly read:

(5) *Charge on property.* A document issued by the Federal Court evidencing a certificate in respect of a debtor registered under subsection (3), a writ of that Court issued pursuant to the certificate or any notification of the document or writ (such document, writ or notification in this section referred to as a "memorial") may be filed, registered or otherwise recorded for the purpose of creating a charge, lien or priority on, or a binding interest in, property in a province, or any interest in such property, held by the debtor in the same manner as a document evidencing

► 223(6) ◄

(6) Creation of charge. If a memorial has been filed, registered or otherwise recorded under subsection (5),

(*a*) a charge, lien or priority is created on, or a binding interest is created in, property in the province, or any interest in, or for civil law any right in, such property, held by the debtor, or

(*b*) such property, or interest or right in the property, is otherwise bound,

in the same manner and to the same extent as if the memorial were a document evidencing a judgment referred to in paragraph (5)(*a*) or an amount referred to in paragraph (5)(*b*), and the charge, lien, priority or binding interest created shall be subordinate to any charge, lien, priority or binding interest in respect of which all steps necessary to make it effective against other creditors were taken before the time the memorial was filed, registered or otherwise recorded.

History: S. 223(6) was replaced by S.C. 2013, c. 34, s. 160(2), in force June 26, 2013, and formerly read:

(6) *Creation of charge.* If a memorial has been filed, registered or otherwise recorded under subsection (5),

(*a*) a charge, lien or priority is created on, or a binding interest is created in, property in the province, or any interest in such property, held by the debtor, or

(*b*) such property or interest in the property is otherwise bound,

in the same manner and to the same extent as if the memorial were a document evidencing a judgment referred to in paragraph (5)(*a*) or an amount referred to in paragraph (5)(*b*), and the charge, lien, priority or binding interest created shall be subordinate to any charge, lien, priority or binding interest in respect of which all steps necessary to make it effective against other creditors were taken before the time the memorial was filed, registered or otherwise recorded.

► 223(7) ◄

(7) Proceedings in respect of memorial. If a memorial is filed, registered or otherwise recorded in a province under subsection (5), proceedings may be taken in the province in respect of the memorial, including proceedings

(*a*) to enforce payment of the amount evidenced by the memorial, interest on the amount and all costs and charges paid or incurred in respect of

(i) the filing, registration or other recording of the memorial, and

(ii) proceedings taken to collect the amount,

(*b*) to renew or otherwise prolong the effectiveness of the filing, registration or other recording of the memorial,

(*c*) to cancel or withdraw the memorial wholly or in respect of any of the property, or interests or rights, affected by the memorial, or

(*d*) to postpone the effectiveness of the filing, registration or other recording of the memorial in favour of any right, charge, lien or priority that has been or is intended to be filed, registered or otherwise recorded in respect of any property, or interest or right, affected by the memorial,

in the same manner and to the same extent as if the memorial were a document evidencing a judgment referred to in paragraph (5)(*a*) or an amount referred to in paragraph (5)(*b*), except that if in any such proceeding or as a condition precedent to any such proceeding any order, consent or ruling is required under the law of the province to be made or given by the superior court of the province or a judge or official of the court, a like order, consent or ruling may be made or given by the Federal Court or a judge or official of the Federal Court and, when so made or given, has the same effect for the purposes of the proceeding as if it were made or given by the superior court of the province or a judge or official of the court.

History: S. 223(7)(*c*) and (*d*) were replaced by S.C. 2013, c. 34, s. 160(3), in force June 26, 2013, and formerly read:

(*c*) to cancel or withdraw the memorial wholly or in respect of any of the property or interests affected by the memorial, or

(*d*) to postpone the effectiveness of the filing, registration or other recording of the memorial in favour of any right, charge, lien or priority that has been or is intended to be filed, registered or otherwise recorded in respect of any property or interest affected by the memorial,

► 223(8) ◄

(8) Presentation of documents. If

(*a*) a memorial is presented for filing, registration or other recording under subsection (5) or a document relating to the memorial is presented for filing, registration or other recording for the purpose of any proceeding described in subsection (7) to any official in the land registry system, personal property or movable property registry system, or other registry system, of a province, it shall be accepted for filing, registration or other recording, or

(*b*) access is sought to any person, place or thing in a province to make the filing, registration or other recording, the access shall be granted

in the same manner and to the same extent as if the memorial or document relating to the memorial were a document evidencing a judgment referred to in paragraph (5)(*a*) or an amount referred to in paragraph (5)(*b*) for the purpose of a like proceeding, as the case may be, except that, if the memorial or document is issued by the Federal Court or signed or certified by a judge or official of the Court, any affidavit, declaration or other evidence required under the law of the province to be provided with or to accompany the memorial or document in the proceedings is deemed to have been provided with or to have accompanied the memorial or document as so required.

History: S. 223(8)(*a*) was replaced by S.C. 2013, c. 34, s. 160(4), in force June 26, 2013, and formerly read:

(*a*) a memorial is presented for filing, registration or other recording under subsection (5) or a document relating to the memorial is presented for filing, registration or other recording for the purpose of any proceeding described in subsection (7) to any official in the land, personal property or other registry system of a province, it shall be accepted for filing, registration or other recording, or

▶ 223(9) ◀

(9) Sale, etc. Notwithstanding any law of Canada or of a province, a sheriff or other person shall not, without the written consent of the Minister, sell or otherwise dispose of any property, or publish any notice or otherwise advertise in respect of any sale or other disposition of any property pursuant to any process issued or charge, lien, priority or binding interest created in any proceeding to collect an amount certified in a certificate made under subsection (2), interest on the amount and costs, but if that consent is subsequently given, any property that would have been affected by such a process, charge, lien, priority or binding interest if the Minister's consent had been given at the time the process was issued or the charge, lien, priority or binding interest was created, as the case may be, shall be bound, seized, attached, charged or otherwise affected as it would be if that consent had been given at the time the process was issued or the charge, lien, priority or binding interest was created, as the case may be.

▶ 223(10) ◀

(10) Completion of notices, etc. If information required to be set out by any sheriff or other person in a minute, notice or document required to be completed for any purpose cannot, by reason of subsection (9), be so set out, the sheriff or other person shall complete the minute, notice or document to the extent possible without that information and, when the consent of the Minister is given under that subsection, a further minute, notice or document setting out all the information shall be completed for the same purpose, and the sheriff or other person having complied with this subsection is deemed to have complied with the Act, regulation or rule requiring the information to be set out in the minute, notice or document.

▶ 223(11) ◀

(11) Application for an order. A sheriff or other person who is unable, by reason of subsection (9) or (10), to comply with any law or rule of court is bound by any order made by a judge of the Federal Court, on an *ex parte* application by the Minister, for the purpose of giving effect to the proceeding, charge, lien, priority or binding interest.

▶ 223(11.1) ◀

(11.1) Deemed security. When a charge, lien, priority or binding interest created under subsection (6) by filing, registering or otherwise recording a memorial under subsection (5) is registered in accordance with subsection 87(1) of the *Bankruptcy and Insolvency Act*, it is deemed

(*a*) to be a claim that is secured by a security and that, subject to subsection 87(2) of that Act, ranks as a secured claim under that Act; and

(*b*) to also be a claim referred to in paragraph 86(2)(*a*) of that Act.

▶ 223(12) ◀

(12) Details in certificates and memorials. Notwithstanding any law of Canada or of a province, in any certificate made under subsection (2) in respect of a debtor, in any memorial evidencing the certificate or in any writ or document issued for the purpose of collecting an amount certified, it is sufficient for all purposes

(*a*) to set out, as the amount payable by the debtor, the total of amounts payable by the debtor without setting out the separate amounts making up that total; and

(*b*) to refer to the rate of interest to be charged on the separate amounts making up the amount payable in general terms as interest at the rate prescribed under this Act applicable from time to time on amounts payable to the Receiver General without indicating the specific rates of interest to be charged on each of the separate amounts or to be charged for any particular period of time.

Related Regulations: 4301.

SECTION 223.1: Application of ss. 223(1) to (8) and (12)

▶ 223.1(1) ◀

(1) Application of ss. 223(1) to (8) and (12). Subsections 223(1) to (8) and (12) are applicable with respect to certificates made under section 223 or section 223 of the *Income Tax Act*, chapter 148 of the Revised Statutes of Canada, 1952, after 1971 and documents evidencing such certificates that were issued by the Federal Court and that were filed, registered or otherwise recorded after 1977 under the laws of a province, except that, where any such certificate or document was the subject of an action pending in a court on February 10, 1988 or the subject of a court decision given on or before that date, section 223 shall be read, for the purposes of applying it with respect to that certificate or document, as section 223 of the *Income Tax Act*, chapter 148 of the Revised Statutes of Canada, 1952, read at the time the certificate was registered or the document was issued, as the case may be.

▶ 223.1(2) ◀

(2) Application of ss. 223(9) to (11). Subsections 223(9) to (11) are applicable with respect to certificates made under section 223, or section 223 of the *Income Tax Act*, chapter 148 of the Revised Statutes of Canada, 1952, after September 13, 1988.

SECTION 224: Garnishment

▶ 224(1) ◀

(1) Garnishment. Where the Minister has knowledge or suspects that a person is, or will be within one year, liable to make a payment to another person who is liable to make a payment under this Act (in this subsection and subsections (1.1) and (3) referred to as the "tax debtor"), the Minister may in writing require the person to pay forthwith, where the moneys are immediately payable, and in any other case as and when the moneys become payable, the moneys otherwise payable to the tax debtor in whole or in part to the Receiver General on account of the tax debtor's liability under this Act.

Related Sections: S. 225.1 Collection restrictions.

Information Circulars: IC 98-1R4 Collections Policies.

Cases: A lawyer drew cheques payable to himself on his trust account and directed his financial institution to deposit them into a joint account that he held with another lawyer. Since the financial institution was not liable to make a payment solely to the taxpayer, it was not required to comply with s. 224(1) requirements to pay. *Canada Trustco Mortgage Company v. The Queen*, 2011 DTC 5112 (S.C.C.), reversing 2009 DTC 5171 (F.C.A.) and 2008 DTC 4752 (T.C.C.).

► 224(1.1) ◄

(1.1) Idem. Without limiting the generality of subsection (1), where the Minister has knowledge or suspects that within 90 days

(*a*) a bank, credit union, trust company or other similar person (in this section referred to as the "institution") will lend or advance moneys to, or make a payment on behalf of, or make a payment in respect of a negotiable instrument issued by, a tax debtor who is indebted to the institution and who has granted security in respect of the indebtedness, or

(*b*) a person, other than an institution, will lend or advance moneys to, or make a payment on behalf of, a tax debtor who the Minister knows or suspects

(i) is employed by, or is engaged in providing services or property to, that person or was or will be, within 90 days, so employed or engaged, or

(ii) where that person is a corporation, is not dealing at arm's length with that person,

the Minister may in writing require the institution or person, as the case may be, to pay in whole or in part to the Receiver General on account of the tax debtor's liability under this Act the moneys that would otherwise be so lent, advanced or paid and any moneys so paid to the Receiver General shall be deemed to have been lent, advanced or paid, as the case may be, to the tax debtor.

Related Sections: S. 225.1 Collection restrictions.

Cases: Private arrangements between taxpayers cannot affect the rights of the Crown under s. 224(1.2). The Crown acquires rights by operation of law and the issuance of a Requirement to Pay; its rights too cannot be displaced by private arrangements. *Manitoba Housing Renewal Corp. v. Able Eavestroughing Ltd. et al.*, 2017 DTC 5016 (MBQB)

Inasmuch as no outstanding payroll deductions had been made prior to an assignment of inventory, a bank's security created by such an assignment took priority over the Crown's deemed trust in the unremitted source deductions since the bank had legal title to that inventory. *The Queen v. Royal Bank of Canada*, 97 DTC 5089 (S.C.C.).

► 224(1.2) ◄

(1.2) Garnishment. Notwithstanding any other provision of this Act, the *Bankruptcy and Insolvency Act*, any other enactment of Canada, any enactment of a province or any law, but subject to subsections 69(1) and 69.1(1) of the *Bankruptcy and Insolvency Act* and section 11.09 of the *Companies' Creditors Arrangement Act*, if the Minister has knowledge or suspects that a particular person is, or will become within one year, liable to make a payment

(*a*) to another person (in this subsection referred to as the "tax debtor") who is liable to pay an amount assessed under subsection 227(10.1) or a similar provision, or

(*b*) to a secured creditor who has a right to receive the payment that, but for a security interest in favour of the secured creditor, would be payable to the tax debtor,

the Minister may in writing require the particular person to pay forthwith, where the moneys are immediately payable, and in any other case as and when the moneys become payable, the moneys otherwise payable to the tax debtor or the secured creditor in whole or in part to the Receiver General on account of the tax debtor's liability under subsection 227(10.1) or the similar provision, and on receipt of that requirement by the particular person, the amount of those moneys that is so required to be paid to the Receiver General shall, notwithstanding any security interest in those moneys, become the property of Her Majesty to the extent of that liability as assessed by the Minister and shall be paid to the Receiver General in priority to any such security interest.

Related Sections: S. 224(1.3), "secured creditor", "security interest", "similar provision"; s. 227(10.1) Assessment — failure to remit tax; s. 248(1) Definitions.

Cases: A Requirement to Pay issued under s. 224(1.2) takes priority over secured creditors. In this context, a "secured creditor" does not include any person who owns property absolutely. However, a general assignment of book debts does not confer absolute ownership. It is collateral security, and falls within the definition of "security interest" set out in s. 224(1.3). *The Queen v. Province of Alberta Treasury Branches et al.*, 96 DTC 6245 (S.C.C.), reversing 94 DTC 6650 (Alta. C.A.)

Under the very clearly worded provisions of ss. 224(1.1)–(1.3), Revenue Canada's third party demand took priority over a bank, in its capacity as a secured creditor, notwithstanding the decision of the Alberta Court of Appeal to the contrary in *Lloyds Bank v. International Warranty Co. Ltd.*, a case involving an identical fact situation which was wrongly decided. *The Royal Bank of Canada v. Saskatchewan Power Corp. et al.*, 90 DTC 6330 (Sask. Q.B.), affirmed by (Sask. C.A.), [1991]1 W.W.R. 1

The Minister could issue third party demands to the the taxpayer's debtors, notwithstanding the fact that it had previously filed a bankruptcy proposal. *Air Atonabee Ltd. v. The Queen*, 90 DTC 6573 (Ont. S.C.).

► 224(1.3) ◄

(1.3) Definitions. In subsection (1.2),

"secured creditor" —"secured creditor" means a person who has a security interest in the property of another person or who acts for or on behalf of that person with respect to the security interest and includes a trustee appointed under a trust deed relating to a security interest, a receiver or receiver-manager appointed by a secured creditor or by a court on the application of a secured creditor, a sequestrator or any other person performing a similar function;

"security interest" —"security interest" means any interest in, or for civil law any right in, property that secures payment or performance of an obligation and includes an interest, or for civil law a right, created by or arising out of a debenture, mortgage, hypothec, lien, pledge, charge, deemed or actual trust, assignment or encumbrance of any kind whatever, however or whenever arising, created, deemed to arise or otherwise provided for;

History: S. 224(1.3), the definition "security interest" was replaced by S.C. 2013, c. 34, s. 161, in force June 26, 2013, and formerly read:

"security interest" —"security interest" means any interest in property that secures payment or performance of an obligation and includes an interest created by or arising out of a debenture, mortgage, hypothec, lien, pledge, charge, deemed or actual trust, assignment or encumbrance of any kind whatever, however or whenever arising, created, deemed to arise or otherwise provided for;

Cases: To secure a line of credit, a corporation made a $200,000 deposit with a Caisse Populaire under a compensation agreement. When the corporation went bankrupt, the Caisse set off this deposit against the corporation's debt, purportedly by way of "compensation" under Quebec law. Regardless of the form of the agreement, a "security interest" under s. 224(1.3) arises as long as the creditor's interest in the debtor's property secures payment or performance of an obligation. *Caisse populaire Desjardins de l'Est de Drummond v. The Queen*, 2009 DTC 5106 (S.C.C.), affirming 2007 DTC 5220 (F.C.A.), affirming 2007 DTC 5664 (F.C.) and 2006 DTC 6385 (F.C.)

"similar provision" —"similar provision" means a provision, similar to subsection 227(10.1), of any Act of a province that imposes a tax similar to the tax imposed under this Act, where the province has entered into an agreement with the Minister of Finance for the collection of the taxes payable to the province under that Act.

► 224(1.4) ◄

(1.4) Garnishment. Provisions of this Act that provide that a person who has been required to do so by the Minister must pay to the Receiver General an amount that would otherwise be lent, advanced or paid to a taxpayer who is liable to make a payment under this Act, or to that taxpayer's secured creditor, apply to Her Majesty in right of Canada or a province.

► 224(2) ◄

(2) Minister's receipt discharges original liability. The receipt of the Minister for moneys paid as required under this section is a good and sufficient discharge of the original liability to the extent of the payment.

► 224(3) ◄

(3) Idem. Where the Minister has, under this section, required a person to pay to the Receiver General on account of a liability under this Act of a tax debtor moneys otherwise payable by the person to the tax debtor as interest, rent, remuneration, a dividend, an annuity or other periodic payment, the requirement applies to all such payments to be made by the person to the tax debtor until the liability under this Act is satisfied and operates to require payments to the Receiver General out of each such payment of such amount as is stipulated by the Minister in the requirement.

► 224(4) ◄

(4) Failure to comply with s. (1), (1.2) or (3) requirement. Every person who fails to comply with a requirement under subsection (1), (1.2) or (3) is liable to pay to Her Majesty an amount equal to the amount that the person was required under subsection (1), (1.2) or (3), as the case may be, to pay to the Receiver General.

► 224(4.1) ◄

(4.1) Failure to comply with s. (1.1) requirement. Every institution or person that fails to comply with a requirement under subsection (1.1) with respect to moneys to be lent, advanced or paid is liable to pay to Her Majesty an amount equal to the lesser of

(*a*) the total of moneys so lent, advanced or paid, and

(*b*) the amount that the institution or person was required under that subsection to pay to the Receiver General.

► 224(5) ◄

(5) Service of garnishee. Where a person carries on business under a name or style other than the person's own name, notification to the person of a requirement under subsection (1), (1.1) or (1.2) may be addressed to the name or style under which the person carries on business and, in the case of personal service, shall be deemed to be validly served if it is left with an adult person employed at the place of business of the addressee.

► 224(6) ◄

(6) Idem. Where persons carry on business in partnership, notification to the persons of a requirement under subsection (1), (1.1) or (1.2) may be addressed to the partnership name and, in the case of personal service, shall be deemed to be validly served if it is served on one of the partners or left with an adult person employed at the place of business of the partnership.

Related Sections: S. 248(1), "business", "employee", "employer"; s. 251(1), "arm's length"; ITAR s. 65.1 Part XV of amended Act.

SECTION 224.1: Recovery by deduction or set-off

Where a person is indebted to Her Majesty under this Act or under an Act of a province with which the Minister of Finance has entered into an agreement for the collection of the taxes payable to the province under that Act, the Minister may require the retention by way of deduction or set-off of such amount as the Minister may specify out of any amount that may be or become payable to the person by Her Majesty in right of Canada.

Related Sections: S. 225.1 Collection restrictions.

Tax Topics: No. 1901, Narrowing of the Collection Restrictions — Set-Off Can Occur!.

Information Circulars: IC 98-1R4 Collections policies.

Cases: Set-off was denied where the Minister failed to follow the correct procedure. *Clarkson Co. Ltd. as Receiver and Manager of Aero Trades (Western) Ltd. v. The Queen*, 89 DTC 5050 (F.C.A.), reversing in part 88 DTC 6256 (F.C.T.D.)

SECTION 224.2: Acquisition of debtor's property

For the purpose of collecting debts owed by a person to Her Majesty under this Act or under an Act of a province with which the Minister of Finance has entered into an agreement for the collection of taxes payable to the province under that Act, the Minister may purchase or otherwise acquire any interest in, or for civil law any right in, the person's property that the Minister is given a right to acquire in legal proceedings or under a court order or that is offered for sale or redemption and may dispose of any interest or right so acquired in such manner as the Minister considers reasonable.

History: S. 224.2 was replaced by S.C. 2013, c. 34, s. 162, in force June 26, 2013, and formerly read:

S. 224.2 *Acquisition of debtor's property.* For the purpose of collecting debts owed by a person to Her Majesty under this Act or under an Act of a province with which the Minister of Finance has entered into an agreement for the collection of taxes payable to the province under that Act, the Minister may purchase or otherwise acquire any interest in the person's property that the Minister is given a right to acquire in legal proceedings or under a court order or that is offered for sale or redemption and may dispose of any interest so acquired in such manner as the Minister considers reasonable.

Information Circulars: IC 98-1R4 Collections policies.

SECTION 224.3: Payment of moneys seized from tax debtor

► 224.3(1) ◄

(1) Payment of moneys seized from tax debtor. Where the Minister has knowledge or suspects that a particular person is holding moneys that were seized by a police officer in the course of administering or enforcing the criminal law of Canada from another person (in this section referred to as the "tax debtor") who is liable to make a payment under this Act or under an Act of a province with which the Minister of Finance has entered into an agreement for the collection of taxes payable to the province under that Act and that are restorable to the tax debtor, the Minister may in writing require the particular person to turn over the moneys otherwise restorable to the tax debtor in whole or in part to the Receiver General on account of the tax debtor's liability under this Act or under the Act of the province, as the case may be.

Related Sections: S. 225.1 Collection restrictions.

Information Circulars: IC 98-1R4 Collections policies.

► 224.3(2) ◄

(2) Receipt of Minister. The receipt of the Minister for moneys turned over as required by this section is a good and sufficient discharge of the requirement to restore the moneys to the tax debtor to the extent of the amount so turned over.

SECTION 225: Seizure of goods, chattels or movable property

► 225(1) ◄

(1) Seizure of goods, chattels or movable property. If a person has failed to pay an amount as required by this Act, the Minister may give 30 days notice to the person by registered mail addressed to the person's latest known address of the Minister's intention to direct that the person's goods and chattels, or movable property, be seized and sold, and, if the person fails to make the payment before the expiration of the 30 days, the Minister may issue a certificate of the failure and direct that the person's goods and chattels, or movable property, be seized.

History: S. 225(1) was replaced by S.C. 2013, c. 34, s. 163(1), in force June 26, 2013, and formerly read:

(1) *Seizure of chattels.* Where a person has failed to pay an amount as required by this Act, the Minister may give 30 days notice to the person by registered mail addressed to the person's latest known address of the Minister's intention to direct that the person's goods and chattels be seized and sold, and, if the person fails to make the payment before the expiration of the 30 days, the Minister may issue a certificate of the failure and direct that the person's goods and chattels be seized.

Related Sections: S. 225.1 Collection restrictions.

Information Circulars: IC 98-1R4 Collections Policies.

Cases: The seizure of paintings and objects of art was valid against a third party claiming to be the owner of the art. The third party was unable to provide even approximate details of ownership or acquisition of the art. *In re assessment by M.N.R. v. Levine et al.,* 89 DTC 5295 (F.C.T.D.)

► 225(2) ◄

(2) Sale of seized property. Property seized under this section shall be kept for 10 days at the cost and charges of the owner and, if the owner does not pay the amount owing together with the costs and charges within the 10 days, the property seized shall be sold by public auction.

Related Sections: S. 226 Taxpayer leaving Canada.

► 225(3) ◄

(3) Notice of sale. Except in the case of perishable goods, notice of the sale setting out the time and place thereof, together with a general description of the property to be sold shall, a reasonable time before the goods are sold, be published at least once in one or more newspapers of general local circulation.

► 225(4) ◄

(4) Surplus returned to owner. Any surplus resulting from the sale after deduction of the amount owing and all costs and charges shall be paid or returned to the owner of the property seized.

► 225(5) ◄

(5) Exemptions from seizure. Goods and chattels, or movable property, of any person in default that would be exempt from seizure under a writ of execution issued out of a superior court of the province in which the seizure is made are exempt from seizure under this section.

History: S. 225(5) was replaced by S.C. 2013, c. 34, s. 163(2), in force June 26, 2013, and formerly read:

(5) *Exemptions from seizure.* Such goods and chattels of any person in default as would be exempt from seizure under a writ of execution issued out of a superior court of the province in which the seizure is made are exempt from seizure under this section.

Related Sections: S. 226(2) Taxpayer leaving Canada — seizure; s. 248(1), "assessment", "property", "province"; ITAR s. 65.1 Part XV of amended Act.

SECTION 225.1: Collection restrictions

► 225.1(1) ◄

(1) Collection restrictions. If a taxpayer is liable for the payment of an amount assessed under this Act, other than an amount assessed under subsection 152(4.2), 169(3) or 220(3.1), the Minister shall not, until after the collection-commencement day in respect of the amount, do any of the following for the purpose of collecting the amount:

(*a*) commence legal proceedings in a court,

(*b*) certify the amount under section 223,

(*c*) require a person to make a payment under subsection 224(1),

(*d*) require an institution or a person to make a payment under subsection 224(1.1),

(*e*) (Repealed by S.C. 2006, c. 4, s. 166(1).)

(*f*) require a person to turn over moneys under subsection 224.3(1), or

(*g*) give a notice, issue a certificate or make a direction under subsection 225(1).

Related Sections: S. 164(1.1) Repayment on objections and appeals; s. 179.1 No reasonable grounds for appeal; s. 225.2(2) Authorization to proceed forthwith; s. 248(1), "assessment".

Tax Profile: April 2003 — The Clock is Ticking for the Tax Man!.

Tax Topics: No. 1901, Narrowing of the Collection Restrictions — Set-Off Can Occur!.

Information Circulars: IC 07-1 Taxpayer Relief Provisions; IC 98-1R4 Collections Policies.

Cases: Federal income tax collection proceedings are subject to the limitation period in s. 32 of the *Crown Liability and Proceedings Act.* In addition, s. 3(5) of the *B.C. Limitation Act* barred the Crown from collecting the taxpayer's provincial tax debt. *The Queen v. Markevich et al.,* 2003 DTC 5185 (S.C.C.), affirming 2001 DTC 5305 (F.C.A.), reversing 99 DTC 5136 (F.C.T.D.).

► 225.1(1.1) ◄

(1.1) Collection-commencement day. The collection-commencement day in respect of an amount is

(*a*) in the case of an amount assessed under subsection 188(1.1) in respect of a notice of intention to revoke given under subsection 168(1) or any of subsections 149.1(2) to (4.1), one year after the day on which the notice was mailed;

(*b*) in the case of an amount assessed under section 188.1, one year after the day on which the notice of assessment was sent; and

(*c*) in any other case, 90 days after the day on which the notice of assessment was sent.

History: S. 225.1(1.1)(*b*) and (*c*) were replaced by S.C. 2010, c. 25, s. 66(1), in force on Royal Assent, December 15, 2010. S. 225.1(1.1)(*b*) and (*c*) formerly read:

(*b*) in the case of an amount assessed under section 188.1, one year after the day on which the notice of assessment was mailed; and

(*c*) in any other case, 90 days after the day on which the notice of assessment was mailed.

► 225.1(2) ◄

(2) No action by Minister. If a taxpayer has served a notice of objection under this Act to an assessment of an amount payable under this Act, the Minister shall not, for the purpose of collecting the amount in controversy, take any of the actions described in paragraphs (1)(*a*) to (*g*) until after the day that is 90 days after the day on which notice is sent to the taxpayer that the Minister has confirmed or varied the assessment.

History: S. 225.1(2) was replaced by S.C. 2010, c. 25, s. 66(2), in force on Royal Assent, December 15, 2010. S. 225.1(2) formerly read:

(2) *Idem.* Where a taxpayer has served a notice of objection under this Act to an assessment of an amount payable under this Act, the Minister shall not, for the purpose of collecting the amount in controversy, take any of the actions described in paragraphs (1)(*a*) to (*g*) until after the day that is 90 days after the day on which notice is mailed to the taxpayer that the Minister has confirmed or varied the assessment.

Related Sections: S. 248(1), "assessment".

► 225.1(3) ◄

(3) Idem. Where a taxpayer has appealed from an assessment of an amount payable under this Act to the Tax Court of Canada, the Minister shall not, for the purpose of collecting the amount in controversy, take any of the actions described in paragraphs (1)(*a*) to (*g*) before the day of mailing of a copy of the decision of the Court to the taxpayer or the day on which the taxpayer discontinues the appeal, whichever is the earlier.

Cases: A taxpayer was bound by the terms of an abeyance letter signed on his behalf by his authorized agent. *Doyle v. M.N.R.*, 89 DTC 5483 (F.C.T.D.). See also *McCall v. The Queen*, 89 DTC 5148 (F.C.T.D.)

► 225.1(4) ◄

(4) Idem. Where a taxpayer has agreed under subsection 173(1) that a question should be determined by the Tax Court of Canada, or where a taxpayer is served with a copy of an application made under subsection 174(1) to that Court for the determination of a question, the Minister shall not take any of the actions described in paragraphs (1)(*a*) to (*g*) for the purpose of collecting that part of an amount assessed, the liability for payment of which will be affected by the determination of the question, before the day on which the question is determined by the Court.

► 225.1(5) ◄

(5) Idem. Notwithstanding any other provision in this section, where a taxpayer has served a notice of objection under this Act to an assessment or has appealed to the Tax Court of Canada from an assessment and agrees in writing with the Minister to delay proceedings on the objection or appeal, as the case may be, until judgment has been given in another action before the Tax Court of Canada, the Federal Court of Appeal or the Supreme Court of Canada in which the issue is the same or substantially the same as that raised in the objection or appeal of the taxpayer, the Minister may take any of the actions described in paragraphs (1)(*a*) to (*g*) for the purpose of collecting the amount assessed, or a part thereof, determined in a manner consistent with the decision or judgment of the Court in the other action at any time after the Minister notifies the taxpayer in writing that

(*a*) the decision of the Tax Court of Canada in that action has been mailed to the Minister,

(*b*) judgment has been pronounced by the Federal Court of Appeal in that action, or

(*c*) judgment has been delivered by the Supreme Court of Canada in that action,

as the case may be.

Tax Topics: No. 1891, The Collections Implications of an Agreement To Hold an Objection or Appeal in Abeyance.

► 225.1(6) ◄

(6) Where ss. (1) to (4) do not apply. Subsections (1) to (4) do not apply with respect to

(*a*) an amount payable under Part VIII;

(*a*.1) an amount payable under section 281;

(*b*) an amount required to be deducted or withheld, and required to be remitted or paid, under this Act or the Regulations;

(*c*) an amount of tax required to be paid under section 116 or a regulation made under subsection 215(4) but not so paid;

(*d*) the amount of any penalty payable for failure to remit or pay an amount referred to in paragraph (*b*) or (*c*) as and when required by this Act or a regulation made under this Act; and

(*e*) any interest payable under a provision of this Act on an amount referred to in this paragraph or any of paragraphs (*a*) to (*d*).

History: S. 225.1(6)(*a.1*) was added by S.C. 2016, c. 12, s. 60(1), in force July 1, 2017.

► 225.1(7) ◄

(7) One-half collection. If an amount has been assessed under this Act in respect of a corporation for a taxation year in which it was a large corporation, or in respect of a particular amount claimed under section 110.1 or 118.1 where the particular amount was claimed in respect of a tax shelter, then subsections (1) to (4) do not limit any action of the Minister to collect

(*a*) at any time on or before the particular day that is 90 days after the day of the sending of the notice of assessment, $1/2$ of the amount so assessed; and

(*b*) at any time after the particular day, the amount, if any, by which the amount so assessed exceeds the total of

(i) all amounts collected before that time with respect to the assessment, and

(ii) $1/2$ of the amount in controversy at that time.

History: S. 225.1(7), the portion before paragraph (*a*) was replaced by S.C. 2013, c. 33, s. 20(1), applicable in respect of amounts assessed for taxation years that end after 2012, and formerly read:

(7) *Idem — large corporations.* Where an amount has been assessed under this Act in respect of a corporation for a taxation year in which it was a large corporation, subsections (1) to (4) do not apply to limit any action of the Minister to collect

S. 225.1(7)(*a*) was replaced by S.C. 2010, c. 25, s. 66(3), in force on Royal Assent, December 15, 2010. S. 225.1(7)(*a*) formerly read:

(*a*) at any time on or before the particular day that is 90 days after the day of the mailing of the notice of assessment, 1/2 of the amount so assessed; and

Related Sections: S. 248(1), "corporation"; s. 249(1) Definition of "taxation year".

► 225.1(8) ◄

(8) Definition of "large corporation". For the purposes of this section and section 235, a corporation (other than a corporation described in subsection 181.1(3)) is a "large corporation" in a particular taxation year if the total of the taxable capital employed in Canada of the corporation, at the end of the particular taxation year, and the taxable capital employed in Canada of any other corporation, at the end of the other corporation's last taxation year that ends at or before the end of the particular taxation year, if the other corporation is related (within the meaning assigned for the purposes of section 181.5) to the corporation at the end of the particular taxation year, exceeds $10 million, and, for the purpose of this subsection, a corporation formed as a result of the amalgamation or merger of 2 or more predecessor corporations is deemed to be the same corporation as, and a continuation of, each predecessor corporation.

Related Sections: S. 3 Income for taxation year; s. 181.5(1) Capital deduction; s. 248(1), "corporation"; s. 249(1) Definition of "taxation year"; Part I.

SECTION 225.2: [Authorization to proceed before collection-commencement day]

► 225.2(1) ◄

(1) Definition of "judge". In this section, "judge" means a judge or a local judge of a superior court of a province or a judge of the Federal Court.

Related Sections: S. 248(1), "assessment".

Canadian Tax Foundation: Sibson, *Revenue Canada's Long Collection Arm: Jeopardy Orders, Section 160 Assessments, and Directors' Liability*, 1998 Conference Report 26:1–26.

► 225.2(2) ◄

(2) Authorization to proceed forthwith. Notwithstanding section 225.1, where, on *ex parte* application by the Minister, a judge is satisfied that there are reasonable grounds to believe that the collection of all or any part of an amount assessed in respect of a taxpayer would be jeopardized by a delay in the collection of that amount, the judge shall, on such terms as the judge considers reasonable in the circumstances, authorize the Minister to take forthwith any of the actions described in paragraphs 225.1(1)(*a*) to (*g*) with respect to the amount.

Information Circulars: IC 73-10R3 Tax evasion; IC 07-1 Taxpayer Relief Provisions; IC 98-1R4 Collections Policies.

Cases: The Court had no authority to order a taxpayer to appear personally for examination under oath where the taxpayer had applied to the Federal Court for an order vacating the Minister's direction that tax owing be collected forthwith. *Cuffaro v. The Queen*, 89 DTC 5192 (F.C.T.D.)

A motion was dismissed as inappropriate where the taxpayer sought to challenge the Minister's proposed collection of taxes, the assessment of which was disputed by the taxpayer. *McCall v. The Queen*, 88 DTC 6466 (F.C.T.D.)

See also *Neeb v. The Queen*, 90 DTC 6666 (F.C.T.D.)

► 225.2(3) ◄

(3) Notice of assessment not sent. An authorization under subsection (2) in respect of an amount assessed in respect of a taxpayer may be granted by a judge notwithstanding that a notice of assessment in respect of that amount has not been sent to the taxpayer at or before the time the application is made where the judge is satisfied that the receipt of the notice of assessment by the taxpayer would likely further jeopardize the collection of the amount, and for the purposes of sections 222, 223, 224, 224.1, 224.3 and 225, the amount in respect of which an authorization is so granted shall be deemed to be an amount payable under this Act.

► 225.2(4) ◄

(4) Affidavits. Statements contained in an affidavit filed in the context of an application under this section may be based on belief with the grounds therefor.

► 225.2(5) ◄

(5) Service of authorization and of notice of assessment. An authorization granted under this section in respect of a taxpayer shall be served by the Minister on the taxpayer within 72 hours after it is granted, except where the judge orders the authorization to be served at some other time specified in the authorization, and, where a notice of assessment has not been sent to the taxpayer at or before the time of the application, the notice of assessment shall be served together with the authorization.

► 225.2(6) ◄

(6) How service effected. For the purposes of subsection (5), service on a taxpayer shall be effected by

(*a*) personal service on the taxpayer; or

(*b*) service in accordance with directions, if any, of a judge.

► 225.2(7) ◄

(7) Application to judge for direction. Where service on a taxpayer cannot reasonably otherwise be effected as and when required under this section, the Minister may, as soon as practicable, apply to a judge for further direction.

► 225.2(8) ◄

(8) Review of authorization. Where a judge of a court has granted an authorization under this section in respect of a taxpayer, the taxpayer may, on 6 clear days notice to the Deputy Attorney General of Canada, apply to a judge of the court to review the authorization.

► 225.2(9) ◄

(9) Limitation period for review application. An application under subsection (8) shall be made

(*a*) within 30 days from the day on which the authorization was served on the taxpayer in accordance with this section; or

(*b*) within such further time as a judge may allow, on being satisfied that the application was made as soon as practicable.

Cases: The 30-day limitation period set out in s. 225.2(9) does not run during settlement negotiations between the taxpayer and the Department. *M.N.R. v. Rudyk*, 96 DTC 6192 (F.C.T.D.).

► 225.2(10) ◄

(10) Hearing *in camera*. An application under subsection (8) may, on the application of the taxpayer, be heard *in camera*, if the taxpayer establishes to the satisfaction of the judge that the circumstances of the case justify *in camera* proceedings.

► 225.2(11) ◄

(11) Disposition of application. On an application under subsection (8), the judge shall determine the question summarily and may confirm, set aside or vary the authorization and make such other order as the judge considers appropriate.

► 225.2(12) ◄

(12) Directions. Where any question arises as to the course to be followed in connection with anything done or being done under this section and there is no direction in this section with respect thereto, a judge may give such direction with regard thereto as, in the opinion of the judge, is appropriate.

► 225.2(13) ◄

(13) No appeal from review order. No appeal lies from an order of a judge made pursuant to subsection (11).

SECTION 226: Taxpayer leaving Canada

► 226(1) ◄

(1) Taxpayer leaving Canada. Where the Minister suspects that a taxpayer has left or is about to leave Canada, the Minister may, before the day otherwise fixed for payment, by notice served personally or by registered letter addressed to the taxpayer's latest known address, demand payment of the amount of all taxes, interest and penalties for which the taxpayer is liable or would be liable if the time for payment had arrived, and that amount shall be paid forthwith by the taxpayer notwithstanding any other provision of this Act.

Related Regulations: Part XIII.

► 226(2) ◄

(2) Seizure in case of default of payment. If a taxpayer fails to pay, as required, any tax, interest or penalties demanded under this section, the Minister may direct that the goods and chattels, or movable property, of the taxpayer be seized and subsections 225(2) to (5) apply, with respect to the seizure, with any modifications that the circumstances require.

History: S. 226(2) was replaced by S.C. 2013, c. 34, s. 164, in force June 26, 2013, and formerly read:

(2) *Idem.* Where a taxpayer fails to pay, as required, any tax, interest or penalties demanded under this section, the Minister may direct that the goods and chattels of the taxpayer be seized and subsections 225(2) to (5) apply, with respect to the seizure, with such modifications as the circumstances require.

Related Sections: S. 248(1) Definitions; ITAR s. 65.1 Part XV of amended Act.

Cases: Seizure of visitor's chattels for non-payment of tax has been held valid. *Carolus et al. v. M.N.R.*, 76 DTC 6359 (F.C.T.D.).

SECTION 227: Withholding taxes

► 227(1) ◄

(1) Withholding taxes. No action lies against any person for deducting or withholding any sum of money in compliance or intended compliance with this Act.

Tax Topics: No. 2184, JP Morgan – A Road Map Leading in the Wrong Direction?; No. 2178, JP Morgan: Can Taxpayers Use the Judicial Review Process To Challenge Tax Assessments That Are Contrary to the CRA's Administrative Policies?.

► 227(2) ◄

(2) Return filed with person withholding. Where a person (in this subsection referred to as the "payer") is required by regulations made under subsection 153(1) to deduct or withhold from a payment to another person an amount on account of that other person's tax for the year, that other person shall, from time to time as prescribed, file a return with the payer in prescribed form.

Related Regulations: 107(1).

Related Sections: S. 227(3) Failure to file return; s. 235 Penalty for failing to file corporate returns.

Forms: T1213 — Request to Reduce Tax Deductions at Source for Year(s)__; TD1-WS — Worksheet for the __ Personal Tax Credits Return; TD1 — Personal Tax Credits Return.

Information Circulars: IC 98-1R4 Collections Policies.

► 227(3) ◄

(3) Failure to file return. Every person who fails to file a return as required by subsection (2) is liable to have the deduction or withholding under section 153 on account of the person's tax made as though the person were a person who is neither married nor in a common-law partnership and is without dependants.

► 227(4) ◄

(4) Trust for moneys deducted. Every person who deducts or withholds an amount under this Act is deemed, notwithstanding any security interest (as defined in subsection 224(1.3)) in the amount so deducted or withheld, to hold the amount separate and apart from the property of the person and from property held by any secured creditor (as defined in subsection 224(1.3)) of that person that but for the security interest would be property of the person, in trust for Her Majesty and for payment to Her Majesty in the manner and at the time provided under this Act.

Related Regulations: 2201.

Tax Topics: No. 2028, The *Century Services* Case — Getting the Crown's Priorities Straight.

Tax Window Files: Prescribed Security Interest, *January 28, 2014*, CRA Document No. 2013-0506991E5.

Cases: Although the *Companies' Creditors Arrangement Act* and the *Bankruptcy and Insolvency Act* specifically provide that deemed statutory trusts for unremitted source deductions (income tax, CPP and EI) remain effective in insolvency, there is no statutory basis for concluding that GST claims enjoy similar treatment. *Century Services Inc. v. A.G. of Canada*, 2011 DTC 5006 (S.C.C.), reversing *(Re) Ted LeRoy Trucking Ltd. et al.*, 2009 GTC 2020 (B.C.C.A.)

Crown's claim did not take priority over the bank's general security agreement or *Bank Act* security created by an assignment of inventory. *The Queen v. Royal Bank of Canada*, 97 DTC 5089 (S.C.C.)

A claim by a provincial Ministry of Labour in respect of unpaid wages took priority over the Minister of National Revenue's claim for unremitted source deductions. At the time that the trust relied on by Revenue came into existence, the monies had already been impressed with the trust created under the *Payment of Wages Act The Queen in Right of Manitoba (Minister of Labour) v. Coopers & Lybrand, Receiver and Manager of Omega Autobody Ltd. et al.*, 88 DTC 6514 (Man. Q.B.).

► 227(4.1) ◄

(4.1) Extension of trust. Notwithstanding any other provision of this Act, the *Bankruptcy and Insolvency Act* (except sections 81.1 and 81.2 of that Act), any other enactment of Canada, any enactment of a province or any other law, where at any time an amount deemed by subsection (4) to be held by a person in trust for Her Majesty is not paid to Her Majesty in the manner and at the time provided under this Act, property of the person and property held by any secured creditor (as defined in subsection 224(1.3)) of that person that but for a security interest (as defined in subsection 224(1.3)) would be property of the person, equal in value to the amount so deemed to be held in trust is deemed

(*a*) to be held, from the time the amount was deducted or withheld by the person, separate and apart from the property of the person, in trust for Her Majesty whether or not the property is subject to such a security interest, and

(*b*) to form no part of the estate or property of the person from the time the amount was so deducted or withheld, whether or not the property has in fact been kept separate and apart from the estate or property of the person and whether or not the property is subject to such a security interest

and is property beneficially owned by Her Majesty notwithstanding any security interest in such property and in the proceeds thereof, and the proceeds of such property shall be paid to the Receiver General in priority to all such security interests.

Tax Topics: No. 2028, The *Century Services* Case — Getting the Crown's Priorities Straight.

Cases: To secure a line of credit, a corporation made a $200,000 deposit with a Caisse Populaire under a compensation agreement. When the corporation went bankrupt, the Caisse set off this deposit against the corporation's debt, purportedly by way of "compensation" under Quebec law. The compensation agreement gave rise to a "security interest". Therefore, the deposit was subject to a statutory deemed trust in favour of the Crown and the Caisse was liable for an amount equal to the corporation's unremitted source deductions. *Caisse populaire Desjardins de l'Est de Drummond v. The Queen*, 2009 DTC 5106 (S.C.C.), affirming 2007 DTC 5220 (F.C.A.), affirming 2007 DTC 5664 (F.C.) and 2006 DTC 6385 (F.C.)

A deemed trust arises at the time when source deductions are actually made and is similar to a floating charge over all of a tax debtor's assets. As property comes into the possession of the tax debtor, it is caught by the trust, and property disposed of by the tax debtor is released from the trust. The deemed trust, however, does not operate over assets which a tax debtor sells in the ordinary course to third party purchasers. *The Queen v. First Vancouver Finance et al.*, 2002 DTC 6998 (S.C.C.).

► 227(4.2) ◄

(4.2) Meaning of security interest. For the purposes of subsections (4) and (4.1), a security interest does not include a prescribed security interest.

Related Regulations: 2201.

► 227(4.3) ◄

(4.3) Application to Crown. For greater certainty, subsections (4) to (4.2) apply to Her Majesty in right of Canada or a province where Her Majesty in right of Canada or a province is a secured creditor (within the meaning assigned by subsection 224(1.3)) or holds a security interest (within the meaning assigned by that subsection).

► 227(5) ◄

(5) Payments by trustees, etc. Where a specified person in relation to a particular person (in this subsection referred to as the "payer") has any direct or indirect influence over the disbursements, property, business or estate of the payer and the specified person, alone or together with another person, authorizes or otherwise causes a payment referred to in subsection 135(3), 135.1(7) or 153(1), or on or in respect of which tax is payable under Part XII.5 or XIII, to be made by or on behalf of the payer, the specified person

(*a*) is, for the purposes of subsections 135(3) and 153(1), section 215 and this section, deemed to be a person who made the payment;

(*a*.1) is, for the purposes of subsections 135.1(7) and 211.8(2), deemed to be a person who redeemed, acquired or cancelled a share and made the payment as a consequence of the redemption, acquisition or cancellation;

(*b*) is jointly and severally, or solidarily, liable with the payer to pay to the Receiver General

(i) all amounts payable by the payer because of any of subsections 135(3), 135.1(7), 153(1) and 211.8(2) and section 215 in respect of the payment, and

(ii) all amounts payable under this Act by the payer because of any failure to comply with any of those provisions in respect of the payment; and

(*c*) is entitled to deduct or withhold from any amount paid or credited by the specified person to the payer or otherwise recover from the payer any amount paid under this subsection by the specified person in respect of the payment.

History: S. 227(5)(*b*), the portion before subparagraph (i) was replaced by S.C. 2013, c. 34, s. 165(1), in force June 26, 2013, and formerly read:

(*b*) is jointly and severally liable with the payer to pay to the Receiver General

Related Sections: S. 238(2) Compliance orders.

► 227(5.1) ◄

(5.1) Definition of "specified person". In subsection (5), a "specified person" in relation to a particular person means a person who is, in relation to the particular person or the disbursements, property, business or estate of the particular person,

(*a*) a trustee;

(*b*) a liquidator;

(*c*) a receiver;

(*d*) an interim receiver;

(*e*) a receiver-manager;

(*f*) a trustee in bankruptcy or other person appointed under the *Bankruptcy and Insolvency Act*;

(*g*) an assignee;

(*h*) a secured creditor (as defined in subsection 224(1.3));

(*i*) an executor, a liquidator of a succession or an administrator;

(*j*) any person acting in a capacity similar to that of a person referred to in any of paragraphs (*a*) to (*i*);

(*k*) a person appointed (otherwise than as an employee of the creditor) at the request of, or on the advice of, a secured creditor in relation to the particular person to monitor, or provide advice in respect of, the disbursements, property, business or estate of the particular person under circumstances such that it is reasonable to conclude that the person is appointed to protect or advance the interests of the creditor; or (*l*) an agent of a specified person referred to in any of paragraphs (*a*) to (*k*).

▶ 227(5.2) ◀

(5.2) "Person" includes partnership. For the purposes of this section, references in subsections (5) and (5.1) to persons include partnerships.

▶ 227(6) ◀

(6) Excess withheld, returned or applied. Where a person on whose behalf an amount has been paid under Part XII.5 or XIII to the Receiver General was not liable to pay tax under that Part or where the amount so paid is in excess of the amount that the person was liable to pay, the Minister shall, on written application made no later than 2 years after the end of the calendar year in which the amount was paid, pay to the person the amount so paid or such part of it as the person was not liable to pay, unless the person is or is about to become liable to make a payment to Her Majesty in right of Canada, in which case the Minister may apply the amount otherwise payable under this subsection to that liability and notify the person of that action.

History: Per 2013, c. 34, s. 347(31), a written application made under subsection 227(6) in respect of a particular amount that has been paid to the Receiver General is deemed to be filed on time if

(*a*) the application is filed with the Minister of National Revenue by December 23, 2013 [within 180 days after royal assent (June 26, 2013)]; and

(*b*) the particular amount is an amount on which tax would not be payable because of the application of subsection 212(9) if that subsection 212(9) were read without reference to its paragraphs (*a*) to (*c*).

Forms: NR7-R — Application for Refund of Non-Resident Tax Withheld.

Information Circulars: IC 77-16R4 Non-resident income tax (paras. 67 to 77).

▶ 227(6.1) ◀

(6.1) Repayment of non-resident shareholder loan. Where, in respect of a loan from or indebtedness to a corporation or partnership, a person on whose behalf an amount was paid to the Receiver General under Part XIII because of subsection 15(2) and paragraph 214(3)(*a*) repays the loan or indebtedness or a portion of it and it is established by subsequent events or otherwise that the repayment was not made as part of a series of loans or other transactions and repayments, the Minister shall, on written application made no later than 2 years after the end of the calendar year in which the repayment is made, pay to the person an amount equal to the lesser of

(*a*) the amount so paid to the Receiver General in respect of the loan or indebtedness or portion of it, as the case may be, and

(*b*) the amount that would be payable to the Receiver General under Part XIII if a dividend described in paragraph 212(2)(*a*) equal in amount to the amount of the loan or indebtedness repaid were paid by the corporation or partnership to the person at the time of the repayment,

unless the person is or is about to become liable to make a payment to Her Majesty in right of Canada, in which case the Minister may apply the amount otherwise payable under this subsection to that liability and notify the person of that action.

Tax Window Files: Subsections 15(2) and 227(6.1) and Part XIII tax, *April 24, 2015*, CRA Document No. 2014-0560401E5.

▶ 227(6.2) ◀

(6.2) Foreign affiliate dumping — late-filed form. If, in respect of an investment described in subsection 212.3(10), a corporation is deemed by subparagraph 212.3(7)(*d*)(ii) to pay a dividend and the corporation subsequently complies with the requirements of subparagraph 212.3(7)(*d*)(i) in respect of the investment,

(*a*) subject to paragraph (*b*), the Minister shall, on written application made on a particular day that is, or is no more than two years after, the day on which the form described in subparagraph 212.3(7)(*d*)(i) is filed, pay to the corporation an amount equal to the lesser of

(i) the total of all amounts, if any, paid to the Receiver General, on or prior to the particular day, on behalf of a person and in respect of the liability of the person to pay an amount under Part XIII in respect of the dividend, and

(ii) the amount that the person was liable to pay in respect of the dividend under Part XIII;

(*b*) where the corporation or the person is or is about to become liable to make a payment to Her Majesty in right of Canada, the Minister may apply the amount otherwise payable under paragraph (*a*) to that liability and notify the corporation, and, if applicable, the person, of that action; and

(*c*) for the purposes of this Part (other than subparagraph (*a*)(i)), if the amount described in subparagraph (*a*)(ii) exceeds the amount described in subparagraph (*a*)(i), the corporation is deemed to pay that excess to the Receiver General on the day on which the form described in subparagraph 212.3(7)(*d*)(i) is filed.

History: S. 227(6.2) was added by S.C. 2014, c. 39, s. 68(1), applicable in respect of transactions and events that occur after March 28, 2012.

Related Sections: 212.3(7) Reduction of deemed dividend; 227(8.5) No penalty — certain deemed payments.

▶ 227(7) ◀

(7) Application for assessment. Where, on application under subsection (6) by or on behalf of a person to the Minister in respect of an amount paid under Part XII.5 or XIII to the Receiver General, the Minister is not satisfied

(*a*) that the person was not liable to pay any tax under that Part, or

(*b*) that the amount paid was in excess of the tax that the person was liable to pay,

the Minister shall assess any amount payable under that Part by the person and send a notice of assessment to the person, and sections 150 to 163, subsections 164(1) and (1.4) to (7), sections 164.1 to 167 and Division J of Part I apply with any modifications that the circumstances require.

▶ 227(7.1) ◀

(7.1) Application for determination. Where, on application under subsection (6.1) by or on behalf of a person to the Minister in respect of an amount paid under Part XIII to the Receiver General, the Minister is not satisfied that the person is entitled to the amount claimed, the Minister shall, at the person's request, determine, with all due dispatch, the amount, if any, payable under subsection (6.1) to the person and shall send a notice of determination to the person, and sections 150 to 163, subsections 164(1) and (1.4) to (7), sections 164.1 to 167 and Division J of Part I apply with such modifications as the circumstances require.

► 227(8) ◄

(8) Penalty. Subject to subsection (9.5), every person who in a calendar year has failed to deduct or withhold any amount as required by subsection 153(1) or section 215 is liable to a penalty of

(*a*) 10% of the amount that should have been deducted or withheld; or

(*b*) where at the time of the failure a penalty under this subsection was payable by the person in respect of an amount that should have been deducted or withheld during the year and the failure was made knowingly or under circumstances amounting to gross negligence, 20% of that amount.

History: S. 227(8), the portion before paragraph (*a*) was replaced by S.C. 2013, c. 34, s. 351(1), in force June 26, 2013, and formerly read:

(8) *Penalty.* Subject to subsection (8.5), every person who in a calendar year has failed to deduct or withhold any amount as required by subsection 153(1) or section 215 is liable to a penalty of

Related Regulations: Part XLIII.

Related Sections: S. 147.1(3) Deemed registration; s. 153(1) Withholding; s. 215(1) Withholding and remittance of tax; s. 220(3.1) Waiver of penalty or interest; s. 227(8.5) Payments from same establishment; s. 227(9) Penalty; s. 227(10) Assessment — failure to deduct or withhold tax; s. 248(1) Definitions; ITAR s. 62(2) Interest.

Tax Topics: No. 1819, The Implications of Withholding Requirements on Non-Residents Providing Services in Canada.

Information Circulars: IC 75-6R2 Required withholding from amounts paid to non-residents providing services in Canada; IC 77-16R4 Non-resident income tax; IC 07-1 Taxpayer relief provisions.

Interpretation Bulletins: *Secondary* — IT-494 Hire of ships and aircraft from non-residents.

► 227(8.1) ◄

(8.1) Joint and several, or solidary, liability. If a particular person has failed to deduct or withhold an amount as required under subsection 153(1) or section 215 in respect of an amount that has been paid to a non-resident person, the non-resident person is jointly and severally, or solidarily, liable with the particular person to pay any interest payable by the particular person pursuant to subsection (8.3) in respect thereof.

History: S. 227(8.1) was replaced by S.C. 2013, c. 34, s. 165(2), in force June 26, 2013, and formerly read:

(8.1) *Joint and several liability.* Where a particular person has failed to deduct or withhold an amount as required under subsection 153(1) or section 215 in respect of an amount that has been paid to a non-resident person, the non-resident person is jointly and severally liable with the particular person to pay any interest payable by the particular person pursuant to subsection (8.3) in respect thereof.

Related Sections: S. 227(10) Assessment — failure to deduct or withhold tax.

► 227(8.2) ◄

(8.2) Retirement compensation arrangement deductions. Where a person has failed to deduct or withhold any amount as required under subsection 153(1) in respect of a contribution under a retirement compensation arrangement, that person is liable to pay to Her Majesty an amount equal to the amount of the contribution, and each payment on account of that amount is deemed to be, in the year in which the payment is made,

(*a*) for the purposes of paragraph 20(1)(*r*), a contribution by the person to the arrangement; and

(*b*) an amount on account of tax payable by the custodian under Part XI.3.

Related Sections: S. 227(10) Assessment — failure to deduct or withhold tax; s. 248(1), "retirement compensation arrangement".

► 227(8.3) ◄

(8.3) Interest on amounts not deducted or withheld. A person who fails to deduct or withhold any amount as required by subsection 135(3), 135.1(7), 153(1) or 211.8(2) or section 215 shall pay to the Receiver General interest on the amount at the prescribed rate, computed

(*a*) in the case of an amount required by subsection 153(1) to be deducted or withheld from a payment to another person, from the fifteenth day of the month immediately following the month in which the amount was required to be deducted or withheld, or from such earlier day as may be prescribed for the purposes of subsection 153(1), to,

(i) where that other person is not resident in Canada, the day of payment of the amount to the Receiver General, and

(ii) where that other person is resident in Canada, the earlier of the day of payment of the amount to the Receiver General and April 30 of the year immediately following the year in which the amount was required to be deducted or withheld;

(*b*) in the case of an amount required by subsection 135(3) or 135.1(7) or section 215 to be deducted or withheld, from the day on which the amount was required to be deducted or withheld to the day of payment of the amount to the Receiver General; and

(*c*) in the case of an amount required by subsection 211.8(2) to be withheld, from the day on or before which the amount was required to be remitted to the Receiver General to the day of the payment of the amount to the Receiver General.

Related Regulations: 4301.

Related Sections: S. 227(10) Assessment — failure to deduct or withhold tax; s. 248(11) Compound interest.

Information Circulars: IC 77-16R4 Non-resident income tax; IC 07-1 Taxpayer relief provisions.

► 227(8.4) ◄

(8.4) Liability to pay amount not deducted or withheld. A person who fails to deduct or withhold any amount as required under subsection 135(3) or 135.1(7) in respect of a payment made to another person or under subsection 153(1) in respect of an amount paid to another person who is non-resident or who is resident in Canada solely because of paragraph 250(1)(*a*) is liable to pay as tax under this Act on behalf of the other person the whole of the amount that should have been so deducted or withheld and is entitled to deduct or withhold from any amount paid or credited by the person to the other person or otherwise to recover from the other person any amount paid by the person as tax under this Part on behalf of the other person.

Related Sections: S. 227(10) Assessment — failure to deduct or withhold tax.

Canadian Tax Foundation: Boudreault, *Placement Agencies: The Risk in Not Making Source Deductions*, 2015 Canadian Tax Focus 5(1):4.

Tax Topics: No. 1819, The Implications of Withholding Requirements on Non-Residents Providing Services in Canada.

► 227(8.5) ◄

(8.5) No penalty — certain deemed payments. Subsection (8) does not apply to a corporation in respect of

(*a*) an amount of interest deemed by subsection 214(16) to have been paid as a dividend by the corporation unless, if the Act were read without reference to subsection 214(16), a penalty under subsection (8) would have applied in respect of the amount; and

(*b*) an amount deemed by subparagraph 212.3(7)(*d*)(ii) or subsection 247(12) to have been paid as a dividend by the corporation.

History: S. 227(8.5)(*b*) was replaced by S.C. 2014, c. 39, s. 68(2), applicable in respect of transactions and events that occur after March 28, 2012, and formerly read:

(*b*) an amount deemed by subsection 247(12) to have been paid as a dividend by the corporation.

S. 227(8.5) was added by S.C. 2012, c. 31, s. 52(1), applicable to taxation years that end after March 28, 2012.

Related Sections: 212.3(7) Reduction of deemed dividend; 227(6.2) Foreign affiliate dumping — late-filed form.

► 227(8.6) ◄

(8.6) No penalty — qualifying non-resident employers. Subsection (8) does not apply to a *qualifying non-resident employer* (as defined in subsection 153(6)) in respect of a payment made to an employee if, after reasonable inquiry, the employer had no reason to believe at the time of the payment that the employee was not a *qualifying non-resident employee* (as defined in subsection 153(6)).

History: S. 227(8.6) was added by S.C. 2016, c. 7, s. 46(1), applicable in respect of payments made after 2015.

Related Regulations: 200(1.1).

Related Sections: 153(1) Withholding; 153(6) Definitions.

► 227(9) ◄

(9) Penalty. Subject to subsection (9.5), every person who in a calendar year has failed to remit or pay as and when required by this Act or a regulation an amount deducted or withheld as required by this Act or a regulation or an amount of tax that the person is, by section 116 or by a regulation made under subsection 215(4), required to pay is liable to a penalty of

(*a*) subject to paragraph (*b*), if

(i) the Receiver General receives that amount on or before the day it was due, but that amount is not paid in the manner required, 3% of that amount,

(ii) the Receiver General receives that amount

(A) no more than three days after it was due, 3% of that amount,

(B) more than three days and no more than five days after it was due, 5% of that amount, or

(C) more than five days and no more than seven days after it was due, 7% of that amount, or

(iii) that amount is not paid or remitted on or before the seventh day after it was due, 10% of that amount; or

(*b*) where at the time of the failure a penalty under this subsection was payable by the person in respect of an amount that should have been remitted or paid during the year and the failure was made knowingly or under circumstances amounting to gross negligence, 20% of that amount.

Related Regulations: Part VIII; Part XLIII.

Related Sections: S. 116(5) Liability of purchaser; s. 220(3.1) Waiver of penalty or interest; s. 227(8) Penalty; s. 227(9.5) Payment from same establishment; s. 227(10.1) Assessment — failure to remit tax; ITAR s. 62(2) Interest.

Tax Topics: No. 1819, The Implications of Withholding Requirements on Non-Residents Providing Services in Canada.

Information Circulars: IC 07-1 Taxpayer Relief Provisions.

Cases: By the taxpayer's own admission, the payment was late, and the Court was therefore without jurisdiction to grant relief from the penalty assessed on compassionate grounds. *Steen Contractors Ltd. v. M.N.R.*, 91 DTC 145 (T.C.C.)

A penalty for failure to remit taxes imposed after a proposal in bankruptcy was filed could not be proven in bankruptcy. *Re Wosk's Ltd.*, 86 DTC 6243 (B.C.S.C.)

► 227(9.1) ◄

(9.1) Penalty. Notwithstanding any other provision of this Act, any other enactment of Canada, any enactment of a province or any other law, the penalty for failure to remit an amount required to be remitted by a person on or before a prescribed date under subsection 153(1), subsection 21(1) of the *Canada Pension Plan*, subsection 53(1) of the *Unemployment Insurance Act* and subsection 82(1) of the *Employment Insurance Act* shall, unless the person who is required to remit the amount has, knowingly or under circumstances amounting to gross negligence, delayed in remitting the amount or has, knowingly or under circumstances amounting to gross negligence, remitted an amount less than the amount required, apply only to the amount by which the total of all amounts so required to be remitted on or before that date exceeds $500.

Related Sections: S. 153(1) Withholding; s. 248(1) Definitions.

► 227(9.2) ◄

(9.2) Interest on amounts deducted or withheld but not remitted. Where a person has failed to remit as and when required by this Act or a regulation an amount deducted or withheld as required by this Act or a regulation, the person shall pay to the Receiver General interest on the amount at the prescribed rate computed from the day on which the person was so required to remit the amount to the day of remittance of the amount to the Receiver General.

Related Regulations: 4301.

Related Sections: S. 227(10.1) Assessment — failure to remit tax; s. 248(11) Compound interest.

Information Circulars: IC 07-1 Taxpayer Relief Provisions.

► 227(9.3) ◄

(9.3) Interest on certain tax not paid. Where a person fails to pay an amount of tax that, because of section 116, subsection 212(19) or a regulation made under subsection 215(4), the person is required to pay, as and when the person is required to pay it, the person shall pay to the Receiver General interest on the amount at the prescribed rate computed from the day on or before which the amount was required to be paid to the day of payment of the amount to the Receiver General.

Related Regulations: 4301.

Related Sections: S. 116(1) Disposition by non-resident person of certain property; s. 215(4) Regulations creating exceptions; s. 227(10.1) Assessment — failure to remit tax; s. 248(1), "amount"; s. 248(11) Compound interest.

► 227(9.4) ◄

(9.4) Liability to pay amount not remitted. A person who has failed to remit as and when required by this Act or a regulation an amount deducted or withheld from a payment to another person as required by this Act or a regulation is liable to pay as tax under this Act on behalf of the other person the amount so deducted or withheld.

Related Sections: S. 227(10.1) Assessment — failure to remit tax.

Cases: When the taxpayer was dismissed from his employment, he negotiated a settlement of $111,540 from which source deductions were to be withheld. He received the net amount of $72,500 but the employer never remitted the source deductions. The taxpayer was credited with $39,040 under s. 227(9.4). *Suermondt v. The Queen et al.*, 2001 DTC 5389 (F.C.A.), reversing 99 DTC 3513 (T.C.C.).

► 227(9.5) ◄

(9.5) Payment from same establishment. In applying paragraphs (8)(*b*) and (9)(*b*) in respect of an amount required by paragraph 153(1)(*a*) to be deducted or withheld, each establishment of a person shall be deemed to be a separate person.

Related Sections: S. 153(1) Withholding; s. 227(8) Penalty; s. 227(9) Penalty; s. 248(1) Definitions.

► 227(10) ◄

(10) Assessment. The Minister may at any time assess any amount payable under

(*a*) subsection (8), (8.1), (8.2), (8.3) or (8.4) or 224(4) or (4.1) or section 227.1 or 235 by a person,

(*b*) subsection 237.1(7.4) or (7.5) or 237.3(8) by a person or partnership,

(*c*) subsection (10.2) by a person as a consequence of a failure of a non-resident person to deduct or withhold any amount, or

(*d*) Part XIII by a person resident in Canada,

and, where the Minister sends a notice of assessment to that person or partnership, Divisions I and J of Part I apply with any modifications that the circumstances require.

History: S. 227(10)(*b*) was replaced by S.C. 2013, c. 34, s. 351(2), in force June 26, 2013, and formerly read:

(*b*) subsection 237.1(7.4) or (7.5) by a person or partnership,

S. 227(10)(*b*) was replaced by S.C. 2012, c. 19, s. 14, in force on Royal Assent, June 29, 2012. S. 227(10)(*b*) formerly read:

(*b*) subsection 237.1(7.4) by a person or partnership,

Canadian Tax Foundation: Studniberg, *Current Cases: Federal Court of Appeal — JP Morgan: All But Closing the Door on Judicial Oversight of the CRA (Canada (National Revenue) v. JP Morgan Asset Management (Canada) Inc., 2013 FCA 250)*, 2014 Canadian Tax Journal 1:183–192.

► 227(10.01) ◄

(10.01) Part XII.5. The Minister may at any time assess any amount payable under Part XII.5 by a person resident in Canada and, where the Minister sends a notice of assessment to that person, Divisions I and J of Part I apply with any modifications that the circumstances require.

► 227(10.1) ◄

(10.1) Idem. The Minister may at any time assess

(*a*) any amount payable under section 116 or subsection (9), (9.2), (9.3) or (9.4) by any person,

(*a*.1) (Repealed by S.C. 1997, c. 25, s. 67(7).)

(*b*) any amount payable under subsection (10.2) by any person as a consequence of a failure by a non-resident person to remit any amount, and

(*c*) any amount payable under Part XII.5 or XIII by any non-resident person,

and, where the Minister sends a notice of assessment to the person, sections 150 to 163, subsections 164(1) and (1.4) to (7), sections 164.1 to 167 and Division J of Part I apply with such modifications as the circumstances require.

► 227(10.2) ◄

(10.2) Joint and several, or solidary, liability re contributions to RCA. If a non-resident person fails to deduct, withhold or remit an amount as required by subsection 153(1) in respect of a contribution under a retirement compensation arrangement that is paid on behalf of the employees or former employees of an employer with whom the non-resident person does not deal at arm's length, the employer is jointly and severally, or solidarily, liable with the non-resident person to pay any amount payable under subsection (8), (8.2), (8.3), (9), (9.2) or (9.4) by the non-resident person in respect of the contribution.

History: S. 227(10.2) was replaced by S.C. 2013, c. 34, s. 165(3), in force June 26, 2013, and formerly read:

(10.2) *Joint and several liability re contributions to RCA.* Where a non-resident person fails to deduct, withhold or remit an amount as required by subsection 153(1) in respect of a contribution under a retirement compensation arrangement that is paid on behalf of the employees or former employees of an employer with whom the non-resident person does not deal at arm's length, the employer is jointly and severally liable with the non-resident person to pay any amount payable under subsection (8), (8.2), (8.3), (9), (9.2) or (9.4) by the non-resident person in respect of the contribution.

Related Sections: S. 207.6(5) Residents' arrangement.

► 227(10.3)-(10.9) ◄

(10.3)-(10.9) [Tax withholding and remittance] — (Repealed by S.C. 1994, c. 7, Sched. VIII, s. 153.)

► 227(11) ◄

(11) Withholding tax. Provisions of this Act requiring a person to deduct or withhold an amount in respect of taxes from amounts payable to a taxpayer are applicable to Her Majesty in right of Canada or a province.

► 227(12) ◄

(12) Agreement not to deduct void. Where this Act requires an amount to be deducted or withheld, an agreement by the person on whom that obligation is imposed not to deduct or withhold is void.

► 227(13) ◄

(13) Minister's receipt discharges debtor. The receipt of the Minister for an amount deducted or withheld by any person as required by or under this Act is a good and sufficient discharge of the liability of any debtor to the debtor's creditor with respect thereto to the extent of the amount referred to in the receipt.

Cases: The fact that a receipt under former s. 123(13) (now s. 227(13)) may not have discharged the liability of the payer according to the law of the country where the taxpayer is incorporated, does not relieve the payer of his obligation to deduct and remit the tax. *B.C. Electric Railway v. The King*, 2 DTC 839 (P.C.)

► 227(14) ◄

(14) Application of other Parts. Parts IV, IV.1, VI and VI.1 do not apply to any corporation for any period throughout which it is exempt from tax because of section 149.

Interpretation Bulletins: *Secondary* — IT-269R4 Part IV tax on taxable dividends received by a private corporation or a subject corporation.

► 227(15) ◄

(15) Partnership included in "person". In this section, a reference to a "person" with respect to any amount deducted or withheld or required to be deducted or withheld is deemed to include a partnership.

Related Sections: S. 96 General rules; s. 212(13.1) Application of Part XIII tax where payer or payee is a partnership.

► 227(16) ◄

(16) Municipal or provincial corporation excepted. A corporation that at any time in a taxation year would be a corporation described in any of paragraphs 149(1)(*d*) to (*d*.6) but for a provision of an appropriation Act is deemed not to be a private corporation for the purposes of Part IV with respect to that year.

Related Sections: S. 89(1), "private corporation"; s. 104(1) Reference to trust or estate; s. 149(1)(*d*) Corporations owned by the Crown; s. 238(3) Saving; s. 248(1), "amount", "assessment", "corporation", "employer", "prescribed", "regulation", "salary or wages"; s. 255 Canada; ITAR s. 65.1 Part XV of amended Act.

Interpretation Bulletins: *Secondary* — IT-269R4 Part IV tax on taxable dividends received by a private corporation or a subject corporation.

SECTION 227.1: Liability of directors for failure to deduct

► 227.1(1) ◄

(1) Liability of directors for failure to deduct. Where a corporation has failed to deduct or withhold an amount as required by subsection 135(3) or 135.1(7) or section 153 or 215, has failed to remit such an amount or has failed to pay an amount of tax for a taxation year as required under Part VII or VIII, the directors of the corporation at the time the corporation was required to deduct, withhold, remit or pay the amount are jointly and severally, or solidarily, liable, together with the corporation, to pay that amount and any interest or penalties relating to it.

Editorial Note: In certain situations, directors of a corporation are jointly and severally liable with the corporation if the corporation fails to deduct, withhold, remit or pay tax as required by certain provisions of the Act. The potential liability of the director does not extend to the corporation's ordinary Part I tax liability. Rather, the potential liability is limited to cases where the corporation has failed to deduct or withhold taxes pursuant to s. 135(3) or 135.1(7) (patronage dividends), s. 153 (source deductions) or 215 (non-resident withholding), where the corporation has failed to remit such taxes deducted or withheld, or where the corporation has failed to pay the special taxes under Part VII or Part VIII (former SR&ED regimes).

Canadian Tax Foundation: Friedlan and Friedlan, *When Is a Director's Resignation Legally Effective?*, 2017 Tax for the Owner Manager 17(1):5–6; Lewy and Nevsky, *Directors' Liability*, 2014 Canadian Tax Highlights 22(10):10–11; Kreklewetz and Bassindale, *Directors' Liability and Non-Arm's-Length Transfer*, 2014 Canadian Tax Highlights 22(1):4–5.

Tax Topics: No. 1819, The Implications of Withholding Requirements on Non-Residents Providing Services in Canada; No. 1710, Section 227.1 and Director's Liability After the Peoples Decision: A Clarification from Above?; No. 1615, Director's Liability - The Two-Year Rule.

Information Circulars: IC 89-2R3 Directors' Liability.

Cases: Resignation documents were prepared but never executed and contained a blank date field with no instructions as to when they were effective. This was not a written resignation received by the corporation according to the legislation and was not effective. The director, C, did not have a viable due diligence defence based on a reasonable belief she had resigned. *The Queen v. Chriss*, 2016 DTC 5101 (FCA)

A corporate director does not cease to be a director upon the corporation's assignment into bankruptcy. Directors cease to hold office when they die, resign, are removed by the shareholders, or are disqualified. The taxpayer had not resigned or been removed, and he did not claim that the corporation had been liquidated or wound up. The company was not dissolved simply by being expunged from the Quebec business registry. The assessment of the taxpayer for source deduction arrears was valid. *Jobin v. The Queen*, 2015 DTC 1023 (T.C.C.)

The appellant was only a shareholder and not a *de jure* or *de facto* director. He was not liable for payroll deductions or GST remittances. *MacDonald v. The Queen*, 2014 DTC 1212 (T.C.C.)

An inside director tried to ascertain the amount of the company's liabilities and relied on corporate officers and on inaccurate information from Revenue Canada. Given his limited experience in tax and business affairs, it was reasonable for him to accept the Revenue Canada information. The fact that his efforts were unsuccessful does not mean that he failed to act reasonably. *Smith v. The Queen*, 2001 DTC 5226 (F.C.A.), reversing 2000 DTC 1888 (T.C.C.)

The responsibilities of a director require more than merely doing one's best, and complying with the demands of a corporation's most immediately pressing creditors, while ignoring the corporation's tax remittance obligations. On the evidence, the taxpayer failed to show the requisite degree of care, diligence and skill that would enable him to take advantage of the due diligence defence. *Short v. The Queen*, 99 DTC 5348 (F.C.T.D.), affirming 91 DTC 67 (T.C.C.)

The Tax Court did not apply the proper test when it held a director liable for failing to exercise the required standard of care to ensure that the corporation properly calculated and remitted GST. On judicial review, the Federal Court of Appeal referred the case back to the Tax Court for a determination in a manner consistent with the principles enunciated in *Soper. Drover v. The Queen*, 98 DTC 6378 (F.C.A.), reversing unreported (T.C.C.)

Inside directors (i.e., those involved in a corporation's day to day management) are likely to have the most difficulty in establishing a due diligence defence. Conversely, to demonstrate due diligence, outside directors are not required to establish and monitor a trust account to pay unremitted source deductions. They are, however, required to take some action when becoming aware of facts possibly leading to the conclusion that there could be a potential problem with remissions. The extent of the director's business knowledge and experience should also be considered. *Soper v. The Queen*, 97 DTC 5407 (F.C.A.), affirming unreported (T.C.C.).

► 227.1(2) ◄

(2) Limitations on liability. A director is not liable under subsection (1), unless

(*a*) a certificate for the amount of the corporation's liability referred to in that subsection has been registered in the Federal Court under section 223 and execution for that amount has been returned unsatisfied in whole or in part;

(*b*) the corporation has commenced liquidation or dissolution proceedings or has been dissolved and a claim for the amount of the corporation's liability referred to in that subsection has been proved within six months after the earlier of the date of commencement of the proceedings and the date of dissolution; or

(*c*) the corporation has made an assignment or a bankruptcy order has been made against it under the *Bankruptcy and Insolvency Act* and a claim for the amount of the corporation's liability referred to in that subsection has been proved within six months after the date of the assignment or bankruptcy order.

Editorial Note: A director's liability is limited to situations in which (i) a certificate has been registered under s. 223 against the corporation and execution has been returned unsatisfied, (ii) the corporation is dissolved (or has commenced liquidation or dissolution proceedings), or (iii) the corporation is bankrupt. In order for (ii) or (iii) to apply, a claim for the amount of the corporation's liability must be proved within the specified time period.

► 227.1(3) ◄

(3) Idem. A director is not liable for a failure under subsection (1) where the director exercised the degree of care, diligence and skill to prevent the failure that a reasonably prudent person would have exercised in comparable circumstances.

Editorial Note: A director is not liable for the failure of a corporation to remit if he or she exercises the degree of care, diligence and skill to prevent the failure that a reasonable, prudent person would have exercised in comparable circumstances (i.e., the "due diligence" defence). There are numerous cases relating to the due diligence defence, although they tend to turn on a consideration of all the facts and circumstances. Some guiding principles are provided in the cases as follows: (i) there is some uncertainty with respect to the standard of care that is to be applied as the courts have applied an "objective subjective" standard in some circumstances (as enumerated in *Soper v. The Queen*, 97 DTC 5407 (F.C.A.)), which standard can be flexible depending on the director (i.e., "inside" directors will have a higher standard of care than "outside" directors), and in other circumstances, the courts have applied a purely objective standard (as enunciated in *People's Department Stores Ltd. (1992) Inc.*, Re, 2004 SCC 68); (ii) reliance on those to whom the task to remit has been delegated may not be a sufficient due diligence defence; and (iii) the involvement of a trustee in bankruptcy may tie a director's hands.

Tax Topics: No. 2054, *Buckingham v. The Queen* — Stricter Due Diligence Standards for Directors; No. 1710, Section 227.1 and Director's Liability After the Peoples Decision: A Clarification from Above?.

Information Circulars: IC 89-2R3 Directors' Liability.

Cases: The taxpayer's argument that he was a "labourer" and just did what his family asked could not absolve him of his responsibilities as a director. He failed to exercise due diligence and to take any steps to prevent the corporation's failure to make remittances. *Whissell v. The Queen*, 2016 DTC 5109 (FCA)

A director was not held personally liable for unremitted source deductions, because, although he was a lawyer, he was not involved in the day-to-day operation of the corporation and had only limited influence on management. His inquiries and actions met the standard of due diligence required of him in the circumstances. *Cameron v. The Queen*, 2001 DTC 5405 (F.C.A.), reversing 2000 DTC 1495 (T.C.C.)

See *Soper v. The Queen*, 97 DTC 5407 (F.C.A.), after s. 227.1(1).

► 227.1(4) ◄

(4) Limitation period. No action or proceedings to recover any amount payable by a director of a corporation under subsection (1) shall be commenced more than two years after the director last ceased to be a director of that corporation.

Editorial Note: A director is not liable unless the action or proceeding to recover an amount payable has been commenced against him or her within two years after he or she last ceased to be a director of the corporation. If a director's resignation is technically defective, he or she will avoid liability if there are reasonable grounds to support the belief that he or she is no longer a director. Conversely, a person who may have resigned but continues to act as a *de facto* director could still be liable. Further, not knowing or forgetting that one is a director is not sufficient to absolve a director of liability for unremitted taxes.

Cases: The taxpayer provided credible evidence that his resignation as a director took effect in 1993, although a notice of change was not filed until two years later. Even if his resignation was not effective, he actually believed he was no longer a director, which relieved him of liability under s. 227.1. *Alfano v. The Queen*, 2000 DTC 1962 (T.C.C.)

Although the appointment of directors was defective, it was not a nullity and shareholder acquiescence could be considered to have cured the irregularity. In any event, the taxpayers were liable for unremitted source deductions as *de facto* directors. *Parton et al. v. The Queen*, 99 DTC 738 (T.C.C.)

A director's resignation was ineffective under the *Ontario Business Corporations Act* since he had been named in the Articles of Incorporation as the company's first director and no other person had been elected to succeed him at the time at which he had purported to resign. *Zwierschke v. M.N.R.*, 92 DTC 1003 (T.C.C.)

The taxpayers were directors of a company before it obtained a certificate of continuance. They had not acted, nor consented to act, as directors after the continuance and were therefore not liable for unremitted source deductions occurring after that date. *DeWitt et al. v. M.N.R.*, 90 DTC 1027 (T.C.C.).

► 227.1(5) ◄

(5) Amount recoverable. Where execution referred to in paragraph (2)(*a*) has issued, the amount recoverable from a director is the amount remaining unsatisfied after execution.

Editorial Note: The amount recoverable from a director in the case where an execution under s. 223 against the corporation has been returned unsatisfied is only the amount remaining unsatisfied after execution.

► 227.1(6) ◄

(6) Preference. Where a director pays an amount in respect of a corporation's liability referred to in subsection (1) that is proved in liquidation, dissolution or bankruptcy proceedings, the director is entitled to any preference that Her Majesty in right of Canada would have been entitled to had that amount not been so paid and, where a certificate that relates to that amount has been registered, the director is entitled to an assignment of the certificate to the extent of the director's payment, which assignment the Minister is hereby empowered to make.

Editorial Note: If a director pays an amount in respect of the liability of a corporation under s. 227.1(1), which amount is proved in liquidation, dissolution, or bankruptcy proceedings, he or she is given the same preference as a creditor of the corporation as the Crown would have been entitled to if the amount owed by the corporation had remained unpaid.

► 227.1(7) ◄

(7) Contribution. A director who has satisfied a claim under this section is entitled to contribution from the other directors who were liable for the claim.

Editorial Note: A director who has satisfied a claim under s. 227.1 is entitled to contribution from his or her fellow directors who were liable for the claim unless such directors have satisfied the due diligence defence or ceased to be directors for more than two years before the action commenced.

SECTION 228: Applying payments under collection agreements

Where a payment is made to the Minister on account of tax under this Act, an Act of a province that imposes a tax similar to the tax imposed under this Act, or any two or more such Acts, such part of that payment as is applied by the Minister in accordance with the provisions of a collection agreement entered into under Part III of the *Federal-Provincial Fiscal Arrangements and Federal Post-Secondary Education and Health Contributions Act* against the tax payable by a taxpayer for a taxation year under this Act discharges the liability of the taxpayer for that tax only to the extent of the part of the payment so applied, notwithstanding that the taxpayer directed that the payment be applied in a manner other than that provided in the collection agreement or made no direction as to its application.

Related Sections: S. 154 Tax transfer payments.

SECTION 229: Receipt of taxes by banks

(Repealed by R.S.C. 1985, c. 1, 5th Supplement, s. 229.1(1).)

SECTION 229.1: Repeal of s. 229

► 229.1(1) ◄

(1) Repeal of s. 229. Section 229 is repealed.

► 229.1(2) ◄

(2) Coming into force. Subsection (1) shall come into force on a day to be fixed by proclamation.

General

SECTION 230: Records and books

▶ 230(1) ◀

(1) Records and books. Every person carrying on business and every person who is required, by or pursuant to this Act, to pay or collect taxes or other amounts shall keep records and books of account (including an annual inventory kept in prescribed manner) at the person's place of business or residence in Canada or at such other place as may be designated by the Minister, in such form and containing such information as will enable the taxes payable under this Act or the taxes or other amounts that should have been deducted, withheld or collected to be determined.

Related Regulations: Part XVIII.

Related Sections: S. 230(2.1) Records and books — lawyers.

Canadian Tax Foundation: Quigley, *Controlling Tax Information: Limits to Record-Keeping and Disclosure Obligations*, 1999 Canadian Tax Journal 1:1–48.

Tax Topics: No. 2043, Record Retention Policies as a Strategy To Limit Exposure on Audit; No. 1562, Are Your Documentary Records Ready for a Tax Dispute?.

Forms: T137 — Request for Destruction of Books and Records; T183 — Information Return for Electronic Filing.

Information Circulars: IC 77-9R Books, records and other requirements for taxpayers having foreign affiliates; IC 78-10R5 Books and records retention/destruction; IC 05-1R1 Electronic book keeping.

▶ 230(1.1) ◀

(1.1) Idem — (Repealed by 1986, c. 6, s. 120(1).)

▶ 230(2) ◀

(2) Records and books. Every qualified donee referred to in paragraphs (*a*) to (*c*) of the definition "qualified donee" in subsection 149.1(1) shall keep records and books of account — in the case of a qualified donee referred to in any of subparagraphs (*a*)(i) and (iii) and paragraphs (*b*) and (*c*) of that definition, at an address in Canada recorded with the Minister or designated by the Minister — containing

> **Amendment not yet in force**
> **Budget Implementation Act, 2019, No. 1 [S.C. 2019, c. 29]**
>
> **S. 230(2), the portion before paragraph (*a*) was replaced by S.C. 2019, c. 29, s. 41(1), and will read as follows:**
>
> **(2) Records and books.** Every qualified donee referred to in paragraphs (*a*) to (*c*) of the definition "qualified donee" in subsection 149.1(1) shall keep records and books of account — in the case of a qualified donee referred to in any of subparagraphs (*a*)(i) and (iii) and paragraphs (*b*), (*b*.1) and (*c*) of that definition, at an address in Canada recorded with the Minister or designated by the Minister — containing
>
> **Applicable:** In force January 1, 2020.

(*a*) information in such form as will enable the Minister to determine whether there are any grounds for the revocation of its registration under this Act;

(*b*) a duplicate of each receipt containing prescribed information for a donation received by it; and

(*c*) other information in such form as will enable the Minister to verify the donations to it for which a deduction or tax credit is available under this Act.

History: S. 230(2), the portion before paragraph (*a*) was replaced by S.C. 2011, c. 24, s. 70(1), in force January 1, 2012. S. 230(2), the portion before paragraph (*a*) formerly read:

(2) *Idem.* Every registered charity and registered Canadian amateur athletic association shall keep records and books of account at an address in Canada recorded with the Minister or designated by the Minister containing

Related Regulations: Part II; Part XXXV.

Related Sections: S. 149.1(1) "qualified donee".

Cases: A CRA auditor asked a charitable foundation to provide a donor list, which was then used to reassess the donors. The taxpayer was required to collect the information under s. 230(2) and the Minister was entitled to obtain it under s. 231.1. Reassessment of the donors was a logical consequence of the determination that the taxpayer was not operating a valid charitable program, and was a proper exercise of audit powers. No judicial authorization was required since the information was requested to verify the taxpayer's compliance with the Act. *Redeemer Foundation v. M.N.R.*, 2008 DTC 6474 (S.C.C.), affirming 2006 DTC 6712 (F.C.A.), reversing 2005 DTC 5617 (F.C.)

▶ 230(2.1) ◀

(2.1) Idem, lawyers. For greater certainty, the records and books of account required by subsection (1) to be kept by a person carrying on business as a lawyer (within the meaning assigned by subsection 232(1)) whether by means of a partnership or otherwise, include all accounting records of the lawyer, including supporting vouchers and cheques.

▶ 230(3) ◀

(3) Minister's requirement to keep records, etc. Where a person has failed to keep adequate records and books of account for the purposes of this Act, the Minister may require the person to keep such records and books of account as the Minister may specify and that person shall thereafter keep records and books of account as so required.

▶ 230(4) ◀

(4) Limitation period for keeping records, etc. Every person required by this section to keep records and books of account shall retain

(*a*) the records and books of account referred to in this section in respect of which a period is prescribed, together with every account and voucher necessary to verify the information contained therein, for such period as is prescribed; and

(*b*) all other records and books of account referred to in this section, together with every account and voucher necessary to verify the information contained therein, until the expiration of six years from the end of the last taxation year to which the records and books of account relate.

Related Regulations: 5800(1).

Related Sections: S. 168(1) Notice of intention to revoke registration; s. 230.1(3) Application of subsections 230(3) to (8); s. 238(2) Compliance orders; s. 248(1), "amount", "business", "inventory", "prescribed", "registered Canadian amateur athletic association", "registered charity"; s. 255 Canada.

Forms: T137 — Request for Destruction of Books and Records.

Information Circulars: IC 78-10R5 Books and records retention/destruction; IC 05-1R1 Electronic book keeping.

▶ 230(4.1) ◀

(4.1) Electronic records. Every person required by this section to keep records who does so electronically shall retain them in an electronically readable format for the retention period referred to in subsection (4).

Related Sections: S. 231.5(1) Copies; s. 244(9) Proof of documents; s. 248(1), "record".

Tax Topics: No. 1768, Electronic and Other Record-Keeping Requirements — The CRA's Views.

► 230(4.2) ◄

(4.2) Exemptions. The Minister may, on such terms and conditions as are acceptable to the Minister, exempt a person or a class of persons from the requirement in subsection (4.1).

► 230(5) ◄

(5) Exception where no return filed. Where, in respect of any taxation year, a person referred to in subsection (1) has not filed a return with the Minister as and when required by section 150, that person shall retain every record and book of account that is required by this section to be kept and that relates to that taxation year, together with every account and voucher necessary to verify the information contained therein, until the expiration of six years from the day the return for that taxation year is filed.

Forms: T137 — Request for Destruction of Books and Records.

► 230(6) ◄

(6) Exception where objection or appeal. Where a person required by this section to keep records and books of account serves a notice of objection or where that person is a party to an appeal to the Tax Court of Canada under this Act, that person shall retain every record, book of account, account and voucher necessary for dealing with the objection or appeal until, in the case of the serving of a notice of objection, the time provided by section 169 to appeal has elapsed or, in the case of an appeal, until the appeal is disposed of and any further appeal in respect thereof is disposed of or the time for filing any such further appeal has expired.

Forms: T137 — Request for Destruction of Books and Records.

► 230(7) ◄

(7) Exception where demand by Minister. Where the Minister is of the opinion that it is necessary for the administration of this Act, the Minister may, by registered letter or by a demand served personally, require any person required by this section to keep records and books of account to retain those records and books of account, together with every account and voucher necessary to verify the information contained therein, for such period as is specified in the letter or demand.

Forms: T137 — Request for Destruction of Books and Records.

► 230(8) ◄

(8) Permission for earlier disposal. A person required by this section to keep records and books of account may dispose of the records and books of account referred to in this section, together with every account and voucher necessary to verify the information contained therein, before the expiration of the period in respect of which those records and books of account are required to be kept if written permission for their disposal is given by the Minister.

Forms: T137 — Request for Destruction of Books and Records.

Information Circulars: IC 78-10R5 Books and records retention/destruction; IC 05-1R1 Electronic book keeping.

SECTION 230.1: Records re monetary contributions — *Canada Elections Act*

► 230.1(1) ◄

(1) Records re monetary contributions — *Canada Elections Act*. Every agent authorized under the *Canada Elections Act* to accept monetary contributions referred to in that Act shall keep records, sufficient to enable each monetary contribution within the meaning assigned by subsection 127(4.1) that they receive and the expenditures that they make to be verified, (including a duplicate of the receipt referred to in subsection 127(3) for each of those monetary contributions) at

(*a*) in the case of an agent other than an official agent of a candidate, the address recorded in the registry of political parties or of electoral district associations referred to in the *Canada Elections Act*; and

(*b*) in the case of an official agent of a candidate, the agent's address set out in the nomination papers filed under that Act with the returning officer when the candidate was a prospective candidate or any other address that the Minister designates.

History: S. 230.1(1)(*a*) was replaced by S.C. 2014, c. 12, s. 149, in force on December 19, 2014, and formerly read:

(*a*) in the case of an agent other than an official agent of a candidate, the address recorded in the registry of parties or of electoral district associations referred to in the *Canada Elections Act*; and

Related Regulations: Part XX.

Information Circulars: IC 78-10R5 Books and records retention/destruction; IC 05-1R1 Electronic book keeping.

► 230.1(2) ◄

(2) Information return. Each agent to whom subsection (1) applies shall file with the Minister an information return in prescribed form and containing prescribed information. The return is to be filed within the period for the filing of a financial transactions return or an electoral campaign return, as the case may be, under the *Canada Elections Act*.

Related Regulations: 2001.

Forms: T2092 — Contributions to a Registered Party Information Return; T2093 — Contributions to a Candidate at an Election — Information Return.

► 230.1(3) ◄

(3) Application of subsections 230(3) to (8). Subsections 230(3) to (8) apply, with any modifications that the circumstances require, in respect of the keeping of records by agents as required by subsection (1).

Related Regulations: 5800(2).

► 230.1(4) ◄

(4) Reports to chief electoral officer — (Repealed by S.C. 1994, c. 21, s. 106.)

► 230.1(5) ◄

(5) No report to enable identification of contributor — (Repealed by S.C. 1994, c. 21, s. 106.)

► 230.1(6) ◄

(6) Definitions — (Repealed by S.C. 2003, c. 19, s. 74(1).)

► 230.1(7) ◄

(7) Definition of "amount contributed" — (Repealed by S.C. 2003, c. 19, s. 74(1).)

SECTION 231: Definitions

In sections 231.1 to 231.8,

History: S. 231, the portion before the first definition was replaced by S.C. 2018, c. 27, s. 22, in force December 13, 2018, and formerly read:

S. 231. *Definitions.* In sections 231.1 to 231.7,

"authorized person" —"authorized person" means a person authorized by the Minister for the purposes of sections 231.1 to 231.5;

"document" —"document" includes money, a security and a record;

Related Sections: S. 248(1), "Record".

"dwelling-house" —"dwelling-house" means the whole or any part of a building or structure that is kept or occupied as a permanent or temporary residence and includes

(*a*) a building within the curtilage of a dwelling-house that is connected to it by a doorway or by a covered and enclosed passageway, and

(*b*) a unit that is designed to be mobile and to be used as a permanent or temporary residence and that is being used as such a residence;

"judge" —"judge" means a judge of a superior court having jurisdiction in the province where the matter arises or a judge of the Federal Court.

SECTION 231.1: Inspections

► 231.1(1) ◄

(1) Inspections. An authorized person may, at all reasonable times, for any purpose related to the administration or enforcement of this Act,

(*a*) inspect, audit or examine the books and records of a taxpayer and any document of the taxpayer or of any other person that relates or may relate to the information that is or should be in the books or records of the taxpayer or to any amount payable by the taxpayer under this Act, and

(*b*) examine property in an inventory of a taxpayer and any property or process of, or matter relating to, the taxpayer or any other person, an examination of which may assist the authorized person in determining the accuracy of the inventory of the taxpayer or in ascertaining the information that is or should be in the books or records of the taxpayer or any amount payable by the taxpayer under this Act,

and for those purposes the authorized person may

(*c*) subject to subsection (2), enter into any premises or place where any business is carried on, any property is kept, anything is done in connection with any business or any books or records are or should be kept, and

(*d*) require the owner or manager of the property or business and any other person on the premises or place to give the authorized person all reasonable assistance and to answer all proper questions relating to the administration or enforcement of this Act and, for that purpose, require the owner or manager to attend at the premises or place with the authorized person.

Related Sections: S. 232(3.1) Examination of certain documents where privilege claimed; s. 238(2) Compliance orders.

Canadian Tax Foundation: Hu, *BP: Working Papers Held To Be Accessible to CRA*, 2015 Canadian Tax Focus 2(4):3; Suarez and James, *Uncertain Tax Positions Disclosure*, 2015 Canadian Tax Highlights 23(9):2–3; Du Pont and Lubetsky, *The Power To Audit Is the Power To Destroy: Judicial Supervision of the Exercise of Audit Powers*, 2013 Canadian Tax Journal SS:103–121; Plumridge, *CRA's Access to Taxpayer Documents Expanded*, 2013 Canadian Tax Highlights 21(5):11–12; Schmidt, *Limits on the CRA's Power To Access Information*, 2012 Canadian Tax Highlights 20(4):3–4; Kroft, *Recent Developments in CRA's Reach for Information: Questions You Want Answered*, 2011 British Columbia Tax Conference 5:5–11 and 55–63; Kroft, *Recent Developments in CRA's Reach for Information: Questions You Want Answered*, 2011 Ontario Tax Conference 4:5–11 and 55–63; Kreklewetz and Bassindale, *Beware of Warrantless Seizures*, 2011 Tax for the Owner-Manager 11(3):8–9; Henry and Kingissepp, *Managing the Confidentiality of Tax Accrual Working Papers*, 2009 Conference Report 29:1–28; Heddema and Russell, *CRA Requests for Information Under the Income Tax Act: A Review of Sections 231.1 and 231.2*, 2008 British Columbia Tax Conference 1:1–18; Kepes and Winters, *Dealing with the CRA: An Update to the Voluntary Disclosure Program, Taxpayer Relief (Fairness) Provisions, and Matters Related to Dispute Resolution*, 2007 Ontario Tax Conference 5A:2–46; Tari, *Audit, Enforcement and Collection*, 2003 Ontario Tax Conference 19:3–37; Innes and Williams, *Protections Against Self-Incrimination in Income Tax Audits, Investigations, and Inquiries*, 2001 Canadian Tax Journal 6:1459–1485.

Tax Profile: October 2006 — Tax Controversies in Canada: A Variety of Issues.

Tax Topics: No. 2380, *MNR v. Cameco*: Minister's Ability To Compel Oral Interviews in Audit Examined; No. 2262, Taxpayers Obliged to Provide Tax Accrual Working Papers During an Audit; No. 2023-24, 2010 Canadian Tax Foundation CRA Roundtable: Pipelines, Privilege and Working Papers (Again!); No. 1971-72, 2009 Canadian Tax Foundation Conference: Wizards, Tiny Taxes and "Evil" Kirk; No. 1811, CRA's Use of Audit Powers "Redeemed"; No. 1763-64, When Audit Obligations Conflict with Rights to Privilege — Who Wins?.

Guides: RC4024 Enhancing Service to Large Businesses.

Information Circulars: IC 71-14R3 The tax audit; IC 73-10R3 Tax evasion.

Cases: Paragraph 231.1(1)(*d*) does not provide the Minister with an unlimited right to conduct oral interviews. The Minister could not compel the taxpayer's employees, during an audit, to answer oral questions posed by CRA auditors. The time and cost of interviewing 25 individuals in numerous locations was not proportional to the information being sought. Written questions would suffice. *Canada (MNR) v. Cameco*, 2017 DTC 5102 (FC), affirmed *Canada (MNR) v. Cameco*, 2019 DTC 5042 (FCA)

Where the Minister's predominant purpose in issuing a demand is to determine tax liability for civil audit purposes, an individual's Charter rights are neither applicable nor engaged. Only when the predominant purpose is to determine penal liability do sections 7 and 8 of the Charter preclude the Minister from using section 231.1. The totality of the circumstances at the time the request is made, applying the factors set out in *Jarvis* (2002 SCC 73), must be reviewed in making a determination of "predominant purpose". Possible future criminal proceedings do not excuse a taxpayer from compliance. A mere suspicion does not change the predominant purpose of an audit into a criminal investigation. *Minister of National Revenue v. Stankovic*, 2018 DTC 5056 (FC)

A CRA auditor asked a charitable foundation to provide a donor list, which was then used to reassess the donors. The taxpayer was required to collect the information under s. 230(2) and the Minister was entitled to obtain it under s. 231.1. Reassessment of the donors was a logical consequence of the determination that the taxpayer was not operating a valid charitable program, and was a proper exercise of audit powers. No judicial authorization was required since the information was requested to verify the taxpayer's compliance with the Act. *Redeemer Foundation v. M.N.R.*, 2008 DTC 6474 (S.C.C.), affirming 2006 DTC 6712 (F.C.A.), reversing 2005 DTC 5617 (F.C.)

Evidence gathered by the CCRA under s. 231.1(1) and 231.2(1) may be used in a subsequent investigation or prosecution for tax offences. However, where the predominant purpose of a question or inquiry is the determination of criminal liability, CCRA relinquishes the authority to use s. 231.1(1) and 231.2(1). There is no clear formula to determine when an audit inquiry becomes a criminal investigation and there is nothing to prevent the CCRA from carrying out an audit and a criminal investigation simultaneously. *Jarvis v. The Queen et al.*, 2002 DTC 7547 (S.C.C.), affirming 271 A.R. 263, (Alta C.A.) (2000), affirming 98 DTC 6308 (Alta Q.B.). *Ling v. The Queen et al.*, 2002 DTC 7566 (S.C.C.), affirming 149 C.C.C. (3d) 127 (B.C.C.A.), (2000), affirming [1999] 3 C.T.C. 386 (B.C.S.C.)

A requirement for information pursuant to [former] s. 231(3) is not a seizure within s. 8 of the Charter and does not contravene it. Various grounds of attack are available, including failure to provide a reasonable time for production, privileged documents, irrelevancy of documents to the matters in issue and any attempt by the Minister to conduct a "fishing expedition". *The Queen v. McKinlay Transport Ltd.*, 90 DTC 6243 (S.C.C.)

Other Publications: AD-19-02R Obtaining Information for Audit Purposes.

► 231.1(2) ◄

(2) Prior authorization. Where any premises or place referred to in paragraph (1)(*c*) is a dwelling-house, an authorized person may not enter that dwelling-house without the consent of the occupant except under the authority of a warrant under subsection (3).

► 231.1(3) ◄

(3) Application. Where, on *ex parte* application by the Minister, a judge is satisfied by information on oath that

(*a*) there are reasonable grounds to believe that a dwelling-house is a premises or place referred to in paragraph (1)(*c*),

(*b*) entry into the dwelling-house is necessary for any purpose relating to the administration or enforcement of this Act, and

(*c*) entry into the dwelling-house has been, or there are reasonable grounds to believe that entry will be, refused,

the judge may issue a warrant authorizing an authorized person to enter the dwelling-house subject to such conditions as are specified in the warrant but, where the judge is not satisfied that entry into the dwelling-house is necessary for any purpose relating to the administration or enforcement of this Act, the judge may

(*d*) order the occupant of the dwelling-house to provide to an authorized person reasonable access to any document or property that is or should be kept in the dwelling-house, and

(*e*) make such other order as is appropriate in the circumstances to carry out the purposes of this Act,

to the extent that access was or may be expected to be refused and that the document or property is or may be expected to be kept in the dwelling-house.

SECTION 231.2: Requirement to provide documents or information

► 231.2(1) ◄

(1) Requirement to provide documents or information. Notwithstanding any other provision of this Act, the Minister may, subject to subsection (2), for any purpose related to the administration or enforcement of this Act (including the collection of any amount payable under this Act by any person), of a listed international agreement or, for greater certainty, of a tax treaty with another country, by notice served personally or by registered or certified mail, require that any person provide, within such reasonable time as is stipulated in the notice,

Proposed Amendment

2019 Federal Budget Resolutions

The portion of subsection 231.2(1) of the Act before paragraph (*a*) is replaced by the following:

SECTION 231.2 Requirement to provide documents or information.

(1) Notwithstanding any other provision of this Act, the Minister may, subject to subsection (2), for any purpose related to the administration or enforcement of this Act (including the collection of any amount payable under this Act by any person), of a listed international agreement or, for greater certainty, of a tax treaty with another country, by notice sent or served in accordance with subsection (1.1), require that any person provide, within such reasonable time as is stipulated in the notice,

---

Applicable: In force on January 1, 2020.

(*a*) any information or additional information, including a return of income or a supplementary return; or

(*b*) any document.

Proposed Amendment

2019 Federal Budget Resolutions

Section 231.2 of the Act is amended by adding the following after subsection (1):

(1.1) Notice. A notice referred to in subsection (1) may be

(*a*) served personally;

(*b*) sent by registered or certified mail; or

(*c*) sent electronically, in the case of a bank, or credit union, that has provided written consent to receive notices under subsection (1) electronically.

Applicable: In force on January 1, 2020.

History: S. 231.2(1), the portion before paragraph (*a*) was replaced by S.C. 2013, c. 34, s. 353, in force on June 26, 2013, and formerly read:

(1) *Requirement to provide documents or information.* Notwithstanding any other provision of this Act, the Minister may, subject to subsection (2), for any purpose related to the administration or enforcement of this Act (including the collection of any amount payable under this Act by any person), of a comprehensive tax information exchange agreement between Canada and another country or jurisdiction that is in force and has effect or, for greater certainty, of a tax treaty with another country, by notice served personally or by registered or certified mail, require that any person provide, within such reasonable time as is stipulated in the notice,

Related Sections: S. 232(3.1) Examination of certain documents where privilege claimed.

Canadian Tax Foundation: Antel, *Disclosing Information to the CRA About Unnamed Non-Target Persons,* 2013 Canadian Tax Focus 3(1):4; Plumridge, *CRA's Access to Taxpayer Documents Expanded,* 2013 Canadian Tax Highlights 21(5):11–12; Schmidt, *Limits on the CRA's Power To Access Information,* 2012 Canadian Tax Highlights 20(4):3–4; Kroft, *Recent Developments in CRA's Reach for Information: Questions You Want Answered,* 2011 British Columbia Tax Conference 5:11–19; Kroft, *Recent Developments in CRA's Reach for Information: Questions You Want Answered,* 2011 Ontario Tax Conference 4:11–19; Henry and Kingissepp, *Managing the Confidentiality of Tax Accrual Working Papers,* 2009 Conference Report 29:1–28; Lindsay and Robinson, *Requirements To Produce Documents and Information: Policy and Practice,* 2008 Conference Report 12:1–38; Heddema and Russell, *CRA Requests for Information Under the Income Tax Act: A Review of Sections 231.1 and 231.2,* 2008 British Columbia Tax Conference 1:1–18; Thomas, *Current Cases: The Federal Court — Charitable Donations: An Investigation Minefield,* 2006 Canadian Tax Journal 2:457–461; Sidhu, *Current Cases: The Federal Court of Appeal — The Art of Redaction (CCRA v. Artistic Ideas Inc., 2005 DTC 5165),* 2005 Canadian Tax Journal 4:1061–1066; Barsalou, *Transfer-Pricing Audits: Selected Issues,* 2003 Conference Report 12:1–25; Kroft et al., *Legislative, Administrative, and Judicial Developments: Current Cases — Increased Requests for Information,* 2003 Conference Report 9:10–13; Penny, *Accountant-Client Privilege and Section 231.2 Requirements,* 2003 Tax for the Owner-Manager 3(4):1; Wilson, *CCRA Gains Further Access to Taxpayer Information,* 2002 Tax for the Owner-Manager 2(3):20–21; Innes and Williams, *Protections Against Self-Incrimination in Income Tax Audits, Investigations, and Inquiries,* 2001 Canadian Tax Journal 6:1459–1485; Stewart, *CCRA Audits and Use of Audit Information in Criminal Investigations,* 2000 Prairie Provinces Tax Conference 3:1–35; Sturrock, *Revenue Canada Audits and Investigations: Powers, Procedures, Abuses, and Remedies,* 1999 Conference Report 21:1–23; Beninger and Tahara, *Current Cases: Federal Court of Appeal — The Next Step? Charter Remedies in Civil Proceedings (The Queen v. O'Neill Motors Limited, 98 DTC 6424),* 1999 Canadian Tax Journal 4:957–968.

Tax Profile: October 2006 — Tax Controversies in Canada: A Variety of Issues; November 2003 — Current Cases.

Tax Topics: No. 2447, Federal Court Refuses To Authorize a Requirement for Information in Respect of Unnamed Persons; No. 2413, Requirement for Information and Inevitability of a Criminal Investigation: Revisiting *Jarvis*; No. 2319, Section 231.2 Requirements Issued to Lawyers Held Unconstitutional: *Chambre des Notaries du Québec* and *Thompson*; No. 2311, Supreme Court Reaffirms Supremacy of Solicitor-Client Privilege; No. 2023-24, 2010 Canadian Tax Foundation CRA Roundtable: Pipelines, Privilege and Working Papers (Again!); No. 1640, Required Reading Regarding Requirements; No. 1530, The CCRA's Administrative Powers Under the *Income Tax Act* and the Canada-United States Income Tax Convention.

Information Circulars: IC 73-10R3 Tax evasion.

Cases: Any provision which interferes with solicitor-client privilege more than absolutely necessary will be deemed unreasonable. The threshold is quite low. A provision will only withstand Charter scrutiny if its impact is minimal. The Court "read down" s. 231.2(1) and held it was inapplicable to notaries and lawyers in their capacity as legal advisers. *Canada (Attorney General) v. Chambre des notaires du Québec*, 2016 DTC 5067 (SCC)

The Court refused to order an auditor to disclose documents covered by solicitor-client privilege. The documents were not knowingly disclosed to the auditor pursuant to a limited waiver of privilege and, although they were disclosed to third parties, privilege was maintained under the doctrines of common interest and inadvertent disclosure. *M.N.R. v. Grant Thornton*, 2013 DTC 5008 (F.C.)

The taxpayers were required to produce information relating to some of their Canadian customers, in order to verify the customers' compliance with the Act. Although the information was stored electronically on U.S. servers, owned by the taxpayers' parent corporation, it was not "foreign-based information", since it was readily accessible in Canada for the taxpayers' use. *eBay Canada Limited et al. v. M.N.R.*, 2008 DTC 6728 (F.C.A.), affirming 2007 DTC 5573 (F.C.)

Although CCRA Requirements issued against individuals during a criminal investigation violated s. 7 and s. 8 of the Charter, corporations do not have the same rights. Requirements issued to the individual applicants were quashed, whereas those issued to the corporate applicants were upheld. *Kligman et al. v. M.N.R.*, 2003 DTC 5100 (F.C.T.D.)

Evidence gathered by the CCRA under s. 231.1(1) and 231.2(1) may be used in a subsequent investigation or prosecution for tax offences. However, where the predominant purpose of a question or inquiry is the determination of criminal liability, CCRA relinquishes the authority to use s. 231.1(1) and 231.2(1). There is no clear formula to determine when an audit inquiry becomes a criminal investigation and there is nothing to prevent the CCRA from carrying out an audit and a criminal investigation simultaneously. *Jarvis v. The Queen et al.*, 2002 DTC 7547 (S.C.C.), affirming, 271 A.R. 263, (Alta C.A.) (2000), affirming 98 DTC 6308 (Alta Q.B.). *Ling v. The Queen et al.*, 2002 DTC 7566 (S.C.C.), affirming 149 C.C.C. (3d) 127, (B.C.C.A.), (2000), affirming 3 C.T.C. 386 (B.C.S.C.)[1999]

Requirements demanding tax planning information were valid. A requirement can be valid even if its sole purpose is to determine whether there was an avoidance transaction. *Fraser Milner Casgrain LLP et al. v. M.N.R.*, 2002 DTC 7310 (F.C.T.D.)

Subsection 231.2(1) authorizes the Minister to demand responses to written questions. In addition, the applicants were not entitled to any accountant-client privilate. *Tower et al. v. M.N.R. et al.*, 2003 DTC 5540 (F.C.A.), reversing in part 2002 DTC 7315 (F.C.T.D.)

The Minister issued certain requirements for the production of information under s. 231.2(1). The requirements were not stayed pending the outcome of the plaintiff's proceedings against the Crown for certain declaratory relief. *Bisaillon et. al. v. The Queen*, 99 DTC 5695 (F.C.A.), affirming 99 DTC 5270 (F.C.T.D.)

If the required statements concerning the taxpayer's expenses and net worth were communicated to the RCMP while narcotics-related charges against him still remained outstanding, his right to remain silent would be infringed. *Tyler v. M.N.R.*, 91 DTC 5022 (F.C.A.)

The demand for information must provide a reasonable time within which such information or document is to be provided. It has been held that a demand to produce "without delay" does not satisfy this requirement. *Joseph et al. v. M.N.R.*, 85 DTC 5391 (Ont. H.C.)

Other Publications: AD-19-02R Obtaining Information for Audit Purposes.

► 231.2(2) ◄

(2) Unnamed persons. The Minister shall not impose on any person (in this section referred to as a "third party") a requirement under subsection (1) to provide information or any document relating to one or more unnamed persons unless the Minister first obtains the authorization of a judge under subsection (3).

Tax Topics: No. 1917, Requirement Letters and Technology — *eBay Canada Limited*; No. 1913, The *Amex* Decision: Further Expansion of the CRA's Audit Powers and Requirement for Third Parties To Provide Information on Unnamed Persons.

Cases: A CRA auditor asked a charitable foundation to provide a donor list, which was then used to reassess the donors. The taxpayer was required to collect the information under s. 230(2) and the Minister was entitled to obtain it under s. 231.1. Reassessment of the donors was a logical consequence of the determination that the taxpayer was not operating a valid charitable program, and was a proper exercise of audit powers. No judicial authorization was required since the information was requested to verify the taxpayer's compliance with the Act. *Redeemer Foundation v. M.N.R.*, 2008 DTC 6474 (S.C.C.), affirming 2006 DTC 6712 (F.C.A.), reversing 2005 DTC 5617 (F.C.).

► 231.2(3) ◄

(3) Judicial authorization. A judge of the Federal Court may, on application by the Minister and subject to any conditions that the judge considers appropriate, authorize the Minister to impose on a third party a requirement under subsection (1) relating to an unnamed person or more than one unnamed person (in this section referred to as the "group") if the judge is satisfied by information on oath that

(*a*) the person or group is ascertainable; and

(*b*) the requirement is made to verify compliance by the person or persons in the group with any duty or obligation under this Act.

(*c*) (Repealed by 1996, c. 21, s. 58(1).)

(*d*) (Repealed by 1996, c. 21, s. 58(1).)

History: S. 231.2(3), the portion before paragraph (*a*) was replaced by S.C. 2013, c. 33, s. 21(1), applicable to applications made by the Minister of National Revenue after June 26, 2013, and formerly read:

(3) *Judicial authorization.* On *ex parte* application by the Minister, a judge may, subject to such conditions as the judge considers appropriate, authorize the Minister to impose on a third party a requirement under subsection (1) relating to an unnamed person or more than one unnamed person (in this section referred to as the "group") where the judge is satisfied by information on oath that

Tax Topics: No. 2126, Section 8 of the Charter and Requirements to Provide Documents and Information in Respect of Unnamed Persons; No. 1917, Requirement Letters and Technology — *eBay Canada Limited*; No. 1913, The *Amex* Decision: Further Expansion of the CRA's Audit Powers and Requirement for Third Parties To Provide Information on Unnamed Persons; No. 1811, CRA's Use of Audit Powers "Redeemed".

Cases: Authorizations, requiring the taxpayers to produce information about purchasers of a particular insurance product, were quashed since the Minister failed to disclose relevant information on the *ex parte* application and the primary reason for the authorization was to quash the insurance product, not to ensure compliance with the Act. *M.N.R. v. RBC Life Insurance Company*, 2013 DTC 5051 (F.C.A.), affirming 2011 DTC 5172 (F.C.)

An authorization, requiring the taxpayers to produce customer information, was quashed because the Minister had provided inaccurate and misleading information on the *ex parte* application and failed to disclose that there were alternative sources for obtaining the information. *M.N.R. v. Lordco Parts Ltd.*, 2013 DTC 5050 (F.C.A.), reversing 2011 DTC 5035 (F.C.)

Since the Minister was seeking information relating to the tax returns of unidentified taxpayers, prior judicial authorization was required in order for the Minister to proceed by way of s. 231.2(3). *Canadian Forest Products Ltd. et al. v. M.N.R.*, 96 DTC 6506 (F.C.T.D.)

► 231.2(4) ◄

(4) Service of authorization — (Repealed by S.C. 2013, c. 33, s. 21(2).)

History: S. 231.2(4) was repealed by S.C. 2013, c. 33, s. 21(2), applicable to applications made by the Minister of National Revenue after June 26, 2013, and formerly read:

(4) *Service of authorization.* Where an authorization is granted under subsection (3), it shall be served together with the notice referred to in subsection (1).

► 231.2(5) ◄

(5) Review of authorization — (Repealed by S.C. 2013, c. 33, s. 21(2).)

History: S. 231.2(5) was repealed by S.C. 2013, c. 33, s. 21(2), applicable to applications made by the Minister of National Revenue after June 26, 2013, and formerly read:

(5) *Review of authorization.* Where an authorization is granted under subsection (3), a third party on whom a notice is served under subsection (1) may, within 15 days after the service of the notice, apply to the judge who granted the authorization or, where the judge is unable to act, to another judge of the same court for a review of the authorization.

► 231.2(6) ◄

(6) Powers on review — (Repealed by S.C. 2013, c. 33, s. 21(2).)

History: S. 231.2(6) was repealed by S.C. 2013, c. 33, s. 21(2), applicable to applications made by the Minister of National Revenue after June 26, 2013, and formerly read:

(6) *Powers on review.* On hearing an application under subsection (5), a judge may cancel the authorization previously granted if the judge is not then satisfied that the conditions in paragraphs (3)(*a*) and (*b*) have been met and the judge may confirm or vary the authorization if the judge is satisfied that those conditions have been met.

► 231.2(7) ◄

(7) Additional remedy — (Repealed by 1988, c. 55, s. 174.)

SECTION 231.3: Search warrant

► 231.3(1) ◄

(1) Search warrant. A judge may, on *ex parte* application by the Minister, issue a warrant in writing authorizing any person named therein to enter and search any building, receptacle or place for any document or thing that may afford evidence as to the commission of an offence under this Act and to seize the document or thing and, as soon as practicable, bring it before, or make a report in respect of it to, the judge or, where the judge is unable to act, another judge of the same court to be dealt with by the judge in accordance with this section.

Canadian Tax Foundation: Innes and Williams, *Protections Against Self-Incrimination in Income Tax Audits, Investigations, and Inquiries*, 2001 Canadian Tax Journal 6:1459–1485.

Information Circulars: 73-10R3 Tax evasion.

Cases: Although the ITA and ETA handle the subject matter of search warrants somewhat differently than the Criminal Code, they are not inconsistent with it. The Code warrant procedure may be less rigorous, but there was no violation of the taxpayer's Charter rights. *R v. Baudais*, 2014 DTC 5071 (B.C.S.C.)

A stolen safe was recovered by police. Documents from the safe, that were photocopied by police and provided to Revenue Canada, were inadmissible in tax proceedings since they were obtained through unreasonable search, contrary to s. 8 of the Charter and their admission would bring the administration of justice into disrepute. *Law et al v. The Queen*, 2002 DTC 6789 (S.C.C.), reversing 2001 DTC 5664 (N.B.C.A.), which reversed 2001 DTC 5661 (N.B.Q.B.)

Section 231.3 was found to be of no force and effect as a result of the Supreme Court of Canada decision in *Baron v. Her Majesty the Queen*, 93 DTC 5018. As a result of this decision, subsection 231.3(3) was amended, effective June 15, 1994, to replace the word "shall", with the word "may", apparently giving a judge the prerequisite discretion to make the provision valid under the Charter.

► 231.3(2) ◄

(2) Evidence in support of application. An application under subsection (1) shall be supported by information on oath establishing the facts on which the application is based.

► 231.3(3) ◄

(3) Evidence. A judge may issue the warrant referred to in subsection (1) where the judge is satisfied that there are reasonable grounds to believe that

(*a*) an offence under this Act was committed;

(*b*) a document or thing that may afford evidence of the commission of the offence is likely to be found; and

(*c*) the building, receptacle or place specified in the application is likely to contain such a document or thing.

Cases: Section 231.3 was found to be of no force and effect as a result of the Supreme Court of Canada decision in *Baron v. Her Majesty the Queen*, 93 DTC 5018. As a result of this decision, subsection 231.3(3) was amended, effective June 15, 1994, to replace the word "shall", with the word "may", apparently giving a judge the prerequisite discretion to make the provision valid under the Charter.

► 231.3(4) ◄

(4) Contents of warrant. A warrant issued under subsection (1) shall refer to the offence for which it is issued, identify the building, receptacle or place to be searched and the person alleged to have committed the offence and it shall be reasonably specific as to any document or thing to be searched for and seized.

► 231.3(5) ◄

(5) Seizure of document. Any person who executes a warrant under subsection (1) may seize, in addition to the document or thing referred to in that subsection, any other document or thing that the person believes on reasonable grounds affords evidence of the commission of an offence under this Act and shall as soon as practicable bring the document or thing before, or make a report in respect thereof to, the judge who issued the warrant or, where the judge is unable to act, another judge of the same court to be dealt with by the judge in accordance with this section.

► 231.3(6) ◄

(6) Retention of things seized. Subject to subsection (7), where any document or thing seized under subsection (1) or (5) is brought before a judge or a report in respect thereof is made to a judge, the judge shall, unless the Minister waives retention, order that it be retained by the Minister, who shall take reasonable care to ensure that it is preserved until the conclusion of any investigation into the offence in relation to which the document or thing was seized or until it is required to be produced for the purposes of a criminal proceeding.

► 231.3(7) ◄

(7) Return of things seized. Where any document or thing seized under subsection (1) or (5) is brought before a judge or a report in respect thereof is made to a judge, the judge may, of the judge's own motion or on summary application by a person with an interest in the document or thing on three clear days notice of application to the Deputy Attorney General of Canada, order that the document or thing be returned to the person from whom it was seized or the person who is otherwise legally entitled thereto if the judge is satisfied that the document or thing

(*a*) will not be required for an investigation or a criminal proceeding; or

(*b*) was not seized in accordance with the warrant or this section.

► 231.3(8) ◄

(8) Access and copies. The person from whom any document or thing is seized pursuant to this section is entitled, at all reasonable times and subject to such reasonable conditions as may be imposed by the Minister, to inspect the document or thing and to obtain one copy of the document at the expense of the Minister.

Cases: Although search warrants were defective, the evidence obtained was still to be admitted, since, to do so would not "bring the administration of justice into disrepute" within the meaning of s. 24(2) of the Charter. *The Queen v. Hazlewood et al.*, 93 DTC 5406 (S.C. B.C.)

However, the evidence obtained under s. 231.3, in violation of the Charter, was excluded where the Crown could have attempted to return the seized items and immediately seize them properly again. *The Queen v. Agopsowicz*, 93 DTC 5412 (Prov.Ct. Sask.)

SECTION 231.4: Inquiry

► 231.4(1) ◄

(1) Inquiry. The Minister may, for any purpose related to the administration or enforcement of this Act, authorize any person, whether or not the person is an officer of the Canada Revenue Agency, to make such inquiry as the person may deem necessary with reference to anything relating to the administration or enforcement of this Act.

Canadian Tax Foundation: Innes and Williams, *Protections Against Self-Incrimination in Income Tax Audits, Investigations, and Inquiries*, 2001 Canadian Tax Journal 6:1459–1485.

Information Circulars: IC 73-10R3 Tax evasion.

► 231.4(2) ◄

(2) Appointment of hearing officer. Where the Minister, pursuant to subsection (1), authorizes a person to make an inquiry, the Minister shall forthwith apply to the Tax Court of Canada for an order appointing a hearing officer before whom the inquiry will be held.

► 231.4(3) ◄

(3) Powers of hearing officer. For the purposes of an inquiry authorized under subsection (1), a hearing officer appointed under subsection (2) in relation thereto has all the powers conferred on a commissioner by sections 4 and 5 of the *Inquiries Act* and that may be conferred on a commissioner under section 11 thereof.

► 231.4(4) ◄

(4) When powers to be exercised. A hearing officer appointed under subsection (2) in relation to an inquiry shall exercise the powers conferred on a commissioner by section 4 of the *Inquiries Act* in relation to such persons as the person authorized to make the inquiry considers appropriate for the conduct thereof but the hearing officer shall not exercise the power to punish any person unless, on application by the hearing officer, a judge of a superior or county court certifies that the power may be exercised in the matter disclosed in the application and the applicant has given to the person in respect of whom the applicant proposes to exercise the power 24 hours notice of the hearing of the application or such shorter notice as the judge considers reasonable.

► 231.4(5) ◄

(5) Rights of witness at inquiry. Any person who gives evidence in an inquiry authorized under subsection (1) is entitled to be represented by counsel and, on request made by the person to the Minister, to receive a transcript of the evidence given by the person.

► 231.4(6) ◄

(6) Rights of person whose affairs are investigated. Any person whose affairs are investigated in the course of an inquiry authorized under subsection (1) is entitled to be present and to be represented by counsel throughout the inquiry unless the hearing officer appointed under subsection (2) in relation to the inquiry, on application by the Minister or a person giving evidence, orders otherwise in relation to the whole or any part of the inquiry on the ground that the presence of the person and the person's counsel, or either of them, would be prejudicial to the effective conduct of the inquiry.

Cases: The holding of an inquiry and the issuing of *subpoenas duces tecum* cannot be seen as inevitably leading to an unreasonable seizure within the meaning of section 8 of the Charter. As well, inasmuch as the taxpayer had not been subpoenaed, it was premature for him to evoke the self-incrimination provisions of section 7 of the Charter. The inquiry under s. 231.4 was not unconstitutional. *The Queen et al. v. Del Zotto et al.*, 99 DTC 5029 (S.C.C.), reversing 97 DTC 5328 (F.C.A.), and affirming 97 DTC 5145 (F.C.T.D.).

SECTION 231.5: Copies

► 231.5(1) ◄

(1) Copies. Where any document is seized, inspected, audited, examined or provided under any of sections 231.1 to 231.4, the person by whom it is seized, inspected, audited or examined or to whom it is provided or any officer of the Canada Revenue Agency may make, or cause to be made, one or more copies thereof and, in the case of an electronic document, make or cause to be made a print-out of the electronic document, and any document purporting to be certified by the Minister or an authorized person to be a copy of the document, or to be a print-out of an electronic document, made pursuant to this section is evidence of the nature and content of the original document and has the same probative force as the original document would have if it were proven in the ordinary way.

Related Sections: S. 230(4.1) Electronic records; s. 244(9) Proof of documents.

Information Circulars: IC 73-10R3 Tax evasion.

Cases: The copying of a letter during an audit did not violate the Charter as there was no formal search or seizure. *Thyssen Canada Limited v. The Queen*, 84 DTC 6049 (F.C.T.D.)

► 231.5(2) ◄

(2) Compliance. No person shall, physically or otherwise, interfere with, hinder or molest an official (in this subsection having the meaning assigned by subsection 241(10)) doing anything that the official is authorized to do under this Act or attempt to interfere with, hinder or molest any official doing or prevent or attempt to prevent an official from doing, anything that the official is authorized to do under this Act, and every person shall, unless the person is unable to do so, do everything that the person is required to do by or under subsection (1) or sections 231.1 to 231.4.

SECTION 231.6: [Requirement to provide foreign-based information or document]

► 231.6(1) ◄

(1) Definition of "foreign-based information or document". For the purposes of this section, "foreign-based information or document" means any information or document that is available or located outside Canada and that may be relevant to the administration or enforcement of this Act, including the collection of any amount payable under this Act by any person.

Related Sections: S. 231 Definitions; s. 248(1) Definitions.

Canadian Tax Foundation: Kroft, *Recent Developments in CRA's Reach for Information: Questions You Want Answered*, 2011 British Columbia Tax Conference 5:11–29; Kroft, *Recent Developments in CRA's Reach for Information: Questions You Want Answered*, 2011 Ontario Tax Conference 4:11–29; Henry and Kingissepp, *Managing the Confidentiality of Tax Accrual Working Papers*, 2009 Conference Report 29:1–28; Lindsay and Robinson, *Requirements To Produce Documents and Information: Policy and Practice*, 2008 Conference Report 12:1–38; Barsalou, *Transfer-Pricing Audits: Selected Issues*, 2003 Conference Report 12:1–25.

Tax Topics: No. 1917, Requirement Letters and Technology — *eBay Canada Limited*.

Cases: There was no time period in s. 231.6 within which the request for the information had to be made. The Department was therefore not limited to producing the request for information prior to the taxpayer's filing of a notice of objection to a notice of reassessment. *Merko v. M.N.R.*, 90 DTC 6643 (F.C.T.D.)

▶ 231.6(2) ◀

(2) Requirement to provide foreign-based information. Notwithstanding any other provision of this Act, the Minister may, by notice served personally or by registered or certified mail, require that a person resident in Canada or a non-resident person carrying on business in Canada provide any foreign-based information or document.

> **Proposed Amendment**
> **2019 Federal Budget Resolutions**
> **Subsection 231.6(2) of the Act is replaced by the following:**
>
> **(2) Requirement to provide foreign-based information.** Notwithstanding any other provision of this Act, the Minister may, by notice sent or served in accordance with subsection (3.1), require that a person resident in Canada or a non-resident person carrying on business in Canada provide any foreign-based information or document.
>
> **Applicable:** In force on January 1, 2020.

Tax Topics: No. 1917, Requirement Letters and Technology — *eBay Canada Limited*; No. 1739, CRA's Use of Foreign-Based Requirements Under Section 231.6 - Are There Any Limits?; No. 1716, Managing CRA Requirements To Provide Foreign-Based Information; No. 1530, The CCRA's Administrative Powers Under the *Income Tax Act* and the Canada-United States Income Tax Convention.

Information Circulars: IC 77-9R Books, records and other requirements for taxpayers having foreign affiliates.

▶ 231.6(3) ◀

(3) Notice. The notice referred to in subsection (2) shall set out

(*a*) a reasonable period of time of not less than 90 days for the production of the information or document;

(*b*) a description of the information or document being sought; and

(*c*) the consequences under subsection (8) to the person of the failure to provide the information or documents being sought within the period of time set out in the notice.

> **Proposed Amendment**
> **2019 Federal Budget Resolutions**
> **Section 231.6 of the Act is amended by adding the following after subsection (3):**
>
> **(3.1) Notice.** A notice referred to in subsection (2) may be
>
> (*a*) served personally;
>
> (*b*) sent by registered or certified mail; or
>
> (*c*) sent electronically, in the case of a bank, or credit union, that has provided written consent to receive notices under subsection (2) electronically.
>
> **Applicable:** In force on January 1, 2020.

▶ 231.6(4) ◀

(4) Review of foreign information requirement. The person on whom a notice of a requirement is served under subsection (2) may, within 90 days after the service of the notice, apply to a judge for a review of the requirement.

> **Proposed Amendment**
> **2019 Federal Budget Resolutions**
> **Subsection 231.6(4) of the English version of the Act is replaced by the following:**
>
> **(4) Review of foreign information requirement.** The person who is sent or served with a notice of a requirement under subsection (2) may, within 90 days after the notice is sent or served, apply to a judge for a review of the requirement.
>
> **Applicable:** In force on January 1, 2020.

▶ 231.6(5) ◀

(5) Powers on review. On hearing an application under subsection (4) in respect of a requirement, a judge may

(*a*) confirm the requirement;

(*b*) vary the requirement as the judge considers appropriate in the circumstances; or

(*c*) set aside the requirement if the judge is satisfied that the requirement is unreasonable.

Tax Topics: No. 1739, CRA's Use of Foreign-Based Requirements Under Section 231.6 — Are There Any Limits?.

▶ 231.6(6) ◀

(6) Idem. For the purposes of paragraph (5)(*c*), the requirement to provide the information or document shall not be considered to be unreasonable because the information or document is under the control of or available to a non-resident person that is not controlled by the person served with the notice of the requirement under subsection (2) if that person is related to the non-resident person.

> **Proposed Amendment**
> **2019 Federal Budget Resolutions**
> **Subsection 231.6(6) of the English version of the Act is replaced by the following:**
>
> **(6) Idem.** For the purposes of paragraph (5)(*c*), the requirement to provide the information or document shall not be considered to be unreasonable because the information or document is under the control of or available to a non-resident person that is not controlled by the person who is sent or served with the notice of the requirement under subsection (2) if that person is related to the non-resident person.
>
> **Applicable:** In force on January 1, 2020.

▶ 231.6(7) ◀

(7) Time period not to count. The period of time between the day on which an application for review of a requirement is made pursuant to subsection (4) and the day on which the application is finally disposed of shall not be counted in the computation of

(*a*) the period of time set out in the notice of the requirement; and

(*b*) the period of time within which an assessment may be made pursuant to subsection 152(4).

History: S. 231.6(7), the portion before paragraph (*a*) was replaced by S.C. 2018, c. 27, s. 23, in force December 13, 2018, and formerly read:

(7) *Time during consideration not to count.* The period of time between the day on which an application for review of a requirement is made pursuant to subsection (4) and the day on which the review is decided shall not be counted in the computation of

► 231.6(8) ◄

(8) Consequence of failure. If a person fails to comply substantially with a notice served under subsection (2) and if the notice is not set aside by a judge pursuant to subsection (5), any court having jurisdiction in a civil proceeding relating to the administration or enforcement of this Act shall, on motion of the Minister, prohibit the introduction by that person of any foreign-based information or document covered by that notice.

Proposed Amendment
2019 Federal Budget Resolutions
Subsection 231.6(8) of the Act is replaced by the following:

(8) Consequence of failure. If a person fails to comply substantially with a notice sent or served under subsection (2) and if the notice is not set aside by a judge pursuant to subsection (5), any court having jurisdiction in a civil proceeding relating to the administration or enforcement of this Act shall, on motion of the Minister, prohibit the introduction by that person of any foreign-based information or document covered by that notice.

Applicable: In force on January 1, 2020.

Tax Topics: No. 1637, Subsection 231.6(8): Multinationals Beware!!!.

SECTION 231.7: Compliance order

► 231.7(1) ◄

(1) Compliance order. On summary application by the Minister, a judge may, notwithstanding subsection 238(2), order a person to provide any access, assistance, information or document sought by the Minister under section 231.1 or 231.2 if the judge is satisfied that

(*a*) the person was required under section 231.1 or 231.2 to provide the access, assistance, information or document and did not do so; and

(*b*) in the case of information or a document, the information or document is not protected from disclosure by solicitor-client privilege (within the meaning of subsection 232(1)).

Tax Topics: No. 2451, Accounting Firm's Due Diligence Report Ordered Produced to the Canada Revenue Agency; No. 2380, *MNR v. Cameco*: Minister's Ability To Compel Oral Interviews in Audit Examined; No. 2319, Section 231.2 Requirements Issued to Lawyers Held Unconstitutional: *Chambre des Notaries du Québec* and *Thompson*; No. 2311, Supreme Court Reaffirms Supremacy of Solicitor-Client Privilege; No. 2023-24, 2010 Canadian Tax Foundation CRA Roundtable: Pipelines, Privilege and Working Papers (Again!).

Cases: The due diligence report had been prepared for purposes of the transaction under audit. The Minister did not have to demonstrate it was relevant, only that it may be relevant. The Minister met the low threshold for relevance. The dominant or principal purpose when the report was commissioned and generated was to inform the decision of whether to proceed with the transaction and at what price, which was a business purpose, and the report was not protected by solicitor-client privilege. Compelling the taxpayer to provide the report would not offend the principle that a taxpayer is not required to self-audit. *The Minister of National Revenue v. Atlas Tube Canada ULC*, 2018 DTC 5124 (FC)

Solicitor-client privilege is not waived when an opinion provided by a lawyer to one party is disclosed, on a confidential basis, to other parties with sufficient common interest in the same transactions. This applies whether the opinion is first disclosed to the client of the lawyer and then to the other parties, or simultaneously to all. The parties had sufficient common interest in the transactions to warrant finding the impugned memo was protected from disclosure by solicitor-client privilege. *Iggillis Holdings v. The Minister of National Revenue*, 2018 DTC 5027 (FCA)

Other Publications: AD-19-02R Obtaining Information for Audit Purposes.

► 231.7(2) ◄

(2) Notice required. An application under subsection (1) must not be heard before the end of five clear days from the day the notice of application is served on the person against whom the order is sought.

► 231.7(3) ◄

(3) Judge may impose conditions. A judge making an order under subsection (1) may impose any conditions in respect of the order that the judge considers appropriate.

► 231.7(4) ◄

(4) Contempt of court. If a person fails or refuses to comply with an order, a judge may find the person in contempt of court and the person is subject to the processes and the punishments of the court to which the judge is appointed.

► 231.7(5) ◄

(5) Appeal. An order by a judge under subsection (1) may be appealed to a court having appellate jurisdiction over decisions of the court to which the judge is appointed. An appeal does not suspend the execution of the order unless it is so ordered by a judge of the court to which the appeal is made.

Cases: Any provision which interferes with solicitor-client privilege more than absolutely necessary will be deemed unreasonable. The threshold is quite low. A provision will only withstand Charter scrutiny if its impact is minimal. The Court "read down" s. 231.7 and held it was inapplicable to notaries and lawyers in their capacity as legal advisers. *Canada (Attorney General) v. Chambre des notaires du Québec*, 2016 DTC 5067 (SCC)

SECTION 231.8: Time period not to count

The following periods of time shall not be counted in the computation of the period of time within which an assessment may be made for a taxation year of a taxpayer under subsection 152(4):

(*a*) where the taxpayer is served a notice of a requirement under subsection 231.2(1), the period of time between the day on which an application for judicial review in respect of the requirement is made and the day on which the application is finally disposed of; and

Proposed Amendment
2019 Federal Budget Resolutions
Paragraph 231.8(*a*) of the Act is replaced by the following:

(*a*) where the taxpayer is sent or served with a notice of a requirement under subsection 231.2(1), the period of time between the day on which an application for judicial review in respect of the requirement is made and the day on which the application is finally disposed of; and

Applicable: In force on January 1, 2020.

(*b*) where an application is commenced by the Minister under subsection 231.7(1) to order the taxpayer to provide any access, assistance, information or document, the period of time between the day on which the taxpayer files a notice of appearance, or otherwise opposes the application, and the day on which the application is finally disposed of.

History: S. 231.8 was added by S.C. 2018, c. 27, s. 24, in force December 13, 2018.

SECTION 232: [Solicitor-client privilege]

► 232(1) ◄

(1) Definitions. In this section,

Tax Topics: No. 1601, Revisiting Solicitor-Client Privilege.

"custodian" —"custodian" means a person in whose custody a package is placed pursuant to subsection (3);

"judge" —"judge" means a judge of a superior court having jurisdiction in the province where the matter arises or a judge of the Federal Court;

"lawyer" —"lawyer" means, in the province of Quebec, an advocate or notary and, in any other province, a barrister or solicitor;

Related Sections: S. 230(2.1) Records and books — lawyers.

"officer" —"officer" means a person acting under the authority conferred by or under sections 231.1 to 231.5;

"solicitor-client privilege" —"solicitor-client privilege" means the right, if any, that a person has in a superior court in the province where the matter arises to refuse to disclose an oral or documentary communication on the ground that the communication is one passing between the person and the person's lawyer in professional confidence, except that for the purposes of this section an accounting record of a lawyer, including any supporting voucher or cheque, shall be deemed not to be such a communication.

Related Sections: S. 232(10) Directions.

Canadian Tax Foundation: Innes, *Current Cases: The Ontario Court of Appeal — Seizure and Examination of Privileged Materials in Lawyers' Offices (R v. Fink)*, 2001 Canadian Tax Journal 3:727–731; Geddes, *The Fragile Privilege: Establishing and Safeguarding Solicitor-Client Privilege*, 1999 Canadian Tax Journal 4:799–843; Quigley, *Controlling Tax Information: Limits to Record-Keeping and Disclosure Obligations*, 1999 Canadian Tax Journal 1:1–48; Swystun, *Solicitor-Client Privilege Under the Income Tax Act*, 1998 Ontario Tax Conference 15:1–49.

Tax Profile: July 2013 — Solicitor-Client Privilege Not Extended to Accountants; October 2006 — Tax Controversies in Canada: A Variety of Issues.

Tax Topics: No. 2319, Section 231.2 Requirements Issued to Lawyers Held Unconstitutional: *Chambre des Notaries du Québec* and *Thompson*; No. 2311, Supreme Court Reaffirms Supremacy of Solicitor-Client Privilege; No. 1698, Solicitor-Client Privilege: Commonwealth Cases Without Common Ground.

Cases: Solicitor-client privilege is not waived when an opinion provided by a lawyer to one party is disclosed, on a confidential basis, to other parties with sufficient common interest in the same transactions. This applies whether the opinion is first disclosed to the client of the lawyer and then to the other parties, or simultaneously to all. The parties had sufficient common interest in the transactions to warrant finding the impugned memo was protected from disclosure by solicitor-client privilege. *Iggillis Holdings v. The Minister of National Revenue*, 2018 DTC 5027 (FCA)

The purported abrogation of solicitor-client privilege in this section is constitutionally invalid. It permits the state to obtain privileged information to a far greater extent than absolutely necessary for administration of the Act and, as it applies to lawyers and notaries, infringes s. 8 of the Charter and cannot be justified under s. 1. *Canada (MNR) v. Thompson*, 2016 DTC 5069 (SCC)

Any provision which interferes with solicitor-client privilege more than absolutely necessary will be deemed unreasonable. The threshold is quite low. A provision will only withstand Charter scrutiny if its impact is minimal. The exception for a lawyer's accounting records was unconstitutional and invalid since the way it limited privilege was not absolutely necessary to achieve the purposes of the Act. *Canada (Attorney General) v. Chambre des notaires du Québec*, 2016 DTC 5067 (SCC)

Where documents evidencing legal advice obtained by a corporate taxpayer had been provided to its outside firm of auditors to assist in the audit and examination of its financial statements, such waiver did not extent to a waiver for other purposes such as disclosure by the firm in response to a Minister's demand for information. *Interprovincial Pipe Line Inc. et al. v. The Queen*, 95 DTC 5642 (F.C.T.D.)

Under s. 232 Parliament intended that a judge deciding the issue of privilege, should act in his judicial capacity. There was nothing unusual about an issue of solicitor-client privilege arising in a civil or criminal case. It was a routine exercise of judicial power to dispose of the issue. *Herman et al. v. The Deputy Attorney General of Canada*, 78 DTC 6456 (S.C.C.). It was held that the decision of a judge regarding solicitor-client privilege in respect of documents was not subject to appeal. *Herman et al. v. The Deputy Attorney General of Canada*, 79 DTC 5372 (Ont. C.A.).

► 232(2) ◄

(2) Solicitor-client privilege defence. Where a lawyer is prosecuted for failure to comply with a requirement under section 231.2 with respect to information or a document, the lawyer shall be acquitted if the lawyer establishes to the satisfaction of the court

(*a*) that the lawyer, on reasonable grounds, believed that a client of the lawyer had a solicitor-client privilege in respect of the information or document; and

(*b*) that the lawyer communicated to the Minister, or some person duly authorized to act for the Minister, the lawyer's refusal to comply with the requirement together with a claim that a named client of the lawyer had a solicitor-client privilege in respect of the information or document.

Related Sections: S. 232(10) Directions; s. 232(14) Waiver of claim of privilege.

Cases: Section 488.1 of the *Criminal Code* (which is very similar to s. 232 of the *Income Tax Act*) was struck down as unconstitutional. The Court restated the common law principles and guidelines that should be complied with when searching a law office. *The Queen v. Lavallee, Rackel and Heintz et al.*, 2002 DTC 7267 (S.C.C.), affirming (2000) 184 D.L.R. (4th) 25, affirming (1998), 126 C.C.C. (3d) 129 (Alta. Q.B.).

► 232(3) ◄

(3) Seizure of certain documents where privilege claimed. Where, pursuant to section 231.3, an officer is about to seize a document in the possession of a lawyer and the lawyer claims that a named client of the lawyer has a solicitor-client privilege in respect of that document, the officer shall, without inspecting, examining or making copies of the document,

(*a*) seize the document and place it, together with any other document in respect of which the lawyer at the same time makes the same claim on behalf of the same client, in a package and suitably seal and identify the package; and

(*b*) place the package in the custody of the sheriff of the district or county in which the seizure was made or, if the officer and the lawyer agree in writing on a person to act as custodian, in the custody of that person.

Related Sections: S. 232(1), "custodian"; s. 232(4) Application to judge; s. 232(6) Order to deliver or make available; s. 232(12) Prohibition — inspection, examination or seizure of document; s. 232(14) Waiver of claim of privilege.

► 232(3.1) ◄

(3.1) Examination of certain documents where privilege claimed. Where, pursuant to section 231.1, an officer is about to inspect or examine a document in the possession of a lawyer or where, pursuant to section 231.2, the Minister has required provision of a document by a lawyer, and the lawyer claims that a named client or former client of the lawyer has a solicitor-client privilege in respect of the document, no officer shall inspect or examine the document and the lawyer shall

(*a*) place the document, together with any other document in respect of which the lawyer at the same time makes the same claim on behalf of the same client, in a package and suitably seal and identify the package or, if the officer and the lawyer agree, allow the pages of the document to be initialed and numbered or otherwise suitably identified; and

(*b*) retain it and ensure that it is preserved until it is produced to a judge as required under this section and an order is issued under this section in respect of the document.

Related Sections: S. 232(4) Application to judge; s. 232(6) Order to deliver or make available; s. 232(12) Prohibition — inspection, examination or seizure of document; s. 232(14) Waiver of claim of privilege.

► 232(4) ◄

(4) Application to judge. Where a document has been seized and placed in custody under subsection (3) or is being retained under subsection (3.1), the client, or the lawyer on behalf of the client, may

(*a*) within 14 days after the day the document was so placed in custody or commenced to be so retained apply, on three clear days notice of motion to the Deputy Attorney General of Canada, to a judge for an order

(i) fixing a day, not later than 21 days after the date of the order, and place for the determination of the question whether the client has a solicitor-client privilege in respect of the document, and

(ii) requiring the production of the document to the judge at that time and place;

(*b*) serve a copy of the order on the Deputy Attorney General of Canada and, where applicable, on the custodian within 6 days of the day on which it was made and, within the same time, pay to the custodian the estimated expenses of transporting the document to and from the place of hearing and of safeguarding it; and

(*c*) if the client or lawyer has proceeded as authorized by paragraph (*b*), apply at the appointed time and place for an order determining the question.

Related Sections: S. 232(5) Disposition of application; s. 232(6) Order to deliver or make available; s. 232(8) Continuation by another judge.

Guides: T4115 Return of Benefits.

Cases: A law firm (FMC) acted for a group of companies (Group A) that negotiated the formation of two business partnerships with another group of companies (Group B). During the negotiations, FMC communicated orally and in writing with Group B regarding legal matters that were of common interest to both groups. The documents that were disclosed to Group B were protected by a common interest privilege. *Fraser Milner Casgrain LLP et al v. M.N.R.*, 2003 DTC 5048 (B.C.S.C.)

Documents in the possession of a lawyer were seized and placed in custody of the sheriff under the authority of s. 232(2). On an application by the Attorney-General, the judge was satisfied that no application had been pursued under s. 232(4) to establish privilege, and ordered the documents to be delivered to the Minister. The judge's order was held to be proper. *Easton v. Attorney-General of Canada*, 76 DTC 6174 (F.C.A.).

► 232(5) ◄

(5) Disposition of application. An application under paragraph (4)(*c*) shall be heard *in camera*, and on the application

(*a*) the judge may, if the judge considers it necessary to determine the question, inspect the document and, if the judge does so, the judge shall ensure that it is repackaged and resealed; and

(*b*) the judge shall decide the matter summarily and,

(i) if the judge is of the opinion that the client has a solicitor-client privilege in respect of the document, shall order the release of the document to the lawyer, and

(ii) if the judge is of the opinion that the client does not have a solicitor-client privilege in respect of the document, shall order

(A) that the custodian deliver the document to the officer or some other person designated by the Commissioner of Revenue, in the case of a document that was seized and placed in custody under subsection (3), or

(B) that the lawyer make the document available for inspection or examination by the officer or other person designated by the Commissioner of Revenue, in the case of a document that was retained under subsection (3.1),

and the judge shall, at the same time, deliver concise reasons in which the judge shall identify the document without divulging the details thereof.

► 232(6) ◄

(6) Order to deliver or make available. Where a document has been seized and placed in custody under subsection (3) or where a document is being retained under subsection (3.1) and a judge, on the application of the Attorney General of Canada, is satisfied that neither the client nor the lawyer has made an application under paragraph (4)(*a*) or, having made that application, neither the client nor the lawyer has made an application under paragraph (4)(*c*), the judge shall order

(*a*) that the custodian deliver the document to the officer or some other person designated by the Commissioner of Revenue, in the case of a document that was seized and placed in custody under subsection (3); or

(*b*) that the lawyer make the document available for inspection or examination by the officer or other person designated by the Commissioner of Revenue, in the case of a document that was retained under subsection (3.1).

► 232(7) ◄

(7) Delivery by custodian. The custodian shall

(*a*) deliver the document to the lawyer

(i) in accordance with a consent executed by the officer or by or on behalf of the Deputy Attorney General of Canada or the Commissioner of Revenue, or

(ii) in accordance with an order of a judge under this section; or

(*b*) deliver the document to the officer or some other person designated by the Commissioner of Revenue

(i) in accordance with a consent executed by the lawyer or the client, or

(ii) in accordance with an order of a judge under this section.

► 232(8) ◄

(8) Continuation by another judge. Where the judge to whom an application has been made under paragraph (4)(*a*) cannot for any reason act or continue to act in the application under paragraph (4)(*c*), the application under paragraph (4)(*c*) may be made to another judge.

► 232(9) ◄

(9) Costs. No costs may be awarded on the disposition of any application under this section.

► 232(10) ◄

(10) Directions. Where any question arises as to the course to be followed in connection with anything done or being done under this section, other than subsection (2), (3) or (3.1), and there is no direction in this section with respect thereto, a judge may give such direction with regard thereto as, in the judge's opinion, is most likely to carry out the object of this section of allowing solicitor-client privilege for proper purposes.

► 232(11) ◄

(11) Prohibition. The custodian shall not deliver a document to any person except in accordance with an order of a judge or a consent under this section or except to any officer or servant of the custodian for the purposes of safeguarding the document.

► 232(12) ◄

(12) Idem. No officer shall inspect, examine or seize a document in the possession of a lawyer without giving the lawyer a reasonable opportunity of making a claim under this section.

► 232(13) ◄

(13) Authority to make copies. At any time while a document is in the custody of a custodian under this section, a judge may, on an *ex parte* application of the lawyer, authorize the lawyer to examine or make a copy of the document in the presence of the custodian or the judge by an order that shall contain such provisions as may be necessary to ensure that the document is repackaged and that the package is resealed without alteration or damage.

► 232(14) ◄

(14) Waiver of claim of privilege. Where a lawyer has, for the purpose of subsection (2), (3) or (3.1), made a claim that a named client of the lawyer has a solicitor-client privilege in respect of information or a document, the lawyer shall at the same time communicate to the Minister or some person duly authorized to act for the Minister the address of the client last known to the lawyer so that the Minister may endeavour to advise the client of the claim of privilege that has been made on the client's behalf and may thereby afford the client an opportunity, if it is practicable within the time limited by this section, of waiving the claim of privilege before the matter is to be decided by a judge or other tribunal.

► 232(15) ◄

(15) Compliance. No person shall hinder, molest or interfere with any person doing anything that that person is authorized to do by or pursuant to this section or prevent or attempt to prevent any person doing any such thing and, notwithstanding any other Act or law, every person shall, unless the person is unable to do so, do everything the person is required to do by or pursuant to this section.

SECTION 233: Information return

► 233(1) ◄

(1) Information return. Every person shall, on written demand from the Minister served personally or otherwise, whether or not the person has filed an information return as required by this Act or the regulations, file with the Minister, within such reasonable time as is stipulated in the demand, the information return if it has not been filed or such information as is designated in the demand.

Related Regulations: Part II.

Related Sections: S. 162(10) Failure to furnish foreign-based information; s. 221(1)(*d*) Regulations; s. 248(1), "prescribed", "regulation"; ITAR s. 65.1 Part XV of amended Act.

Information Circulars: IC 77-9R Books, records and other requirements for taxpayers having foreign affiliates.

► 233(2) ◄

(2) Partnerships. Every partnership shall, on written demand from the Minister served personally or otherwise on any member of the partnership, file with the Minister, within such reasonable time as is stipulated in the demand, an information return required under section 233.3, 233.4 or 233.6.

Related Regulations: Part II.

Related Sections: S. 248(1), "prescribed", "regulation"; ITAR s. 65.1 Part XV of amended Act.

► 233(3) ◄

(3) Application to members of partnerships. For the purposes of this subsection and subsection (2), a person who is a member of a partnership that is a member of another partnership is deemed to be a member of the other partnership.

Related Regulations: Part II.

Related Sections: S. 248(1), "prescribed", "regulation"; ITAR s. 65.1 Part XV of amended Act.

SECTION 233.1: [Reporting for non-arm's length transactions with non-residents]

► 233.1(1) ◄

(1) Definitions. The definitions in this subsection apply in this section.

"reportable transaction" —"reportable transaction" means

(*a*) in the case of

(i) a reporting person for a taxation year who is not resident in Canada at any time in the year, or

(ii) a reporting partnership for a fiscal period no member of which is resident in Canada in the period,

a transaction or series of transactions that relate in any manner whatever to a business carried on in Canada by the reporting person or partnership in the year or period or a preceding taxation year or period; and

(*b*) in any other case, a transaction or series of transactions that relate in any manner whatever to a business carried on by a reporting person (other than a business carried on by a reporting person as a member of a partnership) or partnership in a taxation year or fiscal period.

Related Sections: S. 249.1(1) Definition of "fiscal period".

"reporting partnership" —"reporting partnership" for a fiscal period means a partnership

(*a*) a member of which is resident in Canada in the period; or

(*b*) that carries on a business in Canada in the period.

"reporting person" —"reporting person" for a taxation year means a person who, at any time in the year,

(*a*) is resident in Canada; or

(*b*) is non-resident and carries on a business (other than a business carried on as a member of a partnership) in Canada.

"transaction" —"transaction" includes an arrangement or event.

► 233.1(2) ◄

(2) Reporting person's information return. Subject to subsection (4), a reporting person for a taxation year shall, on or before the reporting person's filing-due date for the year, file with the Minister, in respect of each non-resident person with whom the reporting person does not deal at arm's length in the year and each partnership of which such a non-resident person is a member, an information return for the year in prescribed form containing prescribed information in respect of the reportable transactions in which the reporting person and the non-resident person or the partnership, as the case may be, participated in the year.

Related Sections: S. 248(1), "Filing-due-date"; s. 251 Arm's length.

Tax Profile: April 2011 — Canadian Tax Issues for Non-Resident Franchisors; August 2010 — Expanded Reporting Requirements under Form T106 — Greater Scrutiny on Transactions with Non-Arm's Length Non-Residents.

► 233.1(3) ◄

(3) Reporting partnership's information return. Subject to subsection (4), a reporting partnership for a fiscal period shall, on or before the day on or before which a return is required by section 229 of the *Income Tax Regulations* to be filed in respect of the period or would be required to be so filed if that section applied to the reporting partnership, file with the Minister, in respect of each non-resident person with whom the reporting partnership, or a member of the reporting partnership, does not deal at arm's length in the period and each partnership of which such a non-resident person is a member, an information return for the period in prescribed form containing prescribed information in respect of the reportable transactions in which the reporting partnership and the non-resident person or the partnership, as the case may be, participated in the period.

Related Sections: S. 249.1(1) Definition of "fiscal period".

Tax Profile: August 2010 — Expanded Reporting Requirements under Form T106 — Greater Scrutiny on Transactions with Non-Arm's Length Non-Residents.

Guides: T4068 Guide for the Partnership Information Return.

► 233.1(4) ◄

(4) *De minimis* exception. A reporting person or partnership that, but for this subsection, would be required under subsection (2) or (3) to file an information return for a taxation year or fiscal period is not required to file the return unless the total of all amounts, each of which is the total fair market value of the property or services that relate to a reportable transaction in which the reporting person or partnership and any non-resident person with whom the reporting person or partnership, or a member of the reporting partnership, does not deal at arm's length in the year or period, or a partnership of which such a non-resident person is a member, as the case may be, participated in the year or period, exceeds $1,000,000.

► 233.1(5) ◄

(5) Deemed member of partnership. For the purposes of this section, a person who is a member of a partnership that is a member of another partnership is deemed to be a member of the other partnership.

Forms: T106 — Information Return of Non-Arm's Length Transactions With Non-Residents.

SECTION 233.2: [Reporting for loans or transfers to non-resident trusts]

► 233.2(1) ◄

(1) Definitions. The definitions in this subsection apply in this section.

Related Sections: S. 248(1), "Foreign retirement arrangement"; s. 248(25), "beneficially interested".

"exempt trust" —"exempt trust" means

(*a*) a trust that is governed by a foreign retirement arrangement;

(*b*) a trust that

(i) is resident in a country under the laws of which an income tax is imposed,

(ii) is exempt under the laws referred to in subparagraph (i) from the payment of income tax to the government of that country,

(iii) is established principally in connection with, or the principal purpose of which is to administer or provide benefits under, one or more superannuation, pension or retirement funds or plans or any funds or plans established to provide employee benefits, and

(iv) is either

(A) maintained primarily for the benefit of non-resident individuals, or

(B) governed by an employees profit sharing plan; or

(*c*) a trust

(i) where the interest of each beneficiary under the trust is described by reference to units, and

(ii) that complies with prescribed conditions.

Related Regulations: 4801.1.

Related Sections: S. 248(1), "Foreign retirement arrangement"; s. 248(25), "beneficially interested".

Canadian Tax Foundation: Dumalski, *T1135 Filing Required for Certain Intercompany Debts*, 2014 Canadian Tax Focus 4(3):1–2; Furney and Vadis, *Foreign Income Verification Statements*, 2013 British Columbia Tax Conference 1:1–2; Hickey, *Foreign Income Reporting More Detailed*, 2013 Canadian Tax Highlights 21(8):4; Netley, *T1135 Filings: Much More Expensive for Clients*, 2013 Canadian Tax Focus 3(4):1–2.

"specified beneficiary" — (Repealed by S.C. 2013, c. 34, s. 21(1).)

History: S. 233.2(1), the definition "specified beneficiary" was repealed by S.C. 2013, c. 34, s. 21(1), applicable to returns in respect of trust taxation years that end after 2006. This amendment also applies to returns in respect of an earlier taxation year of a trust if subsection 94(1) applies to the trust for that earlier taxation year [should be 94(3) - CCH].

S. 233.2(1), the definition "specified beneficiary", formerly read:

"specified beneficiary" —"specified beneficiary" at any time under a trust means

(*a*) any person beneficially interested in the trust who is not at that time

(i) a mutual fund corporation,

(ii) a non-resident-owned investment corporation,

(iii) a person (other than a trust) all of whose taxable income for the person's taxation year that includes that time is exempt from tax under Part I,

(iv) a trust all of the taxable income of which for its taxation year that includes that time is exempt from tax under Part I,

(v) a mutual fund trust,

(vi) a trust described in any of paragraphs (*a*) to (*e*.1) of the definition "trust" in subsection 108(1),

(vii) a registered investment,

(viii) a trust in which all persons beneficially interested are persons described in subparagraphs (i) to (vii),

(ix) a particular person who is beneficially interested in the trust solely because the particular person is beneficially interested in an exempt trust or a trust described in this subparagraph or any of subparagraphs (iv) to (vi), nor

(x) a particular person who is beneficially interested in the trust only because of a right that is subject to a contingency, where at that time the identity of the particular person as a person beneficially interested in the trust is impossible to determine; or

(*b*) any person described at that time in any of subparagraphs (*a*)(i) to (x) who is beneficially interested in the trust, where it is reasonable to consider that the person became beneficially interested in the trust as part of a transaction or event or series of transactions or events one of the purposes of which is to limit the reporting in respect of the trust that would, but for this paragraph, be required under subsection (4).

Related Sections: S. 248(1), "Foreign retirement arrangement"; s. 248(25), "beneficially interested".

"specified foreign trust" — (Repealed by S.C. 2013, c. 34, s. 21(1).)

History: S. 233.2(1), the definition "specified foreign trust" was repealed by S.C. 2013, c. 34, s. 21(1), applicable to returns in respect of trust taxation years that end after 2006. This amendment also applies to returns in respect of an earlier taxation year of a trust if subsection 94(1) applies to the trust for that earlier taxation year [should be 94(3) – CCH].

S. 233.2(1), the definition "specified foreign trust", formerly read:

"specified foreign trust"—"specified foreign trust" at any time means a trust (other than an exempt trust) that is non-resident at that time where either

(*a*) there is a specified beneficiary under the trust who at that time

(i) is resident in Canada,

(ii) is a corporation or trust with which a person resident in Canada does not deal at arm's length, or

(iii) is a controlled foreign affiliate of a person resident in Canada; or

(*b*) at that time the terms or conditions of the trust or any arrangement in respect of the trust

(i) permit persons (other than persons described in any of subparagraphs (*a*)(i) to (viii) of the definition "specified beneficiary") who are not beneficially interested in the trust at that time to become, because of the exercise of any discretion by any person or partnership, beneficially interested in the trust after that time, or

(ii) allow property to be distributed, directly or indirectly, to another trust that immediately after the receipt of the distribution can reasonably be expected to be a specified foreign trust.

Related Sections: S. 248(1), "Foreign retirement arrangement"; s. 248(25), "beneficially interested".

► 233.2(2) ◄

(2) Rule of application. In this section and paragraph 233.5(*c.1*), subsections 94(1), (2) and (10) to (13) apply, except that the reference to the expression "(other than restricted property)" in the definition "arm's length transfer" in subsection 94(1) is to be read as a reference to the expression "(other than property to which paragraph 94(2)(*g*) applies but not including a unit of a mutual fund trust or of a trust that would be a mutual fund trust if section 4801 of the *Income Tax Regulations* were read without reference to paragraph 4801(*b*), a share of the capital stock of a mutual fund corporation, or a particular share of the capital stock of a corporation (other than a closely held corporation) which particular share is identical to a share that is, at the transfer time, of a class that is listed on a designated stock exchange)".

History: S. 233.2(2) was replaced by S.C. 2013, c. 34, s. 21(2), applicable to returns in respect of trust taxation years that end after 2006. This amendment also applies to returns in respect of an earlier taxation year of a trust if subsection 94(1) applies to the trust for that earlier taxation year [should be 94(3) – CCH]. However, the reference to "designated stock exchange" in subsection 233.2(2) is in its application to a time that is before December 14, 2007 to be read as a reference to "prescribed stock exchange".

S. 233.2(2) formerly read:

(2) *Non-arm's length indicators.* For the purpose of this section,

(*a*) a non-arm's length indicator applies to a trust at a particular time with respect to a transfer of property made at an earlier time to the trust or a corporation where

(i) immediately after the earlier time the transferor was

(A) a specified beneficiary under the trust,

(B) a person related to a specified beneficiary under the trust,

(C) an uncle, aunt, nephew or niece of a specified beneficiary under the trust, or

(D) a trust or corporation that had, directly or indirectly in any manner whatever, previously acquired the transferred property from a person described in clause (A), (B) or (C),

(ii) the fair market value at the earlier time of the transferred property was greater than the amount, if any, by which

(A) the total fair market value at the earlier time of the consideration, if any, given to the transferor for the transfer of property at the earlier time

exceeds

(B) the portion of the total described in clause (A) that is attributable to the fair market value of an interest as a beneficiary in the trust or a share or debt issued by the corporation,

(iii) the consideration received by the transferor in respect of the transfer included indebtedness on which

(A) interest was not charged in respect of a period that began before the particular time,

(B) interest was charged in respect of a period that began before the particular time at a rate that was less than the lesser of

(I) the prescribed rate that was in effect at the earlier time, and

(II) the rate that would, having regard to all the circumstances, have been agreed on at the earlier time between parties dealing with each other at arm's length,

(C) any interest that was payable at the end of any calendar year that ended at or before the particular time was unpaid on the day that is 180 days after the end of that calendar year, or

(D) the amount of interest that was payable at the end of any calendar year that ended at or before the particular time was paid on or before the day that is 180 days after the end of that calendar year and it is established, by subsequent events or otherwise, that the payment was made as part of a series of loans or other transactions and repayments,

(iv) the property transferred was a share of the capital stock of a corporation or an interest in another trust and a specified beneficiary under the trust is related to the corporation or the other trust or would be so related if paragraph 80(2)(*j*) applied for the purposes of this subparagraph, or

(v) the transfer was made as part of a series of transactions or events one of the purposes of which was to avoid the application of this paragraph; and

(*b*) a non-arm's length indicator applies to a trust at a particular time with respect to a loan made at an earlier time where

(i) interest was not charged on the loan in respect of a period that began before the particular time,

(ii) interest was charged on the loan in respect of a period that began before the particular time at a rate that was less than the lesser of

(A) the prescribed rate that was in effect at the earlier time, and

(B) the rate that would, having regard to all the circumstances, have been agreed on at the earlier time between parties dealing with each other at arm's length,

(iii) any interest on the loan that was payable at the end of any calendar year that ended at or before the particular time was unpaid on the day that is 180 days after the end of that calendar year,

(iv) the amount of interest on the loan that was payable at the end of any calendar year that ended at or before the particular time was paid on or before the day that is 180 days after the end of that calendar year and it is established, by subsequent events or otherwise, that the payment was made as part of a series of loans or other transactions and repayments, or

(v) the loan was made as part of a series of transactions or events one of the purposes of which was to avoid the application of this paragraph.

► 233.2(3) ◄

(3) Partnerships — (Repealed by S.C. 2013, c. 34, s. 21(2).)

History: S. 233.2(3) was repealed by S.C. 2013, c. 34, s. 21(2), applicable to returns in respect of trust taxation years that end after 2006. This amendment also applies to returns in respect of an earlier taxation year of a trust if subsection 94(1) applies to the trust for that earlier taxation year [should be 94(3) – CCH].

S. 233.2(3) formerly read:

(3) *Partnerships.* For the purpose of this section, where property is transferred or lent at any time by a partnership, the property is deemed to have been transferred or lent at that time by each of the members of the partnership.

► 233.2(4) ◄

(4) Filing information on foreign trusts. A person shall file an information return in prescribed form, in respect of a taxation year of a particular trust (other than an exempt trust or a trust described in any of paragraphs (*c*) to (*h*) of the definition "exempt foreign trust" in subsection 94(1)) with the Minister on or before the person's filing-due date for the person's taxation year in which the particular trust's taxation year ends if

(*a*) the particular trust is non-resident at a specified time in that taxation year of the particular trust;

(*b*) the person is a contributor, a connected contributor or a resident contributor to the particular trust; and

(*c*) the person

(i) is resident in Canada at that specified time, and

(ii) is not, at that specified time,

(A) a mutual fund corporation,

(B) an exempt person,

(C) a mutual fund trust,

(D) a trust described in any of paragraphs (*a*) to (*e.1*) of the definition "trust" in subsection 108(1),

(E) a registered investment,

(F) a trust in which all persons beneficially interested are persons described in clauses (A) to (E), or

(G) a contributor to the particular trust by reason only of being a contributor to another trust that is resident in Canada and is described in any of clauses (B) to (F).

History: S. 233.2(4) was replaced by S.C. 2013, c. 34, s. 21(3), applicable to returns in respect of trust taxation years that end after 2006. This amendment also applies to returns in respect of an earlier taxation year of a trust if subsection 94(1) applies to the trust for that earlier taxation year [should be 94(3) – CCH].

A return required to be filed by a person because of subsection 233.2(4) is deemed to have been filed with the Minister of National Revenue on a timely basis if it is filed with the Minister of National Revenue on or before the person's filing-due date for the person's taxation year that includes June 26, 2013.

S. 233.2(4) formerly read:

(4) *Filing information on specified foreign trusts.* Where

(*a*) at any time (in this subsection referred to as the "transfer time") before the end of a trust's taxation year (in this subsection referred to as the "trust's year"), property was transferred or lent, either directly or indirectly in any manner whatever, by any person (in this subsection referred to as the "transferor") to

(i) the trust, or

(ii) a corporation that, at the transfer time, would have been a controlled foreign affiliate of the trust if the trust had been resident in Canada,

(*b*) the trust was a specified foreign trust at any time in the trust's year, and

(*c*) a non-arm's length indicator applied to the trust at the end of the trust's year in respect of the transfer or loan,

the following rules apply:

(*d*) where the transferor is resident in Canada at the end of the trust's year, the transferor shall make an information return in respect of the trust's year in prescribed form and file it with the Minister on or before the transferor's filing-due date for the transferor's taxation year that includes the end of the trust's year, and

(*e*) where

(i) the transferor was, at the transfer time, a corporation that would have been a controlled foreign affiliate of a particular person if the particular person had been resident in Canada, and

(ii) the particular person is resident in Canada at the end of the trust's year,

the particular person shall make an information return in respect of the trust's year in prescribed form and file it with the Minister on or before the filing-due date for the particular person's taxation year that includes the end of the trust's year.

Tax Profile: January 2003 — Foreign Reporting Requirements in Respect of Non-Resident Trusts.

Forms: T1141 — Information Return in Respect of Transfers or Loans to a Non-Resident Trust.

► 233.2(4.1) ◄

(4.1) Similar arrangements. In this section and sections 162, 163 and 233.5, a person's obligations under subsection (4) (except to the extent that they are waived in writing by the Minister) are to be determined as if a contributor described in paragraph (4)(*b*) were any person who had transferred or loaned property, an arrangement or entity were a non-resident trust throughout the calendar year that includes the time referred to in paragraph (*a*) and that calendar year were a taxation year of the arrangement or entity, if

(*a*) the person at any time, directly or indirectly, transferred or loaned the property to be held

(i) under the arrangement and the arrangement is governed by the laws of a country or a political subdivision of a country other than Canada or exists, was formed or organized, or was last continued under the laws of a country or a political subdivision of a country other than Canada, or

(ii) by the entity and the entity is a non-resident entity (as defined by subsection 94.1(2));

(*b*) the transfer or loan is not an arm's length transfer;

(*c*) the transfer or loan is not solely in exchange for property that would be described in paragraphs (*a*) to (*i*) of the definition "specified foreign property" in subsection 233.3(1) if that definition were read without reference to paragraphs (*j*) to (*q*);

(*d*) the arrangement or entity is not a trust in respect of which the person would, if this Act were read without reference to this subsection, be required to file an information return for a taxation year that includes that time; and

(*e*) the arrangement or entity is, for a taxation year or fiscal period of the arrangement or entity that includes that time, not

(i) an exempt foreign trust (as defined in subsection 94(1)),

(ii) a foreign affiliate in respect of which the person is a reporting entity (within the meaning assigned by subsection 233.4(1)), or

(iii) an exempt trust.

History: S. 233.2(4.1) was added by S.C. 2013, c. 34, s. 21(3), applicable to returns in respect of trust taxation years that end after 2006. This amendment also applies to returns in respect of an earlier taxation year of a trust if subsection 94(1) applies to the trust for that earlier taxation year [should be 94(3) – CCH].

► 233.2(5) ◄

(5) Joint filing. Where information returns in respect of a trust's taxation year would, but for this subsection, be required to be filed under subsection 4 by a particular person and another person, and the particular person identifies the other person in an election filed in writing with the Minister, for the purposes of applying this Act to the particular person

(*a*) the information return filed by the other person shall be treated as if it had been filed by the particular person;

(*b*) the information required to be provided with the return by the particular person shall be deemed to be the information required to be provided by the other person with the return;

(c) the day on or before which the return is required to be filed by the particular person is deemed to be the later of the day on or before which

(i) the return would, but for this subsection, have been required to have been filed by the particular person, and

(ii) the return is required to have been filed by the other person; and

(d) each act and omission of the other person in respect of the return is deemed to be an act or omission of the particular person.

SECTION 233.3: [Reporting for ownership of specified foreign property]

► 233.3(1) ◄

(1) Definitions. The definitions in this subsection apply in this section.

Canadian Tax Foundation: Kujath, *Uncommon Scenarios for T1135 Reporting*, 2015 Tax for the Owner-Manager 15(2):2–3; Dumalski, *T1135 Filing Required for Certain Intercompany Debts*, 2014 Canadian Tax Focus 4(3):1–2.

Tax Window Files: Specified foreign property-jointly held property, *December 9, 2016*, CRA Document No. 2016-0639481E5; Specified foreign property - mineral rights, *March 1, 2016*, CRA Document No. 2016-0631181I7; Specified foreign property - Form T1135, *April 13, 2016*, CRA Document No. 2015-0614371E5; 2015 CTF Q.12 - Form T1135 - Jointly held property, *November 24, 2015*, CRA Document No. 2015-0610641C6; Specified Foreign Property, *April 16, 2015*, CRA Document No. 2014-0561061E5; *Life annuity, October 5, 2011*, CRA Document No. 2010-0361681E5; *US Annuities, August 18, 2010* CRA Document No. 2010-0371161E5; *Respecting Distributions from Non-Resident Trusts, March 23, 2010*, CRA Document No. 2009-0332521I7; Canadian Residency — Section 233.7, *Income Tax Rulings Directorate, Legislative Policy and Regulatory Affairs Branch, July 20, 2009*, CRA Document No. 2009-0315911E5.

"reporting entity" —"reporting entity" for a taxation year or fiscal period means a specified Canadian entity for the year or period where, at any time (other than a time when the entity is non-resident) in the year or period, the total of all amounts each of which is the cost amount to the entity of a specified foreign property of the entity exceeds $100,000.

"specified Canadian entity" —"specified Canadian entity" for a taxation year or fiscal period means

(a) a taxpayer resident in Canada in the year that is not

(i) a mutual fund corporation,

(ii) a non-resident-owned investment corporation,

(iii) a person (other than a trust) all of whose taxable income for the year is exempt from tax under Part I,

(iv) a trust all of the taxable income of which for the year is exempt from tax under Part I,

(v) a mutual fund trust,

(vi) a trust described in any of paragraphs (a) to (e.1) of the definition "trust" in subsection 108(1),

(vii) a registered investment, nor

(viii) a trust in which all persons beneficially interested are persons described in subparagraphs (i) to (vii); and

(b) a partnership (other than a partnership all the members of which are taxpayers referred to in any of subparagraphs (a)(i) to (viii)) where the total of all amounts, each of which is a share of the partnership's income or loss for the period of a non-resident member, is less than 90% of the income or loss of the partnership for the period, and, where the income and loss of the partnership are nil for the period, the income of the partnership for the period is deemed to be $1,000,000 for the purpose of determining a member's share of the partnership's income for the purpose of this paragraph.

"specified foreign property" —"specified foreign property" of a person or partnership means any property of the person or the partnership that is

(a) funds or intangible property, or for civil law incorporeal property, situated, deposited or held outside Canada,

(b) tangible property, or for civil law corporeal property, situated outside Canada,

(c) a share of the capital stock of a non-resident corporation,

(d) an interest in a non-resident trust,

(e) an interest in a partnership that owns or holds specified foreign property,

(f) an interest in, or right with respect to, an entity that is non-resident,

(g) indebtedness owed by a non-resident person,

(h) an interest in, or for civil law a right in, or a right — under a contract in equity or otherwise either immediately or in the future and either absolutely or contingently — to, any property (other than any property owned by a corporation or trust that is not the person) that is specified foreign property, and

(i) property that, under the terms or conditions thereof or any agreement relating thereto, is convertible into, is exchangeable for or confers a right to acquire, property that is specified foreign property,

but does not include

(j) property that is used or held exclusively in the course of carrying on an active business of the person or partnership (determined as if the person or partnership were a corporation resident in Canada),

(k) a share of the capital stock or indebtedness of a non-resident corporation that is a foreign affiliate of the person or partnership for the purpose of section 233.4,

(l) an interest in, or indebtedness of, a non-resident trust that is a foreign affiliate of the person or partnership for the purpose of section 233.4,

(m) an interest in a non-resident trust that was not acquired for consideration by either the person or partnership or a person related to the person or partnership,

(n) an interest in a trust described in paragraph (a) or (b) of the definition "exempt trust" in subsection 233.2(1),

(o) an interest in a partnership that is a specified Canadian entity,

(o.1) a right with respect to, or indebtedness of, an authorized foreign bank that is issued by, and payable or otherwise enforceable at, a branch in Canada of the bank,

(p) personal-use property of the person or partnership, and

(q) an interest in, or for civil law a right in, or a right to acquire, a property that is described in any of paragraphs (j) to (p).

History: S. 233.3(1), paragraph (*d*) of the definition "specified foreign property" was replaced by S.C. 2013, c. 34, s. 22(2), applicable to returns in respect of trust taxation years that end after 2006. It also applies to returns in respect of an earlier taxation year of a trust if subsection 94(1) applies to the trust for that earlier taxation year [should be 94(3) – CCH].

S. 233.3(1), paragraph (*d*) of the definition "specified foreign property" formerly read:

(*d*) an interest in a non-resident trust or a trust that, but for section 94, would be a non-resident trust for the purpose of this section,

S. 233.3(1), paragraphs (*a*) and (*b*) of the definition "specified foreign property" were replaced by S.C. 2013, c. 34, s. 166(4), in force June 26, 2013, and formerly read:

(*a*) funds or intangible property which are situated, deposited or held outside Canada,

(*b*) tangible property situated outside Canada,

S. 233.3(1), paragraph (*h*) of the definition "specified foreign property" were replaced by S.C. 2013, c. 34, s. 166(5), in force June 26, 2013, and formerly read:

(*h*) an interest in or right, under a contract, in equity or otherwise, either immediately or in the future and either absolutely or contingently, to any property (other than any property owned by a corporation or trust that is not the person) that is specified foreign property, and

S. 233.3(1), paragraph (*q*) of the definition "specified foreign property" were replaced by S.C. 2013, c. 34, s. 166(6), in force June 26, 2013, and formerly read:

(*q*) an interest in or right to acquire a property that is described in any of paragraphs (*j*) to (*p*).

Related Sections: S. 248(1), "authorized foreign bank".

Canadian Tax Foundation: Shew and Galloway, *Investing with a Foreign Broker and Buying Canadian Shares*, 2018 Canadian Tax Focus 8(2):11-11.

► 233.3(2) ◄

(2) Application to members of partnerships. For the purpose of this section, a person who is a member of a partnership that is a member of another partnership

(*a*) is deemed to be a member of the other partnership; and

(*b*) the person's share of the income or loss of the other partnership is deemed to be equal to the amount of that income or loss to which the person is directly or indirectly entitled.

► 233.3(3) ◄

(3) Returns respecting foreign property. A reporting entity for a taxation year or fiscal period shall file with the Minister for the year or period a return in prescribed form on or before the day that is

(*a*) where the entity is a partnership, the day on or before which a return is required by section 229 of the Income Tax Regulations to be filed in respect of the fiscal period of the partnership or would be required to be so filed if that section applied to the partnership; and

(*b*) where the entity is not a partnership, the entity's filing-due date for the year.

Related Sections: S. 152(4) Assessment and reassessment.

Canadian Tax Foundation: Cepparo, *Form T1135 and Part I Tax Return Reassessment*, 2016 Canadian Tax Highlights 24(1):8; Tollstam, *New Updates for T1135 Filings*, 2015 Canadian Tax Highlights 23(3):4; Furney and Vadis, *Foreign Income Verification Statements*, 2013 British Columbia Tax Conference 1:1-2; Hickey, *Foreign Income Reporting More Detailed*, 2013 Canadian Tax Highlights 21(8):4; Netley, *T1135 Filings: Much More Expensive for Clients*, 2013 Canadian Tax Focus 3(4):1-2.

Tax Topics: No. 2248, T1135 — The Saga Continues.

Forms: T1135 — Information Return Relating to Foreign Property.

Tax Window Files: T1135 - Normal Reassessment Period, *September 15, 2015*, CRA Document No. 2015-0572771I7.

SECTION 233.4: [Reporting in respect of foreign affiliates]

► 233.4(1) ◄

(1) Reporting entity. For the purpose of this section, "reporting entity" for a taxation year or fiscal period means

(*a*) a taxpayer resident in Canada (other than a taxpayer all of whose taxable income for the year is exempt from tax under Part I) of which a non-resident corporation is a foreign affiliate at any time in the year;

(*b*) a taxpayer resident in Canada (other than a taxpayer all of whose taxable income for the year is exempt from tax under Part I) of which a non-resident trust is a foreign affiliate at any time in the year; and

(*c*) a partnership

(i) where the total of all amounts, each of which is a share of the partnership's income or loss for the period of a member that is not resident in Canada or that is a taxpayer all of whose taxable income for the year in which the period ends is exempt from tax under Part I, is less than 90% of the income or loss of the partnership for the period, and, where the income and loss of the partnership are nil for the period, the income of the partnership for the period is deemed to be $1,000,000 for the purpose of determining a member's share of the partnership's income for the purpose of this subparagraph, and

(ii) of which a non-resident corporation or trust is a foreign affiliate at any time in the fiscal period.

History: S. 233.4(1)(*c*)(i) was replaced by S.C. 2014, c. 39, s. 69(1), applicable in respect of taxation years that end after July 11, 2013, and formerly read:

(i) where the total of all amounts, each of which is a share of the partnership's income or loss for the period of a non-resident member, is less than 90% of the income or loss of the partnership for the period, and, where the income and loss of the partnership are nil for the period, the income of the partnership for the period is deemed to be $1,000,000 for the purpose of determining a member's share of the partnership's income for the purpose of this subparagraph, and

S. 233.4(1)(*c*)(ii) was replaced by S.C. 2013, c. 34, s. 354, in force June 26, 2013, and formerly read:

(ii) of which a non-resident corporation or trust is a foreign affiliate of which at any time in the fiscal period.

Canadian Tax Foundation: Bourque and Bronstetter, *Foreign Affiliate Reporting: The First Filing*, 1998 Conference Report 19:1-25.

Guides: T4068 Guide for the Partnership Information Return.

Tax Window Files: Foreign Reporting Requirement under 233.4, *July 13, 2016*, CRA Document No. 2015-0608671E5.

► 233.4(2) ◄

(2) Rules of application. For the purpose of this section, in determining whether a non-resident corporation or trust is a foreign affiliate or a controlled foreign affiliate of a taxpayer resident in Canada or of a partnership

(*a*) paragraph (*b*) of the definition "equity percentage" in subsection 95(4) shall be read as if the reference to "any corporation" were a reference to "any corporation other than a corporation resident in Canada";

(*b*) the definitions "direct equity percentage" and "equity percentage" in subsection 95(4) shall be read as if a partnership were a person;

(*c*) the definitions "controlled foreign affiliate" and "foreign affiliate" in subsection 95(1) shall be read as if a partnership were a taxpayer resident in Canada; and

(*d*) if the taxpayer is a member of one or more partnerships described in subparagraph (1)(*c*)(i) of which a non-resident corporation or trust is a foreign affiliate, and the taxpayer does not have any direct or indirect interest (determined without reference to subsection 93.1(1)) in the non-resident corporation or trust other than through its interest in the partnerships, then the non-resident corporation or trust is deemed not to be a foreign affiliate of the taxpayer.

History: S. 233.4(2)(*d*) was added by S.C. 2014, c. 39, s. 69(2), applicable in respect of taxation years that end after July 11, 2013.

► 233.4(3) ◄

(3) Application to members of partnerships. For the purpose of this section, a person who is a member of a partnership that is a member of another partnership

(*a*) is deemed to be a member of the other partnership; and

(*b*) the person's share of the income or loss of the other partnership is deemed to be equal to the amount of that income or loss to which the person is directly or indirectly entitled.

► 233.4(4) ◄

(4) Returns respecting foreign affiliates. A reporting entity for a taxation year or fiscal period shall file with the Minister for the year or period a return in prescribed form in respect of each foreign affiliate of the entity in the year or period within 15 months after the end of the year or period.

Amendment not yet in force

Budget Implementation Act, 2018, No. 2 [S.C. 2018, c. 27]

S. 233.4(4) was replaced by S.C. 2018, c. 27, s. 25(1), and will read as follows:

(4) Returns respecting foreign affiliates. A reporting entity for a taxation year or fiscal period shall file with the Minister for the year or period a return in prescribed form in respect of each foreign affiliate of the entity in the year or period within 12 months after the end of the year or period.

Applicable: To taxation years of a taxpayer, and fiscal periods of a partnership, that begin in 2020.

Amendment not yet in force

Budget Implementation Act, 2018, No. 2 [S.C. 2018, c. 27]

S. 233.4(4) was replaced by S.C. 2018, c. 27, s. 25(2), and will read as follows:

(4) Returns respecting foreign affiliates. A reporting entity for a taxation year or fiscal period shall file with the Minister for the year or period a return in prescribed form in respect of each foreign affiliate of the entity in the year or period within 10 months after the end of the year or period.

Applicable: To taxation years of a taxpayer, and fiscal periods of a partnership, that begin after 2020.

Related Sections: S. 249(1) Definition of "taxation year"; s. 249.1(1) Definition of "fiscal period".

Canadian Tax Foundation: Pantaleo and Dell'Aniello, *Foreign Reporting for Foreign Affiliates: A Practical Approach*, 1997 Conference Report 45:1–36.

Forms: T1134 — Information Return Relating to Controlled and Not-Controlled Foreign Affiliates; T1134-B — Information Return Relating to Controlled Foreign Affiliates.

SECTION 233.5: Due diligence exception

The information required in a return filed under section 233.2 or 233.4 does not include information that is not available, on the day on which the return is filed, to the person or partnership required to file the return where

(*a*) there is a reasonable disclosure in the return of the unavailability of the information;

(*b*) before that day, the person or partnership exercised due diligence in attempting to obtain the information;

(*c*) if the return is required to be filed under section 233.2 in respect of a trust, at the time of each transaction, if any, entered into by the person or partnership after March 5, 1996 and before June 23, 2000 that gave rise to the requirement to file a return for a taxation year of the trust that ended before 2007 or that affects the information to be reported in the return, it was reasonable to expect that sufficient information would be available to the person or partnership to comply with section 233.2 in respect of each taxation year of the trust that ended before 2007;

(*c*.1) if the return is required to be filed under section 233.2, at the time of each contribution (determined with reference to subsection 233.2(2)) made by the person or partnership after June 22, 2000 that gives rise to the requirement to file the return or that affects the information to be reported in the return, it was reasonable to expect that sufficient information would be available to the person or partnership to comply with section 233.2;

(*c*.2) if the return is required to be filed under section 233.4 by a person or partnership in respect of a corporation that is a controlled foreign affiliate for the purpose of that section of the person or partnership, at the time of each transaction, if any, entered into by the person or partnership after March 5, 1996 that gives rise to the requirement to file the return or that affects the information to be reported in the return, it was reasonable to expect that sufficient information would be available to the person or partnership to comply with section 233.4; and

(*d*) if the information subsequently becomes available to the person or partnership, it is filed with the Minister not more than 90 days after it becomes so available.

History: S. 233.5(*c*) was amended, and (*c.1*) and (*c.2*) were added, by S.C. 2013, c. 34, s. 23(1), applicable to returns in respect of trust taxation years that end after 2006. This amendment also applies to returns in respect of an earlier taxation year of a trust if subsection 94(1) applies to that earlier taxation year of the trust [should be 94(3) – CCH].

S. 233.5(*c*) formerly read:

(*c*) if

(i) the return is required to be filed under section 233.2, or

(ii) the return is required to be filed under section 233.4 by a person or partnership in respect of a corporation that is a controlled foreign affiliate, for the purpose of that section, of the person or partnership,

it was reasonable to expect, at the time of each transaction, if any, entered into by the person or partnership after March 5, 1996 that gives rise to the requirement to file the return or that affects the information to be reported in the return, that sufficient information would be available to the person or partnership to comply with that section; and

Related Sections: S. 163(2.4) False statement or omission.

SECTION 233.6: Returns respecting distributions from non-resident trusts

► 233.6(1) ◄

(1) Returns respecting distributions from non-resident trusts. Where a specified Canadian entity (as defined by subsection 233.3(1)) for a taxation year or fiscal period receives a distribution of property from, or is indebted to, a non-resident trust (other than a trust that was an excluded trust in respect of the year or period of the entity or an estate that arose on and as a consequence of the death of an individual) in the year or period and the entity is beneficially interested in the trust at any time in the year or period, the entity shall file with the Minister for the year or period a return in prescribed form on or before the day that is

(*a*) where the entity is a partnership, the day on or before which a return is required by section 229 of the *Income Tax Regulations* to be filed in respect of the fiscal period of the partnership or would be required to be so filed if that section applied to the partnership; and

(*b*) where the entity is not a partnership, the entity's filing-due date for the year.

Related Sections: S. 248(25) Beneficially interested.

Forms: T1142 — Information Return in Respect of Distributions from and Indebtedness to a Non-Resident Trust.

► 233.6(2) ◄

(2) Excluded trust defined. For the purpose of subsection (1), an excluded trust in respect of the taxation year or fiscal period of an entity means

(*a*) a trust described in paragraph (*a*) or (*b*) of the definition "exempt trust" in subsection 233.2(1) throughout the portion of the year or period during which the trust was extant;

(*b*) a trust in respect of which the entity is required by section 233.2 to file a return in respect of each taxation year of the trust that ends in the entity's year;

(*c*) a trust an interest in which is at any time in the year or period specified foreign property (as defined by subsection 233.3(1)) of the entity, where the entity is a reporting entity (as defined by subsection 233.3(1)) for the year or period; and

(*d*) a trust in respect of which the entity is required by section 233.4 to file a return for the year or period.

SECTION 233.7: Exception for first-year residents

Notwithstanding sections 233.2, 233.3, 233.4 and 233.6, a person who, but for this section, would be required under any of those sections to file an information return for a taxation year, is not required to file the return if the person is an individual (other than a trust) who first became resident in Canada in the year.

SECTION 233.8: Country-by-country report — definitions

► 233.8(1) ◄

(1) [Definitions]. The following definitions apply in this section.

"business entity" — "business entity" means

(*a*) a person (other than an individual that is not a trust) or partnership; and

(*b*) a business that is carried on through a permanent establishment, if a separate financial statement for the business is prepared for financial reporting, regulatory, tax reporting or internal management control purposes.

"consolidated financial statements" — "consolidated financial statements" means financial statements in which the assets, liabilities, income, expenses and cash flows of the members of a group are presented as those of a single economic entity.

"constituent entity" — "constituent entity", of an MNE group, means

(*a*) any business entity of the MNE group that

(i) is included in the consolidated financial statements of the MNE group for financial reporting purposes, or

(ii) would be required to be included if equity interests in any of the business entities in the MNE group were traded on a public securities exchange; and

(*b*) any business entity that is excluded from the MNE group's consolidated financial statements solely because of size or materiality.

"excluded MNE group" — "excluded MNE group" means two or more business entities that meet the conditions in paragraphs (*a*) and (*b*) of the definition "MNE group", if, with respect to a particular fiscal year of the MNE group, it has a total consolidated group revenue of less than €750 million during the fiscal year immediately preceding the particular fiscal year, as reflected in its consolidated financial statements for the preceding fiscal year.

"fiscal year" — "fiscal year", of an MNE group, means an annual accounting period with respect to which the ultimate parent entity of the MNE group prepares its financial statements.

"multinational enterprise group" — "multinational enterprise group" or "MNE group" means two or more business entities, if

(*a*) they are either required to prepare consolidated financial statements for financial reporting purposes under applicable accounting principles or would be so required if equity interests in any of the business entities were traded on a public securities exchange;

(*b*) one of the business entities is resident in a particular jurisdiction and

(i) another business entity resides in a different jurisdiction, or

(ii) is subject to tax in a different jurisdiction with respect to a business carried on by it through a business entity — described in paragraph (*b*) of the definition "business entity" — in that other jurisdiction; and

(*c*) they are not an excluded MNE group.

"permanent establishment" — "permanent establishment" has the meaning assigned by regulation.

"qualifying competent authority agreement" — "qualifying competent authority agreement" means an agreement that (*a*) is between authorized representatives of those jurisdictions that are parties to a listed international agreement; and

(*b*) requires the automatic exchange of country-by-country reports between the party jurisdictions.

"reporting fiscal year" —"reporting fiscal year" means a fiscal year, if the financial and operational results of the fiscal year are reflected in the country-by-country report.

"surrogate parent entity" —"surrogate parent entity" means a constituent entity of an MNE group that has been appointed by the MNE group — in substitution for the ultimate parent entity — to file the country-by-country report on behalf of the MNE group, if one or more of the conditions in subparagraph (3)(*b*)(ii) applies.

"systemic failure" —"systemic failure" means, with respect to a jurisdiction, that the jurisdiction has a qualifying competent authority agreement in effect with Canada, but

(*a*) has suspended automatic exchange (for reasons other than those that are in accordance with the terms of the agreement); or

(*b*) has persistently failed to automatically provide country-by-country reports in its possession — in respect of MNE groups that have constituent entities in Canada — to Canada.

"ultimate parent entity" —"ultimate parent entity" means a constituent entity of an MNE group that meets the following conditions:

(*a*) the constituent entity holds directly or indirectly a sufficient interest in one or more constituent entities of the MNE group so that it is required to prepare consolidated financial statements under accounting principles generally applied in its jurisdiction of residence, or would be so required if its equity interests were traded on a public securities exchange in its jurisdiction of residence; and

(*b*) no other constituent entity of the MNE group holds, directly or indirectly, an interest in it that is described in paragraph (*a*).

History: S. 233.8(1) was added by S.C. 2016, c. 12, s. 61(1), applicable to reporting fiscal years of MNE groups that begin after 2015.

► 233.8(2) ◄

(2) Determination of residence — ultimate parent entity. For the purposes of this section, if an ultimate parent entity is a partnership, it is deemed to be resident

(*a*) if it is, under the laws of another jurisdiction, resident in that other jurisdiction for tax purposes, in that other jurisdiction; and

(*b*) in any other case, in the jurisdiction under the laws of which it was organized.

History: S. 233.8(2) was added by S.C. 2016, c. 12, s. 61(1), applicable to reporting fiscal years of MNE groups that begin after 2015.

► 233.8(3) ◄

(3) Filing obligations. A report in prescribed form (this report, along with each substantially similar report required to be filed in a jurisdiction other than Canada, collectively referred to in this section as a "country-by-country report"), in respect of a reporting fiscal year of an MNE group, shall be filed in prescribed manner with the Minister on or before the date specified in subsection (6) by

(*a*) the ultimate parent entity of the MNE group, if it is resident in Canada in the reporting fiscal year; or

(*b*) a constituent entity of the MNE group — which is not the ultimate parent entity of the MNE group — with respect to the reporting fiscal year of the MNE group, if the following conditions are satisfied:

(i) the constituent entity is resident in Canada in the reporting fiscal year, and

(ii) one of the following conditions applies:

(A) the ultimate parent entity of the MNE group is not obligated to file a country-by-country report in its jurisdiction of residence,

(B) the jurisdiction of residence of the ultimate parent entity of the MNE group does not have a qualifying competent authority agreement in effect to which Canada is a party on or before the time specified in subsection (6) for filing the country-by-country report for the reporting fiscal year, or

(C) there has been a systemic failure of the jurisdiction of residence of the ultimate parent entity and the Minister has notified the constituent entity of the systemic failure.

History: S. 233.8(3) was added by S.C. 2016, c. 12, s. 61(1), applicable to reporting fiscal years of MNE groups that begin after 2015.

Tax Topics: No. 2363, Canada: More Ready Than Ever for CBC Reporting.

Forms: RC4649 Country-by-Country Report.

Guides: RC4651 Guidance on Country-By-Country Reporting in Canada.

News Releases: Canada–U.S. Tax Convention — Arrangement signed on the exchange of Country-by-Country Reports.

► 233.8(4) ◄

(4) Designation for multiple constituent entities. If more than one constituent entity of an MNE group is described in paragraph (3)(*b*) in respect of a reporting fiscal year, one of those constituent entities may be designated — on or before the date specified in subsection (6) in respect of the reporting fiscal year — so that it is entitled to file a country-by-country report for the reporting fiscal year with the Minister on behalf of all such constituent entities in the MNE group.

History: S. 233.8(4) was added by S.C. 2016, c. 12, s. 61(1), applicable to reporting fiscal years of MNE groups that begin after 2015.

► 233.8(5) ◄

(5) Surrogate filing. Notwithstanding subsection (3), a constituent entity of an MNE group described in paragraph (3)(*b*) is not required to file a country-by-country report with the Minister with respect to a reporting fiscal year if

(*a*) a surrogate parent entity of the MNE group files a country-by-country report in respect of the reporting fiscal year with the tax authority of its jurisdiction of residence on or before the date specified in subsection (6); and

(*b*) the jurisdiction of residence of the surrogate parent entity

(i) requires filing of country-by-country reports,

(ii) has a qualifying competent authority agreement in effect to which Canada is a party on or before the time specified in subsection (6) for filing the country-by-country report in respect of the reporting fiscal year,

(iii) is not in a position of systemic failure, and

(iv) has been notified by the surrogate parent entity that it is the surrogate parent entity.

History: S. 233.8(5) was added by S.C. 2016, c. 12, s. 61(1), applicable to reporting fiscal years of MNE groups that begin after 2015.

► 233.8(6) ◄

(6) Time for filing. A country-by-country report in respect of a reporting fiscal year of an MNE group that is required to be filed by a constituent entity under this section shall be filed on or before the later of

(*a*) if notification of systemic failure has been received by the constituent entity, 30 days after receipt of the notification, and

(*b*) 12 months after the last day of the reporting fiscal year.

History: S. 233.8(6) was added by S.C. 2016, c. 12, s. 61(1), applicable to reporting fiscal years of MNE groups that begin after 2015.

SECTION 234: Ownership certificates

► 234(1) ◄

(1) Ownership certificates. Before the bearer coupon or warrant representing either interest or dividends payable by any debtor or cheque representing dividends or interest payable by a non-resident debtor is negotiated by or on behalf of a resident of Canada, there shall be completed by or on behalf of the resident an ownership certificate in prescribed form.

Related Regulations: 201(3); 201(6); 201(7); 207.

Forms: NR601 — Non-Resident Ownership Certificate (Withholding Tax); NR602 — Non-Resident Ownership Certificate (No Withholding Tax); T600 — Ownership Certificate; T600B — Ownership Certificate.

► 234(2) ◄

(2) Idem. An ownership certificate completed pursuant to subsection (1) shall be delivered in such manner, at such time and at such place as may be prescribed.

► 234(3) ◄

(3) Idem. The operation of this section may be extended by regulation to bearer coupons or warrants negotiated by or on behalf of non-resident persons.

► 234(4) ◄

(4) Idem — (Repealed by 1988, c. 55, s. 177(2).)

► 234(5) ◄

(5) Withholding — (Repealed by 1980-81-82-83, c. 48, s. 106(1).)

► 234(6) ◄

(6) Amount withheld deemed paid or credited — (Repealed by 1980-81-82-83, c. 48, s. 106(1).)

SECTION 234.1: Aviation turbine fuel

(Repealed by 1983-84, c. 1, s. 102(1).)

SECTION 235: Penalty for failing to file corporate returns

Every large corporation (within the meaning assigned by subsection 225.1(8)) that fails to file a return for a taxation year as and when required by section 150 or 190.2 is liable, in addition to any penalty otherwise provided, to a penalty for each such failure equal to the amount determined by the formula

$$A \times B$$

where

A is the total of

(*a*) 0.0005% of the corporation's taxable capital employed in Canada at the end of the taxation year, and

(*b*) 0.25% of the tax that would be payable under Part VI by the corporation for the year if this Act were read without reference to subsection 190.1(3); and

B is the number of complete months, not exceeding 40, from the day on or before which the return was required to be filed to the day on which the return is filed.

Related Sections: S. 150(1) Filing returns of income — general rule; s. 161(11) Interest on penalties; s. 190.1(3) Deduction; s. 190.2 Return; s. 248(1), "corporation".

SECTION 236: Execution of documents by corporations

A return, certificate or other document made by a corporation pursuant to this Act or a regulation shall be signed on its behalf by the President, Secretary or Treasurer of the corporation or by any other officer or person thereunto duly authorized by the Board of Directors or other governing body of the corporation.

Related Sections: S. 248(1), "corporation", "regulation"; ITAR s. 65.1 Part XV of amended Act.

SECTION 237: Social Insurance Number

► 237(1) ◄

(1) Social Insurance Number. Every individual (other than a trust) who was resident or employed in Canada at any time in a taxation year and who files a return of income under Part I for the year, or in respect of whom an information return is to be made by a person pursuant to a regulation made under paragraph 221(1)(*d*), shall,

(*a*) on or before the first day of February of the year immediately following the year for which the return of income is filed, or

(*b*) within 15 days after the individual is requested by the person to provide his Social Insurance Number,

apply to the Canada Employment Insurance Commission in prescribed form and manner for the assignment to the individual of a Social Insurance Number unless the individual has previously been assigned, or made application to be assigned, a Social Insurance Number.

Related Regulations: Part XXXVIII.

Information Circulars: IC 82-2R2 Social insurance number legislation that relates to the preparation of information slips.

► 237(1.1) ◄

(1.1) Production of number. Every person and partnership shall provide their designated number

(*a*) in any return filed under this Act; and

(*b*) to another person or partnership at the request of the other person or partnership, if the other person or partnership is required to make an information return pursuant to this Act or the Regulations requiring the designated number.

History: S. 237(1.1) was replaced by S.C. 2018, c. 12, s. 33(1), applicable to the 2018 and subsequent taxation years, and formerly read:

(1.1) *Production of number.* Every person and partnership shall provide

(*a*) in the case of an individual (other than a trust), the individual's Social Insurance Number, and

(*b*) in any other case, the person's or partnership's business number in any return filed under this Act or, at the request of any person required to make an information return pursuant to this Act or the regulations requiring either number, to that person.

Related Sections: S. 162(6) Failure to provide identification number; s. 221(1)(*d*.1) Regulations; s. 237(2) Number required in information returns; s. 237.1(7) Information return; s. 239(2.3) Offence with respect to an identification number; s. 248(1), "business number".

▶ 237(1.2) ◀

(1.2) Designated number. For the purpose of subsection (1.1), *designated number*, of a person or partnership, means

(*a*) in the case of an individual (other than a trust), their Social Insurance Number;

(*b*) in the case of a trust, its trust account number; and

(*c*) in any other case, the person's or partnership's business number.

History: S. 237(1.2) was added by S.C. 2018, c. 12, s. 33(1), applicable to the 2018 and subsequent taxation years.

▶ 237(2) ◀

(2) Number required in information returns. For the purposes of this Act and the Regulations, a person or partnership required to make an information return requiring a business number, Social Insurance Number or trust account number of another person or partnership

(*a*) shall make a reasonable effort to obtain the number from the other person or partnership; and

(*b*) shall not knowingly use, communicate or allow to be communicated, otherwise than as required or authorized under this Act or a regulation, the number without the written consent of the other person or partnership.

History: S. 237(2) was replaced by S.C. 2018, c. 12, s. 33(1), applicable to the 2018 and subsequent taxation years, and formerly read:

(2) *Number required in information returns.* For the purposes of this Act and the regulations, a person required to make an information return requiring a Social Insurance Number or a business number of a person or partnership

(*a*) shall make a reasonable effort to obtain the number from the person or partnership; and

(*b*) shall not knowingly use, communicate or allow to be communicated, otherwise than as required or authorized under this Act or a regulation, the number without the written consent of the person or partnership.

Related Sections: S. 104(1) Reference to trust or estate; s. 162(5) Failure to provide information on form; s. 162(6) Failure to provide identification number; s. 221(1)(*d*.1) Regulations; s. 237(1.1) Production of number; s. 237.1(7) Information return; s. 239(2.3) Offence with respect to an identification number; s. 248(1), "business number", "individual", "prescribed".

Information Circulars: IC 82-2R2 Social insurance number legislation that relates to the preparation of information slips.

▶ 237(3) ◀

(3) Authority to communicate number. A particular person may communicate, or allow to be communicated, a business number, Social Insurance Number or trust account number to another person related to the particular person where the other person is required, by this Act or the Regulations, to make an information return that requires the number.

History: S. 237(3) was replaced by S.C. 2018, c. 12, s. 33(1), applicable to the 2018 and subsequent taxation years, and formerly read:

(3) *Authority to communicate number.* A particular person may communicate, or allow to be communicated, a Social Insurance Number or business number to another person related to the particular person where the other person is required, by this Act or the Regulations, to make an information return that requires the Social Insurance Number or business number.

▶ 237(4) ◀

(4) Authority to communicate number. An insurance corporation may communicate, or allow to be communicated, to another person the business number, Social Insurance Number or trust account number of a particular person or partnership if

(*a*) the other person became the holder of a share of the capital stock of the insurance corporation, or of a holding corporation (in this subsection having the meaning assigned by subsection 139.1(1)) in respect of the insurance corporation, on the share's issuance in connection with the demutualization (as defined by subsection 139.1(1)) of the insurance corporation;

(*b*) the other person became the holder of the share in the other person's capacity as nominee or agent for the particular person or partnership pursuant to an arrangement established by the insurance corporation or a holding corporation in respect of the insurance corporation; and

(*c*) the other person is required, by this Act or the Regulations, to make an information return, in respect of the disposition of the share or income from the share, that requires the number.

History: S. 237(4), the portion before paragraph (*a*), was replaced by S.C. 2018, c. 12, s. 33(2), applicable to the 2018 and subsequent taxation years, and formerly read:

An insurance corporation may communicate, or allow to be communicated, to another person the Social Insurance Number or business number of a particular person or partnership where

S. 237(4)(*c*) was replaced by S.C. 2018, c. 12, s. 33(3), applicable to the 2018 and subsequent taxation years, and formerly read:

(*c*) the other person is required, by this Act or the Regulations, to make an information return, in respect of the disposition of the share or income from the share, that requires the Social Insurance Number or business number.

Related Sections: S. 248(1), "insurance corporation".

SECTION 237.1: [Tax shelters]

▶ 237.1(1) ◀

(1) Definitions. In this section,

"gifting arrangement" —"gifting arrangement" means any arrangement under which it may reasonably be considered, having regard to statements or representations made or proposed to be made in connection with the arrangement, that if a person were to enter into the arrangement, the person would

(*a*) make a gift to a qualified donee, or a contribution referred to in subsection 127(4.1), of property acquired by the person under the arrangement; or

(*b*) incur a limited-recourse debt, determined under subsection 143.2(6.1), that can reasonably be considered to relate to a gift to a qualified donee or a monetary contribution referred to in subsection 127(4.1);

History: S. 237.1(1), paragraph (*b*) of the definition "gifting arrangement" was replaced by S.C. 2013, c. 34, s. 355(1), applicable in respect of gifts and monetary contributions made after 6:00 p.m. (Eastern Standard Time) on December 5, 2003, and formerly read:

(*b*) incur a limited-recourse amount that can reasonably be considered to relate to a gift to a qualified donee or a contribution referred to in subsection 127(4.1).

Canadian Tax Foundation: Wertschek and Wilson, *Shelter from the Storm: The Current State of the Tax Shelter Rules in Section 237.1*, 2008 Canadian Tax Journal 2:285–336; Templeton and Aiken, *Current Cases: The Tax Court of Canada — No Representations Required? An Interpretation of the Tax Shelter Rules (Maege et al. v. The Queen, 2006 DTC 3193)*, 2007 Canadian Tax Journal 1:130–136; McGowan, *Tax Shelters: An Overview and Update*, 2006 Conference Report 37:1–14.

"person" —"person" includes a partnership;

"promoter" —"promoter" in respect of a tax shelter means a person who in the course of a business (*a*) sells or issues, or promotes the sale, issuance or acquisition of, the tax shelter,

(*b*) acts as an agent or adviser in respect of the sale or issuance, or the promotion of the sale, issuance or acquisition, of the tax shelter, or

(*c*) accepts, whether as a principal or agent, consideration in respect of the tax shelter,

and more than one person may be a tax shelter promoter in respect of the same tax shelter;

"tax shelter" —"tax shelter" means

(*a*) a gifting arrangement described by paragraph (*b*) of the definition "gifting arrangement"; and

(*b*) a gifting arrangement described by paragraph (*a*) of the definition "gifting arrangement", or a property (including any right to income) other than a flow-through share or a prescribed property, in respect of which it can reasonably be considered, having regard to statements or representations made or proposed to be made in connection with the gifting arrangement or the property, that, if a person were to enter into the gifting arrangement or acquire an interest in the property, at the end of a particular taxation year that ends within four years after the day on which the gifting arrangement is entered into or the interest is acquired,

(i) the total of all amounts each of which is

(A) an amount, or a loss in the case of a partnership interest, represented to be deductible in computing the person's income for the particular year or any preceding taxation year in respect of the gifting arrangement or the interest in the property (including, if the property is a right to income, an amount or loss in respect of that right that is stated or represented to be so deductible), or

(B) any other amount stated or represented to be deemed under this Act to be paid on account of the person's tax payable, or to be deductible in computing the person's income, taxable income or tax payable under this Act, for the particular year or any preceding taxation year in respect of the gifting arrangement or the interest in the property, other than an amount so stated or represented that is included in computing a loss described in clause (A),

would equal or exceed

(ii) the amount, if any, by which

(A) the cost to the person of the property acquired under the gifting arrangement, or of the interest in the property at the end of the particular year, determined without reference to section 143.2,

would exceed

(B) the total of all amounts each of which is the amount of any prescribed benefit that is expected to be received or enjoyed, directly or indirectly, in respect of the property acquired under the gifting arrangement, or of the interest in the property, by the person or another person with whom the person does not deal at arm's length.

Related Regulations: 3100; 3101.

Related Sections: S. 163.2 Definitions; s. 239(2.1) Providing incorrect tax shelter identification number; s. 248(1), "prescribed", "property", "taxable income", "taxable income earned in Canada".

Canadian Petroleum Tax Journal: The Tax Shelter Minefield, Vincent M. Bjorndahl, 1997, Vol. 10, No. 1.

Canadian Tax Foundation: Watkins, *The Tax-Shelter Rules: An Update*, 1998 Conference Report 5:1–32.

Tax Profile: August 2011 — Structuring Solar Projects in Canada.

Tax Topics: No. 2266, A Further Revision to the Definition of Tax Shelters; No. 1919-20, 2008 Canadian Tax Foundation Annual Conference — Department of Finance Presentation and CRA Round Table; No. 1837, Tax Shelters — Presumed Cognizant?; No. 1814, 2006 Canadian Tax Foundation Annual Conference CRA Round Table.

Forms: T5001 — Application for Tax Shelter Identification Number and Undertaking to Keep Books and Records.

Income Tax Technical News: Issue No. 41, Definition of "Tax Shelter" — Subsection 237.1(1); Issue No. 41, Donation of Flow-Through Shares — Subparagraph 38(a.1)(i), Subsection 248(35) through (41) and Section 237.1.

Information Circulars: IC 89-4 Tax shelter reporting.

► 237.1(2) ◄

(2) Application. A promoter in respect of a tax shelter shall apply to the Minister in prescribed form for an identification number for the tax shelter unless an identification number therefor has previously been applied for.

Forms: T5001 — Application for Tax Shelter Identification Number and Undertaking to Keep Books and Records.

► 237.1(3) ◄

(3) Identification. On receipt of an application under subsection (2) for an identification number for a tax shelter, together with prescribed information and an undertaking satisfactory to the Minister that books and records in respect of the tax shelter will be kept and retained at a place in Canada that is satisfactory to the Minister, the Minister shall issue an identification number for the tax shelter.

Forms: T5001 — Application for Tax Shelter Identification Number and Undertaking to Keep Books and Records.

► 237.1(4) ◄

(4) Sales prohibited. A person may, at any time, whether as a principal or an agent, sell or issue, or accept consideration in respect of, a tax shelter only if

(*a*) the Minister has issued before that time an identification number for the tax shelter; and

(*b*) that time is during the calendar year designated by the Minister as being applicable to the identification number.

History: S. 237.1(4) was replaced by S.C. 2012, c. 19, s. 15(1), deemed to have come into force on March 29, 2012. S. 237.1(4) formerly read:

(4) *Sales prohibited.* No person shall, whether as a principal or an agent, sell or issue, or accept consideration in respect of, a tax shelter before the Minister has issued an identification number for the tax shelter.

S. 237.1(4)(*b*) was replaced by S.C. 2012, c. 19, s. 15(2), applicable in respect of any tax shelter for which an application for an identification number has been made after March 28, 2012. S. 237.1(4)(*b*) formerly read:

(*b*) that time is before 2014.

Canadian Tax Foundation: Friedlan and Friedlan, *Tax Shelter Penalty Assessment Dismissed on Procedural Grounds*, 2014 Tax for the Owner-Manager 14(2):3–4.

Forms: T5001 — Application for Tax Shelter Identification Number and Undertaking to Keep Books and Records.

► 237.1(5) ◄

(5) Providing tax shelter number. Every promoter in respect of a tax shelter shall

(*a*) make reasonable efforts to ensure that all persons who acquire or otherwise invest in the tax shelter are provided with the identification number issued by the Minister for the tax shelter;

(*b*) prominently display on the upper right-hand corner of any statement of earnings prepared by or on behalf of the promoter in respect of the tax shelter the identification number issued for the tax shelter; and

(*c*) on every written statement made after 1995 by the promoter that refers either directly or indirectly and either expressly or impliedly to the issuance by the Canada Revenue Agency of an identification number for the tax shelter, as well as on the copies of the portion of the information return to be forwarded pursuant to subsection (7.3), prominently display

(i) where the statement or return is wholly or partly in English, the following:

"The identification number issued for this tax shelter shall be included in any income tax return filed by the investor. Issuance of the identification number is for administrative purposes only and does not in any way confirm the entitlement of an investor to claim any tax benefits associated with the tax shelter."

(ii) where the statement or return is wholly or partly in French, the following:

"Le numéro d'inscription attribué à cet abri fiscal doit figurer dans toute déclaration d'impôt sur le revenu produite par l'investisseur. L'attribution de ce numéro n'est qu'une formalité administrative et ne confirme aucunement le droit de l'investisseur aux avantages fiscaux découlant de cet abri fiscal."

and

(iii) where the statement includes neither English nor French, the following:

"The identification number issued for this tax shelter shall be included in any income tax return filed by the investor. Issuance of the identification number is for administrative purposes only and does not in any way confirm the entitlement of an investor to claim any tax benefits associated with the tax shelter."

"Le numéro d'inscription attribué à cet abri fiscal doit figurer dans toute déclaration d'impôt sur le revenu produite par l'investisseur. L'attribution de ce numéro n'est qu'une formalité administrative et ne confirme aucunement le droit de l'investisseur aux avantages fiscaux découlant de cet abri fiscal."

Forms: T5001 — Application for Tax Shelter Identification Number and Undertaking to Keep Books and Records.

Information Circulars: IC 89-4 Tax shelter reporting.

► 237.1(6) ◄

(6) Deductions and claims disallowed. No amount may be deducted or claimed by a person in respect of a tax shelter unless the person files with the Minister a prescribed form containing prescribed information, including the identification number for the tax shelter.

Forms: T5004 — Statement of Tax Shelter Loss or Deduction.

► 237.1(6.1) ◄

(6.1) Deductions and claims disallowed. No amount may be deducted or claimed by any person for any taxation year in respect of a tax shelter of the person where any person is liable to a penalty under subsection (7.4) or 162(9) in respect of the tax shelter or interest on the penalty and

(*a*) the penalty or interest has not been paid; or

(*b*) the penalty and interest have been paid, but an amount on account of the penalty or interest has been repaid under subsection 164(1.1) or applied under subsection 164(2).

► 237.1(6.2) ◄

(6.2) Assessments. Notwithstanding subsections 152(4) to (5), such assessments, determinations and redeterminations may be made as are necessary to give effect to subsection (6.1).

► 237.1(7) ◄

(7) Information return. Every promoter in respect of a tax shelter who accepts consideration in respect of the tax shelter or who acts as a principal or agent in respect of the tax shelter in a calendar year shall, in prescribed form and manner, file an information return for the year containing

(*a*) the name, address and the business number, Social Insurance Number or trust account number of each person who so acquires or otherwise invests in the tax shelter in the year,

(*b*) the amount paid by each of those persons in respect of the tax shelter, and

(*c*) such other information as is required by the prescribed form

unless an information return in respect of the tax shelter has previously been filed.

History: S. 237.1(7)(*a*) was replaced by S.C. 2018, c. 12, s. 34(1), applicable to the 2018 and subsequent taxation years, and formerly read:

(*a*) the name, address and either the Social Insurance Number or business number of each person who so acquires or otherwise invests in the tax shelter in the year,

Related Sections: S. 152(4) Assessment and reassessment; s. 162(6) Failure to provide identification number; s. 221(1)(*d*.1) Regulations; s. 237(1.1) Production of number; s. 237(2) Number required in information returns; s. 239(2.3) Offence with respect to an identification number; s. 248(1), "business number".

Forms: T5003 SUM — Summary of Tax Shelter Information; T5003 — Statement of Tax Shelter Information; T5004 — Statement of Tax Shelter Loss or Deduction.

Information Circulars: IC 89-4 Tax shelter reporting.

► 237.1(7.1) ◄

(7.1) Time for filing return. An information return required under subsection (7) to be filed in respect of the acquisition of an interest in a tax shelter in a calendar year shall be filed with the Minister on or before the last day of February of the following calendar year.

► 237.1(7.2) ◄

(7.2) Time for filing — special case. Notwithstanding subsection (7.1), where a person is required under subsection (7) to file an information return in respect of a business or activity and the person discontinues that business or activity, the return shall be filed on or before the earlier of

(*a*) the day referred to in subsection (7.1); and

(*b*) the day that is 30 days after the day of the discontinuance.

► 237.1(7.3) ◄

(7.3) Copies to be provided. Every person required to file a return under subsection (7) shall, on or before the day on or before which the return is required to be filed with the Minister, forward to each person to whom the return relates 2 copies of the portion of the return relating to that person.

▶ 237.1(7.4) ◀

(7.4) Penalty. Every person who files false or misleading information with the Minister in respect of an application under subsection (2) or, whether as a principal or as an agent, sells, issues or accepts consideration in respect of a tax shelter before the Minister has issued an identification number for the tax shelter is liable to a penalty equal to the greater of

(*a*) $500, and

(*b*) 25% of the greater of

(i) the total of all amounts each of which is the consideration received or receivable from a person in respect of the tax shelter before the correct information is filed with the Minister or the identification number is issued, as the case may be, and

(ii) the total of all amounts each of which is an amount stated or represented to be the value of property that a particular person who acquires or otherwise invests in the tax shelter could donate to a qualified donee, if the tax shelter is a gifting arrangement and consideration has been received or is receivable from the particular person in respect of the tax shelter before the correct information is filed with the Minister or the identification number is issued, as the case may be.

History: S. 237.1(7.4)(*b*) was replaced by S.C. 2012, c. 19, s. 15(3), applicable in respect of any application for an identification number made, any sale or issuance of a tax shelter made and any consideration in respect of a tax shelter accepted, on or after royal assent, June 29, 2012. S. 237.1(7.4)(*b*) formerly read:

(*b*) 25% of the total of all amounts each of which is the consideration received or receivable from a person in respect of the tax shelter before the correct information is filed with the Minister or the identification number is issued, as the case may be.

Related Sections: S. 161(11)(*b*.1) Interest on penalties; s. 161(12) Partnership liable to interest; s. 163.2 Definitions.

▶ 237.1(7.5) ◀

(7.5) Penalty. Every person who is required under subsection (7) to file an information return and who fails to comply with a demand under section 233 to file the return, or to report in the return information required under paragraph (7)(*a*) or (*b*), is liable to a penalty equal to 25% of the greater of

(*a*) the total of all amounts each of which is the consideration received or receivable by the person in respect of the tax shelter from a particular person in respect of whom information required under paragraph (7)(*a*) or (*b*) had not been reported at or before the time that the demand was issued or the return was filed, as the case may be, and

(*b*) if the tax shelter is a gifting arrangement, the total of all amounts each of which is an amount stated or represented to be the value of property that the particular person could donate to a qualified donee.

History: S. 237.1(7.5) was added by S.C. 2012, c. 19, s. 15(4), applicable in respect of any demand made, and any information return filed, on or after royal assent, June 29, 2012.

▶ 237.1(8) ◀

(8) Application of ss. 231 to 231.3. Without restricting the generality of sections 231 to 231.3, where an application under subsection (2) with respect to a tax shelter has been made, notwithstanding that a return of income has not been filed by any taxpayer under section 150 for the taxation year of the taxpayer in which an amount is claimed as a deduction in respect of the tax shelter, sections 231 to 231.3 apply, with such modifications as the circumstances require, for the purpose of permitting the Minister to verify or ascertain any information in respect of the tax shelter.

SECTION 237.2: Application of s. 237.1

Section 237.1 is applicable with respect to interests acquired after August 31, 1989.

SECTION 237.3: [Reporting for tax avoidance transactions]

▶ 237.3(1) ◀

(1) Definitions. The following definitions apply in this section.

"advisor" —"advisor", in respect of a transaction or series of transactions, means each person who provides, directly or indirectly in any manner whatever, any contractual protection in respect of the transaction or series, or any assistance or advice with respect to creating, developing, planning, organizing or implementing the transaction or series, to another person (including any person who enters into the transaction for the benefit of another person).

"avoidance transaction" —"avoidance transaction" has the meaning assigned by subsection 245(3).

"confidential protection" —"confidential protection", in respect of a transaction or series of transactions, means anything that prohibits the disclosure to any person or to the Minister of the details or structure of the transaction or series under which a tax benefit results, or would result but for section 245, but for greater certainty, the disclaiming or restricting of an advisor's liability shall not be considered confidential protection if it does not prohibit the disclosure of the details or structure of the transaction or series.

"contractual protection" —"contractual protection", in respect of a transaction or series of transactions, means

(*a*) any form of insurance (other than standard professional liability insurance) or other protection, including, without limiting the generality of the foregoing, an indemnity, compensation or a guarantee that, either immediately or in the future and either absolutely or contingently,

(i) protects a person against a failure of the transaction or series to achieve any tax benefit from the transaction or series, or

(ii) pays for or reimburses any expense, fee, tax, interest, penalty or similar amount that may be incurred by a person in the course of a dispute in respect of a tax benefit from the transaction or series; and

(*b*) any form of undertaking provided by a promoter, or by any person who does not deal at arm's length with a promoter, that provides, either immediately or in the future and either absolutely or contingently, assistance, directly or indirectly in any manner whatever, to a person in the course of a dispute in respect of a tax benefit from the transaction or series.

"fee" —"fee", in respect of a transaction or series of transactions, means any consideration that is, or could be, received or receivable, directly or indirectly in any manner whatever, by an advisor or a promoter, or any person who does not deal at arm's length with an advisor or promoter, for

(*a*) providing advice or an opinion with respect to the transaction or series;

(*b*) creating, developing, planning, organizing or implementing the transaction or series;

(*c*) promoting or selling an arrangement, plan or scheme that includes, or relates to, the transaction or series;

(*d*) preparing documents supporting the transaction or series, including tax returns or any information returns to be filed under this Act; or

(*e*) providing contractual protection.

"person" —"person" includes a partnership.

"promoter" —"promoter", in respect of a transaction or series of transactions, means each person who

(*a*) promotes or sells (whether as principal or agent and whether directly or indirectly) an arrangement, plan or scheme (referred to in this definition as an "arrangement"), if it may reasonably be considered that the arrangement includes or relates to the transaction or series;

(*b*) makes a statement or representation (whether as principal or agent and whether directly or indirectly) that a tax benefit could result from an arrangement, if it may reasonably be considered that

(i) the statement or representation was made in furtherance of the promoting or selling of the arrangement, and

(ii) the arrangement includes or relates to the transaction or series; or

(*c*) accepts (whether as principal or agent and whether directly or indirectly) consideration in respect of an arrangement referred to in paragraph (*a*) or (*b*).

"reportable transaction" —"reportable transaction", at any time, means an avoidance transaction that is entered into by or for the benefit of a person, and each transaction that is part of a series of transactions that includes the avoidance transaction, if at the time any two of the following paragraphs apply in respect of the avoidance transaction or series:

(*a*) an advisor or a promoter, or any person who does not deal at arm's length with the advisor or promoter, has or had an entitlement, either immediately or in the future and either absolutely or contingently, to a fee that to any extent

(i) is based on the amount of a tax benefit that results, or would result but for section 245, from the avoidance transaction or series,

(ii) is contingent upon the obtaining of a tax benefit that results, or would result but for section 245, from the avoidance transaction or series, or may be refunded, recovered or reduced, in any manner whatever, based upon the failure of the person to obtain a tax benefit from the avoidance transaction or series, or

(iii) is attributable to the number of persons

(A) who participate in the avoidance transaction or series, or in a similar avoidance transaction or series, or

(B) who have been provided access to advice or an opinion given by the advisor or promoter regarding the tax consequences from the avoidance transaction or series, or from a similar avoidance transaction or series;

(*b*) an advisor or promoter in respect of the avoidance transaction or series, or any person who does not deal at arm's length with the advisor or promoter, obtains or obtained confidential protection in respect of the avoidance transaction or series,

(i) in the case of an advisor, from a person to whom the advisor has provided any assistance or advice with respect to the avoidance transaction or series under the terms of an engagement of the advisor by that person to provide such assistance or advice, or

(ii) in the case of a promoter, from a person

(A) to whom an arrangement, plan or scheme has been promoted or sold in the circumstances described in paragraph (*a*) of the definition "promoter",

(B) to whom a statement or representation described in paragraph (*b*) of the definition "promoter" has been made, or

(C) from whom consideration described in paragraph (*c*) of the definition "promoter" has been received; or

(*c*) either

(i) the person (in this subparagraph referred to as the "particular person"), another person who entered into the avoidance transaction for the benefit of the particular person or any other person who does not deal at arm's length with the particular person or with a person who entered into the avoidance transaction for the benefit of the particular person, has or had contractual protection in respect of the avoidance transaction or series, otherwise than as a result of a fee described in paragraph (*a*), or

(ii) an advisor or promoter in respect of the avoidance transaction or series, or any person who does not deal at arm's length with the advisor or promoter, has or had contractual protection in respect of the avoidance transaction or series, otherwise than as a result of a fee described in paragraph (*a*).

"solicitor-client privilege" —"solicitor-client privilege" has the meaning assigned by subsection 232(1).

"tax benefit" —"tax benefit" has the meaning assigned by subsection 245(1).

"transaction" —"transaction" has the meaning assigned by subsection 245(1).

History: S. 237.3(1) was added by S.C. 2013, c. 34, s. 356(1), applicable in respect of avoidance transactions that are entered into after 2010 or that are part of a series of transactions that began before 2011 and is completed after 2010, except that, in its application to an avoidance transaction that is part of a series that began before 2011, the definition "confidential protection" in subsection 237.3(1) is to be read as follows:

" 'confidential protection', in respect of a transaction or series of transactions, means anything that prohibits the disclosure to any person or to the

Minister of the details or structure of the transaction or series under which a tax benefit results, or would result but for section 245, but does not include a prohibition on disclosure that relates to an agreement entered into before March 4, 2010 between an advisor and his or her client for the provision of accounting, legal or similar tax advisory services, and for greater certainty, the disclaiming or restricting of an advisor's liability shall not be considered confidential protection if it does not prohibit the disclosure of the details or structure of the transaction or series."

In addition, if the filing of an information return under section 237.3 would be required before July 1, 2012, the information return is deemed to be filed before that day if it is filed before October 24, 2013 [the day that is 120 days after royal assent].

► 237.3(2) ◄

(2) Application. An information return in prescribed form and containing prescribed information in respect of a reportable transaction must be filed with the Minister by

(*a*) every person for whom a tax benefit results, or would result but for section 245, from the reportable transaction, from any other reportable transaction that is part of a series of transactions that includes the reportable transaction or from the series of transactions;

(*b*) every person who has entered into, for the benefit of a person described in paragraph (*a*), an avoidance transaction that is a reportable transaction;

(*c*) every advisor or promoter in respect of the reportable transaction, or in respect of any other transaction that is part of a series of transactions that includes the reportable transaction, who is or was entitled, either immediately or in the future and either absolutely or contingently, to a fee in respect of any of those transactions that is

(i) described in paragraph (*a*) of the definition "reportable transaction" in subsection (1), or

(ii) in respect of contractual protection provided in circumstances described in paragraph (*c*) of the definition "reportable transaction" in subsection (1); and

(*d*) every person who is not dealing at arm's length with an advisor or promoter in respect of the reportable transaction and who is or was entitled, either immediately or in the future and either absolutely or contingently, to a fee that is referred to in paragraph (*c*).

History: S. 237.3(2) was added by S.C. 2013, c. 34, s. 356(1), applicable in respect of avoidance transactions that are entered into after 2010 or that are part of a series of transactions that began before 2011 and is completed after 2010.

Related Sections: S. 152(4) Assessment and reassessment.

STEP Canada: Paul Lynch and Brett Anderson, "Aggressive Tax Reporting: What it means to STEP Members," PowerPoint presentation to the 15th National Conference of STEP Canada, Toronto, June 10-11, 2013.

► 237.3(3) ◄

(3) Clarification of reporting transactions in series. For greater certainty, and subject to subsection (11), if subsection (2) applies to a person in respect of each reportable transaction that is part of a series of transactions that includes an avoidance transaction, the filing of a prescribed form by the person that reports each transaction in the series is deemed to satisfy the obligation of the person under subsection (2) in respect of each transaction so reported.

History: S. 237.3(3) was added by S.C. 2013, c. 34, s. 356(1), applicable in respect of avoidance transactions that are entered into after 2010 or that are part of a series of transactions that began before 2011 and is completed after 2010.

► 237.3(4) ◄

(4) Application. For the purpose of subsection (2), if any person is required to file an information return in respect of a reportable transaction under that subsection, the filing by any such person of an information return with full and accurate disclosure in prescribed form in respect of the transaction is deemed to have been made by each person to whom subsection (2) applies in respect of the transaction.

History: S. 237.3(4) was added by S.C. 2013, c. 34, s. 356(1), applicable in respect of avoidance transactions that are entered into after 2010 or that are part of a series of transactions that began before 2011 and is completed after 2010.

► 237.3(5) ◄

(5) Time for filing return. An information return required by subsection (2) to be filed by a person for a reportable transaction is to be filed with the Minister on or before June 30 of the calendar year following the calendar year in which the transaction first became a reportable transaction in respect of the person.

History: S. 237.3(5) was added by S.C. 2013, c. 34, s. 356(1), applicable in respect of avoidance transactions that are entered into after 2010 or that are part of a series of transactions that began before 2011 and is completed after 2010.

In addition, if the filing of an information return under section 237.3 would be required before July 1, 2012, the information return is deemed to be filed before that day if it is filed before October 24, 2013 [the day that is 120 days after royal assent].

► 237.3(6) ◄

(6) Tax benefits disallowed. Notwithstanding subsection 245(4), subsection 245(2) is deemed to apply at any time to any reportable transaction in respect of a person described in paragraph (2)(*a*) in relation to the reportable transaction if, at that time,

(*a*) the obligation under subsection (2) of the person in respect of the reportable transaction, or any other reportable transaction that is part of a series of transactions that includes the reportable transaction, has not been satisfied;

(*b*) a person is liable to a penalty under subsection (8) in respect of the reportable transaction or any other reportable transaction that is part of a series of transactions that includes the reportable transaction; and

(*c*) the penalty under subsection (8) or interest on the penalty has not been paid, or has been paid but an amount on account of the penalty or interest has been repaid under subsection 164(1.1) or applied under subsection 164(2).

History: S. 237.3(6) was added by S.C. 2013, c. 34, s. 356(1), applicable in respect of avoidance transactions that are entered into after 2010 or that are part of a series of transactions that began before 2011 and is completed after 2010.

► 237.3(7) ◄

(7) Assessments. Notwithstanding subsections 152(4) to (5), the Minister may make any assessments, determinations and redeterminations that are necessary to give effect to subsection (8).

History: S. 237.3(7) was added by S.C. 2013, c. 34, s. 356(1), applicable in respect of avoidance transactions that are entered into after 2010 or that are part of a series of transactions that began before 2011 and is completed after 2010.

► 237.3(8) ◄

(8) Penalty. Every person who fails to file an information return in respect of a reportable transaction as required under subsection (2) on or before the day required under subsection (5) is liable to a penalty equal to the total of each amount that is a fee to which an advisor or a promoter (or any person who does not deal at arm's length with the advisor or the promoter) in respect of the reportable transaction is or was entitled, either immediately or in the future and either absolutely or contingently, to receive in respect of the reportable transaction, any transaction that is part of the series of transactions that includes the reportable transaction or the series of transactions that includes the reportable transaction, if the fee is

(*a*) described in paragraph (*a*) of the definition "reportable transaction" in subsection (1); or

(*b*) in respect of contractual protection provided in circumstances described in paragraph (*c*) of the definition "reportable transaction" in subsection (1).

History: S. 237.3(8) was added by S.C. 2013, c. 34, s. 356(1), applicable in respect of avoidance transactions that are entered into after 2010 or that are part of a series of transactions that began before 2011 and is completed after 2010.

Related Sections: S. 161(11) Interest on penalties; s. 163(2.9) Partnership liable to penalty.

► 237.3(9) ◄

(9) Joint and several liability. If more than one person is liable to a penalty under subsection (8) in respect of a reportable transaction, each of those persons are jointly and severally, or solidarily, liable to pay the penalty.

History: S. 237.3(9) was added by S.C. 2013, c. 34, s. 356(1), applicable in respect of avoidance transactions that are entered into after 2010 or that are part of a series of transactions that began before 2011 and is completed after 2010.

► 237.3(10) ◄

(10) Joint and several liability — special cases. Notwithstanding subsections (8) and (9), the liability of an advisor or a promoter, or a person with whom the advisor or promoter does not deal at arm's length, to a penalty under those subsections in respect of a reportable transaction shall not exceed the total of each amount that is a fee referred to in subsection (8) to which that advisor or promoter, or a person with whom the advisor or promoter does not deal at arm's length, is or was entitled, either immediately or in the future and either absolutely or contingently, to receive in respect of the reportable transaction.

History: S. 237.3(10) was added by S.C. 2013, c. 34, s. 356(1), applicable in respect of avoidance transactions that are entered into after 2010 or that are part of a series of transactions that began before 2011 and is completed after 2010.

► 237.3(11) ◄

(11) Due diligence. A person required to file an information return in respect of a reportable transaction is not liable for a penalty under subsection (8) if the person has exercised the degree of care, diligence and skill to prevent the failure to file that a reasonably prudent person would have exercised in comparable circumstances.

History: S. 237.3(11) was added by S.C. 2013, c. 34, s. 356(1), applicable in respect of avoidance transactions that are entered into after 2010 or that are part of a series of transactions that began before 2011 and is completed after 2010.

► 237.3(12) ◄

(12) Reporting not an admission. The filing of an information return under this section by a person in respect of a reportable transaction is not an admission by the person that

(*a*) section 245 applies in respect of any transaction; or

(*b*) any transaction is part of a series of transactions.

History: S. 237.3(12) was added by S.C. 2013, c. 34, s. 356(1), applicable in respect of avoidance transactions that are entered into after 2010 or that are part of a series of transactions that began before 2011 and is completed after 2010.

► 237.3(13) ◄

(13) Application of sections 231 to 231.3. Without restricting the generality of sections 231 to 231.3, even if a return of income has not been filed by a taxpayer under section 150 for the taxation year of the taxpayer in which a tax benefit results, or would result but for section 245, from a reportable transaction, sections 231 to 231.3 apply, with such modifications as the circumstances require, for the purpose of permitting the Minister to verify or ascertain any information in respect of that transaction.

History: S. 237.3(13) was added by S.C. 2013, c. 34, s. 356(1), applicable in respect of avoidance transactions that are entered into after 2010 or that are part of a series of transactions that began before 2011 and is completed after 2010.

► 237.3(14) ◄

(14) Tax shelters and flow-through shares. For the purpose of this section, a reportable transaction does not include a transaction that is, or is part of a series of transactions that includes,

(*a*) the acquisition of a tax shelter for which an information return has been filed with the Minister under subsection 237.1(7); or

(*b*) the issuance of a flow-through share for which an information return has been filed with the Minister under subsection 66(12.68).

History: S. 237.3(14) was added by S.C. 2013, c. 34, s. 356(1), applicable in respect of avoidance transactions that are entered into after 2010 or that are part of a series of transactions that began before 2011 and is completed after 2010.

► 237.3(15) ◄

(15) Tax shelters and flow-through shares — penalty. Notwithstanding subsection (8), the amount of the penalty, if any, that applies on a person under that subsection in respect of a reportable transaction shall not exceed the amount determined by the formula

$$A - B$$

where

A is the amount of the penalty imposed on the person under subsection (8), determined without reference to this subsection; and

B is

(a) if the reportable transaction is the acquisition of a tax shelter, the amount of the penalty, if any, that applies on the person under subsection 237.1(7.4) in respect of the tax shelter,

(b) if the reportable transaction is the issuance of a flow-through share, the amount of the penalty, if any, that applies on the person under subsection 66(12.74) in respect of the issuance of the flow-through share, and

(c) in any other case, nil.

History: S. 237.3(15) was added by S.C. 2013, c. 34, s. 356(1), applicable in respect of avoidance transactions that are entered into after 2010 or that are part of a series of transactions that began before 2011 and is completed after 2010.

▶ 237.3(16) ◀

(16) Anti-avoidance. Subsection (14) does not apply to a reportable transaction if it is reasonable, having regard to all of the circumstances, to conclude that one of the main reasons for the acquisition of a tax shelter, or the issuance of a flow-through share, is to avoid the application of this section.

History: S. 237.3(16) was added by S.C. 2013, c. 34, s. 356(1), applicable in respect of avoidance transactions that are entered into after 2010 or that are part of a series of transactions that began before 2011 and is completed after 2010.

▶ 237.3(17) ◀

(17) Solicitor-client privilege. For greater certainty, for the purpose of this section, a lawyer who is an advisor in respect of a reportable transaction is not required to disclose in an information return in respect of the transaction any information in respect of which the lawyer, on reasonable grounds, believes that a client of the lawyer has solicitor-client privilege.

History: S. 237.3(17) was added by S.C. 2013, c. 34, s. 356(1), applicable in respect of avoidance transactions that are entered into after 2010 or that are part of a series of transactions that began before 2011 and is completed after 2010.

Offences and Punishment

SECTION 238: Offences and punishment

▶ 238(1) ◀

(1) Offences and punishment. Every person who has failed to file or make a return as and when required by or under this Act or a regulation or who has failed to comply with subsection 116(3), 127(3.1) or (3.2), 147.1(7) or 153 (1), any of sections 230 to 232, 244.7 and 267 or a regulation made under subsection 147.1(18) or with an order made under subsection (2) is guilty of an offence and, in addition to any penalty otherwise provided, is liable on summary conviction to

(*a*) a fine of not less than $1,000 and not more than $25,000; or

(*b*) both the fine described in paragraph (*a*) and imprisonment for a term not exceeding 12 months.

History: S. 238(1), the portion before paragraph (*a*) was replaced by S.C. 2014, c. 20, s. 27, in force June 19, 2014, and formerly read:

(1) *Offences and punishment.* Every person who has failed to file or make a return as and when required by or under this Act or a regulation or who has failed to comply with subsection 116(3), 127(3.1) or (3.2), 147.1(7) or 153(1), any of sections 230 to 232 or a regulation made under subsection 147.1(18) or with an order made under subsection (2) is guilty of an offence and, in addition to any penalty otherwise provided, is liable on summary conviction to

Information Circulars: IC 98-1R4 Collections Policies.

Cases: Offences under subsection 238(1) are strict liability. Persons accused may avoid conviction by proving, on a balance of probabilities, either that they had an honest but mistaken belief in facts which, if true, would render the act innocent, or that they exercised all reasonable care to avoid committing the offence. The due diligence defence is based on a factual finding, on a balance of probabilities, that the accused person did what a reasonable person would have done in the circumstances to avoid the occurrence of the prohibited act. Delegation does not amount to due diligence. *The Queen v. O'Hara and Gallant*, 2017 DTC 5095 (NSPC)

The failure on each successive day to file a return, after demand, constituted a separate offence. *The Queen v. Subacious*, (Ont. C.A.) 78 DTC 6441

▶ 238(2) ◀

(2) Compliance orders. Where a person has been convicted by a court of an offence under subsection (1) for a failure to comply with a provision of this Act or a regulation, the court may make such order as it deems proper in order to enforce compliance with the provision.

▶ 238(3) ◀

(3) Saving. Where a person has been convicted under this section of failing to comply with a provision of this Act or a regulation, the person is not liable to pay a penalty imposed under section 162 or 227 for the same failure unless the person was assessed for that penalty or that penalty was demanded from the person before the information or complaint giving rise to the conviction was laid or made.

Related Sections: S. 248(1), "assessment", "regulation".

SECTION 239: Other offences and punishment

▶ 239(1) ◀

(1) Other offences and punishment. Every person who has

(*a*) made, or participated in, assented to or acquiesced in the making of, false or deceptive statements in a return, certificate, statement or answer filed or made as required by or under this Act or a regulation,

(*b*) to evade payment of a tax imposed by this Act, destroyed, altered, mutilated, secreted or otherwise disposed of the records or books of account of a taxpayer,

(*c*) made, or assented to or acquiesced in the making of, false or deceptive entries, or omitted, or assented to or acquiesced in the omission, to enter a material particular, in records or books of account of a taxpayer,

(*d*) wilfully, in any manner, evaded or attempted to evade compliance with this Act or payment of taxes imposed by this Act, or

(*e*) conspired with any person to commit an offence described in paragraphs (*a*) to (*d*),

is guilty of an offence and, in addition to any penalty otherwise provided, is liable on summary conviction to

(*f*) a fine of not less than 50%, and not more than 200%, of the amount of the tax that was sought to be evaded, or

(*g*) both the fine described in paragraph (*f*) and imprisonment for a term not exceeding 2 years.

Related Sections: S. 163(2) False statements or omissions; ITAR s. 65.1 Part XV of amended Act.

Canadian Tax Foundation: Cook and Gill, *Potential Civil and Criminal Liability of Promoting Tax Avoidance Products*, 2005 Prairie Provinces Tax Conference 19:1–36.

Tax Topics: No. 1801, The Challenge of Proving Wilful Blindness in Tax Evasion Cases.

Information Circulars: IC 73-10R3 Tax evasion.

Cases: The taxpayer was convicted of offences under the Immigration and Refugee Protection Act, the Criminal Code, and the Income Tax Act, and given an aggregate sentence of 7 years. The immigration offences were a separate endeavor from the personal tax offences and properly subject to a consecutive sentence. The total sentence was not demonstrably inappropriate. *R. v. Wang*, 2016 DTC 5103 (BCCA)

There was reasonable doubt that a taxpayer willfully made false statements or evaded tax where it was unclear whether the taxpayer had ever seen the returns filed by his accountant. *The Queen v. McMahon*, 2013 DTC 5151 (Alta. Prov. Ct.).

The taxpayer, who filed returns using estimates that fell far short of actual income, was convicted of tax evasion. However, it was inappropriate to convict the taxpayer on a second charge of filing false returns based on the same evidence. *The Queen v. Tiffin*, 2013 DTC 5150 (Sask. Prov. Ct.).

The arrangement between a taxpayer company and two other companies involving scientific research expenditures was a scheme where it contained a false budget and was false and misleading. *Schmidt v. The Queen*, 93 DTC 5319 (B.C. C.A.), affirming 91 DTC 5440 (B.C. Prov. Ct.)

Taxpayers were found guilty of tax evasion for creating inflated invoices and backdating documents in order to create the impression that R&D work had been done in Canada. *The Queen v. Cancor Software Corp. et al.*, 94 DTC 6102 (Ont. C.A.), affirming 92 DTC 6090 (Ont. C.J.)

Taxpayer's failure to report income in calendar year was not culpable as he had option of reporting income in fiscal year. *Matthys v. The Queen*, 86 DTC 6385 (Ont. Dist. Ct.).

▶ 239(1.1) ◀

(1.1) Offences re refunds and credits. Every person who obtains or claims a refund or credit under this Act to which the person or any other person is not entitled or obtains or claims a refund or credit under this Act in an amount that is greater than the amount to which the person or other person is entitled

(*a*) by making, or participating in, assenting to or acquiescing in the making of, a false or deceptive statement in a return, certificate, statement or answer filed or made under this Act or a regulation,

(*b*) by destroying, altering, mutilating, hiding or otherwise disposing of a record or book of account of the person or other person,

(*c*) by making, or assenting to or acquiescing in the making of, a false or deceptive entry in a record or book of account of the person or other person,

(*d*) by omitting, or assenting to or acquiescing in an omission to enter a material particular in a record or book of account of the person or other person,

(*e*) wilfully in any manner, or

(*f*) by conspiring with any person to commit any offence under this subsection,

is guilty of an offence and, in addition to any penalty otherwise provided, is liable on summary conviction to

(*g*) a fine of not less than 50% and not more than 200% of the amount by which the amount of the refund or credit obtained or claimed exceeds the amount, if any, of the refund or credit to which the person or other person, as the case may be, is entitled, or

(*h*) both the fine described in paragraph (*g*) and imprisonment for a term not exceeding 2 years.

Information Circulars: IC 73-10R3 Tax evasion.

▶ 239(2) ◀

(2) Prosecution on indictment. Every person who is charged with an offence described in subsection (1) or (1.1) may, at the election of the Attorney General of Canada, be prosecuted on indictment and, if convicted, is, in addition to any penalty otherwise provided, liable to

(*a*) a fine of not less than 100% and not more than 200% of

(i) where the offence is described in subsection (1), the amount of the tax that was sought to be evaded, and

(ii) where the offence is described in subsection (1.1), the amount by which the amount of the refund or credit obtained or claimed exceeds the amount, if any, of the refund or credit to which the person or other person, as the case may be, is entitled; and

(*b*) imprisonment for a term not exceeding 5 years.

Information Circulars: IC 73-10R3 Tax evasion.

▶ 239(2.1) ◀

(2.1) Providing incorrect tax shelter identification number. Every person who wilfully provides another person with an incorrect identification number for a tax shelter is guilty of an offence and, in addition to any penalty otherwise provided, is liable on summary conviction to

(*a*) a fine of not less than 100%, and not more than 200%, of the cost to the other person of that person's interest in the shelter;

(*b*) imprisonment for a term not exceeding 2 years; or

(*c*) both the fine described in paragraph (*a*) and the imprisonment described in paragraph (*b*).

Information Circulars: IC 89-4 Tax shelter reporting.

▶ 239(2.2) ◀

(2.2) Offence with respect to confidential information. Every person who

(*a*) contravenes subsection 241(1), or

(*b*) knowingly contravenes an order made under subsection 241(4.1)

is guilty of an offence and liable on summary conviction to a fine not exceeding $5,000 or to imprisonment for a term not exceeding 12 months, or to both.

Related Sections: S. 239(2.22), "official"; s. 241(1) Provision of information; s. 241(4.1) Measures to prevent unauthorized use or disclosure; s. 241(10), "official".

▶ 239(2.21) ◀

(2.21) Idem. Every person

(*a*) to whom taxpayer information has been provided for a particular purpose under paragraph 241(4)(*b*), (*c*), (*e*), (*h*), (*k*), (*n*), (*o*) or (*p*), or

(*b*) who is an official to whom taxpayer information has been provided for a particular purpose under paragraph 241(4)(*a*), (*d*), (*f*), (*f.1*), (*i*), (*j.1*) or (*j.2*)

and who for any other purpose knowingly uses, provides to any person, allows the provision to any person of, or allows any person access to, that information is guilty of an offence and liable on summary conviction to a fine not exceeding $5,000 or to imprisonment for a term not exceeding 12 months, or to both.

History: S. 239(2.21)(*b*) was replaced by S.C. 2013, c. 40, s. 85(1), in force December 12, 2013, and formerly read:

(*b*) who is an official to whom taxpayer information has been provided for a particular purpose under paragraph 241(4)(*a*), (*d*), (*f*), (*f.1*), (*i*) or (*j.1*)

Related Sections: S. 239(2.22) Definitions; s. 241(4) Where taxpayer information may be disclosed; s. 241(10) Definitions.

▶ 239(2.22) ◀

(2.22) Definitions. In subsection (2.21), "official" and "taxpayer information" have the meanings assigned by subsection 241(10).

Related Sections: S. 241(10), "official".

▶ 239(2.3) ◀

(2.3) Offence with respect to an identification number. Every person to whom the business number of a taxpayer or partnership, to whom the Social Insurance Number of an individual or to whom the trust account number of a trust has been provided under this Act or the Regulations, and every officer, employee and agent of such a person, who without written consent of the individual, taxpayer, partnership or trust, as the case may be, knowingly uses, communicates or allows to be communicated the number (otherwise than as required or authorized by law, in the course of duties in connection with the administration or enforcement of this Act or for a purpose for which it was provided by the individual, taxpayer, partnership or trust, as the case may be) is guilty of an offence and liable on summary conviction to a fine not exceeding $5,000 or to imprisonment for a term not exceeding 12 months, or to both.

History: S. 239(2.3) was replaced by S.C. 2018, c. 12, s. 35(1), applicable to the 2018 and subsequent taxation years, and formerly read:

(2.3) *Offence with respect to an identification number.* Every person to whom the Social Insurance Number of an individual or to whom the business number of a taxpayer or partnership has been provided under this Act or a regulation, and every officer, employee and agent of such a person, who without written consent of the individual, taxpayer or partnership, as the case may be, knowingly uses, communicates or allows to be communicated the number (otherwise than as required or authorized by law, in the course of duties in connection with the administration or enforcement of this Act or for a purpose for which it was provided by the individual, taxpayer or partnership, as the case may be) is guilty of an offence and liable on summary conviction to a fine not exceeding $5,000 or to imprisonment for a term not exceeding 12 months, or to both.

Related Sections: S. 162(6) Failure to provide identification number; s. 221(1)(*d*.1) Regulations; s. 237(1.1) Production of number; s. 237(2) Number required in information returns; s. 237.1(7) Information return; s. 248(1), "business number".

Information Circulars: IC 82-2R2 Social insurance number legislation that relates to the preparation of information slips.

► 239(2.31) ◄

(2.31) Offence: section 149.01 — (Repealed by S.C. 2017, c. 12, s. 13.)

History: S. 239(2.31) was repealed by S.C. 2017, c. 12, s. 13, in force June 19, 2017, and formerly read:

(2.31) *Offence: section 149.01.* Every labour organization or labour trust that contravenes section 149.01 is guilty of an offence and liable on summary conviction to a fine of $1,000 for each day that it fails to comply with that section, to a maximum of $25,000.

S. 239(2.31) was added by S.C. 2015, c. 41, s. 2, applicable in respect of fiscal periods that begin after December 31, 2015.

Related Sections: 149.01(2) Information return.

► 239(3) ◄

(3) Penalty on conviction. If a person is convicted under this section, the person is not liable to pay a penalty imposed under any of sections 162, 163, 163.2 and 163.3 for the same contravention unless the penalty is assessed before the information or complaint giving rise to the conviction was laid or made.

History: S. 239(3) was replaced by S.C. 2013, c. 40, s. 85(2), in force January 1, 2014, and formerly read:

(3) *Penalty on conviction.* Where a person is convicted under this section, the person is not liable to pay a penalty imposed under section 162, 163 or 163.2 for the same contravention unless the penalty is assessed before the information or complaint giving rise to the conviction was laid or made.

Information Circulars: IC 73-10R3 Tax evasion.

► 239(4) ◄

(4) Stay of appeal. Where, in any appeal under this Act, substantially the same facts are at issue as those that are at issue in a prosecution under this section, the Minister may file a stay of proceedings with the Tax Court of Canada and thereupon the proceedings before that Court are stayed pending final determination of the outcome of the prosecution.

Related Sections: S. 248(1), "assessment", "regulation"; ITAR s. 65.1 Part XV of amended Act.

► 239(5) ◄

(5) Offence and punishment without reference to subsection 120(2.2). In determining whether an offence under this Act, for which a person may on summary conviction or indictment be liable for a fine or imprisonment, has been committed, and in determining the punishment for such an offence, this Act is to be read without reference to subsection 120(2.2).

SECTION 239.1: [Electronic suppression of sales — offences]

► 239.1(1) ◄

(1) Definitions. The definitions in subsection 163.3(1) apply in this section.

History: S. 239.1(1) was added by S.C. 2013, c. 40, s. 86(1), in force January 1, 2014.

► 239.1(2) ◄

(2) Offences. Every person that, without lawful excuse, the proof of which lies on the person,

(*a*) uses an electronic suppression of sales device or a similar device or software in relation to records that are required to be kept by any person under section 230,

(*b*) acquires or possesses an electronic suppression of sales device, or a right in respect of an electronic suppression of sales device, that is, or is intended to be, capable of being used in relation to records that are required to be kept by any person under section 230,

(*c*) designs, develops, manufactures, possesses for sale, offers for sale, sells, transfers or otherwise makes available to another person an electronic suppression of sales device that is, or is intended to be, capable of being used in relation to records that are required to be kept by any person under section 230,

(*d*) supplies installation, upgrade or maintenance services for an electronic suppression of sales device that is, or is intended to be, capable of being used in relation to records that are required to be kept by any person under section 230, or

(*e*) participates in, assents to or acquiesces in the commission of, or conspires with any person to commit, an offence described in any of paragraphs (*a*) to (*d*),

is guilty of an offence and, in addition to any penalty otherwise provided, is liable on summary conviction to a fine of not less than $10,000 and not more than $500,000 or to imprisonment for a term not exceeding two years, or to both.

History: S. 239.1(2) was added by S.C. 2013, c. 40, s. 86(1), in force January 1, 2014.

► 239.1(3) ◄

(3) Prosecution on indictment. Every person that is charged with an offence described in subsection (2) may, at the election of the Attorney General of Canada, be prosecuted on indictment and, if convicted, is, in addition to any penalty otherwise provided, liable to a fine of not less than $50,000 and not more than $1,000,000 or to imprisonment for a term not exceeding five years, or to both.

History: S. 239.1(3) was added by S.C. 2013, c. 40, s. 86(1), in force January 1, 2014.

► 239.1(4) ◄

(4) Penalty on conviction. A person that is convicted of an offence under this section is not liable to pay a penalty imposed under any of sections 162, 163, 163.2 and 163.3 for the same action unless a notice of assessment for that penalty was issued before the information or complaint giving rise to the conviction was laid or made.

History: S. 239.1(4) was added by S.C. 2013, c. 40, s. 86(1), in force January 1, 2014.

► 239.1(5) ◄

(5) Stay of appeal. If, in any appeal under this Act, substantially the same facts are at issue as those that are at issue in a prosecution under this section, the Minister may file a stay of proceedings with the Tax Court of Canada and, upon that filing, the proceedings before that Court are stayed pending final determination of the outcome of the prosecution.

History: S. 239.1(5) was added by S.C. 2013, c. 40, s. 86(1), in force January 1, 2014.

SECTION 240: [Offence — interest coupons]

► 240(1) ◄

(1) Definition of "taxable obligation" and "non-taxable obligation". In this section, "taxable obligation" means any bond, debenture or similar obligation the interest on which would, if paid by the issuer to a non-resident person, be subject to the payment of tax under Part XIII by that non-resident person at the rate provided in subsection 212(1) (otherwise than by virtue of subsection 212(6)), and "non-taxable obligation" means any bond, debenture or similar obligation the interest on which would not, if paid by the issuer to a non-resident person, be subject to the payment of tax under Part XIII by that non-resident person.

► 240(2) ◄

(2) Interest coupon to be identified in prescribed manner — offence and punishment. Every person who, at any time after July 14, 1966, issues

(*a*) any taxable obligation, or

(*b*) any non-taxable obligation

the right to interest on which is evidenced by a coupon or other writing that does not form part of, or is capable of being detached from, the evidence of indebtedness under the obligation is, unless the coupon or other writing is marked or identified in prescribed manner by the letters "AX" in the case of a taxable obligation, and by the letter "F" in the case of a non-taxable obligation, on the face thereof, guilty of an offence and liable on summary conviction to a fine not exceeding $500.

Related Regulations: 807.

Related Sections: S. 248(1), "non-resident", "prescribed"; ITAR s. 65.1 Part XV of amended Act.

SECTION 241: Provision of information

► 241(1) ◄

(1) Provision of information. Except as authorized by this section, no official or other representative of a government entity shall

(*a*) knowingly provide, or knowingly allow to be provided, to any person any taxpayer information;

(*b*) knowingly allow any person to have access to any taxpayer information; or

(*c*) knowingly use any taxpayer information otherwise than in the course of the administration or enforcement of this Act, the *Canada Pension Plan*, the *Unemployment Insurance Act* or the *Employment Insurance Act* or for the purpose for which it was provided under this section.

History: S. 241(1), the portion before paragraph (*a*) was replaced by S.C. 2009, c. 2, s. 75(1), in force on Royal Assent, March 12, 2009. S. 241(1), the portion before paragraph (*a*) formerly read:

(1) *Provision of information.* Except as authorized by this section, no official shall

Related Sections: S. 149.1(15) Information may be communicated; s. 230.1(4) Reports to chief electoral officer; s. 239(2.2) Offence with respect to confidential information; s. 241(3) Communication where proceedings have been commenced; s. 241(3.1) Circumstances involving danger; s. 241(9) Offence; s. 241(10), "official"; s. 241(11) References to Petroleum and Gas Revenue Tax Act.

Canadian Tax Foundation: Bendin, *The Requirement of Confidentiality Under the Income Tax Act and Its Effect on the Conduct of Appeals Before the Tax Court of Canada*, 1996 Canadian Tax Journal 3:680–722.

Information Circulars: IC 94-4R International Transfer Pricing: Advance Pricing Arrangements (APAs).

SR&ED Publications: 95-04R, Conflict of Interest.

Cases: Although s. 241 does not preclude the Minister from disclosing taxpayer information in a legal proceeding, s. 37 of the *Evidence Act* may prevent the disclosure if there is a specified public interest that outweighs the public interest in the disclosure of the information. *The Queen et al. v. Harris*, 2001 DTC 5247 (F.C.A.), reversing in part 2001 DTC 5058 (F.C.T.D.)

In divorce proceedings in which it was alleged that a taxpayer had kidnapped the children of the marriage and was in contempt of custody orders, it was not within the power of the Court to order the Minister to release the addresses of the taxpayer and of the co-respondent. Neither the judge nor the petitioner in the divorce proceedings was a person "otherwise entitled" to such information. *Glover v. M.N.R.*, 82 DTC 6035 (S.C.C.)

► 241(2) ◄

(2) Evidence relating to taxpayer information. Notwithstanding any other Act of Parliament or other law, no official or other representative of a government entity shall be required, in connection with any legal proceedings, to give or produce evidence relating to any taxpayer information.

History: S. 241(2) was replaced by S.C. 2009, c. 2, s. 75(2), in force on Royal Assent, March 12, 2009. S. 241(2) formerly read:

(2) *Idem.* Notwithstanding any other Act of Parliament or other law, no official shall be required, in connection with any legal proceedings, to give or produce evidence relating to any taxpayer information.

Related Sections: S. 241(3) Communication where proceedings have been commenced; s. 241(10), "official".

► 241(3) ◄

(3) Communication where proceedings have been commenced. Subsections (1) and (2) do not apply in respect of

(*a*) criminal proceedings, either by indictment or on summary conviction, that have been commenced by the laying of an information or the preferring of an indictment, under an Act of Parliament; or

(*b*) any legal proceedings relating to the administration or enforcement of this Act, the *Canada Pension Plan*, the *Unemployment Insurance Act* or the *Employment Insurance Act* or any other Act of Parliament or law of a province that provides for the imposition or collection of a tax or duty.

Related Sections: S. 241(11) References to Petroleum and Gas Revenue Tax Act.

Cases: Confidential information was admissible in bankruptcy proceedings since it fell within the exception contained in s. 241(3), the text or context of which was simply too broad to support the argument that the only proceedings it envisaged were the ones expressly provided for in Part XV of the *Income tax Act*. *Slattery v. Doane Raymond Limited*, 93 DTC 5443 (S.C.C.)

► 241(3.1) ◄

(3.1) Circumstances involving danger. The Minister may provide to appropriate persons any taxpayer information relating to imminent danger of death or physical injury to any individual.

Related Sections: S. 241(10) Definitions.

► 241(3.2) ◄

(3.2) Registered charities and registered Canadian amateur athletic associations. An official may provide to any person the following taxpayer information relating to another person (in this subsection referred to as the "registrant") that was at any time a registered charity or registered Canadian amateur athletic association:

> **Amendment not yet in force**
>
> **Budget Implementation Act, 2019, No. 1 [S.C. 2019, c. 29]**
>
> **S. 241(3.2), the portion before paragraph (*a*), was replaced by S.C. 2019, c. 29, s. 42(1), and will read as follows:**
>
> **(3.2) Certain qualified donees.** An official may provide to any person the following taxpayer information relating to another person (in this subsection referred to as the "registrant") that was at any time a registered charity, registered Canadian amateur athletic association or registered journalism organization:
>
> **Applicable:** In force on January 1, 2020.

(*a*) a copy of the registrant's governing documents, including its statement of purpose, and function in the case of a Canadian amateur athletic association;

(*b*) any information provided in prescribed form to the Minister by the registrant on applying for registration under this Act;

(*c*) the names of the persons who at any time were the registrant's directors and the periods during which they were its directors;

(*d*) a copy of the notification of the registrant's registration, including any conditions and warnings;

(*e*) if the registration of the registrant has been revoked or annulled, a copy of the entirety of or any part of any letter sent by or on behalf of the Minister to the registrant relating to the grounds for the revocation or annulment;

(*f*) financial statements required to be filed with an information return referred to in subsection 149.1(14);

> **Amendment not yet in force**
>
> **Budget Implementation Act, 2019, No. 1 [S.C. 2019, c. 29]**
>
> **S. 241(3.2)(*f*) was replaced by S.C. 2019, c. 29, s. 42(2), and will read as follows:**
>
> (*f*) financial statements required to be filed with an information return referred to in subsection 149.1(14) or (14.1);
>
> **Applicable:** In force on January 1, 2020.

(*g*) a copy of the entirety of or any part of any letter or notice by the Minister to the registrant relating to a suspension under section 188.2 or an assessment of tax or penalty under this Act (other than the amount of a liability under subsection 188(1.1)); and

(*h*) in the case of a registrant that is a charity, an application by the registrant, and information filed in support of the application, for a designation, determination or decision by the Minister under any of subsections 149.1(5), (6.3), (7), (8) and (13).

History: S. 241(3.2) was replaced by S.C. 2011, c. 24, s. 71(2), in force January 1, 2012. S. 241(3.2) formerly read:

(3.2) *Registered charities.* An official may provide to any person the following taxpayer information relating to another person that was at any time a registered charity (in this subsection referred to as the "charity"):

(*a*) a copy of the charity's governing documents, including its statement of purpose;

(*b*) any information provided in prescribed form to the Minister by the charity on applying for registration under this Act;

(*c*) the names of the persons who at any time were the charity's directors and the periods during which they were its directors;

(*d*) a copy of the notification of the charity's registration, including any conditions and warnings;

(*e*) if the registration of the charity has been revoked or annulled, a copy of the entirety of or any part of any letter sent by or on behalf of the Minister to the charity relating to the grounds for the revocation or annulment;

(*f*) financial statements required to be filed with an information return referred to in subsection 149.1(14);

(*g*) a copy of the entirety of or any part of any letter or notice by the Minister to the charity relating to a suspension under section 188.2 or an assessment of tax or penalty under this Act (other than the amount of a liability under subsection 188(1.1)); and

(*h*) an application by the charity, and information filed in support of the application, for a designation, determination or decision by the Minister under subsection 149.1(5), (6.3), (7), (8) or (13).

S. 241(3.2)(*h*) was replaced by S.C. 2011, c. 24, s. 71(1), applicable in respect of documents that, after May 13, 2005, are sent by the Minister of National Revenue; or are filed or required to be filed with that Minister. S. 241(3.2)(*h*) formerly read:

(*h*) an application by the charity, and information filed in support of the application, for a designation, determination or decision by the Minister under subsection 149.1(6.3), (7), (8) or (13).

► 241(3.3) ◄

(3.3) Information may be communicated. The Minister of Canadian Heritage may communicate or otherwise make available to the public, in any manner that that Minister considers appropriate, the following taxpayer information in respect of a Canadian film or video production certificate (as defined under subsection 125.4(1)) that has been issued or revoked:

(*a*) the title of the production for which the Canadian film or video production certificate was issued;

(*b*) the name of the taxpayer to whom the Canadian film or video production certificate was issued;

(*c*) the names of the producers of the production;

(*d*) the names of the individuals in respect of whom and places in respect of which that Minister has allotted points in respect of the production in accordance with regulations made for the purpose of section 125.4;

(*e*) the total number of points so allotted; and

(*f*) any revocation of the Canadian film or video production certificate.

Editorial Note: Subsection 241(3.3) provides authority to the Minister of Canadian Heritage to publish certain information relevant to the Canadian film or video tax credit program. Allowable information includes the title of the film or video production for which a certificate has been issued or revoked by that Minister, and the names of producers and artists for which the minister has allotted "points" in determining whether the production is a "Canadian film or video production."

History: S. 241(3.3) was added by S.C. 2014, c. 39, s. 70(1), in force December 16, 2014.

Related Regulations: 1106.

Related Sections: 125.4 [Film or video production tax credit].

► 241(3.4) ◄

(3.4) Information may be communicated. The Minister may communicate or otherwise make available to the public, in any manner that the Minister considers appropriate, the following taxpayer information:

(*a*) the names of each organization with respect to which an individual can be entitled to a deduction under subsection 118.02(2); and

(*b*) the start and, if applicable, end of the period in which paragraph (*a*) applies in respect of any particular organization.

Editorial Note: Subsection 241(3.4) provides authority to the Minister to publish certain information relevant to the digital news subscription tax credit. Allowable information includes the names of each organization to which an individual may apply any deductions, as well as the start and end period when a taxpayer is entitled to the deduction for each organization.

History: S. 241(3.4) was added by S.C. 2019, c. 29, s. 42(3), in force June 21, 2019.

► 241(4) ◄

(4) Where taxpayer information may be disclosed. An official may

(*a*) provide to any person taxpayer information that can reasonably be regarded as necessary for the purposes of the administration or enforcement of this Act, the *Canada Pension Plan*, the *Unemployment Insurance Act* or the *Employment Insurance Act*, solely for that purpose;

(*b*) provide to any person taxpayer information that can reasonably be regarded as necessary for the purposes of determining any tax, interest, penalty or other amount that is or may become payable by the person, or any refund or tax credit to which the person is or may become entitled, under this Act or any other amount that is relevant for the purposes of that determination;

(*c*) provide to the person who seeks a certification referred to in paragraph 147.1(10)(*a*) the certification or a refusal to make the certification, solely for the purposes of administering a registered pension plan;

(*d*) provide taxpayer information

(i) to an official of the Department of Finance solely for the purposes of the formulation or evaluation of fiscal policy,

(ii) to an official solely for the purposes of the initial implementation of a fiscal policy or for the purposes of the administration or enforcement of an Act of Parliament that provides for the imposition and collection of a tax or duty,

(iii) to an official solely for the purposes of the administration or enforcement of a law of a province that provides for the imposition or collection of a tax or duty,

(iv) to an official of the government of a province solely for the purposes of the formulation or evaluation of fiscal policy,

(v) to an official of the Department of Natural Resources or of the government of a province solely for the purposes of the administration or enforcement of a program of the Government of Canada or of the province relating to the exploration for or exploitation of Canadian petroleum and gas resources,

(vi) to an official of the government of a province that has received or is entitled to receive a payment referred to in this subparagraph, or to an official of the Department of Natural Resources, solely for the purposes of the provisions relating to payments to a province in respect of the taxable income of corporations earned in the offshore area with respect to the province under the *Canada-Nova Scotia Offshore Petroleum Resources Accord Implementation Act*, chapter 28 of the Statutes of Canada, 1988, the *Canada–Newfoundland and Labrador Atlantic Accord Implementation Act*, chapter 3 of the Statutes of Canada, 1987, or similar Acts relating to the exploration for or exploitation of offshore Canadian petroleum and gas resources,

Proposed Amendment

Bill C-74, Canada–Quebec Gulf of St. Lawrence Petroleum Resources Accord Implementation Act (June 18, 2015)

Subparagraph 241(4)(*d*)(vi) of the Act is replaced by the following:

(vi) to an official of the government of a province that has received or is entitled to receive a payment referred to in this subparagraph, or to an official of the Department of Natural Resources, solely for the purposes of the provisions relating to payments to a province in respect of the taxable income of corporations earned, as the case may be, in the Nova Scotia offshore area under the *Canada–Nova Scotia Offshore Petroleum Resources Accord Implementation Act*, in the Newfoundland offshore area under the *Canada–Newfoundland and Labrador Atlantic Accord Implementation Act*, in the joint management area under the *Canada–Quebec Gulf of St. Lawrence Petroleum Resources Accord Implementation Act* or in similar areas under similar Acts relating to the exploration for or exploitation of offshore Canadian petroleum and gas resources,

Applicable: On Royal Assent.

(vi.1) to an official of the Department of Natural Resources solely for the purpose of determining whether property is prescribed energy conservation property or whether an outlay or expense is a Canadian renewable and conservation expense,

(vii) to an official solely for the purposes of the administration or enforcement of the *Pension Benefits Standards Act, 1985*, the *Pooled Registered Pension Plans Act* or a similar law of a province,

(vii.1) to an official solely for the purpose of the administration or enforcement of the *Canada Education Savings Act* or a designated provincial program as defined in subsection 146.1(1), (vii.2) to an official solely for the purposes of the administration and enforcement of Part 1 of the *Energy Costs Assistance Measures Act*,

(vii.3) to an official solely for the purposes of the administration and enforcement of the *Children's Special Allowances Act* or the evaluation or formation of policy for that Act,

(vii.4) to an official solely for the purposes of the administration and enforcement of the *Universal Child Care Benefit Act* or the evaluation or formation of policy for that Act,

(vii.5) to an official solely for the purposes of the administration or enforcement of the *Canada Disability Savings Act* or a designated provincial program as defined in subsection 146.4(1),

(viii) to an official of the Department of Veterans Affairs solely for the purposes of the administration of the *War Veterans Allowance Act*, the *Veterans Well-being Act* or Part XI of the *Civilian War-related Benefits Act*,

(ix) to an official of a department or agency of the Government of Canada or of a province as to the name, address, telephone number, occupation, size or type of business of a taxpayer, solely for the purpose of enabling that department or agency to obtain statistical data for research and analysis,

(x) to an official of the Canada Employment Insurance Commission or the Department of Employment and Social Development, solely for the purpose of the administration or enforcement of the *Employment Insurance Act*, an employment program of the Government of Canada (including, for greater certainty, any activity relating to a program for temporary foreign workers for which the administration or enforcement is the responsibility of the Minister of Employment and Social Development under the *Immigration and Refugee Protection Regulations*) or the evaluation or formation of policy for that Act or program,

(x.1) to an official of the Department of Employment and Social Development solely for the purpose of the administration or enforcement of a program established under the authority of the *Department of Employment and Social Development Act* in respect of children who are deceased or missing as a result of an offence, or a probable offence, under the *Criminal Code*,

(xi) to an official of the Department of Agriculture and Agri-Food or of the government of a province solely for the purposes of the administration or enforcement of a program of the Government of Canada or of the province established under an agreement entered into under the *Farm Income Protection Act*,

(xii) to a member of the Canadian Cultural Property Export Review Board or an official of the Administrative Tribunals Support Service of Canada solely for the purposes of administering sections 32 to 33.2 of the *Cultural Property Export and Import Act*,

(xiii) to an official solely for the purposes of setting off against any sum of money that may be due or payable by Her Majesty in right of Canada a debt due to

(A) Her Majesty in right of Canada, or

(B) Her Majesty in right of a province,

(xiv) to an official solely for the purposes of section 7.1 of the *Federal-Provincial Fiscal Arrangements and Federal Post-Secondary Education and Health Contributions Act*,

(xv) to an official of the Financial Transactions and Reports Analysis Centre of Canada solely for the purpose of enabling the Centre to evaluate the usefulness of information provided by the Centre to the Canada Revenue Agency under the *Proceeds of Crime (Money Laundering) and Terrorist Financing Act*;

(xvi) to a person employed or engaged in the service of an office or agency, of the Government of Canada or of a province, whose mandate includes the provision of assistance (as defined in subsection 125.4(1) or 125.5(1)) in respect of film or video productions or film or video production services, solely for the purpose of the administration or enforcement of the program under which the assistance is offered,

(xvi.1) to a person employed or engaged in the service of an office or agency, of the Government of Canada or of a province, whose mandate includes the provision of "assistance" (as defined in subsection 125.6(1)) in respect of qualified Canadian journalism organizations, solely for the purpose of the administration or enforcement of the program under which the assistance is offered,

(xvi.2) to a body referred to in paragraph (*b*) of the definition "qualified Canadian journalism organization" in subsection 248(1), solely for the purpose of determining eligibility for designation under that paragraph,

(xvii) to an official of the Canadian Radio-television and Telecommunications Commission, solely for the purpose of the administration or enforcement of a regulatory function of that Commission, or

(xviii) to an official of the Canada Revenue Agency solely for the purpose of the collection of amounts owing to Her Majesty in right of Canada or of a province under the *Government Employees Compensation Act*, the *Canada Labour Code*, the *Merchant Seamen Compensation Act*, the *Canada Student Loans Act*, the *Canada Student Financial Assistance Act*, the *Postal Services Continuation Act, 1997*, the *Wage Earner Protection Program Act*, the *Apprentice Loans Act* or a law of a province governing the granting of financial assistance to students at the post-secondary school level;

(*e*) provide taxpayer information, or allow the inspection of or access to taxpayer information, as the case may be, under, and solely for the purposes of,

(i) subsection 36(2) or section 46 of the *Access to Information Act*,

(ii) section 13 of the *Auditor General Act*,

(iii) section 92 of the *Canada Pension Plan*,

(iv) a warrant issued under subsection 21(3) of the *Canadian Security Intelligence Service Act*,

(v) an order made under subsection 462.48(3) of the *Criminal Code*,

(vi) section 26 of the *Cultural Property Export and Import Act*,

(vii) section 79 of the *Family Orders and Agreements Enforcement Assistance Act*,

(viii) paragraph 33.1(*a*) of the *Old Age Security Act*,

(ix) subsection 34(2) or section 45 of the *Privacy Act*,

(x) section 24 of the *Statistics Act*,

(xi) section 9 of the *Tax Rebate Discounting Act*,

(xii) a provision contained in a tax treaty with another country or in a listed international agreement, or

(xiii) an order made under the *Mutual Legal Assistance in Criminal Matters Act* to gather or send information, for the purposes of an investigation or prosecution relating to an act or omission that, if it had occurred in Canada, would constitute an offence for which an order could be obtained under subsection 462.48(3) of the *Criminal Code*, in response to a request made pursuant to

(A) an administrative arrangement entered into under section 6 of the *Mutual Legal Assistance in Criminal Matters Act*, or

(B) a bilateral agreement for mutual legal assistance in criminal matters to which Canada is a party;

(*f*) provide taxpayer information solely for the purposes of sections 23 to 25 of the *Financial Administration Act;*

(*f*.1) provide taxpayer information to an official for the purposes of the administration and enforcement of the *Charities Registration (Security Information) Act*, and where an official has so received taxpayer information, the official may provide that information to another official as permitted by subsection (9.1);

(*g*) use taxpayer information to compile information in a form that does not directly or indirectly reveal the identity of the taxpayer to whom the information relates;

(*h*) use, or provide to any person, taxpayer information solely for a purpose relating to the supervision, evaluation or discipline of an authorized person by Her Majesty in right of Canada in respect of a period during which the authorized person was employed by or engaged by or on behalf of Her Majesty in right of Canada to assist in the administration or enforcement of this Act, the *Canada Pension Plan*, the *Unemployment Insurance Act* or the *Employment Insurance Act*, to the extent that the information is relevant for the purpose;

(*i*) provide access to records of taxpayer information to the Librarian and Archivist of Canada or a person acting on behalf of or under the direction of the Librarian and Archivist, solely for the purposes of section 12 of the *Library and Archives of Canada Act*, and transfer such records to the care and control of such persons solely for the purposes of section 13 of that Act;

(*j*) use taxpayer information relating to a taxpayer to provide information to the taxpayer;

(*j*.1) provide taxpayer information to an official or a designated person solely for the purpose of permitting the making of an adjustment to a social assistance payment made on the basis of a means, needs or income test if the purpose of the adjustment is to take into account

(i) the amount determined in respect of a person for C in subsection 122.61(1), as it read before July 20 2018, in respect of a "base taxation year" (as defined in section 122.6) before 2017, or

(ii) an amount determined in respect of a person under subsection 122.61(1) or (1.1) in respect of a "base taxation year" (as defined in section 122.6) after 2014;

(*j*.2) provide information obtained under section 122.62 to an official of the government of a province solely for the purposes of the administration or enforcement of a prescribed law of the province;

(*k*) provide, or allow inspection of or access to, taxpayer information to or by any person otherwise legally entitled to it under an Act of Parliament solely for the purposes for which that person is entitled to the information;

(*l*) subject to subsection (9.2), provide to a representative of a government entity the business number of, the name of (including any trade name or other name used by), and any contact information, corporate information and registration information in respect of, the holder of a business number (other than an excluded individual), if the information is provided solely for the purposes of the administration or enforcement of

(i) an Act of Parliament or of a legislature of a province, or

(ii) a by-law of a municipality in Canada or a law of an aboriginal government;

(*m*) provide taxpayer information to an official of the government of a province solely for use in the management or administration by that government of a program relating to payments under subsection 164(1.8);

(*n*) provide taxpayer information to any person, solely for the purposes of the administration or enforcement of a law of a province that provides for workers' compensation benefits;

(*o*) provide taxpayer information to any person solely for the purpose of enabling the Chief Statistician, within the meaning assigned by section 2 of the *Statistics Act*, to provide to a statistical agency of a province data concerning business activities carried on in the province, where the information is used by the agency solely for research and analysis and the agency is authorized under the law of the province to collect the same or similar information on its own behalf in respect of such activities;

(*p*) provide taxpayer information to a police officer (within the meaning assigned by subsection 462.48(17) of the *Criminal Code*) solely for the purpose of investigating whether an offence has been committed under the *Criminal Code*, or the laying of an information or the preferring of an indictment, where

(i) such information can reasonably be regarded as being necessary for the purpose of ascertaining the circumstances in which an offence under the *Criminal Code* may have been committed, or the identity of the person or persons who may have committed an offence, with respect to an official, or with respect to any person related to that official,

(ii) the official was or is engaged in the administration or enforcement of this Act, and

(iii) the offence can reasonably be considered to be related to that administration or enforcement;

(*q*) provide taxpayer information to an official of the government of a province solely for the use in the management or administration by that government of a program relating to earning supplementation or income support;

(*r*) provide taxpayer information to a person who has — under a program administered by the Canada Revenue Agency to obtain information relating to tax non-compliance — entered into a contract to provide information to the Canada Revenue Agency, to the extent necessary to inform the person of any amount they may be entitled to under the contract and of the status of their claim under the contract;

(*s*) provide taxpayer information, solely for the purpose of ensuring compliance with Part 1 of the *Proceeds of Crime (Money Laundering) and Terrorist Financing Act*, to an official of the Financial Transactions and Reports Analysis Centre of Canada, if the information

(i) can reasonably be considered to be relevant to a determination of whether a reporting entity (as defined in section 244.1) has complied with a duty or obligation under Part XV.1, and

(ii) does not directly or indirectly reveal the identity of a client (as defined in section 244.1); or

(*t*) provide taxpayer information to an official solely for the purpose of enabling the Chief Actuary of the Office of the Superintendent of Financial Institutions to conduct actuarial reviews of pension plans established under the *Old Age Security Act* as required by the *Public Pensions Reporting Act*.

Editorial Note: Subsection 241(4) authorizes the limited communication of information to government officials outside of the CRA.

History: S. 241(4)(*d*)(xvi.1) and (xvi.2) were added by S.C. 2019, c. 29, s. 42(3), in force June 21, 2019.

S. 241(4)(*e*)(xiii) was added by S.C. 2018, c. 27, s. 26, in force December 13, 2018.

S. 241(4)(*j*.1) was replaced by S.C. 2018, c. 12, s. 36(1), in force July 1, 2018, and formerly read:

(*j*.1) provide taxpayer information to an official or a designated person solely for the purpose of permitting the making of an adjustment to a social assistance payment made on the basis of a means, needs or income test if the purpose of the adjustment is to take into account the amount determined for C in subsection 122.61(1) in respect of a person for a taxation year;

S. 241(4)(*d*)(viii) was replaced by S.C. 2017, c. 20, s. 29(1), in force April 1, 2018, and formerly read:

(viii) to an official of the Department of Veterans Affairs solely for the purposes of the administration of the *War Veterans Allowance Act*, the *Canadian Forces Members and Veterans Re-establishment and Compensation Act* or Part XI of the *Civilian War-related Benefits Act*,

S. 241(4)(*d*)(xviii) was added by S.C. 2016, c. 7, s. 47(1), in force June 22, 2016.

S. 241(4)(*t*) was added by S.C. 2016, c. 7, s. 47(2), in force June 22, 2016.

S. 241(4)(*d*)(vi) was amended by S.C. 2014, c. 13, s. 115(*f*)(i) by replacing the *Canada-Newfoundland Atlantic Accord Implementation Act* with the *Canada–Newfoundland and Labrador Atlantic Accord Implementation Act*, in force December 31, 2014.

S. 241(4)(*d*)(xvi) and (xvii) were added by S.C. 2014, c. 39, s. 70(2), in force December 16, 2014.

S. 241(4)(*d*)(xii) was replaced by S.C. 2014, c. 20, s. 458, proclaimed in force November 1, 2014, and formerly read:

(xii) to an official of the Department of Canadian Heritage or a member of the Canadian Cultural Property Export Review Board solely for the purposes of administering sections 32 to 33.2 of the *Cultural Property Export and Import Act*,

S. 241(4)(*d*)(xv) was added by S.C. 2014, c. 20, s. 28(1), in force June 19, 2014.

S. 241(4)(*r*) and (*s*) were added by S.C. 2014, c. 20, s. 28(2), in force June 19, 2014.

S. 241(4)(*d*)(ix) and (x) were replaced by S.C. 2013, c. 40, s. 87(1), in force December 12, 2013, and formerly read:

(ix) to an official of a department or agency of the Government of Canada or of a province as to the name, address, occupation, size or type of business of a taxpayer, solely for the purposes of enabling that department or agency to obtain statistical data for research and analysis,

(x) to an official of the Canada Employment Insurance Commission or the Department of Human Resources and Skills Development, solely for the purpose of the administration or enforcement of the *Employment Insurance Act*, an employment program of the Government of Canada or the evaluation or formation of policy for that Act or program,

S. 241(4)(*j.1*) was replaced and s. 241(4)(*j.2*) was added by S.C. 2013, c. 40, s. 87(2), in force December 12, 2013. S. 241(4)(*j.1*) formerly read:

(*j*.1) provide taxpayer information to an official or a designated person solely for the purpose of permitting the making of an adjustment to

(i) a social assistance payment made on the basis of a means, needs or income test, or

(ii) a payment pursuant to a prescribed law of a province in respect of a child within the meaning of the prescribed law,

where the purpose of the adjustment is to take into account the amount determined for C in subsection 122.61(1) in respect of a person for a taxation year;

S. 241(4)(*e*)(xii) was replaced by S.C. 2013, c. 34, s. 357(1), in force June 26, 2013, and formerly read:

(xii) a provision contained in a tax treaty with another country or in a comprehensive tax information exchange agreement between Canada and another country or jurisdiction that is in force and has effect;

S. 241(4)(*d*)(x.1) was replaced by S.C. 2012, c. 27, s. 36(3), in force March 1, 2013, and formerly read:

(x.1) to an official of the Department of Human Resources and Skills Development solely for the purpose of the administration or enforcement of a program established under the authority of the *Department of Social Development Act* in respect of children who are deceased or missing as a result of an offence, or a probable offence, under the *Criminal Code*,

S. 241(4)(*d*)(x.1) was added by S.C. 2012, c. 27, s. 29, in force December 14, 2012.

S. 241(4)(*d*)(vii) was replaced by S.C. 2012, c. 31, s. 53(1), in force December 14, 2012. S. 241(4)(*d*)(vii) formerly read:

(vii) to an official solely for the purposes of the administration or enforcement of the *Pension Benefits Standards Act, 1985* or a similar law of a province,

S. 241(4)(*d*)(x) was replaced by S.C. 2012, c. 19, s. 692, in force March 1, 2013. S. 241(4)(*d*)(x) formerly read:

(x) to an official of the Canada Employment Insurance Commission, the Department of Human Resources and Skills Development or the Department of Social Development, solely for the purpose of the administration or enforcement of the *Employment Insurance Act*, an employment program of the Government of Canada or the evaluation or formation of policy for that Act or program,

S. 241(4)(*e*)(viii) was replaced by S.C. 2012, c. 19, s. 302, in force March 1, 2013. S. 241(4)(*e*)(viii) formerly read:

(viii) paragraph 33.11(*a*) of the *Old Age Security Act*,

S. 241(4)(*d*)(vii.1) was replaced by S.C. 2010, c. 12, s. 21(1), applicable to the 2009 and subsequent taxation years. S. 241(4)(*d*)(vii.1) formerly read:

(vii.1) to an official solely for the purpose of the administration or enforcement of the *Canada Education Savings Act* or a program administered pursuant to an agreement entered into under section 12 of that Act,

S. 241(4)(*d*)(vii.5) was replaced by S.C. 2010, c. 12, s. 21(2), applicable to the 2009 and subsequent taxation years. S. 241(4)(*d*)(vii.5) formerly read:

(vii.5) to an official solely for the purposes of the administration and enforcement of the *Canada Disability Savings Act*,

S. 241(4)(*l*) was replaced by S.C. 2009, c. 2, s. 75(3), in force on Royal Assent, March 12, 2009. S. 241(4)(*l*) formerly read:

(*l*) provide the business number, name, address, telephone number and facsimile number of a holder of a business number to an official of a department or agency of the Government of Canada or of a province solely for the purpose of the administration or enforcement of an Act of Parliament or a law of a province, if the holder of the business number is required by that Act or that law to provide the information (other than the business number) to the department or agency;

Related Regulations: 3004; 8200.1.

Related Sections: S. 66.1(6) Definitions; s. 125.6(1) "assistance"; s. 146.1(14) Former Act; s. 147.1(10)(*a*) Past service benefits; s. 241(10), "authorized person", "official"; s. 241(11) References to Petroleum and Gas Revenue Tax Act; s. 248(1), "business number"; s. 248(1), "qualified Canadian journalism organization".

► 241(4.1) ◄

(4.1) Measures to prevent unauthorized use or disclosure. The person who presides at a legal proceeding relating to the supervision, evaluation or discipline of an authorized person may order such measures as are necessary to ensure that taxpayer information is not used or provided to any person for any purpose not relating to that proceeding, including

(*a*) holding a hearing *in camera*;

(*b*) banning the publication of the information;

(*c*) concealing the identity of the taxpayer to whom the information relates; and

(*d*) sealing the records of the proceeding.

History:

Related Sections: S. 241(10), "authorized person".

► 241(5) ◄

(5) Disclosure to taxpayer or on consent. An official or other representative of a government entity may provide taxpayer information relating to a taxpayer

(*a*) to the taxpayer; and

(*b*) with the consent of the taxpayer, to any other person.

History: S. 241(5), the portion before paragraph (*a*) was replaced by S.C. 2009, c. 2, s. 75(4), in force on Royal Assent, March 12, 2009. S. 241(5), the portion before paragraph (*a*) formerly read:

(5) *Disclosure to taxpayer or on consent.* An official may provide taxpayer information relating to a taxpayer

Forms: RC59 — Business Consent Form; T1013 — Consent Form; T1153 — Consent and Request Form.

► 241(6) ◄

(6) Appeal from order or direction. An order or direction that is made in the course of or in connection with any legal proceedings and that requires an official, other representative of a government entity or authorized person to give or produce evidence relating to any taxpayer information may, by notice served on all interested parties, be appealed forthwith by the Minister or by the person against whom the order or direction is made to

(*a*) the court of appeal of the province in which the order or direction is made, in the case of an order or direction made by a court or other tribunal established by or pursuant to the laws of the province, whether or not that court or tribunal is exercising a jurisdiction conferred by the laws of Canada; or

(*b*) the Federal Court of Appeal, in the case of an order or direction made by a court or other tribunal established by or pursuant to the laws of Canada.

History: S. 241(6), the portion before paragraph (*a*) was replaced by S.C. 2009, c. 2, s. 75(5), in force on Royal Assent, March 12, 2009. S. 241(6), the portion before paragraph (*a*) formerly read:

(6) *Appeal from order or direction.* An order or direction that is made in the course of or in connection with any legal proceedings and that requires an official or authorized person to give or produce evidence relating to any taxpayer information may, by notice served on all interested parties, be appealed forthwith by the Minister or by the person against whom the order or direction is made to

Related Sections: S. 241(10), "authorized person", "official".

► 241(7) ◄

(7) Disposition of appeal. The court to which an appeal is taken pursuant to subsection (6) may allow the appeal and quash the order or direction appealed from or dismiss the appeal, and the rules of practice and procedure from time to time governing appeals to the courts shall apply, with such modifications as the circumstances require, to an appeal instituted pursuant to that subsection.

► 241(8) ◄

(8) Stay of order or direction. An appeal instituted pursuant to subsection (6) shall stay the operation of the order or direction appealed from until judgment is pronounced.

► 241(9) ◄

(9) Threats to security. An official may provide to the head of a recipient Government of Canada institution listed in Schedule 3 to the *Security of Canada Information Disclosure Act*, or to an official designated for the purposes of that Act by the head of that recipient institution,

(*a*) publicly accessible charity information;

(*b*) taxpayer information, if there are reasonable grounds to suspect that the information would be relevant to

(i) an investigation of whether the activity of any person may constitute threats to the security of Canada, as defined in section 2 of the *Canadian Security Intelligence Service Act*, or

(ii) an investigation of whether any of the following offences may have been committed:

(A) a terrorism offence as defined in section 2 of the *Criminal Code*, and

(B) an offence under section 462.31 of the *Criminal Code*, if that investigation is related to a terrorism offence as defined in section 2 of that Act; and

(*c*) information setting out the reasonable grounds referred to in paragraph (*b*), to the extent that any such grounds rely on information referred to in paragraph (*a*) or (*b*).

History: S. 241(9), the portion before paragraph (*a*) was replaced by S.C. 2019, c. 13, s. 124, effective June 21, 2019, and formerly read:

(9) *Threats to security.* An official may provide to the head, or their delegate, of a recipient Government of Canada institution listed in Schedule 3 to the *Security of Canada Information Sharing Act*

S. 241(9), the portion before paragraph (*c*), was amended by S.C. 2015, c. 20, s. 6(1), in force August 1, 2015, and formerly read:

(9) **Threats to security.** An official may provide, to an official of the Canadian Security Intelligence Service, of the Royal Canadian Mounted Police or of the Financial Transactions and Reports Analysis Centre of Canada,

(*a*) publicly accessible charity information;

(*b*) designated taxpayer information, if there are reasonable grounds to suspect that the information would be relevant to

(i) an investigation by the Canadian Security Intelligence Service of whether the activity of any person may constitute threats to the security of Canada, as defined in section 2 of the *Canadian Security Intelligence Service Act*,

(ii) an investigation of whether an offence may have been committed under

(A) Part II.1 of the *Criminal Code*, or

(B) section 462.31 of the *Criminal Code*, if that investigation is related to an offence under Part II.1 of that Act, or

(iii) the prosecution of an offence referred to in subparagraph (ii); and

► 241(9.1) ◄

(9.1) Threats to security. Information — other than designated donor information — provided to an official of the Canadian Security Intelligence Service or the Royal Canadian Mounted Police, as permitted by paragraph (4)(*f*.1), may be used by such an official, or communicated by such an official to another official of the Canadian Security Intelligence Service or the Royal Canadian Mounted Police for use by that other official, for the purpose of

(*a*) investigating whether an offence may have been committed, ascertaining the identity of a person or persons who may have committed an offence, or prosecuting an offence, which offence is

(i) described in Part II.1 of the *Criminal Code*, or

(ii) described in section 462.31 of the *Criminal Code*, if that investigation, ascertainment or prosecution is related to an investigation, ascertainment or prosecution in respect of an offence described in Part II.1 of that Act; or

(*b*) investigating whether the activities of any person may constitute threats to the security of Canada, as defined in section 2 of the *Canadian Security Intelligence Service Act*.

► 241(9.2) ◄

(9.2) Restrictions on information sharing. No information may be provided to a representative of a government entity under paragraph (4)(*l*) in connection with a program, activity or service provided or undertaken by the government entity unless the government entity uses the business number as an identifier in connection with the program, activity or service.

History: S. 241(9.2) was added by S.C. 2009, c. 2, s. 75(6), in force on Royal Assent, March 12, 2009.

► 241(9.3) ◄

(9.3) Public disclosure. The Minister may, in connection with a program, activity or service provided or undertaken by the Minister, make available to the public the business number of, and the name of (including any trade name or other name used by), the holder of a business number (other than an excluded individual).

History: S. 241(9.3) was added by S.C. 2009, c. 2, s. 75(6), in force on Royal Assent, March 12, 2009.

► 241(9.4) ◄

(9.4) Public disclosure by representative of government entity. A representative of a government entity may, in connection with a program, activity or service provided or undertaken by the government entity, make available to the public the business number of, and the name of (including any trade name or other name used by), the holder of a business number (other than an excluded individual), if

(*a*) a representative of the government entity was provided with that information pursuant to paragraph (4)(*l*); and

(*b*) the government entity uses the business number as an identifier in connection with the program, activity or service.

History: S. 241(9.4) was added by S.C. 2009, c. 2, s. 75(6), in force on Royal Assent, March 12, 2009.

► 241(9.5) ◄

(9.5) Serious offences. An official may provide to a law enforcement officer of an appropriate police organization

(*a*) taxpayer information, if the official has reasonable grounds to believe that the information will afford evidence of an act or omission in or outside of Canada that, if committed in Canada, would be

(i) an offence under any of

(A) section 3 of the *Corruption of Foreign Public Officials Act*,

(B) sections 119 to 121, 123 to 125 and 426 of the *Criminal Code*,

(C) section 465 of the *Criminal Code* as it relates to an offence described in clause (B), and

(D) sections 144, 264, 271, 279, 279.02, 281 and 333.1, paragraphs 334(*a*) and 348(1)(*e*) and sections 349, 435 and 462.31 of the *Criminal Code*,

(ii) a terrorism offence or a criminal organization offence, as those terms are defined in section 2 of the *Criminal Code*, for which the maximum term of imprisonment is 10 years or more, or

(iii) an offence

(A) that is punishable by a minimum term of imprisonment,

(B) for which the maximum term of imprisonment is 14 years or life, or

(C) for which the maximum term of imprisonment is 10 years and that

(I) resulted in bodily harm,

(II) involved the import, export, trafficking or production of drugs, or

(III) involved the use of a weapon; and

(*b*) information setting out the reasonable grounds referred to in paragraph (*a*), to the extent that any such grounds rely on information referred to in that paragraph.

History: S. 241(9.5) was added by S.C. 2014, c. 20, s. 28(3), in force June 19, 2014.

Canadian Tax Foundation: D'Aoust, *Release of Taxpayer Information to Police: Possible Legal Conflicts*, 2014 Canadian Tax Focus 4(3):8; Kneis, *Release of Taxpayer Information to Police*, 2014 Canadian Tax Focus 4(3):7–8.

► 241(10) ◄

(10) Definitions. In this section,

"aboriginal government"—"aboriginal government" means an aboriginal government as defined in subsection 2(1) of the *Federal-Provincial Fiscal Arrangements Act*;

History: S. 241(10), the definition "aboriginal government" was added by S.C. 2009, c. 2, s. 75(8), in force on Royal Assent, March 12, 2009.

"authorized person"—"authorized person" means a person who is engaged or employed, or who was formerly engaged or employed, by or on behalf of Her Majesty in right of Canada to assist in carrying out the provisions of this Act, the *Canada Pension Plan*, the *Unemployment Insurance Act* or the *Employment Insurance Act*;

Related Sections: S. 241(11) References to Petroleum and Gas Revenue Tax Act; s. 248(1), "employed".

"business number"—(Repealed by S.C. 1998, c. 19, s. 236(9).)

"contact information"—"contact information", in respect of a holder of a business number, means the name, address, telephone number, facsimile number and preferred language of communication of the holder, or similar information as specified by the Minister in respect of the holder, and includes such information in respect of one or more

(*a*) trustees of the holder, if the holder is a trust,

(*b*) members of the holder, if the holder is a partnership,

(*c*) officers of the holder, if the holder is a corporation, or

(*d*) officers or members of the holder, if the holder is not described by any of paragraphs (*a*) to (*c*);

History: S. 241(10), the definition "contact information" was added by S.C. 2009, c. 2, s. 75(8), in force on Royal Assent, March 12, 2009.

"corporate information"—"corporate information", in respect of a holder of a business number that is a corporation, means the name (including the number assigned by the incorporating authority), date of incorporation, jurisdiction of incorporation and any information on the dissolution, reorganization, amalgamation, winding-up or revival of the corporation;

History: S. 241(10), the definition "corporate information" was added by S.C. 2009, c. 2, s. 75(8), in force on Royal Assent, March 12, 2009.

"court of appeal"—"court of appeal" has the meaning assigned by the definition "court of appeal" in section 2 of the *Criminal Code*;

"designated donor information"—"designated donor information" means information of a charity, or of a person who has at any time made an application for registration as a registered charity, that is directly attributable to a gift that has been made or proposed to be made to the charity or applicant and that is presented in any form that directly or indirectly reveals the identity of the donor or prospective donor, other than a donor or prospective donor who is not resident in Canada and is neither a citizen of Canada nor a person described in subsection 2(3);

"designated person"—"designated person" means any person who is employed in the service of, who occupies a position of responsibility in the service of, or who is engaged by or on behalf of,

(*a*) a municipality in Canada, or

(*b*) a public body performing a function of government in Canada,

or any person who was formerly so employed, who formerly occupied such a position or who was formerly so engaged;

"designated taxpayer information"(Repealed by S.C. 2015, c. 20, s. 6(2).)

History: S. 241(10), the definition "designated taxpayer information" was repealed by S.C. 2015, c. 20, s. 6(2), in force August 1, 2015, and formerly read:

"designated taxpayer information"—"designated taxpayer information" means taxpayer information — other than designated donor information — of a registered charity, or of a person who has at any time made an application for registration as a registered charity, that is

(*a*) in respect of a financial transaction

(i) relating to the importation or exportation of currency or monetary instruments by the charity or applicant, or

(ii) in which the charity or applicant has engaged a person to whom section 5 of the *Proceeds of Crime (Money Laundering) and Terrorist Financing Act* applies,

(*b*) information provided to the Minister by the Canadian Security Intelligence Service, the Royal Canadian Mounted Police or the Financial Transactions and Reports Analysis Centre of Canada,

(*c*) the name, address, date of birth and citizenship of any current or former director, trustee or like official, or of any agent, mandatary or employee, of the charity or applicant,

(*d*) information submitted by the charity or applicant in support of an application for registration as a registered charity that is not publicly accessible charity information,

(*e*) publicly available, including commercially available databases, or

(*f*) information prepared from publicly accessible charity information and information referred to in paragraphs (*a*) to (*e*);

"excluded individual"—"excluded individual" means an individual who is a holder of a business number solely because the individual is required under this Act to deduct or withhold an amount from an amount paid or credited or deemed to be paid or credited;

History: S. 241(10), the definition "excluded individual" was added by S.C. 2009, c. 2, s. 75(8), in force on Royal Assent, March 12, 2009.

"government entity"—"government entity" means

(*a*) a department or agency of the government of Canada or of a province,

(*b*) a municipality in Canada,

(*c*) an aboriginal government,

(*d*) a corporation all of the shares (except directors' qualifying shares) of the capital stock of which are owned by one or more persons each of which is

(i) Her Majesty in right of Canada,

(ii) Her Majesty in right of a province,

(iii) a municipality in Canada, or

(iv) a corporation described in this paragraph, or

(*e*) a board or commission, established by Her Majesty in right of Canada or Her Majesty in right of a province, that performs an administrative or regulatory function of government, or by one or more municipalities in Canada, that performs an administrative or regulatory function of a municipality;

History: S. 241(10), the definition "government entity" was added by S.C. 2009, c. 2, s. 75(8), in force on Royal Assent, March 12, 2009.

"official" —"official" means any person who is employed in the service of, who occupies a position of responsibility in the service of, or who is engaged by or on behalf of,

(*a*) Her Majesty in right of Canada or a province, or

(*b*) an authority engaged in administering a law of a province similar to the *Pension Benefits Standards Act, 1985* or the *Pooled Registered Pension Plans Act*,

or any person who was formerly so employed, who formerly occupied such a position or who was formerly so engaged and, for the purposes of subsection 239(2.21), subsections (1) and (2), the portion of subsection (4) before paragraph (*a*), and subsections (5) and (6), includes a designated person;

History: S. 241(10), paragraph (*b*) of the definition "official" was replaced by S.C. 2012, c. 31, s. 53(2), in force December 14, 2012. S. 241(10), paragraph (*b*) of the definition "official" formerly read:

(*b*) an authority engaged in administering a law of a province similar to the *Pension Benefits Standards Act, 1985*,

Related Sections: S. 241(11) References to Petroleum and Gas Revenue Tax Act; s. 248(1), "employed".

"publicly accessible charity information" —"publicly accessible charity information" means taxpayer information that is

(*a*) described in subsection (3.2), or that would be described in that subsection if the words "that was at any time a registered charity" were read as "that has at any time made an application for registration as a registered charity",

(*b*) information — other than designated donor information — submitted to the Minister with, or required to be contained in, any public information return filed or required to be filed under subsection 149.1(14), or

(*c*) information prepared from information referred to in paragraph (*a*) or (*b*);

"registration information" —"registration information", in respect of a holder of a business number, means

(*a*) any information pertaining to the legal form of the holder,

(*b*) the type of activities carried on or proposed to be carried on by the holder,

(*c*) each date on which

(i) the business number was issued to the holder,

(ii) the holder began activities,

(iii) the holder ceased or resumed activities, or

(iv) the business number assigned to the holder was changed, and

(*d*) the reasons for the cessation, resumption or change referred to in subparagraph (*c*)(iii) or (iv);

History: S. 241(10), the definition "registration information" was added by S.C. 2009, c. 2, s. 75(8), in force on Royal Assent, March 12, 2009.

"representative" —"representative" of a government entity means a person who is employed in the service of, who occupies a position of responsibility in the service of, or who is engaged by or on behalf of, a government entity, and includes, for the purposes of subsections (1), (2), (5) and (6), a person who was formerly so employed, who formerly occupied such a position or who formerly was so engaged;

History: S. 241(10), the definition "representative" was added by S.C. 2009, c. 2, s. 75(8), in force on Royal Assent, March 12, 2009.

"taxpayer information" —"taxpayer information" means information of any kind and in any form relating to one or more taxpayers that is

(*a*) obtained by or on behalf of the Minister for the purposes of this Act, or

(*b*) prepared from information referred to in paragraph (*a*),

but does not include information that does not directly or indirectly reveal the identity of the taxpayer to whom it relates and, for the purposes of applying subsections (2), (5) and (6) to a representative of a government entity that is not an official, taxpayer information includes only the information referred to in paragraph (4)(*l*).

History: S. 241(10), the portion of the definition "taxpayer information" following paragraph (*b*) was replaced by S.C. 2009, c. 2, s. 75(7), in force on Royal Assent, March 12, 2009. S. 241(10), the portion of the definition "taxpayer information" following paragraph (*b*) formerly read:

but does not include information that does not directly or indirectly reveal the identity of the taxpayer to whom it relates.

Related Sections: S. 248(1), "employed", "prescribed".

▶ 241(11) ◀

(11) References to "this Act". The references in subsections (1), (3), (4) and (10) to "this Act" shall be read as references to "this Act or the *Federal-Provincial Fiscal Arrangements Act* ".

> **Proposed Amendment**
> **Bill C-74, Canada–Quebec Gulf of St. Lawrence Petroleum Resources Accord Implementation Act (June 18, 2015)**
> **Subsection 241(11) of the Act is replaced by the following:**
>
> **(11) References to "this Act".** The references in subsections (1), (3), (4) and (10) to "this Act" are to be read as references to "this Act, the *Federal–Provincial Fiscal Arrangements Act* or Part 3 of the *Canada–Quebec Gulf of St. Lawrence Petroleum Resources Accord Implementation Act*".
>
> **Applicable:** On Royal Assent.

History: S. 241(11) was replaced by S.C. 2013, c. 34, s. 357(2), in force June 26, 2013, and formerly read:

(11) *References to Petroleum and Gas Revenue Tax Act.* The references in subsections (1), (3), (4) and (10) to "this Act" shall be read as references to "this Act or the *Petroleum and Gas Revenue Tax Act*".

S. 241(4)(*d*)(x.1) was replaced by S.C. 2012, c. 27, s. 36(3), in force March 1, 2013, and formerly read:

(x.1) to an official of the Department of Human Resources and Skills Development solely for the purpose of the administration or enforcement of a program established under the authority of the *Department of Social Development Act* in respect of children who are deceased or missing as a result of an offence, or a probable offence, under the *Criminal Code*,

SECTION 242: Officers, etc., of corporations

Where a corporation commits an offence under this Act, any officer, director or agent of the corporation who directed, authorized, assented to, acquiesced in or participated in the commission of the offence is a party to and guilty of the offence and is liable on conviction to the punishment provided for the offence whether or not the corporation has been prosecuted or convicted.

Related Sections: S. 248(1), "corporation"; ITAR s. 65.1 Part XV of amended Act.

Information Circulars: IC 73-10R3 Tax evasion.

Cases: Although failure to remit is a strict liability offence, the Crown must still prove that the officer participated in the commission of the offence. *The Queen v. Swendson*, 87 DTC 5335 (Alta. Q.B.)

SECTION 243: Power to decrease punishment

Notwithstanding the *Criminal Code* or any other statute or law in force on June 30, 1948, the court has, in any prosecution or proceeding under this Act, no power to impose less than the minimum fine or imprisonment fixed by this Act or to suspend sentence.

Related Sections: ITAR s. 65.1 Part XV of amended Act.

Procedure and Evidence

SECTION 244: Information or complaint

▶ 244(1) ◀

(1) Information or complaint. An information or complaint under this Act may be laid or made by any officer of the Canada Revenue Agency, by a member of the Royal Canadian Mounted Police or by any person thereto authorized by the Minister and, where an information or complaint purports to have been laid or made under this Act, it shall be deemed to have been laid or made by a person thereto authorized by the Minister and shall not be called in question for lack of authority of the informant or complainant except by the Minister or by a person acting for the Minister or Her Majesty.

▶ 244(2) ◀

(2) Two or more offences. An information or complaint in respect of an offence under this Act may be for one or more offences and no information, complaint, warrant, conviction or other proceeding in a prosecution under this Act is objectionable or insufficient by reason of the fact that it relates to two or more offences.

▶ 244(3) ◀

(3) Venue. An information or complaint in respect of an offence under this Act may be heard, tried or determined by any court, judge or justice if the accused is resident, carrying on business, found or apprehended or is in custody within the territorial jurisdiction of the court, judge or justice, as the case may be, although the matter of the information or complaint did not arise within that jurisdiction.

▶ 244(4) ◀

(4) Limitation period. An information or complaint under the provisions of the *Criminal Code* relating to summary convictions, in respect of an offence under this Act, may be laid or made at any time within but not later than 8 years after the day on which the matter of the information or complaint arose.

Cases: An application to quash a subpoena to be issued to a Director of Taxation for the purpose of challenging the Minister's certificate as to when sufficient evidence to justify prosecution became available for the purposes of the one-year limitation period was dismissed on the basis of the taxpayer's intention to raise at trial a Charter right to equality*Giles v. Print Three Inc.*, 87 DTC 5462 (S.C. Ont.)

▶ 244(5) ◀

(5) Proof of service by mail. Where, by this Act or a regulation, provision is made for sending by mail a request for information, notice or demand, an affidavit of an officer of the Canada Revenue Agency, sworn before a commissioner or other person authorized to take affidavits, setting out that the officer has knowledge of the facts in the particular case, that such a request, notice or demand was sent by registered letter on a named day to the person to whom it was addressed (indicating the address) and that the officer identifies as exhibits attached to the affidavit the post office certificate of registration of the letter or a true copy of the relevant portion thereof and a true copy of the request, notice or demand, shall, in the absence of proof to the contrary, be received as evidence of the sending and of the request, notice or demand.

▶ 244(6) ◀

(6) Proof of personal service. Where, by this Act or a regulation, provision is made for personal service of a request for information, notice or demand, an affidavit of an officer of the Canada Revenue Agency, sworn before a commissioner or other person authorized to take affidavits, setting out that the officer has knowledge of the facts in the particular case, that such a request, notice or demand was served personally on a named day on the person to whom it was directed and that the officer identifies as an exhibit attached to the affidavit a true copy of the request, notice or demand, shall, in the absence of proof to the contrary, be received as evidence of the personal service and of the request, notice or demand.

Proposed Amendment
2019 Federal Budget Resolutions

Section 244 of the Act is amended by adding the following after subsection (6):

(6.1) Proof of electronic delivery. If, by this Act or a regulation, provision is made for sending a notice to a person electronically, an affidavit of an officer of the Canada Revenue Agency sworn before a commissioner or other person authorized to take affidavits, shall, in the absence of proof to the contrary, be received as evidence of the sending and of the notice if the affidavit sets out that

(*a*) the officer has knowledge of the facts in the particular case;

(*b*) the notice was sent electronically to the person on a named day; and

(*c*) the officer identifies as exhibits attached to the affidavit copies of

(i) an electronic message confirming the notice has been sent to the person, and

(ii) the notice.

Applicable: In force on January 1, 2020.

▶ 244(7) ◀

(7) Proof of failure to comply. Where, by this Act or a regulation, a person is required to make a return, statement, answer or certificate, an affidavit of an officer of the Canada Revenue Agency, sworn before a commissioner or other person authorized to take affidavits, setting out that the officer has charge of the appropriate records and that after a careful examination and search of those records the officer has been unable to find in a given case that the return, statement, answer or certificate, as the case may be, has been made by that person, shall, in the absence of proof to the contrary, be received as evidence that in that case that person did not make the return, statement, answer or certificate, as the case may be.

▶ 244(8) ◀

(8) Proof of time of compliance. Where, by this Act or a regulation, a person is required to make a return, statement, answer or certificate, an affidavit of an officer of the Canada Revenue Agency, sworn before a commissioner or other person authorized to take affidavits, setting out that the officer has charge of the appropriate records and that after careful examination of those records the officer has found that the return, statement, answer or certificate was filed or made on a particular day, shall, in the absence of proof to the contrary, be received as evidence that it was filed or made on that day and not prior thereto.

▶ 244(9) ◀

(9) Proof of documents. An affidavit of an officer of the Canada Revenue Agency, sworn before a commissioner or other person authorized to take affidavits, setting out that the officer has charge of the appropriate records and that a document annexed to the affidavit is a document or true copy of a document, or a print-out of an electronic document, made by or on behalf of the Minister or a person exercising a power of the Minister or by or on behalf of a taxpayer, is evidence of the nature and contents of the document.

Related Sections: S. 230(4.1) Electronic records; s. 231.5(1) Copies.

▶ 244(10) ◀

(10) Proof of no appeal. An affidavit of an officer of the Canada Revenue Agency, sworn before a commissioner or other person authorized to take affidavits, setting out that the officer has charge of the appropriate records and has knowledge of the practice of the Agency and that an examination of those records shows that a notice of assessment for a particular taxation year or a notice of determination was mailed or otherwise communicated to a taxpayer on a particular day under this Act and that, after careful examination and search of those records, the officer has been unable to find that a notice of objection or of appeal from the assessment or determination or a request under subsection 245(6), as the case may be, was received within the time allowed, shall, in the absence of proof to the contrary, be received as evidence of the statements contained in it.

▶ 244(11) ◀

(11) Presumption. Where evidence is offered under this section by an affidavit from which it appears that the person making the affidavit is an officer of the Canada Revenue Agency, it is not necessary to prove the person's signature or that the person is such an officer nor is it necessary to prove the signature or official character of the person before whom the affidavit was sworn.

▶ 244(12) ◀

(12) Judicial notice. Judicial notice shall be taken of all orders or regulations made under this Act without those orders or regulations being specially pleaded or proven.

▶ 244(13) ◀

(13) Proof of documents. Every document purporting to have been executed under, or in the course of the administration or enforcement of, this Act over the name in writing of the Minister, the Deputy Minister of National Revenue, the Commissioner of Customs and Revenue, the Commissioner of Revenue or an officer authorized to exercise a power or perform a duty of the Minister under this Act is deemed to have been signed, made and issued by the Minister, the Deputy Minister, the Commissioner of Customs and Revenue, the Commissioner of Revenue or the officer unless it has been called in question by the Minister or by a person acting for the Minister or Her Majesty.

▶ 244(13.1) ◀

(13.1) Revenue Canada, Taxation — (Repealed by S.C. 1994, c. 13, s. 10.)

▶ 244(14) ◀

(14) Mailing or sending date. For the purposes of this Act, where any notice or notification described in subsection 149.1(6.3), 152(3.1), 165(3) or 166.1(5) or any notice of assessment or determination is mailed, or sent electronically, it shall be presumed to be mailed or sent, as the case may be, on the date of that notice or notification.

History: S. 244(14) was replaced by S.C. 2010, c. 25, s. 67, in force on Royal Assent, December 15, 2010. S. 244(14) formerly read:

(14) *Mailing date.* For the purposes of this Act, where any notice or notification described in subsection 149.1(6.3), 152(3.1), 165(3) or 166.1(5) or any notice of assessment or determination is mailed, it shall be presumed to be mailed on the date of that notice or notification.

Related Sections: S. 248(7) Receipt of things mailed.

▶ 244(14.1) ◀

(14.1) Date when electronic notice sent. For the purposes of this Act, if a notice or other communication in respect of a person or partnership is made available in electronic format such that it can be read or perceived by a person or a computer system or other similar device, the notice or other communication is presumed to be sent to the person or partnership and received by the person or partnership on the date that an electronic message is sent, to the electronic address most recently provided before that date by the person or partnership to the Minister for the purposes of this subsection, informing the person or partnership that a notice or other communication requiring the person or partnership's immediate attention is available in the person or partnership's secure electronic account. A notice or other communication is considered to be made available if it is posted by the Minister in the person or partnership's secure electronic account and the person or partnership has authorized that notices or other communications may be made available in this manner and has not before that date revoked that authorization in a manner specified by the Minister.

History: S. 244(14.1) was added by S.C. 2010, c. 25, s. 67, in force on Royal Assent, December 15, 2010.

► 244(15) ◄

(15) Date when assessment made. If any notice of assessment or determination has been sent by the Minister as required by this Act, the assessment or determination is deemed to have been made on the day of sending of the notice of the assessment or determination.

History: S. 244(15) was replaced by S.C. 2010, c. 25, s. 67, in force on Royal Assent, December 15, 2010. S. 244(15) formerly read:

(15) *Date when assessment made.* Where any notice of assessment or determination has been sent by the Minister as required by this Act, the assessment or determination is deemed to have been made on the day of mailing of the notice of the assessment or determination.

► 244(16) ◄

(16) Forms prescribed or authorized. Every form purporting to be a form prescribed or authorized by the Minister shall be deemed to be a form authorized under this Act by the Minister unless called in question by the Minister or by a person acting for the Minister or Her Majesty.

Related Sections: S. 150.1(2) Filing of return by electronic transmission.

► 244(17) ◄

(17) Proof of return in prosecution for offence. In any prosecution for an offence under this Act, the production of a return, certificate, statement or answer required by or under this Act or a regulation, purporting to have been filed or delivered by or on behalf of the person charged with the offence or to have been made or signed by or on behalf of that person shall, in the absence of proof to the contrary, be received as evidence that the return, certificate, statement or answer was filed or delivered, or was made or signed, by or on behalf of that person.

► 244(18) ◄

(18) Idem, in proceedings under Division J of Part I. In any proceedings under Division J of Part I, the production of a return, certificate, statement or answer required by or under this Act or a regulation, purporting to have been filed or delivered, or to have been made or signed, by or on behalf of the taxpayer shall, in the absence of proof to the contrary, be received as evidence that the return, certificate, statement or answer was filed or delivered, or was made or signed, by or on behalf of the taxpayer.

► 244(19) ◄

(19) Proof of statement of non-receipt. In any prosecution for an offence under this Act, an affidavit of an officer of the Canada Revenue Agency, sworn before a commissioner or other person authorized to take affidavits, setting out that the officer has charge of the appropriate records and that an examination of those records shows that an amount required under this Act to be remitted to the Receiver General on account of tax for a year has not been received by the Receiver General, shall, in the absence of proof to the contrary, be received as evidence of the statements contained therein.

Related Sections: S. 248(1), "amount", "assessment", "business", "employee", "prescribed", "regulation".

► 244(20) ◄

(20) Members of partnerships. For the purposes of this Act,

(*a*) a reference in any notice or other document to the firm name of a partnership shall be read as a reference to all the members thereof; and

(*b*) any notice or other document shall be deemed to have been provided to each member of a partnership if the notice or other document is mailed to, served on or otherwise sent to the partnership

(i) at its latest known address or place of business, or

(ii) at the latest known address

(A) where it is a limited partnership, of any member thereof whose liability as a member is not limited, or

(B) in any other case, of any member thereof.

Cases: All notices or documents sent to a partnership at its place of business or to the general partner of a limited partnership are considered to have been provided to each member of the partnership. That presumption is conclusive, and such deeming provisions are absolute and do not create a rebuttable presumption. *Menzies v. The Queen*, 2016 DTC 1055 (TCC)

► 244(21) ◄

(21) Proof of return filed. For the purposes of this Act, a document presented by the Minister purporting to be a print-out of the information in respect of a taxpayer received under section 150.1 by the Minister from a person shall be received as evidence and, in the absence of evidence to the contrary, is proof of the return filed by the person under that section.

Related Sections: S. 150.1(1) Definition of "electronic filing".

► 244(22) ◄

(22) Filing of information returns. Where a person who is required by this Act or a regulation to file an information return in prescribed form with the Minister meets the criteria specified in writing by the Minister, the person may at any time file the information return with the Minister by way of electronic filing (within the meaning assigned by subsection 150.1(1)) and the person shall be deemed to have filed the information return with the Minister at that time, and a document presented by the Minister purporting to be a print-out of the information so received by the Minister shall be received as evidence and, in the absence of evidence to the contrary, is proof of the information return so deemed to have been filed.

Related Sections: S. 150.1(1) Definition of "electronic filing"; s. 248(1), "prescribed".

Part XV.1
Reporting of Electronic Funds Transfer

SECTION 244.1: Definitions

The following definitions apply in this Part.

"cash" —"cash" means coins referred to in section 7 of the *Currency Act*, notes issued by the Bank of Canada pursuant to the *Bank of Canada Act* that are intended for circulation in Canada or coins or bank notes of countries other than Canada.

History: S. 244.1, the definition "cash" was added by S.C. 2014, c. 20, s. 29(1), applicable in respect of electronic funds transfers made after 2014.

"casino" —"casino" means

(*a*) the government of a province that, in accordance with paragraph 207(1)(*a*) of the *Criminal Code*,

(i) in a permanent establishment that is held out to be a casino, conducts and manages a lottery scheme that includes games of roulette or card games, or

(ii) in any other permanent establishment, conducts and manages games that are operated on or through a "slot machine", as defined in subsection 207(4.01) of that Act, or any other similar electronic gaming device, if there are more than 50 of those machines or other devices in the establishment;

(*b*) the government of a province that, in accordance with paragraph 207(1)(*a*) of the *Criminal Code*, conducts and manages a lottery scheme, other than bingo or the sale of lottery tickets, that is accessible to the public through the Internet or other digital network, except if the network is an internal network within an establishment referred to in subparagraph (*a*)(ii);

(*c*) an organization that, in accordance with paragraph 207(1)(*b*) of the *Criminal Code*, in a permanent establishment that is held out to be a casino, conducts and manages a lottery scheme that includes games of roulette or card games, unless the organization is a registered charity and the lottery scheme is conducted or managed for a period of not more than two consecutive days at a time; and

(*d*) the board of a fair or of an exhibition, or the operator of a concession leased by such a board, that, in accordance with paragraph 207(1)(*c*) of the *Criminal Code*, in a permanent establishment that is held out to be a casino, conducts and manages a lottery scheme that includes games of roulette or card games.

History: S. 244.1, subparagraph (*a*)(ii) of the definition "casino" was replaced by S.C. 2018, c. 29, s. 78(2), in force December 13, 2018, and formerly read:

(ii) in any other permanent establishment, conducts and manages games that are operated on or through a slot machine, as defined in subsection 198(3) of that Act, or any other similar electronic gaming device, if there are more than 50 of those machines or other devices in the establishment;

S. 244.1, the definition "casino" was replaced by S.C. 2014, c. 20, s. 29(3), in force June 17, 2017, and formerly read:

"casino"—"casino" means an entity that is licensed, registered, permitted or otherwise authorized to do business under any of paragraphs 207(1)(*a*) to (*g*) of the *Criminal Code* and that conducts its business activities in a permanent establishment

(*a*) that the entity holds out to be a casino and in which roulette or card games are carried on; or

(*b*) where there is a slot machine, which, for the purposes of this definition, does not include a video lottery terminal.

A casino does not include an entity that is a registered charity and is licensed, registered, permitted or otherwise authorized to carry on business temporarily for charitable purposes, if the business is carried out in the establishment of the casino for not more than two consecutive days at a time under the supervision of the casino.

S. 244.1, the definition "casino" was added by S.C. 2014, c. 20, s. 29(1), applicable in respect of electronic funds transfers made after 2014.

"client" —"client" means a particular entity that engages in a financial transaction or activity with a reporting entity and includes an entity on whose behalf the particular entity is acting.

History: S. 244.1, the definition "client" was added by S.C. 2014, c. 20, s. 29(1), applicable in respect of electronic funds transfers made after 2014.

"credit union central" —"credit union central" means a central cooperative credit society, as defined in section 2 of the *Cooperative Credit Associations Act*, or a credit union central or a federation of credit unions or caisses populaires that is regulated by a provincial Act other than one enacted by the legislature of Quebec.

History: S. 244.1, the definition "credit union central" was added by S.C. 2014, c. 20, s. 29(1), applicable in respect of electronic funds transfers made after 2014.

"electronic funds transfer" —"electronic funds transfer" means the transmission — through any electronic, magnetic or optical device, telephone instrument or computer — of instructions for the transfer of funds, other than the transfer of funds within Canada. In the case of Society for Worldwide Interbank Financial Telecommunication messages, only SWIFT MT 103 messages are included.

History: S. 244.1, the definition "electronic funds transfer" was added by S.C. 2014, c. 20, s. 29(1), applicable in respect of electronic funds transfers made after 2014.

"entity" —"entity" means an individual, a body corporate, a partnership, a fund or an unincorporated association or organization.

History: S. 244.1, the definition "entity" was added by S.C. 2014, c. 20, s. 29(1), applicable in respect of electronic funds transfers made after 2014.

"funds" —"funds" means cash, currency or securities, or negotiable instruments or other financial instruments, in any form, that indicate an entity's title or interest, or for civil law a right, in them.

History: S. 244.1, the definition "funds" was added by S.C. 2014, c. 20, s. 29(1), applicable in respect of electronic funds transfers made after 2014.

"money services business" —"money services business" means an entity engaged in the business of foreign exchange dealing, of remitting funds or transmitting funds by any means or through any entity or electronic funds transfer network, or of issuing or redeeming money orders, traveller's cheques or other similar negotiable instruments except for cheques payable to a named entity.

Amendment not yet in force
Economic Action Plan 2014 Act, No. 1 [S.C. 2014, c. 20]

S. 244.1, the definition "money services business" was replaced by S.C. 2014, c. 20, s. 29(4)(*a*) and will read as follows:

"money services business" —"money services business" means an entity

(*a*) that has a place of business in Canada and that is engaged in the business of providing at least one of the following services:

(i) foreign exchange dealing,

(ii) remitting funds or transmitting funds by any means or through any entity or electronic funds transfer network,

(iii) issuing or redeeming money orders, traveller's cheques or other similar negotiable instruments except for cheques payable to a named entity,

(iv) dealing in virtual currencies, as defined by regulation, or

(v) a prescribed service; or

(*b*) that does not have a place of business in Canada, that is engaged in the business of providing at least one of the following services that is directed at entities in Canada, and that provides those services to their customers in Canada:

(i) foreign exchange dealing,

(ii) remitting funds or transmitting funds by any means or through any entity or electronic funds transfer network,

(iii) issuing or redeeming money orders, traveller's cheques or other similar negotiable instruments except for cheques payable to a named entity,

(iv) dealing in virtual currencies, as defined by regulation, or

(v) a prescribed service.

Applicable: If subsection 256(2) of the *Economic Action Plan 2014 Act, No. 1* [S.C. 2014, c. 20] comes into force (the amendment to paragraph 5(*h*) of the *Proceeds of Crime (Money Laundering) and Terrorist Financing Act*), then on the later of January 1, 2015 and the day on which subsection 256(2) comes into force.

History: S. 244.1, the definition "money services business" was added by S.C. 2014, c. 20, s. 29(1), applicable in respect of electronic funds transfers made after 2014.

"reporting entity" —"reporting entity" means an entity that is

(*a*) an authorized foreign bank within the meaning of section 2 of the *Bank Act* in respect of its business in Canada, or a bank to which that Act applies;

(*b*) a cooperative credit society, savings and credit union or caisse populaire regulated by a provincial Act;

(*c*) a financial services cooperative regulated by *An Act respecting financial services cooperatives*, R.S.Q., c. C-67.3, or *An Act respecting the Mouvement Desjardins*, S.Q. 2000, c. 77;

(*d*) an association regulated by the *Cooperative Credit Associations Act*;

(*e*) a company to which the *Trust and Loan Companies Act* applies;

(*f*) a trust company regulated by a provincial Act;

(*g*) a loan company regulated by a provincial Act;

(*h*) a money services business;

(*i*) a casino, including a casino owned or controlled by Her Majesty;

(*j*) a department or an agent of Her Majesty in right of Canada or of a province that is engaged in the business of accepting deposit liabilities in the course of providing financial services to the public; or

(*k*) a credit union central in respect of financial services it offers to an entity, other than an entity that is referred to in any of paragraphs (*a*) to (*g*) and (*j*) and is a member of that credit union central.

History: S. 244.1, the definition "reporting entity" was added by S.C. 2014, c. 20, s. 29(1), applicable in respect of electronic funds transfers made after 2014.

SECTION 244.2: [Electronic funds transfer]

► 244.2(1) ◄

(1) Electronic funds transfer. Every reporting entity shall file with the Minister an information return in prescribed form in respect of

(*a*) the sending out of Canada, at the request of a client, of an electronic funds transfer of $10,000 or more in the course of a single transaction; or

(*b*) the receipt from outside Canada of an electronic funds transfer, sent at the request of a client, of $10,000 or more in the course of a single transaction.

History: S. 244.2(1) was added by S.C. 2014, c. 20, s. 29(1), applicable in respect of electronic funds transfers made after 2014.

Related Sections: S. 241(4) Where taxpayer information may be disclosed.

► 244.2(2) ◄

(2) Transfer within Canada. For greater certainty and subject to subsection (3), subsection (1) does not apply to a reporting entity in respect of an electronic funds transfer if the entity

(*a*) sends the transfer to an entity in Canada, even if the final recipient is outside Canada; or

(*b*) receives the transfer from an entity in Canada, even if the initial sender is outside Canada.

History: S. 244.2(2) was added by S.C. 2014, c. 20, s. 29(1), applicable in respect of electronic funds transfers made after 2014.

► 244.2(3) ◄

(3) Intermediary. Subsection (1) applies to a reporting entity in respect of an electronic funds transfer if the entity

(*a*) orders another reporting entity to send, at the request of a client, the transfer out of Canada, unless it provides the other reporting entity with the name and address of the client; or

(*b*) receives the transfer for a beneficiary in Canada from another reporting entity in circumstances where the initial sender is outside Canada, unless the transfer contains the name and address of the beneficiary.

History: S. 244.2(3) was added by S.C. 2014, c. 20, s. 29(1), applicable in respect of electronic funds transfers made after 2014.

► 244.2(4) ◄

(4) Transfer conducted by agent. If a particular reporting entity is an agent of or is authorized to act on behalf of another reporting entity in respect of an electronic funds transfer, subsection (1) applies, in respect of the transfer, to the other reporting entity and not to the particular reporting entity.

Amendment not yet in force
Economic Action Plan 2014 Act, No. 1 [S.C. 2014, c. 20]

S. 244.2(5) was added by S.C. 2014, c. 20, s. 29(4)(*b*) and will read as follows:

(5) Entities outside Canada. Subsection (1) does not apply to an entity described in paragraph (b) of the definition "money services business" in respect of the services it provides to entities outside Canada.

Applicable: If subsection 256(2) of the *Economic Action Plan 2014 Act, No. 1* [S.C. 2014, c. 20] comes into force (the amendment to paragraph 5(*h*) of the *Proceeds of Crime (Money Laundering) and Terrorist Financing Act*), then on the later of January 1, 2015 and the day on which subsection 256(2) comes into force.

History: S. 244.2(4) was added by S.C. 2014, c. 20, s. 29(1), applicable in respect of electronic funds transfers made after 2014.

SECTION 244.3: Casino

An electronic funds transfer in respect of which subsection 244.2(1) applies that occurs in the course of a business, temporarily conducted for charitable purposes in the establishment of a casino by a registered charity carried on for not more than two consecutive days at a time under the supervision of the casino, shall be reported by the supervising casino.

History: S. 244.3 was added by S.C. 2014, c. 20, s. 29(1), applicable in respect of electronic funds transfers made after 2014.

SECTION 244.4: [Single transaction]

► 244.4(1) ◄

(1) Single transaction. For the purposes of this Part, two or more electronic funds transfers of less than $10,000 each that are made within 24 consecutive hours and that total $10,000 or more are considered to be made in the course of a single transaction of $10,000 or more if

(*a*) an individual, other than a trust, who is a reporting entity knows that the transfers are conducted by, or on behalf of, the same entity; and

(*b*) an employee of a reporting entity, other than an entity described in paragraph (*a*), knows that the transfers are conducted by, or on behalf of, the same entity.

History: S. 244.4(1) was added by S.C. 2014, c. 20, s. 29(1), applicable in respect of electronic funds transfers made after 2014.

► 244.4(2) ◄

(2) Exception. For greater certainty, subsection (1) does not apply in respect of an electronic funds transfer sent to two or more beneficiaries if the transfer is requested by

(*a*) an administrator of a pension fund that is regulated by or under an Act of Parliament or of the legislature of a province;

(*b*) a department or agent of Her Majesty in right of Canada or of a province;

(*c*) an incorporated city, town, village, metropolitan authority, township, district, county, rural municipality or other incorporated municipal body or an agent of any of them;

(*d*) an organization that operates a public hospital and that is designated by the Minister as a hospital authority under the *Excise Tax Act*, or an agent of such an organization; or

(*e*) a corporation that has minimum net assets of $75 million on its last audited balance sheet, whose shares are traded on a Canadian stock exchange or a designated stock exchange and that operates in a country that is a member of the Financial Action Task Force on Money Laundering established in 1989.

History: S. 244.4(2) was added by S.C. 2014, c. 20, s. 29(1), applicable in respect of electronic funds transfers made after 2014.

SECTION 244.5: Foreign currency

If an electronic funds transfer is carried out by a reporting entity in a foreign currency, the amount of the transfer is to be converted into Canadian dollars using

(*a*) the official conversion rate of the Bank of Canada for the currency published in the Bank of Canada's *Daily Memorandum of Exchange Rates* that is in effect at the time of the transfer; or

(*b*) if no official conversion rate is set out in that publication for the currency, the conversion rate that the entity would use for the currency in the normal course of business at the time of the transfer.

History: S. 244.5 was added by S.C. 2014, c. 20, s. 29(1), applicable in respect of electronic funds transfers made after 2014.

SECTION 244.6: Filing of return

An information return in respect of an electronic funds transfer that is required to be filed by a reporting entity under this Part shall be filed

(*a*) not later than five working days after the day of the transfer; and

(*b*) using electronic media, in the manner specified by the Minister, if the entity has the technical capabilities to do so.

History: S. 244.6 was added by S.C. 2014, c. 20, s. 29(1), applicable in respect of electronic funds transfers made after 2014.

SECTION 244.7: [Record keeping]

► 244.7(1) ◄

(1) Record keeping. Every reporting entity that is required to file an information return under this Part shall keep such records as will enable the Minister to determine whether the entity has complied with its duties and obligations under this Part.

History: S. 244.7(1) was added by S.C. 2014, c. 20, s. 29(1), applicable in respect of electronic funds transfers made after 2014.

Related Sections: S. 238(1) Offences and punishment

► 244.7(2) ◄

(2) Form of records. A record that is required to be kept under this Part may be kept in machine-readable or electronic form if a paper copy can be readily produced from it.

History: S. 244.7(2) was added by S.C. 2014, c. 20, s. 29(1), applicable in respect of electronic funds transfers made after 2014.

► 244.7(3) ◄

(3) Retention of records. A reporting entity that is required to keep records under this Part in respect of an electronic funds transfer shall retain those records for a period of at least five years from the day of the transfer.

History: S. 244.7(3) was added by S.C. 2014, c. 20, s. 29(1), applicable in respect of electronic funds transfers made after 2014.

Part XVI
Tax Avoidance

SECTION 245: [General anti-avoidance rule]

► 245(1) ◄

(1) Definitions. In this section,

Interpretation Bulletins: *Secondary* — IT-532 Part I.3 — Tax on large corporations.

Tax Window Files: 2016 CALU CRA roundtable Q1-LIA Policies, *May 3, 2016*, CRA Document No. 2016-0632601C6; Loss consolidation, *15XXXX*, CRA Document No. 2014-0554411R3.

Canadian Tax Foundation: Guindon, *If GAAR Applies, When Does Interest Start To Accrue?*, 2015 Canadian Tax Focus 1(1):6; Powrie, *GAAR: A Planner's Perspective*, 2010 Conference Report 8:1–30; Hickey, *GAAR Applied More Often, Fewer Appeals Allowed*, 2010 Canadian Tax Highlights 18(1):5; Miller and Irvine, *Current Cases: Tax Court of Canada — Lehigh Cement Limited v. The Queen (2009 DTC 776)*, 2009 Canadian Tax Journal 3:579–585; Templeton, *Current Cases: Supreme Court of Canada — The Supreme Court Revisits GAAR (Lipson v. Canada, 2009 SCC 1)*, 2009 Canadian Tax Journal 1:59–66; Hickey, *GAAR Update: CRA Stats*, 2009 Canadian Tax Highlights 17(1):4; Kroft and Olsen, *GAAR: Recent Developments*, 2008 Conference Report 1:1–22; Kopstein and Sidhu, *Current Cases: Tax Court of Canada — You Know It When You See It? (Copthorne Holdings Ltd. v. The Queen, 2007 DTC 1230)*, 2008 Canadian Tax Journal 2:485–499; Carr and Milot, *Copthorne: Series of Transactions Revisited*, 2008 Canadian Tax Journal 1:243–268; Larin et al., *Policy Forum: Responses to Aggressive Tax Planning — A Study Framework*, 2008 Canadian Tax Journal 1:143–159; Nitikman, *A Year's Worth of GAAR Cases*, 2008 British Columbia Tax Conference 7:1–23; McDonnell, *GAAR: Meaning of "Avoidance Transaction"*, 2008 Tax for the Owner-Manager 8(2):9–10; Schwartz, *Understanding What the Supreme Court of Canada Said in Canada Trustco*, 2006 Conference Report 3:1–39; Thivierge, *GAAR Redux: After Canada Trustco*, 2006 Conference Report 4:1–21; McDonnell, *Current Cases: Tax Court of Canada — GAAR Applied To Reverse Attribution Plan (Lipson et al. v. The Queen, 2006 DTC 148)*, 2006 Canadian Tax Journal 3:711–719; Thomas, *Current Cases: The Supreme Court of Canada — A Disciplined Approach to GAAR*, 2006 Canadian Tax Journal 1:221–227; Jack et al., *General Anti-Avoidance Rule and Audit Issues and Concerns (Canada Revenue Agency Round Table)*, 2005 Conference Report 6A:32–34; Spiro et al., *Legislative, Administrative, and Judicial Developments: Current Cases*, 2005 Conference Report 5:1–4; Arnold et al., *The Future of GAAR*, 2005 Conference Report 4:1–16; McDonnell, *Current Cases: Federal Court of Appeal — The GAAR: Avoidance Transaction — Real Issue Avoided (The Queen v. Imperial Oil Limited, 2004 FCA 36)*, 2004 Canadian Tax Journal 2:555–563; Meredith, *GAAR in Quotes: Section 245 Cases from the Past Twelve Months*, 2003 Conference Report 2:1–19; McDonnell, *Current Cases: Tax Court of Canada — The GAAR: Limited-Recourse Defeased Lease Survives Review (Canada Trustco Mortgage Company v. The Queen, 2003 DTC 587)*, 2003 Canadian Tax Journal 4:1618–1629; Thomas, *Current Cases: The Tax Court of Canada — GAAR Update (Loyens et al. v. The Queen, 2003 DTC 355)*, 2003 Canadian Tax Journal 3:1301–1305; Bienvenue, *GAAR and the Concept of Tax Benefit*, 2003 Tax for the Owner-Manager 3(3):6–7; Jones, *Current Cases: The Tax Court of Canada — Reference to GAAR on Notice of Assessment (STB Holdings Ltd. v. The Queen, 2002 DTC 1254)*, 2002 Canadian Tax Journal 3:1141–1144; McDonnell, *GAAR Update*, 2002 Tax for the Owner-Manager 2(4):32; Bienvenue, *GAAR not Applicable to the ITA Regulations*, 2002 Tax for the Owner-Manager 2(1):3; Mitchell, *GAAR: A Snapshot*, 2001 Conference Report 2:1–5; Kroft, *Tax Avoidance Update*, 2001 British Columbia Tax Conference 3:1–31; Beaubier and Stack, *The General Anti-Avoidance Rule: Recent Developments*, 2001 Prairie Provinces Tax Conference 4:1–50; Thomas, *Current Cases: The Tax Court of Canada — The Focus of GAAR is Sharpened (Canadian Pacific Limited v. The Queen, 2000 DTC 2428)*, 2000 Canadian Tax Journal 6:1861–1868; Belley, *The Corporate Veil in Tax Law: In Praise of Judicial Circumspection*, 2000 Canadian Tax Journal 3:929–978; Mitchell, *GAAR — What We May Expect*, 2000 Prairie Provinces Tax Conference 2:1–6; Taylor, *The Supreme Court of Canada: Principles of Adjudication of Tax-Avoidance Appeals from Stubart to Shell Canada*, 1999 Conference Report 17:1–53; Kroft, *Tax Avoidance in the Next Millenium — An Update*, 1999 British Columbia Tax Conference 4:1–32; Tari, *G-r-r-r: Its GAAR*, 1999 Ontario Tax Conference 4:1–21; Owen, *Statutory Interpretation and the General Anti-Avoidance Rule: A Practitioner's Perspective*, 1998 Canadian Tax Journal 2:233–273.

"tax benefit" — "tax benefit" means a reduction, avoidance or deferral of tax or other amount payable under this Act or an increase in a refund of tax or other amount under this Act, and includes a reduction, avoidance or deferral of tax or other amount that would be payable under this Act but for a tax treaty or an increase in a refund of tax or other amount under this Act as a result of a tax treaty;

Cases: Subsection 39(2) applies to deem the capital loss on the taxpayer's share disposition to be a capital loss from the disposition of currency rather than a capital loss from the disposition of shares. As subsection 112(3.1) reduces losses from the disposition of shares and not losses from the disposition of currency, it would not have applied, and the taxpayer did not and could not have received a tax benefit by avoiding a loss reduction. In the absence of a tax benefit, there was no basis for a GAAR reassessment. *Bank of Montreal v. The Queen*, 2018 DTC 1131 (TCC) [under appeal]

"tax consequences" — "tax consequences" to a person means the amount of income, taxable income, or taxable income earned in Canada of, tax or other amount payable by or refundable to the person under this Act, or any other amount that is relevant for the purposes of computing that amount;

"transaction" — "transaction" includes an arrangement or event.

Related Sections: S. 248(1); s. 248(10) Series of transactions.

Information Circulars: IC 73-10R3 Tax evasion; IC 88-2 General anti-avoidance rule — Section 245 of the Income Tax Act.

► 245(1.1) ◄

(1.1) Idem — (Repealed by 1988, c. 55, s. 185(1).)

► 245(2) ◄

(2) General anti-avoidance provision. Where a transaction is an avoidance transaction, the tax consequences to a person shall be determined as is reasonable in the circumstances in order to deny a tax benefit that, but for this section, would result, directly or indirectly, from that transaction or from a series of transactions that includes that transaction.

Editorial Note: Section 245 sets out the general anti-avoidance rule (the "GAAR"). The GAAR was enacted partially in response to the Supreme Court of Canada's decision in *Stubart* (84 DTC 6305) that the *Income Tax Act* does not require that a transaction have a business purpose to be effective, and, more generally, for the purpose of combating abusive tax avoidance transactions and arrangements which technically comply with the provisions of the Act.

Avoidance Transaction: The GAAR applies to any transaction that is an "avoidance transaction". An "avoidance transaction" is defined in s. 245(3) as a transaction that results in a tax benefit or a transaction that is part of a series of transactions that results in a tax benefit. However, it does not include a transaction arranged primarily for *bona fide* purposes other than to obtain a tax benefit (see *Evans*, 2005 DTC 1762 (T.C.C.)). A tax benefit is defined in s. 245(1) as a reduction, avoidance or deferral of tax, an increase in a deferral of tax or an increase in a refund of tax, under the Act or under a tax treaty. The existence of an alternative transaction that may have resulted in additional tax may be considered when determining whether there is an avoidance transaction, but that it is not determinative (see *Spruce Credit Union*, 2014 DTC 5079 (F.C.A.)), affirming 2012 DTC 1295 (T.C.C.)). Where there are both tax and non-tax purposes for undertaking a transaction, the focus is on the primary purpose of the transaction (see *OSFC Holdings Ltd.*, 2001 DTC 5471 (F.C.A.)) In addition, the GAAR only applies to a transaction that results directly or indirectly in a misuse of the provisions of the Act, the Regulations, or a tax treaty or an abuse of those provisions other than s. 245 read as a whole.

Three-Step Framework: In *Canada Trustco* (2005 DTC 5523), the Supreme Court established a three-step frame work for determining whether the GAAR applies to a transaction or a series of transactions. This framework was reasserted by the Supreme Court in several cases, including *Copthorne Holdings* (2012 DTC 5007) and *Lipson* (2009 DTC 5015). The first step is to inquire into the existence of a "tax benefit". For there to be a tax benefit, a transaction or series of transactions must result in "a reduction, avoidance or deferral of tax or other amount" or an "increase in a refund of tax or other amount". The second step is to determine whether the tax benefit is an avoidance transaction within the meaning of s. 245(3). The third step is to determine whether the avoidance transaction giving rise to the tax benefit is abusive under s. 245(4). The abuse inquiry involves, first, interpreting the relevant provisions of the Act to determine their object, spirit and purpose and, second, determining whether the transactions fall within or frustrate the object, spirit and purposes of those provisions. The existence of abusive tax avoidance must be clear, and if it is not clear, the benefit of the doubt goes to the taxpayer. In addition, the Minister bears the burden of establishing abusive tax avoidance.

Statutory Interpretation: There are a large number of court decisions, including Supreme Court of Canada decisions, which have considered the GAAR. Despite these decisions, the applicability of the GAAR to a specific fact pattern is difficult to predict because in many cases, it is not clear whether a tax benefit realized by a taxpayer is inconsistent with the object, spirit and purpose of a provision of the Act, or the Act read as a whole. The Supreme Court has stated that courts should not seek to give effect to an unexpressed parliamentary intention or purpose to restrict a clear and unambiguous provision (see *65302 British Columbia Limited*, 99 DTC 5799). The GAAR cannot be used to fill a perceived gap in the legislation (see *Gwartz*, 2013 DTC 1122 (T.C.C.)).

Artificial Transactions: The court will take an objective approach as to whether a particular transaction is an "artificial transaction" under the spirit, purpose and object of the Act. For example, limited partners entering into a complicated series of transactions lacking any commercial purpose solely to generate a tax loss had deductions for such losses disallowed (see *Carson* 88 DTC 1249 (T.C.C.)).

Other Provisions: The Act contains numerous specific anti-avoidance provisions, such as s. 69, which deals with property transferred to a person not at arm's length; s. 74.1 to 74.5, which deal with transfers of property or income between spouses or between an adult and a non-arm's length minor; s. 15, which deals with benefits conferred by a corporation; s. 110.6, which deals with the capital gains exemption; and s. 40(3.3) and 54, which stop certain losses from being claimed. The GAAR supplements the specific anti-avoidance provisions in the Act and normally is a provision of last resort.

Related Sections: S. 248(10) Series of transactions.

Canadian Tax Foundation: Wang, *GAAR: The Search for Object, Spirit, and Purpose*, 2018 Tax for the Owner Manager 18(3):5–6; Hamelin, *GAAR and Capital Gains Splits Between Spouses*, 2018 Tax for the Owner Manager 18(2):8–9; Dolson, *The GAAR Post-Copthorne: Where We've Come From, and Current Applications*, 2017 Prairie Provinces Tax Conference 6:1–37; Morin, *Pre- and Post-Acquisition PUC Planning: GAARable?*, 2015 Canadian Tax Highlights 23(2):8–9; Morin, *Series of Transactions and GAAR*, 2014 Canadian Tax Focus 4(1):7; Man et al., *Current Cases: Tax Court of Canada — GAARguments in the Tax Court of Canada: Crown Must Disclose Policy Supporting GAAR Assessments (Birchcliff Energy Ltd. v. The Queen, Docket no. 2012-1087(IT)G)*, 2013 Canadian Tax Journal 2:440–442; Li and Hwong, *GAAR in Action: An Empirical Exploration of Tax Court of Canada Cases (1997-2009) and Judicial Decision Making*, 2013 Canadian Tax Journal 2:321–366; Lacroix, *GAAR: Observations on the Concept of Abuse*, 2013 Canadian Tax Journal SS:181–194; Blackler and Nitikman, *Case Comment: Daishowa-Marubeni International Ltd. v. The Queen, 2013 DTC 5085*, 2013 British Columbia Tax Conference 2:1–5; Bartucci, *Gwartz: GAAR Doesn't Upset Old Kiddie Tax Plan*, 2013 Tax for the Owner-Manager 13(6):4–6; McDonnell, *Dividend Stripping and GAAR*, 2013 Tax for the Owner-Manager 13(1):8–9; Hickey, *CRA's GAAR Update*, 2013 Canadian Tax Highlights 21(1):3–4; MacKnight, *Recent Cases*, 2012 Ontario Tax Conference 2A:1–21; Chiang, *GAAR: Avoidance Transaction Required*, 2012 Canadian Tax Highlights 20(12):8–9; Baker and Trossman, *Copthorne: SCC Applies GAAR*, 2012 Canadian Tax Highlights 20(1):3–5; Kearl and Lemons, *GAAR in the Tax Court After Canada Trustco: A Practitioner's Guide*, 2007 Canadian Tax Journal 4:745–776; Arnold, *Policy Forum: Confusion Worse Confounded — The Supreme Court's GAAR Decisions*, 2006 Canadian Tax Journal 1:167–209; Li, *"Economic Substance": Drawing the Line Between Legitimate Tax Minimization and Abusive Tax Avoidance*, 2006 Canadian Tax Journal 1:23–56; Sandler, *The Minister's Burden Under GAAR*, 2006 Canadian Tax Journal 1:3–22; Wilkie, *Policy Forum: Canada Trustco and Beyond*, 2005 Canadian Tax Journal 4:1007–1009; Arnold, *The Long, Slow, Steady Demise of the General Anti-Avoidance Rule*, 2004 Canadian Tax Journal 2:488–511.

Tax Profile: January 2019 — Tax Court of Canada Provides Useful Commentary on Treaty Shopping in ALTA Energy Luxembourg S.A.R.L. v. The Queen; May 2013 — Current International Tax Issues In Cross-Border Corporate Finance and Capital Markets; January 2012 — Highlights from the 2011 Ontario Tax Conference: Q&A with the Tax Administration Panel; August 2007 — Case Comment on MIL (Investments) S.A.; December 2006 — GAAR and Treaty Shopping: A Taxpayer Victory; March 2005 — GAAR and Treaty Shopping — An International Perspective.

Tax Topics: No. 2441-42, FCA Upholds GAAR Assessment in Respect of Complex Transactions That Abused Section 84.1; No. 2429, Transactions Inappropriately Inflating Paid-Up Capital Do Not Constitute Misuse or Abuse Until Associated Tax Savings Are Realized by Shareholder; No. 2357, 1245989 Alberta Ltd.: Tax Court Applies GAAR to PUC Averaging Transaction; No. 2206, What is an "Avoidance Transaction"? The Federal Court of Appeal Finds for the Taxpayer in Spruce Credit Union; No. 2104, Pipeline Planning Alive and Well After All?; No. 1976, Quebec Gets Tough on Aggressive Tax Planning; No. 1927, Quebec Putting the Screws on Aggressive Tax Planning; No. 1845, MIL (Investments) — A Resounding Win for the Taxpayer; No. 1780, Claude Desmarais: The Latest Float in the GAAR Parade; No. 1669, GAAR: Clear And Unambiguous Policy An Ever So Elusive Target For The Crown.

Income Tax Technical News: Issue No. 34, General Anti-Avoidance Rule and Audit Issues/Concerns; Issue No. 32, Update on GAAR Reviews; Issue No. 30, Tax Avoidance.

Information Circulars: IC 73-10R3 Tax evasion; IC 88-2 General anti-avoidance rule — Section 245 of the Income Tax Act.

Tax Window Files: Neuman Type Situation, *March 14, 2016*, CRA Document No. 2016-0626781E5; 2015 TEI Meeting Q7 Donations to qualifying US charity, *November 17, 2015*, CRA Document No. 2015-0614251C6; 2015 CTF Q.6(b) Loss Consolidation and Section 55, *November 24, 2015*, CRA Document No. 2015-0610671C6; Postmortem Hybrid/Partial Pipeline Planning, *15XXXX*, CRA Document No. 2015-0606721R3; ACB increase in paragraph 55(3)(a) reorganization, *January 13, 2016*, CRA Document No. 2015-0604521E5; Loss Consolidation Arrangement, *15XXXX*, CRA Document No. 2015-0604071R3; Loss utilization, *15XXXX*, CRA Document No. 2015-0582101R3; Standard Loss Consolidation, *15XXXX*, CRA Document No. 2015-0576421R3; Loss consolidation arrangements, *August 19, 2015*, CRA Document No. 2015-0589611E5; Loss consolidation, *15XXXX*, CRA Document No. 2014-0554411R3; Post-Mortem Pipeline Planning, *15XXXX*, CRA Document No. 2014-0545531R3; loss consolidation, *14XXXX*, CRA Document No. 2014-0543911R3; Postmortem Pipeline Planning, *15XXXX*, CRA Document No. 2014-0552071R3; Reorganization, *14XXXX*, CRA Document No. 2013-0516071R3.

Cases: The corporate taxpayer undertook a recapitalization and restart transaction in which its assets and liabilities were moved to a new corporation. The remaining corporate shell was used to raise funds through an initial public offering and certain tax attributes previously earned by the corporation, including tax losses and investment tax credits, were used to shelter income earned by the new business. No change of control had occurred, as the transactions were carefully structured to avoid an acquisition of control under the relevant provisions. The transactions resulted in a reduction of tax and a tax benefit to the taxpayer. Based on a textual and contextual analysis of the object, spirit, and purpose of the tax attribute streaming restrictions and the corporate control rules, the transactions did not constitute an abuse of such provisions. *Deans Knight v. The Queen*, 2019 DTC 1059 (TCC)

The taxpayers argued that interest began to accrue only from the date of the GAAR assessments. GAAR provisions may apply retrospectively, and there was nothing in s. 245 to suggest the application of GAAR should be suspended until an assessment is issued. *J.K. Read Engineering Ltd. v. The Queen*, 2014 DTC 1216 (T.C.C.)

The taxpayer, a credit union, was a member of two deposit insurance corporations, CUDIC and STAB. Due to regulatory changes, CUDIC was required to increase its deposit protection funds. STAB paid out dividends to its shareholders to help fund the assessments made by CUDIC to increase its funds. The taxpayer deducted the dividends under s. 112. GAAR did not apply. The existence of an alternative transaction that may have resulted in additional tax is only one factor to consider. A transaction may be undertaken for both tax and non-tax purposes; in determining whether there is an avoidance transaction the primary purpose of the transaction must be considered. *The Queen v. Spruce Credit Union*, 2014 DTC 5079 (F.C.A.), affirming 2012 DTC 1295 (T.C.C.)

Sections 3, 4, 9, and 111 are not intended to apply to all business losses, but only to those involving an air of economic or business reality, which the losses in this case did not have. They were artificial and resulted from a paper shuffle. These transactions constituted abusive tax avoidance, which defeated the rationale underlying these provisions. *The Queen v. Global Equity Fund Ltd.*, 2013 DTC 5007 (F.C.A.), reversing 2011 DTC 1350 (T.C.C.), leave to appeal refused (S.C.C.)

The taxpayer implemented a "reverse freeze" in which artificially devalued shares were transferred to a person within the same economic unit to create an artificial capital loss. GAAR was used to deny the capital loss deduction since the primary purpose of the series of transactions was to obtain a tax benefit. The transactions amounted to abusive tax avoidance because they defeated the underlying rationale of the capital loss provisions. *Triad Gestco Ltd. v. The Queen*, 2012 DTC 5156 (F.C.A.), affirming 2011 DTC 1254 (T.C.C.)

A Canadian corporation borrowed $140 million. The loan was later amended to separate the right to receive the principal from the right to receive interest. An arm's length Belgian bank purchased the right to receive the interest payments, which were exempt from Part XIII withholding tax under s. 212(1)(*b*)(vii). GAAR did not apply since this was not a misuse of s. 212(1)(*b*)(vii). *Lehigh Cement Limited v. The Queen*, 2010 DTC 5081 (F.C.A.), reversing 2009 DTC 1148 (T.C.C.)

Rather than doing a vertical amalgamation, a parent and subsidiary became directly owned by the same shareholder and then did a horizontal amalgamation, thereby preserving $67 million in PUC. A subsequent share redemption, which was part of the same series of transactions, resulted in a tax benefit through distribution of the PUC. This frustrated and defeated the purpose of s. 87(3) and was therefore abusive tax avoidance. In determining whether a transaction is a part of a series, s. 248(10) is to be read both prospectively and retrospectively. *Copthorne Holdings Ltd. v. The Queen*, 2012 DTC 5007 (S.C.C.), affirming 2009 DTC 5101 (F.C.A.) and 2007 DTC 1230 (T.C.C.)

The taxpayer's wife obtained a bank loan to purchase shares of a family corporation from him. He used the proceeds to buy a new house. They then took out a mortgage on the house and used it to pay off the bank loan. The mortgage interest was deducted from her dividend income and the resulting loss was attributed to him under s. 74.1(1). This was not an abuse of s. 20(1)(*c*) or 20(3). However, it was an abuse of the attribution rules. *Lipson et al. v. The Queen*, 2009 DTC 5015 (S.C.C.), affirming 2007 DTC 5172 (F.C.A.), affirming 2006 DTC 2687 (T.C.C.)

Using a unified textual, contextual, and purposive approach to the interpretation of s. 18(13) and s. 96, the Court concluded that using these provisions to preserve and sell an unrealized loss to an arm's length party constituted abusive tax avoidance under s. 245(4). *Mathew v. The Queen (sub nom. Kaulius v. The Queen)*, 2005 DTC 5538 (S.C.C.), affirming 2003 DTC 5644 (F.C.A.), affirming 2002 DTC 1637 (T.C.C.)

Purchasing equipment and circuitously leasing it back to the vendor, in order to generate CCA with minimal financial risk, was not an abuse or misuse of the Act. The onus is on the Minister to establish abusive tax avoidance. Determinations of misuse and abuse are not separate inquiries. In analyzing s. 245(4), a unified textual, contextual, and purposive analysis of the relevant provisions must be conducted. The Court must then determine whether the avoidance transaction has frustrated the object, spirit, or purpose of the provisions. *The Queen v. Canada Trustco Mortgage Company*, 2005 DTC 5523 (S.C.C.), affirming 2004 DTC 6119 (F.C.A.), affirming 2003 DTC 587 (T.C.C.)

The non-resident taxpayer had a substantial capital gain which was exempt from Canadian tax under the Canada-Luxembourg Tax Convention. GAAR did not apply due to a lack of evidence that the tax benefit was an abuse or misuse of the Act or the treaty. Crown arguments justifying the taxation of the gain in Canada based on the lack of taxation in Luxembourg were inappropriate in the context of the GAAR. *The Queen v. MIL (Investments) S.A.*, 2007 DTC 5437 (F.C.A.), affirming 2006 DTC 3307 (T.C.C.)

The liquidator of an insolvent trust company transferred some of the company's non-performing mortgages to a partnership at an ACB in excess of market value. The trust company's interest in the partnership was later sold in an arm's length transaction, thereby allowing the corporate purchaser to deduct the losses. This was a series of avoidance transactions. The tax benefit does not have to be enjoyed by the party entering into the impugned transactions. *OSFC Holdings Ltd. v. The Queen*, 2001 DTC 5471 (F.C.A.), affirming 99 DTC 1044 (T.C.C.)

► 245(3) ◄

(3) Avoidance transaction. An avoidance transaction means any transaction

(*a*) that, but for this section, would result, directly or indirectly, in a tax benefit, unless the transaction may reasonably be considered to have been undertaken or arranged primarily for *bona fide* purposes other than to obtain the tax benefit; or

(*b*) that is part of a series of transactions, which series, but for this section, would result, directly or indirectly, in a tax benefit, unless the transaction may reasonably be considered to have been undertaken or arranged primarily for *bona fide* purposes other than to obtain the tax benefit.

Related Sections: S. 248(10) Series of transactions.

Canadian Tax Foundation: Humphries, *GAAR Applied to Loss-Utilization Strategy*, 2015 Canadian Tax Highlights 23(12):7–8; Couzin, *Subsection 245(3): A Framework*, 1997 Conference Report 4:1–15.

Tax Topics: No. 2386, FCA Finds Tax Plan Not Abusive Under GAAR as Alternative Transaction Would Lead to Same Result; No. 2357, 1245989 Alberta Ltd.: Tax Court Applies GAAR to PUC Averaging Transaction; No. 2145, GAAR Trilogy — Federal Court Of Appeal Strikes Down Stock Dividend "Value Shift" Planning; No. 1886, *MacKay:* A Potential Threat to the Duke; No. 1806, Expanding GAAR to Tax Treaties? Or Not; No. 1692, Income Tax Implications of Buy-Sell Provisions; No. 1669, GAAR: Clear And Unambiguous Policy An Ever So Elusive Target For The Crown; No. 1578, After REOP, Where Do We GAAR From Here?.

Cases: The taxpayer, a credit union, was a member of two deposit insurance corporations, CUDIC and STAB. Due to regulatory changes, CUDIC was required to increase its deposit protection funds. STAB paid out dividends to its shareholders to help fund the assessments made by CUDIC to increase its funds. The taxpayer deducted the dividends under s. 112. GAAR did not apply. The existence of an alternative transaction that may have resulted in additional tax is only one factor to consider. A transaction may be undertaken for both tax and non-tax purposes; in determining whether there is an avoidance transaction the primary purpose of the transaction must be considered. *The Queen v. Spruce Credit Union*, 2014 DTC 5079, affirming 2012 DTC 1295 (T.C.C.)

The taxpayer acquired common shares of a new corporation and then received a stock dividend of class B shares of the corporation, which reduced the value of the common shares to a nominal amount. The capital loss sustained when the common shares were transferred to a family trust resulted in abusive tax avoidance contrary to the object, spirit, and purpose of s. 38(*b*), 39(1)(*b*), and 40(1)(*b*). Although credit-proofing was the alleged basis for the series of transactions, not all transactions within the series had that purpose. *1207192 Ontario Limited v. The Queen*, 2012 DTC 5157 (F.C.A.), affirming 2011 DTC 1301 (T.C.C.), leave to appeal refused (S.C.C.)

A partnership acquired a shopping centre from a bank as part of foreclosure proceedings. The partnership wrote down the value of the property to its FMV, realizing a $6 million loss. Although the series of transactions, as a whole, had a *bona fide* business purpose, the transactions that resulted in the transfer of the accrued loss from the bank to the partnership comprised an abusive avoidance transaction and the partnership losses were denied. *The Queen v. MacKay et al.*, 2008 DTC 6238 (F.C.A.), reversing 2007 DTC 425 (T.C.C.)

The taxpayer's wife borrowed $2.3 million from a bank and used it to buy shares from the taxpayer. He used the proceeds to pay down a shareholder loan, thus avoiding having it included in income. Her interest and loan guarantee fees resulted in losses that were attributed back to him since he didn't elect to avoid the application of s. 73(1). There may have been a tax benefit, but GAAR could not be used to disallow his deduction of losses since there was no avoidance transaction or abuse of the Act. *Overs v. The Queen*, 2006 DTC 2192 (T.C.C.)

In return for an interest-bearing promissory note, the taxpayer sold shares of his professional corporation to a partnership consisting of his wife and children. All dividends received by the partnership were used to pay the taxpayer interest and capital repayments on the note. The Minister was not justified in using GAAR to re-characterize these interest and capital repayments as dividends from a surplus strip. *Evans v. The Queen*, 2005 DTC 1762 (T.C.C.)

The taxpayer, Univar, was a subsidiary of UC. Univar incorporated B, a Barbadian subsidiary. B used the money received from Univar's share subscription to purchase a debt from UC. After paying 2.5% Barbadian tax on interest received on this debt, B paid dividends to Univar. The Minister could not use s. 95(6) and s. 245 to re-characterize these dividends as interest since his premise that the debt was purchased by Univar, rather than by B, was not true. *Univar Canada Ltd. v. The Queen*, 2005 DTC 1478 (T.C.C.)

A series of agreements were used to effect a sale of the taxpayers' beneficial interests in real property while utilizing the losses of a corporation owned by the taxpayers. Although the primary purpose of the transactions was to obtain a tax benefit, they were in accordance with normal business practices, and were entered into for *bona fide* purposes. There was no misuse or abuse of the Act. *Loyens et al. v. The Queen*, 2003 DTC 355 (T.C.C.)

The taxpayer borrowed Australian currency (at a higher rate than it could have borrowed in Canadian currency) as part of a series of transactions resulting in a large foreign exchange gain. This was not an avoidance transaction. It was arranged primarily to raise capital which is a *bona fide* business purpose even though it resulted in significant tax benefits. In addition, deducting the excess interest did not result in an abuse of the Act as a whole. *The Queen v. Canadian Pacific Limited*, 2002 DTC 6742 (F.C.A.), affirming 2000 DTC 2428 (T.C.C.)

► 245(4) ◄

(4) Application of subsection (2). Subsection (2) applies to a transaction only if it may reasonably be considered that the transaction

(*a*) would, if this Act were read without reference to this section, result directly or indirectly in a misuse of the provisions of any one or more of

(i) this Act,

(ii) the *Income Tax Regulations*,

(iii) the *Income Tax Application Rules*,

(iv) a tax treaty, or

(v) any other enactment that is relevant in computing tax or any other amount payable by or refundable to a person under this Act or in determining any amount that is relevant for the purposes of that computation; or

(*b*) would result directly or indirectly in an abuse having regard to those provisions, other than this section, read as a whole.

Canadian Tax Foundation: Samtani and Kutyan, *GAAR Revisited: From Instinctive Reaction to Intellectual Rigour*, 2014 Canadian Tax Journal 2:401–428; Schwartz and Yip, *Policy Forum: Defending Against a GAAR Reassessment*, 2014 Canada Tax Journal 1:129–146; Arnold, *Policy Forum: Some Thoughts on the Supreme Court's Approach to the Determination of Abuse Under the General Anti-Avoidance Rule*, 2014 Canadian Tax Journal 1:113–127; Baxter et al., *Surplus Stripping — What's Acceptable, What's Not, and What Should Be?*, 2014 British Columbia Tax Conference 12:1–A5; Gilbert and Dolson, *Accessing Surplus: What Works, What Doesn't, What's Left*, 2014 Prairie Provinces Tax Conference 9:1–57; Darmo and Fournier, *Recent Developments Regarding the Application of Subsection 245(4)*, 2011 Conference Report 37:1–26; Arnold, *Reflections on the Relationship Between Statutory Interpretation and Tax Avoidance*, 2001 Canadian Tax Journal 11:1–33.

Tax Profile: March 2011 — The General Anti-Avoidance Rule — The Burden on the Crown under Subsection 245(4); March 2011 — Canada 2010 — Year in Review.

Tax Topics: No. 2167, Form Still Matters... Right?!; No. 2145, GAAR Trilogy — Federal Court Of Appeal Strikes Down Stock Dividend "Value Shift" Planning; No. 2080, "He Who Wants a Rose Must Respect the (Cop)Thorn(e)"; No. 2069, The GAAR Saga; No. 1949, GAAR in the Gaps: *Collins & Aikman Products Co. et al. v. The Queen*; No. 1947, Case Comment: *Copthorne Holdings Ltd. v. The Queen,* 2009 DTC 5101; No. 1924, Lipson (SCC) — A Unanimously Divided Supreme Court; No. 1883, Supreme Court To Consider GAAR in *Lipson Appeal*; No. 1856, *Copthorne Holdings Ltd. v. The Queen:* Backward Contemplation Bad for the Taxpayer; No. 1833, Lipson (FCA): All-Purpose Logic?; No. 1806, Expanding GAAR to Tax Treaties? Or Not; No. 1782, Walk the Line — *Lipson v. The Queen*; No. 1767, U.K. Decision Challenges Rule Against Treaty Shopping; No. 1756, The Supreme Court on GAAR: "The Line is Far from Bright" (No Kidding); No. 1578, After REOP, Where Do We GAAR From Here?.

Income Tax Technical News: Issue No. 34, Loss Consolidation — Provincial Tax.

Cases: The corporate taxpayer entered into a series of transactions using offsetting capital gains and losses to minimize the amount of tax in connection with the sale of a property. The goal was to distribute the full proceeds to the individual shareholders as a tax-free distribution. There had been a "tax benefit" and there were "avoidance transactions". By deliberately triggering specific anti-avoidance provisions, the taxpayer achieved a result that led to significant over-integration and, but for GAAR, allowed it to pay a capital dividend equal to the entire capital gain. The statutory provisions were not intended to allow a taxpayer to achieve this tax benefit. The result was inconsistent with the rationale underlying the provisions and inconsistent with the capital dividend account mechanism. *The Gladwin Realty Corporation v. The Queen,* 2019 DTC 1048 (TCC)

The corporate taxpayer undertook a recapitalization and restart transaction in which its assets and liabilities were moved to a new corporation. The remaining corporate shell was then used to raise funds through an initial public offering and certain tax attributes previously earned by the corporation, including tax losses and investment tax credits, were used to shelter income earned by the new business. No change of control had occurred, as the transactions were carefully structured to avoid an acquisition of control under the relevant provisions. The transactions resulted in a reduction of tax and a tax benefit to the taxpayer. Based on a textual and contextual analysis of the object, spirit, and purpose of the tax attribute streaming restrictions and the corporate control rules, the transactions did not constitute an abuse of such provisions. *Deans Knight v. The Queen,* 2019 DTC 1059 (TCC)

It is contrary to the object, spirit, or purposes of subsection 96(1) to use that provision to allocate taxable income in a manner that does not assist the organizational structure of the partnership or the efficient conduct of the partnership business. The taxpayer's actions amounted to abusive tax avoidance. *The Queen v. 594710 British Columbia Ltd.,* 2018 DTC 5111 (FCA)

The corporate taxpayer, a resident of Luxembourg, received a capital gain from the sale of its shares of a wholly-owned Canadian subsidiary and claimed the gain was exempt from tax under Article 13(5) of the *Canada-Luxembourg Income Tax Convention* (1999). Canada has the right to tax capital gains from the disposition of shares where those shares derive their value principally from immovable property located in Canada, except for excluded property where the business of the corporation is carried on in the property. A resource property qualifies as excluded property when developed in accordance with the industry's best practices. The taxpayer used the best practices of the industry to develop its reserves at each stage of development. All of the taxpayer's interest in the Canadian resource property qualified as excluded property, and GAAR did not apply to preclude the taxpayer from claiming the available treaty exemption. *Alta Energy Luxembourg S.A.R.L v. The Queen,* 2018 DTC 1120 (TCC) [under appeal]

While the corporate reorganization changed the tax attributes of a class of preferred shares in a way which created the potential for a tax-free distribution of retained earnings, that potential had not, to date, been realized. Because the tax-free distribution of retained earnings which section 84.1 was intended to prevent had not occurred, there was no evidence that the section had been misused or abused and GAAR did not apply. *1245989 Alberta Ltd. et al v. Attorney General of Canada,* 2018 DTC 5067 (FCA)

The transactions involved rolling three real estate properties through a tiered partnership structure, increasing the adjusted cost base of the partnership interests. Those interests were then sold to tax-exempt entities without tax being paid on the latent recapture and accrued gains in the property held by the partnerships. The elimination of the capital gain on the sale of the partnership interests to exempt entities by the use of "bumps" under sections 88 and 98, and the consequential avoidance of recapture under section 100, frustrated those provisions and were abusive. *The Queen v. Oxford Properties,* 2018 DTC 5017 (FCA)

The choice of a different year-end for federal and provincial tax purposes allowed the taxpayers to avoid paying Quebec income tax, which is contrary to the object and spirit of the tax provision allowing taxpayers to select their taxation year-end. This was an abusive tax avoidance allowing the taxpayers not to pay income tax on their capital gains and capital cost allowance recaptures. *Développements Iberville Ltée v. Quebec,* 2017 DTC 5088 (QCCQ)

The purpose of section 212.1 is not to prevent the removal from Canada by an arm's length purchaser of a Canadian corporation of any surplus such corporation accumulated prior to the acquisition of control. The transactions did not clearly frustrate the object, spirit, and purpose of section 212.1 as it was written in 2007, and 2016 amendments could not be used to make a finding that the avoidance transaction was abusive. *Univar v. The Queen,* 2017 DTC 5119 (FCA)

The purpose and spirit of subsections 73(1) and 74.2(1) are to insure that a gain or loss related to a spousal rollover remains that of the transferor. The taxpayer and W, by resorting to the identical property rules in subsection 47(1), were able to split the capital gain resulting from the disposition of the taxpayer's shares, which circumvented subsections 73(1) and 74.2. The entire portion of this gain ought to have been attributed to the taxpayer. *Gervais v. The Queen,* 2018 DTC 5005 (CAF)

There was a series of transactions involving tax avoidance. The husband's election to take advantage of the rollover provisions of s. 73(1) resulted in the application of s. 47(1) at the time that the wife sold 2 million shares. As a result, a portion of the taxable capital gain that would normally have been attributed to the husband accrued to the wife. Subsection 74.2(1) was intended to avoid this result, and the series of transactions constituted abusive tax avoidance. GAAR was used to attribute back to the husband the capital gain reported by his wife on the sale of the shares. *Gervais et al. v. The Queen,* 2016 DTC 1166 (CCI). [Under Appeal]

The transactions in issue were all similar, in that the taxpayer incorporated a new corporation, received its common shares at fair market value, received a preferred share stock dividend (on the common shares) with a high redemptive value and a low paid-up capital, and then disposed of the common shares at a loss. These transactions constitute an abuse of s. 34(1)(*b*), 38(*b*), and 39(1)(b) contrary to the GAAR. *Barrasso v. The Queen,* 2014 DTC 1130 (T.C.C.)

The taxpayers implemented a series of transactions which allowed them to use the pre-1971 value of a corporation's shares to indirectly distribute a portion of its surplus tax-free. This violated the object and spirit of s. 84.1. Although the Minister did not initially plead s. 84.1, the taxpayers were not prejudiced by the Court's reliance on it. *Descarries et al. v. The Queen,* 2014 DTC 1143 (T.C.C.)

A series of transactions were undertaken to convert corporate surplus into capital gains which were then allocated to minor beneficiaries of a family trust, thereby avoiding the tax on split income under s. 120.4 (which did not apply to capital gains at the time). It was reasonable to infer that Parliament did not intend for s. 120.4 to apply to all types of income splitting with minors. There is no broad policy against surplus stripping or income splitting grounded in the Act. The GAAR cannot be used to fill a perceived gap in the legislation. *Gwartz v. The Queen,* 2013 DTC 1122 (T.C.C.)

The taxpayer implemented a "reverse freeze" in which artificially devalued shares were transferred to a person within the same economic unit to create an artificial capital loss. GAAR was used to deny the capital loss deduction since the primary purpose of the series of transactions was to obtain a tax benefit. The transactions amounted to abusive tax avoidance because they defeated the underlying rationale of the capital loss provisions. *Triad Gestco Ltd. v. The Queen,* 2012 DTC 5156 (F.C.A.), affirming 2011 DTC 1254 (T.C.C.)

A Canadian corporation borrowed $140 million. The loan was later amended to separate the right to receive the principal from the right to receive interest. An arm's length Belgian bank purchased the right to receive the interest payments, which were exempt from Part XIII withholding tax under s. 212(1)(*b*)(vii). GAAR did not apply since this was not a misuse of s. 212(1)(*b*)(vii). *Lehigh Cement Limited v. The Queen,* 2010 DTC 5081 (F.C.A.), reversing 2009 DTC 1148 (T.C.C.)

The whole series of transactions clearly violated the spirit and purpose of ss. 80 and 80.01, constituted abusive tax avoidance, and led to the Minister's reassessments, which were justified. *Pièces Automobiles LeCavalier Inc. v. The Queen,* 2013 DTC 1245 (T.C.C.)

Sections 3, 4, 9, and 111 are not intended to apply to all business losses, but only to those involving an air of economic or business reality, which the losses in this case did not have. They were artificial and resulted from a value shift involving a paper shuffle. These transactions constituted abusive tax avoidance, which defeated the rationale underlying these provisions. *The Queen v. Global Equity Fund Ltd.,* 2013 DTC 5007 (F.C.A.), reversing 2011 DTC 1350 (T.C.C.)

Rather than doing a vertical amalgamation, a parent and subsidiary became directly owned by the same shareholder and then did a horizontal amalgamation, thereby preserving $67 million in PUC. A subsequent share redemption, which was part of the same series of transactions, resulted in a tax benefit through distribution of the PUC. This frustrated and defeated the purpose of s. 87(3) and was therefore abusive tax avoidance. *Copthorne Holdings Ltd. v. The Queen,* 2012 DTC 5007 (S.C.C.), affirming 2009 DTC 5101 (F.C.A.) and 2007 DTC 1230 (T.C.C.)

The taxpayer's wife obtained a bank loan to purchase shares of a family corporation from him. He used the proceeds to buy a new house. They then took out a mortgage on the house and used it to pay off the bank loan. The mortgage interest was deducted from her dividend income and the resulting loss was attributed to him under s. 74.1(1). This was not an abuse of s. 20(1)(*c*) or 20(3). However, it was an abuse of the attribution rules. *Lipson et al. v. The Queen,* 2009 DTC 5015 (S.C.C.), affirming 2007 DTC 5172 (F.C.A.), affirming 2006 DTC 2687 (T.C.C.)

Purchasing equipment and circuitously leasing it back to the vendor, in order to generate CCA with minimal financial risk, was not an abuse or misuse of the Act. The onus is on the Minister to establish abusive tax avoidance. Determinations of misuse and abuse are not separate inquiries. In analyzing s. 245(4), a unified textual, contextual, and purposive analysis of the relevant provisions must be conducted. The Court must then determine whether the avoidance transaction has frustrated the object, spirit, or purpose of the provisions. *The Queen v. Canada Trustco Mortgage Company*, 2005 DTC 5523 (S.C.C.), affirming 2004 DTC 6119 (F.C.A.), affirming 2003 DTC 587 (T.C.C.)

Using a unified textual, contextual, and purposive approach to the interpretation of s. 18(13) and s. 96, the Court concluded that using these provisions to preserve and sell an unrealized loss to an arm's length party constitutes abusive tax avoidance under s. 245(4). *Mathew v. The Queen (sub nom. Kaulius v. The Queen)*, 2005 DTC 5538 (S.C.C.), affirming 2003 DTC 5644 (F.C.A.), affirming 2002 DTC 1637 (T.C.C.)

The taxpayer made loans to subsidiaries of two banks. Since the subsidiaries were not "financial institutions", the loans were included in the taxpayer's investment allowance, thereby reducing taxable capital. This was not an abuse or misuse of the Act. *The Queen v. Imperial Oil Limited*, 2004 DTC 6044 (F.C.A.), affirming 2002 DTC 1954 (T.C.C.)

▶ 245(5) ◀

(5) Determination of tax consequences. Without restricting the generality of subsection (2), and notwithstanding any other enactment,

(*a*) any deduction, exemption or exclusion in computing income, taxable income, taxable income earned in Canada or tax payable or any part thereof may be allowed or disallowed in whole or in part,

(*b*) any such deduction, exemption or exclusion, any income, loss or other amount or part thereof may be allocated to any person,

(*c*) the nature of any payment or other amount may be recharacterized, and

(*d*) the tax effects that would otherwise result from the application of other provisions of this Act may be ignored,

in determining the tax consequences to a person as is reasonable in the circumstances in order to deny a tax benefit that would, but for this section, result, directly or indirectly, from an avoidance transaction.

▶ 245(6) ◀

(6) Request for adjustments. Where with respect to a transaction

(*a*) a notice of assessment, reassessment or additional assessment involving the application of subsection (2) with respect to the transaction has been sent to a person, or

(*b*) a notice of determination pursuant to subsection 152(1.11) has been sent to a person with respect to the transaction,

any person (other than a person referred to in paragraph (*a*) or (*b*)) shall be entitled, within 180 days after the day of sending of the notice, to request in writing that the Minister make an assessment, reassessment or additional assessment applying subsection (2) or make a determination applying subsection 152(1.11) with respect to that transaction.

History: S. 245(6), the portion after paragraph (*b*) was replaced by S.C. 2010, c. 25, s. 68, in force on Royal Assent, December 15, 2010. S. 245(6), the portion after paragraph (*b*) formerly read:

any person (other than a person referred to in paragraph (*a*) or (*b*)) shall be entitled, within 180 days after the day of mailing of the notice, to request in writing that the Minister make an assessment, reassessment or additional assessment applying subsection (2) or make a determination applying subsection 152(1.11) with respect to that transaction.

Related Sections: S. 166.1 Extension of time by Minister.

▶ 245(7) ◀

(7) Exception. Notwithstanding any other provision of this Act, the tax consequences to any person, following the application of this section, shall only be determined through a notice of assessment, reassessment, additional assessment or determination pursuant to subsection 152(1.11) involving the application of this section.

▶ 245(8) ◀

(8) Duties of Minister. On receipt of a request by a person under subsection (6), the Minister shall, with all due dispatch, consider the request and, notwithstanding subsection 152(4), assess, reassess or make an additional assessment or determination pursuant to subsection 152(1.11) with respect to that person, except that an assessment, reassessment, additional assessment or determination may be made under this subsection only to the extent that it may reasonably be regarded as relating to the transaction referred to in subsection (6).

SECTION 246: Benefit conferred on a person

▶ 246(1) ◀

(1) Benefit conferred on a person. Where at any time a person confers a benefit, either directly or indirectly, by any means whatever, on a taxpayer, the amount of the benefit shall, to the extent that it is not otherwise included in the taxpayer's income or taxable income earned in Canada under Part I and would be included in the taxpayer's income if the amount of the benefit were a payment made directly by the person to the taxpayer and if the taxpayer were resident in Canada, be

(*a*) included in computing the taxpayer's income or taxable income earned in Canada under Part I for the taxation year that includes that time; or

(*b*) where the taxpayer is a non-resident person, deemed for the purposes of Part XIII to be a payment made at that time to the taxpayer in respect of property, services or otherwise, depending on the nature of the benefit.

Interpretation Bulletins: *Secondary* — IT-432R2 Benefits conferred on shareholders.

▶ 246(2) ◀

(2) Arm's length. Where it is established that a transaction was entered into by persons dealing at arm's length, *bona fide* and not pursuant to, or as part of, any other transaction and not to effect payment, in whole or in part, of an existing or future obligation, no party thereto shall be regarded, for the purpose of this section, as having conferred a benefit on a party with whom the first-mentioned party was so dealing.

Related Sections: S. 251 Arm's length.

Part XVI.1
Transfer Pricing

SECTION 247: [Transfer pricing adjustment]

▶ 247(1) ◀

(1) Definitions. The definitions in this subsection apply in this section.

Canadian Tax Foundation: Wang, *Current Cases: Supreme Court of Canada — Supreme Court Provides Transfer-Pricing Guidance (Canada v. GlaxoSmithKline Inc., 2012 SCC 52)*, 2013 Canadian Tax Journal 1:187–193; Couzin, *Policy Forum: The End of Transfer Pricing?*, 2013 Canadian Tax Journal 1:159–178; Love, *OECD Transfer-Pricing Guidelines — Part 2*, 2012 Canadian Tax Highlights 20(11):2–3; McMechan, *GlaxoSmithKline at the SCC*, 2012 Canadian Tax Highlights 20(11):1–2; Love, *OECD Transfer-Pricing Guidelines — Part 1*, 2012 Canadian Tax Highlights 20(6):5–6; Barsalou and Chalmers, *Transfer Pricing Impact?*, 2012 Canadian Tax Highlights 20(6):2–3; Steeves, *Business Restructurings: Recent Changes to the OECD Transfer-Pricing Guidelines*, 2011 Canadian Tax Journal 1:151–166; Murray, *Transfer Pricing: Current Issues and Developments in Arbitration under the Canada-U.S. Tax Convention*, 2010 Conference Report 23:1–16; Purdy and Tang, *Transfer Pricing for Financial Services*, 2009 Conference Report 23:1–34; McCrodan and Borraccia, *The Dilemma of GlaxoSmithKline: Unreasonable in the Circumstances?*, 2008 Conference Report 23:1–21; Colborne and McLaren, *Current Cases: Tax Court of Canada — Transfer Pricing (GlaxoSmithKline Inc. v. The Queen, 2008 TCC 324)*, 2008 Canadian Tax Journal 4:930–936; Sambrook and Noble, *An Individual's Exposure to Transfer Pricing*, 2008 Canadian Tax Journal 3:753–770; Oatway, *Current Issues in Transfer Pricing*, 2007 Conference Report 22:1–22; Kerr, *Intellectual Property and Intangibles: Global Tax Planning Update*, 2007 Conference Report 8:1–22; Skretkowicz and Diebel, *Canadian Competent Authority Update*, 2006 Conference Report 18:1–22; Maclagan, *Transfer-Pricing Update, 2006*, 2006 Conference Report 17:1–15; Noble and Turner, *Competent Authority Update*, 2005 Conference Report 29:1–27; McCrodan and Williams, *Recent Developments in Transfer Pricing: Corporate Restructuring Issues, The Proposed U.S. Regulations on Services and Intangible Property, and Other General Developments*, 2004 Conference Report 27:1–28; Praulins and McCart, *Transfer-Pricing Audits: Emerging Issues*, 2003 Conference Report 13:1–14; Barsalou, *Transfer-Pricing Audits: Selected Issues*, 2003 Conference Report 12:1–25; Turner, *Transfer-Pricing Compliance Standards*, 2003 Conference Report 11:1–60; Hoffman et al., *Transfer Pricing: A Critique of the CCRA's position on Range Issues*, 2003 Canadian Tax Journal 4:1630–1646; Bienvenue, *Transfer-Pricing Rules Revisited*, 2003 Tax for the Owner-Manager 3(4):8–9; Golla et al., *How to Deal with Transfer-Pricing Disputes*, 2002 Conference Report 23:1–41; McMechan, *How to Deal with Transfer-Pricing Disputes: Appeals to the Tax Court of Canada*, 2002 Conference Report 22:1–23; Vincent, *Transfer Pricing: Range and Multiple-Year Data in Perspective*, 2002 Conference Report 16:1–16; Simkover, *Transfer Pricing: Acceptable Arm's-Length Prices Within the Range*, 2002 Conference Report 17:1–10; Nitikman, *Obtaining Disclosure of Secret Comparables in Canadian Transfer-Pricing Litigation: Policy and Practice*, 2002 Canadian Tax Journal 1:28–53; Lénik, *Prix de Transfert et Accords de Répartition des Coûts: Nouveaux enjeux — Nouvelles perspectives — Nouveaux défis*, 2000 Canadian Tax Journal 4:1078–1137; Brodie and Denusik, *Transfer Pricing — Current Issues*, 2000 British Columbia Tax Conference 13:1–13; Tamaki, *Selected Issues in Transfer Pricing*, 1999 Conference Report 44:1–15; Wilkie and Raizenne, *International Tax Policy Directions: Some Thoughts On Recent Canadian Experience*, 1999 Conference Report 42:1–38; Ward, *Tax Treaties: An Eroding Set of Rules*, 1999 Conference Report 41:1–21; Glicklich et al., *Lessons in Avoiding Transfer-Pricing Penalties: DHL Corp.*, 1999 Canadian Tax Journal 2:382–390; Humphreys and Plener, *Transfer Pricing for the Owner-Managed Business: Not Just a Big Company Problem!*, 1998 Conference Report 40:1–26; Chalmers, *International Transfer Pricing: The Australian Approach and Lessons for Canada*, 1998 Canadian Tax Journal 2:303–340; Hadari, *Resolution of International Transfer-Pricing Disputes*, 1998 Canadian Tax Journal 1:29–57; McLachlan, *Transfer Pricing*, 1998 Prairie Provinces Tax Conference 12:1–27; Robertson, *Transfer Pricing — A Common Sense Guide to Management Fees and Intra-Group Services*, 1998 British Columbia Tax Conference 20:1–22; Birnkrant, *Lessons from the United States: Transfer-Pricing Documentation and Penalties — IRC Sections 482 and 6662 and Regulations*, 1997 Conference Report 40B:1–16; McCart, *Panel Discussion on Transfer Pricing: Note from the Chair*, 1997 Conference Report 40A:1; Vincent and Freedman, *Transfer Pricing in Canada: The Arm's-Length Principle and the New Rules*, 1997 Canadian Tax Journal 6:1213–1242; Meister, *Transfer Pricing and Flow-Through Entities*, 1997 Prairie Provinces Tax Conference 11:1–50.

Information Circulars: IC 87-2R International Transfer Pricing; IC 94-4R International Transfer Pricing: Advance Pricing Arrangements (APAs).

Transfer Pricing Memoranda: TPM-15 Intra-group Services and Section 247 of the Income Tax Act.

"arm's length allocation" — "arm's length allocation" means, in respect of a transaction, an allocation of profit or loss that would have occurred between the participants in the transaction if they had been dealing at arm's length with each other.

"arm's length transfer price" — "arm's length transfer price" means, in respect of a transaction, an amount that would have been a transfer price in respect of the transaction if the participants in the transaction had been dealing at arm's length with each other.

Editorial Note: The "arm's length standard" is at the heart of the transfer pricing rules in jurisdictions that are member states of the OECD, including Canada. However, s. 247 does not define how the arm's length transfer prices are to be determined. Instead, the CRA has publicly endorsed the methods of determining an arm's length transfer price used by the OECD in its published *Guidelines for Multinational Enterprises*. (See IC 87-2R as amended by TPM-14).

"documentation-due date" — "documentation-due date" for a taxation year or fiscal period of a person or partnership means

(*a*) in the case of a person, the person's filing-due date for the year; or

(*b*) in the case of a partnership, the day on or before which a return is required by section 229 of the *Income Tax Regulations* to be filed in respect of the period or would be required to be so filed if that section applied to the partnership.

Related Sections: S. 150 Filing returns of income — general rule; s. 248(1), "filing due date".

"qualifying cost contribution arrangement" — "qualifying cost contribution arrangement" means an arrangement under which reasonable efforts are made by the participants in the arrangement to establish a basis for contributing to, and to contribute on that basis to, the cost of producing, developing or acquiring any property, or acquiring or performing any services, in proportion to the benefits which each participant is reasonably expected to derive from the property or services, as the case may be, as a result of the arrangement.

Related Sections: S. 247(3) Penalty; s. 247(4) Contemporaneous documentation.

Canadian Petroleum Tax Journal: High Tech in the Oil Patch: Planning Considerations For Transferring Technology Offshore, Derek A. Kurrant, 2000, Vol. 13, No. 1.

Tax Profile: June 2008 — International Tax Planning for the Owner-Manager; March 2006 — Some Tax Considerations for Investing in Silicon Valley North.

Tax Topics: No. 2140, Newly Released CRA Transfer Pricing Memoranda TPM-13 AND TPM-14.

"tax benefit" — "tax benefit" has the meaning assigned by subsection 245(1).

Information Circulars: IC 88-2 General anti-avoidance rule — Section 245 of the Income Tax Act.

"transaction" — "transaction" includes an arrangement or event.

"transfer price" — "transfer price" means, in respect of a transaction, an amount paid or payable or an amount received or receivable, as the case may be, by a participant in the transaction as a price, a rental, a royalty, a premium or other payment for, or for the use, production or reproduction of, property or as consideration for services (including services provided as an employee and the insurance or reinsurance of risks) as part of the transaction.

"transfer pricing capital adjustment" —"transfer pricing capital adjustment" of a taxpayer for a taxation year means the total of

(*a*) all amounts each of which is

(i) 1/2 of the amount, if any, by which the adjusted cost base to the taxpayer of a capital property (other than a depreciable property) is reduced in the year because of an adjustment made under subsection (2), or

(ii) (Repealed by S.C. 2016, c. 12, s. 62(1).)

(iii) the amount, if any, by which the capital cost to the taxpayer of a depreciable property is reduced in the year because of an adjustment made under subsection (2); and

(*b*) all amounts each of which is that proportion of the total of

(i) 1/2 of the amount, if any, by which the adjusted cost base to a partnership of a capital property (other than a depreciable property) is reduced in a fiscal period that ends in the year because of an adjustment made under subsection (2), and

(ii) (Repealed by S.C. 2016, c. 12, s. 62(1).)

(iii) the amount, if any, by which the capital cost to a partnership of a depreciable property is reduced in the period because of an adjustment made under subsection (2),

that

(iv) the taxpayer's share of the income or loss of the partnership for the period

is of

(v) the income or loss of the partnership for the period,

and where the income and loss of the partnership are nil for the period, the income of the partnership for the period is deemed to be $1,000,000 for the purpose of determining a taxpayer's share of the partnership's income for the purpose of this definition.

History: S. 247(1), subparagraph (ii) of paragraph (*a*) of the definition "transfer pricing capital adjustment" was repealed by S.C. 2016, c. 12, s. 62(1), in force January 1, 2017, and formerly read:

(ii) 3/4 of the amount, if any, by which the adjusted cost base to the taxpayer of an eligible capital expenditure of the taxpayer in respect of a business is reduced in the year because of an adjustment made under subsection (2), or

S. 247(1), subparagraph (ii) of paragraph (*b*) of the definition "transfer pricing capital adjustment" was repealed by S.C. 2016, c. 12, s. 62(2), in force January 1, 2017, and formerly read:

(ii) 3/4 of the amount, if any, by which the adjusted cost base to a partnership of an eligible capital expenditure of the partnership in respect of a business is reduced in a fiscal period that ends in the year because of an adjustment made under subsection (2), and

"transfer pricing capital setoff adjustment" —"transfer pricing capital setoff adjustment" of a taxpayer for a taxation year means the amount, if any, that would be the taxpayer's transfer pricing capital adjustment for the year if the references, in the definition "transfer pricing capital adjustment", to "reduced" were read as "increased".

"transfer pricing income adjustment" —"transfer pricing income adjustment" of a taxpayer for a taxation year means the total of all amounts each of which is the amount, if any, by which an adjustment made under subsection (2) (other than an adjustment included in determining a transfer pricing capital adjustment of the taxpayer for a taxation year) would result in an increase in the taxpayer's income for the year or a decrease in a loss of the taxpayer for the year from a source if that adjustment were the only adjustment made under subsection (2).

"transfer pricing income setoff adjustment" —"transfer pricing income setoff adjustment" of a taxpayer for a taxation year means the total of all amounts each of which is the amount, if any, by which an adjustment made under subsection (2) (other than an adjustment included in determining a transfer pricing capital setoff adjustment of the taxpayer for a taxation year) would result in a decrease in the taxpayer's income for the year or an increase in a loss of the taxpayer for the year from a source if that adjustment were the only adjustment made under subsection (2).

Editorial Note: Part XVI.1 contains Canada's transfer pricing tax legislation which consists of three principal components that may apply where transactions are entered into between Canadian taxpayers and non-arm's length non-residents. Firstly, these provisions allow the Minister to make adjustments to the determination of amounts in respect of a taxpayer or a partnership that are part of a transaction with a non-arm's length non-resident that are not made in accordance with the internationally recognized arm's length standard (the "primary adjustment"). The primary adjustment will normally result in the Canadian taxpayer having an increase of income or a decrease in its deductions. Secondly, these provisions impose penalties on a taxpayer where a transfer pricing adjustment is made in excess of certain thresholds and where the taxpayer has failed to make reasonable efforts to determine arm's length transfer prices or allocations in respect of a transaction. Thirdly, the provisions provide a "secondary adjustment" which allows the Minister to deem the non-arm's length non-resident to have received a dividend, subject to Part XIII withholding tax equal to the primary adjustment because the non-resident has received a benefit unless the non-resident is a controlled foreign affiliate for the purposes of s. 17. In certain situations, the deemed dividend can be avoided, if the amount of the primary adjustment is paid back to the Canadian taxpayer.

Proposed Amendment

2019 Federal Budget Resolutions

Section 247 of the Act is amended by adding the following after subsection (1):

(1.1) Order of applying provisions. For the purpose of applying the provisions of this Act, the adjustments under Part XVI. 1 shall be made before any other provision of the Act is applied.

Applicable: To taxation years that begin on or after March 19, 2019.

► 247(2) ◄

(2) Transfer pricing adjustment. Where a taxpayer or a partnership and a non-resident person with whom the taxpayer or the partnership, or a member of the partnership, does not deal at arm's length (or a partnership of which the non-resident person is a member) are participants in a transaction or a series of transactions and (*a*) the terms or conditions made or imposed, in respect of the transaction or series, between any of the participants in the transaction or series differ from those that would have been made between persons dealing at arm's length, or

(*b*) the transaction or series

(i) would not have been entered into between persons dealing at arm's length, and

(ii) can reasonably be considered not to have been entered into primarily for *bona fide* purposes other than to obtain a tax benefit,

any amounts that, but for this section and section 245, would be determined for the purposes of this Act in respect of the taxpayer or the partnership for a taxation year or fiscal period shall be adjusted (in this section referred to as an "adjustment") to the quantum or nature of the amounts that would have been determined if,

(*c*) where only paragraph (*a*) applies, the terms and conditions made or imposed, in respect of the transaction or series, between the participants in the transaction or series had been those that would have been made between persons dealing at arm's length, or

(*d*) where paragraph (*b*) applies, the transaction or series entered into between the participants had been the transaction or series that would have been entered into between persons dealing at arm's length, under terms and conditions that would have been made between persons dealing at arm's length.

Editorial Note: The transfer pricing adjustment provisions may apply to any transaction between a taxpayer or a partnership and a non-resident person with whom the taxpayer or the partnership or a member of the partnership does not deal at arm's length.

Adjustments may be made by the Minister so that transactions entered into by the taxpayer better reflect terms and conditions that arm's length parties would have agreed to.

The Minister also has the power to recharacterize transactions where it is concluded that transactions would not have been entered into by arm's length parties and were entered into by the parties primarily to obtain a tax benefit. Prior to issuing a reassessment resulting from a recharacterization, the Transfer Pricing Review Committee must approve it (see TPM-13). The Minister has the ability to make these adjustments three years after the typical limitation periods for reassessment expire pursuant to s. 152(4)(*b*)(iii). Transfer pricing adjustments can create the potential for double taxation where a corresponding adjustment is not made in the jurisdiction of the non-resident, and Canada's income tax treaties generally contain mutual agreement procedures whereby the two competent authorities can attempt to resolve any double taxation that may result from a transfer pricing adjustment.

See also the following CRA Transfer Memorandums: TPM-02 Repatriation of Funds by Non-residents — Part XIII Assessments; TPM-03 Downward Transfer Pricing Adjustments Under Subsection 247(2); TPM-04 Third-Party Information; TPM-05R Requests for Contemporaneous Documentation; TPM-06 Bundled Transactions; TPM-09 Reasonable Efforts under Section 247 of the *Income Tax Act*; TPM-11 Advance Pricing Arrangement Rollback; TPM-12 Accelerated Competent Authority Procedure; TPM-13 Referrals to the Transfer Pricing Review Committee; TPM-14 2010 Update of the OECD Transfer Pricing Guidelines.

Related Sections: S. 115.2(4) Transfer pricing s. 152(4)(*b*)(iii) Assessment and reassessment; s. 247(3) Penalty; s. 247(6) Deemed member of partnership; s. 247(7) Exclusion for loans to certain controlled foreign affiliates.

Canadian Petroleum Tax Journal: Canada Customs and Revenue Agency 1999 Roundtable Questions and Answers, Question 3, 2000, Vol. 13, No. 1.

Canadian Tax Foundation: Marcotte and Tan, *Cameco: A Transfer-Pricing Win for Taxpayers*, 2018 Canadian Tax Focus 8(4):9–9; Markham, *Advance Pricing Arrangements: Are Australia's Recent Reforms Relevant to Canada?*, 2013 Canadian Tax Journal 2:387–409; Wang, *Current Cases: Supreme Court of Canada — Supreme Court Provides Transfer-Pricing Guidance (Canada v. GlaxoSmithKline Inc., 2012 SCC 52)*, 2013 Canadian Tax Journal 1:187–193; Blackler and Nitikman, *Case Comment: GlaxoSmithKline Inc. v. The Queen*, 2013 British Columbia Tax Conference 2:6–11; Evans, *The Discretionary Nature of Downward Transfer-Pricing Adjustments*, 2013 Canadian Tax Focus 3(4):5–6; Akin and Siegal, *GlaxoSmithKline: Study of a Supreme Court Decision*, 2012 Conference Report 24:1–22; Rheault, *Recharacterization of Transactions in Transfer-Pricing Audits and Appeals: Recourse and Strategies*, 2011 Conference Report 21:1–16; Bloom and Vincent, *Canada's (Two) Transfer-Pricing Rules: A Tax Policy and Legal Analysis*, 2011 Conference Report 20:1–40; Oatway and Berthaudin, *Transfer Pricing: Current Issues and Developments*, 2010 Conference Report 22:1–15; Mawani and Reid, *Transfer Pricing and Employee Stock Options*, 2005 Canadian Tax Journal 3:607–639; Turner, *Transfer-Pricing Compliance Standards*, 2003 Conference Report 11:1–60; Vincent, *Transfer Pricing: Range and Multiple-Year Data in Perspective*, 2002 Conference Report 16:1–16.

International Tax: No. 103, The Canada Revenue Agency's Interpretation of the 2017 OECD Transfer Pricing Guidelines.

Tax Profile: December 2018 — *Cameco Corporation v. The Queen*: A Lesson in Sham and Canadian Transfer Pricing Adjustments; January 2015 — Marzen Aluminum — The CRA Win on Transfer Pricing; January 2015 — McKesson Canada — The Saga Continues; May 2013 — Current International Tax Issues In Cross-Border Corporate Finance and Capital Markets; February 2011 — Canada's Transfer Pricing Rules; September 2010 — Taxpayer Wins Major Transfer Pricing Case; January 2009 — Enhancing Canada's International Tax Advantage; June 2008 — International Tax Planning for the Owner-Manager; October 2006 — Tax Controversies in Canada: A Variety of Issues; January 2005 — CRA Threatens Use of Transfer Pricing in Non-Commercial Transactions.

Tax Topics: No. 2197, Can Transfer Pricing Rules Be Applied to an Arm's Length Sale?; No. 2185, Important Developments in Canadian Transfer Pricing; No. 2140, Newly Released CRA Transfer Pricing Memoranda TPM-13 AND TPM-14; No. 2136, Another View of the *GlaxoSmithKline* Decision; No. 2130, Transfer Pricing — What Does the *GlaxoSmithKline* Decision Mean?; No. 2111, IFA 2012 Tax Seminar Roundtables; No. 2036, CRA To Adopt OECD's Revised Transfer Pricing Guidelines; No. 2011, Competent Authority Program Reports Reveal Transfer Pricing Trends; No. 2009, The Federal Court of Appeal Decision in *GlaxoSmithKline Inc. v. The Queen*; No. 1957, A Policy of Disengagement: How Subsection 247(2) Relates to the Act's Income-Modifying Rules; No. 1895, Transfer Pricing Decision — GlaxoSmithKline Inc. v. The Queen; No. 1897, Unmasking "Management Fees" — What's in a Name?; No. 1885, OECD Reviews Transfer Pricing Methodologies — Will the CRA Follow Suit?; No. 1783, Paragraph 247(2)(*b*) Demystified; No. 1717, OECD Transfer Pricing Updates; No. 1687, Proposed U.S. Regulations on Services and Intangible Property: Implications for Canada; No. 1687, PATA Releases Guidance Documents Re Transfer Pricing; No. 1664, How Comparable Are Your CUPs?; No. 1661, Intercompany Interest Rates: an Overlooked Transfer Pricing Issue; No. 1634, Repatriation of Funds by Non-Residents — Part XIII Assessments; No. 1567, Contract Manufacturing Strategies: Tax-Saving Options for Intercompany Profit Allocation; No. 1566, Third Party Civil Penalties: Caution Needed When Filing T2 and T106 Returns; No. 1536, Transfer Pricing: An Outline of the Canadian Rules; No. 1534, Revised Circular on Advance Pricing Arrangements: The Rebirth of the APA Program?.

Income Tax Technical News: Issue No. 41, Transfer Pricing and Dispute Resolution; Issue No. 34, Update on Transfer Pricing; Issue No. 32, Application of Penalties.

Information Circulars: IC 87-2R International Transfer Pricing; IC 94-4R International Transfer Pricing: Advance Pricing Arrangements (APAs); IC 06-1 Income Tax Transfer Pricing and Customs Valuation.

Tax Window Files: Subsection 247(2), surplus, and FAPI, *October 27, 2017*, CRA Document No. 2017-0694231I7; Transfer pricing adjustments and gross revenue, *September 1, 2015*, CRA Document No. 2013-0507381I7; Transfer pricing for FAPI calculation, *June 14, 2017*, CRA Document No. 2017-0691191C6.

Transfer Pricing Memoranda: TPM-16 Role of Multiple Year Data in Transfer Pricing Analyses.

Cases: The methodology used by one of the taxpayer's experts to analyze the prices charged provided the most reliable and objectively reasonable assessment of those prices. That analysis reflected a reasonable assessment of the terms and conditions arm's length parties would have reached in the same circumstances and showed the prices charged were well within an arm's length range. No transfer pricing adjustment was warranted. *Cameco Corporation v. The Queen*, 2018 DTC 1138 (TCC)

Taking into account the OECD Guidelines 1995, an arm's length party would have paid an amount in excess of the amount the parties actually paid, but less than the amount reassessed by the Minister. *Marzen Artistic Aluminum Ltd. v. The Queen*, 2016 DTC 5018 (F.C.A.)

The taxpayer entered into a receivable sales agreement with its parent company wherein the parent agreed to purchase all of its receivables for the next five years at a discount. The taxpayer then deducted the discount from its income as a financing charge. The Minister was entitled to decrease the discount from 2.206% to 1.013%, which was more realistic and reflected the discount the parties would have reached had they been at arm's length.

McKesson Canada Corporation v. The Queen, 2014 DTC 1040 (T.C.C.) (FCA appeal discontinued)

A pharmaceutical company purchased an active ingredient from a related non-resident supplier for $1600/kg. The Tax Court held that this was not a reasonable price since generic drug manufacturers were purchasing the same ingredient for $200-$300/kg. However, since the judge misunderstood the test for reasonableness and failed to consider the terms of a licensing agreement, his judgment was set aside and the matter was referred back for redetermination. *GlaxoSmithKline Inc. v. The Queen*, 2012 DTC 5147 (S.C.C.), confirming 2010 DTC 5124 (F.C.A.), reversing 2008 DTC 3957 (T.C.C.)

The Minister could not use s. 247(2) to deny the taxpayer's deduction of fees it paid to its U.S. parent company, for guaranteeing its capital market borrowings, since the fees did not exceed the price that would have been paid by an arm's length party. *The Queen v. General Electric Capital Canada Inc.*, 2011 DTC 5011 (F.C.A.), affirming 2010 DTC 1007 (T.C.C.)

▶ 247(3) ◀

(3) Penalty. A taxpayer (other than a taxpayer all of whose taxable income for the year is exempt from tax under Part I) is liable to a penalty for a taxation year equal to 10% of the amount determined under paragraph (*a*) in respect of the taxpayer for the year, where

(*a*) the amount, if any, by which

(i) the total of

(A) the taxpayer's transfer pricing capital adjustment for the year, and

(B) the taxpayer's transfer pricing income adjustment for the year

exceeds the total of

(ii) the total of all amounts each of which is the portion of the taxpayer's transfer pricing capital adjustment or transfer pricing income adjustment for the year that can reasonably be considered to relate to a particular transaction, where

(A) the transaction is a qualifying cost contribution arrangement in which the taxpayer or a partnership of which the taxpayer is a member is a participant, or

(B) in any other case, the taxpayer or a partnership of which the taxpayer is a member made reasonable efforts to determine arm's length transfer prices or arm's length allocations in respect of the transaction, and to use those prices or allocations for the purposes of this Act, and

(iii) the total of all amounts, each of which is the portion of the taxpayer's transfer pricing capital setoff adjustment or transfer pricing income setoff adjustment for the year that can reasonably be considered to relate to a particular transaction, where

(A) the transaction is a qualifying cost contribution arrangement in which the taxpayer or a partnership of which the taxpayer is a member is a participant, or

(B) in any other case, the taxpayer or a partnership of which the taxpayer is a member made reasonable efforts to determine arm's length transfer prices or arm's length allocations in respect of the transaction, and to use those prices or allocations for the purposes of this Act,

is greater than

(*b*) the lesser of

(i) 10% of the amount that would be the taxpayer's gross revenue for the year if this Act were read without reference to subsection (2), subsections 69(1) and (1.2) and section 245, and

(ii) $5,000,000.

Editorial Note: The transfer pricing penalty provision serves two purposes. It provides a deterrent to non-compliance with the arm's length standard on transfer pricing and it encourages the preparation of contemporaneous documentation to support transfer prices without actually requiring it. The penalty is imposed at a rate of 10% of the transfer pricing adjustment and because the penalty is a function of the income adjustment and not the tax payable, the penalty cannot be sheltered and accrues non-deductible interest from the date of assessment.

Related Sections: S. 152(4)(*b*)(iii) Assessment and reassessment; s. 247(5) Partner's gross revenue; s. 247(6) Deemed member of partnership; s. 247(9) Anti-avoidance; s. 247(11) Provisions applicable to Part.

Canadian Tax Foundation: Pandher, *Transfer-Pricing Penalty Update*, 2017 Canadian Tax Focus 7(2):9; Colborne et al., *International Tax Planning — Subsection 247(3): What Are "Reasonable Efforts"?*, 2016 Canadian Tax Journal 1:229–243; Pandher, *Transfer-Pricing Penalties Now at Issue*, 2016 Canadian Tax Focus 6(3):8–9; Nanji, *TCC: Transfer-Pricing Structure Unsupportable*, 2014 Canadian Tax Focus 4(3):10–11; Sorensen et al., *Non-Criminal Penalties Under the Income Tax Act*, 2013 Ontario Tax Conference 12:1–50.

Tax Topics: No. 2140, Newly Released CRA Transfer Pricing Memoranda TPM-13 AND TPM-14; No. 1536, Transfer Pricing: An Outline of the Canadian Rules.

Information Circulars: IC 94-4R International Transfer Pricing: Advance Pricing Arrangements (APAs); IC 06-1 Income Tax Transfer Pricing and Customs Valuation.

▶ 247(4) ◀

(4) Contemporaneous documentation. For the purposes of subsection (3) and the definition "qualifying cost contribution arrangement" in subsection (1), a taxpayer or a partnership is deemed not to have made reasonable efforts to determine and use arm's length transfer prices or arm's length allocations in respect of a transaction or not to have participated in a transaction that is a qualifying cost contribution arrangement, unless the taxpayer or the partnership, as the case may be,

(*a*) makes or obtains, on or before the taxpayer's or partnership's documentation-due date for the taxation year or fiscal period, as the case may be, in which the transaction is entered into, records or documents that provide a description that is complete and accurate in all material respects of

(i) the property or services to which the transaction relates,

(ii) the terms and conditions of the transaction and their relationship, if any, to the terms and conditions of each other transaction entered into between the participants in the transaction,

(iii) the identity of the participants in the transaction and their relationship to each other at the time the transaction was entered into,

(iv) the functions performed, the property used or contributed and the risks assumed, in respect of the transaction, by the participants in the transaction,

(v) the data and methods considered and the analysis performed to determine the transfer prices or the allocations of profits or losses or contributions to costs, as the case may be, in respect of the transaction, and

(vi) the assumptions, strategies and policies, if any, that influenced the determination of the transfer prices or the allocations of profits or losses or contributions to costs, as the case may be, in respect of the transaction;

(*b*) for each subsequent taxation year or fiscal period, if any, in which the transaction continues, makes or obtains, on or before the taxpayer's or partnership's documentation-due date for that year or period, as the case may be, records or documents that completely and accurately describe each material change in the year or period to the matters referred to in any of subparagraphs (*a*)(i) to (vi) in respect of the transaction; and

(*c*) provides the records or documents described in paragraphs (*a*) and (*b*) to the Minister within 3 months after service, made personally or by registered or certified mail, of a written request therefor.

Editorial Note: This deeming provision provides that a taxpayer or partnership will be deemed not to have made reasonable efforts to determine and use arm's length transfer prices in respect of a transaction (and thereby be exposed to the potential for penalties under s. 247(3)) unless the taxpayer makes or obtains on or before the taxpayer's or partnership's documentation-due date for the taxation year in which the transaction was entered into, records or documents that accurately describe the details of the transaction as set out in ss. 247(4)(*a*)(i) to (vi). While these documents are not filed with the CRA, the taxpayer must provide these records and documents to the CRA within three months after service of a written request for them from the Minister. This section deems a taxpayer who has not complied with the conditions specified therein to have not made reasonable efforts. The corollary is not true. The Minister has the authority to conclude that a taxpayer has not made reasonable efforts and is subject to a penalty, even where contemporaneous documentation has been prepared and provided to the Minister within the applicable time limits.

It is important to understand that transfer pricing documentation is not compulsory in Canada. However, the failure to prepare such documentation will result in a penalty if the penalty thresholds set out in s. 247(3) are met. See also Pacific Association of Tax Administrators (PATA) Transfer Pricing Documentation Package.

Related Sections: S. 248(1), "record".

Tax Profile: April 2011 — Canadian Tax Issues for Non-Resident Franchisors; February 2011 — Canada's Transfer Pricing Rules.

Tax Topics: No. 1860, Transfer Pricing — How Long Does the Canada Revenue Agency Have To Reassess a Taxpayer?; No. 1860, Transfer Pricing — Shareholder Costs: To Allocate or Not To Allocate, Thatls the Question; No. 1765, Canadian Distributors, Marketing Intangibles and Profit: The Transfer Pricing Connection; No. 1762, Foreign Exchange Fluctuations and Transfer Pricing Analysis; No. 1761, Transfer Pricing — Defending Intra-Group Service Charges under Audit; No. 1597, PATA Transfer Pricing Documentation Proposal Confuses Rather Than Clarifies; No. 1536, Transfer Pricing: An Outline of the Canadian Rules.

Forms: T106 — Information Return of Non-Arm's Length Transactions With Non-Residents.

Information Circulars: IC 87-2R International Transfer Pricing; 94-4R International Transfer Pricing: Advance Pricing Arrangements (APAs).

► 247(5) ◄

(5) Partner's gross revenue. For the purpose of subparagraph (3)(*b*)(i), where a taxpayer is a member of a partnership in a taxation year, the taxpayer's gross revenue for the year as a member of the partnership from any activities carried on by means of the partnership is deemed to be that proportion of the amount that would be the partnership's gross revenue from the activities if it were a taxpayer (to the extent that amount does not include amounts received or receivable from other partnerships of which the taxpayer is a member in the year), for a fiscal period of the partnership that ends in the year, that

(*a*) the taxpayer's share of the income or loss of the partnership from its activities for the period

is of

(*b*) the income or loss of the partnership from its activities for the period,

and where the income and loss of the partnership from its activities are nil for the period, the income of the partnership from its activities for the period is deemed to be $1,000,000 for the purpose of determining a taxpayer's share of the partnership's income from its activities for the purpose of this subsection.

Related Sections: S. 247(9) Anti-avoidance; s. 248(1), "gross revenue".

► 247(6) ◄

(6) Deemed member of partnership. For the purposes of this section, where a person is a member of a partnership that is a member of another partnership,

(*a*) the person is deemed to be a member of the other partnership; and

(*b*) the person's share of the income or loss of the other partnership is deemed to be equal to the amount of that income or loss to which the person is directly or indirectly entitled.

► 247(7) ◄

(7) Exclusion for loans to certain controlled foreign affiliates. Where, in a taxation year of a corporation resident in Canada, a non-resident person owes an amount to the corporation, the non-resident person is a controlled foreign affiliate of the corporation for the purpose of section 17 throughout the period in the year during which the amount is owing and it is established that the amount owing is an amount owing described in paragraph 17(8)(*a*) or (*b*), subsection (2) does not apply to adjust the amount of interest paid, payable or accruing in the year on the amount owing.

Related Sections: S. 17(8) Exception; S. 17(15) "controlled foreign affiliate".

Tax Topics: No. 1957, A Policy of Disengagement: How Subsection 247(2) Relates to the Act's Income-Modifying Rules.

Tax Window Files: Transfer Pricing Adjustment — Loan to Non-resident Corporation, *Technical Interpretation, International and Trusts Division, February 6, 2004*, CRA Document No. 2003-0033891E5.

► 247(7.1) ◄

(7.1) Exclusion — certain guarantees. Subsection (2) does not apply to adjust an amount of consideration paid, payable or accruing to a corporation resident in Canada (in this subsection referred to as the "parent") in a taxation year of the parent for the provision of a guarantee to a person or partnership (in this subsection referred to as the "lender") for the repayment, in whole or in part, of a particular amount owing to the lender by a non-resident person, if

(*a*) the non-resident person is a controlled foreign affiliate of the parent for the purposes of section 17 throughout the period in the year during which the particular amount is owing; and

(*b*) it is established that the particular amount would be an amount owing described in paragraph 17(8)(*a*) or (*b*) if it were owed to the parent.

History: S. 247(7.1) was added by S.C. 2013, c. 40, s. 88(1), applicable to taxation years that begin after 1997, and in applying subsection 247(7.1) to taxation years that begin before February 24, 1998, section 17 of the Act is to be read as it read on January 24, 2005, except that if a taxpayer elects under this subsection in writing and files the election with the Minister of

National Revenue on or before the taxpayer's filing-due date for the taxation year that includes December 12, 2013 (the day on which this Act receives royal assent),

(*a*) notwithstanding the time limitations in subsection 152(4) of the Act, the Minister of National Revenue may make such assessments, reassessments and determinations under Part I of the Act as are necessary to give effect to this subsection for a taxation year that ends before that day; and

(*b*) if the taxpayer so indicates in the election, the above application does not apply to taxation years of the taxpayer that begin before December 22, 2012.

Related Sections: S. 17(8) Exception; S. 17(15) "controlled foreign affiliate".

Tax Topics: No. 2166, Downstream Loan Guarantees and Subsection 247(7.1) Transfer Pricing Relief.

▶ 247(8) ◀

(8) Provisions not applicable. Where subsection (2) would, if this Act were read without reference to sections 67 and 68 and subsections 69(1) and (1.2), apply to adjust an amount under this Act, sections 67 and 68 and subsections 69(1) and (1.2) shall not apply to determine the amount if subsection (2) is applied to adjust the amount.

Proposed Amendment
2019 Federal Budget Resolutions

Subsection 247(8) of the Act is repealed.

Applicable: To taxation years that begin on or after March 19, 2019.

▶ 247(9) ◀

(9) Anti-avoidance. For the purposes of determining a taxpayer's gross revenue under subparagraph (3)(*b*)(i) and subsection (5), a transaction or series of transactions is deemed not to have occurred, if one of the purposes of the transaction or series was to increase the taxpayer's gross revenue for the purpose of subsection (3).

Related Sections: S. 248(10) Series of transactions.

▶ 247(10) ◀

(10) No adjustment unless appropriate. An adjustment (other than an adjustment that results in or increases a transfer pricing capital adjustment or a transfer pricing income adjustment of a taxpayer for a taxation year) shall not be made under subsection (2) unless, in the opinion of the Minister, the circumstances are such that it would be appropriate that the adjustment be made.

▶ 247(11) ◀

(11) Provisions applicable to Part. Sections 152, 158, 159, 162 to 167 and Division J of Part I apply to this Part, with such modifications as the circumstances require.

▶ 247(12) ◀

(12) Deemed dividends to non-residents. For the purposes of Part XIII, if a particular corporation that is a resident of Canada for the purposes of Part XIII would have a transfer pricing capital adjustment or a transfer pricing income adjustment for a taxation year, if the particular corporation, or a partnership of which the particular corporation is a member, had undertaken no transactions or series of transactions other than those in which a particular non-resident person, or a partnership of which the particular non-resident person is a member, that does not deal at arm's length with the particular corporation (other than a corporation that was for the purposes of section 17 a controlled foreign affiliate of the particular corporation throughout the period during which the transaction or series of transactions occurred) was a participant,

(*a*) a dividend is deemed to have been paid by the particular corporation and received by the particular non-resident person immediately before the end of the taxation year; and

(*b*) the amount of the dividend is the amount, if any, by which

(i) the amount that would be the portion of the total of the particular corporation's transfer pricing capital adjustment and transfer pricing income adjustment for the taxation year that could reasonably be considered to relate to the particular non-resident person if

(A) the only transactions or series of transactions undertaken by the particular corporation were those in which the particular non-resident person was a participant, and

(B) the definition "transfer pricing capital adjustment" in subsection (1) were read without reference to the references therein to "1/2 of" and "3/4 of"

exceeds

(ii) the amount that would be the portion of the total of the particular corporation's transfer pricing capital setoff adjustment, and transfer pricing income setoff adjustment, for the taxation year that could reasonably be considered to relate to the particular non-resident person if

(A) the only transactions or series of transactions undertaken by the particular corporation were those in which the particular non-resident person was a participant, and

(B) the definition "transfer pricing capital adjustment" in subsection (1) were read without reference to the references therein to "1/2 of" and "3/4 of".

Editorial Note: Subsection 247(12) permits the CRA to impose a secondary adjustment if the Canadian taxpayer has overpaid a non-arm's length non-resident or has been underpaid by a non-arm's length non-resident in respect of goods or services. Under s. 247(2), the transfer pricing adjustment (the "primary adjustment") will normally result in an increase of income or a decrease of deduction for the Canadian resident. However, the CRA may also impose a "secondary adjustment" in respect of the Canadian taxpayer's excess payment (or under charging) in respect of the non-resident. Therefore, in addition to increased income for the Canadian resident taxpayer, s. 247(12) deems the non-resident to have received a dividend equal to the primary adjustment which will be subject to Part XIII withholding tax because the non-resident has received a benefit. The secondary adjustment deemed dividend will not apply where the non-arm's length non-resident is a controlled foreign affiliate of the Canadian corporation as defined for the purposes of s. 17.

History: S. 247(12) was added by S.C. 2012, c. 31, s. 54(1), applicable in respect of any transaction that occurs after March 28, 2012.

▶ 247(13) ◀

(13) Repatriation. If a dividend is deemed by subsection (12) to have been paid by a corporation and received by a non-resident person, and a particular amount has been paid with the concurrence of the Minister by the non-resident person to the corporation, (*a*) the amount of the dividend may be reduced by the amount (in this subsection referred to as the "reduction") that the Minister considers appropriate, having regard to all the circumstances, and

(*b*) subsections 227(8.1) and (8.3) apply as if

(i) the amount of the dividend were not reduced, and

(ii) on the day on which the particular amount was paid, the corporation paid to the Receiver General an amount equal to the amount that would be required to be withheld and remitted under Part XIII in respect of the reduction.

Editorial Note: Subsections 247(13) and (14) deal with repatriation. Where s. 247 deems a secondary adjustment dividend to have been paid by a Canadian corporation and received by a non-arm's length non-resident, and the non-resident repatriates the amount of the dividend to the Canadian corporation, the amount of the secondary adjustment deemed dividend is reduced by the amount the Minister considers appropriate, having regard to all the circumstances, if the repatriation is made with the concurrence of the Minister.

History: S. 247(13) was added by S.C. 2012, c. 31, s. 54(1), applicable in respect of any transaction that occurs after March 28, 2012.

► 247(14) ◄

(14) Repatriation — interest. If the amount of a dividend is reduced under paragraph (13)(*a*), the amount of interest payable by a taxpayer because of paragraph (13)(*b*) may be reduced to the amount that the Minister considers appropriate, having regard to all the circumstances, including the provision of reciprocal treatment by the country in which the non-resident person referred to in subsection (13) is resident.

Editorial Note: Pursuant to paragraph 247(13)(*b*), even if the secondary adjustment is cancelled due to a repatriation which is approved by the Minister, interest is payable on amounts required to be withheld until the time of repatriation. Subsection 247(14) provides the Minister with discretion to reduce the amount of the interest, having regard to all of the circumstances, including reciprocal treatment by the country in which the non-resident dividend recipient is resident.

History: S. 247(14) was added by S.C. 2012, c. 31, s. 54(1), applicable in respect of any transaction that occurs after March 28, 2012.

► 247(15) ◄

(15) Non-application of provisions. Section 15, subsections 56(2) and 212.3(2) and section 246 do not apply in respect of an amount to the extent that a dividend is deemed by subsection (12) (determined without reference to subsection (13)) to have been paid in respect of the amount.

History: S. 247(15) was added by S.C. 2012, c. 31, s. 54(1), applicable in respect of any transaction that occurs after March 28, 2012.

Part XVII
Interpretation

SECTION 248: Definitions

► 248(1) ◄

(1) Definitions. In this Act,

"active business" — "active business", in relation to any business carried on by a taxpayer resident in Canada, means any business carried on by the taxpayer other than a specified investment business or a personal services business;

Canadian Tax Foundation: Friedlan, *A Question of Meaning: The Definition of Active Business in Subsection 248(1)*, 2013 Tax for the Owner-Manager 13(3):1–2.

Interpretation Bulletins: *Secondary* — IT-73R6 The small business deduction; IT-373R2 (Consolid.) Woodlots.

"additional voluntary contribution" — "additional voluntary contribution" to a registered pension plan means a contribution that is made by a member to the plan, that is used to provide benefits under a money purchase provision (within the meaning assigned by subsection 147.1(1)) of the plan and that is not required as a general condition of membership in the plan;

Related Sections: S. 8(1)(*m*) Employee's registered pension plan contributions; s. 8(8) Employees' contributions to pension fund for arrears; s. 60.2 Refund of undeducted past service AVCs; s. 147.2(4) Amount of employee's pension contributions deductible.

"adjusted cost base" — "adjusted cost base" has the meaning assigned by section 54;

"adjustment time" — (Repealed by S.C. 2016, c. 12, s. 63(1).)

History: S. 248(1), the definition "adjustment time" was repealed by S.C. 2016, c. 12, s. 63(1), in force January 1, 2017, and formerly read:

"adjustment time" — "adjustment time" has the meaning assigned by subsection 14(5);

Related Sections: S. 54, "adjusted cost base".

"aggregate investment income" — "aggregate investment income" has the meaning assigned by subsection 129(4);

"allowable business investment loss" — "allowable business investment loss" has the meaning assigned by section 38;

"allowable capital loss" — "allowable capital loss" has the meaning assigned by section 38;

"alter ego trust" — "alter ego trust" means a trust to which paragraph 104(4)(*a*) would apply if that paragraph were read without reference to subparagraph 104(4)(*a*)(iii) and clauses 104(4)(*a*)(iv)(B) and (C);

Related Sections: S. 73(1) Inter vivos transfers by individuals; s. 73(1.01) Qualifying transfers; s. 73(1.02) Exception for transfers; s. 104(4) Deemed disposition by trust; s. 104(5.8) Trust transfers; s. 104(6) Deduction in computing income of trust; s. 104(15) Allocable amount for preferred beneficiary; s. 108(1), "trust".

Canadian Tax Foundation: Main and McEachren, *Using Inter Vivos Trusts in Estate and Family Planning: Alter Ego and Joint Spousal and Common-Law Partner Trusts*, 2013 Ontario Tax Conference 9:3–29; Kerr and Sorensen, *Use of Special-Purpose Trusts*, 2007 Conference Report 35:1–47; Bueschkens, *Trusts: Practical Issues, Uses, and Pitfalls*, 2006 Conference Report 34:1–29; Brown, *Alter Ego Joint Conjugal and Self-Benefit Trusts Revisited: Some Troubling Tax Issues and a Search for Better Alternatives*, 2005 Canadian Tax Journal 1:224–244; Hoffstein, *Alter Ego Trusts/Joint Partner Trusts — Tips, Traps & Planning*, 2004 Ontario Tax Conference 12A:1–47.

Tax Profile: February 2002 — Transferring Property to a Trust After the Enactment of Bill C-22.

"amateur athlete trust" — "amateur athlete trust" has the meaning assigned by subsection 143.1(1.2);

History: S. 248(1), the definition "amateur athlete trust" was replaced by S.C. 2009, c. 2, s. 76(2), applicable to the 2008 and subsequent taxation years. S. 248(1), the definition "amateur athlete trust" formerly read:

"amateur athlete trust" — "amateur athlete trust" has the meaning assigned by subsection 143.1(1);

Related Sections: S. 143.1(1) Definitions.

"amortized cost" — "amortized cost" of a loan or lending asset at any time to a taxpayer means the amount, if any, by which the total of

(*a*) in the case of a loan made by the taxpayer, the total of all amounts advanced in respect of the loan at or before that time,

(*b*) in the case of a loan or lending asset acquired by the taxpayer, the cost of the loan or lending asset to the taxpayer,

(*c*) in the case of a loan or lending asset acquired by the taxpayer, the part of the amount, if any, by which

(i) the principal amount of the loan or lending asset at the time it was so acquired

exceeds

(ii) the cost to the taxpayer of the loan or lending asset

that was included in computing the taxpayer's income for any taxation year ending at or before that time,

(*c*.1) the total of all amounts each of which is an amount in respect of the loan or lending asset that was included in computing the taxpayer's income for a taxation year that ended at or before that time in respect of changes in the value of the loan or lending asset attributable to the fluctuation in the value of a currency of a country other than Canada relative to Canadian currency,

(*d*) where the taxpayer is an insurer, any amount in respect of the loan or lending asset that was deemed by reason of paragraph 142(3)(*a*) of the *Income Tax Act*, chapter 148 of the Revised Statutes of Canada, 1952, as it read in its application to the 1977 taxation year, to be a gain for any taxation year ending at or before that time, and

(*e*) the total of all amounts each of which is an amount in respect of the loan or lending asset that was included under paragraph 12(1)(*i*) in computing the taxpayer's income for any taxation year ending at or before that time

exceeds the total of

(*f*) the part of the amount, if any, by which

(i) the amount referred to in subparagraph (*c*)(ii)

exceeds

(ii) the amount referred to in subparagraph (*c*)(i)

that was deducted in computing the taxpayer's income for any taxation year ending at or before that time,

(*f*.1) the total of all amounts each of which is an amount in respect of the loan or lending asset that was deducted in computing the taxpayer's income for a taxation year that ended at or before that time in respect of changes in the value of the loan or lending asset attributable to the fluctuation in the value of a currency of a country other than Canada relative to Canadian currency,

(*g*) the total of all amounts that, at or before that time, the taxpayer had received as or on account or in lieu of payment of or in satisfaction of the principal amount of the loan or lending asset,

(*h*) where the taxpayer is an insurer, any amount in respect of the loan or lending asset that was deemed by reason of paragraph 142(3)(*b*) of the *Income Tax Act*, chapter 148 of the Revised Statutes of Canada, 1952, as it read in its application to the 1977 taxation year, to be a loss for any taxation year ending at or before that time, and

(*i*) the total of all amounts each of which is an amount in respect of the loan or lending asset deducted under paragraph 20(1)(*p*) in computing the taxpayer's income for any taxation year ending at or before that time;

"amount" —"amount" means money, rights or things expressed in terms of the amount of money or the value in terms of money of the right or thing, except that,

(*a*) notwithstanding paragraph (*b*), in any case where subsection 112(2.1), (2.2) or (2.4), or section 187.2 or 187.3 or subsection 258(3) or (5) applies to a stock dividend, the "amount" of the stock dividend is the greater of

(i) the amount by which the paid-up capital of the corporation that paid the dividend is increased by reason of the payment of the dividend, and

(ii) the fair market value of the share or shares paid as a stock dividend at the time of payment,

(*b*) in any case where section 191.1 applies to a stock dividend, the "amount" of the stock dividend for the purposes of Part VI.1 is the greater of

(i) the amount by which the paid-up capital of the corporation that paid the dividend is increased by reason of the payment of the dividend, and

(ii) the fair market value of the share or shares paid as a stock dividend at the time of payment,

and for any other purpose the amount referred to in subparagraph (i), and

(*b*.1) (Repealed by S.C. 2013, c. 34, s. 358(7).)

(*c*) in any other case, the "amount" of any stock dividend is the amount by which the paid-up capital of the corporation that paid the dividend is increased by reason of the payment of the dividend;

History: S. 248(1), paragraph (*b.1*) of the definition "amount" was repealed by S.C. 2013, c. 34, s. 358(7), applicable to taxation years that begin after 2012, and formerly read:

(*b*.1) if a taxpayer files an election in writing with the Minister of National Revenue on or before the taxpayer's filing-due date for the 2012 taxation year, then in the case of each stock dividend declared after July 17, 2005 and paid to the taxpayer before 2013 by a corporation that is, when the dividend is paid, a non-resident corporation, the "amount" of the stock dividend is, except where subsection 95(7) applies to the dividend, the greater of

(i) the amount by which the paid-up capital of the corporation that paid the dividend is increased by reason of the payment of the dividend, and

(ii) the fair market value of the share or shares paid as a stock dividend at the time of payment, and

S. 248(1), paragraph (*b.1*) of the definition "amount" was added by S.C. 2013, c. 34, s. 358(6), deemed to have come into force on July 17, 2005 and, if a taxpayer files an election referred to in paragraph (*b.1*) of the definition "amount" in subsection 248(1) on or before the taxpayer's filing-due date for its taxation year that includes June 26, 2013, the election is deemed to have been filed on time.

Tax Topics: No. 1683, *Imperial Oil Limited v. The Queen.*

Interpretation Bulletins: *Primary* — IT-88R2 Stock dividends.

Cases: Board and lodging received by a ship engineer under his employment contract and in accordance with the *Canada Shipping Act*, was held not to be an amount within the meaning of former s. 139(1)(*a*) [now s. 248(1)]. *Williams v. M.N.R.*, 55 DTC 1006 (Ex. Ct.)

"annuity" —"annuity" includes an amount payable on a periodic basis whether payable at intervals longer or shorter than a year and whether payable under a contract, will or trust or otherwise;

"appropriate percentage" —"appropriate percentage", for a taxation year, means the lowest percentage referred to in subsection 117(2) for the taxation year;

History: S. 248(1), the definition "appropriate percentage" was replaced by S.C. 2016, c. 11, s. 10(1), applicable to the 2016 and subsequent taxation years, and formerly read:

"appropriate percentage"—"appropriate percentage" for a taxation year means the lowest percentage referred to in subsection 117(2) that is applicable in determining tax payable under Part I for the year;

"assessment" —"assessment" includes a reassessment;

"authorized foreign bank" —"authorized foreign bank" has the meaning assigned by section 2 of the *Bank Act*;

Related Sections: S. 18(1)(*v*) Interest — authorized foreign bank; s. 20.2(5) Notional interest; s. 115(1)(*a*)(ii) Non-resident's taxable income in Canada; s. 181.3(3)(*e*) Capital; s. 190.13(*d*) Capital; s. 190.14(1)(*c*) Investment in related institutions; s. 212(13.3) Application of Part XIII to authorized foreign bank; s. 218.2(1) Branch interest tax; s. 218.2(2) Taxable interest expense; s. 219 Branch tax; s. 233.3(1), "specified foreign property".

"automobile" —"automobile" means

(*a*) a motor vehicle that is designed or adapted primarily to carry individuals on highways and streets and that has a seating capacity for not more than the driver and 8 passengers,

but does not include

(*b*) an ambulance,

(*b*.1) a clearly marked emergency-response vehicle that is used in connection with or in the course of an individual's office or employment with a fire department or the police;

(*b*.2) a clearly marked emergency medical response vehicle that is used, in connection with or in the course of an individual's office or employment with an emergency medical response or ambulance service, to carry emergency medical equipment together with one or more emergency medical attendants or paramedics,

(*c*) a motor vehicle acquired primarily for use as a taxi, a bus used in a business of transporting passengers or a hearse used in the course of a business of arranging or managing funerals,

(*d*) except for the purposes of section 6, a motor vehicle acquired to be sold, rented or leased in the course of carrying on a business of selling, renting or leasing motor vehicles or a motor vehicle used for the purpose of transporting passengers in the course of carrying on a business of arranging or managing funerals, and

(*e*) a motor vehicle

(i) of a type commonly called a van or pick-up truck, or a similar vehicle, that has a seating capacity for not more than the driver and two passengers and that, in the taxation year in which it is acquired or leased, is used primarily for the transportation of goods or equipment in the course of gaining or producing income,

(ii) of a type commonly called a van or pick-up truck, or a similar vehicle, the use of which, in the taxation year in which it is acquired or leased, is all or substantially all for the transportation of goods, equipment or passengers in the course of gaining or producing income, or

(iii) of a type commonly called a pick-up truck that is used in the taxation year in which it is acquired or leased primarily for the transportation of goods, equipment or passengers in the course of earning or producing income at one or more locations in Canada that are

(A) described, in respect of any of the occupants of the vehicle, in subparagraph 6(6)(*a*)(i) or (ii), and

(B) at least 30 kilometres outside the nearest point on the boundary of the nearest population centre, as defined by the last census dictionary published by Statistics Canada before the year, that has a population of at least 40,000 individuals as determined in the last census published by Statistics Canada before the year;

History: S. 248(1), clause (*e*)(iii)(B) of the definition "automobile" was replaced by S.C. 2013, c. 40, s. 89(3), applicable to the 2013 and subsequent taxation years, and formerly read:

(B) at least 30 kilometres outside the nearest point on the boundary of the nearest urban area, as defined by the last census dictionary published by Statistics Canada before the year, that has a population of at least 40,000 individuals as determined in the last census published by Statistics Canada before the year.

Editorial Note: Subject to the specified exceptions, an automobile is defined as a motor vehicle primarily designed to carry up to 8 passengers and the driver on highways and streets. A "motor vehicle" is an automotive vehicle designed or adapted to be used on highways and streets but does not include a trolley bus or a vehicle designed or adapted to be operated exclusively on rails.

Application: The definition of "automobile" is relevant, *inter alia*, for the purposes of determining employment standby charges and operating expense benefits for employees (s. 6(1)(*e*) and (*k*)). A vehicle that is not an automobile is not a passenger vehicle and is therefore not subject to the Class 10.1 capital cost allowance limitation, or the limitations on the deduction of interest or leasing costs in s. 67.2 or 67.3.

Specific exceptions: The following are defined not to be automobiles: (a) ambulances; (b) clearly marked emergency-response vehicles used in connection with an office or employment with a fire department, police, or an emergency medical response or ambulance service; (c) vehicles acquired to be used primarily as taxis; (d) buses used in a business of transporting passengers; (e) hearses used in a funeral business; (f) except for the purposes of the employment benefit provisions of s. 6, motor vehicles acquired to be sold, rented, or leased in the course of a business, or motor vehicles used for transporting passengers in a funeral business; (g) vans or pickup trucks with a seating capacity for the driver and (at most) two passengers used primarily for transporting goods or equipment in the course of gaining or producing income in the year of acquisition (see *Ilott et al. v. The Queen*, 2003 DTC 123 (T.C.C.)); (h) vans or pickup trucks used in the year of acquisition (all or substantially all) for transporting goods, equipment, or passengers in the course of gaining or producing income; and (i) pick-up trucks used primarily in the year of acquisition for the transportation of goods, equipment, or passengers in the course of earning or producing income at a remote or special worksite.

Extent of "use": The distance a truck travels for dead head trips — such as travelling a leg of a round trip without cargo — forms part of the use test in subparagraph (*e*)(ii) of the definition for the purpose of determining whether the truck was used all or substantially all for the transportation of goods or equipment (see CRA Document No. 2004-010331117).

Meaning of "goods and equipment": For the purpose of paragraph (*e*) in the definition, "goods or equipment" can include tools. A truck used primarily to transport tools of the trade to various job sites is considered to be transporting "goods or equipment" (CRA Document No. 2004-0064541E5).

Alterations to vehicle: The removal of seating does not affect the legal seating capacity of a vehicle for the purposes of the definition. A delivery van modified to carry merchandise was still designed primarily to carry individuals on highways and streets and was an "automobile". (CRA Document No. 2003-0029355; *Gariépy v. The Queen*, 2007 DTC 1475 (T.C.C.)).

Interpretation Bulletins: *Secondary* — IT-521 Motor vehicle expenses claimed by self-employed individuals; IT-522R Vehicle, travel and sales expenses of employees.

"balance-due day" —"balance-due day" of a taxpayer for a taxation year means,

(*a*) if the taxpayer is a trust,

(i) in the case where the time at which the taxation year ends is determined under paragraph 249(4)(*a*), the day that is

(A) in the case where that time occurs in a calendar year after the end of the trust's particular taxation year that ends on December 15 of that calendar year because of an election made under paragraph 132.11(1)(*a*), the balance-due day of the trust for the particular taxation year,

(B) in the case where clause (A) does not apply and the trust's particular taxation year that begins immediately after that time ends in the calendar year that includes that time, the balance-due day of the trust for the particular taxation year, and

(C) in any other case, 90 days after the end of the calendar year that includes that time, and

(ii) in any other case, the day that is 90 days after the end of the taxation year,

(*b*) where the taxpayer is an individual who died after October in the year and before May in the following taxation year, the day that is 6 months after the day of death,

(*c*) in any other case where the taxpayer is an individual, April 30 in the following taxation year, and

(*d*) where the taxpayer is a corporation,

(i) the day that is three months after the day on which the taxation year (in this subparagraph referred to as the "current year") ends, if

(A) an amount was deducted under section 125 in computing the corporation's tax payable under this Part for the current year or for its preceding taxation year,

(B) the corporation is, throughout the current year, a Canadian-controlled private corporation, and

(C) either

(I) in the case of a corporation that is not associated with another corporation in the current year, its taxable income for its preceding taxation year (determined before taking into consideration the specified future tax consequences for that preceding taxation year) does not exceed its business limit for that preceding taxation year, or

(II) in the case of a corporation that is associated with one or more other corporations in the current year, the total of the taxable incomes of the corporation and of those other corporations for their last taxation years that ended in the last calendar year that ended before the end of the current year (determined before taking into consideration the specified future tax consequences for those last taxation years) does not exceed the total of the business limits of the corporation and of those other corporations for those last taxation years, and

(ii) the day that is two months after the day on which the taxation year ends, in any other case;

History: S. 248(1), paragraph (*a*) of the definition "balance-due day" was replaced by S.C. 2016, c. 12, s. 63(3), deemed to have come into force on March 21, 2013, and formerly read:

(*a*) where the taxpayer is a trust, the day that is 90 days after the end of the year,

Related Sections: 251.2(7) Filing and other deadlines; S. 125.4(3) Tax credit; s. 127.1(1) Refundable investment tax credit; s. 127.41(3) Deemed payment of Part I tax; s. 153(2) Deemed withholding; s. 156.1 No instalment required; s. 157(1) Payment by corporations; s. 161(2.2) Contra interest; s. 161(6.2) Flow-through share renunciations.

Information Circulars: IC 98-1R4 Collections Policies.

"bank" —"bank" means a bank within the meaning assigned by section 2 of the *Bank Act* (other than a federal credit union) or an authorized foreign bank;

History: S. 248(1), the definition "bank" was replaced by S.C. 2010, c. 12, s. 2109(1), in force December 19, 2012 (P.C. 2012-1623, SI/2012-99). S. 248(1), the definition "bank" formerly read:

"bank"—"bank" means a bank within the meaning assigned by section 2 of the *Bank Act* or an authorized foreign bank;

Related Sections: S. 20.2 Interest — authorized foreign bank — interpretation.

"bankrupt" —"bankrupt" has the meaning assigned by the *Bankruptcy and Insolvency Act*;

Related Sections: 181.1(3) Where tax not payable; 186.1 Exempt corporations.

"benefit under a deferred profit sharing plan" —"benefit under a deferred profit sharing plan" received by a taxpayer in a taxation year means the total of all amounts each of which is an amount received by the taxpayer in the year from a trustee under the plan, minus any amounts deductible under subsections 147(11) and (12) in computing the income of the taxpayer for the year;

"bituminous sands" —"bituminous sands" means sands or other rock materials containing naturally occurring hydrocarbons (other than coal) which hydrocarbons have

(*a*) a viscosity, determined in a prescribed manner, equal to or greater than 10,000 centipoise, or

(*b*) a density, determined in a prescribed manner, equal to or less than 12 degrees API;

Related Regulations: 1107.

"borrowed money" —"borrowed money" includes the proceeds to a taxpayer from the sale of a post-dated bill drawn by the taxpayer on a bank;

Interpretation Bulletins: *Secondary* — IT-533 Interest deductibility and related issues.

"business" —"business" includes a profession, calling, trade, manufacture or undertaking of any kind whatever and, except for the purposes of paragraph 18(2)(*c*), section 54.2, subsection 95(1) and paragraph 110.6(14)(*f*), an adventure or concern in the nature of trade but does not include an office or employment;

Related Sections: S. 18(2)(*c*) Limit on certain interest and property tax; s. 54.2 Certain shares deemed to be capital property; s. 110.6(14) Related persons, etc.

Income Tax Technical News: Issue No. 41, Meaning of "Business".

Interpretation Bulletins: *Primary* — IT-459 Adventure or concern in the nature of trade. *Secondary* — IT-218R Profit, capital gains and losses from the sale of real estate, including farmland and inherited land and conversion of real estate from capital property to inventory and vice versa.

Cases: In determining whether a taxpayer's conduct constituted an adventure in the nature of trade, the critical factor is the intention of the taxpayer at the time the property in question is acquired, and such intention is to be ascertained from the taxpayer's whole course of conduct. The taxpayer, who was employed in the securities industry for several years, was found to be trading in securities personally as a business activity, or at least as part of an adventure in the nature of trade. *Andrew Foote v. The Queen*, 2017 DTC 1032 (TCC)

The taxpayers participated extensively in sports lotteries using a methodology that increased their potential payout and risk significantly. Although they lost 95% of the time, they had net winnings of $5,523,088. However, they were not professional gamblers who had a system to assess and minimize risks. The winnings were not business income but tax-exempt capital gains. *Leblanc et al. v. The Queen*, 2007 DTC 307 (T.C.C.)

The meaning of an "adventure in the nature of trade" has been discussed at length in *M.N.R. v. Taylor*, 56 DTC 1125 (Ex. Ct.)

"business limit" —"business limit" of a corporation for a taxation year means the amount determined under section 125 to be its business limit for the year;

Related Sections: S. 87(2)(*oo*.1) Refundable investment tax credit and balance-due day; s. 88(1)(*e*.9) Winding-up.

"business number" —"business number" means the number (other than a Social Insurance Number or trust account number) used by the Minister to identify

(*a*) a corporation or partnership, or

(*b*) any other association or taxpayer that carries on a business or is required by this Act to deduct or withhold an amount from an amount paid or credited or deemed to be paid or credited under this Act

and of which the Minister has notified the corporation, partnership, association or taxpayer;

History: S. 248(1), the portion of the definition "business number" before paragraph (*a*), was replaced by S.C. 2018, c. 12, s. 37(1), applicable to the 2018 and subsequent taxation years, and formerly read:

"business number" means the number (other than a Social Insurance Number) used by the Minister to identify

Related Sections: S. 162(6) Failure to provide identification number; s. 221(1) Regulations; s. 237(1.1) Production of number; s. 237(2) Number required in information returns; s. 237.1(7) Information return; s. 239(2.3) Offence with respect to an identification number; s. 241(4) Where taxpayer information may be disclosed.

"Canadian banking business" —"Canadian banking business" means the business carried on by an authorized foreign bank through a permanent establishment (as defined by regulation) in Canada, other than business conducted through a representative office registered or required to be registered under section 509 of the *Bank Act*;

Related Regulations: 8201.

Related Sections: S. 18(5), "outstanding debts to specified non residents"; s. 20.2 Interest — authorized foreign bank — interpretation; s. 33.1(1), "foreign bank"; s. 115(1)(*a*)(ii) Non-resident's taxable income in Canada; s. 116(6)(*f*) Definition of "excluded property"; s. 126(1.1) Authorized foreign bank; s. 142.7(3) Branch-establishment rollover; s. 142.7(7) Reserves; s. 142.7(8) Assumption of debt obligation; s. 181.3(3)(*e*) Capital of financial institution; s. 181.3(4)(*c*) Investment allowance of financial institution; s. 190.13(*d*) Capital; s. 190.14(1)(*c*) Investment in related institutions; s. 212(13.3) Application of Part XIII to authorized foreign bank; s. 218.2(2)(*a*) Taxable interest expense.

"Canadian-controlled private corporation" —"Canadian-controlled private corporation" has the meaning assigned by subsection 125(7);

"Canadian corporation" —"Canadian corporation" has the meaning assigned by subsection 89(1);

"Canadian development expense" —"Canadian development expense" has the meaning assigned by subsection 66.2(5);

Interpretation Bulletins: *Secondary* — IT-458R2 Canadian-controlled private corporation.

"Canadian exploration and development expenses" — "Canadian exploration and development expenses" has the meaning assigned by subsection 66(15);

"Canadian exploration expense" —"Canadian exploration expense" has the meaning assigned by subsection 66.1(6);

"Canadian field processing" —"Canadian field processing" means, except as otherwise prescribed,

(*a*) the processing in Canada of raw natural gas at a field separation and dehydration facility,

(*b*) the processing in Canada of raw natural gas at a natural gas processing plant to any stage that is not beyond the stage of natural gas that is acceptable to a common carrier of natural gas,

(*c*) the processing in Canada of hydrogen sulphide derived from raw natural gas to any stage that is not beyond the marketable sulphur stage,

(*d*) the processing in Canada of natural gas liquids, at a natural gas processing plant where the input is raw natural gas derived from a natural accumulation of natural gas, to any stage that is not beyond the marketable liquefied petroleum stage or its equivalent,

(*e*) the processing in Canada of crude oil (other than heavy crude oil recovered from an oil or gas well or a tar sands deposit) recovered from a natural accumulation of petroleum to any stage that is not beyond the crude oil stage or its equivalent, and

(*f*) prescribed activities

and, for the purposes of paragraphs (*b*) to (*d*),

(*g*) gas is not considered to cease to be raw natural gas solely because of its processing at a field separation and dehydration facility until it is received by a common carrier of natural gas, and

(*h*) where all or part of a natural gas processing plant is devoted primarily to the recovery of ethane, the plant, or the part of the plant, as the case may be, is considered not to be a natural gas processing plant;

Related Sections: S. 125.1(3) Definitions.

Canadian Petroleum Tax Journal: Resource Allowance — The New Certainty?, B. David Nielsen and Nelson M. Whitmore, 1997, Vol. 10, No. 1.

Income Tax Folios: S4-F15-C1 Manufacturing and Processing.

Interpretation Bulletins: *Primary* — IT-476R Capital cost allowance — Equipment used in petroleum and natural gas activities.

"Canadian oil and gas property expense" —"Canadian oil and gas property expense" has the meaning assigned by subsection 66.4(5);

"Canadian partnership" —"Canadian partnership" has the meaning assigned by section 102;

"Canadian real, immovable or resource property" — "Canadian real, immovable or resource property" means

(*a*) a property that would, if this Act were read without reference to the definition "real or immovable property" in subsection 122.1(1), be a real or immovable property situated in Canada,

(*b*) a Canadian resource property,

(*c*) a timber resource property,

(*d*) a share of the capital stock of a corporation, an income or a capital interest in a trust or an interest in a partnership — other than a taxable Canadian corporation, a SIFT trust (determined without reference to subsection 122.1(2)), a SIFT partnership (determined without reference to subsection 197(8)) or a real estate investment trust (as defined in subsection 122.1(1)) — if more than 50% of the fair market value of the share or interest is derived directly or indirectly from one or any combination of properties described in paragraphs (*a*) to (*c*), or

(*e*) any right to or interest in — or, for civil law, any right to or in — any property described in any of paragraphs (*a*) to (*d*);

History: S. 248(1), paragraph (*d*) of the definition "Canadian real, immovable or resource property" was replaced by S.C. 2013, c. 34, s. 358(8), applicable to

(*a*) taxation years of a trust that end after 2006 and before 2011 if

(i) investments in the trust are, in one or more of those taxation years, listed or traded on a stock exchange or other public market, and

(ii) the trust elects, by notifying the Minister of National Revenue in writing on or before its filing due-date for its taxation year that includes June 26, 2013, to have S.C. 2013, c. 34, s. 358(1)-(10) so apply; and

(*b*) the 2011 and subsequent taxation years.

S. 248(1), paragraph (*d*) of the definition "Canadian real, immovable or resource property" formerly read:

(*d*) a share of the capital stock of a corporation, an income or capital interest in a trust or an interest in a partnership (other than a taxable Canadian corporation, a SIFT trust or a SIFT partnership), if more than 50% of the fair market value of the share or interest is derived directly or indirectly from one or any combination of properties described in paragraphs (*a*) to (*c*), or

S. 248(1), paragraph (*d*) of the definition "Canadian real or immovable property" was replaced by S.C. 2009, c. 2, s. 76(3), deemed to have come into force on October 31, 2006. S. 248(1), paragraph (*d*) of the definition "Canadian real or immovable property" formerly read:

(*d*) a share of the capital stock of a corporation, an income or a capital interest in a trust or an interest in a partnership, if more than 50% of the fair market value of the share or interest is derived directly or indirectly from one or any combination of properties described in paragraphs (*a*) to (*c*), or

Related Sections: S. 122.1(1), "non-portfolio property"; s. 248(1), "non-portfolio property".

"Canadian resident partnership" —"Canadian resident partnership" means a partnership that, at any time in respect of which the expression is relevant,

(*a*) is a Canadian partnership,

(*b*) would, if it were a corporation, be resident in Canada (including, for greater certainty, a partnership that has its central management and control in Canada), or

(*c*) was formed under the laws of a province;

Related Sections: S. 102, s. 197(1), "SIFT partnership".

"Canadian resource property" —"Canadian resource property" has the meaning assigned by subsection 66(15);

"capital dividend" —"capital dividend" has the meaning assigned by section 83;

"capital gain" —"capital gain" for a taxation year from the disposition of any property has the meaning assigned by section 39;

"capital interest" —"capital interest" of a taxpayer in a trust has the meaning assigned by subsection 108(1);

"capital loss" —"capital loss" for a taxation year from the disposition of any property has the meaning assigned by section 39;

"capital property" —"capital property" has the meaning assigned by section 54;

"cash method" —"cash method" has the meaning assigned by subsection 28(1);

"cemetery care trust" —"cemetery care trust" has the meaning assigned by subsection 148.1(1);

"common-law partner" —"common-law partner", with respect to a taxpayer at any time, means a person who cohabits at that time in a conjugal relationship with the taxpayer and

(*a*) has so cohabited throughout the 12-month period that ends at that time, or

(*b*) would be the parent of a child of whom the taxpayer is a parent, if this Act were read without reference to paragraphs 252(1)(*c*) and (*e*) and subparagraph 252(2)(*a*)(iii),

and, for the purpose of this definition, where at any time the taxpayer and the person cohabit in a conjugal relationship, they are, at any particular time after that time, deemed to be cohabiting in a conjugal relationship unless they were living separate and apart at the particular time for a period of at least 90 days that includes the particular time because of a breakdown of their conjugal relationship;

History: S. 248(1), the definition "common-law partner" was replaced by S.C. 2013, c. 34, s. 358(1), applicable in determining whether a person is, for the 2001 and subsequent taxation years, a common-law partner of a taxpayer, except that it does not apply to so determine whether a person is a common-law partner of a taxpayer for a taxation year to which an election, made under section 144 of the *Modernization of Benefits and Obligations Act* [S.C. 2000, c. 12], applied before February 27, 2004. However, on and after February 27, 2004, no such election may be made to affect a current or subsequent taxation year.

S. 248(1), the definition "common-law partner" formerly read:

"common-law partner"—"common-law partner", with respect to a taxpayer at any time, means a person who cohabits at that time in a conjugal relationship with the taxpayer and

(*a*) has so cohabited with the taxpayer for a continuous period of at least one year, or

(*b*) would be the parent of a child of whom the taxpayer is a parent, if this Act were read without reference to paragraphs 252(1)(*c*) and (*e*) and subparagraph 252(2)(*a*)(iii),

and, for the purposes of this definition, where at any time the taxpayer and the person cohabit in a conjugal relationship, they are, at any particular time after that time, deemed to be cohabiting in a conjugal relationship unless they were not cohabiting at the particular time for a period of at least 90 days that includes the particular time because of a breakdown of their conjugal relationship;

Income Tax Folios: *Primary* — S1-F3-C1 Child Care Expense Deduction.

Interpretation Bulletins: *Secondary* — IT-307R4 Spousal or common-law partner registered retirement savings plans.

"common-law partnership" —"common-law partnership" means the relationship between two persons who are common-law partners of each other;

"common share" —"common share" means a share the holder of which is not precluded on the reduction or redemption of the capital stock from participating in the assets of the corporation beyond the amount paid up on that share plus a fixed premium and a defined rate of dividend;

Interpretation Bulletins: *Secondary* — IT-116R3 Rights to buy additional shares.

"controlled foreign affiliate" —"controlled foreign affiliate" has, except as expressly otherwise provided in this Act, the meaning assigned by subsection 95(1);

History: S. 248(1), the definition "controlled foreign affiliate" was replaced by S.C. 2013, c. 34, s. 358(2), applicable to taxation years that begin after 2006, and formerly read:

"controlled foreign affiliate"—"controlled foreign affiliate" has the meaning assigned by subsection 95(1);

"corporation" —"corporation" includes an incorporated company;

Canadian Tax Foundation: Boidman and Kandev, *Foreign Entity Classification and the Meaning of "Corporation"/"Société" in the Income Tax Act*, 2009 Canadian Tax Journal 4:880–904.

Tax Profile: October 2007 — Will Canadian Unlimited Liability Companies Survive?; July 2005 — Alberta Introduces Alberta Unlimited Liability Corporations.

Tax Topics: No. 2067, What Is An LLC?.

No. 1836, Oh Say Can You (LL)C? A Case Comment on Boliden Westmin Ltd. v. British Columbia.

Income Tax Technical News: Issue No. 38, Foreign Entity Classification.

Interpretation Bulletins: *Secondary* — IT-432R2 Benefits conferred on shareholders.

Tax Window Files: IFA 2016 Q.1: Classification of U.S. LLPs & LLLPs, *May 26, 2016*, CRA Document No. 2016-0642051C6; 2016 STEP - Q8 - U.S. LLPs & LLLPs Classification, *June 10, 2016*, CRA Document No. 2016-0634951C6; Conversion of Delaware corporation to LLC, *16XXXX*, CRA Document No. 2015-0615041R3; Dutch Cooperative - 93.2 & 95(2)(c), *16XXXX*, CRA Document No. 2015-0571441R3; Classification of a Delaware LLLP, *February 13, 2017*, CRA Document No. 2015-0587691I7; Classification of Florida LLLP, *February 13, 2017*, CRA Document No. 2015-0568011I7; Dutch Co-Op Entity Classification, *June 21, 2016*, CRA Document No. 2015-0581151I7; Netherlands Antilles private foundation, *October 4, 2010*, CRA Document No. 2008-0289461I7.

Cases: A reference in the *Income Tax Act* simply to a "corporation" will include any corporation regardless of where it is incorporated. See *International Fruit Distributors Ltd. v. M.N.R.*, 55 DTC 1186 (S.C.C.)

"corporation incorporated in Canada" —"corporation incorporated in Canada" includes a corporation incorporated in any part of Canada before or after it became part of Canada;

"cost amount" —"cost amount" to a taxpayer of any property at any time means, except as expressly otherwise provided in this Act,

(*a*) where the property was depreciable property of the taxpayer of a prescribed class, the amount that would be that proportion of the undepreciated capital cost to the taxpayer of property of that class at that time that the capital cost to the taxpayer of the property is of the capital cost to the taxpayer of all property of that class that had not been disposed of by the taxpayer before that time if subsection 13(7) were read without reference to paragraph 13(7)(*e*) and if

(i) paragraph 13(7)(*b*) were read as follows:

"(*b*) where a taxpayer, having acquired property for some other purpose, has commenced at a later time to use it for the purpose of gaining or producing income, the taxpayer shall be deemed to have acquired it at that later time at a capital cost to the taxpayer equal to the fair market value of the property at that later time;", and

(ii) subparagraph 13(7)(*d*)(i) were read as follows:

"(i) if the use regularly made by the taxpayer of the property for the purpose of gaining or producing income has increased, the taxpayer shall be deemed to have acquired at that time depreciable property of that class at a capital cost equal to the proportion of its fair market value at that time that the amount of the increase in the use regularly made by the taxpayer of the property for that purpose is of the whole of the use regularly made of the property, and"

(*b*) where the property was capital property (other than depreciable property) of the taxpayer, its adjusted cost base to the taxpayer at that time,

(*c*) where the property was property described in an inventory of the taxpayer, its value at that time as determined for the purpose of computing the taxpayer's income,

(*c*.1) where the taxpayer was a financial institution in its taxation year that includes that time and the property was a mark-to-market property for the year, the cost to the taxpayer of the property,

(*d*) (Repealed.)

(*d*.1) where the property was a loan or lending asset (other than a net income stabilization account or a property in respect of which paragraph (*b*), (*c*), (*c*.1) or (*d*.2) applies), the amortized cost of the property to the taxpayer at that time,

(*d*.2) where the taxpayer was a financial institution in its taxation year that includes that time and the property was a specified debt obligation (other than a mark-to-market property for the year), the tax basis of the property to the taxpayer at that time,

(*e*) where the property was a right of the taxpayer to receive an amount, other than property that is

(i) a debt the amount of which was deducted under paragraph 20(1)(*p*) in computing the taxpayer's income for a taxation year that ended before that time,

(ii) a net income stabilization account,

(iii) a right in respect of which paragraph (*b*), (*c*), (*c*.1), (*d*.1) or (*d*.2) applies, or

(iv) a right to receive production (as defined in subsection 18.1(1)) to which a matchable expenditure (as defined in subsection 18.1(1)) relates,

the amount the taxpayer has a right to receive,

(*e*.1) where the property was a policy loan (within the meaning assigned by subsection 138(12)) of an insurer, nil,

(*e*.2) where the property is an interest of a beneficiary under a qualifying environmental trust, nil, and

(*f*) in any other case, the cost to the taxpayer of the property as determined for the purpose of computing the taxpayer's income, except to the extent that that cost has been deducted in computing the taxpayer's income for any taxation year ending before that time;

and, for the purposes of this definition, "financial institution", "mark-to-market property" and "specified debt obligation" have the meanings assigned by subsection 142.2(1), and "tax basis" has the meaning assigned by subsection 142.4(1);

History: S. 248(1), paragraph (*d*) of the definition of "cost amount" was repealed by S.C. 2016, c. 12, s. 63(4), in force January 1, 2017, and formerly read:

(*d*) where the property was eligible capital property of the taxpayer in respect of a business, 4/3 of the amount that would, but for subsection 14(3), be determined by the formula

$$A \times B/C$$

where

A is the cumulative eligible capital of the taxpayer in respect of the business at that time,

B is the fair market value at that time of the property, and

C is the fair market value at that time of all the eligible capital property of the taxpayer in respect of the business,

Related Sections: S. 13(7) Rules applicable; s. 14(3) Acquisition of eligible capital property; s. 20(1)(*p*) Bad debts; s. 54, "adjusted cost base", "eligible capital property"; s. 132(6) Meaning of "mutual fund trust"; s. 132.2(1) Mutual funds — qualifying exchange; s. 248(1), "adjusted cost base", "amortized cost", "amount", "business", "eligible capital property", "inventory", "lending asset", "net income stabilization account", "property", "qualifying environmental trust", "taxpayer"; s. 257 Negative amounts.

Income Tax Folios: *Primary* — S3-F4-C1 General Discussion of Capital Cost Allowance. *Secondary* — S4-F7-C1 Amalgamations of Canadian Corporations.

Interpretation Bulletins: *Secondary* — IT-291R3 Transfer of property to a corporation under subsection 85(1). *Secondary* — IT-142R3 Settlement of debts on the winding-up of a corporation; IT-528 Transfers of funds between registered plans.

"credit union" — "credit union" has the meaning assigned by subsection 137(6), except for the purposes of Part XV.1;

History: S. 248(1), the definition of "credit union" was replaced by S.C. 2014, c. 20, s. 30(1), in force January 1, 2015, and formerly read:

"credit union" — "credit union" has the meaning assigned by subsection 137(6);

"cumulative eligible capital" — (Repealed by S.C. 2016, c. 12, s. 63(1).)

History: S. 248(1), the definition of "cumulative eligible capital" was repealed by S.C. 2016, c. 12, s. 63(1), in force January 1, 2017, and formerly read:

"cumulative eligible capital" — "cumulative eligible capital" has the meaning assigned by subsection 14(5);

"death benefit" — "death benefit" means the total of all amounts received by a taxpayer in a taxation year on or after the death of an employee in recognition of the employee's service in an office or employment minus

(*a*) where the taxpayer is the only person who has received such an amount and who is a surviving spouse or common-law partner of the employee (which person is, in this definition, referred to as the "surviving spouse or common-law partner"), the lesser of

(i) the total of all amounts so received by the taxpayer in the year, and

(ii) the amount, if any, by which $10,000 exceeds the total of all amounts received by the taxpayer in preceding taxation years on or after the death of the employee in recognition of the employee's service in an office or employment, or

(*b*) where the taxpayer is not the surviving spouse or common-law partner of the employee, the lesser of

(i) the total of all amounts so received by the taxpayer in the year, and

(ii) that proportion of

(A) the amount, if any, by which $10,000 exceeds the total of all amounts received by the surviving spouse or common-law partner of the employee at any time on or after the death of the employee in recognition of the employee's service in an office or employment

that

(B) the amount described in subparagraph (i)

is of

(C) the total of all amounts received by all taxpayers other than the surviving spouse or common-law partner of the employee at any time on or after the death of the employee in recognition of the employee's service in an office or employment;

Related Sections: S. 248(1), "amount", "common-law partner", "employee", "employment", "office"; s. 249(1) Definition of "taxation year".

Interpretation Bulletins: *Primary* — IT-508R Death benefits.

"deferred amount" —"deferred amount" at the end of a taxation year under a salary deferral arrangement in respect of a taxpayer means

(*a*) in the case of a trust governed by the arrangement, any amount that a person has a right under the arrangement at the end of the year to receive after the end of the year where the amount has been received, is receivable or may at any time become receivable by the trust as, on account or in lieu of salary or wages of the taxpayer for services rendered in the year or a preceding taxation year, and

(*b*) in any other case, any amount that a person has a right under the arrangement at the end of the year to receive after the end of the year,

and, for the purposes of this definition, a right under the arrangement shall include a right that is subject to one or more conditions unless there is a substantial risk that any one of those conditions will not be satisfied;

"deferred profit sharing plan" —"deferred profit sharing plan" has the meaning assigned by subsection 147(1);

"depreciable property" —"depreciable property" has the meaning assigned by subsection 13(21);

"derivative forward agreement" —"derivative forward agreement", of a taxpayer, means an agreement entered into by the taxpayer to purchase or sell a capital property if

(*a*) the term of the agreement exceeds 180 days or the agreement is part of a series of agreements with a term that exceeds 180 days,

(*b*) in the case of a purchase agreement, the difference between the fair market value of the property delivered on settlement, including partial settlement, of the agreement and the amount paid for the property is attributable, in whole or in part, to an underlying interest (including a value, price, rate, variable, index, event, probability or thing) other than

(i) revenue, income or cashflow in respect of the property over the term of the agreement, changes in the fair market value of the property over the term of the agreement, or any similar criteria in respect of the property,

Proposed Amendment

2019 Federal Budget Resolutions

Subparagraph (*b*)(i) of the definition *derivative forward agreement in* subsection 248(1) of the Act is replaced by the following:

(i) revenue, income or cashflow in respect of the property over the term of the agreement, changes in the fair market value of the property over the term of the agreement, or any similar criteria in respect of the property unless

(A) the property is

(I) a *Canadian security* (*in* this subparagraph as defined in subsection 39(6)), or

(II) an interest in a partnership the fair market value of which is derived, in whole or in part, from a Canadian security,

(B) the purchase agreement is an agreement to acquire property from

(I) a tax-indifferent investor, or

(II) a *financial institution* (as defined in subsection 142.2(1)), and

(C) it can reasonably be considered that one of the main purposes of the series of transactions or events, or any transaction or event in the series, of which the purchase agreement is part is for all or any portion of the capital gain on a disposition of a Canadian security referred to in clause (A) — as part of the same series of transactions or events — to be attributable to amounts paid or payable on the Canadian security by the issuer of the Canadian security during the term of the purchase agreement as

(I) interest,

(II) dividends, or

(III) income of a trust other than income paid out of the taxable capital gains of the trust,

Applicable: Deemed to have come into force on March 19, 2019. However, it does not apply before 2020 in respect of

(a) an agreement that is entered into after the final settlement of another derivative forward agreement (in this paragraph referred to as the "prior agreement") if

(i) having regard to the source of the funds used to purchase the property to be sold under the agreement, it is reasonable to conclude that the agreement is a continuation of the prior agreement,

(ii) the terms of the agreement and the prior agreement are substantially similar,

(iii) the final settlement date under the agreement is before 2020,

(iv) subsection (1) does not apply to the prior agreement, and

(v) the notional amount of the agreement is at all times less than or equal to the amount determined by the formula

$$(A + B + C + D + E) - (F + G)$$

where

A is the notional amount of the agreement when it is entered into,

B is the total of all amounts each of which is an increase in the notional amount of the agreement, at or before that time, that is attributable to the underlying interest,

C is the amount of the taxpayer's cash on hand immediately before March 19, 2019 that was committed, before March 19, 2019, to be invested under the agreement,

D is the total of all amounts each of which is an increase, at or before that time, in the notional amount of the agreement that is attributable to the final settlement of another derivative forward agreement if subsection (1) does not apply to the other agreement,

E is the lesser of

(A) either

(I) if the prior agreement was entered into before March 19, 2019, the amount, if any, by which the amount determined under subparagraph (i) of the description of F in paragraph (*b*) for the prior agreement immediately before it was finally settled exceeds the total determined under subparagraph (ii) of the description of F in paragraph (*b*) for the prior agreement immediately before it was finally settled, or

(II) in any other case, the amount, if any, by which the amount determined under this clause for the prior agreement immediately before it was finally settled exceeds the total determined under clause (B) for the prior agreement immediately before it was finally settled, and

(B) the total of all amounts each of which is an increase in the notional amount of the agreement before 2020 that is not otherwise described in this formula,

F is the total of all amounts each of which is a decrease in the notional amount of the agreement, at or before that time, that is attributable to the underlying interest, and

G is the total of all amounts each of which is the amount of a partial settlement of the agreement, at or before that time, to the extent that it is not reinvested in the agreement; or

(b) an agreement that is entered into before March 19, 2019, unless at any time on or after March 19, 2019, the notional amount of the agreement exceeds the amount determined by the formula

$$(A + B + C + D + E + F) - (G + H)$$

where

A is the notional amount of the agreement immediately before March 19, 2019,

B is the total of all amounts each of which is an increase in the notional amount of the agreement, on or after March 19, 2019 and at or before that time, that is attributable to the underlying interest,

C is the amount of the taxpayer's cash on hand immediately before March 19, 2019 that was committed, before March 19, 2019, to be invested under the agreement,

D is the amount, if any, of an increase, on or after March 19, 2019 and at or before that time, in the notional amount of the agreement as a consequence of the exercise of an over-allotment option granted before March 19, 2019,

E is the total of all amounts each of which is an increase, on or after March 19, 2019 and at or before that time, in the notional amount of the agreement that is attributable to the final settlement of another derivative forward agreement if subsection (1) does not apply to the other agreement,

F is the lesser of

(i) 5% of the notional amount of the agreement immediately before March 19, 2019, and

(ii) the total of all amounts each of which is an increase in the notional amount of the agreement on or after March 19, 2019 and before 2020 that is not otherwise described in this formula,

G is the total of all amounts each of which is a decrease in the notional amount of the agreement, on or after March 19, 2019 and at or before that time, that is attributable to the underlying interest, and

H is the total of all amounts each of which is the amount of a partial settlement of the agreement, on or after March 19, 2019 and at or before that time, to the extent that it is not reinvested in the agreement.

The notional amount of a derivative forward agreement at any time is the fair market value at that time of the property that would be acquired under the agreement if the agreement were finally settled at that time.

(ii) if the purchase price is denominated in the currency of a country other than Canada, changes in the value of the Canadian currency relative to that other currency, or

(iii) an underlying interest that relates to a purchase of currency, if it can reasonably be considered that the purchase is agreed to by the taxpayer in order to reduce its risk of fluctuations in the value of the currency in which a purchase or sale by the taxpayer of a capital property is denominated, in which an obligation that is a capital property of the taxpayer is denominated or from which a capital property of the taxpayer derives its value, and

(*c*) in the case of a sale agreement,

(i) the difference between the sale price of the property and the fair market value of the property at the time the agreement is entered into by the taxpayer is attributable, in whole or in part, to an underlying interest (including a value, price, rate, variable, index, event, probability or thing) other than

(A) revenue, income or cashflow in respect of the property over the term of the agreement, changes in the fair market value of the property over the term of the agreement, or any similar criteria in respect of the property,

(B) if the sale price is denominated in the currency of a country other than Canada, changes in the value of the Canadian currency relative to that other currency, or

(C) an underlying interest that relates to a sale of currency, if it can reasonably be considered that the sale is agreed to by the taxpayer in order to reduce its risk of fluctuations in the value of the currency in which a purchase or sale by the taxpayer of a capital property is denominated, in which an obligation that is a capital property of the taxpayer is denominated or from which a capital property of the taxpayer derives its value, and

(ii) the agreement is part of an arrangement that has the effect — or would have the effect if the agreements that are part of the arrangement and that were entered into by persons or partnerships not dealing at arm's length with the taxpayer were entered into by the taxpayer instead of non-arm's length persons or partnerships — of eliminating a majority of the taxpayer's risk of loss and opportunity for gain or profit in respect of the property for a period of more than 180 days;

Editorial Note: Paragraph 12(1)(*z.7*) requires a taxpayer to include in income any profit derived from the acquisition or disposition of property under a derivative forward agreement. Conversely, where the purchase or sale under a derivative forward agreement results in a loss, a deduction is available under 20(1)(*xx*).

History: S. 248(1), subparagraph (*b*)(iii) of the definition "derivative forward agreement" was added by S.C. 2017, c. 33, s. 77(1), deemed in force March 21, 2013.

S. 248(1), clause (*c*)(i)(C) of the definition "derivative forward agreement" was added by S.C. 2017, c. 33, s. 77(2), deemed in force March 21, 2013.

S. 248(1), the definition "derivative forward agreement", was added by S.C. 2013, c. 40, s. 89(5), deemed to have come into force on March 21, 2013.

Related Sections: S. 12(1)(*z.7*) Derivative forward agreement; s. 20(1)(*xx*) Derivative forward agreement; s. 53(1)(*s*) [Adjustments to cost base — Derivative forward agreement]; s. 53(1)(*t*) [Adjustments to cost base — Derivative forward agreement]; s. 53(2)(*w*) [Amounts to be deducted — Derivative forward agreement]; s. 53(2)(*x*) [Amounts to be deducted — Derivative forward agreement].

Canadian Tax Foundation: Miller and Milet, *Derivative Forward Agreements and Synthetic Disposition Arrangements,* 2013 Conference Report 10:1-50.

Tax Profile: June 2013 — Exchangeable Shares and UPREITS — At Risk in Canada; June 2013 — 2013 Federal Budget.

"designated insurance property" —"designated insurance property" has the meaning assigned by subsection 138(12);

Related Sections: S. 85(1.1) Definition of "eligible property"; s. 115(1)*(b)* Non-resident's taxable income in Canada; s. 219 Branch tax.

"designated stock exchange" —"designated stock exchange" means a stock exchange, or that part of a stock exchange, for which a designation by the Minister of Finance under section 262 is in effect;

"designated surplus" — (Repealed by 1977-78, c. 1, s. 98(1).)

"disposition" —"disposition" of any property, except as expressly otherwise provided, includes

(*a*) any transaction or event entitling a taxpayer to proceeds of disposition of the property,

(*b*) any transaction or event by which,

(i) where the property is a share, bond, debenture, note, certificate, mortgage, hypothecary claim, agreement of sale or similar property, or interest, or for civil law a right, in it, the property is in whole or in part redeemed, acquired or cancelled,

(ii) where the property is a debt or any other right to receive an amount, the debt or other right is settled or cancelled,

(iii) where the property is a share, the share is converted because of an amalgamation or merger,

(iv) where the property is an option to acquire or dispose of property, the option expires, and

(v) a trust, that can reasonably be considered to act as agent for all the beneficiaries under the trust with respect to all dealings with all of the trust's property (unless the trust is described in any of paragraphs (*a*) to (*e*.1) of the definition "trust" in subsection 108(1)), ceases to act as agent for a beneficiary under the trust with respect to any dealing with any of the trust's property,

(*b*.1) where the property is an interest in a life insurance policy, a disposition within the meaning of section 148,

(*c*) any transfer of the property to a trust or, where the property is property of a trust, any transfer of the property to any beneficiary under the trust, except as provided by paragraph (*f*) or (*k*), and

(*d*) where the property is, or is part of, a taxpayer's capital interest in a trust, except as provided by paragraph (*h*) or (*i*), a payment made after 1999 to the taxpayer from the trust that can reasonably be considered to have been made because of the taxpayer's capital interest in the trust,

but does not include

(*e*) any transfer of the property as a consequence of which there is no change in the beneficial ownership of the property, except where the transfer is

(i) from a person or a partnership to a trust for the benefit of the person or the partnership,

(ii) from a trust to a beneficiary under the trust, or

(iii) from one trust maintained for the benefit of one or more beneficiaries under the trust to another trust maintained for the benefit of the same beneficiaries,

(*f*) any transfer of the property as a consequence of which there is no change in the beneficial ownership of the property, where

(i) the transferor and the transferee are trusts that are, at the time of the transfer, resident in Canada,

(ii) (Repealed by S.C. 2013, c. 34, s. 358(11).)

(iii) the transferee does not receive the property in satisfaction of the transferee's right as a beneficiary under the transferor trust,

(iv) the transferee held no property immediately before the transfer (other than property the cost of which is not included, for the purposes of this Act, in computing a balance of undeducted outlays, expenses or other amounts in respect of the transferee),

(v) the transferee does not file a written election with the Minister on or before the filing-due date for its taxation year in which the transfer is made (or on such later date as is acceptable to the Minister) that this paragraph not apply,

(vi) if the transferor is an amateur athlete trust, a cemetery care trust, an employee trust, a trust deemed by subsection 143(1) to exist in respect of a congregation that is a constituent part of a religious organization, a related segregated fund trust (in this paragraph having the meaning assigned by section 138.1), a trust described in paragraph 149(1)(*o.4*) or a trust governed by an eligible funeral arrangement, an employees profit sharing plan, a registered disability savings plan, a registered education savings plan, a registered supplementary unemployment benefit plan or a TFSA, the transferee is the same type of trust, and

(vii) the transfer results, or is part of a series of transactions or events that results, in the transferor ceasing to exist and, immediately before the time of the transfer or the beginning of that series, as the case may be, the transferee never held any property or held only property having a nominal value,

(*g*) (Repealed.)

(*h*) where the property is part of a capital interest of a taxpayer in a trust (other than a personal trust or a trust prescribed for the purpose of subsection 107(2)) that is described by reference to units issued by the trust, a payment after 1999 from the trust in respect of the capital interest, where the number of units in the trust that are owned by the taxpayer is not reduced because of the payment,

(*i*) where the property is a taxpayer's capital interest in a trust, a payment to the taxpayer after 1999 in respect of the capital interest to the extent that the payment

(i) is out of the income of the trust (determined without reference to subsection 104(6)) for a taxation year or out of the capital gains of the trust for the year, if the payment was made in the year or the right to the payment was acquired by the taxpayer in the year, or

(ii) is in respect of an amount designated in respect of the taxpayer by the trust under subsection 104(20),

(*j*) any transfer of the property for the purpose only of securing a debt or a loan, or any transfer by a creditor for the purpose only of returning property that had been used as security for a debt or a loan,

(*k*) any transfer of the property to a trust as a consequence of which there is no change in the beneficial ownership of the property, where the main purpose of the transfer is

(i) to effect payment under a debt or loan,

(ii) to provide assurance that an absolute or contingent obligation of the transferor will be satisfied, or

(iii) to facilitate either the provision of compensation or the enforcement of a penalty, in the event that an absolute or contingent obligation of the transferor is not satisfied,

(*l*) any issue of a bond, debenture, note, certificate, mortgage or hypothecary claim,

(*m*) any issue by a corporation of a share of its capital stock, or any other transaction that, but for this paragraph, would be a disposition by a corporation of a share of its capital stock, and

(*n*) a redemption, an acquisition or a cancellation of a share or of a right to acquire a share (which share or which right, as the case may be, is referred to in this paragraph as the "security") of the capital stock of a corporation (referred to in this paragraph as the "issuing corporation") held by another corporation (referred to in this paragraph as the "disposing corporation") if

(i) the redemption, acquisition or cancellation occurs as part of a merger or combination of two or more corporations (including the issuing corporation and the disposing corporation) to form one corporate entity (referred to in this paragraph as the "new corporation"),

(ii) the merger or combination

(A) is an amalgamation (within the meaning assigned by subsection 87(1)) to which subsection 87(11) does not apply,

(B) is an amalgamation (within the meaning assigned by subsection 87(1)) to which subsection 87(11) applies, if the issuing corporation and the disposing corporation are described by subsection 87(11) as the parent and the subsidiary, respectively,

(C) is a foreign merger (within the meaning assigned by subsection 87(8.1)), or

(D) would be a foreign merger (within the meaning assigned by subsection 87(8.1)) if subparagraph 87(8.1)(*c*)(ii) were read without reference to the words "that was resident in a country other than Canada", and

(iii) either

(A) the disposing corporation receives no consideration for the security, or

(B) in the case where the merger or combination is described by clause (ii)(C) or (D), the disposing corporation receives no consideration for the security other than property that was, immediately before the merger or combination, owned by the issuing corporation and that, on the merger or combination, becomes property of the new corporation;

History: S. 248(1), subparagraph (*f*)(vi) of the definition "disposition" was replaced by S.C. 2014, c. 39, s. 71(1), applicable to the 2016 and subsequent taxation years, and formerly read:

(vi) if the transferor is an amateur athlete trust, a cemetery care trust, an employee trust, an *inter vivos* trust deemed by subsection 143(1) to exist in respect of a congregation that is a constituent part of a religious organization, a related segregated fund trust (in this paragraph having the meaning assigned by section 138.1), a trust described in paragraph 149(1)(*o.4*) or a trust governed by an eligible funeral arrangement, an employees profit sharing plan, a registered disability savings plan, a registered education savings plan, a registered supplementary unemployment benefit plan or a TFSA, the transferee is the same type of trust, and

S. 248(1), subparagraph (*b*)(i) of the definition "disposition" was replaced by S.C. 2013, c. 34, s. 358(9), applicable to redemptions, acquisitions and cancellations that occur after December 23, 1998, and formerly read:

(i) where the property is a share, bond, debenture, note, certificate, mortgage, agreement of sale or similar property, or an interest in it, the property is redeemed in whole or in part or is cancelled,

S. 248(1), paragraph (*b.1*) of the definition "disposition" was added by S.C. 2013, c. 34, s. 358(10), applicable to taxation years that begin after 2006.

S. 248(1), subparagraph (*f*)(i) of the definition "disposition" was replaced by S.C. 2013, c. 34, s. 358(11), applicable to transfers that occur after February 27, 2004, and formerly read:

(i) the transferor and the transferee are trusts,

S. 248(1), subparagraph (*f*)(ii) of the definition "disposition" was repealed by S.C. 2013, c. 34, s. 358(11), applicable to transfers that occur after February 27, 2004, and formerly read:

(ii) the transfer is not by a trust resident in Canada to a non-resident trust,

S. 248(1), paragraph (*n*) of the definition "disposition" was added by S.C. 2013, c. 34, s. 358(12), applicable to redemptions, acquisitions and cancellations that occur after December 23, 1998.

Related Sections: S. 13(21), "proceeds of disposition"; s. 43(2) Ecological gifts; s. 54, "proceeds of disposition"; s. 52(6) Cost of right to receive from trust; s. 107(2) Distribution by personal trust; s. 107(2.1) Other distributions; s. 107.4(1) Qualifying disposition; s. 108(1), "capital interest"; s. 248(25.1) Trust-to-trust transfers; s. 248(25.2) Trusts to ensure obligations fulfilled.

Canadian Tax Foundation: Ewens and Flatters, *Toward a More Coherent Theory of Dispositions*, 1995 Canadian Tax Journal 5:1377–1411; Arnold and Ward, *Dispositions — A Critique of Revenue Canada's Interpretation*, 1980 Canadian Tax Journal 5:559.

Tax Profile: February 2002 — Transferring Property to a Trust After the Enactment of Bill C-22.

Tax Topics: No. 1663, Vive la Différence: The Tax Consequences of Conditional Obligations Under Civil Law and Common Law.

Income Tax Folios: *Primary* — S3-F4-C1 General Discussion of Capital Cost Allowance. *Secondary* — S4-F7-C1 Amalgamations of Canadian Corporations.

Interpretation Bulletins: *Primary* — IT-146R4 Shares entitling shareholders to choose taxable or capital dividends; IT-170R Sale of property — When included in income computation; IT-325R2 Property transfers after separation, divorce and annulment; IT-444R Corporations — Involuntary Dissolutions; IT-460 Dispositions — Absence of consideration. *Secondary* — IT-96R6 Options granted by corporations to acquire shares, bonds or debentures; IT-102R2 Conversion of property, other than real property, from or to inventory; IT-124R6 Contributions to registered retirement savings plans; IT-125R4 Disposition of resource properties; IT-126R2 Meaning of "winding-up"; IT-170R Sale of property — When included in income computation; IT-218R Profit, capital gains and losses from the sale of real estate, including farmland and inherited land and conversion of real estate from capital property to inventory and vice versa.

Tax Window Files: Whether re-designation of LPUs is a disposition., *17XXXX*, CRA Document No. 2017-0687061R3; Assignment of right to purchase, *March 7, 2016*, CRA Document No. 2015-0608211E5.

"dividend" —"dividend" includes a stock dividend (other than a stock dividend that is paid to a corporation or to a mutual fund trust by a non-resident corporation);

Interpretation Bulletins: *Primary* — IT-88R2 Stock dividends.

"dividend rental arrangement" —"dividend rental arrangement", of a person or a partnership (each of which is referred to in this definition as the *person*), means

(*a*) any arrangement entered into by the person where it can reasonably be considered that

(i) the main reason for the person entering into the arrangement was to enable the person to receive a dividend on a share of the capital stock of a corporation, other than a dividend on a prescribed share or on a share described in paragraph (*e*) of the definition *term preferred share* in this subsection or an amount deemed by subsection 15(3) to be received as a dividend on a share of the capital stock of a corporation, and

(ii) under the arrangement someone other than that person bears the risk of loss or enjoys the opportunity for gain or profit with respect to the share in any material respect,

(*b*) for greater certainty, any arrangement under which

(i) a corporation at any time receives on a particular share a taxable dividend that would, if this Act were read without reference to subsection 112(2.3), be deductible in computing its taxable income or taxable income earned in Canada for the taxation year that includes that time, and

(ii) the corporation or a partnership of which the corporation is a member is obligated to pay to another person or partnership an amount

(A) that is compensation for

(I) the dividend described in subparagraph (i),

(II) a dividend on a share that is identical to the particular share, or

(III) a dividend on a share that, during the term of the arrangement, can reasonably be expected to provide to a holder of the share the same or substantially the same proportionate risk of loss or opportunity for gain as the particular share, and

(B) that, if paid, would be deemed by subsection 260(5.1) to have been received by that other person or partnership, as the case may be, as a taxable dividend,

(*c*) any synthetic equity arrangement, in respect of a DRA share of the person, and

(*d*) one or more agreements or arrangements (other than agreements or arrangements described in paragraph (*c*)) entered into by the person, the connected person referred to in paragraph (*a*) of the definition *synthetic equity arrangement* or, for greater certainty, by any combination of the person and connected persons, if

(i) the agreements or arrangements have the effect, or would have the effect if each agreement or arrangement entered into by a connected person were entered into by the person, of eliminating all or substantially all of the person's risk of loss and opportunity for gain or profit in respect of a DRA share of the person,

(ii) as part of a series of transactions that includes these agreements or arrangements, a tax-indifferent investor, or a group of tax-indifferent investors each member of which is affiliated with every other member, obtains all or substantially all of the risk of loss and opportunity for gain or profit in respect of the DRA share or an *identical share* (as defined in subsection 112(10)), and

(iii) it is reasonable to conclude that one of the purposes of the series of transactions is to obtain the result described in subparagraph (ii);

Editorial Note: See the Editorial Note to s. 112(2.3).

History: S. 248(1), the definition "dividend rental arrangement" was replaced by S.C. 2016, c. 7, s. 48(1), applicable to

(*a*) dividends that are paid or become payable after April 2017; and

(*b*) dividends that are paid or become payable at any time after October 2015 and before May 2017 on a share if

(i) there is a synthetic equity arrangement, or one or more agreements or arrangements described by paragraph (*d*) of the definition *dividend rental arrangement* in subsection 248(1) in respect of the share at that time, and

(ii) after April 21, 2015 and before that time, all or any part of the synthetic equity arrangement, or the agreements or arrangements, referred to in subparagraph (i) — including an option, swap, futures contract, forward contract or other financial or commodity contract or instrument as well as a right or obligation under the terms of such a contract or instrument — that contributes or could contribute to the effect of providing all or substantially all of the risk of loss and opportunity for gain or profit, in respect of the share, to one or more persons or partnerships is

(A) entered into, acquired, extended or renewed after April 21, 2015, or

(B) in the case of a right to increase the notional amount under an agreement that is or is part of the synthetic equity arrangement, is exercised or acquired after April 21, 2015.

S. 248(1), the definition "dividend rental arrangement" formerly read:

"dividend rental arrangement"—"dividend rental arrangement", of a person or a partnership (each of which is referred to in this definition as the "person"),

(*a*) means any arrangement entered into by the person where it can reasonably be considered that

(i) the main reason for the person entering into the arrangement was to enable the person to receive a dividend on a share of the capital stock of a corporation, other than a dividend on a prescribed share or on a share described in paragraph (*e*) of the definition "term preferred share" in this subsection or an amount deemed by subsection 15(3) to be received as a dividend on a share of the capital stock of a corporation, and

(ii) under the arrangement someone other than that person bears the risk of loss or enjoys the opportunity for gain or profit with respect to the share in any material respect, and

(*b*) includes, for greater certainty, any arrangement under which

(i) a corporation at any time receives on a particular share a taxable dividend that would, if this Act were read without reference to subsection 112(2.3), be deductible in computing its taxable income or taxable income earned in Canada for the taxation year that includes that time, and

(ii) the corporation or a partnership of which the corporation is a member is obligated to pay to another person or partnership an amount

(A) that is compensation for

(I) the dividend described in subparagraph (i),

(II) a dividend on a share that is identical to the particular share, or

(III) a dividend on a share that, during the term of the arrangement, can reasonably be expected to provide to a holder of the share the same or substantially the same proportionate risk of loss or opportunity for gain as the particular share, and

(B) that, if paid, would be deemed by subsection 260(5.1) to have been received by that other person or partnership, as the case may be, as a taxable dividend;

S. 248(1), the definition "dividend rental arrangement" was replaced by S.C. 2013, c. 34, s. 358(3), applicable to arrangements made after December 20, 2002 and, subject to the application below, to an arrangement made after

November 2, 1998 and before December 21, 2002 if the parties to the arrangement jointly so elect in writing and file the election with the Minister of National Revenue by September 24, 2013 [within 90 days after royal assent] except that the reference to "subsection 260(5.1)" in clause (*b*)(ii)(B) of the definition "dividend rental arrangement" in subsection 248(1) is to be, in the application of that definition to any of those arrangements made before 2002, read as a reference to "subsection 260(5)".

S. 248(1), the definition "dividend rental arrangement" formerly read:

"dividend rental arrangement"—"dividend rental arrangement" of a person means any arrangement entered into by the person where it may reasonably be considered that

(*a*) the main reason for the person entering into the arrangement was to enable the person to receive a dividend on a share of the capital stock of a corporation, other than a dividend on a prescribed share or a share described in paragraph (*e*) of the definition "term preferred share" in this subsection or an amount deemed to be received as a dividend on a share of the capital stock of a corporation by reason of subsection 15(3), and

(*b*) under the arrangement someone other than that person bears the risk of loss or enjoys the opportunity for gain or profit with respect to the share in any material respect;

and for greater certainty includes any arrangement under which

(*c*) a corporation at any time receives on a particular share a taxable dividend that would, but for subsection 112(2.3), be deductible in computing its taxable income or taxable income earned in Canada for the taxation year that includes that time, and

(*d*) the corporation is obligated to pay to another person an amount as compensation for

(i) that dividend,

(ii) a dividend on a share that is identical to the particular share, or

(iii) a dividend on a share that, during the term of the arrangement, can reasonably be expected to provide to a holder of the share the same or substantially the same proportionate risk of loss or opportunity for gain as the particular share,

that, if paid, would be deemed by subsection 260(5.1) to have been received by that other person as a taxable dividend;

S. 248(1), the portion of paragraph (*d*) after subparagraph (iii) of the definition "dividend rental arrangement" was replaced by S.C. 2013, c. 34, s. 358(13), applicable to arrangements made after 2001 and before December 21, 2002, other than to an arrangement to which the above election applies.

S. 248(1), the portion of paragraph (*d*) after subparagraph (iii) of the definition "dividend rental arrangement" formerly read:

that, if paid, would be deemed by subsection 260(5) to have been received by that other person as a taxable dividend;

Related Sections: 82(1)(c); 112(2.3) Where no deduction permitted; 248(1) synthetic equity arrangement.

"DRA share"—"DRA share", of a person or partnership, means a share

(*a*) that is owned by the person or partnership,

(*b*) in respect of which the person or partnership is deemed to have received a dividend under subsection 260(5.1) and is provided with all or substantially all of the risk of loss and opportunity for gain or profit under an agreement or arrangement,

(*c*) that is held by a trust under which the person or partnership is a beneficiary and in respect of which the person or partnership is deemed to have received a dividend as a result of a designation by the trust under subsection 104(19),

(*d*) in respect of which the person or partnership is deemed to have received a dividend under subsection 82(2), or

(*e*) in any other case, in respect of which the person or partnership is (or would be in the absence of subsection 112(2.3)) entitled to a deduction under subsection 112(1) in respect of dividends received on the share;

Editorial Note: This definition is relevant to the meaning of "synthetic equity arrangement", which is a type of dividend rental arrangement; see the editorial note to subsection 112(2.3).

History: S. 248(1), the definition "DRA share" was added by S.C. 2016, c. 7, s. 48(2), deemed to have come into force on April 22, 2015.

"eligible capital amount" — (Repealed by S.C. 2016, c. 12, s. 63(1).)

History: S. 248(1), the definition "eligible capital amount" was repealed by S.C. 2016, c. 12, s. 63(1), in force January 1, 2017, and formerly read:

"eligible capital amount"—"eligible capital amount" has the meaning assigned by subsection 14(1);

"eligible capital expenditure" — (Repealed by S.C. 2016, c. 12, s. 63(1).)

History: S. 248(1), the definition "eligible capital expenditure" was repealed by S.C. 2016, c. 12, s. 63(1), in force January 1, 2017, and formerly read:

"eligible expenditure"—"eligible capital expenditure" has the meaning assigned by subsection 14(5);

Interpretation Bulletins: *Secondary* — IT-143R3 Meaning of eligible capital expenditure.

"eligible capital property" — (Repealed by S.C. 2016, c. 12, s. 63(1).)

History: S. 248(1), the definition "eligible capital property" was repealed by S.C. 2016, c. 12, s. 63(1), in force January 1, 2017, and formerly read:

"eligible capital property"—"eligible capital property" has the meaning assigned by section 54;

"eligible dividend"—"eligible dividend" has the meaning assigned by subsection 89(1);

"eligible funeral arrangement"—"eligible funeral arrangement" has the meaning assigned by subsection 148.1(1);

"eligible relocation"—"eligible relocation" means a relocation of a taxpayer in respect of which the following apply:

(*a*) the relocation occurs to enable the taxpayer

(i) to carry on a business or to be employed at a location (in section 62 and this definition referred to as "the new work location") that is, except if the taxpayer is absent from but resident in Canada, in Canada, or

(ii) to be a student in full-time attendance enrolled in a program at a post-secondary level at a location of a university, college or other educational institution (in section 62 and in this definition referred to as "the new work location"),

(*b*) the taxpayer ordinarily resided before the relocation at a residence (in section 62 and this definition referred to as "the old residence") and ordinarily resided after the relocation at a residence (in section 62 and this definition referred to as "the new residence"),

(*c*) except if the taxpayer is absent from but resident in Canada, both the old residence and the new residence are in Canada, and

(*d*) the distance between the old residence and the new work location is not less than 40 kilometres greater than the distance between the new residence and the new work location;

History: S. 248(1), the definition "eligible relocation" was replaced by S.C. 2013, c. 34, s. 358(4), applicable to taxation years that end after October 31, 2011, and formerly read:

"eligible relocation"—"eligible relocation" means a relocation of a taxpayer where

(*a*) the relocation occurs to enable the taxpayer

(i) to carry on a business or to be employed at a location in Canada (in section 62 and this subsection referred to as "the new work location"), or

(ii) to be a student in full-time attendance enrolled in a program at a post-secondary level at a location of a university, college or other educational institution (in section 62 and in this subsection referred to as "the new work location"), (*b*) both the residence at which the taxpayer ordinarily resided before the relocation (in section 62 and this subsection referred to as "the old residence") and the residence at which the taxpayer ordinarily resided after the relocation (in section 62 and this subsection referred to as "the new residence") are in Canada, and

(*c*) the distance between the old residence and the new work location is not less than 40 kilometres greater than the distance between the new residence and the new work location

except that, in applying subsections 6(19) to (23) and section 62 in respect of a relocation of a taxpayer who is absent from but resident in Canada, this definition shall be read without reference to the words "in Canada" in subparagraph (*a*)(i), and without reference to paragraph (*b*);

Related Sections: S. 6(22) Eligible housing loss; s. 62(1) Moving expenses; s. 62(2) Moving expenses of students; s. 64.1 Individuals absent from Canada; s. 80.4(1.1) Loan or debt from office or employment; s. 115(2)(*f*) Non-resident's taxable income in Canada; s. 248(1), "home relocation loan".

Cases: The distance from home must be determined by the shortest route that one might travel to work, as long as it is a normal route used by the public. In this case, the urban route was clearly a shorter route and a commonly used one. *Hauser v. The Queen*, 2015 DTC 1011 (T.C.C.)

"emissions allowance" —"emissions allowance" means an allowance, credit or similar instrument that represents a unit of emissions that can be used to satisfy a requirement under the laws of Canada or a province governing emissions of a regulated substance, such as greenhouse gas emissions;

History: S. 248(1), the definition "emissions allowance" was added by S.C. 2016, c. 12, s. 63(7), in force January 1, 2017. However, if a taxpayer elects under subsection 10(2) of the *Budget Implementation Act, 2016, No. 2* (Bill C-29), this amendment applies in respect of emissions allowances acquired by the taxpayer in taxation years that end after 2012.

Related Regulations: 7300.

Related Sections: 27.1(3) Expense restriction.

"emissions obligation" —"emissions obligation" means an obligation to surrender an emissions allowance, or an obligation that can otherwise be satisfied through the use of an emissions allowance, under a law of Canada or a province governing emissions of a regulated substance;

History: S. 248(1), the definition "emissions obligation" was added by S.C. 2016, c. 12, s. 63(7), in force January 1, 2017. However, if a taxpayer elects under subsection 10(2) of the *Budget Implementation Act, 2016, No. 2* (Bill C-29), this amendment applies in respect of emissions allowances acquired by the taxpayer in taxation years that end after 2012.

Related Regulations: 7300.

Related Sections: 27.1(3) Expense restriction.

"employed" —"employed" means performing the duties of an office or employment;

Related Sections: S. 54, "eligible capital property".

"employee" —"employee" includes officer;

"employee benefit plan" —"employee benefit plan" means an arrangement under which contributions are made by an employer or by any person with whom the employer does not deal at arm's length to another person (in this Act referred to as the "custodian" of an employee benefit plan) and under which one or more payments are to be made to or for the benefit of employees or former employees of the employer or persons who do not deal at arm's length with any such employee or former employee (other than a payment that, if section 6 were read without reference to subparagraph 6(1)(*a*)(ii) and paragraph 6(1)(*g*), would not be required to be included in computing the income of the recipient or of an employee or former employee), but does not include any portion of the arrangement that is

(*a*) a fund, plan or trust referred to in subparagraph 6(1)(*a*)(i) or paragraph 6(1)(*d*) or (*f*),

Proposed Amendment

Legislative Proposals Relating to the Income Tax Act, Employee Life and Health Trusts (May 27, 2019)

The portion of the definition *employee benefit plan* in subsection 248(1) of the Act before paragraph (*b*) is replaced by the following:

employee benefit plan *—employee benefit plan* means an arrangement under which contributions are made by an employer or by any person with whom the employer does not deal at arm's length to another person (in this Act referred to as the "custodian" of an employee benefit plan) and under which one or more payments are to be made to or for the benefit of employees or former employees of the employer or persons who do not deal at arm's length with any such employee or former employee (other than a payment that, if section 6 were read without reference to its subparagraphs (1)(*a*)(i) and (ii) and paragraph (1)(*g*), would not be required to be included in computing the income of the recipient or of an employee or former employee), but does not include any portion of the arrangement that is

(*a*) a deferred profit sharing plan, an employee life and health trust, an employees profit sharing plan, a pooled registered pension plan, a registered pension plan or a supplementary unemployment benefit plan,

(*a*.1) a plan (other than a plan that is administered or provided by a trust) that is a group sickness or accident insurance plan, a group term life insurance policy or a private health services plan,

Applicable: In force on January 1, 2021.

(*b*) a trust described in paragraph 149(1)(*y*),

(*c*) an employee trust,

(*c*.1) a salary deferral arrangement, in respect of a taxpayer, under which deferred amounts are required to be included as benefits under paragraph 6(1)(*a*) in computing the taxpayer's income,

(*c*.2) a retirement compensation arrangement,

(*d*) an arrangement the sole purpose of which is to provide education or training for employees of the employer to improve their work or work-related skills and abilities, or

(*e*) a prescribed arrangement;

History: S. 248(1), the portion of the definition "employee benefit plan" before paragraph (*a*) was replaced by S.C. 2013, c. 34, s. 358(14), deemed to have come into force on November 1, 2011, and formerly read:

"employee benefit plan"—"employee benefit plan" means an arrangement under which contributions are made by an employer or by any person with whom the employer does not deal at arm's length to another person (in this Act referred to as the "custodian" of an employee benefit plan) and under which one or more payments are to be made to or for the benefit of employees or former employees of the employer or persons who do not deal at arm's length with any such employee or former employee (other than a payment that, if section 6 were read without reference to subparagraph 6(1)(*a*)(ii) and paragraph 6(1)(*g*), would not be required to be included in computing the income of the recipient), but does not include any portion of the arrangement that is

S. 248(1), the definition "employee benefit plan" was replaced by S.C. 2010, s. 25, s. 69(1), applicable after 2009. S. 248(1), the definition "employee benefit plan" formerly read:

"employee benefit plan"—"employee benefit plan" means an arrangement under which contributions are made by an employer or by any person with whom the employer does not deal at arm's length to another person (in this Act referred to as the "custodian" of an employee benefit plan) and under which one or more payments are to be made to or for the benefit of employees or former employees of the employer or persons who do not deal at arm's length with any such employee or former employee (other than a payment that, if section 6 were read without reference to subparagraph 6(1)(*a*)(ii) and paragraph 6(1)(*g*), would not be required to be included in computing the income of the recipient), but does not include

(*a*) a fund or plan referred to in subparagraph 6(1)(*a*)(i) or paragraph 6(1)(*d*) or (*f*),

(*b*) a trust described in paragraph 149(1)(*y*),

(*c*) an employee trust,

(*c*.1) a salary deferral arrangement, in respect of a taxpayer, under which deferred amounts are required to be included as benefits under paragraph 6(1)(*a*) in computing the taxpayer's income,

(*c*.2) a retirement compensation arrangement,

(*d*) an arrangement the sole purpose of which is to provide education or training for employees of the employer to improve their work or work-related skills and abilities, or

(*e*) a prescribed arrangement;

Related Regulations: 6800.

Canadian Tax Foundation: Horner, *Canadian Taxation and Cross-Border Pensions*, 2009 Canadian Tax Journal 4:905–930.

Interpretation Bulletins: *Secondary* — IT-499R Superannuation or pension benefits; IT-502 Employee benefit plans and employee trusts.

"employee life and health trust" —"employee life and health trust" has the meaning assigned by subsection 144.1(2);

History: S. 248(1), the definition "employee life and health trust" was added by S.C. 2010, c. 25, s. 69(4), applicable after 2009.

"employee trust" —"employee trust" means an arrangement (other than an employees profit sharing plan, a deferred profit sharing plan or a plan referred to in subsection 147(15) as a "revoked plan") established after 1979

(*a*) under which payments are made by one or more employers to a trustee in trust solely to provide to employees or former employees of

(i) the employer, or

(ii) a person with whom the employer does not deal at arm's length,

benefits the right to which vests at the time of each such payment and the amount of which does not depend on the individual's position, performance or compensation as an employee,

(*b*) under which the trustee has, since the commencement of the arrangement, each year allocated to individuals who are beneficiaries thereunder, in such manner as is reasonable, the amount, if any, by which the total of all amounts each of which is

(i) an amount received under the arrangement by the trustee in the year from an employer or from a person with whom the employer does not deal at arm's length,

(ii) the amount that would, if this Act were read without reference to subsection 104(6), be the income of the trust for the year (other than a taxable capital gain from the disposition of property) from a property or other source other than a business, or

(iii) a capital gain of the trust for the year from the disposition of property

exceeds the total of all amounts each of which is

(iv) the loss of the trust for the year (other than an allowable capital loss from the disposition of property) from a property or other source other than a business, or

(v) a capital loss of the trust for the year from the disposition of property, and

(*c*) the trustee of which has elected to qualify the arrangement as an employee trust in its return of income filed within 90 days from the end of its first taxation year;

Interpretation Bulletins: *Secondary* — IT-502 Employee benefit plans and employee trusts.

"employees profit sharing plan" —"employees profit sharing plan" has the meaning assigned by subsection 144(1);

"employer" —"employer", in relation to an officer, means the person from whom the officer receives the officer's remuneration;

"employment" —"employment" means the position of an individual in the service of some other person (including Her Majesty or a foreign state or sovereign) and "servant" or "employee" means a person holding such a position;

Cases: Dancers at the Royal Winnipeg Ballet were independent contractors, not employees. Although the company exercised extensive control over their work, this was required to stage a season of performances. The understanding of the parties as to the nature of their legal relationship was relevant, although not conclusive. *The Royal Winnipeg Ballet v. M.N.R.*, 2006 DTC 6323 (F.C.A.), reversing 2004 DTC 390 (T.C.C.)

The Federal Court of Appeal laid down its view of the prevailing Canadian tests for determining whether a relationship is one of employment in *Wiebe Door Services Ltd. v. M.N.R.*, 87 DTC 5025 (F.C.A.).

"estate" —"estate" has the meaning assigned by subsection 104(1) and includes, for civil law, a succession;

History: S. 248(1), the definition "estate" was replaced by S.C. 2013, c. 40, s. 89(2), in force December 12, 2013, and formerly read:

"estate"—"estate" has the meaning assigned by subsection 104(1);

Related Sections: S. 104(1) Reference to trust or estate.

"estate of the bankrupt" —"estate of the bankrupt" has the same meaning as in the *Bankruptcy and Insolvency Act*;

"excessive eligible dividend designation" —"excessive eligible dividend designation" has the meaning assigned by subsection 89(1);

"exempt income" —"exempt income" means property received or acquired by a person in such circumstances that it is, because of any provision of Part I, not included in computing the person's income, but does not include a dividend on a share or a support amount (as defined in subsection 56.1(4));

Related Sections: S. 18(1)(*c*) Limitation re exempt income.

"farming" —"farming" includes tillage of the soil, livestock raising or exhibiting, maintaining of horses for racing, raising of poultry, fur farming, dairy farming, fruit growing and the keeping of bees, but does not include an office or employment under a person engaged in the business of farming;

Canadian Tax Foundation: Bodie et al., *Farming Taxation, With An Emphasis On Farm Succession*, 2017 Prairie Provinces Tax Conference 14:1–33; Hanson and Yaskowich, *There is more to the Family Farm than Meets the Eye*, 2014 Prairie Provinces Tax Conference 5:1–28.

Income Tax Folios: *Primary* — S4-F11-C1 Meaning of Farming and Farming Business.

Interpretation Bulletins: *Secondary* — IT-268R4 Inter vivos transfer of farm property to child; IT-433R Farming or fishing — Use of cash method.

Cases: The breeding of dogs to be sold as pets and the operation of a kennel are not considered as farming activities. *Partington v. M.N.R.*, 91 DTC 347 (T.C.C.)

Buying cattle and feeding them for sale is included in "livestock raising" and therefore constitutes farming. *Stringham v. M.N.R.*, 54 DTC 45 (T.A.B.)

"farm loss" —"farm loss" has the meaning assigned by subsection 111(8);

"federal credit union" —"federal credit union" has the meaning assigned by section 2 of the *Bank Act*;

History: S. 248(1), the definition "federal credit union" was added by S.C. 2010, c. 12, s. 2109(2), in force December 19, 2012 (P.C. 2012-1623, SI/2012-99).

"filing-due date" —"filing-due date" for a taxation year of a taxpayer means the day on or before which the taxpayer's return of income under Part I for the year is required to be filed or would be required to be filed if tax under that Part were payable by the taxpayer for the year;

"fiscal period" — (Repealed by S.C. 1996, c. 21, s. 60(1).)

"fishing" —"fishing" includes fishing for or catching shellfish, crustaceans and marine animals but does not include an office or employment under a person engaged in the business of fishing;

Cases: The taxpayer's appeal was dismissed when he failed to show that he was engaged in fishing with a reasonable expectation of profit. *Smith v. M.N.R.*, 80 DTC 1220 (T.R.B.)

"flow-through share" —"flow-through share" has the meaning assigned by subsection 66(15);

"foreign accrual property income" —"foreign accrual property income" has the meaning assigned by section 95;

History: S. 248(1), the definition "foreign accrual property income" was added by S.C. 2011, c. 24, s. 72(4), applicable to taxation years that begin after 2006.

"foreign affiliate" —"foreign affiliate" has the meaning assigned by subsection 95(1);

"foreign currency" —"foreign currency" means currency of a country other than Canada;

Related Sections: S. 76.1 Non-resident moving debt from Canadian business; s. 142.7(8) Assumption of debt obligation.

"foreign currency debt" —"foreign currency debt" has the meaning assigned by subsection 111(8);

History: S. 248(1), the definition "foreign currency debt" was added by S.C. 2009, c. 2, s. 76(4), applicable after 2005.

"foreign exploration and development expenses" —"foreign exploration and development expenses" has the meaning assigned by subsection 66(15);

"foreign resource expense" —"foreign resource expense" has the meaning assigned by subsection 66.21(1);

"foreign resource pool expenses" —"foreign resource pool expenses" of a taxpayer means the taxpayer's foreign resource expenses in respect of all countries and the taxpayer's foreign exploration and development expenses;

"foreign resource property" —"foreign resource property" has the meaning assigned by subsection 66(15), and a foreign resource property in respect of a country means a foreign resource property that is

(*a*) a right, licence or privilege to explore for, drill for or take petroleum, natural gas or related hydrocarbons in that country,

(*b*) a right, licence or privilege to

(i) store underground petroleum, natural gas or related hydrocarbons in that country, or

(ii) prospect, explore, drill or mine for minerals in a mineral resource in that country,

(*c*) an oil or gas well in that country or real or immovable property in that country the principal value of which depends on its petroleum or natural gas content (but not including depreciable property),

(*d*) any right to a rental or royalty computed by reference to the amount or value of production from an oil or gas well in that country, or from a natural accumulation of petroleum or natural gas in that country, if the payer of the rental or royalty has an interest in, or for civil law a right in, the well or accumulation, as the case may be, and 90% or more of the rental or royalty is payable out of, or from the proceeds of, the production from the well or accumulation,

(*e*) any right to a rental or royalty computed by reference to the amount or value of production from a mineral resource in that country, if the payer of the rental or royalty has an interest in, or for civil law a right in, the mineral resource and 90% or more of the rental or royalty is payable out of, or from the proceeds of, the production from the mineral resource,

(*f*) a real or immovable property in that country the principal value of which depends upon its mineral resource content (but not including depreciable property),

(*g*) a right to or an interest in — or for civil law a right to or in — any property described in any of paragraphs (*a*) to (*e*), other than a right or an interest that the taxpayer has because the taxpayer is a beneficiary under a trust or a member of a partnership, or

(*h*) an interest in real property described in paragraph (*f*) or a real right in an immovable described in that paragraph, other than an interest or a right that the taxpayer has because the taxpayer is a beneficiary under a trust or a member of a partnership;

History: S. 248(1), paragraph (*c*) of the definition "foreign resource property" was replaced by S.C. 2013, c. 34, s. 167(1), in force June 26, 2013, and formerly read:

(*c*) an oil or gas well in that country or real property in that country the principal value of which depends on its petroleum or natural gas content (but not including depreciable property),

S. 248(1), paragraphs (*f*) and (*g*) of the definition "foreign resource property" were replaced by S.C. 2013, c. 34, s. 167(2), in force June 26, 2013, and formerly read:

(*f*) a real property in that country the principal value of which depends upon its mineral resource content (but not including depreciable property), or

(*g*) a right to or interest in any property described in any of paragraphs (*a*) to (*f*), other than such a right or interest that the taxpayer has by reason of being a beneficiary of a trust;

S. 248(1), paragraph (*h*) of the definition "foreign resource property" was added by S.C. 2013, c. 34, s. 167(2), in force June 26, 2013.

S. 248(1), paragraphs (*d*) and (*e*) of the definition "foreign resource property" were replaced by S.C. 2013, c. 34, s. 358(15), applicable to property acquired after December 20, 2002, and formerly read:

(*d*) a rental or royalty computed by reference to the amount or value of production from an oil or gas well in that country or from a natural accumulation of petroleum or natural gas in that country,

(*e*) a rental or royalty computed by reference to the amount or value of production from a mineral resource in that country,

"foreign retirement arrangement" —"foreign retirement arrangement" means a prescribed plan or arrangement;

Related Regulations: 6803.

Related Sections: S. 12(11) Definitions; s. 60(*j*) Transfer of superannuation benefits; s. 81(1)(*r*) Foreign retirement arrangements.

Cases: The taxpayer was the beneficiary of his father's U.S. individual retirement account ("IRA"). Following his father's death, the taxpayer's share of that IRA was rolled over to an IRA in his name. Funds from that IRA were distributed to him and amounts withheld for U.S. income taxes. While amounts distributed from an estate do not trigger tax, the taxpayer received the amount from an IRA and not from his father's estate. A payment out of a "foreign retirement arrangement" is included in computing the income of a taxpayer, and the payment from the IRA to the taxpayer was clearly a payment out of a foreign retirement arrangement and must be included in income. *Owen v. The Queen*, 2019 DTC 2071 (TCC)

"former business property" —"former business property", in respect of a taxpayer, means a capital property of the taxpayer that was used by the taxpayer or a person related to the taxpayer primarily for the purpose of gaining or producing income from a business, and that was real or immovable property of the taxpayer, an interest of the taxpayer in real property, a right of the taxpayer in an immovable or a property that is the subject of an election under subsection 13(4.2), but does not include

(*a*) a rental property of the taxpayer,

(*b*) land subjacent to a rental property of the taxpayer,

(*c*) land contiguous to land referred to in paragraph (*b*) that is a parking area, driveway, yard or garden or that is otherwise necessary for the use of the rental property referred to in that paragraph, or

(*d*) a leasehold interest in any property described in paragraphs (*a*) to (*c*),

and for the purpose of this definition, "rental property" of a taxpayer means real or immovable property owned by the taxpayer, whether jointly with another person or otherwise, and used by the taxpayer in the taxation year in respect of which the expression is being applied principally for the purpose of gaining or producing gross revenue that is rent (other than property leased by the taxpayer to a person related to the taxpayer and used by that related person principally for any other purpose), but, for greater certainty, does not include a property leased by the taxpayer or the related person to a lessee, in the ordinary course of a business of the taxpayer or the related person of selling goods or rendering services, under an agreement by which the lessee undertakes to use the property to carry on the business of selling or promoting the sale of the goods or services of the taxpayer or the related person;

Proposed Amendment
2019 Federal Budget Resolutions

Subsection 248(1) of the Act is amended by adding the following in alphabetical order:

fully collateralized arrangement —*fully collateralized arrangement* means a securities lending arrangement or a specified securities lending arrangement if, throughout the term of the arrangement, the borrower

(*a*) has provided the lender under the arrangement with money in an amount of, or securities described in paragraph (*c*) of the definition *qualified security in* subsection 260(1) that have a fair market value of, not less than 95% of the fair market value of the security that is transferred or lent under the arrangement, and

(*b*) is entitled to enjoy, directly or indirectly, the benefits of all or substantially all income derived from, and opportunity for gain in respect of, the money or securities provided;

Applicable: Deemed to have come into force on March 19, 2019.

History: S. 248(1), the portion of the definition "former business property" after paragraph (*d*) was replaced by S.C. 2013, c. 34, s. 167(3), in force June 26, 2013, and formerly read:

and, for the purpose of this definition, "rental property" of a taxpayer means real property owned by the taxpayer, whether jointly with another person or otherwise, and used by the taxpayer in the taxation year in respect of which the expression is being applied principally for the purpose of gaining or producing gross revenue that is rent (other than property leased by the taxpayer to a person related to the taxpayer and used by that related person principally for any other purpose), but, for greater certainty, does not include a property leased by the taxpayer or the related person to a lessee, in the ordinary course of a business of the taxpayer or the related person of selling goods or rendering services, under an agreement by which the lessee undertakes to use the property to carry on the business of selling or promoting the sale of the goods or services of the taxpayer or the related person;

S. 248(1), the portion of the definition "former business property" before paragraph (*a*) was replaced by S.C. 2013, c. 34, s. 358(16), applicable in respect of dispositions and terminations that occur after December 20, 2002, and formerly read:

"former business property" —"former business property" of a taxpayer means a capital property of the taxpayer that was used by the taxpayer or a person related to the taxpayer primarily for the purpose of gaining or producing income from a business, and that was real property of the taxpayer or an interest of the taxpayer in real property, but does not include

Related Sections: S. 13(4) Exchanges of property; s. 44 Exchanges of property.

Interpretation Bulletins: *Primary* — IT-491 Former business property.

"functional currency" — (Repealed by S.C. 2009, c. 2, s. 76(1).)

History: S. 248(1), the definition "functional currency" was repealed by S.C. 2009, c. 2, s. 76(1), applicable in respect of taxation years that begin after December 13, 2007. S. 248(1), the definition "functional currency" formerly read:

"functional currency" —"functional currency" of a taxpayer for a particular taxation year has the meaning assigned by section 261;

"general rate income pool" —"general rate income pool" has the meaning assigned by subsection 89(1);

"goods and services tax" —"goods and services tax" means the tax payable under Part IX of the *Excise Tax Act*;

"graduated rate estate" —"graduated rate estate", of an individual at any time, means the estate that arose on and as a consequence of the individual's death if

(*a*) that time is no more than 36 months after the death,

(*b*) the estate is at that time a testamentary trust,

(*c*) the individual's Social Insurance Number (or if the individual had not, before the death, been assigned a Social Insurance Number, such other information as is acceptable to the Minister) is provided in the estate's return of income under Part I for the taxation year that includes that time and for each of its earlier taxation years that ended after 2015,

(*d*) the estate designates itself as the graduated rate estate of the individual in its return of income under Part I for its first taxation year that ends after 2015, and

(*e*) no other estate designates itself as the graduated rate estate of the individual in a return of income under Part I for a taxation year that ends after 2015;

History: S. 248(1), the definition "graduated rate estate" was added by S.C. 2014, c. 39, s. 71(6), in force December 31, 2015.

Related Sections: 118.1(5.1) Gifts by graduated rate estate; 249(1) Definition of "taxation year"; 249(5) Graduated rate estate; 249.1(4) Alternative method.

Canadian Tax Foundation: Frajman, *Graduated Rate Estate: Current Debt*, 2015 Canadian Tax Highlights 23(3):9–10.

Tax Window Files: 2016 STEP - Q3- Estate beneficiary of IV Trust, *June 10, 2016*, CRA Document No. 2016-0634891C6; 2016 STEP - Q2 - GRE and multiple wills, *June 10, 2016*, CRA Document No. 2016-0634881C6; 2015 STEP – Q2 – Meaning of Graduated Rate Estates, *June 18, 2015*, CRA Document No. 2015-0572091C6.

"grandfathered share" —"grandfathered share" means

(*a*) a share of the capital stock of a corporation issued after 8:00 p.m. Eastern Daylight Saving Time,

June 18, 1987 pursuant to an agreement in writing entered into before that time,

(*b*) a share of the capital stock of a corporation issued after 8:00 p.m. Eastern Daylight Saving Time, June 18, 1987 and before 1988 as part of a distribution to the public made in accordance with the terms of a prospectus, preliminary prospectus, registration statement, offering memorandum or notice filed before 8:00 p.m. Eastern Daylight Saving Time, June 18, 1987 with a public authority pursuant to and in accordance with the securities legislation of the jurisdiction in which the shares are distributed,

(*c*) a share (in this paragraph referred to as the "new share") of the capital stock of a corporation that is issued after 8:00 p.m. Eastern Daylight Saving Time, June 18, 1987 in exchange for

(i) a share of a corporation that was issued before 8:00 p.m. Eastern Daylight Saving Time, June 18, 1987 or is a grandfathered share, or

(ii) a debt obligation of a corporation that was

(A) issued before 8:00 p.m. Eastern Daylight Saving Time, June 18, 1987, or

(B) issued after 8:00 p.m. Eastern Daylight Saving Time, June 18, 1987 under an agreement in writing entered into before that time, or after that time and before 1988 as part of a distribution to the public made in accordance with the terms of a prospectus, preliminary prospectus, registration statement, offering memorandum or notice filed before that time with a public authority under and in accordance with the securities legislation of the jurisdiction in which the debt obligation is distributed,

where the right to the exchange and all or substantially all the terms and conditions of the new share were established in writing before that time, and

(*d*) a share of a class of the capital stock of a Canadian corporation listed on a designated stock exchange that is issued after 8:00 p.m. Eastern Daylight Saving Time, June 18, 1987 on the exercise of a right that

(i) was issued before that time, that was issued after that time under an agreement in writing entered into before that time or that was issued after that time and before 1988 as part of a distribution to the public made in accordance with the terms of a prospectus, preliminary prospectus, registration statement, offering memorandum or notice filed before that time with a public authority under and in accordance with the securities legislation of the jurisdiction in which the rights were distributed, and

(ii) was listed on a designated stock exchange,

where all or substantially all the terms and conditions of the right and the share were established in writing before that time,

except that a share that is deemed under the definition "short-term preferred share", "taxable preferred share" or "term preferred share" in this subsection or under subsection 112(2.22) to have been issued at any time is deemed after that time not to be a grandfathered share for the purposes of that provision;

Related Sections: S. 87(4.2) Exchanged shares — amalgamations after November 27, 1986; s. 87(4.3) Exchanged rights; s. 112(2.21) Exceptions; s. 187.3(2)(*c*) Time of acquisition of share; s. 258(3) Deemed interest on preferred shares; s. 262 Designated stock exchanges.

"gross revenue" —"gross revenue" of a taxpayer for a taxation year means the total of

(*a*) all amounts received in the year or receivable in the year (depending on the method regularly followed by the taxpayer in computing the taxpayer's income) otherwise than as or on account of capital, and

(*b*) all amounts (other than amounts referred to in paragraph (*a*)) included in computing the taxpayer's income from a business or property for the year because of subsection 12(3) or (4) or section 12.2 of this Act or subsection 12(8) of the *Income Tax Act*, chapter 148 of the Revised Statutes of Canada, 1952.

"group term life insurance policy" —"group term life insurance policy" means a group life insurance policy under which the only amounts payable by the insurer are

(*a*) amounts payable on the death or disability of individuals whose lives are insured in respect of, in the course of or because of, their office or employment or former office or employment, and

(*b*) policy dividends or experience rating refunds;

Related Regulations: Part XIV.

Related Sections: S. 138(15) Definition not to apply.

"highest individual percentage" —"highest individual percentage", for a taxation year, means the highest percentage referred to in subsection 117(2) for the taxation year;

History: S. 248(1), the definition "highest individual percentage" was added by S.C. 2016, c. 11, s. 10(2), applicable to the 2016 and subsequent taxation years.

"home relocation loan" —"home relocation loan" means a loan received by an individual or the individual's spouse or common-law partner in circumstances where the individual has commenced employment at a location in Canada (in this definition referred to as the "new work location") and by reason thereof has moved from the residence in Canada at which, before the move, the individual ordinarily resided (in this definition referred to as the "old residence") to a residence in Canada at which, after the move, the individual ordinarily resided (in this definition referred to as the "new residence") if

(*a*) the distance between the old residence and the new work location is at least 40 kilometres greater than the distance between the new residence and the new work location,

(*b*) the loan is used to acquire a dwelling, or a share of the capital stock of a cooperative housing corporation acquired for the sole purpose of acquiring the right to inhabit a dwelling owned by the corporation, where the dwelling is for the habitation of the individual and is the individual's new residence,

(*c*) the loan is received in the circumstances described in subsection 80.4(1), or would have been so received if subsection 80.4(1.1) had applied to the loan at the time it was received, and

(*d*) the loan is designated by the individual to be a home relocation loan, but in no case shall more than one loan in respect of a particular move, or more than one loan at any particular time, be designated as a home relocation loan by the individual;

Related Sections: S. 80.4(1.1) Loan or debt from office or employment; s. 110(1)(*j*) Home relocation loan; s. 115(2)(*f*) Non-resident's taxable income in Canada; s. 248(1), "common-law partner", "eligible relocation".

"income-averaging annuity contract" —"income-averaging annuity contract" of an individual means, except for the purposes of section 61, a contract

(*a*) that is an income-averaging annuity contract within the meaning assigned by subsection 61(4), and

(*b*) in respect of which the individual has made a deduction under section 61 in computing the individual's income for a taxation year;

"income bond" or "income debenture" —"income bond" or"income debenture" of a corporation (in this definition referred to as the "issuing corporation") means a bond or debenture in respect of which interest or dividends are payable only to the extent that the issuing corporation has made a profit before taking into account the interest or dividend obligation and that was issued

(*a*) before November 17, 1978,

(*b*) after November 16, 1978 and before 1980 pursuant to an agreement in writing to do so made before November 17, 1978 (in this definition referred to as an "established agreement"), or

(*c*) by an issuing corporation resident in Canada for a term that may not, in any circumstances, exceed 5 years,

(i) as part of a proposal to or an arrangement with its creditors that had been approved by a court under the *Bankruptcy and Insolvency Act*,

(ii) at a time when all or substantially all of its assets were under the control of a receiver, receiver-manager, sequestrator or trustee in bankruptcy, or

(iii) at a time when, by reason of financial difficulty, the issuing corporation or another corporation resident in Canada with which it does not deal at arm's length was in default, or could reasonably be expected to default, on a debt obligation held by a person with whom the issuing corporation or the other corporation was dealing at arm's length and the bond or debenture was issued either wholly or in substantial part and either directly or indirectly in exchange or substitution for that obligation or a part thereof,

and, in the case of a bond or debenture issued after November 12, 1981, the proceeds from the issue may reasonably be regarded as having been used by the issuing corporation or a corporation with which it was not dealing at arm's length in the financing of its business carried on in Canada immediately before the bond or debenture was issued,

and, for the purposes of this definition,

(*d*) where the terms or conditions of an established agreement were amended after November 16, 1978, the agreement shall be deemed to have been made after that date, and

(*e*) where

(i) at any particular time the terms or conditions of a bond or debenture issued pursuant to an established agreement or of any agreement relating to such a bond or debenture have been changed,

(ii) under the terms or conditions of a bond or debenture acquired in the ordinary course of the business carried on by a specified financial institution or a partnership or trust (other than a testamentary trust) or under the terms or conditions of any agreement relating to any such bond or debenture (other than an agreement made before October 24, 1979 to which the issuing corporation or any person related thereto was not a party), the owner thereof could at any particular time after November 16, 1978 require, either alone or together with one or more taxpayers, the repayment, acquisition, cancellation or conversion of the bond or debenture otherwise than by reason of a failure or default under the terms or conditions of the bond or debenture or any agreement that related to, and was entered into at the time of, the issuance of the bond or debenture,

(iii) at any particular time after November 16, 1978, the maturity date of a bond or debenture was extended or the terms or conditions relating to the repayment of the principal amount thereof were changed,

(iv) at a particular time a specified financial institution (or a partnership or trust of which a specified financial institution or a person related to the institution is a member or beneficiary) acquires a bond or debenture that

(A) was issued before November 17, 1978 or under an established agreement,

(B) was issued to a person other than a corporation that was, at the time of issue,

(I) described in any of paragraphs (*a*) to (*e*) of the definition "specified financial institution", or

(II) a corporation that was controlled by one or more corporations described in subclause (I) and, for the purpose of this subclause, one corporation is controlled by another corporation if more than 50% of its issued share capital (having full voting rights under all circumstances) belongs to the other corporation, to persons with whom the other corporation does not deal at arm's length, or to the other corporation and persons with whom the other corporation does not deal at arm's length,

(C) was acquired from a person that was, at the time the person last acquired the bond or debenture and at the particular time, a person other than a corporation described in any of paragraphs (*a*) to (*f*) of that definition, and

(D) was acquired otherwise than under an agreement in writing made before October 24, 1979, or

(v) at a particular time after November 12, 1981, a specified financial institution (or a partnership or trust of which a specified financial institution or a person related to the institution is a member or beneficiary) acquires a bond or debenture that

(A) was not a bond or debenture referred to in paragraph (*c*),

(B) was acquired from a person that was, at the particular time, a corporation described in any of paragraphs (*a*) to (*f*) of the definition "specified financial institution", and

(C) was acquired subject to or conditional on a guarantee agreement (within the meaning that would be assigned by subsection 112(2.2) if the reference in that subsection to a "share" were read as a reference to an "income bond" or "income debenture") that was entered into after November 12, 1981,

the bond or debenture shall, for the purposes of determining at any time after the particular time whether it is an income bond or income debenture, be deemed to have been issued at the particular time otherwise than pursuant to an established agreement;

Interpretation Bulletins: *Secondary* — IT-527 Distress preferred shares.

"income interest" — "income interest" of a taxpayer in a trust has the meaning assigned by subsection 108(1);

"indexed debt obligation" — "indexed debt obligation" means a debt obligation the terms or conditions of which provide for an adjustment to an amount payable in respect of the obligation for a period during which the obligation was outstanding that is determined by reference to a change in the purchasing power of money;

Related Sections: S. 248(1), "amount".

"indexed security" — (Repealed by 1986, c. 6, s. 126(1).)

"indexed security investment plan" — (Repealed by 1986, c. 6, s. 126(1).)

"individual" — "individual" means a person other than a corporation;

"insurance corporation" — "insurance corporation" means a corporation that carries on an insurance business;

"insurance policy" — "insurance policy" includes a life insurance policy;

Related Sections: S. 138(12), "life insurance policy".

"insurer" — "insurer" has the meaning assigned by this subsection to the expression "insurance corporation";

"international shipping" — "international shipping" means the operation of a ship owned or leased by a person or partnership (in this definition referred to as the "operator") that is used, either directly or as part of a pooling arrangement, primarily in transporting passengers or goods in international traffic — determined as if, except where paragraph (*c*) of the definition "international traffic" in this subsection applies, any port or other place on the Great Lakes or St. Lawrence River is in Canada — including the chartering of the ship, provided that one or more persons related to the operator (if the operator and each such person is a corporation), or persons or partnerships affiliated with the operator (in any other case), has complete possession, control and command of the ship, and any activity incident to or pertaining to the operation of the ship, but does not include

(*a*) the offshore storing or processing of goods,

(*b*) fishing,

(*c*) laying cable,

(*d*) salvaging,

(*e*) towing,

(*f*) tug-boating,

(*g*) offshore oil and gas activities (other than the transportation of oil and gas), including exploration and drilling activities,

(*h*) dredging, or

(*i*) leasing a ship by a lessor to a lessee that has complete possession, control and command of the ship, unless the lessor or a corporation, trust or partnership affiliated with the lessor has an eligible interest (as defined in subsection 250(6.04)) in the lessee;

History: S. 248(1), the definition "international shipping" was added by S.C. 2014, c. 39, s. 71(6), applicable to taxation years that begin after July 12, 2013.

Related Sections: 81(1)(c) Ship or aircraft of non-residents; 250(6) Residence of international shipping corporation.

Tax Window Files: International shipping, *December 24, 2015*, CRA Document No. 2014-0560831I7.

"international traffic" — "international traffic" means, in respect of a person or partnership carrying on the business of transporting passengers or goods, a voyage made in the course of that business if the principal purpose of the voyage is to transport passengers or goods

(*a*) from Canada to a place outside Canada,

(*b*) from a place outside Canada to Canada, or

(*c*) from a place outside Canada to another place outside Canada;

History: S. 248(1), the portion of the definition "international traffic" before paragraph (*a*) was replaced by S.C. 2014, c. 39, s. 71(2), applicable to taxation years that begin after July 12, 2013, and formerly read:

"international traffic" — "international traffic" means, in respect of a non-resident person carrying on the business of transporting passengers or goods, any voyage made in the course of that business where the principal purpose of the voyage is to transport passengers or goods

Related Sections: S. 108(1), "inter vivos trust"; s. 248(3) Property subject to certain Quebec institutions and arrangements.

"inter vivos trust" — "inter vivos trust" has the meaning assigned by subsection 108(1);

"inventory" — "inventory" means a description of property the cost or value of which is relevant in computing a taxpayer's income from a business for a taxation year or would have been so relevant if the income from the business had not been computed in accordance with the cash method and includes

(*a*) with respect to a farming business, all of the livestock held in the course of carrying on the business, and

(*b*) an emissions allowance;

History: S. 248(1), the definition "inventory" was replaced by S.C. 2016, c. 12, s. 63(2), in force January 1, 2017, except that paragraph (*b*) of the definition "inventory" does not apply in respect of emissions allowances acquired in taxation years that begin before 2017. In addition, if a taxpayer elects under subsection 10(2) of the *Budget Implementation Act, 2016, No. 2* (Bill C-29), this amendment applies in respect of emissions allowances acquired by the taxpayer in taxation years that end after 2012.

S. 248(1), the definition "inventory" formerly read:

"inventory"—"inventory" means a description of property the cost or value of which is relevant in computing a taxpayer's income from a business for a taxation year or would have been so relevant if the income from the business had not been computed in accordance with the cash method and, with respect to a farming business, includes all of the livestock held in the course of carrying on the business;

Interpretation Bulletins: *Secondary* — IT-51R2 Supplies on hand at the end of a fiscal period; IT-92R2 Income of contractors; IT-102R2 Conversion of property, other than real property, from or to inventory; IT-457R Election by professionals to exclude work in progress from income; IT-473R Inventory valuation.

"investment corporation"—"investment corporation" has the meaning assigned by subsection 130(3);

"investment tax credit"—"investment tax credit" has the meaning assigned by subsection 127(9);

Proposed Amendment

Bill C-74, Canada–Quebec Gulf of St. Lawrence Petroleum Resources Accord Implementation Act (June 18, 2015)

Subsection 248(1) of the Act is amended by adding the following in alphabetical order:

"joint management area"—"joint management area" means the submarine areas within the limits described in Schedule 1 to the *Canada–Quebec Gulf of St. Lawrence Petroleum Resources Accord Implementation Act*;

Applicable: To taxation years that begin after the day on which an administration agreement in respect of tax imposed under section 235 of the *Canada–Quebec Gulf of St. Lawrence Petroleum Resources Accord Implementation Act* comes into effect.

"joint spousal or common-law partner trust"—"joint spousal or common-law partner trust" means a trust to which paragraph 104(4)(*a*) would apply if that paragraph were read without reference to subparagraph 104(4)(*a*)(iii) and clause 104(4)(*a*)(iv)(A);

Related Sections: S. 73(1) Inter vivos transfers by individuals; s. 73(1.01) Qualifying transfers; s. 73(1.02) Exception for transfers; s. 104(4) Deemed disposition by trust; s. 104(5.8) Trust transfers; s. 104(6) Deduction in computing income of trust; s. 104(15) Allocable amount for preferred beneficiary; s. 107(4) Trusts in favour of spouse, common-law partner or self; s. 108(1), "trust".

Canadian Tax Foundation: Brown, *Alter Ego Joint Conjugal and Self-Benefit Trusts Revisited: Some Troubling Tax Issues and a Search for Better Alternatives*, 2005 Canadian Tax Journal 1:224–244; Hoffstein, *Alter Ego Trusts/Joint Partner Trusts — Tips, Traps & Planning*, 2004 Ontario Tax Conference 12A:1–47.

Tax Profile: February 2002 — Transferring Property to a Trust After the Enactment of Bill C-22.

Tax Window Files: 2014 STEP CRA Roundtable Question, *June 16, 2014*, CRA Document No. 2014-0523031C6.

"lawyer"—"lawyer" has the meaning assigned by subsection 232(1);

"legal representative"—"legal representative" of a taxpayer means a trustee in bankruptcy, an assignee, a liquidator, a curator, a receiver of any kind, a trustee, an heir, an administrator, an executor, a liquidator of a succession, a committee, or any other like person, administering, winding up, controlling or otherwise dealing in a representative or fiduciary capacity with the property that belongs or belonged to, or that is or was held for the benefit of, the taxpayer or the taxpayer's estate;

Related Sections: S. 34.1(9) Death of partner or proprietor; s. 34.2(8) Death of partner or proprietor; s. 150(1)(*b*) Deceased individuals; s. 150(1)(*d*) Individuals; 159(1) Person acting for another; 159(2) Certificate before distribution; 159(3) Personal liability; 159(3.1) Appropriation of property.

"lending asset"—"lending asset" means a bond, debenture, mortgage, hypothecary claim, note, agreement of sale or any other indebtedness or a prescribed share, but does not include a prescribed property;

Related Regulations: 6209.

Related Sections: S. 20(1)(*l*) Doubtful or impaired debts; s. 20(1)(*p*) Bad debts; s. 95(1), "lending of money"; s. 248(1), "cost amount".

"LIA policy"—"LIA policy" means a life insurance policy (other than an annuity) where

(*a*) a particular person or partnership becomes obligated after March 20, 2013 to repay an amount to another person or partnership (in this definition referred to as the "lender") at a time determined by reference to the death of a particular individual whose life is insured under the policy, and

(*b*) the lender is assigned an interest in

(i) the policy, and

(ii) an annuity contract the terms of which provide that payments are to continue for a period that ends no earlier than the death of the particular individual;

History: S. 248(1), the definition "LIA policy", was added by S.C. 2013, c. 40, s. 89(5), applicable to taxation years that end after March 20, 2013.

Canadian Tax Foundation: Everett, *Life Insurance Planning After the 2013 Budget*, 2013 Conference Report 32:1–23; Marino, *Impact of the 2013 Federal Budget on Life Insurance Planning for Individuals and Private Companies*, 2013 Ontario Tax Conference 13B:1–12.

"licensed annuities provider"—"licensed annuities provider" has the meaning assigned by subsection 147(1);

"life insurance business"—"life insurance business" includes

(*a*) an annuities business, and

(*b*) the business of issuing contracts all or any part of the issuer's reserves for which vary in amount depending on the fair market value of a specified group of assets,

carried on by a life insurance corporation or a life insurer;

"life insurance capital dividend"—"life insurance capital dividend" has the meaning assigned by subsection 83(2.1);

"life insurance corporation"—"life insurance corporation" means a corporation that carries on a life insurance business that is not a business described in paragraph (*a*) or (*b*) of the definition "life insurance business" in this subsection, whether or not the corporation also carries on a business described in either of those paragraphs;

"life insurance policy"—"life insurance policy" has the meaning assigned by subsection 138(12);

"life insurance policy in Canada"—"life insurance policy in Canada" has the meaning assigned by subsection 138(12);

"life insurer"—"life insurer" has the meaning assigned by this subsection to the expression "life insurance corporation";

"limited partnership loss"—"limited partnership loss" has the meaning assigned by subsection 96(2.1);

"limited-recourse amount"—"limited-recourse amount" means an amount that is a limited-recourse amount under section 143.2.

"listed international agreement"—"listed international agreement" means (*a*) the *Convention on Mutual Administrative Assistance in Tax Matters*, concluded at Strasbourg on January 25, 1988, as amended from time to time by a protocol, or other international instrument, as ratified by Canada, or

(*b*) a comprehensive tax information exchange agreement that Canada has entered into and that has effect, in respect of another country or jurisdiction;

History: S. 248(1), the definition of "listed international agreement" was added by S.C. 2013, c. 34, s. 358(20), in force June 26, 2013.

"listed personal property" —"listed personal property" has the meaning assigned by section 54;

"low rate income pool" —"low rate income pool" has the meaning assigned by subsection 89(1);

"majority-interest partner" —"majority-interest partner", of a particular partnership at any time, means a person or partnership (in this definition referred to as the "taxpayer")

(*a*) whose share of the particular partnership's income from all sources for the last fiscal period of the particular partnership that ended before that time (or, if the particular partnership's first fiscal period includes that time, for that period) would have exceeded 1/2 of the particular partnership's income from all sources for that period if the taxpayer had held throughout that period each interest in the partnership that the taxpayer or a person affiliated with the taxpayer held at that time, or

(*b*) whose share, if any, together with the shares of every person with whom the taxpayer is affiliated, of the total amount that would be paid to all members of the particular partnership (otherwise than as a share of any income of the partnership) if it were wound up at that time exceeds 1/2 of that amount;

History: S. 248(1), the portion of the definition of "majority interest partner" before paragraph (*a*) was replaced by S.C. 2013, c. 40, s. 89(4), in force December 12, 2013, and formerly read:

"majority interest partner" —"majority interest partner" of a particular partnership at any time means a person or partnership (in this definition referred to as the "taxpayer")

"mineral" —"mineral" includes ammonite gemstone, bituminous sands, calcium chloride, coal, kaolin, oil shale and silica, but does not include petroleum, natural gas or a related hydrocarbon not expressly referred to in this definition;

Interpretation Bulletins: *Secondary* — IT-125R4 Disposition of resource properties.

"mineral resource" —"mineral resource" means

(*a*) a base or precious metal deposit,

(*b*) a coal deposit,

(*c*) a bituminous sands deposit or oil shale deposit, or

(*d*) a mineral deposit in respect of which

(i) the Minister of Natural Resources has certified that the principal mineral extracted is an industrial mineral contained in a non-bedded deposit,

(ii) the principal mineral extracted is ammonite gemstone, calcium chloride, diamond, gypsum, halite, kaolin or sylvite, or

(iii) the principal mineral extracted is silica that is extracted from sandstone or quartzite;

Income Tax Folios: S4-F15-C1 Manufacturing and Processing.

Interpretation Bulletins: *Secondary* — IT-125R4 Disposition of resource properties.

Tax Window Files: Mineral resource certification - Jade nephrite, *December 28, 2018*, CRA Document No. 2018-0785211E5.

"minerals" — (Repealed by S.C. 1994, c. 21, s. 109(1).)

"mining reclamation trust" — (Repealed by S.C. 1998, c. 19, s. 66(1).)

"Minister" —"Minister" means the Minister of National Revenue;

"money purchase limit" —"money purchase limit" for a calendar year has the meaning assigned by subsection 147.1(1);

"mortgage investment corporation" —"mortgage investment corporation" has the meaning assigned by subsection 130.1(6);

"motor vehicle" —"motor vehicle" means an automotive vehicle designed or adapted to be used on highways and streets but does not include

(*a*) a trolley bus, or

(*b*) a vehicle designed or adapted to be operated exclusively on rails;

Interpretation Bulletins: *Secondary* — IT-521R Motor vehicle expenses claimed by self-employed individuals; IT-522R Vehicle, travel and sales expenses of employees.

"mutual fund corporation" —"mutual fund corporation" has the meaning assigned by subsection 131(8);

"mutual fund trust" —"mutual fund trust" has the meaning assigned by subsection 132(6);

"net capital loss" —"net capital loss" has the meaning assigned by subsection 111(8), except as otherwise expressly provided;

"net corporate income tax rate" —"net corporate income tax rate" in respect of a SIFT trust or SIFT partnership for a taxation year means the amount, expressed as a decimal fraction, by which

(*a*) the percentage rate of tax provided under paragraph 123(1)(*a*) for the taxation year

exceeds

(*b*) the total of

(i) the percentage that would, if the SIFT trust or SIFT partnership were a corporation, be its general rate reduction percentage, within the meaning assigned by subsection 123.4(1), for the taxation year, and

(ii) the percentage deduction from tax provided under subsection 124(1) for the taxation year;

Related Sections: S. 122(1) Tax payable by inter vivos trust; s. 197(2) Tax on partnership income.

"net income stabilization account" —"net income stabilization account" means an account of a taxpayer

(*a*) under the net income stabilization account program under the *Farm Income Protection Act*, or

(*b*) that is a prescribed account;

History: S. 248(1), the definition "net income stabilization account" was replaced by S.C. 2011, c. 24, s. 72(1), applicable to the 2011 and subsequent taxation years. S. 248(1), the definition "net income stabilization account" formerly read:

"net income stabilization account" —"net income stabilization account" means an account of a taxpayer under the net income stabilization account program under the *Farm Income Protection Act*;

Related Regulations: 5503(2).

Related Sections: S. 12(10.2) NISA receipts; s. 12(10.3) Amount credited or added not included in income; s. 12(10.4) Acquisition of control — corporate NISA Fund No. 2.

Guides: RC4060 Farming Income and the AgriStability and AgriInvest Program Guide; RC4408 Farming Income and the AgriStability and AgriInvest Programs Harmonized Guide.

"Newfoundland offshore area" —"Newfoundland offshore area" has the meaning assigned to the expression "offshore area" by the *Canada–Newfoundland and Labrador Atlantic Accord Implementation Act*, chapter 3 of the Statutes of Canada, 1987;

History: S. 248(1), the definition "Newfoundland offshore area" was amended by amended by S.C. 2014, c. 13, s. 115(*f*)(ii) by replacing the *Canada-Newfoundland Atlantic Accord Implementation Act* with the *Canada–Newfoundland and Labrador Atlantic Accord Implementation Act*, in force December 31, 2014.

"NISA Fund No. 2" —"NISA Fund No. 2" means the portion of a taxpayer's net income stabilization account

(*a*) that is described in paragraph 8(2)(*b*) of the *Farm Income Protection Act* or is a prescribed fund, and

(*b*) that can reasonably be considered to be attributable to a program that allows the funds in the account to accumulate;

History: S. 248(1), paragraph (*a*) of the definition "NISA Fund No. 2" was replaced by S.C. 2011, c. 24, s. 72(3), applicable to the 2011 and subsequent taxation years. S. 248(1), paragraph (*a*) of the definition "NISA Fund No. 2" formerly read:

(*a*) that is described in paragraph 8(2)(*b*) of the *Farm Income Protection Act*, and

Related Regulations: 5503(1).

"non-capital loss" —"non-capital loss" has the meaning assigned by subsection 111(8);

"non-portfolio property" —"non-portfolio property" has the same meaning as in subsection 122.1(1);

"non-resident" —"non-resident" means not resident in Canada;

"non-resident-owned investment corporation" —"non-resident-owned investment corporation" has the meaning assigned by subsection 133(8);

"Nova Scotia offshore area" —"Nova Scotia offshore area" has the meaning assigned to the expression "offshore area" by the *Canada-Nova Scotia Offshore Petroleum Resources Accord Implementation Act*, chapter 28 of the Statutes of Canada, 1988;

"office" —"office" means the position of an individual entitling the individual to a fixed or ascertainable stipend or remuneration and includes a judicial office, the office of a minister of the Crown, the office of a member of the Senate or House of Commons of Canada, a member of a legislative assembly or a member of a legislative or executive council and any other office, the incumbent of which is elected by popular vote or is elected or appointed in a representative capacity and also includes the position of a corporation director, and "officer" means a person holding such an office;

Tax Window Files: Fixed or ascertainable stipend or remuneration, *November 7, 2014*, CRA Document No. 2014-0549861I7.

Cases: A member of a regulatory body held an "office", since she was entitled to receive *per diem* payments when she worked that were fixed or ascertainable stipends. Even though she received nothing when there was no work, the entitlement requirement means nothing more than a position for pay. *M.N.R. v. Real Estate Council of Alberta*, 2012 DTC 5099 (F.C.A.), reversing 2011 UDTC 1 (T.C.C.)

It has been held that the position of mayor or alderman of a city is an "office" (*Badanai v. M.N.R.*, 51 DTC 378 (T.A.B.); *Mitchell v. M.N.R.*, 51 DTC 380 (T.A.B.)). It has also been held that a professor delivering a series of lectures for a fixed remuneration occupies an office. *Blatz v. M.N.R.*, 51 DTC 382 (T.A.B.)

"oil or gas well" —"oil or gas well" means any well (other than an exploratory probe or a well drilled from below the surface of the earth) drilled for the purpose of producing petroleum or natural gas or of determining the existence, location, extent or quality of a natural accumulation of petroleum or natural gas, but, for the purpose of applying sections 13 and 20 and any regulations made for the purpose of paragraph 20(1)(*a*) in respect of property acquired after March 6, 1996, does not include a well for the extraction of material from a deposit of bituminous sands or oil shales;

Interpretation Bulletins: *Secondary* — IT-125R4 Disposition of resource properties.

"OSFI risk-weighting guidelines" —"OSFI risk-weighting guidelines" means the guidelines, issued by the Superintendent of Financial Institutions under the authority of section 600 of the *Bank Act*, requiring an authorized foreign bank to provide to the Superintendent on a periodic basis a return of the bank's risk-weighted on-balance sheet assets and off-balance sheet exposures, that apply as of August 8, 2000;

Related Sections: S. 181.3(3) Capital of financial institution; s. 181.3(4) Investment allowance of financial institution; s. 190.13 Capital; s. 190.14 Investment in related institutions.

"overseas Canadian Forces school staff" —"overseas Canadian Forces school staff" means personnel employed outside Canada whose services are acquired by the Minister of National Defence under a prescribed order relating to the provision of educational facilities outside Canada;

Related Regulations: Part LXVI.

"paid-up capital" —"paid-up capital" has the meaning assigned by subsection 89(1);

Related Sections: S. 89(1), "paid-up capital".

"paid-up capital deficiency" — (Repealed by 1977-78, c. 1, s. 98(5).)

"Part VII refund" —"Part VII refund" has the meaning assigned by subsection 192(2);

"Part VIII refund" —"Part VIII refund" has the meaning assigned by subsection 194(2);

"participant" — (Repealed by 1986, c. 6, s. 126(1).)

"passenger vehicle" —"passenger vehicle" means an automobile

(*a*) acquired after June 17, 1987, other than an automobile that is acquired after that date pursuant to an obligation in writing entered into before June 18, 1987 or that is a zero-emission vehicle, or

(*b*) leased under a lease entered into, extended or renewed after June 17, 1987;

History: S. 248(1), the definition "passenger vehicle" was replaced by S.C. 2019, c. 29, s. 43(1), deemed to have come in force on March 19, 2019, and former read:

"passenger vehicle"—"passenger vehicle" means an automobile acquired after June 17, 1987 (other than an automobile acquired after that date pursuant to an obligation in writing entered into before June 18, 1987) and an automobile leased under a lease entered into, extended or renewed after June 17, 1987;

Related Sections: S. 13(2) Recaptured depreciation for passenger vehicle; s. 20(16.1) Terminal loss for passenger vehicle.

Interpretation Bulletins: *Secondary* — IT-521R Motor vehicle expenses claimed by self-employed individuals; IT-522R Vehicle, travel and sales expenses of employees.

"past service pension adjustment" —"past service pension adjustment" of a taxpayer for a calendar year in respect of an employer has the meaning assigned by regulation;

Related Regulations: 8303; 8304.

Interpretation Bulletins: *Secondary* — IT-528 Transfers of funds between registered plans.

"pension adjustment" —"pension adjustment" of a taxpayer for a calendar year in respect of an employer has the meaning assigned by regulation;

Related Regulations: 8301; 8308(4) Period of Reduced Services — Retroactive Benefits; 8308(5) Period of Reduced Services — Retroactive Contributions; 8308(6) Commitment to Make Retroactive Contributions.

"person" —"person", or any word or expression descriptive of a person, includes any corporation, and any entity exempt, because of subsection 149(1), from tax under Part I on all or part of the entity's taxable income and the heirs, executors, liquidators of a succession, administrators or other legal representatives of such a person, according to the law of that part of Canada to which the context extends;

Related Sections: S. 149(1) Miscellaneous exemptions; s. 248(1), "corporation"; s. 255 Canada.

"personal or living expenses" —"personal or living expenses" includes

(*a*) the expenses of properties maintained by any person for the use or benefit of the taxpayer or any person connected with the taxpayer by blood relationship, marriage or common-law partnership or adoption, and not maintained in connection with a business carried on for profit or with a reasonable expectation of profit,

(*b*) the expenses, premiums or other costs of a policy of insurance, annuity contract or other like contract if the proceeds of the policy or contract are payable to or for the benefit of the taxpayer or a person connected with the taxpayer by blood relationship, marriage or common-law partnership or adoption, and

(*c*) expenses of properties maintained by an estate or trust for the benefit of the taxpayer as one of the beneficiaries;

Related Sections: S. 251(6) Blood relationship, etc.

Income Tax Folios: *Secondary* — S4-F11-C1 Meaning of Farming and Farming Business.

Interpretation Bulletins: *Secondary* — IT-322R Farm losses.

"personal services business" —"personal services business" has the meaning assigned by subsection 125(7);

Related Sections: S. 125(7) Definitions.

"personal trust" —"personal trust" means a trust (other than a trust that is, or was at any time after 1999, a unit trust) that is

(*a*) a graduated rate estate, or

(*b*) a trust in which no beneficial interest was acquired for consideration payable directly or indirectly to

(i) the trust, or

(ii) any person or partnership that has made a contribution to the trust by way of transfer, assignment or other disposition of property;

History: S. 248(1), paragraph (*a*) of the definition "personal trust" was replaced by S.C. 2014, c. 39, s. 71(3), applicable to the 2016 and subsequent taxation years, and formerly read:

(*a*) a testamentary trust, or

S. 248(1), the portion of paragraph (*b*) of the definition "personal trust" before subparagraph (i) was replaced by S.C. 2014, c. 39, s. 71(4), applicable to the 2016 and subsequent taxation years, and formerly read:

(*b*) an *inter vivos* trust no beneficial interest in which was acquired for consideration payable directly or indirectly to

S. 248(1), the definition "personal trust" was replaced by S.C. 2009, c. 2, s. 76(2), applicable after July 14, 2008. S. 248(1), the definition "personal trust" formerly read:

"personal trust"—"personal trust" means

(*a*) a testamentary trust, or

(*b*) an *inter vivos* trust, no beneficial interest in which was acquired for consideration payable directly or indirectly to

(i) the trust, or

(ii) any person who has made a contribution to the trust by way of transfer, assignment or other disposition of property,

but, after 1999, does not include a unit trust;

Related Sections: 248(1) graduated rate estate; S. 53(2)(*h*) Amounts to be deducted — Capital interest in a trust; S. 104(1) Reference to trust or estate; s. 108(1), "inter vivos trust"; s. 108(6) Variation of trusts; s. 108(7) Interests acquired for consideration; s. 248(1), "individual", "inter vivos trust", "property", "testamentary trust", "trust"; s. 248(3) Property subject to certain Quebec institutions and arrangements; s. 248(25) Beneficially interested; s. 251(2) Definition of "related persons"; s. 252(1) Extended meaning of "child".

Interpretation Bulletins: *Secondary* — IT-342R Trusts — Income payable to beneficiaries.

"personal-use property" —"personal-use property" has the meaning assigned by section 54;

Related Sections: S. 54 Definitions.

"pooled pension plan" —"pooled pension plan" has the same meaning as in subsection 147.5(1);

History: S. 248(1), the definition "pooled pension plan" was added by S.C. 2012, c. 31, s. 55(5), in force December 14, 2012.

"pooled registered pension plan" or "PRPP" —"pooled registered pension plan" or "PRPP" has the same meaning as in subsection 147.5(1);

History: S. 248(1), the definition "pooled registered pension plan" or "PRPP" was added by S.C. 2012, c. 31, s. 55(5), in force December 14, 2012.

"post-1971 spousal or common-law partner trust" — "post-1971 spousal or common-law partner trust" means a trust that would be described in paragraph 104(4)(*a*) if that paragraph were read without reference to subparagraph 104(4)(*a*)(iv);

"preferred share" —"preferred share" means a share other than a common share;

"prescribed" —"prescribed" means

(*a*) in the case of a form, the information to be given on a form or the manner of filing a form, authorized by the Minister,

(*a*.1) in the case of the manner of making or filing an election, authorized by the Minister, and

(*b*) in any other case, prescribed by regulation or determined in accordance with rules prescribed by regulation;

"principal amount" —"principal amount", in relation to any obligation, means the amount that, under the terms of the obligation or any agreement relating thereto, is the maximum amount or maximum total amount, as the case may be, payable on account of the obligation by the issuer thereof, otherwise than as or on account of interest or as or on account of any premium payable by the issuer conditional on the exercise by the issuer of a right to redeem the obligation before the maturity thereof;

Editorial Note: See s. 20(1)(*c*) for Department of Finance comfort letter dated October 24, 2001 regarding a reserve for a premium on a bond issue.

Interpretation Bulletins: *Secondary* — IT-142R3 Settlement of debts on the winding-up of a corporation.

Cases: The principal amount of a convertible debenture is the value of the debt as reflected under the terms of the trust indenture. The principal amount can not fluctuate between the date of issuance and the date of redemption. *Provigo Inc. et al. v. The Queen*, 2008 DTC 6601 (F.C.A.), affirming 2007 DTC 3232 (T.C.C.).

"private corporation" —"private corporation" has the meaning assigned by subsection 89(1);

Related Sections: S. 89(1), "private corporation".

Interpretation Bulletins: *Secondary* — IT-458R2 Canadian-controlled private corporation.

"private foundation" —"private foundation" has the meaning assigned by section 149.1;

"private health services plan" —"private health services plan" means

(*a*) a contract of insurance in respect of hospital expenses, medical expenses or any combination of such expenses, or

(*b*) a medical care insurance plan or hospital care insurance plan or any combination of such plans,

except any such contract or plan established by or pursuant to

(*c*) a law of a province that establishes a health care insurance plan as defined in section 2 of the *Canada Health Act*, or

(*d*) an Act of Parliament or a regulation made thereunder that authorizes the provision of a medical care insurance plan or hospital care insurance plan for employees of Canada and their dependants and for dependants of members of the Royal Canadian Mounted Police and the regular force where such employees or members were appointed in Canada and are serving outside Canada;

Related Sections: S. 6(1)(*a*) Value of benefits; s. 20.01(1) PHSP premiums; s. 118.2(2) Medical expenses.

Canadian Tax Foundation: Cheng and Shah, *Private Health Services Plans for Small Businesses*, 2015 Canadian Tax Focus 2(4):2–3; Bordeleau et al., *Change in Position: Employee Bonus Allocated to Health-Care Spending Account (Canada Revenue Agency and Revenu Québec Round Table, Questions 10 and 11)*, 2011 Conference Report 4:7–8.

Interpretation Bulletins: *Primary* — IT-339R2 Meaning of "private health services plan".

Tax Window Files: private health services plans, *September 25, 2018*, CRA Document No. 2016-0636871E5.

"professional corporation" —"professional corporation" means a corporation that carries on the professional practice of an accountant, dentist, lawyer, medical doctor, veterinarian or chiropractor;

Related Sections: S. 249.1 Definition of "fiscal period".

Canadian Tax Foundation: Baron, *Selected Considerations in the Use of Professional Corporations*, 2013 Canadian Tax Journal 4:1167–1192.

Tax Profile: May 2006 — Professional Corporations for Physicians and Dentists in Ontario.

"profit sharing plan" —"profit sharing plan" has the meaning assigned by subsection 147(1);

"property" —"property" means property of any kind whatever whether real or personal, immovable or movable, tangible or intangible, or corporeal or incorporeal and, without restricting the generality of the foregoing, includes

(*a*) a right of any kind whatever, a share or a chose in action,

(*b*) unless a contrary intention is evident, money,

(*c*) a timber resource property,

(*d*) the work in progress of a business that is a profession, and

(*e*) the goodwill of a business, as referred to in subsection 13(34);

History: S. 248(1), paragraph (*e*) of the definition "property" was added by S.C. 2016, c. 12, s. 63(5), in force January 1, 2017.

S. 248(1), the portion of the definition "property" before paragraph (*a*) was replaced by S.C. 2013, c. 34, s. 167(4), in force June 26, 2013, and formerly read:

"property"—"property" means property of any kind whatever whether real or personal or corporeal or incorporeal and, without restricting the generality of the foregoing, includes

Tax Topics: No. 1827, The Nature of "Property" Remains Open to Question.

Interpretation Bulletins: *Secondary* — IT-432R2 Benefits conferred on shareholders.

Cases: Under a government program, a commercial fisherman received $2,583,465 for transferring his fishing licences to an aboriginal organization. Since the licences were not "property", the payment was not included in his income as a capital gain. *Haché v. The Queen*, 2010 DTC 1088 (T.C.C.)

The right to compete is not "property", and therefore payments under a non-competition agreement are non-taxable capital receipts. *Manrell v. The Queen*, 2003 DTC 5225 (F.C.A.), reversing 2002 DTC 1222 (T.C.C.).

"Province" — (Repealed by 1980-81-82-83, c. 48, s. 108(8).)

"provincial SIFT tax factor" — (Repealed by S.C. 2008, c. 28, s. 34(1).)

Related Regulations: 414(3).

Related Sections: S. 122(1) Tax payable by inter vivos trust; s. 197(2) Tax on partnership income.

"provincial SIFT tax rate" —"provincial SIFT tax rate" of a SIFT trust or a SIFT partnership for a taxation year means the prescribed amount determined in respect of the SIFT trust or SIFT partnership for the taxation year;

Related Regulations: 414(3).

Related Sections: S. 122(1) Tax payable by inter vivos trust; s. 122.1(1), "SIFT trust"; s. 197(1), "SIFT partnership"; s. 197(2) Tax on partnership income.

"public corporation" —"public corporation" has the meaning assigned by subsection 89(1);

Interpretation Bulletins: *Secondary* — IT-458R2 Canadian-controlled private corporation.

"public foundation" —"public foundation" has the meaning assigned by section 149.1;

"public market" —"public market" has the same meaning as in subsection 122.1(1);

"qualified Canadian journalism organization" —"qualified Canadian journalism organization", at any time, means a corporation, partnership or trust that

(*a*) meets the following conditions:

(i) in the case of a corporation,

(A) it is incorporated under the laws of Canada or a province,

(B) the chairperson or other presiding officer, and at least 3/4 of the directors or other similar officers, are citizens of Canada, and

(C) it is resident in Canada,

(ii) in the case of a partnership,

(A) it is formed under the laws of a province, and

(B) individuals who are citizens of Canada or persons, or partnerships, described in any of subparagraphs (i) to (iii) hold interests in the partnership

(I) representing in value at least 75% of the total value of the partnership property, and

(II) that result in at least 75% of each income or loss of the partnership from any source being included in the determination of their incomes,

(iii) in the case of a trust,

(A) it is formed under the laws of a province,

(B) it is resident in Canada, and

(C) if interests as a beneficiary under the trust are held by one or more persons or partnerships, at least 75% of the fair market value of all interests as a beneficiary under the trust are held by

(I) individuals who are citizens of Canada, or

(II) persons or partnerships described in any of subparagraphs (i) to (iii),

(iv) it operates in Canada, including that its content is edited, designed and, except in the case of digital content, published in Canada,

(v) it is primarily engaged in the production of original news content, which

(A) must be primarily focused on matters of general interest and reports of current events, including coverage of democratic institutions and processes, and

(B) must not be primarily focused on a particular topic such as industry-specific news, sports, recreation, arts, lifestyle or entertainment,

(vi) it regularly employs two or more journalists who deal at arm's length with the organization in the production of its content,

(vii) it is not significantly engaged in the production of content

(A) to promote the interests, or report on the activities, of an organization, an association or its members,

(B) for a government, Crown corporation or government agency, or

(C) to promote goods or services, and

(viii) it is not a Crown corporation, municipal corporation or government agency, and

(*b*) is designated at that time by the Minister and, for this purpose, the Minister shall take into account any recommendations of a body established for the purpose of this definition;

History: S. 248(1), the definition "qualified Canadian journalism organization" was added by S.C. 2019, c. 29, s. 43(2), deemed to have come into force on January 1, 2019.

"qualified donee" —"qualified donee" has the meaning assigned by subsection 149.1(1).

"qualifying environmental trust" —"qualifying environmental trust" has the meaning assigned by subsection 211.6(1);

History: S. 248(1), the definition "qualifying environmental trust" was replaced by S.C. 2011, c. 24, s. 72(1), applicable to the 2012 and subsequent taxation years. S. 248(1), the definition "qualifying environmental trust" formerly read:

"qualifying environmental trust" —"qualifying environmental trust" at any time means a trust resident in a province and maintained at that time for the sole purpose of funding the reclamation of a site in the province that had been used primarily for, or for any combination of, the operation of a mine, the extraction of clay, peat, sand, shale or aggregates (including dimension stone and gravel) or the deposit of waste, where the maintenance of the trust is or may become required under the terms of a contract entered into with Her Majesty in right of Canada or the province or is or may become required under a law of Canada or the province and the contract was entered into or that law was enacted, as the case may be, on or before the later of January 1, 1996 and the day that is one year after the day on which the trust was created, but does not include a trust

(*a*) that relates at that time to the reclamation of a well,

(*b*) that is not maintained at that time to secure the reclamation obligations of one or more persons or partnerships that are beneficiaries under the trust,

(*c*) that at that time has a trustee other than

(i) Her Majesty in right of Canada or the province, or

(ii) a corporation resident in Canada that is licensed or otherwise authorized under the laws of Canada or a province to carry on in Canada the business of offering to the public its services as trustee,

(*d*) that borrows money at that time,

(*e*) that acquired at that time any property that is not described in any of paragraphs (*a*), (*b*) and (*f*) of the definition "qualified investment" in section 204,

(*f*) to which the first contribution was made before 1992,

(*g*) from which any amount was distributed before February 23, 1994,

(*h*) if that time is before 1998 and the trust is not a mining reclamation trust at that time,

(i) to which the first contribution was made before 1996,

(ii) from which any amount was distributed before February 19, 1997, or

(iii) any interest in which was disposed of before February 19, 1997,

(*i*) that elected in writing filed with the Minister, before 1998 or before April of the year following the year in which the first contribution to the trust was made, never to have been a qualifying environmental trust, or

(*j*) that was at any previous time during its existence not a qualifying environmental trust;

Related Sections: S. 12(1)(*z*.1) Qualifying environmental trusts; s. 12(1)(*z*.2) Dispositions of interests in qualifying environmental trusts; s. 20(1)(*ss*) Qualifying environmental trusts; s. 20(1)(*tt*) Acquisition of interests in qualifying environmental trusts; s. 39(1) Meaning of capital gain and capital loss; s. 75(3) Exceptions; s. 107.3 Treatment of beneficiaries under qualifying environmental trusts; s. 149(1)(*z*) Qualifying environmental trust; s. 211.6(1) Tax on qualifying environmental trusts; s. 250(7) Residence of a qualifying environmental trust.

"qualifying share" —"qualifying share" has the meaning assigned by subsection 192(6);

"qualifying trust annuity" —"qualifying trust annuity" has the meaning assigned by subsection 60.011(2);

History: S. 248(1), the definition "qualifying trust annuity" was added by S.C. 2013, c. 34, s. 358(20), deemed to have come into force on January 1, 1989.

"recognized derivatives exchange" —"recognized derivatives exchange" means a person or partnership recognized or registered under the securities laws of a province to carry on the business of providing the facilities necessary for the trading of options, swaps, futures contracts or other financial contracts or instruments whose market price, value, delivery obligations, payment obligations or settlement obligations are derived from, referenced to or based on an underlying interest;

Editorial Note: Certain agreements that are traded on a "recognized derivatives exchange" are excluded from the definition of "synthetic equity arrangement" and therefore are not subject to the dividend rental arrangement rules of subsection 112(2.3).

History: S. 248(1), the definition "recognized derivatives exchange" was added by S.C. 2016, c. 7, s. 48(2), deemed to have come into force on April 22, 2015.

"recognized stock exchange" —"recognized stock exchange" means

(*a*) a designated stock exchange, and

(*b*) any other stock exchange, if that other stock exchange is located in Canada or in a country that is a member of the Organisation for Economic Co-operation and Development and that has a tax treaty with Canada;

"record" —"record" includes an account, an agreement, a book, a chart or table, a diagram, a form, an image, an invoice, a letter, a map, a memorandum, a plan, a return, a statement, a telegram, a voucher, and any other thing containing information, whether in writing or in any other form;

Related Sections: S. 230(4.1) Electronic records; s. 231, "document".

Tax Topics: No. 2043, Record Retention Policies as a Strategy To Limit Exposure on Audit; No. 1562, Are Your Documentary Records Ready for a Tax Dispute?.

"refundable Part VII tax on hand" —"refundable Part VII tax on hand" has the meaning assigned by subsection 192(3);

"refundable Part VIII tax on hand" —"refundable Part VIII tax on hand" has the meaning assigned by subsection 194(3);

"registered Canadian amateur athletic association" — "registered Canadian amateur athletic association" means a Canadian amateur athletic association within the meaning assigned by subsection 149.1(1) that has applied to the Minister in prescribed form for registration, that has been registered and whose registration has not been revoked;

History: S. 248(1), the definition "registered Canadian amateur athletic association" was replaced by S.C. 2011, c. 24, s. 72(1), in force January 1, 2012. S. 248(1), the definition "registered Canadian amateur athletic association" formerly read:

"registered Canadian amateur athletic association"—"registered Canadian amateur athletic association" means an association that was created under any law in force in Canada, that is resident in Canada and that

(*a*) is a person described in paragraph 149(1)(*l*), and

(*b*) has, as its primary purpose and its primary function, the promotion of amateur athletics in Canada on a nation-wide basis,

that has applied to the Minister in prescribed form for registration, that has been registered and whose registration has not been revoked under subsection 168(2);

Forms: T1189 — Application to Register a Canadian Amateur Athletic Association under the Income Tax Act.

Interpretation Bulletins: *Secondary* — IT-496R Non-profit organizations.

"registered charity" —"registered charity" at any time means

(*a*) a charitable organization, private foundation or public foundation, within the meanings assigned by subsection 149.1(1), that is resident in Canada and was either created or established in Canada, or

(*b*) a branch, section, parish, congregation or other division of an organization or foundation described in paragraph (*a*), that is resident in Canada and was either created or established in Canada and that receives donations on its own behalf,

that has applied to the Minister in prescribed form for registration and that is at that time registered as a charitable organization, private foundation or public foundation;

Forms: T2050 — Application to Register Charity Under the Income Tax Act.

Guides: T4063 Registering a Charity for Income Tax Purposes.

Interpretation Bulletins: *Secondary* — IT-496R Non-profit organizations.

"registered disability savings plan" or "RDSP" —"registered disability savings plan" or "RDSP" has the same meaning as in subsection 146.4(1);

History: S. 248(1), the definition "registered disability savings plan" was replaced by S.C. 2012, c. 31, s. 55(1), in force December 14, 2012. S. 248(1), the definition "registered disability savings plan" formerly read:

"registered disability savings plan"—"registered disability savings plan" has the same meaning as in subsection 146.4(1);

"registered education savings plan" or "RESP" —"registered education savings plan" or "RESP" has the same meaning as in subsection 146.1(1);

History: S. 248(1), the definition "registered education savings plan" was replaced by S.C. 2012, c. 31, s. 55(1), in force December 14, 2012. S. 248(1), the definition "registered education savings plan" formerly read:

"registered education savings plan"—"registered education savings plan" has the meaning assigned by subsection 146.1(1);

Related Sections: S. 146.1 Registered education savings plans.

"registered home ownership savings plan" — (Repealed by 1986, c. 6, s. 126(1).)

"registered investment" —"registered investment" has the meaning assigned by subsection 204.4(1);

> **Amendment not yet in force**
>
> **Budget Implementation Act, 2019, No. 1 [S.C. 2019, c. 29]**
>
> **S. 248(1), the definition "registered journalism organization" was added by S.C. 2019, c. 29, s. 43(3), and will read as follows:**
>
> ***"registered journalism organization"*** —"registered journalism organization" means a "qualifying journalism organization" (as defined in subsection 149.1(1)) that has applied to the Minister in prescribed form for registration, that has been registered and whose registration has not been revoked;
>
> **Applicable:** Comes into force on January 1, 2020.

"registered labour-sponsored venture capital corporation" —"registered labour-sponsored venture capital corporation" means a corporation that was registered under subsection 204.81(1), the registration of which has not been revoked;

"registered national arts service organization" —"registered national arts service organization", at any time, means a national arts service organization that has been registered by the Minister under subsection 149.1(6.4), which registration has not been revoked;

Related Sections: S. 56(1)(*aa*) Value of benefits; s. 149.1(6.4) National arts service organizations; s. 149.1(6.5) Revocation of designation.

"registered pension fund or plan" — (Repealed by 1990, c. 35, s. 27(1).)

"registered pension plan" —"registered pension plan" means a pension plan (other than a pooled pension plan) that has been registered by the Minister for the purposes of this Act and whose registration has not been revoked;

History: S. 248(1), the definition "registered pension plan" was replaced by S.C. 2012, c. 31, s. 55(1), in force December 14, 2012. S. 248(1), the definition "registered pension plan" formerly read:

"registered pension plan"—"registered pension plan" means a pension plan that has been registered by the Minister for the purposes of this Act, which registration has not been revoked;

Related Sections: S. 147.1 Registered pension plans; s. 147.2 Pension contributions deductible — employer contributions; s. 147.3 Transfer — money purchase to money purchase, RRSP or RRIF.

Forms: T510 — Application for Registration of a Pension Plan.

Interpretation Bulletins: *Secondary* — IT-528 Transfers of funds between registered plans.

Tax Window Files: General Info re IPPs, *July 23, 2015*, CRA Document No. 2014-0553991E5.

Cases: A company pension plan was held not to qualify as a registered pension plan because the company did not carry on an active business and had no employees. Accordingly, funds transferred to the plan from the RPP of another company were not sheltered under the rollover provisions of s. 60(*j*), nor were payments from the plan eligible for the pension income tax credit. *Feldstein et al. v. M.N.R.*, 92 DTC 1015 (T.C.C.)

"registered retirement income fund" or "RRIF" —"registered retirement income fund or RRIF" have the same meaning as "registered retirement income fund" in subsection 146.3(1);

History: S. 248(1), the definition "registered retirement income fund" was replaced by the definition "registered retirement income fund" or "RRIF" by S.C. 2011, c. 24, s. 72(1), deemed to have come into force on March 23, 2011. S. 248(1), the definition "registered retirement income fund" formerly read:

"registered retirement income fund"—"registered retirement income fund" has the meaning assigned by subsection 146.3(1);

"registered retirement savings plan" or "RRSP"—"registered retirement savings plan or RRSP" have the same meaning as "registered retirement savings plan" in subsection 146(1);

History: S. 248(1), the definition "registered retirement savings plan" was replaced by the definition "registered retirement savings plan" or "RRSP" by S.C. 2011, c. 24, s. 72(1), deemed to have come into force on March 23, 2011. S. 248(1), the definition "registered retirement savings plan" formerly read:

"registered retirement savings plan"—"registered retirement savings plan" has the meaning assigned by subsection 146(1);

"registered securities dealer"—"registered securities dealer" means a person registered or licensed under the laws of a province to trade in securities, in the capacity of an agent or principal, without any restriction as to the types or kinds of securities in which that person may trade;

"registered supplementary unemployment benefit plan"—"registered supplementary unemployment benefit plan" has the meaning assigned by subsection 145(1);

"regulation"—"regulation" means a regulation made by the Governor in Council under this Act;

"relevant factor"—"relevant factor" means

(*a*) for taxation years that end before 2010, 3, and

(*b*) for taxation years that end after 2009, the amount determined by the formula

$$1/(A - B)$$

where

A is the percentage set out in paragraph 123(1)(*a*), and

B is the percentage that is the corporation's general rate reduction percentage (as defined by section 123.4) for the taxation year;

History: S. 248(1), the definition of "relevant factor" was added by S.C. 2013, c. 34, s. 358(20), applicable to the 2003 and subsequent taxation years.

"restricted farm loss"—"restricted farm loss" has the meaning assigned by subsection 31(1.1);

"restricted financial institution"—"restricted financial institution" means

(*a*) a bank,

(*b*) a corporation licensed or otherwise authorized under the laws of Canada or a province to carry on in Canada the business of offering to the public its services as trustee,

(*c*) a credit union,

(*d*) an insurance corporation,

(*e*) a corporation whose principal business is the lending of money to persons with whom the corporation is dealing at arm's length or the purchasing of debt obligations issued by such persons or a combination thereof,

(*e*.1) a corporation described in paragraph (*g*) of the definition "financial institution" in subsection 181(1), or

(*f*) a corporation that is controlled by one or more corporations described in any of paragraphs (*a*) to (*e*.1);

Related Sections: S. 142.2(1), "Financial institution".

"retirement compensation arrangement"—"retirement compensation arrangement" means a plan or arrangement under which contributions (other than payments made to acquire an interest in a life insurance policy) are made by an employer or former employer of a taxpayer, or by a person with whom the employer or former employer does not deal at arm's length, to another person or partnership (in this definition and in Part XI.3 referred to as the "custodian") in connection with benefits that are to be or may be received or enjoyed by any person on, after or in contemplation of any substantial change in the services rendered by the taxpayer, the retirement of the taxpayer or the loss of an office or employment of the taxpayer, but does not include

(*a*) a registered pension plan,

(*a*.1) a pooled registered pension plan,

(*b*) a disability or income maintenance insurance plan under a policy with an insurance corporation,

(*c*) a deferred profit sharing plan,

(*d*) an employees profit sharing plan,

(*e*) a registered retirement savings plan,

(*f*) an employee trust,

(*f*.1) an employee life and health trust,

(*g*) a group sickness or accident insurance plan,

(*h*) a supplementary unemployment benefit plan,

(*i*) a vacation pay trust described in paragraph 149(1)(*y*),

(*j*) a plan or arrangement established for the purpose of deferring the salary or wages of a professional athlete for his services as such with a team that participates in a league having regularly scheduled games (in this definition referred to as an "athlete's plan"), where

(i) the plan or arrangement would, but for paragraph (*j*) of the definition "salary deferral arrangement" in this subsection, be a salary deferral arrangement, and

(ii) in the case of a Canadian team, the custodian of the plan or arrangement carries on business through a fixed place of business in Canada and is licensed or otherwise authorized under the laws of Canada or a province to carry on in Canada the business of offering to the public its services as trustee,

(*k*) a salary deferral arrangement, whether or not deferred amounts thereunder are required to be included as benefits under paragraph 6(1)(*a*) in computing a taxpayer's income,

(*l*) a plan or arrangement (other than an athlete's plan) that is maintained primarily for the benefit of non-residents in respect of services rendered outside Canada, (*m*) an insurance policy, or

(*n*) a prescribed plan or arrangement,

and, for the purposes of this definition, where a particular person holds property in trust under an arrangement that, if the property were held by another person, would be a retirement compensation arrangement, the arrangement shall be deemed to be a retirement compensation arrangement of which the particular person is the custodian;

History: S. 248(1), paragraph (*a.1*) of the definition "retirement compensation arrangement" was added by S.C. 2012, c. 31, s. 55(2), in force December 14, 2012.

S. 248(1), paragraph (*f.1*) of the definition "retirement compensation arrangement" was added by S.C. 2010, c. 25, s. 69(2), applicable after 2009.

Related Regulations: 6802.

Canadian Petroleum Tax Journal: Current Trends in Executive Compensation Structures and Their Taxation, Rachel Colabella and Denise McMullen, 2000, Vol. 13, No. 1.

Canadian Tax Foundation: Kahane et al., *A Fresh Look at Retirement Compensation Arrangements: A Flexible Vehicle for Retirement Planning*, 2013 Canadian Tax Journal 2:479–502; Bernstein, *Retirement Compensation Arrangements*, 2012 Canadian Tax Highlights 20(7):9–10; Bernstein, *RCAs under Attack*, 2010 Canadian Tax Highlights 18(8):7–8; Bank, *Deferred Income Plans for the Owner Manager*, 2009 British Columbia Tax Conference 13:1–37; Horner, *Canadian Taxation and Cross-Border Pensions*, 2009 Canadian Tax Journal 4:905–930.

Tax Profile: May 2012 — Retirement Compensation Arrangements.

Tax Topics: No. 2108, Existing Retirement Compensation Arrangements Under Attack.

Income Tax Technical News: Issue No. 34, Retirement Compensation Arrangements.

"retirement income fund" —"retirement income fund" has the meaning assigned by subsection 146.3(1);

"retirement savings plan" —"retirement savings plan" has the meaning assigned by subsection 146(1);

"retiring allowance" —"retiring allowance" means an amount (other than a superannuation or pension benefit, an amount received as a consequence of the death of an employee or a benefit described in subparagraph 6(1)(*a*)(iv)) received

(*a*) on or after retirement of a taxpayer from an office or employment in recognition of the taxpayer's long service, or

(*b*) in respect of a loss of an office or employment of a taxpayer, whether or not received as, on account or in lieu of payment of, damages or pursuant to an order or judgment of a competent tribunal,

by the taxpayer or, after the taxpayer's death, by a dependant or a relation of the taxpayer or by the legal representative of the taxpayer;

Tax Profile: August 2011 — Retiring Allowances for Owners/Managers.

Income Tax Folios: *Primary* — S2-F1-C2 Retiring Allowances.

Interpretation Bulletins: *Secondary* — IT-365R2 Damages, settlement, and similar receipts.

Cases: When the taxpayer's employment as a university dean was terminated, he sued and was awarded $90,000 in damages. This was not a "retiring allowance" since it did not relate to his past service as dean, but was made for the loss of a future instructor position that he had elected to pursue. *Schewe v. The Queen*, 2010 DTC 1056 (T.C.C.)

The taxpayer was demoted by his employer due to the interference of the employer's major customer. When the taxpayer sued the customer, the damage award he received was not a "retiring allowance" since it was not related to loss of employment. *Ahmad v. The Queen*, 2002 DTC 2065 (T.C.C.)

Severance pay received by a taxpayer upon his retirement in 1991 after 26 years of service in the Public Service constituted a "retiring allowance" within the meaning of s. 248(1) and was included in his income. *Adler v. The Queen*, 94 DTC 6605 (F.C.A.).

"RRSP deduction limit" —"RRSP deduction limit" has the meaning assigned by subsection 146(1);

"RRSP dollar limit" —"RRSP dollar limit" has the meaning assigned by subsection 146(1);

"salary deferral arrangement" —"salary deferral arrangement", in respect of a taxpayer, means a plan or arrangement, whether funded or not, under which any person has a right in a taxation year to receive an amount after the year where it is reasonable to consider that one of the main purposes for the creation or existence of the right is to postpone tax payable under this Act by the taxpayer in respect of an amount that is, or is on account or in lieu of, salary or wages of the taxpayer for services rendered by the taxpayer in the year or a preceding taxation year (including such a right that is subject to one or more conditions unless there is a substantial risk that any one of those conditions will not be satisfied), but does not include

(*a*) a registered pension plan,

(*a*.1) a pooled registered pension plan,

(*b*) a disability or income maintenance insurance plan under a policy with an insurance corporation,

(*c*) a deferred profit sharing plan,

(*d*) an employees profit sharing plan,

(*e*) an employee trust,

(*e*.1) an employee life and health trust,

(*f*) a group sickness or accident insurance plan,

(*g*) a supplementary unemployment benefit plan,

(*h*) a vacation pay trust described in paragraph 149(1)(*y*),

(*i*) a plan or arrangement the sole purpose of which is to provide education or training for employees of an employer to improve their work or work-related skills and abilities,

(*j*) a plan or arrangement established for the purpose of deferring the salary or wages of a professional athlete for the services of the athlete as such with a team that participates in a league having regularly scheduled games,

(*k*) a plan or arrangement under which a taxpayer has a right to receive a bonus or similar payment in respect of services rendered by the taxpayer in a taxation year to be paid within 3 years following the end of the year, or

(*l*) a prescribed plan or arrangement;

History: S. 248(1), paragraph (*a.1*) of the definition "salary deferral arrangement" was added by S.C. 2012, c. 31, s. 55(3), in force December 14, 2012.

S. 248(1), paragraph (*e.1*) of the definition "salary deferral arrangement" was added by S.C. 2010, c. 25, s. 69(3), applicable after 2009.

Related Regulations: 6801.

Canadian Tax Foundation: Horner, *Canadian Taxation and Cross-Border Pensions*, 2009 Canadian Tax Journal 4:905–930.

Tax Topics: No. 2108, Existing Retirement Compensation Arrangements Under Attack.

Tax Window Files: Deferred Salary Early Retirement Plan, *February 7, 2017*, CRA Document No. 2017-0728851E5; Amendment to DSU plan, *April 29, 2015*, CRA Document No. 2015-0565181E5; Election under DSU Plan, *April 10, 2015*, CRA Document No. 2014-0535951E5.

"salary or wages" —"salary or wages", except in sections 5 and 63 and the definition "death benefit" in this subsection, means the income of a taxpayer from an office or employment as computed under subdivision a of Division B of Part I and includes all fees received for services not rendered in the course of the taxpayer's business but does not include superannuation or pension benefits or retiring allowances;

Cases: Stock option benefits granted by the taxpayer to its employees fell within the definition of "salary or wages". *Alcatel Canada Inc. v. The Queen*, 2005 DTC 387 (T.C.C.).

"scientific research and experimental development" —"scientific research and experimental development" means systematic investigation or search that is carried out in a field of science or technology by means of experiment or analysis and that is

(*a*) basic research, namely, work undertaken for the advancement of scientific knowledge without a specific practical application in view,

(*b*) applied research, namely, work undertaken for the advancement of scientific knowledge with a specific practical application in view, or

(*c*) experimental development, namely, work undertaken for the purpose of achieving technological advancement for the purpose of creating new, or improving existing, materials, devices, products or processes, including incremental improvements thereto,

and, in applying this definition in respect of a taxpayer, includes

(*d*) work undertaken by or on behalf of the taxpayer with respect to engineering, design, operations research, mathematical analysis, computer programming, data collection, testing or psychological research, where the work is commensurate with the needs, and directly in support, of work described in paragraph (*a*), (*b*), or (*c*) that is undertaken in Canada by or on behalf of the taxpayer,

but does not include work with respect to

(*e*) market research or sales promotion,

(*f*) quality control or routine testing of materials, devices, products or processes,

(*g*) research in the social sciences or the humanities,

(*h*) prospecting, exploring or drilling for, or producing, minerals, petroleum or natural gas,

(*i*) the commercial production of a new or improved material, device or product or the commercial use of a new or improved process,

(*j*) style changes, or

(*k*) routine data collection;

Related Regulations: 2900.

Related Sections: S. 37 Scientific research and experimental development; s. 127 [Investment tax credit, etc.]; s. 149 Miscellaneous exemptions.

Canadian Tax Foundation: Regan and Cepparo, *CRA Loses*, 2015 Canadian Tax Highlights 23(5):6–7.

Guides: Claiming Scientific Research and Experimental Development Expenditures 1998.

Information Circulars: IC 97-1 Scientific research and experimental development administrative guidelines for software development.

SR&ED Publications: Contract Expenditures for SR&ED Performed on Behalf of a Claimant Policy; SR&ED Overhead and Other Expenditures Policy.

Cases: The corporate taxpayer expended amounts on two projects involving the removal of linings from large metal pipes used to transport bitumen. The taxpayer did not meet the last of the five criteria set out in *Northwest Hydraulic Consultants Ltd. v. The Queen*— the need to keep detailed records of hypotheses, tests, and results of the SR&ED work done. The handwritten notes did not contain any hypotheses and could not be used to replicate or confirm any of the results obtained from the taxpayer's SR&ED work. *Mac & Mac v. The Queen*, 2018 DTC 1008 (TCC)

The following criteria determine whether SR&ED activities have been undertaken: there must be a technical risk or uncertainty, specific hypotheses must be established to reduce or eliminate that uncertainty, true scientific methodology must be used in testing these hypotheses, a technological advance must be achieved, and detailed records of this testing process must be maintained. The taxpayer's work met all of these criteria. *ACSIS EHR v. The Queen*, 2015 DTC 1212 (TCC)

"In respect of" is to be interpreted broadly. The sole purpose of the expenditures was to facilitate the projects by arranging for the cattle to be delivered to the feedlots, where the research (which was accepted as SR&ED) was carried out. The expenditures provided the subjects of the research and as such were in respect of the SR&ED. *Feedlot Health Management Services Ltd. v. Her Majesty the Queen*, 2015 DTC 1083 (T.C.C.)

The taxpayer's development projects met the SR&ED criteria set out in *C.W. Agencies Inc. v. Canada* and, hence, qualified for SR&ED treatment. *Les Abeilles Service de Conditionnement Inc. v. The Queen*, 2014 DTC 1219 (T.C.C.)

"scientific research and experimental development financing contract" —"scientific research and experimental development financing contract" has the meaning assigned by subsection 194(6);

"scientific research and experimental development tax credit" —"scientific research and experimental development tax credit" of a taxpayer for a taxation year has the meaning assigned by subsection 127.3(2);

"securities lending arrangement" —"securities lending arrangement" has the meaning assigned by subsection 260(1);

"self-contained domestic establishment" —"self-contained domestic establishment" means a dwelling-house, apartment or other similar place of residence in which place a person as a general rule sleeps and eats;

Interpretation Bulletins: *Secondary* — IT-352R2 Employee's expenses, including work space in home expenses.

"separation agreement" —"separation agreement" includes an agreement by which a person agrees to make payments on a periodic basis for the maintenance of a former spouse or common-law partner, children of the marriage or common-law partnership or both the former spouse or common-law partner and children of the marriage or common-law partnership, after the marriage or common-law partnership has been dissolved, whether the agreement was made before or after the marriage or common-law partnership was dissolved;

Related Sections: S. 248(1), "common-law partner".

Tax Topics: No. 1702, Income Tax Issues To Be Considered in Negotiating Marriage Contracts.

"share" —"share", except as the context otherwise requires, means a share or a fraction of a share of the capital stock of a corporation and, for greater certainty, a share of the capital stock of a corporation includes a share of the capital of a cooperative corporation (within the meaning assigned by subsection 136(2)), a share of the capital of an agricultural cooperative corporation (within the meaning assigned by subsection 135.1(1)) and a share of the capital of a credit union;

History: S. 248(1), the definition "share" was replaced by S.C. 2013, c. 34, s. 358(5), applicable to taxation years that begin after 2006, and formerly read:

"share"—"share" means a share or fraction of a share of the capital stock of a corporation and, for greater certainty, a share of the capital stock of a corporation includes a share of the capital of a cooperative corporation (within the meaning assigned by subsection 136(2)) and a share of the capital of a credit union;

Interpretation Bulletins: *Secondary* — IT-116R3 Right to buy additional shares.

Tax Window Files: Mandatory redeemable preferred shares, *January 8, 2016*, CRA Document No. 2015-0604491I7.

"shareholder" —"shareholder" includes a member or other person entitled to receive payment of a dividend;

Income Tax Folios: *Secondary* — S4-F7-C1 Amalgamations of Canadian Corporations.

Interpretation Bulletins: *Secondary* — IT-116R3 Rights to buy additional shares; IT-432R2 Benefits conferred on shareholders.

"share-purchase tax credit" —"share-purchase tax credit" of a taxpayer for a taxation year has the meaning assigned by subsection 127.2(6);

"short-term preferred share" —"short-term preferred share" of a corporation at any particular time means a share, other than a grandfathered share, of the capital stock of the corporation issued after December 15, 1987 that at that particular time

(*a*) is a share where, under the terms and conditions of the share, any agreement relating to the share or any modification of those terms and conditions or that agreement, the corporation or a specified person in relation to the corporation is or may, at any time within 5 years after the date of its issue, be required to redeem, acquire or cancel, in whole or in part, the share (unless the requirement to redeem, acquire or cancel the share arises only in the event of the death of the shareholder or by reason only of a right to convert or exchange the share) or to reduce the paid-up capital of the share, and for the purposes of this paragraph

(i) an agreement in respect of a share of the capital stock of a corporation shall be read without reference to that part of the agreement under which a person agrees to acquire the share for an amount

(A) in the case of a share (other than a share that would, but for that part of the agreement, be a taxable preferred share) the agreement in respect of which provides that the share is to be acquired within 60 days after the day on which the agreement was entered into, that does not exceed the greater of the fair market value of the share at the time the agreement was entered into, determined without reference to the agreement, and the fair market value of the share at the time of the acquisition, determined without reference to the agreement, or

(B) that does not exceed the fair market value of the share at the time of the acquisition, determined without reference to the agreement, or for an amount determined by reference to the assets or earnings of the corporation where that determination may reasonably be considered to be used to determine an amount that does not exceed the fair market value of the share at the time of the acquisition, determined without reference to the agreement, and

(ii) "shareholder" includes a shareholder of a shareholder, or

(*b*) is a share that is convertible or exchangeable at any time within 5 years after the date of its issue, unless

(i) it is convertible into or exchangeable for

(A) another share of the corporation or a corporation related to the corporation that, if issued, would not be a short-term preferred share,

(B) a right or warrant that, if exercised, would allow the person exercising it to acquire only a share of the corporation or a corporation related to the corporation that, if issued, would not be a short-term preferred share, or

(C) both a share described in clause (A) and a right or warrant described in clause (B), and

(ii) all the consideration receivable for the share on the conversion or exchange is the share described in clause (i)(A) or the right or warrant described in clause (i)(B) or both, as the case may be, and for the purposes of this subparagraph, where a taxpayer may become entitled on the conversion or exchange of a share to receive any particular consideration (other than consideration described in any of clauses (i)(A) to (C)) in lieu of a fraction of a share, the particular consideration shall be deemed not to be consideration unless it may reasonably be considered that the particular consideration was receivable as part of a series of transactions or events one of the main purposes of which was to avoid or limit the application of Part IV.1 or VI.1,

and, for the purposes of this definition,

(*c*) where at any particular time after December 15, 1987, otherwise than pursuant to a written arrangement to do so entered into before December 16, 1987, the terms or conditions of a share of the capital stock of a corporation that are relevant to any matter referred to in any of paragraphs (*a*), (*b*), (*f*) and (*h*) are established or modified, or any agreement in respect of any such matter to which the corporation or a specified person in relation to the corporation is a party, is changed or entered into, the share shall be deemed after that particular time to have been issued at that particular time,

(*d*) where at any particular time after December 15, 1987 a particular share of the capital stock of a corporation has been issued or its terms or conditions have been modified or an agreement in respect of the share is modified or entered into, and it may reasonably be considered, having regard to all the circumstances, including the rate of interest on any debt obligation or the dividend provided on any short-term preferred share, that

(i) but for the existence at any time of such a debt obligation or such a short-term preferred share, the particular share would not have been issued or its terms or conditions modified or the agreement in respect of the share would not have been modified or entered into, and

(ii) one of the main purposes for the issue of the particular share or the modification of its terms or conditions or the modification or entering into the agreement in respect of the share was to avoid or limit the tax payable under subsection 191.1(1),

the particular share shall be deemed after that particular time to have been issued at that particular time and to be a short-term preferred share of the corporation, (*e*) where at any particular time after December 15, 1987, otherwise than pursuant to a written arrangement to do so entered into before December 16, 1987, the terms or conditions of a share of the capital stock of a corporation are modified or established or any agreement in respect of the share has been changed or entered into, and as a consequence thereof the corporation or a specified person in relation to the corporation may reasonably be expected to redeem, acquire or cancel (otherwise than by reason of the death of the shareholder or by reason only of a right to convert or exchange the share that would not cause the share to be a short-term preferred share by reason of paragraph (*b*)), in whole or in part, the share, or to reduce its paid-up capital, within 5 years after the particular time, the share shall be deemed to have been issued at that particular time and to be a short-term preferred share of the corporation after the particular time until the time that that reasonable expectation ceases to exist and, for the purposes of this paragraph,

(i) an agreement in respect of a share of the capital stock of a corporation shall be read without reference to that part of the agreement under which a person agrees to acquire the share for an amount

(A) in the case of a share (other than a share that would, but for that part of the agreement, be a taxable preferred share) the agreement in respect of which provides that the share is to be acquired within 60 days after the day on which the agreement was entered into, that does not exceed the greater of the fair market value of the share at the time the agreement was entered into, determined without reference to the agreement, and the fair market value of the share at the time of the acquisition, determined without reference to the agreement, or

(B) that does not exceed the fair market value of the share at the time of the acquisition, determined without reference to the agreement, or for an amount determined by reference to the assets or earnings of the corporation where that determination may reasonably be considered to be used to determine an amount that does not exceed the fair market value of the share at the time of the acquisition, determined without reference to the agreement, and

(ii) "shareholder" includes a shareholder of a shareholder,

(*f*) if a share of the capital stock of a corporation was issued after December 15, 1987 and at the time the share was issued the existence of the corporation was, or there was an arrangement under which it could be, limited to a period that was within five years from the date of its issue, the share is deemed to be a short-term preferred share of the corporation unless

(i) the share is a grandfathered share and the arrangement is a written arrangement entered into before December 16, 1987, or

(ii) the share is issued to an individual after April 14, 2005 under an agreement referred to in subsection 7(1), if when the individual last acquired a right under the agreement to acquire a share of the capital stock of the corporation, the existence of the corporation was not, and no arrangement was in effect under which it could be, limited to a period that was within five years from the date of that last acquisition,

(*g*) where a share of the capital stock of a corporation is acquired at any time after December 15, 1987 by the corporation or a specified person in relation to the corporation and the share is at any particular time after that time acquired by a person with whom the corporation or a specified person in relation to the corporation was dealing at arm's length if this Act were read without reference to paragraph 251(5)(*b*), from the corporation or a specified person in relation to the corporation, the share shall be deemed after that particular time to have been issued at that particular time,

(*h*) where at any particular time after December 15, 1987, otherwise than pursuant to a written arrangement to do so entered into before December 16, 1987, as a result of the terms or conditions of a share of the capital stock of a corporation or any agreement entered into by the corporation or a specified person in relation to the corporation, any person (other than the corporation or an individual other than a trust) was obligated, either absolutely or contingently and either immediately or in the future, to effect any undertaking within 5 years after the day on which the share was issued (in this paragraph referred to as a "guarantee agreement") including any guarantee, covenant or agreement to purchase or repurchase the share, and including the lending of funds or the placing of amounts on deposit with, or on behalf of the shareholder or a specified person in relation to the shareholder given

(i) to ensure that any loss that the shareholder or a specified person in relation to the shareholder may sustain, by reason of the ownership, holding or disposition of the share or any other property is limited in any respect, and

(ii) as part of a transaction or event or series of transactions or events that included the issuance of the share,

the share shall be deemed after that particular time to have been issued at the particular time and to be at and immediately after the particular time a short-term preferred share, and for the purposes of this paragraph, where a guarantee agreement in respect of a share is given at any particular time after December 15, 1987, otherwise than pursuant to a written arrangement to do so entered into before December 16, 1987, the share shall be deemed to have been issued at the particular time and the guarantee agreement shall be deemed to have been given as part of a series of transactions that included the issuance of the share, (*i*) a share that is, at the time a dividend is paid thereon, a share described in paragraph (*e*) of the definition "term preferred share" in this subsection during the applicable time period referred to in that paragraph or a prescribed share shall, notwithstanding any other provision of this definition, be deemed not to be a short-term preferred share at that time, and

(*j*) "specified person" has the meaning assigned by paragraph (*h*) of the definition "taxable preferred share" in this subsection;

History: S. 248(1), paragraph (*f*) of the definition "short-term preferred share" was replaced by S.C. 2013, c. 34, s. 358(17), applicable to shares issued after April 14, 2005, and formerly read:

(*f*) where a share of the capital stock of a corporation was issued after December 15, 1987 and at the time the share was issued the existence of the corporation was, or there was an arrangement under which it could be, limited to a period that was within 5 years after the date of its issue, the share shall be deemed to be a short-term preferred share of the corporation unless the share is a grandfathered share and the arrangement is a written arrangement entered into before December 16, 1987,

Related Sections: S. 248(10) Series of transactions.

Canadian Tax Foundation: Jung, *The Taxable Preferred Share Rules and the Private Corporation*, 2017 Ontario Tax Conference 12:1–20; Diep, *Preferred Share Rules: The Expected, Unexpected and Unintended*, 2017 Prairie Provinces Tax Conference 13:1–29.

"SIFT partnership" —"SIFT partnership" has the meaning assigned by section 197;

"SIFT partnership balance-due day" —"SIFT partnership balance-due day", in respect of a taxation year of a SIFT partnership, means the day on or before which the partnership is required to file a return for the taxation year under section 229 of the *Income Tax Regulations*;

"SIFT trust" —"SIFT trust" has the meaning assigned by section 122.1;

"SIFT trust wind-up event" —"SIFT trust wind-up event" means a distribution by a particular trust resident in Canada of property to a taxpayer in respect of which the following conditions are met:

(*a*) the distribution occurs before 2013,

(*b*) there is a resulting disposition of all of the taxpayer's interest as a beneficiary under the particular trust,

(*c*) the particular trust is

(i) a SIFT wind-up entity,

(ii) a trust whose only beneficiary throughout the period (referred to in this definition as the "qualifying period") that begins on July 14, 2008 and that ends at the time of the distribution is another trust that throughout the qualifying period

(A) is resident in Canada, and

(B) is a SIFT wind-up entity or a trust described by this subparagraph, or

(iii) a trust whose only beneficiary at the time of distribution is another trust that throughout the qualifying period

(A) is resident in Canada,

(B) is a SIFT wind-up entity or a trust described by subparagraph (ii), and

(C) is a majority interest beneficiary (within the meaning that would be assigned by section 251.1 if the references in the definition "majority interest beneficiary" in subsection 251.1(3) to "50%" were read as references to "25%") of the particular trust,

(*d*) the particular trust ceases to exist immediately after the distribution or immediately after the last of a series of SIFT trust wind-up events (determined without reference to this paragraph) of the particular trust that includes the distribution, and

(*e*) the property was not acquired by the particular trust as a result of a transfer or an exchange

(i) that is

(A) a "qualifying exchange" as defined in subsection 132.2(1) or a "qualifying disposition" as defined in subsection 107.4(1),

(B) made after February 2, 2009, and

(C) from any person other than a SIFT wind-up entity, or

(ii) to which any of sections 51, 85, 85.1, 86, 87, 88, 107.4 or 132.2 applies, of another property acquired as a result of a transfer or an exchange described by subparagraph (i) or this subparagraph;

History: S. 248(1), the definition "SIFT trust wind-up event" was added by S.C. 2009, c. 2, s. 76(4), applicable after December 19, 2007.

Related Sections: S. 80.01(5.1) Deemed settlement on SIFT trust wind-up event; s. 88.1 SIFT trust wind-up event; s. 107(2) Distribution by personal trust; s. 107(3) Application of subsection (3.1); s. 107(3.1) SIFT trust wind-up event; s. 122.1(1), "SIFT trust"; s. 248(1), "SIFT wind-up entity", "SIFT wind-up corporation"; s. 256(7)(*f*) Acquiring control.

"SIFT wind-up corporation" —"SIFT wind-up corporation", in respect of a SIFT wind-up entity, means at any particular time a corporation

(*a*) that, at any time that is after July 13, 2008 and before the earlier of the particular time and January 1, 2013, owns all of the equity in the SIFT wind-up entity, or

(*b*) shares of the capital stock of which are at or before the particular time distributed on a SIFT trust wind-up event of the SIFT wind-up entity;

History: S. 248(1), the definition "SIFT wind-up corporation" was added by S.C. 2009, c. 2, s. 76(4), applicable after December 19, 2007.

Related Sections: S. 54, "superficial loss"; s. 80.01(5.1) Deemed settlement on SIFT trust wind-up event; s. 85.1(8) Rollover on SIFT unit for share exchange; s. 87(2)(*s.1*) Deemed SIFT wind-up corporation; s. 88(1)(*e.2*) Winding-up — Application of amalgamation provisions; s. 88.1 SIFT trust wind-up event; s. 107(2) Distribution by personal trust; s. 107(3.1) SIFT trust wind-up event; s. 132.2(2), "qualifying exchange"; s. 248(1), "SIFT wind-up entity", "SIFT trust wind-up event"; s. 256(7)(*f*) Acquiring control.

"SIFT wind-up entity" —"SIFT wind-up entity" means a trust or partnership that at any time in the period that began on October 31, 2006 and that ends on July 14, 2008 is

(*a*) a SIFT trust (determined without reference to subsection 122.1(2)),

(*b*) a SIFT partnership (determined without reference to subsection 197(8)), or

(*c*) a real estate investment trust (as defined in subsection 122.1(1));

History: S. 248(1), the definition "SIFT wind-up entity" was added by S.C. 2009, c. 2, s. 76(4), applicable after December 19, 2007.

Related Sections: S. 7(1.4)(*b*)(vi) Exchange of options; s. 54, "superficial loss"; s. 80.01(5.1) Deemed settlement on SIFT trust wind-up event; s. 85.1(8) Rollover on SIFT unit for share exchange; s. 88.1 SIFT trust wind-up event; s. 107(3.1) SIFT trust wind-up event; s. 248(1), "SIFT wind-up entity", "SIFT wind-up corporation".

"SIFT wind-up entity equity" —"SIFT wind-up entity equity", or equity in a SIFT wind-up entity, means

(*a*) if the SIFT wind-up entity is a trust, a capital interest (determined without reference to subsection (25)) in the trust, and

(*b*) if the SIFT wind-up entity is a partnership, an interest as a member of the partnership where, by operation of any law governing the arrangement in respect of the partnership, the liability of the member as a member of the partnership is limited,

except that if all of the interests described in paragraph (*a*) or (*b*), as the case may be, in the SIFT wind-up entity are described by reference to units, it means the part of the interest represented by such a unit;

History: S. 248(1), the definition "SIFT wind-up entity equity" was added by S.C. 2009, c. 2, s. 76(4), applicable after December 19, 2007.

Related Sections: S. 85.1(8) Rollover on SIFT unit for share exchange; s. 108(1), "capital interest"; s. 116(6)(*b*)(ii) Definition of "excluded property"; s. 248(1), "capital interest"; s. 248(1), "SIFT wind-up entity", "SIFT wind-up corporation"; s. 248(25), "beneficially interested".

"small business bond" —"small business bond" has the meaning assigned by section 15.2;

"small business corporation" —"small business corporation", at any particular time, means, subject to subsection 110.6(15), a particular corporation that is a Canadian-controlled private corporation all or substantially all of the fair market value of the assets of which at that time is attributable to assets that are

(*a*) used principally in an active business carried on primarily in Canada by the particular corporation or by a corporation related to it,

(*b*) shares of the capital stock or indebtedness of one or more small business corporations that are at that time connected with the particular corporation (within the meaning of subsection 186(4) on the assumption that the small business corporation is at that time a "payer corporation" within the meaning of that subsection), or

(*c*) assets described in paragraphs (*a*) and (*b*),

including, for the purpose of paragraph 39(1)(*c*), a corporation that was at any time in the 12 months preceding that time a small business corporation, and, for the purpose of this definition, the fair market value of a net income stabilization account shall be deemed to be nil;

Editorial Note: Small business corporation status is a prerequisite for a number of important income tax incentives, including the capital gains exemption and ABILs. The CRA's position is that "all or substantially all" means 90% or more, although case law has supported a lesser proportion. Per paragraph (*b*), a corporation is generally connected with another corporation if it controls that other corporation (within the extended meaning of s. 186(2)) or owns shares representing more than 10% of both votes and value. The CRA has issued a large number of technical interpretations as to circumstances in which particular types of assets are considered to be used in a business.

Related Regulations: 4900(12).

Related Sections: S. 15.1 Interest on small business development bonds; s. 39(1)(*c*) Meaning of capital gain and capital loss; s. 40(1.1) Reserve — property disposed of to a child; s. 44.1 Reserve — property disposed of to a child; s. 48.1 Gain when small business corporation becomes public; s. 74.4(2) Transfers and loans to corporations; s. 110.6(2.1) Capital gains deduction — qualified small business corporation shares; s. 110.6(15) Value of assets of corporations; s. 125(7), "Canadian-controlled private corporation"; s. 186(4) Corporations connected with particular corporation; s. 248(1), "active business", "Canadian-controlled private corporation", "corporation", "net income stabilization account"; s. 255 Canada; s. 256(6.1) Simultaneous control.

Canadian Tax Foundation: Campbell, *Current Cases: Legislative Interpretation — Looking to the substance and intent (Ollenberger)*, 2013 Atlantic Provinces Tax Conference 1C:4–5.

Income Tax Folios: S4-F8-C1 Business Investment Losses.

Interpretation Bulletins: *Secondary* — IT-349R3 Intergenerational transfers of farm property on death.

Cases: It is sufficient for a business to be carried on in order for it to be carried on *actively*. The taxpayer remained active during the years preceding its dissolution to sell off merchandise inventory. The business was being actively carried on, although in a minimal way. *Hébert v. The Queen*, 2018 DTC 1049 (TCC)

"Active business" simply means "any business carried on by the taxpayer". A corporation pursuing oil and gas ventures was carrying on an active business and was therefore a small business corporation, allowing the taxpayer to claim an ABIL deduction for money he loaned to it. *Ollenberger v. The Queen*, 2013 DTC 5064 (F.C.A.), reversing 2012 DTC 1094 (T.C.C.)

"small business development bond" —"small business development bond" has the meaning assigned by section 15.1;

"specified employee" —"specified employee" of a person means an employee of the person who is a specified shareholder of the person or who does not deal at arm's length with the person;

Related Regulations: 2900(5).

Related Sections: S. 37(9) Salary or wages.

"specified financial institution" —"specified financial institution", at any time, means

(*a*) a bank,

(*b*) a corporation licensed or otherwise authorized under the laws of Canada or a province to carry on in Canada the business of offering to the public its services as trustee,

(*c*) a credit union,

(*d*) an insurance corporation,

(*e*) a corporation whose principal business is the lending of money to persons with whom the corporation is dealing at arm's length or the purchasing of debt obligations issued by such persons or a combination thereof,

(*e*.1) a corporation described in paragraph (*g*) of the definition "financial institution" in subsection 181(1),

(*f*) a corporation that is controlled by one or more corporations described in any of paragraphs (*a*) to (*e*.1) and, for the purpose of this paragraph, one corporation is controlled by another corporation if more than 50% of its issued share capital (having full voting rights under all circumstances) belongs to the other corporation, to persons with whom the other corporation does not deal at arm's length, or to the other corporation and persons with whom the other corporation does not deal at arm's length, or

(*g*) a corporation that is related to a particular corporation described in any of paragraphs (*a*) to (*f*), other than a particular corporation described in paragraph (*e*) or (*e*.1) the principal business of which is the factoring of trade accounts receivable that

(i) the particular corporation acquired from a related person,

(ii) arose in the course of an active business carried on by a person (in this paragraph referred to as the "business entity") related at that time to the particular corporation, and

(iii) at no particular time before that time were held by a person other than a person who was related to the business entity;

Related Sections: S. 112(2.1) Where no deduction permitted; s. 112(2.2) Guaranteed shares; s. 187.1 Definition of "excepted dividend"; s. 191(1), "private holding corporation"; s. 248(14) Related corporations.

"specified future tax consequence" —"specified future tax consequence" for a taxation year means

(*a*) the consequence of the deduction or exclusion of an amount referred to in paragraph 161(7)(*a*),

(*b*) the consequence of a reduction under subsection 66(12.73) of a particular amount purported to be renounced by a corporation after the beginning of the year to a person or partnership under subsection 66(12.6) or (12.601) because of the application of subsection 66(12.66), determined as if the purported renunciation would, but for subsection 66(12.73), have been effective only where

(i) the purported renunciation occurred in January, February or March of a calendar year,

(ii) the effective date of the purported renunciation was the last day of the preceding calendar year,

(iii) the corporation agreed in that preceding calendar year to issue a flow-though share to the person or partnership,

(iv) the particular amount does not exceed the amount, if any, by which the consideration for which the share is to be issued exceeds the total of all other amounts purported by the corporation to have been renounced under subsection 66(12.6) or (12.601) in respect of that consideration,

(v) paragraphs 66(12.66)(*c*) and (*d*) are satisfied with respect to the purported renunciation, and

(vi) the form prescribed for the purpose of subsection 66(12.7) in respect of the purported renunciation is filed with the Minister before May of the calendar year; and

(*c*) the consequence of an adjustment or a reduction described in subsection 161(6.1);

Related Sections: S. 88(1)(*e*.9) Winding-up; s. 127(10.2) Expenditure limit determined; s. 127.1(2) Definitions; s. 156.1(1.1) Values of A and B in "net tax owing"; s. 156.1(1.2) Value of D in "net tax owing"; s. 157(2) Special case; s. 157(2.1) $3,000 threshold; s. 161(4) Limitation — farmers and fishermen; s. 161(6.2) Flow-through share renunciations.

"specified individual" —"specified individual" has the meaning assigned by subsection 120.4(1);

"specified investment business" —"specified investment business" has the meaning assigned by subsection 125(7);

"specified member" —"specified member" of a partnership in a fiscal period or taxation year of the partnership, as the case may be, means

(*a*) any member of the partnership who is a limited partner (within the meaning assigned by subsection 96(2.4)) of the partnership at any time in the period or year, and

(*b*) any member of the partnership, other than a member who is

(i) actively engaged in those activities of the partnership business that are other than the financing of the partnership business, or

(ii) carrying on a similar business as that carried on by the partnership in its taxation year, otherwise than as a member of a partnership,

on a regular, continuous and substantial basis throughout that part of the period or year during which the business of the partnership is ordinarily carried on and during which the member is a member of the partnership;

"specified mutual fund trust" —"specified mutual fund trust", at any time, means a mutual fund trust other than a mutual fund trust for which it can reasonably be considered, having regard to all the circumstances, including the terms and conditions of the units of the trust, that the total of all amounts each of which is the fair market value, at that time, of a unit issued by the trust and held by a person exempt from tax under section 149 is all or substantially all of the total of all amounts each of which is the fair market value, at that time, of a unit issued by the trust;

Editorial Note: This definition is relevant to the meaning of "synthetic equity arrangement", which is a type of dividend rental arrangement; see the editorial note to subsection 112(2.3).

History: S. 248(1), the definition "specified mutual fund trust" was added by S.C. 2016, c. 7, s. 48(2), deemed to have come into force on April 22, 2015.

"specified pension plan" —"specified pension plan" means a prescribed arrangement;

History: S. 248(1), the definition "specified pension plan" was added by S.C. 2011, c. 24, s. 72(4), applicable after 2009.

Related Regulations: 7800.

"specified proportion" —"specified proportion", of a member of a partnership for a fiscal period of the partnership, means the proportion that the member's share of the total income or loss of the partnership for the partnership's fiscal period is of the partnership's total income or loss for that period and, for the purpose of this definition, where that income or loss for a period is nil, that proportion shall be computed as if the partnership had income for that period in the amount of $1,000,000;

Proposed Amendment

2019 Federal Budget Resolutions

Subsection 248(1) of the Act is amended by adding the following in alphabetical order:

specified securities lending arrangement —*specified securities lending arrangement* has the meaning assigned by subsection 260(1);

Applicable: Deemed to have come into force on March 19, 2019.

History: S. 248(1), the definition of "specified proportion" was added by S.C. 2013, c. 34, s. 358(20), applicable after December 20, 2002.

"specified shareholder" —"specified shareholder" of a corporation in a taxation year means a taxpayer who owns, directly or indirectly, at any time in the year, not less than 10% of the issued shares of any class of the capital stock of the corporation or of any other corporation that is related to the corporation and, for the purposes of this definition,

(*a*) a taxpayer shall be deemed to own each share of the capital stock of a corporation owned at that time by a person with whom the taxpayer does not deal at arm's length,

(*b*) each beneficiary of a trust shall be deemed to own that proportion of all such shares owned by the trust at that time that the fair market value at that time of the beneficial interest of the beneficiary in the trust is of the fair market value at that time of all beneficial interests in the trust,

(*c*) each member of a partnership shall be deemed to own that proportion of all the shares of any class of the capital stock of a corporation that are property of the partnership at that time that the fair market value at that time of the member's interest in the partnership is of the fair market value at that time of the interests of all members in the partnership,

(*d*) an individual who performs services on behalf of a corporation that would be carrying on a personal services business if the individual or any person related to the individual were at that time a specified shareholder of the corporation shall be deemed to be a specified shareholder of the corporation at that time if the individual, or any person or partnership with whom the individual does not deal at arm's length, is, or by virtue of any arrangement may become, entitled, directly or indirectly, to not less than 10% of the assets or the shares of any class of the capital stock of the corporation or any corporation related thereto, and

(*e*) notwithstanding paragraph (*b*), where a beneficiary's share of the income or capital of the trust depends on the exercise by any person of, or the failure by any person to exercise, any discretionary power, the beneficiary shall be deemed to own each share of the capital stock of a corporation owned at that time by the trust;

Related Sections: S. 7(9) Meaning of "qualifying acquisition"; s. 18(5), "specified shareholder"; s. 18(5.1) Specified shareholder or specified beneficiary; s. 104(1) Reference to trust or estate; s. 125(7) Definitions; s. 248(1), "corporation", "individual", "property", "share", "trust"; s. 249(1) Definition of "taxation year"; s. 251(1) Arm's length; s. 251(2) Definition of "related persons".

Interpretation Bulletins: *Secondary* — IT-73R6 The small business deduction; IT-432R2 Benefits conferred on shareholders.

"specified synthetic equity arrangement" —"specified synthetic equity arrangement", in respect of a DRA share of a person or partnership, means one or more agreements or other arrangements that

(*a*) have the effect of providing to a person or partnership all or any portion of the risk of loss or opportunity for gain or profit in respect of the DRA share and, for greater certainty, opportunity for gain or profit includes rights to, benefits from and distributions on a share, and

(*b*) can reasonably be considered to have been entered into in connection with a synthetic equity arrangement, in respect of the DRA share, or in connection with another specified synthetic equity arrangement, in respect of the DRA share;

History: S. 248(1), the definition "specified synthetic equity arrangement" was added by S.C. 2016, c. 7, s. 48(2), deemed to have come into force on April 22, 2015.

"specified unitholder" —"specified unitholder", of a partnership or trust (referred to in this definition as the "entity"), the interests in which are described by reference to units, means a taxpayer who would be a specified shareholder of the entity if the entity were a corporation and each unit of the entity were a share of a class of the corporation having the same attributes as the unit;

History: S. 248(1), the definition "specified unitholder" was added by S.C. 2012, c. 31, s. 55(5), in force December 14, 2012.

"split income" —"split income" has the meaning assigned by subsection 120.4(1);

"stock dividend" —"stock dividend" includes any dividend (determined without reference to the definition "dividend" in this subsection) paid by a corporation to the extent that it is paid by the issuance of shares of any class of the capital stock of the corporation;

"subsidiary controlled corporation" —"subsidiary controlled corporation" means a corporation more than 50% of the issued share capital of which (having full voting rights under all circumstances) belongs to the corporation to which it is subsidiary;

"subsidiary wholly-owned corporation" —"subsidiary wholly-owned corporation" means a corporation all the issued share capital of which (except directors' qualifying shares) belongs to the corporation to which it is subsidiary;

Related Sections: S. 87(1.4), "subsidiary wholly-owned corporation".

"superannuation or pension benefit" —"superannuation or pension benefit" includes any amount received out of or under a superannuation or pension fund or plan (including, except for the purposes of subparagraph 56(1)(*a*)(i), a pooled registered pension plan) and, without restricting the generality of the foregoing, includes any payment made to a beneficiary under the fund or plan or to an employer or former employer of the beneficiary under the fund or plan

(*a*) in accordance with the terms of the fund or plan,

(*b*) resulting from an amendment to or modification of the fund or plan, or

(*c*) resulting from the termination of the fund or plan;

History: S. 248(1), the portion of the definition "superannuation or pension benefit" before paragraph (*a*) was replaced by S.C. 2012, c. 31, s. 55(4), in force December 14, 2012. The portion of the definition "superannuation or pension benefit" before paragraph (*a*) formerly read:

> *"superannuation or pension benefit"*—"superannuation or pension benefit" includes any amount received out of or under a superannuation or pension fund or plan and, without restricting the generality of the foregoing, includes any payment made to a beneficiary under the fund or plan or to an employer or former employer of the beneficiary thereunder

"supplementary unemployment benefit plan" —"supplementary unemployment benefit plan" has the meaning assigned by subsection 145(1);

"synthetic disposition arrangement" —"synthetic disposition arrangement", in respect of a property owned by a taxpayer, means one or more agreements or other arrangements that

(a) are entered into by the taxpayer or by a person or partnership that does not deal at arm's length with the taxpayer,

(b) have the effect, or would have the effect if entered into by the taxpayer instead of the person or partnership, of eliminating all or substantially all the taxpayer's risk of loss and opportunity for gain or profit in respect of the property for a definite or indefinite period of time, and

(c) can, in respect of any agreement or arrangement entered into by a person or partnership that does not deal at arm's length with the taxpayer, reasonably be considered to have been entered into, in whole or in part, with the purpose of obtaining the effect described in paragraph (b);

Editorial Note: See the editorial note under s. 80.6(1).

History: S. 248(1), the definition "synthetic disposition arrangement", was added by S.C. 2013, c. 40, s. 89(5), deemed to have come into force on March 21, 2013.

Related Sections: S. 80.6 [Synthetic disposition]; s. 112(8) Synthetic disposition — holding period; s. 126(4.5) Synthetic disposition — holding period.

Canadian Tax Foundation: Miller and Milet, *Derivative Forward Agreements and Synthetic Disposition Arrangements*, 2013 Conference Report 10:1–50; Panasiuk, *Synthetic Dispositions: Get Cash Now, Pay Tax Later*, 2013 Canadian Tax Focus 13(2):10.

Tax Profile: June 2013 — 2013 Federal Budget.

"synthetic disposition period" —"synthetic disposition period", of a synthetic disposition arrangement, means the definite or indefinite period of time during which the synthetic disposition arrangement has, or would have, the effect described in paragraph (b) of the definition "synthetic disposition arrangement" in this subsection;

History: S. 248(1), the definition "synthetic disposition period", was added by S.C. 2013, c. 40, s. 89(5), deemed to have come into force on March 21, 2013.

"synthetic equity arrangement" —"synthetic equity arrangement" in respect of a DRA share of a person or partnership (referred to in this definition as the *particular person*),

(a) means one or more agreements or other arrangements that

(i) are entered into by the particular person, by a person or partnership that does not deal at arm's length with, or is affiliated with, the particular person (referred to in this definition as a *connected person*) or, for greater certainty, by any combination of the particular person and connected persons, with one or more persons or partnerships (referred to in this definition as a *counterparty* and in subsection 112(2.32) as a *counterparty* or an *affiliated counterparty* as appropriate),

(ii) have the effect, or would have the effect, if each agreement entered into by a connected person were entered into by the particular person, of providing all or substantially all of the risk of loss and opportunity for gain or profit in respect of the DRA share to a counterparty or a group of counterparties each member of which is affiliated with every other member and, for greater certainty, opportunity for gain or profit includes rights to, benefits from and distributions on a share, and

(iii) if entered into by a connected person, can reasonably be considered to have been entered into with the knowledge, or where there ought to have been the knowledge, that the effect described in subparagraph (ii) would result, and

(b) does not include

(i) an agreement that is traded on a recognized derivatives exchange unless it can reasonably be considered that, at the time the agreement is entered into,

(A) the particular person or the connected person, as the case may be, knows or ought to know that the agreement is part of a series of transactions that has the effect of providing all or substantially all of the risk of loss and opportunity for gain or profit in respect of the DRA share to a tax-indifferent investor, or a group of tax-indifferent investors each member of which is affiliated with every other member, or

(B) one of the main reasons for entering into the agreement is to obtain the benefit of a deduction in respect of a payment, or a reduction of an amount that would otherwise have been included in income, under the agreement, that corresponds to an expected or actual dividend in respect of a DRA share,

(ii) one or more agreements or other arrangements that, but for this subparagraph, would be a synthetic equity arrangement, in respect of a share owned by the particular person (in this subparagraph referred to as the *synthetic short position*), if

(A) the particular person has entered into one or more other agreements or other arrangements (other than, for greater certainty, an agreement under which the share is acquired or an agreement or arrangement under which the particular person receives a deemed dividend and is provided with all or substantially all of the risk of loss and opportunity for gain or profit in respect of the share) that have the effect of providing all or substantially all of the risk of loss and opportunity for gain or profit in respect of the share to the particular person (in this subparagraph referred to as the *synthetic long position*),

(B) the synthetic short position has the effect of offsetting all amounts included or deducted in computing the income of the particular person with respect to the synthetic long position, and

(C) the synthetic short position was entered into for the purpose of obtaining the effect referred to in clause (B), and

(iii) an agreement to purchase the shares of a corporation, or a purchase agreement that is part of a series of agreements to purchase the shares of a corporation, under which a counterparty or a group of counterparties each member of which is affiliated with every other member acquires control of the corporation that has issued the shares being purchased, unless the main reason for establishing, incorporating or operating the corporation is to have this subparagraph apply;

Editorial Note: A synthetic equity arrangement in respect of a DRA share is a type of dividend rental arrangement. As a result, a dividend received on a share in respect of the arrangement is potentially subject to the denial of the intercorporate dividend deduction under subsection 112(2.3).

History: S. 248(1), the definition "synthetic equity arrangement" was added by S.C. 2016, c. 7, s. 48(2), deemed to have come into force on April 22, 2015.

Related Sections: 82(1)(c); 112(2.3) Where no deduction permitted; 248(1) dividend rental arrangement.

"synthetic equity arrangement chain" —"synthetic equity arrangement chain", in respect of a share owned by a person or partnership, means a synthetic equity arrangement — or a synthetic equity arrangement in combination with one or more specified synthetic equity arrangements — where

(*a*) no party to the synthetic equity arrangement or a specified synthetic equity arrangement, if any, is a tax-indifferent investor, and

(*b*) each other party to these agreements or arrangements is affiliated with the person or partnership;

History: S. 248(1), the definition "synthetic equity arrangement chain" was added by S.C. 2016, c. 7, s. 48(2), deemed to have come into force on April 22, 2015.

"tar sands" —"tar sands" means bituminous sands or oil shales extracted, otherwise than by a well, from a mineral resource, but, for the purpose of applying sections 13 and 20 and any regulations made for the purpose of paragraph 20(1)(*a*) in respect of property acquired after March 6, 1996, includes material extracted by a well from a deposit of bituminous sands or oil shales;

"tax-indifferent investor" —"tax-indifferent investor", at any time, means a person or partnership that is at that time

(*a*) a person exempt from tax under section 149,

(*b*) a non-resident person, other than a person to which all amounts paid or credited under a synthetic equity arrangement or a specified synthetic equity arrangement may reasonably be attributed to the business carried on by the person in Canada through a permanent establishment (as defined by regulation) in Canada,

(*c*) a trust resident in Canada (other than a specified mutual fund trust) if any of the interests as a beneficiary under the trust is not a *fixed interest* (as defined in subsection 251.2(1)) in the trust (in this definition referred to as a *discretionary trust*),

(*d*) a partnership more than 10% of the fair market value of all interests in which can reasonably be considered to be held, directly or indirectly through one or more trusts or partnerships, by any combination of persons described in paragraphs (*a*) to (*c*), or

(*e*) a trust resident in Canada (other than a specified mutual fund trust or a discretionary trust) if more than 10% of the fair market value of all interests as beneficiaries under the trust can reasonably be considered to be held, directly or indirectly through one or more trusts or partnerships, by any combination of persons described in paragraph (*a*) or (*c*);

History: S. 248(1), the definition "tax-indifferent investor" was added by S.C. 2016, c. 7, s. 48(2), deemed to have come into force on April 22, 2015.

"tax shelter" —"tax shelter" has the meaning assigned by subsection 237.1(1);

"tax treaty" —"tax treaty" with a country at any time means a comprehensive agreement or convention for the elimination of double taxation on income, between the Government of Canada and the government of the country, which has the force of law in Canada at that time;

Related Sections: S. 126(1) Foreign tax deduction — non-business income; s. 126(2.1) Amount determined for purposes of para. (2)(b); s. 126(7), "tax-exempt income"; s. 250(5) Deemed non-resident.

Tax Window Files: Canada-Hong Kong Tax Agreement, *March 25, 2015*, CRA Document No. 2014-0560351E5.

"taxable Canadian corporation" —"taxable Canadian corporation" has the meaning assigned by subsection 89(1);

Related Sections: S. 89(1), "taxable Canadian corporation".

"taxable Canadian property" —"taxable Canadian property" of a taxpayer at any time in a taxation year means a property of the taxpayer that is

(*a*) real or immovable property situated in Canada,

(*b*) property used or held by the taxpayer in, property included in Class 14.1 of Schedule II to the *Income Tax Regulations* in respect of, or property described in an inventory of, a business carried on in Canada, other than

(i) property used in carrying on an insurance business, and

(ii) where the taxpayer is non-resident, ships and aircraft used principally in international traffic and personal or movable property pertaining to their operation if the country in which the taxpayer is resident does not impose tax on gains of persons resident in Canada from dispositions of such property,

(*c*) if the taxpayer is an insurer, its designated insurance property for the year,

(*d*) a share of the capital stock of a corporation (other than a mutual fund corporation) that is not listed on a designated stock exchange, an interest in a partnership or an interest in a trust (other than a unit of a mutual fund trust or an income interest in a trust resident in Canada), if, at any particular time during the 60-month period that ends at that time, more than 50% of the fair market value of the share or interest, as the case may be, was derived directly or indirectly (otherwise than through a corporation, partnership or trust the shares or interests in which were not themselves taxable Canadian property at the particular time) from one or any combination of

(i) real or immovable property situated in Canada,

(ii) Canadian resource properties,

(iii) timber resource properties, and

(iv) options in respect of, or interests in, or for civil law rights in, property described in any of subparagraphs (i) to (iii), whether or not the property exists,

(*e*) a share of the capital stock of a corporation that is listed on a designated stock exchange, a share of the capital stock of a mutual fund corporation or a unit of a mutual fund trust, if, at any particular time during the 60-month period that ends at that time,

(i) 25% or more of the issued shares of any class of the capital stock of the corporation, or 25% or more of the issued units of the trust, as the case may be, were owned by or belonged to one or any combination of

(A) the taxpayer,

(B) persons with whom the taxpayer did not deal at arm's length, and

(C) partnerships in which the taxpayer or a person referred to in clause (B) holds a membership interest directly or indirectly through one or more partnerships, and

(ii) more than 50% of the fair market value of the share or unit, as the case may be, was derived directly or indirectly from one or any combination of properties described under subparagraphs (*d*)(i) to (iv), or

(*f*) an option in respect of, or an interest in, or for civil law a right in, a property described in any of paragraphs (*a*) to (*e*), whether or not the property exists,

and, for the purposes of section 2, subsection 107(2.001) and sections 128.1 and 150, and for the purpose of applying paragraphs 85(1)(*i*) and 97(2)(*c*) to a disposition by a non-resident person, includes

(*g*) a Canadian resource property,

(*h*) a timber resource property,

(*i*) an income interest in a trust resident in Canada,

(*j*) a right to a share of the income or loss under an agreement referred to in paragraph 96(1.1)(*a*), and

(*k*) a life insurance policy in Canada;

Editorial Note: Applicable after March 4, 2010, the definition of taxable Canadian property was narrowed, particularly as the definition relates to shares in Canadian resident corporations. Previously, there was no requirement that more than 50% of the fair market value of those shares be derived from real estate in Canada or Canadian resource or timber resource properties. The amendment is consistent with most of Canada's tax treaties, which generally limit Canada's right to tax a non-resident's capital gains from the disposition of shares in a corporation to those cases where the value of those shares is derived principally from real property located in Canada.

History: S. 248(1), the portion of paragraph (*b*) of the definition "taxable Canadian property" before subparagraph (i) was replaced by S.C. 2016, c. 12, s. 63(6), in force January 1, 2017, and formerly read:

(*b*) property used or held by the taxpayer in, eligible capital property in respect of, or property described in an inventory of, a business carried on in Canada, other than

S. 248(1), subparagraph (*e*)(i)(C) of the definition "taxable Canadian property" was added by S.C. 2014, c. 39, s. 71(5), applicable in determining after July 11, 2013 whether a property is taxable Canadian property of a taxpayer.

S. 248(1), the portion of paragraph (*d*) of the definition "taxable Canadian property" before subparagraph (i) was replaced by S.C. 2013, c. 34, s. 358(18), applicable in determining after March 4, 2010 whether a property is taxable Canadian property of a taxpayer, and formerly read:

(*d*) a share of the capital stock of a corporation (other than a mutual fund corporation) that is not listed on a designated stock exchange, an interest in a partnership or an interest in a trust (other than a unit of a mutual fund trust or an income interest in a trust resident in Canada), if, at any particular time during the 60-month period that ends at that time, more than 50% of the fair market value of the share or interest, as the case may be, was derived directly or indirectly from one or any combination of

S. 248(1), the definition "taxable Canadian property" was replaced by S.C. 2010, c. 12, s. 22(1), applicable in determining after March 4, 2010 whether a property is taxable Canadian property of a taxpayer. S. 248(1), the definition "taxable Canadian property" formerly read:

"taxable Canadian property"—"taxable Canadian property" of a taxpayer at any time in a taxation year means a property of the taxpayer that is

(*a*) real property situated in Canada,

(*b*) property used or held by the taxpayer in, eligible capital property in respect of, or property described in an inventory of, a business carried on in Canada, other than

(i) property used in carrying on an insurance business, and

(ii) where the taxpayer is non-resident, ships and aircraft used principally in international traffic and personal property pertaining to their operation if the country in which the taxpayer is resident does not impose tax on gains of persons resident in Canada from dispositions of such property,

(*c*) if the taxpayer is an insurer, its designated insurance property for the year,

(*d*) a share of the capital stock of a corporation resident in Canada (other than a non-resident-owned investment corporation if, on the first day of the year, the corporation owns neither taxable Canadian property nor property referred to in any of paragraphs (*m*) to (*o*), or a mutual fund corporation) that is not listed on a designated stock exchange,

(*e*) a share of the capital stock of a non-resident corporation that is not listed on a designated stock exchange if, at any particular time during the 60-month period that ends at that time,

(i) the fair market value of all of the properties of the corporation each of which was

(A) a taxable Canadian property,

(B) a Canadian resource property,

(C) a timber resource property,

(D) an income interest in a trust resident in Canada, or

(E) an interest in or option in respect of a property described in any of clauses (B) to (D), whether or not the property exists,

was greater than 50% of the fair market value of all of its properties, and

(ii) more than 50% of the fair market value of the share was derived directly or indirectly from one or any combination of

(A) real property situated in Canada,

(B) Canadian resource properties, and

(C) timber resource properties,

(*f*) a share that is listed on a designated stock exchange and that would be described in paragraph (*d*) or (*e*) if those paragraphs were read without reference to the words "that is not listed on a designated stock exchange", or a share of the capital stock of a mutual fund corporation, if at any time during the 60-month period that ends at that time the taxpayer, persons with whom the taxpayer did not deal at arm's length, or the taxpayer together with all such persons owned 25% or more of the issued shares of any class of the capital stock of the corporation that issued the share,

(*g*) an interest in a partnership if, at any particular time during the 60-month period that ends at that time, the fair market value of all of the properties of the partnership each of which was

(i) a taxable Canadian property,

(ii) a Canadian resource property,

(iii) a timber resource property,

(iv) an income interest in a trust resident in Canada, or

(v) an interest in or option in respect of a property described in any of subparagraphs (ii) to (iv), whether or not that property exists,

was greater than 50% of the fair market value of all of its properties,

(*h*) a capital interest in a trust (other than a unit trust) resident in Canada,

(*i*) a unit of a unit trust (other than a mutual fund trust) resident in Canada,

(*j*) a unit of a mutual fund trust if, at any time during the 60-month period that ends at that time, not less than 25% of the issued units of the trust belonged to the taxpayer, to persons with whom the taxpayer did not deal at arm's length, or to the taxpayer and persons with whom the taxpayer did not deal at arm's length,

(*k*) an interest in a non-resident trust if, at any particular time during the 60-month period that ends at that time,

(i) the fair market value of all of the properties of the trust each of which was

(A) a taxable Canadian property,

(B) a Canadian resource property,

(C) a timber resource property,

(D) an income interest in a trust resident in Canada, or

(E) an interest in or option in respect of a property described in any of clauses (B) to (D), whether or not that property exists

was greater than 50% of the fair market value of all of its properties, and

(ii) more than 50% of the fair market value of the interest was derived directly or indirectly from one or any combination of

(A) real property situated in Canada,

(B) Canadian resource properties, and

(C) timber resource properties, or

(*l*) an interest in or option in respect of a property described in any of paragraphs (*a*) to (*k*), whether or not that property exists, and, for the purposes of section 2, subsection 107(2.001) and sections 128.1 and 150, and for the purpose of applying paragraphs 85(1)(*i*) and 97(2)(*c*) to a disposition by a non-resident person, includes

(*m*) a Canadian resource property,

(*n*) a timber resource property,

(*o*) an income interest in a trust resident in Canada,

(*p*) a right to a share of the income or loss under an agreement referred to in paragraph 96(1.1)(*a*), and

(*q*) a life insurance policy in Canada;

Related Sections: 87(8.4) Taxable Canadian property — conditions for rollover; S. 55(6) Unlisted shares deemed listed; S. 115(1) Non-resident's taxable income in Canada; s. 116(6) Definition of "excluded property"; s. 250(5.1) Continued corporation.

Canadian Petroleum Tax Journal: Taxable Canadian Property, Tony Van Rooyen, 2000, Vol. 13, No. 1.

Canadian Tax Foundation: Kakkar, *CRA's Position on TCP Makes "Simple Planning" Look Good,* 2015 Tax for the Owner-Manager 15(1):4–5; Troup, *Purchasing Private Corporation Shares: Hazards if the Vendor Is Non-Resident,* 2013 Canadian Tax Focus 3(4):4–5; Bernstein and Gucciardo, *TCP Proposal Overshoots Objective?,* 2013 Canadian Tax Highlights 21(8):4; Bordeleau et al., *Determination of Whether Shares Derive Their Value Principally from Real Property (Canada Revenue Agency and Revenu Québec Round Table, Questions 23 and 24),* 2011 Conference Report 4:17–19; Bowman, *Taxable Canadian Property,* 2010 Conference Report 32:1–24; Raizenne and Nikolakakis, *Taxable Canadian Property*, 1996 Conference Report 46:1–72.

Tax Profile: September 2013 — Proposal to Amend "Taxable Canadian Property" Overly Expansive; October 2012 — Exchangeable Shares in Canada; fAugust 2012 — U.S. Purchases and Sales of Canadian Businesses: Tax and Corporate Issues; June 2012 — Use of Canadian Partnerships by Non-Residents; August 2011 — Canadian Share Dispositions by a Non-Resident — Taxable in Canada?; March 2011 — Canada 2010 — Year in Review; September 2010 — Recent Tax Developments Affecting Non-Residents.

Tax Topics: No. 2315, Canada Revenue Agency Views on Taxable Canadian Property Determinations Involving Subsidiaries; No. 2111, IFA 2012 Tax Seminar Roundtables; No. 2075, 2011 Canadian Tax Foundation Roundtable.

Interpretation Bulletins: *Secondary* — IT-420R3 Non-residents — Income earned in Canada.

Tax Window Files: Assignment of right to purchase, *March 7, 2016,* CRA Document No. 2015-0608211E5; 248(1)(e)(ii) of the definition of TCP, *May 1, 2017,* CRA Document No. 2015-0624511I7.

"taxable capital gain" — "taxable capital gain" has the meaning assigned by section 38;

"taxable dividend" — "taxable dividend" has the meaning assigned by subsection 89(1);

"taxable income" — "taxable income" has the meaning assigned by subsection 2(2), except that in no case may a taxpayer's taxable income be less than nil;

"taxable income earned in Canada" — "taxable income earned in Canada" means a taxpayer's taxable income earned in Canada determined in accordance with Division D of Part I, except that in no case may a taxpayer's taxable income earned in Canada be less than nil;

Related Sections: S. 115(1) Non-resident's taxable income in Canada.

"taxable net gain" — "taxable net gain" from dispositions of listed personal property has the meaning assigned by section 41;

"taxable preferred share" — "taxable preferred share" at any particular time means

(*a*) a share issued after December 15, 1987 that is a short-term preferred share at that particular time, or

(*b*) a share (other than a grandfathered share) of the capital stock of a corporation issued after 8:00 p.m Eastern Daylight Saving Time, June 18, 1987 where, at that particular time by reason of the terms or conditions of the share or any agreement in respect of the share or its issue to which the corporation, or a specified person in relation to the corporation, is a party,

(i) it may reasonably be considered, having regard to all the circumstances, that the amount of the dividends that may be declared or paid on the share (in this definition referred to as the "dividend entitlement") is, by way of a formula or otherwise

(A) fixed,

(B) limited to a maximum, or

(C) established to be not less than a minimum (including any amount determined on a cumulative basis) and with respect to the dividend that may be declared or paid on the share there is a preference over any other dividend that may be declared or paid on any other share of the capital stock of the corporation,

(ii) it may reasonably be considered, having regard to all the circumstances, that the amount that the shareholder is entitled to receive in respect of the share on the dissolution, liquidation or winding-up of the corporation or on the redemption, acquisition or cancellation of the share (unless the requirement to redeem, acquire or cancel the share arises only in the event of the death of the shareholder or by reason only of a right to convert or exchange the share) or on a reduction of the paid-up capital of the share by the corporation or by a specified person in relation to the corporation (in this definition referred to as the "liquidation entitlement") is, by way of a formula or otherwise

(A) fixed,

(B) limited to a maximum, or

(C) established to be not less than a minimum,

and, for the purposes of this subparagraph, "shareholder" includes a shareholder of a shareholder,

(iii) the share is convertible or exchangeable at any time, unless

(A) it is convertible into or exchangeable for

(I) another share of the corporation or a corporation related to the corporation that, if issued, would not be a taxable preferred share,

(II) a right or warrant that, if exercised, would allow the person exercising it to acquire only a share of the corporation or a corporation related to the corporation that, if issued, would not be a taxable preferred share, or

(III) both a share described in subclause (I) and a right or warrant described in subclause (II), and

(B) all the consideration receivable for the share on the conversion or exchange is the share described in subclause (A)(I) or the right or warrant described in subclause (A)(II) or both, as the case may be, and, for the purposes of this clause, where a taxpayer may become entitled on the conversion or exchange of a share to receive any particular consideration (other than consideration described in any of subclauses (A)(I) to (III)) in lieu of a fraction of a share, the particular consideration shall be deemed not to be consideration unless it may reasonably be considered that the particular consideration was receivable as part of a series of transactions or events one of the main purposes of which was to avoid or limit the application of Part IV.1 or VI.1, or

(iv) any person (other than the corporation) was, at or immediately before that particular time, obligated, either absolutely or contingently, and either immediately or in the future, to effect any undertaking (in this subparagraph referred to as a "guarantee agreement"), including any guarantee, covenant or agreement to purchase or repurchase the share, and including the lending of funds to or the placing of amounts on deposit with, or on behalf of, the shareholder or any specified person in relation to the shareholder given

(A) to ensure that any loss that the shareholder or a specified person in relation to the shareholder may sustain by reason of the ownership, holding or disposition of the share or any other property is limited in any respect, or

(B) to ensure that the shareholder or a specified person in relation to the shareholder will derive earnings by reason of the ownership, holding or disposition of the share or any other property,

and the guarantee agreement was given as part of a transaction or event or a series of transactions or events that included the issuance of the share and, for the purposes of this paragraph, where a guarantee agreement in respect of a share is given at any particular time after 8:00 p.m. Eastern Daylight Saving Time, June 18, 1987, otherwise than pursuant to a written arrangement to do so entered into before 8:00 p.m. Eastern Daylight Saving Time, June 18, 1987, the share shall be deemed to have been issued at the particular time and the guarantee agreement shall be deemed to have been given as part of a series of transactions that included the issuance of the share,

but does not include a share that is at the particular time a prescribed share or a share described in paragraph (*e*) of the definition "term preferred share" in this subsection during the applicable time period referred to in that paragraph and, for the purposes of this definition,

(*c*) the dividend entitlement of a share of the capital stock of a corporation shall be deemed not to be fixed, limited to a maximum or established to be not less than a minimum where all dividends on the share are determined solely by reference to the dividend entitlement of another share of the capital stock of the corporation or of another corporation that controls the corporation that would not be a taxable preferred share if

(i) this definition were read without reference to paragraph (*f*),

(ii) the other share were issued after June 18, 1987, and

(iii) the other share were not a grandfathered share, a prescribed share or a share described in paragraph (*e*) of the definition "term preferred share" in this subsection,

(*d*) the liquidation entitlement of a share of the capital stock of a corporation shall be deemed not to be fixed, limited to a maximum or established to be not less than a minimum where all the liquidation entitlement is determinable solely by reference to the liquidation entitlement of another share of the capital stock of the corporation or of another corporation that controls the corporation that would not be a taxable preferred share if

(i) this definition were read without reference to paragraph (*f*),

(ii) the other share were issued after June 18, 1987, and

(iii) the other share were not a grandfathered share, a prescribed share or a share described in paragraph (*e*) of the definition "term preferred share" in this subsection,

(*e*) where at any particular time after 8:00 p.m. Eastern Daylight Saving Time, June 18, 1987, otherwise than pursuant to a written arrangement to do so entered into before 8:00 p.m. Eastern Daylight Saving Time, June 18, 1987, the terms or conditions of a share of the capital stock of a corporation that are relevant to any matter referred to in any of subparagraphs (*b*)(i) to (iv) are established or modified or any agreement in respect of any such matter, to which the corporation or a specified person in relation to the corporation is a party, is changed or entered into, the share shall, for the purpose of determining after the particular time whether it is a taxable preferred share, be deemed to have been issued at that particular time, unless

(i) the share is a share described in paragraph (*b*) of the definition "grandfathered share" in this subsection, and

(ii) the particular time is before December 16, 1987 and before the time at which the share is first issued,

(*f*) an agreement in respect of a share of the capital stock of a corporation shall be read without reference to that part of the agreement under which a person agrees to acquire the share for an amount

(i) in the case of a share the agreement in respect of which provides that the share is to be acquired within 60 days after the day on which the agreement was entered into, that does not exceed the greater of the fair market value of the share at the time the agreement was entered into, determined without reference to the agreement, and the fair market value of the share at the time of the acquisition, determined without reference to the agreement, or

(ii) that does not exceed the fair market value of the share at the time of the acquisition, determined without reference to the agreement, or for an amount determined by reference to the assets or earnings of the corporation where that determination may reasonably be considered to be used to determine an amount that does not exceed the fair market value of the share at the time of the acquisition, determined without reference to the agreement,

(*g*) where

(i) it may reasonably be considered that the dividends that may be declared or paid to a shareholder at any time on a share (other than a prescribed share or a share described in paragraph (*e*) of the definition "term preferred share" in this subsection during the applicable time period referred to in that paragraph) of the capital stock of a corporation issued after December 15, 1987 or acquired after June 15, 1988 are derived primarily from dividends received on taxable preferred shares of the capital stock of another corporation, and

(ii) it may reasonably be considered that the share was issued or acquired as part of a transaction or event or series of transactions or events one of the main purposes of which was to avoid or limit the application of Part IV.1 or VI.1,

the share shall be deemed at that time to be a taxable preferred share, and

(*h*) "specified person", in relation to any particular person, means another person with whom the particular person does not deal at arm's length or any partnership or trust of which the particular person or the other person is a member or beneficiary, respectively;

Related Sections: S. 248(10) Series of transactions.

Canadian Tax Foundation: Jung, *The Taxable Preferred Share Rules and the Private Corporation*, 2017 Ontario Tax Conference 12:1–20; Diep, *Preferred Share Rules: The Expected, Unexpected and Unintended*, 2017 Prairie Provinces Tax Conference 13:1–29; Moskowitz, *The Preferred Share Rules: Yes They Can Apply to You!*, 1997 Conference Report 9:1–47.

"taxable RFI share" —"taxable RFI share" at any particular time means a share of the capital stock of a corporation issued before 8:00 p.m. Eastern Daylight Saving Time, June 18, 1987 or a grandfathered share of the capital stock of a corporation, where at the particular time under the terms or conditions of the share or any agreement in respect of the share,

(*a*) it may reasonably be considered, having regard to all the circumstances, that the amount of the dividends that may be declared or paid on the share (in this definition referred to as the "dividend entitlement") is, by way of a formula or otherwise

(i) fixed,

(ii) limited to a maximum, or

(iii) established to be not less than a minimum, or

(*b*) it may reasonably be considered, having regard to all the circumstances, that the amount that the shareholder is entitled to receive in respect of the share on the dissolution, liquidation or winding-up of the corporation (in this definition referred to as the "liquidation entitlement") is, by way of formula or otherwise

(i) fixed,

(ii) limited to a maximum, or

(iii) established to be not less than a minimum,

but does not include a share that is at the particular time a prescribed share, a term preferred share, a share described in paragraph (*e*) of the definition "term preferred share" in this subsection during the applicable time period referred to in that paragraph or a taxable preferred share and, for the purposes of this definition,

(*c*) the dividend entitlement of a share of the capital stock of a corporation shall be deemed not to be fixed, limited to a maximum or established to be not less than a minimum where all dividends on the share are determined solely by reference to the dividend entitlement of another share of the capital stock of the corporation or of another corporation that controls the corporation that would not be a taxable preferred share if

(i) the definition "taxable preferred share" in this subsection were read without reference to paragraph (*f*) of that definition,

(ii) the other share were issued after June 18, 1987, and

(iii) the other share were not a grandfathered share, a prescribed share or a share described in paragraph (*e*) of the definition "term preferred share" in this subsection,

(*d*) the liquidation entitlement of a share of the capital stock of a corporation shall be deemed not to be fixed, limited to a maximum or established to be not less than a minimum where all the liquidation entitlement is determinable solely by reference to the liquidation entitlement of another share of the capital stock of the corporation or of another corporation that controls the corporation that would not be a taxable preferred share if

(i) the definition "taxable preferred share" in this subsection were read without reference to paragraph (*f*) of that definition,

(ii) the other share were issued after June 18, 1987, and

(iii) the other share were not a grandfathered share, a prescribed share or a share described in paragraph (*e*) of the definition "term preferred share" in this subsection, and

(*e*) where

(i) it may reasonably be considered that the dividends that may be declared or paid to a shareholder at any time on a share (other than a prescribed share or a share described in paragraph (*e*) of the definition "term preferred share" in this subsection during the applicable time period referred to in that paragraph) of the capital stock of a corporation issued after December 15, 1987 or acquired after June 15, 1988 are derived primarily from dividends received on taxable RFI shares of the capital stock of another corporation, and

(ii) it may reasonably be considered that the share was issued or acquired as part of a transaction or event or series of transactions or events one of the main purposes of which was to avoid or limit the application of Part IV.1,

the share shall be deemed at that time to be a taxable RFI share;

Related Regulations: 6201(4); 6201(5), (10), (11).

Related Sections: S. 248(10) Series of transactions.

"taxpayer" —"taxpayer" includes any person whether or not liable to pay tax;

Cases: The Supreme Court of Canada denied a Part I deduction premised on the assumption that a non-resident company was a "taxpayer", although the company was clearly subject to non-resident withholding tax. *Lea-Don Canada Ltd. v. M.N.R.*, 70 DTC 6271 (S.C.C.)

"tax-paid undistributed surplus on hand" — (Repealed by 1977-78, c. 1, s. 98(6).)

"term preferred share" —"term preferred share" of a corporation (in this definition referred to as the "issuing corporation") means a share of a class of the capital stock of the issuing corporation if the share was issued or acquired after June 28, 1982 and, at the time the share was issued or acquired, the existence of the issuing corporation was, or there was an arrangement under which it could be, limited or, in the case of a share issued after November 16, 1978 if

(*a*) under the terms or conditions of the share, any agreement relating to the share or any modification of those terms or conditions or that agreement,

(i) the owner thereof may cause the share to be redeemed, acquired or cancelled (unless the owner of the share may cause the share to be redeemed, acquired or cancelled by reason only of a right to convert or exchange the share) or cause its paid-up capital to be reduced,

(ii) the issuing corporation or any other person or partnership is or may be required to redeem, acquire or cancel, in whole or in part, the share (unless the requirement to redeem, acquire or cancel the share arises by reason only of a right to convert or exchange the share) or to reduce its paid-up capital,

(iii) the issuing corporation or any other person or partnership provides or may be required to provide any form of guarantee, security or similar indemnity or covenant (including the lending of funds to or the placing of amounts on deposit with, or on behalf of, the holder thereof or any person related thereto) with respect to the share, or

(iv) the share is convertible or exchangeable unless

(A) it is convertible into or exchangeable for

(I) another share of the issuing corporation or a corporation related to the issuing corporation that, if issued, would not be a term preferred share,

(II) a right or warrant that, if exercised, would allow the person exercising it to acquire only a share of the issuing corporation or a corporation related to the issuing corporation that, if issued, would not be a term preferred share, or

(III) both a share described in subclause (I) and a right or warrant described in subclause (II), and

(B) all the consideration receivable for the share on the conversion or exchange is the share described in subclause (A)(I) or the right or warrant described in subclause (A)(II) or both, as the case may be, and, for the purposes of this clause, where a taxpayer may become entitled on the conversion or exchange of a share to receive any particular consideration (other than consideration described in any of subclauses (A)(I) to (III)) in lieu of a fraction of a share, the particular consideration shall be deemed not to be consideration unless it may reasonably be considered that the particular consideration was receivable as part of a series of transactions or events one of the main purposes of which was to avoid or limit the application of subsection 112(2.1) or 258(3), or

(*b*) the owner thereof acquired the share after October 23, 1979 and is

(i) a corporation described in any of paragraphs (*a*) to (*e*.1) of the definition "specified financial institution",

(ii) a corporation that is controlled by one or more corporations described in subparagraph (i),

(iii) a corporation that acquired the share after December 11, 1979 and is related to a corporation referred to in subparagraph (i) or (ii), or

(iv) a partnership or trust of which a corporation referred to in subparagraph (i) or (ii) or a person related thereto is a member or a beneficiary,

that (either alone or together with any of such corporations, partnerships or trusts) controls or has an absolute or contingent right to control or to acquire control of the issuing corporation,

but does not include a share of the capital stock of a corporation

(*c*) that was issued after November 16, 1978 and before 1980 pursuant to an agreement in writing to do so made before November 17, 1978 (in this definition referred to as an "established agreement"),

(*d*) that was issued as a stock dividend

(i) before April 22, 1980 on a share of the capital stock of a public corporation that was not a term preferred share, or

(ii) after April 21, 1980 on a share that was, at the time the stock dividend was paid, a share prescribed for the purposes of paragraph (*f*),

(*d*.1) that is listed on a designated stock exchange in Canada and was issued before April 22, 1980 by

(i) a corporation referred to in any of paragraphs (*a*) to (*d*) of the definition "specified financial institution" in this subsection,

(ii) a corporation whose principal business is the lending of money or the purchasing of debt obligations or a combination thereof, or

(iii) an issuing corporation associated with a corporation described in subparagraph (i) or (ii),

(*e*) for a period not exceeding ten years and, in the case of a share issued after November 12, 1981, for a period not exceeding five years, from the date of its issuance, which share was issued by a corporation resident in Canada,

(i) as part of a proposal to, or an arrangement with, its creditors that had been approved by a court under the *Bankruptcy and Insolvency Act*,

(ii) at a time when all or substantially all of its assets were under the control of a receiver, receiver-manager, sequestrator or trustee in bankruptcy, or

(iii) at a time when, by reason of financial difficulty, the issuing corporation or another corporation resident in Canada with which it does not deal at arm's length was in default, or could reasonably be expected to default, on a debt obligation held by a person with whom the issuing corporation or the other corporation was dealing at arm's length and the share was issued either wholly or in substantial part and either directly or indirectly in exchange or substitution for that obligation or a part thereof,

and, in the case of a share issued after November 12, 1981, the proceeds from the issue may reasonably be regarded as having been used by the issuing corporation or a corporation with which it was not dealing at arm's length in the financing of its business carried on in Canada immediately before the share was issued,

(*f*) that is a prescribed share, or

(*f*.1) that is a taxable preferred share held by a specified financial institution that acquired the share

(i) before December 16, 1987, or

(ii) before 1989 pursuant to an agreement in writing entered into before December 16, 1987,

other than a share deemed by paragraph (*c*) of the definition "short-term preferred share" in this subsection or by paragraph (*i*.2) to have been issued after December 15, 1987 or a share that would be deemed by paragraph (*e*) of the definition "taxable preferred share" in this subsection to have been issued after December 15, 1987 if the references therein to "8:00 p.m. Eastern Daylight Saving Time, June 18, 1987" were read as references to "December 15, 1987",

and, for the purposes of this definition,

(*g*) where the terms or conditions of an established agreement were amended after November 16, 1978, the agreement shall be deemed to have been made after that date,

(*h*) where

(i) at any particular time the terms or conditions of a share issued pursuant to an established agreement or of any agreement relating to such a share have been changed,

(ii) under the terms or conditions of

(A) a share of a class of the capital stock of the issuing corporation issued before November 17, 1978 (other than a share that was listed on November 16, 1978 on a prescribed stock exchange in Canada),

(B) a share issued pursuant to an established agreement,

(C) any agreement between the issuing corporation and the owner of a share described in clause (A) or (B), or

(D) any agreement relating to a share described in clause (A) or (B) made after October 23, 1979,

the owner thereof could at any particular time after November 16, 1978 require, either alone or together with one or more taxpayers, the redemption, acquisition, cancellation, conversion or reduction of the paid-up capital of the share otherwise than by reason of a failure or default under the terms or conditions of the share or any agreement that related to, and was entered into at the time of, the issuance of the share,

(iii) in respect of a share issued before November 17, 1978, at any particular time after November 16, 1978 the redemption date was extended or the terms or conditions relating to its redemption, acquisition, cancellation, conversion or reduction of its paid-up capital were changed,

(iv) at a particular time after October 23, 1979 and before November 13, 1981, a specified financial institution (or a partnership or trust of which a specified financial institution or a person related to the institution is a member or beneficiary) acquired a share that

(A) was issued before November 17, 1978 or under an established agreement,

(B) was issued to a person other than a corporation that was, at the time of issue,

(I) described in any of paragraphs (*a*) to (*e*) of the definition "specified financial institution", or

(II) a corporation that was controlled by one or more corporations described in subclause (I) and, for the purpose of this subclause, one corporation is controlled by another corporation if more than 50% of its issued share capital (having full voting rights under all circumstances) belongs to the other corporation, to persons with whom the other corporation does not deal at arm's length, or to the other corporation and persons with whom the other corporation does not deal at arm's length,

(C) was acquired from a person that was, at the particular time, a person other than a corporation described in subclause (B)(I) or (II), and

(D) was acquired otherwise than under an agreement in writing made before October 24, 1979,

(v) at any particular time after November 12, 1981

(A) in respect of

(I) a share (other than a share referred to in paragraph (*e*) or a share listed on November 13, 1981 on a prescribed stock exchange in Canada) issued after November 16, 1978 and before November 13, 1981, or

(II) a share issued after November 12, 1981 and before 1983 pursuant to an agreement in writing to do so made before November 13, 1981 (in this definition referred to as a "specified agreement")

the owner thereof could require, either alone or together with one or more taxpayers, the redemption, acquisition, cancellation, conversion or reduction of the paid-up capital of the share otherwise than by reason of a failure or default under the terms or conditions of the share or any agreement that related to, and was entered into at the time of, the issuance of the share, or

(B) the redemption date of

(I) a share issued after November 16, 1978 and before November 13, 1981 or

(II) a share issued pursuant to a specified agreement

was extended or the terms or conditions relating to its redemption, acquisition, cancellation, conversion or reduction of its paid-up capital were changed, or

(vi) at a particular time after November 12, 1981, a specified financial institution (or a partnership or trust of which a specified financial institution or a person related to the institution is a member or beneficiary) acquired a share (other than a share referred to in paragraph (*e*)) that

(A) was issued before November 13, 1981 or under a specified agreement,

(B) was acquired from a partnership or person, other than a person that was, at the particular time, a corporation described in any of paragraphs (*a*) to (*f*) of the definition "specified financial institution" in this subsection,

(C) was acquired in an acquisition that was not subject to nor conditional on a guarantee agreement, within the meaning assigned by subsection 112(2.2), entered into after November 12, 1981, and

(D) was acquired otherwise than under an agreement in writing made before October 24, 1979 or a specified agreement,

the share shall, for the purposes of determining at any time after the particular time whether it is a term preferred share, be deemed to have been issued at the particular time otherwise than pursuant to an established or specified agreement,

(*i*) where the terms or conditions of a share of the capital stock of the issuing corporation are modified or established after June 28, 1982 and as a consequence thereof the issuing corporation, any person related thereto or any partnership or trust of which the issuing corporation or a person related thereto is a member or a beneficiary may reasonably be expected at any time to redeem, acquire or cancel, in whole or in part, the share or to reduce its paid-up capital, the share shall be deemed as from the date of the modification or as from the date of the establishment, as the case may be, to be a share described in paragraph (*a*),

(*i*.1) where

(i) it may reasonably be considered that the dividends that may be declared or paid at any time on a share (other than a prescribed share or a share described in paragraph (*e*) during the applicable time period referred to in that paragraph) of the capital stock of a corporation issued after December 15, 1987 or acquired after June 15, 1988 are derived primarily from dividends received on term preferred shares of the capital stock of another corporation, and

(ii) it may reasonably be considered that the share was issued or acquired as part of a transaction or event or series of transactions or events one of the main purposes of which was to avoid or limit the application of subsection 112(2.1) or 138(6),

the share shall be deemed at that time to be a term preferred share acquired in the ordinary course of business,

(*i*.2) where at any particular time after December 15, 1987, otherwise than pursuant to a written arrangement to do so entered into before December 16, 1987, the terms or conditions of a taxable preferred share of the capital stock of a corporation relating to any matter referred to in subparagraphs (*a*)(i) to (iv) have been modified or established, or any agreement in respect of the share relating to any such matter has been changed or entered into by the corporation or a specified person (within the meaning assigned by paragraph (*h*) of the definition "taxable preferred share" in this subsection) in relation to the corporation, the share shall be deemed after that particular time to have been issued at that particular time, and,

(*j*) where a particular share of the capital stock of a corporation has been issued or its terms and conditions have been modified and it may reasonably be considered, having regard to all circumstances (including the rate of interest on any debt or the dividend provided on any term preferred share), that

(i) but for the existence at any time of the debt or the term preferred share, the particular share would not have been issued or its terms or conditions modified, and

(ii) one of the main purposes for the issue of the particular share or for the modification of its terms or conditions was to avoid a limitation provided by subsection 112(2.1) or 138(6) in respect of a deduction,

the particular share shall be deemed after December 31, 1982 to be a term preferred share of the corporation;

Related Regulations: 6201 Prescribed Shares.

Related Sections: S. 87(4.1) Exchanged shares — amalgamations after November 16, 1978; s. 248(10) Series of transactions.

Canadian Tax Foundation: Diep, *Preferred Share Rules: The Expected, Unexpected and Unintended,* 2017 Prairie Provinces Tax Conference 13:1–29; Hanly and McCay, *Current Cases: The Tax Court of Canada — Convertible Preferred Shares Not Term Preferred Shares (Citibank Canada v. The*

Queen, 2001 DTC 111), 2001 Canadian Tax Journal 4:368–372; Moskowitz, *The Preferred Share Rules: Yes They Can Apply to You!*, 1997 Conference Report 9:1–47.

Interpretation Bulletins: *Secondary* — IT-527 Distress preferred shares.

Cases: The taxpayer acquired preferred shares that included the right to convert to common shares at a ratio determined at the time of conversion. The conversion right did not constitute a "form of guarantee, security or similar indemnity or covenant". Therefore the shares were not "term preferred shares" and the taxpayer was entitled to deduct the dividends received thereon*The Queen v. Citibank Canada*, 2002 DTC 6876 (F.C.A.), affirming 2001 DTC 111 (T.C.C.).

"termination payment" — (Repealed by 1980-81-82-83, c. 140, s. 128(13).)

"testamentary trust" —"testamentary trust" has the meaning assigned by subsection 108(1);

Related Sections: S. 248(3) Property subject to certain Quebec institutions and arrangements.

"TFSA" —"TFSA", being a tax-free savings account, has the meaning assigned by subsection 146.2(5);

History: S. 248(1), the definition "TFSA" was replaced by S.C. 2009, c. 2, s. 76(2), applicable to the 2009 and subsequent taxation years. S. 248(1), the definition "TFSA" formerly read:

"TFSA"—"TFSA", being a tax-free savings account, has the meaning assigned by subsection 146.2(3);

"timber resource property" —"timber resource property" has the meaning assigned by subsection 13(21);

"total pension adjustment reversal" —"total pension adjustment reversal" of a taxpayer for a calendar year has the meaning assigned by regulation;

Related Regulations: 8304.1.

Related Sections: S. 146(1), "RRSP deduction limit"; s. 147.1(18) Regulations; s. 204.2(1.1) Cumulative excess amount in respect of RRSPs.

"Treasury Board" —"Treasury Board" means the Treasury Board established by section 5 of the *Financial Administration Act*;

"treaty-protected business" —"treaty-protected business" of a taxpayer at any time means a business in respect of which any income of the taxpayer for a period that includes that time would, because of a tax treaty with another country, be exempt from tax under Part I;

Related Sections: S. 111(9) Exception; s. 115(1) Non-resident's taxable income in Canada; s. 248(1), "treaty-protected property".

Forms: T2 SCH 91 — Information Concerning Claims for Treaty-based Exemptions.

"treaty-protected property" —"treaty-protected property" of a taxpayer at any time means property any income or gain from the disposition of which by the taxpayer at that time would, because of a tax treaty with another country, be exempt from tax under Part I;

Related Sections: S. 13(4.1) Replacement for a former property; s. 44(5) Replacement property; s. 80(1), "excluded property"; s. 111(9) Exception; s. 115(1) Non-resident's taxable income in Canada; s. 128.1(1)(c.1) Deemed dividend to immigrating corporation; s. 248(1), "treaty-protected business".

Forms: T2 SCH 91 — Information Concerning Claims for Treaty-based Exemptions.

"trust" —"trust" has the meaning assigned by subsection 104(1) and, unless the context otherwise requires, includes an estate;

History: S. 248(1), the definition "trust" was replaced by S.C. 2013, c. 40, s. 89(1), in force December 12, 2013, and formerly read:

"trust"—"trust" has the meaning assigned by subsection 104(1);

Related Sections: S. 248(3) Property subject to certain Quebec institutions and arrangements.

Tax Topics: No. 2087, Is an Estate Not a Trust For All Purposes of the Income Tax Act?.

Tax Window Files: Netherlands Antilles private foundation, *October 4, 2010*, CRA Document No. 2008-0289461I7.

trust account number —trust account number means the number (other than a business number)

(*a*) used by the Minister to identify a trust, and

(*b*) of which the Minister has notified the trust;

History: S. 248(1), the definition "trust account number" was added by S.C. 2018, c. 12, s. 37(2), applicable to the 2018 and subsequent taxation years.

"undepreciated capital cost" —"undepreciated capital cost" to a taxpayer of depreciable property of a prescribed class has the meaning assigned by subsection 13(21);

"unit trust" —"unit trust" has the meaning assigned by subsection 108(2);

"unused RRSP deduction room" —"unused RRSP deduction room" of a taxpayer at the end of a taxation year has the meaning assigned by subsection 146(1);

"unused scientific research and experimental development tax credit" —"unused scientific research and experimental development tax credit" of a taxpayer for a taxation year has the meaning assigned by subsection 127.3(2);

"unused share-purchase tax credit" —"unused share-purchase tax credit" of a taxpayer for a taxation year has the meaning assigned by subsection 127.2(6).

"zero-emission passenger vehicle" —"zero-emission passenger vehicle", of a taxpayer, means an automobile of the taxpayer that is included in Class 54 of Schedule II to the *Income Tax Regulations*;

History: S. 248(1), the definition "zero-emission passenger vehicle", was added by S.C. 2019, c. 29, s. 43(4), deemed to have come into force on March 19, 2019.

Related Regulations: Schedule II Class 54.

Related Sections: 248(17) Application of subsection (16) to certain vehicles and aircraft; 248(17.1) Application of subsection (16.1) to certain vehicles and aircraft.

"zero-emission vehicle" —"zero-emission vehicle", of a taxpayer, means a motor vehicle that

(*a*) is a plug-in hybrid that meets prescribed conditions or is fully

(i) electric, or

(ii) powered by hydrogen,

(*b*) is acquired, and becomes available for use, by the taxpayer after March 18, 2019 and before 2028, and

(*c*) is not a vehicle

(i) that has been used, or acquired for use, for any purpose before it was acquired by the taxpayer, or

(ii) in respect of which

(A) the taxpayer has, at any time, made an election under subsection 1103(2j) of the *Income Tax Regulations*,

(B) assistance has been paid by the Government of Canada under a prescribed program, or

(C) an amount has been deducted under paragraph 20(1)(*a*) or subsection 20(16) by another person or partnership.

History: S. 248(1), the definition "zero-emission vehicle", was added by S.C. 2019, c. 29, s. 43(4), deemed to have come into force on March 19, 2019.

Related Regulations: 1102(26); 1103(2j).

Related Sections: 20(1)(a) Capital cost of property; 20(16) Terminal loss.

"10/8 policy" —"10/8 policy" means a life insurance policy (other than an annuity) where (*a*) an amount is or may become

(i) payable, under the terms of a borrowing, to a person or partnership that has been assigned an interest in the policy or in an investment account in respect of the policy, or

(ii) payable (within the meaning assigned by the definition "amount payable" in subsection 138(12)) under a policy loan (as defined in subsection 148(9)) made in accordance with the terms and conditions of the policy, and

(*b*) either

(i) the return credited to an investment account in respect of the policy

(A) is determined by reference to the rate of interest on the borrowing or policy loan, as the case may be, described in paragraph (*a*), and

(B) would not be credited to the account if the borrowing or policy loan, as the case may be, were not in existence, or

(ii) the maximum amount of an investment account in respect of the policy is determined by reference to the amount of the borrowing or policy loan, as the case may be, described in paragraph (*a*);

History: S. 248(1), the definition "10/8 policy", was added by S.C. 2013, c. 40, s. 89(5), applicable to taxation years that end after March 20, 2013.

Canadian Tax Foundation: Everett, *Life Insurance Planning After the 2013 Budget*, 2013 Conference Report 32:1–23.

"1971 capital surplus on hand" — (Repealed by 1977-78, c. 1, s. 98(7).)

"1971 undistributed income on hand" — (Repealed by 1977-78, c. 1, s. 98(7).)

► 248(1.1) ◄

(1.1) Non-disposition before December 24, 1998. A redemption, an acquisition or a cancellation, at any particular time after 1971 and before December 24, 1998, of a share or of a right to acquire a share (which share or which right, as the case may be, is referred to in this subsection as the "security") of the capital stock of a corporation (referred to in this subsection as the "issuing corporation") held by another corporation (referred to in this subsection as the "disposing corporation") is not a disposition (within the meaning of the definition "disposition" in section 54 as that section read in its application to transactions and events that occurred at the particular time) of the security if

(*a*) the redemption, acquisition or cancellation occurred as part of a merger or combination of two or more corporations (including the issuing corporation and the disposing corporation) to form one corporate entity (referred to in this subsection as the "new corporation");

(*b*) the merger or combination

(i) is an amalgamation (within the meaning assigned by subsection 87(1) as it read at the particular time) to which subsection 87(11) if in force, and as it read, at the particular time did not apply,

(ii) is an amalgamation (within the meaning assigned by subsection 87(1) as it read at the particular time) to which subsection 87(11) if in force, and as it read, at the particular time applies, if the issuing corporation and the disposing corporation are described by subsection 87(11) (if in force, and as it read, at the particular time) as the parent and the subsidiary, respectively,

(iii) occurred before November 13, 1981 and is a merger of corporations that is described by subsection 87(8) (as it read in respect of the merger or combination), or

(iv) occurred after November 12, 1981 and

(A) is a foreign merger (within the meaning assigned by subsection 87(8.1) as it read in respect of the merger or combination), or

(B) all of the following conditions are met:

(I) the merger or combination is not a foreign merger (within the meaning assigned by subsection 87(8.1) as it read in respect of the merger or combination),

(II) subsection 87(8.1), as it read in respect of the merger or combination, contained a subparagraph (*c*)(ii), and

(III) the merger or combination would be a foreign merger (within the meaning of subsection 87(8.1), as it read in respect of the merger or combination) if that subparagraph 87(8.1)(*c*)(ii) were read as follows:

"(ii) if, immediately after the merger, the new foreign corporation was controlled by another foreign corporation (in this subsection referred to as the "parent corporation"), shares of the capital stock of the parent corporation,";

and

(*c*) either

(i) the disposing corporation received no consideration for the security, or

(ii) in the case where the merger or combination is described by subparagraph (*b*)(iv), the disposing corporation received no consideration for the security other than property that was, immediately before the merger or combination, owned by the issuing corporation and that, on the merger or combination, became property of the new corporation.

History: S. 248(1.1) was added by S.C. 2013, c. 34, s. 358(21), in force June 26, 2013.

► 248(2) ◄

(2) Tax payable. In this Act, the tax payable by a taxpayer under any Part of this Act by or under which provision is made for the assessment of tax means the tax payable by the taxpayer as fixed by assessment or reassessment subject to variation on objection or on appeal, if any, in accordance with the provisions of that Part.

► 248(3) ◄

(3) Property subject to certain Quebec institutions and arrangements. For the purposes of this Act, if property is subject to an institution or arrangement that is described by this subsection and that is governed by the laws of the Province of Quebec, the following rules apply in respect of the property:

(*a*) if at any time property is subject to a usufruct, right of use or habitation, or substitution,

(i) the usufruct, right of use or habitation, or substitution, as the case may be, is deemed to be at that time

(A) a trust, and

(B) where the usufruct, right of use or habitation, or substitution, as the case may be, is created by will, a trust created by will,

(ii) the property is deemed

(A) where the usufruct, right of use or habitation, or substitution, as the case may be, arises on the death of a testator, to have been transferred to the trust on and as a consequence of the death of the testator, and not otherwise, and

(B) where the usufruct, right of use or habitation, or substitution, as the case may be, arises otherwise, to have been transferred (at the time it first became subject to the usufruct, right of use or habitation, or substitution, as the case may be) to the trust by the person that granted the usufruct, right of use or habitation, or substitution, and

(iii) the property is deemed to be, throughout the period in which it is subject to the usufruct, right of use or habitation, or substitution, as the case may be, held by the trust, and not otherwise;

(*b*) an arrangement (other than a partnership, a qualifying arrangement or an arrangement that is a trust determined without reference to this paragraph) is deemed to be a trust and property subject to rights and obligations under the arrangement is, if the arrangement is deemed by this paragraph to be a trust, deemed to be held in trust and not otherwise, where the arrangement

(i) is established before October 31, 2003 by or under a written contract that

(A) is governed by the laws of the Province of Quebec, and

(B) provides that, for the purposes of this Act, the arrangement shall be considered to be a trust, and

(ii) creates rights and obligations that are substantially similar to the rights and obligations under a trust (determined without reference to this subsection);

(*c*) if the arrangement is a qualifying arrangement,

(i) the arrangement is deemed to be a trust,

(ii) any property contributed at any time to the arrangement by an annuitant, a holder or a subscriber of the arrangement, as the case may be, is deemed to have been transferred, at that time, to the trust by the contributor, and

(iii) property subject to rights and obligations under the arrangement is deemed to be held in trust and not otherwise;

(*d*) a person who has a right (whether immediate or future and whether absolute or contingent) to receive all or part of the income or capital in respect of property that is referred to in paragraph (*a*) or (*b*) is deemed to be beneficially interested in the trust; and

(*e*) notwithstanding that a property is at any time subject to a servitude, the property is deemed to be beneficially owned by a person at that time if, at that time, the person has in relation to the property

(i) the right of ownership,

(ii) a right as a lessee under an emphyteusis, or

(iii) a right as a beneficiary in a trust.

History: S. 248(3) was replaced by S.C. 2009, c. 2, s. 76(5), applicable to taxation years that begin after October 30, 2003 except that for taxation years that end before 2008, subparagraph 248(3)(*c*)(ii) shall be read without reference to the expression "a holder".

For taxation years that begin after 1988 and before October 31, 2003, paragraph 248(3)(*d*) shall, in its application to each arrangement that is entered into between an individual and a corporation licensed or otherwise authorized under the laws of Canada or a province to carry on in Canada the business of offering to the public its services as trustee and that is accepted by the Minister for registration under section 146 or 146.3, be read without reference to

(a) clause (i)(B) of that paragraph, if the arrangement is presented as a declaration of trust but does not provide that, for the purposes of the Act, the arrangement shall be considered to be a trust; and

(b) subparagraph (ii) of that paragraph.

S. 248(3) formerly read:

(3) *Rules applicable in relation to the Province of Quebec.* For the purposes of the application of this Act in relation to the Province of Quebec,

(*a*) a usufruct shall be deemed to be a trust, created by will where the usufruct was so established, and property subject to a usufruct shall be deemed to have been transferred to the trust, on the death of the testator and as a consequence thereof where the usufruct arises on death, and to be held in trust and not otherwise;

(*b*) a right of use or habitation shall be deemed to be a trust, created by will where the right was so established, and property subject to such a right shall be deemed to have been transferred to the trust, on the death of the testator and as a consequence thereof where the right arises on death, and to be held in trust and not otherwise;

(*c*) a substitution shall be deemed to be a trust, created by will where the substitution was so established, and property subject to a substitution shall be deemed to have been transferred to the trust, on the death of the testator and as a consequence thereof where the substitution arises on death, and to be held in trust and not otherwise;

(*d*) property subject to rights and obligations under an arrangement (other than a trust) that

(i) is established by or under a written contract that

(A) is governed by the laws of the Province of Quebec, and

(B) provides that, for the purposes of this Act, the arrangement shall be considered to be a trust, and

(ii) creates rights and obligations that are substantially similar to the rights and obligations under a trust (determined without reference to this subsection),

shall be deemed to be held in trust and not otherwise, and such an arrangement shall be deemed to be a trust;

(*e*) a person who has a right (whether immediate or future and whether absolute or contingent) to receive all or any part of the income or capital in respect of property referred to in paragraph (*a*), (*b*), (*c*) or (*d*) shall be deemed to be beneficially interested in the trust referred to in that paragraph; and

(*f*) property in relation to which any person has, at any time,

(i) the right of ownership,

(ii) a right as a lessee in an emphyteutic lease, or

(iii) a right as a beneficiary in a trust

shall, notwithstanding that such property is subject to a servitude, be deemed to be beneficially owned by the person at that time.

Related Sections: S. 108(1), "beneficiary", "trust".

Canadian Tax Foundation: Brender, *Beneficial Ownership in Canadian Income Tax Law: Required Reform and Impact on Harmonization of Quebec Civil Law and Federal Legislation,* 2003 Canadian Tax Journal 1:311–354.

Tax Profile: December 2003 — Non-Resident Trust Rules To Apply To Usufructs And Foundations.

Income Tax Folios: *Secondary* — S1-F3-C2 Principal Residence.

▶ 248(3.1) ◀

(3.1) Gift of bare ownership of immovables. Subsection (3) does not apply in respect of a usufruct or a right of use of an immovable in circumstances where a taxpayer disposes of the bare ownership of the immovable by way of a gift to a qualified donee and retains, for life, the usufruct or the right of use.

History: S. 248(3.1) was replaced by S.C. 2011, c. 24, s. 72(5), in force January 1, 2012. S. 248(3.1) formerly read:

(3.1) *Gift of bare ownership of immovables.* Subsection (3) does not apply in respect of a usufruct or a right of use of an immovable in circumstances where a taxpayer disposes of the bare ownership of the immovable by way of a gift to a donee described in the definition "total charitable gifts", "total Crown gifts" or "total ecological gifts" in subsection 118.1(1) and retains, for life, the usufruct or the right of use.

S. 248(3.1) was added by S.C. 2009, c. 2, s. 76(5), applicable to dispositions that occur after July 18, 2005.

▶ 248(3.2) ◀

(3.2) Qualifying arrangement. For the purposes of paragraphs 248(3)(*b*) and (*c*), an arrangement is a qualifying arrangement if it is

(*a*) entered into with a corporation that is licensed or otherwise authorized under the laws of Canada or a province to carry on in Canada the business of offering to the public its services as trustee;

(*b*) established by or under a written contract that is governed by the laws of the Province of Quebec;

(*c*) presented as a declaration of trust or provides that, for the purposes of this Act, it shall be considered to be a trust; and

(*d*) presented as an arrangement in respect of which the corporation is to take action for the arrangement to become a registered disability savings plan, a registered education savings plan, a registered retirement income fund, a registered retirement savings plan or a TFSA.

History: S. 248(3.2) was added by S.C. 2009, c. 2, s. 76(5), applicable to taxation years that begin after October 30, 2003 except that for taxation years that end before 2008, paragraph 248(3.2)(*d*) shall be read without reference to registered disability savings plans and TFSAs; and for taxation years that end in 2008, paragraph 248(3.2)(*d*) shall be read without reference to TFSAs.

▶ 248(4) ◀

(4) Interest in real property. In this Act, an interest in real property includes a leasehold interest in real property but does not include an interest as security only derived by virtue of a mortgage, agreement for sale or similar obligation.

History: S. 248(4) was replaced by S.C. 2013, c. 34, s. 167(5), in force June 26, 2013, and formerly read:

(4) *Interest in real property.* In this Act, an interest in real property includes a leasehold interest in real property but does not include an interest as security only derived by virtue of a mortgage, hypothecary claim, agreement for sale or similar obligation.

Related Sections: S. 43.1(1) Life estates in real property; s. 85(1.1) Definition of "eligible property"; s. 108(2) When trust is a unit trust; s. 131(8) Meaning of "mutual fund corporation"; s. 132(6) Meaning of "mutual fund trust"; s. 216(1) Alternatives re rents and timber royalties; s. 216(5) Disposition by non-resident of interest in real property, timber resource property or timber limit.

▶ 248(4.1) ◀

(4.1) Real right in immovables. In this Act, a real right in an immovable includes a lease but does not include a security right derived by virtue of a hypothec, agreement for sale or similar obligation.

History: S. 248(4.1) was added by S.C. 2013, c. 34, s. 167(5), in force June 26, 2013.

▶ 248(5) ◀

(5) Substituted property. For the purposes of this Act, other than paragraph 98(1)(*a*),

(*a*) where a person has disposed of or exchanged a particular property and acquired other property in substitution therefor and subsequently, by one or more further transactions, has effected one or more further substitutions, the property acquired by any such transaction shall be deemed to have been substituted for the particular property; and

(*b*) any share received as a stock dividend on another share of the capital stock of a corporation shall be deemed to be property substituted for that other share.

Related Sections: S. 248(1), "stock dividend".

Interpretation Bulletins: *Secondary* — IT-244R3 Gifts by individuals of life insurance policies as charitable donations; IT-369R Attribution of trust income to settlor; IT-511R Interspousal and certain other transfers and loans of property.

▶ 248(6) ◀

(6) "Class" of shares issued in series. In its application in relation to a corporation that has issued shares of a class of its capital stock in one or more series, a reference in this Act to the "class" shall be read, with such modifications as the circumstances require, as a reference to a "series of the class."

▶ 248(7) ◀

(7) Receipt of things mailed. For the purposes of this Act,

(*a*) anything (other than a remittance or payment described in paragraph (*b*)) sent by first class mail or its equivalent shall be deemed to have been received by the person to whom it was sent on the day it was mailed; and

(*b*) the remittance or payment of an amount

(i) deducted or withheld, or

(ii) payable by a corporation,

as required by this Act or a regulation shall be deemed to have been made on the day on which it is received by the Receiver General.

Related Sections: S. 150.1(3) Deemed date of filing; s. 244(14) Mailing date.

Tax Window Files: Timing of Income Recognition — Cheques Mailed to Taxpayer, *Technical Interpretation, Business and Partnerships Division, December 23, 2003*, CRA Document No. 2003-0049497. No receipt of employment income where cheques were mailed but not actually received by taxpayer.

▶ 248(8) ◀

(8) Occurrences as a consequence of death. For the purpose of this Act,

(*a*) a transfer, distribution or acquisition of property under or as a consequence of the terms of the will or other testamentary instrument of a taxpayer or the taxpayer's spouse or common-law partner or as a consequence of the law governing the intestacy of a taxpayer or the taxpayer's spouse or common-law partner shall be considered to be a transfer, distribution or acquisition of the property as a consequence of the death of the taxpayer or the taxpayer's spouse or common-law partner, as the case may be;

(*b*) a transfer, distribution or acquisition of property as a consequence of a disclaimer, release or surrender by a person who was a beneficiary under the will or other testamentary instrument or on the intestacy of a taxpayer or the taxpayer's spouse or common-law partner shall be considered to be a transfer, distribution or acquisition of the property as a consequence of the death of the taxpayer or the taxpayer's spouse or common-law partner, as the case may be; and

(*c*) a release or surrender by a beneficiary under the will or other testamentary instrument or on the intestacy of a taxpayer with respect to any property that was property of the taxpayer immediately before the taxpayer's death shall be considered not to be a disposition of the property by the beneficiary.

Related Sections: S. 248(1), "common-law partner".

Interpretation Bulletins: *Secondary* — IT-305R4 Establishment of testamentary spouse trust; IT-349R3 Intergenerational transfers of farm property on death; IT-313R2 Eligible capital property — Rules where a taxpayer has ceased carrying on a business or has died.

▶ 248(9) ◀

(9) Definitions. In subsection (8),

"disclaimer" — "disclaimer" includes a renunciation of a succession made under the laws of the Province of Quebec that is not made in favour of any person, but does not include any disclaimer made after the period ending 36 months after the death of the taxpayer unless written application therefor has been made to the Minister by the taxpayer's legal representative within that period and the disclaimer is made within such longer period as the Minister considers reasonable in the circumstances;

Interpretation Bulletins: *Secondary* — IT-305R4 Establishment of testamentary spouse trust; IT-313R2 Eligible capital property — Rules where a taxpayer has ceased carrying on a business or has died.

"release or surrender" — "release or surrender" means

(*a*) a release or surrender made under the laws of a province (other than the Province of Quebec) that does not direct in any manner who is entitled to benefit therefrom, or

(*b*) a gift *inter vivos* made under the laws of the Province of Quebec of an interest in, or right to property of, a succession that is made to the person or persons who would have benefited if the donor had made a renunciation of the succession that was not made in favour of any person,

and that is made within the period ending 36 months after the death of the taxpayer or, where written application therefor has been made to the Minister by the taxpayer's legal representative within that period, within such longer period as the Minister considers reasonable in the circumstances.

Interpretation Bulletins: *Secondary* — IT-305R4 Establishment of testamentary spouse trust.

▶ 248(9.1) ◀

(9.1) How trust created. For the purposes of this Act, a trust shall be considered to be created by a taxpayer's will if the trust is created

(*a*) under the terms of the taxpayer's will; or

(*b*) by an order of a court in relation to the taxpayer's estate made under any law of a province that provides for the relief or support of dependants.

Related Sections: S. 104(1) Reference to trust or estate; s. 248(1), "estate", "trust"; s. 248(3) Property subject to certain Quebec institutions and arrangements.

▶ 248(9.2) ◀

(9.2) Vested indefeasibly. For the purposes of this Act, property shall be deemed not to have vested indefeasibly

(*a*) in a trust under which a taxpayer's spouse or common-law partner is a beneficiary, where the trust is created by the will of the taxpayer, unless the property vested indefeasibly in the trust before the death of the spouse or common-law partner; and

(*b*) in an individual (other than a trust), unless the property vested indefeasibly in the individual before the death of the individual.

Related Sections: S. 104(1) Reference to trust or estate; s. 248(1), "common-law partner", "individual", "property", "trust"; s. 252(4) Extended meaning of spouse.

▶ 248(10) ◀

(10) Series of transactions. For the purposes of this Act, where there is a reference to a series of transactions or events, the series shall be deemed to include any related transactions or events completed in contemplation of the series.

Related Sections: S. 212(1)(*b*) Interest; s. 212.2(1) Application.

Canadian Petroleum Tax Journal: Recent Developments in Tax Jurisprudence, Edward Rowe and Catherine Bradley, 2002, Vol. 15, No. 1.

Canadian Tax Foundation: Alarie and Lockhart, *The Importance of Family Resemblance: Series of Transactions After Copthorne*, 2014 Canadian Tax Journal 1:69–109; Kepes et al., *The Meaning and Effect of the Copthorne Decision on "Series of Transactions" for the Non-GAAR Provisions of the Income Tax Act*, 2012 Conference Report 12:1–37; Carr and Milot, *Copthorne: Series of Transactions Revisited*, 2008 Canadian Tax Journal 1:243–268; Brender, *Series of Transactions: A Case for a Purposive Interpretation*, 2007 Canadian Tax Journal 1:210–234; Prendergast, *Current Case Law: An Update on Recent Court Decisions of Interest to Tax Practitioners*, 2004 Prairie Provinces Tax Conference 1:1–53.

Tax Profile: March 2012 — Supreme Court Elaborates on GAAR.

Tax Topics: No. 2080, "He Who Wants a Rose Must Respect the (Cop)Thorn(E)"; No. 1947, Case Comment: *Copthorne Holdings Ltd. v. The Queen*, 2009 DTC 5101; No. 1856, *Copthorne Holdings Ltd. v. The Queen:* Backward Contemplation Bad for the Taxpayer; No. 1775, Series of Transactions After Canada Trustco: When Does Paragraph 55(3)(a) Apply?.

Cases: A transaction completed after a separate series of transactions can be said to have been "completed in contemplation of the series," and therefore be included in that series under s. 248(10), if the subsequent transaction was undertaken "in relation to" or "because of" the series. *Copthorne Holdings Ltd. v. The Queen*, 2012 DTC 5007 (S.C.C.), affirming 2009 DTC 5101 (F.C.A.) and 2007 DTC 1230 (T.C.C.).

▶ 248(11) ◀

(11) Compound interest. Interest computed at a prescribed rate under any of subsections 129(2.1) and (2.2), 131(3.1) and (3.2), 132(2.1) and (2.2), 133(7.01) and (7.02), 159(7), 160.1(1), 161(1), (2) and (11), 161.1(5), 164(3) to (4), 181.8(1) and (2) (as those two subsections read in their application to the 1991 and earlier taxation years), 185(2), 187(2) and 189(7), section 190.23 (as it read in its application to the 1991 and earlier taxation years) and subsections 193(3), 195(3), 202(5) and 227(8.3), (9.2) and (9.3) of this Act and subsection 182(2) of the *Income Tax Act*, chapter 148 of the Revised Statutes of Canada, 1952 (as that subsection read in its application to taxation years beginning before 1986) and subsection 191(2) of that Act (as that subsection read in its application to the 1984 and earlier taxation years) shall be compounded daily and, where interest is computed on an amount under any of those provisions and is unpaid or unapplied on the day it would, but for this subsection, have ceased to be computed under that provision, interest at the prescribed rate shall be computed and compounded daily on the unpaid or unapplied interest from that day to the day it is paid or applied and shall be paid or applied as would be the case if interest had continued to be computed under that provision after that day.

Related Regulations: 4301.

► 248(12) ◄

(12) Identical properties. For the purposes of this Act, one bond, debenture, bill, note or similar obligation issued by a debtor is identical to another such obligation issued by that debtor if both are identical in respect of all rights (in equity or otherwise, either immediately or in the future and either absolutely or contingently) attaching thereto, except as regards the principal amount thereof.

Related Sections: S. 14(13) Deemed identical property; s. 18(16) Deemed identical property; s. 40(3.5) Deemed identical property; S. 212(1)(*b*) Interest.

Interpretation Bulletins: *Secondary* — IT-387R2 (Consolid.) Meaning of "identical properties".

► 248(13) ◄

(13) Interests in trusts and partnerships. Where after November 12, 1981 a person has an interest in a trust or partnership, whether directly or indirectly through an interest in any other trust or partnership or in any manner whatever, the person shall, for the purposes of the definitions "income bond", "income debenture" and "term preferred share" in subsection (1), paragraph (*h*) of the definition "taxable preferred share" in that subsection, subsections 84(4.2) and (4.3) and 112(2.6) and section 258, be deemed to be a beneficiary of the trust or a member of the partnership, as the case may be.

► 248(14) ◄

(14) Related corporations. For the purpose of paragraph (g) of the definition "specified financial institution" in subsection (1), where in the case of 2 or more corporations it can reasonably be considered, having regard to all the circumstances, that one of the main reasons for the separate existence of those corporations in a taxation year is to limit or avoid the application of subsection 112(2.1) or (2.2) or 138(6), the 2 or more corporations shall be deemed to be related to each other and to each other corporation to which any such corporation is related.

► 248(15) ◄

(15) Goods and services tax — change of use. For the purposes of this Act, where a liability for the goods and services tax is incurred in respect of a change of use at any time of a property, the liability so incurred shall be deemed to have been incurred immediately after that time in respect of the acquisition of the property.

► 248(16) ◄

(16) Goods and services tax — input tax credit and rebate. For the purposes of this Act, other than this subsection and subsection 6(8), an amount claimed by a taxpayer as an input tax credit or rebate with respect to the goods and services tax in respect of a property or service is deemed to be assistance from a government in respect of the property or service that is received by the taxpayer

(*a*) where the amount was claimed by the taxpayer as an input tax credit in a return under Part IX of the *Excise Tax Act* for a reporting period under that Act,

(i) at the particular time that is the earlier of the time that the goods and services tax in respect of the input tax credit was paid and the time that it became payable,

(A) if the particular time is in the reporting period, or

(B) if,

(I) the taxpayer's threshold amount, determined in accordance with subsection 249(1) of the *Excise Tax Act*, is greater than $500,000 for the taxpayer's fiscal year (within the meaning assigned by that Act) that includes the particular time, and

(II) the taxpayer claimed the input tax credit at least 120 days before the end of the normal reassessment period, as determined under subsection 152(3.1), for the taxpayer in respect of the taxation year that includes the particular time,

(ii) at the end of the reporting period, if

(A) subparagraph (i) does not apply, and

(B) the taxpayer's threshold amount, determined in accordance with subsection 249(1) of the *Excise Tax Act*, is $500,000 or less for the fiscal year (within the meaning assigned by that Act) of the taxpayer that includes the particular time, and

(iii) in any other case, on the last day of the taxpayer's earliest taxation year

(A) that begins after the taxation year that includes the particular time, and

(B) for which the normal reassessment period, as determined under subsection 152(3.1), for the taxpayer ends at least 120 days after the time that the input tax credit was claimed; or

(*b*) where the amount was claimed as a rebate with respect to the goods and services tax, at the time the amount was received or credited.

History: S. 248(16) was replaced by S.C. 2013, c. 34, s. 358(23), applicable in respect of input tax credits that become eligible to be claimed in taxation years that begin after December 20, 2002, and formerly read:

(16) *Goods and services tax — input tax credit and rebate.* For the purposes of this Act, other than this subsection and subsection 6(8), an amount claimed by a taxpayer as an input tax credit or rebate with respect to the goods and services tax in respect of a property or service shall be deemed to be assistance from a government in respect of the property or service that is received by the taxpayer

(*a*) where the amount was claimed by the taxpayer as an input tax credit in a return under Part IX of the *Excise Tax Act* for a reporting period under that Act,

(i) at the time the goods and services tax in respect of the input tax credit was paid or became payable, if the tax was paid or became payable in the reporting period, or

(ii) if no such tax was paid or became payable in respect of the input tax credit in the reporting period, at the end of the reporting period; or

(*b*) where the amount was claimed as a rebate with respect to the goods and services tax, at the time the amount was received or credited.

Related Sections: 248(17) Application of subsection (16) to certain vehicles and aircraft.

Interpretation Bulletins: *Secondary* — IT-273R2 Government assistance — General comments.

► 248(16.1) ◄

(16.1) Quebec input tax refund and rebate. For the purpose of this Act, other than this subsection and subsection 6(8), an amount claimed by a taxpayer as an input tax refund or a rebate with respect to the Quebec sales tax in respect of a property or service is deemed to be assistance from a government in respect of the property or service that is received by the taxpayer

(*a*) where the amount was claimed by the taxpayer as an input tax refund in a return under *An Act respecting the Québec sales tax*, R.S.Q., c. T-0.1, for a reporting period under that Act,

(i) at the particular time that is the earlier of the time that the Quebec sales tax in respect of the input tax refund was paid and the time that it became payable,

(A) if the particular time is in the reporting period, or

(B) if,

(I) the taxpayer's threshold amount, determined in accordance with section 462 of that Act is greater than $500,000 for the taxpayer's fiscal year (within the meaning assigned by that Act) that includes the particular time, and

(II) the taxpayer claimed the input tax refund at least 120 days before the end of the normal reassessment period, as determined under subsection 152(3.1), for the taxpayer in respect of the taxation year that includes the particular time,

(ii) at the end of the reporting period, if

(A) subparagraph (i) does not apply, and

(B) the taxpayer's threshold amount, determined in accordance with section 462 of that Act is $500,000 or less for the fiscal year (within the meaning assigned by that Act) of the taxpayer that includes the particular time, and

(iii) in any other case, on the last day of the taxpayer's earliest taxation year

(A) that begins after the taxation year that includes the particular time, and

(B) for which the normal reassessment period, as determined under subsection 152(3.1), for the taxpayer ends at least 120 days after the time that the input tax refund was claimed; or

(*b*) where the amount was claimed as a rebate with respect to the Quebec sales tax, at the time the amount was received or credited.

History: S. 248(16.1) was added by S.C. 2013, c. 34, s. 358(24), applicable in respect of input tax refunds and rebates that become eligible to be claimed in taxation years that begin after February 27, 2004.

Related Sections: 248(17.1) Application of subsection (16.1) to certain vehicles and aircraft.

► 248(17) ◄

(17) Application of subsection (16) to certain vehicles and aircraft. If the input tax credit of a taxpayer under Part IX of the *Excise Tax Act* in respect of a passenger vehicle, zero-emission passenger vehicle or aircraft is determined with reference to subsection 202(4) of that Act, subparagraphs (16)(*a*)(i) to (iii) are to be read as they apply in respect of the vehicle or aircraft, as the case may be, as follows:

(i) at the beginning of the first taxation year or fiscal period of the taxpayer commencing after the end of the taxation year or fiscal period, as the case may be, in which the goods and services tax in respect of such property was considered for the purposes of determining the input tax credit to be payable, if the tax was considered for the purposes of determining the input tax credit to have become payable in the reporting period, or

(ii) if no such tax was considered for the purposes of determining the input tax credit to have become payable in the reporting period, at the end of the reporting period; or

History: S. 248(17) was replaced by S.C. 2019, c. 29, s. 43(5), deemed to have come into force on March 19, 2019, and formerly read:

(17) *Application of subsection (16) to passenger vehicles and aircraft.* If the input tax credit of a taxpayer under Part IX of the *Excise Tax Act* in respect of a passenger vehicle or aircraft is determined with reference to subsection 202(4) of that Act, subparagraphs (16)(*a*)(i) to (iii) are to be read as they apply in respect of the passenger vehicle or aircraft, as the case may be, as follows:

"(i) at the beginning of the first taxation year or fiscal period of the taxpayer commencing after the end of the taxation year or fiscal period, as the case may be, in which the goods and services tax in respect of such property was considered for the purposes of determining the input tax credit to be payable, if the tax was considered for the purposes of determining the input tax credit to have become payable in the reporting period, or

(ii) if no such tax was considered for the purposes of determining the input tax credit to have become payable in the reporting period, at the end of the reporting period; or"

S. 248(17), the portion before the portion enclosed by quotation marks was replaced by S.C. 2013, c. 34, s. 358(25), applicable in respect of input tax credits that become eligible to be claimed in taxation years that begin after December 20, 2002, and formerly read:

(17) *Application of s. (16) to passenger vehicles and aircraft.* Where the input tax credit of a taxpayer under Part IX of the *Excise Tax Act* in respect of a passenger vehicle or aircraft is determined with reference to subsection 202(4) of the *Excise Tax Act*, subparagraphs (16)(*a*)(i) and (ii) shall, as they apply in respect of such property, be read as follows:

Related Sections: 248(16) Goods and services tax — input tax credit and rebate; 248(1) "zero-emission passenger vehicle".

► 248(17.1) ◄

(17.1) Application of subsection (16.1) to certain vehicles and aircraft. If the input tax refund of a taxpayer under *An Act respecting the Québec sales tax*, R.S.Q., c. T-0.1, in respect of a passenger vehicle, zero-emission passenger vehicle or aircraft is determined with reference to section 252 of that Act, subparagraphs (16.1)(*a*)(i) to (iii) are to be read as they apply in respect of the vehicle or aircraft, as the case may be, as follows:

(i) at the beginning of the first taxation year or fiscal period of the taxpayer that begins after the end of the taxation year or fiscal period, as the case may be, in which the Quebec sales tax in respect of such property was considered for the purposes of determining the input tax refund to be payable, if the tax was considered for the purposes of determining the input tax refund to have become payable in the reporting period, or

(ii) if no such tax was considered for the purposes of determining the input tax refund to have become payable in the reporting period, at the end of the reporting period; or

History: S. 248(17.1) was replaced by S.C. 2019, c. 29, s. 43(5), deemed to have come into force on March 19, 2019, and formerly read:

(17.1) *Application of subsection (16.1) to passenger vehicles and aircraft.* If the input tax refund of a taxpayer under *An Act respecting the Québec sales tax*, R.S.Q., c. T-0.1, in respect of a passenger vehicle or aircraft is determined with reference to section 252 of that Act, subparagraphs (16.1)(*a*)(i) to (iii) are to be read as they apply in respect of the passenger vehicle or aircraft, as the case may be, as follows:

"(i) at the beginning of the first taxation year or fiscal period of the taxpayer that begins after the end of the taxation year or fiscal period, as the case may be, in which the Quebec sales tax in respect of such property was considered for the purposes of determining the input tax refund to be payable, if the tax was considered for the purposes of determining the input tax refund to have become payable in the reporting period, or

(ii) if no such tax was considered for the purposes of determining the input tax refund to have become payable in the reporting period, at the end of the reporting period; or".

S. 248(17.1) was added by S.C. 2013, c. 34, s. 358(26), applicable in respect of input tax refunds and rebates that become eligible to be claimed in taxation years that begin after February 27, 2004.

Related Sections: 248(16.1) Quebec input tax refund and rebate; 248(1) "zero-emission passenger vehicle".

► 248(17.2) ◄

(17.2) Input tax credit on assessment. An amount in respect of an input tax credit that is deemed by subsection 296(5) of the *Excise Tax Act* to have been claimed in a return or application filed under Part IX of that Act is deemed to have been so claimed for the reporting period under that Act that includes the time when the Minister makes the assessment referred to in that subsection.

History: S. 248(17.2) was added by S.C. 2013, c. 34, s. 358(26), applicable in respect of input tax credits that become eligible to be claimed in taxation years that begin after December 20, 2002.

► 248(17.3) ◄

(17.3) Quebec input tax refund on assessment. An amount in respect of an input tax refund that is deemed by section 30.5 of the *Tax Administration Act*, R.S.Q., c. A-6.002, to have been claimed is deemed to have been so claimed for the reporting period under *An Act respecting the Québec sales tax*, R.S.Q., c. T-0.1, that includes the day on which an assessment is issued to the taxpayer indicating that the refund has been allocated under that section 30.5.

History: S. 248(17.3) was added by S.C. 2013, c. 34, s. 358(26), applicable in respect of input tax refunds and rebates that become eligible to be claimed in taxation years that begin after February 27, 2004, except that, before April 1, 2011, the reference to "the *Tax Administration Act*, R.S.Q., c. A-6.002" in subsection 248(17.3) is to be read as a reference to "*An Act respecting the Ministère du Revenu*, R.S.Q., c. M-31".

► 248(18) ◄

(18) Goods and services tax — repayment of input tax credit. For the purposes of this Act, where an amount is added at a particular time in determining the net tax of a taxpayer under Part IX of the *Excise Tax Act* in respect of an input tax credit relating to property or a service that had been previously deducted in determining the net tax of the taxpayer, that amount shall be deemed to be assistance repaid at the particular time in respect of the property or service pursuant to a legal obligation to repay all or part of that assistance.

► 248(18.1) ◄

(18.1) Repayment of Quebec input tax refund. For the purposes of this Act, if an amount is added at a particular time in determining the net tax of a taxpayer under *An Act respecting the Québec sales tax*, R.S.Q., c. T-0.1, in respect of an input tax refund relating to property or service that had been previously deducted in determining the net tax of the taxpayer, that amount is deemed to be assistance repaid at the particular time in respect of the property or service under a legal obligation to repay all or part of that assistance.

History: S. 248(18.1) was added by S.C. 2013, c. 34, s. 358(27), deemed to have come into force on February 28, 2004.

► 248(19) ◄

(19) When property available for use. Except as otherwise provided, property shall be considered to have become available for use for the purposes of this Act at the time at which it has, or would have if it were depreciable property, become available for use for the purpose of subsection 13(26).

Related Sections: S. 13(26) Restriction on deduction before available for use; s. 37(1.2) Deemed time of capital expenditure; s. 127(11.2) Time of expenditure and acquisition.

► 248(20) ◄

(20) Partition of property. Subject to subsections (21) to (23), for the purposes of this Act, if at any time a property owned by two or more persons is the subject of a partition, the following rules apply, notwithstanding any retroactive or declaratory effect of the partition:

(*a*) each such person who had, immediately before that time, an interest in, or for civil law a right in, the property (which interest or right in the property is referred to in this subsection and subsection (21) as an "interest" or a "right", as the case may be) is deemed not to have disposed at that time of that proportion, not exceeding 100%, of the interest or right that the fair market value of that person's interest or right in the property immediately after that time is of the fair market value of that person's interest or right in the property immediately before that time,

(*b*) each such person who has an interest or a right in the property immediately after that time is deemed not to have acquired at that time that proportion of the interest or right that the fair market value of that person's interest or right in the property immediately before that time is of the fair market value of that person's interest or right in the property immediately after that time,

(*c*) each such person who had an interest or a right in the property immediately before that time is deemed to have had until that time, and to have disposed at that time of, that proportion of the person's interest or right to which paragraph (*a*) does not apply,

(*d*) each such person who has an interest or a right in the property immediately after that time is deemed not to have had before that time, and to have acquired at that time, that proportion of the person's interest or right to which paragraph (*b*) does not apply, and

(*e*) paragraphs (*a*) to (*d*) do not apply if the interest or right of the person is an interest or a right in fungible tangible property, or for civil law fungible corporeal property described in that person's inventory,

and, for the purposes of this subsection, if an interest or a right in the property is an undivided interest or right, the fair market value of the interest or right at any time is deemed to be equal to that proportion of the fair market value of the property at that time that the interest or right is of all the undivided interests or rights in the property.

History: S. 248(20) was replaced by S.C. 2013, c. 34, s. 167(6), in force June 26, 2013, and formerly read:

(20) *Partition of property.* Subject to subsections (21) to (23), for the purposes of this Act, where at any time a property owned by two or more persons is the subject of a partition, the following rules apply, notwithstanding any retroactive or declaratory effect of the partition:

(*a*) each such person who had an interest in the property immediately before that time shall be deemed not to have disposed at that time of that proportion, not exceeding 100%, of the interest that the fair market value of that person's interest in the property immediately after that time is of the fair market value of that person's interest in the property immediately before that time,

(*b*) each such person who has an interest in the property immediately after that time shall be deemed not to have acquired at that time that proportion of the interest that the fair market value of that person's interest in the property immediately before that time is of the fair market value of that person's interest in the property immediately after that time,

(*c*) each such person who had an interest in the property immediately before that time shall be deemed to have had until that time, and to have disposed at that time of, that proportion of the person's interest to which paragraph (*a*) does not apply,

(*d*) each such person who has an interest in the property immediately after that time shall be deemed not to have had before that time, and to have acquired at that time, that proportion of the person's interest to which paragraph (*b*) does not apply, and

(*e*) paragraphs (*a*) to (*d*) do not apply where the interest of the person is an interest in fungible tangible property described in that person's inventory,

and, for the purposes of this subsection, where an interest in the property is an undivided interest, the fair market value of the interest at any time shall be deemed to be equal to that proportion of the fair market value of the property at that time that the interest is of all the undivided interests in the property.

▶ 248(21) ◀

(21) Subdivision of property. If a property that was owned by two or more persons is the subject of a partition among those persons and, as a consequence of it, each such person has, in the property, a new interest or right the fair market value of which immediately after the partition, expressed as a percentage of the fair market value of all the new interests or rights in the property immediately after the partition, is equal to the fair market value of that person's undivided interest or right immediately before the partition, expressed as a percentage of the fair market value of all the undivided interests or rights in the property immediately before the partition,

(*a*) subsection (20) does not apply to the property, and

(*b*) the new interest or right of each such person is deemed to be a continuation of that person's undivided interest or right in the property immediately before the partition,

and, for the purposes of this subsection,

(*c*) subdivisions of a building or of a parcel of land that are established in the course of, or in contemplation of, a partition and that are co-owned by the same persons who co-owned the building or the parcel of land, or by their assignee, shall be regarded as one property, and

(*d*) if an interest or a right in the property is or includes an undivided interest or right, the fair market value of the interest or right shall be determined without regard to any discount or premium that applies to a minority or majority interest or right in the property.

History: S. 248(21) was replaced by S.C. 2013, c. 34, s. 167(6), in force June 26, 2013, and formerly read:

(21) *Subdivision of property.* Where a property that was owned by two or more persons is the subject of a partition among those persons and, as a consequence thereof, each such person has, in the property, a new interest the fair market value of which immediately after the partition, expressed as a percentage of the fair market value of all the new interests in the property immediately after the partition, is equal to the fair market value of that person's undivided interest immediately before the partition, expressed as a percentage of the fair market value of all the undivided interests in the property immediately before the partition,

(*a*) subsection (20) does not apply to the property, and

(*b*) the new interest of each such person shall be deemed to be a continuation of that person's undivided interest in the property immediately before the partition,

and, for the purposes of this subsection,

(*c*) subdivisions of a building or of a parcel of land that are established in the course of, or in contemplation of, a partition and that are co-owned by the same persons who co-owned the building or the parcel of land, or by their assignee, shall be regarded as one property, and

(*d*) where an interest in the property is or includes an undivided interest, the fair market value of the interest shall be determined without regard to any discount or premium that applies to a minority or majority interest in the property.

▶ 248(22) ◀

(22) Matrimonial regimes. Where at any time property could, as a consequence of the dissolution of a matrimonial regime between 2 spouses or common-law partners, be the subject of a partition, for the purposes of this Act

(*a*) where that property was owned by one of the spouses or common-law partners immediately before it became subject to that regime and had not subsequently been disposed of before that time, it shall be deemed to be owned at that time by that spouse or common-law partner and not by the other spouse or common-law partner; and

(*b*) in any other case, the property shall be deemed to be owned by the spouse or common-law partner who has the administration of that property at that time and not by the other spouse or common-law partner.

Related Sections: S. 252(3) Extended meaning of "spouse" and "former spouse".

▶ 248(23) ◀

(23) Dissolution of a matrimonial regime. Where, immediately after the dissolution of a matrimonial regime (other than a dissolution occurring as a consequence of death), the owner of a property that was subject to that regime is not the person, or the estate of the person, who is deemed by subsection (22) to have been the owner of the property immediately before the dissolution, the person shall be deemed for the purposes of this Act to have transferred the property to the person's spouse or common-law partner immediately before the dissolution.

▶ 248(23.1) ◀

(23.1) Transfers after death. If, as a consequence of the laws of a province relating to spouses' or common-law partners' interests or rights in respect of property as a result of marriage or common-law partnership, property is, after the death of a taxpayer,

(*a*) transferred or distributed to a person who was the taxpayer's spouse or common-law partner at the time of the death, or acquired by that person, the property shall be deemed to have been so transferred, distributed or acquired, as the case may be, as a consequence of the death; or

(*b*) transferred or distributed to the taxpayer's estate, or acquired by the taxpayer's estate, the property shall be deemed to have been so transferred, distributed or acquired, as the case may be, immediately before the time that is immediately before the death.

History: S. 248(23.1), the portion before paragraph (*a*) was replaced by S.C. 2013, c. 34, s. 167(7), in force June 26, 2013, and formerly read:

(23.1) *Transfers after death.* Where, as a consequence of the laws of a province relating to spouses' or common-law partners' interests in respect of property as a result of marriage or common-law partnership, property is, after the death of a taxpayer,

Interpretation Bulletins: *Secondary* — IT-313R2 Eligible capital property — Rules where a taxpayer has ceased carrying on a business or has died.

► 248(24) ◄

(24) Accounting methods. For greater certainty, it is hereby declared that, unless specifically required, neither the equity nor the consolidation method of accounting shall be used to determine any amount for the purposes of this Act.

Income Tax Technical News: Issue No. 42, International financial reporting standards.

► 248(25) ◄

(25) Beneficially interested. For the purposes of this Act,

(*a*) a person or partnership beneficially interested in a particular trust includes any person or partnership that has any right (whether immediate or future, whether absolute or contingent or whether conditional on or subject to the exercise of any discretion by any person or partnership) as a beneficiary under a trust to receive any of the income or capital of the particular trust either directly from the particular trust or indirectly through one or more trusts or partnerships;

(*b*) except for the purpose of this paragraph, a particular person or partnership is deemed to be beneficially interested in a particular trust at a particular time where

(i) the particular person or partnership is not beneficially interested in the particular trust at the particular time,

(ii) because of the terms or conditions of the particular trust or any arrangement in respect of the particular trust at the particular time, the particular person or partnership might, because of the exercise of any discretion by any person or partnership, become beneficially interested in the particular trust at the particular time or at a later time, and

(iii) at or before the particular time, either

(A) the particular trust has acquired property, directly or indirectly in any manner whatever, from

(I) the particular person or partnership,

(II) another person with whom the particular person or partnership, or a member of the particular partnership, does not deal at arm's length,

(III) a person or partnership with whom the other person referred to in subclause (II) does not deal at arm's length,

(IV) a controlled foreign affiliate of the particular person or of another person with whom the particular person or partnership, or a member of the particular partnership, does not deal at arm's length, or

(V) a non-resident corporation that would, if the particular partnership were a corporation resident in Canada, be a controlled foreign affiliate of the particular partnership, or

(B) a person or partnership described in any of subclauses (A)(I) to (V) has given a guarantee on behalf of the particular trust or provided any other financial assistance whatever to the particular trust; and

(*c*) a member of a partnership that is beneficially interested in a trust is deemed to be beneficially interested in the trust.

Related Sections: s. 233.6(1) Returns respecting distributions from non-resident trusts; s. 248(1), "trust"; s. 248(3) Property subject to certain Quebec institutions and arrangements.

Canadian Tax Foundation: Fortin, *Strangers in Strange Lands: The Hidden Traps of Offshore Trusts*, 1999 Conference Report 40:1–68.

Tax Profile: March 2010 — Association Through A Trust: When is A Person A Beneficiary?.

Interpretation Bulletins: *Secondary* — IT-394R2 Preferred beneficiary election.

► 248(25.1) ◄

(25.1) Trust-to-trust transfers. If, at any time, a particular trust transfers property to another trust (other than a trust governed by a registered retirement savings plan or by a registered retirement income fund) in circumstances to which paragraph (*f*) of the definition "disposition" in subsection (1) applies, without affecting the personal liabilities under this Act of the trustees of either trust or the application of subsection 104(5.8),

(*a*) the other trust is deemed to be after that time the same trust as, and a continuation of, the particular trust; and

(*b*) for greater certainty, if, as a result of a transaction or event, the property was deemed to be taxable Canadian property of the particular trust by any of paragraphs 51(1)(*f*), 85(1)(*i*) and 85.1(1)(*a*), subsection 85.1(5), paragraph 85.1(8)(*b*), subsections 87(4) and (5) and paragraphs 97(2)(*c*) and 107(3.1)(*d*), the property is also deemed to be, at any time that is within 60 months after the transaction or event, taxable Canadian property of the other trust.

History: S. 248(25.1), the portion before paragraph (*a*) was replaced by S.C. 2014, c. 39, s. 71(7), applicable to the 2016 and subsequent taxation years, and formerly read:

(25.1) *Trust-to-trust transfers.* If, at any time, a particular trust transfers property to another trust (other than a trust governed by a registered retirement savings plan or by a registered retirement income fund) in circumstances to which paragraph (*f*) of the definition "disposition" in subsection (1) applies, without affecting the personal liabilities under this Act of the trustees of either trust or the application of subsection 104(5.8) and paragraph 122(2)(*f*),

S. 248(25.1) was replaced by S.C. 2010, c. 12, s. 22(2), applicable in determining after March 4, 2010 whether a property is taxable Canadian property of a taxpayer. S. 248(25.1) formerly read:

(25.1) *Trust-to-trust transfers.* Where at any time a particular trust transfers property to another trust (other than a trust governed by a registered retirement savings plan or by a registered retirement income fund) in circumstances to which paragraph (*f*) of the definition "disposition" in subsection (1) applies, without affecting the personal liabilities under this Act of the trustees of either trust or the application of subsection 104(5.8) and paragraph 122(2)(*f*), the other trust is deemed to be after that time the same trust as, and a continuation of, the particular trust, and, for greater certainty, if the property was deemed to be taxable Canadian property of the particular trust by paragraph 51(1)(*f*), 85(1)(*i*) or 85.1(1)(*a*) or (8)(*b*), subsection 85.1(5) or

87(4) or (5) or paragraph 97(2)(*c*) or 107(2)(*d.1*) or (3.1)(*d*), the property is deemed to be taxable Canadian property of the other trust.

S. 248(25.1) was replaced by S.C. 2009, c. 2, s. 76(6), applicable after December 19, 2007. S. 248(25.1) formerly read:

(25.1) *Trust-to-trust transfers.* Where at any time a particular trust transfers property to another trust (other than a trust governed by a registered retirement savings plan or by a registered retirement income fund) in circumstances to which paragraph (*f*) of the definition "disposition" in subsection (1) applies, without affecting the personal liabilities under this Act of the trustees of either trust or the application of subsection 104(5.8) and paragraph 122(2)(*f*), the other trust is deemed to be after that time the same trust as, and a continuation of, the particular trust.

► 248(25.2) ◄

(25.2) Trusts to ensure obligations fulfilled. Except for the purpose of this subsection, where at any time property is transferred to a trust in circumstances to which paragraph (*k*) of the definition "disposition" in subsection (1) applies, the trust is deemed to deal with the property as agent for the transferor throughout the period that begins at the time of the transfer and ends at the time of the first change after that time in the beneficial ownership of the property.

► 248(25.3) ◄

(25.3) Cost of trust interest. The cost to a taxpayer of a particular unit of a trust is deemed to be equal to the amount described in paragraph (*a*) where

(*a*) the trust issues the particular unit to the taxpayer directly in satisfaction of a right to enforce payment of an amount by the trust in respect of the taxpayer's capital interest in the trust;

(*b*) at the time that the particular unit is issued, the trust is neither a personal trust nor a trust prescribed for the purpose of subsection 107(2); and

(*c*) either

(i) the particular unit is capital property and the amount is not proceeds of disposition of a capital interest in the trust, or

(ii) the particular unit is not capital property and subparagraph 53(2)(*h*)(i.1) does not apply in respect of the amount described in paragraph (*a*) but would so apply if that subparagraph were read without reference to clauses 53(2)(*h*)(i.1)(A) and (B).

History: S. 248(25.3)(*c*)(i) was replaced by S.C. 2013, c. 34, s. 358(29), applicable to units issued after December 20, 2002, and formerly read:

(i) the particular unit is capital property and subparagraph 53(2)(*h*)(i.1) applies in respect of the amount described in paragraph (*a*), or would apply if that subparagraph were read without reference to clauses 53(2)(*h*)(i.1)(A) and (B), or

► 248(25.4) ◄

(25.4) Where acquisition by another of right to enforce. If at a particular time a taxpayer's capital interest in a trust includes a right to enforce payment of an amount by the trust, the amount shall be added at the particular time to the cost otherwise determined to the taxpayer of the capital interest where

(*a*) immediately after the particular time there is a disposition by the taxpayer of the capital interest;

(*b*) as a consequence of the disposition, the right to enforce payment of the amount is acquired by another person or partnership; and

(*c*) if the right to enforce payment of the amount had been satisfied by a payment to the taxpayer by the trust, there would have been no disposition of that right for the purposes of this Act because of the application of paragraph (*i*) of the definition "disposition" in subsection (1).

► 248(26) ◄

(26) Debt obligations. For greater certainty, where at any time a person or partnership (in this subsection referred to as the "debtor") becomes liable to repay money borrowed by the debtor or becomes liable to pay an amount (other than interest)

(*a*) as consideration for any property acquired by the debtor or services rendered to the debtor, or

(*b*) that is deductible in computing the debtor's income,

for the purposes of applying the provisions of this Act relating to the treatment of the debtor in respect of the liability, the liability shall be considered to be an obligation, issued at that time by the debtor, that has a principal amount at that time equal to the amount of the liability at that time.

► 248(27) ◄

(27) Parts of debt obligations. For greater certainty,

(*a*) unless the context requires otherwise, an obligation issued by a debtor includes any part of a larger obligation that was issued by the debtor;

(*b*) the principal amount of that part shall be considered to be the portion of the principal amount of that larger obligation that relates to that part; and

(*c*) the amount for which that part was issued shall be considered to be the portion of the amount for which that larger obligation was issued that relates to that part.

► 248(28) ◄

(28) Limitation respecting inclusions, deductions and tax credits. Unless a contrary intention is evident, no provision of this Act shall be read or construed

(*a*) to require the inclusion or permit the deduction, either directly or indirectly, in computing a taxpayer's income, taxable income or taxable income earned in Canada, for a taxation year or in computing a taxpayer's income or loss for a taxation year from a particular source or from sources in a particular place, of any amount to the extent that the amount has already been directly or indirectly included or deducted, as the case may be, in computing such income, taxable income, taxable income earned in Canada or loss, for the year or any preceding taxation year;

(*b*) to permit the deduction, either directly or indirectly, in computing a taxpayer's tax payable under any Part of this Act for a taxation year of any amount to the extent that the amount has already been directly or indirectly deducted in computing such tax payable for the year or any preceding taxation year; or

(*c*) to consider an amount to have been paid on account of a taxpayer's tax payable under any Part of this Act for a taxation year to the extent that the amount has already been considered to have been paid on account of such tax payable for the year or any preceding taxation year.

Related Sections: S. 20(12.1) Foreign tax where no economic profit; s. 62(1) Moving expenses; s. 126(4.1) No economic profit.

▶ 248(29) ◀

(29) Farming or fishing business. For the purposes of subsection 40(1.1) and sections 70, 73 and 110.6, if at any time a person or partnership carries on a farming business and a fishing business, a property used at that time principally in a combination of the activities of the farming business and the fishing business is deemed to be used at that time principally in the course of carrying on a farming or fishing business.

History: S. 248(29) was added by S.C. 2014, c. 39, s. 71(8), applicable in respect of property disposed of, or transferred, in the 2014 and subsequent taxation years.

Related Regulations: 3200 (repealed); 3201 (repealed).

Related Sections: 40(1.1) Reserve — property disposed of to a child; 70(9.1) When subsection (9.11) applies; 73(3) When subsection (3.1) applies; 110.6(1.3) Farming or fishing property — conditions.

▶ 248(30) ◀

(30) Intention to give. The existence of an amount of an advantage in respect of a transfer of property does not in and by itself disqualify the transfer from being a gift to a qualified donee if

(*a*) the amount of the advantage does not exceed 80% of the fair market value of the transferred property; or

(*b*) the transferor of the property establishes to the satisfaction of the Minister that the transfer was made with the intention to make a gift.

Editorial Note: A gift must be made voluntarily and with the intention to gift. At common law, if the donor of the gift receives any form of benefit or consideration, the gift is presumed not to have been made as the intention is deemed not to be present. S. 248(30) to (40) apply to rebut this presumption and allow for a donor to receive a tax benefit regarding a gift (under s. 110.1 or 118.1) even where a gift involves an advantage to the donor, provided the advantage does not exceed 80% of the fair market value of the transferred property. An "advantage" received by the donor in respect of a gift is defined in s. 248(32) and generally includes any consideration or other benefit received by the donor in exchange for the gift. Where the advantage exceeds 80%, it is still possible to establish an intention to give by way of application to the Minister of National Revenue. S. 248(40) provides an exception for inter-charity transfers.

History: S. 248(30) was added by S.C. 2013, c. 34, s. 358(30), applicable in respect of gifts and monetary contributions made after December 20, 2002.

Income Tax Folios: *Primary* — S7-F1-C1 Split-receipting and Deemed Fair Market Value.

▶ 248(31) ◀

(31) Eligible amount of gift or monetary contribution. The eligible amount of a gift or monetary contribution is the amount by which the fair market value of the property that is the subject of the gift or monetary contribution exceeds the amount of the advantage, if any, in respect of the gift or monetary contribution.

Editorial Note: The eligible amount of a gift for the purposes of receiving a tax credit or deduction (see s. 110.1 and 118.1) is the amount by which the fair market value of the gifted property exceeds the amount of any advantage received by the donor. "Advantage" is defined in s. 248(32) and generally includes any consideration or benefits received by the donor. S. 248(35) to (39) set out anti-avoidance rules for determining the eligible amount of a gift where gifted property was acquired under a tax shelter, was acquired from a non-arm's length party, or was disposed of and reacquired.

History: S. 248(31) was added by S.C. 2013, c. 34, s. 358(30), applicable in respect of gifts and monetary contributions made after December 20, 2002.

▶ 248(32) ◀

(32) Amount of advantage. The amount of the advantage in respect of a gift or monetary contribution by a taxpayer is the total of

(*a*) the total of all amounts, other than an amount referred to in paragraph (*b*), each of which is the value, at the time the gift or monetary contribution is made, of any property, service, compensation, use or other benefit that the taxpayer, or a person or partnership who does not deal at arm's length with the taxpayer, has received, obtained or enjoyed, or is entitled, either immediately or in the future and either absolutely or contingently, to receive, obtain, or enjoy

(i) that is consideration for the gift or monetary contribution,

(ii) that is in gratitude for the gift or monetary contribution, or

(iii) that is in any other way related to the gift or monetary contribution, and

(*b*) the limited-recourse debt, determined under subsection 143.2(6.1), in respect of the gift or monetary contribution at the time the gift or monetary contribution is made.

Editorial Note: Any advantage received by a donor in respect of making a gift or contribution is deducted from the fair market value of the gift in determining the eligible amount for a tax benefit. The amount of any such advantage is essentially the total value of all property, services, compensation or other benefits to which the donor of a property (or a non-arm's length party) is entitled (this does not include the tax benefit of making the gift). An advantage need not be received at the time of gift or contribution, but instead may be part of a series of transactions. Paragraph 248(32)(*b*) includes as an advantage any limited-recourse debt in respect of the gift or contribution. For additional details regarding limited-recourse debt, see s. 143.2(6.1) and s. 248(34) of the Act.

History: S. 248(32) was added by S.C. 2013, c. 34, s. 358(30), applicable in respect of gifts and monetary contributions made after December 20, 2002, except that it is to be read without reference to

(*a*) its paragraph (*b*) in respect of gifts and monetary contributions made before February 19, 2003, and

(*b*) its subparagraph (*a*)(iii) in respect of gifts and monetary contributions made before 6:00 p.m. (Eastern Standard Time) on December 5, 2003.

▶ 248(33) ◀

(33) Cost of property acquired by donor. The cost to a taxpayer of a property, acquired by the taxpayer in circumstances where subsection (32) applies to include the value of the property in computing the amount of the advantage in respect of a gift or monetary contribution, is equal to the fair market value of the property at the time the gift or monetary contribution is made.

History: S. 248(33) was added by S.C. 2013, c. 34, s. 358(30), applicable in respect of gifts and monetary contributions made after December 20, 2002.

▶ 248(34) ◀

(34) Repayment of limited-recourse debt. If at any time in a taxation year a taxpayer has paid an amount (in this subsection referred to as the "repaid amount") on account of the principal amount of an indebtedness which was, before that time, an unpaid principal amount that was a limited-recourse debt referred to in subsection 143.2(6.1) (in this subsection referred to as the "former limited-recourse debt") in respect of a gift or monetary contribution (in this subsection referred to as the "original gift" or "original monetary contribution", respectively, as the case may be) of the taxpayer (otherwise than by way of an assignment or transfer of a guarantee, security or similar indemnity or covenant, or by way of a payment in respect of which any taxpayer referred to in subsection 143.2(6.1) has incurred an indebtedness that would be a limited-recourse debt referred to in that subsection if that indebtedness were in respect of a gift or monetary contribution made at the time that that indebtedness was incurred), the following rules apply:

(*a*) if the former limited-recourse debt is in respect of the original gift, for the purposes of sections 110.1 and 118.1, the taxpayer is deemed to have made in the taxation year a gift to a qualified donee, the eligible amount of which deemed gift is the amount, if any, by which

(i) the amount that would have been the eligible amount of the original gift, if the total of all such repaid amounts paid at or before that time were paid immediately before the original gift was made,

exceeds

(ii) the total of

(A) the eligible amount of the original gift, and

(B) the eligible amount of all other gifts deemed by this paragraph to have been made before that time in respect of the original gift; and

(*b*) if the former limited-recourse debt is in respect of the original monetary contribution, for the purposes of subsection 127(3), the taxpayer is deemed to have made in the taxation year a monetary contribution referred to in that subsection, the eligible amount of which is the amount, if any, by which

(i) the amount that would have been the eligible amount of the original monetary contribution, if the total of all such repaid amounts paid at or before that time were paid immediately before the original monetary contribution was made,

exceeds

(ii) the total of

(A) the eligible amount of the original monetary contribution, and

(B) the eligible amount of all other monetary contributions deemed by this paragraph to have been made before that time in respect of the original monetary contribution.

Editorial Note: A repayment of the principal amount of a limited-recourse debt in respect of a gift or monetary contribution is deemed to be a gift in the year it is paid. However, in some circumstances the total amount of limited-recourse debt and other advantages received by a donor may exceed the fair market value of the property donated, resulting in no eligible amount of a gift or contribution for the purposes of receiving a tax benefit (s. 248(31)). In this case, the donor must pay off the excess amount before any amount will be allowed as a gift. Also, a payment financed by other limited-recourse debt or made by way of assignment or transfer of a guarantee, security or similar indemnity or covenant is not recognized for these purposes.

History: S. 248(34) was added by S.C. 2013, c. 34, s. 358(30), applicable in respect of gifts and monetary contributions made after December 20, 2002, except that it does not apply in respect of gifts and monetary contributions made before February 19, 2003.

▶ 248(35) ◀

(35) Deemed fair market value. For the purposes of subsection (31), paragraph 69(1)(*b*) and subsections 110.1(2.1) and (3) and 118.1(5.4), (6) and (13.2), the fair market value of a property that is the subject of a gift made by a taxpayer to a qualified donee is deemed to be the lesser of the fair market value of the property otherwise determined and the cost or, in the case of capital property, the adjusted cost base or, in the case of a life insurance policy in respect of which the taxpayer is a policyholder, the adjusted cost basis (as defined in subsection 148(9)), of the property to the taxpayer immediately before the gift is made if

(*a*) the taxpayer acquired the property under a gifting arrangement that is a tax shelter as defined in subsection 237.1(1); or

(*b*) except where the gift is made as a consequence of the taxpayer's death,

(i) the taxpayer acquired the property less than three years before the day that the gift is made, or

(ii) the taxpayer acquired the property less than 10 years before the day that the gift is made and it is reasonable to conclude that, at the time the taxpayer acquired the property, one of the main reasons for the acquisition was to make a gift of the property to a qualified donee.

Editorial Note: For the purposes of determining the eligible amount of a gift for tax credit or deduction, s. 248(35) deems the fair market value of a gift to be the lesser of its actual fair market value and its cost where the gifted property was acquired as part of a gifting arrangement under a tax shelter (see s. 237.1) or (unless the gift was made as a consequence of the taxpayer's death) the property was acquired less than three years prior to its donation, or less than 10 years, if it is reasonable to conclude that one of the main reasons for its acquisition was to make a gift to a qualified donee. Where a non-arm's length party owned the property during the prior three-year or 10-year period, s. 248(36) deems the donor's cost to be the lesser of actual cost and former cost to the non-arm's length party. S. 248(37) provides for exceptions to the rule in s. 248(35) for certain types of gifted property. S. 248(38) and (39) set out anti-avoidance rules where gifted property is disposed of and reacquired or disposed of with proceeds being donated.

History: S. 248(35), the portion before paragraph (*a*) was replaced by S.C. 2013, c. 34, s. 358(31), deemed to have come into force on October 24, 2012, and formerly read:

(35) *Deemed fair market value.* For the purposes of subsection (31), paragraph 69(1)(*b*) and subsections 110.1(2.1) and (3) and 118.1(5.4) and (6), the fair market value of a property that is the subject of a gift made by a taxpayer to a qualified donee is deemed to be the lesser of the fair market value of the property otherwise determined and the cost or, in the case of capital property, the adjusted cost base or, in the case of a life insurance policy in respect of which the taxpayer is a policyholder, the adjusted cost basis (as defined in subsection 148(9)), of the property to the taxpayer immediately before the gift is made if

S. 248(35) was added by S.C. 2013, c. 34, s. 358(30), applicable in respect of gifts and monetary contributions made after December 20, 2002, except that it applies only in respect of gifts made on or after 6:00 p.m. (Eastern Standard Time) on December 5, 2003.

Related Sections: S. 87(2)(*m.2*) Gift of predecessor's property.

▶ 248(36) ◀

(36) Non-arm's length transaction. If a taxpayer acquired a property, otherwise than by reason of the death of an individual, that is the subject of a gift to which subsection (35) applies because of subparagraph (35)(*b*)(i) or (ii) and the property was, at any time within the 3-year or 10-year period, respectively, that ends when the gift was made, acquired by a person or partnership with whom the taxpayer does not deal at arm's length, for the purpose of applying subsection (35) to the taxpayer, the cost, or in the case of capital property, the adjusted cost base, of the property to the taxpayer immediately before the gift is made is deemed to be equal to the lowest amount that is the cost, or in the case of capital property, the adjusted cost base, to the taxpayer or any of those persons or partnerships immediately before the property was disposed of by that person or partnership.

Editorial Note: S. 248(35) deems the fair market value of a gift to be the lesser of actual fair market value and the cost of the property where a property was acquired less than three years prior to its donation or within 10 years if gifting was one of the purposes of the acquisition. If s. 248(35) applies because the donor acquired the property within the prior three-year or 10-year period and a non-arm's length person owned that property within that period, the cost of the gift to the donor will be the lower of the donor's cost and the lowest cost to any such non-arm's length person.

History: S. 248(36) was added by S.C. 2013, c. 34, s. 358(30), applicable in respect of gifts and monetary contributions made after December 20, 2002, except that it does not apply in respect of gifts or monetary contributions made before July 18, 2005.

Income Tax Folios: *Primary* — S7-F1-C1 Split-receipting and Deemed Fair Market Value.

Tax Window Files: CLHIA 2017 Q4 - Gift of a life insurance policy, *May 18, 2017*, CRA Document No. 2017-0692361C6.

► 248(37) ◄

(37) Non-application of subsection (35). Subsection (35) does not apply to a gift

(*a*) of inventory;

(*b*) of real property or an immovable situated in Canada;

(*c*) of an object referred to in subparagraph 39(1)(*a*)(i.1), other than an object acquired under a gifting arrangement (as defined in subsection 237.1(1)) that is a tax shelter;

(*d*) of property to which paragraph 38(*a.1*) or (*a.2*) applies;

(*e*) of a share of the capital stock of a corporation if

(i) the share was issued by the corporation to the donor,

(ii) immediately before the gift, the corporation was controlled by the donor, a person related to the donor or a group of persons each of whom is related to the donor, and

(iii) subsection (35) would not have applied in respect of the consideration for which the share was issued had that consideration been donated by the donor to the qualified donee when the share was so donated;

(*f*) by a corporation of property if

(i) the property was acquired by the corporation in circumstances to which subsection 85(1) or (2) applied,

(ii) immediately before the gift, the shareholder from whom the corporation acquired the property controlled the corporation or was related to a person or each member of a group of persons that controlled the corporation, and

(iii) subsection (35) would not have applied in respect of the property had the property not been transferred to the corporation and had the shareholder made the gift to the qualified donee when the corporation so made the gift; or

(*g*) of a property that was acquired in circumstances where subsection 70(6) or (9) or 73(1), (3) or (4) applied, unless subsection (36) would have applied if this subsection were read without reference to this paragraph.

Editorial Note: The anti-avoidance rule in s. 248(35) of the Act will not apply where the property that is the subject of a gift is an ecological gift, inventory, real property situated in Canada, publicly traded securities or certified cultural property (unless acquired under a tax shelter).

History: S. 248(37)(*c*) was replaced by S.C. 2014, c. 20, s. 30(2), applicable to gifts made after February 10, 2014, and formerly read:

(*c*) of an object referred to in subparagraph 39(1)(*a*)(i.1);

S. 248(37) was added by S.C. 2013, c. 34, s. 358(30), applicable in respect of gifts and monetary contributions made after December 20, 2002, except that it applies only in respect of gifts made on or after 6:00 p.m. (Eastern Standard Time) on December 5, 2003 but in respect of gifts made after that time but before March 18, 2007, paragraph 248(37)(*d*) is to be read as follows:

"(*d*) of property to which paragraph 38(*a.1*) or (*a.2*) would apply, if those paragraphs were read without reference to 'other than a private foundation';"

► 248(38) ◄

(38) Artificial transactions. The eligible amount of a particular gift of property by a taxpayer is nil if it can reasonably be concluded that the particular gift relates to a transaction or series of transactions

(*a*) one of the purposes of which is to avoid the application of subsection (35) to a gift of any property; or

(*b*) that would, if this Act were read without reference to this paragraph, result in a tax benefit to which subsection 245(2) applies.

Editorial Note: Subsection 248(38) is an anti-avoidance rule that prevents donors from artificially inflating the cost base of a gifted property by disposing of and reacquiring it before gifting it to a qualified donee. Where one of the purposes of a transaction or series of transactions is to defeat the "lower of fair market value and adjusted cost base" rule in s. 248(35) regarding the eligible amount of a gift, s. 248(35) deems the eligible amount of that gift to be nil. This provision also applies where transaction(s) would otherwise result in a s. 245(2) GAAR applicable tax benefit.

History: S. 248(38) was added by S.C. 2013, c. 34, s. 358(30), applicable in respect of gifts and monetary contributions made after December 20, 2002, except that it applies only in respect of gifts made on or after 6:00 p.m. (Eastern Standard Time) on December 5, 2003 but in respect of gifts made after that time but before July 18, 2005, it is to be read as follows:

"(38) If it can reasonably be concluded that one of the reasons for a series of transactions, that includes a disposition or acquisition of a property of a taxpayer that is the subject of a gift by the taxpayer, is to increase the amount that would be deemed by subsection (35) to be the fair market value of the property, the cost of the property for the purpose of that subsection is deemed to be the lowest cost to the taxpayer to acquire that property or an identical property at any time."

► 248(39) ◄

(39) Substantive gift. If a taxpayer disposes of a property (in this subsection referred to as the "substantive gift") that is a capital property of the taxpayer, to a recipient that is a registered party, a registered association or a candidate, as those terms are defined in the *Canada Elections Act*, or that is a qualified donee, subsection (35) would have applied in respect of the substantive gift if it had been the subject of a gift by the taxpayer to a qualified donee, and all or a part of the proceeds of disposition of the substantive gift are (or are substituted, directly or indirectly in any manner whatever, for) property that is the subject of a gift or monetary contribution by the taxpayer to the recipient or any person dealing not at arm's length with the recipient, the following rules apply:

(*a*) for the purpose of subsection (31), the fair market value of the property that is the subject of the gift or monetary contribution made by the taxpayer is deemed to be that proportion of the lesser of the fair market value of the substantive gift and the cost, or if the substantive gift is capital property of the taxpayer, the adjusted cost base, of the substantive gift to the taxpayer immediately before the disposition to the recipient, that the fair market value otherwise determined of the property that is the subject of the gift or monetary contribution is of the proceeds of disposition of the substantive gift; and (*b*) if the substantive gift is capital property of the taxpayer, for the purpose of the definitions "proceeds of disposition" of property in subsection 13(21) and section 54, the sale price of the substantive gift is to be reduced by the amount by which the fair market value of the property that is the subject of the gift (determined without reference to this section) exceeds the fair market value determined under paragraph (*a*).

(*c*) (Repealed by S.C. 2016, c. 12, s. 63(9).)

Editorial Note: S. 248(39) prevents donors from avoiding the application of s. 248(35) in determining fair market value of gifted property where a donor disposes of property to a qualified donee and then donates the proceeds of disposition, rather than donating the property itself.

History: S. 248(39), the portion before paragraph (*a*) was replaced by S.C. 2016, c. 12, s. 63(8), in force January 1, 2017, and formerly read:

(39) *Substantive gift.* If a taxpayer disposes of a property (in this subsection referred to as the "substantive gift") that is a capital property or an eligible capital property of the taxpayer, to a recipient that is a registered party, a registered association or a candidate, as those terms are defined in the *Canada Elections Act*, or that is a qualified donee, subsection (35) would have applied in respect of the substantive gift if it had been the subject of a gift by the taxpayer to a qualified donee, and all or a part of the proceeds of disposition of the substantive gift are (or are substituted, directly or indirectly in any manner whatever, for) property that is the subject of a gift or monetary contribution by the taxpayer to the recipient or any person dealing not at arm's length with the recipient, the following rules apply:

S. 248(39)(*c*) was repealed by S.C. 2016, c. 12, s. 63(9), in force January 1, 2017, and formerly read:

(*c*) if the substantive gift is eligible capital property of the taxpayer, the amount determined under paragraph (*a*) in the description of E in the definition "cumulative eligible capital" in subsection 14(5) in respect of the substantive gift is to be reduced by the amount by which the fair market value of the property that is the subject of the gift (determined without reference to this section) exceeds the fair market value determined under paragraph (*a*).

S. 248(39) was added by S.C. 2013, c. 34, s. 358(30), applicable in respect of gifts and monetary contributions made after December 20, 2002, except that it does not apply in respect of gifts or monetary contributions made before February 27, 2004.

► 248(40) ◄

(40) Inter-charity gifts. Subsection (30) does not apply in respect of a gift received by a qualified donee from a registered charity.

Editorial Note: Subsection 248(30) does not apply to transfers made by a registered charity to a qualified donee.

History: S. 248(40) was added by S.C. 2013, c. 34, s. 358(30), applicable in respect of gifts and monetary contributions made after December 20, 2002, except that it does not apply in respect of gifts made before November 9, 2006.

► 248(41) ◄

(41) Information not provided. Notwithstanding subsection (31), the eligible amount of a gift or monetary contribution made by a taxpayer is nil if the taxpayer does not — before a receipt referred to in subsection 110.1(2), 118.1(2) or 127(3), as the case may be, is issued in respect of the gift or monetary contribution — inform the qualified donee or the recipient, as the case may be, of any circumstances in respect of which subsection (31), (35), (36), (38) or (39) requires that the eligible amount of the gift or monetary contribution be less than the fair market value, determined without reference to subsections (35), 110.1(3) and 118.1(6), of the property that is the subject of the gift or monetary contribution.

Editorial Note: Unless the information required to issue a proper charitable receipt to a donor is provided to the donee, the eligible amount of a gift will be zero.

History: S. 248(41) was added by S.C. 2013, c. 34, s. 358(30), applicable in respect of gifts and monetary contributions made after December 20, 2002, except that it does not apply in respect of gifts and monetary contributions made before 2006.

► 248(42) ◄

(42) Synthetic equity arrangements – disaggregation. For the purposes of the definition *synthetic equity arrangement* in subsection (1), paragraphs (*c*) and (*d*) of the definition *dividend rental arrangement* in subsection (1) and subsections 112(2.31), (2.32) and (10), an arrangement that reflects the fair market value of more than one type of *identical share* (as defined in subsection 112(10)) is considered to be a separate arrangement with respect to each type of identical share the value of which the arrangement reflects.

History: S. 248(42) was added by S.C. 2016, c. 7, s. 48(3), deemed to have come into force on April 22, 2015.

SECTION 249: Definition of "taxation year"

► 249(1) ◄

(1) Definition of "taxation year". In this Act, except as expressly otherwise provided, a "taxation year" is

(*a*) in the case of a corporation or Canadian resident partnership, a fiscal period;

(*b*) in the case of a graduated rate estate, the period for which the accounts of the estate are made up for purposes of assessment under this Act; and

(*c*) in any other case, a calendar year.

Editorial Note: In the case of an individual other than a testamentary trust, the taxation year is the calendar year. Similarly, an individual carrying on a business must normally have a calendar year fiscal period (see s. 249.1(1)(*b*)). However, if the individual chooses to use the "alternative method" of computing business income, he or she may choose a fiscal period for his or her business other than the calendar year. However, an individual using the alternative method must make the additional computations under s. 34.1 to account for income occurring in the period between the end of the fiscal period and the taxation year, if any.

In the case of a corporation, the taxation year is the corporation's fiscal period. The corporation's fiscal period may not exceed a period of 53 weeks. However, if the taxation year (and fiscal period) exceeds 365 days and overlaps two calendar year ends, there will be a deemed year end at the end of the second calendar year; see s. 249(3).

The taxation year of a testamentary trust including an estate is defined as its fiscal period. Effective for 2016, all testamentary trusts that are not "graduated rate estates" or "qualified disability trusts" will be required to have taxation years that coincide with the calendar year.

History: S. 249(1)(*b*) and (*c*) were replaced by S.C. 2014, c. 39, s. 72(1), applicable to the 2016 and subsequent taxation years, and formerly read:

(*b*) in the case of an individual (other than a testamentary trust), a calendar year; and

(*c*) in the case of a testamentary trust, the period for which the accounts of the trust are made up for purposes of assessment under this Act.

S. 249(1) was replaced by S.C. 2013, c. 34, s. 359(1), deemed to have come into force on December 21, 2002, except that paragraph 249(1)(*a*) is to be read before October 31, 2006 without reference to "or Canadian resident partnership". S. 249(1) formerly read:

(1) *Definition of "taxation year".* For the purpose of this Act, a "taxation year" is

in the case of a corporation or Canadian resident partnership, a fiscal period, and

(*b*) in the case of an individual, a calendar year,

and when a taxation year is referred to by reference to a calendar year, the reference is to the taxation year or years coinciding with, or ending in, that year.

Related Sections: 70(1) Death of a taxpayer; 104(23) Deceased beneficiary of graduated rate estate; 128(2)(d); 128(2)(d.1); 128(2)(d.2); s. 248(1), definition of "Canadian resident partnership".

Interpretation Bulletins: *Secondary* — IT-184R Deferred cash purchase tickets issued for grain.

► 249(1.1) ◄

(1.1) References to calendar year. When a taxation year is referred to by reference to a calendar year, the reference is to the taxation year or taxation years that coincide with, or that end in, that calendar year.

History: S. 249(1.1) was added by S.C. 2013, c. 34, s. 359(1), deemed to have come into force on December 21, 2002.

► 249(2) ◄

(2) References to certain taxation years and fiscal periods. For the purposes of this Act,

(*a*) a reference to a taxation year ending in another year includes a reference to a taxation year ending coincidentally with that other year; and

(*b*) a reference to a fiscal period ending in a taxation year includes a reference to a fiscal period ending coincidentally with that year.

► 249(3) ◄

(3) Fiscal period exceeding 365 days. If a fiscal period of a corporation exceeds 365 days and for that reason the corporation does not have a taxation year that ends in a particular calendar year, for the purposes of this Act,

(*a*) the corporation's first taxation year that would otherwise end in the immediately following calendar year is deemed to end on the last day of the particular calendar year and its next taxation year is deemed to commence on the first day of the immediately following calendar year; and

(*b*) the corporation's first fiscal period that would otherwise end in the immediately following calendar year is deemed to end on the last day of the particular calendar year and its next fiscal period is deemed to commence on the first day of the immediately following calendar year.

History: S. 249(3) was replaced by S.C. 2013, c. 34, s. 359(2), applicable to the 2012 and subsequent taxation years, and formerly read:

(3) *Deemed year end where fiscal period exceeds 365 days.* Notwithstanding subsection (1), where the fiscal period of a corporation exceeds 365 days and by reason thereof the corporation does not have a taxation year that ends in a particular calendar year, for the purposes of this Act, the corporation's first taxation year ending in the immediately following calendar year shall be deemed to end on the last day of the particular calendar year.

Related Sections: S. 248(1), definition of "corporation", "individual"; s. 249.1(1) definition of "fiscal period".

► 249(3.1) ◄

(3.1) Year end on status change. If at any time a corporation becomes or ceases to be a Canadian-controlled private corporation, otherwise than because of an acquisition of control to which subsection (4) would, if this Act were read without reference to this subsection, apply,

(*a*) subject to paragraph (*c*), the corporation's taxation year that would, if this Act were read without reference to this subsection, include that time is deemed to end immediately before that time;

(*b*) a new taxation year of the corporation is deemed to begin at that time;

(*c*) notwithstanding subsections (1) and (3), the corporation's taxation year that would, if this Act were read without reference to this subsection, have been its last taxation year that ended before that time is deemed instead to end immediately before that time if

(i) were this Act read without reference to this paragraph, that taxation year would, otherwise than because of paragraph 128(1)(*d*), section 128.1 and paragraphs 142.6(1)(*a*) or 149(10)(*a*), have ended within the 7-day period that ended immediately before that time,

(ii) within that 7-day period no person or group of persons acquired control of the corporation, and the corporation did not become or cease to be a Canadian-controlled private corporation, and

(iii) the corporation elects, in its return of income under Part I for that taxation year to have this paragraph apply; and

(*d*) for the purpose of determining the corporation's fiscal period after that time, the corporation is deemed not to have established a fiscal period before that time.

Editorial Note: This provision deems a year-end immediately before a change of status to/from a CCPC (s. 249(3.1)(*a*)). A new taxation year of the corporation is deemed to have commenced at the time such change of status occurs (s. 249(3.1)(*b*)); starting with that new taxation year, the corporation may adopt a new fiscal period (s. 249(3.1)(*d*)). Generally, by virtue of s. 249(3.1)(*c*), where the corporation had a taxation year that ended within seven days before the change of status, the corporation may elect in its tax return for that year to extend that year so that it ends immediately before the change of status. By such an election, the corporation can avoid having an additional taxation year in the period before the change of status. (Although an election in letter form may be prudent, arguably, the election may be made by reporting its results on the relevant income tax return — see *Dhaliwal*, (2012 DTC 1122 (TCC).) This election will not apply if the last taxation year ended within the seven-day period because of bankruptcy, emigration, becoming or ceasing to be a financial institution or exempt from tax, or by virtue of a previous acquisition of control or change of status. Situations triggering subsection 249(3.1) include where there is an agreement to acquire control of the corporation by a public company and/or a non-resident (see s. 251(5)(*b*)), the corporation becomes public, or the controlling shareholder becomes non-resident. This provision permits the small business deduction and RDTOH build-up for the stub taxation year preceding the change of status, since CCPC status would be maintained throughout that year. Opening GRIP/LRIP accounts (re: eligible dividends) are calculated (using a "tax balance sheet" approach) immediately before the end of the stub taxation year (see ss. 89(4) and (8)). S. 249(3.1) does not apply where s. 249(4) applies (providing a separate deemed year-end on an acquisition of *de jure* control) — but it can apply in addition to s. 249(4), nor does it apply to "change of status" elections/revocations re: s. 89(11) or 89(12) (provided that the s. 89(11) election is not late filed — see CRA Document No. 2010-0377251E5). See also the editorial note under s. 249(4).

Related Sections: S. 89(11) Election: non-CCPC; s. 125(5) Special rules for business limit; s. 125(7), "Canadian-controlled private corporation"; s. 249(4) Loss restriction event – year end; s. 251(5)(*b*) Control by related groups, options, etc.

Tax Profile: November 2009 — Purchase and Sale of a Canadian Business.

► 249(4) ◄

(4) Loss restriction event — year end. If at any time a taxpayer is subject to a loss restriction event (other than a foreign affiliate, of a taxpayer resident in Canada, that did not carry on a business in Canada at any time in its last taxation year that began before that time), then for the purposes of this Act,

(*a*) subject to paragraph (*b*), the taxpayer's taxation year that would, but for this paragraph, have included that time is deemed to end immediately before that time, a new taxation year of the taxpayer is deemed to begin at that time and, for the purpose of determining the taxpayer's fiscal period after that time, the taxpayer is deemed not to have established a fiscal period before that time; and

(*b*) subject to paragraph 128(1)(*d*), section 128.1 and paragraphs 142.6(1)(*a*) and 149(10)(*a*), and notwithstanding subsections (1) and (3), if the taxpayer is a corporation and the taxpayer's taxation year that would, but for this subsection, have been its last taxation year that ended before that time, would, but for this paragraph, have ended within the seven-day period that ended immediately before that time, that taxation year is, except if the taxpayer is subject to a loss restriction event within that period, deemed to end immediately before that time, provided that the taxpayer so elects in its return of income under Part I for that taxation year.

Editorial Note: This provision gives rise to a deemed year-end immediately before the time when a taxpayer entity (other than a described foreign affiliate) is subject to a "loss restriction event". Subsection 249(4) previously referred to the impacts when control of a taxpayer corporation was acquired by a person or group of persons; the subsection was broadened in applicability (primarily to also encapsulate trusts) for loss restriction events that occur on or after March 21, 2013. A new taxation year of the taxpayer entity is deemed to have commenced immediately before the loss restriction event occurred; starting with that new taxation year, the taxpayer entity may adopt a new fiscal period. Generally, where the taxpayer entity had a taxation year that ended within seven days before the loss restriction event, the taxpayer entity, unless it is a trust, may elect in its tax return for that year to extend that year so that it ends immediately before the loss restriction event. By such an election, the taxpayer entity can avoid having an additional taxation year in the period before the loss restriction event; this election will not apply if (another) loss restriction event also occurred within that seven day period. (Although an election in letter form may be prudent, arguably, the election may be made by reporting its results on the relevant income tax return — see *Dhaliwal*, 2012 DTC 1122 (TCC).) In Document No. 2011-0416871E5, the CRA confirmed that, with a s. 249(4) election, it is possible to have a taxation year in excess of 53 weeks.

The application of s. 249(4) will give rise to the consequences which normally follow taxation year end, such as the filing of the corporate tax return and the payment of taxes due, as well as the acceleration of various limitation periods, such as the repayment of shareholder loans. See also Document No. 2008-0285461C6 for the failure of a corporate return to recognize a s. 249(4) year end; among other things, filing based on a non-existent year end means the non-application of assessment limitation period. The deemed year end per s. 249(4) does not apply to a foreign affiliate that did not carry on a business in Canada at any time in its last taxation year beginning before the acquisition of control.

If a s. 249(4) election could be made, consideration should be given to CCPC status — see Document No. 2010-0388101E5 (in which s. 249(3.1) triggered a year end, with a s. 249(4) extension thereof being considered). Another alternative may be the filing of a s. 89(11) election (see also the editorial note for s. 89(11)). See also Document No. 2011-0424446E5 on the juxtaposition of s. 249(3.1) and (4) in a "sign and close" transaction (see also "Interaction of Subsections 249(3.1) and (4) on a Sale of a CCPC", Friedlan, *Tax for the Owner-Manager*, April 2012 and "Corporate Reorganizations — An Update on Recent Issues", Gamble and Christian, 2011 British Columbia Tax Conference p.6:1-16).

History: S. 249(4)(*b*) was replaced by S.C. 2016, c. 12, s. 64(1), deemed to have come into force on March 21, 2013, and formerly read:

(*b*) subject to paragraph 128(1)(*d*), section 128.1 and paragraphs 142.6(1)(*a*) and 149(10)(*a*), and notwithstanding subsections (1) and (3), if the taxpayer's taxation year that would, but for this subsection, have been its last taxation year that ended before that time, would, but for this paragraph, have ended within the seven-day period that ended immediately before that time, that taxation year is, except if the taxpayer is subject to a loss restriction event within that period, deemed to end immediately before that time, provided that the taxpayer so elects in its return of income under Part I for that taxation year.

S. 249(4) was replaced by S.C. 2013, c. 40, s. 90(1), deemed to have come into force on March 21, 2013, and formerly read:

(4) *Year end on change of control.* Where at any time control of a corporation (other than a corporation that is a foreign affiliate of a taxpayer resident in Canada and that did not carry on a business in Canada at any time in its last taxation year beginning before that time) is acquired by a person or group of persons, for the purposes of this Act,

(*a*) subject to paragraph (*c*), the taxation year of the corporation that would, but for this paragraph, have included that time shall be deemed to have ended immediately before that time;

(*b*) a new taxation year of the corporation shall be deemed to have commenced at that time;

(*c*) subject to paragraph 128(1)(*d*), section 128.1, and paragraphs 142.6(1)(*a*) and 149(10)(*a*), and notwithstanding subsections (1) and (3), where the taxation year of the corporation that would, but for this subsection, have been its last taxation year that ended before that time would, but for this paragraph, have ended within the 7-day period that ended immediately before that time, that taxation year shall, except where control of the corporation was acquired by a person or group of persons within that period, be deemed to end immediately before that time where the corporation so elects in its return of income under Part I for that taxation year; and

(*d*) for the purpose of determining the corporation's fiscal period after that time, the corporation shall be deemed not to have established a fiscal period before that time.

Related Sections: 251.2(7) Filing and other deadlines; 111(4) Loss restriction event — capital losses; 111(5) Loss restriction event — non-capital losses and farm losses; 125(5) Special rules for business limit; 127(9.1) Loss restriction event before end of year; 127(9.2) Loss restriction event after end of year; 249(3.1) Year end on status change; 250(5.1) Continued corporation; 251.2(2) Loss restriction event; 256(7) Acquiring control; 256.1 [Corporate tax-attribute trading].

Canadian Tax Foundation: Jung and McIntyre, *Current Issues: Change of Trustee and Control*, 2013 Ontario Tax Conference 1:28–30; Bodie and Novotny, *Acquisitions of Control Under the Income Tax Act — Recent Developments*, 2013 Prairie Provinces Tax Conference 6:1–27.

Tax Profile: August 2012 — U.S. Purchases and Sales of Canadian Businesses: Tax and Corporate Issues; November 2009 — Purchase and Sale of a Canadian Business.

Tax Window Files: Clarification STEP Roundtable Q3 — Deemed Year End, *February 17, 2011*, CRA Document No. 2010-0388081E5; STEP Roundtable Q3, *June 8, 2010*, CRA Document No. 2010-0363081C6; Deemed Year Ends, *October 5, 2007*, CRA Document No. 2007-0243341C6.

► 249(4.1) ◄

(4.1) Trust transition from graduated rate estate. For a particular trust that is a testamentary trust,

(*a*) its taxation year that otherwise includes a particular time is deemed to end immediately before the particular time if

(i) the particular trust is an estate and the particular time is the first time after 2015 at which the estate is not a graduated rate estate, or

(ii) the particular trust is not an estate and the particular time is immediately after 2015; and

(*b*) if the particular trust exists at the particular time,

(i) a new taxation year of the particular trust is deemed to begin at the particular time, and

(ii) for the purpose of determining the particular trust's fiscal period after the particular time, the particular trust is deemed not to have established a fiscal period before that time.

History: S. 249(4.1) was added by S.C. 2014, c. 39, s. 72(2), in force December 31, 2015.

Tax Window Files: 2015 STEP Q1- Tax Year of Graduated Rate Estate, *June 18, 2015*, CRA Document No. 2015-0572131C6.

► 249(5) ◄

(5) Graduated rate estate. The period for which the accounts of a graduated rate estate are made up for the purposes of an assessment under this Act may not exceed 12 months, and no change in the time when that period ends may be made for the purposes of this Act without the concurrence of the Minister.

History: S. 249(5) was replaced by S.C. 2014, c. 39, s. 72(3), applicable to the 2016 and subsequent taxation years, and formerly read:

(5) *Testamentary trusts.* The period for which the accounts of a testamentary trust are made up for the purposes of an assessment under this Act may not exceed 12 months, and no change in the time when such a period ends may be made for the purposes of this Act without the concurrence of the Minister.

Related Sections: 248(1) graduated rate estate.

► 249(6) ◄

(6) Loss of testamentary trust status — (Repealed by S.C. 2014, c. 39, s. 72(4).)

History: S. 249(6) was repealed by S.C. 2014, c. 39, s. 72(4), applicable to transactions and events that occur after 2015, and formerly read:

(6) *Loss of testamentary trust status.* If at a particular time after December 20, 2002 a transaction or event, described in any of paragraphs (*b*) to (*d*) of the definition "testamentary trust" in subsection 108(1), occurs and as a result of that occurrence a trust or estate is not a testamentary trust, the following rules apply:

(*a*) the fiscal period for a business or property of the trust or estate that would, if this Act were read without reference to this subsection and those paragraphs, have included the particular time is deemed to have ended immediately before the particular time;

(*b*) the taxation year of the trust or estate that would, if this Act were read without reference to this subsection and those paragraphs, have included the particular time is deemed to have ended immediately before the particular time;

(*c*) a new taxation year of the trust or estate is deemed to have started at the particular time; and

(*d*) in determining the fiscal period for a business or property of the trust or estate after the particular time, the trust or estate is deemed not to have established a fiscal period before that time.

S. 249(6) was added by S.C. 2013, c. 34, s. 359(3), deemed to have come into force on July 19, 2005 and, if a trust or estate so elects in writing by filing the election with the Minister of National Revenue on or before its filing-due date for its taxation year that includes June 26, 2013, it also applies to that trust or estate, as the case may be, after December 20, 2002.

In addition, the following application applies a trust or estate (referred to in this application as the "trust") for a particular taxation year of the trust that ends in the period that begins on December 21, 2002 and ends on October 24, 2012 (in this application referred to as the "relevant period"), if

(*a*) the particular taxation year would have — if paragraph (*d*) of the definition "testamentary trust", as contained in section 100 of Bill C-10 of the second session of the 39th Parliament as passed by the House of Commons on October 29, 2007 [reproduced below], had applied to the particular taxation year — been deemed by paragraph 249(6)(*b*), to have ended on a day (referred to in this application as the "deemed year-end day") in the relevant period; and

(*b*) the trust filed, before October 24, 2012, a return of income for the particular taxation year.

If the above conditions apply to a trust for a particular taxation year, for purposes of the Act

(*a*) the particular taxation year is deemed to have ended on the deemed year-end day and not at any other time;

(*b*) the trust is deemed to be an *inter vivos* trust for the purpose of determining each of the trust's taxation years that ends

(i) after the particular taxation year and in the relevant period, and

(ii) unless the trust elects under paragraph (*c*), after October 24, 2012; and

(*c*) if the trust so elects — by filing an election in writing with the Minister of National Revenue on or before its filing-due date for its taxation year which includes June 26, 2013 — for each of the trust's taxation years that ends after October 24, 2012 the period for which the accounts of the trust are made up for purposes of assessment under the Act is deemed to be the period for which the accounts of the trust were made up for purposes of the Act for the trust's last taxation year that ended before the particular taxation year.

Paragraph (*d*) of the definition "testamentary trust", as contained in section 100 of Bill C-10 of the second session of the 39th Parliament as passed by the House of Commons on October 29, 2007, and referred to above, read as follows:

(*d*) a trust that, at any time after December 20, 2002 and before the end of the taxation year, incurs a debt or any other obligation owed to, or guaranteed by, a beneficiary or any other person or partnership (which beneficiary, person or partnership is referred to in this paragraph as the "specified party") with whom any beneficiary of the trust does not deal at arm's length, other than a debt or other obligation

(i) incurred by the trust in satisfaction of the specified party's right as a beneficiary under the trust

(A) to enforce payment of an amount of the trust's income or capital gains payable at or before that time by the trust to the specified party, or

(B) to otherwise receive any part of the capital of the trust,

(ii) owed to the specified party, if the debt or other obligation arose because of a service (for greater certainty, not including any transfer or loan of property) rendered by the specified party to, for or on behalf of the trust, or

(iii) owed to the specified party, if

(A) the debt or other obligation arose because of a payment made by the specified party for or on behalf of the trust,

(B) in exchange for the payment, the trust transfers property, the fair market value of which is not less than the principal amount of that debt or other obligation, to the specified party within 12 months after the payment was made (or, where written application has been made to the Minister by the trust within that 12 months, within any longer period that the Minister considers reasonable in the circumstances), and

(C) it is reasonable to conclude that the specified party would have been willing to make the payment if the specified party dealt at arm's length with the trust, except where the trust is the individual's estate and that payment was made within the first 12 months after the individual's death (or, where written application has been made to the Minister by the estate within that 12 months, within any longer period that the Minister considers reasonable in the circumstances);

SECTION 249.1: Definition of "fiscal period"

► 249.1(1) ◄

(1) Definition of "fiscal period". For the purposes of this Act, a "fiscal period" of a business or a property of a person or partnership means the period for which the person's or partnership's accounts in respect of the business or property are made up for purposes of assessment under this Act, but no fiscal period may end

(*a*) in the case of a corporation, more than 53 weeks after the period began,

(*b*) in the case of

(i) an individual (other than an individual to whom section 149 or 149.1 applies or a trust),

(i.1) a trust (other than a mutual fund trust if the fiscal period is one to which paragraph 132.11(1)(*c*) applies or a graduated rate estate),

(ii) a partnership of which

(A) an individual (other than an individual to whom section 149 or 149.1 applies or a graduated rate estate),

(B) a professional corporation, or

(C) a partnership to which this subparagraph applies,

would, if the fiscal period ended at the end of the calendar year in which the period began, be a member of the partnership in the period, or

(iii) a professional corporation that would, if the fiscal period ended at the end of the calendar year in which the period began, be in the period a member of a partnership to which subparagraph (ii) applies,

after the end of the calendar year in which the period began unless, in the case of a business, the business is not carried on in Canada,

(*c*) in the case of a partnership (other than a partnership to which subparagraph (*b*)(ii) or subsection (9) applies) that is a member of a partnership or has a member that is a partnership, after the end of the calendar year in which it began, if at the end of the calendar year

(i) a corporation has a significant interest, as defined in section 34.2, in the partnership,

(ii) the partnership is a member of another partnership in which a corporation has a significant interest as defined in section 34.2,

(iii) a membership interest in the partnership is held directly, or indirectly through one or more partnerships, by a partnership described in subparagraph (i) or (ii), or

(iv) the partnership holds directly, or indirectly through one or more partnerships, a membership interest in a partnership described in any of subparagraphs (i) to (iii), or

(*d*) in any other case, more than 12 months after the period began,

and, for the purpose of this subsection, the activities of a person to whom section 149 or 149.1 applies are deemed to be a business.

Editorial Note: Beginning in 2016, testamentary trusts other than graduated rate estates must have a taxation year and fiscal period that ends on December 31.

History: S. 249.1(1)(*b*), the portion before clause (ii)(B) was replaced by S.C. 2014, c. 39, s. 73(1), applicable to the 2016 and subsequent taxation years, and formerly read:

(*b*) in the case of

(i) an individual (other than an individual to whom section 149 or 149.1 applies or a testamentary trust),

(i.1) a fiscal period of an *inter vivos* trust (other than a fiscal period to which paragraph 132.11(1)(*c*) applies),

(ii) a partnership of which

(A) an individual (other than a testamentary trust or an individual to whom section 149 or 149.1 applies),

S. 249.1(1)(*b*), the portion after subparagraph (iii) was replaced by S.C. 2013, c. 34, s. 360(1), applicable to fiscal periods that begin after June 26, 2013, and formerly read:

after the end of the calendar year in which the period began unless, in the case of a business, the business is not carried on in Canada, is a prescribed business or is carried on by a prescribed person or partnership,

S. 249.1(1)(*c*) was replaced, and paragraph (*d*) was added by S.C. 2011, c. 24, s. 73(1), applicable to fiscal periods that end in or after 2011. S. 249.1(1)(*c*) formerly read:

(*c*) in any other case, more than 12 months after the period began,

Related Sections: 248(1) graduated rate estate; S. 10(1) Valuation of inventory; s. 11(2) Reference to "taxation year"; s. 13(3) "Taxation year", "year" and "income" of individual; s. 34.1 Additional business income; s. 99(4), "professional corporation"; s. 125(5) Special rules for business limit; s. 128.1(1)(*a*) Year-end, fiscal period; s. 128.1(4)(*a*) Year-end, fiscal period; s. 132.11(1) Taxation year of mutual fund trust; s. 248(1) "graduated rate estate"; s. 249(3) Deemed year end where fiscal period exceeds 365 days.

Tax Profile: April 2011 — Proposed Changes to Canada's Tax Laws — The Canadian Government Reacts To Close Perceived Abuses.

Tax Topics: No. 2039, Eliminating the Corporate Tax Deferral Using Partnerships — Resolution 41 of the 2011 Federal Budget; No. 1889, Taxation Year of a Foreign Affiliate.

Tax Window Files: Multi-tier alignment election and new partnership, *April 3, 2013*, CRA Document No. 2012-0470921E5.

► 249.1(2) ◄

(2) Not a member of a partnership. For the purpose of subparagraph (1)(*b*)(ii) and subsection (4), a person or partnership that would not have a share of any income or loss of a partnership for a fiscal period of the partnership, if the period ended at the end of the calendar year in which the period began, is deemed not to be a member of the partnership in that fiscal period.

► 249.1(3) ◄

(3) Subsequent fiscal periods. Where a fiscal period of a business or a property of a person or partnership ends at any time, the subsequent fiscal period, if any, of the business or property of the person or partnership is deemed to begin immediately after that time.

► 249.1(4) ◄

(4) Alternative method. Paragraph (1)(*b*) does not apply to a fiscal period of a business carried on, throughout the period of time that began at the beginning of the fiscal period and ended at the end of the calendar year in which the fiscal period began,

(*a*) by an individual (otherwise than as a member of a partnership), or

(*b*) by an individual as a member of a partnership, where throughout that period

(i) each member of the partnership is an individual, and

(ii) the partnership is not a member of another partnership,

where

(*c*) in the case of an individual

(i) who is referred to in paragraph (*a*), or

(ii) who is a member of a partnership no member of which is a graduated rate estate,

an election in prescribed form to have paragraph (1)(*b*) not apply is filed with the Minister by the individual on or before the individual's filing-due date, and with the individual's return of income under Part I, for the taxation year that includes the first day of the first fiscal period of the business that begins after 1994, and

(*d*) in the case of an individual who is a member of a partnership a member of which is a graduated rate estate, an election in prescribed form to have paragraph (1)(*b*) not apply is filed with the Minister by the individual on or before the earliest of the filing-due dates of the members of the partnership for a taxation year that includes the first day of the first fiscal period of the business that begins after 1994.

History: S. 249.1(4)(*c*)(ii) was replaced by S.C. 2014, c. 39, s. 73(2), applicable to the 2016 and subsequent taxation years, and formerly read:

(ii) who is a member of a partnership no member of which is a testamentary trust,

S. 249.1(4)(*d*) was replaced by S.C. 2014, c. 39, s. 73(3), applicable to the 2016 and subsequent taxation years, and formerly read:

(*d*) in the case of an individual who is a member of a partnership a member of which is a testamentary trust, an election in prescribed form to have paragraph (1)(*b*) not apply is filed with the Minister by the individual on or before the earliest of the filing-due dates of the members of the partnership for a taxation year that includes the first day of the first fiscal period of the business that begins after 1994.

Related Sections: S. 96(3) Agreement or election of partnership members; s. 99(2) Fiscal period of terminated partnership for individual member.

Forms: T1139 — Reconciliation of Business Income for Tax Purposes.

► 249.1(5) ◄

(5) Alternative method not applicable to tax shelter investments. Subsection (4) does not apply to a particular fiscal period of a business where, in a preceding fiscal period or throughout the period of time that began at the beginning of the particular period and ended at the end of the calendar year in which the particular period began, the expenditures made in the course of carrying on the business were primarily the cost or capital cost of tax shelter investments (as defined in subsection 143.2(1)).

► 249.1(6) ◄

(6) Revocation of election. Subsection (4) does not apply to fiscal periods of a business carried on by an individual that begin after the beginning of a particular taxation year of the individual where (*a*) an election in prescribed form to revoke an election filed under subsection (4) in respect of the business is filed with the Minister, and

(*b*) the election to revoke is filed

(i) in the case of an individual

(A) who is not a member of a partnership, or

(B) who is a member of a partnership no member of which is a graduated rate estate,

by the individual on or before the individual's filing-due date, and with the individual's return of income under Part I, for the particular taxation year, and

(ii) in the case of an individual who is a member of a partnership a member of which is a graduated rate estate, by the individual on or before the earliest of the filing-due dates of the members of the partnership for a taxation year that includes the first day of the first fiscal period of the business that begins after the beginning of the particular year.

History: S. 249.1(6)(*b*)(i)(B) was replaced by S.C. 2014, c. 39, s. 73(4), applicable to the 2016 and subsequent taxation years, and formerly read:

(B) who is a member of a partnership no member of which is a testamentary trust,

S. 249.1(6)(*b*)(ii) was replaced by S.C. 2014, c. 39, s. 73(5), applicable to the 2016 and subsequent taxation years, and formerly read:

(ii) in case of an individual who is a member of a partnership a member of which is a testamentary trust, by the individual on or before the earliest of the filing-due dates of the members of the partnership for a taxation year that includes the first day of the first fiscal period of the business that begins after the beginning of the particular year.

Related Sections: S. 96(3) Agreement or election of partnership members.

► 249.1(7) ◄

(7) Change of fiscal period. No change in the time when a fiscal period ends may be made for the purposes of this Act without the concurrence of the Minister.

► 249.1(8) ◄

(8) Single-tier fiscal period alignment. The members of a partnership that has a fiscal period that begins before March 22, 2011 and that would, if this Act were read without reference to this subsection and subsection (10), end on a day after March 22, 2011, may elect to end that fiscal period on a particular day that is before the day on which the fiscal period would otherwise end (in this subsection and subsection (10) referred to as a "single-tier alignment election") if

(*a*) each member of the partnership is, on the particular day, a corporation that is not a professional corporation;

(*b*) the partnership is not, on the particular day, a member of another partnership;

(*c*) at least one member of the partnership is, on the particular day, a corporation that has a significant interest, as defined in section 34.2, in the partnership;

(*d*) at least one member of the partnership referred to in paragraph (*c*) has a taxation year that ends on a day that differs from the day on which the fiscal period of the partnership would end if this Act were read without reference to this subsection and subsection (10);

(*e*) the particular day is after March 22, 2011 and no later than the latest day that is the last day of the first taxation year that ends after March 22, 2011 of any corporation that has been a member of the partnership continuously since March 21, 2011; and

(*f*) subsection (10) applies to the single-tier alignment election.

History: S. 249.1(8) was added by S.C. 2011, c. 24, s. 73(2), applicable to fiscal periods that end in or after 2011.

Related Sections: S. 34.2(1), "single-tier alignment".

Canadian Tax Foundation: Oldewening and Carr, *Limitation on Deferral of Partnership Income by a Corporation*, 2012 Canadian Tax Journal 1:219–256.

► 249.1(9) ◄

(9) Multi-tier fiscal period alignment — one-time election. The members of a partnership to which paragraph (1)(*c*) would apply if it were read without reference to this subsection may elect (in this subsection and subsections (10) and (11) referred to as a "multi-tier alignment election") to end a fiscal period of the partnership on a particular day if

(*a*) as a consequence of the multi-tier alignment election, the fiscal period of the partnership, and of each other partnership described in relation to the partnership by any of subparagraphs (1)(*c*)(ii) to (iv), ends on the particular day;

(*b*) the particular day is before March 22, 2012; and

(*c*) subsection (10) applies to the multi-tier alignment election.

History: S. 249.1(9) was added by S.C. 2011, c. 24, s. 73(2), applicable to fiscal periods that end in or after 2011.

Related Sections: S. 34.2(1), "single-tier alignment".

Canadian Tax Foundation: Oldewening and Carr, *Limitation on Deferral of Partnership Income by a Corporation*, 2012 Canadian Tax Journal 1:219–256.

► 249.1(9.1) ◄

(9.1) When subsection (9) ceases to apply. If paragraph (1)(*c*) did not apply to end the fiscal period of a partnership on December 31 of a calendar year (in this subsection referred to as the "preceding year") because subsection (9) applies to the partnership, and to each other partnership described in relation to the partnership by any of subparagraphs (1)(*c*)(ii) to (iv), (in this subsection referred to collectively as the "aligned multi-tier partnerships" and each individually as an "aligned multi-tier partnership"),

(*a*) subsection (9) ceases to apply — for the purpose of applying paragraph (1)(*c*) to each of the aligned multi-tier partnerships — in the calendar year following the preceding year (in this subsection referred to as the "current year") if another partnership (in this subsection referred to as the "new partnership") becomes in the current year a member of any of the aligned multi-tier partnerships, or any of the aligned multi-tier partnerships becomes in the current year a member of the new partnership, unless

(i) the fiscal period of the new partnership, and each other partnership described in relation to the new partnership by any of subparagraphs

(1)(*c*)(ii) to (iv), ends in the current year on the same day as the fiscal period of each of the aligned multi-tier partnerships, and

(ii) each member (other than a partnership) of each aligned multi-tier partnership — or a subsidiary wholly-owned corporation of such a member — has been a member of the aligned multi-tier partnership from the end of the last fiscal period ending in the preceding year until the time at which the new partnership becomes a member of an aligned multi-tier partnership, or any of the aligned multi-tier partnerships becomes a member of the new partnership, as the case may be; and

(*b*) if paragraph (*a*) does not apply because the conditions in subparagraphs (*a*)(i) and (ii) are met, the new partnership is deemed — for the purpose of applying paragraph (1)(*c*) to each of the aligned multi-tier partnerships and the new partnership in the current year and subsequent years — to have made the multi-tier alignment election referred to in subsection (9).

History: S. 249.1(9.1) was added by S.C. 2017, c. 33, s. 78(1), applicable to fiscal periods of partnerships that end after March 2014.

► 249.1(10) ◄

(10) Conditions to align a partnership fiscal period. This subsection applies to a single-tier alignment election or a multi-tier alignment election, as the case may be, for a partnership if

(*a*) the election is filed in writing and in prescribed form with the Minister

(i) in the case of a single-tier alignment election, by a corporation that is a member of the partnership on or before the day that is the earliest filing-due date of any corporation that is a member of the partnership for its first taxation year ending after March 22, 2011, and

(ii) in the case of a multi-tier alignment election,

(A) by a corporation that is a member of the partnership, or of a partnership described in relation to the partnership by any of subparagraphs (1)(*c*)(ii) to (iv), and

(B) on or before the day that is the earliest filing-due date of any corporation that is a member of a partnership referred to in clause (A) for the first taxation year of the corporation ending after March 22, 2011;

(*b*) as a consequence of the election, the fiscal period of each partnership to which the election applies is 12 months or less;

(*c*) the election was made by a corporation that has the authority to act for the members of the partnership and each member of any other partnership described in relation to the partnership in subparagraph (1)(*c*)(ii) to (iv); and

(*d*) no other election is filed with the Minister to end the fiscal period of the partnership, or of any other partnership described in relation to the partnership in subparagraph (1)(*c*)(ii) to (iv), on a day other than the particular day referred to in subsection (8) or (9), as the case may be.

History: S. 249.1(10) was added by S.C. 2011, c. 24, s. 73(2), applicable to fiscal periods that end in or after 2011, except that an election referred to in subsection 249.1(10) of the Act is deemed to be filed on time if it is filed in writing with the Minister of National Revenue on or before January 31, 2012. The application provision for this amendment was amended by 2013, c. 34, s. 375, and formerly read: "applicable to the 2011 and subsequent fiscal periods".

► 249.1(11) ◄

(11) Deemed multi-tier alignment election. For the purposes of this Act, if paragraph (1)(*c*) applies to end the fiscal period of a partnership on December 31, 2011, a multi-tier alignment election under subsection (9) is deemed to have been made to end the fiscal period of the partnership on December 31, 2011.

History: S. 249.1(11) was added by S.C. 2011, c. 24, s. 73(2), applicable to fiscal periods that end in or after 2011.

Related Sections: S. 34.2(1), "single-tier alignment".

SECTION 250: Person deemed resident

► 250(1) ◄

(1) Person deemed resident. For the purposes of this Act, a person shall, subject to subsection (2), be deemed to have been resident in Canada throughout a taxation year if the person

(*a*) sojourned in Canada in the year for a period of, or periods the total of which is, 183 days or more;

(*b*) was, at any time in the year, a member of the Canadian Forces;

(*c*) was, at any time in the year,

(i) an ambassador, minister, high commissioner, officer or servant of Canada, or

(ii) an agent-general, officer or servant of a province,

and was resident in Canada immediately prior to appointment or employment by Canada or the province or received representation allowances in respect of the year;

(*d*) performed services, at any time in the year, in a country other than Canada under a prescribed international development assistance program of the Government of Canada and was resident in Canada at any time in the 3 month period preceding the day on which those services commenced;

(*d*.1) was, at any time in the year, a member of the overseas Canadian Forces school staff who filed his or her return for the year on the basis that the person was resident in Canada throughout the period during which the person was such a member;

(*e*) (Repealed by 1999, c. 22, s. 82(1).)

(*f*) was at any time in the year a child of, and dependent for support on, an individual to whom paragraph (*b*), (*c*), (*d*) or (*d*.1) applies and the person's income for the year did not exceed the amount used under paragraph (*c*) of the description of B in subsection 118(1) for the year;

(*g*) was at any time in the year, under an agreement or a convention with one or more other countries that has the force of law in Canada, entitled to an exemption from an income tax otherwise payable in any of those countries in respect of income from any source (unless all or substantially all of the person's income from all sources was not so exempt), because at that time the person was related to or a member of the family of an individual (other than a trust) who was resident in Canada.

Editorial Note: S. 250(1)(*a*) extends residency status by deeming a person who "sojourns" in Canada for a period of 183 days or more in a taxation year to be resident in Canada throughout that year and therefore taxable on his or her worldwide income. The CRA's position is that a "day" means any part of a day and that "sojourn" means a temporary stay, even if of a very short duration. If an individual is in Canada less than 183 days, he or she may still be a part or full-time resident under the common law test.

The remainder of s. 250(1) specifies other deemed residents, who may include members of the Canadian Forces (s. 250(1)(*b*)), federal or provincial employees (s. 250(1)(*c*)), service providers under a prescribed international assistance program (s. 250(1)(*d*)), overseas Canadian Forces school staff (s. 250(1)(*d.1*)), dependent children of the foregoing (s. 250(1)(*f*)), or persons exempt from foreign income tax under a tax agreement (s. 250(1)(*g*)). If a person ceases to be subject to ss. 250(1)(*b*) to (*d.1*), s. 250(2) deems that person (and his or her dependent children) to have been resident in Canada only during the part of the year preceding that time, unless common-law residence applies.

Related Regulations: 2601(5); 3400.

Related Sections: S. 2 Tax payable by persons resident in Canada; s. 6(1)(*b*)(iii) Personal or living expenses; s. 114 Individual resident in Canada for only part of year; s. 122.5(2) Persons not eligible individuals, qualified relations or qualified dependants; s. 122.6, "eligible individual"; s. 227(8.4) Liability to pay amount not deducted or withheld; s. 252(1) Extended meaning of "child".

Canadian Tax Foundation: Lefebvre, *Canadas Jurisdiction to Tax: Residency and the Thomson Decision 60 Years Later*, 2006 Canadian Tax Journal 3:762–780.

Tax Profile: November 2012 — Canadian Residency Traps for Former Canadian Residents; June 2002 — Canadian Residency Update for Individuals.

Tax Topics: No. 2151, "All-American" Professionals: Tax Court of Canada Reviews the Centre of Vital Interests Concept in the Canada-US Treaty Tie-Breaker Rules.

Forms: T1248 — Information About Your Residency Status; NR73 — Determination of Residency Status (Leaving Canada); NR74 — Determination of Residency Status (Entering Canada).

Income Tax Folios: *Primary* — S5-F1-C1 Determining an Individual's Residence Status. *Secondary* — S1-F3-C4 Moving Expenses; S1-F2-C2 Tuition Tax Credit.

Interpretation Bulletins: *Primary* — IT-106R3 Crown corporation employees abroad. *Secondary* — IT-451R Deemed disposition and acquisition on ceasing to be or becoming resident in Canada.

Tax Window Files: Representation or other special allowances, *January 31, 2019*, CRA Document No. 2017-0695931E5.

Cases: The taxpayer was (a) subject to tax in Canada despite being deemed a resident of the United Kingdom under the Canada-UK Tax Convention; and (b) subject to tax in Canada under Article 27(2) of the Convention on the taxpayer's non-UK income, not just income that arose in Canada. *Black v. The Queen*, 2015 DTC 5024 (T.C.C.)

In calculating the number of days that a taxpayer sojourned in Canada during a taxation year, the Minister may not count fractional days where the taxpayer was present for only for one hour. *Stephens v. M.N.R.*, 88 DTC 1170 (T.C.C.)

► 250(2) ◄

(2) Idem. Where at any time in a taxation year a person described in paragraph (1)(*b*), (*c*) or (*d*) ceases to be a person so described, or a person described in paragraph (1)(*d*.1) ceases to be a member of the overseas Canadian Forces school staff, that person shall be deemed to have been resident in Canada throughout the part of the year preceding that time and the spouse or common-law partner and child of that person who by reason of paragraph (1)(*e*) or (*f*) would, but for this subsection, be deemed to have been resident in Canada throughout the year shall be deemed to have been resident in Canada throughout that part of the year.

Editorial Note: See the editorial note to s. 250(1).

► 250(3) ◄

(3) Ordinarily resident. In this Act, a reference to a person resident in Canada includes a person who was at the relevant time ordinarily resident in Canada.

Editorial Note: This provision is relevant to the common law test of residence, per s. 2(1).

Related Sections: S. 2(1) Tax payable by persons resident in Canada; s. 128.1(1) Immigration; s. 128.1(2) Paid-up capital adjustment; s. 128.1(4) Emigration.

Tax Profile: November 2012 — Canadian Residency Traps for Former Canadian Residents; December 2008 — Tax Planning for Emigration from Canada to the United States; June 2002 — Canadian Residency Update for Individuals.

► 250(4) ◄

(4) Corporation deemed resident. For the purposes of this Act, a corporation shall be deemed to have been resident in Canada throughout a taxation year if

(*a*) in the case of a corporation incorporated after April 26, 1965, it was incorporated in Canada;

(*b*) in the case of a corporation that

(i) was incorporated before April 9, 1959,

(ii) was, on June 18, 1971, a foreign business corporation (within the meaning of section 71 of the *Income Tax Act*, chapter 148 of the Revised Statutes of Canada, 1952, as it read in its application to the 1971 taxation year) that was controlled by a corporation resident in Canada,

(iii) throughout the 10 year period ending on June 18, 1971, carried on business in any one particular country other than Canada, and

(iv) during the period referred to in subparagraph (iii), paid dividends to its shareholders resident in Canada on which its shareholders paid tax to the government of the country referred to in that subparagraph,

it was incorporated in Canada and, at any time in the taxation year or at any time in any preceding taxation year commencing after 1971, it was resident in Canada or carried on business in Canada; and

(*c*) in the case of a corporation incorporated before April 27, 1965 (other than a corporation to which subparagraphs (*b*)(i) to (iv) apply), it was incorporated in Canada and, at any time in the taxation year or at any time in any preceding taxation year of the corporation ending after April 26, 1965, it was resident in Canada or carried on business in Canada.

Editorial Note: Unless a corporation was incorporated before April 27, 1965, s. 250(4)(*a*) stipulates that a corporation incorporated in Canada is deemed to be resident therein throughout a taxation year (so that the case law on residence does not need to be analyzed). A corporation incorporated in Canada on before April 26, 1965 is deemed resident if it was otherwise resident or carried on business in Canada at any time in a taxation year ending after that date (s. 250(4)(*c*)); s. 250(4)(*b*) deems certain "foreign business corporations" to be resident. Residence under a tax treaty (s. 250(5)) "trumps" this subsection, as does continuation to another jurisdiction (once this has occurred — s. 250(5.1)). Of course, a corporation may also be resident under common law tests (central management and control).

Related Sections: S. 2(1) Tax payable by persons resident in Canada; s. 89(1), "private corporation"; s. 133(8), "non-resident-owned investment corporation"; s. 248(1), "corporation incorporated in Canada"; s. 250(4) Corporation deemed resident; s. 250(5) Deemed non-resident; ITAR s. 59(2) Non-resident-owned investment corporation.

Canadian Tax Foundation: Baker and Gamble, *Corporate Residence*, 2010 Conference Report 24:1–22.

Tax Profile: June 2002 — Canadian Residency Update for Individuals.

Cases: The residency of the corporation (incorporated in the Netherlands) was based on the common law test of central management and control. A review of the ownership structure of the company and the locus of decision-making authority determined the corporation was a resident of Canada and liable for Part 1 tax. *Landbouwbedrijf v. The Queen*, 2018 DTC 1104 (TCC)

A Canadian company acted as an intermediary for an associated U.S. company. Although incorporated before April 26, 1965, the corporation subsequently carried on business in Canada and was consequently deemed to be resident. *The Queen v. Gurd's Products Co. Ltd.*, 85 DTC 5314 (F.C.A.)

► 250(5) ◄

(5) Deemed non-resident. Notwithstanding any other provision of this Act (other than paragraph 126(1.1)(*a*)), a person is deemed not to be resident in Canada at a time if, at that time, the person would, but for this subsection and any tax treaty, be resident in Canada for the purposes of this Act but is, under a tax treaty with another country, resident in the other country and not resident in Canada.

Editorial Note: S. 250(5) deems a person not to be resident in Canada if the person qualifies as a resident of Canada under the *Income Tax Act* but at the same time is a non-resident under one of Canada's tax treaties. This rule "trumps" nearly all other *Income Tax Act* provisions. Therefore, the cessation of residence because of the application of a treaty could trigger a deemed disposition under s. 128.1(4); in addition Part XIII would apply.

Related Sections: S. 2(1) Tax payable by persons resident in Canada; s. 89(1), "Canadian corporation", "private corporation"; s. 128.1(4) Emigration; s. 248(1), "tax treaty".

Tax Profile: February 2013 — The Purchase of US Businesses by Canadians; December 2008 — Tax Planning for Emigration from Canada to the United States; June 2002 — Canadian Residency Update for Individuals; April 2002 — Tax Considerations for Canadian Businesses Expanding to the U.S.

Tax Topics: No. 1962, Another NRT seeks Judicial Review: *Morris and Smith v. M.N.R.*.

Forms: T2Sch97 — Additional Information on Non-Resident Corporations in Canada; T1248 — Information About Your Residency Status.

Income Tax Folios: *Secondary* — S5-F1-C1 Determining an Individual's Residence Status.

Cases: The issue was the date the taxpayer resumed Canadian residency, as any amounts received after would constitute income for Canadian tax purposes. At the time, the taxpayer was a resident of both the US and Canada. The taxpayer's habitual abode was in the US on the date he received the 401(k) proceeds and he was taxed in the US as a resident. As a dual treaty resident he was a resident of the US and not Canada by virtue of the tie-breaker rule in section 2(b) of Article IV of the *Canada-U.S. Income Tax Convention* and the income from the 401(k) was not taxable in Canada. *Davis v. The Queen*, 2018 DTC 1085 (TCC)

► 250(5.1) ◄

(5.1) Continued corporation. Where a corporation is at any time (in this subsection referred to as the "time of continuation") granted articles of continuance (or similar constitutional documents) in a particular jurisdiction, the corporation shall

(*a*) for the purposes of applying this Act (other than subsection (4)) in respect of all times from the time of continuation until the time, if any, of continuation in a different jurisdiction, be deemed to have been incorporated in the particular jurisdiction and not to have been incorporated in any other jurisdiction; and

(*b*) for the purpose of applying subsection (4) in respect of all times from the time of continuation until the time, if any, of continuation in a different jurisdiction, be deemed to have been incorporated in the particular jurisdiction at the time of continuation and not to have been incorporated in any other jurisdiction.

Editorial Note: A corporation may be continued or "exported" into a foreign jurisdiction, so that it becomes subject to the corporate law of the particular (new) jurisdiction rather than applicable Canadian corporate law. Generally, a continued corporation will be treated as incorporated in the new jurisdiction and not incorporated in Canada (or any other jurisdiction) for the purposes of applying the Act (other than s. 250(4)) from the time of continuation until the time the corporation is continued in a different jurisdiction (s. 250(5.1)(*a*)). For the purposes of applying the deemed residence rules in s. 250(4) from the time of continuation until the time the corporation is continued in a different jurisdiction, the continued corporation is deemed to have been incorporated in the new jurisdiction at the time of continuation (s. 250(5.1)(*b*)); however, the corporation may nonetheless be resident in Canada under the common law residence test (central management and control) unless s. 250(5) (residence for treaty purposes) applies to "trump" this.

S. 250(5.1) also applies to corporations continued into Canada, so that such a corporation would be deemed to be Canadian resident, as it would be considered to be incorporated in Canada for the purposes of s. 250(4) as at the date of continuance into Canada (again, unless s. 250(5) applies). S. 250(5.1) affects the status of a corporation as a "Canadian corporation" (and therefore its potential status as a "Canadian-controlled private corporation" and a "taxable Canadian corporation"), but not necessarily its residence.

Related Sections: S. 44(2)(*d*) Time of disposition and of receipt of proceeds; s. 52(8) Cost of shares of immigrant corporation; s. 54 Definitions; s. 89(1), "Canadian corporation"; s. 128.1 Immigration; s. 128.2 Cross-border mergers — treatment of resident predecessor; s. 219.1 Corporate emigration; s. 248(1), "corporation incorporated in Canada", "taxable Canadian property"; ITAR s. 26(10) Where paragraph 128.1(1)(b) of amended Act applies.

Tax Profile: February 2009 — Tax Consequences of a Corporate Continuance.

Forms: T2Sch97 — Additional Information on Non-Resident Corporations in Canada.

► 250(6) ◄

(6) Residence of international shipping corporation. For the purposes of this Act, a corporation that was incorporated or otherwise formed under the laws of a country other than Canada or of a state, province or other political subdivision of such a country is deemed to be resident in that country throughout a taxation year and not to be resident in Canada at any time in the year, if

(*a*) the corporation

(i) has international shipping as its principal business in the year, or

(ii) holds eligible interests in one or more eligible entities throughout the year and at no time in the year is the total of the cost amounts to it of all those eligible interests and of all debts owing to it by an eligible entity in which an eligible interest is held by it, by a person related to it or by a partnership affiliated with it less than 50% of the total of the cost amounts to it of all its property;

(*b*) all or substantially all the corporation's gross revenue for the year consists of any one or more of

(i) gross revenue from international shipping,

(ii) gross revenue from an eligible interest held by it in an eligible entity, and

(iii) interest on a debt owing by an eligible entity in which an eligible interest is held by it, by a person related to it or by a partnership affiliated with it; and

(*c*) the corporation was not granted articles of continuance in Canada before the end of the year.

History: S. 250(6)(*b*), the portion before paragraph (*c*) was replaced by S.C. 2014, c. 39, s. 74(1), applicable to taxation years that begin after July 12, 2013, and formerly read:

(6) *Residence of international shipping corporation.* For the purposes of this Act, a corporation that was incorporated or otherwise formed under the laws of a country other than Canada or of a state, province or other political subdivision of such a country shall be deemed to be resident in that country throughout a taxation year and not to be resident in Canada at any time in the year, where

(*a*) the corporation

(i) has as its principal business in the year the operation of ships that are used primarily in transporting passengers or goods in international traffic (determined on the assumption that the corporation is non-resident and that, except where paragraph (*c*) of the definition "international traffic" in subsection 248(1) applies, any port or other place on the Great Lakes or St. Lawrence River is in Canada), or

(ii) holds throughout the year shares of one or more other corporations, each of which

(A) is a subsidiary wholly-owned corporation of the corporation as defined by subsection 87(1.4), and

(B) is deemed by this subsection to be resident in a country other than Canada throughout the year,

and at no time in the year is the total of the cost amounts to the corporation of all those shares less than 50% of the total of the cost amounts to it of all its property;

(*b*) all or substantially all of the corporation's gross revenue for the year consists of

(i) gross revenue from the operation of ships in transporting passengers or goods in that international traffic,

(ii) dividends from one or more other corporations each of which

(A) is a subsidiary wholly-owned corporation of the corporation, as defined by subsection 87(1.4), and

(B) is deemed by this subsection to be resident in a country other than Canada throughout each of its taxation years that began after February 1991 and before the last time at which it paid any of those dividends, or

(iii) a combination of amounts described in subparagraph (i) or (ii); and

Related Sections: 248(1) international shipping; 250(6.03) Service providers; 250(6.04) Definitions.

Forms: T2Sch97 — Additional Information on Non-Resident Corporations in Canada.

► 250(6.01) ◄

(6.01) Partner's gross revenue. For the purposes of paragraph (6)(*b*), an amount of profit allocated from a partnership to a member of the partnership for a taxation year is deemed to be gross revenue of the member from member's interest in the partnership for the year.

History: S. 250(6.01) was added by S.C. 2014, c. 39, s. 74(2), applicable to taxation years that begin after July 12, 2013.

► 250(6.02) ◄

(6.02) Service providers. Subsection (6.03) applies to a corporation, trust or partnership (in this subsection and subsection (6.03) referred to as the "relevant entity") for a taxation year if

(*a*) the relevant entity does not satisfy the condition in subparagraph (6)(*a*)(i), determined without reference to subsection (6.03);

(*b*) all or substantially all the gross revenue of the relevant entity for the year consists of any one or more of

(i) gross revenue from the provision of services to one or more eligible entities, other than services described in any of paragraphs (*a*) to (*h*) of the definition "international shipping" in subsection 248(1),

(ii) gross revenue from international shipping,

(iii) gross revenue from an eligible interest held by it in an eligible entity, and

(iv) interest on a debt owing by an eligible entity in which an eligible interest is held by it or a person related to it;

(*c*) either the relevant entity is a subsidiary wholly-owned corporation (as defined in subsection 87(1.4)) of the eligible entity referred to in paragraph (*b*) or an eligible interest in each eligible entity referred to in paragraph (*b*) is held throughout the year by

(i) the relevant entity,

(ii) one or more persons related to the relevant entity (if the relevant entity and each such person is a corporation), or persons or partnerships affiliated with the relevant entity (in any other case), or

(iii) any combination of the relevant entity and persons or partnerships described in subparagraph (ii); and

(*d*) all or substantially all the shares of the capital stock of, or interests in, the relevant entity are held, directly or indirectly through one or more subsidiary wholly-owned corporations (as defined in subsection 87(1.4)), throughout the year by one or more corporations, trusts or partnerships that would be eligible entities if they did not own shares of, or interests in, the relevant entity.

History: S. 250(6.02) was added by S.C. 2014, c. 39, s. 74(2), applicable to taxation years that begin after July 12, 2013.

► 250(6.03) ◄

(6.03) Service providers. If this subsection applies for a taxation year, then for the purposes of subsection (6) and paragraph 81(1)(*c*),

(*a*) the relevant entity is deemed to have international shipping as its principal business in the year; and

(*b*) the gross revenue described in subparagraph (6.02)(*b*)(i) is deemed to be gross revenue from international shipping.

History: S. 250(6.03) was added by S.C. 2014, c. 39, s. 74(2), applicable to taxation years that begin after July 12, 2013.

Related Sections: 250(6.02) Service providers.

► 250(6.04) ◄

(6.04) Definitions. The following definitions apply in this subsection and subsections (6) to (6.03).

History: S. 250(6.04) was added by S.C. 2014, c. 39, s. 74(2), applicable to taxation years that begin after July 12, 2013.

"eligible entity" —"eligible entity", for a taxation year, means

(*a*) a corporation that is deemed by subsection (6) to be resident in a country other than Canada for the year; or

(*b*) a partnership or trust, if

(i) it satisfies the conditions in subparagraph (6)(*a*)(i) or (ii), and

(ii) all or substantially all its gross revenue for the year consists of any combination of amounts described in any of subparagraphs (6)(*b*)(i) to (iii).

"eligible interest" —"eligible interest" means

(*a*) in respect of a corporation, shares of the capital stock of the corporation that

(i) give the holders of those shares not less than 25% of the votes that could be cast at an annual meeting of the shareholders of the corporation, and

(ii) have a fair market value that is not less than 25% of the fair market value of all the issued and outstanding shares of the capital stock of the corporation;

(*b*) in respect of a trust, an interest as a beneficiary (as defined in subsection 108(1)) under the trust with a fair market value that is not less than 25% of the fair market value of all the interests of all beneficiaries under the trust; and

(*c*) in respect of a partnership, an interest as a member of the partnership with a fair market value that is not less than 25% of the fair market value of all the membership interests in the partnership.

▶ 250(6.05) ◀

(6.05) Holdings in eligible entities. For the purpose of determining whether a person or partnership (in this subsection referred to as the "holder") holds an eligible interest in an eligible entity in subsections (6) to (6.04), the holder is deemed to hold all of the shares or interests, as the case may be, in the eligible entity held by

(*a*) the holder;

(*b*) if the holder is a corporation,

(i) each corporation related to the holder, and

(ii) each person, other than a corporation, or partnership that is affiliated with the holder; and

(*c*) if the holder is not a corporation, each person or partnership affiliated with the holder.

History: S. 250(6.05) was added by S.C. 2014, c. 39, s. 74(2), applicable to taxation years that begin after July 12, 2013.

▶ 250(6.1) ◀

(6.1) Residence of inter vivos trusts. For the purposes of provisions of this Act that apply to a trust for a taxation year only where the trust has been resident in Canada throughout the year, where a particular trust ceases at any time to exist and the particular trust was resident in Canada immediately before that time, the particular trust is deemed to be resident in Canada throughout the period that begins at that time and ends at the end of the year.

▶ 250(7) ◀

(7) Residence of a qualifying environmental trust — (Repealed by S.C. 2011, c. 24, s. 74(1).)

History: S. 250(7) was repealed by S.C. 2011, c. 24, s. 74(1), applicable to the 2012 and subsequent taxation years. S. 250(7) formerly read:

(7) *Residence of a qualifying environmental trust* For the purposes of this Act, where a trust resident in Canada would be a qualifying environmental trust at any time if it were resident at that time in the province in which the site to which the trust relates is situated, the trust is deemed to be resident at that time in that province and in no other province.

Related Sections: S. 12(1)(*z*.1) Qualifying environmental trusts; s. 12(1)(*z*.2) Dispositions of interests in qualifying environmental trusts; s. 20(1)(*ss*) Qualifying environmental trusts; s. 20(1)(*tt*) Acquisition of interests in qualifying environmental trusts; s. 107.3 Treatment of beneficiaries under qualifying environmental trusts; s. 149(1)(*z*) Qualifying environmental trust; s. 248(1), "qualifying environmental trust".

SECTION 250.1: Non-resident person's taxation year and income

For greater certainty, unless the context requires otherwise

(*a*) a taxation year of a non-resident person shall be determined, except as otherwise permitted by the Minister, in the same manner as the taxation year of a person resident in Canada; and

(*b*) a person for whom income for a taxation year is determined in accordance with this Act includes a non-resident person.

Related Sections: S. 212(1)(*c*) Estate or trust income; s. 216(1)(*b*) Alternatives re rents and timber royalties; s. 217(3) Taxable income earned in Canada.

Tax Topics: No. 1889, Taxation Year of a Foreign Affiliate.

SECTION 251: Arm's length

▶ 251(1) ◀

(1) Arm's length. For the purposes of this Act,

(*a*) related persons shall be deemed not to deal with each other at arm's length;

(*b*) a taxpayer and a personal trust (other than a trust described in any of paragraphs (*a*) to (*e*.1) of the definition "trust" in subsection 108(1)) are deemed not to deal with each other at arm's length if the taxpayer, or any person not dealing at arm's length with the taxpayer, would be beneficially interested in the trust if subsection 248(25) were read without reference to subclauses 248(25)(*b*)(iii)(A)(II) to (IV); and

(*c*) in any other case, it is a question of fact whether persons not related to each other are, at a particular time, dealing with each other at arm's length.

Editorial Note: The term "arm's length" is used in many sections of the Act. Section 251(1) determines when persons do not deal at arm's length. Most of these provisions are designed to prevent tax avoidance, which otherwise might arise by reason of collusion between taxpayers. In some cases, these provisions do more than prevent tax avoidance and, in effect, impose a penalty upon persons who do not deal with others at arm's length. In certain specified circumstances, taxpayers are conclusively deemed not to deal with others at arm's length, and in other circumstances, it will be a question of fact whether persons are dealing at arm's length.

Deemed not to deal at arms-length: Paragraph 251(1)(*a*) provides that "related persons" shall be *deemed* not to deal with each other at arm's length. The circumstances in which persons are considered to be "related persons" are determined under s. 251(2) to 251(6). It has been held that the word "deemed" means "conclusively and irrebuttably presumed", and that it does not merely create a presumption which can be rebutted by evidence that the parties are actually dealing at arm's length (see previous decisions under the former Income Tax Appeal Board: *No. 25 v. M.N.R.*, 51 DTC 331; *Western Printers Association Limited v. M.N.R.*, 51 DTC 345; *No. 116 v M.N.R.*, 53 DTC 344; *Benedet v. M.N.R.*, 54 DTC 51). The Canada Revenue Agency's views on when unrelated parties deal at arm's length are set out in the May 2014 Income Tax Folio S1-F5-C1 at paragraphs 1.30 to 1.54.

Circumstances where persons are not dealing at arms-length: A taxpayer shall be deemed not to deal at arm's length with a personal trust under which the taxpayer, or any person not dealing at arm's length with the taxpayer, is beneficially interested or would be beneficially interested if s. 248(25)(*b*)(iii)(A)(II) to (IV) did not apply. Each of the following taxpayers is deemed not to deal at arm's length with a personal trust:

(1) a person or partnership that has any right (whether immediate or future, whether absolute or contingent and whether conditional on or subject to the exercise of any discretion by any person or partnership) as a beneficiary under the trust to receive any of the income or capital of the particular trust either directly from the particular trust or indirectly through one or more trusts or partnerships;

(2) a person or partnership from whom the trust has acquired property directly or indirectly in any manner whatever, and who might, because of the terms of the trust or any arrangement in respect of the trust and

upon the exercise of any discretion by any person or partnership, acquire a right referred to in paragraph 248(25)(*a*);

(3) a member of a partnership that is beneficially interested in the trust under paragraphs 1 or 2 above; and

(4) a person or partnership that does not deal at arm's length with a person or partnership referred to in paragraphs 1, 2, or 3 above.

History: S. 251(1)(*c*) was replaced by S.C. 2013, c. 34, s. 361(1), deemed to have come into force on December 24, 1998, and formerly read:

(*c*) where paragraph (*b*) does not apply, it is a question of fact whether persons not related to each other are at a particular time dealing with each other at arm's length.

Related Regulations: 231(6); 1100; 1100A; 1101; 1102; Part XII; 4605; 4800.1; Part XLIX; Part LI; Part LXII; Part LXVII; Part LXVIII; Part LXXXV.

Related Sections: S. 7 Agreement to issue securities to employees; s. 13(7)(*e*) Rules applicable; s. 14(5), "cumulative eligible capital"; s. 15(2.1) Persons connected with a shareholder; s. 18(2) Limit on certain interest and property tax; s. 18(5) Definitions; s. 18(5.1) Specified shareholder or specified beneficiary; s. 18(6) Loans made on condition; s. 39(1)(*c*) Meaning of capital gain and capital loss; s. 40(2)(*g*)(ii) Limitations; s. 55 Definitions; s. 56(4) Transfer of rights to income; s. 56(4.1) Interest free or low interest loans; S. 56.4 Restrictive Covenants; s. 69 Inadequate considerations; s. 74.1(2) Transfers and loans to minors; s. 80.4 Loans; s. 84(8) Where s. (3) does not apply; s. 84.1 Non-arm's length sale of shares; s. 88 Winding-up; s. 94 [Non-resident trusts]; s. 94.1 Offshore investment fund property; s. 95 Foreign accrual property income; s. 103(1.1) Agreement to share income, etc., in unreasonable proportions; s. 112 Deduction of taxable dividends received by corporation resident in Canada; s. 149.1(1) Definitions (various definitions); s. 160 Tax liability re property transferred not at arm's length; s. 186(2) When corporation controlled; s. 212(1)(*b*) Interest; s. 212(4) Interpretation of "management or administration fee or charge"; s. 212.1 Non-arm's length sales of shares by non-residents s. 246 Benefit conferred on a person; s. 248(1), "specified employee", "specified financial institution"; "specified shareholder"; s. 248(25) Beneficially interested; s. 248(36) Non-arm's length transaction; s. 251(2) Definition of "related persons"; s. 251(3) Corporations related through a third corporation; s. 251(3.1) Relation where amalgamation or merger; s. 251(3.2) Amalgamation of related corporations; s. 251(4) Definitions concerning groups; s. 251(5) Control by related groups, options, etc; s. 251(6) Blood relationship, etc; s. 260 Definitions.

Canadian Tax Foundation: Dueck and Daniels, *Update and Review of the Related, Affiliated, and Associated Rules: Overlaps, Differences, and Their Significance*, 2014 British Columbia Tax Conference 10:1–77; Stack, *Arm's Length as a Question of Fact*, 1997 Conference Report 16:1–15.

Tax Topics: No. 1977, Whether Parties Were At Arm's Length.

Income Tax Folios: *Secondary*— S1-F3-C1 Child Care Expense Deduction; *Primary*— S1-F5-C1 Related Persons and Dealing at Arm's Length.

Interpretation Bulletins: *Secondary* — IT-64R4 (Consolid.) Corporations: Association and control.

Cases: The issue was whether the appellant and transferor were dealing at arm's length at the time of the transfer. Looking at the history of employment and the business relationship between the parties, they were not dealing at arm's length. At some point they developed a common-law relationship. The transferor was the controlling mind behind the transaction, and the goal was to provide the transferor with a vehicle without it being subject to collection. *McKay v. The Queen*, 2016 DTC 1185 (TCC)

► 251(2) ◄

(2) Definition of "related persons". For the purpose of this Act, "related persons", or persons related to each other, are

(*a*) individuals connected by blood relationship, marriage or common-law partnership or adoption;

(*b*) a corporation and

(i) a person who controls the corporation, if it is controlled by one person,

(ii) a person who is a member of a related group that controls the corporation, or

(iii) any person related to a person described in subparagraph (i) or (ii); and

(*c*) any two corporations

(i) if they are controlled by the same person or group of persons,

(ii) if each of the corporations is controlled by one person and the person who controls one of the corporations is related to the person who controls the other corporation,

(iii) if one of the corporations is controlled by one person and that person is related to any member of a related group that controls the other corporation,

(iv) if one of the corporations is controlled by one person and that person is related to each member of an unrelated group that controls the other corporation,

(v) if any member of a related group that controls one of the corporations is related to each member of an unrelated group that controls the other corporation, or

(vi) if each member of an unrelated group that controls one of the corporations is related to at least one member of an unrelated group that controls the other corporation.

Editorial Note: This subsection, supplemented by s. 251(3) to (6), provides a series of rules as to when individuals and corporations are related for the purposes of the Act. The status of being related has itself various consequences under the Act. Additionally, related persons are deemed not to deal at arm's length for the purposes of the Act. The concepts of associated corporations, affiliated persons, and connected corporations also rely on the concept of related persons.

Individuals: Individuals are related if they are connected by blood, marriage or common-law partnership, or adoption; these terms are defined in s. 251(6). An individual's niece, nephew, aunt, uncle, or cousin is not connected by blood, marriage or common-law partnership, or adoption to the individual, and is therefore not related to the individual.

A trust and a beneficiary of the trust are typically non-arm length persons because of paragraph 251(1)(*b*). In terms of whether a trust is related to a beneficiary, the Canada Revenue Agency ("CRA") has stated that, if the beneficiary is an individual who is connected by blood relationship, marriage or common-law partnership or adoption to the trustee, the trust and the beneficiary will be related (CRA Document No. 2009-0311891I7).

Control of corporation: For the purposes of determining whether a corporation is controlled under the relationship rules of s. 251(2)(*b*) and (*c*), *de jure* control applies, and the *de facto* control rules in s. 256(5.1) do not apply. *De jure* control has been interpreted by the courts to mean ownership of enough shares carrying a majority of votes in the election of the directors of the corporation (*Buckerfield's v. M.N.R.*, 64 DTC 5301 (Ex. Ct.), confirmed in *M.N.R. v. Dworkin Furs (Pembroke) Ltd. et al.*, 67 DTC 5035 (S.C.C.)). In *The Queen v. Imperial General Properties Ltd.*, 85 DTC 5500 (S.C.C.), one company held shares which gave it the right to wind-up the other company. It therefore controlled the other company, notwithstanding the fact that it only held 50% of the voting rights.

See also s. 251(5)(*b*), under which a person who has a right to acquire shares in a corporation, to cause the corporation to redeem or cancel its shares, or to acquire voting rights, is generally deemed to be in the same position of control as if the right had been exercised. The CRA has stated that s. 251(5)(*b*) will not normally be applied solely because of a "right of first refusal" or a "shotgun arrangement" (see CRA document no. 2005-0121951E5 and Income Tax Folio S1-F5-C1, paragraph 1.28).

Since s. 104(2) deems a trust to be an individual in respect of the trust property, it will be a person to which s. 251 applies. Thus, for example, where a trust owns a majority of the voting shares of a corporation such that the trustee(s) of the trust control the corporation, the trust and the corporation will be related persons by virtue of s. 251(2)(*b*). See paragraphs 1.45 through 1.47 of Income Tax Folio S1-F5-C1, *Related Persons and Dealing at Arm's Length*, which contains the CRA views on this and other aspects of the concept of related persons (as well as the concept of non-arm's length).

Control by related partners: Where a related group of partners owns a controlling interest in a partnership, each member of that related group will not be considered to deal at arm's length with the partnership (Income Tax Folio S1-F5-C1, paragraph 1.43).

Effect of control by trust on trustee: The control of a corporation by a trust may also result in a trustee of the trust being related to the corporation because of that trustee's ownership of the shares of, and control of, the corporation (see the examples in Income Tax Folio S1-F5-C1, paragraphs 1.47 to 1.49).

Related Regulations: 4901(2); Part LI; 5907(1); Part LXXXV.

Related Sections: S. 6 Amounts to be included as income from office or employment; s. 15 Benefit conferred on shareholder; s. 17 Amount owing by non-resident; s. 40(2)(*e.1*) Limitations; s. 44.1 Reserve — property disposed of to a child; s. 51(2) Limitation of rollover benefit; s. 53(1)(*c*) Adjustments to cost base — Contributions of capital; s. 53(1)(*e*) Adjustments to cost base — Interest in a partnership; s. 54, "personal use property; s. 55 Definitions; s. 74.4(2) Transfers and loans to corporations; s. 80 Definitions; s. 80.01(6) Specified obligation in relation to debt parking; s. 80.04 Definitions; s. 80.4 Loans; s. 83(2.4) Capital dividend — exception to anti-avoidance rule; s. 85(1)(*e.2*) Transfer of property to corporation by shareholders; s. 86(1) Exchange of shares by a shareholder in course of reorganization of capital; s. 86(2) Disposition of old shares and benefit; s. 87(4) Computation of adjusted cost base; s. 88(1) Winding-up; s. 88(3) Dissolution of foreign affiliate; s. 94 [Non-resident trusts]; s. 95 Application of certain provisions to trusts not resident in Canada; s. 110.6(1), "qualified small business corporation share"; s. 112(2.21) Exceptions; s. 112(2.4) Where no deduction permitted; s. 120.4 Definitions; s. 125(7), "personal services business"; s. 127 [Investment tax credit, etc.]; s. 147(2) Acceptance of plan for registration; s. 191(2) Substantial interest; s. 191(3) Substantial interest — anti-avoidance rule; s. 191.3(1) Agreement respecting liability for tax; s. 191.3(4) Related corporations; s. 248(1), "small business corporation", "specified financial institution", "specified shareholder", "term preferred share"; s. 251(1) Arm's length; s. 251(3) Corporations related through a third corporation; s. 251(3.1) Relation where amalgamation or merger; s. 251(3.2) Amalgamation of related corporations; s. 251(4) Definitions concerning groups; s. 251(5) Control by related groups, options, etc; s. 251(6) Blood relationship, etc; s. 256(1) Associated corporations; s. 256(6.1) Simultaneous control; s. 256(7) Acquiring control.

Canadian Tax Foundation: Bodie and Novotny, *Acquisitions of Control Under the Income Tax Act— Recent Developments*, 2013 Prairie Provinces Tax Conference 6:1–27; Nitikman, *Who Has De Jure Control of a Corporation when its Shares are Held by a Limited Partnership?*, 2011 Canadian Tax Journal 4:765–782; Brender, *Developments in the Concept of Corporate Control*, 2007 Conference Report 31:1–49; Diep, *"Associated", "Affiliated", and "Related" Transactions, Part 1: A Technical Overview*, 2005 Conference Report 38:1–12; Marquette, *Selected Income Tax Issues of Particular Relevance to Shareholders Agreements: Part 1*, 2001 Canadian Tax Journal 1:182–208; Hiseler, *Corporate Control*, 1988 Conference Report 12:1–33.

Tax Topics: No. 2461-2462, Part 3: Shareholders Agreements, the Act, and the Non-Specialist Advisor: The Impact of Control; No. 2460, Part 2: Shareholders Agreements, the Act, and the Non-Specialist Advisor: The Impact of Control; No. 2457, Part 1: Shareholders Agreements, the Act, and the Non-Specialist Advisor: The Impact of Control; No. 2040, CRA Roundtable at Association de planification fiscale et financière (APFF) 2010 Conference; No. 1692, Income Tax Implications of Buy-Sell Provisions.

Income Tax Folios: *Primary* — S1-F5-C1 Related Persons and Dealing at Arm's Length.

Interpretation Bulletins: *Secondary* — IT-64R4 (Consolid.) Corporations: Association and control.

Tax Window Files: Half-brothers and related persons, *July 12, 2018*, CRA Document No. 2018-0755471E5.

Cases: A corporation was a CCPC even though more than 50% of its common shares were held by various non-residents. There was no sufficient common link or interest amongst the shareholders, or evidence that they acted together to exert control. *Silicon Graphics Limited v. The Queen*, 2002 DTC 7112 (F.C.A.), reversing 2001 DTC 379 (T.C.C.)

Although the parent company did not have *de facto* over both corporations, it did have *de jure* control, and that was sufficient to allow the non-capital losses to be transferred from one corporation to the other. *Duha Printers (Western) Ltd.*, 98 DTC 6334 (S.C.C.), reversing 96 DTC 6323 (F.C.A.), which reversed 95 DTC 828 (T.C.C.)

Two corporations were not associated by virtue of the *de jure* or "voting control" test and the attempt to show that one corporation enjoyed *de facto* control of the other corporation through its unexercised right, under certain circumstances, to force the redemption of its preferred shares was ill-conceived. *Harvard International Resources Ltd. v. Prov. Treasurer of Ontario*, 93 DTC 5254 (Alta. Q.B.)

One company held shares which gave it the right to wind-up the other company. It therefore controlled the other company, notwithstanding the fact that it only held 50% of the voting rights. *The Queen v. Imperial General Properties Ltd.*, 85 DTC 5500 (S.C.C.), reversing 83 DTC 5055 (F.C.A.), affirming 81 DTC 5191 (F.C.T.D.)

A group of shareholders was held to control several corporations because they had the right to authorize the surrender of the company's letters patent. These circumstances were sufficient to vest control in the group even though they only held 50% of the voting power. *Oakfield Developments (Toronto) Ltd. v. M.N.R.*, 71 DTC 5175 (S.C.C.), affirming 69 DTC 5175 (Ex. Ct.)

If a group of shareholders owns a majority of the voting shares of a company, and the same group owns a majority of the voting shares of a second company, that fact is sufficient to constitute the two companies associated. Moreover, in determining *de jure* control more than one group of persons can be aptly described as a "group of persons". It is immaterial whether other combinations of shareholders may own a majority of voting shares in either company. *Vina-Rug (Canada) Limited v. M.N.R.*, 68 DTC 5021 (S.C.C.), affirming 66 DTC 5373 (Ex. Ct)

Control means *de jure* control, and not *de facto*. The right of control rests in ownership of such a number of shares as carries with it the right to a majority of the votes in the election of the Board of Directors. The fact that a particular shareholder has a second or casting vote in the case of an equality of votes does not give that shareholder control of the company. *M.N.R. v. Dworkin Furs (Pembroke) Limited et al.*, 67 DTC 5035 (S.C.C.), affirming 65 DTC 5277 (Ex.Ct.), 66 DTC 5244 (Ex.Ct.), 66 DTC 5263 (Ex.Ct.) and 66 DTC 5303 (Ex.Ct.)

Where two individuals each owned half the shares of three companies either through personal holding or through ownership of two intermediary companies, the three companies were deemed controlled by the same group of persons. *Vineland Quarries and Crushed Stone Ltd. v. M.N.R.*, 67 DTC 5283 (S.C.C.), affirming 66 DTC 5092 (Ex. Ct.)

The word "controlled" contemplates the right of control that rests in ownership of such a number of shares as carries with it the right to a majority of the votes in the election of the Board of Directors. *Buckerfield's Limited v. M.N.R.*, 64 DTC 5301 (Ex. Ct.).

► 251(3) ◄

(3) Corporations related through a third corporation. Where two corporations are related to the same corporation within the meaning of subsection (2), they shall, for the purposes of subsections (1) and (2), be deemed to be related to each other.

Editorial Note: See the Editorial Note to s. 251(2).

Related Regulations: Part XXXI.

Income Tax Folios: *Primary* — S1-F5-C1 Related Persons and Dealing at Arm's Length.

► 251(3.1) ◄

(3.1) Relation where amalgamation or merger. Where there has been an amalgamation or merger of two or more corporations and the new corporation formed as a result of the amalgamation or merger and any predecessor corporation would have been related immediately before the amalgamation or merger if the new corporation were in existence at that time, and if the persons who were the shareholders of the new corporation immediately after the amalgamation or merger were the shareholders of the new corporation at that time, the new corporation and any such predecessor corporation shall be deemed to have been related persons.

Income Tax Folios: *Secondary* — S4-F7-C1 Amalgamations of Canadian Corporations.

► 251(3.2) ◄

(3.2) Amalgamation of related corporations. Where there has been an amalgamation or merger of 2 or more corporations each of which was related (otherwise than because of a right referred to in paragraph (5)(*b*)) to each other immediately before the amalgamation or merger, the new corporation formed as a result of the amalgamation or merger and each of the predecessor corporations is deemed to have been related to each other.

Related Sections: S. 251.1(2) Affiliation where amalgamation or merger.

Income Tax Folios: *Secondary* — S4-F7-C1 Amalgamations of Canadian Corporations.

► 251(4) ◄

(4) Definitions concerning groups. In this Act,

"related group" — "related group" means a group of persons each member of which is related to every other member of the group;

"unrelated group" — "unrelated group" means a group of persons that is not a related group.

► 251(5) ◄

(5) Control by related groups, options, etc. For the purposes of subsection (2) and the definition "Canadian-controlled private corporation" in subsection 125(7),

(*a*) where a related group is in a position to control a corporation, it shall be deemed to be a related group that controls the corporation whether or not it is part of a larger group by which the corporation is in fact controlled;

(*b*) where at any time a person has a right under a contract, in equity or otherwise, either immediately or in the future and either absolutely or contingently,

(i) to, or to acquire, shares of the capital stock of a corporation or to control the voting rights of such shares, the person shall, except where the right is not exercisable at that time because the exercise thereof is contingent on the death, bankruptcy or permanent disability of an individual, be deemed to have the same position in relation to the control of the corporation as if the person owned the shares at that time,

(ii) to cause a corporation to redeem, acquire or cancel any shares of its capital stock owned by other shareholders of the corporation, the person shall, except where the right is not exercisable at that time because the exercise thereof is contingent on the death, bankruptcy or permanent disability of an individual, be deemed to have the same position in relation to the control of the corporation as if the shares were so redeemed, acquired or cancelled by the corporation at that time;

(iii) to, or to acquire or control, voting rights in respect of shares of the capital stock of a corporation, the person is, except where the right is not exercisable at that time because its exercise is contingent on the death, bankruptcy or permanent disability of an individual, deemed to have the same position in relation to the control of the corporation as if the person could exercise the voting rights at that time, or

(iv) to cause the reduction of voting rights in respect of shares, owned by other shareholders, of the capital stock of a corporation, the person is, except where the right is not exercisable at that time because its exercise is contingent on the death, bankruptcy or permanent disability of an individual, deemed to have the same position in relation to the control of the corporation as if the voting rights were so reduced at that time; and

(*c*) where a person owns shares in two or more corporations, the person shall as shareholder of one of the corporations be deemed to be related to himself, herself or itself as shareholder of each of the other corporations.

Editorial Note: S. 251(5) expands the control concept, for the purposes (only) of related person (and consequently non-arm's length) status and the CCPC definition in s. 125(7) (but a change of status to/from a CCPC may in turn trigger a deemed year-end per s. 249(3.1)). (A similar provision, s. 256(1.4), applies re associated corporation status.) S. 251(5) does not apply, for example, to s. 111(5) (loss streaming) or 249(4) (deemed year-end). S. 251(5)(*b*) applies to rights under contract (e.g., shareholders' or share purchase agreements), in equity or otherwise, including contingent rights, to acquire shares, control voting rights, or to cause a corporation to redeem/acquire shares owned by others. Exceptions apply to rights contingent on death, bankruptcy or permanent disability of an individual. The CRA's longstanding policy excludes a right of first refusal or shotgun arrangement, but it has indicated that it is not prepared to extend administrative concessions to other situations in shareholders agreements (see Document No. 2007-0243211C6; but see also Document No. 2010-0380571E5 re events beyond control the control of shareholders including fraud). See also 2009-0329941C6 where the CRA indicated that s. 251(5)(*b*) could include a situation where a capital beneficiary of a trust has an "absolute right" to eventually receive shares (and a partner has a right under a partnership agreement to receive shares on the dissolution of the partnership), but declined to opine for a shareholder who had 49% of the share with the power to determine who could acquire the remaining 51%. A number of ITA provisions based on related-person status exclude rights under s. 251(5)(*b*). S. 110.6(14)(*b*) ignores rights under a share purchase and sale agreement which might otherwise jeopardize the availability of the capital gains exemption. S. 256(8) may treat such s. 251(5)(*b*) rights as exercised, if acquired to avoid/affect specified provisions.

Related Regulations: 1100(2.2); 1100(19); 1100(28); 1101(1ad); 1102(1); 1102(14); 1102(14.1); 5202; 6204(3).

Related Sections: S. 13(25) Affiliation – subsection (24); s. 13(30) Transfers of property; s. 13(31) Transfers of property — continuity of ownership; s. 17(11.1) Determination of whether persons related; s. 17(11.3) Determination of whether persons related; s. 17(13) Extended definition of controlled foreign affiliate; s. 37(1.1) Business of related corporations; s. 53(5)(*c*) Recomputation of adjusted cost base on other transfer; s. 55(5)(*e*)(iv) Applicable rules; s. 56.4(1), "eligible corporation"; s. 56.4(3) Non-application of subsection (2); s. 56.4(8)(*a*) Application of subsection (7) and section 69 — special rules; s. 66(11.5)(*b*) Affiliation – subsection (24); s. 66(15), "principal business corporation"; s. 69(14)(*b*) New taxpayer; s. 80.01(6)(*a*)(ii) Specified obligation in relation to debt parking; s. 80.04(2) Eligible transferee; s. 83(2.4) Capital dividend — exception to anti-avoidance rule; s. 85(1.2)(*a*) Application of subsection (1); s. 85.1(2)(*a*) Where s. (1) does not apply; s. 85.1(6)(*a*) Where subsection (5) does not apply; s. 88(1)(*d.4*) Winding-up; s. 89(1), "designated property"; s. 94.1(1), "exempt property", "investment property", "significant interest"; s. 95(1), "investment business", "investment property"; s. 95(2) Determination of certain components of foreign accrual property income; s. 110.6(14)(*b*) Related persons, etc; s. 112(2.21) Exceptions; s. 112(2.4)(*b*) Where no deduction permitted; s. 125(7), "Canadian-controlled private corporation"; s. 142.2(2)(*a*) Significant interest; s. 142.2(3)(*a*) Rules re significant interest; s. 149.1(1), "relevant person"; s. 181.5(6) Government-controlled corporation; s. 186(4)(*a*) Corporations connected with particular corporation; s. 190.15(6) Government-controlled corporation; s. 191(2) Substantial interest; s. 191(3) Substantial interest — anti-avoidance rule; s. 191.3(1) Agreement respecting liability for tax; s. 212.1(1) Non-arm's length sales of shares by non-residents; s. 248(1), "short-term preferred share"; s. 251(2) Definition of "related persons"; s. 256(6) Saving provision — controlled corporations; s. 256(6.1) Simultaneous control; s. 256(7) Acquiring control; s. 256(8) Deemed exercise of right.

Canadian Tax Foundation: Cepparo, *Letter of Intent Causes Loss of CCPC Status?*, 2015 Canadian Tax Highlights 23(11):7.

STEP Canada: Mark Chartrand and Bryan McNulty, "Shareholders' Agreements: The Hard Stuff," PowerPoint presentation to the 15th National Conference of STEP Canada, Toronto, June 10-11, 2013.

Tax Profile: January 2010 — Shareholders' Agreements — A Survey of Income Tax Issues; April 2006 — Concept of Control.

Tax Topics: No. 2075, 2011 Canadian Tax Foundation Roundtable; No. 1867-68, 2007 Canadian Tax Foundation Annual Conference CRA Round Table; No. 1692, Income Tax Implications of Buy-Sell Provisions; No. 1650, Family Shareholders' Agreements - Succession Planning's Missing Link?.

Income Tax Folios: *Primary* — S1-F5-C1 Related Persons and Dealing at Arm's Length.

Secondary — S3-F8-C1 Principal-business Corporations in the Resource Industries.

Income Tax Technical News: Issue No. 38, Canadian Controlled Private Corporation (CCPC) Determination — Impact of the Sedona Decision; Issue No. 38, Paragraph 251(5)(b) — Conditional Agreements.

Information Circulars: IC 72-25R4 Business equity valuations; IC 89-3 Policy statement on business equity valuations.

Interpretation Bulletins: *Secondary* — IT-64R4 (Consolid.) Corporations: Association and control; IT-302R3 Losses of a corporation — The effect on their deductibility of changes in control, amalgamation and winding-up; IT-458R2 Canadian-controlled private corporation.

Tax Window Files: Application de 251(5)(b)(ii) et 256(1.4)(b), *March 16, 2011*, CRA Document No. 2010-0380571E5; 251(5)(b) and 256(1.4), *October 9, 2009*, CRA Document No. 2009-0329941C6.

Cases: The taxpayer corporation argued that options to acquire shares in a corporation, if exercised, would have been contrary to the provisions of a certain provincial statute. The Court rejected the taxpayer's argument that, since paragraph 251(5)(*b*) deemed the options to be exercised, the options were void such that the corporation could qualify as a Canadian-controlled private corporation. *Line Durocher v. The Queen*, 2017 DTC 5050 (FCA)

Although the majority of its voting shares were held by non-residents, a corporation was a CCPC since a unanimous shareholder agreement prevented the non-resident shareholders from electing a majority of the board of directors, thereby giving *de jure* control to the Canadian shareholders. *The Queen v. Price Waterhouse Coopers Inc.*, 2013 DTC 5123 (F.C.A.), affirming 2013 DTC 1048 (T.C.C.)

Sedona Networks Corporation v. The Queen, 2007 DTC 5359 addresses the situation where rights are held by a number of persons, indicating that paragraph 251(5)(*b*) "is directed at the concept of ownership, not control ... [and that if paragraph 251(5)(*b*) is applicable to a person who has treasury share options] ... it is necessary to assume that the option is exercised and the related shares are actually acquired by" the option holder [paragraph 27]. This statement is not consistent with the CRA's pre-existing position, which is that, while the "fully diluted" approach is used in respect of subsection 256(1.4), it is not used for the purposes of paragraph 251(5)(*b*): in that case, "the determination of the control of a corporation must be determined person by person" ignoring rights of others (see, for example, Doc. No. 2004-008676). At the Round Table presented at the 2007 Canadian Tax Foundation Annual Conference, the CRA indicated that it does not believe that *Sedona* precludes it from applying its pre-existing position. See also 2011 RCRT Q. 2 (Status of CCPC — options held by non-residents).

► 251(6) ◄

(6) Blood relationship, etc. For the purposes of this Act, persons are connected by

(*a*) blood relationship if one is the child or other descendant of the other or one is the brother or sister of the other;

(*b*) marriage if one is married to the other or to a person who is so connected by blood relationship to the other;

(*b*.1) common-law partnership if one is in a common-law partnership with the other or with a person who is connected by blood relationship to the other; and

(*c*) adoption if one has been adopted, either legally or in fact, as the child of the other or as the child of a person who is so connected by blood relationship (otherwise than as a brother or sister) to the other.

Related Sections: S. 8(1)(*e*) Expenses of railway employees; s. 118.2(2) Medical expenses; s. 146.1(2) Conditions for registration; s. 204.9(4) New beneficiary; s. 248(1), "corporation", "individual", "share", "shareholder"; s. 256(6.1) Simultaneous control.

Canadian Tax Foundation: Cepparo, *Stepbrothers Blood-Related*, 2016 Canadian Tax Highlights 24(3):9.

Income Tax Folios: *Secondary*— S1-F3-C1 Child Care Expense Deduction; *Primary*— S1-F5-C1 Related Persons and Dealing at Arm's Length.

Tax Window Files: Half-brothers and related persons, *July 12, 2018*, CRA Document No. 2018-0755471E5.

SECTION 251.1: Definition of "affiliated persons"

► 251.1(1) ◄

(1) Definition of "affiliated persons". For the purposes of this Act, "affiliated persons", or persons affiliated with each other, are

(*a*) an individual and a spouse or common-law partner of the individual;

(*b*) a corporation and

(i) a person by whom the corporation is controlled,

(ii) each member of an affiliated group of persons by which the corporation is controlled, and

(iii) a spouse or common-law partner of a person described in subparagraph (i) or (ii);

(*c*) two corporations, if

(i) each corporation is controlled by a person, and the person by whom one corporation is controlled is affiliated with the person by whom the other corporation is controlled,

(ii) one corporation is controlled by a person, the other corporation is controlled by a group of persons, and each member of that group is affiliated with that person, or

(iii) each corporation is controlled by a group of persons, and each member of each group is affiliated with at least one member of the other group;

(*d*) a corporation and a partnership, if the corporation is controlled by a particular group of persons each member of which is affiliated with at least one member of a majority-interest group of partners of the partnership, and each member of that majority-interest group is affiliated with at least one member of the particular group;

(*e*) a partnership and a majority-interest partner of the partnership;

(*f*) two partnerships, if

(i) the same person is a majority-interest partner of both partnerships,

(ii) a majority-interest partner of one partnership is affiliated with each member of a majority-interest group of partners of the other partnership, or

(iii) each member of a majority-interest group of partners of each partnership is affiliated with at least one member of a majority-interest group of partners of the other partnership;

(*g*) a person and a trust, if the person

(i) is a majority-interest beneficiary of the trust, or

(ii) would, if this subsection were read without reference to this paragraph, be affiliated with a majority-interest beneficiary of the trust; and

(*h*) two trusts, if a contributor to one of the trusts is affiliated with a contributor to the other trust and

(i) a majority-interest beneficiary of one of the trusts is affiliated with a majority-interest beneficiary of the other trust,

(ii) a majority-interest beneficiary of one of the trusts is affiliated with each member of a majority-interest group of beneficiaries of the other trust, or

(iii) each member of a majority-interest group of beneficiaries of each of the trusts is affiliated with at least one member of a majority-interest group of beneficiaries of the other trust.

Editorial Note: The concept of an "affiliated person" was introduced into the Act in 1995 primarily in support of a number of anti-avoidance provisions, most of which deal with "stop-losses". Apparently, the Department of Finance determined that the application of these anti-avoidance provisions required a concept that in some ways would be more focused than the existing arm's length and related concepts (only a person and the person's spouse can be affiliated to one another) and in some cases broader than these concepts (e.g., the concept of control used in the definition is *de facto* control; see s. 251.1(3) and 256(5.1)). Detailed rules are provided as to when persons, corporations, partnerships and trusts (see the editorial note for the definition of "majority-interest beneficiary" below) will be affiliated with one another.

History: S. 251.1(1)(*e*) was replaced by S.C. 2013, c. 40, s. 91(1), in force December 12, 2013, and formerly read:

(*e*) a partnership and a majority interest partner of the partnership;

Related Sections: S. 13(21.2) Loss on certain transfers; s. 13(24) Loss restriction event; s. 14(12) Loss on certain transfers; 18(13) When s. (15) applies to money lenders; 18(14) When s. (15) applies to adventurers in trade; 18(15) Loss on certain properties; s. 18.1(8) Non-arm's length disposition s. 18.1(10) Amount of deduction if non-arm's length disposition; s. 20.01(2) Limit; s. 40(3.3) When subsection (3.4) applies; s. 40(3.4) Loss on certain properties; s. 40(3.5) Deemed identical property; s. 40(3.6) Loss on shares; s. 40(3.61) Exception — estate loss carried back; s. 54(1), "superficial loss; s. 66(11.4) Loss restriction event; s. 66(11.5) Affiliation – subsection (24); s. 69(11) Acquisition of control; s. 69(14) New taxpayer; s. 73(1) Inter vivos transfers by individuals; s. 84(2) Distribution on winding-up, etc; s. 84(3) Redemption, etc; s. 84(9) Shares disposed of on redemptions, etc; s. 84.1(1) Non-arm's length sale of shares; s. 107(6) Loss reduction; s. 115.2 Definitions; s. 118.1(18) Non-qualifying security defined; s. 122.1(1) Definitions; s. 248(1), "majority interest partner"; s. 251(2) Definition of "related persons"; s. 251(3) Corporations related through a third corporation; s. 251(3.1) Relation where amalgamation or merger; s. 251(3.2) Amalgamation of related corporations; s. 251(4) Definitions concerning groups; s. 256(5.1) Control in fact.

Canadian Tax Foundation: Dueck and Daniels, *Update and Review of the Related, Affiliated, and Associated Rules: Overlaps, Differences, and Their Significance*, 2014 British Columbia Tax Conference 10:1–77; Micallef, *"Associated", "Affiliated", and "Related" Transactions, Part 2: The Practical Applications of the Terms*, 2005 Conference Report 39:1–14; Diep, *"Associated", "Affiliated", and "Related" Transactions, Part 1: A Technical Overview*, 2005 Conference Report 38:1–12; Ireland, *The New Trust Affiliation Rule*, 2005 Prairie Provinces Tax Conference 8:1–15.

Tax Profile: September 2004 — Review of Tax Implications of Corporate-Owned Life Insurance Buy-Sell Arrangements.

Tax Topics: No. 2461-2462, Part 3: Shareholders Agreements, the Act, and the Non-Specialist Advisor: The Impact of Control; No. 2460, Part 2: Shareholders Agreements, the Act, and the Non-Specialist Advisor: The Impact of Control; No. 2457, Part 1: Shareholders Agreements, the Act, and the Non-Specialist Advisor: The Impact of Control; No. 1692, Income Tax Implications of Buy-Sell Provisions.

Interpretation Bulletins: *Secondary* — IT-291R3 Transfer of property to a corporation under subsection 85(1).

Tax Window Files: Superficial Loss, *January 22, 2009*, CRA Document No. 2008-0299661E5; Majority-interest Beneficiaries of an Estate, *2006 STEP Conference — Question 15, September 11, 2006*, CRA Document No. 2006-0185581C6; Affiliation of Unadministered Estate With Others, *Technical Interpretation, International & Trusts Division, March 30, 2006*, CRA Document No. 2004-0105471E5.

► 251.1(2) ◄

(2) Affiliation where amalgamation or merger. Where at any time 2 or more corporations (in this subsection referred to as the "predecessors") amalgamate or merge to form a new corporation, the new corporation and any predecessor are deemed to have been affiliated with each other where they would have been affiliated with each other immediately before that time if

(*a*) the new corporation had existed immediately before that time; and

(*b*) the persons who were the shareholders of the new corporation immediately after that time had been the shareholders of the new corporation immediately before that time.

Related Sections: S. 251(3.2) Amalgamation of related corporations.

► 251.1(3) ◄

(3) Definitions. The definitions in this subsection apply in this section.

"affiliated group of persons" —"affiliated group of persons" means a group of persons each member of which is affiliated with every other member.

"beneficiary" —"beneficiary", under a trust, includes a person beneficially interested in the trust.

"contributor" —"contributor", to a trust, means a person who has at any time made a loan or transfer of property, either directly or indirectly, in any manner whatever, to or for the benefit of the trust other than, if the person deals at arm's length with the trust at that time and is not immediately after that time a majority-interest beneficiary of the trust,

(*a*) a loan made at a reasonable rate of interest; or

(*b*) a transfer made for fair market value consideration.

"controlled" —"controlled" means controlled, directly or indirectly in any manner whatever.

"majority-interest beneficiary" —"majority-interest beneficiary", of a trust at any time, means a person whose interest as a beneficiary, if any, at that time

(*a*) in the income of the trust has, together with the interests as a beneficiary in the income of the trust of all persons with whom the person is affiliated, a fair market value that is greater than 50% of the fair market value of all the interests as a beneficiary in the income of the trust; or

(*b*) in the capital of the trust has, together with the interests as a beneficiary in the capital of the trust of all persons with whom the person is affiliated, a fair market value that is greater than 50% of the fair market value of all the interests as a beneficiary in the capital of the trust.

Editorial Note: A person and a trust will be affiliated pursuant to s. 251.1(1)(*g*) where the person is a majority-interest beneficiary of the trust or is affiliated with such a person. Similarly two trusts will be affiliated pursuant to s. 251.1(1)(*h*) where "contributors" are affiliated and where a majority-interest beneficiary of each trust, majority-interest beneficiary of one trust and a majority-interest group of beneficiaries of another trust or two majority-interest groups of beneficiaries are affiliated with one another. In addition, notwithstanding the level of detail in s. 251.1(1)(*g*) and 251.1(1)(*h*), these provisions are not intended to comprehensively deal with all situations involving the affiliated person rules and trusts. For example, a trust and a corporation that the trust controls will be considered to be affiliated pursuant to the general rules in s. 251.1(1)(*b*)(i). Otherwise, per s. 251.1(4)(*c*), the affiliated person rules ignore the identity of the trustees or executors of a trust or estate.

A beneficiary will be a majority-interest beneficiary at any particular time if the beneficiary together with all person's affiliated to the beneficiary hold either an income interest or a capital interest having a fair market value in excess of, respectively, 50% of the fair market value of all income interests in the trust or 50% of the fair market value of all capital interests in the trust. S. 251.1(4)(*d*)(i) deems discretionary powers to receive income or capital to be fully exercised in favour of each beneficiary of a trust. Consequently, in a garden variety discretionary *inter-vivos* trust each beneficiary will usually be deemed to be entitled to 100% of the income or capital of the trust and will be a majority-interest beneficiary of the trust affiliated with the trust. Since interests in estates tend to be fixed as opposed to discretionary, except where under the terms of a will a particular beneficiary receives a bequest that would cause the beneficiary to control a particular corporation, s. 256.1(4)(*d*)(i) will tend not to be as problematic in the estates arena.

Related Sections: S. 251.1(1)(*g*) and (*h*); s. 251.1(3), "majority interest group of beneficiaries; 251.1(4) Interpretation.

Tax Window Files: Majority-interest Beneficiaries of an Estate, *2006 STEP Conference — Question 15, September 11, 2006*, CRA Document No. 2006-0185581C6; Affiliation of Unadministered Estate With Others, *Technical Interpretation, International & Trusts Division, March 30, 2006*, CRA Document No. 2004-0105471E5.

"majority-interest group of beneficiaries" —"majority-interest group of beneficiaries", of a trust at any time, means a group of persons each of whom is a beneficiary under the trust at that time such that

(*a*) if one person held the interests as a beneficiary of all of the members of the group, that person would be a majority-interest beneficiary of the trust; and

(*b*) if any member of the group were not a member, the test described in paragraph (*a*) would not be met.

"majority-interest group of partners" —"majority-interest group of partners" of a partnership means a group of persons each of whom has an interest in the partnership such that

(*a*) if one person held the interests of all members of the group, that person would be a majority-interest partner of the partnership; and

(*b*) if any member of the group were not a member, the test described in paragraph (*a*) would not be met.

History: S. 251.1(3), paragraph (*a*) of the definition "majority-interest group of partners" was replaced by S.C. 2013, c. 40, s. 91(2), in force December 12, 2013, and formerly read:

(*a*) if one person held the interests of all members of the group, that person would be a majority interest partner of the partnership; and

► 251.1(4) ◄

(4) Interpretation. For the purposes of this section,

(*a*) persons are affiliated with themselves;

(*b*) a person includes a partnership;

(*c*) notwithstanding subsection 104(1), a reference to a trust does not include a reference to the trustee or other persons who own or control the trust property; and

(*d*) in determining whether a person is affiliated with a trust,

(i) if the amount of income or capital of the trust that a person may receive as a beneficiary under the trust depends on the exercise by any person of, or the failure by any person to exercise, a discretionary power, that person is deemed to have fully exercised, or to have failed to exercise, the power, as the case may be,

(ii) the interest of a person in a trust as a beneficiary is disregarded in determining whether the person deals at arm's length with the trust if the person would, in the absence of the interest as a beneficiary, be considered to deal at arm's length with the trust,

(iii) a trust is not a majority interest beneficiary of another trust unless the trust has an interest as a beneficiary in the income or capital, as the case may be, of the other trust, and

(iv) in determining whether a contributor to one trust is affiliated with a contributor to another trust, individuals connected by blood relationship, marriage, common-law partnership or adoption are deemed to be affiliated with one another.

History: S. 251.1(4)(*d*)(iv) was replaced by S.C. 2013, c. 40, s. 91(3), in force December 12, 2013, and formerly read:

(iv) in determining whether a contributor to one trust is affiliated with a contributor to another trust, individuals connected by blood, marriage, common-law partnership or adoption are deemed to be affiliated with one another.

SECTION 251.2: [Loss restriction events]

► 251.2(1) ◄

(1) Definitions. The following definitions apply in this section.

History: S. 251.2(1) was added by S.C. 2013, c. 40, s. 92(1), deemed to have come into force on March 21, 2013.

"beneficiary" —"beneficiary" has the same meaning as in subsection 251.1(3).

"equity" —"equity" has the same meaning as in subsection 122.1(1) read without reference to paragraph (*e*) of the definition "equity" in that subsection.

"equity value" —"equity value" has the same meaning as in subsection 122.1(1).

"fixed interest" —"fixed interest", at any time of a person in a trust, means an interest of the person as a beneficiary (in this definition, determined without reference to subsection 248(25)) under the trust provided that no amount of the income or capital of the trust to be distributed at any time in respect of any interest in the trust depends on the exercise by any person of, or the failure by any person to exercise, any discretionary power, other than a power in respect of which it is reasonable to conclude that

(*a*) the power is consistent with normal commercial practice;

(*b*) the power is consistent with terms that would be acceptable to the beneficiaries under the trust if the beneficiaries were dealing with each other at arm's length; and

(*c*) the exercise of, or failure to exercise, the power will not materially affect the value of an interest as a beneficiary under the trust relative to the value of other such interests under the trust.

History: S. 251.2(1), the definition "fixed interest" was added by S.C. 2014, c. 39, s. 75(1), deemed to have come into force on March 21, 2013, except that if a trust elects in writing and files the election with the Minister of National Revenue on or before the trust's filing-due date for its last taxation year that ends before January 1, 2015, then the amendment is deemed to have come into force in respect of that trust on January 1, 2014.

"investment fund" —"investment fund", at any time, means a trust, if

(*a*) at all times throughout the period that begins at the later of March 21, 2013 and the end of the calendar year in which it is created and that ends at that time, the trust has a class of units outstanding that complies with the conditions prescribed for the purposes of paragraph 132(6)(*c*) determined without reference to paragraph 4801(*b*) of the *Income Tax Regulations;* and

(*b*) at all times throughout the period that begins at the later of March 21, 2013 and the time of its creation and that ends at that time, the trust

(i) is resident in Canada,

(ii) has no beneficiaries who may for any reason receive directly from the trust any of the income or capital of the trust, other than beneficiaries whose interests as beneficiaries under the trust are fixed interests described by reference to units of the trust,

(iii) follows a reasonable policy of investment diversification,

(iv) limits its undertaking to the investing of its funds in property,

(v) does not alone, or as a member of a group of persons, control a corporation, and

(vi) does not hold

(A) property that the trust, or a person with which the trust does not deal at arm's length, uses in carrying on a business,

(B) real or immovable property, an interest in real property or an immovable, or a real right in an immovable,

(C) Canadian resource property, foreign resource property, or an interest or right in Canadian resource property or foreign resource property, or

(D) more than 20% of the securities of any class of securities of a person (other than an investment fund or a mutual fund corporation that would meet the conditions in this paragraph, other than in subparagraph (ii), if it were a trust), unless at that time

(I) the securities (other than liabilities) of the person held by the trust have a total fair market value that is no more than 10% of the equity value of the person, and

(II) the liabilities of the person held by the trust have a total fair market value that is no more than 10% of the fair market value of all of the liabilities of the person.

History: S. 251.2(1), the definition "investment fund" was replaced by S.C. 2016, c. 12, s. 65(2), deemed to have come into force on March 21, 2013, except that

(a) if a trust elects in writing to have paragraph 251.2(3)(*f*) apply as of the first day of the trust's 2014 taxation year and files the election with the Minister of National Revenue on or before the trust's filing-due date for its last 2014 taxation year, then this amendment is deemed to have come into force in respect of that trust on the first day of the trust's first 2014 taxation year;

(b) if a trust elects in writing to have paragraph 251.2(3)(*f*) apply as of the first day of the trust's 2015 taxation year and files the election with the Minister of National Revenue on or before the trust's filing-due date for its last 2014 taxation year, then this amendment is deemed to have come into force in respect of that trust on the first day of the trust's first 2015 taxation year; and

(c) in applying paragraph (*a*) of the definition "investment fund" to a trust created before 2016, the expression "and the end of the calendar year" is to be read as "and 90 days after the end of the calendar year".

S. 251.2(1), the definition "investment fund" formerly read:

"investment fund"—"investment fund", at any time, means a trust that

(*a*) is at that time a portfolio investment fund; and

(*b*) is, at all times throughout the period that begins at the later of March 21, 2013 and the time of its creation and that ends at that time,

(i) a mutual fund trust, or

(ii) a trust

(A) that would be a mutual fund trust if section 4801 of the *Income Tax Regulations* were read without reference to its paragraph (*b*), and

(B) if the only beneficiaries who may for any reason receive directly from the trust any of the income or capital of the trust are beneficiaries whose interests as beneficiaries under the trust are fixed interests.

S. 251.2(1), the definition "investment fund" was added by S.C. 2014, c. 39, s. 75(1), deemed to have come into force on March 21, 2013, except that if a trust elects in writing and files the election with the Minister of National Revenue on or before the trust's filing-due date for its last taxation year that ends before January 1, 2015, then the amendment is deemed to have come into force in respect of that trust on January 1, 2014.

"majority-interest beneficiary" —"majority-interest beneficiary" has the same meaning as in subsection 251.1(3) read without reference to the expression ", if any," in the definition "majority-interest beneficiary" in that subsection.

History: S. 251.2(1), the definition "majority-interest beneficiary" was replaced by S.C. 2016, c. 12, s. 65(2), deemed to have come into force on March 21, 2013, except that:

(a) if a trust elects in writing to have paragraph 251.2(3)(*f*) apply as of the first day of the trust's 2014 taxation year and files the election with the Minister of National Revenue on or before the trust's filing-due date for its last 2014 taxation year, then this amendment is deemed to have come into force in respect of that trust on the first day of the trust's first 2014 taxation year; and

(b) if a trust elects in writing to have paragraph 251.2(3)(*f*) apply as of the first day of the trust's 2015 taxation year and files the election with the Minister of National Revenue on or before the trust's filing-due date for its last 2014 taxation year, then this amendment is deemed to have come into force in respect of that trust on the first day of the trust's first 2015 taxation year.

S. 251.2(1), the definition "majority-interest beneficiary" formerly read:

"majority-interest beneficiary"—"majority-interest beneficiary" has the same meaning as in subsection 251.1(3).

"majority-interest group of beneficiaries" —"majority-interest group of beneficiaries" has the same meaning as in subsection 251.1(3).

"majority-interest group of partners" —"majority-interest group of partners" has the same meaning as in subsection 251.1(3).

"person" —"person" includes a partnership.

"portfolio investment fund" — (Repealed by S.C. 2016, c. 12, s. 65(1).)

History: S. 251.2(1), the definition "portfolio investment fund" was repealed by S.C. 2016, c. 12, s. 65(1), deemed to have come into force on March 21, 2013, except that:

(a) if a trust elects in writing to have paragraph 251.2(3)(*f*) apply as of the first day of the trust's 2014 taxation year and files the election with the Minister of National Revenue on or before the trust's filing-due date for its last 2014 taxation year, then this amendment is deemed to have come into force in respect of that trust on the first day of the trust's first 2014 taxation year; and

(b) if a trust elects in writing to have paragraph 251.2(3)(*f*) apply as of the first day of the trust's 2015 taxation year and files the election with the Minister of National Revenue on or before the trust's filing-due date for its last 2014 taxation year, then this amendment is deemed to have come into force in respect of that trust on the first day of the trust's first 2015 taxation year.

S. 251.2(1), the definition "portfolio investment fund" formerly read:

"portfolio investment fund"—"portfolio investment fund", at any time, means an entity that at that time would be a portfolio investment entity as defined in subsection 122.1(1) if

(*a*) the references to "subject entity" in paragraph (a) of the definition "non-portfolio property" in subsection 122.1(1) were read as references to "entity";

(*b*) the definition "Canadian real, immovable or resource property" in subsection 248(1) were read as though

(i) its paragraph (*a*) were read without reference to "situated in Canada",

(ii) its paragraph (*b*) were read as "a Canadian resource property or a foreign resource property", and

(iii) "timber resource property" in paragraph (*c*) were defined as extending to rights in respect of property outside Canada; and

(*c*) paragraph (*c*) of the definition "non-portfolio property" in subsection 122.1(1) were read without reference to "in Canada".

S. 251.2(1), the definition "portfolio investment fund" was added by S.C. 2014, c. 39, s. 75(1), deemed to have come into force on March 21, 2013, except that if a trust elects in writing and files the election with the Minister of National Revenue on or before the trust's filing-due date for its last taxation year that ends before January 1, 2015, then the amendment is deemed to have come into force in respect of that trust on January 1, 2014.

"specified right" —"specified right", held at any time by a person in respect of a trust, means a right under a contract, in equity or otherwise, to acquire, either immediately or in the future and either absolutely or contingently, equity of the trust, or to cause the trust to redeem or cancel equity of the trust, unless the right is not exercisable at that time because its exercise is contingent on the death, bankruptcy or permanent disability of an individual.

"subsidiary" —"subsidiary", of a particular person at any time, means a corporation, partnership or trust (in this definition referred to as the "subject entity") where

(*a*) the particular person holds at that time property

(i) that is equity of the subject entity, or

(ii) that derives all or part of its fair market value, directly or indirectly, from equity of the subject entity; and

(*b*) the total of the following amounts is at that time equal to more than 50% of the equity value of the subject entity:

(i) each amount that is the fair market value at that time of equity of the subject entity that is held at that time by the particular person or a person with whom the particular person is affiliated, and

(ii) each amount (other than an amount described in subparagraph (i)) that is the portion of the fair market value at that time — derived directly or indirectly from equity of the subject entity — of a property that is held at that time by the particular person or a person with whom the particular person is affiliated.

► 251.2(2) ◄

(2) Loss restriction event. For the purposes of this Act, a taxpayer is at any time subject to a loss restriction event if

(*a*) the taxpayer is a corporation and at that time control of the corporation is acquired by a person or group of persons; or

(*b*) the taxpayer is a trust and

(i) that time is after March 20, 2013 and after the time at which the trust is created, and

(ii) at that time a person becomes a majority-interest beneficiary, or a group of persons becomes a majority-interest group of beneficiaries, of the trust.

Editorial Note: Various loss restriction rules under the Act prevent the utilization of losses and other tax attributes upon a change of control of a corporation. For example, upon the acquisition of control of a corporation, many provisions deny or restrict the utilization of certain pre-acquisition-of-control losses, credits, deductions, and similar amounts in the period after the acquisition of control. The taxation year of the corporation has a deemed taxation year end immediately before the acquisition of control. The denied or restricted amounts include pools such as net capital and non-capital losses, eligible capital expenditures, resource-related exploration and development expenditures, scientific research and experimental development expenditures, and investment tax credits. Certain streaming rules allow some amounts such as non-capital losses to be utilized after the acquisition of control, as long as the corporation continues to carry on the same or similar business.

Until 251.2 was introduced, there were no such rules in the Act dealing with the acquisition of control or similar event of a trust. Basically, under new section 251.2, a trust will be subject to various acquisition of control provisions that have applied to corporations noted above. The triggering event for the application of the provisions, termed a "loss restriction event" of the trust, will occur at any time at which a person becomes a majority-interest beneficiary or a group of persons becomes a majority-interest group of beneficiaries of the trust. The "majority-interest" condition is generally met if the person or group has an interest or interests in the income of the trust whose value is more than 50% of the value of all the interests in the income of the trust, or an interest or interests in the trust whose value is more than 50% of all of the interests in the capital of the trust.

History: S. 251.2(2) was added by S.C. 2013, c. 40, s. 92(1), deemed to have come into force on March 21, 2013.

Related Sections: S. 111(4) Loss restriction event — capital losses; s. 111(5) Loss restriction event — non-capital losses and farm losses; s. 127(9.1) Loss restriction event before end of year; s. 127(9.2) Loss restriction event after end of year; s. 249(4) Loss restriction event — year end; s. 256(7) Acquiring control.

Canadian Tax Foundation: Kirby et al., *When Is A Loss a Loss and When Can You Claim a Loss?*, 2015 Prairie Provinces Tax Conference 11:1–37; Jiang, *Loss Restriction Events for the Family Trust*, 2015 Canadian Tax Highlights 23(1):6–7; Burghardt and Chiu, *"Loss" Is Just a Four-Letter Word: Policy, Practice, and Proposals*, 2013 Conference Report 14:1–43.

Tax Topics: No. 2461-2462, Part 3: Shareholders Agreements, the Act, and the Non-Specialist Advisor: The Impact of Control; No. 2460, Part 2: Shareholders Agreements, the Act, and the Non-Specialist Advisor: The Impact of Control; No. 2457, Part 1: Shareholders Agreements, the Act, and the Non-Specialist Advisor: The Impact of Control.

► 251.2(3) ◄

(3) Trusts — exceptions. For the purposes of paragraph (2)(*b*), a person is deemed not to become a majority-interest beneficiary, and a group of persons is deemed not to become a majority-interest group of beneficiaries, as the case may be, of a particular trust solely because of

(*a*) the acquisition of equity of the particular trust by

(i) a particular person from another person with whom the particular person was affiliated immediately before the acquisition,

(ii) a particular person who was affiliated with the particular trust immediately before the acquisition,

(iii) an estate from an individual, if the estate arose on and as a consequence of the death of the individual and the estate acquired the equity from the individual as a consequence of the death, or

(iv) a particular person from an estate that arose on and as a consequence of the death of an individual, if the estate acquired the equity from the individual as a consequence of the death and the individual was affiliated with the particular person immediately before the death;

(*b*) a variation in the terms of the particular trust, the satisfaction of, or failure to satisfy, a condition under the terms of the particular trust, the exercise by any person of, or the failure by any person to exercise, a power, or (without limiting the generality of the foregoing) the redemption, surrender or termination of equity of the particular trust at any time, if each majority-interest beneficiary, and each member of a majority-interest group of beneficiaries, of the particular trust immediately after that time was affiliated with the particular trust immediately before

(i) that time, or

(ii) in the case of the redemption or surrender of equity of the particular trust that was held, immediately before that time, by an estate and that was acquired by the estate from an individual as described in subparagraph (*a*)(iii), the individual's death;

(*c*) the transfer at any time of all the equity of the particular trust to a corporation, partnership or another trust (in this paragraph referred to as the "acquirer"), if

(i) the only consideration for the transfer is equity (determined without reference to paragraph (*d*) of the definition "equity" in subsection 122.1(1)) of the acquirer,

(ii) at all times before that time the acquirer held no property or held only property having a nominal value, and

(iii) immediately after that time the acquirer is neither

(A) a subsidiary of any person, nor

(B) a corporation controlled, directly or indirectly in any manner whatever, by a person or group of persons;

(*d*) the transfer at any time of equity of the particular trust to a corporation, partnership or another trust (in this paragraph referred to as the "acquirer"), if

(i) immediately before that time a person was a majority-interest beneficiary, or a group of persons was a majority-interest group of beneficiaries, of the particular trust,

(ii) immediately after that time the person, or group of persons, as the case may be, described in subparagraph (i) in respect of the particular trust, and no other person or group of persons, is

(A) if the acquirer is a corporation, a person by whom, or a group of persons by which, the corporation is controlled directly or indirectly in any manner whatever,

(B) if the acquirer is a partnership, a majority-interest partner, or a majority-interest group of partners, of the partnership, and

(C) if the acquirer is a trust, a majority-interest beneficiary, or a majority-interest group of beneficiaries, of the trust, and

(iii) at no time during a series of transactions or events that includes the transfer does the person or group of persons, as the case may be, described in subparagraph (i) in respect of the particular trust, cease to be a person or group of persons described in any of clauses (ii)(A) to (C) in respect of the acquirer;

(*e*) a transaction (other than a transaction one or more of the parties to which may be excused from completing as a result of changes to this Act) the parties to which are obligated to complete under the terms of an agreement in writing between the parties entered into before March 21, 2013; or

(*f*) the acquisition or disposition of equity of the particular trust at any time if

(i) the particular trust is an investment fund immediately before that time, and

(ii) the acquisition or disposition, as the case may be, is not part of a series of transactions or events that includes the particular trust ceasing to be an investment fund.

Editorial Note: Subsection 251.2(3) effectively provides various exceptions to the application of the loss restriction rules as they apply to trusts. Under the provision, a person is deemed not to become a majority-interest beneficiary of a trust, or a group of persons is deemed not to become a majority-interest group of beneficiaries of a trust, solely because of any of the transactions or events listed in paragraphs (*a*) through (*f*). If a person (or group of persons) does not becomes a majority-interest beneficiary (beneficiaries), paragraph 251.2(5)(*b*) does not apply, such that the loss restriction rules do not apply.

History: S. 251.2(3)(*f*) was replaced by S.C. 2016, c. 12, s. 65(3), deemed to have come into force on March 21, 2013, except that

(a) if a trust elects in writing to have paragraph 251.2(3)(*f*) apply as of the first day of the trust's 2014 taxation year and files the election with the Minister of National Revenue on or before the trust's filing-due date for its last 2014 taxation year, then this amendment is deemed to have come into force in respect of that trust on the first day of the trust's first 2014 taxation year; and

(b) if a trust elects in writing to have paragraph 251.2(3)(*f*) apply as of the first day of the trust's 2015 taxation year and files the election with the Minister of National Revenue on or before the trust's filing-due date for its last 2014 taxation year, then this amendment is deemed to have come into force in respect of that trust on the first day of the trust's first 2015 taxation year.

S. 251.2(3)(*f*) formerly read:

(*f*) the acquisition of equity of the particular trust by a person or group of persons if

(i) immediately before the acquisition, the particular trust is an investment fund, and

(ii) the acquisition is not part of a series of transactions or events that includes the particular trust becoming a portfolio investment fund, or ceasing to be an investment fund.

S. 251.2(3)(*f*) was added by S.C. 2014, c. 39, s. 75(2), deemed to have come into force on March 21, 2013, except that if a trust elects in writing and files the election with the Minister of National Revenue on or before the trust's filing-due date for its last taxation year that ends before January 1, 2015, then the amendment is deemed to have come into force in respect of that trust on January 1, 2014.

S. 251.2(3) was added by S.C. 2013, c. 40, s. 92(1), deemed to have come into force on March 21, 2013.

Related Sections: S. 122.1(1) Definitions; s. 248(10) Series of transactions; s. 251.1(1) Definition of "affiliated persons"; s. 256(5.1) Control in fact.

▶ 251.2(4) ◀

(4) Trusts — additional cases. For the purposes of paragraph (2)(*b*) and subject to subsection (3), a person is deemed to become at a particular time a majority-interest beneficiary of a particular trust if

(*a*) a particular person is at and immediately before the particular time a majority-interest beneficiary, or a member of a majority-interest group of beneficiaries, of the particular trust, and the particular person is at the particular time, but is not immediately before the particular time, a subsidiary of another person (in this paragraph referred to as the "acquirer"), unless

(i) the acquirer is immediately before the particular time affiliated with the particular trust, or

(ii) this paragraph previously applied to deem a person to become a majority-interest beneficiary of the particular trust because the particular person became, as part of a series of transactions or events that includes the particular person becoming at the particular time a subsidiary of the acquirer, a subsidiary of another person that is at the particular time a subsidiary of the acquirer; or

(*b*) at the particular time, as part of a series of transactions or events, two or more persons acquire equity of the particular trust in exchange for or upon a redemption or surrender of equity of, or as a consequence of a distribution from, a corporation, partnership or another trust, unless

(i) a person affiliated with the corporation, partnership or other trust was immediately before the particular time a majority-interest beneficiary of the particular trust,

(ii) if all the equity of the particular trust that was acquired at or before the particular time as part of the series were acquired by one person, the person would not at the particular time be a majority-interest beneficiary of the particular trust, or

(iii) this paragraph previously applied to deem a person to become a majority-interest beneficiary of the particular trust because of an acquisition of equity of the particular trust that was part of the series.

Editorial Note: See the note for subsection 251.2(3).

History: S. 251.2(4) was added by S.C. 2013, c. 40, s. 92(1), deemed to have come into force on March 21, 2013.

Related Sections: S. 122.1(1) Definitions; s. 248(10) Series of transactions; s. 256(7) Acquiring control.

► 251.2(5) ◄

(5) Trusts — special rules of application. For the purposes of this section,

(*a*) in determining whether persons are affiliated with each other

(i) except for the purposes of paragraph (*b*) of the definition "subsidiary" in subsection (1), section 251.1 is to be read without reference to the definition "controlled" in subsection 251.1(3),

(ii) in determining whether an individual (other than a trust) is affiliated with another individual (other than a trust), individuals connected by blood relationship, marriage or common-law partnership or adoption are deemed to be affiliated with one another, and

(iii) if, at any time as part of a series of transactions or events a person acquires equity of a corporation, partnership or trust, and it can reasonably be concluded that one of the reasons for the acquisition, or for making any agreement or undertaking in respect of the acquisition, is to cause a condition in paragraph (3)(*a*) or (*b*) or subparagraph (4)(*a*)(i) or (*b*)(i) regarding affiliation to be satisfied at a particular time, the condition is deemed not to be satisfied at the particular time;

(*b*) in determining whether a particular person becomes at any time a majority-interest beneficiary, or a particular group of persons becomes at any time a majority-interest group of beneficiaries, of a trust, the fair market value of each person's equity of the trust is to be determined at and immediately before that time

(i) without reference to the portion of that fair market value that is attributable to property acquired if it can reasonably be concluded that one of the reasons for the acquisition is to cause paragraph (2)(*b*), or any provision that applies by reference to a trust being subject to a loss restriction event at any time, not to apply,

(ii) without reference to the portion of that fair market value that is attributable to a change in the fair market value of all or part of any equity of the trust if it can reasonably be concluded that one of the reasons for the change is to cause paragraph (2)(*b*), or any provision that applies by reference to a trust being subject to a loss restriction event at any time, not to apply, and

(iii) as if each specified right held immediately before that time by the particular person, or by a member of the particular group, in respect of the trust is at that time exercised if it can reasonably be concluded that one of the reasons for the acquisition of the right is to cause paragraph (2)(*b*), or any provision that applies by reference to a trust being subject to a loss restriction event at any time, not to apply; and

(*c*) if, at any time as part of a series of transactions or events a person acquires a "security" (as defined in subsection 122.1(1)) and it can reasonably be concluded that one of the reasons for the acquisition, or for making any agreement or undertaking in respect of the acquisition, is to cause a condition in subparagraph (*b*)(v) or clause (*b*)(vi)(D) of the definition "investment fund" in subsection (1) to be satisfied at a particular time in respect of a trust, the condition is deemed not to be satisfied at the particular time in respect of the trust.

Editorial Note: For the purposes of s. 251.2, in determining whether an individual (other than a trust) is affiliated with another individual (other than a trust), individuals connected by blood relationship, marriage or common-law partnership, or adoption are deemed to be affiliated with one another (subparagraph 251.2(5)(*a*)(ii)). This expands the affiliated person concept that applies for other purposes, under which individuals (other than trusts) are considered to be affiliated with each other only if they are spouses or common-law partners, and an individual is considered to be affiliated with himself or herself. In terms of the affiliated person rules as they relate to corporations, control of the corporation does not generally include *de facto* control, as is usually the case under the affiliated person rules (subparagraph 251.2(5)(*a*)(i)).

Additionally, for the purposes of s. 251.2, where, at any time as part of a series of transactions or events, a person acquires equity of a corporation, partnership, or trust (shares or interests, as the case may be), and it can reasonably be concluded that one of the reasons for the acquisition, or for making any agreement or undertaking in respect of the acquisition, is to cause a condition in paragraph 3(*a*) or (*b*) or subparagraph 4(*a*)(i) or (*b*)(i) regarding affiliation to be satisfied, the condition is deemed not to be satisfied (subparagraph 251.2(5)(*a*)(iii))

History: S. 251.2(5)(*c*) was added by S.C. 2016, c. 12, s. 65(4), deemed to have come into force on March 21, 2013, except that:

(a) if a trust elects in writing to have paragraph 251.2(3)(*f*) apply as of the first day of the trust's 2014 taxation year and files the election with the Minister of National Revenue on or before the trust's filing-due date for its last 2014 taxation year, then this amendment is deemed to have come into force in respect of that trust on the first day of the trust's first 2014 taxation year; and

(b) if a trust elects in writing to have paragraph 251.2(3)(*f*) apply as of the first day of the trust's 2015 taxation year and files the election with the Minister of National Revenue on or before the trust's filing-due date for its last 2014 taxation year, then this amendment is deemed to have come into force in respect of that trust on the first day of the trust's first 2015 taxation year.

S. 251.2(5) was added by S.C. 2013, c. 40, s. 92(1), deemed to have come into force on March 21, 2013.

► 251.2(6) ◄

(6) Trusts — time of day. For the purposes of this Act, if a trust is subject to a loss restriction event at a particular time during a day, the trust is deemed to be subject to the loss restriction event at the beginning of that day and not at the particular time unless the trust elects in its return of income under Part I filed for its taxation year that ends immediately before the loss restriction event to have this subsection not apply.

Editorial Note: A similar rule to that in subsection 251.2(6) is found in subsection 256(9); it applies to a corporation the control of which has been acquired.

History: S. 251.2(6) was added by S.C. 2013, c. 40, s. 92(1), deemed to have come into force on March 21, 2013.

Related Regulations: 600.

▶ 251.2(7) ◀

(7) Filing and other deadlines. If at any time a trust is subject to a loss restriction event, in respect of the trust for its taxation year that ends immediately before that time,

(*a*) the reference in paragraph 132(2.1)(*a*) to "the day that is 90 days after the end of the year" is to be read as "the balance-due day of the trust for the year";

(*b*) the reference in subsection 132(6.1) to "before the 91st day after the end of is to be read as "on or before the balance-due day of the trust for";

(*c*) the reference in paragraph 150(1)(*c*) to "within 90 days from the end of is to be read as "on or before the balance-due day of the trust for";

(*d*) the reference in subsection 204.7(1) to "Within 90 days from the end of each taxation year commencing after 1980" is to be read as "On or before the balance-due day of the trust for each taxation year";

(*e*) the reference in subsection 210.2(5), and in subsection 221(2) of the *Income Tax Regulations*, to "within 90 days after the end of is to be read as "on or before the balance-due day of the trust for"; and

(*f*) the references in subsections 202(8) and 204(2) of the *Income Tax Regulations* to "within 90 days from the end of are to be read as "on or before the balance-due day of the trust for".

Editorial Note: Where a trust undergoes a loss restriction event (LRT) at a particular time, the taxation year that includes that time is deemed to end immediately before that time (pre-LRT year), and a deemed new taxation year that begins at that time. Basically, subsection 251.2(7) provides that the filing deadline in respect of certain filing requirements for the pre-LRT year is 90 days after the calendar year in which the pre-LRT ends.

History: S. 251.2(7) was replaced by S.C. 2016, c. 12, s. 65(5), deemed to have come into force on March 21, 2013, and formerly read:

(7) *Timing of filing.* If a trust is subject to a loss restriction event in a taxation year, subsection 249(4) does not apply to end the year for the purpose of this subsection or to determine the end of that year in applying subsection 132(6.1), paragraph 150(1)(*c*), paragraph (a) of the definition "balance-due day" in subsection 248(1) and subsection 204(2) of the *Income Tax Regulations* to the trust in respect of the year.

S. 251.2(7) was added by S.C. 2014, c. 39, s. 75(3), deemed to have come into force on March 21, 2013, except that if a trust elects in writing and files the election with the Minister of National Revenue on or before the trust's filing-due date for its last taxation year that ends before January 1, 2015, then the amendment is deemed to have come into force in respect of that trust on January 1, 2014.

SECTION 252: Extended meaning of "child"

▶ 252(1) ◀

(1) Extended meaning of "child". In this Act, words referring to a child of a taxpayer include

(*a*) a person of whom the taxpayer is the legal parent;

(*b*) a person who is wholly dependent on the taxpayer for support and of whom the taxpayer has, or immediately before the person attained the age of 19 years had, in law or in fact, the custody and control;

(*c*) a child of the taxpayer's spouse or common-law partner; and

(*d*) (Repealed.)

(*e*) a spouse or common-law partner of a child of the taxpayer.

Related Sections: S. 63(3), "eligible child"; s. 248(1), "common-law partner".

Income Tax Folios: *Secondary*— S1-F2-C2 Tuition Tax Credit; S1-F3-C1 Child Care Expense Deduction; *Primary*— S1-F5-C1 Related Persons and Dealing at Arm's Length.

Interpretation Bulletins: *Secondary* — IT-268R4 Inter vivos transfer of farm property to child; IT-349R3 Intergenerational transfers of farm property on death; IT-394R2 Preferred beneficiary election.

▶ 252(2) ◀

(2) Relationships. In this Act, words referring to

(*a*) a parent of a taxpayer include a person

(i) whose child the taxpayer is,

(ii) whose child the taxpayer had previously been within the meaning of paragraph (1)(*b*), or

(iii) who is a parent of the taxpayer's spouse or common-law partner;

(*b*) a brother of a taxpayer include a person who is

(i) the brother of the taxpayer's spouse or common-law partner, or

(ii) the spouse or common-law partner of the taxpayer's sister;

(*c*) a sister of a taxpayer include a person who is

(i) the sister of the taxpayer's spouse or common-law partner, or

(ii) the spouse or common-law partner of the taxpayer's brother;

(*d*) a grandparent of a taxpayer include a person who is

(i) the grandfather or grandmother of the taxpayer's spouse or common-law partner, or

(ii) the spouse or common-law partner of the taxpayer's grandfather or grandmother;

(*e*) an aunt or uncle of a taxpayer include the spouse or common-law partner of the taxpayer's aunt or uncle, as the case may be;

(*f*) a great-aunt or great-uncle of a taxpayer include the spouse or common-law partner of the taxpayer's great-aunt or great-uncle, as the case may be; and

(*g*) a niece or nephew of a taxpayer include the niece or nephew, as the case may be, of the taxpayer's spouse or common-law partner.

Related Sections: S. 248(1) Definitions.

Income Tax Folios: *Secondary*— S1-F2-C2 Tuition Tax Credit; S1-F3-C1 Child Care Expense Deduction; *Primary*— S1-F5-C1 Related Persons and Dealing at Arm's Length.

Interpretation Bulletins: *Secondary* — IT-349R3 Intergenerational transfers of farm property on death.

▶ 252(3) ◀

(3) Extended meaning of "spouse" and "former spouse". For the purposes of paragraph 56(1)(*b*), section 56.1, paragraphs 60(*b*) and (*j*), section 60.1, subsections 70(6) and (6.1), 73(1) and (5) and 104(4), (5.1) and (5.4), the definition "pre-1972 spousal trust" in subsection 108(1), subsection 146(16), the definition "survivor" in subsection 146.2(1), subparagraph 146.3(2)(*f*)(iv), subsections 146.3(14), 147(19) and 147.3(5) and (7), section 147.5, subsections 148(8.1) and (8.2), the definition "qualifying transfer" in subsection 207.01(1), and subsections 210(1) and 248(22) and (23), "spouse" and "former spouse" of a particular individual include another individual who is a party to a void or voidable marriage with the particular individual.

History: S. 252(3) was amended by S.C. 2013, c. 34, s. 362(1), by replacing "subparagraph 210(*c*)(ii) and subsections 248(22) and (23)" with "and subsections 210(1) and 248(22) and (23)", applicable to the 1996 and subsequent taxation years.

S. 252(3) was replaced by S.C. 2012, c. 31, s. 56(1), in force December 14, 2012. S. 252(3) formerly read:

(3) *Extended meaning of "spouse" and "former spouse".* For the purposes of paragraph 56(1)(*b*), section 56.1, paragraphs 60(*b*) and (*j*), section 60.1, subsections 70(6) and (6.1), 73(1) and (5) and 104(4), (5.1) and (5.4), the definition "pre-1972 spousal trust" in subsection 108(1), subsection 146(16), the definition "survivor" in subsection 146.2(1), subparagraph 146.3(2)(*f*)(iv), subsections 146.3(14), 147(19), 147.3(5) and (7) and 148(8.1) and (8.2), the definition "small business property" in subsection 206(1), the definition "qualifying transfer" in subsection 207.01(1), subparagraph 210(*c*)(ii) and subsections 248(22) and (23), "spouse" and "former spouse" of a particular individual include another individual who is a party to a void or voidable marriage with the particular individual.

Related Sections: S. 148(8.1) Inter vivos transfer to spouse; s. 148(8.2) Transfer to spouse at death; s. 248(22) Matrimonial regimes; s. 248(23) Dissolution of a matrimonial regime.

Interpretation Bulletins: *Secondary* — IT-307R4 Spousal registered retirement savings plans.

► 252(4) ◄

(4) Idem — (Repealed by S.C. 2000, c. 12, s. 141(2).)

Related Sections: S. 248(1), "individual".

Interpretation Bulletins: *Secondary* — IT-307R4 Spousal or common-law partner registered retirement savings plan; IT-313R2 Eligible capital property — Rules where a taxpayer has ceased carrying on a business or has died; IT-394R2 Preferred beneficiary election; IT-528 Transfers of funds between registered plans.

SECTION 252.1: Union employer

All the structural units of a trade union, including each local, branch, national and international unit, shall be deemed to be a single employer and a single entity for the purposes of the provisions of this Act and the regulations relating to

(*a*) pension adjustments and past service pension adjustments for years after 1994;

(*b*) the determination of whether a pension plan is, in a year after 1994, a multi-employer plan or a specified multi-employer plan (within the meanings assigned by subsection 147.1(1));

(*c*) the determination of whether a contribution made under a plan or arrangement is a resident's contribution (within the meaning assigned by subsection 207.6(5.1)); and

(*d*) the deduction or withholding and the remittance of any amount as required by subsection 153(1) in respect of a contribution made after 1991 under a retirement compensation arrangement.

Related Regulations: 8500(1); 8510(3).

Related Sections: S. 227(8) Penalty; s. 227(9) Penalty.

SECTION 253: Extended meaning of "carrying on business"

For the purposes of this Act, where in a taxation year a person who is a non-resident person or a trust to which Part XII.2 applies

(*a*) produces, grows, mines, creates, manufactures, fabricates, improves, packs, preserves or constructs, in whole or in part, anything in Canada whether or not the person exports that thing without selling it before exportation,

(*b*) solicits orders or offers anything for sale in Canada through an agent or servant, whether the contract or transaction is to be completed inside or outside Canada or partly in and partly outside Canada, or

(*c*) disposes of

(i) Canadian resource property, except where an amount in respect of the disposition is included under paragraph 66.2(1)(*a*) or 66.4(1)(*a*),

(ii) property (other than depreciable property) that is a timber resource property, an option in respect of a timber resource property or an interest in, or for civil law a right in, a timber resource property, or

(iii) property (other than capital property) that is real or immovable property situated in Canada, including an option in respect of such property or an interest in, or for civil law a real right in, such property, whether or not the property is in existence,

the person shall be deemed, in respect of the activity or disposition, to have been carrying on business in Canada in the year.

History: S. 253(*c*)(ii) and (iii) were replaced by S.C. 2013, c. 34, s. 168, in force June 26, 2013, and formerly read:

(ii) property (other than depreciable property) that is a timber resource property or an interest therein or option in respect thereof, or

(iii) property (other than capital property) that is real property situated in Canada, including an interest therein or option in respect thereof, whether or not the property is in existence,

Related Sections: S. 248(1), "business", "non-resident"; s. 255 Canada.

Tax Profile: January 2013 — Canadian Taxation of E-Commerce — An Overview; April 2011 — Canadian Tax Issues for Non-Resident Franchisors; June 2008 — International Tax Planning for the Owner-Manager; August 2007 — Professionals and Other Service Providers Beware — A Canadian Trap; August 2005 — Canada Revenue Agency's Recent Attack on U.S. Companies; August 2003 — Distributorships-A Canadian Perspective.

Interpretation Bulletins: *Secondary* — IT-420R3 Non-residents — Income earned in Canada.

Tax Window Files: Carrying on business in Canada and PE, *15XXXX*, CRA Document No. 2014-0542411R3; Permanent Establishment, *15XXXX*, CRA Document No. 2014-0550611R3.

Cases: An American insurance company was not carrying on business in Canada and all the matters which might suggest otherwise resulted solely from the requirements of the Superintendent of Insurance. *Capitol Life Insurance Company v. The Queen*, 86 DTC 6164 (F.C.A.), affirming 84 DTC 6087 (F.C.T.D.)

A non-resident taxpayer who merely accepted offers to participate in the money-lending activities of a resident broker was not carrying on business in Canada. *Pullman v. The Queen*, 83 DTC 5080 (F.C.T.D.)

SECTION 253.1: [Investments in limited partnerships]

► 253.1(1) ◄

(1) Investments in limited partnerships. For the purposes of subparagraph 108(2)(*b*)(ii), paragraphs 130.1(6)(*b*), 131(8)(*b*), 132(6)(*b*) and 146.1(2.1)(*c*), subsection 146.2(6), paragraph 146.4(5)(*b*), subsection 147.5(8), paragraph 149(1)(*o*.2), the definition "private holding corporation" in subsection 191(1), the definition "investment fund" in subsection 251.2(1) and regulations made for the purposes of paragraphs 149(1)(*o*.3) and (*o*.4), if a trust or corporation holds an interest as a member of a partnership and, by operation of any law governing the arrangement in respect of the partnership, the liability of the member as a member of the partnership is limited, the member shall not, solely because of its acquisition and holding of that interest, be considered to carry on any business or other activity of the partnership.

History: S. 253.1(1) was replaced by S.C. 2016, c. 12, s. 66(1), deemed to have come into force on March 21, 2013, and formerly read:

(1) *Investments in limited partnerships.* For the purposes of subparagraph 108(2)(*b*)(ii), paragraphs 130.1(6)(*b*), 131(8)(*b*), 132(6)(*b*) and 146.1(2.1)(*c*), subsection 146.2(6), paragraph 146.4(5)(*b*), subsection 147.5(8), paragraph 149(1)(*o.2*), the definition "private holding corporation" in subsection 191(1) and regulations made for the purposes of paragraphs 149(1)(*o.3*) and (*o.4*), if a trust or corporation holds an interest as a member of a partnership and, by operation of any law governing the arrangement in respect of the partnership, the liability of the member as a member of the partnership is limited, the member shall not, solely because of its acquisition and holding of that interest, be considered to carry on any business or other activity of the partnership.

S. 253.1 was renumbered as s. 253.1(1) by 2016, c. 7, s. 49(1), applicable in respect of investments in limited partnerships that are made or acquired after April 20, 2015.

S. 253.1 was replaced by S.C. 2013, c. 34, s. 426(5)(*a*), applicable on the first day on which the *Pooled Registered Pension Plans Act* [S.C. 2012, c. 16] is in force [December 14, 2012] and on which both the *Technical Amendments Act 2012* [S.C. 2013, c. 34] and the Jobs and Growth Act, 2012 [S.C. 2012, c. 31] have received royal assent [June 26, 2013]. S. 253.1 formerly read:

S. 253.1 *Investments in limited partnerships.* For the purposes of subparagraph 108(2)(*b*)(ii), paragraphs 130.1(6)(*b*), 131(8)(*b*), 132(6)(*b*) and 146.1(2.1)(*c*), subsection 146.2(6), paragraphs 146.4(5)(*b*) and 149(1)(*o.2*), the definition "private holding corporation" in subsection 191(1) and regulations made for the purposes of paragraphs 149(1)(*o.3*) and (*o.4*), if a trust or corporation holds an interest as a member of a partnership and, by operation of any law governing the arrangement in respect of the partnership, the liability of the member as a member of the partnership is limited, the member shall not, solely because of its acquisition and holding of that interest, be considered to carry on any business or other activity of the partnership.

S. 253.1 was replaced by S.C. 2013, c. 34, s. 363(1), deemed to have come into force on January 1, 1998, except that

(*a*) for taxation years that end after December 16, 1999 and before 2003, section 253.1 is to be read as follows:

S. 253.1 "For the purposes of subparagraph 108(2)(*b*)(ii), paragraphs 130.1(6)(*b*), 131(8)(*b*), 132(6)(*b*), 146.1(2.1)(*c*) and 149(1)(*o.2*), the definition "private holding corporation" in subsection 191(1) and regulations made for the purposes of paragraphs 149(1)(*o.3*) and (*o.4*), if a trust or corporation is a member of a partnership and, by operation of any law governing the arrangement in respect of the partnership, the liability of the member as a member of the partnership is limited, the member is deemed

(*a*) to undertake an investing of its funds because of its acquisition and holding of its interest as a member of the partnership; and

(*b*) not to carry on any business or other activity of the partnership."

(*b*) for taxation years that end after 2002 and before 2008, section 253.1 is to be read without reference to "146.4(5)(*b*)"; and

(*c*) for taxation years that end after 2002 and before 2009, section 253.1 is to be read without reference to "subsection 146.2(6), paragraphs".

S. 253.1 formerly read:

S. 253.1 *Investments in limited partnerships.* For the purposes of subparagraph 108(2)(*b*)(ii), paragraphs 130.1(6)(*b*), 131(8)(*b*) and 132(6)(*b*), subsection 146.2(4), paragraphs 146.4(5)(*b*) and 149(1)(*o.2*), the definition "private holding corporation" in subsection 191(1) and regulations made for the purposes of paragraphs 149(1)(*o.3*) and (*o.4*), if a trust or corporation holds an interest as a member of a partnership and, by operation of any law governing the arrangement in respect of the partnership, the liability of the member as a member of the partnership is limited, the member shall not, solely because of its acquisition and holding of that interest, be considered to carry on any business or other activity of the partnership.

S. 253.1 was replaced by S.C. 2012, c. 31, s. 57(1), in force December 14, 2012. However, this amendment was repealed and deemed never to have come into force by S.C. 2013, c. 34, s. 426(5)(*b*). S. 253.1, as it was replaced by S.C. 2012, c. 31, read as follows:

S. "253.1 *Investments in limited partnerships.* For the purposes of subparagraph 108(2)(*b*)(ii), paragraphs 130.1(6)(*b*), 131(8)(*b*) and 132(6)(*b*), subsection 146.2(6), paragraph 146.4(5)(*b*), subsection 147.5(8), paragraph 149(1)(*o.2*), the definition "private holding corporation" in subsection 191(1) and regulations made for the purposes of paragraphs 149(1)(*o.3*) and (*o.4*), if a trust or corporation holds an interest as a member of a partnership and, by operation of any law governing the arrangement in respect of the partnership, the liability of the member as a member of the partnership is limited, the member shall not, solely because of its acquisition and holding of that interest, be considered to carry on any business or other activity of the partnership."

S. 253.1, prior to amendments by S.C. 2012, c. 31 and 2013, c. 34, formerly read:

S. 253.1 *Investments in limited partnerships.* For the purposes of subparagraph 108(2)(*b*)(ii), paragraphs 130.1(6)(*b*), 131(8)(*b*) and 132(6)(*b*), subsection 146.2(4), paragraphs 146.4(5)(*b*) and 149(1)(*o.2*), the definition "private holding corporation" in subsection 191(1) and regulations made for the purposes of paragraphs 149(1)(*o.3*) and (*o.4*), if a trust or corporation holds an interest as a member of a partnership and, by operation of any law governing the arrangement in respect of the partnership, the liability of the member as a member of the partnership is limited, the member shall not, solely because of its acquisition and holding of that interest, be considered to carry on any business or other activity of the partnership.

S. 253.1 was replaced by S.C. 2009, c. 2, s. 77(1), applicable to the 2009 and subsequent taxation years. S. 253.1 formerly read:

S. 253.1 *Investments in limited partnerships.* For the purposes of subparagraph 108(2)(*b*)(ii), paragraphs 130.1(6)(*b*), 131(8)(*b*) and 132(6)(*b*), subsection 146.2(4), paragraphs 146.4(5)(*b*) and 149(1)(*o.2*), the definition "private holding corporation" in subsection 191(1) and regulations made for the purposes of paragraphs 149(1)(*o.3*) and (*o.4*), if a trust or corporation holds an interest as a member of a partnership and, by operation of any law governing the arrangement in respect of the partnership, the liability of the member as a member of the partnership is limited, the member shall not, solely because of its acquisition and holding of that interest, be considered to carry on any business or other activity of the partnership.

► 253.1(2) ◄

(2) Investments in limited partnerships. For the purposes of section 149.1 and subsections 188.1(1) and (2), if a registered charity or a registered Canadian amateur athletic association holds an interest as a member of a partnership, the member shall not, solely because of its acquisition and holding of that interest, be considered to carry on any business of the partnership if

Amendment not yet in force

Budget Implementation Act, 2019, No. 1 [S.C. 2019, c. 29]

S. 253.1(2), the portion before paragraph (*a*), is replaced by S.C. 2019, c. 29, s. 44(1), and will read as follows:

(2) Investments in limited partnerships. For the purposes of section 149.1 and subsections 188.1(1) and (2), if a registered charity, a registered Canadian amateur athletic association or a registered journalism organization holds an interest as a member of a partnership, the member shall not, solely because of its acquisition and holding of that interest, be considered to carry on any business of the partnership if

Applicable: In force on January 1, 2020.

(*a*) by operation of any law governing the arrangement in respect of the partnership, the liability of the member as a member of the partnership is limited;

(*b*) the member deals at arm's length with each general partner of the partnership; and

(*c*) the member, or the member together with persons and partnerships with which it does not deal at arm's length, holds interests in the partnership that have a fair market value of not more than 20% of the fair market value of the interests of all members in the partnership.

History: S. 253.1(2) was added by 2016, c. 7, s. 49(1), applicable in respect of investments in limited partnerships that are made or acquired after April 20, 2015.

Related Sections: 149.1(11) Partnership look-through rule.

SECTION 254: Contract under pension plan

Where a document has been issued or a contract has been entered into before July 31, 1997 purporting to create, to establish, to extinguish or to be in substitution for, a taxpayer's right to an amount or amounts, immediately or in the future, out of or under a superannuation or pension fund or plan,

(*a*) if the rights provided for in the document or contract are rights provided for by the superannuation or pension plan or are rights to a payment or payments out of the superannuation or pension fund, and the taxpayer acquired an interest under the document or in the contract before that day, any payment under the document or contract is deemed to be a payment out of or under the superannuation or pension fund or plan and the taxpayer is deemed not to have received, by the issuance of the document or entering into the contract, an amount out of or under the superannuation or pension fund or plan; and

(*b*) if the rights created or established by the document or contract are not rights provided for by the superannuation or pension plan or a right to payments out of the superannuation or pension fund, an amount equal to the value of the rights created or established by the document or contract shall be deemed to have been received by the taxpayer out of or under the superannuation or pension fund or plan when the document was issued or the contract was entered into.

Related Sections: S. 147.4 RPP annuity contract; s. 248(1), "amount".

Forms: T2037 — Notice of Purchase of Annuity with Plan Funds.

Information Circulars: IC 72-13R8 Employees' pension plans; IC 74-1R5 Form T2037, notice of purchase of annuity with "plan" funds.

Interpretation Bulletins: *Secondary* — IT-499R Superannuation or pension benefits.

SECTION 255: "Canada"

For the purposes of this Act, "Canada" is hereby declared to include and to have always included

(*a*) the sea bed and subsoil of the submarine areas adjacent to the coasts of Canada in respect of which the Government of Canada or of a province grants a right, licence or privilege to explore for, drill for or take any minerals, petroleum, natural gas or any related hydrocarbons; and

(*b*) the seas and airspace above the submarine areas referred to in paragraph (*a*) in respect of any activities carried on in connection with the exploration for or exploitation of the minerals, petroleum, natural gas or hydrocarbons referred to in that paragraph.

Canadian Petroleum Tax Journal: Offshore Oil & Gas Interests: A Perspective on Exploration & Development of Offshore Petroleum and Natural Gas Resources in Eastern Canada, Michael R. Smith, CA and B. David Nielsen, CA, 2000, Vol. 13, No. 1.

Interpretation Bulletins: *Secondary* — IT-494 Hire of ships and aircraft from non-residents.

Tax Window Files: Definition of "Outside Canada" - Water Boundaries, *July 18, 2013*, CRA Document No. 2013-0493081E5.

SECTION 256: Associated corporations

► 256(1) ◄

(1) Associated corporations. For the purposes of this Act, one corporation is associated with another in a taxation year if, at any time in the year,

(*a*) one of the corporations controlled, directly or indirectly in any manner whatever, the other;

(*b*) both of the corporations were controlled, directly or indirectly in any manner whatever, by the same person or group of persons;

(*c*) each of the corporations was controlled, directly or indirectly in any manner whatever, by a person and the person who so controlled one of the corporations was related to the person who so controlled the other, and either of those persons owned, in respect of each corporation, not less than 25% of the issued shares of any class, other than a specified class, of the capital stock thereof;

(*d*) one of the corporations was controlled, directly or indirectly in any manner whatever, by a person and that person was related to each member of a group of persons that so controlled the other corporation, and that person owned, in respect of the other corporation, not less than 25% of the issued shares of any class, other than a specified class, of the capital stock thereof; or

(*e*) each of the corporations was controlled, directly or indirectly in any manner whatever, by a related group and each of the members of one of the related groups was related to all of the members of the other related group, and one or more persons who were members of both related groups, either alone or together, owned, in respect of each corporation, not less than 25% of the issued shares of any class, other than a specified class, of the capital stock thereof.

Editorial Note: The primary purpose of the associated corporation rules is to restrict corporate groups that meet certain tests of common "control" set out in s. 256(1) from improperly accessing a number of specific tax incentives generally available to qualifying Canadian-controlled private corporations, such as the small business deduction in s. 125(1), and certain refundable and enhanced investment tax credits, such as those in ss. 127 and 127.1. For purposes of the associated corporation rules, the concept of control is broader than voting control (subject to certain expanded concepts in the case law, voting control is usually referred to as *de jure* control). It includes specific expanded concepts of control set out in s. 256(1.2) as well as a factual analysis of indirect factors that evidence control (referred to as *de facto* control). See, in particular, ss. 256(5.1)–(6.2).

Related Sections: S. 15.1(6) Disqualification; s. 15.1(7) Exception; s. 15.2(3) Definitions; s. 15.2(7) Deemed eligible issuer; s. 18(2.2) Base level deduction; s. 18(2.3) Associated corporations; s. 18(2.4) Failure to file agreement; s. 18(2.5) Special rules for base level deduction; s. 37(9.2) Associated corporations; s. 37(9.3) Agreement among associated corporations; s. 37(9.4) Filing; s. 37(9.5) Deemed corporation; s. 66(12.6011) Taxable capital amount; s. 66(12.6012) Taxable capital employed in Canada; s. 66(12.6013) Amalgamations and mergers; s. 66(12.602) Deemed non-renunciation of Canadian development expenses; s. 87(2)(*oo.1*) Refundable investment tax credit and balance-due day; s. 88(1) Winding-up; s. 125 Small business deduction; s. 126.1 Definitions; s. 127 [Investment tax credit, etc.]; s. 127.1 Refundable investment tax credit; s. 129(6) Investment income from associated corporation deemed to be active business income; s. 157(1.3) Taxable income — small-CCPC; s. 157(1.4) Taxable capital — small-CCPC; s. 181.5(7) Related corporations that are not associated; s. 191.1 Tax on taxable dividends; s. 248(1), "balance due day", "term preferred share"; 256(1.1) Definition of "specified class"; 256(1.2) Control, etc; 256(1.3) Parent deemed to own shares; 256(1.4) Options and rights; 256(1.5) Person related to himself, herself or itself; 256(1.6) Exception; 256(2) Corporations associated through a third corporation; 256(2.1) Anti-avoidance; 256(3) Saving provision; 256(4) Saving provision; 256(5) Idem; 256(5.1) Control in fact; 256(5.11) Factual control — interpretation; 256(6) Idem; 256(6.1) Simultaneous control.

Canadian Tax Foundation: Singh, *De Facto Control Broadened: More Than a Board of Directors Test*, 2015 Canadian Tax Focus 5(1):10–11; Truster, *Fees Charged to a Controlled Foreign Corporation*, 2015 Tax for the Owner-Manager 15(4):5; Micallef, *"Associated", "Affiliated", and "Related" Transactions, Part 2: The Practical Applications of the Terms*, 2005 Conference Report 39:1–14; Diep, *"Associated", "Affiliated", and "Related" Transactions, Part 1: A Technical Overview*, 2005 Conference Report 38:1–12; Couzin, *Some Reflections on Corporate Control*, 2005 Canadian Tax Journal 2:305–332; Prieur and Mayer, *Le fait et la théorie de l'influence*, 2005 Canadian Tax Journal 1:62–106; Finkelstein and Nixon, *Takeovers*, 2004 Conference Report 21:1–48; Smith, *De Facto Control: An Update*, 2004 Tax for the Owner-Manager 4(4):1–2; Kroft et al., *Legislative, Administrative, and Judicial Developments: Current Cases — Control in Fact*, 2003 Conference Report 9:1–5; Anderson, *Current Cases: The Tax Court of Canada — De Facto Control: The Franchise Exception Revisited (Lenester Sales Ltd. et al. v. The Queen, 2003 DTC 997)*, 2003 Canadian Tax Journal 6:2282–2286; Truster, *De Facto Control: Subsection 256(5.1)*, 2003 Tax for the Owner-Manager 3(3):2–3; McMahon, *Current Cases: Control In Fact*, 2002 British Columbia Tax Conference 6:14–22; Nightingale, *Selected Small Business Issues: De Facto Control*, 2002 Ontario Tax Conference 2:1–12; Marquette, *Selected Income Tax Issues of Particular Relevance to Shareholders Agreements: Part 1*, 2001 Canadian Tax Journal 1:182–208; Donnelly and Young, *The Associated Corporation Rules: Getting Tax Reduction Under "Control"*, 1998 Canadian Tax Journal 3:589–625.

Tax Topics: No. 2461-2462, Part 3: Shareholders Agreements, the Act, and the Non-Specialist Advisor: The Impact of Control; No. 2460, Part 2: Shareholders Agreements, the Act, and the Non-Specialist Advisor: The Impact of Control; No. 2457, Part 1: Shareholders Agreements, the Act, and the Non-Specialist Advisor: The Impact of Control; No. 1692, Income Tax Implications of Buy-Sell Provisions.

Forms: T2 SCH 9 — Related and Associated Corporations.

Interpretation Bulletins: *Primary* — IT-64R4 (Consolid.) Corporations: Association and control.

Tax Window Files: Expenditure Limit, *November 15, 2011*, CRA Document No. 2011-0423671E5; Associated corporations, Debt Forgiveness,*February 18, 2013*, CRA Document No. 2012-0439781E5; Small Business Deduction, *April 26, 2010*, CRA Document No. 2012-0467121E5.

Cases: Two corporations were under the *de facto* control of a third corporation, and hence associated with it. Relevant factors included economic dependency, operational control and familial connection amongst the shareholders of all three corporations. *De jure* and *de facto* control can co-exist. *9044-2807 Québec Inc. v. The Queen*, 2004 DTC 6141 (F.C.A.), affirming 2003 DTC 817 (T.C.C.)

One company held shares which gave it the right to wind-up the other company. It therefore controlled the other company, notwithstanding the fact that it only held 50% of the voting rights. *The Queen v. Imperial General Properties Ltd.*, 85 DTC 5500 (S.C.C.), reversing 83 DTC 5055 (F.C.A.), affirming 81 DTC 5191 (F.C.T.D.)

A group of shareholders was held to control several corporations because they had the right to authorize the surrender of the company's letters patent. These circumstances were sufficient to vest control in the group even though they only held 50% of the voting power. *Oakfield Developments (Toronto) Ltd. v. M.N.R.*, 71 DTC 5175 (S.C.C.), affirming 69 DTC 5175 (Ex. Ct.)

If a group of shareholders owns a majority of the voting shares of a company, and the same group owns a majority of the voting shares of a second company, that fact is sufficient to constitute the two companies associated. Moreover, in determining *de jure* control more than one group of persons can be aptly described as a "group of persons". It is immaterial whether other combinations of shareholders may own a majority of voting shares in either company. *Vina-Rug (Canada) Limited v. M.N.R.*, 68 DTC 5021 (S.C.C.), affirming 66 DTC 5373 (Ex. Ct)

Control means *de jure* control, and not *de facto*. The right of control rests in ownership of such a number of shares as carries with it the right to a majority of the votes in the election of the Board of Directors. The fact that a particular shareholder has a second or casting vote in the case of an equality of votes does not give that shareholder control of the company. *M.N.R. v. Dworkin Furs (Pembroke) Limited et al.*, 67 DTC 5035 (S.C.C.), affirming 65 DTC 5277 (Ex.Ct.), 66 DTC 5244 (Ex.Ct.), 66 DTC 5263 (Ex.Ct.) and 66 DTC 5303 (Ex.Ct.)

Where two individuals each owned half the shares of three companies either through personal holding or through ownership of two intermediary companies, the three companies were deemed controlled by the same group of persons. *Vineland Quarries and Crushed Stone Ltd. v. M.N.R.*, 67 DTC 5283 (S.C.C.), affirming 66 DTC 5092 (Ex. Ct.)

The word "controlled" contemplates the right of control that rests in ownership of such a number of shares as carries with it the right to a majority of the votes in the election of the Board of Directors. *Buckerfield's Limited v. M.N.R.*, 64 DTC 5301 (Ex. Ct.)

Note that although the common law concept of control as determined in these cases is applicable for the purposes of s. 256(1), the concept of control under s. 256(1) is actually broader than the common law concept, owing to the statutory rules in the remainder of s. 256

► 256(1.1) ◄

(1.1) Definition of "specified class". For the purposes of subsection (1), "specified class" means a class of shares of the capital stock of a corporation where, under the terms or conditions of the shares or any agreement in respect thereof,

(*a*) the shares are not convertible or exchangeable;

(*b*) the shares are non-voting;

(*c*) the amount of each dividend payable on the shares is calculated as a fixed amount or by reference to a fixed percentage of an amount equal to the fair market value of the consideration for which the shares were issued;

(*d*) the annual rate of the dividend on the shares, expressed as a percentage of an amount equal to the fair market value of the consideration for which the shares were issued, cannot in any event exceed,

(i) where the shares were issued before 1984, the rate of interest prescribed for the purposes of subsection 161(1) at the time the shares were issued, and

(ii) where the shares were issued after 1983, the prescribed rate of interest at the time the shares were issued; and

(*e*) the amount that any holder of the shares is entitled to receive on the redemption, cancellation or acquisition of the shares by the corporation or by any person with whom the corporation does not deal at arm's length cannot exceed the total of an amount equal to the fair market value of the consideration for which the shares were issued and the amount of any unpaid dividends thereon.

Editorial Note: Meeting "specified class" status per the above requirements will be helpful in avoiding associated corporation status, as shares of a specified class are ignored for the purposes of the 25% cross-ownership provisions of ss. 256(1)(*c*)–(*e*), as well as the deeming provisions of s. 256(1.2) (per s. 256(1.6)(*b*)). To avoid associating corporations in the course of implementing estate freezes, freeze shares could be designed to comply with s. 256(1.1). The CRA has indicated that a dividend rate "up to" a percentage amount will not qualify under s. 256(1.1)(*c*) (Document No. 9309595).

Related Regulations: 4301.

Related Sections: S. 94(14)(*a*); s. 256(1) Associated corporations; s. 256(1.2) Control, etc.; s. 256(1.6) Exception.

► 256(1.2) ◄

(1.2) Control, etc. For the purposes of this subsection and subsections (1), (1.1) and (1.3) to (5),

(*a*) a group of persons in respect of a corporation means any two or more persons each of whom owns shares of the capital stock of the corporation;

(*b*) for greater certainty,

(i) a corporation that is controlled by one or more members of a particular group of persons in respect of that corporation shall be considered to be controlled by that group of persons, and

(ii) a corporation may be controlled by a person or a particular group of persons notwithstanding that the corporation is also controlled or deemed to be controlled by another person or group of persons;

(*c*) a corporation shall be deemed to be controlled by another corporation, a person or a group of persons at any time where

(i) shares of the capital stock of the corporation having a fair market value of more than 50% of the fair market value of all the issued and outstanding shares of the capital stock of the corporation, or

(ii) common shares of the capital stock of the corporation having a fair market value of more than 50% of the fair market value of all the issued and outstanding common shares of the capital stock of the corporation

are owned at that time by the other corporation, the person or the group of persons, as the case may be;

(*d*) where shares of the capital stock of a corporation are owned, or deemed by this subsection to be owned, at any time by another corporation (in this paragraph referred to as the "holding corporation"), those shares shall be deemed to be owned at that time by any shareholder of the holding corporation in a proportion equal to the proportion of all those shares that

(i) the fair market value of the shares of the capital stock of the holding corporation owned at that time by the shareholder

is of

(ii) the fair market value of all the issued shares of the capital stock of the holding corporation outstanding at that time;

(*e*) where, at any time, shares of the capital stock of a corporation are property of a partnership, or are deemed by this subsection to be owned by the partnership, those shares shall be deemed to be owned at that time by each member of the partnership in a proportion equal to the proportion of all those shares that

(i) the member's share of the income or loss of the partnership for its fiscal period that includes that time

is of

(ii) the income or loss of the partnership for its fiscal period that includes that time

and for this purpose, where the income and loss of the partnership for its fiscal period that includes that time are nil, that proportion shall be computed as if the partnership had had income for that period in the amount of $1,000,000;

(*f*) where shares of the capital stock of a corporation are owned, or deemed by this subsection to be owned, at any time by a trust,

(i) (Repealed.)

(ii) where a beneficiary's share of the accumulating income or capital therefrom depends on the exercise by any person of, or the failure by any person to exercise, any discretionary power, those shares are deemed to be owned at that time by the beneficiary,

(iii) in any case where subparagraph (ii) does not apply, a beneficiary is deemed at that time to own the proportion of those shares that the fair market value of the beneficial interest in the trust of the beneficiary is of the fair market value of all beneficial interests in the trust, and

(iv) in the case of a trust referred to in subsection 75(2), the person referred to in that subsection from whom property of the trust or property for which it was substituted was directly or indirectly received shall be deemed to own those shares at that time; and

(*g*) in determining the fair market value of a share of the capital stock of a corporation, all issued and outstanding shares of the capital stock of the corporation shall be deemed to be non-voting.

Editorial Note: This provision expands a number of key concepts in the association rules, including that of a group (paragraphs (*a*) and (*b*)); control (paragraph (*c*), which establishes a control test based on greater than 50% of the fair market value of all shares), or 50% of the fair market value of the common shares only. The CRA does not consider this provision to take precedence over s. 256(9) — see Document Nos. 9525315, 2009-0330131C6); ownership (paragraphs (*d*), (*e*) and (*f*) provide look-through rules for corporations, partnerships and trusts; see *The Queen v. Propep Inc.*, 2010 DTC 5008 (F.C.A.), in which the FCA found that a beneficially interested party that could become a beneficiary upon the exercise of the discretion of the trustee was a beneficiary — a conclusion that has been subject to significant critical commentary); and valuation (paragraph (*g*) provides that, in determining fair market value, all shares are deemed to be non-voting). Further expansion of the ownership and control concepts is found in s. 256(1.3), which deems shares owned by a child under 18 to be owned by a parent, unless the child manages the business on an independent basis, and s. 256(1.4), which expands the concepts of ownership and control in respect of rights to acquire shares, control voting rights, or cause a corporation to redeem/acquire shares owned by others.

History: S. 256(1.2)(*f*)(i) was repealed and s. 256(1.2)(*f*)(ii) and (iii) were replaced by S.C. 2014, c. 39, s. 76(1), applicable to the 2016 and subsequent taxation years, and formerly read:

(i) in the case of a testamentary trust under which one or more beneficiaries were entitled to receive all of the income of the trust that arose before the date of death of one or the last surviving of those beneficiaries (in this paragraph referred to as the "distribution date") and no other person could, before the distribution date, receive or otherwise obtain the use of any of the income or capital of the trust,

(A) where any such beneficiary's share of the income or capital therefrom depends on the exercise by any person of, or the failure by any person to exercise, any discretionary power, those shares shall be deemed to be owned at any time before the distribution date by the beneficiary, and

(B) where clause (A) does not apply, those shares shall be deemed to be owned at any time before the distribution date by any such beneficiary in a proportion equal to the proportion of all those shares that the fair market value of the beneficial interest in the trust of the beneficiary is of the fair market value of the beneficial interests in the trust of all those beneficiaries,

(ii) where a beneficiary's share of the accumulating income or capital therefrom depends on the exercise by any person of, or the failure by any person to exercise, any discretionary power, those shares shall be deemed to be owned at that time by the beneficiary, except where subparagraph (i) applies and that time is before the distribution date,

(iii) in any case where subparagraph (ii) does not apply, a beneficiary shall be deemed at that time to own the proportion of those shares that the fair market value of the beneficial interest in the trust of the beneficiary is of the fair market value of all beneficial interests in the trust, except where subparagraph (i) applies and that time is before the distribution date, and

Related Sections: S. 127(10.22) Deemed non-association of corporations; s. 127.1(2.2) Refundable investment tax credit — associated CCPCs; s. 248(25) Beneficially interested. s. 256(1) Associated corporations; s. 256(1.1) Definition of "specified class"; s. 256(1.3) Parent deemed to own shares; s. 256(1.4) Options and rights; s. 256(1.5) Person related to himself, herself or itself; s. 256(1.6) Exception.

Canadian Tax Foundation: Hamelin, *Discretionary Trusts and Associated Corporations*, 2018 Tax for the Owner Manager 18(3):8–9.

Tax Profile: March 2010 — Association Through A Trust: When is A Person A Beneficiary?.

Income Tax Technical News: Issue No. 38, Control of Corporation Owned by Income Trust — Impact of Change in Trustees.

Interpretation Bulletins: *Primary* — IT-64R4 (Consolid.) Corporations: Association and control.

Cases: For the purposes of the associated corporations rule, beneficiaries of the trusts were deemed to hold the corporate shares held by the trusts despite clause 256(1.2)(*f*)(ii). *Moules Industriels (C.H.F.G.) Inc. et al v. The Queen*, 2018 DTC 1069 (TCC)

► 256(1.3) ◄

(1.3) Parent deemed to own shares. Where at any time shares of the capital stock of a corporation are owned by a child who is under 18 years of age, for the purpose of determining whether the corporation is associated at that time with any other corporation that is controlled, directly or indirectly in any manner whatever, by a parent of the child or by a group of persons of which the parent is a member, the shares shall be deemed to be owned at that time by the parent unless, having regard to all the circumstances, it can reasonably be considered that the child manages the business and affairs of the corporation and does so without a significant degree of influence by the parent.

Editorial Note: See the editorial note to s. 256(1.2).

Related Sections: S. 256(1) Associated corporations; s. 256(1.2) Control, etc.; s. 256(1.4) Options and rights; s. 256(5.1) Control in fact.

► 256(1.4) ◄

(1.4) Options and rights. For the purpose of determining whether a corporation is associated with another corporation with which it is not otherwise associated, where a person or any partnership in which the person has an interest has a right at any time under a contract, in equity or otherwise, either immediately or in the future and either absolutely or contingently,

(*a*) to, or to acquire, shares of the capital stock of a corporation, or to control the voting rights of shares of the capital stock of a corporation, the person or partnership shall, except where the right is not exercisable at that time because the exercise thereof is contingent on the death, bankruptcy or permanent disability of an individual, be deemed to own the shares at that time, and the shares shall be deemed to be issued and outstanding at that time; or

(*b*) to cause a corporation to redeem, acquire or cancel any shares of its capital stock owned by other shareholders of a corporation, the person or partnership shall, except where the right is not exercisable at that time because the exercise thereof is contingent on the death, bankruptcy or permanent disability of an individual, be deemed at that time to have the same position in relation to control of the corporation and ownership of shares of its capital stock as if the shares were redeemed, acquired or cancelled by the corporation.

Editorial Note: This provision, which is similar to s. 251(5)(*b*), expands the concepts of ownership and control in respect of the association rules. S. 256(1.4) applies to rights under contract (e.g., shareholders' or share purchase agreements), in equity or otherwise, including contingent rights, to acquire shares, control voting rights, or cause a corporation to redeem/acquire shares owned by others. Exceptions apply to rights contingent on death, bankruptcy or permanent disability of an individual. Although s. 256(1.4) may be broad enough to include almost any "buy-sell" agreement, the CRA has indicated that it will not normally apply the provision solely because of a "right of first refusal" or a "shotgun arrangement" contained in a shareholder agreement. See also the editorial note to s. 251(5).

Related Regulations: 5100(3).

Related Sections: S. 251(5) Control by related groups, options, etc; s. 256(1) Associated corporations; s. 256(1.2) Control, etc.; s. 256(1.3) Parent deemed to own shares; s. 256(1.5) Person related to himself, herself or itself; s. 256(1.6) Exception.

Canadian Tax Foundation: Schusheim, *Shareholders' Agreements*, 2012 Ontario Tax Conference 12:1–23.

STEP Canada: Mark Chartrand and Bryan McNulty, "Shareholders' Agreements: The Hard Stuff," PowerPoint presentation to the 15th National Conference of STEP Canada, Toronto, June 10-11, 2013.

Tax Profile: May 2017 — Buy-Sell Provisions in Shareholders' Agreements and Their Effect on Association; January 2010 — Shareholders' Agreements — A Survey of Income Tax Issues; November 2003 — Current Cases.

Tax Topics: No. 1650, Family Shareholders' Agreements - Succession Planning's Missing Link?.

Cases: See the note on *Sedona Networks*, at subsection 251(5)

► 256(1.5) ◄

(1.5) Person related to himself, herself or itself. For the purposes of subsections (1) to (1.4) and (1.6) to (5), where a person owns shares in two or more corporations, the person shall as shareholder of one of the corporations be deemed to be related to himself, herself or itself as shareholder of each of the other corporations.

► 256(1.6) ◄

(1.6) Exception. For the purposes of subsection (1.2) and notwithstanding subsection (1.4), any share that is

(*a*) described in paragraph (*e*) of the definition "term preferred share" in subsection 248(1) during the applicable time referred to in that paragraph, or

(*b*) a share of a specified class within the meaning of subsection (1.1)

shall be deemed not to have been issued and outstanding and not to be owned by any shareholder and an amount equal to the greater of the paid-up capital of the share and the amount, if any, that any holder of the share is entitled to receive on the redemption, cancellation or acquisition of the share by the corporation shall be deemed to be a liability of the corporation.

► 256(2) ◄

(2) Corporations associated through a third corporation. For the purposes of

(*a*) this Act, subject to paragraph (*b*), two corporations are deemed to be associated with each other at a particular time if

(i) they would, but for this subsection, not be associated with each other at the particular time, and

(ii) each corporation is associated with, or is deemed by this subsection to be associated with, the same corporation (in this subsection referred to as the "third corporation") at the particular time; and

(*b*) section 125,

(i) if the third corporation is not a Canadian-controlled private corporation at the particular time, the two corporations are deemed not to be associated with each other at the particular time, and

(ii) if the third corporation is a Canadian-controlled private corporation that elects in prescribed form to apply this subparagraph in its taxation year that includes the particular time, the two corporations are deemed not to be associated with each other at the particular time and the business limit of the third corporation for its taxation year that includes the particular time is deemed to be nil.

Editorial Note: This subsection provides that where two corporations not otherwise associated are associated with the same third corporation, they are deemed to be associated with one another for the purposes of the Act, subject to the comments below regarding the section 125 small business deduction.

For taxation years that begin before March 22, 2016, for the purposes of the small business deduction, an exception applies where the third corporation is not a CCPC, or where it elects not to be associated with either of the other corporations, in which case the third corporation cannot claim the small business deduction. Multiple section 256(2) elections can be made in situations involving more than three corporations (see Document Nos. 2003-0038235, 2004-0108311E5).

For taxation years that begin after March 21, 2016, for the purposes of the small business deduction, where the third corporation is not a CCPC or where it elects not to be associated under subsection 256(2), the two corporations are deemed not to be associated with each other, but remain associated with the third corporation.

History: S. 256(2) was replaced by S.C. 2016, c. 12, s. 67(1), applicable to taxation years that begin after March 21, 2016, and formerly read:

(2) *Corporations associated through a third corporation.* Where two corporations

(*a*) would, but for this subsection, not be associated with each other at any time, and

(*b*) are associated, or are deemed by this subsection to be associated, with the same corporation (in this subsection referred to as the "third corporation") at that time,

they shall, for the purposes of this Act, be deemed to be associated with each other at that time, except that, for the purposes of section 125, where the third corporation is not a Canadian-controlled private corporation at that time or elects, in prescribed form, for its taxation year that includes that time not to be associated with either of the other two corporations, the third corporation shall be deemed not to be associated with either of the other two corporations in that taxation year and its business limit for that taxation year shall be deemed to be nil.

Related Sections: S. 125(2) Business limit.

Forms: T2 SCH 28 — Election not to be an Associated Corporation.

► 256(2.1) ◄

(2.1) Anti-avoidance. For the purposes of this Act, where, in the case of two or more corporations, it may reasonably be considered that one of the main reasons for the separate existence of those corporations in a taxation year is to reduce the amount of taxes that would otherwise be payable under this Act or to increase the amount of refundable investment tax credit under section 127.1, the two or more corporations shall be deemed to be associated with each other in the year.

Editorial Note: This subsection may associate two or more corporations where it may reasonably be considered that one of the main reasons for the separate existence of those corporations in a taxation year is to reduce the amount of taxes or increase the investment tax credit under s. 127.1. This longstanding provision has become less frequently used by the CRA in recent years, particularly in view of the CRA's success in applying the *de facto* control provisions in s. 256(5.1).

Related Sections: S. 127.1 Refundable investment tax credit; s. 256(5.1) Control in fact.

Tax Profile: August 2009 — Structuring a Services Business.

Cases: A corporation underwent a reorganization resulting in the creation of five separate holding companies, one for each of the children of the founder, designed to allow each company to claim the small business deduction. One holding company claimed the small business deduction for 2012–2013, which was denied on assessment. The burden was on the taxpayer to show reducing tax was not one of the main reasons for its separate existence, and it had not met that burden. Documentary evidence indicated that tax reduction was one of the main reasons for the use of the holding companies. The small business limit available to the taxpayers was nil. *Jencal Holdings Ltd. v. The Queen*, 2019 DTC 1019 (TCC).

The corporate taxpayers were deemed associated since the main reason for separate corporate existence was to avoid tax by each claiming a small business deduction. The owners had obtained tax advice about the benefits of maintaining separate corporate entities, and there was no evidence of their claim that marital difficulties accounted for their separate existence. *Maintenance Euréka Ltée v. The Queen*, 2011 DTC 1319 (T.C.C.).

► 256(3) ◄

(3) Saving provision. Where one corporation (in this subsection referred to as the "controlled corporation") would, but for this subsection, be associated with another corporation in a taxation year by reason of being controlled, directly or indirectly in any manner whatever, by the other corporation or by reason of both of the corporations being controlled, directly or indirectly in any manner whatever, by the same person at a particular time in the year (which corporation or person so controlling the controlled corporation is in this subsection referred to as the "controller") and it is established to the satisfaction of the Minister that

(*a*) there was in effect at the particular time an agreement or arrangement enforceable according to the terms thereof, under which, on the satisfaction of a condition or the happening of an event that it is reasonable to expect will be satisfied or happen, the controlled corporation will

(i) cease to be controlled, directly or indirectly in any manner whatever, by the controller, and

(ii) be or become controlled, directly or indirectly in any manner whatever, by a person or group of persons, with whom or with each of the members of which, as the case may be, the controller was at the particular time dealing at arm's length, and

(*b*) the purpose for which the controlled corporation was at the particular time so controlled was the safeguarding of rights or interests of the controller in respect of

(i) any indebtedness owing to the controller the whole or any part of the principal amount of which was outstanding at the particular time, or

(ii) any shares of the capital stock of the controlled corporation that were owned by the controller at the particular time and that were, under the agreement or arrangement, to be redeemed by the controlled corporation or purchased by the person or group of persons referred to in subparagraph (*a*)(ii),

the controlled corporation and the other corporation with which it would otherwise be so associated in the year shall be deemed, for the purpose of this Act, not to be associated with each other in the year.

▶ 256(4) ◀

(4) Saving provision. Where one corporation would, but for this subsection, be associated with another corporation in a taxation year by reason of both of the corporations being controlled by the same executor, liquidator of a succession or trustee and it is established to the satisfaction of the Minister

(*a*) that the executor, liquidator or trustee did not acquire control of the corporations as a result of one or more estates or trusts created by the same individual or two or more individuals not dealing with each other at arm's length, and

(*b*) that the estate or trust under which the executor, liquidator or trustee acquired control of each of the corporations arose only on the death of the individual creating the estate or trust,

the two corporations are deemed, for the purposes of this Act, not to be associated with each other in the year.

Editorial Note: This provision, if applicable, relieves association between two corporations controlled by an executor, liquidator or trustee. However, it will not avoid the association rules where an individual executor, liquidator or trustee controls one or more corporations other than as an executor, i.e., he or she is the owner-manager of a corporation. Also the applicability of paragraphs (*a*) and (*b*) must be established to the satisfaction of the CRA.

▶ 256(5) ◀

(5) Idem. Where one corporation would, but for this subsection, be associated with another corporation in a taxation year, by reason only that the other corporation is a trustee under a trust pursuant to which the corporation is controlled, the two corporations shall be deemed, for the purposes of this Act, not to be associated with each other in the year unless, at any time in the year, a settlor of the trust controlled or is a member of a related group that controlled the other corporation that is the trustee under the trust.

Editorial Note: S. 256(5) may relieve association between a corporate executor and a controlled corporation. However, this provision does not speak to other effects of control. For example, CCPC status could be lost. The CRA's policy is generally to ignore this issue where control passes to an executor which has "public corporation" status, provided there is no undue delay in disposing of the shares (see paragraph 14 of IT-391R) (archived, as it doesn't meet current government web standards). However, in the 2007 STEP Round Table, the CRA indicated that this policy is "under consideration" (Q. 12, Document No. 2007-0240431C6).

Related Sections: S. 256(1.2) Control, etc.; s. 256(1.5) Person related to himself, herself or itself.

▶ 256(5.1) ◀

(5.1) Control in fact. For the purposes of this Act, where the expression "controlled, directly or indirectly in any manner whatever," is used, a corporation shall be considered to be so controlled by another corporation, person or group of persons (in this subsection referred to as the "controller") at any time where, at that time, the controller has any direct or indirect influence that, if exercised, would result in control in fact of the corporation, except that, where the corporation and the controller are dealing with each other at arm's length and the influence is derived from a franchise, licence, lease, distribution, supply or management agreement or other similar agreement or arrangement, the main purpose of which is to govern the relationship between the corporation and the controller regarding the manner in which a business carried on by the corporation is to be conducted, the corporation shall not be considered to be controlled, directly or indirectly in any manner whatever, by the controller by reason only of that agreement or arrangement.

Editorial Note: S. 256(5.1), which applies throughout the *Income Tax Act*, requires the application of the *de facto* control test as specified in this subsection, whenever the expression "controlled, directly or indirectly in any manner whatever" is used in respect of control of a corporation. Potentially applying where *de jure* control does not, the CRA has increasingly relied on this provision to associate corporations. The *Silicon Graphics* case (2002 DTC 7112 (F.C.A.)) indicates that *de facto* control requires the ability to effect a significant change in the board of directors or its powers, or to influence in a very direct way the shareholders who otherwise have the ability to elect the board. However, other cases have focused on a broader test relating to operational and economic dependency. It has been stated that the courts will consider a wide range of facts including the shareholders, the constating documents, the make-up of the board of directors, family relationships, and commercial relationships between corporations including economic dependence and degree of integration. The courts will also examine who is making operational and managerial decisions and where board of director decision-making lies.

The CRA is of the view close family ties especially lend themselves to the development of significant influences. The composition of the board of directors and the control of day-to-day management and operation of the business would be considered. Further, the CRA often indicates that jurisprudence has established that control in fact of a corporation could generally result from three major types of influence: moral influence, economic influence and contractual influence, and that *de facto* control may even exist without the ownership of any shares. But the CRA's overall view is that *de facto* control is a question of facts and circumstances. (See, for example, Document No. 2010-0382381E5; also Document Nos. 2007-0253591I7, 2008-0285211C6.) An exception in s. 256(5.1) pertains to arm's length situations where influence derives only from an agreement or arrangement (e.g., a franchise) the main purpose of which is to govern the manner in which a business is conducted.

Note the addition of subsection 256(5.11) to the Act effective for taxation years that begin after March 21, 2017, to clarify that all factors that are relevant in the circumstances should be taken into account in determining whether a taxpayer has any direct or indirect influence which, if exercised, would result in control in fact of a corporation.

Related Regulations: 1106(2); 2902(*e*)(i); 5100(3).

Related Sections: S. 20(8)(*c*) No deduction in respect of property in certain circumstances; s. 24(2) Business carried on by spouse or controlled corporation; s. 40(2) Limitations; s. 44(7) Where subpara. (1)(*e*)(iii) does not apply; 83(2.2) Where s. 83(2.1) does not apply; 83(2.4) Idem; s. 87(2)(*kk*) Disposition of shares of controlled corporation; s. 89(1), "capital dividend account"; s. 89(1.1) Capital dividend account where control acquired; s. 125(6.2) Specified partnership income deemed nil; s. 125(7), "Canadian-controlled private corporation"; s. 125.5(1), "eligible production corporation"; s. 127.1(2), "excluded corporation"; 149(1)(*t*) Farmers' and fishermen's insurer; 149(1.3) Votes or de facto control; s. 149.1(1), "public foundation", "charitable organization"; 149(4.1) Income exempt under 149(1)(*t*); 149(4.2) Idem; s. 251.1(3), "controlled"; 256(1) Associated corporations; 256(1.1) Definition of "specified class"; 256(1.2) Control, etc; 256(1.3) Parent deemed to own shares; 256(1.4) Options and rights; 256(1.5) Person related to himself, herself or itself; 256(1.6) Exception; 256(2) Corporations associated through a third corporation; 256(2.1) Anti-avoidance; 256(3) Saving provision; 256(4) Saving provision; 256(5) Idem; 256(5.1) Control in fact; 256(5.11) Factual control — interpretation; 256(6) Idem; 256(6.1) Simultaneous control; 256(6.2) Application to control in fact.

Canadian Tax Foundation: Friedlan and Friedlan, *256(5.1) — De Facto Control: A Return to the Past*, 2017 Ontario Tax Conference 5:1–17; Singh, *FCA Reinstates Narrow View of De Facto Control*, 2016 Canadian Tax Focus 6(3):11–12; Plecko and Williams, *Various Aspects of Control, Including De Facto Control*, 2015 British Columbia Tax Conference 11:1–13; Friedlan and Friedlan, *De Facto Control Delineated*, 2015 Tax for the Owner-Manager 15(2):3–4; Brender, *Developments in the Concept of Corporate Control*, 2007 Conference Report 31:1–49.

Tax Topics: No. 2461-2462, Part 3: Shareholders Agreements, the Act, and the Non-Specialist Advisor: The Impact of Control; No. 2460, Part 2: Shareholders Agreements, the Act, and the Non-Specialist Advisor: The Impact of Control; No. 2457, Part 1: Shareholders Agreements, the Act, and the Non-Specialist Advisor: The Impact of Control; No. 2420, More From the Federal Court of Appeal on *De Facto* Control; No. 2245, *De Facto* Control: Do We Know What It Means — Yet? (PT II); No. 2244, *De Facto* Control: Do We Know What It Means — Yet? (PT I); No. 1978, *De Facto* Control; No. 1700, 2004 Canadian Tax Foundation Conference — CRA Round Table.

Income Tax Technical News: Issue No. 32, Control in Fact: Impact of Recent Jurisprudence; Issue No. 25, Silicon Graphics Ltd. v. The Queen.

Interpretation Bulletins: *Primary* — IT-64R4 (Consolid.) Corporations: Association and control. *Secondary* — IT-291R3 Transfer of property to a corporation under subsection 85(1); IT-313R2 Eligible capital property —

Rules where a taxpayer has ceased carrying on a business or has died; IT-458R2 Canadian-controlled private corporation.

Cases: The Tax Court erred in premising its *de facto* control decision on factors *McGillivray* determined to be irrelevant. It also erred by considering the fact the companies were related and not dealing at arm's length before the relevant time period. However, the errors were immaterial since the agreement the taxpayer entered into constituted a legally-enforceable arrangement capable of establishing control in fact. *Aeronautic Development Corp. v. The Queen*, 2018 DTC 5044 (FCA)

The taxpayer was not a CCPC since a public corporation had *de facto* control over it, as the taxpayer could not have survived without the public corporation's financial support. *De facto* and *de jure* control can exist simultaneously for purposes of the Act without any specific provision to that effect. *Lyrtech RD Inc. v. The Queen*, 2013 DTC 1054 (T.C.C.)

B was the sole shareholder and director of one corporate taxpayer and her husband K was the controlling shareholder and director of the other corporate taxpayer. The taxpayers were associated corporations under the *de facto* control provisions of s. 256(5.1) since K had actual influence over board decisions of B's company and B's company was economically dependent on K's company, which was its sole customer. *Taber Solids Control (1998) Ltd. et al. v. The Queen*, 2009 DTC 1343 (T.C.C.)

There was nothing in franchise arrangements, including the documents, shareholders' agreements, leases, and franchise agreements, that could result in the franchisor having control in fact of its franchisees. *The Queen v. Lenester Sales Ltd. et al.*, 2004 DTC 6461 (F.C.A.), affirming 2003 DTC 997 (T.C.C.)

Two corporations were under the *de facto* control of a third corporation, and hence associated with it. Relevant factors included economic dependency, operational control and familial connection amongst the shareholders of all three corporations. *De jure* and *de facto* control can co-exist. *9044-2807 Québec Inc. v. The Queen*, 2004 DTC 6141 (F.C.A.), affirming 2003 DTC 817 (T.C.C.).

► 256(5.11) ◄

(5.11) Factual control — interpretation. For the purposes of the Act, the determination of whether a taxpayer has, in respect of a corporation, any direct or indirect influence that, if exercised, would result in control in fact of the corporation, shall

(*a*) take into consideration all factors that are relevant in the circumstances; and

(*b*) not be limited to, and the relevant factors need not include, whether the taxpayer has a legally enforceable right or ability to effect a change in the board of directors of the corporation, or its powers, or to exercise influence over the shareholder or shareholders who have that right or ability.

History: S. 256(5.11) was added by S.C. 2017, c. 33, s. 79(1), applicable to taxation years that begin after March 21, 2017.

► 256(6) ◄

(6) Idem. For the purposes of this Act, where a corporation (in this subsection referred to as the "controlled corporation") would, but for this subsection, be regarded as having been controlled or controlled, directly or indirectly in any manner whatever, by a person or partnership (in this subsection referred to as the "controller") at a particular time and it is established that

(*a*) there was in effect at the particular time an agreement or arrangement enforceable according to the terms thereof, under which, on the satisfaction of a condition or the happening of an event that it is reasonable to expect will be satisfied or happen, the controlled corporation will

(i) cease to be controlled, or controlled, directly or indirectly in any manner whatever, as the case may be, by the controller, and

(ii) be or become controlled, or controlled, directly or indirectly in any manner whatever, as the case may be, by a person or group of persons, with whom or with each of the members of which, as the case may be, the controller was at the particular time dealing at arm's length, and

(*b*) the purpose for which the controlled corporation was at the particular time so controlled, or controlled, directly or indirectly in any manner whatever, as the case may be, was the safeguarding of rights or interests of the controller in respect of

(i) any indebtedness owing to the controller the whole or any part of the principal amount of which was outstanding at the particular time, or

(ii) any shares of the capital stock of the controlled corporation that were owned by the controller at the particular time and that were, under the agreement or arrangement, to be redeemed by the controlled corporation or purchased by the person or group of persons referred to in subparagraph (*a*)(ii),

the controlled corporation is deemed not to have been controlled by the controller at the particular time.

Related Sections: S. 256(6.1) Simultaneous control.

Interpretation Bulletins: *Secondary* — IT-458R2 Canadian-controlled private corporation.

► 256(6.1) ◄

(6.1) Simultaneous control. For the purposes of this Act and for greater certainty,

(*a*) where a corporation (in this paragraph referred to as the "subsidiary") would be controlled by another corporation (in this paragraph referred to as the "parent") if the parent were not controlled by any person or group of persons, the subsidiary is controlled by

(i) the parent, and

(ii) any person or group of persons by whom the parent is controlled; and

(*b*) where a corporation (in this paragraph referred to as the "subject corporation") would be controlled by a group of persons (in this paragraph referred to as the "first-tier group") if no corporation that is a member of the first-tier group were controlled by any person or group of persons, the subject corporation is controlled by

(i) the first-tier group, and

(ii) any group of one or more persons comprised of, in respect of every member of the first-tier group, either the member, or a person or group of persons by whom the member is controlled.

Editorial Note: S. 256(6.1) (which applies for the entire ITA) provides that control in a multi-tiered corporate structure is to be determined at each level in the corporate chain: a lower-tier corporation can be controlled by more than one person or group of persons higher up the chain. This provision effectively overrides *Parthenon Investments Ltd. v. MNR*, 97 DTC 5343 (F.C.A.), which held that *de jure* control means ultimate control.

Related Sections: S. 125(7), "Canadian-controlled private corporation"; s. 248(1), "small business corporation"; s. 251(2) Definition of "related persons"; s. 251(5) Control by related groups, options, etc; s. 251(6) Blood relationship, etc.

► 256(6.2) ◄

(6.2) Application to control in fact. In its application to subsection (5.1), subsection (6.1) shall be read as if the references in subsection (6.1) to "controlled" were references to "controlled, directly or indirectly in any manner whatever,".

► 256(7) ◄

(7) Acquiring control. For the purposes of this subsection, of section 55, subsections 66(11), 66.5(3), 66.7(10) and (11), 85(1.2), 88(1.1) and (1.2), 110.1(1.2) and 111(5.4) and paragraph 251.2(2)(*a*) and of subsection 5905(5.2) of the *Income Tax Regulations*,

(*a*) control of a particular corporation shall be deemed not to have been acquired solely because of

(i) the acquisition at any time of shares of any corporation by

(A) a particular person who acquired the shares from a person to whom the particular person was related (otherwise than because of a right referred to in paragraph 251(5)(*b*)) immediately before that time,

(B) a particular person who was related to the particular corporation (otherwise than because of a right referred to in paragraph 251(5)(*b*)) immediately before that time,

(C) an estate that acquired the shares because of the death of a person,

(D) a particular person who acquired the shares from an estate that arose on and as a consequence of the death of an individual, if the estate acquired the shares from the individual as a consequence of the death and the individual was related to the particular person immediately before the death,

(E) a corporation on a distribution (within the meaning assigned by subsection 55(1)) by a specified corporation (within the meaning assigned by that subsection) if a dividend, to which subsection 55(2) does not apply because of paragraph 55(3)(*b*), is received in the course of the reorganization in which the distribution occurs,

(ii) the redemption or cancellation at any particular time of, or a change at any particular time in the rights, privileges, restrictions or conditions attaching to, shares of the particular corporation or of a corporation controlling the particular corporation, where each person and each member of each group of persons that controls the particular corporation immediately after the particular time was related (otherwise than because of a right referred to in paragraph 251(5)(*b*)) to the corporation

(A) immediately before the particular time, or

(B) immediately before the death of a person, where the shares were held immediately before the particular time by an estate that acquired the shares because of the person's death, or

(iii) the acquisition at any time of shares of the particular corporation if

(A) the acquisition of those shares would otherwise result in the acquisition of control of the particular corporation at that time by a related group of persons, and

(B) each member of each group of persons that controls the particular corporation at that time was related (otherwise than because of a right referred to in paragraph 251(5)(*b*)) to the particular corporation immediately before that time;

(*b*) where at any time 2 or more corporations (each of which is referred to in this paragraph as a "predecessor corporation") have amalgamated to form one corporate entity (in this paragraph referred to as the "new corporation"),

(i) control of a corporation is deemed not to have been acquired by any person or group of persons solely because of the amalgamation unless it is deemed by subparagraph (ii) or (iii) to have been so acquired,

(ii) a person or group of persons that controls the new corporation immediately after the amalgamation and did not control a predecessor corporation immediately before the amalgamation is deemed to have acquired immediately before the amalgamation control of the predecessor corporation and of each corporation it controlled immediately before the amalgamation (unless the person or group of persons would not have acquired control of the predecessor corporation if the person or group of persons had acquired all the shares of the predecessor corporation immediately before the amalgamation), and

(iii) control of a predecessor corporation and of each corporation it controlled immediately before the amalgamation is deemed to have been acquired immediately before the amalgamation by a person or group of persons

(A) unless the predecessor corporation was related (otherwise than because of a right referred to in paragraph 251(5)(*b*)) immediately before the amalgamation to each other predecessor corporation,

(B) unless, if one person had immediately after the amalgamation acquired all the shares of the new corporation's capital stock that the shareholders of the predecessor corporation, or of another predecessor corporation that controlled the predecessor corporation, acquired on the amalgamation in consideration for their shares of the predecessor corporation or of the other predecessor corporation, as the case may be, the person would have acquired control of the new corporation as a result of the acquisition of those shares, or

(C) unless this subparagraph would, but for this clause, deem control of each predecessor corporation to have been acquired on the amalgamation where the amalgamation is an amalgamation of

(I) two corporations, or

(II) two corporations (in this subclause referred to as the "parents") and one or more other corporations (each of which is in this subclause referred to as a "subsidiary") that would, if all the shares of each subsidiary's capital stock that were held immediately before the amalgamation by the parents had been held by one person, have been controlled by that person;

(*c*) subject to paragraph (*a*), where 2 or more persons (in this paragraph referred to as the "transferors") dispose of shares of the capital stock of a particular corporation in exchange for shares of the capital stock of another corporation (in this paragraph referred to as the "acquiring corporation"), control of the acquiring corporation and of each corporation controlled by it immediately before the exchange is deemed to have been acquired at the time of the exchange by a person or group of persons unless

(i) the particular corporation and the acquiring corporation were related (otherwise than because of a right referred to in paragraph 251(5)(*b*)) to each other immediately before the exchange, or

(ii) if all the shares of the acquiring corporation's capital stock that were acquired by the transferors on the exchange were acquired at the time of the exchange by one person, the person would not control the acquiring corporation;

(*c*.1) subject to paragraph (*a*), if, at any particular time, as part of a series of transactions or events, two or more persons acquire shares of a corporation (in this paragraph referred to as the "acquiring corporation") in exchange for or upon a redemption or surrender of interests in, or as a consequence of a distribution from, a SIFT trust (determined without reference to subsection 122.1(2)), SIFT partnership (determined without reference to subsection 197(8)) or real estate investment trust (as defined in subsection 122.1(1)), control of the acquiring corporation and of each corporation controlled by it immediately before the particular time is deemed to have been acquired by a person or group of persons at the particular time unless

(i) in respect of each of the corporations, a person (in this subparagraph referred to as a "relevant person") affiliated (within the meaning assigned by section 251.1 read without reference to the definition "controlled" in subsection 251.1(3)) with the SIFT trust, SIFT partnership or real estate investment trust owned shares of the particular corporation having a total fair market value of more than 50% of the fair market value of all the issued and outstanding shares of the particular corporation at all times during the period that

(A) begins on the latest of July 14, 2008, the date the particular corporation came into existence and the time of the last acquisition of control, if any, of the particular corporation by a relevant person, and

(B) ends immediately before the particular time,

(ii) if all the securities (in this subparagraph as defined in subsection 122.1(1)) of the acquiring corporation that were acquired as part of the series of transactions or events at or before the particular time were acquired by one person, the person would

(A) not at the particular time control the acquiring corporation, and

(B) have at the particular time acquired securities of the acquiring corporation having a fair market value of not more than 50% of the fair market value of all the issued and outstanding shares of the acquiring corporation, or

(iii) this paragraph previously applied to deem an acquisition of control of the acquiring corporation upon an acquisition of shares that was part of the same series of transactions or events;

(*c*.2) subject to paragraph (*a*), if, at any particular time, as part of a series of transactions or events, two or more persons acquire shares of a corporation (in this paragraph referred to as the "acquiring corporation") in exchange for or upon a redemption or surrender of interests in, or as a consequence of a distribution from, a partnership or trust, control of the acquiring corporation and of each corporation controlled by it immediately before the particular time is deemed to have been acquired by a person or group of persons at the particular time unless

(i) in respect of each of the corporations, a person affiliated with the partnership or trust owned immediately before the particular time shares of the particular corporation having a total fair market value of more than 50% of the fair market value of all the issued and outstanding shares of the particular corporation immediately before the particular time,

(ii) if all the *securities* (in this subparagraph as defined in subsection 122.1(1)) of the acquiring corporation that were acquired at or before the particular time as part of the series were acquired by one person, the person would

(A) not at the particular time control the acquiring corporation, and

(B) have at the particular time acquired securities of the acquiring corporation having a fair market value of not more than 50% of the fair market value of all the issued and outstanding shares of the acquiring corporation, or

(iii) paragraph (*c*.1) applies, or this paragraph or paragraph (*c*.1) previously applied, to deem an acquisition of control of the acquiring corporation upon an acquisition of shares that was part of the same series of transactions or events;

(*d*) where at any time shares of the capital stock of a particular corporation are disposed of to another corporation (in this paragraph referred to as the "acquiring corporation") for consideration that includes shares of the acquiring corporation's capital stock and, immediately after that time, the acquiring corporation and the particular corporation are controlled by a person or group of persons who

(i) controlled the particular corporation immediately before that time, and

(ii) did not, as part of the series of transactions or events that includes the disposition, cease to control the acquiring corporation,

control of the particular corporation and of each corporation controlled by it immediately before that time is deemed not to have been acquired by the acquiring corporation solely because of the disposition;

(*e*) control of a particular corporation and of each corporation controlled by it immediately before a particular time is deemed not to have been acquired at the particular time by a corporation (in this paragraph referred to as the "acquiring corporation") if at the particular time, the acquiring corporation acquires shares of the particular corporation's capital stock for consideration that consists solely of shares of the acquiring corporation's capital stock, and if

(i) immediately after the particular time

(A) the acquiring corporation owns all the shares of each class of the particular corporation's capital stock (determined without reference to shares of a specified class, within the meaning assigned by paragraph 88(1)(*c.8*)),

(B) the acquiring corporation is not controlled by any person or group of persons, and

(C) the fair market value of the shares of the particular corporation's capital stock that are owned by the acquiring corporation is not less than 95% of the fair market value of all of the assets of the acquiring corporation, or

(ii) any of clauses (i)(A) to (C) do not apply and the acquisition occurs as part of a plan of arrangement that, on completion, results in

(A) the acquiring corporation (or a new corporation that is formed on an amalgamation of the acquiring corporation and a subsidiary wholly-owned corporation of the acquiring corporation) owning all the shares of each class of the particular corporation's capital stock (determined without reference to shares of a specified class, within the meaning assigned by paragraph 88(1)(*c.8*)),

(B) the acquiring corporation (or the new corporation) not being controlled by any person or group of persons, and

(C) the fair market value of the shares of the particular corporation's capital stock that are owned by the acquiring corporation (or the new corporation) being not less than 95% of the fair market value of all of the assets of the acquiring corporation (or the new corporation);

(*f*) if a particular trust is the only beneficiary of another trust, the particular trust is described in paragraph (*c*) of the definition "SIFT trust wind-up event", the particular trust would, in the absence of this paragraph, acquire control of a corporation solely because of a SIFT trust wind-up event that is a distribution of shares of the capital stock of the corporation by the other trust, and the other trust controlled the corporation immediately before the distribution, the particular trust is deemed not to acquire control of the corporation because of the distribution;

(*g*) a corporation (in this paragraph referred to as the "acquiring corporation") that acquires shares of another corporation on a distribution that is a SIFT trust wind-up event of a SIFT wind-up entity is deemed not to acquire control of the other corporation because of that acquisition if the following conditions are met:

(i) the SIFT wind-up entity is a trust whose only beneficiary immediately before the distribution is the acquiring corporation,

(ii) the SIFT wind-up entity controlled the other corporation immediately before the distribution,

(iii) as part of a series of transactions or events under which the acquiring corporation became the only beneficiary under the trust, two or more persons acquired shares in the acquiring corporation in exchange for their interests as beneficiaries under the trust, and

(iv) if all the shares described in subparagraph (iii) had been acquired by one person, the person would

(A) control the acquiring corporation, and

(B) have acquired shares of the acquiring corporation having a fair market value of more than 50% of the fair market value of all the issued and outstanding shares of the acquiring corporation,

(*h*) if at any time after September 12, 2013 a trust is subject to a loss restriction event and immediately before that time the trust, or a group of persons a member of which is the trust, controls a corporation, control of the corporation and of each corporation controlled by it immediately before that time is deemed to have been acquired at that time by a person or group of persons; and

(*i*) if at any time after September 12, 2013 a trust controls a corporation, control of the corporation is deemed not to be acquired solely because of a change in the trustee or legal representative having ownership or control of the trust's property if

(i) the change is not part of a series of transactions or events that includes a change in the beneficial ownership of the trust's property, and

(ii) no amount of income or capital of the trust to be distributed, at any time at or after the change, in respect of any interest in the trust depends upon the exercise by any person or partnership, or the failure of any person or partnership, to exercise any discretionary power.

Editorial Note: Without s. 256(7), any acquisition of control (e.g., by a related person or a holding company) could trigger a number of anti-avoidance rules which rely on this concept. Subsection 256(7) provides for a number of exceptions which vitiate the effects of an acquisition of control for the purposes of the provisions enumerated at the beginning of the subsection. These may include transactions in respect of related persons, to and from an estate, qualifying share-for-share exchanges, and amalgamations.

History: S. 256(7)(*c.2*) was added by S.C. 2017, c. 33, s. 79(2), applicable to transactions completed after September 15, 2016, other than transactions the parties to which are obligated to complete pursuant to the terms of an agreement in writing between the parties entered into before September 16, 2016. However, for this purpose, the parties to a transaction shall be considered not to be obligated to complete the transaction if one or more of those parties may be excused from completing the transaction as a result of amendments to the Act.

S. 256(7), the portion before paragraph (*a*) was replaced by S.C. 2013, c. 40 , s. 93(1), deemed to have come into force on March 21, 2013, and formerly read:

(7) *Acquiring control.* For the purposes of this subsection, of subsections 10(10), 13(21.2) and (24), 14(12) and 18(15), sections 18.1 and 37, subsection 40(3.4), the definition "superficial loss" in section 54, section 55, subsections 66(11), (11.4) and (11.5), 66.5(3) and 66.7(10) and (11), section 80, paragraph 80.04(4)(*h*), subsections 85(1.2), 88(1.1) and (1.2) and 110.1(1.2), sections 111 and 127 and subsection 249(4) and of subsection 5905(5.2) of the *Income Tax Regulations*,

S. 256(7)(*a*)(i)(D) was replaced by S.C. 2013, c. 40 , s. 93(2), deemed to have come into force on September 13, 2013, and formerly read:

(D) a particular person who acquired the shares from an estate that arose on the death of another person to whom the particular person was related, or

S. 256(7)(*h*) and (*i*) were added by S.C. 2013, c. 40 , s. 93(3), deemed to have come into force on March 21, 2013.

S. 256(7), the portion before paragraph (*a*) was replaced by S.C. 2013, c. 34, s. 37(1), deemed to have come into force on December 19, 2009.

Any assessment of a taxpayer's tax, interest and penalties payable under the Act for any taxation year that ends before June 26, 2013 that would, in the absence of this section, be precluded because of subsections 152(4) to (5) of the Act, shall be made to the extent necessary to take into account this amendment, if the taxpayer

(i) elects in writing in respect of all of its foreign affiliates that this section apply in respect of that provision, and

(ii) files that election with the Minister of National Revenue on or before December 26, 2013 [the day that is six months after royal assent].

S. 256(7), the portion before paragraph (*a*) formerly read:

Acquiring control For the purposes of subsections 10(10), 13(21.2) and (24), 14(12) and 18(15), sections 18.1 and 37, subsection 40(3.4), the definition "superficial loss" in section 54, section 55, subsections 66(11), (11.4) and (11.5), 66.5(3) and 66.7(10) and (11), section 80, paragraph 80.04(4)(*h*), subsections 85(1.2), 88(1.1) and (1.2) and 110.1(1.2), sections 111 and 127, subsection 249(4) and this subsection,

S. 256(7)(*a*)(i)(E) was added by S.C. 2013, c. 34, s. 364(2), applicable to acquisitions of shares that occur after 2000.

S. 256(7)(*a*)(iii) was added by S.C. 2013, c. 34, s. 364(3), applicable to acquisitions of shares that occur after 2000.

S. 256(7)(*c.1*) was added by S.C. 2013, c. 34, s. 364(4), applicable to transactions undertaken after 4:00 p.m. Eastern Standard Time March 4, 2010, other than transactions the parties to which are obligated to complete pursuant to the terms of an agreement in writing between the parties entered into before that time. However, the parties to a transaction shall be considered not to be obligated to complete the transaction if one or more of those parties may be excused from completing the transaction as a result of amendments to the Act.

S. 256(7)(*c.1*) also applies to transactions completed or agreed to in writing in the period that begins on July 14, 2008 and ends at 4:00 pm Eastern Standard Time March 4, 2010 if the parties to the transactions jointly elect in writing to the Minister of National Revenue on or before

(*a*) if a party to the transactions is a partnership, the day that is the later of

(i) the day that is the latest on which a return is required by section 229 of the *Income Tax Regulations* to be filed in respect of the partnership's fiscal period that includes June 26, 2013, and

(ii) the day that is the latest filing-due date of any party for its taxation year that includes June 26, 2013, and

(*b*) if none of the parties to the transaction is a partnership, the day that is the latest filing-due date of any party for its taxation year that includes June 26, 2013.

For the purposes of the application above, the parties shall be considered to be the relevant SIFT trust, SIFT partnership, real estate investment trust and acquiring corporation described in paragraph 256(7)(*c.1*).

S. 256(7)(*e*) was replaced by S.C. 2013, c. 34, s. 364(5), applicable in respect of shares acquired after 1999, and formerly read:

(*e*) where at any time all the shares of the capital stock of a particular corporation are disposed of to another corporation (in this paragraph referred to as the "acquiring corporation") for consideration that consists solely of shares of the acquiring corporation's capital stock and, immediately after that time,

(i) the acquiring corporation is not controlled by any person or group of persons, and

(ii) the fair market value of the shares of the capital stock of the particular corporation is not less than 95% of the fair market value of all the assets of the acquiring corporation,

control of the particular corporation and of each corporation controlled by it immediately before that time is deemed not to have been acquired by the acquiring corporation solely because of the disposition; and

S. 256(7)(*g*) was added by S.C. 2013, c. 34, s. 364(6), applicable to transactions undertaken after 4:00 p.m. Eastern Standard Time March 4, 2010, other than transactions the parties to which are obligated to complete pursuant to the terms of an agreement in writing between the parties entered into before that time. However, the parties to a transaction shall be considered not to be obligated to complete the transaction if one or more of those parties may be excused from completing the transaction as a result of amendments to the Act.

S. 256(7)(*g*) also applies to transactions completed or agreed to in writing in the period that begins on July 14, 2008 and ends at 4:00 pm Eastern Standard Time March 4, 2010 if the parties to the transactions jointly elect in writing to the Minister of National Revenue on or before

(*a*) if a party to the transactions is a partnership, the day that is the later of

(i) the day that is the latest on which a return is required by section 229 of the *Income Tax Regulations* to be filed in respect of the partnership's fiscal period that includes June 26, 2013, and

(ii) the day that is the latest filing-due date of any party for its taxation year that includes June 26, 2013, and

(*b*) if none of the parties to the transaction is a partnership, the day that is the latest filing-due date of any party for its taxation year that includes June 26, 2013.

For the purposes of the application above, the parties shall be considered to be the relevant SIFT trust, SIFT partnership, real estate investment trust and acquiring corporation described in paragraph 256(7)(*g*).

S. 256(7)(*f*) was added by S.C. 2009, c. 2, s. 78(1), applicable after July 14, 2008.

Related Sections: S. 139.1(18) Acquisition of control; s. 256(8.1) Corporations without share capital; s. 256.1 [Corporate tax-attribute trading].

Canadian Petroleum Tax Journal: Recent Developments in Corporate Reorganizations and International Transactions, Doug Richardson and Edward Rowe, 2000, Vol. 13, No. 1.

Canadian Tax Foundation: Jung and McIntyre, *Current Issues: Change of Trustee and Control*, 2013 Ontario Tax Conference 1:28–30; Bodie and Novotny, *Acquisitions of Control Under the Income Tax Act — Recent Developments*, 2013 Prairie Provinces Tax Conference 6:1–27; Dolson, *Provincial Residency — Trusts*, 2013 Prairie Provinces Tax Conference 4A:1–17; Hickey, *Acquisition of Control: Change of Trustee*, 2013 Canadian Tax Highlights 21(11):6–7.

Tax Profile: June 2011 — Summary of Canada Revenue Agency Round Table Held at the 13th National STEP Canada Conference; June 2003 — The December 20, 2002 Technical Amendments to the Income Tax Act.

Tax Topics: No. 2407, Tax Court Finds That the GAAR Applied To Deny Non-Capital Loss Carryforwards in Amalgamated Company.

Income Tax Folios: *Secondary* — S4-F7-C1 Amalgamations of Canadian Corporations.

Income Tax Technical News: Issue No. 34, Change in Trustees and Control.

Interpretation Bulletins: *Secondary* — IT-302R3 Losses of a corporation — The effect that acquisitions of control, amalgamations, and windings-up have on their deductibility — After January 15, 1987.

Cases: Subsection 111(5) limits the ability to deduct unused business losses where there has been a change of control of the corporation. There is no change of control as a result of an amalgamation unless one of subparagraphs 256(7)(*b*)(ii) or (iii) deems it. Neither applied in this case. However, the series of transactions involved in the amalgamation was not undertaken primarily for purposes other than to obtain a tax benefit in the form of the losses being claimed, which made it an "avoidance transaction". The insertion of the short-lived Class B shares, whose only purpose was to be converted into common shares, constituted the manipulation of the shareholdings of a predecessor contrary to subsection 256(7). This constituted an abuse of that provision. The solution was to ignore the Class B shares, with the result that there was a change of control immediately before the amalgamation, which justified the refusal to permit the taxpayer to deduct pre-amalgamation accumulated non-capital losses. *Birchcliff Energy Ltd. v. The Queen*, 2017 DTC 1151 (TCC)

▶ 256(8) ◀

(8) Deemed exercise of right. Where at any time a taxpayer acquires a right referred to in paragraph 251(5)(*b*) in respect of a share and it can reasonably be concluded that one of the main purposes of the acquisition is

(*a*) to avoid any limitation on the deductibility of any non-capital loss, net capital loss, farm loss or any expense or other amount referred to in subsection 66(11), 66.5(3) or 66.7(10) or (11),

(*b*) to avoid the application of subsection 10(10) or 13(24), paragraph 37(1)(*h*) or subsection 55(2) or 66(11.4) or (11.5), paragraph 88(1)(*c.3*) or subsection 111(4), (5.1) or (5.3), 181.1(7), 190.1(6) or 251.2(2),

(*c*) to avoid the application of paragraph (*j*) or (*k*) of the definition "investment tax credit" in subsection 127(9),

(*d*) to avoid the application of section 251.1, or

(*e*) to affect the application of section 80,

the taxpayer is deemed to be in the same position in relation to the control of the corporation as if the right were immediate and absolute and as if the taxpayer had exercised the right at that time for the purpose of determining whether control of a corporation has been acquired for the purposes of subsections 10(10) and 13(24), section 37, subsections 55(2), 66(11), (11.4) and (11.5), 66.5(3), 66.7(10) and (11), section 80, paragraph 80.04(4)(*h*), subparagraph 88(1)(*c*)(vi), paragraph 88(1)(*c.3*), subsections 88(1.1) and (1.2), sections 111 and 127, subsections 181.1(7), 190.1(6) and 249(4) and paragraph 251.2(2)(*a*) and in determining for the purposes of section 251.1, paragraph (*b*) of the definition "investment fund" in subsection 251.2(1) and paragraphs 251.2(3)(*c*) and (*d*) and 256(7)(*i*) whether a corporation is controlled by any other person or group of persons.

Editorial Note: S. 256(8) treats rights under s. 251(5)(*b*) as having been exercised if one of the main purposes of the acquisition of such rights is to avoid/affect specified provisions (including loss streaming and debt forgiveness rules). S. 251(5)(*b*) applies to rights (including contingent rights) to acquire shares, control voting rights, or cause a corporation to redeem/acquire shares owned by others.

History: S. 256(8)(*b*) was replaced by S.C. 2016, c. 12, s. 67(3), in force January 1, 2017, and formerly read:

> (*b*) to avoid the application of subsection 10(10) or 13(24), paragraph 37(1)(*h*) or subsection 55(2) or 66(11.4) or (11.5), paragraph 88(1)(*c.3*) or subsection 111(4), (5.1), (5.2) or (5.3), 181.1(7), 190.1(6) or 251.2(2),

S. 256(8), the portion after paragraph (*e*) was replaced by S.C. 2016, c. 12, s. 67(4), deemed to have come into force on March 21, 2013, and formerly read:

> the taxpayer is deemed to be in the same position in relation to the control of the corporation as if the right were immediate and absolute and as if the taxpayer had exercised the right at that time for the purpose of determining whether control of a corporation has been acquired for the purposes of subsections 10(10) and 13(24), section 37, subsections 55(2), 66(11), (11.4) and (11.5), 66.5(3), 66.7(10) and (11), section 80, paragraph 80.04(4)(*h*), subparagraph 88(1)(*c*)(vi), paragraph 88(1)(*c.3*), subsections 88(1.1) and (1.2), sections 111 and 127, subsections 181.1(7), 190.1(6) and 249(4) and paragraph 251.2(2)(*a*) and in determining for the purposes of section 251.1 and paragraphs 251.2(3)(*c*) and (*d*) whether a corporation is controlled by any other person or group of persons.

S. 256(8)(*b*) was replaced by S.C. 2013, c. 40, s. 93(5), deemed to have come into force on March 21, 2013, and formerly read:

> (*b*) to avoid the application of subsection 10(10) or 13(24), paragraph 37(1)(*h*) or subsection 55(2) or 66(11.4) or (11.5), paragraph 88(1)(*c.3*) or subsection 111(4), (5.1), (5.2) or (5.3), 181.1(7) or 190.1(6),

S. 256(8), the portion after paragraph (*e*) was replaced by S.C. 2013, c. 40, s. 93(6), deemed to have come into force on March 21, 2013, and formerly read:

> the taxpayer is deemed to be in the same position in relation to the control of the corporation as if the right were immediate and absolute and as if the taxpayer had exercised the right at that time for the purpose of determining whether control of a corporation has been acquired for the purposes of subsections 10(10) and 13(24), section 37, subsections 55(2), 66(11), (11.4) and (11.5), 66.5(3), 66.7(10) and (11), section 80, paragraph 80.04(4)(*h*), subparagraph 88(1)(*c*)(vi), paragraph 88(1)(*c.3*), sections 111 and 127 and subsections 181.1(7), 190.1(6) and 249(4), and in determining for the purpose of section 251.1 whether a corporation is controlled by any person or group of persons.

Related Sections: 181.5(6) Idem; 190.15(6) Idem; s. 251(5) Control by related groups, options, etc; s. 256(8.1) Corporations without share capital.

▶ 256(8.1) ◀

(8.1) Corporations without share capital. For the purposes of subsections (7) and (8),

(*a*) a corporation incorporated without share capital is deemed to have a capital stock of a single class;

(*b*) each member, policyholder and other participant in the corporation is deemed to be a shareholder of the corporation; and

(*c*) the membership, policy or other interest in the corporation of each of those participants is deemed to be the number of shares of the corporation's capital stock that the Minister considers reasonable in the circumstances, having regard to the total number of participants in the corporation and the nature of their participation.

▶ 256(9) ◀

(9) Date of acquisition of control. For the purposes of this Act, other than for the purposes of determining if a corporation is, at any time, a small business corporation or a Canadian-controlled private corporation, where control of a corporation is acquired by a person or group of persons at a particular time on a day, control of the corporation shall be deemed to have been acquired by the person or group of persons, as the case may be, at the beginning of that day and not at the particular time unless the corporation elects in its return of income under Part I filed for its taxation year that ends immediately before the acquisition of control not to have this subsection apply.

Editorial Note: S. 256(9) (which applies for the entire ITA) provides that, unless a corporation otherwise elects (in its income tax return for the year ending immediately before acquisition of control), control is deemed to have been acquired at the beginning of the particular day in question. See T4012 (T2 Corporation — Income Tax Guide) lines 063 and 065 for CRA views on making the election. See also editorial comments under s. 249(4), particularly for events which can trigger multiple year-ends. The subsection does not apply for the purpose of determining if a corporation is, at any time, a small business corporation or a Canadian-controlled private corporation. As a result, if control of an otherwise qualifying corporation is acquired from a Canadian-resident individual by a public corporation and/or non-residents, the individual may be able to claim the capital gain exemption without the election being made. Effective March 21, 2013, a similar rule in subsection 251.2(6) applies to a trust that is subject to a loss restriction event, which occurs when a person has become a majority-interest beneficiary, or a group of persons has become a majority-interest group of beneficiaries, of the trust.

History: S. 256(9) was replaced by S.C. 2009, c. 2, s. 78(2), applicable in respect of an acquisition of control of a corporation that occurs after 2005, other than in respect of such an acquisition of control that occurs before January 28, 2009 and in respect of which the taxpayer elects in writing, filed with the Minister of National Revenue on or before the taxpayer's filing-due date for the taxpayer's 2009 taxation year, that subsection 256(9) not apply.

A taxpayer is deemed to have made the election described above in respect of an acquisition of control of a corporation that occurs before January 28, 2009 if it can reasonably be considered, having regard to a return of income, notice of objection, or notice of appeal, filed or served by the taxpayer under the Act before January 28, 2009, that the taxpayer has interpreted and applied subsection 256(9) for the purposes of determining if the corporation was a small business corporation or a Canadian-controlled private corporation at the time of the transfer of shares of the corporation that caused the acquisition of control to occur.

S. 256(9) formerly read:

(9) *Date of acquisition of control.* For the purposes of this Act, where control of a corporation is acquired by a person or group of persons at a particular time on a day, control of the corporation shall be deemed to have been acquired by the person or group of persons, as the case may be, at the commencement of that day and not at the particular time unless the corporation elects in its return of income under Part I filed for its taxation year ending immediately before the acquisition of control not to have this subsection apply.

Related Regulations: 600; 6204(4).

Related Sections: s. 88(1)(*c.6*) Winding-up; s. 125(7), "Canadian-controlled private corporation"; s. 110.6(2.1) Capital gains deduction — qualified small business corporation shares; s. 220(3.2) Late, amended or revoked elections; s. 248(1) "small business corporation"; s. 249(4) Loss restriction event – year end.

Tax Profile: August 2012 — U.S. Purchases and Sales of Canadian Businesses: Tax and Corporate Issues.

Tax Topics: No. 1881, Parallel Universe: La Survivance and the Capital Gains Exemption; No. 1879, Interaction of Subsections 110.6(2.1) and 256(9).

SECTION 256.1: [Corporate tax-attribute trading]

► 256.1(1) ◄

(1) Definitions. The following definitions apply in this section.

History: S. 256.1(1) was added by S.C. 2013, c. 40, s. 94(1), deemed to have come into force on March 21, 2013, except that it does not apply to an event or transaction that occurs

(*a*) before March 21, 2013, or

(*b*) after March 20, 2013 pursuant to an obligation created by the terms of an agreement in writing entered into between parties before March 21, 2013, and for the purposes of this paragraph, parties will be considered not to be obligated if one or more of those parties may be excused from fulfilling the obligation as a result of changes to the Act.

"attribute trading restriction"—"attribute trading restriction" means a restriction on the use of a tax attribute arising on the application, either alone or in combination with other provisions, of any of this section, subsections 10(10) and 13(24), section 37, subsections 66(11.4) and (11.5), 66.7(10) and (11), 69(11) and 88(1.1) and (1.2), sections 111 and 127 and subsections 181.1(7), 190.1(6), 249(4) and 256(7).

"person"—"person" includes a partnership.

"specified provision"—"specified provision" means any of subsections 10(10) and 13(24), paragraph 37(1)(*h*), subsections 66(11.4) and (11.5), 66.7(10) and (11), 69(11) and 111(4), (5), (5.1) and (5.3), paragraphs (j) and (*k*) of the definition "investment tax credit" in subsection 127(9), subsections 181.1(7) and 190.1(6) and any provision of similar effect.

History: S. 256.1(1), the definition "specified provision" was replaced by S.C. 2016, c. 12, s. 68(1), in force January 1, 2017, and formerly read:

"specified provision"—"specified provision" means any of subsections 10(10) and 13(24), paragraph 37(1)(*h*), subsections 66(11.4) and (11.5), 66.7(10) and (11), 69(11) and 111(4), (5), (5.1), (5.2) and (5.3), paragraphs (*j*) and (*k*) of the definition "investment tax credit" in subsection 127(9), subsections 181.1(7) and 190.1(6) and any provision of similar effect.

► 256.1(2) ◄

(2) Application of subsection (3). Subsection (3) applies at a particular time in respect of a corporation if

(*a*) shares of the capital stock of the corporation held by a person, or the total of all shares of the capital stock of the corporation held by members of a group of persons, as the case may be, have at the particular time a fair market value that exceeds 75% of the fair market value of all the shares of the capital stock of the corporation;

(*b*) shares, if any, of the capital stock of the corporation held by the person, or the total of all shares, if any, of the capital stock of the corporation held by members of the group, have immediately before the particular time a fair market value that does not exceed 75% of the fair market value of all the shares of the capital stock of the corporation;

(*c*) the person or group does not control the corporation at the particular time; and

(*d*) it is reasonable to conclude that one of the main reasons that the person or group does not control the corporation is to avoid the application of one or more specified provisions.

History: S. 256.1(2) was added by S.C. 2013, c. 40, s. 94(1), deemed to have come into force on March 21, 2013, except that it does not apply to an event or transaction that occurs

(*a*) before March 21, 2013, or

(*b*) after March 20, 2013 pursuant to an obligation created by the terms of an agreement in writing entered into between parties before March 21, 2013, and for the purposes of this paragraph, parties will be considered not to be obligated if one or more of those parties may be excused from fulfilling the obligation as a result of changes to the Act.

► 256.1(3) ◄

(3) Deemed acquisition of control. If this subsection applies at a particular time in respect of a corporation, then for the purposes of the attribute trading restrictions,

(*a*) the person or group referred to in subsection (2)

(i) is deemed to acquire control of the corporation, and each corporation controlled by the corporation, at the particular time, and

(ii) is not deemed to have control of the corporation, and each corporation controlled by the corporation, at any time after the particular time solely because this paragraph applied at the particular time; and

(*b*) during the period that the condition in paragraph (2)(*a*) is satisfied, each corporation referred to in paragraph (*a*) — and any corporation incorporated or otherwise formed subsequent to that time and controlled by that corporation — is deemed not to be related to, or affiliated with, any person to which it was related to, or affiliated with, immediately before paragraph (*a*) applies.

Editorial Note: Section 256.1 deems an acquisition of control to have occurred where a person or group of persons (which may include partnerships) acquires (without control otherwise having been acquired) shares holding more than 75% of the fair market value of all the capital stock of a corporation, for the purpose of specified provisions throughout the Act restricting the use of corporate tax attributes (such as losses) upon a change of control. For example, this provision is designed to eliminate the benefit of certain corporate loss trading or utilization structures designed to circumvent loss restriction rules. For the purposes of the fair market value threshold, shareholdings are to be determined on a fully diluted basis (by including potential holdings from all rights, options, warrants, etc.). In addition, subsection 256.1(4) sets out a broad anti-avoidance rule such that, where it may reasonably be considered that one of the purposes of a transaction or event is to avoid having a person or group of persons meet this threshold of FMV holdings, such transaction or event may be ignored for the purpose of applying this deeming rule. Where the value of a corporation's shares is nil, subsection 256.1(5) provides a deemed valuation.

History: S. 256.1(3) was added by S.C. 2013, c. 40, s. 94(1), deemed to have come into force on March 21, 2013, except that it does not apply to an event or transaction that occurs

(*a*) before March 21, 2013, or

(*b*) after March 20, 2013 pursuant to an obligation created by the terms of an agreement in writing entered into between parties before March 21, 2013, and for the purposes of this paragraph, parties will be considered not to be obligated if one or more of those parties may be excused from fulfilling the obligation as a result of changes to the Act.

Canadian Tax Foundation: Burghardt and Chiu, *"Loss" Is Just a Four-Letter Word: Policy, Practice, and Proposals*, 2013 Conference Report 14:1–43; Jamal, *Revisiting Affiliated Group Loss Consolidations: Effective Strategies & Techniques*, 2013 British Columbia Tax Conference 3:1–34.

Tax Profile: May 2015 — Loss Restriction Event.

▶ 256.1(4) ◀

(4) Special rules. For the purpose of applying paragraph (2)(*a*) in respect of a person or group of persons,

(*a*) if it is reasonable to conclude that one of the reasons that one or more transactions or events occur is to cause a person or group of persons not to hold shares having a fair market value that exceeds 75% of the fair market value of all the shares of the capital stock of a corporation, the paragraph is to be applied without reference to those transactions or events; and

(*b*) the person, or each member of the group, is deemed to have exercised each right that is held by the person or a member of the group and that is referred to in paragraph 251(5)(*b*) in respect of a share of the corporation referred to in paragraph (2)(*a*).

History: S. 256.1(4) was added by S.C. 2013, c. 40, s. 94(1), deemed to have come into force on March 21, 2013, except that it does not apply to an event or transaction that occurs

(*a*) before March 21, 2013, or

(*b*) after March 20, 2013 pursuant to an obligation created by the terms of an agreement in writing entered into between parties before March 21, 2013, and for the purposes of this paragraph, parties will be considered not to be obligated if one or more of those parties may be excused from fulfilling the obligation as a result of changes to the Act.

▶ 256.1(5) ◀

(5) Deeming rules — if share value nil. For the purposes of subsections (2) to (4), if the fair market value of the shares of the capital stock of a corporation is nil at any time, then for the purpose of determining the fair market value of those shares, the corporation is deemed, at that time, to have assets net of liabilities equal to $100,000 and to have $100,000 of income for the taxation year that includes that time.

History: S. 256.1(5) was added by S.C. 2013, c. 40, s. 94(1), deemed to have come into force on March 21, 2013, except that it does not apply to an event or transaction that occurs

(*a*) before March 21, 2013, or

(*b*) after March 20, 2013 pursuant to an obligation created by the terms of an agreement in writing entered into between parties before March 21, 2013, and for the purposes of this paragraph, parties will be considered not to be obligated if one or more of those parties may be excused from fulfilling the obligation as a result of changes to the Act.

▶ 256.1(6) ◀

(6) Deemed acquisition of control. If, at any time as part of a transaction or event or series of transactions or events, control of a particular corporation is acquired by a person or group of persons and it can reasonably be concluded that one of the main reasons for the acquisition of control is so that a specified provision does not apply to one or more corporations, the attribute trading restrictions are deemed to apply to each of those corporations as if control of each of those corporations were acquired at that time.

History: S. 256.1(6) was added by S.C. 2013, c. 40, s. 94(1), deemed to have come into force on March 21, 2013, except that it does not apply to an event or transaction that occurs

(*a*) before March 21, 2013, or

(*b*) after March 20, 2013 pursuant to an obligation created by the terms of an agreement in writing entered into between parties before March 21, 2013, and for the purposes of this paragraph, parties will be considered not to be obligated if one or more of those parties may be excused from fulfilling the obligation as a result of changes to the Act.

SECTION 257: Negative amounts

Except as specifically otherwise provided, where an amount or a number is required under this Act to be determined or calculated by or in accordance with an algebraic formula, if the amount or number when so determined or calculated would, but for this section, be a negative amount or number, it shall be deemed to be nil.

Related Regulations: Part II; Part XXXI; Part XXXII.

Cases: "Taxable income" as defined in subsection 2(2) could not be negative, since "minus" therein was used in its ordinary and grammatical sense. Accordingly, a forward averaging calculation could not be made on the assumption that taxable income was negative. *Capling Estate v. M.N.R.*, 87 DTC 344 (T.C.C.)

SECTION 258: Deemed dividend on term preferred share

▶ 258(1) ◀

(1) Deemed dividend on term preferred share — (Repealed by 1988, c. 55, s. 193(1).)

▶ 258(2) ◀

(2) Idem. Notwithstanding subsection 15(3), an amount paid or payable after 1978 as interest on or as an amount in lieu of interest in respect of

(*a*) any interest or dividend payable after November 16, 1978 on an income bond or an income debenture issued before November 17, 1978 or pursuant to an agreement in writing made before that date, or

(*b*) a dividend that became payable or in arrears after November 16, 1978 on a share of the capital stock of a corporation that is not a term preferred share by reason of having been issued before November 17, 1978 or pursuant to an agreement in writing made before that date,

shall, for the purposes of subsections 112(2.1) and 138(6), be deemed to be a dividend received on a term preferred share.

Related Sections: S. 89(1), "taxable Canadian corporation"; s. 248(1), "amount", "dividend", "income bond", "specified financial institution", "term preferred share".

▶ 258(3) ◀

(3) Deemed interest on preferred shares. Subject to subsection (4), for the purposes of paragraphs 12(1)(*c*) and (*k*) and sections 113 and 126, each amount that is a dividend received in a taxation year on

(*a*) a term preferred share by a specified financial institution resident in Canada from a corporation not resident in Canada, or

(*b*) any other share that

(i) is a grandfathered share, or

(ii) was issued before 8:00 p.m. Eastern Daylight Saving Time, June 18, 1987 and is not deemed by subsection 112(2.22) to have been issued after that time

by a corporation from a corporation not resident in Canada, if the dividend would have been a dividend in respect of which no deduction could have been made under subsection 112(1) or (2) or 138(6) because of subsection 112(2.2) of the *Income Tax Act*, chapter 148 of the Revised Statutes of Canada, 1952, as it read on June 17, 1987, if the corporation that paid the dividend were a taxable Canadian corporation

shall be deemed to be interest received in the year and not a dividend received on a share of the capital stock of a corporation.

Related Sections: S. 12(1)(*c*) Interest; s. 12(1)(*k*) Dividends from other corporations; s. 89(1)(*l*), "taxable Canadian corporation"; s. 112(1) Deduction of taxable dividends received by corporation resident in Canada; s. 112(2) Dividends received from non-resident corporation; s. 112(2.2) Guaranteed shares; s. 113(1) Deduction in respect of dividend received from foreign affiliate; s. 126(1) Foreign tax deduction — non-business income; s. 138(6) Deduction for dividends from taxable corporations; s. 248(1), "corporation", "dividend", "grandfathered share", "taxable Canadian corporation"; s. 249(1) Definition of "taxation year"; s. 250(4) Corporation deemed resident; s. 250(5) Deemed non-resident; s. 258(4) Exception.

Interpretation Bulletins: *Secondary* — IT-88R2 Stock dividends.

► 258(4) ◄

(4) Exception. Subsection (3) does not apply to a dividend described in paragraph (3)(*a*)

(*a*) if the share on which the dividend was paid was not acquired in the ordinary course of the business carried on by the corporation; or

(*b*) to the extent that the dividend would be described by subparagraph 53(2)(*b*)(ii) if the corporation not resident in Canada were not a foreign affiliate of the corporation.

History: S. 258(4) was replaced by S.C. 2013, c. 34, s. 76(1), applicable to dividends paid after August 19, 2011.

Any assessment of a taxpayer's tax, interest and penalties payable under the Act for any taxation year that ends before June 26, 2013 that would, in the absence of this section, be precluded because of subsections 152(4) to (5) of the Act shall be made to the extent necessary to take into account the amendments by S.C. 2013, c. 34, s. 54 to 89.

S. 258(4) formerly read:

(4) *Exception.* Subsection (3) is not applicable to a dividend described in paragraph (3)(*a*) if the share on which the dividend was paid was not acquired in the ordinary course of the business carried on by the corporation.

► 258(5) ◄

(5) Deemed interest on certain shares. For the purposes of paragraphs 12(1)(*c*) and (*k*) and sections 113 and 126, a dividend received after June 18, 1987 and in a taxation year from a corporation not resident in Canada, other than a corporation in which the recipient had or would have, if the corporation were a taxable Canadian corporation, a substantial interest (within the meaning assigned by section 191), on a share, if the dividend would have been a dividend in respect of which no deduction could have been made under subsection 112(1) or (2) or 138(6) by reason of subsection 112(2.2) or (2.4) if the corporation that paid the dividend were a taxable Canadian corporation, shall be deemed to be interest received in the year and not a dividend received on a share of the capital stock of the payer corporation.

► 258(6) ◄

(6) Exception. Subsection (5) does not apply to a dividend described in that subsection to the extent that the dividend would be described by subparagraph 53(2)(*b*)(ii) if the corporation not resident in Canada were not a foreign affiliate of the recipient.

History: S. 258(6) was added by S.C. 2013, c. 34, s. 76(2), applicable to dividends paid after August 19, 2011.

See the application for the amendment to s. 258(4) for the extension of assessment periods to take into account the amendments by S.C. 2013, c. 34, s. 54 to 89.

SECTION 259: Proportional holdings in trust property

► 259(1) ◄

(1) Proportional holdings in trust property. For the purposes of designated provisions, if at any time a specified taxpayer acquires, holds or disposes of a particular unit in a qualified trust and the qualified trust elects for any period that includes that time to have this subsection apply,

(*a*) the taxpayer shall be deemed not to acquire, hold or dispose of at that time, as the case may be, the particular unit;

(*b*) where the taxpayer holds the particular unit at that time, the taxpayer shall be deemed to hold at that time that proportion (referred to in this subsection as the "specified portion") of each property (in this subsection referred to as a "relevant property") held by the trust at that time that one (or, where the particular unit is a fraction of a whole unit, that fraction) is of the number of units of the trust outstanding at that time;

(*c*) (Repealed.)

(*d*) where that time is the later of

(i) the time the trust acquires the relevant property, and

(ii) the time the taxpayer acquires the particular unit,

the taxpayer shall be deemed to acquire the specified portion of a relevant property at that time;

(*e*) where that time is the time the specified portion of a relevant property is deemed by paragraph (*d*) to have been acquired, the fair market value of the specified portion of the relevant property at that time shall be deemed to be the specified portion of the fair market value of the relevant property at the time of its acquisition by the trust;

(*f*) where that time is the time immediately before the time the trust disposes of a particular relevant property, the taxpayer shall be deemed to dispose of, immediately after that time, the specified portion of the particular relevant property for proceeds equal to the specified portion of the proceeds of disposition to the trust of the particular relevant property;

(*g*) where that time is the time immediately before the time the taxpayer disposes of the particular unit, the taxpayer shall be deemed to dispose of, immediately after that time, the specified portion of each relevant property for proceeds equal to the specified portion of the fair market value of that relevant property at that time; and (*h*) where the taxpayer is deemed because of this subsection

(i) to have acquired a portion of a relevant property as a consequence of the acquisition of the particular unit by the taxpayer and the acquisition of the relevant property by the trust, and

(ii) subsequently to have disposed of the specified portion of the relevant property,

the specified portion of the relevant property shall, for the purposes of determining the consequences under this Act of the disposition and without affecting the proceeds of disposition of the specified portion of the relevant property, be deemed to be the portion of the relevant property referred to in subparagraph (i).

History: S. 259(1), the portion before paragraph (*a*) was replaced by S.C. 2011, c. 24, s. 75(1), applicable after 1999. S. 259(1), the portion before paragraph (*a*) formerly read:

(1) *Proportional holdings in trust property.* For the purposes of subsections 146(6), (10) and (10.1), 146.2(6) and 146.3(7), (8) and (9) and Parts X, X.2 and XI to XI.1, if at any time a taxpayer that is a registered investment or that is described in any of paragraphs 149(1)(*r*), (*s*), (*u*) to (*u.2*) or (*x*) acquires, holds or disposes of a particular unit in a qualified trust and the qualified trust elects for any period that includes that time to have this subsection apply,

S. 259(1), the portion before paragraph (*a*) was replaced by S.C. 2009, c. 2, s. 79(1), applicable to the 2009 and subsequent taxation years. S. 259(1), the portion before paragraph (*a*) formerly read:

(1) *Proportional holdings in trust property.* For the purposes of subsections 146(6), (10) and (10.1), 146.2(4) and 146.3(7), (8) and (9) and Parts X, X.2 and XI to XI.1, if at any time a taxpayer that is a registered investment or that is described in any of paragraphs 149(1)(*r*), (*s*), (*u*) to (*u.2*) or (*x*) acquires, holds or disposes of a particular unit in a qualified trust and the qualified trust elects for any period that includes that time to have this subsection apply,

Forms: T1024 — Election to Deem a Proportional Holding in a Qualified Trust Property.

► 259(2) ◄

(2) Proportional holdings in corporate property — (Repealed by S.C. 2005, c. 30, s. 18(3).)

► 259(3) ◄

(3) Election. An election by a qualified trust under subsection (1) shall be made by the qualified trust filing a prescribed form with the Minister and shall apply for the period

(*a*) that begins on the later of

(i) the day that is 15 months before the day on which the election is filed, and

(ii) the day, if any, that is designated by the qualified trust in the election; and

(*b*) that ends on the earlier of

(i) the day on which the qualified trust files with the Minister a notice of revocation of the election, and

(ii) the day, if any, that is designated by the qualified trust in the notice of revocation and that is not before the day that is 15 months before the day on which the notice of revocation is filed.

Related Regulations: 5103(1).

Forms: T1024 — Election to Deem a Proportional Holding in a Qualified Trust Property.

► 259(4) ◄

(4) Requirement to provide information. Where a qualified trust elects under subsection (1),

(*a*) it shall provide notification of the election

(i) within 30 days after making the election, to each person who held a unit in the qualified trust at any time in the period before the election was made and during which the election is applicable, and

(ii) at the time of acquisition, to each person who acquires a unit in the qualified trust at any time in the period after the election was made and during which the election is applicable; and

(*b*) if a person who holds a unit in the qualified trust at any time in the period during which the election is applicable makes a written request to the qualified trust for information that is necessary for the purpose of determining the consequences under this Act of the election for that person, the qualified trust shall provide to the person that information within 30 days after receiving the request.

► 259(5) ◄

(5) Definitions. In this section,

"designated provisions" — "designated provisions" means sections 146 and 146.1 to 146.4 and Parts X, XI.01 and XI.1, as they apply in respect of investments that are not qualified investments for a trust, and Part X.2;

History: S. 259(5), the definition "designated provisions" was replaced by S.C. 2017, c. 33, s. 80(1), deemed in force March 23, 2017, and formerly read:

"designated provisions" — "designated provisions" means sections 146 and 146.1 to 146.4 and Parts X and XI to XI.1, as they apply in respect of investments that are not qualified investments for a trust, and Part X.2;

S. 259(5), the definition "designated provisions" was added by S.C. 2011, c. 24, s. 75(2), applicable after 1999, except that

(i) in its application to taxation years that begin before 2005, is to be read as follows:

" *'designated provisions'* — 'designated provisions' means subsections 146(6), (10) and (10.1), 146.1(2.1), 146.3(7), (8) and (9), and Parts X, X.2, XI and XI.1;"

(ii) in its application to taxation years that begin after 2004 and before 2008, is to be read as follows:

" *'designated provisions'* — 'designated provisions' means subsections 146(6), (10) and (10.1), 146.1(2.1), 146.3(7), (8) and (9), and Parts X, X.2 and XI.1;"

(iii) in its application to taxation years that begin after 2007 and before 2009, is to be read as follows:

" *'designated provisions'* — 'designated provisions' means subsections 146(6), (10) and (10.1), 146.1(2.1), 146.3(7), (8) and (9), and 146.4(5), and Parts X, X.2, XI and XI.1;"

(iv) in its application to taxation years that begin after 2008 and end before March 23, 2011, is to be read as follows:

" *'designated provisions'* — 'designated provisions' means subsections 146(6), (10) and (10.1), 146.1(2.1), 146.2(6), 146.3(7), (8) and (9), and 146.4(5), and Parts X, X.2 and XI to XI.1;"

"qualified corporation" — (Repealed by S.C. 2005, c. 30, s. 18(5).)

Related Regulations: 5103(1).

Related Sections: S. 104(1) Reference to trust or estate; s. 204.4(1), "registered investment"; s. 248(1), "corporation", "registered pension plan", "trust"; s. 248(10) Series of transactions.

"qualified trust" — "qualified trust" at any time means a trust (other than a registered investment or a trust that is prescribed to be a small business investment trust) where

(*a*) each trustee of the trust at that time is a corporation that is licensed or otherwise authorized under the laws of Canada or a province to carry on in Canada the business of offering to the public its services as a trustee or a person who is a trustee of a trust governed by a registered pension plan,

(*b*) all the interests of the beneficiaries under the trust at that time are described by reference to units of the trust all of which are at that time identical to each other,

(*c*) it has never before that time borrowed money except where the borrowing was for a term not exceeding 90 days and the borrowing was not part of a series of loans or other transactions and repayments, and

(*d*) it has never before that time accepted deposits.

Related Regulations: 5103(1).

Related Sections: S. 104(1) Reference to trust or estate; s. 204.4(1), "registered investment"; s. 248(1), "corporation", "registered pension plan", "trust"; s. 248(10) Series of transactions.

"specified taxpayer" —"specified taxpayer" means a taxpayer that is a registered investment or that is described in any of paragraphs 149(1)(*r*), (*s*), (*u*) to (*u*.2) and (*x*).

History: S. 259(5), the definition "specified taxpayer" was added by S.C. 2011, c. 24, s. 75(2), applicable after 1999, except that

(i) in its application to taxation years that begin before 2005, is to be read as follows:

" *'specified taxpayer'* — 'specified taxpayer' means a taxpayer described in section 205."

(ii) in its application to taxation years that begin after 2004 and before 2008, is to be read as follows:

" *'specified taxpayer'* — 'specified taxpayer' means a taxpayer that is a registered investment or that is described in any of paragraphs 149(1)(*r*), (*s*), (*u*) and (*x*)."

(iii) in its application to taxation years that begin after 2007 and before 2009, is to be read as follows:

" *'specified taxpayer'* — 'specified taxpayer' means a taxpayer that is a registered investment or that is described in any of paragraphs 149(1)(*r*), (*s*), (*u*), (*u*.1) and (*x*)."

SECTION 260: [Securities lending arrangements]

► 260(1) ◄

(1) Definitions. In this section,

"dealer compensation payment" —"dealer compensation payment" means an amount received by a taxpayer as compensation, for an underlying payment,

(*a*) from a registered securities dealer resident in Canada who paid the amount in the ordinary course of a business of trading in securities, or

(*b*) in the ordinary course of the taxpayer's business of trading in securities, where the taxpayer is a registered securities dealer resident in Canada;

History: S. 260(1), the definition "dealer compensation payment" was added by S.C. 2013, c. 34, s. 365(5), applicable to arrangements made after 2001.

"qualified security" —"qualified security" means

(*a*) a share of a class of the capital stock of a corporation that is listed on a stock exchange or of a class of the capital stock of a corporation that is a public corporation by reason of the designation of the class by the corporation in an election made under subparagraph (*b*)(i) of the definition "public corporation" in subsection 89(1) or by the Minister in a notice to the corporation under subparagraph (*b*)(ii) of that definition,

(*b*) a bond, debenture, note or similar obligation of a corporation described in paragraph (*a*) or of a corporation that is controlled by such a corporation,

(*c*) a bond, debenture, note or similar obligation of or guaranteed by the government of any country, province, state, municipality or other political subdivision, or a corporation, commission, agency or association controlled by any such person,

(*d*) a warrant, right, option or similar instrument with respect to a share described in paragraph (*a*), or

(*e*) a qualified trust unit;

History: S. 260(1), paragraph (*e*) of the definition "qualified security" was added by S.C. 2013, c. 34, s. 365(1), applicable to arrangements made after 2001.

"qualified trust unit" —"qualified trust unit" means an interest, as a beneficiary under a trust, that is listed on a stock exchange;

History: S. 260(1), the definition "qualified trust unit" was added by S.C. 2013, c. 34, s. 365(5), applicable to arrangements made after 2001, except that, the definition "qualified trust unit" in subsection 260(1) is to be read,

(i) in its application to arrangements made before October 24, 2012, as follows:

" 'qualified trust unit' means a unit of a mutual fund trust that is listed on a stock exchange;"

and

(ii) before December 14, 2007 as though the reference to "stock exchange" in the read-as text in subparagraph (i) were a reference to "prescribed stock exchange".

"securities lending arrangement" —"securities lending arrangement" means an arrangement under which

(*a*) a person (in this section referred to as the "lender") transfers or lends at any particular time a qualified security to another person (in this section referred to as the "borrower"),

(*b*) it may reasonably be expected, at the particular time, that the borrower will transfer or return after the particular time to the lender a security (in this section referred to as an "identical security") that is identical to the security so transferred or lent,

(*c*) the borrower is obligated to pay to the lender amounts equal to and as compensation for all amounts, if any, paid on the security that would have been received by the borrower if the borrower had held the security throughout the period that begins after the particular time and that ends at the time an identical security is transferred or returned to the lender,

(*d*) the lender's risk of loss or opportunity for gain or profit with respect to the security is not changed in any material respect, and

(*e*) if the lender and the borrower do not deal with each other at arm's length, it is intended that neither the arrangement nor any series of securities lending arrangements, loans or other transactions of which the arrangement is a part be in effect for more than 270 days,

but does not include an arrangement one of the main purposes of which may reasonably be considered to be to avoid or defer the inclusion in income of any gain or profit with respect to the security.

History: S. 260(1), paragraph (*a*) of the definition "securities lending arrangement" was replaced by S.C. 2013, c. 34, s. 365(2), applicable to arrangements made after 2002, and formerly read:

(*a*) a person (in this section referred to as the "lender") transfers or lends at any particular time a qualified security to another person (in this section referred to as the "borrower") with whom the lender deals at arm's length,

S. 260(1), paragraph (*c*) of the definition "securities lending arrangement" was replaced by S.C. 2013, c. 34, s. 365(3), applicable to arrangements made after 2001, and formerly read:

(*c*) where the qualified security is a share of the capital stock of a corporation, the borrower is obligated to pay to the lender amounts equal to and as compensation for all dividends, if any, paid on the security that would have been received by the borrower if the borrower had held the security throughout the period beginning after the particular time and ending at the time an identical security is transferred or returned to the lender, and

S. 260(1), paragraph (*e*) of the definition "securities lending arrangement" was added by S.C. 2013, c. 34, s. 365(4), applicable to arrangements made after 2002.

Tax Profile: November 2006 — Structuring and Taxation of Canadian Hedge Funds; February 2005 — The Canadian Treatment of Derivatives.

"security distribution" —"security distribution" means an amount that is

(*a*) an underlying payment, or

(*b*) an SLA compensation payment, or a dealer compensation payment, that is deemed by subsection (5.1) to be an amount received as an amount described by any of paragraphs (5.1)(*a*) to (*c*);

History: S. 260(1), the definition "security distribution" was added by S.C. 2013, c. 34, s. 365(5), applicable to arrangements made after 2001.

"SLA compensation payment" —"SLA compensation payment" means an amount paid pursuant to

(*a*) a securities lending arrangement as compensation for an underlying payment; or

(*b*) a specified securities lending arrangement as compensation for an underlying payment, including, if the property transferred or lent is described in subparagraph (*a*)(ii) of the definition specified securities lending arrangement, as compensation for a taxable dividend paid on a share described in subparagraph (*a*)(i) of that definition;

History: S. 260(1), the definition "SLA compensation payment" was replaced by S.C. 2018, c. 27, s. 27(1), applicable in respect of amounts paid or payable, or received or receivable, as compensation for dividends after February 26, 2018. However, the amendment does not apply in respect of amounts paid or payable, or received or receivable, as compensation for dividends after February 26, 2018 and before October 2018, if they are pursuant to a written 2018. The definition "SLA compensation payment" formerly read:

"SLA compensation payment"—"SLA compensation payment" means an amount paid pursuant to a securities lending arrangement as compensation for an underlying payment;

S. 260(1), the definition "SLA compensation payment" was added by S.C. 2013, c. 34, s. 365(5), applicable to arrangements made after 2001.

"specified securities lending arrangement"means an arrangement, other than a securities lending arrangement, under which

(*a*) a particular person (referred to in this definition as a "transferor") transfers or lends at any particular time a property to another person (referred to in this definition as a "transferee") and the property is

(i) a particular share described in paragraph (*a*) of the definition qualified security, or

(ii) a property in respect of which the following conditions are met:

(A) the property is

(I) an interest in a partnership, or

(II) an interest as a beneficiary under a trust, and

(B) all or any part of the fair market value of the property, immediately before the particular time, is derived, directly or indirectly, from a share described in subparagraph (i),

(*b*) it may reasonably be expected, at the particular time, that the transferee — or a person that does not deal at arm's length with, or is affiliated with, the transferee — will transfer or return after the particular time to the transferor — or a person that does not deal at arm's length with, or is affiliated with, the transferor (referred to in this definition as a "substitute transferor") — a property that is identical or substantially identical to the property so transferred or lent, and

(*c*) the transferor's (together with any substitute transferor's) risk of loss or opportunity for gain or profit with respect to the particular property is not changed in any material respect;

History: S. 260(1), the definition "specified securities lending arrangement" was added by S.C. 2018, c. 27, s. 27(2), applicable in respect of amounts paid or payable, or received or receivable, as compensation for dividends after February 26, 2018. However, the amendment does not apply in respect of amounts paid or payable, or received or receivable, as compensation for dividends after February 26, 2018 and before October 2018, if they are pursuant to a written arrangement entered into before February 27, 2018.

"underlying payment" —"underlying payment" means an amount paid on a qualified security by the issuer of the security.

History: S. 260(1), the definition "underlying payment" was added by S.C. 2013, c. 34, s. 365(5), applicable to arrangements made after 2001.

▶ 260(1.1) ◀

(1.1) Eligible dividend. This subsection applies to an amount if the amount is received by a person who is resident in Canada, the amount is deemed under subsection (5.1) to be a taxable dividend, and the amount is either

(*a*) received as compensation for an eligible dividend, within the meaning assigned by subsection 89(1); or

(*b*) received as compensation for a taxable dividend (other than an eligible dividend) paid by a corporation to a non-resident shareholder in circumstances where it is reasonable to consider that the corporation would, if that shareholder were resident in Canada, have designated the dividend to be an eligible dividend under subsection 89(14).

Proposed Amendment

2019 Federal Budget Resolutions

Section 260 of the Act is amended by adding the following after subsection (1.1):

(1.2) References — borrower and lender. For the purposes of subsections (8), (8.1), (8.2), (8.3), (8.4) and (9.1) and 212(2.1) and (3), in respect of a specified securities lending arrangement,

(*a*) a reference to a borrower includes a transferee; and

(*b*) a reference to a lender includes a transferor.

Applicable: Deemed to have come into force on March 19, 2019.

History: S. 260(1.1), the portion before paragraph (*a*) was replaced by S.C. 2013, c. 34, s. 365(6), applicable to amounts received as compensation for dividends paid after 2005, and formerly read:

(1.1) *Eligible dividend.* This subsection applies to an amount if the amount is received by a person who is resident in Canada, the amount is deemed under subsection (5) to be a taxable dividend, and the amount is either

► 260(2) ◄

(2) Non-disposition. Subject to subsections (3) and (4), for the purposes of this Act, any transfer or loan by a lender of a security under a securities lending arrangement shall be deemed not to be a disposition of the security and the security shall be deemed to continue to be property of the lender and, for the purposes of this subsection, a security shall be deemed to include an identical security that has been transferred or returned to the lender under the arrangement.

► 260(3) ◄

(3) Disposition of right. Where, at any time, a lender receives property (other than an identical security or an amount deemed by subsection (4) to have been received as proceeds of disposition) in satisfaction of or in exchange for the lender's right under a securities lending arrangement to receive the transfer or return of an identical security, for the purposes of this Act the lender shall be deemed to have disposed at that time of the security that was transferred or lent for proceeds of disposition equal to the fair market value of the property received for the disposition of the right (other than any portion thereof that is deemed to have been received by the lender as a taxable dividend), except that section 51, 85.1, 86 or 87, as the case may be, shall apply in computing the income of the lender with respect to any such disposition as if the security transferred or lent had continued to be the lender's property and the lender had received the property directly.

► 260(4) ◄

(4) Idem. Where, at any time, it may reasonably be considered that a lender would have received proceeds of disposition for a security that was transferred or lent under a securities lending arrangement, if the security had not been transferred or lent, the lender shall be deemed to have disposed of the security at that time for those proceeds of disposition.

► 260(5) ◄

(5) Where subsection (5.1) applies. Subsection (5.1) applies to a taxpayer for a taxation year in respect of a particular amount (other than an amount received as proceeds of disposition or an amount received by a person under an arrangement where it may reasonably be considered that one of the main reasons for the person entering into the arrangement was to enable the person to receive an SLA compensation payment pursuant to a securities lending arrangement, or a dealer compensation payment, that would be deductible in computing the taxable income, or not included in computing the income, for any taxation year of the person) received by the taxpayer in the taxation year

(*a*) as an SLA compensation payment,

(i) from a person resident in Canada, or

(ii) from a non-resident person who paid the particular amount in the course of carrying on business in Canada through a permanent establishment as defined by regulation; or

(*b*) as a dealer compensation payment.

History: S. 260(5), the portion before paragraph (*a*) was replaced by S.C. 2018, c. 27(3), applicable in respect of amounts paid or payable, or received or receivable, as compensation for dividends after February 26, 2018. However, the amendment does not apply in respect of amounts paid or payable, or received or receivable, as compensation for dividends after February 26, 2018 and before October 2018, if they are pursuant to a written arrangement entered into before February 27, 2018, and formerly read:

Where subsection (5.1) applies Subsection (5.1) applies to a taxpayer for a taxation year in respect of a particular amount (other than an amount received as proceeds of disposition or an amount received by a person under an arrangement where it may reasonably be considered that one of the main reasons for the person entering into the arrangement was to enable the person to receive an SLA compensation payment or a dealer compensation payment that would be deductible in computing the taxable income, or not included in computing the income, for any taxation year of the person) received by the taxpayer in the taxation year

S. 260(5) was replaced by S.C. 2013, c. 34, s. 365(7), applicable to arrangements made after 2001, and formerly read:

(5) *Deemed dividend.* For the purposes of this Act, any amount received (other than an amount received as proceeds of disposition or an amount received by a corporation under an arrangement where it may reasonably be considered that one of the main reasons for the corporation entering into the arrangement was to enable it to receive an amount that would otherwise have been deemed by this subsection to be a dividend)

(*a*) under a securities lending arrangement from a person resident in Canada, or a person not resident in Canada where the amount was paid in the course of carrying on business in Canada through a permanent establishment as defined by regulation, or

(*b*) by or from a person who is a registered securities dealer resident in Canada, where the amount is received or paid, as the case may be, in the ordinary course of the business of trading in securities carried on by the dealer,

as compensation for a taxable dividend paid on a share of the capital stock of a public corporation that is a qualified security shall, to the extent of the amount of that dividend, be deemed to have been received as a taxable dividend and, if subsection (1.1) applies to the amount, as an eligible dividend on the share from the corporation.

Related Regulations: 8201.

Tax Profile: February 2005 — The Canadian Treatment of Derivatives.

► 260(5.1) ◄

(5.1) Deemed character of compensation payments. If this subsection applies in respect of a particular amount received by a taxpayer in a taxation year as an SLA compensation payment or as a dealer compensation payment, the particular amount is deemed, to the extent of the underlying payment to which the amount relates, to have been received by the taxpayer in the taxation year as,

(*a*) where the underlying payment is a taxable dividend paid on a share of the capital stock of a public corporation (other than an underlying payment to which paragraph (*b*) applies), a taxable dividend on the share and, if subsection (1.1) applies to the particular amount, an eligible dividend on the share;

(*b*) where the underlying payment is paid by a trust on a qualified trust unit issued by the trust,

(i) an amount of the trust's income that was, to the extent that subsection 104(13) applied to the underlying payment,

(A) paid by the trust to the taxpayer as a beneficiary under the trust, and

(B) designated by the trust in respect of the taxpayer to the extent of a valid designation, if any, by the trust under this Act in respect of the recipient of the underlying payment, and

(ii) to the extent that the underlying payment is a distribution of a property from the trust, a distribution of that property from the trust; or

(*c*) in any other case, interest.

History: S. 260(5.1) was added by S.C. 2013, c. 34, s. 365(7), applicable to arrangements made after 2001, except that,

(a) if the parties to an arrangement jointly so elect in writing and file the election with the Minister of National Revenue by September 24, 2013 [within 90 days after royal assent] subsection 260(5.1) is to be read, in its application to SLA compensation payments or dealer compensation payments received under the arrangement before February 28, 2004, without reference to paragraph 260(5.1)(b) or (c), or to both of those paragraphs, as specified by the parties in the election;

(b) for amounts received as compensation for dividends paid before 2006, paragraph 260(5.1)(a) is to be read without reference to "and, if subsection (1.1) applies to the amount, an eligible dividend on the share from the corporation".

Related Sections: S. 18(1)(w) Underlying payments on qualified securities.

► 260(6) ◄

(6) Deductibility. In computing the income of a taxpayer under Part I from a business or property for a taxation year, there may be deducted a particular amount, paid by the taxpayer in the year as an SLA compensation payment or as a dealer compensation payment, that is equal to

(a) if the taxpayer is a registered securities dealer and the particular amount is deemed by subsection (5.1) to have been received as a taxable dividend, no more than 2/3 of the particular amount (unless, for greater certainty, the particular amount is an amount for which a deduction in computing income may be claimed under subsection (6.1) by the taxpayer); or

(b) if the particular amount is in respect of an amount other than an amount that is, or is deemed by subsection (5.1) to have been, received as a taxable dividend,

(i) where the taxpayer disposes of the borrowed security and includes the gain or loss, if any, from the disposition in computing its income from a business, the particular amount, or

(ii) in any other case, the lesser of

(A) the particular amount, and

(B) the amount, if any, in respect of the security distribution to which the SLA compensation payment or dealer compensation payment relates that is included in computing the income, and not deducted in computing the taxable income, for any taxation year of the taxpayer or of any person to whom the taxpayer is related.

History: S. 260(6)(a) was replaced by S.C. 2018, c. 27, s. 27(4), applicable in respect of amounts paid or payable, or received or receivable, as compensation for dividends after February 26, 2018. However, the amendment does not apply in respect of amounts paid or payable, or received or receivable, as compensation for dividends after February 26, 2018 and before October 2018, if they are pursuant to a written arrangement entered into before February 27, 2018, and formerly read:

(a) if the taxpayer is a registered securities dealer and the particular amount is deemed by subsection (5.1) to have been received as a taxable dividend, no more than 2/3 of the particular amount; or

S. 260(6) was replaced by S.C. 2013, c. 34, s. 365(7), applicable to arrangements made after 2001, and formerly read:

(6) *Non-deductibility.* In computing a taxpayer's income under Part I from a business or property

(a) where the taxpayer is not a registered securities dealer, no deduction shall be made in respect of an amount that, if paid, would be deemed by subsection (5) to have been received by another person as a taxable dividend; and

(b) where the taxpayer is a registered securities dealer, no deduction shall be made in respect of more than $^2/_3$ of that amount.

► 260(6.1) ◄

(6.1) Deductible amount. There may be deducted in computing a corporation's income under Part I from a business or property for a taxation year an amount equal to the lesser of

(a) the total of all amounts each of which is an amount that the corporation becomes obligated in the taxation year to pay to another person under an arrangement described in paragraph (b) of the definition "dividend rental arrangement" in subsection 248(1) that, if paid, would be deemed by subsection (5.1) to have been received by another person as a taxable dividend, and

(b) the amount of the dividends received by the corporation under the arrangement that were identified in its return of income under Part I for the year as an amount in respect of which no amount was deductible because of subsection 112(2.3) in computing the taxpayer's taxable income or taxable income earned in Canada.

History: S. 260(6.1), the portion before paragraph (a) was replaced by S.C. 2018, c. 27, s. 27(5), applicable in respect of amounts paid or payable, or received or receivable, as compensation for dividends after February 26, 2018. However, the amendment does not apply in respect of amounts paid or payable, or received or receivable, as compensation for dividends after February 26, 2018 and before October 2018, if they are pursuant to a written arrangement entered into before February 27, 2018, and formerly read:

(6.1) *Deductible amount.* Notwithstanding subsection (6), there may be deducted in computing a corporation's income under Part I from a business or property for a taxation year an amount equal to the lesser of

S. 260(6.1)(a) was replaced by S.C. 2013, c. 34, s. 365(8), applicable to

(a) arrangements made after December 20, 2002;

(b) an arrangement made after November 2, 1998 and before December 21, 2002 if the parties to the arrangement have made the election under the definition "dividend rental arrangement" in s. 248(1), except that, in its application to an arrangement made before 2002, the reference to "subsection (5.1)" in paragraph 260(6.1)(a) is to be read as a reference to "subsection (5)"; and

(c) an arrangement, other than an arrangement to which paragraph (b) applies, made after 2001 and before December 21, 2002, except that, in its application before December 21, 2002, paragraph 260(6.1)(a) is to be read as follows:

"(a) the amount that the corporation is obligated to pay to another person under an arrangement described in paragraphs (c) and (d) of the definition 'dividend rental arrangement' in subsection 248(1) that, if paid, would be deemed by subsection (5.1) to have been received by another person as a taxable dividend, and"

S. 260(6.1)(a) formerly read:

(a) the amount that the corporation is obligated to pay to another person under an arrangement described in paragraphs (c) and (d) of the definition "dividend rental arrangement" in subsection 248(1) that, if paid, would be deemed by subsection (5) to have been received by another person as a taxable dividend, and

► 260(7) ◄

(7) Dividend refund. For the purpose of section 129, if a corporation pays an amount for which no deduction in computing the corporation's income may be claimed under subsection (6.1) and subsection (5.1) deems the amount to have been received by another person as a taxable dividend,

(a) the corporation is deemed to have paid the amount as a taxable dividend, where the corporation is not a registered securities dealer; and

(b) the corporation is deemed to have paid 1/3 of the amount as a taxable dividend, where the corporation is a registered securities dealer.

History: S. 260(7) was replaced by S.C. 2013, c. 34, s. 365(9), applicable to arrangements made after 2001, and formerly read:

(7) *Dividend refund.* For the purposes of section 129,

(a) any amount paid by a corporation that is not a registered securities dealer (other than an amount for which a deduction in computing income may be claimed under subsection (6.1)), and (*b*) $^{1}/_{3}$ of any amount paid by a corporation that is a registered securities dealer (other than an amount for which a deduction in computing income may be claimed under subsection (6.1))

that is deemed by subsection (5) to have been received by another person as a taxable dividend shall be deemed to have been paid by the corporation as a taxable dividend.

► 260(8) ◄

(8) Non-resident withholding tax. For the purpose of Part XIII, any amount paid or credited under a securities lending arrangement by or on behalf of the borrower to the lender

(*a*) as an SLA compensation payment is, subject to paragraph (*b*) or (*c*), deemed to be a payment of interest made by the borrower to the lender;

(*b*) as an SLA compensation payment in respect of a security that is a qualified trust unit, is deemed, to the extent of the amount of the underlying payment to which the SLA compensation payment relates, to be an amount paid by the trust and having the same character and composition as the underlying payment;

(*c*) as an SLA compensation payment, if the security is not a qualified trust unit and throughout the term of the securities lending arrangement, the borrower has provided the lender under the arrangement with money in an amount of, or securities described in paragraph (*c*) of the definition "qualified security" in subsection (1) that have a fair market value of, not less than 95% of the fair market value of the security and the borrower is entitled to enjoy, directly or indirectly, the benefits of all or substantially all income derived from, and opportunity for gain with respect of, the money or securities,

(i) is, to the extent of the amount of the interest or dividend paid in respect of the security, deemed to be a payment made by the borrower to the lender of interest or a dividend, as the case may be, payable on the security, and

(ii) is, to the extent of the amount of the interest, if any, paid in respect of the security, deemed to have been payable on a security described in paragraph (*a*) of the definition "fully exempt interest" in subsection 212(3) if the security is described in paragraph (*c*) of the definition "qualified security" in subsection (1); and

(*d*) as, on account of, in lieu of payment of or in satisfaction of, a fee for the use of the security is deemed to be a payment of interest made by the borrower to the lender.

Proposed Amendment
2019 Federal Budget Resolutions
Subsection 260(8) of the Act is replaced by the following:

(8) Non-resident withholding tax. For the purpose of Part XIII, any amount paid or credited under a securities lending arrangement or a specified securities lending arrangement by or on behalf of the borrower to the lender

(*a*) as an SLA compensation payment in respect of a security that is not a qualified trust unit, is deemed

(i) to the extent of the amount of the interest paid in respect of the security, to be a payment made by the borrower to the lender of interest, and

(ii) to the extent of the amount of the dividend paid in respect of the security, to be a payment made by the borrower to the lender of a dividend payable on the security;

(*b*) as an SLA compensation payment in respect of a security that is a qualified trust unit, is deemed, to the extent of the amount of the underlying payment to which the SLA compensation payment relates, to be an amount paid by the trust and having the same character and composition as the underlying payment; and

(*c*) as, on account of, in lieu of payment of or in satisfaction of, a fee for the use of the security is deemed to be a payment of interest made by the borrower to the lender.

Applicable: In respect of amounts paid or credited as SLA compensation payments on or after March 19, 2019. However, this does not apply in respect of amounts paid or credited as SLA compensation payments on or after March 19, 2019 and before October 2019, if they are pursuant to a written arrangement entered into before March 19, 2019.

History: S. 260(8) was replaced by S.C. 2013, c. 34, s. 365(9), applicable to arrangements made after 2001, except that, before 2008, subparagraph 260(8)(*c*)(ii) is to be read as follows:

"(ii) is, to the extent of the amount of the interest, if any, paid in respect of the security, deemed

(A) for the purpose of subparagraph 212(1)(*b*)(vii) to have been payable by the issuer of the security, and

(B) to have been payable on a security that is a security described in subparagraph 212(1)(*b*)(ii) where the security is a security described in paragraph (*c*) of the definition "qualified security" in subsection (1); and"

S. 260(8) formerly read:

(8) *Non-resident withholding tax.* For the purposes of Part XIII,

(*a*) any amount paid or credited under a securities lending arrangement by or on behalf of the borrower to the lender as compensation for any interest or dividend paid in respect of the security shall be deemed to be a payment made by the borrower to the lender of interest, except that where, throughout the term of the securities lending arrangement, the borrower has provided the lender under the arrangement with money in an amount of, or securities described in paragraph (*c*) of the definition "qualified security" in subsection (1) that have a fair market value of, not less than 95% of the fair market value of the security and the borrower is entitled to enjoy, directly or indirectly, the benefits of all or substantially all income derived from, and opportunity for gain in respect of, the money or securities,

(i) the amount paid or credited shall, to the extent of the amount of the interest or dividend paid in respect of the security, be deemed to be a payment made by the borrower to the lender of interest or a dividend, as the case may be, payable on the security, and

(ii) the security is deemed to be a security described in paragraph (*a*) of the definition "fully exempt interest" in subsection 212(3) if the security is described in paragraph (*c*) of the definition "qualified security" in subsection (1), and

(iii) (Repealed.)

(*b*) any amount paid or credited under a securities lending arrangement by or on behalf of the borrower to the lender as, on account of, in lieu of payment of or in satisfaction of, a fee for the use of the security shall be deemed to be a payment made by the borrower to the lender of interest and, for the purpose of this paragraph, where the borrower has at any time provided the lender with money, either as collateral or consideration for the security, and the borrower does not under the arrangement pay or credit a reasonable amount to the lender as, on account of, in lieu of payment of or in satisfaction of, a fee for the use of the security, the amount, if any, by which

(i) interest on the money computed at the prescribed rates in effect during the term of the arrangement

exceeds

(ii) the amount, if any, by which any amount that the lender pays or credits to the borrower under the arrangement exceeds the amount of the money shall be deemed to be an amount paid under the arrangement by the borrower to the lender as a fee for the use of the security, at the time that an identical security is or can reasonably be expected to be transferred or returned to the lender,

and, for the purposes of Part XIII and any agreement or convention between the Government of Canada and the government of another country that has the force of law in Canada, any amount deemed by this subsection (other than subparagraph (*a*)(i) or (ii)) to be a payment of interest shall be deemed not to be payable on or in respect of the security.

► 260(8.1) ◄

(8.1) Deemed fee for borrowed security. For the purpose of paragraph (8)(*d*), if under a securities lending arrangement the borrower has at any time provided the lender with money, either as collateral or consideration for the security, and the borrower does not, under the arrangement, pay or credit a reasonable amount to the lender as, on account of, in lieu of payment of or in satisfaction of, a fee for the use of the security, the borrower is deemed to have, at the time that an identical security is or can reasonably be expected to be transferred or returned to the lender, paid to the lender under the arrangement an amount as a fee for the use of the security equal to the amount, if any, by which

Proposed Amendment
2019 Federal Budget Resolutions

The portion of subsection 260(8.1) of the Act before paragraph (*a*) is replaced by the following:

(8.1) Deemed fee for borrowed security. For the purpose of paragraph (8)(*c*), if under a securities lending arrangement or a specified securities lending arrangement the borrower has at any time provided the lender with money, either as collateral or consideration for the security, and the borrower does not, under the arrangement, pay or credit a reasonable amount to the lender as, on account of, in lieu of payment of or in satisfaction of, a fee for the use of the security, the borrower is deemed to have, at the time that an identical or substantially identical security is or can reasonably be expected to be transferred or returned to the lender, paid to the lender under the arrangement an amount as a fee for the use of the security equal to the amount, if any, by which

Applicable: In respect of amounts paid or credited as SLA compensation payments on or after March 19, 2019. However, this does not apply in respect of amounts paid or credited as SLA compensation payments on or after March 19, 2019 and before October 2019, if they are pursuant to a written arrangement entered into before March 19, 2019.

(*a*) the interest on the money computed at the prescribed rates in effect during the term of the arrangement

exceeds

(*b*) the amount, if any, by which any amount that the lender pays or credits to the borrower under the arrangement exceeds the amount of the money.

History: S. 260(8.1) was added by S.C. 2013, c. 34, s. 365(9), applicable to arrangements made after 2001.

► 260(8.2) ◄

(8.2) Effect for tax treaties. In applying subsection (8), any amount, paid or credited under a securities lending arrangement by or on behalf of the borrower to the lender, that is deemed by paragraph (8)(*a*), (*b*) or (*d*) to be a payment of interest, is deemed for the purposes of any tax treaty not to be payable on or in respect of the security.

Proposed Amendment
2019 Federal Budget Resolutions

Subsection 260(8.2) of the Act is replaced by the following:

(8.2) Effect for tax treaties — interest. In applying subparagraph (8)(*a*)(i), if a securities lending arrangement or specified securities lending arrangement is a fully collateralized arrangement, any SLA compensation payment deemed to be a payment made by the borrower to the lender of interest is deemed for the purposes of any tax treaty to be payable on the security.

Applicable: In respect of amounts paid or credited as SLA compensation payments on or after March 19, 2019. However, this does not apply in respect of amounts paid or credited as SLA compensation payments on or after March 19, 2019 and before October 2019, if they are pursuant to a written arrangement entered into before March 19, 2019.

Proposed Amendment
2019 Federal Budget Resolutions

Section 260 of the Act is amended by adding the following after subsection (8.2):

(8.3) Effect for tax treaties — dividend. In applying subparagraph (8)(*a*)(ii), if the security is a share of a class of the capital stock of a corporation resident in Canada (in this subsection referred to as the "Canadian share"), for the purposes of determining the rate of tax that Canada may impose on a dividend because of the dividend article of a tax treaty,

(*a*) any SLA compensation payment deemed to be a payment made by the borrower to the lender of a dividend is deemed to be paid by the issuer of the Canadian share and not by the borrower;

(*b*) the lender is deemed to be the beneficial owner of the Canadian share; and

(*c*) the shares of the capital stock of the issuer owned by the lender are deemed to give it less than 10% of the votes that could be cast at an annual meeting of the shareholders of the issuer and have less than 10% of the fair market value of all of the issued and outstanding shares of the capital stock of the issuer, if

(i) the securities lending arrangement or the specified securities lending arrangement is not a fully collateralized arrangement, and

(ii) the borrower and the lender are not dealing at arm's length.

(8.4) Idem. In applying subparagraph (8)(*a*)(ii), if the security is a share of a class of the capital stock of a non-resident corporation, for the purposes of determining the rate of tax that Canada may impose on a dividend because of the dividend article of a tax treaty, the shares of the capital stock of the borrower owned by the lender are deemed to give it less than 10% of the votes that could be cast at an annual meeting of the shareholders of the borrower, and the lender is deemed to hold less than 10% of the fair market value of all of the issued and outstanding shares of the capital stock of the borrower if

(*a*) the securities lending arrangement or the specified securities lending arrangement is not a fully collateralized arrangement; and

(*b*) the borrower and the lender are not dealing at arm's length.

Applicable: In respect of amounts paid or credited as SLA compensation payments on or after March 19, 2019. However, this does not apply in respect of amounts paid or credited as SLA compensation payments on or after March 19, 2019 and before October 2019, if they are pursuant to a written arrangement entered into before March 19, 2019.

History: S. 260(8.2) was added by S.C. 2013, c. 34, s. 365(9), applicable to arrangements made after 2001.

▶ 260(9) ◀

(9) Restricted financial institution. For the purposes of subsection 187.3(1), where at any time a dividend is received by a restricted financial institution on a share that was last acquired before that time pursuant to an obligation of a borrower to return or transfer a share under a securities lending arrangement, an acquisition of the share under the arrangement shall be deemed at and after that time not to be an acquisition of the share.

▶ 260(9.1) ◀

(9.1) Non-arm's length compensation payment. For the purpose of Part XIII, where the lender under a securities lending arrangement is not dealing at arm's length with either the borrower under the arrangement or the issuer of the security that is transferred or lent under the arrangement, or both, and subsection (8) deems an amount to be a payment of interest by a person to the lender in respect of that security, the lender is deemed, in respect of that payment, not to be dealing at arm's length with that person.

Proposed Amendment
2019 Federal Budget Resolutions
Subsection 260(9.1) of the Act is replaced by the following:

(9.1) Non-arm's length compensation payment. For the purpose of Part XIII, if the lender under a securities lending arrangement or a specified securities lending arrangement is not dealing at arm's length with either the borrower under the arrangement or the issuer of the security that is transferred or lent under the arrangement, or both, and subsection (8) deems an amount to be a payment of interest by a person to the lender, the lender is deemed, in respect of that payment, not to be dealing at arm's length with that person.

Applicable: In respect of amounts paid or credited as SLA compensation payments on or after March 19, 2019. However, this does not apply in respect of amounts paid or credited as SLA compensation payments on or after March 19, 2019 and before October 2019, if they are pursuant to a written arrangement entered into before March 19, 2019.

History: S. 260(10) was renumbered as s. 260(9.1) by S.C. 2013, c. 34, s. 365(10), deemed to have come into force on January 1, 2008.

▶ 260(10) ◀

(10) Partnerships. For the purpose of this section,

(*a*) a person includes a partnership; and

(*b*) a partnership is deemed to be a registered securities dealer if each member of the partnership is a registered securities dealer.

History: S. 260(10) was added by S.C. 2013, c. 34, s. 365(11), applicable to

(*a*) arrangements made after December 20, 2002; and

(*b*) an arrangement made after November 2, 1998 and before December 21, 2002 if the parties to the arrangement have made the election under the definition "dividend rental arrangement" in s. 248(1).

▶ 260(11) ◀

(11) Corporate members of partnerships. A corporation that is, in a taxation year, a member of a partnership is deemed

(*a*) for the purpose of applying subsection (5) in respect of the taxation year,

(i) to receive its specified proportion, for each fiscal period of the partnership that ends in the taxation year, of each amount received by the partnership in that fiscal period, and

(ii) in respect of the receipt of its specified proportion of that amount, to be the same person as the partnership;

(*b*) for the purpose of applying paragraph (6.1)(*a*) in respect of the taxation year, to become obligated to pay its specified proportion, for each fiscal period of the partnership that ends in the taxation year, of the amount the partnership becomes, in that fiscal period, obligated to pay to another person under the arrangement described in that paragraph; and

(*c*) for the purpose of applying section 129 in respect of the taxation year, to have paid

(i) if the partnership is not a registered securities dealer, the corporation's specified proportion, for each fiscal period of the partnership that ends in the taxation year, of each amount paid by the partnership (other than an amount for which a deduction in computing income may be claimed under subsection (6.1) by the corporation), and

(ii) if the partnership is a registered securities dealer, 1/3 of the corporation's specified proportion, for each fiscal period of the partnership that ends in the taxation year, of each amount paid by the partnership (other than an amount for which a deduction in computing income may be claimed under subsection (6.1) by the corporation).

History: S. 260(11) was added by S.C. 2013, c. 34, s. 365(11), applicable to

(*a*) arrangements made after December 20, 2002; and

(*b*) an arrangement made after November 2, 1998 and before December 21, 2002 if the parties to the arrangement have made the election under the definition "dividend rental arrangement" in s. 248(1).

▶ 260(12) ◀

(12) Individual members of partnerships. An individual that is, in a taxation year, a member of a partnership is deemed

(*a*) for the purpose of applying subsection (5) in respect of the taxation year,

(i) to receive the individual's specified proportion, for each fiscal period of the partnership that ends in the taxation year, of each amount received by the partnership in that fiscal period, and

(ii) in respect of the receipt of the individual's specified proportion of that amount, to be the same person as the partnership; and

(*b*) for the purpose of subsection 82(1), to have paid the individual's specified proportion, for each fiscal period of the partnership that ends in the year, of each amount paid by the partnership in that fiscal period that is deemed by subsection (5.1) to have been received by another person as a taxable dividend.

History: S. 260(12) was added by S.C. 2013, c. 34, s. 365(11), applicable to

(*a*) arrangements made after December 20, 2002; and

(*b*) an arrangement made after November 2, 1998 and before December 21, 2002 if the parties to the arrangement have made the election under the definition "dividend rental arrangement" in s. 248(1).

except that, in its application to an arrangement made before 2002, the reference to "subsection (5.1)" in paragraph 260(12)(*b*) is to be read as a reference to "subsection (5)".

SECTION 261: [Functional currency reporting]

► 261(1) ◄

(1) Definitions. The following definitions apply in this section.

History: S. 261(1), the portion before the definitions was replaced by S.C. 2009, c. 2, s. 80(1), applicable in respect of taxation years that begin after December 13, 2007. S. 261(1), the portion before the definitions formerly read:

(1) *Definitions.* The definitions in this subsection apply in this section.

Canadian Tax Foundation: Barnicke and Huynh, *Functional Currency and FAs*, 2009 Canadian Tax Highlights 17(4):7; Hickey, *Functional Currency Tax Reporting*, 2007 Canadian Tax Highlights 15(11):6–7.

Income Tax Folios: *Primary* — S5-F4-C1 Income Tax Reporting Currency.

"Canadian currency year" —"Canadian currency year" of a taxpayer means a taxation year that precedes the first functional currency year of the taxpayer.

History: S. 261(1), the definition "Canadian currency year" was replaced by S.C. 2009, c. 2, s. 80(1), applicable in respect of taxation years that begin after December 13, 2007. S. 261(1), the definition "Canadian currency year" formerly read:

"Canadian currency year"—"Canadian currency year" of a taxpayer means a taxation year of the taxpayer in respect of which subsection (4) did not apply to the taxpayer.

"Canadian tax results" —"Canadian tax results" of a taxpayer for a taxation year means

(*a*) the amount of the income, taxable income or taxable income earned in Canada of the taxpayer for the taxation year;

(*b*) the amount (other than an amount payable on behalf of another person under subsection 153(1) or section 215) of tax or other amount payable under this Act by the taxpayer in respect of the taxation year;

(*c*) the amount (other than an amount refundable on behalf of another person in respect of amounts payable on behalf of that person under subsection 153(1) or section 215) of tax or other amount refundable under this Act to the taxpayer in respect of the taxation year; and

(*d*) any amount that is relevant in determining the amounts described in respect of the taxpayer under paragraphs (*a*) to (*c*).

History: S. 261(1), the definition "Canadian tax results" was replaced by S.C. 2009, c. 2, s. 80(1), applicable for all taxation years. S. 261(1), the definition "Canadian tax results" formerly read:

"Canadian tax results"—"Canadian tax results" of a taxpayer for a particular taxation year of the taxpayer means

(*a*) the amount of the income of the taxpayer for the particular taxation year;

(*b*) the amount of the taxable income of the taxpayer for the particular taxation year;

(*c*) the amount (other than an amount payable on behalf of another person under subsection 153(1) or section 215) of tax or other amount payable under this Act by the taxpayer in respect of the particular taxation year;

(*d*) the amount (other than an amount refundable on behalf of another person in respect of amounts payable on behalf of that person under subsection 153(1) or section 215) of tax or other amount refundable under this Act to the taxpayer in respect of the particular taxation year; and

(*e*) any amount that is relevant in determining the amounts described in respect of the taxpayer under paragraphs (*a*) to (*d*).

"consolidated financial statements" — (Repealed by S.C. 2009, c. 2, s. 80(1).)

History: S. 261(1), the definition "consolidated financial statements" was repealed by S.C. 2009, c. 2, s. 80(1), applicable in respect of taxation years that begin after December 13, 2007. S. 261(1), the definition "consolidated financial statements" formerly read:

"consolidated financial statements"—"consolidated financial statements" of a taxpayer for a taxation year means the financial statements of the taxpayer that are prepared in accordance with generally accepted accounting principles that are applicable to that taxation year.

"currency exchange rate" — (Repealed by S.C. 2009, c. 2, s. 80(1).)

History: S. 261(1), the definition "currency exchange rate" was repealed by S.C. 2009, c. 2, s. 80(1), applicable in respect of taxation years that begin after December 13, 2007. S. 261(1), the definition "currency exchange rate" formerly read:

"currency exchange rate"—"currency exchange rate" on a particular day means, in respect of a conversion of an amount determined in a particular currency into an amount determined in another currency, the average, for the 12 month period ending on the particular day,

(*a*) where the particular currency is Canadian currency, of the rate of exchange (calculated by reference to the rate of exchange quoted by the Bank of Canada at noon on each business day in the period) for the exchange of the Canadian dollar for a unit of the other currency or such rate or rates of exchange acceptable to the Minister;

(*b*) where the other currency is Canadian currency, of the rate of exchange (calculated by reference to the rate of exchange quoted by the Bank of Canada at noon on each business day in the period) for the exchange of a unit of the particular currency for the Canadian dollar or such rate or rates of exchange acceptable to the Minister; or

(*c*) where neither the particular currency nor the other currency is Canadian currency, of the rate of exchange (calculated by reference to the rates of exchange quoted by the Bank of Canada at noon on each business day in the period for the exchange of the Canadian dollar for a unit of each of those currencies) for the exchange of a unit of the particular currency for a unit of the other currency or such rate or rates of exchange acceptable to the Minister.

"elected functional currency" —"elected functional currency" of a taxpayer means the currency of a country other than Canada that was the functional currency of the taxpayer for its first taxation year in respect of which it made an election under paragraph (3)(*b*).

History: S. 261(1), the definition "elected functional currency" was added by S.C. 2009, c. 2, s. 80(1), applicable in respect of taxation years that begin after December 13, 2007.

"functional currency" —"functional currency" of a taxpayer for a taxation year means the currency of a country other than Canada if that currency is, throughout the taxation year,

(*a*) a qualifying currency; and

(*b*) the primary currency in which the taxpayer maintains its records and books of account for financial reporting purposes.

History: S. 261(1), the definition "functional currency" was replaced by S.C. 2009, c. 2, s. 80(1), applicable in respect of taxation years that begin after December 13, 2007. S. 261(1), the definition "functional currency" formerly read:

"functional currency"—"functional currency" of a taxpayer for a particular taxation year of the taxpayer means the currency of a country other than Canada if that currency is

(*a*) a qualifying currency;

(*b*) the currency that is, more often than any other currency, used in the conduct of the taxpayer's principal business activities in the particular taxation year; and

(*c*) the currency in which the financial results of the taxpayer for the particular taxation year are computed in the taxpayer's consolidated financial statements and legal-entity financial statements for the particular taxation year.

Tax Window Files: Functional Currency Tax Reporting - CTF 2010, *November 28, 2010*, CRA Document No. 2010-0385891C6.

"functional currency year" —"functional currency year" of a taxpayer means a taxation year in respect of which subsection (5) applies to the taxpayer.

History: S. 261(1), the definition "functional currency year" was replaced by S.C. 2009, c. 2, s. 80(1), applicable in respect of taxation years that begin after December 13, 2007. S. 261(1), the definition "functional currency year" formerly read:

"functional currency year"—"functional currency year" of a taxpayer means a taxation year of the taxpayer in respect of which subsection (4) applies to the taxpayer.

"generally accepted accounting principles" — (Repealed by S.C. 2009, c. 2, s. 80(1).)

History: S. 261(1), the definition "generally accepted accounting principles" was repealed by S.C. 2009, c. 2, s. 80(1), applicable in respect of taxation years that begin after December 13, 2007. S. 261(1), the definition "generally accepted accounting principles" formerly read:

"generally accepted accounting principles"—"generally accepted accounting principles" means the accounting principles established or recommended by the Accounting Standards Board of Canada or such other accounting principles as are determined to be acceptable by the Minister.

"initial functional currency year" — (Repealed by S.C. 2009, c. 2, s. 80(1).)

History: S. 261(1), the definition "initial functional currency year" was repealed by S.C. 2009, c. 2, s. 80(1), applicable in respect of taxation years that begin after December 13, 2007. S. 261(1), the definition "initial functional currency year" formerly read:

"initial functional currency year"—"initial functional currency year" of a taxpayer means a functional currency year of the taxpayer if the particular taxation year of the taxpayer ending immediately before the beginning of that functional currency year of the taxpayer was a Canadian currency year of the taxpayer.

"initial reversionary year" — (Repealed by S.C. 2009, c. 2, s. 80(1).)

History: S. 261(1), the definition "initial reversionary year" was repealed by S.C. 2009, c. 2, s. 80(1), applicable in respect of taxation years that begin after December 13, 2007. S. 261(1), the definition "initial reversionary year" formerly read:

"initial reversionary year"—"initial reversionary year" of a taxpayer means the first taxation year of the taxpayer that begins immediately after the last functional currency year of the taxpayer.

"last Canadian currency year" — (Repealed by S.C. 2009, c. 2, s. 80(1).)

History: S. 261(1), the definition "last Canadian currency year" was repealed by S.C. 2009, c. 2, s. 80(1), applicable in respect of taxation years that begin after December 13, 2007. S. 261(1), the definition "last Canadian currency year" formerly read:

"last Canadian currency year"—"last Canadian currency year" of a taxpayer means the last taxation year of the taxpayer that ends before the beginning of the initial functional currency year of the taxpayer.

"last functional currency year" — (Repealed by S.C. 2009, c. 2, s. 80(1).)

History: S. 261(1), the definition "last functional currency year" was repealed by S.C. 2009, c. 2, s. 80(1), applicable in respect of taxation years that begin after December 13, 2007. S. 261(1), the definition "last functional currency year" formerly read:

"last functional currency year"—"last functional currency year" of a taxpayer means a functional currency year of the taxpayer if the particular taxation year of the taxpayer beginning immediately after the end of that functional currency year is a Canadian currency year of the taxpayer.

"legal-entity financial statements" — (Repealed by S.C. 2009, c. 2, s. 80(1).)

History: S. 261(1), the definition "legal-entity financial statements" was repealed by S.C. 2009, c. 2, s. 80(1), applicable in respect of taxation years that begin after December 13, 2007. S. 261(1), the definition "legal-entity financial statements" formerly read:

"legal-entity financial statements"—"legal-entity financial statements" of a taxpayer for a taxation year means the financial statements of the taxpayer that would be prepared for that taxation year in accordance with generally accepted accounting principles that are applicable to that taxation year if those generally accepted accounting principles did not require consolidation.

"pre-reversion debt" —"pre-reversion debt" of a taxpayer means a debt obligation of the taxpayer that was issued by the taxpayer before the beginning of the taxpayer's first reversionary year.

History: S. 261(1), the definition "pre-reversion debt" was added by S.C. 2009, c. 2, s. 80(1), applicable in respect of taxation years that begin after December 13, 2007.

"pre-transition debt" —"pre-transition debt" of a taxpayer means a debt obligation of the taxpayer that was issued by the taxpayer before the beginning of the taxpayer's first functional currency year.

History: S. 261(1), the definition "pre-transition debt" was added by S.C. 2009, c. 2, s. 80(1), applicable in respect of taxation years that begin after December 13, 2007.

"qualifying currency" —"qualifying currency" at any time means each of

(*a*) the currency of the United States of America;

(*b*) the currency of the European Monetary Union;

(*c*) the currency of the United Kingdom;

(*d*) the currency of Australia; and

(*e*) a prescribed currency.

History: S. 261(1), the definition "qualifying currency" was replaced by S.C. 2009, c. 2, s. 80(1), applicable in respect of taxation years that begin after December 13, 2007. S. 261(1), the definition "qualifying currency" formerly read:

"qualifying currency"—"qualifying currency" of a taxpayer for a taxation year means each of

(*a*) the currency of the United States of America;

(*b*) the currency of the European Monetary Union;

(*c*) the currency of the United Kingdom; and

(*d*) a prescribed currency.

"relevant spot rate" —"relevant spot rate", for a particular day, means, in respect of a conversion of an amount from a particular currency to another currency,

(*a*) if the particular currency or the other currency is Canadian currency, the rate quoted by the Bank of Canada on the particular day (or, if the Bank of Canada ordinarily quotes such a rate, but there is no such rate quoted for the particular day, the closest preceding day for which such a rate is quoted) for the exchange of the particular currency for the other currency, or, in applying paragraphs (2)(*b*) and (5)(*c*), another rate of exchange that is acceptable to the Minister; and

(*b*) if neither the particular currency nor the other currency is Canadian currency, the rate — calculated by reference to the rates quoted by the Bank of Canada on the particular day (or, if the Bank of Canada ordinarily quotes such rates, but either of such rates is not quoted for the particular day, the closest preceding day for which both such rates are quoted) for the exchange of Canadian currency for each of those currencies — for the exchange of the particular currency for the other currency, or, in applying paragraphs (2)(*b*) and (5)(*c*), another rate of exchange that is acceptable to the Minister.

Editorial Note: The "relevant spot rate" is relevant for the functional currency reporting rules of section 216. The relevant spot rate for a particular day means, in respect of a conversion of an amount from a particular currency to another currency, if the particular currency or the other currency is Canadian currency, the rate quoted by the Bank of Canada on the particular day (or, if there is no such rate quoted for the particular day and the Bank of Canada ordinarily quotes the rate, the closest preceding day for which such a rate is quoted), for the exchange of the particular currency for the other currency. If neither the particular currency nor the other currency is Canadian currency, the relevant spot rate is the rate, calculated by reference to the rates quoted by the Bank of Canada on the particular day (or, if either of such rates is not quoted for the particular day, the closest preceding day for which both such rates are quoted) for the exchange of Canadian currency for each of those currencies, for the exchange of the particular currency for the other currency. (Prior to March 1, 2017 the Bank of Canada made two quotes per day, such that the quote on noon of the day was the relevant quote.)

History: S. 261(1), the definition "relevant spot rate" was replaced by S.C. 2017, c. 33, s. 81(1), deemed in force March 1, 2017, and formerly read:

"relevant spot rate"—"relevant spot rate" for a particular day means, in respect of a conversion of an amount from a particular currency to another currency,

(*a*) if the particular currency or the other currency is Canadian currency, the rate quoted by the Bank of Canada for noon on the particular day (or, if there is no such rate quoted for the particular day, the closest preceding day for which such a rate is quoted) for the exchange of the particular currency for the other currency, or, in applying paragraphs (2)(*b*) and (5)(*c*), another rate of exchange that is acceptable to the Minister; and

(*b*) if neither the particular currency nor the other currency is Canadian currency, the rate — calculated by reference to the rates quoted by the Bank of Canada for noon on the particular day (or, if either of such rates is not quoted for the particular day, the closest preceding day for which both such rates are quoted) for the exchange of Canadian currency for each of those currencies — for the exchange of the particular currency for the other currency, or, in applying paragraphs (2)(*b*) and (5)(*c*), another rate of exchange that is acceptable to the Minister.

S. 261(1), the definition "relevant spot rate" was added by S.C. 2009, c. 2, s. 80(1), applicable in respect of taxation years that begin after December 13, 2007.

Tax Window Files: Guidance on Relevant Spot Rate Acceptable to the Minister, *May 3, 2017*, CRA Document No. 2017-0684831I7.

"reversionary exchange rate" — (Repealed by S.C. 2009, c. 2, s. 80(1).)

History: S. 261(1), the definition "reversionary exchange rate" was repealed by S.C. 2009, c. 2, s. 80(1), applicable in respect of taxation years that begin after December 13, 2007. S. 261(1), the definition "reversionary exchange rate" formerly read:

"reversionary exchange rate"—"reversionary exchange rate" of a taxpayer for a functional currency year of the taxpayer means the average, for the 12-month period ending on the last day of the functional currency year of the taxpayer, of the rate of exchange (quoted by the Bank of Canada at noon on each business day in the period) for the exchange of a unit of the functional currency of the taxpayer for the functional currency year for the Canadian dollar.

"reversionary year" —"reversionary year" of a taxpayer means a taxation year that begins after the last functional currency year of the taxpayer.

History: S. 261(1), the definition "reversionary year" was added by S.C. 2009, c. 2, s. 80(1), applicable in respect of taxation years that begin after December 13, 2007.

"tax credit" — (Repealed by S.C. 2009, c. 2, s. 80(1).)

History: S. 261(1), the definition "tax credit" was repealed by S.C. 2009, c. 2, s. 80(1), applicable in respect of taxation years that begin after December 13, 2007. S. 261(1), the definition "tax credit" formerly read:

"tax credit"—"tax credit" means an amount deductible in computing a taxpayer's tax payable, or deemed to have been paid on account of a taxpayer's tax payable, under any Part of this Act for a taxation year.

"tax reporting currency" —"tax reporting currency" of a taxpayer for a taxation year, and at any time in the taxation year, means the currency in which the taxpayer's Canadian tax results for the taxation year are to be determined.

History: S. 261(1), the definition "tax reporting currency" was added by S.C. 2009, c. 2, s. 80(1), applicable in respect of taxation years that begin after December 13, 2007.

"transitional exchange rate" — (Repealed by S.C. 2009, c. 2, s. 80(1).)

History: S. 261(1), the definition "transitional exchange rate" was repealed by S.C. 2009, c. 2, s. 80(1), applicable in respect of taxation years that begin after December 13, 2007. S. 261(1), the definition "transitional exchange rate" formerly read:

"transitional exchange rate"—"transitional exchange rate" of a taxpayer means the average, for the 12-month period ending on the last day of the last Canadian currency year of the taxpayer, of the rate of exchange (calculated by reference to the rate of exchange quoted by the Bank of Canada at noon on each business day in the period) for the exchange of the Canadian dollar for a unit of the functional currency of the taxpayer for the initial functional currency year of the taxpayer.

▶ 261(2) ◀

(2) Canadian currency requirement. In determining the Canadian tax results of a taxpayer for a particular taxation year,

(*a*) subject to this section, other than this subsection, Canadian currency is to be used; and

(*b*) subject to this section, other than this subsection, subsections 20(14.2) and 79(7) and paragraphs 80(2)(*k*) and 142.7(8)(*b*), if a particular amount that is relevant in computing those Canadian tax results is expressed in a currency other than Canadian currency, the particular amount is to be converted to an amount expressed in Canadian currency using the relevant spot rate for the day on which the particular amount arose.

Editorial Note: The original version of the functional currency reporting rules in s. 261 was enacted by Bill C-28; S.C. 2007, c. 35. However, the entire provision was re-drafted to address certain concerns in the original enactment, including, *inter alia*, an asymmetry in foreign exchange calculations used in the reporting of debt obligations and assets for corporations converting to the functional currency regime, and also to provide more comprehensive rules in respect of windings-up and amalgamations and more comprehensive anti-avoidance rules. The re-written s. 261 was passed into law by Bill C-10; S.C. 2009, c. 2, and is generally effective for taxation years ending after December 13, 2007, such that it entirely replaces the original version of the provision on a retroactive basis.

Owing to the re-writing of the provision, there are a couple of transitional rules. First, where a taxpayer has, on or before June 27, 2008, made an election under s. 261(3)(*b*) to enter into the functional currency reporting regime, if the taxpayer makes a further election in writing on or before the taxpayer's filing-due date for the taxpayer's taxation year that includes March 12, 2009 (the day the rewritten provision received Royal Assent as part of Bill C-10), the relevant spot rate for a particular day is deemed, for the purposes of ss. 261(7) to (10), to be the average of the rates that would, in the absence of this transitional rule, be the relevant spot rates for each day in the 12-month period that ends on the particular day; furthermore, ss. 261(20) and (21) apply to the taxpayer in respect of taxation years that begin after June 27, 2008. Second, in applying s. 261(3)(*b*) (the paragraph providing the election into the functional currency regime), if the day that is six months before the end of the particular taxation year referred to in that paragraph is before December 15, 2008, the reference in that paragraph to "the day that is six months before the end of the particular taxation year" is, in respect of that particular taxation year, to be read as a reference to "December 15, 2008". This second transitional rule effectively extends the deadline for the functional currency regime election to December 15, 2008 if the deadline would otherwise occur before that date under current s. 261(3)(*b*).

History: S. 261(2)(*b*) was replaced by S.C. 2016, c. 12, s. 69(1), in force January 1, 2017, and formerly read:

(*b*) subject to this section, other than this subsection, subsection 79(7) and paragraphs 80(2)(*k*) and 142.7(8)(*b*), if a particular amount that is relevant in computing those Canadian tax results is expressed in a currency other than Canadian currency, the particular amount is to be converted to an amount expressed in Canadian currency using the relevant spot rate for the day on which the particular amount arose.

S. 261(2) was replaced by S.C. 2009, c. 2, s. 80(1), applicable for all taxation years. S. 261(2) formerly read:

(2) *Canadian currency requirement.* Subject to subsections (3) to (10),

(*a*) the Canadian tax results of a taxpayer for a particular taxation year are to be determined using Canadian currency; and

(*b*) subject to subsection 79(7), paragraphs 80(2)(*k*) and 142.7(8)(*b*), if a particular amount that is relevant in computing the taxpayer's Canadian tax results for the particular taxation year is an amount expressed in a currency other than Canadian currency, that amount is to be converted to an amount expressed in Canadian currency using the rate of exchange quoted by the Bank of Canada at noon on the day on which that amount first arose for the exchange of a unit of that other currency for a unit of Canadian currency or such other rate of exchange as is acceptable to the Minister.

Canadian Tax Foundation: Thung and Pham, *Issues for MNEs with the New "Relevant Spot Rate"*, 2017 Canadian Tax Focus 7(2):2–3.

Tax Topics: No. 2149, Foreign Exchange Revisited.

Income Tax Folios: *Primary* — S5-F4-C1 Income Tax Reporting Currency.

Tax Window Files: 2015 CTF Q.10 Thin cap - foreign currency debt, *November 24, 2015*, CRA Document No. 2015-0610601C6; FX Loss on Disposition of Cash, *January 6, 2009*, CRA Document No. 2008-0280111I7.

▶ 261(3) ◀

(3) Application of subsection (5). Subsection (5) applies to a taxpayer in respect of a particular taxation year if

(*a*) the taxpayer is, throughout the particular taxation year, a corporation (other than an investment corporation, a mortgage investment corporation or a mutual fund corporation) resident in Canada;

(*b*) the taxpayer has elected that subsection (5) apply to the taxpayer and has filed that election with the Minister in prescribed form and manner on or before the day that is 60 days after the first day of the particular taxation year;

(*c*) there is a functional currency of the taxpayer for the first taxation year of the taxpayer in respect of which subsection (5) would, if this subsection were read without reference to this paragraph, apply;

(*d*) the taxpayer has not filed another election under paragraph (*b*); and

(*e*) a revocation by the taxpayer under subsection (4) does not apply to the particular taxation year.

History: S. 261(3)(*b*) was replaced by S.C. 2014, c. 39, s. 77(1), applicable to taxation years that begin after July 12, 2013.

In addition, any assessment of a taxpayer's tax, interest and penalties payable under the Act for any taxation year that ends before the day on which this amendment receives royal assent [December 16, 2014] that would, in the absence of this section, be precluded because of the time references in subsection 152(4) of the Act is to be made to the extent necessary to take into account this amendment.

S. 261(3)(*b*) formerly read:

(*b*) the taxpayer has elected that subsection (5) apply to the taxpayer and has filed that election with the Minister in prescribed form and manner on or before the day that is six months before the end of the particular taxation year;

S. 261(3) was replaced by S.C. 2009, c. 2, s. 80(1), applicable in respect of taxation years that begin after December 13, 2007, except that in applying paragraph 261(3)(*b*), if the day that is six months before the end of the particular taxation year referred to in that paragraph is before December 15, 2008, the reference in that paragraph to "the day that is six months before the end of the particular taxation year" is, in respect of that particular taxation year, to be read as a reference to "December 15, 2008". S. 261(3) formerly read:

(3) *Application of subsection (4).* Subsection (4) applies to a taxpayer in respect of a particular taxation year of the taxpayer if

(*a*) the taxpayer is, throughout the particular taxation year, a corporation (other than an investment corporation, a mortgage investment corporation or a mutual fund corporation) resident in Canada;

(*b*) the taxpayer has elected that subsection (4) apply to the taxpayer in respect of the particular taxation year, or a preceding taxation year, and each subsequent taxation year of the taxpayer and has filed that election with the Minister in prescribed form and manner on or before the taxpayer's filing due date

(i) for the taxation year immediately preceding the first taxation year in respect of which the election was made, or

(ii) where there was not a taxation year immediately preceding the first taxation year in respect of which the election was made, for the first taxation year in respect of which the election was made;

(*c*) there is a functional currency of the taxpayer for the particular taxation year;

(*d*) where the taxpayer's taxation year immediately preceding the particular taxation year was a functional currency year of the taxpayer, the functional currency of the taxpayer for that preceding taxation year is the same as the functional currency of the taxpayer for the particular taxation year; and

(*e*) where the taxpayer's taxation year immediately preceding the particular taxation year was a Canadian currency year of the taxpayer, no preceding taxation year of the taxpayer was a functional currency year of the taxpayer.

Related Sections: 261(1) functional currency.

Tax Topics: No. 1919-20, 2008 Canadian Tax Foundation Annual Conference — Department of Finance Presentation and CRA Round Table; No. 1918, New and Improved Functional Currency Proposals.

Forms: T1296 — Election, or Revocation of an Election, to Report in a Functional Currency.

Income Tax Folios: *Primary* — S5-F4-C1 Income Tax Reporting Currency.

Income Tax Technical News: Issue No. 44, Foreign Currency Reporting.

Tax Window Files: Functional Currency Tax Reporting, *February 11, 2010*, CRA Document No. 2009-0345361C6.

▶ 261(4) ◀

(4) Revocation of election. A taxpayer may revoke its election under paragraph (3)(*b*) by filing, on a day that is in a functional currency year of the taxpayer (other than its first functional currency year), a notice of revocation in prescribed form and manner. The revocation applies to each taxation year of the taxpayer that begins on or after the day that is six months after that day.

History: S. 261(4) was replaced by S.C. 2009, c. 2, s. 80(1), applicable in respect of taxation years that begin after December 13, 2007. S. 261(4) formerly read:

(4) *Functional currency reporting.* If, because of subsection (3), this subsection applies to a taxpayer for a particular taxation year of the taxpayer,

(*a*) the taxpayer's Canadian tax results for the particular taxation year are to be determined using the taxpayer's functional currency for the particular taxation year;

(*b*) each reference in the Act or the regulations to a particular amount expressed in Canadian dollars is to be read as a reference to a particular amount expressed in the taxpayer's functional currency for the particular taxation year determined by applying the currency exchange rate in respect of the conversion of Canadian currency into that functional currency as of the first day of the particular taxation year;

(*c*) subject to subsection 79(7), paragraphs 80(2)(*k*) and 142.7(8)(*b*), if a particular amount that is relevant in computing the taxpayer's Canadian tax results for the particular taxation year is an amount expressed in a currency other than the taxpayer's functional currency for the particular taxation year, that amount is to be converted to an amount expressed in the taxpayer's functional currency for the particular taxation year by using the rates of exchange quoted by the Bank of Canada at noon on the day that the particular amount first arose for the exchange of the Canadian dollar for a unit of each of those currencies or such other rate of exchange as is acceptable to the Minister;

(*d*) each reference in subsection 79(7), paragraph 80(2)(*k*) and subsections 80.01(11) and 80.1(8) to "Canadian currency" is to be read as a reference to "the taxpayer's functional currency";

(*e*) the reference in subsection 39(2) to "the value of the currency or currencies of one or more countries other than Canada relative to Canadian currency, a taxpayer has made a gain or sustained a loss in a taxation year" is to be read as reference to "the value of the currency or currencies of one or more countries (other than the taxpayer's functional currency for the taxation year) relative to a taxpayer's functional currency for a taxation year, the taxpayer has made a gain or sustained a loss in the taxation year" and the references in that subsection to "currency of a country other than Canada" shall be read as references to "currency other than the taxpayer's functional currency for the taxation year";

(*f*) the definition "foreign currency" in subsection 248(1) is, in respect of the taxpayer, to be, at any time in the particular taxation year, read as:

"foreign currency" in respect of a taxpayer, at any time in a particular taxation year, means a currency other than the taxpayer's functional currency for the particular taxation year;

(*g*) where a taxation year of a foreign affiliate of the taxpayer ends in the particular taxation year of the taxpayer, the references in section 95 and in regulations made for the purposes of that section (other than subsection 5907(6) of the Regulations) to "Canadian currency" shall be read, in respect of the foreign affiliate, as a reference to "the taxpayer's functional currency for the particular taxation year".

Tax Topics: No. 1863, Functional Currency: Proposed Election.

Forms: T1296 — Election, or Revocation of an Election, to Report in a Functional Currency.

► 261(5) ◄

(5) Functional currency tax reporting. If this subsection applies to a taxpayer in respect of a particular taxation year,

(*a*) the taxpayer's Canadian tax results for the particular taxation year are to be determined using the taxpayer's elected functional currency;

(*b*) unless the context otherwise requires, each reference in this Act or the regulations to an amount (other than in respect of a penalty or fine) that is described as a particular number of Canadian dollars is to be read, in respect of the taxpayer and the particular taxation year, as a reference to that amount expressed in the taxpayer's elected functional currency using the relevant spot rate for the first day of the particular taxation year;

(*c*) subject to paragraph (9)(*b*), subsection (15), subsections 20(14.2) and 79(7) and paragraphs 80(2)(*k*) and 142.7(8)(*b*), if a particular amount that is relevant in computing the taxpayer's Canadian tax results for the particular taxation year is expressed in a currency other than the taxpayer's elected functional currency, the particular amount is to be converted to an amount expressed in the taxpayer's elected functional currency using the relevant spot rate for the day on which the particular amount arose;

(*d*) the definition "exchange rate" in subsection 111(8) is, in respect of the taxpayer and the particular taxation year, and with such modifications as the context requires, to be read as follows:

"'exchange rate' at any time in respect of a particular currency other than the taxpayer's elected functional currency means the relevant spot rate, for the day that includes that time, in respect of the conversion of an amount from the particular currency to the taxpayer's elected functional currency, or a rate of exchange acceptable to the Minister;"

(*e*) except in applying paragraph 95(2)(*f.15*) in respect of a taxation year, of a foreign affiliate of the taxpayer, that is a functional currency year of the foreign affiliate within the meaning of subsection (6.1), each reference in subsection 39(2) to "Canadian currency" is to be read, in respect of the taxpayer and the particular taxation year, and with such modifications as the context requires, as a reference to "the taxpayer's elected functional currency";

(*f*) each reference in

(i) section 76.1, subsections 20(14.2) and 79(7), paragraph 80(2)(*k*), subsections 80.01(11), 80.1(8), 93(2.01) to (2.31), 142.4(1) and 142.7(8) and the definition "amortized cost" in subsection 248(1), and subparagraph 231(6)(*a*)(iv) of the *Income Tax Regulations*, to "Canadian currency" is, in respect of the taxpayer and the particular taxation year, and with such modifications as the context requires, to be read as "the taxpayer's elected functional currency", and

(ii) subparagraph 94.1(1)(*b*)(vii), the definition "foreign currency debt" in subsection 111(8), subsection 142.4(1), and the definition "amortized cost" in subsection 248(1) to "currency of a country other than Canada" is, in respect of the taxpayer and the particular taxation year, and with such modifications as the context requires, to be read as a reference to "currency other than the taxpayer's elected functional currency";

(*g*) the definition "foreign currency" in subsection 248(1) is, in respect of the taxpayer and the taxation year, and with such modifications as the context requires, to be read as follows:

"'foreign currency' in respect of a taxpayer, at any time in a taxation year, means a currency other than the taxpayer's elected functional currency;"

(*h*) where a taxation year, of a foreign affiliate of the taxpayer, is a functional currency year of the foreign affiliate within the meaning of subsection (6.1),

(i) the references in section 95 (other than paragraph 95(2)(*f.15*)) and the references in regulations made for the purposes of section 95 or 113 to

(A) "Canadian currency" are to be read, in respect of the foreign affiliate and the taxation year, and with such modifications as the context requires, as references to "the taxpayer's elected functional currency", and

(B) "currency of a country other than Canada" are to be read, in respect of the foreign affiliate and the taxation year, and with such modifications as the context requires, as references to "currency other than the taxpayer's elected functional currency", and

(ii) the reference in paragraph 95(2)(*f.*13) to "the rate of exchange quoted by the Bank of Canada on" is to be read, in respect of the foreign affiliate and the taxation year, and with such modifications as the context requires, as a reference to "the relevant spot rate for".

Editorial Note: Subsection 261(5) provides the basic machinery for a taxation year for which a corporation has elected to use a functional currency other than Canadian currency under subsection 261(3). Among the consequences: The Canadian tax results for the taxation year are to be determined using the elected functional currency for that year; all Canadian dollar amounts set out in the Act are to be converted to the taxpayer's elected functional currency for the year using the relevant spot rate on the first day of the year; and, subject to certain exceptions, if a particular amount is determined in a currency other than the elected functional currency for the year and it is relevant in determining the taxpayer's Canadian tax results, that amount must be converted to the taxpayer's elected functional currency using the relevant spot rate on the day that the amount arose.

See also the editorial note to the definition of "relevant spot rate" in subsection 261(1).

History: S. 261(5)(*h*)(ii) was replaced by S.C. 2017, c. 33, s. 81(2), deemed in force March 1, 2017, and formerly read:

(ii) the reference in paragraph 95(2)(*f.13*) to "the rate of exchange quoted by the Bank of Canada at noon on" is to be read, in respect of the foreign affiliate and the taxation year, and with such modifications as the context requires, as a reference to "the relevant spot rate for".

S. 261(5)(*c*) was replaced by S.C. 2016, c. 12, s. 69(2), in force January 1, 2017, and formerly read:

(*c*) subject to paragraph (9)(*b*), subsection (15), subsection 79(7) and paragraphs 80(2)(*k*) and 142.7(8)(*b*), if a particular amount that is relevant in computing the taxpayer's Canadian tax results for the particular taxation year is expressed in a currency other than the taxpayer's elected functional currency, the particular amount is to be converted to an amount expressed in the taxpayer's elected functional currency using the relevant spot rate for the day on which the particular amount arose;

S. 261(5)(*f*)(i) was replaced by S.C. 2016, c. 12, s. 69(3), in force January 1, 2017, and formerly read:

(i) section 76.1, subsection 79(7), paragraph 80(2)(*k*), subsections 80.01(11), 80.1(8), 93(2.01) to (2.31), 142.4(1) and 142.7(8) and the definition "amortized cost" in subsection 248(1), and subparagraph 231(6)(*a*)(iv) of the *Income Tax Regulations*, to "Canadian currency" is, in respect of the taxpayer and the particular taxation year, and with such modifications as the context requires, to be read as "the taxpayer's elected functional currency", and

S. 261(5)(*h*)(i), the portion before clause (A) was replaced by S.C. 2013, c. 34, s. 38(1), applicable to taxation years of a foreign affiliate of a taxpayer that begin after December 18, 2009.

Any assessment of a taxpayer's tax, interest and penalties payable under the Act for any taxation year that ends before June 26, 2013 that would, in the absence of this section, be precluded because of subsections 152(4) to (5) of the Act, shall be made to the extent necessary to take into account this amendment, if the taxpayer

(i) elects in writing in respect of all of its foreign affiliates that this section apply in respect of that provision, and

(ii) files that election with the Minister of National Revenue on or before December 26, 2013 [the day that is six months after royal assent].

S. 261(5)(*h*)(i), the portion before clause (A) formerly read:

(i) the references in section 95 (other than paragraph 95(2)(*f.15*)) and the references in regulations made for the purposes of section 95 or 113 (other than subsection 5907(6) of the Regulations) to

S. 261(5)(*e*) was replaced by S.C. 2013, c. 34, s. 77(1), applicable in respect of gains made and losses sustained in taxation years that begin after August 19, 2011.

Any assessment of a taxpayer's tax, interest and penalties payable under the Act for any taxation year that ends before June 26, 2013 that would, in the absence of this section, be precluded because of subsections 152(4) to (5) of the Act shall be made to the extent necessary to take into account the amendments by S.C. 2013, c. 34, s. 54 to 89.

S. 261(5)(*e*) formerly read:

(*e*) except in applying paragraph 95(2)(*f.15*) in respect of a taxation year, of a foreign affiliate of the taxpayer, that is a functional currency year of the foreign affiliate within the meaning of subsection (6.1), each reference in subsection 39(2)

(i) to "the value of the currency or currencies of one or more countries other than Canada relative to Canadian currency, a taxpayer" is to be read, in respect of the taxpayer and the particular taxation year, and with such modifications as the context requires, as a reference to "the value of the currency or currencies of one or more countries (other than the taxpayer's elected functional currency) relative to a taxpayer's elected functional currency, the taxpayer", and

(ii) to "currency of a country other than Canada" is to be read, in respect of the taxpayer and the particular taxation year, and with such modifications as the context requires, as a reference to "currency other than the taxpayer's elected functional currency";

S. 261(5)(*f*)(i) was replaced by S.C. 2013, c. 34, s. 77(2), applicable In respect of taxation years that begin after December 13, 2007.

See the application for the amendment to s. 261(5)(*e*) (above) for the extension of assessment periods to take into account the amendments by S.C. 2013, c. 34, s. 54 to 89.

S. 261(5)(*f*)(i) formerly read:

(i) section 76.1, subsection 79(7), paragraph 80(2)(*k*), subsections 80.01(11), 80.1(8), 142.4(1) and 142.7(8) and the definition "amortized cost" in subsection 248(1), and subparagraph 231(6)(*a*)(iv) of the Regulations, to "Canadian currency" is, in respect of the taxpayer and the particular taxation year, and with such modifications as the context requires, to be read as a reference to "the taxpayer's elected functional currency", and

S. 261(5) was replaced by S.C. 2009, c. 2, s. 80(1), applicable in respect of taxation years that begin after December 13, 2007. S. 261(5) formerly read:

(5) *Converting Canadian currency amounts.* In applying this Act to a taxpayer for a particular functional currency year of the taxpayer

(*a*) subject to subparagraph (10)(*b*)(iii), in determining the amount (expressed in the taxpayer's functional currency for the particular functional currency year) that may be deducted, or relevant in determining the amount that may be deducted, under subsection 37(1) or 66(4), section 110.1 or 111 or subsection 126(2), 127(5), 129(1), 181.1(4) or 190.1(3) in the particular functional currency year, each amount (determined in Canadian currency) that is relevant to the determination and that was determined for a taxation year of the taxpayer that preceded the initial functional currency year of the taxpayer, is to be converted to the taxpayer's functional currency for the particular functional currency year using the transitional exchange rate of the taxpayer;

(*b*) in determining, at any time in the particular functional currency year, the cost (expressed in the taxpayer's functional currency for the particular functional currency year) to the taxpayer of a property that was acquired by the taxpayer before the beginning of the taxpayer's initial functional currency year, the cost (determined in Canadian currency) to the taxpayer of the property at the end of the last Canadian currency year of the taxpayer is to be converted to the taxpayer's functional currency for the particular functional currency year using the transitional exchange rate of the taxpayer;

(*c*) in determining, at any time in the particular functional currency year, the adjusted cost base (expressed in the taxpayer's functional currency for the particular functional currency year) to the taxpayer of a capital property that was acquired by the taxpayer before the beginning of the taxpayer's initial functional currency year, each amount (determined in Canadian currency) that was required by section 53 to be added or deducted in computing, at any time before the beginning of the initial functional currency year of the taxpayer, the adjusted cost base of the property to the taxpayer is to be converted to the taxpayer's functional currency for the particular functional currency year using the transitional exchange rate of the taxpayer;

(*d*) in determining, at any time in the particular functional currency year, the amount (expressed in the taxpayer's functional currency for the particular functional currency year) of the taxpayer's undepreciated capital cost of depreciable property of a prescribed class, cumulative eligible capital in respect of a business, cumulative Canadian exploration expense (within the meaning assigned by subsection 66.1(6)), cumulative Canadian development expense (within the meaning assigned by subsection 66.2(5)), cumulative foreign resource expense in respect of a country other than Canada (within the meaning assigned by subsection 66.21(1)) and cumulative Canadian oil and gas property expense (within the meaning assigned by subsection 66.4(5)), (each of which is referred to in this paragraph as a "pool amount") each amount (determined in Canadian currency) that was added to or deducted from a particular pool amount of the taxpayer in respect of a taxation year of the taxpayer preceding the initial functional currency year of the taxpayer is to be converted to the taxpayer's functional currency for the particular functional currency year using the transitional exchange rate of the taxpayer;

(*e*) in determining any amount (expressed in the taxpayer's functional currency for the particular functional currency year) that has been deducted or claimed as a reserve in computing the income of the taxpayer for its last Canadian currency year, that amount (determined in Canadian currency) deducted or claimed as a reserve is to be converted to the taxpayer's functional currency for the particular functional currency year using the transitional exchange rate of the taxpayer;

(*f*) in determining the amount (expressed in the taxpayer's functional currency for the particular functional currency year) of any outlay or expense referred to in subsection 18(9) that was made or incurred by the taxpayer and the amount that was deducted in respect of that outlay or expense in respect of a taxation year preceding the initial functional currency year of the taxpayer, such amounts of outlay or expense or deductions (determined in Canadian currency for those years) are to be converted to the taxpayer's functional currency for the particular functional currency year using the transitional exchange rate of the taxpayer;

(*g*) in determining, at any time in the particular functional currency year, the amount (expressed in the taxpayer's functional currency for the particular functional currency year) of the taxpayer's paid-up capital in respect of any class of shares of its capital stock, any amount (determined in Canadian currency) added or deducted in computing the taxpayer's paid-up capital in respect of the class in a taxation year preceding the initial functional currency year of the taxpayer is to be converted to the taxpayer's functional currency for the particular functional currency year using the transitional exchange rate of the taxpayer;

(*h*) where the taxpayer issued a debt obligation in a taxation year of the taxpayer preceding the initial functional currency year of the taxpayer, in determining the amount (expressed in the taxpayer's functional currency for the particular functional currency year) for which the obligation was issued, the principal amount (expressed in the taxpayer's functional currency for the particular functional currency year) of the obligation, any amount (expressed in the taxpayer's functional currency for the particular functional currency year) paid in satisfaction of the principal amount of the obligation in a taxation year of the taxpayer preceding the initial functional currency year of the taxpayer, and the amount (determined in the taxpayer's functional currency for the particular functional currency year) of any gain or loss attributable to the fluctuation in the values of currencies,

(i) where the obligation was issued in the taxpayer's functional currency for the particular functional currency year, the amount (determined in the taxpayer's functional currency for the particular functional currency year) for which the obligation was issued, the principal amount (determined in the taxpayer's functional currency for the particular functional currency year) of the obligation and the amounts (determined in the taxpayer's functional currency for the particular functional currency year) paid in satisfaction of the principal amount of the obligation, in a taxation year of the taxpayer preceding the initial functional currency year of the taxpayer are those amounts determined in those years in the taxpayer's functional currency for the particular functional currency year,

(ii) where the obligation was issued in Canadian currency, the amount for which the obligation was issued (determined in Canadian currency), the principal amount (determined in Canadian currency) of the obligation and the amounts (determined in Canadian currency) paid in satisfaction of the principal amount of the obligation, in a taxation year preceding the initial functional currency year are to be converted to the taxpayer's functional currency for the particular functional currency year using the transitional exchange rate of the taxpayer, and

(iii) where the obligation was issued in a currency (referred to in this subparagraph as the "third currency") other than Canadian currency or the taxpayer's functional currency for the particular functional currency year, the amount (determined in the third currency) for which the obligation was issued, the principal amount (determined in the third currency) of the obligation and the amounts (determined in the third currency) paid in satisfaction of the principal amount of the obligation in a taxation year of the taxpayer preceding the initial functional currency year of the taxpayer, are to be converted to the taxpayer's functional currency for the particular functional currency year using the currency exchange rate in respect of a conversion of an amount determined in the third currency into an amount determined in the taxpayer's functional currency for the particular functional currency year on the last day of the last Canadian currency year of the taxpayer;

(*i*) in determining the amount (expressed in the taxpayer's functional currency for the particular functional currency year) of tax payable under Part I for a Canadian currency year for the purpose of determining the taxpayer's first instalment base or second instalment base for the taxpayer's initial functional currency year, the amount (determined in Canadian currency) of tax payable is to be converted to the taxpayer's functional currency for the particular functional currency year using the transitional exchange rate of the taxpayer; and

(*j*) any amount (expressed in Canadian currency), other than an amount referred to in paragraphs (*a*) to (*i*), determined under the provisions of this Act in or in respect of a taxation year preceding the initial functional currency year of the taxpayer that is relevant in determining the Canadian tax results (expressed in the taxpayer's functional currency for the particular functional currency year) of the taxpayer for the particular functional currency year is to be converted to the taxpayer's functional currency for the particular functional currency year using the transitional exchange rate of the taxpayer.

Related Sections: 261(1) Canadian tax results; 261(1) elected functional currency; relevant spot rate; 261(3) Application of subsection (5).

Canadian Tax Foundation: Wach, *Paid-Up Capital of Shares Held by a Functional-Currency Reporter: How Do We Resolve the Conflicts?*, 2017 Canadian Tax Journal 4:1001–1020.

Tax Topics: No. 1918, New and Improved Functional Currency Proposals.

Income Tax Folios: *Primary* — S5-F4-C1 Income Tax Reporting Currency.

Income Tax Technical News: Issue No. 41, Functional Currency Tax Reporting Rules.

► 261(6) ◄

(6) Partnerships. For the purposes of computing the Canadian tax results of a particular taxpayer for each taxation year that is a functional currency year or a reversionary year of the particular taxpayer, this section is to be applied as if each partnership of which the particular taxpayer is a member at any time in the taxation year were a taxpayer that

(*a*) had as its first functional currency year its first fiscal period, if any, that

(i) is a fiscal period at any time during which the particular taxpayer is a member of the partnership,

(ii) begins after December 13, 2007, and

(iii) begins on or after the first day of the particular taxpayer's first functional currency year;

(*b*) had as its last Canadian currency year its last fiscal period, if any, that ends before its first functional currency year;

(*c*) had as its first reversionary year its first fiscal period, if any, that begins after the particular taxpayer's last functional currency year;

(*d*) is subject to subsection (5) for each of its fiscal periods that is, or begins after, its first functional currency year and that ends before its first reversionary year;

(*e*) had as its elected functional currency in respect of each fiscal period described in paragraph (*d*) the elected functional currency of the particular taxpayer; and

(*f*) had as its last functional currency year its last fiscal period, if any, that ends before its first reversionary year.

History: S. 261(6)(*a*)(iii) was replaced by S.C. 2014, c. 39, s. 77(2), applicable to taxation years that begin after July 12, 2013.

In addition, any assessment of a taxpayer's tax, interest and penalties payable under the Act for any taxation year that ends before the day on which this amendment receives royal assent [December 16, 2014] that would, in the absence of this section, be precluded because of the time references in subsection 152(4) of the Act is to be made to the extent necessary to take into account this amendment.

S. 261(6)(*a*)(iii) formerly read:

(iii) ends at least six months after the day that is six months before the end of the particular taxpayer's first functional currency year;

S. 261(6) was replaced by S.C. 2009, c. 2, s. 80(1), applicable in respect of taxation years that begin after December 13, 2007. S. 261(6) formerly read:

(6) *Deferred amounts relating to debt.* In applying this Act to a taxpayer for a particular functional currency year of the taxpayer

(*a*) where, at any time in the particular functional currency year, the taxpayer has made a particular payment (expressed in the taxpayer's functional currency for the particular functional currency year) on account of the principal amount (expressed in the taxpayer's functional currency for the particular functional currency year) of a debt obligation that was issued by the taxpayer in a Canadian currency year of the taxpayer that ended before the beginning of the initial functional currency year of the taxpayer

(i) the taxpayer is deemed to have a capital gain under paragraph 39(2)(*a*) or income, as the case may be, attributable to the fluctuation in the values of currencies in respect of the particular payment for the particular functional currency year equal to the amount determined by the formula

$$A \times B/C$$

where

A is the amount determined by the formula

$$D \times E$$

where

D is the amount (expressed in Canadian currency), if any, that would have been determined to be the taxpayer's capital gain under paragraph 39(2)(*a*) or income, as the case may be, if the principal amount of the debt obligation outstanding (determined in Canadian currency), immediately before the end of the last Canadian currency year of the taxpayer, had been settled by a payment by the taxpayer to the holder of the obligation of an amount equal to that outstanding principal amount at that time, and

E is the transitional exchange rate of the taxpayer,

B is the amount of the particular payment (expressed in the taxpayer's functional currency for the particular functional currency year), and

C is the principal amount of the debt obligation outstanding (determined in the taxpayer's functional currency for the particular functional currency year) at the beginning of the initial functional currency year of the taxpayer,

(ii) the taxpayer is deemed to have a capital loss under paragraph 39(2)(*b*) or a loss, as the case may be, attributable to the fluctuation in the values of currencies in respect of the particular payment for the particular functional currency year equal to the amount determined by the formula

$$F \times G/H$$

where

F is the amount determined by the formula

$$I \times J$$

where

I is the amount (expressed in Canadian currency), if any, that would have been determined to be the taxpayer's capital loss under paragraph 39(2)(*b*) or loss, as the case may be, if the principal amount of the debt obligation outstanding (determined in Canadian currency), immediately before the end of the last Canadian currency year of the taxpayer, had been settled by a payment by the taxpayer to the holder of the obligation of an amount equal to that outstanding principal amount at that time, and

J is the transitional exchange rate of the taxpayer,

G is the amount of the particular payment (expressed in the taxpayer's functional currency for the particular functional currency year), and

H is the principal amount of the debt obligation outstanding (determined in the taxpayer's functional currency for the particular functional currency year) at the beginning of the initial functional currency year of the taxpayer, and

(iii) where a debt obligation is denominated in a currency other than the taxpayer's functional currency for the particular functional currency year, any amount determined under element B in the formula in subparagraph (i) or element G in the formula in subparagraph (ii) is to be determined with reference to the relative value of that currency and the taxpayer's functional currency for the particular functional currency year at the beginning of the initial functional currency year of the taxpayer, and

(*b*) notwithstanding paragraph 80(2)(*k*), where an obligation of the taxpayer was issued in a taxation year of the taxpayer preceding the initial functional currency year of the taxpayer in a currency other than the taxpayer's functional currency for the particular functional currency year, a forgiven amount arising at any time in the particular functional currency year in respect of the obligation is to be determined by reference to the currency exchange rate on the last day of the taxpayer's last Canadian currency year in respect of a conversion of an amount determined in the other currency into an amount determined in the taxpayer's functional currency for the particular functional currency year.

Tax Window Files: Functional currency election and partnerships, *May 31, 2016*, CRA Document No. 2016-0642011E5; Functional Currency Tax Reporting, *June 5, 2009*, CRA Document No. 2009-0324161C6.

► 261(6.1) ◄

(6.1) Foreign affiliates. For the purposes of computing the foreign accrual property income of a foreign affiliate of a particular taxpayer, in respect of the particular taxpayer, for each taxation year that is a functional currency year or a reversionary year of the particular taxpayer, this section is to be applied as if

(*a*) the foreign affiliate were a taxpayer that

(i) had, as its first functional currency year, its first taxation year that

(A) is a taxation year at any time during which the foreign affiliate is a foreign affiliate of the particular taxpayer,

(B) begins after December 13, 2007, and

(C) begins on or after the first day of the particular taxpayer's first functional currency year,

(ii) had as its last Canadian currency year its last taxation year, if any, that ends before its first functional currency year,

(iii) had as its first reversionary year its first taxation year, if any, that begins after the particular taxpayer's last functional currency year,

(iv) is subject to subsection (5) for each of its taxation years that is, or begins after, its first functional currency year and that ends before its first reversionary year,

(v) had as its elected functional currency in respect of each taxation year described in subparagraph (iv) the elected functional currency of the particular taxpayer, and

(vi) had as its last functional currency year its last taxation year, if any, that ends before its first reversionary year; and

(*b*) the Canadian tax results of the foreign affiliate for each taxation year that is a functional currency year or a reversionary year of the foreign affiliate, within the meaning of paragraph (*a*), were its foreign accrual property income, in respect of the particular taxpayer, for that taxation year and any amount that is relevant in determining such foreign accrual property income.

History: S. 261(6.1)(*a*)(i)(C) was replaced by S.C. 2014, c. 39, s. 77(3), applicable to taxation years that begin after July 12, 2013.

In addition, any assessment of a taxpayer's tax, interest and penalties payable under the Act for any taxation year that ends before the day on which this amendment receives royal assent [December 16, 2014] that would, in the absence of this section, be precluded because of the time references in subsection 152(4) of the Act is to be made to the extent necessary to take into account this amendment.

S. 261(6.1)(*a*)(i)(C) formerly read:

(C) ends at least six months after the day that is six months before the end of the particular taxpayer's first functional currency year,

S. 261(6.1) was added by S.C. 2009, c. 2, s. 80(1), applicable in respect of taxation years that begin after December 13, 2007.

► 261(7) ◄

(7) Converting Canadian currency amounts. In applying this Act to a taxpayer for a particular functional currency year of the taxpayer, the following amounts are to be converted from Canadian currency to the taxpayer's elected functional currency using the relevant spot rate for the last day of the taxpayer's last Canadian currency year:

(*a*) each particular amount that

(i) is, or is relevant to the determination of, an amount that may be deducted under subsection 37(1) or 66(4), variable F or F.1 in the definition "foreign accrual property income" in subsection 95(1), section 110.1 or 111 or subsection 126(2), 127(5), 129(1), 181.1(4) or 190.1(3), in the particular functional currency year, and

(ii) was determined for a Canadian currency year of the taxpayer;

(*b*) the cost to the taxpayer of a property that was acquired by the taxpayer in a Canadian currency year of the taxpayer;

(*c*) an amount that was required by section 53 to be added or deducted in computing, at any time in a Canadian currency year of the taxpayer, the adjusted cost base to the taxpayer of a capital property that was acquired by the taxpayer in such a year;

(*d*) an amount that

(i) is in respect of the taxpayer's undepreciated capital cost of depreciable property of a prescribed class, "cumulative Canadian exploration expense" (as defined in subsection 66.1(6)), "cumulative

Canadian development expense" (as defined in subsection 66.2(5)), "cumulative foreign resource expense" in respect of a country other than Canada (as defined in subsection 66.21(1)) or "cumulative Canadian oil and gas property expense" (as defined in subsection 66.4(5)) (each of which is referred to in this paragraph as a "pool amount"), and

(ii) was added to or deducted from a pool amount of the taxpayer in respect of a Canadian currency year of the taxpayer;

(*e*) an amount that has been deducted or claimed as a reserve in computing the income of the taxpayer for its last Canadian currency year;

(*f*) an outlay or expense referred to in subsection 18(9) that was made or incurred by the taxpayer in respect of a Canadian currency year of the taxpayer, and any amount that was deducted in respect of the outlay or expense in computing the income of the taxpayer for such a year;

(*g*) an amount that was added or deducted in computing the taxpayer's paid-up capital in respect of a class of shares of its capital stock in a Canadian currency year of the taxpayer; and

(*h*) any amount (other than an amount referred to in any of paragraphs (*a*) to (*g*) or any of subsections (6), (6.1) and (8)) determined under the provisions of this Act in or in respect of a Canadian currency year of the taxpayer that is relevant in determining the Canadian tax results of the taxpayer for the particular functional currency year.

History: S. 261(7)(*d*)(i) was replaced by S.C. 2016, c. 12, s. 69(4), in force January 1, 2017, and formerly read:

(i) is in respect of the taxpayer's undepreciated capital cost of depreciable property of a prescribed class, cumulative eligible capital in respect of a business, cumulative Canadian exploration expense (within the meaning assigned by subsection 66.1(6)), cumulative Canadian development expense (within the meaning assigned by subsection 66.2(5)), cumulative foreign resource expense in respect of a country other than Canada (within the meaning assigned by subsection 66.21(1)) or cumulative Canadian oil and gas property expense (within the meaning assigned by subsection 66.4(5)) (each of which is referred to in this paragraph as a "pool amount"), and

S. 261(7)(*a*)(i) was replaced by S.C. 2013, c. 34, s. 77(3), deemed to have come into force on August 20, 2011.

See the application for the amendment to s. 261(5)(*e*) for the extension of assessment periods to take into account the amendments by S.C. 2013, c. 34, s. 54 to 89.

S. 261(7)(*a*)(i) formerly read:

(i) is, or is relevant to the determination of, an amount that may be deducted under subsection 37(1) or 66(4), element F in the definition "foreign accrual property income" in subsection 95(1), section 110.1 or 111 or subsection 126(2), 127(5), 129(1), 181.1(4) or 190.1(3), in the particular functional currency year, and

S. 261(7) was replaced by S.C. 2009, c. 2, s. 80(1), applicable in respect of taxation years that begin after December 13, 2007, except that where a taxpayer has, on or before June 27, 2008, made an election under paragraph 261(3)(*b*), if the taxpayer makes a further election in writing, and files it with the Minister of National Revenue on or before the taxpayer's filing-due date for the taxpayer's taxation year that includes the day on which this Act is assented to [R.A. March 12, 2009], the relevant spot rate for a particular day is deemed, for the purposes of subsections 261(7) to (10), to be the average of the rates that would, in the absence of this election, be the relevant spot rates for each day in the 12-month period that ends on the particular day. S. 261(7) formerly read:

(7) *Amounts payable or refundable in respect of a functional currency year.* Notwithstanding subsection (4),

(*a*) if, at any particular time, an amount (determined in the taxpayer's functional currency for the particular functional currency year) first becomes payable under this Act by a taxpayer to the Receiver General in respect of a particular functional currency year of the taxpayer,

(i) that amount (determined in the taxpayer's functional currency for the particular functional currency year) is to be converted to Canadian currency using the currency exchange rate on the earlier of the day the amount is so paid and the day that includes the particular time in respect of a conversion of an amount determined in the taxpayer's functional currency for the particular functional currency year into an amount determined in Canadian currency, and

(ii) the amount so determined in Canadian currency under subparagraph (i) is to be paid to the Receiver General in Canadian currency; and

(*b*) if, at any particular time, an amount (determined in a taxpayer's functional currency for the particular functional currency year) first becomes payable under this Act to the taxpayer by the Minister, for a particular functional currency year of the taxpayer, or is deemed to be paid on account of an amount payable by the taxpayer under the Act for that particular functional currency year,

(i) that amount (determined in the taxpayer's functional currency for the particular functional currency year) is to be converted to Canadian currency using the currency exchange rate on the day that includes the particular time in respect of the conversion of an amount determined in the taxpayer's functional currency for the particular functional currency year into an amount determined in Canadian currency, and

(ii) the amount so determined in Canadian currency under subparagraph (i) is to be paid to the taxpayer by the Minister or is deemed to have been paid to the taxpayer by the Minister, as the case may be, in Canadian currency.

Canadian Tax Foundation: Barnicke and Huynh, *Functional Currency and FAs*, 2009 Canadian Tax Highlights 17(4):7; Hickey, *Functional Currency Tax Reporting*, 2007 Canadian Tax Highlights 15(11):6–7.

Tax Topics: No. 1918, New and Improved Functional Currency Proposals.

Income Tax Folios: *Primary* — S5-F4-C1 Income Tax Reporting Currency.

► 261(8) ◄

(8) Converting pre-transition debts. In determining, at any time in a particular functional currency year of a taxpayer, the amount for which a pre-transition debt of the taxpayer (other than a pre-transition debt denominated in the taxpayer's elected functional currency) was issued and its principal amount at the beginning of the taxpayer's first functional currency year,

(*a*) where the pre-transition debt is denominated in Canadian currency, those amounts are to be converted to the taxpayer's elected functional currency using the relevant spot rate for the last day of the taxpayer's last Canadian currency year; and

(*b*) where the pre-transition debt is denominated in a currency (referred to in this paragraph as the "debt currency") that is neither Canadian currency nor the taxpayer's elected functional currency, those amounts are to be converted from the debt currency to the taxpayer's elected functional currency using the relevant spot rate for the last day of the taxpayer's last Canadian currency year.

History: S. 261(8) was replaced by S.C. 2009, c. 2, s. 80(1), applicable in respect of taxation years that begin after December 13, 2007, except that where a taxpayer has, on or before June 27, 2008, made an election under paragraph 261(3)(*b*), if the taxpayer makes a further election in writing, and files it with the Minister of National Revenue on or before the taxpayer's filing-due date for the taxpayer's taxation year that includes the day on which this Act is assented to [R.A. March 12, 2009], the relevant spot rate for a particular day is deemed, for the purposes of subsections 261(7) to (10), to be the average of the rates that would, in the absence of this election, be the relevant spot rates for each day in the 12-month period that ends on the particular day. S. 261(8) formerly read:

(8) *Application of subsection (9).* Subsection (9) applies to a taxpayer for a particular Canadian currency year that begins after the last functional currency year of the taxpayer.

Income Tax Technical News: Issue No. 41, Functional Currency Tax Reporting Rules.

► 261(9) ◄

(9) Pre-transition debts. A pre-transition debt of a taxpayer that is denominated in a currency other than the taxpayer's elected functional currency is deemed to have been issued immediately before the taxpayer's first functional currency year for the purposes of

(*a*) determining the amount of the taxpayer's income, gain or loss, for a functional currency year of the taxpayer (other than an amount that subsection (10) deems to arise), that is attributable to a fluctuation in the value of a currency; and

(*b*) applying paragraph 80(2)(*k*) in respect of a functional currency year of the taxpayer.

History: S. 261(9) was replaced by S.C. 2009, c. 2, s. 80(1), applicable in respect of taxation years that begin after December 13, 2007, except that where a taxpayer has, on or before June 27, 2008, made an election under paragraph 261(3)(*b*), if the taxpayer makes a further election in writing, and files it with the Minister of National Revenue on or before the taxpayer's filing-due date for the taxpayer's taxation year that includes the day on which this Act is assented to [R.A. March 12, 2009], the relevant spot rate for a particular day is deemed, for the purposes of subsections 261(7) to (10), to be the average of the rates that would, in the absence of this election, be the relevant spot rates for each day in the 12-month period that ends on the particular day. S. 261(9) formerly read:

(9) *Converting functional currency amounts.* Where, because of subsection (8), this subsection applies to a taxpayer for a particular Canadian currency year of the taxpayer, in applying this Act to the taxpayer for that particular Canadian currency year, the following rules apply:

(*a*) subject to subparagraph (10)(*a*)(iii), in determining the amount (expressed in Canadian currency) that may be deducted, or relevant in determining the amount that may be deducted, under subsection 37(1) or 66(4), section 110.1 or 111 or subsection 126(2), 127(5), 129(1), 181.1(4) or 190.1(3) in the particular Canadian currency year,

(i) each amount (determined in the taxpayer's functional currency for the functional currency year of the taxpayer) that is relevant to the determination and that was first required to be determined in a functional currency year of the taxpayer that preceded the particular Canadian currency year, is to be converted to Canadian currency using the reversionary exchange rate of the taxpayer for that functional currency year, and

(ii) each amount (determined in Canadian currency) that is relevant to the determination and that was first required to be determined in a Canadian currency year of the taxpayer preceding the particular Canadian currency year is the amount that was so determined in Canadian currency in that Canadian currency year;

(*b*) in determining, at any time in the particular Canadian currency year, the cost (expressed in Canadian currency) to the taxpayer of a property,

(i) where the property was acquired by the taxpayer in a functional currency year of the taxpayer preceding the particular Canadian currency year, the cost (determined in the taxpayer's functional currency for the functional currency year) to the taxpayer of the property is to be converted to Canadian currency using the reversionary exchange rate of the taxpayer for that functional currency year, and

(ii) where the property was acquired by the taxpayer in a Canadian currency year of the taxpayer preceding the particular Canadian currency year, the cost (determined in Canadian currency) to the taxpayer of the property is the cost so determined in Canadian currency in that Canadian currency year;

(*c*) in determining, at any time in the particular Canadian currency year, the adjusted cost base (expressed in Canadian currency) to the taxpayer of a capital property

(i) each amount (determined in the taxpayer's functional currency for the functional currency year) that is required by section 53 to be added or deducted in computing the adjusted cost base of the property to the taxpayer and was first required by that section to be added or deducted at any time in a functional currency year of the taxpayer preceding the particular Canadian currency year is to be converted to Canadian currency using the reversionary exchange rate of the taxpayer for that functional currency year, and

(ii) each amount (determined in Canadian currency) that is required by section 53 to be added or deducted in computing the adjusted cost base of the property to the taxpayer and was first required by that section to be added or deducted at any time in a Canadian currency year of the taxpayer preceding the particular Canadian currency year is the amount that was so determined in Canadian currency in that Canadian currency year;

(*d*) in determining, at any time in the particular Canadian currency year, the amount (expressed in Canadian currency) of the taxpayer's undepreciated capital cost of depreciable property of a prescribed class, cumulative eligible capital in respect of a business, cumulative Canadian exploration expense (within the meaning assigned by subsection 66.1(6)), cumulative Canadian development expense (within the meaning assigned by subsection 66.2(5)), cumulative foreign resource expense in respect of a country other than Canada (within the meaning assigned by subsection 66.21(1)) and cumulative Canadian oil and gas property expense (within the meaning assigned by subsection 66.4(5)), (each of which is referred to in this paragraph as a "pool amount"),

(i) each amount (determined in the taxpayer's functional currency for the functional currency year) that is required to be added to or deducted from a particular pool amount of the taxpayer and was first required to be added or deducted in respect of a functional currency year of the taxpayer preceding the particular Canadian currency year is to be converted to Canadian currency using the reversionary exchange rate of the taxpayer for that functional currency year, and

(ii) each amount (determined in Canadian currency) that is required to be added to or deducted from a particular pool amount of the taxpayer and was first required to be added or deducted in respect of a Canadian currency year of the taxpayer preceding the particular Canadian currency year is the amount that was so determined in Canadian currency in that Canadian currency year;

(*e*) in determining any amount (expressed in Canadian currency) that has been deducted or claimed as a reserve in computing the income of the taxpayer for its last functional currency year preceding the particular Canadian currency year, that amount (determined in the taxpayer's functional currency for the last functional currency year) deducted or claimed as a reserve for that last functional currency year is to be converted to Canadian currency using the reversionary exchange rate of the taxpayer for that last functional currency year;

(*f*) in determining the amount (expressed in Canadian currency) of any outlay or expense referred to in subsection 18(9) that was made or incurred by the taxpayer and the amount that was deducted by the taxpayer in respect of that outlay or expense in respect of a taxation year of the taxpayer preceding the particular Canadian currency year,

(i) such of those amounts (determined in the taxpayer's functional currency for the functional currency year) that were first made or incurred or deducted by the taxpayer in or in respect of a functional currency year of the taxpayer preceding the particular Canadian currency year are to be converted to Canadian currency using the reversionary exchange rate of the taxpayer for that functional currency year, and

(ii) such of those amounts (determined in Canadian currency) that were first made or incurred or deducted by the taxpayer in or in respect of a Canadian currency year of the taxpayer preceding the particular Canadian currency year are the amounts that were so determined in Canadian currency in that Canadian currency year;

(*g*) in determining, at any time in the particular Canadian currency year, the amount (expressed in Canadian currency) of the taxpayer's paid-up capital in respect of any class of shares of its capital stock,

(i) any amount (determined in the taxpayer's functional currency for the functional currency year) that was first added or deducted in computing the taxpayer's paid-up capital in respect of the class in a functional currency year of the taxpayer preceding the particular Canadian currency year is to be converted to Canadian currency using the reversionary exchange rate of the taxpayer for that functional currency year, and

(ii) any amount (determined in Canadian currency) that was first added or deducted in computing the taxpayer's paid-up capital in respect of the class in a Canadian currency year of the taxpayer preceding the particular Canadian currency year is the amount that was so determined in Canadian currency in that Canadian currency year;

(*h*) where an obligation was issued in a taxation year of the taxpayer preceding the initial reversionary year of the taxpayer, in determining, at any time in the particular Canadian currency year, the amount (expressed in Canadian currency) for which an obligation was issued, the principal amount (expressed in Canadian currency) of the obligation, the amounts (expressed in Canadian currency) paid in satisfaction of the principal amount of the obligation, and the amount (determined in Canadian currency), if any, of any gain or loss attributable to the fluctuation in the value of the Canadian currency relative to the value of the currency in which the obligation was issued,

(i) subject to paragraph (*i*), where the obligation was issued in a currency other than Canadian currency,

(A) the amount (determined in the currency in which the obligation was issued) for which the obligation was issued and the principal amount (determined in the currency in which the obligation was issued) of the obligation are

(I) where the taxation year of the taxpayer in which the obligation was issued was a Canadian currency year of the taxpayer, the amounts (determined in Canadian currency) that were so determined in Canadian currency in that Canadian currency year, or

(II) where the taxation year of the taxpayer in which the obligation was issued was a functional currency year of the taxpayer, the amounts determined by converting those amounts (determined in the taxpayer's functional currency for the functional currency year) to Canadian currency by using the reversionary exchange rate of the taxpayer for that functional currency year, and

(B) the amounts (determined in the currency in which the obligation was issued) paid at any time in a taxation year of the taxpayer preceding the initial reversionary year of the taxpayer in satisfaction of the principal amount of the obligation are

(I) where the taxation year of the taxpayer in which an amount was paid was a Canadian currency year of the taxpayer, the amount (determined in Canadian currency) that was so determined in Canadian currency in that Canadian currency year, or

(II) where the taxation year of the taxpayer in which an amount was paid was a functional currency year of the taxpayer, the amount determined by converting that amount (determined in the taxpayer's functional currency for the functional currency year) to Canadian currency by using the reversionary exchange rate of the taxpayer for that functional currency year, and

(ii) where the obligation was issued in Canadian currency, the amount (determined in Canadian currency) for which the obligation was issued, the principal amount (determined in Canadian currency) of the obligation and the amounts (determined in Canadian currency) paid, in a taxation year of the taxpayer preceding the initial reversionary year of the taxpayer, in satisfaction of the principal amount of the obligation, are the amounts so determined in Canadian currency in those preceding years;

(*i*) where an obligation was issued in a currency other than Canadian currency in a taxation year of the taxpayer preceding the initial reversionary year of the taxpayer, in determining, in respect of subsection 79(7) or paragraph 80(2)(*k*) or 142.7(8)(*b*), the amount (expressed in Canadian currency) for which the obligation was issued, the principal amount (determined in Canadian currency) of the obligation, and the amounts (determined in Canadian currency) paid in satisfaction of the principal amount of the obligation, at any time in the particular Canadian currency year, those amounts are to be determined as if subsections (1) to (7) had not applied to the taxpayer for any preceding taxation year;

(*j*) where the particular Canadian currency year is the initial reversionary year of the taxpayer, for the purpose of determining the taxpayer's first instalment base or second instalment base in the particular Canadian currency year, the amount (determined in the taxpayer's functional currency for the functional currency year) of tax payable by the taxpayer under Part I for the last functional currency year of the taxpayer is to be converted to Canadian currency using the reversionary exchange rate of the taxpayer for that last functional currency year; and

(*k*) in determining any amount (determined in Canadian currency and referred to in this paragraph as the "specified amount"), at any time in the particular Canadian currency year, other than an amount referred to in paragraphs (*a*) to (*j*), that is relevant in determining the Canadian tax results of the taxpayer for the particular Canadian currency year

(i) any amount (determined in the taxpayer's functional currency for the functional currency year) that is relevant in determining the specified amount and was first determined in or in respect of a functional currency year of the taxpayer preceding the particular Canadian currency year, is to be converted to Canadian currency using the reversionary exchange rate of the taxpayer for that functional currency year, and

(ii) any amount (determined in Canadian currency) that is relevant in determining the specified amount and was first determined in or in respect of a Canadian currency year of the taxpayer preceding the particular Canadian currency year is the amount that was so determined in Canadian currency in that Canadian currency year.

Tax Topics: No. 1918, New and Improved Functional Currency Proposals.

Income Tax Technical News: Issue No. 41, Functional Currency Tax Reporting Rules.

▶ 261(10) ◀

(10) Deferred amounts relating to pre-transition debts. If a taxpayer has, at any time in a taxation year that is a functional currency year or a reversionary year of the taxpayer, made a particular payment on account of the principal amount of a pre-transition debt of the taxpayer:

(*a*) where the taxpayer would have made a gain — or, if the pre-transition debt was not on account of capital, would have had income — (referred to in this paragraph as the "hypothetical gain or income") attributable to a fluctuation in the value of a currency if the pre-transition debt had been settled by the taxpayer's having paid, immediately before the end of its last Canadian currency year, an amount equal to the principal amount (expressed in the currency in which the pre-transition debt is denominated, which currency is referred to in this subsection as the "debt currency") at that time, the taxpayer is deemed to make a gain or to have income, as the case may be, for the taxation year equal to the amount determined by the formula

$$A \times B/C$$

where

A is

(i) if the taxation year is a functional currency year of the taxpayer, the amount of the hypothetical gain or income converted to the taxpayer's elected functional currency using the relevant spot rate for the last day of the taxpayer's last Canadian currency year, and

(ii) if the taxation year is a reversionary year of the taxpayer, the amount determined under subparagraph (i) converted to Canadian currency using the relevant spot rate for the last day of the taxpayer's last functional currency year,

B is the amount of the particular payment (expressed in the debt currency), and

C is the principal amount of the pre-transition debt at the beginning of the taxpayer's first functional currency year (expressed in the debt currency); and

(*b*) where the taxpayer would have sustained a loss — or, if the pre-transition debt was not on account of capital, would have had a loss — (referred to in this paragraph as the "hypothetical loss") attributable to a fluctuation in the value of a currency if the pre-transition debt had been settled by the taxpayer's having paid, immediately before the end of its last Canadian currency year, an amount equal to the principal amount (expressed in the debt currency) at that time, the taxpayer is deemed to sustain or to have a loss in respect of the particular payment for the taxation year equal to the amount that would be determined by the formula in paragraph (*a*) if the reference in the description of A in that paragraph to "hypothetical gain or income" were read as a reference to "hypothetical loss".

History: S. 261(10) was replaced by S.C. 2009, c. 2, s. 80(1), applicable in respect of taxation years that begin after December 13, 2007, except that where a taxpayer has, on or before June 27, 2008, made an election under paragraph 261(3)(*b*), if the taxpayer makes a further election in writing, and files it with the Minister of National Revenue on or before the taxpayer's filing-due date for the taxpayer's taxation year that includes the day on which this Act is assented to [R.A. March 12, 2009], the relevant spot rate for a particular day is deemed, for the purposes of subsections 261(7) to (10), to be the average of the rates that would, in the absence of this election, be the relevant spot rates for each day in the 12-month period that ends on the particular day. S. 261(10) formerly read:

(10) *Functional currency and Canadian currency amounts carried back.* In determining an amount that a taxpayer may claim under section 111 or

subsection 126(2), 127(5), 181.1(4) or 190.1(3), for a particular taxation year of the taxpayer, the following rules apply:

(*a*) if the particular taxation year is a Canadian currency year of the taxpayer, the amount that may be claimed (determined in Canadian currency) is to be determined,

(i) by converting each amount (determined in the taxpayer's functional currency for the particular functional currency year) of a loss incurred, tax credit arising and expenditure made in or in respect of a particular functional currency year of the taxpayer that ends after the particular taxation year to Canadian currency using the currency exchange rate in respect of the conversion of an amount determined in the taxpayer's functional currency for the particular functional currency year into an amount determined in Canadian currency on the last day of that particular functional currency year,

(ii) as if each amount (determined in Canadian currency) of a loss incurred, tax credit arising, expenditure made and deduction claimed in or in respect of a Canadian currency year of the taxpayer were the amount of that loss incurred, tax credit arising, expenditure made and deduction claimed in Canadian currency in or in respect of that Canadian currency year of the taxpayer, and

(iii) by converting each amount (determined in the taxpayer's functional currency for the particular functional currency year) claimed in or in respect of a particular functional currency year of the taxpayer preceding the initial reversionary year of the taxpayer (in respect of an amount of loss incurred, tax credit arising or expenditure made by a taxpayer in or in respect of a Canadian currency year) to Canadian currency using the currency exchange rate on the last day of the Canadian currency year of the taxpayer in or in respect of which the amount claimed arose in respect of the conversion of an amount determined in the taxpayer's functional currency for the particular functional currency year to an amount determined in Canadian currency; and

(*b*) if the particular taxation year is a functional currency year of the taxpayer, the amount that may be claimed (determined in the taxpayer's functional currency for the particular taxation year) is to be determined,

(i) by converting each amount (determined in Canadian currency) of a loss incurred, tax credit arising and expenditure made in or in respect of a particular Canadian currency year of the taxpayer that ends after the particular taxation year to the taxpayer's functional currency for the particular taxation year using the currency exchange rate in respect of the conversion of an amount determined in Canadian currency into an amount determined in the taxpayer's functional currency for the particular taxation year on the last day of that particular Canadian currency year,

(ii) as if each amount (determined in the taxpayer's functional currency for the particular taxation year) of a loss incurred, tax credit arising, expenditure made and deduction claimed in or in respect of a functional currency year of the taxpayer were the amount of that loss incurred, tax credit arising, expenditure made and deduction claimed in the taxpayer's functional currency for the particular taxation year, and

(iii) by converting each amount (determined in Canadian currency) claimed in or in respect of a particular Canadian currency year of the taxpayer preceding the initial functional currency year of the taxpayer (in respect of an amount of loss incurred, tax credit arising or expenditure made by a taxpayer in or in respect of a functional currency year of the taxpayer) to the taxpayer's functional currency for the particular taxation year using the currency exchange rate on the last day of the functional currency year of the taxpayer in or in respect of which the amount claimed arose in respect of the conversion of an amount determined in Canadian currency to an amount determined in the taxpayer's functional currency for the particular taxation year.

Tax Topics: No. 1918, New and Improved Functional Currency Proposals.

Income Tax Technical News: Issue No. 41, Functional Currency Tax Reporting Rules.

▶ 261(10.1) ◀

(10.1) Debt parking — foreign exchange. For the purposes of determining a taxpayer's gain under subsection (10), if at a particular time a pre-transition debt of the taxpayer (referred to in this subsection as the "debtor") that is denominated in a currency other than Canadian currency becomes a parked obligation (within the meaning assigned by subsection 39(2.02)), the debtor is deemed to have made, at that time, a particular payment on account of the principal amount of the debt equal to

(*a*) if the debt has become a parked obligation at that particular time as a result of its acquisition by the holder of the debt, the portion of the amount paid by the holder to acquire the debt that can reasonably be considered to relate to the principal amount of the debt at the particular time; and

(*b*) in any other case, the portion of the fair market value of the debt that can reasonably be considered to relate to the principal amount of the debt at the particular time.

Editorial Note: In general terms, subsection 261(10.1) provides special rules for determining a taxpayer's foreign exchange income or loss, or capital gain or capital loss, in respect of the repayment of a debt by the taxpayer in a functional currency year that was issued by the taxpayer in a previous Canadian currency year. In this regard, if such a debt has become a "parked debt" (see the editorial note to subsection 39(2.02)), the taxpayer is deemed to make a repayment of the debt at that time, and the amount of the repayment is the amount in either paragraph 261(10.1)(*a*) or (*b*).

History: S. 261(10.1) was added by S.C. 2016, c. 12, s. 69(5), deemed to have come into force on March 22, 2016. However, this amendment does not apply to a debtor in respect of a debt owing by that debtor at the time that the debt meets the conditions to become a parked obligation under subsection 39(2.02), because of a written agreement entered into before March 22, 2016, if that time is before 2017.

▶ 261(11) ◀

(11) Determination of amounts payable. Notwithstanding subsections (5) and (7), for the purposes of applying this Act in respect of a functional currency year (referred to in this subsection as the "particular taxation year") of a taxpayer,

(*a*) for the purposes of determining the taxpayer's payment obligations under paragraph 157(1)(*a*) or (1.1)(*a*),

(i) the estimated amounts, each of which is described in subparagraph 157(1)(*a*)(i) or (1.1)(*a*)(i), that are payable by the taxpayer for the particular taxation year are to be determined by converting those amounts, as determined in the taxpayer's elected functional currency, to Canadian currency using the relevant spot rate for the day on which those amounts are due,

(ii) the taxpayer's first instalment base (within the meaning assigned by subsection 157(4)) for the particular taxation year is to be determined

(A) if the particular taxation year is the taxpayer's first functional currency year, without reference to this section, and

(B) in any other case, as if the taxes payable by the taxpayer for the taxpayer's functional currency year (referred to in this paragraph as the "first base year") immediately preceding the particular taxation year were the total of

(I) the total of the taxpayer's payment obligations under paragraph 157(1)(*a*) or (1.1)(*a*), as determined with reference to this subparagraph or subparagraph (i) or (iii), as the case may be, in respect of the first base year, and

(II) the amount, if any, of the remainder of the taxes payable by the taxpayer under paragraph 157(1)(*b*) or (1.1)(*b*), as determined under paragraph (*b*), in respect of the first base year, and

(iii) the taxpayer's second instalment base (within the meaning assigned by subsection 157(4)) for the particular taxation year is to be determined

(A) if the particular taxation year is the taxpayer's first functional currency year or its taxation year that immediately follows its first functional currency year, without reference to this section, and

(B) in any other case, as if the taxes payable by the taxpayer for the taxpayer's functional currency year (referred to in this subparagraph as the "second base year") immediately preceding the first base year were the total of

(I) the total of the taxpayer's payment obligations under paragraph 157(1)(*a*) or (1.1)(*a*), as determined with reference to this subparagraph or subparagraph (i) or (ii), as the case may be, in respect of the second base year, and

(II) the amount, if any, of the remainder of the taxes payable by the taxpayer under paragraph 157(1)(*b*) or (1.1)(*b*), as determined under paragraph (*b*), in respect of the second base year;

(*b*) the remainder of the taxes payable by the taxpayer under paragraph 157(1)(*b*) or (1.1)(*b*) for the particular taxation year is the amount, if any, determined by

(i) computing the amount, if any, by which

(A) the total of the taxes payable by the taxpayer under Parts I, VI, VI.1 and XIII.1 for the particular taxation year, as determined in the taxpayer's elected functional currency

exceeds

(B) the total of all amounts each of which is the amount determined by converting the amount of a payment obligation — determined by paragraph 157(1)(*a*) or (1.1)(*a*), as the case may be, with reference to subparagraph (*a*)(i), (ii) or (iii), as the case may be — of the taxpayer in respect of the particular taxation year to the taxpayer's elected functional currency using the relevant spot rate for the day on which the payment obligation was due, and

(ii) converting the amount, if any, determined by subparagraph (i) to Canadian currency using the relevant spot rate for the taxpayer's balance-due day for the particular taxation year;

(*c*) for the purposes of determining any amount (other than tax) that is payable by the taxpayer under Part I, VI, VI.1 or XIII.1 for the particular taxation year, the taxpayer's tax payable under the Part for the particular taxation year is deemed to be equal to the total of

(i) the total of the taxpayer's payment obligations under paragraph 157(1)(*a*) or (1.1)(*a*), in respect of the Part, as determined with reference to subparagraph (*a*)(i), (ii) or (iii), as the case may be, in respect of the particular taxation year, and

(ii) the amount, if any, of the remainder of the taxes payable by the taxpayer under paragraph 157(1)(*b*) or (1.1)(*b*), in respect of the Part, as determined under paragraph (*b*), in respect of the particular taxation year;

(*d*) amounts of tax that are payable under this Act (except under Parts I, VI, VI.1 and XIII.1) by the taxpayer for the particular taxation year are to be determined by converting those amounts, as determined in the taxpayer's elected functional currency, to Canadian currency using the relevant spot rate for the day on which those amounts are due;

(*e*) if a particular amount that is determined in the taxpayer's elected functional currency is deemed to be paid at any time on account of an amount payable by the taxpayer under this Act for the particular taxation year, the particular amount is to be converted to Canadian currency using the relevant spot rate for the day that includes that time;

(*f*) the following amounts are to be determined in the taxpayer's elected functional currency and converted to Canadian currency using the relevant spot rate for the taxpayer's balance-due day for the particular taxation year:

(i) amounts described in paragraph 163(1)(*a*) in respect of the particular taxation year, and

(ii) the amount of the taxpayer's taxable capital employed in Canada, for the purpose of applying section 235; and

(*g*) for greater certainty, all amounts payable by the taxpayer under this Act in respect of the particular taxation year are to be paid in Canadian currency.

History: S. 261(11)(*b*)(i)(A) was replaced by S.C. 2014, c. 39, s. 77(4), applicable to taxation years that begin after December 13, 2007.

In addition, any assessment of a taxpayer's tax, interest and penalties payable under the Act for any taxation year that ends before the day on which this amendment receives royal assent [December 16, 2014] that would, in the absence of this section, be precluded because of the time references in subsection 152(4) of the Act is to be made to the extent necessary to take into account this amendment.

S. 261(11)(*b*)(i)(A) formerly read:

(A) the total of the taxes payable by the taxpayer under this Part and Parts VI, VI.1 and XIII.1 for the particular taxation year, as determined in the taxpayer's elected functional currency

S. 261(11)(*c*), the portion before subparagraph (i) was replaced by S.C. 2014, c. 39, s. 77(5), applicable to taxation years that begin after December 13, 2007.

In addition, any assessment of a taxpayer's tax, interest and penalties payable under the Act for any taxation year that ends before the day on which this amendment receives royal assent [December 16, 2014] that would, in the absence of this section, be precluded because of the time references in subsection 152(4) of the Act is to be made to the extent necessary to take into account this amendment.

S. 261(11)(*c*), the portion before subparagraph (i) formerly read:

(*c*) for the purposes of determining any amount (other than tax) that is payable by the taxpayer under this Part or Part VI, VI.1 or XIII.1 for the particular taxation year, the taxpayer's tax payable under the Part for the particular taxation year is deemed to be equal to the total of

S. 261(11)(*d*) was replaced by S.C. 2014, c. 39, s. 77(6), applicable to taxation years that begin after December 13, 2007.

In addition, any assessment of a taxpayer's tax, interest and penalties payable under the Act for any taxation year that ends before the day on which this amendment receives royal assent [December 16, 2014] that would, in the absence of this section, be precluded because of the time references in subsection 152(4) of the Act is to be made to the extent necessary to take into account this amendment.

S. 261(11)(*d*) formerly read:

(*d*) amounts of tax that are payable under this Act (except under this Part and Parts VI, VI.1 and XIII.1) by the taxpayer for the particular taxation year are to be determined by converting those amounts, as determined in the taxpayer's elected functional currency, to Canadian currency using the relevant spot rate for the day on which those amounts are due;

S. 261(11) was replaced by S.C. 2009, c. 2, s. 80(1), applicable in respect of taxation years that begin after December 13, 2007. S. 261(11) formerly read:

(11) *Subsection 88(1) wind-ups — effect on subsidiary.* Subsection (12) applies to a corporation (referred to in this subsection and subsection (12) as the "subsidiary") that has been wound up into another corporation (referred to in this subsection as the "parent") if

(*a*) subsection 88(1) applied to the subsidiary and the parent in respect of the winding-up of the subsidiary;

(*b*) the taxation year of the subsidiary (referred to in this subsection and subsection (12) as the "distribution year of the subsidiary") in which any portion of a property (such portion of the property referred to in this subsection as the "distributed property") of the subsidiary was distributed to the parent, or any portion of an obligation (such portion of the obligation referred to in this subsection as the "assumed obligation") of the subsidiary was assumed by the parent, on the winding-up of the subsidiary would, were this section read without reference to this subsection, be a functional currency year of the subsidiary; and

(*c*) either

(i) where the taxation year of the parent (referred to in this paragraph as the "acquisition year of the parent") in which the subsidiary distributed the distributed property to the parent, or the assumed obligation of the subsidiary was assumed by the parent, on the winding-up of the subsidiary was a functional currency year of the parent, the functional currency for the acquisition year of the parent was not the functional currency of the subsidiary for the distribution year of the subsidiary, or

(ii) the acquisition year of the parent was not a functional currency year of the parent.

Tax Window Files: Functional Currency Tax Reporting, *September 15, 2009*, CRA Document No. 2009-0332771E5.

▶ 261(12) ◀

(12) Application of subsections (7) and (8) to reversionary years. In applying this Act to a reversionary year of a taxpayer, subsections (7) and (8) are to be read as if the references in those subsections to

(*a*) "Canadian currency" were references to "the taxpayer's elected functional currency";

(*b*) "Canadian currency year" were references to "functional currency year";

(*c*) "functional currency year" were references to "reversionary year";

(*d*) "first functional currency year" were references to "first reversionary year";

(*e*) "last Canadian currency year" were references to "last functional currency year";

(*f*) "pre-transition debt" were references to "pre-reversion debt"; and

(*g*) "the taxpayer's elected functional currency" were references to "Canadian currency".

History: S. 261(12) was replaced by S.C. 2009, c. 2, s. 80(1), applicable in respect of taxation years that begin after December 13, 2007. S. 261(12) formerly read:

(12) *Taxation year of subsidiary.* Where, because of subsection (11), this subsection applies to the subsidiary, for the purposes of this section

(*a*) the last taxation year of the subsidiary that ends before the beginning of the distribution year of the subsidiary is deemed to be the last functional currency year of the subsidiary; and

(*b*) subsection (4) is deemed not to apply to the subsidiary for each taxation year of the subsidiary commencing after the end of the last functional currency year of the subsidiary described in paragraph (*a*).

▶ 261(13) ◀

(13) Pre-reversion debts. A pre-reversion debt of a taxpayer that is denominated in a currency other than Canadian currency is deemed to have been issued immediately before the taxpayer's first reversionary year for the purposes of

(*a*) determining the amount of the taxpayer's income, gain or loss, for a reversionary year of the taxpayer (other than an amount that subsection (14) deems to arise), that is attributable to a fluctuation in the value of a currency; and

(*b*) applying paragraph 80(2)(*k*) in respect of a reversionary year of the taxpayer.

History: S. 261(13) was replaced by S.C. 2009, c. 2, s. 80(1), applicable in respect of taxation years that begin after December 13, 2007. S. 261(13) formerly read:

(13) *Amalgamations — effect on predecessor corporations.* Subsection (14) applies to a corporation (referred to in this subsection and subsection (14) as the "specified predecessor") that has merged with one or more other corporations to form one corporate entity (referred to in this subsection as the "new corporation") if

(*a*) the merger was an amalgamation (within the meaning assigned by subsection 87(1));

(*b*) the taxation year of the specified predecessor (referred to in this subsection and subsection (14) as the "last taxation year of the specified predecessor") that ended immediately before the amalgamation would, were this section read without reference to subsection (14), be a functional currency year of the specified predecessor; and

(*c*) either

(i) where the taxation year of the new corporation (referred to in this paragraph as the "first taxation year of the new corporation") that began at the time of the amalgamation was a functional currency year of the new corporation, the functional currency of the new corporation for the first taxation year of the new corporation was not the functional currency of the specified predecessor for the last taxation year of the specified predecessor, or

(ii) the first taxation year of the new corporation was not a functional currency year of the new corporation.

▶ 261(14) ◀

(14) Deferred amounts relating to pre-reversion debts. If a taxpayer has, at any time in a reversionary year of the taxpayer, made a particular payment on account of the principal amount of a pre-reversion debt of the taxpayer:

(*a*) where the taxpayer would have made a gain — or, if the pre-reversion debt was not on account of capital, would have had income — (referred to in this paragraph as the "hypothetical gain or income") attributable to a fluctuation in the value of a currency if the pre-reversion debt had been settled by the taxpayer's having paid, immediately before the end of its last functional currency year, an amount equal to the principal amount (expressed in the currency in which the pre-reversion debt is denominated, which currency is referred to in this subsection as the "debt currency") at that time, the taxpayer is deemed to make a gain or to have income, as the case may be, for the reversionary year equal to the amount determined by the formula

$$A \times B/C$$

where

A is the amount of the hypothetical gain or income converted to Canadian currency using the relevant spot rate for the last day of the taxpayer's last functional currency year,

B is the amount of the particular payment (expressed in the debt currency), and

C is the principal amount of the pre-reversion debt at the beginning of the taxpayer's first reversionary year (expressed in the debt currency); and

(*b*) where the taxpayer would have sustained a loss — or, if the pre-reversion debt was not on account of capital, would have had a loss — (referred to in this paragraph as the "hypothetical loss") attributable to a fluctuation in the value of a currency if the pre-reversion debt had been settled by the taxpayer's having paid, immediately before the end of its last functional currency year, an amount equal to the principal amount (expressed in the debt currency) at that time, the taxpayer is deemed to sustain or to have a loss in respect of the particular payment for the reversionary year equal to the amount that would be determined by the formula in paragraph (*a*) if the reference in the description of A in that paragraph to "hypothetical gain or income" were read as a reference to "hypothetical loss".

History: S. 261(14) was replaced by S.C. 2009, c. 2, s. 80(1), applicable in respect of taxation years that begin after December 13, 2007. S. 261(14) formerly read:

(14) *Taxation year of specified predecessor.* Where, because of subsection (13), this subsection applies to the specified predecessor, for the purposes of this section

(*a*) the taxation year of the specified predecessor that ends immediately before the beginning of the last taxation year of the specified predecessor is deemed to be the last functional currency year of the specified predecessor; and

(*b*) subsection (4) is deemed not to apply to the specified predecessor corporation for each taxation year of the specified predecessor commencing after the end of the last functional currency year of the specified predecessor described in paragraph (*a*).

► 261(14.1) ◄

(14.1) Debt parking — foreign exchange. For the purposes of determining a taxpayer's gain under subsection (14), if at a particular time a pre-reversion debt of the taxpayer (referred to in this subsection as the "debtor") that is denominated in a currency other than the taxpayer's elected functional currency becomes a parked obligation (within the meaning assigned by subsection 39(2.02)), the debtor is deemed to have made, at that time, a particular payment on account of the principal amount of the debt equal to

(*a*) if the debt has become a parked obligation at that particular time as a result of its acquisition by the holder of the debt, the portion of the amount paid by the holder to acquire the debt that can reasonably be considered to relate to the principal amount of the debt at the particular time; and

(*b*) in any other case, the portion of the fair market value of the debt that can reasonably be considered to relate to the principal amount of the debt at the particular time.

Editorial Note: In general terms, subsection 261(14.1) provides special rules for determining a taxpayer's foreign exchange income or loss, or capital gain or capital loss, in respect of the repayment of a debt by the taxpayer in a particular year (which is not a functional currency year) that was issued by the taxpayer in a previous functional currency year (a "pre-reversion debt"). In this regard, if such a debt has become a "parked debt" (see the editorial note to subsection 39(2.02)), the taxpayer is deemed to make a repayment of the debt at that time, and the amount of the repayment is the amount in either paragraph 261(14.1)(*a*) or (*b*).

History: S. 261(14.1) was added by S.C. 2016, c. 12, s. 69(6), deemed to have come into force on March 22, 2016. However, this amendment does not apply to a debtor in respect of a debt owing by that debtor at the time that the debt meets the conditions to become a parked obligation under subsection 39(2.02), because of a written agreement entered into before March 22, 2016, if that time is before 2017.

► 261(15) ◄

(15) Amounts carried back. For the purposes of determining the amount that may be deducted, in respect of a particular amount that arises in a taxation year (referred to in this subsection as the "later year") of a taxpayer, under section 111 or subsection 126(2), 127(5), 181.1(4) or 190.1(3) in computing the taxpayer's Canadian tax results for a taxation year (referred to in this subsection as the "current year") that ended before the later year, and for the purposes of determining the amount by which the amount included under subsection 91(1) for the current year is reduced because of a reduction referred to in paragraph 152(6.1)(*b*) in respect of the later year,

(*a*) if the later year is a functional currency year of the taxpayer and the current year is a Canadian currency year of the taxpayer, the following amounts (expressed in the taxpayer's elected functional currency) are to be converted to Canadian currency using the relevant spot rate for the last day of the taxpayer's last Canadian currency year:

(i) the particular amount, and

(ii) any amount so deducted in computing the taxpayer's Canadian tax results for another functional currency year of the taxpayer;

(*b*) if the later year is a reversionary year of the taxpayer and the current year is a functional currency year of the taxpayer,

(i) the following amounts (expressed in Canadian currency) are to be converted to the taxpayer's elected functional currency using the relevant spot rate for the last day of the taxpayer's last functional currency year:

(A) the particular amount, and

(B) any amount so deducted in computing the taxpayer's Canadian tax results for another reversionary year of the taxpayer, and

(ii) any amount (expressed in Canadian currency) so deducted in computing the taxpayer's Canadian tax results for a Canadian currency year of the taxpayer is to be converted to the taxpayer's elected functional currency using the relevant spot rate for the last day of the taxpayer's last Canadian currency year;

(*c*) if the later year is a reversionary year of the taxpayer and the current year is a Canadian currency year of the taxpayer, the following amounts (expressed in the taxpayer's elected functional currency) are to be converted to Canadian currency using the relevant spot rate for the last day of the taxpayer's last Canadian currency year:

(i) the amount that would be determined under clause (*b*)(i)(A) in respect of the particular amount if the current year were a functional currency year of the taxpayer, and

(ii) any amount so deducted in computing the taxpayer's Canadian tax results for a functional currency year of the taxpayer; and (*d*) in any other case, this subsection does not apply.

History: S. 261(15), the portion before paragraph (*a*) was replaced by S.C. 2013, c. 34, s. 38(2), deemed to have come into force on December 14, 2007.

Any assessment of a taxpayer's tax, interest and penalties payable under the Act for any taxation year that ends before June 26, 2013 that would, in the absence of this section, be precluded because of subsections 152(4) to (5) of the Act, shall be made to the extent necessary to take into account this amendment, if the taxpayer

(i) elects in writing in respect of all of its foreign affiliates that this section apply in respect of that provision, and

(ii) files that election with the Minister of National Revenue on or before December 26, 2013 [the day that is six months after royal assent].

S. 261(15), the portion before paragraph (*a*) formerly read:

Amounts carried back For the purposes of determining the amount that may be deducted, in respect of a particular amount that arises in a taxation year (referred to in this subsection as the "later year") of a taxpayer, under section 111 or subsection 126(2), 127(5), 181.1(4) or 190.1(3) in computing the taxpayer's Canadian tax results for a taxation year (referred to in this subsection as the "current year") that ended before the later year,

S. 261(15) was replaced by S.C. 2009, c. 2, s. 80(1), applicable after December 13, 2007. S. 261(15) formerly read:

(15) *Deemed continuation on winding-up or amalgamation.* For the purpose of this section,

(*a*) subject to subsection (16), where there has been a winding-up of a taxpayer (referred to in this subsection and subsection (16) as the "subsidiary") into another taxpayer (referred to in this subsection and subsection (16) as the "parent") to which subsection 88(1) has applied, the parent is deemed to be the same corporation as and a continuation of the subsidiary; and

(*b*) subject to subsection (17), where there has been an amalgamation (within the meaning assigned by subsection 87(1)) of two or more corporations (each such taxpayer referred to in this subsection and subsection (17) as a "predecessor") to form one corporate entity (referred to in this subsection and subsection (17) as the "new corporation") the new corporation is deemed to be the same corporation as and a continuation of each such predecessor corporation.

► 261(16) ◄

(16) Windings-up. If a winding-up described in subsection 88(1) commences at any time (referred to in this subsection as the "commencement time") and the parent and the subsidiary referred to in that subsection would, in the absence of this subsection, have different tax reporting currencies at the commencement time, the following rules apply for the purposes of determining the subsidiary's Canadian tax results for its taxation years that end after the commencement time:

(*a*) where the subsidiary's tax reporting currency is Canadian currency,

(i) notwithstanding subsection (3), subsection (5) is deemed to apply to the subsidiary in respect of its taxation year that includes the commencement time and each of its subsequent taxation years, if any,

(ii) the subsidiary is deemed to have as its elected functional currency the parent's tax reporting currency, and

(iii) if the subsidiary's taxation year that includes the commencement time would, in the absence of this subsection, be a reversionary year of the subsidiary, this section is to be read with any modifications that the circumstances require; and

(*b*) where the subsidiary's tax reporting currency is not Canadian currency,

(i) the subsidiary is deemed to have filed, at the time that is six months and one day before the beginning of its taxation year that includes the commencement time, in prescribed form and manner, a notice of revocation described in subsection (4), and

(ii) if the parent's tax reporting currency is not Canadian currency,

(A) the subsidiary's first reversionary year is deemed to have ended at the particular time that is immediately after the time at which it began,

(B) a new taxation year of the subsidiary is deemed to have begun immediately after the particular time,

(C) notwithstanding subsection (3), subsection (5) is deemed to apply to the subsidiary in respect of its taxation year that includes the commencement time and each of its subsequent taxation years, if any, and

(D) the subsidiary is deemed to have as its elected functional currency the parent's tax reporting currency.

History: S. 261(16) was replaced by S.C. 2009, c. 2, s. 80(1), applicable in respect of taxation years that begin after December 13, 2007. S. 261(16) formerly read:

(16) *Exception to deemed continuation — winding-up.* Where the parent would not, in a taxation year of the parent ending after the time the subsidiary was wound up, satisfy the requirements of paragraph (3)(*e*) because the last functional currency year of the subsidiary referred to in subsection (12) in respect of the winding-up is, because of paragraph (15)(*a*), the last functional currency year of the parent, paragraph (15)(*a*) shall not apply, for the purposes of paragraph (3)(*e*), to the parent in respect of the subsidiary if the total of all amounts each of which is the cost amount, at the end of the taxation year of the parent in which the property of the subsidiary was distributed to the parent in the course of winding-up, to the parent of a property that was distributed to the parent on the winding-up (or property substituted for such property) is less than 50% of the total of all amounts each of which is the cost amount, at the end of that taxation year, to the parent of a property of the parent.

Tax Topics: No. 1918, New and Improved Functional Currency Proposals.

► 261(17) ◄

(17) Amalgamations. If a predecessor corporation and the new corporation, in respect of an amalgamation within the meaning of subsection 87(1), have different tax reporting currencies for their last and first taxation years, respectively, paragraphs (16)(*a*) and (*b*) apply, for the purposes of determining the predecessor corporation's Canadian tax results for its last taxation year, as if the tax reporting currencies referred to in those paragraphs were the tax reporting currencies referred to in this subsection and as if the references in those paragraphs to

(*a*) "subsidiary" were references to "predecessor corporation";

(*b*) "parent" were references to "new corporation"; and

(*c*) "taxation year that includes the commencement time" were references to "last taxation year".

History: S. 261(17) was replaced by S.C. 2009, c. 2, s. 80(1), applicable in respect of taxation years that begin after December 13, 2007. S. 261(17) formerly read:

(17) *Exception to deemed continuation — amalgamation.* Where the new corporation would not, in a taxation year of the new corporation commencing on or after the time of the amalgamation, satisfy the requirements of paragraph (3)(*e*) because the last functional currency year of the predecessor referred to in subsection (14) in respect of the amalgamation is, because of paragraph (15)(*b*) the last functional currency year of the new corporation, paragraph (15)(*b*) shall not apply, for the purposes of paragraph (3)(*e*), to the new corporation in respect of the predecessor if the total of all amounts each of which is the cost amount, at the end of the taxation year of the new corporation that began at the time of the amalgamation, to the new corporation of a property that, immediately before the amalgama-

tion, was a property of the predecessor (or property substituted for such property) is less than 50% of the total of all amounts each of which is the cost amount, at the end of that taxation year of the new corporation, to the new corporation of a property of the new corporation.

Tax Topics: No. 1918, New and Improved Functional Currency Proposals.

► 261(17.1) ◄

(17.1) Amalgamation — deemed application of subsection (5). Notwithstanding subsection (3), if each predecessor corporation in respect of an amalgamation (within the meaning assigned by subsection 87(1)) has the same elected functional currency for its last taxation year, then, unless a predecessor corporation has filed a notice of revocation under subsection (4) on or before the day that is six months before the end of its last taxation year,

(*a*) the new corporation formed as a result of the amalgamation is deemed to have made an election under paragraph (3)(*b*) and to have filed that election on the first day of its first taxation year; and

(*b*) that elected functional currency is deemed to be the new corporation's functional currency for its first taxation year.

History: S. 261(17.1) was added by S.C. 2014, c. 39, s. 77(7), applicable in respect of amalgamations that occur after July 12, 2013.

In addition, any assessment of a taxpayer's tax, interest and penalties payable under the Act for any taxation year that ends before the day on which this amendment receives royal assent [December 16, 2014] that would, in the absence of this section, be precluded because of the time references in subsection 152(4) of the Act is to be made to the extent necessary to take into account this amendment.

► 261(18) ◄

(18) Anti-avoidance. The Canadian tax results of a corporation for any one or more taxation years shall be determined using a particular currency if

(*a*) at any time (referred to in this subsection as the "transfer time") one or more properties are directly or indirectly transferred

(i) by the corporation to another corporation (referred to in this subsection as the "transferor" and the "transferee", respectively), or

(ii) by another corporation to the corporation (referred to in this subsection as the "transferor" and the "transferee", respectively);

(*b*) the transferor and the transferee are related at the transfer time or become related in the course of a series of transactions or events that includes the transfer;

(*c*) the transfer time

(i) is, or would in the absence of subsections (16) and (17) be, in a functional currency year of the transferor and the transferor and the transferee have, or would in the absence of those subsections have, different tax reporting currencies at the transfer time, or

(ii) is, or would in the absence of those subsections be, in a reversionary year of the transferor and is not in a reversionary year of the transferee;

(*d*) it can reasonably be considered that one of the main purposes of the transfer or of any portion of a series of transactions or events that includes the transfer is to change, or to enable the changing of, the currency in which the Canadian tax results in respect of the property, or property substituted for it, for a taxation year would otherwise be determined; and

(*e*) the Minister directs that those Canadian tax results be determined in the particular currency.

History: S. 261(18) was replaced by S.C. 2009, c. 2, s. 80(1), applicable in respect of taxation years that begin after December 13, 2007. S. 261(18) formerly read:

(18) *Anti-avoidance.* Where, at any time, all or substantially all of the property (referred to in this subsection as the "transferred property") of a business (referred to in this subsection as the "transferred business") of a taxpayer has been disposed of by the taxpayer (referred to in this subsection as the "transferor") and acquired, either directly or indirectly by a corporation resident in Canada (referred to in this subsection as the "transferee") that, immediately after the acquisition, was related to the taxpayer, and a taxation year of the transferor beginning before that time was a functional currency year of the transferor, for the purposes of this section, the transferee is deemed to be the same corporation as and a continuation of the transferor if the total of all amounts each of which is the cost amount, at the end of the taxation year of the transferee in which the transferred business was transferred, to the transferee of a property that was a transferred property (or property substituted for such property) is greater than 50% of the total of all amounts each of which is the cost amount, at the end of that taxation year of the transferree, to the transferree of a property of the transferee.

Tax Topics: No. 1918, New and Improved Functional Currency Proposals.

► 261(19) ◄

(19) Mergers. For the purposes of subsection (18), if one corporate entity (referred to in this subsection as the "new corporation") is formed at a particular time by the amalgamation or other merger of two or more corporations (each of which is referred to in this subsection as a "predecessor corporation"),

(*a*) the predecessor corporation is deemed to have transferred to the new corporation at the time (referred to in this subsection as the "merger transfer time") that is immediately before the particular time each property that was held at the merger transfer time by the predecessor corporation and at the particular time by the new corporation;

(*b*) the new corporation is deemed to exist, and to be related to the predecessor corporation, at the merger transfer time; and

(*c*) the new corporation is deemed to have as its tax reporting currency at the merger transfer time its tax reporting currency at the particular time.

History: S. 261(19) was added by S.C. 2009, c. 2, s. 80(1), applicable in respect of taxation years that begin after December 13, 2007.

► 261(20) ◄

(20) Application of subsection (21). Subsection (21) applies in determining a taxpayer's income, gain or loss for a taxation year in respect of a transaction (referred to in this subsection and subsection (21) as a "specified transaction") if

(*a*) the specified transaction was entered into, directly or indirectly, at any time by the taxpayer and a corporation (referred to in this subsection as the "related corporation") to which the taxpayer is at that time related;

(*b*) the taxpayer and the related corporation had different tax reporting currencies at any time during the period (referred to in this subsection as the "accrual period") in which the income, gain or loss accrued; and

(*c*) it would, in the absence of this subsection and subsection (21), be reasonable to consider that a fluctuation at any time in the accrual period in the value of the taxpayer's tax reporting currency relative to the value of the related corporation's tax reporting currency

(i) increased the taxpayer's loss in respect of the specified transaction,

(ii) reduced the taxpayer's income or gain in respect of the specified transaction, or

(iii) caused the taxpayer to have a loss, instead of income or a gain, in respect of the specified transaction.

History: S. 261(20) was added by S.C. 2009, c. 2, s. 80(1), applicable in respect of taxation years that begin after December 13, 2007, except that where a taxpayer has, on or before June 27, 2008, made an election under paragraph 261(3)(*b*), subsection 261(20) applies in respect of taxation years that begin after June 27, 2008.

▶ 261(21) ◀

(21) Income, gain or loss determinations. If this subsection applies, each fluctuation in value referred to in paragraph (20)(*c*) is, for the purposes of determining the taxpayer's income, gain or loss in respect of the specified transaction and notwithstanding any other provision of this Act, deemed not to have occurred.

History: S. 261(21) was added by S.C. 2009, c. 2, s. 80(1), applicable in respect of taxation years that begin after December 13, 2007, except that where a taxpayer has, on or before June 27, 2008, made an election under paragraph 261(3)(*b*), subsection 261(21) applies in respect of taxation years that begin after June 27, 2008.

Tax Window Files: Denial of foreign exchange loss on loan from foreign affiliate, *June 14, 2017*, CRA Document No. 2017-0691211C6; ITA 261(21) anti-avoidance, *March 9, 2016*, CRA Document No. 2015-0612501I7.

▶ 261(22) ◀

(22) Partnership transactions. For the purposes of this subsection and subsections (18) to (21),

(*a*) if a property is directly or indirectly transferred to or by a partnership, the property is deemed to have been transferred to or by (as the case may be) each member of the partnership; and

(*b*) if a partnership is a party to a transaction, each member of the partnership is deemed to be that party to that transaction.

History: S. 261(22) was added by S.C. 2009, c. 2, s. 80(1), applicable in respect of taxation years that begin after December 13, 2007.

SECTION 262: Authority to designate stock exchange

▶ 262(1) ◀

(1) Authority to designate stock exchange. The Minister of Finance may designate a stock exchange, or a part of a stock exchange, for the purposes of this Act.

▶ 262(2) ◀

(2) Revocation of designation. The Minister of Finance may revoke the designation of a stock exchange, or a part of a stock exchange, designated under subsection (1).

▶ 262(3) ◀

(3) Timing. A designation under subsection (1) or a revocation under subsection (2) shall specify the time at and after which it is in effect, which time may, for greater certainty, precede the time at which the designation or revocation is made.

▶ 262(4) ◀

(4) Publication. The Minister of Finance shall cause to be published, by posting on the Internet website of the Department of Finance or by any other means that the Minister of Finance considers appropriate, the names of those stock exchanges, or parts of stock exchanges, as the case may be, that are or at any time were designated under subsection (1).

▶ 262(5) ◀

(5) Transition. The Minister of Finance is deemed to have designated under subsection (1) each stock exchange and each part of a stock exchange that was, immediately before the day on which this section came into force, a prescribed stock exchange, with effect on and after that day.

Part XVIII
Enhanced International Information Reporting

SECTION 263: [Enhanced international information reporting]

► 263(1) ◄

(1) Definitions. The following definitions apply in this Part.

Canadian Tax Foundation: Berg, *Canadian FATCA Challenge*, 2015 Canadian Tax Highlights 23(9):11–12; Wright, *FATCA Comes to Canada: The Basics*, 2014 Canadian Tax Focus 4(3):2–3.

"agreement" —"agreement" has the same meaning as in section 2 of the *Canada–United States Enhanced Tax Information Exchange Agreement Implementation Act*.

History: S. 263(1), the definition "agreement" was added by S.C. 2014, c. 20, s. 101(1), in force on July 1, 2014.

"electronic filing" —"electronic filing" means using electronic media in a manner specified by the Minister.

History: S. 263(1), the definition "electronic filing" was added by S.C. 2014, c. 20, s. 101(1), in force on July 1, 2014.

"listed financial institution" —"listed financial institution" means a financial institution that is

(*a*) an authorized foreign bank within the meaning of section 2 of the *Bank Act* in respect of its business in Canada, or a bank to which that Act applies;

(*b*) a cooperative credit society, a savings and credit union or a caisse populaire regulated by a provincial Act;

(*c*) an association regulated by the *Cooperative Credit Associations Act*;

(*d*) a central cooperative credit society, as defined in section 2 of the *Cooperative Credit Associations Act*, or a credit union central or a federation of credit unions or caisses populaires that is regulated by a provincial Act other than one enacted by the legislature of Quebec;

(*e*) a financial services cooperative regulated by *An Act respecting financial services cooperatives*, R.S.Q., c. C-67.3, or *An Act respecting the Mouvement Desjardins*, S.Q. 2000, c. 77;

(*f*) a life company or a foreign life company to which the *Insurance Companies Act* applies or a life insurance company regulated by a provincial Act;

(*g*) a company to which the *Trust and Loan Companies Act* applies;

(*h*) a trust company regulated by a provincial Act;

(*i*) a loan company regulated by a provincial Act;

(*j*) an entity authorized under provincial legislation to engage in the business of dealing in securities or any other financial instruments, or to provide portfolio management, investment advising, fund administration, or fund management, services;

(*k*) an entity that is represented or promoted to the public as a collective investment vehicle, mutual fund, exchange traded fund, private equity fund, hedge fund, venture capital fund, leveraged buyout fund or similar investment vehicle that is established to invest or trade in financial assets and that is managed by an entity referred to in paragraph (*j*);

(*l*) an entity that is a clearing house or clearing agency; or

(*m*) a department or an agent of Her Majesty in right of Canada or of a province that is engaged in the business of accepting deposit liabilities.

History: S. 263(1), the definition "listed financial institution" was added by S.C. 2014, c. 20, s. 101(1), in force on July 1, 2014.

"non-reporting Canadian financial institution" —"non-reporting Canadian financial institution" means any Canadian financial institution or other entity resident in Canada that

(*a*) is described in any of paragraphs C, D and G to J of section III of Annex II to the agreement;

(*b*) makes a reasonable determination that it is described in any of paragraphs A, B, E and F of section III of Annex II to the agreement;

(*c*) qualifies as an exempt beneficial owner under relevant U.S. Treasury Regulations in effect on the date of signature of the agreement; or

(*d*) makes a reasonable determination that it qualifies as a deemed-compliant FFI under relevant U.S. Treasury Regulations in effect on the date of signature of the agreement.

History: S. 263(1), the definition "non-reporting Canadian financial institution" was added by S.C. 2014, c. 20, s. 101(1), in force on July 1, 2014.

"U.S. reportable account" —"U.S. reportable account" means a financial account that, under the agreement, is to be treated as a U.S. reportable account.

History: S. 263(1), the definition "U.S. reportable account" was added by S.C. 2014, c. 20, s. 101(1), in force on July 1, 2014.

► 263(2) ◄

(2) Financial institution. For the purposes of this Part, "Canadian financial institution" and "reporting Canadian financial institution" each have the meaning that would be assigned by the agreement, and the definition "non-reporting Canadian financial institution" in subsection (1) has the meaning that would be assigned by that subsection, if the definition "Financial Institution" in subparagraph 1(g) of Article 1 of the agreement were read as follows:

"(g) The term "**Financial Institution**" means any Entity that is a Custodial Institution, a Depository Institution, an Investment Entity or a Specified Insurance Company, and that is a listed financial institution within the meaning of Part XVIII of the *Income Tax Act*."

History: S. 263(2) was added by S.C. 2014, c. 20, s. 101(1), in force on July 1, 2014.

► 263(3) ◄

(3) Financial account. For the purposes of this Part, the agreement is to be read as if the definition "Financial Account" in subparagraph 1(*s*) of Article 1 of the agreement included the following subparagraph after subparagraph (1):

(1.1) an account that is a client name account maintained by a person or entity that is authorized under provincial legislation to engage in the business of dealing in securities or any other financial instruments, or to provide portfolio management or investment advising services.

History: S. 263(3) was added by S.C. 2014, c. 20, s. 101(1), in force on July 1, 2014.

▶ 263(4) ◀

(4) Identification number. For the purposes of this Part, a reference in the agreement to "Canadian TIN" or "taxpayer identification number" is to be read as including a reference to Social Insurance Number.

History: S. 263(4) was added by S.C. 2014, c. 20, s. 101(1), in force on July 1, 2014.

▶ 263(5) ◀

(5) Term defined in agreement. In this Part, a term has the meaning that is defined in, or assigned by, the agreement unless the term is defined in this Part.

History: S. 263(5) was added by S.C. 2014, c. 20, s. 101(1), in force on July 1, 2014.

▶ 263(6) ◀

(6) Amending instrument. No person shall be liable for a failure to comply with a duty or obligation imposed by this Act that results from an amendment to the agreement unless at the date of the alleged failure,

(*a*) the text of the instrument that effected the amendment had been published in the *Canada Gazette*; or

(*b*) reasonable steps had been taken to bring the purport of the amendment to the notice of those persons likely to be affected by it.

History: S. 263(6) was added by S.C. 2014, c. 20, s. 101(1), in force on July 1, 2014.

SECTION 264: [Designation of account]

▶ 264(1) ◀

(1) Designation of account. Subject to subsection (2), a reporting Canadian financial institution may designate a financial account to not be a U.S. reportable account for a calendar year if the account is

(*a*) a preexisting individual account described in paragraph A of section II of Annex I to the agreement;

(*b*) a new individual account described in paragraph A of section III of Annex I to the agreement;

(*c*) a preexisting entity account described in paragraph A of section IV of Annex I to the agreement; or

(*d*) a new entity account described in paragraph A of section V of Annex I to the agreement.

History: S. 264(1) was added by S.C. 2014, c. 20, s. 101(1), in force July 1, 2014.

Tax Window Files: Canada-U.S. Enhanced TIEA, *August 20, 2018*, CRA Document No. 2018-0759081E5.

▶ 264(2) ◀

(2) U.S. reportable account. A reporting Canadian financial institution may not designate a financial account for a calendar year unless the account is part of a clearly identifiable group of accounts all of which are designated for the year.

History: S. 264(2) was added by S.C. 2014, c. 20, s. 101(1), in force on July 1, 2014.

▶ 264(3) ◀

(3) Applicable rules. The rules in paragraph C of section VI of Annex I to the agreement apply in determining whether a financial account is described in any of paragraphs (1)(*a*) to (*d*).

History: S. 264(3) was added by S.C. 2014, c. 20, s. 101(1), in force on July 1, 2014.

SECTION 265: [Identification obligation — financial accounts]

▶ 265(1) ◀

(1) Identification obligation — financial accounts. Every reporting Canadian financial institution shall establish, maintain and document the due diligence procedures set out in subsections (2) and (3).

History: S. 265(1) was added by S.C. 2014, c. 20, s. 101(1), in force on July 1, 2014.

Canadian Tax Foundation: Berg, *Canadian FATCA Challenge*, 2015 Canadian Tax Highlights 23(9):11–12; Wright, *FATCA Comes to Canada: The Basics*, 2014 Canadian Tax Focus 4(3):2–3.

Tax Profile: February 2015 — Canada-US Agreement to Implement FATCA Reporting Obligations Enters into Force.

▶ 265(2) ◀

(2) Due diligence — general. Every reporting Canadian financial institution shall have the following due diligence procedures:

(*a*) for preexisting individual accounts that are lower value accounts, other than accounts described in paragraph A of section II of Annex I to the agreement, the procedures described in paragraphs B and C of that section, subject to paragraph F of that section;

(*b*) for preexisting individual accounts that are high value accounts, other than accounts described in paragraph A of section II of Annex I to the agreement, the procedures described in paragraphs D and E of that section, subject to paragraph F of that section;

(*c*) for new individual accounts, other than accounts described in paragraph A of section III of Annex I to the agreement, the procedures described in paragraph B of section III of Annex I to the agreement;

(*d*) for preexisting entity accounts, other than accounts described in paragraph A of section IV of Annex I to the agreement, the procedures described in paragraphs D and E of that section; and

(*e*) for new entity accounts, other than accounts described in paragraph A of section V of Annex I to the agreement, the procedures described in paragraphs B to E of that section.

History: S. 265(2)(*c*) was replaced by S.C. 2016, c. 12, s. 70(1), in force on July 1, 2017, and formerly read:

(*c*) for new individual accounts, other than accounts described in paragraph A of section III of Annex I to the agreement,

(i) the procedures described in paragraph B of section III of Annex I to the agreement, or

(ii) in respect of a clearly identifiable group of accounts, the procedures that would be applicable if the accounts were preexisting individual accounts that were lower value accounts, with such modifications as the circumstances require, including procedures to review any documentary evidence obtained by the institution in connection with the opening of the accounts for the U.S. indicia described in subparagraph B(1) of section II of Annex I to the agreement;

S. 265(2) was added by S.C. 2014, c. 20, s. 101(1), in force on July 1, 2014.

► 265(3) ◄

(3) Due diligence — no designation. If a reporting Canadian financial institution does not designate a financial account under subsection 264(1) for a calendar year, the institution shall have the following due diligence procedures with respect to the account:

(*a*) if the account is a preexisting individual account described in paragraph A of section II of Annex I to the agreement, the procedures described in paragraphs B and C of that section, subject to paragraph F of that section;

(*b*) if the account is a new individual account described in paragraph A of section III of Annex I to the agreement, the procedures described in paragraph B of section III of Annex I to the agreement;

(*c*) if the account is a preexisting entity account described in paragraph A of section IV of Annex I to the agreement, the procedures described in paragraphs D and E of that section; and

(*d*) if the account is a new entity account described in paragraph A of section V of Annex I to the agreement, the procedures described in paragraphs B to E of that section.

History: S. 265(3)(*b*) was replaced by S.C. 2016, c. 12, s. 70(2), in force on July 1, 2017, and formerly read:

(*b*) if the account is a new individual account described in paragraph A of section III of Annex I to the agreement,

(i) the procedures described in paragraph B of section III of Annex I to the agreement, or

(ii) in respect of an account that is part of a clearly identifiable group of accounts, the procedures that would be applicable if the account were a preexisting individual account that was a lower value account, with such modifications as the circumstances require, including procedures to review any documentary evidence obtained by the institution in connection with the opening of the account for the U.S. indicia described in subparagraph B(1) of section II of Annex I to the agreement;

S. 265(3) was added by S.C. 2014, c. 20, s. 101(1), in force on July 1, 2014.

► 265(4) ◄

(4) Rules and definitions. For the purposes of subsections (2) and (3), subparagraphs B(1) to (3) of section I, and section VI, of Annex I to the agreement apply except that

(*a*) in applying paragraph C of that section VI, an account balance that has a negative value is deemed to be nil; and

(*b*) the definition "NFFE" in subparagraph B(2) of that section VI is to be read as follows:

"2. **NFFE**–An "NFFE" means any Non-U.S. Entity that is not an FFI as defined in relevant U.S. Treasury Regulations or is an Entity described in subparagraph B(4)(j) of this section, and also includes any Non-U.S. Entity

a) that is resident in Canada and is not a listed financial institution within the meaning of Part XVIII of the Income Tax Act; or

b) that is resident in a Partner Jurisdiction other than Canada and is not a Financial Institution."

History: S. 265(4) was added by S.C. 2014, c. 20, s. 101(1), in force on July 1, 2014.

► 265(5) ◄

(5) U.S. indicia. For the purposes of paragraphs (2)(*a*) and (*b*), subparagraph (2)(*c*)(ii), paragraph (3)(*a*) and subparagraph (3)(*b*)(ii), subparagraph B(3) of section II of Annex I to the agreement is to be read as follows:

"3. If any of the U.S indicia listed in subparagraph B(1) of this section are discovered in the electronic search, or if there is a change in circumstances that results in one or more U.S. indicia being associated with the account, then the Reporting Canadian Financial Institution must seek to obtain or review the information described in the portion of subparagraph B(4) of this section that is relevant in the circumstances and must treat the account as a U.S. Reportable Account unless one of the exceptions in subparagraph B(4) applies with respect to that account."

History: S. 265(5) was added by S.C. 2014, c. 20, s. 101(1), in force on July 1, 2014.

► 265(6) ◄

(6) Financial institution. For the purpose of applying the procedures referred to in paragraphs (2)(*d*) and (*e*) and (3)(*c*) and (*d*) to a financial account of an account holder that is resident in Canada, the definition "Financial Institution" in subparagraph 1(g) of Article 1 of the agreement is to be read as follows:

"g) The term "**Financial Institution**" means any Entity that is a Custodial Institution, a Depository Institution, an Investment Entity or a Specified Insurance Company, and that is a listed financial institution within the meaning of Part XVIII of the *Income Tax Act*."

History: S. 265(6) was added by S.C. 2014, c. 20, s. 101(1), in force on July 1, 2014.

► 265(7) ◄

(7) Dealer accounts. Subsection (8) applies to a reporting Canadian financial institution in respect of a client name account maintained by the institution if

(*a*) property recorded in the account is also recorded in a financial account (in this subsection and subsection (8) referred to as the "related account") maintained by a financial institution (in this subsection and subsection (8) referred to as the "dealer") that is authorized under provincial legislation to engage in the business of dealing in securities or any other financial instrument, or to provide portfolio management or investment advising services; and

(*b*) the dealer has advised the institution whether the related account is a U.S. reportable account.

However, subsection (8) does not apply if it can reasonably be concluded by the institution that the dealer has failed to comply with its obligations under this section.

History: S. 265(7) was added by S.C. 2014, c. 20, s. 101(1), in force on July 1, 2014.

▶ 265(8) ◀

(8) Dealer accounts. If this subsection applies to a reporting Canadian financial institution in respect of a client name account,

(*a*) subsections (1) to (4) do not apply to the institution in respect of the account; and

(*b*) the institution shall rely on the determination of the dealer in respect of the related account in determining whether the account is a U.S. reportable account.

History: S. 265(8) was added by S.C. 2014, c. 20, s. 101(1), in force on July 1, 2014.

SECTION 266: [Reporting — U.S. reportable accounts]

▶ 266(1) ◀

(1) Reporting — U.S. reportable accounts. Every reporting Canadian financial institution shall file with the Minister, before May 2 of each calendar year, an information return in prescribed form relating to each U.S. reportable account maintained by the institution at any time during the immediately preceding calendar year and after June 29, 2014.

Editorial Note: Part XVIII of the Act requires certain Canadian financial institutions to report specified information to the CRA regarding accounts held by certain U.S. persons or by foreign entities controlled by U.S. persons. S. 265 sets out due diligence procedures required to be followed by financial institutions for identifying reportable accounts. S. 266 requires reporting financial institutions to file annual information returns by May 1 of each year. S. 267 provides for record-keeping requirements for reporting institutions. An anti-avoidance rule related to reporting obligations is set out in s. 268. Certain deposit-taking institutions such as small credit unions are exempt from reporting requirements, and certain accounts such as RRSPs, RRIFs, PRPPs, RPPs, TFSAs, RDSPs, RESPs, and DPSPs are exempt from being reportable accounts. Penalties apply for failing to file a return or to keep records under s. 238(1).

Under the *Canada-United States Enhanced Information Exchange Agreement* made under the Canada-U.S. treaty, the CRA and IRS will exchange certain reported information. This agreement was made in relation to the U.S. *Foreign Account Tax Compliance Act* ("FACTA"), which would otherwise have required Canadian financial institutions to report certain information directly to the IRS had the information exchange agreement and related *Income Tax Act* provisions not been enacted.

History: S. 266(1) was added by S.C. 2014, c. 20, s. 101(1), in force on July 1, 2014.

Related Sections: S. 162(6) Failure to provide identification number; S. 238(1) Offences and punishment.

▶ 266(2) ◀

(2) Reporting — nonparticipating financial institutions. Every reporting Canadian financial institution shall file with the Minister, before May 2 of each calendar year, an information return in prescribed form relating to payments, to a nonparticipating financial institution that is the holder of a financial account maintained by the reporting Canadian financial institution, during the immediately preceding calendar year if the immediately preceding year is 2015 or 2016.

History: S. 266(2) was added by S.C. 2014, c. 20, s. 101(1), in force on July 1, 2014.

▶ 266(3) ◀

(3) Filing of return. An information return required under subsection (1) or (2) shall be filed by way of electronic filing.

History: S. 266(3) was added by S.C. 2014, c. 20, s. 101(1), in force on July 1, 2014.

SECTION 267: [Record keeping]

▶ 267(1) ◀

(1) Record keeping. Every reporting Canadian financial institution shall keep, at the institution's place of business or at such other place as may be designated by the Minister, records that the institution obtains or creates for the purpose of complying with this Part, including self-certifications and records of documentary evidence.

History: S. 267(1) was added by S.C. 2014, c. 20, s. 101(1), in force on July 1, 2014.

Related Sections: S. 238(1) Offences and punishment.

▶ 267(2) ◀

(2) Form of records. Every reporting Canadian financial institution required by this Part to keep records that does so electronically shall retain them in an electronically readable format for the retention period referred to in subsection (3).

History: S. 267(2) was added by S.C. 2014, c. 20, s. 101(1), in force on July 1, 2014.

▶ 267(3) ◀

(3) Retention of records. Every reporting Canadian financial institution that is required to keep, obtain, or create records under this Part shall retain those records for a period of at least six years following

(*a*) in the case of a self-certification, the last day on which a related financial account is open; and

(*b*) in any other case, the end of the last calendar year in respect of which the record is relevant.

History: S. 267(3) was added by S.C. 2014, c. 20, s. 101(1), in force on July 1, 2014.

SECTION 268: Anti-avoidance

If a person enters into an arrangement or engages in a practice, the primary purpose of which can reasonably be considered to be to avoid an obligation under this Part, the person is subject to the obligation as if the person had not entered into the arrangement or engaged in the practice.

History: S. 268 was added by S.C. 2014, c. 20, s. 101(1), in force on July 1, 2014.

SECTION 269: Deemed-compliant FFI

If a Canadian financial institution makes a reasonable determination that it is to be treated as a deemed-compliant FFI under Annex II to the agreement, this Part applies to the institution, with such modifications as the circumstances require, to the extent that the agreement imposes due diligence and reporting obligations on the institution.

History: S. 269 was added by S.C. 2014, c. 20, s. 101(1), in force on July 1, 2014.

Part XIX
Common Reporting Standards

SECTION 270: Definitions

► 270(1) ◄

(1) [Definitions]. The following definitions apply in this Part.

"account holder" —"account holder" means

(*a*) the person listed or identified as the holder of a financial account by the financial institution that maintains the account, other than a person (other than a financial institution) holding a financial account for the benefit of, or on behalf of, another person as agent, custodian, nominee, signatory, investment advisor or intermediary; and

(*b*) in the case of a cash value insurance contract or an annuity contract,

(i) any person entitled to access the cash value or change the beneficiary,

(ii) if no person can access the cash value or change the beneficiary,

(A) any person named as the owner in the contract, and

(B) any person with a vested entitlement to payment under the terms of the contract, and

(iii) upon maturity of the cash value insurance contract or annuity contract, each person entitled to receive a payment under the contract.

History: S. 270, the definition "account holder" was added by S.C. 2016, c. 12, s. 71(1), in force on July 1, 2017.

"active NFE" —"active NFE" means, at any time, a non-financial entity that meets any of the following criteria:

(*a*) less than 50% of the NFE's gross income for the preceding fiscal period is passive income and less than 50% of the assets held by the NFE during the preceding fiscal period are assets that produce or are held for the production of passive income;

(*b*) either

(i) interests in the NFE are regularly traded on an established securities market, or

(ii) the NFE is a related entity of an entity interests in which are regularly traded on an established securities market;

(*c*) the NFE is

(i) a governmental entity,

(ii) an international organization,

(iii) a central bank, or

(iv) an entity wholly owned by one or more entities described in subparagraphs (i) to (iii);

(*d*) both

(i) all or substantially all of the activities of the NFE consist of holding (in whole or in part) the outstanding stock of, or providing financing and services to, one or more of its subsidiaries that engage in trades or businesses other than the business of a financial institution, and

(ii) the NFE does not function as (and is not represented or promoted to the public as) an investment fund, including

(A) a private equity fund,

(B) a venture capital fund,

(C) a leveraged buyout fund, and

(D) an investment vehicle whose purpose is to acquire or fund companies and then hold interests in those companies as capital assets for investment purposes;

(*e*) the NFE

(i) is not yet operating a business,

(ii) has no prior operating history,

(iii) is investing capital into assets with the intent to operate a business other than that of a financial institution, and

(iv) was initially organized no more than 24 months prior to that time;

(*f*) the NFE has not been a financial institution in any of the past five years and is in the process of liquidating its assets or is reorganizing with the intent to continue or recommence operations in a business other than that of a financial institution;

(*g*) the NFE primarily engages in financing and hedging transactions with, or for, related entities that are not financial institutions, and does not provide financing or hedging services to any entity that is not a related entity, provided that the group of those related entities is primarily engaged in a business other than that of a financial institution; and

(*h*) the NFE meets all of the following requirements:

(i) it

(A) is established and operated in its jurisdiction of residence exclusively for religious, charitable, scientific, artistic, cultural, athletic or educational purposes, or

(B) is established and operated in its jurisdiction of residence and it is a professional organization, business league, chamber of commerce, labour organization, agricultural or horticultural organization, civic league or an organization operated exclusively for the promotion of social welfare,

(ii) it is exempt from income tax in its jurisdiction of residence,

(iii) it has no shareholders or members who have a proprietary or beneficial interest in its income or assets,

(iv) the applicable laws of the NFE's jurisdiction of residence or the NFE's formation documents do not permit any income or assets of the NFE to be distributed to, or applied for the benefit of, a private person or non-charitable entity other than pursuant to the conduct of the NFE's charitable activities, or as payment of reasonable compensation for services rendered, or as payment representing the fair market value of property which the NFE has purchased, and

(v) the applicable laws of the NFE's jurisdiction of residence or the NFE's formation documents require that, upon the NFE's liquidation or dissolution, all of its assets be distributed to a governmental entity or other non-profit organization, or escheat to the government of the NFE's jurisdiction of residence or any political subdivision thereof.

Editorial Note: Active non-financial entities are considered to be at a low risk of non-compliance and accounts held by them are not subject to reporting. The term encompasses active businesses but also includes other low-risk entities, such as government entities, charities, and publicly-listed companies (other than financial institutions). This definition should be read in conjunction with the definition of "non-financial entity" or "NFE" set out below.

History: S. 270, the definition "active NFE" was added by S.C. 2016, c. 12, s. 71(1), in force on July 1, 2017.

"annuity contract" —"annuity contract" means a contract under which the issuer agrees to make payments for a period of time determined in whole or in part by reference to the life expectancy of one or more individuals and includes a contract

(*a*) that is considered to be an annuity contract in accordance with the law, regulation or practice of the jurisdiction in which the contract was issued; and

(*b*) under which the issuer agrees to make payments for a term of years.

History: S. 270, the definition "annuity contract" was added by S.C. 2016, c. 12, s. 71(1), in force on July 1, 2017.

"anti-money laundering and know your customer procedures" "anti-money laundering and know your customer procedures" or "AML/KYC procedures" means the record keeping, verification of identity, reporting of suspicious transactions and registration requirements required of a reporting financial institution under the *Proceeds of Crime (Money Laundering) and Terrorist Financing Act*.

History: S. 270, the definition "anti-money laundering and know your customer procedures" was added by S.C. 2016, c. 12, s. 71(1), in force on July 1, 2017.

"broad participation retirement fund" —"broad participation retirement fund" means a fund that is established to provide retirement, disability or death benefits to beneficiaries that are current or former employees (or persons designated by those employees) of one or more employers in consideration for services rendered, if the fund

(*a*) does not have a single beneficiary with a right to more than 5% of the fund's assets;

(*b*) is subject to government regulation and provides information reporting to the Minister; and

(*c*) satisfies at least one of the following requirements:

(i) the fund is generally exempt from tax on investment income, or taxation of investment income is deferred or taxed at a reduced rate, due to its status as a retirement or pension plan,

(ii) the fund receives at least 50% of its total contributions (other than transfers of assets from broad participation retirement funds, narrow participation retirement funds or from retirement and pension accounts described in paragraph (*a*) of the definition "excluded account") from the sponsoring employers,

(iii) distributions or withdrawals from the fund are

(A) allowed only upon the occurrence of specified events related to retirement, disability or death (except rollover distributions to broad participation retirement funds, narrow participation retirement funds and pension funds of a governmental entity, international organization or central bank or retirement and pension accounts described in paragraph (*a*) of the definition "excluded account"), or

(B) subject to penalties if they are made before such specified events, and

(iv) contributions (other than permitted make-up contributions) by an employee to the fund

(A) are limited by reference to the employee's remuneration, or

(B) must not exceed 50,000 USD annually, applying the rules set forth in subsection 277(3).

History: S. 270, the definition "broad participation retirement fund" was added by S.C. 2016, c. 12, s. 71(1), in force on July 1, 2017.

"Canadian financial institution" —"Canadian financial institution" means a financial institution that is

(*a*) either

(i) resident in Canada, but excluding any branch of the financial institution that is located outside Canada, or

(ii) a branch of a financial institution that is not resident in Canada, if the branch is located in Canada; and

(*b*) a "listed financial institution" as defined in subsection 263(1).

History: S. 270, the definition "Canadian financial institution" was added by S.C. 2016, c. 12, s. 71(1), in force on July 1, 2017.

"cash value" —"cash value", in respect of a contract held by a policyholder, means the greater of the amount that the policyholder is entitled to receive upon surrender or termination of the contract (determined without reduction for any surrender charge or policy loan) and the amount the policyholder can borrow under or with regard to the contract, but does not include an amount payable under an insurance contract

(*a*) solely by reason of the death of an individual insured under a life insurance contract;

(*b*) as a personal injury or sickness benefit, or other benefit, providing indemnification of an economic loss incurred upon the occurrence of an event insured against;

(*c*) as a refund of a previously paid premium (less any cost of insurance charges whether or not actually imposed) under an insurance contract (other than an investment-linked life insurance or annuity contract) due to the cancellation or termination of the contract, a decrease in risk exposure during the effective period of the contract or arising from the correction of a posting or similar error with regard to the premium for the contract;

(*d*) as a policyholder dividend (other than a termination dividend) if the dividend relates to an insurance contract under which the only benefits payable are described in paragraph (*b*); or

(*e*) as a return of an advance premium or premium deposit for an insurance contract for which the premium is payable at least annually, if the amount of the advance premium or premium deposit does not exceed the next annual premium that will be payable under the contract.

History: S. 270, the definition "cash value" was added by S.C. 2016, c. 12, s. 71(1), in force on July 1, 2017.

"cash value insurance contract" —"cash value insurance contract" means an insurance contract (other than an indemnity reinsurance contract between two insurance companies) that has a cash value.

History: S. 270, the definition "cash value insurance contract" was added by S.C. 2016, c. 12, s. 71(1), in force on July 1, 2017.

"central bank" —"central bank" means an institution that is, by law or government sanction, the principal authority, other than the government of the jurisdiction itself, issuing instruments intended to circulate as currency and may include an instrumentality that is separate from the government of the jurisdiction, whether or not owned in whole or in part by the jurisdiction.

History: S. 270, the definition "central bank" was added by S.C. 2016, c. 12, s. 71(1), in force on July 1, 2017.

"controlling persons" —"controlling persons", in respect of an entity, means the natural persons who exercise control over the entity (interpreted in a manner consistent with the *Financial Action Task Force Recommendations — International Standards on Combating Money Laundering and the Financing of Terrorism and Proliferation*, adopted in February 2012 and as amended from time to time) and includes

(*a*) in the case of a trust,

(i) its settlors,

(ii) its trustees,

(iii) its protectors (if any),

(iv) its beneficiaries (for this purpose, a discretionary beneficiary of a trust will only be considered a beneficiary of the trust in a calendar year if a distribution has been paid or made payable to the discretionary beneficiary in the calendar year), and

(v) any other natural persons exercising ultimate effective control over the trust; and

(*b*) in the case of a legal arrangement other than a trust, persons in equivalent or similar positions to those described in paragraph (*a*).

Editorial Note: This definition is intended to correspond to the term "beneficial owner" in Recommendation 10 and the Interpretative Note on Recommendation 10 of the FATF Recommendations.

History: S. 270, the definition "controlling persons" was added by S.C. 2016, c. 12, s. 71(1), in force on July 1, 2017.

"custodial account" —"custodial account" means an account (other than an insurance contract or annuity contract) that holds one or more financial assets for the benefit of another person.

History: S. 270, the definition "custodial account" was added by S.C. 2016, c. 12, s. 71(1), in force on July 1, 2017.

"custodial institution" —"custodial institution" means an entity, if the entity's gross income attributable to the holding of financial assets for the account of others and related financial services equals or exceeds 20% of the entity's gross income during the shorter of

(*a*) the three-year period that ends at the end of the entity's last fiscal period, and

(*b*) the period during which the entity has been in existence.

History: S. 270, the definition "custodial institution" was added by S.C. 2016, c. 12, s. 71(1), in force on July 1, 2017.

"depository account" —"depository account" includes

(*a*) any commercial, chequing, savings, time or thrift account, or an account that is evidenced by a certificate of deposit, thrift certificate, investment certificate, certificate of indebtedness or other similar instrument maintained by a financial institution in the ordinary course of a banking or similar business; and

(*b*) an amount held by an insurance company under a guaranteed investment contract or similar agreement to pay or credit interest on the contract.

Editorial Note: The explanatory notes to Bill C-29 indicate that an account that is evidenced by a passbook would generally be considered a depository account, while debt instruments traded on a regulated or over-the-counter market and distributed and held through financial institutions would be financial assets that would not generally be considered depository accounts.

History: S. 270, the definition "depository account" was added by S.C. 2016, c. 12, s. 71(1), in force on July 1, 2017.

"depository institution" —"depository institution" means any entity that accepts deposits in the ordinary course of a banking or similar business.

History: S. 270, the definition "depository institution" was added by S.C. 2016, c. 12, s. 71(1), in force on July 1, 2017.

"documentary evidence" —"documentary evidence" includes

(*a*) a certificate of residence issued by an authorized government body (such as a government or agency thereof, or a municipality) of the jurisdiction in which the payee claims to be a resident;

(*b*) with respect to an individual (other than a trust), any valid identification issued by an authorized government body that includes the individual's name and is typically used for identification purposes;

(*c*) with respect to an entity, any official documentation issued by an authorized government body that includes the name of the entity and either the address of its principal office in the jurisdiction in which it claims to be resident or the jurisdiction in which the entity was incorporated or organized; and (*d*) any audited financial statement, third-party credit report, bankruptcy filing or securities regulator's report.

History: S. 270, the definition "documentary evidence" was added by S.C. 2016, c. 12, s. 71(1), in force on July 1, 2017.

"entity" —"entity" means a person (other than a natural person) or a legal arrangement, such as a corporation, partnership, trust or foundation,

Editorial Note: The definition of "entity" is deliberately broad in scope and includes, for instance, a unit, business, or office of a financial institution that is treated as a branch under the regulatory regime of a jurisdiction, or that is otherwise regulated under the laws of a jurisdiction as separate from other offices, units, or branches of the financial institution. For this purpose, all units, businesses, or offices of a reporting financial institution in a single jurisdiction are treated as a single branch.

History: S. 270, the definition "entity" was added by S.C. 2016, c. 12, s. 71(1), in force on July 1, 2017.

"equity or debt interest" —"equity or debt interest" includes, in the case of a partnership that is a financial institution, either a capital or profits interest in the partnership,

History: S. 270, the definition "equity or debt interest" was added by S.C. 2016, c. 12, s. 71(1), in force on July 1, 2017.

"established securities market" —"established securities market" means an exchange that

(*a*) is officially recognized and supervised by a governmental authority in which the market is located; and

(*b*) has an annual value of shares traded on the exchange (or a predecessor exchange) exceeding one billion USD during each of the three calendar years immediately preceding the calendar year in which the determination is being made. For this purpose, if an exchange has more than one tier of market level on which stock may be separately listed or traded, each of those tiers must be treated as a separate exchange.

History: S. 270, the definition "established securities market" was added by S.C. 2016, c. 12, s. 71(1), in force on July 1, 2017.

"excluded account" —"excluded account" means

(*a*) a retirement or pension account that satisfies the following requirements:

(i) the account is

(A) subject to regulation as a personal retirement account, or

(B) part of a registered or regulated retirement or pension plan for the provision of retirement or pension benefits (including disability or death benefits),

(ii) the account is tax-favoured in that

(A) contributions to the account that would otherwise be subject to tax are deductible or excluded from the gross income of the account holder or taxed at a reduced rate, or

(B) taxation of investment income within the account is deferred or investment income within the account is taxed at a reduced rate,

(iii) information reporting to the Minister is required with respect to the account,

(iv) withdrawals are

(A) conditioned on reaching a specified retirement age, disability or death, or

(B) subject to penalties if made before the events specified in clause (A), and

(v) after applying the rules in subsection 277(3) to all similar accounts, annual contributions to the account are limited to 50,000 USD or less or there is a maximum lifetime contribution limit to the account of 1,000,000 USD or less (and an account that otherwise satisfies this requirement will not fail to satisfy this requirement solely because the account may receive assets or funds transferred from one or more accounts that meet the requirements of this paragraph or paragraph (*b*) or from one or more broad participation retirement funds, narrow participation retirement funds or pension funds of a governmental entity, international organization or central bank);

(*b*) an account that satisfies the following requirements:

(i) the account is

(A) both

(I) subject to regulation as an investment vehicle for purposes other than for retirement, and

(II) regularly traded on an established securities market, or

(B) subject to regulation as a savings vehicle for purposes other than for retirement,

(ii) the account is tax-favoured in that

(A) contributions to the account that would otherwise be subject to tax are deductible or excluded from the gross income of the account holder or taxed at a reduced rate, or

(B) taxation of investment income within the account is deferred or investment income within the account is taxed at a reduced rate,

(iii) withdrawals are

(A) conditioned on meeting specific criteria related to the purpose of the investment or savings account (including the provision of educational or medical benefits), or

(B) subject to penalties if made before the criteria in clause (A) are met, and

(iv) annual contributions are, after applying the rules in subsection 277(3) to all similar accounts, limited to 50,000 USD or less (and an account that otherwise satisfies this requirement will not fail to satisfy this requirement solely because the account may receive assets or funds transferred from one or more accounts that meet the requirements of paragraph (*a*) or this paragraph or from one or more broad participation retirement funds, narrow participation retirement funds or pension funds of a governmental entity, international organization or central bank);

(*c*) a life insurance contract with a coverage period that ends before the insured individual attains age 90, if the contract satisfies the following requirements:

(i) periodic premiums, which do not decrease over time, are payable at least annually until the earlier of

(A) the end of the period in which the contract is in existence, and

(B) the date that the insured attains age 90,

(ii) the contract has no contract value that any person can access (by withdrawal, loan or otherwise) without terminating the contract,

(iii) the amount (other than a death benefit) payable upon cancellation or termination of the contract must not exceed the amount determined by the formula

$$A - (B + C)$$

where

A is the aggregate premiums paid for the contract,

B is the total of all mortality, morbidity and expense charges (whether or not actually imposed) for the period or periods of the contract's existence, and

C is the total of all amounts paid prior to the cancellation or termination of the contract, and

(iv) the contract has not been acquired by a transferee for value;

(*d*) an account held solely by an estate of a deceased individual, if the documentation for the account includes a copy of the will or death certificate of the individual;

(*e*) an account established in connection with any of the following:

(i) a court order or judgement,

(ii) a sale, exchange or lease of property, if the account satisfies the following requirements:

(A) the account is funded

(I) solely with a down payment, earnest money, deposit in an amount appropriate to secure an obligation directly related to the transaction or a similar payment, or

(II) with a financial asset that is deposited in the account in connection with the sale, exchange or lease of the property,

(B) the account is established and used solely to secure the obligation of

(I) the purchaser to pay the purchase price for the property,

(II) the seller to pay any contingent liability, or

(III) the lessor or lessee to pay for any damages relating to the leased property as agreed under the lease,

(C) the assets of the account, including the income earned on the account, will be paid or otherwise distributed for the benefit of the purchaser, seller, lessor or lessee (including to satisfy such person's obligation) when the property is sold, exchanged or surrendered or the lease terminates,

(D) the account is not a margin or similar account established in connection with a sale or exchange of a financial asset, and

(E) the account is not associated with an account described in paragraph (*f*),

(iii) an obligation of a financial institution servicing a loan secured by real or immovable property to set aside a portion of a payment solely to facilitate the payment of taxes or insurance related to the property at a later time, or

(iv) an obligation of a financial institution solely to facilitate the payment of taxes at a later time;

(*f*) a depository account that satisfies the following requirements:

(i) the account exists solely because a customer makes a payment in excess of a balance due with respect to a credit card or other revolving credit facility and the overpayment is not immediately returned to the customer, and

(ii) after June 2017, policies and procedures are in effect relating to overpayments (for this purpose, a customer overpayment does not include credit balances to the extent of disputed charges but does include credit balances resulting from merchandise returns) to either

(A) prevent a customer from making an overpayment in excess of 50,000 USD, or

(B) ensure that any customer overpayment in excess of 50,000 USD is refunded to the customer within 60 days; and

(*g*) a prescribed account.

Editorial Note: An excluded account is considered to be at a low risk of non-compliance and is not subject to being reported. Included are certain retirement accounts, estate accounts, certain escrow accounts, and "prescribed accounts". The following accounts are prescribed in section 9006 of the *Income Tax Regulations* to be excluded accounts:

- a registered retirement savings plan;
- a registered retirement income fund;
- a pooled registered pension plans;
- a registered pension plan;
- a registered disability savings plan;
- a registered education savings plan;
- a deferred profit sharing plan;
- a net income stabilization account, including a NISA Fund No. 2;
- an eligible funeral arrangement;
- a dormant account if the balance or value of the account does not exceed 1,000 USD; and
- a TFSA.

History: S. 270, the definition "excluded account" was added by S.C. 2016, c. 12, s. 71(1), in force on July 1, 2017.

Related Regulations: 9006 Prescribed Excluded Accounts.

"exempt collective investment vehicle" —"exempt collective investment vehicle" means an investment entity that is regulated as a collective investment vehicle, provided that all of the interests in the collective investment vehicle are held by or through individuals or entities (other than a passive NFE with a controlling person who is a reportable person) that are not reportable persons.

Editorial Note: The term "collective investment vehicle" is used to describe funds that are widely-held, hold a diversified portfolio of securities, and are subject to investor-protection regulations in the country in which they are established. The term would include "master" and "feeder" funds that are part of "fund of funds" structures where the master fund holds a diversified portfolio of investments. However, for example, private equity funds and hedge funds would generally not fall within the definition of collective investment vehicle.

History: S. 270, the definition "exempt collective investment vehicle" was added by S.C. 2016, c. 12, s. 71(1), in force on July 1, 2017.

"financial account" — "financial account" means an account maintained by a financial institution, and

(*a*) includes

(i) a depository account,

(ii) a custodial account,

(iii) in the case of an investment entity, any equity or debt interest in the financial institution, except that it does not include any equity or debt interest in an entity that is an investment entity solely because it,

(A) renders investment advice to, and acts on behalf of, a customer for the purpose of investing, managing or administering financial assets deposited in the name of the customer with a financial institution other than such entity, or

(B) manages portfolios for, and acts on behalf of, a customer for the purpose of investing, managing, or administering financial assets deposited in the name of the customer with a financial institution other than such entity,

(iv) any equity or debt interest in the financial institution if one of the purposes of establishing the class of interests was to avoid reporting in accordance with section 271, except that it does not include any equity or debt interest in an entity that is an investment entity solely because it meets the conditions described in clauses (iii)(A) or (B),

(v) any cash value insurance contract and any annuity contract issued or maintained by a financial institution, other than a non-investment-linked, non-transferable immediate life annuity that is issued to an individual and monetizes a pension or disability benefit provided under an account that is an excluded account, and

(vi) an account that is a client name account maintained by a person or entity that is authorized under provincial legislation to engage in the business of dealing in securities or any other financial instruments, or to provide portfolio management or investment advising services; and

(*b*) despite paragraph (*a*), does not include an excluded account.

History: S. 270, the definition "financial account" was added by S.C. 2016, c. 12, s. 71(1), in force on July 1, 2017.

"financial asset" — "financial asset"

(*a*) includes

(i) a security, such as

(A) a share of the capital stock of a corporation,

(B) an income or capital interest in a widely held or publicly traded trust, or

(C) a note, bond, debenture or other evidence of indebtedness,

(ii) a partnership interest,

(iii) a commodity,

(iv) a swap (such as interest rate swaps, currency swaps, basis swaps, interest rate caps, interest rate floors, commodity swaps, equity swaps, equity index swaps and similar agreements),

(v) an insurance contract or annuity contract, and

(vi) any interest (including a futures or forward contract or option) in a security, partnership interest, commodity, swap, insurance contract or annuity contract; and

(*b*) does not include a non-debt, direct interest in real or immovable property.

Editorial Note: The definition "financial asset", which is an "inclusive" definition, is intended to encompass any assets that may be held in an account maintained by a financial institution. Negotiable debt instruments that are traded on a regulated market (or on an over-the-counter market and distributed and held through financial institutions) and shares or units in a real estate investment trust, would generally be considered financial assets.

History: S. 270, the definition "financial asset" was added by S.C. 2016, c. 12, s. 71(1), in force on July 1, 2017.

"financial institution" — "financial institution" means an entity, other than a passive NFE, that is a custodial institution, a depository institution, an investment entity or a specified insurance company.

Editorial Note: The definition of "financial institution" excludes "passive NFEs", thereby excluding professionally managed personal trusts and investment holding companies. (See editorial note to "investment entity".)

History: S. 270, the definition "financial institution" was added by S.C. 2016, c. 12, s. 71(1), in force on July 1, 2017.

Related Sections: 270(4) Equity or debt interest — deeming rule.

"governmental entity" — "governmental entity" means the government of a jurisdiction, any political subdivision of a jurisdiction (which, for greater certainty, includes a state, province, county or municipality), a public body performing a function of government in a jurisdiction or any agency or instrumentality of a jurisdiction wholly owned by one or more of the foregoing, unless it is not an integral part or a controlled entity of a jurisdiction (or a political subdivision of a jurisdiction) and for these purposes

(*a*) an integral part of a jurisdiction means any person, organization, agency, bureau, fund, instrumentality or other body, however designated, that constitutes a governing authority of a jurisdiction and where the net earnings of the governing authority are credited to its own account or to other accounts of the jurisdiction, with no portion inuring to the benefit of any private person, except that an integral part does not include any individual who is a sovereign, official or administrator acting in a private or personal capacity;

(*b*) a controlled entity means an entity that is separate in form from the jurisdiction or that otherwise constitutes a separate juridical entity, provided that

(i) the entity is wholly owned and controlled by one or more governmental entities directly or indirectly through one or more controlled entities,

(ii) the entity's net earnings are credited to its own account or to the accounts of one or more governmental entities, with no portion of its income inuring to the benefit of any private person, and

(iii) the entity's assets vest in one or more governmental entities upon liquidation and dissolution; and

(c) for the purposes of paragraphs (a) and (b),

(i) income is deemed not to inure to the benefit of private persons if such persons are the intended beneficiaries of a governmental program and the program activities are performed for the general public with respect to the common welfare or relate to the administration of government, and

(ii) income is deemed to inure to the benefit of private persons if the income is derived from the use of a governmental entity to conduct a commercial business that provides financial services to private persons.

History: S. 270, the definition "governmental entity" was added by S.C. 2016, c. 12, s. 71(1), in force on July 1, 2017.

"group annuity contract" —"group annuity contract" means an annuity contract under which the obligees are individuals who are associated through an employer, trade association, labour union or other association or group.

History: S. 270, the definition "group annuity contract" was added by S.C. 2016, c. 12, s. 71(1), in force on July 1, 2017.

"group cash value insurance contract" —"group cash value insurance contract" means a cash value insurance contract that

(a) provides coverage on individuals who are associated through an employer, trade association, labour union or other association or group; and

(b) charges a premium for each member of the group (or member of a class within the group) that is determined without regard to the individual health characteristics other than age, gender and smoking habits of the member (or class of members) of the group.

History: S. 270, the definition "group cash value insurance contract" was added by S.C. 2016, c. 12, s. 71(1), in force on July 1, 2017.

"high value account" —"high value account" means a preexisting individual account with an aggregate balance or value that exceeds 1 million USD on June 30, 2017 or on December 31 of any subsequent year.

Editorial Note: Once an account becomes a high value account, it maintains its status as such until the date of its closure and, therefore, can no longer be considered a lower-value account at any point in the future.

History: S. 270, the definition "high value account" was added by S.C. 2016, c. 12, s. 71(1), in force on July 1, 2017.

Related Sections: 277(3) Aggregation rules.

"insurance contract" —"insurance contract" means a contract (other than an annuity contract) under which the issuer agrees to pay an amount upon the occurrence of a specified contingency involving mortality, morbidity, accident, liability or property risk.

History: S. 270, the definition "insurance contract" was added by S.C. 2016, c. 12, s. 71(1), in force on July 1, 2017.

"international organization" —"international organization" means any intergovernmental organization (or wholly owned agency or instrumentality thereof), including a supranational organization

(a) that is comprised primarily of governments;

(b) that has in effect a headquarters or substantially similar agreement with a jurisdiction; and

(c) the income of which does not inure to the benefit of private persons.

History: S. 270, the definition "international organization" was added by S.C. 2016, c. 12, s. 71(1), in force on July 1, 2017.

"investment entity" —"investment entity" means any entity (other than an entity that is an "active NFE" because of any of paragraphs (d) to (g) of that definition)

(a) that primarily carries on as a business one or more of the following activities or operations for or on behalf of a customer:

(i) trading in money market instruments (such as cheques, bills, certificates of deposit and derivatives), foreign exchange, transferable securities or commodity futures, exchange, interest rate and index instruments,

(ii) individual and collective portfolio management, or

(iii) otherwise investing, administering or managing financial assets or money on behalf of other persons; or

(b) the gross income of which is primarily attributable to investing, reinvesting or trading in financial assets, if the entity is managed by another entity that is a depository institution, a custodial institution, a specified insurance company or an investment entity described in paragraph (a).

Editorial Note: An investment entity is generally a "financial institution" and therefore possibly has due diligence and reporting obligations. Note that passive investment vehicles, like personal trusts and investment holding companies that are professionally managed and described in paragraph (b) are considered "passive NFEs" under the definition of that term later in this subsection and are therefore carved out from the definition of "financial institution". Although they do not have reporting obligations themselves because of this, accounts they hold at a financial institution may be reportable under the definition of "reportable account" if one or more of their "controlling persons" are "reportable persons".

See also subsection 270(3).

History: S. 270, the definition "investment entity" was added by S.C. 2016, c. 12, s. 71(1), in force on July 1, 2017.

Related Sections: 270(3) Interpretation — investment entity.

"lower value account" —"lower value account" means a preexisting individual account with an aggregate balance or value as of June 30, 2017 that does not exceed 1 million USD.

History: S. 270, the definition "lower value account" was added by S.C. 2016, c. 12, s. 71(1), in force on July 1, 2017.

Related Sections: 277(3) Aggregation rules.

"narrow participation retirement fund" —"narrow participation retirement fund" means a fund that is established to provide retirement, disability or death benefits to beneficiaries who are current or former employees (or persons designated by those employees) of one or more employers in consideration for services rendered, if

(a) the fund has fewer than 50 participants;

(b) the fund is sponsored by one or more employers that are not investment entities or passive NFEs;

(c) the employee and employer contributions to the fund (other than transfers of assets from retirement and pension accounts described in paragraph (a) of the definition "excluded account") are limited by reference to the employee's remuneration;

(*d*) participants that are not resident in Canada are not entitled to more than 20% of the fund's assets; and

(*e*) the fund is subject to government regulation and provides information reporting to the Minister.

History: S. 270, the definition "narrow participation retirement fund" was added by S.C. 2016, c. 12, s. 71(1), in force on July 1, 2017.

"natural person" —"natural person" means an individual other than a trust.

History: S. 270, the definition "natural person" was added by S.C. 2016, c. 12, s. 71(1), in force on July 1, 2017.

"new account" —"new account" means a financial account maintained by a reporting financial institution opened after June 2017.

History: S. 270, the definition "new account" was added by S.C. 2016, c. 12, s. 71(1), in force on July 1, 2017.

"new entity account" —"new entity account" means a new account held by one or more entities.

History: S. 270, the definition "new entity account" was added by S.C. 2016, c. 12, s. 71(1), in force on July 1, 2017.

"new individual account" —"new individual account" means a new account held by one or more individuals (other than trusts).

History: S. 270, the definition "new individual account" was added by S.C. 2016, c. 12, s. 71(1), in force on July 1, 2017.

"non-financial entity or NFE" —"non-financial entity or NFE" means an entity if

(*a*) in the case of an entity that is resident in Canada, it is not a Canadian financial institution; and

(*b*) in the case of a non-resident entity, it is not a financial institution.

Editorial Note: An NFE can be either a passive NFE or an active NFE.

History: S. 270, the definition "non-financial entity or NFE" was added by S.C. 2016, c. 12, s. 71(1), in force on July 1, 2017.

"non-reporting financial institution" —"non-reporting financial institution" means a Canadian financial institution that is

(*a*) the Bank of Canada;

(*b*) a governmental entity or international organization, other than with respect to a payment that is derived from an obligation held in connection with a commercial financial activity of a type engaged in by a specified insurance company, custodial institution or depository institution;

(*c*) a broad participation retirement fund, a narrow participation retirement fund, a pension fund of a governmental entity, international organization or central bank, or a qualified credit card issuer;

(*d*) an exempt collective investment vehicle;

(*e*) a trust if a trustee of the trust is a reporting financial institution and reports all information required to be reported under this Part with respect to all reportable accounts of the trust; or

(*f*) a prescribed entity.

History: S. 270, the definition "non-reporting financial institution" was added by S.C. 2016, c. 12, s. 71(1), in force on July 1, 2017.

"participating jurisdiction" —"participating jurisdiction" means

(*a*) Canada; and

(*b*) each jurisdiction identified as a participating jurisdiction by the Minister on the Internet website of the Canada Revenue Agency or by any other means that the Minister considers appropriate.

Editorial Note: The term "participating jurisdiction" is used in respect of jurisdictions where there is an information agreement in place to share the information that is collected pursuant to the Common Reporting Standard. These will be listed by the Minister of National Revenue on the CRA website (cra-arc.gc.ca).

History: S. 270, the definition "participating jurisdiction" was added by S.C. 2016, c. 12, s. 71(1), in force on July 1, 2017.

"participating jurisdiction financial institution" —"participating jurisdiction financial institution" means

(*a*) a financial institution that is resident in a participating jurisdiction, but excludes a branch of that financial institution that is located outside a participating jurisdiction; and

(*b*) a branch of a financial institution that is not resident in a participating jurisdiction, if that branch is located in a participating jurisdiction.

History: S. 270, the definition "participating jurisdiction financial institution" was added by S.C. 2016, c. 12, s. 71(1), in force on July 1, 2017.

"passive NFE" —"passive NFE" means

(*a*) a non-financial entity that is not an active NFE; and

(*b*) an entity that is

(i) described in paragraph (*b*) of the definition "investment entity", and

(ii) not a participating jurisdiction financial institution.

Editorial Note: Notably, the definition of "passive NFE" includes "investment entities" described in paragraph (*b*) of that definition that are professionally managed passive investment holding companies and personal trusts. (See editorial note to "investment entity".) Accounts held by a passive NFE at a financial institution may be reportable under the definition of "reportable account" if one or more of their "controlling persons" are "reportable persons".

History: S. 270, the definition "passive NFE" was added by S.C. 2016, c. 12, s. 71(1), in force on July 1, 2017.

"pension fund of a governmental entity, international organization or central bank" —"pension fund of a governmental entity, international organization or central bank" means a fund that is established by a governmental entity, international organization or central bank to provide retirement, disability or death benefits to beneficiaries or participants

(*a*) that are current or former employees (or persons designated by those employees); or

(*b*) that are not current or former employees, if the benefits provided to them are in consideration of personal services performed for the governmental entity, international organization or central bank.

History: S. 270, the definition "pension fund of a governmental entity, international organization or central bank" was added by S.C. 2016, c. 12, s. 71(1), in force on July 1, 2017.

"preexisting account" —"preexisting account" means

(*a*) a financial account maintained by a reporting financial institution on June 30, 2017; and

(*b*) a financial account of an account holder (other than a financial account described in paragraph (*a*)) maintained by a reporting financial institution if

(i) the account holder also holds with the reporting financial institution (or with a related entity within Canada) a financial account that is a preexisting account under paragraph (*a*),

(ii) the reporting financial institution (and, as applicable, the related entity within Canada) treats both of the aforementioned financial accounts, and any other financial accounts of the account holder that are preexisting accounts under this paragraph, as a single financial account for the purposes of

(A) satisfying the standards and knowledge requirements set forth under this Part, and

(B) determining the balance or value of any of the financial accounts, when applying any of the account thresholds,

(iii) with respect to a financial account that is subject to AML/KYC procedures, the reporting financial institution is permitted to satisfy those AML/KYC procedures for the financial account by relying upon the AML/KYC procedures performed for the preexisting account described in paragraph (*a*), and

(iv) the opening of the financial account does not require the provision of new, additional or amended customer information by the account holder other than for purposes of this Part.

History: S. 270, the definition "preexisting account" was added by S.C. 2016, c. 12, s. 71(1), in force on July 1, 2017.

"preexisting entity account" —"preexisting entity account" means a preexisting account held by one or more entities.

History: S. 270, the definition "preexisting entity account" was added by S.C. 2016, c. 12, s. 71(1), in force on July 1, 2017.

"preexisting individual account" —"preexisting individual account" means a preexisting account held by one or more individuals (other than trusts).

History: S. 270, the definition "preexisting individual account" was added by S.C. 2016, c. 12, s. 71(1), in force on July 1, 2017.

"qualified credit card issuer" —"qualified credit card issuer" means a financial institution that satisfies the following requirements:

(*a*) the financial institution is a financial institution solely because it is an issuer of credit cards that accepts deposits only when a customer makes a payment in excess of a balance due with respect to the card and the overpayment is not immediately returned to the customer; and

(*b*) the financial institution has policies and procedures either to prevent a customer from making an overpayment in excess of 50,000 USD or to ensure that any customer overpayment in excess of 50,000 USD is refunded to the customer within 60 days, in each case applying the rules set forth in subsection 277(3) for account aggregation, and, for the purposes of this paragraph, a customer overpayment does not refer to credit balances to the extent of disputed charges but does include credit balances resulting from merchandise returns.

History: S. 270, the definition "qualified credit card issuer" was added by S.C. 2016, c. 12, s. 71(1), in force on July 1, 2017.

"related entity" —"related entity", in respect of an entity, means an entity if either entity controls the other entity or the two entities are controlled by the same entity or individual (and in the case of two entities that are investment entities described under paragraph (*b*) of the definition "investment entity", the two entities are under common management and such management fulfils the due diligence obligations of the investment entities). For this purpose, control includes direct or indirect ownership of

(*a*) in the case of a corporation, shares of the capital stock of a corporation that

(i) give their holders more than 50% of the votes that could be cast at the annual meeting of the shareholders of the corporation, and

(ii) have a fair market value of more than 50% of the fair market value of all the issued and outstanding shares of the capital stock of the corporation;

(*b*) in the case of a partnership, an interest as a member of the partnership that entitles the member to more than 50% of

(i) the income or loss of the partnership, or

(ii) the assets (net of liabilities) of the partnership if it were to cease to exist; and

(*c*) in the case of a trust, an interest as a beneficiary under the trust with a fair market value that is greater than 50% of the fair market value of all interests as a beneficiary under the trust.

History: S. 270, the definition "related entity" was added by S.C. 2016, c. 12, s. 71(1), in force on July 1, 2017.

"reportable account" —"reportable account" means an account that

(*a*) is held by

(i) one or more reportable persons, or

(ii) by a passive NFE, if one or more controlling persons of the passive NFE is a reportable person; and

(*b*) has been identified as meeting the conditions in paragraph (*a*) in accordance with the due diligence procedures described in sections 272 to 277.

History: S. 270, the definition "reportable account" was added by S.C. 2016, c. 12, s. 71(1), in force on July 1, 2017.

"reportable jurisdiction" —"reportable jurisdiction" means a jurisdiction other than Canada and the United States of America.

Editorial Note: The US is excluded from these rules as there are separate "FATCA" rules for reporting to the US that are set forth in Part XVIII.

History: S. 270, the definition "reportable jurisdiction" was added by S.C. 2016, c. 12, s. 71(1), in force on July 1, 2017.

"reportable jurisdiction person" —"reportable jurisdiction person" means a natural person or entity that is resident in a reportable jurisdiction under the tax laws of that jurisdiction, or an estate of an individual who was a resident of a reportable jurisdiction under the tax laws of that jurisdiction immediately before death. For this purpose, an entity that has no residence for tax purposes is deemed to be resident in the jurisdiction in which its place of effective management is situated.

History: S. 270, the definition "reportable jurisdiction person" was added by S.C. 2016, c. 12, s. 71(1), in force on July 1, 2017.

"reportable person" —"reportable person" means a reportable jurisdiction person other than

(*a*) a corporation the stock of which is regularly traded on one or more established securities markets;

(*b*) any corporation that is a related entity of a corporation described in paragraph (*a*);

(*c*) a governmental entity;

(*d*) an international organization;

(*e*) a central bank; or

(*f*) a financial institution.

History: S. 270, the definition "reportable person" was added by S.C. 2016, c. 12, s. 71(1), in force on July 1, 2017.

"reporting financial institution" —"reporting financial institution" means a Canadian financial institution that is not a non-reporting financial institution.

History: S. 270, the definition "reporting financial institution" was added by S.C. 2016, c. 12, s. 71(1), in force on July 1, 2017.

"specified insurance company" —"specified insurance company" means any entity that is an insurance company (or the holding company of an insurance company) that issues, or is obligated to make payments with respect to, cash value insurance contracts or annuity contracts.

History: S. 270, the definition "specified insurance company" was added by S.C. 2016, c. 12, s. 71(1), in force on July 1, 2017.

"TIN" —"TIN" means

(*a*) the number used by the Minister to identify an individual or entity, including

(i) a social insurance number,

(ii) a business number, and

(iii) an account number issued to a trust; and

(*b*) in respect of a jurisdiction other than Canada, a taxpayer identification number used in that jurisdiction to identify an individual or entity (or a functional equivalent in the absence of a taxpayer identification number).

History: S. 270, the definition "TIN" was added by S.C. 2016, c. 12, s. 71(1), in force on July 1, 2017.

"USD" —"USD" means dollars of the United States of America.

History: S. 270, the definition "USD" was added by S.C. 2016, c. 12, s. 71(1), in force on July 1, 2017.

► 270(2) ◄

(2) Interpretation. This Part relates to the implementation of the *Common Reporting Standard* set out in the *Standard for Automatic Exchange of Financial Account Information in Tax Matters* approved by the Council of the Organisation for Economic Co-operation and Development and, unless the context otherwise requires, the provisions in this Part are to be interpreted consistently with the *Common Reporting Standard*, as amended from time to time.

Editorial Note: This subsection links Part XIX to the model Common Reporting Standard developed and approved by the Organisation for Economic Co-operation and Development (OECD). It provides that, unless the context requires otherwise, the provisions of Part XIX are to be interpreted consistently with the Common Reporting Standard and associated commentary published by the OECD and as amended from time to time. This documentation is available at http://www.oecd.org/tax/automatic-exchange/common-reporting-standard/.

History: S. 270(2) was added by S.C. 2016, c. 12, s. 71(1), in force on July 1, 2017.

► 270(3) ◄

(3) Interpretation — investment entity. For the purposes of the definition "investment entity" in subsection (1), an entity is considered to be primarily carrying on as a business one or more of the activities described in paragraph (*a*) of that definition, or an entity's gross income is primarily attributable to investing, reinvesting or trading in financial assets for the purposes of paragraph (*b*) of that definition, if the entity's gross income attributable to the relevant activities equals or exceeds 50% of the entity's gross income during the shorter of

(*a*) the three-year period that ends at the end of the entity's last fiscal period, and

(*b*) the period during which the entity has been in existence.

History: S. 270(3) was added by S.C. 2016, c. 12, s. 71(1), in force on July 1, 2017.

► 270(4) ◄

(4) Equity or debt interest — deeming rule. In the case of a trust that is a financial institution,

(*a*) an equity interest is deemed to be held by any person treated as a settlor or beneficiary of all or a portion of the trust or any other natural person exercising ultimate effective control over the trust, and

(*b*) a reportable person is treated as a beneficiary of a trust if the reportable person has the right to receive directly or indirectly (such as through a nominee) a mandatory distribution from the trust or may receive, directly or indirectly, a discretionary distribution from the trust.

History: S. 270(4) was added by S.C. 2016, c. 12, s. 71(1), in force on July 1, 2017.

Editorial Note: Part XIX imports the Common Reporting Standard ("CRS") for the automatic international exchange of tax information developed by the OECD into Canadian law, effective January 1, 2017. The CRS is based on the "FATCA" requirements found in the Canada–US Enhanced Information Exchange Agreement, which Canada entered into with the US on February 5, 2014, and Part XVIII of the *Income Tax Act*, with the key differences being that the CRS will apply to all countries who agree to the tax information exchange, not just the US, and that it is based on residency, as opposed to both residency and citizenship.

Essentially, financial institutions will be required to identify the tax residency of their clients and report certain FATCA-like account information to the CRA starting on July 1, 2017. The CRA will stockpile this information and, once information exchange agreements have been formalized with other countries and the CRA has verified that the country in question has appropriate information safeguards in place, exchange the information relating to tax residents of that country on a bilateral reciprocal basis with the tax enforcement agency of the country.

Part XIX contains the rules that reporting financial institutions must follow. There is a substantial definitions section in section 270, which, among other things, is important in determining the application of the rules, followed by general reporting requirements in section 271 and generally applicable due diligence rules in section 272. Following that are the specific due diligence procedures that apply to "pre-existing" (a defined term, but basically accounts in existence on June 30, 2017) individual accounts in section 273, including an enhanced review that is required for high-value accounts thought to be at greater risk of non-compliance; due diligence procedures that apply to new individual accounts in section 274; due diligence procedures applicable to pre-existing entity accounts in section 275; and due diligence procedures for new entity accounts in section 276. There are special rules that apply to all types of accounts in section 277 and general administrative provisions in sections 278–281.

SECTION 271: [General reporting requirements]

► 271(1) ◄

(1) General reporting requirements. Subject to subsections (3) and (4), each reporting financial institution must report the following information to the Minister with respect to each of its reportable accounts:

(*a*) the name, address, jurisdiction of residence, TIN and date of birth (in the case of a natural person) of each reportable person that is an account holder of the account;

(*b*) in the case of any entity that is an account holder of the account and that, after applying the due diligence procedures in sections 275 to 277, is identified as having one or more controlling persons that is a reportable person,

(i) the name, address, jurisdiction of residence and TIN of the entity, and

(ii) the name, address, jurisdiction of residence, TIN and date of birth of each of those controlling persons;

(*c*) the account number (or functional equivalent in the absence of an account number) of the account;

(*d*) the name and identifying number (if any) of the reporting financial institution;

(*e*) the account balance or value (including, in the case of a cash value insurance contract or annuity contract, the cash value or surrender value)

(i) at the end of the relevant calendar year or other appropriate reporting period, or

(ii) if the account was closed during the relevant calendar year or period, on closure of the account;

(*f*) in the case of any custodial account,

(i) the total gross amount of interest, the total gross amount of dividends and the total gross amount of other income generated with respect to the assets held in the account, in each case paid or credited to the account (or with respect to the account) during the calendar year or other appropriate reporting period, and

(ii) the total gross proceeds from the sale or redemption of financial assets paid or credited to the account during the calendar year or other appropriate reporting period with respect to which the reporting financial institution acted as a custodian, broker, nominee or otherwise as an agent for the account holder;

(*g*) in the case of any depository account, the total gross amount of interest paid or credited to the account during the calendar year or other appropriate reporting period; and

(*h*) in the case of any account not described in paragraph (*f*) or (*g*), the total gross amount paid or credited to the account holder with respect to the account during the calendar year or other appropriate reporting period with respect to which the reporting financial institution is the obligor or debtor, including the aggregate amount of any redemption payments made to the account holder during the calendar year or other appropriate reporting period.

History: S. 271(1) was added by S.C. 2016, c. 12, s. 71(1), in force on July 1, 2017.

Tax Topics: No. 2454, Common Reporting Standards in Canadian Tax; No. 2427, What Is the Common Reporting Standard and What Does It Mean for Canadian Financial Institutions?.

► 271(2) ◄

(2) Currency. The information reported must identify the currency in which each amount is denominated.

History: S. 271(2) was added by S.C. 2016, c. 12, s. 71(1), in force on July 1, 2017.

► 271(3) ◄

(3) TIN and date of birth. With respect to each reportable account that is a preexisting account,

(*a*) notwithstanding paragraphs (1)(*a*) and (*b*), the TIN or date of birth are not required to be reported if the TIN or the date of birth (as appropriate)

(i) are not in the records of the reporting financial institution, and

(ii) are not otherwise required to be collected by the reporting financial institution under the Act; and

(*b*) a reporting financial institution is required to use reasonable efforts to obtain the TIN and the date of birth with respect to a preexisting account by the end of the second calendar year following the year in which the preexisting account is identified as a reportable account.

Editorial Note: See section 281.

History: S. 271(3) was added by S.C. 2016, c. 12, s. 71(1), in force on July 1, 2017.

► 271(4) ◄

(4) Exceptions. Notwithstanding paragraphs (1)(*a*) and (*b*), a TIN of a reportable person is not required to be reported if

(*a*) the relevant reportable jurisdiction does not issue TINs; or

(*b*) the domestic law of the relevant reportable jurisdiction does not require the collection of the TIN issued by such reportable jurisdiction.

History: S. 271(4) was added by S.C. 2016, c. 12, s. 71(1), in force on July 1, 2017.

SECTION 272: [General due diligence rules]

► 272(1) ◄

(1) General due diligence rules. An account is treated as a reportable account as of the date it is identified as a reportable account under the due diligence procedures set out in this section and in sections 273 to 277.

History: S. 272(1) was added by S.C. 2016, c. 12, s. 71(1), in force on July 1, 2017.

► 272(2) ◄

(2) Timing — determination of balance or value. The balance or value of an account is determined on the last day of the calendar year or other appropriate reporting period.

Editorial Note: While the balance or value of an account is part of the information to be reported, it is also relevant for other purposes, such as determining the appropriate due diligence procedures for preexisting entity accounts and the account balance aggregation rules.

History: S. 272(2) was added by S.C. 2016, c. 12, s. 71(1), in force on July 1, 2017.

► 272(3) ◄

(3) Determination — balance or value. For the purpose of determining whether the balance or value of an account exceeds a particular threshold on the last day of a calendar year, the balance or value must be determined on the last day of the last reporting period that ends on or before the end of the calendar year.

History: S. 272(3) was added by S.C. 2016, c. 12, s. 71(1), in force on July 1, 2017.

► 272(4) ◄

(4) Service provider. A reporting financial institution may use service providers to fulfil its reporting and due diligence obligations imposed, but these obligations shall remain the responsibility of the reporting financial institution.

History: S. 272(4) was added by S.C. 2016, c. 12, s. 71(1), in force on July 1, 2017.

► 272(5) ◄

(5) Optional due diligence procedures. A reporting financial institution may, either with respect to all preexisting accounts or, separately, with respect to any clearly identified group of those accounts, apply the due diligence procedures

(*a*) for new accounts to preexisting accounts (with the other rules for preexisting accounts continuing to apply); and

(*b*) for high value accounts to lower value accounts.

History: S. 272(5) was added by S.C. 2016, c. 12, s. 71(1), in force on July 1, 2017.

► 272(6) ◄

(6) Documentation of due diligence procedures. Every reporting financial institution shall establish, maintain and document the due diligence procedures set out in this section and sections 273 to 277.

History: S. 272(6) was added by S.C. 2016, c. 12, s. 71(1), in force on July 1, 2017.

SECTION 273: [Due diligence for preexisting individual accounts]

► 273(1) ◄

(1) Due diligence for preexisting individual accounts. A preexisting individual account that is a cash value insurance contract or an annuity contract is not required to be reviewed, identified or reported, if the reporting financial institution is effectively prevented by law from selling those contracts to residents of a reportable jurisdiction.

History: S. 273(1) was added by S.C. 2016, c. 12, s. 71(1), in force on July 1, 2017.

► 273(2) ◄

(2) Lower value accounts. The following review procedures apply with respect to lower value accounts that are preexisting individual accounts:

(*a*) if the reporting financial institution has in its records the address of the individual account holder's current residence (in this section, their "current residence address") based on documentary evidence, the reporting financial institution may treat the individual account holder as being a resident for tax purposes of the jurisdiction in which the address is located for purposes of determining whether the individual account holder is a reportable person;

Editorial Note: Paragraph 273(2)(*a*) provides an alternate test that can be used by a financial institution for determining the jurisdiction of residence of an individual account holder if the financial institution has a current residence address for the account holder in its records. See 270(1) for the definition of "documentary evidence".

(*b*) if the reporting financial institution does not rely on a current residence address for the individual account holder based on documentary evidence as described in paragraph (*a*), the reporting financial institution must review electronically searchable data maintained by the reporting financial institution for any of the following indicia and apply paragraphs (*c*) to (*f*):

(i) identification of the account holder as a resident of a reportable jurisdiction,

(ii) current mailing or residence address (including post office box) in a reportable jurisdiction,

(iii) one or more telephone numbers in a reportable jurisdiction and no telephone number in the jurisdiction of the reporting financial institution,

(iv) standing instructions (other than with respect to a depository account) to transfer funds to an account maintained in a reportable jurisdiction,

(v) currently effective power of attorney or signatory authority granted to a person with an address in a reportable jurisdiction, and

(vi) a hold mail instruction or in-care-of address in a reportable jurisdiction if the reporting financial institution does not have any other address on file for the account holder;

(*c*) if none of the indicia listed in paragraph (*b*) are discovered in the electronic search, then no further review is required until the earlier of

(i) a change in circumstances that results in one or more of the indicia referred to in paragraph (*b*) being associated with the account, and

(ii) the account becoming a high value account;

Editorial Note: See editorial note to paragraph 273(2)(*d*).

(*d*) if any of the indicia listed in subparagraphs (*b*)(i) to (v) are discovered in the electronic search or if there is a change in circumstances that results in one or more of the indicia in paragraph (*b*) being associated with the account, then the reporting financial institution must treat the account holder as a resident for tax purposes of each reportable jurisdiction for which an indicium is identified, unless one of the exceptions in paragraph (*f*) applies with respect to that account;

Editorial Note: A "change in circumstances" includes any change that results in the addition of information relevant to a person's status or otherwise conflicts with such person's status. It also includes any change or addition of information to the account holder's account (including the addition, substitution, or other change of an account holder) or any change or addition of information to any account associated with such account (applying the account aggregation rules) if such change or addition of information affects the status of the account holder.

(*e*) if a hold mail instruction or in-care-of address in a reportable jurisdiction is discovered in the electronic search and no other address and none of the other indicia listed in subparagraphs (*b*)(i) to (v) are identified for the account holder, then

(i) the reporting financial institution must do one (if the relevant information is obtained) or both (in the order most appropriate to the circumstances) of the following:

(A) apply the paper record search described in paragraph (3)(*b*), and

(B) seek to obtain from the account holder a self-certification or documentary evidence to establish the residence for tax purposes of the account holder, and

(ii) if the paper record search referred to in clause (i)(A) fails to establish an indicium and the attempt to obtain the self-certification or documentary evidence referred to in clause (i)(B) is not successful, then the reporting financial institution must report the account as an undocumented account; and

(*f*) notwithstanding the discovery of indicia under paragraph (*b*), a reporting financial institution is not required to treat an account holder as a resident of a reportable jurisdiction if

(i) both

(A) the account holder information contains

(I) a current mailing or residence address in the reportable jurisdiction,

(II) one or more telephone numbers in the reportable jurisdiction (and no telephone number in the jurisdiction of the reporting financial institution), or

(III) standing instructions (with respect to financial accounts other than depository accounts) to transfer funds to an account maintained in a reportable jurisdiction, and

(B) the reporting financial institution obtains, or has previously reviewed and currently maintains a record of,

(I) a self-certification from the account holder of the jurisdictions of residence of the account holder that does not include the reportable jurisdiction, and

(II) documentary evidence establishing the account holder's non-reportable status in relation to that jurisdiction, or

(ii) both

(A) the account holder information contains a currently effective power of attorney or signatory authority granted to a person with an address in the reportable jurisdiction, and

(B) the reporting financial institution obtains, or has previously reviewed and currently maintains a record of,

(I) a self-certification from the account holder of the jurisdictions of residence of the account holder that does not include the reportable jurisdiction, or

(II) documentary evidence establishing the account holder's non-reportable status in relation to that jurisdiction.

Editorial Note: Paragraph 273(2)(*f*) contains a procedure for curing a finding of *indicia* under paragraph 273(2)(*b*). A self-certification or documentary evidence that has been previously reviewed may be relied upon for purposes of the curing procedure unless the reporting financial institution knows or has reasons to know that the self-certification or documentary evidence is incorrect or unreliable.

History: S. 273(2) was added by S.C. 2016, c. 12, s. 71(1), in force on July 1, 2017.

Related Sections: 270(1) "excluded account".

► 273(3) ◄

(3) Enhanced review procedure — high value accounts. The following enhanced review procedures apply with respect to high value accounts that are preexisting individual accounts:

(*a*) the reporting financial institution must review electronically searchable data maintained by the reporting financial institution for any of the indicia described in paragraph (2)(*b*);

(*b*) subject to paragraph (*c*), the reporting financial institution must review for any of the indicia described in paragraph (2)(*b*)

(i) the current customer master file, and

(ii) the following documents associated with the account, and obtained by the reporting financial institution within the last five years, to the extent that they are not contained in the current customer master file:

(A) the most recent documentary evidence collected with respect to the account,

(B) the most recent account opening contract or documentation,

(C) the most recent documentation obtained by the reporting financial institution in accordance with AML/KYC procedures or for other regulatory purposes,

(D) any power of attorney or signature authority forms currently in effect, and

(E) any standing instructions (other than with respect to a depository account) to transfer funds currently in effect;

(*c*) a reporting financial institution is not required to perform the paper record search described in paragraph (*b*) to the extent that the reporting financial institution's electronically searchable information includes the following:

(i) the account holder's residence status,

(ii) the account holder's residence address and mailing address currently on file with the reporting financial institution,

(iii) the account holder's telephone number currently on file, if any, with the reporting financial institution,

(iv) in the case of financial accounts other than depository accounts, whether there are standing instructions to transfer funds in the account to another account (including an account at another branch of the reporting financial institution or at another financial institution),

(v) whether there is a hold mail instruction or current in-care-of address for the account holder, and

(vi) whether there is any power of attorney or signatory authority for the account;

(*d*) in addition to the electronic and paper record searches described in paragraphs (*a*) to (*c*), the reporting financial institution must treat as a reportable account any high value account assigned to a relationship manager (including any financial accounts aggregated with that high value account under section 277) if the relationship manager has actual knowledge that the account holder is a reportable person;

Editorial Note: A "relationship manager" is an officer or other employee of a reporting financial institution who is assigned responsibility for specific account holders on an on-going basis (including as an officer or employee of a financial institution's private banking department), advises account holders regarding their banking, investment, trust, fiduciary, estate planning, or philanthropic needs, and recommends, makes referrals to, or arranges for the provision of financial products, services, or other assistance by internal or external providers to meet those needs.

(*e*) with respect to the enhanced review of high value accounts described in paragraphs (*a*) to (*d*),

(i) if none of the indicia listed in paragraph (2)(*b*) are discovered in the enhanced review and the account is not identified as being held by a reportable person in paragraph (*d*), then further action is not required until there is a change in circumstances that results in one or more indicia being associated with the account,

(ii) if any of the indicia listed in subparagraphs (2)(*b*)(i) through (v) are discovered in the enhanced review, or if there is a subsequent change in circumstances that results in one or more indicia being associated with the account, then the reporting financial institution must treat the account as a reportable account with respect to each reportable jurisdiction for which an indicium is identified unless one of the exceptions in paragraph (2)(*f*) applies with respect to that account, and

(iii) if a hold mail instruction or in-care-of address is discovered in the enhanced review and no other address or other indicia listed in subparagraphs (2)(*b*)(i) to (v) are identified for the account holder, then the reporting financial institution must

(A) obtain from the account holder a self-certification or documentary evidence to establish the residence for tax purposes of the account holder, and

(B) if the reporting financial institution cannot obtain a self-certification or documentary evidence, report the account as an undocumented account;

Editorial Note: It is important to note that an *indicium* discovered in one review procedure, such as the paper record search or the relationship manager inquiry, cannot be used to cure an *indicium* identified in another review procedure, such as the electronic record search. For example, a current residence address in a reportable jurisdiction within the knowledge of the relationship manager cannot be used to cure a different residence address currently on file with the reporting financial institution discovered in the paper record search.

(*f*) if a preexisting individual account is not a high value account on June 30, 2017, but becomes a high value account as of the last day of a subsequent calendar year,

(i) the reporting financial institution must complete the enhanced review procedures described in this subsection with respect to the account within the calendar year following the year in which the account becomes a high value account, and

(ii) if the account is identified as a reportable account based on the review in subparagraph (i), the reporting financial institution must report the required information about the account with respect to the year in which it is identified as a reportable account (and subsequent years on an annual basis, unless the account holder ceases to be a reportable person);

(*g*) if a reporting financial institution applies the enhanced review procedures described in this subsection to a high value account in a year, then the reporting financial institution is not required to reapply those procedures — other than the relationship manager inquiry described in paragraph (*d*) — to the same high value account in any subsequent year unless the account is undocumented, in which case the reporting financial institution must reapply them annually until the account ceases to be undocumented;

(*h*) if there is a change of circumstances with respect to a high value account that results in one or more indicia described in paragraph (2)(*b*) being associated with the account, then the reporting financial institution must treat the account as a reportable account with respect to each reportable jurisdiction for which an indicium is identified unless one of the exceptions in paragraph (2)(*f*) applies with respect to that account; and

(*i*) a reporting financial institution must implement procedures to ensure that a relationship manager identifies any change in circumstances of an account.

Editorial Note: Subsection 273(3) contains the review procedures that apply to high-value accounts. These are the electronic record search that also applies to lower value accounts, plus a paper record search and relationship manager inquiry.

History: S. 273(3) was added by S.C. 2016, c. 12, s. 71(1), in force on July 1, 2017.

Related Sections: 270(1) "excluded account".

► 273(4) ◄

(4) Timing of review. Each preexisting individual account must be reviewed in accordance with subsection (2) or (3) before

(*a*) 2019, if the account is a high value account; or

(*b*) 2020, if the account is a lower value account.

History: S. 273(4) was added by S.C. 2016, c. 12, s. 71(1), in force on July 1, 2017.

▶ 273(5) ◀

(5) Reportable preexisting individual accounts. Any preexisting individual account that has been identified as a reportable account under this section must be treated as a reportable account in all subsequent years, unless the account holder ceases to be a reportable person.

History: S. 273(5) was added by S.C. 2016, c. 12, s. 71(1), in force on July 1, 2017.

Editorial Note: This section contains the due diligence procedures which must be applied to preexisting individual accounts in order to identify those accounts that must be reported. The procedures are different for lower-value accounts and high-value accounts, with an enhanced level of due diligence procedures provided for the latter. The reason for this enhanced review is that there is a much greater risk of tax evasion with high value accounts.

SECTION 274: [Due diligence — new individual accounts]

▶ 274(1) ◀

(1) Due diligence - new individual accounts. Upon opening a new individual account, the reporting financial institution must obtain a self-certification (which may be a part of the account opening documentation) that allows the reporting financial institution to

(*a*) determine the account holder's residence for tax purposes; and

(*b*) confirm the reasonableness of the self-certification taking into account information obtained by the reporting financial institution in connection with the opening of the account, including any documentation collected in accordance with the AML/KYC procedures.

Editorial Note: No specific format is required for the required self-certification, which may be included as part of the account opening documentation.

History: S. 274(1) was added by S.C. 2016, c. 12, s. 71(1), in force on July 1, 2017.

▶ 274(2) ◀

(2) Determination of reportable account. If the self-certification for a new individual account establishes that the account holder is resident for tax purposes in a reportable jurisdiction, then

(*a*) the reporting financial institution must treat the account as a reportable account; and

(*b*) the self-certification must also include the account holder's TIN with respect to the reportable jurisdiction (subject to subsection 271(4)) and the account holder's date of birth.

History: S. 274(2) was added by S.C. 2016, c. 12, s. 71(1), in force on July 1, 2017.

Related Sections: 270(1) "excluded account".

▶ 274(3) ◀

(3) Requirement to obtain new self-certification. If there is a change in circumstances with respect to a new individual account that causes the reporting financial institution to know, or have reason to know, that the original self-certification is incorrect or unreliable, then the reporting financial institution

(*a*) cannot rely on the original self-certification; and

(*b*) must obtain a valid self-certification that establishes the residence for tax purposes of the account holder.

Editorial Note: See editorial note to paragraph 273(2)(*d*) for what constitutes a change of circumstances.

History: S. 274(3) was added by S.C. 2016, c. 12, s. 71(1), in force on July 1, 2017.

Editorial Note: Section 274 sets out the due diligence procedures applicable to the opening of new accounts for individuals. They essentially require that a self-certification be obtained from the client and that the financial institution confirm that it is reasonable.

SECTION 275: [Due diligence — preexisting entity accounts]

▶ 275(1) ◀

(1) Due diligence — preexisting entity accounts. Unless the reporting financial institution elects otherwise — either with respect to all preexisting entity accounts or, separately, with respect to any clearly identified group of those accounts — a preexisting entity account with an aggregate account balance or value that does not exceed 250,000 USD on June 30, 2017 is not required to be reviewed, identified or reported as a reportable account until the aggregate account balance or value exceeds 250,000 USD on the last day of any subsequent calendar year.

History: S. 275(1) was added by S.C. 2016, c. 12, s. 71(1), in force on July 1, 2017.

Related Sections: 277(3) Aggregation rules.

▶ 275(2) ◀

(2) Application of subsection (4). The review procedures set forth in subsection (4) apply to a preexisting entity account if it has an aggregate account balance or value that exceeds 250,000 USD on

(*a*) June 30, 2017; or

(*b*) the last day of any subsequent calendar year.

History: S. 275(2) was added by S.C. 2016, c. 12, s. 71(1), in force on July 1, 2017.

▶ 275(3) ◀

(3) Determination of reportable accounts. With respect to preexisting entity accounts described in subsection (2), the only accounts that shall be treated as reportable accounts are accounts that are held by

(*a*) one or more entities that are reportable persons; or

(*b*) passive NFEs with one or more controlling persons who are reportable persons.

History: S. 275(3) was added by S.C. 2016, c. 12, s. 71(1), in force on July 1, 2017.

Related Sections: 270(1) "passive NFE"; 270(1) "controlling person"; 270(1) "excluded account".

▶ 275(4) ◀

(4) Review procedures — preexisting entity account. If this subsection applies to a preexisting entity account, a reporting financial institution must apply the following review procedures to determine whether the account is held by one or more reportable persons or by passive NFEs with one or more controlling persons who are reportable persons:

(*a*) review information maintained for regulatory or customer relationship purposes (including information collected in accordance with AML/KYC procedures) to determine whether the information indicates that the account holder is resident in a reportable jurisdiction and, if so, the reporting financial institution must treat the account as a reportable account unless it

(i) obtains a self-certification from the account holder to establish that the account holder is not a reportable person, or

(ii) reasonably determines, based on information in its possession or that is publicly available, that the account holder is not a reportable person; and

(*b*) with respect to an account holder of a preexisting account (including an entity that is a reportable person), the reporting financial institution must determine whether the account holder is a passive NFE with one or more controlling persons who are reportable persons and for the purposes of

(i) determining whether the account holder is a passive NFE, the reporting financial institution must obtain a self-certification from the account holder to establish its status, unless it has information in its possession or information is publicly available, based on which it can reasonably determine that the account holder is

(A) an active NFE, or

(B) a financial institution other than an entity described in paragraph (*b*) of the definition "investment entity" that is not a participating jurisdiction financial institution,

(ii) determining the controlling persons of an account holder, a reporting financial institution may rely on information collected and maintained in accordance with AML/KYC procedures, and

(iii) determining whether a controlling person of a passive NFE is a reportable person, a reporting financial institution may rely on

(A) information collected and maintained in accordance with AML/KYC procedures in the case of a preexisting entity account held by one or more NFEs with an aggregate account balance or value that does not exceed 1 million USD, or

(B) a self-certification from the account holder or the controlling person indicating the jurisdiction in which the controlling person is resident for tax purposes.

History: S. 275(4) was added by S.C. 2016, c. 12, s. 71(1), in force on July 1, 2017.

► 275(5) ◄

(5) Timing of review. Each preexisting entity account must be reviewed in accordance with subsection (4) before

(*a*) 2020, if the account has an aggregate account balance or value that exceeds 250,000 USD on June 30, 2017; or

(*b*) the end of the calendar year following the year in which the aggregate account balance or value exceeds 250,000 USD on December 31, if paragraph (*a*) does not apply.

History: S. 275(5) was added by S.C. 2016, c. 12, s. 71(1), in force on July 1, 2017.

► 275(6) ◄

(6) Change of circumstances. If there is a change of circumstances with respect to a preexisting entity account that causes the reporting financial institution to know, or have reason to know, that the self-certification or other documentation associated with the account is incorrect or unreliable, the reporting financial institution must redetermine the status of the account in accordance with subsection (4).

Editorial Note: See editorial note to paragraph 273(2)(*c*) for what constitutes a change of circumstances.

History: S. 275(6) was added by S.C. 2016, c. 12, s. 71(1), in force on July 1, 2017.

Editorial Note: Section 275 sets out the due diligence procedures that apply to preexisting entity accounts. Subsections 275(1)–(3) and (6) set out the accounts subject to review, while subsection 275(4) sets out the procedures to be followed and subsection 275(5) sets out the timing.

SECTION 276: Due diligence for new entity accounts

For new entity accounts, a reporting financial institution must apply the following review procedures to determine whether the account is held by one or more reportable persons or by passive NFEs with one or more controlling persons who are reportable persons:

(*a*) the reporting financial institution must

(i) obtain a self-certification (which may be part of the account opening documentation) that allows the reporting financial institution to determine the account holder's residence for tax purposes and confirm the reasonableness of the self-certification based on the information obtained by the reporting financial institution in connection with the opening of the account, including any documentation collected in accordance with AML/KYC procedures, and

(ii) if the self-certification referred to in subparagraph (i) indicates that the account holder is resident in a reportable jurisdiction, treat the account as a reportable account unless it reasonably determines, based on information in its possession or information that is publicly available, that the account holder is not a reportable person with respect to the reportable jurisdiction; and

(*b*) with respect to an account holder of a new entity account (including an entity that is a reportable person), the reporting financial institution must determine whether the account holder is a passive NFE with one or more controlling persons who are reportable persons and, if so, treat the account as a reportable account and, for the purposes of

(i) determining whether the account holder is a passive NFE, the reporting financial institution must obtain a self-certification from the account holder to establish its status, unless it has information in its possession or information is publicly available, based on which it can reasonably determine that the account holder is

(A) an active NFE, or

(B) a financial institution other than an entity that

(I) is an "investment entity" because of paragraph (*b*) of that definition, and

(II) is not a participating jurisdiction financial institution,

(ii) determining the controlling persons of an account holder, a reporting financial institution may rely on information collected and maintained in accordance with AML/KYC procedures, and

(iii) determining whether a controlling person of a passive NFE is a reportable person, a reporting financial institution may rely on a self-certification from the account holder or the controlling person.

Editorial Note: See editorial note to paragraph 273(2)(*c*) for what constitutes a change of circumstances.

History: S. 276 was added by S.C. 2016, c. 12, s. 71(1), in force on July 1, 2017.

SECTION 277: [Special due diligence rules]

► 277(1) ◄

(1) Special due diligence rules. A reporting financial institution may not rely on a self-certification or documentary evidence if the reporting financial institution knows or has reason to know that the self-certification or documentary evidence is incorrect or unreliable.

History: S. 277(1) was added by S.C. 2016, c. 12, s. 71(1), in force on July 1, 2017.

► 277(2) ◄

(2) Exception — individual beneficiary receiving death benefit. A reporting financial institution may presume that an individual beneficiary (other than the owner) of a cash value insurance contract or an annuity contract receiving a death benefit is not a reportable person and may treat the financial account as other than a reportable account unless it has actual knowledge, or reason to know, that the beneficiary is a reportable person.

History: S. 277(2) was added by S.C. 2016, c. 12, s. 71(1), in force on July 1, 2017.

► 277(3) ◄

(3) Aggregation rules. For the purposes of

(*a*) determining the aggregate balance or value of financial accounts held by an individual or entity,

(i) a reporting financial institution is required to aggregate all financial accounts maintained by the reporting financial institution, or by a related entity, but only to the extent that the reporting financial institution's computerized systems

(A) link the financial accounts by reference to a data element such as a client number or TIN, and

(B) allow account balances or values to be aggregated, and

(ii) each holder of a jointly held financial account shall be attributed the entire balance or value of the jointly held financial account; and

(*b*) determining the aggregate balance or value of financial accounts held by an individual in order to determine whether a financial account is a high value account, a reporting financial institution is also required — in the case of any financial accounts that a relationship manager knows, or has reason to know, are directly or indirectly owned, controlled or established (other than in a fiduciary capacity) by the same individual — to aggregate all such accounts.

Editorial Note: The dollar thresholds for the various due diligence procedures all refer to aggregated account balances. Subsection 277(3) provides the rules to be used for arriving at this number.

History: S. 277(3) was added by S.C. 2016, c. 12, s. 71(1), in force on July 1, 2017.

► 277(4) ◄

(4) Dealer accounts. Subsection (5)

(*a*) applies to a reporting financial institution in respect of a client name account maintained by the institution if

(i) property recorded in the account is also recorded in a financial account (in this subsection and subsection (5) referred to as the *related account*) maintained by a financial institution (in this subsection and subsection (5) referred to as the "dealer") that is authorized under provincial legislation

(A) to engage in the business of dealing in securities or any other financial instrument, or

(B) to provide portfolio management or investment advising services, and

(ii) the dealer has advised the institution whether the related account is a reportable account; and

(*b*) does not apply, despite paragraph (*a*), if it can reasonably be concluded by the institution that the dealer has failed to comply with its obligations under this Part.

Editorial Note: See editorial note to subsection 277(5).

History: S. 277(4) was added by S.C. 2016, c. 12, s. 71(1), in force on July 1, 2017.

► 277(5) ◄

(5) Dealer accounts. If this subsection applies to a reporting financial institution in respect of a client name account,

(*a*) sections 272 to 276 do not apply to the institution in respect of the account; and

(*b*) the institution shall rely on the determination of the dealer in respect of the related account in determining whether the account is a reportable account.

Editorial Note: Subsections 277(4) and (5) provide equivalent rules for "client name accounts" held by both a financial institution and a dealer to the rules for FATCA that are found in subsections 265(7) and (8). The rules essentially provide that a financial institution can rely on the determination made by the dealer as to whether or not client name accounts are reportable accounts, unless it can "reasonably conclude" that the dealer has failed to comply with its due diligence obligations.

History: S. 277(5) was added by S.C. 2016, c. 12, s. 71(1), in force on July 1, 2017.

► 277(6) ◄

(6) Group insurance and annuities. A reporting financial institution may treat a financial account that is a member's interest in a group cash value insurance contract or group annuity contract as a financial account that is not a reportable account until the day on which an amount becomes payable to the employee, certificate holder or beneficiary, if the financial account meets the following requirements:

(*a*) the group cash value insurance contract or group annuity contract is issued to an employer and covers 25 or more employees or certificate holders;

(*b*) the employees or certificate holders are entitled to

(i) receive any contract value related to their interest, and

(ii) name beneficiaries for the benefit payable upon the employee's or certificate holder's death; and (*c*) the aggregate amount payable to any employee or certificate holder or beneficiary does not exceed 1 million USD.

Editorial Note: Subsection 277(6) provides an alternative procedure that applies to certain group insurance contracts and group annuity contracts.

History: S. 277(6) was added by S.C. 2016, c. 12, s. 71(1), in force on July 1, 2017.

Editorial Note: The rules in this section apply to all types of accounts.

SECTION 278: [Reporting]

► 278(1) ◄

(1) Reporting. Every reporting financial institution shall file with the Minister, before May 2 of each calendar year, an information return in prescribed form relating to each reportable account maintained by the institution at any time during the immediately preceding calendar year and after June 30, 2017.

Editorial Note: Subsection 278(1) provides the reporting deadline.

History: S. 278(1) was added by S.C. 2016, c. 12, s. 71(1), in force on July 1, 2017.

► 278(2) ◄

(2) Electronic filing. The information return required under subsection (1) shall be filed by way of electronic filing.

Editorial Note: The OECD has developed an xml schema to be used for electronic filing.

History: S. 278(2) was added by S.C. 2016, c. 12, s. 71(1), in force on July 1, 2017.

SECTION 279: [Record keeping]

► 279(1) ◄

(1) Record keeping. Every reporting financial institution shall keep, at the institution's place of business or at such other place as may be designated by the Minister, records that the institution obtains or creates for the purpose of complying with this Part, including self-certifications and records of documentary evidence.

History: S. 279(1) was added by S.C. 2016, c. 12, s. 71(1), in force on July 1, 2017.

► 279(2) ◄

(2) Form of records. Every reporting financial institution required by this Part to keep records that does so electronically shall retain them in an electronically readable format for the retention period referred to in subsection (3).

History: S. 279(2) was added by S.C. 2016, c. 12, s. 71(1), in force on July 1, 2017.

► 279(3) ◄

(3) Retention of records. Every reporting financial institution that is required to keep, obtain or create records under this Part shall retain those records for a period of at least six years following

(*a*) in the case of a self-certification, the last day on which a related financial account is open; and

(*b*) in any other case, the end of the last calendar year in respect of which the record is relevant.

History: S. 279(3) was added by S.C. 2016, c. 12, s. 71(1), in force on July 1, 2017.

SECTION 280: Anti-avoidance

If a person enters into an arrangement or engages in a practice, the primary purpose of which can reasonably be considered to be to avoid an obligation under this Part, the person is subject to the obligation as if the person had not entered into the arrangement or engaged in the practice.

History: S. 280 was added by S.C. 2016, c. 12, s. 71(1), in force on July 1, 2017.

SECTION 281: [Production of TIN]

► 281(1) ◄

(1) Production of TIN. Every reportable person shall provide their TIN at the request of a reporting financial institution that is required under this Part to make an information return requiring the TIN.

History: S. 281(1) was added by S.C. 2016, c. 12, s. 71(1), in force on July 1, 2017.

Related Sections: 271(3) TIN and date of birth; 271(4) Exceptions.

► 281(2) ◄

(2) Confidentiality of TIN. A person required to make an information return referred to in subsection (1) shall not knowingly use, communicate or allow to be communicated, otherwise than as required or authorized under this Act or a regulation, the TIN without the written consent of the reportable person.

History: S. 281(2) was added by S.C. 2016, c. 12, s. 71(1), in force on July 1, 2017.

► 281(3) ◄

(3) Penalty for failure to provide TIN. Every reportable person who fails to provide on request their TIN to a reporting financial institution that is required under this Part to make an information return requiring the TIN is liable to a penalty of $500 for each such failure, unless

(*a*) an application for the assignment of the TIN is made to the relevant reportable jurisdiction not later than 90 days after the request was made and the TIN is provided to the reporting financial institution that requested it within 15 days after the reportable person received it; or

(*b*) the reportable person is not eligible to obtain a TIN from the relevant reportable jurisdiction (including because the relevant reportable jurisdiction does not issue TINs).

History: S. 281(3) was added by S.C. 2016, c. 12, s. 71(1), in force on July 1, 2017.

► 281(4) ◄

(4) Assessment. The Minister may at any time assess any amount payable under subsection (3) by any person and, if the Minister sends a notice of assessment to the person, sections 150 to 163, subsections 164(1) and (1.4) to (7), sections 165 to 167 and Division J of Part I apply with such modifications as the circumstances require.

Editorial Note: Note that since subsections 164(1.1)–(1.3) are excluded from this provision, reportable persons will not be entitled to any repayment of a penalty in dispute by filing an objection.

History: S. 281(4) was added by S.C. 2016, c. 12, s. 71(1), in force on July 1, 2017.

Schedule
Listed Corporations

Schedule: ***(Subsection 181(1))***

Ally Credit Canada Limited/Ally Crédit Canada Limitée

AmeriCredit Financial Services of Canada Ltd.

AVCO Financial Services Quebec Limited

Bombardier Capital Ltd.

Canaccord Capital Credit Corporation/Corporation de crédit Canaccord capital

Canaccord Financial Holdings Inc./Corporation financière Canaccord Inc.

Canadian Cooperative Agricultural Financial Services

Canadian Home Income Plan Corporation

Citibank Canada Investment Funds Limited

Citicapital Commercial Corporation/Citicapital Corporation Commerciale

Citi Cards Canada Inc./Cartes Citi Canada Inc.

Citi Commerce Solutions of Canada Ltd.

CitiFinancial Canada East Corporation/CitiFinancière, corporation du Canada Est

CitiFinancial Canada, Inc./CitiFinancière Canada, Inc.

Citigroup Finance Canada Inc.

Crédit Industriel Desjardins

CU Credit Inc.

Ford Credit Canada Limited

GMAC Residential Funding of Canada, Limited

Household Commercial Canada Inc.

Household Finance Corporation Limited

Household Finance Corporation of Canada

Household Realty Corporation Limited

Hudson's Bay Company Acceptance Limited

John Deere Credit Inc./Crédit John Deere Inc.

Merchant Retail Services Limited

PACCAR Financial Ltd./Compagnie Financière Paccar Ltée

Paradigm Fund Inc./Le Fonds Paradigm Inc.

Prêts étudiants Atlantique Inc./Atlantic Student Loans Inc.

Principal Fund Incorporated

RT Mortgage-Backed Securities Limited

RT Mortgage-Backed Securities II Limited

State Farm Finance Corporation of Canada/Corporation de Crédit State Farm du Canada

Trans Canada Credit Corporation

Trans Canada Retail Services Company/Société de services de détails trans Canada

Wells Fargo Financial Canada Corporation

History: The schedule was amended by S.C. 2013, c. 34, s. 366(5), by removing from the list, as of the dates set out below, the following corporations:

(*a*) GE Card Services Canada Inc./GE Services Cartes du Canada Inc., January 1, 2003;

(*b*) 2419726 Canada Inc., March 31, 2002;

(*c*) CitiFinancial Mortgage Corporation/CitiFinancière, corporation de prêts hypothécaires, March 31, 2002; and

(*d*) CitiFinancial Mortgage East Corporation/CitiFinancière, corporation de prêts hypothécaires de l'Est, April 1, 2002.

The schedule was added by S.C. 2013, c. 34, s. 366(1), deemed to have come into force on December 20, 2002. In addition, it is deemed to have come into force so as to, as of the dates set out below, list each of the following corporations in the schedule:

(*a*) 2419726 Canada Inc., January 1, 1998, except that, in its application

(i) after May 1999 and before April 2002, the reference in the schedule to that corporation is to be read as a reference to "CitiFinancial Canada, Inc./CitiFinancière Canada, Inc.", and

(ii) after 1997 and before June 1999, the reference in the schedule to that corporation is to be read as a reference to "Commercial Credit Corporation CCC Limited/Corporation De Credit Commerciale CCC Limitee";

(*b*) Ally Credit Canada Limited/Ally Crédit Canada Limitée, January 1, 1991, except that, in its application after 1990 and before August 23, 2010, the reference in the schedule to that corporation is to be read as a reference to "General Motors Acceptance Corporation of Canada Limited";

(*c*) AmeriCredit Financial Services of Canada Ltd., June 30, 2001;

(*d*) Canaccord Capital Credit Corporation/Corporation de crédit Canaccord capital, September 25, 2000;

(*e*) Canaccord Financial Holdings Inc./Corporation financière Canaccord Inc., January 1, 2004;

(*f*) Citibank Canada Investment Funds Limited, December 31, 2001;

(*g*) Citicapital Commercial Corporation/Citicapital Corporation Commerciale, January 1, 2000, except that, in its application after 1999 and before July 2001, the reference in the schedule to that corporation is to be read as a reference to "Associates Commercial Corporation of Canada Ltd./Les Associés, Corporation Commerciale du Canada Ltee";

(*h*) Citi Cards Canada Inc./Cartes Citi Canada Inc., September 25, 2003;

(*i*) Citi Commerce Solutions of Canada Ltd., January 1, 2003;

(*j*) CitiFinancial Canada East Company/CitiFinancière, corporation du Canada Est, December 23, 1997, except that, in its application

(i) after April 2001 and before April 2002, the reference in the schedule to that corporation is to be read as a reference to "CitiFinancial Services of Canada East Company/CitiFinancière, compagnie de services du Canada Est",

(ii) after September 26, 1999 and before May 2001, the reference in the schedule to that corporation is to be read as a reference to "Associates Financial Services of Canada East Company/Les Associés, Compagnie de Services Financiers du Canada Est",

(iii) after February 12, 1998 and before September 27, 1999, the reference in the schedule to that corporation is to be read as a reference to "Avco Financial Services Canada East Company/Compagnie Services Financiers Avco Canada Est",

(iv) after December 29, 1997 and before February 13, 1998, the reference in the schedule to that corporation is to be read as a reference to "Avco Financial Services Canada East Company/Services Financiers Avco Canada Est Compagnie", and

(v) after December 22, 1997 and before December 30, 1997, the reference in the schedule to that corporation is to be read as a reference to "Avco Financial Services Canada East Company";

(*k*) CitiFinancial Canada, Inc./CitiFinancière Canada, Inc., March 2, 1998, except that, in its application

(i) after April 2001 and before April 2002, the reference in the schedule to that corporation is to be read as a reference to "CitiFinancial Services of Canada, Ltd./CitiFinancière, services du Canada, Ltée", and

(ii) after March 1, 1998 and before May 2001, the reference in the schedule to that corporation is to be read as a reference to "Associates Financial Services of Canada Ltd./Les Associés, Services Financières du Canada Ltée";

(*l*) CitiFinancial Mortgage Corporation/CitiFinancière, corporation de prêts hypothécaires, March 2, 1998, except that, in its application after March 1, 1998 and before May 2001, the reference in the schedule to that corporation is to be read as a reference to "Associates Mortgage Corporation/Les Associés, Corporation de Prêts Hypothécaires";

(*m*) CitiFinancial Mortgage East Corporation/CitiFinancière, corporation de prêts hypothécaires de l'Est, December 23, 1997, except that, in its application

(i) after November 2, 1999 and before May 2001, the reference in the schedule to that corporation is to be read as a reference to "Associates Mortgage East Corporation/Les Associés, Corporation de Prêts Hypothécaires de l'Est",

(ii) after September 27, 1999 and before November 3, 1999, the reference in the schedule to that corporation is to be read as a reference to "Associates Mortgage East Corporation/Les Associés, Corporation de Financiers du Prêts Hypothécaires de l'Est",

(iii) after February 12, 1998 and before September 28, 1999, the reference in the schedule to that corporation is to be read as a reference to "Avco Financial Services Realty East Company/Compagnie Services Financiers Immobiliers Avco Est",

(iv) after December 29, 1997 and before February 13, 1998, the reference in the schedule to that corporation is to be read as a reference to "Avco Financial Services Realty East Company/Services Financiers Immobiliers Avco Est Compagnie", and

(v) after December 22, 1997 and before December 30, 1997, the reference in the schedule to that corporation is to be read as a reference to "Avco Financial Services Realty East Company";

(*n*) Citigroup Finance Canada Inc., January 1, 1998, except that, in its application after 1997 and before June 11, 2003, the reference in the schedule to that corporation is to be read as a reference to "Associates Capital Corporation of Canada/Corporation de capital associés du Canada";

(*o*) Ford Credit Canada Limited, December 23, 1997;

(*p*) GE Card Services Canada Inc./GE Services de Cartes du Canada Inc., August 2, 2000;

(*q*) GMAC Residential Funding of Canada, Limited, January 1, 2003;

(*r*) John Deere Credit Inc./Crédit John Deere Inc., January 1, 1999;

(*s*) PACCAR Financial Ltd./Compagnie Financière Paccar Ltée, January 1, 2003;

(*t*) Paradigm Fund Inc./Le Fonds Paradigm Inc., January 1, 2002;

(*u*) Prêts étudiants Atlantique Inc./Atlantic Student Loans Inc., January 1, 1998, except that, in its application after 1997 and before June 13, 2002, the reference in the schedule to that corporation is to be read as a reference to "Prêts étudiants Acadie Inc./Acadia Student Loans Inc.";

(*v*) State Farm Finance Corporation of Canada/ Corporation de Crédit State Farm du Canada, January 1, 2002, except that, in its application after 2001 and before May 2002, the reference in the schedule to that corporation is to be read as a reference to "VNB Financial Services Inc./Services financiers VNB, Inc.";

(*w*) Trans Canada Retail Services Company/Société de services de détails trans Canada, January 1, 1999, except that, in its application after 1998 and before January 15, 2002, the reference in the schedule to that corporation is to be read as a reference to "National Retail Credit Services Company/Société de services de crédit aux détaillants national"; and

(*x*) Wells Fargo Financial Canada Corporation, January 1, 1999, except that, in its application after 1998 and before September 7, 2001, the reference in the schedule to that corporation is to be read as a reference to "Norwest Financial Canada Company".

In addition, Ford Credit Canada Limited is deemed to have been, from July 1, 1989 to December 22, 1997, prescribed by a regulation made under paragraph 181(1)(*g*).

Income Tax Application Rules

R.S.C. 1985 (5th Supp.), c. 2,

[The Income Tax Application Rules enacted as R.S.C. 1985, c. 2, (5th Supp.) deal with the coming into force of the revised Income Tax Act. The Income Tax Act Application Rules set forth special transitional rules, as well as special rules that apply in the case of certain taxpayers having taxation years not coinciding with calendar years.]

Short Title

7. Short title

This Act may be cited as the *Income Tax Application Rules*.

Part I

Income Tax Application Rules, 1971

Interpretation

8. Definitions

In this Act,

"amended Act" —"amended Act" means, according to the context in which that expression appears,

(*a*) the *Income Tax Act*, chapter 148 of the Revised Statutes of Canada, 1952, as amended by section 1 of chapter 63 of the Statutes of Canada, 1970-71-72, and by any subsequent Act, and

(*b*) the *Income Tax Act*, as amended from time to time;

"former Act" —"former Act" means the *Income Tax Act*, chapter 148 of the Revised Statutes of Canada, 1952, as it was before being amended by section 1 of chapter 63 of the Statutes of Canada, 1970-71-72.

Application of 1970-71-72, c. 63, s. 1

9. Application of 1970-71-72, c. 63, s. 1

Subject to the amended Act and this Act, section 1 of chapter 63 of the Statutes of Canada, 1970-71-72, applies to the 1972 and subsequent taxation years.

9.1. Application of Part VIII of amended Act (Repealed by 1977-78, c. 1, s. 102(1).)

Application of Part XIII of Amended Act

10. Application of Part XIII of Amended Act

(1) (Repealed by 1985, c. 45, s. 127.)

► 10(2) ◄

(2) Idem — (Repealed by 1985, c. 45, s. 127.)

► 10(3) ◄

(3) Idem — (Repealed by 1985, c. 45, s. 127.)

► 10(4) ◄

(4) Application of Part XIII of Amended Act. Where an amount is paid or credited by a person resident in Canada to a non-resident person

(*a*) who is resident in a prescribed country, and

(*b*) with whom the person resident in Canada was dealing at arm's length,

as, on account of, in lieu of payment of or in satisfaction of, interest payable on any bond, debenture, mortgage, note or similar obligation issued before 1976 by the person resident in Canada to the non-resident person, for the purposes of computing the tax under Part XIII of the amended Act payable by the non-resident person on the amount, the reference in subsection 212(1) of that Act to "25%" shall be read as a reference to "15%".

Related Regulations: Part XVI.

Information Circulars: IC 77-16R4 Non-resident income tax.

► 10(5) ◄

(5) Certificates of exemption — (Repealed by S.C. 2007, c. 35, s. 69(1).)

History: S. 10(5) was repealed by S.C. 2007, c. 35, s. 69(1), appliable after 2007. S. 10(5) formerly read:

(5) *Certificates of exemption.* Any certificate of exemption issued by the Minister under subsection 106(9) of the former Act that was in force on December 31, 1971 shall, for the purposes of subparagraph 212(1)(*b*)(iv) of the amended Act,

(*a*) be deemed to have been issued under subsection 212(14) of the amended Act; and

(*b*) be deemed

(i) in respect of interest payable on any bond, debenture or similar obligation acquired on or before December 31, 1971 by the person to whom the certificate was issued, to have been in force on January 1, 1972 and thereafter without interruption,

except that if the person to whom the certificate was issued ceased at any time after 1971 to be exempt, under the laws of the country of which the person is a resident, from the payment of income tax to the government of that country, the certificate ceases to be in force

(iii) in respect of interest described in subparagraph (i), on the day on which the person first so ceased to be exempt.

► 10(6) ◄

(6) Limitation on non-resident's tax rate. Notwithstanding any provision of the amended Act, where an agreement or convention between the Government of Canada and the government of any other country that has the force of law in Canada provides that where an amount is paid or credited, or deemed to be paid or credited, to a resident of that other country the rate of tax imposed thereon shall not exceed a specified rate,

(*a*) any reference in Part XIII of the amended Act to a rate in excess of the specified rate shall, in respect of such an amount, be read as a reference to the specified rate; and (*b*) except where the amount can reasonably be attributed to a business carried on by that person in Canada, that person shall, for the purpose of the agreement or convention in respect of the amount, be deemed not to have a permanent establishment in Canada.

11. Application of Part XIV of amended Act

(1) (Repealed by 1985, c. 45, s. 128(1).)

▶ 11(2) ◀

(2) Idem — (Repealed by 1985, c. 45, s. 128(1).)

▶ 11(3) ◀

(3) Idem — (Repealed by 1985, c. 45, s. 128(1).)

▶ 11(4) ◀

(4) Idem — (Repealed by 1985, c. 45, s. 128(2).)

References and Continuation of Provisions

12. Definitions

In this section and sections 13 to 18,

"enactment" —"enactment" has the meaning assigned by section 2 of the *Interpretation Act*;

"old law" —"old law" means the *Income War Tax Act, The 1948 Income Tax Act*, and the *Income Tax Act*, chapter 148 of the Revised Statutes of Canada, 1952, as amended from time to time otherwise than by section 1 of chapter 63 of the Statutes of Canada, 1970-71-72, or any subsequent Act;

"The 1948 Income Tax Act" —"The 1948 Income Tax Act" means *The Income Tax Act*, chapter 52 of the Statutes of Canada, 1948, together with all Acts passed in amendment thereof.

13. References relating to same subject-matter

(1) Subject to this Act and unless the context otherwise requires, a reference in any enactment to a particular Part or provision of the amended Act shall be construed, as regards any transaction, matter or thing to which the old law applied, to include a reference to the Part or provision, if any, of the old law relating to, or that may reasonably be regarded as relating to, the same subject-matter.

Related Sections: ITAR 11(4).

14. Part IV of former Act

Part IV of the former Act is continued in force but does not apply in respect of gifts made after 1971.

15. Part VIII of former Act

Part VIII of the former Act is continued in force but as though the references in that Part that, according to the context in which they appear, are references to or to provisions of the *Income Tax Act* were read as references to or to provisions of the *Income Tax Act*, chapter 148 of the Revised Statutes of Canada, 1952, as amended from time to time otherwise than by section 1 of chapter 63 of the Statutes of Canada, 1970-71-72, or any subsequent Act.

16. Construction of certain references

In any enactment, a reference by number to any provision of the *Income Tax Act* that, according to the context in which the reference appears, is a reference to

(*a*) a provision of Part IV of the former Act,

(*b*) a provision of Part VIII of the former Act, or

(*c*) a provision of the amended Act having the same number as a provision described in paragraph (*a*) or (*b*),

shall, for greater certainty, be read as reference to the provision described in paragraph (*a*), (*b*) or (*c*), as the case may be, and not to any other provision of the *Income Tax Act*, or the *Income Tax Act*, chapter 148 of the Revised Statutes of Canada, 1952, having the same number.

17. Income War Tax Act, s. 8

(1) A taxpayer may deduct from the tax otherwise payable under Part I of the amended Act for a taxation year such amount as would, if the *Income War Tax Act* applied to the taxation year, be deductible from tax because of subsections 8(6), (7) and (7A) of the *Income War Tax Act*.

▶ 17(2) ◀

(2) S.C. 1947, c. 63, s. 16. There may be deducted in computing income for a taxation year under Part I of the amended Act an amount that would be deductible under section 16 of chapter 63 of the Statutes of Canada, 1947, from income as defined by the *Income War Tax Act* if that Act applied to the taxation year.

▶ 17(3) ◀

(3) Idem. There may be deducted from the tax for a taxation year otherwise payable under Part I of the amended Act an amount that would be deductible under section 16 of chapter 63 of the Statutes of Canada, 1947, from the total of taxes payable under the *Income War Tax Act* and *The Excess Profits Tax Act, 1940*, if those Acts applied to the taxation year.

▶ 17(4) ◀

(4) Retrospection. Where there is a reference in the amended Act to any act, matter or thing done or existing before a taxation year, it shall be deemed to include a reference to the act, matter or thing, even though it was done or existing before the commencement of that Act.

▶ 17(5) ◀

(5) Amount not previously included as income. Where, on the application of a method adopted by a taxpayer for computing income from a business, other than a business that is a profession, or farm or property for a taxation year to which the amended Act applies, an amount received in the year would not be included in computing the taxpayer's income for the year because on the application of that method it would have been included in computing the taxpayer's income for the purposes of the *Income Tax Act* or the *Income Tax Act*, chapter 148 of the Revised Statutes of Canada, 1952, for a preceding taxation year in respect of which it was receivable, if the amount was not included in computing the income for the preceding year, it shall be included in computing the income for the year in which it was received.

▶ 17(6) ◀

(6) S.C. 1949 (2nd S.), c. 25, s. 53. There may be deducted in computing income for a taxation year under Part I of the amended Act an amount that would be deductible under section 53 of chapter 25 of the Statutes of Canada, 1949 (Second Session), in computing income under *The 1948 Income Tax Act* if that Act applied to the taxation year.

► 17(7) ◄

(7) Idem. There may be deducted from the tax for a taxation year otherwise payable under Part I of the amended Act an amount that would be deductible under section 53 of chapter 25 of the Statutes of Canada, 1949 (Second Session), from the tax payable under Part I of *The 1948 Income Tax Act* if that Act applied to the taxation year.

► 17(8) ◄

(8) Registered pension plan. A reference in the amended Act to a registered pension plan shall, in respect of a period while the plan was an approved superannuation or pension fund or plan, be construed as a reference to that approved superannuation or pension fund or plan.

18. General depreciation provisions

(1) Where the capital cost to a taxpayer of any depreciable property that was acquired by the taxpayer before 1972 was required by any provision of the old law to be determined for the purpose of computing the amount of any deduction under any such provision in respect of that property, or would have been required by any provision of the old law to be determined for that purpose if any deduction under any such provision had been claimed by the taxpayer in respect of that property, the amount of the capital cost so required to be determined or that would have been so required to be determined, as the case may be, shall be deemed, for all purposes of the amended Act, to be the capital cost to the taxpayer of that property.

► 18(2) ◄

(2) Idem. Where a taxpayer acquired depreciable property before the beginning of the 1949 taxation year, for the purposes of section 13 of the amended Act and any regulations made under paragraph 20(1)(*a*) of that Act an amount equal to the total of

(*a*) all deductions allowed in computing the taxpayer's income for the purpose of the *Income War Tax Act* as "special depreciation", "extra depreciation" or allowances in lieu of depreciation for property the taxpayer had at the beginning of the 1949 taxation year (except deductions allowed under subparagraph 6(1)(*n*)(ii) of that Act), and

(*b*) 1/2 of all amounts allowed to the taxpayer under subparagraph 6(1)(*n*)(ii) of that Act for property that the taxpayer had at the beginning of the 1949 taxation year,

shall be deemed to have been allowed to the taxpayer under regulations made under paragraph 20(1)(*a*) of the amended Act in computing income for a taxation year before the 1949 taxation year.

► 18(3) ◄

(3) Provisoes not applicable. The second and third provisoes to paragraph 6(1)(*n*) of the *Income War Tax Act* do not apply with respect to sales made after the beginning of the 1949 taxation year.

► 18(4) ◄

(4) Reference to depreciation. Reference in this section to depreciation shall be deemed to include a reference to allowances in respect of depreciable property of a taxpayer made under paragraph 5(1)(*a*) of the *Income War Tax Act*.

► 18(5) ◄

(5) Deduction deemed depreciation. An amount deducted under paragraph 5(1)(*u*) of the *Income War Tax Act* in respect of amounts of a capital nature shall, for the purpose of this section, be deemed to be depreciation taken into account in ascertaining the taxpayer's income for the purpose of that Act or in ascertaining the taxpayer's loss for the taxation year for which it was deducted.

ITARs

Special Transitional Rules

19. Income maintenance payments

(1) Notwithstanding section 9, paragraph 6(1)(*f*) of the amended Act does not apply in respect of amounts received by a taxpayer in a taxation year that were payable to the taxpayer in respect of the loss, in consequence of an event occurring before 1974, of all or any part of the taxpayers income from an office or employment, under a plan, described in that paragraph, that was established before June 19, 1971.

Interpretation Bulletins: *Secondary* — IT-85R2 Health and welfare trusts for employees; IT-428 Wage loss replacement plans.

► 19(2) ◄

(2) Effect of certain changes made in plan established before June 19, 1971. For the purposes of this section, a plan described in paragraph 6(1)(*f*) of the amended Act that was in existence before June 19, 1971 does not cease to be a plan established before that date solely because of changes made therein on or after that date for the purpose of ensuring that the plan qualifies as one entitling the employer of persons covered under the plan to a reduction, as provided for by subsection 50(2) of the *Unemployment Insurance Act*, in the amount of the employer's premium payable under that Act in respect of insured persons covered under the plan.

20. Depreciable property

► 20(1) ◄

(1) Depreciable property. If the capital cost to a taxpayer of any depreciable property (other than a property that was, at any time, "eligible capital property" as defined in the amended Act at that time) acquired by the taxpayer before 1972 and owned by the taxpayer without interruption from December 31, 1971 until such time after 1971 as the taxpayer disposed of it is less than the fair market value of the property on valuation day and less than the proceeds of disposition thereof otherwise determined,

(*a*) for the purposes of section 13 of the amended Act, subdivision c of Division B of Part I of that Act and any regulations made under paragraph 20(1)(*a*) of that Act, the taxpayers proceeds of disposition of the property shall be deemed to be an amount equal to the total of its capital cost to the taxpayer and the amount, if any, by which the proceeds of disposition thereof otherwise determined exceed the fair market value of the property on valuation day, (*b*) where the property has, by one or more transactions or events (other than the death of a taxpayer to which subsection 70(5) of the amended Act applies) between persons not dealing at arms length, become vested in another taxpayer

(i) for the purposes of the amended Act (other than, where paragraph 13(7)(*e*) of that Act applies in determining the capital cost to that other taxpayer of the property, for the purposes of paragraphs 8(1)(*j*) and (*p*) and sections 13 and 20 of that Act), that other taxpayer shall be deemed to have acquired the property at a capital cost equal to the proceeds deemed to have been received for the property by the person from whom that other taxpayer acquired the property, and

(ii) for the purposes of this subsection, that other taxpayer shall be deemed to have acquired the property before 1972 at a capital cost equal to the capital cost of the property to the taxpayer who actually owned the property at the end of 1971, and to have owned it without interruption from December 31, 1971 until such time after 1971 as that other taxpayer disposed of it, and

(*c*) where the disposition occurred because of an election under subsection 110.6(19) of the amended Act,

(i) for the purposes of that Act (other than paragraphs 8(1)(*j*) and (*p*) and sections 13 and 20 of that Act), the taxpayer is deemed to have reacquired the property at a capital cost equal to

(A) where the amount designated in respect of the property in the election did not exceed 110% of the fair market value of the property at the end of February 22, 1994, the taxpayer's proceeds of disposition determined under paragraph (*a*) in respect of the disposition of the property that immediately preceded the reacquisition minus the amount, if any, by which the amount designated in respect of the property in the election exceeded that fair market value, and

(B) in any other case, the amount otherwise determined under subsection 110.6(19) of that Act to be the cost to the taxpayer of the property immediately after the reacquisition referred to in that subsection minus the amount by which the fair market value of the property on valuation day exceeded the capital cost of the property at the time it was last acquired before 1972, and

(ii) for the purposes of this subsection, the taxpayer's capital cost of the property after the reacquisition shall be deemed to be equal to the taxpayer's capital cost of the property before the reacquisition and the taxpayer shall be considered to have owned the property without interruption from December 31, 1971 until such time after February 22, 1994 as the taxpayer disposes of it.

History: S. 20(1), the portion before paragraph (*a*) was replaced by S.C. 2016, c. 12, s. 72(1), in force January 1, 2017, and formerly read:

(1) Where the capital cost to a taxpayer of any depreciable property acquired by the taxpayer before 1972 and owned by the taxpayer without interruption from December 31, 1971 until such time after 1971 as the taxpayer disposed of it is less than the fair market value of the property on valuation day and less than the proceeds of disposition thereof otherwise determined,

Interpretation Bulletins: *Secondary* — IT-209R Inter-vivos gifts of capital property to individuals directly or through trusts; IT-268R4 Inter vivos transfer of farm property to child; IT-349R3 Intergenerational transfers of farm property on death; IT-432R2 Benefits conferred on shareholders.

► 20(1.1) ◄

(1.1) Where depreciable property disposed of to spouse, trust or child. Subsection (1) does not apply in any case where

(*a*) subsection 70(6) or 73(1) of the amended Act applies in respect of the disposition by a taxpayer of any depreciable property of a prescribed class to the spouse, common-law partner, trust or transferee, as the case may be, referred to therein, and

(*b*) subsection 70(9) of the amended Act applies in respect of the disposition by a taxpayer of any depreciable property of a prescribed class to a child referred to therein,

except that where the spouse, common-law partner, trust, transferee or child, as the case may be, subsequently disposes of the property at any time, subsection (1) applies as if the spouse, common-law partner, trust, transferee or child, as the case may be, had acquired the property before 1972 and owned it without interruption from December 31, 1971 until that time.

History: Sec. 147(3), Chap. 12, S.C. 2000

(3) Where a taxpayer and a person have jointly elected pursuant to section 144 of this Act in respect of the 1998, 1999 or 2000 taxation years, subsection (1) applies to the taxpayer and the person in respect of the applicable taxation year and subsequent taxation years.

S. 20(1.11) was added by 1973-74, c. 14, s. 71(2).

S. 20(1.1) was amended by 1977-78 c. 32, S. 57(1), applicable in respect of dispositions of property by a taxpayer after 1977, by adding the word "transferee" wherever it occurs.

S. 20(1.1) was amended by 1973-74, c. 14, S. 71(2). S. 20(1.1) formerly read:

(1.1) Subsection (1) is not applicable in any case in which subsection 70(6) or 73(1) of the disposition by a taxpayer of any depreciable amended Act is applicable in respect of the property of a prescribed class to the spouse or trust, as the case may be, referred to therein, except that where the spouse or trust, as case may be, subsequently disposes of the property at any time, subsection (1) is applicable as if the spouse or trust, as the case may be, had acquired the property before 1972, and owned it without interruption from December 31, 1971 until that time.

Interpretation Bulletins: *Secondary* — IT-209R Inter-vivos gifts of capital property to individuals directly or through trusts; IT-349R3 Intergenerational transfers of farm property on death.

► 20(1.11) ◄

(1.11) Extended meaning of "child". For the purposes of subsection (1.1), "child" of a taxpayer includes

(*a*) a child of the taxpayer's child;

(*b*) a child of the taxpayer's child's child; and

(*c*) a person who, at any time before attaining the age of 21 years, was wholly dependent on the taxpayer for support and of whom the taxpayer had, at that time, in law or in fact, the custody and control.

► 20(1.2) ◄

(1.2) Other transfers of depreciable property. Where, because of a transaction or an event in respect of which any of subsections 70(5), 85(1), (2) and (3), 87(2), section 88, subsections 97(2), 98(3) and (5) and 107(2) of the amended Act applies, a taxpayer has at any particular time after 1971 acquired any depreciable property of a prescribed class from a person who acquired the property before 1972 and owned it without interruption from December 31, 1971 until the particular time, for the purposes of subsection (1) the taxpayer shall be deemed to have acquired the property before 1972 and to have owned it without interruption from December 31, 1971 until such time after 1971 as the taxpayer disposed of it.

Interpretation Bulletins: *Secondary* — IT-209R Capital property owned on December 31, 1971 — Depreciable property.

► 20(1.3) ◄

(1.3) Transfers before 1972 not at arm's length. Without restricting the generality of section 18, if any depreciable property (other than a property that was, at any time, "eligible capital property" as defined in the amended Act at that time) has been transferred before 1972 in circumstances such that subsection 20(4) of the former Act would, if that provision applied to transfers of property made in the 1972 taxation year, apply, paragraph 69(1)(*b*) of the amended Act does not apply to the transfer and subsection 20(4) of the former Act applies thereto.

History: S. 20(1.3) was replaced by S.C. 2016, c. 12, s. 72(2), in force January 1, 2017, and formerly read:

(1.3) *Transfers before 1972 not at arm's length.* Without restricting the generality of section 18, where any depreciable property has been transferred before 1972 in circumstances such that subsection 20(4) of the former Act would, if that provision applied to transfers of property made in the 1972 taxation year, apply, paragraph 69(1)(*b*) of the amended Act does not apply to the transfer and subsection 20(4) of the former Act applies thereto.

► 20(1.4) ◄

(1.4) Depreciable property received as dividend in kind. The capital cost to a taxpayer, as of any particular time after 1971, of any depreciable property (other than depreciable property referred to in subsection (1.3) or deemed by subparagraph (1)(*b*)(ii) to have been acquired by the taxpayer before 1972 or a property that was, at any time, "eligible capital property" as defined in the amended Act at that time) acquired by the taxpayer before 1972 as, on account of, in lieu of payment of or in satisfaction of, a dividend payable in kind (other than a stock dividend) in respect of a share owned by the taxpayer of the capital stock of a corporation, is deemed to be the fair market value of that property at the time the property was so received.

History: S. 20(1.4) was replaced by S.C. 2016, c. 12, s. 72(2), in force January 1, 2017, and formerly read:

(1.4) *Depreciable property received as dividend in kind.* The capital cost to a taxpayer, as of any particular time after 1971, of any depreciable property (other than depreciable property referred to in subsection (1.3) or deemed by subparagraph (1)(*b*)(ii) to have been acquired by the taxpayer before 1972) acquired by the taxpayer before 1972 as, on account of, in lieu of payment of or in satisfaction of, a dividend payable in kind (other than a stock dividend) in respect of a share owned by the taxpayer of the capital stock of a corporation, shall be deemed to be the fair market value of that property at the time the property was so received.

S. 20(1.4) was added by 1973-74, c. 14, S. 71(3).

► 20(2) ◄

(2) Recapture of capital cost allowances. In determining a taxpayer's income for a taxation year from farming or fishing, subsection 13(1) of the amended Act does not apply in respect of the disposition by the taxpayer of property (other than a property that was, at any time, "eligible capital property" as defined in the amended Act at that time) acquired by the taxpayer before 1972 unless the taxpayer has elected to make a deduction for that or a preceding taxation year, in respect of the capital cost of property acquired by the taxpayer before 1972, under regulations made under paragraph 20(1)(*a*) of that Act other than a regulation providing solely for an allowance for computing income from farming or fishing.

History: S. 20(2) was replaced by S.C. 2016, c. 12, s. 72(2), in force January 1, 2017, and formerly read:

(2) *Recapture of capital cost allowances.* In determining a taxpayer's income for a taxation year from farming or fishing, subsection 13(1) of the amended Act does not apply in respect of the disposition by the taxpayer of property acquired by the taxpayer before 1972 unless the taxpayer has elected to make a deduction for that or a preceding taxation year, in respect of the capital cost of property acquired by the taxpayer before 1972, under regulations made under paragraph 20(1)(*a*) of that Act other than a regulation providing solely for an allowance for computing income from farming or fishing.

► 20(3) ◄

(3) Depreciable property of partnership of prescribed class. For the purposes of the amended Act, where a partnership had, on December 31, 1971, partnership property that was depreciable property of a prescribed class,

(*a*) the capital cost to the partnership of each property of that class shall be deemed to be an amount determined as follows:

(i) determine, for each person who, because of having been a member of the partnership on the later of June 18, 1971 and the day the partnership was created, and thereafter without interruption until December 31, 1971, can reasonably be regarded as having had an interest in the property of that class on December 31, 1971, the persons acquisition cost in respect of property of that class,

(ii) determine, for each such person, the amount that is that proportion of the person's acquisition cost in respect of property of that class that 100% is of the person's percentage in respect of property of that class,

(iii) select the amount determined under subparagraph (ii) for a person described therein that is not greater than any amount so determined for any other such person, and

(iv) determine that proportion of the amount selected under subparagraph (iii) (in this subsection referred to as the "capital cost of that class") that the fair market value on December 31, 1971 of that property is of the fair market value on that day of all property of that class,

and the amount determined under subparagraph (iv) is the capital cost to the partnership of that property;

(*b*) for the purposes of sections 13 and 20 of the amended Act and any regulations made under paragraph 20(1)(*a*) of that Act, the undepreciated capital cost to the partnership of property of that class as of any time after 1971 shall be computed as though the amount, if any, by which the capital cost of that class to the partnership exceeds the undepreciated cost to the partnership of that class had been allowed to the partnership in respect of property of that class under regulations made under para-

ITARs

graph 20(1)(*a*) of the amended Act in computing income for taxation years before that time;

(*c*) in computing the income for the 1972 and subsequent taxation years of each person who was a member of the partnership on June 18, 1971 and thereafter without interruption until December 31, 1971, there may be deducted such amount as the person claims for the year, not exceeding the amount, if any, by which the total of

(i) the lesser of

(A) the amount, if any, by which the amount that was the capital cost to the person of all property of that class exceeds the percentage, equal to the person's percentage in respect of property of that class, of the capital cost of that class to the partnership, and

(B) the amount that was the undepreciated capital cost to the person of property of that class as of December 31, 1971, and

(ii) the amount, if any, by which

(A) the undepreciated capital cost to the person of property of that class as of December 31, 1971, less the amount, if any, determined under subparagraph (i) in respect of property of that class;

exceeds

(B) the percentage, equal to the person's percentage in respect of property of that class, of the undepreciated cost to the partnership of that class,

exceeds the total of all amounts deducted under this paragraph in computing the persons income for preceding taxation years, and, for the purposes of section 3 of the amended Act, the amount so claimed shall be deemed to be a deduction permitted by subdivision e of Division B of Part I of that Act; and

(*d*) notwithstanding paragraph (*c*), a person who became a member of the partnership after June 18, 1971 and who was a member of the partnership thereafter without interruption until December 31, 1971 shall be deemed to be a person described in paragraph (*c*) and the amount that may be claimed thereunder as a deduction in computing the person's income for any taxation year shall not exceed 10% of the total of the amounts determined under subparagraphs (*c*)(i) and (ii).

Related Regulations: Part LII.

► 20(4) ◄

(4) Definitions. In subsection (3),

"acquisition cost" —"acquisition cost" of a person who was a member of a partnership on December 31, 1971 in respect of depreciable property of a prescribed class that was partnership property of the partnership on December 31, 1971 means the total of the undepreciated capital cost to the person of property of that class as of December 31, 1971 and the total depreciation allowed to the person before 1972 in respect of property of that class;

"percentage" —"percentage" of a member of a partnership in respect of any depreciable property of a prescribed class that was partnership property of the partnership on December 31, 1971 means the interest of the member of the partnership in property of that class, expressed as a percentage of the total of the interests of all members of the partnership in property of that class on that day;

"undepreciated cost to the partnership" —"undepreciated cost to the partnership" of any class of depreciable property means an amount determined as follows:

(*a*) determine, for each person who, because of having been a member of the partnership on the later of June 18, 1971 and the day the partnership was created, and thereafter without interruption until December 31, 1971, can reasonably be regarded as having had an interest in property of that class on December 31, 1971, the amount, if any, by which the undepreciated capital cost to the person of property of that class as of December 31, 1971 exceeds the amount, if any, determined under subparagraph (3)(*c*)(i) for the person in respect of property of that class,

(*b*) determine, for each such person, the amount that is that proportion of the amount determined under paragraph (*a*) that 100% is of the person's percentage in respect of property of that class, and

(*c*) select the amount determined under paragraph (*b*) for a person described therein that is not greater than any amount so determined for any other such person,

and the amount selected under paragraph (*c*) is the undepreciated cost to the partnership of that class.

► 20(5) ◄

(5) Other depreciable property of partnership. For the purposes of the amended Act, where a partnership had, on December 31, 1971, any particular partnership property that was depreciable property other than depreciable property of a prescribed class,

(*a*) the cost to the partnership of the particular property shall be deemed to be the amount that would be determined under paragraph (3)(*a*) to be the capital cost thereof if

(i) the particular property constituted a prescribed class of property, and

(ii) the acquisition cost of each person described therein in respect of the particular property were its actual cost to the person or the amount at which the person was deemed by subsection 20(6) of the former Act to have acquired it, as the case may be;

(*b*) for the purposes of sections 13 and 20 of the amended Act and any regulations made under paragraph 20(1)(*a*) of that Act, the undepreciated capital cost of property of any class as of any particular time after 1971 shall be computed as if the amount, if any, by which

(i) the amount determined under paragraph (*a*) to have been the cost to the partnership of the particular property,

exceeds

(ii) the amount that would be determined under the definition "undepreciated cost to the partnership" in subsection (4) to be the undepreciated cost to the partnership of any class of depreciable property comprising the particular property if

(A) paragraph (*a*) of that definition were read without reference to the words "the later of June 18, 1971 and the day the partnership was created, and thereafter without interruption until",

(B) the amount determined under subparagraph (3)(*c*)(i) for any person in respect of that class were nil, and

(C) the undepreciated capital cost to each person described in the definition "acquisition cost" in subsection (4) of the particular property as of December 31, 1971 were the amount, if any, by which the amount assumed by subparagraph (*a*)(ii) to have been the acquisition cost of the person in respect of the property exceeds the total of all allowed to the person in respect of the property under regulations made under paragraph 11(1)(*a*) of the former Act in computing income for taxation years ending before 1972,

had been allowed to the partnership in respect of the particular property under regulations made under paragraph 20(1)(*a*) of the amended Act in computing income for taxation years ending before the particular time; and

(*c*) in computing the income for the 1972 and subsequent taxation years of each person who was, on December 31, 1971, a member of the partnership, there may be deducted such amount as the person claims for the year, not exceeding the amount, if any, by which

(i) the amount by which

(A) the amount assumed by clause (*b*)(ii)(C) to have been the undepreciated capital cost to the person of the particular property as of December 31, 1971

exceeds

(B) a percentage of the amount determined under subparagraph (*b*)(ii) in respect of the particular property, equal to the percentage that would be the person's percentage (within the meaning assigned by subsection (4)) in respect of the particular property if that property constituted a prescribed class,

exceeds

(ii) the total of all amounts deducted under this paragraph in computing the person's income for preceding taxation years,

and for the purposes of section 3 of the amended Act the amount so claimed shall be deemed to be a deduction permitted by subdivision e of Division B of Part I of that Act.

Related Regulations: Part XVII; Part LII.

Income Tax Folios: *Primary* — S3-F4-C1 General Discussion of Capital Cost Allowance.

21. Goodwill and other nothings

► 21(1) ◄

(1) Government right. If as a result of a disposition occurring after 1971 a taxpayer has or may become entitled to receive an amount (in this section referred to as the "actual amount") that may reasonably be considered to be consideration received by the taxpayer for the disposition of, or for allowing the expiration of, a government right, in respect of a business carried on by the taxpayer throughout the period beginning January 1, 1972 and ending immediately after the disposition occurred, for the purposes of the amended Act the amount that the taxpayer has or may become entitled to receive is deemed to be the amount, if any, by which the actual amount exceeds the greater of

(*a*) the total of all amounts each of which is an outlay or expenditure made or incurred by the taxpayer as a result of a transaction that occurred before 1972 for the purpose of acquiring the government right, or the taxpayer's original right in respect of the government right, to the extent that the outlay or expenditure was not otherwise deducted in computing the income of the taxpayer for any taxation year and would, if made or incurred by the taxpayer as a result of a transaction that occurred after 1971, be an eligible capital expenditure of the taxpayer; and

(*b*) the fair market value to the taxpayer on December 31, 1971 of the taxpayer's specified right in respect of the government right, if no outlay or expenditure was made or incurred by the taxpayer for the purpose of acquiring the right or, if an outlay or expenditure was made or incurred, if that outlay or expenditure would have been an eligible capital expenditure of the taxpayer if it had been made or incurred as a result of a transaction that occurred after 1971.

History: S. 21(1) was replaced by S.C. 2016, c. 12, s. 73(1), in force January 1, 2017, and formerly read:

(1) Where as a result of a disposition occurring after 1971 a taxpayer has or may become entitled to receive an amount (in this section referred to as the "actual amount") in respect of a business carried on by the taxpayer throughout the period beginning January 1, 1972 and ending immediately after the disposition occurred, for the purposes of section 14 of the amended Act the amount that the taxpayer has or may become entitled to receive shall be deemed to be the total of

(*a*) an amount equal to a percentage, equal to 40% plus the percentage (not exceeding 60%) obtained when 5% is multiplied by the number of full calendar years ending in the period and before the transaction occurred, of the amount, if any, by which the actual amount exceeds the portion thereof referred to in subparagraph (*b*)(i), and

(*b*) an amount equal to the lesser of

(i) the percentage, described in paragraph (*a*), of such portion, if any, of the actual amount as may reasonably be considered as being the consideration received by the taxpayer for the disposition of, or for allowing the expiration of, a government right, and

(ii) the amount, if any, by which the portion described in subparagraph (i) exceeds the greater of

(A) the total of all amounts each of which is an outlay or expenditure made or incurred by the taxpayer as a result of a transaction that occurred before 1972 for the purpose of acquiring the government right, or the taxpayer's original right in respect of the government right, to the extent that the outlay or expenditure was not otherwise

ITARs

deducted in computing the income of the taxpayer for any taxation year and would, if made or incurred by the taxpayer as a result of a transaction that occurred after 1971, be an eligible capital expenditure of the taxpayer, and

(B) the fair market value to the taxpayer as at December 31, 1971 of the taxpayers specified right in respect of the government right, if no outlay or expenditure was made or incurred by the taxpayer for the purpose of acquiring the right or, if an outlay or expenditure was made or incurred, if that outlay or expenditure would have been an eligible capital expenditure of the taxpayer if it had been made or incurred as a result of a transaction that occurred after 1971.

Interpretation Bulletins: *Secondary* — IT-123R6 Disposition of and transactions involving eligible capital property; IT-268R4 Inter vivos transfer of farm property to child; IT-313R2 Eligible capital property — Rules where a taxpayer has ceased carrying on a business or has died.

► 21(2) ◄

(2) Idem. Where the taxpayer and the person by whom the actual amount has become payable to the taxpayer were not dealing with each other at arm's length, for the purposes of computing the income of that person the portion of the actual amount in excess of the amount deemed by subsection (1) to be the amount that has become payable to the taxpayer shall be deemed not to have been an outlay, expense or cost, as the case may be, of that person.

Interpretation Bulletins: *Secondary* — IT-268R4 Inter vivos transfer of farm property to child.

► 21(2.1) ◄

(2.1) Idem. Where after 1971 a taxpayer has acquired a particular government right referred to in subsection (1)

(*a*) from a person with whom the taxpayer was not dealing at arm's length, or

(*b*) under an agreement with a person with whom the taxpayer was not dealing at arm's length, if under the terms of the agreement that person allowed the right to expire so that the taxpayer could acquire a substantially similar right from the authority that had issued the right to that person,

and an actual amount subsequently becomes payable to the taxpayer as consideration for the disposition by the taxpayer of, or for the taxpayer allowing the expiration of, the particular government right or any other government right acquired by the taxpayer for the purpose of effecting the continuation, without interruption, of rights that are substantially similar to the rights that the taxpayer had under the particular government right, for the purpose of the amended Act, the amount that has so become payable to the taxpayer shall be deemed to be the amount that would, if that person and the taxpayer had at all times been the same person, be determined under subsection (1) to be the amount that would have become so payable to the taxpayer.

History: S. 21(2.1), the portion after paragraph (*b*) was replaced by S.C. 2016, c. 12, s. 73(2), in force January 1, 2017, and formerly read:

> and an actual amount subsequently becomes payable to the taxpayer as consideration for the disposition by the taxpayer of, or for the taxpayer allowing the expiration of, the particular government right or any other government right acquired by the taxpayer for the purpose of effecting the continuation, without interruption, of rights that are substantially similar to the rights that the taxpayer had under the particular government right, for the purpose of section 14 of the amended Act, the amount that has so become payable to the taxpayer shall be deemed to be the amount that would, if that person and the taxpayer had at all times been the same person, be determined under subsection (1) to be the amount that would have become so payable to the taxpayer.

► 21(2.2) ◄

(2.2) Amalgamations. For the purposes of this section, an amalgamation (within the meaning of section 87 of the amended Act) of two or more Canadian corporations shall be deemed to be a transaction between persons not dealing at arm's length.

► 21(3) ◄

(3) Definitions. In this section,

"government right" —"government right" of a taxpayer means a right or licence

(*a*) that enables the taxpayer to carry on a business activity in accordance with a law of Canada or of a province or Canadian municipality, to an extent to which the taxpayer would otherwise be unable to carry it on in accordance therewith,

(*b*) that was granted or issued by Her Majesty in right of Canada or a province or a Canadian municipality, or by a department, board, agency or any other body authorized by or under a law of Canada, a province or a Canadian municipality to grant or issue such a right or licence, and

(*c*) that was acquired by the taxpayer

(i) as a result of a transaction that occurred before 1972, or

(ii) at a particular time for the purpose of affecting the continuation, without interruption, of rights that are substantially similar to the rights that the taxpayer had under a government right held by the taxpayer before the particular time;

"original right" —"original right" of a taxpayer in respect of a government right means a right or licence

(*a*) described in the definition "government right" in this subsection, and

(*b*) acquired by the taxpayer as a result of a transaction that occurred before 1972 for a purpose other than the purpose described in subparagraph (*c*)(ii) of that definition,

if the government right was acquired by the taxpayer for the purpose of effecting the continuation, without interruption, of rights that are substantially similar to the rights that the taxpayer had under the right or licence;

"specified right" —"specified right" of a taxpayer in respect of a government right means a right owned by a taxpayer on December 31, 1971 that was

(*a*) an original right, or

(*b*) a government right that was acquired by the taxpayer in substitution for the original right or that was one of a series of government rights acquired by the taxpayer for the purpose of effecting the continuation, without interruption, of rights that are substantially similar to the rights that the taxpayer had under the original right.

22. Deduction of interest by certain corporations

(1) (Repealed by 1985, c. 45, s. 129.)

▶ 22(2) ◀

(2) Idem — (Repealed by 1985, c. 45, s. 129.)

23. Rules applicable

▶ 23(1) ◀

(1) Income from professional business — (Repealed by 1985, c. 45, s. 130.)

▶ 23(2) ◀

(2) Valuation of work in progress — (Repealed by 1985, c. 45, s. 130.)

▶ 23(3) ◀

(3) Rules applicable. For the purposes of computing the income of a taxpayer for a taxation year ending after 1971 from a business that is a profession,

(*a*) there may be deducted such amount as the taxpayer claims, not exceeding the lesser of

(i) the amount deducted under this paragraph in computing the taxpayer's income from the business for the preceding taxation year, and

(ii) the taxpayer's investment interest in the business at the end of the year;

(*b*) where the taxation year is the taxpayer's 1972 taxation year, the amount deducted under paragraph (*a*) in computing the taxpayer's income for the preceding taxation year from the business shall be deemed to be an amount equal to the taxpayer's 1971 receivables in respect of the business;

(*c*) there shall be included the amount deducted under paragraph (*a*) in computing the taxpayer's income for the preceding taxation year from the business; and

(*d*) there shall be included amounts received by the taxpayer in the year on account of debts in respect of the business that were established by the taxpayer to have become bad debts before the end of the 1971 fiscal period of the business.

Related Regulations: Part II.

Interpretation Bulletins: *Secondary* — IT-212R3 Income of deceased persons — Rights or things; IT-242R Retired partners; IT-278R2 Death of a partner or of a retired partner.

▶ 23(4) ◀

(4) Application of para. (3)(*a*). Paragraph (3)(*a*) does not apply to allow a deduction in computing the income of a taxpayer from a business that is a profession

(*a*) for the taxation year in which the taxpayer died; or

(*b*) for any taxation year, if,

(i) in the case of a taxpayer who at no time in the year was resident in Canada, the taxpayer ceased to carry on the business, or

(ii) in the case of any other taxpayer, the taxpayer ceased to be resident in Canada and ceased to carry on the business

at any time in the year or the following year.

Interpretation Bulletins: *Secondary* — IT-242R Retired partners; IT-278R2 Death of a partner or of a retired partner.

▶ 23(4.1) ◀

(4.1) Certain persons deemed to be carrying on business by means of partnership. For the purposes of paragraph (*a*) of the definition investment interest in subsection (5),

(*a*) where subsection 98(1) of the amended Act applies, the persons who are deemed not to have ceased to be members of a partnership because of that subsection shall be deemed to be carrying on business in Canada by means of that partnership; and

(*b*) a taxpayer who has a residual interest in a partnership (within the meaning assigned by section 98.1 of the amended Act) shall be deemed to be carrying on business in Canada by means of that partnership.

▶ 23(5) ◀

(5) Definitions. In this section,

"investment interest" — "investment interest" in a business at the end of a taxation year of a taxpayer means

(*a*) in the case of a taxpayer other than a corporation, the total of all amounts each of which is an amount in respect of a proprietorship or partnership by means of which the taxpayer carried on that business in Canada in the year, equal to,

(i) in respect of each such proprietorship, the amount, if any, by which

(A) the total of such of the amounts that were included in computing the taxpayer's income for that or a preceding taxation year as were receivable by the taxpayer at the end of the fiscal period of the proprietorship ending in the taxation year,

exceeds

(B) the amount claimed under paragraph 20(1)(*l*) of the amended Act as a reserve for doubtful debts in computing the taxpayer's income from the business for the fiscal period of the proprietorship ending in the year, and

(ii) in respect of each such partnership, the adjusted cost base to the taxpayer of the taxpayer's interest in the partnership immediately after the end of the fiscal period of the partnership ending in the year,

(*b*) in the case of a taxpayer that is a corporation, the lesser of

(i) the amount thereof that would be determined under paragraph (*a*) in respect of the corporation if that paragraph applied to a taxpayer that is a corporation, and

(ii) that proportion of its 1971 receivables in respect of the business that

(A) the amount, if any, by which 10 exceeds the number of its taxation years ending after 1971

ITARs

and either before or coincidentally with the taxation year,

is of

(B) 10;

"1971 receivables" —"1971 receivables" in respect of a business of a taxpayer means the total of

(*a*) all amounts that became receivable by the taxpayer in respect of property sold or services rendered in the course of the business (within the meaning given that expression in section 34 of the amended Act) in taxation years ending before 1972 and that were not included in computing the taxpayer's income for any such taxation year, other than debts that were established by the taxpayer to have become bad debts before the end of the 1971 fiscal period of the business, and

(*b*) the total of all amounts each of which is an amount, in respect of each partnership by means of which the taxpayer carried on that business before 1972, equal to such portion of the total that would be determined under paragraph (*a*) in respect of the partnership, if the references in that paragraph to "the taxpayer" were read as references to "the partnership", as is designated by the taxpayer in the taxpayer's return of income under Part I of the amended Act for the year to be attributable to the taxpayer, except that where the total of the portions so designated by all members of the partnership is less than the total that would be so determined under paragraph (*a*) in respect of the partnership, the Minister may designate the portion of that total that is attributable to the taxpayer, in which case the portion so designated by the Minister in respect of the taxpayer shall be deemed to be the portion so designated by the taxpayer.

24. Definition of "valuation day" for capital gains and losses

In this Act, "valuation day" means

(*a*) December 22, 1971, in relation to any property prescribed to be a publicly-traded share or security; and

(*b*) December 31, 1971, in relation to any other property.

Related Regulations: Part XLIV.

26. Capital gains subject to tax

(1) The provisions of subdivision c of Division B of Part I of the amended Act apply to dispositions of property made after 1971 and to transactions or events occurring after 1971 because of which any disposition of property was made or deemed to have been made in accordance with the provisions of that subdivision.

Income Tax Folios: *Primary* — S4-F5-C1 Share for Share Exchange.

Interpretation Bulletins: *Secondary* — IT-450R Share for Share Exchange.

▶ 26(1.1) ◀

(1.1) Principal amount of certain obligations. For the purposes of subsection 39(3) and section 80 of the amended Act, the principal amount of any debt or other obligation of a taxpayer to pay an amount that was outstanding on January 1, 1972 (in this subsection referred to as an "obligation") shall be deemed to be the lesser of

(*a*) the principal amount, otherwise determined for the purposes of the amended Act, of the obligation, and

(*b*) the fair market value, on valuation day, of the obligation,

and in applying paragraph 39(3)(*a*) of the amended Act to an obligation, the reference in that paragraph to "the amount for which the obligation was issued" shall be read as a reference to "the lesser of the principal amount of the obligation and the amount for which the obligation was issued".

Interpretation Bulletins: *Secondary* — IT-293R Debtor's gain on settlement of debt.

▶ 26(2) ◀

(2) Listed personal property — (Repealed by 1985, c. 45, s. 131(1).)

▶ 26(3) ◀

(3) Cost of acquisition of capital property owned on Dec. 31, 1971. For the purpose of computing the adjusted cost base to a taxpayer of any capital property (other than depreciable property or an interest in a partnership) that was owned by the taxpayer on December 31, 1971 and thereafter without interruption until such time as the taxpayer disposed of it, its cost to the taxpayer shall be deemed to be the amount that is neither the greatest nor the least of the following three amounts, namely,

(*a*) its actual cost to the taxpayer or, if the property was an obligation, its amortized cost to the taxpayer on January 1, 1972,

(*b*) its fair market value on valuation day, and

(*c*) the amount, if any, by which the total of

(i) the taxpayer's proceeds of disposition of the property, determined without reference to subsection 13(21.1) of the amended Act,

(ii) all amounts required by subsection 53(2) of the amended Act to be deducted in computing its adjusted cost base to the taxpayer immediately before the disposition, and

(iii) all amounts described in clause (5)(*c*)(ii)(B) that are relevant in computing its adjusted cost base to the taxpayer immediately before the disposition,

exceeds the total of

(iv) all amounts required by subsection 53(1) of the amended Act (other than paragraphs 53(1)(*f*.1) to (*f*.2)) to be added in computing its adjusted cost base to the taxpayer immediately before the disposition, and

(v) all amounts described in clause (5)(*c*)(i)(B) that are relevant in computing its adjusted cost base to the taxpayer immediately before the disposition,

except that where two or more of the amounts determined under paragraphs (*a*) to (*c*) in respect of any property are the same amount, that amount shall be deemed to be its costs to the taxpayer.

Interpretation Bulletins: *Primary* — IT-65 Stock splits and consolidations. *Secondary* — IT-96R6 Options granted by corporations to acquire shares, bonds or debentures; IT-209R Inter-vivos gifts of capital property to individuals directly or through trusts; IT-268R4 Inter vivos transfer of farm property to child; IT-349R3 Intergenerational transfers of farm property on death.

▶ 26(4) ◀

(4) Determination of cost where property not disposed of. For the purpose of computing the adjusted cost base to a taxpayer of any capital property (other than depreciable property or an interest in a partnership) at any particular time before the taxpayer disposed of it, where the property was owned by the taxpayer on December 31, 1971 and thereafter without interruption until the particular time, its costs to the taxpayer shall be deemed to be the amount that would be determined under subsection (3) to be its cost to the taxpayer if the taxpayer had disposed of it at the particular time and the taxpayer's proceeds of disposition had been its fair market value at that time.

Interpretation Bulletins: *Secondary* — IT-209R Inter-vivos gifts of capital property to individuals directly or through trusts.

▶ 26(5) ◀

(5) Where property disposed of in transaction not at arm's length. Where any capital property (other than depreciable property or an interest in a partnership) that was owned by a taxpayer (in this subsection referred to as the "original owner") on June 18, 1971 has, by one or more transactions or events between persons not dealing at arm's length, become vested in another taxpayer (in this subsection referred to as the "subsequent owner") and the original owner has not elected under subsection (7) in respect of the property, notwithstanding the provisions of the amended Act, for the purposes of computing, at any particular time after 1971, the adjusted cost base of the property to the subsequent owner,

(*a*) the subsequent owner shall be deemed to have owned the property on June 18, 1971 and thereafter without interruption until the particular time;

(*b*) for the purposes of this section, the actual cost of the property to the subsequent owner or, if the property was an obligation, its amortized cost to the subsequent owner on January 1, 1972 shall be deemed to be the amount that was its actual cost or amortized cost, on January 1, 1972, as the case may be, to the original owner; and

(*c*) where the property became vested in the subsequent owner after 1971, there shall be added to the cost to the subsequent owner of the property (as determined under subsection (3)) the amount, if any, by which

(i) the total of all amounts each of which is

(A) a capital gain (other than any amount deemed by subsection 40(3) of the amended Act to be a capital gain) from the disposition after 1971 of the property by a person who owned the property before it so became vested in the subsequent owner,

(B) an amount required by subsection 53(1) of the amended Act to be added in computing the adjusted cost base of the property to a person (other than the subsequent owner) described in clause (A),

(C) an amount determined under paragraph 88(1)(*d*) of the amended Act in computing the cost of the property to the subsequent owner or a person who owned the property before it became vested in the subsequent owner, or

(D) an amount by which a gain otherwise determined of a person who owned the property before it became so vested in the subsequent owner was reduced because of paragraph 40(2)(*b*) or (*c*) of the amended Act,

exceeds

(ii) the total of all amounts each of which is

(A) a capital loss or an amount that would, but for paragraph 40(2)(*e*) and subsection 85(4) of the amended Act (as that Act read in its application to property disposed of on or before April 26, 1995) and paragraphs 40(2)(*e*.1) and (*e*.2) and subsection 40(3.3) of the amended Act, be a capital loss from the disposition to a corporation after 1971 of the property by a person who owned the property before it became vested in the subsequent owner, or

(B) an amount required by subsection 53(2) of the amended Act to be deducted in computing the adjusted cost base of the property to a person (other than the subsequent owner) described in clause (A),

and there shall be deducted from the cost to the subsequent owner of the property the amount, if any, by which the total determined under subparagraph (ii) exceeds the total determined under subparagraph (i).

Interpretation Bulletins: *Secondary* — IT-209R Inter-vivos gifts of capital property to individuals directly or through trusts; IT-268R4 Inter vivos transfer of farm property to child; IT-349R3 Intergenerational transfers of farm property on death; IT-432R2 Benefits conferred on shareholders.

▶ 26(5.1) ◀

(5.1) Idem. For the purposes of subsection (5), an amalgamation (within the meaning assigned by section 87 of the amended Act) of two or more Canadian corporations shall be deemed to be a transaction between persons not dealing at arm's length.

▶ 26(5.2) ◀

(5.2) Transfer of capital property to a corporation. For the purposes of subsection (5), where a taxpayer has disposed of capital property after May 6, 1974 to a corporation in respect of which an election under section 85 of the amended Act was made, the disposition shall be deemed to be a transaction between persons not dealing at arm's length.

▶ 26(6) ◀

(6) Reacquired property. Where a taxpayer has, at any time after June 18, 1971 and before 1972, disposed of any property owned by the taxpayer on that day and has, within 30 days after that time, reacquired the same property or acquired a substantially identical property, for the purposes of this section

ITARs

(*a*) the taxpayer shall be deemed to have owned the property so reacquired or the substantially identical property so acquired, as the case may be, on June 18, 1971 and thereafter without interruption until the time the taxpayer so reacquired or acquired it as the case may be;

(*b*) where the property was property so reacquired, its actual cost or its amortized cost on January 1, 1972, as the case may be, to the taxpayer shall be determined as if the taxpayer had not so disposed of and so reacquired it; and

(*c*) where the property was substantially identical property so acquired, its actual cost or its amortized cost on January 1, 1972, as the case may be, to the taxpayer shall be deemed to be the amount that was the actual cost or the amortized cost on January 1, 1972, as the case may be, to the taxpayer of the property so disposed of by the taxpayer.

► 26(7) ◄

(7) Election re cost. Where, but for this subsection, the cost to an individual of any property actually owned by the individual on December 31, 1971 would be determined under subsection (3) or (4) otherwise than because of subsection (5) and the individual has so elected, in prescribed manner and not later than the day on or before which the individual is required by Part I of the amended Act to file a return of income for the first taxation year in which the individual disposes of all or any part of the property, other than

(*a*) personal-use property of the individual that was not listed personal property or real property,

(*b*) listed personal property, if the individual's gain or loss, as the case may be, from the disposition thereof was, because of subsection 46(1) or (2) of the amended Act, nil,

(*c*) the individual's principal residence, if the individual's gain from the disposition thereof was, because of paragraph 40(2)(*b*) of the amended Act, nil,

(*d*) personal-use property of the individual that was real property (other than the individual's principal residence), if the individual's gain from the disposition thereof was, because of subsection 46(1) or (2) of the amended Act, nil, or

(*e*) any other property, the proceeds of disposition of which are equal to its fair market value on valuation day,

the cost to the individual of each capital property (other than depreciable property, an interest in a partnership or any property described in any of paragraphs (*a*) to (*e*) that was disposed of by the individual before that taxation year) actually owned by the individual on December 31, 1971 shall be deemed to be its fair market value on valuation day.

Related Regulations: Part XLVII.

Forms: T2076 — Valuation Day Value Election for Capital Properties Owned on December 31, 1971.

► 26(8) ◄

(8) Identical properties. For the purposes of computing, at any particular time after 1971, the adjusted cost base to a taxpayer of any capital property (other than depreciable property or an interest in a partnership) that was owned by the taxpayer on December 31, 1971 and thereafter without interruption until the particular time, if the property was one of a group of identical properties owned by the taxpayer on December 31, 1971,

(*a*) section 47 of the amended Act does not apply;

(*b*) where the property was an obligation,

(i) for the purpose of paragraph (3)(*a*), its amortized cost to the taxpayer on January 1, 1972 shall be deemed to be that proportion of the total of the amortized costs to the taxpayer on January 1, 1972 of all obligations of that group that the principal amount of the obligation is of the total of the principal amounts of all obligations of that group, and

(ii) for the purpose of paragraph (3)(*b*), its fair market value on valuation day shall be deemed to be that proportion of the fair market value on that day of all obligations of that group that the principal amount of the obligation is of the total of the principal amounts of all obligations of that group;

(*c*) where the property was not an obligation,

(i) for the purpose of paragraph (3)(*a*), its actual cost to the taxpayer shall be deemed to be the quotient obtained when the total of the actual costs to the taxpayer of all properties of that group is divided by the number of properties of that group, and

(ii) for the purpose of paragraph (3)(*b*), its fair market value on valuation day shall be deemed to be the quotient obtained when the fair market value on that day of all properties of that group is divided by the number of properties of that group;

(*d*) for the purpose of distinguishing any such property from an otherwise identical property acquired and disposed of by the taxpayer before 1972, properties acquired by the taxpayer at any time shall be deemed to have been disposed of by the taxpayer before properties acquired by the taxpayer after that time; and

(*e*) for the purposes of distinguishing any such property from an otherwise identical property acquired by the taxpayer after 1971, properties owned by the taxpayer on December 31, 1971 shall be deemed to have been disposed of by the taxpayer before properties acquired by the taxpayer at a later time.

Interpretation Bulletins: *Secondary* — IT-88R2 Stock dividends; IT-115R2 Fractional interests in shares; IT-387R2 (Consolid.) Meaning of "identical properties"; IT-489R Non-arm's length sale of shares to a corporation.

► 26(8.1) ◄

(8.1) Idem. For the purposes of subsection (8), any property of a life insurance corporation that would, but for this subsection, be identical to any other property of the corporation shall be deemed not to be identical to that other property unless both properties are (*a*) included in the same segregated fund of the corporation;

(*b*) non-segregated property used in the year in, or held in the course of, carrying on a life insurance business in Canada; or

(*c*) non-segregated property used in the year in, or held in the course of, carrying on an insurance business in Canada, other than a life insurance business.

Interpretation Bulletins: *Secondary* — IT-387R2 (Consolid.) Meaning of "identical properties".

► 26(8.2) ◄

(8.2) Idem. For the purposes of subsection (8), any bond, debenture, bill, note or other similar obligation issued by a debtor is identical to any other such obligation issued by that debtor if both are identical in respect of all rights (in equity or otherwise, either immediately or in the future and either absolutely or contingently) attaching thereto, except as regards the principal amount thereof.

Interpretation Bulletins: *Secondary* — IT-387R2 (Consolid.) Meaning of "identical properties".

► 26(8.3) ◄

(8.3) Idem. Where a corporation resident in Canada has, after 1971, received a stock dividend in respect of a share owned on June 18, 1971 and December 31, 1971 by it or by a corporation with which it did not deal at arm's length of the capital stock of a foreign affiliate of that corporation and the share or shares received as the stock dividend are identical to the share in respect of which the stock dividend was received, the share or shares received as the stock dividend may, at the option of the corporation, be deemed for the purposes of subsection (5) to be capital property owned by it on June 18, 1971 and for the purposes of this subsection, paragraph (3)(*c*) and subsection (8) to be capital property owned by it on June 18, 1971 and December 31, 1971 and not to be property acquired by the corporation after 1971 for the purposes of paragraph (8)(*e*).

Interpretation Bulletins: *Secondary* — IT-88R2 Stock dividends.

► 26(8.4) ◄

(8.4) Idem. Where a corporation resident in Canada has, after 1971, received a stock dividend in respect of a share acquired by it after June 18, 1971 from a person with whom it was dealing at arm's length and owned by it on December 31, 1971 of the capital stock of a foreign affiliate of that corporation and the share or shares received as the stock dividend are identical to the share in respect of which the stock dividend was received, the share or shares received as the stock dividend may, at the option of the corporation, be deemed for the purposes of this subsection, paragraph (3)(*c*) and subsection (8) to be capital property owned by it on December 31, 1971 and not to be property acquired by the corporation after 1971 for the purposes of paragraph (8)(*e*).

Interpretation Bulletins: *Secondary* — IT-88R2 Stock dividends.

► 26(8.5) ◄

(8.5) Amalgamation. For the purposes of subsections (8.3) and (8.4), where there has been an amalgamation (within the meaning of section 87 of the amended Act), the new corporation shall be deemed to be the same corporation as, and a continuation of, each predecessor corporation.

► 26(9) ◄

(9) Cost of interest in partnership. For the purpose of computing, at any particular time after 1971, the adjusted cost base to a taxpayer of an interest in a partnership of which the taxpayer was a member on December 31, 1971 and thereafter without interruption until the particular time, the cost to the taxpayer of the interest shall be deemed to be the amount that is neither the greatest nor the least of the following three amounts, namely,

(*a*) its actual cost to the taxpayer as of the particular time,

(*b*) the amount determined under subsection (9.1) in respect of the interest as of the particular time, and

(*c*) the amount, if any, by which the total of the fair market value of the interest at the particular time and all amounts required by subsection 53(2) of the amended Act to be deducted in computing its adjusted cost base to the taxpayer immediately before the particular time exceeds the total of all amounts required by subsection 53(1) of the amended Act to be added in computing its adjusted cost base to the taxpayer immediately before the particular time,

except that where two or more of the amounts determined under paragraphs (*a*) to (*c*) in respect of the interest are the same amount, that amount shall be deemed to be its cost to the taxpayer.

Related Regulations: Part II.

► 26(9.1) ◄

(9.1) Determination of amounts for purpose of s. (9). For the purposes of subsection (9), the amount determined under this subsection in respect of a taxpayer's interest in a partnership as of a particular time is the amount, if any, by which the total of

(*a*) the taxpayer's share, determined at the beginning of the first fiscal period of the partnership ending after 1971, of the tax equity of the partnership at the particular time,

(*b*) such part of any contribution of capital made by the taxpayer to the partnership (otherwise than by way of loan) before 1972 and after the beginning of the partnership's first fiscal period ending after 1971, as cannot reasonably be regarded as a gift made to, or for the benefit of, any other member of the partnership who was related to the taxpayer, and

(*c*) the amount of any consideration that became payable by the taxpayer after 1971 to any other person to acquire, after 1971, any right in respect of the partnership, the sole purpose of the acquisition of which was to increase the taxpayer's interest in the partnership,

exceeds the total of

(*d*) all amounts received by the taxpayer before 1972 and after the beginning of the partnership's first fiscal period ending after 1971 as, on account of, in lieu of payment of or in satisfaction of, a distribution of the taxpayer's share of the partnership profits or partnership capital, and

ITARs

(*e*) all amounts each of which is an amount in respect of the disposition by the taxpayer after 1971 and before the particular time of a part of the taxpayer's interest in the partnership, equal to such portion of the adjusted cost base to the taxpayer of the interest immediately before the disposition as may reasonably be regarded as attributable to the part so dispose of.

▶ 26(9.2) ◀

(9.2) Where interest acquired before 1972 and after beginning of 1st fiscal period ending after 1971. Where a taxpayer has, before 1972 and after the beginning of the first fiscal period of a partnership ending after 1971, acquired an interest in the partnership from another person, subsection (9.1) applies as if, for the purposes of paragraphs (*a*), (*b*) and (*d*) thereof, the taxpayer had had in respect of the interest, throughout the period beginning at the beginning of that fiscal period and ending at the time the taxpayer acquired the interest, the same position in relation to the partnership as the taxpayer would have had in relation thereto if, throughout that period, the taxpayer had been the owner of the interest.

▶ 26(9.3) ◀

(9.3) Amounts deemed to be required to be deducted in respect of interest in partnership. For the purpose of computing, at any particular time after 1971, the adjusted cost base to a taxpayer of an interest in a partnership of which the taxpayer was a member on December 31, 1971 and thereafter without interruption until the particular time, the lesser of

(*a*) the amount, if any, by which

(i) the total of all amounts in respect of the interest determined under paragraph (9.1)(*d*)

exceeds

(ii) the total of

(A) the taxpayer's share, determined at the beginning of the first fiscal period of the partnership ending after 1971, of the tax equity of the partnership at the particular time, and

(B) the amount in respect of the interest determined under paragraph (9.1)(*b*), and

(*b*) the amount, if any, by which

(i) the total of all amounts in respect of the interest determined as of the particular time under paragraphs (14)(*e*) to (*g*)

exceeds

(ii) the total of all amounts in respect of the interest determined as of the particular time under paragraphs (14)(*a*) to (*d*),

shall be deemed to be required by subsection 53(2) of the amended Act to be deducted.

▶ 26(9.4) ◀

(9.4) Application of s. 53 of amended Act in respect of interest in partnership. For the purpose of computing, at any particular time after 1971, the adjusted cost base to a taxpayer of an interest in a partnership of which the taxpayer was a member on December 31, 1971 and thereafter without interruption until the particular time,

(*a*) the reference in clause 53(1)(*e*)(i)(B) of the amended Act to "relating to" shall be read as a reference to "relating to section 14 or to"; and

(*b*) clause 53(2)(*c*)(i)(B) of the amended Act shall be read as follows:

"(B) paragraphs 12(1)(*o*) and (*z*.5), 18(1)(*m*) and 20(1)(*v*.1), section 31, subsection 40(2), section 55 and subsections 69(6) and (7) of this Act, paragraphs 20(1)(*gg*) and 81(1)(*r*) and (*s*) of the *Income Tax Act*, chapter 148 of the Revised Statutes of Canada, 1952, and the provisions of the *Income Tax Application Rules* relating to section 14, and"

▶ 26(10) ◀

(10) Where paragraph 128.1(1)(*b*) of amended Act applies. Where subsection 48(3) of the amended Act, as it read in its application before 1993, or paragraph 128.1(1)(*b*) of the amended Act applies for the purpose of determining the cost to a taxpayer of any property, this section does not apply for that purpose.

▶ 26(11) ◀

(11) Fair market value of publicly-traded securities. For the purposes of this section, the fair market value on valuation day of any property prescribed to be a publicly-traded share or security shall be deemed to be the greater of the amount, if any, prescribed in respect of that property and the fair market value of that property, otherwise determined, on valuation day.

Related Regulations: Part XLIV.

▶ 26(11.1) ◀

(11.1) Fair market value of share of foreign affiliate. For the purposes of computing the fair market value

(*a*) on December 31, 1971, or

(*b*) at any subsequent time for the purposes of subsection (4),

of any shares owned by a taxpayer resident in Canada of the capital stock of a foreign affiliate of the taxpayer, the fair market value at that time of any asset owned by the foreign affiliate at that time

(*c*) that was subsequently acquired by the taxpayer from the foreign affiliate

(i) as a dividend payable in kind,

(ii) as a benefit the amount of which was deemed by paragraph 80.1(4)(*b*) of the amended Act to have been received by the taxpayer as a dividend from the foreign affiliate, or

(iii) as consideration for the settlement or extinguishment of an obligation described in subsection 80.1(5) of the amended Act, and

(*d*) in respect of which subsection 80.1(4) or (5), as the case may be, of the amended Act applies because of an election described in that subsection made by the taxpayer,

shall be deemed to be the principal amount of that asset.

► 26(11.2) ◄

(11.2) Idem. For the purposes of computing the fair market value on December 31, 1971 of any shares owned by a taxpayer resident in Canada of the capital stock of a foreign affiliate of the taxpayer, the fair market value on that day of any asset owned by the foreign affiliate on that day

(*a*) that was subsequently acquired by the taxpayer from the foreign affiliate as described in paragraph 80.1(6)(*a*) or (*b*) of the amended Act, and

(*b*) in respect of which subsection 80.1(1) of the amended Act applies because of an election described in subsection 80.1(6) of that Act made by the taxpayer,

shall be deemed to be the principal amount of that asset.

► 26(12) ◄

(12) Definitions. In this section,

"amortized cost"—"amortized cost" to a taxpayer of any obligation on January 1, 1972 means

(*a*) the principal amount of the obligation, if its actual cost to the taxpayer was less than 100% but not less than 95% of that principal amount and the obligation was issued before November 8, 1969,

(*b*) the actual cost to the taxpayer of the obligation, if the actual cost to the taxpayer thereof was less than 105% but not less than 100% of the principal amount thereof, and

(*c*) in any other case, the actual cost to the taxpayer of the obligation, plus that proportion of the discount or minus that proportion of the premium, as the case may be, in respect thereof that

(i) the number of full months in the period commencing with the day the taxpayer last acquired the obligation and ending with valuation day,

is of

(ii) the number of full months in the period commencing with the day the taxpayer last acquired the obligation and ending with the date of its maturity;

"capital property"—"capital property" of a taxpayer means any depreciable property of the taxpayer, and any property (other than depreciable property) any gain or loss from the disposition of which would, if the property were disposed of after 1971, be a capital gain or a capital loss, as the case may be, of the taxpayer;

"discount"—"discount" in respect of any obligation owned by a taxpayer means the amount, if any, by which the principal amount thereof exceeds its actual cost to the taxpayer, determined without reference to subsection (3);

"eligible capital property"—"eligible capital property" of a taxpayer means any property, 1/2 of any amount payable to the taxpayer as consideration for the disposition of which would, if the property were disposed of after 1971, be eligible capital amount in respect of business within the meaning assigned by subsection 14(1) of the amended Act;

"obligation"—"obligation" means a bond, debenture, bill, note, mortgage, hypothecary claim or agreement of sale;

"premium"—"premium" in respect of any obligation owned by a taxpayer means the amount, if any, by which its actual cost to the taxpayer determined without reference to subsection (3) exceeds the principal amount thereof;

"tax equity"—"tax equity" of a partnership at any particular time means the amount, if any, by which the total of all amounts each of which is

(*a*) the amount of any money of the partnership on hand at the beginning of its first fiscal period ending after 1971,

(*b*) the cost amount to the partnership, at the beginning of that fiscal period, of any partnership property other than capital property or eligible capital property,

(*c*) an amount in respect of any property (other than depreciable property) that was, at the beginning of that fiscal period, capital property of the partnership, equal to,

(i) where the property was disposed of before 1972, the proceeds of disposition thereof,

(ii) where the property was disposed of after 1971 and before the particular time, the amount determined under this section to be its cost to the partnership for the purposes of computing its adjusted cost base to the partnership immediately before it was disposed of, and

(iii) in any other case, the amount determined under this section to be its cost to the partnership for the purposes of computing its adjusted cost base to the partnership immediately before the particular time,

(*d*) an amount in respect of any prescribed class of depreciable property of the partnership, equal to the amount, if any, by which the total of the undepreciated capital cost to the partnership of property of that class as of January 1, 1972 exceeds the capital cost to the partnership of property of that class acquired by it after the beginning of that fiscal period and before 1972,

(*e*) an amount in respect of any other depreciable property of the partnership at the beginning of that fiscal period, equal to the amount by which

(i) the actual cost of the property to the partnership, or the amount at which the partnership was deemed to have acquired the property under subsection 20(6) of the former Act as it read in its application to the 1971 taxation year, as the case may be,

exceeds

(ii) the total of all amounts in respect of the cost of the property that were allowed under paragraph 11(1)(*a*) of the former Act as it read in computing the income from the partnership of the

ITARs

members thereof for taxation years ending before 1972,

(*f*) an amount in respect of any property that was, at the beginning of that fiscal period, partnership property that was depreciable property, equal to

(i) where the property was disposed of before 1972, the proceeds of disposition thereof minus the amount, if any, by which the lesser of

(A) the proceeds of disposition thereof, and

(B) the capital cost of the property,

exceeds

(C) in respect of depreciable property of a prescribed class, the undepreciable capital cost of all of the property of that class at the time of the disposition, or

(D) in respect of any other depreciable property, the amount that would be determined under paragraph (*e*) if the words "at the beginning of that fiscal period" were read as "at the time of the disposition",

(ii) where the property was disposed of after 1971 and before the particular time, the amount, if any, by which the lesser of

(A) the proceeds of disposition thereof, and

(B) the fair market value of the property on valuation day,

exceeds the capital cost to the partnership of the property, and

(iii) in any other case, the amount, if any, by which

(A) the lesser of the fair market value of the property on valuation day and its fair market value at the particular time

exceeds

(B) the capital cost to the partnership of the property, or

(*g*) an amount in respect of any business carried on by the partnership in its 1971 fiscal period and thereafter without interruption until the particular time, equal to the amount, if any, by which

(i) 2 times the eligible capital amounts (within the meaning assigned by section 14 of the amended Act) in respect of the business (computed without reference to section 21 of this Act) that would have become payable to the partnership

would exceed

(ii) the amount that would be deemed by subsection 21(1) to be the amount that had become payable to the partnership

if the partnership had disposed of the business at the particular time for an amount equal to its fair market value at that time,

exceeds the total of all amounts each of which is the amount of any debt owing by the partnership, or of any other obligation of the partnership to pay an amount, that was outstanding at the beginning of the partnership's first fiscal period ending after 1971, minus such part, if any, thereof as would, if the amount had been paid by the partnership in that fiscal period, have been deductible in computing its income for that fiscal period.

► 26(13) ◄

(13) Meaning of "actual cost". For the purposes of this section, the "actual cost" to a person of any property means, except as expressly otherwise provided in this section, the amount, if any, by which

(*a*) its cost to the person computed without regard to the provisions of this section

exceeds

(*b*) such part of that cost as was deductible in computing the person's income for any taxation year ending before 1972.

► 26(14) ◄

(14) Idem. For the purposes of this section, the "actual cost" to a taxpayer, as of any particular time after 1971, of an interest in a partnership of which the taxpayer was a member on December 31, 1971 and thereafter without interruption until the particular time means the amount, if any, by which the total of

(*a*) the cost to the taxpayer of the interest, computed as of the particular time without regard to the provisions of this section,

(*b*) the total of all amounts each of which is an amount in respect of a fiscal period of the partnership that ended before 1972, equal to the total of

(i) the amount that the taxpayer's income from the partnership for the taxation year of the taxpayer in which the period ended would have been, if the former Act had been read without reference to subsection 83(5) of that Act, and

(ii) the taxpayer's share, determined at the end of the period, of all profits made from dispositions in the period of capital assets that were partnership property of the partnership, to the extent that those profits were not included in computing the income or loss, as the case may be, from the partnership, of any member thereof,

(*c*) where the taxpayer had, before 1972, made a contribution of capital to the partnership otherwise than by way of loan, such part of the contribution as cannot reasonably be regarded as a gift made to, or for the benefit of, any other member of the partnership who was related to the taxpayer, and

(*d*) where, by means of the partnership, the taxpayer carried on before 1972 a business that was a profession, the amount that the taxpayer's 1971 receivables (within the meaning assigned by subsection 23(5)) in respect of the business would have been if, before 1972, the taxpayer had carried on no businesses except by means of the partnership,

exceeds the total of

(*e*) all amounts each of which is an amount in respect of the disposition by the taxpayer before the particular time of a part of the taxpayer's interest in the partnership, equal to such portion of,

(i) where the disposition was made before 1972, the actual cost to the taxpayer of the interest, and

(ii) in any other case, the adjusted cost base to the taxpayer of the interest immediately before the disposition,

as can reasonably be regarded as attributable to the part so disposed of,

(*f*) all amounts each of which is an amount in respect of a fiscal period of the partnership that ended before 1972, equal to the total of

(i) the amount that would have been the taxpayer's loss from the partnership for the taxation year of the taxpayer in which the period ended if the former Act had been read without reference to subsection 83(5) of that Act,

(ii) the taxpayer's share, determined the end of the period, of all losses sustained from dispositions in the period of capital assets that were partnership property of the partnership, to the extent that those losses were not included in computing the loss or income, as the case may be, from the partnership, of any member thereof, and

(iii) the taxpayer's share, determined at the end of the period, of such of the drilling and exploration expenses, including all general geological and geophysical expenses, incurred by the partnership while the taxpayer was a member thereof, on or in respect of exploring or drilling for petroleum or natural gas in Canada as were incurred in the period and after 1948, to the extent that those expenses were not deducted in computing the taxpayer's income from the partnership for the taxpayer's 1971 or any preceding taxation year, and

(*g*) all amounts received by the taxpayer before 1972 as, on account of, in lieu of payment of or in satisfaction of, a distribution of the taxpayer's share of the partnership profits or partnership capital.

► 26(15) ◄

(15) Idem. For the purposes of this section and subsection 88(2.1) of the amended Act, the "actual cost" to a taxpayer, as of any particular time after 1971, of any shares (in this subsection referred to as "new shares") of any class of the capital stock of a new corporation formed as a result of an amalgamation of two or more corporations (within the meaning of section 85I of the former Act as it read in its application to the 1971 taxation year) that were

(*a*) owned by the taxpayer on December 31, 1971, and thereafter without interruption until the particular time, and

(*b*) acquired by the taxpayer by the conversion, because of the amalgamation, of shares of the capital stock of a predecessor corporation into shares of the capital stock of the new corporation,

means that proportion of the actual cost to the taxpayer of any shares owned by the taxpayer that were so converted because of the amalgamation that the fair market value, immediately after the amalgamation, of the new shares of that class so acquired by the taxpayer is of the fair market value, immediately after the amalgamation, of all of the shares of the capital stock of the new corporation so acquired by the taxpayer.

► 26(16) ◄

(16) Idem. For the purposes of this section, the "actual cost" to an individual, as of any particular time after 1971, of any share of the capital stock of a corporation that was

(*a*) owned by the individual on December 31, 1971 and thereafter without interruption until the particular time, and

(*b*) acquired by the individual in a taxation year before 1972 under an agreement referred to in subsection 85A(1) of the former Act as it read in its application to that taxation year,

means an amount equal to the greater of

(*c*) the actual cost to the individual of the share computed without regard to this subsection, and

(*d*) the fair market value of the share at the time the individual so acquired it.

► 26(17) ◄

(17) Idem. For the purposes of this section and subsection 88(2.1) of the amended Act, the "actual cost" to a taxpayer, as of any particular time after 1971, of any capital property received by the taxpayer before 1972 and owned by the taxpayer thereafter without interruption until the particular time means,

(*a*) where the property was so received as, on account of, in lieu of payment of or in satisfaction of, a dividend payable in kind (other than a stock dividend) in respect of a share owned by the taxpayer of the capital stock of a corporation, the fair market value of that property at the time the property was so received;

(*b*) where the property so received was a share of the capital stock of a corporation received by the taxpayer as a stock dividend, the amount that, because of the receipt of the share, was deemed by subsection 81(3) of the former Act to have been received by the taxpayer as a dividend; and

(*c*) where the property was so received from a pension fund or plan, an employees profit sharing plan, a retirement savings plan, a deferred profit sharing plan or a supplementary unemployment benefit plan, the fair market value of that property at the time the property was so received.

Interpretation Bulletins: *Secondary* — IT-88R2 Stock dividends.

► 26(17.1) ◄

(17.1) Application. Where a taxpayer is deemed to have acquired a property because of subsection 138(11.3) of the amended Act, this section does not apply in respect of any subsequent disposition or deemed disposition of the property.

► 26(18) ◄

(18) Transfer of farm land by a farmer to his child at death. Where

(*a*) a taxpayer owned, on December 31, 1971 and thereafter without interruption until the taxpayer's death, any land referred to in subsection 70(9) of the amended Act, (*b*) the land has, on or after the death of the taxpayer and as a consequence thereof, been transferred or distributed to a child of the taxpayer who was resident in Canada immediately before the death of the taxpayer, and

(*c*) it can be shown, within the period ending 36 months after the death of the taxpayer or, where written application therefor has been made to the Minister by the legal representative of the taxpayer within that period, within such longer period as the Minister considers reasonable in the circumstances, that the land has become vested indefeasibly in the child,

the following rules apply:

(*d*) paragraph 70(9)(*b*) of the amended Act does not apply for the purpose of determining the cost to the child of the land or part thereof, as the case may be, and

(*e*) subsection (5) applies in respect of the transfer or distribution of the land to the child as if the references in that subsection to "June 18, 1971" were references to "December 31, 1971".

Interpretation Bulletins: *Secondary* — IT-349R3 Intergenerational transfers of farm property on death.

▶ 26(19) ◀

(19) Inter vivos transfer of farm land by farmer to child. Where a taxpayer owned, on December 31, 1971, and thereafter without interruption until a transfer thereof by the taxpayer to the taxpayer's child, in circumstances to which subsection 73(3) of the amended Act applies, land referred to in that subsection,

(*a*) paragraph 73(3)(*d*) of the amended Act does not apply for the purpose of determining the cost to the child of the land; and

(*b*) subsection (5) shall apply in respect of the transfer of the land to the child as if the references in that subsection to "June 18, 1971" were references to "December 31, 1971".

Interpretation Bulletins: *Secondary* — IT-268R4 Inter vivos transfer of farm property to child.

▶ 26(20) ◀

(20) Extended meaning of "child". For the purposes of subsections (18) and (19), "child" of a taxpayer includes

(*a*) a child of the taxpayer's child;

(*b*) a child of the taxpayer's child's child; and

(*c*) a person who, at any time before attaining the age of 21 years, was wholly dependent on the taxpayer for support and of whom the taxpayer had, at that time, in law or in fact, the custody and control.

▶ 26(21) ◀

(21) Shares received on amalgamation. Where, after May 6, 1974, there has been an amalgamation (within the meaning assigned by section 87 of the amended Act) of two or more corporations (each of which is in this subsection referred to as a "predecessor corporation") to form one corporate entity (in this subsection referred to as the "new corporation"), and

(*a*) any shareholder (except any predecessor corporation) owned shares of the capital stock of a predecessor corporation on December 31, 1971 and thereafter without interruption until immediately before the amalgamation,

(*b*) any shares referred to in paragraph (*a*) were shares of one class of the capital stock of a predecessor corporation (in this subsection referred to as the "old shares"),

(*c*) no consideration was received by the shareholder for the disposition of the old shares on the amalgamation other than shares of one class of the capital stock of the new corporation (in this subsection referred to as the "new shares"), and

(*c*.1) the cost of the new shares received by the shareholder because of the amalgamation was determined otherwise than because of paragraph 87(4)(*e*) of the amended Act,

notwithstanding any other provision of this Act or of the amended Act, for the purposes of subsection 88(2.1) of the amended Act and of determining the cost to the taxpayer and the adjusted cost base to the taxpayer of the new shares,

(*d*) the property that was the old shares shall be deemed not to have been disposed of by the shareholder because of the amalgamation but to have been altered, in form only, because of the amalgamation and to have continued in existence in the form of the new shares, and

(*e*) the property that is the new shares shall be deemed not to have been acquired by the shareholder because of the amalgamation but to have been in existence prior thereto in the form of the old shares that were altered, in form only, because of the amalgamation.

▶ 26(22) ◀

(22) Options received on amalgamations. Where, after May 6, 1974, there has been an amalgamation (within the meaning assigned by section 87 of the amended Act) of two or more corporations (each of which is in this subsection referred to as a "predecessor corporation") to form one corporate entity (in this subsection referred to as the "new corporation") and a taxpayer has acquired an option to acquire capital property that was shares of the capital stock of the new corporation (in this subsection referred to as the "new option") as sole consideration for the disposition on the amalgamation of an option to acquire shares of the capital stock of a predecessor corporation (in this subsection referred to as the "old option") owned by the taxpayer on December 31, 1971 and thereafter without interruption until immediately before the amalgamation, notwithstanding any other provision of this Act or of the amended Act, for the purposes of subsection 88(2.1) of the amended Act and of determining the cost to the taxpayer and the adjusted cost base to the taxpayer of the new option,

(*a*) the property that was the old option shall be deemed not to have been disposed of by the taxpayer because of the amalgamation but to have been altered, in form only, because of the amalgamation and to have continued in existence in the form of the new option; and

(*b*) the property that is the new option shall be deemed not to have been acquired by the taxpayer because of the amalgamation but to have been in existence prior thereto in the form of the old option that was altered, in form only, because of the amalgamation.

► 26(23) ◄

(23) Obligations received on amalgamations. Where, after May 6, 1974, there has been an amalgamation (within the meaning assigned by section 87 of the amended Act) of two or more corporations (each of which is in this subsection referred to as a "predecessor corporation") to form one corporate entity (in this subsection referred to as the "new corporation") and a taxpayer has acquired a capital property that was a bond, debenture, note, mortgage, hypothecary claim or other similar obligation of the new corporation (in this subsection referred to as the "new obligation") as sole consideration for the disposition on the amalgamation of a bond, debenture, note, mortgage, hypothecary claim or other similar obligation respectively of a predecessor corporation (in this subsection referred to as the "old obligation") owned by the taxpayer on December 31, 1971 and thereafter without interruption until immediately before the amalgamation, notwithstanding any other provision of this Act or of the amended Act, for the purposes of subsection 88(2.1) of the amended Act and of determining the cost to the taxpayer and the adjusted cost base to the taxpayer of the new obligation,

(*a*) the property that was the old obligation shall be deemed not to have been disposed of by the taxpayer because of the amalgamation but to have been altered, in form only, because of the amalgamation and to have continued in existence in the form of the new obligation; and

(*b*) the property that is the new obligation shall be deemed not to have been acquired by the taxpayer because of the amalgamation but to have been in existence prior thereto in the form of the old obligation that was altered, in form only, because of the amalgamation.

► 26(24) ◄

(24) Convertible properties. Where there has been an exchange to which subsection 51(1) of the amended Act applies on which a taxpayer has acquired shares of one class of the capital stock of a corporation (in this subsection referred to as the "new shares") in exchange for a share, bond, debenture or note of the corporation (in this subsection referred to as the "old property") owned by the taxpayer on December 31, 1971 and thereafter without interruption until immediately before the time of the exchange, notwithstanding any other provision of this Act or of the amended Act, for the purposes of subsection 88(2.1) of the amended Act and, where the exchange occurred after May 6, 1974, for the purposes of determining the cost to the taxpayer and the adjusted cost base to the taxpayer of the new shares,

(*a*) the property that was the old property shall be deemed not to have been disposed of by the taxpayer because of the exchange but to have been altered, in form only, because of the exchange and to have continued in existence in the form of the new shares; and

(*b*) the property that is the new shares shall be deemed not to have been acquired by the taxpayer because of the exchange but to have been in existence prior thereto in the form of the old property that was altered, in form only, because of the exchange.

Interpretation Bulletins: *Secondary* — IT-146R4 Shares entitling shareholders to choose taxable or capital dividends.

► 26(25) ◄

(25) Bond conversion. Where, after May 6, 1974, there has been an exchange to which section 51.1 of the amended Act applies on which a taxpayer has acquired a bond of a debtor (in this subsection referred to as the "new bond") in exchange for another bond of the same debtor (in this subsection referred to as the "old bond") owned by the taxpayer on December 31, 1971 and thereafter without interruption until immediately before the exchange, notwithstanding any other provision of this Act or of the amended Act, for the purposes of subsection 88(2.1) of the amended Act and of determining the cost to the taxpayer and the adjusted cost base to the taxpayer of the new bond,

(*a*) the property that was the old bond shall be deemed not to have been disposed of by the taxpayer because of the exchange but to have been altered, in form only, because of the exchange and to have continued in existence in the form of the new bond; and

(*b*) the property that is the new bond shall be deemed not to have been acquired by the taxpayer because of the exchange but to have been in existence prior thereto in the form of the old bond that was altered, in form only, because of the exchange.

► 26(26) ◄

(26) Share for share exchange. Where, after May 6, 1974, there has been an exchange to which subsection 85.1(1) of the amended Act applies on which a taxpayer has acquired shares of any particular class of the capital stock of a corporation (in this subsection referred to as the "new shares") in exchange for shares of any particular class of the capital stock of another corporation (in this subsection referred to as the "old shares") owned by the taxpayer on December 31, 1971 and thereafter without interruption until immediately before the exchange, notwithstanding any other provision of this Act or of the amended Act, for the purposes of subsection 88(2.1) of the amended Act and of determining the cost to the taxpayer and the adjusted cost base to the taxpayer of the new shares,

(*a*) the property that was the old shares shall be deemed not to have been disposed of by the taxpayer because of the exchange but to have been altered, in form only, because of the exchange and to have continued in existence in the form of the new shares; and (*b*) the property that is the new shares shall be deemed not to have been acquired by the taxpayer because of the exchange but to have been in existence prior thereto in the form of the old shares that were altered, in form only, because of the exchange.

► 26(27) ◄

(27) Reorganization of capital. Where, after May 6, 1974, there has been a reorganization of the capital of a corporation to which section 86 of the amended Act applies on which a taxpayer has acquired shares of a particular class of the capital stock of the corporation (in this subsection referred to as the "new shares") as the sole consideration for the disposition on the reorganization of shares of another class of the capital stock of the corporation (in this subsection referred to as the "old shares") owned by the taxpayer on December 31, 1971 and thereafter without interruption until immediately before the reorganization and the cost to the taxpayer of the new shares was determined otherwise than because of subsection 86(2) of the amended Act, notwithstanding any other provision of this Act or of the amended Act, for the purposes of subsection 88(2.1) of the amended Act and of determining the cost to the taxpayer and the adjusted cost base to the taxpayer of the new shares,

(*a*) the property that was the old shares shall be deemed not to have been disposed of by the taxpayer because of the reorganization but to have been altered, in form only, because of the reorganization and to have continued in existence in the form of the new shares; and

(*b*) the property that is the new shares shall be deemed not to have been acquired by the taxpayer because of the reorganization but to have been in existence prior thereto in the form of the old shares that were altered, in form only, because of the reorganization.

► 26(28) ◄

(28) Idem. Where a taxpayer acquired a property (in this subsection referred to as the "first property") in circumstances to which any of subsections (5) and (21) to (27) applied and subsequently acquires, in exchange for or in consideration for the disposition of the first property, another property in circumstances to which any of subsections (21) to (27) would apply if the taxpayer had owned the first property on December 31, 1971 and thereafter without interruption until the time of the subsequent acquisition, for the purposes of applying subsections (21) to (27) in respect of that subsequent acquisition, the taxpayer shall be deemed to have owned the first property on December 31, 1971 and thereafter without interruption until the time of the subsequent acquisition.

► 26(29) ◄

(29) Effect of election under subsection 110.6(19). Where subsection 110.6(19) of the amended Act applies to a particular property, for the purposes of determining the cost and the adjusted cost base to a taxpayer of any property at any time after February 22, 1994, the particular property shall be deemed not to have been owned by any taxpayer on December 31, 1971.

► 26(30) ◄

(30) Additions to taxable Canadian property. Subsections (1.1) to (29) do not apply to a disposition by a non-resident person of a property

(*a*) that the person last acquired before April 27, 1995;

(*b*) that would not be a taxable Canadian property immediately before the disposition if section 115 of the amended Act were read as it applied to dispositions that occurred on April 26, 1995; and

(*c*) that would be a taxable Canadian property immediately before the disposition if section 115 of the amended Act were read as it applied to dispositions that occurred on January 1, 1996.

26.1. Change of use of property before 1972

(1) For the purposes of paragraph 40(2)(*b*) and the definition "principal residence" in section 54 of the amended Act, where a taxpayer owned, on December 31, 1971, a property that is a housing unit, a leasehold interest in a housing unit or a share of the capital stock of a cooperative housing corporation, if the housing unit was, or if the share was acquired for the sole purpose of acquiring the right to inhabit, a housing unit owned by the corporation that was ordinarily inhabited by the taxpayer, the taxpayer began at any time thereafter but before 1972 to use the property for the purpose of gaining or producing income therefrom, or for the purpose of gaining or producing income from a business, and the taxpayer elected in the taxpayer's return of income for the 1974 or 1975 taxation year as if the taxpayer had begun to use the property for the purpose of gaining or producing income therefrom or for the purpose of gaining or producing income from a business on January 1, 1972, the taxpayer shall be deemed to have made an election under subsection 45(2) of the amended Act in the taxpayer's return of income for the 1972 taxation year and to have so begun to use the property.

Income Tax Folios: *Secondary* — S1-F3-C2 Principal Residence.

► 26.1(2) ◄

(2) No capital cost allowance while election in force. Where the taxpayer has made the election described in subsection (1), no amount may be deducted under paragraph 20(1)(*a*) of the amended Act for the 1974 and subsequent taxation years in respect of property referred to in that subsection while the election remains in force.

27. Moving expenses

(Repealed by 1985, c. 45, s. 132.)

28. Income derived from operation of mine

(1) (Repealed by 1985, c. 45, s. 132.)

► 28(1.1) ◄

(1.1) "Income derived from the operation of a mine" defined — (Repealed by 1985, c. 45, s. 132.)

► 28(2) ◄

(2) Definitions — (Repealed by 1985, c. 45, s. 132.)

29. Deduction from income of petroleum or natural gas corporation

(1) A corporation whose principal business is production, refining or marketing of petroleum, petroleum products or natural gas or exploring or drilling for petroleum or natural gas may deduct, in computing its income for a taxation year, the lesser of

(*a*) the total of such of the drilling and exploration expenses, including all general geological and geophysical expenses, incurred by it on or in respect of exploring or drilling for petroleum or natural gas in Canada as were incurred during the calendar years 1949 to 1952, to the extent that they were not deductible in computing income for a preceding taxation year, and

(*b*) of that total, an amount equal to its income for the taxation year if no deduction were allowed under this section or section 65, 66 or 66.1 of the amended Act minus the deductions allowed for the year under subsections (9), (10) and (25) of this section and sections 112 and 113 of the amended Act.

Related Regulations: Part XI; Part XII.

► 29(2) ◄

(2) Deduction from income of mining corporation. A corporation whose principal business is mining or exploring for minerals may deduct, in computing its income for a taxation year, the lesser of

(*a*) the total of such of the prospecting, exploration and development expenses incurred by it in searching for minerals in Canada as were incurred during 1952, to the extent that they were not deductible in computing income for a preceding taxation year, and

(*b*) of that total, an amount equal to its income for the taxation year if no deduction were allowed under this section or section 65, 66 or 66.1 of the amended Act minus the deductions allowed for the year under subsections (9), (10) and (25) of this section and sections 112 and 113 of the amended Act,

if the corporation has filed certified statements of those expenses and has satisfied the Minister that it has been actively engaged in prospecting and exploring for minerals in Canada by means of qualified persons and has incurred the expenses for those purposes.

Related Regulations: Part XII.

► 29(3) ◄

(3) Deduction from income of petroleum or natural gas corporation or mining corporation. A corporation whose principal business is

(*a*) production, refining or marketing of petroleum, petroleum products or natural gas, or exploring or drilling for petroleum or natural gas, or

(*b*) mining or exploring for minerals,

may deduct, in computing its income for a taxation year, the lesser of

(*c*) the total of such of

(i) the drilling and exploration expenses, including all general geological and geophysical expenses, incurred by it on or in respect of exploring or drilling for petroleum or natural gas in Canada, and

(ii) the prospecting, exploration and development expenses incurred by it in searching for minerals in Canada,

as were incurred after 1952 and before April 11, 1962, to the extent that they were not deductible in computing income for a preceding taxation year, and

(*d*) of that total, an amount equal to its income for the taxation year if no deduction were allowed under this section or section 65, 66 or 66.1 of the amended Act minus the deductions allowed for the year under subsections (1), (2), (9), (10) and (25) of this section and sections 112 and 113 of the amended Act.

Related Regulations: Part XII.

► 29(4) ◄

(4) Deduction from income of petroleum corporation, etc. A corporation whose principal business is

(*a*) production, refining or marketing of petroleum, petroleum products or natural gas, or exploring or drilling for petroleum or natural gas,

(*b*) mining or exploring for minerals,

(*c*) processing mineral ores for the purpose of recovering metals therefrom,

(*d*) a combination of

(i) processing mineral ores for the purpose of recovering metals therefrom, and

(ii) processing metals recovered from the ores so processed,

(*e*) fabricating metals, or

(*f*) operating a pipeline for the transmission of oil or natural gas,

may deduct, in computing its income for a taxation year, the lesser of

(*g*) the total of such of

(i) the drilling and exploration expenses, including all general geological and geophysical expenses, incurred by it on or in respect of exploring or drilling for petroleum or natural gas in Canada, and

(ii) the prospecting, exploration and development expenses incurred by it in searching for minerals in Canada,

as were incurred after April 10, 1962 and before 1972, to the extent that they were not deductible in computing income for a preceding taxation year, and

(*h*) of that total, an amount equal to its income for the taxation year if no deduction were allowed under this subsection or section 65, 66 or 66.1 of the amended Act minus the deductions allowed for the year under subsection 66(2) and sections 112 and 113 of the amended Act.

Related Regulations: Part XII.

▶ 29(5) ◀

(5) Application of para. (4)(*g*). In applying paragraph (4)(*g*) to a corporation described in paragraph (4)(*f*), the reference in paragraph (4)(*g*) to "April 10, 1962" shall be read as a reference to "June 13, 1963".

▶ 29(6) ◀

(6) Joint exploration corporation may renounce expenses — (Repealed by 1997, c. 25, s. 73(1).)

▶ 29(7) ◀

(7) Idem — (Repealed by 1997, c. 25, s. 73(1).)

▶ 29(8) ◀

(8) Definitions — (Repealed by 1997, c. 25, s. 73(1).)

▶ 29(9) ◀

(9) Deduction from income from businesses of associations, etc. There may be deducted in computing the income of a taxpayer for a taxation year from the businesses of all associations, partnerships or syndicates formed for the purpose of exploring or drilling for petroleum or natural gas and of which the taxpayer was a member or partner, the lesser of

(*a*) the total of the taxpayer's share of such of the drilling and exploration expenses, including all general geological and geophysical expenses, incurred by all those associations, partnerships or syndicates while the taxpayer was a member or partner thereof, on or in respect of exploring or drilling for petroleum or natural gas in Canada as were incurred after 1948 and before April 11, 1962, to the extent that they were not deductible in computing the taxpayer's income for a preceding taxation year, and

(*b*) of that total, an amount equal to the taxpayer's income from the businesses of all those associations, partnerships or syndicates for the taxation year, computed before making any deduction under this section or section 65, 66 or 66.1 of the amended Act.

▶ 29(10) ◀

(10) Idem. There may be deducted in computing the income of a taxpayer for a taxation year from the businesses of all associations, partnerships or syndicates formed for the purpose of exploring or drilling for petroleum or natural gas and of which the taxpayer was a member or partner, the lesser of

(*a*) the total of the taxpayer's share of such of the drilling and exploration expenses, including all general geological and geophysical expenses incurred by all those associations, partnerships or syndicates while the taxpayer was a member or partner thereof, on or in respect of exploring or drilling for petroleum or natural gas in Canada as were incurred after April 10, 1962 and before 1972, to the extent that they were not deductible in computing the taxpayer's income for a preceding taxation year, and

(*b*) of that total, an amount equal to the taxpayer's income from the businesses of all those associations, partnerships or syndicates for the taxation year computed before making any deduction under this section or section 65, 66 or 66.1 of the amended Act, minus the deduction allowed for the year under subsection (9) of this section.

▶ 29(11) ◀

(11) Deduction from income of corporation. A corporation, other than a corporation described in subsection (4), may deduct, in computing its income for a taxation year, the lesser of

(*a*) the total of such of

(i) the drilling and exploration expenses, including all general geological and geophysical expenses, incurred by it on or in respect of exploring or drilling for petroleum or natural gas in Canada, and

(ii) the prospecting, exploration and development expenses incurred by it in searching for minerals in Canada,

as were incurred after April 10, 1962 and before 1972, to the extent that they were not deductible in computing income for a preceding taxation year, and

(*b*) of that total, an amount that would be equal to the total of

(i) its income for the taxation year from operating an oil or gas well in Canada in which the corporation has an interest,

(ii) its income for the taxation year from royalties in respect of an oil or gas well in Canada,

(iii) any amount included in computing its income for the taxation year because of subsection (17), and

(iv) the amount, if any, included under paragraph 59(3.2)(*b*) or (*c*) of the amended Act in computing its income for the year,

if no deduction were allowed under this section or section 65, 66 or 66.1 of the amended Act minus the deductions allowed for the year under subsections (9) and (10) of this section and subsection 66(2) of the amended Act.

▶ 29(12) ◀

(12) Deduction by individual of exploration expenses. There may be deducted, in computing an individual's income for a taxation year, the lesser of

(*a*) the total of such of

(i) the drilling and exploration expenses, including all general geological and geophysical expenses, incurred by the individual on or in respect of exploring or drilling for petroleum or natural gas in Canada, and

(ii) the individual's share of the drilling and exploration expenses, including all general geological and geophysical expenses, incurred by all associations, partnerships or syndicates described in subsection (9), while the individual was a member or partner thereof, on or in respect of exploring or drilling for petroleum or natural gas in Canada,

as were incurred after April 10, 1962 and before 1972, to the extent that they were not deductible in computing the individual's income for a preceding taxation year, and

(*b*) of that total, an amount that would be equal to the total of

(i) the individual's income for the taxation year from a business that consisted of the operation of an oil or gas well in Canada in which the individual had an interest,

(ii) the individual's income for the taxation year from royalties in respect of an oil or gas well in Canada,

(iii) any amount included in computing the individual's income for the taxation year because of subsection (17), and

(iv) the amount, if any, included under paragraph 59(3.2)(*b*) or (*c*) of the amended Act in computing the individual's income for the year,

if no deduction were allowed under this section or section 65, 66 or 66.1 of the amended Act, minus the deductions allowed for the year under subsections (9) and (10) of this section.

► 29(13) ◄

(13) Limitation re payments for exploration and drilling rights. In computing a deduction under subsection (1), (3) or (9), no amount shall be included in respect of a payment for or in respect of a right, licence or privilege to explore for, drill for or take petroleum or natural gas, acquired before April 11, 1962, other than an annual payment not exceeding $1 per acre.

► 29(14) ◄

(14) Exploration and drilling rights; payments deductible. Where an association, partnership or syndicate described in subsection (9) or a corporation or individual has, after April 10, 1962 and before 1972, acquired under an agreement or other contract or arrangement a right, licence or privilege to explore for, drill for or take in Canada petroleum, natural gas or other related hydrocarbons (except coal) under which agreement, contract or arrangement there was not acquired any other right to, over or in respect of the land in respect of which such right, licence or privilege was so acquired except the right

(*a*) to explore for, drill for or take materials and substances (whether liquid or solid and whether hydrocarbons or not) produced in association with the petroleum, natural gas or other related hydrocarbons (except coal) or found in any water contained in an oil or gas reservoir, or

(*b*) to enter on, use and occupy as much of the land as is necessary for the purpose of exploiting the right, licence or privilege,

an amount paid in respect of the acquisition thereof that was paid

(*c*) before 1972, shall, for the purposes of subsections (4), (7), (10), (11) and (12), be deemed to be a drilling or exploration expense on or in respect of exploring or drilling for petroleum or natural gas in Canada incurred at the time of its payment,

(*d*) after 1971 and before May 7, 1974, shall, for the purposes of the amended Act, be deemed to be Canadian exploration and development expenses (within the meaning assigned by subsection 66(15) of the amended Act) incurred at the time of its payment, and

(*e*) after May 6, 1974, shall, for the purposes of the amended Act, be deemed to be a Canadian development expense (within the meaning assigned by subsection 66.2(5) of the amended Act) incurred at the time of its payment.

► 29(15) ◄

(15) Idem. In applying subsection (14) for the purposes of subsection (7), the expression "after April 10, 1962 and before 1972" in subsection (14) shall be read as "after April 10, 1962 and before April 27, 1965".

► 29(16) ◄

(16) Receipts for exploration or drilling rights included in income. Where a right, licence or privilege to explore for, drill for or take in Canada petroleum, natural gas or other related hydrocarbons (except coal) was disposed of after April 10, 1962 and before October 23, 1968

(*a*) by a corporation described in subsection (4),

(*b*) by a corporation, other than a corporation described in subsection (4), that was at the time of acquisition of the right, licence or privilege a corporation described in subsection (4), or

(*c*) by an association, partnership or syndicate described in subsection (9),

any amount received by the corporation, association, partnership or syndicate as consideration for the disposition thereof shall be included in computing its income for its fiscal period in which the amount was received, unless the corporation, association, partnership or syndicate

(*d*) acquired the right, licence or privilege by inheritance or bequest, or

(*e*) acquired the right, licence or privilege before April 11, 1962 and disposed of it before November 9, 1962.

► 29(17) ◄

(17) Idem. Where a right, licence or privilege to explore for, drill for or take in Canada petroleum, natural gas or other related hydrocarbons (except coal) that was acquired after April 10, 1962 and before 1972 by an individual or a corporation other than a corporation described in subsection (4), was subsequently disposed of before October 23, 1968, any amount received by the taxpayer as consideration for the disposition thereof shall be included in computing the taxpayer's income for the taxation year in which the amount was received, unless the right, licence or privilege was acquired by the taxpayer by inheritance or bequest.

► 29(18) ◄

(18) Idem. Subsections (16) and (17) do not apply to any disposition by an association, partnership or syndicate described in subsection (9) or a corporation or an indi-

ITARs

vidual of any right, licence or privilege described in subsection (14) or (16) unless the right, licence or privilege was acquired by the association, partnership, syndicate or corporation or individual, as the case may be, under an agreement, contract or arrangement described in subsection (14).

► 29(19) ◄

(19) Idem. For the purposes of subsections (16) and (17),

(*a*) where an association, partnership or syndicate described in subsection (9) or a corporation or an individual has disposed of any interest in land that includes a right, licence or privilege described in subsection (14) that was acquired under an agreement, contract or arrangement described in that subsection, the proceeds of disposition of the interest shall be deemed to be proceeds of disposition of the right, licence or privilege; and

(*b*) where an association, partnership or syndicate described in subsection (9) or a corporation or an individual has acquired a right, licence or privilege described in subsection (14) under an agreement, contract or arrangement described in that subsection and subsequently disposes of any interest

(i) in the right, licence or privilege, or

(ii) in the production of wells situated on the land to which the right, licence or privilege relates,

the proceeds of disposition of the interest shall be deemed to be proceeds of disposition of the right, licence or privilege.

► 29(20) ◄

(20) Idem. Subsections (11), (12) and (17) do not apply in computing the income for a taxation year of a taxpayer whose business includes trading or dealing in rights, licences or privileges to explore for, drill for or take in Canada petroleum, natural gas or other related hydrocarbons (except coal).

► 29(21) ◄

(21) Bonus payments. Notwithstanding subsection (13), where a corporation whose principal business is of the class described in paragraph (3)(*a*) or (*b*) or an association, partnership or syndicate formed for the purpose of exploring or drilling for petroleum or natural gas has after 1952 paid an amount (other than a rental or royalty) to the government of Canada or a province for

(*a*) the right to explore for petroleum or natural gas on a specified parcel of land in Canada (which right is, for greater certainty, declared to include a right of the type commonly referred to as a "licence", "permit" or "reservation"), or

(*b*) a legal lease of the right to take or remove petroleum or natural gas from a specified parcel of land in Canada,

and before April 11, 1962 acquired the rights in respect of which the amount was so paid and, before any well came into production on the land in reasonable commercial quantities, the corporation, association, partnership or syndicate surrendered all the rights so acquired (including, in respect of a right of the kind described in paragraph (*a*), all rights thereunder to any lease and all rights under any lease made thereunder) without receiving any consideration therefor or repayment of any part of the amount so paid, the amount so paid shall, for the purposes of subsections (3), (4), (7), (9) and (10) of this section, and for the purposes of subsections 66(1), (10) and (10.1) and the definitions "Canadian exploration and development expenses" in subsection 66(15) and "Canadian exploration expense" in subsection 66.1(6) of the amended Act, be deemed to have been a drilling or exploration expense on or in respect of exploring or drilling for petroleum or natural gas in Canada or a Canadian exploration expense described in paragraph (*a*) of the definition "Canadian exploration expense" in subsection 66.1(6) of the amended Act, as the case may be, incurred by the corporation, association, partnership or syndicate during the taxation year in which the rights were so surrendered.

► 29(22) ◄

(22) Idem. In applying the provisions of subsection (25) to determine the amount that may be deducted by a successor corporation in computing its income for a taxation year, where the predecessor corporation has paid an amount (other than a rental or royalty) to the government of Canada or a province for

(*a*) the right to explore for petroleum or natural gas on a specified parcel of land in Canada (which is, for greater certainty, declared to include a right of the type commonly referred to as a "licence", "permit" or "reservation"), or

(*b*) a legal lease of the right to take or remove petroleum or natural gas from a specified parcel of land in Canada,

if, before the predecessor corporation was entitled, because of subsection (21), to any deduction in computing its income for a taxation year in respect of the amount so paid, the property of the predecessor corporation was acquired by the successor corporation before April 11, 1962 in the manner set out in subsection (25), and the successor corporation did, before any well came into production in reasonable commercial quantities on the land referred to in paragraph (*a*) or (*b*), surrender all the rights so acquired by the predecessor corporation (including in respect of a right of the kind described in paragraph (*a*), all rights thereunder to any lease and all rights under any lease made thereunder) without receiving any consideration therefor or payment of any part of the amount so paid by the predecessor corporation, the amount so paid by the predecessor corporation shall be added to the amount determined under paragraph (25)(*c*).

► 29(23) ◄

(23) Expenses incurred for specified considerations not deductible. For the purposes of this section and section 53 of chapter 25 of the Statutes of Canada, 1949 (Second Session), it is declared that expenses incurred before 1972 by a corporation, association, partnership or syndicate on or in respect of exploring or drilling for petroleum or natural gas in Canada or in searching for minerals in Canada do not and never did include expenses so incurred by that corporation, association, partnership or syndicate under an agreement under which it undertook to incur those expenses in consideration for

(*a*) shares of the capital stock of a corporation that owned or controlled the mineral rights;

(*b*) an option to purchase shares of the capital stock of a corporation that owned or controlled the mineral rights; or

(*c*) a right to purchase shares of the capital stock of a corporation that was to be formed for the purpose of acquiring or controlling the mineral rights.

► 29(24) ◄

(24) Exception. Notwithstanding subsection (23), a corporation whose principal business is

(*a*) production, refining or marketing of petroleum, petroleum products or natural gas or exploring or drilling for petroleum or natural gas, or

(*b*) mining or exploring for minerals,

may deduct, in computing its income for a taxation year, the lesser of

(*c*) the total of such of

(i) the drilling and exploration expenses, including all general geological and geophysical expenses, incurred by it on or in respect of exploring or drilling for petroleum or natural gas in Canada, and

(ii) the prospecting, exploration and development expenses incurred by it in searching for minerals in Canada,

as were incurred after 1953 and before 1972,

(iii) under an agreement under which it undertook to incur those expenses for a consideration mentioned in paragraph (23)(*a*), (*b*) or (*c*), and

(iv) to the extent that they were not deductible in computing income for a preceding taxation year, and

(*d*) of that total, an amount equal to its income for the taxation year if no deduction were allowed under this subsection or subsection (4) or under section 65, 66 or 66.1 of the amended Act minus the deductions allowed for the year under subsection 66(2) and sections 112 and 113 of the amended Act,

but where a corporation has incurred expenses in respect of which this subsection authorizes deduction from income for a taxation year, no deduction in respect of those expenses may be made in computing the income of any other corporation or from the business of an association, partnership or syndicate for any taxation year.

► 29(25) ◄

(25) Successor rule. Notwithstanding subsection (24) and subject to subsections 66.7(6) and (7) of the amended Act, where a corporation (in this subsection referred to as the "successor") whose principal business is

(*a*) production, refining or marketing of petroleum, petroleum products or natural gas, or exploring or drilling for petroleum or natural gas, or exploring or drilling for petroleum or natural gas, or

(*b*) mining or exploring for minerals,

has, at any time after 1954, acquired a particular Canadian resource property (whether by way of a purchase, amalgamation, merger, winding-up or otherwise) from another person whose principal business was a business described in paragraph (*a*) or (*b*), there may be deducted by the successor in computing its income for a taxation year an amount not exceeding the total of all amounts each of which is an amount determined in respect of an original owner of the particular property that is the lesser of

(*c*) the total of

(i) the drilling and exploration expenses, including all general geological and geophysical expenses, incurred before 1972 by the original owner on or in respect of exploring or drilling for petroleum or natural gas in Canada, and

(ii) the prospecting, exploration and development expenses incurred before 1972 by the original owner in searching for minerals in Canada,

to the extent that those expenses

(iii) were not otherwise deducted in computing the income of the successor for the year, were not deducted in computing the income of the successor for any preceding taxation year and were not deductible by the original owner or deducted by any predecessor owner of the particular property in computing income for any taxation year, and

(iv) would, but for the provisions of any of this subsection and paragraphs (1)(*b*), (2)(*b*), (3)(*a*), (4)(*h*) and (24)(*d*), have been deductible in computing the income of the original owner or any predecessor owner of the particular property for the taxation year preceding the taxation year in which the particular property was acquired by the successor, and

(*d*) the amount, if any, by which

(i) the part of its income for the year that can reasonably be regarded as being attributable to

(A) the amount included in computing its income for the year under paragraph 59(3.2)(*c*) of the amended Act that can reasonably be regarded as being attributable to the disposition by it in the year or a preceding taxation year of any Canadian resource properties owned by the original owner and each predecessor owner of the particular property before the acquisition of the particular property by the successor to the extent that the proceeds of the disposition have not been included in determining an amount under this clause or clause 66.7(1)(*b*)(i)(A) or (3)(*b*)(i)(A) or paragraph 66.7(10)(*g*) of the amended Act for a preceding taxation year, or

(B) production from the particular property,

computed as if no deduction were allowed under this section or subdivision e of Division B of Part I of the amended Act,

exceeds

(ii) the total of all other amounts deducted under this subsection and subdivision e of Division B of Part I of the amended Act for the year that can reasonably be regarded as attributable to the part of its income for the year described in subparagraph (i) in respect of the particular property.

► 29(25.1) ◄

(25.1) Definitions. For the purposes of subsection (25), the terms "Canadian resource property", "original owner", "predecessor owner" and "production" have the meanings assigned by subsection 66(15) of the amended Act.

► 29(26) ◄

(26) Processing or fabricating corporation. A reference in subsection (3), (21), (24) or (25) to a corporation whose principal business is mining or exploring for minerals shall, for the purposes of this section, be deemed to include a reference to a corporation whose principal business is

(*a*) processing mineral ores for the purpose of recovering metals therefrom,

(*b*) a combination of

(i) processing mineral ores for the purpose of recovering metals therefrom, and

(ii) processing metals recovered from the ores so processed, or

(*c*) fabricating metals,

but in applying the provisions of this section to any such corporation the references, respectively, in subsections (3), (21), (24) and (25) to the years 1952, 1953 and 1954 shall be read as a reference in each case to the year 1956.

► 29(27) ◄

(27) Meaning of "drilling and exploration expenses". For the purposes of this section, "drilling and exploration expenses" incurred on or in respect of exploring or drilling for petroleum or natural gas in Canada include expenses incurred on or in respect of

(*a*) drilling or converting a well for the disposal of waste liquids from a petroleum or natural gas well in Canada;

(*b*) drilling for water or gas for injection into a petroleum or natural gas formation in Canada; and

(*c*) drilling or converting a well for the injection of water or gas to assist in the recovery of petroleum or natural gas from another well in Canada.

► 29(28) ◄

(28) Deduction from expenses. For the purposes of this section, there shall be deducted in computing

(*a*) drilling and exploration expenses incurred by a taxpayer on or in respect of exploring or drilling for petroleum or natural gas in Canada, and

(*b*) prospecting, exploration and development expenses incurred by a taxpayer in searching for minerals in Canada,

any amount paid to the taxpayer before 1972 under the *Northern Mineral Exploration Assistance Regulations* made under an appropriation Act that provides for payments in respect of the Northern Mineral Grants Program, and there shall be included in computing those expenses any amount, except an amount in respect of interest, paid by the taxpayer before 1972 under those Regulations to Her Majesty in right of Canada.

► 29(29) ◄

(29) Property acquired by second successor corporation — (Repealed by 1987, c. 46, s. 73(2).)

► 29(30) ◄

(30) Inclusion in "drilling and exploration expenses". For the purposes of this section, "drilling and exploration expenses" incurred on or in respect of exploring or drilling for petroleum or natural gas in Canada include an annual payment made for the preservation of a right, licence or privilege described in subsection (14).

► 29(31) ◄

(31) General limitation. Where a corporation, association, partnership or syndicate has incurred expenses the deduction of which from income is authorized under more than one provision of this section, it is not entitled to make the deduction under more than one provision but is entitled to select the provision under which to make the deduction.

► 29(32) ◄

(32) Deduction for provincial tax. Where a corporation whose principal business is production, refining or marketing of petroleum, petroleum products or natural gas or exploring or drilling for petroleum or natural gas could have deducted an amount in respect of expenditures of the corporation in connection with exploration or drilling for petroleum or natural gas incurred in a preceding taxation year from the tax payable under a provincial statute for the 1952 or a subsequent taxation year if the provincial statute were applicable to that year, the corporation may deduct from the tax otherwise payable by it under Part I of the amended Act for the year an amount not exceeding the amount that would have been so deductible.

► 29(33) ◄

(33) Definition of "provincial statute". For the purposes of subsection (32), "provincial statute" means a statute imposing a tax on the incomes of corporations enacted by the legislature of a province in 1949 and, for the purpose of that subsection, an amount deductible thereunder for one year shall, for the purpose of computing the deduction for a subsequent year, be deemed to have been deductible under the provincial statute.

► 29(34) ◄

(34) Expenses deductible under certain enactments deemed not otherwise deductible. Where expenses are or have been, under this section, section 8 of the *Income War Tax Act*, section 16 of chapter 63 of the Statutes of Canada, 1947, section 16 of chapter 53 of the Statutes of Canada, 1948, section 53 of chapter 25 of the Statutes of Canada, 1949 (Second Session) or section 83A of the former Act, deductible from or in computing a taxpayer's income, or where any amount is or has been deductible in respect of expenses under any of those provisions from taxes otherwise payable, it is declared that no amount in respect of the same expenses is or has been deductible under any other authority in computing the income or from the income of that taxpayer or any other taxpayer for any taxation year.

30. Reference to this Act in amended Act

► 30(1) ◄

(1) References in amended Act to Income Tax Application Rules, 1971 — (Repealed by 1987, c. 46, s. 74(1).)

► 30(2) ◄

(2) Idem — (Repealed by 1977-78, c. 1, s. 107(1).)

► 30(3) ◄

(3) [Reference to this Act in amended Act]. In subsection 66(14) of the amended Act, "any amount deductible under the *Income Tax Application Rules*" in respect of that subsection means any amount deductible under section 29 of this Act.

31. Application of s. 67 of amended Act

In respect of any outlay or expense made or incurred by a taxpayer before 1972, section 67 of the amended Act shall be read without reference to the words "in respect of which any amount is".

32. Application of para. 69(1)(*a*) of amended Act

(1) Paragraph 69(1)(*a*) of the amended Act does not apply to deem a taxpayer by whom anything was acquired at any time before 1972 to have acquired it at its fair market value at that time, unless, if subsection 17(1) of the former Act had continued to apply, that fair market value would have been deemed to have been paid or to be payable therefor for the purpose of computing the taxpayer's income from a business.

► 32(2) ◄

(2) Application of para. 69(1)(*b*) of amended Act. Paragraph 69(1)(*b*) of the amended Act does not apply to deem a taxpayer by whom anything was disposed of at any time before the 1972 taxation year to have received proceeds of disposition therefor equal to its fair market value at that time.

► 32(3) ◄

(3) Application of para. 69(1)(*c*) of amended Act. For greater certainty, paragraph 69(1)(*c*) of the amended Act applies to property acquired by a taxpayer before, at or after the end of 1971.

32.1. Capital dividend account

► 32.1(1) ◄

(1) Election respecting surplus — (Repealed by 1977-78, c. 1, s. 108(1).)

► 32.1(2) ◄

(2) Idem — (Repealed by 1977-78, c. 1, s. 108(1).)

► 32.1(3) ◄

(3) Late filed elections — (Repealed by 1985, c. 45, s. 134(1).)

► 32.1(3.1) ◄

(3.1) Request for election — (Repealed by 1985, c. 45, s. 134(1).)

► 32.1(3.2) ◄

(3.2) Penalty — (Repealed by 1985, c. 45, s. 134(1).)

► 32.1(4) ◄

(4) [Capital dividend account]. Where a dividend became payable, or was paid if that time was earlier, by a corporation in a taxation year at a particular time that was before May 7, 1974, for the purpose of computing the corporation's capital dividend account immediately before the particular time, all amounts each of which is an amount in respect of a capital loss from the disposition of property in the taxation year and before the particular time shall be deemed to be nil.

► 32.1(5) ◄

(5) Late-filed section 85 elections — (Repealed by 1985, c. 45, s. 134(2).)

► 32.1(6) ◄

(6) Late-filed subsection 97(2) and 98(3) elections — (Repealed by 1985, c. 45, s. 134(2).)

33. Deemed dividends

(Repealed by 1985, c. 45, s. 135.)

34. Amalgamations

(1) Notwithstanding section 9, subsections 85I(1) and (2) of the former Act continue to apply with such modifications as, in the circumstances, are necessary because of this Act, in respect of any amalgamation of two or more corporations before 1972.

► 34(2) ◄

(2) Idem — (Repealed by 1985, c. 45, s. 136(1).)

► 34(3) ◄

(3) Idem — (Repealed by 1985, c. 45, s. 136(1).)

► 34(4) ◄

(4) Idem [Amalgamations]. In applying the provisions of subsection 29(25) to determine the amount that may be deducted by the successor or second successor corporation, as the case may be, in computing its income under Part I of the amended Act for a taxation year, where a predecessor corporation has paid an amount (other than a rental or royalty) to the government of Canada or a province for

(*a*) the right to explore for petroleum or natural gas on a specified parcel of land in Canada (which right is, for greater certainty, declared to include a right of the type commonly referred to as a "licence", "permit" or "reservation"), or

(*b*) a legal lease of the right to take or remove petroleum or natural gas from a specified parcel of land in Canada

and before April 11, 1962 acquired the rights in respect of which the amount was so paid, if, before the predecessor corporation was entitled because of subsection 29(21) to any deduction in computing its income for a taxation year in respect of the amount so paid, the property of the predecessor corporation was acquired by the successor or second successor corporation, as the case may be, and at any time, before any well came into production in reasonable commercial quantities on the land referred to in paragraph (*a*)

ITARs

or (*b*), the successor or second successor corporation, as the case may be, surrendered all rights so acquired by the predecessor corporation (including, in respect of a right of the kind described in paragraph (*a*), all rights thereunder to any lease and all rights under any lease made thereunder) without receiving any consideration therefor or payment of any part of the amount so paid by the predecessor corporation, the amount so paid by the predecessor corporation shall be added at that time to the amount determined under subparagraph 29(25)(*c*)(i).

▶ 34(5) ◀

(5) Tax payable — (Repealed by 1985, c. 45, s. 136(2).)

▶ 34(6) ◀

(6) Paid-up capital deemed liability — (Repealed by 1985, c. 45, s. 136(2).)

▶ 34(7) ◀

(7) Definition of "amalgamation". In this section, "amalgamation" has the meaning assigned by section 85I of the former Act.

▶ 34(8) ◀

(8) Provisions applicable to ss. (5) — (Repealed by 1985, c. 45, s. 136(3).)

35. Foreign affiliates

(1) Section 26 does not apply in determining for the purposes of section 91 of the amended Act the amount of any taxable capital gain or allowable capital loss of a foreign affiliate of a taxpayer.

▶ 35(2) ◀

(2) Idem. Any corporation that was a foreign affiliate of a taxpayer on January 1, 1972 shall be deemed, for the purposes of subdivision i of Division B of Part I of the amended Act, to have become a foreign affiliate of the taxpayer on that day.

▶ 35(3) ◀

(3) Idem — (Repealed by 1985, c. 45, s. 137.)

▶ 35(4) ◀

(4) Idem. Any corporation that was deemed to be a foreign affiliate of a taxpayer at any time prior to May 7, 1974 because of an election made by the taxpayer in accordance with subparagraph 95(1)(*b*)(iv) of the amended Act, as it read before being amended by chapter 26 of the Statutes of Canada, 1974-75-76, shall be deemed to have been a foreign affiliate of the taxpayer at that time.

35.1. Trusts not resident in Canada

(Repealed by 1985, c. 45, s. 138.)

36. Application of paras. 107(2)(*b*) and (*d*) of amended Act

In computing the income of a taxpayer for the taxpayer's 1972 or any subsequent taxation year, paragraphs 107(2)(*b*) to (*d*) of the amended Act do not apply in respect of any property of a trust distributed by the trust to the taxpayer at any time before the commencement of the taxpayer's 1972 taxation year.

37. Loss carry-overs

(1) (Repealed by 1985, c. 45, s. 139.)

▶ 37(2) ◀

(2) Idem — (Repealed by 1985, c. 45, s. 139.)

▶ 37(3) ◀

(3) Idem — (Repealed by 1985, c. 45, s. 139.)

▶ 37(4) ◀

(4) Reference to preceding taxation year — (Repealed by 1985, c. 45, s. 139.)

▶ 37(5) ◀

(5) Non-capital losses — (Repealed by 1985, c. 45, s. 139.)

▶ 37(6) ◀

(6) Restricted farm loss — (Repealed by 1985, c. 45, s. 139.)

▶ 37(7) ◀

(7) Non-capital loss and restricted farm loss — (Repealed by 1985, c. 45, s. 139.)

38. Averaging provisions

(1) (Repealed by 1985, c. 45, s. 139.)

▶ 38(2) ◀

(2) Idem — (Repealed by 1985, c. 45, s. 139.)

39. Specific averaging provisions: part payments

(1) (Repealed by 1985, c. 45, s. 139.)

▶ 39(2) ◀

(2) Idem — (Repealed by 1985, c. 45, s. 139.)

▶ 39(3) ◀

(3) Idem — (Repealed by 1985, c. 45, s. 139.)

40. Payments out of pension funds, etc

(1) In the case of

(*a*) a single payment

(i) out of or under a superannuation or pension fund or plan

(A) on the death, withdrawal or retirement from employment of an employee or former employee,

(B) on the winding-up of the fund or plan in full satisfaction of all rights of the payee in or under the fund or plan, or

(C) to which the payee is entitled because of an amendment to the plan although the payee continues to be an employee to whom the plan applies,

(ii) on retirement of an employee in recognition of long service and not made out of or under a superannuation fund or plan,

(iii) under an employees profit sharing plan in full satisfaction of all rights of the payee in or under the plan, to the extent that the amount thereof would otherwise be included in computing the payee's income for the year in which the payment was received, or

(iv) under a deferred profit sharing plan on the death, withdrawal or retirement from employment of an employee or former employee, to the extent that the amount thereof would otherwise be included in computing the payee's income for the year in which the payment was received,

(*b*) a payment or payments made by an employer to an employee or former employee on or after retirement in respect of loss of office or employment, if made in the year of retirement or within one year after that year, or

(*c*) a payment or payments made as a death benefit, if made in the year of death or within one year after that year,

the payment or payments made in a taxation year ending after 1971 and before 1974 may, at the option of the taxpayer by whom it is or they are received, be deemed not to be income of the taxpayer for the purpose of Part I of the amended Act, in which case the taxpayer shall pay, in addition to any other tax payable for the year, a tax on the payment or total of the payments equal to the proportion thereof that

(*d*) the total of the taxes otherwise payable by the employee under that Part for the 3 years immediately preceding the taxation year (before making any deduction under section 120, 121 or 126 or subsection 127(3) of the amended Act),

is of

(*e*) the total of the employee's incomes for those 3 years.

Information Circulars: IC 74-21R Payments out of pension and deferred profit sharing plans — ITAR 40.

▶ 40(2) ◀

(2) Employee not resident in Canada. Where a taxpayer has elected that a payment or payments of one of the classes described in paragraphs (1)(*a*) to (*c*) in respect of an employee or former employee who was not resident in Canada throughout the whole of the 3 years referred to in paragraph (1)(*e*) shall be deemed not to be income of the taxpayer for the purpose of Part I of the amended Act, the tax payable under this section is that proportion of the amount on which the tax is payable that

(*a*) the total of the taxes that would have been payable by the employee under that Part for the 3 years referred to in paragraph (1)(*e*) (before making any deduction under section 120, 121 or 126 or subsection 127(3) of the amended Act) if the employee had been resident in Canada throughout those years and the employee's incomes for those years had been from sources in Canada,

is of

(*b*) the total of the employee's incomes for those 3 years,

and, in such a case, the election is not valid unless the taxpayer has filed with the election, a return of the employee's incomes for each of the 3 years in the same form and containing the same information as the return that the employee, or the employee's legal representative, would have been required to file under that Part if the employee had been resident in Canada in those years.

▶ 40(3) ◀

(3) Determination of amount of payment. In determining the amount of any payment or payments made in a taxation year out of or under a superannuation or pension fund or plan, under a deferred profit sharing plan or as a retiring allowance that is deemed, for the purposes of this section, not to be income of the taxpayer by whom it is or they are received, there shall be subtracted from the amount of the payment or payments so made

(*a*) the total of all amounts deductible under paragraph 60(*j*) of the amended Act in computing the taxpayer's income for that year; and

(*b*) any amount deductible under paragraph 60(*m*) of the amended Act because of that payment or those payments in computing the taxpayer's income for that year.

▶ 40(4) ◀

(4) Idem. In determining the amount of any payment or payments made in a taxation year as a death benefit that is deemed, for the purpose of this section, not to be income of the taxpayer by whom it is or they are received, there shall be subtracted from the amount of the payment or payments so made any amount deductible under paragraph 60(*m*) of the amended Act because of that payment or those payments in computing the taxpayer's income for that year.

▶ 40(5) ◀

(5) Maximum amount for election. For the purpose of determining the amount of any payment or payments of one or more of the classes described in subsection (1) made in a taxation year that may be deemed, for the purposes of this section, not to be income of the taxpayer by whom it is or they are received, the maximum amount in respect of which an election may be made by the taxpayer under subsection (1) for the taxation year in respect of the payment or payments is,

(*a*) in the case of a payment or payments of a class described in subsection (1) made to the taxpayer on the death of an employee or former employee in respect of whom the payment or payments are made, the amount of the payment or the total amount of the payments, as the case may be, minus any amount subtracted therefrom under subsection (3) or (4);

(*b*) in the case of one or more single payments of a class described in subparagraph (1)(*a*)(i), (iii) or (iv), other than a payment described in paragraph (*a*) of this subsection, the lesser of

(i) the amount of the payment or the total amount of the payments, as the case may be, minus any amount subtracted therefrom under subsection (3), and

(ii) the amount by which

(A) the product obtained by multiplying $1,500 by the number of consecutive 12 month periods included in the period throughout which the taxpayer was a member of any plan or plans described in subparagraph (1)(*a*)(i), (iii) or (iv) (in this subsection referred to as a "retirement plan"),

(I) out of or under which a payment was made to the taxpayer in the taxation year or a pre-

ITARs

ceding taxation year ending after April 26, 1965, and

(II) to which an employer of the taxpayer has made a contribution on behalf of the taxpayer,

exceeds

(B) the total of all amounts each of which is an amount that, because of a payment to the taxpayer after April 26, 1965,

(I) out of or under a retirement plan to which the employer referred to in subclause (A)(II) made a contribution on behalf of the taxpayer, or

(II) by the employer referred to in subclause (A)(II),

was deemed not to be income of the taxpayer for the purpose of Part I of the amended Act for a preceding taxation year because of an election made by the taxpayer under subsection (1); and

(*c*) in the case of a payment or payments of the class described in subparagraph (1)(*a*)(ii) or paragraph (1)(*b*), other than a payment described in paragraph (*a*) or (*b*) of this subsection, the lesser of

(i) the amount of the payment or the total amount of the payments, as the case may be, minus any amount subtracted therefrom pursuant to subsection (3), and

(ii) the amount by which

(A) the product obtained by multiplying $ 1,000 by the number of years during which the taxpayer was an employee of the employer who made the payment

exceeds

(B) the total of

(I) the total of all amounts each of which is an amount that, because of a payment to the taxpayer after April 26, 1965 by an employer referred to in clause (A) or a payment to the taxpayer after that date out of or under a retirement plan to which such an employer made a contribution on behalf of the taxpayer, was deemed not to be income of the taxpayer for the purpose of Part I of the amended Act for a preceding taxation year by reason of an election made by the taxpayer under subsection (1), and

(II) the total of all amounts each of which is an amount that, because of a payment to the taxpayer after April 26, 1965 out of or under a retirement plan to which an employer referred to in clause (A) made a contribution on behalf of the taxpayer, may be deemed, by subsection (1), not to be income of the taxpayer for the purpose of that Part for the taxation year.

▶ 40(6) ◀

(6) Idem. For the purpose of subsection (5),

(*a*) where all or substantially all of the property used in carrying on the business of a person who was an employer of an employee (in this subsection referred to as the "former employer")

(i) has been purchased by a person who, because of the purchase, or

(ii) has been acquired by bequest or inheritance, or because of an amalgamation (within the meaning assigned by section 85I of the former Act), by a person who, because of the acquisition,

became an employer of the employee, and who subsequently made a payment of a class described in paragraph (5)(*c*) in respect of the employee or former employee, the employee or former employee shall be deemed to have been an employee of that employer throughout the period he or she was an employee of the former employer; and

(*b*) a taxpayer may, in computing the number of years during which the taxpayer was a member of a superannuation or pension fund or plan (in this subsection referred to as the "subsequent plan"), include the number of years during which the taxpayer was a member of another plan (in this subsection referred to as the "former plan") if the taxpayer had received an amount out of or under the former plan all or part of which amount was deductible under paragraph 60(*j*) of the amended Act in computing the taxpayer's income for the taxation year in which the amount was received, because of the fact that all or part of the amount, as the case may be, was paid by the taxpayer to or under the subsequent plan as described in clause 60(*j*)(i)(A) of the *Income Tax Act*, chapter 148 of the Revised Statutes of Canada, 1952, as it read in its application to the 1978 and preceding taxation years.

▶ 40(7) ◀

(7) Limitation. This section applies in respect of any payment or payments described in subparagraph (1)(*a*)(i) or (iv) made in a taxation year ending after 1973, except that the amount of the payment or the total amount of the payments, as the case may be, shall be deemed to be the lesser of the amount thereof otherwise determined and the total of the amounts that the taxpayer would have received out of or under the plan described in subparagraph (1)(*a*)(i) or (iv), as the case may be, if

(*a*) the taxpayer had withdrawn from the plan on January 1, 1972;

(*b*) there had been no change in the terms and conditions of the plan after June 18, 1971 and before January 2, 1972; and

(*c*) any term or condition of the plan that would, in the event that the taxpayer had withdrawn from the plan on January 1, 1972, have reduced the amount of any payment or payments that would, if the tax-

ITARs

payer remained a member of the plan for a specified period of time after December 31, 1971, have been made to the taxpayer in respect of years ending before 1972 were not a term or condition of the plan.

► 40(8) ◄

(8) Application rule. For the purposes of paragraphs (1)(*d*) and (2)(*a*), there may be deducted from the total referred to in those paragraphs 9% of the portion of that total that is attributable to the 1974, 1975 or 1976 taxation year.

41. Fiscal periods ending in same year

(1) (Repealed by 1985, c. 45, s. 140.)

► 41(2) ◄

(2) "Earnings period" defined — (Repealed by 1985, c. 45, s. 140.)

► 41(3) ◄

(3) Earnings periods ending in same year — (Repealed by 1985, c. 45, s. 140.)

► 41(4) ◄

(4) Election — (Repealed by 1985, c. 45, s. 140.)

► 41(5) ◄

(5) Idem — (Repealed by 1985, c. 45, s. 140.)

42. Election

(1) (Repealed by 1985, c. 45, s. 140.)

► 42(2) ◄

(2) Idem — (Repealed by 1985, c. 45, s. 140.)

► 42(3) ◄

(3) Non-residents — (Repealed by 1985, c. 45, s. 140.)

43. Authors

(Repealed by 1985, c. 45, s. 140.)

44. Benefits to employees

(1) (Repealed by 1985, c. 45, s. 140.)

► 44(2) ◄

(2) Idem — (Repealed by 1985, c. 45, s. 140.)

45. Sale of inventory

(Repealed by 1985, c. 45, s. 140.)

45.1. Included reference

(Repealed by 1974-75-76, c. 26, s. 138.)

46. Accounts receivable

(Repealed by 1985, c. 45, s. 140.)

47. Death of a taxpayer: amount receivable

(Repealed by 1985, c. 45, s. 140.)

48. Incorrect valuation of inventory: election

(Repealed by 1985, c. 45, s. 140.)

49. Tax deemed payable under amended Act

(1) Where, because of section 40, any tax is payable in addition to or in lieu of any amount of tax payable under Part I of the amended Act for a taxation year, that tax shall be deemed to be payable under Part I of the amended Act for that taxation year.

► 49(2) ◄

(2) Application of s. 13. In applying section 13 to section 40, subsection 13(1) shall be read without reference to the words "subject to this Act and unless the context otherwise requires".

► 49(3) ◄

(3) Computation of tax deemed payable under amended Act. In computing, under section 40 of this Act or any of section 39 and sections 41 to 48 of the *Income Tax Act*, chapter 148 of the Revised Statutes of Canada, 1952, any tax that is payable in addition to or in lieu of any amount of tax payable under Part I of the amended Act by an individual for a taxation year,

(*a*) a reference to section 120 of the amended Act does not include a reference to paragraph 33(1)(*a*) of the former Act; and

(*b*) for the purposes of paragraph 33(1)(*a*) of the former Act and subsection 120(1) of the amended Act, all of the income of the individual for that or any preceding taxation year shall be deemed to have been income earned in the year in a province.

50. Status of certain corporations

(1) For the purposes of the amended Act, a corporation that was, throughout that portion of its 1972 taxation year that is in 1972, a private corporation, a Canadian-controlled private corporation or a public corporation shall be deemed to have been throughout that taxation year a private corporation, a Canadian-controlled private corporation or a public corporation, as the case may be.

► 50(2) ◄

(2) Election to be public corporation. For the purposes of the definition "public corporation" in subsection 89(1) of the amended Act, where at any particular time before 1973 a corporation elected in the manner referred to in subparagraph (*b*)(i) of that definition to be a public corporation and at any time after 1971 and before the time of the election the corporation complied with the conditions referred to in that subparagraph, the corporation shall,

(*a*) at such time after 1971 and before the particular time as is specified in the election to be the effective date thereof, or

(*b*) where no time described in paragraph (*a*) is specified in the election to be the effective date thereof, at the particular time,

be deemed to have elected in the manner referred to in that subparagraph to be a public corporation and to have complied with the conditions referred to therein.

► 50(3) ◄

(3) Designation by Minister. For the purposes of the definition "public corporation" in subsection 89(1) of the amended Act, where at any particular time before March 22, 1972 the Minister, by notice in writing to a corporation, designated the corporation to be a public corporation or not to be a public corporation, as the case may be, and at the time of the designation the corporation complied with the conditions referred to in subparagraph (*b*)(i) or (*c*)(i) of that definition, as the case may be, the corporation shall, at such time as is specified by the Minister in the notice, be deemed

(*a*) to have been designated by the Minister, by notice in writing to the corporation, to be a public corporation or not to be a public corporation, as the case may be; and

(*b*) to have complied with the conditions referred to in subparagraph (*b*)(i) or (*c*)(i) of that definition, as the case may be.

51. Tax payable by corporation with fiscal period other than calendar year 1972

(1) (Repealed by 1985, c. 45, s. 141.)

▶ 51(2) ◀

(2) Determination of amount taxable — (Repealed by 1985, c. 45, s. 141.)

▶ 51(3) ◀

(3) Definitions — (Repealed by 1985, c. 45, s. 141.)

52. Tax payable by corporations for particular years

(Repealed by 1985, c. 45, s. 141.)

53. Deduction from corporate tax for 1977 taxation year

(Repealed by 1974-75-76, c. 26, s. 139.)

54. Small business deduction for particular years

(Repealed by 1985, c. 45, s. 141.)

55. Foreign-tax carryover

(1) (Repealed by 1985, c. 45, s. 141.)

▶ 55(2) ◀

(2) Idem — (Repealed by 1985, c. 45, s. 141.)

56. Refundable dividend tax on hand

(Repealed by 1985, c. 45, s. 141.)

56.01. Capital gains dividend of a mutual fund corporation

(1) (Repealed by 1985, c. 45, s. 141.)

▶ 56.01(2) ◀

(2) Idem — (Repealed by 1985, c. 45, s. 141.)

56.1. Mutual fund trusts

(Repealed by 1985, c. 45, s. 141.)

57. Capital dividend account

▶ 57(1) ◀

(1) Specified personal corporations — (Repealed by 1985, c. 45, s. 142(1).)

▶ 57(2) ◀

(2) Dividends received — (Repealed by 1985, c. 45, s. 142(1).)

▶ 57(3) ◀

(3) Amount included in income of shareholder — (Repealed by 1985, c. 45, s. 142(1).)

▶ 57(4) ◀

(4) Valuation of transferred property — (Repealed by 1985, c. 45, s. 142(1).)

▶ 57(5) ◀

(5) Transfers — (Repealed by 1985, c. 45, s. 142(1).)

▶ 57(6) ◀

(6) Taxable dividends — (Repealed by 1985, c. 45, s. 142(1).)

▶ 57(7) ◀

(7) Foreign taxes — (Repealed by 1985, c. 45, s. 142(1).)

▶ 57(8) ◀

(8) Tax-paid undistributed income — (Repealed by 1977-78, c. 1, s. 111(1).)

▶ 57(9) ◀

(9) [Capital dividend account]. In computing a specified personal corporation's capital dividend account at any time after the end of its 1972 taxation year, there shall be added to the total of the amounts described in paragraphs (*a*) and (*b*) of the definition "capital dividend account" in subsection 89(1) of the amended Act the total of its net capital gains (within the meaning assigned by subsection 51(3) of the *Income Tax Application Rules, 1971*, Part III of chapter 63 of the Statutes of Canada, 1970-71-72, as it read before October 29, 1985) for its 1972 taxation year and that proportion of the total of its incomes for that year, other than

(*a*) any taxable capital gains of the corporation for the year from dispositions of property, and

(*b*) any amounts that were, because of subsection 57(3) of the *Income Tax Application Rules, 1971*, Part III of chapter 63 of the Statutes of Canada, 1970-71-72, as it read before October 29, 1985 or under the provisions of subsection 67(1) of the former Act that applied because of subsection 57(12) of those Rules as it read before that date, required to be included in computing the income of the specified personal corporation for its 1972 taxation year,

that the number of days in that portion of the 1972 taxation year that is in 1972 is of the number of days in the whole year.

▶ 57(10) ◀

(10) Statement to be filed — (Repealed by 1985, c. 45, s. 142(2).)

▶ 57(11) ◀

(11) Meaning of "specified personal corporation". For the purposes of this section, a corporation is a specified personal corporation if

(*a*) part of its 1972 taxation year was before and part thereof after the beginning of 1972; and

(*b*) during the whole of the period beginning on the earlier of June 18, 1971 and the beginning of its 1972 taxation year and ending at the end of its 1972 taxation year, it was a personal corporation within the meaning assigned by section 68 of the former Act.

▶ 57(12) ◀

(12) Rule where corporation's 1971 taxation year ends in shareholder's 1972 taxation year — (Repealed by 1985, c. 45, s. 142(3).)

57.1. Cooperative corporations

(1) (Repealed by 1985, c. 45, s. 143.)

▶ 57.1(2) ◀

(2) Ss. 51(1) not applicable — (Repealed by 1985, c. 45, s. 143.)

▶ 57.1(3) ◀

(3) "Amount taxable" defined — (Repealed by 1985, c. 45, s. 143.)

58. Credit unions

(1) For the purpose of computing the income of a credit union for the 1972 and subsequent taxation years,

(*a*) property of the credit union that is a bond, debenture, mortgage or agreement of sale owned by it at the beginning of its 1972 taxation year shall be valued at its actual cost to the credit union,

(i) plus a reasonable amount in respect of the amortization of the amount by which the principal amount of the property at the time it was acquired by the credit union exceeds its actual cost to the credit union, or

(ii) minus a reasonable amount in respect of the amortization of the amount by which its actual cost to the credit union exceeds the principal amount of the property, at the time it was acquired by the credit union;

(*b*) property of the credit union that is a debt owing to the credit union (other than property described in paragraph (*a*) or a debt that became a bad debt before its 1972 taxation year) acquired by it before the beginning of its 1972 taxation year shall be valued at any time at the amount thereof outstanding at that time;

(*c*) any depreciable property acquired by the credit union in a taxation year ending before 1972 shall be deemed to have been acquired by it on the last day of its 1971 taxation year at a capital cost equal to

(i) in the case of any building or automotive equipment owned by it on the last day of its 1971 taxation year, the amount, if any, by which the depreciable cost to the credit union of the building or equipment, as the case may be, exceeds the product obtained when the number of full taxation years in the period beginning on the first day of the taxation year following the taxation year in which the building or equipment, as the case may be, was acquired by it and ending with the last day of its 1971 taxation year is multiplied by, in the case of a building, 2 1/2%, and in the case of equipment, 15%, of its depreciable cost (and for the purposes of this subparagraph, a capital improvement or capital addition to a building owned by a credit union shall be deemed not to be part of the building but to be a separate and distinct building acquired by it, if the cost to the credit union of the improvement or addition, as the case may be, exceeded $10,000),

(ii) in the case of any leasehold interest, the proportion of the capital cost thereof to the credit union (determined without regard to this subparagraph) that

(A) the number of months in the period beginning with the first day of the credit union's 1972 taxation year and ending with the day on which the leasehold interest expires

is of

(B) the number of months in the period beginning with the day on which the credit union acquired the leasehold interest and ending with the day on which the leasehold interest expires,

and

(iii) in the case of any property (other than a building, automotive equipment or leasehold interest) acquired by the credit union after 1961, the amount, if any, by which the depreciable cost to the credit union of the property exceeds the product obtained when the number of full taxation years beginning with the first day of the taxation year following the taxation year in which the property was acquired by it and ending with the last day of its 1971 taxation year is multiplied by 1/2 the relevant percentage of the depreciable cost to the credit union of the property; and

(*d*) the undepreciated capital cost to the credit union as of the first day of its 1972 taxation year of depreciable property of a prescribed class acquired by it before that taxation year is the total of the amounts determined under paragraph (*c*) to be the capital costs to it as of that day of all property of that class.

Related Regulations: Part VI.

▶ 58(1.1) ◀

(1.1) Exception. For the purpose of computing a capital gain from the disposition of depreciable property acquired by a credit union in a taxation year ending before 1972, the capital cost of the property shall be its capital cost determined without reference to paragraph (1)(*c*).

▶ 58(2) ◀

(2) Deemed deductions — (Repealed by 1985, c. 45, s. 144(1).)

▶ 58(3) ◀

(3) Special rule applicable to 1972 taxation year — (Repealed by 1985, c. 45, s. 144(1).)

▶ 58(3.1) ◀

(3.1) Additional deductions for 1973 to 1976 taxation years — (Repealed by 1985, c. 45, s. 144(1).)

▶ 58(3.2) ◀

(3.2) Determination of maximum cumulative reserve at end of taxation year. Notwithstanding the definition "maximum cumulative reserve" in subsection 137(6) of the amended Act, for the purposes of section 137 of the amended Act a credit union's maximum cumulative reserve at the end of any particular taxation

ITARs

year is the amount, if any, by which its maximum cumulative reserve at that time, determined under that definition without regard to this subsection, exceeds the lesser of

(*a*) its maximum cumulative reserve, determined under that definition without regard to this subsection, at the end of its 1971 taxation year, and

(*b*) the amount, if any, by which its 1971 reserve exceeds the total of the amounts deemed by subsection 58(2) of the *Income Tax Application Rules, 1971*, Part III of chapter 63 of the Statutes of Canada, 1970-71-72, to have been deducted by it in computing its income for its 1971 taxation year.

▶ 58(3.3) ◀

(3.3) Idem. Notwithstanding subsection (3.2), where at any time after May 6, 1974 there has been an amalgamation (within the meaning assigned by section 87 of the amended Act) of two or more credit unions to form a new credit union, the maximum cumulative reserve of the new credit union shall be deemed to be the amount by which its maximum cumulative reserve, determined under the definition of that term in subsection 137(6) of the amended Act, exceeds the total of all amounts, if any, each of which is the lesser of the amounts referred to in paragraphs (3.2)(*a*) and (*b*) in respect of each of the predecessor corporations.

▶ 58(3.4) ◀

(3.4) Idem. Notwithstanding subsection (3.2), where a credit union (in this subsection referred to as the acquirer) has, at any time after May 6, 1974, acquired otherwise than by way of amalgamation all or substantially all of the assets of another credit union, the maximum cumulative reserve of the acquirer shall be the amount by which the acquirer's maximum cumulative reserve, determined under the definition of that term in subsection 137(6) of the amended Act, exceeds the total of

(*a*) the lesser of the amounts determined under paragraphs (3.2)(*a*) and (*b*) in respect of the acquirer, and

(*b*) the lesser of the amounts determined under paragraphs (3.2)(*a*) and (*b*) in respect of the other credit union.

▶ 58(4) ◀

(4) Amounts not to be deducted — (Repealed by 1985, c. 45, s. 144(2).)

▶ 58(4.1) ◀

(4.1) Amount of non-capital loss — (Repealed by 1985, c. 45, s. 144(2).)

▶ 58(5) ◀

(5) Definitions. In this section,

"depreciable cost" — "depreciable cost" to a credit union of any property means the actual cost to it of the property or the amount at which it is deemed by subsection 13(7) of the amended Act to have acquired the property, as the case may be;

"relevant percentage" — "relevant percentage" in relation to a prescribed class of property is the percentage prescribed in respect of that class by any regulations made under paragraph 11(1)(*a*) of the former Act;

"1971 reserve" — "1971 reserve" of a credit union means the amount, if any, by which the total of all amounts each of which is

(*a*) the amount of any money of the credit union on hand at the beginning of its 1972 taxation year,

(*b*) an amount in respect of any property described in paragraph (1)(*a*) or (*b*), equal to the amount at which it is required by those paragraphs to be valued at the beginning of its 1972 taxation year,

(*c*) an amount in respect of depreciable property of a prescribed class owned by the credit union on the first day of its 1972 taxation year, equal to the amount determined under paragraph (1)(*d*) to be the undepreciated capital cost thereof to the credit union as of that day, or

(*d*) an amount in respect of any capital property (other than depreciable property) owned by the credit union at the beginning of its 1972 taxation year, equal to its cost to the credit union computed without reference to the provisions of section 26,

exceeds the total of all amounts each of which is

(*e*) the amount of any debt owing by the credit union or of any other obligation of the credit union to pay an amount, that was outstanding at the beginning of its 1972 taxation year, excluding, for greater certainty, any share in the credit union of any member thereof, or

(*f*) the amount, as of the beginning of the credit union's 1972 taxation year, of any share in the credit union of any member thereof.

59. Non-resident-owned investment corporation

(1) (Repealed by 1985, c. 45, s. 145.)

▶ 59(2) ◀

(2) [Non-resident-owned investment corporation]. In its application to the 1972 and subsequent taxation years of a corporation, section 133 of the amended Act shall be read as if, in respect of such portion of any period described in the definition "non-resident-owned investment corporation" in subsection 133(8) of that Act as ended before the beginning of the corporation's 1976 taxation year, paragraph (*a*) of that definition were read as follows:

(*a*) at least 95% of the total value of its issued shares, and all of its bonds, debentures and other funded indebtedness, were

(i) beneficially owned by non-resident persons (other than any foreign affiliate of a taxpayer resident in Canada),

(ii) owned by trustees for the benefit of non-resident persons or their unborn issue, or

(iii) owned by a corporation, whether incorporated in Canada or elsewhere, at least 95% of the total value of the issued shares of which and all of the bonds, debentures and other funded indebtedness of which were beneficially owned by non-resident persons or owned by trustees for the benefit of non-resident persons or their unborn issue, or by two or more such corporations,

60. Taxes payable by insurer under Part IA of former Act

For the purposes of the description of F in the definition "surplus funds derived from operations" in subsection 138(12) of the amended Act, the reference in that description to "this Part" shall be deemed to be a reference to "this Part and Part IA of the former Act".

History: Former s. 60.1, which was added by 1973-74, c. 14, s. 86, was renumbered as s. 60 in the revised Act.

61. Registered retirement savings plans

(1) For the purposes of the definition "non-qualified investment" in subsection 146(1) of the amended Act, property acquired after June 18, 1971 and before 1972 by a trust governed by a registered retirement savings plan shall, if owned or held by the trust on January 1, 1972, be deemed to have been acquired by the trust on January 1, 1972.

62. Assessments

(1) Subsections 152(4) and (5) of the amended Act apply in respect of any assessment made after December 23, 1971, except that subsection 152(5) of that Act does not apply in respect of any such assessment made in consequence of a waiver filed with the Minister before December 23, 1971 in the form and within the time referred to in subsection 152(4) of that Act.

► 62(2) ◄

(2) Interest. Subsections 161(1) and (2), 164(3) and (4), 202(5) and 227(8) and (9) of the amended Act, subsection 183(2) of the *Income Tax Act*, chapter 148 of the Revised Statutes of Canada, 1952, and subsection 195(1) of that Act as it read in its application in respect of dividends paid or received before April 1, 1977, in so far as those subsections relate to the rate of interest payable thereunder, apply in respect of interest payable in respect of any period after December 23, 1971.

► 62(3) ◄

(3) Penalties — (Repealed by 1988, c. 55, s. 198.)

► 62(4) ◄

(4) Objections to assessment. Subsection 165(3) of the amended Act applies in respect of any notice of objection served on the Minister after December 23, 1971.

► 62(5) ◄

(5) Appeals. Division J of Part I of the amended Act applies in respect of any appeal or application instituted or made, as the case may be, after December 23, 1971.

► 62(6) ◄

(6) Appeals to Federal Court. Any appeal to the Federal Court instituted, within 2 years after December 23, 1971 and in accordance with Division J of Part I of the former Act and any rules made thereunder (as those rules read immediately before December 23, 1971), shall be deemed to have been instituted in the manner provided by the amended Act, and any document served on the Minister or a taxpayer in connection with an appeal so instituted in the manner provided in that Division and those rules shall be deemed to have been served in the manner provided by the amended Act.

63. Part II of amended Act

(Repealed by 1977-78, c. 1, s. 112(1).)

64. Preferred-rate amount

(Repealed by 1984, c. 45, s. 98(1).)

64.1. Life insurance corporation's control period earnings

(Repealed by 1977-78, c. 1, s. 113(1).)

64.2. Parts VII and VIII of amended Act

(Repealed by 1977-78, c. 1, s. 113(1).)

64.3. Retroactive Part IX election

(Repealed by 1974-75-76, c. 26, s. 141(1).)

65. Part XI of amended Act

(1)

Forms: T3F — Investments Prescribed to be Qualified or not to be Foreign Property Information Return.

► 65(1.1) ◄

(1.1) Idem — (Repealed by S.C. 2005, c. 30, s. 21(1).)

► 65(2) ◄

(2) Definition of "foreign investment limit" — (Repealed by S.C. 2005, c. 30, s. 21(1).)

► 65(3) ◄

(3) Foreign property acquired by registered retirement savings plan — (Repealed by S.C. 2005, c. 30, s. 21(1).)

► 65(4) ◄

(4) Definition of "foreign reinvestment limit" — (Repealed by S.C. 2005, c. 30, s. 21(1).)

► 65(5) ◄

(5) Shares of a mutual fund corporation received on amalgamation — (Repealed by S.C. 2005, c. 30, s. 21(1).)

65.1. Part XV of amended Act

For greater certainty,

(*a*) section 9 does not apply in respect of the repeal, by section 1 of chapter 63 of the Statutes of Canada, 1970-71-72, of Part V of the former Act and the substitution therefor, by that section, of Part XV of the amended Act, and

(*b*) in its application in respect of any offence described in subsection 239(1) of the amended Act that was committed before December 23, 1971, paragraph 239(1)(*f*) of the amended Act shall be read as follows:

(*f*) a fine of not less than $25 and not more than $ 10,000 plus, in an appropriate case, an amount not exceeding double the amount of the tax that should have been shown to be payable or that was sought to be evaded, or

66. Part of former Act

(1) For greater certainty, Part II of the former Act applies only in respect of elections made thereunder before 1972.

► 66(2) ◄

(2) Idem — (Repealed by 1977-78, c. 1, s. 114(1).)

67. Prescription of unpaid amounts

(5) Her Majesty in right of Canada is not liable, and no action shall be taken, for or in respect of any unrefunded instalment of tax paid under Part IID of the former Act or any interest thereon where

(*a*) a repayment date with respect to the instalment was prescribed by regulation and reasonable efforts were made thereafter to locate the corporation or trust entitled to the refund;

(*b*) at least 5 years have elapsed since publication in the *Canada Gazette* of the regulation referred to in paragraph (*a*); and

(*c*) no claim whatever has been received by or on behalf of Her Majesty from the corporation or trust entitled to the refund.

Part II
Transitional Concerning The 1985 Statute Revision

Definitions

69. Definitions

In this Act and the *Income Tax Act*, unless the context otherwise requires,

"Income Tax Act, chapter 148 of the Revised Statutes of Canada, 1952," —"Income Tax Act, chapter 148 of the Revised Statutes of Canada, 1952," means that Act as amended by section 1 of chapter 63 of the Statutes of Canada, 1970-71-72, and by any subsequent Act that received royal assent before December, 1991;

"Income Tax Application Rules, 1971, Part III of chapter 63 of the Statutes of Canada, 1970-71-72," —"Income Tax Application Rules, 1971, Part III of chapter 63 of the Statutes of Canada, 1970-71-72," means that Act as amended by any subsequent Act that received royal assent before December, 1991.

Application of the 1971 Acts and the Revised Acts

70. Application of *Income Tax Application Rules, 1971*, 1970-71-72, c. 63

Subject to this Act and the *Income Tax Act* and unless the context otherwise requires,

(*a*) sections 7 to 9 and 12 to 68 of the *Income Tax Application Rules, 1971*, Part III of chapter 63 of the Statutes of Canada, 1970-71-72, apply with respect to taxation years that ended before December, 1991; and

(*b*) section 10 of the *Income Tax Application Rules, 1971*, Part III of chapter 63 of the Statutes of Canada, 1970-71-72, applies with respect to amounts paid or credited before December, 1991.

71. Application of this Act

Subject to this Act and the *Income Tax Act* and unless the context otherwise requires,

(*a*) sections 7 to 9 and 12 to 78 of this Act apply with respect to taxation years that end after November, 1991; and

(*b*) section 10 of this Act applies with respect to amounts paid or credited after November, 1991.

72. Application of Income Tax Act, R.S.C., 1952, c. 148

Subject to this Act and the *Income Tax Act* and unless the context otherwise requires, the *Income Tax Act*, chapter 148 of the Revised Statutes of Canada, 1952, applies as follows:

(*a*) Parts I, I.1, I.2, I.3, II.1, IV, IV.1, V, VI, VI.1, VII, VIII, IX, XI.3, XII, XII.1, XII.2, XII.3 and XIV of that Act apply with respect to taxation years that ended before December 1991;

(*b*) Part III of that Act applies with respect to dividends that became payable before December, 1991;

(*c*) Parts X, X.1, X.2, XI, XI.1 and XI.2 of that Act apply with respect to calendar years that ended before December, 1991;

(*d*) Part XIII of that Act applies with respect to amounts paid or credited before December, 1991; and

(*e*) Parts XV, XVI and XVII of that Act apply before December, 1991.

73. Application of Income Tax Act

Subject to this Act and the *Income Tax Act* and unless the context otherwise requires, the *Income Tax Act* applies as follows:

(*a*) Parts I, I.1, I.2, I.3, II.1, IV, IV.1, V, VI, VI.1, VII, VIII, IX, XI.3, XII, XII.1, XII.2, XII.3 and XIV of that Act apply with respect to taxation years that end after November 1991;

(*b*) Part III of that Act applies with respect to dividends that become payable after November, 1991;

(*c*) Parts X, X.1, X.2, XI, XI.1 and XI.2 of that Act apply with respect to calendar years that end after November, 1991;

(*d*) Part XIII of that Act applies with respect to amounts paid or credited after November, 1991; and

(*e*) Parts XV, XVI and XVII of that Act apply after November, 1991.

Application of Certain Provisions

74. Definition of "provision"

In sections 75 to 78, "provision" means the whole or part of a provision.

75. Continued effect of amending and application provisions

For greater certainty, where an enactment passed after 1971 in amendment of the *Income Tax Application Rules,*

1971, Part III of chapter 63 of the Statutes of Canada, 1970-71-72, or of the *Income Tax Act*, chapter 148 of the Revised Statutes of Canada, 1952, contains an amending, repeal, application or other provision that, immediately before the coming into force of the fifth supplement to the Revised Statutes of Canada, 1985, has any effect on, or in connection with, the application of either or both of those Acts, that provision has, on the coming into force of that supplement, the same effect on, or in connection with, the application of either this Act or the *Income Tax Act* or both.

76. Application of s. 75

Section 75 is applicable whether or not this Act or the *Income Tax Act*, as the case may be, contains, or contains the tenor of or any reference to,

(*a*) the amending, repeal, application or other provision referred to in that section; or

(*b*) any provision of the *Income Tax Application Rules, 1971*, Part III of chapter 63 of the Statutes of Canada, 1970-71-72, or the *Income Tax Act*, chapter 148 of the Revised Statutes of Canada, 1952, expressed or intended to be the subject of or otherwise affected by that amending, repeal, application or other provision.

77. Continued effect of repealed provisions

For greater certainty, where a provision of the *Income Tax Application Rules, 1971*, Part III of chapter 63 of the Statutes of Canada, 1970-71-72, or the *Income Tax Act*, chapter 148 of the Revised Statutes of Canada, 1952, was repealed at any time after 1971 but, immediately before the coming into force of the fifth supplement to the Revised Statutes of Canada, 1985, continues to be applied to any extent or otherwise to have any effect on, or in connection with, the application of either or both of those Acts, the repealed provision, on the coming into force of that supplement, continues to be so applied or to have that effect on, or in connection with, the application of either this Act or the *Income Tax Act* or both.

78. Application of s. 77

Section 77 is applicable whether or not this Act or the *Income Tax Act*, as the case may be, contains any reference to the repealed provision referred to in that section or to the subject-matter of that provision.

79. Effect of amendments on former ITA

(1) Where a provision of an enactment amends the *Income Tax Act* or affects the application of the *Income Tax Act* and the provision applies to or with respect to a period, transaction or event to which the *Income Tax Act*, chapter 148 of the Revised Statutes of Canada, 1952, applies, the *Income Tax Act*, chapter 148 of the Revised Statutes of Canada, 1952, shall be read as if it had been amended or its application had been affected by the provision, with such modifications as the circumstances require, to the extent of the provision's application to or with respect to that period, transaction or event.

► 79(2) ◄

(2) Effect of amendments on former ITAR. Where a provision of an enactment amends this Act or affects the application of this Act and the provision applies to or with respect to a period, transaction or event to which the *Income Tax Application Rules, 1971*, Part III of chapter 63 of the Statutes of Canada, 1970-71-72, apply, the *Income Tax Application Rules, 1971*, Part III of chapter 63 of the Statutes of Canada, 1970-71-72, shall be read as if they had been amended or their application had been affected by the provision, with such modifications as the circumstances require, to the extent of the provision's application to or with respect to that period, transaction or event.

ITARs

Income Tax Regulations

The Income Tax Regulations (Consolidated Regulations of Canada, 1978, c. 945) were issued by P.C. 1979–1933, proclaimed in force August 15, 1979, superseding the former consolidation, as amended. Since the Regulations were consolidated only to December 31, 1977, a Special Issue of the *Canada Gazette*, dated December 31, 1978 but issued shortly after the appearance of the C.R.C. in August, 1979, was published to allow the updating of the Consolidation to reflect those 1978 Regulations that amend or revoke Regulations found in the Consolidation. These revisions and all subsequent revisions have been incorporated in place in the Regulations with appropriate historical notes.

TABLE OF CONTENTS

SECTIONAL LIST OF THE INCOME TAX REGULATIONS

[Consolidated Regulations of Canada, c. 945, as amended.]

PART I
TAX DEDUCTIONS

PART II
INFORMATION RETURNS

PART III
ANNUITIES AND LIFE INSURANCE POLICIES

PART IV
TAXABLE INCOME EARNED IN A PROVINCE BY A CORPORATION

Section	Subject
407	Airline Corporations
408	Grain Elevator Operators
409	Bus and Truck Operators
410	Ship Operators
411	Pipeline Operators
412	Divided Businesses
413	Non-Resident Corporations
413.1	(Revoked.)
414	Provincial SIFT Tax Rate
415	(Repealed.)

PART V
NON-RESIDENT-OWNED INVESTMENT CORPORATIONS

500	Elections
501	Elections Revoked
502	Certificates of Changes of Ownership
503	(Revoked.)

PART VI
ELECTIONS

600	[Prescribed provisions for late, amended or revoked elections]

PART VII
LOGGING TAXES ON INCOME

700	Logging

PART VIII
NON-RESIDENT TAXES

800	Registered Non-Resident Insurers
801	Filing of Returns by Registered Non-Resident Insurers
802	Amounts Taxable
803	Payment of Tax by Registered Non-Resident Insurers
803.1	(Repealed.)
804	Interpretation
805	Other Non-Resident Persons
805.1	Payee Certificate
806	International Organizations and Agencies
806.1	International Organizations and Agencies (Repealed.)
806.2	Prescribed Obligation
807	Identification of Obligations
808	Allowances in Respect of Investment in Property in Canada
809	Reduction of Certain Amounts to be Deducted or Withheld
810	(Repealed.)

PART IX
DELEGATION OF THE POWERS AND DUTIES OF THE MINISTER [REPEALED.]

900	(Repealed.)

PART X
ELECTIONS IN RESPECT OF DECEASED TAXPAYERS

1000	Property Dispositions
1000.1	Realization of Options
1001	Annual Instalments

PART XI
CAPITAL COST ALLOWANCES

DIVISION I DEDUCTIONS ALLOWED

1100	[Capital cost allowance – deductions allowed]
1100(1)(*a*)	Rates
1100(1)(*a*.1)	Class 1
1100(1)(*a*.2)	Class 1
1100(1)(*b*)	Class 13 — [Leasehold interest]
1100(1)(*c*)	Class 14 — [Patent, franchise, concession or licence]
1100(1)(*c*.1)	Additional Allowances — Class 14.1
1100(1)(*d*)	In lieu of double depreciation
1100(1)(*e*)	Timber limits and cutting rights
1100(1)(*f*)	Class 15 — [Woods assets]
1100(1)(*g*)	Industrial mineral mines
1100(1)(*h*)	(Revoked.)
1100(1)(*i*)	Additional allowances — Fishing vessels
1100(1)(*j*)	(Revoked.)
1100(1)(*k*)	(Revoked.)
1100(1)(*l*)	Additional allowances — Certified productions
1100(1)(*m*)	Additional allowance — Canadian film or video production
1100(1)(*n*)	Class 19 — [Accelerated allowances]
1100(1)(*o*)	Class 19 — [Accelerated allowances]

DIVISION II SEPARATE CLASSES

Regulations

Regulations

DIVISION VIII DETERMINATION OF VISCOSITY AND DENSITY

Section	Subject
1107	[Bituminous sands]

PART XII
RESOURCE AND PROCESSING ALLOWANCES

Section	Subject
1200	[Deductions allowed]
1201	Earned Depletion Allowances
1202	Earned Depletion Allowances
1203	Mining Exploration Depletion
1204	Resource Profits
1205	Earned Depletion Base
1206	Interpretation
1207	Frontier Exploration Allowances
1208	Additional Allowances in Respect of Certain Oil or Gas Wells
1209	Additional Allowances in Respect of Certain Mines
1210	Resource Allowance
1210.1	Resource Allowance
1211	Prescribed Amounts
1212	Supplementary Depletion Allowances
1213	Prescribed Deductions
1214	Amalgamations and Windings-up
1215	(Revoked.)
1216	Prescribed Persons
1217	Prescribed Canadian Exploration Expense
1218	Prescribed Canadian Development Expense
1219	Canadian Renewable and Conservation Expense

PART XIII
ELECTIONS IN RESPECT OF TAXPAYERS CEASING TO BE RESIDENT IN CANADA

Section	Subject
1300	Elections to Defer Capital Gains
1301	Elections to Defer Payment of Taxes
1302	Elections to Realize Capital Gains

PART XIV
INSURANCE BUSINESS POLICY RESERVES

DIVISION 1 POLICY RESERVES

Section	Subject
1400	Non-Life Insurance Business

DIVISION 2 AMOUNTS DETERMINED

Section	Subject
1401	Life Insurance Business

DIVISION 3 SPECIAL RULES

Section	Subject
1402	Non-Life and Life Insurance Businesses
1402.1	Non-Life and Life Insurance Businesses
1403	Non-Life and Life Insurance Businesses

DIVISION 4 LIFE INSURANCE POLICY RESERVES

Section	Subject
1404	[Reserve amounts]
1405	[Reserve for unpaid claims]
1406	[Calculation of amount]
1407	[Negative amounts]

DIVISION 5 INTERPRETATION

Section	Subject
1408	Insurance Businesses

PART XV
PROFIT SHARING PLANS

DIVISION I EMPLOYEES PROFIT SHARING PLANS

Section	Subject
1500	[Elections]

DIVISION II DEFERRED PROFIT SHARING PLANS

Section	Subject
1501	Registration of Plans
1502	(Revoked.)

DIVISION III ELECTIONS IN RESPECT OF CERTAIN SINGLE PAYMENTS

Section	Subject
1503	[Election by beneficiary]

PART XVI
PRESCRIBED COUNTRIES

Section	Subject
1600	[Prescribed countries]

PART XVII
CAPITAL COST ALLOWANCES, FARMING AND FISHING

DIVISION I DEDUCTIONS ALLOWED

Section	Subject
1700(1)	Rates
1700(2)	Taxation Years Less Than 12 Months
1700(3)	Property Disposed of During Year
1700(4)	Leasehold Interests

DIVISION II MAXIMUM DEDUCTIONS

Section	Subject
1701	[Maximum deduction]

DIVISION III PROPERTY NOT INCLUDED

Section	Subject
1702	[Excluded property]

DIVISION IV INTERPRETATION

Section	Subject
1703(1)	Taxation Years for Individuals in Business
1703(2)	Depreciable Cost
1703(3)	Depreciable Cost
1703(4)	Personal Use of Property
1703(5)	Grants, Subsidies or Other Government Assistance
1703(6)	Transactions Not at Arm's Length
1703(7)	Property Acquired From a Parent
1703(8)	Property Acquired by Gift

DIVISION V APPLICATION OF THIS PART

Section	Subject
1704	[Application of Part]

PART XVIII
INVENTORIES

Section	Subject
1800	Manner of Keeping Inventories
1801	Valuation
1802	Valuation of animals

PART XIX
INVESTMENT INCOME TAX

Section	Subject
1900	Interpretation

PART XX
POLITICAL CONTRIBUTIONS

Section	Subject
2000	Contents of Receipts
2001	[Information Returns] (Repealed.)
2002	Interpretation

PART XXI
ELECTIONS IN RESPECT OF SURPLUSES

Section	Subject
2100	Reduction of Tax-Paid Undistributed Surplus on Hand or 1971 Capital Surplus on Hand
2101	Capital Dividends and Life Insurance Capital Dividends Payable by Private Corporations
2102	Tax on 1971 Undistributed Income on Hand
2104	Capital Gains Dividends Payable by Mutual Fund Corporations, Investment Corporations and Mortgage Investment Corporations
2104.1	Capital Gains Dividends Payable by Mutual Fund Corporations, Investment Corporations and Mortgage Investment Corporations
2105	Capital Gains Dividends Payable by Non-Resident-Owned Investment Corporations
2106	Alternative to Additional Tax on Excessive Elections
2107	Tax-deferred Preferred Series

PART XXIX
SCIENTIFIC RESEARCH AND EXPERIMENTAL DEVELOPMENT

Section	Subject
2900(1)	Interpretation
2900(2)	[Expenditures directly attributable to SR&ED]
2900(3)	[Expenditures directly attributable to premises, facilities and equipment]
2900(4)	[Calculation of prescribed proxy amount]
2900(5)	[All or substantially all salaries or wages]
2900(6)	[Maximum prescribed proxy amount]
2900(7)	[Restrictions for specified employees]
2900(8)	[Specified employee employed by an associated corporation]
2900(9)	[Exclusions to salary base]
2900(10)	[Deemed associated corporation]
2900(11)	[Prescribed depreciable property]
2901	Prescribed Expenditures
2902	Prescribed Expenditures
2903	Special-Purpose Buildings (Repealed.)

PART XXX
COMMUNICATION OF INFORMATION [REPEALED]

Section	Subject
3000	(Repealed.)
3001	(Repealed.)
3002	(Repealed.)
3003	Prescribed Laws of the Province of Quebec (Repealed.)
3004	(Repealed.)

PART XXXI
TAX SHELTER

Section	Subject
3100	Prescribed benefits
3101	Prescribed property

PART XXXII
PRESCRIBED PAYMENTS [REPEALED.]

Section	Subject
3200	(Repealed.)
3201	(Repealed.)
3202	(Repealed.)

PART XXXIII
TAX TRANSFER PAYMENTS

Section	Subject
3300	[Prescribed rate]

PART XXXIV
INTERNATIONAL DEVELOPMENT ASSISTANCE PROGRAMS

Section	Subject
3400	[Prescribed programs]

PART XXXV
GIFTS

Section	Subject
3500	Interpretation
3501	Contents of Receipts
3501.1	Contents of Information Returns
3502	Employees' Charity Trusts
3503	Universities Outside Canada (Repealed.)
3504	[Prescribed Donees]
3505	Conditions (Repealed.)

PART XXXVI
RESERVES FOR SURVEYS

Section	Subject
3600	[Reserve amount]

PART XXXVII
REGISTERED CHARITIES

Section	Subject
3700	(Repealed.)
3701	Disbursement Quota
3702	Determination of Value

Section	Subject	Section	Subject

PART XXXVIII
SOCIAL INSURANCE NUMBER APPLICATIONS

3800	[Prescribed form]		

PART XXXIX
MINING TAXES

3900	[Mining taxes]		

PART XL
BORROWED MONEY COSTS

4000	(Revoked.)		
4001	Interest on Insurance Policy Loans		

PART XLI
REPRESENTATION EXPENSES

4100	[Election]		

PART XLII
VALUATION OF ANNUITIES AND OTHER INTERESTS

4200			

PART XLIII
INTEREST RATES

4300	[Interpretation]		
4301	Prescribed Rate of Interest		
4302	[Prescribed Leasing Interest Rate]		

PART XLIV
PUBLICLY-TRADED SHARES OR SECURITIES

4400	[Publicly-traded shares or securities]		

PART XLV
ELECTIONS IN RESPECT OF EXPROPRIATION ASSETS

4500	[Election]		

PART XLVI
INVESTMENT TAX CREDIT

4600	Qualified Property	4607	Prescribed Designated Regions
4601	Qualified Transportation Equipment	4608	Prescribed Expenditure for Qualified Canadian Exploration Expenditure
4602	Certified Property	4609	Prescribed offshore Region
4603	Qualified Construction Equipment	4610	Prescribed Area
4604	Approved Project Property		
4605	Prescribed Activities		
4606	Prescribed Amount		

PART XLVII
ELECTION IN RESPECT OF CERTAIN PROPERTY OWNED ON DECEMBER 31, 1971

4700	[Election]		

PART XLVIII
STATUS OF CORPORATIONS AND TRUSTS

4800	[Public corporation]	4801.01	[Mutual fund trust]
4800.1	[Prescribed trusts]	4801.02	[Labour sponsored venture capital corporation]
4801	[Mutual fund trust]	4801.1	[Exempt foreign trust]
4801.001	[Mutual fund trust]		

PART XLIX
REGISTERED PLANS – INVESTMENTS

PART L
TAX-FREE SAVINGS ACCOUNTS — PROHIBITED INVESTMENTS [REPEALED]

PART LI
DEFERRED INCOME PLANS, INVESTMENTS IN SMALL BUSINESS

PART LII
CANADIAN MANUFACTURING AND PROCESSING PROFITS

PART LIII
INSTALMENT BASE

PART LIV
DEBTOR'S GAINS ON SETTLEMENT OF DEBTS [REPEALED.]

PART LV
PRESCRIBED PROGRAMS AND BENEFITS

PART LVI
PRESCRIBED DISTRIBUTIONS

PART LVII
MEDICAL EXPENSE TAX CREDIT

Regulations

Section	Subject	Section	Subject

PART LVIII
RETENTION OF BOOKS AND RECORDS

Section	Subject
5800	[Required retention period]

PART LIX
FOREIGN AFFILIATES

Section	Subject	Section	Subject
5900	Dividends Out of Exempt, Taxable and Pre-Acquisition Surplus	5906	Carrying on Business in a Country
5901	Order of Surplus Distributions	5907	Interpretation
5902	Election in Respect of Capital Gains	5908	[Partnerships]
5903	Deductible Loss	5909	Prescribed Circumstances (Repealed.)
5903.1	[Foreign accrual capital losses]	5910	[Foreign oil and gas businesses]
5904	Participating Percentage	5911	[Elections]
5905	Special Rules		

PART LX
PRESCRIBED ACTIVITIES

Section	Subject
6000	[Overseas employment tax credit]

PART LXI
RELATED SEGREGATED FUND TRUSTS

Section	Subject
6100	[Election]

PART LXII
PRESCRIBED SECURITIES, SHARES AND DEBT OBLIGATIONS

Section	Subject	Section	Subject
6200	Prescribed Securities	6206	Prescribed Shares
6201	Prescribed Shares	6207	Prescribed Shares
6202	Prescribed Shares	6208	Prescribed Shares
6202.1	Prescribed Shares	6209	Prescribed Shares
6203	Prescribed Shares	6210	Prescribed Shares
6204	Prescribed Shares		
6205	Prescribed Shares		

PART LXIII
CHILD TAX BENEFITS

Section	Subject
6300	Interpretation
6301	Non-Application of Presumption
6302	Factors

PART LXIV
PRESCRIBED DATES

Section	Subject
6400	Child Tax Credits
6401	Quebec Tax Abatement

PART LXV
PRESCRIBED LAWS

Section	Subject
6500	[Prescribed laws of the Province of Quebec]
6501	[Prescribed provision of the law of a province]
6502	[Prescribed class of persons]
6503	[Prescribed pension legislation]

PART LXVI
PRESCRIBED ORDER

Section	Subject
6600	[Overseas Canadian Forces school staff]

Regulations

Section	Subject	Section	Subject

PART LXVII
PRESCRIBED VENTURE CAPITAL CORPORATIONS, LABOUR-SPONSORED VENTURE CAPITAL CORPORATIONS, INVESTMENT CONTRACT CORPORATIONS, QUALIFYING CORPORATIONS AND PRESCRIBED STOCK SAVINGS PLANS

Section	Subject
6700	[Prescribed venture capital corporations]
6700.1	[Prescribed venture capital corporations]
6700.2	[Prescribed venture capital corporations]
6701	[Prescribed labour-sponsored venture capital corporation]
6701.1	[Exception for registration after March 2013] (Repealed.)
6702	[Prescribed assistance]
6703	[Prescribed investment contract corporation]
6704	[Prescribed qualifying corporation]
6705	[Prescribed stock savings plan]
6706	[Prescribed condition]
6707	[Prescribed provision of a law of a province]
6708	[Prescribed wind-up rule]
6709	[Prescribed provisions of a provincial law]

PART LXVIII
PRESCRIBED PLANS, ARRANGEMENTS AND CONTRIBUTIONS

Section	Subject
6800	[Prescribed arrangement – employee benefit plan]
6801	[Prescribed plan or arrangement – salary deferral arrangement]
6802	[Prescribed plan or arrangement – retirement compensation arrangement]
6802.1	[Prescribed plan or arrangement – pension plans]
6803	[Prescribed plan or arrangement – foreign retirement arrangement]
6804(1)	Definitions
6804(2)	Electing Employer
6804(3)	Election by Union
6804(4)	Contributions Made Before 1992
6804(5)	Contributions Made in 1992, 1993 or 1994
6804(6)	Contributions Made after 1994
6804(7)	Replacement Plan

PART LXIX
PRESCRIBED OFFSHORE INVESTMENT FUND PROPERTIES

Section	Subject
6900	[Prescribed offshore investment fund property]

PART LXX
ACCRUED INTEREST ON DEBT OBLIGATIONS

Section	Subject
7000	Prescribed Debt Obligations
7001	Indexed Debt Obligations

PART LXXI
PRESCRIBED FEDERAL CROWN CORPORATIONS

Section	Subject
7100	[Prescribed federal Crown corporations]

PART LXXII
CUMULATIVE DEDUCTION ACCOUNT [REPEALED.]

Section	Subject
7200	(Repealed.)

PART LXXIII
PRESCRIBED AMOUNTS AND AREAS

Section	Subject
7300	[Prescribed amount – inducement, reimbursement, etc.]
7301	(Repealed.)
7302	(Revoked.)
7303	(Revoked.)
7303.1	[Prescribed northern and intermediate zones]
7304	[Prescribed amount – northern residents deduction]
7305	[Prescribed drought regions]
7305.01	(Repealed.)
7305.02	[Prescribed flood regions]
7305.1	[Prescribed amount – automobile operating expense benefit]
7306	[Prescribed amount – automobile allowance]
7307	[Prescribed amount – automobile deduction limits]
7308	[Prescribed factor – retirement income fund]
7309	[Prescribed penalties]
7310	[Prescribed trade]

Regulations

Section	Subject
8301(7)	Pension Credit — Defined Benefit Provision of a Multi-Employer Plan
8301(8)	Non-Vested Termination from RPP
8301(9)	Multi-Employer Plans
8301(10)	Transition Rule — Money Purchase Offsets
8301(11)	Timing of Contributions
8301(12)	Indirect Contributions
8301(13)	Apportionment of Payments
8301(14)	Non-Compliance by Contributing Entity
8301(15)	Transferred Amounts
8301(16)	Subsequent Events
8302(1)	Benefit Entitlement
8302(2)	Benefit Accrual for Year
8302(3)	Normalized Pensions
8302(4)	Optional Forms
8302(5)	Termination of Entitlement to Benefits
8302(6)	Defined Benefit Offset
8302(7)	Offset of Specified Multi-Employer Plan Benefits
8302(8)	Transition Rule — Career Average Benefits
8302(9)	Transition Rule — Benefit Rate Greater Than 2 Per Cent
8302(10)	Period of Reduced Remuneration
8302(11)	Anti-Avoidance
8303(1)	PSPA with Respect to Employer
8303(2)	Accumulated PSPA for Year
8303(2.1)	1991 Past Service Events and Certifications
8303(3)	Provisional PSPA
8303(4)	Redetermined Benefit Entitlement
8303(5)	Normalized Pension
8303(6)	Qualifying Transfers
8303(6.1)	Exclusion for Pre-1990 Benefits
8303(7)	Deemed Payment
8303(7.1)	Excess Money Purchase Transfer
8303(8)	Specified Multi-Employer Plan
8303(9)	Conditional Contributions
8303(10)	Benefits in Respect of Foreign Service
8304(1)	Replacement of Defined Benefits
8304(2)	Replacement of Money Purchase Benefits
8304(3)	Past Service Benefits in Year of Past Service Event
8304(4)	Exceptions
8304(5)	Modified PSPA Calculation
8304(5.1)	Definitions for Subsection
8304(6)	Reinstatement of Pre-1997 Benefits
8304(7)	Two or More Employers
8304(8)	Two or More Employers (Repealed.)
8304(9)	Specified Multi-Employer Plans
8304(10)	Individual Pension Plans
8304(11)	Individual Pension Plans
8304.1(1)	Total Pension Adjustment Reversal
8304.1(2)	Termination in 1997
8304.1(3)	PAR — Deferred Profit Sharing Plan
8304.1(4)	PAR — Money Purchase Provision
8304.1(5)	PAR — Defined Benefit Provision
8304.1(6)	Defined Benefit Pension Credits
8304.1(7)	Grossed-up PSPA Amount
8304.1(8)	Specified Distribution
8304.1(9)	Property Made Available
8304.1(10)	PA Transfer Amount
8304.1(11)	Special 1997 PA Transfer Amount
8304.1(12)	Subsequent Membership
8304.1(13)	Termination Conditions — Deferred Profit Sharing Plan
8304.1(14)	Termination Conditions — Registered Pension Plan
8304.1(15)	Breakdown of Marriage or Common-law Partnership
8305	Association of Benefits with Employers
8306	Exemption from Certification
8307(1)	Application for Certification
8307(2)	Prescribed Condition
8307(3)	Qualifying Withdrawals
8307(4)	Eligibility of Withdrawn Amount for Designation
8307(5)	PSPA Withdrawals
8307(6)	Prescribed Withdrawal
8307(7)	Prescribed Premium
8308(1)	Benefits Provided Before Registration
8308(2)	Prescribed Amount for Connected Persons
8308(3)	Remuneration for Prior Years
8308(4)	Period of Reduced Services — Retroactive Benefits
8308(5)	Period of Reduced Services — Retroactive Contributions
8308(6)	Commitment to Make Retroactive Contributions
8308(7)	Loaned Employees
8308(8)	Successor Plans
8308(9)	Special Downsizing Benefits
8308.1(1)	Definition
8308.1(2)	Pension Credit
8308.1(2.1)	Pension Credit — Tax Treaty
8308.1(3)	Pension Credit — Alternative Determination
8308.1(4)	Pension Credits for 1992, 1993 and 1994
8308.1(4.1)	Pension Credits — 1996 to 2002
8308.1(5)	Foreign Plan PSPA
8308.1(6)	Foreign Plan PSPA — Alternative Determination
8308.2(1)	Prescribed Amount
8308.2(2)	Prescribed Amount
8308.3(1)	Definition
8308.3(2)	Pension Credit
8308.3(3)	Pension Credit — Alternative Determination
8308.3(3.1)	Pension Credits — 1996 to 2002
8308.3(4)	Specified Retirement Arrangement PSPA
8308.3(5)	Specified Retirement Arrangement PSPA — Alternative Determination
8308.4(1)	Definitions
8308.4(2)	Prescribed Amount
8309	Prescribed Amount for Lieutenant Governors and Judges
8310	Minister's Powers
8311	Rounding of Amounts

PART LXXXIV
RETIREMENT AND PROFIT-SHARING PLANS — REPORTING AND PROVISION OF INFORMATION

Section	Subject
8400	Definitions
8401	Pension Adjustment
8402	Past Service Pension Adjustment
8402.01(1)	Deferred Profit Sharing Plan
8402.01(2)	Deferred Profit Sharing Plan — Employer Reporting
8402.01(3)	Benefit Provision of a Registered Pension Plan
8402.01(4)	Extended Deadline — PA Transfer Amount
8402.01(5)	Calendar Year Quarter
8402.1	Government-Sponsored Retirement Arrangements
8403	Connected Persons
8404	Reporting to Individuals
8405	Discontinuance of Business
8406	Provision of Information
8407	Qualifying Withdrawals
8408	Requirement to Provide Minister with Information
8409	Annual Information Returns
8410	Actuarial Reports

PART LXXXV
REGISTERED PENSION PLANS

Section	Subject
8500	Interpretation
8501(1)	Conditions for Registration
8501(2)	Conditions Applicable to Registered Pension Plans
8501(3)	Permissive Rules
8501(4)	Supplemental Plans
8501(5)	Benefits Payable after the Breakdown of the Marriage or Common-law Partnership
8501(6)	Indirect Contributions
8501(6.1)	Member Contributions for Unfunded Liability
8501(6.2)	Prescribed Eligible Contributions
8501(7)	Benefits Provided with Surplus on Plan Wind-up
8502	Conditions Applicable to All Plans
8502(*a*)	Primary purpose
8502(*b*)	Permissible contributions
8502(*c*)	Permissible benefits
8502(*d*)	Permissible distributions
8502(*e*)	Payment of pension
8502(*f*)	Assignment of rights
8502(*g*)	Funding media
8502(*h*)	Investments
8502(*i*)	Borrowing
8502(*j*)	Determination of amounts
8502(*k*)	Transfer of property between provisions
8502(*l*)	Appropriate pension adjustments
8502(*m*)	Participants in GSRAs
8503(1)	Net Contribution Accounts
8503(2)	Permissible Benefits
8503(2)(*a*)	Lifetime retirement benefits
8503(2)(*b*)	Bridging benefits
8503(2)(*c*)	Guarantee period
8503(2)(*d*)	Post-retirement survivor benefits
8503(2)(*e*)	Pre-retirement survivor benefits
8503(2)(*f*)	Pre-retirement survivor benefits — Alternative rule
8503(2)(*g*)	Pre-retirement survivor benefits — Guarantee period
8503(2)(*h*)	Lump sum payments on termination
8503(2)(*i*)	Payment of commuted value of benefits on death before retirement
8503(2)(*j*)	Lump sum payments on death
8503(2)(*k*)	Additional post-retirement death benefits
8503(2)(*l*)	Additional bridging benefits
8503(2)(*l*.1)	Survivor bridging benefits
8503(2)(*m*)	Commutation of benefits
8503(2)(*n*)	[Idem]
8503(2.1)	Rule for Commutation of Benefits
8503(3)	Conditions Applicable to Benefits
8503(3)(*a*)	Eligible service
8503(3)(*b*)	Benefit accruals after pension commencement
8503(3)(*c*)	Early retirement
8503(3)(*d*)	Increased benefits for disabled member
8503(3)(*e*)	Pre-1991 benefits
8503(3)(*f*)	Determination of retirement benefits
8503(3)(*g*)	Benefit accrual rate
8503(3)(*h*)	Increase in accrued benefits
8503(3)(*i*)	[Idem]
8503(3)(*j*)	Offset benefits
8503(3)(*k*)	Bridging benefits — Cross-plan restriction
8503(3)(*l*)	Division of benefits on breakdown of the marriage or common-law partnership
8503(4)	Additional Conditions
8503(4)(*a*)	Member contributions
8503(4)(*b*)	Pre-payment of member contributions
8503(4)(*c*)	Reduction in benefits and return of contributions
8503(4)(*d*)	Undue deferral of payment
8503(4)(*e*)	Evidence of disability
8503(4)(*f*)	Idem
8503(5)	Waiver of Member Contribution Condition
8503(6)	Pre-Retirement Death Benefits
8503(7)	Commutation of Lifetime Retirement Benefits
8503(7.1)	Bridging Benefits and Election
8503(8)	Suspension or Cessation of Pension
8503(9)	Re-Employed Member
8503(10)	Re-Employed Member — Special Rules Not Applicable
8503(11)	Re-Employed Member — Anti-Avoidance
8503(11.1)	Special Rules for Member Aged 70 or 71 in 2007
8503(12)	Limits Dependent On Consumer Price Index
8503(13)	Statutory Plans — Special Rules
8503(14)	Artificially Reduced Pension Adjustments
8503(15)	Past Service Employer Contributions
8503(16)	Definitions
8503(17)	Bridging Benefits Payable on a Stand-alone Basis
8503(18)	Rules of Application
8503(19)	Benefit Accruals After Pension Commencement
8503(20)	Redetermination of Benefits
8503(21)	Rules of Application
8503(22)	Anti-avoidance
8503(23)	Cross-plan Rules
8503(24)	Associated Defined Benefit Provisions
8503(25)	Subsection
8503(26)	IPP — Minimum Withdrawal
8504(1)	Lifetime Retirement Benefits
8504(2)	Highest Average Compensation
8504(2.1)	Predecessor Employer
8504(3)	Alternative Compensation Rules
8504(4)	Part-Time Employees
8504(5)	Retirement Benefits Before Age 65
8504(6)	Pre-1990 Benefits
8504(7)	Limit Not Applicable
8504(8)	Cross-Plan Restrictions
8504(9)	Associated Defined Benefit Provisions
8504(10)	Excluded Benefits
8504(11)	[Idem]
8504(12)	[Idem]
8504(13)	Alternative CPI Indexing
8504(14)	[Idem]
8504(15)	[Idem]
8505(1)	Downsizing Program
8505(2)	Applicability of Downsizing Rules
8505(2.1)	Qualifying Individual — Exclusion
8505(3)	Additional Lifetime Retirement Benefits
8505(3.1)	Re-employed Members
8505(4)	Early Retirement Reduction
8505(5)	Exception for Future Benefits
8505(6)	Alternative CPI Indexing
8505(7)	Exclusion from Maximum Pension Rules
8505(8)	Exemption from Past Service Contribution Rule
8506(1)	Permissible Benefits
8506(1)(*a*)	Lifetime retirement benefits
8506(1)(*b*)	Bridging benefits
8506(1)(*c*)	Guarantee period
8506(1)(*d*)	Post-retirement survivor benefits
8506(1)(*e*)	Pre-retirement survivor benefits
8506(1)(*e*.1)	Variable benefits
8506(1)(*f*)	Payment from account
8506(1)(*g*)	Payment from account after death
8506(1)(*h*)	Commutation of benefits
8506(1)(*i*)	[Idem]
8506(2)	Additional Conditions
8506(2)(*a*)	Employer contributions acceptable to Minister

Section	Subject
8506(2)(*b*)	Employer contributions with respect to particular members
8506(2)(*b*.1)	Allocation of employer contributions
8506(2)(*c*)	Employer contributions not permitted
8506(2)(*c*.1)	Contributions not permitted
8506(2)(*d*)	Return of contributions
8506(2)(*e*)	Allocation of earnings
8506(2)(*f*)	Payment or reallocation of forfeited amounts
8506(2)(*g*)	Retirement benefits
8506(2)(*h*)	Undue deferral of payment — Death of member
8506(2)(*i*)	Undue deferral of payment — Death of specified beneficiary
8506(2.1)	Alternative Method for Allocating Employer Contributions
8506(3)	Reallocation of Forfeitures
8506(4)	Non-payment of Minimum Amount — Plan Revocable
8506(5)	Minimum Amount
8506(6)	Determination of Account Balance
8506(7)	Special Rules for Minimum Amount
8506(8)	Specified Beneficiary
8506(9)	Recontribution — Adjusted Minimum Amount for 2008
8506(10)	Conditions Referred to in Subsection
8506(11)	Recontribution for 2015
8506(12)	Conditions Referred to in Subsection
8507(1)	Prescribed Compensation
8507(2)	Additional Compensation in Respect of Qualifying Period
8507(3)	Qualifying Periods and Periods of Parenting
8507(4)	Cumulative Additional Compensation Fraction
8507(5)	Additional Compensation Fraction
8507(6)	Exclusion of Subperiods
8507(7)	Complete Period of Reduced Pay
8508	Salary Deferral Leave Plan
8509(1)	Prescribed Conditions Applicable Before 1992 to Grandfathered Plan
8509(2)	Conditions Applicable After 1991 to Benefits Under Grandfathered Plan
8509(3)	Additional Prescribed Condition for Grandfathered Plan After 1991
8509(4)	Defined Benefits Under Grandfathered Plan Exempt From Conditions
8509(4.1)	Benefits under Grandfathered Plan — Pre-1992 Disability
8509(5)	Conditions Not Applicable to Grandfathered Plan
8509(6)	PA Limits for Grandfathered Plan for 1991
8509(7)	Limit on Pre-Age 65 Benefits
8509(8)	Benefit Accrual Rate Greater Than 2 Per Cent
8509(9)	Benefits Under Plan Other Than Grandfathered Plan
8509(10)	Money Purchase Benefits Exempt From Conditions
8509(10.1)	Stipulation Not Required for Pre-1992 Plans
8509(11)	Benefits Acceptable to Minister
8509(12)	PA Limits — 1996 to 2002
8509(13)	Maximum Benefits Indexed Before 2005
8510(1)	Definition of "Multi-Employer Plan"
8510(2)	Definition of "Specified Multi-Employer Plan"
8510(3)	Qualification as a Specified Multi-Employer Plan
8510(4)	Minister's Notice
8510(5)	Special Rules — Multi-Employer Plan
8510(6)	Special Rules — Specified Multi-Employer Plan
8510(7)	Additional Prescribed Conditions
8510(8)	Purchase of Additional Benefits
8510(9)	Special Rules — Member-funded Pension Plans
8511	Conditions Applicable to Amendments
8512	Registration and Amendment
8513	Designated Laws
8514	Prohibited Investments
8515(1)	Designated Plans
8515(2)	Designated Plan in Previous Year
8515(3)	Exceptions
8515(3.1)	Exceptions
8515(4)	Specified Individuals
8515(5)	Eligible Contributions
8515(6)	Funding Restriction
8515(7)	Maximum Funding Valuation
8515(8)	Restricted-Funding Members
8515(9)	Member Contributions
8516(1)	Prescribed Contribution
8516(2)	Funding on Termination Basis
8516(3)	Contributions Required by Pension Benefits Legislation
8517(1)	Prescribed Amount
8517(2)	Minimum Prescribed Amount
8517(3)	Underfunded Pension
8517(3.02)	Underfunded Pension
8517(3.1)	Benefits Provided With Surplus on Plan Wind-up
8517(4)	Amount of Lifetime Retirement Benefits Commuted
8517(5)	Normalized Pensions
8517(6)	Optional Forms
8517(7)	Replacement Benefits
8518	Transfer — Defined Benefit to Money Purchase
8519	Association of Benefits with Time Periods
8520	Minister's Actions

PART LXXXVI
TAXABLE CAPITAL EMPLOYED IN CANADA

8600	[Definitions]
8601	[Prescribed proportion of taxable capital]
8602	[Prescribed proportion re Canadian surtax]
8603	[Interpretation]
8604	(Repealed.)
8605	[Prescribed amount – financial institution]

PART LXXXVII
NATIONAL ARTS SERVICE ORGANIZATIONS

8700	[Prescribed conditions]

PART LXXXVIII
DISABILITY-RELATED MODIFICATIONS AND APPARATUS

8800	[Prescribed renovations and alterations]
8801	[Prescribed devices and equipment]

PART LXXXIX
ENTITIES PRESCRIBED WITH RESPECT TO CERTAIN RULES

PART XC
FINANCIAL INSTITUTIONS — PRESCRIBED ENTITIES AND PROPERTIES

PART XCI
FINANCIAL INSTITUTIONS — INCOME FROM SPECIFIED DEBT OBLIGATIONS

PART XCII
FINANCIAL INSTITUTIONS — DISPOSITION OF SPECIFIED DEBT OBLIGATIONS

PART XCIII
FILM OR VIDEO PRODUCTION SERVICES TAX CREDIT

PART XCIV
PRESCRIBED CHILDREN'S PROGRAMS [REPEALED.]

PART XCV
EMPLOYEE LIFE AND HEALTH TRUSTS

Regulations

Section	Subject	Section	Subject

PART XCVI

SCHOOL SUPPLIES TAX CREDIT

Section	Subject
9600	Prescribed durable goods

SCHEDULE I

(SS. 100, 102 AND 106)

SCHEDULE II

CAPITAL COST ALLOWANCES

SCHEDULE III

CAPITAL COST ALLOWANCES, CLASS 13

SCHEDULE IV

CAPITAL COST ALLOWANCES, CLASS 15

SCHEDULE V

CAPITAL COST ALLOWANCES, INDUSTRIAL MINERAL MINES

SCHEDULE VI

CAPITAL COST ALLOWANCES, TIMBER LIMITS AND CUTTING RIGHTS

SCHEDULE VII

PUBLICLY-TRADED SHARES OR SECURITIES

SCHEDULE VIII

UNIVERSITIES OUTSIDE CANADA [REPEALED.]

SCHEDULE IX

PRESCRIBED AREAS — 1987 TO 1992 [REVOKED.]

SCHEDULE X

PRESCRIBED AREAS [REVOKED.]

Income Tax Regulations

C.R.C., c. 945, as amended

Consolidated to December 31, 1977 by P.C. 1979-1933, dated July 19, 1979 and proclaimed in force August 15, 1979 by P.C. 1979-1934, SI/79-131, dated and gazetted August 8, 1979; originally issued as P.C. 6471, SOR/49-573, dated December 22, 1949, published December 28, 1949, and applicable to the 1949 and subsequent taxation years; first consolidated by Order in Council P.C. 1954-1917, SOR/54-682, dated December 8, 1954, published January 12, 1955.

1. Short title

These Regulations may be cited as the *Income Tax Regulations*.

2. Interpretation

In these Regulations, "Act" means the *Income Tax Act*.

Regulations

Part I
Tax Deductions

100. Interpretation

(1) In this Part and in Schedule I,

"employee" means any person receiving remuneration;

"employer" means any person paying remuneration;

"estimated deductions" means, in respect of a taxation year, the total of the amounts estimated to be deductible by an employee for the year under any of paragraphs 8(1)(*f*), (*h*), (*h*.1), (*i*) and (*j*) of the Act and determined by the employee for the purpose of completing the form referred to in subsection 107(2);

"exemptions"

"pay period" includes

(*a*) a day,

(*b*) a week,

(*c*) a two week period,

(*d*) a semi-monthly period,

(*e*) a month,

(*f*) a four week period,

(*g*) one tenth of a calendar year, or

(*h*) one twenty-second of a calendar year;

"personal credits" means, in respect of a particular taxation year, the greater of

(*a*) the amount referred to in paragraph 118(1)(*c*) of the Act, and

(*b*) the aggregate of the credits which the employee would be entitled to claim for the year under

(i) subsections 118(1), (2) and (3) of the Act if the description of A in those subsections were read as "is equal to one",

(ii) subsections 118.3(1) and (2) of the Act if the description of A in subsection 118.3(1) of the Act were read as "is equal to one" and if subsection 118.3(1) of the Act were read without reference to paragraph (*c*) thereof,

(iii) subsections 118.5(1) and 118.6(2) of the Act if subsection 118.5(1) of the Act were read without reference to "the product obtained when the appropriate percentage for the year is multiplied by" and the description of A in subsection 118.6(2) of the Act were read as "is equal to one", and after deducting from the aggregate of the amounts determined under those subsections the excess over $3,000 of the aggregate of amounts that the employee claims to expect to receive in the year on account of a scholarship, fellowship or bursary,

(iv) section 118.8 of the Act if the formula A + B - C in that section were read as

$$(A + B) / C$$

where

A is the value of A in that section,

B is the value of B in that section, and

C is the appropriate percentage for the year.

(v) section 118.9 of the Act if the formula A - B in section 118.81 of the Act were read as

$$A/B$$

where

A is the value of A set out in that section, and

B is the appropriate percentage for the year.

➔ ***"remuneration"*** includes any payment that is

(*a*) in respect of

(i) salary or wages, or

(ii) commissions or other similar amounts fixed by reference to the volume of the sales made or the contracts negotiated (referred to as "commissions" in this Part),

paid to an officer or employee or former officer or employee,

(*a*.1) in respect of an employee's gratuities required under provincial legislation to be declared to the employee's employer, (*b*) a superannuation or pension benefit (including an annuity payment made pursuant to or under a superannuation or pension fund or plan) other than a distribution

(i) that is made from a pooled registered pension plan and is not required to be included in computing a taxpayer's income under paragraph 56(1)(*z.3*) of the Act, or

(ii) that subsection 147.5(14) of the Act deems to have been made,

(*b*.1) an amount of a distribution out of or under a retirement compensation arrangement,

(*c*) a retiring allowance,

(*d*) a death benefit,

(*e*) a benefit under a supplementary unemployment benefit plan,

(*f*) a payment under a deferred profit sharing plan or a plan referred to in section 147 of the Act as a "revoked plan", reduced, if applicable, by amounts determined under subsections 147(10.1), (11) and (12) of the Act,

(*g*) a benefit under the *Employment Insurance Act*,

(*g*.1) an amount that is required by paragraph 56(1)(*a.3*) of the Act to be included in computing a taxpayer's income,

(*h*) an amount that is required by paragraph 56(1)(*r*) of the Act to be included in computing a taxpayer's income, except the portion of the amount that relates to child care expenses and tuition costs,

(*i*) a payment made during the lifetime of an annuitant referred to in the definition "annuitant" in subsection 146(1) of the Act out of or under a registered retirement savings plan of that annuitant, other than

(i) a periodic annuity payment, or

(ii) a payment made by a person who has reasonable grounds to believe that the payment may be deducted under subsection 146(8.2) of the Act in computing the income of any taxpayer,

(*j*) a payment out of or under a plan referred to in subsection 146(12) of the Act as an "amended plan" other than

(i) a periodic annuity payment, or

(ii) where paragraph 146(12)(*a*) of the Act applied to the plan after May 25, 1976, a payment made in a year subsequent to the year in which that paragraph applied to the plan,

(*j*.1) a payment made during the lifetime of an annuitant referred to in the definition "annuitant" in subsection 146.3(1) of the Act under a registered retirement income fund of that annuitant, other than a particular payment to the extent that

(i) the particular payment is in respect of the minimum amount (in this paragraph having the meaning assigned by subsection 146.3(1) of the Act) under the fund for a year, or

(ii) where the fund governs a trust, the particular payment would be in respect of the minimum amount under the fund for a year if each amount that, at the beginning of the year, is scheduled to be paid after the time of the particular payment and in the year to the trust under an annuity contract that is held by the trust both at the beginning of the year and at the time of the particular payment, is paid to the trust in the year,

(*k*) a benefit described in section 5502,

(*l*) an amount as, on account or in lieu of payment of, or in satisfaction of, proceeds of the surrender, cancellation or redemption of an income-averaging annuity contract,

(*m*) in respect of an amount that can reasonably be regarded as having been received, in whole or in part, as consideration or partial consideration for entering into a contract of service, where the service is to be performed in Canada, or for an undertaking not to enter into such a contract with another party,

(*n*) a payment out of a registered education savings plan other than

(i) a refund of payments,

(ii) an educational assistance payment, or

(iii) an amount, up to $50,000, of an accumulated income payment that is made to a subscriber, as defined in subsection 204.94(1) of the Act, or if there is no subscriber at that time, that is made to a person that has been a spouse or common-law partner of an individual who was a subscriber, if

(A) that amount is transferred to an RRSP in which the annuitant is either the recipient of the payment or the recipient's spouse or common-law partner, and

(B) it is reasonable for the person making the payment to believe that that amount is deductible for the year by the recipient of the payment within the limits provided for in subsection 146(5) or (5.1) of the Act, or

(*o*) an amount of a disability assistance payment made under a registered disability savings plan that is required by paragraph 56(1)(*q.1*) of the Act to be included in computing a taxpayer's income;

"total remuneration" means, in respect of a taxation year, the total of all amounts each of which is an amount referred to in paragraph (*a*) or (*a*.1) of the definition "remuneration".

History: S. 100(1), paragraph (*o*) of the definition "remuneration" was added by SOR/2016-30, s. 1, applicable July 1, 2015.

S. 100(1), paragraph (*g.1*) of the definition "remuneration" was added by S.C. 2012, c. 27, s. 30(1), in force January 1, 2013.

S. 100(1), paragraph (*b*) of the definition "remuneration" was replaced by S.C. 2012, c. 31, s. 58(1), in force December 14, 2012, and formerly read:

(*b*) a superannuation or pension benefit (including an annuity payment made pursuant to or under a superannuation or pension fund or plan),

Information Circulars: IC 98-1R4 Collections policies.

Tax Window Files: Source Deductions — Employee Working Abroad, *Technical Interpretation, International and Trust Division, November 14, 2007*, CRA Document No. 2007-0245631E5; Financial Assistance to Disabled Persons — Withholding and Reporting, *Technical Interpretation, Business and Partnerships Division, February 12, 2007*, CRA Document No. 2006-0205981E5.

(2) Where the amount of any credit referred to in paragraph (*a*) or (*b*) of the definition "personal credits" in subsection (1) is subject to an annual adjustment under section 117.1 of the Act, such amount shall, in a particular taxation year, be subject to that annual adjustment.

(3) For the purposes of this Part, where an employer deducts or withholds from a payment of remuneration to an employee one or more amounts each of which is

(*a*) a contribution to or under a pooled registered pension plan, a registered pension plan or a specified pension plan, or

(*b*) dues described in subparagraph 8(1)(*i*)(iv), (v) or (vi) of the Act paid on account of the employee,

(*b*.1) a contribution by the employee under subparagraph 8(1)(*m*.2) of the Act,

(*c*) a premium under a registered retirement savings plan, to the extent that the employer believes on reasonable grounds that the premium is deductible under paragraph 60(*j*.1) or subsection 146(5) or (5.1) of the Act in computing the employee's income for the taxation year in which the payment of remuneration is made, or

(*d*) an amount that is deductible under paragraph 60(*b*) of the Act,

the balance remaining after deducting or withholding this amount, as the case may be, shall be deemed to be the amount of that payment of remuneration.

History: S. 100(3)(*a*) was replaced by S.C. 2012, c. 31, s. 58(2), in force December 14, 2012, and formerly read:

(*a*) a contribution to or under a registered pension plan,

(3.1) For the purposes of this Part, where an employee has claimed a deduction for a taxation year under paragraph 110.7(1)(*b*) of the Act as shown on the return most recently filed by the employee with the employee's employer pursuant to subsection 227(2) of the Act, the amount of remuneration otherwise determined, including the amount deemed by subsection (3) to be the amount of that payment of remuneration, paid to the employee for a pay period shall be reduced by an amount equal to the amount of the deduction divided by the maximum number of pay periods in the year in respect of the appropriate pay period.

(3.2) (Repealed by P.C. 2001-1053, SOR/2001-209.)

(4) For the purposes of this Part, where an employee is not required to report for work at any establishment of the employer, he shall be deemed to report for work

(*a*) in respect of remuneration that is salary, wages or commissions, at the establishment of the employer from which the remuneration is paid;

or

(*b*) in respect of remuneration other than salary, wages or commissions, at the establishment of the employer in the province where the employee resides at the time the remuneration is paid but, if the employer does not have an establishment in that province at that time, he shall, for the purposes of this paragraph, be deemed to have an establishment in that province.

(5) For the purposes of this Part, where an employer deducts or withholds from a payment of remuneration to an employee an amount in respect of the acquisition by the employee of an approved share, as defined in subsection 127.4(1) of the Act, there shall be deducted from the amount determined under paragraph 102(1)(*e*) or (2)(*e*), as the case may be, in respect of that payment the lesser of

(*a*) $750, and

(*b*) 15% of the amount deducted or withheld in respect of the acquisition of an approved share.

101. Deductions and Remittances

Every person who makes a payment described in subsection 153(1) of the Act in a taxation year shall deduct or withhold therefrom, and remit to the Receiver General, such amount, if any, as is determined in accordance with rules prescribed in this Part.

102. Periodic Payments

(1) Except as otherwise provided in this Part, the amount to be deducted or withheld by an employer

(*a*) from any payment of remuneration (in this subsection referred to as the "payment") made to an employee in his taxation year where he reports for work at an establishment of the employer in a province, in Canada beyond the limits of any province or outside Canada, and

(*b*) for any pay period in which the payment is made by the employer

shall be determined for each payment in accordance with the following rules:

(*c*) an amount that is a notional remuneration for the year in respect of

(i) a payment to the employee, and

(ii) the amount, if any, of gratuities referred to in paragraph (*a*.1) of the definition "remuneration" in subsection 100(1)

is deemed to be the amount determined by the formula

$$A \times B$$

where

A is the amount that is deemed for the purpose of this paragraph to be the mid-point of the applicable range of remuneration for the pay period, as provided in Schedule I, in which falls the total of

(A) the payment referred to in subparagraph (i) made in the pay period, and

(B) the amount of gratuities referred to in subparagraph (ii) declared by the employee for the pay period, and

B is the maximum number of such pay periods in that year;

(*d*) if the employee is not resident in Canada at the time of the payment, no personal credits will be allowed for the purposes of this subsection and, if the employee is resident in Canada at the time of the payment, the employee's personal credits for the year are deemed to be the mid-point of the range of amounts of personal credits for a taxation year as provided for in section 2 of Schedule I;

(*e*) an amount (in this subsection referred to as the "notional tax for the year") shall be computed in respect of that employee by

(i) calculating the amount of tax payable for the year, as if that amount were calculated under subsection 117(2) of the Act and adjusted annually pursuant to section 117.1 of the Act, on the amount determined in accordance with paragraph (*c*) as if that amount represented the employee's amount taxable for that year,

and deducting the aggregate of

(ii) the amount determined in accordance with paragraph (*d*) multiplied by the appropriate percentage for the year,

(iii) an amount equal to

(A) the amount determined in accordance with paragraph (c) multiplied by the employee's premium rate for the year under the *Employment Insurance Act*, not exceeding the maximum amount of the premiums payable by the employee for the year under that Act,

multiplied by

(B) the appropriate percentage for the year, and

(iv) an amount equal to

(A) the product obtained when the difference between the amount determined in accordance with paragraph (c) and the amount determined under section 20 of the *Canada Pension Plan* for the year is multiplied by the employee's contribution rate for the year under the *Canada Pension Plan* or under a provincial pension plan as defined in subsection 3(1) of that Act, not exceeding the maximum amount of such contributions payable by the employee for the year under the plan,

multiplied by

(B) the appropriate percentage for the year;

(*f*) the amount determined in accordance with paragraph (*e*) shall be increased by, where applicable, the tax as determined under subsection 120(1) of the Act;

(*g*) where the amount of notional remuneration for the year is income earned in the Province of Quebec, the amount determined in accordance with paragraph (*e*) shall be reduced by an amount that is the aggregate of

(i) the amount that is deemed to be paid under subsection 120(2) of the Act as if there were no other source of income or loss for the year, and

(ii) the amount by which the amount referred to in subparagraph (i) is increased by virtue of section 27 of the *Federal-Provincial Fiscal Arrangements and Federal Post-Secondary Education and Health Contributions Act*; and

(*h*) (Revoked.)

(*i*) the amount to be deducted or withheld shall be computed by

(i) dividing the amount of the notional tax for the year by the maximum number of pay periods for the year in respect of the appropriate pay period, and

(ii) rounding the amount determined under subparagraph (i) to the nearest multiple of five cents or, if such amount is equidistant from two such multiples, to the higher multiple.

Canadian Tax Foundation: Dumalski, *Accessing Statute-Barred Corporate Refunds Through Employee Refunds: Regulation 102*, 2015 Canadian Tax Focus 2(4):1.

Tax Profile: May 2011 — Creating a Canada-U.S. Service Joint Venture; January 2009 — Enhancing Canada's International Tax Advantage; August 2007 — Professionals and Other Service Providers Beware — A Canadian Trap; August 2005 — Canada Revenue Agency's Recent Attack on U.S. Companies.

Tax Topics: No. 2289, Update on the Exemption for Non-Residents from Payroll Withholding; No. 2127, CRA Panel: Rulings Update and Other Department News; No. 1818, Withholding Tax Obligations on Remuneration Paid to Non-Residents of Canada.

(2) Where an employee has elected pursuant to subsection 107(2) and has not revoked such election, the amount to be deducted or withheld by the employer from any payment of remuneration (in this subsection referred to as the "payment") that is

(*a*) a payment in respect of commissions or is a combined payment of commissions and salary or wages, or

(*b*) a payment in respect of salary or wages where that employee receives a combined payment of commissions and salary or wages,

made to that employee in his taxation year where he reports for work at an establishment of the employer in a province, in Canada beyond the limits of any province or outside Canada, shall be determined for each payment in accordance with the following rules:

(*c*) an employee's "estimated annual taxable income" shall be determined by using the formula

$$A - B$$

where

A is the amount of that employee's total remuneration in respect of the year as recorded by the employee on the form referred to in subsection 107(2), and

B is the amount of that employee's expenses in respect of the year as recorded by that employee on that form;

(*d*) if the employee is not resident in Canada at the time of the payment, no personal credits will be allowed for the purposes of this subsection and if the employee is resident in Canada at the time of the payment, the employee's personal credits for the year shall be the total claim amount as recorded by that employee on the return for the year referred to in subsection 107(1);

(*e*) an amount (in this subsection referred to as the "notional tax for the year") shall be calculated in respect of that employee by using the formula

$$C - [(D + E + F) \times G] + H - I$$

where

C is the amount of tax payable for the year, calculated as if that amount of tax were computed under subsection 117(2) of the Act and adjusted annually pursuant to section 117.1 of the Act, on the amount determined under paragraph (*c*) as if that amount represented the employee's amount taxable for that year,

D is the amount determined in accordance with paragraph (*d*),

E is the amount determined in the description of A in paragraph (*c*) multiplied by the employee's premium rate for the year under the *Employ-*

ment Insurance Act, not exceeding the maximum amount of the premiums payable by the employee for the year under that Act,

F is the amount determined in the description of A in paragraph (*c*) less the amount for the year determined under section 20 of the *Canada Pension Plan* multiplied by the employee's contribution rate for the year under that Act or under a provincial pension plan as defined in section 3 of that Act, not exceeding the maximum amount of such contributions payable by the employee for the year under the plan,

G is the appropriate percentage for the year,

H is, where applicable, the tax as determined under subsection 120(1) of the Act,

I is, where the amount of total remuneration for the year is income earned in the Province of Quebec, an amount equal to the aggregate of

(i) the amount that would be deemed to have been paid under subsection 120(2) of the Act with respect to the employee if the notional tax for the year for the employee were determined without reference to the elements H, I and J [*sic*.] in this formula and if that tax were that employee's tax payable under Part I of the Act for that year, as if there were no other source of income or loss for the year, and

(ii) the amount by which the amount referred to in subparagraph (i) is increased by virtue of section 27 of the *Federal–Provincial Fiscal Arrangements Act*;

(*f*) the employee's notional rate of tax for a year is calculated by dividing the amount determined under paragraph (*e*) by the amount referred to in the description of A in paragraph (*c*) in respect of that employee and expressed as a decimal fraction rounded to the nearest hundredth, or where the third digit is equidistant from two consecutive one-thousandths, to the higher thereof;

(*g*) the amount to be deducted or withheld in respect of any payment made to that employee shall be determined by multiplying the payment by the appropriate decimal fraction determined pursuant to paragraph (*f*).

(3) (Revoked by P.C. 1989-2105, SOR/89-508.)

(4) (Revoked.)

(5) Notwithstanding subsections (1) and (2), no amount shall be deducted or withheld in the year by an employer from a payment of remuneration to an employee in respect of commissions earned by the employee in the immediately preceding year where those commissions were previously reported by the employer as remuneration of the employee in respect of that year on an information return.

(6) Despite subsection (1), no amount shall be deducted or withheld in the year by an employer from an amount determined in accordance with subparagraph 110(1)(*f*)(iii), (iv) or (v) of the Act.

History: S. 102(6) and the heading before it were replaced by S.C. 2014, c. 39, s. 78(1), applicable to amounts paid on or after July 12, 2013.

In addition, any assessment of a taxpayer's tax, interest and penalties payable under the Act for any taxation year that ends before the day on which this amendment receives royal assent [December 16, 2014] that would, in the absence of this section, be precluded because of the time references in subsection 152(4) of the Act is to be made to the extent necessary to take into account this amendment.

S. 102(6) formerly read:

(6) *Canadian Forces and Police — Exception.* Despite subsection (1), no amount shall be deducted or withheld in the year by an employer from an amount determined in accordance with subparagraph 110(1)(*f*)(v) of the Act.

103. Non-Periodic Payments

(1) Where a payment in respect of a bonus or retroactive increase in remuneration is made by an employer to an employee whose total remuneration from the employer (including the bonus or retroactive increase) may reasonably be expected not to exceed $5,000 in the taxation year of the employee in which the payment is made, the employer shall deduct or withhold, in the case of an employee who reports for work at an establishment of the employer

(*a*) in any province, 10 percent, or

(*b*) in Canada beyond the limits of any province or outside Canada, 15 percent,

of such payment in lieu of the amount determined under section 102.

(2) Where a payment in respect of a bonus is made by an employer to an employee whose total remuneration from the employer (including the bonus) may reasonably be expected to exceed $5,000 in the taxation year of the employee in which the payment is made, the amount to be deducted or withheld therefrom by the employer is

(*a*) the amount determined under section 102 in respect of an assumed remuneration equal to the aggregate of

(i) the amount of regular remuneration paid by the employer to the employee in the pay period in which the remuneration is paid, and

(ii) an amount equal to the bonus payment divided by the number of pay periods in the taxation year of the employee in which the payment is made

minus

(*b*) the amount determined under section 102 in respect of the amount of regular remuneration paid by the employer to the employee in the pay period

multiplied by

(*c*) the number of pay periods in the taxation year of the employee in which the payment is made.

(3) Where a payment in respect of a retroactive increase in remuneration is made by an employer to an employee whose total remuneration from the employer (including the retroactive increase) may reasonably be expected to exceed $5,000 in the taxation year of the employee in which the payment is made, the amount to be deducted or withheld therefrom by the employer is

(*a*) the amount determined under section 102 in respect of the new rate of remuneration

minus

(*b*) the amount determined under section 102 in respect of the previous rate of remuneration

multiplied by

(*c*) the number of pay periods in respect of which the increase in remuneration is retroactive.

Regulations

(4) Subject to subsection (5), where a lump sum payment is made by an employer to an employee who is a resident of Canada,

(*a*) if the payment does not exceed $5,000, the employer shall deduct or withhold therefrom, in the case of an employee who reports for work at an establishment of the employer

(i) in Quebec, 5 percent,

(ii) in any other province, 7 percent, or

(iii) in Canada beyond the limits of any province or outside Canada, 10 percent,

of such payment in lieu of the amount determined under section 102;

(*b*) if the payment exceeds $5,000 but does not exceed $15,000, the employer shall deduct or withhold therefrom, in the case of an employee who reports for work at an establishment of the employer

(i) in Quebec, 10 percent,

(ii) in any other province, 13 percent, or

(iii) in Canada beyond the limits of any province or outside Canada, 20 percent,

of such payment in lieu of the amount determined under section 102; and

(*c*) if the payment exceeds $15,000, the employer shall deduct or withhold therefrom, in the case of an employee who reports for work at an establishment of the employer

(i) in Quebec, 15 percent,

(ii) in any other province, 20 percent, or

(iii) in Canada beyond the limits of any province or outside Canada, 30 percent,

of such payment in lieu of the amount determined under section 102.

Tax Topics: No. 1706, Retiring Allowances and E.I. Reimbursements: How Many Times Do You Have To Withhold?.

(5) Where the payment referred to in subsection (4) would be pension income or qualified pension income of the employee in respect of which subsection 118(3) of the Act would apply if the definition "pension income" in subsection 118(7) of the Act were read without reference to subparagraphs (*a*)(ii) and (iii) thereof, the payment shall be deemed to be the amount of the payment minus

(*a*) where the payment does not exceed the amount taxable referred to in paragraph 117(2)(*a*) of the Act, as adjusted annually pursuant to section 117.1 of the Act, the lesser of $1,000 and the amount of the payment;

(*b*) where the payment exceeds the amount referred to in paragraph (*a*) but does not exceed $61,509, $727;

(*c*) where the payment exceeds $61,509 but does not exceed $100,000, $615; and

(*d*) where the payment exceeds $100,000, $552.

(6) For the purposes of subsection (4), a "lump sum payment" means a payment that is

(*a*) a payment described in subparagraph 40(1)(*a*)(i) or (iii) or paragraph 40(1)(*c*) of the *Income Tax Application Rules*,

(*b*) a payment under a deferred profit sharing plan or a plan referred to in section 147 of the Act as a "revoked plan", except a payment referred to in subparagraph 147(2)(*k*)(v) of the Act,

(*c*) a payment made during the lifetime of an annuitant referred to in the definition "annuitant" in subsection 146(1) of the Act out of or under a registered retirement savings plan of that annuitant, other than

(i) a periodic annuity payment, or

(ii) a payment made by a person who has reasonable grounds to believe that the payment may be deducted under subsection 146(8.2) of the Act in computing the income of any taxpayer,

(*d*) a payment out of or under a plan referred to in subsection 146(12) of the Act as an "amended plan" other than

(i) a periodic annuity payment, or

(ii) where paragraph 146(12)(*a*) of the Act applied to the plan after May 25, 1976, a payment made in a year subsequent to the year in which that paragraph applied to the plan,

(*d*.1) a payment made during the lifetime of an annuitant referred to in the definition "annuitant" in subsection 146.3(1) of the Act under a registered retirement income fund of that annuitant, other than a payment to the extent that it is in respect of the minimum amount (within the meaning assigned by subsection 146.3(1) of the Act) under the fund for a year,

(*e*) a retiring allowance,

(*f*) a payment of an amount as, on account or in lieu of payment of, or in satisfaction of, proceeds of the surrender, cancellation or redemption of an income-averaging annuity contract, or

(*g*) a payment described in paragraph (*n*) of the definition "remuneration" in subsection 100(1).

(7) For the purposes of subsection 153(1) of the Act, the amount to be deducted or withheld by a person shall be 50 per cent

(*a*) of the contribution made by the person under a retirement compensation arrangement, other than

(i) a contribution made by the person as an employee,

(ii) a contribution made to a plan or arrangement that is a prescribed plan or arrangement for the purposes of subsection 207.6(6) of the Act, or

(iii) a contribution made by way of a transfer from another retirement compensation arrangement under circumstances in which subsection 207.6(7) of the Act applies; or

(*b*) of the payment by the person to a resident of Canada of an amount on account of the purchase price of an interest in a retirement compensation arrangement.

(8) Every employer making a payment described in paragraph (*n*) of the definition "remuneration" in subsection 100(1) shall withhold — in addition to any other amount required to be withheld under Part I of these Regulations — on account of the tax payable under Part X.5 of the Act, an amount equal to (*a*) where the amount is paid in the province of Quebec, 12 per cent of the payment, and

(*b*) in any other case, 20 per cent of the payment.

(9) The amount to be deducted or withheld by a person from any payment of an amount described in paragraph 56(1)(*z.4*) of the Act is

(*a*) in the case of a payment to a resident of Quebec, 30% of the payment; or

(*b*) in the case of a payment to a resident of Canada who is not a resident of Quebec, 50% of the payment.

History: S. 103(9) was added by S.C. 2014, c. 20, s. 32, in force June 19, 2014.

103.1. (1) For the purpose of the description of C in subsection (2), "plan payment" means

(*a*) in the case of a disability assistance payment that is a lifetime disability assistance payment, the total amount of all the lifetime disability assistance payments that have been made or that may reasonably be expected to be made to the employee under the plan in their taxation year and that the employer has reasonable grounds to believe are described in paragraph (*o*) of the definition "remuneration" in subsection 100(1); or

(*b*) in the case of a disability assistance payment that is other than a lifetime disability assistance payment, the amount of the payment that is made to the employee under the plan and that is described in paragraph (*o*) of the definition "remuneration" in subsection 100(1).

History: S. 103.1(1) was added by SOR/2016-30, s. 2, applicable July 1, 2015.

(2) If an employer makes a disability assistance payment under a registered disability savings plan to an employee who is a resident of Canada, the employer shall, in lieu of the amount determined under section 102, deduct or withhold from the payment an amount determined by the formula

$$(A - B) \times C$$

where

A is the amount of the disability assistance payment that is made to the employee and that is described in paragraph (*o*) of the definition "remuneration" in subsection 100(1);

B is

(*a*) if the beneficiary of the plan is deceased, nil, or

(*b*) the amount by which the total of the following amounts exceeds the total amount of all the disability assistance payments previously made to the employee in their taxation year and that are described in paragraph (*o*) of the definition "remuneration" in subsection 100(1):

(i) the amount used under paragraph (*c*) of the description of B in subsection 118(1) of the Act for the taxation year, and

(ii) the amount used under the description of B in subsection 118.3(1) of the Act for the taxation year; and

C is

(*a*) if the plan payment does not exceed $5,000 and the amount is paid

(i) in Quebec, 5 per cent,

(ii) in any other province, 7 per cent, or

(iii) in Canada beyond the limits of any province or outside Canada, 10 per cent,

(*b*) if the plan payment exceeds $5,000 but does not exceed $15,000 and the amount is paid

(i) in Quebec, 10 per cent,

(ii) in any other province, 13 per cent, or

(iii) in Canada beyond the limits of any province or outside Canada, 20 per cent, or

(*c*) if the plan payment exceeds $15,000 and the amount is paid

(i) in Quebec, 15 per cent,

(ii) in any other province, 20 per cent, or

(iii) in Canada beyond the limits of any province or outside Canada, 30 per cent.

History: S. 103.1(2) was added by SOR/2016-30, s. 2, applicable July 1, 2015.

104. Deductions Not Required

(1) (Repealed by P.C. 2001-1115, SOR/2001-221.)

(2) No amount shall be deducted or withheld from a payment in accordance with any of sections 102 to 103.1 in respect of an employee who was neither employed nor resident in Canada at the time of payment except in respect of

(*a*) remuneration described in subparagraph 115(2)(*e*)(i) of the Act that is paid to a non-resident person who has in the year, or had in any previous year, ceased to be resident in Canada; or

(*b*) remuneration reasonably attributable to the duties of any office or employment performed or to be performed in Canada by the non-resident person.

History: S. 104(2), the portion before paragraph (*a*), was replaced by SOR/2016-30, s. 3, applicable July 1, 2015.

(3) No amount shall be deducted or withheld from a payment made by a person during the lifetime of an annuitant referred to in paragraph (*a*) of the definition "annuitant" in subsection 146(1) of the Act out of or under a registered retirement savings plan of the annuitant where, at the time of the payment, the annuitant has certified in prescribed form to the person that

(*a*) a written agreement has been entered into to acquire a home by either

(i) the annuitant, or

(ii) a disabled person who is related to the annuitant and who is entitled to the credit for mental or physical impairment under subsection 118.3(1) of the Act;

(*b*) the annuitant intends that the home be used as a principal place of residence in Canada for the annuitant or the disabled person, as the case may be, within one year after its acquisition;

(*c*) the home has not been previously owned by the annuitant, the annuitant's spouse or common-law partner, the disabled person or the spouse or common-law partner of that person;

(*d*) the annuitant was resident in Canada;

(*e*) the total amount of the payment and all other such payments received by the annuitant in respect of the home at or before the time of the payment does not exceed the dollar amount specified in paragraph (*h*)

Regulations

of the definition "regular eligible amount" in subsection 146.01(1) of the Act;

(*f*) except where the annuitant certifies that he or she is a disabled person entitled to the credit for mental or physical impairment under subsection 118.3(1) of the Act or certifies that the payment is being withdrawn for the benefit of such a disabled person, the annuitant is a qualifying homebuyer at the time of the certification; and

(*g*) where the annuitant has withdrawn an eligible amount, within the meaning assigned by subsection 146.01(1) of the Act, before the calendar year of the certification, the total of all eligible amounts received by the annuitant before that calendar year does not exceed the total of all amounts previously designated under subsection 146.01(3) of the Act or included in computing the annuitant's income under subsection 146.01(4) or (5) of the Act.

History: S. 104(3)(*e*) was replaced by S.C. 2013, c. 34, s. 376(1), deemed to have come into force on January 28, 2009, and formerly read:

(*e*) the total amount of the payment and all other such payments received by the annuitant in respect of the home at or before the time of payment does not exceed $20,000;

(3.01) For the purpose of subsection (3), the annuitant is a qualifying homebuyer at a particular time unless

(*a*) the annuitant had an owner-occupied home in the period beginning on January 1 of the fourth calendar year preceding the particular time, and ending on the thirty-first day before the particular time; or

(*b*) the annuitant's spouse or common-law partner, in the period referred to in paragraph (*a*), had an owner-occupied home that was inhabited by the annuitant at any time during the annuitant's marriage to the spouse or the annuitant's common-law partnership with the common-law partner.

(3.1) For the purpose of subsection (3.01), an individual shall be considered to have had an owner-occupied home at any time where the home was owned, whether jointly with another person or otherwise, by the individual at that time and inhabited by the individual as the individual's principal place of residence at that time.

(4) For the purposes of subsections (3), (3.01) and (3.1), "home" means

(*a*) a housing unit;

(*b*) a share of the capital stock of a cooperative housing corporation, where the holder of the share is entitled to possession of a housing unit; and

(*c*) where the context so requires, the housing unit to which a share described in paragraph (*b*) relates.

Forms: TD1 — Personal Tax Credits Return.

104.1. Lifelong Learning Plan

(1) No amount shall be deducted or withheld from a payment made by a person during the lifetime of an annuitant referred to in paragraph (*a*) of the definition "annuitant" in subsection 146(1) of the Act out of or under a registered retirement savings plan of the annuitant where, at the time of the payment, the annuitant has certified in prescribed form to the person that

(*a*) at the time of certification, the annuitant or the annuitant's spouse or common-law partner

(i) is a full-time student in a qualifying educational program,

(ii) is a part-time student in a qualifying educational program and is entitled to the credit for mental or physical impairment under subsection 118.3(1) of the Act, or

(iii) has received notification in writing of his or her entitlement, either absolutely or conditionally, to enrol before March of the year that follows the year of certification as

(A) a full-time student in a qualifying educational program, or

(B) a part-time student in a qualifying educational program where the annuitant or the annuitant's spouse or common-law partner is entitled to the credit for mental or physical impairment under subsection 118.3(1) of the Act;

(*b*) the annuitant is resident in Canada;

(*c*) the total amount of the payment and all other such payments received by the annuitant for a year at or before that time does not exceed $10,000; and

(*d*) the total payments received by the annuitant do not exceed $20,000 throughout the period in which the annuitant participates in the Lifelong Learning Plan.

(2) For the purpose of subsection (1), a "qualifying educational program" means a qualifying educational program at a designated educational institution (as those expressions are defined in subsection 118.6(1) of the Act), except that a reference to a "qualifying educational program" shall be read

(*a*) without reference to paragraphs (*a*) and (*b*) of that definition; and

(*b*) as if the reference to "3 consecutive weeks" in that definition were a reference to "3 consecutive months".

105. Non-Residents

(1) Every person paying to a non-resident person a fee, commission or other amount in respect of services rendered in Canada, of any nature whatever, shall deduct or withhold 15 per cent of such payment.

(2) Subsection (1) does not apply to a payment

(*a*) described in the definition "remuneration" in subsection 100(1);

(*b*) made to a registered non-resident insurer (within the meaning assigned by section 804); or

(*c*) made to an authorized foreign bank in respect of its Canadian banking business.

History: S. 105(2) was replaced by P.C. 2009-1869, SOR/2009-302, dated November 19, 2009, published in the *Canada Gazette* December 9, 2009, applicable to payments made after June 27, 1999, except that in its application to payments made before August 8, 2009 (the day on which this text is published in Part I of the *Canada Gazette*), paragraph 105(2)(*c*) is to be read as follows:

(*c*) made to an authorized foreign bank.

S. 105(2) formerly read:

(2) Subsection (1) does not apply to a payment described in the definition "remuneration" in subsection 100(1).

Tax Profile: September 2012 — Canadian Refundable Withholding Taxes — Traps; May 2011 — Creating a Canada-U.S. Service Joint Venture; April 2011 — Canadian Tax Issues for Non-Resident Franchisors;

October 2009 — New Rules under the Canada — U.S. Treaty and Canadian Withholding Taxes on Cross-Border Services; August 2009 — Structuring a Services Business; January 2009 — Enhancing Canada's International Tax Advantage; November 2008 — 2008 Cross-Border Developments in Canada; August 2007 — Professionals and Other Service Providers Beware — A Canadian Trap; July 2007 — Canadian Tax Traps; August 2005 — Canada Revenue Agency's Recent Attack on U.S. Companies; September 2002 — Canadian Withholding Taxes Update.

Tax Topics: No. 1953, Regulation 105 — Where are we now?; No. 1902, Regulation 105 Withholding for Services Rendered By a Canadian Subcontractor; No. 1819, The Implications of Withholding Requirements on Non-Residents Providing Services in Canada; No. 1818, Withholding Tax Obligations on Remuneration Paid to Non-Residents of Canada; No. 1719, Withholding Taxes — Purchase of Software from a Non-Resident; No. 1575, CCRA's Comments on Administration of Regulation 105.

Forms: R105 — Regulation 105 Waiver Application; T1261 — Application for a Canada Revenue Agency Individual Tax Number (ITN) for Non-Residents; T4A-NR Supp — Statement of Fees, Commissions, or Other Amounts Paid to Non-Residents for Services Rendered in Canada; NR4 — Statement of Amounts Paid or Credited to Non-Residents of Canada; NR4 Sum — Return of Amounts Paid or Credited to Non-Residents of Canada; NR4 Seg — NR4 Segment.

Information Circulars: IC 75-6R2 Required withholding from amounts paid to non-residents providing services in Canada.

Tax Window Files: Carrying on business in Canada and PE, *15XXXX*, CRA Document No. 2014-0542411R3.

Cases: A U.S. resident produced a figure skating show which took place in facilities owned by the taxpayers. After each show, the taxpayers paid the net revenues to the producer. Because the payments were in respect of services provided in Canada, the taxpayers were liable for tax which they should have withheld under paragraph 153(1)(*g*). *Ogden Palladium Services (Canada) Inc. et al. v. The Queen*, 2002 DTC 7378 (F.C.A.), affirming 2001 DTC 345 (T.C.C.)

105.1. Fishermen's Election

(1) Notwithstanding section 100, in this section,

"amount of remuneration" paid to a fisherman means

(*a*) where a boat crewed by one or more fishermen engaged in making a catch is owned, together with the gear, by a person, other than a member of the crew, to whom the catch is to be delivered for subsequent sale or other disposition, such portion of the proceeds from the disposition of the catch that is payable to the fisherman in accordance with an arrangement under which the proceeds of disposition of the catch are to be distributed (in this section referred to as a "share arrangement");

(*b*) where the boat or gear used in making a catch is owned or leased by a fisherman who alone or with another individual engaged under a contract of service makes the catch, such portion of the proceeds from the disposition of the catch that remains after deducting therefrom

(i) the amount in respect of any portion of the catch not caught by the fisherman or the other individual,

(ii) the amount payable to the other individual under the contract of service, and

(iii) the amount of such proportionate share of the catch as is attributable to the expenses of the operation of the boat or its gear pursuant to their share arrangement;

(*c*) where a crew includes the owner of the boat or gear (in this paragraph referred to as the "owner") and any other fisherman engaged in making a catch, such portion of the proceeds from the disposition of the catch that remains after deducting therefrom

(i) in the case of an owner,

(A) the amount in respect of that portion of the catch not caught by the crew or an owner,

(B) the aggregate of all amounts each of which is an amount payable to a crew member (other than the owner) pursuant to their share arrangement or to an individual engaged under a contract of service, and

(C) the amount of such proportionate share of the catch as is attributable to the expenses of the owner's operation of the boat or its gear pursuant to their share arrangement, or

(ii) in the case of any other crew member, such proceeds from the disposition of the catch as is payable to him in accordance with their share arrangement; or

(*d*) in any other case, the proceeds of disposition of the catch payable to the fisherman;

"catch" means a catch of shell fish, crustaceans, aquatic animals or marine plants caught or taken from any body of water;

"crew" means one or more fishermen engaged in making a catch;

"fisherman" means an individual engaged in making a catch other than under a contract of service.

(2) Every person paying at any time in a taxation year an amount of remuneration to a fisherman who, pursuant to paragraph 153(1)(*n*) of the Act, has elected for the year in prescribed form in respect of all such amounts shall deduct or withhold 20% of each such amount paid to the fisherman while the election is in force.

106. Variations in Deductions

(1) Where an employer makes a payment of remuneration to an employee in his taxation year

(*a*) for a period for which no provision is made in Schedule I, or

(*b*) for a pay period referred to in Schedule I in an amount that is greater than any amount provided for therein,

the amount to be deducted or withheld by the employer from any such payment is that proportion of the payment that the tax that may reasonably be expected to be payable under the Act by the employee with respect to the aggregate of all remuneration that may reasonably be expected to be paid by the employer to the employee in respect of that taxation year is of such aggregate.

(2) (Revoked by P.C. 1984-3684, SOR/84-913.)

(3) (Revoked by P.C. 1984-3684, SOR/84-913.)

107. Employee's Returns

(1) The return required to be filed by an employee under subsection 227(2) of the Act shall be filed by the employee with the employer when the employee commences employment with that employer and a new return shall be filed thereunder within 7 days after the date on which a change occurs that may reasonably be expected to result in a change in the employee's personal credits for the year.

Forms: TD1 — Personal Tax Credits Return.

Information Circulars: IC 98-1R4 Collections policies.

(2) Notwithstanding subsection (1), where, in a year, an employee receives payments in respect of commissions or in respect of commissions and salary or wages, and the employee elects to file a prescribed form for the year in addition to the return referred to in that subsection, that form shall be filed with the employee's continuing employer on or before January 31 of that year and, where applicable, within one month after the employee commences employment with a new employer or within one month after the date on which a change occurs that may reasonably be expected to result in a substantial change in the employee's estimated total remuneration for the year or estimated deductions for the year.

Forms: TD1X — Statement of Commission Income and Expenses for Payroll Tax Deductions.

(3) Where, in a taxation year, an employee has elected to file the prescribed form referred to in subsection (2) and has filed such form with his employer, the employee may at any time thereafter in the year revoke that election and such revocation is effective from the date that he notifies his employer in writing of his intention.

108. Remittances to Receiver General

(1) Subject to subsections (1.1) to (1.13), amounts deducted or withheld in a month under subsection 153(1) of the Act shall be remitted to the Receiver General on or before the 15th day of the following month.

History: S. 108(1) was replaced by S.C. 2015, c. 36, s. 20(1), applicable in respect of amounts deducted or withheld after 2015, and formerly read:

(1) Subject to subsections (1.1), (1.11) and (1.12), amounts deducted or withheld in a month under subsection 153(l) of the Act shall be remitted to the Receiver General on or before the 15th day of the following month.

Related Regulations: 108(1.13).

(1.1) Subject to subsection (1.11), where the average monthly withholding amount of an employer for the second calendar year preceding a particular calendar year is

(*a*) equal to or greater than $25,000 and less than $100,000, all amounts deducted or withheld from payments described in the definition "remuneration" in subsection 100(1) that are made in a month in the particular calendar year by the employer shall be remitted to the Receiver General

(i) in respect of payments made before the 16th day of the month, on or before the 25th day of the month, and

(ii) in respect of payments made after the 15th day of the month, on or before the 10th day of the following month; or

(*b*) equal to or greater than $100,000, all amounts deducted or withheld from payments described in the definition "remuneration" in subsection 100(1) that are made in a month in the particular calendar year by the employer shall be remitted to the Receiver General on or before the third day, not including a Saturday or holiday, after the end of the following periods in which the payments were made,

(i) the period beginning on the first day and ending on the 7th day of the month,

(ii) the period beginning on the 8th day and ending on the 14th day of the month,

(iii) the period beginning on the 15th day and ending on the 21st day of the month, and

(iv) the period beginning on the 22nd day and ending on the last day of the month.

History: S. 108(1.1)(*a*), the portion before subparagraph (i) was replaced by S.C. 2014, c. 20, s. 33(1), applicable to amounts deducted or withheld after 2014, and formerly read:

(*a*) equal to or greater than $15,000 and less than $50,000, all amounts deducted or withheld from payments described in the definition "remuneration" in subsection 100(1) that are made in a month in the particular calendar year by the employer shall be remitted to the Receiver General

S. 108(1.1)(*b*), the portion before subparagraph (i) was replaced by S.C. 2014, c. 20, s. 33(2), applicable to amounts deducted or withheld after 2014, and formerly read:

(*b*) equal to or greater than $50,000, all amounts deducted or withheld from payments described in the definition "remuneration" in subsection 100(1) that are made in a month in the particular calendar year by the employer shall be remitted to the Receiver General on or before the third day, not including a Saturday or holiday, after the end of the following periods in which the payments were made,

(1.11) Where an employer referred to in paragraph (1.1)(*a*) or (*b*) would otherwise be required to remit in accordance with that paragraph the amounts withheld or deducted under subsection 153(1) of the Act in respect of a particular calendar year, the employer may elect to remit those amounts

(*a*) in accordance with subsection (1), if the average monthly withholding amount of the employer for the calendar year preceding the particular calendar year is less than $25,000 and the employer has advised the Minister that the employer has so elected; or

(*b*) if the average monthly withholding amount of the employer for the calendar year preceding the particular calendar year is equal to or greater than $25,000 and less than $100,000 and the employer has advised the Minister that the employer has so elected,

(i) in respect of payments made before the 16th day of a month in the particular calendar year, on or before the 25th day of the month, and

(ii) in respect of payments made after the 15th day of a month in particular calendar year, on or before the 10th day of the following month.

History: S. 108(1.11)(*a*) was replaced by S.C. 2014, c. 20, s. 33(3), applicable to amounts deducted or withheld after 2014, and formerly read:

(*a*) in accordance with subsection (1), if the average monthly withholding amount of the employer for the calendar year preceding the particular calendar year is less than $15,000 and the employer has advised the Minister that the employer has so elected; or

S. 108(1.11)(*b*), the portion before subparagraph (i) was replaced by S.C. 2014, c. 20, s. 33(4), applicable to amounts deducted or withheld after 2014, and formerly read:

(*b*) if the average monthly withholding amount of the employer for the calendar year preceding the particular calendar year is equal to or greater than $15,000 and less than $50,000 and the employer has advised the Minister that the employer has so elected,

(1.12) If at any time

(*a*) the average monthly withholding amount in respect of an employer for either the first or the second calendar year before the particular calendar year that includes that time is less than $3,000,

(*b*) throughout the 12-month period before that time, the employer has remitted, on or before the day on or before which the amounts were required to be remitted, all amounts each of which was required to be remitted under subsection 153(1) of the Act, under subsection 21(1) of the *Canada Pension Plan*, under subsection 82(1) of the *Employment Insurance Act* or under Part IX of the *Excise Tax Act*, and

(*c*) throughout the 12-month period before that time, the employer has filed all returns each of which was required to be filed under this Act or Part IX of the *Excise Tax Act* on or before the day on or before which those returns were required to be filed under those Acts,

all amounts deducted or withheld from payments described in the definition "remuneration" in subsection 100(1) that are made by the employer in a month that ends after that time and that is in the particular calendar year may be remitted to the Receiver General

(*d*) in respect of such payments made in January, February and March of the particular calendar year, on or before the 15th day of April of the particular year,

(*e*) in respect of such payments made in April, May and June of the particular calendar year, on or before the 15th day of July of the particular year,

(*f*) in respect of such payments made in July, August and September of the particular calendar year, on or before the 15th day of October of the particular year, and

(*g*) in respect of such payments made in October, November and December of the particular calendar year, on or before the 15th day of January of the year following the particular year.

(1.13) If an employer is a new employer throughout a particular month in a particular calendar year, all amounts deducted or withheld from payments described in the definition "remuneration" in subsection 100(1) that are made by the employer in the month may be remitted to the Receiver General

(*a*) in respect of such payments made in January, February and March of the particular calendar year, on or before the 15th day of April of the particular calendar year;

(*b*) in respect of such payments made in April, May and June of the particular calendar year, on or before the 15th day of July of the particular calendar year;

(*c*) in respect of such payments made in July, August and September of the particular calendar year, on or before the 15th day of October of the particular calendar year; and

(*d*) in respect of such payments made in October, November and December of the particular calendar year, on or before the 15th day of January of the year following the particular calendar year.

History: S. 108(1.13) was added by S.C. 2015, c. 36, s. 20(2), applicable in respect of amounts deducted or withheld after 2015.

Related Regulations: 108(1); 108(1.21); 108(1.4); 108(1.41).

(1.2) For the purposes of this section, average monthly withholding amount, in respect of an employer for a particular calendar year, is the quotient obtained when

(*a*) the aggregate of all amounts each of which is an amount required to be remitted with respect to the particular year under

(i) subsection 153(1) of the Act and a similar provision of a law of a province which imposes a tax upon the income of individuals, where the province has entered into an agreement with the Minister of Finance for the collection of taxes payable to the province, in respect of payments described in the definition "remuneration" in subsection 100(1),

(ii) subsection 21(1) of the *Canada Pension Plan*, or

(iii) subsection 82(1) of the *Employment Insurance Act*,

by the employer or, where the employer is a corporation, by each corporation associated with the corporation in a taxation year of the employer ending in the second calendar year following the particular year

is divided by

(*b*) the number of months in the particular year, not exceeding twelve, for which such amounts were required to be remitted by the employer and, where the employer is a corporation, by each corporation associated with it in a taxation year of the employer ending in the second calendar year following the particular year.

History: S. 108(1.2)(*a*)(iii) was replaced by S.C. 2014, c. 20, s. 33(5), in force June 19, 2014, and formerly read:

(iii) subsection 82(1) of the *Employment Insurance Act* or subsection 53(1) of the *Unemployment Insurance Act*,

(1.21) For the purposes of subsection (1.4), the monthly withholding amount, in respect of an employer for a month, is the total of all amounts each of which is an amount required to be remitted with respect to the month by the employer or, if the employer is a corporation, by each corporation associated with the corporation, under

(*a*) subsection 153(1) of the Act and a similar provision of a law of a province which imposes a tax upon the income of individuals, if the province has entered into an agreement with the Minister of Finance for the collection of taxes payable to the province, in respect of payments described in the definition "remuneration" in subsection 100(1);

(*b*) subsection 21(1) of the *Canada Pension Plan*; or

(*c*) subsection 82(1) of the *Employment Insurance Act*.

History: S. 108(1.21) was added by S.C. 2015, c. 36, s. 20(3), applicable in respect of amounts deducted or withheld after 2015.

(1.3) For the purposes of subsection (1.2), where a particular employer that is a corporation has acquired in a taxation year of the corporation ending in a particular calendar year all or substantially all of the property of another employer used by the other employer in a business

(*a*) in a transaction in respect of which an election was made under subsection 85(1) or (2) of the Act,

(*b*) by virtue of an amalgamation within the meaning assigned to that term by section 87 of the Act, or

(*c*) as the result of a winding-up in respect of which subsection 88(1) of the Act is applicable,

the other employer shall be deemed to be a corporation associated with the particular employer in the taxation year and each taxation year ending at any time in the next two following calendar years.

(1.4) For the purposes of subsection (1.13) an employer

(*a*) becomes a new employer at the beginning of any month after 2015 in which the employer first becomes an employer; and

(*b*) ceases to be a new employer at a specified time in a particular year, if in a particular month the employer does not meet any of the following conditions:

Regulations

(i) the monthly withholding amount in respect of the employer for the particular month is less than $1,000,

(ii) throughout the 12-month period before that time, the employer has remitted, on or before the day on or before which the amounts were required to be remitted, all amounts each of which was required to be remitted under subsection 153(1) of the Act, subsection 21(1) of the *Canada Pension Plan*, subsection 82(1) of the *Employment Insurance Act* or Part IX of the *Excise Tax Act*, and

(iii) throughout the 12-month period before that time, the employer has filed all returns each of which was required to be filed under the Act or Part IX of the *Excise Tax Act* on or before the day on or before which those returns were required to be filed under those Acts.

History: S. 108(1.4) was added by S.C. 2015, c. 36, s. 20(4), applicable in respect of amounts deducted or withheld after 2015.

(1.41) For the purposes of subsection (1.4), the specified time is the end of

(*a*) March of the particular year, if the particular month is January, February or March of that year;

(*b*) June of the particular year, if the particular month is April, May or June of that year;

(*c*) September of the particular year, if the particular month is July, August or September of that year; and

(*d*) December of the particular year, if the particular month is October, November or December of that year.

History: S. 108(1.41) was added by S.C. 2015, c. 36, s. 20(4), applicable in respect of amounts deducted or withheld after 2015.

(2) Where an employer has ceased to carry on business, any amount deducted or withheld under subsection 153(1) of the Act that has not been remitted to the Receiver General shall be paid within 7 days of the day when the employer ceased to carry on business.

(3) Remittances made to the Receiver General under subsection 153(1) of the Act shall be accompanied by a return in prescribed form.

Forms: PD24 — Statement of Overpayment and Application for Refund.

(4) Amounts deducted or withheld under subsection 153(4) of the Act shall be remitted to the Receiver General within 60 days after the end of the taxation year subsequent to the 12-month period referred to in that subsection.

Information Circulars: IC 71-9R Unclaimed dividends.

109. Elections to Increase Deductions

(1) Any election under subsection 153(1.2) of the Act shall be made by filing with the person making the payment or class of payments referred to therein (in this section referred to as the "payer") the form prescribed by the Minister for that purpose.

(2) A taxpayer who has made an election in the manner prescribed by subsection (1) may require that the amount deducted or withheld pursuant to that election be varied by filing with the payer the form prescribed by the Minister for that purpose.

(3) An election made in the manner prescribed by subsection (1) or a variation made pursuant to subsection (2) need not be taken into account by the payer in respect of the first payment to be made to the taxpayer after the election or variation, as the case may be, unless the election or variation, as the case may be, is made within such time, in advance of the payment, as may reasonably be required by the payer.

Forms: TD1 — Personal Tax Credits Return.

110. Prescribed Persons

(1) The following are prescribed persons for the purposes of subsection 153(1) of the Act:

(*a*) an employer who is required, under subsection 153(1) of the Act and in accordance with paragraph 108(1.1)(*b*), to remit amounts deducted or withheld; and

(*b*) a person or partnership who, acting on behalf of one or more employers, remits the following amounts in a particular calendar year and whose average monthly remittance, in respect of those amounts, for the second calendar year preceding the particular calendar year, is equal to or greater than $50,000,

(i) amounts required to be remitted under subsection 153(1) of the Act and a similar provision of a law of a province that imposes a tax on the income of individuals, where the province has entered into an agreement with the Minister of Finance for the collection of taxes payable to the province, in respect of payments described in the definition "remuneration" in subsection 100(1),

(ii) amounts required to be remitted under subsection 21(1) of the *Canada Pension Plan*, and

(iii) amounts required to be remitted under subsection 82(1) of the *Employment Insurance Act* or subsection 53(1) of the *Unemployment Insurance Act*.

(2) For the purposes of paragraph (1)(*b*), the average monthly remittance made by a person or partnership on behalf of all the employers for whom that person or partnership is acting, for the second calendar year preceding the particular calendar year, is the quotient obtained when the aggregate, for that preceding year, of all amounts referred to in subparagraphs (1)(*b*)(i) to (iii) remitted by the person or partnership on behalf of those employers is divided by the number of months, in that preceding year, for which the person or partnership remitted those amounts.

Regulations

Part II
Information Returns

200. Remuneration and Benefits

(1) Subject to subsection (1.1), every person who makes a payment described in subsection 153(1) of the Act (including an amount paid that is described in subparagraph 153(1)(*a*)(ii) of the Act) shall make an information return in prescribed form in respect of the payment unless an information return in respect of the payment has been made under sections 202, 214, 237 or 238.

History: S. 200(1) was amended by S. C. 2016, c. 7, s. 55(1), applicable in respect of payments made after 2015, and formerly read:

(1) Every person who makes a payment described in subsection 153(1) of the Act (other than an annuity payment in respect of an interest in an annuity contract to which subsection 201(5) applies) shall make an information return in prescribed form in respect of the payment unless an information return in respect of the payment has been made under sections 202, 214, 237 or 238.

Information Circulars: IC 82-2R2 Social insurance number legislation that relates to the preparation of information slips; IC 97-2R15 Customized forms.

(1.1) Subsection (1) does not apply in respect of

(*a*) an annuity payment in respect of an interest in an annuity contract to which subsection 201(5) applies; or

(*b*) an amount paid by a qualifying non-resident employer to a qualifying non-resident employee that is exempted under subparagraph 153(1)(*a*)(ii) of the Act if the employer, after reasonable inquiry, has no reason to believe that the employee's total amount of taxable income earned in Canada under Part I of the Act during the calendar year that includes the time of this payment (including an amount described in paragraph 110(1)(*f*) of the Act) is more than $10,000.

History: S. 200(1.1) was added by S. C. 2016, c. 7, s. 55(1), applicable in respect of payments made after 2015.

(2) Every person who makes a payment as or on account of, or who confers a benefit or allocates an amount that is,

(*a*) a scholarship, fellowship or bursary, or a prize for achievement in a field of endeavour ordinarily carried on by the recipient thereof (other than a prize prescribed by section 7700),

(*b*) a grant to enable the recipient thereof to carry on research or any similar work,

(*b*.1) an amount that is required by paragraph 56(1)(*n*.1) of the Act to be included in computing a taxpayer's income,

(*c*) an amount that is required by paragraph 56(1)(*r*) of the Act to be included in computing a taxpayer's income,

(*d*) a benefit under regulations made under an *Appropriation Act* providing for a scheme of transitional assistance benefits to persons employed in the production of products to which the *Canada–United States Agreement on Automotive Products*, signed on January 16, 1965, applies,

(*e*) a benefit described in section 5502,

(*f*) an amount payable to a taxpayer on a periodic basis in respect of the loss of all or any part of his income from an office or employment, pursuant to

(i) a sickness or accident insurance plan,

(ii) a disability insurance plan, or

(iii) an income maintenance insurance plan,

to or under which his employer has made a contribution,

(*g*) an amount or benefit the value of which is required by paragraph 6(1)(*a*), (*e*) or (*h*) or subsection 6(9) of the Act to be included in computing a taxpayer's income from an office or employment, other than a payment referred to in subsection (1),

(*h*) a benefit the amount of which is required by virtue of subsection 15(5) of the Act to be included in computing a shareholder's income,

(*i*) a benefit deemed by subsection 15(9) of the Act to be a benefit conferred on a shareholder by a corporation, or

(*j*) a payment out of a registered education savings plan, other than a refund of payments,

shall make an information return in prescribed form in respect of such payment or benefit except where subsection (3) or (4) applies with respect to the payment or benefit.

History: S. 200(2)(*b*.1) was added by P.C. 2015-862, SOR/2015-170, s. 1(1), dated June 19, 2015, published in the *Canada Gazette*, Part II on July 1, 2015, applicable July 1, 2015.

Forms: T4 Sum. — Summary of Remuneration Paid; T4A Sum. — Summary of Pension, Retirement Annuity, and Other Income; T4A Seg. — T4A Segment; T4 — Statement of Remuneration Paid; T4A — Statement of Pension, Retirement, Annuity, and Other Income; T4 Seg. — T4 Segment; T4F Sum. — Summary of Fishing Income; T4F — Statement of Fishing Income.

Income Tax Folios: *Secondary* — S1-F2-C3 Scholarships, Research Grants and Other Education Assistance.

Information Circulars: IC 74-21R Payments out of pension and deferred profit sharing plans--ITAR 40; IC 75-6R2 Required withholding from amounts paid to non-residents providing services in Canada; IC 77-1R5 Deferred profit sharing plan; IC 82-2R2 Social insurance number legislation that relates to the preparation of information slips; IC 97-2R15 Customized forms.

(3) Where a benefit is included in computing a taxpayer's income from an office or employment pursuant to paragraph 6(1)(*a*) or (*e*) of the Act in respect of an automobile made available to the taxpayer or to a person related to the taxpayer by a person related to the taxpayer's employer, the employer shall make an information return in prescribed form in respect of the benefit.

(4) Where a benefit is included in computing the income of a shareholder of a corporation by virtue of subsection 15(5) of the Act in respect of an automobile made available to the shareholder or to a person related to the shareholder by a person related to the corporation, the corporation shall make an information return in prescribed form in respect of the benefit.

(5) Where a particular qualifying person (within the meaning assigned by subsection 7(7) of the Act) has agreed to sell or issue a security (within the meaning assigned by that subsection) of the particular qualifying person (or of a qualifying person with which it does not deal at arm's length) to a taxpayer who is an employee of the particular qualifying person (or of a qualifying person with which it does not deal at arm's length) and the taxpayer has acquired the security under the agreement in circumstances to which subsection 7(8) of the Act applied, each of the particular qualifying person, the qualifying person of which the security is acquired and the qualifying person which is the taxpayer's employer shall, for the particular taxation year in which the security is acquired, make an information return in the prescribed form in respect of the benefit from employment that the taxpayer would be deemed to have received in the particular taxation year in respect of the acquisition of the security if the Act were read without reference to subsection 7(8) and, for this purpose, an information return made by one of the qualifying persons in respect of the taxpayer's acquisition of the security is deemed to have been made by each of the qualifying persons.

(6) Every person who makes a payment as or on account of an amount that is required by subsection 56(6) of the Act to be included in computing a taxpayer's income shall make an information return in prescribed form in respect of that payment.

History: S. 200(6) was added by P.C. 2015-862, SOR/2015-170, s. 1(2), dated June 19, 2015, published in the *Canada Gazette*, Part II on July 1, 2015, applicable July 1, 2015.

Canadian Tax Foundation: Cepparo, *Information Returns but No Withholding Tax*, 2015 Canadian Tax Highlights 23(12):4.

Regulations

201. Investment Income

(1) Every person who makes a payment to a resident of Canada as or on account of

(*a*) a dividend or an amount deemed by the Act to be a dividend (other than a dividend deemed to have been paid to a person under any of subsections 84(1) to (4) of the Act where, pursuant to subsection 84(8) of the Act, those subsections do not apply to deem the dividend to have been received by the person),

(*b*) interest (other than the portion of the interest to which any of subsections (4) to (4.2) applies)

(i) on a fully registered bond or debenture,

(ii) in respect of

(A) money on loan to an association, corporation, institution, organization, partnership or trust,

(B) money on deposit with an association, corporation, institution, organization, partnership or trust, or

(C) property deposited or placed with an association, corporation, institution, organization, partnership or trust,

(iii) in respect of an account with an investment dealer or broker,

(iv) paid by an insurer in connection with an insurance policy or an annuity contract, or

(v) on an amount owing in respect of compensation for property expropriated,

(*c*) a royalty payment in respect of the use of a work or invention or a right to take natural resources,

(*d*) a payment referred to in subsection 16(1) of the Act that can reasonably be regarded as being in part a payment of interest or other payment of an income nature and in part a payment of a capital nature, where the payment is made by a corporation, association, organization or institution,

(*e*) an amount paid from a person's NISA Fund No. 2,

(*f*) an amount that is required by subsection 148.1(3) of the Act to be added in computing a person's income for a taxation year, or

(*g*) the portion of the price for which a debt obligation was assigned or otherwise transferred that is deemed by subsection 20(14.2) of the Act to be interest that accrued on the debt obligation to which the transferee has become entitled to for a period commencing before the time of the transfer and ending at that particular time that is not payable until after that particular time if the payment is made by a person that is a "financial company" (whether acting as principal or as agent for the transferee) for the purposes of section 211

shall make an information return in prescribed form in respect of the portion of such payment for which an information return has not previously been made under this section.

History: S. 201(1)(*b*)(ii) was replaced by S.C. 2018, c. 12 s. 42(1), applicable to the 2018 and subsequent taxation years, and formerly read:

(ii) in respect of

(A) money on loan to,

(B) money on deposit with, or

(C) property of any kind deposited or placed with,

a corporation, association, organization or institution,

S. 201(1)(*g*) was added by S.C. 2016, c. 12, s. 74(1), in force January 1, 2017.

Forms: T5 Sum. — Return of Investment Income; T5 — Statement of Investment Income; T619 — Magnetic Media Transmittal.

Information Circulars: IC 71-9R Unclaimed dividends; IC 82-2R2 Social insurance number legislation that relates to the preparation of information slips; IC 97-2R14 Customized forms.

(2) Every person who receives as nominee or agent for a person resident in Canada a payment to which subsection (1) applies shall make an information return in prescribed form in respect of such payment.

(3) Where a person negotiates a bearer coupon, warrant or cheque representing interest or dividends referred to in subsection 234(1) of the Act for another person resident in Canada and the name of the beneficial owner of the interest or dividends is not disclosed on an ownership certificate completed pursuant to that subsection, the person negotiating the coupon, warrant or cheque, as the case may be, shall make an information return in prescribed form in respect of the payment received.

(4) A person or partnership that is indebted in a calendar year under a debt obligation in respect of which subsection 12(4) of the Act and paragraph (1)(*b*) apply with respect to a taxpayer shall make an information return in prescribed form in respect of the amount (other than an amount to which paragraph (1)(*g*) applies) that would, if the year were a taxation year of the taxpayer, be included as interest in respect of the debt obligation in computing the taxpayer's income for the year.

History: S. 201(4) was replaced by S.C. 2016, c. 12, s. 74(2), in force January 1, 2017, and formerly read:

(4) A person or partnership that is indebted in a calendar year under a debt obligation in respect of which subsection 12(4) of the Act and paragraph (1)(*b*) apply with respect to a taxpayer shall make an information return in prescribed form in respect of the amount that would, if the year were a taxation year of the taxpayer, be included as interest in respect of the debt obligation in computing the taxpayer's income for the year.

(4.1) A person or partnership that is indebted in a calendar year under an indexed debt obligation in respect of which paragraph (1)(*b*) applies shall, for each taxpayer who holds an interest in the debt obligation at any time in the year, make an information return in prescribed form in respect of the amount that would, if the year were a taxation year of the taxpayer, be included as interest in respect of the debt obligation in computing the taxpayer's income for the year.

(4.2) Where, at any time in a calendar year, a person or partnership holds, as nominee or agent for a taxpayer resident in Canada, an interest in a debt obligation referred to in paragraph (1)(*b*) that is

(*a*) an obligation in respect of which subsection 12(4) of the Act applies with respect to the taxpayer, or

(*b*) an indexed debt obligation,

that person or partnership shall make an information return in prescribed form in respect of the amount that would, if the year were a taxation year of the taxpayer, be included as interest in respect of the debt obligation in computing the taxpayer's income for the year.

(5) Every insurer, within the meaning assigned by paragraph 148(10)(*a*) of the Act, who is a party to a life insurance policy in respect of which an amount is to be included in computing a taxpayer's income under subsection 12.2(1) or (5) of the Act shall make an information return in prescribed form in respect of that amount.

History: S. 201(5) was replaced by P.C. 2010-548, SOR/2010-93, dated April 29, 2010, published in the *Canada Gazette* May 12, 2010, applicable to contracts last acquired after 1989. S. 201(5) formerly read:

(5) Every insurer (within the meaning assigned by paragraph 148(10)(*a*) of the Act) who is a party to a life insurance policy (within the meaning assigned by paragraph 138(12)(*f*) [subsection 138(12) "life insurance policy"] of the Act) in respect of which an amount is to be included in computing a taxpayer's income pursuant to subsection 12.2(1), (3) or (5) or paragraph 56(1)(*d*.1) of the Act shall make an information return in prescribed form in respect of that amount.

(5.1) Subsection (5) applies to an insurer in respect of an LIA policy in respect of a calendar year only if

(*a*) the insurer is notified in writing — before the end of the calendar year and by, or on behalf, of the policyholder — that the policy is an LIA policy; or

(*b*) it is reasonable to conclude that the insurer knew, or ought to have known, before the end of the calendar year, that the policy is an LIA policy.

History: S. 201(5.1) was added by S.C. 2013, c. 40, s. 96(1), applicable to taxation years that end after March 20, 2013.

(6) Every person who makes a payment to, or acts as a nominee or agent for, an individual resident in Canada in respect of the disposition or redemption of a debt obligation in bearer form shall make an information return in prescribed form in respect of the transaction indicating the proceeds of disposition or the redemption amount and such other information as may be required by the prescribed form.

(7) For the purposes of subsection (6), "debt obligation in bearer form" means any debt obligation in bearer form other than

(*a*) a debt obligation that is redeemed for the amount for which the debt obligation was issued;

(*b*) a debt obligation described in paragraph 7000(1)(*b*); and

(*c*) a coupon, warrant or cheque referred to in subsection 207(1).

202. Payments to Non-Residents

(1) In addition to any other return required by the Act or these Regulations, every person resident in Canada shall make an information return in prescribed form in respect of any amount that the person pays or credits, or is deemed under Part I, XIII or XIII.2 of the Act to pay or credit, to a non-resident person as, on account or in lieu of payment of, or in satisfaction of,

(*a*) a management or administration fee or charge;

(*b*) interest;

(*c*) income of or from an estate or trust;

(*d*) rent, royalty or a similar payment referred to in paragraph 212(1)(*d*) of the Act, including any payment described in any of subparagraphs 212(1)(*d*)(i) to (viii) of the Act;

(*e*) a timber royalty as described in paragraph 212(1)(*e*) of the Act;

(*f*) an assessable distribution, as defined in subsection 218.3(1) of the Act;

(*g*) a dividend, including a patronage dividend as described in paragraph 212(1)(*g*) of the Act; or

(*h*) a payment for a right in or to the use of

(i) a motion picture film, or

(ii) a film or video tape for use in connection with television.

History: S. 202(1), the portion before paragraph (*a*) was replaced by P.C. 2011-936, SOR/2011-188, dated September 22, 2011, published in the *Canada Gazette* October 12, 2011, applicable after February 18, 2011. S. 202(1), the portion before paragraph (*a*) formerly read:

(1) Every person resident in Canada who pays or credits, or is deemed by Part I or Part XIII of the Act to pay or credit, to a non-resident person an amount as, on account or in lieu of payment of, or in satisfaction of,

S. 202(1)(*f*) was added by P.C. 2011-936, SOR/2011-188, dated September 22, 2011, published in the *Canada Gazette* October 12, 2011, applicable after February 18, 2011.

S. 202(1), the portion following paragraph (*h*) was repealed by P.C. 2011-936, SOR/2011-188, dated September 22, 2011, published in the *Canada Gazette* October 12, 2011, applicable after February 18, 2011. S. 202(1), the portion following paragraph (*h*) formerly read:

shall, in addition to any other return required by the Act or these Regulations, make an information return in prescribed form in respect of such amount.

Forms: NR4 Sum. — Return of Amounts Paid or Credited to Non-Residents of Canada; NR4 — Statement of Amounts Paid or Credited to Non-Residents of Canada.

Information Circulars: IC 77-16R4 Non-resident income tax (paras. 55 to 57); IC 97-2R14 Customized forms.

(1.1) Every person who pays or credits an amount, or provides a benefit to or on behalf of a person who is either a non-resident individual who is an actor or that is a corporation related to such an individual, for the provision in Canada of acting services of the actor in a film or video production, shall, in addition to any other return required by the Act or these Regulations, make an information return in prescribed form in respect of such payment, credit or benefit.

(2) Every person resident in Canada who pays or credits, or is deemed by Part I or Part XIII of the Act to pay or credit, to a non-resident person an amount as, on account or in lieu of payment of, or in satisfaction of,

(*a*) a payment of a superannuation or pension benefit,

(*b*) a payment of any allowance or benefit described in any of subparagraphs 56(1)(*a*)(ii) to (vi) of the Act,

Regulations

(*c*) a payment by a trustee under a registered supplementary unemployment benefit plan,

(*d*) a payment out of or under a registered retirement savings plan or a plan referred to in subsection 146(12) of the Act as an amended plan,

(*e*) a payment under a deferred profit sharing plan or a plan referred to in subsection 147(15) of the Act as a revoked plan,

(*f*) a payment under an income-averaging annuity contract, any proceeds of the surrender, cancellation, redemption, sale or other disposition of an income-averaging annuity contract, or any amount deemed by subsection 61.1(1) of the Act to have been received by the non-resident person as proceeds of the disposition of an income-averaging annuity contract,

(*g*) an annuity payment not described in any other paragraph of this subsection or subsection (1),

(*h*) a payment to which paragraph 212(1)(*p*) of the Act applies,

(*i*) a payment out of or under a registered retirement income fund,

(*j*) a payment that is or that would be, if paragraph 212(1)(*r*) of the Act were read without reference to subparagraph 212(1)(*r*)(ii), a payment described in that paragraph in respect of a registered education savings plan,

(*k*) a grant under a program prescribed for the purposes of paragraph 212(1)(*s*) of the Act,

(*l*) a payment described in paragraph 212(1)(*j*) of the Act in respect of a retirement compensation arrangement,

(*m*) a payment described in paragraph 212(1)(*v*) or (*x*) of the Act, or

(*n*) a payment described in paragraph 212(1)(*r.1*) of the Act,

shall, in addition to any other return required by the Act or these Regulations, make an information return in prescribed form in respect of such amount.

History: S. 202(2)(*n*) was added by SOR/2016-30, s. 4, applicable July 1, 2015.

S. 202(2)(*m*) was replaced by S.C. 2014, c. 20, s. 34, in force June 19, 2014, and formerly read:

(*m*) a payment described in paragraph 212(1)(*v*) of the Act,

S. 202(2)(*h*) was replaced by S.C. 2009, c. 2, s. 83(1), applicable to the 2009 and subsequent taxation years. S. 202(2)(*h*) formerly read:

(*h*) a payment of a portion thereof, to which paragraph 212(1)(*p*) of the Act applies, out of or under a fund, plan, or trust that was on December 31, 1985 a registered home ownership savings plan (within the meaning assigned by paragraph 146.2(1)(*h*) of the Act as it read in its application to the 1985 taxation year),

Forms: NR4 Sum. — Return of Amounts Paid or Credited to Non-Residents of Canada; NR4 — Statement of Amounts Paid or Credited to Non-Residents of Canada.

(2.1) Every person resident in Canada who pays an amount to a non-resident person from a NISA Fund No. 2 shall, in addition to any other return required by the Act or these Regulations, make an information return in prescribed form in respect of the amount.

(3) Every person who is paid or credited with an amount referred to in subsection (1), (2) or (2.1) for or on behalf of a non-resident person shall make an information return in prescribed form in respect of the amount.

(4) A non-resident person who is deemed, under subsection 212(13) of the Act, to be a person resident in Canada for the purposes of section 212 of the Act shall be deemed, in the same circumstances, to be a person resident in Canada for the purposes of subsections (1) and (2).

(5) A partnership that is deemed, under paragraph 212(13.1)(*a*) of the Act, to be a person resident in Canada for the purposes of Part XIII of the Act shall be deemed, in the same circumstances, to be a person resident in Canada for the purposes of subsections (1) and (2).

(6) A non-resident person who is deemed, under subsection 212(13.2) of the Act, to be a person resident in Canada for the purposes of Part XIII of the Act shall be deemed, in the same circumstances, to be a person resident in Canada for the purposes of subsections (1) and (2).

(6.1) A trust that is deemed by subsection 94(3) of the Act to be resident in Canada for a taxation year for the purposes of computing its income, is deemed, in respect of amounts (other than an exempt amount as defined in subsection 94(1) of the Act) paid or credited by it, to be a person resident in Canada for the taxation year for the purposes of subsections (1) and (2).

History: S. 202(6.1) was added by S.C. 2013, c. 34, s. 27(1), applicable to amounts paid or credited after August 27, 2010.

(7) Subject to subsection (8), an information return required under this section shall be filed on or before March 31 and shall be in respect of the preceding calendar year.

(8) Where an amount referred to in subsection (1) or (2) is income of or from an estate or trust, the information return required under this section in respect thereof shall be filed within 90 days from the end of the taxation year of the estate or trust in which the amount was paid or credited and shall be in respect of that taxation year.

203. Requirement to file

Every institution that is a *designated educational institution* (as defined in subsection 118.6(1) of the Act) because of paragraph (*a*) of that definition shall make an information return in prescribed form in respect of each individual enrolled at that institution who is a *qualifying student* (as defined in subsection 118.6(1)) for a month in a taxation year.

History: S. 203 was added by S.C. 2018, c. 27, s. 35(1), applicable to the 2019 and subsequent taxation years.

Related Sections: 118.6(1), "designated educational institution".

204. Estates and Trusts

(1) Every person having the control of, or receiving income, gains or profits in a fiduciary capacity, or in a capacity analogous to a fiduciary capacity, shall make a return in prescribed form in respect thereof.

Forms: T3 — Statement of Trust Income Allocations or Designations; T3S — Supplementary Unemployment Benefit Plan Information and Income Tax Return; T3D — Income Tax Return for Deferred Profit Sharing Plan (DPSP or Revoked DPSP); T3P — Employee's Pension Plan Information and Income Tax Return; T3GR — Group Income Tax and Information Return for RRSP, RRIF, RESP or RDSP Trusts; T3S — Supplementary Unemployment Benefit Plan Information and Income Tax Return.

Information Circulars: IC 73-13 Investment clubs; IC 77-1R5 Deferred profit sharing plan; IC 78-5R3 Communal organizations; IC 78-14R4 Guidelines for trust companies and other persons responsible for filing T3GR, T3D, T3P, T3S, T3RI, and T3F returns; IC 82-2R2 Social insurance number legislation that relates to the preparation of information slips; IC 97-2R14 Customized Forms.

(2) The return required under this section shall be filed within 90 days from the end of the taxation year and shall be in respect of the taxation year.

Related Sections: 251.2(7) Filing and other deadlines.

(3) Subsection (1) does not require a trust to make a return for a taxation year at the end of which it is

(*a*) governed by a deferred profit sharing plan or by a plan referred to in subsection 147(15) of the Act as a revoked plan;

(*b*) governed by an employees profit sharing plan;

(*c*) a registered charity;

(*d*) governed by an eligible funeral arrangement;,

(*d*.1) a cemetery care trust;

(*e*) governed by a registered education savings plan;

(*f*) governed by a TFSA or by an arrangement that is deemed by paragraph 146.2(9)(*a*) of the Act to be a TFSA; or

(g) governed by a registered disability savings plan, except if paragraph 146.4(5)(*a*) or (*b*) of the Act applies.

History: S. 204(3)(*g*) was added by SOR/2016-30, s. 5, applicable July 1, 2015.

S. 204(3)(*f*) was added by S.C. 2009, c. 2, s. 84(1), applicable to the 2009 and subsequent taxation years.

204.1. Estates and Trusts

(1) Interpretation. The following definitions apply in this section.

"public investment trust", at any time, means a public trust all or substantially all of the fair market value of the property of which is, at that time, attributable to the fair market value of property of the trust that is

(*a*) units of public trusts;

(*b*) partnership interests in public partnerships (as defined in subsection 229.1(1));

(*c*) shares of the capital stock of public corporations; or

(*d*) any combination of properties referred to in paragraphs (*a*) to (*c*).

"public trust", at any time, means a mutual fund trust the units of which are, at that time, listed on a designated stock exchange in Canada.

(2) Required Information Disclosure. A trust that is, at any time in a taxation year of the trust, a public trust shall, within the time required by subsection (3),

(*a*) make public, in prescribed form, information in respect of the trust for the taxation year by posting that prescribed form, in a manner that is accessible to the general public, on the Internet website of CDS Innovations Inc.; and

(*b*) notify the Minister in writing as to when the posting of the prescribed form, as required by paragraph (*a*), has been made.

(3) Required Disclosure Time. The time required for a public trust to satisfy the requirements of subsection (2) in respect of the public trust for a taxation year of the public trust is

(*a*) subject to paragraph (*b*), on or before the day that is 60 days after the end of the taxation year; and

(*b*) where the public trust is, at any time in the taxation year, a public investment trust, on or before the day that is 67 days after the end of the calendar year in which the taxation year ends.

Proposed Amendment

Legislative Proposals Relating to Income Tax Act and Other Legislation (July 27, 2018)

The Regulations are amended by adding the following after section 204.1:

204.2 Additional reporting trusts.

(1) For the purposes of subsection 150(1) of the Act, every person having the control of, or receiving income, gains or profits in a fiduciary capacity, or in a capacity analogous to a fiduciary capacity, shall provide information in respect of a trust, unless the trust is subject to one of the exceptions listed in paragraphs 150(1.2)(*a*) to (*n*) of the Act, that includes the name, address, date of birth (in the case of an individual other than a trust), jurisdiction of residence and *TIN* (as defined in subsection 270(1) of the Act) for each person who, in the year,

(*a*) is a trustee, beneficiary (subject to subsection (2)) or *settlor* (as defined in subsection 17(15) of the Act) of the trust; or

(*b*) has the ability (through the terms of the trust or a related agreement) to exert influence over trustee decisions regarding the appointment of income or capital of the trust.

(2) For the purposes of subsection (1), the requirement in paragraph (1)(*a*) to provide required information in respect of beneficiaries of a trust in a return is met if

(*a*) the required information is provided in respect of each beneficiary of the trust whose identity is known or ascertainable with reasonable effort by the person making the return at the time of filing the return; and

(*b*) in respect of beneficiaries not described in paragraph (*a*), the person making the return provides sufficiently detailed information to determine with certainty whether any particular person is a beneficiary of the trust.

Applicable: To taxation years that end after December 30, 2021.

205. Date Returns to be Filed

(1) All returns required under this Part shall be filed with the Minister without notice or demand and, unless otherwise specifically provided, on or before the last day of February in each year and shall be in respect of the preceding calendar year.

(2) Where a person who is required to make a return under this Part discontinues his business or activity, the return shall be filed within 30 days of the day of the discontinuance of the business or activity and shall be in respect of any calendar year or a portion thereof prior to the discontinuance of the business or activity for which a return has not previously been filed.

(3) For the purpose of subsection 162(7.01) of the Act, the following types of information returns are prescribed:

Government Service Contract Payments	T1204
International Electronic Funds Transfer Report	
International Exchange of Information on Financial Accounts Information Return (Part XVIII of the Act)	
Past Service Pension Adjustment (PSPA) Exempt from Certification	T215
Pension Adjustment Reversal (PAR)	T10
Pooled Registered Pension Plan (PRPP) Information Return	
Registered Retirement Savings Plan (RRSP) Contribution Information Return	
Statement of Amounts Paid or Credited to Non-residents of Canada	NR4

Regulations

Statement of Benefits	T5007
Statement of Canada Pension Plan Benefits	T4A(P)
Statement of Contract Payments	T5018
Statement of Distributions from a Retirement Compensation Arrangement (RCA)	T4A-RCA
Statement of Employee Profit Sharing Plan Allocations and Payments	T4PS
Statement of Employment Insurance and Other Benefits	T4E
Statement of Farm-support Payments	AGR-1
Statement of Fees, Commissions, or Other Amounts Paid to Non-residents for Services Rendered in Canada	T4A-NR
Statement of Income from a Registered Retirement Income Fund	T4RIF
Statement of Investment Income	T5
Statement of Old Age Security	T4A(OAS)
Statement of Pension, Retirement, Annuity and Other Income	T4A
Statement of Registered Retirement Savings Plan (RRSP) Income	T4RSP
Statement of Remuneration Paid	T4
Statement of Securities Transactions	T5008
Statement of Trust Income Allocations and Designations	T3
Tax-free Savings Account (TFSA) Annual Information Return	
Tuition and Enrolment Certificate	
Universal Child Care Benefit Statement	RC62

History: S. 205(3) was amended by S.C. 2018, c. 27, s. 36(1), by adding "Tuition and Enrolment Certificate", in force on January 1, 2019.

S. 205(3) was amended by SOR/2015-170, s. 2, by adding "International Electronic Funds Transfer Report" and "International Exchange of Information on Financial Accounts Information Return (Part XVIII of the Act)", applicable July 1, 2015.

S. 205(3) was amended by SOR/2013-199, s. 1(2), by adding "Pooled Registered Pension Plan (PRPP) Information Return", applicable after December 13, 2012.

S. 205(3) was added by SOR/2013-199, s. 1(1), applicable after December 31, 2011.

Related Sections: 162(7.01) Late filing penalty — prescribed information returns.

205.1. Electronic Filing

(1) For the purpose of subsection 162(7.02) of the Act, the following types of information returns are prescribed and must be filed by Internet if more than 50 information returns of that type are required to be filed for a calendar year:

Government Service Contract Payments	T1204
International Electronic Funds Transfer Report	
Part XVIII Information Return — International Exchange of Information on Financial Accounts	
Pooled Registered Pension Plan (PRPP) Information Return	
Registered Retirement Savings Plan (RRSP) Contribution Information Return	
Registered Retirement Savings Plans and Registered Retirement Income Funds Non-qualified Investments	
Statement of Amounts Paid or Credited to Non-residents of Canada	NR4
Statement of Benefits	T5007
Statement of Canada Pension Plan Benefits	T4A(P)
Statement of Contract Payments	T5018
Statement of Employment Insurance and Other Benefits	T4E
Statement of Farm-support Payments	AGR-1
Statement of Fees, Commissions, or Other Amounts Paid to Non-residents for Services Rendered in Canada	T4A-NR
Statement of Income from a Registered Retirement Income Fund (RIF)	T4RIF
Statement of Investment Income	T5
Statement of Old Age Security	T4A(OAS)
Statement of Partnership Income	T5013
Statement of Pension, Retirement, Annuity and Other Income	T4A
Statement of Remuneration Paid	T4
Statement of Registered Retirement Savings Plan (RRSP) Income	T4RSP
Statement of Securities Transactions	T5008
Statement of Trust Income Allocations and Designations	T3
Tax-free Savings Account (TFSA) Annual Information Return	
Tuition and Enrolment Certificate	
Universal Child Care Benefit Statement	RC62

History: S. 205.1(1) was amended by S.C. 2018, c. 27, s. 37(1), by adding "Tuition and Enrolment Certificate", in force on January 1, 2019.

S. 205.1 was amended by P.C. 2015-787, SOR/2015-140, dated June 10, 2015, published in the *Canada Gazette*, Part II on July 1, 2015, in force on June 10, 2015, and formerly read:

(1) A person who is required to make an information return under this Part, or who files an information return on behalf of a person who is required to make an information return under this Part, shall file the information return with the Minister in an electronic format if more than 500 such returns are to be filed for the calendar year.

S. 205.1 was renumbered as s. 205.1(1) by P.C. 2011-1531, SOR/2011-295, dated December 8, 2011, published in the *Canada Gazette*, Part II on December 21, 2012, effective for taxation years ending after 2009.

(2) For purposes of subsection 150.1(2.1) of the Act, a "prescribed corporation" is any corporation whose gross revenue exceeds $1 million except

(*a*) an insurance corporation as defined in subsection 248(1) of the Act;

(*b*) a non-resident corporation;

(*c*) a corporation reporting in functional currency as defined in subsection 261(1) of the Act; or

(*d*) a corporation that is exempt under section 149 of the Act from tax payable.

History: S. 205.1(2) was added by P.C. 2011-1531, SOR/2011-295, dated December 8, 2011, published in the*Canada Gazette*, Part II on December 21, 2012, effective for taxation years ending after 2009.

206. Legal Representatives and Others

(1) Where a person, who is required to make a return under this Part, has died, such return shall be filed by his legal representative within 90 days of the date of death and shall be in respect of any calendar year or a portion thereof prior to the date of death for which a return has not previously been filed.

(2) Every trustee in bankruptcy, assignee, liquidator, curator, receiver, trustee or committee and every agent or other person administering, managing, winding-up, controlling or otherwise dealing with the property, business, estate or income of a person who has not filed a return as required by this Part shall file such return.

207. Ownership Certificates

(1) An ownership certificate completed pursuant to section 234 of the Act shall be delivered to the debtor or encashing agent at the time the coupon, warrant or cheque referred to in that section is negotiated.

Forms: T600 — Ownership Certificate; T600B — Ownership Certificate.

Information Circulars: IC 82-2R2 Social insurance number legislation that relates to the preparation of information slips.

(2) The debtor or encashing agent to whom an ownership certificate has been delivered pursuant to subsection (1) shall forward it to the Minister on or before the

15th day of the month following the month the coupon, warrant or cheque, as the case may be, was negotiated.

(3) The operation of section 234 of the Act is extended to a bearer coupon or warrant negotiated by or on behalf of a non-resident person who is subject to tax under Part XIII of the Act in respect of such a coupon or warrant.

Forms: NR601 — Non-Resident Ownership Certificate (Withholding Tax); NR602 — Non-Resident Ownership Certificate (No Withholding Tax).

Information Circulars: IC 77-16R4 Non-resident income tax; IC 97-2R14 Customized forms.

208. (Repealed.)

History: S. 208 and the heading before it were repealed by P.C. 2010-548, SOR/2010-93, dated April 29, 2010, in force May 12, 2010, date of publication in the *Canada Gazette.* S. 208 and the heading before it formerly read:

Dispositions of Income-Averaging Annuity Contracts

208. Every person who carries on a business referred to in paragraph 61(4)(*b*) [subsection 61(4) "life insurance policy"] of the Act shall make an information return in prescribed form in respect of

(*a*) any amount paid by that person to a resident of Canada as, on account or in lieu of payment of, or in satisfaction of, proceeds of the surrender, cancellation, redemption, sale or other disposition of an income-averaging annuity contract; or

(*b*) any amount deemed by subsection 61.1(1) of the Act to have been received by an individual resident in Canada as proceeds of the disposition of an income-averaging annuity contract that was made with that person.

209. Distribution of Taxpayers' Portions of Returns

(1) A person who is required by section 200, 201, 202, 203, 204, 212, 214, 215, 217 or 218, subsection 223(2) or section 228, 229, 230, 232, 233 or 234 to make an information return shall forward to each taxpayer to whom the return relates two copies of the portion of the return that relates to that taxpayer.

History: S. 209(1) was replaced by S.C. 2018, c. 27, s. 38(1), in force on January 1, 2019, and formerly read:

209. *Distribution of Taxpayers' Portions of Returns.*

(1) A person who is required by section 200, 201, 202, 204, 212, 214, 215, 217 or 218, subsection 223(2) or section 228, 229, 230, 232, 233 or 234 to make an information return shall forward to each taxpayer to whom the return relates two copies of the portion of the return that relates to that taxpayer.

S. 209(1) was replaced by P.C. 2010-548, SOR/2010-93, dated April 29, 2010, in force May 12, 2010, date of publication in the *Canada Gazette.* S. 209(1) formerly read:

(1) A person who is required by section 200, 201, 202, 204, 208, 212, 214, 215, 217 or 218, subsection 223(2) or section 228, 229, 230, 232, 233 or 234 to make an information return shall forward to each taxpayer to whom the return relates two copies of the portion of the return that relates to that taxpayer.

S. 209(1) was replaced by S.C. 2009, c. 2, s. 85(1), applicable to the 2009 and subsequent taxation years. S. 209(1) formerly read:

(1) Every person who is required by section 200, 201, 202, 204, 208, 212, 214, 215, 217, 218, 223, 226, 227, 228, 229, 230, 232, 233 or 234 to make an information return shall forward to each taxpayer to whom the return relates two copies of the portion of the return that relates to that taxpayer.

(2) The copies referred to in subsection (1) shall be sent to the taxpayer at his last known address or delivered to him in person, on or before the date the return is required to be filed with the Minister.

(3) A person may send a document, as required under subsection (1), in an electronic format if the person has received the express consent of the taxpayer, and in that case, the person shall send a single copy to the taxpayer, on or before the date on which the return referred to in subsection (1) is to be filed with the Minister.

(4) In subsection (3), "express consent" means consent given in writing or in an electronic format.

(5) A person may provide a Statement of Remuneration Paid (T4) information return or a Tuition and Enrolment Certificate, as required under subsection (1), as a single document in an electronic format (instead of the two copies required under subsection (1)) to the taxpayer to whom the return relates, on or before the date on which the return is to be filed with the Minister, unless

(*a*) the specified criteria referred to in section 221.01 of the Act are not met;

(*b*) the taxpayer has requested that the information return be provided in paper format; or

(*c*) at the time the return is required to be issued,

(i) if the return is a T4, the taxpayer is on extended leave or is no longer an employee of the person, or

(ii) the taxpayer cannot reasonably be expected to have access to the information return in electronic format.

History: S. 209(5) was replaced by S.C. 2018, c. 27, s. 38(2), in force on January 1, 2019, and formerly read:

(5) A person may provide a Statement of Remuneration Paid (T4) information return, as required under subsection (1), as a single document in an electronic format (instead of the two copies required under subsection (1)) to the taxpayer to whom the return relates, on or before the date on which the return is to be filed with the Minister, unless

(*a*) the specified criteria referred to in section 221.01 of the Act are not met;

(*b*) the taxpayer has requested that the information return be provided in paper format; or

(*c*) at the time the return is required to be issued,

(i) the taxpayer is on extended leave or is no longer an employee of the person, or

(ii) the taxpayer cannot reasonably be expected to have access to the information return in electronic format.

S. 209(5) was added by S.C. 2017, c. 20, s. 31(1), applicable in respect of information returns that are required to be filed after 2017.

Related Sections: 221.01 Providing information returns in electronic format.

210. Tax Deduction Information

Every person who makes a payment described in section 153 of the Act (including an amount paid that is described in subparagraph 153(1)(*a*)(ii) of the Act), or who pays or credits, or is deemed by any of Part I, XIII and XIII.2 of the Act to have paid or credited, an amount described in that section, Part XIII or XIII.2 of the Act, shall, on demand by registered letter from the Minister, make an information return in prescribed form containing the information required in the return and shall file the return with the Minister within such reasonable time as is stipulated in the registered letter.

History: S. 210 was amended by S. C. 2016, c. 7, s. 56(1), applicable in respect of payments made after 2015, and formerly read:

210. *Tax Deduction Information.* Every person who makes a payment described in section 153 of the Act, or who pays or credits, or is deemed by any of Part I, XIII and XIII.2 of the Act to have paid or credited, an amount described in that section, Part XIII or XIII.2 of the Act, shall, on demand by registered letter from the Minister, make an information return in prescribed form containing the information required in the return and shall file the return with the Minister within such reasonable time as is stipulated in the registered letter.

S. 210 was replaced by P.C. 2011-936, SOR/2011-188, dated September 22, 2011, published in the *Canada Gazette* October 12, 2011, applicable after February 18, 2011. S. 210 formerly read:

210. Every person who makes or has at any time made a payment described in section 153 of the Act and every person who pays or credits or has at any time paid or credited, or is deemed by Part I or Part XIII of the Act

Regulations

to pay or credit or to have at any time paid or credited, an amount described in Part XIII of the Act shall, on demand by registered letter from the Minister make an information return in prescribed form containing the information required therein and shall file the return with the Minister within such reasonable time as may be stipulated in the registered letter.

211. Accrued Bond Interest

(1) Every financial company making a payment in respect of accrued interest by virtue of redemption, assignment or other transfer of a bond, debenture or similar security (other than an income bond, an income debenture or an investment contract in respect of which subsection 201(4) applies) shall make an information return in prescribed form.

Forms: T600 — Ownership Certificate; T600B — Ownership Certificate.

Information Circulars: IC 82-2R2 Social insurance number legislation that relates to the preparation of information slips.

(2) The return referred to in subsection (1) shall be forwarded to the Minister on or before the 15th day of the month following the month in which the payment referred to in subsection (1) is made.

(3) For the purposes of this section, a financial company includes a bank, an investment dealer, a stockbroker, a trust company and an insurance company.

(4) The provisions of subsection (1) do not apply to a payment made by one financial company to another financial company.

Regulations

212. Employees Profit Sharing Plans

(1) Every trustee of an employees profit sharing plan shall make an information return in prescribed form.

Forms: T4PS Sum. — Return of Allocations and Payments Under Employees Profit Sharing Plan; T4PS — Statement of Employee Profit Sharing Plan Allocations and Payments.

Information Circulars: IC 82-2R2 Social insurance number legislation that relates to the preparation of information slips; IC 97-2R14 Customized Forms.

Interpretation Bulletins: *Secondary* — IT-280R Employees profit sharing plans — Payments computed by reference to profits.

(2) Notwithstanding subsection (1), the return required under this section may be filed by the employer instead of by the trustee.

213. Pooled Registered Pension Plans

An administrator of a PRPP must file with the Minister an information return for each calendar year in prescribed form in respect of the PRPP

(*a*) if an agreement concerning annual information returns has been entered into by the Minister and an authority responsible for the supervision of the PRPP under the *Pooled Registered Pension Plans Act* or a similar law of a province, on or before the day on which an information return required by that authority is to be filed for the calendar year; and

(*b*) in any other case, on or before May 1 of the following calendar year.

History: S. 213 was added by S.C. 2012, c. 31, s. 59(1), in force December 14, 2012.

S. 213 and the heading before it were repealed by P.C. 2010-548, SOR/2010-93, dated April 29, 2010, published in the *Canada Gazette* May 12, 2010, applicable to the 2009 and subsequent taxation years. S. 213 and the heading before it formerly read:

Electric, Gas or Steam Corporations

213.

(1) Every corporation engaged in the distribution or generation of electrical energy, gas or steam shall make an information return in prescribed form in respect of each taxation year of the corporation.

(2) The return required under this section shall be filed within six months from the end of the taxation year in respect of which the return is made.

214. Registered Retirement Savings Plans

(1) Every person who pays any of the following amounts shall make an information return in prescribed form:

(*a*) an amount that is required by subsection 146(8) of the Act to be included in computing the income of a taxpayer for a taxation year;

(*b*) an amount that is an eligible amount, within the meaning of subsection 146.01(1) of the Act; or

(*c*) an amount that is an eligible amount, within the meaning of subsection 146.02(1) of the Act.

Forms: T4RSP Sum. — Summary of Income from a Registered Retirement Savings Plan; T4RSP Supp. — Statement of Registered Retirement Savings Plan Income.

Information Circulars: IC 82-2R2 Social insurance number legislation that relates to the preparation of information slips; IC 97-2R14 Customized forms.

(2) If, in a taxation year, subsection 146(7), (9) or (10) of the Act or, in relation to a non-qualified investment, subsection 207.04(1) or (4) of the Act applies in respect of a trust governed by a registered retirement savings plan, the trustee of the plan shall make an information return in prescribed form.

History: S. 214(2) was replaced by S.C. 2011, c. 24, s. 76(1), applicable in respect of investments acquired after March 22, 2011. S. 214(2) formerly read:

(2) Where, in a taxation year, subsection 146(6), (7), (9), or (10) of the Act is applicable in respect of a trust governed by a registered retirement savings plan, the trustee of such a plan shall make an information return in prescribed form.

Forms: T3GR — Group Income Tax and Information Return for RRSP, RRIF, RESP or RDSP Trusts.

(3) Where, in respect of an amended plan referred to in subsection 146(12) of the Act, an amount is required to be included in computing the income of a taxpayer for a taxation year, the issuer of the plan shall make an information return in prescribed form.

(4) Where subsection 146(8.8) of the Act deems an amount to be received by an annuitant as a benefit out of or under a registered retirement savings plan and such amount is required by subsection 146(8) of the Act to be included in computing the income of that annuitant for a taxation year, the issuer of the plan shall make an information return in prescribed form.

Forms: T4RSP Sum. — Summary of Income from a Registered Retirement Savings Plan; T4RSP Supp. — Statement of Registered Retirement Savings Plan Income.

(5) If a payment or transfer of property to which paragraph 146(16)(*b*) of the Act applies is made from a plan, the issuer of the plan shall make an information return in prescribed form in respect of the payment or transfer.

(6) Where an amount may be deducted under subsection 146(8.92) of the Act in computing the income of a deceased annuitant under a registered retirement savings plan, the issuer of the plan shall make an information return in prescribed form in respect of the amount.

History: S. 214(6) was added by S.C. 2009, c. 2, s. 86(1), applicable after 2008.

(7) In this section, "annuitant" and "issuer" have the meanings assigned by subsection 146(1) of the Act.

214.1. Registered Retirement Savings Plans

(1) The issuer of a registered retirement savings plan shall make an information return in prescribed form in respect of the amounts that have been paid by the annuitant, or by the spouse or common-law partner of the annuitant, under the plan in a contribution year

(*a*) as consideration for any contract referred to in paragraph (*a*) of the definition "retirement savings plan" in subsection 146(1) of the Act to pay a retirement income; or

(*b*) as a contribution or deposit referred to in paragraph (*b*) of that definition for the purpose stated in that paragraph.

(2) For greater certainty and for the purposes of subsection (1), amounts that have been paid do not include amounts that have been paid or transferred under the plan in accordance with subsection 146(16) of the Act, or those that have been transferred under the plan in accordance with any of subsections 146(21), 146.3(14), 147(19) or 147.3(1), (4) or (5) to (7) of the Act.

(3) The return shall be filed with the Minister on or before the 1st day of May of the year in which the contribution year ends and shall be in respect of the contribution year.

(4) The following definitions apply in this section.

"contribution year" means the period beginning on the 61st day of one year and ending on the 60th day of the following year.

"issuer" has the same meaning as in subsection 146(1) of the Act, with any modifications that the circumstances require.

215. Registered Retirement Income Funds

(1) In this section, "annuitant" and "carrier" have the meanings assigned by subsection 146.3(1) of the Act.

(2) Every carrier of a registered retirement income fund who pays out of or under it an amount any portion of which is required under subsection 146.3(5) of the Act to be included in computing the income of a taxpayer shall make an information return in prescribed form in respect of the amount.

(3) If subsection 146.3(4), (7) or (10) of the Act or, in relation to a non-qualified investment, subsection 207.04(1) or (4) of the Act applies in respect of any transaction or event with respect to property of a registered retirement income fund, the carrier of the fund shall make an information return in prescribed form in respect of the transaction or event.

History: S. 215(3) was replaced by S.C. 2011, c. 24, s. 77(1), applicable in respect of investments acquired after March 22, 2011. S. 215(3) formerly read:

(3) Where subsection 146.3(4), (7), (8) or (10) of the Act applies in respect of any transaction or event with respect to property of a registered retirement income fund, the carrier of the fund shall make an information return in prescribed form in respect of the transaction or event.

(4) Where an amount is deemed under subsection 146.3(6) or (12) of the Act to be received by an annuitant out of or under a registered retirement income fund, the carrier of the fund shall make an information return in prescribed form in respect of the amount.

(5) If a transfer of an amount to which subsection 146.3(14) of the Act applies is made from a fund, the carrier of the fund shall make an information return in prescribed form in respect of the transfer.

Forms: T4RIF — Statement of Income from a Registered Retirement Income; T4RIF Sum. — T4RIF Summary.

Information Circulars: IC 78-18R6 Registered retirement income funds; IC 82-2R2 Social insurance number legislation that relates to the preparation of information slips; IC 97-2R14 Customized forms.

(6) Where an amount may be deducted under subsection 146.3(6.3) of the Act in computing the income of a deceased annuitant under a registered retirement income fund, the carrier of the fund shall make an information return in prescribed form in respect of the amount.

History: S. 215(6) was added by S.C. 2009, c. 2, s. 87(1), applicable after 2008.

216. (Repealed.)

History: S. 216 and the heading before it were repealed by S.C. 2011, c. 24, s. 78(1), applicable to fiscal periods of registered Canadian amateur athletic associations that begin on or after January 1, 2012. S. 216 formerly read:

Registered Canadian Amateur Athletic Associations

216.

(1) Every registered Canadian amateur athletic association shall make an information return in prescribed form for each fiscal period of the association within six months after the end of the fiscal period.

(2) For the purposes of this section, "fiscal period" means the period for which the accounts of the registered Canadian amateur athletic association have been ordinarily made up and, in the absence of an established practice, the fiscal period is that adopted by the association but no such fiscal period shall exceed 12 months.

Forms: T2052 — Registered Canadian Amateur Athletic Association Return of Information.

217. Disposition of Interest in Annuities and Life Insurance Policies

(1) In this section,

"disposition" has the meaning assigned by subsection 148(9) of the Act and includes anything deemed to be a disposition of a life insurance policy under subsection 148(2) of the Act;

"insurer" has the meaning assigned by paragraph 148(10)(*a*) of the Act;

"life insurance policy" (Repealed.)

History: S. 217(1), the definition "life insurance policy" was repealed by P.C. 2011-936, SOR/2011-188, dated September 22, 2011, published in the *Canada Gazette* October 12, 2011, applicable after February 18, 2011. S. 217(1), the definition "life insurance policy" formerly read:

"life insurance policy" has the meaning assigned by subsection 138(12) of the Act.

(2) Where by reason of a disposition of an interest in a life insurance policy an amount is required, pursuant to paragraph 56(1)(*j*) of the Act, to be included in computing the income of a taxpayer and the insurer that is the issuer of the policy is a party to, or is notified in writing of, the disposition, the insurer shall make an information return in prescribed form in respect of the amount.

Forms: T5 Sum. — Return of Investment Income; T5 — Statement of Investment Income; T619 — Magnetic Media Transmittal.

Information Circulars: IC 82-2R2 Social insurance number legislation that relates to the preparation of information slips; IC 97-2R14 Customized forms.

218. Patronage Payments

(1) Every person who, within the meaning of section 135 of the Act, makes payments to residents of Canada pursuant to an allocation in proportion to patronage shall make an information return in prescribed form in respect of payments so made.

(2) Every person who receives a payment referred to in subsection (1) as nominee or agent for another person resident in Canada shall make an information return in prescribed form in respect of the payment so received.

219. (Repealed.)

220. Cash Bonus Payments on Canada Savings Bonds

(1) Every person authorized to redeem Canada Savings Bonds (in this section referred to as the "redemption agent") who pays an amount in respect of a Canada Savings Bond as a cash bonus that the Government of Canada has undertaken to pay (other than an amount of interest, bonus or principal agreed to be paid at the time of the issue of the bond under the terms of the bond) shall make an information return in prescribed form in respect of such payment.

Information Circulars: IC 82-2R2 Social insurance number legislation that relates to the preparation of information slips; IC 97-2R14 Customized forms.

(2) Every redemption agent required by subsection (1) to make an information return shall

(*a*) issue to the payee, at the time the cash bonus is paid, two copies of the portion of the return relating to him; and

(*b*) file the return with the Minister on or before the 15th day of the month following the month in which the cash bonus was paid.

221. Qualified Investments

(1) In this section, "reporting person" means

(*a*) a mutual fund corporation;

(*b*) an investment corporation;

(*c*) a mutual fund trust;

(*d*) (Repealed by P.C. 2005-1508, SOR/2005-264.)

(*e*) (Repealed by P.C. 2005-1508, SOR/2005-264.)

(*f*) a trust that would be a mutual fund trust if Part XLVIII were read without reference to paragraph 4801(*b*); or

(*g*) (Repealed by P.C. 2005-1508, SOR/2005-264.)

(*h*) a small business investment trust (within the meaning assigned by subsection 5103(1));

(*i*) (Repealed by P.C. 2005-1508, SOR/2005-264.)

History: S. 221(1) was amended by P.C. 2010-548, SOR/2010-93, by adding the word "or" at the end of paragraph (*f*) and by striking out the word "or" at the end of paragraph (*h*), dated April 29, 2010, in force May 12, 2010, date of publication in the *Canada Gazette*.

(2) Where in any taxation year a reporting person (other than a registered investment) claims that a share of its capital stock issued by it, or an interest as a beneficiary under it, is a qualified investment under section 146, 146.1, 146.3, 146.4, 204 or 207.01 of the Act, the reporting person shall, in respect of the year and within 90 days after the end of the year, make an information return in prescribed form.

History: S. 221(2) was replaced by S.C. 2017, c. 33, s. 83(1), deemed in force March 23, 2017, and formerly read:

(2) Where in any taxation year a reporting person (other than a registered investment) claims that a share of its capital stock issued by it, or an interest as a beneficiary under it, is a qualified investment under section 146, 146.1, 146.3, 204, 205 or 207.01 of the Act, the reporting person shall, in respect of the year and within 90 days after the end of the year, make an information return in prescribed form.

S. 221(2) was replaced by S.C. 2009, c. 2, s. 88(1), applicable to the 2009 and subsequent taxation years. S. 221(2) formerly read:

(2) Where in any taxation year a reporting person (other than a registered investment) claims that a share of its capital stock issued by it, or an interest as a beneficiary under it, is a qualified investment under section 146, 146.1, 146.3, 204 or 205 of the Act, the reporting person shall, in respect of the year and within 90 days after the end of the year, make an information return in prescribed form.

Related Sections: 146.4(1) qualified investment.

Forms: T3F — Investments Prescribed to be Qualified or not to be Foreign Property Information Return.

Information Circulars: IC 78-14R4 Guidelines for trust companies and other persons responsible for filing T3GR, T3D, T3P, T3S, T3RI, and T3F returns.

(3) (Repealed by P.C. 2005-1508, SOR/2005-264.)

222. The issuer of a RDSP, or the promoter of a RESP, that governs a trust shall notify the holders of the RDSP, or subscribers of the RESP, in prescribed form and manner before March of a calendar year if, at any time during the preceding calendar year,

(*a*) the trust acquires or disposes of property that is a not a qualified investment for the trust; or

(*b*) property held by the trust becomes or ceases to be a qualified investment for the trust.

History: S. 222 was added by S.C. 2017, c. 33, s. 84(1), deemed in force March 23, 2017.

Related Sections: 207.01(1) non-qualified investment; 207.01 qualified investment.

223. TFSAs

(1) An issuer of a TFSA shall make an information return for each calendar year in prescribed form in respect of the TFSA.

History: S. 223(1) and the heading before it were replaced by S.C. 2009, c. 2, s. 89(1), applicable to the 2009 and subsequent taxation years. S. 223(1) and the heading before it formerly read:

Registered Home Ownership Savings Plans

223.

(1) Every person who, before May 23, 1985, pays an amount out of or under a registered home ownership savings plan to a resident of Canada as a beneficiary under the plan shall make an information return in prescribed form.

(2) An issuer of a TFSA who makes a payment of an amount that is required because of paragraph 146.2(9)(*b*) of the Act to be included in computing the income of a taxpayer for a taxation year shall make an information return in prescribed form.

History: S. 223(2) was replaced by S.C. 2009, c. 2, s. 89(1), applicable to the 2009 and subsequent taxation years. S. 223(2) formerly read:

(2) Every trustee or depositary that is party to a registered home ownership savings plan the registration of which is revoked during a taxation year pursuant to subsection 146.2(7) or (7.1) of the Act shall make an information return in prescribed form with respect to any amount that is deemed by subsection 146.2(8) of the Act to have been received by the beneficiary of that plan.

(3) An issuer of a TFSA that governs a trust shall notify the holder of the TFSA in prescribed form and manner before March of a calendar year if, at any time during the preceding calendar year,

(*a*) the trust acquires or disposes of property that is a non-qualified investment for the trust; or

(*b*) property held by the trust becomes or ceases to be a non-qualified investment for the trust.

History: S. 223(3) was replaced by S.C. 2009, c. 2, s. 89(1), applicable to the 2009 and subsequent taxation years. S. 223(3) formerly read:

(3) Every trustee or depositary that is party to a registered home ownership savings plan, the beneficiary of which is a resident of Canada and has been deemed by subsection 146.2(9) of the Act to have received an amount during a taxation year and before May 23, 1985, shall make an information return in prescribed form.

(3.1) (Repealed by S.C. 2009, c. 2, s. 89(1).)

History: S. 223(3.1) was repealed by S.C. 2009, c. 2, s. 89(1), applicable to the 2009 and subsequent taxation years. S. 223(3.1) formerly read:

(3.1) Every trustee or depositary that, after May 22, 1985 and before 1986, was a party to a registered home ownership savings plan, any of the income of which is required by subsection 146.2(22) of the Act to be included in computing the income of a taxpayer for the 1985 taxation year, shall make an information return in prescribed form.

(4) (Repealed by S.C. 2009, c. 2, s. 89(1).)

History: S. 223(4) was repealed by S.C. 2009, c. 2, s. 89(1), applicable to the 2009 and subsequent taxation years. S. 223(4) formerly read:

(4) Every trustee of a trust governed by a registered home ownership savings plan shall make an information return in prescribed form, where in a taxation year a taxpayer who is a beneficiary under the plan

(*a*) is required pursuant to subsection 146.2(12) or (15) of the Act to include an amount in computing his income; or

(*b*) is allowed pursuant to subsection 146.2(13) or (16) of the Act to deduct an amount in computing his income.

(5) (Repealed by S.C. 2009, c. 2, s. 89(1).)

History: S. 223(5) was repealed by S.C. 2009, c. 2, s. 89(1), applicable to the 2009 and subsequent taxation years. S. 223(5) formerly read:

(5) In this section,

"beneficiary" has the meaning assigned by paragraph 146.2(1)(*a*) of the Act as it read in its application to the 1985 taxation year;

"depositary" has the meaning assigned by subparagraph 146.2(1)(*d*)(ii) of the Act as it read in its application to the 1985 taxation year;

"registered home ownership savings plan" has the meaning assigned by paragraph 146.2(1)(*h*) of the Act as it read in its application to the 1985 taxation year.

224. Canadian Home Insulation Program and Canada Oil Substitution Program

Where an amount has been paid to a person pursuant to a program prescribed for the purposes of paragraphs 12(1)(*u*), 56(1)(*s*) and 212(1)(*s*) of the Act, the payor shall

(*a*) make an information return in prescribed form in respect of such payment; and

(*b*) forward to the person at his latest known address on or before the date the return is required to be filed with the Minister two copies of the portion of the return relating to that person.

225. Certified Films and Video Tapes

(1) Where principal photography or taping of a film or tape (within the meanings assigned by subsection 1100(21)) has occurred during a year or has been completed within 60 days after the end of the year, the producer of the film or tape or production company that produced the film or tape, or an agent of the producer or production company, shall

(*a*) make an information return in prescribed form in respect of any person who owns an interest in the film or tape at the end of the year; and

(*b*) forward to the person referred to in paragraph (*a*) at his latest known address on or before the date the return is required to be filed with the Minister two copies of the portion of the return relating to that person.

(2) The return required under this section shall be filed on or before March 31 and shall be in respect of the preceding calendar year.

226. Scientific Research Tax Credits

(1) In this section,

"administrator" has the meaning assigned by paragraph 47.1(1)(*a*) [repealed by S.C. 1986, c. 6, s. 20(1)] of the Act;

"designated security" means a security issued or granted by a corporation in respect of which the corporation has designated an amount pursuant to subsection 194(4) of the Act;

"first purchaser", in relation to a designated security, means the first person (other than a trader or dealer in securities) to be the registered holder of the designated security;

"security" means

(*a*) a share of the capital stock of a corporation,

(*b*) a debt obligation issued by a corporation, or

(*c*) a right granted by a corporation under a scientific research financing contract;

"trader or dealer in securities" has the meaning assigned by paragraph 47.1(1)(*l*) [repealed by S.C. 1986, c. 6, s. 20(1)] of the Act.

(2) Each corporation that has designated an amount under subsection 194(4) of the Act in respect of a security issued or granted by it shall make an information return in prescribed form in respect of each such security.

(3) Each trader or dealer in securities who has acquired and disposed of a designated security during the course of the primary distribution thereof pursuant to a public offering shall make an information return in prescribed form in respect of each such designated security.

(4) Each bank, credit union and trust company that, as agent, acquired a designated security for the first purchaser thereof shall make an information return in prescribed form in respect of each such designated security.

(5) Each trader or dealer in securities who, as administrator of an indexed security investment plan, acquired a designated security for the first purchaser thereof shall make an information return in prescribed form in respect of each such designated security.

(6) Notwithstanding subsection 205(1), any return required to be made

(*a*) under subsection (2), in respect of a security issued by a corporation before March 1, 1984,

(*b*) under subsection (3), in respect of a designated security disposed of as described in subsection (3) before March 1, 1984, or

(*c*) under subsection (4) or (5), in respect of a designated security acquired as described in subsection (4) or (5), as the case may be, before March 1, 1984,

shall be filed on or before March 31, 1984.

227. Share Purchase Tax Credits

(1) In this section,

"administrator" has the meaning assigned by paragraph 47.1(1)(*a*) [repealed by S.C. 1986, c. 6, s. 20(1)] of the Act;

"designated share" means a share of the capital stock of a corporation in respect of which the corporation has designated an amount pursuant to subsection 192(4) of the Act;

"first purchaser", in relation to a designated share, means the first person (other than a trader or dealer in securities) to be the registered holder of the share;

"trader or dealer in securities" has the meaning assigned by paragraph 47.1(1)(*l*) [repealed by S.C. 1986, c. 6, s. 20(1)] of the Act.

(2) Each corporation that has designated an amount under subsection 192(4) of the Act in respect of a share issued by it shall make an information return in prescribed form in respect of each such share.

(3) Each trader or dealer in securities who has acquired and disposed of a designated share during the course of the primary distribution thereof pursuant to a public offering shall make an information return in prescribed form in respect of each such designated share.

(4) Each bank, credit union and trust company that, as agent, acquired a designated share for the first purchaser thereof shall make an information return in prescribed form in respect of each such designated share.

(5) Each trader or dealer in securities who, as administrator of an indexed security investment plan, acquired a designated share for the first purchaser thereof shall make an information return in prescribed form in respect of each such designated share.

228. Resource Flow-Through Shares

(1) Each corporation that has renounced an amount under subsection 66(12.6), (12.601), (12.62) or (12.64) of the Act to a person shall make an information return in prescribed form in respect of the amount renounced.

(2) The return required under subsection (1) shall be filed with the Minister together with the prescribed form required to be filed under subsection 66(12.7) of the Act in respect of the amount renounced.

229. Partnership Return

(1) Every member, of a partnership that carries on a business in Canada at any time in a fiscal period of the partnership (other than a member that is, because of subsection 115.2(2) of the Act, not considered to be carrying on business in Canada at that time), or of a partnership that is at any time in a fiscal period of the partnership, a Canadian partnership or a SIFT partnership, shall make for that period an information return in prescribed form containing the following information:

(*a*) the income or loss of the partnership for the fiscal period;

(*b*) in respect of each member of the partnership who is entitled to a share referred to in paragraph (*c*) or (*d*) for the fiscal period, the member's

(i) name,

(ii) address, and

(iii) business number, Social Insurance Number or trust account number, as the case may be;

(*c*) the share of each member of the income or loss of the partnership for the fiscal period;

(*d*) the share of each member for the fiscal period of each deduction, credit or other amount in respect of the partnership that is relevant in determining the member's income, taxable income, tax payable or other amount under the Act;

(*e*) the prescribed information contained in the form prescribed for the purposes of subsection 37(1) of the Act, where the partnership has made an expenditure in respect of scientific research and experimental development in the fiscal period; and

(*f*) such other information as may be required by the prescribed form.

History: S. 229(1)(*b*) was replaced by S.C. 2018, c. 12 s. 43(1), applicable to the 2018 and subsequent taxation years, and formerly read:

(*b*) the name, address and, in the case of an individual, the social insurance number of each member of the partnership who is entitled to a share referred to in paragraph (*c*) or (*d*) for the fiscal period;

S. 229(1), the portion before paragraph (*a*) was replaced by S.C. 2013, c. 34, s. 377(1), applicable to fiscal periods that end after 2007, and formerly read:

(1) Every member of a partnership that carries on a business in Canada, or that is a Canadian partnership or a SIFT partnership, at any time in a fiscal period of the partnership shall make for that period an information return in prescribed form containing the following information:

Canadian Tax Foundation: Baron, *Current Issues: Partnership Returns*, 2012 Ontario Tax Conference 1A:1–8.

Tax Topics: No. 1831, Should You File a Partnership Information Return?.

Forms: T5011 — Application for a Partnership's Filer Identification Number; T5013 Sum. — Partnership Information Return; T5013 Supp. — Statement of Partnership Income; T5014 — Partnership Capital Cost Allowance Schedule; T5015 — Reconciliation of Partner's Capital Account; T5017 — Calculation of Deduction for Cumulative Eligible Capital of a Partnership.

Income Tax Technical News: Issue No. 38, Filing requirements for T5013, Partnership Information Return.

Information Circulars: IC 73-13 Investment clubs; IC 82-2R2 Social insurance number legislation that relates to the preparation of information slips; IC 97-2R14 Customized forms.

(2) For the purposes of subsection (1), an information return made by any member of a partnership shall be deemed to have been made by each member of the partnership.

(3) Every person who holds an interest in a partnership as nominee or agent for another person shall make an information return in prescribed form in respect of that interest.

(4) (Revoked.)

(5) Subject to subsection (6), a return required by this section shall be filed with the Minister without notice or demand

(*a*) in the case of a fiscal period of a partnership all the members of which are corporations throughout the fiscal period, within five months after the end of the fiscal period;

(*b*) in the case of a fiscal period of a partnership all the members of which are individuals throughout the fiscal period, on or before the last day of March in the calendar year immediately following the calendar year in which the fiscal period ended or with which the fiscal period ended coincidentally; and

(*c*) in the case of any other fiscal period of a partnership, on or before the earlier of

(i) the day that is five months after the end of the fiscal period, and

(ii) the last day of March in the calendar year immediately following the calendar year in which the fiscal period ended or with which the fiscal period ended coincidentally.

(6) Where a partnership discontinues its business or activity, the return required under this section shall be filed, in respect of any fiscal period or portion thereof prior to the discontinuance of the business or activity for which a return has not previously been filed under this section, on or before the earlier of

(*a*) the day that is 90 days after the discontinuance of the business or activity, and

(*b*) the day the return is required to be filed under subsection (5).

229.1. Definitions

(1) Definitions. The definitions in this subsection apply in this section.

"public investment partnership", at any time, means a public partnership all or substantially all of the fair market value of the property of which is, at that time, attributable to the fair market value of property of the partnership that is

(*a*) units of public trusts (as defined in subsection 204.1(1));

(*b*) partnership interests in public partnerships;

(*c*) shares of the capital stock of public corporations; or

(*d*) any combination of properties referred to in paragraphs (*a*) to (*c*).

"public partnership", at any time, means a partnership the partnership interests in which are, at that time, listed on a designated stock exchange in Canada if, at that time, the partnership carries on a business in Canada or is a Canadian partnership.

(2) Required Information Disclosure. Every member of a partnership that is, at any time in a fiscal period of the partnership, a public partnership shall, within the time required by subsection (3),

(*a*) make public, in prescribed form, information in respect of the public partnership for the fiscal period by posting the prescribed form, in a manner that is accessible to the general public, on the Internet website of CDS Innovations Inc.; and

(*b*) notify the Minister in writing as to when the posting of the prescribed form, as required by paragraph (*a*), has been made.

(3) Required Disclosure Time. The time required for the members of a public partnership to satisfy the requirements of subsection (2) in respect of the public partnership for a fiscal period of the public partnership is

(*a*) subject to paragraph (*b*), on or before the day that is the earlier of

(i) 60 days after the end of the calendar year in which the fiscal period ends, and

(ii) four months after the end of the fiscal period; and

(*b*) where the public partnership is, at any time in the fiscal period, a public investment partnership, on or before the day that is 67 days after the end of the calendar year in which the fiscal period ends.

(4) Obligation Fulfilled By One Partner Deemed Fulfilled By All. Every member of a partnership that is required to satisfy the requirements of subsection (2) in respect of the partnership for a fiscal period of the partnership will be deemed to have satisfied those requirements if a particular member of the partnership, who has authority to act for the partnership, has satisfied those requirements in respect of the partnership for the fiscal period.

230. Security Transactions

(1) In this section,

"publicly traded" means, with respect to any security,

(*a*) a security that is listed or posted for trading on a stock exchange, commodity exchange, futures exchange or any other exchange, or

(*b*) a security in respect of the sale and distribution of which a prospectus, registration statement or similar document has been filed with a public authority;

"sale" includes the granting of an option and a short sale;

"security" means

(*a*) a publicly traded share of the capital stock of a corporation,

(*b*) a publicly traded debt obligation;

(*c*) a debt obligation of or guaranteed by

(i) the Government of Canada,

(ii) the government of a province or an agent thereof,

(iii) a municipality in Canada,

(iv) a municipal or public body performing a function of government in Canada, or

(v) the government of a foreign country or of a political subdivision of a foreign country or a local authority of such a government;

(*c*.1) a debt obligation that is, at any time, described in paragraph 7000(1)(*d*),

(*d*) a publicly traded interest in a trust,

(*e*) a publicly traded interest in a partnership,

(*f*) an option or contract in respect of any property described in any of paragraphs (*a*) to (*e*), or

(*g*) a publicly traded option or contract in respect of any property including any commodity, financial futures, foreign currency or precious metal or in respect of any index relating to any property;

"trader or dealer in securities" means

(*a*) a person who is registered or licensed under the laws of a province to trade in securities, or

(*b*) a person who in the ordinary course of business makes sales of securities as agent on behalf of others.

History: S. 230(1), paragraph (*c.1*) of the definition "security" was added by S.C. 2016, c. 12, s. 75(1), in force January 1, 2017.

Tax Window Files: Section 230 of the Regulations, *November 8, 2016*, CRA Document No. 2016-0673361E5.

(2) Every trader or dealer in securities who, in a calendar year, purchases a security as principal or sells a security as agent for any vendor shall make an information return for the year in prescribed form in respect of the purchase or sale.

Forms: T5008 — Statement of Securities Transactions; T5008Sum — Return of Securities Transactions.

Information Circulars: IC 82-2R2 Social insurance number legislation that relates to the preparation of information slips.

(3) Every person (other than an individual who is not a trust) who in a calendar year redeems, acquires or cancels in any manner whatever any securities issued by that person shall make an information return for the year in prescribed form in respect of each such transaction, other than a transaction to which section 51, 51.1, 86 (if there is no consideration receivable other than new shares) or 87 or subsection 98(3) or (6) of the Act applies.

Information Circulars: IC 82-2R2 Social insurance number legislation that relates to the preparation of information slips.

(4) Subsection (3) applies to

(*a*) Her Majesty in right of Canada or a province;

(*b*) a municipal or public body performing a function of government in Canada; and

(*c*) an agent of a person referred to in paragraph (*a*) or (*b*).

(5) Every person who, in the ordinary course of a business of buying and selling precious metals in the form of certificates, bullion or coins, makes a payment in a calendar year to another person in respect of a sale by that other person of any such property shall make an information return for that year in prescribed form in respect of each such sale.

Information Circulars: IC 82-2R2 Social insurance number legislation that relates to the preparation of information slips.

(6) Every person who, while acting as nominee or agent for another person in respect of a sale or other transaction to which subsection (2), (3) or (5) applies, receives the proceeds of the sale or other transaction shall, where the transaction is carried out in the name of the nominee or agent, make an information return in prescribed form in respect of the sale or other transaction.

Information Circulars: IC 82-2R2 Social insurance number legislation that relates to the preparation of information slips.

(7) This section does not apply in respect of

(*a*) a purchase of a security by a trader or dealer in securities from another trader or dealer in securities other than a non-resident trader or dealer in securities;

(*b*) a sale of currencies or precious metals in the form of jewellery, works of art or numismatic coins;

(*c*) a sale of precious metals by a person who, in the ordinary course of business, produces or sells precious metals in bulk or in commercial quantities;

(*d*) a sale of securities by a trader or dealer in securities on behalf of a person who is exempt from tax under Part I of the Act; or

(*e*) a redemption by the issuer or an agent of the issuer of a debt obligation where

(i) the debt obligation was issued for its principal amount,

(ii) the redemption satisfies all of the issuer's obligations in respect of the debt obligation,

(iii) each person with an interest in the debt obligation is entitled in respect thereof to a proportion of all payments of principal equal to the proportion to which the person is entitled of all payments other than principal, and

(iv) an information return is required under another section of this Part to be made as a result of the redemption in respect of each person with an interest in the debt obligation.

231. (Repealed.)

History: S. 231 and the heading before it were repealed by P.C. 2011-936, SOR/2011-188, dated September 22, 2011, published in the *Canada Gazette* October 12, 2011, applicable after February 18, 2003. S. 231 formerly read:

Information Respecting Tax Shelters

231.

(1) In this section, "promoter" in respect of a tax shelter and "tax shelter" have the meanings assigned by subsection 237.1(1) of the Act.

(2) An information return made under subsection 237.1(7) of the Act in respect of the acquisition of an interest in a tax shelter in a calendar year shall be filed with the Minister on or before the last day of February of the immediately following calendar year.

(3) Where a person who is required to make an information return under subsection 237.1(7) of the Act discontinues the business or activity by reason of which the person is required to make the return, the return shall be filed within 30 days after the day of the discontinuance of the business or activity in respect of any calendar year or portion thereof prior to the discontinuance for which such a return has not previously been filed.

(4) Every person required to make a return under subsection 237.1(7) of the Act shall, on or before the day on or before which the return is required to be filed with the Minister, forward to each person to whom the return relates two copies of the portion of the return relating to that person.

(5) Every promoter with respect to a tax shelter shall

(*a*) on every written statement made by the promoter that refers either directly or indirectly and either expressly or impliedly to the issuance by the Department of National Revenue of an identification number for the tax shelter, as well as on the copies of the portion of the information return to be forwarded pursuant to subsection (4), include the following statement:

"The identification number issued for this tax shelter shall be included in any income tax return filed by the investor. Issuance of the identification number is for administrative purposes only and does not in any way confirm the entitlement of an investor to claim any tax benefits associated with the tax shelter"; and

(*b*) prominently display on the upper right-hand corner of any statement of earnings prepared by the promoter in respect of the tax shelter the identification number issued for the tax shelter.

(6) For the purposes of paragraph (*b*) of the definition "tax shelter" in subsection 237.1(1) of the Act, "prescribed benefit" in respect of an interest in a property means any amount that may reasonably be expected, having regard to statements or representations made in respect of the interest, to be received or enjoyed by a person (in this subsection referred to as "the purchaser") who acquires the interest, or a person with whom the purchaser does not deal at arm's length, which receipt or enjoyment would have the effect of reducing the impact of any loss that the purchaser may sustain in respect of the interest, and includes such an amount

(*a*) that is, either immediately or in the future, owed to any other person by the purchaser or a person with whom the purchaser does not deal at arm's length, to the extent that

(i) liability to pay that amount is contingent,

(ii) payment of that amount is or will be guaranteed by, security is or will be provided by, or an agreement to indemnify the other person to whom the amount is owed is or will be entered into by

(A) a promoter in respect of the interest,

(B) a person with whom the promoter does not deal at arm's length, or

(C) a person who is to receive a payment (other than a payment made by the purchaser) in respect of the guarantee, security or agreement to indemnify,

(iii) the rights of that other person against the purchaser, or against a person with whom the purchaser does not deal at arm's length, in respect of the collection of all or part of the purchase price are limited to a maximum amount, are enforceable only against certain property, or are otherwise limited by agreement, or

(iv) payment of that amount is to be made in a foreign currency or is to be determined by reference to its value in a foreign currency and it may reasonably be considered, having regard to the history of the exchange rate between the foreign currency and Canadian currency, that the aggregate of all such payments, when converted to Canadian currency at the exchange rate expected to prevail at the date on which each such payment would be required to be made, will be substantially less than that aggregate would be if each such payment was converted to Canadian currency at the time that each such payment became owing,

(*b*) that the purchaser or a person with whom the purchaser does not deal at arm's length is entitled at any time to, directly or indirectly, receive or have available

(i) as a form of assistance from a government, municipality or other public authority, whether as a grant, subsidy, forgiveable loan, deduction from tax or investment allowance, or as any other form of assistance, or

(ii) by reason of a revenue guarantee or other agreement in respect of which revenue may be earned by the purchaser or a person with whom the purchaser does not deal at arm's length, to the extent that the revenue guarantee or other agreement may reasonably be considered to ensure that the purchaser or person will receive a return of all or a portion of the purchaser's outlays in respect of the interest,

(*c*) that is the proceeds of disposition to which the purchaser may be entitled by way of an agreement or other arrangement under which the purchaser has a right, either absolutely or contingently, to dispose of the interest (otherwise than as a consequence of the purchaser's death), including the fair market value of any property that the agreement or arrangement provides for the acquisition of in exchange for all or any part of the interest, and

(*d*) that is owed to a promoter, or a person with whom the promoter does not deal at arm's length, by the purchaser or a person with whom the purchaser does not deal at arm's length in respect of the interest,

but, except as otherwise provided in subparagraph (*b*)(ii), does not include profits earned in respect of the interest.

(6.1) For the purpose of paragraph (*b*) of the definition "tax shelter" in subsection 237.1(1) of the Act, "prescribed benefit" in respect of an interest in a property includes an amount that is a limited-recourse amount because of subsection 143.2(1), (7) or (13) of the Act, but does not include an amount of indebtedness that is a limited-recourse amount

(*a*) solely because it is not required to be repaid within 10 years from the time the indebtedness arose where the debtor would, if the interest were acquired by the debtor immediately after that time, be

(i) a partnership

Regulations

(A) at least 90% of the fair market value of the property of which is attributable to the partnership's tangible capital property located in Canada, and

(B) at least 90% of the value of all interests in which are held by limited partners (within the meaning assigned by subsection 96(2.4) of the Act) of the partnership,

except where it is reasonable to conclude that one of the main reasons for the acquisition of one or more properties by the partnership, or for the acquisition of one or more interests in the partnership by limited partners, is to avoid the application of this subsection, or

(ii) a member of a partnership having fewer than six members, except where

(A) the partnership is a member of another partnership,

(B) there is a limited partner (within the meaning assigned by subsection 96(2.4) of the Act) of the partnership,

(C) less than 90% of the fair market value of the partnership's property is attributable to the partnership's tangible capital property located in Canada, or

(D) it is reasonable to conclude that one of the main reasons for the existence of one of two or more partnerships, one of which is the partnership, or the acquisition of one or more properties by the partnership, is to avoid the application of this section to the member's indebtedness,

(*b*) of a partnership

(i) where

(A) the indebtedness is secured by and used to acquire the partnership's tangible capital property located in Canada (other than rental property, within the meaning assigned by subsection 1100(14), leasing property, within the meaning assigned by subsection 1100(17), or specified energy property, within the meaning assigned by subsection 1100(25)), and

(B) the person to whom the indebtedness is repayable is a member of the Canadian Payments Association, and

(ii) throughout the period during which any amount is outstanding in respect of the indebtedness,

(A) at least 90% of the fair market value of the property of which is attributable to tangible capital property located in Canada of the partnership,

(B) at least 90% of the value of all interests in which are held by limited partners (within the meaning assigned by subsection 96(2.4) of the Act) that are corporations, and

(C) the principal business of each such limited partner is related to the principal business of the partnership,

except where it is reasonable to conclude that one of the main reasons for the acquisition of one or more properties by the partnership, or for the acquisition of one or more interests in the partnership by limited partners, is to avoid the application of this subsection, or

(*c*) of a corporation where the amount is a *bona fide* business loan made to the corporation for the purpose of financing a business that the corporation operates and the loan is made pursuant to a loan program of the Government of Canada or of a province the purpose of which is to extend financing to small- and medium-sized Canadian businesses.

(7) For the purposes of the definition "tax shelter" in subsection 237.1(1) of the Act, "prescribed property" in relation to a tax shelter means property that is a registered pension plan, a registered retirement savings plan, a deferred profit sharing plan, a registered retirement income fund, a registered education savings plan or a property in respect of which paragraph 40(2)(*i*) of the Act is applicable.

232. Worker's Compensation

(1) Every person who pays an amount in respect of compensation described in subparagraph 110(1)(*f*)(ii) of the Act shall make an information return in prescribed form in respect of that payment.

(2) Where a worker's compensation board, or a similar body, adjudicates a claim for compensation described in subparagraph 110(1)(*f*)(ii) of the Act and stipulates the amount of the award, that board or body shall make an information return in prescribed form in respect of the amount of the award.

(3) A return required under this section must be filed on or before the last day of February of each year and shall be in respect of

(*a*) the preceding calendar year, if the return is required under subsection (1); and

(*b*) the amount of the award that pertains to the preceding calendar year, if the return is required under subsection (2).

(4) Subsections (1) and (2) are not applicable in respect of a payment or an award in respect of

(*a*) medical expenses incurred by or on behalf of the employee;

(*b*) funeral expenses in respect of the employee;

(*c*) legal expenses in respect of the employee;

(*d*) job training or counselling of the employee; or

(*e*) the death of the employee, other than periodic payments made after the death of the employee.

233. Social Assistance

(1) Every person who makes a payment described in paragraph 56(1)(*u*) of the Act shall make an information return in prescribed form in respect of the payment.

(2) Subsection (1) is not applicable in respect of a payment that

(*a*) is in respect of medical expenses incurred by or on behalf of the payee;

(*b*) is in respect of child care expenses, as defined in subsection 63(3) of the Act, incurred by or on behalf of the payee or a person related to the payee;

(*c*) is in respect of funeral expenses in respect of a person related to the payee;

(*d*) is in respect of legal expenses incurred by or on behalf of the payee or a person related to the payee;

(*e*) is in respect of job training or counselling of the payee or a person related to the payee;

(*f*) is paid in a particular year as a part of a series of payments, the total of which in the particular year does not exceed $500; or

(*g*) is not a part of a series of payments.

History: S. 233(2)(*b*) was replaced by P.C. 2010-548, SOR/2010-93, dated April 29, 2010, in force May 12, 2010, date of publication in the *Canada Gazette*. S. 233(2)(*b*) formerly read:

(*b*) is in respect of child care expenses, within the meaning assigned by paragraph 63(3)(*a*) [subsection 63(3) "child care expense"] of the Act, incurred by or on behalf of the payee or a person related to the payee;

234. Farm Support Payments

(1) Every government, municipality or municipal or other public body (in sections 235 and 236 referred to as the "government payer") or producer organization or association that makes a payment of an amount that is a farm support payment (other than an amount paid out of a net income stabilization account) to a person or partnership shall make an information return in prescribed form in respect of the amount.

(2) For the purposes of subsection (1) "farm support payment" includes

(*a*) a payment that is computed with respect to an area of farm land;

(*b*) a payment that is made in respect of a unit of farm commodity grown or disposed of or a farm animal raised or disposed of; and

(*c*) a rebate of, or compensation for, all or a portion of

(i) a cost or capital cost incurred in respect of farming, or

Regulations

(ii) unsowed or unplanted land or crops, or destroyed crops, farm animals or other farm output.

235. Identifier Information

Every corporation or trust for which an information return is required to be made under these Regulations by a government payer or by a producer organization or association shall provide its legal name, address and income tax identification number to the government payer or the producer organization or association, as the case may be.

236. Identifier Information

Every person who is a member of a partnership for which an information return is required to be made under these Regulations by a government payer or by a producer organization or association shall provide the government payer or the producer organization or association, as the case may be, with the following information:

(*a*) the person's legal name, address and Social Insurance Number, or, where the person is a trust or is not an individual, the person's income tax identification number; and

(*b*) the partnership's name and business address.

Information Circulars: IC 82-2R2 Social insurance number legislation that relates to the preparation of information slips.

237. Contract for Goods and Services

(1) The definitions in this subsection apply in this section.

"federal body" means a department or a Crown corporation, within the meaning of section 2 of the *Financial Administration Act*.

"payee" means a person or partnership to whom an amount is paid or credited in respect of goods for sale or lease, or services rendered, by or on behalf of the person or the partnership.

(2) A federal body that pays or credits an amount to a payee shall file an information return in prescribed form in respect of the amount on or before March 31 in each year in respect of the preceding calendar year.

Forms: T1204 — Government Service Contract Payments; T1204 Sum. — Government Service Contract Payments.

(3) Subsection (2) does not apply in respect of an amount

(*a*) all or substantially all of which is paid or credited in the year in respect of goods for sale or lease by the payee;

(*b*) to which section 212 of the Act applies;

(*c*) that is not required to be included in computing the income of the payee, if the payee is an employee of the federal body;

(*d*) that is paid or credited in respect of services rendered outside Canada by a payee who was not resident in Canada during the period in which the services were rendered; or

(*e*) that is paid or credited in respect of a program administered under the *Witness Protection Program Act* or any other similar program.

238. Reporting of Payments in respect of Construction Activities

(1) In this section, "construction activities" includes the erection, excavation, installation, alteration, modification, repair, improvement, demolition, destruction, dismantling or removal of all or any part of a building, structure, surface or sub-surface construction, or any similar property.

Tax Window Files: Requirement to file T5018 information returns, *June 10, 2013*, CRA Document No. 2012-0458651E5.

(2) Every person or partnership that pays or credits, in a reporting period, an amount in respect of goods or services rendered on their behalf in the course of construction activities shall make an information return in the prescribed form in respect of that amount, if the person's or partnership's business income for that reporting period is derived primarily from those activities.

Forms: T5018 — Statement of Contract Payments.

(3) The reporting period may be either on a calendar year basis or a fiscal period basis. Once a period is chosen, it cannot be changed for subsequent years, unless the Minister authorizes it.

(4) The return shall be filed within six months after the end of the reporting period to which it pertains.

(5) Subsection (2) does not apply in respect of an amount

(*a*) all of which is paid or credited in the reporting period in respect of goods for sale or lease by the person or partnership;

(*b*) to which section 212 of the Act applies; or

(*c*) that is paid or credited in respect of services rendered outside Canada by a person or partnership who was not resident in Canada during the period in which the services were rendered.

Part III
Annuities and Life Insurance Policies

300. Capital Element of Annuity Payments

(1) For the purposes of paragraphs 32.1(3)(*b*) and 60(*a*) of the Act, where an annuity is paid under a contract (other than an income-averaging annuity contract or an annuity contract purchased pursuant to a deferred profit sharing plan or pursuant to a plan referred to in subsection 147(15) of the Act as a "revoked plan") at a particular time, that part of the annuity payment determined in prescribed manner to be a return of capital is that proportion of a taxpayer's interest in the annuity payment that the adjusted purchase price of the taxpayer's interest in the contract at that particular time is of his interest, immediately before the commencement under the contract of payments to which paragraph 56(1)(*d*) of the Act applies, in the total of the payments

(*a*) to be made under the contract, in the case of a contract for a term of years certain; or

(*b*) expected to be made under the contract, in the case of a contract under which the continuation of the payments depends in whole or in part on the survival of an individual.

Interpretation Bulletins: *Secondary* — IT-500R Registered retirement savings plans — Death of annuitant.

(1.1) For the purposes of subsections (1) and (2), "annuity payment" does not include any portion of a payment under a contract the amount of which cannot be reasonably determined immediately before the commencement of payments under the contract except where the payment of such portion cannot be so determined because the continuation of the annuity payments under the contract depends in whole or in part on the survival of an individual.

(2) For the purposes of this section, if the continuance of the annuity payments under a contract depends in whole or in part on the survival of an individual,

(*a*) the total of the payments expected to be made under the contract is

(i) in the case of a contract that provides for equal payments and does not provide for a guaranteed period of payment, to be equal to the product obtained by multiplying the total of the annuity payments expected to be received throughout a year under the contract by the complete expectations of life determined

(A) using the table of mortality known as the *1971 Individual Annuity Mortality Table* as published in Volume XXIII of the *Transactions of the Society of Actuaries*, if the annuity rates in respect of the contract were fixed and determined before 2017, and

(I) annuity payments under the contract commenced before 2017, or

(II) on December 31, 2016, the contract would be a prescribed annuity contract if paragraph 304(1)(*c*) were read without reference to its subparagraph (i) and the contract cannot be terminated other than on the death of an individual on whose life payments under the contract are contingent, and

(B) in any other case, using the table of mortality known as the *Annuity 2000 Basic Table* as published in the *Transactions of Society of Actuaries, 1995-96 Reports*, and

(ii) in any other case, to be calculated in accordance with subparagraph (i) with such modifications as the circumstances may require;

(*b*) the age of the individual on any particular date as of which a calculation is being made is

(i) if the life insured was determined by the insurer that issued the contract to be a substandard life at the time the contract was issued and the *Annuity 2000 Basic Table* as published in the *Transactions of Society of Actuaries, 1995-96 Reports* applies to determine the total of the payments expected to be made under the contract, the age that is equal to the total of the age used for the purpose of determining the annuity rate under the policy at the date of issue of the contract and the number determined by subtracting the calendar year in which the contract was issued from the calendar year in which the particular date occurs, and

(ii) in any other case, determined by subtracting the calendar year of the individual's birth from the calendar year in which the particular date occurs; and

(*c*) if, in the event of the death of the individual before the annual payments total a stated sum, the contract provides that the unpaid balance of the stated sum is to be paid in a lump sum or instalments, then for the purpose of determining the expected term of the contract, the contract is deemed to provide for the continuance of the payments under the contract for a minimum term certain equal to the nearest whole number of years required to complete the payment of the stated sum.

History: S. 300(2) was replaced by S.C. 2014, c. 39, s. 79, in force December 16, 2014, and formerly read:

(2) For the purposes of this section,

(*a*) where the continuance of the annuity payments under any contract depends in whole or in part on the survival of an individual, the total of the payments expected to be made under the contract

(i) shall, in the case of a contract that provides for equal payments and does not provide for a guaranteed period of payment, be equal to the product obtained by multiplying the aggregate of the annuity payments expected to be received throughout a year under the contract by the complete expectations of life using the table of mortality known as the *1971 Individual Annuity Mortality Table* as published in Volume XXIII of the *Transactions of the Society of Actuaries*, or

(ii) shall, in any other case, be calculated in accordance with subparagraph (i) with such modifications as the circumstances may require;

(*b*) subject to subsections (3) and (4), "adjusted purchase price" of a taxpayer's interest in an annuity contract at a particular time means the amount that would be determined at that time in respect of that interest under the definition "adjusted cost basis" in subsection 148(9) of the Act if the formula in that definition were read without reference to variable K;

(*c*) where the continuance of the annual payments under any contract depends on the survival of a person, the age of that person on any date as of which a calculation is being made shall be determined by subtracting the calendar year of his birth from the calendar year in which such date occurs; and

(*d*) where the continuance of the annual payments under any contract depends on the survival of a person, and where, in the event of the death of that person before the annual payments aggregate a stated sum, the contract provides that the unpaid balance of the stated sum shall be paid, either in a lump sum or instalments, then, for the purpose of determining the expected term of the contract, the contract shall be

Regulations

deemed to provide for the continuance of the payments thereunder for a minimum term certain equal to the nearest integral number of years required to complete the payment of the stated sum.

(*e*) (Revoked.)

S. 300(2), the portion before paragraph (*a*) was replaced by P.C. 2011-936, SOR/2011-188, dated September 22, 2011, published in the *Canada Gazette* October 12, 2011, applicable with respect to annuity contracts and life insurance policies last acquired after 1989. S. 300(2), the portion before paragraph (*a*) formerly read:

(2) For the purposes of this section and section 305,

S. 300(2)(*b*) was replaced by P.C. 2011-936, SOR/2011-188, dated September 22, 2011, published in the *Canada Gazette* October 12, 2011, applicable after February 1994. S. 300(2)(*b*) formerly read:

(*b*) except as provided in subsections (3) and (4), "adjusted purchase price" of a taxpayer's interest in an annuity contract at a particular time means the amount that would be determined at that time in respect of that interest under paragraph 148(9)(*a*) [subsection 148(9) "adjusted cost basis"] of the Act if that paragraph were read without reference to subparagraph (viii) [subsection 148(9) "adjusted cost basis", item K] thereof;

Interpretation Bulletins: *Secondary* — IT-500R Registered retirement savings plans — Death of annuitant.

(3) Where

(*a*) an annuity contract is a life annuity contract entered into before November 17, 1978 under which the annuity payments commence on the death of an individual,

(*a*.1) (Revoked.)

(*b*) an annuity contract (other than an annuity contract described in paragraph (*a*)) is

(i) a life annuity contract entered into before October 23, 1968, or

(ii) any other annuity contract entered into before January 4, 1968,

under which the annuity payments commence

(iii) on the expiration of a term of years, and

(iv) before the later of January 1, 1970 and the tax anniversary date of the annuity contract,

the adjusted purchase price of a taxpayer's interest in the annuity contract shall be

(*c*) the lump sum, if any, that the person entitled to the annuity payments might have accepted in lieu thereof, at the date the annuity payments commence;

(*d*) if no lump sum described in paragraph (*c*) is provided for in the contract, the sum ascertainable from the contract as the present value of the annuity at the date the annuity payments commence; and

(*e*) if no lump sum described in paragraph (*c*) is provided for in the contract and no sum is ascertainable under paragraph (*d*),

(i) in the case of a contract issued under the *Government Annuities Act*, the premiums paid, accumulated with interest at the rate of four per cent per annum to the date the annuity payments commence, and

(ii) in the case of any other contract, the present value of the annuity payments at the date on which payments under the contract commence, computed by applying

(A) a rate of interest of four per cent per annum where the payments commence before 1972 and $5^1/_2$ per cent per annum where the payments commence after 1971, and

(B) the provisions of subsection (2) where the payments depend on the survival of a person.

Interpretation Bulletins: *Secondary* — IT-500R Registered retirement savings plans — Death of annuitant.

(4) Where an annuity contract would be described in paragraph (3)(*b*) if the reference in subparagraph (iv) thereof to "before the later of" were read as a reference to "on or after the later of", the adjusted purchase price of a taxpayer's interest in the annuity contract at a particular time shall be the greater of

(*a*) the aggregate of

(i) the amount that would be determined in respect of that interest under paragraph (3)(*c*), (*d*) or (*e*), as the case may be, if the date referred to therein was the tax anniversary date of the contract and not the date the annuity payments commence, and

(ii) the adjusted purchase price that would be determined in respect of that interest if the expression "before that time" in the descriptions of A, B, C, D and H in the definition "adjusted cost basis" in subsection 148(9) of the Act were read as "before that time and after the tax anniversary date"; and

(*b*) the amount determined under paragraph (2)(*b*) in respect of that interest.

History: S. 300(4)(*a*)(ii) was replaced by P.C. 2011-936, SOR/2011-188, dated September 22, 2011, published in the *Canada Gazette* October 12, 2011, applicable after February 1994. S. 300(4)(*a*)(ii) formerly read:

(ii) the adjusted purchase price that would be determined in respect of that interest if the words "and after the tax anniversary date" were inserted in each of subparagraphs 148(9)(*a*)(i) to (iii.1) and (vi) [subsection 148(9) "adjusted cost basis", items A to D and H] of the Act immediately following the words "before that time" in each of those subparagraphs; and

Interpretation Bulletins: *Secondary* — IT-500R Registered retirement savings plans — Death of annuitant.

301. Life Annuity Contracts

(1) For the purposes of this Part and section 148 of the Act, "life annuity contract" means a contract under which a person authorized under the laws of Canada or of a province to carry on in Canada an annuities business agrees to make annuity payments to one person or partnership (in this section referred to as "the annuitant") or jointly to two or more annuitants, which annuity payments are, under the terms of the contract,

(*a*) to be paid annually or at more frequent periodic intervals;

(*b*) to commence on a specified day; and

(*c*) to continue throughout the lifetime of one or more individuals (each of whom is referred to in this section as "the identified individual").

History: S. 301(1) was replaced by P.C. 2011-936, SOR/2011-188, dated September 22, 2011, published in the *Canada Gazette* October 12, 2011, applicable to taxation years that end after 1996, and for those taxation years the adjusted cost basis of a policy holder's interest in a life insurance policy is to be determined as if s. 301(1) also applied to taxation years that begin after 1980. S. 301(1) formerly read:

(1) For the purposes of this Part and section 148 of the Act, "life annuity contract" means any contract under which a person authorized under the laws of Canada or a province to carry on in Canada an annuities business agrees to make annuity payments to an individual (in this section referred to as "the annuitant") or jointly to two or more individuals (each of whom is referred to as "the annuitant" in this section), which payments are, by the terms of the contract,

(*a*) to be paid annually or at more frequent periodic intervals;

(*b*) to commence on a specified day; and

(*c*) to continue throughout the lifetime of the annuitant or one or more of the annuitants.

(2) For the purposes of subsection (1), a contract shall not fail to be a life annuity contract by reason that (*a*) the contract provides that the annuity payments may be assigned by the annuitant or owner;

(*b*) the contract provides for annuity payments to be made for a period ending on the death of the identified individual or for a specified period of not less than 10 years, whichever is the lesser;

(*c*) the contract provides for annuity payments to be made for a specified period or throughout the lifetime of the identified individual, whichever is longer, to the annuitant and, if the specified period is longer, to a specified person after that period;

(*d*) the contract provides, in addition to the annuity payments to be made throughout the lifetime of the identified individual, for a payment to be made on the death of the identified individual;

(*e*) the contract provides that the date

(i) on which the annuity payments commence, or

(ii) on which the contract holder becomes entitled to proceeds of the disposition,

may be changed with respect to the whole contract or any portion thereof at the option of the annuitant or owner; or

(*f*) the contract provides that all or a portion of the proceeds payable at any particular time under the contract may be received in the form of an annuity contract other than a life annuity contract.

History: S. 301(2)(*b*) to (*d*) were replaced by P.C. 2011-936, SOR/2011-188, dated September 22, 2011, published in the *Canada Gazette* October 12, 2011, applicable to taxation years that end after 1996, and for those taxation years the adjusted cost basis of a policy holder's interest in a life insurance policy is to be determined as if s. 301(2)(*b*) to (*d*) also applied to taxation years that begin after 1980. S. 301(2)(*b*) to (*d*) formerly read:

(*b*) the contract provides for annuity payments to be made for a period ending upon the death of the annuitant or for a specified period of not less than 10 years, whichever is the lesser;

(*c*) the contract provides for annuity payments to be made for a specified period or throughout the lifetime of the annuitant, whichever is longer, to the annuitant and thereafter, if the specified period is the longer, to a specified person;

(*d*) the contract provides, in addition to the annuity payments to be made throughout the lifetime of the annuitant, for a payment to be made upon the annuitant's death;

302. (Repealed.)

303. Life Annuity Contracts

(1) Where in a taxation year the rights of a holder under an annuity contract cease upon termination or cancellation of the contract and

(*a*) the aggregate of all amounts, each of which is an amount in respect of the contract that was included in computing the income of the holder for the year or any previous taxation year by virtue of subsection 12(3) of the Act

exceeds the aggregate of

(*b*) such proportion of the amount determined under paragraph (*a*) that the annuity payments made under the contract before the rights of the holder have ceased is of the total of the payments expected to be made under the contract, and

(*c*) the aggregate of all amounts, each of which is an amount in respect of the contract that was deductible in computing the income of the holder for the year or any previous year by virtue of subsection (2),

the amount of such excess may be deducted by the holder under subsection 20(19) of the Act in computing his income for the year.

(2) For the purposes of subsection 20(19) of the Act, where an annuity contract was acquired after December 19, 1980 and annuity payments under the contract commenced before 1982, the amount that may be deducted by a holder under that subsection in respect of an annuity contract for a taxation year is that proportion of

(*a*) the aggregate of all amounts, each of which is an amount that was included in computing the income of the holder for any previous taxation year by virtue of subsection 12(3) of the Act in respect of the contract

that

(*b*) the aggregate of all annuity payments received by the holder in the year in respect of the contract

is of

(*c*) the total of the payments determined under paragraph 300(1)(*a*) or (*b*) in respect of the holder's interest in the contract.

304. Prescribed Annuity Contracts

(1) For the purposes of this Part and of subsections 12.2(1) and 20(20) and paragraph 148(2)(*b*) of the Act, "prescribed annuity contract", for a taxation year, means

(*a*) an annuity contract that is, or is issued pursuant to, an arrangement described in any of paragraphs 148(1)(*a*) to (*b.3*) and (*d*) of the Act;

(*b*) an annuity contract described in paragraph 148(1)(*c*) or (*e*) of the Act; and

(*c*) an annuity contract

(i) under which annuity payments have commenced in the taxation year or a preceding taxation year,

(ii) issued by any one of the following (referred to in this section as the "issuer"):

(A) a life insurance corporation,

(B) a registered charity,

(C) a corporation referred to in any of paragraphs (*a*) to (*c*) of the definition "specified financial institution" in subsection 248(1) of the Act,

(D) a corporation referred to in subparagraph (*b*)(ii) of the definition "retirement savings plan" in subsection 146(1) of the Act, and

(E) a corporation (other than a mutual fund corporation or a mortgage investment corporation) the principal business of which is the making of loans,

(iii) each holder of which

(A) is

(I) an individual other than a trust,

(II) a trust described in paragraph 104(4)(*a*) of the Act (in this paragraph referred to as a "specified trust"),

(III) a trust that is a qualified disability trust (as defined in subsection 122(3) of the Act) for the taxation year in which the annuity is issued, or

(IV) if the annuity is issued before 2016, a trust that is a testamentary trust at the time the annuity is issued,

(B) is an annuitant under the contract, and

(C) throughout the taxation year, dealt at arm's length with the issuer,

Regulations

(iv) the terms and conditions of which require that, from the time the contract meets the requirements of this paragraph,

(A) all payments made out of the contract be equal annuity payments made at regular intervals but not less frequently than annually, subject to the holder's right to vary the frequency and quantum of payments to be made out of the contract in any taxation year without altering the present value at the beginning of the year of the total payments to be made in that year out of the contract,

(B) the annuity payments thereunder continue for a fixed term or

(I) if the holder is an individual (other than a trust), for the life of the first holder or until the day of the later of the death of the first holder and the death of any of the spouse, common-law partner, former spouse, former common-law partner, brothers and sisters (in this subparagraph referred to as "the survivor") of the first holder, or

(II) if the holder is a trust

1. in the case of a specified trust, for the life of an individual referred to in paragraph 104(4)(*a*) of the Act who is entitled to receive all of the income of the trust that arose before the individual's death, or, in the case of a joint spousal or common-law partner trust, until the day of the later of the death of the individual and the death of the beneficiary under the trust who is the individual's spouse or common-law partner,

2. in the case of a qualified disability trust, for the life of an individual who is an electing beneficiary (as defined in subsection 122(3) of the Act) of the trust for the taxation year in which the annuity is issued,

3. in the case of a trust (other than a qualified disability trust or specified trust) where the annuity is issued before October 24, 2012, for the life of an individual who is entitled to receive income from the trust, and

4. in the case of a trust (other than a qualified disability trust or specified trust) where the annuity is issued after October 23, 2012, for the life of an individual who was entitled when the contract was first held to receive all of the trust's income that is from an amount received by the trust on or before the individual's death as a payment under the annuity,

(C) if the annuity payments are to be made over a term that is guaranteed or fixed, the guaranteed or fixed term not exceed 91 years minus the age, when the contract was first held, in whole years of the following individual:

(I) if the holder is not a trust, the individual who is

1. in the case of a joint and last survivor annuity, the younger of the first holder and the survivor,

2. in the case of a contract that is held jointly, the younger of the first holders, and

3. in any other case, the first holder,

(II) if the holder is a specified trust, the individual who is

1. in the case of a joint and last survivor annuity held by a joint spousal or common-law partner trust, the younger of the individuals referred to in paragraph 104(4)(*a*) of the Act who are in combination entitled to receive all of the income of the trust that arose before the later of their deaths, and

2. in the case of an annuity that is not a joint and last survivor annuity, the individual referred to in paragraph 104(4)(*a*) of the Act who is entitled to receive all of the income of the trust that arose before the individual's death,

(III) if the holder is a qualified disability trust, an individual who is an electing beneficiary of the trust for the taxation year in which the annuity is issued, and

(IV) if the holder is a trust (other than a qualified disability trust or specified trust) and the annuity is issued before 2016, the individual who was the youngest beneficiary under the trust when the contract was first held,

(D) no loans exist under the contract,

(E) the holder's rights under the contract not be disposed of otherwise than

(I) if the holder is an individual, on the holder's death,

(II) if the holder is a specified trust (other than a joint spousal or common-law partner trust), on the death of the individual referred to in paragraph 104(4)(*a*) of the Act who is entitled to receive all of the income of the trust that arose before the individual's death,

(III) if the holder is a specified trust that is a joint spousal or common-law partner trust, on the later of the deaths of the individuals referred to in paragraph 104(4)(*a*) of the Act who are in combination entitled to receive all of the income of the trust that arose before the later of their deaths, and

(IV) if the holder is a trust, other than a specified trust, and the contract is first held after October 2011, on the earlier of

1. the time at which the trust ceases to be a testamentary trust, and

2. the death of the individual referred to in subclause (B)(II) or (C)(III) or (IV), as the case may be, in respect of the trust, and

(F) no payments be made out of the contract other than as permitted by this section,

Regulations

(v) none of the terms and conditions of which provide for any recourse against the issuer for failure to make any payment under the contract, and

(vi) where annuity payments under the contract have commenced

(A) before 1987, in respect of which a holder thereof has notified the issuer in writing, before the end of the taxation year, that the contract is to be treated as a prescribed annuity contract,

(B) after 1986, in respect of which a holder thereof has not notified the issuer in writing, before the end of the taxation year in which the annuity payments under the contract commenced, that the contract is not to be treated as a prescribed annuity contract, or

(C) after 1986, in respect of which a holder thereof has notified the issuer in writing, before the end of the taxation year in which the annuity payments under the contract commenced, that the contract is not to be treated as a prescribed annuity contract and a holder thereof has rescinded the notification by so notifying the issuer in writing before the end of the taxation year.

History: S. 304(1)(*c*)(iii)(A) was replaced by S.C. 2014, c. 39, s. 80(1), applicable to the 2016 and subsequent taxation years, and formerly read:

(A) is an individual, other than a trust that is neither a trust described in paragraph 104(4)(*a*) of the Act (in this paragraph referred to as a "specified trust") nor a testamentary trust,

S. 304(1)(*c*)(iv)(B)(II)2 and 3 were replaced by S.C. 2014, c. 39, s. 80(2), applicable to the 2016 and subsequent taxation years, and formerly read:

2. in the case of a testamentary trust (other than a specified trust) where the annuity is issued before October 24, 2012, for the life of an individual who is entitled to receive income from the trust, and

3. in the case of any other testamentary trust other than a specified trust, for the life of an individual who was entitled when the contract was first held to receive all of the income of the trust that arose before the individual's death,

S. 304(1)(*c*)(iv)(B)(II)4 was added by S.C. 2014, c. 39, s. 80(2), applicable to the 2016 and subsequent taxation years.

S. 304(1)(*c*)(iv)(C)(III) was replaced by S.C. 2014, c. 39, s. 80(3), applicable to the 2016 and subsequent taxation years, and formerly read:

(III) if the holder is a testamentary trust other than a specified trust, the individual who was the youngest beneficiary under the trust when the contract was first held,

S. 304(1)(*c*)(iv)(C)(IV) was added by S.C. 2014, c. 39, s. 80(3), applicable to the 2016 and subsequent taxation years.

S. 304(1)(*c*)(iv)(E)(IV) was replaced by S.C. 2014, c. 39, s. 80(4), applicable to the 2016 and subsequent taxation years, and formerly read:

(IV) if the holder is a testamentary trust, other than a specified trust, and the contract was first held after October 2011, on the earlier of

1. the time at which the trust ceases to be a testamentary trust, and

2. the death of the individual referred to in subclause (B)(II) or (C)(III), as the case may be, in respect of the trust, and

S. 304(1)(*c*)(iv)(B)(II) was replaced by S.C. 2013, c. 34, s. 378(1), applicable to the 2000 and subsequent taxation years, except that with regard to a contract held by a trust created by a taxpayer at a particular time in 2000 for the benefit of another individual, subclause 304(1)(*c*)(iv)(B)(II) is to be read without reference to "or common-law partner", unless, because of an election made under section 144 of the *Modernization of Benefits and Obligations Act*, chapter 12 of the Statutes of Canada, 2000, sections 130 to 142 of that Act apply at the particular time to the taxpayer and the other individual.

S. 304(1)(*c*)(iv)(B)(II) formerly read:

(II) if the holder is a specified trust, for the life of the spouse or common-law partner who is entitled to receive the income of the trust,

S. 304(1)(*c*)(iv)(C) to (E) were replaced by S.C. 2013, c. 34, s. 378(2), applicable to the 2000 and subsequent taxation years, except that with regard to a contract held by a trust created by a taxpayer at a particular time in 2000 for the benefit of another individual, subclause 304(1)(*c*)(iv)(C)(II) is to be read without reference to "or common-law partner", unless, because of an election made under section 144 of the *Modernization of Benefits and Obligations Act*, chapter 12 of the Statutes of Canada, 2000, sections 130 to 142 of that Act apply at the particular time to the taxpayer and the other individual.

S. 304(1)(*c*)(iv)(C) to (E) formerly read:

(C) where the annuity payments are to be made over a term that is guaranteed or fixed, the guaranteed or fixed term not extend beyond the time at which

(I) in the case of a joint and last survivor annuity, the younger of the first holder and the survivor,

(II) if the holder is a specified trust, the spouse or common-law partner who is entitled to receive the income of the trust,

(III) if the holder is a testamentary trust other than a specified trust, the youngest beneficiary under the trust,

(IV) where the contract is held jointly, the younger of the first holders, or

(V) in any other case, the first holder,

would, if he survived, attain the age of 91 years,

(D) no loans exist under the contract and the holder's rights under the contract not be disposed of otherwise than on the holder's death or, if the holder is a specified trust, on the death of the spouse or common-law partner who is entitled to receive the income of the trust, and

(E) no payments be made out of the contract other than as permitted by this section,

S. 304(1)(*c*)(iv)(F) was added by S.C. 2013, c. 34, s. 378(2), applicable to the 2000 and subsequent taxation years.

S. 304(1)(*a*) was replaced by S.C. 2012, c. 31, s. 60(1), in force December 14, 2012, and formerly read:

(*a*) an annuity contract that is, or is issued pursuant to, an arrangement described in any of paragraphs 148(1)(*a*) to (*b.2*) and (*d*) of the Act;

S. 304(1), the portion before paragraph (*a*) was replaced by P.C. 2011-936, SOR/2011-188, dated September 22, 2011, published in the *Canada Gazette* October 12, 2011, applicable after February 18, 2011, except that the replacement of the references to subsections 12.2(1), (3) and (4) in subsection 304(1) the Regulations with the reference to subsection 12.2(1) that results from the enactment of the portion of s. 304(1) before paragraph (*a*) applies to life insurance policies last acquired after 1989. S. 304(1), the portion before paragraph (*a*) formerly read:

(1) For the purposes of this Part and subsections 12.2(1), (3) and (4) and paragraph 148(2)(*b*) of the Act, prescribed annuity contract for a taxation year means

S. 304(1)(*c*)(ii) was replaced by P.C. 2009-1212, SOR/2009-222, dated July 30, 2009, published in the *Canada Gazette* August 19, 2009, applicable after February 22, 1994. S. 304(1)(*c*)(ii) formerly read:

(ii) issued by a corporation described in any of paragraphs 39(5)(*b*) to (*d*) or clause 146(1)(*j*)(ii)(B) of the Act, a life insurance corporation, a registered charity or a corporation (other than a mutual fund corporation or a mortgage investment corporation) the principal business of which is the making of loans (which corporation or charity is in this section referred to as an "issuer"),

S. 304(1)(*a*) was replaced by S.C. 2009, c. 2, s. 90(1), applicable to annuity contracts issued after 2008. S. 304(1)(*a*) formerly read:

(*a*) an annuity contract purchased pursuant to a registered pension plan, a registered retirement savings plan, a deferred profit sharing plan or a plan referred to in subsection 147(15) of the Act as a revoked plan;

(2) Notwithstanding subsection (1), an annuity contract shall not fail to be a prescribed annuity contract by reason that

(*a*) where the contract provides for a joint and last survivor annuity or is held jointly, the terms and conditions thereof provide that there will be a decrease in the amount of the annuity payments to be made under the contract from the time of death of one of the annuitants thereunder;

(*b*) the terms and conditions thereof provide that where the holder thereof dies at or before the time he attains the age of 91 years, the contract will terminate and an amount will be paid out of the contract not exceeding the amount, if any, by which the total premiums paid under the contract exceeds the total annuity payments made under the contract;

(*c*) where the annuity payments are to be made over a term that is guaranteed or fixed, the terms and conditions thereof provide that as a consequence of the death of the holder thereof during the guaranteed or fixed term any payments that, but for the death of the holder, would be made during the term may be commuted into a single payment; or

(*d*) the terms and conditions thereof, as they read on December 1, 1982 and at all subsequent times, provide that the holder participates in the investment earnings of the issuer and that the amount of such participation is to be paid within 60 days after the end of the year in respect of which it is determined.

(3) For the purposes of this section, the annuitant under an annuity contract is deemed to be the holder of the contract where

(*a*) the contract is held by another person in trust for the annuitant; or

(*b*) the contract was acquired by the annuitant under a group term life insurance policy under which life insurance was effected on the life of another person in respect of, in the course of, or by virtue of the office or employment or former office or employment of that other person.

(4) In this section, "annuitant" under an annuity contract, at any time, means a person who, at that time, is entitled to receive annuity payments under the contract.

(5) For the purpose of this section, "spouse" and "former spouse" of a particular individual include another individual who is a party to a void or voidable marriage with the particular individual.

305. (Repealed.)

History: S. 305 and the heading before it were repealed by P.C. 2011-936, SOR/2011-188, dated September 22, 2011, published in the *Canada Gazette* October 12, 2011, applicable with respect to annuity contracts and life insurance policies last acquired after 1989. S. 305 formerly read:

Unallocated Income Accrued Before 1982

305.

(1) For the purposes of section 12.2 and paragraph 56(1)(*d*.1) of the Act, the amount at any time of "unallocated income accrued in respect of the interest before 1982, as determined in prescribed manner", in respect of a taxpayer's interest in an annuity contract (other than an interest last acquired after December 1, 1982) or in a life insurance policy referred to in subsection (3), means the amount, if any, by which

(*a*) the accumulating fund at December 31, 1981 in respect of the interest exceeds the aggregate of

(*b*) his adjusted cost basis (within the meaning assigned by paragraph 148(9)(*a*) [subsection 148(9) "adjusted cost basis"] of the Act) at December 31, 1981 in respect of the interest; and

(*c*) that proportion of the amount, if any, by which the amount determined under paragraph (*a*) exceeds the amount determined under paragraph (*b*) that

(i) the aggregate of all amounts each of which is the amount of an annuity payment received before that time in respect of the interest

is of

(ii) the taxpayer's interest, immediately before the commencement of payments under the contract, in the total of the annuity payments

(A) to be made under the contract, in the case of a contract for a term of years certain, or

(B) expected to be made under the contract, in the case of a contract under which the continuation of the payments depends in whole or in part on the survival of an individual.

(2) For the purposes of paragraph (1)(*c*), "annuity payment" does not include any portion of a payment under a contract the amount of which cannot be reasonably determined immediately before the commencement of payments under the contract except where such portion cannot be so determined because the continuation of the annuity payments under the contract depends in whole or in part on the survival of an individual.

(3) For the purposes of this section, an interest in an annuity contract to which subsection 12.2(9) of the Act applies shall be deemed to be a continuation of the interest in the life insurance policy in respect of which it was issued.

306. Exempt Policies

(1) For the purposes of this Part and subsection 12.2(11) of the Act, "exempt policy" at any time means a life insurance policy (other than an annuity contract, LIA policy or a deposit administration fund policy) in respect of which the following conditions are met at that time:

(*a*) if that time is a policy anniversary of the policy, the accumulating fund of the policy at that time (determined without regard to any policy loan) does not exceed the total of the accumulating funds at that time of the exemption test policies issued at or before that time in respect of the policy;

(*b*) assuming that the terms and conditions of the policy do not change from those in effect on the last policy anniversary of the policy at or before that time and, where necessary, making reasonable assumptions about all other factors (including, in the case of a participating life insurance policy within the meaning assigned by subsection 138(12) of the Act, the assumption that the amounts of dividends paid will be as shown in the dividend scale),

(i) if the policy is issued before 2017, it is reasonable to expect that the condition in paragraph (*a*) will be met on each policy anniversary of the policy on which the policy could remain in force after that time and before the endowment date of the exemption test policies issued in respect of the policy, and

(ii) if the policy is issued after 2016, it is reasonable to expect — without reference to any automatic adjustments under the policy that may be made after that time to ensure that the policy is an exempt policy and, where applicable, making projections using the most recent values that are used to calculate the accumulating fund in respect of the policy or in respect of each exemption test policy issued in respect of a coverage under the policy, as the case may be — that the condition in paragraph (*a*) will be met on the policy's next policy anniversary;

(*c*) the condition in paragraph (*a*) was met on all policy anniversaries of the policy before that time; and

(*d*) the condition in paragraph (*b*) was met at all times on and after the first policy anniversary of the policy and before that time.

History: S. 306(1)(*b*) was replaced by S.C. 2014, c. 39, s. 81(1), in force December 16, 2014, and formerly read:

(*b*) assuming that the terms and conditions of the policy do not change from those in effect on the last policy anniversary of the policy at or before that time and, where necessary, making reasonable assumptions about all other factors (including, in the case of a participating life insurance policy within the meaning assigned by subsection 138(12) of the Act, the assumption that the amounts of dividends paid will be as shown in the dividend scale), it is reasonable to expect that the condition in paragraph (*a*) will be met on each policy anniversary of the policy on which the policy could remain in force after that time and before the date determined under subparagraph (3)(*d*)(ii) with respect to the exemption test policies issued in respect of the policy;

S. 306(1), the portion before paragraph (*a*) was replaced by S.C. 2013, c. 40, s. 97(1), applicable to taxation years that end after March 20, 2013, and formerly read:

(1) For the purposes of this Part and subsection 12.2(11) of the Act, "exempt policy" at any time means a life insurance policy (other than an annuity contract or a deposit administration fund policy) in respect of which the following conditions are met at that time:

Related Sections: 148(11) Loss of grandfathering.

Interpretation Bulletins: *Secondary* — IT-87R2 Policyholders' income from life insurance policies.

(2) For the purposes of subsection (1), a life insurance policy that is an exempt policy on its first policy anniversary shall be deemed to have been an exempt policy from the time of its issue until that anniversary.

(3) For the purposes of this section and section 307,

(*a*) in the case of a life insurance policy issued before 2017, a separate exemption test policy is deemed, subject to subsection (7), to be issued in respect of the life insurance policy

(i) on the date of issue of the life insurance policy, and

(ii) on each policy anniversary of the life insurance policy on which

(A) the amount of the benefit on death under the life insurance policy

exceeds

(B) 108% of the amount of the benefit on death under the life insurance policy on the later of the life insurance policy's date of issue and the date of the life insurance policy's preceding policy anniversary, if any; and

(*b*) in the case of a life insurance policy issued after 2016, a separate exemption test policy is deemed, subject to subsection (7), to be issued in respect of each coverage under the life insurance policy

(i) on the date of

(A) issue of the life insurance policy, if the coverage is issued before the first policy anniversary of the life insurance policy,

(B) issue of the coverage, if the coverage is issued on a policy anniversary of the life insurance policy, or

(C) the life insurance policy's preceding policy anniversary, if the coverage is issued on any date that is after the policy's first policy anniversary and that is not a policy anniversary,

(ii) on each policy anniversary of the life insurance policy on which

(A) the amount of the benefit on death under the coverage on that policy anniversary

exceeds

(B) 108% of the amount of the benefit on death under the coverage, on the later of the coverage's date of issue and the date of the life insurance policy's preceding policy anniversary (or, if there is no preceding policy anniversary, the coverage's date of issue), and

(iii) on each policy anniversary of the life insurance policy — except to the extent that another exemption test policy has been issued on that date under this subparagraph in respect of a coverage under the life insurance policy — on which

(A) the amount by which the fund value benefit under the life insurance policy on that policy anniversary exceeds the fund value benefit under the life insurance policy on the life insurance policy's preceding policy anniversary (or, if there is no preceding policy anniversary, the date of issue of the policy)

exceeds

(B) the amount by which

(I) 8% of the amount of the benefit on death under the life insurance policy on the life insurance policy's preceding policy anniversary (or, if there is no preceding policy anniversary, the date of issue of the policy)

exceeds

(II) the total of all amounts each of which is, in respect of a coverage under the policy, the lesser of

1. the amount by which the amount of the benefit on death under the coverage on that policy anniversary exceeds the amount of the benefit on death under the coverage on the later of the coverage's date of issue and the date of the life insurance policy's preceding policy anniversary (or, if there is no preceding policy anniversary, the coverage's date of issue), and

2. 8% of the amount of the benefit on death under the coverage on the later of the coverage's date of issue and the date of the life insurance policy's preceding policy anniversary (or, if there is no preceding policy anniversary, the coverage's date of issue).

History: S. 306(3)(*a*), the portion before subparagraph (i) was replaced by S.C. 2017, c. 33, s. 85(1), in force December 14, 2017, and formerly read:

(*a*) in the case of a life insurance policy issued before 2017 or at a particular time determined under subsection 148(11) of the Act, a separate exemption test policy is deemed, subject to subsection (7), to be issued in respect of the life insurance policy

S. 306(3)(*a*)(ii), the portion before clause (A) was replaced by S.C. 2017, c. 33, s. 85(2), in force December 14, 2017, and formerly read:

(ii) on each policy anniversary (that ends before the particular time, if any, determined under subsection 148(11) of the Act in respect of the policy) of the life insurance policy on which

S. 306(3)(*b*), the portion before clause (i)(A) was replaced by S.C. 2017, c. 33, s. 85(3), in force December 14, 2017, and formerly read:

(*b*) in the case of a life insurance policy issued after 2016 (including, for greater certainty, at a particular time determined under subsection 148(11) of the Act in respect of the policy), a separate exemption test policy is deemed, subject to subsection (7), to be issued in respect of each coverage under the life insurance policy

(i) unless the particular time when the policy is issued is determined under subsection 148(11) of the Act and the coverage was issued before the particular time, on the date of

S. 306(3)(*b*)(ii), the portion before clause (A), was replaced by S.C. 2017, c. 33, s. 85(4), in force December 14, 2017, and formerly read:

(ii) on each policy anniversary of the life insurance policy (except that, if a particular time when the policy is issued has been determined under subsection 148(11) of the Act, only on a policy anniversary that ends at or after the particular time) on which

S. 306(3)(*b*)(iii), the portion before clause (A) was replaced by S.C. 2017, c. 33, s. 85(5), in force December 14, 2017, and formerly read:

(iii) on each policy anniversary of the life insurance policy (except that, if a particular time when the policy is issued has been determined under subsection 148(11) of the Act, only on a policy anniversary that ends at or after the particular time) — except to the extent that another exemption test policy has been issued on that date under this subparagraph in respect of a coverage under the life insurance policy — on which

S. 306(3) was replaced by S.C. 2014, c. 39, s. 81(2), in force December 16, 2014, and formerly read:

(3) For the purposes of this section and section 307, a separate exemption test policy shall be deemed to have been issued to a policyholder in respect of a life insurance policy

(*a*) on the date of issue of the life insurance policy, and

(*b*) on each policy anniversary of the life insurance policy where the amount of the benefit on death thereunder exceeds 108 per cent of the amount of the benefit on death thereunder on the later of the date of its issue and the date of its preceding anniversary, if any,

and, for the purpose of determining whether the accumulating fund of the life insurance policy on any particular policy anniversary meets the condition in paragraph (1)(*a*), each such exemption test policy shall be deemed

Regulations

(*c*) to have a benefit on death that is uniform throughout the term of the exemption test policy and equal to

(i) where the exemption test policy is the first such policy issued in respect of the life insurance policy, the amount on that policy anniversary of the benefit on death of the life insurance policy less the total of all amounts each of which is the amount on that policy anniversary of the benefit on death of another exemption test policy issued on or before that policy anniversary in respect of the life insurance policy, and

(ii) in any other case, the amount by which the benefit on death of the life insurance policy on the date the exemption test policy was issued exceeds 108 per cent of the amount of the benefit on death of the life insurance policy on the later of the date of issue of the life insurance policy and the date of its preceding policy anniversary, if any;

(*d*) to pay the amount of its benefit on death on the earlier of

(i) the date of death of the person whose life is insured under the life insurance policy, and

(ii) the later of

(A) ten years after the date of issue of the life insurance policy, and

(B) the date that the person whose life is insured would, if he survived, attain the age of 85 years; and

(*e*) to be a life insurance policy in Canada issued by a life insurer that carried on its life insurance business in Canada.

(4) For the purpose of determining whether the condition in paragraph (1)(*a*) is met on a policy anniversary of a life insurance policy, each exemption test policy issued in respect of the life insurance policy, or in respect of a coverage under the life insurance policy, is deemed

(*a*) to have a benefit on death that is uniform throughout the term of the exemption test policy and that, subject to subsection (5), is equal to

(i) if the date on which the exemption test policy is issued is determined by subparagraph (3)(*a*)(i), the amount by which the amount on that policy anniversary of the benefit on death under the life insurance policy exceeds the total of all amounts each of which is the amount, if any, on that policy anniversary of the benefit on death under another exemption test policy issued on or before that policy anniversary in respect of the life insurance policy,

(ii) if the date on which the exemption test policy is issued is determined by subparagraph (3)(*a*)(ii), the amount of the excess referred to in that subparagraph on that date in respect of the life insurance policy,

(iii) if the date on which the exemption test policy is issued is determined by subparagraph (3)(*b*)(i), the amount determined by the formula

$$A + B - C$$

where

A is the amount on that policy anniversary of the benefit on death under the coverage,

B is

(A) if the benefit on death under the life insurance policy includes a fund value benefit on that policy anniversary, the portion of the fund value benefit on that policy anniversary that is equal to the lesser of

(I) the maximum amount of the fund value benefit that could be payable on that policy anniversary if no other coverage were offered under the life insurance policy and the life insurance policy were an exempt policy, and

(II) the amount by which the fund value benefit on that policy anniversary exceeds the total of all amounts each of which is the portion of the fund value benefit allocated to other coverages under the life insurance policy, and

(B) in any other case, nil, and

C is the total of all amounts each of which is the amount, if any, on that policy anniversary of the benefit on death under another exemption test policy issued on or before that policy anniversary in respect of the coverage,

(iv) if the date on which the exemption test policy is issued is determined by subparagraph (3)(*b*)(ii), the amount of the excess referred to in that subparagraph on that date in respect of the coverage, and

(v) if the date on which the exemption test policy is issued is determined by subparagraph (3)(*b*)(iii), the lesser of

(A) the amount by which the amount determined under clause (3)(*b*)(iii)(A) exceeds the amount determined under clause (3)(*b*)(iii)(B) on that date in respect of the coverage, and

(B) the amount determined in respect of the coverage under subclause (A)(I) of the description of B in subparagraph (iii) on that date; and

(*b*) to pay the amount of its benefit on death on the earlier of

(i) if the life insurance policy

(A) is issued before 2017, the date of death of the individual whose life is insured under the life insurance policy, or

(B) is issued after 2016,

(I) if two or more lives are jointly insured under the coverage, the date at which the benefit would be payable as a result of the death of any of the lives, and

(II) in any other case, the date of death of the individual whose life is insured under the coverage, and

(ii) the exemption test policy's endowment date.

History: S. 306(4), the portion before, paragraph (*a*) was replaced by S.C. 2017, c. 33, s. 85(6), in force December 14, 2017, and formerly read:

(4) Subject to subsection (10), for the purpose of determining whether the condition in paragraph (1)(*a*) is met on a policy anniversary of a life insurance policy, each exemption test policy issued in respect of the life insurance policy, or in respect of a coverage under the life insurance policy, is deemed

S. 306(4) was replaced by S.C. 2014, c. 39, s. 81(2), in force December 16, 2014, and formerly read:

(4) Notwithstanding subsections (1) to (3),

(*a*) where at any particular time the amount of the benefit on death of a life insurance policy is reduced, an amount equal to such reduction (such amount is in this paragraph referred to as "the reduction") shall be applied at that time to reduce the amount of the benefit on death of exemption test policies issued before that time in respect of the life insurance policy (other than the exemption test policy issued in respect thereof pursuant to paragraph (3)(*a*)), in the order in which the dates of their issuance are proximate to the particular time, by an amount equal to the lesser of

(i) the portion, if any, of the reduction not applied to reduce the benefit on death of one or more other such exemption test policies, and

(ii) the amount, immediately before that time, of the benefit on death of the relevant exemption test policy;

(*b*) where on the tenth or on any subsequent policy anniversary of a life insurance policy, the accumulating fund thereof (computed without regard to any policy loan then outstanding in respect of the policy) exceeds 250 per cent of the accumulating fund thereof on its third preceding policy anniversary (computed without regard to any policy loan then outstanding in respect of the policy), each exemption test policy deemed by subsection (3) to have been issued before that time in respect of the life insurance policy shall be deemed to have been issued on the later of the date of that third preceding policy anniversary and the date on which it was deemed by subsection (3) to have been issued; and

(*c*) where at one or more times after December 1, 1982

(i) a prescribed premium has been paid by a taxpayer in respect of an interest in a life insurance policy (other than an annuity contract or a deposit administration fund policy) last acquired on or before that date, or

(ii) an interest in a life insurance policy (other than an annuity contract or a deposit administration fund policy) issued on or before that date has been acquired by a taxpayer from the person who held the interest continuously since that date,

the policy shall be deemed to have been an exempt policy from the date of its issue until the earliest of those times that occurred after December 1, 1982; and

(*d*) a life insurance policy that ceases to be an exempt policy (other than by reason of its conversion into an annuity contract) on a policy anniversary shall be deemed to be an exempt policy on that anniversary

(i) if, had that anniversary occurred 60 days after the date on which it did in fact occur, the policy would have been an exempt policy on that later date, or

(ii) if the person whose life is insured under the policy dies on that anniversary or within 60 days thereafter.

(5) For the purpose of determining the amount of a benefit on death under an exemption test policy,

(*a*) if the exemption test policy is issued in respect of a life insurance policy issued before 2017 and at any time the amount of a benefit on death under the life insurance policy is reduced, a particular amount that is equal to the reduction is to be applied at that time to reduce the amount of the benefit on death under each exemption test policy issued before that time in respect of the life insurance policy (other than the exemption test policy the date of issue of which is determined under subparagraph (3)(*a*)(i)) in the order in which the dates of their issuance are proximate to that time, by an amount equal to the lesser of

(i) the portion, if any, of the particular amount not applied to reduce the benefit on death under one or more other such exemption test policies, and

(ii) the amount, immediately before that time, of the benefit on death under the relevant exemption test policy; and

(*b*) if the exemption test policy is issued in respect of a coverage under a life insurance policy issued after 2016 and at any time there is a particular reduction in the amount of a benefit on death under the coverage, or the portion, if any, of the fund value benefit referred to in clause (A) of the description of B in subparagraph (4)(*a*)(iii) in respect of the coverage, the amount of the benefit on death under each exemption test policy issued before that time in respect of the coverage (other than the exemption test policy the date of issue of which is determined under subparagraph (3)(*b*)(i)) is reduced at that time by an amount equal to the least of

(i) the particular reduction,

(ii) the amount, immediately before that time, of the benefit on death under the relevant exemption test policy, and

(iii) the portion, if any, of the particular reduction not applied to reduce the benefit on death under one or more other such exemption test policies issued on or after the date of issue of the relevant exemption test policy.

History: S. 306(5), the portion before paragraph (*a*) was replaced by S.C. 2017, c. 33, s. 85(7), in force December 14, 2017, and formerly read:

(5) Subject to subsection (10), for the purpose of determining the amount of a benefit on death under an exemption test policy,

S. 306(5) was added by S.C. 2014, c. 39, s. 81(2), in force December 16, 2014.

(6) Subsection (7) applies at any time in respect of a life insurance policy if

(*a*) that time is on its tenth or a later policy anniversary;

(*b*) the accumulating fund (computed without regard to any amount payable in respect of a policy loan) in respect of the policy at that time exceeds 250% of

(i) in the case where the particular time at which the policy is issued is determined under subsection 148(11) of the Act and the policy's third preceding policy anniversary is before the particular time, the accumulating fund (computed without regard to any amount payable in respect of a policy loan and as though the policy were issued after 2016) in respect of the policy on that third preceding policy anniversary, and

(ii) in any other case, the accumulating fund (computed without regard to any amount payable in respect of a policy loan) in respect of the policy on its third preceding policy anniversary; and

(*c*) where that time is after 2016,

(i) the accumulating fund (computed without regard to any amount payable in respect of a policy loan) in respect of the policy at that time exceeds the total of all amounts each of which is

(A) if the policy is issued before 2017, 3/20 of the accumulating fund, at that time, in respect of an exemption test policy issued in respect of the policy, and

(B) if the policy is issued after 2016, 3/8 of the accumulating fund, at that time, in respect of an exemption test policy issued in respect of a coverage under the policy, and

(ii) subsection (7) did not apply on any of the policy's six preceding policy anniversaries.

History: S. 306(6)(*b*) was replaced by S.C. 2017, c. 33, s. 85(8), in force December 14, 2017, and formerly read:

(*b*) the accumulating fund (computed without regard to any amount payable in respect of a policy loan) in respect of the policy at that time exceeds 250% of the accumulating fund (computed without regard to any amount payable in respect of a policy loan) in respect of the policy on its third preceding policy anniversary; and

S. 306(6) was added by S.C. 2014, c. 39, s. 81(2), in force December 16, 2014.

(7) If this subsection applies at any time in respect of a life insurance policy, each exemption test policy issued before that time in respect of the life insurance policy is at and after that time deemed to be issued (except for purposes of this subsection, paragraph (4)(*a*) and subsection (5))

(*a*) on the later of

(i) the date of the third preceding policy anniversary described in paragraph (6)(*b*) in respect of the policy, and

(ii) the date on which it was deemed by subsection (3) or (10), as the case may be, to be issued (determined immediately before that time); and

(*b*) not at any other time.

History: S. 306(7)(*a*)(ii) was replaced by S.C. 2017, c. 33, s. 85(9), in force December 14, 2017, and formerly read:

Regulations

(ii) the date on which it was deemed by subsection (3) to be issued (determined immediately before that time); and

S. 306(7) was added by S.C. 2014, c. 39, s. 81(2), in force December 16, 2014.

(8) A life insurance policy that would, in the absence of this subsection, cease (other than by reason of its conversion into an annuity contract) on a policy anniversary of the policy to be an exempt policy is deemed to be an exempt policy on that policy anniversary if

(*a*) had that policy anniversary occurred on the particular day that is 60 days after that policy anniversary, the policy would have been an exempt policy on the particular day; or

(*b*) the person whose life is insured under the policy dies on that policy anniversary or within 60 days after that policy anniversary.

History: S. 306(8) was added by S.C. 2014, c. 39, s. 81(2), in force December 16, 2014.

(9) A life insurance policy (other than an annuity contract or deposit administration fund policy) issued before December 2, 1982 is deemed to be an exempt policy at all times from the date of its issue until the first time after December 1, 1982 at which

(*a*) a prescribed premium is paid by a taxpayer in respect of an interest, last acquired before December 2, 1982, in the policy; or

(*b*) an interest in the policy is acquired by a taxpayer from the person who held the interest continuously since December 1, 1982.

History: S. 306(9) was added by S.C. 2014, c. 39, s. 81(2), in force December 16, 2014.

(10) Notwithstanding subsections (3) and (4), if a life insurance policy is issued for any purpose at a particular time determined under subsection 148(11) of the Act, then for the purposes of applying this section (other than this subsection and subsection (9)) and section 307 in respect of the life insurance policy at and after the particular time,

(*a*) in respect of each coverage issued before the particular time under the life insurance policy, a separate exemption test policy is deemed to be issued in respect of a coverage under the life insurance policy

(i) on the date of issue of the life insurance policy, and

(ii) on each policy anniversary that ends before the particular time of the life insurance policy on which

(A) the amount of the benefit on death under the life insurance policy

exceeds

(B) 108% of the amount of the benefit on death under the life insurance policy on the later of the life insurance policy's date of issue and the date of the life insurance policy's preceding policy anniversary, if any;

(*b*) in respect of each coverage issued before the particular time under the life insurance policy, subsection (3) does not apply to deem an exemption test policy to be issued in respect of the policy, or in respect of a coverage under the policy, at any time before the particular time;

(*c*) in respect of each exemption test policy the date of issuance of which is determined under subparagraph (*a*)(i), the references in subparagraph (4)(*a*)(iii) and paragraph (5)(*b*) to "subparagraph (3)(*b*)(i)" are to be read as references to "subparagraph (10)(*a*)(i)";

(*d*) in respect of each exemption test policy the date of issuance of which is determined under subparagraph (*a*)(ii), subparagraph (4)(*a*)(iv) is to be read as follows:

(iv) if the date on which the exemption test policy is issued is determined by subparagraph (10)(*a*)(ii) at a time before a particular time, the portion of the amount - that amount being the amount that would be determined, at the time immediately before the particular time, under subparagraph (*a*)(ii), if the exemption test policy were issued in respect of the policy on the same date as the date determined for it under subparagraph (10)(*a*)(ii) - that can be reasonably allocated to the coverage in the circumstances (and for these purposes, an allocation is considered not to be reasonable if the total of the amounts determined for A and B in subparagraph (*a*)(iii) is less than the amount determined for C in that subparagraph in respect of the exemption test policy the date of issuance of which is determined under subparagraph (10)(*a*)(i) in respect of the coverage), and

and

(*e*) in applying paragraph (5)(*b*), the reference in that paragraph to "any time" is to be read as "any time at or after the particular time referred to in subsection (10) in respect of the life insurance policy".

History: S. 306(10) was replaced by S.C. 2017, c. 33, s. 85(10), in force December 14, 2017, and formerly read:

(10) If a particular time when a life insurance policy is issued has been determined under subsection 148(11) of the Act, in applying subsections (4) and (5) at or after the particular time to an exemption test policy issued before the particular time in respect of the policy,

(*a*) subparagraphs (4)(*a*)(iii) and (iv), and not subparagraph (4)(*a*)(i) or (ii), apply to the exemption test policy; and

(*b*) for greater certainty, paragraph (5)(*b*), and not paragraph (5)(*a*), applies to the exemption test policy.

S. 306(10) was added by S.C. 2014, c. 39, s. 81(2), in force December 16, 2014.

307. Accumulating Funds

(1) For the purposes of this Part and sections 12.2 and 148 of the Act, "accumulating fund", at any particular time, means

(*a*) in respect of a taxpayer's interest in an annuity contract (other than a contract issued by a life insurer), the amount that is the greater of

(i) the amount, if any, by which the cash surrender value of the taxpayer's interest at that time exceeds the amount payable, if any, in respect of a loan outstanding at that time made under the contract in respect of the interest, and

(ii) the amount, if any, by which

(A) the present value at that time of future payments to be made out of the contract in respect of the taxpayer's interest

exceeds

(B) the total of

(I) the present value at that time of future premiums to be paid under the contract in respect of the taxpayer's interest, and

(II) the amount payable, if any, in respect of a loan outstanding at that time, made under the contract in respect of the taxpayer's interest;

(*b*) in respect of a taxpayer's interest in a life insurance policy (other than an exemption test policy or an annuity contract to which paragraph (1)(*a*) applies), the product obtained when,

(i) where the policy is not a deposit administration fund policy and the particular time is immediately after the death of any person on whose life the life insurance policy is issued or effected, the aggregate of the maximum amounts that could be determined by the life insurer immediately before the death in respect of the policy under paragraph 1401(1)(*c*) and subparagraph 1401(1)(*d*)(i) if the mortality rates used were adjusted to reflect the assumption that the death would occur at the time and in the manner that it did occur, and

(ii) in any other case, the maximum amount that could be determined at that particular time by the life insurer under paragraph 1401(1)(*a*), computed as though there were only one deposit administration fund policy, or under paragraph 1401(1)(*c*), as the case may be, in respect of the policy

is multiplied by

(iii) the taxpayer's proportionate interest in the policy; and

(*c*) in respect of an exemption test policy,

(i) if the particular time is during the exemption test policy's pay period, the amount determined by the formula

$$A \times B/C$$

where

A is the amount that would be determined under subparagraph (ii) in respect of the exemption test policy

(A) if the exemption test policy's pay period is determined by subparagraph (*b*)(i) or (ii) of the definition "pay period" in section 310, on the first policy anniversary that is on or after the day on which the individual whose life is insured would, if the individual survived, attain the age of 105 years, as defined under the terms of the policy, and

(B) in any other case, on the exemption test policy's policy anniversary represented by the adjectival form of the number of years in its pay period,

B is the number of years since the exemption test policy was issued, and

C is the number of years in the exemption test policy's pay period,

(ii) if the particular time is after the exemption test policy's pay period and before its endowment date, the amount that is the present value at the particular time of the future benefit on death under the exemption test policy, and

(iii) if the particular time is on or after the exemption test policy's endowment date and the relevant life insurance policy is issued after 2016, the amount that is the benefit on death under the exemption test policy at the particular time.

History: S. 307(1), the portion before paragraph (*b*) was replaced by S.C. 2014, c. 39, s. 82(1), in force December 16, 2014, and formerly read:

(1) For the purposes of this Part and sections 12.2 and 148 of the Act, "accumulating fund", at any particular time, means,

(*a*) in respect of a taxpayer's interest in an annuity contract (other than a contract issued by a life insurer), the amount that is the greater of

(i) the amount, if any, by which the cash surrender value of his interest at that time exceeds the amount payable, if any, in respect of a loan outstanding at that time made under the contract in respect of the interest, and

(ii) the amount, if any, by which

(A) the present value at that time of future payments to be made out of the contract in respect of his interest

exceeds the aggregate of

(B) the present value at that time of future premiums to be paid under the contract in respect of his interest, and

(C) the amount payable, if any, in respect of a loan outstanding at that time, made under the contract in respect of his interest;

S. 307(1), the portion after subparagraph (*b*)(ii) was replaced by S.C. 2014, c. 39, s. 82(2), in force December 16, 2014, and formerly read:

is multiplied by

(iii) the taxpayer's proportionate interest in the policy,

assuming for the purposes of this paragraph that the life insurer carried on its life insurance business in Canada, its taxation year ended at the particular time and the policy was a life insurance policy in Canada; and

(*c*) in respect of an exemption test policy,

(i) where the policy was issued at least 20 years before the particular time, the amount that would be determined at that particular time by the life insurer under clause 1401(1)(*c*)(ii)(A) in respect of the policy if the insurer's taxation year ended at that particular time, and

(ii) in any other case, the product obtained when the amount that would be determined under subparagraph (i) in respect of the policy on its twentieth policy anniversary is multiplied by the quotient obtained when the number of years since the policy was issued is divided by 20.

S. 307(1), the portion before paragraph (*a*) was replaced by P.C. 2011-936, SOR/2011-188, dated September 22, 2011, published in the *Canada Gazette* October 12, 2011, applicable with respect to annuity contracts and life insurance policies last acquired after 1989. S. 307(1), the portion before paragraph (*a*) formerly read:

(1) For the purposes of this Part and section 12.2, paragraph 56(1)(*d*.1) and section 148 of the Act, "accumulating fund" at any particular time means,

(2) For the purposes of subsection (1), when computing the accumulating fund in respect of

(*a*) an interest described in paragraph (1)(*a*), the amounts determined under clauses (1)(*a*)(ii)(A) and (B) are to be computed using,

(i) where an interest rate for a period used by the issuer when the contract was issued in determining the terms of the contract was less than any rate so used for a subsequent period, the single rate that would, if it applied for each period, have produced the same terms, and

(ii) in any other case, the rates used by the issuer when the contract was issued in determining the terms of the contract;

(*b*) an interest described in paragraph (1)(*b*) in respect of a life insurance policy issued before 2017 or an annuity contract, if an interest rate used for a period by a life insurer in computing the relevant amounts in paragraph 1403(1)(*a*) or (*b*) is determined under paragraph 1403(1)(*c*), (*d*) or (*e*), as the case may be, and that rate is less than an interest rate so determined for a subsequent period, the single rate that could, if it applied for each period, have been used in determining the premiums for the policy is to be used;

(*c*) an exemption test policy issued in respect of a life insurance policy issued before 2017,

Regulations

(i) the rates of interest and mortality used and the age of the person whose life is insured shall be the same as those used in computing the amounts described in paragraph 1403(1)(*a*) or (*b*) in respect of the life insurance policy in respect of which the exemption test policy was issued except that

(A) where the life insurance policy is one to which paragraph 1403(1)(*e*) applies and the amount determined under subparagraph 1401(1)(*c*)(i) in respect of that policy is greater than the amount determined under subparagraph 1401(1)(*c*)(ii) in respect thereof, the rates of interest and mortality used may be those used in computing the cash surrender values of that policy, and

(B) where an interest rate for a period otherwise determined under this subparagraph in respect of that interest is less than an interest rate so determined for a subsequent period, the single rate that could, if it applied for each period, have been used in determining the premiums for the life insurance policy shall be used, and

(ii) notwithstanding subparagraph (i),

(A) where the rates referred to in subparagraph (i) do not exist, the minimum guaranteed rates of interest used under the life insurance policy to determine cash surrender values and the rates of mortality under the *Commissioners 1958 Standard Ordinary Mortality Table*, as published in Volume X of the *Transactions of the Society of Actuaries*, relevant to the person whose life is insured under the life insurance policy shall be used, or

(B) where, in respect of the life insurance policy, the particular period over which the amount determined under clause (B) of the description of A in subparagraph 1401(1)(*c*)(ii) does not extend to the exemption test policy's endowment date, the weighted arithmetic mean of the interest rates used to determine the amount is to be used for the period that is after the particular period and before that date,

(iii) notwithstanding subparagraphs (i) and (ii), no rate of interest used for the purpose of determining the accumulating fund in respect of an exemption test policy issued in respect of the life insurance policy is to be less than

(A) if the life insurance policy is issued after April 1985, 4% per annum, and

(B) if the life insurance policy is issued before May 1985, 3% per annum, and

(iv) each amount of a benefit on death is to be determined net of any portion in respect of the benefit on death of the exemption test policy related to a segregated fund; and

(*d*) an exemption test policy issued in respect of a coverage under a life insurance policy issued after 2016,

(i) the rates of interest and mortality used and the age of the individual whose life is insured under the coverage are to be the same as those used in computing amounts under paragraph 1401(1)(*c*) in respect of the policy, and

(ii) each amount of a benefit on death is to be determined net of any portion in respect of the benefit on death of the exemption test policy related to a segregated fund.

History: S. 307(2), the portion before subparagraph (*a*)(i) was replaced by S.C. 2014, c. 39, s. 82(3), in force December 16, 2014, and formerly read:

(2) For the purposes of subsection (1), when computing the accumulating fund of an interest described in

(*a*) paragraph (1)(*a*), the amounts determined under clauses (1)(*a*)(ii)(A) and (B) shall be computed using,

S. 307(2)(*b*) was replaced by S.C. 2014, c. 39, s. 82(5), in force December 16, 2014, and formerly read:

(*b*) paragraph (1)(*b*), where an interest rate used for a period by a life insurer in computing the relevant amounts in paragraph 1403(1)(*a*) or (*b*) is determined under paragraph 1403(1)(*c*), (*d*) or (*e*), as the case may be, and that rate is less than an interest rate so determined for a subsequent period, the single rate that could, if it applied for each period, have been used in determining the premiums for the policy shall be used; and

S. 307(2)(*c*), the portion before subparagraph (i) was replaced by S.C. 2014, c. 39, s. 82(6), in force December 16, 2014, and formerly read:

(*c*) paragraph (1)(*c*),

S. 307(2), the portion after clause (*c*)(ii)(A) was replaced by S.C. 2014, c. 39, s. 82(7), in force December 16, 2014, and formerly read:

(B) where, in respect of the life insurance policy in respect of which the exemption test policy was issued, the period over which the amount determined under clause 1401(1)(*c*)(ii)(A) does not extend to the date determined under subparagraph 306(3)(*d*)(ii), the weighted arithmetic mean of the interest rates used to determine such amount shall be used for the period that is after that period and before that date.

(3) (Repealed.)

History: S. 307(3) was repealed by S.C. 2014, c. 39, s. 82(8), in force December 16, 2014, and formerly read:

(3) Notwithstanding paragraph (2)(*c*),

(*a*) in the case of a life insurance policy issued after April 30, 1985, no rate of interest used for the purpose of determining the accumulating fund in respect of an exemption test policy issued in respect thereof shall be less than 4 per cent per annum; and

(*b*) in the case of a life insurance policy issued before May 1, 1985, no rate of interest used for the purpose of determining the accumulating fund in respect of an exemption test policy issued in respect thereof shall be less than 3 per cent per annum.

(4) (Repealed.)

History: S. 307(4) was repealed by S.C. 2014, c. 39, s. 82(8), in force December 16, 2014, and formerly read:

(4) For the purposes of paragraph (1)(*c*),

(*a*) where on the date of issue of an exemption test policy the person whose life is insured has attained the age of 75 years, the references in paragraph (1)(*c*) to "20" and "twentieth" shall be read as references to "10" and "tenth" respectively; and

(*b*) where on the date of issue of an exemption test policy the person whose life is insured has attained the age of 66 years but not the age of 75 years, the references in paragraph (1)(*c*) to "20" and "twentieth" shall be read as references to

(i) the number obtained when the number of years by which the age of the person whose life is insured exceeds 65 years is subtracted from 20, and

(ii) the adjectival form of the number obtained by performing the computation described in subparagraph (i),

respectively.

(5) In this section, any amount determined by reference to section 1401 shall be determined

(*a*) without regard to section 1402; and

(*b*) as if each reference to "policy loan" in section 1401 were read as a reference to "policy loan, as defined in subsection 148(9) of the Act,".

(*c*) (Repealed.)

History: S. 307(5)(*c*) was repealed by S.C. 2014, c. 39, s. 82(9), in force December 16, 2014, and formerly read:

(*c*) as if clauses 1401(1)(*c*)(i)(B) and 1401(1)(*c*)(ii)(C) were read without reference to the expression "or the interest thereon that has accrued to the insurer at the end of the year".

S. 307(5)(*b*) was replaced by P.C. 2011-936, SOR/2011-188, dated September 22, 2011, published in the *Canada Gazette* October 12, 2011, applicable after February 1994. S. 307(5)(*b*) formerly read:

(*b*) as if each reference therein to the term "policy loan" were read as if that term had the meaning assigned by paragraph 148(9)(*e*) [subsection 148(9) "policy loan"] of the Act; and

308. Net Cost of Pure Insurance and Mortality Gains And Losses

(1) For the purposes of subparagraph 20(1)(*e*.2)(ii) and paragraph (*a*) of the description of L in the definition "adjusted cost basis" in subsection 148(9) of the Act, the net cost of pure insurance for a year in respect of a taxpayer's interest in a life insurance policy is

(*a*) if, determined at the end of the year, the policy was issued before 2017, the amount determined by the formula

$$A \times (B - C)$$

where

A is the probability, computed on the basis of the rates of mortality under the 1969-75 mortality tables of the Canadian Institute of Actuaries published in Volume XVI of the *Proceedings of the Canadian Institute of Actuaries*, or on the basis described in subsection (1.1), that an individual who has the same relevant characteristics as the individual whose life is insured will die in the year,

B is the benefit on death in respect of the interest at the end of the year, and

C is the accumulating fund (determined without regard to any amount payable in respect of the policy loan) in respect of the interest at the end of the year or the interest's cash surrender value at the end of the year, depending on the method regularly followed by the life insurer in computing amounts under this subsection; and

(*b*) if, determined at the end of the year, the policy was issued after 2016, the total of all amounts each of which is an amount determined in respect of a coverage in respect of the interest by the formula

$$A \times (B - C)$$

where

A is the probability, computed on the basis of the rates of mortality determined in accordance with paragraph 1401(4)(*b*), or on the basis described in subsection (1.2), that an individual whose life is insured under the coverage will die in the year,

B is the benefit on death under the coverage in respect of the interest at the end of the year, and

C is the amount determined by the formula

$$D + E$$

where

D is the portion, in respect of the coverage in respect of the interest, of the amount that would be the present value, determined for the purposes of section 307, on the last policy anniversary that is on or before the last day of the year, of the fund value of the coverage if the fund value of the coverage were equal to the fund value of the coverage at the end of the year, and

E is the portion, in respect of the coverage in respect of the interest, of the amount that would be determined, on that policy anniversary, for paragraph (*a*) of the description of C in the definition "net premium reserve" in subsection 1401(3) in respect of the coverage, if the benefit on death under the coverage, and the fund value of the coverage, on that policy anniversary were equal to the benefit on death under the coverage and the fund value of the coverage, respectively, at the end of the year.

History: S. 308(1) was replaced by S.C. 2014, c. 39, s. 83, in force December 16, 2014, and formerly read:

(1) For the purposes of subparagraph 20(1)(*e*.2)(ii) and paragraph (*a*) of the description of L in the definition "adjusted cost basis" in subsection 148(9) of the Act, the net cost of pure insurance for a year in respect of a taxpayer's interest in a life insurance policy is the product obtained when the probability, computed on the basis of the rates of mortality under the 1969-75 mortality tables of the Canadian Institute of Actuaries published in Volume XVI of the proceedings of the Canadian Institute of Actuaries or on the basis described in subsection (1.1), that a person who has the same relevant characteristics as the person whose life is insured will die in the year is multiplied by the amount by which

(*a*) the benefit on death in respect of the taxpayer's interest at the end of the year

exceeds

(*b*) the accumulating fund (determined without regard to any policy loan outstanding) in respect of the taxpayer's interest in the policy at the end of the year or the cash surrender value of such interest at the end of the year, depending on the method regularly followed by the life insurer in computing net cost of pure insurance.

Interpretation Bulletins: *Secondary* — IT-309R2 Premiums on life insurance used as collateral.

(1.1) If premiums for a life insurance policy do not depend directly on smoking or sex classification, the probability referred to in paragraph (1)(*a*) may be determined using rates of mortality otherwise determined, provided that for each age for the policy, the expected value of the aggregate net cost of pure insurance, calculated using those rates of mortality, is equal to the expected value of the aggregate net cost of pure insurance, calculated using the rates of mortality under the 1969-75 mortality tables of the Canadian Institute of Actuaries published in Volume XVI of the *Proceedings of the Canadian Institute of Actuaries*.

History: S. 308(1.1) was replaced by S.C. 2014, c. 39, s. 83, in force December 16, 2014, and formerly read:

(1.1) Where premiums for a particular class of life insurance policy offered by a life insurer do not depend directly on smoking or sex classification, the probability referred to in subsection (1) may be determined using rates of mortality otherwise determined provided that for each age for such class of life insurance policy, the expected value of the aggregate net cost of pure insurance, calculated using such rates of mortality, is equal to the expected value of the aggregate net cost of pure insurance, calculated using the rates of mortality under the 1969-75 mortality tables of the Canadian Institute of Actuaries published in Volume XVI of the Proceedings of the Canadian Institute of Actuaries.

(1.2) If premiums or costs of insurance charges for a coverage under a life insurance policy do not depend directly on smoking or sex classification, the probability referred to in paragraph (1)(*b*) may be determined using rates of mortality otherwise determined, provided that for each age for the coverage, the expected value of the aggregate net cost of pure insurance, calculated using those rates of mortality, is equal to the expected value of the aggregate net cost of pure insurance, calculated using the rates of mortality that would be calculated under paragraph (1)(*b*) in respect of the coverage using the mortality tables described in paragraph 1401(4)(*b*).

History: S. 308(1.2) was added by S.C. 2014, c. 39, s. 83, in force December 16, 2014.

(2) Subject to subsection (4), for the purposes of this section and of the description of G in the definition "adjusted cost basis" in subsection 148(9) of the Act, a "mortality gain" immediately before the end of any cal-

Regulations

endar year after 1982 in respect of a taxpayer's interest in a life annuity contract means such reasonable amount in respect of the taxpayer's interest in the life annuity contract at that time that the life insurer determines to be the increase to the accumulating fund in respect of the interest that occurred during that year as a consequence of the survival to the end of the year of one or more of the annuitants under the life annuity contract.

History: S. 308(2) was replaced by P.C. 2011-936, SOR/2011-188, dated September 22, 2011, published in the *Canada Gazette* October 12, 2011, applicable after February 1994. S. 308(2) formerly read:

(2) Subject to subsection (4), for the purposes of this section and subparagraph 148(9)(*a*)(v.1) [subsection 148(9) "adjusted cost basis", item G] of the Act, a "mortality gain" immediately before the end of any calendar year after 1982 in respect of a taxpayer's interest in a life annuity contract means such reasonable amount in respect of his interest therein at that time that the life insurer determines to be the increase to the accumulating fund in respect of the interest that occurred during that year as a consequence of the survival to the end of the year of one or more of the annuitants thereunder.

(3) Subject to subsection (4), for the purposes of this section and of paragraph (*c*) of the description of L in the definition "adjusted cost basis" in subsection 148(9) of the Act, a "mortality loss" immediately before a particular time after 1982 in respect of an interest in a life annuity contract disposed of immediately after that particular time as a consequence of the death of an annuitant under the life annuity contract means such reasonable amount that the life insurer determines to be the decrease, as a consequence of the death, in the accumulating fund in respect of the interest assuming that, in determining such decrease, the accumulating fund immediately after the death is determined in the manner described in subparagraph 307(1)(*b*)(i).

History: S. 308(3) was replaced by P.C. 2011-936, SOR/2011-188, dated September 22, 2011, published in the *Canada Gazette* October 12, 2011, applicable after February 1994. S. 308(3) formerly read:

(3) Subject to subsection (4), for the purposes of this section and subparagraph 148(9)(*a*)(xi) [subsection 148(9) "adjusted cost basis", item L(*c*)] of the Act, a "mortality loss" immediately before a particular time after 1982 in respect of an interest in a life annuity contract disposed of immediately after that particular time as a consequence of the death of an annuitant thereunder means such reasonable amount that the life insurer determines to be the decrease, as a consequence of the death, in the accumulating fund in respect of the interest assuming that, in determining such decrease, the accumulating fund immediately after the death is determined in the manner described in subparagraph 307(1)(*b*)(i).

(4) In determining an amount for a year in respect of an interest in a life annuity contract under subsection (2) or (3), the expected value of the mortality gains in respect of the interest for the year shall be equal to the expected value of the mortality losses in respect of the interest for the year and the mortality rates for the year used in computing those expected values shall be those that would be relevant to the interest and that are specified under such of paragraphs 1403(1)(*c*), (*d*) and (*e*) as are applicable.

309. Prescribed Premiums and Prescribed Increases

(1) For the purposes of this section and section 306, and of subsection 89(2) of the Act, a premium at any time under a life insurance policy is a "prescribed premium" if the total amount of one or more premiums paid at that time under the policy exceeds the amount of premium that, under the policy, was scheduled to be paid at that time and that was fixed and determined on or before December 1, 1982, adjusted for such of the following transactions and events that have occurred after that date in respect of the policy:

(*a*) a change in underwriting class;

(*b*) a change in premium due to a change in frequency of premium payments within a year that does not alter the present value, at the beginning of the year, of the total premiums to be paid under the policy in the year;

(*c*) an addition or deletion of accidental death or guaranteed purchase option benefits or disability benefits that provide for annuity payments or waiver of premiums;

(*d*) a premium adjustment as a result of interest, mortality or expense considerations, or of a change in the benefit on death under the policy relating to an increase in the Consumer Price Index (as published by Statistics Canada under the authority of the *Statistics Act*) where such adjustment

(i) is made by the life insurer on a class basis pursuant to the policy's terms as they read on December 1, 1982, and

(ii) is not made as a result of the exercise of a conversion privilege under the policy;

(*e*) a change arising from the provision of an additional benefit on death under a participating life insurance policy, as defined in subsection 138(12) of the Act, as, on account or in lieu of payment of, or in satisfaction of

(i) policy dividends or other distributions of the life insurer's income from its participating life insurance business, or

(ii) interest earned on policy dividends that are held on deposit by the life insurer;

(*f*) redating lapsed policies, if the policy was reinstated not later than 60 days after the end of the calendar year in which the lapse occurred, or redating for policy loan indebtedness;

(*g*) a change in premium due to a correction of erroneous information contained in the application for the policy;

(*h*) payment of a premium after its due date, or payment of a premium no more than 30 days before its due date, as established on or before December 1, 1982; and

(*i*) the payment of interest described in paragraph (*a*) of the definition "premium" in subsection 148(9) of the Act.

History: S. 309(1)(*e*)(i) was replaced by S.C. 2013, c. 34, s. 379(1), applicable to taxation years that begin after October 31, 2011, and formerly read:

(i) policy dividends or other distributions of the life insurer's income from its participating life insurance business as determined under section 2402, or

S. 309(1), the portion before paragraph (*a*) was replaced by P.C. 2011-936, SOR/2011-188, dated September 22, 2011, published in the *Canada Gazette* October 12, 2011, applicable with respect to life insurance policies last acquired after 1989. S. 309(1), the portion before paragraph (*a*) formerly read;

(1) For the purposes of subsections 12.2(9) and 89(2) of the Act, section 306 and this section, a premium at any time under a life insurance policy is a "prescribed premium" if the total amount of one or more premiums paid at that time under the policy exceeds the amount of premium that, under the policy, was scheduled to be paid at that time and that was fixed and determined on or before December 1, 1982, adjusted for such of the following transactions and events that have occurred after that date in respect of the policy:

S. 309(1)(*e*), the portion before subparagraph (i) was replaced by P.C. 2011-936, SOR/2011-188, dated September 22, 2011, published in the *Canada Gazette* October 12, 2011, applicable after February 1994. S. 309(1)(*e*), the portion before subparagraph (i) formerly read:

(*e*) a change arising from the provision of an additional benefit on death under a participating life insurance policy (within the meaning assigned by paragraph 138(12)(*k*) [subsection 138(12) "participating life insurance policy"] of the Act) as, on account or in lieu of payment of, or in satisfaction of

S. 309(1)(*f*) was replaced by P.C. 2011-936, SOR/2011-188, dated September 22, 2011, published in the *Canada Gazette* October 12, 2011, applicable after February 1994. S. 309(1)(*f*) formerly read:

(*f*) redating lapsed policies within the reinstatement period referred to in subparagraph 148(9)(*c*)(vi) [subsection 148(9) "disposition", paragraph (*g*)] of the Act or redating for policy loan indebtedness;

S. 309(1)(*i*) was replaced by P.C. 2011-936, SOR/2011-188, dated September 22, 2011, published in the *Canada Gazette* October 12, 2011, applicable after February 1994. S. 309(1)(*i*) formerly read:

(*i*) the payment of an amount described in subparagraph 148(9)(*e*.1)(i) [subsection 148(9) "premium", paragraph (*a*)] of the Act.

Interpretation Bulletins: *Secondary* — IT-87R2 Policyholders' income from life insurance policies.

(2) For the purposes of subsections 12.2(9) and 89(2) of the Act, a "prescribed increase" in a benefit on death under a life insurance policy has occurred at any time where the amount of the benefit on death under the policy at that time exceeds the amount of the benefit on death at that time under the policy that was fixed and determined on or before December 1, 1982, adjusted for such of the following transactions and events that have occurred after that date in respect of the policy:

(*a*) an increase resulting from a change described in paragraph (1)(*e*);

(*b*) a change as a result of interest, mortality or expense considerations, or an increase in the Consumer Price Index (as published by Statistics Canada under the authority of the *Statistics Act*) where such change is made by the life insurer on a class basis pursuant to the policy's terms as they read on December 1, 1982;

(*c*) an increase in consequence of the prepayment of premiums (other than prescribed premiums) under the policy where such increase does not exceed the aggregate of the premiums that would otherwise have been paid;

(*d*) an increase in respect of a policy for which

(i) the benefit on death was, at December 1, 1982, a specific mathematical function of the policy's cash surrender value or factors including the policy's cash surrender value, and

(ii) that function has not changed since that date,

unless any part of such increase is attributable to a prescribed premium paid in respect of a policy or to income earned on such a premium; and

(*e*) an increase that is granted by the life insurer on a class basis without consideration and not pursuant to any term of the contract.

(3) For the purposes of subsections (1) and (2), a life insurance policy that is issued as a result of the exercise of a renewal privilege provided under the terms of another policy as they read on December 1, 1982 shall be deemed to be a continuation of that other policy.

(4) For the purposes of subsection (2), a life insurance policy that is issued as a result of the exercise of a conversion privilege provided under the terms of another policy as they read on December 1, 1982 shall be deemed to be a continuation of that other policy except that any portion of the policy relating to the portion of the benefit on death, immediately before the conversion, that arose as a consequence of an event occurring after December 1, 1982 and described in paragraph (1)(*e*) shall be deemed to be a separate life insurance policy issued at the time of the conversion.

Income Tax Folios: *Primary* — S3-F2-C1 Capital Dividends.

Interpretation Bulletins: *Secondary* — IT-87R2 Policyholders' income from life insurance policies.

309.1. Income From Participating Life Insurance Businesses

For the purpose of subparagraph 309(1)(*e*)(i), in computing a life insurer's income for a taxation year from its participating life insurance business carried on in Canada,

(*a*) there shall be included the amount determined by the formula

$$A \times B/C$$

where

A is the insurer's gross Canadian life investment income (in this section as defined in subsection 2400(1)) for the year,

B is the total of

(i) the insurer's mean maximum tax actuarial reserve (in this section as defined in subsection 2400(1)) for the year in respect of participating life insurance policies in Canada, and

(ii) 1/2 of the total of

(A) all amounts on deposit with the insurer as at the end of the year in respect of policies described in subparagraph (i), and

(B) all amounts on deposit with the insurer as at the end of the immediately preceding taxation year in respect of policies described in subparagraph (i), and

C the total of all amounts, each of which is

(i) the insurer's mean maximum tax actuarial reserve for the year in respect of a class of life insurance policies in Canada, or

(ii) 1/2 of the total of

(A) all amounts on deposit with the insurer as at the end of the year in respect of a class of policies described in subparagraph (i), and

(B) all amounts on deposit with the insurer as at the end of the immediately preceding taxation year in respect of a class of policies described in subparagraph (i);

(*b*) there shall be included

(i) the insurer's maximum tax actuarial reserve for the immediately preceding taxation year in respect of participating life insurance policies in Canada, and

(ii) the maximum amount deductible by the insurer under subparagraph 138(3)(*a*)(ii) of the Act in computing its income for the immediately preceding taxation year in respect of participating life insurance policies in Canada;

(*c*) there shall not be included any amount in respect of the insurer's participating life insurance policies in Canada that was deducted under subparagraph 138(3)(*a*)(i) or (ii) of the Act in computing its income for the immediately preceding taxation year;

(*d*) subject to paragraph (*a*),

(i) there shall not be included any amount

Regulations

(A) as a reserve that was deducted under paragraph 20(1)(*l*) of the Act in computing the insurer's income for the immediately preceding taxation year, or

(B) that was included in determining the insurer's gross Canadian life investment income for the year, and

(ii) no deduction shall be made in respect of any amount

(A) taken into account in determining the insurer's gross Canadian life investment income for the year, or

(B) deductible under paragraph 20(1)(*l*) of the Act in computing the insurer's income for the year;

(*e*) there shall be deducted

(i) the insurer's maximum tax actuarial reserve for the year in respect of participating life insurance policies in Canada, and

(ii) the maximum amount deductible by the insurer under subparagraph 138(3)(*a*)(ii) of the Act in computing its income for the year in respect of participating life insurance policies in Canada;

(*f*) no deduction shall be made in respect of any amount deductible under subparagraph 138(3)(*a*)(iii) of the Act in computing the insurer's income for the year;

(*g*) except as otherwise provided in paragraph (*e*), no deduction shall be made in respect of a reserve deductible under subparagraph 138(3)(*a*)(i) or (ii) of the Act in computing the insurer's income for the year; and

(*h*) except as otherwise provided in this section, the provisions of the Act relating to the computation of income from a source shall apply.

History: S. 309.1 was added by S.C. 2013, c. 34, s. 380(1), applicable to taxation years that begin after October 31, 2011, except that if a taxpayer has deducted an amount under subparagraph 138(3)(*a*)(iv), as it read in its application to the taxpayer's last taxation year that began before November 1, 2011, in computing the taxpayer's income for that taxation year, then for the taxpayer's first taxation year that begins after October 31, 2011 paragraph 309.1(*b*) is to be read as follows:

"(*b*) there shall be included

(i) the amount deducted by the insurer under subparagraph 138(3)(*a*)(iv) of the Act, as it read in its application to the insurer's last taxation year that began on or before October 31, 2011, in computing its income for the immediately preceding taxation year,

(ii) the insurer's maximum tax actuarial reserve for the immediately preceding taxation year in respect of participating life insurance policies in Canada, and

(iii) the maximum amount deductible by the insurer under subparagraph 138(3)(*a*)(ii) of the Act in computing its income for the immediately preceding taxation year in respect of participating life insurance policies in Canada;"

310. Interpretation

The following definitions apply for the purposes of this section and sections 300, 301 and 304 to 309.

"adjusted purchase price" — "adjusted purchase price", of a taxpayer's interest in an annuity contract at any time, means, subject to subsections 300(3) and (4), the amount that would be determined at that time in respect of the interest under the definition "adjusted cost basis" in subsection 148(9) of the Act if the formula in that definition were read without reference to K.

History: S. 310, the definition "adjusted purchase price" was added by S.C. 2014, c. 39, s. 84(2), in force December 16, 2014.

"amount payable" — "amount payable" has the same meaning as in subsection 138(12) of the Act.

"benefit on death" — "benefit on death" has the same meaning as in subsection 1401(3).

History: S. 310, the definition "benefit on death" was replaced by S.C. 2014, c. 39, s. 84(1), in force December 16, 2014, and formerly read:

benefit on death—"benefit on death" does not include policy dividends, or any interest on a policy dividend, held on deposit by an insurer or any additional amount payable as a result of accidental death.

"cash surrender value" — "cash surrender value" has the same meaning as in subsection 148(9) of the Act.

"coverage" — "coverage", under a life insurance policy,

(*a*) for the purposes of section 306, means all life insurance (other than a fund value benefit) under the policy in respect of a specific life, or two or more specific lives jointly insured; and

(*b*) for the purposes of sections 307 and 308, has the same meaning as in subsection 1401(3).

History: S. 310, the definition "coverage" was added by S.C. 2014, c. 39, s. 84(2), in force December 16, 2014.

"endowment date" — "endowment date", of an exemption test policy, means

(*a*) where the exemption test policy is issued in respect of a life insurance policy issued before 2017, the later of

(i) 10 years after the date of issue of the life insurance policy, and

(ii) the first policy anniversary that is on or after the day on which the individual whose life is insured under the life insurance policy would, if the individual survived, attain the age of 85 years, as defined under the terms of the policy; and

(*b*) where the exemption test policy is issued in respect of a coverage under a life insurance policy issued after 2016,

(i) if two or more lives are jointly insured under the coverage, the date that would be determined under subparagraph (ii) using the equivalent single age, determined on the coverage's date of issue and in accordance with accepted actuarial principles and practices, that reasonably approximates the mortality rates of those lives, and

(ii) in any other case, the later of

(A) the earlier of

(I) 15 years after the date of issue of the exemption test policy, and

(II) the first policy anniversary that is on or after the day on which the individual whose life is insured under the coverage would, if the individual survived, attain the age of 105 years, as defined under the terms of the policy, and

(B) the first policy anniversary that is on or after the day on which the individual whose life is insured under the coverage would, if the individual survived, attain the age of 90 years, as defined under the terms of the policy.

History: S. 310, the definition "endowment date" was added by S.C. 2014, c. 39, s. 84(2), in force December 16, 2014.

"fund value benefit" — "fund value benefit" has the same meaning as in subsection 1401(3).

History: S. 310, the definition "fund value benefit" was added by S.C. 2014, c. 39, s. 84(2), in force December 16, 2014.

"fund value of a coverage" —"fund value of a coverage" has the same meaning as in subsection 1401(3).

History: S. 310, the definition "fund value of a coverage" was added by S.C. 2014, c. 39, s. 84(2), in force December 16, 2014.

"pay period" —"pay period", of an exemption test policy, means

(*a*) where the exemption test policy is issued in respect of a life insurance policy issued before 2017,

(i) if on the date of issue of the exemption test policy, the individual whose life is insured has attained the age of 66 years, as defined under the terms of the policy, but not the age of 75 years, as defined under the terms of the policy, the period that starts on that date and that ends after the number of years obtained when the number of years by which the age of the individual exceeds 65 years, as defined under the terms of the policy, is subtracted from 20,

(ii) if on the date of issue of the exemption test policy, the individual whose life is insured has attained the age of 75 years, as defined under the terms of the policy, the 10-year period that starts on that date, and

(iii) in any other case, the 20-year period that starts on the date of issue of the exemption test policy; and

(*b*) where the exemption test policy is issued in respect of a coverage under a life insurance policy issued after 2016,

(i) subject to subparagraph (ii), if the individual whose life is insured under the coverage would, if the individual survived, attain the age of 105 years, as defined under the terms of the policy, within the eight-year period that starts on the date of issue of the exemption test policy, the period that starts on that date and that ends on the first policy anniversary that is on or after the day on which the individual would, if the individual survived, attain the age of 105 years, as defined under the terms of the policy,

(ii) if two or more lives are jointly insured under the coverage and an individual of an age equal to the equivalent single age on the date of the issue of the coverage would, if the individual survived, attain the age of 105 years, as defined under the terms of the policy, within the eight-year period that starts on the date of issue of the exemption test policy, the period that starts on that date and that ends on the first policy anniversary that is on or after the day on which the individual would, if the individual survived, attain the age of 105 years, as defined under the terms of the policy, and

(iii) in any other case, the eight-year period that starts on the date of issue of the exemption test policy.

History: S. 310, the definition "pay period" was added by S.C. 2014, c. 39, s. 84(2), in force December 16, 2014.

"policy anniversary" —"policy anniversary" includes, in the case of a life insurance policy that is in existence throughout a calendar year and that would not otherwise have a policy anniversary for the calendar year, the end of the calendar year.

"policy loan" —"policy loan" has the same meaning as in subsection 148(9) of the Act.

"proceeds of the disposition" —"proceeds of the disposition" has the same meaning as in subsection 148(9) of the Act.

"tax anniversary date" —"tax anniversary date", in relation to an annuity contract, means the second anniversary date of the contract to occur after October 22, 1968.

History: S. 310 was replaced by P.C. 2011-936, SOR/2011-188, dated September 22, 2011, published in the *Canada Gazette* October 12, 2011, applicable after February 1994. S. 310 formerly read:

310. For the purposes of sections 300, 301 and 304 to 309 and this section,

"amount payable" has the meaning assigned by paragraph 138(12)(*b*.1) [subsection 138(12) "amount payable"] of the Act;

"benefit on death" does not include policy dividends or any interest thereon held on deposit by an insurer or any additional amount payable as a result of accidental death;

"cash surrender value" has the meaning assigned by paragraph 148(9)(*b*) [148(9) "cash surrender value"] of the Act;

"life insurance policy" has the meaning assigned by paragraph 138(12)(*f*) [subsection 138(12) "life insurance policy"] of the Act;

"life insurance policy in Canada" has the meaning assigned by paragraph 138(12)(*g*) [subsection 138(12) "life insurance policy in Canada"] of the Act;

"policy anniversary" includes, where a life insurance policy was in existence throughout a calendar year and there would not otherwise be a policy anniversary in the year in respect of the policy, the end of the calendar year;

"policy loan" has the meaning assigned by paragraph 148(9)(*e*) [subsection 148(9) "policy loan"] of the Act;

"proceeds of the disposition" has the meaning assigned by paragraph 148(9)(*e*.2) [subsection 148(9) "proceeds of disposition"] of the Act;

"tax anniversary date" in relation to an annuity contract means the second anniversary date of the contract to occur after October 22, 1968.

Regulations

Part IV
Taxable Income Earned in a Province by a Corporation

400. Interpretation

(1) In applying the definition "taxable income earned in the year in a province" in subsection 124(4) of the Act for a corporation's taxation year

(*a*) the prescribed rules referred to in that definition are the rules in this Part; and

(*b*) the amount determined under those prescribed rules means the total of all amounts each of which is the taxable income of the corporation earned in the taxation year in a particular province as determined under this Part.

History: S. 400(1) was replaced by S.C. 2009, c. 2, s. 91(1), applicable to the 2009 and subsequent taxation years. S. 400(1) formerly read:

(1) For the purposes of paragraph 124(4)(*a*) [subsection 124(4), "taxable income earned in the year in a province"] of the Act, a corporation's "taxable income earned in the year in a province" means the aggregate of the taxable incomes of the corporation earned in the year in each of the provinces.

Interpretation Bulletins: *Secondary* — IT-177R2 (Consolid.) Permanent establishment of a corporation in a province and of a foreign enterprise in Canada.

(1.1) (Repealed by S.C. 2013, c. 33, s. 32(1).)

History: S. 400(1.1) was repealed by S.C. 2013, c. 33, s. 32(1), applicable to taxation years that begin after March 20, 2013, and formerly read:

(1.1) In this Part, a corporation's taxable income for a taxation year is equal to the total of

(*a*) the corporation's taxable income for the taxation year (determined without reference to this subsection) or the corporation's taxable income earned in Canada for the taxation year, as the case may be, and

(*b*) the positive or negative amount determined by the formula

$$A - B$$

where

A is the total of all amounts that are, because of the application of section 33.1 of the Act, not required to be added in computing the corporation's income for the taxation year, and

B is the total of all amounts that are, because of the application of section 33.1 of the Act, not allowed to be deducted in computing the corporation's income for the taxation year.

S. 400(1.1) was added by S.C. 2009, c. 2, s. 91(1), applicable to the 2009 and subsequent taxation years.

(2) For the purposes of this Part, "permanent establishment" in respect of a corporation means a fixed place of business of the corporation, including an office, a branch, a mine, an oil well, a farm, a timberland, a factory, a workshop or a warehouse, and

(*a*) where the corporation does not have any fixed place of business it means the principal place in which the corporation's business is conducted;

(*b*) where a corporation carries on business through an employee or agent, established in a particular place, who has general authority to contract for his employer or principal or who has a stock of merchandise owned by his employer or principal from which he regularly fills orders which he receives, the corporation shall be deemed to have a permanent establishment in that place;

(*c*) an insurance corporation is deemed to have a permanent establishment in each province and country in which the corporation is registered or licensed to do business;

(*d*) where a corporation, otherwise having a permanent establishment in Canada, owns land in a province, such land shall be deemed to be a permanent establishment;

(*e*) where a corporation uses substantial machinery or equipment in a particular place at any time in a taxation year it shall be deemed to have a permanent establishment in that place;

(*e*.1) if, but for this paragraph, a corporation would not have a permanent establishment, the corporation is deemed to have a permanent establishment at the place designated in its incorporating documents or bylaws as its head office or registered office;

(*f*) the fact that a corporation has business dealings through a commission agent, broker or other independent agent or maintains an office solely for the purchase of merchandise shall not of itself be held to mean that the corporation has a permanent establishment; and

(*g*) the fact that a corporation has a subsidiary controlled corporation in a place or a subsidiary controlled corporation engaged in trade or business in a place shall not of itself be held to mean that the corporation is operating a permanent establishment in that place.

History: S. 400(2)(*e*.1) was added by S.C. 2009, c. 2, s. 91(2), applicable to the 2009 and subsequent taxation years.

Tax Topics: No. 1737, Why Tax Lawyers Should Care that the Toronto Blue Jays Struck Out.

Income Tax Technical News: Issue No. 41, Provincial income allocation — Section 400 of the Income Tax Regulations; Issue No. 34, Permanent establishments.

Interpretation Bulletins: *Secondary* — IT-177R2 (Consolid.) Permanent establishment of a corporation in a province.

401. Computation of Taxable Income

This Part applies to determine the amount of taxable income of a corporation earned in a taxation year in a particular province.

History: S. 401 was replaced by S.C. 2009, c. 2, s. 92(1), applicable to the 2009 and subsequent taxation years. S. 401 formerly read:

401. The amount of taxable income of a corporation earned in a year in a particular province shall be determined in accordance with the provisions of this Part.

402. General Rules

(1) Where, in a taxation year, a corporation had a permanent establishment in a particular province and had no permanent establishment outside that province, the whole of its taxable income for the year shall be deemed to have been earned therein.

Interpretation Bulletins: *Secondary* — IT-177R2 (Consolid.) Permanent establishment of a corporation in a province and of a foreign enterprise in Canada.

(2) Where, in a taxation year, a corporation had no permanent establishment in a particular province, no part of its taxable income for the year shall be deemed to have been earned therein.

Interpretation Bulletins: *Secondary* — IT-177R2 (Consolid.) Permanent establishment of a corporation in a province and of a foreign enterprise in Canada.

(3) Except as otherwise provided, where, in a taxation year, a corporation had a permanent establishment in a province and a permanent establishment outside that province, the amount of its taxable income that shall be deemed to have been earned in the year in the province is

(*a*) in any case other than a case specified in paragraph (*b*) or (*c*), 1/2 the aggregate of

(i) that proportion of its taxable income for the year that the gross revenue for the year reasonably attributable to the permanent establishment in the province is of its total gross revenue for the year, and

(ii) that proportion of its taxable income for the year that the aggregate of the salaries and wages paid in the year by the corporation to employees of the permanent establishment in the province is of the aggregate of all salaries and wages paid in the year by the corporation;

(*b*) in any case where the gross revenue for the year of the corporation is nil, that proportion of its taxable income for the year that the aggregate of the salaries and wages paid in the year by the corporation to employees of the permanent establishment in the province is of the aggregate of all salaries and wages paid in the year by the corporation; and

(*c*) in any case where the aggregate of the salaries and wages paid in the year by the corporation is nil, that proportion of its taxable income for the year that the gross revenue for the year reasonably attributable to the permanent establishment in the province is of its total gross revenue for the year.

Interpretation Bulletins: *Secondary* — IT-177R2 (Consolid.) Permanent establishment of a corporation in a province and of a foreign enterprise in Canada.

Tax Window Files: Transfer pricing adjustments and gross revenue, *September 1, 2015*, CRA Document No. 2013-0507381I7.

(4) For the purpose of determining the gross revenue for the year reasonably attributable to a permanent establishment in a province or country other than Canada, within the meaning of subsection (3), the following rules shall apply:

(*a*) where the destination of a shipment of merchandise to a customer to whom the merchandise is sold is in the particular province or country, the gross revenue derived therefrom shall be attributable to the permanent establishment in the province or country;

(*b*) except as provided in paragraph (*c*), where the destination of a shipment of merchandise to a customer to whom the merchandise is sold is in a province or country other than Canada in which the taxpayer has no permanent establishment, if the person negotiating the sale may reasonably be regarded as being attached to the permanent establishment in the particular province or country, the gross revenue derived therefrom shall be attributable to that permanent establishment;

(*c*) where the destination of a shipment of merchandise to a customer to whom the merchandise is sold is in a country other than Canada in which the taxpayer has no permanent establishment,

(i) if the merchandise was produced or manufactured or produced and manufactured, entirely in the particular province by the taxpayer, the gross revenue derived therefrom shall be attributable to the permanent establishment in the province, or

(ii) if the merchandise was produced or manufactured, or produced and manufactured, partly in the particular province and partly in another place by the taxpayer, the gross revenue derived therefrom attributable to the permanent establishment in the province shall be that proportion thereof that the salaries and wages paid in the year to employees of the permanent establishment in the province where the merchandise was partly produced or manufactured (or partly produced and manufactured) is of the aggregate of the salaries and wages paid in the year to employees of the permanent establishments where the merchandise was produced or manufactured (or produced and manufactured);

(*d*) where a customer to whom merchandise is sold instructs that shipment be made to some other person and the customer's office with which the sale was negotiated is located in the particular province or country, the gross revenue derived therefrom shall be attributable to the permanent establishment in the province or country;

(*e*) except as provided in paragraph (*f*), where a customer to whom merchandise is sold instructs that shipment be made to some other person and the customer's office with which the sale was negotiated is located in a province or country other than Canada in which the taxpayer has no permanent establishment, if the person negotiating the sale may reasonably be regarded as being attached to the permanent establishment in the particular province or country, the gross revenue derived therefrom shall be attributable to that permanent establishment;

(*f*) where a customer to whom merchandise is sold instructs that shipment be made to some other person and the customer's office with which the sale was negotiated is located in a country other than Canada in which the taxpayer has no permanent establishment,

(i) if the merchandise was produced or manufactured, or produced and manufactured, entirely in the particular province by the taxpayer, the gross revenue derived therefrom shall be attributable to the permanent establishment in the province, or

(ii) if the merchandise was produced or manufactured, or produced and manufactured, partly in the particular province and partly in another place by the taxpayer, the gross revenue derived therefrom attributable to the permanent establishment in the province shall be that proportion thereof that the salaries and wages paid in the year to employees of the permanent establishment in the province where the merchandise was partly produced or manufactured (or partly produced

Regulations

and manufactured) is of the aggregate of the salaries and wages paid in the year to employees of the permanent establishments where the merchandise was produced or manufactured (or produced and manufactured);

(*g*) where gross revenue is derived from services rendered in the particular province or country, the gross revenue shall be attributable to the permanent establishment in the province or country;

(*h*) where gross revenue is derived from services rendered in a province or country other than Canada in which the taxpayer has no permanent establishment, if the person negotiating the contract may reasonably be regarded as being attached to the permanent establishment of the taxpayer in the particular province or country, the gross revenue shall be attributable to that permanent establishment;

(*i*) where standing timber or the right to cut standing timber is sold and the timber limit on which the timber is standing is in the particular province or country, the gross revenue from such sale shall be attributable to the permanent establishment of the taxpayer in the province or country; and

(*j*) gross revenue which arises from leasing land owned by the taxpayer in a province and which is included in computing its income under Part I of the Act shall be attributable to the permanent establishment, if any, of the taxpayer in the province where the land is situated.

Interpretation Bulletins: *Secondary* — IT-177R2 (Consolid.) Permanent establishment of a corporation in a province and of a foreign enterprise in Canada.

(4.1) For the purposes of subsections (3) and (4), where, in a taxation year,

(*a*) the destination of a shipment of merchandise to a customer to whom the merchandise is sold by a corporation is in a country other than Canada or the customer to whom merchandise is sold by a corporation instructs that the shipment of merchandise be made by the corporation to another person and the customer's office with which the sale was negotiated is located in a country other than Canada,

(*b*) the corporation has a permanent establishment in the other country, and

(*c*) the corporation is not subject to taxation on its income under the laws of the other country, or its gross revenue derived from the sale is not included in computing the income or profit or other base for income or profits taxation by the other country, because of

(i) the provisions of any taxing statute of the other country, or

(ii) the operation of any tax treaty or convention between Canada and the other country,

the following rules apply:

(*d*) with respect to the gross revenue derived from the sale,

(i) paragraphs (4)(*a*) and (*d*) do not apply,

(ii) that portion of paragraph (4)(*c*) preceding subparagraph (i) thereof shall be read as follows:

"(*c*) where the destination of a shipment of merchandise to a customer to whom the merchandise is sold is in a country other than Canada," and

(iii) that portion of paragraph (4)(*f*) preceding subparagraph (i) thereof shall be read as follows:

"(*f*) where a customer to whom the merchandise is sold instructs that shipment be made to some other person and the customer's office with which the sale was negotiated is located in a country other than Canada,"; and

(*e*) for the purposes of subparagraph (3)(*a*)(ii), paragraph (3)(*b*) and subparagraphs (4)(*c*)(ii) and (*f*)(ii), salaries and wages paid in the year to employees of any permanent establishment of the corporation located in that other country shall be deemed to be nil.

(5) For the purposes of subsection (3), "gross revenue" does not include interest on bonds, debentures or mortgages, dividends on shares of capital stock, or rentals or royalties from property that is not used in connection with the principal business operations of the corporation.

Income Tax Technical News: Issue No. 41, Provincial Income Allocation — Section 400 of the Income Tax Regulations.

Interpretation Bulletins: *Secondary* — IT-177R2 (Consolid.) Permanent establishment of a corporation in a province and of a foreign enterprise in Canada.

(6) For the purposes of subsection (3), where part of the corporation's operations were conducted in partnership with one or more other persons

(*a*) the corporation's gross revenue for the year, and

(*b*) the salaries and wages paid in the year by the corporation,

shall include, in respect of those operations, only that proportion of

(*c*) the total gross revenue of the partnership for its fiscal period ending in or coinciding with the year, and

(*d*) the total salaries and wages paid by the partnership in its fiscal period ending in or coinciding with the year,

respectively, that

(*e*) the corporation's share of the income or loss of the partnership for the fiscal period ending in or coinciding with the year,

is of

(*f*) the total income or loss of the partnership for the fiscal period ending in or coinciding with the year.

Interpretation Bulletins: *Secondary* — IT-177R2 (Consolid.) Permanent establishment of a corporation in a province and of a foreign enterprise in Canada.

(7) Where a corporation pays a fee to another person under an agreement pursuant to which that other person or employees of that other person perform services for the corporation that would normally be performed by employees of the corporation, the fee so paid shall be deemed to be salary paid in the year by the corporation and that part of the fee that may reasonably be regarded as payment in respect of services rendered at a particular permanent establishment of the corporation shall be deemed to be salary paid to an employee of that permanent establishment.

Income Tax Folios: S4-F15-C1 Manufacturing and Processing.

Income Tax Technical News: Issue No. 44, Central Paymaster Rules.

Interpretation Bulletins: *Secondary* — IT-177R2 (Consolid.) Permanent establishment of a corporation in a province and of a foreign enterprise in Canada.

(8) For the purposes of subsection (7), a fee does not include a commission paid to a person who is not an employee of the corporation.

Interpretation Bulletins: *Secondary* — IT-177R2 (Consolid.) Permanent establishment of a corporation in a province and of a foreign enterprise in Canada.

402.1. Central Paymaster

(1) In this Part, if an individual (referred to in this section as the "employee") is employed by a person (referred to in this section as the "employer") and performs a service in a particular province for the benefit of or on behalf of a corporation that is not the employer, an amount that may reasonably be regarded as equal to the amount of salary or wages earned by the employee for the service (referred to in this section as the "particular salary") is deemed to be salary paid by the corporation to an employee of the corporation in the corporation's taxation year in which the particular salary is paid if

(*a*) at the time the service is performed,

(i) the corporation and the employer do not deal at arm's length, and

(ii) the corporation has a permanent establishment in the particular province;

(*b*) the service

(i) is performed by the employee in the normal course of the employee's employment by the employer,

(ii) is performed for the benefit of or on behalf of the corporation in the ordinary course of a business carried on by the corporation, and

(iii) is of a type that could reasonably be expected to be performed by employees of the corporation in the ordinary course of the business referred to in subparagraph (ii); and

(*c*) the amount is not otherwise included in the aggregate, determined for the purposes of this Part, of the salaries and wages paid by the corporation.

(2) In this Part, an amount deemed under subsection (1) to be salary paid by a corporation to an employee of the corporation for a service performed in a particular province is deemed to have been paid,

(*a*) if the service was performed at one or more permanent establishments of the corporation in the particular province, to an employee of the permanent establishment or establishments; or

(*b*) if paragraph (*a*) does not apply, to an employee of any other permanent establishment (as is reasonably determined in the circumstances) of the corporation in the particular province.

(3) In determining under this Part the amount of salaries and wages paid in a year by an employer, there shall be deducted the total of all amounts each of which is a particular salary paid by the employer in the year.

(4) Despite subparagraph (1)(*a*)(i), this section applies to a corporation and an employer that deal at arm's length if the Minister determines that the corporation and the employer have entered into an arrangement the purpose of which is to reduce, through the provision of services as described in subsection (1), the total amount of income tax payable by the corporation under a law of the particular province referred to in subsection (1).

(5) For the purposes of this section, a partnership is deemed to be a corporation and the corporation's taxation year is deemed to be the partnership's fiscal period.

History: S. 402.1 and the heading before it were replaced by S.C. 2009, c. 2, s. 93(1), applicable to the 2009 and subsequent taxation years. S. 402.1 and the heading before it formerly read:

Transitional — Taxable Income Earned in the 1978 Taxation Year in the Northwest Territories

402.1 Where in its 1978 taxation year a corporation had a permanent establishment in the Northwest Territories, its taxable income earned in the year in the Northwest Territories is that proportion of the amount thereof otherwise determined in accordance with this Part that the number of days in that portion of the 1978 taxation year of the corporation that is in 1978 is of the number of days in the whole of that taxation year.

Income Tax Technical News: Issue No. 44, Central Paymaster Rules.

402.2. (Repealed.)

History: S. 402.2 was repealed by S.C. 2009, c. 2, s. 93(1), applicable to the 2009 and subsequent taxation years. S. 402.2 formerly read:

Transitional — Taxable Income Earned in the 1980 Taxation Year in the Yukon Territory

402.2 Where in its 1980 taxation year a corporation had a permanent establishment in the Yukon Territory, its taxable income earned in the year in the Yukon Territory is that proportion of the amount thereof otherwise determined in accordance with this Part that the number of days in that portion of the 1980 taxation year of the corporation that is in 1980 is of the number of days in the whole of that taxation year.

403. Insurance Corporations

(1) Notwithstanding subsections 402(3) and (4), the amount of taxable income that shall be deemed to have been earned in a taxation year in a particular province by an insurance corporation is that proportion of its taxable income for the year that the aggregate of

(*a*) its net premiums for the year in respect of insurance on property situated in the province, and

(*b*) its net premiums for the year in respect of insurance, other than on property, from contracts with persons resident in the province,

is of the total of such of its net premiums for the year as are included in computing its income for the purposes of Part I of the Act.

(2) In this section, "net premiums" of a corporation for a taxation year means the aggregate of the gross premiums received by the corporation in the year (other than consideration received for annuities), minus the aggregate for the year of

(*a*) premiums paid for reinsurance,

(*b*) dividends or rebates paid or credited to policyholders, and

(*c*) rebates or returned premiums paid in respect of the cancellation of policies,

by the corporation.

(3) For the purposes of subsection (1), where an insurance corporation had no permanent establishment in a taxation year in a particular province,

(*a*) each net premium for that year in respect of insurance on property situated in the particular province shall be deemed to be a net premium in respect of insurance on property situated in the province in which the permanent establishment of the corporation to which the net premium is reasonably attributable is situated; and

Regulations

(*b*) each net premium for that year in respect of insurance, other than on property, from contracts with persons resident in the particular province shall be deemed to be a net premium in respect of insurance, other than on property, from contracts with persons resident in the province in which the permanent establishment of the corporation to which the net premium is reasonably attributable is situated.

(4) For the purposes of subsection (1), if in a taxation year an insurance corporation has no permanent establishment in a particular country other than Canada, but provides insurance on property in the particular country or has a contract for insurance, other than on property, with a person resident in the particular country, each net premium for the taxation year in respect of the insurance is deemed to be a net premium in respect of insurance on property situated in, or from contracts with persons resident in, as the case may be, the province in Canada or country other than Canada in which is situated the permanent establishment of the corporation to which the net premium is reasonably attributable in the circumstances.

History: S. 403(4) was added by S.C. 2009, c. 2, s. 94(1), applicable to the 2009 and subsequent taxation years.

404. Banks

(1) Notwithstanding subsections 402(3) and (4), the amount of taxable income that is deemed to have been earned by a bank in a taxation year in a province in which it had a permanent establishment is $^1/_3$ of the total of

(*a*) the proportion of its taxable income for the year that the total of the salaries and wages paid in the year by the bank to employees of its permanent establishment in the province is of the total of all salaries and wages paid in the year by the bank; and

(*b*) twice the proportion of its taxable income for the year that the total amount of loans and deposits of its permanent establishment in the province for the year is of the total amount of all loans and deposits of the bank for the year.

History: S. 404(1)(*a*) and (*b*) were replaced by S.C. 2017, c. 33, s. 86(2), deemed in force September 16, 2016, and formerly read:

(*a*) that proportion of its taxable income for the year that the aggregate of the salaries and wages paid in the year by the bank to employees of its permanent establishment in the province is of the aggregate of all salaries and wages paid in the year by the bank; and

(*b*) twice that proportion of its taxable income for the year that the aggregate amount of loans and deposits of its permanent establishment in the province for the year is of the aggregate amount of all loans and deposits of the bank for the year.

The heading before s. 404 was replaced by P.C. 2009-1869, SOR/2009-302, dated November 19, 2009, published in the *Canada Gazette* December 9, 2009, applicable after June 27, 1999. The heading before s. 404 formerly read "Chartered Banks".

S. 404(1), the portion before paragraph (*a*) was replaced by P.C. 2009-1869, SOR/2009-302, dated November 19, 2009, published in the *Canada Gazette* December 9, 2009, applicable after June 27, 1999. S. 404(1), the portion before paragraph (*a*) formerly read:

(1) Notwithstanding subsections 402(3) and (4), the amount of taxable income that shall be deemed to have been earned by a chartered bank in a taxation year in a province in which it had a permanent establishment is $^1/_3$ of the aggregate of

(2) For the purposes of subsection (1), the amount of loans for a taxation year is $^1/_{12}$ of the total of the amounts outstanding, on the loans made by the bank, at the close of business on the last day of each month in the year.

History: S. 404(2) was replaced by S.C. 2017, c. 33, s. 86(3), deemed in force September 16, 2016, and formerly read:

(2) For the purposes of subsection (1), the amount of loans for a taxation year is $^1/_{12}$ of the aggregate of the amounts outstanding, on the loans made by the bank, at the close of business on the last day of each month in the year.

(3) For the purposes of subsection (1), the amount of deposits for a taxation year is $^1/_{12}$ of the total of the amounts on deposit with the bank at the close of business on the last day of each month in the year.

History: S. 404(3) was replaced by S.C. 2017, c. 33, s. 86(3), deemed in force September 16, 2016, and formerly read:

(3) For the purposes of subsection (1), the amount of deposits for a taxation year is $^1/_{12}$ of the aggregate of the amounts on deposit with the bank at the close of business on the last day of each month in the year.

(4) For the purposes of subsections (2) and (3), loans and deposits do not include bonds, stocks, debentures, items in transit and deposits in favour of Her Majesty in right of Canada.

404.1. (1) Notwithstanding subsections 402(3) and (4), the amount of taxable income that is deemed to have been earned by a federal credit union in a taxation year in a province in which it had a permanent establishment is $^1/_3$ of the total of

(*a*) the proportion of its taxable income for the year that the total of the salaries and wages paid in the year by the federal credit union to employees of its permanent establishment in the province is of the total of all salaries and wages paid in the year by the federal credit union, and

(*b*) twice the proportion of its taxable income for the year that the total amount of loans and deposits of its permanent establishment in the province for the year is of the total amount of all loans and deposits of the federal credit union for the year.

History: S. 404.1(1) was added by S.C. 2017, c. 33, s. 87(1), deemed in force September 16, 2016.

(2) For the purposes of subsection (1), the amount of loans for a taxation year is $^1/_{12}$ of the total of the amounts outstanding, on the loans made by the federal credit union, at the close of business on the last day of each month in the year.

History: S. 404.1(2) was added by S.C. 2017, c. 33, s. 87(1), deemed in force September 16, 2016.

(3) For the purposes of subsection (1), the amount of deposits for a taxation year is $^1/_{12}$ of the total of the amounts on deposit with the federal credit union at the close of business on the last day of each month in the year.

History: S. 404.1(3) was added by S.C. 2017, c. 33, s. 87(1), deemed in force September 16, 2016.

(4) For the purposes of subsections (2) and (3), loans and deposits do not include bonds, stocks, debentures, items in transit and deposits in favour of Her Majesty in right of Canada.

History: S. 404.1(4) was added by S.C. 2017, c. 33, s. 87(1), deemed in force September 16, 2016.

405. Trust and Loan Corporations

(1) Notwithstanding subsections 402(3) and (4), the amount of taxable income that shall be deemed to have been earned in a taxation year by a trust and loan corporation, trust corporation or loan corporation in a province in which it had a permanent establishment is that proportion of its taxable income for the year that the gross revenue for the year of its permanent establishment in the province is of the total gross revenue for the year of the corporation.

(2) In subsection (1), "gross revenue for the year of its permanent establishment in the province" means the aggregate of the gross revenue of the corporation for the year arising from

(*a*) loans secured by lands situated in the province;

(*b*) loans, not secured by land, to persons residing in the province;

(*c*) loans

(i) to persons residing in a province or country other than Canada in which the corporation has no permanent establishment, and

(ii) administered by a permanent establishment in the province,

except loans secured by land situated in a province or country other than Canada in which the corporation has a permanent establishment; and

(*d*) business conducted at the permanent establishment in the province, other than revenue in respect of loans.

406. Railway Corporations

(1) Notwithstanding subsections 402(3) and (4), the amount of taxable income that shall be deemed to have been earned by a railway corporation in a taxation year in a province in which it had a permanent establishment is, unless subsection (2) applies, 1/2 the aggregate of

(*a*) that proportion of the taxable income of the corporation for the year that the equated track miles of the corporation in the province is of the equated track miles of the corporation in Canada; and

(*b*) that proportion of the taxable income of the corporation for the year that the gross ton miles of the corporation for the year in the province is of the gross ton miles of the corporation for the year in Canada.

(2) Where a corporation to which subsection (1) would apply, if this subsection did not apply thereto, operates an airline service, ships or hotels or receives substantial revenues that are petroleum or natural gas royalties, or does a combination of two or more of those things, the amount of its taxable income that shall be deemed to have been earned in a taxation year in a province in which it had a permanent establishment is the aggregate of the amounts computed

(*a*) by applying the provisions of section 407 to that part of its taxable income for the year that may reasonably be considered to have arisen from the operation of the airline service;

(*b*) by applying the provisions of section 410 to that part of its taxable income for the year that may reasonably be considered to have arisen from the operation of the ships;

(*c*) by applying the provisions of section 402 to that part of its taxable income for the year that may reasonably be considered to have arisen from the operation of the hotels;

(*d*) by applying the provisions of section 402 to that part of its taxable income for the year that may reasonably be considered to have arisen from the ownership by the taxpayer of petroleum or natural gas rights or any interest therein; and

(*e*) by applying the provisions of subsection (1) to the remaining portion of its taxable income for the year.

(3) In this section, "equated track miles" in a specified place means the aggregate of

(*a*) the number of miles of first main track,

(*b*) 80 per cent of the number of miles of other main tracks, and

(*c*) 50 per cent of the number of miles of yard tracks and sidings,

in that place.

(4) For the purpose of making an allocation under paragraph (2)(*b*), a reference in section 410 to "salaries and wages paid in the year by the corporation to employees" shall be read as a reference to salaries and wages paid by the corporation to employees employed in the operation of permanent establishments (other than ships) maintained for the shipping business.

(5) For the purpose of making an allocation under paragraph (2)(*c*),

(*a*) a reference in section 402 to "gross revenue for the year reasonably attributable to the permanent establishment in the province" shall be read as a reference to the gross revenue of the taxpayer from operating hotels therein;

(*b*) a reference in section 402 to "total gross revenue for the year" shall be read as a reference to the total gross revenue of the taxpayer for the year from operating hotels; and

(*c*) a reference in section 402 to "salaries and wages paid in the year by the corporation to employees" shall be read as a reference to salaries and wages paid to employees engaged in the operations of its hotels.

(6) Notwithstanding subsection 402(5), for the purpose of making an allocation under paragraph (2)(*d*),

(*a*) a reference in section 402 to "gross revenue for the year reasonably attributable to the permanent establishment in the province" shall be read as a reference to the gross revenue of the taxpayer from the ownership by the taxpayer of petroleum and natural gas rights in lands in the province and any interest therein;

(*b*) a reference in section 402 to "total gross revenue for the year" shall be read as a reference to the total gross revenue of the taxpayer from ownership by the taxpayer of petroleum and natural gas rights and any interest therein; and

(*c*) a reference in section 402 to "salaries and wages paid in the year by the corporation to employees" shall be read as a reference to salaries and wages paid to employees employed in connection with the corporation's petroleum and natural gas rights and interests therein.

407. Airline Corporations

(1) Notwithstanding subsections 402(3) and (4), the amount of taxable income that shall be deemed to have been earned in a taxation year by an airline corporation in a province in which it had a permanent establishment is the amount that is equal to 1/4 of the aggregate of

(*a*) that proportion of its taxable income for the year that the capital cost of all the corporation's fixed assets, except aircraft, in the province at the end of the year is of the capital cost of all its fixed assets, except aircraft, in Canada at the end of the year; and

(*b*) that proportion of its taxable income for the year that three times the number of revenue plane miles flown by its aircraft during the year in the province is of the total of all amounts, each of which is the total number of revenue plane miles flown by its aircraft during the year in a province in which the corporation had a permanent establishment.

History: S. 407(1)(*b*) was replaced by S.C. 2013, c. 34, s. 381(1), applicable to taxation years that end after October 24, 2012, and formerly read:

(*b*) that proportion of its taxable income for the year that three times the number of revenue plane miles flown by its aircraft in the province during the year is of the total number of revenue plane miles flown by its aircraft in Canada during the year other than miles flown in a province in which the corporation had no permanent establishment.

(2) For the purposes of this section, "revenue plane miles flown" shall be weighted according to take-off weight of the aircraft operated.

(3) For the purposes of this section, "take-off weight" of an aircraft means

(*a*) for an aircraft in respect of which an application form for a Certificate of Airworthiness has been submitted to and accepted by the Department of Transport, the maximum permissible take-off weight, in pounds, shown on the form; and

(*b*) for any other aircraft, the weight, in pounds, that may reasonably be considered to be the equivalent of the weight referred to in paragraph (*a*).

408. Grain Elevator Operators

Notwithstanding subsections 402(3) and (4), the amount of taxable income of a corporation whose chief business is the operation of grain elevators that shall be deemed to have been earned by that corporation in a taxation year in a province in which it had a permanent establishment is 1/2 of the aggregate of

(*a*) that proportion of its taxable income for the year that the number of bushels of grain received in the year in the elevators operated by the corporation in the province is of the total number of bushels of grain received in the year in all the elevators operated by the corporation; and

(*b*) that proportion of its taxable income for the year that the aggregate of salaries and wages paid in the year by the corporation to employees of its permanent establishment in the province is of the aggregate of all salaries and wages paid in the year by the corporation.

409. Bus and Truck Operators

Notwithstanding subsections 402(3) and (4), the amount of taxable income of a corporation whose chief business is the transportation of goods or passengers (other than by the operation of a railway, ship or airline service) that shall be deemed to have been earned by that corporation in a taxation year in a province in which it had a permanent establishment is 1/2 of the aggregate of

(*a*) that proportion of its taxable income for the year that the number of kilometres driven by the corporation's vehicles, whether owned or leased, on roads in the province in the year is of the total number of kilometres driven by those vehicles in the year on roads other than roads in provinces or countries in which the corporation had no permanent establishment; and

(*b*) that proportion of its taxable income for the year that the aggregate of salaries and wages paid in the year by the corporation to employees of its permanent establishment in the province is of the aggregate of all salaries and wages paid in the year by the corporation.

410. Ship Operators

(1) Notwithstanding subsections 402(3) and (4), the amount of taxable income of a corporation whose chief business is the operation of ships that shall be deemed to have been earned by the corporation in a taxation year in a province in which it had a permanent establishment is the aggregate of,

(*a*) that proportion of its allocable income for the year that its port-call-tonnage in the province is of its total port-call-tonnage in all the provinces in which it had a permanent establishment; and

(*b*) if its taxable income for the year exceeds its allocable income for the year, that proportion of the excess that the aggregate of the salaries and wages paid in the year by the corporation to employees of the permanent establishment (other than a ship) in the province is of the aggregate of salaries and wages paid in the year by the corporation to employees of its permanent establishments (other than ships) in Canada.

(2) In this section,

(*a*) "allocable income for the year" means that proportion of the taxable income of the corporation for the year that its total port-call-tonnage in Canada is of its total port-call-tonnage in all countries; and

(*b*) "port-call-tonnage" in a province or country means the aggregate of the products obtained by multiplying, for each ship operated by the corporation, the number of calls made in the year by that ship at ports in that province or country by the number of tons of the registered net tonnage of that ship.

411. Pipeline Operators

Notwithstanding subsections 402(3) and (4), the amount of taxable income of a corporation whose chief business is the operation of a pipeline that shall be deemed to have been earned by that corporation in a taxation year in a province in which it had a permanent establishment is 1/2 of the aggregate of

(*a*) that proportion of its taxable income for the year that the number of miles of pipeline of the corporation in the province is of the number of miles of pipeline of the corporation in all the provinces in which it had a permanent establishment; and

(*b*) that proportion of its taxable income for the year that the aggregate of the salaries and wages paid in the year by the corporation to employees of its permanent establishment in the province is of the aggregate of salaries and wages paid in the year by the corporation to employees of its permanent establishments in Canada.

412. Divided Businesses

If part of the business of a corporation for a taxation year, other than a corporation described in any of sections 403, 404, 404.1, 405, 406, 407, 408, 409, 410 and 411, consisted of operations normally conducted by a corporation described in one of those sections, the corporation and the Minister may agree to determine the amount of taxable income deemed to have been earned in the year in a particular province to be the total of the amounts computed

(*a*) by applying the provisions of such of those sections as would have been applicable if it had been a corporation described therein to the portion of its taxable income for the year that might reasonably be considered to have arisen from that part of the business; and

(*b*) by applying the provisions of section 402 to the remaining portion of its taxable income for the year.

History: S. 412, the portion before paragraph (*a*), was replaced by S.C. 2017, c. 33, s. 88(1), deemed in force September 16, 2016, and formerly read:

412 *Divided Businesses.* Where part of the business of a corporation for a taxation year, other than a corporation described in section 403, 404, 405, 406, 407, 408, 409, 410 or 411, consisted of operations normally conducted by a corporation described in one of those sections, the corporation and the Minister may agree to determine the amount of taxable income deemed to have been earned in the year in a particular province to be the aggregate of the amounts computed

S. 306(6) was added by S.C. 2014, c. 39, s. 81(2), in force December 16, 2014.

413. Non-Resident Corporations

(1) In this Part, if a corporation is not resident in Canada

(*a*) "salaries and wages paid in the year" by the corporation does not include salaries and wages paid to employees of a permanent establishment outside Canada; and

(*b*) "taxable income" of the corporation is deemed to refer to the corporation's taxable income earned in Canada.

History: S. 413(1) was replaced by S.C. 2013, c. 33, s. 33(1), applicable to taxation years that begin after March 20, 2013, and formerly read:

(1) In this Part, if a corporation is not resident in Canada, "salaries and wages paid in the year" by the corporation does not include salaries and wages paid to employees of a permanent establishment outside Canada.

S. 413(1) was replaced by S.C. 2009, c. 2, s. 95(1), applicable to the 2009 and subsequent taxation years. S. 413(1) formerly read:

(1) For the purposes of this Part, where a corporation is not resident in Canada, "salaries and wages paid in the year" by the corporation does not include salaries and wages paid to employees of a permanent establishment outside Canada and "taxable income" shall be deemed to refer to taxable income earned in Canada as determined under section 115 of the Act.

(2) For the purposes of paragraph 402(3)(*a*), where a corporation is not resident in Canada, "total gross revenue for the year" of the corporation does not include gross revenue reasonably attributable to a permanent establishment outside Canada.

(3) For the purpose of paragraph 404(1)(*b*), in the case of an authorized foreign bank, "all loans and deposits of the bank for the year" is to be read as a reference to "all loans and deposits of the bank for the year in respect of its Canadian banking business".

History: S. 413(3) was added by P.C. 2009-1869, SOR/2009-302, dated November 19, 2009, published in the *Canada Gazette* December 9, 2009, applicable after June 27, 2009.

413.1. (Revoked by S.C. 2013, c. 33, s. 34(1).)

History: S. 413.1 and the preceding heading were repealed by S.C. 2013, c. 33, s. 34(1), applicable to taxation years that begin after March 20, 2013, and formerly read:

413.1 *International Banking Centre Exception.* Despite any other provision in this Part, a corporation's taxable income earned in a taxation year in a particular province is equal to the total of

(*a*) the corporation's taxable income earned in the taxation year in the particular province (determined without reference to this section), and

(*b*) the positive or negative amount determined by the formula

$$A - B$$

where

A is the total of all amounts that are, because of the application of section 33.1 of the Act to a business carried on in a branch or office situated in the particular province, not allowed to be deducted in computing the corporation's income for the taxation year, and

B is the total of all amounts that are, because of the application of section 33.1 of the Act to a business carried on in a branch or office situated in the particular province, not required to be added in computing the corporation's income for the taxation year.

S. 413.1 and the heading before it were added by S.C. 2009, c. 2, s. 96(1), applicable to the 2009 and subsequent taxation years.

414. Provincial SIFT Tax Rate

(1) The following definitions apply in this section.

"general corporate income tax rate", in a province for a taxation year, means

(*a*) for Quebec, 0%;

(*b*) for the Newfoundland offshore area, the highest percentage rate of tax imposed under the laws of Newfoundland and Labrador on the taxable income of a public corporation earned in the taxation year in Newfoundland and Labrador;

(*c*) for the Nova Scotia offshore area, the highest percentage rate of tax imposed under the laws of Nova Scotia on the taxable income of a public corporation earned in the taxation year in Nova Scotia; and

(*d*) for each other province, the highest percentage rate of tax imposed under the laws of the province on the taxable income of a public corporation earned in the taxation year in the province.

"province" includes the Newfoundland offshore area and the Nova Scotia offshore area.

"taxable SIFT distributions", for a taxation year, means

(*a*) in the case of a SIFT trust, its non-deductible distributions amount for the taxation year; and

(*b*) in the case of a SIFT partnership, its taxable non-portfolio earnings for the taxation year.

(2) In determining the amount of a SIFT trust's or SIFT partnership's taxable SIFT distributions for a taxation year earned in a province

(*a*) except as provided in paragraph (*b*), this Part applies in respect of the SIFT trust or SIFT partnership as though

(i) each reference to "corporation" (other than in the expression "subsidiary controlled corporation") were read as a reference to "SIFT trust" or "SIFT partnership", as the case may be,

(ii) each reference to "taxable income" were read as a reference to "taxable SIFT distributions",

(iii) each reference to "its incorporating documents or bylaws" were read as a reference to "the agreement governing the SIFT trust" or "the agreement governing the SIFT partnership", as the case may be, and

(iv) "subsidiary controlled corporation" in respect of a SIFT trust or a SIFT partnership meant a corporation more than 50% of the issued share capital of which (having full voting rights under all circumstances) belongs to the SIFT trust or SIFT partnership, as the case may be; and

(*b*) subsection 400(1), section 401, subsections 402(1) and (2) and sections 403 to 413 do not apply.

(3) Subject to subsection (4), in applying the definition "provincial SIFT tax rate" in subsection 248(1) of the Act in respect of a SIFT trust or SIFT partnership for a taxation year, the prescribed amount determined in respect of the SIFT trust or SIFT partnership for the taxation year is

(*a*) if the SIFT trust or SIFT partnership has no permanent establishment in a province in the taxation year, 0.10;

(*b*) if the SIFT trust or SIFT partnership has a permanent establishment in a province in the taxation year and has no permanent establishment outside that province in the taxation year, the decimal fraction equivalent of the general corporate income tax rate in the province for the taxation year; and

(*c*) if the SIFT trust or SIFT partnership has a permanent establishment in the taxation year in a province, and has a permanent establishment outside that province in the taxation year, the amount, expressed as a decimal fraction, determined by the formula

$$A + B$$

where

A is the total of all amounts, if any, each of which is in respect of a province in which the SIFT trust or SIFT partnership has a permanent establishment in the taxation year and is determined by the formula

$$C/D \times E$$

where

C is its taxable SIFT distributions for the taxation year earned in the province,

D is its total taxable SIFT distributions for the taxation year, and

E is the decimal fraction equivalent of the general corporate income tax rate in the province for the taxation year, and

B is the amount determined by the formula

$$(1 - F/D) \times 0.1$$

where

F is the total of all amounts each of which is an amount determined under the description of C in the description of A in respect of a province in which the SIFT trust or SIFT partnership has a permanent establishment in the taxation year.

(4) If a SIFT trust or a SIFT partnership has a permanent establishment in Quebec in a taxation year, paragraph (*a*) of the definition "general corporate income tax rate" in subsection (1) does not apply in determining the prescribed amount under subsection (3) in respect of the SIFT trust or the SIFT partnership for the taxation year for the purposes of applying the definition "provincial SIFT tax rate" in determining:

(*a*) in the case of the SIFT partnership, the amount of a dividend deemed by paragraph 96(1.11)(*b*) of the Act to have been received by it in the taxation year; and

(*b*) in the case of the SIFT trust, the amount of its taxable SIFT trust distributions for the taxation year.

History: S. 414 and the heading before it were replaced by S.C. 2009, c. 2, s. 97(1), applicable to the 2007 and subsequent taxation years, except that paragraph 414(4)(*b*) shall not apply for the taxation years of a SIFT trust that end on or before February 3, 2009. S. 414 and the heading before it formerly read:

Nova Scotia Offshore Area

414. For the purpose of subsection 123(2) of the Act, the "amount taxable earned by the corporation in the year in the Nova Scotia offshore area", in respect of a corporation for a taxation year, means the amount of taxable income of the corporation earned in the year that would be allocated under this Part to the Nova Scotia offshore area if the reference to the word "province" in this Part were read as "Nova Scotia offshore area".

415. (Repealed.)

History: S. 415 was repealed by S.C. 2009, c. 2, s. 97(1), applicable to the 2007 and subsequent taxation years. S. 415 formerly read:

415. For the purposes of this Part and subsection 123(2) of the Act, "Nova Scotia offshore area" has the meaning assigned to the expression "offshore area" by subsection 63(1) of the *Canada-Nova Scotia Oil and Gas Agreement Act*.

Part V
Non-Resident-Owned Investment Corporations

500. Elections

Any election by a corporation to be taxed under section 133 of the Act shall be made by forwarding by registered mail to the Director–Taxation at the District Office of the Department of National Revenue, Taxation that serves the area in which the head office of the corporation is located the following documents:

(*a*) a letter stating that the corporation elects to be taxed under the said section 133;

(*b*) a certified copy of the resolution of the directors of the corporation authorizing the election to be made; and

(*c*) a certified list showing

(i) the names and addresses of the registered shareholders and the number of shares of each class held by each,

(ii) the names and addresses of the holders of the corporation's bonds, debentures, or other funded indebtedness, if any, and

(iii) the names and addresses of the beneficial owners of shares, bonds, debentures, or other funded indebtedness in cases where the registered shareholders or holders, as the case may be, are not the beneficial owners.

501. Elections Revoked

Any election to be taxed under section 133 of the Act shall be revoked by a corporation by forwarding by registered mail to the Deputy Minister of National Revenue for Taxation at Ottawa the following documents in duplicate:

(*a*) a letter stating that the corporation revokes its election; and

(*b*) a certified copy of the resolution of the directors of the corporation authorizing the election to be revoked.

502. Certificates of Changes of Ownership

A corporation which is taxable under section 133 of the Act shall attach to its return of income required to be filed under subsection 150(1) of the Act, a certified statement showing any changes during the taxation year in the information referred to in paragraph 500(*c*).

503. (Revoked.)

Regulations

Part VI
Elections

600. [Prescribed provisions for late, amended or revoked elections]

For the purposes of paragraphs 220(3.2)(*a*) and (*b*) of the Act, the following are prescribed provisions:

(*a*) section 21 of the Act;

(*b*) subsections 13(4), (7.4) and (29), 20(24), 44(1) and (6), 45(2) and (3), 50(1), 53(2.1), 56.4(13), 70(6.2), (9.01), (9.11), (9.21) and (9.31), 72(2), 73(1), 80.1(1), 82(3), 83(2), 91(1.4), 104(14), 107(2.001), 143(2), 146.01(7), 146.02(7), 164(6) and (6.1), 184(3), 251.2(6) and 256(9) of the Act;

(*c*) paragraphs 12(2.2)(*b*), 66.7(7)(*c*), (*d*) and (*e*) and (8)(*c*), (*d*) and (*e*), 80.01(4)(*c*), 86.1(2)(*f*) and 128.1(4)(*d*), (6)(*a*) and (*c*), (7)(*d*) and (*g*) and (8)(*c*) of the Act;

(*d*) subsections 1103(1), (2) and (2d) and 5907(2.1) of these Regulations.

History: S. 600(*b*) was replaced by S.C. 2017, c. 33, s. 89(1), deemed in force July 12, 2013, and formerly read:

(*b*) subsections 13(4), (7.4) and (29), 20(24), 44(1) and (6), 45(2) and (3), 50(1), 53(2.1), 56.4(13), 70(6.2), (9.01), (9.11), (9.21) and (9.31), 72(2), 73(1), 80.1(1), 82(3), 83(2), 104(14), 107(2.001), 143(2), 146.01(7), 146.02(7), 164(6) and (6.1), 184(3), 251.2(6) and 256(9) of the Act;

S. 600(*b*) was replaced by S.C. 2016, c. 12, s. 76(1), in force January 1, 2017, and formerly read:

(*b*) subsections 13(4), (7.4) and (29), 14(6), 20(24), 44(1) and (6), 45(2) and (3), 50(1), 53(2.1), 56.4(13), 70(6.2), (9.01), (9.11), (9.21) and (9.31), 72(2), 73(1), 80.1(1), 82(3), 83(2), 104(14), 107(2.001), 143(2), 146.01(7), 146.02(7), 164(6) and (6.1), 184(3), 251.2(6) and 256(9) of the Act;

S. 600(*b*) was replaced by S.C. 2013, c. 40, s. 98(1), deemed to have come into force on March 21, 2013, and formerly read:

(*b*) subsections 13(4), (7.4) and (29), 14(6), 20(24), 44(1) and (6), 45(2) and (3), 50(1), 53(2.1), 56.4(13), 70(6.2), (9.01), (9.11), (9.21) and (9.31), 72(2), 73(1), 80.1(1), 82(3), 83(2), 104(14), 107(2.001), 143(2), 146.01(7), 146.02(7), 164(6) and (6.1), 184(3) and 256(9) of the Act;

S. 600(*b*) was replaced by S.C. 2013, c. 34, s. 382(2), deemed to have come into force on November 1, 2011, and formerly read:

(*b*) subsections 7(10), 13(4), (7.4) and (29), 14(6), 20(24), 44(1) and (6), 45(2) and (3), 50(1), 53(2.1), 56.4(13), 70(6.2), (9.01), (9.11), (9.21) and (9.31), 72(2), 73(1), 80.1(1), 82(3), 83(2), 104(5.3) and (14), 107(2.001), 143(2), 146.01(7), 146.02(7), 164(6) and (6.1), 184(3) and 256(9) of the Act;

S. 600(*b*) was replaced by S.C. 2013, c. 34, s. 382(1), deemed to have come into force on May 13, 2010, and formerly read:

(*b*) subsections 7(10), 13(4), (7.4) and (29), 14(6), 20(24), 44(1) and (6), 45(2) and (3), 50(1), 53(2.1), 70(6.2), (9.01), (9.11), (9.21) and (9.31), 72(2), 73(1), 80.1(1), 82(3), 83(2), 104(5.3) and (14), 107(2.001), 143(2), 146.01(7), 146.02(7), 164(6) and (6.1), 184(3) and 256(9) of the Act;

S. 600(*b*) was replaced by P.C. 2010-551, SOR/2010-96, dated April 29, 2010, published in the *Canada Gazette* May 12, 2010, applicable in respect of dispositions of property on or after May 2, 2006. S. 600(*b*) formerly read:

(*b*) subsections 7(10), 12.2(4) , 13(4), (7.4) and (29), 14(6), 20(24), 44(1) and (6), 45(2) and (3), 50(l), 53(2.1), 70(6.2), (9), (9.1), (9.2) and (9.3), 72(2), 73(l), 80.1(1), 82(3), 83(2), 104(5.3) and (14), 107(2.001), 143(2), 146.01(7), 164(6) and (6.1), 184(3) and 256(9) of the Act;

S. 600(*b*) was amended by P.C. 2010-551, SOR/2010-96, dated April 29, 2010, by adding the reference "146.02(7)," in numerical order, in force May 12, 2010, date published in the *Canada Gazette*.

S. 600(*b*) was amended by P.C. 2010-551, SOR/2010-96, dated April 29, 2010, by striking out the reference to "12.2(4)", in force May 12, 2010, date published in the *Canada Gazette*.

Information Circulars: IC 07-1 Taxpayer relief provisions.

Part VII
Logging Taxes on Income

700. Logging

(1) Except as provided in subsection (2), for the purposes of paragraph 127(2)(*a*) [subsection 127(2) "income for the year from logging operations in the province"] of the Act "income for the year from logging operations in the province" means the aggregate of (*a*) where standing timber is cut in the province by the taxpayer or logs cut from standing timber in the province are acquired by the taxpayer and the logs so obtained are sold by the taxpayer in the province before or on delivery to a sawmill, pulp or paper plant or other place for processing logs, the taxpayer's income for the year from the sale, other than any portion thereof that was included in computing the taxpayer's income from logging operations in the province for a previous year;

(*b*) where standing timber in the province or the right to cut standing timber in the province is sold by the taxpayer, the taxpayer's income for the year from the sale, other than any portion thereof that was included in computing the taxpayer's income from logging operations in the province for a previous year;

(*c*) where standing timber is cut in the province by the taxpayer or logs cut from standing timber in the province are acquired by the taxpayer, if the logs so obtained are

(i) exported from the province and are sold by him prior to or on delivery to a sawmill, pulp or paper plant or other place for processing logs, or

(ii) exported from Canada,

the amount computed by deducting from the value, as determined by the province, of the logs so exported in the year, the aggregate of the costs of acquiring, cutting, transporting and selling the logs; and

(*d*) where standing timber is cut in the province by the taxpayer or logs cut from standing timber in the province are acquired by the taxpayer, if the logs are processed by the taxpayer or by a person on his behalf in a sawmill, pulp or paper plant or other place for processing logs in Canada, the income of the taxpayer for the year from all sources minus the aggregate of

(i) his income from sources other than logging operations carried on in Canada and other than the processing in Canada by him or on his behalf and sale by him of logs, timber and products produced therefrom,

(ii) each amount included in the aggregate determined under this subsection by virtue of paragraph (*a*), (*b*) or (*c*), and

(iii) an amount equal to eight per cent of the original cost to him of properties described in Schedule II used by him in the year in the processing of logs or products derived therefrom or, if the amount so determined is greater than 65 per cent of the income remaining after making the deductions under subparagraphs (i) and (ii), 65 per cent of the income so remaining or, if the amount so determined is less than 35 per cent of the income so remaining, 35 per cent of the income so remaining.

(2) Where the taxpayer cuts standing timber or acquires logs cut from standing timber in more than one province, for the purposes of paragraph 127(2)(*a*) [subsection 127(2) "income for the year from logging operations in the province"] of the Act "income for the year from logging operations in the province" means the aggregate of

(*a*) the amounts determined in respect of that province in accordance with paragraphs (1)(*a*), (*b*) and (*c*); and

(*b*) where the logs are processed by the taxpayer or by a person on his behalf in a sawmill, pulp or paper plant or other place for processing logs in Canada, an amount equal to the proportion of the income of the taxpayer for the year from all sources minus the aggregate of

(i) his income from sources other than logging operations carried on in Canada and other than the processing in Canada by him or on his behalf and sale by him of logs, timber and products produced therefrom,

(ii) the aggregate of amounts determined in respect of each province in accordance with paragraphs (1)(*a*), (*b*) and (*c*), and

(iii) an amount equal to eight per cent of the original cost to him of properties described in Schedule II used by him in the year in the processing of logs or products derived therefrom or, if the amount so determined is greater than 65 per cent of the income remaining after making the deductions under subparagraphs (i) and (ii), 65 per cent of the income so remaining or, if the amount so determined is less than 35 per cent of the income so remaining, 35 per cent of the income so remaining,

that

(iv) the quantity of standing timber cut in the province in the year by the taxpayer and logs cut from standing timber in the province acquired by the taxpayer in the year,

is of

(v) the total quantity of standing timber cut and logs acquired in the year by the taxpayer.

(3) For the purpose of the definition "logging tax" in subsection 127(2) of the Act, each of the following is declared to be a tax of general application on income from logging operations:

(*a*) the tax imposed by the Province of British Columbia under the *Logging Tax Act*, R.S.B.C. 1996, c. 277; and

(*b*) the tax imposed by the Province of Quebec under Part VII of the *Taxation Act*, R.S.Q., c. I-3.

History: S. 700(3) was replaced by P.C. 2010-548, SOR/2010-93, dated April 29, 2010, in force May 12, 2010, date of publication in the *Canada Gazette*. S. 700(3) formerly read:

(3) For the purposes of paragraph 127(2)(*b*) [subsection 127(2) "logging tax"] of the Act, the tax imposed by the legislature of

(*a*) the Province of British Columbia under the *Logging Tax Act* of that province, and

(*b*) (Revoked.)

(*c*) the Province of Quebec under Part VII of the *Taxation Act* of that province,

are each declared to be a tax of general application on income from logging operations.

Part VIII
Non-Resident Taxes

800. Registered Non-Resident Insurers

Subsections 215(1), (2) and (3) of the Act do not apply to amounts paid or credited to a registered non-resident insurer.

History: S. 800 was replaced by P.C. 2009-1869, SOR/2009-302, dated November 19, 2009, published in the *Canada Gazette* December 9, 2009, applicable to taxation years that end after June 27, 1999. S. 800 formerly read:

800. For the purposes of subsection 215(4) of the Act, subsections 215(1), (2) and (3) of the Act do not apply to amounts paid or credited to a registered non-resident insurer.

801. Filing of Returns by Registered Non-Resident Insurers

A taxpayer that is a registered non-resident insurer in a taxation year shall file a return for the taxation year in prescribed form with the Minister on or before its filing-due date for the taxation year.

History: S. 801 was replaced by P.C. 2009-1869, SOR/2009-302, dated November 19, 2009, published in the *Canada Gazette* December 9, 2009, applicable to taxation years that end after June 27, 1999.

TIME EXTENSION — SECTIONS 801 AND 803

Returns required to be filed by an authorized foreign bank under section 801 and amounts required to be paid by an authorized foreign bank under section 803 are deemed to have been filed or paid, as the case may be, with the Minister of National Revenue in a timely manner if they are so filed and paid on or before the later of

(a) the day on or before which they would, but for this section, be required to be filed or paid; and

(b) the day that is six months after the day on which these Regulations are published in Part II of the *Canada Gazette*.

S. 801 formerly read:

Filing of Returns by Non-Resident Insurers

801. For the purposes of subsection 215(4) of the Act, where a taxpayer is a registered non-resident insurer in a taxation year, the taxpayer shall file a return in respect thereof in prescribed form with the Minister within the six month period immediately following the end of the year.

Forms: T2016 — Part XIII Tax Return — Tax On Income from Canada of Approved Non-Resident Insurers.

802. Amounts Taxable

The amounts that are taxable under Part XIII of the Act in a taxation year of a taxpayer that is a registered non-resident insurer in the taxation year are amounts paid or credited to the taxpayer in the taxation year other than amounts included under Part I of the Act in computing the taxpayer's income from a business carried on by it in Canada.

History: S. 802 was replaced by P.C. 2009-1869, SOR/2009-302, dated November 19, 2009, published in the *Canada Gazette* December 9, 2009, applicable to taxation years that end after June 27, 1999. S. 802 formerly read:

Amounts Taxable

802. For the purposes of paragraph 214(13)(*c*) of the Act, the amounts taxable under Part XIII of the Act in a relevant taxation year of a taxpayer are amounts paid or credited to the taxpayer in the relevant taxation year other than amounts included pursuant to Part I of the Act in computing the taxpayer's income from a business carried on by it in Canada.

803. Payment of Tax by Registered Non-Resident Insurers

A taxpayer that is a registered non-resident insurer in a taxation year shall pay to the Receiver General, on or before its filing-due date for the taxation year, the tax payable by it under Part XIII of the Act in the taxation year.

History: S. 803 was replaced by P.C. 2009-1869, SOR/2009-302, dated November 19, 2009, published in the *Canada Gazette* December 9, 2009, applicable to taxation years that end after June 27, 1999.

TIME EXTENSION — SECTIONS 801 AND 803

Returns required to be filed by an authorized foreign bank under section 801 and amounts required to be paid by an authorized foreign bank under section 803 are deemed to have been filed or paid, as the case may be, with the Minister of National Revenue in a timely manner if they are so filed and paid on or before the later of

(a) the day on or before which they would, but for this section, be required to be filed or paid; and

(b) the day that is six months after the day on which these Regulations are published in Part II of the *Canada Gazette*.

S. 803 formerly read:

Payment of Tax by Non-Resident Insurers

803. For the purposes of subsection 215(4) of the Act, a taxpayer shall pay to the Receiver General, on or before the last day on which the return in respect of a relevant taxation year is required to be filed pursuant to section 801, the tax payable by the taxpayer under Part XIII of the Act on amounts referred to in section 802 in respect of the relevant taxation year.

803.1. (Repealed.)

History: S. 803.1 was repealed by P.C. 2009-1869, SOR/2009-302, dated November 19, 2009, published in the *Canada Gazette* December 9, 2009, applicable in respect of amounts paid or credited on or after August 8, 2009. S. 803.1 formerly read:

803.1 Sections 800 to 803 apply in respect of amounts paid or credited to an authorized foreign bank as if the references in those sections to a registered non-resident insurer were references to the authorized foreign bank.

S. 803.1 was added by P.C. 2009-1869, SOR/2009-302, dated November 19, 2009, published in the *Canada Gazette* December 9, 2009, applicable to amounts that are paid or credited before August 8, 2009 and in a taxation year that ends after June 27, 1999.

804. Interpretation

In this Part, "registered non-resident insurer" means a non-resident corporation approved to carry on business in Canada under the *Insurance Companies Act*.

805. Other Non-Resident Persons

Subject to section 802, every non-resident person who carries on business in Canada is taxable under Part XIII of the Act on all amounts otherwise taxable under that Part except those amounts that

(*a*) may reasonably be attributed to the business carried on by the person through a permanent establishment (within the meaning assigned by section 8201) in Canada; or

(*b*) are required by subparagraph 115(1)(*a*)(iii.3) of the Act to be included in computing the person's taxable income earned in Canada for the year.

History: S. 805 was replaced by P.C. 2009-1869, SOR/2009-302, dated November 19, 2009, published in the *Canada Gazette* December 9, 2009, applicable to taxation years that end after June 27, 1999, except that for taxation years that begin before August 8, 2009, paragraph 805(*a*) is to be read as follows:

"(*a*) may reasonably be attributed to the business carried on by the person through a permanent establishment (within the meaning that would be assigned by subsection 400(2) if that subsection applied to the person) in Canada; or"

S. 805 formerly read:

(1) Every non-resident person who carries on business in Canada shall be taxable under Part XIII of the Act on all amounts otherwise taxable under that Part except those amounts that

(*a*) may reasonably be attributed to the business carried on by him through a permanent establishment (within the meaning assigned by subsection 400(2) or that would be assigned by that subsection if he were a corporation) in Canada; or

(*b*) are required by subparagraph 115(1)(*a*)(iii.3) of the Act to be included in computing his taxable income earned in the year in Canada.

(2) Where the Minister is satisfied that under subsection (1) an amount is not taxable under Part XIII of the Act, he may permit payment to be made to the non-resident person without any deduction being made under section 215 of the Act.

Regulations

(3) Subsections (1) and (2) do not apply in respect of amounts upon which tax under Part XIII of the Act is payable in a relevant taxation year by a taxpayer required by section 801 to file the return described in that section in respect of that year.

Tax Topics: No. 1965, Potential Double Taxation of Rental Income to Non-Residents?.

Information Circulars: IC 77-16R4 Non-resident income tax (para. 53).

Interpretation Bulletins: *Secondary* — IT-432R2 Benefits conferred on shareholders.

805.1. Payee Certificate

If a person (in this section referred to as the "payee") files an application under this section with the Minister in respect of the anticipated payment or crediting of an amount to the payee, and the Minister determines that the amount is an amount described in paragraph 805(*a*) or (*b*), the Minister shall issue to the payee a certificate that records that determination.

History: S. 805.1 was added by P.C. 2009-1869, SOR/2009-302, dated November 19, 2009, published in the *Canada Gazette* December 9, 2009, applicable after August 8, 2009.

Regulations

806. For the purposes of paragraph (*c*) of the definition *fully exempt interest* in subsection 212(3) of the Act, the Bank for International Settlements and the European Bank for Reconstruction and Development are prescribed.

History: S. 806 was replaced by S.C. 2017, c. 33, s. 90(1), deemed in force January 1, 2008, and formerly read:

806 *International Organizations and Agencies.* For the purposes of clause 212(1)(*b*)(ii)(B) of the Act, the following international organizations and agencies are hereby prescribed:

(*a*) Bank for International Settlements;

(*b*) European Fund;

(*c*) International Bank for Reconstruction and Development;

(*d*) International Development Association;

(*e*) International Finance Corporation; and

(*f*) International Monetary Fund.

S. 306(6) was added by S.C. 2014, c. 39, s. 81(2), in force December 16, 2014.

Information Circulars: IC 77-16R4 Non-resident income tax (para. 53).

806.1. International Organizations and Agencies

(Repealed.)

History: S. 806.1 was repealed by S.C. 2017, c. 33, s. 90(1), deemed in force January 1, 2008, and formerly read:

806.1 *International Organizations and Agencies.* For the purposes of subparagraph 212(1)(*b*)(x) of the Act, the Bank for International Settlements and the European Bank for Reconstruction and Development are prescribed international agencies.

Information Circulars: IC 77-16R4 Non-resident income tax (para. 53).

806.2. Prescribed Obligation

For the purposes of the definition "participating debt interest" in subsection 212(3) of the Act, an obligation is a prescribed obligation if it is an indexed debt obligation and no amount payable in respect of it is

(*a*) contingent or dependent upon the use of, or production from, property in Canada; or

(*b*) computed by reference to

(i) revenue, profit, cash flow, commodity price or any other similar criterion, other than a change in the purchasing power of money, or

(ii) dividends paid or payable to shareholders of any class of shares.

History: S. 806.2, the portion before paragraph (*a*) was replaced by S.C. 2013, c. 40, s. 99(1), deemed to have come into force on January 1, 2008, and formerly read:

806.2 *Prescribed Obligation.* For the purpose of paragraph 212(1)(*b*) of the Act, an obligation is a prescribed obligation if it is an indexed debt obligation and no amount payable in respect of it is

807. Identification of Obligations

For the purposes of subsection 240(2) of the Act, the letters "AX" or the letter "F", as the case may be, shall be clearly and indelibly printed in gothic or similar style capital letters of seven point or larger size either as a prefix to the coupon number or on the lower right hand corner of each coupon or other writing issued in evidence of a right to interest on an obligation referred to in that subsection.

808. Allowances in Respect of Investment in Property in Canada

(1) For the purposes of paragraph 219(1)(*j*) of the Act, the allowance of a corporation (other than an authorized foreign bank) for a taxation year in respect of its investment in property in Canada is prescribed to be the amount, if any, by which

(*a*) the corporation's qualified investment in property in Canada at the end of the year,

exceeds

(*b*) the amount determined under this paragraph for the immediately preceding taxation year.

History: S. 808(1)(*b*) was replaced by P.C. 2010-548, SOR/2010-93, dated April 29, 2010, published in the *Canada Gazette* May 12, 2010, applicable to the 2009 and subsequent taxation years. S. 808(1)(*b*) formerly read:

(*b*) the aggregate of

(i) all allowances computed under this section as it read in its application to each of the taxation years of the corporation that ended before 1972 to the extent that for those taxation years such allowances reduced the amount on which the corporation was taxable under subsection 110B(1) of the Act as it read in its application to those taxation years, and

(ii) the capital investment of the corporation in property in Canada at the end of the corporation's 1960 taxation year, determined under this section as it read in its application to the 1961 taxation year.

S. 808(1), the portion before paragraph (*a*) was replaced by P.C. 2009-1869, SOR/2009-302, dated November 19, 2009, published in the *Canada Gazette* December 9, 2009, applicable to taxation years that begin after 1995, except that in applying the portion of subsection 808(1) before its paragraph (*a*) to taxation years that end before June 28, 1999, it is to be read without reference to "(other than an authorized foreign bank)".

S. 808(1), the portion before paragraph (*a*) formerly read:

(1) For the purposes of paragraph 219(1)(*h*) [paragraph 219(1)(*j*)] of the Act, a corporation's allowance for a taxation year in respect of its investment in property in Canada is hereby prescribed to be the amount, if any, by which

Interpretation Bulletins: *Secondary* — IT-137R3 Additional tax on certain corporations carrying on business in Canada.

(1.1) Notwithstanding subsections (1) and (8), for the purpose of paragraph 219(1)(*j*) of the Act, the allowance of a corporation that becomes resident in Canada at any time is, in respect of its investment in property in Canada for its last taxation year that ends before that time, prescribed to be nil.

History: S. 808(1.1) was added by P.C. 2009-1869, SOR/2009-302, dated November 19, 2009, published in the *Canada Gazette* December 9, 2009, applicable to corporations that become resident in Canada after February 23, 1998, except that before June 28, 1999, subsection 808(1.1) is to be read as follows:

"(1.1) Notwithstanding subsection (1), for the purpose of paragraph 219(1)(*j*) of the Act, the allowance of a corporation that becomes resident in Canada at any time is, in respect of its investment in property in Canada for its last taxation year that ends before that time, prescribed to be nil."

(2) For the purposes of subsection (1), where, at the end of a taxation year, a corporation is not a member of a partnership that was carrying on business in Canada at any time in the year, the corporation's "qualified investment in property in Canada at the end of the year" is the amount, if any, by which the aggregate of (*a*) the cost amount to the corporation, at the end of the year, of land in Canada owned by it at that time for the purpose of gaining or producing income from a business carried on by it in Canada, other than land that is

(i) described in the corporation's inventory,

(ii) depreciable property,

(iii) a Canadian resource property, or

(iv) land the cost of which is or was deductible in computing the corporation's income,

(*b*) an amount equal to the aggregate of the cost amount to the corporation, immediately after the end of the year, of each depreciable property in Canada owned by it for the purpose of gaining or producing income from a business carried on by it in Canada,

(*c*) (Repealed.)

(*d*) where the corporation is not a principal-business corporation, within the meaning assigned by subsection 66(15) of the Act, an amount equal to the total of the corporation's

(i) Canadian exploration and development expenses incurred by the corporation before the end of the year, except to the extent that those expenses were deducted in computing the corporation's income for the year or for a previous taxation year, and

(ii) cumulative Canadian exploration expense, within the meaning assigned by subsection 66.1(6) of the Act, at the end of the year minus any deduction under subsection 66.1(3) of the Act in computing the corporation's income for the year,

(*d*.1) an amount equal to the corporation's cumulative Canadian development expense, within the meaning assigned by subsection 66.2(5) of the Act, at the end of the year minus any deduction under subsection 66.2(2) of the Act in computing the corporation's income for the year,

(*d*.2) an amount equal to the corporation's cumulative Canadian oil and gas property expense, within the meaning assigned by subsection 66.4(5) of the Act, at the end of the year minus any deduction under subsection 66.4(2) of the Act in computing the corporation's income for the year,

(*e*) an amount equal to the aggregate of the cost amount to the corporation at the end of the year of each debt owing to it, or any other right of the corporation to receive an amount, that was outstanding as a result of the disposition by it of property in respect of which an amount would be included, by virtue of paragraph (*a*), (*b*) or (*h*), in its qualified investment in property in Canada at the end of the year if the property had not been disposed of by it before the end of that year,

(*f*) an amount equal to the aggregate of the cost amount to the corporation at the end of the year of each property, other than a Canadian resource property, that was described in the corporation's inventory in respect of a business carried on by it in Canada,

(*g*) an amount equal to the aggregate of the cost amount to the corporation at the end of the year of each debt (other than a debt referred to in paragraph (*e*) or a debt the amount of which was deducted under paragraph 20(1)(*p*) of the Act in computing the corporation's income for the year) owing to it

(i) in respect of any transaction by virtue of which an amount has been included in computing its income for the year or for a previous year from a business carried on by it in Canada, or

(ii) where any part of its ordinary business carried on in Canada was the lending of money, in respect of a loan made by the corporation in the ordinary course of that part of its business, and

(*h*) (Repealed.)

(*i*) an amount equal to the allowable liquid assets of the corporation at the end of the year,

exceeds the aggregate of

(*j*) an amount equal to the total of all amounts each of which is an amount deducted under paragraph 20(1)(*l*), (*l.1*) or (*n*) of the Act in computing the corporation's income for the year from a business carried on by the corporation in Canada,

(*k*) an amount equal to the aggregate of all amounts each of which is an amount deducted by the corporation in the year under subparagraph 40(1)(*a*)(iii) or 44(1)(*e*)(iii) of the Act in respect of a debt referred to in paragraph (*e*);

(*l*) an amount equal to the aggregate of each amount owing by the corporation at the end of the year on account of

(i) the purchase price of property that is referred to in paragraph (*a*), (*b*) or (*f*) or that would be so referred to but for the fact that it has been disposed of before the end of the year,

(ii) Canadian exploration and development expenses, Canadian exploration expense, Canadian development expense or Canadian oil and gas property expense, or

(iii) (Repealed.)

(iv) any other outlay or expense made or incurred by the corporation to the extent that it was deducted in computing its income for the year or for a previous taxation year from a business carried on by it in Canada;

(*m*) an amount equal to the aggregate of all amounts each of which is an amount equal to that proportion of the amount owing (other than an amount owing on account of an outlay or expense referred to in paragraph (*l*)) by the corporation at the end of the year on account of an obligation outstanding at any time in the year in respect of which interest is stipulated to be payable by it that

(i) the interest paid or payable on the obligation by the corporation in respect of the year that is deductible, or would be deductible but for subsection 18(2), (3.1) or (4) or section 21 of the Act, in computing its income for the year from a business carried on by it in Canada,

is of

Regulations

(ii) the interest paid or payable on the obligation by the corporation in respect of the year;

(*n*) the amount, if any, by which

(i) the amount (referred to in this paragraph as "Part I liability"), if any, by which the tax payable for the year by the corporation under Part I of the Act exceeds the amount, if any, paid by the corporation before the end of the year on account thereof,

exceeds

(ii) that proportion of the Part I liability that the amount, if any, in respect of the corporation for the year that is the lesser of

(A) the amount, if any, by which the total of all amounts each of which is a taxable capital gain of the corporation for the year from a disposition of a taxable Canadian property that was not used or held by it in the year in the course of carrying on business in Canada exceeds the total of all amounts each of which is an allowable capital loss of the corporation for the year from a disposition of such a property, and

(B) the amount that would be determined under clause (A) for the year if it were read without reference to the expression "that was not used or held by it in the year in the course of carrying on business in Canada",

is of the corporation's taxable income earned in Canada for the year; and

(iii) (Repealed.)

(*o*) the amount, if any, by which

(i) the amount (referred to in this paragraph as "provincial tax liability"), if any, by which any income taxes payable for the year by the corporation to the government of a province (to the extent that such taxes were not deductible under Part I of the Act in computing the corporation's income for the year from a business carried on by it in Canada) exceeds the amount, if any, paid by the corporation before the end of the year on account thereof,

exceeds

(ii) that proportion of the provincial tax liability that the amount, if any, in respect of the corporation for the year that is the lesser of

(A) the amount, if any, by which the total of all amounts each of which is a taxable capital gain of the corporation for the year from a disposition of a taxable Canadian property that was not used or held by it in the year in the course of carrying on business in Canada exceeds the total of all amounts each of which is an allowable capital loss of the corporation for the year from a disposition of such a property, and

(B) the amount that would be determined under clause (A) for the year if it were read without reference to the expression "that was not used or held by it in the year in the course of carrying on business in Canada",

is of the corporation's taxable income earned in Canada for the year.

(iii) (Repealed.)

(*p*) (Repealed.)

History: S. 808(2)(*c*) was repealed by S.C. 2016, c. 12, s. 77(1), in force January 1, 2017, and formerly read:

(*c*) an amount equal to $^4/_3$ of the cumulative eligible capital of the corporation immediately after the end of the year in respect of each business carried on by it in Canada,

S. 808(2)(*e*) was replaced by S.C. 2016, c. 12, s. 77(2), in force January 1, 2017, and formerly read:

(*e*) an amount equal to the aggregate of the cost amount to the corporation at the end of the year of each debt owing to it, or any other right of the corporation to receive an amount, that was outstanding as a result of the disposition by it of property in respect of which an amount would be included, by virtue of paragraph (*a*), (*b*), (*c*) or (*h*), in its qualified investment in property in Canada at the end of the year if the property had not been disposed of by it before the end of that year,

S. 808(2)(*l*)(iii) was repealed by S.C. 2016, c. 12, s. 77(3), in force January 1, 2017, and formerly read:

(iii) an eligible capital expenditure made or incurred by the corporation before the end of the year in respect of a business carried on by it in Canada, or

S. 808(2)(*j*) was replaced by P.C. 2010-548, SOR/2010-93, dated April 29, 2010, published in the *Canada Gazette* May 12, 2010, applicable with respect to dispositions occurring after November 12, 1981 otherwise than under the terms of an agreement in writing made or entered into on or before that date. S. 808(2)(*j*) formerly read:

(*j*) an amount equal to the aggregate of each amount deducted by the corporation under paragraph 20(1)(*l*), (*l*.1) or (*n*) or subsection 64(1), (1.1) or (1.2) of the Act, in computing its income for the year from a business carried on by it in Canada,

S. 808(2)(*d*) to (*d*.2) were replaced by P.C. 2009-1869, SOR/2009-302, dated November 19, 2009, published in the *Canada Gazette* December 9, 2009, in force November 19, 2009. S. 808(2)(*d*) to (*d*.2) formerly read:

(*d*) where the corporation is not a principal-business corporation, within the meaning assigned by paragraph 66(15)(*h*) [subsection 66(15) "principal-business corporation"] of the Act, an amount equal to the aggregate of the corporation's

(i) Canadian exploration and development expenses, within the meaning assigned by paragraph 66(15)(*b*) [subsection 66(15) "Canadian exploration and development expenses"] of the Act, incurred by the corporation before the end of the year except to the extent that such expenses were deducted by the corporation in computing its income for the year or for a previous taxation year, and

(ii) cumulative Canadian exploration expense, within the meaning assigned by paragraph 66.1(6)(*b*) [subsection 66.1(6) "cumulative Canadian exploration expense"] of the Act, at the end of the year minus any deduction under subsection 66.1(3) of the Act in computing the corporation's income for the year,

(*d*.1) an amount equal to the corporation's cumulative Canadian development expense, within the meaning assigned by paragraph 66.2(5)(*b*) [subsection 66.2(5) "cumulative Canadian development expense"] of the Act, at the end of the year minus any deduction under subsection 66.2(2) of the Act in computing the corporation's income for the year,

(*d*.2) an amount equal to the corporation's cumulative Canadian oil and gas property expense, within the meaning assigned by paragraph 66.4(5)(*b*) [subsection 66.4(5) "cumulative Canadian oil and gas property expense"] of the Act, at the end of the year minus any deduction under subsection 66.4(2) of the Act in computing the corporation's income for the year,

S. 808(2)(*h*) was repealed by P.C. 2009-1869, SOR/2009-302, dated November 19, 2009, published in the *Canada Gazette* December 9, 2009, applicable to taxation years that begin after 1995. S. 808(2)(*h*) formerly read:

(*h*) where the corporation was resident in Canada at any time in the year, an amount equal to the aggregate of the cost amount to the corporation at the end of the year of any property in Canada owned by it

(i) the cost amount of which is not included in its qualified investment in property in Canada at the end of the year by virtue of paragraph (*a*) or (*b*) or subparagraph (*g*)(i), but would be so included if those provisions were read without the phrase "from a business carried on by it in Canada",

(ii) that is a share of the capital stock of a corporation that was not described in the corporation's inventory in respect of a business carried on by it in Canada, or

(iii) that is a bond, debenture, bill, note, mortgage or similar obligation that was not described in the corporation's inventory in respect of a business carried on by it in Canada (other than an obligation referred to in subparagraph (3)(*a*)(iii), a debt referred to in paragraph (*e*) or (*g*) or a debt the amount of which was deducted under paragraph 20(1)(*p*) of the Act in computing the corporation's income for the year), and

Regulations

S. 808(2)(*l*)(i) was replaced by P.C. 2009-1869, SOR/2009-302, dated November 19, 2009, published in the *Canada Gazette* December 9, 2009, applicable to taxation years that begin after 1995. S. 808(2)(*l*)(i) formerly read:

(i) the purchase price of property that is referred to in paragraph (*a*), (*b*), (*f*) or (*h*) or that would be so referred to but for the fact that it has been disposed of before the end of the year,

S. 808(2)(*l*)(ii) was replaced by P.C. 2009-1869, SOR/2009-302, dated November 19, 2009, published in the *Canada Gazette* December 9, 2009, in force November 19, 2009. S. 808(2)(*l*)(ii) formerly read:

(ii) Canadian exploration and development expenses, Canadian exploration expense, Canadian development expense or Canadian oil and gas property expense, within the meanings assigned by paragraphs 66(15)(*b*) [subsection 66(15) "Canadian exploration and development expenses"], 66.1(6)(*a*) [subsection 66.1(6) "Canadian exploration expense"], 66.2(5)(*a*) [subsection 66.2(5) "Canadian development expense"] and 66.4(5)(*a*) [subsection 66.4(5) "Canadian oil and gas property expense"] of the Act, respectively,

S. 808(2)(*n*)(ii) and (iii) were replaced by P.C. 2009-1869, SOR/2009-302, dated November 19, 2009, published in the *Canada Gazette* December 9, 2009, applicable to taxation years that begin after 1995. S. 808(2)(*n*)(ii) and (iii) formerly read:

(ii) where the corporation was, throughout the year, not resident in Canada, that proportion of the Part I liability that the amount, if any, determined under paragraph 219(1)(*d*) of the Act in respect of the corporation for the year is of the corporation's amount taxable (within the meaning given to that expression in section 123 of the Act) for the year, or

(iii) in any other case, nil;

S. 808(2)(*o*)(ii) was replaced, and subparagraph (iii) was repealed, by P.C. 2009-1869, SOR/2009-302, dated November 19, 2009, published in the *Canada Gazette* December 9, 2009, applicable to taxation years that begin after 1995. S. 808(2)(*o*)(ii) and (iii) formerly read:

(ii) where the corporation was, throughout the year, not resident in Canada, that proportion of the provincial tax liability that the amount, if any, determined under paragraph 219(1)(*d*) of the Act in respect of the corporation for the year is of the corporation's amount taxable (within the meaning given to that expression in section 123 of the Act) for the year, or

(iii) in any other case, nil; and

S. 808(2)(*p*) was repealed by P.C. 2009-1869, SOR/2009-302, dated November 19, 2009, published in the *Canada Gazette* December 9, 2009, applicable to taxation years that begin after 1995. S. 808(2)(*p*) formerly read:

(*p*) where the corporation was resident in Canada at any time in the year, an amount equal to the aggregate of

(i) an amount equal to the aggregate of each amount deducted by the corporation in the year under paragraph 20(1)(*l*) or (*l*.1) or subsection 64(1), (1.1) or (1.2) of the Act in computing its income for the year from a source other than

(A) a business carried on by it in Canada, or

(B) a property situated outside Canada,

(ii) an amount equal to the aggregate of each amount owing by the corporation at the end of the year on account of any outlay or expense made or incurred by the corporation to the extent that it was deducted in computing its income for the year or for a previous taxation year from a source other than

(A) a business carried on by it in Canada, or

(B) a property situated outside Canada, and

(iii) an amount equal to the aggregate of all amounts each of which is an amount equal to that proportion of the amount owing (other than an amount owing on account of an outlay or expense referred to in subparagraph (ii) or paragraph (*l*)) by the corporation at the end of the year on account of an obligation outstanding at any time in the year in respect of which interest is stipulated to be payable by it that

(A) the interest paid or payable on the obligation by the corporation in respect of the year that is deductible, or would be deductible but for subsection 18(2), (3.1) or (4) or section 21 of the Act, in computing its income for the year from a source other than

(I) a business carried on by it in Canada, or

(II) a property situated outside Canada,

is of

(B) the interest paid or payable on the obligation by the corporation in respect of the year.

(3) For the purposes of paragraph (2)(*i*), the "allowable liquid assets of the corporation at the end of the year" is an amount equal to the lesser of

(*a*) the aggregate of

(i) the amount of Canadian currency owned by the corporation at the end of that year,

(ii) the balance standing to the credit of the corporation at the end of that year as or on account of amounts deposited with a branch or other office in Canada of

(A) a bank,

(B) a corporation licenced or otherwise authorized under the laws of Canada or a province to carry on in Canada the business of offering to the public its services as trustee, or

(C) a credit union, and

(iii) an amount equal to the aggregate of the cost amount to the corporation at the end of that year of each bond, debenture, bill, note, mortgage or similar obligation that was not described in the corporation's inventory in respect of a business carried on by it in Canada (other than a debt referred to in paragraph (2)(*e*) or (*g*) or a debt the amount of which was deducted under paragraph 20(1)(*p*) of the Act in computing the corporation's income for the year), that was issued by a person resident in Canada with whom the corporation was dealing at arm's length and that matures within one year after the date on which it was acquired by the corporation,

to the extent that such amounts are attributable to the profits of the corporation from carrying on a business in Canada, or are used or held by the corporation in the year in the course of carrying on a business in Canada; and

(*b*) an amount equal to 4/3 of the quotient obtained by dividing

(i) the aggregate of all amounts that would otherwise be determined under subparagraphs (*a*)(i), (ii) and (iii) if the references therein to "at the end of that year" were read as references to "at the end of each month in that year",

by

(ii) the number of months in that year.

(4) For the purposes of subsection (1), where, at the end of a taxation year, a corporation is a member of a partnership that was carrying on business in Canada at any time in that year, the corporation's qualified investment in property in Canada at the end of the year is an amount equal to the aggregate of

(*a*) the amount, if any, that would be determined under subsection (2) if the corporation were not, at the end of the year, a member of a partnership that was carrying on business in Canada at any time in the year; and

(*b*) an amount equal to the portion of the amount of the partnership's qualified investment in property in Canada at the end of the last fiscal period of the partnership ending in the taxation year of the corporation that may reasonably be attributed to the corporation, having regard to all the circumstances including the rights the corporation would have, if the partnership ceased to exist, to share in the distribution of the property owned by the partnership for the purpose of gaining or producing income from a business carried on by it in Canada.

Regulations

(5) For the purposes of subsection (4), a partnership's "qualified investment in property in Canada" at the end of a fiscal period is the amount, if any, by which the aggregate of

(*a*) the cost amount to the partnership, at the end of the fiscal period, of land in Canada owned by it at that time for the purpose of gaining or producing income from a business carried on by it in Canada, other than land that is

(i) described in the inventory of the partnership,

(ii) depreciable property,

(iii) a Canadian resource property, or

(iv) land the cost of which is or was deductible in computing the income of the partnership or the income of a member of the partnership,

(*b*) an amount equal to the aggregate of the cost amount to the partnership, immediately after the end of the fiscal period, of each depreciable property in Canada owned by it for the purpose of gaining or producing income from a business carried on by it in Canada,

(*c*) an amount equal to 4/3 of the cumulative eligible capital of the partnership immediately after the end of the fiscal period in respect of each business carried on by it in Canada,

(*d*) an amount equal to the aggregate of the cost amount to the partnership at the end of the fiscal period of each debt owing to it, or any other right of the partnership to receive an amount, that was outstanding as a result of the disposition by it of property in respect of which an amount would be included, by virtue of paragraph (*a*), (*b*) or (*c*), in its qualified investment in property in Canada at the end of the fiscal period if the property had not been disposed of by it before the end of that fiscal period,

(*e*) an amount equal to the aggregate of the cost amount to the partnership at the end of the fiscal period of each property, other than a Canadian resource property, that was described in the partnership's inventory in respect of a business carried on by it in Canada,

(*f*) an amount equal to the aggregate of the cost amount to the partnership at the end of the fiscal period of each debt (other than a debt referred to in paragraph (*d*) or a debt the amount of which was deducted under paragraph 20(1)(*p*) of the Act in computing the partnership's income for the fiscal period) owing to it

(i) in respect of any transaction by virtue of which an amount has been included in computing its income for the fiscal period or for a previous fiscal period or in computing the income of a member of the partnership for a previous taxation year from a business carried on in Canada by the partnership, or

(ii) where any part of its ordinary business carried on in Canada was the lending of money, in respect of a loan made by the partnership in the ordinary course of that part of its business, and

(*g*) an amount equal to the allowable liquid assets of the partnership at the end of the fiscal period,

exceeds the aggregate of

(*h*) an amount equal to the total of all amounts each of which is an amount deducted under paragraph 20(1)(*l*), (*l.1*) or (*n*) of the Act in computing the partnership's income for the fiscal period from a business carried on by the partnership in Canada;

(*i*) an amount equal to the aggregate of all amounts each of which is an amount deducted by the partnership in the fiscal period under subparagraph 40(1)(*a*)(iii) or 44(1)(*e*)(iii) of the Act in respect of a debt referred to in paragraph (*d*);

(*j*) an amount equal to the aggregate of each amount owing by the partnership at the end of the fiscal period on account of

(i) the purchase price of property that is referred to in paragraph (*a*), (*b*) or (*e*) or that would be so referred to but for the fact that it has been disposed of before the end of the fiscal period,

(ii) Canadian exploration and development expenses, Canadian exploration expense, Canadian development expense or Canadian oil and gas property expense,

(iii) an eligible capital expenditure made or incurred by the partnership before the end of the fiscal period in respect of a business carried on by it in Canada, or

(iv) any other outlay or expense made or incurred by the partnership to the extent that it was deducted in computing its income for the fiscal period or for a previous fiscal period, or in computing the income of a member of the partnership for a previous taxation year, from a business carried on in Canada by the partnership; and

(*k*) an amount equal to the aggregate of all amounts each of which is an amount equal to that proportion of the amount owing (other than an amount owing on account of an outlay or expense referred to in paragraph (*j*)) by the partnership at the end of the fiscal period on account of an obligation outstanding at any time in the period in respect of which interest is stipulated to be payable by it that

(i) the interest paid or payable on the obligation by the partnership in respect of the fiscal period that is deductible, or would be deductible but for subsection 18(2) or (3.1) or section 21 of the Act, in computing its income for the fiscal period from a business carried on by it in Canada,

is of

(ii) the interest paid or payable on the obligation by the partnership in respect of the fiscal period.

History: S. 808(5)(*h*) was replaced by P.C. 2010-548, SOR/2010-93, dated April 29, 2010, published in the *Canada Gazette* May 12, 2010, applicable with respect to dispositions occurring after November 12, 1981 otherwise than under the terms of an agreement in writing made or entered into on or before that date. S. 808(5)(*h*) formerly read:

(*h*) an amount equal to the aggregate of each amount deducted by the partnership under paragraph 20(1)(*l*), (*l.1*) or (*n*) or subsection 64(1), (1.1) or (1.2) of the Act in computing its income for the fiscal period from a business carried on by it in Canada,

S. 808(5)(*j*)(ii) was replaced by P.C. 2009-1869, SOR/2009-302, dated November 19, 2009, published in the *Canada Gazette* December 9, 2009, in force November 19, 2009. S. 808(5)(*j*)(ii) formerly read:

(ii) Canadian exploration and development expenses, Canadian exploration expense, Canadian development expense or Canadian oil and gas property expense, within the meanings assigned by paragraphs 66(15)(*b*) [subsection 66(15) "Canadian exploration and development expenses"], 66.1(6)(*a*) [subsection 66.1(6) "Canadian exploration expense"], 66.2(5)(*a*) [subsection 66.2(5) "Canadian development expense"] and 66.4(5)(*a*) [subsection 66.4(5) "Canadian oil and gas property expense"] of the Act, respectively.

(6) For the purposes of paragraph (5)(*g*), the "allowable liquid assets of the partnership at the end of the fiscal period" is an amount equal to the lesser of

(*a*) the total of the following amounts (to the extent that those amounts are attributable to the profits of the partnership from carrying on a business in Canada, or are used or held by the partnership in the year in the course of carrying on a business in Canada):

(i) the amount of Canadian currency owned by the partnership at the end of that fiscal period,

(ii) the balance standing to the credit of the partnership at the end of that fiscal period as or on account of amounts deposited with a branch or other office in Canada of

(A) a bank,

(B) a corporation licensed or otherwise authorized under the laws of Canada or a province to carry on in Canada the business of offering to the public its services as trustee, or

(C) a credit union, and

(iii) an amount equal to the aggregate of the cost amount to the partnership at the end of that fiscal period of each bond, debenture, bill, note, mortgage, hypothec or similar obligation that was not described in the partnership's inventory in respect of a business carried on by it in Canada (other than a debt referred to in paragraph (5)(*d*) or (*f*) or a debt the amount of which was deducted under paragraph 20(1)(*p*) of the Act in computing the partnership's income for the fiscal period), that was issued by a person resident in Canada with whom all the members of the partnership were dealing at arm's length and that matures within one year after the date on which it was acquired by the partnership; and

(*b*) an amount equal to 4/3 of the quotient obtained by dividing

(i) the aggregate of all amounts that would otherwise be determined under subparagraphs (*a*)(i), (ii) and (iii) if the references therein to "at the end of that fiscal period" were read as references to "at the end of each month in that fiscal period",

by

(ii) the number of months in that fiscal period.

History: S. 808(6)(*a*), the portion before subparagraph (i) was replaced by P.C. 2009-1869, SOR/2009-302, dated November 19, 2009, published in the *Canada Gazette* December 9, 2009, deemed to have come into force on August 8, 2000. S. 808(6)(*a*), the portion before subparagraph (i) formerly read:

(*a*) the aggregate of

(7) Subsections (4) to (6) shall be read and construed as if each of the assumptions in paragraphs 96(1)(*a*) to (*g*) of the Act were made.

(8) For the purpose of paragraph 219(1)(*j*) of the Act, the allowance of an authorized foreign bank for a taxation year in respect of its investment in property in Canada is prescribed to be the amount, if any, by which

(*a*) the average of all amounts, each of which is the amount for a calculation period (within the meaning assigned by subsection 20.2(1) of the Act) of the bank for the year that is the greater of

(i) the amount determined by the formula

$$0.05 \times A$$

where

A is the amount of the element A in the formulae in subsection 20.2(3) of the Act for the period, and

(ii) the amount by which

(A) the total of the cost amount to the bank, at the end of the period (or, in the case of depreciable property or eligible capital property, immediately after the end of the year), of each asset in respect of the bank's Canadian banking business that is an asset recorded in the books of account of the business in a manner consistent with the manner in which it is required to be treated for the purpose of the branch financial statements (within the meaning assigned by subsection 20.2(1) of the Act) for the year

exceeds

(B) the amount equal to the total of

(I) the amount determined by the formula

$$L + BA$$

where

L is the amount of the element L in the formulae in subsection 20.2(3) of the Act for the period, and

BA is the amount of the element BA in the formulae in subsection 20.2(3) of the Act for the period, and

(II) the amount claimed by the bank under clause 20.2(3)(*b*)(ii)(A) of the Act

exceeds

(*b*) the total of all amounts each of which is an amount that would be determined under paragraph (2)(*j*), (*k*), (*n*) or (*o*) if that provision applied to the bank for the year, except to the extent that the amount reflects a liability of the bank that has been included in the element L in the formulae in subsection 20.2(3) of the Act for the bank's last calculation period for the year.

History: S. 808(8) was added by P.C. 2009-1869, SOR/2009-302, dated November 19, 2009, published in the *Canada Gazette* December 9, 2009, applicable after June 27, 1999.

809. Reduction of Certain Amounts to be Deducted or Withheld

(1) Subject to subsection (2), where a non-resident person (in this section referred to as the "payee") has filed with the Minister the payee's required statement for the year, the amount otherwise required by subsections 215(1) to (3) of the Act to be deducted or withheld from any qualifying payment paid or credited by a person resident in Canada (in this section referred to as the "payer") to the payee in the year and after the required statement for the year was so filed is hereby reduced by the amount determined in accordance with the following rules:

(*a*) determine the amount by which

Regulations

(i) the amount that would, if the payee does not make an election in respect of the year under section 217 of the Act, be the tax payable by the payee under Part XIII of the Act on the aggregate of the amounts estimated by him in his required statement for the year pursuant to paragraph (*a*) of the definition "required statement" in subsection (4),

exceeds

(ii) the amount that would, if the payee makes the election referred to in subparagraph (i), be the tax payable (on the assumption that no portion of the payee's income for the year was income earned in the year in a province) by the payee under Part I of the Act on his estimated taxable income calculated by him in his required statement for the year pursuant to paragraph (*b*) of the definition "required statement" in subsection (4),

(*b*) determine the percentage that the amount determined under paragraph (*a*) is of the aggregate of the amounts estimated by him in his required statement for the year pursuant to paragraph (*a*) of the definition "required statement" in subsection (4),

(*c*) where the determination of a percentage under paragraph (*b*) results in a fraction, disregard the fraction for the purposes of paragraph (*d*),

(*d*) multiply the percentage determined under paragraph (*b*) by the amount of the qualifying payment,

and the product obtained under paragraph (*d*) is the amount by which the amount required to be deducted or withheld is reduced.

(2) Subsection (1) does not apply to reduce the amount to be deducted or withheld from a qualifying payment if, after the qualifying payment has been paid or credited by the payer, the aggregate of all qualifying payments that the payer has paid or credited to the payee in the year would exceed the amount estimated, in respect of that payer, by the payee in his required statement for the year pursuant to paragraph (*a*) of the definition "required statement" in subsection (4).

(3) Where a payee has filed with the Minister a written notice indicating that certain information or estimates in the payee's required statement for the year are incorrect and setting out the correct information or estimates that should be substituted therefor or where the Minister is satisfied that certain information or estimates in a payee's required statement for the year are incorrect and that the Minister has the correct information or estimates that should be substituted therefor, for the purposes of making the calculations in subsection (1) with respect to any qualifying payment paid or credited to the payee after the time when he has filed that notice or after the time when the Minister is so satisfied, as the case may be, the incorrect information or estimates shall be disregarded and the required statement for the year shall be deemed to contain only the correct information or estimates.

(4) In this section,

"qualifying payment" in relation to a non-resident person means any amount

(*a*) paid or credited, or to be paid or credited, to him as, on account or in lieu of payment of, or in satisfaction of, any amount described in paragraph 212(1)(*f*) or (*h*) or in any of paragraphs 212(1)(*j*), (*k*), (*l*), (*m*) or (*q*) of the Act, and

(*b*) on which tax under Part XIII of the Act is, or would be, but for an election by him under section 217 of the Act, payable by him;

"required statement" of a payee for a taxation year means a written statement signed by him that contains, in respect of the payee,

(*a*) the name and address of each payer of a qualifying payment in the year and, in respect of each such payer, an estimate by the payee of the aggregate of such qualifying payments, and

(*b*) a calculation by him of his estimated taxable income earned in Canada for the year, on the assumption that he makes the election in respect of the year under section 217 of the Act, and such information as may be necessary for the purpose of estimating such income.

Forms: NR5 — Application by a Non-Resident of Canada for a Reduction by a Non-Resident Receiving Rent from Real Property or Receiving a Timber Royalty for Tax Year.

Information Circulars: IC 77-16R4 Non-resident income tax (para. 53).

810. (Repealed.)

History: S. 810 and the heading before it were repealed by P.C. 2009-1869, SOR/2009-302, dated November 19, 2009, published in the *Canada Gazette* December 9, 2009, P.C. 2009-1869, SOR/2009-302, dated November 19, 2009, published in the *Canada Gazette* December 9, 2009, applicable after June 27, 1999. S. 810 and the heading before it formerly read:

Excluded Property of Non-Resident Persons

810.

(1) For the purposes of paragraph 116(6)(*e*) of the Act, any property that is

(*a*) property of a non-resident insurer that is a qualified insurance corporation,

(*b*) an option in respect of property referred to in any of paragraphs 116(6)(*a*) to (*d*) of the Act and paragraph (*a*) whether or not such property is in existence, or

(*c*) an interest in property referred to in paragraph 116(6)(*a*), (*c*) or (*d*) of the Act or paragraph (*a*) or (*b*),

is prescribed to be excluded property.

(2) For the purposes of this section, a non-resident insurer is a "qualified insurance corporation" throughout the period during which it

(*a*) was licenced or otherwise authorized under the laws of Canada or a province to carry on an insurance business in Canada; and

(*b*) carried on an insurance business, within the meaning of subsection 138(1) of the Act, in Canada.

Part IX
Delegation of the Powers and Duties of the Minister [Repealed.]

900. (Repealed.)

Part X
Elections in Respect of Deceased Taxpayers

1000. Property Dispositions

(1) Any election under subsection 164(6) of the Act shall be made by the legal representative of a deceased taxpayer by filing with the Minister the following documents:

(*a*) a letter from the legal representative specifying

(i) the part of the one or more capital losses from the disposition of properties, if any, under paragraph 164(6)(*c*) of the Act, and

(ii) the part of the amount, if any, under paragraph 164(6)(*d*) of the Act

in respect of which the election is made;

(*b*) where an amount is specified under subparagraph (*a*)(i), a schedule of the capital losses and capital gains referred to in paragraph 164(6)(*a*) of the Act;

(*c*) where an amount is specified under subparagraph (*a*)(ii),

(i) a schedule of the amounts of undepreciated capital cost described in paragraph 164(6)(*b*) of the Act,

(ii) a statement of the amount that, but for subsection 164(6) of the Act, would be the non-capital loss of the estate for its first taxation year, and

(iii) a statement of the amount that, but for subsection 164(6) of the Act, would be the farm loss of the estate for its first taxation year.

(2) The documents referred to in subsection (1) shall be filed not later than the day that is the later of

(*a*) the last day provided by the Act for the filing of a return that the legal representative of a deceased taxpayer is required or has elected to file under the Act in respect of the income of that deceased taxpayer for the taxation year in which he died; and

(*b*) the day the return of the income for the first taxation year of the deceased taxpayer's estate is required to be filed under paragraph 150(1)(*c*) of the Act.

1000.1. Realization of Options

(1) An election under subsection 164(6.1) of the Act shall be made by the legal representative of a deceased taxpayer by filing with the Minister a letter from the legal representative setting out the following:

(*a*) the amount of the benefit referred to in subparagraph 164(6.1)(*a*)(i) of the Act;

(*b*) the value of the right, and the amount paid for the right, referred to in subparagraph 164(6.1)(*a*)(ii) of the Act;

(*c*) the deducted amount, referred to in subparagraph 164(6.1)(*a*)(iii) of the Act; and

(*d*) the amount of the loss referred to in paragraph 164(6.1)(*b*) of the Act.

(2) The letter shall be filed not later than the day that is the later of

(*a*) the last day provided by the Act for the filing of a return that the legal representative of a deceased taxpayer is required or has elected to file under the Act in respect of the income of that deceased taxpayer for the taxation year in which he or she died, and

(*b*) the day the return of the income for the first taxation year of the deceased taxpayer's estate is required to be filed under paragraph 150(1)(*c*) of the Act.

1001. Annual Instalments

Any election by a deceased taxpayer's legal representative under subsection 159(5) of the Act shall be made by filing with the Minister the prescribed form on or before the day on or before which payment of the first of the "equal consecutive annual instalments" referred to in that subsection is required to be made.

Forms: T2075 — Election to Defer Payment of Income Tax, Under Subsection 159(5) of the Income Tax Act by a Deceased Taxpayer's Legal Representative or Trustee.

Regulations

Part XI
Capital Cost Allowances

Division I
Deductions Allowed

1100. [Capital cost allowance – deductions allowed]

(1) For the purposes of paragraphs 8(1)(*j*) and (*p*) and 20(1)(*a*) of the Act, the following deductions are allowed in computing a taxpayer's income for each taxation year:

Income Tax Folios: *Primary* — S3-F4-C1 General Discussion of Capital Cost Allowance.

(a) Rates — subject to subsection (2), such amount as the taxpayer may claim in respect of property of each of the following classes in Schedule II not exceeding in respect of property

(i) of Class 1, 4 per cent,
(ii) of Class 2, 6 per cent,
(iii) of Class 3, 5 per cent,
(iv) of Class 4, 6 per cent,
(v) of Class 5, 10 per cent,
(vi) of Class 6, 10 per cent,
(vii) of Class 7, 15 per cent,
(viii) of Class 8, 20 per cent,
(ix) of Class 9, 25 per cent,
(x) of Class 10, 30 per cent,
(x.1) of Class 10.1, 30 per cent,
(xi) of Class 11, 35 per cent,
(xii) of Class 12, 100 per cent,
(xii.1) of Class 14.1, 5 per cent,
(xiii) of Class 16, 40 per cent,
(xiv) of Class 17, 8 per cent,
(xv) of Class 18, 60 per cent,
(xvi) of Class 22, 50 per cent,
(xvii) of Class 23, 100 per cent,
(xviii) of Class 25, 100 per cent,
(xix) of Class 26, 5 per cent,
(xx) of Class 28, 30 per cent,
(xxi) of Class 30, 40 per cent,
(xxii) of Class 31, 5 per cent,
(xxiii) of Class 32, 10 per cent,
(xxiv) of Class 33, 15 per cent,
(xxv) of Class 35, 7 per cent,
(xxvi) of Class 37, 15 per cent,
(xxvii) of Class 41, 25 per cent,
(xxvii.1) of Class 41.1, 25 per cent,
(xxvii.2) of Class 41.2, 25 per cent,
(xxviii) of Class 42, 12 per cent,
(xxix) of Class 43, 30 per cent,
(xxix.1) of Class 43.1, 30 per cent,
(xxix.2) of Class 43.2, 50 per cent,
(xxx) of Class 44, 25 per cent,
(xxxi) of Class 45, 45 per cent,
(xxxii) of Class 46, 30 per cent,
(xxxiii) of Class 47, 8 per cent,
(xxxiv) of Class 48, 15 per cent,
(xxxv) of Class 49, 8 per cent,
(xxxvi) of Class 50, 55 per cent,
(xxxvii) of Class 51, 6 per cent,
(xxxviii) of Class 52, 100 per cent,
(xxxix) of Class 53, 50 per cent,
(xl) of Class 54, 30 per cent, and
(xli) of Class 55, 40 per cent,

of the undepreciated capital cost to the taxpayer as of the end of the taxation year (before making any deduction under this subsection for the taxation year) of property of the class;

History: S. 1100(1)(*a*)(xl) and (xli) were added by S.C. 2019, c. 29, s. 52(1), effective June 21, 2019.

S. 1100(1)(*a*)(xii.1) was added by S.C. 2016, c. 12, s. 78(1), in force January 1, 2017.

S. 1100(1)(*a*)(xxxix) was added by S.C. 2015, c. 36, s. 21, in force on Royal Assent, June 23, 2015.

S. 1100(1)(*a*)(xxvii.2) was added by S.C. 2013, c. 40, s. 100(1), applicable to taxation years that end after March 20, 2013.

S. 1100(1)(*a*)(xxvii.1) was added by P.C. 2011-44, SOR/2011-9, dated February 4, 2011, published in the *Canada Gazette* February 16, 2011, applicable to taxation years that end after March 18, 2007.

S. 1100(1)(*a*)(xxxviii) was added by P.C. 2009-660, SOR/2009-126, dated April 30, 2009, applicable in respect of property acquired after January 27, 2009.

S. 1100(1)(*a*), the portion before subparagraph (i) was replaced by P.C. 2009-581, SOR/2009-115, dated April 23, 2009, deemed to have come into force on March 19, 2007. S. 1100(1)(*a*), the portion before subparagraph (i) formerly read:

> (*a*) subject to subsection (2), such amount as he may claim in respect of property of each of the following classes in Schedule II not exceeding in respect of property

S. 1100(1)(*a*)(xxxvi) and (xxxvii) were added by P.C. 2009-581, SOR/2009-115, dated April 23, 2009, deemed to have come into force on March 19, 2007.

S. 1100(1)(*a*), the portion following subparagraph (xxxvii) was replaced by P.C. 2009-581, SOR/2009-115, dated April 23, 2009, deemed to have come into force on March 19, 2007. S. 1100(1)(*a*), the portion following subparagraph (xxxvii), formerly read:

> of the undepreciated capital cost to him as of the end of the taxation year (before making any deduction under this subsection for the taxation year) of property of the class;

Canadian Tax Foundation: Hickey, *Building Additions Attract 6 percent CCA*, 2013 Canadian Tax Highlights 21(9):14–15.

Income Tax Folios: *Primary* — S3-F4-C1 General Discussion of Capital Cost Allowance. *Secondary* — S4-F7-C1 Amalgamations of Canadian Corporations.

Interpretation Bulletins: *Secondary* — IT-472 Capital cost allowance — Class 8 property; IT-521R Motor vehicle expenses claimed by self-employed individuals; IT-522R Vehicle, travel and sales expenses of employees.

(a.1) Class 1 — where a separate class is prescribed by subsection 1101(5b.1) for a property of a taxpayer that is a building and at least 90 per cent of the floor space of the building is used at the end of the taxation year for the manufacturing or processing in Canada of goods for sale or lease, such amount as the taxpayer may claim not exceeding six per cent of the undepreciated capital cost to the taxpayer of the property of that class as of the end of the taxation year (before making any deduction under this subsection for the taxation year);

History: S. 1100(1)(*a.1*) was added by P.C. 2009-581, SOR/2009-115, dated April 23, 2009, applicable to property acquired on or after March 19, 2007.

Income Tax Folios: S4-F15-C1 Manufacturing and Processing.

(a.2) Class 1 — where a separate class is prescribed by subsection 1101(5b.1) for a property of a taxpayer that is a building, at least 90 per cent of the floor space of the building is used at the end of the taxation year for a non-residential use in Canada and an additional allowance is not allowed for the year under paragraph (a.1) in respect of the property, such amount as the taxpayer may claim not exceeding two per cent of the undepreciated capital cost to the taxpayer of the property of that class as of the end of the taxation year (before making any deduction under this subsection for the taxation year);

History: S. 1100(1)(*a.2*) was added by P.C. 2009-581, SOR/2009-115, dated April 23, 2009, applicable to property acquired on or after March 19, 2007.

(*a*.3) any additional amount that the taxpayer may claim in respect of property that is used as part of an eligible liquefaction facility for which a separate class is prescribed by subsection 1101(5b.2), not exceeding the lesser of

(i) the income for the taxation year from the taxpayer's eligible liquefaction activities in respect of the eligible liquefaction facility (taking into consideration any deduction under paragraph (*yb*) and before making any deduction under this paragraph), and

(ii) 6% of the undepreciated capital cost to the taxpayer of property of that separate class as of the end of the taxation year (before making any deduction under this subsection for the taxation year);

History: S. 1100(1)(*a.3*) was added by P.C. 2015-629, SOR/2015-117, s. 1(1), dated May 29, 2015, deemed to have come into force on February 19, 2015.

(b) Class 13 — [Leasehold interest] — such amount as the taxpayer may claim in respect of the capital cost to the taxpayer of property of Class 13 in Schedule II, not exceeding

(i) if the capital cost of the property was incurred in the taxation year and after November 12, 1981,

(A) if the property is an accelerated investment incentive property and the capital cost of the property was incurred before 2024, the lesser of

(I) 150 per cent of the amount for the year calculated in accordance with Schedule III, and

(II) the amount determined for paragraph 1(*b*) of Schedule III, and

(B) if the property is not an accelerated investment incentive property and is not described in any of subparagraphs (*b*)(iii) to (v) of the description of F in subsection (2), 50 per cent of the amount for the year calculated in accordance with Schedule III, and

(ii) in any other case, the amount for the year calculated in accordance with Schedule III,

and, for the purposes of this paragraph and Schedule III, the capital cost to a taxpayer of a property shall be deemed to have been incurred at the time at which the property became available for use by the taxpayer;

History: S. 1100(1)(*b*)(i) was replaced by S.C. 2019, c. 29, s. 52(2), effective June 21, 2019, and formerly read:

> (i) where the capital cost of the property, other than property described in subparagraph (2)(*a*)(v), (vi) or (vii), was incurred in the taxation year and after November 12, 1981, 50 per cent of the amount for the year calculated in accordance with Schedule III, and

Interpretation Bulletins: *Secondary* — IT-464R Capital cost allowance — Leasehold interests.

(c) Class 14 — [Patent, franchise, concession or licence] — such amount as he may claim in respect of property of Class 14 in Schedule II not exceeding the lesser of

(i) the total of

(A) the aggregate of the amounts for the year obtained by apportioning the capital cost to the taxpayer of each property over the life of the property remaining at the time the cost was incurred, and

(B) if the property is accelerated investment incentive property, the portion of the amount determined under clause (A) that is in respect of the property multiplied by

(I) 0.5, if the property becomes available for use in the year and before 2024, and

(II) 0.25, if the property becomes available for use in the year and after 2023, and

(ii) the undepreciated capital cost to him as of the end of the taxation year (before making any deduction under this subsection for the taxation year) of property of the class;

History: S. 1100(1)(*c*)(i) was replaced by S.C. 2019, c. 29, s. 52(3), effective June 21, 2019, and formerly read:

> (i) the aggregate of the amounts for the year obtained by apportioning the capital cost to him of each property over the life of the property remaining at the time the cost was incurred, and

Interpretation Bulletins: *Secondary* — IT-143R3 Meaning of eligible capital expenditure; IT-477 (Consolid.) Capital cost allowance — Patents, franchises, concessions and licences.

(c.1) Additional Allowances — Class 14.1 — for a taxation year that ends before 2027, such additional amount as the taxpayer may claim in respect of property of Class 14.1 of Schedule II not exceeding

(i) 2% of the particular amount by which the undepreciated capital cost of the class at the beginning of 2017 exceeds the total of all amounts each of which is

(A) the amount of a deduction taken under paragraph 20(1)(*a*) of the Act in respect of the class for a preceding taxation year, and

(B) equal to three times the amount of the capital cost of a property deemed by subsection 13(39) of the Act to be acquired by the taxpayer in the year or a preceding year, and

(ii) the amount determined by the formula

$$A - B$$

where

A is the lesser of

(A) $ 500, and

(B) the undepreciated capital cost of the class to the taxpayer as of the end of the year (before making any deduction under paragraph 20(1)(*a*) of the Act in respect of the class for the year), and

B is the total of all amounts deductible for the year under paragraph 20(1)(*a*) of the Act in respect of the class because of subparagraph (i) or (*a*)(xii.1);

History: S. 1100(1)(c.1) was added by S.C. 2016, c. 12, s. 78(2), in force January 1, 2017.

(d) In lieu of double depreciation — such additional amount as he may claim not exceeding in the case of property described in each of the classes in Schedule II, the lesser of

(i) one-half the amount that would have been allowed to him in respect of property of that class under subparagraph 6(*n*)(ii) of the *Income War Tax Act* if that Act were applicable to the taxation year, and

(ii) the undepreciated capital cost to him as of the end of the taxation year (before making any deduction under this paragraph for the taxation year) of property of the class;

(e) Timber limits and cutting rights — such amount as he may claim not exceeding the amount calculated in accordance with Schedule VI in respect of the capital cost to him of a property, other than a timber resource property, that is a timber limit or a right to cut timber from a limit;

Interpretation Bulletins: *Secondary* — IT-481 (Consolid.) Timber resource property and timber limits.

(f) Class 15 — [Woods assets] — such amount as he may claim not exceeding the amount calculated in accordance with Schedule IV in respect of the capital cost to him of property of Class 15 in Schedule II;

(g) Industrial mineral mines — such amount as he may claim not exceeding the amount calculated in accordance with Schedule V in respect of the capital cost to him of a property that is an industrial mineral mine or a right to remove industrial minerals from an industrial mineral mine;

Interpretation Bulletins: *Secondary* — IT-492 Capital cost allowance — Industrial mineral mines.

(h) (Revoked.)

(i) Additional allowances — Fishing vessels — such additional amount as he may claim in the case of property of a separate class prescribed by subsection 1101(2) not exceeding the lesser of

(i) the amount by which the depreciation that could have been taken on the property, if the Orders in Council referred to in that subsection were applicable to the taxation year, exceeds the amount allowed under paragraph (*a*) in respect of the property, and

(ii) the undepreciated capital cost to him as of the end of the taxation year (before making any deduction under this paragraph for the taxation year) of property of the class.

(j) (Revoked.)

(k) (Revoked.)

(l) Additional allowances — Certified productions — such additional amount as he may claim in respect of property for which a separate class is prescribed by subsection 1101(5k) not exceeding the lesser of

(i) the aggregate of his income for the year from that property and from property described in paragraph (*n*) of Class 12 in Schedule II, determined before making any deduction under this paragraph, and

(ii) the undepreciated capital cost to him of property of that separate class as of the end of the year before making any deduction under this paragraph for the year;

(m) Additional allowance — Canadian film or video production — such additional amount as the taxpayer claims in respect of property for which a separate class is prescribed by subsection 1101(5k.1) not exceeding the lesser of

(i) the taxpayer's income for the year from the property, determined before making any deduction under this paragraph, and

(ii) the undepreciated capital cost to the taxpayer of the property of that separate class at the end of the year (before making any deduction under this paragraph for the year and computed without reference to subsection (2));

(n) Class 19 — [Accelerated allowances] — where the taxpayer is a corporation that had a degree of Canadian ownership in the taxation year, or is an individual who was resident in Canada in the taxation year for not less than 183 days, such amount as he may claim in respect of property of Class 19 in Schedule II that was acquired in a particular taxation year not exceeding the lesser of

(i) 50 per cent of the capital cost thereof to him, and

(ii) the amount by which the capital cost thereof to him exceeds the aggregate of the amounts deducted in respect thereof in computing his income for previous taxation years,

but the aggregate of amounts deductible for a taxation year in respect of property acquired in each of the particular taxation years, under this paragraph, shall not exceed the undepreciated capital cost to him as of the end of the taxation year (before making any deduction under this subsection for the taxation year) of property of the class;

(o) Class 19 — [Accelerated allowances] — where the taxpayer is not entitled to make a deduction under paragraph (*n*) in computing his income for a taxation year, such amount as he may claim in respect of property of Class 19 in Schedule II not exceeding 20 per cent of the undepreciated capital cost to him as of the end of the taxation year (before making any deduction under this subsection for the taxation year) of property of the class;

(p) Class 20 — [Accelerated allowances] — such amount as he may claim in respect of property of Class 20 in Schedule II that was acquired in a particular taxation year not exceeding the lesser of

(i) 20 per cent of the capital cost thereof to him, and

(ii) the amount by which the capital cost thereof to him exceeds the aggregate of the amounts deducted in respect thereof in computing his income for previous taxation years,

but the aggregate of amounts deductible for a taxation year in respect of property acquired in each of the particular taxation years, under this paragraph, shall not exceed the undepreciated capital cost to him as of the end of the taxation year (before making any deduction under this subsection for the taxation year) of property of the class;

(q) Class 21 — [Accelerated allowances] — such amount as he may claim in respect of property of Class 21 in Schedule II that was acquired in a particular taxation year not exceeding the lesser of

(i) 50 per cent of the capital cost thereof to him, and

(ii) the amount by which the capital cost thereof to him exceeds the aggregate of the amounts deducted in respect thereof in computing his income for previous taxation years,

but the aggregate of amounts deductible for a taxation year in respect of property acquired in each of the particular taxation years, under this paragraph, shall not exceed the undepreciated capital cost to him as of the end of the taxation year (before making any deduction under this subsection for the taxation year) of property of the class;

(sb) [Additional allowances — Grain storage facilities and grain elevators] — such additional amount as he may claim in respect of property included in Class 3, 6 or 8 in Schedule II

(i) that is

(A) a grain elevator situated in that part of Canada that is defined in section 2 of the *Canada Grain Act* as the "Eastern Division" the principal use of which

(I) is the receiving of grain directly from producers for storage or forwarding or both,

(II) is the receiving and storing of grain for direct manufacture or processing into other products, or

(III) has been certified by the Minister of Agriculture to be the receiving of grain that has not been officially inspected or weighed,

(B) an addition to a grain elevator described in clause (A),

(C) fixed machinery installed in a grain elevator in respect of which, or in respect of an addition to which, an additional amount has been or may be claimed under this paragraph,

(D) fixed machinery, designed for the purpose of drying grain, installed in a grain elevator described in clause (A),

(E) machinery designed for the purpose of drying grain on a farm, or

(F) a building or other structure designed for the purpose of storing grain on a farm,

(ii) that was acquired by the taxpayer in the taxation year or in one of the three immediately preceding taxation years, at a time that was after April 1, 1972 but before August 1, 1974, and

(iii) that was not used for any purpose whatever before it was acquired by the taxpayer,

not exceeding the lesser of

(iv) where the property is included in Class 3, 22 per cent of the capital cost thereof, where the property is included in Class 6, 20 per cent of the capital cost thereof or where the property is included in Class 8,

(A) 14 per cent of the capital cost thereof in the case of property referred to in clause (i)(C), (D) or (F), and

(B) 14 per cent of the lesser of $15,000 and the capital cost thereof in the case of property described in clause (i)(E), and

(v) the undepreciated capital cost to him as of the end of the taxation year (before making any deduction under this paragraph for the taxation year) of property of the class;

(t) Classes 24, 27, 29 and 34 — for the taxation year that includes November 12, 1981, such amount as he may claim in respect of property of each of Classes 24, 27, 29 and 34 in Schedule II not exceeding the aggregate of

(i) 50 per cent of the lesser of

(A) the capital cost to him of all designated property of the class acquired by him in the year, and

(B) the undepreciated capital cost to him of property of the class as of the end of the year (computed as if no amount were included in respect of property, other than designated property of the class, acquired after November 12, 1981 and before making any deduction under this paragraph for the year),

(ii) the amount, if any, by which the amount determined under clause (i)(B) in respect of the class exceeds the amount determined under clause (i)(A) in respect of the class, and

(iii) the lesser of

(A) 25 per cent of the capital cost to him of all property, other than designated property, of the class acquired by him in the year, and

(B) the undepreciated capital cost to him of property of the class as of the end of the year (before making any deduction under this paragraph for the year);

(ta) [Classes 24, 27, 29 and 34 — Taxation years commencing after November 12, 1981] — for taxation years commencing after November 12,

Regulations

1981, such amount as he may claim in respect of property of each of Classes 24, 27, 29 and 34 in Schedule II not exceeding the aggregate of

(i) the aggregate of

(A) the lesser of

(I) 50 per cent of the capital cost to him of all designated property of the class acquired by him in the year, and

(II) the undepreciated capital cost to him of property of the class as of the end of the year (before making any deduction under this paragraph for the year and, where any of the property referred to in subclause (I) was acquired by virtue of a specified transaction, computed as if no amount were included in respect of property, other than designated property of the class acquired by him in the year), and

(B) 25 per cent of the lesser of

(I) the undepreciated capital cost to him of property of the class as of the end of the year (computed as if no amount were included in respect of designated property of the class acquired by him in the year and before making any deduction under this paragraph for the year), and

(II) the capital cost to him of all property, other than designated property, of the class acquired by him in the year, and

(ii) the lesser of

(A) the amount, if any, by which

(I) the undepreciated capital cost to him of property of the class as of the end of the year (before making any deduction under this paragraph for the year)

exceeds

(II) the capital cost to him of all property of the class acquired by him in the year, and

(B) an amount equal to the aggregate of

(I) 50 per cent of the capital cost to him of all property of the class acquired by him in the immediately preceding taxation year, other than designated property of the class acquired in a specified transaction, and

(II) the amount, if any, by which the amount determined under clause (A) for the year with respect to the class exceeds the aggregate of 75 per cent of the capital cost to him of all property, other than designated property, of the class acquired by him in the immediately preceding taxation year and 50 per cent of the capital cost to him of designated property of the class acquired by him in the immediately preceding taxation year, other than designated property of the class acquired in a specified transaction,

and for the purposes of this paragraph and paragraph (*t*), "designated property" of a class means

(iii) property of the class acquired by him before November 13, 1981,

(iv) property deemed to be designated property of the class by virtue of paragraph (2.1)(*g*) or (2.2)(*j*), and

(v) property described in any of subparagraphs (*b*)(iii) to (v) of the description of F in subsection (2),

and, for the purposes of this paragraph,

(vi) "specified transaction" means a transaction to which subsection 85(5), 87(1), 88(1), 97(4) or 98(3) or (5) of the Act applies, and

(vii) subject to paragraph (2.2)(*j*), a property shall be deemed to have been acquired by a taxpayer at the time at which the property became available for use by the taxpayer;

History: S. 1100(1)(*ta*)(v) was replaced by S.C. 2019, c. 29, s. 52(4), effective June 21, 2019, and formerly read:

(v) property described in subparagraph (2)(*a*)(v), (vi) or (vii).

Related Regulations: 1100(2).

Income Tax Folios: S4-F15-C1 Manufacturing and Processing.

(v) Canadian vessels — such amount as the taxpayer may claim in respect of property that is

(i) a vessel described in subsection 1101(2a),

(ii) included in a separate prescribed class because of subsection 13(14) of the Act, or

(iii) a property that has been constituted a prescribed class by subsection 24(2) of Chapter 91 of the Statutes of Canada, 1966-67,

not exceeding the lesser of

(iv) the capital cost of the property to the taxpayer multiplied by

(A) 50 per cent, in the case of an accelerated investment incentive property acquired in the year and before 2024,

(B) 16 2/3 per cent, in the case of property acquired in the year, other than

(I) accelerated investment incentive property, and

(II) property described in any of subparagraphs (*b*)(iii) to (v) of the description of F in subsection (2), and

(C) 33 1/3 per cent, in any other case, and

(v) the undepreciated capital cost to the taxpayer as of the end of the taxation year (before making any deduction under this paragraph for the taxation year) of property of the class,

and, for the purposes of subparagraph (iv), a property shall be deemed to have been acquired by a taxpayer at the time at which the property became available for use by the taxpayer for the purposes of the Act;

History: S. 1100(1)(*v*)(iv) was replaced by S.C. 2019, c. 29, s. 52(5), effective June 21, 2019, and formerly read:

(iv) where the property, other than property described in subparagraph (2)(*a*)(v), (vi) or (vii), was acquired in the taxation year and after November 12, 1981, $16^2/_3$ per cent of the capital cost thereof to the taxpayer and, in any other case, $33^1/_3$ per cent of the capital cost thereof to the taxpayer, and

Related Regulations: 1100(2).

Interpretation Bulletins: *Secondary* — IT-267R2 Capital cost allowance — Vessels.

(va) Additional allowances — Offshore drilling vessels — such additional amount as he may claim in respect of property for which a separate class is prescribed by subsection 1101(2b) not exceeding 15 per cent of the undepreciated capital cost to him of property of that class as of the end of the taxation year (before making any deduction under this subsection for the taxation year);

Interpretation Bulletins: *Secondary* — IT-267R2 Capital cost allowance — Vessels.

(w) Additional allowances — Class 28 — subject to section 1100A, such additional amount as he may claim in respect of property described in Class 28 acquired for the purpose of gaining or producing income from a mine or in respect of property acquired for the purpose of gaining or producing income from a mine and for which a separate class is prescribed by subsection 1101(4a), not exceeding the lesser of

(i) the taxpayer's income for the taxation year from the mine, before making any deduction under this paragraph, paragraph (*x*), (*y*), (*y.1*), (*y.2*), (*ya*), (*ya.1*) or (*ya.2*), section 65, 66, 66.1, 66.2 or 66.7 of the Act or section 29 of the *Income Tax Application Rules*, and

(ii) the undepreciated capital cost to the taxpayer of property of that class as of the end of the taxation year (computed without reference to subsection (2) and before making any deduction under this paragraph for the taxation year);

History: S. 1100(1)(*w*)(i) was replaced by S.C. 2013, c. 40, s. 100(2), applicable to taxation years that end after March 20, 2013, and formerly read:

> (i) the taxpayer's income for the year from the mine, before making any deduction under this paragraph, paragraph (*x*), (*y*), (*y.1*), (*ya*) or (*ya.1*), section 65, 66, 66.1, 66.2 or 66.7 of the Act or section 29 of the *Income Tax Application Rules*, and

S. 1100(1)(*w*)(i) was replaced by P.C. 2011-44, SOR/2011-9, dated February 4, 2011, published in the *Canada Gazette* February 16, 2011, applicable to taxation years that end after March 18, 2007. S. 1100(1)(*w*)(i) formerly read:

> (i) the taxpayer's income for the year from the mine, before making any deduction under this paragraph, paragraph (*x*), (*y*) or (*ya*), section 65, 66, 66.1, 66.2 or 66.7 of the Act or section 29 of the *Income Tax Application Rules*, and

(x) [Additional allowances — Class 28 — More than one mine] — subject to section 1100A, such additional amount as he may claim in respect of property acquired for the purpose of gaining or producing income from more than one mine and for which a separate class is prescribed by subsection 1101(4b), not exceeding the lesser of

(i) the taxpayer's income for the taxation year from the mines, before making any deduction under this paragraph, paragraph (*ya*), (*ya.1*) or (*ya.2*), section 65, 66, 66.1, 66.2 or 66.7 of the Act or section 29 of the *Income Tax Application Rules*, and

(ii) the undepreciated capital cost to him of property of that class as of the end of the taxation year (before making any deduction under this paragraph for the taxation year);

History: S. 1100(1)(*x*)(i) was replaced by S.C. 2013, c. 40, s. 100(3), applicable to taxation years that end after March 20, 2013, and formerly read:

> (i) the taxpayer's income for the year from the mines, before making any deduction under this paragraph, paragraph (*ya*) or (*ya.1*), section 65, 66, 66.1, 66.2 or 66.7 of the Act or section 29 of the *Income Tax Application Rules*, and

S. 1100(1)(*x*)(i) was replaced by P.C. 2011-44, SOR/2011-9, dated February 4, 2011, published in the *Canada Gazette* February 16, 2011, applicable to taxation years that end after March 18, 2007. S. 1100(1)(*x*)(i) formerly read:

> (i) the taxpayer's income for the year from the mines, before making any deduction under this paragraph, paragraph (*ya*), section 65, 66, 66.1, 66.2 or 66.7 of the Act or section 29 of the *Income Tax Application Rules*, and

(y) Additional allowances — Class 41 — such additional amount as the taxpayer may claim in respect of property acquired for the purpose of gaining or producing income from a mine and for which a separate class is prescribed by subsection 1101(4c), not exceeding the lesser of

(i) the taxpayer's income for the taxation year from the mine, before making any deduction under this paragraph, paragraph (*x*), (*ya*), (*ya.1*) or (*ya.2*), section 65, 66, 66.1, 66.2 or 66.7 of the Act or section 29 of the *Income Tax Application Rules*, and

(ii) the undepreciated capital cost to the taxpayer of property of that class as of the end of the taxation year (computed without reference to subsection (2) and before making any deduction under this paragraph for the taxation year);

History: S. 1100(1)(*y*)(i) was replaced by S.C. 2013, c. 40, s. 100(4), applicable to taxation years that end after March 20, 2013, and formerly read:

> (i) the taxpayer's income for the year from the mine, before making any deduction under this paragraph, paragraph (*x*), (*ya*) or (*ya.1*), section 65, 66, 66.1, 66.2 or 66.7 of the Act or section 29 of the *Income Tax Application Rules*, and

S. 1100(1)(*y*)(i) was replaced by P.C. 2011-44, SOR/2011-9, dated February 4, 2011, published in the *Canada Gazette* February 16, 2011, applicable to taxation years that end after March 18, 2007. S. 1100(1)(*y*)(i) formerly read:

> (i) the taxpayer's income for the year from the mine, before making any deduction under this paragraph, paragraph (*x*) or (*ya*), section 65, 66, 66.1, 66.2 or 66.7 of the Act or section 29 of the *Income Tax Application Rules*, and

Canadian Petroleum Tax Journal: Canada Customs and Revenue Agency 1999 Roundtable Questions and Answers, Question 21, Vol. 13, No. 1, 2000.

Interpretation Bulletins: *Secondary* — IT-476R Capital cost allowance — Equipment used in petroleum and natural gas activities.

(y.1) Additional Allowances — Class 41.1 — such additional amount as the taxpayer may claim in respect of property acquired for the purpose of gaining or producing income from a mine and for which a separate class is prescribed by subsection 1101(4e), not exceeding the amount determined by the formula

$$A \times B$$

where

A is the lesser of

(i) the taxpayer's income for the taxation year from the mine, before making any deduction under this paragraph, paragraph (*x*), (*y*), (*y.2*), (*ya*), (*ya.1*) or (*ya.2*), section 65, 66, 66.1, 66.2 or 66.7 of the Act or section 29 of the *Income Tax Application Rules*, and

Regulations

(ii) the undepreciated capital cost to the taxpayer of property of that class as of the end of the taxation year computed

(A) without reference to subsection (2),

(B) after making any deduction under paragraph (*a*) for the taxation year, and

(C) before making any deduction under this paragraph; and

B is the percentage that is the total of

(i) that proportion of 100% that the number of days in the taxation year that are before 2011 is of the number of days in the taxation year,

(ii) that proportion of 90% that the number of days in the taxation year that are in 2011 is of the number of days in the taxation year,

(iii) that proportion of 80% that the number of days in the taxation year that are in 2012 is of the number of days in the taxation year,

(iv) that proportion of 60% that the number of days in the taxation year that are in 2013 is of the number of days in the taxation year,

(v) that proportion of 30% that the number of days in the taxation year that are in 2014 is of the number of days in the taxation year, and

(vi) 0%, if one or more days in the year are after 2014;

History: S. 1100(1)(*y.1*), subparagraph (i) of the description of A was replaced by S.C. 2013, c. 40, s. 100(5), applicable to taxation years that end after March 20, 2013, and formerly read:

> (i) the taxpayer's income for the year from the mine, before making any deduction under this paragraph, paragraph (*x*), (*y*), (*ya*) or (*ya.1*), section 65, 66, 66.1, 66.2 or 66.7 of the Act or section 29 of the *Income Tax Application Rules*, and

S. 1100(1)(*y.1*), subparagraph (vi) of the description of B was added by S.C. 2013, c. 40, s. 100(6), applicable to taxation years that end after March 20, 2013.

S. 1100(1)(*y.1*) was added by P.C. 2011-44, SOR/2011-9, dated February 4, 2011, published in the *Canada Gazette* February 16, 2011, applicable to taxation years that end after March 18, 2007.

(y.2) Additional Allowances — Class 41.2 — Single Mine Properties — such additional amount as the taxpayer may claim in respect of property acquired for the purpose of gaining or producing income from a mine and for which a separate class is prescribed by subsection 1101(4g), not exceeding the amount determined by the formula

$$A \times B$$

where

A is the lesser of

(i) the taxpayer's income for the taxation year from the mine, before making any deduction under this paragraph, paragraph (*x*), (*y*), (*ya*), (*ya.1*) or (*ya.2*), section 65, 66, 66.1, 66.2 or 66.7 of the Act or section 29 of the *Income Tax Application Rules*, and

(ii) the undepreciated capital cost to the taxpayer of property of that class as of the end of the year computed

(A) without reference to subsection (2),

(B) after making any deduction under paragraph (*a*) for the year, and

(C) before making any deduction under this paragraph, and

B is the percentage that is the total of

(i) that proportion of 100% that the number of days in the year that are before 2017 is of the number of days in the year,

(ii) that proportion of 90% that the number of days in the year that are in 2017 is of the number of days in the year,

(iii) that proportion of 80% that the number of days in the year that are in 2018 is of the number of days in the year,

(iv) that proportion of 60% that the number of days in the year that are in 2019 is of the number of days in the year,

(v) that proportion of 30% that the number of days in the year that are in 2020 is of the number of days in the year, and

(vi) 0%, if one or more days in the year are after 2020;

History: S. 1100(1)(*y.2*) was added by S.C. 2013, c. 40, s. 100(7), applicable to taxation years that end after March 20, 2013.

(ya) [Additional allowances — Class 41 — More than one mine] — such additional amount as the taxpayer may claim in respect of property acquired for the purpose of gaining or producing income from more than one mine and for which a separate class is prescribed by subsection 1101(4d), not exceeding the lesser of

(i) the taxpayer's income for the year from the mines, before making any deduction under this paragraph, section 65, 66, 66.1, 66.2 or 66.7 of the Act or section 29 of the *Income Tax Application Rules*, and

(ii) the undepreciated capital cost to the taxpayer of property of that class as of the end of the taxation year (computed without reference to subsection (2) and before making any deduction under this paragraph for the taxation year);

Canadian Petroleum Tax Journal: Canada Customs and Revenue Agency 1999 Roundtable Questions and Answers, Question 21, Vol. 13, No. 1, 2000.

Interpretation Bulletins: *Secondary* — IT-476R Capital cost allowance — Equipment used in petroleum and natural gas activities.

(ya.1) Additional Allowances — Class 41.1 — Multiple Mine Properties — such additional amount as the taxpayer may claim in respect of property acquired for the purpose of gaining or producing income from more than one mine and for which a separate class is prescribed by subsection 1101(4f), not exceeding the amount determined by the formula

$$A \times B$$

where

A is the lesser of

(i) the taxpayer's income for the taxation year from the mines, before making any deduction under this paragraph, paragraph (*ya*) or (*ya.2*), section 65, 66, 66.1, 66.2 or 66.7 of the

Act or section 29 of the *Income Tax Application Rules*, and

(ii) the undepreciated capital cost to the taxpayer of property of that class as of the end of the taxation year computed

(A) without reference to subsection (2),

(B) after making any deduction under paragraph (*a*) for the taxation year, and

(C) before making any deduction under this paragraph; and

B is the percentage that is the total of

(i) that proportion of 100% that the number of days in the taxation year that are before 2011 is of the number of days in the taxation year,

(ii) that proportion of 90% that the number of days in the taxation year that are in 2011 is of the number of days in the taxation year,

(iii) that proportion of 80% that the number of days in the taxation year that are in 2012 is of the number of days in the taxation year,

(iv) that proportion of 60% that the number of days in the taxation year that are in 2013 is of the number of days in the taxation year,

(v) that proportion of 30% that the number of days in the taxation year that are in 2014 is of the number of days in the taxation year, and

(vi) 0%, if one or more days in the year are after 2014;

History: S. 1100(1)(*ya.1*), subparagraph (i) of the description of A was replaced by S.C. 2013, c. 40, s. 100(8), applicable to taxation years that end after March 20, 2013, and formerly read:

(i) the taxpayer's income for the year from the mines, before making any deduction under this paragraph, paragraph (*ya*), section 65, 66, 66.1, 66.2 or 66.7 of the Act or section 29 of the *Income Tax Application Rules*, and

S. 1100(1)(*ya.1*), subparagraph (vi) of the description of B was added by S.C. 2013, c. 40, s. 100(9), applicable to taxation years that end after March 20, 2013.

S. 1100(1)(*ya.2*) was added by S.C. 2013, c. 40, s. 100(10), applicable to taxation years that end after March 20, 2013.

S. 1100(1)(*ya.1*) was added by P.C. 2011-44, SOR/2011-9, dated February 4, 2011, published in the *Canada Gazette* February 16, 2011, applicable to taxation years that end after March 18, 2007.

(ya.2) Additional allowances Class 41.2 — Multiple Mine Properties — such additional amount as the taxpayer may claim in respect of a property acquired for the purpose of gaining or producing income from more than one mine and for which a separate class is prescribed by subsection 1101(4h), not exceeding the amount determined by the formula

$$A \times B$$

where

A is the lesser of

(i) the taxpayer's income for the taxation year from the mines, before making any deduction under this paragraph, paragraph (*ya*), section 65, 66, 66.1, 66.2 or 66.7 of the Act or section 29 of the *Income Tax Application Rules*, and

(ii) the undepreciated capital cost to the taxpayer of property of that class as of the end of the year computed

(A) without reference to subsection (2),

(B) after making any deduction under paragraph (*a*) for the year, and

(C) before making any deduction under this paragraph, and

B is the percentage that is the total of

(i) that proportion of 100% that the number of days in the year that are before 2017 is of the number of days in the year,

(ii) that proportion of 90% that the number of days in the year that are in 2017 is of the number of days in the year,

(iii) that proportion of 80% that the number of days in the year that are in 2018 is of the number of days in the year,

(iv) that proportion of 60% that the number of days in the year that are in 2019 is of the number of days in the year,

(v) that proportion of 30% that the number of days in the year that are in 2020 is of the number of days in the year, and

(vi) 0%, if one or more days in the year are after 2020;

History: S. 1100(1)(*ya.2*) was added by S.C. 2013, c. 40, s. 100(10), applicable to taxation years that end after March 20, 2013.

(yb) Additional Allowance — Class 47 — any additional amount as the taxpayer may claim in respect of property used as part of an eligible liquefaction facility for which a separate class is prescribed by subsection 1101(4i), not exceeding the lesser of

(i) the income for the taxation year from the taxpayer's eligible liquefaction activities in respect of the eligible liquefaction facility (taking into consideration any deduction under paragraph (*a.3*) and before making any deduction under this paragraph), and

(ii) 22% of the undepreciated capital cost to the taxpayer of property of that separate class as of the end of the taxation year (before making any deduction under this subsection for the taxation year);

History: S. 1100(1)(*yb*) was added by P.C. 2015-629, SOR/2015-117, s. 1(2), dated May 29, 2015, deemed to have come into force on February 19, 2015.

(z) Additional allowances — Railway cars — such additional amount as the taxpayer may claim in respect of property for which a separate class is prescribed by paragraph 1101(5d)(*c*) not exceeding eight per cent of the undepreciated capital cost to the taxpayer of property of that class as of the end of the taxation year (before making any deduction under this subsection for the taxation year);

(z.1a) Additional allowances — Railway cars — such additional amount as the taxpayer may claim in respect of property for which a separate class is prescribed by paragraph 1101(5d)(*d*), (*e*) or (*f*), not exceeding six per cent of the undepreciated capital cost to the taxpayer of property of that class as of the end of the taxation year (before making any deduction under this subsection for the taxation year);

(z.1b) Additional allowances — Railway cars — where throughout the taxation year the taxpayer was a common carrier that owned and operated a railway, such additional amount as the taxpayer may claim in respect of property for which a separate class is prescribed by subsection 1101(5d.1), not exceeding three per cent of the undepreciated capital cost to the taxpayer of property of that class as of the end of the year (before making any deduction under this subsection for the year);

(z.1c) Additional allowances — Railway cars — where throughout the taxation year the taxpayer was a common carrier that owned and operated a railway, such additional amount as the taxpayer may claim in respect of property for which a separate class is prescribed by subsection 1101(5d.2), not exceeding six percent of the undepreciated capital cost to the taxpayer of property of that class as of the end of the year (before making any deduction under this subsection for the year);

(za) Additional allowances — Railway track and related property — such additional amount as he may claim in respect of property for which a separate class is prescribed by subsection 1101(5e) not exceeding 4% of the undepreciated capital cost to him of property of that class as of the end of the taxation year (before making any deduction under this subsection for the taxation year);

(za.1) Additional allowances — Railway track and related property — where throughout the taxation year the taxpayer was a common carrier that owned and operated a railway, such additional amount as the taxpayer may claim in respect of property for which a separate class is prescribed by subsection 1101(5e.1), not exceeding six per cent of the undepreciated capital cost to the taxpayer of property of that class as of the end of the year (before making any deduction under this subsection for the year);

(za.2) Additional allowances — Railway track and related property — where throughout the taxation year the taxpayer was a common carrier that owned and operated a railway, such additional amount as the taxpayer may claim in respect of property for which a separate class is prescribed by subsection 1101(5e.2), not exceeding five per cent of the undepreciated capital cost to the taxpayer of property of that class as of the end of the year (before making any deduction under this subsection for the year);

(zb) Additional allowances — Railway track and related property — such additional amount as he may claim in respect of property for which a separate class is prescribed by subsection 1101(5f) not exceeding 3% of the undepreciated capital cost to him of property of that class as of the end of the taxation year (before making any deduction under this subsection for the taxation year);

(zc) Additional allowances — Railway expansion and modernization property — where the taxpayer owns and operates a railway as a common carrier, such additional amount as he may claim in respect of property of a class in Schedule II (in this paragraph referred to as "designated property" of the class)

(i) that is

(A) included in Class 1 in Schedule II by virtue of paragraph (*h*) or (*i*) of that Class,

(B) a bridge, culvert, subway or tunnel included in Class 1 in Schedule II that is ancillary to railway track and grading,

(C) a trestle included in Class 3 in Schedule II that is ancillary to railway track and grading,

(D) included in Class 6 in Schedule II by virtue of paragraph (*j*) of that Class,

(E) machinery or equipment included in Class 8 in Schedule II that is ancillary to

(I) railway track and grading, or

(II) railway traffic control or signalling equipment, including switching, block signalling, interlocking, crossing protection, detection, speed control or retarding equipment, but not including property that is principally electronic equipment or systems software therefor,

(F) machinery or equipment included in Class 8 in Schedule II that

(I) was acquired principally for the purpose of maintaining or servicing, or

(II) is ancillary to and used as part of, a railway locomotive or railway car,

(G) included in Class 10 in Schedule II by virtue of subparagraph (*m*)(i), (ii) or (iii) of that Class,

(H) included in Class 28 in Schedule II by virtue of subparagraph (*d*)(ii) of that Class (other than property referred to in subparagraph (*m*)(iv) of Class 10), or

(I) included in Class 35 in Schedule II,

(ii) that was acquired by him principally for use in or is situated in Canada,

(iii) that was acquired by him in respect of the railway in the taxation year or in one of the four immediately preceding taxation years, at a time that was after April 10, 1978 but before 1988, and

(iv) that was not used for any purpose whatever before it was acquired by him,

not exceeding the lesser of

(v) 6 per cent of the aggregate of the capital cost to him of the designated property of the class, and

(vi) the undepreciated capital cost to him as of the end of the taxation year (after making all deductions claimed by him under other provisions of this subsection for the taxation year but before making any deduction under this paragraph for the taxation year) of property of the class.

(zd) Class 38 — such amount as the taxpayer may claim in respect of property of Class 38 in Schedule II not exceeding that percentage which is the aggregate of

(i) that proportion of 40 per cent that the number of days in the taxation year that are in 1988 is of the number of days in the taxation year that are after 1987,

(ii) that proportion of 35 per cent that the number of days in the taxation year that are in 1989 is of the number of days in the taxation year, and

(iii) that proportion of 30 per cent that the number of days in the taxation year that are after 1989 is of the number of days in the taxation year

of the undepreciated capital cost to the taxpayer of property of that class as of the end of the taxation year (before making any deduction under this paragraph for the taxation year);

(ze) Class 39 — such amount as the taxpayer may claim in respect of property of Class 39 in Schedule II not exceeding that percentage which is the aggregate of

(i) that proportion of 40 per cent that the number of days in the taxation year that are in 1988 is of the number of days in the taxation year that are after 1987,

(ii) that proportion of 35 per cent that the number of days in the taxation year that are in 1989 is of the number of days in the taxation year,

(iii) that proportion of 30 per cent that the number of days in the taxation year that are in 1990 is of the number of days in the taxation year, and

(iv) that proportion of 25 per cent that the number of days in the taxation year that are after 1990 is of the number of days in the taxation year

of the undepreciated capital cost to the taxpayer of property of that class as of the end of the taxation year (before making any deduction under this paragraph for the taxation year);

(zf) Class 40 — such amount as the taxpayer may claim in respect of property of Class 40 in Schedule II not exceeding that percentage which is the aggregate of

(i) that proportion of 40 per cent that the number of days in the taxation year that are in 1988 is of the number of days in the taxation year that are after 1987,

(ii) that proportion of 35 per cent that the number of days in the taxation year that are in 1989 is of the number of days in the taxation year, and

(iii) that proportion of 30 per cent that the number of days in the taxation year that are in 1990 is of the number of days in the taxation year

of the undepreciated capital cost to the taxpayer of property of that class as of the end of the taxation year (before making any deduction under this paragraph for the taxation year).

(zg) Additional allowance — Year 2000 computer hardware and systems software — where the taxpayer

(i) has elected for the year in prescribed manner,

(ii) was not in the year a large corporation, as defined in subsection 225.1(8) of the Act, or a partnership any member of which was such a corporation in a taxation year that included any time that is in the partnership's year, and

(iii) acquired property included in paragraph (*f*) of Class 10 in Schedule II

(A) in the year,

(B) after 1997 and before November 1999, and

(C) for the purpose of replacing property that was acquired before 1998 that has a material risk of malfunctioning because of the change of the calendar year to 2000 and that is described in paragraph (*f*) of Class 10, or paragraph (*o*) of Class 12, in Schedule II,

such additional amount as the taxpayer claims in respect of all property described in subparagraph (iii) not exceeding the least of

(iv) the amount, if any, by which $50,000 exceeds the total of

(A) the total of all amounts each of which is an amount claimed by the taxpayer under this paragraph for a preceding taxation year,

(B) the total of all amounts each of which is an amount claimed by the taxpayer for the year or a preceding taxation year under paragraph (*zh*), and

(C) the total of all amounts each of which is an amount claimed under this paragraph or paragraph (*zh*) by a corporation for a taxation year in which it was associated with the taxpayer,

(v) 85% of the capital cost to the taxpayer of all property described in subparagraph (iii), and

(vi) the undepreciated capital cost to the taxpayer as of the end of the year (computed without reference to subsection (2) and after making all deductions claimed under other provisions of this subsection for the year but before making any deduction under this paragraph for the year) of property included in Class 10 in Schedule II; and

(zh) Additional allowance — Year 2000 computer software — where the taxpayer

(i) has elected for the year in prescribed manner,

(ii) was not in the year a large corporation, as defined in subsection 225.1(8) of the Act, or a partnership any member of which was such a corporation in a taxation year that included any time that is in the partnership's year, and

(iii) acquired property included in paragraph (*o*) of Class 12 in Schedule II

(A) in the year,

(B) after 1997 and before November 1999, and

(C) for the purpose of replacing property that was acquired before 1998 that has a material risk of malfunctioning because of the change of the calendar year to 2000 and that is described in paragraph (*f*) of Class 10, or paragraph (*o*) of Class 12, in Schedule II,

Regulations

such additional amount as the taxpayer claims in respect of all property described in subparagraph (iii) not exceeding the least of

(iv) the amount, if any, by which $50,000 exceeds the total of

(A) the total of all amounts each of which is an amount claimed by the taxpayer under this paragraph for a preceding taxation year,

(B) the total of all amounts each of which is an amount claimed by the taxpayer for the year or a preceding taxation year under paragraph (*zg*), and

(C) the total of all amounts each of which is an amount claimed under this paragraph or paragraph (*zg*) by a corporation for a taxation year in which it was associated with the taxpayer,

(v) 50% of the capital cost to the taxpayer of all property described in subparagraph (iii), and

(vi) the undepreciated capital cost to the taxpayer as of the end of the year (computed without reference to subsection (2) and after making all deductions claimed under other provisions of this subsection for the year but before making any deduction under this paragraph for the year) of property included in Class 12 in Schedule II.

Regulations

(1.1) [Specified leasing property – amount deductible]. Notwithstanding subsections (1) and (3), the amount deductible by a taxpayer for a taxation year in respect of a property that is a specified leasing property at the end of the year is the lesser of

(*a*) the amount, if any, by which the aggregate of

(i) all amounts that would be considered to be repayments in the year or a preceding year on account of the principal amount of a loan made by the taxpayer if

(A) the taxpayer had made the loan at the time that the property last became a specified leasing property and in a principal amount equal to the fair market value of the property at that time,

(B) interest had been charged on the principal amount of the loan outstanding from time to time at the rate, determined in accordance with section 4302, in effect at the earlier of

(I) the time, if any, before the time referred to in subclause (II), at which the taxpayer last entered into an agreement to lease the property, and

(II) the time that the property last became a specified leasing property

(or, where a particular lease provides that the amount paid or payable by the lessee of the property for the use of, or the right to use, the property varies according to prevailing interest rates in effect from time to time, and the taxpayer so elects, in respect of all of the property that is the subject of the particular lease, in the taxpayer's return of income under Part I of the Act for the taxation year of the taxpayer in which the particular lease was entered into, the rate determined in accordance with section 4302 that is in effect at the beginning of the period for which the interest is being calculated), compounded semi-annually not in advance, and

(C) the amounts that were received or receivable by the taxpayer before the end of the year for the use of, or the right to use, the property before the end of the year and after the time it last became a specified leasing property were blended payments of principal and interest, calculated in accordance with clause (B), on the loan applied firstly on account of interest on principal, secondly on account of interest on unpaid interest, and thirdly on account of principal, and

(ii) the amount that would have been deductible under this section for the taxation year (in this subparagraph referred to as the "particular year") that includes the time (in this subparagraph referred to as the "particular time") at which the property last became a specified leasing property of the taxpayer, if

(A) the property had been transferred to a separate prescribed class at the later of

(I) the beginning of the particular year, and

(II) the time at which the property was acquired by the taxpayer,

(B) the particular year had ended immediately before the particular time, and

(C) where the property was not a specified leasing property immediately before the particular time, subsection (3) had applied,

exceeds

(iii) the aggregate of all amounts deducted by the taxpayer in respect of the property by reason of this subsection before the commencement of the year and after the time at which it last became a specified leasing property; and

(*b*) the amount, if any, by which,

(i) the aggregate of all amounts that would have been deducted by the taxpayer under this Part in respect of the property under paragraph 20(1)(*a*) of the Act in computing the income of the taxpayer for the year and all preceding taxation years had this subsection and subsections (11) and (15) not applied, and had the taxpayer, in each such year, deducted under paragraph 20(1)(*a*) of the Act the maximum amount allowed under this Part, read without reference to this subsection and subsections (11) and (15), in respect of the property,

exceeds

(ii) the total depreciation allowed to the taxpayer before the commencement of the year in respect of the property.

(1.11) [Specified leasing property – meaning]. In this section and subsection 1101(5n), "specified leasing property" of a taxpayer at any time means depreciable property (other than exempt property) that is

(*a*) used at that time by the taxpayer or a person with whom the taxpayer does not deal at arm's length principally for the purpose of gaining or producing gross revenue that is rent or leasing revenue,

(*b*) the subject of a lease at that time to a person with whom the taxpayer deals at arm's length and that, at the time the lease was entered into, was a lease for a term of more than one year, and

(*c*) the subject of a lease of property where the tangible property, other than exempt property, that was the subject of the lease had, at the time the lease was entered into, an aggregate fair market value in excess of $25,000,

but, for greater certainty, does not include intangible property, or for civil law incorporeal property, (including systems software and property referred to in paragraph (*w*) of Class 10 or paragraph (*n*) or (*o*) of Class 12 in Schedule II).

History: S. 1100(1.11), the portion following paragraph (*c*) was replaced by P.C. 2010-548, SOR/2010-93, dated April 29, 2010, in force May 12, 2010, date of publication in the *Canada Gazette*. S. 1100(1.11), the portion following paragraph (*c*) formerly read:

> but, for greater certainty, does not include intangible property (including systems software and property referred to in paragraph (*w*) of Class 10 or paragraph (*n*) or (*o*) of Class 12 in Schedule II).

(1.12) [Specified leasing property – acquisition of property]. Notwithstanding subsections (1) and (1.1), where, in a taxation year, a taxpayer has acquired a property that was not used by the taxpayer for any purpose in that year and the first use of the property by the taxpayer is a lease of the property in respect of which subsection (1.1) applies, the amount allowed to the taxpayer under subsection (1) in respect of the property for the year shall be deemed to be nil.

(1.13) [Specified leasing property – interpretation]. For the purposes of this section,

(*a*) "exempt property" means

(i) general purpose office furniture or office equipment included in Class 8 in Schedule II (including for greater certainty, mobile office equipment such as cellular telephones and pagers) or general purpose electronic data processing equipment and ancillary data processing equipment, included in paragraph (*f*) of Class 10 in Schedule II, other than any individual piece thereof having a capital cost to the taxpayer in excess of $1,000,000,

(i.1) general-purpose electronic data processing equipment and ancillary data processing equipment, included in Class 45, 50 or 52 in Schedule II, other than any individual item of that type of equipment having a capital cost to the taxpayer in excess of $1,000,000,

(ii) furniture, appliances, television receivers, radio receivers, telephones, furnaces, hot-water heaters and other similar properties, designed for residential use,

(iii) a property that is a motor vehicle that is designed or adapted primarily to carry individuals on highways and streets and that has a seating capacity for not more than the driver and eight passengers, or a motor vehicle of a type commonly called a van or pick-up truck, or a similar vehicle,

(iv) a truck or tractor that is designed for hauling freight on highways,

(v) a trailer that is designed for hauling freight and to be hauled under normal operating conditions by a truck or tractor described in subparagraph (iv),

(vi) a building or part thereof included in Class 1, 3, 6, 20, 31 or 32 in Schedule II (including component parts such as electric wiring, plumbing, sprinkler systems, air-conditioning equipment, heating equipment, lighting fixtures, elevators and escalators) other than a building or part thereof leased primarily to a lessee that is

(A) a person who is exempt from tax by reason of section 149 of the Act,

(B) a person who uses the building in the course of carrying on a business the income from which is exempt from tax under Part I of the Act by reason of any provision of the Act, or

(C) a Canadian government, municipality or other Canadian public authority,

who owned the building or part thereof at any time before the commencement of the lease (other than at any time during a period ending not later than one year after the later of the date the construction of the building or part thereof was completed and the date the building or part thereof was acquired by the lessee),

(vii) vessel mooring space, and

(viii) property that is included in Class 35 in Schedule II,

and for the purposes of subparagraph (i), where a property is owned by two or more persons or partnerships, or any combination thereof, the capital cost of the property to each such person or partnership shall be deemed to be the total of all amounts each of which is the capital cost of the property to such a person or partnership;

(*a*.1) notwithstanding paragraph (*a*), "exempt property" does not include property that is the subject of a lease if that property had, at the time the lease was entered into, an aggregate fair market value in excess of $1,000,000 and the lessee of the property is

(i) a person who is exempt from tax by reason of section 149 of the Act,

(ii) a person who uses the property in the course of carrying on a business, the income from which is exempt from tax under Part I of the Act by reason of any provision of the Act,

(iii) a Canadian government, or

(iv) a person not resident in Canada, except if the person uses the property primarily in the course of carrying on a business in Canada that is not a treaty-protected business;

Regulations

(*a.2*) for the purposes of paragraph (*a.1*), if it is reasonable, having regard to all the circumstances, to conclude that one of the main reasons for the existence of two or more leases was to avoid the application of paragraph (*a.1*) by reason of each such lease being a lease of property where the property that was the subject of the lease had an aggregate fair market value, at the time the lease was entered into, not in excess of $1,000,000, each such lease shall be deemed to be a lease of property that had, at the time the lease was entered into, an aggregate fair market value in excess of $1,000,000;

(*b*) property shall be deemed to be the subject of a lease for a term of more than one year at any time where, at that time

(i) the property had been leased by the lessee thereunder, a person with whom the lessee does not deal at arm's length, or any combination thereof, for a period of more than one year ending at that time, or

(ii) it is reasonable, having regard to all the circumstances, to conclude that the lessor thereunder knew or ought to have known that the lessee thereunder, a person with whom the lessee does not deal at arm's length, or any combination thereof, would lease the property for more than one year; and

(*c*) for the purposes of paragraph (1.11)(*c*), where it is reasonable, having regard to all the circumstances, to conclude that one of the main reasons for the existence of two or more leases was to avoid the application of subsection (1.1) by reason of each such lease being a lease of property where the tangible property, other than exempt property, that was the subject of the lease had an aggregate fair market value, at the time the lease was entered into, not in excess of $25,000, each such lease shall be deemed to be a lease of tangible property that had, at the time the lease was entered into, an aggregate fair market value in excess of $25,000.

History: S. 1100(1.13)(*a.1*) and (*a.2*) were added by S.C. 2013, c. 34, s. 383(1), applicable to property that is the subject of a lease entered into after 4:00 p.m. Eastern Standard Time, March 4, 2010.

S. 1100(1.13)(*a*)(i.1) was replaced by P.C. 2009-660, SOR/2009-126, dated April 30, 2009, applicable in respect of property acquired after January 27, 2009. S. 1100(1.13)(*a*)(i.1) formerly read:

(i.1) general-purpose electronic data processing equipment and ancillary data processing equipment, included in Class 45 or 50 in Schedule II, other than any individual item of that type of equipment having a capital cost to the taxpayer in excess of $1,000,000,

S. 1100(1.13)(*a*)(i.1) was replaced by P.C. 2009-581, SOR/2009-115, dated April 23, 2009, applicable to property acquired on or after March 19, 2007. S. 1100(1.13)(*a*)(i.1) formerly read:

(i.1) general-purpose electronic data processing equipment and ancillary data processing equipment, included in Class 45 in Schedule II, other than any individual item of that type of equipment having a capital cost to the taxpayer in excess of $1,000,000,

(1.14) [Specified leasing property – interpretation]. For the purposes of subsection (1.11) and notwithstanding subsection (1.13), where a taxpayer referred to in subsection (16) so elects in the taxpayer's return of income under Part I of the Act for a taxation year in respect of the year and all subsequent taxation years, all of the property of the taxpayer that is the subject of leases entered into in those years shall be deemed not to be exempt property for those years and the aggregate fair market value of all of the tangible property that is the subject of each such lease shall be deemed to have been, at the time the lease was entered into, in excess of $25,000.

(1.15) [Specified leasing property – term of more than one year]. Subject to subsection (1.16) and for the purposes of subsection (1.11), where at any time a taxpayer acquires property that is the subject of a lease with a remaining term at that time of more than one year from a person with whom the taxpayer was dealing at arm's length, the taxpayer shall be deemed to have entered into a lease of the property at that time for a term of more than one year.

(1.16) [Specified leasing property – amalgamation or non-arm's length]. Where, at any time, a taxpayer acquires from a person with whom the taxpayer is not dealing at arm's length, or by virtue of an amalgamation (within the meaning assigned by subsection 87(1) of the Act), property that was specified leasing property of the person from whom the taxpayer acquired it, the taxpayer shall, for the purposes of paragraph (1.1)(*a*) and for the purpose of computing the income of the taxpayer in respect of the lease for any period after the particular time, be deemed to be the same person as, and a continuation of, that person.

(1.17) [Specified leasing property – replacement property]. For the purposes of subsections (1.1) and, (1.11), where at any particular time a property (in this subsection referred to as a "replacement property") is provided by a taxpayer to a lessee for the remaining term of a lease as a replacement for a similar property of the taxpayer (in this subsection referred to as the "original property") that was leased by the taxpayer to the lessee, and the amount payable by the lessee for the use of, or the right to use, the replacement property is the same as the amount that was so payable in respect of the original property, the following rules apply:

(*a*) the replacement property shall be deemed to have been leased by the taxpayer to the lessee at the same time and for the same term as the original property;

(*b*) the amount of the loan referred to in clause (1.1)(*a*)(i)(A) shall be deemed to be equal to the amount of that loan determined in respect of the original property;

(*c*) the amount determined under subparagraph (1.1)(*a*)(ii) in respect of the replacement property shall be deemed to be equal to the amount so determined in respect of the original property;

(*d*) all amounts received or receivable by the taxpayer for the use of, or the right to use, the original property before the particular time shall be deemed to have been received or receivable, as the case may be, by the taxpayer for the use of, or the right to use, the replacement property; and

(*e*) the original property shall be deemed to have ceased to be subject to the lease at the particular time.

(1.18) [Specified leasing property – breakdown of property]. For the purposes of subsection (1.1), where for any period of time any amount that would have been received or receivable by a taxpayer during that period in respect of the use of, or the right to use, a property of the taxpayer during that period is not received or receivable by the taxpayer as a consequence of a breakdown of the property during that period and before the lease of that property is terminated, that amount shall be deemed to have been received or receivable, as the case may be, by the taxpayer.

(1.19) [Specified leasing property – addition or alteration or property]. For the purposes of subsections (1.1) and (1.11), where at any particular time

(*a*) an addition or alteration (in this subsection referred to as "additional property") is made by a taxpayer to a property (in this subsection referred to as the "original property") of the taxpayer that is a specified leasing property at the particular time, and

(*b*) as a consequence of the addition or alteration, the aggregate amount receivable by the taxpayer after the particular time for the use of, or the right to use, the original property and the additional property exceeds the amount so receivable in respect of the original property,

the following rules apply:

(*c*) the taxpayer shall be deemed to have leased the additional property to the lessee at the particular time,

(*d*) the term of the lease of the additional property shall be deemed to be greater than one year,

(*e*) the prescribed rate in effect at the particular time in respect of the additional property shall be deemed to be equal to the prescribed rate in effect in respect of the lease of the original property at the particular time,

(*f*) subsection (1.11) shall be read without reference to paragraph (*c*) thereof in respect of the additional property, and

(*g*) the excess described in paragraph (*b*) shall be deemed to be an amount receivable by the taxpayer for the use of, or the right to use, the additional property.

(1.2) [Specified leasing property – renegotiation of lease]. For the purposes of subsections (1.1) and (1.11), where at any time

(*a*) a lease (in this subsection referred to as the "original lease") of property is renegotiated in the course of a *bona fide* renegotiation, and

(*b*) as a result of the renegotiation, the amount paid or payable by the lessee of the property for the use of, or the right to use, the property is altered in respect of a period after that time (otherwise than by reason of an addition or alteration to which subsection (1.19) applies),

the following rules apply:

(*c*) the original lease shall be deemed to have expired and the renegotiated lease shall be deemed to be a new lease of the property entered into at that time, and

(*d*) paragraph (1.13)(*b*) shall not apply in respect of any period before that time during which the property was leased by the lessee or a person with whom the lessee did not deal at arm's length.

(1.3) [Specified leasing property – lease of building]. For the purposes of subsections (1.1) and (1.11), where a taxpayer leases to another person a building or part thereof that is not exempt property, the references to "one year" in paragraphs (1.11)(*b*) and (1.13)(*b*), subsection (1.15) and paragraph (1.19)(*d*) shall in respect of that building or part thereof be read as references to "three years".

(2) The amount that a taxpayer may deduct for a taxation year under subsection (1) in respect of property of a class in Schedule II is to be determined as if the undepreciated capital cost to the taxpayer at the end of the taxation year (before making any deduction under subsection (1) for the taxation year) of property of the class were adjusted by adding the positive or negative amount determined by the formula

$$A(B) - 0.5(C)$$

where

A is, in respect of property of the class that became available for use by the taxpayer in the taxation year and that is accelerated investment incentive property or property included in Class 54 or 55,

(*a*) if the property is not included in paragraph (1)(*v*) or in any of Classes 12, 13, 14, 15, 43.1, 43.2, 53, 54 and 55 or in Class 43 in the circumstances described in paragraph (*d*),

(i) 1/2, for property that became available for use by the taxpayer before 2024, and

(ii) nil, for property that became available for use by the taxpayer after 2023,

(*b*) if the class is Class 43.1,

(i) 2 1/3, for property that became available for use by the taxpayer before 2024,

(ii) 1 1/2, for property that became available for use by the taxpayer in 2024 or 2025, and

(iii) 5/6, for property that became available for use by the taxpayer after 2025,

(*c*) if the class is Class 43.2,

(i) 1, for property that became available for use by the taxpayer before 2024,

(ii) 1/2, for property that became available for use by the taxpayer in 2024, and

(iii) nil, in any other case,

(*d*) if the property is included in Class 53 or — for property acquired after 2025 — is included in Class 43 and would have been included in Class 53 if it had been acquired in 2025,

(i) 1, for property that became available for use by the taxpayer before 2024,

(ii) 1/2, for property that became available for use by the taxpayer in 2024 or 2025, and

(iii) 5/6, for property that became available for use by the taxpayer after 2025,

(*e*) if the class is Class 54,

(i) 2 1/3, for property that became available for use by the taxpayer before 2024,

(ii) 1 1/2, for property that became available for use by the taxpayer in 2024 or 2025, and

(iii) 5/6, for property that became available for use by the taxpayer after 2025,

(*f*) if the class is Class 55,

(i) 1 1/2, for property that became available for use by the taxpayer before 2024,

(ii) 7/8, for property that became available for use by the taxpayer in 2024 or 2025, and

(iii) 3/8, for property that became available for use by the taxpayer after 2025, and

(*g*) in any other case, nil;

B is the amount determined, in respect of the class, by the formula

$$D - E$$

where

D is the total of all amounts, if any, each of which is an amount included in the description of A in the definition "undepreciated capital cost" in subsection 13(21) of the Act in respect of property of the class that became available for use by the taxpayer in the taxation year and that is accelerated investment incentive property or property included in Class 54 or 55, as the case may be, and

E is the amount, if any, by which the amount determined for G exceeds the amount determined for F in the description of C; and

C is the amount determined, in respect of the class, by the formula

$$F - G$$

where

F is the total of all amounts each of which

(*a*) is an amount added to the undepreciated capital cost to the taxpayer of property of the class

(i) because of element A in the definition "undepreciated capital cost" in subsection 13(21) of the Act in respect of property (other than accelerated investment incentive property) that was acquired, or became available for use, by the taxpayer in the taxation year, or

(ii) because of element C or D in the definition "undepreciated capital cost" in subsection 13(21) of the Act in respect of an amount that was repaid in the taxation year, and

(*b*) is not in respect of

(i) property included in paragraph (1)(*v*), in paragraph (*w*) of Class 10 or in any of paragraphs (*a*) to (*c*), (*e*) to (*i*), (*k*), (*l*) and (*p*) to (*s*) of Class 12,

(ii) property included in any of Classes 13, 14, 15, 23, 24, 27, 29, 34, 52, 54 and 55,

(iii) where the taxpayer was a corporation described in subsection (16) throughout the taxation year, property that was specified leasing property of the taxpayer at that time,

(iv) property that was deemed to have been acquired by the taxpayer in a preceding taxation year by reason of the application of paragraph 16.1(1)(*b*) of the Act in respect of a lease to which the property was subject immediately before the time at which the taxpayer last acquired the property, or

(v) property considered to have become available for use by the taxpayer in the taxation year by reason of paragraph 13(27)(*b*) or (28)(*c*) of the Act, and

G is the total of all amounts each of which is an amount deducted from the undepreciated capital cost to the taxpayer of property of the class

(*a*) because of element F or G in the definition "undepreciated capital cost" in subsection 13(21) of the Act in respect of property disposed of in the taxation year, or

(*b*) because of element J in the definition "undepreciated capital cost" in subsection 13(21) of the Act in respect of an amount the taxpayer received or was entitled to receive in the taxation year.

History: S. 1100(2) was replaced by S.C. 2019, c. 29, s. 52(6), effective June 21, 2019, and formerly read:

(2) *Property Acquired in the Year.* The amount that a taxpayer may deduct for a taxation year under subsection (1) in respect of property of a class in Schedule II is to be determined as if the undepreciated capital cost to the taxpayer at the end of the taxation year (before making any deduction under subsection (1) for the taxation year) of property of the class were reduced by an amount equal to 50 per cent of the amount, if any, by which

(*a*) the total of all amounts, each of which is an amount added

(i) because of element A in the definition "undepreciated capital cost" in subsection 13(21) of the Act in respect of property that was acquired in the year or that became available for use by the taxpayer in the year, or

(ii) because of element C or D in the definition "undepreciated capital cost" in subsection 13(21) of the Act in respect of an amount that was repaid in the year,

to the undepreciated capital cost to the taxpayer of property of a class in Schedule II, other than

(iii) property included in paragraph (1)(*v*), in paragraph (*w*) of Class 10 or in any of paragraphs (*a*) to (*c*), (*e*) to (*i*), (*k*), (*l*) and (*p*) to (*s*) of Class 12,

(iv) property included in any of Classes 13, 14, 15, 23, 24, 27, 29, 34 and 52,

(v) where the taxpayer was a corporation described in subsection (16) throughout the year, property that was specified leasing property of the taxpayer at that time,

(vi) property that was deemed to have been acquired by the taxpayer in a preceding taxation year by reason of the application of paragraph 16.1(1)(*b*) of the Act in respect of a lease to which the property was subject immediately before the time at which the taxpayer last acquired the property, and

(vii) property considered to have become available for use by the taxpayer in the year by reason of paragraph 13(27)(*b*) or (28)(*c*) of the Act

exceeds

(*b*) the total of all amounts, each of which is an amount deducted from the undepreciated capital cost to the taxpayer of property of the class

(i) because of element F or G in the definition "undepreciated capital cost" in subsection 13(21) of the Act in respect of property disposed of in the year, or

(ii) because of element J in the definition "undepreciated capital cost" in subsection 13(21) of the Act in respect of an amount the taxpayer received or was entitled to receive in the year.

S. 1100(2)(*a*), the portion before subparagraph (v) was replaced by P.C. 2009-660, SOR/2009-126, dated April 30, 2009, applicable in respect of property acquired after January 27, 2009. S. 1100(2)(*a*), the portion before subparagraph (v) formerly read:

(2) Where at the end of a taxation year of a taxpayer

(*a*) the aggregate of all amounts, each of which is an amount added

(i) by reason of subparagraph 13(21)(*f*)(i) [subsection 13(21) "undepreciated capital cost", item A] of the Act in respect of a property acquired in the year or that became available for use by the taxpayer in the year, or

(ii) by reason of subparagraph 13(21)(*f*)(ii.1) or (ii.2) [subsection 13(21) "undepreciated capital cost", items C and D] of the Act in respect of an amount repaid in the year

to the undepreciated capital cost to the taxpayer of property of a class in Schedule II, other than

(iii) property included in paragraph (1)(*v*), paragraph (*w*) of Class 10 or any of paragraphs (*a*) to (*c*), (*e*) to (*i*), (*k*), (*1*) and (*p*) to (*s*) of Class 12,

(iv) property included in any of Classes 13, 14, 15, 23, 24, 27, 29 and 34,

S. 1100(2), the portion following paragraph (*a*) was replaced by P.C. 2009-660, SOR/2009-126, dated April 30, 2009, applicable in respect of property acquired after January 27, 2009. S. 1100(2), the portion following paragraph (*a*) formerly read:

exceeds

(*b*) the aggregate of all amounts, each of which is an amount deducted

(i) by virtue of subparagraph 13(21)(*f*)(iv) or (v) [subsection 13(21) "undepreciated capital cost", items F and G] of the Act in respect of property disposed of in the year, or

(ii) by virtue of subparagraph 13(21)(*f*)(viii) [subsection 13(21) "undepreciated capital cost", item J] of the Act in respect of an amount the taxpayer received or was entitled to receive in the year

from the undepreciated capital cost to him of property of the class,

the amount that the taxpayer may deduct for the year under subsection (1) in respect of property of the class shall be determined as if the undepreciated capital cost to him as of the end of the year (before making any deduction under subsection (1) for the year) of property of the class were reduced by an amount equal to 50 per cent of the amount by which the aggregate determined under paragraph (*a*) exceeds the aggregate determined under paragraph (*b*).

Related Regulations: 1100(1); 1100(2.01) Straddle years; 1100(2.02) Expenditures before November 21, 2018.

Tax Topics: No. 2439, Accelerated CCA and Other Measures From the 2018 Fall Economic Statement.

Interpretation Bulletins: *Secondary* — IT-469R Capital cost allowance — Earth-moving equipment; IT-522R Vehicle, travel and sales expenses of employees.

(2.01) Straddle years. For the purposes of subsection (2),

(*a*) if a taxation year begins in 2023 and ends in 2024, the factor determined for A in subsection (2) is to be replaced by the factor determined by the formula

(A(B) + C(D))/(B + D)

where

A is the factor otherwise determined for A in subsection (2) for 2023,

B is the amount that would be determined for D in subsection (2) if the only property that became available for use by the taxpayer in the taxation year were property that became available for use by the taxpayer in 2023,

C is the factor otherwise determined for A in subsection (2) for 2024, and

D is the amount that would be determined for D in subsection (2) if the only property that became available for use by the taxpayer in the taxation were property that became available for use by the taxpayer in 2024; and

(*b*) if a taxation year begins in 2025 and ends in 2026, the factor determined for A in subsection (2) is to be replaced by the factor determined by the formula

(A(B) + C(D))/(B + D)

where

A is the factor otherwise determined for A in subsection (2) for 2025,

B is the amount that would be determined for D in subsection (2) if the only property that became available for use by the taxpayer in the taxation year were property that became available for use by the taxpayer in 2025,

C is the factor otherwise determined for A in subsection (2) for 2026, and

D is the amount that would be determined for D in subsection (2) if the only property that became available for use by the taxpayer in the taxation year were property that became available for use by the taxpayer in 2026.

History: S. 1100(2.01) was added by S.C. 2019, c. 29, s. 52(6), effective June 21, 2019.

Related Regulations: 1100(2).

(2.02) Expenditures before November 21, 2018. For the purposes of subsection (2), in respect of property of a class in Schedule II that is accelerated investment incentive property of a taxpayer solely because of subparagraph 1104(4)(*b*)(i),

(*a*) no amount is to be included in respect of the property in determining the amount for D in subsection (2) in respect of the class to the extent that the amount includes expenditures incurred by any person or partnership before November 21, 2018, unless the person or partnership from which the taxpayer acquired the property dealt at arm's length with the taxpayer and held the property as inventory; and

(*b*) any amount excluded from the amount determined for D in subsection (2) in respect of the class because of paragraph (*a*) is to be included in determining the amount for F in subsection (2) in respect of the class, unless no amount in respect of the property would be so included if the property were not accelerated investment incentive property of the taxpayer.

History: S. 1100(2.02) was added by S.C. 2019, c. 29, s. 52(6), effective June 21, 2019.

Related Regulations: 1100(2); 1104(4).

(2.1) Property Acquired in the Year. Where a taxpayer has, after November 12, 1981 and before 1983, acquired or incurred a capital cost in respect of a property of a class in Schedule II and

(*a*) he was obligated to acquire the property under the terms of an agreement in writing entered into before November 13, 1981 (or, where the property is a property described in Class 31 in Schedule II, before 1982),

Regulations

(*b*) he or a person with whom he was not dealing at arm's length commenced the construction, manufacture or production of the property before November 13, 1981 (or, where the property is a property described in Class 31 in Schedule II, before 1982),

(*c*) he or a person with whom he was not dealing at arm's length had made arrangements, evidenced in writing for the construction, manufacture or production of the property that were substantially advanced before November 13, 1981 and the construction, manufacture or production commenced before June 1, 1982, or

(*d*) he was obligated to acquire the property under the terms of an agreement in writing entered into before June 1, 1982 where arrangements, evidenced in writing, for the acquisition or leasing of the property were substantially advanced before November 13, 1981,

the following rules apply:

(*e*) no amount shall be included under paragraph (2)(*a*) in respect of the property;

(*f*) where the property is a property to which paragraph (1)(*b*) applies, that paragraph shall be read, in respect of the property, as "such amount, not exceeding the amount for the year calculated in accordance with Schedule III, as he may claim in respect of the capital cost to him of property of Class 13 in Schedule II";

(*g*) where the property is a property of a class to which paragraph (1)(*t*) or (*ta*) applies, the property shall be deemed to be designated property of the class; and

(*h*) where the property is a property described in paragraph (1)(*v*), subparagraph (iv) thereof shall be read, in respect of the property, as "33⅓ per cent of the capital cost thereof to him, and".

Income Tax Folios: *Primary* — S3-F4-C1 General Discussion of Capital Cost Allowance. S4-F15-C1 Manufacturing and Processing.

Interpretation Bulletins: *Secondary* — IT-464R Capital cost allowance — Leasehold interests.

(2.2) Property Acquired in the Year. Where a property of a class in Schedule II is acquired by a taxpayer

(*a*) in the course of a reorganization in respect of which, if a dividend were received by a corporation in the course of the reorganization, subsection 55(2) of the Act would not be applicable to the dividend by reason of the application of paragraph 55(3)(*b*) of the Act, or

(*b*) (Revoked.)

(*c*) (Revoked.)

(*d*) (Revoked.)

(*e*) from a person with whom the taxpayer was not dealing at arm's length (otherwise than by virtue of a right referred to in paragraph 251(5)(*b*) of the Act) at the time the property was acquired,

and where

(*f*) the property was depreciable property of the person from whom it was acquired and was owned continuously by that person for the period from

(i) a day that was at least 364 days before the end of the taxation year of the taxpayer during which he acquired the property, or

(ii) November 12, 1981

to the day it was acquired by the taxpayer, or

(*g*) the rules provided in subsection (2.1) or this subsection applied in respect of the property for the purpose of determining the allowance under subsection (1) to which the person from whom the taxpayer acquired the property was entitled,

the following rules apply:

(*h*) no amount shall be included in determining an amount for F in subsection (2) in respect of the property;

(*i*) where the property is a property to which paragraph (1)(*b*) applies, that paragraph shall be read, in respect of the property, as "such amount, not exceeding the amount for the year calculated in accordance with Schedule III, as he may claim in respect of the capital cost to him of property of Class 13 in Schedule II";

(*j*) where the property is a property of a class to which paragraph (1)(*ta*) applies,

(i) the property shall be deemed to be designated property of the class,

(ii) for the purposes of computing the amount determined under paragraph (1)(*ta*) for any taxation year of the taxpayer ending after the time the property was actually acquired by the taxpayer, the property shall be deemed, other than for the purposes of paragraph (*f*), to have been acquired by the taxpayer immediately after the commencement of the taxpayer's first taxation year that commenced after the time that is the earlier of

(A) the time the property was last acquired by the transferor of the property, and

(B) where the property was transferred in a series of transfers to which this subsection applies, the time the property was last acquired by the first transferor in that series,

unless

(C) where clause (A) applies, the property was acquired by the taxpayer before the end of the taxation year of the transferor of the property that includes the time at which that transferor acquired the property, or

(D) where clause (B) applies, the property was acquired by the taxpayer before the end of the taxation year of the first transferor that includes the time at which that transferor acquired the property,

(iii) where the taxpayer is a corporation that was incorporated or otherwise formed after the end of the transferor's, or where applicable, the first transferor's, taxation year in which the transferor last acquired the property, the taxpayer shall be deemed, for the purposes of subparagraph (ii),

(A) to have been in existence throughout the period commencing immediately before the end of that year and ending immediately after the taxpayer was incorporated or otherwise formed, and

(B) to have had, throughout the period referred to in clause (A), fiscal periods ending on the day of the year on which the taxpayer's first fiscal period ended, and

(iv) the property shall be deemed to have become available for use by the taxpayer at the earlier of

(A) the time it became available for use by the taxpayer, and

(B) if applicable,

(I) the time it became available for use by the person from whom the taxpayer acquired the property, determined without reference to paragraphs 13(27)(*c*) and (28)(*d*) of the Act, or

(II) the time it became available for use by the first transferor in a series of transfers of the same property to which this subsection applies, determined without reference to paragraphs 13(27)(*c*) and (28)(*d*) of the Act; and

(*k*) if the property is a property described in paragraph (1)(*v*), its subparagraph (iv) shall be read, in respect of the property, as "33 1/3 per cent of the capital cost of the property to the taxpayer, and".

History: S. 1100(2.2)(*h*) was replaced by S.C. 2019, c. 29, s. 52(7), effective June 21, 2019, and formerly read:

(*h*) no amount shall be included under paragraph (2)(*a*) in respect of the property;

S. 1100(2.2)(*k*) was replaced by S.C. 2019, c. 29, s. 52(8), effective June 21, 2019, and formerly read:

(*k*) where the property is a property described in paragraph (1)(*v*), subparagraph (iv) thereof shall be read, in respect of the property, as "33 1/3 per cent of the capital cost thereof to him, and".

Income Tax Folios: *Primary* — S3-F4-C1 General Discussion of Capital Cost Allowance. S4-F15-C1 Manufacturing and Processing.

(2.21) Property Acquired in the Year. Where a taxpayer is deemed by a provision of the Act to have disposed of and acquired or reacquired a property,

(*a*) for the purposes of paragraph (2.2)(*e*) and subsections (19), 1101(1ad) and 1102(14) and (14.1), the acquisition or reacquisition shall be deemed to have been from a person with whom the taxpayer was not dealing at arm's length at the time of the acquisition or reacquisition; and

(*b*) for the purposes of paragraphs (2.2)(*f*) and (*g*), the taxpayer shall be deemed to be the person from whom the taxpayer acquired or reacquired the property.

Interpretation Bulletins: *Secondary* — IT-476R Capital cost allowance — Equipment used in petroleum and natural gas activities.

(2.3) If a taxpayer has disposed of a property and, because of paragraph (2.2)(*h*), no amount is required to be included in determining an amount for F in subsection (2) in respect of the property by the person that acquired the property, no amount shall be included by the taxpayer in determining an amount for G in subsection (2) in respect of the disposition of the property.

History: S. 1100(2.3) was replaced by S.C. 2019, c. 29, s. 52(9), effective June 21, 2019, and formerly read:

(2.3) *Property Acquired in the Year.* Where a taxpayer has disposed of a property and, by virtue of paragraph (2.2)(*h*), no amount is required to be included under paragraph (2)(*a*) in respect of the property by the person that acquired the property, no amount shall be included by the taxpayer under paragraph (2)(*b*) in respect of the disposition of the property.

(2.4) Property Acquired in the Year. For the purposes of subsection (2), where a taxpayer has disposed of property described in Class 10 of Schedule II that would qualify as property described in paragraph (*e*) of Class 16 of Schedule II if the property had been acquired by the taxpayer after November 12, 1981, the proceeds of disposition of the property shall be deemed to be proceeds of disposition of property described in Class 16 of Schedule II and not of property described in Class 10 of Schedule II.

Interpretation Bulletins: *Secondary* — IT-522R Vehicle, travel and sales expenses of employees.

(2.5) Property Acquired in the Year. Where in a particular taxation year a taxpayer disposes of a property included in Class 10.1 in Schedule II that was owned by the taxpayer at the end of the immediately preceding taxation year,

(*a*) the deduction allowed under subsection (1) in respect of the property in computing the taxpayer's income for the year shall be determined as if the property had not been disposed of in the particular year and the number of days in the particular year were one-half of the number of days in the particular year otherwise determined; and

(*b*) no amount shall be deducted under subsection (1) in respect of the property in computing the taxpayer's income for any subsequent taxation year.

(3) Taxation Years Less Than 12 Months. Where a taxation year is less than 12 months, the amount allowed as a deduction under this section, other than under any of paragraphs (1)(*c*), (*e*), (*f*), (*g*), (*l*), (*m*), (*w*), (*x*), (*y*), (*ya*), (*zg*) and (*zh*), shall not exceed that proportion of the maximum amount otherwise allowable that the number of days in the taxation year is of 365.

Income Tax Folios: *Primary* — S3-F4-C1 General Discussion of Capital Cost Allowance. S4-F15-C1 Manufacturing and Processing.

Interpretation Bulletins: *Secondary* — IT-434R Rental of real property by individual.

(4) Reserved.

(5) (Revoked.)

(6) (Revoked.)

(7) Reserved.

(8) Railway Sidings. Where a taxpayer, other than an operator of a railway system, has made a capital expenditure pursuant to a contract or arrangement with an operator of a railway system under which a railway siding that does not become the taxpayer's property is constructed to provide service to the taxpayer's place of business or to a property acquired by the taxpayer for the purpose of gaining or producing income, there is hereby allowed to the taxpayer, in computing income for the taxation year from the business or property, as the case may be, a deduction equal to such amount as he may claim not exceeding four per cent of the amount remaining, if any, after deducting from the capital expenditure the aggregate of all amounts

Regulations

previously allowed as deductions in respect of the expenditure.

(9) Patents. Where a part or all of the cost of a patent is determined by reference to the use of the patent, in lieu of the deduction allowed under paragraph (1)(*c*), a taxpayer, in computing his income for a taxation year from a business or property, as the case may be, may deduct such amount as he may claim in respect of property of Class 14 in Schedule II not exceeding the lesser of

(*a*) the aggregate of

(i) that part of the capital cost determined by reference to the use of the patent in the year, and

(ii) the amount that would be computed under subparagraph (1)(*c*)(i) if the capital cost of the patent did not include the amounts determined by reference to the use of the patent in that year and previous years; and

(*b*) the undepreciated capital cost to him as of the end of the taxation year (before making any deduction under this subsection for the taxation year) of property of the class.

Tax Profile: July 2012 — Intangibles.

Tax Topics: No. 1528, Tax planning opportunities for intellectual property rights.

Income Tax Folios: S4-F15-C1 Manufacturing and Processing.

Interpretation Bulletins: *Secondary* — IT-477 (Consolid.) Capital cost allowance — Patents, franchises, concessions and licences.

(9.1) Patents. Where a part or all of the capital cost to a taxpayer of property that is a patent, or a right to use patented information, is determined by reference to the use of the property and that property is included in Class 44 in Schedule II, in lieu of the deduction allowed under paragraph (1)(*a*), there may be deducted in computing the taxpayer's income for a taxation year from a business or property such amount as the taxpayer may claim in respect of property of the class not exceeding the lesser of

(*a*) the total of

(i) that part of the capital cost that is determined by reference to the use of the property in the year, and

(ii) the amount that would be deductible for the year by reason of paragraph (1)(*a*) in respect of property of the class if the capital cost of property of the class did not include the amounts determined under subparagraph (i) for the year and preceding taxation years; and

(*b*) the undepreciated capital cost to the taxpayer as of the end of the taxation year (before making any deduction under this subsection for the taxation year) of property of the class.

(10) Reserved.

(11) Rental Properties. Notwithstanding subsection (1), in no case shall the aggregate of deductions, each of which is a deduction in respect of property of a prescribed class owned by a taxpayer that includes rental property owned by him, otherwise allowed to the taxpayer by virtue of subsection (1) in computing his income for a taxation year, exceed the amount, if any, by which

(*a*) the aggregate of amounts each of which is

(i) his income for the year from renting or leasing a rental property owned by him, computed without regard to paragraph 20(1)(*a*) of the Act, or

(ii) the income of a partnership for the year from renting or leasing a rental property of the partnership, to the extent of the taxpayer's share of such income,

exceeds

(*b*) the aggregate of amounts each of which is

(i) his loss for the year from renting or leasing a rental property owned by him, computed without regard to paragraph 20(1)(*a*) of the Act, or

(ii) the loss of a partnership for the year from renting or leasing a rental property of the partnership, to the extent of the taxpayer's share of such loss.

Guides: T4036 Rental Income.

Interpretation Bulletins: *Primary* — IT-195R4 Rental property — Capital cost allowance restrictions. *Secondary* — IT-274R Rental properties — Capital cost of $50,000 or more; IT-304R2 Condominiums.

(12) Rental Properties. Subject to subsection (13), subsection (11) does not apply in respect of a taxation year of a taxpayer that was, throughout the year,

(*a*) a life insurance corporation, or a corporation whose principal business was the leasing, rental, development or sale, or any combination thereof, of real property owned by it; or

(*b*) a partnership each member of which was

(i) a corporation described in paragraph (*a*), or

(ii) another partnership described in this paragraph.

History: S. 1100(12)(*b*) was replaced by S.C. 2013, c. 40, s. 100(11), applicable to fiscal periods that end after October 2010, and formerly read:

(*b*) a partnership each member of which was a corporation described in paragraph (*a*).

Interpretation Bulletins: *Primary* — IT-371 Rental property — Meaning of "principal business"; IT-195R4 Rental property — Capital cost allowance restrictions.

(13) Rental Properties. For the purposes of subsection (11), where a taxpayer or partnership has a leasehold interest in a property that is property of Class 1, 3 or 6 in Schedule II by virtue of subsection 1102(5) and the property is leased by the taxpayer or the partnership to a person who owns the land, an interest therein or an option in respect thereof, on which the property is situated, this section shall be read without reference to subsection (12) with respect to that property.

Interpretation Bulletins: *Primary* — IT-195R4 Rental property — Capital cost allowance restrictions.

(14) Rental Properties. In this section and section 1101, "rental property" of a taxpayer or a partnership means

(*a*) a building owned by the taxpayer or the partnership, whether owned jointly with another person or otherwise, or

(*b*) a leasehold interest in real property, if the leasehold interest is property of Class 1, 3, 6 or 13 in Schedule II and is owned by the taxpayer or the partnership,

if, in the taxation year in respect of which the expression is being applied, the property was used by the taxpayer or the partnership principally for the purpose of gaining or producing gross revenue that is rent, but, for greater certainty, does not include a property leased by the taxpayer or the partnership to a lessee, in the ordinary course of the taxpayer's or partnership's business of selling goods or rendering services, under an agreement by which the lessee undertakes to use the property to carry on the business of selling, or promoting the sale of, the taxpayer's or partnership's goods or services.

Tax Profile: March 2004 — Loss Utilization By Individuals.

Income Tax Folios: S4-F15-C1 Manufacturing and Processing.

Interpretation Bulletins: *Primary* — IT-195R4 Rental property — Capital cost allowance restrictions. *Secondary* — IT-274R Rental properties — Capital cost of $50,000 or more; IT-304R2 Condominiums.

(14.1) Rental Properties. For the purposes of subsection (14), gross revenue derived in a taxation year from

(*a*) the right of a person or partnership, other than the owner of a property, to use or occupy the property or a part thereof, and

(*b*) services offered to a person or partnership that are ancillary to the use or occupation by the person or partnership of the property or the part thereof

shall be considered to be rent derived in that year from the property.

Income Tax Folios: S4-F15-C1 Manufacturing and Processing.

Interpretation Bulletins: *Primary* — IT-195R4 Rental property — Capital cost allowance restrictions.

(14.2) Rental Properties. Subsection (14.1) does not apply in any particular taxation year to property owned by

(*a*) a corporation, where the property is used in a business carried on in the year by the corporation;

(*b*) an individual, where the property is used in a business carried on in the year by the individual in which he is personally active on a continuous basis throughout that portion of the year during which the business is ordinarily carried on; or

(*c*) a partnership, where the property is used in a business carried on in the year by the partnership if at least ⅔ of the income or loss, as the case may be, of the partnership for the year is included in the determination of the income of

(i) members of the partnership who are individuals that are personally active in the business of the partnership on a continuous basis throughout that portion of the year during which the business is ordinarily carried on, and

(ii) members of the partnership that are corporations.

Interpretation Bulletins: *Primary* — IT-195R4 Rental property — Capital cost allowance restrictions.

(15) Leasing Properties. Notwithstanding subsection (1), in no case shall the aggregate of deductions, each of which is a deduction in respect of property of a prescribed class that is leasing property owned by a taxpayer, otherwise allowed to the taxpayer under subsection (1) in computing his income for a taxation year, exceed the amount, if any, by which

(*a*) the aggregate of amounts each of which is

(i) his income for the year from renting, leasing or earning royalties from, a leasing property or a property that would be a leasing property but for subsection (18), (19) or (20) where such property is owned by him, computed without regard to paragraph 20(1)(*a*) of the Act, or

(ii) the income of a partnership for the year from renting, leasing or earning royalties from, a leasing property or a property that would be a leasing property but for subsection (18), (19) or (20) where such property is owned by the partnership, to the extent of the taxpayer's share of such income,

exceeds

(*b*) the aggregate of amounts each of which is

(i) his loss for the year from renting, leasing or earning royalties from, a property referred to in subparagraph (*a*)(i), computed without regard to paragraph 20(1)(*a*) of the Act, or

(ii) the loss of a partnership for the year from renting, leasing or earning royalties from, a property referred to in subparagraph (*a*)(ii), to the extent of the taxpayer's share of such loss.

Tax Profile: March 2004 — Loss Utilization By Individuals.

Income Tax Folios: S4-F15-C1 Manufacturing and Processing.

Interpretation Bulletins: *Primary* — IT-443 Leasing property — Capital cost allowance restrictions. *Secondary* — IT-195R4 Rental property — Capital cost allowance restrictions.

(16) Leasing Properties. Subsection (15) does not apply in respect of a taxation year of a taxpayer that was, throughout the year,

(*a*) a corporation whose principal business was

(i) renting or leasing of leasing property or property that would be leasing property but for subsection (18), (19) or (20), or

(ii) renting or leasing of property referred to in subparagraph (i) combined with selling and servicing of property of the same general type and description,

if the gross revenue of the corporation for the year from such principal business was not less than 90 per cent of the gross revenue of the corporation for the year from all sources; or

(*b*) a partnership each member of which was

(i) a corporation described in paragraph (*a*), or

(ii) another partnership described in this paragraph.

History: S. 1100(16)(*b*) was replaced by S.C. 2013, c. 40, s. 100(12), applicable to fiscal periods that end after October 2010, and formerly read:

(*b*) a partnership each member of which was a corporation described in paragraph (*a*).

Interpretation Bulletins: *Secondary* — IT-267R2 Capital cost allowance — Vessels; IT-443 Leasing property — Capital cost allowance restrictions.

(17) Leasing Properties. Subject to subsection (18), in this section and section 1101, "leasing property" of a taxpayer or a partnership means depreciable property other than

(*a*) rental property,

(*b*) computer tax shelter property, or

(*c*) property referred to in paragraph (*w*) of Class 10 or in paragraph (*n*) of Class 12 in Schedule II,

Regulations

where such property is owned by the taxpayer or the partnership, whether jointly with another person or otherwise, if, in the taxation year in respect of which the expression is being applied, the property was used by the taxpayer or the partnership principally for the purpose of gaining or producing gross revenue that is rent, royalty or leasing revenue, but for greater certainty, does not include a property leased by the taxpayer or the partnership to a lessee, in the ordinary course of the taxpayer's or partnership's business of selling goods or rendering services, under an agreement by which the lessee undertakes to use the property to carry on the business of selling, or promoting the sale of, the taxpayer's or partnership's goods or services.

History: S. 1100(17)(*b*) was replaced by P.C. 2009-581, SOR/2009-115, dated April 23, 2009, applicable to property acquired on or after March 19, 2007. S. 1100(17)(*b*) formerly read:

(*b*) computer software tax shelter property, or

Interpretation Bulletins: *Secondary* — IT-195R4 Rental property—Capital cost allowance restrictions; IT-443 Leasing property—Capital cost allowance restrictions.

(17.1) Leasing Properties. For the purposes of subsection (17), where, in a taxation year, a taxpayer or a partnership has acquired a property

(*a*) that was not used for any purpose in that year, and

(*b*) the first use of the property by the taxpayer or the partnership was principally for the purpose of gaining or producing gross revenue that is rent, royalty or leasing revenue,

the property shall be deemed to have been used in the taxation year in which it was acquired principally for the purpose of gaining or producing gross revenue that is rent, royalty or leasing revenue.

Interpretation Bulletins: *Secondary* — IT-443 Leasing property—Capital cost allowance restrictions.

(17.2) Leasing Properties. For the purposes of subsections (1.11) and (17), gross revenue derived in a taxation year from

(*a*) the right of a person or partnership, other than the owner of a property, to use or occupy the property or a part thereof, and

(*b*) services offered to a person or partnership that are ancillary to the use or occupation by the person or partnership of the property or the part thereof

shall be considered to be rent derived in the year from the property.

Interpretation Bulletins: *Secondary* — IT-443 Leasing property—Capital cost allowance restrictions.

(17.3) Leasing Properties. Subsection (17.2) does not apply in any particular taxation year to property owned by

(*a*) a corporation, where the property is used in a business carried on in the year by the corporation;

(*b*) an individual, where the property is used in a business carried on in the year by the individual in which he is personally active on a continuous basis throughout that portion of the year during which the business is ordinarily carried on; or

(*c*) a partnership, where the property is used in a business carried on in the year by the partnership if at least 2/3 of the income or loss, as the case may be, of the partnership for the year is included in the determination of the income of

(i) members of the partnership who are individuals that are personally active in the business of the partnership on a continuous basis throughout that portion of the year during which the business is ordinarily carried on, and

(ii) members of the partnership that are corporations.

Interpretation Bulletins: *Secondary* — IT-443 Leasing property—Capital cost allowance restrictions.

(18) Leasing Properties. Leasing property of a taxpayer or a partnership referred to in subsection (17) does not include

(*a*) property that the taxpayer or the partnership acquired before May 26, 1976 or was obligated to acquire under the terms of an agreement in writing entered into before May 26, 1976;

(*b*) property the construction, manufacture or production of which was commenced by the taxpayer or the partnership before May 26, 1976 or was commenced under an agreement in writing entered into by the taxpayer or the partnership before May 26, 1976; or

(*c*) property that the taxpayer or the partnership acquired on or before December 31, 1976 or was obligated to acquire under the terms of an agreement in writing entered into on or before December 31, 1976, if

(i) arrangements, evidenced by writing, respecting the acquisition, construction, manufacture or production of the property had been substantially advanced before May 26, 1976, and

(ii) the taxpayer or the partnership had before May 26, 1976 demonstrated a *bona fide* intention to acquire the property for the purpose of gaining or producing gross revenue that is rent, royalty or leasing revenue.

Interpretation Bulletins: *Secondary* — IT-443 Leasing property—Capital cost allowance restrictions.

(19) Leasing Properties. Notwithstanding subsection (17), a property acquired by a taxpayer

(*a*) in the course of a reorganization in respect of which, if a dividend were received by a corporation in the course of the reorganization, subsection 55(2) of the Act would not be applicable to the dividend by reason of the application of paragraph 55(3)(*b*) of the Act, or

(*b*) from a person with whom the taxpayer was not dealing at arm's length (otherwise than by virtue of a right referred to in paragraph 251(5)(*b*) of the Act) at the time the property was acquired,

that would otherwise be leasing property of the taxpayer, shall be deemed not to be leasing property of the taxpayer if immediately before it was so acquired by the taxpayer, it was, by virtue of subsection (18) or (20) or this subsection, not a leasing property of the person from whom the property was so acquired.

Interpretation Bulletins: *Secondary* — IT-443 Leasing property—Capital cost allowance restrictions.

(20) Leasing Properties. Notwithstanding subsection (17), a property acquired by a taxpayer or partnership that is a replacement property (within the meaning assigned by subsection 13(4) of the Act), that would otherwise be a leasing property of the taxpayer or partnership, shall be deemed not to be a leasing property of the taxpayer or partnership if the property replaced, referred to in paragraph 13(4)(*a*) or (*b*) of the Act, was, by reason of subsection (18) or (19) or this subsection, not a leasing property of the taxpayer or partnership immediately before it was disposed of by the taxpayer or partnership.

Interpretation Bulletins: *Secondary* — IT-443 Leasing property — Capital cost allowance restrictions.

(20.1) Computer Tax Shelter Property. The total of all amounts each of which is a deduction in respect of computer tax shelter property allowed to the taxpayer under subsection (1) in computing a taxpayer's income for a taxation year shall not exceed the amount, if any, by which

(*a*) the total of all amounts each of which is

(i) the taxpayer's income for the year from a business in which computer tax shelter property owned by the taxpayer is used, computed without reference to any deduction under subsection (1) in respect of such property, or

(ii) the income of a partnership from a business in which computer tax shelter property of the partnership is used, to the extent of the share of such income that is included in computing the taxpayer's income for the year,

exceeds

(*b*) the total of all amounts each of which is

(i) a loss of the taxpayer from a business in which computer tax shelter property owned by the taxpayer is used, computed without reference to any deduction under subsection (1) in respect of such property, or

(ii) a loss of a partnership from a business in which computer tax shelter property of the partnership is used, to the extent of the share of such loss that is included in computing the taxpayer's income for the year.

History: S. 1100(20.1) and the heading before it were replaced by P.C. 2009-581, SOR/2009-115, dated April 23, 2009, applicable to property acquired on or after March 19, 2007. S. 1100(20.1) and the heading before it formerly read:

Computer Software Tax Shelter Property

(20.1) *Computer Software Tax Shelter Property.* The total of all amounts each of which is a deduction in respect of computer software tax shelter property allowed to the taxpayer under subsection (1) in computing a taxpayer's income for a taxation year shall not exceed the amount, if any, by which

(*a*) the total of all amounts each of which is

(i) the taxpayer's income for the year from a business in which computer software tax shelter property owned by the taxpayer is used, computed without reference to any deduction under subsection (1) in respect of such property, or

(ii) the income of a partnership from a business in which computer software tax shelter property owned by the partnership is used, to the extent of the taxpayer's share of such income that is included in computing the taxpayer's income for the year,

exceeds

(*b*) the total of all amounts each of which is

(i) a loss of the taxpayer from a business in which computer software tax shelter property is used, computed without reference to any deduction under subsection (1) in respect of such property, or

(ii) a loss of a partnership from a business in which computer software tax shelter property is used, to the extent of the taxpayer's share of such loss that is included in computing the taxpayer's income for the year.

(20.2) Computer Tax Shelter Property. For the purpose of this Part, computer tax shelter property of a person or partnership is depreciable property of a prescribed class in Schedule II that is computer software or property described in Class 50 or 52 where

(*a*) the person's or partnership's interest in the property is a tax shelter investment (as defined by subsection 143.2(1) of the Act) determined without reference to subsection (20.1); or

(*b*) an interest in the person or partnership is a tax shelter investment (as defined by subsection 143.2(1) of the Act) determined without reference to subsection (20.1).

History: S. 1100(20.2), the portion before paragraph (*a*) was replaced by P.C. 2009-660, SOR/2009-126, dated April 30, 2009, applicable in respect of property acquired after January 27, 2009. S. 1100(20.2), the portion before paragraph (*a*) formerly read:

(20.2) For the purpose of this Part, computer tax shelter property is computer software, and property described in Class 50 in Schedule II, that is depreciable property of a prescribed class of a person or partnership where

S. 1100(20.2), the portion before paragraph (*a*) was replaced by P.C. 2009-581 SOR/2009-115, dated April 23, 2009, applicable to property acquired on or after March 19, 2007. S. 1100(20.2), the portion before paragraph (*a*), formerly read:

(20.2) For the purpose of this Part, computer software tax shelter property is computer software that is depreciable property of a prescribed class of a person or partnership where

(21) Certified Films and Video Tapes. Notwithstanding subsection (1), where a taxpayer (in this subsection and subsection (22) referred to as the "investor") has acquired property of Class 10 or 12 in Schedule II that is a certified feature film or certified production (in this subsection and subsection (22) referred to as the "film or tape"), in no case shall the deduction in respect of property of that class otherwise allowed to the investor by virtue of subsection (1) in computing the investor's income for a particular taxation year exceed the amount that it would be if the capital cost to the investor of the film or tape were reduced by the aggregate of amounts, each of which is

(*a*) where the principal photography or taping of the film or tape is not completed before the end of the particular taxation year, the amount, if any, by which

(i) the capital cost to the investor of the film or tape as of the end of the year exceeds the aggregate of

(ii) where the principal photography or taping of the film or tape is completed within 60 days after the end of the year, the amount that may reasonably be considered to be the investor's proportionate share of the production costs incurred in respect of the film or tape before the end of the year,

(iii) where the principal photography or taping of the film or tape is not completed within 60 days after the end of the year, the amount that may reasonably be considered to be the investor's proportionate share of the lesser of

(A) the production costs incurred in respect of the film or tape before the end of the year, and

(B) the proportion of the production costs incurred to the date the principal photography or taping is completed that the percentage of the principal photography or taping completed as of the end of the year, as certified by the Minister of Communications, is of 100 per cent, and

(iv) the total of amounts determined under paragraphs (*b*) to (*e*) in respect of the film or tape as of the end of the year;

(*b*) where, at any time before the later of

(i) the date the principal photography or taping of the film or tape is completed, and

(ii) the date the investor acquired the film or tape,

a revenue guarantee (other than a revenue guarantee that is certified by the Minister of Communications to be a guarantee under which the person who agrees to provide the revenue is a licensed broadcaster or *bona fide* film or tape distributor) is entered into in respect of the film or tape whereby it may reasonably be considered certain, having regard to all the circumstances, that the investor will receive revenue under the terms of the revenue guarantee, the amount, if any, that may reasonably be considered to be the portion of the revenue that has not been included in the investor's income in the particular taxation year or a previous taxation year;

(*c*) where, at any time, a revenue guarantee, other than

(i) a revenue guarantee in respect of which paragraph (*b*) applies, or

(ii) a revenue guarantee under which the person (in this subsection referred to as the "guarantor") who agrees to provide the revenue under the terms of the guarantee is a person who does not deal at arm's length with either the investor or the person from whom the investor acquired the film or tape (in this subsection referred to as the "vendor") and in respect of which the Minister of Communications certifies that

(A) the guarantor is a licensed broadcaster or *bona fide* film or tape distributor, and

(B) the cost of the film or tape does not include any amount for or in respect of the guarantee,

is entered into in respect of the film or tape, the amount, if any, that may reasonably be considered to be the portion of the revenue that is to be received by the investor under the terms of the revenue guarantee that has not been included in the investor's income in the particular taxation year or a preceding taxation year, if

(iii) the guarantor and the investor are not dealing at arm's length,

(iv) the vendor and the guarantor are not dealing at arm's length, or

(v) the vendor or a person not dealing at arm's length with the vendor undertakes in any way, directly or indirectly, to fulfill all or any part of the guarantor's obligations under the terms of the revenue guarantee;

(*d*) where, at any time, a revenue guarantee, other than a revenue guarantee in respect of which paragraph (*b*) or (*c*) applies, is entered into in respect of the film or tape, the amount, if any, that may reasonably be considered to be the portion of the revenue that is to be received by the investor under the terms of the revenue guarantee that

(i) is not due to the investor until a time that is more than four years after the first day on which the guarantor has the right to the use of the film or tape, and

(ii) has not been included in the investor's income in the particular taxation year or a previous taxation year; and

(*e*) the portion of any debt obligation of the investor outstanding at the end of the particular year that is convertible into an interest in the film or tape or in the investor.

(21.1) Certified Films and Video Tapes. Notwithstanding subsection (1), where a taxpayer has acquired property described in paragraph (*s*) of Class 10 in Schedule II, or in paragraph (*m*) of Class 12 of Schedule II, the deduction in respect of the property otherwise allowed to the taxpayer under subsection (1) in computing the taxpayer's income for a taxation year shall not exceed the amount that it would be if the capital cost to the taxpayer of the property were reduced by the portion of any debt obligation of the taxpayer outstanding at the end of the year that is convertible into an interest in the property or in the taxpayer.

(22) Certified Films and Video Tapes. Notwithstanding subsection (1), where an investor has acquired a film or tape after his 1977 taxation year and before 1979 and the principal photography or taping in respect of the film or tape is completed after a particular taxation year and not later than March 1, 1979, in no case shall the deduction in respect of property of Class 12 in Schedule II otherwise allowed to the investor by virtue of subsection (1) in computing his income for the particular taxation year exceed the amount, otherwise determined, if the capital cost to the investor of the film or tape were reduced by the amount, if any, by which

(*a*) the capital cost to the investor of the film or tape as of the end of the year

exceeds

(*b*) the amount that may reasonably be considered to be the investor's proportionate share of the production costs incurred in respect of the film or tape to March 1, 1979.

(23) Certified Films and Video Tapes. For the purposes of paragraph (21)(*a*),

(*a*) in respect of a film or tape acquired in 1987, other than a film or tape in respect of which paragraph (*b*) applies, the references in paragraph (21)(*a*) to "within 60 days after the end of the year" shall be read as references to "before July, 1988"; and

(*b*) in respect of a film or tape acquired in 1987 or 1988 that is included in paragraph (*n*) of Class 12 in Schedule II and that is part of a series of films or tapes that includes another property included in that paragraph, the references in paragraph (21)(*a*) to "within 60 days after the end of the year" shall be read as references to "before 1989".

(24) Specified Energy Property. Notwithstanding subsection (1), in no case shall the total of deductions, each of which is a deduction in respect of property of Class 34, 43.1, 43.2, 47 or 48 in Schedule II that is specified energy property owned by a taxpayer, otherwise allowed to the taxpayer under subsection (1) in computing the taxpayer's income for a taxation year, exceed the amount, if any, by which

(*a*) the total of all amounts each of which is

(i) the total of

(A) the amount that would be the income of the taxpayer for the year from property described in Class 34, 43.1, 43.2, 47 or 48 in Schedule II (other than specified energy property), or from the business of selling the product of that property, if that income were calculated after deducting the maximum amount allowable in respect of the property for the year under paragraph 20(1)(*a*) of the Act, and

(B) the taxpayer's income for the year from specified energy property or from the business of selling the product of that property, computed without regard to paragraph 20(1)(*a*) of the Act, or

(ii) the total of

(A) the taxpayer's share of the amount that would be the income of a partnership for the year from property described in Class 34, 43.1, 43.2, 47 or 48 in Schedule II (other than specified energy property), or from the business of selling the product of that property, if that income were calculated after deducting the maximum amount allowable in respect of the property for the year under paragraph 20(1)(*a*) of the Act, and

(B) the income of a partnership for the year from specified energy property or from the business of selling the product of that property of the partnership, to the extent of the taxpayer's share of that income,

exceeds

(*b*) the total of all amounts each of which is

(i) the taxpayer's loss for the year from specified energy property or from the business of selling the product of that property, computed without regard to paragraph 20(1)(*a*) of the Act, or

(ii) the loss of a partnership for the year from specified energy property or from the business of selling the product of that property of the partnership, to the extent of the taxpayer's share of that loss.

Canadian Petroleum Tax Journal: Renewable Energy — Tax Developments and Opportunities, Leanne Sereda, 2000, Vol. 13, No. 1.

Income Tax Folios: *Primary* — S3-F8-C2 Tax Incentives for Clean Energy Equipment

(25) Specified Energy Property. Subject to subsections (27) to (29), in this section and section 1101, "specified energy property" of a taxpayer or partnership (in this subsection referred to as "the owner") for a taxation year means property of Class 34 in Schedule II acquired by the owner after February 9, 1988 and property of Class 43.1, 43.2, 47 or 48 in Schedule II, other than a particular property

(*a*) acquired to be used by the owner primarily for the purpose of gaining or producing income from a business carried on in Canada (other than the business of selling the product of the particular property) or from another property situated in Canada, or

(*b*) leased in the year, in the ordinary course of carrying on a business of the owner in Canada, to

(i) a person who can reasonably be expected to use the property primarily for the purpose of gaining or producing income from a business carried on in Canada (other than the business of selling the product of the particular property) or from another property situated in Canada, or

(ii) a corporation or partnership described in subsection (26),

where the owner was

(iii) a corporation whose principal business was, throughout the year,

(A) the renting or leasing of leasing property or property that would be leasing property but for subsection (18), (19) or (20),

(B) the renting or leasing of property referred to in clause (A) combined with the selling and servicing of property of the same general type and description, or

(C) the manufacturing of property described in Class 34, 43.1, 43.2, 47 or 48 in Schedule II that it sells or leases,

and the gross revenue of the corporation for the year from that principal business was not less than 90 per cent of the gross revenue of the corporation for the year from all sources, or

(iv) a partnership each member of which was

(A) a corporation described in subparagraph (iii) or paragraph (26)(*a*), or

(B) another partnership described in this subparagraph.

History: S. 1100(25)(*b*)(iv) was replaced by S.C. 2013, c. 40, s. 100(13), applicable to fiscal periods that end after October 2010, and formerly read:

(iv) a partnership each member of which was a corporation described in subparagraph (iii) or paragraph (26)(*a*).

Income Tax Folios: *Primary* — S3-F8-C2 Tax Incentives for Clean Energy Equipment

(26) Specified Energy Property. Subsection (24) does not apply to a taxation year of a taxpayer that was, throughout the year,

(*a*) a corporation whose principal business throughout the year was

(i) manufacturing or processing,

(ii) mining operations, or

(iii) the sale, distribution or production of electricity, natural gas, oil, steam, heat or any other form of energy or potential energy; or

(*b*) a partnership each member of which was

(i) a corporation described in paragraph (*a*), or

(ii) another partnership described in this paragraph.

History: S. 1100(26)(*b*) was replaced by S.C. 2013, c. 40, s. 100(13), applicable to fiscal periods that end after October 2010, and formerly read:

(*b*) a partnership each member of which was a corporation described in paragraph (*a*).

Income Tax Folios: *Primary* — S3-F8-C2 Tax Incentives for Clean Energy Equipment. S4-F15-C1 Manufacturing and Processing.

(27) Specified Energy Property. Specified energy property of a person or partnership does not include property acquired by the person or partnership after February 9, 1988 and before 1990

(*a*) pursuant to an obligation in writing entered into by the person or partnership before February 10, 1988;

(*b*) pursuant to the terms of a prospectus, preliminary prospectus, registration statement or offering memorandum filed before February 10, 1988 with a public authority in Canada pursuant to and in accordance with the securities legislation of any province;

(*c*) pursuant to the terms of an offering memorandum distributed as part of an offering of securities where

(i) the offering memorandum contained a complete or substantially complete description of the securities contemplated in the offering as well as the terms and conditions of the offering of the securities,

(ii) the offering memorandum was distributed before February 10, 1988,

(iii) solicitations in respect of the sale of the securities contemplated by the offering memorandum were made before February 10, 1988, and

(iv) the sale of the securities was substantially in accordance with the offering memorandum; or

(*d*) as part of a project where, before February 10, 1988,

(i) some of the machinery or equipment to be used in the project had been acquired, or agreements in writing for the acquisition of that machinery or equipment had been entered into, by or on behalf of the person or partnership, and

(ii) an approval had been received by or on behalf of the person or partnership from a government environmental authority in respect of the location of the project.

(28) Specified Energy Property. A property acquired by a taxpayer

(*a*) in the course of a reorganization in respect of which, if a dividend were received by a corporation in the course of the reorganization, subsection 55(2) of the Act would not be applicable to the dividend by reason of the application of paragraph 55(3)(*b*) of the Act, or

(*b*) from a person with whom the taxpayer was not dealing at arm's length (otherwise than by virtue of a right referred to in paragraph 251(5)(*b*) of the Act) at the time the property was acquired

that would otherwise be specified energy property of the taxpayer shall be deemed not to be specified energy property of the taxpayer if, immediately before it was so acquired by the taxpayer, it was not, by virtue of subsection (27), this subsection or subsection (29), specified energy property of the person from whom the property was so acquired.

(29) Specified Energy Property. A property acquired by a taxpayer or partnership that is a replacement property (within the meaning assigned by subsection 13(4) of the Act), that would otherwise be specified energy property of the taxpayer or partnership, shall be deemed not to be specified energy property of the taxpayer or partnership if the property replaced, referred to in paragraph 13(4)(*a*) or (*b*) of the Act, was, by virtue of subsection (27), (28) or this subsection, not specified energy property of the taxpayer or partnership immediately before it was disposed of by the taxpayer or partnership.

1100A. Exempt Mining Income

(1) (Revoked.)

(2) Any election under subparagraph 13(21)(*f*)(vi) of the Act in respect of property of a prescribed class acquired by a corporation for the purpose of gaining or producing income from a mine shall be made by filing with the Minister, not later than the day on or before which the corporation is required to file a return of income pursuant to section 150 of the Act for its taxation year in which the exempt period in respect of the mine ended, one of the following documents in duplicate:

(*a*) where the directors of the corporation are legally entitled to administer the affairs of the corporation, a certified copy of their resolution authorizing the election to be made in respect of that class; and

(*b*) where the directors of the corporation are not legally entitled to administer the affairs of the corporation, a certified copy of the authorization of the making of the election in respect of that class by the person or persons legally entitled to administer the affairs of the corporation.

Division II
Separate Classes

1101. Businesses and Properties

(1) Where more than one property of a taxpayer is described in the same class in Schedule II and where

(*a*) one of the properties was acquired for the purpose of gaining or producing income from a business, and

(*b*) one of the properties was acquired for the purpose of gaining or producing income from another business or from the property,

a separate class is hereby prescribed for the properties that

(*c*) were acquired for the purpose of gaining or producing income from each business; and (*d*) would otherwise be included in the class.

Income Tax Folios: *Primary* — S3-F4-C1 General Discussion of Capital Cost Allowance.

Interpretation Bulletins: *Secondary* — IT-206R Separate businesses; IT-218R Profit, capital gains and losses from the sale of real estate, including farmland and inherited land and conversion of real estate from capital property to inventory and vice versa; IT-474R Amalgamations of Canadian corporations.

(1a) [Insurance business]. For the purposes of subsection (1),

(*a*) a life insurance business, and

(*b*) an insurance business other than a life insurance business,

shall each be regarded as a separate business.

(1ab) [Partnership property]. Where, at the end of 1971, more than one property of a taxpayer who was a member of a partnership at that time is described in the same class in Schedule II and where

(*a*) one of the properties can reasonably be regarded to be the interest of the taxpayer in a depreciable property that is partnership property of the partnership, and

(*b*) one of the properties is property other than property referred to in paragraph (*a*),

a separate class is hereby prescribed for all properties each of which

(*c*) is a property referred to in paragraph (*a*); and

(*d*) would otherwise be included in the class.

(1ac) [Rental property]. Subject to subsection (5h), where more than one property of a taxpayer is described in the same class in Schedule II, and one or more of the properties is a rental property of the taxpayer the capital cost of which to the taxpayer was not less than $50,000, a separate class is hereby prescribed for each such rental property of the taxpayer that would otherwise be included in the same class, other than a rental property that was acquired by the taxpayer before 1972 or that is

(*a*) a building or an interest therein, or

(*b*) a leasehold interest acquired by the taxpayer by reason of the fact that the taxpayer erected a building on leased land,

erection of which building was commenced by the taxpayer before 1972 or pursuant to an agreement in writing entered into by the taxpayer before 1972.

Interpretation Bulletins: *Primary* — IT-274R Rental properties — Capital cost of $50,000 or more. *Secondary* — IT-304R2 Condominiums.

(1ad) [Rental property]. Notwithstanding subsection (1ac), a rental property acquired by a taxpayer

(*a*) in the course of a reorganization in respect of which, if a dividend were received by a corporation in the course of the reorganization, subsection 55(2) of the Act would not be applicable to the dividend by reason of the application of paragraph 55(3)(*b*) of the Act, or

(*b*) from a person with whom the taxpayer was not dealing at arm's length (otherwise than by virtue of a right referred to in paragraph 251(5)(*b*) of the Act) at the time the property was acquired,

that would otherwise be rental property of the taxpayer of a separate class prescribed under subsection (1ac), shall be deemed not to be property of a separate class prescribed under that subsection if, immediately before it was so acquired by the taxpayer, it was a rental property of the person from whom the property was so acquired of a prescribed class other than a separate class prescribed under that subsection.

Interpretation Bulletins: *Secondary* — IT-274R Rental properties — Capital cost of $50,000 or more.

(1ae) [Rental property]. Except in the case of a corporation or partnership described in subsection 1100(12), where more than one property of a taxpayer is described in the same class in Schedule II and where

(*a*) one of the properties is a rental property other than a property of a separate class prescribed under subsection (1ac), and

(*b*) one of the properties is a property other than rental property,

a separate class is hereby prescribed for properties that

(*c*) are described in paragraph (*a*); and

(*d*) would otherwise be included in the class.

Interpretation Bulletins: *Secondary* — IT-195R4 Rental property — Capital cost allowance restrictions; IT-304R2 Condominiums.

(1af) [Passenger vehicle]. A separate class is hereby prescribed for each property included in Class 10.1 in Schedule II.

Income Tax Folios: *Primary* — S3-F4-C1 General Discussion of Capital Cost Allowance.

Interpretation Bulletins: *Secondary* — IT-521R Motor vehicle expenses claimed by self-employed individuals; IT-522R Vehicle, travel and sales expenses of employees.

(1ag) [Franchise, concession or license]. If more than one property of a taxpayer is described in the same class in Schedule II, and one or more of the properties is a property in respect of which the taxpayer is a transferee that has elected under subsection 13(4.2) of the Act (each of which is referred to in this subsection as an "elected property"), a separate class is prescribed for each elected property of the taxpayer that would otherwise be included in the same class.

History: S. 1101(1ag) was added by S.C. 2013, c. 34, s. 384(1), deemed to have come into force on December 21, 2002.

(1b) (Revoked.)

(1c) (Revoked.)

(2) Fishing Vessels. Where a property of a taxpayer that would otherwise be included in Class 7 in Schedule II is a property in respect of which a depreciation allowance could have been taken under Order in Council

(*a*) P.C. 2798 of April 10, 1942,

(*b*) P.C. 7580 of August 26, 1942, as amended by P.C. 3297 of April 22, 1943, or

(*c*) P.C. 3979 of June 1, 1944,

if those Orders in Council were applicable to the taxation year, a separate class is hereby prescribed for each property, including the furniture, fittings and equipment attached thereto.

(2a) Canadian Vessels. A separate class is hereby prescribed for each vessel of a taxpayer, including the furniture, fittings, radiocommunication equipment and other equipment attached thereto, that

(*a*) was constructed in Canada;

(*b*) is registered in Canada; and

(*c*) had not been used for any purpose whatever before it was acquired by the taxpayer.

Interpretation Bulletins: *Secondary* — IT-267R2 Capital cost allowance — Vessels.

(2b) Offshore Drilling Vessels. A separate class is hereby prescribed for all vessels described in Class 7 in Schedule II, including the furniture, fittings, radiocommunication equipment and other equipment attached thereto, acquired by a taxpayer

(*a*) after May 25, 1976 and designed principally for the purpose of

(i) determining the existence, location, extent or quality of accumulations of petroleum or natural gas (other than mineral resources), or

(ii) drilling oil or gas wells; or

(*b*) after May 22, 1979 and designed principally for the purpose of determining the existence, location, extent or quality of mineral resources.

Interpretation Bulletins: *Secondary* — IT-267R2 Capital cost allowance — Vessels.

(2c) Vessels and a Structured Financing Facility. Subsections (2a) and (2b) do not apply to a vessel, nor to the furniture, fittings, radio communications equipment and other equipment attached to the vessel, if a structured financing facility relating to any such property has been agreed to by the Minister of Industry under the *Department of Industry Act*.

(3) Timber Limits and Cutting Rights. For the purposes of this Part and Schedules IV and VI, each property of a taxpayer that is

(*a*) a timber limit other than a timber resource property, or

(*b*) a right to cut timber from a limit other than a right that is a timber resource property,

is hereby prescribed to be a separate class of property.

Interpretation Bulletins: *Secondary* — IT-469R Capital cost allowance — Earth-moving equipment; IT-481 (Consolid.) Timber resource property and timber limits.

(4) Industrial Mineral Mines. For the purposes of this Part and Schedule V, where a taxpayer has

(*a*) more than one industrial mineral mine in respect of which he may claim an allowance under paragraph 1100(1)(g),

(*b*) more than one right to remove industrial minerals from an industrial mineral mine in respect of which he may claim an allowance under that paragraph, or

(*c*) both such a mine and a right,

each such industrial mineral mine and each such right to remove industrial minerals from an industrial mineral mine is hereby prescribed to be a separate class of property.

Interpretation Bulletins: *Secondary* — IT-492 Capital cost allowance — Industrial mineral mines.

(4a) Class 28 — Single Mine Properties. If one or more properties of a taxpayer are described in Class 28 of Schedule II and some or all of the properties were acquired for the purpose of gaining or producing income from one mine and not from any other mine (which properties are referred to as "single mine properties" in this subsection), a separate class is prescribed for the single mine properties that

(*a*) were acquired for the purpose of gaining or producing income from that mine;

(*b*) would otherwise be included in Class 28; and

(*c*) are not included in a separate class by reason of subsection (4b).

History: S. 1101(4a) and the heading before subsection 1101(4a) were replaced by P.C. 2011-44, SOR/2011-9, dated February 4, 2011, published in the *Canada Gazette* February 16, 2011, applicable to taxation years that end after March 18, 2007. S. 1101(4a) and the heading before subsection 1101(4a) formerly read:

New or Expanded Mines Properties

(4a) *New or Expanded Mines Properties.* Where more than one property of a taxpayer is described in Class 28 in Schedule II and

(*a*) one of the properties was acquired for the purpose of gaining or producing income from only one mine, and

(*b*) one of the properties was acquired for the purpose of gaining or producing income from another mine,

a separate class is hereby prescribed for the properties that

(*c*) were acquired for the purpose of gaining or producing income from each mine;

(*d*) would otherwise be included in the class; and

(*e*) are not included in a separate class by virtue of subsection (4b).

(4b) Class 28 — Multiple Mine Properties. If more than one property of a taxpayer is described in Class 28 in Schedule II and some or all of the properties were acquired for the purpose of gaining or producing income from particular mines and not from any other mine (which properties are referred to as "multiple mine properties" in this subsection), a separate class is prescribed for the multiple mine properties that

(*a*) were acquired for the purpose of gaining or producing income from the particular mines; and

(*b*) would otherwise be included in Class 28.

History: S. 1101(4b) was replaced by P.C. 2011-44, SOR/2011-9, dated February 4, 2011, published in the *Canada Gazette* February 16, 2011, applicable to taxation years that end after March 18, 2007. S. 1101(4b) formerly read:

(4b) Where more than one property of a taxpayer is described in Class 28 in Schedule II and

(*a*) one of the properties was acquired for the purpose of gaining or producing income from particular mines, and

(*b*) one of the properties was acquired for the purpose of gaining or producing income from only one mine or more than one mine other than any of the particular mines,

a separate class is hereby prescribed for the properties that

(*c*) were acquired for the purpose of gaining or producing income from the particular mines; and

(*d*) would otherwise be included in the class.

(4c) Class 41 — Single Mine Properties. If one or more properties of a taxpayer are described in paragraph (*a*), (*a.1*) or (*a.2*) of Class 41 of Schedule II and some or all of the properties were acquired for the purpose of gaining or producing income from one mine and not from any other mine (which properties are referred to as "single mine properties" in this subsection), a separate class is prescribed for the single mine properties that

(*a*) were acquired for the purpose of gaining or producing income from that mine;

(*b*) would otherwise be included in Class 41; and

(*c*) are not included in a separate class by reason of subsection (4d).

History: S. 1101(4c) was replaced by P.C. 2011-44, SOR/2011-9, dated February 4, 2011, published in the *Canada Gazette* February 16, 2011, applicable to taxation years that end after March 18, 2007. S. 1101(4c) formerly read:

(4c) Where one or more properties of a taxpayer are described in paragraph (*a*), (*a*.1) or (*a*.2) of Class 41 in Schedule II and

(*a*) where all of the properties were acquired for the purpose of gaining or producing income from only one mine, or

(*b*) where

(i) one or more of the properties were acquired for the purpose of gaining or producing income from a particular mine, and

(ii) one or more of the properties were acquired for the purpose of gaining or producing income from another mine,

a separate class is hereby prescribed for the properties that

(*c*) were acquired for the purpose of gaining or producing income from each mine,

(*d*) would otherwise be included in the class, and

(*e*) are not included in a separate class by reason of subsection (4d).

S. 1101(4b) was replaced by P.C. 2011-44, SOR/2011-9, dated February 4, 2011, published in the *Canada Gazette* February 16, 2011, applicable to taxation years that end after March 18, 2007. S. 1101(4b) formerly read:

Interpretation Bulletins: *Secondary* — IT-476R Capital cost allowance — Equipment used in petroleum and natural gas activities.

(4d) Class 41 — Multiple Mine Properties. If more than one property of a taxpayer is described in paragraph (*a*), (*a.1*) or (*a.2*) of Class 41 in Schedule II and some or all of the properties were acquired for the purpose of gaining or producing income from particular mines and not from any other mine (which properties are referred to as "multiple mine properties" in this subsection), a separate class is prescribed for the multiple mine properties that

(*a*) were acquired for the purpose of gaining or producing income from the particular mines; and

(*b*) would otherwise be included in Class 41.

History: S. 1101(4d) was replaced by P.C. 2011-44, SOR/2011-9, dated February 4, 2011, published in the *Canada Gazette* February 16, 2011, applicable to taxation years that end after March 18, 2007. S. 1101(4d) formerly read:

(4d) Where more than one property of a taxpayer is described in paragraph (*a*), (*a*.1) or (*a*.2) of Class 41 in Schedule II and

(*a*) one of the properties was acquired for the purpose of gaining or producing income from particular mines, and

(*b*) one of the properties was acquired for the purpose of gaining or producing income from only one mine or more than one mine other than any of the particular mines,

a separate class is hereby prescribed for the properties that

(*c*) were acquired for the purpose of gaining or producing income from the particular mines, and

(*d*) would otherwise be included in the class.

Interpretation Bulletins: *Secondary* — IT-476R Capital cost allowance — Equipment used in petroleum and natural gas activities.

(4e) Class 41.1 — Single Mine Properties. If one or more properties of a taxpayer are described in paragraph (*a*) of Class 41.1 of Schedule II and some or all of the properties were acquired for the purpose of gaining or producing income from one mine and not from any other mine (which properties are referred to as "single mine properties" in this subsection), a separate class is prescribed for the single mine properties that

(*a*) were acquired for the purpose of gaining or producing income from that mine;

(*b*) would otherwise be included in Class 41.1, because of paragraph (*a*) of that class; and

(*c*) are not included in a separate class by reason of subsection (4f).

History: S. 1101(4e) was added by P.C. 2011-44, SOR/2011-9, dated February 4, 2011, published in the *Canada Gazette* February 16, 2011, applicable to taxation years that end after March 18, 2007.

(4f) Class 41.1 — Multiple Mine Properties. If more than one property of a taxpayer is described in paragraph (*a*) of Class 41.1 in Schedule II and some or all of the properties were acquired for the purpose of gaining or producing income from particular mines and not from any other mine (which properties are referred to as "multiple mine properties" in this subsection), a separate class is prescribed for the multiple mine properties that

(*a*) were acquired for the purpose of gaining or producing income from the particular mines; and

(*b*) would otherwise be included in Class 41.1 because of paragraph (*a*) of that class.

History: S. 1101(4f) was added by P.C. 2011-44, SOR/2011-9, dated February 4, 2011, published in the *Canada Gazette* February 16, 2011, applicable to taxation years that end after March 18, 2007.

(4g) Class 41.2 — Single Mine Properties. If one or more properties of a taxpayer are described in paragraph (*a*) of Class 41.2 of Schedule II and some or all of the properties were acquired for the purpose of gaining or producing income from one mine and not from any other mine (in this subsection referred to as "single mine properties"), a separate class is prescribed for the single mine properties that

(*a*) were acquired for the purpose of gaining or producing income from that mine;

(*b*) would otherwise be included in Class 41.2 because of paragraph (*a*) of that class; and

(*c*) are not included in a separate class because of subsection (4h).

History: S. 1101(4g) was added by S.C. 2013, c. 40, s. 101(1), applicable to fiscal periods that end after March 20, 2013.

(4h) Class 41.2 — Multiple Mine Properties. If more than one property of a taxpayer is described in paragraph (*a*) of Class 41.2 in Schedule II and some or all of the properties were acquired for the purpose of gaining or producing income from particular mines and not from any other mine (in this subsection referred to as "multiple mine properties"), a separate class is prescribed for the multiple mine properties that

(*a*) were acquired for the purpose of gaining or producing income from the particular mines; and

(*b*) would otherwise be included in Class 41.2 because of paragraph (*a*) of that class.

History: S. 1101(4h) was added by S.C. 2013, c. 40, s. 101(1), applicable to fiscal periods that end after March 20, 2013.

(4i) Class 47 — Liquefaction equipment. If a taxpayer acquires property that is eligible liquefaction equipment to be used as part of an eligible liquefaction facility of the taxpayer, a separate class is prescribed for those properties that were acquired for the purpose of gaining or producing income from that eligible liquefaction facility.

History: S. 1101(4i) was added by P.C. 2015-629, SOR/2015-117, s. 2(1), dated May 29, 2015, deemed to have come into force on February 19, 2015.

(5) Lease Option Agreements. Where, by virtue of an agreement, contract or arrangement entered into on or after May 31, 1954, a taxpayer is deemed by section 18 of the *Income Tax Act*, as enacted by the Statutes of Canada, 1958, Chapter 32, subsection 8(1), to have acquired a property, a separate class is hereby prescribed for each such property and if the taxpayer subsequently actually acquires the property it shall be included in the same class.

(5a) Telecommunication Spacecraft. For the purposes of this Part, each property of a taxpayer that is an

Regulations

unmanned telecommunication spacecraft described in paragraph (*f*.2) of Class 10 or in Class 30 in Schedule II is hereby prescribed to be a separate class of property.

(5b) Multiple-Unit Residential Buildings. For the purposes of this Part, when any property of a taxpayer is a property of Class 31 or 32 in Schedule II and the capital cost of that property to the taxpayer was not less than $50,000, a separate class is hereby prescribed for each such property of the taxpayer that would otherwise be included in the same class.

Interpretation Bulletins: *Secondary* — IT-274R Rental properties — Capital cost of $50,000 or more.

(5b.1) Eligible Non-Residential Building. For the purposes of this Part, a separate class is prescribed for each eligible non-residential building (other than an eligible liquefaction building) of a taxpayer in respect of which the taxpayer has (by letter attached to the return of income of the taxpayer filed with the Minister in accordance with section 150 of the Act for the taxation year in which the building is acquired) elected that this subsection apply.

History: S. 1101(5b.1) was replaced by P.C. 2015-629, SOR/2015-117, s. 2(2), dated May 29, 2015, deemed to have come into force on February 19, 2015, and formerly read:

(5b.1) *Eligible Non-Residential Building.* For the purposes of this Part, a separate class is prescribed for each eligible non-residential building of a taxpayer in respect of which the taxpayer has (by letter attached to the return of income of the taxpayer filed with the Minister in accordance with section 150 of the Act for the taxation year in which the building is acquired) elected that this subsection apply.

S. 1101(5b.1) was added by P.C. 2009-581, SOR/2009-115, dated April 23, 2009, applicable to property acquired on or after March 19, 2007.

If a taxpayer files in writing an election referred to in subsection 1101(5b.1), the election is deemed to have been filed in the manner and by the time required if the election is received by the Minister of National Revenue no later than 90 days after May 13, 2009 (the day on which these Regulations were published in the *Canada Gazette*, Part II).

(5b.2) Liquefaction Buildings. If a taxpayer acquires property that is an eligible liquefaction building to be used as part of an eligible liquefaction facility of the taxpayer, a separate class is prescribed for those properties that were acquired for the purpose of gaining or producing income from that eligible liquefaction facility.

History: S. 1101(5b.2) was added by P.C. 2015-629, SOR/2015-117, s. 2(2), dated May 29, 2015, deemed to have come into force on February 19, 2015.

(5c) Leasing Properties. For the purposes of this Part, except in the case of a corporation or partnership described in subsection 1100(16), where more than one property of a taxpayer is described in the same class in Schedule II and where

(*a*) one of the properties is a leasing property, and

(*b*) one of the properties is a property other than a leasing property,

a separate class is hereby prescribed for properties that

(*c*) are described in paragraph (*a*); and

(*d*) would otherwise be included in the class.

Interpretation Bulletins: *Secondary* — IT-443 Leasing property — Capital cost allowance restrictions.

(5d) Railway Cars. Where more than one property of a taxpayer is a railway car included in Class 35 in Schedule II that was rented, leased or used by the taxpayer in Canada in the taxation year, other than a railway car owned by a corporation, or a partnership any member of which is a corporation, that

(*a*) was at any time in that taxation year a common carrier that owned or operated a railway, or

(*b*) rented or leased the railway cars at any time in that taxation year, by one or more transactions between persons not dealing at arm's length, to an associated corporation that was, at that time, a common carrier that owned or operated a railway,

a separate class is prescribed

(*c*) for all such properties acquired by the taxpayer before February 3, 1990 (other than such properties acquired for rent or lease to another person),

(*d*) for all such properties acquired by the taxpayer after February 2, 1990 (other than such properties acquired for rent or lease to another person),

(*e*) for all such properties acquired by the taxpayer before April 27, 1989 for rent or lease to another person, and

(*f*) for all such properties acquired by the taxpayer after April 26, 1989 for rent or lease to another person.

(5d.1) Railway Cars. A separate class is hereby prescribed for all property included in Class 35 in Schedule II acquired at a time after December 6, 1991 and before February 28, 2000 by a taxpayer that was at that time a common carrier that owned and operated a railway.

(5d.2) Railway Cars. A separate class is hereby prescribed for all property included in Class 35 in Schedule II acquired at a time after February 27, 2000 by a taxpayer that was at that time a common carrier that owned and operated a railway.

(5e) Railway Track and Related Property. A separate class is hereby prescribed for all property included in Class 1 in Schedule II acquired by a taxpayer after March 31, 1977 and before 1988 that is

(*a*) railway track and grading, including components such as rails, ballast, ties and other track material;

(*b*) railway traffic control or signalling equipment, including switching, block signalling, interlocking, crossing protection, detection, speed control or retarding equipment, but not including property that is principally electronic equipment or systems software therefor; or

(*c*) a bridge, culvert, subway or tunnel that is ancillary to railway track and grading.

(5e.1) Railway Track and Related Property. A separate class is hereby prescribed for all property included in Class 1 in Schedule II acquired at a time after December 6, 1991 by a taxpayer that was at that time a common carrier that owned and operated a railway, where the property is

(*a*) railway track and grading, including components such as rails, ballast, ties and other track material;

(*b*) railway traffic control or signalling equipment, including switching, block signalling, interlocking, crossing protection, detection, speed control or retarding equipment, but not including property that is principally electronic equipment or systems software therefor; or (*c*) a bridge, culvert, subway or tunnel that is ancillary to railway track and grading.

(5e.2) Railway Track and Related Property. A separate class is hereby prescribed for all trestles included in Class 3 in Schedule II acquired at a time after December 6, 1991 by a taxpayer that was at that time a common carrier that owned and operated a railway, where the trestles are ancillary to railway track and grading.

(5f) Railway Track and Related Property. A separate class is hereby prescribed for all trestles included in Class 3 in Schedule II acquired by a taxpayer after March 31, 1977 and before 1988 that are ancillary to railway track and grading.

(5g) Deemed Depreciable Property. A separate class is hereby prescribed for each property of a taxpayer described in Class 36 in Schedule II.

(5h) Leasehold Interest in Real Properties. For the purposes of this Part, where more than one property of a taxpayer is described in the same class in Schedule II and where

(*a*) one of the properties is a leasehold interest in real property described in subsection 1100(13), and

(*b*) one of the properties is a property other than a leasehold interest in real property described in subsection 1100(13),

a separate class is hereby prescribed for properties that

(*c*) are described in paragraph (*a*); and

(*d*) would otherwise be included in the class.

(5i) Pipelines. A separate class is hereby prescribed for each property of a taxpayer described in Class 2 in Schedule II that is

(*a*) a pipeline the construction of which was commenced after 1984 and completed after September 1, 1985 and the capital cost of which to the taxpayer is not less than $10,000,000,

(*b*) a pipeline that has been extended or converted where the extension or conversion was completed after September 1, 1985 and the capital cost to the taxpayer of the extension or the cost to him of the conversion, as the case may be, is not less than $10,000,000, or

(*c*) a pipeline that has been extended and converted as part of a single program of extension and conversion of the pipeline where the program was completed after September 1, 1985 and the aggregate of the capital cost to the taxpayer of the extension and the cost to him of the conversion is not less than $10,000,000,

and in respect of which the taxpayer has, by letter attached to the return of his income filed with the Minister in accordance with section 150 of the Act for the taxation year in which the construction, extension, conversion or program, as the case may be, was completed, elected that this subsection apply.

(5j) Pipelines. An election under subsection (5i), (5l) or (5o) shall be effective from the first day of the taxation year in respect of which the election is made and shall continue to be effective for all subsequent taxation years.

(5k) Certified Productions. A separate class is hereby prescribed for all property of a taxpayer included in Class 10 in Schedule II by reason of paragraph (*w*) thereof.

(5k.1) Canadian Film or Video Production. A separate class is hereby prescribed for all property of a corporation included in Class 10 in Schedule II because of paragraph (*x*) of that Class that is property

(*a*) in respect of which the corporation is deemed under subsection 125.4(3) of the Act to have paid an amount on account of its tax payable under Part I of the Act for a taxation year; or

(*b*) acquired by the corporation from another corporation where

(i) the other corporation is deemed under subsection 125.4(3) of the Act to have paid an amount on account of its tax payable under Part I of the Act for a taxation year in respect of the property, and

(ii) the corporations were related to each other throughout the period that began when the other corporation first incurred a qualified labour expenditure (as defined in subsection 125.4(1) of the Act) in respect of the property and ended when the other corporation disposed of the property to the corporation.

Regulations

(5l) Class 38 — Property and Outdoor Advertising Signs. A separate class is hereby prescribed for each property of a taxpayer described in Class 38 in Schedule II or in paragraph (*l*) of Class 8 in Schedule II in respect of which the taxpayer has, by letter attached to the return of income of the taxpayer filed with the Minister in accordance with section 150 of the Act for the taxation year in which the property was acquired, elected that this subsection apply.

Interpretation Bulletins: *Secondary* — IT-469R Capital cost allowance — Earth-moving equipment.

(5m) Specified Energy Property. Where, for any taxation year, a property of a taxpayer or partnership is a specified energy property, a separate class is prescribed in respect of that property for that and subsequent taxation years.

(5n) Specified Energy Property. Notwithstanding subsection (5c), where at the end of any taxation year a property of a taxpayer is specified leasing property, a separate class is prescribed in respect of that property (including any additions or alterations to that property included in the same class in Schedule II) for that year and all subsequent taxation years.

(5o) Specified Energy Property. A separate class is prescribed for one or more properties of a class in Schedule II that are exempt properties, as defined in paragraph 1100(1.13)(*a*), of a taxpayer referred to in subsection 1100(16) in respect of which the taxpayer has, by letter attached to the return of income of the taxpayer filed with the Minister in accordance with section 150 of the Act for the taxation year in which the property or properties were acquired, elected that this subsection apply.

(5p) Rapidly Depreciating Electronic Equipment. Subject to subsection (5q), a separate class is prescribed for one or more properties of a taxpayer acquired in a taxation year and included in the year in Class 8 in Schedule II, where each of the properties has a capital cost to the taxpayer of at least $1,000 and is

(*a*) computer software;

(*b*) a photocopier; or

(*c*) office equipment that is electronic communications equipment, such as a facsimile transmission device or telephone equipment.

(5q) Rapidly Depreciating Electronic Equipment. Each of subsections (5p) and (5s) apply to a property or properties of a taxpayer only if the taxpayer has (by letter attached to the taxpayer's return of income filed with the Minister in accordance with section 150 of the Act for the taxation year in which the property or properties were acquired) elected that the subsection apply to the property or properties, as the case may be.

(5r) Computer Tax Shelter Property. For the purpose of this Part, where

(*a*) more than one property of a taxpayer is described in the same class in Schedule II,

(*b*) one of the properties is a computer tax shelter property, and

(*c*) one of the properties is not a computer tax shelter property,

for properties that are described in paragraph (*b*) and that would otherwise be included in the class, a separate class is prescribed.

History: The heading before s. 1101(5r) was replaced by P.C. 2009-581, SOR/2009-115, dated April 23, 2009, applicable to property acquired on or after March 19, 2007. The heading before s. 1101(5r) formerly read:

Computer Software Tax Shelter Property

S. 1101(5r)(*b*) and (*c*) were replaced by P.C. 2009-581, SOR/2009-115, dated April 23, 2009, applicable to property acquired on or after March 19, 2007. S. 1101(5r)(*b*) and (*c*) formerly read:

(*b*) one of the properties is computer software tax shelter property, and

(*c*) one of the properties is a property other than computer software tax shelter property,

(5s) Manufacturing or Processing Property. Subject to subsection (5q), a separate class is prescribed for one or more properties of a taxpayer

(*a*) that were acquired in a taxation year and included in the year in Class 43 in Schedule II because of paragraph (*a*) of that Class; and

(*b*) that had a capital cost to the taxpayer of at least $1,000.

(5t) (Repealed.)

(5u) Equipment Related to Transmission Pipelines. A separate class is prescribed for one or more properties of a taxpayer that is property included in Class 7 in Schedule II because of paragraph (*j*) or (*k*) of that Class if the taxpayer has (by letter attached to the taxpayer's return of income filed with the Minister in accordance with section 150 of the Act for the taxation year in which the property or properties were acquired) elected that this subsection apply to the property or properties.

History: S. 1101(5u) was replaced by P.C. 2009-660, SOR/2009-126, dated April 30, 2009, applicable in respect of property acquired after February 25, 2008. S. 1101(5u) formerly read:

(5u) A separate class is prescribed for one or more properties of a taxpayer that is property included in Class 7 in Schedule II because of paragraph (*j*) of that Class if the taxpayer has (by letter attached to the taxpayer's return of income filed with the Minister in accordance with section 150 of the Act for the taxation year in which the property or properties were acquired) elected that this subsection apply to the property or properties.

Interpretation Bulletins: *Secondary* — IT-476R Capital cost allowance — Equipment used in petroleum and natural gas activities.

(5v) Transmission Pipelines. A separate class is prescribed for one or more properties of a taxpayer that is property included in Class 49 in Schedule II if the taxpayer has (by letter attached to the taxpayer's return of income filed with the Minister in accordance with section 150 of the Act for the taxation year in which the property or properties were acquired) elected that this subsection apply to the property or properties.

Interpretation Bulletins: *Secondary* — IT-476R Capital cost allowance — Equipment used in petroleum and natural gas activities.

(6) Reference. A reference in this Part to a class in Schedule II includes a reference to the corresponding separate classes prescribed by this section.

Division III
Property Rules

1102. Property Not Included

(1) The classes of property described in this Part and in Schedule II shall be deemed not to include property

(*a*) the cost of which would be deductible in computing the taxpayer's income if the Act were read without reference to sections 66 to 66.4 of the Act;

(*a*.1) the cost of which is included in the taxpayer's Canadian renewable and conservation expense (within the meaning assigned by section 1219);

(*b*) that is described in the taxpayer's inventory;

(*c*) that was not acquired by the taxpayer for the purpose of gaining or producing income;

(*d*) that was acquired by an expenditure in respect of which the taxpayer is allowed a deduction in computing income under section 37 of the Act;

(*e*) that was acquired by the taxpayer after November 12, 1981, other than property acquired from a person with whom the taxpayer was not dealing at arm's length (otherwise than by virtue of a right referred to in paragraph 251(5)(*b*) of the Act) at the time the property was acquired if the property was acquired in circumstances where subsection (14) applies, and is

(i) a print, etching, drawing, painting, sculpture, or other similar work of art, the cost of which to the taxpayer was not less than $200,

(ii) a hand-woven tapestry or carpet or a handmade appliqué, the cost of which to the taxpayer was not less than $215 per square metre,

(iii) an engraving, etching, lithograph, woodcut, map or chart, made before 1900, or

(iv) antique furniture, or any other antique object, produced more than 100 years before the date it was acquired, the cost of which to the taxpayer was not less than $1,000,

other than any property described in subparagraph (i) or (ii) where the individual who created the property was a Canadian (within the meaning assigned by paragraph 1104(10)(*a*)) at the time the property was created;

(*f*) that is property referred to in paragraph 18(1)(*l*) of the Act acquired after December 31, 1974, an outlay or expense for the use or maintenance of which is not deductible by virtue of that paragraph;

(*g*) in respect of which an allowance is claimed and permitted under Part XVII;

(*h*) that is a passenger automobile acquired after June 13, 1963 and before January 1, 1966, the cost to the taxpayer of which, minus the initial transportation charges and retail sales tax in respect thereof, exceeded $5,000, unless the automobile was acquired by a person before June 14, 1963 and has by one or more transactions between persons not dealing at arm's length become vested in the taxpayer;

(*i*) that was deemed by section 18 of the *Income Tax Act*, as enacted by the Statutes of Canada, 1958, Chapter 32, subsection 8(1), to have been acquired by the taxpayer and that did not vest in the taxpayer before the 1963 taxation year;

(*j*) of a life insurer, that is property used by it in, or held by it in the course of, carrying on an insurance business outside Canada; or

(*k*) that is linefill in a pipeline.

Tax Topics: No. 1846, Demolition of Buildings.

Income Tax Folios: *Primary* — S3-F4-C1 General Discussion of Capital Cost Allowance. *Secondary* — S4-F7-C1 Amalgamations of Canadian Corporations.

Interpretation Bulletins: *Secondary* — IT-205 Capital cost allowance — Capital cost of property in a foreign country; IT-218R Profit, capital gains and losses from the sale of real estate, including farmland and inherited land and conversion of real estate from capital property to inventory and vice versa; IT-350R Investigation of site; IT-476R Capital cost allowance — Equipment used in petroleum and natural gas activities.

SR&ED Publications: SR&ED Capital Expenditures Policy.

(1a) Partnership Property. Where the taxpayer is a member of a partnership, the classes of property described in this Part and in Schedule II shall be deemed not to include any property that is an interest of the taxpayer in depreciable property that is partnership property of the partnership.

Income Tax Folios: *Primary* — S3-F4-C1 General Discussion of Capital Cost Allowance.

(2) Land. The classes of property described in Schedule II shall be deemed not to include the land upon which a property described therein was constructed or is situated.

(3) Non-Residents. Where the taxpayer is a non-resident person, the classes of property described in this Part and in Schedule II shall, except for the purpose of determining the foreign accrual property income of the taxpayer for the purposes of subdivision i of Division B of Part I of the Act, be deemed not to include property that is situated outside Canada.

(4) Improvements or Alterations to Leased Properties. Subject to subsection (5), "capital cost" for the purposes of paragraph 1100(1)(*b*) includes any amount expended by a taxpayer for or in respect of an improvement or alteration to a leased property.

(5) Buildings on Leased Properties. Where the taxpayer has a leasehold interest in a property, a reference in Schedule II to a property that is a building or other structure shall include a reference to that leasehold interest to the extent that that interest

(*a*) was acquired by reason of the fact that the taxpayer

(i) erected a building or structure on leased land,

(ii) made an addition to a leased building or structure, or

(iii) made alterations to a leased building or structure that substantially changed the nature of the property; or

(*b*) was acquired after 1975 or, in the case of any property of Class 31 or 32, after November 18, 1974, from a former lessee who had acquired it by reason of the fact that he or a lessee before him

(i) erected a building or structure on leased land,

(ii) made an addition to a leased building or structure, or

(iii) made alterations to a leased building or structure that substantially changed the nature of the property.

Income Tax Folios: *Primary* — S3-F4-C1 General Discussion of Capital Cost Allowance.

Interpretation Bulletins: *Secondary* — IT-464R Capital cost allowance — Leasehold interests.

(5.1) Buildings on Leased Properties. Where a taxpayer has acquired a property that would, if the property had been acquired by a person with whom the taxpayer was not dealing at arm's length at the time the property was acquired by the taxpayer, be described in paragraph (5)(*a*) or (*b*) in respect of that person, a reference in Schedule II to a property that is a building or other structure shall, in respect of the taxpayer, include a reference to that property.

(6) Leasehold Interests Acquired Before 1949. For the purposes of paragraphs 2(*a*) and (*b*) of Schedule III, where an item of capital cost has been incurred before the commencement of the taxpayer's 1949 taxation year, there shall be added to the capital cost of each item the amount that has been allowed in respect thereof as depreciation under the *Income War Tax Act* and has been deducted from the original cost to arrive at the capital cost of the item.

(7) River Improvements. For the purposes of paragraph 1100(1)(*f*), capital cost includes an amount expended on river improvements by the taxpayer for the purpose of facilitating the removal of timber from a timber limit.

(8) Electrical Plant Used for Mining. Where the generating or distributing equipment and plant (including structures) of a producer or distributor of electrical energy were acquired for the purpose of providing power to a consumer for use by the consumer in the operation in Canada of a mine, ore mill, smelter, metal refinery or any combination thereof and at least 80 per cent of the producer's or distributor's output of electrical energy

(*a*) for his 1948 and 1949 taxation years, or

(*b*) for his first two taxation years in which he sold power,

Regulations

whichever period is later, was sold to the consumer for that purpose, the property shall be included in

(*c*) Class 10 in Schedule II if it is property acquired

(i) before 1988, or

(ii) before 1990

(A) pursuant to an obligation in writing entered into by the taxpayer before June 18, 1987,

(B) that was under construction by or on behalf of the taxpayer on June 18, 1987, or

(C) that is machinery or equipment that is a fixed and integral part of a building, structure, plant facility or other property that was under construction by or on behalf of the taxpayer on June 18, 1987, or

(*d*) Class 41, 41.1 or 41.2 in Schedule II in any other case, unless the property would otherwise be included in Class 43.1 or 43.2 in Schedule II and the taxpayer has, by a letter filed with the taxpayer's return of income filed with the Minister in accordance with section 150 of the Act for the taxation year in which the property was acquired, elected to include the property in Class 43.1 or 43.2, as the case may be.

History: S. 1102(8)(*d*) was replaced by S.C. 2013, c. 40, s. 102(1), applicable to property acquired after March 20, 2013.

An election referred to in paragraph 1102(8)(*d*) made by a taxpayer in respect of a property is deemed to have been filed in the manner described in those paragraphs for the taxation year in which the property was acquired if for the taxation year in which the property was acquired if

(*a*) the election is filed with the Minister in writing on or before the day that is 180 days after the day on which this Act receives royal assent; and

(*b*) the property is

(i) an eligible mine development property as defined in subsection 1104(2) of the Regulations, or

(ii) described in Class 41.2 in Schedule II to the Regulations.

S. 1102(8)(*d*) formerly read:

(*d*) Class 41 or 41.1 in Schedule II in any other case, except where the property would otherwise be included in Class 43.1 or 43.2 in Schedule II and the taxpayer has, by a letter filed with the taxpayer's return of income filed with the Minister in accordance with section 150 of the Act for the taxation year in which the property was acquired, elected to include the property in Class 43.1 or 43.2, as the case may be.

S. 1102(8)(*d*) was replaced by P.C. 2011-44, SOR/2011-9, dated February 4, 2011, published in the *Canada Gazette* February 16, 2011, applicable to property acquired after March 18, 2007, except that in respect of property acquired after March 18, 2007 and before May 3, 2010, the expression "for the taxation year in which the property was acquired" in paragraph 1102(8)(*d*) shall be read as "for the taxation year that includes May 3, 2010."

S. 1102(8)(*d*) formerly read:

(*d*) Class 41 in Schedule II in any other case, except where the property would otherwise be included in Class 43.1 or Class 43.2 in Schedule II and the taxpayer has, by a letter filed with the return of income of the taxpayer filed with the Minister in accordance with section 150 of the Act for the taxation year in which the property was acquired, elected to include the property in Class 43.1 or Class 43.2, as the case may be.

(9) Electrical Plant Used for Mining. Where a taxpayer has acquired generating or distributing equipment and plant (including structures) for the purpose of providing power for his own consumption in operating a mine, ore mill, smelter, metal refinery or any combination thereof and at least 80 per cent of the output of electrical energy was so used

(*a*) in his 1948 and 1949 taxation years, or

(*b*) in the first two taxation years in which he so produced power,

whichever period is the later, the property shall be included in

(*c*) Class 10 in Schedule II if it is property acquired

(i) before 1988, or

(ii) before 1990

(A) pursuant to an obligation in writing entered into by the taxpayer before June 18, 1987,

(B) that was under construction by or on behalf of the taxpayer on June 18, 1987, or

(C) that is machinery or equipment that is a fixed and integral part of a building, structure, plant facility or other property that was under construction by or on behalf of the taxpayer on June 18, 1987, or

(*d*) Class 41, 41.1 or 41.2 in Schedule II in any other case, unless the property would otherwise be included in Class 43.1 or 43.2 in Schedule II and the taxpayer has, by a letter filed with the taxpayer's return of income filed with the Minister in accordance with section 150 of the Act for the taxation year in which the property was acquired, elected to include the property in Class 43.1 or 43.2, as the case may be.

History: S. 1102(9)(*d*) was replaced by S.C. 2013, c. 40, s. 102(1), applicable to property acquired after March 20, 2013.

An election referred to in paragraph 1102(9)(*d*) made by a taxpayer in respect of a property is deemed to have been filed in the manner described in those paragraphs for the taxation year in which the property was acquired if for the taxation year in which the property was acquired if

(*a*) the election is filed with the Minister in writing on or before the day that is 180 days after the day on which this Act receives royal assent; and

(*b*) the property is

(i) an eligible mine development property as defined in subsection 1104(2) of the Regulations, or

(ii) described in Class 41.2 in Schedule II to the Regulations.

S. 1102(9)(*d*) formerly read:

(*d*) Class 41 or 41.1 in Schedule II in any other case, except where the property would otherwise be included in Class 43.1 or 43.2 in Schedule II and the taxpayer has, by a letter filed with the taxpayer's return of income filed with the Minister in accordance with section 150 of the Act for the taxation year in which the property was acquired, elected to include the property in Class 43.1 or 43.2, as the case may be.

S. 1102(9)(*d*) was replaced by P.C. 2011-44, SOR/2011-9, dated February 4, 2011, published in the *Canada Gazette* February 16, 2011, applicable to property acquired after March 18, 2007, except that in respect of property acquired after March 18, 2007 and before May 3, 2010, the expression "for the taxation year in which the property was acquired" in paragraph 1102(9)(*d*) shall be read as "for the taxation year that includes May 3, 2010."

S. 1102(9)(*d*) formerly read:

(*d*) Class 41 in Schedule II in any other case, except where the property would otherwise be included in Class 43.1 or Class 43.2 in Schedule II and the taxpayer has, by a letter filed with the return of income of the taxpayer filed with the Minister in accordance with section 150 of the Act for the taxation year in which the property was acquired, elected to include the property in Class 43.1 or Class 43.2, as the case may be.

(9.1) Electrical Plant Used for Mining. In their application to generating or distributing equipment and plant (including structures) that were acquired by the taxpayer before November 8, 1969, subsections (8) and (9) shall be read without reference to a "metal refinery".

(9.2) Electrical Plant Used for Mining. Where a taxpayer acquires property after November 7, 1969 from a person with whom he was not dealing at arm's length that is property referred to in subsection (8) or (9), notwithstanding those subsections, that property shall not be included in Class 10 in Schedule II by the taxpayer unless the property had been included in that class by the person from whom it was acquired, by virtue of subsection (8) or (9) as it read in its application before November 8, 1969.

(10) Railway Companies. (Repealed by S.C. 2013, c. 40, s. 102(3).)

History: S. 1102(10) was repealed by S.C. 2013, c. 40, s. 102(3), applicable in respect of expenditures incurred in taxation years that begin after December 21, 2012, and formerly read:

(10) *Railway Companies.* For the purposes of section 36 of the Act, where a taxpayer is deemed to have acquired depreciable property of a prescribed class at the time a repair, replacement, alteration or renovation expenditure described therein was incurred,

(*a*) if the expenditure was incurred by the taxpayer before May 26, 1976, the class hereby prescribed is Class 4 in Schedule II; and

(*b*) if the expenditure was incurred by the taxpayer after May 25, 1976, the class hereby prescribed is the class in Schedule II in which the depreciable property that was repaired, replaced, altered or renovated would be included if such property had been acquired at the time the expenditure was incurred.

(11) Passenger Automobiles. In paragraph (1)(*h*),

"cost to the taxpayer" of an automobile means, except as provided in subsections (12) and (13),

(*a*) except in any case coming under paragraph (*b*) or (*c*), the capital cost to the taxpayer of the automobile,

(*b*) except in any case coming under paragraph (*c*), where the automobile was acquired by a person (in this section referred to as the "original owner") after June 13, 1963, and has, by one or more transactions between persons not dealing at arm's length, become vested in the taxpayer, the greater of

(i) the actual cost to the taxpayer, and

(ii) the actual cost to the original owner, and

(*c*) where the automobile was acquired by the taxpayer outside Canada for use in connection with a permanent establishment, as defined for the purposes of Part IV or Part XXVI, outside Canada, the lesser of

(i) the actual cost to the taxpayer, and

(ii) the amount that such an automobile would ordinarily cost the taxpayer if he purchased it from a dealer in automobiles in Canada for use in Canada;

"initial transportation charges" in respect of an automobile means the costs incurred by a dealer in automobiles for transporting the automobile (before it had been used for any purpose whatever) from,

(*a*) in the case of an automobile manufactured in Canada, the manufacturer's plant, and

(*b*) in any other case, the place in Canada, if any, at which the automobile was received or stored by a wholesale distributor,

to the dealer's place of business;

"passenger automobile" means a vehicle, other than an ambulance or hearse, that was designed to carry not more than nine persons, and that is

(*a*) an automobile designed primarily for carrying persons on highways and streets, except an automobile that

(i) is designed to accommodate and is equipped with auxiliary folding seats installed between the front and the rear seats,

(ii) was acquired by a person carrying on the business of operating a taxi or automobile rental service, or arranging and managing funerals, for use in such business, and

(iii) is not a vehicle described in paragraph (*b*), or

(*b*) a station wagon or substantially similar vehicle;

"retail sales tax" in respect of an automobile means the aggregate of municipal and provincial retail sales taxes payable in respect of the purchase of the automobile by the taxpayer.

(12) Passenger Automobiles. For the purposes of paragraph (1)(*h*), where an automobile is owned by two or more persons or by partners, a reference to "cost to the taxpayer" shall be deemed to be a reference to the aggregate of the cost, as defined in subsection (11), to each such person or partner.

(13) Passenger Automobiles. In determining the cost to the taxpayer for the purposes of paragraph (1)(*h*), subsection 13(7) of the Act shall not apply unless the automobile was acquired by gift.

(14) Property Acquired by Transfer, Amalgamation or Winding-Up. Subject to subsections (14.11) to (14.13), for the purposes of this Part and Schedule II, if a property is acquired by a taxpayer

(*a*) in the course of a reorganization in respect of which, if a dividend were received by a corporation in the course of the reorganization, subsection 55(2) of the Act would not be applicable to the dividend by reason of the application of paragraph 55(3)(*b*) of the Act, or

(*a*.1) (Revoked by SOR/90-22, s. 3.)

(*b*) (Revoked by SOR/90-22, s. 3.)

(*c*) (Revoked by SOR/90-22, s. 3.)

(*d*) from a person with whom the taxpayer was not dealing at arm's length (otherwise than by virtue of a right referred to in paragraph 251(5)(*b*) of the Act) at the time the property was acquired, and

(*e*) (Revoked by SOR/90-22, s. 3.)

the property, immediately before it was so acquired by the taxpayer, was property of a prescribed class or a separate prescribed class of the person from whom it was so acquired, the property shall be deemed to be property of that same prescribed class or separate prescribed class, as the case may be, of the taxpayer.

History: S. 1102(14), the portion before paragraph (*a*) was replaced by S.C. 2019, c. 29, s. 53(1), deemed in force on March 19, 2019, and formerly read:

(14) *Property Acquired by Transfer, Amalgamation or Winding-Up.* Subject to subsections (14.11) and (14.12), for the purposes of this Part and Schedule II, if a property is acquired by a taxpayer

S. 1102(14), the portion before paragraph (*a*) was replaced by S.C. 2013, c. 40, s. 102(4), applicable to property acquired after March 20, 2013, and formerly read:

(14) *Property Acquired by Transfer, Amalgamation or Winding-Up.* Subject to subsection (14.11), for the purposes of this Part and Schedule II, if a property is acquired by a taxpayer

S. 1102(14), the portion before paragraph (*a*) was replaced by P.C. 2011-44, SOR/2011-9, dated February 4, 2011, published in the *Canada Gazette* February 16, 2011, applicable to property acquired after March 18, 2007. S. 1102(14), the portion before paragraph (*a*) formerly read:

(14) For the purposes of this Part and Schedule II, where a property is acquired by a taxpayer

Related Regulations: 1100(14.13).

Income Tax Folios: *Primary* — S3-F4-C1 General Discussion of Capital Cost Allowance.

Interpretation Bulletins: *Secondary* — IT-147R3 Capital cost allowance — Accelerated write-off of manufacturing and processing machinery and equipment; IT-267R2 Capital cost allowance — Vessels; IT-476R Capital cost allowance — Equipment used in petroleum and natural gas activities; IT-481 (Consolid.) Timber resource property and timber limits.

(14.1) Property Acquired by Transfer, Amalgamation or Winding-Up. For the purposes of this Part and Schedule II, if a taxpayer has acquired, after May 25, 1976, property of a class in Schedule II (in this subsection referred to as the "present class"), that had been previously owned before May 26, 1976 by the taxpayer or by a person with whom the taxpayer was not dealing at arm's length (otherwise than by virtue of a right referred to in paragraph 251(5)(*b*) of the Act) at the time the property was acquired, and at the time the property was previously so owned it was a property of a different class (other than Class 28 or 41) in Schedule II (in this subsection referred to as the "former class"), the property is deemed to be property of the former class and not to be property of the present class.

History: S. 1102(14.1) was replaced by P.C. 2011-44, SOR/2011-9, dated February 4, 2011, published in the *Canada Gazette* February 16, 2011, applicable to property acquired after March 18, 2007. S. 1102(14.1) formerly read:

(14.1) For the purposes of this Part and Schedule II, where a taxpayer has acquired, after May 25, 1976, property of a class in Schedule II (in this subsection referred to as the "present class") that had been previously owned before May 26, 1976 by the taxpayer or by a person with whom the taxpayer was not dealing at arm's length (otherwise than by virtue of a right referred to in paragraph 251(5)(*b*) of the Act) at the time the property was acquired, and at the time the property was previously so owned it was a property of a different class in Schedule II (in this subsection referred to as the "former class"), the property shall be deemed to be property of the former class and not property of the present class.

Interpretation Bulletins: *Secondary* — IT-147R3 Capital cost allowance — Accelerated write-off of manufacturing and processing machinery and equipment; IT-267R2 Capital cost allowance — Vessels.

(14.11) Property Acquired by Transfer, Amalgamation or Winding-Up. If, after March 18, 2007, a taxpayer acquires an oil sands property in circumstances to which subsection (14) applies and the property was depreciable property that was included in Class 41, because of paragraph (*a*), (*a.1*) or (*a.2*) of that Class, by the person or partnership from whom the taxpayer acquired the property, the following rules apply:

(*a*) there may be included in Class 41 of the taxpayer only that portion of the property the capital cost of which portion to the taxpayer is the lesser of the undepreciated capital cost of Class 41 of that person or partnership immediately before the disposition of the property by the person or partnership and the amount, if any, by which that undepreciated capital cost is reduced as a result of that disposition; and

(*b*) there shall be included in Class 41.1 of the taxpayer that portion, if any, of the property that is not the portion included in Class 41 of the taxpayer under paragraph (*a*).

History: S. 1102(14.11) was added by P.C. 2011-44, SOR/2011-9, dated February 4, 2011, published in the *Canada Gazette* February 16, 2011, applicable to property acquired after March 18, 2007.

(14.12) If, after March 20, 2013, a taxpayer acquires a property (other than an oil sands property) in circumstances to which subsection (14) applies and the property was depreciable property that was included in Class 41, because of paragraph (*a*) or (*a.1*) of that Class, by the person or partnership from whom the taxpayer acquired the property, the following rules apply:

(*a*) there may be included in Class 41 of the taxpayer only that portion of the property the capital cost of which portion to the taxpayer is the lesser of the undepreciated capital cost of Class 41 of that person or partnership immediately before the disposition of the property by the person or partnership and the amount, if any, by which that undepreciated capital cost is reduced as a result of that disposition; and

(*b*) there shall be included in Class 41.2 of the taxpayer that portion, if any, of the property that is not the portion included in Class 41 of the taxpayer under paragraph (*a*).

History: S. 1102(14.12) was added by S.C. 2013, c. 40, s. 102(5), applicable to property acquired after March 20, 2013.

(14.13) Subsection (14) does not apply to an acquisition of property by a taxpayer from a person in respect of which the property is a zero-emission vehicle included in Class 54 or 55.

History: S. 1102(14.13) was added by S.C. 2019, c. 29, s. 53(2), deemed in force on March 19, 2019.

Related Regulations: 1100(14) Rental Properties.

(14.2) Townsite Costs. For the purpose of paragraph 13(7.5)(*a*) of the Act, a property is prescribed in respect of a taxpayer where the property would, if it had been acquired by the taxpayer, be property included in Class 10 in Schedule II because of paragraph (*l*) of that Class.

Interpretation Bulletins: *Secondary* — IT-476R Capital cost allowance — Equipment used in petroleum and natural gas activities.

(14.3) Surface Construction and Bridges. For the purpose of paragraph 13(7.5)(*b*) of the Act, prescribed property is any of

(*a*) a road (other than a specified temporary access road), sidewalk, airplane runway, parking area, storage area or similar surface construction;

(*b*) a bridge; and

(*c*) a property that is ancillary to any property described in paragraph (*a*) or (*b*).

Income Tax Folios: *Primary* — S3-F4-C1 General Discussion of Capital Cost Allowance.

(15) Manufacturing and Processing Enterprises. For the purposes of subsection 13(10) of the Act,

(*a*) property is hereby prescribed that is

(i) a building included in Class 3 or 6 in Schedule II, or

(ii) machinery or equipment included in Class 8 in Schedule II,

except

(iii) property that may reasonably be regarded as having been acquired for the purpose of producing coal from a coal mine or oil, gas, metals or industrial minerals from a resource referred to in section 1201 as it read immediately before it was repealed by section 2 of Order in Council P.C. 1975-1323 of June 12, 1975, or

(iv) property acquired for use outside Canada; and

(*b*) a business carried on by the taxpayer is hereby prescribed as a manufacturing or processing business if,

(i) for the fiscal period in which the property was acquired, or

(ii) for the fiscal period in which a reasonable volume of business was first carried on,

whichever was later, the revenue received by the taxpayer, in the course of carrying on the business from

(iii) the sale of goods processed or manufactured by the taxpayer in Canada,

(iv) the leasing or renting of goods that were processed or manufactured by the taxpayer in Canada,

(v) advertisements in a newspaper or magazine that was produced by the taxpayer in Canada, and

(vi) construction carried on by the taxpayer in Canada,

was not less than 2/3 of the revenue of the business for the period.

(16) Manufacturing and Processing Enterprises. For the purposes of paragraph (15)(*b*), "revenue" means gross revenue minus the aggregate of

(*a*) amounts that were paid or credited in the period, to customers of the business, in relation to such revenue as a bonus, rebate or discount or for returned or damaged goods; and

(*b*) amounts included therein by virtue of section 13 or subsection 23(1) of the Act.

(16.1) Election for Certain Manufacturing or Processing Equipments. A taxpayer who acquires a property after March 18, 2007 and before 2016 that is manufacturing or processing machinery or equipment may (by letter attached to the return of income of the taxpayer filed with the Minister in accordance with section 150 of the Act for the taxation year in which the property is acquired) elect to include the property in Class 29 in Schedule II if

(*a*) Class 43.1 or 43.2 in Schedule II would otherwise apply to the property; and

(*b*) Class 29 in Schedule II would apply to the property if that schedule were read without reference to Classes 43.1 and 43.2.

History: S. 1102(16.1), the portion before paragraph (*a*) was replaced by S.C. 2013, c. 33, s. 35(1), deemed to have come into force on January 1, 2012, and formerly read:

(16.1) *Election for Certain Manufacturing or Processing Equipments.* A taxpayer who acquires a property after March 18, 2007 and before 2012 that is manufacturing or processing machinery or equipment may (by letter attached to the return of income of the taxpayer filed with the Minister in accordance with section 150 of the Act for the taxation year in which the property is acquired) elect to include the property in Class 29 in Schedule II if

S. 1102(16.1), the portion before paragraph (*a*) was replaced by P.C. 2009-660, SOR/2009-126, dated April 30, 2009, applicable in respect of property acquired after February 25, 2008. S. 1102(16.1), the portion before paragraph (*a*) formerly read:

(16.1) A taxpayer that acquires a property after March 18, 2007 and before 2009 that is manufacturing or processing machinery or equipment may (by letter attached to the return of income for the taxation year in which the property is acquired) elect to include the property in Class 29 in Schedule II if

S. 1102(16.1) was added by P.C. 2009-581, SOR/2009-115, dated April 23, 2009, deemed to have come into force on March 19, 2007.

If a taxpayer files in writing an election referred to in subsection 1102(16.1), the election is deemed to have been filed in the manner and by the time required if the election is received by the Minister of National Revenue no later than 90 days after May 13, 2009 (the day on which these Regulations were published in the *Canada Gazette*, Part II).

Income Tax Folios: *Primary* — S3-F4-C1 General Discussion of Capital Cost Allowance.

(17) Recreational Property. Property referred to in paragraph (1)(*f*) does not include

(*a*) any property that the taxpayer was obligated to acquire under the terms of an agreement in writing entered into before November 13, 1974; or

(*b*) any property the construction of which was

(i) commenced by the taxpayer before November 13, 1974 or commenced under an agreement in writing entered into by the taxpayer before November 13, 1974, and

(ii) completed substantially according to plans and specifications agreed to by the taxpayer before November 13, 1974.

(18) (Repealed.)

(19) Additions and Alterations. For the purposes of this Part and Schedule II, where

(*a*) a taxpayer acquired a property that is included in a class in Schedule II (in this subsection referred to as the "actual class"),

(*b*) the taxpayer acquires property that is an addition or alteration to the property referred to in paragraph (*a*),

(*c*) the property that is the addition or alteration referred to in paragraph (*b*) would have been property of the actual class if it had been acquired by the taxpayer at the time he acquired the property referred to in paragraph (*a*), and

(*d*) the property referred to in paragraph (*a*) would have been property of a class in Schedule II (in this subsection referred to as the "present class") that is different from the actual class if it had been acquired by the taxpayer at the time he acquired the addition or alteration referred to in paragraph (*b*),

the addition or alteration referred to in paragraph (*b*) shall, except as otherwise provided in this Part or in Schedule II, be deemed to be an acquisition by the taxpayer of property of the present class.

Income Tax Folios: *Primary* — S3-F4-C1 General Discussion of Capital Cost Allowance.

(19.1) Additions and Alterations. For the purposes of this Part and Schedule II, if subsection (19.2) applies to the refurbishment or reconditioning of a railway locomotive of a taxpayer, any property acquired by the taxpayer after February 25, 2008 that is incorporated into the locomotive in the course of the refurbishment or reconditioning is, except as otherwise provided in this Part or in Schedule II, deemed to be included in paragraph (*y*) of Class 10 in Schedule II.

History: S. 1102(19.1) was added by P.C. 2009-660, SOR/2009-126, dated April 30, 2009, applicable in respect of property acquired after February 25, 2008.

(19.2) Additions and Alterations. This subsection applies to the refurbishment or reconditioning of a railway locomotive, of a taxpayer, that

(*a*) is included in a class in Schedule II other than Class 10; and

(*b*) would be included in Class 10 in Schedule II if it had not been used or acquired for use for any purpose by any taxpayer before February 26, 2008.

History: S. 1102(19.2) was added by P.C. 2009-660, SOR/2009-126, dated April 30, 2009, applicable in respect of property acquired after February 25, 2008.

Regulations

(20) Non-arm's Length Exception. For the purposes of subsections 1100(2.2) and (19), 1101(1ad) and 1102(14) (in this subsection referred to as the "relevant subsections"), where, but for this subsection, a taxpayer would be considered to be dealing not at arm's length with another person as a result of a transaction or series of transactions the principal purpose of which may reasonably be considered to have been to cause one or more of the relevant subsections to apply in respect of the acquisition of a property, the taxpayer shall be considered to be dealing at arm's length with the other person in respect of the acquisition of that property.

Interpretation Bulletins: *Secondary* — IT-267R2 Capital cost allowance — Vessels.

(20.1) For the purposes of subsection 1104(4), if, in the absence of this subsection, a taxpayer would be considered to be dealing at arm's length with another person or partnership as a result of a transaction or series of transactions the principal purpose of which may reasonably be considered to have been to cause one or more properties of the taxpayer to qualify as accelerated investment incentive property, the taxpayer shall be considered not to be dealing at arm's length with the other person or partnership in respect of the acquisition of those properties.

History: S. 1102(20.1) was added by S.C. 2019, c. 29, s. 53(3), effective June 21, 2019.

Related Regulations: 1104(4).

(21) Non-arm's Length Exception. Where a taxpayer has acquired a property described in Class 43.1 of Schedule II in circumstances in which clauses (*b*)(iii)(A) and (B) or (*e*)(iii)(A) and (B) of that class apply,

(*a*) the portion of the property, determined by reference to capital cost, that is equal to or less than the capital cost of the property to the person from whom the property was acquired, is included in that class; and

(*b*) the portion of the property, if any, determined by reference to capital cost, that is in excess of the capital cost of the property to the person from whom it was acquired, shall not be included in that class.

Income Tax Folios: *Primary* — S3-F8-C2 Tax Incentives for Clean Energy Equipment.

(22) Non-arm's Length Exception. Where a taxpayer has acquired a property that is described in Class 43.2 in Schedule II in circumstances in which clauses (*b*)(iii)(A) and (B) or (*e*)(iii)(A) and (B) of Class 43.1 in Schedule II apply and the property was included in Class 43.2 in Schedule II of the person from whom the taxpayer acquired the property,

(*a*) the portion of the property, determined by reference to capital cost, that is equal to or less than the capital cost of the property to the person from whom the property was acquired is included in Class 43.2 in Schedule II; and

(*b*) the portion of the property, if any, determined by reference to capital cost, that is in excess of the capital cost of the property to the person from whom it was acquired shall not be included in Class 43.1 or 43.2 in Schedule II.

Income Tax Folios: *Primary* — S3-F8-C2 Tax Incentives for Clean Energy Equipment.

(23) Rules for Additions to and Alterations of Certain Buildings. For the purposes of applying paragraphs 1100(1)(*a.1*) and (*a.2*) and subsection 1101(5b.1), the capital cost of an addition to or an alteration of a taxpayer's building is deemed to be the capital cost to the taxpayer of a separate building if the building to which the addition or alteration was made is not included in a separate class under subsection 1101(5b.1).

History: S. 1102(23) was added by P.C. 2009-581, SOR/2009-115, dated April 23, 2009, applicable to additions and alterations made after March 18, 2007.

(24) Rules for Additions to and Alterations of Certain Buildings. If an addition or an alteration is deemed to be a separate building under subsection (23), the references in paragraphs 1100(1)(*a.1*) and (*a.2*) to "the floor space of the building" shall be read as references to "the total floor space of the separate building and the building to which the addition or alteration was made".

History: S. 1102(24) was added by P.C. 2009-581, SOR/2009-115, dated April 23, 2009, applicable to additions and alterations made after March 18, 2007.

(25) Acquisition Costs of Certain Buildings. For the purposes of this Part and Schedule II, if an eligible non-residential building of a taxpayer was under construction on March 19, 2007, the portion, if any, of the capital cost of the building that was incurred by the taxpayer before March 19, 2007 is deemed to have been incurred by the taxpayer on March 19, 2007 unless the taxpayer elects (by letter attached to the taxpayer's return of income filed with the Minister in accordance with section 150 of the Act for the taxation year in which the building was acquired) that this subsection not apply to that cost.

History: S. 1102(25) was added by P.C. 2009-581, SOR/2009-115, dated April 23, 2009, applicable to additions and alterations made after March 18, 2007.

(26) For the purpose of the definition "zero-emission vehicle" in subsection 248(1) of the Act,

(*a*) it is a prescribed condition that the motor vehicle has a battery capacity of at least 7 kWh; and; and

(*b*) the federal purchase incentive announced on March 19, 2019 is a prescribed program.

History: S. 1102(26) was added by S.C. 2019, c. 29, s. 53(4), deemed in force on March 19, 2019.

Related Sections: 248(1) "zero-emission vehicle".

DIVISION IV
INCLUSIONS IN AND TRANSFERS BETWEEN CLASSES

1103. Elections to Include Properties in Class 1

(1) Elections to Include Properties in Class 1. In respect of properties otherwise included in any of Classes 2 to 10, 11 and 12 in Schedule II, a taxpayer may elect to include in Class 1 in Schedule II all such properties acquired for the purpose of gaining or producing income from the same business.

Income Tax Folios: *Primary* — S3-F4-C1 General Discussion of Capital Cost Allowance.

Information Circulars: IC 07-1 Taxpayer relief provisions.

Interpretation Bulletins: *Secondary* — IT-274R Rental properties — Capital cost of $50,000 or more.

(2) Elections to Include Properties in Class 2, 4 or 17. Where the chief depreciable properties of a taxpayer are included in Class 2, 4 or 17 in Schedule II, the taxpayer may elect to include in Class 2, 4 or 17 in Schedule II, as the case may be, a property that would otherwise be included in another class in Schedule II and that was acquired by him before May 26, 1976 for the purpose of gaining or producing income from the same business as that for which those properties otherwise included in the said Class 2, 4 or 17 were acquired.

Information Circulars: IC 07-1 Taxpayer relief provisions.

(2a) Elections to Include Properties in Class 8. In respect of properties otherwise included in Class 19 or 21 in Schedule II, a taxpayer may, by letter attached to the return of his income for a taxation year filed with the Minister in accordance with section 150 of the Act, elect to include in Class 8 in Schedule II all properties of the said Class 19 or all properties of the said Class 21, as the case may be, owned by him at the commencement of the year.

(2b) Elections to Include Properties in Class 37. In respect of properties that would have been included in Class 37 in Schedule II had they been acquired after the date on which Class 37 became effective, a taxpayer may, by letter attached to the return of his income for a taxation year filed with the Minister in accordance with section 150 of the Act, elect to include in Class 37 all such properties acquired by the taxpayer before that date.

(2c) Elections to Make Certain Transfers. Where a taxpayer has acquired, after May 25, 1976, all or any part of a property of a class in Schedule II (in this subsection referred to as the "present class") and the property or part thereof, if it had been acquired before May 26, 1976, would have been property of a different class in Schedule II (in this subsection referred to as the "former class") and

(*a*) he was obligated to acquire the property under the terms of an agreement in writing entered into before May 26, 1976,

(*b*) he commenced the construction, manufacture or production of the property before May 26, 1976 or the construction, manufacture or production of the property was commenced under an agreement in writing entered into by him before May 26, 1976, or

(*c*) he acquired the property on or before December 31, 1976 or he was obligated to acquire the property under the terms of an agreement in writing entered into on or before December 31, 1976, if

(i) arrangements, evidenced by writing, respecting the acquisition, construction, manufacture or production of the property had been substantially advanced before May 26, 1976, and

(ii) he had, before May 26, 1976, demonstrated a *bona fide* intention to acquire the property,

the taxpayer may, by letter attached to the return of his income filed with the Minister in accordance with section 150 of the Act, for the taxation year in which the property was acquired or for the immediately following taxation year, elect to transfer in the year of acquisition

(*d*) the property or the part thereof, acquired after May 25, 1976, from the present class to the former class; or

(*e*) the part of the property acquired before May 26, 1976, from the former class to the present class.

(2d) Elections to Make Certain Transfers. Where a taxpayer has

(*a*) disposed of a property (in this subsection referred to as the "former property") of a class in Schedule II (in this subsection referred to as the "former class"), and

(*b*) before the end of the taxation year in which the former property was disposed of, acquired property (in this subsection referred to as the "new property") of a class in Schedule II (in this subsection referred to as the "present class") and the present class is neither

(i) the former class, nor

(ii) a separate class described in section 1101, other than subsection 1101(5d),

such that

(*c*) if the former property had been acquired at the time that the new property was acquired and from the person from whom the new property was acquired, the former property would have been included in the present class, and

(*d*) if the new property had been acquired at the time that the former property was acquired and from the person from whom the former property was acquired, the new property would have been included in the former class,

the taxpayer may, by letter attached to the return of income of the taxpayer filed with the Minister in accordance with section 150 of the Act in respect of the taxation year in which the former property was disposed of, elect to transfer the former property from the former class to the present class in the year of its disposition and, for greater certainty, the transfer shall be considered to have been made before the disposition of the property.

Information Circulars: IC 07-1 Taxpayer relief provisions.

Interpretation Bulletins: *Secondary* — IT-469R Capital cost allowance — Earth-moving equipment; IT-476R Capital cost allowance — Equipment used in petroleum and natural gas activities.

(2e) Transfers from Class 40 to Class 10. For the purposes of this Part and Schedule II, where property of a taxpayer would otherwise be included in Class 40 in Schedule II, all such properties owned by the taxpayer shall be transferred from Class 40 to Class 10 immediately after the commencement of the first taxation year of the taxpayer commencing after 1989.

(2f) Elections to Include Properties in Class 1, 3 or 6. In respect of properties otherwise included in Class 20 in Schedule II, a taxpayer may, by letter attached to the return of income of the taxpayer for a taxation year filed with the Minister in accordance with section 150 of the Act, elect to include in Class 1, 3 or 6 in Schedule II, as specified in the letter, all properties of Class 20 in

Regulations

Schedule II owned by the taxpayer at the commencement of the year.

(2g) Transfers to Class 8, Class 10 or Class 43. For the purposes of this Part and Schedule II, where one or more properties of a taxpayer are included in a separate class pursuant to an election filed by the taxpayer in accordance with subsection 1101(5q), all the properties in that class immediately after the beginning of the taxpayer's fifth taxation year beginning after the end of the first taxation year in which a property of the class became available for use by the taxpayer for the purposes of subsection 13(26) of the Act shall be transferred immediately after the beginning of that fifth taxation year from the separate class to the class in which the property would, but for the election, have been included.

(2h) Elections Not to Include Properties in Class 44. A taxpayer may, by letter attached to the taxpayer's return of income filed with the Minister in accordance with section 150 of the Act for the taxation year in which a property was acquired, elect not to include the property in Class 44 in Schedule II.

Regulations

(2i) Election to Include Properties in Class 35. In respect of any property otherwise included in Class 7 in Schedule II because of paragraph (*h*) of that Class and to which paragraph 1100(1)(z.1a) and subsection 1101(5d), or paragraph 1100(1)(z.1c) and subsection 1101(5d.2), would apply if Class 35 of that Schedule applied to the property, the taxpayer may (by letter attached to the taxpayer's return of income filed with the Minister in accordance with section 150 of the Act for the taxation year in which the property was acquired) elect to include the property in Class 35 rather than in Class 7.

(2j) A taxpayer may, in its return of income filed with the Minister on or before its filing-due date for the taxation year in which a property is acquired, elect not to include the property in Class 54 or 55 in Schedule II, as the case may be.

History: S. 1103(2j) was added by S.C. 2019, c. 29, s. 54(1), deemed in force on March 19, 2019.

(3) Election Rules. To be effective in respect of a taxation year, an election under this section must be made not later than the last day on which the taxpayer may file a return of his income for the taxation year in accordance with section 150 of the Act.

(4) Election Rules. An election under paragraph 1102(8)(*d*) or (9)(*d*) or this section shall be effective from the first day of the taxation year in respect of which the election is made and shall continue to be effective for all subsequent taxation years.

(5) Election Rules. An election under subsection (1) or (2) shall be made by sending a letter to that effect by registered mail to the Tax Centre at which the taxpayer customarily files the returns required by section 150 of the Act.

DIVISION V
INTERPRETATION

1104. Definitions

(1) Where the taxpayer is an individual and his income for the taxation year includes income from a business the fiscal period of which does not coincide with the calendar year, in respect of the depreciable properties acquired for the purpose of gaining or producing income from the business, a reference in this Part to

"end of the taxation year" shall be deemed to be a reference to the end of the fiscal period of the business; and

"taxation year" shall be deemed to be a reference to the fiscal period of the business.

Interpretation Bulletins: *Secondary* — IT-492 Capital cost allowance — Industrial mineral mines.

(2) In this Part and in Schedule II,

Canadian Petroleum Tax Journal: Pot Pourri of Income Tax Issues, John Chan, 2001, Vol. 14, No. 1; Canada Customs and Revenue Agency 1999 Roundtable Questions and Answers, Question 20, Vol. 13, No. 1, 2000.

"bitumen development phase" —"bitumen development phase" of a taxpayer's oil sands project means a development phase that expands the oil sands project's capacity to extract and initially process tar sands to produce bitumen or a similar product;

"certified feature film" —"certified feature film" means a motion picture film certified by the Minister of Communications to be a film of not less than 75 minutes running time in respect of which all photography or art work specifically required for the production thereof and all film editing therefor were commenced after November 18, 1974, and either the film was completed before May 26, 1976, or the photography or art work was commenced before May 26, 1976, and certified by him to be

(*a*) a film the production of which is contemplated in a coproduction agreement entered into between Canada and another country, or

(*b*) a film in respect of which

(i) the person who performed the duties of producer was a Canadian,

(ii) no fewer than 2/3 in number of all the persons each of whom

(A) was a person who performed the duties of director, screenwriter, music composer, art director, picture editor or director of photography, or

(B) was the individual in respect of whose services as an actor or actress in respect of the film the highest remuneration or the second highest remuneration was paid or payable,

were Canadians,

(iii) not less than 75 per cent of the aggregate of the remuneration paid or payable to persons for services provided in respect of the film (other than remuneration paid or payable to or in respect of the persons referred to in subparagraphs (i) and (ii) or remuneration paid or payable for processing and final preparation of the film) was paid or payable to Canadians,

(iv) not less than 75 per cent of the aggregate of costs incurred for processing and final preparation of the film including laboratory work, sound recording, sound editing and picture editing (other than remuneration paid or payable to or in respect of persons referred to in subparagraphs (i), (ii) and (iii)), was incurred in respect of services rendered in Canada, and

(v) the copyright protecting its use in Canada is beneficially owned

(A) by a person who is either a Canadian or a corporation incorporated under the laws of Canada or a province, or

(B) jointly or otherwise by two or more persons described in clause (A),

other than a film

(*c*) acquired after the day that is the earlier of

(i) the day of its first commercial use, and

(ii) 12 months after the day the principal photography thereof is completed, or

(*d*) in respect of which certification under this definition has been revoked by the Minister of Communications as provided in paragraph (10)(*b*);

"certified production" —"certified production", in respect of a particular taxation year, means a motion picture film or video tape certified by the Minister of Communications to be a film or tape in respect of which all photography, taping or art work required specifically for the production thereof and all film or tape editing therefor were commenced after May 25, 1976, certified by him to be a film or tape in respect of which the principal photography or taping thereof was commenced before the end of the particular taxation year or was completed no later than 60 days after the end of that year and certified by him to be

(*a*) a film or tape the production of which is contemplated in a coproduction agreement entered into between Canada and another country, or

(*b*) a film or tape in respect of which

(i) the individual who performed the duties of producer was a Canadian,

(ii) the Minister of Communications has allotted not less than an aggregate of six units of production, not less than two of which were allotted by virtue of clause (A) or (B) and not less than one of which was allotted by virtue of clause (C) or (D), for individuals who provided services in respect of the film or tape, in the following manner:

(A) for the director, two units of production,

(B) for the screenwriter, two units of production,

(C) for the actor or actress in respect of whose services for the film or tape the highest remuneration was paid or payable (unless in the opinion of the Minister of Communications the individual did not perform a major role in the film or tape), one unit of production,

(D) for the actor or actress in respect of whose services for the film or tape the second highest remuneration was paid or payable (unless in the opinion of the Minister of Communications the individual did not perform a major role in the film or tape), one unit of production,

(E) for the art director, one unit of production,

(F) for the director of photography, one unit of production,

(G) for the music composer, one unit of production, and

(H) for the picture editor, one unit of production,

shall be allotted, provided the individual in respect of such allotment was a Canadian,

(iii) not less than 75 per cent of the aggregate of all costs (other than costs determined by reference to the amount of income from the film or tape) paid or payable to persons for services provided in respect of producing the film or tape (other than remuneration paid or payable to, or in respect of, individuals referred to in subparagraph (i) or (ii), costs referred to in subparagraph (iv) incurred for processing and final preparation of the film or tape, and amounts paid or payable in respect of insurance, financing, brokerage, legal and accounting fees and similar amounts) was paid or payable to, or in respect of services provided by, Canadians, and

(iv) not less than 75 per cent of the aggregate of all costs (other than costs determined by reference to the amount of income from the film or tape) incurred for processing and final preparation of the film or tape, including laboratory work, sound re-recording, sound editing and picture editing (other than remuneration paid or payable to, or in respect of, individuals referred to in subparagraph (i) or (ii)) was incurred in respect of services provided in Canada,

other than a film or tape

(*c*) acquired after the day that is the earlier of

(i) the day of its first commercial use, and

(ii) 12 months after the day the principal photography or taping thereof is completed,

(*d*) acquired by a taxpayer who has not paid in cash, as of the end of the particular taxation year, to the person from whom he acquired the film or tape, at least 5 per cent of the capital cost to the taxpayer of the film or tape as of the end of the year,

(*e*) acquired by a taxpayer who has issued in payment or part payment thereof, a bond, debenture, bill, note, mortgage or similar obligation in respect of which an amount is not due until a time that is more than four years after the end of the taxation year in which the taxpayer acquired the film or tape,

(*f*) acquired from a non-resident, or

(*g*) in respect of which certification under this definition has been revoked by the Minister of Communications as provided in paragraph (10)(*b*),

and, for the purposes of the application of this definition,

(*h*) in respect of a film or tape acquired in 1987, other than a film or tape in respect of which paragraph (*i*) applies, the reference in this definition to "commenced before the end of the particular taxation year or was completed no later than 60 days after the

Regulations

end of that year" shall be read as a reference to "commenced before the end of 1987 or was completed before July, 1988", and

(*i*) in respect of a film or tape acquired in 1987 or 1988 that is included in paragraph (*n*) of Class 12 in Schedule II and that is part of a series of films or tapes that includes another property included in that paragraph, the reference in this definition to "commenced before the end of the particular taxation year or was completed no later than 60 days after the end of that year" shall be read as a reference to "completed before 1989";

"completion"—"completion" of a specified development phase of a taxpayer's oil sands project means the first attainment of a level of average output, attributable to the specified development phase and measured over a sixty day period, equal to at least 60% of the planned level of average daily output (as determined in paragraph (*b*) of the definition "specified development phase") in respect of that phase;

"computer software"—"computer software" includes systems software and a right or licence to use computer software;

"data network infrastructure equipment"—"data network infrastructure equipment" means network infrastructure equipment that controls, transfers, modulates or directs data, and that operates in support of telecommunications applications such as e-mail, instant messaging, audio- and video-over-Internet Protocol or Web browsing, Web searching and Web hosting, including data switches, multiplexers, routers, remote access servers, hubs, domain name servers, and modems, but does not include

(*a*) network equipment (other than radio network equipment) that operates in support of telecommunications applications, if the bandwidth made available by that equipment to a single end-user of the network is 64 kilobits per second or less in either direction,

(*b*) radio network equipment that operates in support of wireless telecommunications applications unless the equipment supports digital transmission on a radio channel,

(*c*) network equipment that operates in support of broadcast telecommunications applications and that is unidirectional,

(*d*) network equipment that is end-user equipment, including telephone sets, personal digital assistants and facsimile transmission devices,

(*e*) equipment that is described in paragraph (*f.2*) or (*v*) of Class 10, or in any of Classes 45, 50 and 52, in Schedule II,

(*f*) wires or cables, or similar property, and

(*g*) structures;

"designated asset"—"designated asset" in respect of a development phase of a taxpayer's oil sands project, means a property that is a building, a structure, machinery or equipment and is, or is an integral and substantial part of,

(*a*) in the case of a bitumen development phase,

(i) a crusher,

(ii) a froth treatment plant,

(iii) a primary separation unit,

(iv) a steam generation plant,

(v) a cogeneration plant, or

(vi) a water treatment plant, or

(*b*) in the case of an upgrading development phase,

(i) a gasifier unit,

(ii) a vacuum distillation unit,

(iii) a hydrocracker unit,

(iv) a hydrotreater unit,

(v) a hydroprocessor unit, or

(vi) a coker;

"designated overburden removal cost"—"designated overburden removal cost" of a taxpayer means any cost incurred by him in respect of clearing or removing overburden from a mine in Canada owned or operated by him where the cost

(*a*) was incurred after November 16, 1978 and before 1988,

(*b*) was incurred after the mine came into production in reasonable commercial quantities,

(*c*) as of the end of the taxation year in which the cost was incurred, has not been deducted by the taxpayer in computing his income, and

(*d*) is not deductible, in whole or in part, by the taxpayer in computing his income for a taxation year subsequent to the taxation year in which the cost was incurred, other than by virtue of paragraph 20(1)(*a*) of the Act;

"designated underground storage cost"—"designated underground storage cost" of a taxpayer means any cost incurred by him after December 11, 1979 in respect of developing a well, mine or other similar underground property for the storage in Canada of petroleum, natural gas or other related hydrocarbons;

Interpretation Bulletins: *Secondary* — IT-476R Capital cost allowance — Equipment used in petroleum and natural gas activities.

"development phase"—"development phase" of a taxpayer's oil sands project means the acquisition, construction, fabrication or installation of a group of assets, by or on behalf of the taxpayer, that may reasonably be considered to constitute a discrete expansion in the capacity of the oil sands project when complete (including, for greater certainty, the initiation of a new oil sands project);

"eligible liquefaction building"—"eligible liquefaction building" of a taxpayer, in respect of an eligible liquefaction facility of the taxpayer, means property (other than property that has been used or acquired for use for any purpose before it was acquired by the taxpayer or a residential building) acquired by the taxpayer after February 19, 2015 and before 2025 that is included in Class 1 in Schedule II because of paragraph (*q*) of that Class and that is used as part of the eligible liquefaction facility;

"eligible liquefaction equipment"—"eligible liquefaction equipment" in respect of an eligible liquefaction facility of a taxpayer, means property of the taxpayer that is used in connection with the liquefaction of natural gas and that

(*a*) is acquired by the taxpayer after February 19, 2015 and before 2025,

(*b*) is included in Class 47 in Schedule II because of paragraph (*b*) of that Class,

(*c*) has not been used or acquired for use for any purpose before it was acquired by the taxpayer,

(*d*) is not excluded equipment, and

(*e*) is used as part of the eligible liquefaction facility;

"eligible liquefaction facility" —"eligible liquefaction facility" of a taxpayer means a self-contained system located in Canada — including buildings, structures and equipment — that is used or intended to be used by the taxpayer for the purpose of liquefying natural gas;

"eligible mine development property" —"eligible mine development property" means a property acquired by a taxpayer after March 20, 2013 and before 2018 for the purpose of gaining or producing income

(*a*) from a new mine or an expansion of a mine, if the property was acquired under a written agreement entered into by the taxpayer before March 21, 2013,

(*b*) from a new mine, if

(i) the construction of the new mine was started by, or on behalf of, the taxpayer before March 21, 2013 (and for this purpose construction does not include obtaining permits or regulatory approvals, conducting environmental assessments, community consultations or impact benefit studies, and similar activities), or

(ii) the engineering and design work for the construction of the new mine, as evidenced in writing, was started by, or on behalf of, the taxpayer before March 21, 2013 (and for this purpose engineering and design work does not include obtaining permits or regulatory approvals, conducting environmental assessments, community consultations or impact benefit studies, and similar activities), or

(*c*) from an expansion of a mine, if

(i) the construction for the expansion of the mine was started by, or on behalf of, the taxpayer before March 21, 2013 (and for this purpose construction does not include obtaining permits or regulatory approvals, conducting environmental assessments, community consultations or impact benefit studies, and similar activities), or

(ii) the engineering and design work for the construction of the expansion of the mine, as evidenced in writing, was started by, or on behalf of, the taxpayer before March 21, 2013 (and for this purpose engineering and design work does not include obtaining permits or regulatory approvals, conducting environmental assessments, community consultations or impact benefit studies, and similar activities);

"eligible non-residential building" —"eligible non-residential building" means a taxpayer's building (other than a building that was used, or acquired for use, by any person or partnership before March 19, 2007) that is located in Canada, that is included in Class 1 in Schedule II and that is acquired by the taxpayer on or after March 19, 2007 to be used by the taxpayer, or a lessee of the taxpayer, for a non-residential use;

"excluded equipment" —"excluded equipment" means

(*a*) pipelines (other than pipelines used to move natural gas, or its components that are extracted, within an eligible liquefaction facility during the liquefaction process or used to move liquefied natural gas),

(*b*) equipment used exclusively to regasify liquefied natural gas, and

(*c*) electrical generation equipment;

"gas or oil well equipment" —"gas or oil well equipment" includes

(*a*) equipment, structures and pipelines, other than a well casing, acquired to be used in a gas or oil field in the production therefrom of natural gas or crude oil, and

(*b*) a pipeline acquired to be used solely for transmitting gas to a natural gas processing plant,

but does not include

(*c*) equipment or structures acquired for the refining of oil or the processing of natural gas including the separation therefrom of liquid hydrocarbons, sulphur or other joint products or by-products, or

(*d*) a pipeline for removal or for collection for immediate removal of natural gas or crude oil from a gas or oil field except a pipeline referred to in paragraph (*b*);

Interpretation Bulletins: *Secondary* — IT-476R Capital cost allowance — Equipment used in petroleum and natural gas activities.

"general-purpose electronic data processing equipment" — "general-purpose electronic data processing equipment" means electronic equipment that, in its operation, requires an internally stored computer program that

(*a*) is executed by the equipment,

(*b*) can be altered by the user of the equipment,

(*c*) instructs the equipment to read and select, alter or store data from an external medium such as a card, disk or tape, and

(*d*) depends upon the characteristics of the data being processed to determine the sequence of its execution;

"oil sands project" —"oil sands project" of a taxpayer means an undertaking by the taxpayer for the extraction of tar sands from a mineral resource owned by the taxpayer, which undertaking may include the processing of the tar sands to a stage that is not beyond the crude oil stage or its equivalent;

"oil sands property" —"oil sands property" of a taxpayer means property acquired by the taxpayer for the purpose of earning income from an oil sands project of the taxpayer;

"ore" —"ore" includes ore from a mineral resource that has been processed to any stage that is prior to the prime metal stage or its equivalent;

"preliminary work activity" —"preliminary work activity" means activity that is preliminary to the acquisition, construction, fabrication or installation by or on behalf of a taxpayer of designated assets in respect of the taxpayer's oil sands project including, without limiting the generality of the foregoing, the following activities:

(*a*) obtaining permits or regulatory approvals,

(*b*) performing design or engineering work,

(*c*) conducting feasibility studies,

(*d*) conducting environmental assessments,

(*e*) clearing or excavating land,

(*f*) building roads, and

(*g*) entering into contracts;

"railway system" —"railway system" includes a railway owned or operated by a common carrier, together with all buildings, rolling stock, equipment and other properties pertaining thereto, but does not include a tramway;

"specified development phase" —"specified development phase" of a taxpayer's oil sands project means a bitumen development phase or an upgrading development phase of the oil sands project which can reasonably be expected to result in a planned level of average daily output (where that output is bitumen or a similar product in the case of a bitumen development phase, or synthetic crude oil or a similar product in the case of an upgrading development phase), and in respect of which phase,

(*a*) not including any preliminary work activity, one or more designated assets was, before March 19, 2007,

(i) acquired by the taxpayer, or

(ii) in the process of being constructed, fabricated or installed, by or on behalf of the taxpayer, and

(*b*) the planned level of average daily output is the lesser of,

(i) the level that was the demonstrated intention of the taxpayer as of March 19, 2007 to produce from the specified development phase, and

(ii) the maximum level of output associated with the design capacity, as of March 19, 2007, of the designated asset referred to in paragraph (*a*);

"specified oil sands property" —"specified oil sands property" of a taxpayer means oil sands property, acquired by the taxpayer before 2012, the taxpayer's use of which is reasonably required

(*a*) for a specified development phase of an oil sands project of the taxpayer to reach completion; or

(*b*) as part of a bitumen development phase of an oil sands project of the taxpayer,

(i) to the extent that the output from the bitumen development phase is required for an upgrading development phase that is a specified development phase of the oil sands project to reach completion, and it is reasonable to conclude that all or substantially all of the output from the bitumen development phase will be so used; and

(ii) where it was the demonstrated intention of the taxpayer as of March 19, 2007 to produce, from a mineral resource owned by the taxpayer, the bitumen feedstock required for the upgrading development phase to reach completion;

"specified temporary access road" —"specified temporary access road" means

(*a*) a temporary access road to an oil or gas well in Canada, and

(*b*) a temporary access road the cost of which would, if the definition "Canadian exploration expense" in subsection 66.1(6) of the Act were read without reference to paragraphs (*k.1*) and (*l*) of that definition, be a Canadian exploration expense because of paragraph (*f*) or (*g*) of that definition;

Interpretation Bulletins: *Secondary* — IT-476R Capital cost allowance — Equipment used in petroleum and natural gas activities.

"systems software" —"systems software" means a combination of computer programs and associated procedures, related technical documentation and data that

(*a*) performs compilation, assembly, mapping, management or processing of other programs,

(*b*) facilitates the functioning of a computer system by other programs,

(*c*) provides service or utility functions such as media conversion, sorting, merging, system accounting, performance measurement, system diagnostics or programming aids,

(*d*) provides general support functions such as data management, report generation or security control, or

(*e*) provides general capability to meet widespread categories of problem solving or processing requirements where the specific attributes of the work to be performed are introduced mainly in the form of parameters, constants or descriptors rather than in program logic,

and includes a right or licence to use such a combination of computer programs and associated procedures, related technical documentation and data;

"tar sands ore" —"tar sands ore" means ore extracted from a deposit of bituminous sands or oil shales;

"telegraph system" —"telegraph system" includes the buildings, structures, general plant and communication and other equipment pertaining thereto;

"telephone system" —"telephone system" includes the buildings, structures, general plant and communication and other equipment pertaining thereto;

"television commercial message" —"television commercial message" means a commercial message as defined in the *Television Broadcasting Regulations, 1987* made under the *Broadcasting Act*;

"tramway or trolley bus system" —"tramway or trolley bus system" includes the buildings, structures, rolling stock, general plant and equipment pertaining thereto and where buses other than trolley buses are operated in connection therewith includes the properties pertaining to those bus operations.

"upgrading development phase" —"upgrading development phase" of a taxpayer's oil sands project means a development phase that expands the oil sands project's capacity to process bitumen or a similar feedstock (all or substantially all of which is from a mineral resource owned by the taxpayer) to the crude oil stage or its equivalent.

History: S. 1104(2), the definition "eligible liquefaction building" was added by P.C. 2015-629, SOR/2015-117, s. 3(1), dated May 29, 2015, deemed to have come into force on February 19, 2015.

S. 1104(2), the definition "eligible liquefaction equipment" was added by P.C. 2015-629, SOR/2015-117, s. 3(1), dated May 29, 2015, deemed to have come into force on February 19, 2015.

S. 1104(2), the definition "eligible liquefaction facility" was added by P.C. 2015-629, SOR/2015-117, s. 3(1), dated May 29, 2015, deemed to have come into force on February 19, 2015.

S. 1104(2), the definition "excluded equipment" was added by P.C. 2015-629, SOR/2015-117, s. 3(1), dated May 29, 2015, deemed to have come into force on February 19, 2015.

S. 1104(2), the definition "eligible mine development property" was added by S.C. 2013, c. 40, s. 103(1), deemed to have come into force on March 21, 2013.

S. 1104(2), the definition "bitumen development phase" was added by P.C. 2011-44, SOR/2011-9, dated February 4, 2011, published in the *Canada Gazette* February 16, 2011, applicable after March 18, 2007.

S. 1104(2), the definition "completion" was added by P.C. 2011-44, SOR/2011-9, dated February 4, 2011, published in the *Canada Gazette* February 16, 2011, applicable after March 18, 2007.

S. 1104(2), the definition "designated asset" was added by P.C. 2011-44, SOR/2011-9, dated February 4, 2011, published in the *Canada Gazette* February 16, 2011, applicable after March 18, 2007.

S. 1104(2), the definition "development phase" was added by P.C. 2011-44, SOR/2011-9, dated February 4, 2011, published in the *Canada Gazette* February 16, 2011, applicable after March 18, 2007.

S. 1104(2), the definition "oil sands project" was added by P.C. 2011-44, SOR/2011-9, dated February 4, 2011, published in the *Canada Gazette* February 16, 2011, applicable after March 18, 2007.

S. 1104(2), the definition "oil sands property" was added by P.C. 2011-44, SOR/2011-9, dated February 4, 2011, published in the *Canada Gazette* February 16, 2011, applicable after March 18, 2007.

S. 1104(2), the definition "preliminary work activity" was added by P.C. 2011-44, SOR/2011-9, dated February 4, 2011, published in the *Canada Gazette* February 16, 2011, applicable after March 18, 2007.

S. 1104(2), the definition "specified development phase" was added by P.C. 2011-44, SOR/2011-9, dated February 4, 2011, published in the *Canada Gazette* February 16, 2011, applicable after March 18, 2007.

S. 1104(2), the definition "specified oil sands property" was added by P.C. 2011-44, SOR/2011-9, dated February 4, 2011, published in the *Canada Gazette* February 16, 2011, applicable after March 18, 2007.

S. 1104(2), paragraph (*b*) of the definition "specified temporary access road" was replaced by P.C. 2011-44, SOR/2011-9, dated February 4, 2011, published in the *Canada Gazette* February 16, 2011, applicable after March 5, 1996. S. 1104(2), paragraph (*b*) of the definition "specified temporary access road" formerly read:

> (*b*) a temporary access road the cost of which would, if the definition "Canadian exploration expense" in subsection 66.1(6) of the Act were read without reference to paragraph (*l*) of that definition, be a Canadian exploration expense because of paragraph (*f*) or (*g*) of that definition;

S. 1104(2), the definition "upgrading development phase" was added by P.C. 2011-44, SOR/2011-9, dated February 4, 2011, published in the *Canada Gazette* February 16, 2011, applicable after March 18, 2007.

S. 1104(2), paragraph (*e*) of the definition "data network infrastructure equipment" was replaced by P.C. 2009-660, SOR/2009-126, dated April 30, 2009, applicable in respect of property acquired after January 27, 2009. S. 1104(2), paragraph (*e*) of the definition "data network infrastructure equipment" formerly read:

> (*e*) equipment that is described in paragraph (*f*.2) or (*v*) of Class 10 or in Class 45 or 50, in Schedule II,

S. 1104(2), paragraph (*e*) of the definition "data network infrastructure equipment" was replaced by P.C. 2009-581 SOR/2009-115, dated April 23, 2009, deemed to have come into force on March 19, 2007. S. 1104(2), paragraph (*e*) of the definition "data network infrastructure equipment" formerly read:

> (*e*) equipment that is described in paragraph (*f*.2) or (*v*) of Class 10 or in Class 45,

S. 1104(2), the definition "eligible non-residential building" was added by P.C. 2009-581, SOR/2009-115, dated April 23, 2009, deemed to have come into force on March 19, 2007.

(3) Except as otherwise provided in subsection (6), in this Part and in Schedules II and V,

"industrial mineral mine" includes a peat bog or deposit of peat but does not include a mineral resource;

"mineral" includes peat;

"mining" includes the harvesting of peat.

(4) For the purposes of this Part and Schedules II to VI, *accelerated investment incentive property* means property of a taxpayer (other than property included in Class 54 or 55) that

(*a*) is acquired by the taxpayer after November 20, 2018 and becomes available for use before 2028; and

(*b*) meets either of the following conditions:

(i) the property

(A) has not been used for any purpose before it was acquired by the taxpayer, and

(B) is not a property in respect of which an amount has been deducted under paragraph 20(1)(*a*) or subsection 20(16) of the Act by another person or partnership, or

(ii) the property was not

(A) acquired in circumstances where

(I) the taxpayer was deemed to have been allowed or deducted an amount under paragraph 20(1)(*a*) of the Act in respect of the property in computing income for previous taxation years, or

(II) the undepreciated capital cost of depreciable property of a prescribed class of the taxpayer was reduced by an amount determined by reference to the amount by which the capital cost of the property to the taxpayer exceeds its cost amount, or

(B) previously owned or acquired by the taxpayer or by a person or partnership with which the taxpayer did not deal at arm's length at any time when the property was owned or acquired by the person or partnership.

History: S. 1104(4) was added by S.C. 2019, c. 29, s. 55(1), effective June 21, 2019.

Related Regulations: 1102(20.1).

(5) Mining. For the purposes of paragraphs 1100(1)(*w*) to (*ya.2*), subsections 1101(4a) to (4h) and Classes 10, 28 and 41 to 41.2 of Schedule II, a taxpayer's "income from a mine", or any expression referring to a taxpayer's income from a mine, includes income reasonably attributable to

(*a*) the processing by the taxpayer of

(i) ore (other than iron ore or tar sands ore) all or substantially all of which is from a mineral resource owned by the taxpayer to any stage that is not beyond the prime metal stage or its equivalent,

(ii) iron ore all or substantially all of which is from a mineral resource owned by the taxpayer to any

Regulations

stage that is not beyond the pellet stage or its equivalent,

(iii) tar sands ore all or substantially all of which is from a mineral resource owned by the taxpayer to any stage that is not beyond the crude oil stage or its equivalent, or

(iv) material extracted by a well, all or substantially all of which is from a deposit of bituminous sands or oil shales owned by the taxpayer, to any stage that is not beyond the crude oil stage or its equivalent;

(*b*) the production by the taxpayer of material from a deposit of bituminous sands or oil shales; and

(*c*) the transportation by the taxpayer of

(i) output, other than iron ore or tar sands ore, from a mineral resource owned by the taxpayer that has been processed by him to any stage that is not beyond the prime metal stage or its equivalent,

(ii) iron ore from a mineral resource owned by the taxpayer that has been processed by him to any stage that is not beyond the pellet stage or its equivalent, or

(iii) tar sands ore from a mineral resource owned by the taxpayer that has been processed by him to any stage that is not beyond the crude oil stage or its equivalent,

to the extent that such transportation is effected through the use of property of the taxpayer that is included in Class 10 in Schedule II because of paragraph (*m*) thereof or that would be so included if that paragraph were read without reference to subparagraph (v) thereof and if Class 41 in Schedule II were read without the reference therein to that paragraph.

History: S. 1104(5), the portion before paragraph (*a*) was replaced by S.C. 2013, c. 40, s. 103(2), deemed to have come into force on March 21, 2013, and formerly read:

(5) *Mining.* For the purposes of paragraphs 1100(1)(*w*) to (*ya.1*), subsections 1101(4a) to (4f) and Classes 10, 28, 41 and 41.1 of Schedule II, a taxpayer's "income from a mine", or any expression referring to a taxpayer's income from a mine, includes income reasonably attributable to

S. 1104(5), the portion before paragraph (*a*) was replaced by P.C. 2011-44, SOR/2011-9, dated February 4, 2011, published in the *Canada Gazette* February 16, 2011, applicable after March 18, 2007. S. 1104(5), the portion before paragraph (*a*) formerly read:

(5) For the purposes of paragraphs 1100(1)(*w*) to (*ya*), subsections 1101 (4a) to (4d) and Classes 10, 28 and 41 in Schedule II, a taxpayer's "income from a mine", or any expression referring to a taxpayer's income from a mine, includes income reasonably attributable to

Interpretation Bulletins: *Secondary* — IT-469R Capital cost allowance — Earth-moving equipment; IT-476R Capital cost allowance — Equipment used in petroleum and natural gas activities.

(5.1) Mining. For the purposes of Classes 41 to 41.2 of Schedule II, a taxpayer's "gross revenue from a mine" includes

(*a*) revenue reasonably attributable to the processing by the taxpayer of

(i) ore (other than iron ore or tar sands ore) from a mineral resource owned by the taxpayer to any stage that is not beyond the prime metal stage or its equivalent,

(ii) iron ore from a mineral resource owned by the taxpayer to any stage that is not beyond the pellet stage or its equivalent,

(iii) tar sands ore from a mineral resource owned by the taxpayer to any stage that is not beyond the crude oil stage or its equivalent, and

(iv) material extracted by a well from a mineral resource owned by the taxpayer that is a deposit of bituminous sands or oil shales to any stage that is not beyond the crude oil stage or its equivalent;

(*b*) the amount, if any, by which any revenue reasonably attributable to the processing by the taxpayer of

(i) ore (other than iron ore or tar sands ore) from a mineral resource not owned by the taxpayer, to any stage that is not beyond the prime metal stage or its equivalent,

(ii) iron ore from a mineral resource not owned by the taxpayer to any stage that is not beyond the pellet stage or its equivalent,

(iii) tar sands ore from a mineral resource not owned by the taxpayer to any stage that is not beyond the crude oil stage or its equivalent, and

(iv) material extracted by a well from a mineral resource not owned by the taxpayer that is a deposit of bituminous sands or oil shales to any stage that is not beyond the crude oil stage or its equivalent

exceeds the cost to the taxpayer of the ore or material processed; and

(*c*) revenue reasonably attributable to the production by the taxpayer of material from a deposit of bituminous sands or oil shales.

History: S. 1104(5.1), the portion before paragraph (*a*) was replaced by S.C. 2013, c. 40, s. 103(3), deemed to have come into force on March 21, 2013, and formerly read:

(5.1) *Mining.* For the purposes of Classes 41 and 41.1 of Schedule II, a taxpayer's "gross revenue from a mine" includes

S. 1104(5.1), the portion before paragraph (*a*) was replaced by P.C. 2011-44, SOR/2011-9, dated February 4, 2011, published in the *Canada Gazette* February 16, 2011, applicable after March 18, 2007. S. 1104(5.1), the portion before paragraph (*a*) formerly read:

(5.1) For the purpose of Class 41 in Schedule II, a taxpayer's "gross revenue from a mine" includes

Interpretation Bulletins: *Secondary* — IT-476R Capital cost allowance — Equipment used in petroleum and natural gas activities.

(5.2) Mining. For the purpose of subsection (5.1), "gross revenue from a mine" does not include revenue reasonably attributable to the addition of diluent, for the purpose of transportation, to material extracted from a deposit of bituminous sands or oil shales.

Interpretation Bulletins: *Secondary* — IT-476R Capital cost allowance — Equipment used in petroleum and natural gas activities.

(6) Mining. For the purposes of Class 10 in Schedule II,

(*a*) "income from a mine" includes income reasonably attributable to the processing of

(i) ore, other than iron ore or tar sands ore, from a mineral resource not owned by the taxpayer to any stage that is not beyond the prime metal stage or its equivalent,

(ii) iron ore from a mineral resource not owned by the taxpayer to any stage that is not beyond the pellet stage or its equivalent,

(iii) tar sands ore from a mineral resource not owned by the taxpayer to any stage that is not beyond the crude oil stage or its equivalent, or

(iv) material extracted by a well from a mineral resource not owned by the taxpayer that is a deposit of bituminous sands or oil shales to any stage that is not beyond the crude oil stage or its equivalent; and

(*b*) "mine" includes a well for the extraction of material from a deposit of bituminous sands or oil shales or from a deposit of calcium chloride, halite or sylvite.

Interpretation Bulletins: *Secondary* — IT-469R Capital cost allowance — Earth-moving equipment; IT-476R Capital cost allowance — Equipment used in petroleum and natural gas activities.

(6.1) (Repealed.)

(7) Mining. For the purposes of paragraphs 1100(1)(*w*) to (*ya.2*), subsections 1101(4a) to (4h) and 1102(8) and (9), section 1107 and Classes 12, 28 and 41 to 41.2 of Schedule II,

(*a*) "mine" includes

(i) a well for the extraction of material from a deposit of bituminous sands or oil shales or from a deposit of calcium chloride, halite or sylvite, and

(ii) a pit for the extraction of kaolin or tar sands ore,

but does not include

(iii) an oil or gas well, or

(iv) a sand pit, gravel pit, clay pit, shale pit, peat bog, deposit of peat or a stone quarry (other than a kaolin pit or a deposit of bituminous sands or oil shales);

(*b*) all wells of a taxpayer for the extraction of material from one or more deposits of calcium chloride, halite or sylvite, the material produced from which is sent to the same plant for processing, are deemed to be one mine of the taxpayer; and

(*c*) all wells of a taxpayer for the extraction of material from a deposit of bituminous sands or oil shales that the Minister, in consultation with the Minister of Natural Resources, determines constitute one project, are deemed to be one mine of the taxpayer.

History: S. 1104(7), the portion before paragraph (*a*) was replaced by S.C. 2013, c. 40, s. 103(4), deemed to have come into force on March 21, 2013, and formerly read:

(7) *Mining.* For the purposes of paragraphs 1100(1)(*w*) to (*ya.1*), subsections 1101(4a) to (4f) and 1102(8) and (9), section 1107 and Classes 12, 28, 41 and 41.1 of Schedule II,

S. 1104(7), the portion before paragraph (*a*) was replaced by P.C. 2011-44, SOR/2011-9, dated February 4, 2011, published in the *Canada Gazette* February 16, 2011, applicable after March 18, 2007. S. 1104(7), the portion before paragraph (*a*) formerly read:

(7) For the purposes of paragraphs 1100(1)(*w*) to (*ya*), subsections 1101(4a) to (4d) and 1102(8) and (9), section 1107 and Classes 12, 28 and 41 in Schedule II,

Interpretation Bulletins: *Secondary* — IT-476R Capital cost allowance — Equipment used in petroleum and natural gas activities.

(8) Mining. For the purposes of subsection (7), "stone quarry" includes a mine producing dimension stone or crushed rock for use as aggregates or for other construction purposes.

(8.1) For greater certainty, for the purposes of paragraphs (*c*) and (*e*) of Class 28 and paragraph (*a*) of Classes 41 to 41.2 in Schedule II, "production" means production in reasonable commercial quantities.

History: S. 1104(8.1) was replaced by S.C. 2013, c. 40, s. 103(5), deemed to have come into force on March 21, 2013, and formerly read:

(8.1) *Mining.* For greater certainty, for the purposes of paragraphs (*c*) and (*e*) of Class 28 and paragraph (*a*) of Class 41 and Class 41.1 in Schedule II, production means production in reasonable commercial quantities.

S. 1104(8.1) was replaced by P.C. 2011-44, SOR/2011-9, dated February 4, 2011, published in the *Canada Gazette* February 16, 2011, applicable after March 18, 2007. S. 1104(8.1) formerly read:

(8.1) For greater certainty, for the purposes of paragraphs (*c*) and (*e*) of Class 28 and paragraph (*a*) of Class 41 in Schedule II, production means production in reasonable commercial quantities.

(9) Manufacturing or Processing. For the purposes of paragraph 1100(1)(*a.1*), subsection 1100(26) and Class 29 in Schedule II, "manufacturing or processing" does not include

(*a*) farming or fishing;

(*b*) logging;

(*c*) construction;

(*d*) operating an oil or gas well or extracting petroleum or natural gas from a natural accumulation thereof;

(*e*) extracting minerals from a mineral resource;

(*f*) processing of

(i) ore, other than iron ore or tar sands ore, from a mineral resource to any stage that is not beyond the prime metal stage or its equivalent,

(ii) iron ore from a mineral resource to any stage that is not beyond the pellet stage or its equivalent, or

(iii) tar sands ore from a mineral resource to any stage that is not beyond the crude oil stage or its equivalent;

(*g*) producing industrial minerals;

(*h*) producing or processing electrical energy or steam, for sale;

(*i*) processing natural gas as part of the business of selling or distributing gas in the course of operating a public utility;

(*j*) processing heavy crude oil recovered from a natural reservoir in Canada to a stage that is not beyond the crude oil stage or its equivalent; or

(*k*) Canadian field processing.

History: S. 1104(9), the portion before paragraph (*a*) was replaced by P.C. 2009-581, SOR/2009-115, dated April 23, 2009, deemed to have come into force on March 19, 2007. S. 1104(9), the portion before paragraph (*a*) formerly read:

(9) For the purposes of subsection 1100(26) and Class 29 in Schedule II, "manufacturing or processing" does not include

Income Tax Folios: S4-F15-C1 Manufacturing and Processing.

(10) Certified Films and Video Tapes. For the purposes of subsection 1100(21) and the definitions "certified feature film" and "certified production" in subsection (2),

(*a*) "Canadian" means an individual who was, at all relevant times,

(i) a Canadian citizen as defined in the *Citizenship Act*, or

(ii) a permanent resident within the meaning of the *Immigration Act, 1976*;

Regulations

(*b*) a motion picture film or video tape that has been certified by

(i) the Secretary of State, or

(ii) the Minister of Communications

as a certified feature film or certified production, as the case may be, may have its certification revoked by the Minister of Communications where an incorrect statement was made in the furnishing of information for the purpose of obtaining that certification and a certification that has been so revoked is void from the time of its issue;

(*c*) "remuneration" does not include an amount determined by reference to the amount of income from a motion picture film or video tape;

(*c*.1) "revenue guarantee" means a contract or other arrangement under the terms of which a taxpayer has a right to receive a minimum rental revenue or other fixed revenue in respect of a right to the use, in any manner whatever, of a certified feature film or certified production;

(*c*.2) a screenwriter shall be deemed to be an individual who is a Canadian where

(i) each individual involved in the preparation of the screenplay is a Canadian, or

(ii) the principal screenwriter is an individual who is a Canadian and

(A) the screenplay for the motion picture film or video tape is based upon a work authored by a Canadian,

(B) copyright in the work subsists in Canada, and

(C) the work is published in Canada;

(*d*) "unit of production" means a measure used by the Minister of Communications in determining the weight to be given for each individual Canadian referred to in subparagraph (*b*)(ii) of the definition "certified production" in subsection (2) who provides services in respect of a motion picture film or video tape; and

(*e*) where each individual who performed a service in respect of a motion picture film or video tape as the

(i) director,

(ii) screenwriter,

(iii) actor or actress in respect of whose services for the film or tape the highest remuneration was paid or payable,

(iv) actor or actress in respect of whose services for the film or tape the second highest remuneration was paid or payable,

(v) art director,

(vi) director of photography,

(vii) music composer, or

(viii) picture editor

was a Canadian, the Minister of Communications shall be deemed to have allotted six units of production in respect of the film or tape for the purposes of the definition "certified production" in subsection (2).

(11) Certified Class 34 Properties. For the purposes of paragraph (*h*) of Class 34 in Schedule II, a certificate issued under

(*a*) subparagraph (*d*)(i) of that class may be revoked by the Minister of Industry, Trade and Commerce, or

(*b*) subparagraph (*d*)(ii) or paragraph (*g*) of that class, as the case may be, may be revoked by the Minister of Energy, Mines and Resources

where

(*c*) an incorrect statement was made in the furnishing of information for the purpose of obtaining the certificate, or

(*d*) the taxpayer does not conform to the plan described in subparagraph (*d*)(i) or (*d*)(ii) of that class, as the case may be,

and a certificate that has been so revoked shall be void from the time of its issue.

(12) Amusement Parks. For the purposes of Class 37 in Schedule II, "amusement park" means a park open to the public where amusements, rides and audio-visual attractions are permanently situated.

(13) Classes 43.1 and 43.2 — Energy Conservation Property. The definitions in this subsection apply for the purposes of this subsection, subsections (14) to (17) and Classes 43.1 and 43.2 in Schedule II.

Income Tax Folios: *Primary* — S3-F8-C2 Tax Incentives for Clean Energy Equipment.

"basic oxygen furnace gas" —"basic oxygen furnace gas" means the gas that is produced intermittently in a basic oxygen furnace of a steel mill by the chemical reaction of carbon in molten steel and pure oxygen.

"biogas" —"biogas" means the gas produced by the anaerobic digestion of organic waste that is food and animal waste, manure, plant residue, pulp and paper by-product, separated organics, wood waste or sludge from an eligible sewage treatment facility.

"bio-oil" —"bio-oil" means liquid fuel that is created from wood waste or plant residues using a thermo-chemical conversion process that takes place in the absence of oxygen.

"blast furnace gas" —"blast furnace gas" means the gas produced in a blast furnace of a steel mill, by the chemical reaction of carbon (in the form of coke, coal or natural gas), the oxygen in air and iron ore.

"digester gas" —"digester gas" means a mixture of gases that are produced from the decomposition of organic waste in a digester and that are extracted from an eligible sewage treatment facility for that organic waste.

"distribution equipment" —"distribution equipment" means equipment (other than transmission equipment) used to distribute electrical energy generated by electrical generating equipment.

"district energy equipment" means property that is part of a district energy system and that consists of pipes or pumps used to collect and distribute an energy transfer medium, meters, control equipment, chillers and heat exchangers that are attached to the main distribution line of a district energy system, but does not include

(*a*) property used to distribute water that is for consumption, disposal or treatment; or

(*b*) property that is part of the internal heating or cooling system of a building.

"district energy system" —"district energy system" means a system that is used primarily to provide heating or cooling by continuously circulating, from a central generation unit to one or more buildings through a system of interconnected pipes, an energy transfer medium that is heated or cooled using thermal energy.

"eligible landfill site" —"eligible landfill site" means a landfill site that is situated in Canada, or a former landfill site that is situated in Canada, and, if a permit or licence in respect of the site is or was required under any law of Canada or of a province, for which the permit or licence has been issued.

"eligible sewage treatment facility" —"eligible sewage treatment facility" means a sewage treatment facility that is situated in Canada and for which a permit or licence is issued under any law of Canada or of a province.

"eligible waste fuel" —"eligible waste fuel" means biogas, bio-oil, digester gas, landfill gas, municipal waste, plant residue, pulp and paper waste and wood waste.

"eligible waste management facility" —"eligible waste management facility" means a waste management facility that is situated in Canada and for which a permit or licence is issued under any law of Canada or of a province.

"enhanced combined cycle system" —"enhanced combined cycle system" means an electrical generating system in which thermal waste from one or more natural gas compressor systems is recovered and used to contribute at least 20 per cent of the energy input of a combined cycle process in order to enhance the generation of electricity, but does not include the natural gas compressor systems.

"food and animal waste" —"food and animal waste" means organic waste that is disposed of in accordance with the laws of Canada or a province and that is

(*a*) generated during the preparation or processing of food or beverage for human or animal consumption;

(*b*) food or beverage that is no longer fit for human or animal consumption; or

(*c*) animal remains.

"food waste" —"food waste"(Repealed.)

"fossil fuel" —"fossil fuel" means a fuel that is petroleum, natural gas or related hydrocarbons, basic oxygen furnace gas, blast furnace gas, coal, coal gas, coke, coke oven gas, lignite or peat.

"landfill gas" —"landfill gas" means a mixture of gases that are produced from the decomposition of organic waste and that are extracted from an eligible landfill site.

"municipal waste" —"municipal waste" means the combustible portion of waste material (other than waste material that is considered to be toxic or hazardous waste pursuant to any law of Canada or of a province) that is generated in Canada and that is accepted at an eligible landfill site or an eligible waste management facility and that, when burned to generate energy, emits only those fluids or other emissions that are in compliance with the law of Canada or of a province.

"plant residue" —"plant residue" means residue of plants (not including wood waste and waste that no longer has the chemical properties of the plants of which it is a residue) that would otherwise be waste material and that is used

(*a*) in a system that converts biomass into bio-oil or biogas; or

(*b*) as an eligible waste fuel.

"producer gas" —"producer gas" means fuel the composition of which, excluding its water content, is all or substantially all non-condensable gases that is generated primarily from eligible waste fuel using a thermochemical conversion process and that is not generated using any fuels other than eligible waste fuel or fossil fuel.

"pulp and paper by-product" —"pulp and paper by-product" means tall oil soaps and crude tall oil that are produced as by-products of the processing of wood into pulp or paper and the by-product of a pulp or paper plant's effluent treatment or its de-inking processes.

"pulp and paper waste" —"pulp and paper waste" means

(*a*) tall oil soaps, crude tall oil and turpentine that are produced as by-products of the processing of wood into pulp or paper; and

(*b*) the by-product of a pulp or paper plant's effluent treatment, or its de-inking processes, if that by-product has a solid content of at least 40 per cent before combustion.

"separated organics" —"separated organics" means organic waste (other than waste that is considered to be toxic or hazardous waste under any law of Canada or a province) that could, but for its use in a system that converts biomass into biogas, be disposed of in an eligible waste management facility or eligible landfill site.

"solution gas" —"solution gas" means a fossil fuel that is gas that would otherwise be flared and has been extracted from a solution of gas and produced oil.

"spent pulping liquor" —"spent pulping liquor" means the by-product of a chemical process of transforming wood into pulp, consisting of wood residue and pulping agents.

"thermal waste" —"thermal waste" means waste heat energy extracted from a distinct point of rejection in an industrial process that would otherwise

(*a*) be vented to the atmosphere or transferred to a liquid, and

(*b*) not be used for a useful purpose.

"transmission equipment" —"transmission equipment" means equipment used to transmit more than 75 per cent of the annual electrical energy generated by electrical generating equipment, but does not include a building.

"wood waste" —"wood waste" includes scrap wood, sawdust, wood chips, bark, limbs, saw-ends and hog fuel,

Regulations

but does not include spent pulping liquor and any waste that no longer has the physical or chemical properties of wood.

History: S. 1104(13), the definition "producer gas" was added by S.C. 2014, c. 39, s. 85(1), deemed to have come into force on February 11, 2014.

S. 1104(13), the definition "biogas" was replaced by S.C. 2013, c. 40, s. 103(6), applicable in respect of property acquired after March 20, 2013 that has not been used or acquired for use before March 21, 2013., and formerly read:

"biogas"—"biogas" means the gas produced by the anaerobic digestion of organic waste that is sludge from an eligible sewage treatment facility, food and animal waste, manure, plant residue or wood waste.

S. 1104(13), paragraphs (*a*) and (*b*) of the definition "food and animal waste" was replaced by S.C. 2013, c. 40, s. 103(7), applicable in respect of property acquired after March 20, 2013 that has not been used or acquired for use before March 21, 2013., and formerly read:

(*a*) generated during the preparation or processing of food for human or animal consumption;

(*b*) food that is no longer fit for human or animal consumption; or

S. 1104(13), the portion before the definition "basic oxygen furnace" was replaced by S.C. 2012, c. 31, s. 61(1), deemed to have come into force March 29, 2012, and formerly read:

(13) *Classes 43.1 and 43.2 — Energy Conservation Property.* The definitions in this subsection apply for the purposes of this subsection, subsections (14) to (16) and Classes 43.1 and 43.2 in Schedule II.

S. 1104(13), the definition "eligible waste fuel" was replaced by S.C. 2012, c. 31, s. 61(2), deemed to have come into force March 29, 2012, and formerly read:

"eligible waste fuel" means biogas, bio-oil, digester gas, landfill gas, municipal waste, pulp and paper waste and wood waste.

S. 1104(13), the definition "plant residue" was replaced by S.C. 2012, c. 31, s. 61(2), deemed to have come into force March 29, 2012, and formerly read:

"plant residue" means the residue of plants that would, but for its use in a system that converts biomass into bio-oil or biogas, be waste material, but does not include wood waste or waste that no longer has the chemical properties of the plants of which it is a residue.

S. 1104(13), the definition "thermal waste" was replaced by S.C. 2011, c. 24, s. 79(1), applicable in respect of property acquired on or after March 22, 2011. S. 1104(13), the definition "thermal waste" formerly read:

"thermal waste" means heat energy extracted from a distinct point of rejection in an industrial process.

S. 1104(13), the definition "biogas" was replaced by S.C. 2010, c. 25, s. 76(2), applicable to property acquired after February 25, 2008. S. 1104(13), the definition "biogas" formerly read:

"biogas" means the gas produced by the anaerobic digestion of organic waste that is manure, food waste, plant residue or wood waste.

S. 1104(13), the definition "district energy system" was replaced by S.C. 2010, c. 25, s. 76(2), applicable to property acquired after March 3, 2010. S. 1104(13), the definition "district energy system" formerly read:

"district energy system" means a system that is used primarily to provide heating or cooling by continuously circulating, from a central generation unit to one or more buildings through a system of interconnected pipes, an energy transfer medium that is heated or cooled using thermal energy that is primarily produced by electrical cogeneration equipment that meets the requirements of paragraphs (*a*) to (*c*) of Class 43.1, or paragraph (*a*) of Class 43.2, in Schedule II.

S. 1104(13), the definition "eligible waste fuel" was replaced by S.C. 2010, c. 25, s. 76(2), applicable to property acquired after February 25, 2008. S. 1104(13), the definition "eligible waste fuel" formerly read:

"eligible waste fuel" means bio-oil, digester gas, landfill gas, municipal waste, pulp and paper waste, and wood waste.

S. 1104(13), the definition "food and animal waste" was added by S.C. 2010, c. 25, s. 76(3), applicable to property acquired after February 25, 2008.

S. 1104(13), the definition "food waste" was repealed by S.C. 2010, c. 25, s. 76(1), applicable to property acquired after February 25, 2008. S. 1104(13), the definition "food waste" formerly read:

"food waste" means organic waste that is

(*a*) generated during the preparation or processing of food for human or animal consumption; or

(*b*) food that is no longer fit for human or animal consumption.

S. 1104(13), the definition "biogas" was added by P.C. 2009-581, SOR/2009-115, dated April 23, 2009, applicable to property acquired on or after March 19, 2007.

S. 1104(13), the definition "eligible waste fuel" was added by P.C. 2009-581, SOR/2009-115, dated April 23, 2009, applicable to property acquired on or after March 19, 2007.

S. 1104(13), the definition "food waste" was added by P.C. 2009-581, SOR/2009-115, dated April 23, 2009, applicable to property acquired on or after March 19, 2007.

S. 1104(13), the definition "plant residue" was replaced by P.C. 2009-581, SOR/2009-115, dated April 23, 2009, applicable to property acquired on or after March 19, 2007. S. 1104(13), the definition "plant residue", formerly read:

"plant residue" means the residue of plants that would, but for its use in a system to convert biomass into bio-oil, be waste material, but does not include wood waste or waste that no longer has the chemical properties of the plants of which it is a residue.

S. 1104(13), the definition "pulp and paper waste" was added by P.C. 2009-581, SOR/2009-115, dated April 23, 2009, applicable to property acquired on or after March 19, 2007.

(14) Classes 43.1 and 43.2 — Energy Conservation Property. Where property of a taxpayer is not operating in the manner required by paragraph (*c*) of Class 43.1, or paragraph (*a*) of Class 43.2, in Schedule II solely because of a deficiency, failing or shutdown that is beyond the control of the taxpayer of the system of which it is a part and that previously operated in the manner required by that paragraph, as the case may be, that property is deemed, for the purpose of that paragraph, to be operating in the manner required under that paragraph during the period of the deficiency, failing or shutdown, if the taxpayer makes all reasonable efforts to rectify the circumstances within a reasonable time.

Related Regulations: 1104(13).

Income Tax Folios: *Primary* — S3-F8-C2 Tax Incentives for Clean Energy Equipment.

(15) Classes 43.1 and 43.2 — Energy Conservation Property. For the purpose of subsection (14), a taxpayer's system referred to in that subsection that has at any particular time operated in the manner required by paragraph (*c*) of Class 43.1, or paragraph (*a*) of Class 43.2, in Schedule II includes at any time after the particular time a property of another person or partnership if

(*a*) the property would reasonably be considered to be part of the taxpayer's system were the property owned by the taxpayer;

(*b*) the property utilizes steam obtained from the taxpayer's system primarily in an industrial process (other than the generation of electrical energy);

(*c*) the operation of the property is necessary for the taxpayer's system to operate in the manner required by paragraph (*c*) of Class 43.1, or paragraph (*a*) of Class 43.2, in Schedule II, as the case may be; and

(*d*) at the time that the taxpayer's system first became operational, the deficiency, failing or shutdown in the operation of the property could not reasonably have been anticipated by the taxpayer to occur within five years after that time.

Income Tax Folios: *Primary* — S3-F8-C2 Tax Incentives for Clean Energy Equipment.

(16) Classes 43.1 and 43.2 — Energy Conservation Property. For the purpose of subsection (14), a district energy system is deemed to satisfy the requirements of paragraph (*c*) of Class 43.1, or paragraph (*a*) of Class 43.2, in Schedule II, as the case may be, if the electrical cogeneration equipment that produces the thermal energy used by the system is deemed by subsection (14) to meet the requirements of paragraph (*c*) of Class 43.1, or paragraph (*a*) of Class 43.2, in Schedule II, as the case may be.

Regulations

(17) Classes 43.1 and 43.2 — Energy Conservation Property. A property that would otherwise be eligible for inclusion in Class 43.1 or Class 43.2 in Schedule II by a taxpayer is deemed not to be eligible for inclusion in either of those classes if

(*a*) the property is

(i) included in Class 43.1 because of its subparagraph (*c*)(i), or

(ii) described in

(A) any of subparagraphs (*d*)(vii) to (ix), (xi), (xiii), (xiv), (xvi) and (xvii) of Class 43.1, or

(B) paragraph (a) of Class 43.2; and

(*b*) at the time the property becomes available for use by the taxpayer, the taxpayer has not satisfied the requirements of all environmental laws, by-laws and regulations

(i) of Canada, a province or a municipality in Canada, or

(ii) of a municipal or public body performing a function of government in Canada

applicable in respect of the property.

History: S. 1104(17)(*a*) was replaced by S.C. 2019, c. 29, s. 55(2), applicable to property acquired after March 21, 2016 that has not been used or acquired for use before March 22, 2016. However, in respect of property acquired before March 22, 2017, clause 1104(17)(*a*)(ii)(A) is to be read as follows:

"(A) any of subparagraphs (*d*)(viii), (ix), (xi), (xiii), (xiv), (xvi) and (xvii) of Class 43.1, or"

S. 1104(17)(*a*) formerly read:

(*a*) the property is included in Class 43.1 because of its subparagraph (*c*)(i) or is described in any of subparagraphs *d*(vii) to (ix), (xi), (xiii), (xiv) and (xvi) of Class 43.1 and paragraph (*a*) of Class 43.2; and

S. 1104(17)(*a*) was replaced by S.C. 2017, c. 33, s. 91(1), applicable in respect of property acquired for use after March 21, 2017 that has not been used or acquired for use before March 22, 2017, and formerly read:

(*a*) the property is included in Class 43.1 because of its subparagraph (*c*)(i) or is described in any of subparagraphs (*d*)(viii), (ix), (xi), (xiii), (xiv) and (xvi) of Class 43.1 and paragraph (*a*) of Class 43.2; and

S. 1104(17)(*a*) was replaced by S.C. 2014, c. 39, s. 85(2), applicable to property acquired after February 10, 2014, and formerly read:

(*a*) the property is included in Class 43.1 because of its subparagraph (*c*)(i) or is described in any of subparagraphs (*d*)(viii), (ix), (xi) and (xiii) of Class 43.1 and paragraph (*a*) of Class 43.2; and

S. 1104(17) was added by S.C. 2012, c. 31, s. 61(3), deemed to have come into force March 29, 2012.

Income Tax Folios: *Primary* — S3-F8-C2 Tax Incentives for Clean Energy Equipment.

(18) Classes 1 and 47 — Liquefaction property. For the purposes of paragraphs 1100(1)(*a.3*) and (*yb*), a taxpayer's income for a taxation year from eligible liquefaction activities in respect of an eligible liquefaction facility of the taxpayer is determined as if

(*a*) the taxpayer carried on a separate business

(i) the only income of which is any combination of:

(A) in the case of natural gas that is owned by the taxpayer at the time it enters the taxpayer's eligible liquefaction facility, income from the sale by the taxpayer of the natural gas that has been liquefied, whether sold as liquefied natural gas or regasified natural gas, and

(B) in any other case, income reasonably attributable to the liquefaction of natural gas at the taxpayer's eligible liquefaction facility, and

(ii) in respect of which the only permitted deductions in computing the separate business' income are those deductions that are attributable to income described in subparagraph (i) and, in the case of income described in clause (i)(A), that are reasonably attributable to income derived after the natural gas enters the eligible liquefaction facility; and

(*b*) in the case of income described in clause (*a*)(i)(A), the taxpayer acquired the natural gas that has been liquefied at a cost equal to the fair market value of the natural gas at the time it entered the eligible liquefaction facility.

History: S. 1104(18) was added by P.C. 2015-629, SOR/2015-117, s. 3(2), dated May 29, 2015, deemed to have come into force on February 19, 2015.

DIVISION VI
CLASSES PRESCRIBED

1105. [Classes prescribed]

The classes of property provided in this Part and in Schedule II are hereby prescribed for the purposes of the Act.

DIVISION VII
CERTIFICATES ISSUED BY THE MINISTER OF CANADIAN HERITAGE

1106. Interpretation

(1) The following definitions apply in this Division and in paragraph (*x*) of Class 10 in Schedule II.

"application for a certificate of completion", in respect of a film or video production, means an application by a prescribed taxable Canadian corporation in respect of the production, filed with the Minister of Canadian Heritage before the day (in this Division referred to as "the production's application deadline") that is the later of

(*a*) the day that is 24 months after the end of the corporation's taxation year in which the production's principal photography began, or

(*b*) the day that is 18 months after the day referred to in paragraph (*a*), if the corporation has filed, with the Canada Revenue Agency, and provided to the Minister of Canadian Heritage a copy of, a waiver described in subparagraph 152(4)(*a*)(ii) of the Act, within the normal reassessment period for the corporation in respect of the first and second taxation years ending after the production's principal photography began.

History: S. 1106(1), paragraph (*b*) of the definition "application for a certificate of completion" was amended by P.C. 2010-551, SOR/2010-96, dated April 29, 2010, by replacing "Canada Customs and Revenue Agency" with "Canada Revenue Agency", in force May 12, 2010, date of publication in the *Canada Gazette*.

"Canadian" means a person that is

(*a*) an individual who is

(i) a citizen, as defined in subsection 2(1) of the *Citizenship Act*, of Canada, or

(ii) a permanent resident, as defined in subsection 2(1) of the *Immigration and Refugee Protection Act*, or

(*b*) a corporation that is a Canadian-controlled entity, as determined under sections 26 to 28 of the *Investment Canada Act*.

"Canadian government film agency" means a federal or provincial government agency whose mandate is related to the provision of assistance to film productions in Canada.

"certificate of completion", in respect of a film or video production of a corporation, means a certificate certifying that the production has been completed, issued by the Minister of Canadian Heritage before the day (in this Division referred to as "the production's certification deadline") that is six months after the production's application deadline.

"copyright owner", of a film or video production, at any time means

(*a*) the maker, as defined in section 2 of the *Copyright Act*, who at that time owns copyright, in relation to the production, within the meaning of section 3 of that Act; or

(*b*) a person to whom that copyright has been assigned, under an assignment described in section 13 of the *Copyright Act*, either wholly or partially, by the maker or by another owner to whom this paragraph applied before the assignment.

History: S. 1106(1), the definition "copyright owner" was added by SOR/2015-61, s. 1(2), deemed to have come into force November 13, 2014. However, this definition does not apply in respect of a prescribed taxable Canadian corporation's film or video production if before that day

(*a*) the Minister of Canadian Heritage has revoked a certificate or refused to issue a certificate of completion in respect of the production; or

(*b*) the Minister of National Revenue has assessed a return of income of the corporation on the basis that the production is not a Canadian film or video production and that assessment's basis is not vacated or varied on or after that particular day.

"excluded production" means a film or video production, of a particular corporation that is a prescribed taxable Canadian corporation,

(*a*) in respect of which

(i) the particular corporation has not filed an application for a certificate of completion before the production's application deadline,

(ii) a certificate of completion has not been issued before the production's certification deadline,

(iii) if the production is not a treaty co-production, a person (other than the particular corporation or a prescribed person)

(A) is a copyright owner of the production for any commercial exploitation purposes at any time during the 25-year period that begins at the earliest time after the production was completed that it is commercially exploitable, or

(B) controls the initial licensing of commercial exploitation,

(iv) there is not an agreement in writing, for consideration at fair market value, to have the production shown in Canada within the 2-year period that begins at the earliest time after the production was completed that it is commercially exploitable,

(A) with a corporation that is a Canadian and is a distributor of film or video productions, or

(B) with a corporation that holds a broadcasting license issued by the Canadian Radio-television and Telecommunications Commission for television markets, or

(v) distribution is made in Canada within the 2-year period that begins at the earliest time after the production was completed that it is commercially exploitable by a person that is not a Canadian, or

(*b*) that is

(i) news, current events or public affairs programming, or a programme that includes weather or market reports,

(ii) (Repealed.)

(iii) a production in respect of a game, questionnaire or contest (other than a production directed primarily at minors),

(iv) a sports event or activity,

(v) a gala presentation or an awards show,

(vi) a production that solicits funds,

(vii) reality television,

(viii) pornography,

(ix) advertising,

(x) a production produced primarily for industrial, corporate or institutional purposes, or

(xi) a production, other than a documentary, all or substantially all of which consists of stock footage.

History: S. 1106(1), subparagraph (*b*)(ii) of the definition "excluded production" was repealed by SOR/2016-262, s. 1, applicable in respect of film or video productions for which principal photography begins after February 16, 2016, and formerly read:

(ii) a talk show,

S. 1106(1), subparagraph (*a*)(iii) of the definition "excluded production" was replaced by SOR/2015-61, s. 1(1), deemed to have come into force November 13, 2014. However, this amendment does not apply in respect of a prescribed taxable Canadian corporation's film or video production if before that day

(*a*) the Minister of Canadian Heritage has revoked a certificate or refused to issue a certificate of completion in respect of the production; or

(*b*) the Minister of National Revenue has assessed a return of income of the corporation on the basis that the production is not a Canadian film or video production and that assessment's basis is not vacated or varied on or after that particular day.

S. 1106(1), subparagraph (*a*)(iii) of the definition "excluded production", formerly read:

(iii) where the production is not a treaty co-production, neither the particular corporation nor another prescribed taxable Canadian corporation related to the particular corporation

(A) is, except to the extent of an interest in the production held by a prescribed taxable Canadian corporation as a co-producer of the production or by a prescribed person, the exclusive worldwide copyright owner in the production for all commercial exploitation purposes for the 25-year period that begins at the earliest time after the production was completed that it is commercially exploitable, and

"producer" means a producer of a film or video production, except that it does not include a person unless the person is the individual who

(*a*) controls and is the central decision maker in respect of the production;

(*b*) is directly responsible for the acquisition of the production story or screenplay and the development, creative and financial control and exploitation of the production; and

(*c*) is identified in the production as being the producer of the production.

"remuneration" means remuneration other than an amount determined by reference to profits or revenues.

"twinning arrangement" means the pairing of two distinct film or video productions, one of which is a Canadian film or video production and the other of which is a foreign film or video production.

(2) Prescribed Taxable Canadian Corporation. For the purposes of section 125.4 of the Act and this Division, "prescribed taxable Canadian corporation" means a taxable Canadian corporation that is a Canadian, other than a corporation that is

(*a*) controlled directly or indirectly in any manner whatever by one or more persons all or part of whose taxable income is exempt from tax under Part I of the Act; or

(*b*) a prescribed labour-sponsored venture capital corporation, as defined in section 6701.

(3) Treaty Co-Production. For the purpose of this Division, "treaty co-production" means a film or video production whose production is contemplated under any of the following instruments, and to which the instrument applies:

(*a*) a co-production treaty entered into between Canada and another State;

(*b*) the Memorandum of Understanding between the Government of Canada and the Government of the Hong Kong Special Administrative Region of the People's Republic of China on Film and Television Co-Production;

(*c*) the Common Statement of Policy on Film, Television and Video Co-Productions between Japan and Canada;

(*d*) the Memorandum of Understanding between the Government of Canada and the Government of the Republic of Korea on Television Co-Production;

(*e*) the Memorandum of Understanding between the Government of Canada and the Government of the Republic of Malta on Audio-Visual Relations; and

(*f*) the Memorandum of Understanding between the Government of Canada and the Respective Governments of the Flemish, French and German-Speaking Communities of the Kingdom of Belgium concerning Audiovisual Coproduction.

History: S. 1106(3)(*f*) was added by S.C. 2019, c. 29, s. 56(1), deemed in force on March 12, 2018.

(4) Canadian Film or Video Production. Subject to subsections (6) to (9), for the purposes of section 125.4 of the Act, this Part and Schedule II, "Canadian film or video production" means a film or video production, other than an excluded production, of a prescribed taxable Canadian corporation in respect of which the Minister of Canadian Heritage has issued a certificate (other than a certificate that has been revoked under subsection 125.4(6) of the Act) and that is

(*a*) a treaty co-production; or

(*b*) a film or video production

(i) whose producer is a Canadian at all times during its production,

(ii) in respect of which the Minister of Canadian Heritage has allotted not less than six points in accordance with subsection (5),

(iii) in respect of which not less than 75% of the total of all costs for services provided in respect of producing the production (other than excluded costs) was payable in respect of services provided to or by individuals who are Canadians, and for the purpose of this subparagraph, excluded costs are

(A) costs determined by reference to the amount of income from the production,

(B) remuneration payable to, or in respect of, the producer or individuals described in any of subparagraphs (5)(*a*)(i) to (viii) and (*b*)(i) to (vi) and paragraph (5)(*c*) (including any individuals that would be described in paragraph (5)(*c*) if they were Canadians),

(C) amounts payable in respect of insurance, financing, brokerage, legal and accounting fees, and similar amounts, and

(D) costs described in subparagraph (iv), and

(iv) in respect of which not less than 75% of the total of all costs incurred for the post-production of the production, including laboratory work, sound re-recording, sound editing and picture editing, (other than costs that are determined by reference to the amount of income from the production and remuneration that is payable to, or in respect of, the producer or individuals described in any of subparagraphs (5)(*a*)(i) to (viii) and (*b*)(i) to (vi) and paragraph (5)(*c*), including any individuals that would be described in paragraph (5)(*c*) if they were Canadians) was incurred in respect of services provided in Canada.

(5) Canadian Film or Video Production. For the purposes of this Division, the Minister of Canadian Heritage shall allot, in respect of a film or video production

(*a*) that is not an animation production, in respect of each of the following persons if that person is an individual who is a Canadian,

(i) for the director, two points,

(ii) for the screenwriter, two points,

(iii) for the lead performer for whose services the highest remuneration was payable, one point,

(iv) for the lead performer for whose services the second highest remuneration was payable, one point,

(v) for the art director, one point,

(vi) for the director of photography, one point,

(vii) for the music composer, one point, and

(viii) for the picture editor, one point;

(*b*) that is an animation production, in respect of each of the following persons if that person is an individual who is a Canadian,

(i) for the director, one point,

Regulations

(ii) for the lead voice for which the highest or second highest remuneration was payable, one point,

(iii) for the design supervisor, one point,

(iv) for the camera operator where the camera operation is done in Canada, one point,

(v) for the music composer, one point, and

(vi) for the picture editor, one point;

(*c*) that is an animation production, one point if both the principal screenwriter and the storyboard supervisor are individuals who are Canadians; and

(*d*) that is an animation production, in respect of each of the following places if that place is in Canada,

(i) for the place where the layout and background work is done, one point,

(ii) for the place where the key animation is done, one point, and

(iii) for the place where the assistant animation and in-betweening is done, one point.

(6) Canadian Film or Video Production. A production (other than a production that is an animation production or a treaty co-production) is a Canadian film or video production only if there is allotted in respect of the production two points under subparagraph (5)(*a*)(i) or (ii) and one point under subparagraph (5)(*a*)(iii) or (iv).

(7) Canadian Film or Video Production. An animation production (other than a production that is a treaty co-production) is a Canadian film or video production only if there is allotted, in respect of the production,

(*a*) one point under subparagraph (5)(*b*)(i) or paragraph (5)(*c*);

(*b*) one point under subparagraph (5)(*b*)(ii); and

(*c*) one point under subparagraph (5)(*d*)(ii).

(8) Lead Performer/Screenwriter. For the purposes of this Division,

(*a*) a lead performer in respect of a production is an actor or actress who has a leading role in the production having regard to the performer's remuneration, billing and time on screen;

(*b*) a lead voice in respect of an animation production is the voice of the individual who has a leading role in the production having regard to the length of time that the individual's voice is heard in the production and the individual's remuneration; and

(*c*) where a person who is not a Canadian participates in the writing and preparation of the screenplay for a production, the screenwriter is not a Canadian unless the principal screenwriter is an individual who is otherwise a Canadian, the screenplay for the production is based upon a work authored by a Canadian, and the work is published in Canada.

(9) Documentary Production. A documentary production that is not an excluded production, and that is allotted less than six points because one or more of the positions referred to in paragraph (5)(*a*) is unoccupied, is a Canadian film or video production if all of the positions described in that paragraph that are occupied in respect of the production are occupied by individuals who are Canadians.

(10) Prescribed Person. For the purpose of section 125.4 of the Act and this Division, "prescribed person" means any of the following:

(*a*) a corporation that holds a television, specialty or pay-television broadcasting licence issued by the Canadian Radio-television and Telecommunications Commission;

(*b*) a corporation that holds a broadcast undertaking licence and that provides production funding as a result of a "significant benefits" commitment given to the Canadian Radio-television and Telecommunications Commission;

(*c*) a person to which paragraph 149(1)(*l*) of the Act applies and that has a fund that is used to finance Canadian film or video productions;

(*d*) a Canadian government film agency;

(*e*) in respect of a film or video production, a non-resident person that does not carry on a business in Canada through a permanent establishment in Canada and whose interest (or, for civil law, right) in the production is acquired to comply with the certification requirements of a treaty co-production twinning arrangement;

(*f*) a person

(i) to which paragraph 149(1)(*f*) of the Act applies,

(ii) that has a fund that is used to finance Canadian film or video productions, all or substantially all of which financing is provided by way of a direct ownership interest (or, for civil law, right) in those productions, and

(iii) that, after 1996, has received donations only from persons described in any of paragraphs (*a*) to (*e*);

(*g*) a prescribed taxable Canadian corporation;

(*h*) an individual who is a Canadian; and

(*i*) a partnership, each member of which is described in any of paragraphs (*a*) to (*h*).

History: S. 1106(10), paragraphs (*g*), (*h*) and (*i*), were added by SOR/2015-61, s. 1(3), deemed to have come into force November 13, 2014. However, these paragraphs do not apply in respect of a prescribed taxable Canadian corporation's film or video production if before that day

(*a*) the Minister of Canadian Heritage has revoked a certificate or refused to issue a certificate of completion in respect of the production; or

(*b*) the Minister of National Revenue has assessed a return of income of the corporation on the basis that the production is not a Canadian film or video production and that assessment's basis is not vacated or varied on or after that particular day.

S. 1106(10), paragraphs (*e*) and (*f*), were replaced by SOR/2015-61, s. 1(3), deemed to have come into force November 13, 2014. However, this amendment does not apply in respect of a prescribed taxable Canadian corporation's film or video production if before that day

(*a*) the Minister of Canadian Heritage has revoked a certificate or refused to issue a certificate of completion in respect of the production; or

(*b*) the Minister of National Revenue has assessed a return of income of the corporation on the basis that the production is not a Canadian film or video production and that assessment's basis is not vacated or varied on or after that particular day.

S. 1106(10), paragraphs (*e*) and (*f*), formerly read:

(*e*) in respect of a film or video production, a non-resident person that does not carry on a business in Canada through a permanent establishment in Canada where the person's interest in the production is acquired to comply with the certification requirements of a treaty co-production twinning arrangement; and

(*f*) a person

(i) to which paragraph 149(1)(*f*) of the Act applies,

(ii) that has a fund that is used to finance Canadian film or video productions, all or substantially all of which financing is provided by way of a direct ownership interest in those productions, and

(iii) that, after 1996, has received donations only from persons described in paragraphs (*a*) to (*e*).

(11) Prescribed Amount. For the purpose of the definition "assistance" in subsection 125.4(1) of the Act, "prescribed amount" means an amount paid or payable to a taxpayer under the License Fee Program of the Canadian Television Fund or as a licence-fee top-up contribution from the Canada Media Fund.

History: S. 1106(11) was replaced by SOR/2015-61, s. 1(4), deemed to have come into force on April 1, 2010, and formerly read:

(11) **Prescribed Amount.** For the purpose of the definition "assistance" in subsection 125.4(1) of the Act, "prescribed amount" means an amount paid or payable to a taxpayer under the License Fee Program of the Canada Media Fund.

S. 1106(11) was replaced by S.C. 2013, c. 34, s. 385(1), deemed to have come into force on April 1, 2010, and formerly read:

(11) *Prescribed Amount.* For the purpose of the definition "assistance" in subsection 125.4(1) of the Act, "prescribed amount" means an amount paid or payable to a taxpayer under the License Fee Program of the Canada Television and Cable Production Fund or the Canada Television Fund/Fonds canadien de télévision.

(12) Copyright Owner. For the purpose of the definition "copyright owner" in subsection (1),

(*a*) the right of a person to share in the revenues from or proceeds of disposition of an interest or, for civil law, a right, in a film or video production is not, in and by itself, an interest or right as a copyright owner of the production; and

(*b*) for greater certainty, a grant of an exclusive licence, within the meaning assigned by the *Copyright Act*, is not an assignment of a copyright.

History: S. 1106(12) was added by SOR/2015-61, s. 1(4), deemed to have come into force November 13, 2014. However, this subsection does not apply in respect of a prescribed taxable Canadian corporation's film or video production if before that day

(*a*) the Minister of Canadian Heritage has revoked a certificate or refused to issue a certificate of completion in respect of the production; or

(*b*) the Minister of National Revenue has assessed a return of income of the corporation on the basis that the production is not a Canadian film or video production and that assessment's basis is not vacated or varied on or after that particular day.

DIVISION VIII

DETERMINATION OF VISCOSITY AND DENSITY

1107. [Bituminous sands]

For the purpose of the definition "bituminous sands" in subsection 248(1) of the Act, viscosity or density of hydrocarbons shall be determined using a number of individual samples (constituting a representative sampling of that deposit or those deposits, as the case may be, from which the taxpayer is committed to produce by means of one mine) tested

(*a*) at atmospheric pressure;

(*b*) at a temperature of 15.6 degrees Celsius; and

(*c*) free of solution gas.

Part XII
Resource and Processing Allowances

1200. [Deductions allowed]

For the purposes of section 65 of the Act, there may be deducted in computing the income of a taxpayer for a taxation year such of the amounts determined in accordance with sections 1201 to 1209 and 1212 as are applicable.

1201. Earned Depletion Allowances

In computing a taxpayer's income for a taxation year there may be deducted such amount as he may claim not exceeding the lesser of

(*a*) the aggregate of

(i) 25 per cent of the amount, if any, by which the taxpayer's resource profits for the year exceed four times the total of amounts, if any, deducted under subsection 1202(2) in computing the taxpayer's income for the year, and

(ii) the amount, if any, by which the aggregate of amounts included in computing the taxpayer's income for the year under paragraphs 59(3.3)(*a*) and (*b*) of the Act exceeds the aggregate of amounts, if any, that may reasonably be considered to have been deducted under subsection 1202(2) by reason of subparagraph (*b*)(ii) thereof in computing the taxpayer's income for the year; and

(*b*) the aggregate of

(i) the taxpayer's earned depletion base as of the end of the year, and

(ii) the amount, if any, by which

(A) the aggregate determined under paragraph 1202(4)(*a*) in respect of the taxpayer for the year

exceeds

(B) the amount, if any, by which

(I) the aggregate of all amounts that would be determined under paragraphs 1205(1)(*e*) to (*k*)

exceeds

(II) 33¹/₃ per cent of the aggregate of all amounts that would be determined under paragraphs 1205(1)(*a*) to (*d*.2)

in computing the taxpayer's earned depletion base as of the end of the year.

1202. Earned Depletion Allowances

(1) For the purposes of computing the earned depletion base of a corporation, control of which has been acquired under circumstances described in subsection 66(11) of the Act, the amount by which the earned depletion base of the corporation at the time referred to in that subsection exceeds the aggregate of amounts otherwise deducted under section 1201 in computing its income for taxation years ending after that time and before control was so acquired shall be deemed to have been deducted under section 1201 by the corporation in computing its income for taxation years ending before such acquisition of control.

(2) Subject to subsections (5) and (6), where after November 7, 1969 a corporation (in this subsection referred to as the "successor") acquired a particular property (whether by way of a purchase, amalgamation, merger, winding-up or otherwise), there may be deducted by the successor in computing its income for a taxation year an amount not exceeding the aggregate of all amounts each of which is an amount determined in respect of an original owner of the particular property that is the lesser of

(*a*) the earned depletion base of the original owner immediately after the original owner disposed of the particular property (determined as if, in the case of a disposition after April 28, 1978 as a result of an amalgamation described in section 87 of the Act, the original owner existed after the time of disposition and no property was acquired or disposed of in the course of the amalgamation) to the extent of the amount thereof that was not

(i) deducted by the original owner or any predecessor owner of the particular property in computing income for any taxation year,

(ii) deducted by the successor in computing income for a preceding taxation year, or

(iii) otherwise deducted by the successor in computing income for the taxation year, and

(*b*) 25 per cent of the amount, if any, by which

(i) the part of the successor's income for the year that can reasonably be regarded as attributable to

(A) the part of any amount included under paragraph 59(3.2)(*c*) of the Act in computing its income for the year that can reasonably be regarded as attributable to the disposition by it in the year or a preceding taxation year of any interest in or right to the particular property, to the extent that the proceeds of the disposition have not been included in determining an amount under this clause, paragraph (7)(*g*), clause 29(25)(*d*)(i)(A) of the *Income Tax Application Rules* or clause 66.7(1)(*b*)(i)(A) or (3)(*b*)(i)(A) or paragraph 66.7(10)(*g*) of the Act for a preceding taxation year,

(B) its reserve amount for the year in respect of the original owner and each predecessor owner, if any, of the particular property,

(C) production from the particular property, or

(D) processing described in subparagraph 1204(1)(*b*)(iii), (iv) or (v) with the particular property

computed as if no deduction were allowed under section 29 of the *Income Tax Application Rules* or under any of sections 65 to 66.7 of the Act and as if that income did not include any amount designated under clause 66.7(2)(*b*)(ii)(A) of the Act,

exceeds

(ii) the total of

(A) four times the total of all other amounts deducted under this subsection for the year that can reasonably be regarded as attributable to the part of the successor's income for the year described in subparagraph (i), and

(B) the total of all amounts each of which is an amount deducted under subsection 66.7(1), (3), (4) or (5) of the Act or subsection 29(25) of the *Income Tax Application Rules* for the year that can reasonably be regarded as attributable to the part of the successor's income for the year described in subparagraph (i).

(2.1) (Revoked.)

(3) Where in a taxation year ending after February 17, 1987 an original owner of a property disposes of the property in circumstances in which subsection (2) applies,

(*a*) the amount of the earned depletion base of the original owner determined immediately after the time of that disposition shall be deducted in determining the earned depletion base of the original owner at any time after the time that is immediately after the disposition;

(*b*) for the purposes of paragraph (2)(*a*), the earned depletion base of the original owner determined immediately after the original owner disposed of the property that was deducted in computing the original owner's income for the year shall be deemed to be equal to the lesser of

(i) the amount deducted in respect of the disposition under paragraph (*a*), and

(ii) the amount, if any, by which

(A) the specified amount determined under subsection (4) in respect of the original owner for the year

exceeds

(B) the aggregate of all amounts each of which is an amount determined under this paragraph in respect of any disposition made by the original owner before the disposition and in the year; and

(*c*) for greater certainty, any amount (other than the amount determined under paragraph (*b*)) that was deducted under section 1201 by the original owner for the year or a subsequent taxation year shall, for the purposes of paragraph (2)(*a*), be deemed not to be in respect of the earned depletion base of the original owner determined immediately after the original owner disposed of the particular property.

(3.1) (Revoked.)

(3.2) (Revoked.)

(4) Where in a taxation year ending after February 17, 1987 an original owner of a property disposes of the property in circumstances in which subsection (2) applies, the lesser of

(*a*) the total of all amounts each of which is the amount, if any, by which

(i) an amount deducted under paragraph (3)(*a*) in respect of such a disposition in the year by the original owner

exceeds

(ii) the amount, if any, designated by the original owner in a prescribed form filed with the Minister within six months after the end of the year in respect of the amount determined under subparagraph (i), and

(*b*) the amount, if any, deducted under section 1201 in computing the income of the original owner for the taxation year

is the specified amount in respect of the original owner for the year for the purposes of paragraphs (3)(*b*) and 1205(1)(*d*.2).

(5) Subsections (2), 1203(3), 1207(7) and 1212(4) do not apply

(*a*) in respect of a property acquired by way of an amalgamation or winding-up to which section 1214 applies;

(*b*) to permit, in respect of the acquisition by a corporation before February 18, 1987 of a property, a deduction by the corporation of an amount that the corporation would not have been entitled to deduct under this Part, if this Part, as it read in its application to taxation years ending before February 18, 1987, applied to taxation years ending after February 17, 1987; or

(*c*) in respect of a property acquired by purchase, amalgamation, merger, winding-up or otherwise, from a person who is exempt from tax under Part I of the Act on that person's taxable income.

(6) Subsections (2), 1203(3), 1207(7) and 1212(4) apply only to a corporation that has acquired a particular property

(*a*) where it acquired the particular property in a taxation year commencing before 1985 and, at the time it acquired the particular property, the corporation acquired the specified property of the person from whom it acquired the particular property;

(*b*) where it acquired the particular property from a person in a taxation year commencing after 1984 and, at the time it acquired the particular property, the corporation acquired

(i) all or substantially all of the Canadian resource properties of that person, or

(ii) where subparagraph (i) does not apply, the specified property of the person;

(*c*) where it acquired (other than in circumstances in which subparagraph (*b*)(ii) applies) the particular property after November 16, 1978 and in a taxation year ending before February 18, 1987 by any means other than by way of an amalgamation or winding-up and it and the person from whom it acquired the particular property have filed with the Minister a joint election under and in accordance with any of subsections 66(6), 66.1(4), 66.1(5), 66.2(3), 66.2(4), 66.4(3), and 66.4(4) of the Act as those subsections read in their application to that year;

(*d*) where it acquired the particular property after June 5, 1987 by way of an amalgamation or winding-

Regulations

up (other than in circumstances in which subparagraph (*b*)(ii) applies) and it has filed an election in the form prescribed for the purposes of paragraph 66.7(7)(*c*) of the Act with the Minister on or before the day on or before which the corporation is required to file a return of income pursuant to section 150 of the Act for its taxation year in which it acquired the particular property;

(*e*) where it acquired the particular property (other than by means of an amalgamation or winding-up or in circumstances in which subparagraph (*b*)(ii) applies) in a taxation year ending after February 17, 1987 and it and the person from whom it acquired the particular property have filed a joint election in the form prescribed for the purposes of paragraph 66.7(7)(*e*) of the Act with the Minister on or before the earlier of the days on or before which either of them is required to file a return of income pursuant to section 150 of the Act in respect of their respective taxation years that include the time of acquisition of the particular property; and

(*f*) where it acquired (other than by way of an amalgamation or winding-up) the particular property in circumstances in which subparagraph (*b*)(ii) applies and it and the person from whom it acquired the particular property agree to have subsection (2), 1203(3), 1207(7) or 1212(4), as the case may be, apply to them and notify the Minister in writing of the agreement in their returns of income under Part I of the Act for their respective taxation years that include the time of acquisition of the particular property.

(7) Where at any time after November 12, 1981

(*a*) control of a corporation is considered for the purposes of subsection 66.7(10) of the Act to have been acquired by a person or group of persons, or

(*b*) a corporation ceases to be exempt from tax under Part I of the Act on its taxable income,

for the purposes of section 1201, this section and section 1205,

(*c*) the corporation shall be deemed after that time to be a successor (within the meaning assigned by subsection (2)) that had, at that time, acquired all the properties owned by the corporation immediately before that time from an original owner thereof;

(*d*) a joint election shall be deemed to have been filed in accordance with subsection (6) in respect of the acquisition;

(*e*) the earned depletion base of the corporation immediately before that time shall be deemed not to be the earned depletion base of the corporation immediately after that time but to be the earned depletion base of the original owner immediately after that time;

(*f*) (Revoked.)

(*g*) where the corporation (in this paragraph referred to as the "transferee") was, immediately before and at that time,

(i) a parent corporation (within the meaning assigned by subsection 87(1.4) of the Act), or

(ii) a subsidiary wholly-owned corporation (within the meaning assigned by subsection 87(1.4) of the Act)

of a particular corporation (in this paragraph referred to as the "transferor"), if both corporations agree to have this paragraph apply to them in respect of a taxation year of the transferor ending after that time and notify the Minister in writing of the agreement in the return of income under Part I of the Act of the transferor for that year, the transferor may, if throughout that year the transferee was such a parent corporation or subsidiary wholly-owned corporation of the transferor, designate in favour of the transferee, in respect of that year, for the purpose of making a deduction under subsection (2) in respect of expenditures incurred by the transferee before that time and when it was such a parent corporation or subsidiary wholly-owned corporation of the transferor, an amount not exceeding such portion of the amount that would be its income for the year, if no deductions were allowed under any of section 29 of the *Income Tax Application Rules* and sections 65 to 66.7 of the Act, that may reasonably be regarded as being attributable to

(iii) the production from Canadian resource properties owned by the transferor immediately before that time,

(iv) the disposition in the year of any Canadian resource properties owned by the transferor immediately before that time, and

(v) such processing as is described in subparagraph 1204(1)(*b*)(iii), (iv), or (v) with property owned by the transferor immediately before that time to the extent that such portion of the amount so designated is not designated under this paragraph in favour of any other taxpayer or under paragraph 66.7(10)(*g*) of the Act in favour of any taxpayer, and the amount so designated shall be deemed, for the purposes of determining the amount under subsection (2),

(vi) to be income from the sources described in subparagraph (iii), (iv) or (v), as the case may be, of the transferee for its taxation year in which that taxation year of the transferor ends, and

(vii) not to be income from the sources described in subparagraph (iii), (iv) or (v), as the case may be, of the transferor for that year;

(*h*) where, immediately before and at that time, the corporation (in this paragraph referred to as the "transferee") and another corporation (in this paragraph referred to as the "transferor") were both subsidiary wholly-owned corporations (within the meaning assigned by subsection 87(1.4) of the Act) of a particular parent corporation (within the meaning assigned by subsection 87(1.4) of the Act), if the transferee and the transferor agree to have this paragraph apply to them in respect of a taxation year of the transferor ending after that time and notify the Minister in writing of the agreement in the return of income under Part I of the Act of the transferor for that year, paragraph (*g*) shall apply for that year to the transferee and transferor as though one were the parent corporation (within the meaning assigned by subsection 87(1.4) of the Act) of the other; and

(*i*) where that time is after January 15, 1987 and at that time the corporation was a member of a partnership that owned a property at that time

(i) for the purposes of paragraph (*c*), the corporation shall be deemed to have owned immediately before that time that portion of the property owned by the partnership at that time that is equal to its percentage share of the aggregate of amounts that would be paid to all members of the partnership if it were wound up at that time, and

(ii) for the purposes of clauses (2)(*b*)(i)(C) and (D) for a taxation year ending after that time, the lesser of

(A) its share of the part of the income of the partnership for the fiscal period of the partnership ending in the year that may reasonably be regarded as being attributable to the production from the property or to such processing as is described in subparagraph 1204(1)(*b*)(iii), (iv) or (v) with the property, and

(B) an amount that would be determined under clause (A) for the year if its share of the income of the partnership for the fiscal year of the partnership were determined on the basis of the percentage share referred to in subparagraph (i)

shall be deemed to be income of the corporation for the year that may reasonably be attributable to production from the property or to such processing as is described in subparagraph 1204(1)(*b*)(iii), (iv) or (v) with the property.

(8) For the purposes of subsections (1) and (7), where a corporation acquired control of another corporation after November 12, 1981 and before 1983 by reason of the acquisition of shares of the other corporation pursuant to an agreement in writing concluded on or before November 12, 1981, the corporation shall be deemed to have acquired such control on or before November 12, 1981.

(9) Where, at any time,

(*a*) control of a taxpayer that is a corporation has been acquired by a person or group of persons,

(*b*) a taxpayer has disposed of all or substantially all of the taxpayer's Canadian resource properties, or

(*c*) a taxpayer has disposed of the specified property of the taxpayer,

and, before that time, the taxpayer or a partnership of which the taxpayer was a member acquired a property and it may reasonably be considered that one of the main purposes of the acquisition was to avoid any limitation provided in subsection (2) on the deduction in respect of the earned depletion base of the taxpayer or of a corporation referred to as a transferee in paragraph (7)(*g*) or (*h*), the taxpayer or the partnership, as the case may be, shall be deemed, for the purposes of applying subsection (2) to or in respect of the taxpayer, not to have acquired the property.

(10) Where in a particular taxation year a predecessor owner of a property disposes of it to a corporation in circumstances in which subsection (2) applies, for the purposes of applying subsection (2) to the predecessor owner for a taxation year ending after February 17, 1987 in respect of its acquisition of the property, the predecessor owner shall be deemed, after the disposition, never to have acquired the property except for the purposes of making a deduction under subsection (2) for the particular year.

(11) Where at any time a property is acquired by a person in circumstances in which subsection (2) does not apply, every person who was an original owner or predecessor owner of the property by reason of having disposed of the property before that time shall, for the purposes of applying this Part to or in respect of the person or any other person who after that time acquires the property, be deemed after that time not to be an original owner or predecessor owner of the property by reason of having disposed of the property before that time.

1203. Mining Exploration Depletion

(1) In computing a taxpayer's income for a taxation year there may be deducted such amount as he may claim not exceeding the lesser of

(*a*) the amount, if any, by which

(i) the aggregate of

(A) 25 per cent of his income for the year, computed in accordance with Part I of the Act without reference to paragraph 59(3.3)(*f*) thereof and on the assumption that no deduction were allowed under section 65 thereof, and

(B) the amount, if any, included in computing his income for the year by virtue of paragraph 59(3.3)(*f*) of the Act

exceeds

(ii) the aggregate of amounts deducted under sections 1201, 1202, 1207 and 1212 in computing his income for the year; and

Regulations

(*b*) his mining exploration depletion base as of the end of the year (before making any deduction under this subsection for the year).

(2) For the purposes of this section, "mining exploration depletion base" of a taxpayer as of a particular time means the amount by which the aggregate of

(*a*) 33⅓ per cent of the amount by which

(i) the aggregate of all amounts each of which was the stated percentage of an expenditure that is, or but for paragraph 66(12.61)(*b*) of the Act would be, incurred by the taxpayer after April 19, 1983 and before the particular time and each of which was a Canadian exploration expense

(A) described in subparagraph 66.1(6)(*a*)(iii) [subsection 66.1(6) "Canadian exploration expense"] of the Act, or

(B) that would have been described in subparagraph 66.1(6)(*a*)(iv) or (v) [subsection 66.1(6) "Canadian exploration expense"] of the Act if the references in those subparagraphs to "any of subparagraphs (i) to (iii.1) [subsection 66.1(6) 'Canadian exploration expense']" were read as "subparagraph (iii) [subsection 66.1(6) 'Canadian exploration expense']",

other than an expense described in clause (A) or (B) that was

(C) an expense renounced by the taxpayer under subsection 66(10.1) or (12.6) of the Act,

(D) an amount that was a Canadian exploration and development overhead expense of the taxpayer,

(E) an amount that was in respect of financing, including any cost incurred prior to the commencement of carrying on a business, or

(F) an eligible expense within the meaning of the *Canadian Exploration Incentive Program Act* in respect of which the taxpayer, a partnership of which the taxpayer was a member or a principal-business corporation of which the taxpayer was a shareholder, has received, is deemed to have received, is entitled to receive or may reasonably be expected to receive at any time an incentive under that Act,

exceeds

(ii) the aggregate of all amounts each of which is the stated percentage of an amount of assistance (within the meaning assigned by paragraph 66(15)(*a*.1) [subsection 66(15) "assistance"] of the Act) that any person has received, is entitled to receive or, at any time, becomes entitled to receive in respect of an expense that would be described in subparagraph (i) if that subparagraph were read without reference to clause (C) thereof, other than such an amount in respect of an expense renounced under subsection 66(10.1) or (12.6) of the Act

(A) by a corporation in favour of the taxpayer, where the amount of that assistance is excluded from the aggregate in respect of which the expense is so renounced, or

(B) by the taxpayer, where the amount of that assistance is not excluded from the aggregate in respect of which the expense is so renounced, and

(*b*) where the taxpayer is a successor corporation, any amount required by paragraph (3)(*a*) to be added before the particular time in computing the taxpayer's mining exploration depletion base

exceeds the aggregate of

(*c*) all amounts each of which is an amount deducted by the taxpayer under subsection (1) in computing his income for a taxation year ending before the particular time; and

(*d*) where the taxpayer is a predecessor, all amounts required by paragraph (3)(*b*) to be deducted before the particular time in computing the taxpayer's mining exploration depletion base.

(3) Subject to subsections 1202(5) and (6), where a corporation (in this section referred to as the "successor corporation") has at any time (in this subsection referred to as the "time of acquisition") after April 19, 1983 and in a taxation year (in this subsection referred to as the "transaction year") acquired a property from another person (in this subsection referred to as the "predecessor"), the following rules apply:

(*a*) for the purpose of computing the mining exploration depletion base of the successor corporation as of any time after the time of acquisition, there shall be added an amount equal to the amount required by paragraph (*b*) to be deducted in computing the mining exploration depletion base of the predecessor; and

(*b*) for the purpose of computing the mining exploration depletion base of the predecessor as of any time after the transaction year of the predecessor, there shall be deducted the amount, if any, by which

(i) the mining exploration depletion base of the predecessor immediately after the time of acquisition (assuming for this purpose that, in the case of an acquisition as a result of an amalgamation described in section 87 of the Act, the predecessor existed after the time of acquisition and no property was acquired or disposed of in the course of the amalgamation)

exceeds

(ii) the amount, if any, deducted under subsection (1) in computing the income of the predecessor for the transaction year of the predecessor.

Regulations

(3.1) (Revoked.)

(4) For greater certainty, where an expense incurred before a particular time is included in the aggregate calculated under subparagraph (2)(*a*)(i) in respect of a taxpayer and subsequent to the particular time any person becomes entitled to receive an amount of assistance (within the meaning assigned by paragraph 66(15)(*a*.1) [subsection 66(15) "assistance"] of the Act) that is included in the aggregate calculated under subparagraph (2)(*a*)(ii), the stated percentage of the amount of assistance shall be included in the amounts referred to in subparagraph (2)(*a*)(ii) in respect of the taxpayer at the time the expense was incurred.

1204. Resource Profits

(1) For the purposes of this Part, "gross resource profits" of a taxpayer for a taxation year means the amount, if any, by which the total of

(*a*) the amount, if any, by which the aggregate of

(i) the aggregate of amounts, if any, that would be included in computing the taxpayer's income for the year by virtue of subsection 59(2) and paragraphs 59(3.2)(*b*) and 59.1(*b*) of the Act if subsection 59(2) were read without reference to subsection 64(1) therein, and

(i.1) the amount, if any, by which the amount included in computing his income for the year by virtue of paragraph 59(3.2)(*c*) of the Act exceeds the proceeds of disposition of property described in clause 66(15)(*c*)(ii)(A) [subsection 66(15) "Canadian resource property"] of the Act that became receivable in the year or a preceding taxation year and after December 31, 1982 to the extent that such proceeds have not been deducted in determining the amount under this subparagraph for a preceding taxation year

exceeds

(ii) the aggregate of amounts, if any, deducted in computing his income for the year by virtue of paragraph 59.1(*a*) and subsections 64(1.1) and (1.2) of the Act,

(*b*) the amount, if any, of the aggregate of his incomes for the year from

(i) the production of petroleum, natural gas, related hydrocarbons or sulphur from

(A) oil or gas wells in Canada operated by the taxpayer, or

(B) natural accumulations (other than mineral resources) of petroleum or natural gas in Canada operated by the taxpayer,

(ii) the production and processing in Canada of

(A) ore, other than iron ore or tar sands ore, from mineral resources in Canada operated by him to any stage that is not beyond the prime metal stage or its equivalent,

(B) iron ore from mineral resources in Canada operated by him to any stage that is not beyond the pellet stage or its equivalent, and

(C) tar sands ore from mineral resources in Canada operated by him to any stage that is not beyond the crude oil stage or its equivalent,

(iii) the processing in Canada of

(A) ore, other than iron ore or tar sands ore, from mineral resources in Canada not operated by him to any stage that is not beyond the prime metal stage or its equivalent,

(B) iron ore from mineral resources in Canada not operated by him to any stage that is not beyond the pellet stage or its equivalent, and

(C) tar sands ore from mineral resources in Canada not operated by him to any stage that is not beyond the crude oil stage or its equivalent,

(iv) the processing in Canada of

(A) ore, other than iron ore or tar sands ore, from mineral resources outside Canada to any stage that is not beyond the prime metal stage or its equivalent,

(B) iron ore from mineral resources outside Canada to any stage that is not beyond the pellet stage or its equivalent, and

(C) tar sands ore from mineral resources outside Canada to any stage that is not beyond the crude oil stage or its equivalent,

(v) the processing in Canada of heavy crude oil recovered from an oil or gas well in Canada to any stage that is not beyond the crude oil stage or its equivalent, and

(vi) Canadian field processing,

(*b*.1) the total of all amounts (other than an amount included because of paragraph (*b*) in computing the taxpayer's gross resource profits for the year) each of which is an amount included in computing the taxpayer's income for the year as a rental or royalty computed by reference to the amount or value of production from a natural accumulation of petroleum or natural gas in Canada, an oil or gas well in Canada or a mineral resource in Canada, and

(*c*) if the taxpayer owns all the issued and outstanding shares of the capital stock of a railway company throughout the year, the amount that may reasonably be considered to be the railway company's income for its taxation year ending in the year from the transportation of such of the taxpayer's ore as is described in clause (*b*)(ii)(A), (B) or (C),

exceeds the aggregate of the taxpayer's losses for the year from the sources described in paragraph (*b*), where the taxpayer's incomes and losses are computed in accordance with the Act on the assumption that the taxpayer had during the year no incomes or losses except from those

Regulations

sources and was allowed no deductions in computing the taxpayer's income for the year other than

(*d*) amounts deductible under section 66 of the Act (other than amounts in respect of foreign exploration and development expenses) or subsection 17(2) or (6) or section 29 of the *Income Tax Application Rules* for the year;

(*e*) the amounts deductible or deducted, as the case may be, under section 66.1, 66.2 (other than an amount that is in respect of a property described in clause 66(15)(*c*)(ii)(A) [subsection 66(15) "Canadian resource property"] of the Act), 66.4, 66.5 or 66.7 (other than subsection (2) thereof) of the Act for the year; and

(*f*) any other deductions for the year that can reasonably be regarded as applicable to the sources of income described in paragraph (*b*) or (*b*.1), other than a deduction under paragraph 20(1)(*ss*) or (*tt*) of the Act or section 1201 or subsection 1202(2), 1203(1), 1207(1) or 1212(1).

(1.1) For the purposes of this Part, "resource profits" of a taxpayer for a taxation year means the amount, if any, by which the taxpayer's gross resource profits for the year exceeds the total of

(*a*) all amounts deducted in computing the taxpayer's income for the year other than

(i) an amount deducted in computing the taxpayer's gross resource profits for the year,

(ii) an amount deducted under any of section 8, paragraphs 20(1)(*ss*) and (*tt*), sections 60 to 64 and subsections 66(4), 66.7(2) and 104(6) and (12) of the Act and section 1201 and subsections 1202(2), 1203(1), 1207(1) and 1212(1) in computing the taxpayer's income for the year,

(iii) an amount deducted under section 66.2 of the Act in computing the taxpayer's income for the year, to the extent that it is attributable to any right, licence or privilege to store underground petroleum, natural gas or related hydrocarbons in Canada,

(iv) an amount deducted in computing the taxpayer's income for the year from a business, or other source, that does not include any resource activity of the taxpayer, and

(v) an amount deducted in computing the taxpayer's income for the year, to the extent that the amount

(A) relates to an activity

(I) that is not a resource activity of the taxpayer, and

(II) that is

1. the production, processing, manufacturing, distribution, marketing, transportation or sale of any property,

2. carried out for the purpose of earning income from property, or

3. the rendering of a service by the taxpayer to another person for the purpose of earning income of the taxpayer, and

(B) does not relate to a resource activity of the taxpayer,

(*b*) all amounts each of which is the amount, if any, by which

(i) the amount that would have been charged to the taxpayer by a person or partnership with whom the taxpayer was not dealing at arm's length if the taxpayer and that person or partnership had been dealing at arm's length

(A) for the use after March 6, 1996 and in the year of a property (other than money) owned by that person or partnership, or

(B) for the provision after March 6, 1996 and in the year by that person or partnership of a service to the taxpayer

exceeds the total of

(ii) the amount charged to the taxpayer for the use of that property or the provision of that service in that period, and

(iii) the portion of the amount described in subparagraph (i) that, if it had been charged, would not have been deductible in computing the taxpayer's resource profits, and

(*c*) where the year ends after February 21, 1994, all amounts added under subsection 80(13) of the Act in computing the taxpayer's gross resource profits for the year.

(1.2) For the purposes of paragraph (1.1)(*b*) and this subsection,

(*a*) a taxpayer is considered not to deal at arm's length with a partnership where the taxpayer does not deal at arm's length with any member of the partnership;

(*b*) a partnership is considered not to deal at arm's length with another partnership where any member of the first partnership does not deal at arm's length with any member of the second partnership;

(*c*) where a taxpayer is a member, or is deemed by this paragraph to be a member, of a partnership that is a member of another partnership, the taxpayer is deemed to be a member of the other partnership; and

(*d*) the provision of a service to a taxpayer does not include the provision of a service by an individual in the individual's capacity as an employee of the taxpayer.

(2) For greater certainty, for the purposes of this section, in computing the income or loss of a trust for a taxation year from the sources described in paragraphs (1)(*b*) and (*b*.1), no deduction shall be made in respect of amounts deductible by the trust pursuant to subsection 104(6) or (12) of the Act.

(3) A taxpayer's income or loss from a source described in paragraph (1)(*b*) does not include

(*a*) any income or loss derived from transporting, transmitting or processing (other than processing described in clause (1)(*b*)(ii)(C), (iii)(C) or (iv)(C) or subparagraph (1)(*b*)(v) or (vi)) petroleum, natural gas or related hydrocarbons or sulphur from a natural accumulation of petroleum or natural gas;

(*b*) any income or loss arising because of the application of paragraph 12(1)(*z*.1) or (*z*.2) or section 107.3 of the Act; and

(*c*) any income or loss that can reasonably be attributable to a service rendered by the taxpayer (other than processing described in subparagraph (1)(*b*)(iii), (iv), (v) or (vi) or activities carried out by the taxpayer as a coal mine operator).

(4) (Repealed.)

(5) (Repealed.)

(6) (Repealed.)

1205. Earned Depletion Base

(1) For the purposes of this Part "earned depletion base" of a taxpayer as of a particular time means the amount by which 33¹/₃ per cent of the aggregate of

(*a*) all amounts, in respect of expenditures (other than expenditures to acquire property under circumstances that entitled the taxpayer to a deduction under section 1202 or would so entitle the taxpayer if the amounts referred to in paragraphs 1202(2)(*a*) and (*b*) were sufficient for the purpose) incurred by the taxpayer after November 7, 1969 and before the particular time, each of which was

(i) a Canadian exploration and development expense or would have been such an expense if it had been incurred after 1971 and was actually incurred before May 7, 1974, other than

(A) a cost of borrowing capital, including any cost incurred prior to the commencement of carrying on a business, that was a Canadian exploration expense or an exploration, prospecting and development expense, as the case may be, of the taxpayer,

(B) the cost to the taxpayer of any Canadian resource property acquired by the taxpayer,

(C) a Canadian exploration and development expense that was incurred after a mine had come into production in reasonable commercial quantities and may reasonably be considered to be related to the mine or to a potential or actual extension thereof,

(D) an expense that would have been described in clause (C) if it had been incurred after 1971,

(E) an expense renounced by the taxpayer under subsection 66(10) of the Act or subsection 29(7) of the *Income Tax Application Rules*,

(F) an amount that, by virtue of subparagraph 66(15)(*b*)(iv) [subsection 66(15) "Canadian exploration and development expenses"] of the Act, was a Canadian exploration and development expense or would have been such an expense if it had been incurred after 1971, if such amount was a cost or expense referred to in clause (A), (B), (C), (D) or (E) that was incurred by an association, partnership or syndicate referred to in that subparagraph, or

(G) an amount that, by virtue of subparagraph 66(15)(*b*)(v) [subsection 66(15) "Canadian exploration and development expenses"] of the Act, was a Canadian exploration and development expense or would have been such an expense if it had been incurred after 1971, if such amount was a cost or expense referred to in clause (A), (B), (C), (D) or (E) that the taxpayer incurred pursuant to an agreement referred to in that subparagraph,

(ii) the stated percentage of a Canadian exploration expense other than

(A) a cost of borrowing capital, including any cost incurred prior to the commencement of carrying on a business, that was a Canadian exploration expense of the taxpayer,

(B) an expense renounced by the taxpayer under subsection 66(10.1) of the Act,

(C) an amount that, by virtue of subparagraph 66.1(6)(*a*)(iv) [subsection 66.1(6) "Canadian exploration expense"] of the Act, was a Canadian exploration expense, if such amount was an expense referred to in clause (A), (B), (E), (F), (G) or (H) that was incurred by a partnership referred to in that subparagraph,

(D) an amount that, by virtue of subparagraph 66.1(6)(*a*)(v) [subsection 66.1(6) "Canadian exploration expense"] of the Act, was a Canadian exploration expense, if such amount was an expense referred to in clause (A), (B), (E), (F), (G), or (H) that the taxpayer incurred pursuant to an agreement referred to in that subparagraph,

(E) an amount described in clause 66.1(6)(*a*)(ii)(B) or (ii.1)(B) [subsection 66.1(6) "Canadian exploration expense"] of the Act,

Regulations

(F) an amount that was a Canadian exploration and development overhead expense of the taxpayer,

(G) an amount that was a Canadian oil and gas exploration expense of the taxpayer, or

(H) an expense described in subparagraph 66.1(6)(*a*)(iii) [subsection 66.1(6) "Canadian exploration expense"] of the Act incurred after April 19, 1983,

(iii) a Canadian development expense incurred before 1981 other than

(A) a cost of borrowing capital, including any cost incurred prior to the commencement of carrying on a business, that was a Canadian development expense of the taxpayer,

(B) an expense renounced by the taxpayer under subsection 66(10.2) of the Act,

(C) an amount referred to in subparagraph 66.2(5)(*a*)(iii) [subsection 66.2(5) "Canadian development expense"] of the Act,

(D) an amount that, by virtue of subparagraph 66.2(5)(*a*)(iv) [subsection 66.2(5) "Canadian development expense"] of the Act, was a Canadian development expense, if such amount was an expense referred to in clause (A), (B) or (C) that was incurred by a partnership referred to in that subparagraph, or

(E) an amount that, by virtue of subparagraph 66.2(5)(*a*)(v) [subsection 66.2(5) "Canadian development expense"] of the Act, was a Canadian development expense, if such amount was an expense referred to in clause (A), (B) or (C) that the taxpayer incurred pursuant to an agreement referred to in that subparagraph,

(iv) the stated percentage of the capital cost to the taxpayer of any processing property acquired by the taxpayer principally for the purpose of

(A) processing in Canada

(I) ore, other than iron ore or tar sands ore, from a qualified resource to any stage that is not beyond the prime metal stage or its equivalent,

(II) iron ore from a qualified resource to any stage that is not beyond the pellet stage or its equivalent, or

(III) tar sands ore from a qualified resource to any stage that is not beyond the crude oil stage or its equivalent, or

(B) processing in Canada

(I) ore, other than iron ore or tar sands ore, from an exporting resource beyond the furthest stage to which such ore or similar ore from that resource was ordinarily processed in Canada before such acquisition but not beyond the prime metal stage or its equivalent,

(II) iron ore from an exporting resource beyond the furthest stage to which such ore or similar ore from that resource was ordinarily processed in Canada before such acquisition but not beyond the pellet stage or its equivalent, or

(III) tar sands ore from an exporting resource beyond the furthest stage to which such ore or similar ore from that resource was ordinarily processed in Canada before such acquisition but not beyond the crude oil stage or its equivalent,

(v) where the taxpayer is a corporation that incurred a Canadian oil and gas exploration expense in respect of conventional lands in a calendar year after 1980 and before 1984, the specified percentage for that year of such expense to the extent that it is not an amount or expense referred to in clause (ii)(A), (B) or (F) or an expense that would be referred to in clause (ii)(C) or (D) if the references in those clauses to "clause (A), (B), (E), (F), (G) or (H)" were read as "clause (A), (B) or (F)", or

(vi) where the taxpayer is a corporation,

(A) the specified percentage in respect of a Canadian oil and gas exploration expense in respect of non-conventional lands incurred in a calendar year after 1980 and before 1985 to the extent that it is not an amount or expense referred to in clause (ii)(A), (B) or (F) or an expense that would be referred to in clause (ii)(C) or (D) if the references in those clauses to "clause (A), (B), (E), (F), (G) or (H)" were read as "clause (A), (B) or (F)",

(B) the stated percentage of a Canadian development expense incurred after 1980 in respect of a qualified tertiary oil recovery project of the taxpayer to the extent that such expense is not

(I) an amount or expense described in any of clauses (iii)(A) to (E),

(II) an amount that was a Canadian exploration and development overhead expense of the taxpayer, or

(III) an eligible expense within the meaning of the *Canadian Exploration and Development Incentive Program Act* in respect of which the taxpayer, a partnership of which the taxpayer was a member, a principal-business corporation of which the taxpayer was a shareholder or a joint exploration corporation of which the taxpayer was a shareholder corporation has received, is entitled to receive or may reasonably be expected to receive at any time an incentive under that Act,

Regulations

(B.1) the stated percentage of a Canadian exploration expense incurred after 1981 in respect of a qualified tertiary oil recovery project of the taxpayer that

(I) would be referred to in subparagraph 66.1(6)(*a*)(ii) or (ii.1) [subsection 66.1(6) "Canadian exploration expense"] of the Act if subparagraph 66.1(6)(*a*)(ii) were read without reference to clause (B) [subsection 66.1(6) "Canadian exploration expense"] thereof, or

(II) would be referred to in subparagraph 66.1(6)(*a*)(iv) or (v) [subsection 66.1(6) "Canadian exploration expense"] of the Act if the Act were read without reference to clause 66.1(6)(*a*)(ii)(B) [subsection 66.1(6) "Canadian exploration expense"] and subparagraphs 66.1(6)(*a*)(i) [subsection 66.1(6) "Canadian exploration expense"], (i.1) [subsection 66.1(6) "Canadian exploration expense"], (ii.2) [subsection 66.1(6) "Canadian exploration expense"], (iii) [subsection 66.1(6) "Canadian exploration expense"] and (iii.1) [subsection 66.1(6) "Canadian exploration expense"],

other than the portion of such expense referred to in subclause (I) or (II) that is

(III) described in any of clauses (ii)(A) to (D) and (F),

(IV) included in the amount determined under subparagraph (v) or clause (vi)(A),

(V) described in subclause (B)(III), or

(VI) an eligible expense within the meaning of the *Canadian Exploration Incentive Program Act* in respect of which the taxpayer, a partnership of which the taxpayer was a member or a principal-business corporation of which the taxpayer was a shareholder corporation, has received, is entitled to receive or may reasonably be expected to receive at any time an incentive under that Act,

(C) the stated percentage of the capital cost to it of property that is tertiary recovery equipment, and

(D) the stated percentage of the capital cost to it of property that is, or but for Class 41 of Schedule II would be, included in Class 10 in Schedule II by virtue of paragraph (*u*) of the description of that Class, other than the capital cost to it of property that had, before the property was acquired by it, been used for any purpose whatever by any person with whom it was not dealing at arm's length,

(*b*) all amounts, in respect of expenditures (other than expenditures referred to in paragraph (*a*) or expenditures to acquire property under circumstances that entitled the taxpayer to a deduction under section 1202 or would so entitle the taxpayer if the amounts referred to in paragraphs 1202(2)(*a*) and (*b*) were sufficient for the purpose) incurred by the taxpayer after May 8, 1972 and before the particular time, each of which was the stated percentage of the capital cost to the taxpayer of property that is or, but for Class 41, would be included in Class 10 in Schedule II because of paragraph (*k*) of the description of that Class and that was acquired for the purpose of processing in Canada

(i) ore (other than iron ore or tar sands ore), after its extraction from a mineral resource, to any stage that is not beyond the prime metal stage or its equivalent,

(ii) iron ore, after its extraction from a mineral resource, to any stage that is not beyond the pellet stage or its equivalent, or

(iii) tar sands ore, after its extraction from a mineral resource, to any stage that is not beyond the crude oil stage or its equivalent,

other than the capital cost to him of property that had, before the property was acquired by the taxpayer, been used for any purpose whatever by any person with whom the taxpayer was not dealing at arm's length,

(*c*) all amounts, in respect of expenditures (other than expenditures referred to in paragraph (*a*) or (*b*) or expenditures to acquire property under circumstances that entitled the taxpayer to a deduction under section 1202 or would so entitle the taxpayer if the amounts referred to in paragraphs 1202(2)(*a*) and (*b*) were sufficient for the purpose) incurred by the taxpayer before the particular time, each of which was the stated percentage of the capital cost to the taxpayer of property (other than property that had, before it was acquired by the taxpayer, been used for any purpose whatever by any person with whom the taxpayer was not dealing at arm's length) that is included in Class 28 or paragraph (*a*) of Class 41, in Schedule II, other than property so included

(i) by virtue of the first reference in Class 28 to paragraph (*l*) of Class 10 in Schedule II, where the property was acquired by the taxpayer before November 17, 1978,

(ii) by virtue of the reference in Class 28 to paragraph (*m*) of Class 10 in Schedule II,

(iii) that is bituminous sands equipment acquired by an individual, or

(iv) that is bituminous sands equipment acquired by a corporation before 1981,

(*d*) all expenditures (other than expenditures referred to in paragraph (*a*), (*b*) or (*c*)) each of which was incurred by him before November 8, 1969 relating to a mine that came into production in reasonable

Regulations

commercial quantities before that date and that were incurred for the purpose of

(i) exploration in respect of, or

(ii) development of the mine for the purpose of gaining or producing income from the extraction of material from,

a bituminous sands deposit, an oil sands deposit or an oil shale deposit,

(*d*.1) three times the total of all amounts each of which is an amount equal to the lesser of

(i) the amount that would be determined under subsection 1210(1) in computing the taxpayer's income for a taxation year that ends before the particular time, if the amount determined for C under that subsection were nil, and

(ii) the amount determined for C under subsection 1210(1) in respect of the taxpayer for that year, and

(*d*.2) three times the aggregate of all amounts each of which is the specified amount determined under subsection 1202(4) in respect of the taxpayer for a taxation year ending after February 17, 1987 and before the particular time,

exceeds the aggregate of

(*e*) all amounts deducted by the taxpayer under section 1201 in computing his income for all taxation years ending after May 6, 1974 and before the particular time;

(*f*) 33¹/₃ per cent of the aggregate of all amounts, each of which is the stated percentage of a cost of borrowing capital, including any cost incurred prior to the commencement of carrying on a business, that was

(i) included in the capital cost to him of depreciable property described in subparagraph (*a*)(iv), clause (*a*)(vi)(C) or (D) or paragraph (*b*) or (*c*), or

(ii) an expenditure described in paragraph (*d*);

(*g*) 33¹/₃ per cent of the aggregate of all amounts, each of which is an amount

(i) that became receivable by the taxpayer after April 28, 1978 and before the earlier of December 12, 1979 and the particular time, and

(ii) in respect of which the consideration given by the taxpayer therefor was a property (other than a share, or a property that would have been a Canadian resource property if it had been acquired by the taxpayer at the time the consideration was given) or services, the cost of which may reasonably be regarded as having been primarily an expenditure that was added in computing

(A) the taxpayer's earned depletion base by reason of subparagraph (*a*)(i), (ii) or (iii) or paragraph (*d*), or

(B) the earned depletion base of an original owner of a property by reason of subparagraph (*a*)(i), (ii) or (iii) or paragraph (*d*) as it applied to the original owner, where the taxpayer acquired the property in circumstances in which subsection 1202(2) applies,

(*h*) 33¹/₃ per cent of the aggregate of all amounts, each of which is

(i) an amount in respect of a disposition of property (other than a disposition of property that had been used by the taxpayer to any person with whom the taxpayer was not dealing at arm's length) of the taxpayer after April 28, 1978 and before the earlier of December 12, 1979 and the particular time, the capital cost of which was added in computing

(A) the taxpayer's earned depletion base by reason of subparagraph (*a*)(iv) or paragraph (*b*) or (*c*), or

(B) the earned depletion base of an original owner of a property by reason of subparagraph (*a*)(iv) or paragraph (*b*) or (*c*) as it applied to the original owner, where the taxpayer acquired the property in circumstances in which subsection 1202(2) applies, and

(ii) equal to the lesser of

(A) the proceeds of disposition of the property, and

(B) the capital cost of the property to the taxpayer, where clause (i)(A) applies, or the original owner, where clause (i)(B) applies, computed as if no amount had been included therein that is a cost of borrowing capital, including any cost incurred prior to the commencement of carrying on a business,

(*i*) any amount required by paragraph 1202(2)(*b*) (as it read in its application to taxation years ending before February 18, 1987) or paragraph 1202(3)(*a*) to be deducted at or before the particular time in computing the taxpayer's earned depletion base,

(*j*) 33¹/₃ per cent of the aggregate of all amounts, each of which is in respect of an amount of assistance or benefit in respect of Canadian exploration expenses or Canadian development expenses or that may reasonably be related to Canadian exploration activities or Canadian development activities, whether such amount is by way of a grant, subsidy, rebate, forgivable loan, deduction from royalty or tax, rebate of royalty or tax, investment allowance or any other form of assistance or benefit that

(i) the taxpayer before the particular time has received or was entitled to receive, or that the taxpayer at or after the particular time becomes entitled to receive, or

Regulations

(ii) an original owner or predecessor owner of a property before the particular time has received or was entitled to receive, or at or after the particular time becomes entitled to receive, where the original owner or the predecessor owner received, became entitled to receive or becomes entitled to receive that amount

(A) at or after the time at which the property was acquired by the taxpayer in circumstances in which subsection 1202(2) applies, and

(B) before the time at which the taxpayer becomes a predecessor owner of the property,

and that is equal to

(iii) where the assistance or benefit was in respect of an amount added by reason of subparagraph (*a*)(ii) or clause (*a*)(vi)(B) or (B.1) in computing

(A) the earned depletion base of the taxpayer (other than such portion thereof included in determining an amount described in paragraph 1202(2)(*a*) before the particular time), or

(B) the portion of the earned depletion base of the original owner included in determining an amount described in paragraph 1202(2)(*a*) before the particular time,

the stated percentage of the amount of the assistance or benefit, and

(iv) where the assistance or benefit was in respect of an amount of Canadian oil and gas exploration expense added by reason of subparagraph (*a*)(v) or clause (*a*)(vi)(A) in computing

(A) the earned depletion base of the taxpayer (other than such portion thereof included in determining an amount described in paragraph 1202(2)(*a*) before the particular time), or

(B) the portion of the earned depletion base of the original owner included in determining an amount described in paragraph 1202(2)(*a*) before the particular time,

the amount equal to the product obtained when the amount of the assistance or benefit is multiplied by the specified percentage in respect of the expense for the calendar year in which the taxpayer or the original owner, as the case may be, incurred the expense, and

(*k*) the amount, if any, by which

(i) the aggregate of all amounts that would be determined under paragraphs 1212(3)(*d*) to (*i*)

exceeds

(ii) the aggregate of all amounts that would be determined under paragraphs 1212(3)(*a*) to (*c*)

in computing his supplementary depletion base at the particular time.

(2) Where an expense is incurred before the particular time referred to in subsection (1) and a person at or after the particular time becomes entitled to receive an amount of assistance or benefit in respect of the expense, the amount of such assistance or benefit shall be included in "the amount of the assistance or benefit" referred to in subparagraphs (1)(*j*)(iii) and (iv) as of the particular time.

1206. Interpretation

(1) In this Part,

"bituminous sands equipment" —"bituminous sands equipment" means property of a taxpayer that

(*a*) is included in Class 28 or in paragraph (*a*) of Class 41 in Schedule II, other than property so included

(i) by virtue of the first reference in Class 28 to paragraph (*l*) of Class 10 in Schedule II, where the property was acquired by the taxpayer before November 17, 1978, or

(ii) by virtue of the reference in Class 28 to paragraph (*m*) of Class 10 in Schedule II, and

(*b*) was acquired by the taxpayer after April 10, 1978 principally for the purpose of gaining or producing income from one or more mines, each of which is a location in a bituminous sands deposit, oil sands deposit or oil shale deposit from which material is extracted;

"Canadian exploration and development overhead expense" —"Canadian exploration and development overhead expense" of a taxpayer means a Canadian exploration expense or a Canadian development expense of the taxpayer made or incurred after 1980 that is not a Canadian renewable and conservation expense (in this definition having the meaning assigned by subsection 66.1(6) of the Act) nor a taxpayer's share of a Canadian renewable and conservation expense incurred by a partnership and

(*a*) that was in respect of the administration, management or financing of the taxpayer,

(*b*) that was in respect of the salary, wages or other remuneration or related benefits paid in respect of a person employed by the taxpayer whose duties were not all or substantially all directed towards exploration or development activities,

(*c*) that was in respect of the upkeep or maintenance of, taxes or insurance in respect of, or rental or leasing of, property other than property all or substantially all of the use of which by the taxpayer was for the purposes of exploration or development activities, or

(*d*) that may reasonably be regarded as having been in respect of

(i) the use of or the right to use any property in which any person who was connected with the taxpayer had an interest,

(ii) compensation for the performance of a service for the benefit of the taxpayer by any person who was connected with the taxpayer, or

(iii) the acquisition of any materials, parts or supplies from any person who was connected with the taxpayer

to the extent that the expense exceeds the least of amounts, each of which was the aggregate of the costs incurred by a person who was connected with the taxpayer

(iv) in respect of the property,

(v) in respect of the performance of the service, or

(vi) in respect of the materials, parts or supplies;

"Canadian oil and gas exploration expense"—"Canadian oil and gas exploration expense", of a taxpayer, means an outlay or expense that is made or incurred after 1980 and that would be a Canadian exploration expense, as defined in subsection 66.1(6) of the Act, of the taxpayer (other than an outlay or expense in respect of a qualified tertiary oil recovery project that is a Canadian exploration expense of the taxpayer because of subparagraph (*c*)(ii) or (*d*)(ii) of that definition) if

(*a*) that definition were read without reference to its paragraphs (*f*) to (*g*.4),

(*b*) the reference in paragraph (*h*) of that definition to "any of paragraphs (*a*) to (*d*) and (*f*) to (*g*.4)" were read as "any of paragraphs (*a*) to (*e*)", and

(*c*) the reference in paragraph (*i*) of that definition to "any of paragraphs (*a*) to (*g*)" were read as "any of paragraphs (*a*) to (*e*)";

History: S. 1206(1), the definition "Canadian oil and gas exploration expense" was replaced by SOR/2016-276, dated October 21, 2016, deemed to have come into force on November 7, 1994, except that paragraphs (*a*) and (*b*) of the definition "Canadian oil and gas exploration expense" in subsection 1206(1) of the Regulations are

(a) before December 6, 1996, to be read as follows:

(*a*) that definition were read without reference to its paragraphs (*f*) and (*g*),

(*b*) the reference in paragraph (*h*) of that definition to "any of paragraphs (*a*), (*b*), (*c*), (*d*), (*f*) and (*g*)" were read as "any of paragraphs (*a*) to (*e*)", and

(b) after December 5, 1996 and before March 21, 2011, to be read as follows:

(*a*) that definition were read without reference to its paragraphs (*f*) to (*g*.1),

(*b*) the reference in paragraph (*h*) of that definition to "any of paragraphs (*a*) to (*d*) and (*f*) to (*g*.1)" were read as "any of paragraphs (*a*) to (*e*)", and

(c) after March 20, 2011 and before March 20, 2013, to be read as follows:

(*a*) that definition were read without reference to its paragraphs (*f*) to (*g*.2),

(*b*) the reference in paragraph (*h*) of that definition to "any of paragraphs (*a*) to (*d*) and (*f*) to (*g*.2)" were read as "any of paragraphs (*a*) to (*e*)", and

S. 1206(1), the definition "Canadian oil and gas exploration expense" formerly read:

"Canadian oil and gas exploration expense"—"Canadian oil and gas exploration expense" of a taxpayer means an outlay or expense made or incurred after 1980 that would be a Canadian exploration expense of the taxpayer within the meaning assigned by paragraph 66.1(6)(*a*) of the Act if that paragraph were read without reference to subparagraphs (iii) and (iii.1) thereof and if the reference in subparagraphs (iv) and (v) thereof to "any of subparagraphs (i) to (iii.1)" were read as a reference to "any of subparagraphs (i) to (ii.2)", other than an outlay or expense that was a Canadian exploration expense by virtue of clause 66.1(6)(*a*)(ii)(B) or (ii.1)(B) of the Act that was in respect of a qualified tertiary oil recovery project;

"coal mine operator"—"coal mine operator" means a person who undertakes all or substantially all of the activities involved in the production of coal from a resource;

"conventional lands"—"conventional lands" means lands situated in Canada other than non-conventional lands;

"disposition of property"—"disposition of property" has the meaning assigned by paragraph 13(21)(*c*) [subsection 248(1) "disposition"] of the Act;

"enhanced recovery equipment"—"enhanced recovery equipment" means property of a taxpayer that

(*a*) is included in Class 10 in Schedule II by virtue of paragraph (*j*) of the description of that Class, and

(*b*) was acquired by the taxpayer after April 10, 1978 and before 1981 for use in the production of oil, from a reservoir or a deposit of bituminous sand, oil sand or oil shale in Canada operated by the taxpayer, that is incremental to oil that would be recovered using primary recovery techniques alone,

other than property

(*c*) used by the taxpayer as part of a primary recovery process prior to the use described in paragraph (*b*),

(*d*) that had, before it was acquired by the taxpayer, been used for any purpose whatever by any person with whom the taxpayer was not dealing at arm's length, or

(*e*) that has been used by any person before April 11, 1978 in the production of oil, from a reservoir in Canada, that is incremental to oil that would be recovered using primary recovery techniques alone;

"exempt partnership"—"exempt partnership"(Repealed.)

"exporting resource"—"exporting resource" means, in relation to a particular processing property of a taxpayer, a resource the ore or any portion thereof produced from which during the year immediately preceding the day on which the property was acquired by the taxpayer was ordinarily processed outside Canada to any stage that is not beyond the prime metal stage or its equivalent;

"mine"—"mine" means any location where material is extracted from a resource but does not include a well for the extraction of material from a deposit of bituminous sand, oil sand or oil shale;

"non-conventional lands"—"non-conventional lands" means lands that belong to Her Majesty in right of Canada, or in respect of which Her Majesty in right of Canada has the right to dispose of or exploit the natural resources, situated in

(*a*) the Yukon Territory, the Northwest Territories, or Sable Island or (*b*) those submarine areas, not within a province, adjacent to the coast of Canada and extending throughout the natural prolongation of the land territory of Canada to the outer edge of the continental margin or to a distance of two hundred nautical miles from the baselines from which the breadth of the territorial sea of Canada is measured, whichever is the greater;

"ore" —"ore" includes ore from a mineral resource that has been processed to any stage that is prior to the prime metal stage or its equivalent;

"original owner" —"original owner" of a property means a person

(*a*) who owned the property and disposed of it to a corporation that acquired it in circumstances in which subsection 1202(2) applies, or would apply if the corporation had continued to own the property, to the corporation in respect of the property, and

(*b*) who would, but for paragraph 1202(2)(*b*) (as it read in its application to taxation years ending before February 18, 1987) or paragraph 1202(3)(*a*), as the case may be, be entitled in computing the person's income for a taxation year ending after the person disposed of the property to a deduction under section 1201 in respect of expenditures that were incurred by the person before the person disposed of the property;

"predecessor owner" —"predecessor owner" of a property means a corporation

(*a*) that acquired the property in circumstances in which subsection 1202(2) applies, or would apply if the corporation had continued to own the property, to the corporation in respect of the property,

(*b*) that disposed of the property to another corporation that acquired it in circumstances in which subsection 1202(2) applies, or would apply if the other corporation had continued to own the property, to the other corporation in respect of the property, and

(*c*) that would, but for subsection 1202(10), be entitled in computing its income for a taxation year after it disposed of the property to a deduction under subsection 1202(2) in respect of expenditures incurred by an original owner of the property;

"primary recovery" —"primary recovery" means the recovery of oil from a reservoir as a result of utilizing the natural energy of the reservoir to move the oil toward a producing well;

"proceeds of disposition" —"proceeds of disposition" of property has the meaning assigned by paragraph 13(21)(*d*) [subsection 13(21) "proceeds of disposition"] of the Act;

"processing property" —"processing property" means property

(*a*) that is included in Class 10 in Schedule II because of paragraph (*g*) of the description of that Class or would be so included if that paragraph were read without reference to subparagraph (ii) of that paragraph and Schedule II were read without reference to Class 41, or

(*b*) that is included in Class 10 in Schedule II because of paragraph (*k*) of the description of that Class or would be so included if that paragraph were read without reference to the words following subparagraph (ii) of that paragraph and Schedule II were read without reference to Class 41,

other than property that had, before it was acquired by a taxpayer, been used for any purpose whatever by any person with whom the taxpayer was not dealing at arm's length;

"production royalty" —"production royalty"(Repealed.)

"qualified resource" —"qualified resource" means, in relation to a particular processing property of a taxpayer, a resource that, within a reasonable time after the property was acquired by him,

(*a*) came into production in reasonable commercial quantities, or

(*b*) was the subject of a major expansion whereby the greatest designed capacity, measured in weight of input of ore, of the mill that processed ore from the resource was not less than 25% greater in the year immediately following the expansion than it was in the year immediately preceding the expansion;

"qualified tertiary oil recovery project" —"qualified tertiary oil recovery project" in respect of an expense incurred in a taxation year means a project that uses a method (including a method that uses carbon dioxide miscible, hydrocarbon miscible, thermal or chemical processes but not including a secondary recovery method) that is designed to recover oil from an oil well in Canada that is incremental to oil that would be recovered therefrom by primary recovery and a secondary recovery method, if

(*a*) a specified royalty provision applies in the year or in the immediately following taxation year in respect of the production, if any, or any portion thereof from the project or in respect of the ownership of property to which such production relates,

(*b*) the project is on a reserve within the meaning of the *Indian Act*, or

(*c*) the project is located in the Province of Ontario;

"resource" —"resource" means any mineral resource in Canada;

"resource activity" —"resource activity" of a taxpayer means

(*a*) the production by the taxpayer of petroleum, natural gas or related hydrocarbons or sulphur from

Regulations

(i) an oil or gas well in Canada, or

(ii) a natural accumulation (other than a mineral resource) of petroleum or natural gas in Canada,

(*b*) the production and processing in Canada by the taxpayer or the processing in Canada by the taxpayer of

(i) ore (other than iron ore or tar sands ore) from a mineral resource in Canada to any stage that is not beyond the prime metal stage or its equivalent,

(ii) iron ore from a mineral resource in Canada to any stage that is not beyond the pellet stage or its equivalent, and

(iii) tar sands ore from a mineral resource in Canada to any stage that is not beyond the crude oil stage or its equivalent,

(*c*) the processing in Canada by the taxpayer of heavy crude oil recovered from an oil or gas well in Canada to any stage that is not beyond the crude oil stage or its equivalent,

(*c*.1) Canadian field processing carried on by the taxpayer,

(*d*) the processing in Canada by the taxpayer of

(i) ore (other than iron ore or tar sands ore) from a mineral resource outside Canada to any stage that is not beyond the prime metal stage or its equivalent,

(ii) iron ore from a mineral resource outside Canada to any stage that is not beyond the pellet stage or its equivalent, and

(iii) tar sands ore from a mineral resource outside Canada to any stage that is not beyond the crude oil stage or its equivalent, or

(*e*) the ownership by the taxpayer of a right to a rental or royalty computed by reference to the amount or value of production from a natural accumulation of petroleum or natural gas in Canada, an oil or gas well in Canada or a mineral resource in Canada,

and, for the purposes of this definition,

(*f*) the production of a substance by a taxpayer includes exploration and development activities of the taxpayer with respect to the substance, whether or not extraction of the substance has begun or will ever begin,

(*g*) the production or the processing, or the production and processing, of a substance by a taxpayer includes activities performed by the taxpayer that are ancillary to, or in support of, the production or the processing, or the production and processing, of that substance by the taxpayer,

(*h*) the production or processing of a substance by a taxpayer includes an activity (including the ownership of property) that is undertaken before the extraction of the substance and that is undertaken for the purpose of extracting or processing the substance,

(*i*) the production or the processing, or the production and processing, of a substance by a taxpayer includes activities that the taxpayer undertakes as a consequence of the production or the processing or the production and processing, of that substance, whether or not the production, the processing or the production and processing of the substance has ceased, and

(*j*) notwithstanding paragraphs (*a*) to (*i*), the production, the processing or the production and processing of a substance does not include any activity of a taxpayer that is part of a source described in paragraph 1204(1)(*b*), where

(i) the activity

(A) is the transporting, transmitting or processing (other than processing described in subparagraph (*b*)(iii), paragraph (*c*) or (*c*.1) or subparagraph (*d*)(iii)) of petroleum, natural gas or related hydrocarbons or of sulphur, or

(B) can reasonably be attributed to a service rendered by the taxpayer, and

(ii) revenues derived from the activity are not taken into account in computing the taxpayer's gross resource profits;

"secondary recovery method" —"secondary recovery method" means a method to recover from a reservoir oil that is incremental to oil that would be recovered therefrom by primary recovery, by supplying energy to supplement or replace the natural energy of the reservoir through the use of technically proven methods, including waterflooding;

"specified development well"

"specified percentage" —"specified percentage" for a calendar year

(*a*) in respect of a Canadian oil and gas exploration expense of a taxpayer for that year incurred in respect of conventional lands means,

(i) for the 1981 calendar year, 100 per cent,

(ii) for the 1982 calendar year, 60 per cent, and

(iii) for the 1983 calendar year, 30 per cent, and

(*b*) in respect of a Canadian oil and gas exploration expense of a taxpayer for that year incurred in respect of non-conventional lands means,

(i) for the 1981 and 1982 calendar years, 100 per cent,

(ii) for the 1983 calendar year, 60 per cent, and

(iii) for the 1984 calendar year, 30 per cent;

"specified property" —"specified property" of a person means all or substantially all of the property used by the person in carrying on in Canada such of the businesses described in subparagraphs 66(15)(*h*)(i) to (vii) [subsection 66(15) "principal-business corporation"] of the Act as were carried on by the person;

"specified royalty" —"specified royalty"(Repealed.)

"stated percentage" —"stated percentage" means

(*a*) where the taxpayer is an individual other than a trust, in respect of subparagraph 1203(2)(*a*)(i),

(i) 100 per cent in respect of an expenditure incurred before 1989,

(ii) 50 per cent in respect of an expenditure incurred after 1988 and before 1990, and

(iii) 0 per cent in respect of an expenditure incurred after 1989,

(*b*) in respect of subparagraph 1203(2)(a)(i) (where paragraph (*a*) is not applicable) and paragraphs 1205(1)(*a*), (*b*), (*c*) and (*f*)

(i) 100 per cent in respect of an expenditure incurred or a cost incurred in borrowing capital before July 1, 1988,

(ii) 50 per cent in respect of an expenditure incurred or a cost incurred in borrowing capital after June 30, 1988 and before 1990, and

(iii) 0 per cent in respect of an expenditure incurred or a cost incurred in borrowing capital after 1989,

(*c*) where the taxpayer is an individual other than a trust, in respect of subparagraph 1203(2)(*a*)(ii) and subsection 1203(4),

(i) 100 per cent in respect of any assistance that relates to expenditures incurred before 1989,

(ii) 50 per cent in respect of any assistance that relates to expenditures incurred after 1988 and before 1990, and

(iii) 0 per cent in respect of any assistance that relates to expenditures incurred after 1989, and

(*d*) in respect of subparagraph 1203(2)(*a*)(ii) (if paragraph (*c*) is not applicable), subsection 1203(4) (if paragraph (*c*) is not applicable) and subparagraph 1205(1)(*j*)(iii),

(i) 100 per cent in respect of any assistance or benefit that relates to expenditures incurred before July 1, 1988,

(ii) 50 per cent in respect of any assistance or benefit that relates to expenditures incurred after June 30, 1988 and before 1990, and

(iii) 0 per cent in respect of any assistance or benefit that relates to expenditures incurred after 1989;

"tar sands ore" —"tar sands ore" means ore extracted, other than through a well, from a mineral resource that is a deposit of bituminous sand, oil sand or oil shale;

"tertiary recovery equipment" —"tertiary recovery equipment" means property of a taxpayer that

(*a*) is, or but for Class 41 in Schedule II would be, included in Class 10 in Schedule II by virtue of paragraph (*j*) of the description of that Class,

(*b*) was acquired by the taxpayer after 1980 for use in a qualified tertiary oil recovery project,

other than property

(*c*) used by the taxpayer for another use prior to the use described in paragraph (*b*), or

(*d*) that had, before it was acquired by the taxpayer, been used for any purpose whatever by any person with whom the taxpayer was not dealing at arm's length.

(2) In this Part, "joint exploration corporation", "principal-business corporation", "production from a Canadian resource property", "reserve amount" and "shareholder corporation" have the meanings assigned by subsection 66(15) of the Act.

(3) For the purposes of sections 1201 to 1209 and 1212, where at the end of a fiscal period of a partnership, a taxpayer was a member thereof

(*a*) the resource profits of the partnership for the fiscal period, to the extent of the taxpayer's share thereof, shall be included in computing his resource profits for his taxation year in which the fiscal period ended;

(*b*) any property acquired or disposed of by the partnership shall be deemed to have been acquired or disposed of by the taxpayer to the extent of his share thereof;

(*c*) any property deemed by paragraph (*b*) to have been acquired or disposed of by the taxpayer shall be deemed to have been acquired or disposed of by him on the day the property was acquired or disposed of by the partnership;

(*d*) any amount that has become receivable by the partnership and in respect of which the consideration given by the partnership therefor was property (other than property referred to in paragraph 59(2)(*a*), (*c*) or (*d*) of the Act or a share or interest therein or right thereto) or services, all or part of the original cost of which to the partnership may reasonably be regarded primarily as an exploration or development expense of the taxpayer, shall be deemed to be an amount receivable by the taxpayer to the extent of his share thereof, and the consideration so given by the partnership shall, to the extent of the taxpayer's share thereof, be deemed to have been given by the taxpayer for the amount deemed to be receivable by him;

(*e*) any expenditure incurred or deemed to have been incurred by the partnership shall be deemed to have

Regulations

been incurred by the taxpayer to the extent of the taxpayer's share thereof; and

(*f*) any amount or expenditure deemed by paragraph (*d*) or (*e*) to have been receivable or incurred, as the case may be, by the taxpayer shall be deemed to have become receivable or been incurred, as the case may be, by the taxpayer on the day the amount became receivable or the expenditure was incurred or deemed to have been incurred by the partnership.

(3.1) For the purposes of sections 1201 to 1203, 1205, 1217 and 1218, where a taxpayer was a member of a partnership at the end of a fiscal period of the partnership, the taxpayer shall be deemed to receive or to become entitled to receive any amount of assistance or benefit, whether such amount is by way of a grant, subsidy, rebate, forgivable loan, deduction from royalty or tax, rebate of royalty or tax, investment allowance or any other form of assistance or benefit, that the partnership at any time receives or becomes entitled to receive in respect of expenses incurred in that fiscal period of the partnership, to the extent of,

(*a*) where the partnership in the fiscal period receives or becomes entitled to receive the amount, the taxpayer's share thereof, or

(*b*) where the partnership after the fiscal period becomes entitled to receive the amount, what would have been the taxpayer's share thereof if the partnership had in the fiscal period received or become entitled to receive the amount,

and the time at which the taxpayer is deemed to receive or become entitled to receive such share of the amount shall be the time that the partnership receives or becomes entitled to receive the amount.

(4) Where an expense incurred after November 7, 1969 that was a Canadian exploration and development expense or that would have been such an expense if it had been incurred after 1971 (other than an amount included therein that is in respect of financing or the cost of any Canadian resource property acquired by a joint exploration corporation or any property acquired by a joint exploration corporation that would have been a Canadian resource property if it had been acquired after 1971), a Canadian exploration expense (other than an amount included therein that is in respect of financing) or a Canadian development expense (other than an amount included therein that is in respect of financing or an amount referred to in subparagraph 66.2(5)(*a*)(iii) [subsection 66.2(5) "Canadian development expense"] of the Act) has been renounced in favour of a taxpayer and was deemed to be an expense of the taxpayer for the purposes of subsection 66(10), (10.1) or (10.2) of the Act or subsection 29(7) of the *Income Tax Application Rules*, the expense shall

(*a*) for the purposes of sections 1203 and 1205, be deemed to have been such an expense incurred by the taxpayer at the time the expense was incurred by the joint exploration corporation; and

(*b*) for the purposes of sections 1204 and 1210 and paragraphs 1217(2)(*e*) and 1218(2)(*e*), be deemed to have been such an expense incurred by the taxpayer at the time it was deemed to have been incurred by the taxpayer for the purposes of subsection 66(10), (10.1) or (10.2) of the Act or subsection 29(7) of the *Income Tax Application Rules*, as the case may be.

(4.1) An expense that is a Canadian exploration and development overhead expense of the joint exploration corporation referred to in subsection (4), or would be such an expense if the references to "connected with the taxpayer" in paragraph (*d*) of the definition "Canadian exploration and development overhead expense" in subsection (1) were read as "connected with the shareholder corporation in favour of whom the expense was renounced for the purposes of subsection 66(10.1) or (10.2) of the Act", that may reasonably be considered to be included in a Canadian exploration expense or Canadian development expense that is deemed by subsection (4) to be a Canadian exploration expense or Canadian development expense of the shareholder corporation, shall be deemed to be a Canadian exploration and development overhead expense of the shareholder corporation incurred by it at the time the expense was deemed by subsection (4) to have been incurred by it and shall be deemed at and after that time not to be a Canadian exploration and development overhead expense incurred by the joint exploration corporation.

(4.2) For the purposes of paragraphs 66(12.6)(*b*), (12.601)(*d*) and (12.62)(*b*) of the Act, a prescribed Canadian exploration and development overhead expense of a corporation is

(*a*) a Canadian exploration and development overhead expense of the corporation;

(*b*) an expense that would be a Canadian exploration and development overhead expense of the corporation if the references to "connected with the taxpayer" in paragraph (*d*) of the definition "Canadian exploration and development overhead expense" in subsection (1) were read as "connected with the person to whom the expense is renounced under subsection 66(12.6), (12.601) or (12.62) of the Act"; and

(*c*) an expense that would be a Canadian exploration and development overhead expense of the corporation if the references to "person who was connected with the taxpayer" in paragraph (*d*) of the definition "Canadian exploration and development overhead expense" in subsection (1) were read as "person to whom the expense is renounced under subsection 66(12.6), (12.601) or (12.62) of the Act".

(4.3) For the purposes of subsections (4.2) and (5), a partnership shall be deemed to be a person and its taxation year shall be deemed to be its fiscal period.

Regulations

(5) For the purposes of subsection (6) and the definition "Canadian exploration and development overhead expense" in subsection (1),

(*a*) a person and a particular corporation are connected with each other if

(i) the person and the particular corporation are not dealing at arm's length,

(ii) the person has an equity percentage in the particular corporation that is not less than 10 per cent, or

(iii) the person is a corporation in which another person has an equity percentage that is not less than 10 per cent and the other person has an equity percentage in the particular corporation that is not less than 10 per cent;

(*a*.1) a person and another person that is not a corporation are connected with each other if they are not dealing at arm's length; and

(*b*) "costs incurred by a person" shall not include

(i) an outlay or expense described in any of paragraphs (*a*) to (*c*) of that definition made or incurred by the person if the references in those paragraphs to "taxpayer" were read as references to "person",

(ii) an outlay or expense made or incurred by the person to the extent that it is not reasonably attributable to the use of a property by, the performance of a service for, or any materials, parts, or supplies acquired by, the taxpayer referred to in that definition, and

(iii) an amount in respect of the capital cost to the person of a property, other than, where the property is a depreciable property of the person, that proportion of the capital allowance of the person for his taxation year in respect of the property that may reasonably be considered attributable to the use of the property by, or in the performance of a service for, the taxpayer referred to in that definition.

(6) For the purpose of subparagraph (5)(*b*)(iii), the "capital allowance" of a person (in this subsection referred to as the "owner") for his taxation year in respect of a property owned by him means that proportion of an amount not exceeding 20 per cent of the amount that is

(*a*) in the case of a property owned by the owner on December 31, 1980, the lesser of

(i) the capital cost of the property to the owner computed as if no amount had been included therein that is a cost of borrowing capital, including any cost incurred prior to the commencement of carrying on a business, and

(ii) the fair market value of the property on December 31, 1980,

(*b*) in the case of a property acquired by the owner after December 31, 1980 that was previously owned by a person connected with the owner, the lesser of

(i) the capital cost of the property, computed as if no amount had been included therein that is a cost of borrowing capital, including any cost incurred prior to the commencement of carrying on a business, to the person, who was connected with the owner, who was the first person to acquire the property from a person with whom the owner was not connected, and

(ii) the fair market value of the property at the time it was acquired by the owner, and

(*c*) in any other case, the capital cost of the property to the owner computed as if no amount had been included therein that is a cost of borrowing capital, including any cost incurred prior to the commencement of carrying on a business,

that the number of days in the taxation year during which the property was owned by the owner is of 365.

(7) For the purposes of paragraph (5)(*a*), "equity percentage" has the meaning assigned by paragraph 95(4)(*b*) [subsection 95(4) "equity percentage"] of the Act.

(8) For the purposes of the definition "qualified tertiary oil recovery project" in subsection (1), a "specified royalty provision" means:

(*a*) the *Experimental Project Petroleum Royalty Regulation* of Alberta (Alta. Reg. 36/79);

(*b*) *The Experimental Oil Sands Royalty Regulations* of Alberta (Alta. Reg. 287/77);

(*c*) section 4.2 of the *Petroleum Royalty Regulations* of Alberta (Alta. Reg. 93/74);

(*d*) section 58A of the *Petroleum and Natural Gas Regulations, 1969* of Saskatchewan (Saskatchewan Regulation 8/69);

(*e*) section 204 of *The Freehold Oil And Gas Production Tax Regulations, 1983* of Saskatchewan (Saskatchewan Regulation 11/83);

(*f*) item 9 of section 2 of the *Petroleum and Natural Gas Royalty Regulations* of British Columbia (B.C. Reg. 549/78);

(*g*) the *Freehold Mineral Taxation Act* of Alberta;

(*h*) the *Freehold Mineral Rights Tax Act* of Alberta;

(*i*) Order in Council 427/84 pursuant to section 9(*a*) of the *Mines and Minerals Act* of Alberta;

(*j*) Order in Council 966/84 pursuant to section 9 of the *Mines and Minerals Act* of Alberta; or

(*k*) Order in Council 870/84 pursuant to section 9 of the *Mines and Minerals Act* of Alberta.

(8.1) For the purpose of paragraph (*a*) of the definition "qualified tertiary oil recovery project" in subsection (1), a specified royalty provision is deemed to apply as of a particular time if, at the particular time, unconditional approval for the specified royalty provision to apply at a time after the particular time is given by

(*a*) Her Majesty in right of Canada or of a province;

(*b*) an agent of Her Majesty in right of Canada or of a province; or

(*c*) a corporation, a commission or an association that is controlled by Her Majesty in right of Canada or of a province or by an agent of Her Majesty in right of Canada or of a province.

(9) (Repealed.)

1207. Frontier Exploration Allowances

(1) A taxpayer may deduct in computing his income for a taxation year such amount as he may claim not exceeding the lesser of

(*a*) his income for the year, computed in accordance with Part I of the Act, if no deduction were allowed under this subsection; and

(*b*) his frontier exploration base as of the end of the year (before making any deduction under this subsection for the year).

(2) For the purposes of this section, "frontier exploration base" of a taxpayer as of a particular time means the amount by which the aggregate of

(*a*) the aggregate of all amounts, each of which is an amount in respect of a particular oil or gas well in Canada equal to 66⅔ per cent of the amount by which

(i) expenses incurred after March, 1977 and before April, 1980 and before the particular time in respect of the well (other than expenses that may reasonably be regarded as having been incurred as consideration for services rendered to the taxpayer after March, 1980) if those expenses would be included in the Canadian exploration expense of the taxpayer within the meaning of paragraph 66.1(6)(*a*) [subsection 66.1(6) "Canadian exploration expense"] of the Act (if that paragraph were read without reference to subparagraphs (iii) and (iii.1) [subsection 66.1(6) "Canadian exploration expense"] thereof and without reference to the words "within six months after the end of the year, the drilling of the well is completed and" in subparagraph (ii) [subsection 66.1(6) "Canadian exploration expense"] thereof, and if the reference in subparagraphs (iv) and (v) [subsection 66.1(6) "Canadian exploration expense"] thereof to "any of subparagraphs (i) to (iii.1) [subsection 66.1(6) 'Canadian exploration expense']" were read as a reference to "subparagraph (i) or (ii) [subsection 66.1(6) 'Canadian exploration expense']") other than

(A) a cost of borrowing capital, including any cost incurred prior to the commencement of carrying on a business, that was a Canadian exploration expense of the taxpayer,

(B) an expense renounced by the taxpayer under subsection 66(10.1) of the Act,

(C) an amount that, by virtue of subparagraph 66.1(6)(*a*)(iv) [subsection 66.1(6) "Canadian exploration expense"] of the Act, was a Canadian exploration expense, if such amount was an expense referred to in clause (A) or (B) that was incurred by a partnership referred to in that subparagraph, or

(D) an amount that, by virtue of subparagraph 66.1(6)(*a*)(v) [subsection 66.1(6) "Canadian exploration expense"] of the Act, was a Canadian exploration expense, if such amount was an expense referred to in clause (A) or (B) that the taxpayer incurred pursuant to an agreement referred to in that subparagraph,

exceeds

(ii) the taxpayer's threshold amount in respect of the well, minus the amount that would be determined under subparagraph (i) in respect of the taxpayer for the well if the reference therein to "after March, 1977 and before April, 1980" were read as "after June, 1976 and before April, 1977", and

(*a*.1) where the taxpayer is a successor corporation, any amount required by paragraph (7)(*a*) to be added before the particular time in computing the taxpayer's frontier exploration base,

exceeds the aggregate of

(*b*) all amounts deducted by the taxpayer under subsection (1) in computing his income for taxation years ending before the particular time;

(*c*) 66⅔ per cent of the aggregate of all amounts, each of which is an amount that became receivable by the taxpayer after March 28, 1979 and before the earlier of December 12, 1979 and the particular time, and in respect of which the consideration given by the taxpayer therefor was a property (other than a share, or a property that would have been a Canadian resource property if it had been acquired by the taxpayer at the time the consideration was given) or services the cost of which may reasonably be regarded as having been primarily an expenditure in respect of an oil or gas well for which an amount was added in computing the taxpayer's frontier exploration base by virtue of paragraph (*a*) or in computing the frontier exploration base of a predecessor by virtue of paragraph (*a*) as it applied to the predecessor where the taxpayer is a successor corporation to the predecessor, as the case may be; and

(*d*) where the taxpayer is a predecessor, any amount required by paragraph (7)(*b*) to be deducted before the particular time in computing the taxpayer's frontier exploration base.

(3) For the purposes of subparagraph (2)(*a*)(ii), a taxpayer's "threshold amount" in respect of an oil or gas well means

(*a*) where the taxpayer and one or more other persons have filed an agreement with the Minister in prescribed form in respect of the well and

(i) the amount allocated to each such person in the agreement does not exceed the amount that would be determined, at the time the agreement is filed, under subparagraph (2)(*a*)(i) in respect of that person for the well, if the reference in that subparagraph to "March, 1977" were read as "June, 1976", and

(ii) the aggregate of the amounts allocated by the agreement is $5 million,

the amount allocated to the taxpayer in the agreement, but if no amount is allocated to the taxpayer in the agreement, nil;

(*b*) where such an agreement has been filed in respect of the well by one or more persons other than the taxpayer, nil; or

(*c*) where no such agreement has been filed in respect of the well, $5 million.

(4) Where as a result of mechanical or geological difficulties the drilling of a particular oil or gas well does not achieve its stated geological objectives under the drilling authority issued by the relevant government body and a further well, including a relief well, is drilled on the same geological formation and may reasonably be regarded as a continuation of or a substitution for the particular oil or gas well, the expenses in respect of the drilling of the further well shall, for the purposes of this section, be deemed to be expenses in respect of the drilling of the particular oil or gas well.

(5) For the purposes of this section,

(*a*) when a shareholder corporation is deemed to have incurred a Canadian exploration expense by virtue of an election made by a joint exploration corporation pursuant to subsection 66(10.1) of the Act, that expense shall be deemed to have been incurred by the shareholder corporation at the time when it was incurred by the joint exploration corporation; and

(*b*) when a member of a partnership is deemed to have incurred a Canadian exploration expense by virtue of subparagraph 66.1(6)(*a*)(iv) [subsection 66.1(6) "Canadian exploration expense"] of the Act, that expense shall be deemed to have been incurred by the member at the time when it was incurred by the partnership.

(6) For the purposes of this section, "oil or gas well" means any well drilled for the purpose of producing petroleum or natural gas or of determining the existence, location, extent or quality of an accumulation of petroleum or natural gas, other than a mineral resource.

(7) Subject to subsections 1202(5) and (6), where a corporation (in this section referred to as the "successor corporation") has at any time (in this subsection referred to as the "time of acquisition") after April 19, 1983 and in a taxation year (in this subsection referred to as the "transaction year") acquired a property from another person (in this subsection referred to as the "predecessor"), the following rules apply:

(*a*) for the purpose of computing the frontier exploration base of the successor corporation as of any time after the time of acquisition, there shall be added an amount equal to the amount required by paragraph (*b*) to be deducted in computing the frontier exploration base of the predecessor; and

(*b*) for the purpose of computing the frontier exploration base of the predecessor as of any time after the transaction year of the predecessor, there shall be deducted the amount, if any, by which

(i) the frontier exploration base of the predecessor immediately after the time of acquisition (assuming for this purpose that, in the case of an acquisition as a result of an amalgamation described in section 87 of the Act, the predecessor existed after the time of acquisition and no property was acquired or disposed of in the course of the amalgamation)

exceeds

(ii) the amount, if any, deducted under subsection (1) in computing the income of the predecessor for the transaction year of the predecessor.

(8) (Revoked.)

1208. Additional Allowances in Respect of Certain Oil or Gas Wells

(1) Subject to subsections (3) and (4) where a taxpayer has income for a taxation year from an oil or gas well that is outside Canada, or where an individual has income for a taxation year from an oil or gas well in Canada, in computing his income for the year he may deduct the lesser of

(*a*) the aggregate of drilling costs incurred by him in that year and previous taxation years in respect of the well (not including the cost of land, leases or other rights and not including indirect expenses such as general exploration, geological and geophysical expenses) minus the aggregate of all amounts deductible in respect thereof in computing his income for previous years; and

(*b*) that part of his income for the year that may reasonably be regarded as income from the well.

(2) Where a taxpayer has more than one oil or gas well to which subsection (1) applies, the allowance in respect of the drilling costs of each well shall be computed separately.

Regulations

(3) Where an individual has income for a taxation year from an oil or gas well in Canada, no deduction may be made under this section in computing such income in respect of drilling costs of that well incurred after April 10, 1962.

(4) Where a taxpayer has income for a taxation year from an oil or gas well that is outside Canada, no deduction may be made under this section in computing such income in respect of drilling costs of that well incurred after 1971.

1209. Additional Allowances in Respect of Certain Mines

(1) Subject to subsection (3), where a taxpayer operates in Canada a mine for the production of materials from a resource he may deduct, in computing his income for a taxation year, such amount as he may claim not exceeding 25 per cent of the amount computed under subsection (2).

(2) The amount referred to in subsection (1) is the aggregate of all expenditures made or incurred by the taxpayer before 1972 that are reasonably attributable to the prospecting and exploration for and the development of the mine prior to the coming into production of the mine in reasonable commercial quantities, except to the extent that the expenditures were

(*a*) expenditures in respect of which a deduction from, or in computing, a taxpayer's income tax or excess profits tax was provided by section 8 of the *Income War Tax Act*;

(*b*) expenditures in respect of which an amount was deducted in computing a taxpayer's income under section 16 of chapter 63, S.C., 1947 or section 16 of chapter 53, S.C., 1947-48 or, if the expenditure was incurred prior to 1953, under section 53 of chapter 25, S.C., 1949 (Second Session);

(*c*) expenditures incurred after 1952 in respect of which a deduction was or is provided by section 53 of chapter 25, S.C., 1949 (Second Session), section 83A of the Act as it read in its application to the 1971 taxation year or section 29 of the *Income Tax Application Rules*;

(*d*) expenditures deducted in computing the income of the taxpayer in the year they were incurred;

(*e*) the cost to the taxpayer of property in respect of which an allowance is provided under paragraph 20(1)(*a*) of the Act; or

(*f*) the cost to the taxpayer of a leasehold interest.

(3) The amount deductible under subsection (1) shall not exceed the amount computed under subsection (2) minus the aggregate of

(*a*) amounts deducted under subsection (1) in computing the income of the taxpayer for previous taxation years; and

(*b*) similar amounts deducted in computing the income of the taxpayer for the purposes of the *Income War Tax Act* and *The 1948 Income Tax Act* (as defined in paragraph 12(*d*) of the *Income Tax Application Rules*).

1210. Resource Allowance

(1) (Repealed.)

(2) (Repealed.)

(3) (Repealed.)

(4) (Repealed.)

Tax Window Files: Geothermal Energy Project, *July 17, 2018*, CRA Document No. 2018-0747311E5.

1210.1. Resource Allowance

(Repealed.)

1211. Prescribed Amounts

(Repealed.)

1212. Supplementary Depletion Allowances

(1) In computing a taxpayer's income for a taxation year there may be deducted

(*a*) where the taxpayer is a corporation, such amount as it may claim not exceeding the lesser of

(i) the aggregate of

(A) 50 per cent of its income for the year, computed in accordance with Part I of the Act without reference to paragraphs 59(3.3)(*c*) and (*d*) thereof, if no deduction were allowed under this subsection or subsection 1207(1), and

(B) the amount, if any, included in its income for the year by virtue of paragraphs 59(3.3)(*c*) and (*d*) of the Act, and

(ii) its supplementary depletion base as of the end of the year (before making any deduction under this subsection for the year); and

(*b*) where the taxpayer is not a corporation, such amount as he may claim not exceeding the lesser of

(i) the aggregate of

(A) 25 per cent of the amount, if any, by which his resource profits for the year exceed four times the amount, if any, deducted by virtue of subparagraph 1201(*a*)(i) in computing his income for the year, and

(B) the amount, if any, included in his income for the year by virtue of paragraphs 59(3.3)(*c*) and (*d*) of the Act, and

(ii) his supplementary depletion base as of the end of the year (before making any deduction under this subsection for the year).

(2) For the purpose of computing the supplementary depletion base of a corporation, where, after the corporation last ceased to carry on active business, control of the corporation is considered, for the purposes of subsection 66(11) of the Act, to have been acquired by a person or persons who did not control the corporation at the time when it so ceased to carry on active business, the amount

by which the supplementary depletion base of the corporation at the time it last ceased to carry on active business exceeds the aggregate of amounts otherwise deducted under subsection (1) in computing its income for taxation years ending after that time and before control was so acquired, shall be deemed to have been deducted under subsection (1) by the corporation in computing its income for taxation years ending before control was so acquired.

(3) For the purposes of this section, "supplementary depletion base" of a taxpayer as of a particular time means the amount by which the aggregate of

(*a*) 50 per cent of the aggregate of all expenditures each of which was incurred by him before the particular time and each of which was the capital cost to him of property that is enhanced recovery equipment,

(*b*) 33$^1/_3$ per cent of the aggregate of all expenditures each of which was incurred by him before the particular time and each of which was the capital cost to him of property (other than property that had, before it was acquired by him, been used for any purpose whatever by any person with whom he was not dealing at arm's length) that is bituminous sands equipment acquired by him before 1981, and

(*c*) where the taxpayer is a successor corporation, any amount required by paragraph (4)(*a*) to be added before the particular time in computing the taxpayer's supplementary depletion base,

exceeds the aggregate of

(*d*) all amounts deducted by the taxpayer under subsection (1) in computing his income for taxation years ending before the particular time;

(*e*) 50 per cent of the aggregate of all amounts, each of which is a cost of borrowing capital, including any cost incurred prior to the commencement of carrying on a business, included in the capital cost to him of depreciable property described in paragraph (*a*);

(*f*) 33$^1/_3$ per cent of the aggregate of all amounts, each of which is a cost of borrowing capital, including any cost incurred prior to the commencement of carrying on a business, included in the capital cost to him of depreciable property described in paragraph (*b*);

(*g*) 50 per cent of the aggregate of all amounts, each of which is an amount in respect of a disposition of property (other than a disposition of property, that had been used by the taxpayer, to any person with whom the taxpayer was not dealing at arm's length) of the taxpayer before the earlier of December 12, 1979 and the particular time, the capital cost of which was added in computing the taxpayer's supplementary depletion base by virtue of paragraph (*a*) or in computing the supplementary depletion base of a predecessor by virtue of paragraph (*a*) as it applied to the predecessor where the taxpayer is a successor corporation to the predecessor, as the case may be, and each of which is the amount that is equal to the lesser of

(i) the proceeds of disposition of the property, and

(ii) the capital cost of the property to the taxpayer or the predecessor, as the case may be, computed as if no amount had been included therein that is a cost of borrowing capital, including a cost incurred prior to the commencement of carrying on a business;

(*h*) 33$^1/_3$ per cent of the aggregate of all amounts, each of which is an amount in respect of a disposition of property (other than a disposition of property, that had been used by the taxpayer, to any person with whom the taxpayer was not dealing at arm's length) of the taxpayer before the earlier of December 12, 1979 and the particular time, the capital cost of which was added in computing the taxpayer's supplementary depletion base by virtue of paragraph (*b*) or in computing the supplementary depletion base of a predecessor by virtue of paragraph (*b*) as it applied to the predecessor where the taxpayer is a successor corporation to the predecessor, as the case may be, and each of which is the amount that is equal to the lesser of

(i) the proceeds of disposition of the property, and

(ii) the capital cost of the property to the taxpayer or the predecessor, as the case may be, computed as if no amount had been included therein that is a cost of borrowing capital, including any cost incurred prior to the commencement of carrying on a business; and

(*i*) where the taxpayer is a predecessor, any amount required by paragraph (4)(*b*) to be deducted before the particular time in computing the taxpayer's supplementary depletion base.

(4) Subject to subsections 1202(5) and (6), where a corporation (in this section referred to as the "successor corporation") has at any time (in this subsection referred to as the "time of acquisition") after April 19, 1983 and in a taxation year (in this subsection referred to as the "transaction year") acquired a property from another person (in this subsection referred to as the "predecessor"), the following rules apply:

(*a*) for the purpose of computing the supplementary depletion base of the successor corporation as of any time after the time of acquisition, there shall be added an amount equal to the amount required by paragraph (*b*) to be deducted in computing the supplementary depletion base of the predecessor; and

(*b*) for the purpose of computing the supplementary depletion base of the predecessor as of any time after the transaction year of the predecessor, there shall be deducted the amount, if any, by which

Regulations

(i) the supplementary depletion base of the predecessor immediately after the time of acquisition (assuming for this purpose that, in the case of an acquisition as a result of an amalgamation described in section 87 of the Act, the predecessor existed after the time of acquisition and no property was acquired or disposed of in the course of the amalgamation)

exceeds

(ii) the amount, if any, deducted under subsection (1) in computing the income of the predecessor for the transaction year of the predecessor.

(5) (Revoked.)

1213. Prescribed Deductions

For the purposes of subparagraph 66.1(2)(*a*)(ii) of the Act, "prescribed deduction" in respect of a corporation for a taxation year means an amount deducted under subsection 1202(2) by the corporation in computing its income for the year.

1214. Amalgamations and Windings-up

(1) Where a particular corporation amalgamates with another corporation to form a new corporation, or the assets of a subsidiary are transferred to its parent corporation on the winding-up of the subsidiary, and subsection 87(1.2) or 88(1.5) of the Act is applicable to the new corporation or the parent corporation, as the case may be, the new corporation or the parent corporation, as the case may be, shall be deemed to be the same corporation as, and a continuation of, the particular corporation or the subsidiary, as the case may be, for the purposes of

(*a*) computing the mining exploration depletion base (within the meaning assigned by subsection 1203(2)), the earned depletion base, the frontier exploration base (within the meaning assigned by subsection 1207(2)) and the supplementary depletion base (within the meaning assigned by subsection 1212(3)) of the new corporation or the parent corporation, as the case may be; and

(*b*) determining the amounts, if any, that may be deducted under subsection 1202(2) in computing the income of the new corporation or the parent corporation, as the case may be, for a particular taxation year.

(2) Where there has been an amalgamation (within the meaning assigned by subsection 87(1) of the Act) of two or more particular corporations to form one corporate entity, that entity shall be deemed to be the same corporation as, and a continuation of, each of the particular corporations for the purposes of subsection 1202(9).

(3) Where a taxable Canadian corporation (in this subsection referred to as the "subsidiary") has been wound up in circumstances in which subsection 88(1) of the Act applies in respect of the subsidiary and another taxable Canadian corporation (in this subsection referred to as the "parent"), the parent shall be deemed to be the same corporation as, and a continuation of, the subsidiary for the purposes of subsection 1202(9).

1215. (Revoked.)

1216. Prescribed Persons

For the purpose of subsection 208(1) of the Act, a person described in any of paragraphs 149(1)(*d*) to (*d*.6) of the Act is a prescribed person.

1217. Prescribed Canadian Exploration Expense

(1) For the purposes of subsection 66(14.1) of the Act, the prescribed Canadian exploration expense of a corporation for a taxation year is the amount, if any, by which its total specified exploration expenses for the year exceed its total exploration assistance for the year.

(2) For the purposes of subsection (1), the total specified exploration expenses of a particular corporation for a particular taxation year are the aggregate of

(*a*) all expenses (other than expenses referred to in paragraph (*b*) or (*c*)) that are described in any of subparagraphs 66.1(6)(*a*)(i) to (ii) [subsection 66.1(6) "Canadian exploration expense"] of the Act and that were incurred by the particular corporation in the particular year and after March 1985 and before October 1986,

(*b*) where the particular corporation is a shareholder corporation of a joint exploration corporation, all expenses described in any of subparagraphs 66.1(6)(*a*)(i) to (ii) [subsection 66.1(6) "Canadian exploration expense"] of the Act that were incurred by the joint exploration corporation after March 1985 and before October 1986 and in the taxation year of the joint exploration corporation ending in the particular year and that were deemed under paragraph 66(10.1)(*c*) of the Act to be Canadian exploration expenses incurred by the particular corporation in the particular year, and

(*c*) all expenses that would be described in subparagraph 66.1(6)(*a*)(iv) or (v) [subsection 66.1(6) "Canadian exploration expense"] of the Act if the references in those subparagraphs to "any of subparagraphs (i) to (iii.1) [subsection 66.1(6) 'Canadian exploration expense'] incurred" were read as "any of subparagraphs (i) to (ii) [subsection 66.1(6) 'Canadian exploration expense'] incurred after March 1985 and before October 1986" and that were incurred by the particular corporation in the particular year or by a partnership in a fiscal period of the partnership that ended in the particular year if, at the end of that fiscal period, the particular corporation was a member of the partnership,

other than

(*d*) expenses renounced by the corporation at any time under subsection 66(10.1) or (12.6) of the Act, (*e*) Canadian exploration and development overhead expenses of the corporation or of a partnership of which the corporation was a member, or

(*f*) expenses incurred or deemed to have been incurred by the corporation in a period during which it was exempt from tax on its taxable income under Part I of the Act.

(3) For the purposes of subsection (1), the total exploration assistance of a corporation for a taxation year is the aggregate of all amounts each of which is an amount of assistance or benefit that the corporation has received or is entitled to receive in the year from a government, municipality or other public authority in respect of an expense that is included in its total specified exploration expenses for the year by virtue of paragraph (2)(*a*) or (*c*), whether such amount is by way of a grant, subsidy, rebate, forgivable loan, deduction from royalty or tax, rebate of royalty or tax, investment allowance or any other form of assistance or benefit.

1218. Prescribed Canadian Development Expense

(1) For the purposes of subsection 66(14.2) of the Act, prescribed Canadian development expense of a corporation for a taxation year is the amount, if any, by which its total specified development expenses for the year exceed its total development assistance for the year.

(2) For the purposes of subsection (1), the total specified development expenses of a particular corporation for a particular taxation year is the aggregate of

(*a*) all expenses (other than expenses referred to in paragraph (*b*) or (*c*)) that are described in subparagraph 66.2(5)(*a*)(i) or (i.1) [subsection 66.2(5) "Canadian development expense"] of the Act and that were incurred by the corporation in the particular year and after March 1985 and before October 1986,

(*b*) where the particular corporation is a shareholder corporation of a joint exploration corporation, all expenses that are described in subparagraph 66.2(5)(*a*)(i) or (i.1) [subsection 66.2(5) "Canadian development expense"] of the Act, that were incurred by the joint exploration corporation after March 1985 and before October 1986 and in the taxation year of the joint exploration corporation ending in the particular year and that were deemed under paragraph 66(10.2)(*c*) of the Act to be Canadian development expenses incurred by the particular corporation in the particular year, and

(*c*) all expenses that would be described in subparagraph 66.2(5)(*a*)(iv) or (v) [subsection 66.2(5) "Canadian development expense"] of the Act if the references in those subparagraphs to "any of subparagraphs (i) to (iii) [subsection 66.2(5) 'Canadian development expense'] incurred" were read as "subparagraph (i) or (i.1) [subsection 66.2(5) 'Canadian development expense'] incurred after March 1985 and before October 1986" and that were incurred by the particular corporation in the particular year or by a partnership in a fiscal period of the partnership that ended in the particular year if, at the end of that fiscal period, the particular corporation was a member of the partnership,

other than

(*d*) expenses renounced by the corporation at any time under subsection 66(10.2), (12.601) or (12.62) of the Act,

(*e*) Canadian exploration and development overhead expenses of the corporation or of a partnership of which the corporation was a member, or

(*f*) expenses incurred or deemed to have been incurred by the corporation in a period during which it was exempt from tax on its taxable income under Part I of the Act.

(3) For the purposes of subsection (1), the total development assistance of a corporation for a taxation year is the aggregate of all amounts each of which is an amount of assistance or benefit that the corporation has received or is entitled to receive in the year from a government, municipality or other public authority in respect of an expense that is included in its total specified development expenses for the year by virtue of paragraph (2)(*a*) or (*c*), whether such amount is by way of a grant, subsidy, rebate, forgivable loan, deduction from royalty or tax, rebate of royalty or tax, investment allowance or any other form of assistance or benefit.

1219. Canadian Renewable and Conservation Expense

(1) Subject to subsections (2) to (4), for the purpose of subsection 66.1(6) of the Act, "Canadian renewable and conservation expense" means an expense incurred by a taxpayer, and payable to a person or partnership with whom the taxpayer is dealing at arm's length, in respect of the development of a project for which it is reasonable to expect that at least 50% of the capital cost of the depreciable property to be used in the project would be the capital cost of any property that is included in Class 43.1 or 43.2 in Schedule II, or that would be so included if this Part were read without reference to this section, and includes such an expense incurred by the taxpayer

(*a*) for the purpose of making a service connection to the project for the transmission of electricity to a purchaser of the electricity, to the extent that the expense so incurred was not incurred to acquire property of the taxpayer;

(*b*) for the construction of a temporary access road to the project site;

(*c*) for a right of access to the project site before the earliest time at which a property described in Class 43.1 or 43.2 in Schedule II is used in the project for the purpose of earning income;

Regulations

(*d*) for clearing land to the extent necessary to complete the project;

(*e*) for process engineering for the project, including

(i) collection and analysis of site data,

(ii) calculation of energy, mass, water, or air balances,

(iii) simulation and analysis of the performance and cost of process design options, and

(iv) selection of the optimum process design;

(*f*) for the drilling or completion of a well for the project, other than

(i) a well that is, or can reasonably be expected to be, used for the installation of underground piping that is included in paragraph (*d*) of Class 43.1 or paragraph (*b*) of Class 43.2 in Schedule II, or

(ii) a well referred to in paragraph (*h*);

(*g*) for a test wind turbine that is part of a wind farm project of the taxpayer; or

(*h*) if at least 50% of the depreciable property to be used in the project, determined by reference to its capital cost, is described in subparagraph (d)(vii) of Class 43.1,

(i) for the drilling of a well, or

(ii) solely for the purpose of determining the extent and quality of a geothermal resource.

History: S. 1219(1)(*f*) was replaced by S.C. 2017, c. 33, s. 92(1), applicable in respect of expenses incurred after March 21, 2017, and formerly read:

(*f*) for the drilling or completion of a well for the project, other than a well that is, or can reasonably be expected to be, used for the installation of underground piping that is included in paragraph (*d*) of Class 43.1 or paragraph (*b*) of Class 43.2 in Schedule II; or

S. 1219(1)(*h*) was added by S.C. 2017, c. 33, s. 92(2), applicable in respect of expenses incurred after March 21, 2017.

S. 1219(1)(*f*) was replaced by S.C. 2010, c. 25, s. 77(1), applicable to expenses incurred after May 2, 2010. S. 1219(1)(*f*) formerly read:

(*f*) for the drilling or completion of a well for the project; or

Related Regulations: 1219(3).

Tax Profile: August 2011 — Structuring Solar Projects in Canada.

Income Tax Folios: *Primary* — S3-F8-C2 Tax Incentives for Clean Energy Equipment.

(2) A Canadian renewable and conservation expense does not include any expense that

(*a*) is described in paragraphs 20(1)(*c*), (*d*), (*e*) or (*e*.1) of the Act; or

(*b*) is incurred by a taxpayer directly or indirectly and is

(i) for the acquisition of, or the use of or the right to use, land, except as provided by paragraph (1)(*b*), (*c*) or (*d*),

(ii) for grading or levelling land or for landscaping, except as provided by paragraph (1)(*b*),

(iii) payable to a non-resident person or a partnership other than a Canadian partnership (other than an expense described in paragraph (1l)(*g*)),

(iv) included in the capital cost of property that, but for this section, would be depreciable property (other than property that would be included in Class 14.1 of Schedule II), except as provided by paragraph (1)(*b*), (*d*), (*e*), (*f*), (*g*) or (*h*),

(v) included in the capital cost of property that, but for this section, would be property included in Class 14.1 of Schedule II, except as provided by any of paragraphs (1)(*a*) to (*e*) or subparagraph (*h*)(ii),

(vi) included in the cost of inventory of the taxpayer,

(vii) an expenditure on or in respect of scientific research and experimental development,

(viii) a Canadian development expense or a Canadian oil and gas property expense,

(ix) incurred, for a project, in respect of any time at or after the earliest time at which a property described in Class 43.1 or 43.2 in Schedule II was used in the project for the purpose of earning income,

(x) incurred in respect of the administration or management of a business of the taxpayer, or

(xi) a cost attributable to the period of the construction, renovation or alteration of depreciable property, other than property described in Class 43.1 or 43.2 in Schedule II, that relates to

(A) the construction, renovation or alteration of the property, except as provided by paragraph (1)(*b*), (*f*), (*g*) or (*h*), or

(B) the ownership of land during the period, except as provided by paragraph (1)(*b*), (*c*) or (*d*).

History: S. 1219(2)(*b*)(iv) and (v) were replaced by S.C. 2017, c. 33, s. 92(3), applicable in respect of expenses incurred after March 21, 2017, and formerly read:

(iv) included in the capital cost of property that, but for this section, would be depreciable property (other than property that would be included in Class 14.1 of Schedule II), except as provided by paragraph (1)(*b*), (*d*), (*e*), (*f*), or (*g*),

(v) included in the capital cost of property that, but for this section, would be property included in Class 14.1 of Schedule II, except as provided by any of paragraphs (1)(*a*) to (*e*),

S. 1219(2)(*b*)(xi)(A) was replaced by S.C. 2017, c. 33, s. 92(4), applicable in respect of expenses incurred after March 21, 2017, and formerly read:

(A) the construction, renovation or alteration of the property, except as provided by paragraph (1)(*b*), (*f*), or (*g*), or

S. 1219(2)(*b*)(iv) and (v) were replaced by S.C. 2016, c. 12, s. 79(1), in force January 1, 2017, and formerly read:

(iv) included in the capital cost of property that, but for this section, would be depreciable property, except as provided by paragraph (1)(*b*), (*d*), (*e*), (*f*) or (*g*),

(v) an expenditure that, but for this section, would be an eligible capital expenditure, except as provided by any of paragraphs (1)(*a*) to (*e*),

Income Tax Folios: *Primary* — S3-F8-C2 Tax Incentives for Clean Energy Equipment.

(3) For the purpose of paragraph (1)(*g*), "test wind turbine" means a fixed location device that is a wind energy conversion system that would, if this Part were read without reference to this section, be property included in Class 43.1 in Schedule II because of subparagraph (*d*)(v) of that Class, or in Class 43.2 in Schedule II because of paragraph (*b*) of that Class, in respect of which the Minister, in consultation with the Minister of Natural Resources, determines that

(*a*) the device is installed as part of a wind farm project of the taxpayer at which the electrical energy produced from wind by the device, and by all other test wind turbines that are part of the project, does not exceed

(i) one third of the project's planned nameplate capacity if

(A) the Minister of Natural Resources determines that the project's planned nameplate capacity is limited from an engineering or scientific perspective, and

(B) the project's planned nameplate capacity does not exceed six megawatts, or

(ii) 20% of the project's planned nameplate capacity, in any other case;

(*b*) the project does not share with any other project a point of interconnection to an electrical energy transmission or distribution system;

(*c*) if the project does not have a point of interconnection to an electrical energy transmission or distribution system, the project has a point of interconnection to an electrical system

(i) of the taxpayer

(A) which system is more than 10 kilometres from any transmission system and from any distribution system, and

(B) from which system at least 90% of the electrical energy produced by the project is used in a business carried on by the taxpayer, or

(ii) of another person or partnership that deals at arm's length with the taxpayer

(A) which system is more than 10 kilometres from any transmission system and from any distribution system, and

(B) from which system at least 90% of the electrical energy produced by the project is used in a business carried on by the other person or partnership;

(*d*) the primary purpose for installing the device is to test the level of electrical energy produced by the device from wind at the place of installation;

(*e*) no other test wind turbine is installed within 1500 metres of the device; and

(*f*) no other wind energy conversion system is installed within 1500 metres of the device until the level of electrical energy produced from wind by the device has been tested for at least 120 calendar days.

Income Tax Folios: *Primary* — S3-F8-C2 Tax Incentives for Clean Energy Equipment.

(4) For greater certainty, a Canadian Renewable and Conservation Expense includes an expense incurred by a taxpayer to acquire a fixed location device that is a wind energy conversion system only if the device is described in paragraph (1)(*g*).

(5) A Canadian renewable and conservation expense does not include an expense incurred by a taxpayer at any time that is in respect of a geothermal project

(*a*) that at that time is described in paragraph (1)(*h*); and

(*b*) in respect of which the taxpayer is not at that time in compliance with the requirements of all environmental laws, by-laws and regulations of

(i) Canada,

(ii) a province or a municipality in Canada, or

(iii) a municipal or public body performing a function of government in Canada.

History: S. 1219(5) was added by S.C. 2017, c. 33, s. 92(5), applicable in respect of expenses incurred after March 21, 2017.

Part XIII
Elections in Respect of Taxpayers Ceasing to be Resident in Canada

1300. Elections to Defer Capital Gains

(1) Any election by an individual under paragraph 48(1)(*c*) of the Act shall be made by filing with the Minister the prescribed form on or before the day on or before which the return of income for the year in which the taxpayer ceased to be resident in Canada is required to be filed under section 150 of the Act.

Income Tax Folios: *Secondary* — S1-F3-C2 Principal Residence.

(2) Any election by a Canadian corporation under paragraph 48(1)(*c*) of the Act shall be made by filing with the Minister, on or before the day on or before which the return of income for the year in which the corporation ceased to be resident in Canada is required to be filed under section 150 of the Act, the following documents in duplicate:

(*a*) the form prescribed by the Minister;

(*b*) where the directors of the corporation are legally entitled to administer the affairs of the corporation, a certified copy of their resolution authorizing the election to be made; and

(*c*) where the directors of the corporation are not legally entitled to administer the affairs of the corporation, a certified copy of the authorization of the making of the election by the person or persons legally entitled to administer the affairs of the corporation.

Forms: T2061 — Election by an Emigrant to defer Deemed Disposition of Property and Capital Gains Thereon.

Interpretation Bulletins: *Secondary* — IT-434R Rental of real property by individual; IT-451R Deemed disposition and acquisition on ceasing to be or becoming resident in Canada.

1301. Elections to Defer Payment of Taxes

(1) Any election by an individual under subsection 159(4) of the Act shall be made by filing with the Minister the prescribed form on or before the day on or before which the return of income for the year in which the taxpayer ceased to be resident in Canada is required to be filed under section 150 of the Act.

(2) Any election by a Canadian corporation under subsection 159(4) of the Act shall be made by filing with the Minister, on or before the day on or before which the return of income for the year in which the corporation ceased to be resident in Canada is required to be filed under section 150 of the Act, the following documents in duplicate:

(*a*) the form prescribed by the Minister;

(*b*) where the directors of the corporation are legally entitled to administer the affairs of the corporation, a certified copy of their resolution authorizing the election to be made; and

(*c*) where the directors of the corporation are not legally entitled to administer the affairs of the corporation, a certified copy of the authorization of the making of the election by the person or persons legally entitled to administer the affairs of the corporation.

1302. Elections to Realize Capital Gains

Any election by an individual under paragraph 48(1)(*a*) of the Act shall be made by filing with the Minister the prescribed form on or before the day on or before which the return of income for the year in which the taxpayer ceased to be resident in Canada is required to be filed under section 150 of the Act.

Part XIV
Insurance Business Policy Reserves

Division 1
Policy Reserves

1400. Non-Life Insurance Business

(1) For the purpose of paragraph 20(7)(*c*) of the Act, the amount prescribed in respect of an insurer for a taxation year is

(*a*) the amount determined under subsection (3) in respect of the insurer for the year, where that amount is greater than nil, and

(*b*) nil, in any other case.

(2) For the purpose of paragraph 12(1)(*e*.1) of the Act, the amount prescribed in respect of an insurer for a taxation year is

(*a*) the absolute value of the amount determined under subsection (3) in respect of the insurer for the year, where that amount is less than nil, and

(*b*) nil, in any other case.

(3) For the purposes of paragraphs (1)(*a*) and (2)(*a*), the amount determined under this subsection in respect of an insurer for a taxation year is the amount, which may be positive or negative, determined by the formula

$$A + B + C + D + E + F + G + H + I + J + K + L$$

where

A is the total of all amounts each of which is the unearned portion at the end of the year of the premium paid by the policyholder for a policy (other than a policy that insures a risk in respect of

(*a*) a financial loss of a lender on a loan made on the security of real property,

(*b*) a home warranty,

(*c*) a lease guarantee, or

(*d*) an extended motor vehicle warranty),

which is determined by apportioning the premium paid by the policyholder equally over the period to which that premium relates;

B is the total of all amounts each of which is an amount determined in respect of a policy referred to in paragraph (*a*), (*b*), (*c*) or (*d*) of the description of A equal to the lesser of

(*a*) the amount of the reported reserve of the insurer at the end of the year in respect of the unearned portion at the end of the year of the premium paid by the policyholder for the policy, and

(*b*) a reasonable amount as a reserve determined as at the end of the year in respect of the unearned portion at the end of the year of the premium paid by the policyholder for the policy;

C is the total of all amounts each of which is the amount in respect of a policy, where all or a portion of a risk under the policy was reinsured, equal to the unearned portion at the end of the year of a reinsurance commission in respect of the policy determined by apportioning the reinsurance commission equally over the period to which it relates;

D is the amount, in respect of policies (other than policies in respect of which an amount can be determined under the description of E) under which

(*a*) a claim that was incurred before the end of the year has been reported to the insurer before the end of the year and in respect of which the insurer is, or may be, required to make a payment or incur an expense after the year, or

(*b*) there may be a claim incurred before the end of the year that has not been reported to the insurer before the end of the year,

equal to 95% of the lesser of

(*c*) the total of the reported reserves of the insurer at the end of the year in respect of such claims or possible claims, and

(*d*) the total of the claim liabilities of the insurer at the end of the year in respect of such claims or possible claims;

E is the amount in respect of policies under which

(*a*) a claim that was incurred before the end of the year has been reported to the insurer before the end of the year,

(*b*) the claim is in respect of damages for personal injury or death, and

(*c*) the insurer has agreed to a structured settlement of the claim,

equal to the lesser of

(*d*) the total of the reported reserves of the insurer at the end of the year in respect of such claims, and

(*e*) the total of the claim liabilities of the insurer at the end of the year in respect of such claims;

F is an additional amount, in respect of policies that insure a fidelity risk, a surety risk, a nuclear risk or a risk related to a financial loss of a lender on a loan made on the security of real property, equal to the lesser of

(*a*) the total of the reported reserves of the insurer at the end of the year in respect of such risks (other than an amount included in determining the value of A, B, C, D, E, G, H, I, J, K or L), and

(*b*) a reasonable amount as a reserve determined as at the end of the year in respect of such risks (other than an amount included in determining the value of A, B, C, D, E, G, H, I, J, K or L);

G is the amount of a guarantee fund at the end of the year provided for under an agreement in writing between the insurer and Her Majesty in right of Canada under which Her Majesty has agreed to guarantee the obligations of the insurer under a policy that insures a risk related to a financial loss of a lender on a loan made on the security of real property;

H is the amount in respect of risks under pre-1996 non-cancellable or guaranteed renewable accident and sickness policies equal to

(*a*) where the amounts determined under each of subparagraphs (i) and (ii) are greater than nil, the lesser of

(i) the total of the reported reserves of the insurer at the end of the year in respect of such risks (other than an amount included in determining the value of A, B, C, D, E, F, G, I, J, K or L), and

(ii) a reasonable amount as a reserve determined as at the end of the year in respect of such risks (other than an amount included in determining the value of A, B, C, D, E, F, G, I, J, K or L), and

(*b*) nil, in any other case;

I is the amount in respect of risks under post-1995 non-cancellable or guaranteed renewable accident and sickness policies equal to the lesser of

(*a*) the total of the reported reserves of the insurer at the end of the year in respect of such risks (other than an amount included in determining the value of A, B, C, D, E, F, G, H, J, K or L), and

(*b*) the total of the policy liabilities of the insurer at the end of the year in respect of such risks (other than an amount included in determining the value of A, B, C, D, E, F, G, H, J, K or L);

J is the total of all amounts (other than an amount deductible under subsection 140(1) of the Act) each of which is the amount, which is the least of P, Q and R, in respect of a dividend, refund of premiums or refund of premium deposits provided for under the terms of a group accident and sickness insurance policy that will be

(*a*) used by the insurer to reduce or eliminate a future adverse claims experience under the policy,

(*b*) paid or unconditionally credited to the policyholder by the insurer, or

(*c*) applied in discharge, in whole or in part, of a liability of the policyholder to pay premiums to the insurer under the policy,

where

P is a reasonable amount as a reserve determined as at the end of the year in respect of the dividend,

Regulations

refund of premiums or refund of premium deposits,

Q is 25% of the amount of the premium payable under the terms of the policy for the 12-month period ending

(*i*) if the policy is terminated in the year, on the day the policy is terminated, and

(*ii*) in any other case, at the end of the year, and

R is the reported reserve of the insurer at the end of the year in respect of the dividend, refund of premiums or refund of premium deposits; and

K is the total of all amounts each of which is the amount, in respect of a policy under which a portion of the particular amount paid or payable by the policyholder for the policy before the end of the year is deducted under paragraph 1408(4)(*b*), equal to the portion of that particular amount that the insurer has determined will, after the end of the year, be returned to or credited to the account of the policyholder on the termination of the policy; and

L is an amount in respect of policies that insure earthquake risks in Canada equal to the lesser of

(*a*) the portion of the reported reserve of the insurer at the end of the year in respect of those risks that is attributable to accumulations from premiums in respect of those risks (other than an amount included in determining the value of A, B, C, D, E, F, G, H, I, J or K), and

(*b*) a reasonable amount as a reserve determined as at the end of the year in respect of those risks (other than an amount included in determining the value of A, B, C, D, E, F, G, H, I, J or K).

(4) Where the relevant authority does not require an insurer (other than an insurer that is required by law to report to the Superintendent of Financial Institutions) to determine its liabilities in respect of claims referred to in the description of D or E in subsection (3) in accordance with actuarial principles,

(*a*) the value of D is deemed to be 95% of the amount determined under paragraph (*c*) of the description of D; and

(*b*) the value of E is deemed to be the amount determined under paragraph (*d*) of the description of E.

(5) (Repealed.)

DIVISION 2
AMOUNTS DETERMINED

1401. Life Insurance Business

(1) For the purposes of applying section 307 and subsection 211.1(3) of the Act at any time, the amounts determined under this subsection are,

(*a*) in respect of a deposit administration fund policy, the total of the insurer's liabilities under the policy calculated in the manner that

(i) if the insurer is required to file an annual report with its relevant authority for a period that includes that time, is required to be used in preparing that report, and

(ii) in any other case, is required to be used in preparing its annual financial statements for the period that includes that time;

(*b*) in respect of a group term life insurance policy that provides insurance for a period not exceeding 12 months, the unearned portion of the premium paid by the policyholder for the policy at that time determined by apportioning the premium paid by the policyholder equally over the period to which that premium pertains;

(*c*) in respect of a life insurance policy, other than a policy referred to in paragraph (*a*) or (*b*), the greater of

(i) the amount determined by the formula

$$A - B$$

where

A is

(A) if the policy is issued after 2016 and is not an annuity contract, the cash surrender value of the policy at that time determined without reference to surrender charges, and

(B) in any other case, the cash surrender value of the policy at that time, and

B is the total of all amounts each of which is an amount payable at that time in respect of a policy loan in respect of the policy, and

(ii) the amount determined by the formula

$$A - (B + C)$$

where

A is

(A) if the policy is issued after 2016 and is not an annuity contract, the net premium reserve in respect of the policy at that time, and

(B) in any other case, the present value at that time of the future benefits provided by the policy,

B is

(A) if the policy is issued after 2016 and is not an annuity contract, nil, and

(B) in any other case, the present value at that time of any future modified net premiums in respect of the policy, and

C is the total of all amounts each of which is an amount payable at that time in respect of a policy loan in respect of the policy;

(*c*.1) in respect of a group life insurance policy, the amount (other than an amount in respect of which a deduction may be claimed by the insurer under subsection 140(1) of the Act because of subparagraph 138(3)(*a*)(v) of the Act in computing the insurer's income for its taxation year that includes that time) in respect of a dividend, refund of premiums or refund of premium deposits provided for under the terms of the policy that will be used by the insurer to reduce or eliminate a future adverse claims experience under the policy or that will be paid or unconditionally credited to the policyholder by the insurer or applied in discharge, in whole or in part, of a liability of the policyholder to pay premiums to the insurer, which is the least of

(i) a reasonable amount in respect of such a dividend, refund of premiums or refund of premium deposits,

(ii) 25% of the amount of the premium payable under the terms of the policy for the 12-month period ending at that time, and

(iii) the amount of the reserve or liability in respect of such a dividend, refund of premiums or refund of premium deposits that

(A) if the insurer is required to file an annual report with its relevant authority for a period that includes that time, is used in preparing that report, and

(B) in any other case, is used in preparing its annual financial statements for the period that includes that time; and

(*d*) in respect of a policy, other than a policy referred to in paragraph (*a*), in respect of a benefit, risk or guarantee that is

(i) an accidental death benefit,

(ii) a disability benefit,

(iii) an additional risk as a result of insuring a substandard life,

(iv) an additional risk in respect of the conversion of a term policy or the conversion of the benefits under a group policy into another policy after that time,

(v) an additional risk under a settlement option,

(vi) an additional risk under a guaranteed insurability benefit,

(vii) a guarantee in respect of a segregated fund policy, or

(viii) any other benefit that is ancillary to the policy, subject to the prior approval of the Minister on the advice of the Superintendent of Insurance for Canada,

but is not

(ix) a benefit, risk or guarantee in respect of which an amount has been claimed under any other paragraph of this subsection by the insurer as a deduction in computing its income for its taxation year that includes that time,

equal to the lesser of

(x) a reasonable amount in respect of the benefit, risk or guarantee, and

(xi) the reserve in respect of the benefit, risk or guarantee that

(A) if the insurer is required to file an annual report with its relevant authority for a period that includes that time, is used in preparing that report, and

(B) in any other case, is used in preparing its annual financial statements for the period that includes that time.

(*d*.1) (Repealed by S.C. 2009, c. 2, s. 99(5).)

(*d*.2) (Repealed by S.C. 2009, c. 2, s. 99(5).)

(*e*) (Repealed by S.C. 2009, c. 2, s. 99(5).)

History: S. 1401(1), the portion before subparagraph (*c.1*)(i) was replaced by S.C. 2014, c. 39, s. 86(1), in force December 16, 2014, and formerly read:

(1) For the purposes of section 307 of the Regulations and subsection 211.1(3) of the Act, the amounts determined under this subsection are,

(*a*) in respect of deposit administration fund policies, the aggregate of the insurer's liabilities under those policies calculated in the manner required for the purposes of the insurer's annual report to the relevant authority for the year or, where the insurer was throughout the year subject to the supervision of the relevant authority but was not required to file an annual report with the relevant authority for the year, in its financial statements for the year;

(*b*) in respect of a group term life insurance policy that provides coverage for a period not exceeding 12 months, the unearned portion of the premium paid by the policyholder for the policy at the end of the year determined by apportioning the premium paid by the policyholder equally over the period to which that premium pertains;

(*c*) in respect of a life insurance policy, other than a policy referred to in paragraph (*a*) or (*b*), the greater of

(i) the amount, if any, by which

(A) the cash surrender value of the policy at the end of the year exceeds

(B) the aggregate of all amounts each of which is an amount payable in respect of a policy loan outstanding at the end of the year in respect of the policy or the interest thereon that has accrued to the insurer at the end of the year, and

(ii) the amount, if any, by which

(A) the present value at the end of the year of the future benefits provided by the policy

exceeds the aggregate of

(B) the present value at the end of the year of any future modified net premiums in respect of the policy, and

(C) the aggregate of all amounts each of which is an amount payable in respect of a policy loan outstanding at the end of the year in respect of the policy or the interest thereon that has accrued to the insurer at the end of the year;

(*c*.1) in respect of a group life insurance policy, the amount (other than an amount in respect of which a deduction may be claimed by the insurer pursuant to subsection 140(1) of the Act because of subparagraph 138(3)(*a*)(v) of the Act in computing its income for the year) in respect of a dividend, refund of premiums or refund of premium deposits provided for under the terms of the policy that will be used by the insurer to reduce or eliminate a future adverse claims experience under the policy or that will be paid or unconditionally credited to the policyholder by the insurer or applied in discharge, in whole or in part, of a liability of the policyholder to pay premiums to the insurer, which is the least of

S. 1401(1)(*c.1*)(ii) and (iii) were replaced by S.C. 2014, c. 39, s. 86(2), in force December 16, 2014, and formerly read:

(ii) 25 per cent of the amount of the premium payable under the terms of the policy for the 12-month period ending

(A) if the policy is terminated in the year, on the day the policy is terminated, and

(B) in any other case, at the end of the year, and

(iii) the amount of the reserve or liability in respect of such a dividend, refund of premiums or refund of premium deposits reported by the insurer in its annual report for the year to the relevant authority or, where the insurer was throughout the year subject to the supervision of the relevant authority for the year but was not required to file an

Regulations

annual report with the relevant authority for the year, in its financial statements for the year; and

S. 1401(1)(*d*)(iv) was replaced by S.C. 2014, c. 39, s. 86(3), in force December 16, 2014, and formerly read:

(iv) an additional risk in respect of the conversion of a term policy or the conversion of the benefits under a group policy into another policy after the end of the year,

S. 1401(1)(*d*)(ix) was replaced by S.C. 2014, c. 39, s. 86(4), in force December 16, 2014, and formerly read:

(ix) a benefit, risk or guarantee in respect of which an amount has been claimed under any other paragraph of this subsection, other than paragraphs (*d*.1) and (*d*.2), by the insurer as a deduction in computing its income for the year,

S. 1401(1)(*d*)(xi) was replaced by S.C. 2014, c. 39, s. 86(5), in force December 16, 2014, and formerly read:

(xi) the reserve in respect of the benefit, risk or guarantee, reported by the insurer in its annual report to the relevant authority for the year or, where the insurer was throughout the year subject to the supervision of the relevant authority but was not required to file an annual report with the relevant authority for the year, in its financial statements for the year.

The heading before s. 1401 was replaced by S.C. 2009, c. 2, s. 98(1), applicable to taxation years that begin after September 2006. That heading formerly read "Policy Reserves For Pre-1996 Policies"

S. 1401(1), the portion before subparagraph (*c*)(i) was replaced by S.C. 2009, c. 2, s. 99(1), applicable to taxation years that begin after September 2006. That portion formerly read:

(1) For the purpose of subparagraph 138(3)(*a*)(i) of the Act, in computing a life insurer's income for a taxation year from carrying on its life insurance business in Canada, there may be deducted in respect of

(*a*) deposit administration fund policies, such amount as the insurer may claim that is a reasonable amount in respect of the aggregate of the insurer's liabilities under the policies as at the end of the year and does not exceed the aggregate of the insurer's liabilities under those policies calculated in the manner required for the purposes of the insurer's annual report to the relevant authority for the year or, where the insurer was throughout the year subject to the supervision of the relevant authority but was not required to file an annual report with the relevant authority for the year, in its financial statements for the year;

(*b*) a group term life insurance policy that provides coverage for a period not exceeding 12 months, such amount as the insurer may claim not exceeding the unearned portion of the premium paid by the policyholder for the policy at the end of the year determined by apportioning the premium paid by the policyholder equally over the period to which that premium pertains;

(*c*) a life insurance policy, other than a policy referred to in paragraph (*a*) or (*b*), such amount as the insurer may claim not exceeding the greater of

S. 1401(1)(*c*.1), the portion before subparagraph (i) was replaced by S.C. 2009, c. 2, s. 99(2), applicable to taxation years that begin after September 2006. That portion formerly read:

(*c*.1) a group life insurance policy, such amount as the insurer may claim as an amount (other than an amount in respect of which a deduction may be claimed by the insurer pursuant to subsection 140(1) of the Act by reason of subparagraph 138(3)(*a*)(v) of the Act in computing its income for the year) in respect of a dividend, refund of premiums or refund of premium deposits provided for under the terms of the policy that will be used by the insurer to reduce or eliminate a future adverse claims experience under the policy or that will be paid or unconditionally credited to the policyholder by the insurer or applied in discharge, in whole or in part, of a liability of the policyholder to pay premiums to the insurer, not exceeding the least of

S. 1401(1)(*d*), the portion before subparagraph (i) was replaced by S.C. 2009, c. 2, s. 99(3), applicable to taxation years that begin after September 2006. That portion formerly read:

(*d*) a policy, other than a policy referred to in paragraph (*a*), such amount as the insurer may claim in respect of a benefit, risk or guarantee that is

S. 1401(1)(*d*), the portion after subparagraph (ix) and before subparagraph (x) was replaced by S.C. 2009, c. 2, s. 99(4), applicable to taxation years that begin after September 2006. That portion formerly read:

not exceeding the lesser of

S. 1401(1)(*d*.1) to (*e*) were repealed by S.C. 2009, c. 2, s. 99(5), applicable to taxation years that begin after September 2006. S. 1401(1)(*d*.1) to (*e*) formerly read:

(*d*.1) a policy referred to in paragraph (*b*) where, after the end of the year, a claim under the policy is made in respect of a death that occurred before the end of the year, such amount as the insurer may claim, not exceeding the lesser of

(i) the present value, at the end of the year, of the payments to be made in respect of the claim made under the policy or such estimate of such payments to be made in respect of the claim as is reasonable in the circumstances, and

(ii) 95 per cent of the amount of the reserve in respect of the claim reported by the insurer in its annual report to the relevant authority for the year or, where the insurer was throughout the year subject to the supervision of the relevant authority for the year but was not required to file an annual report with the relevant authority for the year, in its financial statements for the year;

(*d*.2) a policy referred to in paragraph (*c*) where, after the end of the year, a claim under the policy is made in respect of a death that occurred before the end of the year, such amount as the insurer may claim, not exceeding the lesser of

(i) the amount, if any, by which

(A) the present value, at the end of the year, of the payments to be made in respect of the claim made under the policy or such estimate of such payments to be made in respect of the claim as is reasonable in the circumstances

exceeds

(B) the maximum amounts that may be claimed by the insurer for the year in respect of the policy under paragraph (*c*) or (*d*), and

(ii) 95 per cent of the amount of the reserve in respect of the claim reported by the insurer in its annual report to the relevant authority for the year or, where the insurer was throughout the year subject to the supervision of the relevant authority but was not required to file an annual report with the relevant authority for the year, in its financial statements for the year; and

(*e*) a qualified annuity, such amount as the insurer may claim not exceeding the amount, if any, by which

(i) the amount that would have been determined pursuant to paragraph (*c*) for the year if the rate of interest used (or deemed by section 1403 to have been used) by the insurer in determining the premium for the annuity were reduced by one-half of one percentage point,

exceeds

(ii) the maximum amount that may be claimed by the insurer in respect of the annuity under paragraph (*c*).

(1.1) (Repealed by S.C. 2009, c. 2, s. 99(6).)

History: S. 1401(1.1) was repealed by S.C. 2009, c. 2, s. 99(6), applicable to taxation years that begin after September 2006. S. 1401(1.1) formerly read:

(1.1) An amount may be deducted under subsection (1) only in respect of a life insurance policy in Canada that is a pre-1996 life insurance policy.

(2) For the purposes of subsection (1), (except in respect of subparagraph (*d*)(vii) thereof), any amount claimed by an insurer for the year shall not include an amount in respect of a liability of a segregated fund (within the meaning assigned "segregated fund" by section 138.1 of the Act).

(3) The following definitions apply in this section.

"benefit on death" — "benefit on death" includes the amount of an endowment benefit but does not include

(*a*) any additional amount payable as a result of accidental death; and

(*b*) where interest, if any, on an amount held on deposit by an insurer is included in computing the income of a policyholder for a taxation year, the amount held on deposit and interest on the deposit.

"coverage" — "coverage", under a life insurance policy, means each life insurance (other than a fund value benefit) under the policy in respect of a specific life, or two or more specific lives jointly insured, and in respect of which a particular schedule of premium or cost of insurance rates applies. For greater certainty, each such insurance is a separate coverage.

"fund value benefit" —"fund value benefit", under a life insurance policy at any time, means a benefit under the policy the amount of which is the amount by which the fund value of the policy at that time exceeds the total of all amounts each of which is a fund value of a coverage under the policy at that time.

"fund value of a coverage" —"fund value of a coverage", under a life insurance policy at any time, means the total of all amounts each of which is the amount at that time of an investment account in respect of the policy that reduces the net amount at risk as determined for the purpose of calculating the cost of insurance charges for the coverage during the period over which those charges are incurred or would be incurred if they were to apply until the termination of the coverage.

"fund value of a policy" —"fund value of a policy", at any time, means the total of all amounts each of which is the amount at that time of an investment account in respect of the policy and, for greater certainty,

(*a*) includes, where interest, if any, on an amount held on deposit by an insurer is not included in computing the income of a policyholder for a taxation year, the amount held on deposit and interest on the deposit; and

(*b*) excludes, where interest, if any, on an amount held on deposit by an insurer is included in computing the income of a policyholder for a taxation year, the amount held on deposit and interest on the deposit.

"future benefits to be provided" —"future benefits to be provided", in respect of a coverage under a life insurance policy at any time, means

(*a*) if there is a fund value of the coverage at that time, each benefit on death that would be payable under the coverage at a particular time after that time determined as if the amount of the benefit were equal to the amount by which the benefit on death at that time exceeds the fund value of the coverage at that time; and

(*b*) in any other case, each benefit on death payable under the coverage at a particular time after that time.

"future net premiums or cost of insurance charges" — "future net premiums or cost of insurance charges", in respect of a coverage at any time, means

(*a*) for the purposes of paragraph (*a*) of the description of C in the definition "net premium reserve" in this subsection, each amount determined by the formula

$$A \times B/C$$

where

A is future premiums or cost of insurance charges in respect of the coverage at that time,

B is the present value at the date of issue of the coverage of future benefits to be provided in respect of the coverage on that date, and

C is the present value at the date of issue of the coverage of future premiums or cost of insurance charges in respect of the coverage on that date; and

(*b*) for the purposes of paragraph (*b*) of the description of C in the definition "net premium reserve" in this subsection,

(i) each amount determined by the formula

$$A \times (B + C)/(D + E)$$

where

A is future premiums or cost of insurance charges in respect of the coverage at that time,

B is the present value at the date of issue of the coverage of future benefits to be provided in respect of the coverage on the particular day that is one year after that date and, if the coverage has a fund value on that date, determined as if the fund value of the coverage were nil on that date,

C is the present value at the date of issue of the coverage of future benefits to be provided in respect of the coverage on the particular day that is two years after that date and, if the coverage has a fund value on that date, determined as if the fund value of the coverage were nil on that date,

D is the present value at the date of issue of the coverage of future premiums or cost of insurance charges in respect of the coverage on the particular day that is one year after that date and, if the coverage has a fund value on that date, determined as if the fund value of the coverage were nil on that date, and

E is the present value at the date of issue of the coverage of future premiums or cost of insurance charges in respect of the coverage on the particular day that is two years after that date and, if the coverage has a fund value on that date, determined as if the fund value of the coverage were nil on that date, and

(ii) notwithstanding subparagraph (i), in respect of the second year of the coverage, the amount determined by the formula

$$(A + B)/2$$

where

A is the amount determined under subparagraph (i), and

B is the amount of a one-year term insurance premium or cost of insurance charge that would be payable in respect of the coverage if

Regulations

the benefit on death were equal to the amount by which the benefit on death at the end of the first year of the coverage exceeds the fund value of the coverage, if any, at the end of the first year of the coverage.

"future premiums or cost of insurance charges"—"future premiums or cost of insurance charges", in respect of a coverage at any time, means

(*a*) if there is a fund value of the coverage at that time, each cost of insurance charge in respect of the coverage that would be incurred at a particular time after that time determined as if the net amount at risk under the coverage after that time were equal to the amount by which the benefit on death under the coverage at that time exceeds the fund value of the coverage at that time; and

(*b*) in any other case, each premium in respect of the coverage that is fixed and determined on the date of issue of the coverage that will become payable, or each cost of insurance charge in respect of the coverage that will be incurred, as the case may be, at a particular time after that time.

"interpolation time"—"interpolation time", of a coverage, means the time that is the earlier of

(*a*) the time that is eight years after the date of issue of the coverage; and

(*b*) the first time at which no premiums are payable or cost of insurance charges are incurred, as the case may be, in respect of the coverage.

"net premium reserve"—"net premium reserve", in respect of a life insurance policy at any time, means the amount determined by the formula

$$A + B + C$$

where

A is the total of all amounts, if any, each of which is the present value at that time of the fund value of a coverage under the policy at that time;

B is the amount, if any, of the fund value benefit under the policy at that time; and

C is

(*a*) in applying paragraph (1)(*c*) for the purposes of section 307, the total of all amounts each of which is, in respect of a coverage under the policy,

(i) if that time is at or after the interpolation time of the coverage, the amount determined by the formula

$$D - E$$

where

D is the present value at that time of future benefits to be provided in respect of the coverage at that time, and

E is the present value at that time of future net premiums or cost of insurance charges in respect of the coverage at that time, and

(ii) if that time is before the interpolation time of the coverage, the amount determined by the formula

$$F/G \times (H - I)$$

where

F is the number of years that the coverage has been in effect as of that time,

G is the number of years that the coverage would have been in effect if that time were the interpolation time,

H is the present value at the interpolation time of future benefits to be provided in respect of the coverage at the interpolation time and, if the coverage has a fund value at that time, determined as if the amount of the benefit on death under the coverage at the interpolation time were equal to the amount by which the benefit on death at that time exceeds the fund value of the coverage at that time, and

I is the present value at the interpolation time of future net premiums or cost of insurance charges in respect of the coverage at the interpolation time and, if the coverage has a fund value at that time, determined as if the net amount at risk under the coverage after the interpolation time were equal to the amount by which the benefit on death at that time exceeds the fund value of the coverage at that time, and

(*b*) in applying paragraph (1)(*c*) for the purposes of subsection 211.1(3) of the Act, the total of all amounts each of which is, in respect of a coverage under the policy, the amount determined by the formula

$$J - K$$

where

J is the present value at that time of future benefits to be provided in respect of the coverage at that time, and

K is the present value at that time of future net premiums or cost of insurance charges in respect of the coverage at that time.

"policy anniversary"—"policy anniversary" has the same meaning as in section 310.

History: S. 1401(3) was added by S.C. 2014, c. 39, s. 86(6), in force December 16, 2014.

S. 1401(3) was repealed by S.C. 2009, c. 2, s. 99(7), applicable to taxation years that begin after September 2006. S. 1401(3) formerly read:

(3) In computing the amount that a life insurer may deduct under subparagraph 138(3)(*a*)(i) of the Act in computing its taxable income for a taxation year, there shall be deducted from the aggregate of the amounts determined under subsection (1), the aggregate of all amounts each of which is the lesser of the following amounts determined in respect of a life insurance policy referred to in paragraph (1)(*c*):

(*a*) the amount, if any, by which

(i) the amount that would be determined under clause (1)(*c*)(i)(B) in respect of the policy

exceeds

(ii) the amount that would be determined under clause (1)(*c*)(i)(A) in respect of the policy, and

(*b*) the amount, if any, by which

(i) the aggregate of the amounts that would be determined under clauses (1)(*c*)(ii)(B) and (C) in respect of the policy

exceeds

(ii) the amount that would be determined under clause (1)(*c*)(ii)(A) in respect of the policy.

(4) In applying paragraph (1)(*c*) for the purposes of section 307 in respect of a life insurance policy (other than an annuity contract) issued after 2016, the following rules apply:

(*a*) in computing present values

(i) an annual interest rate of 3.5% is to be used, and

(ii) mortality rates are to be used;

(*b*) in determining the mortality rates that apply to a life insured under a coverage under the policy,

(i) if a single life is insured under the coverage,

(A) the age that is to be used is the age of the life insured at the time at which the coverage was issued, or that which is attained on the birthday of the life insured nearest to the time at which the coverage was issued, depending on the method used by the insurer that issued the policy in determining the premium or cost of insurance rates in respect of the life insured,

(B) if the life insured was determined by the insurer that issued the policy to be a standard life at the time the coverage was issued, the *Proposed CIA Mortality Tables, 1986-1992* included in the *May 17, 1995 Canadian Institute of Actuaries Memorandum*, extended to include select mortality rates from age 81 to age 90 developed using the methodology used by the Canadian Institute of Actuaries to derive select mortality rates from age 71 to age 80, applicable for an individual who has the same relevant characteristics as the life insured, are to be used, and

(C) if the life insured was determined by the insurer that issued the policy to be a substandard life at the time the coverage was issued, the mortality rates that apply are to be equal to, depending on the method used by the insurer for the purpose of determining the premium or cost of insurance rates in respect of the coverage,

(I) the lesser of one and the product of the rating attributed to the life by the insurer and the mortality rates that would be determined under clause (B) if the life were not a substandard life, or

(II) the mortality rates that would have been determined under clause (B) had the life insured been a standard life and the age of the life insured been the age used by the life insurer for the purpose of determining the premium or cost of insurance rates in respect of the coverage, and

(ii) if two or more lives are jointly insured under the coverage, the mortality rates to be used are those determined by applying the methodology used by the insurer that issued the policy to estimate the mortality rates of the lives jointly insured for the purpose of determining the premium or cost of insurance rates in respect of the coverage to the *Proposed CIA Mortality Tables, 1986-1992* included in the *May 17, 1995 Canadian Institute of Actuaries Memorandum*, extended to include select mortality rates from age 81 to age 90 developed using the methodology used by the Canadian Institute of Actuaries to derive select mortality rates from age 71 to age 80; and

(*c*) in determining the net premium reserve in respect of the policy, the present value of future net premiums or cost of insurance charges is to be calculated as if a premium or cost of insurance charge payable or incurred on a policy anniversary were payable or incurred, as the case may be, one day after the policy anniversary.

History: S. 1401(4) was added by S.C. 2014, c. 39, s. 86(6), in force December 16, 2014.

S. 1401(4) was repealed by S.C. 2009, c. 2, s. 99(7), applicable to taxation years that begin after September 2006. S. 1401(4) formerly read:

(4) For the purpose of subparagraph 138(3)(*a*)(ii) of the Act, there may be deducted, in computing a life insurer's income for a taxation year, the amount it claims as a reserve in respect of unpaid claims received by it before the end of the year under life insurance policies in Canada that are pre-1996 life insurance policies, not exceeding the present value at the end of the year, computed using a rate of interest that is reasonable in the circumstances, of a reasonable amount in respect of those unpaid claims.

(5) In applying paragraph (1)(*c*) for the purposes of subsection 211.1(3) of the Act in respect of a life insurance policy (other than an annuity contract)

(*a*) if the policy is issued after 2016,

(i) the rates of interest, mortality and lapses described in subsection 1403(1) are to be used in computing present values, determined as if

(A) subsections 1403(2) to (8) did not apply, and

(B) the reference to "premiums for the policy" in paragraph 1403(1)(*e*) were read as a reference to "premiums or cost of insurance charges in respect of a coverage under the policy",

(ii) subparagraph (1)(*c*)(i) is to be read without reference to "determined without reference to surrender charges", and

(iii) in determining the net premium reserve in respect of the policy, the present value of future net premiums or cost of insurance charges is to be calculated as if a premium or cost of insurance charge payable or incurred on a policy anniversary were payable or incurred, as the case may be, one day after the policy anniversary; and

(*b*) if the policy is issued before 2017 and at a particular time after 2016 life insurance — in respect of a

Regulations

life, or two or more lives jointly insured, and in respect of which a particular schedule of premium or cost of insurance rates applies — is added to the policy or is term insurance that is converted into permanent life insurance within the policy, then that insurance is deemed to be a separate life insurance policy issued at the particular time unless

(i) the insurance is part of a rider deemed by subsection 211(2) of the Act to be a separate life insurance policy issued at the particular time, or

(ii) in the case of insurance added to the policy,

(A) the insurance is medically underwritten

(I) to obtain a reduction in the premium or cost of insurance rates under the policy, or

(II) before 2017, or

(B) the insurance is paid for with policy dividends or is reinstated.

History: S. 1401(5)(*b*), the portion before subparagraph (i), was replaced by S.C. 2017, c. 33, s. 93, in force December 14, 2017, and formerly read:

(*b*) if the policy is issued before 2017 and at a particular time after 2016 life insurance — in respect of a life, or two or more lives jointly insured, and in respect of which a particular schedule of premium or cost of insurance rates applies — is converted (other than only because of a change in premium or cost of insurance rates) into another type of life insurance under the policy or is added to the policy, then that insurance is deemed to be a separate life insurance policy issued at the particular time unless

S. 1401(5) was added by S.C. 2014, c. 39, s. 86(6), in force December 16, 2014.

DIVISION 3
SPECIAL RULES

1402. Non-Life and Life Insurance Businesses

Any amount determined under section 1400 or 1401 shall be determined

(*a*) net of relevant reinsurance recoverable amounts; and

(*b*) without reference to any amount in respect of a deposit accounting insurance policy.

History: S. 1402 was replaced by S.C. 2010, c. 25, s. 78(1), to taxation years that begin after 2010. S. 1402 formerly read:

1402. Any amount determined under section 1400 or 1401 shall be determined on a net of reinsurance ceded basis.

1402.1. Non-Life and Life Insurance Businesses

For greater certainty, any amount referred to or determined under section 1400 may be equal to, or less than, nil.

1403. Non-Life and Life Insurance Businesses

(1) Subject to subsections (2) and (3), for the purposes of applying paragraph 1401(1)(*c*) in respect of a life insurance policy issued before 2017 or an annuity contract, a modified net premium and an amount determined by paragraph 1401(1)(*c*) are to be computed

(*a*) in the case of a lapse-supported policy effected after 1990, based on rates of interest, mortality and policy lapse only, and

(*b*) in any other case, based on rates of interest and mortality only,

using

(*c*) in respect of the modified net premiums and benefits (other than a benefit described in paragraph (*d*)) of a participating life insurance policy (other than an annuity contract) under the terms of which the policyholder is entitled to receive a specified amount in respect of the policy's cash surrender value, the rates used by the insurer when the policy was issued in computing the cash surrender values of the policy;

(*d*) in respect of any benefit provided

(i) in lieu of a cash settlement on the termination or maturity of a policy, or

(ii) in satisfaction of a dividend on a policy,

the rates used by the insurer in determining the amount of such benefit; and

(*e*) in respect of all or part of any other policy, the rates used by the insurer in determining the premiums for the policy.

History: S. 1403(1), the portion before paragraph (*a*) was replaced by S.C. 2014, c. 39, s. 87(1), in force December 16, 2014, and formerly read:

(1) For the purposes of paragraph 1401(1)(*c*) and subject to subsections (2) and (3), a modified net premium and an amount claimed by an insurer for a taxation year shall be computed

(2) For the purposes of subsection (1), where a rate of mortality or other probability used by an insurer in determining the premium for a policy is not reasonable in the circumstances, the Minister on the advice of the Superintendent of Insurance for Canada may make such revision to the rate as is reasonable in the circumstances and the revised rate shall be deemed to have been used by the insurer in determining the premium.

(3) For the purposes of subsection (1), where the present value of the premiums for a policy as at the date of issue of the policy is less than the aggregate of

(*a*) the present value, at that date, of the benefits provided for by the policy, and

(*b*) the present value, at that date, of all outlays and expenses made or incurred by the insurer or outlays and expenses that the insurer reasonably estimates it will make or incur in respect of the policy (except outlays and expenses to maintain the policy after all premiums under the policy have been paid and for which explicit provision has not been made in calculating the premiums) and such part of any other outlays and expenses made or incurred by the insurer that may reasonably be regarded as applicable thereto,

an increased rate of interest shall be determined by multiplying the rate of interest used in determining the premiums by a constant factor so that when the increased rate of interest is used,

(*c*) the present value of the premiums at the date of issue of the policy

shall equal

(*d*) the aggregate of the present values of the benefits, outlays and expenses referred to in paragraphs (*a*) and (*b*),

and the increased rate of interest shall be deemed to have been used by the insurer in determining the premiums for the policy.

(4) For the purposes of subsection (3), a "present value" referred to in that subsection shall be computed by using the rates of mortality and other probabilities used by the insurer in determining its premiums, after making any revision required by subsection (2).

(5) For the purposes of subsection (1), where a record of the rate of interest or mortality used by an insurer in determining the premiums for a policy is not available,

(*a*) the insurer may, if the policy was issued before 1978, make a reasonable estimate of the rate; and

(*b*) the Minister, on the advice of the Superintendent of Insurance for Canada, may

(i) if the policy was issued before 1978 and the insurer has not made the estimate referred to in paragraph (*a*), or

(ii) if the policy was issued after 1977,

make a reasonable estimate of the rate.

(6) Notwithstanding paragraph 1401(1)(*c*), a life insurer in computing its income for a taxation year may, in respect of any class of life insurance policies issued before its 1988 taxation year, other than policies referred to in paragraph 1401(1)(*a*) or (*b*), use a method of approximation to convert the reserve in respect of such policies reported by the insurer in its annual report to the relevant authority for the year to an amount that is a reasonable estimate of the amount that would otherwise be determined for such policies under paragraph 1401(1)(*c*), provided that that method of approximation is acceptable to the Minister on the advice of the relevant authority.

(7) For the purposes of subsection (1) and notwithstanding any other provision of this section, where

(*a*) an individual annuity contract was issued prior to 1969 by a life insurer, or

(*b*) a benefit was purchased prior to 1969 under a group annuity contract issued by a life insurer, and

the contract

(*c*) is a policy in respect of which the provisions of paragraph 1401(1)(*c*) as it read in its application to the insurer's 1977 taxation year applied,

the rates of interest and mortality used by the insurer in computing its reserve for the policy under that paragraph for its 1977 taxation year shall be used by the insurer in respect of that policy.

(8) Subsections (9) and (10) apply to an insurer if

(*a*) in a taxation year of the insurer, there has been a disposition to the insurer by another person with whom the insurer was dealing at arm's length in respect of which subsection 138(11.92) of the Act applied;

(*b*) as a result of the disposition, the insurer assumed obligations under life insurance policies (in this subsection and subsections (9) and (10) referred to as the "transferred policies") in respect of which an amount may be claimed by the insurer as a reserve under paragraph 1401(1)(*c*) for the taxation year;

(*c*) the amount (referred to in this subsection and subsections (9) and (10) as the "reserve deficiency") determined by the following formula is a positive amount:

$$(A - B) - C$$

where

A is the total of all amounts received or receivable by the insurer from the other person in respect of the transferred policies,

B is the total of all amounts paid or payable by the insurer to the other person in respect of commissions in respect of the amounts referred to in the description of A, and

C is the total of the maximum amounts that may be claimed by the insurer as a reserve under 1401(1)(*c*) (determined without reference to this subsection) in respect of the transferred policies for the taxation year; and

(*d*) the reserve deficiency can reasonably be attributed to the fact that the rates of interest, mortality or policy lapse used by the issuer of the transferred policies in determining the cash surrender values or premiums under the transferred policies are no longer reasonable in the circumstances.

History: S. 1403(8) was replaced by S.C. 2013, c. 34, s. 386(1), applicable to dispositions that occur after November 1999, and formerly read:

(8) For the purposes of subsection (1), where

(*a*) in a taxation year of an insurer, there has been a disposition to the insurer by another person with whom the insurer was dealing at arm's length in respect of which subsection 138(11.92) of the Act applied,

(*b*) as a result of the disposition, the insurer assumed obligations under life insurance policies (in this subsection referred to as the "transferred policies") in respect of which an amount may be claimed by the insurer as a reserve under paragraph 1401(1)(*c*) for the taxation year,

(*c*) the amount, if any, by which

(i) the aggregate of all amounts received or receivable by the insurer from the other person in respect of the transferred policies referred to in paragraph (*b*)

exceeds

(ii) the aggregate of all amounts paid or payable by the insurer to the other person in respect of commissions in respect of the amounts referred to in subparagraph (i)

exceeds the total of the maximum amounts that may be claimed by the insurer as a reserve under paragraph 1401(1)(*c*) (determined without reference to this subsection) in respect of the transferred policies for the taxation year, and

(*d*) the amount determined under paragraph (*c*) (in this subsection referred to as "reserve deficiency") can reasonably be attributed to the fact that the rates of interest or mortality used by the issuer of the transferred policies in determining the cash surrender values or premiums under such policies are no longer reasonable in the circumstances,

the Minister, on the request of the insurer and with the advice of the relevant authority, may make such revision to the rates of interest or mortality to eliminate all or any part of that reserve deficiency, and those revised rates shall be deemed to have been used by the issuer of the transferred policies in determining the cash surrender value or premiums under the policies.

Regulations

(9) If this subsection applies to an insurer in respect of transferred policies for which there was a reserve deficiency, then, for the purposes of subsection (1) and subject to subsection (10),

(*a*) the insurer may make such revisions to the rates of interest, mortality or policy lapse used by the issuer of the transferred policies to eliminate all or any part of the reserve deficiency; and

(*b*) the revised rates are deemed to have been used by the issuer of the transferred policies in determining the cash surrender value or premiums under the policies.

History: S. 1403(9) was added by S.C. 2013, c. 34, s. 386(1), applicable to dispositions that occur after November 1999.

(10) If, under subsection (9), an insurer has revised the rates of interest, mortality or policy lapse used by the issuer of transferred policies, the Minister may, for the purposes of subsection (1) and paragraph (9)(*b*), make further revisions to the revised rates to the extent that the insurer's revisions to those rates are not reasonable in the circumstances.

History: S. 1403(10) was added by S.C. 2013, c. 34, s. 386(1), applicable to dispositions that occur after November 1999.

Regulations

DIVISION 4

LIFE INSURANCE POLICY RESERVES

1404. [Reserve amounts]

(1) For the purpose of subparagraph 138(3)(*a*)(i) of the Act, there may be deducted, in computing a life insurer's income from carrying on its life insurance business in Canada for a taxation year in respect of its life insurance policies in Canada, the amount the insurer claims, not exceeding

(*a*) the amount determined under subsection (3) in respect of the insurer for the year, where that amount is greater than nil; and

(*b*) nil, in any other case.

(2) For the purpose of paragraph 138(4)(*b*) of the Act, the amount prescribed in respect of an insurer for a taxation year, in respect of its life insurance policies in Canada, is

(*a*) the absolute value of the amount determined under subsection (3) in respect of the insurer for the year, where that amount is less than nil; and

(*b*) nil, in any other case.

(3) For the purposes of paragraphs (1)(*a*) and (2)(*a*), the amount determined under this subsection in respect of an insurer for a taxation year, in respect of its life insurance policies in Canada, is the amount, which may be positive or negative, determined by the formula

$$A + B + C + D - M$$

where

A is the amount (except to the extent the amount is determined in respect of a claim, premium, dividend or refund in respect of which an amount is included in determining the value of B, C or D), in respect of the insurer's life insurance policies in Canada, equal to the lesser of

(*a*) the total of the reported reserves of the insurer at the end of the year in respect of those policies, and

(*b*) the total of the policy liabilities of the insurer at the end of the year in respect of those policies;

B is the amount, in respect of the insurer's life insurance policies in Canada under which there may be claims incurred before the end of the year that have not been reported to the insurer before the end of the year, equal to 95% of the lesser of

(*a*) the total of the reported reserves of the insurer at the end of the year in respect of the possibility that there are such claims, and

(*b*) the total of the policy liabilities of the insurer at the end of the year in respect of the possibility that there are such claims;

C is the total of all amounts each of which is the unearned portion at the end of the year of the premium paid by the policyholder for the policy, determined by apportioning the premium paid by the policyholder equally over the period to which that premium relates, where the policy is a group term life insurance policy that

(*a*) provides coverage for a period that does not exceed 12 months, and

(*b*) is a life insurance policy in Canada;

D is the total of all amounts (other than an amount deductible under subparagraph 138(3)(*a*)(v) of the Act) each of which is the amount, which is the least of P, Q and R, in respect of a dividend, refund of premiums or refund of premium deposits provided for under the terms of a group life insurance policy that is a life insurance policy in Canada that will be

(*a*) used by the insurer to reduce or eliminate a future adverse claims experience under the policy,

(*b*) paid or unconditionally credited to the policyholder by the insurer, or

(*c*) applied in discharge, in whole or in part, of a liability of the policyholder to pay premiums to the insurer under the policy,

where

P is a reasonable amount as a reserve determined as at the end of the year in respect of the dividend, refund of premiums or refund of premium deposits provided for under the terms of the policy,

Q is 25% of the amount of the premium under the terms of the policy for the 12-month period ending

(*a*) on the day the policy is terminated, if the policy is terminated in the year, and

(*b*) at the end of the year, in any other case, and

R is the amount of the reported reserve of the insurer at the end of the year in respect of the dividend, refund of premiums or refund of premium deposits provided for under the terms of the policy; and

M is the total of all amounts determined in respect of a life insurance policy in Canada each of which is

(*a*) an amount payable in respect of a policy loan under the policy, or

(*b*) interest that has accrued to the insurer to the end of the year in respect of a policy loan under the policy.

(4) (Repealed by SOR/2002-123, s. 4(*b*).)

(5) (Repealed by SOR/99-269, 6.)

(6) (Repealed by SOR/99-269, 6.)

History: S. 1404 and the headings before it were replaced by S.C. 2009, c. 2, s. 100(1), applicable to taxation years that begin after September 2006. S. 1404 and the headings before it formerly read:

Division 4 *Policy Reserves For Post-1995 Policies*

1404. *Life Insurance Business.*

(1) For the purpose of subparagraph 138(3)(*a*)(i) of the Act, there may be deducted, in computing a life insurer's income from carrying on its life insurance business in Canada for a taxation year in respect of its life insurance policies in Canada that are post-1995 life insurance policies, the amount the insurer claims, not exceeding

(*a*) the amount determined under subsection (3) in respect of the insurer for the year, where that amount is greater than nil, and

(*b*) nil, in any other case.

(2) For the purpose of paragraph 138(4)(*b*) of the Act, the amount prescribed in respect of an insurer for a taxation year, in respect of its life insurance policies in Canada that are post-1995 life insurance policies, is

(*a*) the absolute value of the amount determined under subsection (3) in respect of the insurer for the year, where that amount is less than nil, and

(*b*) nil, in any other case.

(3) For the purposes of paragraphs (1)(*a*) and (2)(*a*), the amount determined under this subsection in respect of an insurer for a taxation year, in respect of its life insurance policies in Canada that are post-1995 life insurance policies, is the amount, which may be positive or negative, determined by the formula

$$A + B + C + D - M$$

where

A is the amount (except to the extent the amount is determined in respect of a claim, premium, dividend or refund in respect of which an amount is included in determining the value of B, C or D), in respect of the insurer's life insurance policies in Canada that are post-1995 life insurance policies, equal to the lesser of

(*a*) the total of the reported reserves of the insurer at the end of the year in respect of those policies, and

(*b*) the total of the policy liabilities of the insurer at the end of the year in respect of those policies;

B is the amount, in respect of the insurer's life insurance policies in Canada that are post-1995 life insurance policies under which there may be claims incurred before the end of the year that have not been reported to the insurer before the end of the year, equal to 95% of the lesser of

(*a*) the total of the reported reserves of the insurer at the end of the year in respect of the possibility that there are such claims, and

(*b*) the total of the policy liabilities of the insurer at the end of the year in respect of the possibility that there are such claims;

C is the total of all amounts each of which is the unearned portion at the end of the year of the premium paid by the policyholder for the policy where the policy is a group term life insurance policy that

(*a*) provides coverage for a period that does not exceed 12 months,

(*b*) is a life insurance policy in Canada, and

(*c*) is a post-1995 life insurance policy,

determined by apportioning the premium paid by the policyholder equally over the period to which that premium relates;

D is the total of all amounts (other than an amount deductible under subparagraph 138(3)(*a*)(v) of the Act) each of which is the amount, which is the least of P, Q and R, in respect of a dividend, refund of premiums or refund of premium deposits provided for under the terms of a group life insurance policy that is a life insurance policy in Canada that is a post-1995 life insurance policy that will be

(*a*) used by the insurer to reduce or eliminate a future adverse claims experience under the policy,

(*b*) paid or unconditionally credited to the policyholder by the insurer, or

(*c*) applied in discharge, in whole or in part, of a liability of the policyholder to pay premiums to the insurer under the policy,

where

P is a reasonable amount as a reserve determined as at the end of the year in respect of the dividend, refund of premiums or refund of premium deposits provided for under the terms of the policy,

Q is 25% of the amount of the premium under the terms of the policy for the 12-month period ending

(*i*) on the day the policy is terminated, if the policy is terminated in the year, and

(*ii*) at the end of the year, in any other case, and

R is the amount of the reported reserve of the insurer at the end of the year in respect of the dividend, refund of premiums or refund of premium deposits provided for under the terms of the policy; and

M is the total of all amounts determined in respect of a life insurance policy in Canada that is a post-1995 life insurance policy each of which is

(*a*) an amount payable in respect of a policy loan under the policy, or

(*b*) interest that has accrued to the insurer to the end of the year in respect of a policy loan under the policy.

1405. [Reserve for unpaid claims]

For the purpose of subparagraph 138(3)(*a*)(ii) of the Act, there may be deducted, in computing a life insurer's income for a taxation year, the amount it claims as a reserve in respect of an unpaid claim received by the insurer before the end of the year under a life insurance policy in Canada, not exceeding the lesser of

(*a*) the reported reserve of the insurer at the end of the year in respect of the claim, and

(*b*) the policy liability of the insurer at the end of the year in respect of the claim.

History: S. 1405 was replaced by S.C. 2009, c. 2, s. 100(1), applicable to taxation years that begin after September 2006. S. 1405 formerly read:

1405. For the purpose of subparagraph 138(3)(*a*)(ii) of the Act, there may be deducted in computing a life insurer's income for a taxation year the amount it claims as a reserve in respect of an unpaid claim received by the insurer before the end of the year under a life insurance policy in Canada that is a post-1995 life insurance policy, not exceeding the lesser of

(*a*) the reported reserve of the insurer at the end of the year in respect of the claim, and

(*b*) the policy liability of the insurer at the end of the year in respect of the claim.

1406. [Calculation of amount]

Any amount determined under section 1404 or 1405 shall be determined

(*a*) net of relevant reinsurance recoverable amounts;

(*b*) by excluding any obligation to pay a benefit under a segregated fund policy if

(i) the amount of the benefit varies with the fair market value of the segregated fund at the time the benefit becomes, or may become, payable, and

(ii) the benefit is not in respect of a guarantee given by the insurer under a segregated fund policy; and

(*c*) without reference to any amount in respect of a deposit accounting insurance policy.

History: S. 1406(*b*) was replaced by S.C. 2013, c. 34, s. 387(1), applicable to the 2012 and subsequent taxation years, and formerly read:

(*b*) without reference to any liability in respect of a segregated fund (other than a liability in respect of a guarantee in respect of a segregated fund policy); and

S. 1406 was replaced by S.C. 2010, c. 25, s. 79(1), applicable to taxation years that begin after 2010. S. 1406 formerly read:

1406. Any amount determined under section 1404 or 1405 shall be determined

(*a*) on a net of reinsurance ceded basis; and

(*b*) without reference to any liability in respect of a segregated fund (other than a liability in respect of a guarantee in respect of a segregated fund policy).

1407. [Negative amounts]

For greater certainty, any amount referred to in or determined under section 1404 or 1405 may be equal to, or less than, nil.

DIVISION 5
INTERPRETATION

1408. Insurance Businesses

(1) The definitions in this subsection apply in this Part.

"acquisition costs" —"acquisition costs" (Repealed.)

"amount payable" —"amount payable", in respect of a policy loan at a particular time, means the amount of the policy loan and the interest that is outstanding on the policy loan at that time.

"benefit" —"benefit", in respect of a policy, includes

(*a*) a policy dividend (other than a policy dividend in respect of a policy described in paragraph 1403(1)(*c*)) in respect of the policy to the extent that the dividend was specifically treated as a benefit by the insurer in determining a premium for the policy, and

(*b*) an expense of maintaining the policy after all premiums in respect of the policy have been paid to the extent that the expense was specifically provided for by the insurer in determining a premium for the policy,

but does not include

(*c*) a policy loan,

(*d*) interest on funds left on deposit with the insurer under the terms of the policy, and

(*e*) any other amount under the policy that was not specifically provided for by the insurer in determining a premium for the policy.

"capital tax" —"capital tax" means a tax imposed under Part I.3 or VI of the Act or a similar tax imposed under an Act of the legislature of a province.

"cash surrender value" —"cash surrender value" has the meaning assigned by subsection 148(9) of the Act.

"claim liability" —"claim liability" of an insurer at the end of a taxation year means

(*a*) in respect of a claim reported to the insurer before that time under an insurance policy, the amount, if any, by which

(i) the present value at that time, computed using a rate of interest that is reasonable in the circumstances, of a reasonable estimate, determined in accordance with accepted actuarial practice, of the insurer's future payments and claim adjustment expenses in respect of the claim

exceeds

(ii) the present value at that time, computed using a rate of interest that is reasonable in the circumstances, of a reasonable estimate, determined in accordance with accepted actuarial practice, of the amounts that the insurer will recover after that time in respect of the claim because of salvage, subrogation or any other reason; and

(*b*) in respect of the possibility that there are claims under an insurance policy incurred before that time that have not been reported to the insurer before that time, the amount, if any, by which

(i) the present value at that time, computed using a rate of interest that is reasonable in the circumstances, of a reasonable estimate, determined in accordance with accepted actuarial practice, of the insurer's payments and claim adjustment expenses in respect of those claims

exceeds

(ii) the present value at that time, computed using a rate of interest that is reasonable in the circumstances, of a reasonable estimate, determined in accordance with accepted actuarial practice, of the amounts that the insurer will recover in respect of those claims because of salvage, subrogation or any other reason.

"deposit accounting insurance policy" —"deposit accounting insurance policy" has the meaning assigned by subsection 138(12) of the Act.

History: S. 1408(1), the definition "deposit accounting insurance policy" was added by S.C. 2010, c. 25, s. 80(1), applicable to taxation years that begin after 2010.

"extended motor vehicle warranty" —"extended motor vehicle warranty" means an agreement under which a person agrees to provide goods or render services in respect of the repair or maintenance of a motor vehicle manufactured by the person or a corporation related to the person where

(*a*) the agreement is in addition to a basic or limited warranty in respect of the vehicle;

(*b*) the basic or limited warranty has a term of 3 or more years, although it may expire before the end of such term on the vehicle's odometer registering a specified number of kilometres or miles;

(*c*) more than 50% of the expenses to be incurred under the agreement are reasonably expected to be incurred after the expiry of the basic or limited warranty; and

(*d*) the person's risk under the agreement is insured by an insurer that is subject to the supervision of a relevant authority.

"general amending provision" —"general amending provision", of an insurance policy, means a provision of the policy that allows it to be amended with the consent of the policyholder.

"interest" —"interest", in relation to a policy loan, has the meaning assigned by subsection 138(12) of the Act.

"lapse-supported policy" —"lapse-supported policy" means a life insurance policy that would require materially higher premiums if premiums were determined using policy lapse rates that are zero after the fifth policy year.

"life insurance policy" —"life insurance policy" has the same meaning as defined in subsection 138(12) of the Act.

History: S. 1408(1), the definition "life insurance policy" was added by S.C. 2009, c. 2, s. 101(2), applicable to taxation years that begin after November 7, 2007.

"life insurance policy in Canada" —"life insurance policy in Canada" has the same meaning as defined in subsection 138(12) of the Act.

History: S. 1408(1), the definition "life insurance policy in Canada" was replaced by S.C. 2009, c. 2, s. 101(1), applicable to taxation years that begin after November 7, 2007. That definition formerly read:

"life insurance policy in Canada" means a life insurance policy issued or effected by an insurer on the life of a person resident in Canada at the time the policy was issued or effected.

"modified net premium" —"modified net premium", in respect of a premium under a policy (other than a prepaid premium under a policy that cannot be refunded except on termination of the policy), means

(*a*) where all benefits (other than policy dividends) and premiums (other than the frequency of payment of premiums) in respect of the policy are determined at the date of issue of the policy, the amount determined by the formula

$$A \times [(B + C)/(D + E)]$$

where

A is the amount of the premium,

B is the present value, at the date of the issue of the policy, of the benefits to be provided under the terms of the policy after the day that is one year after the date of the issue of the policy,

C is the present value, at the date of the issue of the policy, of the benefits to be provided under the terms of the policy after the day that is two years after the date of the issue of the policy,

D is the present value, at the date of the issue of the policy, of the premiums payable under the terms of the policy on or after the day that is one year after the date of the issue of the policy, and

E is the present value, at the date of the issue of the policy, of the premiums payable under the terms of the policy on or after the day that is two years after the date of the issue of the policy,

except that the amount determined by the formula in respect of the premium for the second year of a policy is deemed to be the amount that is 50% of the total of

(i) the amount that would otherwise be determined under the formula, and

(ii) the amount of a one-year term insurance premium (determined without regard to the frequency of payment of the premium) that would be payable under the policy; and

(*b*) in any other case, the amount that would be determined under paragraph (*a*) if that paragraph applied and the amount were adjusted in a manner that is reasonable in the circumstances.

"net premium for the policy" —"net premium for the policy" (Repealed.)

"non-cancellable or guaranteed renewable accident and sickness policy" —"non-cancellable or guaranteed renewable accident and sickness policy", includes a non-cancellable or guaranteed renewable accident and sickness benefit under a group policy.

"participating life insurance policy" —"participating life insurance policy" has the meaning assigned by subsection 138(12) of the Act.

"policy liability" —"policy liability" of an insurer at the end of the taxation year in respect of an insurance policy or a claim, possible claim or risk under an insurance policy means the positive or negative amount of the insurer's reserve in respect of its potential liability in respect of the policy, claim, possible claim or risk at the end of the year determined in accordance with accepted actuarial practice, but without reference to projected income and capital taxes (other than the tax payable under Part XII.3 of the Act).

"policy loan" —"policy loan" has the meaning assigned by subsection 138(12) of the Act.

"post-1995 life insurance policy" —"post-1995 life insurance policy" means a life insurance policy that is not a pre-1996 life insurance policy.

"post-1995 non-cancellable or guaranteed renewable accident and sickness policy" —"post-1995 non-cancellable or guaranteed renewable accident and sickness policy" means a non-cancellable or guaranteed renewable accident and sickness policy that is not a pre-1996 non-cancellable or guaranteed renewable accident and sickness policy.

"pre-1996 life insurance policy" —"pre-1996 life insurance policy", at any time, means a life insurance policy where

(*a*) the policy was issued before 1996; and

(*b*) before that time and after 1995 there has been no change, except in accordance with the provisions (other than a general amending provision) of the policy as they existed on December 31, 1995, to

(i) the amount of any benefit under the policy,

(ii) the amount of any premium or other amount payable under the policy, or

Regulations

(iii) the number of premium or other payments under the policy.

"pre-1996 non-cancellable or guaranteed renewable accident and sickness policy" —"pre-1996 non-cancellable or guaranteed renewable accident and sickness policy", at any time, means a non-cancellable or guaranteed renewable accident and sickness policy where

(*a*) the policy was issued before 1996; and

(*b*) before that time and after 1995 there has been no change, except in accordance with the provisions (other than a general amending provision) of the policy as they existed on December 31, 1995, to

(i) the amount of any benefit under the policy,

(ii) the amount of any premium or other amount payable under the policy, or

(iii) the number of premium or other payments under the policy.

"qualified annuity" —"qualified annuity" means an annuity contract issued before 1982, other than a deposit administration fund policy or a policy referred to in paragraph 1403(7)(*c*),

(*a*) in respect of which regular periodic annuity payments have commenced;

(*b*) in respect of which a contract or certificate has been issued that provides for regular periodic annuity payments to commence within one year after the date of issue of the contract or certificate;

(*c*) that is not issued as or under a registered retirement savings plan, registered pension plan or deferred profit sharing plan and that

(i) does not provide for a guaranteed cash surrender value at any time, and

(ii) provides for regular periodic annuity payments to commence not later than the attainment of age 71 by the annuitant; or

(*d*) that is issued as or under a registered retirement savings plan, registered pension plan or deferred profit sharing plan, if the interest rate is guaranteed for at least 10 years and the plan does not provide for any participation in profits, directly or indirectly.

"reinsurance commission" —"reinsurance commission", in respect of a policy, means

(*a*) where the risk under the policy is fully reinsured, the amount, if any, by which

(i) the premium paid by the policyholder for the policy

exceeds

(ii) the consideration payable by the insurer in respect of the reinsurance of the risk; and

(*b*) where the risk under the policy is not fully reinsured, the amount, if any, by which

(i) the portion of the premium paid by the policyholder for the policy that may reasonably be considered to be in respect of the portion of the risk that is reinsured with a particular reinsurer

exceeds

(ii) the consideration payable by the insurer to the particular reinsurer in respect of the risk assumed by the reinsurer.

"reinsurance recoverable amount" —"reinsurance recoverable amount" of an insurer means an amount reported as a reinsurance asset of the insurer as at the end of a taxation year in respect of an amount recoverable from a reinsurer.

History: S. 1408(1), the definition "reinsurance recoverable amount" was added by S.C. 2010, c. 25, s. 80(1), applicable to taxation years that begin after 2010.

"relevant authority" —"relevant authority" of an insurer means

(*a*) the Superintendent of Financial Institutions, if the insurer is required by law to report to the Superintendent of Financial Institutions; and

(*b*) in any other case, the Superintendent of Insurance or other similar officer or authority of the province under whose laws the insurer is incorporated.

"reported reserve" —"reported reserve" of an insurer at the end of a taxation year in respect of an insurance policy or a claim, possible claim, risk, dividend, premium, refund of premiums or refund of premium deposits under an insurance policy means the amount equal to

(*a*) where the insurer is required to file an annual report with its relevant authority for a period ending coincidentally with the year, the positive or negative amount of the reserve that would be reported in that report in respect of the insurer's potential liability under the policy if the reserve were determined without reference to projected income and capital taxes (other than the tax payable under Part XII.3 of the Act);

(*b*) where the insurer is, throughout the year, subject to the supervision of its relevant authority and paragraph (*a*) does not apply, the positive or negative amount of the reserve that would be reported in its financial statements for the year in respect of the insurer's potential liability under the policy if

(i) those statements were prepared in accordance with generally accepted accounting principles, and

(ii) the reserve were determined without reference to projected income and capital taxes (other than the tax payable under Part XII.3 of the Act);

(*c*) where the insurer is the Canada Mortgage and Housing Corporation or a foreign affiliate of a taxpayer resident in Canada, the positive or negative amount of the reserve that would be reported in its financial statements for the year in respect of the insurer's potential liability under the policy if

(i) those statements were prepared in accordance with generally accepted accounting principles, and

(ii) the reserve were determined without reference to projected income and capital taxes (other than the tax payable under Part XII.3 of the Act); and

(*d*) in any other case, nil.

"segregated fund" —"segregated fund" has the meaning assigned by subsection 138.1(1) of the Act.

"segregated fund policy" —"segregated fund policy" has the meaning assigned by subsection 138.1(1) of the Act.

(2) The definition "group term life insurance policy" in subsection 248(1) of the Act does not apply to this Part.

(3) For the purpose of the formula referred to in the definition "modified net premium" in subsection (1), it may be assumed that premiums are payable annually in advance.

(4) For the purposes of this Part,

(*a*) a reference to a "premium paid by the policyholder" shall, depending on the method regularly followed by the insurer in computing its income, be read as a reference to a "premium paid or payable by the policyholder"; and

(*b*) in determining the premium paid by a policyholder for a policy, there may be deducted by the insurer the portion, if any, of the premium that

(i) can reasonably be considered, at the time the policy is issued, to be a deposit that, pursuant to the terms of the policy or the by-laws of the insurer, will be returned to the policyholder, or credited to the account of the policyholder, by the insurer on the termination of the policy, and

(ii) was not otherwise deducted under section 140 of the Act.

(5) For the purposes of this Part, any rider that is attached to a life insurance policy and that provides for additional life insurance or for an annuity is a separate life insurance policy.

(6) For the purposes of this Part, any rider that is attached to a policy and that provides for additional non-cancellable or guaranteed renewable accident and sickness insurance, as the case may be, is a separate non-cancellable or guaranteed renewable accident and sickness policy.

(7) For the purposes of the definitions "pre-1996 life insurance policy" and "pre-1996 non-cancellable or guaranteed renewable accident and sickness policy" in subsection (1), a change in the amount of any benefit or in the amount or number of any premiums or other amounts payable under a policy is deemed not to have occurred where the change results from

(*a*) a change in an underwriting class;

(*b*) a change in frequency of premium payments within a year that does not alter the present value, at the beginning of the year, of the total premiums to be paid under the policy in the year;

(*c*) the deletion of a rider;

(*d*) the correction of erroneous information;

(*e*) the reinstatement of the policy after its lapse, if the reinstatement occurs not later than 60 days after the end of the calendar year in which the lapse occurred;

(*f*) the redating of the policy for policy loan indebtedness; or

(*g*) a change in the amount of a benefit under the policy that is granted by the insurer on a class basis, where

(i) no consideration was payable by the policyholder or any other person for the change, and

(ii) the change was not made because of the terms or conditions of the policy or any other policy or contract to which the insurer is a party.

(8) A reference in this Part to an amount or item reported as an asset or a liability of an insurer as at the end of a taxation year means

(*a*) if reporting by the insurer to the insurer's relevant authority is required at the end of the year, an amount or item that is reported, as at the end of the year, as an asset or a liability in the insurer's non-consolidated balance sheet accepted by the insurer's relevant authority; and

(*b*) in any other case, an amount or item that is reported as an asset or a liability in a non-consolidated balance sheet that is prepared in a manner consistent with the requirements that would have applied had reporting to the insurer's relevant authority been required at the end of the year.

History: S. 1408(8) was added by S.C. 2010, c. 25, s. 80(2), applicable to taxation years that begin after 2010.

Regulations

Part XV
Profit Sharing Plans

Division I
Employees Profit Sharing Plans

1500. [Elections]

(1) An election under subsection 144(4.1) of the Act by the trustee of a trust governed by an employees profit sharing plan shall be made by filing with the Minister the prescribed form in duplicate.

Forms: T3009 — Election from Deemed Disposition and Reacquisition of any Capital Property of an Employees Profit Sharing Plan under Subsection 144(4.2).

Interpretation Bulletins: *Secondary* — IT-280R Employees profit sharing plans — Payments computed by reference to profits.

(2) An election under subsection 144(4.2) of the Act by the trustee of a trust governed by an employees profit sharing plan shall be made by filing with the Minister the prescribed form in duplicate on or before the last day of a taxation year of the trust in respect of any capital property deemed to have been disposed of in that taxation year by virtue of the election.

Forms: T3009 — Election from Deemed Disposition and Reacquisition of any Capital Property of an Employees Profit Sharing Plan Under Subsection 144(4.2).

(3) An election under subsection 144(10) of the Act shall be made by sending the following documents by registered mail to the Commissioner of Revenue at Ottawa:

(*a*) a letter from the employer stating that he elects to have the arrangement qualify as an employees profit sharing plan;

(*b*) if the employer is a corporation,

(i) where the directors of the corporation are legally entitled to administer the affairs of the corporation, a certified copy of their resolution authorizing the election to be made, and

(ii) where the directors of the corporation are not legally entitled to administer the affairs of the corporation, a certified copy of the authorization of the making of the election by the person or persons legally entitled to administer the affairs of the corporation; and

(*c*) a copy of the agreement and any supplementary agreement setting out the plan.

Division II
Deferred Profit Sharing Plans

1501. Registration of Plans

For the purpose of the definition "deferred profit sharing plan" in subsection 147(1) of the Act, an application for registration of a plan shall be made by sending the following documents by registered mail to the Commissioner of Revenue at Ottawa:

(*a*) a letter from the trustee and the employer whereby the trustee and the employer apply for the registration of the plan as a deferred profit sharing plan;

(*b*) if the employer is a corporation, a certified copy of a resolution of the directors authorizing the application to be made; and

(*c*) a copy of the agreement and any supplementary agreement setting out the plan.

Information Circulars: IC 77-1R5 Deferred profit sharing plan.

1502. (Revoked.)

Division III
Elections in Respect of Certain Single Payments

1503. [Election by beneficiary]

Any election by a beneficiary under subsection 147(10.1) of the Act shall be made by filing the prescribed form in duplicate as follows:

(*a*) one form shall be filed by the beneficiary with the trustee of the deferred profit sharing plan not later than 60 days after the end of the taxation year in which the beneficiary received the payment referred to in subsection 147(10.1) of the Act; and

(*b*) the other form shall be filed by the beneficiary with the Minister on or before the day on which the beneficiary is required to file a return of income pursuant to section 150 of the Act for the taxation year in which the beneficiary received the payment referred to in subsection 147(10.1) of the Act.

Forms: T2078 — Election Under Subsection 147(10.1) in Respect of a Single Payment Received from a Deferred Profit Sharing Plan.

Part XVI
Prescribed Countries

1600. [Prescribed countries]

For the purposes of subsection 10(4) of the *Income Tax Application Rules*, the following countries are hereby prescribed:

(*a*) Commonwealth of Australia;

(*b*) Kingdom of Denmark;

(*c*) Republic of Finland;

(*d*) French Republic;

(*e*) Federal Republic of Germany;

(*f*) Ireland;

(*g*) Jamaica;

(*h*) Japan;

(*i*) Kingdom of the Netherlands;

(*j*) New Zealand;

(*k*) Kingdom of Norway;

(*l*) Republic of South Africa;

(*m*) Kingdom of Sweden;

(*n*) Trinidad and Tobago;

(*o*) United Kingdom of Great Britain and Northern Ireland; and

(*p*) United States of America.

Part XVII
Capital Cost Allowances, Farming and Fishing

Division I
Deductions Allowed

1700. Rates

(1) For the purposes of paragraph 20(1)(*a*) of the Act, there is hereby allowed to a taxpayer, in computing his income from farming or fishing, as the case may be, a deduction for each taxation year in respect of each property that was used for the purpose of gaining or producing income from farming or fishing equal to such amount as he may claim, not exceeding in the case of

(*a*) a building or other structure, not described elsewhere in this subsection, including component parts such as electric wiring, plumbing, sprinkler systems, air-conditioning equipment, heating equipment, lighting fixtures, elevators and escalators, 2½ per cent,

(*b*) a building or other structure of

(i) frame,

(ii) log,

(iii) stucco on frame,

(iv) galvanized iron, or

(v) corrugated iron,

construction including component parts such as electric wiring, plumbing, sprinkler systems, air-conditioning equipment, heating equipment, lighting fixtures, elevators and escalators, 5 per cent,

(*c*) a fence, 5 per cent,

(*d*) a scow or a vessel, including furniture, fittings or equipment attached thereto, but not including radiocommunication equipment, 7½ per cent,

(*e*) nonautomotive equipment and machinery, 10 per cent,

(*f*) automotive equipment, a sleigh or a wagon, 15 per cent,

(*g*) radiocommunication equipment, 15 per cent,

(*h*) tile drainage acquired before the 1965 taxation year, 10 per cent,

(*i*) a water storage tank, 5 per cent,

(*j*) a gas well that is part of the equipment of a farm and from which the gas produced is not sold, 10 per cent, and

(*k*) a tool costing less than $100, 100 per cent,

of the depreciable cost to the taxpayer of the property.

Forms: T1175 — Farming — Calculation of Capital Cost Allowance (CCA) and Business Use-of-Home Expenses.

Guides: RC4408 Farming Income and the AgriStability and AgriInvest Programs Harmonized Guide.

Interpretation Bulletins: *Secondary* — IT-268R4 Inter vivos transfer of farm property to child; IT-349R3 Intergenerational transfers of farm property on death.

(2) Taxation Years Less Than 12 Months. Where a taxation year is less than 12 months, the amount allowed as a deduction under subsection (1) shall not exceed that proportion of the maximum amount otherwise allowable that the number of days in the taxation year is of 365.

(3) Property Disposed of During Year. Where a taxpayer has disposed of a property before the end of a taxation year, the amount allowed as a deduction under subsection (1) in respect of that property for the year shall not exceed that proportion of the maximum amount otherwise allowable that the number of months in the taxation year during which the property was owned by the taxpayer is of 12.

(4) Leasehold Interests. Where a taxpayer has property that was used for the purpose of gaining or producing income from farming or fishing and that would be included in Class 13 in Schedule II if he had claimed an allowance under Part XI, he may deduct, in computing his income from farming or fishing for a taxation year, an amount not exceeding the amount he could have deducted in respect of that property for the year under paragraph 1100(1)(*b*).

Division II
Maximum Deductions

1701. [Maximum deduction]

(1) The amount allowed as a deduction under section 1700 in respect of a property shall not exceed the amount by which the capital cost of the property to the taxpayer exceeds the aggregate of the deductions from income allowed under this Part in respect of the property for previous taxation years.

(2) In respect of the 1972 and subsequent taxation years, where subsection 20(5) of the *Income Tax Application Rules* applies to a particular property, notwithstanding subsection (1), the amount allowed as a deduction under section 1700 in respect of the property shall not exceed the amount by which (*a*) the amount determined to be the undepreciated capital cost of the property, under paragraph 20(5)(*b*) of the *Income Tax Application Rules*,

exceeds

(*b*) the aggregate of the deductions from income allowed under this Part in respect of the property for previous taxation years ending after 1971.

Interpretation Bulletins: *Secondary* — IT-349R3 Intergenerational transfers of farm property on death.

DIVISION III

PROPERTY NOT INCLUDED

1702. [Excluded property]

(1) Nothing in this Part shall be construed as allowing a deduction in respect of a property

(*a*) the cost of which is deductible in computing the taxpayer's income;

(*b*) that is described in the taxpayer's inventory;

(*c*) that was acquired by an expenditure in respect of which the taxpayer is allowed a deduction from income under section 37 of the Act;

(*d*) that has been constituted a prescribed class by subsection 24(2) of chapter 91, S.C. 1966-67;

(*e*) that is included in a separate prescribed class established under subsection 13(14) of the Act;

(*f*) that was not used in the business during the year;

(*g*) that is

(i) an animal, or

(ii) a tree, shrub, herb or similar growing thing;

(*h*) that was not acquired by the taxpayer for the purpose of gaining or producing income from farming or fishing;

(*i*) that has been included at any time by the taxpayer in a class prescribed under Part XI;

(*j*) that is a passenger automobile acquired after June 13, 1963, and before January 1, 1966, the cost to the taxpayer of which, minus the initial transportation charges and retail sales tax in respect thereof, exceeded $5,000, unless the automobile was acquired by a person before June 14, 1963 and has, by one or more transactions between persons not dealing at arm's length, become vested in the taxpayer; or

(*k*) that was acquired by the taxpayer after 1971.

(2) Where a taxpayer is a member of a partnership, the properties referred to in this Part shall be deemed not to include any property that is an interest of the taxpayer in depreciable property that is partnership property of the partnership.

(3) The properties referred to in section 1700 shall be deemed not to include the land upon which a property described therein was constructed or is situated.

(4) Where the taxpayer is a non-resident person, the properties referred to in section 1700 shall be deemed not to include property that is situated outside Canada.

(5) The provisions of subsections 1102(11), (12) and (13) are applicable *mutatis mutandis* to paragraph (1)(*j*).

Interpretation Bulletins: *Secondary* — IT-349R3 Intergenerational transfers of farm property on death.

DIVISION IV

INTERPRETATION

1703. Taxation Years for Individuals in Business

(1) Where a taxpayer is an individual and his income for the taxation year includes income from a business the fiscal period of which does not coincide with the calendar year, in respect of depreciable properties acquired for the purpose of gaining or producing income from the business, a reference in this Part to

(*a*) "the taxation year" shall be deemed to be a reference to the fiscal period of the business; and

(*b*) "the end of the taxation year" shall be deemed to be a reference to the end of the fiscal period of the business.

(2) Depreciable Cost. In this Part, "depreciable cost" to a taxpayer of property means, except as otherwise provided, the actual cost of the property to the taxpayer or the amount at which he is deemed under subsection 13(7) of the Act to have acquired the property, as the case may be.

(3) Depreciable Cost. Notwithstanding the other provisions of this section, in the case of property the cost of which to a partnership has been determined under paragraph 20(5)(*a*) of the *Income Tax Application Rules*, the depreciable cost to the taxpayer of the property for the purposes of this Part shall be deemed to be an amount equal to the cost to the partnership of the particular property as determined under that paragraph.

(4) Personal Use of Property. Where a taxpayer has, in a taxation year, regularly used a property in part for the purpose of gaining or producing income from farming or fishing and in part for a purpose other than gaining or producing income, the depreciable cost to the taxpayer of the property for the purposes of this Part is the proportion of the amount that would otherwise be the depreciable cost that the use regularly made of the property for the purpose of gaining or producing income from farming or fishing is of the whole use regularly made of the property.

(5) Grants, Subsidies or Other Government Assistance. Where a taxpayer has received or is entitled to receive a grant, subsidy or other assistance from a government, municipality or other public authority in respect of or for the acquisition of property, the depreciable cost to the taxpayer of the property for the purposes of this Part is the amount that would otherwise be the depreciable cost minus the amount of the grant, subsidy or other assistance.

(6) Transactions Not at Arm's Length. Where property did belong to a person (in this subsection referred to as the "original owner") and has, by one or more transactions between persons not dealing at arm's length, become vested in a taxpayer, the depreciable cost to the taxpayer of the property for the purposes of this Part is the lesser of

(*a*) the actual capital cost of the property to the taxpayer; and

(*b*) the amount by which the actual capital cost of the property to the original owner exceeds the aggregate of

(i) the total amount of depreciation for the property that, since the commencement of 1917, has been or should have been taken into account in accordance with the practice of the Department of National Revenue in ascertaining the income of the original owner and all intervening owners for the purposes of the *Income War Tax Act* or in ascertaining a loss for a year when there was no income under that Act,

(ii) any accumulated depreciation reserves that the original owner or an intervening owner had for the property at the commencement of 1917 and that were recognized by the Minister for the purposes of the *Income War Tax Act*, and

(iii) the aggregate of the deductions, if any, allowed under this Part in respect of the property to the original owner and all intervening owners.

(7) Property Acquired From a Parent. Notwithstanding subsection (6), where depreciable property has been acquired by a taxpayer under such circumstances that the provisions of section 85H of the Act as it read in its application to the 1971 and prior taxation years are applicable for the determination of the capital cost of the property, the depreciable cost to the taxpayer of the property for the purposes of this Part is the capital cost as determined under that section.

(8) Property Acquired by Gift. Subsection (6) does not apply in respect of property which a taxpayer has acquired by gift.

Interpretation Bulletins: *Secondary* — IT-349R3 Intergenerational transfers of farm property on death.

Division V
Application of This Part

1704. [Application of Part]

This Part shall apply only to a taxpayer who, in computing his income, has never claimed an allowance under Part XI in respect of a property at a time when an allowance could have been claimed under this Part in respect of that property, other than an allowance claimed by the taxpayer under Part XI that may be claimed in respect of a property described in

(*a*) paragraph 1100(1)(*r*) as enacted by Order in Council P.C. 1965-1118 of June 18, 1965 and as amended by Order in Council P.C. 1965-2320 of December 29, 1965;

(*b*) paragraph 1100(1)(*sa*) as enacted by Order in Council P.C. 1968-2261 of December 10, 1968;

(*c*) paragraph 1100(1)(*v*); or

(*d*) Class 20 in Schedule II.

Interpretation Bulletins: *Secondary* — IT-349R3 Intergenerational transfers of farm property on death.

Part XVIII
Inventories

1800. Manner of Keeping Inventories

For the purposes of section 230 of the Act, an inventory shall show quantities and nature of the properties that should be included therein in such a manner and in sufficient detail that the property may be valued in accordance with this Part or section 10 of the Act.

Interpretation Bulletins: *Secondary* — IT-504R2 (Consolid.) Visual artists and writers.

1801. Valuation

Except as provided in section 1802, for the purpose of computing the income of a taxpayer from a business, all the property described in all the inventories of the business may be valued at its fair market value.

Interpretation Bulletins: *Secondary* — IT-473 Inventory valuation.

1802. Valuation of animals

(1) Except as provided in subsection (2), a taxpayer who is carrying on a business that includes the breeding and raising of animals may elect in prescribed form for a taxation year and subsequent taxation years to value each animal of a particular species (except a registered animal, an animal purchased for feedlot or similar operations, or an animal purchased by a drover or like person for resale) included in his inventory in respect of the business at a unit price determined in accordance with this section.

Forms: T2034 — Election to Establish Inventory Unit Prices for Animals.

(2) An election made in accordance with subsection (1) may be revoked in writing by the taxpayer, but where a taxpayer has made a revocation in accordance with this subsection a further election may not be made under subsection (1) except with the concurrence of the Minister.

(3) The unit price with respect to an animal of a particular class of animal shall be determined in accordance with the following rules:

(*a*) where animals of a particular class of animal were included in the inventory of a taxpayer at the end of the taxation year immediately preceding the first year in respect of which the taxpayer elected under subsection (1), the unit price of an animal of that class shall be computed by dividing the total value of all animals of the class in the inventory of the preceding year by the number of animals of the class described in that inventory; and

(*b*) in any other case, the unit price of an animal of a class shall be determined by the Minister, having regard, among other things, to the unit prices of animals of a comparable class of animal used in valuing the inventories of other taxpayers in the district.

(4) Notwithstanding subsection (1), where the aggregate value of the animals of a particular class determined in accordance with that subsection exceeds the market value of those animals, the animals of that class may be valued at fair market value.

(5) In this section,

"class of animal" means a group of animals of a particular species segregated on the basis of age, breed or other recognized division, as determined by the taxpayer at the time of election under this section;

"district" means the territory served by a Tax Centre of the Canada Revenue Agency;

"registered animal" means an animal for which a certificate of registration has been issued by the registrar of the breed to which the animal belongs or by the registrar of the Canadian National Livestock Records;

a reference to "taxation year" shall be deemed to include a reference to the fiscal period of a business.

Part XIX

Investment Income Tax

Editorial Note: The provisions in Part XIX are applicable to taxation years commencing after June 17, 1987 and before 1990 that end after 1987.

1900. Interpretation

(1) In this Part,

"benefit"—"benefit" under a policy includes a policy dividend, an experience rating refund, a refund of premiums and any amount deemed by paragraph 138.1(1)(*g*) of the Act for the purposes of Part I of the Act to be a payment under the terms and conditions of the policy, but does not include a policy loan or interest on funds left on deposit with the insurer under the terms of the policy;

"excluded arrangement"—"excluded arrangement" of an insurer at any time means

(*a*) a life insurance policy in Canada issued by the insurer (or in respect of which the insurer has assumed the obligations of the issuer of the policy to the policyholder), which is at that time a registered life insurance policy, an annuity contract (including a settlement annuity), a group term life insurance policy or an existing guaranteed life insurance policy,

(*b*) a registered pension fund or plan in respect of which the insurer is at that time a plan sponsor, or a retirement compensation arrangement in respect of which the insurer is the custodian,

(*c*) a life insurance policy (other than a life insurance policy in Canada) issued by the insurer before that time (or in respect of which the insurer has before that time assumed the obligations of the issuer of the policy to the policyholder), and

(*d*) a reinsurance arrangement under which the insurer has before that time assumed, directly or indirectly, risks under life insurance policies (other than policies issued by the insurer or in respect of which the insurer has assumed the obligations of the issuer of the policy to the policyholder), to the extent that the arrangement relates to those risks;

"existing guaranteed life insurance policy"—"existing guaranteed life insurance policy" at any time means a non-participating life insurance policy in Canada in respect of which the amount of every premium that became payable before that time and after March 2, 1988 was fixed and determined on or before March 2, 1988, adjusted for any specified transaction or event that occurs after March 2, 1988 in respect of the policy;

"group term life insurance policy"—"group term life insurance policy" is a group life insurance policy under which

(*a*) no amount (other than a policy dividend, an experience rating refund or a refund of premiums) may become payable to any person, except in the event of the death or disability of a person whose life was insured under the policy, and

(*b*) no amount may become payable to a person (other than the group policyholder) in respect of a policy dividend, an experience rating refund or a refund of premiums that has been funded by contributions made to or under the policy by another person;

"guaranteed interest"—"guaranteed interest" in respect of a life insurance policy for a taxation year means

(*a*) in respect of a life insurance policy (other than a pre-funded group life insurance policy), the total of all amounts each of which is the amount in respect of a guaranteed benefit in respect of which an amount is determined under paragraph 1401(1)(*a*), (*c*) or (*d*) for the year, where that benefit is provided under the terms and conditions of the policy as they existed on March 2, 1988, determined by multiplying the greater of

(i) the rate of interest used by the issuer of the policy in respect of the year in determining the amount of the benefit, and

(ii) 4%

by $^1/_2$ of the total of

(iii) the maximum amount that would be deductible under subparagraph 138(3)(*a*)(i) of the Act pursuant to paragraph 1401(1)(*a*), (*c*) or (*d*), as the case may be, in respect of the benefit in computing the insurer's income for the year, if that amount were determined without reference to any policy loan or reinsurance arrangement, and

(iv) the maximum amount that would have been deductible under subparagraph 138(3)(*a*)(i) of the Act pursuant to paragraph 1401(1)(*a*), (*c*) or (*d*), as the case may be, in respect of the benefit in computing the insurer's income for the immediately preceding taxation year, if that amount were determined without reference to any policy loan or reinsurance arrangement, and

(*b*) in respect of a pre-funded group life insurance policy, 80 per cent of the amount that would be determined under paragraph (*a*) in respect of the policy for the year, if that paragraph were read without reference to the words "(other than a pre-funded group life insurance policy)";

"life insurance policy"—"life insurance policy" does not include

(*a*) that part of a policy in respect of which the policyholder is deemed by paragraph 138.1(1)(*e*) of the Act to have an interest in a segregated fund trust, or

(*b*) a reinsurance arrangement;

"life insurance policy in Canada"—"life insurance policy in Canada" does not include

(*a*) that part of a policy in respect of which the policyholder is deemed by paragraph 138.1(1)(*e*) of the Act to have an interest in a segregated fund trust, or

(*b*) a reinsurance arrangement;

Regulations

"maximum tax actuarial reserve"—"maximum tax actuarial reserve" has the meaning assigned by subsection 138(12) of the Act;

"mortality experience"—"mortality experience" of an insurer for a taxation year means the positive or negative amount, as the case may be, determined by the formula

(A - B - C)

where

A is the total of all amounts each of which is the amount that became payable in the year by the insurer under a taxable life insurance policy of the insurer as a consequence of the receipt of a claim in respect of the death of a person whose life was insured under the policy, determined without reference to any policy loan,

B is the total of all amounts each of which is the amount of a reserve that would be determined in accordance with paragraph 1401(1)(*a*), (*c*) or (*d*), if that amount were determined without reference to any policy loan or reinsurance arrangement, in respect of a taxable life insurance policy of the insurer that would have been released in the year as a consequence of the receipt of a claim in respect of the death of a person whose life was insured under the policy, and

C is 90 per cent of the total of all amounts, each of which is the net cost of pure insurance determined in accordance with section 308 for the year in respect of an interest in a taxable life insurance policy of the insurer;

"mortality loss adjustment account"—"mortality loss adjustment account" of an insurer at the end of a taxation year is the positive amount, if any, determined by the formula

A + B - C

where

A is the mortality loss adjustment account of the insurer for the immediately preceding taxation year,

B is

(*a*) where the mortality experience of the insurer for the year is a negative amount, the amount of the mortality experience of the insurer for the year, and

(*b*) in any other case, the amount, if any, by which the amount claimed by the insurer under the description of F in computing the amount determined under subsection (6) for the year exceeds the amount of the mortality loss adjustment account of the insurer for the immediately preceding taxation year, and

C is 1.2 times the amount, if any, by which

(*a*) the net cost of insurance of the insurer for the year

exceeds

(*b*) the total of all amounts each of which is the net cost of pure insurance determined in accordance with section 308 for the year in respect of an interest in a taxable life insurance policy of the insurer;

"net cost of insurance"—"net cost of insurance" of an insurer for a taxation year means the amount, if any, by which

(*a*) the amount determined in the description of A in the definition "mortality experience" in respect of the insurer for the year

exceeds

(*b*) the amount determined in the description of B in the definition "mortality experience" in respect of the insurer for the year;

"net level premium"—"net level premium" in respect of a particular premium under a policy (other than a prepaid premium that cannot be refunded except on termination or cancellation of the policy) means

(*a*) where benefits (other than policy dividends) and premiums (other than the frequency of payment thereof) in respect of the policy have been determined at the date of issue of the policy, the amount determined by the formula

$$A \times (B / C)$$

where

A is the amount of the particular premium,

B is the present value, at the date of issue of the policy, of the amount of the benefits (other than policy dividends) to be provided under the terms of the policy after the issue of the policy, and

C is the present value, at the date of issue of the policy, of the amount of the premiums payable under the terms of the policy on or after the issue of the policy, and

(*b*) where the amounts of the benefits or premiums in respect of the policy are not determined at the date of issue of the policy, the amount that would be determined under paragraph (*a*) in respect of the particular premium if the amount were adjusted in a manner that is reasonable in the circumstances and consistent with the manner of the adjustment referred to in the definition "modified net premium" in subsection 1404(2) in respect of the particular premium;

"net level premium reserve"—"net level premium reserve" in respect of a life insurance policy for a taxation year means the maximum amount that would be deductible under subparagraph 138(3)(*a*)(i) of the Act pursuant to paragraph 1401(1)(*c*) in respect of the policy in computing the insurer's income for the year, if any reference to "modified net premium" in sections 1401, 1403 and 1404 were a reference to "net level premium";

"non-participating life insurance policy"—"non-participating life insurance policy" means a life insurance policy other than a participating life insurance policy within the meaning assigned by subsection 138(12) of the Act;

"policy loan"—"policy loan" has the meaning assigned by subsection 138(12) of the Act;

Regulations

"pre-funded group life insurance policy" —"pre-funded group life insurance policy" means a group term life insurance policy, other than a policy under which each premium payable is in respect of coverage for a period, including the day on which the premium becomes payable, that does not exceed twelve months;

"premium" —"premium" includes

(*a*) consideration received for settlement annuities,

(*b*) amounts received by an insurer in respect of employee contributions under registered pension funds or plans in respect of which the insurer is a plan sponsor or a retirement compensation arrangement in respect of which the insurer is the custodian, and

(*c*) any amount deemed by paragraph 138.1(1)(*h*) of the Act for the purposes of Part I of the Act to be a premium received by an insurer,

but does not include amounts received in respect of the repayment of a policy loan or in respect of interest on a policy loan and, for greater certainty, the amount of a premium is not reduced by the amount of a refund of premiums;

"registered life insurance policy" —"registered life insurance policy" has the meaning assigned by section 211 of the Act;

"reinsurance arrangement" —"reinsurance arrangement" does not include an arrangement under which an insurer has assumed the obligations of the issuer of a life insurance policy to the policyholder;

"segregated fund" —"segregated fund" has the meaning assigned by subsection 138(12) of the Act;

"specified transaction or event" —"specified transaction or event" in respect of a life insurance policy means

(*a*) a change in underwriting class,

(*b*) a change in premium due to a change in frequency of premium payments within a year that does not alter the present value, at the beginning of the year, of the total premiums to be paid under the policy in the year,

(*c*) an addition under the terms of the policy as they existed on March 2, 1988, of accidental death, dismemberment, disability or guaranteed purchase option benefits,

(*d*) a deletion of a rider,

(*e*) redating lapsed policies within 60 days after the end of the calendar year in which the lapse occurred, or redating for policy loan indebtedness,

(*f*) a change in premium due to a correction of erroneous information,

(*g*) the payment of a premium after its due date, or no more than 30 days before its due date, as established on or before March 2, 1988, or

(*h*) the payment of an amount of interest described in subparagraph 148(9)(*e*.1) (i) [subsection 148(9), paragraph (*a*) of the definition of "premium"] of the Act;

"taxable life insurance policy" —"taxable life insurance policy" of an insurer at any time means a life insurance policy in Canada issued by the insurer (or in respect of which the insurer has assumed the obligations of the issuer of the policy to the policyholder), other than a policy that is at that time an excluded arrangement.

(2) For the purposes of this Part,

(*a*) any rider added, at any time after March 2, 1988, to a life insurance policy shall be deemed to be a separate life insurance policy issued at that time; and

(*b*) in respect of an insurer's first taxation year that commences after June 17, 1987 and ends after 1987, the maximum amount that would have been deductible under subparagraph 138(3)(*a*)(i), (ii) or (iv) of the Act, as the case may be, in computing the insurer's income for the immediately preceding year shall be determined as though the provisions that apply in determining that maximum amount for that first taxation year were applicable in respect of that immediately preceding year.

(3) Prescribed Provisions. For the purposes of paragraph (*b*) of the description of C in subsection 211.1(3) of the Act, as it read in its application to taxation years beginning before 1990, the provisions of the Act that are prescribed are paragraphs 12(1)(*i*), (*i*.1), (*n*), (*n*.1), (*n*.2), (*n*.3), (*o*), (*t*) and (*v*) and subsections 13(1), 59(3.2) and (3.3), 138(4.4) and 140(2).

(4) Prescribed Arrangements. For the purposes of the description of D in subsection 211.1(3) of the Act, as it read in its application to taxation years beginning before 1990, prescribed arrangements in respect of an insurer are

(*a*) life insurance policies in Canada issued by the insurer (or in respect of which the insurer has assumed the obligations of the issuer of the policy to the policyholder) that are group term life insurance policies or existing guaranteed life insurance policies;

(*b*) life insurance policies (other than life insurance policies in Canada) issued by the insurer (or in respect of which the insurer has assumed the obligations of the issuer of the policy to the policyholder);

(*c*) retirement compensation arrangements in respect of which the insurer is the custodian; and

(*d*) reinsurance arrangements under which the insurer has assumed or ceded risks insured under life insurance policies (other than policies issued by the insurer or in respect of which the insurer has assumed the obligations of the issuer of the policy to the policyholder).

(5) Prescribed Rules for Determining Amounts. The amount in the description of D in subsection 211.1(3) of the Act, as it read in its application to taxation years beginning before 1990, in respect of a life insurer for a taxation year is determined by the formula

$$A - B + C - D - E - F$$

where

A is the total of all amounts each of which is the maximum amount that would be deductible under subparagraph 138(3)(*a*)(i), (ii) or (iv) of the Act in respect of an excluded arrangement of the insurer in computing

Regulations

the insurer's income for the year, if that amount were determined without reference to any policy loan;

B is the total of all amounts each of which is the maximum amount that would have been deductible under subparagraph 138(3)(*a*)(i), (ii) or (iv) of the Act in respect of an excluded arrangement of the insurer in computing the insurer's income for the immediately preceding year, if that amount were determined without reference to any policy loan;

C is the total of all amounts each of which is the amount of a benefit, determined on a net of reinsurance ceded basis, that has become payable by the insurer in the year in respect of an excluded arrangement of the insurer, to the extent that the benefit is deducted in computing the insurer's income for the year under Part I of the Act from carrying on a life insurance business in Canada;

D is the total of all amounts each of which is the amount of a premium, determined on a net of reinsurance ceded basis, that has become receivable by the insurer in the year in respect of an excluded arrangement of the insurer, to the extent that the premium is included in computing the insurer's income for the year under Part I of the Act from carrying on a life insurance business in Canada;

E is the positive or negative amount, as the case may be, in respect of the insurer for the year determined by the formula

$$(G - H) - (I - J) + (K - L) - (M - N)$$

where

G is the total of all amounts each of which is the maximum amount that would be deductible under subparagraph 138(3)(*a*)(i), (ii) or (iv) of the Act in respect of a taxable life insurance policy of the insurer in computing the insurer's income for the year, if that amount were determined without reference to any policy loan or reinsurance arrangement,

H is the total of all amounts each of which is the maximum amount that would be deductible under subparagraph 138(3)(*a*)(i), (ii) or (iv) of the Act in respect of a taxable life insurance policy of the insurer in computing the insurer's income for the year, if that amount were determined without reference to any policy loan,

I is the total of all amounts each of which is the maximum amount that would have been deductible under subparagraph 138(3)(*a*)(i), (ii) or (iv) of the Act in respect of a taxable life insurance policy of the insurer in computing the insurer's income for the immediately preceding taxation year, if that amount were determined without reference to any policy loan or reinsurance arrangement,

J is the total of all amounts each of which is the maximum amount that would have been deductible under subparagraph 138(3)(*a*)(i), (ii) or (iv) of the Act in respect of a taxable life insurance policy of the insurer in computing the insurer's income for the immediately preceding taxation year, if that amount were determined without reference to any policy loan,

K is the total of all amounts each of which is the amount of a benefit that has become payable in the year by the insurer under a taxable life insurance policy of the insurer,

L is the total of all amounts each of which is the amount of a benefit, determined on a net of reinsurance ceded basis, that has become payable by the insurer under a taxable life insurance policy of the insurer, to the extent that it is deducted in computing the insurer's income from carrying on a life insurance business in Canada for the year,

M is the total of all amounts each of which is the amount of a premium that has become receivable by the insurer in the year under a taxable life insurance policy of the insurer, and

N is the total of all amounts each of which is the amount of a premium, determined on net of reinsurance ceded basis, that has become receivable by the insurer in the year under a taxable life insurance policy of the insurer, to the extent that the premium is included in computing the insurer's income from carrying on a life insurance business in Canada for the year; and

F is the positive or negative amount, as the case may be, determined by the formula

$$O + P - Q - R$$

where

O is the total of all amounts each of which is an amount in respect of a group term life insurance policy equal to the lesser of

(*a*) the amount of interest credited by the insurer in the year on account of the policy (other than interest payable in respect of the period ending on its first anniversary date after March 2, 1988), and

(*b*) the amount, if any, by which the maximum amount that would be deductible under subparagraph 138(3)(*a*)(i) of the Act pursuant to paragraph 1401(1)(*c.1*) in respect of the policy in computing the insurer's income for the year, if that amount were determined without reference to any reinsurance arrangement, exceeds the maximum amount that would have been so deductible in computing the insurer's income for the immediately preceding year,

P is 80 per cent of the total of all amounts each of which is the amount in respect of a liability of the insurer, a benefit, a risk or a guarantee, in respect of which an amount is determined under paragraph 1401(1)(*a*), (*c*) or (*d*) for the year, in respect of a pre-funded group life insurance policy of the insurer, determined by multiplying

(*a*) the rate of interest used in determining the amount under paragraph 1401(1)(*a*), (*c*) or (*d*), as the case may be, for the year in respect of the liability, benefit, risk or guarantee, as the case may be,

by 1/2 of the total of

(*b*) the maximum amount that would be deductible under subparagraph 138(3)(*a*)(i) of the Act pursuant to paragraph 1401(1)(*a*), (*c*) or (*d*), as the case may be, in respect of the liability, benefit, risk or guarantee, as the case may be, in computing the insurer's income for the year if that amount were determined without reference to any policy loan or reinsurance arrangement, and

(*c*) the maximum amount that would have been deductible under subparagraph 138(3)(*a*)(i) of the Act pursuant to paragraph 1401(1)(*a*), (*c*) or (*d*), as the case may be, in respect of the liability, benefit, risk or guarantee, as the case may be, in computing the insurer's income for the immediately preceding taxation year if that amount were determined without reference to any policy loan or reinsurance arrangement,

Q is the total of all amounts each of which is the amount determined for the year in respect of a taxable life insurance policy of the insurer by multiplying

(*a*) the rate of interest used in determining the maximum amount deductible under subparagraph 138(3)(*a*)(i) of the Act pursuant to paragraph 1401(1)(*c*) in respect of the policy in computing the insurer's income for the year,

by 1/2 of the total of

(*b*) the maximum amount that would be deductible under subparagraph 138(3)(*a*)(ii) of the Act in respect of the policy in computing the insurer's income for the year, if that amount were determined without reference to any reinsurance arrangement, and

(*c*) the maximum amount that would have been deductible under subparagraph 138(3)(*a*)(ii) of the Act in respect of the policy in computing the insurer's income for the immediately preceding taxation year, if that amount were determined without reference to any reinsurance arrangement, and

R is the total of all amounts each of which is an amount in respect of a group term life insurance policy equal to the amount, if any, by which

(*a*) the total of all amounts determined in respect of the insurer under the description of O in respect of the policy for taxation years ending before the year

exceeds the total of

(*b*) the total of all amounts determined in respect of the insurer under the description of R in respect of the policy for taxation years ending before the year, and

(*c*) the maximum amount that would be deductible under subparagraph 138(3)(*a*)(i) of the Act pursuant to paragraph 1401(1)(*c*.1) in respect of the policy in computing the insurer's income for the year, if that amount were determined without reference to any reinsurance arrangement.

(6) Prescribed Rules for Determining Amounts. The amount of the term insurance component in the description of E in subsection 211.1(3) of the Act, as it read in its application to taxation years beginning before 1990, in respect of a life insurer for a taxation year is determined by the formula

$$A + B + C - D + E - F + G + H$$

where

A is the amount determined by multiplying 0.0035 by the total of all amounts each of which is the amount of new insurance effected in the year (other than amounts rescinded in the year) under a taxable life insurance policy of the insurer;

B is the amount determined by multiplying 0.0002 by 1/2 of the total of

(*a*) all amounts of insurance in force at the end of the year under taxable life insurance policies of the insurer (other than paid-up policies), and

(*b*) all amounts of insurance in force at the end of the immediately preceding taxation year under taxable life insurance policies of the insurer (other than paid-up policies);

C is the amount determined by multiplying 0.20 by the net cost of insurance in respect of the insurer for the year;

D is the greater of

(*a*) the lesser of $2,500,000 and the amount, if any, by which

(i) the total of the amounts determined under the descriptions of A, B, C and E in respect of the insurer for the year

exceeds

(ii) 50 per cent of the amount that would be determined under the description of N in subsection (5) in respect of the insurer for the year, if that amount were determined without reference to any reinsurance arrangement, and

(*b*) the amount, if any, by which

(i) the total of the amounts determined under the descriptions of A, B, C and E in respect of the insurer for the year

exceeds

(ii) 75 per cent of the amount that would be determined under the description of N in subsection (5) in respect of the insurer for the year, if that amount were determined without reference to any reinsurance arrangement;

E is the amount determined under the description of D in respect of the insurer for the immediately preceding taxation year;

F is such amount as the insurer may claim, not exceeding the positive amount, if any, determined by adding

Regulations

(*a*) the mortality experience of the insurer for the year, and

(*b*) the amount determined under the description of G in respect of the insurer for the year;

G is the mortality loss adjustment account of the insurer for the immediately preceding year; and

H is 1 per cent of the total of all amounts each of which is the amount of a premium that has become receivable by the insurer in the year under a taxable life insurance policy of the insurer in respect of which a positive amount of guaranteed interest is determined for the year under subsection (8).

(7) Prescribed Rules for Determining Amounts. The amount of the amortization adjustment amount in the description of E in subsection 211.1(3) of the Act, as it read in its application to taxation years beginning before 1990, in respect of life insurer for a taxation year is determined by the formula

$$(A - B) - (C - D)$$

where

A is the total of all amounts each of which is the amount that would be the net level premium reserve for the year in respect of a taxable life insurance policy of the insurer (other than a policy in respect of which a positive amount of guaranteed interest is determined for the year under subsection (8)), if that amount were determined without reference to any policy loan or reinsurance agreement;

B is the total of all amounts each of which is the amount that would be the net level premium reserve for the immediately preceding taxation year in respect of a taxable life insurance policy of the insurer (other than a policy in respect of which a positive amount of guaranteed interest is determined for the year under subsection (8)), if that amount were determined without reference to any policy loan or reinsurance arrangement;

C is the total of all amounts each of which is the maximum amount that would be deductible under subparagraph 138(3)(*a*)(i) of the Act pursuant to paragraph 1401(1)(*c*) in computing the insurer's income for the year, in respect of a taxable life insurance policy of the insurer (other than a policy in respect of which a positive amount of guaranteed interest is determined for the year under subsection (8)), if that amount were determined without reference to any policy loan or reinsurance arrangement; and

D is the total of all amounts each of which is the maximum amount that would have been deductible under subparagraph 138(3)(*a*)(i) of the Act pursuant to paragraph 1401(1)(*c*) in computing the insurer's income for the immediately preceding taxation year, in respect of a taxable life insurance policy of the insurer (other than a policy in respect of which a positive amount of guaranteed interest is determined for the year under subsection (8)), if that amount were determined without reference to any policy loan or reinsurance arrangement.

(8) Prescribed Rules for Determining Amounts. The amount of guaranteed interest in the description of F in subsection 211.1(3) of the Act, as it read in its application to taxation years beginning before 1990, in respect of a life insurer for a taxation year is the total of all amounts each of which is guaranteed interest for the year in respect of

(*a*) a life insurance policy in Canada (other than a policy that was at any time an excluded arrangement), or

(*b*) a pre-funded group life insurance policy,

where the policy was issued by the insurer (or in respect of which the insurer has assumed the obligations of the issuer of the policy to the policyholder) and the terms and conditions of the policy relating to premiums and benefits were determined on or before March 2, 1988, except that where, at any time after March 2, 1988, the terms and conditions of the policy relating to premiums and benefits have been changed (other than to give effect to terms and conditions which were determined prior to March 3, 1988 or pursuant to a specified transaction or event), the amount of guaranteed interest in respect of the policy for the year in which the change is made and any subsequent taxation year is deemed to be nil.

(9) Prescribed Portion. The prescribed portion of an amount referred to in the description of G in subsection 211.1(3) of the Act, as it read in its application to taxation years beginning before 1990, for a taxation year is

(*a*) where the amount is in respect of a life insurance policy (other than a policy in respect of which a positive amount of guaranteed interest is determined for the year under subsection (8)), 100 per cent of the amount; and

(*b*) in any other case, nil.

(10) Prescribed Arrangements. For the purposes of the description of G in subsection 211.1(3) of the Act, as it read in its application to taxation years beginning before 1990, prescribed arrangements of an insurer are life insurance policies in Canada issued by the insurer (or in respect of which the insurer has assumed the obligations of the issuer of the policy to the policyholder) that are group term life insurance policies or policies that, at any time, were existing guaranteed life insurance policies.

Regulations

Part XX
Political Contributions

2000. Contents of Receipts

(1) Every official receipt issued by a particular person who is a registered agent of a registered party or an electoral district agent of a registered association, to an individual who makes a monetary contribution to the registered party or registered association, as the case may be, shall contain a statement that it is an official receipt for income tax purposes and shall, in a manner that cannot readily be altered, show clearly

(*a*) the name of the registered party or registered association, as the case may be;

(*b*) the serial number of the receipt;

(*c*) the name of the particular person, as recorded in the registry maintained by the Chief Electoral Officer under section 374 or 403.08 of the *Canada Elections Act*;

(*d*) the date on which the receipt is issued;

(*e*) the date on which the monetary contribution is received;

(*f*) the individual's name and address;

(*g*) the amount of the monetary contribution;

(*h*) a description of the advantage, if any, in respect of the monetary contribution and the amount of that advantage; and

(*i*) the eligible amount of the monetary contribution.

History: S. 2000(1) was replaced by S.C. 2013, c. 34, s. 388(1), applicable in respect of receipts issued after June 26, 2013, and formerly read:

(1) Every official receipt issued by a registered agent of a registered party shall contain a statement that it is an official receipt for income tax purposes and shall, in a manner that cannot readily be altered, show clearly

(*a*) the full name of the registered party;

(*b*) the serial number of the receipt;

(*c*) the name of the registered agent as recorded in the registry maintained by the Chief Electoral Officer pursuant to subsection 13.1(1) of the *Canada Elections Act*;

(*d*) the day on which the receipt was issued;

(*e*) where the person making the contribution is

(i) a person other than an individual, the day on which the contribution was received where that day differs from the day referred to in paragraph (*d*), or

(ii) an individual, the calendar year during which the contribution was received;

(*f*) the place or locality where the receipt was issued;

(*g*) the name and address of the person making the contribution including, in the case of an individual, his first name or initial;

(*h*) the amount of the contribution; and

(*i*) the signature of the registered agent.

Information Circulars: IC 75-2R8 Contributions To a Registered Political Party or To a Candidate at a Federal Election.

(2) Subject to subsection (3), every official receipt issued by an official agent of a candidate to an individual who makes a monetary contribution to the candidate shall contain a statement that it is an official receipt for income tax purposes and shall, in a manner that cannot readily be altered, show clearly

(*a*) the name of the candidate, as it appears in the candidate's nomination papers;

(*b*) the serial number of the receipt;

(*c*) the name of the official agent;

(*d*) the date on which the receipt is issued;

(*e*) the date on which the monetary contribution is received;

(*f*) the polling day;

(*g*) the individual's name and address;

(*h*) the amount of the monetary contribution;

(*i*) a description of the advantage, if any, in respect of the monetary contribution and the amount of that advantage; and

(*j*) the eligible amount of the monetary contribution.

History: S. 2000(2) was replaced by S.C. 2013, c. 34, s. 388(1), applicable in respect of receipts issued after June 26, 2013, and formerly read:

(2) Subject to subsection (3), every official receipt issued by an official agent of an officially nominated candidate shall contain a statement that it is an official receipt for income tax purposes and shall, in a manner that cannot readily be altered, show clearly

(*a*) the name of the officially nominated candidate;

(*b*) the serial number of the receipt;

(*c*) the name of the official agent as recorded with the Minister;

(*d*) the day on which the receipt was issued;

(*e*) the day on which the contribution was received where that day differs from the day referred to in paragraph (*d*);

(*f*) the polling day;

(*g*) the name and address of the person making the contribution including, in the case of an individual, his first name or initial;

(*h*) the amount of the contribution; and

(*i*) the signature of the official agent.

(3) The information required by paragraph (2)(*f*) may be shown by use of a code on an official receipt form issued by the Chief Electoral Officer, provided that the Minister is advised of the meaning of the code used.

(4) For the purposes of subsections (1) and (2), an official receipt issued to replace an official receipt previously issued shall show clearly that it replaces the original receipt and, in addition to its own serial number, shall show the serial number of the receipt originally issued.

(5) A spoiled official receipt form shall be marked "cancelled" and, together with its duplicate, shall be filed by the electoral district agent, the official agent or the registered agent, as the case may be, together with the information return required to be filed with the Minister under subsection 230.1(2) of the Act.

History: S. 2000(5) was replaced by S.C. 2013, c. 34, s. 388(2), applicable in respect of receipts issued after June 26, 2013, and formerly read:

(5) A spoiled official receipt form shall be marked "cancelled" and such form, together with the duplicate thereof, shall be filed by the registered

Regulations

agent or the official agent, as the case may be, together with the duplicates of receipts required to be filed with the Minister pursuant to subsection 230.1(2) of the Act.

(6) An official receipt form on which any of the following is incorrectly or illegibly entered is to be regarded as spoiled:

(*a*) the date on which the monetary contribution is received;

(*b*) the amount of the monetary contribution;

(*c*) a description of the advantage, if any, in respect of the monetary contribution and the amount of that advantage; and

(*d*) the eligible amount of the monetary contribution.

History: S. 2000(6) was replaced by S.C. 2013, c. 34, s. 388(2), applicable in respect of receipts issued after June 26, 2013, and formerly read:

(6) Every official receipt form on which

(*a*) the day on which the contribution was received,

(*b*) the year during which the contribution was received, or

(*c*) the amount of the contribution,

was incorrectly or illegibly entered shall be regarded as spoiled.

2001. [Information Returns]

(Repealed by S.C. 2013, c. 34, s. 389(1).)

History: S. 2001 and the preceding heading were repealed by S.C. 2013, c. 34, s. 389(1), deemed to have come into force on January 1, 2004, and formerly read:

2001. *Information Returns.* The return of information referred to in subsection 230.1(2) of the Act shall be filed by a registered agent on or before the last day of March in each year and shall be in respect of the preceding calendar year.

Information Circulars: IC 75-2R8 Contributions To a Registered Political Party or To a Candidate at a Federal Election.

2002. Interpretation

(1) The following definitions apply in this Part.

"Chief Electoral Officer" —"Chief Electoral Officer" means the person named as chief electoral officer or substitute chief electoral officer under section 13 or 14 of the *Canada Elections Act*.

"nomination paper" —"nomination paper" means, in respect of a candidate, a nomination paper filed in respect of the candidate under the *Canada Elections Act*, with the corrections, if any, made under that Act to the nomination paper after its filing.

"official receipt" —"official receipt" means a receipt issued for the purposes of subsection 127(3) of the Act containing the information that is required under that subsection.

"official receipt form" —"official receipt form" means

(*a*) in the case of an official receipt issued by an electoral district agent or a registered agent under subsection 2000(1), any printed form that an electoral district agent or a registered agent, as the case may be, has that is capable of being completed, or that originally was intended to be completed, as an official receipt of the electoral district agent or registered agent; and

(*b*) in the case of an official receipt issued by an official agent under subsection 2000(2), the official form prescribed under section 477 of the *Canada Elections Act*.

History: S. 2002(1) was replaced by S.C. 2013, c. 34, s. 390, in force June 26, 2013, and formerly read:

(1) In this Part,

"contribution" means an amount contributed within the meaning assigned by subsection 127(4.1) of the Act;

"official receipt" means a receipt for the purposes of subsection 127(3) of the Act containing information as provided in subsection 2000(1) or (2), as the case may be;

"official receipt form" means any printed form that a registered agent or an official agent, as the case may be, has that is capable of being completed, or that originally was intended to be completed, as an official receipt of the registered agent or official agent, as the case may be.

Information Circulars: IC 75-2R8 Contributions To a Registered Political Party or To a Candidate at a Federal Election.

(2) In this Part, "official agent", "polling day" and "registered agent" have the meanings assigned to them by the *Canada Elections Act*.

History: S. 2002(2) was replaced by S.C. 2013, c. 34, s. 390(1), in force June 26, 2013, and formerly read:

(2) In this Part, "official agent", "polling day", "registered agent" and "registered party" have the meanings assigned to them by section 2 of the *Canada Elections Act* and "officially nominated candidate" means a person in respect of whom a nomination paper and deposit have been filed as referred to in the definition "official nomination" in that section of that Act.

Part XXI
Elections in Respect of Surpluses

2100. Reduction of Tax-Paid Undistributed Surplus on Hand or 1971 Capital Surplus on Hand

Any election under subsection 83(1) of the Act in respect of a dividend payable before 1979 by a Canadian corporation shall be made by filing with the Minister the following documents:

(*a*) the form prescribed by the Minister;

(*b*) where the directors of the corporation are legally entitled to administer the affairs of the corporation, a certified copy of their resolution authorizing the election to be made;

(*c*) where the directors of the corporation are not legally entitled to administer the affairs of the corporation, a certified copy of the authorization of the making of the election by the person or persons legally entitled to administer the affairs of the corporation;

(*d*) where paragraph (*e*) is not applicable, schedules showing the computation of the amount, immediately before the election, of the corporation's

(i) tax-paid undistributed surplus on hand, if any,

(ii) 1971 capital surplus on hand, if any, and

(iii) 1971 undistributed income on hand, if any; and

(*e*) where subsection 83(3) of the Act is applicable, schedules showing the computation of the amount, immediately before the dividend became payable, of the corporation's

(i) tax-paid undistributed surplus on hand, if any,

(ii) 1971 capital surplus on hand, if any, and

(iii) 1971 undistributed income on hand, if any.

2101. Capital Dividends and Life Insurance Capital Dividends Payable by Private Corporations

Any election under subsection 83(2) of the Act in respect of a dividend payable by a private corporation shall be made by filing with the Minister the following documents:

(*a*) the form prescribed by the Minister;

(*b*) where the directors of the corporation are legally entitled to administer the affairs of the corporation, a certified copy of their resolution authorizing the election to be made;

(*c*) where the directors of the corporation are not legally entitled to administer the affairs of the corporation, a certified copy of the authorization of the making of the election by the person or persons legally entitled to administer the affairs of the corporation;

(*d*) where the election has been made under subsection 83(2) of the Act and paragraph (*e*) is not applicable, schedules showing the computation of the amount, immediately before the election, of the corporation's

(i) capital dividend account, and

(ii) 1971 undistributed income on hand, if any, if the dividend was payable on or prior to March 31, 1977; and

(*e*) where the election has been made under subsection 83(2) of the Act and subsection 83(3) of the Act is applicable, schedules showing the computation of the amount, immediately before the dividend became payable, of the corporation's

(i) capital dividend account, and

(ii) 1971 undistributed income on hand, if any, if the dividend was payable on or prior to March 31, 1977.

Forms: T2054 — Election for a Capital Dividend Under Subsection 83(2).

Income Tax Folios: *Primary* — S3-F2-C1 Capital Dividends.

2102. Tax on 1971 Undistributed Income on Hand

(1) (Revoked.)

(2) Any retroactive election by a corporation under subsection 196(1.1) of the Act, in respect of a dividend payable before 1979 in respect of which an election was made under section 83 of the Act, shall be made by filing with the Minister the following documents:

(*a*) the form prescribed by the Minister;

(*b*) where the directors of the corporation are legally entitled to administer the affairs of the corporation, a certified copy of their resolution authorizing the election to be made;

(*c*) where the directors of the corporation are not legally entitled to administer the affairs of the corporation, a certified copy of the authorization of the making of the election by the person or persons legally entitled to administer the affairs of the corporation; and

(*d*) a schedule showing the computation of the amount, immediately before the time immediately before the specified election referred to in subsection 196(1.1) of the Act was made, of the corporation's 1971 undistributed income on hand.

2104. Capital Gains Dividends Payable by Mutual Fund Corporations, Investment Corporations and Mortgage Investment Corporations

Any election under subsection 131(1) of the Act in respect of a dividend payable by a mutual fund corporation or an investment corporation shall be made by filing with the Minister the following documents:

(*a*) the form prescribed by the Minister;

(*b*) where the directors of the corporation are legally entitled to administer the affairs of the corporation, a certified copy of their resolution authorizing the election to be made;

(*c*) where the directors of the corporation are not legally entitled to administer the affairs of the corporation, a certified copy of the authorization of the making of the election by the person or persons legally entitled to administer the affairs of the corporation;

(*d*) where paragraph (*f*) is not applicable, a schedule showing the computation of the amount, immediately before the election, of the corporation's capital gains dividend account; and

(*e*) (Revoked.)

Regulations

(*f*) where subsection 131(1.1) of the Act is applicable, a schedule showing the computation of the amount, immediately before the earlier of

(i) the date the dividend became payable, and

(ii) the first day on which any part of the dividend was paid,

of the corporation's capital gains dividend account.

Forms: T2055 — Election in respect of a Capital Gains Dividend Under Subsection 131(1).

2104.1. Capital Gains Dividends Payable by Mutual Fund Corporations, Investment Corporations and Mortgage Investment Corporations

Any election under subsection 130.1(4) of the Act in respect of a dividend payable by a mortgage investment corporation shall be made by filing with the Minister the following documents:

(*a*) the documents referred to in paragraphs 2104(*a*) to (*c*); and

(*b*) a schedule showing the computation of the capital gains dividend in accordance with paragraph 130.1(4)(*a*) of the Act.

2105. Capital Gains Dividends Payable by Non-Resident-Owned Investment Corporations

Any election under subsection 133(7.1) of the Act in respect of a dividend payable by a non-resident-owned investment corporation shall be made by filing with the Minister the following documents:

(*a*) the form prescribed by the Minister;

(*b*) where the directors of the corporation are legally entitled to administer the affairs of the corporation, a certified copy of their resolution authorizing the election to be made;

(*c*) where the directors of the corporation are not legally entitled to administer the affairs of the corporation, a certified copy of the authorization of the making of the election by the person or persons legally entitled to administer the affairs of the corporation;

(*d*) where paragraph (*e*) is not applicable, a schedule showing the computation of the amount, immediately before the election, of the corporation's capital gains dividend account; and

(*e*) where subsection 133(7.3) of the Act is applicable, a schedule showing the computation of the amount, immediately before the earlier of

(i) the date the dividend became payable, and

(ii) the first day on which any part of the dividend was paid,

of the corporation's capital gains dividend account.

Forms: T2063 — Election in Respect of a Capital Gains Dividend Under Subsection 133(7.1).

2106. Alternative to Additional Tax on Excessive Elections

Any election under subsection 184(3) of the Act in respect of a dividend that was paid or payable by a corporation shall be made by

(*a*) filing with the Minister the following documents:

(i) a letter stating that the corporation elects under subsection 184(3) of the Act in respect of the said dividend,

(ii) where the directors of the corporation are legally entitled to administer the affairs of the corporation, a certified copy of

(A) their resolution authorizing the election to be made, and

(B) their declaration that the election is made with the concurrence of all shareholders who received or were entitled to receive all or any portion of the said dividend and whose addresses were known to the corporation,

(iii) where the directors of the corporation are not legally entitled to administer the affairs of the corporation, a certified copy of

(A) the authorization of the making of the election, and

(B) the declaration that the election is made with the concurrence of all shareholders who received or were entitled to receive all or any portion of the said dividend and whose addresses were known to the corporation

by the person or persons legally entitled to administer the affairs of the corporation,

(iv) a schedule showing the following information:

(A) the date of the notice of assessment of the tax that would, but for the election, have been payable under Part III of the Act,

(B) the full amount of the said dividend,

(C) the date the said dividend became payable, or the first day on which any part of the said dividend was paid if that day is earlier,

(D) the portion, if any, of the said dividend described in paragraph 184(3)(*a*) of the Act,

(E) the portion, if any, of the said dividend that the corporation is claiming for the purposes of an election in respect thereof under subsection 83(1) or (2), 130.1(4) or 131(1) of the Act pursuant to paragraph 184(3)(*b*) of the Act, and

(F) the portion, if any, of the said dividend that is deemed by paragraph 184(3)(*c*) of the Act to be a separate dividend that is a taxable dividend; and

(*b*) making an election in prescribed manner and prescribed form in respect of any amount claimed under paragraph 184(3)(*b*) of the Act.

Income Tax Folios: *Primary* — S3-F2-C1 Capital Dividends.

2107. Tax-deferred Preferred Series

The following series of classes of capital stock are hereby prescribed for the purposes of subsection 83(6) of the Act to be tax-deferred preferred series:

(*a*) The Algoma Steel Corporation, Limited, 8% Tax Deferred Preference Shares Series A;

(*b*) Aluminum Company of Canada, Limited, $2.00 Tax Deferred Retractable Preferred Shares;

(*c*) Brascan Limited, 8½% Tax Deferred Preferred Shares Series A;

(*d*) Canada Permanent Mortgage Corporation, 6¾% Tax Deferred Convertible Preference Shares Series A; and

(*e*) Cominco Ltd., $2.00 Tax Deferred Exchangeable Preferred Shares Series A.

Part XXII
Security Interests

2200. [Discharge of security]

Where, under subsection 220(4) of the Act, the Minister has accepted, as security for payment of taxes, a mortgage or other security or guarantee, he may, by a document in writing, discharge such mortgage or other security or guarantee.

2201. [Prescribed security interest]

(1) For the purpose of subsection 227(4.2) of the Act, "prescribed security interest", in relation to an amount deemed by subsection 227(4) of the Act to be held in trust by a person, means that part of a mortgage securing the performance of an obligation of the person, that encumbers land or a building, where the mortgage is registered pursuant to the appropriate land registration system before the time the amount is deemed to be held in trust by the person.

(2) For the purpose of subsection (1), where, at any time after 1999, the person referred to in subsection (1) fails to pay an amount deemed by subsection 227(4) of the Act to be held in trust by the person, as required under the Act, the amount of the prescribed security interest referred to in subsection (1) is deemed not to exceed the amount by which the amount, at that time, of the obligation outstanding secured by the mortgage exceeds the total of

(*a*) all amounts each of which is the value determined at the time of the failure, having regard to all the circumstances including the existence of any deemed trust for the benefit of Her Majesty pursuant to subsection 227(4) of the Act, of all the rights of the secured creditor securing the obligation, whether granted by the person or not, including guarantees or rights of set-off but not including the mortgage referred to in subsection (1), and

(*b*) all amounts applied after the time of the failure on account of the obligation,

so long as any amount deemed under any enactment administered by the Minister, other than the *Excise Tax Act*, to be held in trust by the person, remains unpaid.

(3) For greater certainty, a prescribed security interest includes the amount of insurance or expropriation proceeds relating to land or a building that is the subject of a registered mortgage interest, adjusted after 1999 in accordance with subsection (2), but does not include a lien, a priority or any other security interest created by statute, an assignment or hypothec of rents or leases, or a mortgage interest in any equipment or fixtures that a mortgagee or any other person has the right absolutely or conditionally to remove or dispose of separately from the land or building.

Part XXIII
Principal Residences

2300. [Election]

Any election by a taxpayer under subparagraph 40(2)(*c*)(ii) of the Act shall be made by attaching to the return of income required by section 150 of the Act to be filed by him for his taxation year in which the disposition of the land, including the property that was his principal residence, occurred, a letter signed by the taxpayer

(*a*) stating that he is electing under that subparagraph;

(*b*) stating the number of taxation years ending after the acquisition date (within the meaning assigned by paragraph 40(2)(*b*) of the Act) for which the property was his principal residence and during which he was resident in Canada; and

(*c*) giving a description of the property sufficient to identify it with the property designated as his principal residence.

2301. [Designation]

Any designation by a taxpayer under subparagraph 54(*g*)(iii) [section 54, "principal residence"] of the Act shall be made in the return of income required by section 150 of the Act to be filed by him for any taxation year of the taxpayer in which

(*a*) he has disposed of a property that is to be designated as his principal residence; or

(*b*) he has granted an option to acquire such property.

Forms: T2091 — Designation of a Property as a Principal Residence by an Individual (Other than a Personal Trust).

Part XXIV
Insurers

2400. Definitions

(1) The definitions in this subsection apply in this Part.

"attributed surplus" —"attributed surplus" of a non-resident insurer for a taxation year is the total of

(*a*) the insurer's property and casualty surplus for the year, and

(*b*) either,

(i) if the insurer elects for the year in prescribed form and manner, 50% of the total of

Regulations

(A) the amount that would have been determined at the end of the year in respect of the insurer under subparagraph (*a*)(ii) of the definition "Canadian investment fund", and

(B) the amount that would have been determined at the end of the preceding taxation year in respect of the insurer under subparagraph (*a*)(ii) of the definition "Canadian investment fund",

each amount being calculated as if throughout the year and the preceding taxation year the insurer had been a life insurer resident in Canada and had not carried on any insurance business other than a life insurance business or an accident and sickness insurance business, or

(ii) if the insurer does not elect under subparagraph (i) for the year, 120% of the total of all amounts each of which is 50% of the amount determined in accordance with regulations or guidelines made under Part XIII of the *Insurance Companies Act* to be the margin of assets in Canada over liabilities in Canada required to be maintained by the insurer as at the end of the year or as at the end of the preceding taxation year in respect of an insurance business carried on in Canada (other than a property and casualty insurance business).

"Canadian business property" —"Canadian business property" of an insurer for a taxation year in respect of an insurance business means

(*a*) if the insurer was resident in Canada throughout the year and did not carry on an insurance business outside Canada in the year, property used or held by it in the year in the course of carrying on the business in Canada; and

(*b*) in any other case, designated insurance property of the insurer for the year in respect of the business.

"Canadian equity property" —"Canadian equity property" of a person or partnership (in this definition referred to as the "taxpayer") at any time means property of the taxpayer that is

(*a*) a share of the capital stock of, or an income bond, income debenture, small business development bond or small business bond issued by, a person (other than a corporation affiliated with the taxpayer) resident in Canada or a Canadian partnership; or

(*b*) that proportion of property that is shares of the capital stock of an entity that is a corporation affiliated with the taxpayer or an interest in an entity that is a partnership or trust that

(i) the total value for the taxation year or fiscal period of the entity that includes that time of Canadian equity property of the entity

is of

(ii) the total value for the year or period of all property of the entity.

"Canadian investment fund" —"Canadian investment fund" of an insurer at the end of a taxation year means

(*a*) in the case of a life insurer resident in Canada, the total of

(i) the amount determined by the formula

$$A - B$$

where

A is the amount of the insurer's Canadian reserve liabilities as at the end of the year (to the extent that the amount exceeds the amount of surplus appropriations included in that amount), and

B is the amount of the insurer's Canadian outstanding premiums and policy loans as at the end of the year (to the extent that the amount of the premiums and loans are in respect of policies referred to in paragraphs (*a*) to (*c*) of the description of A in the definition "Canadian reserve liabilities" and were not otherwise deducted in computing the amount of the insurer's Canadian reserve liabilities as at the end of the year), and

(ii) the greater of

(A) the amount determined by the formula

$$C + ((D - E + F) \times (G/H))$$

where

C is 8% of the amount determined under subparagraph (i),

D is the total of all amounts each of which is the amount of a deferred realized net gain or an amount expressed as a negative number of a deferred realized net loss of the insurer as at the end of the year,

E is the total of all amounts each of which is the amount of an item reported as an asset that is owned by the insurer at the end of the year and is a share of the capital stock of, or a debt owing to the insurer by, a financial institution affiliated with the insurer,

F is the total of all amounts each of which is the amount as at the end of the year of a debt assumed or incurred by the insurer in respect of the acquisition of an asset described in E (or another property for which an asset described in E is a substituted property),

G is the amount of the insurer's weighted Canadian liabilities as at the end of the year, and

H is the amount of the insurer's weighted total liabilities as at the end of the year, and

(B) the amount determined by the formula

$$(I - J + K + L) \times (M/N)$$

where

I is the total of all amounts each of which is the amount of an item reported as an asset of the insurer as at the end of the year (other than an item that at no time in the year was used or held by the insurer in the course of carrying on an insurance business),

J is the total of all amounts each of which is the amount of an item reported as a liability of the insurer (other than a liability that was at any time in the year connected with an asset that was not used or held by the insurer in the course of carrying on an insurance business at any time in the year) as at the end of the year in respect of an insurance business carried on by the insurer in the year,

K is the total of all amounts each of which is an amount of an item reported by the insurer as at the end of the year as a general provision or allowance for impairment in respect of investment property of the insurer for the year,

L is the total of all amounts each of which is an amount of a deferred realized net gain or an amount expressed as a negative number of a deferred realized net loss of the insurer as at the end of the year,

M is the amount of the insurer's weighted Canadian liabilities as at the end of the year, and

N is the amount of the insurer's weighted total liabilities as at the end of the year; and

(*b*) in the case of a non-resident insurer, the total of

(i) the amount, if any, by which the amount of the insurer's Canadian reserve liabilities as at the end of the year exceeds the total of

(A) the amount of the insurer's Canadian outstanding premiums and policy loans (to the extent that the amount of the premiums or loans are in respect of policies referred to in paragraphs (*a*) to (*c*) of the description of A in the definition "Canadian reserve liabilities" and were not otherwise deducted in computing the amount of the insurer's Canadian reserve liabilities as at the end of the year), and

(B) the amount of the insurer's deferred acquisition expenses as at the end of the year in respect of its property and casualty insurance business carried on in Canada, and

(ii) the greatest of

(A) the total of

(I) 8% of the amount determined under subparagraph (i), and

(II) the total of all amounts each of which is an amount of a deferred realized net gain or an amount expressed as a negative number of a deferred realized net loss of the insurer as at the end of the year in respect of an insurance business carried on by the insurer in Canada,

(B) the amount, if any, by which the total of

(I) the amount of the insurer's surplus funds derived from operations as at the end of its preceding taxation year,

(II) the total determined under subclause (A)(II) to the extent not included in subclause (I), and

(III) the total of all amounts in respect of which the insurer made an election under subsection 219(4) or (5.2) of the Act, each of which is an amount included in the total determined in respect of the insurer under subparagraph 219(4)(*a*)(i.1) of the Act as at the end of its preceding taxation year

exceeds

(IV) the total of amounts determined in respect of the insurer under subparagraphs 219(4)(*a*)(ii), (iii), (iv) and (v) of the Act, as at the end of the year, and

(C) the total of

(I) the amount of the insurer's attributed surplus for the year, and

(II) if the amount under subclause (I) was determined without the taxpayer electing under subparagraph (*b*)(i) of the definition "attributed surplus", the amount determined under subclause (A)(II).

"Canadian investment property" — "Canadian investment property" of an insurer for a taxation year means an investment property of the insurer for the year (other than, if the insurer is non-resident, property established by the insurer as not being effectively connected with its insurance businesses carried on in Canada in the year) that is, at any time in the year,

(*a*) real property situated in Canada;

(*b*) depreciable property situated in Canada or leased to a person resident in Canada for use inside and outside of Canada;

(*c*) a mortgage, a hypothec, an agreement of sale or any other form of indebtedness in respect of property described in paragraph (*a*) or (*b*);

(*d*) a Canadian equity property;

(*e*) a Canadian resource property;

(*f*) a deposit balance of the insurer that is in Canadian currency;

(*g*) a bond, debenture or other form of indebtedness, in Canadian currency, issued by

(i) a person resident in Canada or a Canadian partnership, or

(ii) the government of Canada, a province or any of their political subdivisions;

(*h*) a property that is

(i) a share of the capital stock of a corporation resident in Canada that is affiliated with the insurer, if at least 75% of the total value for the year of all property of the corporation is attributable to property that would be Canadian investment property if it were owned by an insurer, or

(ii) an interest in a Canadian partnership, or a trust resident in Canada, if at least 75% of the total value for the year of all property of the partnership or trust, as the case may be, is attributable to property that would be Canadian investment property if it were owned by an insurer; or

(*i*) an amount due or an amount accrued to the insurer on account of income that

(i) is from designated insurance property for the year that is Canadian investment property of the insurer for the year because of any of paragraphs (*a*) to (*h*), and

(ii) was assumed in computing the insurer's Canadian reserve liabilities for the year.

Regulations

"Canadian outstanding premiums"—"Canadian outstanding premiums" of an insurer at any time means the total of all amounts each of which is the amount of an outstanding premium of the insurer with respect to an insurance policy at that time, to the extent that the amount of the premium has been assumed to have been paid in computing the insurer's Canadian reserve liabilities as at that time.

"Canadian reserve liabilities"—"Canadian reserve liabilities" of an insurer as at the end of a taxation year means the amount determined by the formula

A - B

where

A is the total of the insurer's liabilities and reserves (other than liabilities and reserves in respect of a segregated fund) as at the end of the year in respect of

(*a*) life insurance policies in Canada,

(*b*) fire insurance policies issued or effected in respect of property situated in Canada, and

(*c*) insurance policies of any other class covering risks ordinarily within Canada at the time the policy was issued or effected; and

B is the total of the reinsurance recoverable reported as a reinsurance asset by the insurer as at the end of the year relating to its liabilities and reserves in A.

"deposit balance"—"deposit balance" of an insurer means an amount standing to the insurer's credit as or on account of amounts deposited with a corporation authorized to accept deposits or to carry on the business of offering to the public its services as a trustee.

"equity limit"—"equity limit" of an insurer for a taxation year means

(*a*) in respect of a life insurer resident in Canada, that proportion of the total of all amounts each of which is the value for the year of an equity property of the insurer that

(i) the insurer's weighted Canadian liabilities as at the end of the year

is of

(ii) the insurer's weighted total liabilities as at the end of the year;

(*b*) in respect of a non-resident insurer (other than a life insurer), 25% of the total of

(i) the amount, if any, by which the insurer's mean Canadian reserve liabilities for the year exceeds 50% of the total of its premiums receivable and deferred acquisition expenses as at the end of the year and its premiums receivable and deferred acquisition expenses as at the end of its preceding taxation year to the extent that those amounts were included in the insurer's Canadian reserve liabilities for the year or the preceding taxation year, as the case may be, in respect of the insurer's business in Canada, and

(ii) the insurer's property and casualty surplus for the year; and

(*c*) in respect of a non-resident life insurer, the total of

(i) either,

(A) if the insurer makes an election referred to in subparagraph (*b*)(i) of the definition "attributed surplus" for the year, the greater of

(I) that proportion of the total of all amounts each of which is the value for the year of an equity property of the insurer that

1. the insurer's weighted Canadian liabilities as at the end of the year

is of

2. the insurer's weighted total liabilities as at the end of year, and

(II) 8% of the insurer's mean Canadian investment fund for the year, or

(B) if the insurer does not make this election for the year, 8% of the insurer's mean Canadian investment fund for the year,

(ii) 25% of the amount, if any, by which

(A) the insurer's mean Canadian reserve liabilities for the year (determined on the assumption that the insurer's property and casualty insurance business carried on in Canada during the year was its only insurance business carried on in Canada that year)

exceeds

(B) 50% of the total of its premiums receivable and deferred acquisition expenses as at the end of the year and its premiums receivable and deferred acquisition expenses as at the end of its preceding taxation year, to the extent that those amounts were included in the insurer's Canadian reserve liabilities as at the end of the year or the preceding taxation year, as the case may be, (determined on the assumption that the insurer's property and casualty insurance business carried on in Canada during the year was its only insurance business carried on in Canada that year), and

(iii) 25% of the insurer's property and casualty surplus for the year.

"equity property"—"equity property" of a person or partnership (in this definition referred to as the "taxpayer") at any time means property of the taxpayer that is

(*a*) a share of the capital stock of, or an income bond, income debenture, small business development bond or small business bond issued by, another person (other than a corporation affiliated with the taxpayer) or partnership; or

(*b*) that proportion of property that is shares of the capital stock of a corporation affiliated with the taxpayer or an interest in a partnership or trust that

(i) the total value for the taxation year or fiscal period of the corporation, partnership or trust that includes that time of equity property of the corporation, partnership or trust, as the case may be,

is of

(ii) the total value for the year or period of all property of the corporation, partnership or trust, as the case may be.

Regulations

"financial institution" — "financial institution" means a corporation that is

(*a*) a corporation described in any of paragraphs (*a*) to (*e*) of the definition "restricted financial institution" in subsection 248(1) of the Act; or

(*b*) a particular corporation all or substantially all of the value of the assets of which is attributable to shares or indebtedness of one or more corporations described in paragraph (*a*) to which the particular corporation is affiliated.

"foreign policy loan" — "foreign policy loan" means an amount advanced by an insurer to a policyholder in accordance with the terms and conditions of a life insurance policy, other than a life insurance policy in Canada.

"gross Canadian life investment income" — "gross Canadian life investment income" of a life insurer for a taxation year means the amount, if any, by which

(*a*) the total of all amounts each of which is

(i) the insurer's gross investment revenue for the year, to the extent that the revenue is from Canadian business property of the insurer for the year in respect of the insurer's life insurance business,

(ii) the amount included in computing the insurer's income for the year under paragraph 138(9)(*b*) of the Act,

(iii) the portion of the amount deducted under paragraph 20(1)(*l*) of the Act in computing the insurer's income for its preceding taxation year that was in respect of Canadian business property of the insurer for that year in respect of the insurer's life insurance business,

(iv) the amount included under section 142.4 of the Act in computing the insurer's income for the year in respect of property disposed of by the insurer that was, in the taxation year of disposition, Canadian business property of the insurer for that year in respect of the insurer's life insurance business,

(v) the insurer's gain for the year from the disposition of a Canadian business property of the insurer for the year in respect of the insurer's life insurance business, other than a capital property or a property in respect of the disposition of which section 142.4 of the Act applies, or

(vi) the insurer's taxable capital gain for the year from the disposition of a Canadian business property of the insurer for the year in respect of the insurer's life insurance business

exceeds

(*b*) the total of all amounts each of which is

(i) the portion of the amount deducted under paragraph 20(1)(*l*) of the Act in computing the insurer's income for the year that is in respect of Canadian business property of the insurer for the year in respect of the insurer's life insurance business,

(ii) the amount deductible under section 142.4 of the Act in computing the insurer's income for the year in respect of a property disposed of by the insurer that was, in the taxation year of disposition, a Canadian business property of the insurer for that year in respect of the insurer's life insurance business,

(iii) the insurer's loss for the year from the disposition of a Canadian business property of the insurer for the year in respect of the insurer's life insurance business, other than a capital property or a property in respect of the disposition of which section 142.4 of the Act applies, or

(iv) the insurer's allowable capital loss for the year from the disposition of a Canadian business property of the insurer for the year in respect of the insurer's life insurance business.

"investment property" — "investment property" of an insurer for a taxation year means non-segregated property owned by the insurer, other than a policy loan payable to the insurer, at any time in the year that is

(*a*) property acquired by the insurer for the purpose of earning gross investment revenue in the year, other than property that is

(i) property, a proportion of which is investment property of the insurer for the year because of paragraph (*b*),

(ii) a share of the capital stock of, or a debt owing to the insurer by, a corporation affiliated with the insurer, or

(iii) an interest in a partnership or trust;

(*b*) that proportion, if any, of property of the insurer that is land, depreciable property or property that would have been depreciable property if it had been situated in Canada and used or held by the insurer in the year in the course of carrying on an insurance business in Canada that

(i) the use made of the property by the insurer in the year for the purpose of earning gross investment revenue in the year

is of

(ii) the whole use made of the property by the insurer in the year;

(*c*) if the insurer is a life insurer, property described in any of paragraphs 138(4.4)(*a*) to (*d*) of the Act;

(*d*) either

(i) a share of the capital stock of, or a debt owing to the insurer by, a corporation (other than a corporation that is a financial institution) affiliated with the insurer, if the total value for the year of all investment property of the corporation for the year is not less than 75% of the total value for the year of all its property, or

(ii) an interest in a partnership or trust, if the total value for the year of all investment property of the partnership or trust, as the case may be, for the year is not less than 75% of the total value for the year of all its property,

and for the purpose of this paragraph (other than for the purpose of determining whether a corporation is a financial institution) every corporation, partnership and trust is deemed to be an insurer; or

(*e*) an amount due or an amount accrued to the insurer on account of income that

Regulations

(i) is from designated insurance property for the year that is investment property of the insurer for the year because of any of paragraphs (*a*) to (*d*), and

(ii) was assumed in computing the insurer's Canadian reserve liabilities for the year.

"mean Canadian outstanding premiums" —"mean Canadian outstanding premiums" of an insurer for a taxation year means 50% of the total of

(*a*) its Canadian outstanding premiums as at the end of the year, and

(*b*) its Canadian outstanding premiums as at the end of its preceding taxation year.

"mean Canadian reserve liabilities" —"mean Canadian reserve liabilities" of an insurer for a taxation year means 50% of the total of

(*a*) its Canadian reserve liabilities as at the end of the year, and

(*b*) its Canadian reserve liabilities as at the end of its preceding taxation year.

"mean maximum tax actuarial reserve" —"mean maximum tax actuarial reserve" in respect of a particular class of life insurance policies of an insurer for a taxation year means 50% of the total of

(*a*) its maximum tax actuarial reserve for that class of policies for the year, and

(*b*) its maximum tax actuarial reserve for that class of policies for its preceding taxation year.

"mean policy loans" —"mean policy loans" of an insurer for a taxation year means 50% of the total of

(*a*) its policy loans as at the end of the year, and

(*b*) its policy loans as at the end of its preceding taxation year.

"outstanding premiums" —"outstanding premiums" of an insurer with respect to an insurance policy at any time means premiums due to the insurer under the policy at that time but unpaid.

"property and casualty surplus" —"property and casualty surplus" of an insurer for a taxation year means the total of

(*a*) 7.5% of the total of

(i) its unearned premium reserve as at the end of the year (net of reinsurance recoverables in respect of the reserve) in respect of its property and casualty insurance business,

(ii) its unearned premium reserve as at the end of its preceding taxation year (net of reinsurance recoverables in respect of the reserve) in respect of its property and casualty insurance business,

(iii) its provision for unpaid claims and adjustment expenses as at the end of the year (net of reinsurance recoverables in respect of the provision) in respect of its property and casualty insurance business, and

(iv) its provision for unpaid claims and adjustment expenses as at the end of its preceding taxation year (net of reinsurance recoverables in respect of the provision) in respect of its property and casualty insurance business, and

(*b*) 50% of the total of

(i) its investment valuation reserve as at the end of the year in respect of its property and casualty insurance business, and

(ii) its investment valuation reserve as at the end of its preceding taxation year in respect of its property and casualty insurance business.

"reinsurance recoverable" —"reinsurance recoverable" of an insurer means the total of all amounts each of which is an amount reported as a reinsurance asset of the insurer as at the end of a taxation year in respect of an amount recoverable from a reinsurer.

"value" —"value" for a taxation year of a property of a person or partnership (in this definition referred to as the "owner") means

(*a*) in the case of a property that is a mortgage, hypothec, an agreement of sale or an investment property that is a deposit balance, the amount, if any, by which

(i) the amount obtained when the gross investment revenue of the owner for the year from the property is divided by the average rate of interest earned by the owner (expressed as an annual rate) on the amortized cost of the property during the year

exceeds

(ii) the amount obtained when the interest payable by the owner, for the period in the year during which the property was held by the owner, on debt assumed or incurred by the owner in respect of the acquisition of the property (or another property for which the property is a substituted property) is divided by the average rate of interest payable by the owner (expressed as an annual rate) on the debt for the year;

(*b*) in the case of a property that is an amount due or an amount accrued to the owner, the total of the amounts due or accrued at the end of each day in the year divided by the number of days in the year;

(*c*) in the case of a property (other than a property referred to in paragraph (*a*) or (*b*)) that was not owned by the owner throughout the year, the amount, if any, by which

(i) that proportion of

(A) the carrying value of the property as at the end of the preceding taxation year, if the property was owned by the owner at that time,

(B) the carrying value of the property as at the end of the year, if the property was owned by the owner at that time and not at the end of the preceding taxation year, and

(C) in any other case, the cost of the property to the owner when it was acquired,

that the number of days that are in the year and at the end of which the owner owned the property is of the number of days in the year,

exceeds

(ii) the amount obtained when the interest payable by the owner, for the period in the year during which the property was held by the owner, on debt assumed or incurred by the owner in respect of the acquisition of the property (or another property for which the property is a substituted property) is divided by the average rate of interest payable by the owner (expressed as an annual rate) on the debt for the year; and

(*d*) in the case of any other property, the amount, if any, by which

(i) 50% of the total of

(A) the carrying value of the property as at the end of the year, and

(B) the carrying value of the property as at the end of the preceding taxation year

exceeds

(ii) the amount obtained when the interest payable by the owner, for the period in the year during which the property was held by the owner, on debt assumed or incurred by the owner in respect of the acquisition of the property (or another property for which the property is a substituted property) is divided by the average rate of interest payable by the owner (expressed as an annual rate) on the debt for the year.

"weighted Canadian liabilities" —"weighted Canadian liabilities" of an insurer as at the end of a taxation year means the total of

(*a*) 300% of the amount, if any, by which

(i) the total of all amounts each of which is an amount that is in respect of an insurance business carried on by the insurer in Canada and that is reported as a liability (other than a liability in respect of an amount payable out of a segregated fund) of the insurer in respect of a life insurance policy in Canada (other than an annuity) or an accident and sickness insurance policy as at the end of the year

exceeds

(ii) the total of

(A) the insurer's policy loans (other than policy loans in respect of annuities) as at the end of the year, and

(B) the reinsurance recoverable reported by the insurer as at the end of the year relating to its liabilities described in subparagraph (i), and

(*b*) the amount, if any, by which

(i) the total of all amounts each of which is an amount in respect of an insurance business carried on by the insurer in Canada that is reported as a liability of the insurer as at the end of the year, except to the extent that the amount is

(A) in respect of an insurance policy (other than an annuity) described in subparagraph (*a*)(i),

(B) a liability in respect of an amount payable out of a segregated fund, or

(C) a debt incurred or assumed by the insurer to acquire a property of the insurer,

exceeds

(ii) the total of

(A) the insurer's policy loans in respect of annuities as at the end of the year, and

(B) the reinsurance recoverable reported by the insurer as at the end of the year relating to its liabilities described in subparagraph (i).

"weighted total liabilities" —"weighted total liabilities" of an insurer as at the end of a taxation year means the total of

(*a*) 300% of the amount, if any, by which

(i) the total of all amounts each of which is an amount that is in respect of an insurance business carried on by the insurer and that is reported as a liability (other than a liability in respect of an amount payable out of a segregated fund) of the insurer in respect of a life insurance policy (other than an annuity) or an accident and sickness insurance policy

exceeds

(ii) the total of

(A) the insurer's policy loans and foreign policy loans (other than policy loans and foreign policy loans in respect of annuities) as at the end of the year, and

(B) the reinsurance recoverable reported by the insurer as at the end of the year relating to its liabilities described in subparagraph (i), and

(*b*) the amount, if any, by which

(i) the total of all amounts each of which is an amount that is in respect of an insurance business carried on by the insurer and that is reported as a liability of the insurer as at the end of the year, except to the extent that the amount is

(A) in respect of an insurance policy (other than an annuity) described in subparagraph (*a*)(i),

(B) a liability in respect of an amount payable out of a segregated fund, or

(C) a debt incurred or assumed by the insurer to acquire a property of the insurer,

exceeds

(ii) the total of

(A) the insurer's policy loans and foreign policy loans in respect of annuities as at the end of the year, and

(B) the reinsurance recoverable reported by the insurer as at the end of the year relating to its liabilities described in subparagraph (i).

History: S. 2400(1), the description of B in subparagraph (*a*)(i) of the definition "Canadian investment fund" was replaced by S.C. 2010, c. 25, s. 81(2), applicable to taxation years that begin after 2010. S. 2400(1), the description of B in subparagraph (*a*)(i) of the definition "Canadian investment fund" formerly read:

B is the amount of the insurer's Canadian outstanding premiums and policy loans as at the end of the year (to the extent that the amount of the premiums and loans are in respect of policies referred to in paragraphs (*a*) to (*c*) of the definition "Canadian reserve liabilities" and were not otherwise deducted in computing the amount of the insurer's Canadian reserve liabilities as at the end of the year), and

S. 2400(1), clause (*b*)(i)(A) of the definition "Canadian investment fund" was replaced by S.C. 2010, c. 25, s. 80(3), applicable to taxation years that begin after 2010. S. 2400(1), clause (*b*)(i)(A) of the definition "Canadian investment fund" formerly read:

(A) the amount of the insurer's Canadian outstanding premiums, policy loans and reinsurance recoverables as at the end of the year (to the extent that the amount of the premiums, loans or recoverables are in respect of policies referred to in paragraphs (*a*) to (*c*) of the definition "Canadian reserve liabilities" and were not otherwise deducted in computing the amount of the insurer's Canadian reserve liabilities as at the end of the year), and

S. 2400(1), the definition "Canadian reserve liabilities" was replaced by S.C. 2010, c. 25, s. 81(1), applicable to taxation years that begin after 2010. S. 2400(1), the definition "Canadian reserve liabilities" formerly read:

"Canadian reserve liabilities" of an insurer as at the end of a taxation year means the total amount of the insurer's liabilities and reserves (other than liabilities and reserves in respect of a segregated fund) in respect of

(*a*) life insurance policies in Canada;

(*b*) fire insurance policies issued or effected in respect of property situated in Canada; or

(*c*) insurance policies of any other class covering risks ordinarily within Canada at the time the policy was issued or effected.

S. 2400(1), subparagraph (*b*)(i) of the definition "equity limit" was replaced by S.C. 2010, c. 25, s. 81(4), applicable to taxation years that begin after 2010. S. 2400(1), subparagraph (*b*)(i) of the definition "equity limit" formerly read:

(i) the amount, if any, by which the insurer's mean Canadian reserve liabilities for the year exceeds the total of

(A) 50% of the total of its premiums receivable and deferred acquisition expenses as at the end of the year and its premiums receivable and deferred acquisition expenses as at the end of its preceding taxation year to the extent that those amounts were included in the insurer's Canadian reserve liabilities for the year or the preceding taxation year, as the case may be, in respect of the insurer's business in Canada, and

(B) 50% of the total of its reinsurance recoverables as at the end of the year and its reinsurance recoverables as at the end of the preceding taxation year that are in respect of policies referred to in paragraphs (*b*) and (*c*) of the definition "Canadian reserve liabilities", and

S. 2400(1), the definition "reinsurance recoverable" was replaced by S.C. 2010, c. 25, s. 81(1), applicable to taxation years that begin after 2010. S. 2400(1), the definition "reinsurance recoverable" formerly read:

"reinsurance recoverable" means

(*a*) in respect of an insurance business (other than a life insurance business) of a non-resident insurer, the total of all amounts each of which is an item reported as an asset of the insurer as at the end of a taxation year in respect of an amount recoverable from a reinsurer for unearned premiums or unpaid claims and adjustment expenses in respect of the reinsurance of a policy that was issued in the course of carrying on the insurance business to the extent that the amount is included in the insurer's Canadian reserve liabilities at that time and the amount is not an outstanding premium, policy loan or investment property; and

(*b*) in any other case, nil.

S. 2400(1), subparagraph (*a*)(ii) of the definition "weighted Canadian liabilities" was replaced by S.C. 2010, c. 25, s. 81(5), applicable to taxation years that begin after 2010. S. 2400(1), subparagraph (*a*)(ii) of the definition "weighted Canadian liabilities" formerly read:

(ii) the total of the insurer's policy loans (other than policy loans in respect of annuities) as at the end of the year, and

S. 2400(1), subparagraph (*b*)(ii) of the definition "weighted Canadian liabilities" was replaced by S.C. 2010, c. 25, s. 81(6), applicable to taxation years that begin after 2010. S. 2400(1), subparagraph (*b*)(ii) of the definition "weighted Canadian liabilities" formerly read:

(ii) the total of the insurer's policy loans in respect of annuities as at the end of the year.

S. 2400(1), subparagraph (*a*)(ii) of the definition "weighted total liabilities" was replaced by S.C. 2010, c. 25, s. 81(7), applicable to taxation years that begin after 2010. S. 2400(1), subparagraph (*a*)(ii) of the definition "weighted total liabilities" formerly read:

(ii) the total of the insurer's policy loans and foreign policy loans (other than policy loans and foreign policy loans in respect of annuities) as at the end of the year, and

S. 2400(1), subparagraph (*b*)(ii) of the definition "weighted total liabilities" was replaced by S.C. 2010, c. 25, s. 81(8), applicable to taxation years that begin after 2010. S. 2400(1), subparagraph (*b*)(ii) of the definition "weighted total liabilities" formerly read:

(ii) the total of the insurer's policy loans and foreign policy loans in respect of annuities as at the end of the year.

(2) Carrying Value. For the purposes of this Part, the carrying value of a taxpayer's property for a taxation year, except as otherwise provided in this Part, means

(*a*) if the taxpayer is an insurer, the amounts reflected in the taxpayer's non-consolidated balance sheet as at the end of the taxation year accepted (or, if that non-consolidated balance sheet was not prepared, the taxpayer's non-consolidated balance sheet as at the end of the year that would have been accepted) by the Superintendent of Financial Institutions, in the case of an insurer that is required under the *Insurance Companies Act* to report to that Superintendent, or by the superintendent of insurance or other similar officer or authority of the province under the laws of which the insurer is incorporated or otherwise formed, in the case of an insurer that is required by law to report to that officer or authority; and

(*b*) in any other case, the amounts that would be reflected in the taxpayer's non-consolidated balance sheet as at the end of the taxation year if that balance sheet were prepared in accordance with generally accepted accounting principles.

(3) Amount or Item Reported. A reference in this Part to an amount or item reported as an asset or a liability of a taxpayer as at the end of a taxation year means an amount or item that is reported as an asset or a liability in the taxpayer's non-consolidated balance sheet as at the end of the year accepted (or, if that non-consolidated balance sheet was not prepared, the taxpayer's non-consolidated balance sheet as at the end of the year that would have been accepted) by the Superintendent of Financial Institutions, in the case of an insurer that is required under the *Insurance Companies Act* to report to that Superintendent, or by the superintendent of insurance or other similar officer or authority of the province under the laws of which the insurer is incorporated or otherwise formed, in the case of an insurer that is required by law to report to that officer or authority.

(4) Application of Certain Definitions. For the purposes

(*a*) of subsection 138(14) of the Act, the expressions "Canadian investment fund for a taxation year", "specified Canadian assets" and "value for the taxation year" have the meanings prescribed for them by subsection 2404(1) as it read in its application to the 1977 taxation year; and

(*b*) of subsection 219(7) of the Act, the expressions "attributed surplus" and "Canadian investment fund" have the meaning prescribed for them by subsection (1).

(5) Deeming Rules for Certain Assets. For the purposes of this Part, other than subsection 2401(6), an asset of an insurer is deemed not to have been used or held by the insurer in a taxation year in the course of carrying on an insurance business if the asset

(*a*) is owned by the insurer at the end of the year; and

(*b*) is a share of the capital stock of, or a debt owing to the insurer by, a financial institution affiliated with the insurer during each of the days in the year during which the insurer owned the asset.

(6) Deeming Rules for Certain Assets. For the purposes of clause (*a*)(ii)(B) of the definition "Canadian investment fund" in subsection (1), an asset of an insurer is deemed not to have been used or held by the insurer in a taxation year in the course of carrying on an insurance business if the asset

(*a*) is owned by the insurer at the end of the year; and

(*b*) is

(i) goodwill, or

(ii) real property (or the portion of real property) owned by the insurer and occupied by the insurer for the purposes of carrying on an insurance business.

History: S. 2400(6)(*b*)(i) was replaced by P.C. 2011-936, SOR/2011-188, dated September 22, 2011, published in the *Canada Gazette* October 12, 2011, applicable to taxation years that begin after October 12, 2011, and, where a taxpayer so elects and notifies the Minister of National Revenue in writing with the taxpayer's return of income under Part I of the Act for the taxation year that includes that day, subsection 2400(6) applies in respect of the taxpayer to the 2005 and subsequent taxation years. S. 2400(6)(*b*)(i) formerly read:

(i) goodwill which arose as a result of an amalgamation, a winding-up of an affiliated financial institution, or the assumption by the insurer of any obligation of another insurer with which the insurer deals at arm's length if a reserve in respect of the obligation

(A) may be claimed by the insurer under paragraph 20(7)(*c*) or subparagraph 138(3)(*a*)(i) or (ii) of the Act, or

(B) could be claimed by the insurer under paragraph 20(7)(*c*) or subparagraph 138(3)(*a*)(i) or (ii) of the Act if the obligations were insurance policies in Canada, or

(7) No Double Counting. For greater certainty, a particular property or a particular proportion of a property shall not, directly or indirectly, be used or included more than once in determining, for a particular taxation year, the Canadian equity property or the equity property of a person or partnership.

(8) Transition Year. A computation that is required to be made under this Part in respect of an insurer's taxation year that included September 30, 2006 and that is relevant to a computation (in this subsection referred to as the "transition year computation") that is required to be made under this Part in respect of the insurer's first taxation year that begins after that date shall, for the purposes only of the transition year computation, be made using the same definitions, rules and methodologies that are used in the transition year computation.

History: S. 2400(8) was added by S.C. 2009, c. 2, s. 102(1), applicable to taxation years that begin after September 2006.

(9) Transition Year. A computation that is required to be made under this Part in respect of an insurer's taxation year that included December 31, 2010 and that is relevant to a computation (in this subsection referred to as the "transition year computation") that is required to be made under this Part in respect of the insurer's first taxation year that begins after that date shall, for the purposes only of the transition year computation, be made using the same definitions, rules and methodologies that are used in the transition year computation.

History: S. 2400(9) was added by S.C. 2010, c. 25, s. 81(9), applicable to taxation years that begin after 2010.

2401. Designated Insurance Property

(1) Designated Insurance Property. For the purposes of the definition "designated insurance property" in subsection 138(12) of the Act, "designated insurance property" of an insurer for a taxation year means property that is designated in accordance with subsections (2) to (7) for the year

(*a*) by the insurer in its return of income under Part I of the Act for the year; or

(*b*) if the Minister determines that the insurer has not made a designation that is in accordance with the prescribed rules found in this section, by the Minister.

(2) Designation Rules. For the purposes of subsection (1), an insurer, or the Minister if paragraph (1)(*b*) applies,

(*a*) shall designate for a taxation year investment property of the insurer for the year with a total value for the year equal to the amount, if any, by which the insurer's mean Canadian reserve liabilities for the year in respect of its life insurance business in Canada exceeds the total of the insurer's mean Canadian outstanding premiums and mean policy loans for the year in respect of that business (to the extent that the amount of the mean policy loans was not otherwise deducted in computing the insurer's mean Canadian reserve liabilities for the year);

(*b*) shall designate for a taxation year investment property of the insurer for the year with a total value for the year equal to the amount, if any, by which the insurer's mean Canadian reserve liabilities for the year in respect of its accident and sickness insurance business in Canada exceeds the insurer's mean Canadian outstanding premiums for the year in respect of that business;

(*c*) shall designate for a taxation year in respect of the insurer's insurance business in Canada (other than a life insurance business or an accident and sickness insurance business) investment property of the insurer for the year with a total value for the year equal to the amount, if any, by which the insurer's mean Canadian reserve liabilities for the year in respect of that business exceeds 50% of the total of all amounts each of which is the amount, as at the end of the year or as at the end of its preceding taxation year, of a premium receivable or a deferred acquisition expense (to the extent that it is included in the insurer's Canadian reserve liabilities as at the end of the year or preceding taxation year, as the case may be) of the insurer in respect of that business;

(*d*) if

(i) the insurer's mean Canadian investment fund for a taxation year

exceeds

(ii) the total value for the year of all property required to be designated under paragraph (*a*), (*b*) or (*c*) for the year,

shall designate for the year, in respect of a particular insurance business that the insurer carries on in Canada, investment property of the insurer for the year with a total value for the year equal to that excess;

(*e*) for greater certainty, under each of paragraphs (*a*), (*b*), (*c*) and (*d*), shall designate for the taxation year investment property with a total value for the year equal to the amount, if any, determined under each of those paragraphs, and no investment property, or portion of investment property, designated for the year under any of paragraphs (*a*) to (*d*) may be designated for the year under any other paragraph; and

(*f*) may designate for a taxation year a portion of a particular investment property if the designation of the entire property would result in a designation of property with a total value for the year exceeding that required to be designated under paragraphs (*a*) to (*d*) for the year.

History: S. 2401(2)(*b*) and (*c*) were replaced by S.C. 2010, c. 25, s. 82(1), applicable to taxation years that begin after 2010. S. 2401(2)(*b*) and (*c*) formerly read:

(*b*) shall designate for a taxation year investment property of the insurer for the year with a total value for the year equal to the amount, if any, by which the insurer's mean Canadian reserve liabilities for the year in respect of its accident and sickness insurance business in Canada exceeds the total of

(i) the insurer's mean Canadian outstanding premiums for the year in respect of that business, and

(ii) 50% of the total of all amounts, each of which is its total reinsurance recoverables, as at the end of the year or as at the end of the preceding taxation year, that are in respect of that business;

(*c*) shall designate for a taxation year in respect of the insurer's insurance business in Canada (other than a life insurance business or an accident and sickness insurance business) investment property of the insurer for the year with a total value for the year equal to the amount, if any, by which the insurer's mean Canadian reserve liabilities for the year in respect of that business exceeds the total of

(i) 50% of the total of all amounts each of which is the amount, as at the end of the year or as at the end of its preceding taxation year, of a premium receivable or a deferred acquisition expense (to the extent that it is included in the insurer's Canadian reserve liabilities as at the end of the year or preceding taxation year, as the case may be) of the insurer in respect of that business, and

(ii) 50% of the total of all amounts, each of which is its total reinsurance recoverables, as at the end of the year or as at the end of the preceding taxation year, that are in respect of that business;

(3) Order of Designation of Properties. For the purpose of subsection (2), investment property of an insurer for a taxation year shall be designated for the year in respect of the insurer's insurance businesses carried on by it in Canada in the following order:

(*a*) Canadian investment property of the insurer for the year owned by the insurer at the beginning of the year that was designated insurance property of the insurer for its preceding taxation year, except that such property shall be designated in the following order:

(i) real and depreciable property,

(ii) mortgages, hypothecs, agreements of sale and other forms of indebtedness in respect of real property situated in Canada or depreciable property situated in Canada or depreciable property leased to a person resident in Canada for use inside and outside of Canada, and

(iii) other property;

(*b*) investment property (other than Canadian investment property of the insurer for the year) owned by the insurer at the beginning of the year that was designated insurance property of the insurer for its preceding taxation year;

(*c*) Canadian investment property of the insurer for the year (other than property included in paragraph (*a*)) in the order set out in subparagraphs (*a*)(i) to (iii); and

(*d*) other investment property.

(4) Equity Limit for the Year. Notwithstanding subsections (2) and (3),

(*a*) the total value for the year of Canadian equity property of an insurer that may be designated in respect of the insurer's insurance businesses for a taxation year shall not exceed the insurer's equity limit for the year; and

(*b*) for a taxation year a portion of a particular Canadian equity property of an insurer may be designated if the designation of the entire property would result in a designation of Canadian equity property of the insurer for the year with a total value for the year exceeding the insurer's equity limit for the year.

(5) Exchanged Property. For the purposes of subsection (3), property acquired by an insurer in a particular taxation year is deemed to be designated insurance property of the insurer in respect of a particular business of the insurer for its preceding taxation year and to have been owned by the insurer at the beginning of the particular taxation year if the property was acquired

(*a*) by reason of

(i) a transaction to which any of sections 51, 51.1, 85.1 and 86 of the Act applies,

(ii) a transaction in respect of which an election is made under subsection 85(1) or (2) of the Act,

(iii) an amalgamation (within the meaning assigned by subsection 87(1) of the Act), or

(iv) a winding-up of a corporation to which subsection 88(1) of the Act applies, and

(*b*) as consideration for or in exchange for property of the insurer that was designated insurance property of the insurer in respect of the particular insurance business for its preceding taxation year.

(6) Non-investment Property. Non-segregated property owned by an insurer at any time in a taxation year (other than investment property of the insurer for the year) that is used or held by the insurer in the year in the course of carrying on an insurance business in Canada is deemed to be designated insurance property of the insurer for the year in respect of the business.

(7) Policy Loan Excluded from Designated Property. Notwithstanding any other provision in this Part, a policy loan payable to an insurer is not designated insurance property of the insurer.

2402. [Income From Participating Life Insurance Businesses]

(Repealed by S.C. 2013, c. 34, s. 391(1).)

History: S. 2402 and the preceding heading were repealed by S.C. 2013, c. 34, s. 391(1), applicable to taxation years that begin after October 31, 2011, and formerly read:

2402. *Income From Participating Life Insurance Businesses.* For the purposes of clause 138(3)(*a*)(iii)(B) of the Act and subparagraph 309(1)(*e*)(i), in computing a life insurer's income for a taxation year from its participating life insurance business carried on in Canada,

(*a*) there shall be included that proportion of the insurer's gross Canadian life investment income for the year that

(i) the aggregate of the insurer's mean maximum tax actuarial reserve for the year in respect of participating life insurance policies in Canada and the mean amount on deposit with the insurer for the year in respect of those policies

is of

(ii) the aggregate of amounts, each of which is

(A) the insurer's mean maximum tax actuarial reserve for the year in respect of a class of life insurance policies in Canada, or

(B) the mean amount on deposit with the insurer for the year in respect of a class of policies described in clause (A);

(*a*.1) there shall be included the amount determined by the formula

$$(A + B) \times C/D$$

where

A is the amount required by subsection 142.5(5) of the Act to be included in computing the insurer's income for the year,

B is the amount deemed by subsection 142.5(7) of the Act to be a taxable capital gain of the insurer for the year from the disposition of property,

C is the amount determined under subparagraph (*a*)(i) for the taxation year of the insurer that includes October 31, 1994, and

D is the amount determined under subparagraph (*a*)(ii) for the taxation year of the insurer that includes October 31, 1994;

(*b*) there shall be included

(i) the amount deducted by the insurer under subparagraph 138(3)(*a*)(iv) of the Act in computing its income for the immediately preceding taxation year,

(ii) the insurer's maximum tax actuarial reserve for the immediately preceding taxation year in respect of participating life insurance policies in Canada, and

(iii) the maximum amount deductible by the insurer under subparagraph 138(3)(*a*)(ii) of the Act in computing its income for the immediately preceding taxation year in respect of participating life insurance policies in Canada;

(iv) (Repealed.)

(*c*) there shall not be included any amount in respect of the insurer's participating life insurance policies in Canada that was deducted under subparagraph 138(3)(*a*)(i) or (ii) of the Act in computing its income for the immediately preceding taxation year;

(*d*) except as otherwise provided in paragraph (*a*), there shall not be included any amount as a reserve that was deducted under paragraph 20(1)(*l*) of the Act in computing the insurer's income for the immediately preceding taxation year;

(*e*) except as provided in paragraph (*a*), there shall not be included any amount that was included in determining the insurer's gross Canadian life investment income for the year;

(*e*.1) except as provided in paragraph (*a*.1), there shall not be included the amounts referred to in the descriptions of A and B in that paragraph;

(*e*.2) if the year includes October 31, 1994, there shall be deducted the amount determined by the formula

$$(A + B) \times C/D$$

where

A is the amount deducted under subsection 142.5(4) of the Act in computing the insurer's income for the year,

B is the amount deemed by subsection 142.5(6) of the Act to be an allowable capital loss of the insurer for the year from the disposition of property,

C is the amount determined under subparagraph (*a*)(i) for the year, and

D is the amount determined under subparagraph (*a*)(ii) for the year;

(*f*) there shall be deducted

(i) the insurer's maximum tax actuarial reserve for the year in respect of participating life insurance policies in Canada, and

(ii) the maximum amount deductible by the insurer under subparagraph 138(3)(*a*)(ii) of the Act in computing its income for the year in respect of participating life insurance policies in Canada;

(iii) (Repealed.)

(*g*) no deduction shall be made in respect of any amount deductible under subparagraph 138(3)(*a*)(iii) or (iv) of the Act in computing the insurer's income for the year;

(*h*) except as provided in paragraph (*a*), no deduction shall be made in respect of

(i) any amount taken into account in determining the insurer's gross Canadian life investment income for the year, or

(ii) any amount deductible under paragraph 20(1)(*l*) of the Act in computing the insurer's income for the year;

(*h*.1) except as provided in paragraph (*e*.2), no deduction shall be made in respect of the amounts referred to in the descriptions of A and B in that paragraph;

(*i*) except as otherwise provided in paragraph (*f*), no deduction shall be made in respect of a reserve deductible under subparagraph 138(3)(*a*)(i) or (ii) of the Act in computing the insurer's income for the year; and

(*j*) except as otherwise provided in this section, the provisions of the Act relating to the computation of income from a source shall apply.

S. 2402(*a*.1) was added by P.C. 2009-1212, SOR/2009-222, dated July 30, 2009, published in the *Canada Gazette* August 19, 2009, applicable to taxation years that end after October 30, 1994.

S. 2402(*b*)(iv) was repealed by P.C. 2009-1212, SOR/2009-222, dated July 30, 2009, published in the *Canada Gazette* August 19, 2009, applicable to taxation years that begin after 1992. S. 2402(*b*)(iv) formerly read:

(iv) that proportion of the amount included in income by the insurer for the year under section 12.3 that

(A) the amount determined under clause (*f*)(iii)(A) for its first taxation year that begins after June 17, 1987 and ends after 1987

is of

(B) the amount determined under clause (*f*)(iii)(B) for its first taxation year that begins after June 17, 1987 and ends after 1987;

S. 2402(*e*) was replaced by P.C. 2009-1212, SOR/2009-222, dated July 30, 2009, published in the *Canada Gazette* August 19, 2009, applicable to taxation years that end after February 22, 1994. S. 2402(*e*) formerly read:

(*e*) except as otherwise provided in paragraph (*a*), there shall not be included

(i) any amount that was included in income for the year by the insurer pursuant to paragraph 138(4)(*b*) or (*c*) of the Act, or

(ii) any amount that was included in computing the insurer's gains or taxable capital gains for the year from the disposition of property;

Ss. 2402(*e*.1) and (*e*.2) were added by P.C. 2009-1212, SOR/2009-222, dated July 30, 2009, published in the *Canada Gazette* August 19, 2009, applicable to taxation years that end after October 30, 1994.

S. 2402(*f*)(iii) was repealed by P.C. 2009-1212, SOR/2009-222, dated July 30, 2009, published in the *Canada Gazette* August 19, 2009, applicable to taxation years that begin after 1992. S. 2402(*f*)(iii) formerly read:

(iii) that proportion of the amount deducted from income by the insurer for the year under subsection 20(26) that

(A) the amount determined in respect of the insurer for the year under subparagraph (*a*)(i)

is of

(B) the amount determined in respect of the insurer for the year under subparagraph (*a*)(ii);

S. 2402(*h*) was replaced by P.C. 2009-1212, SOR/2009-222, dated July 30, 2009, published in the *Canada Gazette* August 19, 2009, applicable to taxation years that end after February 22, 1994. S. 2402(*h*) formerly read:

(*h*) except as otherwise provided in paragraph (*a*), no deduction shall be made in respect of

(i) any amount deductible under paragraph 138(3)(*b*) or (*d*) of the Act in computing the insurer's income for the year,

(ii) any amount deductible as a reserve under paragraph 20(1)(*l*) of the Act in computing the insurer's income for the year, or

(iii) any amount included in computing the insurer's losses or allowable capital losses for the year from the disposition of property;

S. 2402(*h*.1) was added by P.C. 2009-1212, SOR/2009-222, dated July 30, 2009, published in the *Canada Gazette* August 19, 2009, applicable to taxation years that end after October 30, 1994.

2403. Branch Tax Elections

(1) An election referred to in subsection 219(4) of the Act shall be made by a non-resident insurer in respect of a taxation year by filing, with its return of income required by subsection 150(1) of the Act to be filed for the year, a letter in duplicate stating

(*a*) the insurer elects under subsection 219(4) of the Act; and

(*b*) the amount the insurer elects to deduct under subsection 219(4) of the Act.

(2) Where a joint election referred to in subsection 219(5.2) of the Act is made by a non-resident insurer and a qualified related corporation (within the meaning assigned by subsection 219(8) of the Act) of the non-resident insurer in respect of a taxation year of the non-resident insurer, it shall be made by filing, with the non-resident insurer's return of income required by subsection 150(1) of the Act to be filed for the year in which the event to which the election relates occurred, a letter in duplicate signed by an authorized officer of the non-resident insurer and an authorized officer of the qualified related corporation stating

(*a*) whether paragraphs 219(5.2)(*a*) and (*b*) of the Act apply; and

(*b*) the amount elected under subsection 219(5.2) of the Act.

2404. Currency Conversions

(Repealed by S.C. 2013, c. 34, s. 392(1).)

History: S. 2404 and the preceding heading were repealed by S.C. 2013, c. 34, s. 392(1), applicable to taxation years that begin after October 31, 2011, and formerly read:

2404. *Currency Conversions.* For the purposes of this Part, where any amount is determined in a currency other than Canadian currency, that amount shall be converted to Canadian currency using the current rate of exchange, as required for the purposes of the relevant authority, on the date in respect of which the amount is determined.

2405. Interpretation

(1) (Repealed by S.C. 2013, c. 34, s. 392(1).)

History: S. 2405(1) was repealed by S.C. 2013, c. 34, s. 392(1), applicable to taxation years that begin after October 31, 2011, and formerly read:

(1) In this Part,

(*a*) "total depreciation" has the meaning assigned by paragraph 13(21)(*e*) [subsection 13(21) "total depreciation"] of the Act;

(*b*) "accumulated 1968 deficit", "amount payable", "gross investment revenue", "life insurance policy", "life insurance policy in Canada", "maximum tax actuarial reserve", "non-segregated property", "participating life insurance policy", "policy loan" and "surplus funds derived from operations" have the meanings assigned by subsection 138(12) of the Act; and

(*c*) "segregated fund" and "segregated fund policies" have the meanings assigned by subsection 138.1(1) of the Act.

(2) (Repealed by S.C. 2013, c. 34, s. 392(1).)

History: S. 2405(1) was repealed by S.C. 2013, c. 34, s. 392(1), applicable to taxation years that begin after October 31, 2011, and formerly read:

(2) For the purposes of subsection 138(14) of the Act, the expressions "Canadian investment fund for a taxation year", "specified Canadian assets" and "value for the taxation year" have the meanings prescribed therefor by subsection 2404(1) as it read in its application to the 1977 taxation year.

(3) (Repealed by S.C. 2013, c. 34, s. 392(1).)

History: S. 2405(3), the definition "attributed surplus for the year" was repealed by S.C. 2013, c. 34, s. 392(1), applicable to taxation years that begin after October 31, 2011, and formerly read:

"attributed surplus for the year", for a taxation year in respect of a non-resident insurer, means the aggregate of

(*a*) its property and casualty surplus for the year, and

(*b*) an amount equal to the percentage (that is the life surplus factor for the year) of the amount for the year determined under clause (*a*)(i)(B) of the definition "life surplus factor" in this subsection;

S. 2405(3), the definition "Canadian business property" was repealed by S.C. 2013, c. 34, s. 392(1), applicable to taxation years that begin after October 31, 2011, and formerly read:

"Canadian business property" of an insurer for a taxation year in respect of an insurance business means

(*a*) if the insurer was resident in Canada throughout the year and either did not carry on a life insurance business in the year or did not carry on an insurance business outside Canada in the year, the property used or held by it in the year in the course of carrying on the business in Canada, and

(*b*) in any other case, the property designated under subsection 2400(1) for the year in respect of the business;

S. 2405(3), the definition "Canadian equity property" was repealed by S.C. 2013, c. 34, s. 392(1), applicable to taxation years that begin after October 31, 2011, and formerly read:

"Canadian equity property" means

(*a*) a share of the capital stock of, or an income bond, income debenture, small business development bond or small business bond issued by, a person (other than a designated corporation) or partnership, as the case may be, resident in Canada, or

(*b*) that proportion of shares of the capital stock of a designated corporation or an interest in a partnership or trust that

(i) the aggregate value for the year of Canadian equity property owned by the designated corporation or the partnership or trust, as the case may be,

is of

(ii) the aggregate value for the year of all property owned by the designated corporation, or partnership or trust, as the case may be;

S. 2405(3), the definition "Canadian investment fund" was repealed by S.C. 2013, c. 34, s. 392(1), applicable to taxation years that begin after October 31, 2011, and formerly read:

"Canadian investment fund", as at the end of a taxation year, in respect of

(*a*) a life insurer resident in Canada, means the positive amount determined by the formula

$$[(A / B) \times (C - D)] - E$$

where

A is the mount of the insurer's Canadian reserve liabilities as at the end of the year,

B is the amount of the insurer's total reserve liabilities as at the end of the year,

C is the total of

(i) the aggregate amount of policy loans and foreign policy loans of the insurer as at the end of the year, and

(ii) the valuation of all property of the insurer as at the end of the year each of which is

(A) an investment property,

(B) money, or

(C) a balance (other than a property included under clause (A) or (B)) standing to the insurer's credit as or on account of amounts deposited with a corporation authorized to accept deposits or to carry on the business of offering to the public its services as a trustee,

D is the total of

(i) the aggregate of all amounts each of which is an amount outstanding as at the end of the year in respect of a debt (other than a debt referred to in paragraph (*h*) of the definition "valuation" in this subsection or an amount referred to in subparagraph (ii)) owing by the insurer in respect of money borrowed by the insurer (other than money used by the insurer for the purpose of earning income from a source that is not an insurance business), and

(ii) the aggregate of all amounts each of which is the amount of a cheque outstanding at the end of the year drawn on an account of the insurer maintained with a corporation authorized to accept deposits or to carry on the business of offering to the public its services as a trustee, and

E is the aggregate amount of the policy loans of the insurer as at the end of the year, and

(*b*) a non-resident insurer, means the amount, if any, by which the aggregate of amounts each of which is

(i) a maximum tax actuarial reserve of the insurer for the year,

(i.1) the maximum amount that the insurer is entitled to claim under subparagraph 138(3)(*a*)(ii) of the Act for the year,

(ii) the maximum amount that the insurer is entitled to deduct under paragraph 20(7)(*c*) of the Act in computing its income for the year determined on the assumption that it carried on no other than life insurance business other than an accident and sickness insurance business,

(iii) the amount of policy dividends, to the extent that such dividends were not included under subparagraph (i) or (ii), that will, according to the annual report of the insurer filed with the relevant authority for the year or, where the insurer was throughout the year subject to the supervision of the relevant authority but was not required to file an annual report with the relevant authority for the year, according to its financial statements for the year, as at the end of the year, become payable by the insurer in the immediately following year under its participating life insurance policies,

(iv) a liability (other than debt referred to in paragraph (*h*) of the definition "valuation" in this subsection) or a reserve (other than the insurer's investment valuation reserve) as reported by the insurer in its annual report for the year to the relevant authority or, where the insurer was throughout the year subject to the supervision of the relevant authority but was not required to file an annual report with the relevant authority for the year, in its financial statements for the year, that was incurred or provided for in the course of carrying on the insurer's property and casualty insurance business in Canada except to the extent that those amounts are already included under subparagraph (ii),

(v) a debt (other than a debt referred to in paragraph (*h*) of the definition "valuation" in this subsection) owing by the insurer at that time that was incurred in the course of carrying on an insurance business (other than a property and casualty insurance business) in Canada, except to the extent that those amounts are already included under subparagraph (i), (i.1) or (iii), or

(vi) the amount that is the greater of

(A) the amount, if any, by which the aggregate of

(I) the insurer's surplus funds derived from operations computed as at the end of the immediately preceding taxation year, and

(II) the aggregate of amounts in respect of which the insurer has made an election under subsection 219(4) or (5.2) of the Act, each of which is an amount included in the aggregate determined in respect of the insurer under subparagraph 219(4)(*a*)(i.1) of the Act at the end of the immediately preceding taxation year

exceeds

(III) the aggregate of amounts determined in respect of the insurer under subparagraphs 219(4)(*a*)(ii), (iii), (iv) and (v) of the Act, as at the end of the taxation year, and

(B) the insurer's attributed surplus for the year,

exceeds the aggregate of

Regulations

(vii) the aggregate valuation of all non-segregated property referred to in paragraph 2400(1)(*e*) at the end of the year in respect of all the insurer's insurance businesses carried on in Canada other than property that is

(A) money, or

(B) a balance standing to the insurer's credit as or on account of amounts deposited with a corporation authorized to accept deposits or to carry on the business of offering to the public its services as a trustee, and

(viii) the aggregate amount of the insurer's deferred acquisition expenses in respect of its property and casualty insurance business in Canada reported by the insurer in its annual report for the year to the relevant authority or, where the insurer was throughout the year subject to the supervision of the relevant authority but was not required to file an annual report with the relevant authority for the year, in its financial statements for the year;

S. 2405(3), the definition "Canadian investment fund for the year" was repealed by S.C. 2013, c. 34, s. 392(1), applicable to taxation years that begin after October 31, 2011, and formerly read:

"Canadian investment fund for the year", for a taxation year in respect of a life insurer resident in Canada and a non-resident insurer, means the amount determined under section 2412;

S. 2405(3), the definition "Canadian investment property" was repealed by S.C. 2013, c. 34, s. 392(1), applicable to taxation years that begin after October 31, 2011, and formerly read:

"Canadian investment property" of an insurer for a taxation year means an investment property (unless the insurer is a non-resident insurer and it is established by the insurer that the investment property is not effectively connected with its Canadian insurance businesses) that is

(*a*) land or depreciable property situated in Canada and, for that purpose, depreciable property of an insurer leased by a person resident in Canada for use inside and outside of Canada shall be deemed to be depreciable property situated in Canada,

(*b*) a Canadian equity property,

(*c*) a Canadian resource property,

(*d*) a mortgage, an agreement of sale or any other form of indebtedness in respect of property referred to in paragraph (*a*),

(*e*) an amount in Canadian currency standing to the insurer's credit as or on account of amounts deposited with a corporation resident in Canada authorized to accept deposits or to carry on the business of offering to the public its services as a trustee,

(*f*) a bond, debenture or other form of indebtedness (other than a property described in paragraph (*d*) or (*e*)) in Canadian currency issued by

(i) a person resident in Canada, a Canadian partnership or a partnership an interest in which is an investment property described in paragraph (*g*),

(ii) the Government of Canada,

(iii) the government of a province of Canada, or

(iv) any other political subdivision of Canada or of any province of Canada, or

(*g*) a property (to the extent it is not a property described in paragraph (*b*)) that is

(i) a share of a designated corporation resident in Canada,

(ii) an interest in a partnership, or

(iii) an interest in a trust resident in Canada,

where not less than 75 per cent for the aggregate value for the year of all property of the corporation, partnership or trust, as the case may be, is in respect of property each of which is property described in paragraphs (*a*) to (*f*);

S. 2405(3), the definition "Canadian reserve liabilities" was repealed by S.C. 2013, c. 34, s. 392(1), applicable to taxation years that begin after October 31, 2011, and formerly read:

"Canadian reserve liabilities" of an insurer, as at the end of a taxation year, means the aggregate amount of the insurer's liabilities and reserves (other than liabilities and reserves in respect of amounts payable out of segregated funds) in respect of its insurance policies in Canada, as determined for the purposes of the relevant authority at the end of the year or as would be determined at that time if the relevant authority required such a determination;

S. 2405(3), the definition "designated corporation" was repealed by S.C. 2013, c. 34, s. 392(1), applicable to taxation years that begin after October 31, 2011, and formerly read:

"designated corporation", in respect of an insurer, at any time in a taxation year, means a corporation in respect of which the insurer or the insurer and persons or partnerships that do not deal at arm's length with the insurer held, at any time in the year, shares that represented 30 per cent or more of the common shares of the corporation outstanding at that time;

S. 2405(3), the definition "equity limit for the year" was repealed by S.C. 2013, c. 34, s. 392(1), applicable to taxation years that begin after October 31, 2011, and formerly read:

"equity limit for the year", for a taxation year, means

(*a*) in respect of a life insurer resident in Canada, the greater of

(i) that proportion of the aggregate value for the year of all the insurer's equity property that

(A) the amount, if any, by which the insurer's mean Canadian reserve liabilities exceed the aggregate of the insurer's mean policy loans for the year and 1/2 of the aggregate of outstanding premiums of the insurer in respect of its insurance businesses in Canada as determined for the purposes of the relevant authority at the end of the year and the immediately preceding taxation year,

is of

(B) the amount, if any, by which the insurer's mean total reserve liabilities exceed the aggregate of the insurer's mean policy loans and foreign policy loans for the year and 1/2 of the aggregate of outstanding premiums of the insurer in respect of its insurance businesses as determined for the purposes of the relevant authority at the end of the year and the immediately preceding taxation year, and

(ii) 8 per cent of the insurer's Canadian investment fund for the year,

(*b*) in respect of a non-resident insurer (other than a life insurer), 1/4 of the aggregate of

(i) the amount, if any, by which the insurer's mean Canadian reserve liabilities exceed 1/2 of the aggregate of the amounts of the insurer's deferred acquisition expenses and premiums receivable at the end of the year and the immediately preceding year to the extent that those amounts were included in the insurer's Canadian reserve liabilities for those years in respect of the insurer's business in Canada as determined for the purposes of the relevant authority, and

(ii) the insurer's property and casualty surplus for the year, and

(*c*) in respect of a non-resident life insurer, the aggregate of

(i) the insurer's life equity limit for the year, and

(ii) 1/4 of the aggregate of

(A) the amount, if any, by which the insurer's mean Canadian reserve liabilities for the year exceed 1/2 of the aggregate of the amounts of the insurer's deferred acquisition expenses and premiums receivable at the end of the year and the immediately preceding year in respect of the insurer's business in Canada as determined for the purposes of the relevant authority to the extent that those amounts were included in the insurer's Canadian reserve liabilities for those years (determined on the assumption that the only insurance business carried on in Canada by the insurer was a property and casualty insurance business), and

(B) the insurer's property and casualty surplus for the year;

S. 2405(3), the definition "equity property" was repealed by S.C. 2013, c. 34, s. 392(1), applicable to taxation years that begin after October 31, 2011, and formerly read:

"equity property" means

(*a*) a share of the capital stock of, or an income bond, income debenture, small business development bond or small business bond issued by, a person (other than a designated corporation) or partnership, as the case may be, or

(*b*) that proportion of shares of the capital stock of a designated corporation or an interest in a partnership or trust that

(i) the aggregate value for the year of equity property owned by the designated corporation or the partnership or trust, as the case may be,

is of

(ii) the aggregate value for the year of all property owned by the designated corporation or the partnership or trust, as the case may be;

S. 2405(3), the definition "foreign policy loan" was repealed by S.C. 2013, c. 34, s. 392(1), applicable to taxation years that begin after October 31, 2011, and formerly read:

"foreign policy loan" means an amount advanced at a particular time by an insurer to a policyholder in accordance with the terms and conditions of a life insurance policy, other than a life insurance policy in Canada;

S. 2405(3), the definition "gross Canadian life investment income" was repealed by S.C. 2013, c. 34, s. 392(1), applicable to taxation years that begin after October 31, 2011, and formerly read:

"gross Canadian life investment income" of a life insurer for a taxation year means the amount, if any, by which the aggregate of

(*a*) the insurer's gross investment revenue for the year, to the extent that the revenue is from Canadian business property of the insurer for the year in respect of the insurer's life insurance business,

(*b*) the amount included in computing the insurer's income for the year under paragraph 138(9)(*b*) of the Act,

(*c*) (Repealed.)

(*d*) the portion of the amount deducted under paragraph 20(1)(*l*) of the Act in computing the insurer's income for the preceding taxation year that

Regulations

was in respect of Canadian business property of the insurer for that year in respect of the insurer's life insurance business,

(*d*.1) the total of all amounts each of which is an amount included under section 142.4 of the Act in the insurer's income for the year in respect of a property disposed of by the insurer that was, in the taxation year of disposition, a Canadian business property of the insurer for that year in respect of the insurer's life insurance business,

(*e*) the total of all amounts each of which is the insurer's gain for the year from the disposition of a Canadian business property of the insurer for the year in respect of the insurer's life insurance business, other than a capital property or a property in respect of which section 142.4 of the Act applies, and

(*f*) the total of all amounts each of which is the insurer's taxable capital gain for the year from the disposition of a Canadian business property of the insurer for the year in respect of the insurer's life insurance business,

(*g*) (Repealed.)

exceeds the aggregate of

(*h*) (Repealed.)

(*i*) the portion of the amount deducted under paragraph 20(1)(*l*) of the Act in computing the insurer's income for the year that is in respect of debt obligations that are Canadian business property of the insurer for the year in respect of the insurer's life insurance business,

(*i*.1) the total of all amounts each of which is an amount deductible under section 142.4 of the Act in computing the insurer's income for the year in respect of a property disposed of by the insurer that was, in the taxation year of disposition, a Canadian business property of the insurer for that year in respect of the insurer's life insurance business,

(*j*) the total of all amounts each of which is the insurer's loss for the year from the disposition of a Canadian business property of the insurer for the year in respect of the insurer's life insurance business, other than a capital property or a property in respect of which section 142.4 of the Act applies, and

(*k*) the total of all amounts each of which is the insurer's allowable capital loss for the year from the disposition of a Canadian business property of the insurer for the year in respect of the insurer's life insurance business;

S. 2405(3), the definition "insurance policy in Canada" was repealed by S.C. 2013, c. 34, s. 392(1), applicable to taxation years that begin after October 31, 2011, and formerly read:

"insurance policy in Canada", in respect of an insurer, means, in the case of

(*a*) a life insurance policy, a life insurance policy in Canada,

(*b*) a fire insurance policy, a policy issued or effected upon property situated in Canada, and

(*c*) any other class of insurance policy, a policy where the risks covered by the policy were ordinarily within Canada at the time the policy was issued or effected;

S. 2405(3), the definition "investment property" was repealed by S.C. 2013, c. 34, s. 392(1), applicable to taxation years that begin after October 31, 2011, and formerly read:

"investment property" of an insurer for a taxation year means non-segregated property that is

(*a*) property acquired by the insurer for the purpose of earning gross investment revenue, other than property that is

(i) property, a portion of which is investment property pursuant to paragraph (*b*) or (*c*),

(ii) a share of a designated corporation,

(iii) a debt owing to the insurer by a designated corporation,

(iv) an interest in a partnership, or

(v) an interest in a trust,

(*b*) the portion, if any, of property of the insurer (other than property a portion of which is investment property pursuant to paragraph (*c*)) that is

(i) land,

(ii) depreciable property, or

(iii) property that would have been depreciable property if it had been situated in Canada and used in the year in, or held in the year in the course of, carrying on an insurance business in Canada,

that

(iv) the use made of the property in the year for the purpose of earning gross investment revenue therefrom

is of

(v) the whole use made of the property in the year,

(*c*) the portion, if any, of property of the insurer that is not used in the year for the purpose of earning gross investment revenue that is

(i) land,

(ii) depreciable property, or

(iii) property that would be depreciable property if it had been situated in Canada and used in the year in, or held in the year in the course of, carrying on an insurance business in Canada,

to the extent that the property is held for resale or development or is expected to be used in a subsequent taxation year for the purpose of earning gross investment revenue, or

(*d*) property of the insurer that is

(i) a share of, or a debt owing to the insurer by a designated corporation other than a corporation that carries on a business of insurance, banking or offering its services to the public as a trustee or whose principal business is the making of loans,

(ii) an interest in a partnership, or

(iii) an interest in a trust,

if

(iv) the aggregate value for the year of all investment property of the corporation, partnership or trust, as the case may be, is not less than 75 per cent of the aggregate value for the year of all its property, and

(v) the gross investment revenue for the year from the investment property referred to in subparagraph (iv) (other than gross investment revenue from persons with whom the corporation, partnership or trust, as the case may be, did not deal at arm's length) is not less than 90 per cent of the gross revenue for the year of the corporation, partnership or trust, as the case may be,

assuming for the purposes of subparagraphs (iv) and (v) that the definition "gross investment revenue" in paragraph 138(12)(*e*) [subsection 138(12) "gross investment revenue"] of the Act and this definition apply to a corporation, partnership or trust, referred to in those subparagraphs, as though the corporation, partnership or trust, as the case may be, were an insurer;

S. 2405(3), the definition "life equity limit" was repealed by S.C. 2013, c. 34, s. 392(1), applicable to taxation years that begin after October 31, 2011, and formerly read:

"life equity limit" of a non-resident life insurer for a taxation year means

(*a*) where the insurer makes an election in respect of its life surplus factor for the year in the manner described in subsection 2401(1), the amount that would have been the insurer's equity limit for the year if the insurer had been a life insurer resident in Canada registered under the *Canadian and British Insurance Companies Act* to carry on an insurance business in Canada and it had carried on no other than life insurance business other than an accident and sickness insurance business,

(*b*) where the insurer does not make an election referred to in paragraph (*a*) in respect of the year, but

(i) has made such an election in respect of one of the four immediately preceding taxation years, and

(ii) the insurer's life surplus factor for the year is not determined pursuant to paragraph (*c*) of the definition "life surplus factor" in this subsection,

the amount that would have been the insurer's equity limit for the year if the insurer had been a life insurer resident in Canada registered under the *Canadian and British Insurance Companies Act* to carry on an insurance business in Canada and it had carried on no other than life insurance business other than an accident and sickness insurance business, using the amount, in respect of the most recent taxation year for which such an election was made, determined under subparagraph (*a*)(i) of the definition, in this subsection, "equity limit for the year", and

(*c*) in any other case, 8 per cent of the amount of the insurer's Canadian investment fund for the year;

S. 2405(3), the definition "life surplus factor" was repealed by S.C. 2013, c. 34, s. 392(1), applicable to taxation years that begin after October 31, 2011, and formerly read:

"life surplus factor" of a non-resident life insurer for a taxation year means

(*a*) subject to subsection 2401(2), where the insurer elects in respect of the year in the manner described in subsection 2401(1), the proportion (expressed as a percentage) that

(i) the amount, if any, by which

(A) the amount that would have been the insurer's Canadian investment fund for the year if the insurer had been a life insurer resident in Canada registered under the *Canadian and British Insurance Companies Act* to carry on an insurance business in Canada and it had carried on no other than life insurance business other than an accident and sickness insurance business

exceeds

(B) the amount, if any, by which $^1/_2$ of the aggregate of

(I) the aggregate of the amounts described in subparagraphs (*b*)(i), (i.1), (ii), (iii) and (v) of the definition "Canadian investment fund" in this subsection in respect of a non-resident insurer, as at the end of the year, and

(II) the aggregate of those amounts as at the end of the immediately preceding taxation year,

exceeds the aggregate value for the year of all the insurer's non-segregated property referred to in paragraph 2400(1)(*e*) in respect of all the insurer's insurance businesses (other than its property and casualty insurance business) carried on in Canada, other than property that is

(III) money, or

(IV) a balance standing to the insurer's credit as or on account of amounts deposited with a corporation authorized to accept deposits or to carry on the business of offering to the public its services as a trustee

is of

(ii) the amount determined under clause (i)(B),

(*b*) where the insurer does not make an election referred to in paragraph (*a*) in respect of the year, but

(i) has made such an election in respect of one of the four immediately preceding taxation years, and

(ii) has not, since making the most recent election referred to in subparagraph (i), selected pursuant to this paragraph the percentage referred to in paragraph (*c*) as its life surplus factor for a year prior to the taxation year,

the percentage, as shall be selected by the insurer, that is the percentage

(iii) determined under paragraph (*a*) in respect of the most recent taxation year for which the insurer made an election, or

(iv) referred to in paragraph (*c*), and

(*c*) in any other case, 10 per cent;

S. 2405(3), the definition "mean amount on deposit" was repealed by S.C. 2013, c. 34, s. 392(1), applicable to taxation years that begin after October 31, 2011, and formerly read:

"mean amount on deposit" with an insurer for a taxation year in respect of life insurance policies means 1/2 of the aggregate of

(*a*) all amounts on deposit with the insurer as at the end of the year in respect of those policies, and

(*b*) all amounts on deposit with the insurer as at the end of the immediately preceding taxation year in respect of those policies;

S. 2405(3), the definition "mean Canadian reserve liabilities" was repealed by S.C. 2013, c. 34, s. 392(1), applicable to taxation years that begin after October 31, 2011, and formerly read:

"mean Canadian reserve liabilities" of an insurer for a taxation year means 1/2 of the aggregate of

(*a*) the insurer's Canadian reserve liabilities as at the end of the year, and

(*b*) the insurer's Canadian reserve liabilities as at the end of the immediately preceding taxation year;

S. 2405(3), the definition "mean maximum tax actuarial reserve" was repealed by S.C. 2013, c. 34, s. 392(1), applicable to taxation years that begin after October 31, 2011, and formerly read:

"mean maximum tax actuarial reserve", in respect of a particular class of life insurance policies of an insurer for a taxation year, means 1/2 of the aggregate of

(*a*) the insurer's maximum tax actuarial reserve for that class of policies for the year, and

(*b*) the insurer's maximum tax actuarial reserve for that class of policies for the immediately preceding taxation year;

S. 2405(3), the definition "mean policy loans" was repealed by S.C. 2013, c. 34, s. 392(1), applicable to taxation years that begin after October 31, 2011, and formerly read:

"mean policy loans", of an insurer for a taxation year, means 1/2 of the aggregate of

(*a*) the insurer's policy loans as at the end of the year, and

(*b*) the insurer's policy loans as at the end of the immediately preceding taxation year;

S. 2405(3), the definition "mean policy loans and foreign policy loans" was repealed by S.C. 2013, c. 34, s. 392(1), applicable to taxation years that begin after October 31, 2011, and formerly read:

"mean policy loans and foreign policy loans", of an insurer for a taxation year, means 1/2 of the aggregate of

(*a*) the insurer's policy loans and foreign policy loans as at the end of the year, and

(*b*) the insurer's policy loans and foreign policy loans as at the end of the immediately preceding taxation year;

S. 2405(3), the definition "mean total reserve liabilities" was repealed by S.C. 2013, c. 34, s. 392(1), applicable to taxation years that begin after October 31, 2011, and formerly read:

"mean total reserve liabilities" of an insurer for a taxation year means 1/2 of the aggregate of

(*a*) the insurer's total reserve liabilities as at the end of the year, and

(*b*) the insurer's total reserve liabilities as at the end of the immediately preceding taxation year;

S. 2405(3), the definition "property and casualty surplus" was repealed by S.C. 2013, c. 34, s. 392(1), applicable to taxation years that begin after October 31, 2011, and formerly read:

"property and casualty surplus" of an insurer for a taxation year means the aggregate of

(*a*) 15 per cent of 1/2 of the aggregate of

(i) the insurer's unearned premium reserve as at the end of the year, and

(ii) the insurer's unearned premium reserve as at the end of the immediately preceding taxation year,

as reported to the relevant authority in respect of its property and casualty insurance business,

(*b*) 15 per cent of 1/2 of the aggregate of

(i) the insurer's provision for unpaid claims and adjustment expenses as at the end of the year, and

(ii) the insurer's provision for unpaid claims and adjustment expenses as at the end of the immediately preceding taxation year,

as reported to the relevant authority in respect of its property and casualty insurance business, and

(*c*) 1/2 of the aggregate of

(i) the insurer's investment valuation reserve as at the end of the year, and

(ii) the insurer's investment valuation reserve as at the end of the immediately preceding taxation year,

as reported to the relevant authority in respect of its property and casualty insurance business;

S. 2405(3), the definition "relevant authority" was repealed by S.C. 2013, c. 34, s. 392(1), applicable to taxation years that begin after October 31, 2011, and formerly read:

"relevant authority" means

(*a*) the Superintendent of Financial Institutions, if the insurer is required by law to report to the Superintendent of Financial Institutions, or

(*b*) in any other case, the Superintendent of Insurance or other similar officer or authority of the province under whose laws the insurer is incorporated;

S. 2405(3), the definition "total reserve liabilities" was repealed by S.C. 2013, c. 34, s. 392(1), applicable to taxation years that begin after October 31, 2011, and formerly read:

"total reserve liabilities" of an insurer, as at the end of a taxation year, means the aggregate amount of the insurer's liabilities and reserves (other than liabilities and reserves in respect of amounts payable out of segregated funds) in respect of all its insurance policies, as determined for the purposes of the relevant authority at the end of the year;

S. 2405(3), the definition "valuation" was repealed by S.C. 2013, c. 34, s. 392(1), applicable to taxation years that begin after October 31, 2011, and formerly read:

"valuation", in respect of a property of an insurer, designated corporation, partnership or trust (in this definition referred to as an "owner") at a particular time, means, in the case of

(*a*) land, the cost thereof to the owner,

(*b*) depreciable property of a prescribed class (other than a property referred to in paragraph (*f*)), the proportion of the owner's undepreciated capital cost at that time of property of the class that

(i) the owner's capital cost of the property

is of

(ii) the owner's capital cost of all property of the class,

(*c*) property that would have been depreciable property of a prescribed class if it had been situated in Canada and used in the year in, or held in the year in the course of, carrying on an insurance business in Canada, the amount, if any, by which

(i) the owner's capital cost of the property

exceeds

(ii) the amount that would have been the total depreciation allowed to the owner before the particular time in respect of the property if it had been the owner's only depreciable property of the class and the owner had claimed the maximum amount allowable under paragraph 20(1)(*a*) of the Act in respect of property of that class for each year in which the owner owned the property,

(*d*) a share of a corporation (other than a designated corporation), the cost thereof to the owner,

(*e*) a bond, debenture, mortgage, hypothec or agreement of sale (other than a property referred to in paragraph (*f*)), the book value thereof in the accounts of the owner as determined for the purposes of the relevant authority or that would have been so determined if the owner had been a life insurer resident in Canada and registered under the *Canadian and British Insurance Companies Act* to carry on an insurance business in Canada,

(*e*.1) a balance standing to the owner's credit as or on account of amounts deposited with a corporation authorized to accept deposits or to carry on the business of offering to the public its services as a trustee, the amount thereof,

Regulations

(*f*) a property acquired and disposed of in a taxation year, the cost thereof to the owner, and

(*g*) a property (other than a property referred to in any of paragraphs (*a*) to (*f*)), the maximum value of the property as determined for the purposes of the relevant authority or that would have been so determined if the owner had been a life insurer resident in Canada and registered under the *Canadian and British Insurance Companies Act* to carry on an insurance business in Canada,

minus

(*h*) in respect of a particular property referred to in any of paragraphs (*a*) to (*g*), the amount of any debt that was incurred or assumed by the owner to acquire that particular property and that was owing by the owner at that time;

S. 2405(3), the definition "value for the year" was repealed by S.C. 2013, c. 34, s. 392(1), applicable to taxation years that begin after October 31, 2011, and formerly read:

"value for the year", in respect of a property of an insurer, designated corporation, partnership or trust (in this definition referred to as an "owner") for a taxation year, means, in the case of

(*a*) a property that is a mortgage, a hypothec, an agreement of sale or an investment property that is a balance standing to the insurer's credit as or on account of amounts deposited with a corporation authorized to accept deposits or to carry on the business of offering to the public its services as a trustee, the amount, if any, by which

(i) the amount obtained when the gross investment revenue for the year from the property is divided by the average rate of interest earned by the owner (expressed as an annual rate) on the amortized cost of the property during the year if that rate of interest were expressed as a fraction

exceeds

(ii) the amount obtained when the interest paid or payable for the year on a debt incurred for the purposes of acquiring the property is divided by the average rate of interest paid or payable by the owner (expressed as an annual rate) on the debt for the year if that rate of interest were expressed as a fraction,

(*b*) a property (other than a property referred to in paragraph (*a*)) that was not owned by the owner throughout the year, the proportion of

(i) the valuation of the property as at the end of the immediately preceding taxation year, where the property was owned by the owner at that time, and

(ii) the valuation of the property, where it was acquired by the owner during the year,

that

(iii) the number of days that the property may reasonably be considered to have been owned by the owner during the taxation year

is of

(iv) the number of days in the taxation year, and

(*c*) a property (other than a property referred to in paragraph (*a*) or (*b*)), 1/2 of the aggregate of

(i) the valuation of the property as at the end of the year, and

(ii) the valuation of the property as at the end of the immediately preceding taxation year.

S. 2405(3), the definition "Canadian business property" was added by P.C. 2009-1212, SOR/2009-222, dated July 30, 2009, published in the *Canada Gazette* August 19, 2009, applicable to taxation years that end after February 22, 1994 and before 1999.

S. 2405(3), paragraph (*a*) of the definition "gross Canadian life investment income" was replaced by P.C. 2009-1212, SOR/2009-222, dated July 30, 2009, published in the *Canada Gazette* August 19, 2009, applicable to taxation years that end after June 1, 1995 and before 1999. S. 2405(3), paragraph (*a*) of the definition "gross Canadian life investment income" formerly read:

(*a*) the insurer's gross investment revenue for the year to the extent that that revenue is from non-segregated property of the insurer used by it in the year in, or held by it in the year in the course of, carrying on its life insurance business in Canada,

S. 2405(3), paragraph (*c*) of the definition "gross Canadian life investment income" was repealed, and paragraph (*d*) was replaced, by P.C. 2009-1212, SOR/2009-222, dated July 30, 2009, published in the *Canada Gazette* August 19, 2009, applicable to taxation years that begin after February 22, 1994 and end before 1999. S. 2405(3), paragraphs (*c*) and (*d*) of the definition "gross Canadian life investment income" formerly read:

(*c*) the amounts included in computing the insurer's income for the year under paragraphs 138(4)(*b*) and (*c*) of the Act,

(*d*) that portion of the amount included in computing the insurer's income for the year under paragraph 12(1)(*d*) of the Act in respect of amounts deducted in computing the insurer's income under paragraph 20(1)(*l*) of the Act in the immediately preceding taxation year in respect of a Canada security (within the meaning assigned by paragraph 138(12)(*c*) [subsection 138(12) "Canada security"] of the Act) owned by the insurer,

S. 2405(3), paragraph (*d*.1) of the definition "gross Canadian life investment income" was added, and paragraph (*e*) was replaced, by P.C. 2009-1212, SOR/2009-222, dated July 30, 2009, published in the *Canada Gazette* August 19, 2009, applicable to dispositions of property that occur after February 22, 1994 in taxation years that end before 1999 except that, in its application to property disposed of in a taxation year that ends before June 2, 1995, paragraph (*e*) of the definition "gross Canadian life investment income" in subsection 2405(3) is to be read as follows:

"(*e*) the amount included in computing the insurer's gains for the year from the disposition of property (other than capital property or property in respect of which section 142.4 of the Act applies), and"

S. 2405(3), paragraph (*e*) of the definition "gross Canadian life investment income" formerly read:

(*e*) the amount included in computing the insurer's gains for the year from the disposition of property (other than a Canada security or capital property),

S. 2405(3), paragraph (*f*) of the definition "gross Canadian life investment income" was replaced by P.C. 2009-1212, SOR/2009-222, dated July 30, 2009, published in the *Canada Gazette* August 19, 2009, applicable to taxation years that end after October 30, 1994 and before 1999, except that in its application to property disposed of in a taxation year that ends before June 2, 1995, paragraph (*f*) of the definition "gross Canadian life investment income" in subsection 2405(3) is to be read as follows:

"(*f*) the amount included in computing the insurer's taxable capital gains for the year from the disposition of property (other than an amount included because of subsection 142.5(7) of the Act),"

S. 2405(3), paragraph (*f*) of the definition "gross Canadian life investment income" formerly read:

(*f*) the amount included in computing the insurer's taxable capital gains for the year from the disposition of property, and

S. 2405(3), paragraph (*g*) of the definition "gross Canadian life investment income" was repealed by P.C. 2009-1212, SOR/2009-222, dated July 30, 2009, published in the *Canada Gazette* August 19, 2009, applicable to taxation years that begin after February 22, 1994 and end before 1999. S. 2405(3), paragraph (*g*) of the definition "gross Canadian life investment income" formerly read:

(*g*) the amount deducted in computing the insurer's income for the immediately preceding taxation year under paragraph 138(3)(*c*) of the Act (as it read in its application to taxation years commencing before June 17, 1987 or ending before 1988),

S. 2405(3), paragraph (*h*) of the definition "gross Canadian life investment income" was repealed by P.C. 2009-1212, SOR/2009-222, dated July 30, 2009, published in the *Canada Gazette* August 19, 2009, applicable to taxation years that begin after February 22, 1994 and end before 1999. S. 2405(3), paragraph (*h*) of the definition "gross Canadian life investment income" formerly read:

(*h*) the amounts deducted in computing the insurer's income for the year under paragraphs 138(3)(*b*) and (*d*) of the Act,

S. 2405(3), paragraph (*i*) of the definition "gross Canadian life investment income" was replaced by P.C. 2009-1212, SOR/2009-222, dated July 30, 2009, published in the *Canada Gazette* August 19, 2009, applicable to taxation years that end after February 22, 1994 and before 1999. S. 2405(3), paragraph (*i*) of the definition "gross Canadian life investment income" formerly read:

(*i*) the amount deducted in computing the insurer's income for the year under paragraph 20(1)(*l*) of the Act in respect of a Canada security (within the meaning assigned by paragraph 138(12)(*c*) [subsection 138(12) "Canada security"] of the Act) owned by the insurer,

S. 2405(3), paragraph (*i*.1) of the definition "gross Canadian life investment income" was added, and paragraph (*j*) was replaced, by P.C. 2009-1212, SOR/2009-222, dated July 30, 2009, published in the *Canada Gazette* August 19, 2009, applicable to dispositions of property that occur after February 22, 1994 in taxation years that end before 1999 except that, in its application to property disposed of in a taxation year that ends before June 2, 1995, paragraph (*j*) of the definition "gross Canadian life investment income" in subsection 2405(3) is to be read as follows:

"(*j*) the amount included in computing the insurer's losses for the year from the disposition of property (other than capital property or property in respect of which section 142.4 of the Act applies), and"

S. 2405(3), paragraph (*j*) of the definition "gross Canadian life investment income" formerly read:

(*j*) the amount included in computing the insurer's losses for the year from the disposition of property (other than a Canada security or capital property), and

S. 2405(3), paragraph (*k*) of the definition "gross Canadian life investment income" was replaced by P.C. 2009-1212, SOR/2009-222, dated July 30, 2009, published in the *Canada Gazette* August 19, 2009, applicable to taxation years that end after October 30, 1994 and before 1999, except that in its application to property disposed of in a taxation year that ends before June 2, 1995, paragraph (*k*) of the definition "gross Canadian life investment income" in subsection 2405(3) is to be read as follows:

"(*k*) the amount included in computing the insurer's allowable capital losses for the year from the disposition of property (other than an amount included because of subsection 142.5(6) of the Act);"

S. 2405(3), paragraph (*k*) of the definition "gross Canadian life investment income" formerly read:

(*k*) the amount included in computing the insurer's allowable capital losses for the year from the disposition of property;

(4) (Repealed by S.C. 2013, c. 34, s. 392(1).)

History: S. 2405(4) was repealed by S.C. 2013, c. 34, s. 392(1), applicable to taxation years that begin after October 31, 2011, and formerly read:

(4) For the purposes of the definition in subsection (3), "Canadian investment fund" in respect of a life insurer resident in Canada, notwithstanding the definitions "Canadian reserve liabilities" and "total reserve liabilities" in that subsection, the insurer shall determine its liabilities and reserves in respect of its insurance policies outside Canada in a manner consistent with that used in determining its liabilities and reserves in respect of its insurance policies in Canada.

(5) (Repealed by S.C. 2013, c. 34, s. 392(1).)

History: S. 2405(5) was repealed by S.C. 2013, c. 34, s. 392(1), applicable to taxation years that begin after October 31, 2011, and formerly read:

(5) For the purposes of subsection (3), the cost of a property shall be determined without regard to subsection 142.5(2) of the Act.

S. 2405(5) was added by P.C. 2009-1212, SOR/2009-222, dated July 30, 2009, published in the *Canada Gazette* August 19, 2009, applicable to taxation years that end after October 30, 1994 and before 1999.

2406. Interpretation

(Repealed by S.C. 2013, c. 34, s. 392(1).)

History: S. 2406 was repealed by S.C. 2013, c. 34, s. 392(1), applicable to taxation years that begin after October 31, 2011, and formerly read:

2406. *Interpretation.* Sections 2404 and 2405 do not apply to the 1999 and subsequent taxation years.

2407. 1977 Excess Policy Dividend Deduction

(Repealed by S.C. 2013, c. 34, s. 392(1).)

History: S. 2407 was repealed by S.C. 2013, c. 34, s. 392(1), applicable to taxation years that begin after October 31, 2011, and formerly read:

2407. *1977 Excess Policy Dividend Deduction.* For the purposes of paragraph 138(3.1)(*b*) of the Act, a life insurer's 1977 excess policy dividend deduction is hereby prescribed to be the amount that is the lesser of

(*a*) the amount, if any, by which

(i) the amount determined under clause 138(3)(*a*)(iii)(A) of the Act for the insurer's 1977 taxation year (determined without reference to paragraph 138(3.1)(*b*) of the Act),

exceeds

(ii) the amount determined under clause 138(3)(*a*)(iii)(B) of the Act for the insurer's 1977 taxation year; and

(*b*) the amount, if any, by which

(i) the insurer's maximum tax actuarial reserve for its participating life insurance policies in Canada for its 1977 taxation year,

exceeds the aggregate of

(ii) the amount that would have been the insurer's maximum tax actuarial reserve for its participating life insurance policies in Canada for its 1977 taxation year if that reserve had been determined on the basis of the rules applicable to its 1978 taxation year,

(iii) the aggregate of all amounts payable to the insurer in respect of policy loans outstanding at the end of its 1977 taxation year in respect of participating life insurance policies in Canada, and

(iv) the amount, if any, by which

(A) the insurer's maximum tax actuarial reserve for its participating life insurance policies in Canada for its 1968 taxation year,

exceeds the aggregate of

(B) the amount that would have been the insurer's maximum tax actuarial reserve for its participating life insurance policies in Canada for its 1968 taxation year if that reserve had been determined on the basis of the rules applicable to its 1978 taxation year, and

(C) the aggregate of all amounts payable to the insurer in respect of policy loans outstanding at the end of its 1968 taxation year in respect of participating life insurance policies in Canada.

2408. 1977 Carryforward Deduction

(Repealed by S.C. 2013, c. 34, s. 392(1).)

History: S. 2408 was repealed by S.C. 2013, c. 34, s. 392(1), applicable to taxation years that begin after October 31, 2011, and formerly read:

2408. *1977 Carryforward Deduction.* For the purposes of subparagraph 138(4.2)(*a*)(iv) of the Act, a life insurer's 1977 carryforward deduction is hereby prescribed to be the amount, if any, by which

(*a*) the aggregate of

(i) the aggregate of amounts, each of which is an amount determined under paragraph 13(23)(*b*) of the Act in respect of property of a prescribed class of the insurer,

(ii) the aggregate of amounts each of which is a non-capital loss of the insurer for a taxation year ending after 1972 and before 1978 that would have been deductible by the insurer in computing its taxable income for a taxation year ending after 1977 if the Act were read without reference to subsection 111(7.2) thereof,

(iii) the amount prescribed by section 2407 to be the insurer's 1977 excess policy dividend deduction,

(iv) the amount determined under subparagraph 138(4.2)(*b*)(ii) of the Act in respect of the insurer,

(v) the amount determined under subparagraph 138(4.2)(*c*)(ii) of the Act in respect of the insurer,

(vi) the amount, if any, by which

(A) the aggregate of the insurer's maximum tax actuarial reserves for its 1977 taxation year,

exceeds

(B) the aggregate of the amounts deducted by the insurer for its 1977 taxation year under subparagraph 138(3)(*a*)(i) of the Act, and

(vii) the amount, if any, by which

(A) the maximum amount deductible by the insurer for its 1977 taxation year under subparagraph 138(3)(*a*)(ii) of the Act,

exceeds

(B) the amount deducted by the insurer for its 1977 taxation year under subparagraph 138(3)(*a*)(ii) of the Act,

exceeds

(*b*) the amount, if any, by which the aggregate of

(i) the lesser of

(A) the insurer's accumulated 1968 deficit, and

(B) the amount, if any, determined under subparagraph (vi),

(ii) the aggregate of the insurer's maximum tax actuarial reserves for its 1977 taxation year, other than reserves or any portions thereof in respect of segregated fund policies, and

(iii) the maximum amount deductible by the insurer for its 1977 taxation year under subparagraph 138(3)(*a*)(ii) of the Act,

exceeds the aggregate of

(iv) the aggregate of the amounts that would have been the insurer's maximum tax actuarial reserves for its 1977 taxation year if those reserves had been determined on the basis of the rules applicable to its 1978 taxation year,

(v) the aggregate of all amounts payable to the insurer in respect of policy loans outstanding at the end of its 1977 taxation year, and

(vi) the amount, if any, by which

(A) the aggregate of the insurer's maximum tax actuarial reserves for its 1968 taxation year, other than reserves or any portions thereof in respect of segregated fund policies,

exceeds the aggregate of

(B) the aggregate of the amounts that would have been the insurer's maximum tax actuarial reserves for its 1968 taxation year if those reserves had been determined on the basis of the rules applicable to its 1978 taxation year, and

(C) the aggregate of all amounts payable to the insurer in respect of policy loans outstanding at the end of its 1968 taxation year.

2409. Transitional

(1) (Repealed by S.C. 2013, c. 34, s. 392(1).)

History: S. 2409(1) was repealed by S.C. 2013, c. 34, s. 392(1), applicable to taxation years that begin after October 31, 2011, and formerly read:

(1) For the purposes of this Part, except as expressly otherwise provided therein, where the expression "immediately preceding taxation year" refers to an insurer's 1977 taxation year, this Part shall be read as though the definitions therein applied to the insurer's 1977 taxation year.

(2) (Repealed by S.C. 2013, c. 34, s. 392(1).)

History: S. 2409(2) was repealed by S.C. 2013, c. 34, s. 392(1), applicable to taxation years that begin after October 31, 2011, and formerly read:

(2) For the purposes of applying the provisions of paragraph 2400(1)(*c*) in respect of the 1978 taxation year of an insurer that was subject to the provisions of subsection 138(9) of the Act in respect of its 1977 taxation year, the following rules apply:

(*a*) this Part shall be read as though the definitions therein applied to the insurer's 1977 taxation year;

(*b*) such portion of the insurer's Canadian equity property owned by it at the end of its 1977 taxation year as is designated by the insurer in respect of a particular insurance business, in its return of income required by subsection 150(1) of the Act to be filed for the 1978 taxation year, shall be deemed to be investment property of the prior year in respect of the particular insurance business, but the aggregate valuation as at the end of the insurer's 1977 taxation year of the Canadian equity property so designated in respect of all its insurance businesses carried on in Canada shall not exceed

(i) in the case of a life insurer resident in Canada, or a non-resident life insurer that has made the election referred to in subsection 2401(1) in respect of its 1978 taxation year, that proportion of

(A) the insurer's Canadian investment fund as at the end of its 1977 taxation year (determined on the basis of the rules applicable to its 1978 taxation year),

that

(B) the aggregate valuation of the insurer's equity property as at the end of the insurer's 1977 taxation year

is of

(C) the aggregate valuation of the insurer's investment property as at the end of the insurer's 1977 taxation year,

(ii) in the case of a non-resident life insurer, other than an insurer referred to in subparagraph (i), eight per cent of its Canadian investment fund as at the end of its 1977 taxation year (determined on the basis of the rules applicable to its 1978 taxation year), and

(iii) in any other case, 25 per cent of the insurer's Canadian investment fund as at the end of its 1977 taxation year (determined on the basis of the rules applicable to its 1978 taxation year);

(*c*) where the insurer made an election under subsection 138(9) of the Act in respect of its 1977 taxation year, investment property (other than a Canadian equity property) owned by the insurer at the end of its 1977 taxation year that was designated in respect of a particular insurance business by the insurer in its return of income for the 1977 taxation year pursuant to paragraph 138(12)(*l*) [subsection 138(12) "property used by it in the year in, or held by it in the year in the course of"] of the Act as it read in its application to that year shall be deemed to be insurance property of the particular insurance business in the 1977 taxation year;

(*d*) where the insurer did not make the election referred to in paragraph (*c*) and carried on only one insurance business in Canada in its 1977 taxation year, investment property (other than a Canadian equity property) owned by the insurer at the end of its 1977 taxation year that is a specified Canadian asset of the insurer within the meaning of subsection 2405(1) as it read in its application to the 1977 taxation year shall be deemed to be insurance property of that insurance business in the 1977 taxation year; and

(*e*) where the insurer did not make the election referred to in paragraph (*c*) and carried on an other than life insurance business in Canada and a life insurance business in Canada in its 1977 taxation year, investment property (other than a Canadian equity property) owned by the insurer at the end of its 1977 taxation year each of which is a specified Canadian asset of the insurer, within the meaning of subsection 2405(1) as it read in its application to the 1977 taxation year, in respect of which the aggregate value for the year in respect of the insurer's 1978 taxation year is equal to the amount, if any, by which

(i) the insurer's mean Canadian reserve liabilities for its 1978 taxation year in respect of its other than life insurance business

exceeds

(ii) the aggregate value for the year in respect of the insurer's 1978 taxation year of its insurance property of its other than life insurance business as determined for the purposes of clause 2400(1)(*c*)(ii)(C),

shall be deemed to be insurance property of the other than life insurance business in the 1977 taxation year and any other such investment property that is a specified Canadian asset of the insurer shall be deemed to be insurance property of the life insurance business in the 1977 taxation year.

(3) (Repealed by S.C. 2013, c. 34, s. 392(1).)

History: S. 2409(3) was repealed by S.C. 2013, c. 34, s. 392(1), applicable to taxation years that begin after October 31, 2011, and formerly read:

(3) For the purposes of applying the provisions of section 2402 in respect of the 1978 taxation year of a life insurer, the following rules apply:

(*a*) for the purposes of subparagraphs 2402(*a*)(i) and (*b*)(ii), the insurer's maximum tax actuarial reserve for its 1977 taxation year in respect of participating life insurance policies in Canada shall be deemed to be the amount referred to in subparagraph 2407(*b*)(ii);

(*b*) for the purposes of clause 2402(*a*)(ii)(A), the insurer's maximum tax actuarial reserve for its 1977 taxation year in respect of a class of life insurance policies in Canada shall be deemed to have been determined on the basis of the rules applicable to its 1978 taxation year; and

(*c*) for the purposes of subparagraph 2402(*b*)(i), the amount deducted by the insurer under subparagraph 138(3)(*a*)(iv) of the Act in computing its income for the 1977 taxation year shall be deemed to be the amount that is the aggregate determined under paragraph 138(4.2)(*b*) of the Act in respect of the insurer.

(4) (Repealed by S.C. 2013, c. 34, s. 392(1).)

History: S. 2409(4) was repealed by S.C. 2013, c. 34, s. 392(1), applicable to taxation years that begin after October 31, 2011, and formerly read:

(4) Except as expressly otherwise provided in this Part, where the expression "immediately preceding taxation year" occurs in a provision of this Part (other than section 2402) and refers to the insurer's 1987 taxation year, the provision shall be read as though the definitions in this Part applied in respect of the insurer's 1987 taxation year.

2410. Prescribed Amount

For the purpose of subsection 138(4.4) of the Act, the amount prescribed in respect of an insurer's cost or capital cost, as the case may be, of a property for a period in a taxation year is the amount determined by the formula

$$[(A \times B) \times C/365] - D$$

where

A is the average annual rate of interest determined by reference to rates of interest prescribed in section 4301 for the months or portion thereof in the period;

B is the amount, if any, by which, the average cost or average capital cost, as the case may be, of the property for the period exceeds the average amount of debt relating to the acquisition of the property outstanding during the period that bears a fair market interest rate and, for that purpose,

(*a*) the average cost or average capital cost, as the case may be, of a property is the total of

(i) the aggregate of all amounts each of which is the cost or capital cost, as the case may be, if any, immediately before the beginning of the period in respect of the property, and

(ii) the aggregate of all amounts each of which is the proportion of any expenditure incurred on any day in the period in respect of the cost or capital cost, as the case may be, of the property that

(A) the number of days from that day to the end of the period

is of

(B) the number of days in the period, and

(*b*) the average amount of debt relating to the acquisition of a property is the amount, if any, by which the total of

(i) the aggregate of all amounts each of which is an indebtedness relating to the acquisition that was outstanding at the beginning of the period, and

(ii) the aggregate of all amounts each of which is the proportion of an indebtedness relating to the acquisition that was incurred on any day in the period that

(A) the number of days from that day to the end of the period

is of

(B) the number of days in the period,

exceeds

(iii) the aggregate of all amounts each of which is the proportion of an amount that was paid in respect of any indebtedness referred to in subparagraph (i) or (ii) on any day in the period (other than a payment of interest in respect thereof) that

(A) the number of days from that day to the end of the period

is of

(B) the number of days in the period;

C is the number of days in the period; and

D is the income derived from the property in the period by the person or partnership that owned the property.

(2) (Repealed by P.C. 2000-1714, SOR/2000-413.)

2411. Prescribed Amount

(1) Subject to subsection (2), the amount prescribed in respect of an insurer for a taxation year for the purposes of paragraph 138(9)(*b*) of the Act shall be the amount determined by the formula

$$A - (B + B.1 + C)$$

where

A is the positive or negative amount, as the case may be, determined in respect of the insurer for the year under subsection (3);

B is the positive or negative amount, as the case may be, determined in respect of the insurer for the year under subsection (4) in respect of the insurer's investment property for the year that is designated insurance property of the insurer for the year;

B.1 is the positive or negative amount, as the case may be, determined in respect of the insurer for the year under subsection (4.1) in respect of property disposed of by the insurer in a taxation year for which it was designated insurance property of the insurer; and

C is the amount claimed by the insurer for the year in respect of any balance of its cumulative excess account at the end of the year.

(2) Where an amount computed under subsection (1) in respect of an insurer is a negative amount, that amount shall be deemed to be nil.

(3) The positive or negative amount, as the case may be, determined under this subsection in respect of an insurer for a taxation year shall be

(*a*) if the value for the year of the insurer's foreign investment property that is designated insurance property for the year is not greater than 5% of the amount of the insurer's mean Canadian investment fund for the year and the insurer so elects in its return of income under Part I of the Act for the year, the amount determined by the formula

$$\{[((A + A.1)/B) \times (C + J)] + [(D \times F)/E]\}$$

or

(*b*) in any other case, the amount determined by the formula

$$\{[((A + A.1)/B) \times C] + [(D \times F)/E] + [((G + G.1)/H) \times J]\}$$

where

A is the positive or negative amount, as the case may be, determined in respect of the insurer for the year under subsection (4) in respect of Canadian investment property (other than Canadian equity property) owned by the insurer at any time in the year;

A.1 is the positive or negative amount, as the case may be, determined in respect of the insurer for the year under subsection (4.1) in respect of Canadian investment property (other than Canadian equity property) disposed of by the insurer in the year or a preceding taxation year;

B is the total value for the year of Canadian investment property (other than Canadian equity property and any property described in paragraph (*i*) of the definition "Canadian investment property" in subsection 2400(1)) owned by the insurer at any time in the year;

C is the total value for the year of the insurer's Canadian investment property for the year (other than Canadian equity property and any property described in paragraph (*i*) of the definition "Canadian investment property" in subsection 2400(1)) that is designated insurance property of the insurer for the year;

D is the positive or negative amount, as the case may be, determined in respect of the insurer for the year under subsection (4) in respect of Canadian investment property that is Canadian equity property owned by the insurer at any time in the year;

E is the total value for the year of Canadian investment property that is Canadian equity property (other than any property described in paragraph (*i*) of the definition "Canadian investment property" in subsection 2400(1)) owned by the insurer at any time in the year;

F is the total value for the year of the insurer's Canadian investment property (other than any property described in paragraph (*i*) of the definition "Canadian investment property" in subsection 2400(1)) for the year that is Canadian equity property that is designated insurance property of the insurer for the year;

G is the positive or negative amount, as the case may be, determined in respect of the insurer for the year under subsection (4) in respect of foreign investment property owned by the insurer at any time in the year;

G.1 is the positive or negative amount, as the case may be, determined in respect of the insurer for the year under subsection (4.1) in respect of foreign investment property disposed of by the insurer in the year or a preceding taxation year;

H is the total value for the year of foreign investment property (other than any property described in paragraph (*e*) of the definition "investment property" in subsection 2400(1)) owned by the insurer at any time in the year; and

J is the total value for the year of the insurer's foreign investment property (other than any property described in paragraph (*e*) of the definition "investment property" in subsection 2400(1)) that is designated insurance property of the insurer for the year.

History: S. 2411(3), the description of A.1 was replaced by P.C. 2009-1212, SOR/2009-222, dated July 30, 2009, published in the *Canada Gazette* August 19, 2009, applicable to the 1995 and subsequent taxation years. S. 2411(3), the description of A.1 formerly read:

Regulations

A.1 is the positive or negative amount, as the case may be, determined in respect of the insurer for the year under subsection (4.1) in respect of Canadian investment property (other than Canadian equity property) disposed of by the insurer in the year or preceding year;

(4) The positive or negative amount, as the case may be, determined under this subsection in respect of an insurer for a taxation year in respect of property shall be the amount determined by the formula

A - B

where

A is the total of the following amounts determined in respect of the property for the year, or that would be determined in respect of the property for the year if the property were designated insurance property of the insurer in respect of an insurance business in Canada for each taxation year in which the property was held by the insurer:

(*a*) the insurer's gross investment revenue for the year (other than taxable dividends that were or would be deductible in computing the insurer's taxable income for the year under section 112 or subsection 138(6) of the Act) derived from the property,

(*b*) (Repealed by P.C. 2009-1212, SOR/2009-222.)

(*c*) all amounts that were or would be included in computing the insurer's taxable capital gains for the year from the disposition of the property,

(*c*.1) all amounts that were or would be included under paragraph 142.4(5)(*e*) of the Act in respect of the property in computing the insurer's income for the year,

(*d*) all amounts that were or would be included in computing the insurer's income for the year as gains from the disposition of such of the property as is not capital property or a specified debt obligation (as defined in subsection 142.2(1) of the Act),

(*e*) all amounts that were or would be included in computing the insurer's income for the year under subsection 13(1) of the Act in respect of the property,

(*f*) all amounts that were or would be included in computing the insurer's income for the year under paragraph 12(1)(*d*), (*d*.1) or (*i*) of the Act in respect of the property,

(*g*) all amounts that were or would be included in computing the insurer's income for the year under subsection 59(3.2) or (3.3) of the Act in respect of the property, and

(*h*) (Repealed by S.C. 2016, c. 12, s. 80(1).)

(*i*) all other amounts that were or would be included in computing the insurer's income for the year in respect of the property otherwise than because of subsection 142.4(4) of the Act; and

B is the total of the following amounts determined in respect of the property for the year, or that would be determined in respect of the property for the year if the property were designated insurance property of the insurer in respect of an insurance business in Canada for each taxation year in which the property was held by the insurer:

(*a*) all amounts that were or would be included in computing the insurer's allowable capital losses for the year from the disposition of the property,

(*a*.1) all amounts that were or would be deductible under paragraph 142.4(5)(*f*) of the Act in respect of the property in computing the insurer's income for the year,

(*b*) all amounts that were or would be deductible in computing the insurer's income for the year as losses from the disposition of such of the property as is not capital property or a specified debt obligation (as defined in subsection 142.2(1) of the Act),

(*c*) (Repealed by P.C. 2009-1212, SOR/2009-222.)

(*d*) all amounts that were or would be deductible in computing the insurer's income for the year under paragraph 20(1)(*a*) of the Act in respect of the capital cost of the property or under paragraphs 20(1)(*c*) and (*d*) of the Act in respect of interest paid or payable on borrowed money used to acquire the property,

(*e*) where any such property is rental property or leasing property (within the meaning assigned by subsections 1100(14) and (17), respectively), all amounts that were or would be deductible in computing the insurer's income for the year in respect of expenses directly related to the earning of rental income derived from the property,

(*f*) all amounts that were or would be deductible by the insurer in computing the insurer's income for the year under paragraph 20(1)(*l*), (*l*.1) or (*p*) of the Act as a reserve or bad debt in respect of the property,

(*g*) all amounts that were deducted or would be deductible in computing the insurer's income for the year under section 66, 66.1, 66.2 or 66.4 of the Act in respect of the property, and

(*h*) (Repealed by S.C. 2016, c. 12, s. 80(2).)

(*i*) all amounts that were or would be deductible in computing the insurer's income for the year in respect of other expenses directly related to the earning of gross investment revenue derived from the property.

History: S. 2411(4), paragraph (*h*) of the description of A was repealed by S.C. 2016, c. 12, s. 80(1), in force January 1, 2017, and formerly read:

(*h*) all amounts that were or would be included in computing the insurer's income for the year under subsection 14(1) of the Act in respect of the property, and

S. 2411(4), paragraph (*h*) of the description of B was repealed by S.C. 2016, c. 12, s. 80(2), in force January 1, 2017, and formerly read:

(*h*) all amounts that were or would be deductible in computing the insurer's income for the year under paragraph 20(1)(*b*) of the Act in respect of the property, and

S. 2411(4), paragraph (*b*) of the description of A was repealed by P.C. 2009-1212, SOR/2009-222, dated July 30, 2009, published in the *Canada Gazette* August 19, 2009, applicable to taxation years that begin after February 22, 1994. S. 2411(4), paragraph (*b*) of the description of A formerly read:

(*b*) all amounts that were or would be included in computing the insurer's income for the year under paragraphs 138(4)(*b*) and (*c*) of the Act in respect of the property,

S. 2411(4), paragraph (*c*.1) of the description of A was added, and paragraph (*d*) was replaced, by P.C. 2009-1212, SOR/2009-222, dated July 30, 2009, published in the *Canada Gazette* August 19, 2009, applicable to dispositions of property that occur after February 22, 1994. S. 2411(4), paragraph (*d*) of the description of A formerly read:

(*d*) all amounts that were or would be included in computing the insurer's gains for the year from the disposition of the property (other than a Canada security or capital property),

S. 2411(4), paragraph (*i*) of the description of A was replaced by P.C. 2009-1212, SOR/2009-222, dated July 30, 2009, published in the *Canada Gazette* August 19, 2009, applicable to taxation years that end after February 22, 1994. S. 2411(4), paragraph (*i*) of the description of A formerly read:

(*i*) all other amounts that were or would be included in computing the insurer's income for the year in respect of the property; and

S. 2411(4), the portion of the description of B before paragraph (*a*) was replaced by P.C. 2009-1212, SOR/2009-222, dated July 30, 2009, published in the *Canada Gazette* August 19, 2009, applicable to taxation years that end after June 1, 1995. S. 2411(4), the portion of the description of B before paragraph (*a*) formerly read:

B is the aggregate of the following amounts determined in respect of the property for the year or that would be determined in respect of the property for the year if it were insurance property of the insurer for the year in respect of an insurance business in Canada:

S. 2411(4), the portion of the description of B before paragraph (*a*) was replaced by P.C. 2009-1212, SOR/2009-222, dated July 30, 2009, published in the *Canada Gazette* August 19, 2009, applicable to the 1999 and subsequent taxation years. S. 2411(4), the portion of the description of B before paragraph (*a*) formerly read:

B is the total of the following amounts determined in respect of the property for the year, or that would be determined in respect of the property for the year if it were insurance property of the insurer for the year in respect of an insurer business in Canada and if it had been insurance property of the insurer in respect of an insurance business in Canada for each preceding taxation year in which it was held by the insurer:

S. 2411(4), paragraph (*a*.1) of the description of B was added, and paragraph (*b*) was replaced, by P.C. 2009-1212, SOR/2009-222, dated July 30, 2009, published in the *Canada Gazette* August 19, 2009, applicable to dispositions of property that occur after February 22, 1994. S. 2411(4), paragraph (*b*) of the description of B formerly read:

(*b*) all amounts that were or would be included in computing the insurer's losses for the year from the disposition of the property (other than a Canada security or capital property),

S. 2411(4), paragraph (*c*) of the description of B was repealed by P.C. 2009-1212, SOR/2009-222, dated July 30, 2009, published in the *Canada Gazette* August 19, 2009, applicable to taxation years that begin after February 22, 1994. S. 2411(4), paragraph (*c*) of the description of B formerly read:

(*c*) all amounts that were or would be deductible in computing the insurer's income for the year under paragraphs 138(3)(*b*) and (*d*) of the Act in respect of the property,

(4.1) The positive or negative amount, as the case may be, determined under this subsection in respect of an insurer for a taxation year in respect of property disposed of by the insurer in the year or a preceding taxation year is the amount determined by the formula

$$A - B$$

where

A is the total of the amounts included under paragraphs 142.4(4)(*a*) and (*c*) of the Act in the insurer's income for the year in respect of the property, or that would be so included if the property were designated insurance property of the insurer in respect of an insurance business in Canada for each taxation year in which it was held by the insurer; and

B is the total of the amounts deductible under paragraphs 142.4(4)(*b*) and (*d*) of the Act in respect of the property in computing the insurer's income for the year, or that would be so deductible if the property were designated insurance property of the insurer in respect of an insurance business in Canada for each taxation year in which it was held by the insurer.

(5) (Repealed by P.C. 2009-1212, SOR/2009-222.)

History: S. 2411(5) was repealed by P.C. 2009-1212, SOR/2009-222, dated July 30, 2009, published in the *Canada Gazette* August 19, 2009, applicable to taxation years that begin after February 22, 1994. S. 2411(5) formerly read:

(5) For the purposes of subsection (4), a property that has not been designated by the insurer for the year pursuant to subsection 2400(1) as investment property used by it in the year in, or held by it in the year in the course of, carrying on an insurance business in Canada shall be deemed to be a property used by it in the year in, or held by it in the year in the course of, carrying on that insurance business in respect of which the property has been reported by the insurer in its annual report for the year to the relevant authority or, where the insurer was throughout the year subject to the supervision of the relevant authority but was not required to file an annual report with the relevant authority for the year, that insurance business in respect of which the property would have been reported by the insurer in an annual report for the year if it had been so required by the relevant authority.

(6) For the purposes of subsection (1), the balance of an insurer's cumulative excess account at the end of a taxation year shall be determined as the amount, if any, by which

(*a*) the aggregate of all amounts each of which is a positive amount, if any, determined in respect of each of such of its seven immediately preceding taxation years that began after June 17, 1987 and ended after 1987 by the formula

$$B - A$$

where A and B are the amounts determined under subsection (1) in respect of the insurer for such immediately preceding taxation year,

exceeds

(*b*) the aggregate of all amounts each of which is an amount claimed by the insurer under subsection (1) in respect of its cumulative excess account for a preceding taxation year that can be attributed to a positive amount determined under paragraph (*a*) for that year and, for the purpose of this paragraph, a positive amount determined in respect of a taxation year shall be deemed to have been claimed before a positive amount determined in respect of any subsequent taxation year.

(7) (Repealed by P.C. 2000-1714, SOR/2000-413.)

(8) For the purposes of this section, "foreign investment property" of an insurer means investment property of the insurer (unless the insurer is a non-resident insurer and it is established by the insurer that the investment property is not effectively connected with its Canadian insurance businesses) that is not Canadian investment property of the insurer.

2412. Mean Canadian Investment Fund

(1) For the purposes of this Part, the mean Canadian investment fund of an insurer for a particular taxation year is the total of

(*a*) 50% of the total of

(i) its Canadian investment fund at the end of the particular year, and

(ii) either,

(A) if the insurer is resident in Canada, its Canadian investment fund at the end of its preceding taxation year, or

(B) if the insurer is non-resident, its Canadian investment fund at the end of its preceding taxation year determined as if its attributed surplus for that preceding taxation year were its attributed surplus for the particular year, and

(*b*) the insurer's cash-flow adjustment for the particular year.

(2) Cash-flow Adjustment. An insurer's cash-flow adjustment for a taxation year is the amount equal to

(*a*) if the year ended two months or more after it began, the positive or negative amount determined by the formula

$$50\% \times (A - B/C)$$

where

Regulations

A is the total of all amounts each of which is the amount determined under subsection (3) in respect of a full month in the year (or in respect of the part of the month that ends after the last full month in the year, if that part is greater than 15 days),

B is the total of all amounts each of which is the amount determined in respect of a full month in the year (or in respect of the part of the month that ends after the last full month in the year, if that part is greater than 15 days) by the formula

$$D \times (1 + 2E)$$

where

D is the amount determined under subsection (3) in respect of the month or part of the month, and

E is the number of months in the year that ended before the beginning of the month or part of the month, and

C is the number of full months in the year (plus 1, if the year ends more than 15 days after the end of the last full month in the year); and

(*b*) if the year ended less than two months after it began, nil.

(3) Amounts Paid and Received. The amount determined in respect of an insurer for a particular month or part of a month (in this subsection referred to as a "month") in a taxation year is the positive or negative amount determined by the formula

$$G - H$$

where

G is the total of all amounts each of which is

(*a*) the amount of a premium or consideration received by the insurer in the month in respect of a contract of insurance (including a settlement annuity) entered into in the course of carrying on its insurance businesses in Canada,

(*b*) an amount received by the insurer in the month in respect of interest on or a repayment in respect of a policy loan made under a life insurance policy in Canada, or

(*c*) an amount received by the insurer in the month in respect of reinsurance (other than reinsurance undertaken to effect a transfer of a business in respect of which subsection 138(11.5), (11.92) or (11.94) of the Act applies) arising in the course of carrying on its insurance businesses in Canada; and

H is the total of all amounts each of which is

(*a*) the amount of a claim or benefit (including a payment under an annuity or settlement annuity, a payment of a policy dividend and an amount paid on a lapsed or terminated policy), a refund of premiums, a premium or a commission paid by the insurer in the month under a contract of insurance in the course of carrying on its insurance businesses in Canada,

(*b*) the amount of a policy loan made by the insurer in the month under a life insurance policy in Canada, or

(*c*) an amount paid by the insurer in the month in respect of reinsurance (other than reinsurance undertaken to effect a transfer of a business in respect of which subsection 138(11.5), (11.92) or (11.94) of the Act applies) in the course of carrying on its insurance businesses in Canada.

(4) Amounts Paid and Received. A reference to a "month" in this section means

(*a*) if an insurer's taxation year does not begin on the first day of a calendar month and the insurer elects to have this paragraph apply for the year, the period beginning on the day in a calendar month that has the same calendar number as the particular day on which the taxation year began and ending

(i) on the day immediately before the day in the next calendar month that has the same calendar number as the particular day, or

(ii) if the next calendar month does not have a day that has the same calendar number as the particular day, the last day of that next calendar month; and

(*b*) in any other case, a calendar month.

(5) (Repealed by P.C. 2000-1714, SOR/2000-413.)

Part XXV
Special T1 Tax Table for Individuals

2500. **(1)** For the purposes of subsection 117(6) of the Act,

(*a*) $55,605, adjusted for each taxation year after 1989 in the manner set out in subsection 117.1(1) of the Act, is the prescribed amount; and

(*b*) an "individual of a prescribed class" for a taxation year is

(i) an estate or trust,

(ii) an individual who was a non-resident person throughout the year, other than an individual

(A) whose amount taxable for the year was from

(I) the duties of an office or employment performed in one province,

(II) the carrying on of a business in one province, or

(III) any combination of sources described in subclauses (I) and (II) if all of those sources are located in one province, and

(B) who was not subject to any other provision of this subsection,

(iii) an individual who, on the last day of the year, resided in a province and had income for the year from a business with a permanent establishment, as defined in subsection 2600(2), outside the province,

(iv) an individual whose tax otherwise payable for the year under Part I of the Act is reduced by virtue of any of the following provisions of the Act:

(A) subsection 117(7),

(B) section 121,

(C) section 122.3, or

(D) section 126,

(v) an individual who makes an election in respect of the year under subsection 119(1) of the Act,

(vi) an individual eligible to pay tax at a reduced rate pursuant to subsection 40(7) of the *Income Tax Application Rules* on a payment made to him in the year, or

(vii) an individual who makes an election in respect of the year under subsection 110.4(2) of the Act.

(2) For the purposes of subsection 117(6) of the Act, a table of the tax payable for a taxation year shall be prepared in accordance with the following rules:

(*a*) the table shall be divided into ranges of amounts taxable not exceeding $10 each and shall specify the tax payable in respect of each range;

(*b*) the tax payable on an amount taxable within any range referred to in paragraph (*a*) shall be equal to the tax payable thereon for the year computed under subsection 117(2) of the Act and, where applicable, adjusted annually pursuant to section 117.1 of the Act; and

(*c*) the tax payable referred to in paragraph (*b*) shall be calculated as if the amount taxable is equal to the average of the highest and lowest amounts taxable in the range and, where the resulting tax payable is not a multiple of one dollar, it shall be rounded to the nearest multiple of one dollar or, if it is equidistant from two such multiples, to the higher thereof.

(3) For the purposes of subsection 117(6) of the Act, a table of the additional tax for income not earned in a province, the individual surtax and the refundable Quebec abatement for a taxation year shall be prepared in accordance with the following rules:

(*a*) the table shall be divided into ranges of tax payable not exceeding $2 each and shall specify, in respect of each range,

(i) the individual surtax payable,

(ii) where applicable, the additional tax for income not earned in a province, and

(iii) where applicable, the refundable Quebec abatement,

on every amount of tax payable within that range;

(*b*) the tax payable referred to in paragraph (*a*) is the tax payable determined by the table prepared pursuant to subsection (2) less the allowable non-refundable credits under sections 118 to 118.9 of the Act;

(*c*) the individual surtax in respect of an amount of tax payable within any range referred to in paragraph (*a*) shall be the amount that is equal to the surtax thereon computed under subsection 180.1(1) of the Act;

(*d*) the additional tax for income not earned in a province in respect of an amount of tax payable within any range referred to in paragraph (*a*) shall be the amount that is equal to the tax determined thereon under subsection 120(1) of the Act;

(*e*) the refundable Quebec abatement in respect of an amount of tax payable within any range referred to in paragraph (*a*) shall be the amount that is equal to the abatement determined under subsection 120(2) of the Act and in accordance with section 27 of the *Federal-Provincial Fiscal Arrangements and Federal Post-Secondary Education and Health Contributions Act*;

(*f*) the amount referred to in paragraph (*c*) or (*d*) shall be calculated as if the tax payable is equal to the average of the highest and lowest amounts in the range and, where the resulting amount is not a multiple of one dollar, it shall be rounded to the nearest multiple of one dollar or, if it is equidistant from two such multiples, to the higher thereof; and

(*g*) the amount referred to in paragraph (*e*) shall be calculated as if the tax payable is equal to the average of the highest and lowest amounts in the range and, where the resulting amount is not a multiple of one tenth of one dollar, it shall be rounded to the nearest multiple of one tenth of one dollar or, if it is equidistant from two such multiples, to the higher thereof.

2501. In this Part, "amount taxable" has the meaning assigned by subsection 117(2) of the Act.

Part XXVI
Income Earned in a Province by an Individual

2600. Interpretation

(1) In applying the definition "income earned in the year in a province" in subsection 120(4) of the Act for an individual's taxation year

(*a*) the prescribed rules referred to in that definition are the rules in this Part; and

(*b*) the amount determined under those prescribed rules means the total of all amounts each of which is the individual's income earned in the taxation year in a particular province as determined under this Part.

History: S. 2600(1) was replaced by S.C. 2009, c. 2, s. 103(1), applicable to the 2009 and subsequent taxation years. S. 2600(1) formerly read:

(1) For the purposes of paragraph 120(4)(*a*) of the Act, "income earned in the year in a province" by an individual means the aggregate of his incomes earned in the taxation year in each province as determined in accordance with this Part.

(2) In this Part, "permanent establishment" means a fixed place of business of the individual, including an office, a branch, a mine, an oil well, a farm, a timberland, a factory, a workshop or a warehouse, and

(*a*) where an individual carries on business through an employee or agent, established in a particular place, who has general authority to contract for his employer or principal or who has a stock of merchandise owned by his employer or principal from which he regularly fills orders which he receives, the individual shall be deemed to have a permanent establishment in that place;

(*b*) where an individual uses substantial machinery or equipment in a particular place at any time in a taxation year he shall be deemed to have a permanent establishment in that place; and

(*c*) the fact that an individual has business dealings through a commission agent, broker or other independent agent or maintains an office solely for the purchase of merchandise, shall not of itself be held to mean that the individual has a permanent establishment.

(3) (Revoked.)

Forms: T2203 — Provincial and Territorial Taxes — Multiple Jurisdictions.

Interpretation Bulletins: *Secondary* — IT-242R Retired partners; IT-434R Rental of real property by individual.

2601. Residents of Canada

(1) If an individual resides in a particular province on the last day of a taxation year and has no income for the taxation year from a business with a permanent establishment outside the province, the individual's income earned in the taxation year in the particular province is the individual's income for the taxation year.

History: S. 2601(1) was replaced by P.C. 2010-548, SOR/2010-93, dated April 29, 2010, in force May 12, 2010, date of publication in the *Canada Gazette*. S. 2601(1) formerly read:

2601.

(1) Where an individual resided in a particular province on the last day of a taxation year and had no income for the year from a business with a permanent establishment outside the province, his income earned in the taxation year in the province is his income for the year.

(2) If an individual resides in a particular province on the last day of a taxation year and has income for the taxation year from a business with a permanent establishment outside the particular province, the individual's income earned in the taxation year in the particular province is the amount, if any, by which

(*a*) the individual's income for the taxation year

exceeds

(*b*) the total of all amounts each of which is the individual's income for the taxation year from carrying on a business that is earned in a province other than the particular province or in a country other than Canada, determined in accordance with this Part.

History: S. 2601(2) was replaced by P.C. 2010-548, SOR/2010-93, dated April 29, 2010, in force May 12, 2010, date of publication in the *Canada Gazette*. S. 2601(2) formerly read:

(2) Where an individual resided in a particular province on the last day of a taxation year and had income for the year from a business with a permanent establishment outside the province, his income earned in the taxation year in the province is the amount, if any, by which

(*a*) his income for the year

exceeds

(*b*) the aggregate of his income for the year from carrying on business earned in each other province and each country other than Canada determined as hereinafter set forth in this Part.

(3) If an individual, who resides in Canada on the last day of a taxation year and who has carried on business in a particular province at any time in the taxation year, does not reside in the particular province on the last day of the taxation year, the individual's income earned in the taxation year in the particular province is the individual's income for the taxation year from carrying on business earned in the particular province, determined in accordance with this Part.

History: S. 2601(3) was replaced by P.C. 2010-548, SOR/2010-93, dated April 29, 2010, in force May 12, 2010, date of publication in the *Canada Gazette*. S. 2601(3) formerly read:

(3) Where an individual, who resided in Canada on the last day of a taxation year and who carried on business in a particular province at any time in the year, did not reside in the province on the last day of the year, his income earned in the taxation year in the province is his income for the year from carrying on business earned in the province, determined as hereinafter set forth in this Part.

(4) If an individual resides in Canada on the last day of a taxation year and carried on business in another country at any time in the taxation year, the individual's income earned in the taxation year in that other country is the individual's income for the taxation year from carrying on business earned in the other country, determined in accordance with this Part.

History: S. 2601(4) was replaced by P.C. 2010-548, SOR/2010-93, dated April 29, 2010, in force May 12, 2010, date of publication in the *Canada Gazette*. S. 2601(4) formerly read:

(4) Where an individual resided in Canada on the last day of a taxation year and carried on business in another country at any time in the year, his income earned in the taxation year in that other country is his income for the year from carrying on business earned in the other country, determined as hereinafter set forth in this Part.

(5) In this section, a reference to the "last day of a taxation year" is deemed to be a reference to

(*a*) the "last day in the year on which the individual resided in Canada", in the case of an individual who resided in Canada at any time in the year but ceased to reside in Canada before the end of the year; and

(*b*) the "day in the year on which the individual would have ceased to reside in Canada, if the Act were read without reference to paragraphs 250(1)(*d*.1) and (*f*) of the Act,", in the case of a particular individual described in paragraph 250(1)(*d*.1) of the Act, or of another individual who is a spouse, common-law partner or child of the particular individual, who

(i) was resident in Canada at any time in the year,

(ii) would have ceased to be resident in Canada before the end of the year, if the Act were read without reference to paragraphs 250(1)(*d*.1) and (*f*) of the Act, and

(iii) is, pursuant to paragraph 250(1)(*d*.1) or (*f*) of the Act, deemed to have been resident in Canada throughout the year.

2602. Non-Residents

(1) Subject to subsection (2), if an individual does not reside in Canada at any time in a taxation year, the individual's income earned in the taxation year in a province is the total of

(*a*) the portion of the taxpayer's income from an office or employment that is included in the taxpayer's taxable income earned in Canada for the taxation year under subparagraph 115(1)(*a*)(i) of the Act and that is reasonably attributable to the duties performed by the taxpayer the province; and

(*b*) the taxpayer's income for the taxation year from carrying on business earned in the province, determined in accordance with this Part.

History: S. 2602(1) was replaced by P.C. 2010-548, SOR/2010-93, dated April 29, 2010, in force May 12, 2010, date of publication in the *Canada Gazette*. S. 2602(1) formerly read:

(1) Except as provided in subsection (2), where an individual did not reside in Canada at any time in a taxation year, his income earned in the taxation year in a particular province is the aggregate of

(*a*) that part of the amount of his income from an office or employment, that is included in computing his taxable income earned in Canada for the year by virtue of subparagraph 115(1)(*a*)(i) of the Act, that is reasonably attributable to the duties performed by him in the province; and

(*b*) his income for the year from carrying on business earned in the province, determined as hereinafter set forth in this Part.

Interpretation Bulletins: *Secondary* — IT-434R Rental of real property by individual.

(2) Where the aggregate of the amounts of an individual's income as determined under subsection (1) for all provinces for a taxation year exceeds the aggregate of the amounts of his income described in subparagraphs 115(1)(*a*)(i) and (ii) of the Act, the amount of his income earned in the taxation year in a particular province shall be that proportion of his income so described that the amount of his income earned in the taxation year in the province as determined under subsection (1) is of the aggregate of all such amounts.

2603. Income from Business

(1) Where, in a taxation year, an individual had a permanent establishment in a particular province or a country other than Canada and had no permanent establishment outside that province or country, the whole of his income from carrying on business for the year shall be deemed to have been earned therein.

(2) Where, in a taxation year, an individual had no permanent establishment in a particular province or country other than Canada, no part of his income for the year from carrying on business shall be deemed to have been earned therein.

(3) Except as otherwise provided, where, in a taxation year, an individual had a permanent establishment in a particular province or in a particular country other than Canada and had a permanent establishment outside that particular province or particular country, the amount of the individual's income for the taxation year from carrying on business that is deemed to have been earned in the particular province or particular country is half of the total of

(*a*) that proportion of the individual's income for the year from carrying on business that the gross revenue for the fiscal period that ends in the taxation year that is reasonably attributable to the permanent establishment in the particular province or particular country is of the individual's total gross revenue for that period from the business; and

(*b*) that proportion of the individual's income for the taxation year from carrying on business that the total of all amounts that are salaries and wages paid in the fiscal period that ends in the taxation year to employees of the permanent establishment in the particular province or particular country is of the total of all amounts that are salaries and wages paid in that period to employees of the business.

History: S. 2603(3) was replaced by P.C. 2011-951, SOR/2011-195, dated September 22, 2011, published in the *Canada Gazette* October 12, 2011, in force October 12, 2011. S. 2603(3) formerly read:

(3) Except as otherwise provided, where, in a taxation year, an individual had a permanent establishment in a particular province or country other than Canada and a permanent establishment outside that province or country, the amount of his income for the year from carrying on business that shall be deemed to have been earned in the province or country is 1/2 the aggregate of

(*a*) that proportion of his income for the year from carrying on business that the gross revenue for the fiscal period ending in the year reasonably attributable to the permanent establishment in the province or country is of his total gross revenue for that period from the business; and

(*b*) that proportion of his income for the year from carrying on business that the aggregate of the salaries and wages paid in the fiscal period ending in the year to employees of the permanent establishment in the province or country is of the aggregate of all salaries and wages paid in that period to employees of the business.

(4) For the purpose of determining the gross revenue for the year reasonably attributable to the permanent establishment in a particular province or country other than Canada within the meaning of paragraph (3)(*a*), the following rules shall apply:

(*a*) where the destination of a shipment of merchandise to a customer to whom the merchandise is sold is in the particular province or country, the gross revenue derived therefrom shall be attributable to the permanent establishment in the province or country;

(*b*) except as provided in paragraph (*c*), where the destination of a shipment of merchandise to a customer to whom the merchandise is sold is in a province or country other than Canada in which the taxpayer has no permanent establishment, if the person negotiating the sale may reasonably be regarded as being attached to the permanent establishment in the particular province or country, the gross revenue derived therefrom shall be attributable to that permanent establishment;

(*c*) where the destination of a shipment of merchandise to a customer to whom the merchandise is sold is in a country other than Canada in which the taxpayer has no permanent establishment,

(i) if the merchandise was produced or manufactured, or produced and manufactured, entirely in the particular province by the taxpayer, the gross revenue derived therefrom shall be attributable to the permanent establishment in the province, or

Regulations

(ii) if the merchandise was produced or manufactured, or produced and manufactured, partly in the particular province and partly in another place by the taxpayer, the gross revenue derived therefrom attributable to the permanent establishment in the province shall be that proportion thereof that the salaries and wages paid in the year to employees of the permanent establishment in the province where the merchandise was partly produced or manufactured (or partly produced and manufactured) is of the aggregate of the salaries and wages paid in the year to employees of the permanent establishments where the merchandise was produced or manufactured (or produced and manufactured);

(*d*) where a customer to whom merchandise is sold instructs that shipment be made to some other person and the customer's office with which the sale was negotiated is located in the particular province or country, the gross revenue derived therefrom shall be attributable to the permanent establishment in the province or country;

(*e*) except as provided in paragraph (*f*), where a customer to whom merchandise is sold instructs that shipment be made to some other person and the customer's office with which the sale was negotiated is located in a province or country other than Canada in which the taxpayer has no permanent establishment, if the person negotiating the sale may reasonably be regarded as being attached to the permanent establishment in the particular province or country, the gross revenue derived therefrom shall be attributable to that permanent establishment;

(*f*) where a customer to whom merchandise is sold instructs that shipment be made to some other person and the customer's office with which the sale was negotiated is located in a country other than Canada in which the taxpayer has no permanent establishment,

(i) if the merchandise was produced or manufactured, or produced and manufactured, entirely in the particular province by the taxpayer, the gross revenue derived therefrom shall be attributable to the permanent establishment in the province, or

(ii) if the merchandise was produced or manufactured, or produced and manufactured, partly in the particular province and partly in another place by the taxpayer, the gross revenue derived therefrom attributable to the permanent establishment in the province shall be that proportion thereof that the salaries and wages paid in the year to employees of the permanent establishment in the province where the merchandise was partly produced or manufactured (or partly produced and manufactured) is of the aggregate of the salaries and wages paid in the year to employees of the permanent establishments where the merchandise was produced or manufactured (or produced and manufactured);

(*g*) where gross revenue is derived from services rendered in the particular province or country, the gross revenue shall be attributable to the permanent establishment in the province or country;

(*h*) where gross revenue is derived from services rendered in a province or country other than Canada in which the taxpayer has no permanent establishment, if the person negotiating the contract may reasonably be regarded as being attached to the permanent establishment of the taxpayer in the particular province or country, the gross revenue shall be attributable to that permanent establishment;

(*i*) where standing timber or the right to cut standing timber is sold and the timber limit on which the timber is standing is in the particular province or country, the gross revenue from such sale shall be attributable to the permanent establishment of the taxpayer in the province or country; and

(*j*) where land is a permanent establishment of the taxpayer in the particular province, the gross revenue which arises from leasing the land shall be attributable to that permanent establishment.

(5) Where an individual pays a fee to another person under an agreement pursuant to which that other person or employees of that other person perform services for the individual that would normally be performed by employees of the individual, the fee so paid shall be deemed to be salary paid by the individual and that part of the fee that may reasonably be regarded as payment in respect of services rendered at a particular permanent establishment of the individual shall be deemed to be salary paid to an employee of that permanent establishment.

(6) For the purposes of subsection (5), a fee does not include a commission paid to a person who is not an employee of the individual.

2604. Bus and Truck Operators

Notwithstanding subsections 2603(3) and (4), the amount of income that shall be deemed to have been earned in a particular province or country other than Canada by an individual from carrying on the business of transportation of goods or passengers (other than by the operation of a railway, ships or an airline service) is $1/2$ of the aggregate of

(*a*) that proportion of his income therefrom for the year that the number of miles travelled by his vehicles in the province or country in the fiscal period ending in the year is of the total number of miles travelled by his vehicles in that period; and

(*b*) that proportion of his income therefrom for the year that the aggregate of salaries and wages paid in the fiscal period ending in the year to employees of the permanent establishment in the province or country is of the aggregate of all salaries and wages paid in that period to employees of the business.

2605. More Than One Business

Where an individual operates more than one business, the provisions of sections 2603 and 2604 shall be applied in respect of each business and the amount of income for the year from carrying on business earned in a particular province or country in the year is the aggregate of the amounts so determined.

Interpretation Bulletins: *Secondary* — IT-206R Separate businesses.

2606. Limitations of Business Income

(1) If, in the case of an individual to whom section 2601 applies, the total of the amounts otherwise determined to be the individual's income for a taxation year from carrying on business that is earned in all provinces and countries other than Canada is greater than the individual's income for the year, the individual's income for the year from carrying on business earned in a particular province or country other than Canada is deemed to be that proportion of the individual's income for the year that

(*a*) the individual's income for the year from carrying on business in the particular province or country as otherwise determined

is of

(*b*) that total.

History: S. 2606(1) was replaced by P.C. 2009-1869, SOR/2009-302, dated November 19, 2009, published in the *Canada Gazette* December 9, 2009, applicable to the 1998 and subsequent taxation years. S. 2606(1) formerly read:

(1) Where, in the case of an individual to whom section 2601 applies, the aggregate of the amounts otherwise determined as his income for the taxation year from carrying on business earned in all provinces and countries other than Canada is greater than his income for the year, his income for the year from carrying on business earned in a particular province or country shall be deemed to be that proportion of his income for the year that

(*a*) his income for the year from carrying on business in the province or country as otherwise determined,

is of

(*b*) that aggregate.

(2) If section 114 of the Act applies in respect of an individual for a taxation year, the following rules apply:

(*a*) the portion of subsection (1) before paragraph (*a*) is to be read as follows in respect of the individual for the year:

"**(1)** If, in the case of an individual to whom section 2601 applies, the total of the amounts otherwise determined to be the individual's income for a taxation year from carrying on business that is earned in all provinces and countries other than Canada is greater than the individual's taxable income for the year, the individual's income for the year from carrying on business earned in a particular province or country other than Canada is deemed to be that proportion of the individual's taxable income for the year that"

(*b*) for the purpose of this Part, the individual's income for the year from carrying on a business in any place shall be computed by reference only to the income from that business that is included in computing the individual's taxable income for the year.

History: S. 2606(2) was replaced by P.C. 2009-1869, SOR/2009-302, dated November 19, 2009, published in the *Canada Gazette* December 9, 2009, applicable to the 1998 and subsequent taxation years. S. 2606(2) formerly read:

(2) Where section 114 of the Act is applicable for the purpose of determining the taxable income of an individual for the taxation year, a reference in subsection (1) to "his income for the taxation year" shall be construed as a reference to the amount of his income as determined for the purposes of section 114 of the Act and, for the purposes of this Part, his income for the taxation year from carrying on a business in any place shall be computed by reference only to a business the income from which is included in computing his taxable income for the purposes of section 114 of the Act.

(3) For the purposes of sections 2603 to 2605, where an individual's taxable income for the taxation year is computed in accordance with section 115 of the Act,

(*a*) a reference to a "business" shall be deemed to refer only to a business that was wholly or partly carried on in Canada;

(*b*) a reference to "income for the year from carrying on business" shall be deemed to refer only to income for the year from carrying on a business in Canada, as determined for the purposes of section 115 of the Act;

(*c*) a reference to "salaries and wages paid in the year" shall be deemed to be a reference to salaries and wages paid to employees of his permanent establishments in Canada; and

(*d*) a reference to "total gross revenue for the year" from the business shall be deemed to be a reference to total gross revenue reasonably attributable to his permanent establishments in Canada.

2607. Dual Residence

Where an individual was resident in more than one province on the last day of the taxation year, for the purposes of this Part, he shall be deemed to have resided on that day only in that province which may reasonably be regarded as his principal place of residence.

Tax Topics: No. 1848, Individual Residence for Provincial Income Tax Purposes.

2608. SIFT Trusts

For the purposes of this Part, if the individual is a SIFT trust, a reference to income earned in a taxation year shall be read as a reference to the amount that would, if this Part were read without reference to this section, be the amount, if any, by which its income for the taxation year exceeds its taxable SIFT trust distributions for the taxation year.

Regulations

Part XXVII
Group Term Life Insurance Benefits

2700. Definitions & Interpretation

(1) Definitions. The definitions in this subsection apply in this Part.

"lump-sum premium" in relation to a group term life insurance policy means a premium for insurance under the policy on the life of an individual where all or part of the premium is for insurance that is (or would be if the individual survived) in respect of a period that ends more than 13 months after the earlier of the day on which the premium becomes payable and the day on which it is paid.

"paid-up premium" in relation to a group term life insurance policy means a premium for insurance under the policy on the life of an individual where the insurance is for the remainder of the lifetime of the individual and no further premiums will be payable for the insurance.

"premium category" in relation to term insurance provided under a group term life insurance policy means,

(*a*) where the premium rate applicable in respect of term insurance on the life of an individual depends on the group to which the individual belongs, any of the groups for which a premium rate is established, and

(*b*) in any other case, all individuals on whose lives term insurance is in effect under the policy,

and, for the purpose of this definition, a single premium rate is deemed to apply for all term insurance under a policy in respect of periods in 1994, and where individuals are divided into separate groups solely on the basis of their age, sex, or both, the groups are deemed to be a single group for which a premium rate is established.

"term insurance" in relation to an individual and a group term life insurance policy means insurance under the policy on the life of the individual, other than insurance in respect of which a lump-sum premium has become payable or been paid.

(2) Accidental Death Insurance. For greater certainty, a premium for insurance on the life of an individual does not include an amount for accidental death insurance.

2701. Prescribed Benefit

(1) Subject to subsection (2), for the purpose of subsection 6(4) of the Act, the amount prescribed for a taxation year in respect of insurance under a group term life insurance policy on the life of a taxpayer is the total of

(*a*) the taxpayer's term insurance benefit under the policy for the calendar year in which the taxation year ends,

(*b*) the taxpayer's prepaid insurance benefit under the policy for that calendar year, and

(*c*) the total of all sales and excise taxes payable in respect of premiums paid under the policy in that calendar year for insurance on the life of the taxpayer, other than

(i) taxes paid, directly or by way of reimbursement, by the taxpayer, and

(ii) taxes in respect of premiums for term insurance that, if the taxpayer were to die, would be paid otherwise than

(A) to the taxpayer,

(B) for the benefit of the taxpayer,

(C) as a benefit that the taxpayer desired to have conferred on any person.

(2) Bankrupt Individual. Where a taxpayer who has become a bankrupt has two taxation years ending in a calendar year, for the purpose of subsection 6(4) of the Act, the amount prescribed for the first taxation year in respect of insurance under a group term life insurance policy on the life of the taxpayer is nil.

2702. Term Insurance Benefit

(1) Amount of Benefit. Subject to section 2704, for the purpose of paragraph 2701(1)(*a*), a taxpayer's term insurance benefit under a group term life insurance policy for a calendar year is

(*a*) where

(i) the policyholder elects to determine, under this paragraph, the term insurance benefit for the year of each individual whose life is insured under the policy,

(ii) no premium rate that applies for term insurance provided under the policy on the life of an individual in respect of the year depends on the age or sex of the individual,

(iii) no amounts are payable under the policy for term insurance on the lives of individuals in respect of the year other than premiums payable on a regular basis that are based on the amount of term insurance in force in the year for each individual, and

(iv) the year is after 1995,

the amount determined by the formula

$$A - B$$

where

A is the total of the premiums payable for term insurance provided under the policy on the taxpayer's life in respect of periods in the year, to the extent that each such premium is in respect of term insurance that, if the taxpayer died in the year, would be paid to or for the benefit of the taxpayer or as a benefit that the taxpayer desired to have conferred on any person, and

B is the total amount paid by the taxpayer in respect of term insurance under the policy on the taxpayer's life in respect of the year; and

(*b*) in any other case, the amount, if any, by which

(i) the total of all amounts each of which is, for a day in the year on which term insurance is in effect under the policy on the taxpayer's life, the amount determined by the formula

$$A \times B$$

where

A is the amount of term insurance in effect on that day under the policy on the taxpayer's life, except the portion, if any, of the amount that, if the taxpayer were to die on that day, would be paid otherwise than

(A) to the taxpayer,

(B) to benefit of the taxpayer, or

(C) as a benefit that the taxpayer desired to have conferred on any person, and

B is the average daily cost of insurance for the year for the premium category in which the taxpayer is included on that day

exceeds

(ii) the total amount paid by the taxpayer in respect of term insurance under the policy on the taxpayer's life in respect of the year.

(2) Average Daily Cost of Insurance. The average daily cost of insurance under a group term life insurance policy for a calendar year for a premium category is

(*a*) subject to paragraph (*b*), the amount determined by the formula

$$(A + B - C) / D$$

where

A is the total of the premiums payable for term insurance provided under the policy on the lives of individuals in respect of periods in the year while they are in the premium category,

B is the total of the amounts paid in the year under the policy for term insurance in respect of periods in preceding years (other than amounts that have otherwise been taken into account for the purpose of subsection 6(4) of the Act), to the extent that the total can reasonably be considered to relate to term insurance provided on the lives of individuals in the premium category,

C is the total amount of policy dividends and experience rating refunds paid in the year under the policy and not distributed to individuals whose lives are insured under the policy, to the extent that the total can reasonably be considered to relate to term insurance provided on the lives of individuals in the premium category, and

D is the total of all amounts each of which is the amount of term insurance in force on a day in the year on the lives of individuals in the premium category on that day; or

(*b*) the amount that the policyholder determines using a reasonable method that is substantially similar to the method set out in paragraph (*a*).

(3) Survivor Income Benefits. For the purposes of this section, where the proceeds of term insurance on the life of an individual are payable in the form of periodic payments, and the periodic payments are not an optional form of settlement of a lump-sum amount, the amount of term insurance in effect on the individual's life on any day is the present value, on that day, of the periodic payments that would be made if the individual were to die on that day.

(4) Determination of Present Value. For the purpose of subsection (3), the present value on a day in a calendar year

(*a*) shall be determined using assumptions that are reasonable at some time in the year; and

(*b*) may be determined assuming that an individual on whose life the present value depends is the same age on that day as on another day in the year.

2703. Prepaid Insurance Benefit

(1) Amount of Benefit. Subject to section 2704, for the purpose of paragraph 2701(1)(*b*), a taxpayer's prepaid insurance benefit under a group term life insurance policy for a calendar year is

(*a*) where the taxpayer is alive at the end of the year, the total of all amounts each of which is

(i) a lump-sum premium (other than the taxpayer portion) paid in the year and after February 1994 in respect of insurance under the policy on the life of the taxpayer, other than a paid-up premium paid before 1997, or

(ii) 1/3 of a paid-up premium (other than the taxpayer portion) in respect of insurance under the policy on the life of the taxpayer that was paid

(A) after February 1994 and before 1997, and

(B) in the year or one of the two preceding years; and

(*b*) where the taxpayer died after June 1994 and in the year, the amount, if any, by which

(i) the total of all amounts each of which is a lump-sum premium (other than the taxpayer portion) paid under the policy after February 1994 in respect of insurance on the life of the taxpayer

exceeds

(ii) the portion of that total that was included in computing the taxpayer's prepaid insurance benefit under the policy for preceding years.

(2) Taxpayer Portion of Premiums. For the purpose of subsection (1), the taxpayer portion of a premium is the portion, if any, of the premium that the taxpayer paid, either directly or by way of reimbursement.

2704. Employee-Paid Insurance

(1) For the purpose of subsection 2701(1), where the full cost of insurance under a group term life insurance policy in a calendar year is borne by the individuals whose lives are insured under the policy, each individual's term insurance benefit and prepaid insurance benefit under the policy for the year is deemed to be nil.

(2) Where the premiums for part of the life insurance (in this subsection referred to as the "additional insurance") under a group term life insurance policy are determined separately from the premiums for the rest of the life insurance under the policy, and it is reasonable to consider that the individuals on whose lives the additional insurance is provided bear the full cost of the additional insurance, the additional insurance, the premiums, policy dividends and experience rating refunds in respect of that insurance, and the amounts paid in respect of that insurance by the individuals whose lives are insured, shall not be taken into account for the purposes of this Part.

2705. Prescribed Premium and Insurance

For the purpose of subsection 6(4) of the Act, as it applies to insurance provided in respect of periods that are in 1994 and before July 1994,

(*a*) a lump-sum premium paid under a group term life insurance policy after February 1994 in respect of an individual who is alive at the end of June 1994 is a prescribed premium; and

(*b*) insurance in respect of which a premium referred to in paragraph (*a*) is paid is prescribed insurance.

Part XXVIII
Elections in Respect of Accumulating Incomes of Trusts

2800. [Election filing requirements]

(1) Any election under subsection 104(14) of the Act in respect of a taxation year shall be made by filing with the Minister a written statement

(*a*) in which the election in respect of the year is made;

(*b*) in which is designated the part of the accumulating income in respect of which the election is being made; and

(*c*) that is signed by the preferred beneficiary and a trustee having the authority to make the election.

Interpretation Bulletins: *Secondary* — IT-394R2 Preferred beneficiary election.

(2) The statement shall be filed within 90 days after the end of the trust's taxation year in respect of which the election referred to in subsection (1) is made.

(2.1) (Repealed.)

(3) (Repealed.)

(4) (Repealed.)

Regulations

Part XXIX
Scientific Research and Experimental Development

2900. Interpretation

(1) (Repealed.)

(2) [Expenditures directly attributable to SR&ED]. For the purposes of clause 37(8)(*a*)(i)(B) and subclause 37(8)(*a*)(ii)(A)(II) of the Act, the following expenditures are directly attributable to the prosecution of scientific research and experimental development:

(*a*) the cost of materials consumed or transformed in such prosecution;

(*b*) where an employee directly undertakes, supervises or supports such prosecution, the portion of the amount incurred for salary or wages of the employee that can reasonably be considered to be in respect of such prosecution; and

(*c*) other expenditures, or those portions of other expenditures, that are directly related to such prosecution and that would not have been incurred if such prosecution had not occurred.

SR&ED Publications: Traditional and Proxy Methods Policy; Materials for SR&ED Policy; SR&ED Overhead and Other Expenditures Policy.

(3) [Expenditures directly attributable to premises, facilities and equipment]. For the purposes of subclause 37(8)(*a*)(ii)(A)(II) of the Act, the following expenditures are directly attributable to the provision of premises, facilities or equipment for the prosecution of scientific research and experimental development:

(*a*) the cost of the maintenance and upkeep of such premises, facilities or equipment; and

(*b*) other expenditures, or those portions of other expenditures, that are directly related to that provision and that would not have been incurred if those premises or facilities or that equipment had not existed.

(4) [Calculation of prescribed proxy amount]. For the purposes of the definition "qualified expenditure" in subsection 127(9) of the Act, the prescribed proxy amount of a taxpayer for a taxation year, in respect of a business, in respect of which the taxpayer elects under clause 37(8)(*a*)(ii)(B) of the Act is 55% of the total of all amounts each of which is that portion of the amount incurred in the year by the taxpayer in respect of salary or wages of an employee of the taxpayer who is directly engaged in scientific research and experimental development carried on in Canada that can reasonably be considered to relate to the scientific research and experimental development having regard to the time spent by the employee on the scientific research and experimental development.

History: S. 2900(4) was replaced by S.C. 2012, c. 31, s. 62(1), applicable to taxation years that end after 2012, except that for taxation years that begin before 2014 the reference to "55%" in subsection 2900(4) is to be read as a reference to the percentage that is the total of

(*a*) 65% multiplied by the proportion that the number of days that are in the taxation year and before 2013 is of the number of days in the taxation year,

(*b*) 60% multiplied by the proportion that the number of days that are in the taxation year and in 2013 is of the number of days in the taxation year, and

(*c*) 55% multiplied by the proportion that the number of days that are in the taxation year and after 2013 is of the number of days in the taxation year.

S. 2900(4) formerly read:

(4) For the purposes of the definition "qualified expenditure" in subsection 127(9) of the Act, the prescribed proxy amount of a taxpayer for a taxation year, in respect of a business, in respect of which the taxpayer elects under clause 37(8)(*a*)(ii)(B) of the Act is 65% of the total of all amounts each of which is that portion of the amount incurred in the year by the taxpayer in respect of salary or wages of an employee of the taxpayer who is directly engaged in scientific research and experimental development carried on in Canada that can reasonably be considered to relate to the scientific research and experimental development having regard to the time spent by the employee on the scientific research and experimental development.

SR&ED Publications: Prescribed Proxy Amount Policy.

(5) [All or substantially all salaries or wages]. Subject to subsections (6) to (8), where in subsection (4) the portion of an expenditure is all or substantially all of the expenditure, that portion shall be replaced by the amount of the expenditure.

SR&ED Publications: 96-06, Directly Undertaking, Supervising or Supporting Directly Engaged SR&ED Salary and Wages.

(6) [Maximum prescribed proxy amount]. The amount determined under subsection (4) as the prescribed proxy amount of a taxpayer for a taxation year in respect of a business shall not exceed the amount, if any, by which

(*a*) the total of all amounts deducted in computing the taxpayer's income for the year from the business,

exceeds the total of all amounts each of which is

(*b*) an amount deducted in computing the income of the taxpayer for the year from the business under any of sections 20, 24, 26, 30, 32, 37, 66 to 66.8 and 104 of the Act, or

(*c*) an amount incurred by the taxpayer in the year in respect of any outlay or expense made or incurred for the use of, or the right to use, a building other than a special-purpose building.

(7) [Restrictions for specified employees]. In determining the prescribed proxy amount of a taxpayer for a taxation year, the portion of the amount incurred in the year by the taxpayer in respect of salary or wages of a specified employee of the taxpayer that is included in computing the total described in subsection (4) shall not exceed the lesser of

(*a*) 75% of the amount incurred by the taxpayer in the year in respect of salary or wages of the employee, and

(*b*) the amount determined by the formula

$$2.5 \times A \times B/365$$

where

A is the Year's Maximum Pensionable Earnings (as determined under section 18 of the *Canada Pension Plan*) for the calendar year in which the taxation year ends, and

B is the number of days in the taxation year in which the employee is an employee of the taxpayer.

(8) [Specified employee employed by an associated corporation]. Where

(*a*) a taxpayer is a corporation,

(*b*) the taxpayer employs in a taxation year ending in a calendar year an individual who is a specified employee of the taxpayer,

Regulations

(*c*) the taxpayer is associated with another corporation (referred to as the "associated corporation") in a taxation year of the associated corporation ending in the calendar year, and

(*d*) the individual is an employee of the associated corporation in the taxation year of the associated corporation ending in the calendar year,

the total of all amounts that may be included in computing the total described in subsection (4) in respect of salaries or wages of the individual by the taxpayer in its taxation year ending in the calendar year and by all associated corporations in their taxation years ending in the calendar year shall not exceed the amount that is 2.5 times the Year's Maximum Pensionable Earnings (as determined under section 18 of the *Canada Pension Plan*) for the calendar year.

(9) [Exclusions to salary base]. For the purposes of subsections (4) and (7), an amount incurred in respect of salary or wages of an employee in a taxation year does not include

(*a*) an amount described in section 6 or 7 of the Act;

(*b*) an amount deemed under subsection 78(4) of the Act to have been incurred;

(*c*) bonuses; or

(*d*) remuneration based on profits.

(10) [Deemed associated corporation]. For the purpose of subsection (8),

(*a*) an individual related to a particular corporation, and

(*b*) a partnership any member of which is an individual related to a particular corporation or is a corporation associated with a particular corporation,

shall be deemed to be a corporation associated with the particular corporation.

(11) [Prescribed depreciable property]. The depreciable property of a taxpayer that is prescribed for the purposes of the definition "first term shared-use-equipment" in subsection 127(9) of the Act is

(*a*) a building of the taxpayer;

(*b*) a leasehold interest of the taxpayer in a building;

(*c*) a property of the taxpayer if, at the time it was acquired by the taxpayer, the taxpayer or a person related to the taxpayer intended that it would be used in the prosecution of scientific research and experimental development during the assembly, construction or commissioning of a facility, plant or line for commercial manufacturing, commercial processing or other commercial purposes (other than scientific research and experimental development) and intended

(i) that it would be used during its operating time in its expected useful life primarily for purposes other than scientific research and experimental development, or

(ii) that its value would be consumed primarily in activities other than scientific research and experimental development; and

(*d*) part of a property of the taxpayer if, at the time the part was acquired by the taxpayer, the taxpayer or a person related to the taxpayer intended that the part would be used in the prosecution of scientific research and experimental development during the assembly, construction or commissioning of a facility, plant or line for commercial manufacturing, commercial processing or other commercial purposes (other than scientific research and experimental development), and intended

(i) that it would be used during its operating time in its expected useful life primarily for purposes other than scientific research and experimental development, or

(ii) that its value would be consumed primarily in activities other than scientific research and experimental development.

2901. Prescribed Expenditures

For the purposes of paragraph 37.1(5)(*c*) [Repealed by S.C. 1998, c. 19, s. 87(1).] of the Act, a prescribed expenditure is

(*a*) an expenditure of a current nature incurred by a corporation in respect of

(i) the general administration or management of a business, including

(A) administrative salary or wages and related benefits in respect of a person whose duties are not all or substantially all directed to the prosecution of scientific research and experimental development, except to the extent that such expenditure is described in subsection 2900(2) or (3),

(B) a legal or accounting fee,

(C) an amount described in any of paragraphs 20(1)(*c*) to (*g*) of the Act,

(D) an entertainment expense,

(E) an advertising or selling expense,

(F) a convention expense,

(G) a due or fee in respect of membership in a scientific or technical society or organization, and

(H) a fine or penalty, or

(ii) the maintenance and upkeep of premises, facilities or equipment to the extent that such expenditure is not attributable to the prosecution of scientific research and experimental development,

except any such expenditure incurred by a corporation that derives all or substantially all of its revenue from the prosecution of scientific research or the sale of rights in or arising out of scientific research carried on by it;

(*b*) an expenditure of a capital nature incurred by a corporation in respect of

(i) the acquisition of property, except any such expenditure that was incurred for and was all or substantially all attributable to the prosecution, or to the provision of premises, facilities or equipment for the prosecution, of scientific research and experimental development, or

(ii) the acquisition of property that is qualified property within the meaning assigned by subsection 127(9) of the Act;

(*c*) an expenditure made to acquire rights in, or arising out of, scientific research and experimental development; or

(*d*) an expenditure on scientific research and experimental development in respect of which an amount is deductible under section 110 of the Act.

2902. Prescribed Expenditures

For the purposes of the definition "qualified expenditure" in subsection 127(9) of the Act, a prescribed expenditure is

(*a*) an expenditure of a current nature incurred by a taxpayer in respect of

(i) the general administration or management of a business, including

(A) an administrative salary or wages and related benefits in respect of a person whose duties are not all or substantially all directed to the prosecution of scientific research and experimental development, except to the extent that such expenditure is described in subsection 2900(2) or (3),

(B) a legal or accounting fee,

(C) an amount described in any of paragraphs 20(1)(*c*) to (*g*) of the Act,

(D) an entertainment expense,

(E) an advertising or selling expense,

(F) a conference or convention expense,

(G) a due or fee in respect of membership in a scientific or technical society or organization, and

(H) a fine or penalty, or

(ii) the maintenance and upkeep of premises, facilities or equipment to the extent that such expenditure is not attributable to the prosecution of scientific research, and experimental development,

(*b*) an expenditure incurred by a taxpayer in respect of

(i) the acquisition of property that is qualified property or qualified resource property within the meaning assigned by subsection 127(9) of the Act, or

(ii) the acquisition of property that has been used, or acquired for use or lease, for any purpose whatever before it was acquired by the taxpayer;

(*c*) an expenditure made to acquire rights in, or arising out of, scientific research and experimental development;

(*d*) an expenditure on scientific research and experimental development in respect of which an amount is deductible under section 110.1 or section 118.1 of the Act; or

(*e*) an expenditure of a taxpayer, to the extent that the taxpayer has received or is entitled to receive a reimbursement in respect of it from

(i) a person resident in Canada, other than

(A) Her Majesty in right of Canada or a province,

(B) an agent of Her Majesty in right of Canada or a province,

(C) a corporation, commission or association that is controlled, directly or indirectly in any manner whatever, by Her Majesty in right of Canada or a province or by an agent of her Majesty in right of Canada or a province, or

(D) a municipality in Canada or a municipal or public body performing a function of government in Canada, or

(ii) a person not resident in Canada to the extent that the said reimbursement is deductible by the person in computing his taxable income earned in Canada for any taxation year.

History: S. 2902(*b*)(ii) was replaced by S.C. 2012, c. 31, s. 63(1), applicable in respect of expenditures incurred after March 28, 2012, and formerly read:

(ii) the acquisition of property that is qualified property within the meaning assigned by subsection 127(9) of the Act, or

S. 2902(*b*) was replaced by S.C. 2012, c. 31, s. 63(2), applicable in respect of expenditures incurred after 2013, and formerly read:

(*b*) an expenditure of a capital nature incurred by a taxpayer in respect of

(i) the acquisition of property, except any such expenditure that at the time it was incurred

(A) was for first term shared-use-equipment or second term shared-use-equipment, or

(B) was for the provision of premises, facilities or equipment if, at the time of the acquisition of the premises, facilities or equipment, it was intended

(I) that the premises, facilities or equipment would be used during all or substantially all of the operating time of the premises, facilities or equipment in the expected useful life of the premises, facilities or equipment for the prosecution of scientific research and experimental development in Canada, or

(II) that all or substantially all of the value of the premises, facilities or equipment would be consumed in the prosecution of scientific research and experimental development in Canada,

(ii) the acquisition of property that is qualified property or qualified resource property within the meaning assigned by subsection 127(9) of the Act, or

(iii) the acquisition of property that has been used or acquired for use or lease, for any purpose whatever before it was acquired by the taxpayer;

S. 2902(*e*), the portion before subparagraph (i) was replaced by S.C. 2012, c. 31, s. 63(3), applicable in respect of expenditures incurred after 2013, and formerly read:

(*e*) an expenditure of a current or capital nature, to the extent that the taxpayer has received or is entitled to receive a reimbursement in respect thereof from

Income Tax Folios: *Secondary* — S4-F2-C1 Deductibility of Fines and Penalties.

SR&ED Publications: SR&ED Overhead and Other Expenditures Policy; SR&ED Capital Expenditures Policy; Total Qualified SR&ED Expenditures for Investment Tax Credit Purposes Policy.

2903. Special-Purpose Buildings

(Repealed by S.C. 2012, c. 31, s. 64(1).)

History: S. 2903 was repealed by S.C. 2012, c. 31, s. 64(1), applicable after 2013, and formerly read:

2903. *Special-Purpose Buildings*. For the purposes of this Part and paragraph 37(8)(*d*) of the Act, a special-purpose building is a building the working areas of which are designed and constructed to have a displacement in any direction of not more than .02 micrometre and to have, per .028 cubic metre of interior airspace,

(*a*) not more than 350 airborne particles of a size less than or equal to .1 micrometre in diameter and no airborne particles of a size greater than .1 micrometre in diameter,

(*b*) not more than 75 airborne particles of a size less than or equal to .2 micrometre in diameter and no airborne particles of a size greater than .2 micrometre in diameter,

(*c*) not more than 30 airborne particles of a size less than or equal to .3 micrometre in diameter and no airborne particles of a size greater than .3 micrometre in diameter, or

(*d*) not more than 10 airborne particles of a size less than or equal to .5 micrometre in diameter and no airborne particles of a size greater than .5 micrometre in diameter.

Regulations

Part XXX
Communication of Information [Repealed.]

History: Part XXX was repealed by S.C. 2013, c. 40, s. 105, in force December 12, 2013.

3000. (Repealed.)

3001. (Repealed.)

3002. (Repealed.)

3003. Prescribed Laws of the Province of Quebec (Repealed by S.C. 2013, c. 40, s. 105.)

History: S. 3003 was repealed by S.C. 2013, c. 40, s. 105, in force December 12, 2013, and formerly read:

3003 *Prescribed Laws of the Province of Quebec.* For the purposes of paragraph 122.64(2)(*a*) of the Act, the following are prescribed laws of the Province of Quebec:

(*a*) *An Act respecting Family Benefits,* R.S.Q., c. P-19.1;

(*b*) *An Act respecting the Québec Pension Plan,* R.S.Q., c. R-9; and

(*c*) *Individual and Family Assistance Act,* R.S.Q., c. A-13.1.1, as it relates to the additional amounts for dependent children.

S. 3003(*c*) was replaced by S.C. 2013, c. 40, s. 104(1), deemed to have come into force on January 1, 2007, and formerly read:

(*c*) *An Act respecting Income Support, Employment Assistance and Social Solidarity,* R.S.Q., c. S-32.001, as it relates to the additional amounts for dependent children.

3004. (Repealed by S.C. 2013, c. 40, s. 105.).

History: S. 3004 was repealed by S.C. 2013, c. 40, s. 105, in force December 12, 2013, and formerly read:

3004. For the purposes of subparagraph 241(4)(*j*.1)(ii) of the Act, *An Act Respecting Family Benefits,* S.Q. 1997, c. 57, is, in respect of the Province of Quebec, a prescribed law of a province.

Part XXXI
Tax Shelter

3100. Prescribed benefits

(1) For the purposes of paragraph (*b*) of the definition "tax shelter" in subsection 237.1(1) of the Act, "prescribed benefit", in respect of an interest in a property, means any amount that may reasonably be expected, having regard to statements or representations made in respect of the interest, to be received or enjoyed by a person (in this subsection referred to as "the purchaser") who acquires the interest, or a person with whom the purchaser does not deal at arm's length, which receipt or enjoyment would have the effect of reducing the impact of any loss that the purchaser may sustain in respect of the interest, and includes such an amount

(*a*) that is, either immediately or in the future, owed to any other person by the purchaser or a person with whom the purchaser does not deal at arm's length, to the extent that

(i) liability to pay that amount is contingent,

(ii) payment of that amount is or will be guaranteed by, security is or will be provided by, or an agreement to indemnify the other person to whom the amount is owed is or will be entered into by

(A) a promoter in respect of the interest,

(B) a person with whom the promoter does not deal at arm's length, or

(C) a person who is to receive a payment (other than a payment made by the purchaser) in respect of the guarantee, security or agreement to indemnify,

(iii) the rights of that other person against the purchaser, or against a person with whom the purchaser does not deal at arm's length, in respect of the collection of all or part of the purchase price are limited to a maximum amount, are enforceable only against certain property, or are otherwise limited by agreement, or

(iv) payment of that amount is to be made in a foreign currency or is to be determined by reference to its value in a foreign currency and it may reasonably be considered, having regard to the history of the exchange rate between the foreign currency and Canadian currency, that the total of all such payments, when converted to Canadian currency at the exchange rate expected to prevail at the date on which each such payment would be required to be made, will be substantially less than that total would be if each such payment was converted to Canadian currency at the time that each such payment became owing;

(*b*) that the purchaser or a person with whom the purchaser does not deal at arm's length is entitled at any time to, directly or indirectly, receive or have available

(i) as a form of assistance from a government, municipality or other public authority, whether as a grant, a subsidy, a forgivable loan, a deduction from tax (other than an amount described in clause (*b*)(i)(B) of the definition "tax shelter" in subsection 237.1(1) of the Act) or an investment allowance, or as any other form of assistance, or

(ii) by reason of a revenue guarantee or other agreement in respect of which revenue may be earned by the purchaser or a person with whom the purchaser does not deal at arm's length, to the extent that the revenue guarantee or other agreement may reasonably be considered to ensure that the purchaser or person will receive a return of all or a portion of the purchaser's outlays in respect of the interest;

(*c*) that is the proceeds of disposition to which the purchaser may be entitled by way of an agreement or other arrangement under which the purchaser has a right, either absolutely or contingently, to dispose of the interest (otherwise than as a consequence of the purchaser's death), including the fair market value of any property that the agreement or arrangement provides for the acquisition of in exchange for all or any part of the interest; and (*d*) that is owed to a promoter, or a person with whom the promoter does not deal at arm's length, by the purchaser or a person with whom the purchaser does not deal at arm's length in respect of the interest.

History: S. 3100(1) was added by P.C. 2011-936, SOR/2011-188, dated September 22, 2011, published in the *Canada Gazette* October 12, 2011, applicable after February 18, 2003.

(2) Notwithstanding subsection (1), for the purpose of paragraph (*b*) of the definition "tax shelter" in subsection 237.1(1) of the Act, "prescribed benefit", in respect of an interest in a property, does not, except as otherwise provided in subparagraph (1)(*b*)(ii), include profits earned in respect of the interest.

History: S. 3100(2) was added by P.C. 2011-936, SOR/2011-188, dated September 22, 2011, published in the *Canada Gazette* October 12, 2011, applicable after February 18, 2003.

(3) For the purpose of paragraph (*b*) of the definition "tax shelter" in subsection 237.1(1) of the Act, "prescribed benefit", in respect of an interest in a property, includes an amount that is a limited-recourse amount because of subsection 143.2(1), (7) or (13) of the Act, but does not include an amount of indebtedness that is a limited-recourse amount

(*a*) solely because it is not required to be repaid within 10 years from the time the indebtedness arose where the debtor would, if the interest were acquired by the debtor immediately after that time, be

(i) a partnership

(A) at least 90% of the fair market value of the property of which is attributable to the partnership's tangible capital property located in Canada, and

(B) at least 90% of the value of all interests in which are held by limited partners (within the meaning assigned by subsection 96(2.4) of the Act) of the partnership,

except where it is reasonable to conclude that one of the main reasons for the acquisition of one or more properties by the partnership, or for the acquisition of one or more interests in the partnership by limited partners, is to avoid the application of this subsection, or

(ii) a member of a partnership having fewer than six members, except where

(A) the partnership is a member of another partnership,

(B) there is a limited partner (within the meaning assigned by subsection 96(2.4) of the Act) of the partnership,

(C) less than 90% of the fair market value of the partnership's property is attributable to the partnership's tangible capital property located in Canada, or

(D) it is reasonable to conclude that one of the main reasons for the existence of one of two or more partnerships, one of which is the partnership, or the acquisition of one or more properties by the partnership, is to avoid the application of this section to the member's indebtedness,

(*b*) of a partnership

(i) where

(A) the indebtedness is secured by and used to acquire the partnership's tangible capital property located in Canada (other than rental property, within the meaning assigned by subsection 1100(14), leasing property, within the meaning assigned by subsection 1100(17), or specified energy property, within the meaning assigned by subsection 1100(25)), and

(B) the person to whom the indebtedness is repayable is a member of the Canadian Payments Association, and

(ii) throughout the period during which any amount is outstanding in respect of the indebtedness,

(A) at least 90% of the fair market value of the property of which is attributable to tangible capital property located in Canada of the partnership,

(B) at least 90% of the value of all interests in which are held by limited partners (within the meaning assigned by subsection 96(2.4) of the Act) that are corporations, and

(C) the principal business of each such limited partner is related to the principal business of the partnership,

except where it is reasonable to conclude that one of the main reasons for the acquisition of one or more properties by the partnership, or for the acquisition of one or more interests in the partnership by limited partners, is to avoid the application of this subsection, or

(*c*) of a corporation where the amount is a bona fide business loan made to the corporation for the purpose of financing a business that the corporation operates and the loan is made under a loan program of the Government of Canada or of a province the purpose of which is to extend financing to small- and medium-sized Canadian businesses.

History: S. 3100(3) was added by P.C. 2011-936, SOR/2011-188, dated September 22, 2011, published in the *Canada Gazette* October 12, 2011, applicable after February 18, 2003.

3101. Prescribed property

For the purpose of paragraph (*b*) of the definition "tax shelter" in subsection 237.1(1) of the Act, "prescribed property", in relation to a tax shelter, means property that is a registered pension plan, a registered retirement savings plan, a deferred profit sharing plan, a registered retirement income fund, a registered education savings plan or a property in respect of which paragraph 40(2)(*i*) of the Act applies.

History: S. 3101 was added by P.C. 2011-936, SOR/2011-188, dated September 22, 2011, published in the *Canada Gazette* October 12, 2011, applicable after February 18, 2003.

Part XXXII
Prescribed Payments [Repealed.]

3200. (Repealed.)

History: Part XXXII was repealed by P.C. 2011-936, SOR/2011-188, dated September 22, 2011, published in the *Canada Gazette* October 12, 2011, applicable to taxation years that begin after October 28, 2008. Part XXXII formerly read:

Part XXXII *PRESCRIBED PAYMENTS*

3200. *Patronage dividends.* For the purpose of subsection 135(1.1) of the Act, a payment is prescribed if it is made by Western Co-operative Fertilizers Limited,

(*a*) after March 22, 2004 and before March 31, 2005, to Saskatchewan Wheat Pool;

(*b*) after March 22, 2004 and before November 1, 2007, to United Grain Growers Limited;

(*c*) after March 30, 2005 and before March 13, 2008, to Saskatchewan Wheat Pool Inc.; and

(*d*) after March 12, 2008 and before October 29, 2008, to Viterra Inc.

Part XXXII was added by P.C. 2011-936, SOR/2011-188, dated September 22, 2011, published in the *Canada Gazette* October 12, 2011, applicable to taxation years that end after March 22, 2003. The heading for Part XXXII formerly read:

Prescribed Stock Exchanges and Contingency Funds

Regulations 3200 and 3201 were repealed effective December 14, 2007, as a consequence of the addition of s. 262 of the *Income Tax Act*, which gives the Minister of Finance authority to designate stock exchanges for purposes of the Act.

3201. (Repealed.)

3202. (Repealed.)

History: S. 3202 was repealed by P.C. 2011-936, SOR/2011-188, dated September 22, 2011, published in the *Canada Gazette* October 12, 2011, applicable to taxation years that end after March 22, 2003. S. 3202 formerly read:

Contingency Funds

3202. For the purposes of subparagraph 47.1(1)(*l*)(i) of the Act, the National Contingency Fund is a prescribed contingency fund.

Part XXXIII
Tax Transfer Payments

3300. [Prescribed rate]

For the purposes of subsection 154(2) of the Act, a rate of 45% is prescribed.

Part XXXIV
International Development Assistance Programs

3400. [Prescribed programs]

For the purposes of paragraphs 122.3(1)(*a*) and 250(1)(*d*) of the Act, each international development assistance program of the Canadian International Development Agency that is financed with funds (other than loan assistance funds) provided under External Affairs Vote 30a, *Appropriation Act No. 3, 1977-78*, or another vote providing for such financing, is hereby prescribed as an international development assistance program of the Government of Canada.

Interpretation Bulletins: *Secondary* — IT-497R4 Overseas employment tax credit.

Part XXXV
Gifts

History: The heading before s. 3500 was replaced by S.C. 2011, c. 24, s. 80(1), deemed to have come into force on March 23, 2011. The heading before s. 3500 formerly read: "Part XXXV — Receipts for Donations and Gifts".

3500. Interpretation

In this Part,

"employees' charity trust" means a registered charity that is organized for the purpose of remitting, to other registered charities, donations that are collected from employees by an employer;

"official receipt" means a receipt for the purposes of paragraph 110.1(2)(*a*) or 118.1(2)(*a*) of the Act, containing information required by section 3501 or 3502;

History: S. 3500, the definition "official receipt" was replaced by S.C. 2017, c. 33, s. 94, in force December 14, 2017, and formerly read:

"official receipt" means a receipt for the purposes of subsection 110.1(2) or (3) or 118.1(2), (6) or (7) of the Act, containing information as required by section 3501 or 3502;

"official receipt form" means any printed form that a registered organization or other recipient of a gift has that is capable of being completed, or that originally was intended to be completed, as an official receipt by it;

"other recipient of a gift" means a person, to whom a gift is made by a taxpayer, referred to in any of paragraph 110.1(1)(*c*), subparagraph 110.1(2.1)(*a*)(ii) and paragraphs (*a*) and (*d*) of the definition qualified donee in subsection 149.1(1) of the Act;

History: S. 3500, the definition "other recipient of a gift" was replaced by S.C. 2017, c. 33, s. 94, in force December 14, 2017, and formerly read:

"other recipient of a gift" means a person, to whom a gift is made by a taxpayer, referred to in any of paragraphs (*a*) and (*d*) of the definition "qualified donee" in subsection 149.1(1), paragraph 110.1(1)(*c*) and subparagraph 110.1(3)(*a*)(ii) of the Act;

S. 3500, the definition "other recipient of a gift" was replaced by S.C. 2011, c. 24, s. 81(1), in force January 1, 2012. S. 3500, the definition "other recipient of a gift" formerly read:

"other recipient of a gift" means a person, to whom a gift is made by a taxpayer, referred to in any of subparagraphs 110.1(1)(*a*)(iii) to (vii), paragraphs 110.1(1)(*b*) and (*c*), subparagraph 110.1(3)(*a*)(ii), paragraphs (*c*) to (*g*) of the definition "total charitable gifts" in subsection 118.1(1), the definition "total Crown gifts" in subsection 118.1(1), paragraph (*b*) of the definition "total cultural gifts" in subsection 118.1(1) and paragraph 118.1(6)(*b*) of the Act;

"registered organization" means a registered charity, a registered Canadian amateur athletic association or a registered national arts service organization.

> **Amendment not yet in force**
> **Budget Implementation Act, 2019, No. 1 [S.C. 2019, c. 29]**
>
> **S. 3500, the definition "registered organization" was replaced by S.C. 2019, c. 29, s. 57(1), and will read as follows:**
>
> ***registered organization*** —"registered organization" means a registered charity, a registered Canadian amateur athletic association, registered journalism organization or a registered national arts service organization,
>
> **Applicable:** January 1, 2020.

Interpretation Bulletins: *Secondary* — IT-110R3 Deductible gifts and official donation receipts; IT-226R Gift to a charity of a residual interest in real property or an equitable interest in a trust; IT-504R2 (Consolid.) Visual artists and writers.

3501. Contents of Receipts

(1) Every official receipt issued by a registered organization shall contain a statement that it is an official receipt for income tax purposes and shall show clearly in such a manner that it cannot readily be altered,

(*a*) the name and address in Canada of the organization as recorded with the Minister;

(*b*) the registration number assigned by the Minister to the organization;

(*c*) the serial number of the receipt;

(*d*) the place or locality where the receipt was issued;

(*e*) where the gift is a cash gift, the date on which or the year during which the gift was received;

(*e*.1) where the gift is of property other than cash

(i) the date on which the gift was received,

(ii) a brief description of the property, and

(iii) the name and address of the appraiser of the property if an appraisal is done;

(*f*) the date on which the receipt was issued;

(*g*) the name and address of the donor including, in the case of an individual, the individual's first name and initial;

(*h*) the amount that is

(i) the amount of a cash gift, or

(ii) if the gift is of property other than cash, the amount that is the fair market value of the property at the time that the gift is made;

(*h*.1) a description of the advantage, if any, in respect of the gift and the amount of that advantage;

(*h*.2) the eligible amount of the gift;

(*i*) the signature, as provided in subsection (2) or (3), of a responsible individual who has been authorized by the organization to acknowledge gifts; and

(*j*) the name and Internet website of the Canada Revenue Agency.

Editorial Note: See the CRA's Charities Connection Newsletter No. 3, Service Clubs and Fraternal Societies, No. 8, Keep Your Eye on the Ball and No. 10, The Season of Giving — Things to Remember When Issuing Official Donation Receipts.

History: S. 3501(1)(*e*) and the portion of paragraph (*e.1*) before subparagraph (ii) were replaced by S.C. 2013, c. 34, s. 393(1), applicable in respect of gifts made after December 20, 2002, and formerly read:

(*e*) where the donation is a cash donation, the day on which or the year during which the donation was received;

(*e*.1) where the donation is a gift of property other than cash

(i) the day on which the donation was received,

S. 3501(1)(*f*) was replaced by S.C. 2013, c. 34, s. 393(2), applicable in respect of gifts made after December 20, 2002, and formerly read:

(*f*) the day on which the receipt was issued where that day differs from the day referred to in paragraph (*e*) or (*e*.1);

S. 3501(1)(*g*) and (*h*) were replaced by S.C. 2013, c. 34, s. 393(3), applicable in respect of gifts made after December 20, 2002, and formerly read:

(*g*) the name and address of the donor including, in the case of an individual, his first name and initial;

(*h*) the amount that is

(i) the amount of a cash donation, or

(ii) where the donation is a gift of property other than cash, the amount that is the fair market value of the property at the time that the gift was made;

S. 3501(1)(*h.1*) was added by S.C. 2013, c. 34, s. 393(3), applicable in respect of gifts made after December 20, 2002, except that, in respect of receipts issued before 2013, paragraph 3501(1)(*h.1*) is to be read as follows:

"(*h*.1) the amount of the advantage, if any, in respect of the gift;"

S. 3501(1)(*h.2*) was added by S.C. 2013, c. 34, s. 393(3), applicable in respect of gifts made after December 20, 2002.

S. 3501(1)(*i*) was replaced by S.C. 2013, c. 34, s. 393(4), applicable in respect of gifts made after December 20, 2002, and formerly read:

(*i*) the signature, as provided in subsection (2) or (3), of a responsible individual who has been authorized by the organization to acknowledge donations; and

Income Tax Technical News: Issue No. 26, Proposed Guidelines on Split Receipting.

Interpretation Bulletins: *Secondary* — IT-110R3 Deductible gifts and official donation receipts; IT-226R Gift to a charity of a residual interest in real property or an equitable interest in a trust; IT-288R2 Gifts of capital properties to a charity and others.

(1.1) Every official receipt issued by another recipient of a gift shall contain a statement that it is an official receipt for income tax purposes and shall show clearly in such a manner that it cannot readily be altered,

(*a*) the name and address of the other recipient of the gift;

(*b*) the serial number of the receipt;

(*c*) the place or locality where the receipt was issued;

(*d*) where the gift is a cash gift, the date on which the gift was received;

(*e*) where the gift is of property other than cash

(i) the date on which the gift was received,

(ii) a brief description of the property, and

(iii) the name and address of the appraiser of the property if an appraisal is done;

(*f*) the date on which the receipt was issued;

(*g*) the name and address of the donor including, in the case of an individual, the individual's first name and initial;

(*h*) the amount that is

(i) the amount of a cash gift, or

(ii) if the gift is of property other than cash, the amount that is the fair market value of the property at the time that the gift was made;

(*h*.1) a description of the advantage, if any, in respect of the gift and the amount of that advantage;

(*h*.2) the eligible amount of the gift;

(*i*) the signature, as provided in subsection (2) or (3.1), of a responsible individual who has been authorized by the other recipient of the gift to acknowledge donations; and

(*j*) the name and Internet website of the Canada Revenue Agency.

History: S. 3501(1.1)(*d*) and the portion of paragraph (*e*) before subparagraph (ii) were replaced by S.C. 2013, c. 34, s. 393(5), applicable in respect of gifts made after December 20, 2002, and formerly read:

(*d*) where the donation is a cash donation, the day on which or the year during which the donation was received;

(*e*) where the donation is a gift of property other than cash,

(i) the day on which the donation was received,

S. 3501(1.1)(*f*) was replaced by S.C. 2013, c. 34, s. 393(6), applicable in respect of gifts made after December 20, 2002, and formerly read:

(*f*) the day on which the receipt was issued where that day differs from the day referred to in paragraph (*d*) or (*e*);

S. 3501(1.1)(*g*) and (*h*) were replaced by S.C. 2013, c. 34, s. 393(7), applicable in respect of gifts made after December 20, 2002, and formerly read:

(*g*) the name and address of the donor including, in the case of an individual, his first name and initial;

(*h*) the amount that is

(i) the amount of a cash donation, or

(ii) where the donation is a gift of property other than cash, the amount that is the fair market value of the property at the time that the gift was made;

S. 3501(1.1)(*h.1*) was added by S.C. 2013, c. 34, s. 393(7), applicable in respect of gifts made after December 20, 2002, except that, in respect of receipts issued before 2013, paragraph 3501(1.1)(*h.1*) is to be read as follows:

"(*h*.1) the amount of the advantage, if any, in respect of the gift;"

S. 3501(1.1)(*h.2*) was added by S.C. 2013, c. 34, s. 393(7), applicable in respect of gifts made after December 20, 2002.

Information Circulars: IC 84-3R6 Gifts to certain charitable organizations outside Canada.

(2) Except as provided in subsection (3) or (3.1), every official receipt shall be signed personally by an individual referred to in paragraph (1)(*i*) or (1.1)(*i*).

(3) Where all official receipt forms of a registered organization are

(*a*) distinctively imprinted with the name, address in Canada and registration number of the organization, (*b*) serially numbered by a printing press or numbering machine, and

(*c*) kept at the place referred to in subsection 230(2) of the Act until completed as an official receipt,

the official receipts may bear a facsimile signature.

(3.1) Where all official receipt forms of another recipient of the gift are

(*a*) distinctively imprinted with the name and address of the other recipient of the gift,

(*b*) serially numbered by a printing press or numbering machine, and

(*c*) if applicable, kept at a place referred to in subsection 230(1) of the Act until completed as an official receipt,

the official receipts may bear a facsimile signature.

(4) An official receipt issued to replace an official receipt previously issued shall show clearly that it replaces the original receipt and, in addition to its own serial number, shall show the serial number of the receipt originally issued.

(5) A spoiled official receipt form shall be marked "cancelled" and such form, together with the duplicate thereof, shall be retained by the registered organization or the other recipient of a gift as part of its records.

(6) Every official receipt form on which any of the following is incorrectly or illegibly entered is deemed to be spoiled:

(*a*) the date on which the gift is received;

(*b*) the amount of the gift, in the case of a cash gift;

(*c*) a description of the advantage, if any, in respect of the gift and the amount of that advantage; and

(*d*) the eligible amount of the gift.

History: S. 3501(6) was replaced by S.C. 2013, c. 34, s. 393(8), applicable in respect of gifts made after December 20, 2002, except that, in respect of receipts issued before 2013, paragraph 3501(6)(*c*) is to be read as follows:

"(*c*) the amount of the advantage, if any, in respect of the gift; and"

S. 3501(6) formerly read:

(6) Every official receipt form on which

(*a*) the day on which the donation was received,

(*b*) the year during which the donation was received, or

(*c*) the amount of the donation,

was incorrectly or illegibly entered shall be regarded as spoiled.

Interpretation Bulletins: *Secondary* — IT-226R Gift to a charity of a residual interest in real property or an equitable interest in a trust.

3501.1. Contents of Information Returns

Every information return required to be filed under subsection 110.1(16) or 118.1(27) of the Act in respect of a transfer of property must contain

(*a*) a description of the transferred property;

(*b*) the fair market value of the transferred property at the time of the transfer;

(*c*) the date on which the property was transferred;

(*d*) the name and address of the transferee of the property including, in the case of an individual, their first name and initial; and

(*e*) if the transferor of the property, or a person not dealing at arm's length with the transferor, issued the receipt referred to in subsection 110.1(14) or 118.1(25) of the Act, the information contained in that receipt.

History: S. 3501.1 was added by S.C. 2011, c. 24, s. 82(1), deemed to have come into force on March 23, 2011.

3502. Employees' Charity Trusts

Where

(*a*) a registered organization

(i) is an employees' charity trust, or

(ii) has appointed an employer as agent for the purpose of remitting, to that registered organization, donations that are collected by the employer from the employer's employees, and

(*b*) each copy of the return required by section 200 to be filed for a year by an employer of employees who donated to the registered organization in that year shows

(i) the amount of each employee's donations to the registered organization for the year collected by the employer, and

(ii) the registration number assigned by the Minister to the registered organization,

section 3501 shall not apply and the copy of the portion of the return, relating to each employee who made a donation to the registered organization in that year, that is required by section 209 to be distributed to the employee for filing with the employee's income tax return shall be an official receipt.

Interpretation Bulletins: *Secondary* — IT-226R Gift to a charity of a residual interest in real property or an equitable interest in a trust.

3503. (Repealed.)

History: S. 3503 was repealed by S.C. 2018, c. 12, s. 44(1), deemed in force February 27, 2018, and formerly read:

3503. *Universities Outside Canada.* For the purposes of subparagraph (*a*)(iv) of the definition "qualified donee" in subsection 149.1(1) of the Act, the universities outside Canada named in Schedule VIII are prescribed to be universities the student body of which ordinarily includes students from Canada.

S. 3503 was replaced by S.C. 2011, c. 24, s. 83(1), in force January 1, 2012. S. 3503 formerly read:

3503. For the purposes of subparagraph 110.1(1)(*a*)(vi) and paragraph (*f*) of the definition "total charitable gifts" in subsection 118.1(1) of the Act, the universities outside Canada named in Schedule VIII are hereby prescribed to be universities the student body of which ordinarily includes students from Canada.

Interpretation Bulletins: *Secondary* — IT-226R Gift to a charity of a residual interest in real property or an equitable interest in a trust.

3504. [Prescribed Donees]

For the purposes of subparagraphs 110.1(2.1)(*a*)(ii) and 118.1(5.4)(*a*)(ii) of the Act, the following are prescribed donees:

(*a*) Friends of the Nature Conservancy of Canada, Inc., a charity established in the United States;

(*b*) The Nature Conservancy, a charity established in the United States; and

(*c*) American Friends of Canadian Land Trusts.

History: S. 3504, the portion before paragraph (*a*) was replaced by S.C. 2013, c. 34, s. 394(1), deemed to have come into force on May 2, 2007, and formerly read:

3504. *Prescribed Donees.* For the purposes of subparagraph 110.1(3)(*a*)(ii) and paragraph 118.1(6)(*b*) of the Act, the following are prescribed donees:

S. 3504(*c*) was added by P.C. 2010-1112, SOR/2010-197, dated September 23, 2010, published in the *Canada Gazette* October 13, 2010, applicable to the 2010 and subsequent taxation years.

Interpretation Bulletins: *Secondary* — IT-226R Gift to a charity of a residual interest in real property or an equitable interest in a trust; IT-288R2 Gifts of capital properties to a charity and others.

3505. Conditions

(1) (Repealed by S.C. 2017, c. 20, s. 32(1).)

History: S. 3505(1) was repealed by S.C. 2017, c. 20, s. 32(1), applicable in respect of gifts made after March 21, 2017, and formerly read:

(1) The following conditions are prescribed in respect of a donee for the purposes of paragraph 110.1(8)(*e*) of the Act:

(*a*) the donee has applied to the Minister for International Cooperation (or, if there is no such Minister, the Minister responsible for the Canadian International Development Agency) for a determination that the conditions described in this section have been met;

(*b*) medicines received by the donee for use in charitable activities outside Canada are

(i) delivered outside Canada by the donee for use in its charitable activities, or

(ii) transferred to another registered charity that would meet the conditions contained in this section if that registered charity were a donee described in subsection 110.1(8) of the Act;

(*c*) in the course of delivering medicines outside Canada for use in its charitable activities, the donee acts in a manner consistent with the principles and objectives of the inter-agency *Guidelines for Drug Donations* issued by the World Health Organization, as amended from time to time, (referred to in this section as "the WHO Guidelines");

(*d*) the donee has sufficient expertise in delivering medicines for use in charitable activities carried on outside Canada;

(*e*) the donee carries on a program that includes delivering medicines for use in charitable activities carried on outside Canada and that is

(i) an international development assistance program, or

(ii) an international humanitarian assistance program, responding to situations of international humanitarian crisis (resulting from either natural disaster or complex emergency); and

(*f*) the donee has sufficient expertise to design, implement and monitor each program described in subparagraph (*e*)(i) or (ii) that it carries on, unless the donee has declared that it will not deliver medicines in that program.

(2) (Repealed by S.C. 2017, c. 20, s. 32(1).)

History: S. 3505(2) was repealed by S.C. 2017, c. 20, s. 32(1), applicable in respect of gifts made after March 21, 2017, and formerly read:

(2) Without limiting the application of the WHO Guidelines, for the purposes of paragraph (1)(*c*), a donee does not act in a manner consistent with the principles and objectives of those guidelines if the donee's directors, trustees, officers or like officials have not

(*a*) approved a policy and procedural framework, under which the donee is required to act in a manner consistent with the WHO Guidelines; and

(*b*) declared that the donee acts in compliance with that policy and procedural framework.

(3) (Repealed by S.C. 2017, c. 20, s. 32(1).)

History: S. 3505(3) was repealed by S.C. 2017, c. 20, s. 32(1), applicable in respect of gifts made after March 21, 2017, and formerly read:

(3) A donee is considered not to have sufficient expertise for the purpose of a program to which paragraph (1)(*d*) or (*e*) applies if

(*a*) the program does not address the specific and differentiated needs, interests and vulnerabilities of affected women and men, girls and boys;

(*b*) the program does not incorporate, in the design of projects under the program, consideration for environmental effects of those projects; or

(*c*) the donee does not have policies and practices for the design, implementation and monitoring of the program.

(4) (Repealed by S.C. 2017, c. 20, s. 32(1).)

History: S. 3505(4) was repealed by S.C. 2017, c. 20, s. 32(1), applicable in respect of gifts made after March 21, 2017, and formerly read:

(4) The Minister referred to in subsection (1) may

(*a*) rely on any information or evidence in making a determination under subsection (1); and

(*b*) require the donee to provide any other information or evidence that that Minister considers relevant and sufficient for the purpose of this section.

S. 3505 was added by S.C. 2009, c. 2, s. 104(1), applicable in respect of applications made at any time by donees for determinations in respect of gifts made after June 2008.

Regulations

Part XXXVI
Reserves for Surveys

3600. [Reserve amount]

(1) For the purposes of paragraph 20(1)(*o*) of the Act, the amount hereby prescribed is

(*a*) for the third taxation year preceding the taxation year during which a survey is scheduled to occur, the amount that is 1/4 of the estimate of the expenses of the survey;

(*b*) for the second taxation year preceding the taxation year during which a survey is scheduled to occur, the amount that is 1/2 of the estimate of the expenses of the survey;

(*c*) for the first taxation year preceding the taxation year during which a survey is scheduled to occur, the amount that is 3/4 of the estimate of the expenses of the survey; and

(*d*) for the taxation year during which a survey is scheduled to occur, if the quadrennial or other special surveys have not, at the end of the year, been completed to the extent that the vessel is permitted to proceed on a voyage, the amount remaining after deducting from the estimate of the expenses of the survey the amount of expenses actually incurred in the year in carrying out the survey.

(2) In this section,

"classification society" means a society or association for the classification and registry of shipping approved by the Minister of Transport under the *Canada Shipping Act*;

"estimate of the expenses of survey" means a fair and reasonable estimate, made by a taxpayer at the time of filing his return of income for the third taxation year preceding the taxation year in which a quadrennial survey is scheduled to occur, of the costs, charges and expenses which might be expected to be necessarily incurred by him by reason of that survey and in respect of which he does not have or possess nor is he likely to have or possess any right of reimbursement, recoupment, recovery or indemnification from any other person or source;

"inspector" means a steamship inspector appointed under Part VIII of the *Canada Shipping Act*;

"quadrennial survey" means a periodical survey, not being an annual survey nor a survey coinciding as to time with the construction of a vessel, in accordance with the rules of a classification society or, an extended inspection, not being an annual inspection nor an inspection coinciding as to time with the construction of a vessel, pursuant to the provisions of the *Canada Shipping Act*, and the regulations thereunder;

"survey" means the drydocking of a vessel, the examination and inspection of its hull, boilers, machinery, engines and equipment by an inspector or a surveyor and everything done to such vessel, its hull, boilers, machinery, engines and equipment pursuant to an order, requirement or recommendation given or made by the inspector or surveyor as the result of the examination and inspection so that a safety and inspection certificate might be issued in respect of the vessel pursuant to the provisions of the *Canada Shipping Act*, and the regulations thereunder or, as the case may be, so that the vessel might be entitled to retain the character assigned to it in the registry book of a classification society;

"surveyor" means a surveyor to a classification society.

Part XXXVII
Registered Charities

3700. (Repealed.)

History: S. 3700 was repealed, and the heading before it was replaced, by S.C. 2010, c. 25, s. 83(1), applicable for taxation years that end on or after March 4, 2010. S. 3700 and the heading before it formerly read:

Part XXXVII *Charitable Foundations*

3700. *Interpretation.* In this Part,

"charitable foundation" has the meaning assigned by paragraph 149.1(1)(*a*) [subsection 149.1(1) "charitable foundation"] of the Act;

"limited-dividend housing company" means a limited-dividend housing company described in paragraph 149(1)(*n*) of the Act;

"non-qualified investment" has the meaning assigned by paragraph 149.1(1)(*e*.1) [subsection 149.1(1) "non-qualified investment"] of the Act;

"prescribed stock exchange" (Repealed.)

"taxation year" has the meaning assigned by paragraph 149.1(1)(*l*) [subsection 149.1(1) "taxation year"] of the Act.

3701. Disbursement Quota

(1) For the purposes of the description of B in the definition "disbursement quota" in subsection 149.1(1) of the Act, the prescribed amount for a taxation year of a registered charity is determined as follows:

(*a*) choose a number, not less than two and not more than eight, of equal and consecutive periods that total twenty-four months and that end immediately before the beginning of the year;

(*b*) aggregate for each period chosen under paragraph (*a*) all amounts, each of which is the value, determined in accordance with section 3702, of a property, or a portion of a property, owned by the registered charity, and not used directly in charitable activities or administration, on the last day of the period;

(*c*) aggregate all amounts, each of which is the aggregate of values determined for each period under paragraph (*b*); and

(*d*) divide the aggregate amount determined under paragraph (*c*) by the number of periods chosen under paragraph (*a*).

(2) For the purposes of subsection (1) and subject to subsection (3),

(*a*) the number of periods chosen by a registered charity under paragraph (1)(*a*) shall, unless otherwise authorized by the Minister, be used for the taxation year and for all subsequent taxation years; and

(*b*) a registered charity is deemed to have existed on the last day of each of the periods chosen by it.

(3) The number of periods chosen under paragraph (1)(*a*) may be changed by the registered charity for its first taxation year commencing after 1986 and the new number shall, unless otherwise authorized by the Minister, be used for that taxation year and all subsequent taxation years.

History: S. 3701(1), the portion before paragraph (*a*) was replaced by S.C. 2010, c. 25, s. 84(1), applicable to taxation years that end on or after March 4, 2010. S. 3701(1), the portion before paragraph (*a*) formerly read:

(1) For the purposes of clause 149.1(1)(*e*)(iv)(A) [subsection 149.1(1) "disbursement quota"] of the Act, the prescribed amount referred to therein for a taxation year of a charitable foundation shall be determined in accordance with the following rules:

S. 3701(1)(*b*) was replaced by S.C. 2010, c. 25, s. 84(2), applicable to taxation years that end on or after March 4, 2010. S. 3701(1)(*b*) formerly read:

(*b*) aggregate for each period chosen under paragraph (*a*) all amounts, each of which is the value, determined in accordance with section 3702, of property or a portion thereof owned by the foundation, and not used directly in charitable activities or administration, on the last day of the period;

S. 3701(2) and (3) were replaced by S.C. 2010, c. 25, s. 84(3), applicable to taxation years that end on or after March 4, 2010. S. 3701(2) and (3) formerly read:

(2) For the purposes of subsection (1) and subject to subsection (3),

(*a*) the number of periods chosen by a charitable foundation under paragraph (1)(*a*) shall, unless otherwise authorized by the Minister, be used for the taxation year and for all subsequent taxation years; and

(*b*) a charitable foundation shall be deemed to have existed on the last day of each of the periods chosen by it.

(3) The number of periods chosen under paragraph (1)(*a*) may be changed by the foundation for its first taxation year commencing after 1986 and the new number shall, unless otherwise authorized by the Minister, be used for that taxation year and all subsequent taxation years.

3702. Determination of Value

(1) For the purposes of subsection 3701(1), the value of a property, or a portion of a property, owned by a registered charity, and not used directly in charitable activities or administration, on the last day of a period is determined as of that day to be

(*a*) in the case of a non-qualified investment of a private foundation, the greater of its fair market value on that day and its cost amount to the private foundation;

(*b*) subject to paragraph (*c*), in the case of property other than a non-qualified investment that is

(i) a share of a corporation that is listed on a designated stock exchange, the closing price or the average of the bid and asked prices of that share on that day or, if there is no closing price or bid and asked prices on that day, on the last preceding day for which there was a closing price or bid and asked prices,

(ii) a share of a corporation that is not listed on a designated stock exchange, the fair market value of that share on that day,

(iii) an interest in real property or a real right in an immovable, the fair market value on that day of the interest or right less the amount of any debt of the registered charity incurred in respect of the acquisition of the interest or right and secured by the interest or right, where the debt bears a reasonable rate of interest,

(iv) a contribution that is the subject of a pledge, nil,

(v) an interest, or for civil law a right, in property where the registered charity does not have the present use or enjoyment of the interest or right, nil,

(vi) a life insurance policy, other than an annuity contract, that has not matured, nil, and

(vii) a property not described in any of subparagraphs (i) to (vi), the fair market value of the property on that day; and

(*c*) in the case of any property described in paragraph (*b*) that is owned in connection with the charitable activities of the registered charity and is a share of a limited-dividend housing company referred to in paragraph 149(1)(*n*) of the Act or a loan, that has ceased to be used for charitable purposes and is being held pending disposition or for use in charitable activities, or that has been acquired for use in charitable activities, the lesser of the fair market value of the property on that day and an amount determined by the formula

$$(A / 0.035) \times (12 / B)$$

where

A is the income earned on the property in the period, and

B is the number of months in the period.

History: S. 3702(1) was replaced by S.C. 2010, c. 25, s. 85(1), applicable for taxation years that end on or after March 4, 2010. S. 3702(1) formerly read:

(1) For the purposes of subsection 3701(1), the value of property or a portion thereof owned by a charitable foundation, and not used directly in charitable activities or administration, on the last day of a period shall be determined as of that day and shall be

(*a*) in the case of a non-qualified investment, the greater of its fair market value on that day and its cost amount to the foundation;

(*b*) subject to paragraph (*c*), in the case of property other than a non-qualified investment that is

(i) a share of a corporation that is listed on a designated stock exchange, the closing price or the average of the bid and asked prices of that share on that day or, if there is no closing price or bid and asked prices on that day, on the last preceding day for which there was a closing price or bid and asked prices,

(ii) a share of a corporation that is not listed on a designated stock exchange, the fair market value of that share on that day,

(iii) an interest in real property, the fair market value on that day of the interest less the amount of any debt of the foundation incurred in respect of the acquisition of the interest and secured by the real property or the interest therein, where the debt bears a reasonable rate of interest,

(iv) a contribution that is the subject of a pledge, nil,

(v) an interest in property where the foundation does not have the present use or enjoyment of the interest, nil,

(vi) a life insurance policy, other than an annuity contract, that has not matured, nil, and

(vii) a property not described in any of subparagraphs (i) to (vi), the fair market value of the property on that day; and

(*c*) in the case of any property described in paragraph (*b*)

(i) that is owned in connection with the charitable activities of the foundation and is a share of a limited-dividend housing company or a loan,

(ii) that has ceased to be used for charitable purposes and is being held pending disposition or for use in charitable activities, or

(iii) that has been acquired for use in charitable activities,

the lesser of the fair market value of the property on that day and an amount determined by the formula

$$(A/.045) \times (12/B)$$

where

A is the income earned on the property in the period, and

B is the number of months in the period.

(2) For the purposes of subsection (1), a method that the Minister may accept for the determination of the fair market value of property or a portion thereof on the last day of a period is an independent appraisal made

(*a*) in the case of property described in subparagraph (1)(*b*)(ii) or (iii), not more than three years before that day; and

(*b*) in the case of property described in paragraph (1)(*a*), subparagraph (1)(*b*)(vii) or paragraph (1)(*c*), not more than one year before that day.

Part XXXVIII
Social Insurance Number Applications

3800. [Prescribed form]

Every individual who is required by subsection 237(1) of the Act to apply to the Minister of National Health and Welfare for assignment to him of a Social Insurance Number shall do so by delivering or mailing to the local office of the Canada Employment and Immigration Commission nearest to the individual's residence, a completed application in the form prescribed by the Minister for that purpose.

Information Circulars: IC 82-2R2 Social insurance number legislation that relates to the preparation of information slips.

Part XXXIX
Mining Taxes

3900. [Mining taxes]

(1) The following definitions apply in this section.

"income" of a taxpayer for a taxation year from mining operations in a province means the income, for the taxation year, that is derived from mining operations in the province as computed under the laws of the province that impose an eligible tax described in subsection (3).

"mine" includes any work or undertaking in which a mineral ore is extracted or produced and includes a quarry.

"mineral ore" includes an unprocessed mineral or mineral-bearing substance.

"mining operations" means

(*a*) the extraction or production of mineral ore from or in a mine;

(*b*) the transportation of mineral ore to the point of egress from the mine; and

(*c*) the processing of

(i) mineral ore (other than iron ore) to the prime metal stage or its equivalent, and

(ii) iron ore to a stage that is not beyond the pellet stage or its equivalent.

"non-Crown royalty" means a royalty contingent on production of a mine or computed by reference to the amount or value of production from mining operations in a province but does not include a royalty that is payable to the Crown in right of Canada or a province.

"processing" includes all forms of beneficiation, smelting and refining.

(2) For the purpose of paragraph 20(1)(*v*) of the Act, the amount allowed in respect of taxes on income from mining operations of a taxpayer for a taxation year is the total of all amounts each of which is an eligible tax paid or payable by the taxpayer

(*a*) on the income of the taxpayer for the taxation year from mining operations; or

(*b*) on a non-Crown royalty included in computing the income of the taxpayer for the taxation year.

(3) An eligible tax referred to in subsection (2) is

(*a*) a tax, on the income of a taxpayer for a taxation year from mining operations in a province, that is

(i) levied under a law of the province,

(ii) imposed only on persons engaged in mining operations in the province, and

(iii) paid or payable to

(A) the province,

(B) an agent of Her Majesty in right of the province, or

(C) a municipality in the province, in lieu of taxes on property or on any interest, or for civil law any right, in property (other than in lieu of taxes on residential property or on any interest, or for civil law any right, in residential property); and

(*b*) a tax, on an amount received or receivable by a person as a non-Crown royalty, that is

(i) levied under a law of a province,

(ii) imposed specifically on persons who hold a non-crown royalty on mining operations in the province, and

(iii) paid or payable to the province or to an agent of Her Majesty in right of the province.

Part XL
Borrowed Money Costs

4000. (Revoked.)

4001. Interest on Insurance Policy Loans

For the purposes of subsection 20(2.1) of the Act, the amount of interest to be verified by the insurer in respect of a taxpayer shall be verified in prescribed form no later than the last day on which the taxpayer is required to file his return of income under section 150 of the Act for the taxation year in respect of which the interest was paid.

Part XLI
Representation Expenses

4100. [Election]

For the purposes of subsection 20(9) of the Act, an election shall be made by filing with the Minister the following documents in duplicate:

(*a*) a letter from the taxpayer specifying the amount in respect of which the election is being made; and

(*b*) where the taxpayer is a corporation, a certified copy of the resolution of the directors authorizing the election to be made.

Part XLII
Valuation of Annuities and Other Interests

4200. For the purposes of subparagraph 115E(*f*)(i) of the former Act (within the meaning assigned by paragraph 8(*b*) of the *Income Tax Application Rules*), the value of any income right, annuity, term of years, life or other similar estate or interest in expectancy shall be determined in accordance with the rules and standards, including standards as to mortality and interest, as are prescribed by the *Estate Tax Regulations* pursuant to the provisions of subparagraph 58(1)(*s*)(i) of the *Estate Tax Act*.

Regulations

Part XLIII
Interest Rates

4300. [Interpretation]

For the purposes of this Part,

"quarter" means any of the following periods in a calendar year:

(*a*) the period beginning on January 1 and ending on March 31;

(*b*) the period beginning on April 1 and ending on June 30;

(*c*) the period beginning on July 1 and ending on September 30; and

(*d*) the period beginning on October 1 and ending on December 31.

4301. Prescribed Rate of Interest

Subject to section 4302, for the purposes of

(*a*) every provision of the Act that requires interest at a prescribed rate to be paid to the Receiver General, the prescribed rate in effect during any particular quarter is the total of

(i) the rate that is the simple arithmetic mean, expressed as a percentage per year and rounded to the next higher whole percentage where the mean is not a whole percentage, of all amounts each of which is the average equivalent yield, expressed as a percentage per year, of Government of Canada Treasury Bills that mature approximately three months after their date of issue and that are sold at auctions of Government of Canada Treasury Bills during the first month of the quarter preceding the particular quarter, and

(ii) 4 per cent;

(*b*) every provision of the Act that requires interest at a prescribed rate to be paid or applied on an amount payable by the Minister to a taxpayer, the prescribed rate in effect during any particular quarter is the total of

(i) the rate determined under subparagraph (*a*)(i) in respect of the particular quarter, and

(ii) if the taxpayer is a corporation, zero per cent, and in any other case, 2 per cent;

(*b*.1) subsection 17.1(1) of the Act, the prescribed rate in effect during any particular quarter is the rate that would be determined under paragraph (*a*) in respect of the particular quarter if the reference in subparagraph (*a*)(i) to "the next higher whole percentage where the mean is not a whole percentage" were read as "two decimal points"; and

(*c*) every other provision of the Act in which reference is made to a prescribed rate of interest or to interest at a prescribed rate, the prescribed rate in effect during any particular quarter is the rate determined under subparagraph (*a*)(i) in respect of the particular quarter.

Editorial Note: The interest rate prescribed in Income Tax Regulation s. 4301(*a*) is the base rate of Government of Canada Treasury Bills described in s. 4301(*a*)(i) plus 4%, applicable to late or deficient income tax payments and unremitted withholdings; the interest rate prescribed in s. 4301(*b*) is the base rate described in s. 4301(*a*)(i) plus 2%, applicable to tax refunds on overpayments (other than to corporations as of July 1, 2010); and the interest rate prescribed in s. 4301(*c*), is the base rate described in s. 4301(*a*)(i), applicable to deemed interest on employee and shareholder loans and benefits and effective July 1, 2010, to refunds of tax overpayments to corporations. The interest rate prescribed in s. 4301(*b.1*), in force on March 29, 2012 is the rate specified in s. 4301(*a*) rounded to two decimal points, applicable to a pertinent loan or indebtedness owing by a non-resident to a resident corporation.

Base rate of Government of Canada Treasury Bills described in s. 4301(*a*)(i):

	Quarter			
Year	**(1)**	**(2)**	**(3)**	**(4)**
2019	2%	2%		
2018	1%	2%	2%	2%
2017	1%	1%	1%	1%
2016	1%	1%	1%	1%
2015	1%	1%	1%	1%
2014	1%	1%	1%	1%
2013	1%	1%	1%	2%
2012	1%	1%	1%	1%
2011	1%	1%	1%	1%
2010	1%	1%	1%	1%
2009	2%	1%	1%	1%

History: S. 4301(*b.1*) was added by S.C. 2012, c. 31, s. 65(1), deemed to have come into force on March 29, 2012.

S. 4301(*b*)(ii) was replaced by S.C. 2010, c. 12, s. 23(1), and comes into force, or is deemed to have come into force, on July 1, 2010. S. 4301(*b*)(ii) formerly read:

(ii) 2 per cent; and

Interpretation Bulletins: *Secondary* — IT-153R3 Land developers — Subdivision and development costs and carrying charges on land.

4302. [Prescribed Leasing Interest Rate]

Notwithstanding section 4301, for the purposes of paragraph 16.1(1)(*d*) of the Act and subsection 1100(1.1), the interest rate in effect during any month is the rate that is one percentage point greater than the rate that was, during the month before the immediately preceding month, the average yield, expressed as a percentage per year rounded to two decimal points, prevailing on all outstanding domestic Canadian-dollar Government of Canada bonds on the last Wednesday of that month with a remaining term to maturity of over 10 years, as first published by the Bank of Canada.

Part XLIV
Publicly-traded Shares or Securities

4400. [Publicly-traded shares or securities]

(1) For the purposes of section 24 and subsection 26(11) of the *Income Tax Application Rules*,

(*a*) a share or security named in Schedule VII is hereby prescribed to be a publicly-traded share or security; and

(*b*) for each such share or security, the amount set out in Column II of Schedule VII opposite that share or security is hereby prescribed as the amount, if any, prescribed in respect of that property.

(2) In Schedule VII, the abbreviation

(*a*) "Cl" means "Class";

(*b*) "Com" means "Common";

(*c*) "Cv" means "Convertible";

(*d*) "Cu" means "Cumulative";

(*e*) "Pc" means "Per Cent";

(*f*) "Pr" means "Preferred" or "Preference" as the case may be;

(*g*) "Pt" means "Participating";

(*h*) "Rt" means "Right"; and

(*i*) "Wt" means "Warrant".

Part XLV
Elections in Respect of Expropriation Assets

4500. [Election]

Any election by a taxpayer under subsection 80.1(1), (2), (4), (5), (6) or (9) of the Act shall be made on or before the day on or before which the return of income is required to be filed pursuant to section 150 of the Act for the taxation year in which the assets referred to in the particular election were acquired by him.

Forms: T2079 — Election Re: Expropriation Assets Acquired as Compensation for or a Consideration for Sale of Foreign Property Taken by or Sold to Foreign Issuer.

Part XLVI
Investment Tax Credit

4600. Qualified Property

(1) Property is a prescribed building for the purposes of the definitions "qualified property" and "qualified resource property" in subsection 127(9) of the Act if it is depreciable property of the taxpayer that is a building or grain elevator and it is erected on land owned or leased by the taxpayer,

(*a*) that is included in Class 1, 3, 6, 20, 24 or 27 or paragraph (*c*), (*d*) or (*e*) of Class 8 in Schedule II; or

(*b*) that is included or would, but for Class 28, 41, 41.1 or 41.2 in Schedule II, be included in paragraph (*g*) of Class 10 in Schedule II.

History: S. 4600(1)(*b*) was replaced by S.C. 2013, c. 40, s. 106(1), applicable to property acquired after March 20, 2013, and formerly read:

(*b*) that is included or would, but for Classes 28, 41 or 41.1 in Schedule II, be included in paragraph (*g*) of Class 10 in Schedule II.

S. 4600(1), the portion before paragraph (*a*) was replaced by S.C. 2012, c. 31, s. 66(1), deemed to have come into force March 29, 2012, and formerly read:

(1) Property is a prescribed building for the purposes of the definition "qualified property" in subsection 127(9) of the Act if it is depreciable property of the taxpayer that is a building or grain elevator and it is erected on land owned or leased by the taxpayer,

S. 4600(1)(*b*) was replaced by P.C. 2011-44, SOR/2011-9, dated February 4, 2011, published in the *Canada Gazette* February 16, 2011, applicable to property acquired after March 18, 2007. S. 4600(1)(*b*) formerly read:

(*b*) that is included or would, but for Class 28 or 41 in Schedule II, be included in paragraph (*g*) of Class 10 in Schedule II.

Income Tax Folios: S4-F15-C1 Manufacturing and Processing.

(2) Property is prescribed machinery and equipment for the purposes of the definitions "qualified property" and "qualified resource property" in subsection 127(9) of the Act if it is depreciable property of the taxpayer (other than property referred to in subsection (1)) that is

(*a*) a property included in paragraph (*k*) of Class 1 or paragraph (*a*) of Class 2 in Schedule II;

(*b*) an oil or water storage tank;

(*c*) a property included in Class 8 in Schedule II (other than railway rolling stock);

(*d*) a vessel, including the furniture, fittings and equipment attached thereto;

(*e*) a property included in paragraph (*a*) of Class 10 or Class 22 or 38 in Schedule II (other than a car or truck designed for use on highways or streets);

(*f*) notwithstanding paragraph (*e*), a logging truck acquired after March 31, 1977 to be used in the activity of logging and having a weight, including the weight of property the capital cost of which is included in the capital cost of the truck at the time of its acquisition (but for greater certainty not including the weight of fuel), in excess of 16,000 pounds;

(*g*) a property included in any of paragraphs (*b*) to (*f*), (*h*), (*j*), (*k*), (*o*), (*r*), (*t*) or (*u*) of Class 10 in Schedule II, or property included in paragraph (*b*) of Class 41 in Schedule II and that would otherwise be included in paragraph (*j*), (*k*), (*r*), (*t*) or (*u*) of Class 10 in Schedule II;

(*h*) a property included in paragraph (*n*) of Class 10, or Class 15, in Schedule II (other than a roadway);

(*i*) a property included in any of paragraphs (*a*) to (*f*) of Class 9 in Schedule II;

(*j*) a property included in Class 28, in paragraph (*a*), (*a.1*), (*a.2*) or (*a.3*) of Class 41 or in Class 41.1 or 41.2 in Schedule II that would, but for Class 28, 41, 41.1 or 41.2, as the case may be, be included in paragraph (*k*) or (*r*) of Class 10 of Schedule II;

(*k*) a property included in Class 21, 24, 27, 29, 34, 39, 40, 43, 45, 46, 50, 52 or 53 in Schedule II;

Related Regulations: Schedule II Class 53.

(*l*) a property included in paragraph (*c*) or (*d*) of Class 41 in Schedule II;

(*m*) property included in Class 43.1 in Schedule II because of paragraph (*c*) of that Class; or

(*n*) a property included in Class 43.2 in Schedule II because of paragraph (*a*) of that Class.

History: S. 4600(2)(*k*) was replaced by S.C. 2015, c. 36, s. 22, in force on Royal Assent, June 23, 2015, and formerly read:

(*k*) a property included in Class 21, 24, 27, 29, 34, 39, 40, 43, 45, 46, 50 or 52 in Schedule II;

S. 4600(2)(*j*) was replaced by S.C. 2013, c. 40, s. 106(2), applicable to property acquired after March 20, 2013, and formerly read:

(*j*) a property included in Class 28, in paragraph (*a*), (*a.1*), (*a.2*) or (*a.3*) of Class 41 or in Class 41.1 in Schedule II that would, but for Class 28, 41 or 41.1, as the case may be, be included in paragraph (*k*) or (*r*) of Class 10 of Schedule II;

S. 4600(2)(*k*) was replaced by S.C. 2013, c. 34, s. 395(1), applicable to property acquired after March 18, 2007, except that for property acquired before January 28, 2009, paragraph 4600(2)(*k*) is to be read without reference to Class 52. S. 4600(2)(*k*) formerly read:

(*k*) a property included in Class 21, 24, 27, 29, 34, 39, 40, 43, 45 or 46 in Schedule II;

S. 4600(2), the portion before paragraph (*a*) was replaced by S.C. 2012, c. 31, s. 66(2), deemed to have come into force March 29, 2012, and formerly read:

(2) Property is prescribed machinery and equipment for the purposes of the definition "qualified property" in subsection 127(9) of the Act if it is depreciable property of the taxpayer (other than property referred to in subsection (1)) that is

S. 4600(2)(*j*) was replaced by P.C. 2011-44, SOR/2011-9, dated February 4, 2011, published in the *Canada Gazette* February 16, 2011, applicable to property acquired after March 18, 2007. S. 4600(2)(*j*) formerly read:

(*j*) a property included in Class 28 or paragraph (*a*), (*a*.1), (*a*.2) or (*a*.3) of Class 41 in Schedule II that would, but for Class 28 or 41, as the case may be, be included in paragraph (*k*) or (*r*) of Class 10 of Schedule II;

Forms: T2 SCH 31 — Investment Tax Credit — Corporations; T2038 Ind. — Investment Tax Credit (Individuals).

Information Circulars: IC 78-4R3 Investment tax credit rates.

(3) Property is prescribed energy generation and conservation property for the purposes of the definition "qualified property" in subsection 127(9) of the Act if it is depreciable property of the taxpayer (other than property referred to in subsection (1) or (2)) that is a property included in any of subparagraph (*a.1*)(i) of Class 17 and Classes 43.1, 43.2 and 48 in Schedule II.

History: S. 4600(3) was added by S.C. 2012, c. 31, s. 65(3), in force March 29, 2012.

Income Tax Folios: *Primary* — S3-F8-C2 Tax Incentives for Clean Energy Equipment.

4601. Qualified Transportation Equipment

For the purposes of the definition "qualified transportation equipment" in subsection 127(9) of the Act, the following depreciable property of a taxpayer (other than qualified property as defined by subsection 127(9) of the Act) is prescribed equipment:

(*a*) property that is

(i) included in Class 1 in Schedule II by virtue of paragraph (*h*) or (*i*) of that Class,

(ii) a bridge, culvert, subway or tunnel included in Class 1 in Schedule II that is ancillary to railway track and grading,

(iii) a trestle included in Class 3 in Schedule II that is ancillary to railway track and grading,

(iv) machinery or equipment included in Class 8 in Schedule II that is ancillary to

(A) railway track and grading, or

(B) railway traffic control or signalling equipment, including switching, block signalling, interlocking, crossing protection, detection, speed control or retarding equipment, but not including property that is principally electronic equipment or systems software therefor,

(v) included in Class 10 in Schedule II by virtue of subparagraph (*m*)(i), (ii) or (iii) of that Class, or

(vi) property described in paragraph (*m*) of Class 10 in Schedule II (other than property described in subparagraph (iv) thereof) that is included in Class 28 or 41 in Schedule II;

(*b*) property that is

(i) included in Class 6 in Schedule II by virtue of paragraph (*j*) of that Class,

(ii) machinery or equipment included in Class 8 in Schedule II that

(A) was acquired principally for the purpose of maintaining or servicing, or

(B) is ancillary to and used as part of,

a railway locomotive or railway car, or

(iii) included in Class 35 in Schedule II;

(*c*) property that is

(i) a truck, tractor or trailer that

(A) is included in Class 10 in Schedule II because of paragraph (*e*) of that Class or in Class 16 in Schedule II because of paragraph (*g*) of that Class,

(B) is designed for the purpose of carrying freight, or hauling a trailer that carries freight, on highways, and

(C) (Revoked.)

(D) in the case of a truck or tractor, has a "gross vehicle weight rating" (within the meaning assigned that expression by the *Motor Vehicle Safety Regulations*) of 26,001 pounds or more, and in the case of a trailer, is of a type designed to be hauled under normal operating conditions by a truck or tractor described in this subparagraph,

but for greater certainty,

(E) was not acquired principally for the purpose of carrying or hauling freight locally or making local pickups or deliveries, or

(ii) machinery or equipment included in Class 8 or 10 in Schedule II that is ancillary to and used as part of any property described in subparagraph (i)

Regulations

that is qualified transportation equipment within the meaning of subsection 127(9) of the Act;

(*d*) property included in Class 10 in Schedule II by virtue of paragraph (*a*) of that Class that is a bus designed for the purpose of seating 20 or more passengers and carrying their luggage, but not including

(i) a bus acquired principally for the purpose of transportation within any metropolitan area, city, town, village, municipality or other similar community or area, or

(ii) a school bus;

(*e*) property that is

(i) a vessel included in Class 7 in Schedule II (other than a vessel under construction),

(ii) machinery or equipment included in Class 7 or 8 in Schedule II that is ancillary to and used as part of any property described in subparagraph (i) that is qualified transportation equipment within the meaning of subsection 127(9) of the Act, or

(iii) a vessel included in a separate class prescribed by subsection 1101(2a);

(*f*) property that is

(i) included in Class 9 in Schedule II by virtue of paragraph (*g*) of that Class, or

(ii) machinery or equipment included in Class 9 in Schedule II by virtue of paragraph (*h*) or (*i*) of that Class that is ancillary to and used as part of any property described in subparagraph (i) that is qualified transportation equipment within the meaning of subsection 127(9) of the Act; and

(*g*) property included in Class 8 in Schedule II that is a reusable cargo container designed with external fittings for the purpose of handling, securing or stacking and having a carrying capacity of 500 cubic feet or more.

4602. Certified Property

(1) For the purposes of the definition "certified property" in subsection 127(9) of the Act, each of the following areas is a prescribed area:

(*a*) that portion of the Province of Newfoundland comprising the census divisions 2 to 4 and 7 to 10;

(*b*) that portion of the Province of Prince Edward Island comprising the Kings census division;

(*c*) that portion of the Province of Nova Scotia comprising the census divisions of

(i) Cape Breton,

(ii) Guysborough,

(iii) Inverness,

(iv) Richmond, and

(v) Victoria;

(*d*) that portion of the Province of New Brunswick comprising the census divisions of

(i) Gloucester,

(ii) Kent,

(iii) Madawaska,

(iv) Northumberland, and

(v) Restigouche;

(*e*) that portion of the Province of Quebec comprising

(i) all of the area north of the 50th parallel of latitude, other than the area within the limits of the city of Sept-Iles,

(ii) the Magdalen Islands, and

(iii) the census divisions of

(A) Bonaventure,

(B) Gaspé-Est,

(C) Gaspé-Ouest,

(D) Matane,

(E) Matapédia,

(F) Rimouski, other than the area within the limits of the city of Rimouski,

(G) Rivière-du-Loup, and

(H) Témiscouata;

(*f*) that portion of the Province of Ontario that is north of the 50th parallel of latitude;

(*g*) that portion of the Province of Manitoba comprising the census divisions 19 and 21 to 23, other than the area within the limits of the city of Thompson;

(*h*) that portion of the Province of Saskatchewan comprising the census division of Northern Saskatchewan;

(*i*) that portion of the Province of Alberta comprising the census division of Peace River, other than the area within the limits of the city of Grande Prairie;

(*j*) that portion of the Province of British Columbia comprising the Peace River-Liard census division; and

(*k*) all of the Yukon Territory and the Northwest Territories.

(2) For the purposes of subsection (1), the expression "census divisions" has the same meaning as in the *Dictionary of 1971 Census Terms*, Statistics Canada Catalogue Number 12-540, and the *Census Divisions and Subdivisions*, Statistics Canada Catalogues Numbered 92-704, 92-705, 92-706 and 92-707.

Information Circulars: IC 78-4R3 Investment tax credit rates.

4603. Qualified Construction Equipment

For the purposes of the definition "qualified construction equipment" in subsection 127(9) of the Act, "prescribed equipment" means depreciable property of a taxpayer, other than qualified property as defined by subsection 127(9) of the Act or qualified transportation equipment as defined by subsection 127(9) of the Act, that is

(*a*) a property included in Class 22 or 38 in Schedule II;

(*b*) a crane;

(*c*) a pile driver; or

(*d*) a dredge.

4604. Approved Project Property

(1) For the purposes of paragraphs (*a*) and (*c*) of the definition "approved project property" in subsection 127(9) of the Act, property is a prescribed building if it is depreciable property of the taxpayer that is a building or grain elevator, erected on land owned or leased by the taxpayer,

(*a*) that is included in Class 1, 3, 6, 24, 27 or 37 or paragraph (*c*), (*d*) or (*e*) of Class 8 in Schedule II; or

(*b*) that is included or would, but for Class 28 or Class 41 in Schedule II, be included in paragraph (g) of Class 10 in Schedule II.

(2) For the purposes of paragraphs (*b*) and (*d*) of the definition "approved project property" in subsection 127(9) of the Act, property is prescribed machinery and equipment if it is depreciable property of the taxpayer (other than property referred to in subsection (1)) that is

(*a*) a property included in paragraph (*k*) of Class 1 or paragraph (a) of Class 2 in Schedule II;

(*b*) an oil or water storage tank;

(*c*) a property included in Class 8 in Schedule II (other than railway rolling stock);

(*d*) subject to paragraph (*e*), a property included in paragraph (*a*) of Class 10 or Class 22 or 38 in Schedule II (other than a car or truck designed for use on highways or streets);

(*e*) a logging truck acquired to be used in the activity of logging and having a weight, including the weight of property the capital cost of which is included in the capital cost of the truck at the time of its acquisition (but for greater certainty not including the weight of fuel), in excess of 16,000 pounds;

(*f*) a property included in any of paragraphs (*b*) to (*f*), (*h*) to (*k*), (*o*), (*q*), (*r*), (*t*) or (*u*) of Class 10 in Schedule II;

(*g*) a property included in paragraph (*n*) of Class 10, or Class 15, in Schedule II (other than a roadway);

(*h*) a property included in any of paragraphs (*a*) to (*f*) of Class 9 in Schedule II;

(*i*) a property included in Class 28 or 41 in Schedule II that would, but for those classes, be included in paragraph (*k*) or (*r*) of Class 10 in Schedule II;

(*j*) a property included in any of Classes 21, 24, 27, 29, 34, 39, 40 and 43 in Schedule II;

(*k*) a property included in Class 37 in Schedule II; or

(*l*) a vessel (other than a supply boat, workboat, drilling rig, workover rig or shuttle tanker), including the furniture, fittings and equipment attached thereto, that is used primarily for

(i) heavy-lifting or pipe-laying in the construction of, or

(ii) the provision of lodging services in the servicing of,

an installation, structure, apparatus or artificial island that is used for offshore hydrocarbon exploration or exploitation.

4605. Prescribed Activities

For the purposes of the definition "for an approved purpose" in paragraph (*e*) of the definition "approved project property" in subsection 127(9) of the Act, a prescribed activity of a taxpayer is

(*a*) operating a hotel, motel, camping ground, travel trailer park or any similar lodging facility;

(*b*) providing facilities that are ancillary to a lodging facility referred to in paragraph (*a*) that is owned by the taxpayer and that are intended for the use and enjoyment of the occupants of the lodging facility;

(*c*) providing facilities that are primarily for the receiving, storage and distribution of goods owned by persons with whom the taxpayer deals at arm's length;

(*d*) providing to a business owned by a person with whom the taxpayer deals at arm's length

(i) engineering or architectural services,

(ii) computer services, or

(iii) other technical or scientific services,

but not including financial, legal, accounting, medical or dental services;

(*e*) providing to a business owned by a person with whom the taxpayer deals at arm's length

(i) the services of an employment agency, or

(ii) advertising services, other than advertising services in a medium owned by the taxpayer; or

(*f*) operating a vessel described in paragraph 4604(2)(*l*).

4606. Prescribed Amount

For the purposes of paragraph (*b*) of the definition "contract payment" in subsection 127(9) of the Act, a prescribed amount is an amount received from the Canadian Commercial Corporation in respect of an amount received by that Corporation from a government, municipality or other public authority other than the government of Canada or of a province, a Canadian municipality or other Canadian public authority.

4607. Prescribed Designated Regions

For the purposes of the definition "specified percentage" in subsection 127(9) of the Act, "prescribed designated region" means a region of Canada, other than the Gaspé peninsula and the provinces of Nova Scotia, New Brunswick, Prince Edward Island, and Newfoundland, including Labrador, that was a designated region on December 31, 1984, under the *Regional Development Incentives Designated Region Order, 1974*.

4608. Prescribed Expenditure for Qualified Canadian Exploration Expenditure

(1) In this section,

"joint exploration corporation" has the meaning assigned by paragraph 66(15)(*g*) [subsection 66(15) "joint exploration corporation"] of the Act;

"principal-business corporation" has the meaning assigned by paragraph 66(15)(*h*) [subsection 66(15) "principal-business corporation"] of the Act;

"shareholder corporation" has the meaning assigned by paragraph 66(15)(*i*) [subsection 66(15) "shareholder corporation"] of the Act;

"well" means an exploratory probe or an oil or gas well.

(2) For the purposes of the definition "qualified Canadian exploration expenditure" in subsection 127(9) of the Act, the prescribed expenditure of a taxpayer for a taxation year is the aggregate of all amounts each of which is the amount, if any, by which

(*a*) the specified expenses of the taxpayer for the year in respect of the well

exceed

(*b*) the base amount of the taxpayer at the end of the year in respect of the well.

(3) For the purposes of this section, the specified expenses of a taxpayer for a taxation year in respect of a well that is an exploratory probe is the aggregate of all expenses that

(*a*) would be Canadian exploration expenses of the taxpayer by reason of any of subparagraphs 66.1(6)(*a*)(i), (iv) and (v) [subsection 66.1(6) "Canadian exploration expense"] of the Act if the references in subparagraphs 66.1(6)(*a*)(iv) and (v) [subsection 66.1(6) "Canadian exploration expense"] of the Act (as those subparagraphs read on November 30, 1985) to "any of subparagraphs (i) to (iii.1) [subsection 66.1(6) 'Canadian exploration expense']" were read as references to "subparagraph (i) [subsection 66.1(6) 'Canadian exploration expense']";

(*b*) were incurred

(i) in the year, and

(ii) after November 1985 and before 1991;

(*c*) were incurred in the drilling or completing of the exploratory probe or in building a temporary access road to, or preparing the site in respect of, the probe; and

(*d*) are not non-qualifying expenses of the taxpayer.

(4) For the purposes of this section, the specified expenses of taxpayer for a taxation year in respect of a well that is an oil or gas well is the aggregate of all expenses that

(*a*) would be Canadian exploration expenses of the taxpayer by virtue of any of subparagraphs 66.1(6)(*a*)(ii) to (ii.2), (iv) and (v) [subsection 66.1(6) "Canadian exploration expense"] of the Act if the references in subparagraphs 66.1(6)(*a*)(iv) and (v) [subsection 66.1(6) "Canadian exploration expense"] of the Act (as those subparagraphs read on November 30, 1985) to "subparagraphs (i) to (iii.1) [subsection 66.1(6) 'Canadian exploration expense']" were read as references to "subparagraphs (ii) to (ii.2) [subsection 66.1(6) 'Canadian exploration expense']";

(*b*) were incurred in respect of the well

(i) in the year, and

(ii) after November 1985 and before 1991; and

(*c*) are not non-qualifying expenses of the taxpayer.

(5) For the purposes of subsections (3) and (4), a non-qualifying expense of a taxpayer is an expense that

(*a*) may reasonably be regarded as having been incurred as consideration for services to be rendered after 1990 or for property that cannot reasonably be considered to be for use by the taxpayer before 1991;

(*b*) was or is to be renounced by the taxpayer at any time under subsection 66(10.1) or (12.6) of the Act;

(*c*) is or was a Canadian exploration and development overhead expense, within the meaning of section 1206, of the taxpayer, of a partnership of which the taxpayer was a member or of a joint exploration corporation of which the taxpayer was a shareholder corporation;

(*d*) is an eligible cost or expense within the meaning of the *Petroleum Incentives Program Act* or the *Petroleum Incentives Program Act*, Chapter P-4.1 of the Statutes of Alberta, 1981, in respect of which, or in respect of part of which, the taxpayer, a partnership of which the taxpayer was a member, a joint exploration corporation of which the taxpayer was a shareholder corporation or a principal-business corporation of which the taxpayer was a shareholder, has received, is deemed to have received, is entitled to receive or may reasonably be expected to receive an incentive under either of those Acts; or

(*e*) was included in determining the specified expenses of any other taxpayer for a taxation year.

(6) For the purposes of this section, the base amount of a taxpayer at the end of a particular taxation year in respect of a well is the amount, if any, by which the taxpayer's threshold amount in respect of the well exceeds the aggregate of

(*a*) all amounts that would have been the taxpayer's specified expenses for any taxation year in respect of the well if

(i) the references in subparagraphs (3)(*b*)(ii) and (4)(*b*)(ii) to "after November 1985 and before 1991" were read as "after March 1985 and before December 1985", and

(ii) subsection (5) were read without reference to paragraph (*d*) thereof;

(*b*) all amounts referred to in paragraph (5)(*d*) for the particular taxation year or a preceding taxation year in respect of the well that would have been included in determining the taxpayer's specified expenses for the particular taxation year or the preceding taxation year but for that paragraph; and

(*c*) all amounts that are the taxpayer's specified expenses for any preceding taxation year in respect of the well.

(7) For the purposes of this section, the threshold amount of a taxpayer in respect of a well is

(*a*) where no agreement has been filed with the Minister under subsection (8) in respect of the well, $5,000,000; and

(*b*) where an agreement has been filed with the Minister under subsection (8) in respect of the well, the amount, if any, allocated to the taxpayer under the agreement.

(8) For the purposes of this section, where the aggregate of all expenses in respect of a well, each of which

Regulations

(*a*) would be included in determining the specified expenses of a taxpayer for a taxation year in respect of the well if subsection (5) were read without reference to paragraph (*d*) thereof, or

(*b*) would be included in determining the specified expenses of a taxpayer for a taxation year in respect of the well if

(i) the references in subparagraphs (3)(*b*)(ii) and (4)(*b*)(ii) to "after November 1985 and before 1991" were read as "after March 1985 and before December 1985", and

(ii) subsection (5) were read without reference to paragraph (*d*) thereof

exceeds $5,000,000, all taxpayers who have incurred those expenses or in whose favour or to whom any of those expenses have been renounced under subsection 66(10.1) or (12.6) of the Act may file with the Minister an agreement in writing in the prescribed form in respect of the well allocating amounts to some or all of those taxpayers if

(*c*) the amount allocated to each taxpayer does not exceed the total of such expenses that were incurred by the taxpayer in respect of the well, and that are not to be renounced by the taxpayer under subsection 66(10.1) or (12.6) of the Act in favour of or to any other person, and

(*d*) the aggregate of all amounts so allocated is not less than $5,000,000.

(9) For the purposes of this section, where

(*a*) the drilling of a well (in this subsection referred to as the "abandoned well") is abandoned not because of the results obtained but because of geological or mechanical difficulties and the drilling of a new well (in this subsection referred to as the "new well") is commenced, and

(*b*) having regard to all the circumstances, including the lapse of time between the abandonment of the abandoned well and the commencement of the new well and the proximity of the sites of the wells, it is reasonable to regard the new well as a replacement for the abandoned well,

the abandoned well and the new well shall be deemed to be one well.

(10) For the purpose of this section, where an expense of a joint exploration corporation is deemed by subsection 66(10.1) or (10.2) of the Act to be an expense of a shareholder corporation of the joint exploration corporation, the shareholder corporation shall be deemed to have incurred the expense at the time it was incurred by the joint exploration corporation.

(11) For the purpose of this section, where an expense of a principal-business corporation is deemed by subsection 66(12.61) or (12.63) of the Act to be an expense of a shareholder of the corporation, the shareholder shall be deemed to have incurred the expense at the time it was incurred by the principal-business corporation.

(12) For the purposes of this section, where an expense incurred by a partnership is, under subparagraph 66.1(6)(*a*)(iv) [subsection 66.1(6) "Canadian exploration expense", paragraph (*h*)] of the Act, a Canadian exploration expense of a taxpayer who was a member of the partnership, the taxpayer shall be deemed to have incurred the Canadian exploration expense at the time the expense was incurred by the partnership.

(13) For the purposes of this section, where an expense is a Canadian development expense of a taxpayer that is, under subsection 66.1(9) of the Act, deemed to be a Canadian exploration expense of the taxpayer, the taxpayer shall be deemed to have incurred the Canadian exploration expense at the time the Canadian development expense was incurred.

4609. Prescribed Offshore Region

For the purposes of the definition "specified percentage" in subsection 127(9) of the Act, the following region is a prescribed offshore region:

(*a*) that submarine area, not within a province, adjacent to the coast of Canada and extending throughout the natural prolongation of that portion of the land territory of Canada comprising the Gaspé Peninsula and the provinces of Newfoundland, Prince Edward Island, Nova Scotia and New Brunswick to the outer edge of the continental margin or to a distance of two hundred nautical miles from the baselines from which the territorial sea of Canada is measured, whichever is the greater; and

(*b*) the waters above the submarine area referred to in paragraph (*a*).

4610. Prescribed Area

For the purpose of paragraph (*c*.1) of the definition "qualified property" in subsection 127(9) of the Act, the area prescribed is the area comprising the Provinces of Nova Scotia, New Brunswick, Prince Edward Island and Newfoundland and the Gaspé Peninsula.

Part XLVII
Election in Respect of Certain Property Owned on December 31, 1971

4700. [Election]

Any election by an individual under subsection 26(7) of the *Income Tax Application Rules* shall be made by filing with the Minister the form prescribed.

Forms: T2076 — Valuation Day Value Election for Capital Properties Owned on December 31, 1971.

Part XLVIII
Status of Corporations and Trusts

4800. [Public corporation]

(1) For the purposes of subparagraph (*b*)(i) of the definition "public corporation" in subsection 89(1) of the Act, the following conditions are prescribed in respect of a corporation other than a cooperative corporation (within the meaning assigned by section 136 of the Act) or a credit union:

(*a*) a class of shares of the capital stock of the corporation designated by the corporation in its election or by the Minister in his notice to the corporation, as the case may be, shall be qualified for distribution to the public;

(*b*) there shall be no fewer than

(i) where the shares of that class are equity shares, 150, and

(ii) in any other case, 300

persons, other than insiders of the corporation, each of whom holds

(iii) not less than one block of shares of that class, and

(iv) shares of that class having an aggregate fair market value of not less than $500; and

(*c*) insiders of the corporation shall not hold more than 80 per cent of the issued and outstanding shares of that class.

(2) For the purposes of subparagraph (*c*)(i) of the definition "public corporation" in subsection 89(1) of the Act, the following conditions are prescribed in respect of a corporation:

(*a*) insiders of the corporation shall hold more than 90 per cent of the issued and outstanding shares of each class of shares of the capital stock of the corporation that

(i) was, at any time after the corporation last became a public corporation, listed on a designated stock exchange in Canada, or

(ii) was a class, designated as described in paragraph (1)(*a*), by virtue of which the corporation last became a public corporation;

(*b*) in respect of each class of shares described in subparagraph (*a*)(i) or (ii), there shall be fewer than

(i) where the shares of that class are equity shares, 50, and

(ii) in any other case, 100

persons, other than insiders of the corporation, each of whom holds

(iii) not less than one block of shares of that class, and

(iv) shares of that class having an aggregate fair market value of not less than $500; and

(*c*) there shall be no class of shares of the capital stock of the corporation that is qualified for distribution to the public and complies with the conditions described in paragraphs (1)(*b*) and (*c*).

(3) Where, by virtue of an amalgamation (within the meaning assigned by section 87 of the Act) of predecessor corporations any one or more of which was, immediately before the amalgamation, a public corporation, shares of any class of the capital stock of any such public corporation that was

(*a*) at any time after the corporation last became a public corporation, listed on a designated stock exchange in Canada, or

(*b*) the class, designated as described in paragraph (1)(*a*), by virtue of which the corporation last became a public corporation,

are converted into shares of any class (in this subsection referred to as the "new class") of the capital stock of the new corporation, the new class shall, for the purposes of subsection (2), be deemed to be a class, designated as described in paragraph (1)(*a*), by virtue of which the new corporation last became a public corporation.

(4) Any election under subparagraphs (*b*)(i) or (*c*)(i) of the definition "public corporation" in subsection 89(1) of the Act shall be made by filing with the Minister the following documents:

(*a*) the form prescribed by the Minister;

(*b*) where the directors of the corporation are legally entitled to administer the affairs of the corporation, a certified copy of their resolution authorizing the election to be made;

(*c*) where the directors of the corporation are not legally entitled to administer the affairs of the corporation, a certified copy of the authorization of the making of the election by the person or persons legally entitled to administer the affairs of the corporation; and

(*d*) a statutory declaration made by a director of the corporation stating that, after reasonable inquiry for the purpose of informing himself in that regard, to the best of his knowledge the corporation complies with all the prescribed conditions that must be complied with at the time the election is made.

Forms: T2067 — Election not to be a Public Corporation; T2073 — Election to be a Public Corporation.

Interpretation Bulletins: *Secondary* — IT-320R3 Registered retirement savings plans — Qualified investments.

4800.1. [Prescribed trusts]

For the purposes of paragraph 107(1)(*a*) and subsections 107(1.1), (2) and (4.1) of the Act, the following are prescribed trusts:

(*a*) a trust maintained primarily for the benefit of employees of a corporation or two or more corporations which do not deal at arm's length with each other, where one of the main purposes of the trust is to hold interests in shares of the capital stock of the corporation or corporations, as the case may be, or any corporation not dealing at arm's length therewith;

(*b*) a trust established exclusively for the benefit of one or more persons each of whom was, at the time the trust was created, either a person from whom the trust received property or a creditor of that person, where one of the main purposes of the trust is to secure the payments required to be made by or on behalf of that person to such creditor; and

(*c*) a trust all or substantially all of the properties of which consist of shares of the capital stock of a corporation, where the trust was established pursuant to an agreement between two or more shareholders of the corporation and one of the main purposes of the trust is to provide for the exercise of voting rights in respect of those shares pursuant to that agreement.

History: S. 4800.1, the portion before paragraph (*a*) was replaced by S.C. 2013, c. 34, s. 397(1), deemed to have come into force on January 1, 2000, and formerly read:

4800.1 For the purposes of paragraph 107(1)(*a*), subsections 107(2) and (4.1) and paragraph 108(1)(*c*) [subsection 108(1) "capital interest"] of the Act, the following are prescribed trusts:

4801. [Mutual fund trust]

In applying at any time paragraph 132(6)(*c*) of the Act, the following are prescribed conditions in respect of a trust:

(*a*) either

(i) the following conditions are met:

(A) there has been at or before that time a lawful distribution in a province to the public of units of the trust and a prospectus, registration statement or similar document was not, under the laws of the province, required to be filed in respect of the distribution, and

(B) the trust

(I) was created after 1999 and on or before that time, or

(II) satisfies, at that time, the conditions prescribed in section 4801.001, or

(ii) a class of the units of the trust is, at that time, qualified for distribution to the public; and

(*b*) in respect of a class of the trust's units that meets at that time the conditions described in paragraph (*a*), there are at that time no fewer than 150 beneficiaries of the trust, each of whom holds

(i) not less than one block of units of the class, and

(ii) units of the class having an aggregate fair market value of not less than $500.

History: S. 4801, the portion before subparagraph (*b*)(i) was replaced by S.C. 2013, c. 34, s. 398(1), applicable to the 2000 and subsequent taxation years, except that for the purpose of applying clause 4801(*a*)(i)(B) to taxation years that end before 2004, that clause is to be read as follows:

(B) the trust was created after 1999 and on or before that time, or

S. 4801, the portion before subparagraph (*b*)(i) formerly read:

4801. For the purposes of paragraph 132(6)(*c*) of the Act, the following conditions are hereby prescribed in respect of a trust:

(*a*) either

(i) a class of the units of the trust shall be qualified for distribution to the public, or

(ii) there has been a lawful distribution in a province to the public of units of the trust and a prospectus, registration statement or similar document was not required under the laws of the province to be filed in respect of the distribution; and

(*b*) in respect of any one class of units described in paragraph (*a*), there shall be no fewer than 150 beneficiaries of the trust, each of whom holds

4801.001. [Mutual fund trust]

For the purpose of applying at any particular time subclause 4801(*a*)(i)(B)(II), the following are the prescribed conditions:

(*a*) the trust was created before 2000;

(*b*) the trust was a unit trust on July 18, 2005;

(*c*) the particular time is after 2003; and

(*d*) the trusts elects by notifying the Minister, in writing before the trust's filing-due date for its 2012 taxation year, that this section applies to it.

History: S. 4801.001 was added by S.C. 2013, c. 34, s. 399(1), applicable to the 2004 and subsequent taxation years.

4801.01. [Mutual fund trust]

For the purpose of subsection 132.11(1) of the Act, a trust that is a money market fund as defined in National Instrument 81-102 Mutual Funds, as amended from time to time, of the Canadian Securities Administrators is a prescribed trust.

4801.02. [Labour sponsored venture capital corporation]

For the purposes of the definition "eligible business entity" in subsection 204.8(1), clause 204.82(2.2)(*d*)(i)(B) and paragraph 204.82(6)(*a*) of the Act, a corporation registered under Part III.1 of the *Community Small Business Investment Funds Act*, chapter 18 of the Statutes of Ontario, 1992, is a prescribed corporation.

4801.1. [Exempt foreign trust]

For the purpose of paragraph (*c*) of the definition "exempt trust" in subsection 233.2(1) of the Act, the following conditions are hereby prescribed in respect of a trust:

(*a*) at least 150 beneficiaries of the trust are beneficiaries in respect of the same class of units of the trust; and

(*b*) at least 150 of the beneficiaries in respect of that class each hold

(i) at least one block of units of that class, and

(ii) units of that class having a total fair market value of at least $500.

4802. [Prescribed investment corporations]

(1) For the purposes of clause 149(1)(*o*.2)(iv)(D) of the Act the following are prescribed persons:

(*a*) a trust all the beneficiaries of which are trusts described in clause 149(1)(*o*.2)(iv)(B) of the Act;

(*b*) a corporation incorporated before November 17, 1978 solely in connection with, or for the administration of, a registered pension plan;

(*c*) a trust or corporation established by or arising by virtue of an act of a province the principal activities of which are to administer, manage or invest the monies of a pension fund or plan that is established pursuant to an act of the province or an order or regulation made thereunder;

(*c*.1) the Canada Pension Plan Investment Board;

(*c*.2) the Public Sector Pension Investment Board;

(*c*.3) a pooled registered pension plan;

(*d*) a trust or corporation established by or arising by virtue of an act of a province in connection with a scheme or program for the compensation of workers injured in an accident arising out of or in the course of their employment;

(*e*) Her Majesty in right of a province;

(*f*) a trust all of the beneficiaries of which are any combination of

(i) registered pension plans,

(ii) trusts described in clause 149(1)(*o*.2)(iv)(B) or (C) of the Act, and

(iii) persons described in this subsection; and

(*g*) a corporation all of the shares of the capital stock of which are owned by one or more of the following:

(i) registered pension plans,

(ii) trusts described in clause 149(1)(*o*.2)(iv)(B) or (C) of the Act, and

(iii) persons described in this subsection.

History: S. 4802(1)(*c.3*) was added by S.C. 2012, c. 31, s. 67(1), in force December 14, 2012.

S. 4802(1)(*c*.2) was added by P.C. 2011-936, SOR/2011-188, dated September 22, 2011, published in the *Canada Gazette* October 12, 2011, applicable after September 2003.

(1.1) For the purposes of subparagraph 127.55(*f*)(iii) and paragraph 149(1)(*o.4*) of the Act, a trust is prescribed at any particular time if, at all times after its creation and before the particular time,

> **Proposed Amendment**
>
> **Legislative Proposals Relating to Income Tax Act and Other Legislation (July 27, 2018)**
>
> **The portion of subsection 4802(1.1) of the Regulations before paragraph (*a*) is replaced by the following:**
>
> **(1.1) Master trust.** For the purposes of subparagraph 127.55(*f*)(iii) and paragraphs 149(1)(*o*.4) and 150(1.2)(*h*) of the Act, a trust is prescribed at any particular time if, at all times after its creation and before the particular time,
>
> **Applicable:** To taxation years that end after December 30, 2021.

(*a*) it was resident in Canada;

(*b*) its only undertaking was the investing of its funds;

(*c*) it never borrowed money except where the borrowing was for a term not exceeding 90 days and it is established that the borrowing was not part of a series of loans or other transactions and repayments;

(*d*) it never accepted deposits; and

(*e*) each of the beneficiaries of the trust was a trust governed by a deferred profit sharing plan, a pooled registered pension plan or a registered pension plan.

History: S. 4802(1.1)(*e*) was replaced by S.C. 2012, c. 31, s. 67(2), in force December 14, 2012, and formerly read:

(*e*) each of the beneficiaries of the trust was a trust governed by a registered pension plan or a deferred profit sharing plan.

S. 4802(1.1), the portion before paragraph (*a*) was replaced by P.C. 2011-936, SOR/2011-188, dated September 22, 2011, published in the *Canada Gazette* October 12, 2011, applicable to the 1992 and subsequent taxation years, except that in its application before June 29, 2005, the portion of subsection 4802(1.1) before paragraph (*a*), is to be read without reference to "subparagraph 127.55(*f*)(iii) and". S. 4802(1.1), the portion before paragraph (*a*) formerly read:

(1.1) For the purposes of paragraph 149(1)(*o.4*) of the Act, a trust is a master trust at any time if, at all times after it was created and before that time,

(2) (Repealed by S.C. 2017, c. 20, s. 33(1).)

History: S. 4802(2) was repealed by S.C. 2017, c. 20, s. 33(1), applicable to taxation years that begin after 2018, and formerly read:

(2) For the purposes of paragraph 149(1)(*t*) of the Act, the following are prescribed insurers:

(*a*) Union Québécoise, compagnie d'assurances générales inc.;

(*b*) Les Clairvoyants Compagnie d'Assurance Générale Inc.; and

(*c*) Laurentian Farm Insurance Company Inc.

4803. [Interpretation]

(1) In this Part,

"block of shares" means, with respect to any class of the capital stock of a corporation,

(*a*) 100 shares, if the fair market value of one share of the class is less than $25,

(*b*) 25 shares, if the fair market value of one share of the class is $25 or more but less than $100, and

(*c*) 10 shares, if the fair market value of one share of the class is $100 or more;

"block of units" means, with respect to any class of units of a trust,

(*a*) 100 units, if the fair market value of one unit of the class is less than $25,

(*b*) 25 units, if the fair market value of one unit of the class is $25 or more but less than $100, and

(*c*) 10 units, if the fair market value of one unit of the class is $100 or more;

"equity share" has the meaning assigned by section 204 of the Act;

"insider of a corporation" has the meaning that would be assigned by section 100 of the *Canada Corporations Act*, as it read on June 22, 2009, if the references in that section to "insider of a company", "public company" and "equity shares" were read as references to "insider of a corporation", "corporation" and "shares" respectively, and includes a person who is an employee of the corporation, or of a person who does not deal at arm's length with the corporation, and whose right to sell or transfer any share of the capital stock of the corpora-

Regulations

tion, or to exercise the voting rights, if any, attaching to the share, is restricted by

(*a*) the terms and conditions attaching to the share, or

(*b*) any obligation of the person, under a contract, in equity or otherwise, to the corporation or to any person with whom the corporation does not deal at arm's length.

History: S. 4803(1), the portion of the definition "insider of a corporation" before paragraph (*a*) was replaced by P.C. 2011-936, SOR/2011-188, dated September 22, 2011, published in the *Canada Gazette* October 12, 2011, applicable after February 18, 2011. S. 4803(1), the portion of the definition "insider of a corporation" before paragraph (*a*) formerly read:

"insider of a corporation" has the meaning that would be assigned by section 100 of the *Canada Corporations Act* if the references therein to "public company" and to "equity shares" were read as references to "corporation" and "shares" respectively, except that a person who is an employee of the corporation, or of a person who does not deal at arm's length with the corporation, and whose right to sell or transfer any share of the capital stock of the corporation, or to exercise the voting rights, if any, attaching to the share, is restricted by

S. 4803(1), the portion of the definition "insider of a corporation" in subsection 4803(1) following paragraph (*b*) was repealed by P.C. 2011-936, SOR/2011-188, dated September 22, 2011, published in the *Canada Gazette* October 12, 2011, applicable after February 18, 2011. S. 4803(1), the portion of the definition "insider of a corporation" in subsection 4803(1) following paragraph (*b*) formerly read:

shall be deemed to hold the share as an insider of the corporation.

(2) For the purposes of this Part, a class of shares of the capital stock of a corporation or a class of units of a trust is qualified for distribution to the public only if

(*a*) a prospectus, registration statement or similar document has been filed with, and, where required by law, accepted for filing by, a public authority in Canada pursuant to and in accordance with the law of Canada or of any province and there has been a lawful distribution to the public of shares or units of that class in accordance with that document;

(*b*) the class is a class of shares, any of which were issued by the corporation at any time after 1971 while it was a public corporation in exchange for shares of any other class of the capital stock of the corporation that was, immediately before the exchange, qualified for distribution to the public;

(*c*) in the case of any class of shares, any of which were issued and outstanding on January 1, 1972, the class complied on that date with the conditions described in paragraphs 4800(1)(*b*) and (*c*); or

(*d*) in the case of any class of units, any of which were issued and outstanding on January 1, 1972, the class complied on that date with the condition described in paragraph 4801(*b*).

(3) For the purposes of paragraphs 4800(1)(*b*), 4800(2)(*b*) and 4801(*b*), where a group of persons holds

(*a*) not less than one block of shares of any class of shares of the capital stock of a corporation or one block of units of any class of a trust, as the case may be, and

(*b*) shares or units, as the case may be, of that class having an aggregate fair market value of not less than $500,

that group shall, subject to subsection (4), be deemed to be one person for the purposes of determining the number of persons who hold shares or units, as the case may be, of that class.

(4) In determining under subsection (3) the persons who belong to a group for the purposes of determining the number of persons who hold shares or units, as the case may be, of a particular class, the following rules apply:

(*a*) no person shall be included in more than one group;

(*b*) no person shall be included in a group if he holds

(i) not less than one block of shares or one block of units, as the case may be, of that class, and

(ii) shares or units, as the case may be, of that class having an aggregate fair market value of not less than $500; and

(*c*) the membership of each group shall be determined in the manner that results in the greatest possible number of groups.

Part XLIX
Registered Plans – Investments

History: The heading before s. 4900 was amended by S.C. 2013, c. 40, s. 107(1), deemed to have come into force on March 23, 2011. The heading before s. 4900 formerly read: "Deferred Income Plans, Qualified Investments".

4900. [Prescribed qualified investments]

(1) For the purposes of paragraph (*d*) of the definition *qualified investment* in subsection 146(1) of the Act, paragraph (*e*) of the definition *qualified investment* in subsection 146.1(1) of the Act, paragraph (*c*) of the definition *qualified investment* in subsection 146.3(1) of the Act, paragraph (*d*) of the definition *qualified investment* in subsection 146.4(1) of the Act, paragraph (*h*) of the definition *qualified investment* in section 204 of the Act and paragraph (*c*) of the definition *qualified investment* in subsection 207.01(1) of the Act, each of the following investments is prescribed as a qualified investment for a plan trust at a particular time if at that time it is

(*a*) an interest in a trust or a share of the capital stock of a corporation that was a registered investment for the plan trust during the calendar year in which the particular time occurs or the immediately preceding year;

(*b*) a share of the capital stock of a public corporation other than a mortgage investment corporation;

(*c*) a share of the capital stock of a mortgage investment corporation that does not hold as part of its property at any time during the calendar year in which the particular time occurs any indebtedness, whether by way of mortgage or otherwise, of a person who is a connected person under the governing plan of the plan trust;

(*c*.1) a bond, debenture, note or similar obligation of a public corporation other than a mortgage investment corporation;

(*d*) a unit of a mutual fund trust;

(*d*.1) (Repealed by S.C. 2007, c. 29, s. 32.)

(*d*.2) a unit of a trust if

(i) the trust would be a mutual fund trust if Part XLVIII were read without reference to paragraph 4801(*a*), and

(ii) there has been a lawful distribution in a province to the public of units of the trust and a prospectus, registration statement or similar document was not required under the laws of the province to be filed in respect of the distribution;

(*e*) an option, a warrant or a similar right (each of which is, in this paragraph, referred to as the "security") issued by a person or partnership (in this paragraph referred to as the "issuer") that gives the holder the right to acquire, either immediately or in the future, property all of which is a qualified investment for the plan trust or to receive a cash settlement in lieu of delivery of that property, where

(i) the property is

(A) a share of the capital stock of, a unit of, or a debt issued by, the issuer or another person or partnership that does not, when the security is issued, deal at arm's length with the issuer, or

(B) a warrant issued by the issuer or another person or partnership that does not, when the security is issued, deal at arm's length with the issuer, that gives the holder the right to acquire a share or unit described in clause (A), and

(ii) the issuer is not a connected person under the governing plan of the plan trust;

(*e*.01) (Repealed by S.C. 2007, c. 29, s. 32.)

(*e*.1) a share of, or deposit with, a société d'entraide économique;

(*f*) a share of, or similar interest in a credit union;

(*g*) a bond, debenture, note or similar obligation (in this paragraph referred to as the "obligation") issued by, or a deposit with, a credit union that has not at any time during the calendar year in which the particular time occurs granted any benefit or privilege to a person who is a connected person under the governing plan of the plan trust, as a result of the ownership by

(i) the plan trust of a share or obligation of, or a deposit with, the credit union, or

(ii) a registered investment of a share or obligation of, or a deposit with, the credit union if the plan trust has invested in that registered investment,

and a credit union shall be deemed to have granted a benefit or privilege to a person in a year if at any time in that year that person continues to enjoy a benefit or privilege that was granted in a prior year;

(*h*) a bond, debenture, note or similar obligation (in this paragraph referred to as the "obligation") issued by a cooperative corporation (within the meaning assigned by subsection 136(2) of the Act)

(i) that throughout the taxation year of the cooperative corporation immediately preceding the year in which the obligation was acquired by the plan trust had not less than 100 shareholders or, if all its shareholders were corporations, not less than 50 shareholders,

(ii) whose obligations were, at the end of each month of

(A) the last taxation year, if any, of the cooperative corporation prior to the date of acquisition of the obligation by the plan trust, or

(B) the period commencing three months after the date an obligation was first acquired by any plan trust and ending on the last day of the taxation year of the cooperative corporation in which that period commenced,

whichever of the periods referred to in clause (A) or (B) commences later, held by plan trusts the average number of which is not less than 100 computed on the basis that no two plan trusts

Regulations

shall have the same individual as an annuitant or a beneficiary, as the case may be, and

(iii) that, except where the plan trust is governed by a registered education savings plan, has not at any time during the calendar year in which the particular time occurs granted any benefit or privilege to a person who is a connected person under the governing plan of the plan trust, as a result of the ownership by

(A) the plan trust of a share or obligation of the cooperative corporation, or

(B) a registered investment of a share or obligation of the cooperative corporation if the plan trust has invested in that registered investment,

and a cooperative corporation shall be deemed to have granted a benefit or privilege to a person in a year if at any time in that year that person continues to enjoy a benefit or privilege that was granted in a prior year;

(*i*) a bond, debenture, note or similar obligation (in this paragraph referred to as the "obligation") of a Canadian corporation

(i) if payment of the principal amount of the obligation and the interest on the principal amount is guaranteed by a corporation or a mutual fund trust whose shares or units, as the case may be, are listed on a designated stock exchange in Canada,

(ii) if the corporation is controlled directly or indirectly by

(A) one or more corporations,

(B) one or more mutual fund trusts, or

(C) one or more corporations and mutual fund trusts

whose shares or units, as the case may be, are listed on a designated stock exchange in Canada, or

(iii) if, at the time the obligation is acquired by the plan trust, the corporation that issued the obligation is

(A) a corporation that, in respect of its capital stock, has issued and outstanding share capital carried on its books at not less than $25 million, or

(B) a corporation that is controlled by a corporation described in clause (A)

and has issued and outstanding bonds, debentures, notes or similar obligations having in the aggregate a principal amount of at least $10 million that are held by at least 300 different persons and were issued by the corporation by means of one or more offerings, provided that in respect of each such offering a prospectus, registration statement or similar document was filed with and, where required by law, accepted for filing by a public authority in Canada pursuant to and in accordance with the laws of Canada or a province and there was a lawful distribution to the public of those bonds, debentures, notes or similar obligations in accordance with that document;

(*i*.1) a security of a Canadian corporation

(i) that was issued pursuant to *The Community Bonds Act*, chapter C-16.1 of the Statutes of Saskatchewan, 1990, *The Rural Development Bonds Act*, chapter 47 of the Statutes of Manitoba, 1991-92, the *Community Economic Development Act, 1993*, chapter 26 of the Statutes of Ontario, 1993, or the New Brunswick Community Development Bond Program through which financial assistance is provided under the *Economic Development Act*, chapter E-1.11 of the Acts of New Brunswick, 1975, and

(ii) the payment of the principal amount of which is guaranteed by Her Majesty in right of a province;

(*i*.11) a share of the capital stock of a Canadian corporation that is registered under section 11 of the *Equity Tax Credit Act*, chapter 3 of the Statutes of Nova Scotia, 1993, the registration of which has not been revoked under that Act;

(*i*.12) a share of the capital stock of a Canadian corporation that is registered under section 39 of the *Risk Capital Investment Tax Credits Act*, chapter 22 of the Statutes of the Northwest Territories, 1998, the registration of which has not been revoked under that Act;

(*i*.13) a share of the capital stock of a Canadian corporation that is registered under section 2 of the *Community Development Equity Tax Credit Act*, chapter C-13.01 of the Revised Statutes of Prince Edward Island, 1988, the registration of which has not been revoked under that Act;

(*i*.2) indebtedness of a Canadian corporation (other than a corporation that is a connected person under the governing plan of the plan trust) represented by a bankers' acceptance;

(*i*.3) (Repealed by S.C. 2007, c. 29, s. 32.)

(*j*) a debt obligation of a debtor, or an interest, or for civil law a right, in that debt obligation, where

(i) the debt obligation is fully secured by a mortgage, charge, hypothec or similar instrument in respect of real or immovable property situated in Canada, or would be fully secured were it not for a decline in the fair market value of the property after the debt obligation was issued, and

(ii) the debtor (and any partnership that does not deal at arm's length with the debtor) is not a connected person under the governing plan of the plan trust;

(*j*.1) a debt obligation secured by a mortgage, charge, hypothec or similar instrument in respect of real or immovable property situated in Canada, or an interest, or for civil law a right, in that debt obligation, where the debt obligation is

(i) administered by an approved lender under the *National Housing Act*, and

(ii) insured

(A) under the *National Housing Act*, or

(B) by a corporation that offers its services to the public in Canada as an insurer of mortgages or hypothecary claims and that is approved as a private insurer of mortgages or hypothecary claims by the Superintendent of Financial Institutions under subsection 6(1) of the *Office of the Superintendent of Financial Institutions Act*;

(*j*.2) a certificate evidencing an undivided interest, or for civil law an undivided right, in one or more properties, where

(i) all or substantially all of the fair market value of the certificate is attributable to property that is, or is incidental to, a debt obligation secured by

(A) a mortgage, charge, hypothec or similar instrument in respect of real or immovable property situated in Canada, or

(B) property described in paragraph (*a*) or (*b*) of the definition "qualified investment" in section 204 of the Act that was substituted for the security referred to in clause (A) under the terms of the debt obligation,

(ii) the certificate has, at the time of acquisition by the plan trust, an investment grade rating with a credit rating agency referred to in subsection (2), and

(iii) the certificate is issued as part of an issue of certificates by the issuer for a total amount of at least $25 million;

(*k*) (Repealed by S.C. 2009, c. 2, s. 105.)

(*l*) (Repealed by S.C. 2009, c. 2, s. 105.)

(*m*) (Repealed by S.C. 2007, c. 29, s. 32.)

(*n*) (Repealed by S.C. 2007, c. 29, s. 32.)

(*n*.01) (Repealed by S.C. 2007, c. 29, s. 32.)

(*n*.1) (Repealed by S.C. 2007, c. 29, s. 32.)

(*o*) (Repealed by S.C. 2009, c. 2, s. 105.)

(*p*) (Repealed by S.C. 2007, c. 29, s. 32.)

(*p*.1) (Repealed by S.C. 2007, c. 29, s. 32.)

(*q*) a debt issued by a Canadian corporation (other than a corporation with share capital or a corporation that is a connected person under the governing plan of the plan trust) where

(i) the taxable income of the corporation is exempt from tax under Part I of the Act because of paragraph 149(1)(*l*) of the Act, and

(ii) either

(A) before the particular time and after 1995, the corporation

(I) acquired, for a total consideration of not less than $25 million, property from Her Majesty in right of Canada or a province, and

(II) put that property to a use that is the same as or similar to the use to which the property was put before the acquisition described in subclause (I), or

(B) at the time of the acquisition of the debt by the plan trust, it was reasonable to expect that clause (A) would apply in respect of the debt no later than one year after the time of the acquisition;

(*r*) a debt issued by a Canadian corporation (other than a corporation with share capital or a corporation that is a connected person under the governing plan of the plan trust) if

(i) the taxable income of the corporation is exempt from tax under Part I of the Act because of paragraph 149(1)(*l*) of the Act, and

(ii) either

(A) the debt is issued by the corporation as part of an issue of debt by the corporation for an amount of at least $25 million, or

(B) at the time of the acquisition of the debt by the plan trust, the corporation had issued debt as part of a single issue for an amount of at least $25 million;

(*s*) (Repealed by S.C. 2009, c. 2, s. 105.)

(*t*) a gold or silver legal tender bullion coin

(i) that is of a minimum fineness of 995 parts per 1000 in the case of gold and 999 parts per 1000 in the case of silver,

(ii) that was produced by the Royal Canadian Mint,

(iii) that has a fair market value at the particular time not exceeding 110 per cent of the fair market value of the coin's gold or silver content, and

(iv) that is acquired by the plan trust directly from the Royal Canadian Mint or from a corporation (in paragraphs (*u*) and (*v*) referred to as a "specified corporation")

(A) that is a bank, a trust company, a credit union, an insurance corporation or a registered securities dealer,

(B) that is resident in Canada, and

(C) that is a corporation whose business activities are subject by law to the supervision of a regulating authority that is the Superintendent of Financial Institutions or a similar authority of a province;

(*u*) a gold or silver bullion bar, ingot or wafer

(i) that is of a minimum fineness of 995 parts per 1000 in the case of gold and 999 parts per 1000 in the case of silver,

(ii) that was produced by a metal refiner included in the London Bullion Market Association's good delivery list of acceptable refiners for gold or silver, as the case may be,

(iii) that bears the hallmark of the metal refiner that produced it and a stamp indicating its fineness and its weight, and

(iv) that is acquired by the plan trust either directly from the metal refiner that produced it or from a specified corporation;

(*v*) a certificate issued by a specified corporation or the Royal Canadian Mint representing a claim of the holder of the certificate to property held by the issuer of the certificate, where

(i) the property would be property described in paragraph (*t*) or (*u*) if those paragraphs were read without reference to subparagraphs (*t*)(iv) and (*u*)(iv), respectively, and

(ii) the certificate is acquired by the plan trust directly from the issuer of the certificate or from a specified corporation; or

(*w*) an American Depositary Receipt where the property represented by the receipt is listed on a designated stock exchange.

History: S. 4900(1), the portion before paragraph (*a*) was replaced by S.C. 2017, c. 33, s. 95(1), deemed in force March 23, 2017, and formerly read:

(1) For the purposes of paragraph (*d*) of the definition "qualified investment" in subsection 146(1) of the Act, paragraph (*e*) of the definition "qualified investment" in subsection 146.1(1) of the Act, paragraph (*c*) of the definition "qualified investment" in subsection 146.3(1) of the Act, paragraph (*h*) of the definition "qualified investment" in section 204 of the Act, paragraph (*d*) of the definition "qualified investment" in subsection 205(1) of the Act and paragraph (*c*) of the definition "qualified investment" in subsection 207.01(1) of the Act, each of the following investments is prescribed as a qualified investment for a plan trust at a particular time if at that time it is

S. 4900(1)(*g*), the portion before subparagraph (i) was replaced by S.C. 2017, c. 33, s. 95(2), applicable in respect of (a) any investment acquired after March 22, 2017; and (b) any investment acquired before March 23, 2017 that ceases to be a "qualified investment" (as defined in subsection 146.1(1) of the Act) after March 22, 2017. S. 4900(1)(*g*), the portion before subparagraph (i) formerly read:

(*g*) a bond, debenture, note or similar obligation (in this paragraph referred to as the "obligation") issued by, or a deposit with, a credit union that, except where the plan trust is governed by a registered education savings plan, has not at any time during the calendar year in which the particular time occurs granted any benefit or privilege to a person who is a connected person under the governing plan of the plan trust, as a result of the ownership by

S. 4900(1)(*i*.13) was added by P.C. 2012-1629, SOR/2012-270, dated December 7, 2012, deemed to have come into force on September 1, 2011.

S. 4900(1), the portion before paragraph (*a*) was replaced by S.C. 2009, c. 2, s. 105(1), applicable to the 2009 and subsequent taxation years. S. 4900(1), the portion before paragraph (*a*) formerly read:

(1) For the purposes of paragraph (*d*) of the definition "qualified investment" in subsection 146(1) of the Act, paragraph (*e*) of the definition "qualified investment" in subsection 146.1(1) of the Act, paragraph (*c*) of the definition "qualified investment" in subsection 146.3(1) of the Act, paragraph (*h*) of the definition "qualified investment" in section 204 of the Act and paragraph (*d*) of the definition "qualified investment" in subsection 205(1) of the Act, each of the following investments is prescribed as a qualified investment for a plan trust at a particular time if at that time it is

S. 4900(1)(*i*.3) was repealed by S.C. 2009, c. 2, s. 105(2), applicable to property acquired after March 12, 2009. S. 4900(1)(*i*.3) formerly read:

(*i*.3) a debt obligation issued by a Canadian corporation or a trust resident in Canada, where

(i) the principal purpose of the corporation or trust is to derive income from, or from the disposition of, property that is

(A) a debt obligation, or a lease, that arose in the ordinary course of business between parties dealing with each other at arm's length,

(B) a property described by this paragraph, or

(C) an interest, or for civil law a right, in property described in clause (A) or (B),

(ii) the debt obligation has, at the time of its acquisition by the plan trust, an investment grade rating with a bond rating agency that rates debt in the ordinary course of its business, and

(iii) either

(A) the debt obligation is issued as part of a single issue of debt by the corporation or trust for a total amount of at least $25 million, or

(B) at the time the debt obligation is issued, the corporation or trust has issued and outstanding debt of at least $25 million;

S. 4900(1)(*j*.2)(ii) was replaced by S.C. 2009, c. 2, s. 105(3), applicable to property acquired after March 12, 2009. S. 4900(1)(*j*.2)(ii) formerly read:

(ii) the certificate has, at the time of its acquisition by the plan trust, an investment grade rating with a bond rating agency that rates debt in the ordinary course of its business, and

S. 4900(1)(*k*) and (*l*) were repealed by S.C. 2009, c. 2, s. 105(4), applicable to property acquired after March 12, 2009. S. 4900(1)(*k*) and (*l*) formerly read:

(*k*) an investment, other than a qualified investment described in paragraphs (*a*) to (*j*), that

(i) was, at the end of 1980, a qualified investment for a trust pursuant to subparagraph 204(*e*)(v) [Repealed by S.C. 1980-81-82-83, c. 48, s. 93(2).] of the Act or section 1502, this Part or section 5800, as the case may be, as those provisions read at that time,

(ii) was held on December 31, 1980 and continuously thereafter by the trust until the particular time,

(iii) would have continued to be a qualified investment of the trust from December 31, 1980 until the particular time had the provisions referred to in subparagraph (i) been in force throughout that period of time, and

(iv) was not, at any time before the particular time, an interest in a registered investment;

(*l*) a bond, debenture, note or similar obligation issued or guaranteed by

(i) the International Bank for Reconstruction and Development,

(i.1) The International Finance Corporation,

(ii) the Inter-American Development Bank,

(iii) the Asian Development Bank,

(iv) the Caribbean Development Bank,

(v) the European Bank for Reconstruction and Development, or

(vi) the African Development Bank;

S. 4900(1)(*o*) was repealed by S.C. 2009, c. 2, s. 105(5), applicable to property acquired after March 12, 2009. S. 4900(1)(*o*) formerly read:

(*o*) a bond, debenture, note or similar obligation issued by the government of a country other than Canada and that had, at the time of purchase, an investment grade rating with a bond rating agency that in the ordinary course of its business rates the debt obligations issued by that government;

S. 4900(1)(*s*) was repealed by S.C. 2009, c. 2, s. 105(6), applicable to property acquired after March 12, 2009. S. 4900(1)(*s*) formerly read:

(*s*) where the particular time is before 2002, a security of a corporation (other than a corporation that does not deal at arm's length with a person who is an annuitant, a beneficiary, an employer or a subscriber under the governing plan of the plan trust)

(i) that

(A) was last acquired by the plan trust before September 2000, and

(B) either

(I) at the time of that acquisition was quoted on the OTC Bulletin Board quotation service operated by Nasdaq Stock Market, Inc. or on the OTC quotation service operated by Pink Sheets LLC, or

(II) at the time of that acquisition was a qualified investment for the plan trust and at any time in the period that began at the time of that acquisition and ended before September 2000 was quoted on the OTC Bulletin Board quotation service operated by Nasdaq Stock Market, Inc. or on the OTC quotation service operated by Pink Sheets LLC, or

(ii) that

(A) was acquired by the plan trust after August 2000 from another plan trust under which the annuitant or beneficiary is also the annuitant or beneficiary under the plan trust,

(B) immediately before its acquisition by the plan trust was a qualified investment for the other plan trust, and

(C) would be a qualified investment for the plan trust because of this paragraph if this paragraph were read without reference to this subparagraph and the plan trust had acquired the security before September 2000;

S. 4900(1)(*w*) was added by S.C. 2009, c. 2, s. 105(7), applicable in determining whether a property is, at any time after 2005, a qualified investment, except that in applying paragraph 4900(1)(*w*) before December 14, 2007, it is to be read as follows:

"(*w*) an American Depositary Receipt where the property represented by the receipt is listed on a stock exchange referred to in section 3200 or 3201."

Related Sections: 207.01(1) qualified investment.

Tax Profile: August 2004 — Canadian Tax Treatment of Index Participation Units and Exchange-Traded Index Derivatives.

Income Tax Folios: *Primary* — S3-F10-C1 Qualified Investments - RRSPs, RESPs, RRIFs, RDSPs and TFSAs. *Secondary* — S3-F10-C2 Prohibited Investments - RRSPs, RRIFs and TFSAs.

Information Circulars: IC 77-1R5 Deferred profit sharing plan; IC 78-14R4 Guidelines for trust companies and other persons responsible for filing T3GR, T3D, T3P, T3S, T3RI, and T3F returns.

(2) For the purposes of paragraph (*c*.1) of the definition "qualified investment" in section 204 of the Act, each of the following is a prescribed credit rating agency:

(*a*) A.M. Best Company, Inc.;

(*b*) DBRS Limited;

(*c*) Fitch, Inc.;

(*d*) Moody's Investors Service, Inc.; and

(*e*) Standard & Poor's Financial Services LLC.

History: S. 4900(2)(*b*) was replaced by P.C. 2011-936, SOR/2011-188, dated September 22, 2011, published in the *Canada Gazette* October 12, 2011, applicable after February 19, 2011. S. 4900(2)(*b*) formerly read:

(*b*) Dominion Bond Rating Service Limited;

S. 4900(2)(*e*) was replaced by P.C. 2011-936, SOR/2011-188, dated September 22, 2011, published in the *Canada Gazette* October 12, 2011, applicable after February 19, 2011. S. 4900(2)(*e*) formerly read:

(*e*) the Standard and Poor's Division of the McGraw-Hill Companies, Inc.

(3) For the purpose of paragraph (*h*) of the definition "qualified investment" in section 204 of the Act, a contract with a licensed annuities provider for an annuity payable to an employee who is a beneficiary under a deferred profit sharing plan beginning not later than the end of the year in which the employee attains 71 years of age, the guaranteed term of which, if any, does not exceed 15 years, is prescribed as a qualified investment for a trust governed by such a plan or revoked plan.

(4) (Repealed by P.C. 2001-1106, SOR/2001-216.)

(5) For the purposes of paragraph (*e*) of the definition *qualified investment* in subsection 146.1(1) of the Act, paragraph (*d*) of the definition *qualified investment* in subsection 146.4(1) of the Act and paragraph (*c*) of the definition *qualified investment* in subsection 207.01(1) of the Act, a property is prescribed as a qualified investment for a trust governed by a registered disability savings plan, a registered education savings plan or a TFSA at any time if at that time the property is an interest in a trust or a share of the capital stock of a corporation that was a registered investment for a trust governed by a registered retirement savings plan during the calendar year in which that time occurs or during the preceding year.

History: S. 4900(5) was replaced by S.C. 2017, c. 33, s. 95(3), deemed in force March 23, 2017, and formerly read:

(5) For the purposes of paragraph (*e*) of the definition "qualified investment" in subsection 146.1(1) of the Act, paragraph (*d*) of the definition "qualified investment" in subsection 205(1) of the Act and paragraph (*c*) of the definition "qualified investment" in subsection 207.01(1) of the Act, a property is prescribed as a qualified investment for a trust governed by a registered disability savings plan, a registered education savings plan or a TFSA at any time if at that time the property is an interest in a trust or a share of the capital stock of a corporation that was a registered investment for a trust governed by a registered retirement savings plan during the calendar year in which that time occurs or during the preceding year.

S. 4900(5) was replaced by S.C. 2009, c. 2, s. 105(8), applicable to the 2009 and subsequent taxation years. S. 4900(5) formerly read:

(5) For the purposes of paragraph (*e*) of the definition "qualified investment" in subsection 146.1(1) of the Act and paragraph (*d*) of the definition "qualified investment" in subsection 205(1) of the Act, a property is prescribed as a qualified investment for a trust governed by a registered education savings plan or a trust governed by a registered disability savings plan at any time if at that time the property is an interest in a trust or a share of the capital stock of a corporation that was a registered investment for a trust governed by a registered retirement savings plan during the calendar year in which that time occurs or during the preceding year.

Related Sections: 146.4(1) qualified investment.

(6) Subject to subsection (9), for the purposes of paragraph (*d*) of the definition *qualified investment* in subsection 146(1) of the Act, paragraph (*e*) of the definition *qualified investment* in subsection 146.1(1) of the Act and paragraph (*c*) of the definition *qualified investment* in subsection 146.3(1) of the Act, a property is prescribed as a qualified investment for a trust governed by a registered retirement savings plan, a registered education savings plan and a registered retirement income fund at any time if at that time the property is not a prohibited investment for the trust and is

(*a*) a share of the capital stock of an *eligible corporation* (as defined in subsection 5100(1));

(*b*) an interest of a limited partner in a small business investment limited partnership; or

(*c*) an interest in a small business investment trust.

History: S. 4900(6), the portion before paragraph (*b*) was replaced by S.C. 2017, c. 33, s. 95(4), applicable in respect of (a) any investment acquired after March 22, 2017; and (b) any investment acquired before March 23, 2017 that ceases to be a "qualified investment" (as defined in subsection 146.1(1) of the Act) after March 22, 2017. S. 4900(6), the portion before paragraph (*b*) formerly read:

(6) Subject to subsections (8) and (9), for the purposes of paragraph (*d*) of the definition "qualified investment" in subsection 146(1) of the Act, paragraph (*e*) of the definition "qualified investment" in subsection 146.1(1) of the Act and paragraph (*c*) of the definition "qualified investment" in subsection 146.3(1) of the Act, a property is prescribed as a qualified investment for a trust governed by a registered retirement savings plan, a registered education savings plan and a registered retirement income fund at any time if at that time the property is not a prohibited investment for the trust and is

(*a*) a share of the capital stock of an eligible corporation (as defined in subsection 5100(1)) unless, in the case of a registered education savings plan, a beneficiary or subscriber under the plan is a designated shareholder of the corporation;

S. 4900(6), the portion before paragraph (*b*) was replaced by S.C. 2011, c. 24, s. 84(1), applicable in respect of investments acquired after March 22, 2011. S. 4900(6), the portion before paragraph (*b*) formerly read:

(6) Subject to subsections (8) and (9), for the purposes of paragraph (*d*) of the definition "qualified investment" in subsection 146(1) of the Act, paragraph (*e*) of the definition "qualified investment" in subsection 146.1(1) of the Act and paragraph (*c*) of the definition "qualified investment" in subsection 146.3(1) of the Act, a property is prescribed as a qualified investment for a trust governed by a registered retirement savings plan, a registered education savings plan and a registered retirement income fund at any time if at that time the property is

(*a*) a share of the capital stock of an eligible corporation (within the meaning assigned by subsection 5100(1)), unless a person who is an annuitant, a beneficiary or a subscriber under the plan or fund is a designated shareholder of the corporation;

(7) Subject to subsection (11), for the purposes of paragraph (*h*) of the definition "qualified investment" in section 204 of the Act, a property is prescribed as a qualified investment for a trust governed by a deferred profit sharing plan or revoked plan at any time if at that time the property is an interest

(*a*) of a limited partner in a small business investment limited partnership; or

(*b*) in a small business investment trust.

(8) (Repealed by S.C. 2017, c. 33, s. 95(5).)

History: S. 4900(8) was repealed by S.C. 2017, c. 33, s. 95(5), applicable in respect of (a) any investment acquired after March 22, 2017; and (b) any investment acquired before March 23, 2017 that ceases to be a "qualified

Regulations

investment" (as defined in subsection 146.1(1) of the Act) after March 22, 2017. S. 4900(8) formerly read:

(8) For the purposes of subsection (6), a property that is held by a trust governed by a registered education savings plan ceases to be a qualified investment for the trust immediately before an amount is received if

(*a*) the property is a share referred to in paragraph (6)(*a*), an interest in a small business investment limited partnership that holds a small business security, or an interest in a small business investment trust that holds a small business security;

(*b*) a person who is a beneficiary or subscriber under the plan provides services to or for the issuer of the share or small business security, or to or for a person related to that issuer;

(*c*) the amount is received in respect of the share or small business security; and

(*d*) it can reasonably be considered, having regard to all the circumstances (including the terms and conditions of the share or small business security or of any related agreement, and the rate of interest or the dividend provided on the share or small business security), that the amount is on account, in lieu or in satisfaction of payment for the services.

S. 4900(8) was replaced by S.C. 2011, c. 24, s. 84(2), applicable in respect of investments acquired after March 22, 2011. S. 4900(8) formerly read:

(8) For the purposes of subsection (6), where

(*a*) a trust governed by a registered retirement savings plan, a registered education savings plan or a registered retirement income fund holds

(i) a share of the capital stock of an eligible corporation (within the meaning assigned by subsection 5100(1)),

(ii) an interest in a small business investment limited partnership that holds a small business security, or

(iii) an interest in a small business investment trust that holds a small business security, and

(*b*) a person who is an annuitant, a beneficiary or a subscriber under the plan or fund provides services to or for the issuer of the share or small business security, or to or for a person related to that issuer, and it can reasonably be considered, having regard to all the circumstances (including the terms and conditions of the share or small business security or of any related agreement, and the rate of interest or the dividend provided on the share or small business security), that any amount received in respect of the share or small business security is on account, in lieu or in satisfaction of payment for the services,

the property referred to in subparagraph (*a*)(i), (ii) or (iii) held by the plan or fund shall, immediately before that amount is received, cease to be and shall not thereafter be a qualified investment for the trust governed by the plan or fund.

(9) For the purposes of subsection (6), where

(*a*) a trust governed by a registered retirement savings plan, a registered education savings plan or a registered retirement income fund holds

(i) an interest in a small business investment limited partnership, or

(ii) an interest in a small business investment trust

that holds a small business security (referred to in this subsection as the "designated security") of a corporation, and

(*b*) a person who is an annuitant, a beneficiary or a subscriber under the plan or fund is a designated shareholder of the corporation,

the interest shall not be a qualified investment for the trust governed by the plan or fund unless

(*c*) the designated security is a share of the capital stock of an eligible corporation,

(*d*) the partnership or trust, as the case may be, has no right to set off, assign or otherwise apply, directly or indirectly, the designated security against the interest,

(*e*) no person is obligated in any way, either absolutely or contingently, under any undertaking the intent or effect of which is

(i) to limit any loss that the plan or fund may sustain by virtue of the ownership, holding or disposition of the interest, or

(ii) to ensure that the plan or fund will derive earnings by virtue of the ownership, holding or disposition of the interest,

(*f*) in the case of the partnership, there are more than 10 limited partners and no limited partner or group of limited partners who do not deal with each other at arm's length holds more than 10 per cent of the units of the partnership, and

(*g*) in the case of the trust, there are more than 10 beneficiaries and no beneficiary or group of beneficiaries who do not deal with each other at arm's length holds more than 10 per cent of the units of the trust.

(10) (Repealed by S.C. 2011, c. 24, s. 84(3).)

History: S. 4900(10) was repealed by S.C. 2011, c. 24, s. 84(3), in force on Royal Assent, December 15, 2011. S. 4900(10) formerly read:

(10) For the purposes of paragraphs (9)(*f*) and (*g*), a trust governed by a plan or fund shall be deemed not to deal at arm's length with a trust governed by another plan or fund if a person who is an annuitant, a beneficiary or a subscriber under the plan or fund is the same person as, or does not deal at arm's length with, the annuitant, beneficiary or subscriber under the other plan or fund.

(11) For the purposes of subsection (7), where

(*a*) a trust governed by a deferred profit sharing plan or revoked plan holds

(i) an interest in a small business investment limited partnership, or

(ii) an interest in a small business investment trust

that holds a small business security of a corporation,

(*b*) payments have been made in trust to a trustee under the deferred profit sharing plan or revoked plan for the benefit of beneficiaries thereunder by the corporation or a corporation related thereto, and

(*c*) the small business security is not an equity share described in paragraph (*e*) of the definition "qualified investment" in section 204 of the Act,

the interest referred to in subparagraphs (*a*)(i) and (ii) shall not be a qualified investment for the trust referred to in paragraph (*a*).

(12) (Repealed by S.C. 2017, c. 33, s. 95(6).)

History: S. 4900(12) was repealed by S.C. 2017, c. 33, s. 95(6), applicable in respect of (a) any investment acquired after March 22, 2017; and (b) any investment acquired before March 23, 2017 that ceases to be a "qualified investment" (as defined in subsection 146.1(1) of the Act) after March 22, 2017. S. 4900(12) formerly read:

(12) For the purposes of paragraph (*e*) of the definition "qualified investment" in subsection 146.1(1) of the Act, a property is prescribed as a qualified investment for a trust governed by a registered education savings plan at any time if

(*a*) at the time the property was acquired by the trust,

(i) the property was a share of the capital stock of a specified small business corporation,

(ii) the property was a share of the capital stock of a venture capital corporation described in any of sections 6700 to 6700.2, or

(iii) the property was a qualifying share in respect of a specified cooperative corporation and the plan; and (*b*) immediately after the time the property was acquired by the trust, each person who is a beneficiary or a subscriber under the plan was not a connected shareholder of the corporation.

S. 4900(12) was replaced by S.C. 2011, c. 24, s. 84(4), applicable in respect of investments acquired after March 22, 2011. S. 4900(12) formerly read:

(12) For the purposes of paragraph (*d*) of the definition "qualified investment" in subsection 146(1) of the Act, paragraph (*e*) of the definition "qualified investment" in subsection 146.1(1) of the Act and paragraph (*c*) of the definition "qualified investment" in subsection 146.3(1) of the Act, a property is prescribed as a qualified investment for a trust governed by a registered retirement savings plan, a registered education savings plan or a registered retirement income fund at any time if, at the time the property was acquired by the trust,

(*a*) the property was a share of the capital stock of a specified small business corporation,

(*b*) the property was a share of the capital stock of a venture capital corporation described in any of sections 6700, 6700.1 or 6700.2, or

(*c*) the property was a qualifying share in respect of a specified cooperative corporation and the plan or fund

and, immediately after the time the property was acquired by the trust, each person who is an annuitant, a beneficiary or a subscriber under the plan or fund at that time was not a connected shareholder of the corporation.

S. 4900(12)(*a*) was replaced by S.C. 2009, c. 2, s. 105(9), applicable to the 2009 and subsequent taxation years. S. 4900(12)(*a*) formerly read:

(*a*) the property was a share of the capital stock of a corporation (other than a cooperative corporation) that would, at that time or at the end of the last taxation year of the corporation ending before that time, be a small business corporation if the expression "Canadian-controlled private corporation" in the definition "small business corporation" in subsection 248(1) of the Act were read as "Canadian corporation (other than a corporation controlled at that time, directly or indirectly in any manner whatever, by one or more non-resident persons)",

(13) (Repealed by S.C. 2017, c. 33, s. 95(6).)

History: S. 4900(13) was repealed by S.C. 2017, c. 33, s. 95(6), applicable in respect of (a) any investment acquired after March 22, 2017; and (b) any investment acquired before March 23, 2017 that ceases to be a "qualified investment" (as defined in subsection 146.1(1) of the Act) after March 22, 2017. S. 4900(13) formerly read:

(13) Notwithstanding subsection (12), where

(*a*) a share that is otherwise a qualified investment for the purposes of paragraph (*e*) of the definition "qualified investment" in subsection 146.1(1) of the Act solely because of subsection (12) is held by a trust governed by a registered education savings plan,

(*b*) an individual

(i) provides services to or for,

(ii) acquires goods from, or

(iii) is provided services by

the issuer of the share or a person related to that issuer,

(*c*) an amount is received in respect of the share by the trust, and

(*d*) the amount can reasonably be considered, having regard to all the circumstances, including the terms and conditions of the share, or any agreement relating thereto and any dividend provided on the share to be

(i) on account of, or in lieu or in satisfaction of, payment for the services to or for the issuer or the person related to the issuer, or

(ii) in respect of the acquisition of the goods from, or the services provided by, the issuer or the person related to the issuer,

the share shall, immediately before the amount is received, cease to be and shall not thereafter be a qualified investment for the trust.

S. 4900(13)(*a*) was replaced by S.C. 2011, c. 24, s. 84(5), applicable in respect of investments acquired after March 22, 2011. S. 4900(13)(*a*) formerly read:

(*a*) a share that is otherwise a qualified investment for the purposes of paragraph (*d*) of the definition "qualified investment" in subsection 146(1) of the Act, paragraph (*e*) of the definition "qualified investment" in subsection 146.1(1) of the Act and paragraph (*c*) of the definition "qualified investment" in subsection 146.3(1) of the Act solely because of subsection (12) is held by a trust governed by a registered retirement savings plan, registered education savings plan or registered retirement income fund,

(14) For the purposes of paragraph (*d*) of the definition *qualified investment* in subsection 146(1) of the Act, paragraph (*e*) of the definition *qualified investment* in subsection 146.1(1) of the Act, paragraph (*c*) of the definition *qualified investment* in subsection 146.3(1) of the Act and paragraph (*c*) of the definition *qualified investment* in subsection 207.01(1) of the Act, a property is prescribed as a qualified investment for a trust governed by a RESP, RRIF, RRSP or TFSA at any time if, at the time the property was acquired by the trust, the property

(*a*) was

(i) a share of the capital stock of a specified small business corporation,

(ii) a share of the capital stock of a venture capital corporation described in any of sections 6700 to 6700.2, or

(iii) a qualifying share in respect of a specified cooperative corporation and the RESP, RRIF, RRSP or TFSA; and

(*b*) was not a prohibited investment for the trust.

History: S. 4900(14), the portion before paragraph (*a*) was replaced by S.C. 2017, c. 33, s. 95(7), applicable in respect of (a) any investment acquired after March 22, 2017; and (b) any investment acquired before March 23, 2017 that ceases to be a "qualified investment" (as defined in subsection 146.1(1) of the Act) after March 22, 2017. S. 4900(14), the portion before paragraph (*a*) formerly read:

(14) For the purposes of paragraph (*d*) of the definition "qualified investment" in subsection 146(1) of the Act, paragraph (*c*) of the definition "qualified investment" in subsection 146.3(1) of the Act and paragraph (*c*) of the definition "qualified investment" in subsection 207.01(1) of the Act, a property is prescribed as a qualified investment for a trust governed by a RRIF, RRSP or TFSA at any time if, at the time the property was acquired by the trust, the property

S. 4900(14)(*a*)(iii) was replaced by S.C. 2017, c. 33, s. 95(8), applicable in respect of (a) any investment acquired after March 22, 2017; and (b) any investment acquired before March 23, 2017 that ceases to be a "qualified investment" (as defined in subsection 146.1(1) of the Act) after March 22, 2017. S. 4900(14)(*a*)(iii) formerly read:

(iii) a qualifying share in respect of a specified cooperative corporation and the RRIF, RRSP or TFSA; and

S. 4900(14), the portion before paragraph (*a*) was replaced by S.C. 2011, c. 24, s. 84(6), applicable in respect of investments acquired after March 22, 2011. S. 4900(14), the portion before paragraph (*a*) formerly read:

(14) For the purposes of paragraph (*c*) of the definition "qualified investment" in subsection 207.01(1) of the Act, a property is prescribed as a qualified investment for a trust governed by a TFSA at any time if, at the time the property was acquired by the trust, the property

S. 4900(14)(*a*)(iii) was replaced by S.C. 2011, c. 24, s. 84(7), applicable in respect of investments acquired after March 22, 2011. S. 4900(14)(*a*)(iii) formerly read:

(iii) a qualifying share in respect of a specified cooperative corporation and the TFSA; and

S. 4900(14) was added by S.C. 2009, c. 2, s. 105(10), applicable to the 2009 and subsequent taxation years.

(15) For the purposes of the definition *prohibited investment* in subsection 207.01(1) of the Act, property that is a qualified investment for a trust governed by a RESP, RRIF, RRSP or TFSA solely because of subsection (14) is prescribed property for the trust at any time if, at that time, the property is not described in any of subparagraphs (14)(*a*)(i) to (iii).

History: S. 4900(15) was replaced by S.C. 2017, c. 33, s. 95(9), applicable in respect of (a) any investment acquired after March 22, 2017; and (b) any investment acquired before March 23, 2017 that ceases to be a "qualified investment" (as defined in subsection 146.1(1) of the Act) after March 22, 2017. S. 4900(15) formerly read:

(15) For the purposes of the definition "prohibited investment" in subsection 207.01(1) of the Act, property that is a qualified investment for a trust governed by a RRIF, RRSP or TFSA solely because of subsection (14) is prescribed property for the trust at any time if, at that time, the property is not described in any of subparagraphs (14)(*a*)(i) to (iii).

S. 4900(15) was added by S.C. 2013, c. 40, s. 108(1), deemed to have come into force on March 23, 2011.

Income Tax Folios: *Primary* — S3-F10-C2 Prohibited Investments - RRSPs, RRIFs and TFSAs.

Tax Window Files: Application of subsection 4900(15), *May 28, 2015*, CRA Document No. 2015-0579671E5.

4901. Interpretation

(1) For the purposes of paragraphs 204.4(2)(*b*), (*d*) and (*f*) and of subsection 204.6(1) of the Act, a property is a prescribed investment for a corporation or trust, as the case may be, if it is a qualified investment for a plan or fund described in paragraphs 204.4(1)(*a*) to (*d*) of the Act in respect of which the corporation or trust is seeking registration or has been registered, as the case may be.

(1.1) (Revoked.)

(2) In this Part,

"allocation in proportion to patronage" has the meaning assigned by subsection 135(4) of the Act;

"connected person" under a governing plan of a plan trust means a person who is an annuitant, a beneficiary, an employer or a subscriber under, or a holder of, the governing plan and any person who does not deal at arm's length with that person;

History: S. 4901(2), the definition "connected person" was replaced by S.C. 2009, c. 2, s. 106(2), applicable to the 2009 and subsequent taxation years. S. 4901(2), the definition "connected person" formerly read:

"connected person", in relation to a governing plan of a plan trust, means a person who is an annuitant, a beneficiary, an employer or a subscriber under, or a holder of, the governing plan and any person who does not deal at arm's length with that person;

"connected shareholder" of a corporation at any time is a person (other than an exempt person in respect of the corporation) who owns, directly or indirectly, at that time, not less than 10% of the issued shares of any class of the capital stock of the corporation or of any other corporation that is related to the corporation and, for the purposes of this definition,

(*a*) paragraphs (*a*) to (*e*) of the definition "specified shareholder" in subsection 248(1) of the Act apply, and

(*b*) an exempt person in respect of a corporation is a person who deals at arm's length with the corporation where the total of all amounts, each of which is the cost amount of any share of the capital stock of the corporation, or of any other corporation that is related to it, that the person owns or is deemed to own for the purposes of the definition "specified shareholder" in subsection 248(1) of the Act, is less than $25,000;

"consumer goods or services" has the meaning assigned by subsection 135(4) of the Act;

"designated shareholder" of a corporation at any time means a taxpayer who at that time

(*a*) is, or is related to, a person (other than an exempt person) who owns, directly or indirectly, not less than 10% of the issued shares of any class of the capital stock of the corporation or of any other corporation that is related to the corporation and, for the purposes of this definition,

(i) paragraphs (*a*) to (*e*) of the definition "specified shareholder" in subsection 248(1) of the Act apply, and

(ii) an exempt person in respect of a corporation is a person who deals at arm's length with the corporation where the total of all amounts, each of which is the cost amount of any share of the capital stock of the corporation, or of any other corporation that is related to it, that the person owns or is deemed to own for the purposes of the definition "specified shareholder" in subsection 248(1) of the Act, is less than $25,000,

(*b*) is or is related to a member of a partnership that controls the corporation,

(*c*) is or is related to a beneficiary under a trust that controls the corporation,

(*d*) is or is related to an employee of the corporation or a corporation related thereto, where any group of employees of the corporation or of the corporation related thereto, as the case may be, controls the corporation, except where the group of employees includes a person or a related group that controls the corporation, or

(*e*) does not deal at arm's length with the corporation;

"governing plan" means a deferred profit sharing plan or a revoked plan, a registered disability savings plan, a registered education savings plan, a registered retirement income fund, a registered retirement savings plan or a TFSA;

History: S. 4901(2), the definition "governing plan" was replaced by S.C. 2009, c. 2, s. 106(1), applicable to the 2009 and subsequent taxation years. S. 4901(2), the definition "governing plan" formerly read:

"governing plan" means a registered retirement savings plan, a registered education savings plan, a registered retirement income fund, a registered disability savings plan, a deferred profit sharing plan or a revoked plan;

"plan trust" means a trust governed by a governing plan;

"qualifying share", in respect of a specified cooperative corporation and a governing plan, means a share of the capital or capital stock of the corporation where

(*a*) ownership of the share or a share identical to the share is not a condition of membership in the corporation, or

(*b*) a connected person under the governing plan

(i) has not received a payment from the corporation pursuant to an allocation in proportion to patronage in respect of consumer goods or services, and

(ii) can reasonably be expected not to receive a payment, after the acquisition of the share by the plan trust, from the corporation pursuant to an allocation in proportion to patronage in respect of consumer goods or services;

History: S. 4901(2), the definition "qualifying share" was replaced by S.C. 2009, c. 2, s. 106(1), applicable to the 2009 and subsequent taxation years. S. 4901(2), the definition "qualifying share" formerly read:

"qualifying share", in respect of a specified cooperative corporation and a registered retirement savings plan, registered education savings plan or registered retirement income fund, means a share of the capital or capital stock of the corporation where

(*a*) ownership of the share or a share identical to the share is not a condition of membership in the corporation, or

(*b*) a person who is an annuitant, a beneficiary or a subscriber under the plan or fund (or any other person related to that person)

(i) has not received a payment from the corporation after November 29, 1994 pursuant to an allocation in proportion to patronage in respect of consumer goods or services, and

(ii) can reasonably be expected not to receive a payment, after the acquisition of the share by the trust governed by the plan or fund, from the corporation pursuant to an allocation in proportion to patronage in respect of consumer goods or services;

"revoked plan" has the meaning assigned by section 204 of the Act;

"small business investment limited partnership" has the meaning assigned by subsection 5102(1);

"small business investment trust" has the meaning assigned by subsection 5103(1);

"small business security" has the meaning assigned by subsection 5100(2);

"specified cooperative corporation" means

(*a*) a cooperative corporation within the meaning assigned by subsection 136(2) of the Act, or

(*b*) a corporation that would be a cooperative corporation within the meaning assigned by subsection 136(2) of the Act if the purpose described in that subsection were the purpose of providing employment to the corporation's members or customers;

"specified small business corporation", at any time, means a corporation (other than a cooperative corporation) that would, at that time or at the end of the last taxation year of the corporation that ended before that time, be a small business corporation if the expression "Canadian-controlled private corporation" in the definition "small business corporation" in subsection 248(1) of the Act were read as "Canadian corporation (other than a corporation controlled at that time, directly or indirectly in any manner whatever, by one or more non-resident persons)".

History: S. 4901(2), the definition "specified small business corporation" was added by S.C. 2009, c. 2, s. 106(3), applicable to the 2009 and subsequent taxation years.

(2.1) For the purposes of the definition "connected shareholder" in subsection (2) and of subsection (2.2), each share of the capital of a specified cooperative corporation and all other shares of the capital of the corporation that have attributes identical to the attributes of that share shall be deemed to be shares of a class of the capital stock of the corporation.

(2.2) For the purpose of this Part, a person is deemed to be a connected shareholder of a corporation at any time where the person would be a connected shareholder of the corporation at that time if, at that time,

(*a*) the person had each right that the person would be deemed to own at that time for the purposes of the definition "specified shareholder" in subsection 248(1) of the Act if that right were a share of the capital stock of a corporation;

(*b*) the person owned each share of a class of the capital stock of a corporation that the person had a right at that time under a contract, in equity or otherwise, either immediately or in the future and either absolutely or contingently, to acquire; and

(*c*) the cost amount to the person of a share referred to in paragraph (*b*) were the cost amount to the person of the right to which the share relates.

(2.3) For the purpose of this Part, a person is deemed to be a designated shareholder of a corporation at any time if the person would be a designated shareholder of the corporation at that time if, at that time, paragraphs (2.2)(*a*) to (*c*) applied in respect of that person.

(3) (Repealed.)

Part L

Tax-Free Savings Accounts — Prohibited Investments [Repealed.]

History: Part L was repealed by S.C. 2013, c. 40, s. 109(1), deemed to have come into force on March 23, 2011.

Part L was added by S.C. 2009, c. 2, s. 107(1), applicable to the 2009 and subsequent taxation years.

5000. Non-prohibited investment

(Repealed by S.C. 2013, c. 40, s. 109(1).)

History: S. 5000 was repealed by S.C. 2013, c. 40, s. 109(1), deemed to have come into force on March 23, 2011, and formerly read:

5000. *Non-prohibited investment.* For the purpose of the definition "prohibited investment" in subsection 207.01(1) of the Act, an investment is prescribed excluded property at any time if it is

(*a*) property described in paragraph 4900(1)(*j.1*); or

(*b*) a share of a mutual fund corporation or a unit of a mutual fund trust where

(i) the corporation or trust is a mutual fund that is subject to, and substantially complies with, the requirements of *National Instrument 81-102 Mutual Funds*, as amended from time to time, of the Canadian Securities Administrators, and

(ii) the time is before the end of the second taxation year of the corporation or trust.

S. 5000 was replaced by S.C. 2011, c. 24, s. 85(1), applicable after March 22, 2011 in respect of investments acquired at any time. S. 5000 formerly read:

Investment not prohibited

5000. For the purpose of the portion of the definition "prohibited investment" in subsection 207.01(1) of the Act before paragraph (*a*), property described in paragraph 4900(1)(*j.1*) is prescribed property.

5001. Prohibited investment

(Repealed by S.C. 2013, c. 40, s. 109(1).)

History: S. 5001 was repealed by S.C. 2013, c. 40, s. 109109(1), deemed to have come into force on March 23, 2011, and formerly read:

5001. *Prohibited investment.* For the purpose of the definition "prohibited investment" in subsection 207.01(1) of the Act, property that is a qualified investment for a trust governed by a RRIF, RRSP or TFSA solely because of subsection 4900(14) is prescribed property for the trust at any time if, at that time, it is not described in any of subparagraphs 4900(14)(*a*)(i) to (iii).

S. 5001 was replaced by S.C. 2011, c. 24, s. 85(1), applicable after March 22, 2011 in respect of investments acquired at any time. S. 5001 formerly read:

Prohibited investment

5001. For the purpose of paragraph (*d*) of the definition "prohibited investment" in subsection 207.01(1) of the Act, property that is a qualified investment for a trust governed by a TFSA solely because of subsection 4900(14) is prescribed property for the trust at any time if, at that time, it is not described in any of subparagraphs 4900(14)(*a*)(i) to (iii).

S. 5001 was added by S.C. 2009, c. 2, s. 107(1), applicable to the 2009 and subsequent taxation years.

5002. Prohibited investment

(Repealed.)

Part LI
Deferred Income Plans, Investments in Small Business

5100. [Interpretation]

(1) In this Part,

"designated rate", at any time, means 150 per cent of the highest of the prime rates generally quoted at that time by the banks to which Schedule A to the *Bank Act* applies;

"eligible corporation", at any time, means

(*a*) a particular corporation that is a taxable Canadian corporation all or substantially all of the property of which is at that time

(i) used in a qualifying active business carried on by the particular corporation or by a corporation controlled by it,

(ii) shares of the capital stock of one or more eligible corporations that are related to the particular corporation, or debt obligations issued by those eligible corporations, or

(iii) any combination of the properties described in subparagraphs (i) and (ii),

(*a*.1) a specified holding corporation, or

(*b*) a venture capital corporation described in section 6700,

but does not include

(*c*) a corporation (other than a mutual fund corporation) that is

(i) a trader or dealer in securities,

(ii) a bank,

(iii) a corporation licensed or otherwise authorized under the laws of Canada or a province to carry on in Canada the business of offering to the public its services as a trustee,

(iv) a credit union,

(v) an insurance corporation, or

(vi) a corporation the principal business of which is the lending of money or the purchasing of debt obligations or a combination of them,

(*d*) a corporation controlled by one or more non-resident persons,

(*e*) a venture capital corporation, other than a venture capital corporation described in section 6700, or

(*f*) a corporation that has made an election in respect of a particular taxation year under subparagraph (iv) of the description of B in paragraph 204.82(2.2)(*c*.1) of the Act, if that time is in the 12-month period that begins on the day that is six months after the day on which the particular taxation year ends;

"qualifying active business", at any time, means any business carried on primarily in Canada by a corporation, but does not include

(*a*) a business (other than a business of leasing property other than real property) the principal purpose of which is to derive income from property (including interest, dividends, rent and royalties), or

(*b*) a business of deriving gains from the disposition of property (other than property in the inventory of the business),

and, for the purposes of this definition, a business carried on primarily in Canada by a corporation, at any time, includes a business carried on by the corporation if, at that time,

(*c*) at least 50 per cent of the full time employees of the corporation and all corporations related thereto employed in respect of the business are employed in Canada, or

(*d*) at least 50 per cent of the salaries and wages paid to employees of the corporation and all corporations related thereto employed in respect of the business are reasonably attributable to services rendered in Canada;

"qualifying obligation", at any time, means a bond, debenture, mortgage, note or other similar obligation of a corporation described in paragraph 149(1)(*o*.2) or (*o*.3) of the Act, if

(*a*) the obligation was issued by the corporation after October 31, 1985,

(*b*) the corporation used all or substantially all of the proceeds of the issue of the obligation within 90 days after the receipt thereof to acquire

(i) small business securities,

(ii) interests of a limited partner in small business investment limited partnerships,

(iii) interests in small business investment trusts, or

(iv) any combination of the properties described in subparagraphs (i) to (iii)

and, except as provided in subsection 5104(1), the corporation was the first person (other than a broker or dealer in securities) to have acquired the properties and the corporation has owned the properties continuously since they were so acquired,

(*c*) the corporation does not hold, and no group of persons who do not deal with each other at arm's length and of which it is a member holds, more than 30 per cent of the outstanding shares of any class of voting stock of another corporation, except where all or any part of those shares were acquired in specified circumstances, within the meaning of subsection 5104(2),

(*d*) the recourse of the holder of the obligation against the corporation with respect to the obligation is limited to the properties acquired with the proceeds of the issue of the obligation and any properties substituted therefor, and

(*e*) the properties acquired with the proceeds of the issue of the obligation have not been disposed of, unless the disposition occurred within the 90 day period immediately preceding that time;

Regulations

"specified holding corporation", at any time, means a taxable Canadian corporation where

(*a*) all or substantially all of the collective property of the corporation and of all other corporations controlled by it (each of which other corporations is referred to in this definition as a "controlled corporation"), other than shares in the capital stock of the corporation or of a corporation related to it and debt obligations issued by it or by a corporation related to it, is at that time used in a qualifying active business carried on by the corporation, and

(*b*) all or substantially all of the property of the corporation is at that time

(i) property used in a qualifying active business carried on by the corporation or a controlled corporation,

(ii) shares of the capital stock of one or more controlled corporations or eligible corporations related to the corporation,

(iii) debt obligations issued by one or more controlled corporations or eligible corporations related to the corporation, or

(iv) any combination of the properties described in subparagraphs (i), (ii) and (iii),

and in a determination of whether property is used in a qualifying active business for the purposes of paragraph (*a*),

(*c*) where a business is carried on by a controlled corporation,

(i) the business shall be deemed to be a business carried on only by the corporation, and

(ii) the controlled corporation shall be deemed to be the corporation in the application of paragraphs (*c*) and (*d*) of the definition "qualifying active business", and

(*d*) if a business of the corporation is substantially similar to one or more other businesses of the corporation, all those businesses shall be deemed collectively to be one business of the corporation;

"specified property" means property described in any of paragraphs (*a*), (*b*), (*c*), (*f*) and (*g*) of the definition "qualified investment" in section 204 of the Act.

(2) For the purposes of this Part and clause (*b*)(iii)(A) of the definition "eligible investment" in subsection 204.8(1) of the Act, a small business security of a person, at any time, is property of that person that is, at that time,

(*a*) a share of the capital stock of an eligible corporation,

(*b*) a debt obligation of an eligible corporation (other than a venture capital corporation described in section 6700) that does not by its terms or any agreement related to the obligation restrict the corporation from incurring other debts and that is

(i) secured solely by a floating charge on the assets of the corporation and that by its terms or any agreement related thereto is subordinate to all other debt obligations of the corporation (other than a small business security issued by the corporation, or a debt obligation that is owing by the corporation to a shareholder of the corporation or a person related to a shareholder of the corporation and that is not secured in any manner whatever), or

(ii) not secured in any manner whatever,

other than a debt obligation that

(iii) where the debt obligation specifies an invariant rate of interest, has an effective annual rate of return that exceeds the designated rate for the day on which the obligation was issued, and

(iv) in any other case, may have an effective annual rate of return at a particular time that exceeds the designated rate at the particular time,

(*c*) an option or right granted by an eligible corporation in conjunction with the issue of a share or debt obligation that qualifies as a small business security to acquire a share of the capital stock of the corporation, or

(*d*) an option or right granted for no consideration by an eligible corporation to a holder of a share that qualifies as a small business security to acquire a share of the capital stock of the corporation

if, immediately after the time of acquisition thereof,

(*e*) the aggregate of the cost amounts to the person of all shares, options, rights and debt obligations of the eligible corporation and all corporations associated therewith held by the person does not exceed $10,000,000,

(*f*) the total assets (determined in accordance with generally accepted accounting principles, on a consolidated or combined basis, where applicable) of the eligible corporation and all corporations associated with it do not exceed $50,000,000

and includes

(*g*) property of the person that is, at that time,

(i) a qualifying obligation, or

(ii) (Repealed.)

(iii) a security (in this subparagraph referred to as the "new security") described in any of paragraphs (*a*) to (*d*), where the new security was issued at a particular time

(A) in exchange for, on the conversion of, or in respect of rights pertaining to a security (in this paragraph referred to as the "former security") that would, if this subsection were read without reference to this subparagraph and paragraph (*h*), be a small business security of the person immediately before the particular time, and

(B) pursuant to an agreement entered into before the particular time and at or before the time that the former security was last acquired by the person, or

(*h*) where the person is a small business investment corporation, small business investment limited partnership or small business investment trust, property of the person that is, at that time, a security (in this

Regulations

paragraph referred to as the "new security") described in any of paragraphs (*a*) to (*d*), where the new security was issued at a particular time not more than 5 years before that time in exchange for, on the conversion of, or in respect of rights pertaining to a security that would, if this subsection were read without reference to this paragraph, be a small business security of the person immediately before the particular time.

(2.1) Where all or part of the property of a person consists of the shares of the capital stock of a venture capital corporation described in section 6700, options or rights granted by the corporation, or debt obligations of the corporation,

(*a*) the aggregate of the cost amounts to the person of all such property shall be deemed for the purposes of paragraph (2)(*e*) not to exceed $10,000,000; and

(*b*) the total assets (determined in accordance with generally accepted accounting principles, on a consolidated or combined basis, where applicable) of the corporation and all corporations associated with it shall be deemed for the purposes of paragraph (2)(*f*) not to exceed $50,000,000.

(3) For the purposes of subsection (2),

(*a*) in determining the effective annual rate of return in respect of a debt obligation of an eligible corporation, the value of any right to convert the debt obligation or any part thereof into, or to exchange the debt obligation or any part thereof for, shares of the capital stock of the corporation or an option or right to acquire such shares shall not be considered; and

(*b*) a corporation shall be deemed not to be associated with another at any time where the corporation would not be associated with the other if

(i) the references to "controlled, directly or indirectly, in any manner whatever" in section 256 of the Act (other than subsection (5.1) thereof) were read as references to "controlled", and

(ii) such rights described in subsection 256(1.4) of the Act and shares, as were held at that time by a small business investment corporation, small business investment limited partnership or small business investment trust, were disregarded.

(4) (Repealed.)

5101. [Small business investment corporation]

(1) Subject to subsection (4), for the purposes of this Part and paragraph 149(1)(*o*.3) and paragraph (*b*) of the definition "small business property" in subsection 206(1) of the Act, a corporation is a small business investment corporation at any time if it is a Canadian corporation incorporated after May 22, 1985 and at all times after it was incorporated and before that time

(*a*) all of the shares, and rights to acquire shares, of the capital stock of the corporation were owned by

(i) one or more registered pension plans,

(ii) one or more trusts all the beneficiaries of which were registered pension plans,

(iii) one or more related segregated fund trusts (within the meaning assigned by paragraph 138.1(1)(*a*) of the Act) all the beneficiaries of which were registered pension plans, or

(iv) one or more persons prescribed by section 4802 for the purposes of clause 149(1)(*o*.2)(iv)(D) of the Act;

(*b*) its only undertaking was the investing of its funds and its investments consisted solely of

(i) small business securities,

(ii) interests of a limited partner in small business investment limited partnerships,

(iii) interests in small business investment trusts,

(iv) property (other than a small business security) that is

(A) a share of the capital stock of a corporation (other than a share that is issued to the corporation and that is either a share described in section 66.3 of the Act or a share in respect of which an amount has been designated under subsection 192(4) of the Act), or

(B) a put, call, warrant or other right to acquire or sell a share described by clause (A),

(v) specified properties, or

(vi) any combination of properties described in any of subparagraphs (i) to (v)

and, except as provided in subsection 5104(1), with respect to properties referred to in any of subparagraphs (i) to (iii), the corporation was the first person (other than a broker or dealer in securities) to have acquired the properties and the corporation has owned the properties continuously since they were so acquired;

(*c*) it has complied with subsection (2);

(*d*) it did not hold, and no group of persons who did not deal with each other at arm's length and of which it was a member held, more than 30 per cent of the outstanding shares of any class of voting stock of a corporation, except where

(i) all or any part of those shares were acquired in specified circumstances within the meaning of subsection 5104(2), or

(ii) those shares were of any class of voting stock of a venture capital corporation described in section 6700;

(*e*) it has not borrowed money except from its shareholders; and

(*f*) it has not accepted deposits.

(2) Every small business investment corporation shall at all times hold properties referred to in subparagraphs (1)(*b*)(i) to (iii), the aggregate of the cost amounts of which is not less than 75 per cent of the amount, if any, by which

(*a*) the aggregate of all amounts each of which is the amount of consideration for the issue of shares of its capital stock or debt to its shareholders or the amount of a contribution of capital by its share-

Regulations

holders received by it more than 90 days before that time

exceeds

(*b*) the aggregate of

(i) all amounts paid by it before that time to its shareholders as a return of capital or a repayment of debt, and

(ii) the amount, if any, by which the aggregate of its losses from the disposition of properties disposed of before that time exceeds the aggregate of its gains from the disposition of properties disposed of before that time.

(3) For the purposes of subsection (2), where a small business investment corporation disposes of a property referred to in subparagraphs (1)(*b*)(i) to (iii), it shall be deemed to continue to hold the investment for a period of 90 days following the date of the disposition.

(4) For the purposes of paragraph 149(1)(*o*.3) of the Act, where a small business investment corporation holds an interest in a partnership or trust that qualified as a small business investment limited partnership or small business investment trust, as the case may be, when the interest was acquired and that, but for this subsection, would cease at a subsequent time to so qualify, the interest in the partnership or trust shall be deemed to be an interest in a small business investment limited partnership or small business investment trust, as the case may be, for the 24 months immediately following the subsequent time.

5102. [Small business investment limited partnership]

(1) For the purpose of this Part, a partnership is a small business investment limited partnership at any particular time if at all times after it was formed and before the particular time

(*a*) it had only one general partner,

(*b*) the share of the general partner, as general partner, in any income of the partnership from any source in any place, for any period, was the same as his share, as general partner, in

(i) the income of the partnership from that source in any other place,

(ii) the income of the partnership from any other source,

(iii) the loss of the partnership from any source,

(iv) any capital gain of the partnership, and

(v) any capital loss of the partnership

for that period, except that the share of the general partner, as general partner, in the income or loss of the partnership from specified properties may differ from his share, as general partner, in the income or loss of the partnership from other sources,

(*c*) the share of the general partner, as general partner, in any income or loss of the partnership for any period was not less than his share, as general partner, in the income or loss of the partnership for any preceding period;

(*d*) the interests of the limited partners were described by reference to units of the partnership that were identical in all respects,

(*e*) no limited partner or group of limited partners who did not deal with each other at arm's length held more than 30 per cent of the units of the partnership and, for the purposes of this paragraph,

(i) a small business investment corporation that has not borrowed money and in which no shareholder or group of shareholders who did not deal with each other at arm's length held more than 30 per cent of the outstanding shares of any class of voting stock shall be deemed not to be a limited partner, and

(ii) the general partner shall be deemed not to hold any unit of the partnership as a limited partner,

(*f*) its only undertaking was the investing of its funds and its investments consisted solely of

(i) small business securities where, except as provided in subsection 5104(1), the partnership was the first person (other than a broker or dealer in securities) to have acquired the securities and it has owned the securities continuously since they were so acquired,

(ii) property (other than a small business security) that is

(A) a share of the capital stock of a corporation (other than a share that is issued to the partnership and that is either a share described in section 66.3 of the Act or a share in respect of which an amount has been designated under subsection 192(4) of the Act), or

(B) a put, call, warrant or other right to acquire or sell a share described by clause (A),

(iii) specified properties, or

(iv) any combination of properties described in any of subparagraphs (i) to (iii),

(*g*) it has complied with subsection (2),

(*h*) it has not borrowed money except for the purpose of earning income from its investments and the amount of any such borrowings at any time did not exceed 20 per cent of the partnership capital at that time, and

(*i*) it has not accepted deposits.

(2) The aggregate of the cost amounts to a small business investment limited partnership of small business securities held by it at any time shall not be less than the amount, if any, by which the aggregate of

(*a*) 25 per cent of the amount, if any, by which

(i) the aggregate of all amounts received by it more than 12 months before that time and not more than 24 months before that time as consideration for the issue of its units or in respect of its units

exceeds

(ii) the aggregate of all amounts paid by it before that time to its members and designated by the partnership as a return of the consideration referred to in subparagraph (i),

(*b*) 50 per cent of the amount, if any, by which

(i) the aggregate of all amounts received by it more than 24 months before that time and not more than 36 months before that time as consideration for the issue of its units or in respect of its units

exceeds

(ii) the aggregate of all amounts paid by it before that time to its members and designated by the partnership as a return of the consideration referred to in subparagraph (i), and

(*c*) 75 per cent of the amount, if any, by which

(i) the aggregate of all amounts received by it more than 36 months before that time as consideration for the issue of its units or in respect of its units

exceeds

(ii) the aggregate of all amounts paid by it before that time to its members and designated by the partnership as a return of the consideration referred to in subparagraph (i),

exceeds 75 per cent of the amount, if any, by which the aggregate of its losses from the disposition of properties disposed of before that time exceeds the aggregate of its gains from the disposition of properties disposed of before that time.

(3) For the purposes of subsection (2), where a small business investment limited partnership disposes of a small business security it shall be deemed to continue to hold the investment for a period of 90 days following the date of the disposition.

5103. [Small business investment trust]

(1) For the purposes of this Part and subsection 259(5) of the Act, a trust is a small business investment trust at any particular time if at all times after it was created and before the particular time

(*a*) it was resident in Canada;

(*b*) the interests of the beneficiaries under the trust were described by reference to units of the trust that were identical in all respects; and [*sic*]

(*c*) no beneficiary or group of beneficiaries who did not deal with each other at arm's length held more than 30% of the units of the trust and, for the purposes of this paragraph, a small business investment corporation that has not borrowed money and in which no shareholder or group of shareholders who did not deal with each other at arm's length held more than 30 per cent of the outstanding shares of any class of voting stock shall be deemed not to be a beneficiary;

(*d*) its only undertaking was the investing of its funds and its investments consisted solely of

(i) small business securities where, except as provided in subsection 5104(1), the trust was the first person (other than a broker or dealer in securities) to have acquired the securities and it has owned the securities continuously since they were so acquired,

(ii) property (other than a small business security) that is

(A) a share of the capital stock of a corporation (other than a share that is issued to the trust and that is either a share described in section 66.3 of the Act or a share in respect of which an amount has been designated under subsection 192(4) of the Act), or

(B) a put, call, warrant or other right to acquire or sell a share described by clause (A),

(iii) specified properties, or

(iv) any combination of properties described in any of subparagraphs (i) to (iii);

(*e*) it has complied with subsection (2);

(*f*) it has not borrowed money except for the purpose of earning income from its investments and the amount of any such borrowings at any time did not exceed 20 per cent of the trust capital at that time; and

(*g*) it has not accepted deposits.

(2) The aggregate of the cost amounts to a small business investment trust of small business securities held by it at any time shall not be less than the amount, if any, by which the aggregate of

(*a*) 25 per cent of the amount, if any, by which

(i) the aggregate of all amounts received by it more than 12 months before that time and not more than 24 months before that time as consideration for the issue of its units or in respect of its units

exceeds

(ii) the aggregate of all amounts paid by it before that time to its beneficiaries and designated by the trust as a return of the consideration referred to in subparagraph (i),

(*b*) 50 per cent of the amount, if any, by which

(i) the aggregate of all amounts received by it more than 24 months before that time and not more than 36 months before that time as consideration for the issue of its units or in respect of its units

exceeds

(ii) the aggregate of all amounts paid by it before that time to its beneficiaries and designated by the trust as a return of the consideration referred to in subparagraph (i), and

(*c*) 75 per cent of the amount, if any, by which

(i) the aggregate of all amounts received by it more than 36 months before that time as consideration for the issue of its units or in respect of its units

exceeds

(ii) the aggregate of all amounts paid by it before that time to its beneficiaries and designated by the trust as a return of the consideration referred to in subparagraph (i)

exceeds 75 per cent of the amount, if any, by which the aggregate of its losses from the disposition of properties disposed of before that time exceeds the aggregate of its

Regulations

gains from the disposition of properties disposed of before that time.

(3) For the purposes of subsection (2), where a small business investment trust disposes of a small business security it shall be deemed to continue to hold the investment for a period of 90 days following the date of disposition.

5104. [Interpretation]

(1) Notwithstanding paragraph (*b*) of the definition "qualifying obligation" in subsection 5100(1) and paragraphs 5101(1)(*b*), 5102(1)(*f*) and 5103(1)(*d*), the corporation, partnership or trust, as the case may be, may acquire a small business security that another person (other than a broker or dealer in securities) had previously acquired if

(*a*) the small business security is a share of the capital stock of an eligible corporation having full voting rights under all circumstances; and

(*b*) except where the share was acquired in specified circumstances within the meaning of subsection (2), the share was acquired from an officer or employee of the eligible corporation or a person related to the officer or employee.

(2) For the purposes of this Part,

(*a*) where a person acquires a share of a corporation

(i) as part of a proposal to, or an arrangement with, the corporation's creditors that has been approved by a court under the *Bankruptcy and Insolvency Act* or the *Companies' Creditors Arrangement Act*,

(ii) at a time when all or substantially all of the corporation's assets were under the control of a receiver, receiver-manager, sequestrator or trustee in bankruptcy, or

(iii) at a time when, by reason of financial difficulty, the corporation was in default, or could reasonably be expected to default, on a debt obligation held by a person with whom the corporation was dealing at arm's length,

the person shall be deemed, at any time within 36 months after he acquired the share, to have acquired it in specified circumstances;

(*b*) where a person acquires a share of a corporation for the purposes of facilitating the disposition of the entire investment of the person in the corporation, the person shall be deemed, at any time within 12 months after he acquired the share, to have acquired it in specified circumstances; and

(*c*) a qualified trust (within the meaning assigned by subsection 259(3) of the Act) is deemed not to hold any property for any period in respect of which subsection 259(1) of the Act is applicable.

(3) Where the purchaser of a property that, but for this subsection, would at the time of its acquisition be a small business security (or, where the purchaser is a partnership, a member thereof) knew at the time of acquisition that the issuer of the security would, within the immediately following 12 months, cease to qualify as an eligible corporation, the property shall be deemed never to have been a small business security of the purchaser.

(4) Where a person who holds a share of or an interest in a corporation, partnership or trust that, but for this subsection, would be a small business investment corporation, small business investment limited partnership or small business investment trust knew at the time of issue of the share or interest, as the case may be, or at the time of making any contribution in respect of the share or interest, that

(*a*) a substantial portion of

(i) the consideration for the issue of the share or interest, or

(ii) the contribution in respect of the share or interest

would not be invested by the corporation, partnership or trust, as the case may be, directly or indirectly in small business securities, and

(*b*) all or substantially all of

(i) the consideration for the issue of the share or interest, or

(ii) the contribution in respect of the share or interest

would be returned to the purchaser within the immediately following 24 months,

the corporation, partnership or trust shall be deemed to have ceased at that time to be a small business investment corporation, small business investment limited partnership or small business investment trust.

(5) Where, but for this subsection, a property that qualified as a small business security when it was acquired would cease at a subsequent time to so qualify, the property shall be deemed to be a small business security for the 24 months immediately following the subsequent time.

(6) For the purposes of this Part, a partnership shall be deemed to be a person.

Regulations

Part LII
Canadian Manufacturing and Processing Profits

5200. Basic Formula

Subject to section 5201, for the purposes of paragraph 125.1(3)(*a*) [subsection 125.1(3) "Canadian manufacturing and processing profits"] of the Act, "Canadian manufacturing and processing profits" of a corporation for a taxation year are hereby prescribed to be that proportion of the corporation's adjusted business income for the year that

(*a*) the aggregate of its cost of manufacturing and processing capital for the year and its cost of manufacturing and processing labour for the year,

is of

(*b*) the aggregate of its cost of capital for the year and its cost of labour for the year.

Forms: T2 SCH 27 — Calculation of Canadian Manufacturing and Processing Profits Deduction.

Income Tax Folios: S4-F15-C1 Manufacturing and Processing.

Interpretation Bulletins: *Secondary* — IT-145R (Consolid.) Canadian manufacturing and processing profits — Reduced rate of corporate tax.

5201. Small Manufacturers' Rule

For the purposes of paragraph 125.1(3)(*a*) [subsection 125.1(3) "Canadian manufacturing and processing profits"] of the Act, "Canadian manufacturing and processing profits" of a corporation for a taxation year are hereby prescribed to be equal to the corporation's adjusted business income for the year where

(*a*) the activities of the corporation during the year were primarily manufacturing or processing in Canada of goods for sale or lease;

(*b*) the aggregate of

(i) the aggregate of all amounts each of which is the income of the corporation for the year from an active business minus the aggregate of all amounts each of which is the loss of the corporation for the year from an active business, and

(ii) if the corporation is associated in the year with a Canadian corporation, the aggregate of all amounts each of which is the income of the latter corporation from an active business for its taxation year coinciding with or ending in the year,

did not exceed $200,000;

(*c*) the corporation was not engaged in any of the activities listed in subparagraphs 125.1(3)(*b*)(i) to (ix) [subsection 125.1(3) "manufacturing or processing"] of the Act at any time during the year;

(*c*.1) the corporation was not engaged in the processing of ore (other than iron ore or tar sands) from a mineral resource located outside Canada to any stage that is not beyond the prime metal stage or its equivalent;

(*c*.2) the corporation was not engaged in the processing of iron ore from a mineral resource located outside Canada to any stage that is not beyond the pellet stage or its equivalent;

(*c*.3) the corporation was not engaged in the processing of tar sands located outside Canada to any stage that is not beyond the crude oil stage or its equivalent; and

(*d*) the corporation did not carry on any active business outside Canada at any time during the year.

Income Tax Folios: S4-F15-C1 Manufacturing and Processing.

Interpretation Bulletins: *Secondary* — IT-145R (Consolid.) Canadian manufacturing and processing profits — Reduced rate of corporate tax.

5202. Interpretation

In this Part, except as otherwise provided in section 5203 or 5204,

"adjusted business income" of a corporation for a taxation year means the amount, if any, by which

(*a*) the aggregate of all amounts each of which is the income of the corporation for the year from an active business carried on in Canada

exceeds

(*b*) the aggregate of all amounts each of which is the loss of the corporation for the year from an active business carried on in Canada;

"Canadian resource profits" has the meaning that would be assigned to the expression "resource profits" by section 1204 if

(*a*) section 1204 were read without reference to subparagraph 1204(1)(*b*)(iv), and

(*b*) the definition "resource activity" in subsection 1206(1) were read without reference to paragraph (*d*) of that definition;

"cost of capital" of a corporation for a taxation year means an amount equal to the aggregate of

(*a*) 10 per cent of the aggregate of all amounts each of which is the gross cost to the corporation of a property referred to in paragraph 1100(1)(*e*), (*f*), (*g*) or (*h*), paragraph 1102(1)(*d*) or (*g*) or Schedule II that

(i) was owned by the corporation at the end of the year, and

(ii) was used by the corporation at any time during the year, and

(*b*) the aggregate of all amounts each of which is the rental cost incurred by the corporation during the year for the use of any property a portion of the gross cost of which would be included by virtue of paragraph (*a*) if the property were owned by the corporation at the end of the year,

but for the purposes of this definition, the gross cost of a property or rental cost for the use of any property does not include that portion of those costs that reflects the extent to which the property was used by the corporation during the year

(*c*) in an active business carried on outside Canada, or

(*d*) to earn Canadian investment income or foreign investment income as defined in subsection 129(4) of the Act;

"cost of labour" of a corporation for a taxation year means an amount equal to the aggregate of

(*a*) the salaries and wages paid or payable during the year to all employees of the corporation for services performed during the year, and

(*b*) all other amounts each of which is an amount paid or payable during the year for the performance during the year, by any person other than an employee of the corporation, of functions relating to

(i) the management or administration of the corporation,

(ii) scientific research and experimental development, or

(iii) a service or function that would normally be performed by an employee of the corporation,

but for the purposes of this definition, the salaries and wages referred to in paragraph (*a*) or other amounts referred to in paragraph (*b*) do not include that portion of those amounts that

(*c*) was included in the gross cost to the corporation of a property (other than a property that was manufactured by the corporation and leased during the year by the corporation to another person) that was included in computing the cost of capital of the corporation for the year, or

(*d*) was related to an active business carried on outside Canada by the corporation;

"cost of manufacturing and processing capital" of a corporation for a taxation year means 100/85 of that portion of the cost of capital of the corporation for that year that reflects the extent to which each property included in the calculation thereof was used directly in qualified activities of the corporation during the year, but the amount so calculated shall not exceed the cost of capital of the corporation for the year;

"cost of manufacturing and processing labour" of a corporation for a taxation year means 100/75 of that portion of the cost of labour of the corporation for that year that reflects the extent to which

(*a*) the salaries and wages included in the calculation thereof were paid or payable to persons for the portion of their time that they were directly engaged in qualified activities of the corporation during the year, and

(*b*) the other amounts included in the calculation thereof were paid or payable to persons for the performance of functions that would be directly related to qualified activities of the corporation during the year if those persons were employees of the corporation,

but the amount so calculated shall not exceed the cost of labour of the corporation for the year;

"gross cost" to a particular person of a property at any time means, in respect of property that has become available for use by the particular person for the purposes of subsection 13(26) of the Act, the capital cost to the particular person of the property computed without reference to subsections 13(7.1), (7.4) and (10), sections 21 and 80 and paragraph 111(4)(*e*) of the Act and, in respect of any other property, nil, and where the particular person acquired the property

(*a*) in the course of a reorganization in respect of which, if a dividend were received by the particular person in the course of the reorganization, subsection 55(2) of the Act would not apply to the dividend by reason of the application of paragraph 55(3)(*b*) of the Act, or

(*b*) from another person with whom the particular person was not dealing at arm's length (otherwise than by reason of a right referred to in paragraph 251(5)(*b*) of the Act) immediately after the property was acquired,

the capital cost to the particular person of the property for the purposes of this definition shall be computed as if the property had been acquired at a capital cost equal to the gross cost of the property to the person from whom the property was acquired by the particular person;

"qualified activities" means

(*a*) any of the following activities, when they are performed in Canada in connection with manufacturing or processing (not including the activities listed in subparagraphs 125.1(3)(*b*)(i) to (ix) [subsection 125.1(3) "manufacturing or processing"] of the Act) in Canada of goods for sale or lease:

(i) engineering design of products and production facilities,

(ii) receiving and storing of raw materials,

(iii) producing, assembling and handling of goods in process,

(iv) inspecting and packaging of finished goods,

(v) line supervision,

(vi) production support activities including security, cleaning, heating and factory maintenance,

(vii) quality and production control,

(viii) repair of production facilities, and

(ix) pollution control,

(*b*) all other activities that are performed in Canada directly in connection with manufacturing or processing (not including the activities listed in subparagraphs 125.1(3)(*b*)(i) to (ix) [subsection 125.1(3) "manufacturing or processing"] of the Act) in Canada of goods for sale or lease, and

(*c*) scientific research and experimental development, as defined in section 2900, carried on in Canada,

but does not include any of

(*d*) storing, shipping, selling and leasing of finished goods,

(*e*) purchasing of raw materials,

(*f*) administration, including clerical and personnel activities,

(*g*) purchase and resale operations,

(*h*) data processing, and

(*i*) providing facilities for employees, including cafeterias, clinics and recreational facilities;

"rental cost" of a property means the rents incurred for the use of that property;

"resource profits" has the meaning assigned by section 1204;

"salaries and wages" means salaries, wages and commissions, but does not include any other type of remuneration, any superannuation or pension benefits, any retiring allowances or any amount referred to in section 6 or 7 of the Act;

"specified percentage" for a taxation year means

(*a*) where the year commences after 1998, 100%, and

(*b*) in any other case, the total of

(i) that proportion of 10% that the number of days in the year that are in 1990 is of the number of days in the year,

(ii) that proportion of 20% that the number of days in the year that are in 1991 is of the number of days in the year,

(iii) that proportion of 30% that the number of days in the year that are in 1992 is of the number of days in the year,

(iv) that proportion of 50% that the number of days in the year that are in 1993 is of the number of days in the year,

(v) that proportion of 64.3% that the number of days in the year that are in 1994 is of the number of days in the year,

(vi) that proportion of 71.4% that the number of days in the year that are in 1995 is of the number of days in the year,

(vii) that proportion of 78.6% that the number of days in the year that are in 1996 is of the number of days in the year,

(viii) that proportion of 85.7% that the number of days in the year that are in 1997 is of the number of days in the year,

(ix) that proportion of 92.9% that the number of days in the year that are in 1998 is of the number of days in the year, and

(x) that proportion of 100% that the number of days in the year that are in 1999 is of the number of days in the year.

Income Tax Folios: S4-F15-C1 Manufacturing and Processing.

5203. Resource Income

(1) Where a corporation has resource activities for a taxation year the following rules apply, except as otherwise provided in section 5204:

"adjusted business income" of the corporation for the year means the amount, if any, by which

(*a*) the amount otherwise determined under section 5202 to be the adjusted business income of the corporation for the year

exceeds the total of

(*b*) the amount, if any, by which the corporation's net resource income for the year exceeds the corporation's net resource adjustment for the year, and

(*c*) all amounts each of which is an amount in respect of refund interest included in computing the taxpayer's income for the year, to the extent that the amount is included in the amount determined to be the adjusted business income, within the meaning of section 5202, of the corporation for the year;

(*d*) (Repealed.)

"cost of capital" of the corporation for the year means the amount, if any, by which

(*a*) the amount otherwise determined under section 5202 to be the cost of capital of the corporation for the year

exceeds

(*b*) that portion of the gross cost of property or rental cost for the use of property included in computing the cost of capital of the corporation for the year that reflects the extent to which the property was used by the corporation during the year,

(i) in activities engaged in for the purpose of earning Canadian resource profits of the corporation, or

(ii) in activities referred to in subparagraph 66(15)(*b*)(i), (ii) or (v) [subsection 66(15) "Canadian exploration and development expenses"], subparagraph 66(15)(*e*)(i) or (ii) [subsection 66(15) "Canadian exploration and development expenses"], subparagraph 66.1(6)(*a*)(i), (ii), (iii) or (v) [subsection 66(15) "Canadian exploration and development expenses"] or subparagraph 66.2(5)(*a*)(i), (ii) or (v) [subsection 66(15) "Canadian exploration and development expenses"] of the Act;

"cost of labour" of the corporation for the year means the amount, if any, by which

(*a*) the amount otherwise determined under section 5202 to be the cost of labour of the corporation for the year

Regulations

exceeds

(*b*) that portion of the salaries and wages and other amounts included in computing the cost of labour of the corporation for the year that,

(i) was related to the activities engaged in for the purpose of earning Canadian resource profits of the corporation, or

(ii) was included in the Canadian exploration and development expenses, foreign exploration and development expenses, Canadian exploration expense or Canadian development expense, within the meanings assigned by paragraphs 66(15)(*b*) and (*e*) [subsection 66(15) "Canadian exploration and development expenses", and "foreign exploration and development expenses"], 66.1(6)(*a*) [subsection 66(15) "Canadian exploration expense"] and 66.2(5)(*a*) [subsection 66(15) "Canadian development expense"] of the Act respectively, of the corporation.

(2) For the purposes of subsection (1), a corporation has "resource activities" for a taxation year if

(*a*) in computing its income for the year, an amount is deductible pursuant to any of sections 65 to 66.2 of the Act;

(*b*) the corporation was at any time during the year engaged in activities for the purpose of earning resource profits of the corporation; or

(*c*) in computing the corporation's income for the year, an amount was included pursuant to section 59 of the Act.

(3) In subsection (1), "net resource income" of a corporation for a taxation year means the amount, if any, by which the total of

(*a*) the resource profits of the corporation for the year, and

(*b*) the amount, if any, by which

(i) the total of amounts included in computing the income of the corporation for the year, from an active business carried on in Canada, pursuant to section 59 of the Act (other than amounts that may reasonably be regarded as having been included in computing the resource profits of the corporation for the year),

exceeds

(ii) the total of amounts deducted in computing the income of the corporation for the year under section 64 of the Act, as that section applies with respect to dispositions occurring before November 13, 1981 and to dispositions occurring after November 12, 1981 pursuant to the terms in existence on that date of an offer or agreement in writing made or entered into on or before that date, except those amounts that may reasonably be regarded as having been deducted in computing the resource profits of the corporation for the year,

exceeds the total of

(*c*) the total of amounts deducted in computing the income of the corporation for the year under section 65 of the Act (other than amounts that may reasonably be regarded as having been deducted in computing the resource profits of the corporation for the year), and

(*d*) the specified percentage for the year of the amount, if any, by which

(i) the corporation's resource profits for the year exceeds the total of

(ii) the corporation's Canadian resource profits for the year, and

(iii) the earned depletion base (within the meaning assigned by subsection 1205(1)) of the corporation at the beginning of its immediately following taxation year.

(3.1) In subsection (1), the net resource adjustment of a corporation for a taxation year is the amount determined by the formula

$$A - B$$

where

A is the amount of Canadian resource profits of the corporation for the year, and

B is the amount that would be the Canadian resource profits of the corporation for the year if

(*a*) subsections 1204(1) and (1.1) provided for the computation of negative amounts where the amounts subtracted in computing gross resource profits (as defined by subsection 1204(1)) and resource profits exceed the amounts added in computing those amounts, and

(*b*) paragraph 1206(3)(*a*) applied so that a negative amount of resource profits of a partnership for a fiscal period that ended in the year were, to the extent of the corporation's share thereof, deducted in computing the corporation's resource profits for the year.

(4) For the purpose of subsection (1), "refund interest" means an amount that is received, or that becomes receivable, after March 6, 1996 from an authority (including a government or municipality) situated in Canada as a consequence of the overpayment of a tax that was not deductible under the Act in computing any taxpayer's income and that was imposed by an Act of Canada or a province or a bylaw of a municipality.

Income Tax Folios: S4-F15-C1 Manufacturing and Processing.

5204. Partnerships

Where a corporation is a member of a partnership at any time in a taxation year of the corporation, the following rules apply:

"cost of capital" of the corporation for the year means an amount equal to the aggregate of

(*a*) 10 per cent of the aggregate of all amounts each of which is the gross cost to the corporation of a property referred to in paragraph 1100(1)(*e*), (*f*), (*g*) or (*h*), paragraph 1102(1)(*d*) or (*g*) or Schedule II that

(i) was owned by the corporation at the end of the year, and

(ii) was used by the corporation at any time during the year,

(*b*) the aggregate of all amounts each of which is the rental cost incurred by the corporation during the year for the use of any property a portion of the gross cost of which would be included by virtue of paragraph (*a*) if the property were owned by the corporation at the end of the year, and

(*c*) that proportion of the aggregate of the amounts that would be determined under paragraphs (*a*) and (*b*) in respect of the partnership for its fiscal period coinciding with or ending in the taxation year of the corporation if the references in those paragraphs to "the corporation" were read as references to "the partnership" and the references in those paragraphs to "the year" were read as references to "the fiscal period of the partnership coinciding with or ending in the year", that

(i) the corporation's share of the income or loss of the partnership for that fiscal period

is of

(ii) the income or loss of the partnership for that fiscal period, as the case may be,

but for the purposes of this definition, the gross cost of a property or rental cost for the use of any property does not include that portion of those costs that reflects the extent to which the property was used by the corporation during the year or by the partnership during its fiscal period coinciding with or ending in the year

(*d*) in an active business carried on outside Canada,

(*e*) to earn Canadian investment income or foreign investment income as defined in subsection 129(4) of the Act on the assumption that subsection 129(4) of the Act applied to a partnership as well as to a corporation,

(*f*) in activities engaged in for the purpose of earning Canadian resource profits of the corporation or the partnership, as the case may be, or

(*g*) in activities referred to in subparagraph 66(15)(*b*)(i), (ii) or (v) [subsection 66(15) "foreign exploration and development expenses"], subparagraph 66(15)(*e*)(i) or (ii) [subsection 66(15) "foreign exploration and development expenses"], subparagraph 66.1(6)(*a*)(i), (ii), (iii) or (v) [subsection 66.1(6) "Canadian exploration expense"] or subparagraph 66.2(5)(*a*)(i), (ii) or (v) [subsection 66.2(5) "Canadian development expense"] of the Act;

"cost of labour" of the corporation for the year means an amount equal to the aggregate of

(*a*) the salaries and wages paid or payable during the year to all employees of the corporation for services performed during the year,

(*b*) all other amounts each of which is an amount paid or payable during the year for the performance during the year, by any person other than an employee of the corporation, of functions relating to

(i) the management or administration of the corporation,

(ii) scientific research as defined in section 2900, or

(iii) a service or function that would normally be performed by an employee of the corporation, and

(*c*) that proportion of the aggregate of the amounts that would be determined under paragraphs (*a*) and (*b*) in respect of the partnership for its fiscal period coinciding with or ending in the taxation year of the corporation if the references in those paragraphs to "the corporation" were read as references to "the partnership" and the references in those paragraphs to "the year" were read as references to "the fiscal period of the partnership coinciding with or ending in the year", that

(i) the corporation's share of the income or loss of the partnership for that fiscal period

is of

(ii) the income or loss of the partnership for that fiscal period, as the case may be,

but for the purposes of this definition, the salaries and wages referred to in paragraph (*a*) or other amounts referred to in paragraph (*b*), of the corporation or the partnership, as the case may be, do not include that portion of those amounts that

(*d*) was included in the gross cost to the corporation or partnership of a property (other than a property that was manufactured by the corporation or partnership and leased during the year by the corporation or the partnership to another person) that was included in computing the cost of capital of the corporation for the year,

(*e*) was related to an active business carried on outside Canada by the corporation or the partnership,

(*f*) was related to the activities engaged in for the purpose of earning Canadian resource profits of the corporation or the partnership, as the case may be, or

(*g*) was included in the Canadian exploration and development expenses, foreign exploration and development expenses, Canadian exploration expense or Canadian development expense, within the meanings assigned by paragraphs 66(15)(*b*) [subsection 66(15) "Canadian exploration and development expenses"] and (*e*) [subsection 66(15) "foreign exploration and development expenses"], 66.1(6)(*a*) [subsection 66.1(6) "Canadian exploration expense"] and 66.2(5)(*a*) [subsection 66.2(5) "Canadian development expense"] of the Act respectively, of the corporation;

"cost of manufacturing and processing capital" of the corporation for the year means 100/85 of that portion of the cost of capital of the corporation for that year that

Regulations

reflects the extent to which each property included in the calculation thereof was used directly in qualified activities

(*a*) of the corporation during the year, or

(*b*) of the partnership during its fiscal period coinciding with or ending in the year, as the case may be,

but the amount so calculated shall not exceed the cost of capital of the corporation for the year;

"cost of manufacturing and processing labour" of the corporation for the year means 100/75 of that portion of the cost of labour of the corporation for that year that reflects the extent to which

(*a*) the salaries and wages included in the calculation thereof were paid or payable to persons for the portion of their time that they were directly engaged in qualified activities

(i) of the corporation during the year, or

(ii) of the partnership during its fiscal period coinciding with or ending in the year, and

(*b*) the other amounts included in the calculation thereof were paid or payable to persons for the performance of functions that would be directly related to qualified activities

(i) of the corporation during the year, or

(ii) of the partnership during its fiscal period coinciding with or ending in the year,

if those persons were employees of the corporation or the partnership, as the case may be,

but the amount so calculated shall not exceed the cost of labour of the corporation for the year;

"gross cost" of a property at any time means

(*a*) in respect of a property that has become available for use by the partnership for the purposes of subsection 13(26) of the Act, the capital cost to the partnership of the property computed without reference to subsections 13(7.1), (7.4) and (10) and sections 21 and 80 of the Act, and

(*b*) in respect of any other property of the partnership, nil,

and, for the purposes of paragraph (*a*), if the partnership acquired the property from a person who was a majority-interest partner of the partnership immediately after the property was acquired, the capital cost to the partnership of the property is to be computed as if the property had been acquired at a capital cost equal to the gross cost to the person of the property, except that if the property was partnership property on December 31, 1971, its gross cost is its capital cost to the partnership as determined under subsection 20(3) or (5) of the *Income Tax Application Rules*.

History: S. 5204, the portion of the definition "gross cost" after paragraph (*b*) was replaced by S.C. 2013, c. 40, s. 110, in force December 12, 2013, and formerly read:

and, for the purposes of paragraph (*a*), where the partnership acquired the property from a person who was a majority interest partner of the partnership (within the meaning assigned by subsection 97(3.1) of the Act) immediately after the property was acquired, the capital cost to the partnership of the property shall be computed as if the property had been acquired at a capital cost equal to the gross cost to the person of the property, except that where the property was partnership property on December 31, 1971, its gross cost shall be its capital cost to the partnership as determined under subsection 20(3) or (5) of the *Income Tax Application Rules*.

Part LIII
Instalment Base

5300. Individuals

For the purposes of subsections 155(2), 156(3) and 161(9) of the Act, the instalment base of an individual for a taxation year is the amount by which

(*a*) the individual's tax payable under Part I of the Act for the year, determined before taking into consideration the specified future tax consequences for the year,

exceeds

(*b*) the amount deemed by subsection 120(2) of the Act to have been paid on account of the individual's tax under Part I of the Act for the year, determined before taking into consideration the specified future tax consequences for the year.

5301. Corporations Under Part I of the Act

(1) Subject to subsections (6) and (8), for the purposes of subsections 157(4) and 161(9) of the Act, the first instalment base of a corporation for a particular taxation year means the product obtained when the aggregate of

(*a*) the tax payable under Part I of the Act by the corporation for its taxation year preceding the particular year, and

(*b*) the total of the taxes payable by the corporation under Parts VI, VI.1 and XIII.1 of the Act for its taxation year preceding the particular year

is multiplied by the ratio that 365 is of the number of days in that preceding year.

History: S. 5301(1)(*b*) was replaced by P.C. 2009-1869, SOR/2009-302, dated November 19, 2009, published in the *Canada Gazette* December 9, 2009, applicable to the 2001 and subsequent taxation years, except that for taxation years that began before 2008, paragraph 5301(1)(*b*) is to be read as follows:

"(*b*) the total of the taxes payable by the corporation under Parts I.3, VI, VI.1 and XIII.1 of the Act for its taxation year preceding the particular year"

S. 5301(1)(*b*) formerly read:

(*b*) the total of the taxes payable by the corporation under Parts I.3, VI and VI.1 of the Act for its taxation year preceding the particular year

(2) Subject to subsections (6) and (8), for the purposes of subsections 157(4) and 161(9) of the Act, the "second instalment base" of a corporation for a particular taxation year means the amount of the first instalment base of the corporation for the taxation year immediately preceding the particular year.

(3) For the purposes of subsection (1), where the number of days in the taxation year of a corporation immediately preceding the particular taxation year referred to therein is less than 183, the amount determined for the corporation under that subsection shall be the greater of

(*a*) the amount otherwise determined for it under subsection (1); and

(*b*) the amount that would be determined for it under subsection (1) if the reference in that subsection to "its taxation year preceding the particular year" were read as a reference to "its last taxation year, preceding the particular year, in which the number of days exceeds 182".

(4) Notwithstanding subsections (1) and (2), for the purposes of subsections 157(4) and 161(9) of the Act,

(*a*) where a particular taxation year of a new corporation that was formed as a result of an amalgamation (within the meaning assigned by section 87 of the Act) is its first taxation year,

(i) its "first instalment base" for the particular year means the total of all amounts each of which is equal to the product obtained when the total of

(A) the tax payable under Part I of the Act, and

(B) the total of the taxes payable under Parts VI, VI.1 and XIII.1 of the Act

by a predecessor corporation (as defined in section 87 of the Act) for its last taxation year is multiplied by the ratio that 365 is to the number of days in that year, and

(ii) its "second instalment base" for the particular year means the aggregate of all amounts each of which is an amount equal to the amount of the first instalment base of a predecessor corporation for its last taxation year; and

(*b*) where a particular taxation year of a new corporation referred to in paragraph (*a*) is its second taxation year,

(i) its "first instalment base" for the particular year means

(A) where the number of days in its first taxation year is greater than 182, the amount that would, but for this subsection, be determined under subsection (1) for the year, and

(B) in any other case, the greater of the amount that would, but for this subsection, be determined under subsection (1) for the year and its first instalment base for its first taxation year, and

(ii) its "second instalment base" for the particular year means the amount of the first instalment base of the new corporation for its first taxation year.

History: S. 5301(4)(*a*)(i)(B) was replaced by P.C. 2009-1869, SOR/2009-302, dated November 19, 2009, published in the *Canada Gazette* December 9, 2009, applicable to the 2001 and subsequent taxation years, except that for taxation years that began before 2008, clause 5301(4)(*a*)(i)(B) is to be read as follows:

"(B) the total of the taxes payable under Parts I.3, VI, VI.1 and XIII.1 of the Act"

S. 5301(4)(*a*)(i)(B) formerly read:

(B) the total of the taxes payable under Parts I.3, VI and VI.1 of the Act

(5) For the purposes of subsection (4), where the number of days in the last taxation year of a predecessor corporation is less than 183, the amount determined under subparagraph (4)(*a*)(i) in respect of the predecessor corporation shall be the greater of

(*a*) the amount otherwise determined under subparagraph (4)(*a*)(i) in respect of the predecessor corporation; and

(*b*) the amount of the first instalment base of the predecessor corporation for its last taxation year.

(6) Subject to subsection (7), where a subsidiary within the meaning of subsection 88(1) of the Act is winding up, and, at a particular time in the course of the winding up, all or substantially all of the property of the subsidiary has been distributed to a parent within the meaning of subsection 88(1) of the Act, the following rules apply:

(*a*) there shall be added to the amount of the parent's first instalment base for its taxation year that includes the particular time the amount of the subsidiary's first instalment base for its taxation year that includes the particular time;

(*b*) there shall be added to the amount of the parent's second instalment base for its taxation year that includes the particular time the amount of the subsidiary's second instalment base for its taxation year that includes the particular time;

(*c*) there shall be added to the amount of the parent's first instalment base for its taxation year immediately following its taxation year referred to in paragraph (*a*) the amount that is the proportion of the subsidiary's first instalment base for its taxation year referred to in paragraph (*a*) that

(i) the number of complete months that ended at or before the particular time in the taxation year of the parent that includes the particular time

is of

(ii) 12; and

(*d*) there shall be added to the amount of the parent's second instalment base for its taxation year immediately following its taxation year referred to in paragraph (*a*) the amount of the subsidiary's first instalment base for its taxation year that includes the particular time.

(7) The amount of an instalment of tax for the taxation year referred to in paragraphs (6)(*a*) and (*b*) that a parent is deemed under subsection 161(4.1) of the Act to have been liable to pay before the particular time referred to in subsection (6) shall be determined as if subsection (6) were not applicable in respect of a distribution of property described in that subsection occurring after the day on or before which the instalment was required to be paid.

(8) Subject to subsection (9), if at a particular time a corporation (in this subsection referred as the "transferor") has disposed of all or substantially all of its property to another corporation with which it was not dealing at arm's length (in this subsection and subsection (9) referred to as the "transferee") and subsection 85(1), (2) or 142.7(3) of the Act applied in respect of the disposition of any of the property, the following rules apply:

(*a*) there shall be added to the amount of the transferee's first instalment base for its taxation year that includes the particular time the amount of the transferor's first instalment base for its taxation year that includes the particular time;

(*b*) there shall be added to the amount of the transferee's second instalment base for its taxation year that includes the particular time the amount of the transferor's second instalment base for its taxation year that includes the particular time;

(*c*) there shall be added to the amount of the transferee's first instalment base for its taxation year immediately following its taxation year referred to in paragraph (*a*) the amount that is the proportion of the transferor's first instalment base for its taxation year referred to in paragraph (*a*) that

(i) the number of complete months that ended at or before the particular time in the taxation year of the transferee that includes the particular time

is of

(ii) 12; and

(*d*) there shall be added to the amount of the transferee's second instalment base for its taxation year immediately following its taxation year referred to in paragraph (*a*) the amount of the transferor's first instalment base for its taxation year that includes the particular time.

History: S. 5301(8), the portion before paragraph (*a*) was replaced by P.C. 2009-1869, SOR/2009-302, dated November 19, 2009, published in the *Canada Gazette* December 9, 2009, applicable after June 27, 1999. S. 5301(8), the portion before paragraph (*a*) formerly read:

(8) Subject to subsection (9), where at a particular time a corporation (in this subsection referred to as the "transferor") has disposed of all or substantially all of its property to another corporation with which it was not dealing at arm's length (in this subsection and subsection (9) referred to as the "transferee") and subsection 85(1) or (2) of the Act applied in respect of the disposition of any of the property, the following rules apply:

(9) The amount of an instalment of tax for the taxation year referred to in paragraphs (8)(*a*) and (*b*) that a transferee is deemed under subsection 161(4.1) of the Act to have been liable to pay before the particular time referred to in subsection (8) shall be determined as if subsection (8) were not applicable in respect of a disposition of property described in that subsection occurring after the day on or before which the instalment was required to be paid.

(10) For the purpose of this section, tax payable under Part I, VI or XIII.1 of the Act by a corporation for a taxation year means the corporation's tax payable for the year under the relevant Part, determined before taking into consideration the specified future tax consequences for the year.

History: S. 5301(10) was replaced by P.C. 2009-1869, SOR/2009-302, dated November 19, 2009, published in the *Canada Gazette* December 9, 2009, applicable to the 2001 and subsequent taxation years, except that for taxation years that began before 2008, subsection 5301(10) of the Regulations, as enacted by subsection 10(4), is to be read as follows:

"(10) For the purpose of this section, tax payable under Part I, I.3, VI or XIII.1 of the Act by a corporation for a taxation year means the corporation's tax payable for the year under the relevant Part, determined before taking into consideration the specified future tax consequences for the year."

S. 5301(10) formerly read:

(10) For the purpose of this section, tax payable under Part I, I.3 or VI of the Act by a corporation for a taxation year means the corporation's tax payable for the year under the relevant Part, determined before taking into consideration the specified future tax consequences for the year.

5302. (Revoked.)

5303. (Revoked.)

5304. (Revoked.)

5305. (Revoked.)

Part LIV
Debtor's Gains on Settlement of Debts [Repealed.]

5400. (Repealed.)

History: Section 5400 was repealed by P.C. 2011-936, SOR/2011-188, dated September 22, 2011, published in the *Canada Gazette* October 12, 2011, applicable to any obligation that is settled or extinguished in taxation years that end after February 21, 1994 [Editorial Note: See S.C. 2017, c. 33, s. 105] and that is not exempt from the application of subsection 27(1) of *An Act to amend the Income Tax Act, the Income Tax Application Rules and related Acts*, S.C. 1995, c. 21, by virtue of paragraph 27(2)(*a*) of that Act. S. 5400 formerly read:

(1) Subject to section 5401, the excess referred to in paragraph 80(1)(*b*) of the Act, after deducting the portion thereof required to be applied as provided in paragraph 80(1)(*a*) of the Act, shall be applied at the time the debt or obligation is settled or extinguished, in the following order to reduce to the maximum extent possible

(*a*) the capital cost of depreciable property of a prescribed class or prescribed classes, as the case may be;

(*b*) the capital cost of depreciable property other than depreciable property of a prescribed class;

(*c*) the adjusted cost base at that time of capital property, other than depreciable property and personal-use property;

(*d*) the adjusted cost base at that time of capital property that is listed personal property; and

(*e*) the adjusted cost base at that time of capital property that is personal-use property, other than listed personal property.

(2) Where an amount is to be applied pursuant to subsection (1), the taxpayer may choose any particular property to make the reduction in the order specified therein.

5401. (Repealed.)

History: Section 5401 was repealed by P.C. 2011-936, SOR/2011-188, dated September 22, 2011, published in the *Canada Gazette* October 12, 2011, applicable to any obligation that is settled or extinguished in taxation years that end after February 21, 1994 [Editorial Note: See S.C. 2017, c. 33, s. 105] and that is not exempt from the application of subsection 27(1) of *An Act to amend the Income Tax Act, the Income Tax Application Rules and related Acts*, S.C. 1995, c. 21, by virtue of paragraph 27(2)(*a*) of that Act. S. 5401 formerly read:

(1) For the purposes of paragraph 5400(1)(*a*), the amount to be applied to reduce the capital cost of a property shall not exceed the lesser of

(*a*) the amount by which

(i) the capital cost of the property

exceeds

(ii) all amounts that would have been allowed to the taxpayer in respect of the property, if it had been the only property that was included in a prescribed class, at the rate that was allowed to him in respect of property of the class in which it was included under regulations made under paragraph 20(1)(*a*) of the Act for the taxation years prior to the year in which the debt or obligation was settled or extinguished; and

(*b*) the amount by which

(i) the undepreciated capital cost of the class at the time the debt or obligation was settled or extinguished

exceeds

(ii) the amount or the aggregate of amounts, if any, that has already been determined under this subsection in respect of another property of the class at the time referred to in subparagraph (i).

(2) For the purposes of paragraph 5400(1)(*b*), the amount to be applied to reduce the capital cost of a property shall not exceed

(*a*) the amount by which the capital cost of the property

exceeds

(*b*) the amount that was allowed to the taxpayer by virtue of Part XVII in respect of the property before the debt or obligation was settled or extinguished.

(3) For the purposes of paragraphs 5400(1)(*c*), (*d*) and (*e*), the amount to be applied to reduce the adjusted cost base of a property shall not exceed the amount by which

(*a*) the aggregate of the cost to the taxpayer of the property and all amounts required by subsection 53(1) of the Act to be included in computing the adjusted cost base to him of that property

exceeds

(*b*) the aggregate of all amounts required by subsection 53(2) of the Act (except paragraph (*c*) thereof) to be deducted in computing the adjusted cost base to him of that property,

at the time the debt or obligation was settled or extinguished.

Part LV
Prescribed Programs and Benefits

5500. Canadian Home Insulation Program

For the purposes of paragraphs 12(1)(*u*), 56(1)(*s*) and 212(1)(*s*) of the Act, the Canadian Home Insulation Program, as authorized and described in Vote 11a of *Appropriation Act No. 3, 1977-78*, as amended, Energy, Mines and Resources Vote 35, Main Estimates, 1981-82 as authorized by *Appropriation Act No. 1, 1981-82*, as amended, or the *Canadian Home Insulation Program Act*, is hereby prescribed to be a program of the Government of Canada relating to home insulation.

5501. Canada Oil Substitution Program

For the purposes of paragraphs 12(1)(*u*), 56(1)(*s*) and 212(1)(*s*) of the Act, the Canada Oil Substitution Program, as authorized and described in paragraph (*a*) or (*b*) of Energy, Mines and Resources Vote 45, Main Estimates, 1981-82 as authorized by *Appropriation Act No. 1, 1981-82*, as amended, or the *Oil Substitution and Conservation Act* is hereby prescribed to be a program of the Government of Canada relating to energy conversion.

5502. Benefits under Government Assistance Programs

For the purposes of subparagraph 56(1)(*a*)(vi) and paragraph 153(1)(*m*) of the Act, the following benefits are prescribed:

(*a*) benefits under the *Labour Adjustment Benefits Act*;

(*b*) benefits under programs to provide income assistance payments, established pursuant to agreements under section 5 of the *Department of Labour Act*; and

(*c*) benefits under programs to provide income assistance payments, administered pursuant to agreements under section 5 of the *Department of Fisheries and Oceans Act*.

5503. Stabilization of Farm Income

(1) For the purposes of the definition "NISA Fund No. 2" in subsection 248(1) of the Act, a prescribed fund is Fonds 2 as defined under the Agri-Québec program established by La Financière agricole du Québec.

Regulations

(2) For the purposes of the definition "net income stabilization account" in subsection 248(1) of the Act, a prescribed account is an account created under the Agri-Québec program established by La Financière agricole du Québec.

History: S. 5503 was added by S.C. 2011, c. 24, s. 86(1), applicable to the 2011 and subsequent taxation years.

Part LVI
Prescribed Distributions

5600. [Prescribed distributions of shares]

For the purpose of section 86.1 of the Act, the following distributions of shares are prescribed:

(*a*) the distribution by Active Biotech AB, on May 10, 1999, of shares of Wilhelm Sonesson AB;

(*b*) the distribution by Orckit Communications Ltd., on June 30, 2000, of shares of Tioga Technologies Ltd.;

(*c*) the distribution by Electrolux AB, on June 12, 2006, of shares of Husqvarna AB;

(*d*) the distribution by Fiat S.p.A., on January 1, 2011 to its common shareholders, of common shares of Fiat Industrial S.p.A;

(*e*) the distribution by Foster's Group Limited, on May 9, 2011 to its common shareholders, of common shares of Treasury Wine Estates Limited;

(*f*) the distribution by Telecom Corporation of New Zealand Limited, on November 30, 2011 to its common shareholders, of common shares of Chorus Limited;

(*g*) the distribution by Tyco International Ltd. of Switzerland, on September 28, 2012 to its common shareholders, of common shares of Pentair Ltd. of Switzerland;

(*h*) the distribution by Siemens AG, on July 5, 2013 to its common shareholders, of common shares of OSRAM Licht AG;

(*i*) the distribution by Brambles Limited, on December 18, 2013 to its common shareholders, of common shares of Recall Holdings Limited; and

(*j*) the distribution by BHP Billiton Limited, on May 24, 2015 to its common shareholders, of common shares of South32 Limited.

History: S. 5600(*j*) was added by S.C. 2017, c. 33, s. 96, in force December 14, 2017.

S. 5600(*g*), (*h*), and (*i*) were added by SOR/2015-170, s. 3, published in the *Canada Gazette, Part II*, July 1, 2015, in force July 1, 2015.

S. 5600(*d*), (*e*), and (*f*) were added by S.C. 2013, c. 40, s. 111(1), deemed to have come into force on January 1, 2011.

S. 5600(*c*) was added by P.C. 2011-936, SOR/2011-188, dated September 22, 2011, published in the *Canada Gazette* October 12, 2011, applicable after June 11, 2006.

Part LVII
Medical Expense Tax Credit

5700. [Prescribed devices and equipment]

For the purposes of paragraph 118.2(2)(*m*) of the Act, a device or equipment is prescribed if it is a

(*a*) wig made to order for an individual who has suffered abnormal hair loss owing to disease, medical treatment or accident;

(*b*) needle or syringe designed to be used for the purpose of giving an injection;

(*c*) device or equipment, including a replacement part, designed exclusively for use by an individual suffering from a severe chronic respiratory ailment or a severe chronic immune system disregulation, but not including an air conditioner, humidifier, dehumidifier, heat pump or heat or air exchanger;

(*c*.1) air or water filter or purifier for use by an individual who is suffering from a severe chronic respiratory ailment or a severe chronic immune system disregulation to cope with or overcome that ailment or disregulation;

(*c*.2) electric or sealed combustion furnace acquired to replace a furnace that is neither an electric furnace nor a sealed combustion furnace, where the replacement is necessary solely because of a severe chronic respiratory ailment or a severe chronic immune system disregulation;

(*c*.3) air conditioner acquired for use by an individual to cope with the individual's severe chronic ailment, disease or disorder, to the extent of the lesser of $1,000 and 50% of the amount paid for the air conditioner;

(*d*) device or equipment designed to pace or monitor the heart of an individual who suffers from heart disease;

(*e*) orthopaedic shoe or boot or an insert for a shoe or boot made to order for an individual in accordance with a prescription to overcome a physical disability of the individual;

(*f*) power-operated guided chair installation, for an individual, that is designed to be used solely in a stairway;

(*g*) mechanical device or equipment designed to be used to assist an individual to enter or leave a bathtub or shower or to get on or off a toilet;

(*h*) hospital bed including such attachments thereto as may have been included in a prescription therefor;

(*i*) device that is exclusively designed to assist an individual in walking where the individual has a mobility impairment;

(*j*) external breast prosthesis that is required because of a mastectomy;

(*k*) teletypewriter or similar device, including a telephone ringing indicator, that enables a deaf or mute individual to make and receive telephone calls;

(*l*) optical scanner or similar device designed to be used by a blind individual to enable him to read print;

(*l*.1) device or software designed to be used by a blind individual, or an individual with a severe learning disability, to enable the individual to read print;

(*m*) power-operated lift or transportation equipment designed exclusively for use by, or for, a disabled individual to allow the individual access to different areas of a building or to assist the individual to gain access to a vehicle or to place the individual's wheelchair in or on a vehicle;

(*n*) device designed exclusively to enable an individual with a mobility impairment to operate a vehicle;

(*o*) device or equipment, including a synthetic speech system, braille printer and large print-on-screen device, designed exclusively to be used by a blind individual in the operation of a computer;

(*p*) electronic speech synthesizer that enables a mute individual to communicate by use of a portable keyboard;

(*q*) device to decode special television signals to permit the script of a program to be visually displayed;

(*q*.1) a visual or vibratory signalling device, including a visual fire alarm indicator, for an individual with a hearing impairment;

(*r*) device designed to be attached to infants diagnosed as being prone to sudden infant death syndrome in order to sound an alarm if the infant ceases to breathe;

(*s*) infusion pump, including disposable peripherals, used in the treatment of diabetes or a device designed to enable a diabetic to measure the diabetic's blood sugar level;

(*s*.1) blood coagulation monitor, including disposable peripherals, for use by an individual who requires anti-coagulation therapy;

(*t*) electronic or computerized environmental control system designed exclusively for the use of an individual with a severe and prolonged mobility restriction;

(*u*) extremity pump or elastic support hose designed exclusively to relieve swelling caused by chronic lymphedema;

(*v*) inductive coupling osteogenesis stimulator for treating non-union of fractures or aiding in bone fusion;

(*w*) talking textbook for use by an individual with a perceptual disability in connection with the individual's enrolment at an educational institution in Canada, or a designated educational institution;

(*x*) Bliss symbol board, or similar device, designed to be used to help an individual who has a speech impairment communicate by selecting the symbols or spelling out words;

(*y*) Braille note-taker designed to be used by a blind individual to allow them to take notes (that can be read back to them or printed or displayed in Braille) with the help of a keyboard;

(*z*) page turner, designed to be used by an individual who has a severe and prolonged impairment that markedly restricts their ability to use their arms or hands to turn the pages of a book or other bound document;

(*z*.1) altered auditory feedback device designed to be used by an individual who has a speech impairment;

(*z*.2) electrotherapy device designed to be used by an individual with a medical condition or by an individual who has a severe mobility impairment;

(*z*.3) standing device designed to be used by an individual who has a severe mobility impairment to undertake standing therapy; and

(*z*.4) pressure pulse therapy device designed to be used by an individual who has a balance disorder.

History: S. 5700(s.1) was added by S.C. 2012, c. 19, s. 18(1), applicable to expenses incurred after 2011.

The heading before s. 5700 was replaced by S.C. 2009, c. 2, s. 108(1), deemed to have come into force on February 27, 2008. The heading before s. 5700 formerly read: "Medical Devices and Equipment"

S. 5700(z1) to (z4) were added by S.C. 2009, c. 2, s. 109(1), applicable to the 2008 and subsequent taxation years.

Income Tax Folios: *Secondary* — S1-F1-C1 Medical Expense Tax Credit.

5701. [Prescribed drugs and medicaments]

For the purpose of subparagraph 118.2(2)(*n*)(ii) of the Act, a drug, medicament or other preparation or substance is prescribed if it

(*a*) is manufactured, sold or represented for use in the diagnosis, treatment or prevention of a disease, disorder or abnormal physical state, or its symptoms, or in restoring, correcting or modifying an organic function;

(*b*) is prescribed for a patient by a medical practitioner; and

(*c*) may, in the jurisdiction in which it is acquired, be lawfully acquired for use by the patient only with the intervention of a medical practitioner.

History: S. 5701 was added by S.C. 2009, c. 2, s. 110(1), deemed to have come into force on February 27, 2008.

Regulations

Part LVIII

Retention of Books and Records

5800. [Required retention period]

(1) For the purposes of paragraph 230(4)(*a*) of the Act, the required retention periods for records and books of account of a person are prescribed as follows:

(*a*) in respect of

(i) any record of the minutes of meetings of the directors of a corporation,

(ii) any record of the minutes of meetings of the shareholders of a corporation,

(iii) any record of a corporation containing details with respect to the ownership of the shares of the capital stock of the corporation and any transfers thereof,

(iv) the general ledger or other book of final entry containing the summaries of the year-to-year transactions of a corporation, and

(v) any special contracts or agreements necessary to an understanding of the entries in the general ledger or other book of final entry referred to in subparagraph (iv),

the period ending on the day that is two years after the day that the corporation is dissolved;

(*b*) in respect of all records and books of account that are not described in paragraph (*a*) of a corporation that is dissolved and in respect of the vouchers and accounts necessary to verify the information in such records and books of account, the period ending on the day that is two years after the day that the corporation is dissolved;

(*c*) in respect of

(i) the general ledger or other book of final entry containing the summaries of the year-to-year transactions of a business of a person (other than a corporation), and

(ii) any special contracts or agreements necessary to an understanding of the entries in the general ledger or other book of final entry referred to in subparagraph (i),

the period ending on the day that is six years after the last day of the taxation year of the person in which the business ceased;

(*d*) in respect of

(i) any record of the minutes of meetings of the executive of a registered charity or registered Canadian amateur athletic association,

(ii) any record of the minutes of meetings of the members of a registered charity or registered Canadian amateur athletic association, and

(iii) all documents and by-laws governing a registered charity or registered Canadian amateur athletic association,

(iv) (Repealed.)

the period ending on the day that is two years after the date on which the registration of the registered charity or the registered Canadian amateur athletic association under the Act is revoked;

(*e*) in respect of all records and books of account that are not described in paragraph (*d*) and that relate to a registered charity or registered Canadian amateur athletic association whose registration under the Act is revoked, and in respect of the vouchers and accounts necessary to verify the information in such records and books of account, the period ending on the day that is two years after the date on which the registration of the registered charity or the registered Canadian amateur athletic association under the Act is revoked;

Amendment not yet in force
Budget Implementation Act, 2019, No. 1 [S.C. 2019, c. 29]

S. 5800(1)(*d*) and (*e*) were replaced by S.C. 2019, c. 29, s. 58(1), and will read as follows:

(*d*) in respect of

(i) any record of the minutes of meetings of the executive of a registered charity, registered Canadian amateur athletic association or registered journalism organization,

(ii) any record of the minutes of meetings of the members of a registered charity, registered Canadian amateur athletic association or registered journalism organization, and

(iii) all documents and by-laws governing a registered charity, registered Canadian amateur athletic association or registered journalism organization,

the period ending on the day that is two years after the date on which the registration of the registered charity, the registered Canadian amateur athletic association or the registered journalism organization under the Act is revoked;

(*e*) in respect of all records and books of account that are not described in paragraph (*d*) and that relate to a registered charity, registered Canadian amateur athletic association or registered journalism organization whose registration under the Act is revoked, and in respect of the vouchers and accounts necessary to verify the information in such records and books of account, the period ending on the day that is two years after the date on which the registration of the registered charity, the registered Canadian amateur athletic association or the registered journalism organization under the Act is revoked;

Applicable: January 1, 2020.

(*f*) in respect of duplicates of receipts for gifts that are received by a qualified donee to which subsection 230(2) of the Act applies, the period ending on the day that is two years after the end of the last calendar year to which the receipts relate; and

(*g*) notwithstanding paragraphs (*c*) to (*f*), in respect of all records, books of account, vouchers and accounts of a deceased taxpayer or a trust in respect of which a clearance certificate is issued pursuant to subsection 159(2) of the Act with respect to the distribution of all the property of such deceased taxpayer or trust, the period ending on the day that the clearance certificate is issued.

History: S. 5800(1)(*d*)(iv) was repealed by S.C. 2011, c. 24, s. 87(1), in force January 1, 2012. S. 5800(1)(*d*)(iv) formerly read:

(iv) all records of any donations received by a registered charity that were subject to a direction by the donor that the property given be held by the charity for a period of not less than 10 years,

S. 5800(1)(*f*) was replaced by S.C. 2011, c. 24, s. 87(2), dated December 15, 2011, in force January 1, 2012. S. 5800(1)(*f*) formerly read:

(*f*) in respect of duplicates of receipts for donations (other than donations referred to in subparagraph (*d*)(iv)) that are received by a registered charity or registered Canadian amateur athletic association and are required to be kept by that charity or association pursuant to subsection 230(2) of the Act, the period ending on the day that is two years from the end of the last calendar year to which the receipts relate; and

(2) For the purposes of subsection 230.1(3) of the Act, with respect to the application of paragraph 230(4)(*a*) of the Act, the required retention period for records and books of account that are required to be kept pursuant to section 230.1 of the Act is prescribed to be the period ending on the day that is two years after the end of the last calendar year to which the records or books of account relate.

Information Circulars: IC 05-1 Electronic Record Keeping; IC 78-10R5 Books and Records Retention/Destruction.

Part LIX
Foreign Affiliates

5900. Dividends Out of Exempt, Taxable and Pre-Acquisition Surplus

(1) Where at any time a corporation resident in Canada or a foreign affiliate of the corporation receives a dividend on a share of any class of the capital stock of a foreign affiliate of the corporation,

(*a*) for the purposes of this Part and paragraph 113(1)(*a*) of the Act, the portion of the dividend paid out of the exempt surplus of the affiliate is prescribed to be that proportion of the dividend received that

(i) such portion of the whole dividend paid by the affiliate on the shares of that class at that time as was deemed by section 5901 to have been paid out of the affiliate's exempt surplus in respect of the corporation

is of

(ii) the whole dividend paid by the affiliate on the shares of that class at that time;

(*a*.1) for the purposes of this Part and paragraph 113(1)(*a.1*) of the Act, the portion of the dividend paid out of the hybrid surplus of the affiliate is prescribed to be that proportion of the dividend received that

(i) the portion of the whole dividend paid by the affiliate on the shares of that class at that time that was deemed by section 5901 to have been paid out of the affiliate's hybrid surplus in respect of the corporation

is of

(ii) the whole dividend paid by the affiliate on the shares of that class at that time;

(*b*) for the purposes of this Part and subsection 91(5) and paragraphs 113(1)(*b*) and (*c*) of the Act, the portion of the dividend paid out of the taxable surplus of the affiliate is prescribed to be that proportion of the dividend received that

(i) such portion of the whole dividend paid by the affiliate on the shares of that class at that time as was deemed by section 5901 to have been paid out of the affiliate's taxable surplus in respect of the corporation

is of

(ii) the whole dividend paid by the affiliate on the shares of that class at that time;

(*c*) for the purposes of this Part and paragraph 113(1)(*d*) of the Act, the portion of the dividend paid out of the pre-acquisition surplus of the affiliate is prescribed to be that proportion of the dividend received that

(i) such portion of the whole dividend paid by the affiliate on the shares of that class at that time as was deemed by section 5901 to have been paid out of the affiliate's pre-acquisition surplus in respect of the corporation

is of

(ii) the whole dividend paid by the affiliate on the shares of that class at that time;

(*c*.1) for the purposes of this Part and paragraph 113(1)(*a.1*) of the Act, the foreign tax applicable to the portion of the dividend prescribed to have been paid out of the hybrid surplus of the affiliate is prescribed to be that proportion of the hybrid underlying tax applicable, in respect of the corporation, to the whole dividend paid by the affiliate on the shares of that class at that time that

(i) the amount of the dividend received by the corporation or the affiliate, as the case may be, on that share at that time

is of

(ii) the whole dividend paid by the affiliate on the shares of that class at that time; and

(*d*) for the purposes of this Part and paragraph 113(1)(*b*) of the Act, the foreign tax applicable to the portion of the dividend prescribed to have been paid out of the taxable surplus of the affiliate is prescribed to be that proportion of the underlying foreign tax applicable, in respect of the corporation, to the whole dividend paid by the affiliate on the shares of that class at that time that

(i) the amount of the dividend received by the corporation or the affiliate, as the case may be, on that share at that time

is of

(ii) the whole dividend paid by the affiliate on the shares of that class at that time.

History: S. 5900(1)(*a.1*) was added by S.C. 2013, c. 34, s. 78(1), applicable to dividends received after August 19, 2011.

S. 5900(1)(*c.1*) was added by S.C. 2013, c. 34, s. 78(2), applicable to dividends received after August 19, 2011.

Any assessment of a taxpayer's tax, interest and penalties payable under the Act for any taxation year that ends before June 26, 2013 that would, in the absence of this section, be precluded because of subsections 152(4) to (5) of the Act shall be made to the extent necessary to take into account the amendments by S.C. 2013, c. 34, s. 54 to 89.

(2) Notwithstanding paragraphs (1)(*a*) and (*b*), where at any time a foreign affiliate of a corporation resident in Canada pays a dividend on a share of a class of its capital stock (other than a share in respect of which an election is made under subsection 93(1) of the Act) to the corporation, the corporation may, in its return of income under Part I of the Act for its taxation year in which the dividend was received by it, designate an amount not exceeding the portion of the dividend received that would, but for this subsection, be prescribed to have been paid out of the affiliate's exempt surplus in respect of the corporation and that amount

(*a*) is prescribed to have been paid out of the affiliate's taxable surplus in respect of the corporation and not to have been paid out of that exempt surplus; and (*b*) for the purposes of paragraph (1)(*d*) and the definitions "underlying foreign tax" and "underlying foreign tax applicable" in subsection 5907(1) is deemed to have been paid by the affiliate to the corporation as a separate whole dividend on the shares of that class of the capital stock immediately after that time, and that whole dividend is deemed to have been paid out of the affiliate's taxable surplus in respect of the corporation.

(3) For the purposes of subsection 91(5) of the Act, if a person resident in Canada (other than a corporation) receives a dividend on a share of any class of the capital stock of a foreign affiliate of the person, the dividend is prescribed to have been paid out of the affiliate's taxable surplus.

History: S. 5900(3) was replaced by S.C. 2013, c. 34, s. 40(1), applicable in respect of dividends received after November 1999.

However, any assessment of a taxpayer's tax, interest and penalties payable under the Act for any taxation year that ends before June 26, 2013 that would otherwise be precluded because of subsections 152(4) to (5) of the Act, shall be made to the extent necessary to take into account this amendment, if the taxpayer

(i) elects in writing in respect of all of its foreign affiliates that this section apply in respect of that provision, and

(ii) files that election with the Minister of National Revenue on or before December 26, 2013 [the day that is six months after royal assent].

S. 5900(3) formerly read:

(3) For the purposes of subsection 91(5) of the Act, where at any time an individual resident in Canada receives a dividend on a share of any class of the capital stock of a foreign affiliate of that individual, the affiliate shall be deemed to have an amount of taxable surplus in respect of the individual and the portion of the dividend paid out of the taxable surplus of the affiliate in respect of the individual is prescribed to be an amount equal to the dividend received.

5901. Order of Surplus Distributions

(1) Subject to subsection (1.1), if at any time in its taxation year a foreign affiliate of a corporation resident in Canada has paid a whole dividend on the shares of any class of its capital stock, for the purposes of this Part

(*a*) the portion of the whole dividend deemed to have been paid out of the affiliate's exempt surplus in respect of the corporation at that time is an amount equal to the lesser of

(i) the amount of the whole dividend, and

(ii) the amount, if any, by which the exempt surplus exceeds the total of

(A) the affiliate's hybrid deficit, if any, in respect of the corporation at that time, and

(B) the affiliate's taxable deficit, if any, in respect of the corporation at that time;

(*a.1*) the portion of the whole dividend deemed to have been paid out of the affiliate's hybrid surplus in respect of the corporation at that time is an amount equal to the lesser of

(i) the amount, if any, by which the amount of the whole dividend exceeds the portion determined under paragraph (*a*), and

(ii) the amount, if any, by which the hybrid surplus exceeds

(A) if the affiliate has an exempt deficit and a taxable deficit, in respect of the corporation at that time, the total of the exempt deficit and the taxable deficit,

(B) if the affiliate has an exempt deficit and no taxable deficit, in respect of the corporation at that time, the amount of the exempt deficit, and

(C) if the affiliate has a taxable deficit and no exempt deficit, in respect of the corporation at that time, the amount, if any, by which the taxable deficit exceeds the affiliate's exempt surplus in respect of the corporation at that time;

(*b*) the portion of the whole dividend deemed to have been paid out of the affiliate's taxable surplus in respect of the corporation at that time is an amount equal to the lesser of

(i) the amount, if any, by which the amount of the whole dividend exceeds the total of the portions determined under paragraphs (*a*) and (*a.1*), and

(ii) the amount, if any, by which the taxable surplus exceeds

(A) if the affiliate has an exempt deficit and a hybrid deficit, in respect of the corporation at that time, the total of the exempt deficit and the hybrid deficit,

(B) if the affiliate has an exempt deficit and no hybrid deficit, in respect of the corporation at that time, the amount, if any, by which the exempt deficit exceeds the affiliate's hybrid surplus in respect of the corporation at that time, and

(C) if the affiliate has a hybrid deficit and no exempt deficit, in respect of the corporation at that time, the amount, if any, by which the hybrid deficit exceeds the affiliate's exempt surplus in respect of the corporation at that time; and

(*c*) the portion of the whole dividend deemed to have been paid out of the affiliate's pre-acquisition surplus in respect of the corporation at that time is the amount, if any, by which the whole dividend exceeds the total of the portions determined under paragraphs (*a*) to (*b*).

History: S. 5901(1) was replaced by S.C. 2013, c. 34, s. 79(1), applicable to dividends paid after August 19, 2011 by a foreign affiliate of a corporation.

Any assessment of a taxpayer's tax, interest and penalties payable under the Act for any taxation year that ends before June 26, 2013 that would, in the absence of this section, be precluded because of subsections 152(4) to (5) of the Act shall be made to the extent necessary to take into account the amendments by S.C. 2013, c. 34, s. 54 to 89.

S. 5901(1) formerly read:

(1) Where at any time in its taxation year a foreign affiliate of a corporation resident in Canada has paid a whole dividend on the shares of any class of its capital stock, for the purposes of this Part

(*a*) the portion of the whole dividend deemed to have been paid out of the affiliate's exempt surplus in respect of the corporation at that time is an amount equal to the lesser of

(i) the amount of the whole dividend, and

(ii) the amount by which that exempt surplus exceeds the affiliate's taxable deficit in respect of the corporation at that time;

(*b*) the portion of the whole dividend deemed to have been paid out of the affiliate's taxable surplus in respect of the corporation at that time is an amount equal to the lesser of

(i) the amount, if any, by which the amount of the whole dividend exceeds the portion determined under paragraph (*a*), and

Regulations

(ii) the amount by which that taxable surplus exceeds the affiliate's exempt deficit in respect of the corporation at that time; and

(c) the portion of the whole dividend deemed to have been paid out of the affiliate's pre-acquisition surplus in respect of the corporation at that time is the amount by which the whole dividend exceeds the aggregate of the portions determined under paragraphs (a) and (b).

(1.1) If the corporation resident in Canada that is referred to in subsection (1) elects in writing under this subsection in respect of the whole dividend referred to in subsection (1) and files the election with the Minister on or before the corporation's filing-due date for its taxation year that includes the day the whole dividend was paid, subsection (1) applies in respect of the whole dividend as if its paragraphs (*a.1*) and (*b*) read as follows:

(*a*.1) the portion of the whole dividend deemed to have been paid out of the affiliate's taxable surplus in respect of the corporation at that time is an amount equal to the lesser of

(i) the amount, if any, by which the amount of the whole dividend exceeds the portion determined under paragraph (*a*), and

(ii) the amount, if any, by which the taxable surplus exceeds

(A) if the affiliate has an exempt deficit and a hybrid deficit, in respect of the corporation at that time, the total of the exempt deficit and the hybrid deficit,

(B) if the affiliate has an exempt deficit and no hybrid deficit, in respect of the corporation at that time, the amount of the exempt deficit, and

(C) if the affiliate has a hybrid deficit and no exempt deficit, in respect of the corporation at that time, the amount, if any, by which the hybrid deficit exceeds the affiliate's exempt surplus in respect of the corporation at that time;

(*b*) the portion of the whole dividend deemed to have been paid out of the affiliate's hybrid surplus in respect of the corporation at that time is an amount equal to the lesser of

(i) the amount, if any, by which the amount of the whole dividend exceeds the total of the portions determined under paragraphs (*a*) and (*a.1*),

(ii) the amount, if any, by which the hybrid surplus exceeds

(A) if the affiliate has an exempt deficit and a taxable deficit, in respect of the corporation at that time, the total of the exempt deficit and the taxable deficit,

(B) if the affiliate has an exempt deficit and no taxable deficit, in respect of the corporation at that time, the amount, if any, by which the exempt deficit exceeds the affiliate's taxable surplus in respect of the corporation at that time, and

(C) if the affiliate has a taxable deficit and no exempt deficit, in respect of the corporation at that time, the amount, if any, by which the taxable deficit exceeds the affiliate's exempt surplus in respect of the corporation at that time; and [*sic*]

History: S. 5901(1.1) was added by S.C. 2013, c. 34, s. 79(1), applicable to dividends paid after August 19, 2011 by a foreign affiliate of a corporation.

See the application for the amendment to s. 5901(1) for the extension of assessment periods to take into account the amendments by S.C. 2013, c. 34, s. 54 to 89.

(2) Notwithstanding subsection (1),

(*a*) if a foreign affiliate of a corporation resident in Canada pays a whole dividend (other than a whole dividend referred to in subsection 5902(1)) at any particular time in its taxation year that is more than 90 days after the commencement of that year or at any particular time in its 1972 taxation year that is before January 1, 1972, the portion of the whole dividend that would, in the absence of this paragraph, be deemed to have been paid out of the affiliate's pre-acquisition surplus in respect of the corporation (otherwise than because of an election under paragraph (*b*)) is instead deemed to have been paid out of the exempt surplus, hybrid surplus and taxable surplus of the affiliate in respect of the corporation to the extent that it would have been deemed to have been so paid if, immediately after the end of that year, that portion were paid as a separate whole dividend before any whole dividend paid after the particular time and after any whole dividend paid before the particular time by the affiliate, and for the purposes of determining the exempt deficit, exempt surplus, hybrid deficit, hybrid surplus, hybrid underlying tax, taxable deficit, taxable surplus and underlying foreign tax of the affiliate in respect of the corporation at any time, that portion is deemed to have been paid as a separate whole dividend immediately following the end of the year and not to have been paid at the particular time; and

(*b*) a whole dividend referred to in subsection (1) that is paid at any time by a foreign affiliate of a corporation resident in Canada and that would, in the absence of this paragraph, be deemed under subsection (1) to have been, in whole or in part, paid out of the exempt surplus, hybrid surplus or taxable surplus of the affiliate in respect of the corporation is instead deemed to have been paid out of the pre-acquisition surplus of the affiliate in respect of the corporation if

(i) the corporation, and each other corporation, if any, of which the affiliate would, at that time, be a foreign affiliate if paragraph (*b*) of the definition "equity percentage" in subsection 95(4) of the Act were read as if the reference in that paragraph to "any corporation" were a reference to "any corporation other than a corporation resident in Canada" and that is, at that time, related to the corporation,

(A) where there is no such other corporation, elects in writing under this subparagraph and files the election with the Minister on or before the filing-due date for its taxation year in which the whole dividend is paid, and

(B) in any other case, jointly elect in writing under this subparagraph and file the election with the Minister on or before the earliest of the filing-due dates for their taxation years in which the whole dividend is paid,

(ii) no shareholder of the affiliate is, at that time, a partnership a member of which is

(A) a corporation that would, in the absence of this subparagraph, be eligible to elect under subparagraph (i), or

(B) a foreign affiliate of such a corporation, and

(iii) no particular person or particular partnership — in respect of which the affiliate would, at that time, be a foreign affiliate if paragraph (*b*) of the definition "equity percentage" in subsection 95(4) of the Act were read in the manner required by subparagraph (i) — has elected under subsection 90(3) of the Act in respect of the distribution that is the whole dividend where

(A) in the case of a particular person, the particular person is, or is at that time related to, the corporation, or

(B) in the case of a particular partnership, a member of the particular partnership is, or is at that time related to, the corporation.

History: S. 5901(2) was replaced by S.C. 2013, c. 34, s. 79(1), applicable to dividends paid after August 19, 2011 by a foreign affiliate of a corporation. However,

(*a*) if the corporation and each other corporation (the corporation and those other corporations together referred to in this paragraph as the "elector corporations"), if any, of which the affiliate would be a foreign affiliate if paragraph (*b*) of the definition "equity percentage" in subsection 95(4) of the Act were read as if the reference in that paragraph to "any corporation" were a reference to "any corporation other than a corporation resident in Canada" and that is related to the corporation jointly elect in writing in respect of all of their respective foreign affiliates and file the election with the Minister of National Revenue on or before the day that is the later of the earliest of the filing-due dates for their taxation years that include June 26, 2013 and June 26, 2014, subsections 5901(2) applies to dividends paid after December 20, 2002 by all the respective foreign affiliates of the elector corporations, except that, for such dividends paid on or before August 19, 2011,

(i) paragraph 5901(2)(*a*) of the Regulations is to be read as follows:

"(*a*) if a foreign affiliate of a corporation resident in Canada pays a whole dividend (other than a whole dividend referred to in subsection 5902(1)) at any particular time in its taxation year that is more than 90 days after the commencement of that year or at any particular time in its 1972 taxation year that is before January 1, 1972, the portion of the whole dividend that would, in the absence of this paragraph, be deemed to have been paid out of the affiliate's pre-acquisition surplus in respect of the corporation (otherwise than because of an election under paragraph (*b*)) is instead deemed to have been paid out of the exempt surplus and taxable surplus of the affiliate in respect of the corporation to the extent that it would have been deemed to have been so paid if, immediately after the end of that year, that portion were paid as a separate whole dividend before any whole dividend paid after the particular time and after any whole dividend paid before the particular time by the affiliate, and for the purposes of determining the exempt deficit, exempt surplus, taxable deficit, taxable surplus and underlying foreign tax of the affiliate in respect of the corporation at any time, that portion is deemed to have been paid as a separate whole dividend immediately following the end of the year and not to have been paid at the particular time, and"

(ii) the portion of paragraph 5901(2)(*b*) before subparagraph (i) is to be read as follows:

"(*b*) a whole dividend referred to in subsection (1) that is paid at any time by a foreign affiliate of a corporation resident in Canada and that would, in the absence of this paragraph, be deemed under subsection (1) to have been, in whole or in part, paid out of the exempt surplus or taxable surplus of the affiliate in respect of the corporation is instead deemed to have been paid out of the pre-acquisition surplus of the affiliate in respect of the corporation if"

(iii) paragraph 5901(2)(*b*) is to be read without reference to its subparagraph (iii);

(*b*) any election referred to in subparagraph 5901(2)(*b*)(i) of the Regulations that would otherwise be required to be filed with the Minister of National Revenue before October 24, 2013 [120 days after royal assent] is deemed to have been filed with the Minister on a timely basis if it is filed with the Minister by June 26, 2014 [within 365 days after royal assent.

See the application for the amendment to s. 5901(1) for the extension of assessment periods to take into account the amendments by S.C. 2013, c. 34, s. 54 to 89.

S. 5901(2) formerly read:

(2) Notwithstanding subsection (1), where a foreign affiliate of a corporation resident in Canada pays a whole dividend (other than a whole dividend referred to in subsection 5902(1)) at any particular time in its taxation year that is more than 90 days after the commencement of that year or at any particular time in its 1972 taxation year that is before January 1, 1972, the portion of the whole dividend that would, but for this subsection, be deemed to have been paid out of the affiliate's pre-acquisition surplus in respect of the corporation is deemed to have been paid out of the exempt surplus and taxable surplus of the affiliate in respect of the corporation to the extent that it would have been deemed to have been so paid if, immediately after the end of that year, that portion were paid as a separate whole dividend before any whole dividend paid after the particular time and after any whole dividend paid before the particular time by the affiliate, and for the purposes of determining the exempt deficit, exempt surplus, taxable deficit, taxable surplus and underlying foreign tax of the affiliate in respect of the corporation at any time, that portion is deemed to have been paid as a separate whole dividend immediately following the end of the year and not to have been paid at the particular time.

Tax Profile: July 2008 — International Tax Planning for the Owner-Manager.

Tax Topics: No. 2133, New Foreign Affiliate Capital Distribution Elections: QROCs and Regulation 5901(2)(*b*) Dividends; No. 2079, UpEnding the Surplus Ordering Rules: Implications of the New Regulation 5901(2)(b) Election.

(2.1) Subsection (2.2) applies if, in respect of a whole dividend paid by a foreign affiliate of a corporation resident in Canada,

(*a*) the corporation determined not to make an election under subparagraph (2)(*b*)(i) in respect of the whole dividend before the filing-due date specified in the relevant clause of that subparagraph;

(*b*) the corporation demonstrates that the determination was made using reasonable efforts; and

(*c*) the corporation, whether jointly with one or more other corporations or otherwise, files such an election on or before the day that is 10 years after that filing-due date.

History: S. 5901(2.1) was added by S.C. 2013, c. 34, s. 79(1), applicable to dividends paid after August 19, 2011 by a foreign affiliate of a corporation. However,

(*a*) if the corporation and each other corporation (the corporation and those other corporations together referred to in this paragraph as the "elector corporations"), if any, of which the affiliate would be a foreign affiliate if paragraph (*b*) of the definition "equity percentage" in subsection 95(4) of the Act were read as if the reference in that paragraph to "any corporation" were a reference to "any corporation other than a corporation resident in Canada" and that is related to the corporation jointly elect in writing in respect of all of their respective foreign affiliates and file the election with the Minister of National Revenue on or before the day that is the later of the earliest of the filing-due dates for their taxation years that include June 26, 2013 and June 26, 2014, subsections 5901(2.1) applies to dividends paid after December 20, 2002 by all the respective foreign affiliates of the elector corporations, and

(*b*) any determination referred to in paragraph 5901(2.1)(*a*) of the Regulations that would otherwise be required to be made before October 24, 2013 [120 days after royal assent] is deemed to have been made on a timely basis if it is made by June 26, 2014 [within 365 days after royal assent].

See the application for the amendment to s. 5901(1) for the extension of assessment periods to take into account the amendments by S.C. 2013, c. 34, s. 54 to 89.

(2.2) If this subsection applies and, in the opinion of the Minister, the circumstances are such that it would be just and equitable to permit an election referred to in subsection (2.1) to be filed after the filing-due date specified in the relevant clause of subparagraph (2)(*b*)(i), that election is deemed to have been filed on that filing-due date.

History: S. 5901(2.2) was added by S.C. 2013, c. 34, s. 79(1), applicable to dividends paid after August 19, 2011 by a foreign affiliate of a corporation. However, if the corporation and each other corporation (the corporation and those other corporations together referred to in this paragraph as the "elector corporations"), if any, of which the affiliate would be a foreign affiliate if paragraph (*b*) of the definition "equity percentage" in subsection 95(4) of the Act were read as if the reference in that paragraph to "any corporation" were a reference to "any corporation other than a corporation resident in Canada" and that is related to the corporation jointly elect in writing in respect of all of their respective foreign affiliates and file the election with the Minister of National Revenue on or before the day that is the later of the earliest of the filing-due dates for their taxation years that include June 26, 2013 and June 26, 2014, subsections 5901(2.2) applies to dividends paid after December 20, 2002 by all the respective foreign affiliates of the elector corporations.

See the application for the amendment to s. 5901(1) for the extension of assessment periods to take into account the amendments by S.C. 2013, c. 34, s. 54 to 89.

(3) Notwithstanding subsections (1) and (2), for the purposes of the definitions "exempt deficit", "exempt surplus", "taxable deficit" and "taxable surplus" in subsection 5907(1), any amount designated pursuant to subsection 5900(2) in respect of a dividend paid by a foreign affiliate of a corporation resident in Canada increases the portion of the whole dividend deemed to have been paid out of the affiliate's taxable surplus in respect of the corporation and decreases the portion of the whole dividend deemed to have been paid out of the affiliate's exempt surplus in respect of the corporation.

5902. Election in Respect of Capital Gains

(1) If at any time a dividend (such time and each such dividend, respectively, referred to in this subsection and subsection (2) as the "dividend time" and an "elected dividend") is, by virtue of an election made under subsection 93(1) of the Act by a corporation in respect of a disposition, deemed to have been received on a share (each such share referred to in this subsection as an "elected share") of a class of the capital stock of a particular foreign affiliate of the corporation, the following rules apply:

(*a*) for the purposes of subsection 5900(1), in applying the provisions of subsection 5901(1),

(i) the particular affiliate's exempt surplus or exempt deficit, hybrid surplus or hybrid deficit, hybrid underlying tax, taxable surplus or taxable deficit, underlying foreign tax and net surplus, in respect of the corporation at the dividend time, are deemed to be those amounts that would otherwise be determined immediately before the dividend time if

(A) each other foreign affiliate of the corporation in which the affiliate had an equity percentage (within the meaning assigned by subsection 95(4) of the Act) at the dividend time had, immediately before the time that is immediately before the dividend time, paid a dividend equal to its net surplus in respect of the corporation, determined immediately before the time the dividend was paid, and

(B) any dividend referred to in clause (A) that any other foreign affiliate would have received had been received by it immediately before any such dividend that it would have paid, and

(ii) the particular affiliate is deemed to have paid a whole dividend at the dividend time on the shares of that class of its capital stock in an amount determined by the formula

$$A \times B$$

where

A is the total of all amounts each of which is the amount of an elected dividend, and

B is the greater of

(A) one, and

(B) the quotient determined by the formula

$$C/D$$

where

C is the amount of the particular affiliate's net surplus determined under subparagraph (*a*)(i), and

D is the greater of

(I) one unit of the currency in which the amount determined for C is expressed, and

(II) the amount that would have been received on the elected shares if the particular affiliate had at the dividend time paid dividends, on all shares of its capital stock, the total of which was equal to the amount of its net surplus referred to in subparagraph (*a*)(i); and

(*b*) subject to paragraph 5905(5)(*c*), there is to be included, at the dividend time,

(i) under subparagraph (v) of the description of B in the definition "exempt surplus" in subsection 5907(1) in computing the particular affiliate's exempt surplus or exempt deficit, as the case may be, in respect of the corporation an amount equal to the product obtained when the specified adjustment factor in respect of the disposition is multiplied by the total of all amounts each of which is the portion of any elected dividend that is prescribed by paragraph 5900(1)(*a*) to have been paid out of the exempt surplus of the particular affiliate,

(i.1) under subparagraph (vi) of the description of B in the definition "hybrid surplus" in subsection 5907(1) in computing the particular affiliate's hybrid surplus or hybrid deficit, as the case may be, in respect of the corporation an amount equal to the product obtained when the specified adjustment factor in respect of the disposition is multiplied by the total of all amounts each of which is the portion of any elected dividend that is prescribed by paragraph 5900(1)(*a.1*) to have been paid out of the hybrid surplus of the particular affiliate,

(i.2) under subparagraph (iii) of the description of B in the definition "hybrid underlying tax" in subsection 5907(1) in computing the particular affiliate's hybrid underlying tax in respect of the corporation an amount equal to the product obtained when the specified adjustment factor in respect of the disposition is multiplied by the total of all amounts each of which is the amount prescribed by paragraph 5900(1)(*c.1*) to be the foreign tax applicable to the portion of any elected dividend that is prescribed by paragraph 5900(1)(*a.1*) to have been paid out of the hybrid surplus of the particular affiliate,

(ii) under subparagraph (v) of the description of B in the definition "taxable surplus" in subsection 5907(1) in computing the particular affiliate's taxable surplus or taxable deficit, as the case may be, in respect of the corporation an amount equal to the product obtained when the specified adjustment factor in respect of the disposition is multiplied by the total of all amounts each of which is the portion of any elected dividend that is prescribed by paragraph 5900(1)(*b*) to have been paid out of the taxable surplus of the particular affiliate, and

(iii) under subparagraph (iii) of the description of B in the definition "underlying foreign tax" in subsection 5907(1) in computing the particular affiliate's underlying foreign tax in respect of the corporation an amount equal to the product obtained when the specified adjustment factor in respect of the disposition is multiplied by the total of all amounts each of which is the amount prescribed by paragraph 5900(1)(*d*) to be the foreign tax applicable to such portion of any elected dividend as is prescribed by paragraph 5900(1)(*b*) to have been paid out of the taxable surplus of the particular affiliate.

History: S. 5902(1)(*a*)(i), the portion before clause (A), was replaced by S.C. 2013, c. 34, s. 80(1), applicable in respect of elections in respect of dispositions of shares of the capital stock of a foreign affiliate of a taxpayer that occur after August 19, 2011.

Any assessment of a taxpayer's tax, interest and penalties payable under the Act for any taxation year that ends before June 26, 2013 that would, in the absence of this section, be precluded because of subsections 152(4) to (5) of the Act shall be made to the extent necessary to take into account the amendments by S.C. 2013, c. 34, s. 54 to 89.

S. 5902(1)(*a*)(i), the portion before clause (A) formerly read:

(i) the particular affiliate's exempt surplus or exempt deficit, taxable surplus or taxable deficit, underlying foreign tax and net surplus, in respect of the corporation at the dividend time, are deemed to be those amounts that would otherwise be determined immediately before the dividend time if

S. 5902(1)(*b*)(i.1) and (i.2) were added by S.C. 2013, c. 34, s. 80(2), applicable in respect of elections in respect of dispositions of shares of the capital stock of a foreign affiliate of a taxpayer that occur after August 19, 2011.

See the application provision above for the extension of assessment periods to take into account the amendments by S.C. 2013, c. 34, s. 54 to 89.

S. 5902(1) was replaced by S.C. 2013, c. 34, s. 41(1), applicable in respect of elections made in respect of dispositions that occur after December 18, 2009. However, in applying subsection 5905(5.6) of the Regulations, the portion of subsection 5902(1) of the Regulations before subparagraph (*a*)(ii) applies after December 18, 2009.

Any assessment of a taxpayer's tax, interest and penalties payable under the Act for any taxation year that ends before June 26, 2013, that would otherwise be precluded because of subsections 152(4) to (5) of the Act, shall be made to the extent necessary to take into account this amendment, if the taxpayer

(i) elects in writing in respect of all of its foreign affiliates that this section apply in respect of that provision, and

(ii) files that election with the Minister of National Revenue on or before December 26, 2013 [the day that is six months after royal assent.]

S. 5902(1) formerly read:

(1) Where at any time a dividend is, by virtue of an election made under subsection 93(1) of the Act in respect of a disposition, deemed to have been received on one or more shares of a class of the capital stock of a particular foreign affiliate of a corporation resident in Canada, the following rules apply:

(*a*) determine the amounts that would be the particular affiliate's exempt surplus or exempt deficit, taxable surplus or taxable deficit, underlying foreign tax and net surplus in respect of the corporation at that time if

(i) each other foreign affiliate of the corporation in which the affiliate had an equity percentage had immediately before that time paid a dividend equal to its net surplus in respect of the corporation immediately before the dividend was paid, and

(ii) any dividend referred to in subparagraph (i) that any other foreign affiliate would have received had been received by it immediately before any such dividend that it would have paid;

(*b*) determine the amount that would have been received on the shares (of that class) in respect of which an election is made, if the particular affiliate had at that time paid dividends the aggregate of which on all shares of its capital stock was equal to the amount of its net surplus referred to in paragraph (*a*); and

(*c*) for the purposes only of subsection 5900(1), in applying the provisions of subsection 5901(1)

(i) the particular affiliate's exempt surplus or exempt deficit, taxable surplus or taxable deficit and underlying foreign tax in respect of the corporation shall be deemed to be the respective amounts thereof referred to in paragraph (*a*), and

(ii) the particular affiliate shall be deemed to have paid a whole dividend at that time on the shares of that class of its capital stock in an amount equal to the product obtained when the aggregate of amounts so deemed by subsection 93(1) of the Act to have been received as dividends on shares of that class is multiplied by the greater of

(A) one, and

(B) the proportion that the amount of the particular affiliate's net surplus determined under paragraph (*a*) is of the amount determined under paragraph (*b*), except that where the amount determined under paragraph (*b*) is less than one, the amount determined under paragraph (*b*) is deemed for the purpose of this clause to be one.

Application Provision, S.C. 2013, c. 34, s. 51 [Consolidated Net Surplus Election] Subject to the Modified Consolidated Net Surplus Election (below), if a corporation resident in Canada elects in writing in respect of all of its foreign affiliates and files the election with the Minister of National Revenue on or before the day that is the later of the corporation's filing-due date for the corporation's taxation year that includes June 26, 2013 and June 26, 2014, the following rules apply:

(*a*) if there is an election (referred to as a "designated section 93 election") made by the corporation under subsection 93(1) or (1.2) of the *Income Tax Act* in respect of a disposition of shares (referred to as the "designated shares") of the capital stock of a foreign affiliate of the corporation that occurs after December 20, 2002 and before December 19, 2009, other than a disposition that is required to be made under an agreement in writing made by the vendor before December 21, 2002,

(i) subsection 5902(1) of the Regulations is, in respect of the designated section 93 election, to be read as follows:

"(1) If, at a particular time, one or more shares (each of which is referred to in this subsection as a "disposed share") of a class (referred to in this subsection as the "specified class") of the capital stock of a particular foreign affiliate of a corporation resident in Canada are disposed of by a particular shareholder of the particular foreign affiliate and, because of an election made under subsection 93(1) of the Act in respect of that disposition, a dividend is deemed under subsection 93(1) of the Act to have been received on a disposed share at the time (referred to in this subsection and section 5905 as the "dividend time") that is immediately before the particular time, the following rules apply:

(*a*) the amount of the particular foreign affiliate's exempt surplus, in respect of the corporation resident in Canada, (in this subsection referred to as the "consolidated exempt surplus" in respect of the corporation resident in Canada) at the time (in this section and in section 5905 referred to as the "calculation time") that is immediately before the dividend time, is deemed to be the amount that would be its exempt surplus, in respect of the corporation resident in Canada, at the calculation time if

(i) the particular foreign affiliate and each other foreign affiliate of the corporation resident in Canada in which the particular foreign affiliate had, at the calculation time, an equity percentage (each of which other foreign affiliates is referred to in this section as a "subsidiary affiliate") had (except for the purpose of determining consolidated net surplus in respect of the corporation resident in Canada in subparagraph (iii)), at the calculation time, no amount of exempt deficit, taxable surplus or taxable deficit, in respect of the corporation resident in Canada,

Regulations

(ii) the amount of the exempt surplus, in respect of the corporation resident in Canada, of the particular foreign affiliate were, immediately before the calculation time, increased by the total of all amounts each of which is an amount equal to the particular foreign affiliate's proportionate share of the amount that would be the exempt surplus, in respect of the corporation resident in Canada, of a subsidiary affiliate in which it has, immediately before the calculation time, a direct equity percentage if that exempt surplus were, immediately before the calculation time, determined in the following manner:

(A) the exempt surplus, in respect of the corporation resident in Canada, of the subsidiary affiliate, were increased by the subsidiary affiliate's proportionate share of the exempt surplus of a foreign affiliate of the corporation resident in Canada in which the subsidiary affiliate has, immediately before the time that is immediately before the calculation time, a direct equity percentage, and

(B) the exempt surplus, in respect of the corporation resident in Canada, of a subsidiary affiliate in which another subsidiary affiliate has a direct equity percentage, were increased because of this subparagraph before the increase in that other subsidiary affiliate's exempt surplus in respect of the corporation resident in Canada,

(iii) for the purpose of subparagraph (ii), the proportionate share, at any time, of a foreign affiliate (referred to in this subparagraph as the "calculating foreign affiliate") of the corporation resident in Canada, of the exempt surplus, in respect of the corporation resident in Canada, of another foreign affiliate (referred to in this subparagraph as the "providing foreign affiliate") of the corporation resident in Canada in which the calculating foreign affiliate has a direct equity percentage were equal to the proportion determined by the following formula:

$$A/B$$

where

A is the amount of dividends that would be received, at that time, by the calculating foreign affiliate from the providing foreign affiliate if, at that time, the providing foreign affiliate had paid dividends on all of its shares and the total of those dividends were equal to its consolidated net surplus (determined using the provisions of this subsection on the assumption that the providing foreign affiliate were the particular foreign affiliate), in respect of the corporation resident in Canada, or, where it does not have such a consolidated net surplus, in respect of the corporation resident in Canada, its consolidated exempt surplus (determined in accordance with this paragraph on the assumption that the providing foreign affiliate were the particular foreign affiliate), in respect of the corporation resident in Canada, at that time, and

B is the amount of the providing foreign affiliate's consolidated net surplus (determined using the provisions of this subsection on the assumption that the providing foreign affiliate were the particular foreign affiliate), in respect of the corporation resident in Canada, or, where it does not have such consolidated net surplus, its consolidated exempt surplus (determined in accordance with this paragraph on the assumption that the providing foreign affiliate were the particular foreign affiliate), in respect of the corporation resident in Canada, at that time, and

(iv) in determining, under this paragraph, the particular foreign affiliate's consolidated exempt surplus, in respect of the corporation resident in Canada,

(A) no amount were included, directly or indirectly, in respect of the exempt surplus, in respect of the corporation resident in Canada, of the particular shareholder, of the particular foreign affiliate, that disposed of the disposed share, and

(B) no amount were included, directly or indirectly, in respect of the exempt surplus, in respect of the corporation resident in Canada, of the particular foreign affiliate or any subsidiary affiliate more than once;

(*b*) the amount of the particular foreign affiliate's exempt deficit, in respect of the corporation resident in Canada, (in this subsection referred to as the "consolidated exempt deficit" in respect of the corporation resident in Canada) at the calculation time, is deemed to be the amount that would be its exempt deficit, in respect of the corporation resident in Canada, at that time, if

(i) the particular foreign affiliate and each subsidiary affiliate had (except for the purpose of determining consolidated net surplus, in respect of the corporation resident in Canada, in subparagraph (iii)), at the calculation time, no amount of exempt surplus, taxable surplus or taxable deficit, in respect of the corporation resident in Canada,

(ii) the amount of the exempt deficit, in respect of the corporation resident in Canada, of the particular foreign affiliate, were, immediately before the calculation time, increased by the total of all amounts each of which is an amount equal to the particular foreign affiliate's proportionate share of the exempt deficit, in respect of the corporation resident in Canada, of a subsidiary affiliate in which the particular foreign affiliate has, immediately before the calculation time, a direct equity percentage if that exempt deficit were, immediately before the calculation time, determined in the following manner:

(A) the exempt deficit, in respect of the corporation resident in Canada, of the subsidiary affiliate, were increased by the subsidiary affiliate's proportionate share of the exempt deficit of a foreign affiliate of the corporation resident in Canada in which the subsidiary affiliate has, immediately before the time that is immediately before the calculation time, a direct equity percentage, and

(B) the exempt deficit, in respect of the corporation resident in Canada, of a subsidiary affiliate in which another subsidiary affiliate has a direct equity percentage, were increased because of this subparagraph before the increase in that other subsidiary affiliate's exempt deficit in respect of the corporation resident in Canada,

(iii) for the purpose of subparagraph (ii), the proportionate share, at any time, of a foreign affiliate (referred to in this subparagraph as the "calculating foreign affiliate") of the corporation resident in Canada, of the exempt deficit, in respect of the corporation resident in Canada, of another foreign affiliate (referred to in this subparagraph as the "providing foreign affiliate") of the corporation resident in Canada in which the calculating foreign affiliate has a direct equity percentage were equal to the proportion determined by the following formula:

$$A/B$$

where

A is the amount of dividends that would be received by the calculating foreign affiliate from the providing foreign affiliate if, at that time, the providing foreign affiliate had paid dividends on all of its shares and the total of those dividends were equal to its consolidated net surplus (determined using the provisions of this subsection on the assumption that the providing foreign affiliate were the particular foreign affiliate), in respect of the corporation resident in Canada, or, where it does not have such consolidated net surplus, its exempt deficit (determined in accordance with this paragraph on the assumption that the providing foreign affiliate were the particular foreign affiliate), in respect of the corporation resident in Canada, at that time, and

B is the amount of the providing foreign affiliate's consolidated net surplus (determined using the provisions of this subsection on the assumption that the providing foreign affiliate were the particular foreign affiliate), in respect of the corporation resident in Canada, or, where it does not have such consolidated net surplus, its consolidated exempt deficit (determined in accordance with this paragraph on the assumption that the providing foreign affiliate were the particular foreign affiliate), in respect of the corporation resident in Canada, at that time, and

(iv) in determining, under this paragraph, the particular foreign affiliate's consolidated exempt deficit, in respect of the corporation resident in Canada,

(A) no amount were included, directly or indirectly, in respect of the exempt deficit, in respect of the corporation resident in Canada, of the particular shareholder, of the particular foreign affiliate, that disposed of the disposed share, and

(B) no amount were included, directly or indirectly, in respect of the exempt deficit, in respect of the corporation resident in Canada, of the particular foreign affiliate or any subsidiary affiliate more than once;

(*c*) the amount of the particular foreign affiliate's taxable surplus and underlying foreign tax, in respect of the corporation resident in Canada, (referred to, respectively, in this subsection as the "consolidated taxable surplus", and "consolidated underlying foreign tax", in respect of the corporation resident in Canada) at the calculation time, is deemed to be the amount that would be its taxable surplus, and underlying foreign tax, in respect of the corporation resident in Canada, at that time, if

(i) the particular foreign affiliate and each subsidiary affiliate had (except for the purpose of determining consolidated net surplus, in respect of the corporation resident in Canada, in subparagraph (iii)), at the calculation time, no amount of exempt surplus, exempt deficit or taxable deficit, in respect of the corporation resident in Canada,

(ii) the amount of the taxable surplus, and underlying foreign tax, in respect of the corporation resident in Canada, of the particular foreign affiliate, were, immediately before the calculation time, increased by an amount equal to the total of all amounts each of which is the particular foreign affiliate's proportionate share of the taxable surplus, or underlying foreign tax, as the case may be, in respect of the corporation resident in Canada, of a subsidiary affiliate in which the particular foreign affiliate has, immediately before the calculation time, a direct equity percentage if that taxable surplus and underlying foreign tax were, immediately before the calculation time, determined in the following manner:

(A) the taxable surplus, and underlying foreign tax, in respect of the corporation resident in Canada, of the subsidiary affiliate, were increased by the subsidiary affiliate's proportionate share of the taxable surplus, or underlying foreign tax, respectively, of a foreign affiliate of the corporation resident in Canada in which the subsidiary affiliate had, immediately before the time that is immediately before the calculation time, a direct equity percentage, and

(B) the taxable surplus, and underlying foreign tax, in respect of the corporation resident in Canada, of a subsidiary affiliate in which another subsidiary affiliate has a direct equity percentage, were increased because of this subparagraph before the increase in that other subsidiary affiliate's taxable surplus, and underlying foreign tax, respectively, in respect of the corporation resident in Canada,

(iii) for the purpose of subparagraph (ii), the proportionate share, at any time, of a foreign affiliate (referred to in this subparagraph as the "calculating foreign affiliate") of the corporation resident in Canada, of the taxable surplus, or underlying foreign tax, as the case may be, in respect of the corporation resident in Canada, of another foreign affiliate (referred to in this subparagraph as the "providing foreign affiliate") of the corporation resident in Canada in which the particular foreign affiliate has a direct equity percentage were equal to the proportion determined by the following formula:

$$A/B$$

where

A is the amount of dividends that would be received, at that time, by the calculating foreign affiliate from the providing foreign affiliate if, at that time, the providing foreign affiliate had paid dividends on all of its shares and the total of those dividends were equal to its consolidated net surplus (determined using the provisions of this subsection on the assumption that the providing foreign affiliate were the particular foreign affiliate), in respect of the corporation resident in Canada, or, where it does not have such consolidated net surplus, its consolidated taxable surplus (determined in accordance with this paragraph on the assumption that the providing foreign affiliate were the particular foreign affiliate), in respect of the corporation resident in Canada, at that time, and

B is the amount of the providing foreign affiliate's consolidated net surplus (determined using the provisions of this subsection on the assumption that the providing foreign affiliate were the particular foreign affiliate), in respect of the corporation resident in Canada, or, where it does not have such consolidated net surplus, its consolidated taxable surplus (determined in accordance with this paragraph on the assumption that the providing foreign affiliate were the particular foreign affiliate), in respect of the corporation resident in Canada, at that time, and

(iv) in determining, under this paragraph, the particular foreign affiliate's consolidated taxable surplus, and consolidated underlying foreign tax, in respect of the corporation resident in Canada,

(A) no amount were included, directly or indirectly, in respect of the taxable surplus, and underlying foreign tax, in respect of the corporation resident in Canada, of the particular shareholder, of the particular foreign affiliate, that disposed of the disposed share, and

(B) no amount were included, directly or indirectly, in respect of the taxable surplus, and underlying foreign tax, in respect of the corporation resident in Canada, of the particular foreign affiliate or any subsidiary affiliate more than once;

(*d*) the amount of the particular foreign affiliate's taxable deficit, in respect of the corporation resident in Canada, (in this subsection referred to as the "consolidated taxable deficit" in respect of the corporation resident in Canada) at the calculation time is deemed to be the amount that would be its taxable deficit, in respect of the corporation resident in Canada, at that time if

(i) the particular foreign affiliate and each subsidiary affiliate had (except for the purpose of determining consolidated net surplus, in respect of the corporation resident in Canada, in subparagraph (iii)), at the calculation time, no amount of exempt surplus, exempt deficit or taxable surplus, in respect of the corporation resident in Canada,

(ii) the amount of the taxable deficit, in respect of the corporation resident in Canada, of the particular foreign affiliate, were, immediately before the calculation time, increased by the total of all amounts each of which is an amount equal to the particular foreign affiliate's proportionate share of the taxable deficit, in respect of the corporation resident in Canada, of a subsidiary affiliate in which the particular foreign affiliate has, immediately before the calculation time, a direct equity percentage if that taxable deficit were, immediately before the calculation time, determined in the following manner:

(A) the taxable deficit, in respect of the corporation resident in Canada, of the subsidiary affiliate, were increased by the subsidiary affiliate's proportionate share of the taxable deficit of a foreign affiliate of the corporation resident in Canada in which the subsidiary affiliate had, immediately before the time that is immediately before the calculation time, a direct equity percentage, and

(B) the taxable deficit, in respect of the corporation resident in Canada, of a subsidiary affiliate in which another subsidiary affiliate has a direct equity percentage, were increased because of this subparagraph before the increase in that other subsidiary affiliate's taxable deficit in respect of the corporation resident in Canada,

(iii) for the purpose of subparagraph (ii), the proportionate share, at any time, of a foreign affiliate (referred to in this subparagraph as the "calculating foreign affiliate") of the corporation resident in Canada, of the taxable deficit, in respect of the corporation resident in Canada, of another foreign affiliate (referred to in this subparagraph as the "providing foreign affiliate") of the corporation resident in Canada in which the calculating foreign affiliate has a direct equity percentage were equal to the proportion determined by the following formula:

$$A/B$$

where

A is the amount of dividends that would be received, at that time, by the calculating foreign affiliate from the providing foreign affiliate if, at that time, the providing foreign affiliate had paid dividends on all of its shares and the total of those dividends were equal to its consolidated net surplus (determined using the provisions of this subsection on the assumption that the providing foreign affiliate were the particular foreign affiliate), in respect of the corporation resident in Canada, or, where it does not have such consolidated net surplus, its consolidated taxable deficit (determined in accordance with this paragraph on the assumption that the providing foreign affiliate were the particular foreign affiliate), in respect of the corporation resident in Canada, at that time, and

B is the amount of the providing foreign affiliate's consolidated net surplus (determined using the provisions of this subsection on the assumption that the providing foreign affiliate were the particular foreign affiliate), in respect of the corporation resident in Canada, or, where it does not have such consolidated net surplus, its consolidated taxable deficit (determined in accordance with this paragraph on the assumption that the providing foreign affiliate were the particular foreign affiliate), in respect of the corporation resident in Canada, at that time, and

(iv) in determining, under this paragraph, the particular foreign affiliate's consolidated taxable deficit, in respect of the corporation resident in Canada,

(A) no amount were included, directly or indirectly, in respect of taxable deficit, in respect of the corporation resident in

Canada, of the particular shareholder, of the particular foreign affiliate, that disposed of the disposed share, and

(B) no amount were included, directly or indirectly, in respect of the taxable deficit, in respect of the corporation resident in Canada, of the particular foreign affiliate or any subsidiary affiliate more than once;

(*e*) for the purpose of applying subsection 5901(1) to subsection 5900(1), and for the purpose of paragraph (*f*),

(i) the particular foreign affiliate's exempt surplus, in respect of the corporation resident in Canada, immediately before the dividend time, is deemed to be equal to the amount, if any, by which the particular foreign affiliate's consolidated exempt surplus, in respect of the corporation resident in Canada, exceeds the amount of the particular foreign affiliate's consolidated exempt deficit, in respect of the corporation resident in Canada, at that time (or, if there is no such excess, nil),

(ii) the particular foreign affiliate's exempt deficit in respect of the corporation resident in Canada, immediately before the dividend time, is deemed to be equal to the amount, if any, by which the particular foreign affiliate's consolidated exempt deficit, in respect of the corporation resident in Canada, exceeds the amount of the particular foreign affiliate's consolidated exempt surplus, in respect of the corporation resident in Canada, at that time (or, if there is no such excess, nil),

(iii) the particular foreign affiliate's taxable surplus, in respect of the corporation resident in Canada, immediately before the dividend time, is deemed to be equal to the amount, if any, by which the particular foreign affiliate's consolidated taxable surplus, in respect of the corporation resident in Canada, exceeds the amount of the particular foreign affiliate's consolidated taxable deficit, in respect of the corporation resident in Canada, at that time (or, if there is no such excess, nil),

(iv) the particular foreign affiliate's taxable deficit, in respect of the corporation resident in Canada, immediately before the dividend time, is deemed to be equal to the amount, if any, by which the particular foreign affiliate's consolidated taxable deficit, in respect of the corporation resident in Canada, exceeds the amount of the particular foreign affiliate's consolidated taxable surplus, in respect of the corporation resident in Canada, at that time (or, if there is no such excess, nil),

(v) the particular foreign affiliate's underlying foreign tax, in respect of the corporation resident in Canada, immediately before the dividend time, is deemed to be equal to the amount of the particular foreign affiliate's consolidated underlying foreign tax, in respect of the corporation resident in Canada, at that time, and

(vi) the particular foreign affiliate's consolidated net surplus, in respect of the corporation resident in Canada, immediately before the dividend time, is deemed to be equal to the amount, if any, by which

(A) the total of the particular foreign affiliate's consolidated exempt surplus, in respect of the corporation resident in Canada, at that time, and the particular foreign affiliate's consolidated taxable surplus, in respect of the corporation resident in Canada, at that time,

exceeds

(B) the total of the particular foreign affiliate's consolidated exempt deficit, in respect of the corporation resident in Canada, at that time, and the particular foreign affiliate's consolidated taxable deficit, in respect of the corporation resident in Canada, at that time;

(*f*) the attributed net surplus in respect of a disposed share of the specified class in respect of the particular foreign affiliate's consolidated net surplus, in respect of the corporation resident in Canada, immediately before the dividend time, is deemed to be equal to the amount that would be received by the holder of the disposed share, in respect of the disposed share, at the dividend time, if the particular foreign affiliate paid a dividend, at that time, on all of its shares, the total of which was equal to the amount of its consolidated net surplus, in respect of the corporation resident in Canada, immediately before the dividend time;

(*g*) for the purpose of applying subsection 5901(1) to subsection 5900(1), the amount of the whole dividend paid by the particular foreign affiliate, at the dividend time, on the shares of the specified class is deemed to be equal to the amount obtained when the total of all amounts each of which is an amount deemed by subsection 93(1) of the Act to have been received as a dividend on a disposed share of the specified class is multiplied by the greater of

(i) one, and

(ii) the amount determined by the formula

$$A/B$$

where

A is the amount determined, under subparagraph (*e*)(vi), to be the amount of the particular foreign affiliate's consolidated net surplus in respect of the corporation, immediately before the dividend time, and

B is the greater of

(A) one, and

(B) the total of all amounts each of which is the amount determined, under paragraph (*f*), to be the amount of the attributed net surplus, in respect of a disposed share of the specified class, in respect of the particular foreign affiliate's consolidated net surplus, in respect of the corporation resident in Canada, immediately before the dividend time; and

(*h*) for the purposes of paragraphs (*a*) to (*d*), the consolidated net surplus, at any time, in respect of a corporation resident in Canada, of a particular foreign affiliate of the corporation resident in Canada, is the amount that would be determined in paragraph (*e*) in respect of the particular foreign affiliate if the reference in that paragraph to "immediately before the dividend time" were read as a reference to 'at any time'."

(ii) section 5902 of the Regulations is, in respect of the designated section 93 election, to be read without reference to its subsection (2),

(iii) subsection 5902(3) of the Regulations is, in respect of the designated section 93 election, to be read as follows:

"(3) If a corporation resident in Canada elects, under subsection 93(1) of the Act, in respect of the disposition of a share of the capital stock of a foreign affiliate of the corporation, no adjustment, other than an adjustment referred to in subsection 5905(2), (4), (6) or (8), may be made to the foreign affiliate's

(*a*) exempt surplus in respect of the corporation;

(*b*) exempt deficit in respect of the corporation;

(*c*) taxable surplus in respect of the corporation;

(*d*) taxable deficit in respect of the corporation; or

(*e*) underlying foreign tax in respect of the corporation."

(iv) subsection 5902(6) of the Regulations is, in respect of the designated section 93 election, to be read as follows:

"(6) The amount designated in an election deemed by subsection 93(1.1) of the Act to have been made under subsection 93(1) of the Act is prescribed to be the amount that is the lesser of

(*a*) the capital gain, if any, otherwise determined in respect of the disposition of the share, and

(*b*) the amount of attributed net surplus (as determined under paragraph (1)(*f*)) in respect of the share."

Application Provision, S.C. 2013, c. 34, s. 52 [Modified Consolidated Net Surplus Election.]

(1) The application in subsection (2) (below) applies if

(*a*) a corporation has made the election above; and

(*b*) the corporation has made an election under subsection 93(1) or (1.2) of the Income Tax Act in respect of a disposition of a share of the capital stock of a foreign affiliate of the corporation that occurs after December 20, 2002 and on or before February 27, 2004 (other than a disposition required to be made under an agreement in writing made by a vendor on or before December 20, 2002), or in respect of a disposition that occurs after February 27, 2004 and that is required to be made under an agreement in writing made by a vendor after December 20, 2002 and before February 28, 2004; and

(*c*) the corporation elects in writing to apply subsection (2) (below) in respect of all of its foreign affiliates and files the election with the Minister of National Revenue on or before the day that is the later of the corporation's filing-due date for the corporation's taxation year that includes June 26, 2013 and June 26, 2014;

(2) then the Consolidated Net Surplus Election above does not apply in respect of dispositions referred to in paragraph (*b*) and the Regulations are, in respect of the dispositions, to be read as if section 5902 of the Regulations also contained the following subsection:

"(6.1) If an election under subsection 93(1) of the Act is made at any time by a particular corporation resident in Canada in respect of a share of the capital stock of a foreign affiliate (in this subsection referred to as the "particular affiliate") of the particular corporation that is disposed of to the particular corporation, to another corporation resident in Canada with which the particular corporation does not deal at arm's length or to another foreign affiliate of the particular corporation, the amount of the particular affiliate's exempt surplus or exempt deficit, taxable surplus or taxable deficit, underlying foreign tax and net surplus in respect of the particular corporation at that time

Regulations

is to be determined under paragraph (1)(*a*) as if the amount of any dividend referred to in subparagraph (1)(*a*)(i) or (ii) were nil."

(2) In this section,

(*a*) for the purpose of paragraph (1)(*a*),

(i) if a particular foreign affiliate of a corporation has an equity percentage (within the meaning assigned by subsection 95(4) of the Act) in another foreign affiliate of the corporation that has an equity percentage in the particular affiliate, the exempt surplus or exempt deficit, hybrid surplus or hybrid deficit, hybrid underlying tax, taxable surplus or taxable deficit, underlying foreign tax and net surplus of, and the amount of a dividend paid or received by, the particular affiliate are to be determined in a manner that is

(A) reasonable in the circumstances, and

(B) consistent with the results that would be obtained if a series of actual dividends had been paid and received by the foreign affiliates of the corporation that are relevant to the determination, and

(ii) if any foreign affiliate of a corporation resident in Canada has issued shares of more than one class of its capital stock, the amount that would be paid as a dividend on the shares of any class is the portion of its net surplus that, in the circumstances, it might reasonably be expected to have paid on all the shares of the class, and

(*b*) the specified adjustment factor in respect of a disposition is the percentage determined by the formula

$$A/B$$

where

A is

(i) if the elected dividend is received by the corporation, 100 per cent, and

(ii) if the elected dividend is received by another foreign affiliate of the corporation, the surplus entitlement percentage of the corporation in respect of the other affiliate immediately before the dividend time, and

B is the surplus entitlement percentage of the corporation in respect of the particular affiliate immediately before the dividend time.

History: S. 5902(2)(*a*)(i) and (ii) were replaced by S.C. 2013, c.34, s. 80(3), applicable in respect of elections in respect of dispositions of shares of the capital stock of a foreign affiliate of a taxpayer that occur after August 19, 2011.

See the application for the amendment to s. 5902(1)(*a*)(i) for the extension of assessment periods to take into account the amendments by S.C. 2013, c. 34, s. 54 to 89.

S. 5902(2)(*a*)(i) and (ii) formerly read:

(i) in determining the exempt surplus or exempt deficit, the taxable surplus or taxable deficit, the underlying foreign tax and the net surplus of a particular foreign affiliate of a taxpayer resident in Canada in which any other foreign affiliate of the taxpayer has an equity percentage (within the meaning assigned by subsection 95(4) of the Act), no amount shall be included in respect of any distribution that would be received by the particular affiliate from that other affiliate, and

(ii) if any foreign affiliate of a corporation resident in Canada has issued shares of more than one class of its capital stock, the amount that would be paid as a dividend on the shares of any class is the portion of its exempt surplus or exempt deficit and its taxable surplus (including underlying foreign tax applicable) or taxable deficit (and thus net surplus) that, in the circumstances, would reasonably be expected to have been paid on all the shares of that class; and

S. 5902(2) was replaced by S.C. 2013, c. 34, s. 41(1), applicable in respect of elections made in respect of dispositions that occur after December 18, 2009.

See the Application Provision following s. 5902(1) regarding the override of the statute-barring rules for assessments for taxation years that end before June 26, 2013.

S. 5902(2) formerly read:

(2) For the purposes of paragraphs (1)(*a*) and (*b*),

(*a*) in determining the exempt surplus or exempt deficit, the taxable surplus or taxable deficit, the underlying foreign tax and the net surplus of a particular foreign affiliate of a taxpayer resident in Canada in which any other foreign affiliate of the taxpayer has an equity percentage, no amount shall be included in respect of any distribution that would be received by the particular affiliate from such other affiliate; and

(*b*) if any foreign affiliate of a corporation resident in Canada has issued shares of more than one class of its capital stock, the amount that would be paid as a dividend on the shares of any class is such portion of its exempt surplus or exempt deficit and its taxable surplus (including underlying foreign tax applicable) or taxable deficit (and thus net surplus) as, in the circumstances, it might reasonably be expected to have paid on all the shares of that class.

(3) (Repealed by S.C. 2013, c. 34, s. 41(1).)

History: S. 5902(3) was repealed by S.C. 2013, c. 34, s. 41(1), applicable in respect of elections made in respect of dispositions that occur after December 18, 2009.

See the application following s. 5902(1) regarding the override of the statute-barring rules for assessments for taxation years that end before June 26, 2013.

S. 5902(3) formerly read:

(3) Where an election under subsection 93(1) of the Act is made by a corporation resident in Canada in respect of the disposition of a share of the capital stock of a foreign affiliate of the corporation, no adjustment shall be made to the affiliate's exempt surplus, exempt deficit, taxable surplus, taxable deficit or underlying foreign tax in respect of the corporation as a consequence of the election except as provided in subsections 5905(2), (5) and (8).

(4) (Revoked.)

(5) Any election under subsection 93(1) of the Act by a corporation resident in Canada in respect of any share of the capital stock of a foreign affiliate of the corporation disposed of by it or by another foreign affiliate of the corporation shall be made by filing the prescribed form with the Minister on or before the day that is the later of

(*a*) December 31, 1989; and

(*b*) where the election is made

(i) in respect of a share disposed of by the corporation, the day on or before which the corporation's return of income for its taxation year in which the disposition was made is required to be filed pursuant to subsection 150(1) of the Act, or

(ii) in respect of a share disposed of by another foreign affiliate of the corporation, the day on or before which the corporation's return of income for its taxation year, in which the taxation year of the foreign affiliate in which the disposition was made ends, is required to be filed pursuant to subsection 150(1) of the Act,

as the case may be.

Forms: T2107 — Election in Respect of a Share Disposition in a Foreign Affiliate.

(6) If at any time a corporation resident in Canada is deemed under subsection 93(1.11) of the Act to have made an election under subsection 93(1) of the Act in respect of a disposition of a share of the capital stock of a particular foreign affiliate of the corporation, the prescribed amount is the lesser of

Regulations

(*a*) the capital gain, if any, otherwise determined in respect of the disposition of the share; and

(*b*) the amount that would reasonably be expected to have been received in respect of the share if the particular affiliate had at that time paid dividends, on all shares of its capital stock, the total of which was equal to the amount determined under subparagraph (1)(*a*)(i) to be its net surplus in respect of the corporation for the purposes of the election.

History: S. 5902(6)(*b*) was replaced by S.C. 2013, c. 34, s. 41(2), applicable in respect of elections made in respect of dispositions that occur after December 18, 2009.

See the Application Provision following s. 5902(1) regarding the override of the statute-barring rules for assessments for taxation years that end before June 26, 2013.

S. 5902(6)(*b*) formerly read:

(*b*) the amount that could reasonably be expected to have been received in respect of the share if the particular affiliate had at that time paid dividends the aggregate of which on all shares of its capital stock was equal to the amount determined under paragraph (1)(*a*) to be its net surplus in respect of the corporation for the purposes of the election.

S. 5902(6), the portion before paragraph (*a*) was replaced by S.C. 2013, c. 34, s. 80(4), applicable in respect of elections in respect of dispositions of shares of the capital stock of a foreign affiliate of a corporation that occur after August 19, 2011. However, if the corporation makes the election under the application for s. 5901(2), the portion of subsection 5902(6) before paragraph (*a*) applies in respect of elections in respect of dispositions of shares of the capital stock of all foreign affiliates of the corporation that occur after December 20, 2002.

See the application for the amendment to s. 5902(1)(*a*)(i) for the extension of assessment periods to take into account the amendments by S.C. 2013, c. 34, s. 54 to 89.

S. 5902(6), the portion before paragraph (*a*) formerly read:

(6) Where at any time a corporation resident in Canada is deemed by virtue of subsection 93(1.1) of the Act to have made an election under subsection 93(1) of the Act in respect of a share of the capital stock of a particular foreign affiliate of the corporation disposed of by another foreign affiliate of the corporation, the amount deemed to have been designated in the election is hereby prescribed to be the lesser of

5903. Deductible Loss

(1) For the purposes of the description of F in the definition "foreign accrual property income" in subsection 95(1) of the Act, subject to subsection (2), the prescribed amount for the year (referred to in this subsection and subsection (2) as the "particular year") is the total of all amounts each of which is a portion designated for the particular year by the taxpayer of the foreign accrual property loss of the affiliate for a taxation year of the affiliate that is

(*a*) one of the 20 taxation years of the affiliate that immediately precede the particular year; or

(*b*) one of the three taxation years of the affiliate that immediately follow the particular year.

History: S. 5903(1) was replaced by S.C. 2013, c. 34, s. 42(1), applicable to taxation years of a foreign affiliate of a taxpayer that begin after November 1999, except that the reference to "20 taxation years" in paragraph 5903(1)(*a*) is, in respect of foreign accrual property losses for the foreign affiliate's taxation years that end in taxation years of the taxpayer that end

(i) before March 23, 2004, to be read as "seven taxation years", and

(ii) after March 22, 2004 and before 2006, to be read as "10 taxation years".

Any assessment of a taxpayer's tax, interest and penalties payable under the Act for any taxation year that ends before June 26, 2013 that would otherwise be precluded because of subsections 152(4) to (5) of the Act, shall be made to the extent necessary to take into account this amendment, if the taxpayer

(i) elects in writing in respect of all of its foreign affiliates that this section apply in respect of that provision, and

(ii) files that election with the Minister of National Revenue on or before December 26, 2013 [the day that is six months after royal assent].

S. 5903(1) formerly read:

(1) For the purpose of the description of F in the definition "foreign accrual property income" in subsection 95(1) of the Act, the amount prescribed to be the deductible loss of a particular foreign affiliate of a taxpayer for a taxation year and the five immediately preceding taxation years (each of which preceding taxation years is referred to in this subsection as a "preceding year") is the amount, if any, by which

(*a*) the total of all amounts each of which is the amount, if any, determined in respect of the particular affiliate in respect of a preceding year during which it was a controlled foreign affiliate of the taxpayer or of a person described in any of subparagraphs 95(2)(*f*)(iv) to (vii) of the Act, by which

(i) the total of the amounts determined for D and E in the definition "foreign accrual property income" in subsection 95(1) of the Act in respect of the particular affiliate for the preceding year

exceeds

(ii) the total of the amounts determined for A, B and C in the definition "foreign accrual property income" in subsection 95(1) of the Act in respect of the particular affiliate for the preceding year

exceeds the total of

(*b*) the total of all amounts each of which is an amount determined in respect of the particular affiliate in respect of a preceding year during which it was a controlled foreign affiliate of the taxpayer or of a person described in any of subparagraphs 95(2)(*f*)(iv) to (vii) of the Act and equal to the lesser of

(i) the amount that would be determined for F in the definition "foreign accrual property income" in subsection 95(1) of the Act in respect of the particular affiliate for the preceding year if that amount did not take into account any amount determined for any of A, B, C, D or E in the definition "foreign accrual property income" in subsection 95(1) of the Act in respect of the particular affiliate for any taxation year that is not a preceding taxation year, and

(ii) the amount that would be the foreign accrual property income of the particular affiliate for the preceding year if the formula in the definition "foreign accrual property income" in subsection 95(1) of the Act were read without reference to the variable F; and

(*c*) where a payment has been received by the particular affiliate and the payment can reasonably be considered to relate to a payment described in subsection 5907(1.3) made by another foreign affiliate of the taxpayer in respect of a loss, or any portion of a loss, of the particular affiliate described in the description of D or E of the definition "foreign accrual property income" in subsection 95(1) of the Act in respect of any preceding year of the particular affiliate, the amount of that loss or portion.

(2) For the purposes of this subsection and subsection (1),

(*a*) a portion of a foreign accrual property loss of the affiliate for any taxation year of the affiliate may be designated for the particular year only to the extent that the foreign accrual property loss exceeds the total of all amounts each of which is a portion, of the foreign accrual property loss, designated by the taxpayer for a taxation year of the affiliate that precedes the particular year;

(*b*) no portion of the affiliate's foreign accrual property loss for a taxation year of the affiliate is to be designated for the particular year until the affiliate's foreign accrual property losses for the preceding taxation years referred to in paragraph (1)(*a*) have been fully designated; and

(*c*) if any person or partnership that was, at the end of a taxation year (referred to in this paragraph as the "relevant loss year") of the affiliate, a relevant person or partnership in respect of the taxpayer designates for a taxation year (referred to in this paragraph as the "relevant claim year") of the affiliate a particular portion of the affiliate's foreign accrual property loss for the relevant loss year, there is deemed to have been designated for the relevant claim year by the taxpayer the portion of that loss that is the greater of

(i) the particular portion, and

Regulations

(ii) the greatest of the portions of that loss that are so designated by any other relevant persons or partnerships in respect of the taxpayer.

History: S. 5903(2) was replaced by S.C. 2013, c. 34, s. 42(1), applicable to taxation years of a foreign affiliate of a taxpayer that begin after November 1999, except that subsection 5903(2) is, in its application to taxation years that begin before 2001, to be read without reference to its paragraph (*b*).

See the application following s. 5903(1) regarding the override of the statute-barring rules for assessments for taxation years that end before June 26, 2013.

S. 5903(2) formerly read:

(2) For the purpose of subsection (1), each amount referred to in paragraph (1)(*c*) in respect of a controlled foreign affiliate of a taxpayer resident in Canada that is not otherwise determined in Canadian currency shall be converted to Canadian currency at the rate of exchange prevailing on the last day of the affiliate's taxation year in respect of which the amount determined under subsection (1) is being used to determine the foreign affiliate's foreign accrual property income as defined in subsection 95(1) of the Act.

Information Circulars: IC 77-9R Books, records and other requirements for taxpayers having foreign affiliates.

(3) For the purposes of this section, and subject to subsection (4), "foreign accrual property loss" of the affiliate for a taxation year of the affiliate means

(*a*) where, at the end of the year, the affiliate is a controlled foreign affiliate of a person or partnership that is, at the end of the year, a relevant person or partnership in respect of the taxpayer, the amount, if any, determined by the formula

$$J - (K + L + M + N)$$

where

J is the amount determined for D in the formula in the definition "foreign accrual property income" in subsection 95(1) of the Act in respect of the affiliate for the year,

K is the amount, if any, by which

(i) the amount determined for A in that formula in respect of the affiliate for the year

exceeds

(ii) the amount determined for H in that formula in respect of the affiliate for the year,

L is the amount, if any, by which

(i) the amount determined for B in that formula in respect of the affiliate for the year

exceeds

(ii) the total of

(A) the amount determined for E in that formula in respect of the affiliate for the year, and

(B) the amount determined for F.1 in that formula in respect of the affiliate for the year,

M is the amount determined for C in that formula in respect of the affiliate for the year, and

N is the amount, if any, by which

(i) the total of

(A) the amount determined for A.1 in that formula in respect of the affiliate for the year, and

(B) the amount determined for A.2 in that formula in respect of the affiliate for the year

exceeds

(ii) the amount determined for G in that formula in respect of the affiliate for the year; and

(*b*) in any other case, nil.

History: S. 5903(3)(*a*) was replaced by S.C. 2013, c. 34, s. 81(1), applicable in respect of capital losses of a foreign affiliate of a taxpayer that are incurred in taxation years of the foreign affiliate that end after August 19, 2011.

Any assessment of a taxpayer's tax, interest and penalties payable under the Act for any taxation year that ends before June 26, 2013 that would, in the absence of this section, be precluded because of subsections 152(4) to (5) of the Act shall be made to the extent necessary to take into account the amendments by S.C. 2013, c. 34, s. 54 to 89.

S. 5903(3)(*a*) formerly read:

(*a*) if, at the end of the year, the affiliate is a controlled foreign affiliate of a person or partnership that is, at the end of the year, a relevant person or partnership in respect of the taxpayer, the amount, if any, by which

(i) the total of the amounts determined for D, E, G and H in the formula in the definition "foreign accrual property income" in subsection 95(1) of the Act in respect of the affiliate for the year

exceeds

(ii) the total of the amounts determined for A to C in that formula in that definition in respect of the affiliate for the year; and

S. 5903(3) was replaced by 2013, c. 34, s. 42(1) applicable to taxation years of a foreign affiliate of a taxpayer that begin after November 1999, except that paragraph 5903(3)(*a*) is, in its application to taxation years of the foreign affiliate that begin on or before December 18, 2009, to be read as follows:

"(*a*) where, at the end of the year, the affiliate is a controlled foreign affiliate of a person or partnership that is, at the end of the year, a relevant person or partnership in respect of the taxpayer, the amount, if any, by which

(i) the total of the amounts determined for D and E in the formula in the definition "foreign accrual property income" in subsection 95(1) of the Act in respect of the affiliate for the year

exceeds

(ii) the total of the amounts determined for A, B and C in that formula in that definition in respect of the affiliate for the year; and"

See the application following s. 5903(1) regarding the override of the statute-barring rules for assessments for taxation years that end before June 26, 2013.

S. 5903(3) formerly read:

(3) Where

(*a*) there has been a foreign merger (within the meaning assigned by subsection 87(8.1) of the Act) of two or more foreign affiliates of a taxpayer resident in Canada in respect of each of which the taxpayer's surplus entitlement percentage was not less than 90 per cent immediately before the merger (in this subsection referred to as "predecessor affiliates") to form a new foreign affiliate in respect of which the taxpayer's surplus entitlement percentage immediately after the merger was not less than 90 per cent (in this subsection referred to as the "successor affiliate"), or

(*b*) there has been a dissolution of a foreign affiliate (in this subsection referred to as the "predecessor affiliate") of a taxpayer resident in Canada and on the dissolution property of the predecessor affiliate, the fair market value of which was not less than 90 per cent of the fair market value of all property of the predecessor affiliate immediately before the dissolution, was distributed to another foreign affiliate (in this subsection referred to as the "successor affiliate") of the taxpayer,

the successor affiliate shall, in respect of such part of the amount determined under subsection (1) to be the deductible loss of a predecessor affiliate at the time of the foreign merger or dissolution as may reasonably be considered to have arisen while the taxpayer, a person or persons referred to in any of subparagraphs 95(2)(*f*)(iv) to (vii) of the Act, or the taxpayer together with such a person or persons, had a surplus entitlement percentage in respect of such predecessor affiliate that was not less than 90 per cent, be considered to be the same corporation as, and a continuation of, such predecessor affiliate.

(4) In computing under subsection (3) the foreign accrual property loss of the affiliate for a taxation year, if the affiliate or another corporation receives a payment described in subsection 5907(1.3) from a non-resident corporation that is, at the time of the payment, a foreign affiliate of a relevant person or partnership in respect of the taxpayer and any portion of the payment can reasonably be considered to relate to a loss or portion of a loss of the affiliate for the year described in the description of D in the definition "foreign accrual property income" in subsection 95(1) of the Act, the amount of the loss or portion of the loss is deemed to be nil.

History: S. 5903(4) was replaced by S.C. 2013, c. 34, s. 81(2), applicable in respect of capital losses of a foreign affiliate of a taxpayer that are incurred in taxation years of the foreign affiliate that end after August 19, 2011.

See the application for the amendment to s. 5903(3)(*a*) for the extension of assessment periods to take into account the amendments by S.C. 2013, c. 34 s. 54 to 89.

S. 5903(4) formerly read:

(4) In computing under subsection (3) the affiliate's foreign accrual property loss for a taxation year, if the affiliate or another corporation receives a payment described in subsection 5907(1.3) from a non-resident corporation that is, at the time of the payment, a foreign affiliate of a relevant person or partnership in respect of the taxpayer and any portion of the payment can reasonably be considered to relate to a loss or portion of a loss of the affiliate for the year described in the description of D or E in the definition "foreign accrual property income" in subsection 95(1) of the Act, the amount of the loss or portion of the loss is deemed to be nil.

S. 5903(4) was added by 2013, c. 34, s. 42(1) applicable to taxation years of a foreign affiliate of a taxpayer that begin after November 1999, except that subsection 5903(4) is, in its application to taxation years of the foreign affiliate that begin on or before December 18, 2009, to be read as follows:

"(4) In computing under subsection (3) the affiliate's foreign accrual property loss for a taxation year, if the affiliate or another corporation has received a payment described in subsection 5907(1.3) from another foreign affiliate of the taxpayer and any portion of the payment can reasonably be considered to relate to a loss or portion of a loss of the affiliate for the year described in the description of D or E in the definition "foreign accrual property income" in subsection 95(1) of the Act, the amount of the loss or portion of the loss is deemed to be nil."

See the application following s. 5903(1) regarding the override of the statute-barring rules for assessments for taxation years that end before June 26, 2013.

(5) For the purposes of this section and section 5903.1,

(*a*) if paragraph 95(2)(*d.1*) of the Act applies to a foreign merger, the new foreign corporation referred to in that paragraph is, except in the determination of the foreign accrual property income of a foreign affiliate predecessor referred to in that paragraph, deemed to be the same corporation as, and a continuation of, each foreign affiliate predecessor; and

(*b*) if paragraph 95(2)(*e*) of the Act applies to a liquidation and dissolution, of a disposing affiliate referred to in that paragraph, that is a designated liquidation and dissolution of the disposing affiliate, the shareholder affiliate referred to in that paragraph is, except in the determination of the foreign accrual property income of the disposing affiliate, deemed to be the same corporation as, and a continuation of, the disposing affiliate.

History: S. 5903(5), the portion before paragraph (*a*) was replaced by S.C. 2013, c. 34, s. 81(3), applicable in respect of capital losses of a foreign affiliate of a taxpayer that are incurred in taxation years of the foreign affiliate that end after August 19, 2011.

See the application for the amendment to s. 5903(3)(*a*) for the extension of assessment periods to take into account the amendments by S.C. 2013, c. 34, s. 54 to 89.

S. 5903(5), the portion before paragraph (*a*) formerly read:

(5) For the purpose of this section,

S. 5903(5)(*a*) and (*b*) were replaced by S.C. 2013, c. 34, s. 81(4), applicable in respect of mergers or combinations that occur, and liquidations and dissolutions that begin, in respect of a foreign affiliate of a taxpayer, after August 19, 2011. However

(*a*) if the taxpayer makes the election under the application for s. 95(2)(*d.1*) of the *Income Tax Act*,

(i) paragraph 5903(5)(*a*) also applies in respect of mergers or combinations in respect of all foreign affiliates of the taxpayer that occur after December 20, 2002 and on or before August 19, 2011, and

(ii) that paragraph is, for such mergers or combinations, to be read as follows:

"(*a*) if paragraph 95(2)(*d.1*) of the Act applies to a foreign merger, the new foreign corporation referred to in that paragraph is deemed to be the same corporation as, and a continuation of, each foreign affiliate predecessor; and"

(*b*) if the taxpayer makes the election under the application for s. 95(2)(*e*) of the *Income Tax Act*,

(i) paragraph 5903(5)(*b*) also applies in respect of liquidations and dissolutions of all foreign affiliates of the taxpayer that begin after December 20, 2002 and on or before August 19, 2011, and

(ii) that paragraph is, in respect of such liquidations and dissolutions, to be read as follows:

"(*b*) if paragraph 95(2)(*e*) of the Act applies to a liquidation and dissolution, of a disposing affiliate referred to in that paragraph, that is a designated liquidation and dissolution of the disposing affiliate, the shareholder affiliate referred to in that paragraph is deemed to be the same corporation as, and a continuation of, the disposing affiliate."

See the application for the amendment to s. 5903(3)(*a*) for the extension of assessment periods to take into account the amendments by S.C. 2013, c. 34, s. 54 to 89.

S. 5903(5)(*a*) and (*b*) formerly read:

(*a*) if there is a foreign merger (within the meaning assigned by subsection 87(8.1) of the Act) of two or more foreign affiliates of a taxpayer resident in Canada in respect of each of which the taxpayer's surplus entitlement percentage immediately before the merger is not less than 90 per cent to form one corporate entity in respect of which the taxpayer's surplus entitlement percentage immediately after the merger is not less than 90 per cent, the corporate entity is deemed to be the same corporation as, and a continuation of, each of those predecessor affiliates; and

(*b*) if there is a liquidation and dissolution of a foreign affiliate of a taxpayer resident in Canada in respect of which the taxpayer's surplus entitlement percentage immediately before the liquidation and dissolution is not less than 90 per cent into another foreign affiliate of the taxpayer in respect of which the taxpayer's surplus entitlement percentage immediately before and immediately after the liquidation and dissolution is not less than 90 per cent, the other affiliate is deemed to be the same corporation as, and a continuation of, that predecessor affiliate.

S. 5903(5) was added by 2013, c. 34, s. 42(1) applicable to taxation years of a foreign affiliate of a taxpayer that begin after November 1999.

See the application following s. 5903(1) regarding the override of the statute-barring rules for assessments for taxation years that end before June 26, 2013.

(6) In this section and section 5903.1, a "relevant person or partnership", in respect of the taxpayer at any time, means the taxpayer or a person (other than a designated acquired corporation of the taxpayer), or a partnership, that is at that time

(*a*) a person (other than a partnership) that is resident in Canada and does not, at that time, deal at arm's length (otherwise than because of a right referred to in paragraph 251(5)(*b*) of the Act) with the taxpayer;

(*b*) an antecedent corporation of a relevant person or partnership in respect of the taxpayer;

(*c*) a partnership a member of which is at that time a relevant person or partnership in respect of the taxpayer under this subsection; or

(*d*) where paragraph (1)(*b*) is being applied, a corporation of which the taxpayer is an antecedent corporation.

History: S. 5903(6), the portion before paragraph (*a*) was replaced by S.C. 2013, c. 34, s. 81(5), applicable in respect of capital losses of a foreign affiliate of a taxpayer that are incurred in taxation years of the foreign affiliate that end after August 19, 2011.

See the application for the amendment to s. 5903(3)(*a*) for the extension of assessment periods to take into account the amendments by S.C. 2013, c. 34, s. 54 to 89.

S. 5903(6), the portion before paragraph (*a*) formerly read:

(6) In this section, a "relevant person or partnership" in respect of the taxpayer, at any time, means the taxpayer or a person (other than a designated acquired corporation of the taxpayer), or a partnership, that is at that time

S. 5903(6) was added by 2013, c. 34, s. 42(1) applicable to taxation years of a foreign affiliate of a taxpayer that begin after November 1999, except that subsection 5903(6) is, in its application to taxation years of the foreign affiliate that begin on or before December 18, 2009, to be read as follows:

"(6) In this section, a "relevant person or partnership", in respect of a taxpayer, at any time means

(*a*) the taxpayer;

(*b*) any person with whom the taxpayer was not dealing at arm's length;

(*c*) any person with whom the taxpayer would not have been dealing at arm's length if the person had been in existence after the taxpayer came into existence;

(*d*) any predecessor corporation (within the meaning assigned by subsection 87(1) of the Act) of a person described in any of paragraphs (*a*) to (*c*); or

(*e*) any predecessor corporation (within the meaning assigned by paragraph 87(2)(*l.2*) of the Act) of a person described in any of paragraphs (*a*) to (*c*)."

See the application following s. 5903(1) regarding the override of the statute-barring rules for assessments for taxation years that end before June 26, 2013.

(7) For the purposes of paragraphs (6)(*a*) to (*d*),

(*a*) if a person or partnership (referred to in this paragraph as the "relevant person") is not dealing at arm's length (otherwise than because of a right referred to in paragraph 251(5)(*b*) of the Act) with another person or partnership (referred to in this paragraph as the "particular person") at a particular time, the relevant person is deemed to have existed and not to have dealt at arm's length with the particular person, nor with each antecedent corporation (other than a designated acquired corporation of the particular person) of the particular person, throughout the period that began when the particular person or the antecedent corporation, as the case may be, came into existence and that ends at the particular time; and

(*b*) where paragraph (1)(*b*) is being applied, if a corporation of which a particular person (other than a designated acquired corporation of the corporation) is an antecedent corporation is not dealing at arm's length (otherwise than because of a right referred to in paragraph 251(5)(*b*) of the Act) with another person or partnership at any time, the particular person is deemed to exist and not to be dealing at arm's length with the other person or the partnership, as the case may be, at that time.

History: S. 5903(7) was added by 2013, c. 34, s. 42(1) applicable to taxation years of a foreign affiliate of a taxpayer that begin after November 1999, except that section 5903 is, in its application to taxation years that begin on or before December 18, 2009, to be read without reference to its subsection (7).

See the application following s. 5903(1) regarding the override of the statute-barring rules for assessments for taxation years that end before June 26, 2013.

5903.1. [Foreign accrual capital losses]

(1) For the purposes of the description of F.1 in the definition "foreign accrual property income" in subsection 95(1) of the Act, subject to subsection (2), the prescribed amount for the year (referred to in this subsection and subsection (2) as the "particular year") is the total of all amounts each of which is a portion designated for the particular year by the taxpayer of the foreign accrual capital loss of the affiliate for a taxation year of the affiliate that is

(*a*) one of the twenty taxation years of the affiliate that immediately precede the particular year; or

(*b*) one of the three taxation years of the affiliate that immediately follow the particular year.

History: S. 5903.1(1) was added by S.C. 2013, c. 34, s. 82(1), applicable in respect of capital losses of a foreign affiliate of a taxpayer that are incurred in taxation years of the foreign affiliate that end after August 19, 2011.

Any assessment of a taxpayer's tax, interest and penalties payable under the Act for any taxation year that ends before June 26, 2013 that would, in the absence of this section, be precluded because of subsections 152(4) to (5) of the Act shall be made to the extent necessary to take into account the amendments by S.C. 2013, c. 34, s. 54 to 89.

(2) For the purposes of this subsection and subsection (1),

(*a*) a portion of a foreign accrual capital loss of the affiliate for any taxation year of the affiliate may be designated for the particular year only to the extent that the foreign accrual capital loss exceeds the total of all amounts each of which is a portion, of the foreign accrual capital loss, designated by the taxpayer for a taxation year of the affiliate that precedes the particular year;

(*b*) no portion of the foreign accrual capital loss of the affiliate for a taxation year of the affiliate is to be designated for the particular year until the foreign accrual capital losses of the affiliate for the preceding taxation years referred to in paragraph (1)(*a*) have been fully designated; and

(*c*) if any person or partnership that was, at the end of a taxation year (referred to in this paragraph as the "relevant loss year") of the affiliate, a relevant person or partnership in respect of the taxpayer designates for a taxation year (referred to in this paragraph as the "relevant claim year") of the affiliate a particular portion of the foreign accrual capital loss of the affiliate for the relevant loss year, there is deemed to have been designated for the relevant claim year by the taxpayer the portion of that loss that is the greater of

(i) the particular portion, and

(ii) the greatest of the portions of that loss that are so designated by any other relevant persons or partnerships in respect of the taxpayer.

History: S. 5903.1(2) was added by S.C. 2013, c. 34, s. 82(1), applicable in respect of capital losses of a foreign affiliate of a taxpayer that are incurred in taxation years of the foreign affiliate that end after August 19, 2011.

See the application for the amendment to s. 5903.1(1) for the extension of assessment periods to take into account the amendments by S.C. 2013, c. 34 s. 54 to 89.

(3) For the purposes of this section, and subject to subsection (4), "foreign accrual capital loss" of the affiliate for a taxation year of the affiliate means

(*a*) where, at the end of the year, the affiliate is a controlled foreign affiliate of a person or partnership that is, at the end of the year, a relevant person or partnership in respect of the taxpayer, the amount, if any, by which

(i) the amount determined under paragraph (*a*) of the description of E in the formula in the definition "foreign accrual property income" in subsection 95(1) of the Act in respect of the affiliate for the year

exceeds

Regulations

(ii) the amount determined for E in that formula in respect of the affiliate for the year; and

(*b*) in any other case, nil.

History: S. 5903.1(3) was added by S.C. 2013, c. 34, s. 82(1), applicable in respect of capital losses of a foreign affiliate of a taxpayer that are incurred in taxation years of the foreign affiliate that end after August 19, 2011.

See the application for the amendment to s. 5903.1(1) for the extension of assessment periods to take into account the amendments by S.C. 2013, c. 34 s. 54 to 89.

(4) In computing under subsection (3) the foreign accrual capital loss of the affiliate for a taxation year, if the affiliate or another corporation receives a payment described in subsection 5907(1.3) from a non-resident corporation that is, at the time of the payment, a foreign affiliate of a relevant person or partnership in respect of the taxpayer and any portion of the payment can reasonably be considered to relate to an allowable capital loss or a portion of an allowable capital loss of the affiliate for the year described in the description of E in the definition "foreign accrual property income" in subsection 95(1) of the Act, the amount of the loss or portion of the loss is deemed to be nil.

History: S. 5903.1(4) was added by S.C. 2013, c. 34, s. 82(1), applicable in respect of capital losses of a foreign affiliate of a taxpayer that are incurred in taxation years of the foreign affiliate that end after August 19, 2011.

See the application for the amendment to s. 5903.1(1) for the extension of assessment periods to take into account the amendments by S.C. 2013, c. 34 s. 54 to 89.

5904. Participating Percentage

(1) For the purpose of subparagraph (*b*)(ii) of the definition "participating percentage" in subsection 95(1) of the Act, the participating percentage of a particular share owned by a taxpayer of the capital stock of a corporation in respect of any foreign affiliate of the taxpayer that was, at the end of its taxation year, a controlled foreign affiliate of the taxpayer is prescribed to be the percentage that would be the taxpayer's equity percentage in the affiliate at that time on the assumption that

(*a*) the taxpayer owned no shares other than the particular share;

(*b*) the direct equity percentage of a person in any foreign affiliate of the taxpayer, for which the total of the distribution entitlements of all the shares of all classes of the capital stock of the affiliate was greater than nil, was determined by the following rules and not by the rules contained in the definition "direct equity percentage" in subsection 95(4) of the Act:

(i) for each class of the capital stock of the affiliate, determine that amount that is the proportion of the distribution entitlement of all the shares of that class that the number of shares of that class owned by that person is of all the issued shares of that class, and

(ii) determine the proportion that

(A) the aggregate of the amounts determined under subparagraph (i) for each class of the capital stock of the affiliate

is of

(B) the aggregate of the distribution entitlements of all the issued shares of all classes of the capital stock of the affiliate

and the proportion determined under subparagraph (ii) when expressed as a percentage is that person's direct equity percentage in the affiliate; and

(*c*) the direct equity percentage of a person in any foreign affiliate of the taxpayer, for which the total of the distribution entitlements of all the shares of all classes of the capital stock of the affiliate would not, in the absence of this paragraph, be greater than nil, was determined on the assumption that the amount determined under subparagraph (2)(*b*)(i) were the greater of

(i) the amount of the affiliate's retained earnings, if any, determined at the end of the taxation year under accounting principles that are relevant to the affiliate for the taxation year, and

(ii) the amount determined by the formula

$$A \times B$$

where

A is the amount of the affiliate's total assets determined at the end of the taxation year under accounting principles that are relevant to the affiliate for the taxation year, and

B is 25%.

History: S. 5904(1)(*c*) was replaced by S.C. 2013, c. 34, s. 83(1), applicable in respect of taxation years of a foreign affiliate of a taxpayer that begin after August 19, 2011.

Any assessment of a taxpayer's tax, interest and penalties payable under the Act for any taxation year that ends before June 26, 2013 that would, in the absence of this section, be precluded because of subsections 152(4) to (5) of the Act shall be made to the extent necessary to take into account the amendments by S.C. 2013, c. 34, s. 54 to 89.

S. 5904(1)(*c*) formerly read:

(*c*) the direct equity percentage of a person in any foreign affiliate of the taxpayer, for which the total of the distribution entitlements of all the shares of all classes of the capital stock of the affiliate was not greater than nil, was determined by the rules contained in the definition "direct equity percentage" in subsection 95(4) of the Act.

(2) For the purposes of this section, the distribution entitlement of all the shares of a class of the capital stock of a foreign affiliate of the taxpayer at the end of its taxation year is the aggregate of

(*a*) the distributions made during the year by the affiliate to holders of shares of that class; and

(*b*) the amount that the affiliate might reasonably be expected to distribute to holders of shares of that class immediately after the end of the year if at that time it had distributed to its shareholders an amount equal to the aggregate of

(i) the amount, if any, by which the net surplus of the affiliate in respect of the taxpayer at the end of the year, computed as though any adjustments resulting from the provisions of sections 5902 and 5905 and subsections 5907(2.1) and (2.2) and any references thereto during the year were ignored, exceeds the net surplus of the affiliate in respect of the taxpayer at the end of its immediately preceding taxation year, and

(ii) the amount that the affiliate would receive if at that time each controlled foreign affiliate of the taxpayer in which the affiliate had an equity percentage had distributed to its shareholders an amount equal to the aggregate of

(A) the amount that would be determined under subparagraph (i) for the controlled foreign affiliate if the controlled foreign affiliate were the foreign affiliate referred to in subparagraph (i), for each of the taxation years of the controlled foreign affiliate ending in the taxation year of the affiliate, and

(B) each such amount that the controlled foreign affiliate would receive from any other controlled foreign affiliate of the taxpayer in which it had an equity percentage.

(3) For the purposes of subsection (2),

(*a*) the net surplus of a foreign affiliate of a person resident in Canada is, in respect of that person, to be computed as if that person were a corporation resident in Canada;

(*b*) if a particular foreign affiliate of a corporation has an equity percentage (within the meaning assigned by subsection 95(4) of the Act) in another foreign affiliate of the corporation that has an equity percentage in the particular affiliate, the net surplus of, or the amount of a distribution received by, the particular affiliate is to be determined in a manner that is

(i) reasonable in the circumstances, and

(ii) consistent with the results that would be obtained if a series of actual distributions had been made and received by the foreign affiliates of the corporation that are relevant to the determination;

(*c*) if any controlled foreign affiliate of a taxpayer resident in Canada has issued shares of more than one class of its capital stock, the amount that would be distributed to the holders of shares of any class is such portion of the amount determined under subparagraph (2)(*b*)(ii) as, in the circumstances, it might reasonably be expected to distribute to the holders of those shares; and

(*d*) in determining the distribution entitlement

(i) of a class of shares of the capital stock of a foreign affiliate that is entitled to cumulative dividends, the amount of any distribution referred to in paragraph (2)(*a*) shall be deemed not to include any distribution in respect of such class that is, or would, if it were made, be referable to profits of a preceding taxation year, and

(ii) of any other class of shares of the capital stock of the affiliate, the net surplus of the affiliate at the end of the year referred to in subparagraph (2)(*b*)(i) shall be deemed not to have been reduced by any distribution described in subparagraph (i) with respect to a class of shares that is entitled to cumulative dividends to the extent that the distribution was referable to profits of a preceding taxation year.

History: S. 5904(3)(*a*) was replaced by S.C. 2013, c. 34, s. 43(1), applicable to taxation years of a foreign affiliate of a taxpayer that begin after November 1999.

Any assessment of a taxpayer's tax, interest and penalties payable under the Act for any taxation year that ends before June 26, 2013 that would otherwise be precluded because of subsections 152(4) to (5) of the Act, shall be made to the extent necessary to take into account this amendment, if the taxpayer

(i) elects in writing in respect of all of its foreign affiliates that this section apply in respect of that provision, and

(ii) files that election with the Minister of National Revenue on or before December 26, 2013 [the day that is six months after royal assent].

S. 5904(3)(*a*) formerly read:

(*a*) the net surplus of a foreign affiliate of a taxpayer who is an individual, in respect of that individual, shall be computed as if that individual were a corporation resident in Canada;

S. 5904(3)(*b*) was replaced by S.C. 2013, c. 34, s. 83(2), applicable in respect of taxation years of a foreign affiliate of a taxpayer that begin after August 19, 2011.

Any assessment of a taxpayer's tax, interest and penalties payable under the Act for any taxation year that ends before June 26, 2013 that would, in the absence of this section, be precluded because of subsections 152(4) to (5) of the Act shall be made to the extent necessary to take into account the amendments by S.C. 2013, c. 34, s. 54 to 89.

S. 5904(3)(*b*) formerly read:

(*b*) in computing the net surplus of a particular foreign affiliate of a taxpayer resident in Canada in which any other foreign affiliate of the taxpayer has an equity percentage, no amount shall be included in respect of any distribution that would be received by the particular affiliate from such other affiliate;

5905. Special Rules

(1) If, at any time, there is an acquisition or a disposition of shares of the capital stock of a particular foreign affiliate of a corporation resident in Canada and the surplus entitlement percentage of the corporation in respect of the particular foreign affiliate or any other foreign affiliate (the particular affiliate and those other affiliates each being referred to in this subsection as a "relevant affiliate") of the corporation in which the particular affiliate has an equity percentage (within the meaning assigned by subsection 95(4) of the Act) changes, for the purposes of the definitions "exempt surplus", "hybrid surplus", "hybrid underlying tax", "taxable surplus", and "underlying foreign tax" in subsection 5907(1), each of the opening exempt surplus or opening exempt deficit, opening hybrid surplus or opening hybrid deficit, opening hybrid underlying tax, opening taxable surplus or opening taxable deficit, and opening underlying foreign tax, as the case may be, of the relevant affiliate in respect of the corporation is, except where the acquisition or disposition occurs in a transaction to which paragraph (3)(*a*) or subsection (5) or (5.1) applies, the amount determined at that time by the formula

$$A \times B/C$$

where

A is the amount of that surplus, deficit or tax, as the case may be, as otherwise determined at that time;

B is the corporation's surplus entitlement percentage immediately before that time in respect of the relevant affiliate; and

C is the corporation's surplus entitlement percentage immediately after that time in respect of the relevant affiliate.

History: S. 5905(1), the portion before the formula was replaced by S.C. 2013, c. 34, s. 84(1), applicable in respect of acquisitions and dispositions that occur after August 19, 2011.

Any assessment of a taxpayer's tax, interest and penalties payable under the Act for any taxation year that ends before June 26, 2013 that would, in the absence of this section, be precluded because of subsections 152(4) to (5) of the Act shall be made to the extent necessary to take into account the amendments by S.C. 2013, c. 34, s. 54 to 89.

S. 5905(1), the portion before the formula previously read:

(1) If, at any time, there is an acquisition or a disposition of shares of the capital stock of a particular foreign affiliate of a corporation resident in Canada and the surplus entitlement percentage of the corporation in respect of the particular foreign affiliate or any other foreign affiliate (the particular affiliate and those other affiliates being referred to individually in this subsection as a "relevant affiliate") of the corporation in which the particular affiliate has an equity percentage (within the meaning assigned by subsection 95(4) of the Act) changes, for the purposes of the definitions "exempt surplus", "taxable surplus" and "underlying foreign tax" in subsection 5907(1), each of the opening exempt surplus or opening exempt deficit, opening taxable surplus or opening taxable deficit, and opening underlying foreign tax, as the case may be, of the relevant affiliate in respect of the corporation is, except where the acquisition or disposition occurs in a transaction to which paragraph (3)(*a*) or subsection (5) or (5.1) applies, the amount determined at that time by the formula

S. 5905(1) was replaced by S.C. 2013, c. 34, s. 44(1), applicable In respect of acquisitions and dispositions that occur after December 18, 2009.

Any assessment of a taxpayer's tax, interest and penalties payable under the Act for any taxation year that ends before June 26, 2013 that would otherwise be precluded because of subsections 152(4) to (5) of the Act, shall be made to the extent necessary to take into account this amendment, if the taxpayer

(i) elects in writing in respect of all of its foreign affiliates that this section apply in respect of that provision, and

(ii) files that election with the Minister of National Revenue on or before December 26, 2013 [the day that is six months after royal assent].

S. 5905(1) formerly read:

(1) Where at any time, other than in the course of a transaction to which subsection (2) or (5) applies, a corporation resident in Canada or a foreign affiliate of such a corporation acquires in any manner whatever shares of the capital stock of another corporation that was a foreign affiliate of the corporation immediately before that time (in this subsection referred to as the "acquired affiliate") and as a result thereof the surplus entitlement percentage of the corporation in respect of the acquired affiliate increases, for the purposes of this Part, the exempt surplus or exempt deficit, the taxable surplus or taxable deficit and the underlying foreign tax, in respect of the corporation, of the acquired affiliate and of each other foreign affiliate of the corporation in which the acquired affiliate has an equity percentage (in this subsection referred to as the "other affiliate"), other than an acquired affiliate or other affiliate in respect of which subsection (8) applies, shall at that time be reduced to the proportion of the amount thereof otherwise determined that

(*a*) the surplus entitlement percentage immediately before that time of the corporation in respect of the acquired affiliate or the other affiliate, as the case may be, determined on the assumption that the taxation year of the acquired affiliate or the other affiliate, as the case may be, that otherwise would have included that time had ended immediately before that time,

is of

(*b*) the surplus entitlement percentage immediately after that time of the corporation in respect of the acquired affiliate or the other affiliate, as the case may be, determined on the assumption that the taxation year of the acquired affiliate or the other affiliate, as the case may be, that otherwise would have included that time had ended immediately after that time,

and, for the purposes of the definitions "exempt deficit", "exempt surplus", "taxable deficit", "taxable surplus" and "underlying foreign tax" in subsection 5907(1), those reduced amounts are referred to as the opening exempt deficit, opening exempt surplus, opening taxable deficit, opening taxable surplus and opening underlying foreign tax, as the case may be, of each of those affiliates in respect of the corporation.

Application Provision, S.C. 2013, c. 34, s. 51 [Consolidated Net Surplus Election] Subject to the Modified Consolidated Net Surplus Election (below), if a corporation resident in Canada elects in writing in respect of all of its foreign affiliates and files the election with the Minister of National Revenue on or before the day that is the later of the corporation's filing-due date for the corporation's taxation year that includes June 26, 2013 and June 26, 2014, the following rules apply:

(*b*) in respect of acquisitions that occur after February 27, 2004 and before December 19, 2009, subsection 5905(1) of the Regulations is to be read as follows:

"(1) If, at any time, other than in the course of a transaction to which subsection (2) or (5) applies, a corporation resident in Canada or a foreign affiliate of such a corporation acquires in any manner whatever shares of the capital stock of another corporation that was, immediately after that time, a foreign affiliate of the corporation (in this subsection referred to as the "acquired affiliate") and as a result of that acquisition the surplus entitlement percentage of the corporation in respect of the acquired affiliate and in respect of any other foreign affiliate of the corporation resident in Canada (the acquired affiliate and each such other foreign affiliate each being referred to in this subsection as the "particular relevant foreign affiliate"), increases, the following rules apply:

(*a*) for the purposes of this Part, the amount of the exempt surplus or exempt deficit, the taxable surplus or taxable deficit, and the underlying foreign tax, in respect of the corporation, of the particular relevant foreign affiliate is (unless subsection (8) applies to the particular relevant foreign affiliate because of the acquisition of the shares) to be, at that time, adjusted to become the proportion of that amount, determined without making this adjustment, that

(i) the surplus entitlement percentage, immediately before that time, of the corporation in respect of the particular relevant foreign affiliate, determined on the assumption that the taxation year of the particular relevant foreign affiliate that otherwise would have included that time had ended immediately before that time

is of

(ii) the surplus entitlement percentage, immediately after that time, of the corporation in respect of the particular relevant foreign affiliate, determined on the assumption that the taxation year of the particular relevant foreign affiliate that otherwise would have included that time had ended immediately after that time; and

(*b*) for the purposes of applying the definitions "exempt deficit", "exempt surplus", "taxable deficit", "taxable surplus" and "underlying foreign tax" in subsection 5907(1), the adjusted amounts determined under paragraph (*a*) are deemed to be the opening exempt deficit, opening exempt surplus, opening taxable deficit, opening taxable surplus and opening underlying foreign tax, as the case may be, of the particular relevant foreign affiliate, in respect of the corporation."

(*c*) in respect of dispositions in respect of which a designated section 93 election was made,

(i) subsection 5905(2) of the Regulations is to be read as follows:

"(2) If at any time (referred to in this subsection as the "disposition time") a particular foreign affiliate of a corporation resident in Canada redeems, acquires or cancels (other than a redemption, an acquisition or a cancellation in respect of which an adjustment has previously been made under this subsection or subsection (1) as it read prior to November 13, 1981) in any manner whatever (otherwise than by way of a winding-up) one or more shares (referred to in this subsection and subsections (16) to (23) as "disposed shares") of any class of its capital stock, the following rules apply:

(*a*) if, because of an election made by the corporation under subsection 93(1) of the Act in respect of the disposition of the disposed shares, a dividend (referred to in this subsection and subsections (18) and (21) as the "disposition dividend") is deemed to have been received on the disposed shares, by the corporation or by another foreign affiliate of the corporation, for the purpose of the adjustment required by paragraph (*b*),

(i) in computing the exempt surplus, in respect of the corporation resident in Canada, of the particular foreign affiliate or of another foreign affiliate (the particular foreign affiliate and each such other foreign affiliate being referred to in this subsection and subsections (16) to (23) as the "particular relevant foreign affiliate") of the corporation resident in Canada in which the particular foreign affiliate has an equity percentage at the time (referred to in this subsection and subsections (16) to (22) as the "balance adjustment time") that is immediately before the disposition time, there is to be included, under subparagraph (v) of the description of B in the definition "exempt surplus" in subsection 5907(1), the total of

(A) the amount of the exempt surplus reduction, in respect of the corporation resident in Canada, of the particular relevant foreign affiliate, in respect of the disposed shares,

(B) the amount of the exempt deficit reduction, in respect of the corporation resident in Canada, of the particular relevant foreign affiliate, in respect of the disposed shares, and

(C) the amount of the taxable deficit allocation, in respect of the corporation resident in Canada, of the particular relevant foreign affiliate, in respect of the disposed shares,

(ii) in computing the particular relevant foreign affiliate's taxable surplus, in respect of the corporation resident in Canada, at the balance adjustment time, there is to be included, under subparagraph (v) of the description of B in the definition "taxable surplus" in subsection 5907(1), the total of

(A) an amount equal to the taxable surplus reduction, in respect of the corporation resident in Canada, of the particular relevant foreign affiliate, in respect of the disposed shares,

(B) an amount equal to the taxable deficit reduction, in respect of the corporation resident in Canada, of the particular relevant foreign affiliate, in respect of the disposed shares, and

(C) an amount equal to the exempt deficit allocation, in respect of the corporation resident in Canada, of the particular relevant foreign affiliate, in respect of the disposed shares,

(iii) in computing the particular relevant foreign affiliate's underlying foreign tax, in respect of the corporation resident in Canada, at the balance adjustment time, there is to be included, under subparagraph (iii) of the description of B in the definition "underlying foreign tax" in subsection 5907(1), the total of

(A) the amount determined by the formula (which is deemed to be nil, if, in respect of the particular relevant foreign affiliate, the value determined for B in the formula is nil)

$$A/B \times C \times D$$

where

A is the portion of the particular relevant foreign affiliate's underlying foreign tax, in respect of the corporation resident in Canada, at the balance adjustment time, that may reasonably be considered to have been included in computing the particular foreign affiliate's consolidated underlying foreign tax (as determined under paragraph 5902(1)(*c*)), in respect of the corporation resident in Canada, in respect of the disposition,

B is the particular foreign affiliate's consolidated underlying foreign tax (as determined under paragraph 5902(1)(*c*)), in respect of the corporation resident in Canada, in respect of the disposition,

C is the portion, of the particular foreign affiliate's consolidated underlying foreign tax (as determined under paragraph 5902(1)(*c*)), in respect of the corporation resident in Canada, in respect of the disposition), that is prescribed, by paragraph 5900(1)(*d*), to be applicable to the portion of the whole dividend (as determined, under paragraph 5902(1)(*g*), in respect of the disposition dividend in respect of the disposed shares) paid on shares of the specified class that is prescribed, by paragraph 5900(1)(*c*), to have been paid out of the particular foreign affiliate's consolidated taxable surplus, in respect of the corporation resident in Canada, and

D is the specified adjustment factor in respect of the particular relevant foreign affiliate, and

(B) the amount of the underlying foreign tax reduction in respect of the corporation resident in Canada, of the particular relevant foreign affiliate, in respect of the disposition of the disposed shares,

(iv) in computing the particular relevant foreign affiliate's exempt deficit, in respect of the corporation resident in Canada, at the balance adjustment time, there is to be included, under subparagraph (vi.1) of the description of A in the definition "exempt surplus" in subsection 5907(1), an amount equal to the exempt deficit, in respect of the corporation resident in Canada, of the particular relevant foreign affiliate, immediately before that time, and

(v) in computing the particular relevant foreign affiliate's taxable deficit, in respect of the corporation resident in Canada, at the balance adjustment time, there is to be included, under subparagraph (iv.1) of the description of A in the definition "taxable surplus" in subsection 5907(1), an amount equal to the taxable deficit, in respect of the corporation resident in Canada, of the particular relevant foreign affiliate, immediately before that time;

(*b*) the amount, at the balance adjustment time, of exempt surplus, exempt deficit, taxable surplus, taxable deficit and underlying foreign tax, in respect of the corporation resident in Canada, of the particular relevant foreign affiliate is to be adjusted to become the proportion of that amount, determined without making this adjustment, that

(i) the surplus entitlement percentage, at the balance adjustment time, of the corporation resident in Canada, in respect of the particular relevant foreign affiliate, determined on the assumption that the taxation year, of the particular relevant foreign affiliate, that otherwise would have included that time, had ended immediately before that time

is of

(ii) the surplus entitlement percentage, immediately after the time of the disposition, of the corporation resident in Canada, in respect of the particular relevant foreign affiliate, determined on the assumption that the taxation year, of the particular relevant foreign affiliate, that otherwise would have included the balance adjustment time, had ended at the time of the disposition; and

(*c*) for the purposes of applying the definitions "exempt deficit", "exempt surplus", "taxable deficit", "taxable surplus" and "underlying foreign tax", in subsection 5907(1), the amounts determined under paragraph (*b*), in respect of the particular relevant foreign affiliate, in respect of the corporation resident in Canada, are deemed to be the opening exempt deficit, opening exempt surplus, opening taxable deficit, opening taxable surplus and opening underlying foreign tax, as the case may be, of the particular relevant foreign affiliate, in respect of the corporation resident in Canada."

(ii) subsection 5905(4) of the Regulations is to be read as follows:

"(4) For the purpose of subsection (3),

(*a*) if, at any time, a foreign affiliate of a corporation resident in Canada disposes of one or more shares (referred to in this subsection and subsections (16) to (23) as the "disposed shares") of a class of the capital stock of a predecessor corporation and the foreign affiliate is, because of an election made under subsection 93(1) of the Act, deemed to have received a dividend (referred to in this subsection and subsections (18) and (21) as the "disposition dividend") on the disposed shares, for the purposes of the adjustments required by paragraphs (*b*) and (3)(*b*),

(i) in computing the exempt surplus, in respect of the corporation resident in Canada, of each predecessor corporation and of each other foreign affiliate of the corporation resident in Canada in which a predecessor foreign affiliate has an equity percentage (the particular predecessor corporation and each such other foreign affiliate being referred to in this subsection and subsections (16) to (23) as the "particular relevant foreign affiliate") at the time (referred to in this subsection and subsections (16) to (22) as the "balance adjustment time") that is immediately before the foreign merger, there is to be included under subparagraph (v) of the description of B in the definition "exempt surplus" in subsection 5907(1), the total of

(A) an amount equal to the exempt surplus reduction, in respect of the corporation resident in Canada, of the particular relevant foreign affiliate, in respect of the disposed shares,

(B) an amount equal to the exempt deficit reduction, in respect of the corporation resident in Canada, of the particular relevant foreign affiliate, in respect of the disposed shares, and

(C) an amount equal to the taxable deficit allocation, in respect of the corporation resident in Canada, of the particular relevant foreign affiliate, in respect of the disposed shares,

(ii) in computing the particular relevant foreign affiliate's taxable surplus, in respect of the corporation resident in Canada, at the balance adjustment time, there is to be included, under subparagraph (v) of the description of B in the definition "taxable surplus" in subsection 5907(1), the total of

(A) an amount equal to the taxable surplus reduction, in respect of the corporation resident in Canada, of the particular relevant foreign affiliate, in respect of the disposed shares,

(B) an amount equal to the taxable deficit reduction, in respect of the corporation resident in Canada, of the particular relevant foreign affiliate, in respect of the disposed shares, and

(C) an amount equal to the exempt deficit allocation, in respect of the corporation resident in Canada, of the particular relevant foreign affiliate, in respect of the disposed shares,

(iii) in computing the particular relevant foreign affiliate's underlying foreign tax, in respect of the corporation resident in Canada, at the balance adjustment time, there is to be included, under subparagraph (iii) of the description of B in the definition "underlying foreign tax" in subsection 5907(1), the total of

(A) the amount determined by the formula (which is deemed to be nil, if, in respect of the particular relevant foreign affiliate, the value determined for B in the formula is nil)

$$A/B \times C \times D$$

where

A is the portion of the amount of the particular relevant foreign affiliate's underlying foreign tax, in respect of the corporation resident in Canada, at the balance adjustment time, that may reasonably be considered to have been included in computing the amount of the consolidated underlying foreign tax (as determined under paragraph 5902(1)(*c*)), in respect of the corporation resident in Canada, of the particular predecessor corporation that issued the disposed shares, in respect of the disposition,

B is the amount of the consolidated underlying foreign tax (as determined under paragraph 5902(1)(*c*)), in respect of the corporation resident in Canada, of the particular predecessor corporation that issued the disposed shares, in respect of the disposition,

C is the total of all amounts each of which is the amount, determined by paragraph 5900(1)(*d*), to be the amount of foreign tax applicable to the portion of the disposition dividend prescribed to have been paid out of the taxable surplus of the issuing foreign affiliate, that relates to a disposed share, in respect of the disposition, and

D is the specified adjustment factor, in respect of the corporation resident in Canada, in respect of the particular relevant foreign affiliate of the corporation resident in Canada, of the foreign affiliate of the corporation resident in Canada that disposed of the disposed shares, in respect of the disposition of the disposed shares, and

(B) the amount of the underlying foreign tax reduction in respect of the corporation resident in Canada, of the particular relevant foreign affiliate, in respect of the disposition of the disposed shares,

(iv) in computing the exempt deficit, in respect of the corporation resident in Canada, of the particular relevant foreign affiliate, at the balance adjustment time, there is to be included, under subparagraph (vi.1) of the description of A in the definition "exempt surplus" in subsection 5907(1), an amount equal to the exempt deficit, in respect of the corporation resident in Canada, immediately before that time, of the particular relevant foreign affiliate, and

(v) in computing the particular relevant foreign affiliate's taxable deficit, in respect of the corporation resident in Canada, at the balance adjustment time, there is to be included, under subparagraph (iv.1) of the description of A in the definition "taxable surplus" in subsection 5907(1), an amount equal to the taxable deficit, in respect of the corporation resident in Canada, immediately before that time, of the particular relevant foreign affiliate; and

(*b*) the amount, at the balance adjustment time, of exempt surplus, exempt deficit, taxable surplus, taxable deficit and underlying foreign tax, in respect of the corporation resident in Canada, of the particular relevant foreign affiliate is to be adjusted to become the proportion of that amount, determined without making that adjustment, that

(i) the surplus entitlement percentage, at the balance adjustment time, of the corporation resident in Canada, in respect of the particular relevant foreign affiliate, determined on the assumption that the taxation year, of the particular relevant foreign affiliate that otherwise would have included that time, had ended immediately before that time

is of

(ii) the surplus entitlement percentage, immediately after the time of the disposition, of the corporation resident in Canada, in respect of the particular relevant foreign affiliate, determined on the assumption that the taxation year, of the particular relevant foreign affiliate, that otherwise would have included the balance adjustment time, had ended at the time of the disposition."

(iii) the portion of subsection 5905(5) of the Regulations between paragraphs (*c*) and (*d*) is to be read as follows:

"the following rules apply for the purposes of this Part in respect of the particular affiliate and each other foreign affiliate of the predecessor corporation in which the particular affiliate has an equity percentage (the particular affiliate and each such other foreign affiliate each being referred to in subsections (16) to (23) as the "particular relevant foreign affiliate"):"

(iv) subsection 5905(6) of the Regulations is to be read as follows:

"(6) For the purpose of subsection (5), the following rules apply:

(*a*) if paragraph (5)(*a*) applies and the predecessor corporation is, because of an election made under subsection 93(1) of the Act, deemed to have received a dividend (referred to in this subsection and subsections (18) and (21) as the "disposition dividend") on one or more of the shares (each of which is referred to in this subsection and subsections (16) to (23) as a "disposed share") of the particular foreign affiliate (referred to in this subsection as the "issuing foreign affiliate") disposed of, at that time, for the purpose of the adjustment required by paragraph (*b*),

(i) in computing the exempt surplus, in respect of the predecessor corporation, of a particular relevant foreign affiliate at the time (referred to in this subsection and subsections (16) to (22) as the "balance adjustment time") that is immediately before the disposition time, the following rules apply:

(A) if the particular relevant foreign affiliate has, at the balance adjustment time, an amount of exempt surplus, in respect of the corporation resident in Canada, and the issuing foreign affiliate has, at that time, an amount of consolidated exempt surplus (as determined under paragraph 5902(1)(*a*)), in respect of the corporation resident in Canada, in respect of the disposition of the disposed share that is equal to or greater than the amount of its consolidated exempt deficit (as determined under paragraph 5902(1)(*b*)), in respect of the corporation resident in Canada, in respect of the disposition of the disposed shares, there is to be included under subparagraph (v) of the description of B in the definition "exempt surplus" in subsection 5907(1) the amount determined by the formula

$$A/B \times C/D$$

where

A is the portion of the amount of the particular relevant foreign affiliate's exempt surplus, in respect of the predecessor corporation, at the balance adjustment time, that may reasonably be considered to have been included in computing the amount of the issuing foreign affiliate's consolidated exempt surplus (as determined under paragraph 5902(1)(*a*)), in respect of the predecessor corporation, in respect of the disposition of the disposed shares,

B is the amount of the issuing foreign affiliate's consolidated exempt surplus (as determined under paragraph 5902(1)(*a*)), in respect of the predecessor corporation, in respect of the disposition of the disposed shares,

C is the portion, of the disposition dividend that is, because of an election made under subsection 93(1) of the Act in respect of the disposition of the disposed shares, deemed to be received on the disposed shares by the person that disposed of the disposed shares, that is prescribed by paragraph 5900(1)(*a*) to have been paid out of the issuing foreign affiliate's exempt surplus, in respect of the predecessor corporation, and

D is the surplus entitlement percentage of the predecessor corporation in respect of the particular relevant foreign affiliate at the balance adjustment time, determined on the assumption that the disposed shares were the only shares owned by the predecessor corporation at that time,

(B) if the amount determined, in respect of the particular relevant foreign affiliate, for either B or D in the formula in clause (A) is nil, the amount determined, in respect of the particular relevant foreign affiliate, by that formula is deemed to be nil,

(C) there is to be included under subparagraph (v) of the description of B in the definition "exempt surplus" in subsection 5907(1) the amount of the particular relevant foreign affiliate's exempt surplus, in respect of the corporation resident in Canada, at the balance adjustment time if

(I) the particular relevant foreign affiliate has, at the balance adjustment time, an amount of exempt surplus, in respect of the corporation resident in Canada, and

(II) the issuing foreign affiliate has, at that time, an amount of consolidated exempt deficit (as determined under paragraph 5902(1)(*b*)), in respect of the corporation resident in Canada, in respect of the disposition of the disposed share that is equal to or greater than the amount of its consolidated exempt surplus (as determined under paragraph 5902(1)(*a*)), in respect of the corporation resident in Canada, in respect of the disposition of the disposed shares, and

(D) there is to be included under subparagraph (v) of the description of B in the definition "exempt surplus" in subsection 5907(1) an amount equal to the particular relevant foreign affiliate's taxable deficit allocation in respect of the disposed shares,

(ii) in computing the taxable surplus, in respect of a predecessor corporation, of the particular relevant foreign affiliate, at the balance adjustment time, the following rules apply:

(A) if the particular relevant foreign affiliate has, at the balance adjustment time, an amount of taxable surplus in respect of the corporation resident in Canada, and the issuing foreign affiliate has, at that time, an amount of consolidated taxable surplus (as determined under paragraph 5902(1)(*c*)), in respect of the corporation resident in Canada, in respect of the disposition that is equal to or greater than the amount of the issuing foreign affiliate's consolidated taxable deficit (as determined under paragraph 5902(1)(*d*)), in respect of the corporation resident in Canada, in respect of the disposition of the disposed shares, there is to be included under subparagraph (v) of the description of B in the definition "taxable surplus" in subsection 5907(1) the amount determined by the formula

$$A/B \times C/D$$

where

A is the portion of the amount of the particular relevant foreign affiliate's taxable surplus, in respect of the predecessor corporation, at the balance adjustment time, that may reasonably be considered to have been included in computing the amount of the issuing foreign affiliate's consolidated taxable surplus (as determined under paragraph 5902(1)(*c*)), in respect of the predecessor corporation, in respect of the disposition of the disposed shares,

B is the amount of the issuing foreign affiliate's consolidated taxable surplus (as determined under paragraph 5902(1)(*c*)), in respect of the predecessor corporation, in respect of the disposition of the disposed shares,

C is the portion, of the disposition dividend that is, because of an election made under subsection 93(1) of the Act in respect of the disposition of the disposed shares, deemed to be received on the disposed shares by the person that disposed of the disposed shares, that is prescribed by paragraph 5900(1)(*b*) to have been paid out of the issuing foreign affiliate's taxable surplus, in respect of the predecessor corporation, and

D is the surplus entitlement percentage of the predecessor corporation in respect of the particular relevant foreign affiliate at the balance adjustment time, determined on the assumption that the disposed shares were the only shares owned by the predecessor corporation at that time,

(B) if the amount determined, in respect of the particular relevant foreign affiliate for either B or D in the formula in clause (A) is nil, the amount determined, in respect of the particular relevant foreign affiliate, by that formula is deemed to be nil,

(C) there is to be included, under subparagraph (v) of the description of B in the definition "taxable surplus" in subsection 5907(1), the amount of particular relevant foreign affiliate's taxable surplus, in respect of the corporation resident in Canada, at the balance adjustment time, if

(I) the particular relevant foreign affiliate has, at the balance adjustment time, an amount of taxable surplus in respect of the corporation resident in Canada, and

(II) the issuing foreign affiliate has, at that time, an amount of consolidated taxable deficit (as determined under paragraph 5902(1)(*d*)), in respect of the corporation resident in Canada, in respect of the disposition that is equal to or greater than the amount of the issuing foreign affiliate's consolidated taxable surplus (as determined under paragraph 5902(1)(*c*)), in respect of the corporation resident in Canada, in respect of the disposition of the disposed shares, and

(D) there is to be included in subparagraph (v) of the description of B in the definition "taxable surplus" in subsection 5907(1) an amount equal to the particular relevant foreign affiliate's exempt deficit allocation in respect of the disposed shares,

(iii) in computing the underlying foreign tax, in respect of the predecessor corporation, of the particular relevant foreign affiliate, at the balance adjustment time, there is to be included under subparagraph (iii) of the description of B in the definition "underlying foreign tax" in subsection 5907(1) the total of

(A) the amount determined by the formula (which is deemed to be nil, if, in respect of the particular relevant foreign affiliate, the value determined for either B or D in the formula is nil)

$$A/B \times C/D$$

where

A is the portion of the amount of the particular relevant foreign affiliate's underlying foreign tax, in respect of the predecessor corporation, at the balance adjustment time, that may reasonably be considered to have been included in computing the amount of the issuing foreign affiliate's consolidated underlying foreign tax (as determined under paragraph 5902(1)(*c*)), in respect of the predecessor corporation, in respect of the disposition,

B is the amount of the issuing foreign affiliate's consolidated underlying foreign tax (as determined under paragraph 5902(1)(*c*)), in respect of the predecessor corporation, in respect of the disposition,

C is the total of all amounts each of which is the amount, determined by paragraph 5900(1)(*d*), to be the amount of foreign tax applicable to the portion of the disposition dividend prescribed to have been paid out of the taxable surplus of the issuing foreign affiliate, that relates to a disposed share, in respect of the disposition, and

D is the surplus entitlement percentage of the predecessor corporation in respect of the particular relevant foreign affiliate at the balance adjustment time, determined on the assumption that the disposed shares were the only shares owned by the predecessor corporation at that time, and

(B) the amount determined by the formula

$$A \times (B + C)/D$$

where

A is the underlying foreign tax, in respect of the particular predecessor corporation, at the balance adjustment time, of the particular relevant foreign affiliate in respect of the disposition of the disposed shares,

B is the amount determined under clause (ii)(C) in respect of the particular relevant foreign affiliate, in respect of the predecessor corporation, in respect of the disposition of the disposed shares,

C is the exempt deficit allocation, in respect of the predecessor corporation, of the particular relevant foreign affiliate, in respect of the disposition of the disposed shares, and

D is the taxable surplus in respect of the predecessor corporation, at the balance adjustment time, of the particular relevant foreign affiliate,

(iv) in computing the exempt deficit, in respect of the predecessor corporation, of the particular relevant foreign affiliate, at the balance adjustment time, there is to be included under subparagraph (vi.1) of the description of A in the definition "exempt surplus" in subsection 5907(1) an amount equal to the exempt deficit, in respect of the predecessor corporation, of the particular relevant foreign affiliate, immediately before that time, and

(v) in computing the taxable deficit, in respect of the predecessor corporation, of the particular relevant foreign affiliate, at the balance adjustment time, there is to be included under subparagraph (iv.1) of the description of A in the definition "taxable surplus" in subsection 5907(1) an amount equal to the taxable deficit, in respect of the predecessor corporation, of the particular relevant foreign affiliate, immediately before that time; and

(*b*) the exempt surplus or the exempt deficit, the taxable surplus or the taxable deficit and the underlying foreign tax in respect of a predecessor corporation (within the meaning assigned by subsection (5)) and in respect of the acquiring corporation (within the meaning assigned by subsection (5)) of a particular relevant foreign affiliate is, at the balance adjustment time, to be adjusted to become the proportion of the amount of the surplus, deficit or underlying foreign tax determined without reference to this paragraph that

(i) the surplus entitlement percentage, immediately before the time of the latest of the transactions referred to in paragraphs (5)(*a*), (*b*) and (*c*), of the predecessor corporation or the acquiring corporation, as the case may be, in respect of the particular relevant foreign affiliate, determined on the assumptions

(A) that the taxation year of the particular relevant foreign affiliate that otherwise would have included the balance adjustment time had ended immediately before that time, and

(B) if the transaction is a disposition referred to in paragraph (5)(*a*), that the shares referred to in that paragraph were the only shares owned by the predecessor corporation at the balance adjustment time

is of

(ii) the surplus entitlement percentage, immediately after the time of the latest of the transactions referred to in paragraphs (5)(*a*), (*b*) and (*c*), of the predecessor corporation or the acquiring corporation, as the case may be, in respect of the particular relevant foreign affiliate, determined on the assumption that the taxation year of the particular relevant foreign affiliate that otherwise would have included that time had ended immediately after that time."

(v) subsection 5905(8) of the Regulations is to be read as follows:

"(8) If, at any time, a dividend (referred to in this subsection and subsections (18) and (21) as the "disposition dividend") is, because of an election made by a corporation resident in Canada under subsection 93(1) of the Act, deemed to have been received on one or more shares (each of which is referred to in this subsection and subsections (16) to (23) as a "disposed share") of a class of the capital stock of a particular foreign affiliate (referred to in this subsection as the "issuing foreign affiliate") of the corporation resident in Canada that were disposed (which disposition is referred in this subsection and subsections (16) to (23) as the "disposition") to the corporation resident in Canada or to another corporation that was, immediately after the disposition, a foreign affiliate of the corporation resident in Canada, the following rules apply:

(*a*) for the purpose of the adjustment required by paragraph (*b*),

(i) in computing the exempt surplus, in respect of the corporation resident in Canada, of the issuing foreign affiliate or another foreign affiliate of the corporation resident in Canada in which the issuing foreign affiliate has an equity percentage (the issuing foreign affiliate and each such other foreign affiliate each being referred to in this subsection and subsections (16) to (23) as the "particular relevant foreign affiliate") at the time (referred to in this subsection and subsections (16) to (22) as the "balance adjustment time") that is immediately before the time of the disposition, there is to be included under subparagraph (v) of the description of B in the definition "exempt surplus" in subsection 5907(1), the total of

(A) an amount equal to the exempt surplus reduction, in respect of the corporation resident in Canada, of the particular relevant foreign affiliate, in respect of the disposed shares,

(B) an amount equal to the exempt deficit reduction, in respect of the corporation resident in Canada, of the particular relevant foreign affiliate, in respect of the disposed shares, and

(C) an amount equal to the taxable deficit allocation, in respect of the corporation resident in Canada, of the particular relevant foreign affiliate, in respect of the disposed shares,

(ii) in computing the taxable surplus, in respect of the corporation resident in Canada, of the particular relevant foreign affiliate, at the balance adjustment time, there is to be included under subparagraph (v) of the description of B in the definition "taxable surplus" in subsection 5907(1) the total of

(A) an amount equal to the taxable surplus reduction, in respect of the corporation resident in Canada, of the particular relevant foreign affiliate, in respect of the disposed shares,

(B) an amount equal to the taxable deficit reduction, in respect of the corporation resident in Canada, of the particular relevant foreign affiliate, in respect of the disposed shares, and

(C) an amount equal to the exempt deficit allocation, in respect of the corporation resident in Canada, of the particular relevant foreign affiliate, in respect of the disposed shares,

(iii) in computing the underlying foreign tax, in respect of the corporation resident in Canada, of the particular relevant foreign affiliate, at the balance adjustment time, there is to be included under subparagraph (iii) of the description of B in the definition "underlying foreign tax" in subsection 5907(1) the total of

(A) the amount determined by the formula (which is deemed to be nil, if, in respect of the particular relevant foreign affiliate, the value determined for B in the formula is nil)

$$A/B \times C \times D$$

where

A is the portion of the amount of the particular relevant foreign affiliate's underlying foreign tax, in respect of the corporation resident in Canada, at the balance adjustment time, that may reasonably be considered to have been included in computing the amount of the issuing foreign affiliate's consolidated underlying foreign tax (as determined under paragraph 5902(1)(*c*)), in respect of the corporation resident in Canada, in respect of the disposition,

B is the amount of the issuing foreign affiliate's consolidated underlying foreign tax (as determined under paragraph 5902(1)(*c*)), in respect of the corporation resident in Canada, in respect of the disposition,

C is the total of all amounts each of which is the amount, determined by paragraph 5900(1)(*d*), to be the amount of foreign tax applicable to the portion of the disposition dividend prescribed to have been paid out of the taxable surplus of the issuing foreign affiliate, that relates to a disposed share, in respect of the disposition, and

D is the specified adjustment factor, in respect of the corporation resident in Canada, in respect of the particular relevant foreign affiliate of the corporation resident in Canada, of the foreign affiliate of the corporation resident in Canada that disposed of the disposed shares, in respect of the disposition of the disposed shares, and

(B) the amount of the underlying foreign tax reduction in respect of the corporation resident in Canada, of the particular relevant foreign affiliate, in respect of the disposition of the disposed shares,

(iv) in computing the exempt deficit, in respect of the corporation resident in Canada, of the particular relevant foreign affiliate, at the balance adjustment time, there is to be included under subparagraph (vi.1) of the description of A in the definition "exempt surplus" in subsection 5907(1), an amount equal to the exempt deficit, in respect of the corporation resident in Canada, of the particular relevant foreign affiliate, immediately before that time, and

(v) in computing the taxable deficit, in respect of the corporation resident in Canada, of the particular relevant foreign affiliate, at the balance adjustment time, there is to be included under subparagraph (iv.1) of the description of A in the definition "taxable surplus" in subsection 5907(1), an amount equal to the taxable deficit, in respect of the corporation resident in Canada, of the particular relevant foreign affiliate, immediately before that time;

(*b*) the amount, at the balance adjustment time, of exempt surplus, exempt deficit, taxable surplus, taxable deficit and underlying foreign tax, in respect of the corporation resident in Canada, of the particular relevant foreign affiliate is to be adjusted to become the proportion of that amount, determined without making this adjustment, that

(i) the surplus entitlement percentage, at the balance adjustment time, of the corporation resident in Canada, in respect of the particular relevant foreign affiliate, determined on the assumption that the taxation year, of the particular relevant foreign affiliate that otherwise would have included that time, had ended immediately before that time

is of

(ii) the surplus entitlement percentage, immediately after the time of the disposition, of the corporation resident in Canada, in respect of the particular relevant foreign affiliate, determined on the assumption that the taxation year, of the particular relevant foreign affiliate, that otherwise would have included the balance adjustment time, had ended at the time of the disposition; and

(*c*) for the purposes of applying the definitions "exempt deficit", "exempt surplus", "taxable deficit", "taxable surplus" and "underlying foreign tax", in subsection 5907(1), the amounts determined under paragraph (*b*) are deemed to be the opening exempt deficit, opening exempt surplus, opening taxable deficit, opening taxable surplus, and opening underlying foreign tax, as the case may be, of the particular relevant foreign affiliate, in respect of the corporation resident in Canada."

(vi) section 5905 of the Regulations is to be read as if it also contained the following subsections:

"(16) The exempt deficit allocation, of a particular relevant foreign affiliate in respect of a corporation resident in Canada, in respect of disposed shares of the particular foreign affiliate of the corporation resident in Canada, that issued the disposed shares (in this subsection referred to as the "issuing foreign affiliate") is, if the particular relevant foreign affiliate has, at the balance adjustment time, an amount of taxable surplus in respect of the corporation resident in Canada and the issuing foreign affiliate has, at that time, an amount of consolidated exempt deficit (as determined under paragraph 5902(1)(*b*)), in respect of the corporation resident in Canada, in respect of the disposition of the disposed shares, that exceeds the amount of its consolidated exempt surplus (as determined under paragraph 5902(1)(*a*)), in respect of the corporation resident in Canada, in respect of the disposition of the disposed shares,

(*a*) the amount determined by the formula

$$1/E \times [(A - B) \times C/D]$$

where

A is the amount of the issuing foreign affiliate's consolidated exempt deficit (as determined under paragraph 5902(1)(*b*)), in respect of the corporation resident in Canada, in respect of the disposition of the disposed shares,

B is the amount of the issuing foreign affiliate's consolidated exempt surplus (as determined under paragraph 5902(1)(*a*)), in respect of the corporation resident in Canada, in respect of the disposition of the disposed shares,

C is the portion of the amount of the particular relevant foreign affiliate's taxable surplus, in respect of the corporation resident in Canada, immediately before the disposition of the disposed shares, that can reasonably be considered to have been included in computing the amount of the issuing foreign affiliate's consolidated taxable surplus (as determined under paragraph 5902(1)(*c*)), in respect of the corporation resident in Canada, in respect of the disposition of the disposed shares,

D is the amount of the issuing foreign affiliate's consolidated taxable surplus (as determined under paragraph 5902(1)(*c*)), in respect of the corporation resident in Canada, in respect of the disposition of the disposed shares, and

E is

(i) subject to subparagraph (ii), the surplus entitlement percentage, of the issuing foreign affiliate, in respect of the particular relevant foreign affiliate, that would be determined under subsections 5905(10) to (13) at the balance adjustment time if the issuing foreign affiliate were the corporation resident in Canada referred to in those subsections and the particular relevant foreign affiliate were the particular foreign affiliate referred to in those subsections, and

(ii) if the particular relevant foreign affiliate is the issuing foreign affiliate, 1; and

(*b*) if the amount determined, in respect of the particular relevant foreign affiliate, for the description of D or E in the formula in paragraph (a) is nil, nil.

(17) The exempt deficit reduction, in respect of a corporation resident in Canada, of a particular relevant foreign affiliate of the corporation resident in Canada, in respect of disposed shares, is

(*a*) if the particular relevant foreign affiliate has, at the balance adjustment time, an amount of exempt surplus, in respect of the corporation resident in Canada, and the particular foreign affiliate, of the corporation resident in Canada, that issued the disposed shares (in this subsection referred to as the "issuing foreign affiliate") has, at the balance adjustment time, consolidated exempt surplus (as determined under paragraph 5902(1)(*a*)), in respect of the corporation resident in Canada, in respect of the disposition of the disposed shares, that exceeds the amount of its consolidated exempt deficit (as determined under paragraph 5902(1)(*b*)), in respect of the corporation resident in Canada, in respect of the disposition of the disposed shares,

(i) the amount determined by the formula

$$A/B \times C/D$$

where

A is the portion of the amount of the particular relevant foreign affiliate's exempt surplus, in respect of the corporation resident in Canada, at the balance adjustment time, that can reasonably be considered to have been included in computing the amount of the issuing foreign affiliate's consolidated exempt surplus (as determined under paragraph 5902(1)(*a*)), in respect of the corporation resident in Canada, in respect of the disposition of the disposed shares,

B is the amount of the issuing foreign affiliate's consolidated exempt surplus (as determined under paragraph 5902(1)(*a*)), in respect of the corporation resident in Canada, in respect of the disposition of the disposed shares,

C is the amount of the issuing foreign affiliate's consolidated exempt deficit (as determined under paragraph 5902(1)(*b*)), in respect of the corporation resident in Canada, in respect of the disposition of the disposed shares, and

D is

(A) subject to clause (B), the surplus entitlement percentage, of the issuing foreign affiliate, in respect of the particular relevant foreign affiliate, that, under subsections 5905(10) to (13), would be determined, at the balance adjustment time, where the issuing foreign affiliate were the corporation resident in Canada referred to in those subsections and the particular relevant foreign affiliate were the particular foreign affiliate referred to in those subsections, and

(B) where the particular relevant foreign affiliate is the issuing foreign affiliate, 1, and

(ii) if the value determined, in respect of the particular relevant foreign affiliate, for the description of any of A, B or D in the formula in subparagraph (i) is nil, nil; and

(*b*) the amount of the particular relevant foreign affiliate's exempt surplus, in respect of the corporation resident in Canada, at the balance adjustment time, if

(i) the particular relevant foreign affiliate has, at the balance adjustment time, an amount of exempt surplus, in respect of the corporation resident in Canada, and

(ii) the issuing foreign affiliate has, at that time, an amount of consolidated exempt deficit (as determined under paragraph 5902(1)(*b*)), in respect of the corporation resident in Canada, in respect of the disposition of the disposed shares that is equal to or greater than the amount of its consolidated exempt surplus (as determined under paragraph 5902(1)(*a*)), in respect of the corporation resident in Canada, in respect of the disposition of the disposed shares.

(18) The exempt surplus reduction in respect of a corporation resident in Canada, of a particular relevant foreign affiliate in respect of disposed shares is

(*a*) the amount determined by the formula

$$A/B \times C \times D$$

where

A is the portion of the amount of the particular relevant foreign affiliate's exempt surplus, in respect of the corporation resident in Canada, at the balance adjustment time, that can reasonably be considered to have been included in computing the amount of the consolidated exempt surplus, in respect of the corporation resident in Canada, (as determined under paragraph 5902(1)(*a*)) of the particular foreign affiliate, of the corporation resident in Canada, that issued the disposed shares (referred to in this subsection as the "issuing foreign affiliate"), in respect of the disposition of the disposed shares,

B is the amount of the issuing foreign affiliate's consolidated exempt surplus (as determined under paragraph 5902(1)(*a*)), in respect of the corporation resident in Canada, in respect of the disposition of the disposed shares,

C is the portion of the disposition dividend that is, because of an election made under subsection 93(1) of the Act in respect of the disposition of the disposed shares, received on the disposed shares by the person that disposed of those shares and that is prescribed by paragraph 5900(1)(*a*) to have been paid out of the issuing foreign affiliate's exempt surplus, in respect of the corporation resident in Canada, and

Regulations

D is the specified adjustment factor, in respect of the corporation resident in Canada, in respect of the particular relevant foreign affiliate, of the person that disposed of the disposed shares;

(*b*) if the amount determined, in respect of the particular relevant foreign affiliate, for either of A or B, in the formula in paragraph (*a*) is nil, nil; and

(*c*) if an amount is determined, in respect of the particular relevant foreign affiliate, under paragraph (17)(*b*), nil.

(19) The taxable deficit allocation, of a particular relevant foreign affiliate of a corporation resident in Canada, in respect of disposed shares of the particular foreign affiliate, of the corporation resident in Canada, that issued the disposed shares (in this subsection referred to as the "issuing foreign affiliate") is, if the particular relevant foreign affiliate has, at the balance adjustment time, an amount of exempt surplus in respect of the corporation resident in Canada and the issuing foreign affiliate has, at that time, an amount of consolidated taxable deficit (as determined under paragraph 5902(1)(*d*)), in respect of the corporation resident in Canada, in respect of the disposition of the disposed shares, that exceeds the amount of the issuing foreign affiliate's consolidated taxable surplus (as determined under paragraph 5902(1)(*c*)), in respect of the corporation resident in Canada, in respect of the disposition of the disposed shares,

(*a*) the amount determined by the formula

$$1/E \times [(A - B) \times C/D]$$

where

A is the amount of the issuing foreign affiliate's consolidated taxable deficit (as determined under paragraph 5902(1)(*d*)), in respect of the corporation resident in Canada, in respect of the disposition of the disposed shares,

B is the amount of the issuing foreign affiliate's consolidated taxable surplus (as determined under paragraph 5902(1)(*c*)), in respect of the corporation resident in Canada, in respect of the disposition of the disposed shares,

C is the portion of the amount of the particular relevant foreign affiliate's exempt surplus, in respect of the corporation resident in Canada, immediately before the disposition of the disposed shares, that may reasonably be considered to have been included in computing the amount of the issuing foreign affiliate's consolidated exempt surplus (as determined under paragraph 5902(1)(*a*)), in respect of the corporation resident in Canada, in respect of the disposition of the disposed shares,

D is the amount of the issuing foreign affiliate's consolidated exempt surplus (as determined under paragraph 5902(1)(*a*)), in respect of the corporation resident in Canada, in respect of the disposition of the disposed shares, and

E is

(i) subject to subparagraph (ii), the surplus entitlement percentage, of the issuing foreign affiliate, in respect of the particular relevant foreign affiliate, that would be determined under subsections 5905(10) to (13) at the balance adjustment time, where the issuing foreign affiliate were the corporation resident in Canada referred to in those subsections and the particular relevant foreign affiliate were the particular foreign affiliate referred to in those subsections, and

(ii) where the particular relevant foreign affiliate is the issuing foreign affiliate, 1; and

(*b*) where the amount determined, in respect of the particular relevant foreign affiliate, for the description of D or E in the formula in paragraph (*a*) is nil, nil.

(20) The taxable deficit reduction, in respect of a corporation resident in Canada, of a particular relevant foreign affiliate of the corporation resident in Canada, in respect of disposed shares, is

(*a*) if the particular relevant foreign affiliate has, at the balance adjustment time, an amount of taxable surplus, in respect of the corporation resident in Canada, and the particular foreign affiliate, of the corporation resident in Canada, that issued the disposed shares (in this subsection referred to as the "issuing foreign affiliate") has, at the balance adjustment time, consolidated taxable surplus (as determined under paragraph 5902(1)(*c*)), in respect of the corporation resident in Canada, in respect of the disposition of the disposed shares, that exceeds the amount of the issuing foreign affiliate's consolidated taxable deficit (as determined under paragraph 5902(1)(*d*)), in respect of the corporation resident in Canada, in respect of the disposition of the disposed shares,

(i) the amount determined by the formula

$$A/B \times C/D$$

where

A is the portion of the amount of the particular relevant foreign affiliate's taxable surplus, in respect of the corporation, at the balance adjustment time, that can reasonably be considered to have been included in computing the amount of the issuing foreign affiliate's consolidated taxable surplus (as determined under paragraph 5902(1)(*c*)), in respect of the corporation resident in Canada, in respect of the disposition of the disposed shares,

B is the amount of the issuing foreign affiliate's consolidated taxable surplus (as determined under paragraph 5902(1)(*c*)), in respect of the corporation resident in Canada, in respect of the disposition of the disposed shares,

C is the amount of the issuing foreign affiliate's consolidated taxable deficit (as determined under paragraph 5902(1)(*d*)), in respect of the corporation resident in Canada, in respect of the disposition of the disposed shares, and

D is

(A) subject to clause (B), the surplus entitlement percentage, of the issuing foreign affiliate, in respect of the particular relevant foreign affiliate, that would be determined under subsections 5905(10) to (13) at the balance adjustment time where the issuing foreign affiliate were the corporation resident in Canada referred to in those subsections and the particular relevant foreign affiliate were the particular foreign affiliate referred to in those subsections, and

(B) where the particular relevant foreign affiliate is the issuing foreign affiliate, 1, and

(ii) where the amount determined, in respect of the particular relevant foreign affiliate, for the description of A, B or D in the formula in subparagraph (i) is nil, nil; and

(*b*) the amount of the particular relevant foreign affiliate's taxable surplus, in respect of the corporation resident in Canada, at the balance adjustment time, if

(i) the particular relevant foreign affiliate has, at the balance adjustment time, an amount of taxable surplus in respect of the corporation resident in Canada, and

(ii) the issuing foreign affiliate has, at that time, an amount of consolidated taxable deficit (as determined under paragraph 5902(1)(*d*)), in respect of the corporation resident in Canada, in respect of the disposition that is equal to or greater than the amount of the issuing foreign affiliate's consolidated taxable surplus (as determined under paragraph 5902(1)(*c*)), in respect of the corporation resident in Canada, in respect of the disposition of the disposed shares.

(21) The taxable surplus reduction, in respect of a corporation resident in Canada, of a particular relevant foreign affiliate, in respect of disposed shares, is

(*a*) the amount determined by the formula

$$A/B \times C \times D$$

where

A is the portion of the amount of the particular relevant foreign affiliate's taxable surplus, in respect of the corporation resident in Canada, at the balance adjustment time, that can reasonably be considered to have been included in computing the amount of the consolidated taxable surplus (as determined under paragraph 5902(1)(*c*)), in respect of the corporation resident in Canada, in respect of the disposition of the disposed shares, of the particular foreign affiliate, of the corporation resident in Canada, that issued the disposed shares (in this subsection referred to as the "issuing foreign affiliate"),

B is the amount of the issuing foreign affiliate's consolidated taxable surplus (as determined under paragraph 5902(1)(*c*)), in respect of the corporation resident in Canada, in respect of the disposition of the disposed shares,

C is the portion, of the disposition dividend that is, because of an election made under subsection 93(1) of the Act, in respect of the disposition of the disposed shares, received on the disposed shares by the person that disposed of those shares and that is prescribed by paragraph 5900(1)(*b*) to have been paid out of the issuing foreign affiliate's taxable surplus, in respect of the corporation resident in Canada, and

Regulations

D is the specified adjustment factor, in respect of the corporation resident in Canada, in respect of the particular relevant foreign affiliate, of the person that disposed of the disposed shares;

(*b*) if the amount determined, in respect of the particular relevant foreign affiliate, for the description of A or B in the formula in paragraph (*a*) is nil, nil; and

(*c*) if an amount is determined, in respect of the particular relevant foreign affiliate, under paragraph (20)(*b*), nil.

(22) The underlying foreign tax reduction in respect of the corporation resident in Canada, of a particular relevant foreign affiliate of the corporation resident in Canada, in respect of the disposition of the disposed shares, is the amount determined by the following formula:

$$A \times (B + C)/D$$

where

A is the underlying foreign tax in respect of the corporation resident in Canada, at the balance adjustment time, of the particular relevant foreign affiliate;

B is the taxable deficit reduction, in respect of the corporation resident in Canada, of the particular relevant foreign affiliate of the corporation resident in Canada, in respect of the disposition of the disposed shares;

C is the exempt deficit allocation, in respect of the corporation resident in Canada, of the particular relevant foreign affiliate of the corporation resident in Canada, in respect of the disposition of the disposed shares; and

D is the taxable surplus in respect of the corporation resident in Canada of the particular relevant foreign affiliate, at the balance adjustment time.

(23) The specified adjustment factor, in respect of a corporation resident in Canada, in respect of a particular relevant foreign affiliate of the corporation resident in Canada, of the person that disposed of disposed shares, in respect of the disposition of the disposed shares, is the amount determined by the formula

$$A/B$$

where

A is

(*a*) where the corporation resident in Canada disposed of the disposed shares, 100 per cent, and

(*b*) where another foreign affiliate of the corporation resident in Canada disposed of the disposed shares, the surplus entitlement percentage of the corporation resident in Canada in respect of that other foreign affiliate, immediately before the disposition of the disposed shares; and

B is the surplus entitlement percentage of the corporation resident in Canada in respect of the particular relevant foreign affiliate, immediately before the disposition of the disposed shares."

(*d*) if there is a designated section 93 election,

(i) the Regulations are, in respect of the designated shares, to be read as if they also contained the following section:

"5905.1 (1) The amount prescribed for the purpose of paragraph 92(1.4)(*a*) of the Act, in respect of a relevant share referred to in that paragraph, in respect of a specified section 93 election related to the relevant share, is the lesser of

(*a*) the amount, if any, by which the fair market value of the relevant share, at the election time, exceeds the adjusted cost base, at the time of the disposition, of the relevant share to the holder, and

(*b*) the amount determined by the following formula:

$$A/C \times (C - B)$$

where

A is the amount that would, if the relevant share was the disposed share and the relevant affiliate was the disposed affiliate in respect of the specified section 93 election, be determined under paragraph 5902(1)(*f*) to be the attributed net surplus in respect of the relevant share in respect of the specified section 93 election,

B is the amount that would be determined under subparagraph 5902(1)(*e*)(vi) to be the consolidated net surplus in respect of the relevant affiliate, if

(i) the relevant foreign affiliate was the disposed affiliate referred to in subsection 5902(1),

(ii) the relevant share was the disposed share referred to in subsection 5902(1) that was disposed of, immediately following the disposition of the disposed shares to which the specified section 93 election applied, and

(iii) before that determination, in respect of the relevant foreign affiliate and each foreign affiliate of the particular corporation resident in Canada in which the relevant foreign affiliate had an equity percentage, the adjustments that are required by section 5905 to be made, in respect of the whole dividend referred to in paragraph 5902(1)(*g*) in respect of the specified section 93 election were made, and

C is the amount that would be determined under subparagraph 5902(1)(*e*)(vi) to be the consolidated net surplus in respect of the relevant affiliate in respect of the specified section 93 election, if the relevant foreign affiliate was the disposed foreign affiliate referred to in subsection 5902(1) and the relevant share was the disposed share referred to in subsection 5902(1).

(2) The amount prescribed for the purpose of paragraph 92(1.4)(*b*) of the Act, in respect of a relevant share referred to in that paragraph, in respect of a relevant specified section 93 election related to the relevant share, is the lesser of

(*a*) the amount, if any, by which the adjusted cost base, at the time of the disposition, of the relevant share to the holder exceeds the fair market value of the relevant share, at the election time, and

(*b*) the amount determined by the following formula:

$$A/C \times (C - B)$$

where

A is the amount that would be determined to be the attributed net surplus in respect of the relevant share under paragraph 5902(1)(*f*) in respect of the specified section 93 election, if

(i) the relevant share was the disposed share, and the relevant foreign affiliate was the disposed foreign affiliate, in respect of the specified section 93 election, and

(ii) the consolidated net surplus in respect of the relevant foreign affiliate was the amount, if any, determined, in respect of the relevant foreign affiliate, under the description of C,

B is the amount, if any, by which the total that would be determined under clause 5902(1)(*e*)(vi)(B) exceeds the total that would be determined under clause 5902(1)(*e*)(vi)(A), in respect of the relevant foreign affiliate, if

(i) the relevant foreign affiliate was the disposed affiliate referred to in subsection 5902(1),

(ii) the relevant share was the disposed share referred to in subsection 5902(1) that was disposed of immediately following the disposition of the disposed shares to which the specified section 93 election applied, and

(iii) before that determination, in respect of the relevant foreign affiliate and each foreign affiliate of the particular corporation resident in Canada in which the relevant foreign affiliate had an equity percentage, the adjustments that are required by section 5905 to be made, in respect of the whole dividend referred to in paragraph 5902(1)(*g*) in respect of the specified section 93 election, were made, and

C is the amount, if any, by which the total that would be determined under clause 5902(1)(*e*)(vi)(B) exceeds the total that would be determined under clause 5902(1)(*e*)(vi)(A), in respect of the relevant affiliate in respect of the specified section 93 election, if the relevant foreign affiliate was the disposed foreign affiliate referred to in subsection 5902(1) and the relevant share was the disposed share referred to in subsection 5902(1).

(3) If the amount determined in each of the formulae in paragraphs (1)(*b*) and (2)(*b*) in respect of the relevant share referred to in paragraph 92(1.4)(*a*) of the Act is nil, the amount determined for B in the formula in paragraph (1)(*b*) in respect of the relevant affiliate is greater than nil and the amount determined for C in the formula in paragraph (2)(*b*) in respect of the relevant affiliate is greater than nil, the amount prescribed for the purpose of paragraph 92(1.4)(*a*) of the Act, in respect of the relevant share referred to in that paragraph, in respect of a specified section 93 election related to the relevant share, is the lesser of

(*a*) the amount, if any, by which the fair market value of the relevant share, at the election time, exceeds the adjusted cost base, at the time of the disposition, of the relevant share to the holder, and

(*b*) the amount that would, if the relevant share was the disposed share and the relevant affiliate was the disposed affiliate in respect of the specified section 93 election, be determined

Regulations

under paragraph 5902(1)(f) to be the attributed net surplus in respect of the relevant share if the consolidated net surplus of the relevant foreign affiliate were the amount determined for B in the formula in paragraph (1)(b)."

Application Provision, S.C. 2013, c. 34, s. 52 [Modified Consolidated Net Surplus Election.]

(1) The application in subsection (2) (below) applies if

(a) a corporation has made the election above; and

(b) the corporation has made an election under subsection 93(1) or (1.2) of the Income Tax Act in respect of a disposition of a share of the capital stock of a foreign affiliate of the corporation that occurs after December 20, 2002 and on or before February 27, 2004 (other than a disposition required to be made under an agreement in writing made by a vendor on or before December 20, 2002), or in respect of a disposition that occurs after February 27, 2004 and that is required to be made under an agreement in writing made by a vendor after December 20, 2002 and before February 28, 2004; and

(c) the corporation elects in writing to apply subsection (2) (below) in respect of all of its foreign affiliates and files the election with the Minister of National Revenue on or before the day that is the later of the corporation's filing-due date for the corporation's taxation year that includes June 26, 2013 and June 26, 2014;

(2) then the Consolidated Net Surplus Election above does not apply in respect of dispositions referred to in paragraph (b).

(2) (Repealed by S.C. 2013, c. 34, s. 44(2).)

History: S. 5905(2) was repealed by S.C. 2013, c. 34, s. 44(2), applicable iln respect of redemptions, acquisitions and cancellations that occur after December 18, 2009.

See the application following s. 5905(1) regarding the override of the statute-barring rules for assessments for taxation years that end before June 26, 2013.

S. 5905(2) formerly read:

(2) Where at any time a foreign affiliate of a corporation resident in Canada redeems, acquires or cancels in any manner whatever (otherwise than by way of a winding-up) any of the shares of any class of its capital stock (other than shares redeemed or cancelled that the affiliate had previously purchased or acquired and that were held by it until that time and in respect of which an adjustment has previously been made under this subsection or subsection (1) as it read prior to November 13, 1981), the following rules apply:

(a) where, by virtue of an election made by the corporation under subsection 93(1) of the Act, a dividend is deemed to have been received on one or more of the shares of the foreign affiliate that were disposed of by the corporation or another foreign affiliate of the corporation (in this paragraph referred to as the "transferor") by virtue of the redemption, acquisition or cancellation of such share or shares by the foreign affiliate, for the purposes of the adjustment required by paragraph (b),

(i) immediately before that time there is included under subparagraph (v) of the description of B in the definition "exempt surplus" in subsection 5907(1) in computing the affiliate's exempt surplus or exempt deficit, as the case may be, in respect of the corporation an amount equal to the product obtained when the specified adjustment factor in respect of the disposition is multiplied by the total of all amounts each of which is the portion of any such dividend that is prescribed by paragraph 5900(1)(a) to have been paid out of the exempt surplus of the affiliate,

(ii) immediately before that time there is included under subparagraph (v) of the description of B in the definition "taxable surplus" in subsection 5907(1) in computing the affiliate's taxable surplus or taxable deficit, as the case may be, in respect of the corporation an amount equal to the product obtained when the specified adjustment factor in respect of the disposition is multiplied by the total of all amounts each of which is the portion of any such dividend that is prescribed by paragraph 5900(1)(b) to have been paid out of the taxable surplus of the affiliate, and

(iii) immediately before that time there shall be deducted from the amount, if any, otherwise determined to be the underlying foreign tax of the affiliate in respect of the corporation an amount equal to the product obtained when the specified adjustment factor in respect of the disposition is multiplied by the aggregate of all amounts each of which is the amount prescribed by paragraph 5900(1)(d) to be the foreign tax applicable to such portion of any such dividend as is prescribed by paragraph 5900(1)(b) to have been paid out of the taxable surplus of the affiliate,

and, for the purposes of subparagraphs (i) to (iii), the specified adjustment factor in respect of the disposition is the amount equal to the quotient obtained when,

(iv) where the transferor is the corporation, 100 per cent, and

(v) where the transferor is another foreign affiliate of the corporation, the surplus entitlement percentage of the corporation in respect of the transferor immediately before the disposition,

is divided by

(vi) the surplus entitlement percentage of the corporation in respect of the foreign affiliate immediately before the disposition;

(b) the exempt surplus or exempt deficit, the taxable surplus or taxable deficit and the underlying foreign tax, in respect of the corporation, of the affiliate and of each other foreign affiliate of the corporation in which the affiliate has an equity percentage (in this subsection referred to as the "other affiliate") shall at that time be adjusted to the proportion of the amount thereof otherwise determined that

(i) the surplus entitlement percentage immediately before that time of the corporation in respect of the affiliate or the other affiliate, as the case may be, determined on the assumption that the taxation year of the affiliate or the other affiliate, as the case may be, that otherwise would have included that time had ended immediately before that time,

is of

(ii) the surplus entitlement percentage immediately after that time of the corporation in respect of the affiliate or the other affiliate, as the case may be, determined on the assumption that the taxation year of the affiliate or the other affiliate, as the case may be, that otherwise would have included that time had ended immediately after that time; and

(c) for the purposes of the definitions "exempt deficit", "exempt surplus", "taxable deficit", "taxable surplus" and "underlying foreign tax" in subsection 5907(1), the amounts determined under paragraph (b) are referred to as the opening exempt deficit, opening exempt surplus, opening taxable deficit, opening taxable surplus and opening underlying foreign tax, as the case may be, of the affiliate and each other affiliate in respect of the corporation resident in Canada.

(3) If at any time (referred to in this subsection as the "merger time") a foreign affiliate (referred to in this subsection as the "merged affiliate") of a corporation resident in Canada has been formed as a result of a foreign merger (within the meaning assigned by subsection 87(8.1) of the Act) of two or more corporations (referred to individually in this subsection as a "predecessor corporation"), the following rules apply:

(a) for the purposes of the definitions "exempt surplus", "hybrid surplus", "hybrid underlying tax", "taxable surplus" and "underlying foreign tax" in subsection 5907(1), as they apply in respect of the merged affiliate,

(i) the merged affiliate's opening exempt surplus, in respect of the corporation, shall be the amount, if any, by which the total of all amounts each of which is the exempt surplus of a predecessor corporation, in respect of the corporation, immediately before the merger time exceeds the total of all amounts each of which is the exempt deficit of a predecessor corporation, in respect of the corporation, immediately before the merger time,

(ii) the merged affiliate's opening exempt deficit, in respect of the corporation, shall be the amount, if any, by which the total of all amounts each of which is the exempt deficit of a predecessor corporation, in respect of the corporation, immediately before the merger time exceeds the total of all amounts each of which is the exempt surplus of a predecessor corporation, in respect of the corporation, immediately before the merger time,

(ii.1) the merged affiliate's opening hybrid surplus, in respect of the corporation, shall be the amount, if any, by which the total of all amounts each of which is the hybrid surplus of a predecessor corporation, in respect of the corporation, immediately before the merger time exceeds the total of all amounts each of which is the hybrid deficit of a predecessor corporation, in respect of the corporation, immediately before the merger time,

(ii.2) the merged affiliate's opening hybrid deficit, in respect of the corporation, shall be the amount, if any, by which the total of all amounts each of which is the hybrid deficit of a predecessor corporation, in respect of the corporation, immediately before the merger time exceeds the total of all amounts each of which is the hybrid surplus of a predecessor corporation, in respect of the corporation, immediately before the merger time,

(ii.3) the merged affiliate's opening hybrid underlying tax in respect of the corporation shall be the total of all amounts each of which is the hybrid underlying tax of a predecessor corporation, in respect of the corporation, immediately before the merger time,

(iii) the merged affiliate's opening taxable surplus, in respect of the corporation, shall be the amount, if any, by which the total of all amounts each of which is the taxable surplus of a predecessor corporation, in respect of the corporation, immediately before the merger time exceeds the total of all amounts each of which is the taxable deficit of a predecessor corporation, in respect of the corporation, immediately before the merger time,

(iv) the merged affiliate's opening taxable deficit, in respect of the corporation, shall be the amount, if any, by which the total of all amounts each of which is the taxable deficit of a predecessor corporation, in respect of the corporation, immediately before the merger time exceeds the total of all amounts each of which is the taxable surplus of a predecessor corporation, in respect of the corporation, immediately before the merger time, and

(v) the merged affiliate's opening underlying foreign tax in respect of the corporation shall be the total of all amounts each of which is the underlying foreign tax of a predecessor corporation, in respect of the corporation, immediately before the merger time;

(*b*) for the purposes of paragraph (*a*),

(i) each of the exempt surplus or exempt deficit, hybrid surplus or hybrid deficit, hybrid underlying tax, taxable surplus or taxable deficit and underlying foreign tax, in respect of the corporation, of each predecessor corporation immediately before the merger time is deemed to be the amount determined by the formula

$$A \times B/C$$

where

A is the amount of that surplus, deficit or tax, as the case may be, as otherwise determined,

B is the surplus entitlement percentage of the corporation immediately before the merger time in respect of the predecessor corporation, and

C is the percentage that would be the surplus entitlement percentage of the corporation immediately after the merger time in respect of the merged affiliate if the merged affiliate's net surplus were the total of all amounts each of which is the net surplus of a predecessor corporation immediately before the merger time, but

(ii) the values for A, B and C in the formula in subparagraph (i) shall take into account the application of paragraph 5902(1)(*b*) and subsection 5907(8) in respect of the merger; and

(*c*) in respect of any foreign affiliate (other than a predecessor corporation) of the corporation in which a predecessor corporation had an equity percentage (within the meaning assigned by subsection 95(4) of the Act) immediately before the merger time, for the purposes of subsection (1), there is deemed to be an acquisition or a disposition of shares of the capital stock of that affiliate at the merger time.

History: S. 5905(3)(*a*), the portion before subparagraph (i) was replaced by S.C. 2013, c. 34, s. 84(2), deemed to have come into force on August 20, 2011.

See the application for the amendment to s. 5905(1) before the formula for the extension of assessment periods to take into account the amendments by S.C. 2013, c. 34, s. 54 to 89.

S. 5905(3)(*a*), the portion before subparagraph (i) formerly read:

(*a*) for the purposes of the definitions "exempt surplus", "taxable surplus" and "underlying foreign tax" in subsection 5907(1), as they apply in respect of the merged affiliate,

S. 5905(3)(*a*)(ii.1) to (ii.3) were added by S.C. 2013, c. 34, s. 84(3), deemed to have come into force on August 20, 2011.

See the application for the amendment to s. 5905(1) before the formula for the extension of assessment periods to take into account the amendments by S.C. 2013, c. 34, s. 54 to 89.

S. 5905(3)(*b*)(i), the portion before the formula was replaced by S.C. 2013, c. 34, s. 84(4), deemed to have come into force on August 20, 2011.

See the application for the amendment to s. 5905(1) before the formula for the extension of assessment periods to take into account the amendments by S.C. 2013, c. 34, s. 54 to 89.

S. 5905(3)(*b*)(i), the portion before the formula formerly read:

(i) each of the exempt surplus or exempt deficit, taxable surplus or taxable deficit and underlying foreign tax, in respect of the corporation, of each predecessor corporation immediately before the merger time is deemed to be the amount determined by the formula

S. 5905(3) was replaced by S.C. 2013, c. 34, s. 44(3), applicable in respect of mergers or combinations that occur after December 18, 2009.

See the application following s. 5905(1) regarding the override of the statute-barring rules for assessments for taxation years that end before June 26, 2013.

S. 5905(3) formerly read:

(3) Where at any time a foreign affiliate of a corporation resident in Canada has been formed as a result of a foreign merger (within the meaning assigned by subsection 87(8.1) of the Act) of two or more corporations (each of which in this subsection and subsection (4) is referred to as a "predecessor corporation"), for the purposes of this Part, the following rules apply:

(*a*) in respect of the foreign affiliate,

(i) its opening exempt surplus in respect of the corporation shall be the amount, if any, by which the aggregate of all amounts each of which is the exempt surplus of a predecessor corporation that was a foreign affiliate of the corporation immediately before the merger exceeds the aggregate of all amounts each of which is the exempt deficit of a predecessor corporation that was a foreign affiliate of the corporation immediately before the merger,

(ii) its opening exempt deficit in respect of the corporation shall be the amount, if any, by which the aggregate of all amounts each of which is the exempt deficit of a predecessor corporation that was a foreign affiliate of the corporation immediately before the merger exceeds the aggregate of all amounts each of which is the exempt surplus of a predecessor corporation that was a foreign affiliate of the corporation immediately before the merger,

(iii) its opening taxable surplus in respect of the corporation shall be the amount, if any, by which the aggregate of all amounts each of which is the taxable surplus of a predecessor corporation that was a foreign affiliate of the corporation immediately before the merger exceeds the aggregate of all amounts each of which is the taxable deficit of a predecessor corporation that was a foreign affiliate of the corporation immediately before the merger,

(iv) its opening taxable deficit in respect of the corporation shall be the amount, if any, by which the aggregate of all amounts each of which is the taxable deficit of a predecessor corporation that was a foreign affiliate of the corporation immediately before the merger exceeds the aggregate of all amounts each of which is the taxable surplus of a predecessor corporation that was a foreign affiliate of the corporation immediately before the merger, and

(v) its opening underlying foreign tax in respect of the corporation shall be the aggregate of all amounts each of which is the underlying foreign tax of a predecessor corporation that was a foreign affiliate of the corporation immediately before the merger; and

(*b*) in respect of any other foreign affiliate of the corporation, other than a predecessor corporation, in which a predecessor corporation had an equity percentage immediately before the merger, the exempt surplus or exempt deficit, the taxable surplus or taxable deficit and the underlying foreign tax of the other affiliate in respect of the corporation shall at that time be adjusted to the proportion of the amount thereof otherwise determined that

(i) the surplus entitlement percentage immediately before that time of the corporation in respect of the other affiliate, determined on the assumption that the taxation year of the other affiliate that otherwise would have included that time had ended immediately before that time,

is of

(ii) the surplus entitlement percentage immediately after that time of the corporation in respect of the other affiliate, determined on the assumption that the taxation year of the other affiliate that otherwise would have included that time had ended immediately after that time,

and, for the purposes of the definitions "exempt deficit", "exempt surplus", "taxable deficit", "taxable surplus" and "underlying foreign tax" in subsection 5907(1), the adjusted amounts are referred to as the opening exempt deficit, opening exempt surplus, opening taxable deficit, opening taxable surplus and opening underlying foreign tax, as the case may be, of the other affiliate in respect of the corporation resident in Canada.

(4) (Repealed by S.C. 2013, c. 34, s. 44(3).)

History: S. 5905(4) was repealed by S.C. 2013, c. 34, s. 44(3), applicable in respect of mergers or combinations that occur after December 18, 2009.

See the application following s. 5905(1) regarding the override of the statute-barring rules for assessments for taxation years that end before June 26, 2013.

S. 5905(4) formerly read:

(4) For the purposes of paragraph (3)(*a*), the exempt surplus, exempt deficit, taxable surplus, taxable deficit and underlying foreign tax of each predecessor corporation immediately before the foreign merger shall be deemed to be the proportion of the amount thereof otherwise determined that

(*a*) the surplus entitlement percentage of the corporation resident in Canada immediately before the merger in respect of the predecessor corporation, determined on the assumption that the taxation year of the predecessor corporation that otherwise would have included the time of the merger had ended immediately before that time,

is of

(*b*) the percentage that would be the surplus entitlement percentage of the corporation resident in Canada immediately after the merger in respect of the foreign affiliate of the corporation formed as a result of the merger if the net surplus of such foreign affiliate were the aggregate of all amounts, each of which is the net surplus of a predecessor corporation immediately before the merger.

(5) If there is, at any time, a disposition by a corporation (referred to in this subsection as the "disposing corporation") resident in Canada of any of the shares (referred to in this subsection as the "disposed shares") of the capital stock of a particular foreign affiliate of the disposing corporation to a taxable Canadian corporation (referred to in this subsection as the "acquiring corporation") with which the disposing corporation is not dealing at arm's length,

(*a*) each of the opening exempt surplus or opening exempt deficit, opening hybrid surplus or opening hybrid deficit, opening hybrid underlying tax, opening taxable surplus or opening taxable deficit, and opening underlying foreign tax, in respect of the acquiring corporation, of the particular affiliate and of each foreign affiliate of the disposing corporation in which the particular affiliate has, immediately before that time, an equity percentage (within the meaning assigned by subsection 95(4) of the Act) is deemed to be the amount, if any,

(i) in the case of its opening exempt surplus, by which the total of its exempt surplus in respect of each of the disposing corporation and the acquiring corporation, determined immediately before that time, exceeds the total of its exempt deficit in respect of each of the disposing corporation and the acquiring corporation, determined immediately before that time,

(ii) in the case of its opening exempt deficit, by which the total of its exempt deficit in respect of each of the disposing corporation and the acquiring corporation, determined immediately before that time, exceeds the total of its exempt surplus in respect of each of the disposing corporation and the acquiring corporation, determined immediately before that time,

(ii.1) in the case of its opening hybrid surplus, by which the total of its hybrid surplus in respect of each of the disposing corporation and the acquiring corporation, determined immediately before that time, exceeds the total of its hybrid deficit in respect of each of the disposing corporation and the acquiring corporation, determined immediately before that time,

(ii.2) in the case of its opening hybrid deficit, by which the total of its hybrid deficit in respect of each of the disposing corporation and the acquiring corporation, determined immediately before that time, exceeds the total of its hybrid surplus in respect of each of the disposing corporation and the acquiring corporation, determined immediately before that time,

(ii.3) in the case of its opening hybrid underlying tax, that is the total of its hybrid underlying tax in respect of each of the disposing corporation and the acquiring corporation, determined immediately before that time,

(iii) in the case of its opening taxable surplus, by which the total of its taxable surplus in respect of each of the disposing corporation and the acquiring corporation, determined immediately before that time, exceeds the total of its taxable deficit in respect of each of the disposing corporation and the acquiring corporation, determined immediately before that time,

(iv) in the case of its opening taxable deficit, by which the total of its taxable deficit in respect of each of the disposing corporation and the acquiring corporation, determined immediately before that time, exceeds the total of its taxable surplus in respect of each of the disposing corpo-

Regulations

ration and the acquiring corporation, determined immediately before that time, and

(v) in the case of its opening underlying foreign tax, that is the total of its underlying foreign tax in respect of each of the disposing corporation and the acquiring corporation, determined immediately before that time;

(*b*) for the purposes of paragraph (*a*), each of the exempt surplus or exempt deficit, hybrid surplus or hybrid deficit, hybrid underlying tax, taxable surplus or taxable deficit, and underlying foreign tax of an affiliate in respect of the disposing corporation and the acquiring corporation, determined immediately before that time, is deemed to be the amount determined by the formula

$$A \times B/C$$

where

A is the amount of that surplus, deficit or tax, as the case may be, as determined without reference to this subsection but taking into account the application of subparagraph (*c*)(i), if applicable,

B is the surplus entitlement percentage immediately before that time of the disposing corporation or the acquiring corporation, as the case may be, in respect of the affiliate, determined as if the disposed shares were the only shares owned by the disposing corporation immediately before that time, and

C is the surplus entitlement percentage immediately after that time of the acquiring corporation in respect of the affiliate;

(*c*) if the disposing corporation makes an election under subsection 93(1) of the Act in respect of the disposed shares,

(i) for the purposes of paragraph (*b*), the exempt surplus or exempt deficit, hybrid surplus or hybrid deficit, hybrid underlying tax, taxable surplus or taxable deficit, and underlying foreign tax of an affiliate in respect of the disposing corporation, as determined without reference to this subsection, immediately before that time, shall be adjusted in accordance with paragraph 5902(1)(*b*) as if the disposing corporation's surplus entitlement percentage that is referred to in the description of B in paragraph 5902(2)(*b*) were determined as if the disposed shares were the only shares owned by the disposing corporation immediately before that time, and

(ii) no adjustment shall be made to the amount of the exempt surplus or exempt deficit, hybrid surplus or hybrid deficit, hybrid underlying tax, taxable surplus or taxable deficit, or underlying foreign tax of an affiliate in respect of the disposing corporation under paragraph 5902(1)(*b*) other than for the purpose of paragraph (*b*); and

(*d*) for greater certainty, no adjustment shall be made under subsection (1) to the exempt surplus or exempt deficit, hybrid surplus or hybrid deficit, hybrid underlying tax, taxable surplus or taxable deficit, or underlying foreign tax of an affiliate in respect of the disposing corporation.

History: S. 5905(5)(*a*), the portion before subparagraph (i) was replaced by S.C. 2013, c. 34, s. 84(5), deemed to have come into force on August 20, 2011.

See the application for the amendment to s. 5905(1) before the formula for the extension of assessment periods to take into account the amendments by S.C. 2013, c. 34, s. 54 to 89.

S. 5905(5)(*a*), the portion before subparagraph (i) formerly read

(*a*) each of the opening exempt surplus or opening exempt deficit, opening taxable surplus or opening taxable deficit, and opening underlying foreign tax, in respect of the acquiring corporation, of the particular affiliate and of each foreign affiliate of the disposing corporation in which the particular affiliate has, immediately before that time, an equity percentage (within the meaning assigned by subsection 95(4) of the Act) is deemed to be the amount, if any,

S. 5905(5)(*a*)(ii.1) to (ii.3) were added by S.C. 2013, c. 34, s. 84(6), deemed to have come into force on August 20, 2011.

See the application for the amendment to s. 5905(1) before the formula for the extension of assessment periods to take into account the amendments by S.C. 2013, c. 34, s. 54 to 89.

S. 5905(5)(*b*), the portion before the formula was replaced by S.C. 2013, c. 34, s. 84(7), deemed to have come into force on August 20, 2011.

See the application for the amendment to s. 5905(1) before the formula for the extension of assessment periods to take into account the amendments by S.C. 2013, c. 34, s. 54 to 89.

S. 5905(5)(*b*), the portion before the formula formerly read:

(*b*) for the purpose of paragraph (*a*), each of the exempt surplus or exempt deficit, taxable surplus or taxable deficit, and underlying foreign tax of an affiliate in respect of the disposing corporation and the acquiring corporation, determined immediately before that time, is deemed to be the amount determined by the formula

S. 5905(5)(*c*) and (*d*) were replaced by S.C. 2013, c. 34, s. 84(8), deemed to have come into force on August 20, 2011.

See the application for the amendment to s. 5905(1) before the formula for the extension of assessment periods to take into account the amendments by S.C. 2013, c. 34, s. 54 to 89.

S. 5905(5)(*c*) and (*d*) formerly read:

(*c*) if the disposing corporation makes an election under subsection 93(1) of the Act in respect of the disposed shares,

(i) for the purposes of paragraph (*b*), the exempt surplus or exempt deficit, taxable surplus or taxable deficit, and underlying foreign tax of an affiliate in respect of the disposing corporation, as determined without reference to this subsection, immediately before that time, shall be adjusted in accordance with paragraph 5902(1)(*b*) as if the disposing corporation's surplus entitlement percentage that is referred to in the description of B in paragraph 5902(2)(*b*) were determined as if the disposed shares were the only shares owned by the disposing corporation immediately before that time, and

(ii) no adjustment shall be made to the amount of the exempt surplus or exempt deficit, taxable surplus or taxable deficit, or underlying foreign tax of an affiliate in respect of the disposing corporation under paragraph 5902(1)(*b*) other than for the purpose of paragraph (*b*); and

(*d*) for greater certainty, no adjustment shall be made under subsection (1) to the exempt surplus or exempt deficit, taxable surplus or taxable deficit, or underlying foreign tax of an affiliate in respect of the disposing corporation.

S. 5905(5) was replaced by S.C. 2013, c. 34, s. 44(4) applicable in respect of dispositions and amalgamations that occur, and windings-up that begin, after December 18, 2009.

See the application following s. 5905(1) regarding the override of the statute-barring rules for assessments for taxation years that end before June 26, 2013.

S. 5905(5) formerly read:

(5) Where at any time

(*a*) there is a disposition by a corporation resident in Canada (in this subsection referred to as the "predecessor corporation") of any of the shares owned by it of the capital stock of a particular foreign affiliate of it to a taxable Canadian corporation with which the predecessor corporation was not dealing at arm's length (in this subsection referred to as the "acquiring corporation"),

(*b*) there is an amalgamation, to which section 87 of the Act applies, of two or more corporations (each of which in this subsection is referred to as a "predecessor corporation") to form a new corporation (in this subsection referred to as the "acquiring corporation") as a result of which shares of the capital stock of a particular foreign affiliate of a predecessor corporation become the property of the acquiring corporation, or

Regulations

(*c*) there is a winding-up, to which subsection 88(1) of the Act applies, of a corporation (in this subsection referred to as the "predecessor corporation") into another corporation (in this subsection referred to as the "acquiring corporation") as a result of which shares of the capital stock of a particular foreign affiliate of the predecessor corporation become the property of the acquiring corporation,

the following rules apply for the purposes of this Part in respect of the particular affiliate and each other foreign affiliate of the predecessor corporation in which the particular affiliate has an equity percentage;

(*d*) its opening exempt surplus in respect of the acquiring corporation shall be the amount, if any, by which the aggregate of its exempt surplus in respect of each predecessor corporation and in respect of the acquiring corporation immediately before any of the transactions referred to in paragraph (*a*), (*b*) or (*c*) exceeds the aggregate of its exempt deficit in respect of each predecessor corporation and in respect of the acquiring corporation immediately before any of the transactions referred to in paragraph (*a*), (*b*) or (*c*);

(*e*) its opening exempt deficit in respect of the acquiring corporation shall be the amount, if any, by which the aggregate of its exempt deficit in respect of each predecessor corporation and in respect of the acquiring corporation immediately before any of the transactions referred to in paragraph (*a*), (*b*) or (*c*) exceeds the aggregate of its exempt surplus in respect of each predecessor corporation and in respect of the acquiring corporation immediately before any of the transactions referred to in paragraph (*a*), (*b*) or (*c*);

(*f*) its opening taxable surplus in respect of the acquiring corporation shall be the amount, if any, by which the aggregate of its taxable surplus in respect of each predecessor corporation and in respect of the acquiring corporation immediately before any of the transactions referred to in paragraph (*a*), (*b*) or (*c*) exceeds the aggregate of its taxable deficit in respect of each predecessor corporation and in respect of the acquiring corporation immediately before any of the transactions referred to in paragraph (*a*), (*b*) or (*c*);

(*g*) its opening taxable deficit in respect of the acquiring corporation shall be the amount, if any, by which the aggregate of its taxable deficit in respect of each predecessor corporation and in respect of the acquiring corporation immediately before any of the transactions referred to in paragraph (*a*), (*b*) or (*c*) exceeds the aggregate of its taxable surplus in respect of each predecessor corporation and in respect of the acquiring corporation immediately before any of the transactions referred to in paragraph (*a*), (*b*) or (*c*); and

(*h*) its opening underlying foreign tax in respect of the acquiring corporation shall be the aggregate of its underlying foreign tax in respect of each predecessor corporation and in respect of the acquiring corporation immediately before any of the transactions referred to in paragraph (*a*), (*b*) or (*c*).

(5.1) If there is, at any time, an amalgamation within the meaning of subsection 87(1) of the Act and, as a result of the amalgamation, shares of the capital stock of a particular foreign affiliate of a predecessor corporation become property of the new corporation,

(*a*) each of the opening exempt surplus or opening exempt deficit, opening hybrid surplus or opening hybrid deficit, opening hybrid underlying tax, opening taxable surplus or opening taxable deficit, and opening underlying foreign tax, in respect of the new corporation, of the particular affiliate and of each foreign affiliate of the predecessor corporation in which the particular affiliate has, immediately before that time, an equity percentage (within the meaning assigned by subsection 95(4) of the Act) is deemed to be the amount, if any,

(i) in the case of its opening exempt surplus, by which the total of its exempt surplus in respect of each predecessor corporation, determined immediately before that time, exceeds the total of its exempt deficit in respect of each predecessor corporation, determined immediately before that time,

(ii) in the case of its opening exempt deficit, by which the total of its exempt deficit in respect of each predecessor corporation, determined immediately before that time, exceeds the total of its exempt surplus in respect of each predecessor corporation, determined immediately before that time,

(ii.1) in the case of its opening hybrid surplus, by which the total of its hybrid surplus in respect of each predecessor corporation, determined immediately before that time, exceeds the total of its hybrid deficit in respect of each predecessor corporation, determined immediately before that time,

(ii.2) in the case of its opening hybrid deficit, by which the total of its hybrid deficit in respect of each predecessor corporation, determined immediately before that time, exceeds the total of its hybrid surplus in respect of each predecessor corporation, determined immediately before that time,

(ii.3) in the case of its opening hybrid underlying tax, that is the total of its hybrid underlying tax in respect of each predecessor corporation, determined immediately before that time,

(iii) in the case of its opening taxable surplus, by which the total of its taxable surplus in respect of each predecessor corporation, determined immediately before that time, exceeds the total of its taxable deficit in respect of each predecessor corporation, determined immediately before that time,

(iv) in the case of its opening taxable deficit, by which the total of its taxable deficit in respect of each predecessor corporation, determined immediately before that time, exceeds the total of its taxable surplus in respect of each predecessor corporation, determined immediately before that time, and

(v) in the case of its opening underlying foreign tax, that is the total of its underlying foreign tax in respect of each predecessor corporation, determined immediately before that time; and

(*b*) for the purpose of paragraph (*a*), each of the exempt surplus or exempt deficit, hybrid surplus or hybrid deficit, hybrid underlying tax, taxable surplus or taxable deficit, and underlying foreign tax of an affiliate in respect of a predecessor corporation, determined immediately before that time, is deemed to be the amount determined by the formula

$$A \times B/C$$

where

A is the amount of that surplus, deficit or tax, as the case may be, as determined without reference to this subsection,

B is the predecessor corporation's surplus entitlement percentage immediately before that time in respect of the affiliate, and

C is the new corporation's surplus entitlement percentage immediately after that time in respect of the affiliate.

Regulations

History: S. 5905(5.1)(*a*), the portion before subparagraph (i) was replaced by S.C. 2013, c. 34, s. 84(9), deemed to have come into force on August 20, 2011.

See the application for the amendment to s. 5905(1) before the formula for the extension of assessment periods to take into account the amendments by S.C. 2013, c. 34, s. 54 to 89.

S. 5905(5.1)(*a*), the portion before subparagraph (i) formerly read:

(*a*) each of the opening exempt surplus or opening exempt deficit, opening taxable surplus or opening taxable deficit, and opening underlying foreign tax, in respect of the new corporation, of the particular affiliate and of each foreign affiliate of the predecessor corporation in which the particular affiliate has, immediately before that time, an equity percentage (within the meaning assigned by subsection 95(4) of the Act) is deemed to be the amount, if any,

S. 5905(5.1)(*a*)(ii.1) to (ii.3) were added by S.C. 2013, c. 34, s. 84(10), deemed to have come into force on August 20, 2011.

See the application for the amendment to s. 5905(1) before the formula for the extension of assessment periods to take into account the amendments by S.C. 2013, c. 34, s. 54 to 89.

S. 5905(5.1)(*b*), the portion before the formula was replaced by S.C. 2013, c. 34, s. 84(11), deemed to have come into force on August 20, 2011.

See the application for the amendment to s. 5905(1) before the formula for the extension of assessment periods to take into account the amendments by S.C. 2013, c. 34, s. 54 to 89.

S. 5905(5.1)(*b*), the portion before the formula formerly read:

(*b*) for the purpose of paragraph (*a*), each of the exempt surplus or exempt deficit, taxable surplus or taxable deficit, and underlying foreign tax of an affiliate in respect of a predecessor corporation, determined immediately before that time, is deemed to be the amount determined by the formula

S. 5905(5.1) was added by S.C. 2013, c. 34, s. 44(4), applicable in respect of dispositions and amalgamations that occur, and windings-up that begin, after December 18, 2009.

See the application following s. 5905(1) regarding the override of the statute-barring rules for assessments for taxation years that end before June 26, 2013.

(5.11) (Repealed by S.C. 2013, c. 34, s. 44(5).)

History: S. 5905(5.11) was repealed by S.C. 2013, c. 34, s. 44(5), applicable in respect of acquisitions of control that occur after December 18, 2009, except if the acquisition of control results from an acquisition of shares made under an agreement in writing entered into before December 18, 2009.

S. 5905(5.11) formerly read:

(5.11) Subsection (5.12) applies if

(*a*) in the case of a winding-up, an amount has been designated, under paragraph 88(1)(*d*) of the Act by the corporation (referred to in this subsection and subsection (5.12) as the "parent corporation") described in subsection 88(1) of the Act as the parent, in respect of

(i) shares of the capital stock of a corporation (referred to in this subsection and subsection (5.12) as the "particular affiliate") that is, immediately before the winding-up, a foreign affiliate of the corporation (referred to in this subsection and subsection (5.12) as the "subsidiary corporation") resident in Canada that is described in that subsection 88(1) as the subsidiary, or

(ii) an interest in a partnership that holds shares described in subparagraph (i); or

(*b*) in the case of an amalgamation, an amount has been designated, under paragraph 88(1)(*d*) of the Act by the corporation (referred to in this subsection and subsection (5.12) as the "parent corporation") described in subsection 87(11) of the Act as the parent, in respect of

(i) shares of the capital stock of a corporation (referred to in this subsection and subsection (5.12) as the "particular affiliate") that is, immediately before the amalgamation, a foreign affiliate of the corporation (referred to in this subsection and subsection (5.12) as the "subsidiary corporation") resident in Canada that is described in that subsection 87(11) as the subsidiary, or

(ii) an interest in a partnership that holds shares described in subparagraph (i).

S. 5905(5.11) was added by S.C. 2013, c. 34, s. 44(4), applicable in respect of an amalgamation that occurs, or a winding-up that begins, after February 27, 2004.

See the application following s. 5905(1) regarding the override of the statute-barring rules for assessments for taxation years that end before June 26, 2013.

(5.12) (Repealed by S.C. 2013, c. 34, s. 44(5).)

History: S. 5905(5.12) was repealed by S.C. 2013, c. 34, s. 44(5), applicable in respect of acquisitions of control that occur after December 18, 2009, except if the acquisition of control results from an acquisition of shares made under an agreement in writing entered into before December 18, 2009.

S. 5905(5.12) formerly read:

(5.12) If this subsection applies, the following rules apply for the purposes of subsections (5) and (5.1):

(*a*) each amount of the exempt surplus or exempt deficit, taxable surplus or taxable deficit, and underlying foreign tax, in respect of the subsidiary corporation, of the particular affiliate and of all foreign affiliates of the subsidiary corporation in which the particular affiliate has, immediately before the winding-up or the amalgamation, an equity percentage (within the meaning assigned by subsection 95(4) of the Act) is deemed to be, immediately before the winding-up or the amalgamation, nil; and

(*b*) each amount (referred to individually in this paragraph as a "relevant balance") of the exempt surplus or exempt deficit, taxable surplus or taxable deficit, and underlying foreign tax, in respect of the parent corporation, of the particular affiliate and of all foreign affiliates (referred to individually in this paragraph as a "lower-tier affiliate") of the parent corporation in which the particular affiliate has, immediately before the winding-up or the amalgamation, an equity percentage (within the meaning assigned by subsection 95(4) of the Act) is deemed to be, immediately before the winding-up or the amalgamation, the amount that would be determined to be the relevant balance if

(i) in addition to shares or partnership interests, if any, held by the parent corporation that are relevant in computing any relevant balance of the particular affiliate or of any lower-tier affiliate of the parent corporation, in respect of the parent corporation, any shares of the particular affiliate's capital stock, and any interests in partnerships that hold such shares, that were held by the subsidiary corporation at any time in the period (referred to in this paragraph as the "control period") that begins at the first time referred to in subparagraph 88(1)(*d*)(ii) of the Act and ends immediately before the winding-up or the amalgamation, that are relevant in computing any relevant balance of the particular affiliate or any lower-tier affiliate of the subsidiary corporation, in respect of the subsidiary corporation, were held by the parent corporation at the same time in the control period that they were held by the subsidiary corporation,

(ii) the parent corporation had acquired, at that first time, all the shares and partnership interests held, at that first time, by the subsidiary corporation that are relevant in computing any relevant balance of the particular affiliate or any lower-tier affiliate of the subsidiary corporation, in respect of the subsidiary corporation, and

(iii) where the subsidiary corporation acquired or disposed of any shares or partnership interests in the control period that are relevant in computing any relevant balance of the particular affiliate or of any lower-tier affiliate of the subsidiary corporation, in respect of the subsidiary corporation, the parent corporation is deemed to have acquired or disposed of, as the case may be, the shares or partnership interests at the same time they were acquired or disposed of by the subsidiary corporation.

S. 5905(5.12) was added by S.C. 2013, c. 34, s. 44(4), applicable in respect of an amalgamation that occurs, or a winding-up that begins, after February 27, 2004, except that, if subsection 5905(6) of the Regulations applies in respect of the amalgamation or winding-up, then the portion of subsection 5905(5.12) before paragraph (*a*) is to be read as follows:

"(5.12) If this subsection applies, the following rules apply for the purposes of subsections (5) and (6):"

See the application following s. 5905(1) regarding the override of the statute-barring rules for assessments for taxation years that end before June 26, 2013.

(5.13) (Repealed by S.C. 2013, c. 34, s. 44(5).)

History: S. 5905(5.13) was repealed by S.C. 2013, c. 34, s. 44(5), applicable in respect of acquisitions of control that occur after December 18, 2009, except if the acquisition of control results from an acquisition of shares made under an agreement in writing entered into before December 18, 2009.

S. 5905(5.13) formerly read:

(5.13) For the purposes of clause (B) of subparagraph 88(1)(*d*)(ii) of the Act, the prescribed amount is

(*a*) if the property described in that subparagraph is a share of the capital stock of a foreign affiliate of the subsidiary or if that property is an interest in a partnership that holds one or more such shares, the amount determined by the formula

$$A \times B/C$$

where

A is the total of all amounts each of which is the amount, if any, by which

(i) the amount of a dividend received, after the particular time at which the parent last acquired control of the subsidiary, on any share of the capital stock of the foreign affiliate (or any share of the capital stock of the foreign affiliate for which that share was substituted) held by the subsidiary or the partnership, as the case may be, immediately before the winding-up, that was deductible under paragraph 113(1)(*a*) or (*b*) of the Act in computing the

Regulations

taxable income of the subsidiary or of a corporation with which the subsidiary was not dealing at arm's length (otherwise than because of a right referred to in paragraph 251(5)(*b*) of the Act in respect of the foreign affiliate)

exceeds

(ii) the portion of that dividend that may reasonably be considered to have reduced the foreign affiliate's exempt surplus or taxable surplus in respect of the subsidiary that arose after the particular time (determined as if a dividend were paid out of the foreign affiliate's exempt surplus or taxable surplus, as the case may be, in respect of the subsidiary, in the reverse order to that in which that surplus of the foreign affiliate in respect of the subsidiary arose),

B is the fair market value of the property immediately before the winding-up, and

C is

(i) if the property is a share, the fair market value, immediately before the winding-up, of all of the shares of the capital stock of the foreign affiliate held by the subsidiary immediately before the winding-up, and

(ii) if the property is an interest in a partnership, the fair market value of the interest in the partnership immediately before the winding-up; and

(*b*) in any other case, nil.

S. 5905(5.13) was added by S.C. 2013, c. 34, s. 44(4), applicable in respect of windings-up that begin, and amalgamations that occur, after February 27, 2004.

See the application following s. 5905(1) regarding the override of the statute-barring rules for assessments for taxation years that end before June 26, 2013.

(5.2) If, at a particular time, control of a corporation resident in Canada has been acquired by a person or a group of persons and, at the particular time, the corporation owns shares of the capital stock of a foreign affiliate of the corporation, there shall be included — under subparagraph (v) of the description of B in the definition "exempt surplus" in subsection 5907(1) in computing the affiliate's exempt surplus or exempt deficit, as the case may be, in respect of the corporation at the time that is immediately before the particular time — the amount, if any, determined by the formula

$$(A + B - C)/D$$

where

A is the amount determined by the formula

$$E \times F$$

where

E is the affiliate's tax-free surplus balance in respect of the corporation, determined at the time (referred to in this subsection as the "relevant time") that is immediately before the time that is immediately before the particular time, and

F is the corporation's surplus entitlement percentage in respect of the affiliate determined at the relevant time;

B is the total of all amounts each of which is the corporation's cost amount, determined at the particular time, of a share of the capital stock of the affiliate that is owned by the corporation at the particular time;

C is the total of

(*a*) the fair market value, determined at the particular time, of all of the shares of the capital stock of the affiliate that are owned by the corporation at the particular time, and

(*b*) the amount, if any, determined under paragraph 5908(6)(*b*); and

D is the corporation's surplus entitlement percentage in respect of the affiliate determined at the relevant time.

History: S. 5905(5.2) was added by S.C. 2013, c. 34, s. 44(6), applicable in respect of acquisitions of control that occur after December 18, 2009, except if the acquisition of control results from an acquisition of shares made under an agreement in writing entered into before December 18, 2009.

See the application following s. 5905(1) regarding the override of the statute-barring rules for assessments for taxation years that end before June 26, 2013.

(5.3) The cost amount of a share that is referred to in the description of B in subsection (5.2) shall be determined after taking into account the application of subsection 111(4) of the Act.

History: S. 5905(5.3) was added by S.C. 2013, c. 34, s. 44(6), applicable in respect of acquisitions of control that occur after December 18, 2009, except if the acquisition of control results from an acquisition of shares made under an agreement in writing entered into before December 18, 2009.

See the application following s. 5905(1) regarding the override of the statute-barring rules for assessments for taxation years that end before June 26, 2013.

(5.4) For the purposes of clause (B) of subparagraph 88(1)(*d*)(ii) of the Act, the prescribed amount is

(*a*) if the property described in that subparagraph is a share of the capital stock of a foreign affiliate of the subsidiary, the amount determined by the formula

$$A \times B$$

where

A is the affiliate's tax-free surplus balance, in respect of the subsidiary, determined at the time at which the parent last acquired control of the subsidiary, and

B is the percentage that would be the subsidiary's surplus entitlement percentage, determined at that time, in respect of the affiliate if at that time the subsidiary had owned no shares of the affiliate's capital stock other than the share;

(*b*) if the property described in that subparagraph is an interest in a partnership, the amount determined by subsection 5908(7); and

(*c*) in any other case, nil.

History: S. 5905(5.4) was added by S.C. 2013, c. 34, s. 44(6), applicable in respect of acquisitions of control that occur after December 18, 2009, except if the acquisition of control results from an acquisition of shares made under an agreement in writing entered into before December 18, 2009.

See the application following s. 5905(1) regarding the override of the statute-barring rules for assessments for taxation years that end before June 26, 2013.

(5.5) For the purposes of subsections (5.2), (5.4), (7.2) and (7.3), the "tax-free surplus balance" of a foreign affiliate of a corporation resident in Canada, in respect of the corporation, at any time, is the total of

(*a*) the amount, if any, by which the affiliate's exempt surplus in respect of the corporation at that time exceeds the total of

(i) the affiliate's hybrid deficit, if any, in respect of the corporation at that time, and

(ii) the affiliate's taxable deficit, if any, in respect of the corporation at that time;

(*a*.1) the amount, if any, by which the amount of the affiliate's hybrid surplus in respect of the corporation at that time exceeds the amount determined under subsection (5.7) in respect of the corporation at that time if, at that time, the amount of that hybrid surplus is less than or equal to the amount determined by the formula

$$[A \times (B - 0.5)] + (C \times 0.5)$$

where

A is the affiliate's hybrid underlying tax in respect of the corporation at that time,

B is the corporation's relevant tax factor (within the meaning assigned by subsection 95(1) of the Act) for the corporation's taxation year that includes that time, and

C is the affiliate's hybrid surplus in respect of the corporation at that time; and

(*b*) the lesser of

(i) the amount, if any, determined by the formula

$$A \times B$$

where

A is the affiliate's underlying foreign tax in respect of the corporation at that time, and

B is the amount by which the corporation's relevant tax factor (within the meaning assigned by subsection 95(1) of the Act), for the corporation's taxation year that includes that time, exceeds one, and

(ii) the amount, if any, by which the affiliate's taxable surplus in respect of the corporation at that time exceeds

(A) if the affiliate has an exempt deficit and a hybrid deficit, in respect of the corporation at that time, the total of the exempt deficit and the hybrid deficit,

(B) if the affiliate has an exempt deficit and no hybrid deficit, in respect of the corporation at that time, the amount, if any, by which the exempt deficit exceeds the affiliate's hybrid surplus in respect of the corporation at that time, and

(C) if the affiliate has a hybrid deficit and no exempt deficit, in respect of the corporation at that time, the amount, if any, by which the hybrid deficit exceeds the affiliate's exempt surplus in respect of the corporation at that time.

History: S. 5905(5.5)(*a*) was replaced by S.C. 2013, c. 34, s. 84(12), deemed to have come into force on August 20, 2011.

See the application for the amendment to s. 5905(1) before the formula for the extension of assessment periods to take into account the amendments by S.C. 2013, c. 34, s. 54 to 89.

S. 5905(5.5)(*a*) formerly read:

(*a*) the amount, if any, by which the affiliate's exempt surplus in respect of the corporation at that time exceeds the affiliate's taxable deficit in respect of the corporation at that time; and

S. 5905(5.5)(*a.1*) was added by S.C. 2013, c. 34, s. 84(12), deemed to have come into force on August 20, 2011.

See the application for the amendment to s. 5905(1) before the formula for the extension of assessment periods to take into account the amendments by S.C. 2013, c. 34, s. 54 to 89.

S. 5905(5.5)(*b*)(ii) was replaced by S.C. 2013, c. 34, s. 84(13), deemed to have come into force on August 20, 2011.

See the application for the amendment to s. 5905(1) before the formula for the extension of assessment periods to take into account the amendments by S.C. 2013, c. 34, s. 54 to 89.

S. 5905(5.5)(*b*)(ii) formerly read:

(ii) the amount, if any, by which the affiliate's taxable surplus in respect of the corporation at that time exceeds the affiliate's exempt deficit in respect of the corporation at that time.

S. 5905(5.5) was added by S.C. 2013, c. 34, s. 44(6), deemed to have come into force on December 19, 2009.

See the application following s. 5905(1) regarding the override of the statute-barring rules for assessments for taxation years that end before June 26, 2013.

(5.6) For the purposes of subsection (5.5), the amounts of exempt surplus or exempt deficit, hybrid surplus or hybrid deficit, hybrid underlying tax, taxable surplus or taxable deficit, and underlying foreign tax, of a foreign affiliate of corporation resident in Canada, in respect of the corporation, at a particular time are those amounts that would be determined, at the particular time, under subparagraph 5902(1)(*a*)(i) if that subparagraph were applicable at the particular time and the references in that subparagraph to "the dividend time" were references to the particular time.

History: S. 5905(5.6) was replaced by S.C. 2013, c. 34, s. 84(14), deemed to have come into force on August 20, 2011.

See the application for the amendment to s. 5905(1) before the formula for the extension of assessment periods to take into account the amendments by S.C. 2013, c. 34, s. 54 to 89.

S. 5905(5.6) formerly read:

(5.6) For the purposes of subsection (5.5), the amounts of exempt surplus or exempt deficit, taxable surplus or taxable deficit, and underlying foreign tax of a foreign affiliate of a corporation resident in Canada, in respect of the corporation, at a particular time are those amounts that would be determined, at the particular time, under subparagraph 5902(1)(*a*)(i) if that subparagraph were applicable at the particular time and the references in that subparagraph to "the dividend time" were references to the particular time.

S. 5905(5.6) was added by S.C. 2013, c. 34, s. 44(6), deemed to have come into force on December 19, 2009.

See the application following s. 5905(1) regarding the override of the statute-barring rules for assessments for taxation years that end before June 26, 2013.

(5.7) For the purposes of paragraph (5.5)(*a.1*), the amount determined under this subsection in respect of the corporation at any time is

(*a*) if the affiliate has an exempt deficit and a taxable deficit, in respect of the corporation at that time, the total of the exempt deficit and the taxable deficit;

(*b*) if the affiliate has an exempt deficit and no taxable deficit, in respect of the corporation at that time, the amount of the exempt deficit; and

(*c*) if the affiliate has a taxable deficit and no exempt deficit, in respect of the corporation at that time, the amount, if any, by which the taxable deficit exceeds the affiliate's exempt surplus in respect of the corporation at that time.

History: S. 5905(5.7) was added by S.C. 2013, c. 34, s. 84(14), deemed to have come into force on August 20, 2011.

See the application for the amendment to s. 5905(1) before the formula for the extension of assessment periods to take into account the amendments by S.C. 2013, c. 34, s. 54 to 89.

(6) (Repealed by S.C. 2013, c. 34, s. 44(7).)

History: S. 5905(6) was repealed by S.C. 2013, c. 34, s. 44(7), in respect of dispositions and amalgamations that occur, and windings-up that begin, after December 18, 2009.

S. 5905(6) formerly read:

(6) For the purposes of subsection (5), the following rules apply:

(*a*) where paragraph (5)(*a*) is applicable and the predecessor corporation is, by virtue of an election made under subsection 93(1) of the Act, deemed to have received a dividend on one or more of the shares of the particular affiliate disposed of in the transaction, for the purposes of the adjustment required by paragraph (*b*),

(i) immediately before the time of the transaction there shall be included under subparagraph (v) of the description of B in the definition "exempt surplus" in subsection 5907(1) in computing the particular affiliate's exempt surplus or exempt deficit, as the case may be, in respect of the predecessor corporation an amount equal to the quotient obtained when

(A) such portion of the dividend as is prescribed by paragraph 5900(1)(*a*) to have been paid out of the exempt surplus of the particular affiliate

is divided by

(B) the surplus entitlement percentage of the predecessor corporation in respect of the particular affiliate immediately before the disposition, determined on the assumption that the shares disposed of by the predecessor corporation were the only shares owned by it immediately before the time of the transaction,

(ii) immediately before the time of the transaction there shall be included under subparagraph (v) of the description of B in the definition "taxable surplus" in subsection 5907(1) in computing the particular affiliate's taxable surplus or taxable deficit, as the case may be, in respect of the predecessor corporation an amount equal to the quotient obtained when

(A) such portion of the dividend as is prescribed by paragraph 5900(1)(*b*) to have been paid out of the taxable surplus of the particular affiliate

is divided by

(B) the surplus entitlement percentage referred to in clause (i)(B), and

(iii) immediately before the time of the transaction there shall be deducted from the amount, if any, otherwise determined to be the underlying foreign tax of the particular affiliate in respect of the predecessor corporation an amount equal to the quotient obtained when

(A) the amount prescribed by paragraph 5900(1)(*d*) to be the foreign tax applicable to such portion of the dividend as is prescribed by paragraph 5900(1)(*b*) to have been paid out of the taxable surplus of the particular affiliate

is divided by

(B) the surplus entitlement percentage referred to in clause (i)(B); and

(*b*) the exempt surplus, exempt deficit, taxable surplus, taxable deficit and underlying foreign tax of an affiliate in respect of a predecessor corporation (within the meaning assigned by subsection (5)) and the acquiring corporation (within the meaning assigned by subsection (5)) shall be deemed to be the proportion of the amount thereof otherwise determined that

(i) the surplus entitlement percentage immediately before the time of the latest of the transactions referred to in paragraph (5)(*a*), (*b*) or (*c*) of the predecessor corporation or the acquiring corporation, as the case may be, in respect of the affiliate, determined on the assumption

(A) that the taxation year of the affiliate that otherwise would have included that time had ended immediately before that time, and

(B) where the transaction is one referred to in paragraph (5)(*a*), that the shares referred to therein were the only shares owned by the predecessor corporation immediately before that time,

is of

(ii) the surplus entitlement percentage immediately after the time of the latest of the transactions referred to in paragraph (5)(*a*), (*b*) or (*c*) of the acquiring corporation in respect of the affiliate, determined on the assumption that the taxation year of the affiliate that otherwise would have included that time had ended immediately after that time.

(7) If at any time there has been a liquidation and dissolution of a foreign affiliate (referred to in this subsection as the "dissolved affiliate") of a corporation resident in Canada that is a designated liquidation and dissolution (within the meaning assigned by subsection 95(1) of the Act) of the dissolved affiliate, each other foreign affiliate of the corporation that had a direct equity percentage (within the meaning assigned by subsection 95(4) of the Act) in the dissolved affiliate immediately before that time is, for the purposes of computing its exempt surplus or exempt deficit, hybrid surplus or hybrid deficit, hybrid underlying tax, taxable surplus or taxable deficit, and underlying foreign tax, in respect of the corporation, deemed to have received dividends immediately before that time the total of which is equal to the amount it might reasonably have expected to receive if the dissolved affiliate had, immediately before that time, paid dividends on all shares of its capital stock the total of which was equal to the amount of its net surplus in respect of the corporation immediately before that time, determined on the assumption that the taxation year of the dissolved affiliate that otherwise would have included that time had ended immediately before that time.

History: S. 5905(7) was replaced by S.C. 2013, c. 34, s. 84(15) applicable In respect of liquidations and dissolutions of foreign affiliates of a taxpayer that begin after August 19, 2011. However, if the taxpayer makes the election following s. 95(2)(*e*) of the *Income Tax Act*

(*a*) s. 5905(7) applies in respect of all liquidations and dissolutions of foreign affiliates of the taxpayer that begin after December 20, 2002; and

(*b*) s. 5905(7) is, in respect of all such liquidations and dissolutions that begin on or before August 19, 2011, to be read as follows:

"(7) If at any time there has been a liquidation and dissolution of a foreign affiliate (referred to in this subsection as the "dissolved affiliate") of a corporation resident in Canada that is a designated liquidation and dissolution (within the meaning assigned by subsection 95(1) of the Act) of the dissolved affiliate, each other foreign affiliate of the corporation that had a direct equity percentage (within the meaning assigned by subsection 95(4) of the Act) in the dissolved affiliate immediately before that time is, for the purposes of computing its exempt surplus or exempt deficit, taxable surplus or taxable deficit, and underlying foreign tax, in respect of the corporation, deemed to have received dividends immediately before that time the total of which is equal to the amount it might reasonably have expected to receive if the dissolved affiliate had, immediately before that time, paid dividends on all shares of its capital stock the total of which was equal to the amount of its net surplus in respect of the corporation immediately before that time, determined on the assumption that the taxation year of the dissolved affiliate that otherwise would have included that time had ended immediately before that time."

See the application for the amendment to s. 5905(1) before the formula for the extension of assessment periods to take into account the amendments by S.C. 2013, c. 34, s. 54 to 89.

S. 5905(7) formerly read:

(7) Where at any time there has been a dissolution of a foreign affiliate (in this subsection referred to as the "dissolved affiliate") of a corporation resident in Canada and paragraph 95(2)(*e*.1) of the Act is applicable in respect of the dissolution, each other foreign affiliate of the corporation that had a direct equity percentage in the dissolved affiliate immediately before that time shall, for the purposes of computing its exempt surplus or exempt deficit, taxable surplus or taxable deficit and underlying foreign tax in respect of the corporation, be deemed to have received dividends immediately before that time the aggregate of which is equal to the amount it might reasonably have expected to receive if the dissolved affiliate had, immediately before that time, paid dividends the aggregate of which on all shares of its capital stock was equal to the amount of its net surplus in respect of the corporation immediately before that time, determined on the assumption that the taxation year of the dissolved affiliate that otherwise would have included that time had ended immediately before that time.

(7.1) Subsection (7.2) applies if

(*a*) a foreign affiliate (referred to in this subsection and subsections (7.2) to (7.6) as the "deficit affiliate") of a corporation resident in Canada has an exempt deficit, in respect of the corporation, at a particular time; and

(*b*) at the time (referred to in this paragraph and subsections (7.2) to (7.6) as the "acquisition time") that is immediately after the particular time, shares of the capital stock of a foreign affiliate (referred to in this subsection and subsections (7.2) to (7.6) as an "acquired affiliate") of the corporation in which the deficit affiliate has, at the particular time, an equity percentage (within the meaning assigned by subsection 95(4) of the Act) are acquired by, or otherwise become property of,

(i) the corporation, or

(ii) another foreign affiliate of the corporation, in the case where the percentage that would, if the deficit affiliate were resident in Canada, be the deficit affiliate's surplus entitlement percentage in respect of the acquired affiliate immediately after the acquisition time is less than the percentage that would, if the deficit affiliate were so resident, be its surplus entitlement percentage in respect of the acquired affiliate at the particular time.

History: S. 5905(7.1) was added by S.C. 2013, c. 34, s. 44(8), applicable where a share of the capital stock of a foreign affiliate of a corporation is acquired by, or otherwise becomes property of, a person after December 18, 2009.

See the application following s. 5905(1) regarding the override of the statute-barring rules for assessments for taxation years that end before June 26, 2013.

(7.2) If this subsection applies, there is to be included,

(*a*) at the time (referred to in this subsection and subsections (7.6) and (7.7) and 5908(11) and (12) as the "adjustment time") that is immediately before the time that is immediately before the time that is immediately before the acquisition time, under subparagraph (v) of the description of B in the definition "exempt surplus" in subsection 5907(1) in computing an acquired affiliate's exempt surplus or exempt deficit in respect of the corporation, the amount, if any, equal to the lesser of

(i) the amount determined by the formula

$$A/B$$

where

A is the deficit affiliate's exempt deficit in respect of the corporation immediately before the acquisition time, and

B is the percentage that would, if the deficit affiliate were resident in Canada, be the deficit affiliate's surplus entitlement percentage in respect of the acquired affiliate immediately before the acquisition time, and

(ii) the lesser of

(A) the acquired affiliate's tax-free surplus balance in respect of the corporation immediately before the adjustment time, and

(B) either

(I) if there is more than one acquired affiliate, the amount designated by the corporation, in its return of income for the taxation year in which the taxation year of the acquired affiliate that includes the acquisition time ends, in respect of the acquired affiliate, or

(II) in any other case, the amount determined under clause (A);

(*b*) at the time that is immediately after the acquisition time, under subparagraph (vi.1) of the description of A in the definition "exempt surplus" in subsection 5907(1) in computing the deficit affiliate's exempt deficit in respect of the corporation, the total of all amounts each of which is the amount determined in respect of an acquired affiliate by the formula

$$C \times D$$

where

C is the amount determined under paragraph (*a*) in respect of the acquired affiliate, and

D is the percentage that would, if the deficit affiliate were resident in Canada, be the deficit affiliate's surplus entitlement percentage immediately before the acquisition time in respect of the acquired affiliate; and

(*c*) at the time that is immediately after the acquisition time, under subparagraph (vi.1) of the description of A in the definition "exempt surplus" in subsection 5907(1) in computing the exempt surplus or exempt deficit of any other foreign affiliate (referred to in this paragraph and paragraph (7.6)(*b*) as a "subordinate affiliate") of the corporation, in respect of the corporation, that has immediately before the acquisition time a direct equity percentage (within the meaning assigned by subsection 95(4) of the Act) in the acquired affiliate and in which, immediately before the acquisition time, the deficit affiliate does not have an equity percentage (within the meaning assigned by subsection 95(4) of the Act), the amount determined by the formula

$$E \times F$$

where

E is the amount determined under paragraph (*a*) in respect of the acquired affiliate, and

F is the percentage that would, if the subordinate affiliate were resident in Canada, be the subordinate affiliate's surplus entitlement percentage immediately before the acquisition time in respect of the acquired affiliate if the subordinate affiliate owned no shares of the capital stock of any corporation other than its shares of the capital stock of the acquired affiliate.

History: S. 5905(7.2) was added by S.C. 2013, c. 34, s. 44(8), applicable where a share of the capital stock of a foreign affiliate of a corporation is acquired by, or otherwise becomes property of, a person after December 18, 2009.

See the application following s. 5905(1) regarding the override of the statute-barring rules for assessments for taxation years that end before June 26, 2013.

(7.3) Subsection (7.4) applies if

(*a*) the lesser of

(i) the deficit affiliate's exempt deficit in respect of the corporation immediately before the acquisition time, and

(ii) the total of all amounts each of which is the amount, if any, that is the product obtained by multiplying

(A) the tax-free surplus balance immediately before the acquisition time in respect of the corporation of an acquired affiliate, and

(B) the surplus entitlement percentage of the corporation in respect of that acquired affiliate immediately before the acquisition time

exceeds

(*b*) the total of all amounts each of which is the amount, if any, that is the product obtained by multiplying

Regulations

(i) the amount, if any, actually designated under subclause (7.2)(*a*)(ii)(B)(I) in respect of an acquired affiliate, and

(ii) the surplus entitlement percentage of the corporation in respect of that acquired affiliate immediately before the acquisition time.

History: S. 5905(7.3) was added by S.C. 2013, c. 34, s. 44(8), applicable where a share of the capital stock of a foreign affiliate of a corporation is acquired by, or otherwise becomes property of, a person after December 18, 2009.

See the application following s. 5905(1) regarding the override of the statute-barring rules for assessments for taxation years that end before June 26, 2013.

(7.4) If this subsection applies, the amount designated by the corporation in respect of a particular acquired affiliate is deemed, for the purposes of subclause (7.2)(*a*)(ii)(B)(I),

(*a*) to be the amount determined by the Minister in respect of the particular acquired affiliate; and

(*b*) not to be the amount, if any, actually designated under subclause (7.2)(*a*)(ii)(B)(I).

History: S. 5905(7.4) was added by S.C. 2013, c. 34, s. 44(8), applicable where a share of the capital stock of a foreign affiliate of a corporation is acquired by, or otherwise becomes property of, a person after December 18, 2009.

See the application following s. 5905(1) regarding the override of the statute-barring rules for assessments for taxation years that end before June 26, 2013.

(7.5) Subsection (7.6) applies if

(*a*) subsection (7.2) applies;

(*b*) the deficit affiliate, or any other foreign affiliate of the corporation in which the deficit affiliate has, immediately before the acquisition time, an equity percentage (which percentage has, for the purposes of this subsection, the meaning assigned by subsection 95(4) of the Act and which deficit affiliate or other affiliate is referred to in subsection (7.6) as the "direct holder"), has, immediately before the acquisition time, a direct equity percentage (within the meaning assigned by that subsection 95(4)) in any other foreign affiliate (referred to in paragraph (*c*) and subsection (7.6) as the "subject affiliate") of the corporation; and

(*c*) the subject affiliate is the acquired affiliate or has, immediately before the acquisition time, an equity percentage in the acquired affiliate.

History: S. 5905(7.5) was added by S.C. 2013, c. 34, s. 44(8), applicable where a share of the capital stock of a foreign affiliate of a corporation is acquired by, or otherwise becomes property of, a person after December 18, 2009.

See the application following s. 5905(1) regarding the override of the statute-barring rules for assessments for taxation years that end before June 26, 2013.

(7.6) Subject to paragraph 5908(11)(*c*), for the purposes of paragraph 92(1.1)(*a*) of the Act, if this subsection applies, there shall be added, in computing on and after the adjustment time

(*a*) the direct holder's adjusted cost base of a share of the capital stock of the subject affiliate, the amount determined by the formula

$$A \times B$$

where

A is the amount determined under paragraph (7.2)(*a*) in respect of the acquired affiliate, and

B is the percentage that would, if the direct holder were resident in Canada, be the direct holder's surplus entitlement percentage in respect of the acquired affiliate immediately before the acquisition time if the direct holder owned only the share; and

(*b*) the subordinate affiliate's adjusted cost base of a share of the capital stock of the acquired affiliate, the amount determined by the formula

$$C \times D$$

where

C is the amount determined under paragraph (7.2)(*a*) in respect of the acquired affiliate, and

D is the percentage that would, if the subordinate affiliate were resident in Canada, be the subordinate affiliate's surplus entitlement percentage in respect of the acquired affiliate immediately before the acquisition time if the subordinate affiliate owned only the share.

History: S. 5905(7.6) was added by S.C. 2013, c. 34, s. 44(8), applicable where a share of the capital stock of a foreign affiliate of a corporation is acquired by, or otherwise becomes property of, a person after December 18, 2009.

See the application following s. 5905(1) regarding the override of the statute-barring rules for assessments for taxation years that end before June 26, 2013.

(7.7) For the purposes of paragraph 93(3)(*c*) of the Act, if an amount (referred to in this subsection and subsection 5908(12) as the "adjustment amount") is required by subsection 92(1.1) of the Act to be added in computing, on or after the adjustment time, the adjusted cost base of a share of the capital stock of a foreign affiliate of a corporation resident in Canada,

(*a*) where paragraph 92(1.1)(*a*) of the Act applies, the prescribed amount is the adjustment amount; and

(*b*) where paragraph 92(1.1)(*b*) of the Act applies, the prescribed amount is the amount determined under subsection 5908(12).

History: S. 5905(7.7) was added by S.C. 2013, c. 34, s. 44(8), applicable where a share of the capital stock of a foreign affiliate of a corporation is acquired by, or otherwise becomes property of, a person after December 18, 2009.

See the application following s. 5905(1) regarding the override of the statute-barring rules for assessments for taxation years that end before June 26, 2013.

(8) (Repealed by S.C. 2013, c. 34, s. 44(9).)

History: S. 5905(8) was repealed by S.C. 2013, c. 34, s. 44(9), in respect of dispositions that occur after December 18, 2009.

See the application following s. 5905(1) regarding the override of the statute-barring rules for assessments for taxation years that end before June 26, 2013.

S. 5905(8) formerly read:

(8) Where at any time a dividend is, by virtue of an election made by a corporation under subsection 93(1) of the Act, deemed to have been received on one or more shares of a class of the capital stock of a particular foreign affiliate of the corporation disposed of to the corporation or another foreign affiliate of the corporation, the following rules apply:

(*a*) for the purposes of the adjustment required by paragraph (*b*),

Regulations

(i) immediately before that time there shall be included under subparagraph (v) of the description of B in the definition "exempt surplus" in subsection 5907(1) in computing the particular affiliate's exempt surplus or exempt deficit, as the case may be, in respect of the corporation an amount equal to the product obtained when the specified adjustment factor in respect of the disposition is multiplied by the total of all amounts each of which is the portion of any such dividend that is prescribed by paragraph 5900(1)(*a*) to have been paid out of the exempt surplus of the particular affiliate,

(ii) immediately before that time there shall be included under subparagraph (v) of the description of B in the definition "taxable surplus" in subsection 5907(1) in computing the particular affiliate's taxable surplus or taxable deficit, as the case may be, in respect of the corporation an amount equal to the product obtained when the specified adjustment factor in respect of the disposition is multiplied by the total of all amounts each of which is the portion of any such dividend that is prescribed by paragraph 5900(1)(*b*) to have been paid out of the taxable surplus of the particular affiliate, and

(iii) immediately before that time there shall be deducted from the amount, if any, otherwise determined to be the underlying foreign tax of the particular affiliate in respect of the corporation an amount equal to the product obtained when the specified adjustment factor in respect of the disposition is multiplied by the aggregate of all amounts each of which is the amount prescribed by paragraph 5900(1)(*d*) to be the foreign tax applicable to such portion of any such dividend as is prescribed by paragraph 5900(1)(*b*) to have been paid out of the taxable surplus of the particular affiliate,

and, for the purposes of subparagraphs (i) to (iii), the specified adjustment factor in respect of the disposition is the amount equal to the quotient obtained when

(iv) where the person disposing of the shares is the corporation, 100 per cent, and

(v) where the person disposing of the shares is another foreign affiliate of the corporation, the surplus entitlement percentage of the corporation in respect of that affiliate immediately before the disposition,

is divided by

(vi) the surplus entitlement percentage of the corporation in respect of the particular foreign affiliate immediately before the disposition;

(*b*) the exempt surplus or exempt deficit, the taxable surplus or taxable deficit and the underlying foreign tax in respect of the corporation of the particular affiliate and of each other foreign affiliate of the corporation in which the particular affiliate has an equity percentage (in this subsection referred to as the "other affiliate") shall at that time be adjusted to the proportion of the amount thereof otherwise determined that

(i) the surplus entitlement percentage immediately before that time of the corporation in respect of the particular affiliate or the other affiliate, as the case may be, determined on the assumption that the taxation year of the particular affiliate or the other affiliate, as the case may be, that otherwise would have included that time had ended immediately before that time,

is of

(ii) the surplus entitlement percentage immediately after that time of the corporation in respect of the particular affiliate or the other affiliate, as the case may be, determined on the assumption that the taxation year of the particular affiliate or the other affiliate, as the case may be, that otherwise would have included that time had ended immediately after that time; and

(*c*) for the purposes of the definitions "exempt deficit", "exempt surplus", "taxable deficit", "taxable surplus" and "underlying foreign tax" in subsection 5907(1), the amounts determined under paragraph (*b*) are referred to as the opening exempt deficit, opening exempt surplus, opening taxable deficit, opening taxable surplus and opening underlying foreign tax, as the case may be, of the particular affiliate and each other affiliate in respect of the corporation resident in Canada.

(9) (Repealed by S.C. 2013, c. 34, s. 44(10).)

History: S. 5905(9) was repealed by S.C. 2013, c. 34, s. 44(10), in respect of issuances that occur after December 18, 2009.

See the application following s. 5905(1) regarding the override of the statute-barring rules for assessments for taxation years that end before June 26, 2013.

S. 5905(9) formerly read:

(9) Where at any time a foreign affiliate of a corporation resident in Canada (in this subsection referred to as the "issuing affiliate") issues shares of a class of its capital stock to a person other than the corporation or another foreign affiliate of the corporation and as a result thereof the surplus entitlement percentage of the corporation in respect of the issuing affiliate decreases, for the purposes of this Part, the exempt surplus or exempt deficit, the taxable surplus or taxable deficit and the underlying foreign tax, in respect of the corporation, of the issuing affiliate and of each other foreign affiliate of the corporation in which the issuing affiliate has an equity percentage (in this subsection referred to as the "other affiliate") shall at that time be increased to the proportion of the amount thereof otherwise determined that

(*a*) the surplus entitlement percentage immediately before that time of the corporation in respect of the issuing affiliate or the other affiliate, as the case may be, determined on the assumption that the taxation year of the issuing affiliate or the other affiliate, as the case may be, that otherwise would have included that time had ended immediately before that time,

is of

(*b*) the surplus entitlement percentage immediately after that time of the corporation in respect of the issuing affiliate or other affiliate, as the case may be, determined on the assumption that the taxation year of the issuing affiliate or the other affiliate, as the case may be, that otherwise would have included that time had ended immediately after that time,

and, for the purposes of the definitions "exempt deficit", "exempt surplus", "taxable deficit", "taxable surplus" and "underlying foreign tax" in subsection 5907(1), those increased amounts are referred to as the opening exempt deficit, opening exempt surplus, opening taxable deficit, opening taxable surplus and opening underlying foreign tax, as the case may be, of each of those affiliates in respect of the corporation resident in Canada.

(10) For the purposes of this section, the surplus entitlement at any time of a share owned by a corporation resident in Canada of the capital stock of a foreign affiliate of the corporation in respect of a particular foreign affiliate of the corporation is the portion of

(*a*) the amount that would have been received on the share if the foreign affiliate had at that time paid dividends the aggregate of which on all shares of its capital stock was equal to the amount that would be its net surplus in respect of the corporation at that time assuming that

(i) each other foreign affiliate of the corporation in which the foreign affiliate had an equity percentage had immediately before that time paid a dividend equal to its net surplus in respect of the corporation immediately before the dividend was paid, and

(ii) any dividend referred to in subparagraph (i) that would be received by another foreign affiliate was received by such other foreign affiliate immediately before any such dividend that it would have paid,

that may reasonably be considered to relate to

(*b*) the amount that would be the net surplus of the particular affiliate in respect of the corporation at that time assuming that

(i) each other foreign affiliate of the corporation in which the particular affiliate had an equity percentage had immediately before that time paid a dividend equal to its net surplus in respect of the corporation immediately before the dividend was paid, and

(ii) any dividend referred to in subparagraph (i) that would be received by another foreign affiliate was received by such other foreign affiliate immediately before any such dividend that it would have paid.

(11) For the purposes of subsection (10),

(*a*) if a particular foreign affiliate of a corporation has an equity percentage in another foreign affiliate of the corporation that has an equity percentage in the particular affiliate, the amount that would be the net surplus of, or the amount that would be a dividend received by, the particular affiliate is to be determined in a manner that is

(i) reasonable in the circumstances, and

(ii) consistent with the results that would be obtained if a series of actual dividends had been paid and received by the foreign affiliates of the corporation that are relevant to the determination;

(*b*) if any foreign affiliate of a corporation resident in Canada has issued shares of more than one class of its capital stock, the amount that would be paid as a dividend on the shares of any class is the portion of its net surplus that, in the circumstances, it might reasonably be expected to have paid on all the shares of that class; and

(*c*) if the particular affiliate's net surplus as determined for the purposes of subsection (10) would, in the absence of this paragraph, be nil the particular affiliate's net surplus for the purposes of that subsection is deemed to be the greater of

(i) the amount of the particular affiliate's retained earnings, if any, determined at the end of its last taxation year ending before the time referred to in that subsection under accounting principles that are relevant to the particular affiliate for that year, and

(ii) the amount determined by the formula

$$A \times B$$

where

A is the amount of the particular affiliate's total assets determined at the end of that year under accounting principles that are relevant to the particular affiliate for that year, and

B is 25%.

History: S. 5905(11) was replaced by S.C. 2013, c. 34, s. 84(16), deemed to have come into force on August 20, 2011.

See the application for the amendment to s. 5905(1) before the formula for the extension of assessment periods to take into account the amendments by S.C. 2013, c. 34, s. 54 to 89.

S. 5905(11) formerly read:

(11) For the purposes of subsection (10),

(*a*) in determining the net surplus of, or the amount of a dividend received by, a particular foreign affiliate of a taxpayer resident in Canada in which any other foreign affiliate of the taxpayer has an equity percentage, no amount shall be included in respect of any distribution that would be received by the particular affiliate from such other affiliate; and

(*b*) if any foreign affiliate of a corporation resident in Canada has issued shares of more than one class of its capital stock, the amount that would be paid as a dividend on the shares of any class is such portion of its net surplus as, in the circumstances, it might reasonably be expected to have paid on all the shares of that class.

(12) (Repealed by S.C. 2013, c. 34, s. 84(17).)

History: S. 5905(12) was repealed by S.C. 2013, c. 34, s. 84(17), deemed to have come into force on December 19, 2009.

See the application for the amendment to s. 5905(1) before the formula for the extension of assessment periods to take into account the amendments by S.C. 2013, c. 34, s. 54 to 89.

S. 5905(12) formerly read:

(12) Notwithstanding any other provision of this Part, for the purposes of determining under subsection (10) the net surplus of a foreign affiliate of a corporation resident in Canada in respect of the corporation at any time in a taxation year of the affiliate that would otherwise have included that time (in this subsection referred to as the "normal year"), the exempt earnings or loss and the taxable earnings or loss required to be included in computing the net surplus in respect of any taxation year of the affiliate that is assumed for the purposes of a provision of this section to have ended at that time shall be deemed to be that proportion of such amounts determined for the normal year that the number of days in the taxation year assumed to have ended at that time is of the number of days in the normal year.

(13) For the purposes of the definition "surplus entitlement percentage" in subsection 95(1) of the Act and of this Part, the surplus entitlement percentage at any time of a corporation resident in Canada in respect of a particular foreign affiliate of the corporation is,

(*a*) the percentage that is the corporation's equity percentage in the particular affiliate at that time if

(i) the particular affiliate and each corporation that is relevant to the determination of the corporation's equity percentage in the particular affiliate have, at that time, only one class of issued shares, and

(ii) no foreign affiliate (referred to in this subparagraph as the "upper-tier affiliate") of the corporation that is relevant to the determination of the corporation's equity percentage in the particular affiliate has, at that time, an equity percentage in a foreign affiliate (including, for greater certainty, the particular affiliate) of the corporation that has an equity percentage in the upper-tier affiliate; and

(*b*) in any other case, the proportion of 100 that

(i) the aggregate of all amounts, each of which is the surplus entitlement at that time of a share owned by the corporation of the capital stock of a foreign affiliate of the corporation in respect of the particular foreign affiliate of the corporation

is of

(ii) the amount determined under paragraph (10)(*b*) to be the net surplus of the particular affiliate in respect of the corporation at that time.

History: S. 5905(13)(*a*) was replaced by S.C. 2013, c. 34, s. 84(18), deemed to have come into force on August 20, 2011.

See the application for the amendment to s. 5905(1) before the formula for the extension of assessment periods to take into account the amendments by S.C. 2013, c. 34, s. 54 to 89.

S. 5905(13)(*a*) formerly read:

(*a*) where the particular affiliate and each corporation that is relevant to the determination of the corporation's equity percentage in the particular affiliate have only one class of issued shares at that time, the percentage that is the corporation's equity percentage in the particular affiliate at that time, and

S. 5905(13), the portion after subparagraph (*b*)(ii) was repealed by S.C. 2013, c. 34, s. 84(19), deemed to have come into force on August 20, 2011.

See the application for the amendment to s. 5905(1) before the formula for the extension of assessment periods to take into account the amendments by S.C. 2013, c. 34, s. 54 to 89.

S. 5905(13), the portion after subparagraph (*b*)(ii) formerly read:

except that where the amount determined under subparagraph (ii) is nil, the percentage determined under this paragraph shall be the corporation's equity percentage in the particular affiliate at that time,

and, for the purposes of this subsection, "equity percentage" has the meaning that would be assigned by subsection 95(4) of the Act if the reference in paragraph (*b*) of the definition "equity percentage" in that subsection to "any corporation" were read as a reference to "any corporation other than a corporation resident in Canada".

(14) For the purposes of subsections (10), (11) and (13), "equity percentage" has the meaning that would be assigned by subsection 95(4) of the Act if the reference in paragraph (*b*) of the definition "equity percentage" in that subsection to "any corporation" were read as a reference to "any corporation other than a corporation resident in Canada".

History: S. 5905(14) was added by S.C. 2013, c. 34, s. 84(20), deemed to have come into force on August 20, 2011.

See the application for the amendment to s. 5905(1) before the formula for the extension of assessment periods to take into account the amendments by S.C. 2013, c. 34, s. 54 to 89.

5906. Carrying on Business in a Country

(1) For the purposes of this Part, where a foreign affiliate of a corporation resident in Canada carries on an active business, it shall be deemed to carry on that business

(*a*) in a country other than Canada only to the extent that such business is carried on through a permanent establishment situated therein; and

(*b*) in Canada only to the extent that its income therefrom is subject to tax under Part I of the Act.

(2) The expression "permanent establishment" means

(*a*) for the purposes of paragraph (1)(*a*) and the definition "earnings" in subsection 5907(1) (which paragraph or definition is referred to in this paragraph as a "provision"),

(i) if the expression is given a particular meaning in a tax treaty with a country, a permanent establishment within the meaning assigned by that tax treaty with respect to the business carried on in that country by the foreign affiliate referred to in the provision, and

(ii) in any other case, a fixed place of business of the affiliate, including an office, a branch, a mine, an oil well, a farm, a timberland, a factory, a workshop or a warehouse, or if the affiliate does not have any fixed place of business, the principal place at which the affiliate's business is conducted; and

(*b*) for the purposes of subdivision i of Division B of Part I of the Act,

(i) if the expression is given a particular meaning in a tax treaty with a country, a permanent establishment within the meaning assigned by that tax treaty if the person or partnership referred to in the relevant portion of that subdivision (which person or partnership is referred to in this paragraph and subsection (3) as the "person") is a resident of that country for the purpose of that tax treaty, and

(ii) in any other case, a fixed place of business of the person, including an office, a branch, a mine, an oil well, a farm, a timberland, a factory, a workshop or a warehouse, or if the person does not have any fixed place of business, the principal place at which the person's business is conducted.

History: S. 5906(2) was replaced by S.C. 2013, c. 34, s. 45(1) applicable to taxation years of a foreign affiliate of a taxpayer that end after 1999 except that, for taxation years of the affiliate that end on or before December 18, 2009, the portion of paragraph 5906(2)(*b*) before its subparagraph (i) is to be read as follows:

"(*b*) for the purposes of subdivision i of Division B of Part I (other than the definitions "excluded income" and "excluded revenue" in subsection 95(2.5)) of the Act,"

Any assessment of a taxpayer's tax, interest and penalties payable under the Act for any taxation year that ends before June 26, 2013 that would otherwise be precluded because of subsections 152(4) to (5) of the Act, shall be made to the extent necessary to take into account this amendment, if the taxpayer

(i) elects in writing in respect of all of its foreign affiliates that this section apply in respect of that provision, and

(ii) files that election with the Minister of National Revenue on or before December 26, 2013 [the day that is six months after royal assent].

S. 5906(2) formerly read:

(2) For the purposes of subsection (1), the expression "permanent establishment" has:

(*a*) if the expression is given a particular meaning in a tax treaty with a country, the meaning assigned by that tax treaty with respect to a business carried on in that country; and

(*b*) in any other case, the meaning that would be assigned by subsection 400(2) if that subsection were read without reference to its paragraph (*e.1*).

S. 5906(2) was replaced by S.C. 2009, c. 2, s. 111(1), applicable to the 2009 and subsequent taxation years. S. 5906(2) formerly read:

(2) Where the Government of Canada has concluded an agreement or convention with the government of another country for the avoidance of double taxation that has the force of law in Canada and in which the expression "permanent establishment" is given a particular meaning, for the purposes of subsection (1), that expression has that meaning with respect to a business carried on in that country and, in any other case, has the meaning assigned by subsection 400(2).

(3) For the purposes of subparagraphs (2)(*a*)(ii) and (*b*)(ii),

(*a*) if the affiliate or the person, as the case may be, carries on business through an employee or agent, established in a particular place, who has general authority to contract for the affiliate or the person or who has a stock of merchandise owned by the affiliate or the person from which the employee or agent regularly fills orders, the affiliate or the person is deemed to have a fixed place of business at that place;

(*b*) if the affiliate or the person, as the case may be, is an insurance corporation, the affiliate or the person is deemed to have a fixed place of business in each country in which the affiliate or the person is registered or licensed to do business;

(*c*) if the affiliate or the person, as the case may be, uses substantial machinery or equipment at a particular place at any time in a taxation year, the affiliate or the person is deemed to have a fixed place of business at that place;

(*d*) the fact that the affiliate or the person, as the case may be, has business dealings through a commission agent, broker or other independent agent or maintains an office solely for the purchase of merchandise at a particular place does not of itself mean that the affiliate or the person has a fixed place of business at that place; and

(*e*) the fact that the affiliate or the person, as the case may be, has a subsidiary controlled corporation at a place or a subsidiary controlled corporation engaged in trade or business at a place does not of itself mean that the affiliate or person has a fixed place of business at that place.

History: S. 5906(3) was added by S.C. 2013, c. 34, s. 45(1) applicable to taxation years of a foreign affiliate of a taxpayer that end after 1999.

See the application following s. 5906(2) regarding the override of the statute-barring rules for assessments for taxation years that end before June 26, 2013.

5907. Interpretation

(1) For the purposes of this Part,

Editorial Note: The Global Section 95 Election allows a taxpayer to make an election with respect to a collection of foreign affiliate amendments that are applicable at various times.

See the provision following s. 5905(1) for the application and alternative reading if certain elections are made.

"active business"—"active business" has the meaning assigned by subsection 95(1) of the Act;

"controlled foreign affiliate"—"controlled foreign affiliate" has the meaning assigned by subsection 95(1) of the Act;

"designated person or partnership"—"designated person or partnership", in respect of a taxpayer at any time, means

(*a*) the taxpayer,

(*b*) a person or partnership that is at that time

(i) a person (other than a partnership) that does not, at that time, deal at arm's length with the taxpayer, or

(ii) a partnership a member of which is, at that time, a designated person or partnership in respect of the taxpayer under this definition, and

(*c*) if a foreign affiliate of the taxpayer is an original corporation that undergoes a division in respect of which subsection 15(1.5) of the Act applies, a new corporation in respect of the division;

History: S. 5907(1), the definition of "designated person or partnership" was replaced by S.C. 2018, c. 27, s. 39(1), deemed in force July 27, 2018, and formerly read:

"designated person or partnership"—"designated person or partnership", in respect of a taxpayer at any time, means the taxpayer or a person or partnership that is at that time

(*a*) a person (other than a partnership) that does not, at that time, deal at arm's length with the taxpayer, or

(*b*) a partnership a member of which is, at that time, a designated person or partnership in respect of the taxpayer under this definition;

S. 5907(1), the definition "designated person or partnership" was added by S.C. 2013, c. 34, s. 85(24), deemed to have come into force on August 20, 2011.

Any assessment of a taxpayer's tax, interest and penalties payable under the Act for any taxation year that ends before June 26, 2013 that would, in the absence of this section, be precluded because of subsections 152(4) to (5) of the Act shall be made to the extent necessary to take into account the amendments by S.C. 2013, c. 34, s. 54 to 89.

Related Sections: 15(1.5) Division of corporation under foreign laws.

"earnings"—"earnings" of a foreign affiliate of a taxpayer resident in Canada for a taxation year of the affiliate from an active business means

(*a*) in the case of an active business carried on by it in a country,

(i) the income or profit from the active business for the year computed in accordance with the income tax law of the country in which the affiliate is resident, in any case where the affiliate is required by that law to compute that income or profit,

(ii) the income or profit from the active business for the year computed in accordance with the income tax law of the country in which the business is carried on, in any case not described in subparagraph (i) where the affiliate is required by that law to compute that income or profit, and

(iii) in any other case, the amount that would be the income from the active business for the year under Part I of the Act if the business were carried on in Canada, the affiliate were resident in Canada and the Act were read without reference to subsections 18(4), 80(3) to (12), (15) and (17) and 80.01(5) to (11) and sections 80.02 to 80.04,

adjusted in each case in accordance with subsections (2), (2.1), (2.2) and (2.9) and, for the purpose of this Part, to the extent that the earnings of an affiliate from an active business carried on by it cannot be attributed to a permanent establishment in any particular country, they shall be attributed to the permanent establishment in the country in which the affiliate is resident and, if the affiliate is resident in more than one country, to the permanent establishment in the country that may reasonably be regarded as the affiliate's principal place of residence, and

(*b*) in any other case, the total of all amounts each of which is an amount of income that would be required under paragraph 95(2)(*a*) or subsection 95(2.44) of the Act to be included in computing the affiliate's income or loss from an active business for the year if that income were computed taking into account the rules in subsection (2.03);

History: S. 5907(1), subparagraph (*a*)(iii) of the definition "earnings" was replaced by S.C. 2014, c. 39, s. 88(1), applicable in respect of taxation years of a foreign affiliate of a taxpayer that begin after July 12, 2013. However,

(*a*) if a taxpayer elects in writing under paragraph 88(25)(*a*) of the *Economic Action Plan 2014 Act, No. 2* [S.C. 2014, c. 39] in respect of all its foreign affiliates and files the election with the Minister of National Revenue on or before the day that is the later of the taxpayer's filing-due date for the taxpayer's taxation year that includes the day on which the *Economic Action Plan 2014 Act, No. 2* [S.C. 2014, c. 39] receives royal assent [December 16, 2014] and the day that is one year after the day on which the *Economic Action Plan 2014 Act, No. 2* [S.C. 2014, c. 39] receives royal assent [December 16, 2015], the amendment to subparagraph (*a*)(iii) of the definition "earnings" in s. 5907(1) applies in respect of taxation years of all foreign affiliates of the taxpayer that begin either after 1994 or after December 20, 2002, depending on which is specified by the taxpayer in the election;

(*b*) if a taxpayer elects in writing under paragraph 88(25)(*b*) of the *Economic Action Plan 2014 Act, No. 2* [S.C. 2014, c. 39] in respect of all its foreign affiliates and files the election with the Minister of National Revenue on or before the day that is the later of the taxpayer's filing-due date for the taxpayer's taxation year that includes the day on which the *Economic Action Plan 2014 Act, No. 2* [S.C. 2014, c. 39] receives royal assent [December 16, 2014] and the day that is one year after the day on which the *Economic Action Plan 2014 Act, No. 2* [S.C. 2014, c. 39] receives royal assent [December 16, 2015], the amounts of exempt surplus, exempt deficit, taxable surplus, taxable deficit, underlying foreign tax and, if applicable, hybrid surplus, hybrid deficit and hybrid underlying tax, of all foreign affiliates of the taxpayer for applicable taxation years of the affiliates in which those amounts are relevant are to be determined as if the amendment to subparagraph (*a*)(iii) of the definition "earnings" in s. 5907(1) applied in respect of taxation years of all foreign affiliates of the taxpayer that end after 1975; and

(*c*) for the purposes of paragraph (*b*), the applicable taxation years of the affiliates are

(i) if the taxpayer has not elected under paragraph 88(25)(*a*) of the *Economic Action Plan 2014 Act, No. 2* [S.C. 2014, c. 39], taxation years of all foreign affiliates of the taxpayer that begin after July 12, 2013, and

(ii) if the taxpayer has elected under paragraph 88(25)(*a*) of the *Economic Action Plan 2014 Act, No. 2* [S.C. 2014, c. 39], taxation years of all foreign affiliates of the taxpayer that begin either after 1994 or after December 20, 2002, depending on which is specified in the election made under that paragraph.

In addition, any assessment of a taxpayer's tax, interest and penalties payable under the Act for any taxation year that ends before the day on which this amendment receives royal assent [December 16, 2014] that would, in the absence of this section, be precluded because of the time references in subsection 152(4) of the Act is to be made to the extent necessary to take into account this amendment.

Subparagraph (*a*)(iii) of the definition "earnings" formerly read:

(iii) in any other case, the amount that would be the income from the active business for the year under Part I of the Act if the business were carried on in Canada, the affiliate were resident in Canada and the Act were read without reference to subsections 80(3) to (12), (15) and (17) and 80.01(5) to (11) and sections 80.02 to 80.04,

S. 5907(1), paragraph (*b*) of the definition "earnings" was replaced by S.C. 2014, c. 39, s. 88(2), applicable in respect of taxation years of a foreign affiliate of a taxpayer that begin after October 2012, and formerly read:

(*b*) in any other case, the total of all amounts each of which is an amount of income that would be required under paragraph 95(2)(*a*) of the Act to be included in computing the affiliate's income or loss from an active business for the year if that income were computed taking into account the rules in subsection (2.03);

S. 5907(1), paragraph (*b*) of the definition "earnings" was replaced by S.C. 2013, c. 34, s. 85(1), applicable in respect of taxation years of a foreign affiliate of a taxpayer that end after August 19, 2011.

Any assessment of a taxpayer's tax, interest and penalties payable under the Act for any taxation year that ends before June 26, 2013 that would, in the absence of this section, be precluded because of subsections 152(4) to (5) of the Act shall be made to the extent necessary to take into account the amendments by S.C. 2013, c. 34, s. 54 to 89.

S. 5907(1), paragraph (*b*) of the definition "earnings" formerly read:

(*b*) in any other case, the total of all amounts each of which is an amount of income that is required under paragraph 95(2)(*a*) of the Act to be included in computing the affiliate's income or loss from an active business for the year;

S. 5907(1), paragraph (*b*) of the definition "earnings" was replaced by S.C. 2013, c. 34, s. 46(2). Subject to the application below, paragraph (*b*) of the definition "earnings" applies to taxation years of a foreign affiliate of a taxpayer that end after 1999.

If a taxpayer has elected under a Global Section 95 Election (see the Editorial Note at the beginning of s. 5907), the amendment to this definition also applies to taxation years, of all foreign affiliates of the taxpayer, that begin after 1994 and end before 2000.

Any assessment of a taxpayer's tax, interest and penalties payable under the Act for any taxation year that ends before the day on which this Act is assented to that would, in the absence of this section, be precluded because of subsections 152(4) to (5) of the Act shall be made to the extent necessary to take into account the election noted above.

S. 5907(1), paragraph (*b*) of the definition "earnings" formerly read:

(*b*) in any other case, the total of the amounts by which the income for the year from an active business of the affiliate is increased because of paragraph 95(2)(*a*) of the Act;

"exempt deficit" —"exempt deficit" of a foreign affiliate of a corporation in respect of the corporation at any time means the amount, if any, by which

(*a*) the total of all amounts each of which is an amount determined at that time under any of subparagraphs (i) to (vi) of the description of B in the definition "exempt surplus" in this subsection

exceeds

(*b*) the total of all amounts each of which is an amount determined at that time under any of subparagraphs (i) to (vii) of the description of A in that definition;

"exempt earnings" —"exempt earnings", of a particular foreign affiliate of a particular corporation for a taxation year of the particular affiliate, means, subject to subsection (2.02), the total of all amounts each of which is

(*a*) the amount by which the capital gains of the particular affiliate for the year (other than capital gains included in computing the amount, at any time in the year, of the particular affiliate's hybrid surplus, or hybrid deficit, in respect of the particular corporation) exceed the total of

(i) the amount of the taxable capital gains for the year referred to in the description of B in the definition "foreign accrual property income" in subsection 95(1) of the Act,

(ii) the amount of the taxable capital gains for the year referred to in subparagraphs (*c*)(i), (*e*)(i) and (*f*)(iv) of the definition "net earnings", and

(iii) the portion of any income or profits tax paid to the government of a country for the year by the particular affiliate that can reasonably be regarded as tax in respect of the amount by which the capital gains of the particular affiliate for the year exceed the total of the amounts referred to in subparagraphs (i) and (ii),

(*a*.1) the amount determined by the formula

$$A - B$$

where

A is the total of all amounts each of which is a particular amount that would be included, in respect of a particular business of the particular affiliate, by paragraph (*c*), (*c.1*) or (*c.2*) of the definition "capital dividend account" in subsection 89(1) of the Act in determining the particular affiliate's capital dividend account at the end of the year if

(i) the particular affiliate were the corporation referred to in that definition,

(ii) the references in paragraphs (*c.1*) and (*c.2*) of that definition, and in paragraph (*c*) of that definition as that paragraph (*c*) read in its application to taxation years that ended before February 28, 2000, to "a business" were read as references to a business that

(A) is not an active business (as defined in subsection 95(1) of the Act), or

(B) is an active business (as defined in that subsection 95(1)) the particular affiliate's earnings from which for the year are determined under subparagraph (*a*)(iii) of the definition "earnings", and

(iii) the particular amount did not include any amount that can reasonably be considered to have accrued while no person or partnership that carried on the particular business was a specified person or partnership (within the meaning of section 95 of the Act) in respect of the particular corporation, and

B is the amount determined for A at the end of the particular affiliate's taxation year that immediately precedes the year,

(*b*) where the year is the 1975 or any preceding taxation year of the particular affiliate, the total of all amounts each of which is the particular affiliate's net earnings for the year,

(*c*) where the year is the 1975 or any preceding taxation year of the particular affiliate, the earnings as determined in paragraph (*b*) of the definition "earnings" in this subsection to the extent that those earnings have not been included because of paragraph (*b*) or deducted in determining an amount included in subparagraph (*b*)(i) of the definition "exempt loss" in this subsection,

(*d*) where the year is the 1976 or any subsequent taxation year of the particular affiliate and the particular affiliate is, throughout the year, resident in a designated treaty country,

Regulations

(i) the particular affiliate's net earnings for the year from an active business carried on by it in Canada or a designated treaty country, or

(ii) the particular affiliate's earnings for the year from an active business to the extent that they derive from

(A) income that is required to be included in computing the particular affiliate's income or loss from an active business for the year under subparagraph 95(2)(*a*)(i) of the Act and that would

(I) if earned by the other foreign affiliate referred to in subclause 95(2)(*a*)(i)(A)(I) or (IV) of the Act, be included in computing the exempt earnings or exempt loss of the other foreign affiliate for a taxation year,

(II) if earned by the life insurance corporation referred to in subclause 95(2)(*a*)(i)(A)(II) of the Act and based on the assumptions contained in subclause 95(2)(*a*)(i)(B)(II) of the Act, be included in computing the exempt earnings or exempt loss of the life insurance corporation for a taxation year, or

(III) if earned from the active business activities carried on by the particular affiliate, or the partnership referred to in subclause 95(2)(*a*)(i)(A)(III) of the Act, be included in computing the exempt earnings or exempt loss of the particular affiliate for a taxation year,

(B) income that is required to be included in computing the particular affiliate's income or loss from an active business for the year under clause 95(2)(*a*)(ii)(A) of the Act where the income is derived from amounts that are paid or payable by the life insurance corporation referred to in that clause and are for expenditures that would, if that life insurance corporation were a foreign affiliate of the particular corporation, be deductible in computing its exempt earnings or exempt loss for a taxation year,

(C) income that is required to be included in computing the particular affiliate's income or loss from an active business for the year under clause 95(2)(*a*)(ii)(B) of the Act to the extent that the amounts paid or payable referred to in that clause are for expenditures that are deductible in computing the exempt earnings or exempt loss, for a taxation year, of the other foreign affiliate referred to in that clause,

(D) income that is required to be included in computing the particular affiliate's income or loss from an active business for the year under clause 95(2)(*a*)(ii)(C) of the Act to the extent that the amounts paid or payable referred to in that clause are for expenditures that are deductible in computing its exempt earnings or exempt loss for a taxation year,

(E) income that is required to be included in computing the particular affiliate's income or loss from an active business for the year under clause 95(2)(*a*)(ii)(D) of the Act if

(I) the second and third affiliates referred to in subclause 95(2)(*a*)(ii)(D)(IV) of the Act are each resident in a designated treaty country throughout their relevant taxation years (within the meaning assigned by that subclause), and

(II) that income would be required to be so included if

1. paragraph (*a*) of the definition "excluded property" in subsection 95(1) of the Act were read as follows:

(*a*) used or held by the foreign affiliate principally for the purpose of gaining or producing income from an active business carried on by it in a designated treaty country (within the meaning assigned by subsection 5907(11) of the *Income Tax Regulations*),

2. paragraph (*c*) of that definition "excluded property" were read as follows:

(*c*) property all or substantially all of the income from which is, or would be, if there were income from the property, income from an active business (which, for this purpose, includes income that would be deemed to be income from an active business by paragraph (2)(*a*) if that paragraph were read without reference to subparagraph (v)) that is included in computing the foreign affiliate's exempt earnings, or exempt loss, as defined in subsection 5907(1) of the *Income Tax Regulations*, for a taxation year,

(F) income that is required to be included in computing the particular affiliate's income or loss from an active business for the year under subparagraph 95(2)(*a*)(iii) of the Act to the extent that the trade accounts receivable referred to in that subparagraph arose in the course of an active business carried on by the other foreign affiliate referred to in that subparagraph the income or loss from which is included in computing its exempt earnings or exempt loss for a taxation year,

(G) income that is required to be included in computing the particular affiliate's income or loss from an active business for the year under subparagraph 95(2)(*a*)(iv) of the Act to the extent that the loans or lending assets referred to in that subparagraph arose in the course of an active business carried on by the other foreign affiliate referred to in that subparagraph the income or loss from which is included in computing its exempt earnings or exempt loss for a taxation year,

(H) income that is required to be included in computing the particular affiliate's income or loss from an active business for the year under subparagraph 95(2)(*a*)(v) of the Act, where all or substantially all of its income, from the property described in that subparagraph, is, or would be if there were income from the property, income from an active business (which, for this purpose, includes income that would be deemed to be income from an active business by paragraph 95(2)(*a*) of the Act if that paragraph were read without reference to its subparagraph (v) and, for greater certainty, excludes income arising as a result of the disposition of the property) that is included in computing its exempt earnings or exempt loss for a taxation year,

(I) income that is required to be included in computing the particular affiliate's income or loss from an active business for the year under subparagraph 95(2)(*a*)(vi) of the Act, where the agreement for the purchase, sale or exchange of currency referred to in that subparagraph can reasonably be considered to have been made by the particular affiliate to reduce its risk with respect to an amount of income or loss that is included in computing its exempt earnings or exempt loss for a taxation year, or

(J) an amount that is required to be included in computing the particular affiliate's income from an active business for the year under subsection 95(2.44) of the Act if the amount is in respect of income that would, in the absence of paragraph 95(2)(*a.3*) of the Act, be income from an active business carried on by the particular affiliate in a designated treaty country, or

(*e*) where the year is the 1976 or any subsequent taxation year of the particular affiliate, each amount that is included in the particular affiliate's exempt earnings for the year because of subsection (10),

minus the portion of any income or profits tax paid to the government of a country for the year by the particular affiliate that can reasonably be regarded as tax in respect of the earnings referred to in paragraph (*c*) or in subparagraph (*d*)(ii);

History: S. 5907(1), the portion of paragraph (*a*) of the definition "exempt earnings" after subparagraph (iii) was repealed by S.C. 2014, c. 39, s. 88(3), applicable in respect of dispositions after 2012.

In addition, any assessment of a taxpayer's tax, interest and penalties payable under the Act for any taxation year that ends before the day on which this amendment receives royal assent [December 16, 2014] that would, in the absence of this section, be precluded because of the time references in subsection 152(4) of the Act is to be made to the extent necessary to take into account this amendment.

The portion of paragraph (*a*) of the definition "exempt earnings" after subparagraph (iii) formerly read:

and for the purpose of this paragraph, where the particular affiliate has disposed of capital property that was shares of the capital stock of another foreign affiliate of the particular corporation to any corporation that was, immediately after the disposition, a foreign affiliate of the particular corporation, the capital gains of the particular affiliate for the year shall not include the portion of those gains that is the total of all amounts each of which is an amount equal to the excess of the fair market value at the end of the particular affiliate's 1975 taxation year of one of those shares disposed of over the adjusted cost base of that share,

S. 5907(1), clause (*d*)(ii)(A) of the definition "exempt earnings" was replaced by S.C. 2014, c. 39, s. 88(4), applicable in respect of taxation years of a foreign affiliate of a taxpayer that begin after July 12, 2013. However, if the taxpayer elects under subsection 25(31) of the *Economic Action Plan 2014 Act, No. 2* [S.C. 2014, c. 39],

(*a*) the amendment to clause (*d*)(ii)(A) of the definition "exempt earnings" applies in respect of taxation years of all foreign affiliates of the taxpayer that end after 2007; and

(*b*) clause (*d*)(ii)(A) of the definition "exempt earnings" in subsection 5907(1) of the Regulations is to be read as follows in respect of taxation years of foreign affiliates of the taxpayer that end after 2007 and begin before 2009:

"(A) income that is required to be included in computing the particular affiliate's income or loss from an active business for the year under subparagraph 95(2)(*a*)(i) of the Act and that would

(I) if earned by the non-resident corporation referred to in sub-subclause 95(2)(*a*)(i)(A)(I)1 of the Act and based on the assumptions contained in subclause 95(2)(*a*)(i)(B)(II) of the Act, be included in computing the exempt earnings or exempt loss of the non-resident corporation for a taxation year,

(II) if earned by the other foreign affiliate referred to in sub-subclause 95(2)(*a*)(i)(A)(I)2 or subclause 95(2)(*a*)(i)(A)(IV) of the Act, be included in computing the exempt earnings or exempt loss of the other foreign affiliate for a taxation year,

(III) if earned by the life insurance corporation referred to in subclause 95(2)(*a*)(i)(A)(II) of the Act and based on the assumptions contained in subclause 95(2)(*a*)(i)(B)(II) of the Act, be included in computing the exempt earnings or exempt loss of the life insurance corporation for a taxation year, or

(IV) if earned from the active business activities carried on by the particular affiliate, or the partnership referred to in subclause 95(2)(*a*)(i)(A)(III) of the Act, be included in computing the exempt earnings or exempt loss of the particular affiliate for a taxation year,"

In addition, any assessment of a taxpayer's tax, interest and penalties payable under the Act for any taxation year that ends before the day on which this amendment receives royal assent [December 16, 2014] that would, in the absence of this section, be precluded because of the time references in subsection 152(4) of the Act is to be made to the extent necessary to take into account this amendment.

Clause (*d*)(ii)(A) of the definition "exempt earnings" formerly read:

(A) income that is required to be included in computing the particular affiliate's income or loss from an active business for the year under subparagraph 95(2)(*a*)(i) of the Act and that would

(I) if earned by the other foreign affiliate referred to in subclause 95(2)(*a*)(i)(A)(I) of the Act, be included in computing the exempt earnings or exempt loss of the other foreign affiliate for a taxation year, or

(II) if earned by the life insurance corporation referred to in subclause 95(2)(*a*)(i)(A)(II) of the Act and based on the assumptions contained in subclause 95(2)(*a*)(i)(B)(II) of the Act, be included in computing the exempt earnings or exempt loss of the life insurance corporation for a taxation year,

S. 5907(1), subclause (*d*)(ii)(E)(I) of the definition "exempt earnings" was replaced by S.C. 2014, c. 39, s. 88(5), applicable in respect of taxation years of a foreign affiliate of a taxpayer that end after July 12, 2013.

In addition, any assessment of a taxpayer's tax, interest and penalties payable under the Act for any taxation year that ends before the day on which this amendment receives royal assent [December 16, 2014] that would, in the absence of this section, be precluded because of the time references in subsection 152(4) of the Act is to be made to the extent necessary to take into account this amendment.

Subclause (*d*)(ii)(E)(I) of the definition "exempt earnings" formerly read:

(I) the country referred to in subclause 95(2)(*a*)(ii)(D)(IV) of the Act is a designated treaty country, and

S. 5907(1), clause (*d*)(ii)(J) of the definition "exempt earnings" was added by S.C. 2014, c. 39, s. 88(6), applicable in respect of taxation years of a foreign affiliate of a taxpayer that begin after October 2012.

S. 5907(1), the portion of the definition "exempt earnings" before subparagraph (*a*)(iii) was replaced by S.C. 2013, c. 34, s. 85(2), applicable in respect of taxation years of a foreign affiliate of a taxpayer that end after August 19, 2011, except that, for taxation years of the foreign affiliate that begin before 2013, subparagraph (*a*)(ii) of the definition "exempt earnings" in subsection 5907(1) is to be read as follows:

"(ii) the amount of the taxable capital gains for the year referred to in subparagraphs (*c*)(i), (*d*)(iii), (*e*)(i) and (*f*)(iv) of the definition "net earnings", and"

See the application for the amendment to the portion of the definition "earnings" before subparagraph (*a*)(iii) in s. 5907(1) for the extension of assessment periods to take into account the amendments by S.C. 2013, c. 34, s. 54 to 89.

Regulations

S. 5907(1), the portion of the definition "exempt earnings" before subparagraph (*a*)(iii) formerly read:

"exempt earnings" of a particular foreign affiliate of a particular corporation for a taxation year of the particular affiliate is the total of all amounts each of which is

(*a*) the amount by which the capital gains of the particular affiliate for the year exceed the total of

(i) the amount of the taxable capital gains for the year referred to in the description of B in the definition "foreign accrual property income" in subsection 95(1) of the Act.

(ii) the amount of the taxable capital gains for the year referred to in subparagraphs (*c*)(i), (*d*)(iii), (*e*)(i) and (*f*)(iv) of the definition "net earnings", and

S. 5907(1), subparagraph (*a*)(ii) of the definition "exempt earnings" was replaced by S.C. 2013, c. 34, s. 46(3), applicable in respect of dispositions of property that occur after December 18, 2009.

Any assessment of a taxpayer's tax, interest and penalties payable under the Act for any taxation year that ends before June 26, 2013 that would otherwise be precluded because of subsections 152(4) to (5) of the Act, shall be made to the extent necessary to take into account this amendment, if the taxpayer

(i) elects in writing in respect of all of its foreign affiliates that this section apply in respect of that provision, and

(ii) files that election with the Minister of National Revenue on or before December 26, 2013 [the day that is six months after royal assent].

S. 5907(1), subparagraph (*a*)(ii) of the definition "exempt earnings" formerly read:

(ii) the amount of the taxable capital gains for the year referred to in subparagraphs (*c*)(i) and (*d*)(iii) of the definition "net earnings" in this subsection, and

S. 5907(1), subparagraph (*a.1*) of the definition "exempt earnings" was added by S.C. 2013, c. 34, s. 46(4). Subject to the application below, subparagraph (*a.1*) of the definition "exempt earnings" applies to taxation years of a foreign affiliate of a taxpayer that begin after December 20, 2002, except that the description of A in paragraph (*a.1*) of the definition "exempt earnings" is, in its application to taxation years of the foreign affiliate that begin on or before December 18, 2009, to be read without reference to its subparagraph (iii).

If a taxpayer has elected under a Global Section 95 Election (see the Editorial Note at the beginning of s. 5907), this definition also applies to taxation years, of all foreign affiliates of the taxpayer, that begin after 1994 and end before December 20, 2002.

Any assessment of a taxpayer's tax, interest and penalties payable under the Act for any taxation year that ends before the day on which this Act is assented to that would, in the absence of this section, be precluded because of subsections 152(4) to (5) of the Act shall be made to the extent necessary to take into account the election noted above.

S. 5907(1), paragraph (*d*) of the definition "exempt earnings" was replaced by S.C. 2013, c. 34, s. 46(5). Subject to the application below, paragraph (*d*) of the definition "exempt earnings" applies to taxation years of a foreign affiliate of a taxpayer that end after 1999, except that

(*a*) the portion of paragraph (*d*) of the definition "exempt earnings" in subsection 5907(1) before its subparagraph (i) is, in its application to taxation years of the foreign affiliate that begin on or before December 18, 2009, to be read as follows:

"(*d*) where the year is the 1976 or any subsequent taxation year of the particular affiliate and the particular affiliate is resident in a designated treaty country,"

(*b*) subclause (*d*)(ii)(E)(II) of the definition "exempt earnings" in subsection 5907(1) is, in its application to taxation years of the foreign affiliate that begin after 2008 and on or before June 18, 2010, to be read as follows:

"(II) that income would be required to be so included if paragraph (*c*) of the definition "excluded property" in subsection 95(1) of the Act were read as follows:

(*c*) property all or substantially all of the income from which is deemed, or would be deemed, if there were income from the property, to be income from an active business by paragraph (2)(*a*) (which, for this purpose, includes income that would be deemed to be income from an active business by paragraph (2)(*a*) if that paragraph were read without reference to its subparagraph (v)) that is derived from amounts payable by payers who are, or would be, if they were foreign affiliates of the taxpayer, entitled to deduct the amounts in computing their exempt earnings or exempt loss, as defined in subsection 5907(1) of the *Income Tax Regulations*, for a taxation year,"

(*c*) subject to paragraph (*d*) [below], subparagraph (*d*)(ii) of the definition "exempt earnings" in subsection 5907(1) is, in its application to taxation years of the foreign affiliate that end after 1999 and begin before 2009, to be read as follows:

"(ii) the particular affiliate's earnings for the year from an active business to the extent that they derive from

(A) income that is required to be included in computing the particular affiliate's income or loss from an active business for the year under subparagraph 95(2)(*a*)(i) of the Act and that would,

(I) if earned by the non-resident corporation referred to in sub-subclause 95(2)(*a*)(i)(A)(I)1 of the Act and based on the assumptions contained in subclause 95(2)(*a*)(i)(B)(I) of the Act, be included in computing the exempt earnings or exempt loss of the non-resident corporation for a taxation year,

(II) if earned by the foreign affiliate referred to in sub-subclause 95(2)(*a*)(i)(A)(I)2 of the Act, be included in computing the exempt earnings or exempt loss of that foreign affiliate for a taxation year, or

(III) if earned by the life insurance corporation referred to in subclause 95(2)(*a*)(i)(A)(II) of the Act and based on the assumptions contained in subclause 95(2)(*a*)(i)(B)(I) of the Act, be included in computing the exempt earnings or exempt loss of the life insurance corporation for a taxation year,

(B) income that is required to be included in computing the particular affiliate's income or loss from an active business for the year under clause 95(2)(*a*)(ii)(A) of the Act to the extent that the amounts paid or payable referred to in that clause are for expenditures that would be deductible in computing the exempt earnings or exempt loss for a taxation year of the non-resident corporation or the partnership, as the case may be, referred to in that clause if it were a foreign affiliate of the particular corporation,

(C) income that is required to be included in computing the particular affiliate's income or loss from an active business for the year under clause 95(2)(*a*)(ii)(B) of the Act to the extent that the amounts paid or payable referred to in that clause are for expenditures that

(I) are deductible in computing the exempt earnings or exempt loss, for a taxation year, of the other foreign affiliate referred to in that clause, or

(II) would be deductible in computing the exempt earnings or exempt loss, for a taxation year, of the partnership referred to in that clause if the partnership were a foreign affiliate of the particular corporation,

(D) income that is required to be included in computing the particular affiliate's income or loss from an active business for the year under clause 95(2)(*a*)(ii)(C) of the Act to the extent that the amounts paid or payable referred to in that clause are for expenditures that would be deductible in computing the exempt earnings or exempt loss, for a taxation year, of the partnership referred to in that clause if the partnership were a foreign affiliate of the particular corporation,

(E) income that is required to be included in computing the particular affiliate's income or loss from an active business for the year under clause 95(2)(*a*)(ii)(D) of the Act if

(I) the country referred to in subclause 95(2)(*a*)(ii)(D)(IV) of the Act is a designated treaty country, and

(II) that income would be required to be so included if paragraph (*c*) of the definition "excluded property" in subsection 95(1) of the Act were read as follows:

(*c*) property all or substantially all of the income from which is deemed, or would be deemed if there were income from the property, to be income from an active business by paragraph (2)(*a*) (which, for this purpose, includes income that would be deemed to be income from an active business by paragraph (2)(*a*) if that paragraph were read without reference to its subparagraph (v)) that is derived from amounts payable by payers who are, or would be, if they were foreign affiliates of the taxpayer, entitled to deduct the amounts in computing their exempt earnings or exempt loss, as defined in subsection 5907(1) of the *Income Tax Regulations*, for a taxation year,

(F) income that is required to be included in computing the particular affiliate's income or loss from an active business for the year under clause 95(2)(*a*)(ii)(E) of the Act where the income is derived from amounts that are paid or payable by the life insurance corporation referred to in that clause and are for expenditures that would, if that life insurance corporation were a foreign affiliate of the particular corporation, be deductible in computing its exempt earnings or exempt loss for a taxation year,

(G) income that is required to be included in computing the particular affiliate's income or loss from an active business for the year under subparagraph 95(2)(*a*)(iii) of the Act to the extent that the trade accounts receivable referred to in that subparagraph arose in the course of an active business carried on by the non-resident corporation referred to in that subparagraph the income or loss from which would be included in computing its exempt earnings or exempt loss for a taxation year if it were a foreign affiliate of the particular corporation,

(H) income that is required to be included in computing the particular affiliate's income or loss from an active business for the year under subparagraph 95(2)(*a*)(iv) of the Act to the extent that the loans or lending assets referred to in that subparagraph arose in the course of an active business carried on by the non-resident corporation referred to in that subparagraph the income or loss from which would be included in computing its exempt earnings or exempt loss for a taxation year if it were a foreign affiliate of the particular corporation,

(I) income that is required to be included in computing the particular affiliate's income or loss from an active business for the year under subparagraph 95(2)(*a*)(v) of the Act, where all or substantially all of its income, from the property described in that subparagraph, is, or would be if there were income from the property, income from an active business (which, for this purpose, includes income that would be deemed to be income from an active business by paragraph 95(2)(*a*) of the Act if that paragraph were read without reference to its subparagraph (v) and, for greater certainty, excludes income arising as a result of the disposition of the property) that is included in computing its exempt earnings or exempt loss for a taxation year, or

(J) income that is required to be included in computing the particular affiliate's income or loss from an active business for the year under subparagraph 95(2)(*a*)(vi) of the Act, where the agreement for the purchase, sale or exchange of currency referred to in that subparagraph can reasonably be considered to have been made by the particular affiliate to reduce its risk with respect to an amount of income or loss that is included in computing its exempt earnings or exempt loss for a taxation year, or"

(*d*) subclause (*d*)(ii)(E)(II) of the definition "exempt earnings" in subsection 5907(1) as set out in the read-as text contained in paragraph (c) [above], is, in its application to taxation years of the foreign affiliate that end after 1999 and begin before December 21, 2002, to be read as follows:

"(II) that income would be required to be so included if paragraph (*c*) of the definition "excluded property" in subsection 95(1) of the Act were read without reference to amounts receivable referred to in that paragraph (*c*), where the interest on the amounts is not, or would not be if interest were payable on the amounts, deductible in computing the debtor's exempt earnings or exempt loss for a taxation year,"

If a taxpayer has elected under a Global Section 95 Election (see the Editorial Note at the beginning of s. 5907), subparagraph (*d*)(ii) of the definition of "exempt earnings" in subsection 5907(1) and being read in the manner described in paragraph (*c*) [of the application above] but without reference to paragraph (*d*) [of the application above] also applies to taxation years, of all foreign affiliates of the taxpayer, that begin after 1994 and end before 2000, except that, for those taxation years,

(i) clause (A) of subparagraph (*d*)(ii), as so read, is to be read without reference to its subclause (II),

(ii) if the taxpayer has not elected under the application for s. 95(2)(*a*)(ii)(D), clause (E) of that subparagraph (*d*)(ii), as so read, is to be read as if it also contained a subclause (I.1) that read as follows:

"(I.1) the shares of a foreign affiliate (referred to in this subclause as the "non-qualifying affiliate") that is not resident and subject to income taxation in a designated treaty country are not considered relevant for the purpose of determining whether shares of the third affiliate that is referred to in clause 95(2)(*a*)(ii)(D) of the Act are excluded property unless the shares of the third affiliate would not have been excluded property if the shares of all such non-qualifying affiliates were not excluded property, and"

(iii) each reference to "income or loss" in clauses (H) and (I) of subparagraph (*d*)(ii), as so read, is to be replaced by a reference to "income".

If a taxpayer has not elected under a Global Section 95 election but has elected under the application for clause 95(2)(*a*)(ii)(D), subparagraph (*d*)(ii) of the definition "exempt earnings" in subsection 5907(1) of the Regulations, being read in the manner described in paragraphs (*c*) and (*d*) above, also applies to taxation years, of all foreign affiliates of the taxpayer, that begin after 1994 and end before 2000.

S. 5907(1), paragraph (*d*) of the definition "exempt earnings" formerly read:

(*d*) where the year is the 1976 or any subsequent taxation year of the particular affiliate and the particular affiliate is resident in a designated treaty country, each amount that is

(i) the particular affiliate's net earnings for the year from an active business carried on by it in Canada or a designated treaty country, or

(ii) the earnings of the particular affiliate for the year from an active business to the extent that they derive from

(A) amounts by which the income of the particular affiliate from an active business for the year is increase because of subparagraph 95(2)(*a*)(i) of the Act that are derived by the particular affiliate from activities that could reasonably be considered to be directly related to business activities carried on by a non-resident corporation, to which the particular affiliate and the particular corporation are related throughout the year, in the course of an active business carried on by the non-resident corporation the income from which would, if the non-resident corporation were a foreign affiliate of a corporation, be included in computing the non-resident corporation's exempt earnings or exempt loss,

(B) where the particular corporation is a life insurance corporation resident in Canada throughout the year and the particular affiliate is a foreign affiliate in respect of which the particular corporation has a qualifying interest throughout the year, amounts by which the income of the particular affiliate from an active business for the year is increased because of subparagraph 95(2)(*a*)(i) of the Act that are derived by the particular affiliate from activities that could reasonably be considered to be directly related to business activities carried on by the particular corporation in the course of an active business carried on by the particular corporation in a country other than Canada, the income from which would, if the particular corporation were a foreign affiliate of another corporation and were resident in the country other than Canada in which that active business of the particular corporation is carried on, be included in computing the particular corporation's exempt earnings or exempt loss,

(C) amounts by which the income of the particular affiliate from an active business for the year is increased because of clause 95(2)(*a*)(ii)(A) of the Act that are derived from amounts paid or payable, directly or indirectly, to it or a partnership of which it is a member by a non-resident corporation to which the particular affiliate and the particular corporation are related throughout the year, to the extent that, if the non-resident corporation were a foreign affiliate of a corporation, the amounts paid or payable by the non-resident corporation would be deductible in the year or a subsequent taxation year in computing its exempt earnings or exempt loss,

(D) where a non-resident corporation to which the particular affiliate and the particular corporation are related throughout the year is a member of a particular partnership (other than where the non-resident corporation is a specified member of the particular partnership at any time in a fiscal period of the particular partnership ending in the year), amounts by which the income of the particular affiliate from an active business for the year is increased because of clause 95(2)(*a*)(ii)(A) of the Act that are derived from amounts paid or payable, directly or indirectly, to it or another partnership of which it is a member by the particular partnership to the extent that, if the particular partnership were a foreign affiliate of a corporation and were resident in the country in which the non-resident corporation is resident and subject to income taxation, the amounts paid or payable by the particular partnership would be deductible in the year or a subsequent taxation year in computing its exempt earnings or exempt loss,

(E) amounts by which the income of the particular affiliate from an active business for the year is increased because of clause 95(2)(*a*)(ii)(B) of the Act that are derived from amount paid or payable, directly or indirectly, to it or a partnership of which it is a member by another foreign affiliate of the particular corporation in respect of which the particular corporation has a qualifying interest throughout the year, to the extent that the amounts paid or payable by the other foreign affiliate are deductible in the year or a subsequent taxation year in computing its exempt earnings or exempt loss,

(F) where another foreign affiliate of the particular corporation in respect of which the particular corporation has a qualifying interest throughout the year is a member of a particular partnership (other than where the other foreign affiliate is a specified member of the particular partnership at any time in a fiscal period of the particular partnership ending in the year), amounts by which the income of the particular affiliate from an active business for the year is increased because of clause 95(2)(*a*)(ii)(B) of the Act that are derived from amounts paid or payable, directly or indirectly, to it or another partnership of which it is a member by the particular partnership, to the extent that, if the particular partnership were a foreign affiliate of a corporation and were resident in the country in which the other foreign affiliate is resident and subject to income taxation, the amounts paid or payable by the particular partnership would be deductible in the year or a subsequent taxation year in computing its exempt earnings or exempt loss,

(G) where the particular affiliate is a member of a particular partnership (other than where the particular affiliate is a specified member of the particular partnership as any time in a fiscal period of the particular partnership ending in the year), amounts by which the income of the particular affiliate from an active business for the year is increased because of clause 95(2)(*a*)(ii)(C) of the Act that are derived from amounts paid or payable, directly or indirectly, to it or another partnership of which it is a member by the particular partnership, to the extent that, if the particular partnership were a foreign affiliate of a corporation and were resident in the country in which the particular affiliate is resident and subject to income taxation, the amounts paid or payable by the particular partnership would be deductible in the year or a subsequent taxation year in computing its exempt earnings or exempt loss,

(H) amounts by which the income of the particular affiliate from an active business for the year is increased because of clause 95(2)(*a*)(ii)(D) of the Act that are derived from amounts paid or payable, directly or indirectly, to it or a partnership of which it is a member by another foreign affiliate (in this clause referred to as the "second affiliate") of the particular corporation to which the particular affiliate and the particular corporation are related throughout the year, to the extent that the amounts paid or payable

(I) are on account of interest on borrowed money used for the purpose of earning income from property or interest on an amount payable for property, where

1. the property is shares of a foreign affiliate (in this clause referred to as the "third affiliate") of the particular corporation in respect of which the particular corporation has a qualifying interest throughout the year and that are excluded property, and

2. the second affiliate, the third affiliate and each other affiliate relevant for the purpose of determining whether the shares of the third affiliate are excluded property are resident and subject to income taxation in a designated treaty country, and

(II) are relevant in computing the liability for income taxes, in the designated treaty country in which the second and third affiliates are resident, of the members of a group of corporations composed of the second affiliate and one or more other foreign affiliates (the shares of which are excluded property) of the particular corporation that are resident in that country and in respect of which the particular corporation has a qualifying interest throughout the year,

and, for the purpose of this clause, "excluded property" has the meaning assigned by subsection 95(1) of the Act, except that for that purpose,

(III) the definition "excluded property" in subsection 95(1) of the Act shall be read without reference to amounts receivable referred to in paragraph (*c*) of that definition where the interest on the amounts is not, or would not if interest were payable on the amounts, be deductible in computing the debtor's exempt earnings or exempt loss, and

(IV) the shares of a foreign affiliate (in this subclause referred to as the "non-qualifying affiliate") that is not resident and subject to income taxation in a designated treaty country are not considered relevant for the purpose of determining whether shares of the third affiliate are excluded property unless the shares of the third affiliate would not have been excluded property if the shares of all such non-qualifying affiliates were not excluded property,

(I) where the particular corporation is a life insurance corporation resident in Canada and the particular affiliate is a foreign affiliate in respect of which the particular corporation has a qualifying interest throughout the year, amounts by which the income of the particular affiliate from an active business for the year is increased because of clause 95(2)(*a*)(ii)(E) of the Act that are derived from amounts paid or payable, directly or indirectly, to it or a partnership of which it is a member by the particular corporation in the course of the particular corporation carrying on its life insurance business outside Canada, to the extent that, if the particular corporation were a foreign affiliate of another corporation and were resident in the country in which the particular corporation carried on its life insurance business outside Canada, the amounts paid or payable by the particular corporation would be deductible in the year or in a subsequent taxation year in computing its exempt earnings or exempt loss,

(J) amounts by which the income of the particular affiliate from an active business for the year is increased because of subparagraph 95(2)(*a*)(iii) of the Act that are derived from the factoring of trade accounts receivable acquired by the particular affiliate, or by a partnership of which the particular affiliate was a member, from a non-resident corporation to which the particular affiliate and the particular corporation are related throughout the year, to the extent that the trade accounts receivable arose in the course of an active business carried on by the non-resident corporation any income from which would be included in the exempt earnings of the non-resident corporation if it were a foreign affiliate of a corporation, or

(K) amounts by which the income of the particular affiliate from an active business for the year is increased because of subparagraph 95(2)(*a*)(iv) of the Act that are derived from loans or lending assets acquired by the particular affiliate or a partnership of which the particular affiliate was a member from a non-resident corporation to which the particular affiliate and the particular corporation are related throughout the year, to the extent that the loans or lending assets arose in the course of an active business carried on by the non-resident corporation any income from which would be included in the exempt earnings of the non-resident corporation if it were a foreign affiliate of a corporation, or

"exempt loss" —"exempt loss", of a foreign affiliate of a corporation for a taxation year of the affiliate, means, subject to subsection (2.02), the total of all amounts each of which is

(*a*) the amount by which the capital losses of the affiliate for the year (other than capital losses included in computing the amount, at any time in the year, of the particular affiliate's hybrid surplus, or hybrid deficit, in respect of the particular corporation) exceed the total of

(i) the amount of the allowable capital losses for the year referred to in the description of E in the definition "foreign accrual property income" in subsection 95(1) of the Act,

(ii) the amount of the allowable capital losses for the year referred to in subparagraphs (*c*)(i), (*e*)(i) and (*f*)(iv) of the definition "net loss", and

(iii) the portion of any income or profits tax refunded by the government of a country for the year to the affiliate that can reasonably be regarded as tax refunded in respect of the amount by which the capital losses of the affiliate for the year exceed the total of the amounts referred to in subparagraphs (i) and (ii),

(*a*.1) the total of all amounts each of which is the portion of an eligible capital expenditure of the affiliate, in respect of a business of the affiliate, that was not included at any time in the affiliate's cumulative eligible capital in respect of the business, if

(i) the business

(A) is not an active business (as defined in subsection 95(1) of the Act), or

(B) is an active business (as defined in subsection 95(1) of the Act) the affiliate's earnings from which for the year are determined under subparagraph (*a*)(iii) of the definition "earnings", and

(ii) in computing its income for the year, the affiliate has deducted an amount described in paragraph 24(1)(*a*) of the Act for the year in respect of the business,

(*b*) where the year is the 1975 or any preceding taxation year of the affiliate, the total of all amounts each of which is

(i) the affiliate's net loss for the year from an active business carried on by it in a country, or

(ii) the amount, if any, for the year by which

(A) the amount determined under the description of D in the definition "foreign accrual property income" in subsection 95(1) of the Act for the year

exceeds

(B) the amount determined under the description of A in the definition "foreign accrual property income" in subsection 95(1) of the Act for the year,

(*c*) where the year is the 1976 or any subsequent taxation year of the affiliate and the affiliate is, throughout the year, resident in a designated treaty country,

(i) the affiliate's net loss for the year from an active business carried on by it in Canada or a designated treaty country, or

(ii) the amount by which

(A) the affiliate's loss for the year from an active business to the extent determined under subparagraph (*d*)(ii) of the definition "exempt earnings" in respect of the year with any modifications that the circumstances require

exceeds

(B) the portion of any income or profits tax refunded by the government of a country for the year to the affiliate that can reasonably be regarded as tax that was refunded in respect of the amount determined under clause (A), or

(*d*) where the year is the 1976 or any subsequent taxation year of the affiliate, each amount that is included in the affiliate's exempt loss for the year because of subsection (10);

History: S. 5907(1), the portion of the definition "exempt loss" before subparagraph (*a*)(iii) was replaced by S.C. 2013, c. 34, s. 85(3), applicable in respect of taxation years of a foreign affiliate of a taxpayer that end after August 19, 2011, except that, for taxation years of the foreign affiliate that begin before 2013, subparagraph (*a*)(ii) of the definition "exempt loss" in subsection 5907(1) is to be read as follows:

"(ii) the amount of the allowable capital losses for the year referred to in subparagraphs (*c*)(i), (*d*)(iii), (*e*)(i) and (*f*)(iv) of the definition "net loss", and"

See the application for the amendment to the portion of the definition "earnings" before subparagraph (*a*)(iii) in s. 5907(1) for the extension of assessment periods to take into account the amendments by S.C. 2013, c. 34, s. 54 to 89.

S. 5907(1), the portion of the definition "exempt loss" before subparagraph (*a*)(iii) formerly read:

"exempt loss" of a foreign affiliate of a corporation for a taxation year of the affiliate is the total of all amounts each of which is

(*a*) the amount by which the capital losses of the affiliate for the year exceed the total of

(i) the amount of the allowable capital losses for the year referred to in the description of E in the definition "foreign accrual property income" in subsection 95(1) of the Act,

(ii) the amount of the allowable capital losses for the year referred to in subparagraphs (*c*)(i), (*d*)(iii), (*e*)(i) and (*f*)(iv) of the definition "net loss", and

S. 5907(1), subparagraph (*a*)(ii) of the definition "exempt loss" was replaced by S.C. 2013, c. 34, s. 46(6), applicable in respect of dispositions of property that occur after December 18, 2009.

See the application following the amendment to subparagraph (*a*)(ii) of the definition "exempt earnings" in s. 5907(1), regarding the override of the statute-barring rules for assessments for taxation years that end before June 26, 2013.

S. 5907(1), subparagraph (*a*)(ii) of the definition "exempt loss" formerly read:

(ii) the amount of the allowable capital losses for the year referred to in subparagraphs (*c*)(i) and (*d*)(iii) of the definition "net loss" in this subsection, and

S. 5907(1), paragraph (*a.1*) of the definition "exempt loss" was added by S.C. 2013, c. 34, s. 46(7), applicable to taxation years of a foreign affiliate of a taxpayer that begin after December 18, 2009.

See the application following the amendment to subparagraph (*a*)(ii) of the definition "exempt earnings" in s. 5907(1), regarding the override of the statute-barring rules for assessments for taxation years that end before June 26, 2013.

S. 5907(1), paragraph (*c*) of the definition "exempt loss" was replaced by S.C. 2013, c. 34, s. 46(8). Subject to the application below, paragraph (*c*) of the definition "exempt loss" applies to taxation years of a foreign affiliate of a taxpayer that end after 1999, except that the portion of paragraph (*c*) before subparagraph (i) of the definition "exempt loss" in subsection 5907(1) is, in its application to taxation years of the foreign affiliate that begin on or before December 18, 2009, to be read as follows:

"(*c*) where the year is the 1976 or any subsequent taxation year of the affiliate and the affiliate is, throughout the year, resident in a designated treaty country,"

If a taxpayer has elected under a Global Section 95 Election (see the Editorial Note at the beginning of s. 5907), paragraph (*c*) of the definition "exempt loss", with the portion of paragraph (*c*)(i) being read in the manner described in the application provision above, also applies to taxation years, of all foreign affiliates of the taxpayer, that begin after 1994 and end before 2000.

Any assessment of a taxpayer's tax, interest and penalties payable under the Act for any taxation year that ends before the day on which this Act is assented to that would, in the absence of this section, be precluded because of subsections 152(4) to (5) of the Act shall be made to the extent necessary to take into account the election noted above.

S. 5907(1), paragraph (*c*) of the definition "exempt loss" formerly read:

(*c*) where the year is the 1976 or any subsequent taxation year of the affiliate and the affiliate is resident in a designated treaty country, each amount that is the affiliate's net loss for the year from an active business carried on by it in Canada or in a designated treaty country, or

"exempt surplus" —"exempt surplus", of a foreign affiliate (in this definition referred to as the "subject affiliate") of a corporation in respect of the corporation, at any particular time, means the amount determined by the following formula in respect of the period that begins with the latest of the following times and that ends with the particular time:

(*a*) the first day of the taxation year of the subject affiliate in which it last became a foreign affiliate of the corporation,

(*b*) the last time for which the opening exempt surplus of the subject affiliate in respect of the corporation was required to be determined under section 5905, and

(*c*) the last time for which the opening exempt deficit of the subject affiliate in respect of the corporation was required to be determined under section 5905

$$A - B$$

where

A is the total of all amounts, in respect of the period, each of which is

(i) the opening exempt surplus, if any, of the subject affiliate in respect of the corporation as determined under section 5905, at the time established in paragraph (*b*),

(ii) the exempt earnings of the subject affiliate for any of its taxation years ending in the period,

(iii) the portion of any dividend received in the period and before the particular time by the subject affiliate from another foreign affiliate

Regulations

of the corporation (including, for greater certainty, any dividend deemed by subsection 5905(7) to have been received by the subject affiliate) that was prescribed by paragraph 5900(1)(*a*) to have been paid out of the payer affiliate's exempt surplus in respect of the corporation,

(iv) the portion of any income or profits tax refunded by or the amount of a tax credit paid by the government of a country to the subject affiliate that can reasonably be regarded as having been refunded or paid in respect of any amount referred to in subparagraph (iii) and that was not deducted in determining any amount referred to in subparagraph (iii) of the description of B,

(v) the portion of any taxable dividend received in the period and before the particular time by the subject affiliate that would, if the dividend were received by the corporation, be deductible by it under section 112 of the Act,

(vi) an amount added to the exempt surplus of the subject affiliate or deducted from its exempt deficit in the period and before the particular time under subsection (1.092), (1.1) or (1.2),

(vi.1) each amount that is required, under section 5905, to be included under this subparagraph in the period and before the particular time, or

(vii) an amount added, in the period and before the particular time, to the exempt surplus of the subject affiliate under paragraph (7.1)(*d*) (as that paragraph applied to dividends paid on or before August 19, 2011), and

B is the total of those of the following amounts that apply in respect of the period:

(i) the opening exempt deficit, if any, of the subject affiliate in respect of the corporation as determined under section 5905, at the time established in paragraph (*c*),

(ii) the exempt loss of the subject affiliate for any of its taxation years ending in the period,

(iii) the portion of any income or profits tax paid to the government of a country by the subject affiliate that can reasonably be regarded as having been paid in respect of any amount referred to in subparagraph (iii), (iv) or (v) of the description of A,

(iv) the portion of any whole dividend paid by the subject affiliate in the period and before the particular time deemed by paragraph 5901(1)(*a*) to have been paid out of the subject affiliate's exempt surplus in respect of the corporation,

(v) each amount that is required under section 5902 or 5905 to be included under this subparagraph, or subparagraph (1)(*d*)(xii) as it applies to taxation years that end before February 22, 1994, in the period and before the particular time, or

(vi) an amount, in the period and before the particular time, deducted from the exempt surplus of the subject affiliate or added to its exempt deficit under subsection (1.092), (1.1) or (1.2);

History: S. 5907(1), subparagraph (vi) of the description of A in the definition "exempt surplus" was replaced by S.C. 2014, c. 39, s. 88(7), applicable in respect of taxation years of a foreign affiliate of a taxpayer that end after 2010. However, if a taxpayer elects in writing under subsection 88(30) of the *Economic Action Plan 2014 Act, No. 2* [S.C. 2014, c. 39] in respect of all its foreign affiliates and files the election with the Minister of National Revenue on or before the day that is the later of the taxpayer's filing-due date for the taxpayer's taxation year that includes the day on which the *Economic Action Plan 2014 Act, No. 2* [S.C. 2014, c. 39] receives royal assent [December 16, 2014] and the day that is one year after the day on which the *Economic Action Plan 2014 Act, No. 2* [S.C. 2014, c. 39] receives royal assent [December 16, 2015], the amendment to subparagraph (vi) of the description of A in the definition "exempt surplus" applies in respect of taxation years of all foreign affiliates of the taxpayer that end on or after July 12, 2013.

In addition, any assessment of a taxpayer's tax, interest and penalties payable under the Act for any taxation year that ends before the day on which this amendment receives royal assent [December 16, 2014] that would, in the absence of this section, be precluded because of the time references in subsection 152(4) of the Act is to be made to the extent necessary to take into account this amendment.

Subparagraph (vi) of the description of A in the definition "exempt surplus" formerly read:

> (vi) an amount added to the exempt surplus of the subject affiliate or deducted from its exempt deficit in the period and before the particular time under any provision of subsection (1.1) or (1.2),

S. 5907(1), subparagraph (vi) of the description of B in the definition "exempt surplus" was replaced by S.C. 2014, c. 39, s. 88(8), applicable in respect of taxation years of a foreign affiliate of a taxpayer that end after 2010. However, if a taxpayer elects in writing under subsection 88(30) of the *Economic Action Plan 2014 Act, No. 2* [S.C. 2014, c. 39] in respect of all its foreign affiliates and files the election with the Minister of National Revenue on or before the day that is the later of the taxpayer's filing-due date for the taxpayer's taxation year that includes the day on which the *Economic Action Plan 2014 Act, No. 2* [S.C. 2014, c. 39] receives royal assent [December 16, 2014] and the day that is one year after the day on which the *Economic Action Plan 2014 Act, No. 2* [S.C. 2014, c. 39] receives royal assent [December 16, 2015], the amendment to subparagraph (vi) of the description of B in the definition "exempt surplus" applies in respect of taxation years of all foreign affiliates of the taxpayer that end on or after July 12, 2013.

In addition, any assessment of a taxpayer's tax, interest and penalties payable under the Act for any taxation year that ends before the day on which this amendment receives royal assent [December 16, 2014] that would, in the absence of this section, be precluded because of the time references in subsection 152(4) of the Act is to be made to the extent necessary to take into account this amendment.

Subparagraph (vi) of the description of B in the definition "exempt surplus" formerly read:

> (vi) an amount, in the period and before the particular time, deducted from the exempt surplus of the subject affiliate or added to its exempt deficit under any provision of subsection (1.1) or (1.2);

S. 5907(1), the portion of the definition "exempt surplus" before paragraph (*a*) was replaced by S.C. 2013, c. 34, s. 85(4), deemed to have come into force on August 19, 2011.

See the application for the amendment to the portion of the definition "earnings" before subparagraph (*a*)(iii) in s. 5907(1) for the extension of assessment periods to take into account the amendments by S.C. 2013, c. 34, s. 54 to 89.

S. 5907(1), the portion of the definition "exempt surplus" before paragraph (*a*) formerly read:

> *"exempt surplus"* of a foreign affiliate (in this definition referred to as the "subject affiliate") of a corporation in respect of the corporation is, at any particular time, the amount determined by the formula
>
> A - B
>
> in respect of the period beginning with the time that is the latest of

S. 5907(1), the portion of the definition "exempt surplus" after paragraph (*c*) and before the description of A was replaced by S.C. 2013, c. 34, s. 85(5), deemed to have come into force on August 20, 2011.

See the application for the amendment to the portion of the definition "earnings" before subparagraph (*a*)(iii) in s. 5907(1) for the extension of assessment periods to take into account the amendments by S.C. 2013, c. 34, s. 54 to 89.

S. 5907(1), the portion of the definition "exempt surplus" after paragraph (*c*) and before the description of A formerly read:

and ending with the particular time, where

S. 5907(1), subparagraph (vii) of the description of A in the definition "exempt surplus" was replaced by S.C. 2013, c. 34, s. 85(6), deemed to have come into force on August 20, 2011.

See the application for the amendment to the portion of the definition "earnings" before subparagraph (*a*)(iii) in s. 5907(1) for the extension of assessment periods to take into account the amendments by S.C. 2013, c. 34, s. 54 to 89.

S. 5907(1), subparagraph (vii) of the description of A in the definition "exempt surplus" formerly read:

(vii) an amount added, in the period and before the particular time, to the exempt surplus of the subject affiliate under paragraph (7.1)(*d*), and

S. 5907(1), paragraphs (*b*) and (*c*) of the definition "exempt surplus" were replaced by S.C. 2013, c. 34, s. 46(9), deemed to have come into force on December 1, 1999.

See the application following the amendment to subparagraph (*a*)(ii) of the definition "exempt earnings" in s. 5907(1), regarding the override of the statute-barring rules for assessments for taxation years that end before June 26, 2013.

S. 5907(1), paragraphs (*b*) and (*c*) of the definition "exempt surplus" formerly read:

(*b*) where the corporation is an acquiring corporation referred to in subsection 5905(5) and the subject affiliate is a particular affiliate referred to in that subsection or another foreign affiliate in which such a particular affiliate had an equity percentage at the time referred to in that subsection, the last time at which that subsection was applicable in respect of the subject affiliate, and

(*c*) where the subject affiliate is a foreign affiliate referred to in subsection 5905(1), (2), (8) or (9) or paragraph 5905(3)(*b*), the last time at which any of those subsections or that paragraph was applicable in respect of the subject affiliate

S. 5907(1), subparagraph (i) of the description of A in the definition "exempt surplus" was replaced by S.C. 2013, c. 34, s. 46(10), deemed to have come into force on December 1, 1999.

See the application following the amendment to subparagraph (*a*)(ii) of the definition "exempt earnings" in s. 5907(1), regarding the override of the statute-barring rules for assessments for taxation years that end before June 26, 2013.

S. 5907(1), subparagraph (i) of the description of A in the definition "exempt surplus" formerly read:

(i) the opening exempt surplus of the subject affiliate as determined under subsection 5905(1), (2), (3), (5), (8) or (9), at the time established in paragraph (*a*), (*b*) or (*c*),

S. 5907(1), subparagraph (vi.1) of the description of A in the definition "exempt surplus" was added by S.C. 2013, c. 34, s. 46(11), applicable where a share of the capital stock of a foreign affiliate of a corporation is acquired by, otherwise becomes property of, or is disposed of by, a person after December 20, 2002.

See the application following the amendment to subparagraph (*a*)(ii) of the definition "exempt earnings" in s. 5907(1), regarding the override of the statute-barring rules for assessments for taxation years that end before June 26, 2013.

S. 5907(1), subparagraph (i) of the description of B in the definition "exempt surplus" was replaced by S.C. 2013, c. 34, s. 46(12), deemed to have come into force on December 1, 1999.

See the application following the amendment to subparagraph (*a*)(ii) of the definition "exempt earnings" in s. 5907(1), regarding the override of the statute-barring rules for assessments for taxation years that end before June 26, 2013.

S. 5907(1), subparagraph (i) of the description of B in the definition "exempt surplus" formerly read:

(i) the opening exempt deficit of the subject affiliate as determined under subsection 5905(1), (2), (3), (5), (8) or (9), at the time established in paragraph (*a*), (*b*) or (*c*),

S. 5907(1), subparagraph (v) of the description of B in the definition "exempt surplus" was replaced by S.C. 2013, c. 34, s. 46(13), deemed to have come into force on December 1, 1999.

See the application following the amendment to subparagraph (*a*)(ii) of the definition "exempt earnings" in s. 5907(1), regarding the override of the statute-barring rules for assessments for taxation years that end before June 26, 2013.

S. 5907(1), subparagraph (v) of the description of B in the definition "exempt surplus" formerly read:

(v) each amount that is determined under paragraph 5902(4)(*a*) or subparagraph 5905(2)(*a*)(i), (6)(*a*)(i) or (8)(*a*)(i) in the period and before the particular time, or

"hybrid deficit" —"hybrid deficit", of a foreign affiliate of a corporation in respect of the corporation at any time, means the amount, if any, by which

(*a*) the total of all amounts each of which is an amount determined at that time under any of subparagraphs (i) to (vii) of the description of B in the definition "hybrid surplus"

exceeds

(*b*) the total of all amounts each of which is an amount determined at that time under any of subparagraphs (i) to (v) of the description of A in that definition;

History: S. 5907(1), the definition "hybrid deficit" was added by S.C. 2013, c. 34, s. 85(24), deemed to have come into force on August 20, 2011.

See the application for the amendment to the portion of the definition "earnings" before subparagraph (*a*)(iii) in s. 5907(1) for the extension of assessment periods to take into account the amendments by S.C. 2013, c. 34, s. 54 to 89.

"hybrid surplus" —"hybrid surplus", of a foreign affiliate (in this definition referred to as the "subject affiliate") of a corporation in respect of the corporation, at any particular time, means the amount determined by the following formula in respect of the period that begins with the latest of the following times and that ends with the particular time:

(*a*) the first day of the taxation year of the subject affiliate in which it last became a foreign affiliate of the corporation,

(*b*) the last time for which the opening hybrid surplus of the subject affiliate in respect of the corporation was required to be determined under section 5905, and

(*c*) the last time for which the opening hybrid deficit of the subject affiliate in respect of the corporation was required to be determined under section 5905

$$A - B$$

where

A is the total of all amounts, in respect of the period, each of which is

(i) the opening hybrid surplus, if any, of the subject affiliate in respect of the corporation as determined under section 5905, at the time established in paragraph (*b*),

(ii) the amount of a capital gain (except to the extent that the taxable portion of the capital gain is included under the description of B in the definition "foreign accrual property income" in subsection 95(1) of the Act in respect of the subject affiliate), for a taxation year, of the subject affiliate, or of a partnership of which the subject affiliate is a member (to the extent that the capital gain is reasonably attributable to the subject affiliate), in respect of a disposition, at any time in the period, of

(A) a share of the capital stock of another foreign affiliate of the corporation,

(B) a partnership interest, or

(C) a property, that is an excluded property of the subject affiliate because of para-

Regulations

graph (*c.1*) of the definition "excluded property" in subsection 95(1) of the Act, that related to

(I) an amount that was receivable under an agreement that relates to the sale of a property that is referred to in clause (A) or (B) the capital gain or capital loss from the sale of which is included under this subparagraph or subparagraph (ii) of the description of B, as the case may be, or

(II) an amount payable, or an amount of indebtedness, described in clause (*c.1*)(ii)(B) of that definition "excluded property" arising in respect of the acquisition of an excluded property of the affiliate that is referred to in clause (A) or (B) any capital gain or capital loss from the disposition of which would, if that excluded property were disposed of, be included under this subparagraph or subparagraph (ii) of the description of B, as the case may be,

(iii) the portion of any income or profits tax refunded by the government of a country to the subject affiliate that can reasonably be regarded as having been refunded in respect of an amount referred to in subparagraph (ii) or (iii) of the description of B,

(iv) the portion of any dividend received in the period and before the particular time by the subject affiliate from another foreign affiliate of the corporation (including, for greater certainty, any dividend deemed under subsection 5905(7) to have been received by the subject affiliate) that was prescribed under paragraph 5900(1)(*a.1*) to have been paid out of the payer affiliate's hybrid surplus in respect of the corporation, or

(v) an amount added to the hybrid surplus of the subject affiliate or deducted from its hybrid deficit in the period and before the particular time under subsection (1.092), (1.1) or (1.2), and

B is the total of those of the following amounts that apply in respect of the period:

(i) the opening hybrid deficit, if any, of the subject affiliate in respect of the corporation as determined under section 5905, at the time established in paragraph (*c*),

(ii) the amount of a capital loss (except to the extent that the allowable portion of the capital loss is included under paragraph (*a*) of the description of E in the definition "foreign accrual property income" in subsection 95(1) of the Act in respect of the subject affiliate), for a taxation year, of the subject affiliate, or of a partnership of which the subject affiliate is a member (to the extent that the capital loss is reasonably attributable to the subject affiliate), in respect of a disposition, at any time in the period, of

(A) a share of the capital stock of another foreign affiliate of the corporation,

(B) a partnership interest, or

(C) a property, that is an excluded property of the subject affiliate because of paragraph (*c.1*) of the definition "excluded property" in subsection 95(1) of the Act, that related to

(I) an amount that was receivable under an agreement that relates to the sale of a property that is referred to in clause (A) or (B) the capital gain or capital loss from the sale of which is included under subparagraph (ii) of the description of A or this subparagraph, as the case may be, or

(II) an amount payable, or an amount of indebtedness, described in clause (*c.1*)(ii)(B) of that definition "excluded property" arising in respect of the acquisition of an excluded property of the affiliate that is referred to in clause (A) or (B) any capital gain or capital loss from the disposition of which would, if that excluded property were disposed of, be included under subparagraph (ii) of the description of A or this subparagraph, as the case may be,

(iii) the amount of a capital loss for a taxation year of the subject affiliate that would arise in respect of a disposition, at any time in the period, of a share of the capital stock of another foreign affiliate of the corporation in the course of the liquidation and dissolution of that other affiliate if subclause 95(2)(*e*)(iv)(A)(II) of the Act were read without reference to its sub-subclause 1 and section 93 of the Act were read without reference to its subsection (4),

(iv) the portion of any income or profits tax paid to the government of a country by the subject affiliate that can reasonably be regarded as having been paid in respect of an amount referred to in subparagraph (ii) or (iv) of the description of A,

(v) the portion of any whole dividend paid by the subject affiliate in the period and before the particular time deemed under paragraph 5901(1)(*a.1*) or, if subsection 5901(1.1) applied to the whole dividend, paragraph 5901(1)(*b*) to have been paid out of the subject affiliate's hybrid surplus in respect of the corporation,

(vi) each amount that is required under section 5902 to be included under this subparagraph in the period and before the particular time, or

(vii) an amount deducted from the hybrid surplus of the subject affiliate or added to its hybrid deficit in the period and before the particular time under subsection (1.092), (1.1) or (1.2);

History: S. 5907(1), subparagraph (v) of the description of A in the definition "hybrid surplus" was replaced by S.C. 2014, c. 39, s. 88(9), deemed to have come into force on August 20, 2011. However, if a taxpayer elects in writing under subsection 88(30) of the *Economic Action Plan 2014 Act, No. 2* [S.C. 2014, c. 39], this amendment is instead deemed to have come into force, in respect of the taxpayer, on July 12, 2013.

In addition, any assessment of a taxpayer's tax, interest and penalties payable under the Act for any taxation year that ends before the day on which this amendment receives royal assent [December 16, 2014] that would, in the absence of this section, be precluded because of the time references in subsection 152(4) of the Act is to be made to the extent necessary to take into account this amendment.

Subparagraph (v) of the description of A in the definition "hybrid surplus" formerly read:

(v) an amount added to the hybrid surplus of the subject affiliate or deducted from its hybrid deficit in the period and before the particular time under subsection (1.1) or (1.2), and

S. 5907(1), subparagraph (vii) of the description of B in the definition "hybrid surplus" was replaced by S.C. 2014, c. 39, s. 88(10), deemed to have come into force on August 20, 2011. However, if a taxpayer elects in writing under subsection 88(30) of the *Economic Action Plan 2014 Act, No. 2* [S.C. 2014, c. 39], this amendment is instead deemed to have come into force, in respect of the taxpayer, on July 12, 2013.

In addition, any assessment of a taxpayer's tax, interest and penalties payable under the Act for any taxation year that ends before the day on which this amendment receives royal assent [December 16, 2014] that would, in the absence of this section, be precluded because of the time references in subsection 152(4) of the Act is to be made to the extent necessary to take into account this amendment.

Subparagraph (vii) of the description of B in the definition "hybrid surplus" formerly read:

(vii) an amount, in the period and before the particular time, deducted from the hybrid surplus of the subject affiliate or added to its hybrid deficit under subsection (1.1) or (1.2);

S. 5907(1), the definition "hybrid surplus" was added by S.C. 2013, c. 34, s. 85(24), deemed to have come into force on August 20, 2011. However, in respect of dispositions that occur after August 19, 2011 and before 2013,

(*a*) the portion of subparagraph (ii) of the description of A in the definition "hybrid surplus" in subsection 5907(1) of the Regulations before clause (A) is to be read as follows:

"(ii) the amount of a capital gain (except to the extent that the taxable portion of the capital gain is included under the description of B in the definition "foreign accrual property income" in subsection 95(1) of the Act in respect of the subject affiliate), for a taxation year, of the subject affiliate, or of a partnership of which the subject affiliate is a member (to the extent that the capital gain is reasonably attributable to the subject affiliate), in respect of a disposition, at any time in the period, to a person or partnership that was, at that time, a designated person or partnership in respect of the corporation, of"

(*b*) the portion of subparagraph (ii) of the description of B in the definition "hybrid surplus" in subsection 5907(1) of the Regulations before clause (A) is to be read as follows:

"(ii) the amount of a capital loss (except to the extent that the allowable portion of the capital loss is included under paragraph (a) of the description of E in the definition "foreign accrual property income" in subsection 95(1) of the Act in respect of the subject affiliate), for a taxation year, of the subject affiliate, or of a partnership of which the subject affiliate is a member (to the extent that the capital loss is reasonably attribut- able to the subject affiliate), in respect of a disposition, at any time in the period, to a person or partnership that was, at that time, a designated person or partnership in respect of the corporation, of"

(*c*) section 5907 of the Regulations is to be read as if it contained a subsection (1.001) that reads as follows:

"(1.001) For the purposes of subparagraph (ii) of the description of A, and subparagraph (ii) of the description of B, in the definition "hybrid surplus" in subsection (1)

(*a*) if a foreign affiliate of a corporation redeems, acquires or cancels shares of its capital stock those shares are, for greater certainty, deemed to be disposed of to the affiliate by the person or partnership that, immediately before the redemption, acquisition or cancellation, holds those shares;

(*b*) if a partnership redeems, acquires or cancels interests in the partnership those interests are, for greater certainty, deemed to be disposed of to the partnership by the person or partnership that, immediately before the redemption, acquisition or cancellation, holds those interests; and

(*c*) if a person or partnership is deemed under subsection 40(3) of the Act to have disposed of shares of the capital stock of a corporation, the person or partnership is deemed to have disposed of those shares to itself."

See the application for the amendment to the portion of the definition "earnings" before subparagraph (*a*)(iii) in s. 5907(1) for the extension of assessment periods to take into account the amendments by S.C. 2013, c. 34, s. 54 to 89.

"hybrid underlying tax" —"hybrid underlying tax", of a foreign affiliate (in this definition referred to as the "subject affiliate") of a corporation in respect of the corporation, at any particular time, means the amount determined by the following formula in respect of the period that begins with the later of the following times and that ends with the particular time:

(*a*) the first day of the taxation year of the subject affiliate in which it last became a foreign affiliate of the corporation, and

(*b*) the last time for which the opening hybrid underlying tax of the subject affiliate in respect of the corporation was required to be determined under section 5905

$$A - B$$

where

A is the total of all amounts, in respect of the period, each of which is

(i) the opening hybrid underlying tax, if any, of the subject affiliate in respect of the corporation as determined under section 5905, at the time established in paragraph (*b*),

(ii) the portion of any income or profits tax paid to the government of a country by the subject affiliate that can reasonably be regarded as having been paid in respect of any amount referred to in subparagraph (ii) or (iv) of the description of A in the definition "hybrid surplus",

(iii) each amount that was prescribed by paragraph 5900(1)(*c.1*) to have been the foreign tax applicable to the portion of any dividend received in the period and before the particular time by the subject affiliate from another foreign affiliate of the corporation (including, for greater certainty, any dividend deemed under subsection 5905(7) to have been received by the subject affiliate) that was prescribed by paragraph 5900(1)(*a.1*) to have been paid out of the payer affiliate's hybrid surplus in respect of the corporation, or

(iv) the amount by which the subject affiliate's hybrid underlying tax is required to be increased in the period and before the particular time under subsection (1.092), (1.1) or (1.2),

Regulations

B is the total of those of the following amounts that apply in respect of the period:

(i) the portion of any income or profits tax refunded by the government of a country to the subject affiliate that can reasonably be regarded as having been refunded in respect of an amount referred to in subparagraph (ii) or (iii) of the description of B in the definition "hybrid surplus",

(ii) the hybrid underlying tax applicable to any whole dividend paid by the subject affiliate in the period and before the particular time deemed under paragraph 5901(1)(*a.1*) or, if subsection 5901(1.1) applied to the whole dividend, paragraph 5901(1)(*b*) to have been paid out of the subject affiliate's hybrid surplus in respect of the corporation before that time,

(iii) each amount that is required under section 5902 to be included under this subparagraph in the period and before the particular time, or

(iv) the amount by which the subject affiliate's hybrid underlying tax is required to be decreased in the period and before the particular time under subsection (1.092), (1.1) or (1.2);

History: S. 5907(1), subparagraph (iv) of the description of A in the definition "hybrid underlying tax" was replaced by S.C. 2014, c. 39, s. 88(11), deemed to have come into force on August 20, 2011. However, if a taxpayer elects in writing under subsection 88(30) of the *Economic Action Plan 2014 Act, No. 2* [S.C. 2014, c. 39], this amendment is instead deemed to have come into force, in respect of the taxpayer, on July 12, 2013.

In addition, any assessment of a taxpayer's tax, interest and penalties payable under the Act for any taxation year that ends before the day on which this amendment receives royal assent [December 16, 2014] that would, in the absence of this section, be precluded because of the time references in subsection 152(4) of the Act is to be made to the extent necessary to take into account this amendment.

Subparagraph (iv) of the description of A in the definition "hybrid underlying tax" formerly read:

(iv) the amount by which the subject affiliate's hybrid underlying tax is required to be increased under subsection (1.1) or (1.2),

S. 5907(1), subparagraph (iv) of the description of B in the definition "hybrid underlying tax" was replaced by S.C. 2014, c. 39, s. 88(12), deemed to have come into force on August 20, 2011. However, if a taxpayer elects in writing under subsection 88(30) of the *Economic Action Plan 2014 Act, No. 2* [S.C. 2014, c. 39], this amendment is instead deemed to have come into force, in respect of the taxpayer, on July 12, 2013.

In addition, any assessment of a taxpayer's tax, interest and penalties payable under the Act for any taxation year that ends before the day on which this amendment receives royal assent [December 16, 2014] that would, in the absence of this section, be precluded because of the time references in subsection 152(4) of the Act is to be made to the extent necessary to take into account this amendment.

Subparagraph (iv) of the description of B in the definition "hybrid underlying tax" formerly read:

(iv) the amount by which the subject affiliate's hybrid underlying tax is required to be decreased in the period and before the particular time under subsection (1.1) or (1.2);

S. 5907(1), the definition "hybrid underlying tax" was added by S.C. 2013, c. 34, s. 85(24), deemed to have come into force on August 20, 2011.

See the application for the amendment to the portion of the definition "earnings" before subparagraph (*a*)(iii) in s. 5907(1) for the extension of assessment periods to take into account the amendments by S.C. 2013, c. 34, s. 54 to 89.

"hybrid underlying tax applicable" —"hybrid underlying tax applicable", in respect of a corporation to a whole dividend paid at any time on the shares of any class of the capital stock of a foreign affiliate of the corporation by the affiliate, means the proportion of the hybrid underlying tax of the affiliate at that time in respect of the corporation that

(*a*) the portion of the whole dividend deemed to have been paid out of the affiliate's hybrid surplus in respect of the corporation

is of

(*b*) the affiliate's hybrid surplus at that time in respect of the corporation;

History: S. 5907(1), the definition "hybrid underlying tax applicable" was added by S.C. 2013, c. 34, s. 85(24), deemed to have come into force on August 20, 2011.

See the application for the amendment to the portion of the definition "earnings" before subparagraph (*a*)(iii) in s. 5907(1) for the extension of assessment periods to take into account the amendments by S.C. 2013, c. 34, s. 54 to 89.

"loss" —"loss", of a foreign affiliate of a taxpayer resident in Canada for a taxation year of the affiliate from an active business, means

(*a*) in the case of an active business carried on by it in a country, the amount of its loss for the year from the active business carried on in the country computed by applying the provisions of paragraph (*a*) of the definition "earnings" respecting the computation of earnings from that active business carried on in that country, with any modifications that the circumstances require, and

(*b*) in any other case, the total of all amounts each of which is an amount of a loss that would be required under paragraph 95(2)(*a*) of the Act to be included in computing the affiliate's income or loss from an active business for the year if that loss were computed taking into account the rules in subsection (2.03);

History: S. 5907(1), paragraph (*b*) of the definition "loss" was replaced by S.C. 2013. c. 34, s. 85(7), applicable in respect of taxation years of a foreign affiliate of a taxpayer that end after August 19, 2011.

See the application for the amendment to the portion of the definition "earnings" before subparagraph (*a*)(iii) in s. 5907(1) for the extension of assessment periods to take into account the amendments by S.C. 2013, c. 34, s. 54 to 89.

S. 5907(1), paragraph (*b*) of the definition "loss" formerly read:

(*b*) in any other case, the total of all amounts each of which is an amount of a loss that is required under paragraph 95(2)(*a*) of the Act to be included in computing the affiliate's income or loss from an active business for the year;

S. 5907(1), the definition "loss" was replaced by S.C. 2013, c. 34, s. 46(1), applicable to taxation years of a foreign affiliate of a taxpayer that end after 1999.

If a taxpayer has elected under a Global Section 95 Election (see the Editorial Note at the beginning of s. 5907), the amendment to this definition also applies to taxation years, of all foreign affiliates of the taxpayer, that begin after 1994 and end before 2000.

Any assessment of a taxpayer's tax, interest and penalties payable under the Act for any taxation year that ends before the day on which this Act is assented to that would, in the absence of this section, be precluded because of subsections 152(4) to (5) of the Act shall be made to the extent necessary to take into account the election noted above.

S. 5907(1), the definition "loss" formerly read:

"loss" of a foreign affiliate of a taxpayer resident in Canada for a taxation year of the affiliate from an active business carried on by it in a country is the amount of its loss for the year from that active business carried on in that country computed by applying the provisions of paragraph (*a*) of the definition "earnings" in this subsection respecting the computation of earnings from that active business carried on in that country, with any modifications that the circumstances require;

"net earnings" —"net earnings" of a foreign affiliate of a corporation for a taxation year of the affiliate

(*a*) from an active business carried on by it in a country is the amount of its earnings for the year from that active business carried on in that country minus the portion of any income or profits tax paid to the government of a country for the year by the affiliate that can reasonably be regarded as tax in respect of those earnings,

(*b*) in respect of foreign accrual property income is the amount that would be its foreign accrual property income for the year, if the formula in the definition "foreign accrual property income" in subsection 95(1) of the Act were read without reference to F and F.1 in that formula and the amount determined for E in that formula were the amount determined under paragraph (*a*) of the description of E in that formula, minus the portion of any income or profits tax paid to the government of a country for the year by the affiliate that can reasonably be regarded as tax in respect of that income,

(*c*) from dispositions of property used or held by it principally for the purpose of gaining or producing income from an active business carried on by it in a country that is not a designated treaty country (other than Canada) is the amount, if any, by which

(i) the portion of the affiliate's taxable capital gains for the year from those dispositions that can reasonably be considered to have accrued after November 12, 1981

exceeds

(ii) the portion of any income or profits tax paid to the government of a country for the year by the affiliate that can reasonably be regarded as tax in respect of the amount determined under subparagraph (i),

(*d*) (Repealed by S.C. 2013, c. 34, S. 85(10).)

(*e*) from the disposition of a property that is an excluded property of the affiliate that is described in paragraph (*c*) of the definition "excluded property" in subsection 95(1) of the Act but that would not be an excluded property of the affiliate if that paragraph were read in the manner described in subsubclause (*d*)(ii)(E)(II)2 of the definition "exempt earnings" is the amount, if any, by which

(i) the portion of the affiliate's taxable capital gain for the year from the disposition of the property that accrued after its 1975 taxation year

exceeds

(ii) the portion of any income or profits tax paid to the government of a country for the year by the affiliate that can reasonably be regarded as tax that was paid in respect of the amount determined under subparagraph (i), and

(*f*) from a particular disposition of a property, that is an excluded property of the affiliate because of paragraph (*c.1*) of the definition "excluded property" in subsection 95(1) of the Act, that related to

(i) an amount that was receivable under an agreement that relates to the sale of a particular property the taxable capital gain or allowable capital loss from the sale of which is included under any of paragraphs (*c*) to (*e*) of this definition or of the definition "net loss", as the case may be,

(ii) an amount that was receivable and was a property that was described in paragraph (*c*) of that definition "excluded property" but that would not have been an excluded property of the affiliate if that paragraph were read in the manner described in sub-subclause (*d*)(ii)(E)(II)2 of the definition "exempt earnings", or

(iii) an amount payable, or an amount of indebtedness, described in clause (*c.1*)(ii)(B) of that definition "excluded property" arising in respect of the acquisition of an excluded property of the affiliate any taxable capital gain or allowable capital loss from the disposition of which would, if that excluded property were disposed of, be included under any of paragraphs (*c*) to (*e*) of this definition or of the definition "net loss", as the case may be,

is the amount, if any, by which

(iv) the portion of the affiliate's taxable capital gain for the year from the particular disposition that accrued after its 1975 taxation year

exceeds

(v) the portion of any income or profits tax paid to the government of a country for the year by the affiliate that can reasonably be regarded as tax that was paid for the year in respect of the amount determined under subparagraph (iv);

History: S. 5907(1), paragraph (*d*) of the definition "net earnings" was repealed by S.C. 2013, c. 34, s. 85(10), applicable to taxation years of a foreign affiliate of a taxpayer that begin after 2012.

See the application for the amendment to the portion of the definition "earnings" before subparagraph (*a*)(iii) in s. 5907(1) for the extension of assessment periods to take into account the amendments by S.C. 2013, c. 34, s. 54 to 89.

S. 5907(1), paragraph (*d*) of the definition "net earnings" formerly read:

(*d*) from dispositions of

(i) shares of the capital stock of another foreign affiliate of the corporation that were excluded property of the affiliate (other than dispositions to which any of paragraphs 95(2)(*c*) to (*e*) of the Act was applicable and dispositions in respect of which the amount of the capital gain is included in computing the amount, at any time in the year, of the affiliate's hybrid surplus, or hybrid deficit, in respect of the corporation), or

(ii) partnership interests that were excluded property of the affiliate (other than dispositions in respect of which the amount of the capital gain is included in computing the amount, at any time in the year, of the affiliate's hybrid surplus, or hybrid deficit, in respect of the corporation)

is the amount, if any, by which

(iii) the portion of the affiliate's taxable capital gains for the year from those dispositions that can reasonably be considered to have accrued after its 1975 taxation year

exceeds

(iv) the portion of any income or profits tax paid to the government of a country for the year by the affiliate that can reasonably be regarded as tax in respect of the amount determined under subparagraph (iii);

S. 5907(1), subparagraphs (*d*)(i) and (ii) of the definition "net earnings" were replaced by S.C. 2013, c. 34, s. 85(9), applicable In respect of taxation years of a foreign affiliate of a taxpayer that end after August 19, 2011. However, if the taxpayer makes the election following s. 95(2)(*d.1*) of the

Income Tax Act, this amendment also applies to all mergers or combinations in respect of foreign affiliates of the taxpayer that occur after December 20, 2002 and in taxation years of those foreign affiliates that end on or before August 19, 2011 and, in respect of those mergers or combinations, subparagraphs (*d*)(i) and (ii) of the definition "net earnings" in subsection 5907(1) are to be read as follows:

"(i) shares of the capital stock of another foreign affiliate of the corporation that were excluded property of the affiliate (other than dispositions to which any of paragraphs 95(2)(*c*) to (*e*) of the Act was applicable), or

(ii) partnership interests that were excluded property of the affiliate"

See the application for the amendment to the portion of the definition "earnings" before subparagraph (*a*)(iii) in s. 5907(1) for the extension of assessment periods to take into account the amendments by S.C. 2013, c. 34, s. 54 to 89.

S. 5907(1), subparagraphs (*d*)(i) and (ii) of the definition "net earnings" formerly read:

(i) shares of the capital stock of another foreign affiliate of the corporation that were excluded property of the affiliate (other than dispositions to which paragraph 95(2)(*c*), (*d*) or (*e*) of the Act was applicable), or

(ii) partnership interests that were excluded property of the affiliate

S. 5907(1), paragraph (*b*) of the definition "net earnings" was replaced by S.C. 2013, c. 34, s. 85(8), applicable in respect of taxation years of a foreign affiliate of a taxpayer that end after August 19, 2011.

See the application for the amendment to the portion of the definition "earnings" before subparagraph (*a*)(iii) in s. 5907(1) for the extension of assessment periods to take into account the amendments by S.C. 2013, c. 34, s. 54 to 89.

S. 5907(1), paragraph (*b*) of the definition "net earnings" formerly read:

(*b*) in respect of foreign accrual property income is the amount that would be its foreign accrual property income for the year, if the formula in the definition "foreign accrual property income" in subsection 95(1) of the Act were read without reference to the variable F in that formula, minus the portion of any income or profits tax paid to the government of a country for the year by the affiliate that can reasonably be regarded as tax in respect of that income,

S. 5907(1), paragraph (*e*) and (*f*) of the definition "net earnings" were added by S.C. 2013, c. 34, s. 46(14), applicable in respect of dispositions of property that occur after December 18, 2009.

See the application following the amendment to subparagraph (*a*)(ii) of the definition "exempt earnings" in s. 5907(1), regarding the override of the statute-barring rules for assessments for taxation years that end before June 26, 2013.

"net loss" — "net loss" of a foreign affiliate of a corporation for a taxation year of the affiliate

(*a*) from an active business carried on by it in a country is the amount of its loss for the year from that active business carried on in that country minus the portion of any income or profits tax refunded by the government of a country for the year to the affiliate that can reasonably be regarded as tax refunded in respect of that loss,

(*b*) in respect of foreign accrual property income is the amount, if any, by which

(i) the amount, if any, by which

(A) the total of

(I) the amount determined for D in the formula in the definition "foreign accrual property income" in subsection 95(1) of the Act for the year,

(II) the amount determined under paragraph (*a*) of the description of E in that formula for the year,

(III) the amount determined for G in that formula for the year, and

(IV) the amount determined for H in that formula for the year

exceeds

(B) the total of the amounts determined under the descriptions of A, A.1, A.2, B and C in the definition "foreign accrual property income" in subsection 95(1) of the Act for the year

exceeds

(ii) the portion of any income or profits tax refunded by the government of a country for the year to the affiliate that can reasonably be regarded as tax refunded in respect of the amount determined under subparagraph (i),

(*c*) from dispositions of property used or held by it principally for the purpose of gaining or producing income from an active business carried on by it in a country that is not a designated treaty country (other than Canada) is the amount, if any, by which

(i) the portion of the affiliate's allowable capital losses for the year from those dispositions that can reasonably be considered to have accrued after November 12, 1981

exceeds

(ii) the portion of any income or profits tax refunded by the government of a country for the year to the affiliate that can reasonably be regarded as tax refunded in respect of the amount determined under subparagraph (i),

(*d*) (Repealed by S.C. 2013, c. 34, s. 85(13).)

(*e*) from the disposition of a property, that is an excluded property of the affiliate that is described in paragraph (*c*) of the definition "excluded property" in subsection 95(1) of the Act but that would not be an excluded property of the affiliate if that paragraph were read in the manner described in subsubclause (*d*)(ii)(E)(II)2 of the definition "exempt earnings" is the amount, if any, by which

(i) the portion of the affiliate's allowable capital loss for the year from the disposition of the property that accrued after its 1975 taxation year

exceeds

(ii) the portion of any income or profits tax refunded by the government of a country for the year to the affiliate that can reasonably be regarded as tax that was refunded in respect of the amount determined under subparagraph (i), and

(*f*) from a particular disposition of a property, that is an excluded property of the affiliate because of paragraph (*c.1*) of the definition "excluded property" in subsection 95(1) of the Act, that related to

(i) an amount that was receivable under an agreement that relates to the sale of a particular property the taxable capital gain or allowable capital loss from the sale of which is included under any of paragraphs (*c*) to (*e*) of this definition or of the definition "net earnings", as the case may be,

(ii) an amount that was receivable and was a property that was described in paragraph (*c*) of that definition "excluded property" but that would not have been an excluded property of the affiliate if that paragraph were read in the manner described in sub-subclause (*d*)(ii)(E)(II)2 of the definition "exempt earnings", or

(iii) an amount payable, or an amount of indebtedness, described in clause (*c.1*)(ii)(B) of that definition "excluded property" arising in respect of the acquisition of an excluded property of the affiliate any taxable capital gain or allowable capital loss from the disposition of which would, if that excluded property were disposed of, be included under any of paragraphs (*c*) to (*e*) of this definition or of the definition "net earnings", as the case may be,

is the amount, if any, by which

(iv) the portion of the affiliate's allowable capital loss for the year from the particular disposition that accrued after its 1975 taxation year

exceeds

(v) the portion of any income or profits tax refunded by the government of a country for the year to the affiliate that can reasonably be regarded as tax that was refunded in respect of the amount determined under subparagraph (iv);

History: S. 5907(1), paragraph (*d*) of the definition "net loss" was repealed by S.C. 2013, c. 34, s. 85(13), applicable to taxation years of a foreign affiliate of a taxpayer that begin after 2012.

See the application for the amendment to the portion of the definition "earnings" before subparagraph (*a*)(iii) in s. 5907(1) for the extension of assessment periods to take into account the amendments by S.C. 2013, c. 34, s. 54 to 89.

S. 5907(1), paragraph (*d*) of the definition "net loss" formerly read:

(*d*) from dispositions of

(i) shares of the capital stock of another foreign affiliate of the corporation that were excluded property of the affiliate (other than dispositions to which paragraph 95(2)(*c*), (*d*) or (*e*) of the Act was applicable and dispositions in respect of which the amount of the capital loss is included in computing the amount, at any time in the year, of the affiliate's hybrid surplus, or hybrid deficit, in respect of the corporation), or

(ii) partnership interests that were excluded property of the affiliate (other than dispositions in respect of which the amount of the capital loss is included in computing the amount, at any time in the year, of the affiliate's hybrid surplus, or hybrid deficit, in respect of the corporation)

is the amount, if any, by which

(iii) the portion of the affiliate's allowable capital losses for the year from those dispositions that can reasonably be considered to have accrued after its 1975 taxation year

exceeds

(iv) the portion of any income or profits tax refunded by the government of a country for the year to the affiliate that can reasonably be regarded as tax refunded in respect of the amount determined under subparagraph (iii);

S. 5907(1), subparagraphs (*d*)(i) and (ii) of the definition "net loss" were replaced by S.C. 2013, c. 34, s. 85(12), applicable I respect of taxation years of a foreign affiliate of a taxpayer that end after August 19, 2011.

See the application for the amendment to the portion of the definition "earnings" before subparagraph (*a*)(iii) in s. 5907(1) for the extension of assessment periods to take into account the amendments by S.C. 2013, c. 34, s. 54 to 89.

S. 5907(1), subparagraphs (*d*)(i) and (ii) formerly read:

(i) shares of the capital stock of another foreign affiliate of the corporation that were excluded property of the affiliate (other than dispositions to which paragraph 95(2)(*c*), (*d*) or (*e*) of the Act was applicable), or

(ii) partnership interests that were excluded property of the affiliate

S. 5907(1), clause (*b*)(i)(A) of the definition "net loss" was replaced by S.C. 2013, c. 34, s. 85(11), applicable in respect of taxation years of a foreign affiliate of a taxpayer that end after August 19, 2011.

See the application for the amendment to the portion of the definition "earnings" before subparagraph (*a*)(iii) in s. 5907(1) for the extension of assessment periods to take into account the amendments by S.C. 2013, c. 34, s. 54 to 89.

S. 5907(1), clause (*b*)(i)(A) of the definition "net loss" formerly read:

(A) the total of the amounts determined under the descriptions of D, E and G in the definition "foreign accrual property income" in subsection 95(1) of the Act for the year

S. 5907(1), paragraph (*e*) and (*f*) of the definition "net loss" were added by S.C. 2013, c. 34, s. 46(15), applicable in respect of dispositions of property that occur after December 18, 2009.

See the application following the amendment to subparagraph (*a*)(ii) of the definition "exempt earnings" in s. 5907(1), regarding the override of the statute-barring rules for assessments for taxation years that end before June 26, 2013.

"net surplus" —"net surplus" of a foreign affiliate of a corporation resident in Canada in respect of the corporation is, at any particular time,

(*a*) if the affiliate has no exempt deficit, no hybrid deficit and no taxable deficit, the amount that is the total of its exempt surplus, hybrid surplus and taxable surplus in respect of the corporation,

(*b*) if the affiliate has no exempt deficit but has a hybrid deficit and a taxable deficit, the amount, if any, by which its exempt surplus exceeds the total of its hybrid deficit and taxable deficit in respect of the corporation,

(*c*) if the affiliate has no exempt deficit and no hybrid deficit but has a taxable deficit, the amount, if any, by which the total of its exempt surplus and hybrid surplus exceeds its taxable deficit in respect of the corporation,

(*d*) if the affiliate has no exempt deficit and no taxable deficit but has a hybrid deficit, the amount, if any, by which the total of its exempt surplus and taxable surplus exceeds its hybrid deficit in respect of the corporation,

(*e*) if the affiliate has an exempt deficit but no hybrid deficit or taxable deficit, the amount, if any, by which the total of its hybrid surplus and taxable surplus exceeds its exempt deficit in respect of the corporation,

(*f*) if the affiliate has an exempt deficit and a hybrid deficit but no taxable deficit, the amount, if any, by which its taxable surplus exceeds the total of its exempt deficit and hybrid deficit in respect of the corporation, or

(*g*) if the affiliate has an exempt deficit and a taxable deficit but no hybrid deficit, the amount, if any, by which its hybrid surplus exceeds the total of its exempt deficit and taxable deficit in respect of the corporation,

as the case may be, at that time;

History: S. 5907(1), paragraphs (*a*) to (*c*) of the definition "net surplus" were replaced and paragraphs (*d*) to (*g*) were added by S.C. 2013, c. 34, s. 85(14), deemed to have come into force on August 20, 2011.

See the application for the amendment to the portion of the definition "earnings" before subparagraph (*a*)(iii) in s. 5907(1) for the extension of assessment periods to take into account the amendments by S.C. 2013, c. 34, s. 54 to 89.

S. 5907(1), paragraphs (*a*) to (*c*) of the definition "net surplus" formerly read:

(*a*) if the affiliate has no exempt deficit and no taxable deficit, the amount that is the total of its exempt surplus and taxable surplus in respect of the corporation, (*b*) if the affiliate has no taxable surplus, the amount, if any, by which its exempt surplus exceeds its taxable deficit in respect of the corporation, or

(*c*) if the affiliate has no exempt surplus, the amount, if any, by which its taxable surplus exceeds its exempt deficit in respect of the corporation,

"taxable deficit" —"taxable deficit" of a foreign affiliate of a corporation in respect of the corporation at any time is the amount, if any, by which

(*a*) the total of all amounts each of which is an amount determined at that time under any of subparagraphs (i) to (vi) of the description of B in the definition "taxable surplus" in this subsection

exceeds

(*b*) the total of all amounts each of which is an amount determined at that time under any of subparagraphs (i) to (v) of the description of A in that definition;

"taxable earnings" —"taxable earnings" of a foreign affiliate of a corporation for a taxation year of the affiliate is

(*a*) where the year is the 1975 or any preceding taxation year of the affiliate, nil, and

(*b*) in any other case, the total of all amounts each of which is

(i) the affiliate's net earnings for the year from an active business carried on by it in a country,

(ii) the affiliate's net earnings for the year in respect of its foreign accrual property income,

(iii) the affiliate's earnings for the year as determined under paragraph (*b*) of the definition "earnings" minus the portion of any income or profits tax paid to the government of a country for a year by the affiliate that can reasonably be regarded as tax in respect of those earnings,

(iv) to the extent not included under subparagraph (ii), the affiliate's net earnings for the year determined under paragraphs (*c*) to (*f*) of the definition "net earnings", or

(iv.1) the amount, if any, by which

(A) the total of all amounts each of which is an amount required by paragraph (2.02)(*a*) to be included under this definition for the year

exceeds

(B) the total of all amounts each of which is an amount required by paragraph (2.02)(*b*) to be deducted under this definition for the year,

(v) (Repealed by S.C. 2013, c. 34, S. 46(16).)

but does not include any amount included in the affiliate's exempt earnings for the year;

History: s. 5907(1), subparagraph (*b*)(iv.1) of the definition "taxable earnings" was added by S.C. 2013, c. 34, s. 85(15), applicable in respect of taxation years of a foreign affiliate of a taxpayer that end after August 19, 2011.

See the application for the amendment to the portion of the definition "earnings" before subparagraph (*a*)(iii) in s. 5907(1) for the extension of assessment periods to take into account the amendments by S.C. 2013, c. 34, s. 54 to 89.

S. 5907(1), subparagraph (*b*)(iii) and (iv) of the definition "taxable earnings" were replaced and subparagraph (*b*)(v) was repealed by S.C. 2013, c. 34, s. 46(16), applicable in respect of dispositions of property that occur after December 18, 2009.

See the application following the amendment to subparagraph (*a*)(ii) of the definition "exempt earnings" in s. 5907(1), regarding the override of the statute-barring rules for assessments for taxation years that end before June 26, 2013.

S. 5907(1), subparagraph (*b*)(iii) to (v) of the definition "taxable earnings" formerly read:

(iii) to the extent that they have not been included under subparagraph (i) or deducted in determining an amount included under subparagraph (b)(i) of the definition "taxable loss" in this subsection, the earnings for the year as determined under paragraph (b) of the definition "earnings" in this subsection minus the portion of any income or profit tax paid to the government of a country for the year by the affiliate that can reasonably be regarded as tax in respect of those earnings,

(iv) the affiliate's net earnings for the year from dispositions of property used or held by it principally for the purpose of gaining or producing income from an active business carried on by it in a country that is not a designated treaty country (other than Canada), or

(v) the affiliate's net earnings for the year from dispositions of shares of the capital stock of another foreign affiliate of the corporation that were excluded property of the affiliate (other than dispositions to which paragraph 95(2)(*c*), (*d*) or (*e*) of the Act was applicable) or dispositions of partnership interests that were excluded property of the affiliate,

"taxable loss" —"taxable loss" of a foreign affiliate of a corporation for a taxation year of the affiliate is

(*a*) where the year is 1975 or any preceding taxation year of the affiliate, nil, and

(*b*) in any other case, the total of all amounts each of which is

(i) the affiliate's net loss for the year from an active business carried on by it in a country,

(ii) the affiliate's net loss for the year in respect of foreign accrual property income,

(iii) the affiliate's loss for the year as determined under paragraph (*b*) of the definition "loss" minus the portion of any income or profits tax refunded by the government of a country for a year to the affiliate that can reasonably be regarded as tax refunded in respect of that loss, or

(iv) to the extent not included under subparagraph (ii), the affiliate's net loss for the year determined under paragraphs (*c*) to (*f*) of the definition "net loss",

but does not include any amount included in the affiliate's exempt loss for the year;

History: S. 5907(1), subparagraphs (*b*)(iii) and (iv) of the definition "taxable loss" were replaced by S.C. 2013, c. 34, s. 46(17). Subject to the application below, subparagraphs (*b*)(iii) to (v) of the definition "taxable earnings" apply to taxation years of a foreign affiliate of a taxpayer that end after 1999, except that, in respect of dispositions of property that occur before December 18, 2009, subparagraph (*b*)(iv) of the definition "taxable loss" in subsection 5907(1) is to be read as follows:

"(iv) to the extent not included under subparagraph (ii), the affiliate's net loss for the year determined under paragraphs (*c*) and (*d*) of the definition 'net loss',"

If a taxpayer has elected under a Global Section 95 Election (see the Editorial Note at the beginning of s. 5907), subparagraphs (*b*)(iii) and (iv) of the definition of "taxable loss" (with subparagraph (*b*)(iv) being read in the manner described in the application provision above) also apply to taxation years, of all foreign affiliates of the taxpayer, that begin after 1994 and end before 2000.

Any assessment of a taxpayer's tax, interest and penalties payable under the Act for any taxation year that ends before the day on which this Act is assented to that would, in the absence of this section, be precluded because of subsections 152(4) to (5) of the Act shall be made to the extent necessary to take into account the election noted above.

S. 5907(1), subparagraphs (*b*)(iii) and (iv) of the definition "taxable loss" formerly read:

(iii) the affiliate's net loss for the year from dispositions of property used or held by it principally for the purpose of gaining or producing income from an active business carried on by it in a country that is not a designated treaty county (other than Canada), or

(iv) the affiliate's net loss for the year from dispositions of shares of the capital stock of another foreign affiliate of the corporation that were excluded property of the affiliate (other than dispositions to which paragraph 95(2)(*c*), (*d*) or (*e*) of the Act was applicable) or dispositions of partnership interests that were excluded property of the affiliate,

"taxable surplus" —"taxable surplus", of a foreign affiliate (in this definition referred to as the "subject affiliate") of a corporation in respect of the corporation, at any particular time, means the amount determined by the following formula in respect of the period that begins with the latest of the following times and that ends with the particular time:

(*a*) the first day of the taxation year of the subject affiliate in which it last became a foreign affiliate of the corporation,

(*b*) the last time for which the opening taxable surplus of the subject affiliate in respect of the corporation was required to be determined under section 5905, and

(*c*) the last time for which the opening taxable deficit of the subject affiliate in respect of the corporation was required to be determined under section 5905

$$A - B$$

where

A is the total of all amounts, in respect of the period, each of which is

(i) the opening taxable surplus, if any, of the subject affiliate in respect of the corporation as determined under section 5905, at the time established in paragraph (*b*),

(ii) the taxable earnings of the subject affiliate for any of its taxation years ending in the period,

(iii) the portion of any dividend received in the period and before the particular time by the subject affiliate from another foreign affiliate of the corporation (including, for greater certainty, any dividend deemed by subsection 5905(7) to have been received by the subject affiliate) that was prescribed by paragraph 5900(1)(*b*) to have been paid out of the payer affiliate's taxable surplus in respect of the corporation,

(iv) an amount added to the taxable surplus of the subject affiliate or deducted from its taxable deficit in the period and before the particular time under subsection (1.092), (1.1) or (1.2),

(iv.1) each amount that is required under section 5905 to be included under this subparagraph in the period and before the particular time, or

(v) an amount added, in the period and before the particular time, to the subject affiliate's taxable surplus under paragraph (7.1)(*e*) (as that paragraph applied to dividends paid on or before August 19, 2011), and

B is the total of those of the following amounts that apply in respect of the period:

(i) the opening taxable deficit, if any, of the subject affiliate in respect of the corporation as determined under section 5905, at the time established in paragraph (*c*),

(ii) the taxable loss of the subject affiliate for any of its taxation years ending in the period,

(iii) the portion of any income or profits tax paid to the government of a country by the subject affiliate that can reasonably be regarded as having been paid in respect of that portion of a dividend referred to in subparagraph (iii) of the description of A,

(iv) the portion of any whole dividend paid by the subject affiliate in the period and before the particular time deemed under paragraph 5901(1)(*b*) or, if subsection 5901(1.1) applied to the whole dividend, paragraph 5901(1)(*a.1*) to have been paid out of the subject affiliate's taxable surplus in respect of the corporation,

(v) each amount that is required under section 5902 or 5905 to be included under this subparagraph, or subparagraph (1)(*k*)(xi) as it applies to taxation years that end before February 22, 1994, in the period and before the particular time, or

(vi) an amount, in the period and before the particular time, deducted from the taxable surplus of the subject affiliate or added to its taxable deficit under subsection (1.092), (1.1) or (1.2);

History: S. 5907(1), subparagraph (iv) of the description of A in the definition "taxable surplus" was replaced by S.C. 2014, c. 39, s. 88(13), applicable in respect of taxation years of a foreign affiliate of a taxpayer that end after 2010. However, if a taxpayer elects in writing under subsection 88(30) of the *Economic Action Plan 2014 Act, No. 2* [S.C. 2014, c. 39] in respect of all its foreign affiliates and files the election with the Minister of National Revenue on or before the day that is the later of the taxpayer's filing-due date for the taxpayer's taxation year that includes the day on which the *Economic Action Plan 2014 Act, No. 2* [S.C. 2014, c. 39] receives royal assent [December 16, 2014] and the day that is one year after the day on which the *Economic Action Plan 2014 Act, No. 2* [S.C. 2014, c. 39] receives royal assent [December 16, 2015], the amendment to subparagraph (iv) of the description of A in the definition "taxable surplus" applies in respect of taxation years of all foreign affiliates of the taxpayer that end on or after July 12, 2013.

In addition, any assessment of a taxpayer's tax, interest and penalties payable under the Act for any taxation year that ends before the day on which this amendment receives royal assent [December 16, 2014] that would, in the absence of this section, be precluded because of the time references in subsection 152(4) of the Act is to be made to the extent necessary to take into account this amendment.

Subparagraph (iv) of the description of A in the definition "taxable surplus" formerly read:

> (iv) an amount added to the taxable surplus of the subject affiliate or deducted from its taxable deficit in the period and before the particular time under any provision of subsection (1.1) or (1.2),

S. 5907(1), subparagraph (vi) of the description of B in the definition "taxable surplus" was replaced by S.C. 2014, c. 39, s. 88(14), applicable in respect of taxation years of a foreign affiliate of a taxpayer that end after 2010. However, if a taxpayer elects in writing under subsection 88(30) of the *Economic Action Plan 2014 Act, No. 2* [S.C. 2014, c. 39] in respect of all its foreign affiliates and files the election with the Minister of National Revenue on or before the day that is the later of the taxpayer's filing-due date for the taxpayer's taxation year that includes the day on which the *Economic Action Plan 2014 Act, No. 2* [S.C. 2014, c. 39] receives royal assent [December 16, 2014] and the day that is one year after the day on which the *Economic Action Plan 2014 Act, No. 2* [S.C. 2014, c. 39] receives royal assent [December 16, 2015], the amendment to subparagraph (vi) of the description of B in the definition "taxable surplus" applies in respect of taxation years of all foreign affiliates of the taxpayer that end on or after July 12, 2013.

In addition, any assessment of a taxpayer's tax, interest and penalties payable under the Act for any taxation year that ends before the day on which this amendment receives royal assent [December 16, 2014] that would, in the absence of this section, be precluded because of the time references in subsection 152(4) of the Act is to be made to the extent necessary to take into account this amendment.

Subparagraph (vi) of the description of B in the definition "taxable surplus" formerly read:

(vi) an amount, in the period and before the particular time, deducted from the taxable surplus of the subject affiliate or added to its taxable deficit under any provision of subsection (1.1) or (1.2);

S. 5907(1), the portion of the definition "taxable surplus" before paragraph (*a*) was replaced by S.C. 2013, c. 34, s. 85(16), deemed to have come into force on August 20, 2011.

See the application for the amendment to the portion of the definition "earnings" before subparagraph (*a*)(iii) in s. 5907(1) for the extension of assessment periods to take into account the amendments by S.C. 2013, c. 34, s. 54 to 89.

S. 5907(1), the portion of the definition "taxable surplus" before paragraph (*a*) formerly read:

"taxable surplus" of a foreign affiliate (in this definition referred to as the "subject affiliate") of a corporation in respect of the corporation is, at any particular time, the amount determined by the formula

$$A - B$$

in respect of the period beginning with the time that is the latest of

S. 5907(1), the portion of the definition "taxable surplus" after paragraph (*c*) and before the description of A was replaced by S.C. 2013, c. 34, s. 85(17), deemed to have come into force on August 20, 2011.

See the application for the amendment to the portion of the definition "earnings" before subparagraph (*a*)(iii) in s. 5907(1) for the extension of assessment periods to take into account the amendments by S.C. 2013, c. 34, s. 54 to 89.

S. 5907(1), the portion of the definition "taxable surplus" after paragraph (*c*) and before the description of A formerly read:

and ending with the particular time, where

S. 5907(1), subparagraph (v) or the description of A in the definition "taxable surplus" was replaced by S.C. 2013, c. 34, s. 85(18), deemed to have come into force on August 20, 2011.

See the application for the amendment to the portion of the definition "earnings" before subparagraph (*a*)(iii) in s. 5907(1) for the extension of assessment periods to take into account the amendments by S.C. 2013, c. 34, s. 54 to 89.

S. 5907(1), subparagraph (v) or the description of A in the definition "taxable surplus" formerly read:

(v) an amount added, in the period and before the particular time, to the subject affiliate's taxable surplus under paragraph (7.1)(*e*), and

S. 5907(1), subparagraph (iv) or the description of B in the definition "taxable surplus" was replaced by S.C. 2013, c. 34, s. 85(19), deemed to have come into force on August 20, 2011.

See the application for the amendment to the portion of the definition "earnings" before subparagraph (*a*)(iii) in s. 5907(1) for the extension of assessment periods to take into account the amendments by S.C. 2013, c. 34, s. 54 to 89.

S. 5907(1), subparagraph (iv) or the description of B in the definition "taxable surplus" formerly read:

(iv) the portion of any whole dividend paid by the subject affiliate in the period and before the particular time deemed by paragraph 5901(1)(*b*) to have been paid out of the subject affiliate's taxable surplus in respect of the corporation,

S. 5907(1), paragraphs (*b*) and (*c*) of the definition "taxable surplus" were replaced by S.C. 2013, c. 34, s. 46(18), deemed to have come into force on December 1, 1999.

See the application following the amendment to subparagraph (*a*)(ii) of the definition "exempt earnings" in s. 5907(1), regarding the override of the statute-barring rules for assessments for taxation years that end before June 26, 2013.

S. 5907(1), paragraphs (*b*) and (*c*) of the definition "taxable surplus" formerly read:

(*b*) where the corporation is an acquiring corporation referred to in subsection 5905(5) and the subject affiliate is a particular affiliate referred to in that subsection or another foreign affiliate in which such a particular affiliate had an equity percentage at the time referred to in that subsection, the last time at which that subsection was applicable in respect of the subject affiliate, and

(*c*) where the subject affiliate is a foreign affiliate referred to in subsection 5905(1), (2), (8) or (9) or paragraph 5905(3)(*b*), the last time at which any of those subsections or that paragraph was applicable in respect of the subject affiliate

S. 5907(1), subparagraph (i) of the description of A in the definition "taxable surplus" was replaced by S.C. 2013, c. 34, s. 46(19), deemed to have come into force on December 1, 1999.

See the application following the amendment to subparagraph (*a*)(ii) of the definition "exempt earnings" in s. 5907(1), regarding the override of the statute-barring rules for assessments for taxation years that end before June 26, 2013.

S. 5907(1), subparagraph (i) of the description of A in the definition "taxable surplus" formerly read:

(i) the opening taxable surplus of the subject affiliate as determined under subsection 5905(1), (2), (3), (5), (8) or (9), at the time established in paragraph (*a*), (*b*) or (*c*),

S. 5907(1), subparagraph (iv.1) of the description of A in the definition "taxable surplus" was added by S.C. 2013, c. 34, s. 46(20), applicable where a share of the capital stock of a foreign affiliate of a corporation is acquired by, otherwise becomes property of, or is disposed of by, a person after December 20, 2002.

See the application following the amendment to subparagraph (*a*)(ii) of the definition "exempt earnings" in s. 5907(1), regarding the override of the statute-barring rules for assessments for taxation years that end before June 26, 2013.

S. 5907(1), subparagraph (i) of the description of B in the definition "taxable surplus" was replaced by S.C. 2013, c. 34, s. 46(21), deemed to have come into force on December 1, 1999.

See the application following the amendment to subparagraph (*a*)(ii) of the definition "exempt earnings" in s. 5907(1), regarding the override of the statute-barring rules for assessments for taxation years that end before June 26, 2013.

S. 5907(1), subparagraph (i) of the description of B in the definition "taxable surplus" formerly read:

(i) the opening taxable deficit of the subject affiliate as determined under subsection 5905(1), (2), (3), (5), (8) or (9), at the time established in paragraph (*a*), (*b*) or (*c*),

S. 5907(1), subparagraph (v) of the description of B in the definition "taxable surplus" was replaced by S.C. 2013, c. 34, s. 46(22), deemed to have come into force on December 1, 1999.

See the application following the amendment to subparagraph (*a*)(ii) of the definition "exempt earnings" in s. 5907(1), regarding the override of the statute-barring rules for assessments for taxation years that end before June 26, 2013.

S. 5907(1), subparagraph (v) of the description of B in the definition "taxable surplus" formerly read:

(v) each amount that is determined under paragraph 5902(4)(*b*) or subparagraph 5905(2)(*a*)(ii), (6)(*a*)(ii) or (8)(*a*)(ii) in the period and before the particular time, or

"underlying foreign tax" — "underlying foreign tax", of a foreign affiliate (in this definition referred to as the "subject affiliate") of a corporation in respect of the corporation, at any particular time, means the amount determined by the following formula in respect of the period that begins with the later of the following times and that ends with the particular time:

(*a*) the first day of the taxation year of the subject affiliate in which it last became a foreign affiliate of the corporation, and

(*b*) the last time for which the opening underlying foreign tax of the subject affiliate in respect of the corporation was required to be determined under section 5905

(*c*) (Repealed by S.C. 2013, c. 34, s. 46(23).)

$$A - B$$

where

A is, subject to subsection (1.03), the total of all amounts, in respect of the period, each of which is

(i) the opening underlying foreign tax, if any, of the subject affiliate in respect of the corporation as determined under section 5905, at the time established in paragraph (*b*),

(ii) the portion of any income or profits tax paid to the government of a country by the subject affiliate that can reasonably be regarded as having been paid in respect of the taxable earnings, including for greater certainty any amounts included because of paragraph (2.02)(*a*) in computing the taxable earnings, of the affiliate for a taxation year ending in the period,

(iii) the portion of any income or profits tax referred to in subparagraph (iii) of the description of B in the definition "taxable surplus" in this subsection paid by the subject affiliate in respect of a dividend received from any other foreign affiliate of the corporation,

(iv) each amount that was prescribed by paragraph 5900(1)(*d*) to have been the foreign tax applicable to the portion of any dividend received in the period and before the particular time by the subject affiliate from another foreign affiliate of the corporation (including, for greater certainty, any dividend deemed by subsection 5905(7) to have been received by the subject affiliate) that was prescribed by paragraph 5900(1)(*b*) to have been paid out of the payer affiliate's taxable surplus in respect of the corporation, or

(v) the amount by which the subject affiliate's underlying foreign tax is required to be increased in the period and before the particular time under subsection (1.092), (1.1) or (1.2),

B is the total of those of the following amounts that apply in respect of the period:

(i) the portion of any income or profits tax refunded by the government of a country to the subject affiliate that can reasonably be regarded as having been refunded in respect of the taxable loss of the subject affiliate for a taxation year ending in the period,

(ii) the underlying foreign tax applicable to any whole dividend paid by the subject affiliate in the period and before the particular time deemed under paragraph 5901(1)(*b*) or, if subsection 5901(1.1) applied to the whole dividend, paragraph 5901(1)(*a.1*) to have been paid out of the subject affiliate's taxable surplus in respect of the corporation before that time,

(iii) each amount that is required under section 5902 or 5905 to be included under this subparagraph, or subparagraph (1)(*l*)(x) as it applies to taxation years that end before February 22, 1994, in the period and before the particular time, or

(iv) the amount by which the subject affiliate's underlying foreign tax is required to be decreased in the period and before the particular time under subsection (1.092), (1.1) or (1.2);

History: S. 5907(1), subparagraph (v) of the description of A in the definition "underlying foreign tax" was replaced by S.C. 2014, c. 39, s. 88(15), applicable in respect of taxation years of a foreign affiliate of a taxpayer that end after 2010. However, if a taxpayer elects in writing under subsection 88(30) of the *Economic Action Plan 2014 Act, No. 2* [S.C. 2014, c. 39] in respect of all its foreign affiliates and files the election with the Minister of National Revenue on or before the day that is the later of the taxpayer's filing-due date for the taxpayer's taxation year that includes the day on which the *Economic Action Plan 2014 Act, No. 2* [S.C. 2014, c. 39] receives royal assent [December 16, 2014] and the day that is one year after the day on which the *Economic Action Plan 2014 Act, No. 2* [S.C. 2014, c. 39] receives royal assent [December 16, 2015], the amendment to subparagraph (v) of the description of A in the definition "underlying foreign tax" applies in respect of taxation years of all foreign affiliates of the taxpayer that end on or after July 12, 2013.

In addition, any assessment of a taxpayer's tax, interest and penalties payable under the Act for any taxation year that ends before the day on which this amendment receives royal assent [December 16, 2014] that would, in the absence of this section, be precluded because of the time references in subsection 152(4) of the Act is to be made to the extent necessary to take into account this amendment.

Subparagraph (v) of the description of A in the definition "underlying foreign tax" formerly read:

(v) the amount by which the subject affiliate's underlying foreign tax is required to be increased by any provision of subsection (1.1) or (1.2),

S. 5907(1), subparagraph (iv) of the description of B in the definition "underlying foreign tax" was replaced by S.C. 2014, c. 39, s. 88(16), applicable in respect of taxation years of a foreign affiliate of a taxpayer that end after 2010. However, if a taxpayer elects in writing under subsection 88(30) of the *Economic Action Plan 2014 Act, No. 2* [S.C. 2014, c. 39] in respect of all its foreign affiliates and files the election with the Minister of National Revenue on or before the day that is the later of the taxpayer's filing-due date for the taxpayer's taxation year that includes the day on which the *Economic Action Plan 2014 Act, No. 2* [S.C. 2014, c. 39] receives royal assent [December 16, 2014] and the day that is one year after the day on which the *Economic Action Plan 2014 Act, No. 2* [S.C. 2014, c. 39] receives royal assent [December 16, 2015], the amendment to subparagraph (iv) of the description of B in the definition "underlying foreign tax" applies in respect of taxation years of all foreign affiliates of the taxpayer that end on or after July 12, 2013.

In addition, any assessment of a taxpayer's tax, interest and penalties payable under the Act for any taxation year that ends before the day on which this amendment receives royal assent [December 16, 2014] that would, in the absence of this section, be precluded because of the time references in subsection 152(4) of the Act is to be made to the extent necessary to take into account this amendment.

Subparagraph (iv) of the description of B in the definition "underlying foreign tax" formerly read:

(iv) the amount by which the subject affiliate's underlying foreign tax is required to be decreased in the period and before the particular time by any provision of subsection (1.1) or (1.2);

S. 5907(1), the portion of the description of A in the definition "underlying foreign tax" before subparagraph (i) was replaced by S.C. 2013, c. 34, s. 401(1), applicable to income or profits tax paid, and amounts referred to in subsections 5907(1.1) and (1.2), in respect of the income of a foreign affiliate of a corporation for taxation years of the foreign affiliate that end in taxation years of the corporation that end after March 4, 2010. S. 5907(1), the portion of the description of A in the definition "underlying foreign tax" before subparagraph (i) formerly read:

A is the total of all amounts, in respect of the period, each of which is

S. 5907(1), the portion of the definition "underlying foreign tax" before paragraph (*a*) was replaced by S.C. 2013, c. 34, s. 85(20), deemed to have come into force on August 20, 2011.

See the application for the amendment to the portion of the definition "earnings" before subparagraph (*a*)(iii) in s. 5907(1) for the extension of assessment periods to take into account the amendments by S.C. 2013, c. 34, s. 54 to 89.

S. 5907(1), the portion of the definition "underlying foreign tax" before paragraph (*a*) formerly read:

"underlying foreign tax" of a foreign affiliate (in this definition referred to as the "subject affiliate") of a corporation in respect of the corporation is, at any particular time, the amount, determined by the formula

$$A - B$$

in respect of the period beginning with the time that is the latest of

S. 5907(1), the portion of the definition "underlying foreign tax" after paragraph (*b*) and before the description of A was replaced by S.C. 2013, c. 34, s. 85(21), deemed to have come into force on August 20, 2011.

See the application for the amendment to the portion of the definition "earnings" before subparagraph (*a*)(iii) in s. 5907(1) for the extension of assessment periods to take into account the amendments by S.C. 2013, c. 34, s. 54 to 89.

S. 5907(1), the portion of the definition "underlying foreign tax" after paragraph (*b*) and before the description of A formerly read:

and ending with the particular time, where

S. 5907(1), subparagraph (ii) of the description of A in the definition "underlying foreign tax" was replaced by S.C. 2013, c. 34, s. 85(22), applicable in respect of taxation years of a foreign affiliate of a taxpayer that end after August 19, 2011.

See the application for the amendment to the portion of the definition "earnings" before subparagraph (*a*)(iii) in s. 5907(1) for the extension of assessment periods to take into account the amendments by S.C. 2013, c. 34, s. 54 to 89.

S. 5907(1), subparagraph (ii) of the description of A in the definition "underlying foreign tax" formerly read:

(ii) the portion of any income or profits tax paid to the government of a country by the subject affiliate that can reasonably be regarded as having been paid in respect of the taxable earnings of the subject affiliate for a taxation year ending in the period,

S. 5907(1), subparagraph (ii) of the description of B in the definition "underlying foreign tax" was replaced by S.C. 2013, c. 34, s. 85(23), applicable in respect of taxation years of a foreign affiliate of a taxpayer that end after August 19, 2011.

See the application for the amendment to the portion of the definition "earnings" before subparagraph (*a*)(iii) in s. 5907(1) for the extension of assessment periods to take into account the amendments by S.C. 2013, c. 34, s. 54 to 89.

S. 5907(1), subparagraph (ii) of the description of B in the definition "underlying foreign tax" formerly read:

(ii) the underlying foreign tax applicable to any whole dividend paid by the subject affiliate in the period and before the particular time deemed by paragraph 5901(1)(*b*) to have been paid out of the subject affiliate's taxable surplus in respect of the corporation before that time,

S. 5907(1), paragraph (*b*) of the definition "underlying foreign tax" was replaced and paragraph (*c*) was repealed by S.C. 2013, c. 34, s. 46(23), deemed to have come into force on December 1, 1999.

See the application following the amendment to subparagraph (*a*)(ii) of the definition "exempt earnings" in s. 5907(1), regarding the override of the statute-barring rules for assessments for taxation years that end before June 26, 2013.

S. 5907(1), paragraphs (*b*) and (*c*) of the definition "underlying foreign tax" formerly read:

(*b*) where the corporation is an acquiring corporation referred to in subsection 5905(5) and the subject affiliate is a particular affiliate referred to in that subsection or another foreign affiliate in which such a particular affiliate had an equity percentage at the time referred to in that subsection, the last time at which that subsection was applicable in respect of the subject affiliate, and

(*c*) where the subject affiliate is a foreign affiliate referred to in subsection 5905(1), (2), (8) or (9) or paragraph 5905(3)(*b*), the last time at which any of those subsections or that paragraph was applicable in respect of the subject affiliate

S. 5907(1), subparagraph (i) of the description of A in the definition "underlying foreign tax" was replaced by S.C. 2013, c. 34, s. 46(24), deemed to have come into force on December 1, 1999.

See the application following the amendment to subparagraph (*a*)(ii) of the definition "exempt earnings" in s. 5907(1), regarding the override of the statute-barring rules for assessments for taxation years that end before June 26, 2013.

S. 5907(1), subparagraph (i) of the description of A in the definition "underlying foreign tax" formerly read:

(i) the opening underlying foreign tax of the subject affiliate as determined under subsection 5905(1), (2), (3), (5), (8) or (9), at the time established in paragraph (*a*), (*b*) or (*c*),

S. 5907(1), subparagraph (iii) of the description of B in the definition "underlying foreign tax" was replaced by S.C. 2013, c. 34, s. 46(25), deemed to have come into force on December 1, 1999.

See the application following the amendment to subparagraph (*a*)(ii) of the definition "exempt earnings" in s. 5907(1), regarding the override of the statute-barring rules for assessments for taxation years that end before June 26, 2013.

S. 5907(1), subparagraph (iii) of the description of B in the definition "underlying foreign tax" formerly read:

(iii) each amount that is required by paragraph 5902(4)(*c*) or subparagraph 5905(2)(*a*)(iii), (6)(*a*)(iii) or (8)(*a*)(iii) to be deducted in the period and before the particular time in computing the subject affiliate's underlying foreign tax, or

"underlying foreign tax applicable"—"underlying foreign tax applicable" in respect of a corporation to a whole dividend paid at any time on the shares of any class of the capital stock of a foreign affiliate of the corporation by the affiliate is the total of

(*a*) the proportion of the underlying foreign tax of the affiliate at that time in respect of the corporation that

(i) the portion of the whole dividend deemed to have been paid out of the affiliate's taxable surplus in respect of the corporation

is of

(ii) the affiliate's taxable surplus at that time in respect of the corporation, and

(*b*) any additional amount in respect of the whole dividend that the corporation claims in its return of income under Part I of the Act in respect of the whole dividend, not exceeding the amount that is the lesser of

(i) the amount by which the portion of the whole dividend deemed to have been paid out of the affiliate's taxable surplus in respect of the corporation exceeds the amount determined under paragraph (*a*), and

(ii) the amount by which the affiliate's underlying foreign tax in respect of the corporation immediately before the whole dividend was paid exceeds the amount determined under paragraph (*a*);

History: S. 5907(1), paragraph (*b*) of the definition "underlying foreign tax applicable" was replaced by S.C. 2013, c. 34, s. 46(26), applicable in respect of whole dividends paid on the shares of a class of the capital stock of a foreign affiliate of a corporation after December 18, 2009.

See the application following the amendment to subparagraph (*a*)(ii) of the definition "exempt earnings" in s. 5907(1), regarding the override of the statute-barring rules for assessments for taxation years that end before June 26, 2013.

S. 5907(1), paragraph (*b*) of the definition "underlying foreign tax applicable" formerly read:

(*b*) except with respect to any whole dividend referred to in section 5902, in any case where throughout the taxation year of the affiliate in which the whole dividend was paid

(i) there is no more than one class of shares of the capital stock of the affiliate issued and outstanding,

(ii) the surplus entitlement percentage of the corporation in respect of the affiliate is 100 per cent, or

(iii) there is not more than one shareholder who owns shares of the capital stock of the affiliate,

any additional amount in respect of the whole dividend that the corporation claims in its return of income under Part I of the Act in respect of the whole dividend, not exceeding the amount that is the lesser of

(iv) the amount by which the portion of the whole dividend deemed to have been paid out of the affiliate's taxable surplus in respect of the corporation exceeds the amount determined under paragraph (*a*), and

(v) the amount by which the underlying foreign tax of the affiliate in respect of the corporation immediately before the whole dividend was paid exceeds the amount determined under paragraph (*a*);

"whole dividend"—"whole dividend" paid at any time on the shares of a class of the capital stock of a foreign affiliate of a taxpayer resident in Canada is the total of all amounts each of which is the dividend paid at that time on a share of that class except that

(*a*) where a dividend is paid at the same time on shares of more than one class of the capital stock of an affiliate, for the purpose only of section 5900, the whole dividend referred to in section 5901 paid at that time on the shares of a class of the capital stock of the affiliate is deemed to be the total of all amounts each of which is the dividend paid at that time on a share of the capital stock of the affiliate, (*b*) where a whole dividend is deemed by subparagraph 5902(1)(*a*)(ii) to have been paid at the same time on shares of more than one class of an affiliate's capital stock, for the purpose only of that subparagraph, the whole dividend deemed to have been paid at that time on the shares of a class of the affiliate's capital stock is deemed to be the total of all amounts each of which is a whole dividend deemed to have been paid at that time on the shares of a class of the affiliate's capital stock, and

(*c*) where more than one whole dividend is deemed by paragraph 5900(2)(*b*) to have been paid at the same time on shares of a class of the capital stock of an affiliate, for the purposes only of paragraph 5900(1)(*d*) and the definitions "underlying foreign tax" and "underlying foreign tax applicable" in this subsection, the whole dividend deemed to have been paid at that time on the shares of a class of the capital stock of the affiliate is deemed to be the total of all amounts each of which is a whole dividend deemed to have been paid at that time on the shares of a class of the capital stock of the affiliate and all of that whole dividend shall be deemed to have been paid out of the affiliate's taxable surplus in respect of the corporation.

History: S. 5907(1), paragraph (*b*) of the definition "whole dividend" was replaced by S.C. 2013, c. 34, s. 46(27), applicable to elections made in respect of dispositions that occur after December 18, 2009.

See the application following the amendment to subparagraph (*a*)(ii) of the definition "exempt earnings" in s. 5907(1), regarding the override of the statute-barring rules for assessments for taxation years that end before June 26, 2013.

S. 5907(1), paragraph (*b*) of the definition "whole dividend" formerly read:

(*b*) where a whole dividend is deemed by paragraph 5902(1)(*c*) to have been paid at the same time on shares of more than one class of the capital stock of an affiliate, for the purpose only of that paragraph, the whole dividend deemed to have been paid at that time on the shares of a class of the capital stock of the affiliate is deemed to be the total of all amounts each of which is a whole dividend deemed to have been paid at that time on the shares of a class of the capital stock of the affiliate, and

Application Provision, S.C. 2013, c. 34, s. 51 [Consolidated Net Surplus Election] Subject to the Modified Consolidated Net Surplus Election (below), if a corporation resident in Canada elects in writing in respect of all of its foreign affiliates and files the election with the Minister of National Revenue on or before the day that is the later of the corporation's filing-due date for the corporation's taxation year that includes June 26, 2013 and June 26, 2014, the following rules apply:

(*d*) if there is a designated section 93 election, paragraph (*b*) of the definition "whole dividend" in subsection 5907(1) of the Regulations is, in respect of the designated section 93 election, to be read as follows:

"(*b*) where a whole dividend is deemed by paragraph 5902(1)(*g*) to have been paid at the same time on shares of more than one class of the capital stock of an affiliate, for the purpose only of that paragraph, the whole dividend deemed to have been paid at that time on the shares of a class of the capital stock of the affiliate is deemed to be the total of all amounts each of which is a whole dividend deemed to have been paid at that time on the shares of a class of the capital stock of the affiliate, and"

Application Provision, S.C. 2013, c. 34, s. 52 [Modified Consolidated Net Surplus Election.]

(1) The application in subsection (2) (below) applies if

(*a*) a corporation has made the election above; and

(*b*) the corporation has made an election under subsection 93(1) or (1.2) of the Income Tax Act in respect of a disposition of a share of the capital stock of a foreign affiliate of the corporation that occurs after December 20, 2002 and on or before February 27, 2004 (other than a disposition required to be made under an agreement in writing made by a vendor on or before December 20, 2002), or in respect of a disposition that occurs after February 27, 2004 and that is required to be made under an agreement in writing made by a vendor after December 20, 2002 and before February 28, 2004; and

(*c*) the corporation elects in writing to apply subsection (2) (below) in respect of all of its foreign affiliates and files the election with the Minister of National Revenue on or before the day that is the later of the corporation's filing-due date for the corporation's taxation year that includes June 26, 2013 and June 26, 2014;

(2) then the Consolidated Net Surplus Election above does not apply in respect of dispositions referred to in paragraph (*b*).

Tax Profile: July 2008 — International Tax Planning for the Owner-Manager.

(1.01) For the purposes of section 113 of the Act, "exempt surplus", "hybrid surplus" and "taxable surplus" have the meanings assigned by subsection (1).

History: S. 5907(1.01) was replaced by S.C. 2013, c. 34, s. 85(25), deemed to have come into force on August 20, 2011.

See the application for the amendment to the portion of the definition "earnings" before subparagraph (*a*)(iii) in s. 5907(1) for the extension of assessment periods to take into account the amendments by S.C. 2013, c. 34, s. 54 to 89.

S. 5907(1.01) formerly read:

(1.01) For the purposes of section 113 of the Act, "exempt surplus" and "taxable surplus" have the meanings assigned by subsection (1).

(1.02) For the purposes of paragraph (*d*) of the definition "exempt earnings" and paragraph (*c*) of the definition "exempt loss" in subsection (1), if a foreign affiliate of a corporation becomes a foreign affiliate of the corporation in a taxation year of the affiliate, otherwise than as a result of a transaction between persons that do not deal with each other at arm's length, and the affiliate is resident in a designated treaty country at the end of the year, the affiliate is deemed to be so resident throughout the year.

History: S. 5907(1.02) was added by S.C. 2013, c. 34, s. 46(31), applicable to taxation years of a foreign affiliate of a taxpayer that begin after December 18, 2009.

S. 5907(1.02) was repealed by S.C. 2013, c. 34, s. 46(30), applicable to taxation years of a foreign affiliate of a taxpayer that begin after 2008.

See the application following the amendment to subparagraph (*a*)(ii) of the definition "exempt earnings" in s. 5907(1), regarding the override of the statute-barring rules for assessments for taxation years that end before June 26, 2013.

S. 5907(1.02) formerly read:

(1.02) In paragraph (*d*) of the definition "exempt earnings" in subsection (1), the determination of whether a corporation

(*a*) has a "qualifying interest" in respect of a foreign affiliate throughout a taxation year, or

(*b*) is related to another corporation throughout a taxation year

shall be made as it would for the purpose of paragraph 95(2)(*a*) of the Act.

(1.03) For the purposes of the description of A in the definition "underlying foreign tax" in subsection (1), income or profits tax paid in respect of the taxable earnings of a particular foreign affiliate of a particular corporation or in respect of a dividend received by the particular affiliate from another foreign affiliate of the particular corporation, and amounts by which the underlying foreign tax of the particular affiliate or any other foreign affiliate of the particular corporation is required under any of subsections (1.092), (1.1) and (1.2) to be increased, is not to include any income or profits tax paid, or amounts by which the underlying foreign tax would otherwise be so required to be increased, as the case may be, in respect of the foreign accrual property income of the particular affiliate for a taxation year of the particular affiliate if, at any time in the year, a specified owner in respect of the particular corporation is considered,

(*a*) under the income tax laws (referred to in subsection (1.07) as the "relevant foreign tax law") of any country other than Canada under the laws of which any income of another corporation — that is, at any time in the year, a pertinent person or partnership

Regulations

in respect of the particular affiliate — is subject to income taxation, to own less than all of the shares of the capital stock of the other corporation that are considered to be owned by the specified owner for the purposes of the Act; or

(*b*) under the income tax laws (referred to in subsection (1.08) as the "relevant foreign tax law") of any country other than Canada under the laws of which any income of a particular partnership — that is, at any time in the year, a pertinent person or partnership in respect of the particular affiliate — is subject to income taxation, to have a lesser direct or indirect share of the income of the particular partnership than the specified owner is considered to have for the purposes of the Act.

History: S. 5907(1.03), the portion before paragraph (*a*) was replaced by S.C. 2014, c. 39, s. 88(17), applicable to income or profits tax paid, amounts referred to in subsections 5907(1.1) and (1.2) of the Regulations and amounts referred to in subsection 5907(1.092) of the Regulations in respect of the income of a foreign affiliate of a corporation for taxation years of the foreign affiliate that end in taxation years of the corporation that end after March 4, 2010. However,

(a) if the taxpayer does not elect under subsection 88(30) of the *Economic Action Plan 2014 Act, No. 2* [S.C. 2014, c. 39], for taxation years of the corporation that end before October 25, 2012, the portion of subsection 5907(1.03) of the Regulations before paragraph (*a*), as enacted, is to be read as follows:

"(1.03) For the purposes of the description of A in the definition "underlying foreign tax" in subsection (1), income or profits tax paid in respect of the taxable earnings of a particular foreign affiliate of a corporation or in respect of a dividend received by the particular affiliate from another foreign affiliate of the corporation, and amounts by which the underlying foreign tax of the particular affiliate, or any other foreign affiliate of the corporation, is required under any of subsections (1.092), (1.1) and (1.2) to be increased, is not to include any income or profits tax paid, or amounts by which the underlying foreign tax would otherwise be so required to be increased, as the case may be, in respect of the foreign accrual property income of the particular affiliate that is earned during a period in which"

(*b*) if the taxpayer elects under subsection 88(30) of the *Economic Action Plan 2014 Act, No. 2* [S.C. 2014, c. 39], the amendment to s. 5907(1.03) before paragraph (*a*) instead applies to income or profits tax paid, amounts referred to in subsections 5907(1.1) and (1.2) of the Regulations and amounts referred to in subsection 5907(1.092) of the Regulations in respect of the income of a foreign affiliate of a corporation for taxation years of the foreign affiliate that end in taxation years of the corporation that end on or after July 12, 2013.

In addition, any assessment of a taxpayer's tax, interest and penalties payable under the Act for any taxation year that ends before the day on which this amendment receives royal assent [December 16, 2014] that would, in the absence of this section, be precluded because of the time references in subsection 152(4) of the Act is to be made to the extent necessary to take into account this amendment.

S. 5907(1.03), the portion before paragraph (*a*) formerly read:

(1.03) For the purposes of the description of A in the definition "underlying foreign tax" in subsection (1), income or profits tax paid in respect of the taxable earnings of a particular foreign affiliate of a particular corporation or in respect of a dividend received by the particular affiliate from another foreign affiliate of the particular corporation, and amounts by which the underlying foreign tax of the particular affiliate or any other foreign affiliate of the particular corporation is required under subsection (1.1) or (1.2) to be increased, is not to include any income or profits tax paid, or amounts by which the underlying foreign tax would otherwise be so required to be increased, as the case may be, in respect of the foreign accrual property income of the particular affiliate for a taxation year of the particular affiliate if, at any time in the year, a specified owner in respect of the particular corporation is considered,

S. 5907(1.03) was added by S.C. 2013, c. 34, s. 401(2), applicable to income or profits tax paid, and amounts referred to in subsections 5907(1.1) and (1.2), in respect of the income of a foreign affiliate of a corporation for taxation years of the foreign affiliate that end in taxation years of the corporation that end after March 4, 2010, except that, for taxation years of the corporation that end on or before October 24, 2012, subsection 5907(1.03) is to be read as follows:

"(1.03) For the purposes of the description of A in the definition "underlying foreign tax" in subsection (1), income or profits tax paid in respect of the taxable earnings of a particular foreign affiliate of a corporation or in respect of a dividend received by the particular affiliate from another foreign affiliate of the corporation, and amounts by which the underlying foreign tax of the particular affiliate, or any other foreign affiliate of the corporation, is required under subsection (1.1) or (1.2) to be increased, is not to include any income or profits tax paid, or amounts by which the underlying foreign tax would otherwise be so required to be increased, as the case may be, in respect of the foreign accrual property income of the particular affiliate that is earned during a period in which

(*a*) the corporation is considered, under the income tax laws (referred to in subsection (1.07) as the "relevant foreign tax law") of any country, other than Canada, under the laws of which the income of the particular affiliate is subject to income taxation, to own less than all of the shares of the capital stock of the particular affiliate, of another foreign affiliate of the corporation in which the particular affiliate has an equity percentage, or of another foreign affiliate of the corporation that has an equity percentage in the particular affiliate, that are considered to be owned by the corporation for the purposes of the Act; or

(*b*) the corporation's share of the income of a partnership that owns, based on the assumptions contained in paragraph 96(1)(*c*) of the Act, shares of the capital stock of the particular affiliate is, under the income tax laws (referred to in subsection (1.08) as the "relevant foreign tax law") of any country, other than Canada, under the laws of which the income of the partnership is subject to income taxation, less than its share of the income for the purposes of the Act."

(1.04) For the purposes of subsections (1.03) and (1.07), a "specified owner", at any time, in respect of a corporation means the corporation or a person or partnership that is, at that time,

(*a*) a partnership of which the corporation is a member;

(*b*) a foreign affiliate of the corporation;

(*c*) a partnership a member of which is a foreign affiliate of the corporation; or

(*d*) a person or partnership referred to in any of subparagraphs (1.06)(*a*)(i) to (iii).

History: S. 5907(1.04) was added by S.C. 2013, c. 34, s. 401(2), applicable to income or profits tax paid, and amounts referred to in subsections 5907(1.1) and (1.2), in respect of the income of a foreign affiliate of a corporation for taxation years of the foreign affiliate that end in taxation years of the corporation that end after March 4, 2010, except that, for taxation years of the corporation that end on or before October 24, 2012, section 5907 is to be read without reference to subsection (1.04).

(1.05) For the purposes of this subsection and subsection (1.03), a "pertinent person or partnership", at any time, in respect of a particular foreign affiliate of a corporation means the particular affiliate or a person or partnership that is, at that time,

(*a*) another foreign affiliate of the corporation -

(i) in which the particular affiliate has an equity percentage, or

(ii) that has an equity percentage in the particular affiliate;

(*b*) a partnership a member of which is at that time a pertinent person or partnership in respect of the particular affiliate under this subsection; or

(*c*) a person or partnership referred to in any of subparagraphs (1.06)(*b*)(i) to (iii).

History: S. 5907(1.05) was added by S.C. 2013, c. 34, s. 401(2), applicable to income or profits tax paid, and amounts referred to in subsections 5907(1.1) and (1.2), in respect of the income of a foreign affiliate of a corporation for taxation years of the foreign affiliate that end in taxation years of the corporation that end after March 4, 2010, except that, for taxation years of the corporation that end on or before October 24, 2012, section 5907 is to be read without reference to subsection (1.05).

(1.06) For the purposes of subsections (1.04) and (1.05), if, as part of a series of transactions or events that includes the earning of the foreign accrual property income referred to in subsection (1.03), a foreign affiliate (referred to in this subsection as the "funding affiliate") of the corporation or of a person (referred to in this subsection as the "related person") resident in Canada that is related to the corporation, or a partnership (referred to in this subsection as the "funding partnership") of which such an affiliate is a member, directly or indirectly provided funding to the particular affiliate, or a partnership of which the particular affiliate is a member, otherwise than by way of loans or other indebtedness that are subject to terms or conditions made or imposed, in respect of the loans or other indebtedness, that do not differ from those that would be made or imposed between persons dealing at arm's length or by way of an acquisition of shares of the capital stock of any corporation, then

(*a*) if the funding affiliate is, or the funding partnership has a member that is, a foreign affiliate of the related person, the following persons and partnerships are deemed, at all times during which the foreign accrual property income is earned by the particular affiliate, to be specified owners in respect of the corporation:

(i) the related person,

(ii) each foreign affiliate of the related person, and

(iii) each partnership a member of which is referred to in subparagraph (i) or (ii); and

(*b*) the following persons and partnerships are deemed, at all times during which the foreign accrual property income is earned by the particular affiliate, to be pertinent persons or partnerships in respect of the particular affiliate:

(i) the funding affiliate or the funding partnership,

(ii) a non-resident corporation

(A) in which the funding affiliate has an equity percentage, or

(B) that has an equity percentage in the funding affiliate, and

(iii) a partnership a member of which is a person or partnership referred to in subparagraph (i) or (ii).

History: S. 5907(1.06) was added by S.C. 2013, c. 34, s. 401(2), applicable to income or profits tax paid, and amounts referred to in subsections 5907(1.1) and (1.2), in respect of the income of a foreign affiliate of a corporation for taxation years of the foreign affiliate that end in taxation years of the corporation that end after March 4, 2010, except that, for taxation years of the corporation that end on or before October 24, 2012, section 5907 is to be read without reference to subsection (1.06).

(1.07) For the purposes of paragraph (1.03)(*a*), a specified owner in respect of the particular corporation is not to be considered, under the relevant foreign tax law, to own less than all of the shares of the capital stock of another corporation that are considered to be owned for the purposes of the Act solely because the specified owner or the other corporation is not treated as a corporation under the relevant foreign tax law.

History: S. 5907(1.07) was replaced by S.C. 2017, c. 33, s. 97(1), applicable to income or profits tax paid, and amounts referred to in subsections 5907(1.1) and (1.2) of the Regulations, in respect of the income of a foreign affiliate of a corporation for taxation years of the foreign affiliate that end in taxation years of the corporation that end after October 24, 2012. S. 5907(1.07) formerly read:

(1.07) For the purposes of paragraph (1.03)(*a*), a specified owner in respect of the particular corporation is not to be considered, under the relevant foreign tax law, to own less than all of the shares of the capital stock of another corporation that are considered to be owned for the purposes of the Act solely because the specified owner is not treated as a corporation under the relevant foreign tax law.

S. 5907(1.07) was added by S.C. 2013, c. 34, s. 401(2), applicable to income or profits tax paid, and amounts referred to in subsections 5907(1.1) and (1.2), in respect of the income of a foreign affiliate of a corporation for taxation years of the foreign affiliate that end in taxation years of the corporation that end after March 4, 2010, except that, for taxation years of the corporation that end on or before October 24, 2012, subsection 5907(1.07) is to be read as follows:

"(1.07) For the purposes of paragraph (1.03)(*a*), a corporation is not to be considered, under the relevant foreign tax law, to own less than all of the shares of the capital stock of a foreign affiliate of the corporation that are considered to be owned for the purposes of the Act solely because the corporation or the foreign affiliate is not treated as a corporation under the relevant foreign tax law."

Related Sections: 91(4.5) Exception — hybrid entities.

(1.08) For the purposes of paragraph (1.03)(*b*), a member of a partnership is not to be considered to have a lesser direct or indirect share of the income of the partnership under the relevant foreign tax law than for the purposes of the Act solely because of one or more of the following:

(*a*) a difference between the relevant foreign tax law and the Act in the manner of

(i) computing the income of the partnership, or

(ii) allocating the income of the partnership because of the admission to, or withdrawal from, the partnership of any of its members;

(*b*) the treatment of the partnership as a corporation under the relevant foreign tax law; or

(*c*) the fact that the member is not treated as a corporation under the relevant foreign tax law.

History: S. 5907(1.08) was added by S.C. 2013, c. 34, s. 401(2), applicable to income or profits tax paid, and amounts referred to in subsections 5907(1.1) and (1.2), in respect of the income of a foreign affiliate of a corporation for taxation years of the foreign affiliate that end in taxation years of the corporation that end after March 4, 2010, except that, for taxation years of the corporation that end on or before October 24, 2012, the portion of subsection 5907(1.08) before paragraph (*a*) is to be read as follows:

"(1.08) For the purposes of paragraph (1.03)(*b*), a member of a partnership is not to be considered to have a lesser share of the income of the partnership under the relevant foreign tax law than for the purposes of the Act solely because of one or more of the following:"

(1.09) For the purposes of subsection (1.03), if a specified owner owns, for the purposes of the Act, shares of the capital stock of a corporation and the dividends, or similar amounts, in respect of those shares are treated under the income tax laws of any country other than Canada under the laws of which any income of the corporation is subject to income taxation as interest or another form of deductible payment, the specified owner is deemed to be considered, under those tax laws, to own less than all of the shares of the capital stock of the corporation that are considered to be owned by the specified owner for the purposes of the Act.

History: S. 5907(1.09) was added by S.C. 2013, c. 34, s. 401(2), applicable to income or profits tax paid, and amounts referred to in subsections 5907(1.1) and (1.2), in respect of the income of a foreign affiliate of a corporation for taxation years of the foreign affiliate that end in taxation years of the corporation that end after March 4, 2010, except that, for taxation years of the corporation that end on or before October 24, 2012, section 5907 is to be read without reference to subsection (1.09).

(1.091) Subsection (1.092) applies in respect of income or profits tax paid by, or refunded to, a foreign affiliate (in this subsection and subsection (1.092) referred to as the "shareholder affiliate") of a taxpayer for a taxation year of the shareholder affiliate in respect of its income or profits, or loss, as the case may be, and the income or profits, or loss, as the case may be, of another foreign affiliate (in this subsection and subsection (1.092) referred to as the "transparent affiliate") of the taxpayer if

(*a*) the shareholder affiliate has an equity percentage in the transparent affiliate;

(*b*) the income or profits tax is paid to, or refunded by, a government of a country other than Canada; and

(*c*) under the income tax laws of the country referred to in paragraph (*b*), the shareholder affiliate, and not the transparent affiliate, is liable for that tax payable to, or entitled to that refund from, a government of that country for that year (otherwise than solely because the shareholder affiliate is part of a group of corporations that determines its liabilities for income or profits tax payable to the government of that country on a consolidated or combined basis).

History: S. 5907(1.091) was added by S.C. 2014, c. 39, s. 88(18), applicable in respect of taxation years of a foreign affiliate of a taxpayer that end after 2010. However, if a taxpayer elects in writing under subsection 88(30) of the *Economic Action Plan 2014 Act, No. 2* [S.C. 2014, c. 39] in respect of all its foreign affiliates and files the election with the Minister of National Revenue on or before the day that is the later of the taxpayer's filing-due date for the taxpayer's taxation year that includes the day on which the *Economic Action Plan 2014 Act, No. 2* [S.C. 2014, c. 39] receives royal assent [December 16, 2014] and the day that is one year after the day on which the *Economic Action Plan 2014 Act, No. 2* [S.C. 2014, c. 39] receives royal assent [December 16, 2015], s. 5907(1.091) applies in respect of taxation years of all foreign affiliates of the taxpayer that end on or after July 12, 2013.

In addition, any assessment of a taxpayer's tax, interest and penalties payable under the Act for any taxation year that ends before the day on which this amendment receives royal assent [December 16, 2014] that would, in the absence of this section, be precluded because of the time references in subsection 152(4) of the Act is to be made to the extent necessary to take into account this amendment.

(1.092) If this subsection applies in respect of income or profits tax paid by, or refunded to, a shareholder affiliate for a taxation year

(*a*) in respect of the shareholder affiliate,

(i) any such income or profits tax paid by the shareholder affiliate for the year is deemed not to have been paid and any such refund to the shareholder affiliate of income or profits tax otherwise payable by it for the year is deemed not to have been made,

(ii) any such income or profits tax that would have been payable by the shareholder affiliate for the year if the shareholder affiliate had no other taxation year and had not been liable for income or profits tax in respect of income or profits of the transparent affiliate is deemed to have been paid for the year,

(iii) to the extent that

(A) any such income or profits tax that would otherwise have been payable by the shareholder affiliate for the year on behalf of the shareholder affiliate and the transparent affiliate is reduced because of any loss of the shareholder affiliate for the year or any previous taxation year, the amount of such reduction is deemed to have been received by the shareholder affiliate as a refund for the year of the loss of income or profits tax in respect of the loss, and

(B) the shareholder affiliate receives, in respect of a loss of the shareholder affiliate for the year or a subsequent taxation year, a refund of income or profits tax otherwise payable for the year by the shareholder affiliate on behalf of the shareholder affiliate and the transparent affiliate, the amount of such refund is deemed to have been received by the shareholder affiliate as a refund for the year of the loss of income or profits tax in respect of the loss,

(iv) any such income or profits tax that would have been payable by the transparent affiliate for the year if the transparent affiliate had no other taxation year, had no income or profits other than those that are included in computing the income or profits of the shareholder affiliate under the income tax laws referred to in paragraph (1.091)(*c*) and had been liable, and no other person had been liable, for income or profits tax in respect of income or profits of the transparent affiliate is, at the end of the year,

(A) to the extent that such income or profits tax would otherwise have reduced the net earnings included in the exempt earnings of the transparent affiliate, to be deducted from the exempt surplus or added to the exempt deficit, as the case may be, of the shareholder affiliate,

(B) to the extent that such income or profits tax would otherwise have reduced the hybrid surplus or increased the hybrid deficit of the transparent affiliate,

(I) to be deducted from the hybrid surplus or added to the hybrid deficit, as the case may be, of the shareholder affiliate, and

(II) to be added to the hybrid underlying tax of the shareholder affiliate, and

(C) to the extent that such income or profits tax would otherwise have reduced the net earnings included in the taxable earnings of the transparent affiliate,

(I) to be deducted from the taxable surplus or added to the taxable deficit, as the case may be, of the shareholder affiliate, and

(II) to be added to the underlying foreign tax of the shareholder affiliate, and

(v) to the extent that the income or profits tax that would otherwise have been payable by the shareholder affiliate for the year on behalf of the shareholder affiliate and the transparent affiliate is reduced because of a loss of the transparent affiliate for the year or a previous taxation year, or to the extent that the shareholder affiliate receives, in respect of a loss of the transparent affiliate for the year or a subsequent taxation year, a refund of income or profits tax otherwise payable for the year by the shareholder affiliate on behalf of the shareholder affiliate and the transparent affiliate, the amount of such reduction or refund, as the case may be, is, at the end of the year of the loss,

(A) to the extent that such loss reduces the exempt surplus or increases the exempt deficit of the transparent affiliate, to be added to the exempt surplus or deducted from the exempt deficit, as the case may be, of the shareholder affiliate,

(B) to the extent that such loss reduces the hybrid surplus or increases the hybrid deficit of the transparent affiliate,

(I) to be added to the hybrid surplus or deducted from the hybrid deficit, as the case may be, of the shareholder affiliate, and

(II) to be deducted from the hybrid underlying tax of the shareholder affiliate, and

(C) to the extent that such loss reduces the taxable surplus or increases the taxable deficit of the transparent affiliate,

(I) to be added to the taxable surplus or deducted from the taxable deficit, as the case may be, of the shareholder affiliate, and

(II) to be deducted from the underlying foreign tax of the shareholder affiliate;

(*b*) where, because of the shareholder affiliate being responsible for paying, or claiming a refund of, income or profits tax for the year on behalf of the shareholder affiliate and the transparent affiliate,

(i) an amount is paid to the shareholder affiliate by the transparent affiliate in respect of the income or profits tax that would have been payable by the transparent affiliate for the year had it been liable, and no other person had been liable, for income or profits tax in respect of income or profits of the transparent affiliate,

(A) in respect of the transparent affiliate, the amount so paid is deemed to be a payment of such income or profits tax for the year, and

(B) in respect of the shareholder affiliate,

(I) such portion of the amount so paid as may reasonably be regarded as relating to an amount included in the exempt surplus or deducted from the exempt deficit of the transparent affiliate is, at the end of the year, to be added to the exempt surplus or deducted from the exempt deficit, as the case may be, of the shareholder affiliate,

(II) such portion of the amount so paid as may reasonably be regarded as relating to an amount included in the hybrid surplus or deducted from the hybrid deficit of the transparent affiliate is, at the end of the year, to be added to the hybrid surplus or deducted from the hybrid deficit, as the case may be, of the shareholder affiliate and deducted from the hybrid underlying tax of the shareholder affiliate, and

(III) such portion of the amount so paid as may reasonably be regarded as relating to an amount included in the taxable surplus or deducted from the taxable deficit of the transparent affiliate is, at the end of the year, to be added to the taxable surplus or deducted from the taxable deficit, as the case may be, of the shareholder affiliate and be deducted from the underlying foreign tax of the shareholder affiliate, or

(ii) an amount is paid by the shareholder affiliate to the transparent affiliate in respect of a reduction or refund, because of a loss or a tax credit of the transparent affiliate for a taxation year, of the income or profits tax that would otherwise have been payable by the shareholder affiliate for the year on behalf of the shareholder affiliate and the transparent affiliate,

(A) in respect of the shareholder affiliate,

(I) the portion of the amount so paid that can reasonably be regarded as relating to an amount deducted from the exempt surplus or included in the exempt deficit of the transparent affiliate is, at the end of the year to which the loss or the tax credit relates, to be deducted from the exempt surplus or added to the exempt deficit, as the case may be, of the shareholder affiliate,

(II) the portion of the amount so paid that can reasonably be regarded as relating to an amount deducted from the hybrid surplus or included in the hybrid deficit of the transparent affiliate is, at the end of the year of the loss, to be deducted from the hybrid surplus or added to the hybrid deficit, as the case may be, of the shareholder affiliate and added to the hybrid underlying tax of the shareholder affiliate, and

(III) the portion of the amount so paid that can reasonably be regarded as relating to an amount deducted from the taxable surplus or included in the taxable deficit of the transparent affiliate is, at the end of the year to which the loss or the tax credit relates, to be deducted from the taxable surplus or added to the taxable deficit, as the case may be, of the shareholder affiliate and be added to the underlying foreign tax of the shareholder affiliate, and

(B) in respect of the transparent affiliate, the amount is deemed to be a refund to the transparent affiliate, for the year to which the loss or the tax credit relates, of income or profits tax in respect of the loss or the tax credit; and

(*c*) for the purposes of paragraph (*b*), any amount paid by a particular transparent affiliate in respect of the shareholder affiliate to another transparent affiliate in respect of the shareholder affiliate in respect of any income or profits tax that would have been payable by the particular transparent affiliate for the year had it been liable, and no other person had been liable, for income or profits tax in respect of income or profits of the transparent affiliate is deemed to have been paid in respect of such tax by the particular transparent affiliate to the shareholder affiliate and to have been paid in respect of

Regulations

such tax by the shareholder affiliate to the other transparent affiliate.

History: S. 5907(1.092) was added by S.C. 2014, c. 39, s. 88(18), applicable in respect of taxation years of a foreign affiliate of a taxpayer that end after 2010. However, if a taxpayer elects in writing under subsection 88(30) of the *Economic Action Plan 2014 Act, No. 2* [S.C. 2014, c. 39] in respect of all its foreign affiliates and files the election with the Minister of National Revenue on or before the day that is the later of the taxpayer's filing-due date for the taxpayer's taxation year that includes the day on which the *Economic Action Plan 2014 Act, No. 2* [S.C. 2014, c. 39] receives royal assent [December 16, 2014] and the day that is one year after the day on which the *Economic Action Plan 2014 Act, No. 2* [S.C. 2014, c. 39] receives royal assent [December 16, 2015], s. 5907(1.092) applies in respect of taxation years of all foreign affiliates of the taxpayer that end on or after July 12, 2013.

In addition, any assessment of a taxpayer's tax, interest and penalties payable under the Act for any taxation year that ends before the day on which this amendment receives royal assent [December 16, 2014] that would, in the absence of this section, be precluded because of the time references in subsection 152(4) of the Act is to be made to the extent necessary to take into account this amendment.

(1.1) For the purposes of this Part, if, under, the income tax laws of a country other than Canada, a group (in this subsection referred to as the "consolidated group") of two or more foreign affiliates of a corporation resident in Canada determine their liabilities for income or profits tax payable to the government of that country for a taxation year on a consolidated or combined basis and one of the affiliates (in this subsection referred to as the "primary affiliate") is responsible for paying, or claiming a refund of, such tax on behalf of itself and the other affiliates (in this subsection referred to as the "secondary affiliates") that are members of the consolidated group, the following rules apply:

(*a*) in respect of the primary affiliate,

(i) any such income or profits tax paid by the primary affiliate for the year shall be deemed not to have been paid and any refund to the primary affiliate of income or profits tax otherwise payable by it for the year shall be deemed not to have been made,

(ii) any such income or profits tax that would have been payable by the primary affiliate for the year if the primary affiliate had no other taxation year and had not been a member of the consolidated group shall be deemed to have been paid for the year,

(iii) to the extent that

(A) the income or profits tax that would otherwise have been payable by the primary affiliate for the year on behalf of the consolidated group is reduced by virtue of any loss of the primary affiliate for the year or any previous taxation year, or

(B) the primary affiliate receives, in respect of a loss of the primary affiliate for the year or a subsequent taxation year, a refund of income or profits tax otherwise payable for the year by the primary affiliate on behalf of the consolidated group,

the amount of such reduction or refund, as the case may be, shall be deemed to have been received by the primary affiliate as a refund for the year of the loss of income or profits tax in respect of the loss,

(iv) any such income or profits tax that would have been payable by a secondary affiliate for the year if the secondary affiliate had no other taxation year and had not been a member of the consolidated group shall at the end of the year,

(A) to the extent that such income or profits tax would otherwise have reduced the net earnings included in the exempt earnings of the secondary affiliate, be deducted from the exempt surplus or added to the exempt deficit, as the case may be, of the primary affiliate,

(A.1) to the extent that such income or profits tax would otherwise have reduced the hybrid surplus or increased the hybrid deficit of the secondary affiliate,

(I) be deducted from the hybrid surplus or added to the hybrid deficit, as the case may be, of the primary affiliate, and

(II) be added to the hybrid underlying tax of the primary affiliate, and

(B) to the extent that such income or profits tax would otherwise have reduced the net earnings included in the taxable earnings of the secondary affiliate,

(I) be deducted from the taxable surplus or added to the taxable deficit, as the case may be, of the primary affiliate, and

(II) be added to the underlying foreign tax of the primary affiliate,

(v) to the extent that

(A) the income or profits tax that would otherwise have been payable by the primary affiliate for the year on behalf of the consolidated group is reduced by virtue of a loss of a secondary affiliate for the year or a previous taxation year, or

(B) the primary affiliate receives, in respect of a loss of a secondary affiliate for the year or a subsequent taxation year, a refund of income or profits tax otherwise payable for the year by the primary affiliate on behalf of the consolidated group,

the amount of such reduction or refund, as the case may be, shall at the end of the year of the loss,

(C) where such loss reduces the exempt surplus or increases the exempt deficit, as the case may be, of the secondary affiliate, be added to the exempt surplus or deducted from the exempt deficit, as the case may be, of the primary affiliate,

(C.1) where such loss reduces the hybrid surplus or increases the hybrid deficit, as the case may be, of the secondary affiliate,

(I) be added to the hybrid surplus or deducted from the hybrid deficit, as the case may be, of the primary affiliate, and

(II) be deducted from the hybrid underlying tax of the primary affiliate, and

(D) where such loss reduces the taxable surplus or increases the taxable deficit, as the case may be, of the secondary affiliate,

(I) be added to the taxable surplus or deducted from the taxable deficit, as the case may be, of the primary affiliate, and

(II) be deducted from the underlying foreign tax of the primary affiliate; and

(*b*) where by virtue of the primary affiliate being responsible for paying, or claiming a refund of, income or profits tax for the year on behalf of the consolidated group,

(i) an amount is paid to the primary affiliate by a secondary affiliate in respect of the income or profits tax that would have been payable by the secondary affiliate for the year had it not been a member of the group,

(A) in respect of the secondary affiliate, the amount so paid shall be deemed to be a payment of such income or profits tax for the year, and

(B) in respect of the primary affiliate,

(I) such portion of the amount so paid as may reasonably be regarded as relating to an amount included in the exempt surplus or deducted from the exempt deficit, as the case may be, of the secondary affiliate shall at the end of the year be added to the exempt surplus or deducted from the exempt deficit, as the case may be, of the primary affiliate,

(I.1) such portion of the amount so paid as may reasonably be regarded as relating to an amount included in the hybrid surplus or deducted from the hybrid deficit, as the case may be, of the secondary affiliate is, at the end of the year, to be added to the hybrid surplus or deducted from the hybrid deficit, as the case may be, of the primary affiliate and deducted from the hybrid underlying tax of the primary affiliate, and

(II) such portion of the amount so paid as may reasonably be regarded as relating to an amount included in the taxable surplus or deducted from the taxable deficit, as the case may be, of the secondary affiliate shall at the end of the year be added to the taxable surplus or deducted from the taxable deficit, as the case may be, of the primary affiliate and be deducted from the underlying foreign tax of the primary affiliate, or

(ii) an amount is paid by the primary affiliate to a secondary affiliate in respect of a reduction or refund, because of a loss or a tax credit of the secondary affiliate for a taxation year, of the income or profits tax that would otherwise have been payable by the primary affiliate for the year on behalf of the consolidated group

(A) in respect of the primary affiliate,

(I) the portion of the amount so paid that can reasonably be regarded as relating to an amount deducted from the exempt surplus or included in the exempt deficit, as the case may be, of the secondary affiliate shall, at the end of the year to which the loss or the tax credit relates, be deducted from the exempt surplus or added to the exempt deficit, as the case may be, of the primary affiliate,

(I.1) such portion of the amount so paid as may reasonably be regarded as relating to an amount deducted from the hybrid surplus or included in the hybrid deficit, as the case may be, of the secondary affiliate is, at the end of the year of the loss, to be deducted from the hybrid surplus or added to the hybrid deficit, as the case may be, of the primary affiliate and added to the hybrid underlying tax of the primary affiliate, and

(II) the portion of the amount so paid that can reasonably be regarded as relating to an amount deducted from the taxable surplus or included in the taxable deficit, as the case may be, of the secondary affiliate shall, at the end of the year to which the loss or the tax credit relates, be deducted from the taxable surplus or added to the taxable deficit, as the case may be, of the primary affiliate and be added to the underlying foreign tax of the primary affiliate, and

(B) in respect of the secondary affiliate, the amount is deemed to be a refund to the secondary affiliate, for the year to which the loss or the tax credit relates, of income or profits tax in respect of the loss or the tax credit,

and, for the purposes of this paragraph, any amount paid by a particular secondary affiliate to another secondary affiliate in respect of any income or profits tax that would have been payable by the particular secondary affiliate for the year had it not been a member of the consolidated group shall be deemed to have been paid in respect of such tax by the particular secondary affiliate to the primary affiliate and to have been paid in respect of such tax by the primary affiliate to the other secondary affiliate.

History: S. 5907(1.1), the portion before paragraph (*a*) was replaced by S.C. 2014, c. 39, s. 88(19), applicable in respect of taxation years of a foreign affiliate of a taxpayer that end after 2003.

In addition, any assessment of a taxpayer's tax, interest and penalties payable under the Act for any taxation year that ends before the day on which this amendment receives royal assent [December 16, 2014] that would, in the absence of this section, be precluded because of the time references in subsection 152(4) of the Act is to be made to the extent necessary to take into account this amendment.

S. 5907(1.1), the portion before paragraph (*a*) formerly read:

(1.1) For the purposes of this Part, where, pursuant to the income tax law of a country other than Canada, a group of two or more foreign affiliates (in this subsection referred to as the "consolidated group") of a corporation resident in Canada that are resident in that country determine their liabilities for income or profits tax payable to the government of that country for a taxation year on a consolidated or combined basis and one of the affiliates (in

Regulations

this subsection referred to as the "primary affiliate") is responsible for paying, or claiming a refund of, such tax on behalf of itself and the other members of the consolidated group (hereinafter referred to as the "secondary affiliates"), the following rules apply:

S. 5907(1.1)(*a*)(iv)(A.1) was added by S.C. 2013, c. 34, s. 85(26), applicable in respect of taxation years of a foreign affiliate of a taxpayer that end after August 19, 2011.

S. 5907(1.1)(*a*)(v)(C.1) was added by S.C. 2013, c. 34, s. 85(27), applicable in respect of taxation years of a foreign affiliate of a taxpayer that end after August 19, 2011.

S. 5907(1.1)(*b*)(i)(B)(I.1) was added by S.C. 2013, c. 34, s. 85(28), applicable in respect of taxation years of a foreign affiliate of a taxpayer that end after August 19, 2011.

S. 5907(1.1)(*b*)(ii)(A)(I.1) was added by S.C. 2013, c. 34, s. 85(29), applicable in respect of taxation years of a foreign affiliate of a taxpayer that end after August 19, 2011.

See the application for the amendment to the portion of the definition "earnings" before subparagraph (*a*)(iii) in s. 5907(1) for the extension of assessment periods to take into account the amendments by S.C. 2013, c. 34, s. 54 to 89.

S. 5907(1.1)(*b*)(ii) was replaced by S.C. 2013, c. 34, s. 46(32), applicable in respect of payments made after December 20, 2002.

See the application following the amendment to subparagraph (*a*)(ii) of the definition "exempt earnings" in s. 5907(1), regarding the override of the statute-barring rules for assessments for taxation years that end before June 26, 2013.

S. 5907(1.1)(*b*)(ii) formerly read:

(ii) an amount is paid by the primary affiliate to a secondary affiliate in respect of a reduction or refund by virtue of a loss of the secondary affiliate for a taxation year of the income or profits tax that would otherwise have been payable by the primary affiliate for the year on behalf of the consolidated group,

(A) in respect of the primary affiliate,

(I) such portion of the amount so paid as may reasonably be regarded as relating to an amount deducted from the exempt surplus or included in the exempt deficit, as the case may be, of the secondary affiliate shall at the end of the year of the loss be deducted from the exempt surplus or added to the exempt deficit, as the case may be, of the primary affiliate, and

(II) such portion of the amount so paid as may reasonably be regarded as relating to an amount deducted from the taxable surplus or included in the taxable deficit, as the case may be, of the secondary affiliate shall at the end of the year of the loss be deducted from the taxable surplus or added to the taxable deficit, as the case may be, of the primary affiliate and be added to the underlying foreign tax of the primary affiliate, and

(B) in respect of the secondary affiliate, the amount shall be deemed to be a refund to the secondary affiliate for the year of the loss of income or profits tax in respect of the loss,

(1.11) For the purposes of subsection (1.1), a non-resident corporation is deemed to be, at any time, a foreign affiliate of a particular corporation resident in Canada if at that time the non-resident corporation is a foreign affiliate of another corporation that is resident in Canada and is related (otherwise than because of a right referred to in paragraph 251(5)(*b*) of the Act) to the particular corporation.

History: S. 5907(1.11) was added by S.C. 2014, c. 39, s. 88(20), applicable in respect of taxation years of a foreign affiliate of a taxpayer that end after 2003.

In addition, any assessment of a taxpayer's tax, interest and penalties payable under the Act for any taxation year that ends before the day on which this amendment receives royal assent [December 16, 2014] that would, in the absence of this section, be precluded because of the time references in subsection 152(4) of the Act is to be made to the extent necessary to take into account this amendment.

(1.12) Subsection (1.13) applies in respect of a particular foreign affiliate of a corporation resident in Canada that is a secondary affiliate (within the meaning assigned by subsection (1.1)) and in respect of a foreign affiliate of the corporation that is the primary affiliate (within the meaning assigned by subsection (1.1)) in respect of the particular affiliate if

(*a*) the particular affiliate has an equity percentage in another foreign affiliate (in this subsection and subsection (1.13) referred to as the "transparent affiliate");

(*b*) under the income tax laws of the country referred to in subsection (1.1), if the particular affiliate were not a member of a consolidated group, the particular affiliate, and not the transparent affiliate, would be liable for any tax payable to, or entitled to any refund from, a government of that country for that year in respect of the income or profits, or loss, as the case may be, for the year of the transparent affiliate; and

(*c*) the primary affiliate pays income or profits tax, or receives a refund, in respect of the income or profits, or loss, as the case may be, for the year of the transparent affiliate.

History: S. 5907(1.12) was added by S.C. 2014, c. 39, s. 88(21), applicable in respect of taxation years of a foreign affiliate of a taxpayer that end after 2010. However, if a taxpayer elects in writing under subsection 88(30) of the *Economic Action Plan 2014 Act, No. 2* [S.C. 2014, c. 39] in respect of all its foreign affiliates and files the election with the Minister of National Revenue on or before the day that is the later of the taxpayer's filing-due date for the taxpayer's taxation year that includes the day on which the *Economic Action Plan 2014 Act, No. 2* [S.C. 2014, c. 39] receives royal assent [December 16, 2014] and the day that is one year after the day on which the *Economic Action Plan 2014 Act, No. 2* [S.C. 2014, c. 39] receives royal assent [December 16, 2015], s. 5907(1.12) applies in respect of taxation years of all foreign affiliates of the taxpayer that end on or after July 12, 2013.

In addition, any assessment of a taxpayer's tax, interest and penalties payable under the Act for any taxation year that ends before the day on which this amendment receives royal assent [December 16, 2014] that would, in the absence of this section, be precluded because of the time references in subsection 152(4) of the Act is to be made to the extent necessary to take into account this amendment.

(1.13) If this subsection applies, then in respect of the particular foreign affiliate and the primary affiliate referred to in subsection (1.12)

(*a*) for the purposes of applying subparagraphs (1.1)(*a*)(iv) and (1.1)(*b*)(i), where any income or profits tax that would otherwise be payable by the particular affiliate for the year, if the particular affiliate had no other taxation year and were not a member of the consolidated group referred to in subsection (1.1), is increased because of income or profits of the transparent affiliate referred to in paragraph (1.12)(*a*),

(i) to the extent that the income or profits increases the net earnings included in the exempt earnings of the transparent affiliate,

(A) the amount of any such increase is deemed to have been included in the exempt surplus, or deducted from the exempt deficit, as the case may be, of the particular affiliate, and

(B) any such income or profits tax that would have been payable by the particular affiliate in respect of the income or profits is deemed to be income or profits tax that would otherwise have reduced the net earnings that are included in the exempt earnings of the particular affiliate,

(ii) to the extent that the income or profits increases the hybrid surplus or reduces the hybrid deficit of the transparent affiliate,

(A) the amount of the increase or reduction is deemed to have been included in the hybrid surplus, or deducted from the hybrid deficit, as the case may be, of the particular affiliate, and

(B) any such income or profits tax that would have been payable by the particular affiliate in respect of the income or profits is deemed to be income or profits tax that would otherwise have reduced the hybrid surplus or increased the hybrid deficit, as the case may be, of the particular affiliate, and

(iii) to the extent that the income or profits increases the net earnings included in the taxable earnings of the transparent affiliate,

(A) the amount of any such increase is deemed to have been included in the taxable surplus, or deducted from the taxable deficit, as the case may be, of the particular affiliate, and

(B) any such income or profits tax that would have been payable by the particular affiliate in respect of the income or profits is deemed to be income or profits tax that would otherwise have reduced the net earnings that are included in the taxable earnings of the particular affiliate; and

(*b*) for the purpose of applying subparagraphs (1.1)(*a*)(v) and (1.1)(*b*)(ii), to the extent that the income or profits tax that would otherwise have been payable by the primary affiliate for the year on behalf of the consolidated group is reduced because of a loss, for the year or a previous taxation year, of the transparent affiliate referred to in paragraph (1.12)(*a*), or to the extent that the primary affiliate receives, in respect of a loss of the transparent affiliate for the year or a subsequent taxation year, a refund of income or profits tax otherwise payable for the year by the primary affiliate on behalf of the consolidated group,

(i) such loss is deemed to be a loss of the particular affiliate,

(ii) to the extent that such loss reduces the exempt surplus or increases the exempt deficit of the transparent affiliate, such loss is deemed to reduce the exempt surplus or increase the exempt deficit, as the case may be, of the particular affiliate,

(iii) to the extent that such loss reduces the hybrid surplus or increases the hybrid deficit of the transparent affiliate, such loss is deemed to reduce the hybrid surplus or increase the hybrid deficit, as the case may be, of the particular affiliate, and

(iv) to the extent that such loss reduces the taxable surplus or increases the taxable deficit of the transparent affiliate, such loss is deemed to reduce the taxable surplus or increase the taxable deficit, as the case may be, of the particular affiliate.

History: S. 5907(1.13) was added by S.C. 2014, c. 39, s. 88(21), applicable in respect of taxation years of a foreign affiliate of a taxpayer that end after 2010. However, if a taxpayer elects in writing under subsection 88(30) of the *Economic Action Plan 2014 Act, No. 2* [S.C. 2014, c. 39] in respect of all its foreign affiliates and files the election with the Minister of National Revenue on or before the day that is the later of the taxpayer's filing-due date for the taxpayer's taxation year that includes the day on which the *Economic Action Plan 2014 Act, No. 2* [S.C. 2014, c. 39] receives royal assent [December 16, 2014] and the day that is one year after the day on which the *Economic Action Plan 2014 Act, No. 2* [S.C. 2014, c. 39] receives royal assent [December 16, 2015], s. 5907(1.13) applies in respect of taxation years of all foreign affiliates of the taxpayer that end on or after July 12, 2013.

In addition, any assessment of a taxpayer's tax, interest and penalties payable under the Act for any taxation year that ends before the day on which this amendment receives royal assent [December 16, 2014] that would, in the absence of this section, be precluded because of the time references in subsection 152(4) of the Act is to be made to the extent necessary to take into account this amendment.

(1.2) For the purposes of this Part, where, pursuant to the income tax law of a country other than Canada, a corporation resident in that country that is a foreign affiliate of a corporation resident in Canada (in this subsection referred to as the "taxpaying affiliate") deducts, in computing its income or profits tax payable for a taxation year to a government of that country, a loss of another corporation resident in that country that is a foreign affiliate of the corporation resident in Canada (in this subsection referred to as the "loss affiliate"), the following rules apply:

(*a*) any such income or profits tax paid by the taxpaying affiliate for the year shall be deemed not to have been paid;

(*b*) any such income or profits tax that would have been payable by the taxpaying affiliate for the year if the taxpaying affiliate had not been allowed to deduct such loss shall be deemed to have been paid for the year;

(*c*) to the extent that the income or profits tax that would otherwise have been payable by the taxpaying affiliate for the year is reduced by virtue of such loss, the amount of such reduction shall at the end of the year,

(i) where such loss reduces the exempt surplus or increases the exempt deficit, as the case may be, of the loss affiliate, be added to the exempt surplus or deducted from the exempt deficit, as the case may be, of the taxpaying affiliate,

(i.1) where such loss reduces the hybrid surplus or increases the hybrid deficit, as the case may be, of the loss affiliate,

(A) be added to the hybrid surplus or deducted from the hybrid deficit, as the case may be, of the taxpaying affiliate, and

(B) be deducted from the hybrid underlying tax of the taxpaying affiliate, and

(ii) where such loss reduces the taxable surplus or increases the taxable deficit, as the case may be, of the loss affiliate,

(A) be added to the taxable surplus or deducted from the taxable deficit, as the case may be, of the taxpaying affiliate, and

Regulations

(B) be deducted from the underlying foreign tax of the taxpaying affiliate; and

(*d*) where an amount is paid by the taxpaying affiliate to the loss affiliate in respect of the reduction, by virtue of such loss, of the income or profits tax that would otherwise have been payable by the taxpaying affiliate for the year,

(i) in respect of the taxpaying affiliate,

(A) such portion of the amount as may reasonably be regarded as relating to an amount deducted from the exempt surplus or included in the exempt deficit, as the case may be, of the loss affiliate shall at the end of the year be deducted from the exempt surplus or added to the exempt deficit, as the case may be, of the taxpaying affiliate,

(A.1) such portion of the amount as may reasonably be regarded as relating to an amount deducted from the hybrid surplus or included in the hybrid deficit, as the case may be, of the loss affiliate is, at the end of the year, to be deducted from the hybrid surplus or added to the hybrid deficit, as the case may be, of the taxpaying affiliate and added to the hybrid underlying tax of the taxpaying affiliate, and

(B) such portion of the amount as may reasonably be regarded as relating to an amount deducted from the taxable surplus or included in the taxable deficit, as the case may be, of the loss affiliate shall at the end of the year be deducted from the taxable surplus or added to the taxable deficit, as the case may be, of the taxpaying affiliate and be added to the underlying foreign tax of the taxpaying affiliate, and

(ii) in respect of the loss affiliate, the amount shall be deemed to be a refund to the loss affiliate of income or profits tax in respect of the loss for the taxation year of the loss.

History: S. 5907(1.2)(*c*)(i.1) was added by S.C. 2013, c. 34, s. 85(30), applicable in respect of taxation years of a foreign affiliate of a taxpayer that end after August 19, 2011.

S. 5907(1.2)(*d*)(i)(A.1) was added by S.C. 2013, c. 34, s. 85(31), applicable in respect of taxation years of a foreign affiliate of a taxpayer that end after August 19, 2011.

See the application for the amendment to the portion of the definition "earnings" before subparagraph (*a*)(iii) in s. 5907(1) for the extension of assessment periods to take into account the amendments by S.C. 2013, c. 34, s. 54 to 89.

(1.21) Subsection (1.22) applies if

(*a*) a foreign affiliate of the taxpayer (in this subsection and subsection (1.22) referred to as the "shareholder affiliate") has an equity percentage in another foreign affiliate (in this subsection and subsection (1.22) referred to as the "transparent affiliate"); and

(*b*) under the income tax laws of the country in which the shareholder affiliate is resident, the shareholder affiliate, and not the transparent affiliate, is liable for any tax payable to, or entitled to any refund from, a government of that country for that year in respect of the income or profits, or loss, as the case may be, for the year of the transparent affiliate.

History: S. 5907(1.21) was added by S.C. 2014, c. 39, s. 88(22), applicable in respect of taxation years of a foreign affiliate of a taxpayer that end after 2010. However, if a taxpayer elects in writing under subsection 88(30) of the *Economic Action Plan 2014 Act, No. 2* [S.C. 2014, c. 39] in respect of all its foreign affiliates and files the election with the Minister of National Revenue on or before the day that is the later of the taxpayer's filing-due date for the taxpayer's taxation year that includes the day on which the *Economic Action Plan 2014 Act, No. 2* [S.C. 2014, c. 39] receives royal assent [December 16, 2014] and the day that is one year after the day on which the *Economic Action Plan 2014 Act, No. 2* [S.C. 2014, c. 39] receives royal assent [December 16, 2015], s. 5907(1.21) applies in respect of taxation years of all foreign affiliates of the taxpayer that end on or after July 12, 2013.

In addition, any assessment of a taxpayer's tax, interest and penalties payable under the Act for any taxation year that ends before the day on which this amendment receives royal assent [December 16, 2014] that would, in the absence of this section, be precluded because of the time references in subsection 152(4) of the Act is to be made to the extent necessary to take into account this amendment.

(1.22) If this subsection applies, for the purpose of applying subsection (1.2), any loss of the transparent affiliate, to the extent that the loss is deducted in computing the income, profits or loss of the shareholder affiliate under an income tax law referred to in paragraph (1.21)(*b*),

(*a*) is deemed to be a loss of the shareholder affiliate; and

(*b*) is deemed to

(i) reduce the exempt surplus, or increase the exempt deficit, as the case may be, of the shareholder affiliate to the extent that it reduces the exempt surplus or increases the exempt deficit of the transparent affiliate,

(ii) reduce the hybrid surplus or increase the hybrid deficit, as the case may be, of the shareholder affiliate to the extent that it reduces the hybrid surplus or increases the hybrid deficit of the transparent affiliate, and

(iii) reduce the taxable surplus or increase the taxable deficit, as the case may be, of the shareholder affiliate to the extent that it reduces the taxable surplus or increases the taxable deficit of the transparent affiliate.

History: S. 5907(1.22) was added by S.C. 2014, c. 39, s. 88(22), applicable in respect of taxation years of a foreign affiliate of a taxpayer that end after 2010. However, if a taxpayer elects in writing under subsection 88(30) of the *Economic Action Plan 2014 Act, No. 2* [S.C. 2014, c. 39] in respect of all its foreign affiliates and files the election with the Minister of National Revenue on or before the day that is the later of the taxpayer's filing-due date for the taxpayer's taxation year that includes the day on which the *Economic Action Plan 2014 Act, No. 2* [S.C. 2014, c. 39] receives royal assent [December 16, 2014] and the day that is one year after the day on which the *Economic Action Plan 2014 Act, No. 2* [S.C. 2014, c. 39] receives royal assent [December 16, 2015], s. 5907(1.22) applies in respect of taxation years of all foreign affiliates of the taxpayer that end on or after July 12, 2013.

In addition, any assessment of a taxpayer's tax, interest and penalties payable under the Act for any taxation year that ends before the day on which this amendment receives royal assent [December 16, 2014] that would, in the absence of this section, be precluded because of the time references in subsection 152(4) of the Act is to be made to the extent necessary to take into account this amendment.

(1.3) For the purpose of paragraph (*b*) of the definition "foreign accrual tax" in subsection 95(1) of the Act and subject to subsection (1.4),

(*a*) if under the income tax laws of the country in which the particular affiliate or a shareholder affiliate of the particular affiliate, as the case may be, referred to in that paragraph is resident, the particular affiliate, or shareholder affiliate, and one or more other corporations, each of which is resident in that country, determine their liabilities for income or profits tax payable to the government of that country for a taxation year on a consolidated or combined basis, then any amount paid by the particular affiliate, or shareholder affiliate, to any of those other corporations to the extent that the amount paid may reasonably be regarded as being in respect of income or profits tax that would otherwise have been payable by the particular affiliate, or shareholder affiliate, in respect of a particular amount that is included under subsection 91(1) of the Act in computing the taxpayer's income for a taxation year of the taxpayer in respect of the particular affiliate, if the tax liability of the particular affiliate, or shareholder affiliate, and those other corporations had not been determined on a consolidated or combined basis, is prescribed to be foreign accrual tax applicable to the particular amount; and

(*b*) if, under the income tax laws of the country in which the particular affiliate or a shareholder affiliate of the particular affiliate, as the case may be, referred to in that paragraph is resident, the particular affiliate, or shareholder affiliate, deducts, in computing its income or profits subject to tax in that country for a taxation year, an amount in respect of a loss of another corporation (referred to in this paragraph and paragraph (1.6)(*a*) as the "loss transferor") resident in that country (referred to in this paragraph and paragraph (1.6)(*a*) as the "transferred loss"), then any amount paid by the particular affiliate, or shareholder affiliate, to the loss transferor to the extent that the amount paid may reasonably be regarded as being in respect of income or profits tax that would otherwise have been payable by the particular affiliate, or shareholder affiliate, in respect of a particular amount that is included under subsection 91(1) of the Act in computing the taxpayer's income for a taxation year of the taxpayer in respect of the particular affiliate, if the tax liability of the particular affiliate, or shareholder affiliate, had been determined without deducting the transferred loss, is prescribed to be foreign accrual tax applicable to the particular amount.

History: S. 5907(1.3)(*a*) and (*b*) were replaced by S.C. 2014, c. 39, s. 88(23), applicable in respect of taxation years of a foreign affiliate of a taxpayer that end after 2010. However, if a taxpayer elects in writing under subsection 88(30) of the *Economic Action Plan 2014 Act, No. 2* [S.C. 2014, c. 39] in respect of all its foreign affiliates and files the election with the Minister of National Revenue on or before the day that is the later of the taxpayer's filing-due date for the taxpayer's taxation year that includes the day on which the *Economic Action Plan 2014 Act, No. 2* [S.C. 2014, c. 39] receives royal assent [December 16, 2014] and the day that is one year after the day on which the *Economic Action Plan 2014 Act, No. 2* [S.C. 2014, c. 39] receives royal assent [December 16, 2015], paragraphs (*a*) and (*b*) of s. 5907(1.3) apply in respect of taxation years of all foreign affiliates of the taxpayer that end on or after July 12, 2013.

In addition, any assessment of a taxpayer's tax, interest and penalties payable under the Act for any taxation year that ends before the day on which this amendment receives royal assent [December 16, 2014] that would, in the absence of this section, be precluded because of the time references in subsection 152(4) of the Act is to be made to the extent necessary to take into account this amendment.

S. 5907(1.3)(*a*) and (*b*) formerly read:

(*a*) where, pursuant to the income tax law of the country in which a particular foreign affiliate is resident, the particular affiliate and one or more other corporations, each of which is resident in that country, determine their liabilities for income or profits tax payable to the government of that country for a taxation year on a consolidated or combined basis, any amount paid by the particular affiliate to any of the other corporations to the extent that it may reasonably be regarded as being in respect of income or profits tax that would otherwise have been payable by the particular affiliate in respect of a particular amount included in computing the taxpayer's income by virtue of subsection 91(1) of the Act for a taxation year in respect of the particular affiliate, had the tax liability of the particular affiliate and the other corporations not been determined on a consolidated or combined basis, is hereby prescribed to be foreign accrual tax applicable to the particular amount; and

(*b*) where, pursuant to the income tax law of the country in which a particular foreign affiliate of a taxpayer is resident, the particular affiliate, in computing its income or profits subject to tax in that country for a taxation year, deducts an amount in respect of a loss of another corporation resident in that country, any amount paid by the particular affiliate to the other corporation to the extent that it may reasonably be regarded as being in respect of income or profits tax that would otherwise have been payable by the particular affiliate in respect of a particular amount included in computing the taxpayer's income by virtue of subsection 91(1) of the Act for a taxation year in respect of the particular affiliate, had the tax liability of the particular affiliate been determined without deducting the loss of the other corporation, is hereby prescribed to be foreign accrual tax applicable to the particular amount.

S. 5907(1.3), the portion before paragraph (*a*) was replaced by S.C. 2013, c. 34, s. 46(33), applicable to taxation years of a foreign affiliate of a taxpayer that begin after November 1999.

See the application following the amendment to subparagraph (*a*)(ii) of the definition "exempt earnings" in s. 5907(1), regarding the override of the statute-barring rules for assessments for taxation years that end before June 26, 2013.

S. 5907(1.3), the portion before paragraph (*a*) formerly read:

(1.3) For the purpose of paragraph (*b*) of the definition "foreign accrual tax" in subsection 95(1) of the Act,

(1.4) If the amount prescribed under paragraph (1.3)(*a*) or (*b*), or any portion of the amount, can reasonably be considered to be in respect of a particular loss (other than a capital loss) or a capital loss of another corporation for a taxation year of the other corporation, then the amount so prescribed is to be reduced to the extent that it can reasonably be considered to be in respect of the portion of the particular loss or capital loss, as the case may be, that would, if sections 5903 and 5903.1 were read without reference to their subsection (4), not be a foreign accrual property loss (within the meaning assigned by subsection 5903(3)), or a foreign accrual capital loss (within the meaning assigned by subsection 5903.1(3)), as the case may be, of a controlled foreign affiliate of a person or partnership that is, at the end of that taxation year, a relevant person or partnership (within the meaning assigned by subsection 5903(6)) in respect of the taxpayer.

History: S. 5907(1.4) was replaced by S.C. 2013, c. 34, s. 85(32), applicable in respect of taxation years of a foreign affiliate of a taxpayer that end after August 19, 2011.

See the application for the amendment to the portion of the definition "earnings" before subparagraph (*a*)(iii) in s. 5907(1) for the extension of assessment periods to take into account the amendments by S.C. 2013, c. 34, s. 54 to 89.

S. 5907(1.4) formerly read:

(1.4) If the amount prescribed under paragraph (1.3)(*a*) or (*b*), or any portion of the amount, can reasonably be considered to be in respect of a loss of another corporation for a taxation year of the other corporation, then the amount so prescribed is to be reduced to the extent that it can reasonably be considered to be in respect of the portion of that loss that would, if section 5903 were read without reference to its subsection (4), not be a foreign accrual property loss (within the meaning assigned by subsection 5903(3)) of a controlled foreign affiliate of a person or partnership that is, at the end of that taxation year, a relevant person or partnership (within the meaning assigned by subsection 5903(6)) in respect of the taxpayer.

S. 5907(1.4) was added by S.C. 2013, c. 34, s. 46(34), applicable to taxation years of a foreign affiliate of a taxpayer that begin after November 1999.

See the application following the amendment to subparagraph (*a*)(ii) of the definition "exempt earnings" in s. 5907(1), regarding the override of the statute-barring rules for assessments for taxation years that end before June 26, 2013.

(1.5) If subsection (1.4) applied to reduce an amount that would, in the absence of subsection (1.4), be prescribed by subsection (1.3) to be foreign accrual tax applicable to an amount (referred to in this subsection as the "FAPI amount") included under subsection 91(1) of the Act in computing the taxpayer's income for a taxation year (referred to in subsection (1.6) as the "FAPI year") of the taxpayer in respect of the particular affiliate referred to in paragraph (1.3)(*a*) or (*b*), then an amount equal to that reduction is, for the purposes of paragraph (*b*) of the definition "foreign accrual tax" in subsection 95(1) of the Act, prescribed to be foreign accrual tax applicable to the FAPI amount in the taxpayer's taxation year that includes the last day of the designated taxation year, if any, of the particular affiliate or the shareholder affiliate referred to in paragraph (1.3)(*a*) or (*b*), as the case may be.

History: S. 5907(1.5) was replaced by S.C. 2014, c. 39, s. 88(24), applicable in respect of taxation years of a foreign affiliate of a taxpayer that end after 2010. However, if a taxpayer elects in writing under subsection 88(30) of the *Economic Action Plan 2014 Act, No. 2* [S.C. 2014, c. 39] in respect of all its foreign affiliates and files the election with the Minister of National Revenue on or before the day that is the later of the taxpayer's filing-due date for the taxpayer's taxation year that includes the day on which the *Economic Action Plan 2014 Act, No. 2* [S.C. 2014, c. 39] receives royal assent [December 16, 2014] and the day that is one year after the day on which the *Economic Action Plan 2014 Act, No. 2* [S.C. 2014, c. 39] receives royal assent [December 16, 2015], s. 5907(1.5) applies in respect of taxation years of all foreign affiliates of the taxpayer that end on or after July 12, 2013.

In addition, any assessment of a taxpayer's tax, interest and penalties payable under the Act for any taxation year that ends before the day on which this amendment receives royal assent [December 16, 2014] that would, in the absence of this section, be precluded because of the time references in subsection 152(4) of the Act is to be made to the extent necessary to take into account this amendment.

S. 5907(1.5) formerly read:

(1.5) If subsection (1.4) applied to reduce an amount that would, in the absence of subsection (1.4), be prescribed by paragraph (1.3)(*a*) to be foreign accrual tax applicable to an amount (referred to in this subsection as the "FAPI amount") included in the taxpayer's income under subsection 91(1) of the Act for a taxation year (referred to in subsection (1.6) as the "FAPI year") of the taxpayer, an amount equal to that reduction is, for the purpose of paragraph (*b*) of the definition "foreign accrual tax" in subsection 95(1) of the Act, prescribed to be foreign accrual tax applicable to the FAPI amount in the taxpayer's taxation year that includes the last day of the designated taxation year, if any, of the particular affiliate referred to in paragraph (1.3)(*a*).

S. 5907(1.5) was added by S.C. 2013, c. 34, s. 46(34), applicable to taxation years of a foreign affiliate of a taxpayer that begin after November 1999.

See the application following the amendment to subparagraph (*a*)(ii) of the definition "exempt earnings" in s. 5907(1), regarding the override of the statute-barring rules for assessments for taxation years that end before June 26, 2013.

(1.6) For the purposes of subsection (1.5), the designated taxation year of the particular affiliate or the shareholder affiliate, as the case may be, is a particular taxation year of the particular affiliate, or the shareholder affiliate, if

(*a*) in the particular year, or in the taxation year of the particular affiliate or shareholder affiliate (referred to in this paragraph as the "PATY") ending in the FAPI year and one or more taxation years of the particular affiliate (or shareholder affiliate) each of which follows the PATY and the latest of which is the particular year, all losses of the particular affiliate (or shareholder affiliate) and the other corporations referred to in paragraph (1.3)(*a*) — or of the particular affiliate, the loss transferor and each corporation that would have been permitted to deduct the transferred loss against its income under the income tax laws referred to in paragraph (1.3)(*b*) if the transferred loss had not been deducted by the particular affiliate and if the corporation had taxable income for its taxation years ending in the FAPI year in excess of the transferred loss — for their taxation years ending in the FAPI year would, on the assumption that the particular affiliate (or shareholder affiliate) and each of those other corporations had no foreign accrual property income for any taxation year, reasonably be considered to have been fully deducted (under the tax laws referred to in paragraph (1.3)(*a*) or (*b*)) against income (as determined under those tax laws) of the particular affiliate (or shareholder affiliate) or those other corporations;

(*b*) the taxpayer demonstrates that no other losses of the particular affiliate (or shareholder affiliate) or those other corporations for any taxation year were, or could reasonably have been, deducted under those tax laws against that income; and

(*c*) the last day of the particular year occurs in one of the five taxation years of the taxpayer that immediately follow the FAPI year.

History: S. 5907(1.6) was replaced by S.C. 2014, c. 39, s. 88(24), applicable in respect of taxation years of a foreign affiliate of a taxpayer that end after 2010. However, if a taxpayer elects in writing under subsection 88(30) of the *Economic Action Plan 2014 Act, No. 2* [S.C. 2014, c. 39] in respect of all its foreign affiliates and files the election with the Minister of National Revenue on or before the day that is the later of the taxpayer's filing-due date for the taxpayer's taxation year that includes the day on which the *Economic Action Plan 2014 Act, No. 2* [S.C. 2014, c. 39] receives royal assent [December 16, 2014] and the day that is one year after the day on which the *Economic Action Plan 2014 Act, No. 2* [S.C. 2014, c. 39] receives royal assent [December 16, 2015], s. 5907(1.6) applies in respect of taxation years of all foreign affiliates of the taxpayer that end on or after July 12, 2013.

In addition, any assessment of a taxpayer's tax, interest and penalties payable under the Act for any taxation year that ends before the day on which this amendment receives royal assent [December 16, 2014] that would, in the absence of this section, be precluded because of the time references in subsection 152(4) of the Act is to be made to the extent necessary to take into account this amendment.

S. 5907(1.6) formerly read:

(1.6) For the purposes of subsection (1.5), the designated taxation year of the particular affiliate is a particular taxation year of the particular affiliate if

(*a*) in the particular year, or in the particular affiliate's taxation year (referred to in this paragraph as the "PATY") ending in the FAPI year and one or more taxation years of the particular affiliate each of which follows the PATY and the latest of which is the particular year, all losses of the particular affiliate and the other corporations referred to in paragraph (1.3)(*a*) for their taxation years ending in the FAPI year would, on the assumption that the particular affiliate and each of those other corporations had no foreign accrual property income for any taxation year, reasonably be considered to have been fully deducted (under the tax law referred to in paragraph (1.3)(*a*)) against income (as determined under that tax law) of the particular affiliate or those other corporations;

(*b*) the taxpayer demonstrates that no other losses of the particular affiliate or those other corporations for any taxation year were, or could reasonably have been, deducted under that tax law against that income; and

(*c*) the last day of the particular year occurs in one of the five taxation years of the taxpayer that immediately follow the FAPI year.

S. 5907(1.6) was added by S.C. 2013, c. 34, s. 46(34), applicable to taxation years of a foreign affiliate of a taxpayer that begin after November 1999.

See the application following the amendment to subparagraph (*a*)(ii) of the definition "exempt earnings" in s. 5907(1), regarding the override of the statute-barring rules for assessments for taxation years that end before June 26, 2013.

(1.7) If the amount prescribed under paragraph (1.3)(*a*) or (*b*), or any portion of the amount, can reasonably be considered to be in respect of a capital loss of another corporation for a taxation year of the other corporation, then the amount so prescribed, as reduced by subsection (1.4), if applicable, shall be reduced to the extent that it can reasonably be considered to be in respect of the portion of that capital loss that would not be deductible by the particular affiliate in computing its foreign accrual property income for the year if the capital loss had been incurred by the particular affiliate.

History: S. 5907(1.7) was added by S.C. 2013, c. 34, s. 85(33), applicable in respect of taxation years of a foreign affiliate of a taxpayer that end after August 19, 2011.

See the application for the amendment to the portion of the definition "earnings" before subparagraph (*a*)(iii) in s. 5907(1) for the extension of assessment periods to take into account the amendments by S.C. 2013, c. 34, s. 54 to 89.

(2) In computing the earnings of a foreign affiliate of a taxpayer resident in Canada for a taxation year of the affiliate from an active business carried on by it in a country, there shall be added to the amount thereof determined under subparagraph (*a*)(i) or (ii) of the definition "earnings" in subsection (1) (in this subsection referred to as the "earnings amount") such portion of the following amounts as was deducted or was not included, as the case may be, in computing the earnings amount,

(*a*) any income or profits tax paid to the government of a country by the affiliate so deducted,

(*b*) if established by the taxpayer, the amount by which any amount so deducted in respect of an expenditure made by the affiliate exceeds the amount, if any, by which

(i) the amount of the expenditure

exceeds

(ii) the aggregate of all other deductions in respect of that expenditure made by the affiliate in computing the earnings amounts for preceding taxation years,

(*c*) any loss of the affiliate referred to in the description of D in the definition "foreign accrual property income" in subsection 95(1) of the Act so deducted,

(*d*) any capital loss of the affiliate in respect of the disposition of capital property so deducted (for greater certainty, capital property of the affiliate for the purposes of this paragraph includes all the property of the affiliate other than property referred to in subparagraph 39(1)(*b*)(i) or (ii) of the Act on the assumption for this purpose that the affiliate is a corporation resident in Canada),

(*e*) any loss of the affiliate for a preceding or a subsequent taxation year so deducted,

(*f*) any revenue, income or profit (other than an amount referred to in paragraph (*f*.1), (*h*) or (*i*)) of the affiliate derived in the year from such business carried on in that country to the extent that such revenue, income or profit

(i) is not otherwise required to be included in computing the earnings amount of the affiliate for any taxation year by the income tax law that is relevant in computing that amount, and

(ii) subject to subsections (2.01) and (2.011), does not arise with respect to a disposition (other than a disposition to which subsection (9) applies), of property by the affiliate,

(A) to a person or partnership that was, at the time of the disposition, a designated person or partnership in respect of the taxpayer, and

(B) to which a tax deferral, rollover or similar tax postponement provision of the income tax laws that are relevant in computing the earnings amount of the affiliate applied, and

(*f*.1) any assistance from a government, municipality or other public authority (other than any such assistance that reduced the amount of an expenditure for purposes of computing the earnings amount for any taxation year) that the affiliate received or became entitled to receive in the year in connection with such business carried on in that country that is not otherwise required to be included in computing the earnings amount for the year or for any other taxation year,

and there shall be deducted such portion of the following amounts as were included or were not deducted, as the case may be, in computing the earnings amount,

(*g*) any income or profits tax refunded by the government of a country to the affiliate so included;

(*h*) any capital gain of the affiliate in respect of the disposition of capital property so included (for greater certainty, capital property of the affiliate for the purposes of this paragraph includes all the property of the affiliate other than property referred to in any of subparagraphs 39(1)(*a*)(i) to (iv) of the Act on the assumption for this purpose that the affiliate is a corporation resident in Canada);

(*i*) any amount that is included in the foreign accrual property income of the affiliate so included;

(*j*) any loss, outlay or expense made or incurred in the year by the affiliate for the purpose of gaining or producing such earnings amount to the extent that

(i) such loss, outlay or expense is not otherwise permitted to be deducted in computing the earnings amount of the affiliate for any taxation year by the income tax law that is relevant in computing that amount, or

(ii) such outlay or expense can reasonably be regarded as applicable to any revenue added to the earnings amount of the affiliate under paragraph (*f*),

where such loss, outlay or expense

(iii) subject to subsections (2.01) and (2.011), does not arise with respect to a disposition (other than a disposition to which subsection (9) applies), of property by the affiliate,

(A) to a person or partnership that was, at the time of the disposition, a designated person or partnership in respect of the taxpayer, and

(B) to which a loss deferral or similar loss postponement provision of the income tax laws that are relevant in computing the earnings amount of the affiliate applied, and

(iv) is not

Regulations

(A) a loss referred to in paragraph (*c*) or (*d*),

(B) a capital expenditure other than interest, or

(C) income or profits tax paid to the government of a country;

(*k*) any outlay made in the year in repayment of an amount referred to in paragraph (*f*.1), and

(*l*) if any property of the affiliate that was acquired from a person or partnership that was, at the time of the acquisition, a designated person or partnership in respect of the taxpayer has been disposed of, the amount in respect of that property that may reasonably be considered as having been included under paragraph (*f*) in computing the earnings amount of any foreign affiliate of the taxpayer or of a person or partnership that was, at the time of the disposition, a designated person or partnership in respect of the taxpayer.

History: S. 5907(2)(*f*)(ii), the portion before clause (A) was replaced by S.C. 2018, c. 27, s. 39(2), applicable in respect of dispositions that occur after October 23, 2012, and formerly read:

(ii) subject to subsection (2.01), does not arise with respect to a disposition (other than a disposition to which subsection (9) applies), of property by the affiliate,

S. 5907(2)(*j*)(iii), the portion before clause (A) was replaced by S.C. 2018, c. 27, s. 39(3), applicable in respect of dispositions that occur after October 23, 2012, and formerly read:

(iii) subject to subsection (2.01), does not arise with respect to a disposition (other than a disposition to which subsection (9) applies), of property by the affiliate,

S. 5907(2)(*f*)(ii) was replaced by S.C. 2013, c. 34, s. 85(34), applicable in respect of dispositions of property by a foreign affiliate of a taxpayer that occur after August 19, 2011. However, if the taxpayer has elected under subsection 5907(2.01),

(*a*) subparagraph 5907(2)(*f*)(ii) applies in respect of dispositions of property by all foreign affiliates of the taxpayer that occur after December 20, 2002;

(*b*) subparagraph 5907(2)(*f*)(ii) is, in respect of all such dispositions that occur on or before August 19, 2011, to be read as follows:

"(ii) subject to subsection (2.01), does not arise with respect to a disposition (other than a disposition to which subsection (9) applies) by the affiliate of property to another foreign affiliate of the taxpayer or to a person with whom the taxpayer does not deal at arm's length, to which a tax deferral, rollover or similar tax postponement provision of the income tax law that is relevant in computing the earnings amount of the affiliate applied, and"

See the application for the amendment to the portion of the definition "earnings" before subparagraph (*a*)(iii) in s. 5907(1) for the extension of assessment periods to take into account the amendments by S.C. 2013, c. 34, s. 54 to 89.

S. 5907(2)(*f*)(ii) formerly read:

(ii) does not arise with respect to a disposition (other than a disposition to which subsection (9) applies) by the affiliate of property to another foreign affiliate of the taxpayer or to a person with whom the taxpayer does not deal at arm's length, to which a tax deferral, rollover or similar tax postponement provision of the income tax law that is relevant in computing the earnings amount of the affiliate applied, and

S. 5907(2)(*j*)(iii) was replaced by S.C. 2013, c. 34, s. 85(35), applicable in respect of dispositions of property by a foreign affiliate of a taxpayer that occur after August 19, 2011. However, if the taxpayer has elected under subsection 5907(2.01),

(*a*) subparagraph 5907(2)(*j*)(iii) applies in respect of dispositions of property by all foreign affiliates of the taxpayer that occur after December 20, 2002;

(*c*) subparagraph 5907(2)(*j*)(iii) is, in respect of all such dispositions that occur on or before August 19, 2011, to be read as follows:

"(iii) subject to subsection (2.01), does not arise with respect to a disposition (other than a disposition to which subsection (9) applies) by the affiliate of property to another foreign affiliate of the taxpayer or to a person with whom the taxpayer does not deal at arm's length, to which a loss deferral or similar loss postponement provision of the income tax law that is relevant in computing the earnings amount of the affiliate applied, and"

See the application for the amendment to the portion of the definition "earnings" before subparagraph (*a*)(iii) in s. 5907(1) for the extension of assessment periods to take into account the amendments by S.C. 2013, c. 34, s. 54 to 89.

S. 5907(2)(*j*)(iii) formerly read:

(iii) does not arise with respect to a disposition (other than a disposition to which subsection (9) applies) by the affiliate of property to another foreign affiliate of the taxpayer or to a person with whom the taxpayer does not deal at arm's length, to which a loss deferral or similar loss postponement provision of the income tax law that is relevant in computing the earnings amount of the affiliate applied, and

S. 5907(2)(*l*) was replaced by S.C. 2013, c. 34, s. 85(36), applicable in respect of dispositions of property by a foreign affiliate of a taxpayer that occur after August 19, 2011.

See the application for the amendment to the portion of the definition "earnings" before subparagraph (*a*)(iii) in s. 5907(1) for the extension of assessment periods to take into account the amendments by S.C. 2013, c. 34, s. 54 to 89.

S. 5907(2)(*l*) formerly read:

(*l*) where any property of the affiliate acquired from another foreign affiliate of the taxpayer or from any foreign affiliate of a person resident in Canada with whom the taxpayer does not deal at arm's length has been disposed of, such amount in respect of that property as may reasonably be considered as having been included by virtue of paragraph (*f*) in computing the earnings amount of any foreign affiliate of the taxpayer or of a person resident in Canada with whom the taxpayer does not deal at arm's length.

(2.01) Subparagraphs (2)(*f*)(ii) and (*j*)(iii) and subsection (5.1) do not apply to a particular disposition of property (referred to in this subsection as the "affiliate property") by a particular foreign affiliate of a taxpayer if

(*a*) the only consideration received in respect of the particular disposition is shares of the capital stock of another foreign affiliate of the taxpayer;

(*b*) all of the shares of the capital stock of the other affiliate that are, immediately after the particular disposition, owned by the particular affiliate are disposed of, at a particular time that is within 90 days of the day that includes the time of the particular disposition, to a person or partnership that at the particular time is not a designated person or partnership in respect of the taxpayer; and

(*c*) the affiliate property is not disposed of by the other affiliate as part of a series of transactions or events that includes the particular disposition.

History: S. 5907(2.01) was added by S.C. 2013, c. 34, s. 85(37), applicable to dispositions by a foreign affiliate of a taxpayer that occur after August 19, 2011. However, if the taxpayer elects in writing in respect of all of its foreign affiliates and files the election with the Minister of National Revenue on or before the day that is the later of the taxpayer's filing-due date for the taxpayer's taxation year that includes June 26, 2013 and June 26, 2014, that subsection 5907(2.01) applies to dispositions by all foreign affiliates of the taxpayer that occur after December 20, 2002.

See the application for the amendment to the portion of the definition "earnings" before subparagraph (*a*)(iii) in s. 5907(1) for the extension of assessment periods to take into account the amendments by S.C. 2013, c. 34, s. 54 to 89.

Canadian Tax Foundation: Barnicke and Huynh, *Packaging Rule in Regulation 5907(2.01) Deficient*, 2015 Canadian Tax Highlights 23(10):6.

(2.011) Subparagraphs (2)(*f*)(ii) and (*j*)(iii) and subsection (5.1) do not apply to a particular disposition of property (referred to in this subsection as the "affiliate property") by a particular foreign affiliate of a taxpayer to another foreign affiliate of the taxpayer if

(*a*) the particular disposition is a disposition referred to in subparagraph 15(1.5)(*c*)(i) of the Act;

(*b*) all of the shares of the capital stock of the other affiliate are owned, at a particular time that is within 180 days after the day that includes the time of the particular disposition, by a person or partnership that at the particular time is not a designated person or partnership in respect of the taxpayer; and

(*c*) the affiliate property is not disposed of by the other affiliate as part of a series of transactions or events that includes the particular disposition.

History: S. 5907(2.011) was added by S.C. 2018, c. 27, s. 39(4), in respect of dispositions that occur after October 23, 2012.

Related Sections: 15(1.5) Division of corporation under foreign laws.

(2.02) If an amount or a portion of an amount would, in the absence of this subsection, be included in computing the exempt earnings, or deducted in computing the exempt loss, of a foreign affiliate of a corporation in respect of the corporation for a taxation year of the affiliate and the amount or portion arises from a disposition of property (other than money), at any time, to a person or partnership that was, at that time, a designated person or partnership in respect of the corporation where that disposition is a transaction (within the meaning of subsection 245(1) of the Act) that is, or would be (if the amount or portion were a tax benefit for the purposes of section 245 of the Act), an avoidance transaction (within the meaning of subsection 245(3) of the Act), the following rules apply:

(*a*) the amount or portion is instead to be included in the affiliate's taxable earnings for the year in respect of the corporation; and

(*b*) any income or profits tax relating to the transaction that would otherwise be deducted in computing the exempt earnings, or included in computing the exempt loss, of the affiliate for the year in respect of the corporation, is instead to be deducted from the affiliate's taxable earnings for the year in respect of the corporation.

History: S. 5907(2.02) was added by S.C. 2013, s. 85(37), applicable in respect of transactions (within the meaning of subsection 245(1) of the Act) that are entered into after August 19, 2011.

See the application for the amendment to the portion of the definition "earnings" before subparagraph (*a*)(iii) in s. 5907(1) for the extension of assessment periods to take into account the amendments by S.C. 2013, c. 34, s. 54 to 89.

(2.03) The determination — under subparagraph (*a*)(iii) and paragraph (*b*) of the definition "earnings", and paragraph (*b*) of the definition "loss", in subsection (1) — of the earnings or loss of a foreign affiliate of a taxpayer resident in Canada for a particular taxation year from an active business is to be made as if the affiliate

(*a*) had, in computing its income or loss from the business for each taxation year (referred to in this paragraph as an "earnings or loss year") that is the particular year or is any preceding taxation year that ends after August 19, 2011,

(i) claimed all deductions that it could have claimed under the Act, up to the maximum amount deductible in computing the income or loss from the business for that earnings or loss year, and

(ii) made all claims and elections and taken all steps under applicable provisions of the Act, or of enactments implementing amendments to the Act or its regulations, to maximize the amount of any deduction referred to subparagraph (i); and

(*b*) had, in computing its income or loss from the business for any preceding taxation year that ended on or before August 19, 2011, claimed all deductions, if any, that it actually claimed under the Act, up to the maximum amount deductible, and made all claims and elections, if any, and taken all steps, if any, under applicable provisions of the Act, or of enactments implementing amendments to the Act or its regulations, that it actually made.

History: S. 5907(2.03) was added by S.C. 2013, s. 85(37), applicable in respect of taxation years of a foreign affiliate of a taxpayer that end after August 19, 2011.

See the application for the amendment to the portion of the definition "earnings" before subparagraph (*a*)(iii) in s. 5907(1) for the extension of assessment periods to take into account the amendments by S.C. 2013, c. 34, s. 54 to 89.

(2.1) In computing the earnings of a foreign affiliate of a corporation resident in Canada for a taxation year of the affiliate from an active business carried on by it in Canada or in a designated treaty country, where the affiliate is resident in a designated treaty country and the corporation, together with all other corporations resident in Canada with which the corporation does not deal at arm's length and in respect of which the affiliate is a foreign affiliate, have so elected in respect of the business for the taxation year or any preceding taxation year of the affiliate, the following rules apply:

(*a*) there shall be added to the amount determined under subparagraph (*a*)(i) of the definition "earnings" in subsection (1) after adjustment in accordance with the provisions of subsection (2) (in this subsection and in subsection (2.2) referred to as the "adjusted earnings amount") the total of all amounts each of which is the amount, if any, by which

(i) the amount that can reasonably be regarded as having been deducted in respect of the cost of a capital property or foreign resource property of the affiliate in computing the adjusted earnings amount

exceeds

(ii) the amount that may reasonably be regarded as having been deducted in respect of the cost of that capital property or foreign resource property in computing income or profit of the affiliate for the year from that business in its financial statements prepared in accordance with the laws of the country in which the affiliate is resident;

(*b*) there shall be deducted from the adjusted earnings amount the aggregate of all amounts each of which is the amount, if any, by which

(i) the amount determined under subparagraph (*a*)(ii) in respect of that capital property or foreign resource property

exceeds

(ii) the amount determined under subparagraph (*a*)(i) in respect of that capital property or foreign resource property;

Regulations

(*c*) where any capital property or foreign resource property of the affiliate has been disposed of in the taxation year,

(i) there shall be added to the adjusted earnings amount the aggregate of the amounts deducted pursuant to paragraphs (*b*) and (2.2)(*b*) for preceding taxation years of the affiliate in respect of that capital property or foreign resource property, and

(ii) there shall be deducted from the adjusted earnings amount the aggregate of the amounts added pursuant to paragraphs (*a*) and (2.2)(*a*) for the preceding taxation years of the affiliate in respect of that capital property or foreign resource property; and

(*d*) for the purposes of paragraph (*c*), where the affiliate has merged with one or more corporations to form a new corporation, any capital property or foreign resource property of the affiliate that becomes a property of the new corporation shall be deemed to have been disposed of by the affiliate in its last taxation year before the merger.

Information Circulars: IC 77-9R Books, records and other requirements for taxpayers having foreign affiliates; IC 07-1 Taxpayer relief provisions.

(2.2) Where the taxation year of a foreign affiliate of a particular corporation resident in Canada for which the particular corporation has made an election under subsection (2.1) in respect of an active business carried on by the affiliate is not the first taxation year of the affiliate in which it carried on the business and in which it was a foreign affiliate of the particular corporation or of another corporation resident in Canada with which the particular corporation was not dealing at arm's length at any time (hereinafter referred to as the "non-arm's length corporation"), in computing the earnings of the affiliate from the business for the taxation year for which the election is made, the following rules, in addition to those set out in subsection (2.1), apply:

(*a*) there shall be added to the adjusted earnings amount the aggregate of all amounts each of which is an amount that would have been determined under paragraph (2.1)(*a*) or subparagraph (2.1)(*c*)(i)

(i) for any preceding taxation year of the affiliate in which it was a foreign affiliate of the particular corporation if the particular corporation had made an election under subsection (2.1) for the first taxation year of the affiliate in which it was a foreign affiliate of the particular corporation and carried on the business, and

(ii) for any preceding taxation year of the affiliate (other than a taxation year referred to in subparagraph (i)) in which it was a foreign affiliate of the non-arm's length corporation if the non-arm's length corporation had made an election under subsection (2.1) for the first taxation year of the affiliate in which it was a foreign affiliate of the non-arm's length corporation and carried on the business; and

(*b*) there shall be deducted from the adjusted earnings amount the aggregate of all amounts each of which is an amount that would have been determined under paragraph (2.1)(*b*) or subparagraph (2.1)(*c*)(ii)

(i) for any preceding taxation year of the affiliate in which it was a foreign affiliate of the particular corporation if the particular corporation had made an election under subsection (2.1) for the first taxation year of the affiliate in which it was a foreign affiliate of the particular corporation and carried on the business, and

(ii) for any preceding taxation year of the affiliate (other than a taxation year referred to in subparagraph (i)) in which it was a foreign affiliate of the non-arm's length corporation if the non-arm's length corporation had made an election under subsection (2.1) for the first taxation year of the affiliate in which it was a foreign affiliate of the non-arm's length corporation and carried on the business.

(2.3) For the purposes of this subsection and subsections (2.1) and (2.2), where an election under subsection (2.1) has been made by a corporation resident in Canada (in this subsection and in subsection (2.4) referred to as the "electing corporation") in respect of an active business of a foreign affiliate of the electing corporation and the affiliate subsequently becomes a foreign affiliate of another corporation resident in Canada (in this subsection and in subsection (2.4) referred to as the "subsequent corporation") that does not deal at arm's length with the electing corporation, in computing the earnings of the affiliate from such business in respect of the subsequent corporation for any taxation year of the affiliate ending after the affiliate so became a foreign affiliate of the subsequent corporation, the subsequent corporation shall be deemed to have made an election under subsection (2.1) in respect of the business of the affiliate for the first such taxation year and for the purposes of paragraph (2.1)(*d*), the earnings of the affiliate for all of the preceding taxation years shall be deemed to have been adjusted in accordance with subsections (2.1) and (2.2) in the same manner as if the subsequent corporation had been the electing corporation.

(2.4) For the purposes of subsection (2.3)

(*a*) a corporation formed as a result of a merger, to which section 87 of the Act applies, of the electing corporation and one or more other corporations, or

(*b*) a corporation that has acquired shares of the capital stock of a foreign affiliate, in respect of which an election under subsection (2.1) has been made, from the electing corporation in a transaction in respect of which an election under section 85 of the Act was made

shall be deemed to be a subsequent corporation that does not deal at arm's length with the electing corporation.

(2.5) (Repealed by P.C. 1997-1670, SOR/97-505,.)

(2.6) A corporation resident in Canada, and all other corporations resident in Canada with which the corporation does not deal at arm's length, shall each be considered to have elected under subsection (2.1) in respect of an active business carried on by a non-resident corporation that is a foreign affiliate of each such corporation for a taxation year if there is filed with the Minister on or before the day that is the later of

(*a*) June 30, 1986, and

(*b*) the earliest of the days on or before which any one of the said corporations is required to file a return of income pursuant to section 150 of the Act for its taxation year following the taxation year in which the taxation year of the affiliate in respect of which the election is made ends,

the following information:

(*c*) a description of the active business sufficient to identify the business, and

(*d*) a statement on behalf of each such corporation, signed by an authorized official of the corporation on behalf of which the statement is made, that the corporation is electing under subsection (2.1) in respect of the business.

(2.7) Notwithstanding any other provision of this Part, if an amount (referred to in this subsection as the "inclusion amount") is included in computing the income or loss from an active business of a foreign affiliate of a taxpayer for a taxation year under subparagraph 95(2)(*a*)(i) or (ii) of the Act and the inclusion amount is in respect of a particular amount paid or payable,

(*a*) if clause 95(2)(*a*)(ii)(D) of the Act is applicable, by the second affiliate referred to in that clause,

(i) the particular amount is to be deducted in computing the second affiliate's income or loss from an active business carried on by it in the country in which it is resident for its earliest taxation year in which that amount was paid or payable,

(ii) the second affiliate is deemed to have carried on an active business in that country for that earliest taxation year, and

(iii) in computing the second affiliate's income or loss for a taxation year from any source, no amount is to be deducted in respect of the particular amount except as required under subparagraph (i); and

(*b*) in any other case, by the other foreign affiliate referred to in subparagraph 95(2)(*a*)(i) or (ii) of the Act, as the case may be, or by a partnership of which the other foreign affiliate is a member, the particular amount is, except where it has been deducted under paragraph (2)(*j*) in computing the other foreign affiliate's earnings or loss from an active business,

(i) to be deducted in computing the earnings or loss of the other foreign affiliate or the partnership, as the case may be, from the active business for its earliest taxation year in which the particular amount was paid or payable, and

(ii) not to be deducted in computing its earnings or loss from the active business for any other taxation year.

History: S. 5907(2.7) was replaced by S.C. 2013. c. 34, s. 46(35), applicable to taxation years of a foreign affiliate of a taxpayer that begin after 2008.

See the application following the amendment to subparagraph (*a*)(ii) of the definition "exempt earnings" in s. 5907(1), regarding the override of the statute-barring rules for assessments for taxation years that end before June 26, 2013.

S. 5907(2.7) formerly read:

(2.7) Notwithstanding any other provision of this Part, where

(*a*) an amount is included in computing the income or loss from an active business of a particular foreign affiliate of a taxpayer for a particular taxation year under subparagraph 95(2)(*a*)(i) or ii of the Act, and

(*b*) the amount included is in respect of an amount paid or payable (other than an amount paid or payable that is described in clause 95(2)(*a*)(ii)(D) of the Act) by another non-resident corporation described in subparagraph 95(2)(*a*)(i) or (ii) of the Act or by a partnership of which such a corporation is a member,

the amount (in respect of which an amount was included in the income or loss from an active business of the particular affiliate for the particular year) paid or payable by the non-resident corporation or the partnership shall, except where it has been deducted under paragraph (2)(*j*) in computing the non-resident corporation's earnings or loss from an active business, be deducted in computing the earnings or loss of the non-resident corporation or the partnership, as the case may be, from the active business for its earliest taxation year in which the amount was paid or payable and shall not be deducted in computing its earnings or loss from the active business for any other taxation year.

(2.8) (Repealed by S.C. 2013, c. 34, s. 46(35).)

History: S. 5907(2.8) was repealed by S.C. 2013. c. 34, s. 46(35), applicable to taxation years of a foreign affiliate of a taxpayer that begin after 2008.

See the application following the amendment to subparagraph (*a*)(ii) of the definition "exempt earnings" in s. 5907(1), regarding the override of the statute-barring rules for assessments for taxation years that end before June 26, 2013.

S. 5907(2.8) formerly read:

(2.8) Notwithstanding any other provision of this Part, where

(*a*) an amount is included in computing the income from an active business of a particular foreign affiliate of a taxpayer or a person related to the taxpayer for a particular taxation year under clause 95(2)(*a*)(ii)(D) of the Act, and

(*b*) the amount included is in respect of an amount of interest paid or payable by another non-resident corporation (in this subsection referred to as the "second affiliate") to which the particular affiliate and the taxpayer are related

the following rules apply:

(*c*) that amount of interest shall be deducted in computing the second affiliate's income or loss, from an active business carried on by it in a country in which it is resident and subject to income taxation, for its earliest taxation year in which the amount was paid or payable,

(*d*) the second affiliate is deemed to have carried on an active business in a country in which it was resident and subject to income taxation for each taxation year referred to in paragraph (*c*) in which such an active business was not otherwise carried on by it, and

(*e*) in computing the second affiliate's income for a taxation year from any source, no amount shall be deducted in respect of an amount paid or payable by it that is referred to in paragraph (*c*) except as is required under that paragraph.

(2.9) If paragraph 95(2)(*k.1*) of the Act applies in respect of a particular taxation year of a foreign affiliate of a taxpayer or in respect of a particular fiscal period of a partnership (which foreign affiliate or partnership is referred to in this subsection as the "operator" and which particular taxation year or particular fiscal period is referred to in this subsection as the "specified taxation year") a member of which is, at the end of the period, a foreign affiliate of a taxpayer,

(*a*) in computing the affiliate's earnings or loss from the foreign business referred to in that paragraph for the affiliate's taxation year (referred to in subparagraphs (i) and (ii) as the "preceding taxation year") that includes the day that is immediately before the beginning of the specified taxation year,

(i) there is to be added to the amount determined under paragraph (*a*) of the definition "earnings" in subsection (1), after adjustment in accordance with subsections (2) to (2.2),

Regulations

(A) where the operator is the affiliate, the total of

(I) the amount, if any, by which the total determined under sub-subclause (ii)(A)(I)2 in respect of the operator for the preceding taxation year exceeds the total determined under sub-subclause (ii)(A)(I)1 in respect of the operator for that year, and

(II) if the operator was deemed under paragraph 95(2)(*k.1*) of the Act to have, at the end of the preceding taxation year, disposed of property owned by it that was used or held by it in the course of carrying on the foreign business in that year, the amount that is the total of all amounts each of which is determined by the formula

$$(A - B) - C$$

where

A is the fair market value, immediately before the end of that year, of a property deemed because of that paragraph to have been disposed of,

B is the amount determined under paragraph (*a*) of the definition "relevant cost base" in subsection 95(4) of the Act in respect of the property, in respect of the taxpayer, immediately before the time of the disposition, and

C is the amount, if any, of the capital gain determined in respect of the disposition of the property at that time, and

(B) where the operator is the partnership, the amount determined under subsection 5908(13); and

(ii) there is to be added to the amount determined under paragraph (*a*) of the definition "loss" in subsection (1),

(A) where the operator is the affiliate, the total of

(I) the amount, if any, by which

1. the total of all amounts each of which is an amount deemed under paragraph 95(2)(*k.1*) of the Act to have been claimed under any of paragraphs 20(1)(*l*), (*l.1*) and (7)(*c*), and subparagraphs 138(3)(*a*)(i), (ii) and (iv), of the Act (each of which provisions is referred to in this subparagraph as a "reserve provision") in computing the income from the foreign business for the preceding taxation year

exceeds

2. the total of all amounts each of which is an amount actually claimed by the operator as a reserve in computing its income from the foreign business for that year that can reasonably be considered to be in respect of amounts in respect of which a reserve could have been claimed under a reserve provision on the assumption that the operator could have claimed amounts in respect of the reserve provisions for that year, and

(II) the total of all amounts each of which is the amount, if any, by which the amount determined under the description of B in the formula in subclause (i)(A)(II) in respect of a property described in that subclause exceeds the amount determined under the description of A in the formula in that clause in respect of the property, and

(B) where the operator is the partnership, the amount determined under subsection 5908(13); and

(*b*) any property of the operator that is, under that paragraph, deemed to have been disposed of and reacquired by the operator is, for the purposes of this section, deemed to have been disposed of and reacquired by the operator in the same manner and for the same amounts as if that paragraph applied for the purposes of this section.

History: S. 5907(2.9) was replaced by S.C. 2013, c. 34, s. 85(38), applicable iln respect of taxation years of a foreign affiliate of a taxpayer that begin after December 20, 2002. However, if the taxpayer makes the election for the application in s. 95(2)(*j.1*) to (*k.2*), s. 5907(2.9) applies in respect of taxation years of all foreign affiliates of the taxpayer that begin after 1994.

See the application for the amendment to the portion of the definition "earnings" before subparagraph (*a*)(iii) in s. 5907(1) for the extension of assessment periods to take into account the amendments by S.C. 2013, c. 34, s. 54 to 89.

S. 5907(2.9) formerly read:

(2.9) In computing the earnings from an active business of a foreign affiliate of a corporation resident in Canada for the affiliate's taxation year immediately before the particular taxation year of the affiliate referred to in paragraph 95(2)(*k*) of the Act,

(*a*) there shall be added to the amount determined under subparagraph (*a*)(i) or (ii) of the definition "earnings" in subsection (1) after adjustment in accordance with subsections (2), (2.1) and (2.2) the total of

(i) the amount, if any, by which the total determined in respect of the affiliate in clause (*b*)(i)(B) for the year exceeds the total determined in respect of the affiliate in clause (*b*)(i)(A) for the year,

(ii) where, at the end of the year, the affiliate was deemed because of paragraphs 95(2)(*k*) and 138(11.91)(*e*) of the Act to have disposed of property owned by it that was used or held by it in the course of carrying on the active business in the year, the amount that is the total of all amounts each of which is the amount, if any, by which

(A) the lesser of the fair market value and the cost to the affiliate at the end of the year of a capital property (referred to in this subparagraph and subparagraph (*b*)(ii) as a "particular depreciable asset") owned by it that

(I) was used or held by it in the course of carrying on the active business in the year,

(II) was deemed because of paragraphs 95(2)(*k*) and 138(11.91)(*e*) of the Act to have been disposed of at the end of the year, and

(III) was property in respect of the cost of which amounts were, at any time, deductible in computing the earnings from the active business under subparagraph (*a*)(i) or (ii) of the definition "earnings" in subsection (1)

exceeds

(B) the amount, if any, by which the cost to the affiliate of the particular depreciable asset exceeds the total of all amounts each of which is an amount that can reasonably be regarded as having been deducted in respect of the cost of the particular depreciable asset in computing the earnings (as would be defined in subsection (1) if that definition were read as if the reference in that definition to this subsection did not exist) of the affiliate from the active business in the year or in any preceding taxation year of the affiliate in which it was a foreign affiliate of the corporation or of another corporation resident in Canada with which the corporation was not dealing at arm's length at any time, and

(iii) where, at the end of the year, the affiliate was deemed because of paragraphs 95(2)(*k*) and 138(11.91)(*e*) of the Act to have disposed of property (other than capital property) owned by it that was used or held by it in the course of carrying on the active business in the year, the amount that is the total of all amounts each of which is an amount, if any, by which the fair market value of such a property exceeds the cost to the affiliate of the property at the time that is immediately before the end of the year; and

(*b*) there shall be deducted from the amount determined under su paragraph (*a*)(i) or (ii) of the definition "earnings" in subsection (1) after adjustment in accordance with subsections (2), (2.1) and (2.2) the total of

(i) the amount, if any, by which

(A) the total of all amounts each of which is a maximum amount deemed because of paragraphs 95(2)(*k*) and 138(11.91)(*d*) of the Act to have been claimed under subparagraphs 138(3)(*a*)(i), (ii) and (iv) and paragraphs 20(1)(*1*) and (*l*.1) and 20(7)(*c*) of the Act (each of which provisions is referred to in this subparagraph as a "reserve provision") in the year

exceeds

(B) the total of all amounts each of which is an amount actually claimed by the affiliate as a reserve in the year that can reasonably be considered to be in respect of amounts in respect of which a reserve could have been claimed under a reserve provision on the assumption that the affiliate could have claimed amounts in respect of the reserve provisions in the year,

(ii) the amount that is the total of all amounts each of which is the amount, if any, by which the amount determined under clause (*a*)(ii)(B) in respect of a particular depreciable asset described in clause (*a*)(ii)(A) exceeds the fair market value of the particular depreciable asset at the end of the year, and

(iii) where, at the end of the year, the affiliate was deemed because of paragraphs 95(2)(*k*) and 138(11.91)(*e*) of the Act to have disposed of property (other than capital property) owned by it that was used or held by it in the course of carrying on the active business in the year, the amount that is the total of all amounts each of which is an amount, if any, by which the cost to the affiliate of such a property at the time that is immediately before the end of the year exceeds the fair market value of the property at the end of the year.

(3) For the purposes of this Part, any corporation that was, on January 1, 1972, a foreign affiliate of a taxpayer shall be deemed to have become a foreign affiliate of the taxpayer on that day.

(4) For the purposes of this Part, "government of a country" includes the government of a state, province or other political subdivision of that country.

(5) For the purposes of this section, each capital gain, capital loss, taxable capital gain or allowable capital loss of a foreign affiliate of a taxpayer from the disposition of property is to be computed in accordance with the rules set out in subsection 95(2) of the Act.

History: S. 5907(5) was replaced by S.C. 2013, c. 34, s. 85(39), deemed to have come into force on August 20, 2011.

See the application for the amendment to the portion of the definition "earnings" before subparagraph (*a*)(iii) in s. 5907(1) for the extension of assessment periods to take into account the amendments by S.C. 2013, c. 34, s. 54 to 89.

S. 5907(5) formerly read:

(5) For the purposes of this section, each capital gain, capital loss, taxable capital gain or allowable capital loss of a foreign affiliate of a taxpayer from the disposition of property shall be computed in accordance with the rules set out in subsection 95(2) of the Act and, for the purposes of subsection (6), if any such gain or loss is required to be computed in Canadian currency, the amount of such gain or loss shall be converted from Canadian currency into the currency referred to in subsection (6) at the rate of exchange prevailing on the date of disposition of the property.

S. 5907(5) was replaced by S.C. 2013, c. 34, s. 46(36), applicable to taxation years of a foreign affiliate of a taxpayer that begin after December 18, 2009.

See the application following the amendment to subparagraph (*a*)(ii) of the definition "exempt earnings" in s. 5907(1), regarding the override of the statute-barring rules for assessments for taxation years that end before June 26, 2013.

S. 5907(5) formerly read:

(5) For the purposes of this section, each capital gain and each capital loss of a foreign affiliate of a taxpayer from the disposition of property shall be computed in accordance with the rules set out in subsection 95(2) of the Act and, for the purposes of subsection (6), where any such gain or loss is required to be computed in Canadian currency, the amount of such gain or loss shall be converted from Canadian currency into the currency referred to in subsection (6) at the rate of exchange prevailing on the date of disposition of the property.

(5.01) For the purposes of subsection (6), if any capital gain, capital loss, taxable capital gain or allowable capital loss referred to in subsection (5), or any capital loss referred to in subparagraph (iii) of the description of B in the definition "hybrid surplus" in subsection (1), of a foreign affiliate of a corporation is required to be computed in Canadian currency and the currency referred to in subsection (6) is not Canadian currency, the amount of the gain or loss is to be converted from Canadian currency into the currency referred to in subsection (6) at the rate of exchange prevailing on the date of disposition of the property.

History: S. 5907(5.01) was added by S.C. 2013, c. 34, s. 85(39), deemed to have come into force on August 20, 2011.

See the application for the amendment to the portion of the definition "earnings" before subparagraph (*a*)(iii) in s. 5907(1) for the extension of assessment periods to take into account the amendments by S.C. 2013, c. 34, s. 54 to 89.

(5.1) Notwithstanding subsection (5), if, under the income tax laws of a country other than Canada that are relevant in computing the earnings of a foreign affiliate of a taxpayer resident in Canada from an active business carried on by it in a country, no gain or loss is recognized in respect of a disposition (other than a disposition to which subsection (9) applies) by the affiliate of a capital property used or held principally for the purpose of gaining or producing income from an active business to a person or partnership (in this subsection referred to as the "transferee") that was, at the time of the disposition, a designated person or partnership in respect of the taxpayer, for the purposes of this section,

(*a*) the affiliate's proceeds of disposition of the property shall be deemed to be an amount equal to the aggregate of the adjusted cost base to the affiliate of the property immediately before the disposition and any outlays and expenses to the extent they were made or incurred by the affiliate for the purpose of making the disposition;

(*b*) the cost to the transferee of the property acquired from the affiliate shall be deemed to be an amount equal to the affiliate's proceeds of disposition, as determined under paragraph (*a*); and

(*c*) the transferee shall be deemed to have acquired the property on the date that it was acquired by the affiliate.

History: S. 5907(5.1), the portion before paragraph (*a*) was replaced by S.C. 2013, c. 34, s. 85(40), applicable to dispositions that occur after August 19, 2011.

See the application for the amendment to the portion of the definition "earnings" before subparagraph (*a*)(iii) in s. 5907(1) for the extension of assessment periods to take into account the amendments by S.C. 2013, c. 34, s. 54 to 89.

S. 5907(5.1), the portion before paragraph (*a*) formerly read:

(5.1) Notwithstanding subsection (5) and except as provided in subsection (9), where, under the income tax law of a country other than Canada that is relevant in computing the earnings of a foreign affiliate of a taxpayer resident in Canada from an active business carried on by it in a country, no gain or loss is recognized in respect of a disposition by the affiliate of a capital property used or held principally for the purpose of gaining or producing income from an active business to a person (in this subsection referred to as the "transferee") that is another foreign affiliate of the taxpayer or that is a foreign affiliate of another person with whom the taxpayer does not deal at arm's length, for the purposes of this section,

Regulations

(6) All amounts referred to in subsections (1) and (2) shall be maintained on a consistent basis from year to year in the currency of the country in which the foreign affiliate of the corporation resident in Canada is resident or any currency that the corporation resident in Canada demonstrates to be reasonable in the circumstances.

History: S. 5907(6) was replaced by S.C. 2013, c. 34, s. 46(37), applicable to taxation years of a foreign affiliate of a taxpayer that begin after December 18, 2009.

See the application following the amendment to subparagraph (*a*)(ii) of the definition "exempt earnings" in s. 5907(1), regarding the override of the statute-barring rules for assessments for taxation years that end before June 26, 2013.

S. 5907(6) formerly read:

(6) All amounts referred to in subsections (1) and (2) shall be maintained on a consistent basis from year to year in the currency of the country in which the foreign affiliate of the corporation resident in Canada is itself resident or such currency, other than Canadian currency, as is reasonable in the circumstances.

Information Circulars: IC 77-9R Books, records and other requirements for taxpayers having foreign affiliates.

(7) For the purposes of this Part, the amount of any stock dividend paid by a foreign affiliate of a corporation resident in Canada on a share of a class of its capital stock shall be deemed to be nil.

(7.1) (Repealed by S.C. 2013, c. 34, S. 85(41).)

History: S. 5907(7.1) was repealed by S.C. 2013, c. 34 , s. 85(41), deemed to have come into force on August 20, 2011.

See the application for the amendment to the portion of the definition "earnings" before subparagraph (*a*)(iii) in s. 5907(1) for the extension of assessment periods to take into account the amendments by S.C. 2013, c. 34, s. 54 to 89.

S. 5907(7.1) formerly read:

(7.1) Where, at any time in a taxation year of a corporation resident in Canada, a foreign affiliate of the corporation (in this subsection referred to as the "payor affiliate") pays a dividend on the shares of any class of its capital stock to the corporation (in this subsection referred to as the "particular dividend") and as a result of the payment the corporation is entitled to a tax credit from the government of the country in which the payor affiliate is resident,

(*a*) if the particular dividend was paid on or after the day on which this subsection comes into force, or

(*b*) if the particular dividend was paid before the day on which this subsection comes into force and in a taxation year commencing after 1978 and the corporation elects in respect of the tax credit in its return of income for the 1985, 1986, 1987, 1988 or 1989 taxation year required to be filed pursuant to subsection 150(1) of the Act,

for the purpose of this Part, the following rules apply:

(*c*) the tax credit shall be deemed to be a dividend paid at that time by the payor affiliate on the shares of that class of its capital stock to the corporation,

(*d*) immediately before that time there shall be added to the exempt surplus of the payor affiliate an amount equal to the proportion of the tax credit that

(i) the portion of the particular dividend that would, were the corporation not entitled to the tax credit, be deemed by subsection 5900(1) to have been paid out of the payor affiliate's exempt surplus in respect of the corporation

is of

(ii) the particular dividend,

(*e*) immediately before that time, there shall be added to the taxable surplus of the payor affiliate an amount equal to the proportion of the tax credit that

(i) the portion of the particular dividend that would, were the corporation not entitled to the tax credit, be deemed by subsection 5900(1) to have been paid out of the payor affiliate's taxable surplus in respect of the corporation

is of

(ii) the particular dividend, and

(*f*) the foreign tax applicable to the aggregate of

(i) the portion of the particular dividend determined under subparagraph (*e*)(i), and

(ii) the portion of any amount deemed to be a dividend by virtue of paragraph (*c*) that is deemed by subsection 5900(1) to have been paid out of the payor affiliate's taxable surplus in respect of the corporation

shall, notwithstanding paragraph 5900(1)(*d*), be equal to the amount determined under paragraph 5900(1)(*d*) in respect of the amount referred to in paragraph (i), less the amount determined under paragraph (*e*).

(8) For the purposes of computing the various amounts referred to in this section,

(*a*) the first taxation year of a foreign affiliate, of a corporation resident in Canada, that is formed as a result of a *foreign merger* (within the meaning assigned by subsection 87(8.1) of the Act) is deemed to have commenced at the time of the merger, and a taxation year of a *predecessor corporation* (within the meaning assigned by subsection 5905(3)) that would otherwise have ended after that time is deemed to have ended immediately before that time; and

(*b*) if subsection 91(1.2) of the Act applies at any particular time in respect of a foreign affiliate of a corporation, the various amounts are to be computed, in respect of attributed amounts for the stub period in respect of the particular time, as if

(i) the affiliate's taxation year that would have included the particular time ended at the stub-period end time in respect of the particular time, and

(ii) all transactions or events, giving rise to attributed amounts, that occurred at the particular time, occurred at the stub-period end time in respect of the particular time.

History: S. 5907(8) was replaced by S.C. 2017, c. 33, s. 97(2), deemed to have come into force on July 12, 2013, except that if at any time in the period that begins on July 12, 2013 and ends on September 7, 2017, subsection 91(1.2) of the Act (as enacted by S.C. 2017, c. 33, s. 28(1)) applies in respect of a taxpayer, and the taxpayer and all corporations that are connected persons (within the meaning assigned by paragraph (*a*) of the definition *connected person* in subsection 91(1.3) of the Act (as enacted by S.C. 2017, c. 33, s. 28(1))) to the taxpayer at the time file with the Minister an election in prescribed manner on or before the earliest of the filing-due date of the taxpayer and those corporations for their taxation year that includes the day on which this Act receives royal assent [December 14, 2017], for the taxpayer and those corporations, the amendment to s. 5907(8) is deemed to have come into force on September 8, 2017 and not on July 12, 2013. S. 5907(8) formerly read:

(8) For the purposes of computing the various amounts referred to in this section, the first taxation year of a foreign affiliate, of a corporation resident in Canada, that is formed as a result of a foreign merger (within the meaning assigned by subsection 87(8.1) of the Act) is deemed to have commenced at the time of the merger, and a taxation year of a predecessor corporation (within the meaning assigned by subsection 5905(3)) that would otherwise have ended after that time is deemed to have ended immediately before that time.

S. 5907(8) was replaced by S.C. 2013, c. 34, s. 85(42), applicable in respect of mergers or combinations in respect of a foreign affiliate of a taxpayer that occur after August 19, 2011.

See the application for the amendment to the portion of the definition "earnings" before subparagraph (*a*)(iii) in s. 5907(1) for the extension of assessment periods to take into account the amendments by S.C. 2013, c. 34, s. 54 to 89.

S. 5907(8) formerly read:

(8) For the purposes of computing the various amounts referred to in this section, the first taxation year of a foreign affiliate formed as a result of a merger in the manner described in subsection 5905(3) shall be deemed to have commenced at the time of the merger, and a taxation year of a predecessor corporation (within the meaning assigned by subsection 5905(3)) that would otherwise have ended after the merger shall be deemed to have ended immediately before the merger.

(8.1) The following definitions apply in paragraph 5907(8)(*b*).

attributed amounts, for a stub period, in respect of a particular time referred to in paragraph (8)(*b*), of a foreign affiliate of a corporation, means

(*a*) the amounts of any income, gain or loss of the affiliate for the stub period that are relevant in determining amounts that are to be included or may be deducted under section 91 of the Act in respect of the affiliate for the particular stub period, in computing the income of the corporation;

(*b*) any portion of the affiliate's capital gain or capital loss - from a disposition, in the stub period or at the particular time referred to in paragraph (8)(*b*), of a property that is not an excluded property - that is not described in paragraph (*a*); and

(*c*) any income or profits tax paid to the government of a country, in respect of amounts described in paragraph (*a*) or (*b*).

stub period, in respect of a particular time at which subsection 91(1.2) of the Act applies in respect of a foreign affiliate of a corporation, means a period that ends at the stub-period end time in respect of the particular time and begins immediately after the later of

(*a*) the last time, if any, before the particular time that subsection 91(1.2) applied in respect of the affiliate, and

(*b*) the end of the affiliate's last taxation year before the particular time.

stub-period end time, in respect of a particular time at which subsection 91(1.2) of the Act applies in respect of a foreign affiliate of a corporation, means the time that is immediately before the particular time.

History: S. 5907(8.1) was replaced by S.C. 2017, c. 33, s. 97(2), deemed to have come into force on July 12, 2013, except that if at any time in the period that begins on July 12, 2013 and ends on September 7, 2017, subsection 91(1.2) of the Act (as enacted by S.C. 2017, c. 33, s. 28(1)) applies in respect of a taxpayer, and the taxpayer and all corporations that are connected persons (within the meaning assigned by paragraph (*a*) of the definition *connected person* in subsection 91(1.3) of the Act (as enacted by S.C. 2017, c. 33, s. 28(1))) to the taxpayer at the time file with the Minister an election in prescribed manner on or before the earliest of the filing-due date of the taxpayer and those corporations for their taxation year that includes the day on which this Act receives royal assent [December 14, 2017], for the taxpayer and those corporations, the amendment to s. 5907(8.1) is deemed to have come into force on September 8, 2017 and not on July 12, 2013.

(9) If a foreign affiliate of a taxpayer has been liquidated and dissolved (otherwise than as a result of a foreign merger within the meaning assigned by subsection 87(8.1) of the Act), for the purposes of computing the various amounts referred to in this section, the following rules apply:

(*a*) where, at a particular time, property having a fair market value equal to or greater than 90 percent of the fair market value of all of the property that was owned by the affiliate immediately before the commencement of the liquidation and dissolution has been disposed of by the affiliate in the course of the liquidation and dissolution, the taxation year of the affiliate that otherwise would have included the particular time is deemed to have ended immediately before that time; and

(*b*) each property of the affiliate that was disposed of by the affiliate in the course of the liquidation and dissolution is deemed to have been

(i) disposed of by the affiliate, at the time that is the earlier of the time it was actually disposed of and the time that is immediately before the time that is immediately before the particular time, for proceeds of disposition equal to

(A) if the liquidation and dissolution is one to which subsection 88(3) of the Act applies in respect of the disposition, the amount that would, in the absence of subsection 88(3.3) of the Act, be determined under paragraph 88(3)(*a*) or (*b*) of the Act, as the case may be,

(B) if the liquidation and dissolution is one to which paragraph 95(2)(*e*) of the Act applies in respect of the disposition, the amount determined under subparagraph 95(2)(*e*)(i) or (ii) of the Act, as the case may be, and

(C) in any other case, the fair market value of the property at the time it was actually disposed of, and

(ii) acquired by the person or partnership to which the affiliate disposed of the property, at the time it was actually acquired, at a cost equal to the affiliate's proceeds of disposition of the property.

History: S. 5907(9) was replaced by S.C. 2013, c. 34, s. 85(43), applicable in respect of liquidations and dissolutions of foreign affiliates of a taxpayer that begin after December 20, 2002, except that

(*a*) if the taxpayer has made the election under s. 95(2)(*e*) of the Act, paragraph 5907(9)(*b*) is, in respect of liquidations and dissolutions of all foreign affiliates of the taxpayer that begin on or before February 27, 2004, to be read as follows:

"(*b*) each property of the affiliate that was disposed of by the affiliate in the course of the liquidation and dissolution is, subject to subsection 88(3) of the Act, deemed to have been

(i) disposed of by the affiliate, at the time that is the earlier of the time it was actually disposed of and the time that is immediately before the time that is immediately before the particular time, for proceeds of disposition equal to

(A) if the liquidation and dissolution is one to which paragraph 95(2)(*e*) of the Act applies in respect of the disposition, the amount determined under subparagraph 95(2)(*e*)(i) or (ii) of the Act, and

(B) in any other case, the fair market value of the property at the time it was actually disposed of, and

(ii) acquired by the person or partnership to which the affiliate disposed of the property, at the time it was actually acquired, at a cost equal to the affiliate's proceeds of disposition of the property."

(*b*) if the taxpayer has not has made the election under s. 95(2)(*e*) of the Act, paragraph 5907(9)(*b*) is, in respect of liquidations and dissolutions of foreign affiliates of the taxpayer that

(i) begin on or before February 27, 2004, to be read as follows:

"(*b*) each property of the affiliate that was disposed of by the affiliate in the course of the liquidation and dissolution is, subject to subsection 88(3) and paragraphs 95(2)(*e*) and (*e.1*) of the Act, deemed to have been

(i) disposed of by the affiliate, at the time that is the earlier of the time it was actually disposed of and the time that is immediately before the time that is immediately before the particular time, for proceeds of disposition equal to the fair market value of the property at the time it was actually disposed of, and

(ii) acquired by the person or partnership to which the affiliate disposed of the property, at the time it was actually acquired, at a cost equal to the affiliate's proceeds of disposition of the property."

(ii) begin after February 27, 2004 and on or before August 19, 2011, to be read as follows:

"(*b*) each property of the affiliate that was disposed of by the affiliate in the course of the liquidation and dissolution is, subject to paragraphs 95(2)(*e*) and (*e.1*) of the Act, deemed to have been

(i) disposed of by the affiliate, at the time that is the earlier of the time it was actually disposed of and the time that is immediately before the time that is immediately before the particular time, for proceeds of disposition equal to

(A) if the liquidation and dissolution is one to which subsection 88(3) of the Act applies in respect of the disposition, the amount that would (in the absence of subsection 88(3.3) of the Act) be determined under paragraph 88(3)(*a*) or (*b*) of the Act, as the case may be, and

(B) in any other case, the fair market value of the property at the time it was actually disposed of, and

(ii) acquired by the person or partnership to which the affiliate disposed of the property, at the time it was actually acquired, at a cost equal to the affiliate's proceeds of disposition of the property."

See the application for the amendment to the portion of the definition "earnings" before subparagraph (*a*)(iii) in s. 5907(1) for the extension of assessment periods to take into account the amendments by S.C. 2013, c. 34, s. 54 to 89.

S. 5907(9) formerly read:

(9) Where a foreign affiliate of a taxpayer resident in Canada has been dissolved and paragraph 95(2)(*e.1*) of the Act does not apply, for the purpose of computing the various amounts referred to in this section, the following rules apply:

(*a*) where, at a particular time in the course of the dissolution, all or substantially all of the property owned by the affiliate immediately before that time was distributed to the shareholders of the affiliate, the taxation year of the affiliate that otherwise would have included the particular time shall be deemed to have ended immediately before the particular time;

(*b*) except as provided in paragraph 88(3)(*a*) and subparagraph 95(2)(*e*)(i) of the Act,

(i) each property of the affiliate that was distributed to the shareholders in the course of the dissolution shall be deemed to have been disposed of immediately before the end of the affiliate's taxation year deemed to have ended by paragraph (*a*) for proceeds of disposition equal to the fair market value thereof immediately before the particular time, and

(ii) each property of the affiliate that was otherwise disposed of in the course of the dissolution shall be deemed to have been disposed of by the affiliate for proceeds of disposition equal to the fair market value thereof at the time of disposition; and

(*c*) except as provided in subparagraph 95(2)(*e*)(i) of the Act, each property of the dissolved affiliate that was disposed of or distributed in the course of the dissolution to another foreign affiliate of the taxpayer resident in Canada shall be deemed to have been acquired by that other foreign affiliate at a cost equal to the proceeds of disposition of that property to the dissolved affiliate, as determined in paragraph (*b*).

(9.1) Notwithstanding any other provision of this Part, in determining the earnings or loss of a foreign affiliate of a taxpayer resident in Canada, for a taxation year of the affiliate from an active business carried on by it in a country,

(*a*) from a disposition of property to which paragraph 95(2)(*d.1*) of the Act applies, those earnings or that loss are to be determined using the rules in that paragraph; and

(*b*) from a disposition of property acquired in a transaction to which paragraph 95(2)(*d.1*) of the Act applies, the cost to the affiliate of the property is to be determined using the rules in that paragraph.

History: S. 5907(9.1) was added by S.C. 2013, c. 34, s. 85(43), applicable to mergers or combinations in respect of a foreign affiliate of a taxpayer that occur after August 19, 2011. However, if the taxpayer has made the election following s. 95(2)(*d.1*) of the Act, that subsection 5907(9.1) applies to mergers or combinations in respect of all foreign affiliates of the taxpayer that occur after December 20, 2002.

See the application for the amendment to the portion of the definition "earnings" before subparagraph (*a*)(iii) in s. 5907(1) for the extension of assessment periods to take into account the amendments by S.C. 2013, c. 34, s. 54 to 89.

(10) Where

(*a*) the net earnings or net loss for a taxation year of a foreign affiliate of a corporation resident in Canada from an active business carried on in a country other than Canada would otherwise be included in the affiliate's taxable earnings or taxable loss, as the case may be, for the year,

(*b*) the rate of the income or profits tax to which any earnings of that active business of the affiliate are subjected by the government of that country is, by virtue of a special exemption from or reduction of tax (other than an export incentive) that is provided under a law of such country to promote investments or projects in pursuance of a program of economic development, less than the rate of such tax that would, but for such exemption or reduction, be paid by the affiliate, and

(*c*) the affiliate qualified for such exemption from or reduction of tax in respect of an investment made by it in that country before January 1, 1976 or in respect of an investment made by it or a project undertaken by it in that country pursuant to an agreement in writing entered into before January 1, 1976,

for the purposes of this Part, such net earnings or net loss shall be included in the affiliate's exempt earnings or exempt loss, as the case may be, for the year and not in the affiliate's taxable earnings or taxable loss, as the case may be, for the year.

(11) For the purposes of this Part, a sovereign state or other jurisdiction is a "designated treaty country" for a taxation year of a foreign affiliate of a corporation if Canada has entered into a comprehensive agreement or convention for the elimination of double taxation on income, or a comprehensive tax information exchange agreement, in respect of that sovereign state or jurisdiction, that has entered into force and has effect for that taxation year, but any territory, possession, department, dependency or area of that sovereign state or jurisdiction to which that agreement or convention does not apply is not considered to be part of that sovereign state or jurisdiction for the purpose of determining whether it is a designated treaty country.

History: S. 5907(11) was replaced by S.C. 2009, c. 2, s. 112(1), applicable after 2007. S. 5907(11) formerly read:

(11) For the purpose of this Part, a country is a "designated treaty country" for a taxation year of a foreign affiliate of a corporation where Canada and that country have entered into a comprehensive agreement or convention for the elimination of double taxation on income that has entered into force and has effect for that taxation year of the affiliate, but any territory, possession, department, dependency or area of that country to which that agreement or convention does not apply is not included in that designated treaty country.

(11.1) For the purpose of subsection (11), where a comprehensive agreement or convention between Canada and another country for the elimination of double taxation on income has entered into force, that convention or agreement is deemed to have entered into force and have effect in respect of a taxation year of a foreign affiliate of a corporation any day of which is in the period that begins on the day on which the agreement or convention was signed and that ends on the last day of the last taxation year of the affiliate for which the agreement or convention is effective.

(11.11) For the purpose of applying subsection (11) in respect of a foreign affiliate of a corporation, where a comprehensive tax information exchange agreement enters into force on a particular day, the agreement is deemed to enter into force and to come into effect on the first day of the foreign affiliate's taxation year that includes the particular day.

History: S. 5907(11.11) was added by S.C. 2009, c. 2, s. 112(2), applicable after 2007.

(11.2) For the purposes of this Part, a foreign affiliate of a corporation is, at any time, deemed not to be resident in a country with which Canada has entered into a comprehensive agreement or convention for the elimination of double taxation on income unless

(*a*) the affiliate is, at that time, a resident of that country for the purpose of the agreement or convention;

(*b*) the affiliate would, at that time, be a resident of that country for the purpose of the agreement or convention if the affiliate were treated, for the purpose of income taxation in that country, as a body corporate;

(*c*) where the agreement or convention entered into force before 1995, the affiliate would, at that time, be a resident of that country for the purpose of the agreement or convention but for a provision in the agreement or convention that has not been amended after 1994 and that provides that the agreement or convention does not apply to the affiliate; or

(*d*) the affiliate would, at that time, be a resident of that country, as provided by paragraph (*a*), (*b*) or (*c*) if the agreement or convention had entered into force.

(12) (Repealed by S.C. 2013, c. 34, s. 46(38).)

History: S. 5907(12) was repealed by S.C. 2013, c. 34, s. 46(38), deemed to have come into force on December 19, 2009.

See the application following the amendment to subparagraph (*a*)(ii) of the definition "exempt earnings" in s. 5907(1), regarding the override of the statute-barring rules for assessments for taxation years that end before June 26, 2013.

S. 5907(12) formerly read:

(12) For the purposes of paragraph 95(2)(*j*) of the Act, the adjusted cost base to a foreign affiliate of a taxpayer of an interest in a partnership at any time is prescribed to be the cost thereof otherwise determined at that time except that

(*a*) there shall be added to that cost such of the following amounts as are applicable, namely,

(i) any amount included in the earnings of the affiliate for a taxation year ending after 1971 and before that time that may reasonably be considered to relate to profits of the partnership,

(ii) the affiliate's incomes as described by the description of "A" in the definition "foreign accrual property income" in subsection 95(1) of the Act for a taxation year ending after 1971 and before that time that can reasonably be considered to relate to profits of the partnership,

(iii) any amount included in computing the exempt earnings or taxable earnings, as the case may be, of the affiliate for a taxation year ending after 1971 and before that time that may reasonably be considered to relate to a capital gain of the partnership,

(iv) where the affiliate has, at any time before that time and in a taxation year ending after 1971, made a contribution of capital to the partnership otherwise than by way of a loan, such part of the amount of the contribution as cannot reasonably be regarded as a gift made to or for the benefit of any other member of the partnership who was related to the affiliate, and

(v) such portion of any income or profits tax refunded before that time by the government of a country to the partnership as may reasonably be regarded as tax refunded in respect of an amount described in any of subparagraphs (*b*)(i) to (iii), and

(*b*) there shall be deducted from that cost such of the following amounts as are applicable, namely,

(i) any amount included in the loss of the affiliate for a taxation year ending after 1971 that may reasonably be considered to relate to a loss of the partnership,

(ii) the affiliate's losses as described by the description of D in the definition "foreign accrual property income" in subsection 95(1) of the Act for a taxation year ending after 1971 and before that time that can reasonably be considered to relate to the losses of the partnership,

(iii) any amount included in computing the exempt loss or taxable loss, as the case may be, of the affiliate for a taxation year ending after 1971 and before that time that may reasonably be considered to relate to a capital loss of the partnership,

(iv) any amount received by the affiliate before that time and in a taxation year ending after 1971 as, on account or in lieu of payment of, or in satisfaction of, a distribution of his share of the partnership profits or partnership capital, and

(v) such portion of any income or profits tax paid before that time to the government of a country by the partnership as may reasonably be regarded as tax paid in respect of an amount described in any of subparagraphs (*a*)(i) to (iii),

and, for greater certainty, where any interest of a foreign affiliate in a partnership was reacquired by the affiliate after having been previously disposed of, no adjustment that was required to be made under this subsection before such reacquisition shall be made under this subsection to the cost to the affiliate of the interest as reacquired property of the affiliate.

(13) For the purposes of subparagraph (ii) of paragraph 128.1(1)(*d*) of the Act, the prescribed amount is the amount determined by the formula

$$X + Y$$

where

X is the amount, if any, by which

(*a*) the amount, if any, determined by the formula

$$A - B - (C - D) + (E - F)$$

where

A is the taxable surplus of the foreign affiliate of the other taxpayer referred to in that paragraph, in respect of the other taxpayer, at the end of the year referred to in that subparagraph,

B is the affiliate's net earnings for the year in respect of the affiliate's foreign accrual property income for the year to the extent those net earnings have been included in the amount referred to in the description of A,

C is the total of all amounts each of which is the amount by which the affiliate's underlying foreign tax in respect of the other taxpayer at the end of the year would have increased because of the gain or income of the affiliate that would have arisen if a disposition, deemed under paragraph 128.1(1)(*b*) of the Act, of a property by the affiliate had been an actual disposition of the property by the affiliate,

D is the total of all amounts each of which is the amount otherwise added in computing the affiliate's underlying foreign tax in respect of the other taxpayer at the end of the year in respect of income or profits taxes paid to the government of a country in respect of all or a portion of a gain or an income of the affiliate referred to in the description of C,

E is the total of all amounts each of which is the amount by which the affiliate's underlying foreign tax in respect of the other taxpayer at the end of the year would have decreased because of the loss of the affiliate that would have arisen if a disposition, deemed under paragraph 128.1(1)(*b*) of the Act, of a property by the affiliate had been an actual disposition of the property by the affiliate, and

F is the total of all amounts each of which is the amount otherwise deducted in computing the affiliate's underlying foreign tax in respect of the other taxpayer at the end of the year in respect of income or profits taxes refunded by the government of a country in respect of all or a portion of a loss of the affiliate referred to in the description of E

exceeds

(*b*) the amount, if any, determined by the formula

$$[(G - H) \times (J - 1)] + K$$

where

G is the amount determined by the formula

$$L + M - N$$

where

L is the underlying foreign tax of the affiliate in respect of the other taxpayer at the end of the year,

M is the amount, if any, by which the amount determined under the description of C in paragraph (*a*) exceeds the amount determined under the description of D in that paragraph, and

N is the amount, if any, by which the amount determined under the description of E in paragraph (*a*) exceeds the amount determined under the description of F in that paragraph,

H is the portion of the value of L that can reasonably be considered to relate to the affiliate's net earnings for the year in respect of the affiliate's foreign accrual property income,

J is the other taxpayer's relevant tax factor (within the meaning assigned by subsection 95(1) of the Act) for its taxation year that includes the time that is immediately before the particular time, and

K is the amount, if any, by which

(i) the total of all amounts required by paragraph 92(1)(*a*) of the Act to be added at any time in a preceding taxation year in computing the adjusted cost base to the other taxpayer of the shares of the affiliate owned by the other taxpayer at the end of the year

exceeds

(ii) the total of all amounts required by paragraph 92(1)(*b*) of the Act to be deducted at any time in a preceding taxation year in computing the adjusted cost base to the other taxpayer of the shares of the affiliate owned by the other taxpayer at the end of the year, and

Y is the amount, if any, by which

(*a*) the amount, if any, determined by the formula

$$P - (Q - R) + (S - T)$$

where

P is the affiliate's hybrid surplus in respect of the other taxpayer at the end of the year,

Q is the total of all amounts each of which is the amount by which the affiliate's hybrid underlying tax in respect of the other taxpayer at the end of the year would have increased because of the capital gain of the affiliate that would have arisen if a disposition, deemed under paragraph 128.1(1)(*b*) of the Act, of a property by the affiliate had been an actual disposition of the property by the affiliate,

R is the total of all amounts each of which is the amount otherwise added in computing the affiliate's hybrid underlying tax in respect of the other taxpayer at the end of the year in respect of income or profits taxes paid to the government of a country in respect of all or a portion of a capital gain of the affiliate referred to in the description of Q,

S is the total of all amounts each of which is the amount by which the affiliate's hybrid underlying tax in respect of the other taxpayer at the end of the year would have decreased because of the capital loss of the affiliate that would have arisen if a disposition, deemed under paragraph 128.1(1)(*b*) of the Act, of a property by the affiliate had been an actual disposition of the property by the affiliate, and

T is the total of all amounts each of which is the amount otherwise deducted in computing the affiliate's hybrid underlying tax in respect of the other taxpayer at the end of the year in respect of income or profits taxes refunded by the government of a country in respect of all or a portion of a capital loss of the affiliate referred to in the description of S;

exceeds

(*b*) the amount, if any, determined by the formula

$$[U \times (V - 0.5)] + (W \times 0.5)$$

where

U is the amount determined by the formula

$$U.1 + U.2 - U.3$$

where

U.1 is the hybrid underlying tax of the affiliate in respect of the other taxpayer at the end of the year,

U.2 is the amount, if any, by which the amount determined under the description of Q in paragraph (*a*) exceeds the amount determined under the description of R in that paragraph, and

U.3 is the amount, if any, by which the amount determined under the description of S in paragraph (*a*) exceeds the amount determined under the description of T in that paragraph,

V is the other taxpayer's relevant tax factor (within the meaning assigned by subsection 95(1) of the Act) for its taxation year that includes the time that is immediately before the particular time, and

W is the amount determined under paragraph (*a*).

History: S. 5907(13) was replaced by S.C. 2013, c. 34, s. 85(44), applicable after 1992 in respect of a foreign affiliate of a taxpayer. However,

(*a*) if the foreign affiliate elected in accordance with paragraph 111(4)(*a*) of the Statutes of Canada, 1994, chapter 21, subsection 5907(13) applies to the foreign affiliate from the foreign affiliate's time of continuation (within the meaning assigned by that paragraph);

(*b*) in their application in respect of dispositions that occur on or before August 19, 2011, subject to paragraph (*c*) [below], subsection 5907(13) is to be read as follows:

"(13) For the purposes of subparagraph (ii) of paragraph 128.1(1)(*d*) of the Act, the prescribed amount is the amount determined by the formula

$$X - Z$$

where

X is the amount determined by the formula

$$A - B - (C - D)$$

where

A is the taxable surplus of the foreign affiliate of the other taxpayer referred to in that paragraph, in respect of the other taxpayer, at the end of the year referred to in that subparagraph,

B is the affiliate's net earnings for the year in respect of the affiliate's foreign accrual property income for the year to the extent those net earnings have been included in the amount referred to in the description of A,

C is the total of all amounts each of which is the amount by which the affiliate's underlying foreign tax in respect of the other taxpayer at the end of the year would have increased because of the gain or income of the affiliate that would have arisen if a disposition, deemed under paragraph 128.1(1)(*b*) of the Act, of a property by the affiliate had been an actual disposition of the property by the affiliate, and

D is the total of all amounts each of which is the amount otherwise added in computing the affiliate's underlying foreign tax in respect of the other taxpayer at the end of the year in respect of income or profits taxes paid to the government of a country in respect of all or a portion of a gain or an income of the affiliate referred to in the description of C, and

Z is the amount determined by the formula

$$[(G - H) \times (J - 1)] + K$$

where

G is the amount determined by the formula

$$L + M$$

where

L is the underlying foreign tax of the affiliate in respect of the other taxpayer at the end of the year, and

M is the amount, if any, by which the amount determined under the description of C exceeds the amount determined under the description of D,

H is the portion of the value of L that can reasonably be considered to relate to the affiliate's net earnings for the year in respect of the affiliate's foreign accrual property income,

J is the other taxpayer's relevant tax factor (within the meaning assigned by subsection 95(1) of the Act) for its taxation year that includes the time that is immediately before the particular time, and

K is the amount, if any, by which

(i) the total of all amounts required by paragraph 92(1)(*a*) of the Act to be added at any time in a preceding taxation year in computing the adjusted cost base to the other taxpayer of the shares of the affiliate owned by the other taxpayer at the end of the year

exceeds

(ii) the total of all amounts required by paragraph 92(1)(*b*) of the Act to be deducted at any time in a preceding taxation year in computing the adjusted cost base to the other taxpayer of the shares of the affiliate owned by the other taxpayer at the end of the year."

(*c*) in its application in respect of dispositions that occur on or before February 27, 2004, the description of M in subsection 5907(13), as required to be read by subparagraph (*b*) is instead to be read as follows:

"M is the amount that would be determined to be the amount by which the amount determined under the description of C exceeds the amount determined under the description of D if this section were read without reference to subsection (14), and"

See the application for the amendment to the portion of the definition "earnings" before subparagraph (*a*)(iii) in s. 5907(1) for the extension of assessment periods to take into account the amendments by S.C. 2013, c. 34, s. 54 to 89.

S. 5907(13) formerly read:

(13) For the purpose of subparagraph 128.1(1)(*d*)(ii) of the Act, the amount prescribed to be included in the foreign accrual property income of a foreign affiliate of a taxpayer for a taxation year is the amount, if any, by which

(*a*) the taxable surplus of the affiliate in respect of the taxpayer at the end of the year other than the affiliate's net earnings for the year in respect of the affiliate's foreign accrual property income

exceeds the total of

(*b*) the amount determined by the formula

$$(A - B) \times (C - 1)$$

where

A is the total of the underlying foreign tax of the affiliate in respect of the taxpayer at the end of the year and the amount, to the extent that it is not otherwise included in that underlying foreign tax, that would have been added to that underlying foreign tax if each disposition deemed by paragraph 128.1(1)(*b*) of the Act had been an actual disposition,

B is the part of the value of A that can reasonably be considered to relate to the affiliate's net earnings for the year in respect of the affiliate's foreign accrual property income, and

C is the relevant tax factor, as defined in subsection 95(1) of the Act, and

(*c*) the amount, if any, by which

(i) the total of all amounts required by paragraph 92(1)(*a*) of the Act to be added at any time in a preceding taxation year in computing the adjusted cost base to the taxpayer of the shares of the affiliate owned by the taxpayer at the end of the year

exceeds

(ii) the total of all amounts required by paragraph 92(1)(*b*) of the Act to be deducted at any time in a preceding taxation year in computing the adjusted cost base to the taxpayer of the shares of the affiliate owned by the taxpayer at the end of the year.

Interpretation Bulletins: *Secondary* — IT-451R Deemed disposition and acquisition on ceasing to be or becoming resident in Canada.

(14) For the purposes of the description of C in paragraph (*a*) of the description of X in subsection (13) and the description of Q in paragraph (*a*) of the description of Y in subsection (13), the amount by which the underlying foreign tax or the hybrid underlying tax, as the case may be, of the affiliate in respect of the other taxpayer at the end of the year would have increased if a disposition (referred to in this subsection as the "notional actual disposition") deemed under paragraph 128.1(1)(*b*) of the Act of any property by the affiliate had been an actual disposition of the property by the affiliate is the total of all amounts each of which is the amount, if any, by which

(*a*) the amount (determined on the assumption that the notional actual disposition occurred at the time of the deemed disposition) that can reasonably be considered to be the amount of income or profits tax that the affiliate would, because of the notional actual disposition, have had to pay to the government of a particular country (other than Canada), in addition to any other income or profits tax otherwise payable to that government, in relation to the

Regulations

gain or income of the affiliate from the notional actual disposition

exceeds

(*b*) the amount that can reasonably be considered to be the portion of the notional income or profits tax payable by the affiliate to the government of the particular country in relation to the gain or income of the affiliate from the notional actual disposition (determined on the assumptions that the notional actual disposition occurred immediately after the time that is immediately after the time of the deemed disposition and that the notional income or profits tax payable by the affiliate to the government of the particular country in relation to the notional actual disposition is equal to the amount determined under paragraph (*a*)) that, because of a comprehensive agreement or convention for the elimination of double taxation on income between the government of the particular country and the government of any other country, would not have been payable to the government of the particular country.

History: S. 5907(14) was added by S.C. 2013, c. 34, s. 85(44), applicable after 1992 in respect of a foreign affiliate of a taxpayer. However

(*a*) if the foreign affiliate elected in accordance with paragraph 111(4)(*a*) of the Statutes of Canada, 1994, chapter 21, subsection 5907(14) applies to the foreign affiliate from the foreign affiliate's time of continuation (within the meaning assigned by that paragraph);

(*b*) in their application in respect of dispositions that occur on or before August 19, 2011, the portion of subsection 5907(14) of the Regulations before paragraph (*a*) is to be read as follows:

"(14) For the purposes of the description of C in the description of X in subsection (13), the amount by which the underlying foreign tax of the affiliate in respect of the taxpayer at the end of the year would have increased, if a disposition (referred to in this subsection as the "notional actual disposition") deemed under paragraph 128.1(1)(*b*) of the Act of any property by the affiliate had been an actual disposition of the property by the affiliate, is the total of all amounts each of which is the amount, if any, by which"

See the application for the amendment to the portion of the definition "earnings" before subparagraph (*a*)(iii) in s. 5907(1) for the extension of assessment periods to take into account the amendments by S.C. 2013, c. 34, s. 54 to 89.

(15) For the purposes of the description of E in paragraph (*a*) of the description of X in subsection (13) and the description of S in paragraph (*a*) of the description of Y in subsection (13), the amount by which the underlying foreign tax or the hybrid underlying tax, as the case may be, of the affiliate in respect of the other taxpayer at the end of the year would have decreased if a disposition (referred to in this subsection as the "notional actual disposition") deemed under paragraph 128.1(1)(*b*) of the Act of any property by the affiliate had been an actual disposition of the property by the affiliate is the total of all amounts each of which the amount, if any, by which

(*a*) the amount (determined on the assumption that the notional actual disposition occurred at the time of the deemed disposition) that can reasonably be considered to be the amount of income or profits tax that the affiliate would, because of the notional actual disposition, have had refunded to it by the government of a particular country (other than Canada), in addition to any other income or profits tax otherwise refundable by that government, in relation to the loss or capital loss, as the case may be, of the affiliate from the notional actual disposition

exceeds

(*b*) the amount that can reasonably be considered to be the portion of the notional income or profits tax refundable to the affiliate by the government of the particular country in relation to the loss or capital loss, as the case may be, of the affiliate from the notional actual disposition (determined on the assumptions that the notional actual disposition occurred immediately after the time that is immediately after the time of the deemed disposition and that the notional income or profits tax refundable to the affiliate by the government of the particular country in relation to the notional actual disposition is equal to the amount determined by paragraph (*a*)) that, because of a comprehensive agreement or convention for the elimination of double taxation on income between the government of the particular country and the government of any other country, would not have been refundable by the government of the particular country.

History: S. 5907(15) was added by S.C. 2013, c. 34, s. 85(44), applicable in respect of dispositions that occur after August 19, 2011.

See the application for the amendment to the portion of the definition "earnings" before subparagraph (*a*)(iii) in s. 5907(1) for the extension of assessment periods to take into account the amendments by S.C. 2013, c. 34, s. 54 to 89.

5908. [Partnerships]

(1) For the purposes of this subsection, subsections (2) to (7), paragraph 5902(2)(*b*) and section 5905, if at any time shares of a class of the capital stock of a foreign affiliate of a corporation resident in Canada are, based on the assumptions contained in paragraph 96(1)(*c*) of the Act, owned by a partnership, or are deemed under this subsection to be owned by a partnership, each member of the partnership is deemed to own at that time the number of shares of that class that is determined by the formula

$$A \times B/C$$

where

A is the number of shares of that class that are so owned or so deemed owned by the partnership;

B is the fair market value of the member's interest in the partnership at that time; and

C is the fair market value of all members' interests in the partnership at that time.

History: S. 5908(1) was added by S.C. 2013, c. 34, s. 47(1), applicable to taxation years of a foreign affiliate of a taxpayer that begin after November 1999, except that subsection 5908(1) is, in its application to acquisitions, dispositions, redemptions, cancellations, foreign mergers, amalgamations and issuances that occur, and windings-up that begin, on or before December 18, 2009, to be read as follows:

"(1) In determining,

(*a*) for the purposes of this Part (other than section 5904), the equity percentage at any time of a person in a corporation,

(*b*) for the purposes of this section and section 5905, the surplus entitlement at any time of a share owned by a corporation resident in Canada of the capital stock of a foreign affiliate of the corporation in respect of a particular foreign affiliate of the corporation, and

(*c*) for the purposes of this Part and the definition "surplus entitlement percentage" in subsection 95(1) of the Act, the surplus entitlement percentage at any time of a corporation resident in Canada in respect of a particular foreign affiliate of the corporation,

if at any time shares of a class of the capital stock of a corporation are owned by a partnership or are deemed under this subsection to be owned by a partnership, those shares are deemed to be owned at that time by each member of the partnership in a proportion equal to the proportion of all such shares that

(*d*) the fair market value of the member's interest in the partnership at that time

is of

(*e*) the fair market value of all members' interests in the partnership at that time."

Any assessment of a taxpayer's tax, interest and penalties payable under the Act for any taxation year that ends before June 26, 2013 that would otherwise be precluded because of subsections 152(4) to (5) of the Act, shall be made to the extent necessary to take into account this amendment, if the taxpayer

(i) elects in writing in respect of all of its foreign affiliates that this section apply in respect of that provision, and

(ii) files that election with the Minister of National Revenue on or before December 26, 2013 [the day that is six months after royal assent].

(2) For the purposes of subsections (4) and 5905(1), (5) and (7.1), if a person is deemed by subsection (1) to own at a particular time a different number of shares of a class of the capital stock of a foreign affiliate of a corporation resident in Canada (which shares so deemed owned are referred to in this subsection as "affiliate shares") than the person was deemed by that subsection to have owned immediately before the particular time, the number of affiliate shares equal to that difference is deemed to be

(*a*) disposed of, at the particular time, by the person, when that person is deemed to own fewer affiliate shares at the particular time than immediately before it; and

(*b*) acquired by, at the particular time, the person, when that person is deemed to own more affiliate shares at the particular time than immediately before it.

History: S. 5908(2) was added by S.C. 2013, c. 34, s. 47(1), applicable to taxation years of a foreign affiliate of a taxpayer that begin after November 1999, except that subsection 5908(2) is, in its application to acquisitions, dispositions, redemptions, cancellations, foreign mergers, amalgamations and issuances that occur, and windings-up that begin, on or before December 18, 2009, to be read as follows:

"(2) For the purposes of this section and section 5905, if the number of shares of a class of the capital stock of a foreign affiliate of a corporation resident in Canada deemed by subsection 93.1(1) of the Act to be owned by a person at a particular time is different from the number so deemed immediately before the particular time,

(*a*) where the number of shares of that class deemed to be owned by the person has decreased, the person is deemed to have disposed of, at the particular time, the number of shares of that class equal to the amount of the decrease;

(*b*) where the number of shares of that class deemed to be owned by the person has increased, the person is deemed to have acquired, at the particular time, the number of shares of that class equal to the amount of the increase;

(*c*) a person (referred to in this paragraph as the "seller") that is deemed by paragraph (*a*) to have disposed of, at a particular time, shares of a class of the foreign affiliate's capital stock is deemed to have disposed of those shares to the persons (referred to in this paragraph as the "acquirers") deemed in paragraph (*b*) to have acquired shares of that class at that time and the number of shares of that class deemed to have been acquired at that time by a particular acquirer from the seller shall be determined by the formula

$$A \times B/C$$

where

A is the number of shares of that class acquired by the particular acquirer at that time,

B is the number of shares of that class disposed of by the seller at that time, and

C is the number of shares of that class acquired by all acquirers at that time; and

(*d*) persons (referred to in this paragraph as the "acquirers") that are deemed by paragraph (*b*) to have acquired, at a particular time, shares of a class of the foreign affiliate's capital stock are deemed to have acquired those shares from a person (referred to in this paragraph as the "seller") deemed in paragraph (*a*) to have disposed of shares of that class at that time and the number of shares of that class deemed to have been disposed of by the seller to a particular acquirer at that time shall be determined by the formula

$$A \times B/C$$

where

A is the number of shares of that class disposed of by the seller,

B is the number of shares of that class acquired by the particular acquirer at that time, and

C is the number of shares of that class disposed of by all sellers at that time."

See the application following the addition of s. 5908(1), regarding the override of the statute-barring rules for assessments for taxation years that end before June 26, 2013.

(3) For the purposes of subsection (2),

(*a*) if a partnership of which a person is a member at any time does not own, and (but for this subsection) is not deemed by subsection (1) to own, any shares of a class of the capital stock of the foreign affiliate at that time, subsection (1) is deemed to have applied in respect of the person and to have deemed the person to own, because of subsection (1) in respect of the partnership, no shares of that class at that time; and

(*b*) if a corporation resident in Canada or a foreign affiliate of such a corporation disposes of or acquires its entire interest in a partnership that, based on the assumptions contained in paragraph 96(1)(*c*) of the Act, owns shares of a class of the capital stock of a non-resident corporation, the corporation resident in Canada or the foreign affiliate, as the case may be, is deemed at the time that is immediately after the disposition or immediately before the acquisition, as the case may be, to own, because of subsection (1) in respect of the partnership, no shares of that class.

History: S. 5908(3) was added by S.C. 2013, c. 34, s. 47(1), applicable to taxation years of a foreign affiliate of a taxpayer that begin after December 18, 2009.

See the application following the addition of s. 5908(1), regarding the override of the statute-barring rules for assessments for taxation years that end before June 26, 2013.

(4) For the purposes of subsection 5905(5), if at any time a corporation resident in Canada (referred to in this subsection as the "disposing corporation") disposes of shares of a class of the capital stock of a foreign affiliate of the disposing corporation and, as a consequence of the same transaction or event (other than one to which neither paragraph (2)(*a*) nor paragraph (2)(*b*) applies) that caused the disposition, a taxable Canadian corporation with which the disposing corporation is not, at that time, dealing at arm's length acquires shares of that class, the disposing corporation is, at that time, deemed to have disposed of, to the taxable Canadian corporation, the number of the shares of that class that is determined by the formula

$$A \times B$$

where

A is the number of shares of that class disposed of by the disposing corporation; and

B is

(*a*) if the taxable Canadian corporation acquires, because of paragraph (2)(*b*), shares of that class, the fraction determined by the formula

$$C/D$$

where

C is the number of shares of that class that is deemed by that paragraph to be acquired by the taxable Canadian corporation as a result of the transaction or event, and

Regulations

D is the total of all amounts each of which is the number of shares of that class that is deemed by that paragraph to be acquired by a person as a result of the transaction or event, and

(*b*) in any other case, one.

History: S. 5908(4) was added by S.C. 2013, c. 34, s. 47(1), applicable to taxation years of a foreign affiliate of a taxpayer that begin after December 18, 2009.

See the application following the addition of s. 5908(1), regarding the override of the statute-barring rules for assessments for taxation years that end before June 26, 2013.

(5) For the purposes of subsection 5905(5.1), if a predecessor corporation described in that subsection is, at the time that is immediately before the amalgamation described in that subsection, a member of a particular partnership that, based on the assumptions contained in paragraph 96(1)(*c*) of the Act, owns, at that time, shares of the capital stock of a foreign affiliate of the predecessor corporation and the predecessor corporation's interest in the particular partnership, or in another partnership that is a member of the particular partnership, becomes, upon the amalgamation, property of the new corporation described in that subsection, the shares of the capital stock of the affiliate that are deemed under subsection (1) to be owned by the predecessor corporation at that time are deemed to become property of the new corporation upon the amalgamation.

History: S. 5908(5) was added by S.C. 2013, c. 34, s. 47(1), applicable to taxation years of a foreign affiliate of a taxpayer that begin after December 18, 2009.

See the application following the addition of s. 5908(1), regarding the override of the statute-barring rules for assessments for taxation years that end before June 26, 2013.

(6) In applying subsection 5905(5.2), if the corporation is a member of a partnership that, based on the assumptions contained in paragraph 96(1)(*c*) of the Act, owns shares (referred to individually in paragraph (*a*) as a "relevant share") of the affiliate's capital stock at the particular time,

(*a*) for the purposes of the description of B in subsection 5905(5.2), the corporation's cost amount of each relevant share at the particular time is to be determined by the formula

$$P \times Q/R$$

where

P is the partnership's cost amount of that relevant share at the particular time,

Q is the number of shares of the capital stock of the affiliate that are deemed by subsection (1), in respect of the partnership, to be owned by the corporation at the particular time, and

R is the total number of relevant shares at the particular time; and

(*b*) for the purposes of paragraph (*b*) of the description of C in subsection 5905(5.2), the amount determined under this paragraph is the total of all amounts each of which is the amount that would be the corporation's portion of a gain that would be deemed under subsection 92(5) of the Act to be a gain of the member of the partnership from the disposition of a share of the capital stock of the affiliate by the partnership if that share were disposed of immediately before the particular time.

History: S. 5908(6) was added by S.C. 2013, c. 34, s. 47(1), applicable in respect of acquisitions of control that occur after December 18, 2009, except if the acquisition of control results from an acquisition of shares made under an agreement in writing entered into before December 18, 2009.

See the application following the addition of s. 5908(1), regarding the override of the statute-barring rules for assessments for taxation years that end before June 26, 2013.

(7) For the purposes of paragraph 5905(5.4)(*b*), the amount determined by this subsection is the amount determined by the following formula for shares of the capital stock of a foreign affiliate of the subsidiary that were deemed by subsection (1), in respect of the partnership, to be owned by the subsidiary at the time at which the parent last acquired control of the subsidiary:

$$A \times B$$

where

A is the tax-free surplus balance of the affiliate, in respect of the subsidiary, at that time; and

B is the percentage that would be the subsidiary's surplus entitlement percentage in respect of the affiliate at that time if the only shares of that capital stock that were owned at that time by the subsidiary were the shares of that capital stock that were deemed by subsection (1), in respect of the partnership, to be owned by the subsidiary at the time at which the parent last acquired control of the subsidiary.

History: S. 5908(7) was added by S.C. 2013, c. 34, s. 47(1), applicable in respect of acquisitions of control that occur after December 18, 2009, except if the acquisition of control results from an acquisition of shares made under an agreement in writing entered into before December 18, 2009.

See the application following the addition of s. 5908(1), regarding the override of the statute-barring rules for assessments for taxation years that end before June 26, 2013.

(8) If a particular corporation resident in Canada or a particular foreign affiliate of a particular corporation resident in Canada is a member of a particular partnership, the particular partnership owns (based on the assumptions contained in paragraph 96(1)(*c*) of the Act) shares of a class of the capital stock of a foreign affiliate of the particular corporation and the particular partnership disposes of any of those shares,

(*a*) any reference in this Part (other than subsections 5902(5) and (6)) to subsection 93(1) of the Act is deemed to include a reference to subsection 93(1.2) of the Act;

(*b*) an election under subsection 93(1.2) of the Act by the particular corporation is to be made by filing the prescribed form with the Minister on or before

(i) where the particular corporation is the disposing corporation referred to in that subsection, the particular corporation's filing-due date for its taxation year that includes the last day of the particular partnership's fiscal period in which the disposition was made, and

(ii) where the particular affiliate is the disposing corporation referred to in that subsection, the particular corporation's filing-due date for its taxation year that includes the last day of the particular affiliate's taxation year that includes the last day of the disposing partnership's fiscal period in which the disposition was made; and

(*c*) the prescribed amount for the purposes of subparagraph 93(1.2)(*a*)(ii) of the Act is the lesser of

(i) the taxable capital gain, if any, of the particular affiliate otherwise determined in respect of the disposition, and

(ii) the amount determined by the formula

$$A \times B \times C/D$$

where

A is the fraction referred to in paragraph 38(*a*) of the Act that applies to the particular affiliate's taxation year that includes the last day of the particular partnership's fiscal period that includes the time of the disposition,

B is the amount that could reasonably be expected to have been received in respect of all the shares of that class if the second foreign affiliate referred to in subsection 93(1.2) of the Act had, immediately before that time, paid dividends, on all shares of its capital stock, the total of which was equal to the amount determined under subparagraph 5902(1)(*a*)(i) to be its net surplus in respect of the particular corporation,

C is the number of shares of that class that is determined under subsection 93(1.3) of the Act, and

D is the total number of issued shares of that class immediately before that time.

History: S. 5908(8) was added by S.C. 2013, c. 34, s. 47(1), applicable to elections made under subsection 93(1.2) of the *Income Tax Act* in respect of dispositions that occur after November 1999.

See the application following the addition of s. 5908(1), regarding the override of the statute-barring rules for assessments for taxation years that end before June 26, 2013.

Application Provision, S.C. 2013, c. 34, s. 51 [Consolidated Net Surplus Election]

Subject to the Modified Consolidated Net Surplus Election (below), if a corporation resident in Canada elects in writing under this section in respect of all of its foreign affiliates and files the election with the Minister of National Revenue on or before the day that is the later of the corporation's filing-due date for the corporation's taxation year that includes June 26, 2013 and June 26, 2014, the following rules apply:

(*d*) if there is a designated section 93 election, paragraph 5908(8)(*c*) of the Regulations, as enacted by subsection 47 (1), is, in respect of the designated section 93 election, to be read as follows:

"(*c*) the prescribed amount for the purposes of subparagraph 93(1.2)(*a*)(ii) of the Act is the lesser of

(i) the taxable capital gain, if any, of the particular affiliate otherwise determined in respect of the disposition, and

(ii) the amount that is one-half of the amount referred to in paragraph 5902(6)(*b*)."

Application Provision, S.C. 2013, c. 34, s. 52 [Modified Consolidated Net Surplus Election.]

(1) The application in subsection (2) (below) applies if

(*a*) a corporation has made the election above; and

(*b*) the corporation has made an election under subsection 93(1) or (1.2) of the Income Tax Act in respect of a disposition of a share of the capital stock of a foreign affiliate of the corporation that occurs after December 20, 2002 and on or before February 27, 2004 (other than a disposition required to be made under an agreement in writing made by a vendor on or before December 20, 2002), or in respect of a disposition that occurs after February 27, 2004 and that is required to be made under an agreement in writing made by a vendor after December 20, 2002 and before February 28, 2004; and

(*c*) the corporation elects in writing under this paragraph to apply paragraph (*d*) (below) in respect of all of its foreign affiliates and files the election with the Minister of National Revenue on or before the day that is the later of the corporation's filing-due date for the corporation's taxation year that includes June 26, 2013 and June 26, 2014;

(2) then the Consolidated Net Surplus Election above does not apply in respect of dispositions referred to in paragraph (*b*).

(9) For the purposes of this Part, except to the extent that the context otherwise requires, if a person or partnership is (or is deemed by this subsection to be) a member of a particular partnership that is a member of another partnership, the person or partnership is deemed to be a member of the other partnership.

History: S. 5908(9) was added by S.C. 2013, c. 34, s. 47(1), applicable for taxation years of a foreign affiliate of a taxpayer that begin after November 1999 except that, for the foreign affiliate's taxation years that end on or before August 27, 2010, subsection 5908(9) is to be read as follows:

"(9) For the purposes of this section and paragraph 5907(2.7)(*b*), if any corporation is (or is deemed by this subsection to be) a member of a particular partnership that is a member of another partnership, the corporation is deemed to be a member of the other partnership."

See the application following the addition of s. 5908(1), regarding the override of the statute-barring rules for assessments for taxation years that end before June 26, 2013.

(10) For the purposes of paragraph 95(2)(*j*) of the Act, the adjusted cost base to a foreign affiliate of a taxpayer of an interest in a partnership at any time is prescribed to be the cost to the affiliate of the interest as otherwise determined at that time, and for those purposes

(*a*) there shall be added to that cost such of the following amounts as are applicable:

(i) any amount included in the affiliate's earnings for a taxation year ending after 1971 and before that time that may reasonably be considered to relate to profits of the partnership,

(ii) the affiliate's incomes as described by the description of A in the definition "foreign accrual property income" in subsection 95(1) of the Act for a taxation year ending after 1971 and before that time that can reasonably be considered to relate to profits of the partnership,

(iii) any amount included in computing the exempt earnings or taxable earnings, as the case may be, of the affiliate for a taxation year ending after 1971 and before that time that may reasonably be considered to relate to a capital gain of the partnership,

(iii.1) any amount included in computing the hybrid surplus or hybrid deficit of the affiliate before that time that may reasonably be considered to relate to a capital gain of the partnership,

(iv) where the affiliate has, at any time before that time and in a taxation year ending after 1971, made a contribution of capital to the partnership otherwise than by way of a loan, such part of the amount of the contribution as cannot reasonably be regarded as a gift made to or for the benefit of any other member of the partnership who was related to the affiliate,

(v) such portion of any income or profits tax refunded before that time by the government of a country to the partnership as may reasonably be regarded as tax refunded in respect of an amount described in any of subparagraphs (*b*)(i) to (iii), and

(vi) the amount, if any, determined under paragraph (11)(*b*);

(*b*) there shall be deducted from that cost such of the following amounts as are applicable:

(i) any amount included in the affiliate's loss for a taxation year ending after 1971 that may reasonably be considered to relate to a loss of the partnership,

(ii) the affiliate's losses as described by the description of D in the definition "foreign accrual property income" in subsection 95(1) of the Act for a taxation year ending after 1971 and before that

Regulations

time that can reasonably be considered to relate to the losses of the partnership,

(iii) any amount included in computing the exempt loss or taxable loss, as the case may be, of the affiliate for a taxation year ending after 1971 and before that time that may reasonably be considered to relate to a capital loss of the partnership,

(iii.1) any amount included in computing the hybrid surplus or hybrid deficit of the affiliate before that time that may reasonably be considered to relate to a capital loss of the partnership,

(iv) any amount received by the affiliate before that time and in a taxation year ending after 1971 as, on account or in lieu of payment of, or in satisfaction of, a distribution of the affiliate's share of the partnership profits or partnership capital, and

(v) such portion of any income or profits tax paid before that time to the government of a country by the partnership as may reasonably be regarded as tax paid in respect of an amount described in any of subparagraphs (*a*)(i) to (iii); and

(*c*) for greater certainty, where any interest of a foreign affiliate in a partnership was reacquired by the affiliate after having been previously disposed of, no adjustment that was required to be made under this subsection before such reacquisition shall be made under this subsection to the cost to the affiliate of the interest as reacquired property of the affiliate.

History: S. 5908(10)(*a*)(iii.1) was added by S.C. 2013, c. 34, s. 86(1), deemed to have come into force on August 20, 2011.

S. 5908(10)(*b*)(iii.1) was added by S.C. 2013, c. 34, s. 86(2), deemed to have come into force on August 20, 2011.

Any assessment of a taxpayer's tax, interest and penalties payable under the Act for any taxation year that ends before June 26, 2013 that would, in the absence of this section, be precluded because of subsections 152(4) to (5) of the Act shall be made to the extent necessary to take into account the amendments by S.C. 2013, c. 34, s. 54 to 89.

S. 5908(10) was added by S.C. 2013, c. 34, s. 47(1), deemed to have come into force on December 19, 2009.

See the application following the addition of s. 5908(1), regarding the override of the statute-barring rules for assessments for taxation years that end before June 26, 2013.

(11) If at any time a partnership owns, based on the assumptions contained in paragraph 96(1)(*c*) of the Act, a share of the capital stock of a particular foreign affiliate of a corporation resident in Canada and one or more members of the partnership is at that time a direct holder referred to in paragraph 5905(7.6)(*a*) or a subordinate affiliate referred to in paragraph 5905(7.6)(*b*), the following rules apply:

(*a*) for the purposes of paragraph 92(1.1)(*b*) of the Act, there is to be added, in computing at or after that time the partnership's adjusted cost base of the share, the total of all amounts each of which is the amount determined, in respect of an acquired affiliate referred to in subsection 5905(7.6), by the formula

$$A \times B$$

where

A is the amount, if any, determined under paragraph 5905(7.2)(*a*) in respect of the acquired affiliate, and

B is the percentage that would, if the partnership were a corporation resident in Canada, be the partnership's surplus entitlement percentage in respect of the acquired affiliate, at the adjustment time, if the partnership owned only the share;

(*b*) for the purposes of subparagraph (10)(*a*)(vi), the amount determined under this paragraph, in respect of the interest in the partnership of the direct holder or the subordinate affiliate, is the amount determined by the formula

$$A \times B/C$$

where

A is the total of all amounts each of which is the amount, if any, determined under paragraph (*a*) in respect of a share of the capital stock of the particular affiliate,

B is the fair market value, at the adjustment time, of the interest in the partnership of the direct holder or the subordinate affiliate, as the case may be, and

C is the fair market value, at the adjustment time, of all members' interests in the partnership; and

(*c*) no amount is to be added under subsection 5905(7.6) to the direct holder's or the subordinate affiliate's adjusted cost base of the share.

History: S. 5908(11) was added by S.C. 2013, c. 34, s. 47(1), applicable where a share of the capital stock of a foreign affiliate of a corporation is acquired by, or otherwise becomes property of, a person after December 18, 2009.

See the application following the addition of s. 5908(1), regarding the override of the statute-barring rules for assessments for taxation years that end before June 26, 2013.

(12) For the purposes of paragraph 5905(7.7)(*b*), the amount determined under this subsection is the amount determined by the formula

$$A \times B/C$$

where

A is the adjustment amount;

B is the fair market value, at the adjustment time, of the interest in the partnership that is referred to in paragraph 92(1.1)(*b*) of the Act of the particular foreign affiliate that is referred to in paragraph 93(3)(*c*) of the Act; and

C is the fair market value, at the adjustment time, of all members' interests in the partnership.

History: S. 5908(12) was added by S.C. 2013, c. 34, s. 47(1), applicable where a share of the capital stock of a foreign affiliate of a corporation is acquired by, or otherwise becomes property of, a person after December 18, 2009.

See the application following the addition of s. 5908(1), regarding the override of the statute-barring rules for assessments for taxation years that end before June 26, 2013.

(13) For the purposes of clauses 5907(2.9)(*a*)(i)(B) and (ii)(B), the amount determined under this subsection is, subject to subsection (14), the amount determined by the formula

$$A \times B/C$$

where

A is

(*a*) if clause 5907(2.9)(*a*)(i)(B) applies, the amount determined under clause 5907(2.9)(*a*)(i)(A), and (*b*) if clause 5907(2.9)(*a*)(ii)(B) applies, the amount determined under clause 5907(2.9)(*a*)(ii)(A),

B is the affiliate's direct or indirect share of the partnership's income or loss for the preceding taxation year, and

C is the partnership's income or loss for the preceding taxation year.

History: S. 5908(13) was added by S.C. 2013, c. 34, s. 86(3), applicable in respect of taxation years of a foreign affiliate of a taxpayer that begin after December 20, 2002. However, if the taxpayer has elected under s. 95(2)(*j.1*) to (*k.1*) of the Act, the following rules apply in respect of taxation years of the foreign affiliate that begin after 1994 and before December 21, 2002:

(*a*) the reference to "5908(13)" in clauses 5907(2.9)(*a*)(i)(B) and (ii)(B) is to be read as a reference to "5907.1(1)"; and

(*b*) the *Income Tax Regulations* are to be read as if they contained a section that reads as follows

"5907.1 (1) For the purposes of clauses 5907(2.9)(*a*)(i)(B) and (ii)(B), the amount determined under this subsection is, subject to subsection (2), the amount determined by the formula

$$A \times B/C$$

where

A is

(*a*) if clause 5907(2.9)(*a*)(i)(B) applies, the amount determined under clause 5907(2.9)(*a*)(i)(A), and

(*b*) if clause 5907(2.9)(*a*)(ii)(B) applies, the amount determined under clause 5907(2.9)(*a*)(ii)(A);

B is the affiliate's direct or indirect share of the partnership's income or loss for the preceding taxation year; and

C is the partnership's income or loss for the preceding taxation year.

(2) For the purposes of subsection (1), if both the income and loss of the partnership for the preceding taxation year are nil, the descriptions of B and C in the formula in that subsection are to be applied as if the partnership had income for that year in the amount of $1,000,000."

Any assessment of a taxpayer's tax, interest and penalties payable under the Act for any taxation year that ends before June 26, 2013 that would, in the absence of this section, be precluded because of subsections 152(4) to (5) of the Act shall be made to the extent necessary to take into account the amendments by S.C. 2013, c. 34, s. 54 to 89.

(14) For the purposes of subsection (13), if both the income and loss of the partnership for the preceding taxation year are nil, the descriptions of B and C in the formula in that subsection are to be applied as if the partnership had income for that year in the amount of $1,000,000.

History: S. 5908(14) was added by S.C. 2013, c. 34, s. 86(3), applicable in respect of taxation years of a foreign affiliate of a taxpayer that begin after December 20, 2002. See the history note for the addition of subsection 5908(13) regarding the applicable rules if the taxpayer makes an election under s. 95(2)(*j.1*) to (*k.1*) of the Act.

See the application for the addition of s. 5908(13) for the extension of assessment periods to take into account the amendments by S.C. 2013, c. 34, s. 54 to 89.

Editorial Note: See the provision following s. 5905(1) for the application and alternative reading if certain elections are made.

5909. Prescribed Circumstances

(Repealed by S.C. 2013, c. 34, s. 28(1).)

History: S. 5909 was repealed by S.C. 2013, c. 34, s. 28(1), applicable to trust taxation years that end after 2006, and formerly read:

5909. *Prescribed Circumstances.* For the purposes of subparagraph 94(1)(*b*)(i) of the Act, property shall be considered to have been acquired in prescribed circumstances where it is acquired by virtue of the repayment of a loan.

5910. [Foreign oil and gas businesses]

(1) If a foreign affiliate of a corporation resident in Canada carries on in a particular taxation year an active business that is a foreign oil and gas business in a taxing country, the affiliate is deemed for the purposes of this Part to have paid for the particular year, as an income or profits tax to the government of the taxing country in respect of its earnings from the business for the particular year, an amount equal to the lesser of

(*a*) the amount, if any, determined by the formula

$$(A \times B) - C$$

where

A is the percentage determined under subsection (2) for the particular year,

B is the affiliate's earnings from the business for the particular year, and

C is the total of all amounts each of which is an amount that would, but for this subsection, be an income or profits tax paid to the government of the taxing country by the affiliate for the particular year in respect of its earnings from the business for the particular year; and

(*b*) the affiliate's production tax amount for the business in the taxing country for the particular year.

History: S. 5910(1)(*a*), the description of B was replaced by S.C. 2013, c. 34, s. 87(1), applicable in respect of taxation years of a foreign affiliate of a taxpayer that end after August 19, 2011.

Any assessment of a taxpayer's tax, interest and penalties payable under the Act for any taxation year that ends before June 26, 2013 that would, in the absence of this section, be precluded because of subsections 152(4) to (5) of the Act shall be made to the extent necessary to take into account the amendments by S.C. 2013, c. 34, s. 54 to 89.

S. 5910(1)(*a*), the description of B formerly read:

B is the amount determined under subsection (3) in respect of the business for the particular year, and

S. 5910(1) was added by S.C. 2013, c. 34, s. 48(1), applicable in respect of production tax amounts that become receivable by the government of a taxing country in taxation years of a taxpayer's foreign affiliate that begin after the date (referred to in this subsection as the "application date") that is the earlier of December 31, 2002 and the designated date. The designated date is the later of

(*a*) December 31, 1994; and

(*b*) any date that the taxpayer designates in writing for the purpose of this subsection, if the designation is filed with the Minister of National Revenue on or before the taxpayer's filing-due date for the taxpayer's taxation year that includes June 26, 2013.

Any assessment of a taxpayer's tax, interest and penalties payable under the Act for any taxation year that ends before June 26, 2013 that would otherwise be precluded because of subsections 152(4) to (5) of the Act, shall be made to the extent necessary to take into account this amendment, if the taxpayer

(i) elects in writing in respect of all of its foreign affiliates that this section apply in respect of that provision, and

(ii) files that election with the Minister of National Revenue on or before December 26, 2013 [the day that is six months after royal assent].

(2) The percentage determined under this subsection for the particular year is the percentage determined by the formula

$$P - Q$$

where

P is the percentage set out in paragraph 123(1)(*a*) of the Act for the corporation's taxation year that includes the last day of the particular year; and

Q is the corporation's general rate reduction percentage (within the meaning assigned by subsection 123.4(1) of the Act) for that taxation year of the corporation.

History: S. 5910(2) was added by S.C. 2013, c. 34, s. 48(1), applicable in respect of production tax amounts that become receivable by the government of a taxing country in taxation years of a taxpayer's foreign affiliate that begin after the date (referred to in this subsection as the "application date") that is the earlier of December 31, 2002 and the designated date. The designated date is the later of

(*a*) December 31, 1994; and

(*b*) any date that the taxpayer designates in writing for the purpose of this subsection, if the designation is filed with the Minister of National Revenue on or before the taxpayer's filing-due date for the taxpayer's taxation year that includes June 26, 2013.

However, in its application to taxation years of the foreign affiliate that begin after the application date and on or before December 18, 2009, subsection 5910(2) is to be read as follows:

"(2) The percentage determined under this subsection for the particular year is 40 per cent."

See the application following the addition of s. 5910(1), regarding the override of the statute-barring rules for assessments for taxation years that end before June 26, 2013.

(3) (Repealed by S.C. 2013, c. 34, S. 87(2).)

History: S. 5910(3) was repealed by S.C. 2013, c. 34, s. 87(2), applicable in respect of taxation years of a foreign affiliate of a taxpayer that end after August 19, 2011.

See the application for the amendment to s. 59010(*a*), the description of B for the extension of assessment periods to take into account the amendments by S.C. 2013, c. 34, s. 54 to 89.

S. 5910(3) formerly read:

(3) The amount determined under this subsection in respect of the business for the particular year is

(*a*) if the affiliate's earnings from the business for the particular year are required to be determined under subparagraph (*a*)(iii) of the definition "earnings" in subsection 5907(1), the amount that would be determined to be the affiliate's earnings for the particular year from the business if the affiliate

(i) had, in computing its income from the business for each taxation year (referred to in this subparagraph as an "earnings year") that is the particular year or is any preceding taxation year that begins after December 18, 2009,

(A) claimed all deductions that it could have claimed under the Act, up to the maximum amount deductible in computing the income from the business for that earnings year, and

(B) made all claims and elections and taken all steps under applicable provisions of the Act, or of enactments implementing amendments to the Act or its regulations, to maximize the amount of any deduction referred to clause (A), and

(ii) had, in computing its income from the business for any preceding taxation year that began before December 19, 2009, claimed all deductions, if any, that it actually claimed under the Act, up to the maximum amount deductible, and made all claims and elections, if any, and taken all steps, if any, under applicable provisions of the Act, or of enactments implementing amendments to the Act or its regulations, that it actually made; and

(*b*) in any other case, the affiliate's earnings from the business for the particular year.

S. 5910(3) was added by S.C. 2013, c. 34, s. 48(1), applicable in respect of production tax amounts that become receivable by the government of a taxing country in taxation years of a taxpayer's foreign affiliate that begin after the date (referred to in this subsection as the "application date") that is the earlier of December 31, 2002 and the designated date. The designated date is the later of

(*a*) December 31, 1994; and

(*b*) any date that the taxpayer designates in writing for the purpose of this subsection, if the designation is filed with the Minister of National Revenue on or before the taxpayer's filing-due date for the taxpayer's taxation year that includes June 26, 2013.

However, in its application to taxation years of the foreign affiliate that begin after the application date and on or before December 18, 2009, subsection 5910(3) is to be read as follows:

"(3) The amount determined under this subsection in respect of the business for the particular year is the amount that would, if the definition "earnings" in subsection 5907(1) were read without reference to its subparagraphs (*a*)(i) and (ii), be the foreign affiliate's earnings from the business in the taxing country for the particular year."

See the application following the addition of s. 5910(1), regarding the override of the statute-barring rules for assessments for taxation years that end before June 26, 2013.

(4) In this section, "foreign oil and gas business", "production tax amount" and "taxing country" have the meanings assigned by subsection 126(7) of the Act.

History: S. 5910(4) was added by S.C. 2013, c. 34, s. 48(1), applicable in respect of production tax amounts that become receivable by the government of a taxing country in taxation years of a taxpayer's foreign affiliate that begin after the date (referred to in this subsection as the "application date") that is the earlier of December 31, 2002 and the designated date. The designated date is the later of

(*a*) December 31, 1994; and

(*b*) any date that the taxpayer designates in writing for the purpose of this subsection, if the designation is filed with the Minister of National Revenue on or before the taxpayer's filing-due date for the taxpayer's taxation year that includes June 26, 2013.

See the application following the addition of s. 5910(1), regarding the override of the statute-barring rules for assessments for taxation years that end before June 26, 2013.

5911. [Elections]

(1) A listed election is to be made by the taxpayer and, if applicable, the disposing affiliate by so notifying the Minister in writing on or before

(*a*) if the taxpayer is a partnership, the earliest of the filing-due dates of any member of the partnership for the member's taxation year that includes the last day of the partnership's fiscal period that includes the last day of the foreign affiliate's taxation year that includes the time of distribution of a distributed property; and

(*b*) in any other case, the taxpayer's filing-due date for its taxation year that includes the last day of the foreign affiliate's taxation year that includes the time of distribution of a distributed property.

History: S. 5911(1) was added by S.C. 2013, c. 34, s. 88(1), applicable in respect of liquidations and dissolutions of foreign affiliates of a taxpayer that begin after February 27, 2004. However, any listed election referred to in subsection 5911(1) that would otherwise be required to be filed with the Minister of National Revenue before October 24, 2013 [120 days after royal assent] is deemed to have been filed with the Minister on a timely basis if it is filed with the Minister by June 26, 2014 [within 365 days after royal assent].

Any assessment of a taxpayer's tax, interest and penalties payable under the Act for any taxation year that ends before June 26, 2013 that would, in the absence of this section, be precluded because of subsections 152(4) to (5) of the Act shall be made to the extent necessary to take into account the amendments by S.C. 2013, c. 34, s. 54 to 89.

(2) For the purposes of subsection (1), a listed election is any of the following:

(*a*) an election by the taxpayer under subsection 88(3.1) of the Act in respect of a liquidation and dissolution of a disposing affiliate;

(*b*) an election by the taxpayer under subsection 88(3.3) of the Act in respect of a distribution of distributed property; and

(*c*) a joint election by the taxpayer and a disposing affiliate under subsection 88(3.5) of the Act in respect of a distribution of distributed property.

History: S. 5911(2) was added by S.C. 2013, c. 34, s. 88(1), applicable in respect of liquidations and dissolutions of foreign affiliates of a taxpayer that begin after February 27, 2004.

See the application for the addition of s. 5911(1) for the extension of assessment periods to take into account the amendments by S.C. 2013, c. 34, s. 54 to 89.

(3) Subsection (4) applies if

(*a*) a taxpayer has made an election (referred to in this subsection and subsection (4) as the "initial election") under subsection 88(3.3) of the Act in respect of a distribution of distributed property on or before the filing-due date specified in subsection (1);

(*b*) the taxpayer made reasonable efforts to determine all amounts, in respect of the disposing affiliate, that may reasonably be considered to be relevant in making the claim under the initial election; and

(*c*) the taxpayer amends the initial election on or before the day that is 10 years after the filing-due date referred to in paragraph (*a*).

History: S. 5911(3) was added by S.C. 2013, c. 34, s. 88(1), applicable in respect of liquidations and dissolutions of foreign affiliates of a taxpayer that begin after February 27, 2004.

See the application for the addition of s. 5911(1) for the extension of assessment periods to take into account the amendments by S.C. 2013, c. 34, s. 54 to 89.

(4) If this subsection applies and, in the opinion of the Minister, the circumstances are such that it would be just and equitable to permit the initial election to be amended, the amended election under paragraph (3)(*c*) is deemed to have been made on the day on which the initial election was made and the initial election is deemed not to have been made.

History: S. 5911(4) was added by S.C. 2013, c. 34, s. 88(1), applicable in respect of liquidations and dissolutions of foreign affiliates of a taxpayer that begin after February 27, 2004.

See the application for the addition of s. 5911(1) for the extension of assessment periods to take into account the amendments by S.C. 2013, c. 34, s. 54 to 89.

(5) An election under the definition "relevant cost base" in subsection 95(4) of the Act in respect of a property of a foreign affiliate of a taxpayer, in respect of the taxpayer, is to be made by the taxpayer by so notifying the Minister in writing on or before

(*a*) if the taxpayer is a partnership, the earliest of the filing-due dates of any member of the partnership for the member's taxation year that includes the last day of the partnership's fiscal period that includes the last day of the foreign affiliate's taxation year in which the determination of the relevant cost base of the property, in respect of the taxpayer, is relevant; and

(*b*) in any other case, the taxpayer's filing-due date for its taxation year that includes the last day of the foreign affiliate's taxation year in which the determination of the relevant cost base of the property, in respect of the taxpayer, is relevant.

History: S. 5911(5) was added by S.C. 2013, c. 34, s. 88(1), applicable in respect of determinations in respect of which the definition of "relevant cost base" in s. 95(4) of the Act applies. However, any election referred to in subsection 5911(5) that would otherwise be required to be filed with the Minister of National Revenue before October 24, 2013 [120 days after royal assent] is deemed to have been filed with the Minister on a timely basis if it is filed with the Minister by June 26, 2014 [within 365 days after royal assent].

See the application for the addition of s. 5911(1) for the extension of assessment periods to take into account the amendments by S.C. 2013, c. 34, s. 54 to 89.

(6) An election, or joint election, as the case may be, under subsection 90(3) of the Act in respect of a distribution made by a foreign affiliate of a taxpayer is to be made by the taxpayer, or by the taxpayer and each connected person or partnership referred to in that subsection, as the case may be, by so notifying the Minister in writing on or before

(*a*) in the case of an election by the taxpayer,

(i) if the taxpayer is a partnership, the earliest of the filing-due dates of any member of the partnership for the member's taxation year that includes the last day of the partnership's fiscal period in which the distribution was made, and

(ii) in any other case, the taxpayer's filing-due date for its taxation year that includes the last day of the foreign affiliate's taxation year in which the distribution was made; and

(*b*) in the case of a joint election, the earliest of the filing-due dates that would be determined under paragraph (*a*) for each taxpayer that is required to make the joint election if there were no connected persons or partnerships in respect of the taxpayer.

History: S. 5911(6) was added by S.C. 2013, c. 34, s. 88(1), applicable in respect of distributions made after August 19, 2011. However, any election referred to in subsection 5911(6) that would otherwise be required to be filed with the Minister of National Revenue before October 24, 2013 [120 days after royal assent] is deemed to have been filed with the Minister on a timely basis if it is filed with the Minister by June 26, 2014 [within 365 days after royal assent].

See the application for the addition of s. 5911(1) for the extension of assessment periods to take into account the amendments by S.C. 2013, c. 34, s. 54 to 89.

Part LX
Prescribed Activities

6000. [Overseas employment tax credit]

For the purpose of clause 122.3(1)(*b*)(i)(C) of the Act, a prescribed activity is an activity performed under contract with the United Nations.

Interpretation Bulletins: *Secondary* — IT-497R4 Overseas employment tax credit.

Part LXI
Related Segregated Fund Trusts

6100. [Election]

An election under subsection 138.1(4) of the Act by the trustee of a related segregated fund trust shall be made by filing with the Minister the prescribed form within 90 days from the end of the taxation year of the trust in respect of any capital property deemed to have been disposed of in that taxation year by virtue of the election.

Part LXII
Prescribed Securities, Shares and Debt Obligations

6200. Prescribed Securities

For the purposes of subsection 39(6) of the Act, a prescribed security is, with respect to the taxpayer referred to in subsection 39(4) of the Act,

(*a*) a share of the capital stock of a corporation, other than a public corporation, the value of which is, at the time it is disposed of by that taxpayer, a value that is or may reasonably be considered to be wholly or primarily attributable to

(i) real property, an interest therein or an option in respect thereof,

(ii) Canadian resource property or a property that would have been a Canadian resource property if it had been acquired after 1971,

(iii) foreign resource property or a property that would have been a foreign resource property if it had been acquired after 1971, or

(iv) any combination of properties described in subparagraphs (i) to (iii)

owned by

(v) the corporation,

(vi) a person other than the corporation, or

(vii) a partnership;

(*b*) a bond, debenture, bill, note, mortgage or similar obligation, issued by a corporation, other than a public corporation, if at any time before that taxpayer disposes of the security he does not deal at arm's length with the corporation;

(*c*) a security that is

(i) a share, or

(ii) a bond, debenture, bill, note, mortgage or similar obligation

that was acquired by the taxpayer from a person with whom the taxpayer does not deal at arm's length (other than from a person subject to subsection 39(4) of the Act for the person's taxation year that includes the time of the acquisition);

(*c*.1) a security described in subparagraph (*c*)(i) or (ii) that was acquired by the taxpayer from a person (other than from a person subject to subsection 39(4) of the Act for the person's taxation year that includes the time of the acquisition) in circumstances to which subsection 85(1) or (2) of the Act applied;

(*d*) a share acquired by that taxpayer under circumstances referred to in section 66.3 of the Act; or

(*e*) a security described in subparagraph (*c*)(i) or (ii) that was acquired by the taxpayer

(i) as proceeds of disposition for a security of the taxpayer to which paragraph (*a*), (*b*), (*c*) or (*d*) applied in respect of the taxpayer, or

(ii) as a result of one or more transactions that can reasonably be considered to have been an exchange or substitution of a security of the taxpayer to which paragraph (*a*), (*b*), (*c*) or (*d*) applied in respect of the taxpayer.

Interpretation Bulletins: *Primary* — IT-479R Transactions in securities.

6201. Prescribed Shares

(1) For the purposes of paragraph (*f*) of the definition "term preferred share" in subsection 248(1) of the Act, a share last acquired before June 29, 1982 and of a class of the capital stock of a corporation that is listed on a designated stock exchange in Canada is a prescribed share unless more than 10 per cent of the issued and outstanding shares of that class are owned by

(*a*) the owner of that share; or

(*b*) the owner of that share and persons related to him.

(2) For the purposes of paragraph (*f*) of the definition "term preferred share" in subsection 248(1) of the Act, a share acquired after June 28, 1982 and of a class of the capital stock of a corporation that is listed on a designated stock exchange in Canada is a prescribed share at any particular time with respect to another corporation that receives a dividend at the particular time in respect of the share unless

(*a*) where the other corporation is a restricted financial institution,

(i) the share is not a taxable preferred share,

(ii) dividends (other than dividends received on shares prescribed under subsection (5)) are received at the particular time by the other corporation or by the other corporation and restricted financial institutions with which the other corporation does not deal at arm's length, in respect of more than 5 per cent of the issued and outstanding shares of that class, and

(iii) a dividend is received at the particular time by the other corporation or a restricted financial institution with which the other corporation does not deal at arm's length, in respect of a share (other than a share prescribed under subsection (5)) of that class acquired after December 15, 1987 and before the particular time;

(*b*) where the other corporation is a restricted financial institution, the share

(i) is not a taxable preferred share,

(ii) was acquired after December 15, 1987 and before the particular time, and

(iii) was, by reason of subparagraph (*h*)(i), (ii), (iii) or (v) of the definition "term preferred share" in subsection 248(1) of the Act, deemed to have been issued after December 15, 1987 and before the particular time; or

(*c*) in any case, dividends (other than dividends received on shares prescribed under subsection (5)) are received at the particular time by the other corporation or by the other corporation and persons with whom the other corporation does not deal at arm's length in respect of more than 10 per cent of the issued and outstanding shares of that class.

(3) For the purposes of paragraph 112(2.2)(*g*) of the Act and paragraph (*f*) of the definition "term preferred share" in subsection 248(1) of the Act, a share of any of the following series of preferred shares of the capital stock of Massey-Ferguson Limited issued after July 15, 1981 and before March 23, 1982 is a prescribed share:

(*a*) $25 Cumulative Redeemable Retractable Convertible Preferred Shares, Series C;

(*b*) $25 Cumulative Redeemable Retractable Preferred Shares, Series D; or

(*c*) $25 Cumulative Redeemable Retractable Convertible Preferred Shares, Series E.

(4) For the purposes of the definition "taxable RFI share" in subsection 248(1) of the Act, a share of a class of the capital stock of a corporation that is listed on a designated stock exchange in Canada is a prescribed share at any particular time with respect to another corporation that is a restricted financial institution that receives a dividend at the particular time in respect of the share unless dividends (other than dividends received on shares prescribed under subsection (5.1)) are received at that time by the other corporation, or by the other corporation and restricted financial institutions with which the other corporation does not deal at arm's length, in respect of more than

(*a*) 10 per cent of the shares of that class that were issued and outstanding at the last time, before the particular time, at which the other corporation or a restricted financial institution with which the other corporation does not deal at arm's length acquired a share of that class, where no dividend is received at the particular time by any such corporation in respect of a share (other than a share prescribed under subsection (5.1)) of that class acquired after December 15, 1987 and before the particular time; or

(*b*) 5 per cent of the shares of that class that were issued and outstanding at the last time, before the particular time, at which the other corporation or a restricted financial institution with which the other corporation does not deal at arm's length acquired a share of that class, where a dividend is received at the particular time by any such corporation in respect of a share (other than a share prescribed under subsection (5.1)) of that class acquired after December 15, 1987 and before the particular time.

(5) For the purpose of paragraph (*f*) of the definition "term preferred share" in subsection 248(1) of the Act, a share of a class of the capital stock of a corporation that is listed on a designated stock exchange in Canada is a prescribed share at any particular time with respect to another corporation that is registered or licensed under the laws of a province to trade in securities and that holds the share for the purpose of sale in the course of the business ordinarily carried on by it unless

(*a*) it may reasonably be considered that the share was acquired as part of a series of transactions or events one of the main purposes of which was to avoid or limit the application of subsection 112(2.1) of the Act; or

(*b*) the share was not acquired by the other corporation in the course of an underwriting of shares of that class to be distributed to the public and

(i) dividends are received at the particular time by the other corporation or by the other corporation and corporations controlled by the other corporation in respect of more than 10 per cent of the issued and outstanding shares of that class,

(ii) the other corporation is a restricted financial institution and

(A) the share is not a taxable preferred share,

(B) dividends are received at the particular time by the other corporation or by the other corporation and corporations controlled by the other corporation in respect of more than 5 per cent of the issued and outstanding shares of that class, and

(C) a dividend is received at the particular time by the other corporation or a corporation controlled by the other corporation in respect of a share of that class acquired after December 15, 1987 and before the particular time, or

Regulations

(iii) the other corporation is a restricted financial institution and the share

(A) is not a taxable preferred share,

(B) was acquired after December 15, 1987 and before the particular time, and

(C) was, by reason of subparagraph (*h*)(i), (ii), (iii) or (v) of the definition "term preferred share" in subsection 248(1) of the Act, deemed to have been issued after December 15, 1987 and before the particular time.

(5.1) For the purpose of the definition "taxable RFI share" in subsection 248(1) of the Act, a share of a class of the capital stock of a corporation that is listed on a designated stock exchange in Canada is a prescribed share at any particular time with respect to another corporation that is registered or licensed under the laws of a province to trade in securities and that holds the share for the purpose of sale in the course of the business ordinarily carried on by it unless

(*a*) it may reasonably be considered that the share was acquired as part of a series of transactions or events one of the main purposes of which was to avoid or limit the application of section 187.3 of the Act; or

(*b*) the share was not acquired by the other corporation in the course of an underwriting of shares of that class to be distributed to the public and

(i) dividends are received at the particular time by the other corporation, or by the other corporation and corporations controlled by the other corporation, in respect of more than 10 per cent of the shares of that class issued and outstanding at the last time before the particular time at which any such corporation acquired a share of that class,

(ii) the other corporation is a restricted financial institution and

(A) dividends are received at the particular time by the other corporation, or by the other corporation and corporations controlled by the other corporation, in respect of more than 5 per cent of the shares of that class issued and outstanding at the last time before the particular time at which any such corporation acquired a share of that class, and

(B) a dividend is received at the particular time by the other corporation, or a corporation controlled by the other corporation, in respect of a share of that class acquired after December 15, 1987 and before the particular time, or

(iii) the other corporation is a restricted financial institution and the share

(A) was acquired after December 15, 1987 and before the particular time, and

(B) was, because of subparagraph (*h*)(i), (ii), (iii) or (v) of the definition "term preferred share" in subsection 248(1) of the Act, deemed to have been issued after December 15, 1987 and before the particular time.

(6) For the purposes of paragraph (*f*) of the definition "term preferred share" in subsection 248(1) of the Act, a share of the capital stock of a corporation that is a member institution of a deposit insurance corporation, within the meaning assigned by section 137.1 of the Act, is a prescribed share with respect to the deposit insurance corporation and any subsidiary wholly-owned corporation of the deposit insurance corporation deemed by subsection 137.1(5.1) of the Act to be a deposit insurance corporation.

(7) For the purposes of the definition "taxable preferred share" in subsection 248(1) of the Act, the following shares are prescribed shares at any particular time:

(*a*) the 8.5 per cent Cumulative Redeemable Convertible Class A Preferred Shares of St. Marys Paper Inc. issued on July 7, 1987, where such shares are not deemed, by reason of paragraph (*e*) of the definition "taxable preferred share" in subsection 248(1) of the Act, to have been issued after that date and before the particular time; and

(*b*) the Cumulative Redeemable Preferred Shares of CanUtilities Holdings Ltd. issued before July 1, 1991, unless the amount of the consideration for which all such shares were issued exceeds $300,000,000 or the particular time is after July 1, 2001.

(8) For the purposes of paragraph 112(2.2)(*d*) of the Act, paragraph (*i*) of the definition "short-term preferred share", the definition "taxable preferred share" and paragraph (*f*) of the definition "term preferred share" in subsection 248(1) of the Act, the Exchangeable Preference Shares of Canada Cement Lafarge Ltd. (in this subsection referred to as the "subject shares"), the Exchangeable Preference Shares of Lafarge Canada Inc. and the shares of any corporation formed as a result of an amalgamation or merger of Lafarge Canada Inc. with one or more other corporations are prescribed shares at any particular time where the terms and conditions of such shares at the particular time are the same as, or substantially the same as, the terms and conditions of the subject shares as of June 18, 1987 and, for the purposes of this subsection, the amalgamation or merger of one or more corporations with another corporation formed as a result of an amalgamation or merger of Lafarge Canada Inc. with one or more other corporations shall be deemed to be an amalgamation of Lafarge Canada Inc. with another corporation.

(9) For the purposes of determining under subsections (2), (4), (5) and (5.1) the time at which a share of a class of the capital stock of a corporation was acquired by a taxpayer, shares of that class acquired by the taxpayer at any particular time before a disposition by the taxpayer of shares of that class shall be deemed to have been disposed of before shares of that class acquired by the taxpayer before that particular time.

(10) For the purposes of subsections (2), (4), (5) and (5.1) and this subsection,

(*a*) where a taxpayer is a beneficiary of a trust and an amount in respect of the beneficiary has been designated by the trust in a taxation year pursuant to subsection 104(19) of the Act, the taxpayer shall be deemed to have received the amount so designated at the time it was received by the trust; and

(*b*) where a taxpayer is a member of a partnership and a dividend has been received by the partnership, the taxpayer's share of the dividend shall be deemed to have been received by the taxpayer at the time the dividend was received by the partnership.

(11) For the purposes of subsections (2), (4), (5) and (5.1),

(*a*) a share of the capital stock of a corporation acquired by a person after December 15, 1987 pursuant to an agreement in writing entered into before December 16, 1987 shall be deemed to have been acquired by that person before December 16, 1987;

(*b*) a share of the capital stock of a corporation acquired by a person after December 15, 1987 and before July, 1988 as part of a distribution to the public made in accordance with the terms of a prospectus, preliminary prospectus, registration statement, offering memorandum or notice filed before December 16, 1987 with a public authority pursuant to and in accordance with the securities legislation of the jurisdiction in which the shares were distributed shall be deemed to have been acquired by that person before December 16, 1987;

(*c*) where a share that was owned by a particular restricted financial institution on December 15, 1987 has, by one or more transactions between related restricted financial institutions, been transferred to another restricted financial institution, the share shall be deemed to have been acquired by the other restricted financial institution before that date and after June 28, 1982 unless at any particular time after December 15, 1987 and before the share was transferred to the other restricted financial institution the share was owned by a shareholder who, at that particular time, was a person other than a restricted financial institution related to the other restricted financial institution; and

(*d*) where at any particular time there has been an amalgamation (within the meaning assigned by section 87 of the Act) and

(i) each of the predecessor corporations (within the meaning assigned by section 87 of the Act) was a restricted financial institution throughout the period beginning December 16, 1987 and ending at the particular time and the predecessor corporations were related to each other throughout that period, or

(ii) each of the predecessor corporations and the new corporation (within the meaning assigned by section 87 of the Act) is a corporation described in any of paragraphs (*a*) to (*d*) of the definition "restricted financial institution" in subsection 248(1) of the Act,

a share acquired by the new corporation from a predecessor corporation on the amalgamation shall be deemed to have been acquired by the new corporation at the time it was acquired by the predecessor corporation.

6202. Prescribed Shares

(1) For the purposes of paragraph 66(15)(*d*.1) and subparagraphs 66.1(6)(*a*)(v) [subsection 66.1(6) "Canadian exploration expense"], 66.2(5)(*a*)(v) [subsection 66.2(5) "Canadian development expense"] and 66.4(5)(*a*)(iii) [subsection 66.4(5) "Canadian oil and gas property expense"] of the Act, a share of a class of the capital stock of a corporation (in this section referred to as the "issuing corporation") is a prescribed share if it was issued after December 31, 1982 and

(*a*) the issuing corporation, any person related to the issuing corporation or of whom the issuing corporation has effective management or control or any partnership or trust of which the issuing corporation or a person related thereto is a member or beneficiary (each of which is referred to in this section as a "member of the related issuing group") is or may be required to redeem, acquire or cancel, in whole or in part, the share or to reduce its paid-up capital at any time within five years from the date of its issue,

(*b*) a member of the related issuing group provides or may be required to provide any form of guarantee, security or similar indemnity with respect to the share (other than a guarantee, security or similar indemnity with respect to any amount of assistance or benefit from a government, municipality or other public authority in Canada or with respect to eligibility for such assistance or benefit) that could take effect within five years from the date of its issue,

(*c*) the share (referred to in this section as the "convertible share") is convertible under its terms or conditions at any time within five years from the date of its issue directly or indirectly into debt, or into a share (referred to in this section as the "acquired share") that is, or if issued would be, a prescribed share,

(*d*) immediately after the share was issued, the person to whom the share was issued or a person related to the person to whom the share was issued (either alone or together with a related person, a related group of persons of which he is a member or a partnership or trust of which he is a member or beneficiary) controls directly or indirectly, or has an absolute or contingent right to control directly or indirectly or to acquire direct or indirect control of, the issuing corporation and the issuing corporation has the right under the terms and conditions in respect of which the share was issued to redeem, purchase or otherwise acquire the share within five years from the date of its issue,

(*e*) at the time the share was issued, the existence of the issuing corporation was, or there was an arrangement (other than an amalgamation within the meaning assigned by subsection 87(1) of the Act) under which the existence of the issuing corporation

Regulations

could be, limited to a period that ends within five years from the date of its issue, or

(*f*) the terms or conditions of the share (referred to in this paragraph as the "first share") or of an agreement in existence at the time of its issue provide that a share (referred to in this section as the "substituted share") that is, or if issued would be, a prescribed share may be substituted or exchanged for the first share within five years from the date of issue of the first share,

but does not include a share of the capital stock of a corporation

(*g*) that was issued after December 31, 1982 pursuant to an agreement or offering in writing made on or before December 31, 1982 or in accordance with a prospectus, registration statement or similar document that was filed with and, where required by law, accepted for filing by, a public authority in Canada pursuant to and in accordance with the laws of Canada or of any province on or before December 31, 1982,

(*h*) that would be a prescribed share solely by virtue of one or more of the terms or conditions of an agreement if such terms or conditions are not effective or exercisable until the death, disability or bankruptcy of the person to whom the share is issued,

(*i*) that is

(i) convertible under its terms into one or more shares of a class of the capital stock of the corporation for no consideration other than the share or shares,

(ii) described in paragraph (*a*) solely because

(A) it is to be cancelled on the conversion within five years from the date of its issue,

(B) its paid-up capital is to be reduced on the conversion within five years from the date of its issue, or

(C) both clauses (A) and (B) apply, and

(iii) not described in paragraph (*c*), or

(*j*) that

(i) may have a share substituted or exchanged for it pursuant to its terms or the terms or conditions of an agreement in existence at the time of its issue and no consideration is to be received or receivable for it in respect of the substitution or exchange other than the share substituted or exchanged for it,

(ii) is described in paragraph (*a*) solely because it is to be redeemed, acquired or cancelled on the substitution or exchange within five years from the date of its issue, and

(iii) is not a share to which paragraph (*f*) applies,

and for the purposes of this section,

(*k*) where a person has an interest in a trust, whether directly or indirectly, through an interest in any other trust or in any other manner whatever, the person shall be deemed to be a beneficiary of the trust;

(*l*) in determining whether an acquired share would be a prescribed share if issued,

(i) the references in paragraphs (*a*), (*b*), (*d*) and (*e*) to "date of its issue" shall be read as "date of the issue of the convertible share",

(ii) the reference in paragraph (*f*) to "issue of the first share" shall be read as "issue of the convertible share", and

(iii) this section shall be read without reference to paragraph (*g*) and to the words "after December 31, 1982";

(*m*) in determining whether a substituted share would be a prescribed share if issued,

(i) the references in paragraphs (*a*) to (*e*) to "date of its issue" shall be read as "date of the issue of the first share", and

(ii) this section shall be read without reference to paragraph (*g*) and to the words "after December 31, 1982";

(*m*.1) an excluded obligation in relation to a share of a class of the capital stock of the issuing corporation and an obligation that would be an excluded obligation in relation to the share if the share had been issued after June 17, 1987, shall be deemed not to be a guarantee, security or similar indemnity with respect to the share for the purposes of paragraph (*b*);

(*n*) a guarantee, security or similar indemnity referred to in paragraph (*b*) shall, for greater certainty, not be considered to take effect within five years from the date of issue of a share if the effect of the guarantee, security or indemnity is to provide that a member of the related issuing group will be able to redeem, acquire or cancel the share at a time that is not within five years from the date of issue of the share; and

(*o*) where an expense is incurred partly in consideration for shares (referred to in this section as "first corporation shares") of the capital stock of one corporation and partly in consideration for an interest in, or right to, shares (referred to in this paragraph as "second corporation shares") of the capital stock of another corporation, in determining whether the second corporation shares are prescribed shares, the references in paragraphs (*a*), (*d*) and (*e*) to "date of its issue" shall be read as "date of the issue of the first corporation shares".

(2) For the purposes of paragraph 66(15)(*d*.1) [subsection 66(15) "flow-through share"] of the Act, subsection (1) does not apply in respect of a share of the capital stock of an issuing corporation that is a new share.

6202.1. Prescribed Shares

(1) For the purposes of the definition "flow-through share" in subsection 66(15) of the Act, a new share of the capital stock of a corporation is a prescribed share if, at the time it is issued,

(*a*) under the terms or conditions of the share or any agreement in respect of the share or its issue,

(i) the amount of the dividends that may be declared or paid on the share (in this section referred to as the "dividend entitlement") may reasonably be considered to be, by way of a formula or otherwise,

(A) fixed,

(B) limited to a maximum, or

(C) established to be not less than a minimum (including any amount determined on a cumulative basis), where with respect to the dividends that may be declared or paid on the share there is a preference over any other dividends that may be declared or paid on any other share of the capital stock of the corporation,

(ii) the amount that the holder of the share is entitled to receive in respect of the share on the dissolution, liquidation or winding-up of the corporation, on a reduction of the paid-up capital of the share or on the redemption, acquisition or cancellation of the share by the corporation or by specified persons in relation to the corporation (in this section referred to as the "liquidation entitlement") may reasonably be considered to be, by way of a formula or otherwise, fixed, limited to a maximum or established to be not less than a minimum,

(iii) the share is convertible or exchangeable into another security issued by the corporation unless

(A) it is convertible or exchangeable only into

(I) another share of the corporation that, if issued, would not be a prescribed share,

(II) a right (including a right conferred by a warrant) that

1. if it were issued, would not be a prescribed right, and

2. if it were exercised, would allow the person exercising it to acquire only a share of the corporation that, if the share were issued, would not be a prescribed share, or

(III) both a share described in subclause (I) and a right described in subclause (II), and

(B) all the consideration receivable by the holder on the conversion or exchange of the share is the share described in subclause (A)(I) or the right described in subclause (A)(II), or both, as the case may be, or

(iv) the corporation has, either absolutely or contingently, an obligation to reduce, or any person or partnership has, either absolutely or contingently, an obligation to cause the corporation to reduce, the paid-up capital in respect of the share (other than pursuant to a conversion or exchange of the share, where the right to so convert or exchange does not cause the share to be a prescribed share under subparagraph (iii));

(*b*) any person or partnership has, either absolutely or contingently, an obligation (other than an excluded obligation in relation to the share)

(i) to provide assistance,

(ii) to make a loan or payment,

(iii) to transfer property, or

(iv) otherwise to confer a benefit by any means whatever, including the payment of a dividend,

either immediately or in the future, that may reasonably be considered to be, directly or indirectly, a repayment or return by the corporation or a specified person in relation to the corporation of all or part of the consideration for which the share was issued or for which a partnership interest was issued in a partnership that acquires the share;

(*c*) any person or partnership has, either absolutely or contingently, an obligation (other than an excluded obligation in relation to the share) to effect any undertaking, either immediately or in the future, with respect to the share or the agreement under which the share is issued (including any guarantee, security, indemnity, covenant or agreement and including the lending of funds to or the placing of amounts on deposit with, or on behalf of, the holder of the share or, where the holder is a partnership, the members thereof or specified persons in relation to the holder or the members of the partnership, as the case may be) that may reasonably be considered to have been given to ensure, directly or indirectly, that

(i) any loss that the holder of the share and, where the holder is a partnership, the members thereof or specified persons in relation to the holder or the members of the partnership, as the case may be, may sustain by reason of the holding, ownership or disposition of the share or any other property is limited in any respect, or

(ii) the holder of the share and, where the holder is a partnership, the members thereof or specified persons in relation to the holder or the members of the partnership, as the case may be, will derive earnings by reason of the holding, ownership or disposition of the share or any other property;

(*d*) the corporation or a specified person in relation to the corporation may reasonably be expected

(i) to acquire or cancel the share in whole or in part otherwise than on a conversion or exchange of the share that meets the conditions set out in clauses (*a*)(iii)(A) and (B),

(ii) to reduce the paid-up capital of the corporation in respect of the share otherwise than on a conversion or exchange of the share that meets the conditions set out in clauses (*a*)(iii)(A) and (B), or

(iii) to make a payment, transfer or other provision, (otherwise than pursuant to an excluded obligation in relation to the share), directly or indirectly, by way of a dividend, loan, purchase of shares, financial assistance to any purchaser of the share or, where the purchaser is a partnership, the members thereof or in any other manner whatever, that may reasonably be considered to be a repayment or return of all or part of the consid-

Regulations

eration for which the share was issued or for which a partnership interest was issued in a partnership that acquires the share,

within 5 years after the date the share is issued, otherwise than as a consequence of an amalgamation of a subsidiary wholly-owned corporation, a winding-up of a subsidiary wholly-owned corporation to which subsection 88(1) of the Act applies or the payment of a dividend by a subsidiary wholly-owned corporation to its parent;

(*e*) any person or partnership can reasonably be expected to effect, within 5 years after the date the share is issued, any undertaking which, if it were in effect at the time the share was issued, would result in the share being a prescribed share by reason of paragraph (*c*); or

(*f*) it may reasonably be expected that, within 5 years after the date the share is issued,

(i) any of the terms or conditions of the share or any existing agreement relating to the share or its issue will thereafter be modified, or

(ii) any new agreement relating to the share or its issue will be entered into,

in such a manner that the share would be a prescribed share if it had been issued at the time of the modification or at the time when the new agreement is entered into.

History: S. 6202.1(1)(*a*)(iii)(A) and (B) were replaced by S.C. 2013, c. 34, s. 402(2), applicable to shares and rights issued under an agreement made after December 20, 2002, and formerly read:

(A) it is convertible or exchangeable only into

(I) another share of the corporation that, if issued, would not be a prescribed share,

(II) a right, including a right conferred by a warrant that, if exercised, would allow the person exercising it to acquire only a share of the corporation that, if issued, would not be a prescribed share, or

(III) both a share described in subclause (I) and a right or warrant described in subclause (II), and

(B) all the consideration receivable by the holder on the conversion or exchange of the share is the share described in subclause (A)(I) or the right or warrant described in subclause (A)(II), or both, as the case may be, or

Income Tax Folios: *Primary* — S3-F8-C2 Tax Incentives for Clean Energy Equipment.

(1.1) For the purpose of the definition "flow-through share" in subsection 66(15) of the Act, a new right to acquire a share of the capital stock of a corporation is a prescribed right if, at the time the right is issued,

(*a*) the amount that the holder of the right is entitled to receive in respect of the right on the dissolution, liquidation or winding-up of the corporation or on the redemption, acquisition or cancellation of the right by the corporation or by specified persons in relation to the corporation (referred to in this section as the "liquidation entitlement" of the right) can reasonably be considered to be, by way of a formula or otherwise, fixed, limited to a maximum or established to be not less than a minimum;

(*b*) the right is convertible or exchangeable into another security issued by the corporation unless

(i) the right is convertible or exchangeable only into

(A) a share of the corporation that, if issued, would not be a prescribed share,

(B) another right (including a right conferred by a warrant) that

(I) if it were issued, would not be a prescribed right, and

(II) if it were exercised, would allow the person exercising it to acquire only a share of the corporation that, if the share were issued, would not be a prescribed share, or

(C) both a share described in clause (A) and a right described in clause (B), and

(ii) all the consideration receivable by the holder on the conversion or exchange of the right is the share described in clause (A) or the right described in clause (B), or both, as the case may be;

(*c*) any person or partnership has, either absolutely or contingently, an obligation (other than an excluded obligation in relation to the right)

(i) to provide assistance,

(ii) to make a loan or payment,

(iii) to transfer property, or

(iv) to otherwise confer a benefit by any means whatever, including the payment of a dividend,

either immediately or in the future, that can reasonably be considered to be, directly or indirectly, a repayment or return by the corporation or a specified person in relation to the corporation of all or part of the consideration for which the right was issued or for which a partnership interest was issued in a partnership that acquires the right;

(*d*) any person or partnership has, either absolutely or contingently, an obligation (other than an excluded obligation in relation to the right) to effect any undertaking, either immediately or in the future, with respect to the right or the agreement under which the right is issued (including any guarantee, security, indemnity, covenant or agreement and including the lending of funds to or the placing of amounts on deposit with, or on behalf of, the holder of the right or where the holder is a partnership, the members of the partnership or specified persons in relation to the holder or the members of the partnership, as the case may be) that can reasonably be considered to have been given to ensure, directly or indirectly, that

(i) any loss that the holder of the right and, where the holder is a partnership, the members of the partnership or specified persons in relation to the holder or the members of the partnership, as the case may be, may sustain because of the holding, ownership or disposition of the right or any other property is limited in any respect, or

(ii) the holder of the right and, where the holder is a partnership, the members of the partnership or specified persons in relation to the holder or the members of the partnership, as the case may be, will derive earnings, because of the holding, ownership or disposition of the right or any other property;

(e) the corporation or a specified person in relation to the corporation can reasonably be expected

(i) to acquire or cancel the right in whole or in part otherwise than on a conversion or exchange of the right that meets the conditions set out in subparagraphs (b)(i) and (ii), or

(ii) to make a payment, transfer or other provision (otherwise than pursuant to an excluded obligation in relation to the right), directly or indirectly, by way of a dividend, loan, purchase of rights, financial assistance to any purchaser of the right or, where the purchaser is a partnership, the members of the partnership or in any other manner whatever, that can reasonably be considered to be a repayment or return of all or part of the consideration for which the right was issued or for which a partnership interest was issued in a partnership that acquires the right,

within five years after the date the right is issued, otherwise than as a consequence of an amalgamation of a subsidiary wholly-owned corporation, a winding-up of a subsidiary wholly-owned corporation to which subsection 88(1) of the Act applies or the payment of a dividend by a subsidiary wholly-owned corporation to its parent;

(f) any person or partnership can reasonably be expected to effect, within five years after the day the right is issued, any undertaking which, if it were in effect at the time the right was issued, would result in the right being a prescribed right because of paragraph (d);

(g) it can reasonably be expected that, within five years after the date the right is issued,

(i) any of the terms or conditions of the right or any existing agreement relating to the right or its issue will be modified in such a manner that the right would be a prescribed right if it had been issued at the time of the modification, or

(ii) any new agreement relating to the right or its issue will be entered into in such a manner that the right would be a prescribed right if it had been issued at the time the new agreement is entered into; or

(h) it can reasonably be expected that the right, if exercised, would allow the person exercising the right to acquire a share in a corporation that, if that share were issued, would be a prescribed share within five years after the day the right was issued.

History: S. 6202.1(1.1) was added by S.C. 2013, c. 34, s. 402(3), applicable to shares and rights issued under an agreement made after December 20, 2002.

Income Tax Folios: *Primary* — S3-F8-C2 Tax Incentives for Clean Energy Equipment.

(2) For the purposes of the definition "flow-through share" in subsection 66(15) of the Act, a new share of the capital stock of a corporation is a prescribed share if

(a) the consideration for which the share is to be issued is to be determined more than 60 days after entering into the agreement pursuant to which the share is to be issued;

(b) the corporation or a specified person in relation to the corporation, directly or indirectly,

(i) provided assistance,

(ii) made or arranged for a loan or payment,

(iii) transferred property, or

(iv) otherwise conferred a benefit by any means whatever, including the payment of a dividend,

for the purpose of assisting any person or partnership in acquiring the share or any person or partnership in acquiring an interest in a partnership acquiring the share (otherwise than by reason of an excluded obligation in relation to the share); or

(c) the holder of the share or, where the holder is a partnership, a member thereof, has a right under any agreement or arrangement entered into under circumstances where it is reasonable to consider that the agreement or arrangement was contemplated at or before the time when the agreement to issue the share was entered into,

(i) to dispose of the share, and

(ii) through a transaction or event or a series of transactions or events contemplated by the agreement or arrangement, to acquire a share (referred to in this paragraph as the "acquired share") of the capital stock of another corporation that would be a prescribed share under subsection (1) if the acquired share were issued at the time the share was issued, other than a share that would not be a prescribed share if subsection (1) were read without reference to subparagraphs (a)(iv) and (d)(i) and (ii) thereof where the acquired share is a share

(A) of a mutual fund corporation, or

(B) of a corporation that becomes a mutual fund corporation within 90 days after the acquisition of the acquired share.

Income Tax Folios: *Primary* — S3-F8-C2 Tax Incentives for Clean Energy Equipment.

(2.1) For the purpose of the definition "flow-through share" in subsection 66(15) of the Act, a new right is a prescribed right if

(a) the consideration for which the new right is to be issued is to be determined more than 60 days after entering into the agreement pursuant to which the new right is to be issued;

(b) the corporation or a specified person in relation to the corporation, directly or indirectly, for the purpose of assisting any person or partnership to acquire the new right or any person or partnership to acquire an interest in a partnership acquiring the new right (otherwise than because of an excluded obligation in relation to the new right),

(i) provided assistance,

(ii) made or arranged for a loan or payment,

(iii) transferred property, or

(iv) otherwise conferred a benefit by any means whatever, including the payment of a dividend; or (*c*) the holder of the new right or, where the holder is a partnership, a member of the partnership, has a right under any agreement or arrangement entered into under circumstances where it is reasonable to consider that the agreement or arrangement was contemplated at or before the time the agreement to issue the new right was entered into,

(i) to dispose of the new right, and

(ii) through a transaction or event or a series of transactions or events contemplated by the agreement or arrangement, to acquire

(A) a share (referred to in this paragraph as the "acquired share") of the capital stock of another corporation that would be a prescribed share under subsection (1) if the acquired share were issued at the time the new right was issued, other than a share that would not be a prescribed share if subsection (1) were read without reference to subparagraphs (1)(*a*)(iv) and (1)(*d*)(i) and (ii) where the acquired share is a share

(I) of a mutual fund corporation, or

(II) of a corporation that becomes a mutual fund corporation within 90 days after the acquisition of the acquired share, or

(B) a right (referred to in this paragraph as the "acquired right") to acquire a share of the capital stock of another corporation that would, if it were issued at the time the new right was issued, be a prescribed right, other than a right that would not be a prescribed right if subsection (1.1) were read without reference to subparagraph (1.1)(*e*)(i) where the acquired right is a right to acquire a share of the capital stock

(I) of a mutual fund corporation, or

(II) of a corporation that becomes a mutual fund corporation within 90 days after the acquisition of the acquired right.

History: S. 6202.1(2.1) was added by S.C. 2013, c. 34, s. 402(4), applicable to shares and rights issued under an agreement made after December 20, 2002.

Income Tax Folios: *Primary* — S3-F8-C2 Tax Incentives for Clean Energy Equipment.

(3) For the purposes of subsections (1) and (1.1),

(*a*) the dividend entitlement of a share of the capital stock of a corporation is deemed not to be fixed, limited to a maximum or established to be not less than a minimum where all dividends on the share are determined solely by reference to a multiple or fraction of the dividend entitlement of another share of the capital stock of the corporation, or of another corporation that controls the corporation, where the dividend entitlement of that other share is not described in subparagraph (1)(*a*)(i); and

(*b*) the liquidation entitlement of a share of the capital stock of a corporation, or of a right to acquire a share of the capital stock of the corporation, as the case may be, is deemed not to be fixed, limited to a maximum or established to be not less than a minimum where

(i) all the liquidation entitlement is determinable solely by reference to

(A) the liquidation entitlement of another share of the capital stock of the corporation (or a share of the capital stock of another corporation that controls the corporation), or

(B) the liquidation entitlement of a right to acquire the capital stock of the corporation (or another corporation that controls the corporation),

(ii) the liquidation entitlement described in clause (i)(A), if any, is not described in subparagraph (1)(*a*)(ii), and

(iii) the liquidation entitlement described in clause (i)(B), if any, is not described in paragraph (1.1)(*a*).

History: S. 6202.1(3) was replaced by S.C. 2013, c. 34, s. 402(4), applicable to shares and rights issued under an agreement made after December 20, 2002, and formerly read:

(3) For the purposes of subsection (1),

(*a*) the dividend entitlement of a share of the capital stock of a corporation shall be deemed not to be fixed, limited to a maximum or established to be not less than a minimum where all dividends on the share are determined solely by reference to a multiple or fraction of the dividend entitlement of another share of the capital stock of the corporation, or of another corporation that controls the corporation, where the dividend entitlement of that other share is not described in subparagraph (1)(*a*)(i); and

(*b*) the liquidation entitlement of a share of the capital stock of a corporation shall be deemed not to be fixed, limited to a maximum or established to be not less than a minimum where all the liquidation entitlement is determinable solely by reference to the liquidation entitlement of another share of the capital stock of the corporation, or of another corporation that controls the corporation, where the liquidation entitlement of that other share is not described in subparagraph (1)(*a*)(ii).

(4) For the purposes of paragraphs (1)(*c*) and (*e*) and (1.1)(*d*) and (*f*), an agreement entered into between the first holder of a share or right and another person or partnership for the sale of the share or right to that other person or partnership for its fair market value at the time the share or right is acquired by the other person or partnership (determined without regard to the agreement) is deemed not to be an undertaking with respect to the share or right, as the case may be.

History: S. 6202.1(4) was replaced by S.C. 2013, c. 34, s. 402(4), applicable to shares and rights issued under an agreement made after December 20, 2002, and formerly read:

(4) For the purposes of paragraphs (1)(*c*) and (*e*), an agreement entered into between the first holder of a share and another person or partnership for the sale of the share to that other person or partnership for its fair market value at the time the share is acquired by the other person or partnership (determined without regard to the agreement) shall be deemed not to be an undertaking with respect to the share.

(5) For the purposes of section 6202 and this section, ***"excluded obligation"***, in relation to a share or new right issued by a corporation, means

(*a*) an obligation of the corporation

(i) with respect to eligibility for, or the amount of, any assistance under the *Canadian Exploration and Development Incentive Program Act*, the *Canadian Exploration Incentive Program Act*, the *Ontario Mineral Exploration Program Act*, R.S.O., c. O.27, or *The Mineral Exploration Incentive Program Act*, S.M. 1991-92, c. 45, or

(ii) with respect to the making of an election respecting such assistance and the flowing out of such assistance to the holder of the share or the new right in accordance with any of those Acts,

(*b*) an obligation of the corporation, in respect of the share or the new right, to distribute an amount that represents a payment out of assistance to which the corporation is entitled

(i) as a consequence of the corporation making expenditures funded by consideration received for shares or new rights issued by the corporation in respect of which the corporation purports to renounce an amount under subsection 66(12.6) of the Act, and

(ii) under section 25.1 of the *Income Tax Act*, R.S.B.C., 1996, c. 215, or

(*c*) an obligation of any person or partnership to effect an undertaking to indemnify a holder of the share or the new right or, where the holder is a partnership, a member of the partnership, for an amount not exceeding the amount of any tax payable under the Act or the laws of a province by the holder or the member of the partnership, as the case may be, as a consequence of

(i) the failure of the corporation to renounce an amount to the holder in respect of the share or the new right, or

(ii) a reduction, under subsection 66(12.73) of the Act, of an amount purported to be renounced to the holder in respect of the share or the new right;

Income Tax Folios: *Primary* — S3-F8-C2 Tax Incentives for Clean Energy Equipment.

"new right" means a right that is issued after December 20, 2002 to acquire a share of the capital stock of a corporation, other than a right that is issued at a particular time before 2003

(*a*) pursuant to an agreement in writing made on or before December 20, 2002,

(*b*) as part of a distribution of rights to the public made in accordance with the terms of a prospectus, preliminary prospectus, registration statement, offering memorandum or notice, required by law to be filed before distribution of the rights begins, filed on or before December 20, 2002 with a public authority in Canada in accordance with the securities legislation of the province in which the rights are distributed, or

(*c*) to a partnership interests in which were issued as part of a distribution to the public made in accordance with the terms of a prospectus, preliminary prospectus, registration statement, offering memorandum or notice, required by law to be filed before distribution of the interests begins, filed on or before December 20, 2002 with a public authority in Canada in accordance with the securities legislation of the province in which the interests are distributed, where all interests in the partnership issued at or before the particular time were issued

(i) as part of the distribution, or

(ii) before the beginning of the distribution;

"new share" means a share of the capital stock of a corporation issued after June 17, 1987, other than a share issued at a particular time before 1989

(*a*) pursuant to an agreement in writing entered into before June 18, 1987,

(*b*) as part of a distribution of shares to the public made in accordance with the terms of a prospectus, preliminary prospectus, registration statement, offering memorandum or notice, required by law to be filed before distribution of the shares begins, filed before June 18, 1987 with a public authority in Canada in accordance with the securities legislation of the province in which the shares were distributed, or

(*c*) to a partnership in which interests were issued as part of a distribution to the public made in accordance with the terms of a prospectus, preliminary prospectus, registration statement, offering memorandum or notice, required by law to be filed before distribution of the interests begins, filed before June 18, 1987 with a public authority in Canada in accordance with the securities legislation of the province in which the interests were distributed, where all interests in the partnership issued at or before the particular time were issued as part of the distribution or prior to the beginning of the distribution;

"specified person", in relation to any particular person, means another person with whom the particular person does not deal at arm's length or any partnership or trust of which the particular person or the other person is a member or beneficiary, respectively.

History: S. 6202.1(5), the definition "excluded obligation" was replaced by S.C. 2013, c. 34, s. 402(5), applicable to shares and rights issued under an agreement made after December 20, 2002, and formerly read:

"excluded obligation", in relation to a share issued by a corporation, means

(*a*) an obligation of the corporation

(i) with respect to eligibility for, or the amount of, any assistance under the *Canadian Exploration and Development Incentive Program Act*, the *Canadian Exploration Incentive Program Act*, the *Ontario Mineral Exploration Program Act, 1989*, Statutes of Ontario 1989, c. 40, or the *Mineral Exploration Incentive Program Act (Manitoba)*, Statutes of Manitoba 1990-91, c. 45, or

(ii) with respect to the making of an election respecting such assistance and the flowing out of such assistance to the holder of the share in accordance with any of those Acts,

(*a*.1) an obligation of the corporation, in respect of the share, to distribute an amount that represents a payment out of assistance to which the corporation is entitled

(i) under section 25.1 of the *Income Tax Act*, Revised Statutes of British Columbia, 1996, c. 215, and

(ii) as a consequence of the corporation making expenditures funded by consideration received for shares issued by the corporation in respect of which the corporation purports to renounce an amount under subsection 66(12.6) of the Act, and

(*b*) an obligation of any person or partnership to effect an undertaking to indemnify a holder of the share or, where the holder is a partnership, a member thereof, for an amount not exceeding the amount of any tax payable under the Act or the laws of a province by the holder or the member of the partnership, as the case may be, as a consequence of

(i) the failure of the corporation to renounce an amount to the holder in respect of the share, or

(ii) a reduction, under subsection 66(12.73) of the Act, of an amount purported to be renounced to the holder in respect of the share;

S. 6202.1(5), the definition "new right" was added by S.C. 2013, c. 34, s. 402(6), applicable to shares and rights issued under an agreement made after December 20, 2002.

6203. Prescribed Shares

(1) For the purposes of subsection 192(6) of the Act, a prescribed share of the capital stock of a taxable Canadian corporation is a share (other than a share acquired by a taxpayer under circumstances referred to in section 66.3 of the Act, a share acquired as consideration for a disposition of property in respect of which an election was made under subsection 85(1) or (2) of the Act and a share that can be considered to have been issued, directly or indirectly, for consideration that includes other shares of the capital stock of the corporation) where, at the time it is issued,

(*a*) under the terms or conditions of the share or any agreement in respect of the share or its issue,

(i) the amount of the dividends (in this section referred to as the "dividend entitlement") that the corporation may declare or pay on the share is not limited to a maximum amount or fixed at a minimum amount at that time or at any time thereafter by way of a formula or otherwise,

(ii) the amount (in this section referred to as the "liquidation entitlement") that the holder of the share is entitled to receive on the share on the dissolution, liquidation or winding-up of the corporation is not limited to a maximum amount or fixed at a minimum amount by way of a formula or otherwise,

(iii) the share cannot be converted into any other security, other than into another security of the corporation that would, if it were issued for consideration that does not include other shares of the capital stock of the corporation, be a prescribed share,

(iv) the holder of the share cannot at that time or at any time thereafter cause the share to be redeemed, acquired or cancelled by the corporation or any specified person in relation to the corporation, except where the redemption, acquisition or cancellation is required pursuant to a conversion that is not prohibited by subparagraph (iii),

(v) no person or partnership has, either absolutely or contingently, an obligation to reduce, or to cause the corporation to reduce, at that time or at any time thereafter, the paid-up capital in respect of the share, except where the reduction is required pursuant to a conversion that is not prohibited by subparagraph (iii),

(vi) no person or partnership has, either absolutely or contingently, an obligation at that time or at any time thereafter to

(A) provide assistance to acquire the share,

(B) make a loan or payment,

(C) transfer property, or

(D) otherwise confer a benefit by any means whatever, including the payment of a dividend,

that may reasonably be considered to be, directly or indirectly, a repayment or return by the corporation or a specified person in relation to the corporation of all or part of the consideration for which the share was issued,

(vii) neither the corporation nor any specified person in relation to the corporation has, either absolutely or contingently, the right or obligation to redeem, acquire or cancel, at that time or at any time thereafter, the share in whole or in part other than for an amount that approximates the fair market value of the share (determined without reference to any such right or obligation), and

(viii) no person or partnership has, either absolutely or contingently, an obligation to provide, at that time or at any time thereafter, any form of undertaking with respect to the share (including any guarantee, security, indemnity, covenant or agreement and including the lending of funds to or the placing of amounts on deposit with, or on behalf of, the holder of the share or any specified person in relation to the holder) that may reasonably be considered to have been given to ensure that

(A) any loss that the holder of the share may sustain by virtue of the holding, ownership or disposition of the share is limited in any respect, or

(B) the holder of the share will derive earnings by virtue of the holding, ownership or disposition of the share;

(*b*) the corporation or a specified person in relation to the corporation cannot reasonably be expected to, within two years after the time the share is issued,

(i) acquire or cancel the share in whole or in part,

(ii) reduce the paid-up capital of the corporation in respect of the share, or

(iii) make a payment, transfer or other provision, directly or indirectly, by way of a dividend, loan, purchase of shares, financial assistance to any purchaser of the share or in any other manner whatever, that may reasonably be considered to be a repayment or return of all or part of the consideration for which the share was issued

otherwise than as a consequence of the payment of a dividend paid by a subsidiary wholly-owned corporation to its parent, of an amalgamation of a subsidiary wholly-owned corporation or of a winding-up to which subsection 88(1) of the Act applies;

(*c*) no person or partnership can reasonably be expected to provide, within two years after the time the share is issued, any form of undertaking with respect to the share (including any guarantee, security, indemnity, covenant or agreement and including the lending of funds to, or the placing of amounts on deposit with, or on behalf of, the holder of the share or any specified person in relation to the holder); and

(*d*) it cannot reasonably be expected that any of the terms or conditions of the share or any existing agreement in respect of the share or its issue will

Regulations

thereafter be modified or amended, or that any new agreement in respect of the share or its issue will be entered into, within two years after the time the share is issued, in such a manner that the share would not be a prescribed share if it had been issued at the time of such modification or amendment or at the time the new agreement is entered into.

(2) For the purposes of subsection (1),

(*a*) the dividend entitlement of a share of the capital stock of a corporation shall be deemed not to be limited to a maximum amount or fixed at a minimum amount where it may reasonably be considered that all or substantially all of the dividend entitlement is determinable by reference to the dividend entitlement of another share of the capital stock of the corporation that meets the requirements of subparagraph (1)(*a*)(i);

(*b*) the liquidation entitlement of a share of the capital stock of a corporation shall be deemed not to be limited to a maximum amount or fixed at a minimum amount where it may reasonably be considered that all or substantially all of the liquidation entitlement is determinable by reference to the liquidation entitlement of another share of the capital stock of the corporation that meets the requirements of subparagraph (1)(*a*)(ii);

(*c*) where a corporation has merged or amalgamated with one or more other corporations, the corporation formed as a result of the merger or amalgamation shall be deemed to be the same corporation as, and a continuation of, each of its predecessor corporations and a share issued on the merger or amalgamation as consideration for another share shall be deemed to be the same share as the share for which it was issued but this paragraph does not apply if the share issued on the merger or amalgamation is not a prescribed share at the time of its issue; and

(*d*) an agreement entered into between the first purchaser of a share and another person or partnership, other than a specified person in relation to the corporation issuing the share, for the sale of the share to that other person or partnership shall be deemed not to be an undertaking with respect to the share.

(3) For the purposes of subsections (1) and (2), "specified person", in relation to a corporation or a holder of a share, as the case may be (in this subsection referred to as the "taxpayer"), means any person or partnership with whom the taxpayer does not deal at arm's length or any partnership or trust of which the taxpayer (or a person or partnership with whom the taxpayer does not deal at arm's length) is a member or beneficiary, respectively.

6204. Prescribed Shares

(1) For the purposes of subparagraph 110(1)(*d*)(i.1) of the Act, a share is a prescribed share of the capital stock of a corporation at the time of its sale or issue, as the case may be, if, at that time,

(*a*) under the terms or conditions of the share or any agreement in respect of the share or its issue,

(i) the amount of the dividends (in this section referred to as the "dividend entitlement") that the corporation may declare or pay on the share is not limited to a maximum amount or fixed at a minimum amount at that time or at any time thereafter by way of a formula or otherwise,

(ii) the amount (in this section referred to as the "liquidation entitlement") that the holder of the share is entitled to receive on the share on the dissolution, liquidation or winding-up of the corporation is not limited to a maximum amount or fixed at a minimum amount by way of a formula or otherwise,

(iii) the share cannot be converted into any other security, other than into another security of the corporation or of another corporation with which it does not deal at arm's length that is, or would be at the date of conversion, a prescribed share,

(iv) the holder of the share cannot at that time or at any time thereafter cause the share to be redeemed, acquired or cancelled by the corporation or any specified person in relation to the corporation, except where the redemption, acquisition or cancellation is required pursuant to a conversion that is not prohibited by subparagraph (iii),

(v) no person or partnership has, either absolutely or contingently, an obligation to reduce, or to cause the corporation to reduce, at that time or at any time thereafter, the paid-up capital in respect of the share, except where the reduction is required pursuant to a conversion that is not prohibited by subparagraph (iii), and

(vi) neither the corporation nor any specified person in relation to the corporation has, either absolutely or contingently, the right or obligation to redeem, acquire or cancel, at that time or any later time, the share in whole or in part other than for an amount that approximates the fair market value of the share (determined without reference to any such right or obligation) or a lesser amount;

(*b*) the corporation or a specified person in relation to the corporation cannot reasonably be expected to, within two years after the time the share is sold or issued, as the case may be, redeem, acquire or cancel the share in whole or in part, or reduce the paid-up capital of the corporation in respect of the share, otherwise than as a consequence of

(i) an amalgamation of a subsidiary wholly-owned corporation,

(ii) a winding-up to which subsection 88(1) of the Act applies, or

(iii) a distribution or appropriation to which subsection 84(2) of the Act applies; and

Regulations

Proposed Amendment
Legislative Proposals Relating to the Income Tax Regulations (September 16, 2016)

Paragraph 6204(1)(*b*) of the Regulations is amended by striking out "or" at the end of subparagraph (ii), by adding "or" at the end of subparagraph (iii) and by adding the following after subparagraph (iii):

(iv) an exchange to which subsection 51(1) of the Act applies or a disposition to which subsection 86(1) of the Act applies, if no consideration is provided by the corporation for the share other than shares of the capital stock of the corporation that are prescribed shares; and

Applicable: To the 2012 and subsequent taxation years.

(*c*) it cannot reasonably be expected that any of the terms or conditions of the share or any existing agreement in respect of the share or its sale or issue will be modified or amended, or that any new agreement in respect of the share, its sale or issue will be entered into, within two years after the time the share is sold or issued, in such a manner that the share would not be a prescribed share if it had been sold or issued at the time of such modification or amendment or at the time the new agreement is entered into.

History: S. 6204(1), the portion before paragraph (*a*), was replaced by S.C. 2017, c. 33, s. 98(1), applicable in respect of acquisitions of securities and transfers or dispositions of rights that occur after 4:00 pm Eastern Standard Time on March 4, 2010, and formerly read:

(1) For the purposes of subparagraph 110(1)(*d*)(i) of the Act, a share is a prescribed share of the capital stock of a corporation at the time of its sale or issue, as the case may be, if, at that time,

S. 6204(1), the portion before paragraph (*a*) was replaced by P.C. 2010-548, SOR/2010-93, dated April 29, 2010, in force May 12, 2010, date of publication in the *Canada Gazette*. S. 6204(1), the portion before paragraph (*a*) formerly read:

(1) For the purposes of paragraph 110(1)(*d*) of the Act, a share is a prescribed share of the capital stock of a corporation at the time of its sale or issue, as the case may be, where, at that time,

Canadian Tax Foundation: Heakes, *Employee Share Ownership and Similar Arrangements for CCPCs*, 2017 Ontario Tax Conference 14:1–13; Carbone, *The Stock Option Deduction and Prescribed Shares*, 2017 Canadian Tax Focus 7(4):5.

(2) For the purposes of subsection (1),

(*a*) the dividend entitlement of a share of the capital stock of a corporation shall be deemed not to be limited to a maximum amount or fixed at a minimum amount where it may reasonably be considered that all or substantially all of the dividend entitlement is determinable by reference to the dividend entitlement of another share of the capital stock of the corporation that meets the requirements of subparagraph (1)(*a*)(i),

(*b*) the liquidation entitlement of a share of the capital stock of a corporation shall be deemed not to be limited to a maximum amount or fixed at a minimum amount where it may reasonably be considered that all or substantially all of the liquidation entitlement is determinable by reference to the liquidation entitlement of another share of the capital stock of the corporation that meets the requirements of subparagraph (1)(*a*)(ii), and

(*c*) the determination of whether a share of the capital stock of a particular corporation is a prescribed share shall be made without reference to a right or obligation to redeem, acquire or cancel the share, or to cause the share to be redeemed, acquired or cancelled, where

(i) the person (in this paragraph referred to as the "holder") to whom the share is sold or issued is, at the time the share is sold or issued, dealing at arm's length with the particular corporation and with each corporation with which the particular corporation is not dealing at arm's length,

(ii) the right or obligation is provided for in the terms or conditions of the share or in an agreement in respect of the share or its issue and, having regard to all the circumstances, it can reasonably be considered that

(A) the principal purpose of providing for the right or obligation is to protect the holder against any loss in respect of the share, and the amount payable on the redemption, acquisition or cancellation (in this subparagraph and in subparagraph (iii) referred to as the "acquisition") of the share will not exceed the adjusted cost base of the share to the holder immediately before the acquisition, or

(B) the principal purpose of providing for the right or obligation is to provide the holder with a market for the share, and the amount payable on the acquisition of the share will not exceed the fair market value of the share immediately before the acquisition, and

(iii) having regard to all the circumstances, it can reasonably be considered that no portion of the amount payable on the acquisition of the share is directly determinable by reference to the profits of the particular corporation, or of another corporation with which the particular corporation does not deal at arm's length, for all or any part of the period during which the holder owns the share or has a right to acquire the share, unless the reference to the profits of the particular corporation or the other corporation is only for the purpose of determining the fair market value of the share pursuant to a formula set out in the terms or conditions of the share or the agreement in respect of the share or its issue, as the case may be.

(3) For the purposes of subsection (1), "specified person", in relation to a corporation, means

(*a*) any person or partnership with whom the corporation does not deal at arm's length otherwise than because of a right referred to in paragraph 251(5)(*b*) of the Act that arises as a result of an offer by the person or partnership to acquire all or substantially all of the shares of the capital stock of the corporation, or

(*b*) any partnership or trust of which the corporation (or a person or partnership with whom the corporation does not deal at arm's length) is a member or beneficiary, respectively.

(4) For the purposes of subsection (3), the Act shall be read without reference to subsection 256(9) of the Act.

Interpretation Bulletins: *Secondary* — IT-113R4 Benefits to employees — Stock options.

6205. Prescribed Shares

(1) For the purposes of subsections 110.6(8) and (9) of the Act and subject to subsection (3), a prescribed share is a share of the capital stock of a corporation where

(*a*) under the terms or conditions of the share or any agreement in respect of the share or its issue,

(i) at the time the share is issued,

(A) the amount of the dividends (in this section referred to as the "dividend entitlement") that the corporation may declare or pay on the share is not limited to a maximum amount or fixed at a minimum amount at that time or at any time thereafter by way of a formula or otherwise,

(B) the amount (in this section referred to as the "liquidation entitlement") that the holder of the share is entitled to receive on the share on the dissolution, liquidation or winding-up of the corporation is not limited to a maximum amount or fixed at a minimum amount by way of a formula or otherwise,

(C) the share cannot be converted into any other security, other than into another security of the corporation that is, or would be at the date of conversion, a prescribed share,

(D) the holder of the share does not, at that time or at any time thereafter, have the right or obligation to cause the share to be redeemed, acquired or cancelled by the corporation or a specified person in relation to the corporation, except where the redemption, acquisition or cancellation is required pursuant to a conversion that is not prohibited by clause (C),

(E) no person or partnership has, either absolutely or contingently, an obligation to reduce, or to cause the corporation to reduce, at that time or at any time thereafter, the paid-up capital in respect of the share, otherwise than by way of a redemption, acquisition or cancellation of the share that is not prohibited by this section,

(F) no person or partnership has, either absolutely or contingently, an obligation (other than an excluded obligation in relation to the share, as defined in subsection 6202.1(5)) at that time or any time thereafter to

(I) provide assistance to acquire the share,

(II) make a loan or payment,

(III) transfer property, or

(IV) otherwise confer a benefit by any means whatever, including the payment of a dividend,

that may reasonably be considered to be, directly or indirectly, a repayment or return by the corporation or a specified person in relation to the corporation of all or part of the consideration for which the share was issued, and

(G) neither the corporation nor any specified person in relation to the corporation has, either absolutely or contingently, the right or obligation to redeem, acquire or cancel at that time or at any time thereafter, the share in whole or in part, except where the redemption, acquisition or cancellation is required pursuant to a conversion that is not prohibited by clause (C),

(ii) no person or partnership has, either absolutely or contingently, an obligation (other than an excluded obligation in relation to the share, as defined in subsection 6202.1(5)) to provide, at any time, any form of undertaking with respect to the share (including any guarantee, security, indemnity, covenant or agreement and including the lending of funds to or the placing of amounts on deposit with, or on behalf of, the holder of the share or any specified person in relation to that holder) that may reasonably be considered to have been given to ensure that

(A) any loss that the holder of the share may sustain by virtue of the holding, ownership or disposition of the share is limited in any respect, or

(B) the holder of the share will derive earnings by virtue of the holding, ownership or disposition of the share; and

(*b*) at the time the share is issued, it cannot reasonably be expected, having regard to all the circumstances, that any of the terms or conditions of the share or any existing agreement in respect of the share or its issue will thereafter be modified or amended or that any new agreement in respect of the share or its issue will be entered into, in such a manner that the share would not be a prescribed share if it had been issued at the time of such modification or amendment or at the time the new agreement is entered into.

(2) For the purposes of subsections 110.6(8) and (9) of the Act and subject to subsection (3), a prescribed share is a share of the capital stock of a particular corporation where

(*a*) it is a particular share that is owned by a person and that was issued by the particular corporation as part of an arrangement to that person, to a spouse, common-law partner or parent of that person or, if the person is a trust described in paragraph 104(4)(*a*) of the Act, to the person who created the trust or by whose will the trust was created or, if the person is a corporation, to another person owning all of the issued and outstanding shares of the capital stock of the corporation or to a spouse, common-law partner or parent of that other person, and

(i) the main purpose of the arrangement was to permit any increase in the value of the property of the particular corporation to accrue to other

Regulations

shares that would, at the time of their issue, be prescribed shares if this section were read without reference to this subsection, and

(ii) at the time of the issue of the particular share or at the end of the arrangement,

(A) the other shares were owned by

(I) the person to whom the particular share was issued (in this paragraph referred to as the "original holder"),

(II) a person who did not deal at arm's length with the original holder,

(III) a trust none of the beneficiaries of which were persons other than the original holder or a person who did not deal at arm's length with the original holder, or

(IV) any combination of persons described in subclause (I), (II) or (III),

(B) the other shares were owned by employees of the particular corporation or of a corporation controlled by the particular corporation, or

(C) the other shares were owned by any combination of persons each of whom is described in clause (A) or (B); or

(*b*) it is a share that was issued by a mutual fund corporation.

(*c*) (Revoked.)

(3) For the purposes of subsections 110.6(8) and (9) of the Act, a prescribed share does not include a share of the capital stock issued by a mutual fund corporation (other than an investment corporation) the value of which can reasonably be considered to be, directly or indirectly, derived primarily from investments made by the mutual fund corporation in one or more corporations (in this subsection referred to as an "investee corporation") connected with it (within the meaning of subsection 186(4) of the Act on the assumption that the references in that subsection to "payer corporation" and "particular corporation" were read as references to "investee corporation" and "mutual fund corporation", respectively).

(4) For the purposes of this section,

(*a*) the dividend entitlement of a share of the capital stock of a corporation shall be deemed not to be limited to a maximum amount or fixed at a minimum amount where it may reasonably be considered that

(i) all or substantially all of the dividend entitlement is determinable by reference to the dividend entitlement of another share of the capital stock of the corporation that meets the requirements of clause (1)(*a*)(i)(A), or

(ii) the dividend entitlement cannot be such as to impair the ability of the corporation to redeem another share of the capital stock of the corporation that meets the requirements of paragraph (2)(*a*);

(*b*) the liquidation entitlement of a share of the capital stock of a corporation shall be deemed not to be limited to a maximum amount or fixed at a minimum amount where it may reasonably be considered that all or substantially all of the liquidation entitlement is determinable by reference to the liquidation entitlement of another share of the capital stock of the corporation that meets the requirements of clause (1)(*a*)(i)(B);

(*c*) where two or more corporations (each of which is referred to in this paragraph as a "predecessor corporation") have merged or amalgamated, the corporation formed as a result of the merger or amalgamation (in this paragraph referred to as the "new corporation") shall be deemed to be the same corporation as, and a continuation of, each of the predecessor corporations and a share of the capital stock of the new corporation issued on the merger or amalgamation as consideration for a share of the capital stock of a predecessor corporation shall be deemed to be the same share as the share of the predecessor corporation for which it was issued, but this paragraph does not apply if the share issued on the merger or amalgamation is not a prescribed share at the time of its issue and either

(i) the terms and conditions of that share are not identical to those of the share of the predecessor corporation for which it was issued, or

(ii) at the time of its issue the fair market value of that share is not the same as that of the share of the predecessor corporation for which it was issued;

(*d*) a reference in clauses (1)(*a*)(i)(D) and (G) and subparagraph (1)(*a*)(ii) to a right or obligation of the corporation or a person or partnership does not include a right or obligation provided in a written agreement among shareholders of a private corporation owning more than 50% of its issued and outstanding share capital having full voting rights under all circumstances to which the corporation, person or partnership is a party unless it may reasonably be considered, having regard to all the circumstances, including the terms of the agreement and the number and relationship of the shareholders, that one of the main reasons for the existence of the agreement is to avoid or limit the application of subsection 110.6(8) or (9) of the Act;

(*e*) where at any particular time after November 21, 1985, the terms or conditions of a share are changed or any existing agreement in respect thereof is changed or a new agreement in respect of the share is entered into, the share shall, for the purpose of determining whether it is a prescribed share, be deemed to have been issued at that particular time; and

(*f*) the determination of whether a share of the capital stock of a corporation is a prescribed share for the purposes of subsection (1) shall be made without reference to a right or obligation to redeem, acquire or cancel the share or to cause the share to be redeemed, acquired or cancelled where

(i) the share was issued pursuant to an employee share purchase agreement (in this paragraph referred to as "the agreement") to an employee (in this paragraph referred to as "the holder") of the corporation or of a corporation with which it did not deal at arm's length,

(ii) the holder was dealing at arm's length with each corporation referred to in subparagraph (i) at the time the share was issued, and

(iii) having regard to all the circumstances including the terms of the agreement, it may reasonably be considered that

(A) the amount payable on the redemption, acquisition or cancellation (in this clause and in clause (B) referred to as the "acquisition") of the share will not exceed

(I) the adjusted cost base of the share to the holder immediately before the acquisition, where the acquisition was provided for in the agreement and the principal purpose for its provision was to protect the holder against any loss in respect of the share, or

(II) the fair market value of the share immediately before the acquisition, where the acquisition was provided for in the agreement and the principal purpose for its provision was to provide the holder with a market for the share, and

(B) no portion of the amount payable on the acquisition of the share is directly determinable by reference to the profits of the corporation, or of another corporation with which it does not deal at arm's length, for all or any part of the period during which the holder owned the share or had a right to acquire the share, unless the reference to the profits of the corporation or the other corporation is only for the purpose of determining the fair market value of the share pursuant to a formula set out in the agreement.

(5) For the purposes of this section, "specified person", in relation to a corporation or a holder of a share, as the case may be (in this subsection referred to as the "taxpayer"), means any person or partnership with whom the taxpayer does not deal at arm's length or any partnership or trust of which the taxpayer (or a person or partnership with whom the taxpayer does not deal at arm's length) is a member or beneficiary, respectively.

6206. Prescribed Shares

The Class I Special Shares of Reed Stenhouse Companies Limited, issued before January 1, 1986, are prescribed for the purposes of subsection 84(8) of the Act.

6207. Prescribed Shares

(1) For the purposes of paragraph 183.1(4)(*c*) [Repealed by S.C. 1988, c. 55, s. 149(1)] of the Act (as it read in its application to transactions entered into before September 13, 1988), a share is a prescribed share of the capital stock of an acquiring corporation where, at the time the share is issued

(*a*) under the terms or conditions of the share or any agreement in respect of the share or its issue,

(i) the amount of the dividends (in this section referred to as the "dividend entitlement") that the corporation may declare or pay on the share is not limited to a maximum amount or fixed at a minimum amount at that time or at any time thereafter by way of a formula or otherwise,

(ii) the amount (in this section referred to as the "liquidation entitlement") that the holder of the share is entitled to receive on the share on the dissolution, liquidation or winding-up of the corporation is not limited to a maximum amount or fixed at a minimum amount by way of a formula or otherwise,

(iii) the share cannot be converted into any other security, other than into another security of the corporation or of another corporation with which it does not deal at arm's length that is, or would be at the date of conversion, a prescribed share,

(iv) the holder of the share does not, at that time or at any time thereafter, have the right or obligation to cause the share to be redeemed, acquired or cancelled by the corporation or any specified person in relation to the corporation, except where the redemption, acquisition or cancellation is required pursuant to a conversion that is not prohibited by subparagraph (iii),

(v) no person or partnership has, either absolutely or contingently, an obligation to reduce, or to cause the corporation to reduce, at that time or at any time thereafter, the paid-up capital in respect of the share, otherwise than by way of a redemption, acquisition or cancellation of the share that is not prohibited by this section, and

(vi) neither the corporation nor any specified person in relation to the corporation has, either absolutely or contingently, the right or obligation to redeem, acquire or cancel, at that time or at any time thereafter, the share in whole or in part, except where the redemption, acquisition or cancellation is required pursuant to a conversion that is not prohibited by subparagraph (iii); and

(*b*) it cannot reasonably be expected, having regard to all the circumstances, that any of the terms or conditions of the share or any existing agreement in respect of the share or its issue will be modified or amended, or that any new agreement in respect of the share or its issue will be entered into, in such a manner that the share would not be a prescribed share if it had been issued at the time of such modification or amendment or at the time the new agreement is entered into.

(2) For the purposes of this section,

(*a*) the dividend entitlement of a share of the capital stock of a corporation shall be deemed not to be limited to a maximum amount or fixed at a minimum amount where it may reasonably be considered that all or substantially all the dividend entitlement is determinable by reference to the dividend entitlement of another share of the capital stock of

Regulations

the corporation that meets the requirements of subparagraph (1)(*a*)(i);

(*b*) the liquidation entitlement of a share of the capital stock of a corporation shall be deemed not to be limited to a maximum amount or fixed at a minimum amount where it may reasonably be considered that all or substantially all of the liquidation entitlement is determinable by reference to the liquidation entitlement of another share of the capital stock of the corporation that meets the requirements of subparagraph (1)(*a*)(ii);

(*c*) where at any particular time after June 3, 1987, the terms or conditions of a share are changed or any existing agreement in respect of the share is changed or a new agreement in respect of the share is entered into, the share shall, for the purpose of determining whether it is a prescribed share, be deemed to have been issued at that particular time;

(*d*) the determination of whether a share of the capital stock of a corporation owned by an employee of the corporation or another corporation with which it does not deal at arm's length is a prescribed share shall be made without reference to a right or obligation with respect to an acquisition of the share, the consideration for which is described in subparagraph 183.1(4)(*c*)(i) or (ii) [Repealed by S.C. 1988, c. 55, s. 149(1)] of the Act (as those subparagraphs read in their application to transactions entered into before September 13, 1988) where no portion of the amount payable on the acquisition of the share is directly determinable by reference to the profits of the corporation or the other corporation for all or any part of the period during which the employee owned the share or had a right to acquire the share, unless the reference to the profits of the corporation or the other corporation is only for the purpose of determining the fair market value of the share pursuant to a formula set out in the employee share purchase agreement under which the employee acquired the share; and

(*e*) a reference in subparagraphs (1)(*a*)(iv) and (vi) to a right or obligation of the corporation or a person or partnership does not include a right or obligation provided in a written agreement among shareholders of a private corporation owning more than 50% of its issued and outstanding share capital having full voting rights under all circumstances to which the corporation, person or partnership is a party unless it may reasonably be considered, having regard to all the circumstances including the terms of the agreement and the number and relationship of the shareholders, that one of the main reasons for the existence of the agreement is to avoid or limit the application of subsection 183.1(1) of the Act.

(3) For the purposes of subsection (1), "specified person" in relation to a corporation means any person or partnership with whom the corporation does not deal at arm's length or any partnership or trust of which the corporation (or a person or partnership with whom the corporation does not deal at arm's length) is a member or beneficiary, respectively.

Reg. 6207(3)

6208. Prescribed Shares

(1) For the purposes of clause 212(1)(*b*)(vii)(E) of the Act, a prescribed security with respect to an obligation of a corporation is

(*a*) a share of the capital stock of the corporation unless

(i) under the terms and conditions of the share, any agreement relating to the share or any modification of such terms, conditions or agreement, the corporation or a specified person in relation to the corporation is or may, at any time within 5 years after the date of the issue of the obligation, be required to redeem, acquire or cancel, in whole or in part, the share (unless the share is or may be required to be redeemed, acquired or cancelled by reason only of a right to convert the share into, or exchange the share for, another share of the corporation that, if issued, would be a prescribed security) or to reduce its paid-up capital,

(ii) as a result of the modification or establishment of the terms or conditions of the share or the changing or entering into of any agreement in respect of the share, the corporation or a specified person in relation to the corporation may, within 5 years after the date of the issue of the obligation, reasonably be expected to redeem, acquire or cancel, in whole or in part, the share (unless the share is or may be required to be redeemed, acquired or cancelled by reason only of a right to convert the share into, or exchange the share for, another share of the corporation that, if issued, would be a prescribed security) or to reduce its paid-up capital, or

(iii) as a result of the terms or conditions of the share or any agreement entered into by the corporation or a specified person in relation to the corporation or any modification of such terms, conditions or agreement, any person is required, either absolutely or contingently, within 5 years after the date of the issue of the obligation, to effect any undertaking, including any guarantee, covenant or agreement to purchase or repurchase the share, and including a loan of funds to or the placing of amounts on deposit with, or on behalf of, the shareholder or a specified person in relation to the shareholder given

(A) to ensure that any loss that the shareholder or a specified person in relation to the shareholder may sustain, by reason of the ownership, holding or disposition of the share or any other property, is limited in any respect, and

(B) as part of a transaction or event or series of transactions or events that included the issuance or acquisition of the obligation,

and for the purposes of this subparagraph, where such an undertaking in respect of a share is given at any particular time after the date of the issue of the obligation, the obligation shall be deemed to have been issued at the particular time and the undertaking shall be deemed to have been given as part of a series of transactions that included the issuance or acquisition of the obligation, and

(*b*) a right or warrant to acquire a share of the capital stock of the corporation that would, if issued, be a prescribed security with respect to the obligation,

where all the consideration receivable upon a conversion or exchange of the obligation or the prescribed security, as the case may be, is a share of the capital stock of the corporation described in paragraph (*a*) or a right or warrant described in paragraph (*b*), or both, as the case may be.

(2) For the purposes of this section, where a taxpayer may become entitled upon the conversion or exchange of an obligation or a prescribed security to receive consideration in lieu of a fraction of a share, that consideration shall be deemed not to be consideration unless it may reasonably be considered to be receivable as part of a series of transactions or events one of the main purposes of which is to avoid or limit the application of Part XIII of the Act.

(3) In this section, "specified person", in relation to a corporation or a shareholder, means any person with whom the corporation or the shareholder, as the case may be, does not deal at arm's length or any partnership or trust of which the corporation or the shareholder, as the case may be, or the person is a member or beneficiary, respectively.

6209. Prescribed Shares

For the purposes of the definition "lending asset" in subsection 248(1) of the Act,

(*a*) a share owned by a bank is a prescribed share for a taxation year where it is a preferred share of the capital stock of a corporation that is dealing at arm's length with the bank that may reasonably be considered to be, and is reported as, a substitute or alternative for a loan to the corporation, or another corporation with whom the corporation does not deal at arm's length, in the bank's annual report for the year to the relevant authority or, where the bank was throughout the year subject to the supervision of the relevant authority but was not required to file an annual report for the year with the relevant authority, in its financial statements for the year; and

(*b*) a property is a prescribed property for a taxation year where

(i) the security is a mark-to-market property (as defined in subsection 142.2(1) of the Act) for the year of a financial institution (as defined in subsection 142.2(1) of the Act),

(ii) the security is at any time in the year a property described in an inventory of a taxpayer, or

(iii) the property is a direct financing lease, or is any other financing arrangement, of a taxpayer that is reported as a loan in the taxpayer's financial statement for the year prepared in accordance with generally accepted accounting principles and an amount is deductible under paragraph 20(1)(*a*) of the Act in respect of the property that is the subject of the lease or arrangement in computing the taxpayer's income for the year.

History: Ss. 6209(*b*)(i) and (ii) were replaced by P.C. 2009-1212, SOR/2009-222, dated July 30, 2009, published in the *Canada Gazette* August 19, 2009, applicable to taxation years that end after February 22, 1994. Ss. 6209(*b*)(i) and (ii) formerly read:

(i) in the case of a security held by a bank, the security is reported as part of the bank's trading account in its annual report for the year to the relevant authority or, where the bank was throughout the year subject to the supervision of the relevant authority but was not required to file an annual report for the year with the relevant authority, in its financial statements for the year,

(ii) in the case of a security held by a taxpayer other than a bank, the security is at any time in the year a property described in an inventory of the taxpayer, or

S. 6209(*b*) was amended by P.C. 2009-1212, SOR/2009-222, dated July 30, 2009, published in the *Canada Gazette* August 19, 2009, by striking out "or" at the end of subparagraph (i) and by adding "or" at the end of subparagraph (ii), applicable

(a) to taxation years that end after September 1997; and

(b) to a taxpayer's taxation years that end after 1995 and before October 1997 where the taxpayer has made an election under paragraph 81(11)(*b*) of the *Income Tax Amendments Act, 1997*, S.C. 1998, c. 19 [an election under s. 20(1)(*l*) of the *Income Tax Act* to have been filed before October 1998].

6210. Prescribed Shares

For the purposes of paragraph 38(*a*.1) of the Act, a prescribed debt obligation is a bond, debenture, note, mortgage or similar obligation

(*a*) of or guaranteed by the Government of Canada; or

(*b*) of the government of a province or an agent of that government.

Regulations

Part LXIII
Child Tax Benefits

6300. Interpretation

In this Part, "qualified dependant" has the meaning assigned by section 122.6 of the Act.

6301. Non-Application of Presumption

(1) For the purposes of paragraph (*g*) of the definition "eligible individual" in section 122.6 of the Act, the presumption referred to in paragraph (*f*) of that definition does not apply in the circumstances where

(*a*) the female parent of the qualified dependant declares in writing to the Minister that the male parent, with whom she resides, is the parent of the qualified dependant who primarily fulfils the responsibility for the care and upbringing of each of the qualified dependants who reside with both parents;

(*b*) the female parent is a qualified dependant of an eligible individual and each of them files a notice with the Minister under subsection 122.62(1) of the Act in respect of the same qualified dependant;

(*c*) there is more than one female parent of the qualified dependant who resides with the qualified dependant and each female parent files a notice with the Minister under subsection 122.62(1) of the Act in respect of the qualified dependant; or

(*d*) more than one notice is filed with the Minister under subsection 122.62(1) of the Act in respect of the same qualified dependant who resides with each of the persons filing the notices if such persons live at different locations.

(2) For greater certainty, a person who files a notice referred to in paragraph (1)(*b*), (*c*) or (*d*) includes a person who is not required under subsection 122.62(3) of the Act to file such a notice.

6302. Factors

For the purposes of paragraph (*h*) of the definition "eligible individual" in section 122.6 of the Act, the following factors are to be considered in determining what constitutes care and upbringing of a qualified dependant:

(*a*) the supervision of the daily activities and needs of the qualified dependant;

(*b*) the maintenance of a secure environment in which the qualified dependant resides;

(*c*) the arrangement of, and transportation to, medical care at regular intervals and as required for the qualified dependant;

(*d*) the arrangement of, participation in, and transportation to, educational, recreational, athletic or similar activities in respect of the qualified dependant;

(*e*) the attendance to the needs of the qualified dependant when the qualified dependant is ill or otherwise in need of the attendance of another person;

(*f*) the attendance to the hygienic needs of the qualified dependant on a regular basis;

(*g*) the provision, generally, of guidance and companionship to the qualified dependant; and

(*h*) the existence of a court order in respect of the qualified dependant that is valid in the jurisdiction in which the qualified dependant resides.

Part LXIV
Prescribed Dates

6400. Child Tax Credits

For the purposes of subsection 122.2(1) of the Act, the prescribed date for each of the 1978 and subsequent taxation years is December 31st of that year.

6401. Quebec Tax Abatement

For the purposes of subsection 120(2) of the Act, the prescribed date for each of the 1980 and subsequent taxation years is December 31st of that year.

Part LXV
Prescribed Laws

6500. [Prescribed laws of the Province of Quebec]

For the purposes of paragraph 241(4)(*j*.2) of the Act, the following are prescribed laws of the Province of Quebec:

(*a*) *An Act respecting the Québec Pension Plan*, R.S.Q., c. R-9; and

(*b*) *Individual and Family Assistance Act*, R.S.Q., c. A-13.1.1, as it relates to the additional amounts for dependent children.

History: S. 6500 was added by S.C. 2013, c. 40, s. 112, in force December 12, 2013.

6501. [Prescribed provision of the law of a province]

For the purposes of paragraph 81(1)(*q*) of the Act, "prescribed provision of the law of a province" means

(*a*) in respect of the Province of Alberta

(i) subsections 7(1) and 14(1) of *The Criminal Injuries Compensation Act*, R.S.A. 1970, c. 75, and

(ii) subsections 8(3), 10(2) and 13(8) of *The Motor Vehicle Accident Claims Act*, R.S.A. 1970, c. 243;

(*b*) in respect of the Province of British Columbia

(i) paragraphs 3(1)(*a*) and (*b*) and section 9 of the *Criminal Injury Compensation Act*, R.S.B.C. 1979, c. 83, and

(ii) subsection 106(1) of the *Motor-vehicle Act*, R.S.B.C. 1960, c. 253, as amended by S.B.C. 1965, c. 27;

(*c*) in respect of the Province of Manitoba

(i) subsection 6(1) of *The Criminal Injuries Compensation Act*, S.M. 1970, c. 56, and

(ii) subsections 7(9) and 12(11) of *The Unsatisfied Judgement Fund Act*, R.S.M. 1970, U70;

(*d*) in respect of the Province of New Brunswick

(i) subsections 3(1) and (2) of the *Compensation for Victims of Crime Act*, R.S.N.B. 1973, c. C-14, and

(ii) subsections 319(3), (10) and 321(1) of the *Motor Vehicle Act*, R.S.N.B. 1973, c. M-17;

(*e*) in respect of the Province of Newfoundland

(i) subsection 27(1) of the *Criminal Injuries Compensation Act*, R.S.N. 1970, c. 68, and

(ii) subsection 106(2) of *The Highway Traffic Act*, R.S.N. 1970, c. 152;

(*f*) in respect of the Northwest Territories, subsections 3(1) and 5(2) and section 13 of the *Criminal Injuries Compensation Ordinance*, R.O.N.W.T. 1974, c. C-23;

(*g*) in respect of the Province of Nova Scotia, subsections 190(5) and 191(2) of the *Motor Vehicle Act*, R.S.N.S. 1967, c. 191;

(*h*) in respect of the Province of Ontario

(i) section 5, subsection 7(2) and section 14 of *The Compensation for Victims of Crime Act, 1971*, S.O. 1971, c. 51, and

(ii) subsections 5(3) and 6(1) and section 18 of *The Motor Vehicle Accident Claims Act*, R.S.O. 1970, c. 281;

(*i*) in respect of the Province of Prince Edward Island, subsection 351(3) of the *Highway Traffic Act*, R.S.P.E.I. 1974, c. H-6;

(*j*) in respect of the Province of Quebec

(i) sections 5, 5b and 14 of the *Crime Victims Compensation Act*, S.Q. 1971, c. 18, and

(ii) sections 13 and 26, subsection 37(1) and sections 44 and 54 of the *Automobile Insurance Act*, S.Q. 1977, c. 68;

(*k*) in respect of the Province of Saskatchewan

(i) subsection 10(1) of *The Criminal Injuries Compensation Act*, R.S.S. 1978, c. C-47, and

(ii) subsections 23(1) to (4) and (7), 24(2) to (7) and (9), 25(1), 26(1), 27(1) and (2), 27(5), 51(8) and (9), 54(3) and 55(1) of *The Automobile Accident Insurance Act*, R.S.S. 1978, c. A-35; and

(*l*) in respect of the Yukon Territory, subsection 3(1) of the *Compensation for the Victims of Crime Ordinance*, O.Y.T. 1975 (1st), c. 2 as amended by O.Y.T. 1976 (1st), c. 5.

6502. [Prescribed class of persons]

For the purposes of paragraph 56(1)(*c*.1), section 56.1, paragraph 60(*c*.1) and section 60.1 of the Act, the class of individuals

(*a*) who were parties, whether in a personal capacity or by representation, to proceedings giving rise to an order made in accordance with the laws of the Province of Ontario, and

(*b*) who, at the time the application for the order was made, were persons described in subclause 14(*b*)(i) of the *Family Law Reform Act*, Revised Statutes of Ontario 1980, c. 152,

is prescribed as a class of persons described in the laws of a province.

6503. For the purposes of paragraphs 60(*j*.02) to (*j*.04) of the Act, subsection 41(5) of the *Canadian Forces Superannuation Act*, subsections 39(7) and 42(8) of the *Public Service Superannuation Act* and subsection 24(6) of the *Royal Canadian Mounted Police Superannuation Act* are prescribed.

History: S. 6503 was replaced by S.C. 2017, c. 33, s. 99(1), applicable in respect of repayments made after March 2007, and formerly read:

6503 *[Prescribed pension legislation].* For the purposes of paragraphs 60(*j*.02) to (*j*.04) of the Act, subsections 39(7) and 42(8) of the *Public Service Superannuation Act* and subsection 24(6) of the *Royal Canadian Mounted Police Superannuation Act* are prescribed.

Part LXVI
Prescribed Order

6600. [Overseas Canadian Forces school staff]

For the purpose of the definition "overseas Canadian Forces school staff" in subsection 248(1) of the Act, the *Canadian Forces Overseas Schools Regulations* is prescribed.

History: S. 6600 was replaced by P.C. 2010-548, SOR/2010-93, dated April 29, 2010, in force May 12, 2010, date of publication in the *Canada Gazette*. S. 6600 formerly read:

6600. For the purposes of the definition "overseas Canadian Forces school staff" in subsection 248(1) of the Act, the prescribed order is the "Canadian Forces Overseas Schools Order" made by Order in Council P.C. 1975-3/1054 of 6 May, 1975.

Part LXVII
Prescribed Venture Capital Corporations, Labour-Sponsored Venture Capital Corporations, Investment Contract Corporations, Qualifying Corporations and Prescribed Stock Savings Plans

6700. [Prescribed venture capital corporations]

For the purposes of paragraph 40(2)(*i*), clause 53(2)(*k*)(i)(C), the definition "private corporation" in subsection 89(1), subsection 125(6.2), the definition "Canadian-controlled private corporation" in subsection 125(7), section 186.2 and the definition "financial intermediary corporation" in subsection 191(1) of the Act, the following are prescribed venture capital corporations:

(*a*) a corporation that is registered under the provisions of

(i) *An Act Respecting Corporations for the Development of Quebec Business Firms*, Statutes of Quebec 1976, c. 33,

(ii) the *Small Business Development Corporations Act, 1979*, Statutes of Ontario 1979, c. 22,

(iii) *Manitoba Regulation 194/84*, being a regulation made under *The Loans Act, 1983(2)*, Statutes of Manitoba 1982-83-84, c. 36,

(iv) *The Venture Capital Tax Credit Act*, Statutes of Saskatchewan 1983-84, c. V-4.1,

(v) the *Small Business Equity Corporations Act*, Statutes of Alberta 1984, c. S-13.5,

(vi) the *Small Business Venture Capital Act*, Statutes of British Columbia 1985, c. 56,

(vii) *An Act respecting Quebec business investment companies*, Statutes of Quebec 1985, c. 9,

(viii) *The Venture Capital Act*, Statutes of Newfoundland 1988, c. 15,

(ix) *The Labour-sponsored Venture Capital Corporations Act*, Statutes of Saskatchewan 1986, c. L-0.2,

(x) Part 2 of the *Employee Investment Act*, Revised Statutes of British Columbia, 1996, c. 112,

(xi) Part III of the *Community Small Business Investment Funds Act*, chapter 18 of the Statutes of Ontario, 1992,

(xii) The *Labour-Sponsored Venture Capital Corporations Act*, Continuing Consolidation of the Statutes of Manitoba c. L12,

(xiii) Part II of the *Risk Capital Investment Tax Credits Act*, chapter 22 of the Statutes of the Northwest Territories, 1998, or

(xiv) section 11 or Part II of the *Equity Tax Credit Act*, Statutes of Nova Scotia, 1993, c. 3;

(*b*) the corporation established by *An Act to Establish the Fonds de solidarité des travailleurs du Québec (F.T.Q.)*, Revised Statutes of Québec, F-3.2.1;

(*c*) a corporation that is registered with the Department of Economic Development and Tourism of the Government of the Northwest Territories pursuant to the Venture Capital Policy and Directive issued by the Government of the Northwest Territories on June 27, 1985;

(*d*) a corporation that is a registered labour-sponsored venture capital corporation;

(*e*) the corporation established by *The Manitoba Employee Ownership Fund Corporation Act*, Continuing Consolidation of the Statutes of Manitoba, c. E95;

(*e*.1) the corporation established by *An Act constituting Capital régional et coopératif Desjardins*, R.S.Q., c. C-6.1; or

(*f*) the corporation established by *An Act to establish Fondaction, le Fonds de développement de la Confédération des syndicats nationaux pour la coopération et l'emploi*, Statutes of Québec 1995, c. 48.

(*g*) (Repealed.)

History: S. 6700(*e*.1) was added by P.C. 2011-936, SOR/2011-188, dated September 22, 2011, published in the *Canada Gazette* October 12, 2011, applicable to the 2001 and subsequent taxation years.

Interpretation Bulletins: *Secondary* — IT-73R6 The small business deduction; IT-269R4 Part IV tax on taxable dividends received by a private corporation or a subject corporation; IT-273R2 Government assistance — General comments; IT-458R2 Canadian-controlled private corporation.

6700.1. [Prescribed venture capital corporations]

For the purposes of paragraph 40(2)(*i*) and clause 53(2)(*k*)(i)(C) of the Act, a corporation that has an employee share ownership plan registered under Part 1 of the *Employee Investment Act*, R.S.B.C. 1996, c. 112, is also a prescribed venture capital corporation.

Interpretation Bulletins: *Secondary* — IT-273R2 Government assistance — General comments.

6700.2. [Prescribed venture capital corporations]

For the purposes of paragraph 40(2)(*i*) and clause 53(2)(*k*)(i)(C) of the Act, "prescribed venture capital corporation" at any time includes a corporation that at that time is a corporation registered under the provisions of Part II of the *Community Small Business Investment Funds Act*, chapter 18 of the Statutes of Ontario, 1992, or of Part II of the *Risk Capital Investment Tax Credits Act*, chapter 22 of the Statutes of the Northwest Territories, 1998.

Interpretation Bulletins: *Secondary* — IT-273R2 Government assistance — General comments.

6701. [Prescribed labour-sponsored venture capital corporation]

For the purposes of paragraph 40(2)(i), clause 53(2)(*k*)(i)(C), the definition "public corporation" in subsection 89(1), the definition "specified investment business" in subsection 125(7), the definition "approved share" in subsection 127.4(1), subsections 131(8) and (11), section 186.1, the definition "financial intermediary corporation" in subsection 191(1), the definition "eligible investment" in subsection 204.8(1) and subsection 204.81(8.3) of the Act, "prescribed labour-sponsored venture capital corporation" means, at any particular time,

(*a*) the corporation established by the *Act to establish the Fonds de solidarité des travailleurs du Québec (F.T.Q.)*, Statutes of Québec 1983, c. 58;

(*b*) a corporation that is registered under the provisions of *The Labour-sponsored Venture Capital Corporations Act*, Statutes of Saskatchewan 1986, c. L-0.2;

(*c*) a corporation that is registered under Part 2 of the *Employee Investment Act*, Revised Statutes of British Columbia, 1996, c. 112;

(*d*) a registered labour-sponsored venture capital corporation;

(*e*) a corporation that is registered under Part III of the *Community Small Business Investment Funds Act*, chapter 18 of the Statutes of Ontario, 1992;

(*f*) the corporation established by *The Manitoba Employee Ownership Fund Corporation Act*, Continuing Consolidation of the Statutes of Manitoba, c. E95;

(*f*.1) a corporation that is registered under The *Labour-Sponsored Venture Capital Corporations Act*, Continuing Consolidation of the Statutes of Manitoba c. L12;

(*g*) the corporation established by *An Act to establish Fondaction, le Fonds de développement de la Confédération des syndicats nationaux pour la coopération et l'emploi*, Statutes of Québec 1995, c. 48;

(*h*) a corporation that is registered under Part II of the *Equity Tax Credit Act*, Statutes of Nova Scotia 1993, c. 3; or

(*i*) a corporation that is registered under Part II of the *Risk Capital Investment Tax Credits Act*, chapter 22 of the Statutes of the Northwest Territories, 1998.

History: S. 6701, the portion before paragraph (*a*) was replaced by S.C. 2013, c. 34, s. 403(1), deemed to have come into force on October 24, 2012, and formerly read:

6701. For the purposes of paragraph 40(2)(*i*), clause 53(2)(*k*)(i)(C), the definition "public corporation" in subsection 89(1), the definition "specified investment business" in subsection 125(7), the definition "approved share" in subsection 127.4(1), subsections 131(8) and (11), section 186.1, the definition "financial intermediary corporation" in subsection 191(1) and the definition "eligible investment" in subsection 204.8(1), of the Act, "prescribed labour-sponsored venture capital corporation" means, at any particular time,

Interpretation Bulletins: *Secondary* — IT-73R6 The small business deduction; IT-269R3 Part IV tax on taxable dividends received by a private corporation or a subject corporation; IT-458R2 Canadian-controlled private corporation.

6701.1. [Exception for registration after March 2013]

(Repealed.)

History: S. 6701.1 was repealed by S. C. 2016, c. 7, s. 57(1), deemed to have come into force on March 22, 2016, and formerly read:

6701.1 *[Exception for registration after March 2013].* Notwithstanding section 6701, a corporation that applies after March 20, 2013 for registration under a provincial act listed in that section is not a prescribed labour-sponsored venture capital corporation for the purposes of the definition "approved share" in subsection 127.4(1) of the Act and the definition "eligible investment" in subsection 204.8(1) of the Act.

S. 6701.1 was added by S.C. 2013, c. 40, s. 113(1), deemed to have come into force on March 21, 2013.

6702. [Prescribed assistance]

For the purposes of subparagraph 40(2)(*i*)(ii) and clause 53(2)(k)(*i*)(C) of the Act, each of the following is prescribed assistance:

(*a*) the assistance received from a province that has been provided in respect of, or for the acquisition of, a share of the capital stock of a venture capital corporation described in section 6700;

(*a*.1) the assistance provided under the *Employee Investment Act*, R.S.B.C. 1996, c. 112, in respect of, or for the acquisition of, a share of the capital stock of a venture capital corporation described in section 6700.1;

(*a*.2) the assistance provided under the *Community Small Business Investment Funds Act*, S.O. 1992, c. 18, the *Risk Capital Investment Tax Credits Act*, S.N.W.T. 1998, c. 22, or the *Risk Capital Investment Tax Credits Act*, S.N.W.T. 1998, c. 22, as duplicated for Nunavut, in respect of, or for the acquisition of, a share of the capital stock of a venture capital corporation described in section 6700.2;

(*b*) a tax credit provided in respect of, or for the acquisition of, a share of a labour-sponsored venture capital corporation described in section 6701; and

(*c*) a tax credit provided by a province in respect of, or for the acquisition of, a share of the capital stock of a taxable Canadian corporation (other than a share of the capital stock of a corporation in respect of which an amount has been renounced by the corporation under subsection 66(12.6), (12.601), (12.62) or (12.64) of the Act) that is held in a stock savings plan described in section 6705.

Interpretation Bulletins: *Secondary* — IT-73R6 The small business deduction; IT-269R3 Part IV tax on taxable dividends received by a private corporation or a subject corporation; IT-273R2 Government assistance — General comments.

6703. [Prescribed investment contract corporation]

For the purposes of section 186.1 of the Act, a "prescribed investment contract corporation" means a corporation described in clause 146(1)(*j*)(ii)(B) [subsection 146(1) "retirement savings plan"] of the Act.

Interpretation Bulletins: *Secondary* — IT-73R6 The small business deduction; IT-269R3 Part IV tax on taxable dividends received by a private corporation or a subject corporation.

Regulations

6704. [Prescribed qualifying corporation]

For the purposes of section 186.2 of the Act, a corporation is a prescribed qualifying corporation in respect of dividends received by a shareholder on shares of its capital stock if, when the shares were acquired by the shareholder, they constituted

(*a*) an investment described in sections 33 and 34 of the Act referred to in subparagraph 6700(*a*)(i);

(*b*) an eligible investment under the provisions of an Act referred to in subparagraph 6700(*a*)(ii), (iv), (v), (vi) or (viii) or the regulation referred to in subparagraph 6700(*a*)(iii);

(*c*) a qualified investment under the provisions of the Act referred to in subparagraph 6700(*a*)(vii);

(*d*) an investment in an eligible business under the Venture Capital Policy and Directive referred to in paragraph 6700(*c*); or

(*e*) an investment in an eligible entity described in sections 17 and 18 of *An Act constituting Capital régional et coopératif Desjardins*, R.S.Q., c. C-6.1.

History: S. 6704(*e*) was added by P.C. 2011-936, SOR/2011-188, dated September 22, 2011, published in the *Canada Gazette* October 12, 2011, applicable to the 2001 and subsequent taxation years.

Interpretation Bulletins: *Secondary* — IT-73R6 The small business deduction; IT-269R3 Part IV tax on taxable dividends received by a private corporation or a subject corporation.

6705. [Prescribed stock savings plan]

For the purposes of paragraph 40(2)(*i*) and clause 53(2)(*k*)(i)(C) of the Act, a stock savings plan governed by any of the following is a prescribed stock savings plan:

(*a*) the *Alberta Stock Savings Plan Act*, Statutes of Alberta 1986, c. A-37.7;

(*b*) *The Stock Savings Tax Credit Act*, Statutes of Saskatchewan 1986, c. S-59.1;

(*c*) the *Stock Savings Plan Act*, Revised Statutes of Nova Scotia, 1989, c. 445;

(*d*) the *Stock Savings Tax Credit Act*, Revised Statutes of Newfoundland, 1990, c. S-28; or

(*e*) section 11.6 of the *Income Tax Act*, Continuing Consolidation of the Statutes of Manitoba c. I10.

Information Circulars: IC 87-3 Alberta stock savings plan.

Interpretation Bulletins: *Secondary* — IT-73R6 The small business deduction; IT-269R3 Part IV tax on taxable dividends received by a private corporation or a subject corporation; IT-273R2 Government assistance — General comments.

6706. [Prescribed condition]

For the purpose of clause 204.81(1)(*c*)(v)(F) of the Act, a prescribed condition is that, in respect of a redemption of a Class A share of a corporation's capital stock, the shareholder requires the corporation to withhold an amount in respect of the redemption in accordance with Part XII.5 of the Act.

6707. [Prescribed provision of a law of a province]

For the purpose of subsection 204.82(5) of the Act, a "prescribed provision of a law of a province" means section 25.1 of the *Community Small Business Investment Funds Act*, chapter 18 of the Statutes of Ontario, 1992.

6708. [Prescribed wind-up rule]

For the purposes of paragraph 204.8(2)(*b*), section 27.2 of the *Community Small Business Investment Funds Act, 1992*, S.O. 1992, c. 18, is a prescribed wind-up rule.

History: S. 6708 was replaced by S.C. 2014, c. 20, s. 35(1), deemed to have come into force on November 27, 2013, and formerly read:

6708. *[Prescribed wind-up rule].* For the purpose of paragraph 204.8(2)(*b*) and subsection 204.81(8.3) of the Act, section 27.2 of the *Community Small Business Investment Funds Act, 1992*, S.O. 1992, c. 18, is a prescribed wind-up rule.

S. 6708 was added by S.C. 2013, c. 34, s. 404(1), deemed to have come into force on October 24, 2012.

6709. [Prescribed provisions of a provincial law]

For the purposes of section 211.81 of the Act, sections 1086.14 and 1086.20 of the *Taxation Act*, R.S.Q., c. I-3, are prescribed provisions of a provincial law.

History: S. 6709 was added by S.C. 2013, c. 34, s. 404(1), deemed to have come into force on October 24, 2012.

Part LXVIII

Prescribed Plans, Arrangements and Contributions

6800. [Prescribed arrangement — employee benefit plan]

For the purpose of paragraph (*e*) of the definition "employee benefit plan" in subsection 248(1) of the Act, each of the following is a prescribed arrangement:

(*a*) the Major League Baseball Players Benefit Plan;

(*b*) an arrangement under which all contributions are made pursuant to a law of Canada or a province, where one of the main purposes of the law is to enforce minimum standards with respect to wages, vacation entitlement or severance pay; and

(*c*) an arrangement under which all contributions are made in connection with a dispute regarding the entitlement of one or more persons to benefits to be received or enjoyed by the person or persons.

6801. [Prescribed plan or arrangement — salary deferral arrangement]

For the purposes of paragraph (*l*) of the definition "salary deferral arrangement" in subsection 248(1) of the Act, a prescribed plan or arrangement is an arrangement in writing

(*a*) between an employer and an employee that is established on or after July 28, 1986 where

(i) it is reasonable to conclude, having regard to all the circumstances, including the terms and conditions of the arrangement and any agreement relating thereto, that the arrangement is not established to provide benefits to the employee on or after retirement but is established for the main purpose of permitting the employee to fund, through salary or wage deferrals, a leave of absence from the employee's employment of not less than

(A) where the leave of absence is to be taken by the employee for the purpose of permitting the full-time attendance of the employee at a designated educational institution (within the meaning assigned by subsection 118.6(1) of the Act), three consecutive months, or

(B) in any other case, six consecutive months

that is to commence immediately after a period (in this section referred to as the "deferral period") not exceeding 6 years after the date on which the deferrals for the leave of absence commence,

(ii) the amount of salary or wages deferred by the employee under all such arrangements for the services rendered by the employee to the employer in a taxation year does not exceed 33$^1/_3$ per cent of the amount of the salary or wages that the employee would, but for the arrangements, reasonably be expected to have received in the year in respect of the services,

(iii) the arrangement provides that throughout the period of the leave of absence the employee does not receive any salary or wages from the employer, or from any other person or partnership with whom the employer does not deal at arm's length, other than

(A) the amount by which the employee's salary or wages under the arrangement was deferred or is to be reduced or, amounts that are based on a percentage of the salary or wage scale of employees of the employer, which percentage is fixed in respect of the employee for the deferral period and the leave of absence, and

(B) the reasonable fringe benefits that the employer usually pays to or on behalf of employees,

(iv) the arrangement provides that the amounts deferred in respect of the employee under the arrangement

(A) are held by or for the account of a trust governed by a plan or arrangement that is an employee benefit plan within the meaning of the definition thereof in subsection 248(1) of the Act, and provides that the amount that may reasonably be considered to be the income of the trust for a taxation year that has been earned by it for the benefit of the employee shall be paid in the year to the employee, or

(B) are held by or for the account of any person other than a trust referred to in clause (A), and provides that the amount in respect of interest or other additional amounts that may reasonably be considered to have accrued to or for the benefit of the employee to the end of a taxation year shall be paid in the year to the employee,

(v) the arrangement provides that the employee is to return to his regular employment with the employer or an employer that participates in the same or a similar arrangement after the leave of absence for a period that is not less than the period of the leave of absence, and

(vi) subject to subparagraph (iv), the arrangement provides that all amounts held for the employee's benefit under the arrangement shall be paid to the employee out of or under the arrangement no later than the end of the first taxation year that commences after the end of the deferral period;

(*b*) between an employer and an employee that is established before July 28, 1986 where it is reasonable to conclude, having regard to all the circumstances, including the terms and conditions of the arrangement and any agreement relating thereto, that the arrangement is not established to provide

Regulations

benefits on or after retirement but is established for the main purpose of permitting the employee to fund, through salary or wage deferrals, a leave of absence from the employment and under which the deferrals in respect of the leave of absence commenced before 1987;

(*c*) that is established for the purpose of deferring the salary or wages of a professional on-ice official for his services as such with the National Hockey League if, in the case of an official resident in Canada, the trust or other person who has custody and control of any funds, investments or other property under the arrangement is resident in Canada; or

(*d*) between a corporation and an employee of the corporation or a corporation related thereto under which the employee (or, after the employee's death, a dependant or relation of the employee or the legal representative of the employee) may or shall receive an amount that may reasonably be attributable to duties of an office or employment performed by the employee on behalf of the corporation or a corporation related thereto where

(i) all amounts that may be received under the arrangement shall be received after the time of the employee's death or retirement from, or loss of, the office or employment and no later than the end of the first calendar year commencing thereafter, and

(ii) the aggregate of all amounts each of which may be received under the arrangement depends on the fair market value of shares of the capital stock of the corporation or a corporation related thereto at a time within the period that commences one year before the time of the employee's death or retirement from, or loss of, the office or employment and ends at the time the amount is received,

unless, by reason of the arrangement or a series of transactions that includes the arrangement, the employee or a person with whom the employee does not deal at arm's length is entitled, either immediately or in the future, either absolutely or contingently, to receive or obtain any amount or benefit granted or to be granted for the purpose of reducing the impact, in whole or in part, of any reduction in the fair market value of the shares of the corporation or a corporation related thereto.

Tax Window Files: Information Return — Real Estate Developer, *Technical Interpretation, Business and Partnerships Division, November 15, 2006,* CRA Document No. 2006-0202971I7.

6802. [Prescribed plan or arrangement — retirement compensation arrangement]

For the purposes of paragraph (*n*) of the definition "retirement compensation arrangement" in subsection 248(1) of the Act, a prescribed plan or arrangement is

(*a*) the plan instituted by the *Canada Pension Plan*;

(*b*) a provincial pension plan as defined in section 3 of the *Canada Pension Plan*;

(*c*) a plan instituted by the *Unemployment Insurance Act*;

(*d*) a plan pursuant to an agreement in writing that is established for the purpose of deferring the salary or wages of a professional on-ice official for the official's services as such with the National Hockey League if, in the case of an official resident in Canada, the trust or other person who has custody and control of any funds, investments or other property under the plan is resident in Canada;

(*e*) an arrangement under which all contributions are made pursuant to a law of Canada or a province, where one of the main purposes of the law is to enforce minimum standards with respect to wages, vacation entitlement or severance pay;

(*f*) an arrangement under which all contributions are made in connection with a dispute regarding the entitlement of one or more persons to benefits to be received or enjoyed by the person or persons;

(*g*) a plan or arrangement instituted by the social security legislation of a country other than Canada or of a state, province or other political subdivision of such a country; or

(*h*) a trust established

(i) to hold shares of Air Canada, pursuant to the June 2009 memorandum of understanding between Air Canada and certain trade unions who represent employees of Air Canada, if

(A) the shares are held by the trust for the benefit of the trade unions, and

(B) each of the trade unions may direct the trustee to contribute, from time to time, amounts received or receivable by the trust in respect of the shares, whether as dividends, proceeds of disposition or otherwise, to one or more registered pension plans under which Air Canada is a participating employer, or

(ii) in relation to the wind-up of a registered pension plan sponsored by Fraser Papers Inc., if

(A) shares are held by the trust for the benefit of the registered pension plan, and

(B) the trustee will contribute amounts received or receivable by the trust in respect of the shares, whether as dividends, proceeds of disposition or otherwise, to the registered pension plan, not later than December 31, 2018.

Department of Finance Comfort Letters

(June 19, 2017) [Contributions to a Trust and Partnership deemed not to be a contribution to a Retirement Compensation Agreement]

2017-TL-4

XXXX

Dear XXXX:

I am writing in response to your letter of February 15, 2017 and further discussions in which you outline proposed transactions and identify certain technical issues with the income tax rules that would apply to the transactions.

You advise that your client, XXXX (the "Employer"), XXXX as purchaser (the "Purchaser") XXXX. As part of the XXXX

- XXXX (the "Trust") will be established for the benefit of XXXX registered pension plans ("RPPs") sponsored by the Employer XXXX..
- A partnership (the "Partnership") will be established to hold certain XXXX assets sold to it at fair market value by the Employer in exchange for a promissory note.
- The Trust will be a limited partner receiving 50 per cent of the common units of the Partnership. The other limited partners of the Partnership will receive (in aggregate) 50 per cent of the common units and will be employee life and health trusts ("ELHTs") established to provide non-pension benefits to retirees (and their survivors) of the Employer.
- The Employer will make cash contributions to the RPPs and ELHTs equal to the face amount of the promissory note, 50 per cent to the RPPs ("RPP Contributions") and 50 per cent to the ELHTs ("ELHT Contributions"). The RPPs and ELHTs will use the cash to subscribe for special units of the Partnership. The Partnership will use the proceeds to repay the promissory note.
- It is expected that the Partnership XXXX will make priority distributions on the special units of the Partnership to the RPPs not exceeding the RPP Contributions and to the ELHTs not exceeding the ELHT Contributions.
- Pursuant to the agreement establishing the Trust, the Trust will receive a 50 per cent share of the "balance of the Partnership's income and distributable cash-flow", after the priority distributions made on the special units of the Partnership. The Trust will also receive a portion of dividends and profits that the Purchaser will derive from the ownership or disposition of shares of the Employer.
- The Trust will make cash contributions to the RPPs based on an allocation formula to be determined by provincial regulation.

You note that the RPPs have large solvency deficits and that one of the purposes of the XXXX is to provide additional funding to reduce those deficits.

In this context, you have requested that we recommend amendments to the *Income Tax Regulations* (the "Regulations") which would:

- ensure that the Trust and the Partnership are not considered to be retirement compensation arrangements as defined in the *Income Tax Act*; and
- permit contributions from the Trust to the RPPs without jeopardizing the registration of those plans.

We agree that the requested changes would not raise income tax policy concerns. We are prepared to recommend to the Minister of Finance that he recommend to the Governor General in Council that section 6802 of the Regulations be amended to add the Trust and the Partnership to the list of prescribed arrangements that are excluded from the definition "retirement compensation arrangement" and therefore also from the retirement compensation arrangement rules.

We would also recommend that these proposed amendments apply in respect of a trust and partnership established, and pension contribution made, after May 2017.

While I cannot offer any assurance that the Minister of Finance or the Governor General in Council will agree with our recommendations, I hope that this statement of our intention is helpful to you.

Thank you for writing to us on this matter

Yours sincerely,

Brian Ernewein

General Director, Legislation

Tax Policy Branch

History: S. 6802(*h*) was added by S.C. 2013, c. 34, s. 405(1), deemed to have come into force on January 1, 2009.

6802.1. [Prescribed plan or arrangement — pension plans]

(1) For the purpose of paragraph 8(1)(*m*.2) of the Act, each of the following is a prescribed plan:

(*a*) the pension plan established as a consequence of the establishment, by section 27 of the *Members of Parliament Retiring Allowances Act*, of the Members of Parliament Retirement Compensation Arrangements Account; and

(*b*) the pension plan established by the Retirement Compensation Arrangements Regulations, No. 1.

(2) For the purpose of subsection 207.6(6) of the Act, each of the following is a prescribed plan or arrangement:

(*a*) the pension plan established as a consequence of the establishment, by section 27 of the *Members of Parliament Retiring Allowances Act*, of the Members of Parliament Retirement Compensation Arrangements Account;

(*b*) the pension plan established by the Retirement Compensation Arrangements Regulations, No. 1; and

(*c*) the pension plan established by the Retirement Compensation Arrangements Regulations, No. 2.

6803. [Prescribed plan or arrangement — foreign retirement arrangement]

For the purposes of the definition "foreign retirement arrangement" in subsection 248(1) of the Act, a prescribed plan or arrangement is a plan or arrangement to which subsection 408(*a*), (*b*) or (*h*) of the United States' *Internal Revenue Code of 1986*, as amended from time to time, applies.

6804. Contributions to Foreign Plans

(1) Definitions. The definitions in this subsection apply in this section.

"foreign non-profit organization" means,

(*a*) at any time before 1995, an organization

(i) that at that time meets the conditions in subparagraphs (*b*)(i) to (iii), or

(ii) that at that time is not operated for the purpose of profit, and whose assets are situated primarily outside Canada throughout the calendar year that includes that time, and

(*b*) at any time after 1994, an organization that at that time

(i) is not operated for the purpose of profit,

(ii) has its main place of management outside Canada, and

(iii) carries on its activities primarily outside Canada.

"foreign plan" means a plan or arrangement (determined without regard to subsection 207.6(5) of the Act) that would, but for paragraph (*l*) of the definition "retire-

Regulations

ment compensation arrangement" in subsection 248(1) of the Act, be a retirement compensation arrangement.

"qualifying entity" means a non-resident entity that holds all or part of the assets of a foreign plan where the following conditions are satisfied:

(*a*) the entity is resident in a country under the laws of which an income tax is imposed, and

(*b*) where those laws provide an exemption from tax, a reduced rate of tax or other favourable tax treatment for entities that hold assets of pension or other retirement plans, the entity qualifies for the favourable treatment.

(2) Electing Employer. For the purposes of this section, an employer is an electing employer for a calendar year with respect to a foreign plan where

(*a*) the employer has sent or delivered to the Minister a letter stating that the employer elects to have this section apply with respect to contributions to the foreign plan, and

(*b*) the letter was sent or delivered on or before

(i) the last day of February in the year following the first calendar year after 1991 in which a contribution that is, or would be if subsection 207.6(5.1) of the Act were read without reference to paragraph (*a*) of that subsection, a resident's contribution (as defined in that subsection) was made under the foreign plan in respect of services rendered by an individual to the employer, or

(ii) any later date that is acceptable to the Minister,

except that an employer is not an electing employer for a year with respect to a foreign plan if the Minister has granted written permission for the employer to revoke, for the year or a preceding calendar year, the election made under paragraph (*a*) in respect of the foreign plan.

(3) Election by Union. Except as otherwise permitted in writing by the Minister, an election made by a trade union for the purpose of subsection (2) is valid only if it is made by the highest-level structural unit of the union.

(4) Contributions Made Before 1992. For the purpose of paragraph 207.6(5.1)(*a*) of the Act, a contribution made under a foreign plan by a person or body of persons in a calendar year before 1992 is a prescribed contribution where

(*a*) the contribution is paid to a qualifying entity;

(*b*) each employer (in this subsection referred to as a "contributor") that makes a contribution under the foreign plan in the year is

(i) a non-resident corporation throughout the year,

(ii) a partnership that makes contributions under the foreign plan primarily in respect of services rendered outside Canada to the partnership by non-resident employees, or

(iii) a foreign non-profit organization throughout the year;

(*c*) if a corporation or partnership (other than a corporation or partnership that is a foreign non-profit organization throughout the year) is a contributor, no individual who is entitled (either absolutely or contingently) to benefits under the foreign plan is a member of a registered pension plan, or a beneficiary under a deferred profit sharing plan, to which a contributor, or a person or body of persons not dealing at arm's length with a contributor, makes, or is required to make, contributions in relation to the year;

(*d*) contributions made in the year under the foreign plan for the benefit of individuals resident in Canada are reasonable in relation to contributions made under the plan for the benefit of non-resident individuals; and

(*e*) the foreign plan is not a pension plan the registration of which under the Act has been revoked.

(5) Contributions Made in 1992, 1993 or 1994. For the purpose of paragraph 207.6(5.1)(*a*) of the Act, a contribution made under a foreign plan by a person or body of persons at any time in 1992, 1993 or 1994 in respect of services rendered by an individual to an employer is a prescribed contribution where

(*a*) the contribution is paid to a qualifying entity;

(*b*) the employer is an electing employer for the year with respect to the foreign plan;

(*c*) if the employer is not at that time a foreign non-profit organization, the individual is not a member of a registered pension plan (other than a specified multi-employer plan, as defined in subsection 147.1(1) of the Act), or a deferred profit sharing plan, in which the employer, or a person or body of persons that does not deal at arm's length with the employer, participates; and

(*d*) either

(i) the employer is

(A) a corporation that is not resident in Canada at that time,

(B) a partnership that makes contributions under the foreign plan primarily in respect of services rendered outside Canada to the partnership by non-resident employees, or

(C) a foreign non-profit organization at that time, or

(ii) the individual was non-resident at any time before the contribution is made and became a member of the foreign plan before the end of the month after the month in which the individual became resident in Canada.

(6) Contributions Made after 1994. For the purposes of paragraph 207.6(5.1)(*a*) of the Act, a contribution made under a foreign plan by a person or body of persons at any time in a calendar year after 1994 in respect of services rendered by an individual to an employer is a prescribed contribution where

(*a*) the contribution is paid to a qualifying entity;

(*b*) the employer is an electing employer for the year with respect to the foreign plan;

(*c*) if the employer is at that time a foreign non-profit organization,

(i) the amount that, if subsection 8301(1) were read without reference to paragraph (*b*) of that subsection, would be the individual's pension adjustment for the year in respect of the employer is nil, or

(ii) the amount that would be the individual's pension adjustment for the year in respect of the employer if

(A) all contributions made under the foreign plan in the year in respect of the individual were prescribed by this subsection,

(B) where the year is 1996, section 8308.1 were read without reference to subsection (4.1), and

(C) where the year is 1997, subparagraph 8308.1(2)(*b*)(v) were read as

"(v) the amount, if any, by which 18% of the individual's resident compensation from the employer for the year exceeds $1,000, and"

does not exceed the lesser of

(D) the money purchase limit for the year, and

(E) 18% of the individual's compensation (as defined in subsection 147.1(1) of the Act) for the year from the employer;

(*d*) if

(i) the employer is at that time a foreign non-profit organization, and

(ii) a period in the year throughout which the individual rendered services to the employer would be, under paragraph 8507(3)(*a*), a qualifying period of the individual with respect to another employer if that paragraph were read without reference to subparagraph (iv) of that paragraph,

subsection 8308(7) applies with respect to the determination of the individual's pension adjustment for the year with respect to each employer; and

(*e*) if the employer is not at that time a foreign non-profit organization,

(i) the individual was non-resident at any time before the contribution is made,

(ii) the individual became a member of the foreign plan before the end of the month after the month in which the individual became resident in Canada, and

(iii) the individual is not a member of a registered pension plan, or a deferred profit sharing plan, in which the employer, or a person or body of persons that does not deal at arm's length with the employer, participates.

(7) Replacement Plan. For the purposes of subparagraphs (5)(*d*)(ii) and (6)(*e*)(ii), where benefits provided to an individual under a particular plan or arrangement are replaced by benefits under another plan or arrangement, the other plan or arrangement is deemed, in respect of the individual, to be the same plan or arrangement as the particular plan or arrangement.

Regulations

Part LXIX
Prescribed Offshore Investment Fund Properties

6900. [Prescribed offshore investment fund property]

For the purpose of paragraph 94.1(2)(*a*) [subsection 94.1(2) "designated cost"] of the Act, an offshore investment fund property (within the meaning assigned by subsection 94.1(1) of the Act) of a taxpayer that

(*a*) was acquired by him by way of bequest or inheritance from a deceased person who, throughout the five years immediately preceding his death, was not resident in Canada,

(*b*) had not been acquired by the deceased from a person resident in Canada, and

(*c*) is not property substituted for property acquired by the deceased from a person resident in Canada

is a prescribed offshore investment fund property of the taxpayer.

Part LXX
Accrued Interest on Debt Obligations

7000. Prescribed Debt Obligations

(1) For the purpose of subsection 12(9) of the Act, each of the following debt obligations (other than a debt obligation that is an indexed debt obligation) in respect of which a taxpayer has at any time acquired an interest is a prescribed debt obligation:

(*a*) a particular debt obligation in respect of which no interest is stipulated to be payable in respect of its principal amount;

(*b*) a particular debt obligation in respect of which the proportion of the payments of principal to which the taxpayer is entitled is not equal to the proportion of the payments of interest to which he is entitled;

(*c*) a particular debt obligation, other than one described in paragraph (*a*) or (*b*), in respect of which it can be determined, at the time the taxpayer acquired the interest therein, that the maximum amount of interest payable thereon in a year ending after that time is less than the maximum amount of interest payable thereon in a subsequent year; and

(*d*) a particular debt obligation, other than one described in paragraph (*a*), (*b*) or (*c*), in respect of which the amount of interest to be paid in respect of any taxation year is, under the terms and conditions of the obligation, dependent on a contingency existing after the year;

and, for the purposes of this subsection, a debt obligation includes, for greater certainty, all of the issuer's obligations to pay principal and interest under that obligation.

(2) For the purposes of subsection 12(9) of the Act, the amount determined in prescribed manner that is deemed to accrue to a taxpayer as interest on a prescribed debt obligation in each taxation year during which he holds an interest in the obligation is,

(*a*) in the case of a prescribed debt obligation described in paragraph (1)(*a*), the amount of interest that would be determined in respect thereof if interest thereon for that year were computed on a compound interest basis using the maximum of all rates each of which is a rate computed

(i) in respect of each possible circumstance under which an interest of the taxpayer in the obligation could mature or be surrendered or retracted, and

(ii) using assumptions concerning the interest rate and compounding period that will result in a present value, at the date of purchase of the interest, of all the maximum payments thereunder, equal to the cost thereof to the taxpayer;

(*b*) in the case of a prescribed debt obligation described in paragraph (1)(*b*), the aggregate of all amounts each of which is the amount of interest that would be determined in respect of his interest in a payment under the obligation if interest thereon for that year were computed on a compound interest basis using the specified cost of his interest therein and the specified interest rate in respect of his total interest in the obligation, and for the purposes of this paragraph,

(i) the "specified cost" of his interest in a payment under the obligation is its present value at the date of purchase computed using the specified interest rate, and

(ii) the "specified interest rate" is the maximum of all rates each of which is a rate computed

(A) in respect of each possible circumstance under which an interest of the taxpayer in the obligation could mature or be surrendered or retracted, and

(B) using assumptions concerning the interest rate and compounding period that will result in a present value, at the date of purchase of the interest, of all the maximum payments to the taxpayer in respect of his total interest in the obligation, equal to the cost of that interest to the taxpayer;

(*c*) in the case of a prescribed debt obligation described in paragraph (1)(*c*), other than an obligation in respect of which paragraph (*c*.1) applies, the greater of

(i) the maximum amount of interest thereon in respect of the year, and

(ii) the maximum amount of interest that would be determined in respect thereof if interest thereon for that year were computed on a compound interest basis using the maximum of all rates each of which is a rate computed

(A) in respect of each possible circumstance under which an interest of the taxpayer in the obligation could mature or be surrendered or retracted, and

(B) using assumptions concerning the interest rate and compounding period that will result in a present value, at the date of issue of the obligation, of all the maximum payments thereunder, equal to its principal amount;

(*c*.1) in the case of a prescribed debt obligation described in paragraph (1)(*c*) for which

(i) the rate of interest stipulated to be payable in respect of each period throughout which the obligation is outstanding is fixed at the date of issue of the obligation, and

(ii) the stipulated rate of interest applicable at each time is not less than each stipulated rate of interest applicable before that time,

the amount of interest that would be determined in respect of the year if interest on the obligation for that year were computed on a compound interest basis using the maximum of all rates each of which is the compound interest rate that, for a particular assumption with respect to when the taxpayer's interest in the obligation will mature or be surrendered or retracted, results in a present value (at the date the taxpayer acquires the interest in the obligation) of all payments under the obligation after the acquisition by the taxpayer of the taxpayer's interest in the obligation equal to the principal amount of the obligation at the date of acquisition; and

(*d*) in the case of a prescribed debt obligation described in paragraph (1)(*d*), the maximum amount of interest thereon that could be payable thereunder in respect of that year.

(3) For the purpose of this section, any bonus or premium payable under a debt obligation is considered to be an amount of interest payable under the obligation.

(4) For the purposes of this section, where

(*a*) a taxpayer has an interest in a debt obligation (in this subsection referred to as the "first interest") under which there is a conversion privilege or an option to extend its term upon maturity, and

(*b*) at the time the obligation was issued (or, if later, at the time the conversion privilege or option was added or modified), circumstances could reasonably be foreseen under which the holder of the obligation would, by exercising the conversion privilege or option, acquire an interest in a debt obligation with a principal amount less than its fair market value at the time of acquisition,

the subsequent interest in any debt obligation acquired by the taxpayer by exercising the conversion privilege or option shall be considered to be a continuation of the first interest.

(5) For the purposes of making the computations referred to in paragraphs (2)(*a*), (*b*), (*c*) and (*c*.1), the compounding period shall not exceed one year and any interest rate used shall be constant from the time of acquisition or issue, as the case may be, until the time of maturity, surrender or retraction.

(6) For the purpose of the definition "investment contract" in subsection 12(11) of the Act, a registered retirement savings plan or a registered retirement income fund, other than a plan or fund to which a trust is a party, is a prescribed contract throughout a calendar year where an annuitant (as defined in subsection 146(1) or 146.3(1) of the Act, as the case may be) under the plan or fund is alive at any time in the year or was alive at any time in the preceding calendar year.

Interpretation Bulletins: *Secondary* — IT-396R Interest income.

7001. Indexed Debt Obligations

(1) For the purpose of subparagraph 16(6)(*a*)(i) of the Act, where at any time in a taxation year a taxpayer holds an interest in an indexed debt obligation, there is prescribed as interest receivable and received by the taxpayer in the year in respect of the obligation the total of

(*a*) the amount, if any, by which

(i) the total of all amounts each of which is the amount by which the amount payable in respect of the taxpayer's interest in an indexed payment under the obligation (other than a payment that is an excluded payment with respect to the taxpayer for the year) has, because of a change in the purchasing power of money, increased over an inflation adjustment period of the obligation that ends in the year

exceeds the total of

(ii) that portion of the total, if any, determined under subparagraph (i) that is required, otherwise than by subsection 16(6) of the Act, to be included in computing the taxpayer's income for the year or a preceding taxation year, and

(iii) the total of all amounts each of which is the amount by which the amount payable in respect of the taxpayer's interest in an indexed payment under the obligation (other than a payment that is an excluded payment with respect to the taxpayer for the year) has, by reason of a change in the purchasing power of money, decreased over an inflation adjustment period of the obligation that ends in the year, and

(*b*) where the non-indexed debt obligation associated with the indexed debt obligation is an obligation that is described in any of paragraphs 7000(1)(*a*) to (*d*), the amount of interest that would be determined under subsection 7000(2) to accrue to the taxpayer in respect of the non-indexed debt obligation in the particular period that

(i) begins at the beginning of the first inflation adjustment period of the indexed debt obligation in respect of the taxpayer that ends in the year, and

(ii) ends at the end of the last inflation adjustment period of the indexed debt obligation in respect of the taxpayer that ends in the year

if the particular period were a taxation year of the taxpayer and the taxpayer's interest in the indexed debt obligation were an interest in the non-indexed debt obligation.

Regulations

(2) For the purposes of subparagraph 16(6)(*a*)(ii) of the Act, where at any time in a taxation year a taxpayer holds an interest in an indexed debt obligation, there is prescribed as interest payable and paid by the taxpayer in the year in respect of the obligation the amount, if any, by which

(*a*) the total of the amounts, if any, determined under subparagraphs (1)(*a*)(ii) and (iii) for the year in respect of the taxpayer's interest in the obligation

exceeds

(*b*) the amount, if any, determined under subparagraph (1)(*a*)(i) for the year in respect of the taxpayer's interest in the obligation.

(3) For the purposes of subparagraph 16(6)(*b*)(i) of the Act, where at any time in a taxation year an indexed debt obligation is an obligation of a taxpayer, there is prescribed as interest payable in respect of the year by the taxpayer in respect of the obligation the amount, if any, that would be determined under paragraph (1)(*a*) in respect of the taxpayer for the year if, at each time at which the obligation is an obligation of the taxpayer, the taxpayer were the holder of the obligation and not the debtor under the obligation.

(4) For the purposes of subparagraph 16(6)(*b*)(ii) of the Act, where at any time in a taxation year an indexed debt obligation is an obligation of a taxpayer, there is prescribed as interest receivable and received by the taxpayer in the year in respect of the obligation the amount, if any, that would be determined under subsection (2) in respect of the taxpayer for the year if, at each time at which the obligation is an obligation of the taxpayer, the taxpayer were the holder of the obligation and not the debtor under the obligation.

(5) For the purpose of determining the amount by which an indexed payment under an indexed debt obligation has increased or decreased over a period because of a change in the purchasing power of money, the amount of the indexed payment at any time shall be determined using the method for computing the amount of the payment at the time it is to be made, adjusted in a reasonable manner to take into account the earlier date of computation.

(6) For the purposes of this section, the non-indexed debt obligation associated with an indexed debt obligation is the debt obligation that would result if the indexed debt obligation were amended to eliminate all adjustments determined by reference to changes in the purchasing power of money.

(7) In this section,

"excluded payment" with respect to a taxpayer for a taxation year means an indexed payment under an indexed debt obligation where

(*a*) the non-indexed debt obligation associated with the indexed debt obligation provides for the payment, at least annually, of interest at a single fixed rate, and

(*b*) the indexed payment corresponds to one of the interest payments referred to in paragraph (*a*),

but does not include payments under an indexed debt obligation where, at any time in the year, the taxpayer's proportionate interest in a payment to be made under the obligation after that time differs from the taxpayer's proportionate interest in any other payment to be made under the obligation after that time;

"indexed payment" means, in relation to an indexed debt obligation, an amount payable under the obligation that is determined by reference to the purchasing power of money;

"inflation adjustment period" of an indexed debt obligation means, in relation to a taxpayer,

(*a*) where the taxpayer acquires and disposes of the taxpayer's interest in the obligation in the same regular adjustment period of the obligation, the period that begins when the taxpayer acquires the interest in the obligation and ends when the taxpayer disposes of the interest, and

(*b*) in any other case, each of the following consecutive periods:

(i) the period that begins when the taxpayer acquires the taxpayer's interest in the obligation and ends at the end of the regular adjustment period of the obligation in which the taxpayer acquires the interest in the obligation,

(ii) each succeeding regular adjustment period of the obligation throughout which the taxpayer holds the interest in the obligation, and

(iii) where the taxpayer does not dispose of the interest in the obligation at the end of a regular adjustment period of the obligation, the period that begins immediately after the last period referred to in subparagraphs (i) and (ii) and that ends when the taxpayer disposes of the interest in the obligation;

"regular adjustment period" of an indexed debt obligation means

(*a*) where the terms or conditions of the obligation provide that, while the obligation is outstanding, indexed payments are to be made at regular intervals not exceeding 12 months in length, each of the following periods:

(i) the period that begins when the obligation is issued and ends when the first indexed payment is required to be made, and

(ii) each succeeding period beginning when an indexed payment is required to be made and ending when the next indexed payment is required to be made,

(*b*) where paragraph (*a*) does not apply and the obligation is outstanding for less than 12 months, the period that begins when the obligation is issued and ends when the obligation ceases to be outstanding, and

(*c*) in any other case, each of the following periods:

(i) the 12-month period that begins when the obligation is issued,

(ii) each succeeding 12-month period throughout which the obligation is outstanding, and

(iii) where the obligation ceases to be outstanding at a time other than the end of a 12-month period referred to in subparagraph (i) or (ii), the period that commences immediately after the last period referred to in those subparagraphs and that ends when the obligation ceases to be outstanding.

Regulations

Part LXXI
Prescribed Federal Crown Corporations

7100. [Prescribed federal Crown corporations]

For the purposes of subsections 27(2) and (3), the definition "private corporation" in subsection 89(1) and subsection 124(3) of the Act, the following are prescribed federal Crown corporations:

(*a*) Canada Deposit Insurance Corporation;

(*b*) Canada Hibernia Holding Corporation;

(*c*) Canada Lands Company Limited;

(*d*) Canada Mortgage and Housing Corporation;

(*e*) Canada Post Corporation;

(*f*) Canadian Broadcasting Corporation;

(*g*) Cape Breton Development Corporation;

(*h*) Freshwater Fish Marketing Corporation;

(*i*) Royal Canadian Mint;

(*j*) VIA Rail Canada Inc.; and

(*k*) Project Deliver II Ltd.

History: S. 7100(*k*) was added by P.C. 2018-989, SOR/2018-160 dated July 16, 2018, in force July 25, 2018.

Tax Window Files: Obligation of Crown corporations to file a T106, *March 15, 2016*, CRA Document No. 2014-0549701I7.

Part LXXII
Cumulative Deduction Account [Repealed.]

7200. (Repealed.)

Part LXXIII
Prescribed Amounts and Areas

7300. [Prescribed amount – inducement, reimbursement, etc.]

For the purposes of paragraph 12(1)(*x*) of the Act, "prescribed amount" means

(*a*) an amount paid to a corporation by the Native Economic Development Board created under Order in Council P.C. 1983-3394 of October 31, 1983 pursuant to the Native Economic Development Program or paid to a corporation under the Aboriginal Capital Corporation Program of the Canadian Aboriginal Economic Development Strategy, where all of the shares of the capital stock of the corporation are

(i) owned by aboriginal individuals,

(ii) held in trust for the exclusive benefit of aboriginal individuals,

(iii) owned by a corporation, all the shares of which are owned by aboriginal individuals or held in trust for the exclusive benefit of aboriginal individuals, or

(iv) owned or held in a combination of ownership structures described in subparagraph (i), (ii) or (iii)

and the purpose of the corporation is to provide loans, loan guarantees, bridge financing, venture capital, lease financing, surety bonding or other similar financing services to aboriginal enterprises;

(*b*) prescribed assistance within the meaning assigned by section 6702;

(*c*) an amount that is the portion of a student loan forgiven under section 9.2 of the *Canada Student Financial Assistance Act* or under section 11.1 of the *Canada Student Loans Act*;

(*c*.1) an amount that is the portion of a student loan forgiven under a provincial program that would be a prescribed amount because of paragraph (*c*) if section 11.1 of the *Canada Student Loans Act* or 9.2 of the *Canada Student Financial Assistance Act* applied to loans under that program; or

(*d*) an emissions allowance issued to the taxpayer under the laws of Canada or a province.

History: S. 7300(*c*.1) was added by S.C. 2017, c. 33, s. 100(1), deemed in force January 1, 2013.

S. 7300(*d*) was added by S.C. 2016, c. 12, s. 81(1), applicable in respect of emissions allowances acquired in taxation years that begin after 2016. However, if a taxpayer elects under subsection 10(2) of the *Budget Implementation Act, 2016, No. 2* (Bill C-29), this amendment applies in respect of emissions allowances acquired by the taxpayer in taxation years that end after 2012.

S. 7300(*c*) was added by S.C. 2011, c. 24, s. 88(1), in force January 1, 2013 (P.C. 2012-1591, SI/2012-97).

Related Sections: S. 27.1(3) Expense restriction; s. 248(1) "emissions allowance".

Interpretation Bulletins: *Secondary* — IT-273R2 Government assistance — General comments.

7301. (Repealed.)

7302. (Revoked.)

7303. (Revoked.)

7303.1. [Prescribed northern and intermediate zones]

(1) An area is a prescribed northern zone for a taxation year for the purposes of section 110.7 of the Act where it is

(*a*) the Yukon Territory, the Northwest Territories or Nunavut;

(*b*) those parts of British Columbia, Alberta and Saskatchewan that lie north of 57°30"N latitude;

(*c*) that part of Manitoba that lies

(i) north of 56°20"N latitude, or

(ii) north of 52°30"N latitude and east of 95°25"W longitude;

(*d*) that part of Ontario that lies

(i) north of 52°30"N latitude, or

(ii) north of 51°05"N latitude and east of 89°10"W longitude;

(*e*) that part of Quebec that lies

(i) north of 51°05"N latitude, or

(ii) north of the Gulf of St. Lawrence and east of 63°00"W longitude; or

(*f*) Labrador, including Belle Isle.

Guides: T4039 Northern Residents Deductions.

(2) An area is a prescribed intermediate zone for a taxation year for the purposes of section 110.7 of the Act where it is the Queen Charlotte Islands, Anticosti Island, the Magdalen Islands or Sable Island, or where it is not part of a prescribed northern zone referred to in subsection (1) for the year and is

(*a*) that part of British Columbia that lies

(i) north of 55°35"N latitude

(ii) north of 55°00"N latitude and east of 122°00"W longitude, or

(iii) north of 55°13"N latitude and east of 123°16"W longitude;

(*b*) that part of Alberta that lies north of 55°00"N latitude;

(*c*) that part of Saskatchewan that lies

(i) north of 55°00"N latitude,

(ii) north of 54°15"N latitude and east of 107°00"W longitude, or

(iii) north of 53°20"N latitude and east of 103°00"W longitude;

(*d*) that part of Manitoba that lies

(i) north of 53°20"N latitude,

(ii) north of 52°10"N latitude and east of 97°40"W longitude, or

(iii) north of 51°30"N latitude and east of 96°00"W longitude;

(*e*) that part of Ontario that lies north of 50°35"N latitude; or

(*f*) that part of Quebec that lies

(i) north of 50°35"N latitude and west of 79°00"W longitude,

(ii) north of 49°00"N latitude, east of 79°00"W longitude and west of 74°00"W longitude,

(iii) north of 50°00"N latitude, east of 74°00"W longitude and west of 70°00"W longitude,

(iv) north of 50°45"N latitude, east of 70°00"W longitude and west of 65°30"W longitude, or

(v) north of the Gulf of St. Lawrence, east of 65°30"W longitude and west of 63°00"W longitude.

Guides: T4039 Northern Residents Deductions.

7304. [Prescribed amount – northern residents deduction]

(1) In this section,

"member of the taxpayer's household" includes the taxpayer;

"designated city" means St. John's, Halifax, Moncton, Quebec City, Montreal, Ottawa, Toronto, North Bay, Winnipeg, Saskatoon, Calgary, Edmonton and Vancouver.

(2) For the purposes of this section, the trip cost to a taxpayer in respect of a trip made by an individual who, at the time the trip was made, was a member of the taxpayer's household is the least of

(*a*) the aggregate of

(i) the value of travel assistance, if any, provided by the taxpayer's employer in respect of travelling expenses for the trip, and

(ii) the amount, if any, received by the taxpayer from his employer in respect of travelling expenses for the trip,

(*b*) the aggregate of

(i) the value of travel assistance, if any, provided by the taxpayer's employer in respect of travelling expenses for the trip, and

(ii) travelling expenses incurred by the taxpayer for the trip, and

(*c*) the lowest return airfare ordinarily available, at the time the trip was made, to the individual for flights between the place in which the individual resided immediately before the trip, or the airport nearest thereto, and the designated city that is nearest to that place.

(3) For the purposes of subsection (4), the "period travel cost" to a taxpayer for a period in a taxation year, in respect of an individual who was a member of the taxpayer's household at any time during the period, is the total of the trip costs to the taxpayer in respect of all trips that were made by the individual at a time when the individual was a member of the taxpayer's household where the trips may reasonably be considered to relate to the period.

(4) For the purposes of clause 110.7(1)(*a*)(i)(A) of the Act, the prescribed amount in respect of a taxpayer for a period in a taxation year is the lesser of

(*a*) the total of

(i) the value of travel assistance, if any, provided in the period by the taxpayer's employer in respect of travelling expenses for trips, each of which was made by an individual who, at the time the trip was made, was a member of the taxpayer's household, where the trips may reasonably be considered to relate to the period, and

(ii) the amount, if any, received in the period by the taxpayer from the taxpayer's employer in respect of travelling expenses for trips, each of which was made by an individual who, at the time the trip was made, was a member of the taxpayer's household, where the trips may reasonably be considered to relate to the period; and

(*b*) the total of all the period travel costs to the taxpayer for the period in respect of all individuals who were members of the taxpayer's household at any time in the period.

7305. [Prescribed drought regions]

(1) For the purposes of subsection 80.3(4) of the Act, prescribed drought regions in respect of (*a*) the 1995 calendar year are

(i) in Manitoba, the Local Government Districts of Alonsa, Fisher, Grahamdale, Grand Rapids and Mountain (South), the areas designated under The *Northern Affairs Act* (Manitoba) as the communities of Camperville, Crane River, Duck Bay, Homebrook, Mallard, Meadow Portage, Rock Ridge, Spence Lake and Waterhen, the Rural Municipalities of Eriksdale, Lawrence, Mossey River, Ste. Rose and Siglunes, and Skownan,

(ii) in Saskatchewan, the Rural Municipalities of Antelope Park, Battle River, Beaver River, Biggar, Blaine Lake, Britannia, Buffalo, Cut Knife, Douglas, Eagle Creek, Eldon, Eye Hill, Frenchman Butte, Glenside, Grandview, Grass Lake, Great Bend, Heart's Hill, Hillsdale, Kindersley, Loon Lake, Manitou Lake, Mariposa, Mayfield, Meadow Lake, Medstead, Meeting Lake, Meota, Mervin, Milton, Mountain View, North Battleford, Oakdale, Paynton, Parkdale, Perdue, Pleasant Valley, Prairie, Prairiedale, Progress, Redberry, Reford, Round Hill, Round Valley, Rosemont, Senlac, Spiritwood, Tramping Lake, Turtle River, Wilton and Winslow, and

(iii) in Alberta, the Counties of Beaver, Camrose, Flagstaff, Lamont, Minburn, Paintearth, Smoky Lake, St. Paul, Strathcona, Thorhild, Two Hills and Vermilion River, the Municipal Districts of Bonnyville, MacKenzie, Northern Lights, Provost and Wainwright, and Special Areas 2, 3 and 4;

(*b*) the 1997 calendar year are

(i) in Ontario, the Counties of Hastings and Renfrew,

(ii) Nova Scotia,

(iii) in Manitoba, the Rural Municipalities of Albert, Alonsa, Archie, Arthur, Birtle, Boulton, Brenda, Cameron, Clanwilliam, Dauphin, Edward, Ellice, Glenella, Grahamdale, Harrison, Lakeview, Langford, Lansdowne, Lawrence, McCreary, Miniota, Minto, Morton, Ochre River, Park (South), Pipestone, Rosedale, Rossburn, Russell, Ste. Rose, Shellmouth, Shoal Lake, Sifton, Siglunes, Silver Creek, Strathclair, Turtle Mountain, Wallace, Westbourne, Whitewater and Winchester,

(iv) in Saskatchewan, the Rural Municipalities of Abernethy, Antelope Park, Antler, Argyle, Baildon, Bengough, Benson, Big Stick, Biggar, Bratt's Lake, Brock, Brokenshell, Browning, Buchanan, Calder, Caledonia, Cambria, Cana, Chester, Chesterfield, Churchbridge, Clinworth, Coalfields, Cote, Cymri, Deer Forks, Elcapo, Elmsthorpe, Emerald, Enniskillen, Enterprise, Estevan, Excel, Eye Hill, Fertile Belt, Fillmore, Foam Lake, Francis, Fox Valley, Garry, Glenside, Golden West, Good Lake, Grandview, Grass Lake, Grayson, Griffin, Happyland, Happy Valley, Hart Butte, Hazelwood, Heart's Hill, Indian Head, Insinger, Ituna Bon Accord, Invermay, Kellross, Key West, Keys, Kingsley, Lajord, Lake Alma, Lake Johnston, Lake of The Rivers, Langenburg, Laurier, Lipton, Livingston, Lomond, Maple Creek, Mariposa, Martin, Maryfield, McLeod, Milton, Montmartre, Moose Creek, Moose Jaw, Moose Mountain, Moosomin, Mountain View, Mount Pleasant, North Qu'Appelle, Norton, Oakdale, Orkney, Old Post, Poplar Valley, Prairie, Prairiedale, Progress, Reciprocity, Redburn, Reford, Rocanville, Rosemount, St. Philips, Saltcoats, Scott, Silverwood, Sliding Hills, Souris Valley, South Qu'Appelle, Spy Hill, Stanley, Stonehenge, Storthoaks, Surprise Valley, Tecumseh, Terrell, The Gap, Tramping Lake, Tullymet, Wallace, Walpole, Waverley, Wawken, Wellington, Weyburn, Willow Bunch, Willowdale, Winslow and Wolseley, and

(v) in Alberta, the County of Forty Mile, the Municipal Districts of Acadia Valley, Cypress, Pincher Creek, Provost and Willow Creek, and Special Areas 2, 3 and 4;

(*c*) the 1998 calendar year are

(i) in Ontario, the Counties of Bruce, Grey, Huron and Oxford, and the Districts of Nipissing, Parry Sound, Sudbury and Thunder Bay,

(ii) in Nova Scotia, the Counties of Annapolis, Colchester, Cumberland, Digby, Hants and Kings,

(iii) in Saskatchewan, the Rural Municipalities of Aberdeen, Antelope Park, Arlington, Auvergne, Battle River, Bayne, Beaver River, Biggar, Blaine Lake, Blucher, Bone Creek, Britannia, Buffalo, Canaan, Chaplin, Chesterfield, Clinworth, Corman Park, Coteau, Coulee, Cut Knife, Douglas, Dundurn, Eagle Creek, Eldon, Enfield, Excelsior, Eye Hill, Fertile Valley, Frenchman Butte, Frontier, Glen Bain, Glen McPherson, Glenside, Grandview, Grant, Grass Lake, Grassy Creek, Gravelbourg, Great Bend, Harris, Hart Butte, Heart's Hill, Hillsdale, Kindersley, King George, Lac Pelletier, Lacadena, Laird, Lake of The Rivers, Lawtonia, Lone Tree, Loon Lake, Loreburn, Mankota, Manitou Lake, Maple Bush, Mariposa, Marriott, Mayfield, Meadow Lake, Medstead, Meeting Lake, Meota, Mervin, Milden, Milton, Miry Creek, Monet, Montrose, Morse, Mountain View, Newcombe, North Battleford, Oakdale, Old Post, Parkdale, Paynton, Perdue, Pinto Creek, Pleasant Valley, Poplar Valley, Prairie, Prairiedale, Progress, Redberry, Reford, Reno, Riverside, Rosedale, Rosemount, Round Hill, Round Valley, Rosthern, Rudy, St. Andrews, Saskatchewan Landing, Senlac, Shamrock, Snipe Lake, Stonehenge, Swift Current, Tramping Lake, Turtle River, Val Marie, Vanscoy, Victory, Waverly, Webb, Whiska Creek, White Valley, Willow Bunch, Wilton, Winslow, Wise Creek, and Wood River, and

(iv) in Alberta, the Counties of Beaver, Camrose, Flagstaff, Grande Prairie, Lamont, Minburn, Paintearth, St. Paul, Smoky Lake, Stettler, Two Hills and Vermilion River, the Municipal Districts of Acadia, Big Lakes, Birch Hills, Bonnyville, Clear Hills, East Peace, Fairview, Greenview, Northern Lights, Peace, Provost, Saddle Hills, Smoky River, Spirit River, Starland, Wainwright and Yellowhead, and Special Areas 2, 3 and 4;

Regulations

(*d*) the 1999 calendar year are

(i) in Nova Scotia, the Counties of Annapolis, Colchester, Cumberland, Digby, Hants, Kings and Yarmouth,

(ii) in British Columbia, the Peace River Regional District,

(iii) in Saskatchewan, the Rural Municipalities of Beaver River and Loon Lake, and

(iv) in Alberta, the Counties of Athabaska, Barrhead, Birch Hills, Grande Prairie, Lac Ste. Anne, Lakeland, Lamont, Saddle Hills, Smoky Lake, St. Paul, Thorhild, Two Hills, Westlock and Woodlands, and the Municipal Districts of Big Lakes, Bonnyville, Clear Hills, East Peace, Fairview, Greenview, Lesser Slave Lake, MacKenzie, Northern Lights, Peace, Smoky River and Spirit River;

(*e*) the 2000 calendar year are

(i) in British Columbia, the Regional District of East Kootenay,

(ii) in Saskatchewan, the Rural Municipalities of Antelope Park, Battle River, Big Stick, Biggar, Blaine Lake, Buffalo, Chesterfield, Clinworth, Cut Knife, Deer Forks, Douglas, Duck Lake, Eagle Creek, Enterprise, Eye Hill, Fox Valley, Glenside, Grandview, Grass Lake, Great Bend, Happyland, Hearth's Hill, Kindersley, Laird, Leask, Maple Creek, Mariposa, Marriott, Mayfield, Meeting Lake, Milton, Mountain View, Newcombe, North Battleford, Oakdale, Paynton, Piapot, Pleasant Valley, Prairiedale, Progress, Redberry, Reford, Reno, Rosemount, Rosthern, Round Valley, Senlac, St. Louis, Tramping Lake and Winslow, and

(iii) in Alberta, the Counties of Barrhead, Birch Hills, Cardston, Cypress, Flagstaff, Forty Mile, Grande Prairie, Kneehill, Lac Ste. Anne, Lethbridge, Newell, Paintearth, Saddle Hills, Starland, Stettler, Vulcan, Warner, Wheatland and Woodlands, the Improvement Districts of Kananaskis and Waterton, the Municipal Districts of Acadia, Fairview, Foothills, Greenview, Peace, Pincher Creek, Provost, Ranchland, Smoky River, Spirit River, Taber and Willow Creek, and the Municipality of Crowsnest Pass and Special Areas 2, 3, and 4;

(*f*) the 2001 calendar year are

(i) in Ontario, the Counties of Elgin, Essex, Haldimand, Hastings, Huron, Lambton, Lanark, Lennox and Addington, Middlesex, Norfolk, Northumberland, Oxford and Renfrew, the United Counties of Leeds and Grenville, the Frontenac Management Board, the Regional Municipality of Niagara, the Cities of Brant County, Brantford, Hamilton, Ottawa and Prince Edward County and the Municipality of Chatham-Kent,

(ii) in Quebec, the Magdalen Islands,

(iii) in Nova Scotia, the Counties of Annapolis, Antigonish, Cape Breton, Colchester, Cumberland, Digby, Hants, Inverness, Kings, Pictou, Richmond and Victoria,

(iv) in New Brunswick, the Counties of Albert, Kent and Westmorland,

(v) in Manitoba, the Rural Municipality of Kelsey,

(vi) in British Columbia, the Regional Districts of Central Kootenay, East Kootenay, Kootenay Boundary and Okanagan-Similkameen,

(vii) Prince Edward Island,

(viii) in Saskatchewan, the Rural Municipalities of Aberdeen, Abernethy, Antelope Park, Arborfield, Arlington, Arm River, Auvergne, Baildon, Barrier Valley, Battle River, Bayne, Beaver River, Bengough, Big Arm, Big Quill, Big River, Big Stick, Biggar, Birch Hills, Bjorkdale, Blaine Lake, Blucher, Bone Creek, Bratt's Lake, Britannia, Brokenshell, Buchanan, Buckland, Buffalo, Calder, Caledonia, Cana, Canaan, Canwood, Carmichael, Caron, Chaplin, Chester, Chesterfield, Churchbridge, Clayton, Clinworth, Colonsay, Connaught, Corman Park, Cote, Coteau, Coulee, Craik, Cupar, Cut Knife, Deer Forks, Douglas, Duck Lake, Dufferin, Dundurn, Eagle Creek, Edenwold, Elcapo, Eldon, Elfros, Elmsthorpe, Emerald, Enfield, Enterprise, Excel, Excelsior, Eye Hill, Eyebrow, Fertile Valley, Fish Creek, Flett's Springs, Foam Lake, Fox Valley, Francis, Frenchman Butte, Frontier, Garden River, Garry, Glen Bain, Glen Mcpherson, Glenside, Good Lake, Grandview, Grant, Grass Lake, Grassy Creek, Gravelbourg, Grayson, Great Bend, Gull Lake, Happy Valley, Happyland, Harris, Hart Butte, Hazel Dell, Heart's Hill, Hillsborough, Hillsdale, Hoodoo, Hudson Bay, Humboldt, Huron, Indian Head, Insinger, Invergordon, Invermay, Ituna Bon Accord, Kellross, Kelvington, Key West, Keys, Kindersley, King George, Kingsley, Kinistino, Kutawa, Lac Pelletier, Lacadena, Laird, Lajord, Lake Johnston, Lake Lenore, Lake of The Rivers, Lakeland, Lakeside, Lakeview, Last Mountain Valley, Lawtonia, Leask, Leroy, Lipton, Livingston, Lone Tree, Longlaketon, Loon Lake, Loreburn, Lost River, Lumsden, Manitou Lake, Mankota, Maple Bush, Maple Creek, Mariposa, Marquis, Marriott, Mayfield, Mccraney, Mckillop, McLeod, Meadow Lake, Medstead, Meeting Lake, Meota, Mervin, Milden, Milton, Miry Creek, Monet, Montmartre, Montrose, Moose Jaw, Moose Range, Morris, Morse, Mount Hope, Mountain View, Newcombe, Nipawin, North Battleford, North Qu'Appelle, Norton, Oakdale, Old Post, Orkney, Paddockwood, Parkdale, Paynton, Pense, Perdue, Piapot, Pinto Creek, Pittville, Pleasant Valley, Pleasantdale, Ponass Lake, Poplar Valley, Porcupine, Prairie Rose, Prairiedale, Preeceville, Prince Albert, Progress, Redberry, Redburn, Reford, Reno, Riverside, Rodgers, Rosedale, Rosemount, Rosthern, Round Hill, Round Valley, Rudy, Saltcoats, Sarnia, Saskatchewan Landing, Sasman, Scott, Senlac, Shamrock, Shellbrook, Sherwood,

Sliding Hills, Snipe Lake, South Qu'Appelle, Spalding, Spiritwood, St. Andrews, St. Louis, St. Peter, St. Philips, Stanley, Star City, Stonehenge, Surprise Valley, Sutton, Swift Current, Terrell, The Gap, Three Lakes, Tisdale, Torch River, Touchwood, Tramping Lake, Tullymet, Turtle River, Usborne, Val Marie, Vanscoy, Victory, Viscount, Wallace, Waverley, Webb, Wheatlands, Whiska Creek, White Valley, Willner, Willow Bunch, Willow Creek, Wilton, Winslow, Wise Creek, Wolseley, Wolverine, Wood Creek, Wood River and Wreford,

(ix) Alberta, and

(x) in Newfoundland and Labrador, the island of Newfoundland;

(*g*) the 2002 calendar year are

(i) in Ontario, the Counties of Bruce, Elgin, Lambton and Middlesex, the Municipality of Chatham-Kent, the District of Cochrane and the Regional Municipalities of Halton and Peel,

(ii) in Manitoba, the Rural Municipalities of Albert, Alonsa, Archie, Argyle, Arthur, Birtle, Blanshard, Brenda, Cameron, Clanwilliam, Coldwell, Cornwallis, Daly, Dauphin, Edward, Ellice, Elton, Eriksdale, Ethelbert, Gilbert Plains, Glenella, Glenwood, Grahamdale, Grandview, Hamiota, Harrison, Hillsburg, Kelsey, Langford, Lansdowne, Lawrence, McCreary, Miniota, Minitonas, Minto, Morton, Mossey River, Mountain, North Cypress, Oakland, Ochre River, Odanah, Park, Pipestone, Riverside, Roblin, Rosedale, Rossburn, Russell, Saskatchewan, Shell River, Shellmouth-Boulton, Shoal Lake, Sifton, Siglunes, Silver Creek, South Cypress, St. Laurent, Ste. Rose, Strathclair, Strathcona, Swan River, Turtle Mountain, Wallace, Whitehead, Whitewater, Winchester and Woodworth, and the unorganized territory that is north of the Rural Municipality of Alonsa, between that rural municipality and the south shore of Lake Manitoba,

(iii) in British Columbia, the Peace River Regional District,

(iv) in Saskatchewan, the Rural Municipalities of Aberdeen, Abernethy, Antelope Park, Antler, Arborfield, Argyle, Arlington, Arm River, Auvergne, Baildon, Barrier Valley, Battle River, Bayne, Beaver River, Big Arm, Big Quill, Big River, Big Stick, Biggar, Birch Hills, Bjorkdale, Blaine Lake, Blucher, Bone Creek, Britannia, Buchanan, Buckland, Buffalo, Calder, Cana, Canaan, Canwood, Carmichael, Caron, Chaplin, Chesterfield, Churchbridge, Clayton, Clinworth, Colonsay, Connaught, Corman Park, Cote, Coteau, Coulee, Craik, Cupar, Cut Knife, Deer Forks, Douglas, Duck Lake, Dufferin, Dundurn, Eagle Creek, Edenwold, Elcapo, Eldon, Elfros, Emerald, Enfield, Enniskillen, Enterprise, Excelsior, Eye Hill, Eyebrow, Fertile Belt, Fertile Valley, Fish Creek, Flett's Springs, Foam Lake, Fox Valley, Frenchman Butte, Frontier, Garden River, Garry, Glen Bain, Glen McPherson, Glenside, Good Lake, Grandview, Grant, Grass Lake, Grassy Creek, Gravelbourg, Grayson, Great Bend, Gull Lake, Happyland, Harris, Hazel Dell, Hazelwood, Heart's Hill, Hillsborough, Hillsdale, Hoodoo, Hudson Bay, Humboldt, Huron, Insinger, Invergordon, Invermay, Ituna Bon Accord, Kellross, Kelvington, Keys, Kindersley, King George, Kingsley, Kinistino, Kutawa, Lac Pelletier, Lacadena, Laird, Lake Johnston, Lake Lenore, Lakeland, Lakeside, Lakeview, Langenburg, Last Mountain Valley, Lawtonia, Leask, Leroy, Lipton, Livingston, Lone Tree, Longlaketon, Loon Lake, Loreburn, Lost River, Lumsden, Manitou Lake, Mankota, Maple Bush, Maple Creek, Mariposa, Marquis, Marriott, Martin, Maryfield, Mayfield, McCraney, McKillop, McLeod, Meadow Lake, Medstead, Meeting Lake, Meota, Mervin, Milden, Milton, Miry Creek, Monet, Montrose, Moose Creek, Moose Jaw, Moose Mountain, Moose Range, Moosomin, Morris, Morse, Mount Hope, Mount Pleasant, Mountain View, Newcombe, Nipawin, North Battleford, North Qu'appelle, Oakdale, Orkney, Paddockwood, Parkdale, Paynton, Pense, Perdue, Piapot, Pinto Creek, Pittville, Pleasant Valley, Pleasantdale, Ponass Lake, Porcupine, Prairie Rose, Prairiedale, Preeceville, Prince Albert, Progress, Reciprocity, Redberry, Redburn, Reford, Reno, Riverside, Rocanville, Rodgers, Rosedale, Rosemount, Rosthern, Round Hill, Round Valley, Rudy, Saltcoats, Sarnia, Saskatchewan Landing, Sasman, Senlac, Shamrock, Shellbrook, Sherwood, Silverwood, Sliding Hills, Snipe Lake, Spalding, Spiritwood, Spy Hill, St. Andrews, St. Louis, St. Peter, St. Philips, Stanley, Star City, Storthoaks, Sutton, Swift Current, Three Lakes, Tisdale, Torch River, Touchwood, Tramping Lake, Tullymet, Turtle River, Usborne, Val Marie, Vanscoy, Victory, Viscount, Wallace, Walpole, Waverley, Wawken, Webb, Wheatlands, Whiska Creek, White Valley, Willner, Willow Creek, Willowdale, Wilton, Winslow, Wise Creek, Wolverine, Wood Creek, Wood River and Wreford, and

(v) Alberta;

(*h*) the 2003 calendar year are

(i) in Manitoba, the Rural Municipalities of Albert, Alonsa, Archie, Argyle, Armstrong, Arthur, Bifrost, Birtle, Blanshard, Brenda, Cameron, Clanwilliam, Coldwell, Cornwallis, Daly, Dauphin, Edward, Ellice, Elton, Eriksdale, Ethelbert, Fisher, Gilbert Plains, Gimli, Glenella, Glenwood, Grahamdale, Grandview, Hamiota, Harrison, Hillsburg, Kelsey, Lakeview, Langford, Lansdowne, Lawrence, Louise, McCreary, Miniota, Minitonas, Minto, Morton, Mossey River, Mountain, North Cypress, Oakland, Ochre River, Odanah, Park, Pipestone, Riverside, Roblin, Rockwood, Rosedale, Rossburn, Russell, Saskatchewan, Shell River, Shellmouth-Boulton, Shoal Lake, Sifton, Siglunes, Silver Creek, South Cypress, St. Laurent, Ste. Rose, Strathclair, Strathcona, Swan River, Turtle Mountain, Wallace, Westbourne, Whitehead, Whitewater, Winchester, Woodlands and Woodworth, the town of Grand Rapids and the Manitoba Census Consolidated Subdivision no. 19 (unorganized), as that subdivision was developed by Statistics Canada for the 2001 Census,

(ii) in British Columbia, the Regional Districts of Bulkley-Nechako, Cariboo, Central Kootenay, Central Okanagan, Columbia-Shuswap, East Kootenay, Fort Nelson-Liard, Fraser-Fort George, Kootenay Boundary, North Okanagan, Okanagan-Similkameen, Peace River, Spallumcheen, Squamish-Lillooet and Thompson-Nicola,

(iii) in Saskatchewan, the Rural Municipalities of Aberdeen, Abernethy, Antelope Park, Antler, Arborfield, Argyle, Barrier Valley, Battle River, Bayne, Beaver River, Benson, Big Quill, Big River, Biggar, Birch Hills, Bjorkdale, Blaine Lake, Blucher, Britannia, Brock, Brokenshell, Browning, Buchanan, Buckland, Buffalo, Calder, Cana, Canaan, Canwood, Chesterfield, Churchbridge, Clayton, Clinworth, Coalfields, Colonsay, Connaught, Corman Park, Cote, Coteau, Coulee, Cupar, Cut Knife, Cymri, Deer Forks, Douglas, Duck Lake, Dufferin, Dundurn, Eagle Creek, Edenwold, Elcapo, Eldon, Elfros, Emerald, Enniskillen, Excelsior, Fertile Belt, Fertile Valley, Fish Creek, Flett's Springs, Foam Lake, Frenchman Butte, Garden River, Garry, Glenside, Good Lake, Grandview, Grant, Grayson, Great Bend, Griffin, Happyland, Harris, Hazel Dell, Hazelwood, Hillsdale, Hoodoo, Hudson Bay, Humboldt, Insinger, Invergordon, Invermay, Ituna Bon Accord, Kellross, Kelvington, Keys, Kindersley, King George, Kingsley, Kinistino, Kutawa, Lacadena, Laird, Lake Lenore, Lakeland, Lakeside, Lakeview, Langenburg, Last Mountain Valley, Leask, Leroy, Lipton, Livingston, Longlaketon, Loon Lake, Lumsden, Marriott, Martin, Maryfield, Mayfield, McKillop, McLeod, Meadow Lake, Medstead, Meeting Lake, Meota, Mervin, Milden, Milton, Miry Creek, Monet, Montrose, Moose Creek, Moose Mountain, Moose Range, Moosomin, Morse, Mount Hope, Mount Pleasant, Mountain View, Newcombe, Nipawin, North Battleford, North Qu'appelle, Oakdale, Orkney, Paddockwood, Parkdale, Paynton, Pense, Perdue, Pittville, Pleasant Valley, Pleasantdale, Ponass Lake, Porcupine, Prairie Rose, Prairiedale, Preeceville, Prince Albert, Reciprocity, Redberry, Redburn, Reford, Riverside, Rocanville, Rosemount, Rosthern, Round Hill, Rudy, Saltcoats, Sarnia, Saskatchewan Landing, Sasman, Shellbrook, Sherwood, Silverwood, Sliding Hills, Snipe Lake, Spalding, Spiritwood, Spy Hill, St. Andrews, St. Louis, St. Peter, St. Philips, Stanley, Star City, Storthoaks, Swift Current, Tecumseh, Three Lakes, Tisdale, Torch River, Touchwood, Tullymet, Turtle River, Usborne, Vanscoy, Victory, Viscount, Wallace, Walpole, Wawken, Webb, Weyburn, Willow Creek, Willowdale, Winslow and Wolverine, and

(iv) in Alberta, the Counties of Athabasca, Barrhead, Birch Hills, Brazeau, Cardston, Clearwater, Grande Prairie, Kneehill, Lac Ste. Anne, Lacombe, Lakeland, Leduc, Mountain View, Northern Sunrise, Parkland, Ponoka, Red Deer, Saddle Hills, Starland, Thorhild, Wetaskiwin, Woodlands and Yellowhead, the improvement districts of Banff, Jasper Park, Kananaskis, Waterton and Wilmore Wilderness, the municipal districts of Acadia, Big Lakes, Bighorn, Bonnyville, Clear Hills, Fairview, Greenview, MacKenzie, Northern Lights, Peace, Pincher Creek, Ranchland, Smoky River, Spirit River and Willow Creek, the municipalities of Crowsnest Pass and Jasper, and special areas 3 and 4;

(*i*) in the 2004 calendar year are

(i) in British Columbia, the Regional District of Fort Nelson-Liard, and

(ii) in Alberta, the Counties of Beaver, Camrose, Flagstaff, Paintearth, Starland and Stettler, the Municipal Districts of Acadia, Clear Hills, Fairview, Mackenzie and Northern Lights, and Special Areas 2, 3 and 4;

(*j*) the 2006 calendar year are

(i) in Ontario, the Territorial Districts of Algoma, Kenora, Manitoulin, Rainy River and Thunder Bay,

(ii) in British Columbia, the Regional Districts of Bulkley–Nechako, Cariboo, Fraser–Fort George, Kitimat–Stikine and Peace River,

(iii) in Saskatchewan, the Rural Municipalities of Arlington, Auvergne, Bengough, Big Stick, Bone Creek, Carmichael, Clinworth, Frontier, Glen McPherson, Grassy Creek, Gull Lake, Happy Valley, Hart Butte, Lac Pelletier, Lake Alma, Laurier, Lone Tree, Mankota, Maple Creek, Miry Creek, Old Post, Piapot, Pittville, Poplar Valley, Reno, Surprise Valley, The Gap, Val Marie, Waverley, Webb, Whiska Creek, White Valley, Willow Bunch and Wise Creek, and

(iv) in Alberta, the Counties of Clear Hills, Grande Prairie and Saddle Hills and the Municipal Districts of Greenview and Northern Lights;

(*k*) the 2007 calendar year are

(i) in Ontario, the Cities of Hamilton, Kawartha Lakes and Toronto, the Counties of Brant, Bruce, Dufferin, Elgin, Essex, Frontenac, Grey, Haldimand, Hastings, Huron, Lambton, Lennox and Addington, Middlesex, Northumberland, Norfolk, Oxford, Perth, Peterborough, Prince Edward, Simcoe and Wellington, the Municipality of Chatham-Kent, the Regional Municipalities of Durham, Halton, Niagara, Peel, Waterloo and York, the Territorial Districts of Algoma, Manitoulin and Thunder Bay and the United Counties of Leeds and Grenville,

(ii) in British Columbia, the Regional Districts of Central Kootenay, East Kootenay, Kootenay Boundary and Okanagan-Similkameen,

(iii) in Saskatchewan, the Rural Municipalities of Arlington, Auvergne, Bengough, Big Stick, Bone Creek, Carmichael, Coulee, Excel, Excelsior, Frontier, Glen Bain, Glen McPherson, Grassy Creek, Gull Lake, Happy Valley, Hart Butte, Lac

Pelletier, Lake of the Rivers, Lawtonia, Lone Tree, Mankota, Maple Creek, Miry Creek, Morse, Old Post, Piapot, Pinto Creek, Pittville, Poplar Valley, Reno, Riverside, Saskatchewan Landing, Stonehenge, Swift Current, Val Marie, Waverley, Webb, Whiska Creek, White Valley, Willow Bunch, Wise Creek and Wood River, and

(iv) in Alberta, the Counties of Cardston, Cypress, Forty Mile, Lethbridge and Warner, the Municipal Districts of Pincher Creek, Ranchland, Taber and Willow Creek and the Municipality of Crowsnest Pass;

(*l*) the 2008 calendar year are

(i) in Manitoba, the Municipality of Killarney-Turtle Mountain and the Rural Municipalities of Albert, Arthur, Brenda, Cameron, Edward, Glenwood, Morton, Pipestone, Riverside, Sifton, Whitewater and Winchester,

(ii) in British Columbia, the Regional Districts of Central Kootenay, East Kootenay, Kootenay Boundary and Peace River,

(iii) in Saskatchewan, the Rural Municipalities of Argyle, Arlington, Auvergne, Baildon, Bengough, Benson, Bone Creek, Bratt's Lake, Brokenshell, Browning, Caledonia, Cambria, Caron, Coalfields, Cymri, Elmsthorpe, Enniskillen, Estevan, Excel, Francis, Frontier, Glen Bain, Glen McPherson, Grassy Creek, Gravelbourg, Griffin, Hillsborough, Happy Valley, Hart Butte, Key West, Lac Pelletier, Lajord, Lake Alma, Lake Johnston, Lake of the Rivers, Laurier, Lomond, Lone Tree, Mankota, Marquis, Moose Creek, Moose Jaw, Mount Pleasant, Norton, Old Post, Pense, Pinto Creek, Poplar Valley, Redburn, Reciprocity, Rodgers, Scott, Shamrock, Sherwood, Souris Valley, Surprise Valley, Stonehenge, Storthoaks, Sutton, Tecumseh, Terrell, The Gap, Val Marie, Waverley, Wellington, Weyburn, Whiska Creek, White Valley, Willow Bunch, Wise Creek and Wood River, and

(iv) in Alberta, the Counties of Birch Hills, Clear Hills, Grande Prairie and Saddle Hills and the Municipal Districts of Fairview and Spirit River;

(*m*) the 2009 calendar year are

(i) in Manitoba, the Rural Municipalities of Albert, Archie. Arthur, Birtle, Brenda, Cameron, Clanwilliam, Edward, Ellice, Harrison, Hillsburg, Miniota, Minitonas, Park, Pipestone, Rossburn, Russell, Shellmouth-Boulton, Shell River, Shoal Lake, Sifton, Silver Creek, Strathclair, Swan River, Wallace, Winchester and Woodworth and Census Division No. 20, Unorganized, South Part, as developed by Statistics Canada for the 2006 Census,

(ii) in British Columbia, the Census Subdivisions Bulkley-Nechako B and E, Cariboo D, E, G, H and J to L, Central Kootenay A to E, G, H, J and K, Central Okanagan, Central Okanagan J, Columbia-Shuswap C to F, Kootenay Boundary B to E, North Okanagan B and D to F, Okanagan-Similkameen A to H, Peace River C to E, Spallumcheen, Squamish-Lillooet A to C and Thompson-Nicola A (Wells Gray Country), B (Thompson Headwaters), E (Bonaparte Plateau), I (Blue Sky Country), J (Copper Desert Country), L, M, N, O (Lower North Thompson) and P (Rivers and the Peaks), as these subdivisions were developed by Statistics Canada for the 2006 Census,

(iii) in Saskatchewan, the Rural Municipalities of Aberdeen, Antelope Park, Antler, Argyle, Arlington, Auvergne, Battle River, Beaver River, Benson, Biggar, Blucher, Bone Creek, Britannia, Brock, Browning, Buchanan, Buffalo, Calder, Cana, Canaan, Chaplin, Chesterfield, Churchbridge, Clayton, Clinworth, Coalfields, Corman Park, Cote, Coteau, Coulee, Cut Knife, Deer Forks, Dundurn, Eagle Creek, Elcapo, Eldon, Emerald, Enfield, Enniskillen, Estevan, Excelsior, Eye Hill, Fertile Belt, Fertile Valley, Foam Lake, Fox Valley, Frenchman Butte, Frontier, Garry, Glen Bain, Glen McPherson, Glenside, Good Lake, Grandview, Grant, Grass Lake, Grassy Creek, Gravelbourg, Grayson, Happyland, Harris, Hazel Dell, Hazelwood, Heart's Hill, Hillsdale, Insinger, Invermay, Keys, Kindersley, King George, Kingsley, Lacadena, Lac Pelletier, Lawtonia, Langenburg, Livingston, Lone Tree, Loon Lake, Loreburn, Manitou Lake, Mankota, Maple Bush, Mariposa, Marriott, Martin, Maryfield, Mayfield, McLeod, Meadow Lake, Meota, Mervin, Milden, Milton, Miry Creek, Monet, Montrose, Moose Creek, Moose Mountain, Moosomin, Morse, Mountain View, Mount Pleasant, Newcombe, North Battleford, Oakdale, Orkney, Parkdale, Paynton, Perdue, Pinto Creek, Pittville, Pleasant Valley, Prairiedale, Preeceville, Progress, Reciprocity, Reford, Reno, Riverside, Rocanville, Rosedale, Rosemount, Round Valley, Rudy, Saltcoats, Saskatchewan Landing, Senlac, Shamrock, Silverwood, Sliding Hills, Snipe Lake, Spy Hill, St. Andrews, St. Philips, Stanley, Storthoaks, Swift Current, Tecumseh, Tramping Lake, Turtle River, Val Marie, Vanscoy, Victory, Wallace, Walpole, Waverley, Wawken, Webb, Whiska Creek, White Valley, Willowdale, Wilton, Winslow, Wise Creek and Wood River, and

(iv) in Alberta, the Cities of Calgary and Edmonton, the Counties of Athabasca, Barrhead, Beaver, Birch Hills, Brazeau, Camrose, Clear Hills, Clearwater, Flagstaff, Grande Prairie, Kneehill, Lac La Biche, Lacombe, Lac Ste. Anne, Lamont, Leduc, Minburn, Mountain View, Northern Sunrise, Paintearth, Parkland, Ponoka, Red Deer, Rocky View, Saddle Hills, Smoky Lake, St. Paul, Starland, Stettler, Strathcona, Sturgeon, Thorhild, Two Hills, Vermilion River, Westlock, Wetaskiwin, Wheatland, Woodlands and Yellowhead, Improvement District No. 13, the Municipal Districts of Acadia, Big Lakes, Bonnyville, Fairview, Greenview, Lesser Slave River, Northern Lights, Opportunity, Peace, Provost, Smoky River, Spirit River and Wainwright, Special Areas No. 2, 3 and 4 and the Town of Drumheller;

(*n*) the 2010 calendar year are

(i) in British Columbia, the Census Subdivisions Bulkley-Nechako B to F, Cariboo A to F and I to K, Fraser-Fort George A and C to H and Peace River B to E, as these subdivisions were developed by Statistics Canada for the 2006 Census, and

(ii) in Alberta, the Counties of Birch Hills, Clear Hills, Grande Prairie, Northern Lights, Northern Sunrise, Saddle Hills, Woodlands and Yellowhead, the Improvement District No. 12 and the Municipal Districts of Big Lakes, Fairview, Greenview, Peace, Smoky River and Spirit River; and

(*o*) the 2012 calendar year are

(i) in Ontario, the Census Divisions Brant, Haldimand-Norfolk, Hamilton and Ottawa, as these divisions were developed by Statistics Canada for the 2011 Census, the Counties of Bruce, Dufferin, Frontenac, Grey, Hastings, Huron, Lanark, Lennox and Addington, Northumberland, Oxford, Perth, Prince Edward, Renfrew and Wellington, the Districts of Parry Sound and Rainy River, as these districts were developed by Statistics Canada for the 2011 Census, the District Municipality of Muskoka, the Regional Municipalities of Halton, Niagara and Waterloo, the Territorial Districts of Algoma and Manitoulin and the United Counties of Prescott and Russell,

(ii) in Quebec, the Regional County Municipalities of Les Collines-de-l'Outaouais, Papineau, Pontiac and Temiscamingue and the Town of Gatineau,

(iii) in Manitoba, Census Division No. 1, Unorganized, as developed by Statistics Canada for the 2011 Census, and the Rural Municipalities of De Salaberry, Franklin, Hanover, La Broquerie, Montcalm, Morris, Piney, Reynolds, Rhineland, Ritchot, Ste. Anne, Stuartburn, Tache and Whitemouth,

(iv) in British Columbia, the Peace River Regional District, and

(v) in Alberta, the Counties of Birch Hills, Clear Hills, Grande Prairie, Mackenzie, Northern Lights and Saddle Hills and the Municipal Districts of Fairview, Peace and Spirit River.

History: S. 7305 (*n*) and (*o*) were added by P.C. 2013-1253, SOR/2013-206, s. 1(1), published in the *Canada Gazette* December 4, 2013, deemed to have come into force on March 3, 2011.

S. 7305(*m*)(i) to (iii) were replaced, and subparagraph (iv) was added, by P.C. 2011-205, SOR/2011-32, dated February 10, 2011, published in the *Canada Gazette* March 2, 2011, applicable to the 2009 calendar year.

S. 7305(*m*)(i) to (iii) formerly read:

(i) in British Columbia, the Census Subdivisions Cariboo D, E, G and K, Central Kootenay A to E, G, H, J and K, Central Okanagan, Central Okanagan J, Columbia-Shuswap C to F, Kootenay Boundary B to E, North Okanagan B and D to F, Okanagan-Similkameen A to H, Spallumcheen, Squamish-Lillooet A to C and Thompson-Nicola E (Bonaparte Plateau), I (Blue Sky Country), J (Copper Desert Country), L, M, N, O (Lower North Thompson) and P (Rivers and the Peaks), as these subdivisions were developed by Statistics Canada for the 2006 Census,

(ii) in Saskatchewan, the Rural Municipalities of Antelope Park, Auvergne, Battle River, Biggar, Bone Creek, Britannia, Buffalo, Canaan, Chaplin, Chesterfield, Clinworth, Coteau, Coulee, Cut Knife, Deer Forks, Eagle Creek, Eldon, Enfield, Excelsior, Eye Hill, Fertile Valley, Glen Bain, Glen McPherson, Glenside, Grandview, Grass Lake, Grassy Creek, Gravelbourg, Happyland, Harris, Heart's Hill, Hillsdale, Kindersley, King George, Lacadena, Lac Pelletier, Lawtonia, Lone Tree, Loreburn, Manitou Lake, Mankota, Maple Bush, Mariposa, Marriott, Milden, Milton, Miry Creek, Monet, Montrose, Morse, Mountain View, Newcombe, Oakdale, Paynton, Perdue, Pinto Creek, Pittville, Pleasant Valley, Prairiedale, Progress, Reford, Riverside, Rosedale, Rosemount, Round Valley, Rudy, Saskatchewan Landing, Senlac, Shamrock, Snipe Lake, St. Andrews, Swift Current, Tramping Lake, Turtle River, Val Marie, Vanscoy, Victory, Waverley, Webb, Whiska Creek, Wilton, Winslow, Wise Creek and Wood River, and

(iii) in Alberta, the Cities of Calgary and Edmonton, the Counties of Athabasca, Barrhead, Beaver, Birch Hills, Brazeau, Camrose, Clear Hills, Clearwater, Flagstaff, Kneehill, Lac La Biche, Lacombe, Lac Ste. Anne, Lamont, Leduc, Minburn, Mountain View, Paintearth, Parkland, Ponoka, Red Deer, Rocky View, Smoky Lake, St. Paul, Starland, Stettler, Strathcona, Sturgeon, Thorhild, Two Hills, Vermilion River, Westlock, Wetaskiwin, Wheatland and Woodlands, Improvement District No. 13, the Municipal Districts of Acadia, Big Lakes, Bonnyville, Fairview, Greenview, Lesser Slave River, Northern Lights, Peace, Provost, Smoky River, Spirit River and Wainwright, Special Areas No. 2, 3 and 4 and the Town of Drumheller.

S. 7305(*k*), (*l*) and (*m*) were added by S.C. 2009, c. 31, s. 16, in force on Royal Assent, December 15, 2009.

(2) For the purposes of this section, a city, county, district or other municipality is deemed to include any area that is surrounded by the territory of the city, county, district or other municipality.

History: S. 7305 was renumbered as 7305(1) and s. 7305(2) was added by P.C. 2013-1253, SOR/2013-206, s. 1(2), published in the *Canada Gazette* December 4, 2013, deemed to have come into force on March 3, 2011.

7305.01. **(1)** For the purposes of subsections 80.3(4) and (4.1) of the Act, the following regions are prescribed drought regions or prescribed regions of flood or excessive moisture:

(*a*) in respect of the 2014 calendar year

(i) in Manitoba, Census Divisions No. 17, Unorganized, and No. 20, Unorganized, South Part, as these divisions were developed by Statistics Canada for the 2011 Census, the Municipality of Shoal Lake, the Reserve of Valley River 63A and the Rural Municipalities of Albert, Alonsa, Archie, Arthur, Birtle, Blanshard, Brenda, Cameron, Clanwilliam, Coldwell, Daly, Dauphin, Edward, Ellice, Elton, Eriksdale, Ethelbert, Gilbert Plains, Glenella, Glenwood, Grahamdale, Grandview, Hamiota, Harrison, Hillsburg, Killarney-Turtle Mountain, Lakeview, Langford, Lansdowne, Lawrence, McCreary, Miniota, Minitonas, Minto, Morton, Mossey River, Mountain, North Cypress, North Norfolk, Oakland, Ochre River, Odanah, Park, Pipestone, Portage la Prairie, Riverside, Rosedale, Rossburn, Russell, Saskatchewan, Shell River, Shellmouth-Boulton, Sifton, Siglunes, Silver Creek, South Cypress, St. Laurent, Ste. Rose, Strathclair, Swan River, Wallace, Westbourne, Whitehead, Whitewater, Winchester, Woodlands and Woodworth,

(ii) in British Columbia, the Census Subdvisions of Alberni-Clayoquot A, C and D, Bulkley-Nechako A to G, Capital F, Cariboo A to C and I, Comox Valley A, Cowichan Valley F, Fraser-Fort George A and C to H, Nanaimo C and H, Peace River B to E and Powell River D and Part 2 of Census Subdivision Capital H, as these subdivisions were developed by Statistics Canada for the 2011 Census,

(iii) in Saskatchewan, the Rural Municipalities of Antler, Argyle, Buchanan, Calder, Cana, Churchbridge, Clayton, Cote, Elfros, Emerald, Enniskillen, Fertile Belt, Foam Lake, Garry, Good Lake, Grayson, Hazel Dell, Insinger, Invermay, Ituna

Regulations

Bon Accord, Kelvington, Keys, Lakeview, Langenburg, Livingston, Martin, Maryfield, McLeod, Moose Creek, Moose Mountain, Moosomin, Mount Pleasant, Orkney, Ponass Lake, Preeceville, Reciprocity, Rocanville, Saltcoats, Sasman, Silverwood, Sliding Hills, Spy Hill, St. Philips, Stanley, Storthoaks, Wallace, Walpole, Wawken and Willowdale, and

(iv) in Alberta, the Counties of Birch Hills, Clear Hills, Grande Prairie, Mackenzie, Northern Lights, Northern Sunrise and Saddle Hills and the Municipal Districts of Big Lakes, Fairview, Greenview, Peace, Smoky River and Spirit River;

(*b*) in respect of the 2015 calendar year

(i) in Manitoba, Census Divisions No. 18, Unorganized, East Part, No. 19, Unorganized, No. 20, Unorganized, North and South Parts, and No. 21, Unorganized, as these divisions were developed by Statistics Canada for the 2011 Census, the Municipalities of Ethelbert, Gilbert Plains, Grandview, Minitonas-Bowsman, Mossey River, Roblin, Ste. Rose and Swan Valley West, the Reserve Valley River 63A, the Rural Municipalities of Alonsa, Dauphin, Grahamdale, Lakeshore, Mountain and Riding Mountain West and the portion of the Rural Municipality of West Interlake that corresponds to the territory of the Rural Municipality of Siglunes, as it existed on December 31, 2014,

(ii) in British Columbia, the Census Subdvisions of Abbotsford, Alberni-Clayoquot A to D and F, Bulkley-Nechako A to G, Burnaby, Capital F and G, Cariboo A to L, Central Coast A and C, Central Kootenay A to E, G, H, J and K, Central Okanagan, Central Okanagan J, Central Saanich, Columbia-Shuswap A to F, Comox Valley A, B (Lazo North) and C (Puntledge-Black Creek), Cowichan Valley B, F, G and I, East Kootenay A to C and E to G, Fraser Valley A to G, Greater Vancouver A, Kitimat-Stikine B, Kootenay Boundary B to E, Mount Waddington A to D, Nanaimo (City), Nanaimo C and E to H, North Cowichan, North Okanagan B and D to F, North Saanich, Okanagan-Similkameen A to H, Pitt Meadows, Powell River A to D, Saanich, Squamish-Lillooet A to D, Strathcona A, C and D (Oyster Bay-Buttle Lake), Sunshine Coast A, Thompson-Nicola A (Wells Gray Country), B (Thompson Headwaters), E (Bonaparte Plateau), I (Blue Sky Country), J (Copper Desert Country), L (Grasslands), M (Beautiful Nicola Valley-North), N (Beautiful Nicola Valley-South), O (Lower North Thompson) and P (Rivers and the Peaks), Part 2 of Census Subdivision Capital H, as these subdivisions were developed by Statistics Canada for the 2011 Census,

(iii) in Saskatchewan, the Rural Municipalities of Antelope Park, Arlington, Auvergne, Baildon, Battle River, Beaver River, Bengough, Big River, Big Stick, Biggar, Blaine Lake, Bone Creek, Bratt's Lake, Britannia, Brokenshell, Buffalo, Calder, Caledonia, Canaan, Canwood, Carmichael, Caron, Chaplin, Chester, Chesterfield, Clayton, Clinworth, Corman Park, Cote, Coteau, Coulee, Craik, Cupar, Cut Knife, Deer Forks, Douglas, Dufferin, Dundurn, Eagle Creek, Edenwold, Eldon, Elmsthorpe, Enfield, Enterprise, Excel, Excelsior, Eye Hill, Eyebrow, Fertile Valley, Fillmore, Fox Valley, Francis, Frenchman Butte, Frontier, Glen Bain, Glen McPherson, Glenside, Grandview, Grass Lake, Grassy Creek, Gravelbourg, Great Bend, Gull Lake, Happy Valley, Happyland, Harris, Hart Butte, Hazel Dell, Heart's Hill, Hillsborough, Hillsdale, Hudson Bay, Huron, Indian Head, Kelvington, Key West, Keys, Kindersley, King George, Lac Pelletier, Lacadena, Laird, Lajord, Lake Alma, Lake Johnston, Lake of the Rivers, Laurier, Lawtonia, Leask, Livingston, Lone Tree, Longlaketon, Loon Lake, Loreburn, Lost River, Lumsden, Manitou Lake, Mankota, Maple Bush, Maple Creek, Mariposa, Marquis, Marriott, Mayfield, McKillop, Meadow Lake, Medstead, Meeting Lake, Meota, Mervin, Milden, Milton, Miry Creek, Monet, Montmartre, Montrose, Moose Jaw, Morse, Mountain View, Newcombe, North Battleford, North Qu'Appelle, Norton, Oakdale, Old Post, Parkdale, Paynton, Pense, Perdue, Piapot, Pinto Creek, Pittville, Pleasant Valley, Poplar Valley, Porcupine, Prairiedale, Preeceville, Progress, Redberry, Redburn, Reford, Reno, Riverside, Rodgers, Rosedale, Rosemount, Round Hill, Round Valley, Rudy, Sarnia, Saskatchewan Landing, Scott, Senlac, Shamrock, Sherwood, Snipe Lake, South Qu'Appelle, Spiritwood, St. Andrews, St. Philips, Stonehenge, Surprise Valley, Sutton, Swift Current, Terrell, The Gap, Tramping Lake, Turtle River, Val Marie, Vanscoy, Victory, Waverley, Webb, Wellington, Weyburn, Wheatlands, Whiska Creek, White Valley, Willow Bunch, Wilton, Winslow, Wise Creek and Wood River, and

(iv) in Alberta, the portion of the territory of Alberta that is not included in, nor surrounded by, the Improvement Districts No. 12 and 24 and the Regional Municipality of Wood Buffalo;

(*c*) in respect of the 2016 calendar year

(i) in Ontario, the Cities of Barrie, Belleville, Brampton, Burlington, Clarence-Rockland, Cornwall, Hamilton, Kawartha Lakes, Kingston, Markham, Mississauga, Niagara Falls, Oshawa, Ottawa, Peterborough, Pickering, Port Colborne, Quinte West, St. Catharines, Thorold, Toronto, Vaughan and Welland, the Counties of Haldimand, Norfolk and Prince Edward, the Municipalities of Brighton, Centre Hastings, Clarington, Highlands East, Marmora and Lake, North Grenville, Port Hope, South Dundas, The Nation, Trent Hills, Trent Lakes and Tweed, the Towns of Ajax, Aurora, Bracebridge, Bradford West Gwillimbury, Caledon, East Gwillimbury, Fort Erie, Georgina, Gravenhurst, Greater Napanee, Grimsby, Halton Hills, Innisfil, Lincoln, Milton, Mono, New Tecumseth, Newmarket, Niagara-on-the-Lake, Oakville, Pelham, Richmond Hill,

Regulations

Wasaga Beach, Whitby and Whitchurch-Stouffville, the Townships of Addington Highlands, Adjala-Tosorontio, Alfred and Plantagenet, Algonquin Highlands, Alnwick/Haldimand, Amaranth, Asphodel-Norwood, Athens, Augusta, Beckwith, Brock, Cavan Monaghan, Central Frontenac, Champlain, Clearview, Cramahe, Douro-Dummer, Drummond/North Elmsley, East Hawkesbury, Edwardsburgh/ Cardinal, Elizabethtown-Kitley, Essa, Front of Yonge, Frontenac Islands, Havelock-Belmont-Methuen, King, Lake of Bays, Leeds and the Thousand Islands, Limerick, Loyalist, Madoc, Melancthon, Minden Hills, Montague, Mulmur, North Dundas, North Glengarry, North Kawartha, North Stormont, Oro-Medonte, Otonabee-South Monaghan, Puslinch, Ramara, Rideau Lakes, Russell, Scugog, Selwyn, Severn, South Frontenac, South Glengarry, South Stormont, Springwater, Stirling-Rawdon, Stone Mills, Tay, Tay Valley, Tiny, Tudor and Cashel, Tyendinaga, Uxbridge, Wainfleet, West Lincoln and Wollaston, the United Townships of Dysart, Dudley, Harcourt, Guilford, Harburn, Bruton, Havelock, Eyre and Clyde and the Village of Merrickville-Wolford,

(ii) in Quebec, the Cities of Gatineau, Lachute, Mirabel, Saint-Jérôme and Salaberry-de-Valleyfield, the Municipalities of Boileau, Bowman, Denholm, Duhamel, Elgin, Franklin, Grenville-sur-la-Rouge, Hinchinbrooke, Huberdeau, Kazabazua, La Conception, La Minerve, Labelle, Lac-des-Plages, Lac-Sainte-Marie, Lac-Simon, Les Cèdres, Mayo, Mille-Isles, Montcalm, Montpellier, Morin-Heights, Mulgrave-et-Derry, Namur, Notre-Dame-de-Bonsecours, Notre-Dame-de-la-Paix, Notre-Dame-du-Laus, Oka, Ormstown, Papineauville, Plaisance, Ripon, Saint-Adolphe-d'Howard, Saint-André-Avellin, Saint-André-d'Argenteuil, Saint-Anicet, Saint-Clet, Saint-Faustin-Lac-Carré, Saint-Joseph-du-Lac, Saint-Placide, Saint-Polycarpe, Saint-Sixte, Saint-Stanislas-de-Kostka, Saint-Télesphore, Sainte-Barbe, Sainte-Justine-de-Newton, Sainte-Marthe, Très-Saint-Rédempteur, Val-des-Bois and Wentworth-Nord, the Parishes of Brébeuf and Saint-Louis-de-Gonzague, the Regional County Municipality of Les Collines-de-l'Outaouais, the Towns of Boisbriand, Brownsburg-Chatham, Coteau-du-Lac, Mont-Tremblant, Rigaud, Saint-Colomban, Saint-Eustache, Saint-Sauveur, Sainte-Agathe-des-Monts and Vaudreuil-Dorion, the Townships of Amherst, Arundel, Dundee, Godmanchester, Gore, Harrington, Lochaber, Lochaber-Partie-Ouest, Low and Wentworth and the Census Subdivision of Lac-Ernest (Unorganized), as this subdivision was developed by Statistics Canada for the 2016 Census,

(iii) in Nova Scotia, the Counties of Annapolis and Kings, the Districts of Argyle, Barrington, Chester, Clare, Digby, Lunenburg, Shelburne, West Hants and Yarmouth and the Region of Queens,

(iv) in British Columbia, the Census Subdivisions of East Kootenay A, Kitimat-Stikine A, B and D and of Skeena-Queen Charlotte D and E, as these subdivisions were developed by Statistics Canada for the 2016 Census, and

(v) in Alberta, the City of Calgary, the Counties of Clearwater, Kneehill, Lacombe, Lethbridge, Mackenzie, Mountain View, Newell, Red Deer, Rocky View, Vulcan and Wheatland, the Improvement District No. 9, Kananaskis Improvement District, the Municipality of Crowsnest Pass and the Municipal Districts of Bighorn, Foothills, Pincher Creek, Ranchland, Taber and Willow Creek; and

(*d*) in respect of the 2017 calendar year, the Consolidated Census Subdivisions, based on the 2016 Statistics Canada Census, of

(i) in Quebec, Albertville, Amqui, Auclair, Baie-des-Sables, Biencourt, Cacouna, Causapscal, Dégelis, Esprit-Saint, Kamouraska, La Malbaie, Lac-à-la-Croix, Lac-Alfred, Lac-des-Aigles, Lac-des-Eaux-Mortes, Lac-Huron, Lac-Matapédia, Lejeune, Les Bergeronnes, L'Isle-Verte, Notre-Dame-des-Neiges, Pohénégamook, Rimouski, Rivière-du-Loup, Routhierville, Ruisseau-Ferguson, Sacré-Cœur, Saint-Alexandre-de-Kamouraska, Saint-André, Saint-Antonin, Saint-Arsène, Saint-Bruno-de-Kamouraska, Saint-Clément, Saint-Cléophas, Saint-Cyprien, Sainte-Angèle-de-Mérici, Sainte-Flavie, Sainte-Jeanne-d'Arc, Saint-Éloi, Sainte-Luce, Saint-Elzéar-de-Témiscouata, Saint-Épiphane, Saint-Eusèbe, Saint-Fabien, Saint-Gabriel-de-Rimouski, Saint-Germain, Saint-Guy, Saint-Hubert-de-Rivière-du-Loup, Saint-Jean-de-Dieu, Saint-Léon-le-Grand, Saint-Mathieu-de-Rioux, Saint-Octave-de-Métis, Saint-Pascal, Saint-Simon, Saint-Ulric, Sayabec, Témiscouata-sur-le-Lac and Val-Brillant,

(ii) in British Columbia, Alberni-Calyoquot A, B, D and F, Cariboo A to L, Central Kootenay A to E, G, H, J and K, Central Okanagan, Central Okanagan J, Columbia-Shuswap A and C to F, Comox Valley A, Comox Valley C (Puntledge-Black Creek), East Kootenay A to C and E to G, Fraser Valley B and D to G, Fraser-Fort George C to E, Kootenay Boundary B/Lower Columbia-Old-Glory, Kootenay Boundary D/Rural Grand Forks, Kootenay Boundary E/West Boundary, North Okanagan B and D to F, Okanagan-Similkameen A to H, Spallumcheen, SquamishLillooet B and C, Strathcona D (Oyster Bay-Buttle Lake), Thompson-Nicola A (Wells Gray Country), Thompson-Nicola B (Thompson Headwaters), Thompson-Nicola E (Bonaparte Plateau), Thompson-Nicola I (Blue Sky Country), Thompson-Nicola J (Copper Desert Country), ThompsonNicola L (Grasslands), Thompson-Nicola M (Beautiful Nicola Valley-North), Thompson-Nicola N (Beautiful Nicola Valley-South), ThompsonNicola O (Lower North Thompson) and Thompson-Nicola P (Rivers and the Peaks),

(iii) in Saskatchewan, Aberdeen No. 373, Abernethy No. 186, Antelope Park No. 322, Arlington No. 79, Arm River No. 252, Auvergne No. 76, Baildon No. 131, Bayne No. 371, Bengough No. 40, Benson No. 35, Big Arm No. 251, Big Quill No. 308, Big Stick No. 141, Birch Hills No. 460, Blucher No. 343, Bone Creek No. 108, Bratt's Lake No. 129, Brock No. 64, Brokenshell No. 68, Browning No. 34, Buckland No. 491, Caledonia No. 99, Cambria No. 6, Canaan No. 225, Carmichael No. 109, Caron No. 162, Chaplin No. 164, Chester No. 125, Chesterfield No. 261, Clinworth No. 230, Coalfields No. 4, Colonsay No. 342, Connaught No. 457, Corman Park No. 344, Coteau No. 255, Coulee No. 136, Craik No. 222, Cupar No. 218, Cymri No. 36, Deer Forks No. 232, Dufferin No. 190, Dundurn No. 314, Edenwold No. 158, Elcapo No. 154, Elfros No. 307, Elmsthorpe No. 100, Emerald No. 277, Enfield No. 194, Enterprise No. 142, Estevan No. 5, Excel No. 71, Excelsior No. 166, Eyebrow No. 193, Fertile Valley No. 285, Fillmore No. 96, Fish Creek No. 402, Flett's Springs No. 429, Foam Lake No. 276, Fox Valley No. 171, Francis No. 127, Frontier No. 19, Garden River No. 490, Garry No. 245, Glen Bain No. 105, Glen McPherson No. 46, Golden West No. 95, Grant No. 372, Grassy Creek No. 78, Gravelbourg No. 104, Griffin No. 66, Gull Lake No. 139, Happy Valley No. 10, Happyland No. 231, Harris No. 316, Hart Butte No. 11, Hazelwood No. 94, Hillsborough No. 132, Hoodoo No. 401, Humboldt No. 370, Huron No. 223, Indian Head No. 156, Insinger No. 275, Invergordon No. 430, Ituna Bon Accord No. 246, Kellross No. 247, Key West No. 70, Kindersley No. 290, King George No. 256, Kingsley No. 124, Kinistino No. 459, Lac Pelletier No. 107, Lacadena No. 228, Lajord No. 128, Lake Alma No. 8, Lake Johnston No. 102, Lake Lenore No. 399, Lake of the Rivers No. 72, Lakeside No. 338, Lakeview No. 337, Last Mountain Valley No. 250, Laurier No. 38, Lawtonia No. 135, Leroy No. 339, Lipton No. 217, Lomond No. 37, Lone Tree No. 18, Longlaketon No. 219, Loreburn No. 254, Lost River No. 313, Lumsden No. 189, Mankota No. 45, Maple Bush No. 224, Maple Creek No. 111, Marquis No. 191, Marriott No. 317, McCraney No. 282, McKillop No. 220, McLeod No. 185, Milden No. 286, Milton No. 292, Miry Creek No. 229, Monet No. 257, Montmartre No. 126, Montrose No. 315, Moose Jaw No. 161, Morris No. 312, Morse No. 165, Mount Hope No. 279, Mountain View No. 318, Newcombe No. 260, Nipawin No. 487, North Qu'Appelle No. 187, Norton No. 69, Oakdale No. 320, Old Post No. 43, Paddockwood No. 520, Pense No. 160, Perdue No. 346, Piapot No. 110, Pinto Creek No. 75, Pittville No. 169, Pleasant Valley No. 288, Pleasantdale No. 398, Poplar Valley No. 12, Prairie Rose No. 309, Prairiedale No. 321, Prince Albert No. 461, Redburn No. 130, Reno No. 51, Riverside No. 168, Rodgers No. 133, Rosedale No. 283, Rudy No. 284, Sarnia No. 221, Saskatchewan Landing No. 167, Saskatoon, Scott No. 98, Shamrock No. 134, Sherwood No. 159, Snipe Lake No. 259, Souris Valley No. 7, South Qu'Appelle No. 157, Spalding No. 368, St. Andrews No. 287, St. Louis No. 431, St. Peter No. 369, Stanley No. 215, Star City No. 428, Stonehenge No. 73, Surprise Valley No. 9, Sutton No. 103, Swift Current No. 137, Tecumseh No. 65, Terrell No. 101, The Gap No. 39, Three Lakes No. 400, Torch River No. 488, Touchwood No. 248, Tullymet No. 216, Usborne No. 310, Val Marie No. 17, Vanscoy No. 345, Victory No. 226, Viscount No. 341, Waverley No. 44, Webb No. 138, Wellington No. 97, Weyburn No. 67, Wheatlands No. 163, Whiska Creek No. 106, White Valley No. 49, Willner No. 253, Willow Bunch No. 42, Willow Creek No. 458, Winslow No. 319, Wise Creek No. 77, Wolseley No. 155, Wolverine No. 340, Wood Creek No. 281, Wood River No. 74 and Wreford No. 280, and

(iv) in Alberta, the City of Calgary, the Counties of Cardston, Clearwater, Cypress, Kneehill, Lacombe, Lethbridge, Mountain View, Newell, Red Deer, Rocky View, Starland, Vulcan and Wheatlands, Forty Mile County No. 8, Paintearth County No. 18, Stettler County No. 6, Warner County No. 5, the Municipal Districts of Bighorn No. 8, Foothills No. 31, Pincher Creek No. 9, Ranchland No. 66, Taber and Willow Creek No. 26 and Special Areas No. 2, 3 and 4.

Agriculture and Agri-Food Canada News Release
Livestock producers receive tax relief for 2018

[Reproduced below is an Agriculture and Agri-Food Canada News Release dated January 30, 2019.]

Final List of Designated Regions under the Livestock Tax Deferral Provision Released

The Government of Canada today released the final list of designated regions where livestock tax deferral has been authorized for 2018 due to drought conditions in British Columbia, Alberta, Saskatchewan, Manitoba, Ontario, Quebec and New Brunswick.

On September 14th, 2018, the Government announced the initial list of prescribed regions in British Columbia, Alberta, Saskatchewan, Manitoba, and Quebec eligible for livestock tax deferral. A second designation of eligible regions was made on October 31, 2018. Ongoing analysis of drought conditions has indicated the need to expand the list of designated regions for 2018, with new regions identified for Alberta, Saskatchewan, Manitoba, and Ontario.

The livestock tax deferral provision allows producers in prescribed drought or excess moisture regions to defer a portion of their 2018 sale proceeds of breeding livestock until 2019 to help replenish the herd. The cost of replacing the animals in 2019 will offset the deferred income, thereby reducing the tax burden associated with the original sale.

Eligibility for the tax deferral is limited to those producers located inside the prescribed areas. Producers in those regions can request the tax deferral when filing their 2018 income tax returns.

Quotes

Extreme weather conditions created difficulties for Canada's livestock industry in several provinces this past year. This tax deferral will help farmers manage the impacts of drought and focus on rebuilding their herds and businesses.

- Lawrence MacAulay, Minister of Agriculture and Agri-Food

Quick facts

- Low moisture levels resulted in significant forage shortages for livestock producers in British Columbia, Alberta, Sas-

Regulations

katchewan, Manitoba, Quebec and New Brunswick in 2018. One option for producers is to reduce their breeding herd in order to manage feed supplies.

- In addition to the livestock tax deferral provision, producers have access to assistance through existing Canadian Agricultural Partnership Business Risk Management programs, which include AgriInsurance, AgriStability and AgriInvest.

Related products

- Livestock Tax Deferral Provision – List of Prescribed Regions for 2018

Associated links

- Canadian Agricultural Partnership
- Drought Watch

Contacts

Katie Hawkins
Director of Communications
Office of the Honourable Lawrence MacAulay
613-773-1059
katie.hawkins@agr.gc.ca

Media Relations
Agriculture and Agri-Food Canada
Ottawa, Ontario
613-773-7972
1-866-345-7972
aafc.mediarelations-relationsmedias.aac@canada.ca

History: S. 7305.01(1)(*d*) was added by SOR/2019-247, s. 1, published in the *Canada Gazette* July 10, 2019, applicable to the 2017 and subsequent taxation years.

S. 7305.01(1) was added by SOR/2018-12, s. 1, published in the *Canada Gazette* February 21, 2018, applicable to the 2014 and subsequent taxation years.

S. 7305.01 was repealed by P.C. 2013-1253, SOR/2013-206, s. 2, published in the *Canada Gazette* December 4, 2013, applicable to areas referred to in section 7305 of the *Income Tax Regulations* in respect of the 2014 and subsequent calendar years. S. 7305.01 formerly read:

7305.01 For the purposes of subsection 80.3(4) of the Act, the prescribed drought regions in respect of a year include any particular area that is surrounded by a region or regions prescribed under section 7305 in respect of the year.

(2) For the purpose of this section, "reserve" has the same meaning as assigned by the *Indian Act*.

History: S. 7305.01(2) was added by SOR/2018-12, s. 1, published in the *Canada Gazette* February 21, 2018, applicable to the 2014 and subsequent taxation years.

(3) For the purpose of this section, if a portion of territory is surrounded by the territory of a census division, census subdivision, municipal entity or other geographic designation listed in subsection (1) in respect of a year, that portion of territory is deemed to be listed under that subsection in respect of that year.

History: S. 7305.01(3) was added by SOR/2018-12, s. 1, published in the *Canada Gazette* February 21, 2018, applicable to the 2014 and subsequent taxation years.

7305.02. [Prescribed flood regions]

(1) For the purposes of subsection 80.3(4) of the Act, the following regions are prescribed regions of flood or excessive moisture:

(*a*) in respect of the 2008 calendar year, in Manitoba,

(i) the rural municipalities of Alonsa, Armstrong, Bifrost, Coldwell, Dauphin, Eriksdale, Ethelbert, Fisher, Gimli, Glenella, Grahamdale, Lakeview, Lawrence, McCreary, Mossey River, Mountain South, Ochre River, Rockwood, Siglunes, St. Andrews, St. Laurent, Ste. Rose and Woodlands, and

(ii) any reserve that is contiguous to a rural municipality referred to in subparagraph (i), or that is part of a series of contiguous reserves one of which is contiguous to a rural municipality referred to in subparagraph (i), of the bands designated as Dauphin River, Ebb and Flow, Fisher River, Kinonjeoshtegon First Nation, Lake Manitoba First Nation, Lake St. Martin, Little Saskatchewan, O-Chi-Chak-Ko-Sipi First Nation, Peguis, Pinaymootang First Nation, Sandy Bay and Skownan First Nation;

(*b*) in respect of the 2009 calendar year, in Manitoba, the rural municipalities of Alexander, Alonsa, Armstrong, Bifrost, Brokenead, Coldwell, Eriksdale, Fisher, Gimli, Grahamdale, Lac du Bonnet, Lawrence, Mossey River, Reynolds, Rockwood, St. Andrews, St. Clements, St. Laurent, Siglunes, Whitemouth and Woodlands, and Census Division No. 18, Unorganized, East and West Parts and No. 19, Unorganized, as developed by Statistics Canada for the 2006 Census;

(*c*) in respect of the 2010 calendar year,

(i) in Manitoba, Census Divisions No. 18 and 19, Unorganized and No. 20, Unorganized, North and South Parts, as these divisions were developed by Statistics Canada for the 2006 Census, the Rural Municipalities of Albert, Alexander, Alonsa, Armstrong, Arthur, Bifrost, Brenda, Brokenhead, Cameron, Coldwell, Dauphin, East St. Paul, Edward, Eriksdale, Ethelbert, Fisher, Gilbert Plains, Gimli, Glenella, Grahamdale, Grandview, Hillsburg, Kelsey, Lac du Bonnet, Lawrence, McCreary, Minitonas, Mountain, Mossey River, Ochre River, Pipestone, Reynolds, Rockwood, St. Andrews, St. Clements, St. Laurent, Ste. Rose, Shellmouth-Boulton, Shell River, Sifton, Siglunes, Swan River, West St. Paul, Whitemouth, Winchester and Woodlands and the Valley River 63A reserve, and

(ii) in Saskatchewan, the Rural Municipalities of Aberdeen, Arborfield, Barrier Valley, Bayne, Big Quill, Birch Hills, Bjorkdale, Blaine Lake, Blucher, Buchanan, Buckland, Calder, Cana, Canwood, Churchbridge, Clayton, Colonsay, Connaught, Corman Park, Cote, Cupar, Duck Lake, Dundurn, Elfros, Emerald, Fish Creek, Flett's Springs, Foam Lake, Garden River, Garry, Good Lake, Grant, Great Bend, Hazel Dell, Hoodoo, Hudson Bay, Humboldt, Insinger, Invergordon, Invermay, Ituna Bon Accord, Kellross, Kelvington, Keys, Kinistino, Laird, Lakeland, Lake Lenore, Lakeside, Lakeview, Leask, Leroy, Lipton, Livingston, Lost River, McCraney, Moose Range, Morris, Mount Hope, Nipawin, Orkney, Paddockwood, Pleasantdale, Ponass Lake, Porcupine, Prairie Rose, Preeceville, Prince Albert, Redberry, Rosedale, Rosthern, Saltcoats, Sasman, Shellbrook, Sliding Hills, Spalding, St. Louis, St. Peter, St. Philips, Stanley, Star City, Three Lakes, Tisdale, Torch River, Touchwood, Tullymet, Usborne, Vanscoy, Viscount, Wallace, Willow Creek, Wolverine, Wood Creek and Wreford; and

(*d*) in respect of the 2011 calendar year,

Regulations

(i) in Manitoba, Census Divisions No. 18 and 19, Unorganized, as these divisions were developed by Statistics Canada for the 2006 Census, and the Rural Municipalities of Albert, Alonsa, Archie, Armstrong, Arthur, Bifrost, Brenda, Cameron, Coldwell, Cornwallis, Dauphin, Edward, Eriksdale, Fisher, Gimli, Glenella, Glenwood, Grahamdale, Kelsey, Lakeview, Lawrence, McCreary, Miniota, Morton, Mossey River, Oakland, Ochre River, Pipestone, Portage la Prairie, St. Laurent, Ste. Rose, Sifton, Siglunes, Wallace, Westbourne, Whitehead, Whitewater, Winchester, Woodlands and Woodworth, and

(ii) in Saskatchewan, the Rural Municipalities of Abernethy, Antler, Argyle, Benson, Bratt's Lake, Brock, Brokenshell, Browning, Calder, Caledonia, Cambria, Cana, Chester, Churchbridge, Coalfields, Cymri, Elcapo, Enniskillen, Estevan, Fertile Belt, Fillmore, Francis, Golden West, Grayson, Griffin, Hazelwood, Indian Head, Kingsley, Lake Alma, Lajord, Langenburg, Laurier, Lomond, Martin, Maryfield, McLeod, Montmartre, Moose Creek, Moose Mountain, Moosomin, Mount Pleasant, Norton, Orkney, Reciprocity, Rocanville, Saltcoats, Scott, Silverwood, Souris Valley, Spy Hill, Stanley, Storthoaks, Tecumseh, Tullymet, Wallace, Walpole, Wawken, Wellington, Weyburn, Willowdale and Wolseley.

History: S. 7305.02(1)(*c*) and (*d*) were added by P.C. 2013-1253, SOR/2013-206, s. 3(1), published in the *Canada Gazette* December 4, 2013, deemed to have come into force on March 3, 2011.

S. 7305.02(1)(*b*) was replaced by P.C. 2011-205, SOR/2011-32, dated February 10, 2011, published in the *Canada Gazette* March 2, 2011, applicable to the 2009 calendar year.

S. 7305.02(1)(*b*) formerly read:

(*b*) in respect of the 2009 calendar year, in Manitoba, the rural municipalities of Armstrong, Bifrost, Fisher and Gimli.

S. 7305.02(1) was added by S.C. 2009, c. 31, s. 17(1), deemed to have come into force on January 1, 2008.

S. 7305.02(1)(*b*) formerly read:

(*b*) in respect of the 2009 calendar year, in Manitoba, the rural municipalities of Armstrong, Bifrost, Fisher and Gimli.

(2) For the purpose of this section, "band" and "reserve" have the same meaning as assigned by the *Indian Act*.

History: S. 7305.02(2) was added by S.C. 2009, c. 31, s. 17(1), deemed to have come into force on January 1, 2008.

(3) For the purposes of this section, a city, county, district or other municipality is deemed to include any area that is surrounded by the territory of the city, county, district or other municipality.

History: S. 7305.02(3) was added by P.C. 2013-1253, SOR/2013-206, s. 3(2), published in the *Canada Gazette* December 4, 2013, deemed to have come into force on January 1, 2008.

7305.1. [Prescribed amount – automobile operating expense benefit]

For the purpose of subparagraph (v) of the description of A in paragraph 6(1)(*k*) of the Act, the amount prescribed for a taxation year is

(*a*) if a taxpayer is employed in a taxation year by a particular person principally in selling or leasing automobiles and an automobile is made available in the year to the taxpayer or a person related to the taxpayer by the particular person or a person related to the particular person, 22 cents; and

(*b*) in any other case, 25 cents.

Department of Finance News Release

Government Announces the 2019 Automobile Deduction Limits and Expense Benefit Rates for Businesses

[Reproduced below is an excerpt from a Department of Finance News Release dated December 27, 2018, which announces that the prescribed rates to be used in 2019 for the calculation of taxable benefits relating to automobile operating expenses increased from the previous year.]

* * *

The general prescribed rate that is used to determine the taxable benefit of employees relating to the personal portion of automobile operating expenses paid by their employers will also accordingly be increased by 2 cents to 28 cents per kilometre. For taxpayers who are employed principally in selling or leasing automobiles, the prescribed rate used to determine the employee's taxable benefit will be increased by 2 cents to 25 cents per kilometre.

The amount of this benefit is intended to reflect the costs of operating an automobile. The additional benefit of having an employer-provided vehicle available for personal use (i.e., the automobile standby charge) is calculated separately based on capital costs and is also included in the employee's income.

* * *

History: S. 7305.1(*a*) and (*b*) were replaced by P.C. 2018-335, SOR/2018-56, s. 1, dated March 26, 2018, applicable to kilometres driven after 2016, and formerly read:

(*a*) if a taxpayer is employed in a taxation year by a particular person principally in selling or leasing automobiles and an automobile is made available in the year to the taxpayer or a person related to the taxpayer by the particular person or a person related to the particular person, 23 cents; and

(*b*) in any other case, 26 cents.

S. 7305.1(*a*) and (*b*) were replaced by P.C. 2016-984, SOR/2016-296, s. 1, dated November 18, 2016, applicable to kilometres driven after 2015, and formerly read:

(*a*) if a taxpayer is employed in a taxation year by a particular person principally in selling or leasing automobiles and an automobile is made available in the year to the taxpayer or a person related to the taxpayer by the particular person or a person related to the particular person, 24 cents; and

(*b*) in any other case, 27 cents.

S. 7305.1(*a*) and (*b*) were replaced by P.C. 2014-573, SOR/2014-118, s. 1(2), dated May 16, 2014, applicable to taxation years that end after 2012, and formerly read:

(*a*) if a taxpayer is employed in a taxation year by a particular person principally in selling or leasing automobiles and an automobile is made available in the year to the taxpayer or a person related to the taxpayer by the particular person or a person related to the particular person, 23 cents; and

(*b*) in any other case, 26 cents.

S. 7305.1(*a*) and (*b*) were replaced by P.C. 2014-573, SOR/2014-118, s. 1(1), dated May 16, 2014, applicable to taxation years that end in 2012, and formerly read:

(*a*) if a taxpayer is employed in a taxation year by a particular person principally in selling or leasing automobiles and an automobile is made available in the year to the taxpayer or a person related to the taxpayer by the particular person or a person related to the particular person, 21 cents; and

(*b*) in any other case, 24 cents.

S. 7305.1(*a*) and (*b*) were replaced by S.C. 2009, c. 2, s. 113(1), applicable to taxation years that end after 2007. S. 7305.1(*a*) and (*b*) formerly read:

(*a*) if a taxpayer is employed in a taxation year by a particular person principally in selling or leasing automobiles and an automobile is made available in the year to the taxpayer or a person related to the taxpayer by the particular person or a person related to the particular person, 19 cents; and

(*b*) in any other case, 22 cents.

Regulations

7306. [Prescribed amount – automobile allowance]

For the purposes of paragraph 18(1)(*r*) of the Act, the amount in respect of the use of one or more automobiles in a taxation year by an individual for kilometres driven in the year for the purpose of earning income of the individual is the total of

(*a*) the product of 48 cents multiplied by the number of those kilometres;

(*b*) the product of 6 cents multiplied by the lesser of 5,000 and the number of those kilometres; and

(*c*) the product of 4 cents multiplied by the number of those kilometres driven in the Yukon Territory, the Northwest Territories or Nunavut.

Department of Finance News Release

Government Announces the 2019 Automobile Deduction Limits and Expense Benefit Rates for Businesses

[Reproduced below is an excerpt from a Department of Finance News Release dated December 27, 2018, which announces that the limit for tax-exempt automobile allowances for 2019 increased from the previous year.]

* * *

The limit on the deduction of tax-exempt allowances that are paid by employers to employees who use their personal vehicle for business purposes for 2019 will be increased by 3 cents to 58 cents per kilometre for the first 5,000 kilometres driven, and to 52 cents per kilometre for each additional kilometre. For the Northwest Territories, Nunavut and Yukon, the tax-exempt allowance is 4 cents higher, and will be increased to 62 cents per kilometre for the first 5,000 kilometres driven, and 56 cents per kilometre for each additional kilometre. These allowances are intended to reflect the main costs of owning and operating an automobile, such as depreciation, financing, insurance, maintenance and fuel.

* * *

History: S. 7306(*a*) was replaced by P.C. 2016-984, SOR/2016-296 s. 2, dated November 18, 2016, applicable to kilometres driven after 2015, and formerly read:

(*a*) the product of 49 cents multiplied by the number of those kilometres;

S. 7306(*a*) was replaced by P.C. 2015-634, SOR/2015-122, s. 1, dated May 29, 2015, applicable to kilometres driven after 2014, and formerly read:

(*a*) the product of 48 cents multiplied by the number of those kilometres;

S. 7306(*a*) was replaced by P.C. 2014-573, SOR/2014-118, s. 2(2), dated May 16, 2014, applicable to kilometres driven after 2012, and formerly read:

(*a*) the product of 47 cents multiplied by the number of those kilometres;

S. 7306(*a*) was replaced by P.C. 2014-573, SOR/2014-118, s. 2(1), dated May 16, 2014, applicable to kilometres driven in 2012, and formerly read:

(*a*) the product of 46 cents multiplied by the number of those kilometres;

S. 7306(*a*) was replaced by S.C. 2009, c. 2, s. 114(1), applicable to kilometres driven after 2007. S. 7306(*a*) formerly read:

(*a*) the product of 44 cents multiplied by the number of those kilometres;

7307. [Prescribed amount – automobile deduction limits]

(1) For the purposes of subsection 13(2), paragraph 13(7)(*g*), subparagraph 13(7)(*h*)(iii), subsections 20(4) and (16.1), the description of B in paragraph 67.3(*d*) and subparagraph 85(1)(*e*.4)(i) of the Act, the amount prescribed is

(*a*) with respect to an automobile acquired, or leased under a lease entered into, after August 1989 and before 1991, $24,000; and

(*b*) with respect to an automobile acquired, or leased under a lease entered into, after 1990, the amount determined by the formula

$$A + B$$

where

A is, with respect to an automobile acquired, or leased under a lease entered into,

(i) before 1997, $24,000,

(ii) in 1997, $25,000,

(iii) in 1998 or 1999, $26,000,

(iv) in 2000, $27,000, or

(v) after 2000, $30,000, and

B is the sum that would have been payable in respect of federal and provincial sales taxes on the acquisition of the automobile if it had been acquired, at a cost equal to A before the application of the federal and provincial sales taxes, if the automobile

(i) was acquired, at the time of the acquisition, or

(ii) was leased, at the time the lease was entered into.

Department of Finance News Release

Government Announces the 2019 Automobile Deduction Limits and Expense Benefit Rates for Businesses

[Reproduced below is an excerpt from a Department of Finance News Release dated December 27, 2018, which states that the maximum allowable cost of a passenger vehicle purchased in 2019 remains at $30,000, unchanged since 2001.]

* * *

- The ceiling on the capital cost of passenger vehicles for capital cost allowance (CCA) purposes will remain at $30,000 (plus applicable federal and provincial-territorial sales taxes) for purchases after 2018. This ceiling restricts the cost of a vehicle on which CCA may be claimed for business purposes.

* * *

Interpretation Bulletins: *Secondary* — IT-291R3 Transfer of property to a corporation under subsection 85(1).

(1.1) For the purposes of paragraph 13(7)(i) of the Act, the amount prescribed in respect of a zero-emission passenger vehicle of a taxpayer is the amount determined by the formula

$$A + B$$

where

A is $55,000; and

B is the sum that would have been payable in respect of federal and provincial sales taxes on the acquisition of the vehicle if it had been acquired by the taxpayer at a cost equal to A, before the application of the federal and provincial sales taxes.

History: S. 7307(1.1) was added by S.C. 2019, c. 29, s. 59(1), deemed in force on March 19, 2019.

Related Sections: 13(7)(i).

(2) For the purpose of the description of A in section 67.2 of the Act, the amount prescribed in respect of an automobile that is acquired either after August 1989 and before 1997 or after 2000 is $300.

Department of Finance News Release

Government Announces the 2019 Automobile Deduction Limits and Expense Benefit Rates for Businesses

[Reproduced below is an excerpt from a Department of Finance News Release dated December 27, 2018, which states that the maximum allowable interest deduction on amounts borrowed to purchase a passenger vehicle in 2019 remains at $300, unchanged since 2001.]

* * *

- The maximum allowable interest deduction for amounts borrowed to purchase an automobile will remain at $300 per month for loans related to vehicles acquired after 2018.

* * *

(3) For the purpose of the description of A in paragraph 67.3(*c*) of the Act, the amount prescribed in respect of a taxation year of a lessee is, with respect to an automobile leased under a lease entered into

(*a*) after August 1989 and before 1991, $650; and

(*b*) after 1990, the amount determined by the formula

$$A + B$$

where

A is

(i) for leases entered into after 1990 but before 1997, $650,

(ii) for leases entered into in 1997, $550,

(iii) for leases entered into in 1998 or 1999, $650,

(iv) for leases entered into in 2000, $700, and

(v) for leases entered into after 2000, $800, and

B is the sum of the federal and provincial sales taxes that would have been payable on a monthly payment under the lease in the taxation year of the lessee if, before those taxes, the lease had required monthly payments equal to A.

Department of Finance News Release

Government Announces the 2019 Automobile Deduction Limits and Expense Benefit Rates for Businesses

[Reproduced below is an excerpt from a Department of Finance News Release dated December 27, 2018, which states that the maximum deductible monthly leasing cost for passenger vehicle leases entered into in 2019 remains at $800, unchanged since 2001.]

* * *

- The limit on deductible leasing costs will remain at $800 per month (plus applicable federal and provincial-territorial sales taxes) for leases entered into after 2018. This limit is one of two restrictions on the deduction of automobile lease payments. A separate restriction prorates deductible lease costs where the value of the vehicle exceeds the capital cost ceiling.

* * *

(4) For the purpose of the description of C in paragraph 67.3(*d*) of the Act, the amount prescribed in respect of an automobile leased under a lease entered into after August 1989 is the amount equal to 100/85 of the amount determined in accordance with subsection (1) in respect of the automobile.

Income Tax Folios: *Primary* — S3-F4-C1 General Discussion of Capital Cost Allowance.

7308. [Prescribed factor – retirement income fund]

(1) In this section, "carrier" has the meaning assigned by subsection 146.3(1) of the Act.

(2) For the purposes of this section, a retirement income fund is a qualifying retirement income fund at a particular time if

(*a*) the fund was entered into before 1993 and the carrier has not accepted any property as consideration under the fund after 1992 and at or before the particular time, or

(*b*) the carrier has not accepted any property as consideration under the fund after 1992 and at or before the particular time, other than property transferred from a retirement income fund that, immediately before the time of the transfer, was a qualifying retirement income fund.

(3) For the purposes of the definition "minimum amount" in subsection 146.3(1) of the Act, the prescribed factor in respect of an individual for a year in connection with a retirement income fund that was a qualifying retirement income fund at the beginning of the year is the factor, determined pursuant to the following table, that corresponds to the age in whole years (in the table referred to as "X") attained by the individual at the beginning of that year or that would have been so attained by the individual if the individual had been alive at the beginning of that year.

X	Factor
Under 72	1/(90 - X)
72	0.0540
73	0.0553
74	0.0567
75	0.0582
76	0.0598
77	0.0617
78	0.0636
79	0.0658
80	0.0682
81	0.0708
82	0.0738
83	0.0771
84	0.0808
85	0.0851
86	0.0899
87	0.0955
88	0.1021
89	0.1099
90	0.1192
91	0.1306
92	0.1449
93	0.1634
94	0.1879
95 or older	0.2000

History: The table to s. 7308(3) was replaced by S.C. 2015, c. 36, s. 23(1), applicable to the 2015 and subsequent taxation years, and formerly read:

X	Factor
under 79	1/(90 - X)
79	.0853
80	.0875
81	.0899
82	.0927
83	.0958
84	.0993
85	.1033
86	.1079
87	.1133
88	.1196
89	.1271
90	.1362
91	.1473
92	.1612
93	.1792
94 or older	.2

(4) For the purposes of the definition "minimum amount" in subsection 146.3(1) of the Act and subsection 8506(5), the prescribed factor in respect of an individual for a year in connection with a retirement income fund (other than a fund that was a qualifying retirement income fund at the beginning of the year) or the designated factor in respect of an individual for a year in connection with an account under a money purchase provision of a registered pension plan, as the case may be, is the factor, determined in accordance with the following table, that corresponds to the age in whole years (in the table referred to as "Y") attained by the individual at the beginning of the year or that would have been so attained by the individual if the individual was alive at the beginning of the year.

Y	Factor
under 71	1/(90 - Y)
71	0.0528
72	0.0540
73	0.0553
74	0.0567
75	0.0582
76	0.0598
77	0.0617
78	0.0636
79	0.0658
80	0.0682
81	0.0708
82	0.0738
83	0.0771
84	0.0808
85	0.0851
86	0.0899
87	0.0955
88	0.1021
89	0.1099
90	0.1192
91	0.1306
92	0.1449
93	0.1634
94	0.1879
95 or older	0.2000

History: The table to s. 7308(4) was replaced by S.C. 2015, c. 36, s. 23(2), applicable to the 2015 and subsequent taxation years, and formerly read:

Y	Factor
under 71	1/(90 - Y)
71	.0738
72	.0748
73	.0759
74	.0771
75	.0785
76	.0799
77	.0815
78	.0833
79	.0853
80	.0875
81	.0899
82	.0927
83	.0958
84	.0993
85	.1033
86	.1079
87	.1133
88	.1196
89	.1271
90	.1362
91	.1473
92	.1612
93	.1792
94 or older	.2

Related Regulations: 8506(5).

Information Circulars: IC 78-18R6 Registered retirement income funds.

7309. [Prescribed penalties]

For the purpose of section 67.6 of the Act, penalties imposed under paragraph 110.1(1)(*a*) of the *Excise Act* are prescribed.

History: S. 7309 was replaced by P.C. 2011-935, SOR/2011-187, dated September 22, 2011, published in the *Canada Gazette* October 12, 2011, applicable to taxation years that begin after March 2007. S. 7309 formerly read:

7309. For the purpose of section 67.6 of the Act, penalties imposed under any of the following provisions are prescribed:

(*a*) paragraph 110.1(1)(*a*) of the *Excise Act*;

(*b*) paragraphs 280(1)(*a*), (1.1)(*a*) and (2)(*a*) of the *Excise Tax Act*; and

(*c*) subsection 53(1) of the *Air Travellers Security Charge Act*, as it read before April 2007.

S. 7309 was added by P.C. 2011-935, SOR/2011-187, dated September 22, 2011, published in the *Canada Gazette* October 12, 2011, applicable to penalties imposed after March 22, 2004.

Income Tax Folios: *Secondary* — S4-F2-C1 Deductibility of Fines and Penalties.

7310. [Prescribed trade]

For the purpose of the definition "eligible apprentice" in subsection 127(9) of the Act, a prescribed trade in respect of a province means, at all times in a taxation year, a trade that is, at any time in that taxation year, a Red Seal trade for the province under the Interprovincial Standards Red Seal Program.

Part LXXIV
Prescribed Forest Management Plans for Woodlots

7400. [Prescribed forest management plan]

(1) For the purposes of subsections 70(9), (9.3) and (10) and 73(3) of the Act, a prescribed forest management plan in respect of a woodlot of a taxpayer is a written plan for the management and development of the woodlot that

(*a*) describes the composition of the woodlot, provides for the attention necessary for the growth, health and quality of the trees on the woodlot and is approved in accordance with the requirements of a provincial program established for the sustainable management and conservation of forests; or

(*b*) has been certified in writing by a recognized forestry professional to be a plan that describes the composition of the woodlot, provides for the attention necessary for the growth, health and quality of the trees on the woodlot and includes

(i) a description of, or a map indicating, the location of the woodlot,

(ii) a description of the characteristics of the woodlot, including a map of the woodlot site that shows those characteristics,

(iii) a description of the development of the woodlot, including the activities carried out on the woodlot, since the taxpayer acquired it,

(iv) information acceptable to the recognized forestry professional estimating

(A) the ages and heights of the trees on the woodlot, and their species,

(B) the quantity of wood on the woodlot,

(C) the quality and composition of the soil underlying the woodlot, and

(D) the quantity of wood that the woodlot could yield as a result of the implementation of the plan,

(v) a description of, and the timing for, the activities proposed to be carried out on the woodlot under the plan, including any of those activities that deal with

(A) harvesting,

(B) renewal and regeneration,

(C) the application of silviculture techniques, and

(D) responsible stewardship and the protection of the environment, and

(vi) a description of the objectives and strategies for the management and development of the woodlot over a period of at least five years.

(2) A recognized forestry professional referred to in subsection (1) is a forestry professional who has a degree, diploma or certificate recognized by the Canadian Forestry Accreditation Board, the Canadian Institute of Forestry or the Canadian Council of Technicians and Technologists.

(3) A recognized forestry professional referred to in subsection (1) is not required to express an opinion as to the completeness or correctness of a description of past activities referred to in subparagraph (1)(*b*)(iii) or of information referred to in subparagraph (1)(*b*)(iv) if the information was not prepared by that recognized forestry professional.

Part LXXV
Prescribed Missions [Repealed.]

History: Part LXXV was repealed by S.C. 2013, c. 33, s. 36(1), applicable in respect of missions initiated after September 2012.

7500. (Repealed by S.C. 2013, c. 33, s. 36(1).)

History: S. 7500 was repealed by S.C. 2013, c. 33, s. 36(1), applicable in respect of missions initiated after September 2012, and formerly read:

7500. For the purpose of subclause 110(1)(*f*)(v)(A)(II) of the Act, the following are prescribed missions:

(*a*) Operation Palladium (Bosnia-Herzegovina);

(*b*) Operation Halo (Haiti);

(*c*) Operation Danaca (Middle East — Golan Heights);

(*d*) Operation Calumet (Middle East — Sinai);

(*e*) Operation Jade (Middle East — Jerusalem, Damascus and Egypt);

(*f*) Operation Iraqi Freedom (Kuwait);

(*g*) Operation Solitude (Senegal);

(*h*) Operation Altair (Persian Gulf);

(*i*) Operation Hamlet (Haiti);

(*j*) Operation Structure (Sri Lanka);

(*k*) Operation Habitation (Haiti);

(*l*) Operation Augural (Sudan — Kartoum);

(*m*) Operation Bronze (Bosnia-Herzegovina — North Atlantic Treaty Organization Stabilisation Force);

(*n*) Operation Boreas (Bosnia-Herzegovina — European Union Force);

(*o*) Operation Safari (Sudan — Kartoum);

(*p*) Operation Gladius (Golan Heights);

(*q*) Operation Augural (Ethiopia — Addis Ababa);

(*r*) United Nations Mission in the Sudan — Civilian Policing Component (Sudan — Kartoum);

(*s*) Operation Caribbe (Curacao);

(*t*) Operation Kobold (Balkans – Pristina);

(*u*) Operation Saturn (Ethiopia – Addis Ababa);

(*v*) Operation Enduring Freedom (Kuwait);

(*w*) Seventh Airlift Squadron Operation (Kyrgyzstan); and

(*x*) Operation Slipper (United Arab Emirates).

S. 7500(*s*) was added by P.C. 2013-144, SOR/2013-22, s. 1(1), dated February 14, 2013, deemed to have come into force on October 30, 2007.

S. 7500(*t*) and (*u*) were added by P.C. 2013–144, SOR/2013-22, s. 1(2), dated February 14, 2013, deemed to have come into force on September 1, 2008.

S. 7500(*v*) was added by P.C. 2013-144, SOR/2013-22, s. 1(3), dated February 14, 2013, deemed to have come into force on February 23, 2009.

S. 7500(*w*) was added by P.C. 2013-144, SOR/2013-22, s. 1(4), dated February 14, 2013, deemed to have come into force on February 28, 2009.

S. 7500(*x*) was added by P.C. 2013-144, SOR/2013-22, s. 1(5), dated February 14, 2013, deemed to have come into force on April 14, 2009.

Part LXXVI
Carved-out Property Exclusion

7600. [Prescribed property]

For the purposes of paragraph (*g*) of the definition "carved-out property" in subsection 209(1) of the Act, a prescribed property at any time is

(*a*) any right, licence or privilege to prospect, explore, drill or mine for minerals in a mineral resource (other than a bituminous sands deposit, oil sands deposit or oil shale deposit) in Canada;

(*b*) any rental or royalty computed by reference to the amount or value of production of minerals from a mineral resource (other than a bituminous sands deposit, oil sands deposit or oil shale deposit) in Canada;

(*c*) any real property in Canada the principal value of which depends on its mineral resource content (other than a bituminous sands deposit, oil sands deposit or oil shale deposit);

(*d*) any right to or interest in any property described in any of paragraphs (*a*) to (*c*); or

(*e*) a property acquired before that time by a taxpayer in the circumstances described in paragraph (*c*) of the definition "carved-out property" in subsection 209(1) of the Act, except where it is reasonable to consider that one of the main reasons for the acquisition of the property, or any series of transactions or events in which the property was acquired by the taxpayer was to reduce or postpone tax that would, but for this paragraph, be payable by another taxpayer under Part XII.1 of the Act.

Part LXXVII
Prescribed Prizes

7700. [Prescribed prize]

For the purposes of subparagraph 56(1)(*n*)(i) of the Act, a prescribed prize is any prize that is recognized by the general public and that is awarded for meritorious achievement in the arts, the sciences or service to the public but does not include any amount that can reasonably be regarded as having been received as compensation for services rendered or to be rendered.

Income Tax Folios: *Secondary* — S1-F2-C3 Scholarships, Research Grants and Other Education Assistance.

Interpretation Bulletins: *Secondary* — IT-257R Canada Council grants.

Tax Window Files: Polanyi Prizes - Prescribed prize, *November 20, 2015*, CRA Document No. 2015-0595091E5; Prescribed Prize, *February 8, 2016*, CRA Document No. 2015-0610461I7.

Part LXXVIII
Specified Pension Plans

7800. [Prescribed arrangement]

For the purposes of the definition "specified pension plan" in subsection 248(1) of the Act, a prescribed arrangement is the Saskatchewan Pension Plan established under *The Saskatchewan Pension Plan Act*, chapter S-32.2 of the Statutes of Saskatchewan, 1986, as amended from time to time.

History: S. 7800 and the heading before it were replaced by S.C. 2011, c. 24, s. 89(1), applicable after 2009. S. 7800 formerly read:

Part LXXVIII *Prescribed Provincial Pension Plans*

7800.

(1) For the purposes of clause 56(1)(*a*)(i)(C), subsection 56(2), paragraph 60(*v*), subsection 74.1(1) and paragraph 118(8)(*e*) of the Act, the Saskatchewan Pension Plan is a prescribed provincial pension plan.

(2) For the purpose of subparagraph 60(*v*)(ii) of the Act, the prescribed amount for a taxation year in respect of the Saskatchewan Pension Plan is, for the 1987 taxation year, $1,200, and for the 1988 and subsequent taxation years, $600.

Interpretation Bulletins: *Secondary* — IT-124R6 Contributions to registered retirement savings plans.

Part LXXIX
Prescribed Financial Institutions

7900. [Prescribed financial institutions]

For the purposes of the definitions "excluded income" and "excluded revenue" and "specified deposit" in subsection 95(2.5) of the Act, each of the following is a prescribed financial institution:

(*a*) a member of the Canadian Payments Association; and

(*b*) a credit union that is a shareholder or member of a body corporate or organization that is a central for the purposes of the *Canadian Payments Act*.

History: S. 7900 was replaced by S.C. 2013, c. 33, s. 37(1), applicable to taxation years that begin after March 20, 2013, and formerly read:

7900.

(1) For the purposes of section 33.1 and the definitions "excluded income" and "excluded revenue" and "specified deposit" in subsection 95(2.5) of the Act, each of the following is a prescribed financial institution:

(*a*) a member of the Canadian Payments Association, other than an authorized foreign bank; and

(*b*) a credit union that is a shareholder or member of a body corporate or organization that is a central for the purposes of the *Canadian Payments Act.*

(2) For the purposes of the definitions "excluded income" and "excluded revenue" and "specified deposit" in subsection 95(2.5) of the Act, an authorized foreign bank is a prescribed financial institution.

S. 7900 was replaced by P.C. 2009-1869, SOR/2009-302, dated November 19, 2009, published in the *Canada Gazette* December 9, 2009, applicable after 1997, except that

(a) before June 28, 1999, paragraph 7900(1)(*a*) is to be read as follows:

"(*a*) a member of the Canadian Payments Association; and"

(b) subject to paragraph (*c*) [below], before 2008 the portion of subsection 7900(1) before paragraph (*a*), is to be read as follows:

"(1) For the purposes of section 33.1, the definitions "excluded income" and "excluded revenue" and "specified deposit" in subsection 95(2.5), clause 212(1)(*b*)(iii)(D) and subparagraph 212(1)(*b*)(xi) of the Act, each of the following is a prescribed financial institution:"

(c) for taxation years that began before 2000, the portion of subsection 7900(1) before paragraph (*a*), is to be read as follows:

"(1) For the purposes of section 33.1, paragraph 95(2)(*a*.3), the definition "specified deposit" in subsection 95(2.5), clause 212(1)(*b*)(iii)(D) and subparagraph 212(1)(*b*)(xi) of the Act, each of the following is a prescribed financial institution:"

(d) before October 24, 2001, paragraph 7900(1)(*b*) is to be read as follows:

"(*b*) a credit union that is a shareholder or member of a body corporate or organization that is a central for the purposes of the *Canadian Payments Association Act*"

(e) subject to paragraph (*f*) [below], before 2008 subsection 7900(2) is to be read as follows:

"(2) For the purposes of paragraph 95(2)(*a*.3), the definitions "excluded income" and "excluded revenue" and "specified deposit" in subsection 95(2.5) and clause 212(1)(*b*)(iii)(D) of the Act, an authorized foreign bank is a prescribed financial institution."

and

(f) for taxation years that began before 2000, subsection 7900(2) is to be read as follows:

"(2) For the purposes of paragraph 95(2)(*a*.3), the definition "specified deposit" in subsection 95(2.5) and clause 212(1)(*b*)(iii)(D) of the Act, an authorized foreign bank is a prescribed financial institution."

S. 7900 formerly read:

7900. For the purposes of section 33.1, paragraph 95(2)(*a*.3), clause 212(1)(*b*)(iii)(D) and subparagraph 212(1)(*b*)(xi) of the Act, "prescribed financial institution" means

(*a*) a corporation that is a member of the Canadian Payments Association; or

(*b*) a credit union that is a shareholder or member of a body corporate or organization that is a central for the purposes of the *Canadian Payments Association Act.*

Part LXXX
Prescribed Reserve Amount and Recovery Rate

8000. [Prescribed reserve amount]

For the purpose of clause 20(1)(*l*)(ii)(C) of the Act, the prescribed reserve amount for a taxation year means the aggregate of

(*a*) where the taxpayer is a bank, an amount equal to the lesser of

(i) the amount of the reserve reported in its annual report for the year that is filed with and accepted by the relevant authority or, where the taxpayer was throughout the year subject to the supervision of the relevant authority but was not required to file an annual report for the year with the relevant authority, in its financial statements for the year, as general provisions or as specific provisions, in respect of exposures to designated countries in respect of loans or lending assets of the taxpayer made or acquired by it in the ordinary course of its business, and

(ii) an amount in respect of the loans or lending assets of the taxpayer at the end of the year that were made or acquired by the taxpayer in the ordinary course of its business and reported for the year by the taxpayer to the relevant authority, in accordance with the guidelines established by the relevant authority, as part of the taxpayer's total exposure to designated countries for the purposes of determining the taxpayer's general provisions or specific provisions referred to in subparagraph (i) or that were acquired by the taxpayer after August 16, 1990 and reported for the year by the taxpayer to the relevant authority, in accordance with the guidelines established by the relevant authority, as an exposure to a designated country (in this subparagraph referred to as the "loans") equal to the positive or negative amount, as the case may be, determined by the formula

$$45\% (A + B) - (B + C)$$

where

A is the aggregate of all amounts each of which is the amount that would be the amortized cost of a loan to the taxpayer at the end of the year if the definition "amortized cost" in section 248 of the Act were read without reference to paragraphs (*e*) and (*i*) thereof,

B is the aggregate of all amounts each of which is the amount, if any, by which the principal amount of a loan outstanding at the time it was acquired by the taxpayer exceeds the amortized cost of the loan to the taxpayer immediately after the time it was acquired by the taxpayer, and

C is the aggregate of all amounts each of which is

(A) an amount deducted in respect of a loan under clause 20(1)(*l*)(ii)(B) of the Act in computing the taxpayer's income for the year, or

(B) an amount in respect of a loan determined as the amount, if any, by which

(I) the aggregate of all amounts in respect of the loan deducted under paragraph 20(1)(*p*) of the Act in computing the taxpayer's income for the year or a preceding taxation year

exceeds

(II) the aggregate of all amounts in respect of the loan included under paragraph 12(1)(*i*) of the Act in computing the taxpayer's income for the year or a preceding taxation year, and

(*a*.1) where the taxpayer is a bank, the positive or negative amount that would be determined under the formula in subparagraph (*a*)(ii) in respect of the specified loans owned by the taxpayer at the end of the year if that subparagraph applied to those loans.

(*b*) (Repealed.)

8001. (Repealed.)

8002. [Principal amount and amortized cost]

For the purposes of paragraph 8000(*a*),

(*a*) the principal amount outstanding at any time of a lending asset of a taxpayer that is a share of the capital stock of a corporation is the part of the consideration received by the corporation for the issue of the share that is outstanding at that time;

(*b*) where

(i) a taxpayer realizes a loss from the disposition of a loan or lending asset described in subparagraph 8000(*a*)(ii) or a specified loan described in paragraph 8000(*a*.1) (in this paragraph referred to as the "former loan") for consideration that included another loan or lending asset that was a loan or lending asset described in subparagraph 8000(*a*)(ii) or paragraph 8000(*a*.1) (in this paragraph referred to as the "new loan"), and

(ii) in the case of a former loan that is not a specified loan, the loss is included in computing the taxpayer's provisionable assets as reported for the year to the relevant authority, in accordance with the guidelines established by the relevant authority, for the purpose of determining the taxpayer's general provisions or specific provisions in respect of exposures to designated countries,

the principal amount of the new loan outstanding at the time it was acquired by the taxpayer is deemed to be equal to the principal amount of the former loan outstanding immediately before that time; and

(*c*) where at the end of a particular taxation year a taxpayer owns a specified loan that, at the end of the preceding taxation year, was described in an inventory of the taxpayer, the amortized cost of the specified loan to the taxpayer at the end of the particular year is its value determined under section 10 of the Act at the end of the preceding year for the purpose of computing the taxpayer's income for the preceding year.

8003. [Election]

Where a taxpayer elects to have this section apply by notifying the Minister in writing within 90 days after the day on which this section is published in the *Canada Gazette*, the loans or lending assets of the taxpayer that are described in subparagraph 8000(*a*)(ii) shall not include any loan or lending asset acquired by the taxpayer before November 1988 from a person with whom the taxpayer was dealing at arm's length.

8004. (Repealed.)

8005. [Loan or lending asset of related person]

For the purposes of subparagraph 8000(*a*)(ii), where a loan or lending asset of a person (in this section referred to as the "holder") related to a taxpayer

(*a*) was reported for the year by the taxpayer to the relevant authority, in accordance with the guidelines established by the relevant authority, as an exposure to a designated country,

(*b*) was acquired by the holder or another person related to the taxpayer after August 16, 1990 as part of a series of transactions or events in which the taxpayer or a person related to the taxpayer disposed of a loan or lending asset that

(i) for the taxation year immediately preceding the particular year in which it was disposed of, was a loan or lending asset that was reported by the taxpayer to the relevant authority, in accordance with the guidelines established by the relevant authority, as an exposure to a designated country, and

(ii) was a loan or lending asset a loss arising on the disposition of which would be a loss in respect of which a deduction is permitted under Part I of the Act to the taxpayer or a person related to the taxpayer, and

(*c*) had an amortized cost to the holder, immediately after the time it was acquired by the holder, that was less than 55 per cent of its principal amount,

the following rules apply:

(*d*) the loan or lending asset shall be deemed

(i) to be a loan or lending asset of the taxpayer at the end of the year,

(ii) to be a loan or lending asset of the taxpayer that was acquired by the taxpayer at the time it was acquired by the holder, and

(iii) to have an amortized cost to the taxpayer, at any time, that is equal to its amortized cost to the holder at that time, and

(*e*) any amount in respect of the loan or lending asset deducted under paragraph 20(1)(*p*) of the Act or included under paragraph 12(1)(*i*) of the Act in computing the holder's income for a particular year shall be deemed to have been so deducted or included, as the case may be, in computing the income of the taxpayer for the year in which the particular year ends.

8006. [Definitions]

For the purposes of this Part,

"designated country" has the same meaning as in the Guidelines for banks established pursuant to section 175 of the *Bank Act*, as that section read on May 31, 1992, and issued by the Office of the Superintendent of Financial Institutions, as amended from time to time;

"exposure to a designated country" has the same meaning as in the Guidelines for banks established pursuant to section 175 of the *Bank Act*, as that section read on May 31, 1992, and issued by the Office of the Superintendent of Financial Institutions, as amended from time to time;

"general provisions" has the same meaning as the expression "general country risk provisions" in the Guidelines for banks established pursuant to section 175 of the *Bank Act*, as that section read on May 31, 1992, and issued by the Office of the Superintendent of Financial Institutions, as amended from time to time;

"provisionable assets" has the same meaning as in the Guidelines for banks established pursuant to section 175 of the *Bank Act*, as that section read on May 31, 1992, and issued by the Office of the Superintendent of Financial Institutions, as amended from time to time;

"relevant authority" means the Superintendent of Financial Institutions;

"specific provisions" has the same meaning as in the Guidelines for banks established pursuant to section 175 of the *Bank Act*, as that section read on May 31, 1992, and issued by the Office of the Superintendent of Financial Institutions, as amended from time to time;

"specified loan" means

(*a*) a United Mexican States Collateralized Par Bond due in 2019, or

(*b*) a United Mexican States Collateralized Discount Bond due in 2019;

8007. (Repealed.)

Part LXXXI
Transition for Financial Institutions [Repealed.]

History: Part LXXXI was repealed by S.C. 2013, c. 34, s. 406(1), applicable to taxation years that begin after October 31, 2011.

8100. Transition Deduction in respect of Unpaid Claims Reserve

(Repealed by S.C. 2013, c. 34, s. 406(1).)

History: S. 8100 was repealed by S.C. 2013, c. 34, s. 406(1), applicable to taxation years that begin after October 31, 2011, and formerly read:

8100. *Transition Deduction in respect of Unpaid Claims Reserve.* For the purpose of subsection 20(26) of the Act, an insurer's unpaid claims reserve adjustment for its taxation year that includes February 23, 1994 is the amount, if any, by which

(*a*) the total of all amounts each of which is the maximum amount that, because of paragraph 1400(*e*), was deductible under paragraph 20(7)(*c*) of the Act in respect of an insurance policy in computing the insurer's income for its last taxation year that ended before February 23, 1994

exceeds

(*b*) where the insurer elects, by notifying the Minister in writing, to have this paragraph apply, the total of all amounts each of which is the maximum amount that would, because of paragraph 1400(*e*), have been deductible under paragraph 20(7)(*c*) of the Act in respect of an insurance policy in computing the insurer's income for its last taxation year that ended before February 23, 1994 if the amount "$^1/_3$" in the formula in subparagraph 1400(*e*)(ii), as it read for that year, were replaced by the amount "1", and

(*c*) in any other case, the total of all amount each of which is the maximum amount that would, because of paragraph 1400(*e*) or (*e*.1), have been deductible under paragraph 20(7)(*c*) of the Act in respect of an insurance policy in computing the insurer's income for its last taxation year that ended before February 23, 1994 if paragraph 1400(*e*.1) had applied to that year and paragraphs 1400(*e*) and (*e*.1) were read in their application to that year as they read in their application to the insurer's taxation year that includes February 23, 1994.

8101. Inclusion of Transition Amount in respect of Unpaid Claims Reserve

(Repealed by S.C. 2013, c. 34, s. 406(1).)

History: S. 8101 was repealed by S.C. 2013, c. 34, s. 406(1), applicable to taxation years that begin after October 31, 2011, and formerly read:

(1) In this section, "transition deduction" of an insurer means the amount deducted under subsection 20(26) of the Act in computing the insurer's income for its taxation year that includes February 23, 1994.

(2) Subject to subsection (3), there is prescribed for the purpose of section 12.3 of the Act in respect of an insurer for a taxation year that ends after February 22, 1994 the amount determined by the formula

$$[(.05A + 0.10B + 0.15C)/365] \times D$$

where

A is the total of

(*a*) the number of days in the taxation year that are in 1994 or 1995, and

(*b*) where the taxation year includes February 23, 1994, the number of days in 1994 that are before the first day of the taxation year,

B is the number of days in the taxation year (other than February 29) that are in any of 1996 to 2001,

C is the number of days in the taxation year that are in 2002 or 2003, and

D is the insurer's transition deduction minus the amount, if any, required by subsection (4) or paragraph (5)(*b*) to be subtracted.

(3) Where subsection 88(1) of the Act has applied to the winding-up of an insurer (in this subsection referred to as the "subsidiary"),

(*a*) the values of A, B and C in subsection (2) shall be determined in respect of the subsidiary without including any days that are after the day on which the subsidiary's assets were distributed to its parent on the winding-up; and

(*b*) there is prescribed for the purpose of section 12.3 ot the Act in respect of the parent for its taxation year that includes the day referred to in paragraph (*a*) the total of

(i) the amount that would be determined under subsection (2) in respect of the parent for the year if the parent's transition deduction did not include the subsidiary's transition deduction, and

(ii) the amount that would be determined under subsection (2) in respect of the parent for the year if

(A) the values of A, B and C in that subsection were determined without including the day referred to in paragraph (*a*) and any days before that day, and

(B) the value of D in that subsection were equal to the subsidiary's transition deduction.

(4) Where subsection 138(11.5) or (11.94) of the Act has applied to the transfer of an insurance business by an insurer, there shall be subtracted, in determining the value of D in subsection (2) in respect of the insurer for a taxation year ending after the insurer ceased to carry on all or substantially all of the business, the part of the insurer's transition deduction that can reasonably be attributed to the business.

(5) Where an insurer ceases to carry on all or substantially all of an insurance business, otherwise than as a result of a merger to which subsection 87(2) of the Act applies, a winding-up to which subsection 88(1) of the Act applies or a transfer of the business to which subsection 138(11.5) or (11.94) of the Act applies,

(*a*) there is prescribed for the purpose of section 12.3 of the Act in respect of the insurer for its taxation year in which the cessation of business occurs, in addition to the amount prescribed by subsection (2), the amount, if any, by which

(i) the part of the insurer's transition deduction that can reasonably be attributed to the business

exceeds

(ii) that part of the total of the amounts included under section 12.3 of the Act in computing the income of the insurer for preceding taxation years that can reasonably be considered to be in respect of the amount determined under subparagraph (i); and

(*b*) there shall be subtracted, in determining the value of D in subsection (2) in respect of the insurer for the year or a subsequent taxation year, the amount determined under subparagraph (*a*)(i).

8102. Mark-to-Market — Transition Deduction

(Repealed by S.C. 2013, c. 34, s. 406(1).)

History: S. 8102 was repealed by S.C. 2013, c. 34, s. 406(1), applicable to taxation years that begin after October 31, 2011, and formerly read:

(1) In this section, "excluded property", of a taxpayer, means a mark-to-market property used in a business of the taxpayer in its taxation year that includes October 31, 1994 where it is reasonable to expect that the property would have been valued at its fair market value for the purpose of computing the taxpayer's income from the business for the year if

(*a*) the Act were read without reference to subsection 142.5(2); and

(*b*) the property were held at the end of the year.

(2) For the purpose of subsection 142.5(4) of the Act, the prescribed amount for a taxpayer's taxation year that includes October 31, 1994 is the amount, if any, by which

(*a*) the total of all amounts each of which is the taxpayer's profit from the disposition in the year, because of subsection 142.5(2) of the Act, of a property other than a capital property or an excluded property

exceeds the total of

(*b*) the total of all amounts each of which is the taxpayer's loss from the disposition in the year, because of subsection 142.5(2) of the Act, of a property other than a capital property or an excluded property, and

(*c*) the amount, if any, by which

(i) the total of all amounts each of which is the taxpayer's loss from the disposition in the year of a mark-to-market property (other than a capital property, an excluded property or a property disposed of because of subsection 142.5(2) of the Act)

exceeds

(ii) the total of all amounts each of which is the taxpayer's profit from the disposition in the year of a mark-to-market property (other than a capital property, an excluded property or a property disposed of because of subsection 142.5(2) of the Act).

S. 8102(1) was added by P.C. 2009-1212, SOR/2009-222, dated July 30, 2009, published in the *Canada Gazette* August 19, 2009, applicable to taxation years that end after October 30, 1994.

S. 8102(2) was added by P.C. 2009-1212, SOR/2009-222, dated July 30, 2009, published in the *Canada Gazette* August 19, 2009, applicable to taxation years that end after October 30, 1994.

8103. Mark-to-Market — Transition Inclusion

(Repealed by S.C. 2013, c. 34, s. 406(1).)

History: S. 8103 was repealed by S.C. 2013, c. 34, s. 406(1), applicable to taxation years that begin after October 31, 2011, and formerly read:

(1) In this section, "transition deduction", of a taxpayer, means the amount deducted under subsection 142.5(4) of the Act in computing the taxpayer's income for its taxation year that includes October 31, 1994.

(2) Subject to subsections (3), (5) and (7), there is prescribed for the purpose of subsection 142.5(5) of the Act in respect of a taxpayer for a taxation year that ends after October 30, 1994 the amount determined by the formula

$$A \times B/1825$$

where

A is the number of days (other than February 29) in the year that are before the day that is five years after the first day of the taxation year of the taxpayer that includes October 31, 1994; and

B is the taxpayer's transition deduction minus the amount, if any, required by subsection (4) or paragraph (6)(*b*) to be subtracted.

(3) If subsection 88(1) of the Act has applied to the winding-up of a taxpayer (in this subsection referred to as the "subsidiary"),

(*a*) the value of A in subsection (2) shall be determined in respect of the subsidiary without including any days that are after the day on which the subsidiary's assets were distributed to its parent on the winding-up; and

(*b*) there is prescribed for the purpose of subsection 142.5(5) of the Act in respect of the parent for its taxation year that includes the day referred to in paragraph (*a*) the total of

(i) the amount that would be determined under subsection (2) in respect of the parent for the year if the parent's transition deduction did not include the subsidiary's transition deduction, and

(ii) the amount that would be determined under subsection (2) in respect of the parent for the year if

(A) the value of A in that subsection were determined without including the day referred to in paragraph (*a*) and any days before that day, and

(B) the value of B in that subsection were equal to the subsidiary's transition deduction.

(4) If subsection 138(11.5) or (11.94) of the Act has applied to the transfer of an insurance business by an insurer, there shall be subtracted, in determining the value of B in subsection (2) in respect of the insurer for a taxation year that ends after the insurer ceased to carry on all or substantially all of the business, the part of the insurer's transition deduction that is included, because of paragraph 138(11.5)(*k*) of the Act, in the transition deduction of the person to whom the business was transferred.

(5) If subsection 98(6) of the Act deems a partnership (in this subsection referred to as the "new partnership") to be a continuation of another partnership (in this subsection referred to as the "predecessor partnership"),

(*a*) the value of A in subsection (2) shall be determined in respect of the predecessor partnership without including any days that are after the day on which the predecessor partnership's property was transferred to the new partnership; and

(*b*) there is prescribed for the purpose of subsection 142.5(5) of the Act in respect of the new partnership for its taxation year that includes the day referred to in paragraph (*a*) the total of

(i) the amount that would be determined under subsection (2) in respect of the new partnership for the year if its transition deduction did not include the predecessor partnership's transition deduction, and

(ii) the amount that would be determined under subsection (2) in respect of the new partnership for the year if

(A) the value of A in that subsection were determined without including the day referred to in paragraph (*a*) and any days before that day, and

(B) the value of B in that subsection were equal to the predecessor partnership's transition deduction.

(6) If a taxpayer ceases to carry on all or substantially all of a business, otherwise than as a result of a merger to which subsection 87(2) of the Act applies, a winding-up to which subsection 88(1) of the Act applies or a transfer of the business to which subsection 98(6) or 138(11.5) or (11.94) of the Act applies,

(*a*) there is prescribed for the purpose of subsection 142.5(5) of the Act in respect of the taxpayer for its taxation year in which the cessation of business occurs, in addition to the amount prescribed by subsection (2), the amount, if any, by which

(i) the part of the taxpayer's transition deduction that can reasonably be attributed to the business

exceeds

(ii) that part of the total of the amounts included under subsection 142.5(5) of the Act in computing the income of the taxpayer for preceding taxation years that can reasonably be considered to be in respect of the amount determined under subparagraph (i); and

(*b*) there shall be subtracted, in determining the value of B in subsection (2) in respect of the taxpayer for the year or a subsequent taxation year, the amount determined under subparagraph (*a*)(i).

(7) If a taxpayer ceases at any time to be a financial institution otherwise than because it ceases to carry on a business,

(*a*) there is prescribed for the purpose of subsection 142.5(5) of the Act in respect of the taxpayer for its taxation year that ended immediately before that time, the amount, if any, by which

(i) the taxpayer's transition deduction

exceeds

(ii) the total of the amounts included under subsection 142.5(5) of the Act in computing the taxpayer's income for preceding taxation years; and

(*b*) the amount prescribed for the purpose of subsection 142.5(5) of the Act in respect of the taxpayer for taxation years after the taxation year referred to in paragraph (*a*) is nil.

S. 8103(1) to (7) were added by P.C. 2009-1212, SOR/2009-222, dated July 30, 2009, published in the *Canada Gazette* August 19, 2009, applicable to taxation years that end after October 30, 1994.

8104. Mark-to-Market — Transition Capital Loss

(Repealed by S.C. 2013, c. 34, s. 406(1).)

History: S. 8104 was repealed by S.C. 2013, c. 34, s. 406(1), applicable to taxation years that begin after October 31, 2011, and formerly read:

(1) In this section, "excluded property", of a taxpayer, means a mark-to-market property of the taxpayer for its taxation year that includes October 31, 1994 if

(*a*) the taxpayer had a taxable capital gain or an allowable capital loss for the year from the disposition of the property to which section 142 of the Act applied; or

(*b*) in the case of a taxpayer that was non-resident in the year, the property was a capital property other than a taxable Canadian property.

(2) For the purpose of subsection 142.5(6) of the Act, the prescribed amount for a taxpayer's taxation year that includes October 31, 1994 is the amount, if any, by which

(*a*) the total of all amounts each of which is the taxable capital gain of the taxpayer for the year from the disposition, because of subsection 142.5(2) of the Act, of a property other than an excluded property

exceeds the total of

(*b*) the total of all amounts each of which is the allowable capital loss of the taxpayer for the year from the disposition, because of subsection 142.5(2) of the Act, of a property other than an excluded property, and

(*c*) the amount, if any, by which

(i) the total of all amounts each of which is the allowable capital loss of the taxpayer for the year from the disposition of a mark-to-market property (other than an excluded property or a property disposed of because of subsection 142.5(2) of the Act)

exceeds

(ii) the total of all amounts each of which is the taxable capital gain of the taxpayer for the year from the disposition of a mark-to-market property (other than an excluded property or a property disposed of because of subsection 142.5(2) of the Act).

S. 8104(1) and (2) were added by P.C. 2009-1212, SOR/2009-222, dated July 30, 2009, published in the *Canada Gazette* August 19, 2009, applicable to taxation years that end after October 30, 1994.

8105. Mark-to-Market — Transition Capital Gains

(Revoked by S.C. 2013, c. 34, s. 406(1).)

History: S. 8105 was repealed by S.C. 2013, c. 34, s. 406(1), applicable to taxation years that begin after October 31, 2011, and formerly read:

(1) In this section, "transition loss", of a taxpayer, means the amount elected by the taxpayer under subsection 142.5(6) of the Act to be an allowable capital loss of the taxpayer for its taxation year that includes October 31, 1994.

(2) There is prescribed for the purpose of subsection 142.5(7) of the Act in respect of a taxpayer for a taxation year that ends after October 30, 1994 the amounts that would be prescribed in respect of the taxpayer for the year by section 8103 if the references in subsections 8103(2) to (7) to

(*a*) "subsection 142.5(5)" were read as "subsection 142.5(7)"; and

(*b*) "transition deduction" were read as "transition loss (as defined in subsection 8105(1))".

S. 8105(1) and (2) were added by P.C. 2009-1212, SOR/2009-222, dated July 30, 2009, published in the *Canada Gazette* August 19, 2009, applicable to taxation years that end after October 30, 1994.

Part LXXXII
Prescribed Properties and Permanent Establishments

8200. Prescribed Properties

For the purposes of subsection 16.1(1) of the Act, "prescribed property" means

(*a*) exempt property, within the meaning assigned by paragraph 1100(1.13)(*a*), other than property leased on or before February 2, 1990 that is

(i) a truck or tractor that is designed for use on highways and has a "gross vehicle weight rating" (within the meaning assigned that expression by the Motor Vehicle Safety Regulations) of 11,778 kilograms or more,

(ii) a trailer that is designed for use on highways and is of a type designed to be hauled under normal operating conditions by a truck or tractor described in subparagraph (i), or

(iii) a railway car,

(*b*) property that is the subject of a lease where the tangible property, other than exempt property (within the meaning assigned by paragraph 1100(1.13)(*a*)), that was the subject of the lease had, at the time the lease was entered into, an aggregate fair market value not in excess of $25,000, and

(*c*) intangible property.

8200.1. Prescribed Properties

For the purposes of subsection 13(18.1), the definition "Canadian renewable and conservation expense" in subsection 66.1(6) and subparagraph 241(4)(*d*)(vi.1) of the Act, "prescribed energy conservation property" means property described in Class 43.1 or 43.2 in Schedule II.

History: S. 8200.1 was replaced by S.C. 2013, c. 40, s. 114(1), deemed to have come into force on December 21, 2012, and formerly read:

8200.1 *Prescribed Properties.* For the purposes of subsection 13(18.1) and subparagraph 241(4)(*d*)(vi.1) of the Act, "prescribed energy conservation property" means property described in Class 43.1 or 43.2 in Schedule II.

8201. Permanent Establishments

For the purposes of subsection 16.1(1), the definition "outstanding debts to specified non-residents" in subsection 18(5), subsections 100(1.3) and 112(2), the definition "qualified Canadian transit organization" in subsection 118.02(1), subsections 125.4(1) and 125.5(1), the definition "taxable supplier" in subsection 127(9), subparagraph 128.1(4)(*b*)(ii), paragraphs 181.3(5)(*a*) and 190.14(2)(*b*), section 233.8, the definitions "Canadian banking business" and "tax-indifferent investor" in subsection 248(1) and paragraph 260(5)(*a*) of the Act, a "permanent establishment" of a person or partnership (either of whom is referred to in this section as the person) means a fixed place of business of the person, including an office, a branch, a mine, an oil well, a farm, a timberland, a factory, a workshop or a warehouse if the person has a fixed place of business and, where the person does not have any fixed place of business, the principal place at which the person's business is conducted, and

(*a*) where the person carries on business through an employee or agent, established in a particular place, who has general authority to contract for the person or who has a stock of merchandise owned by the person from which the employee or agent regularly fills orders, the person shall be deemed to have a permanent establishment at that place,

(*b*) where the person is an insurance corporation, the person is deemed to have a permanent establishment in each country in which the person is registered or licensed to do business,

(*c*) where the person uses substantial machinery or equipment at a particular place at any time in a taxation year, the person shall be deemed to have a permanent establishment at that place,

(*d*) the fact that the person has business dealings through a commission agent, broker or other independent agent or maintains an office solely for the purchase of merchandise shall not of itself be held to mean that the person has a permanent establishment, and

(*e*) where the person is a corporation, the fact that the person has a subsidiary controlled corporation at a place or a subsidiary controlled corporation engaged in trade or business at a place shall not of itself be held to mean that the person is operating a permanent establishment at that place,

except that, where the person is resident in a country with which the Government of Canada has concluded a tax treaty in which the expression "permanent establishment" is given a particular meaning, that meaning shall apply.

History: S. 8201, the portion before paragraph (*a*) was replaced by S.C. 2016, c. 12, s. 82(1), deemed to have come into force on January 1, 2016, and formerly read:

8201. For the purposes of subsection 16.1(1), the definition "outstanding debts to specified non-residents" in subsection 18(5), subsections 100(1.3) and 112(2), the definition "qualified Canadian transit organization" in subsection 118.02(1), subsections 125.4(1) and 125.5(1), the definition "taxable supplier" in subsection 127(9), subparagraph 128.1(4)(*b*)(ii), paragraphs 181.3(5)(*a*) and 190.14(2)(*b*), the definitions "Canadian banking business" and "tax-indifferent investor" in subsection 248(1) and paragraph 260(5)(*a*) of the Act, a "permanent establishment" of a person or partnership (either of whom is referred to in this section as the "person") means a fixed place of business of the person, including an office, a branch, a mine, an oil well, a farm, a timberland, a factory, a workshop or a warehouse if the person has a fixed place of business and, where the person does not have any fixed place of business, the principal place at which the person's business is conducted, and

S. 8201, the portion before paragraph (*a*) was replaced by S.C. 2016, c. 7, s. 58(1), deemed to have come into force on April 22, 2015, and formerly read:

8201. *Permanent Establishments.* For the purposes of subsection 16.1(1), the definition "outstanding debts to specified non-residents" in subsection 18(5), subsections 100(1.3) and 112(2), the definition "qualified Canadian transit organization" in subsection 118.02(1), subsections 125.4(1) and 125.5(1), the definition "taxable supplier" in subsection 127(9), subparagraph 128.1(4)(*b*)(ii), paragraphs 181.3(5)(*a*) and 190.14(2)(*b*), the definition "Canadian banking business" in subsection 248(1) and paragraph 260(5)(*a*) of the Act, a "permanent establishment" of a person or partnership (either of whom is referred to in this section as the "person") means a fixed place of business of the person, including an office, a branch, a mine, an oil well, a farm, a timberland, a factory, a workshop or a warehouse if the person has a fixed place of business and, where the person does not have any fixed place of business, the principal place at which the person's business is conducted, and

S. 8201, the portion before paragraph (*a*) was replaced by S.C. 2013, c. 34, s. 427(2)(*g*), applicable to the 2012 and subsequent taxation years, and formerly read:

8201. *Permanent Establishments.* For the purposes of subsection 16.1(1), the definition "outstanding debts to specified non-residents" in subsection 18(5), subsection 112(2), the definition "qualified Canadian transit organization" in subsection 118.02(1), subsections 125.4(1) and 125.5(1), the definition "taxable supplier" in subsection 127(9), subparagraph 128.1(4)(*b*)(ii), paragraphs 181.3(5)(*a*) and 190.14(2)(*b*), the definition "Canadian banking business" in subsection 248(1) and paragraph 260(5)(*a*) of the Act, a "permanent establishment" of a person or partnership (either of whom is referred to in this section as the "person") means a fixed place of business of the person, including an office, a branch, a mine, an oil well, a farm, a timberland, a factory, a workshop or a warehouse if the person has a fixed place of business and, where the person does not have any fixed place of business, the principal place at which the person's business is conducted, and

S. 8201, the portion before paragraph (*a*) was replaced by S.C. 2013, c. 34, s. 49(1), to taxation years that end after 2008, except that, for taxation years that end before December 19, 2009, s. 8201, the portion before paragraph (*a*) is to be read as follows:

"8201. For the purposes of subsection 16.1(1), the definition "outstanding debts to specified non-residents" in subsection 18(5), the definitions "excluded income" and "excluded revenue" in subsection 95(2.5), subsection 112(2), the definition "qualified Canadian transit organization" in subsection 118.02(1), subsections 125.4(1) and 125.5(1), the definition "taxable supplier" in subsection 127(9), subparagraph 128.1(4)(*b*)(ii), paragraphs 181.3(5)(*a*) and 190.14(2)(*b*), the definition "Canadian banking business" in subsection 248(1) and paragraph 260(5)(*a*) of the Act, a "permanent establishment" of a person or partnership (either of whom referred to in this section as the "person") means a fixed place of business of the person, including an office, a branch, a mine, an oil well, a farm, a timberland, a factory, a workshop or a warehouse if the person has a fixed place of business and, where the person does not have any fixed place of business, the principal place at which the person's business is conducted, and"

Any assessment of a taxpayer's tax, interest and penalties payable under the Act for any taxation year that ends before June 26, 2013 that would otherwise be precluded because of subsections 152(4) to (5) of the Act, shall be made to the extent necessary to take into account this amendment, if the taxpayer

(i) elects in writing in respect of all of its foreign affiliates that this section apply in respect of that provision, and

(ii) files that election with the Minister of National Revenue on or before December 26, 2013 [the day that is six months after royal assent].

S. 8201, the portion before paragraph (*a*) formerly read:

8201. *Permanent Establishments.* For the purposes of subsection 16.1(1), the definition "outstanding debts to specified non-residents" in subsection 18(5), the definition "excluded income" and "excluded revenue" in subsection 95(2.5), subsections 100(1.3), 112(2), 125.4(1) and 125.5(1), the definition "taxable supplier" in subsection 127(9), subparagraph 128.1(4)(*b*)(ii), paragraphs 181.3(5)(*a*) and 190.14(2)(*b*), the definition "Canadian banking business" in subsection 248(1) and paragraph 260(5)(*a*) of the Act, a "permanent establishment" of a person or partnership (either of whom is referred to in this section as the "person") means a fixed place of business of the person, including an office, a branch, a mine, an oil well, a farm, a timberland, a factory, a workshop or a warehouse if the person has a fixed place of business and, if the person does not have any fixed place of business, the principal place at which the person's business is conducted, and

S. 8201, the portion before paragraph (*a*) was replaced by S.C. 2012, c. 31, s. 68(1), applicable to the 2012 and subsequent taxation years, and formerly read:

8201. For the purposes of subsection 16.1(1), the definition "outstanding debts to specified non-residents" in subsection 18(5), subsection 34.2(6), the definition "excluded income" and "excluded revenue" in subsection 95(2.5), subsections 112(2), 125.4(1) and 125.5(1), the definition "taxable supplier" in subsection 127(9), subparagraph 128.1(4)(*b*)(ii), paragraphs 181.3(5)(*a*) and 190.14(2)(*b*), the definition "Canadian banking business" in subsection 248(1) and paragraph 260(5)(*a*) of the Act, a "permanent establishment" of a person or partnership (either of whom referred to in this section as the "person") means a fixed place of business of the person, including an office, a branch, a mine, an oil well, a farm, a timberland, a factory, a workshop or a warehouse if the person has a fixed place of business and, where the person does not have any fixed place of business, the principal place at which the person's business is conducted, and

S. 8201, the portion after paragraph (*e*) was replaced by P.C. 2010-548, SOR/2010-93, dated April 29, 2010, published in the *Canada Gazette* May 12, 2010, deemed to have come into force on June 14, 2001. S. 8201, the portion after paragraph (*e*) formerly read:

except that, where the person is resident in a country with which the Government of Canada has concluded an agreement or convention for the avoidance of double taxation that has the force of law in Canada and in which the expression "permanent establishment" is given a particular meaning, that meaning shall apply.

Tax Profile: June 2005 — Are You Sure That You Don't Have a Permanent Establishment?.

Tax Topics: No. 1737, Why Tax Lawyers Should Care that the Toronto Blue Jays Struck Out.

8201.1. Permanent Establishments

(Repealed.)

Regulations

Part LXXXIII
Pension Adjustments, Past Service Pension Adjustments, Pension Adjustment Reversals and Prescribed Amounts

8300. Interpretation

(1) In this Part,

"certifiable past service event", with respect to an individual, means a past service event that is required, by reason of subsection 147.1(10) of the Act, to be disregarded, in whole or in part, in determining the benefits to be paid under a registered pension plan with respect to the individual until a certification of the Minister in respect of the event has been obtained;

"complete period of reduced services" of an individual means a period of reduced services of the individual that is not part of a longer period of reduced services of the individual;

"designated savings arrangement" of an individual means a RRIF or RRSP under which the individual is the annuitant, or the individual's account under a money purchase provision of a registered pension plan;

"excluded contribution" to a registered pension plan means an amount that is transferred to the plan in accordance with any of subsections 146(16), 146.3(14.1), 147(19), 147.3(1) to (4) and 147.3(5) to (7) of the Act;

"flat benefit provision" of a pension plan means a defined benefit provision of the plan under which the amount of lifetime retirement benefits provided to each member is based on the aggregate of all amounts each of which is the product of a fixed rate and either the duration of service of the member or the number of units of output of the member, and, for the purposes of this definition, where

(*a*) the amount of lifetime retirement benefits provided under a defined benefit provision to each member is subject to a limit based on the remuneration received by the member, and

(*b*) the limit may reasonably be considered to be included to ensure that the amount of lifetime retirement benefits provided to each member does not exceed the maximum amount of such benefits that may be provided by a registered pension plan,

the limit shall be disregarded for the purpose of determining whether the provision is a flat benefit provision;

"individual pension plan", in respect of a calendar year, means a registered pension plan that contains a defined benefit provision if, at any time in the year or a preceding year, the plan

(*a*) has fewer than four members and at least one of them is related to a participating employer in the plan, or

(*b*) is a designated plan and it is reasonable to conclude that the rights of one or more members to receive benefits under the plan exist primarily to avoid the application of paragraph (*a*);

Tax Window Files: General Info re IPPs, *July 23, 2015*, CRA Document No. 2014-0553991E5.

"member", in relation to a deferred profit sharing plan or a benefit provision of a registered pension plan, means an individual who has a right (either immediate or in the future and either absolute or contingent) to receive benefits under the plan or the provision, as the case may be, other than an individual who has such a right only because of the participation of another individual in the plan or under the provision, as the case may be;

"PA offset" for a calendar year means

(*a*) for years before 1997, $1,000, and

(*b*) for years after 1996, $600;

"past service event" means any transaction, event or circumstance that occurs after 1989 and as a consequence of which

(*a*) retirement benefits become provided to an individual under a defined benefit provision of a pension plan in respect of a period before the time the transaction, event or circumstance occurs,

(*b*) there is a change to the way in which retirement benefits provided to an individual under a defined benefit provision of a pension plan in respect of a period before the time the transaction, event or circumstance occurs are determined, including a change that is applicable only in specified circumstances, or

(*c*) there is a change in the value of an indexing or other automatic adjustment that enters into the determination of the amount of an individual's retirement benefits under a defined benefit provision of a pension plan in respect of a period before the time the value of the adjustment changes;

"period of reduced services" of an individual means, in connection with a benefit provision of a registered pension plan, a period that consists of one or more periods each of which is

(*a*) an eligible period of reduced pay or temporary absence of the individual with respect to an employer who participates under the provision, or

(*b*) a period of disability of the individual;

"refund benefit" means

(*a*) with respect to an individual and a benefit provision of a pension plan, a return of contributions made by the individual under the provision, and

(*b*) with respect to an individual and a deferred profit sharing plan, a return of contributions made by the individual to the plan,

and includes any interest (computed at a rate not exceeding a reasonable rate) payable in respect of those contributions.

"resident compensation" of an individual from an employer for a calendar year means the amount that would be the individual's compensation from the employer for the year if the definition "compensation" in subsection 147.1(1) of the Act were read without reference to paragraphs (*b*) and (*c*) of that definition.

History: S. 8300(1), the definition "designated savings arrangement" was added by S.C. 2011, c. 24, s. 90(1), deemed to have come into force on March 23, 2011.

S. 8300(1), the definition "individual pension plan" was added by S.C. 2011, c. 24, s. 90(1), deemed to have come into force on March 23, 2011.

(1.1) The Minister may waive in writing the application of the definition "individual pension plan" in subsection (1) if is just and equitable to do so having regard to all the circumstances.

History: S. 8300(1.1) was added by S.C. 2011, c. 24, s. 90(2), deemed to have come into force on March 23, 2011.

(2) The definition "past service event" in subsection (1) is applicable for the purposes of subsection 147.1(1) of the Act.

(3) All words and expressions used in this Part that are defined in sections 147 or 147.1 of the Act or in Part LXXXV have the meanings assigned in those provisions unless a definition in this Part is applicable.

(4) For the purposes of this Part, an officer who receives remuneration for holding an office shall, for any period that the officer holds the office, be deemed to render services to, and to be in the service of, the person from whom the officer receives the remuneration.

(5) For the purposes of this Part (other than the definition "member" in subsection (1)), where an individual has received an interest in an annuity contract in full or partial satisfaction of the individual's entitlement to benefits under a defined benefit provision of a pension plan, any rights of the individual under the contract are deemed to be rights under the defined benefit provision.

(6) For the purposes of this Part and subsection 147.1(10) of the Act, and subject to subsection 8308(1), the following rules apply in respect of the determination of the benefits that are provided to an individual under a defined benefit provision of a pension plan at a particular time:

(*a*) where a term of the defined benefit provision, or an amendment to a term of the provision, is not applicable with respect to the individual before a specified date, the term shall be considered to have been added to the provision, or the amendment shall be considered to have been made to the term, on the specified date;

(*b*) where an alteration to the benefits provided to the individual is conditional on the requirements of subsection 147.1(10) of the Act being met, those requirements shall be assumed to have been met;

(*c*) benefits that will be reinstated if the individual returns to employment with an employer who participates in the plan shall be considered not to be provided until the individual returns to employment; and

(*d*) where benefits under the provision depend on the individual's job category or other circumstances, the only benefits provided to the individual are the benefits that are relevant to the individual's circumstances at the particular time.

(7) For the purposes of subsections 8301(3) and (8), paragraph 8302(3)(*c*), subsections 8302(5) and 8304(5) and (5.1), paragraphs 8304.1(10)(*c*) and (11)(*c*), subparagraph 8306(4)(*a*)(ii) and subsection 8308(3), the benefits to which an individual is entitled at any time under a deferred profit sharing plan or pension plan include benefits to which the individual has only a contingent right because a condition for the vesting of the benefits has not been satisfied.

(8) For the purposes of this Part, such portion of an amount allocated to an individual at any time under a money purchase provision of a registered pension plan as

(*a*) is attributable to

(i) forfeited amounts under the provision or earnings of the plan that are reasonably attributable to those amounts,

(ii) a surplus under the provision,

(iii) property transferred to the provision in respect of the actuarial surplus under a defined benefit provision of the plan or another registered pension plan, or

(iv) property transferred to the provision in respect of the surplus under another money purchase provision of the plan or under a money purchase provision of another registered pension plan, and

(*b*) can reasonably be considered to be allocated in lieu of a contribution that would otherwise have been made under the provision by an employer in respect of the individual

shall be deemed to be a contribution made under the provision by the employer with respect to the individual at that time and not to be an amount attributable to anything referred to in paragraph (*a*).

(9) For the purposes of this Part and Part LXXXV, where property held in connection with a particular benefit provision of a pension plan is made available at any time to pay benefits under another benefit provision of the plan, the property is deemed to be transferred at that time from the particular benefit provision to the other benefit provision.

(10) For the purposes of this Part and Parts LXXXIV and LXXXV, and subject to subsection (11), an individual is considered to have terminated from a deferred profit sharing plan or a benefit provision of a registered pension plan when the individual has ceased to be a member in relation to the plan or the provision, as the case may be.

(11) Where the benefits provided with respect to an individual under a particular defined benefit provision of a registered pension plan depend on benefits provided with respect to the individual under one or more other defined benefit provisions of registered pension plans (each of the particular provision and the other provisions being referred to in this subsection as a "related provision"), for the purposes of this Part and Parts LXXXIV and LXXXV,

(*a*) if the individual ceases, at any particular time after 1996, to be a member in relation to a specific related provision and is, at the particular time, a member in relation to another related provision, the individual is deemed

(i) not to terminate from the specific provision at the particular time, and

Regulations

(ii) to terminate from the specific provision at the earliest subsequent time when the individual is no longer a member in relation to any of the related provisions;

(*b*) if the conditions in subsection 8304.1(14) (read without reference to the words "after 1996 and") are not satisfied with respect to the individual's termination from a related provision, the conditions in that subsection are deemed not to be satisfied with respect to the individual's termination from each of the other related provisions; and

(*c*) a specified distribution (as defined in subsection 8304.1(8)) made at any particular time in respect of the individual and a related provision is deemed, for the purpose of subsection 8304.1(5), also to be a specified distribution made at the particular time in respect of the individual and each of the other related provisions, except to the extent that the Minister has waived the application of this paragraph with respect to the distribution.

(12) For the purposes of this Part, where

(*a*) all or any part of the amounts payable to an individual under a deferred profit sharing plan are paid by a trustee under the plan to a licensed annuities provider to purchase for the individual an annuity described in subparagraph 147(2)(*k*)(vi) of the Act, or

(*b*) an individual has acquired, in full or partial satisfaction of the individual's entitlement to benefits under a benefit provision of a registered pension plan (other than benefits to which the individual was entitled only because of the participation of another individual under the provision), an interest in an annuity contract (other than as a consequence of a transfer of property from the provision to a registered retirement savings plan or a registered retirement income fund under which the individual is the annuitant),

the individual is deemed to continue, from the time of the payment or acquisition, as the case may be, until the individual's death, to be a member in relation to the plan or provision, as the case may be.

(13) For the purposes of this Part and Part LXXXV, where a benefit is to be provided, or may be provided, to an individual under a defined benefit provision of a registered pension plan as a consequence of an allocation that is to be made, or may be made, to the individual of all or part of an actuarial surplus under the provision, the individual is considered not to have any right to receive the benefit under the provision until the time at which the benefit becomes provided under the provision.

8301. Pension Adjustments

(1) Pension Adjustment with Respect to Employer. For the purpose of subsection 248(1) of the Act, "pension adjustment" of an individual for a calendar year with respect to an employer means, subject to paragraphs 8308(4)(*d*) and (5)(*c*), the total of all amounts each of which is

(*a*) the individual's pension credit for the year with respect to the employer under a deferred profit sharing plan or under a benefit provision of a registered pension plan;

(*b*) the individual's pension credit for the year with respect to the employer under a foreign plan, determined under section 8308.1; or

(*c*) the individual's pension credit for the year with respect to the employer under a specified retirement arrangement, determined under section 8308.3.

Interpretation Bulletins: *Secondary* — IT-124R6 Contributions to registered retirement savings plans; IT-307R4 Spousal registered retirement savings plans.

(2) Pension Credit — Deferred Profit Sharing Plan. For the purposes of subsection (1) and Part LXXXV and subsection 147(5.1) of the Act, and subject to subsection 8304(2), an individual's pension credit for a calendar year with respect to an employer under a deferred profit sharing plan is the amount determined by the formula

$$A - B$$

where

A is the total of all amounts each of which is

(*a*) a contribution made to the plan in the year by the employer with respect to the individual, or

(*b*) the portion of an amount allocated in the year to the individual that is attributable to forfeited amounts under the plan or to earnings of the plan in respect of forfeited amounts, except to the extent that the portion

(i) is included in determining the individual's pension credit for the year with respect to any other employer who participates in the plan, or

(ii) is paid to the individual in the year; and

B is nil, unless the conditions in subsection (2.1) are satisfied, in which case it is the total referred to in paragraph (2.1)(*b*).

Related Regulations: 8301(15).

Interpretation Bulletins: *Secondary* — IT-124R6 Contributions to registered retirement savings plans.

(2.1) Conditions Re — Description of B in Subsection (2). The following are conditions for the purpose of the description of B in subsection (2):

(*a*) the total of all amounts, each of which would be the individual's pension credit for the calendar year with respect to the employer under a deferred profit sharing plan if the description of B in subsection (2) were read as "is nil.", is

(i) equal to, or less than, 50% of the money purchase limit for the year,

(ii) greater than 18% of the amount that would be the individual's compensation from the employer for the year if the definition "compensation" in subsection 147.1(1) of the Act were read without reference to paragraph (*b*) of that definition, and

(iii) equal to, or less than, 18% of the amount that would be the individual's compensation from the employer for the preceding year if the definition "compensation" in subsection 147.1(1) of the Act were read without reference to paragraph (*b*) of that definition; and

(*b*) the total of all amounts, each of which is an amount that is paid from the plan to the individual or the employer in the calendar year or in the first two months of the following year that can reasonably be considered to derive from an amount included in the value of A in subsection (2) with respect to the individual and the employer for the year, is greater than nil.

Related Regulations: 8301(15).

(3) Non-Vested Termination from DPSP. For the purposes of subsection (1) and Part LXXXV and subsection 147(5.1) of the Act, where

(*a*) an individual ceased in a calendar year after 1989 and before 1997 to be employed by an employer who participated in a deferred profit sharing plan for the benefit of the individual,

(*b*) as a consequence of the termination of employment, the individual ceased in the year to have any rights to benefits (other than a right to a refund benefit) under the plan,

(*c*) the individual was not entitled to benefits under the plan at the end of the year, or was entitled only to a refund benefit, and

(*d*) no benefit has been paid under the plan with respect to the individual, other than a refund benefit,

the individual's pension credit under the plan for the year with respect to the employer is nil.

Interpretation Bulletins: *Secondary* — IT-124R6 Contributions to registered retirement savings plans.

(4) Pension Credit — Money Purchase Provision. For the purposes of subsection (1) and Part LXXXV and subsection 147.1(9) of the Act, and subject to subsections (4.1) and (8) and 8304(2), an individual's pension credit for a calendar year with respect to an employer under a money purchase provision of a registered pension plan is the total of all amounts each of which is

(*a*) a contribution (other than an additional voluntary contribution made by the individual in 1990, an excluded contribution or a contribution described in paragraph 8308(6)(*e*) or (*g*)) made under the provision in the year by

(i) the individual, except to the extent that the contribution was not made in connection with the individual's employment with the employer and is included in determining the individual's pension credit for the year with respect to any other employer who participates in the plan, or

(ii) the employer with respect to the individual, or

(*b*) such portion of an amount allocated in the year to the individual as is attributable to

(i) forfeited amounts under the provision or earnings of the plan in respect thereof,

(ii) a surplus under the provision,

(ii.1) property transferred to the provision in respect of the actuarial surplus under a defined benefit provision of the plan or another registered pension plan, or

(ii.2) property transferred to the provision in respect of the surplus under another money purchase provision of the plan or under a money purchase provision of another registered pension plan,

except to the extent that that portion is

(iii) included in determining the individual's pension credit for the year with respect to any other employer who participates in the plan,

(iv) paid to the individual in the year, or

(v) where the year is 1990, attributable to amounts forfeited before 1990 or earnings of the plan in respect thereof,

except that the individual's pension credit is nil where the year is before 1990, and, for the purposes of this subsection, the plan administrator shall determine the portion of a contribution made by an individual or an amount allocated to the individual that is to be included in determining the individual's pension credit with respect to each employer.

Related Regulations: 8301(15).

Information Circulars: IC 98-2 Prescribed compensation for registered pension plans.

Interpretation Bulletins: *Secondary* — IT-124R6 Contributions to registered retirement savings plans.

Registered Plans Directorate Newsletters: No. 91-4R, Registration rules for money purchase provisions.

(4.1) Money Purchase Pension Credits Based on Amounts Allocated. Where,

(*a*) under the terms of a money purchase provision of a pension plan, the method for allocating contributions is such that contributions made by an employer with respect to a particular individual may be allocated to another individual, and

(*b*) the Minister has, on the written application of the administrator of the plan, approved in writing a method for determining pension credits under the provision that, for each individual, takes into account amounts allocated to the individual,

each pension credit under the provision is the amount determined in accordance with the method approved by the Minister.

(5) Pension Credit — Defined Benefit Provision of a Specified Multi-Employer Plan. For the purposes of this Part and Part LXXXV and subsection 147.1(9) of the Act, an individual's pension credit for a calendar year with respect to an employer under a defined benefit provision of a registered pension plan that is, in the year, a specified multi-employer plan is the aggregate of

(*a*) the aggregate of all amounts each of which is a contribution (other than an excluded contribution) made under the provision by the individual

(i) in the year, in respect of

(A) the year, or

(B) a plan year ending in the year (other than in respect of such portion of a plan year as is before 1990), or

Regulations

(ii) in January of the year (other than in January, 1990) in respect of the immediately preceding calendar year,

except to the extent that the contribution was not made in connection with the individual's employment with the employer and is included in determining the individual's pension credit for the year with respect to any other employer who participates in the plan,

(*b*) the aggregate of all amounts each of which is a contribution made in the year by the employer in respect of the provision, to the extent that the contribution may reasonably be considered to be determined by reference to the number of hours worked by the individual or some other measure that is specific to the individual, and

(*c*) the amount determined by the formula

$$(A / B) \times (C - B)$$

where

A is the amount determined under paragraph (*b*) for the purpose of computing the individual's pension credit,

B is the aggregate of all amounts each of which is the amount determined under paragraph (*b*) for the purpose of computing the pension credit of an individual for the year with respect to the employer under the provision, and

C is the aggregate of all amounts each of which is a contribution made in the year by the employer in respect of the provision,

except that, where the year is before 1990, the individual's pension credit is nil.

(6) Pension Credit — Defined Benefit Provision. Subject to subsections (7), (8) and (10) and sections 8304 and 8308, for the purposes of this Part and Part LXXXV and subsection 147.1(9) of the Act, an individual's pension credit for a calendar year with respect to an employer under a defined benefit provision of a particular registered pension plan (other than a plan that is, in the year, a specified multi-employer plan) is

(*a*) if the year is after 1989, the amount determined by the formula

$$A - B$$

where

A is 9 times the individual's benefit entitlement under the provision with respect to the employer and the year, and

B is the amount, if any, by which the PA offset for the year exceeds the total of all amounts each of which is the value of B determined under this paragraph for the purpose of computing the individual's pension credit for the year

(i) with respect to the employer under any other defined benefit provision of a registered pension plan,

(ii) with respect to any other employer who at any time in the year does not deal at arm's length with the employer, under a defined benefit provision of a registered pension plan, or

(iii) with respect to any other employer under a defined benefit provision of the particular plan; and

(*b*) if the year is before 1990, nil.

Interpretation Bulletins: *Secondary* — IT-124R6 Contributions to registered retirement savings plans.

(7) Pension Credit — Defined Benefit Provision of a Multi-Employer Plan. Where a registered pension plan is a multi-employer plan (other than a specified multi-employer plan) in a calendar year, the following rules apply, except to the extent that the Minister has waived in writing their application in respect of the plan, for the purpose of determining the pension credit of an individual for the year under a defined benefit provision of the plan:

(*a*) where the individual is employed in the year by more than one participating employer, the pension credit of the individual for the year under the provision with respect to a particular employer shall be determined as if the individual were not employed by any other participating employer;

(*b*) the description of B in paragraph (6)(*a*) shall be read as

"B is the amount determined by the formula

$$(C \times D) - E$$

where

C is the PA offset for the year,

D is

(i) where the member rendered services on a full-time basis throughout the year to the employer, one, and

(ii) in any other case, the fraction (not greater than one) that measures the services that, for the purpose of determining the member's lifetime retirement benefits under the provision, the member is treated as having rendered in the year to the employer, expressed as a proportion of the services that would have been rendered by the member in the year to the employer if the member had rendered services to the employer on a full-time basis throughout the year, and

E is the total of all amounts each of which is the value of B determined under this paragraph for the purpose of computing the individual's pension credit for the year with respect to the employer under any other defined benefit provision of the plan; and;"

(*c*) where a period in the year is a period of reduced services of the individual, the pension credit of the individual for the year under the provision with respect to each participating employer shall be determined as the aggregate of

(i) the pension credit that would be determined if no benefits (other than benefits attributable to services rendered by the individual) had accrued to the individual in respect of periods of reduced services, and

(ii) the pension credit that would be determined if the only benefits that had accrued to the individual were benefits in respect of periods of reduced services, other than benefits attributable to services rendered by the individual during such periods; and

(*d*) subsection (10) shall not apply.

(8) Non-Vested Termination from RPP. For the purposes of this Part and Part LXXXV and subsection 147.1(9) of the Act, and subject to subsection (9), where

(*a*) an individual ceased in a calendar year after 1989 and before 1997 to be employed by an employer who participated in a registered pension plan for the benefit of the individual,

(*b*) as a consequence of the termination of employment, the individual ceased in the year to have any rights to benefits (other than a right to a refund benefit) under a benefit provision of the plan,

(*c*) the individual was not entitled to benefits under the provision at the end of the year, or was entitled only to a refund benefit, and

(*d*) no benefit has been paid under the provision with respect to the individual, other than a refund benefit,

the individual's pension credit under the provision for the year with respect to the employer is

(*e*) where the provision is a money purchase provision, the total of all amounts each of which is a contribution (other than an additional voluntary contribution made by the individual in 1990, an excluded contribution or a contribution described in paragraph 8308(6)(*e*)) made under the provision in the year by the individual, except to the extent that the contribution was not made in connection with the individual's employment with the employer and is included in determining the individual's pension credit for the year with respect to any other employer who participates in the plan, and

(*f*) where the provision is a defined benefit provision, the lesser of

(i) the pension credit that would be determined if this subsection were not applicable, and

(ii) the aggregate of all amounts each of which is a contribution (other than an excluded contribution) made under the provision by the individual in, and in respect of, the year, except to the extent that the contribution was not made in connection with the individual's employment with the employer and is included in determining the individual's pension credit for the year with respect to any other employer who participates in the plan.

Interpretation Bulletins: *Secondary* — IT-124R6 Contributions to registered retirement savings plans.

(9) Multi-Employer Plans. Subsection (8) is not applicable in respect of a registered pension plan that is a multi-employer plan in a calendar year, except where

(*a*) the plan is not a specified multi-employer plan in the year;

(*b*) if the plan contains a defined benefit provision, the Minister has waived in writing the application of paragraph (7)(*b*) in respect of the plan for the year; and

(*c*) the Minister has approved in writing the application of subsection (8) in respect of the plan for the year.

Interpretation Bulletins: *Secondary* — IT-124R6 Contributions to registered retirement savings plans.

(10) Transition Rule — Money Purchase Offsets. Where,

(*a*) throughout the period beginning on January 1, 1981 and ending on December 31 of a particular calendar year after 1989 and before 2000, there has been subtracted, in determining the amount of lifetime retirement benefits under a defined benefit provision of a registered pension plan (other than a specified multi-employer plan), the amount of lifetime retirement benefits under a money purchase provision of the plan or of another registered pension plan,

(*b*) lifetime retirement benefits under the defined benefit provision are determined, at the end of the particular year, in substantially the same manner as they were determined at the end of 1989, and

(*c*) for each individual and each calendar year before 1990, the amount of employer contributions made under the money purchase provision for the year with respect to the individual did not exceed $3,500,

the pension credit of an individual for the particular year with respect to an employer under the defined benefit provision is equal to the amount, if any, by which

(*d*) the amount that would, but for this subsection, be the individual's pension credit

exceeds

(*e*) the lesser of

(i) $2,500, and

(ii) the amount determined by the formula

$$1/10 \times (A - (B \times C))$$

where

A is the balance in the individual's account under the money purchase provision at the end of 1989,

B is the aggregate of all amounts each of which is the duration (measured in years, including any fraction of a year) of a period ending before 1990 that is pensionable service of the individual under the defined benefit provision and that is not part of a longer period ending before 1990 that is pensionable service of the individual under the provision, and

C is the amount that would be the individual's pension credit for 1989 with respect to the employer under the defined benefit provision if subsection (6) were read without reference

Regulations

to the words "if the year is after 1989" in paragraph (6)(*a*) and without reference to paragraph (6)(*b*).

(11) Timing of Contributions. Subject to paragraph (12)(*b*), for the purposes of this Part, a contribution made by an employer in the first two months of a calendar year to a deferred profit sharing plan, in respect of a money purchase provision of a registered pension plan, or in respect of a defined benefit provision of a registered pension plan that was, in the immediately preceding calendar year, a specified multi-employer plan, shall be deemed to have been made by the employer at the end of the immediately preceding calendar year and not to have been made in the year, to the extent that the contribution can reasonably be considered to relate to a preceding calendar year.

Information Circulars: IC 98-2 Prescribed compensation for registered pension plans.

(12) Indirect Contributions. For the purposes of this Part and Part LXXXIV, where a trade union or association of employers (in this subsection and subsections (13) and (14) referred to as the "contributing entity") makes contributions to a registered pension plan,

(*a*) such portion of a payment made to the contributing entity by an employer or an individual as may reasonably be considered to relate to the plan (determined in accordance with subsection (13), where that subsection is applicable) shall be deemed to be a contribution made to the plan by the employer or individual, as the case may be, at the time the payment was made to the contributing entity; and

(*b*) subsection (11) shall not apply in respect of a contribution deemed by paragraph (*a*) to have been made to the plan.

(13) Apportionment of Payments. For the purposes of subsection (12), where employers or individuals make payments in a calendar year to a contributing entity to enable the contributing entity to make contributions to a registered pension plan and the payments are not made solely for the purpose of being contributed to the plan, the contributing entity shall

(*a*) determine, in a manner that is reasonable in the circumstances, the portion of each payment that relates to the plan;

(*b*) make the determination in such a manner that all contributions made by the contributing entity to the plan, other than contributions made by the contributing entity as an employer or former employer of members of the plan, are considered to be funded by payments made to the contributing entity by employers or individuals;

(*c*) in the case of payments remitted to the contributing entity by an employer, notify the employer in writing, by January 31 of the immediately following calendar year, of the portion, or of the method for determining the portion, of each such payment that relates to the plan; and

(*d*) in the case of payments remitted to the contributing entity by an individual, notify the administrator of the plan in writing, by January 31 of the immediately following calendar year, of the total amount of payments made in the year by the individual that relate to the plan.

(14) Non-Compliance by Contributing Entity. Where a contributing entity does not comply with the requirements of subsection (13) as they apply in respect of payments made to the contributing entity in a calendar year to enable the contributing entity to make contributions to a registered pension plan,

(*a*) the plan becomes, on February 1 of the immediately following calendar year, a revocable plan; and

(*b*) the Minister may make any determinations referred to in subsection (13) that the contributing entity failed to make, or failed to make in accordance with that subsection.

(15) Transferred Amounts. For the purposes of subparagraph (*b*)(ii) of the description of A in subsection (2), paragraph (2.1)(*b*) and subparagraph (4)(*b*)(iv), an amount transferred for the benefit of an individual from a registered pension plan or a deferred profit sharing plan directly to a registered pension plan, a registered retirement savings plan, a registered retirement income fund or a deferred profit sharing plan is deemed to be an amount that was not paid to the individual.

(16) Subsequent Events. Except as otherwise expressly provided in this Part, each pension credit of an individual for a calendar year shall be determined without regard to any transactions, events or circumstances that occur subsequent to the year.

8302. Benefit Entitlement

(1) For the purposes of subsection 8301(6), the benefit entitlement of an individual under a defined benefit provision of a registered pension plan in respect of a calendar year and an employer is the portion of the individual's benefit accrual under the provision in respect of the year that can reasonably be considered to be attributable to the individual's employment with that employer.

(2) Benefit Accrual for Year. For the purposes of subsection (1), and subject to subsections (6), (8) and (9), the benefit accrual of an individual under a defined benefit provision of a registered pension plan in respect of a calendar year is the amount computed in accordance with the following rules:

(*a*) determine the portion of the individual's normalized pension under the provision at the end of the year that can reasonably be considered to have accrued in respect of the year;

(*b*) where the year is after 1989 and before 1995, determine the lesser of the amount determined under paragraph (*a*) and

(i) for 1990, $1,277.78,

(ii) for 1991 and for 1992, $1,388.89,

(iii) for 1993, $1,500.00, and

(iv) for 1994, $1,611.11; and

(*c*) where, in determining the amount of lifetime retirement benefits payable to the individual under the provision, there is deducted from the amount of those benefits that would otherwise be payable the amount of lifetime retirement benefits payable to the individual under a money purchase provision of a registered pension plan or the amount of a lifetime annuity payable to the individual under a deferred profit sharing plan, reduce the amount that would otherwise be determined under this subsection by 1/9 of the total of all amounts each of which is the pension credit of the individual for the year under such a money purchase provision or deferred profit sharing plan.

(3) Normalized Pensions. For the purposes of paragraph (2)(*a*), and subject to subsection (11), the normalized pension of an individual under a defined benefit provision of a registered pension plan at the end of a particular calendar year is the amount (expressed on an annualized basis) of lifetime retirement benefits that would be payable under the provision to the individual immediately after the end of the particular year if

(*a*) where lifetime retirement benefits have not commenced to be paid under the provision to the individual before the end of the particular year, they commenced to be paid immediately after the end of the year;

(*b*) where the individual had not attained 65 years of age before the time at which lifetime retirement benefits commenced to be paid (or are assumed by reason of paragraph (*a*) to have commenced to be paid) to the individual, the individual attained that age at that time;

(*c*) all benefits to which the individual is entitled under the provision were fully vested;

(*d*) where the amount of the individual's lifetime retirement benefits would otherwise be determined with a reduction computed by reference to the individual's age, duration of service or both, or with any other similar reduction, no such reduction were applied;

(*d*.1) no reduction in the amount of the individual's lifetime retirement benefits were applied in respect of benefits described in any of clauses 8503(2)(*a*)(vi)(A) to (C);

(*d*.2) no adjustment that is permissible under subparagraph 8503(2)(*a*)(ix) were made to the amount of the individual's lifetime retirement benefits;

(*e*) where the amount of the individual's lifetime retirement benefits depends on the remuneration received by the individual in a calendar year (in this paragraph referred to as the "other year") other than the particular year, the remuneration received by the individual in the other year were determined in accordance with the following rules:

(i) where the individual was remunerated for both the particular year and the other year as a person who rendered services on a full-time basis throughout each of the years, the remuneration received by the individual in the other year is identical to the remuneration received by the individual in the particular year,

(ii) where subparagraph (i) is not applicable and the individual rendered services in the particular year, the remuneration received by the individual in the other year is the remuneration that the individual would have received in the other year (or a reasonable estimate thereof determined by a method acceptable to the Minister) had the individual's rate of remuneration in the other year been the same as the individual's rate of remuneration in the particular year, and

(iii) where subparagraph (i) is not applicable and the individual did not render services in the particular year, the remuneration received by the individual in the other year is the remuneration that the individual would have received in the other year (or a reasonable estimate thereof determined by a method acceptable to the Minister) had the individual's rate of remuneration in the other year been the amount that it is reasonable to consider would have been the individual's rate of remuneration in the particular year had the individual rendered services in the particular year;

(*f*) where the amount of the individual's lifetime retirement benefits depends on the individual's remuneration and all or a portion of the remuneration received by the individual in the particular year is treated under the provision as if it were remuneration received in a calendar year preceding the particular year for services rendered in that preceding year, that remuneration were remuneration for services rendered in the particular year;

(*g*) where the amount of the individual's lifetime retirement benefits depends on the individual's remuneration and the particular year is after 1989 and before 1995, benefits, to the extent that they can reasonably be considered to be in respect of the following range of annual remuneration, were excluded:

(i) where the particular year is 1990, the range from $63,889 to $86,111,

(ii) where the particular year is 1991 or 1992, the range from $69,444 to $86,111,

(iii) where the particular year is 1993, the range from $75,000 to $86,111, and

(iv) where the particular year is 1994, the range from $80,556 to $86,111;

(*h*) where

(i) the amount of the individual's lifetime retirement benefits depends on the individual's remuneration,

(ii) the formula for determining the amount of the individual's lifetime retirement benefits includes an adjustment to the individual's remuneration for one or more calendar years,

(iii) the adjustment to the individual's remuneration for a year (in this paragraph referred to as the "specified year") consists of multiplying the individual's remuneration for the specified year by a factor that does not exceed the ratio of the average wage for the year in which the amount of the individual's lifetime retirement benefits is required to be determined to the average wage for

Regulations

the specified year (or a substantially similar measure of the change in the wage measure), and

(iv) the adjustment may reasonably be considered to be made to increase the individual's remuneration for the specified year to reflect, in whole or in part, increases in average wages and salaries from that year to the year in which the amount of the individual's lifetime retirement benefits is required to be determined,

the formula did not include the adjustment to the individual's remuneration for the specified year;

(*i*) where the amount of the individual's lifetime retirement benefits depends on the Year's Maximum Pensionable Earnings for calendar years other than the particular year, the Year's Maximum Pensionable Earnings for each such year were equal to the Year's Maximum Pensionable Earnings for the particular year;

(*j*) if the amount of the individual's lifetime retirement benefits depends solely on the actual amount of the pension (in this paragraph referred to as the "statutory pension") payable to the individual under paragraph 46(1)(*a*) of the *Canada Pension Plan* or a similar provision of a "provincial pension plan" (as defined in section 3 of that Act), the amount of statutory pension (expressed on an annualized basis) were equal to

(i) 25 per cent of the lesser of the Year's Maximum Pensionable Earnings for the particular year and

(A) in the case of an individual who renders services throughout the particular year on a full-time basis to employers who participate in the plan, the aggregate of all amounts each of which is the individual's remuneration for the particular year from such an employer, and

(B) in any other case, the amount that it is reasonable to consider would be determined under clause (A) if the individual had rendered services throughout the particular year on a full-time basis to employers who participate in the plan, or

(ii) at the option of the plan administrator, any other amount determined in accordance with a method for estimating the statutory pension that can be expected to result in amounts substantially similar to amounts determined under subparagraph (i);

(*j*.1) if the amount of the individual's lifetime retirement benefits depends on the actual amount of the pension (in this paragraph referred to as the "statutory pension") payable to the individual under paragraphs 46(1)(*a*) and (*b*) of the *Canada Pension Plan* or a similar provision of a "provincial pension plan" (as defined in section 3 of that Act), the amount of statutory pension (expressed on an annualized basis) were equal to

(i) the amount determined by the formula

$$A \times B$$

where

A is

(A) for 2018 and preceding years, 0.25,

(B) for 2019, 0.2625,

(C) for 2020, 0.275,

(D) for 2021, 0.29165,

(E) for 2022, 0.3125, and

(F) for 2023 and subsequent years, 1/3, and

B is the lesser of the Year's Maximum Pensionable Earnings for the particular year and,

(A) in the case of an individual who renders services throughout the particular year on a full-time basis to employers who participate in the plan, the aggregate of all amounts each of which is the individual's remuneration for the particular year from such an employer, and

(B) in any other case, the amount that it is reasonable to consider would be determined under clause (A) if the individual had rendered services throughout the particular year on a full-time basis to employers who participate in the plan, or

(ii) at the option of the plan administrator, any other amount determined in accordance with a method for estimating the statutory pension that can be expected to result in amounts substantially similar to amounts determined under subparagraph (i);

(*k*) where the amount of the individual's lifetime retirement benefits depends on a pension (in this paragraph referred to as the "statutory pension") payable to the individual under Part I of the *Old Age Security Act*, the amount of statutory pension payable for each calendar year were equal to the aggregate of all amounts each of which is the amount of the full monthly pension payable under Part I of the *Old Age Security Act* for a month in the particular year;

(*l*) except as otherwise expressly permitted in writing by the Minister, where the amount of the individual's lifetime retirement benefits depends on the amount of benefits (other than public pension benefits or similar benefits of a country other than Canada) payable under another benefit provision of a pension plan or under a deferred profit sharing plan, the amounts of the other benefits were such as to maximize the amount of the individual's lifetime retirement benefits;

(*m*) where the individual's lifetime retirement benefits would otherwise include benefits that the plan is required to provide by reason of a designated provision of the law of Canada or a province (within the meaning assigned by section 8513), or that the plan would be required to provide if each such provision were applicable to the plan with respect to all its members, such benefits were not included;

(*n*) where

(i) the individual attained 65 years of age before lifetime retirement benefits commenced to be paid (or are assumed by reason of paragraph (*a*) to have commenced to be paid) to the individual, and

(ii) an adjustment is made in determining the amount of those benefits for the purpose of offsetting, in whole or in part, the decrease in the value of lifetime retirement benefits that would otherwise result by reason of the deferral of those benefits after the individual attained 65 years of age,

that adjustment were not made, except to the extent that the adjustment exceeds the adjustment that would be made on an actuarially equivalent basis;

(*o*) except as otherwise provided by subsection (4), where the amount of the individual's lifetime retirement benefits depends on

(i) the form of benefits provided with respect to the individual under the provision (whether or not at the option of the individual), including

(A) the benefits to be provided after the death of the individual,

(B) the amount of retirement benefits, other than lifetime retirement benefits, provided to the individual, or

(C) the extent to which the lifetime retirement benefits will be adjusted to reflect changes in the cost of living, or

(ii) circumstances that are relevant in determining the form of benefits,

the form of benefits and the circumstances were such as to maximize the amount of the individual's lifetime retirement benefits on commencement of payment;

(*p*) where the amount of the individual's lifetime retirement benefits depends on whether the individual is totally and permanently disabled at the time at which retirement benefits commence to be paid to the individual, the individual were not so disabled at that time; and

(*q*) where lifetime retirement benefits have commenced to be paid under the provision to the individual before the end of the particular year, benefits payable as a consequence of cost-of-living adjustments described in paragraph 8303(5)(*k*) were disregarded.

History: S. 8302(3)(*j*), the portion before subparagraph (i) was replaced by S.C. 2019, c. 29, s. 60(1), deemed in force on January 1, 2019, and formerly read:

(*j*) where the amount of the individual's lifetime retirement benefits depends on the actual amount of pension (in this paragraph referred to as the "statutory pension") payable to the individual under the *Canada Pension Plan* or a provincial plan (as defined in section 3 of that Act), the amount of statutory pension (expressed on an annualized basis) were equal to

S. 8302(3)(*j*.1) was added by S.C. 2019, c. 29, s. 60(2), deemed in force on January 1, 2019.

(4) Optional Forms. Where the terms of a defined benefit provision of a registered pension plan permit a member to elect to receive additional lifetime retirement benefits in lieu of benefits that would, in the absence of the election, be payable after the death of the member if the member dies after retirement benefits under the provision commence to be paid to the member, paragraph (3)(*o*) applies as if the following elections were not available to the member:

(*a*) an election to receive additional lifetime retirement benefits, not exceeding additional benefits determined on an actuarially equivalent basis, in lieu of all or any portion of a guarantee that retirement benefits will be paid for a minimum period of 10 years or less, and

(*b*) an election to receive additional lifetime retirement benefits in lieu of retirement benefits that would otherwise be payable to an individual who is a spouse or common-law partner or former spouse or common-law partner of the member for a period beginning after the death of the member and ending with the death of the individual, where

(i) the election may be made only if the life expectancy of the individual is significantly shorter than normal and has been so certified in writing by a medical doctor or a nurse practitioner licensed to practise under the laws of a province or of the place where the individual resides, and

(ii) the additional benefits do not exceed additional benefits determined on an actuarially equivalent basis and on the assumption that the individual has a normal life expectancy.

History: S. 8302(4)(*b*)(i) was replaced by S.C. 2017, c. 33, s. 101(1), applicable in respect of certifications made after September 7, 2017, and formerly read:

(i) the election may be made only if the life expectancy of the individual is significantly shorter than normal and has been so certified in writing by a medical doctor licensed to practice under the laws of a province or of the place where the individual resides, and

(5) Termination of Entitlement to Benefits. For the purposes of subsection (3), where an individual ceased in a calendar year to be entitled to all or part of the lifetime retirement benefits provided to the individual under a defined benefit provision of a registered pension plan, the normalized pension of the individual under the provision at the end of the year shall be determined on the assumption that the individual continued to be entitled to those benefits immediately after the end of the year.

(6) Defined Benefit Offset. Where the amount of lifetime retirement benefits provided under a particular defined benefit provision of a registered pension plan to a member of the plan depends on the amount of lifetime retirement benefits provided to the member under one or more other defined benefit provisions of registered pension plans, the benefit accrual of the member under the particular provision in respect of a calendar year is the amount, if any, by which

(*a*) the amount that would, but for this subsection, be the benefit accrual of the member under the particular provision in respect of the year if the benefits provided under the other provisions were provided under the particular provision

exceeds

(*b*) the amount that would be the benefit accrual of the member under the other provisions in respect of

Regulations

the year if the other provisions were a single provision.

(7) Offset of Specified Multi-Employer Plan Benefits. Where the amount of an individual's lifetime retirement benefits under a defined benefit provision (in this subsection referred to as the "supplemental provision") of a registered pension plan depends on the amount of benefits payable under a defined benefit provision of a specified multi-employer plan, the defined benefit provision of the specified multi-employer plan shall be deemed to be a money purchase provision for the purpose of determining the benefit accruals of the individual under the supplemental provision.

(8) Transition Rule — Career Average Benefits. Where

(*a*) on March 27, 1988 lifetime retirement benefits under a defined benefit provision of a pension plan were determined as the greater of benefits computed on a career average basis and benefits computed on a final or best average earnings basis,

(*b*) the method for determining lifetime retirement benefits under the provision was not amended after March 27, 1988 and before the end of a particular calendar year, and

(*c*) it was reasonable to expect, on January 1, 1990, that the lifetime retirement benefits to be paid under the provision to at least 75 per cent of the members of the plan on that date (other than members to whom benefits do not accrue under the provision after that date) will be determined on a final or best average earnings basis,

at the option of the plan administrator, benefit accruals under the provision in respect of the particular year may, where the particular year is before 1992, be determined without regard to the career average formula.

(9) Transition Rule — Benefit Rate Greater Than 2 Per Cent. Subject to subsection (6), where

(*a*) the amount of lifetime retirement benefits provided under a defined benefit provision of a registered pension plan to a member of the plan is determined, in part, by multiplying the member's remuneration (or a function of the member's remuneration) by one or more benefit accrual rates, and

(*b*) the largest benefit accrual rate that may be applicable is greater than 2 per cent,

the member's benefit accrual under the provision in respect of 1990 or 1991 is the lesser of

(*c*) the member's benefit accrual otherwise determined, and

(*d*) 2 per cent of the aggregate of all amounts each of which is the amount that would, if the definition "compensation" in subsection 147.1(1) of the Act were read without reference to subparagraphs (*a*)(iii) and (iv) and paragraphs (*b*) and (*c*) thereof, be the member's compensation for the year from an employer who participated in the plan in the year for the benefit of the member.

(10) Period of Reduced Remuneration. For the purposes of paragraph (9)(*d*), where a member of a registered pension plan is provided with benefits under a defined benefit provision of the plan in respect of a period in 1990 or 1991

(*a*) throughout which, by reason of disability, leave of absence, lay-off or other circumstance, the member rendered no services, or rendered a reduced level of services, to employers who participate in the plan, and

(*b*) throughout which the member received no remuneration, or a reduced rate of remuneration,

the member's compensation shall be determined on the assumption that the member received remuneration for the period equal to the amount of remuneration that it is reasonable to consider the member would have received if the member had rendered services throughout the period on a regular basis (having regard to the services rendered by the member before the period) and the member's rate of remuneration had been commensurate with the member's rate of remuneration when the member did render services on a regular basis.

(11) Anti-Avoidance. Where the terms of a defined benefit provision of a registered pension plan can reasonably be considered to have been established or modified so that a pension credit of an individual for a calendar year under the provision would, but for this subsection, be reduced as a consequence of the application of paragraph (3)(*g*), that paragraph shall not apply in determining the individual's normalized pension under the provision in respect of the year.

8303. Past Service Pension Adjustment

(1) PSPA with Respect to Employer. For the purpose of subsection 248(1) of the Act, "past service pension adjustment" of an individual for a calendar year in respect of an employer means the total of

(*a*) the accumulated past service pension adjustment (in this Part referred to as "accumulated PSPA") of the individual for the year with respect to the employer, determined as of the end of the year,

(*b*) the total of all amounts each of which is the foreign plan PSPA (determined under subsection 8308.1(5) or (6)) of the individual with respect to the employer associated with a modification of benefits in the year under a foreign plan (as defined in subsection 8308.1(1)), and

(*c*) the total of all amounts each of which is the specified retirement arrangement PSPA (determined under subsection 8308.3(4) or (5)) of the individual with respect to the employer associated with a modification of benefits in the year under a specified retirement arrangement (as defined in subsection 8308.3(1)).

Interpretation Bulletins: *Secondary* — IT-124R6 Contributions to registered retirement savings plans; IT-528 Transfers of funds between registered plans.

(2) Accumulated PSPA for Year. For the purposes of this Part, the accumulated PSPA of an individual for a calendar year with respect to an employer, determined as of any time, is the total of all amounts each of which is the individual's provisional past service pension adjustment (in this Part referred to as "provisional PSPA") with respect to the employer that is associated with

(*a*) a past service event (other than a certifiable past service event with respect to the individual) that occurred in the preceding year; or

(*b*) a certifiable past service event with respect to the individual where the Minister has, in the year and before that time, issued a certification for the purposes of subsection 147.1(10) of the Act in respect of the event and the individual.

Interpretation Bulletins: *Secondary* — IT-528 Transfers of funds between registered plans.

(2.1) 1991 Past Service Events and Certifications. For the purposes of subsection (2),

(*a*) a past service event that occurred in 1991 (including, for greater certainty, a past service event that is deemed by paragraph 8304(3)(*b*) to have occurred immediately after the end of 1990) shall be deemed to have occurred on January 1, 1992 and not to have occurred in 1991; and

(*b*) a certification issued by the Minister in 1991 shall be deemed to have been issued on January 1, 1992 and not to have been issued in 1991.

Interpretation Bulletins: *Secondary* — IT-528 Transfers of funds between registered plans.

(3) Provisional PSPA. Subject to subsections (8) and (10) and sections 8304 and 8308, for the purposes of this Part, the provisional PSPA of an individual with respect to an employer that is associated with a past service event that occurs at a particular time in a particular calendar year is the amount determined by the formula

$$A - B - C + D$$

where

A is the aggregate of all amounts each of which is, in respect of a calendar year after 1989 and before the particular year, the amount that would have been the individual's pension credit for the year with respect to the employer under a defined benefit provision of a registered pension plan (other than a plan that is, at the particular time, a specified multi-employer plan) had the individual's benefit entitlement under the provision in respect of the year and the employer been equal to the individual's redetermined benefit entitlement (determined as of the particular time) under the provision in respect of the year and the employer,

B is the aggregate that would be determined for A if the reference in the description of A to "determined as of the particular time" were read as a reference to "determined as of the time immediately before the particular time",

C is such portion of the amount of the individual's qualifying transfers made in connection with the past service event as is not deducted in computing the provisional PSPA of the individual with respect to any other employer, and

D is the total of all amounts each of which is an excess money purchase transfer in relation to the individual and the past service event that is not included in determining any other provisional PSPA of the individual that is associated with the past service event.

Interpretation Bulletins: *Secondary* — IT-528 Transfers of funds between registered plans.

(4) Redetermined Benefit Entitlement. For the purposes of the description of A in subsection (3), an individual's redetermined benefit entitlement under a defined benefit provision of a registered pension plan in respect of a calendar year and an employer, determined as of a particular time, is the amount that would be determined under section 8302 to be the individual's benefit entitlement under the provision in respect of the year and the employer if, for the purpose of computing the benefit accrual of the individual in respect of the year under the provision and, where subsection 8302(6) is applicable, under any other defined benefit provision, the amount determined under paragraph 8302(2)(*a*) in respect of a specific provision were equal to that portion of the individual's normalized pension (computed in accordance with subsection (5)) under the specific provision at the particular time, determined with reference to the year, as may reasonably be considered to have accrued in respect of the year.

Interpretation Bulletins: *Secondary* — IT-528 Transfers of funds between registered plans.

(5) Normalized Pension. For the purposes of subsection (4), the normalized pension of an individual under a defined benefit provision of a registered pension plan at a particular time, determined with reference to a calendar year (in this subsection referred to as the "pension credit year"), is the amount (expressed on an annualized basis) of lifetime retirement benefits, other than excluded benefits, that would be payable to the individual under the provision immediately after the particular time if

(*a*) where lifetime retirement benefits have not commenced to be paid under the provision to the individual before the particular time, they commenced to be paid immediately after the particular time,

(*b*) where the individual had not attained 65 years of age before the time at which lifetime retirement benefits commenced to be paid (or are assumed by reason of paragraph (*a*) to have commenced to be paid) to the individual, the individual attained that age at that time,

(*c*) the amount of the individual's lifetime retirement benefits were determined with regard to all past service events occurring at or before the particular time and without regard to past service events occurring after the particular time,

(*d*) paragraphs 8302(3)(*c*) to (*p*) (other than paragraph 8302(3)(*g*), where subsection 8302(11) was applicable in respect of the pension credit year and the provision or would have been applicable had all benefits provided as a consequence of past service events become provided in the pension credit year) were applied for the purpose of determining the amount of the individual's lifetime retirement benefits and, for the purpose of those paragraphs, the pension credit year were the particular year referred to in those paragraphs, and

(*e*) where

Regulations

(i) the amount of the individual's lifetime retirement benefits under the provision depends on the individual's remuneration, and

(ii) all or part of the individual's lifetime retirement benefits in respect of the pension credit year became provided as a consequence of a past service event pursuant to terms of the provision that enable benefits to be provided to members of the plan in respect of periods of employment with employers who have not participated under the provision,

the remuneration received by the individual from each such employer in respect of a period of employment in respect of which the individual is provided with benefits under the provision were remuneration received from an employer who has participated under the provision for the benefit of the individual,

and, for the purposes of this subsection, the following benefits are excluded benefits:

(*f*) where the formula for determining the amount of lifetime retirement benefits payable under the provision to the individual requires the calculation of an amount that is the product of a fixed rate and the duration of all or part of the individual's pensionable service, benefits payable as a direct consequence of an increase in the value of the fixed rate at any time (in this paragraph referred to as the "time of increase") after the pension credit year, other than benefits

(i) provided as a consequence of a second or subsequent increase in the value of the fixed rate after the time that retirement benefits under the provision commenced to be paid to the individual, or

(ii) that would not have become provided had the value of the fixed rate been increased to the amount determined by the formula

$$A \times (B / C)$$

where

A is the value of the fixed rate immediately before the time of the increase,

B is the average wage for the calendar year that includes the time of the increase, and

C is

(A) if the value of the fixed rate was last increased or established in the calendar year that includes the time of the increase, the average wage for that year, or

(B) otherwise, the average wage for the year immediately preceding the calendar year that includes the time of increase,

(*f*.1) where the formula for determining the amount of lifetime retirement benefits payable under the provision to the individual includes a limit that is the product of the duration of the individual's pensionable service and the lesser of a percentage of the individual's remuneration and a fixed rate, and the value of the fixed rate is increased after the pension credit year to an amount equal to the defined benefit limit for the earlier of the year in which the increase occurs and the year in which retirement benefits under the provision commenced to be paid to the individual, the portion of the benefits payable as a direct consequence of the increase that would not have become provided had the value of the fixed rate been set at the defined benefit limit for the pension credit year, if

(i) the value of the fixed rate was, immediately before the increase, equal to the defined benefit limit for the year in which the value of the fixed rate was last established, and

(ii) where the year in which the value of the fixed rate was last established precedes the year immediately preceding the year in which the increase occurs,

(A) the Minister has approved in writing the application of this paragraph in respect of the past service event,

(B) there are more than nine active members (within the meaning assigned by paragraph 8306(4)(*a*)) under the provision, and

(C) the plan is not a designated plan,

(*f*.2) where the formula for determining the amount of lifetime retirement benefits payable under the provision to the individual includes a limit that is the product of the duration of the individual's pensionable service and the lesser of a percentage of the individual's remuneration and a fixed rate the value of which can reasonably be considered to be fixed each year as a portion of the defined benefit limit for that year, benefits payable as a direct consequence of an increase, after the pension credit year, in the value of the fixed rate to reflect the defined benefit limit for the year in which the increase occurs, if

(i) except as otherwise expressly permitted by the Minister, it is reasonable to consider that, for years after 1989, the ratio of the fixed rate to the defined benefit limit has been, and will remain, constant,

(ii) the benefits are not provided as a consequence of a second or subsequent increase in the value of the fixed rate after the time that retirement benefits under the provision commenced to be paid to the individual,

(iii) the Minister has approved in writing the application of this paragraph in respect of the past service event, and

(iv) the plan is not a designated plan,

(*g*) where

(i) the provision is a flat benefit provision,

(ii) at the particular time, the amount (expressed on an annual basis) of lifetime retirement benefits provided under the provision to each member in respect of pensionable service in each calendar year does not exceed 40 per cent of the defined benefit limit for the year that includes the particular time,

Regulations

(iii) the conditions in subsection 8306(2) are satisfied in respect of the provision and the past service event in connection with which the normalized pension is being calculated, and

(iv) only one fixed rate is applicable in determining the amount of the individual's lifetime retirement benefits,

benefits provided as a direct consequence of an increase in the value of the fixed rate at any time (in this paragraph referred to as the "time of increase") after the pension credit year, other than benefits

(v) provided as a consequence of a second or subsequent increase in the value of the fixed rate after the time that retirement benefits under the provision commenced to be paid to the individual, or

(vi) that would not have become provided had the value of the fixed rate been increased to the greater of

(A) the greatest of all amounts each of which is an amount determined by the formula

$$A \times (B / C)$$

where

A is a value of the fixed rate in the period beginning on January 1, 1984 and ending immediately before the time of increase,

B is the average wage for the calendar year that includes the time of increase, and

C is the average wage for the later of 1984 and the calendar year in which the value of the fixed rate used for A was first effective, and

(B) the amount determined by the formula

$$D + (E \times F)$$

where

D is the value of the fixed rate immediately before the time of increase,

E is the amount by which the value of the fixed rate used for D would have to be increased to provide an increase in the individual's annual lifetime retirement benefits equal to $18 for each year of pensionable service, and

F is the duration (measured in years, including any fraction of a year) of the period beginning on the later of January 1, 1984 and the day on which the value of the fixed rate used for D was first effective and ending on the day that includes the time of increase,

(*h*) where the provision is a flat benefit provision, benefits provided as a direct consequence of an increase at any time (in this paragraph referred to as the "time of increase") after the pension credit year in the value of a fixed rate under the provision where

(i) the value of the fixed rate was increased pursuant to an agreement made before 1992, and

(ii) at the time the agreement was made, it was reasonable to expect that the percentage increase in the value of the fixed rate would approximate or be less than the percentage increase in the average wage from the calendar year in which the value of the fixed rate was last increased before the time of increase (or, if the increase is the first increase, the calendar year in which the initial value of the fixed rate was first applicable) to the calendar year that includes the time of increase,

(*i*) where the provision is a flat benefit provision under which the amount of each member's retirement benefits depends on the member's job category or rate of pay in such a manner that the ratio of the amount of lifetime retirement benefits to remuneration does not significantly increase as remuneration increases, benefits provided as a direct consequence of a change, after the pension credit year, in the individual's job category or rate of pay,

(*j*) where

(i) the individual's pensionable service under the provision ends before the particular time,

(ii) the individual's lifetime retirement benefits under the provision have been adjusted by a cost-of-living or similar adjustment in respect of the period (in this paragraph referred to as the "deferral period") beginning at the latest of

(A) the time the individual's pensionable service under the provision ends,

(B) if the amount of the individual's lifetime retirement benefits depends on the individual's remuneration, the end of the most recent period for which the individual received remuneration that is taken into account in determining the individual's lifetime retirement benefits,

(C) if the amount of the individual's lifetime retirement benefits depends on the individual's remuneration and the remuneration is adjusted as described in paragraph 8302(3)(*h*), the end of the period in respect of which the adjustment is made, and

(D) if the formula for determining the amount of the individual's lifetime retirement benefits requires the calculation of an amount that is the product of a fixed rate and the duration of all or part of the individual's pensionable service (or other measure of services rendered by the individual), the time as of which the value of the fixed rate applicable with respect to the individual was established,

and ending at the earlier of the particular time and the time, if any, at which lifetime retirement benefits commenced to be paid under the provision to the individual, and

(iii) the adjustment is warranted, having regard to all prior such adjustments, by the increase in the Consumer Price Index or in the wage measure from the commencement of the deferral period to the time the adjustment was made,

benefits payable as a consequence of the adjustment,

Regulations

(*k*) benefits payable as a consequence of a cost-of-living adjustment made after the time lifetime retirement benefits commenced to be paid under the provision to the individual, where the adjustment

(i) is warranted, having regard to all prior such adjustments, by the increase in the Consumer Price Index from that time to the time the adjustment was made, or

(ii) is a periodic adjustment described in subparagraph 8503(2)(*a*)(ii), and

(*l*) such portion of the individual's lifetime retirement benefits as

(i) would not otherwise be excluded in determining the individual's normalized pension,

(ii) may reasonably be considered to be attributable to cost-of-living adjustments or to adjustments made by reason of increases in a general measure of salaries and wages (other than increases in such a measure after the time lifetime retirement benefits commenced to be paid under the provision to the individual), and

(iii) is acceptable to the Minister.

History: S. 8303(5)(*f*), clause (A) of the description of C was replaced by P.C. 2011-936, SOR/2011-188, dated September 22, 2011, published in the *Canada Gazette* October 12, 2011, applicable to past service events that occur after February 18, 2011. S. 8303(5)(*f*), clause (A) of the description of C formerly read:

(A) if the value of the fixed rate has previously been increased in the calendar year that includes the time of increase, the average wage for that year, or

Interpretation Bulletins: *Secondary* — IT-528 Transfers of funds between registered plans.

(6) Qualifying Transfers. For the purposes of subsections (3) and 8304(5), (7) and (10), and subject to subsection (6.1) and paragraph 8304(2)(*h*), the amount of an individual's qualifying transfers made in connection with a past service event is the total of all amounts each of which is

(*a*) the portion of an amount transferred to a registered pension plan

(i) in accordance with any of subsections 146(16), 147(19) and 147.3(2), (5) and (7) of the Act, or

(ii) from a specified multi-employer plan in accordance with subsection 147.3(3) of the Act

that is transferred to fund benefits provided to the individual as a consequence of the past service event; or

(*b*) the amount of any property held in connection with a benefit provision of a registered pension plan that is made available to fund benefits provided to the individual under another benefit provision of the plan as a consequence of the past service event, where the transaction by which the property is made so available is such that, if the benefit provisions were in separate registered pension plans, the transaction would constitute a transfer of property from one plan to the other in accordance with any of subsections 147.3(2), (5) and (7) of the Act.

History: S. 8303(6), the portion before paragraph (*a*) was replaced by S.C. 2011, c. 24, s. 91(1), deemed to have come into force on March 23, 2011. S. 8303(6), the portion before paragraph (*a*) formerly read:

(6) For the purposes of subsections (3) and 8304(5) and (7), and subject to subsection (6.1) and paragraph 8304(2)(*h*), the amount of an individual's qualifying transfers made in connection with a past service event is the total of all amounts each of which is

Interpretation Bulletins: *Secondary* — IT-528 Transfers of funds between registered plans.

Registered Plans Directorate Newsletters: 16-1 Qualifying Transfers to Individual Pension Plans.

(6.1) Exclusion for Pre-1990 Benefits. The amount of an individual's qualifying transfers made in connection with a past service event shall be determined under subsection (6) without regard to the portion, if any, of amounts transferred or property made available, as the case may be, that can reasonably be considered to have been transferred or made available to fund benefits provided in respect of periods before 1990.

(7) Deemed Payment. Where

(*a*) an individual has given an irrevocable direction that

(i) an amount be paid to a registered pension plan, or

(ii) property held in connection with a benefit provision of a registered pension plan be made available to fund benefits provided to the individual under another benefit provision of the plan

in the event that the Minister issues a certification for the purposes of subsection 147.1(10) of the Act with respect to the individual and to benefits provided under a defined benefit provision of the plan as a consequence of a past service event, and

(*b*) the amount is to be paid or the property is to be made available, as the case may be,

(i) where subparagraph (ii) does not apply, on or before the day that is 90 days after the day on which the certification is received by the administrator of the plan, and

(ii) where the plan was deemed by paragraph 147.1(3)(*a*) of the Act to be a registered pension plan at the time the direction was given, on or before the day that is 90 days after the later of

(A) the day on which the certification is received by the administrator of the plan, and

(B) the day on which the administrator of the plan receives written notice from the Minister of the registration of the plan for the purposes of the Act,

the amount or property, as the case may be, is deemed, for the purpose of subsection (6), to have been paid or made available, as the case may be, at the time the direction was given.

Interpretation Bulletins: *Secondary* — IT-528 Transfers of funds between registered plans.

(7.1) Excess Money Purchase Transfer. Where lifetime retirement benefits have, as a consequence of a past service event, become provided to an individual under a defined benefit provision of a registered pension plan (other than a specified multi-employer plan) in respect of a period (in this subsection referred to as the "past service period") that

Regulations

(*a*) was previously pensionable service of the individual under a particular defined benefit provision of a registered pension plan (other than a specified multi-employer plan),

(*b*) ceased to be pensionable service of the individual under the particular provision as a result of the payment of a single amount, all or part of which was transferred on behalf of the individual from the particular provision to a registered retirement savings plan, a registered retirement income fund, a money purchase provision of a registered pension plan or a defined benefit provision of a registered pension plan that was, at the time of the transfer, a specified multi-employer plan,

(*c*) has not, at any time after the payment of the single amount and before the past service event, been pensionable service of the individual under any defined benefit provision of a registered pension plan (other than a specified multi-employer plan), and

(*d*) is not, for the purpose of subsection 8304(5), a qualifying past service period in relation to the individual and the past service event,

the amount determined by the formula

$$A - B$$

is, for the purpose of the description of D in subsection (3), an excess money purchase transfer in relation to the individual and the past service event, where

A is the portion of the amount transferred, as described in paragraph (*b*), that can reasonably be considered to be attributable to benefits in respect of the portion of the past service period that is after 1989, and

B is the total of all amounts each of which is the portion of a pension credit, or the grossed-up amount of a provisional PSPA, of the individual that can reasonably be considered to be attributable to benefits previously provided under the particular provision in respect of the past service period.

(8) Specified Multi-Employer Plan. Where, in a calendar year, an individual makes a contribution (other than an excluded contribution) in respect of a defined benefit provision of a registered pension plan that is, in the year, a specified multi-employer plan, and the contribution

(*a*) is made in respect of a period after 1989 and before the year, and

(*b*) is not included in determining the individual's pension credit for the year with respect to any employer under the provision,

the individual's provisional PSPA with respect to an employer who participates in the plan, associated with the payment of the contribution, is the portion of the contribution that is not included in the individual's provisional PSPA with respect to any other employer who participates in the plan, and, for the purpose of this subsection, the plan administrator shall determine the portion of the contribution to be included in the provisional PSPA of the individual with respect to each employer.

Interpretation Bulletins: *Secondary* — IT-528 Transfers of funds between registered plans.

(9) Conditional Contributions. For the purpose of subsection (8), a contribution includes an amount paid by an individual to a registered pension plan where the right of any person to retain the amount on behalf of the plan is conditional on the Minister issuing a certification for the purposes of subsection 147.1(10) of the Act as it applies with respect to the individual and to benefits provided as a consequence of the payment.

Interpretation Bulletins: *Secondary* — IT-528 Transfers of funds between registered plans.

(10) Benefits in Respect of Foreign Service. Where, as a consequence of a past service event, benefits become provided to an individual under a defined benefit provision of a registered pension plan in respect of a period throughout which the individual was employed outside Canada, and the Minister has consented in writing to the application of this subsection, each provisional PSPA of the individual associated with the past service event shall be determined on the assumption that no benefits were provided in respect of the period.

Interpretation Bulletins: *Secondary* — IT-528 Transfers of funds between registered plans.

Registered Plans Directorate Newsletters: No. 93-2, Foreign service newsletter.

Regulations

8304. Past Service Benefits — Additional Rules

(1) Replacement of Defined Benefits. Where

(*a*) an individual ceased, at any time in a calendar year, to have any rights to benefits under a defined benefit provision of a registered pension plan (in this subsection referred to as the "former provision"),

(*b*) benefits became provided at that time to the individual under another defined benefit provision of a registered pension plan (in this subsection referred to as the "current provision") in lieu of the benefits under the former provision,

(*c*) the benefits that became provided at that time to the individual under the current provision in respect of the period in the year before that time are attributable to employment with the same employers as were the individual's benefits in respect of that period under the former provision,

(*d*) no amount was transferred in the year on behalf of the individual from the former provision to a registered retirement savings plan, a registered retirement income fund or a money purchase provision of a registered pension plan, and

(*e*) no benefits became provided under the former provision to the individual in the year and after that time,

each pension credit of the individual under the former provision for the year is nil.

Interpretation Bulletins: *Secondary* — IT-124R6 Contributions to registered retirement savings plans; IT-528 Transfers of funds between registered plans.

(2) Replacement of Money Purchase Benefits. Where

(*a*) an individual ceased, at any time in a calendar year, to have any rights to benefits under a money purchase provision of a registered pension plan or under a deferred profit sharing plan (in this subsection referred to as the "former provision"),

(*b*) benefits became provided at that time to the individual under a defined benefit provision of a registered pension plan (in this subsection referred to as the "current provision") in lieu of benefits under the former provision,

(*c*) the benefits that became provided at that time to the individual under the current provision in respect of the period in the year before that time are attributable to employment with the same employers who made contributions under the former provision in respect of that period on behalf of the individual,

(*d*) no amount was transferred in the year on behalf of the individual from the former provision to a registered retirement savings plan, a registered retirement income fund, a money purchase provision of a registered pension plan or a deferred profit sharing plan,

(*e*) no contributions were made under the former provision by or on behalf of the individual, and no other amounts were allocated under the former provision to the individual, in the year and after that time, and

(*f*) it is reasonable to consider that no excess would, if this subsection did not apply and if the year ended at that time, be determined under any of paragraphs 147(5.1)(*a*) to (*c*), 147.1(8)(*a*) and (*b*) and (9)(*a*) and (*b*) of the Act with respect to the individual for the year,

the following rules apply:

(*g*) each pension credit of the individual under the former provision for the year is nil, and

(*h*) the amount, if any, of the individual's qualifying transfers made in connection with the replacement of the individual's benefits shall be determined under subsection 8303(6) without regard to the portion, if any, of amounts transferred from the former provision to the current provision that can reasonably be considered to relate to an amount that, but for paragraph (*g*), would have been included in determining the individual's pension credit under the former provision for the year.

(3) Past Service Benefits in Year of Past Service Event. Subject to subsection (4), where, as a consequence of a past service event that occurs at a particular time in a calendar year, benefits (in this subsection and subsection (4) referred to as "past service benefits") become provided to an individual under a defined benefit provision of a registered pension plan in respect of a period in the year and before the particular time that, immediately before the past service event, was not pensionable service of the individual under the provision, the following rules apply, except to the extent that the Minister has waived in writing their application in respect of the plan:

(*a*) each pension credit of the individual under the provision for the year shall be determined as if the past service benefits had not become provided to the individual;

(*b*) where the year is 1990, the past service event shall be deemed, for the purposes of this Part, to have occurred immediately after the end of the year;

(*c*) where the year is after 1990, each provisional PSPA of the individual that is associated with the past service event as a consequence of which the past service benefits became provided shall be determined as if the past service event had occurred immediately after the end of the year;

(*d*) where information that is required for the computation of a provisional PSPA referred to in paragraph (*c*) is not determinable until after the time the provisional PSPA is computed, reasonable assumptions shall be made in respect of such information; and

(*e*) subsection 147.1(10) of the Act shall apply in respect of the past service benefits to the extent that that subsection would apply if the past service event had occurred immediately after the end of the year.

(4) Exceptions. Subsection (3) does not apply where

(*a*) the past service benefits become provided in circumstances where subsection (1) or (2) is applicable; or

(*b*) the period in respect of which the past service benefits are provided was not, at any time before the past service event,

(i) pensionable service of the individual under a defined benefit provision of a registered pension plan, or

(ii) a period in respect of which a contribution was made on behalf of, or an amount (other than an amount in respect of earnings of a plan) was allocated to, the individual under a money purchase provision of a registered pension plan or under a deferred profit sharing plan.

(*c*) (Repealed.)

(5) Modified PSPA Calculation. Subject to subsection (10), if

(*a*) lifetime retirement benefits have, as a consequence of a past service event, become provided to an individual under a defined benefit provision of a registered pension plan in respect of one or more qualifying past service periods in relation to the individual and the past service event, and

(*b*) the benefits are considered to be attributable to employment of the individual with a single employer,

the provisional PSPA of the individual with respect to the employer that is associated with the past service event is the amount determined by the formula

$$A + B + C - D$$

where

A is the provisional PSPA that would be determined if

(*a*) this subsection did not apply,

(*b*) all former benefits in relation to the individual and the past service event had ceased to be provided at the time the past service event occurred,

(*c*) all former benefits in relation to the individual and the past service event were considered to be attributable to employment of the individual with the employer, and

(*d*) the value of C in subsection 8303(3) were nil;

B is the total of all amounts each of which is a non-vested PA amount in respect of the individual and the past service event;

C is the total of all amounts each of which is a money purchase transfer in relation to the individual and the past service event; and

D is the amount of the individual's qualifying transfers made in connection with the past service event.

History: S. 8304(5), the portion before paragraph (*a*) was replaced by S.C. 2011, c. 24, s. 92(1), applicable to past service events occurring after March 22, 2011. S. 8304(5), the portion before paragraph (*a*) formerly read:

(5) Where

(5.1) Definitions for Subsection (5). For the purpose of subsection (5), where

(*a*) lifetime retirement benefits (in this subsection referred to as "past service benefits") have, as a consequence of a past service event occurring at a particular time, become provided to an individual under a defined benefit provision of a registered pension plan in respect of a period that

(i) immediately before the particular time, was not pensionable service of the individual under the provision, and

(ii) is, or was, pensionable service of the individual under another defined benefit provision (in this subsection referred to as the "former provision") of a registered pension plan,

(*b*) either

(i) the individual has not, at any time after 1996 and before the particular time, been a member in relation to the former provision,

(ii) the individual ceased, at the particular time, to be a member in relation to the former provision, or

(iii) the past service event is a certifiable past service event and the individual is to cease being a member in relation to the former provision no later than 90 days after the day on which a certification of the Minister is issued for the purposes of subsection 147.1(10) of the Act in respect of the past service benefits, and

(*c*) lifetime retirement benefits to which the individual is or was entitled under the former provision in respect of the period have not been taken into account under subsection (5) as former benefits in determining a provisional PSPA of the individual that is associated with any other past service event,

the following rules apply:

(*d*) the period is a qualifying past service period in relation to the individual and the past service event,

(*e*) lifetime retirement benefits to which the individual is or was entitled under the former provision in respect of the period are former benefits in relation to the individual and the past service event,

(*f*) where subsection 8301(8) has applied in respect of the determination of a pension credit of the individual under the former provision with respect to an employer for a year that includes any part of the period, the amount determined by the formula

$$A - B$$

is a non-vested PA amount in respect of the individual and the past service event, where

A is the amount that would have been the individual's pension credit under the former provision for the year with respect to the employer if subsection 8301(8) had not applied, and

B is the individual's pension credit under the former provision for the year with respect to the employer, and

(*g*) the amount determined by the formula

$$A - B$$

is a money purchase transfer in relation to the individual and the past service event, where

A is the total of all amounts each of which is

(i) an amount that was transferred, at or before the particular time, on behalf of the individual from the former provision to a registered retirement savings plan, a registered retirement income fund, a money purchase provision of a registered pension plan or a defined benefit provision of a registered pension plan that was, at the time of the transfer, a specified multi-employer plan, or

(ii) an amount that is to be paid or otherwise made available under the former provision with respect to the individual after the particular time, other than an amount that is to be transferred to fund the past service benefits or paid directly to the individual,

to the extent that the amount can reasonably be considered to be attributable to benefits in respect of the portion of the period that is after 1989, and

B is the total of all amounts each of which is, in respect of an employer with respect to which a provisional PSPA of the individual that is associated with the past service event is determined under subsection (5), the amount, if any, by which

(i) the portion of the value determined for B in subsection 8303(3), for the purpose of determining the individual's provisional PSPA with respect to the employer, that can reasonably be considered to be attributable to benefits provided in respect of the period

exceeds

Regulations

(ii) the portion of the value determined for A in subsection 8303(3), for the purpose of determining the individual's provisional PSPA with respect to the employer, that can reasonably be considered to be attributable to benefits provided in respect of the period.

(6) Reinstatement of Pre-1997 Benefits. Where lifetime retirement benefits have, as a consequence of a past service event, become provided to an individual under a defined benefit provision of a registered pension plan in respect of a period that

(*a*) was previously pensionable service of the individual under the provision,

(*b*) ceased to be pensionable service of the individual under the provision as a consequence of the individual ceasing before 1997 to be a member in relation to the provision, and

(*c*) has not, at any time after 1996 and before the past service event, been pensionable service of the individual under a defined benefit provision of a registered pension plan,

each provisional PSPA of the individual that is associated with the past service event shall be determined as if all benefits provided to the individual under the provision before 1997 in respect of the period had been provided to the individual under another defined benefit provision of a registered pension plan in relation to which the individual has not, at any time after 1996, been a member.

(7) Two or More Employers. Where

(*a*) lifetime retirement benefits (in this subsection referred to as "past service benefits") provided to an individual under a defined benefit provision of a registered pension plan as a consequence of a past service event are attributable to employment of the individual with two or more employers (each of which is, in this subsection, referred to as a "current employer"), and

(*b*) subsection (5) would, but for paragraph (5)(*b*), apply in respect of the determination of each provisional PSPA of the individual that is associated with the past service event,

each such provisional PSPA shall be determined in accordance with the formula set out in subsection (5), except that

(*c*) in determining the amount A,

(i) the former benefits of the individual shall be considered to be attributable to employment of the individual with the individual's current employers, and

(ii) the portion of the former benefits attributable to employment with each current employer shall be determined by the administrator of the pension plan under which the past service benefits are provided in a manner that is consistent with the association of the past service benefits with each current employer,

(*d*) the amounts B and C shall be included in computing only one provisional PSPA of the individual, as determined by the administrator of the pension plan under which the past service benefits are provided, and

(*e*) the amount D that is deducted in computing the individual's provisional PSPA with respect to a particular employer shall equal such portion of the individual's qualifying transfers made in connection with the past service event as is not deducted in computing the provisional PSPA of the individual with respect to any other employer.

(8) Two or More Employers. (Repealed.)

(9) Specified Multi-Employer Plans. Except in subparagraph (4)(*b*)(i), a reference in this section to a defined benefit provision of a registered pension plan at any time does not, unless expressly provided, include a defined benefit provision of a plan that is, at that time, a specified multi-employer plan.

(10) Individual Pension Plans. If there is a past service event in relation to a defined benefit provision under an individual pension plan, the provisional PSPA of an individual with respect to an employer that is associated with the past service event is the amount, if any, determined by the formula

$$A - B$$

where

A is the greater of

(*a*) the provisional PSPA that would be determined if

(i) this subsection did not apply,

(ii) the value of C in subsection 8303(3) were nil, and

(iii) the value of D in subsection 8304(5) were nil, and

(*b*) the lesser of

(i) the total of

(A) the proportion of the fair market value of all property held in connection with the individual's designated savings arrangements at the time of the past service event, that

(I) the total of all amounts each of which is the duration (measured in years, including any fraction of a year) of a period that is pensionable service of the individual under the provision

is of

(II) the lesser of 35 and the number of years by which the individual's age in whole years at the time of the past service event exceeds 18, and

(B) the individual's unused RRSP deduction room at the end of the year immediately preceding the calendar year that includes the past service event, and

(ii) the actuarial liabilities of the retirement benefits associated with the past service event, determined on the basis of the funding assumptions specified under subsections 8515(6) and (7), at the same effective date as the actuarial valuation that forms the basis for the recommendation referred to in subsection 147.2(2) of the Act that is not earlier than the calendar year of the past service event; and

B is the amount of the individual's qualifying transfers made in connection with the past service event.

History: S. 8304(10) was added by S.C. 2011, c. 24, s. 92(2), applicable to past service events occurring after March 22, 2011.

(11) Individual Pension Plans. Subsection (10) does not apply to a past service event in relation to an individual pension plan if the provisional PSPA of the member determined under subsections 8303(3) and 8304(5) would be nil if no qualifying transfers were made in connection with the past service event, unless it is a past service event that results from the establishment of the plan or from an amendment to the plan to provide additional retirement benefits.

History: S. 8304(11) was added by S.C. 2011, c. 24, s. 92(2), applicable to past service events occurring after March 22, 2011.

8304.1. Pension Adjustment Reversal

(1) Total Pension Adjustment Reversal. For the purpose of subsection 248(1) of the Act, an individual's "total pension adjustment reversal" for a calendar year means the total of all amounts each of which is the pension adjustment reversal (in this Part and Part LXXXIV referred to as "PAR") determined in connection with the individual's termination in the year from a deferred profit sharing plan or from a benefit provision of a registered pension plan.

(2) Termination in 1997. For the purposes of subsection (1) and the description of R in paragraph 8307(2)(*b*), where an individual terminates in 1997 from a deferred profit sharing plan or from a benefit provision of a registered pension plan, the termination is deemed to have occurred in 1998.

(3) PAR — Deferred Profit Sharing Plan. For the purposes of this Part and Part LXXXIV and subject to subsection (12), an individual's PAR determined in connection with the individual's termination from a deferred profit sharing plan is

(*a*) if the conditions in subsection (13) are satisfied with respect to the termination, the total of all amounts each of which is an amount

(i) included in determining a pension credit of the individual under the plan, and

(ii) to which the individual has ceased, at or before the time of the termination, to have any rights,

but does not include any amount to which a spouse or common-law partner or former spouse or common-law partner of the individual has acquired rights as a consequence of a breakdown of their marriage or common-law partnership; and

(*b*) in any other case, nil.

(4) PAR — Money Purchase Provision. For the purposes of this Part and Part LXXXIV and subject to subsection (12), an individual's PAR determined in connection with the individual's termination from a money purchase provision of a registered pension plan is

(*a*) if the conditions in subsection (14) are satisfied with respect to the termination, the total of all amounts each of which is an amount

(i) included in determining a pension credit of the individual under the provision, and

(ii) to which the individual has ceased, at or before the time of the termination, to have any rights,

but does not include any amount to which a spouse or common-law partner or former spouse or common-law partner of the individual has acquired rights as a consequence of a breakdown of their marriage or common-law partnership; and

(*b*) in any other case, nil.

(5) PAR — Defined Benefit Provision. For the purposes of this Part and Part LXXXIV and subject to subsections (6) and (12), an individual's PAR determined in connection with the individual's termination from a defined benefit provision of a registered pension plan is

(*a*) where the conditions in subsection (14) are satisfied with respect to the termination, the amount determined by the formula

$$A + B - C - D$$

where

A is the total of all amounts each of which is, in respect of a particular year that is the year in which the termination occurs or that is a preceding year, the lesser of

(i) the total of all amounts each of which is the pension credit of the individual under the provision for the particular year with respect to an employer, and

(ii) the RRSP dollar limit for the year following the particular year,

B is the total of all amounts each of which is the portion of the grossed-up amount of a provisional PSPA (other than a provisional PSPA determined in accordance with subsection 8303(8)) of the individual that is associated with a past service event occurring before the time of the termination that can reasonably be considered to be attributable to benefits provided under the provision,

C is the total of all amounts each of which is a specified distribution made in respect of the individual and the provision at or before the time of the termination, and

D is the total of all amounts each of which is a PA transfer amount in relation to the individual's termination from the provision; and

(*b*) in any other case, nil.

(6) Defined Benefit Pension Credits. For the purpose of subparagraph (i) of the description of A in paragraph (5)(*a*), in determining an individual's PAR in connection with the individual's termination from a defined benefit provision of a registered pension plan,

Regulations

(*a*) the individual's pension credits under the provision for the year in which the termination occurs shall be determined without regard to benefits provided after the time of the termination; and

(*b*) the individual's pension credits under the provision for each year in which the plan was a specified multi-employer plan are deemed to be nil.

(7) Grossed-up PSPA Amount. For the purposes of the descriptions of B in subsection 8303(7.1) and paragraph (5)(*a*), the grossed-up amount of an individual's provisional PSPA with respect to an employer that is associated with a past service event is the amount that would be the provisional PSPA if

(*a*) the values of C and D in subsections 8303(3) and 8304(5) were nil; and

(*b*) the words "at the time the past service event occurred" in paragraph (*b*) of the description of A in subsection 8304(5) were read as "immediately before the time the past service event occurred".

(8) Specified Distribution. For the purpose of the description of C in paragraph (5)(*a*), an amount paid under a defined benefit provision of a registered pension plan with respect to an individual is a specified distribution made in respect of the individual and the provision at the time it is paid, except to the extent that

(*a*) it can reasonably be considered to be a payment of benefits in respect of any period before 1990;

(*b*) it is transferred to another registered pension plan (other than a plan that is, at the time of the transfer, a specified multi-employer plan) in accordance with subsection 147.3(3) of the Act;

(*c*) it is transferred to another defined benefit provision of the plan where the transfer would, if the provision and the other provision were in separate registered pension plans, constitute a transfer in accordance with subsection 147.3(3) of the Act;

(*d*) it is a payment in respect of an actuarial surplus;

(*e*) it is

(i) a return of contributions made by the individual under the provision, where the contributions are returned pursuant to an amendment to the plan that also reduces the future contributions that would otherwise be required to be made under the provision by members of the plan and that does not reduce benefits provided under the provision, or

(ii) a payment of interest in respect of contributions that are returned as described in subparagraph (i);

(*f*) it can reasonably be considered to be a payment of benefits provided in respect of a period throughout which the plan was a specified multi-employer plan; or

(*g*) it can reasonably be considered to be a payment of benefits provided in respect of a period throughout which the individual was employed outside Canada, where the benefits became provided as a consequence of a past service event in respect of which the Minister had consented to the application of subsection 8303(10) for the purpose of determining the individual's provisional PSPAs.

(9) Property Made Available. Where property held in connection with a particular defined benefit provision of a pension plan is made available at any time to provide benefits with respect to an individual under another benefit provision of a pension plan, subsection (8) applies as if the amount of the property had been paid under the particular provision at that time with respect to the individual.

(10) PA Transfer Amount. Where

(*a*) an individual has terminated, at a particular time after 1996, from a defined benefit provision (in this subsection referred to as the "former provision") of a registered pension plan,

(*b*) lifetime retirement benefits (in this subsection referred to as the "past service benefits") have, as a consequence of a past service event occurring at or before the particular time, become provided to the individual under another defined benefit provision of a registered pension plan in respect of a period that is or was pensionable service of the individual under the former provision, and

(*c*) lifetime retirement benefits to which the individual is or was entitled under the former provision in respect of the period have, under subsection 8304(5), been taken into account as former benefits in determining a provisional PSPA of the individual that is associated with the past service event,

for the purposes of subsection 8406(5) and the description of D in paragraph (5)(a), the lesser of

(*d*) the portion of the value determined for A in subsection 8303(3), for the purpose of determining the provisional PSPA, that can reasonably be considered to be attributable to the past service benefits, and

(*e*) the portion of the value determined for B in subsection 8303(3), for the purpose of determining the provisional PSPA, that can reasonably be considered to be attributable to the former benefits

is a PA transfer amount in relation to the individual's termination from the former provision.

(11) Special 1997 PA Transfer Amount. Where

(*a*) an individual has terminated, at a particular time in 1997, from a particular defined benefit provision of a registered pension plan,

(*b*) lifetime retirement benefits (in this subsection referred to as the "past service benefits") have, as a consequence of a past service event that occurred after the particular time and before 1998, become provided to the individual under the particular provision, or under another defined benefit provision of a registered pension plan, in respect of a period that was previously pensionable service of the individual under the particular provision, and

(*c*) lifetime retirement benefits to which the individual was previously entitled under the particular provision in respect of the period have, under subsection 8304(5), been taken into account as former benefits in determining a provisional PSPA of the individual that is associated with the past service event,

for the purposes of subsection 8406(5) and the description of D in paragraph (5)(a), the lesser of

(*d*) the portion of the value determined for A in subsection 8303(3), for the purpose of determining the provisional PSPA, that can reasonably be considered to be attributable to the past service benefits, and

(*e*) the portion of the value determined for B in subsection 8303(3), for the purpose of determining the provisional PSPA, that can reasonably be considered to be attributable to the former benefits

is a PA transfer amount in relation to the individual's termination from the particular provision at the particular time.

(12) Subsequent Membership. Where an individual has ceased at a particular time to be a member in relation to a deferred profit sharing plan or a benefit provision of a registered pension plan and subsequently becomes a member in relation to the plan or the provision, as the case may be, the following rules apply in determining the individual's PAR in connection with any subsequent termination from the plan or the provision, as the case may be:

(*a*) in the case of a deferred profit sharing plan or money purchase provision, any amounts included in a pension credit of the individual under the plan or provision because of an allocation to the individual before the particular time shall be disregarded; and

(*b*) in the case of a defined benefit provision,

(i) the value of A in paragraph (5)(*a*) shall be determined without regard to any pension credit, or portion of a pension credit, that is attributable to benefits provided under the provision before the particular time,

(ii) the value of B in paragraph (5)(*a*) shall be determined without regard to any provisional PSPA that is associated with a past service event that occurred before the particular time, and

(iii) the value of C in paragraph (5)(a) shall be determined without regard to any specified distribution (as defined in subsection (8)) made at or before the particular time.

(13) Termination Conditions — Deferred Profit Sharing Plan. For the purpose of paragraph (3)(*a*), the conditions with respect to an individual's termination from a deferred profit sharing plan are the following:

(*a*) the termination occurs after 1996 and otherwise than because of death; and

(*b*) no payments described in subparagraph 147(2)(*k*)(v) of the Act have been made out of or under the plan with respect to the individual.

(14) Termination Conditions — Registered Pension Plan. For the purposes of paragraphs (4)(*a*) and (5)(*a*), the conditions with respect to an individual's termination from a benefit provision of a registered pension plan are the following:

(*a*) the termination occurs after 1996 and otherwise than because of death; and

(*b*) no retirement benefits have been paid under the provision with respect to the individual (other than retirement benefits paid with respect to the individual's spouse or common-law partner or former spouse or common-law partner as a consequence of a breakdown of their marriage or common-law partnership).

(15) Breakdown of Marriage or Common-law Partnership. Where

(*a*) before a member terminates from a defined benefit provision of a registered pension plan, there has been a breakdown of the member's marriage or common-law partnership, and

(*b*) as a consequence of the breakdown,

(i) the member has ceased to have rights to all or a portion of the benefits provided under the provision with respect to the member, and

(ii) an individual who is the member's spouse or common-law partner or former spouse or common-law partner has acquired rights under the provision in respect of those benefits,

for the purpose of subsection (8),

(*c*) any amount paid under the provision with respect to the rights acquired by the individual (other than a single amount paid under the provision at or before the time of the member's termination in full satisfaction of the rights acquired by the individual) is deemed not to have been paid with respect to the member, and

(*d*) unless a single amount has been paid under the provision at or before the time of the member's termination in full satisfaction of the rights acquired by the individual, a single amount equal to the present value (at the time the member terminates from the provision) of the benefits to which the member has ceased to have rights as a consequence of the breakdown is deemed to have been paid to the member at that time under the provision in full satisfaction of those benefits.

8305. Association of Benefits with Employers

(1) Where, for the purposes of this Part, it is necessary to determine the portion of an amount of benefits provided with respect to a member of a registered pension plan under a defined benefit provision of the plan that is attributable to the member's employment with a particular employer, the following rules apply, subject to subsection 8308(7):

(*a*) the determination shall be made by the plan administrator;

(*b*) benefits provided as a consequence of services rendered by the member to an employer who participates in the plan shall be regarded as attributable to employment with that employer, whether the benefits become provided at the time the services are rendered or at a subsequent time; and

(*c*) the determination shall be made in a manner that

Regulations

(i) is reasonable in the circumstances,

(ii) is not inconsistent with such determinations made previously, and

(iii) results in the full amount of benefits being attributed to employment with one or more employers who participate in the plan.

(2) Where the administrator of a registered pension plan does not comply with the requirements of subsection (1) in connection with the determination of an amount under this Part at any time,

(*a*) the plan becomes, at that time, a revocable plan; and

(*b*) the Minister shall make any determinations referred to in subsection (1) that the administrator fails to make, or fails to make in accordance with that subsection.

Regulations

8306. Exemption from Certification

(1) For the purposes of subsection 147.1(10) of the Act as it applies in respect of a past service event and the benefits provided under a defined benefit provision of a registered pension plan with respect to a particular member of the plan, a certification of the Minister is not required where

(*a*) each provisional PSPA of the member that is associated with the past service event is nil;

(*b*) the conditions in subsection (2) or (3) are satisfied;

(*c*) the conditions in subsection (2) or (3) are substantially satisfied and the Minister waives in writing the requirement for certification;

(*c*.1) paragraph 8303(5)(*f*.1) was applicable in determining the provisional PSPA of the member that is associated with the past service event; or

(*d*) the past service event is deemed by paragraph 8304(3)(*b*) to have occurred immediately after the end of 1990.

(2) The following are conditions for the purposes of paragraphs (1)(*b*) and (*c*) and 8303(5)(*g*):

(*a*) there are more than 9 active members under the provision;

(*b*) no more than 25 per cent of the active members under the provision are specified active members under the provision;

(*c*) for all or substantially all of the active members under the provision, the amount of lifetime retirement benefits accrued under the provision has increased as a consequence of the past service event;

(*d*) where there is a specified active member under the provision,

(i) the amounts C and D in subparagraph (ii) are greater than nil, and

(ii) the amount determined by the formula A/C does not exceed the amount determined by the formula B/D

where

A is the aggregate of all amounts each of which is the amount of lifetime retirement benefits accrued under the provision, immediately after the past service event, to a specified active member under the provision,

B is the aggregate of all amounts each of which is the amount of lifetime retirement benefits accrued under the provision, immediately after the past service event, to an active member (other than a specified active member) under the provision,

C is the aggregate of all amounts each of which is the amount of lifetime retirement benefits accrued under the provision, immediately before the past service event, to a specified active member under the provision, and

D is the aggregate of all amounts each of which is the amount of lifetime retirement benefits accrued under the provision, immediately before the past service event, to an active member (other than a specified active member) under the provision; and

(*e*) the benefits provided under the provision as a consequence of the past service event to members of the plan who are not active members under the provision are not more advantageous than such benefits provided to active members under the provision.

(3) The following are conditions for the purposes of paragraphs (1)(*b*) and (*c*):

(*a*) the past service event consists of the establishment of the provision;

(*b*) there are more than 9 active members under the provision;

(*c*) no more than 25 per cent of the active members under the provision are specified active members under the provision;

(*d*) the member is not a specified active member under the provision;

(*e*) if the member is not an active member under the provision, for each of the 5 years immediately preceding the calendar year in which the past service event occurs,

(i) the member was not connected at any time in the year with an employer who participates in the plan, and

(ii) the aggregate of all amounts each of which is the remuneration of the member for the year from an employer who participates in the plan did not exceed $2^1/_2$ times the Year's Maximum Pensionable Earnings for the year; and

(*f*) the aggregate of all amounts each of which is a provisional PSPA of the member that is associated with the past service event does not exceed $^7/_2$ of the money purchase limit for the year in which the past service event occurs.

(4) For the purposes of this section as it applies in respect of a past service event,

(*a*) a member of a pension plan is an active member under a defined benefit provision of the plan if

(i) lifetime retirement benefits accrue under the provision to the member in respect of a period that immediately follows the time the past service event occurs, or

(ii) the member is entitled, immediately after the time the past service event occurs, to lifetime retirement benefits under the provision in respect of a period before that time and it is reasonable to expect, at that time, that lifetime retirement benefits will accrue under the provision to the member in respect of a period after that time; and

(*b*) an active member under a defined benefit provision of a pension plan is a specified active member under the provision if

(i) the member is connected, at the time of the past service event, with an employer who participates in the plan, or

(ii) it is reasonable to expect, at the time of the past service event, that the aggregate of all amounts each of which is the remuneration of the member for the calendar year in which the past service event occurs from an employer who participates in the plan will exceed $2^1/_2$ times the Year's Maximum Pensionable Earnings for the year.

8307. Certification in Respect of Past Service Events

(1) Application for Certification. Application for a certification of the Minister for the purposes of subsection 147.1(10) of the Act shall be made in prescribed form by the administrator of the registered pension plan to which the certification relates.

(2) Prescribed Condition. For the purposes of subsection 147.1(10) of the Act in respect of a past service event and benefits with respect to a particular member of a registered pension plan, the prescribed condition is that, at the particular time the Minister issues the certification,

(*a*) the aggregate of all amounts each of which is the member's provisional PSPA with respect to an employer that is associated with the past service event

does not exceed

(*b*) the amount determined by the formula

$$\$8,000 + A + B + C - D + R$$

where

A is the member's unused RRSP deduction room at the end of the year immediately preceding the calendar year (in this paragraph referred to as the "particular year") that includes the particular time,

B is the amount of the member's qualifying withdrawals made for the purposes of the certification, determined as of the particular time,

C is the amount of the member's PSPA withdrawals for the particular year, determined as of the particular time,

D is the aggregate of all amounts each of which is the accumulated PSPA of the member for the particular year with respect to an employer, determined as of the particular time, and

R is the total of all amounts each of which is a PAR determined in connection with the individual's termination in the particular year from a deferred profit sharing plan, or from a benefit provision of a registered pension plan, and in respect of which an information return has been filed under section 8402.01 with the Minister before the particular time.

(3) Qualifying Withdrawals. For the purposes of paragraph (5)(*a*) and the description of B in paragraph (2)(*b*), the amount of an individual's qualifying withdrawals made for the purposes of a certification in respect of a past service event, determined as of a particular time, is the lesser of

(*a*) the aggregate of all amounts each of which is such portion of an amount withdrawn by the individual from a registered retirement savings plan under which the individual was the annuitant (within the meaning assigned by subsection 146(1) of the Act) at the time of the withdrawal as

(i) is eligible, pursuant to subsection (4), to be designated for the purposes of the certification, and

(ii) is designated by the individual for the purposes of the certification by filing a prescribed form containing prescribed information with the Minister before the particular time, and

(*b*) the amount, if any, by which

(i) the aggregate of all amounts each of which is the provisional PSPA of the individual with respect to an employer that is associated with the past service event

exceeds

(ii) the amount, positive or negative, determined by the formula

$$A + C - D + R$$

where A, C, D and R have the same values as they have at the particular time for the purposes of the formula in paragraph (2)(*b*).

Interpretation Bulletins: *Secondary* — IT-124R6 Contributions to registered retirement savings plans.

(4) Eligibility of Withdrawn Amount for Designation. An amount withdrawn by an individual from a registered retirement savings plan is eligible to be designated for the purposes of a certification except to the extent that the following rules provide otherwise:

(*a*) the amount is not eligible to be designated if the amount was

(i) withdrawn from a registered retirement savings plan in a calendar year other than the year in which the designation would be filed with the Minister or either of the 2 immediately preceding calendar years, or

(ii) withdrawn in circumstances that entitle the individual to a deduction under paragraph 60(*l*) of the Act; and

(*b*) the amount is not eligible to be designated to the extent that the amount was

(i) designated by the individual for the purposes of any other certification, or

(ii) deducted under section 60.2 or subsection 146(8.2) or 147.3(13.1) of the Act in computing the individual's income for any taxation year.

Regulations

(5) PSPA Withdrawals. For the purposes of the description of C in paragraph (2)(*b*) and the description of G in the definition "net past service pension adjustment" in subsection 146(1) of the Act, the amount of an individual's PSPA withdrawals for a calendar year, determined as of a particular time, is

(*a*) if the Minister has issued, in the year and before the particular time, a certification for the purposes of subsection 147.1(10) of the Act with respect to the individual, the aggregate of all amounts each of which is the amount of the individual's qualifying withdrawals made for the purposes of a certification that the Minister has issued in the year and before the particular time; and

(*b*) in any other case, nil.

Interpretation Bulletins: *Secondary* — IT-124R6 Contributions to registered retirement savings plans.

(6) Prescribed Withdrawal. For the purposes of subsection (7) and subsections 146(8.2) and 147.3(13.1) of the Act, a prescribed withdrawal is the portion of an amount withdrawn by an individual from a registered retirement savings plan under which the individual is the annuitant (within the meaning assigned by subsection 146(1) of the Act) that is designated in accordance with subparagraph (3)(*a*)(ii) for the purposes of a certification in respect of the individual.

Interpretation Bulletins: *Secondary* — IT-124R6 Contributions to registered retirement savings plans; IT-528 Transfers of funds between registered plans.

(7) Prescribed Premium. For the purpose of subsection 146(6.1) of the Act, a premium paid by a taxpayer under a registered retirement savings plan under which the taxpayer is the annuitant (within the meaning assigned by subsection 146(1) of the Act) at the time the premium is paid is a prescribed premium for a particular taxation year of the taxpayer where the following conditions are satisfied:

(*a*) the taxpayer withdrew an amount (in this subsection referred to as the "withdrawn amount") in the particular year from a registered retirement savings plan for the purposes of a certification in respect of a past service event;

(*b*) all or part of the withdrawn amount is a prescribed withdrawal pursuant to subsection (6);

(*c*) it is subsequently determined that

(i) as a consequence of reasonable error, the taxpayer withdrew a greater amount than necessary for the purposes of the certification, or

(ii) as a consequence of the application of paragraph 147.1(3)(*b*) of the Act, it was not necessary for the taxpayer to withdraw any amount;

(*d*) the premium is paid by the taxpayer in the 12-month period immediately following the time the determination referred to in paragraph (*c*) is made;

(*e*) the amount of the premium does not exceed such portion of the withdrawn amount as is a prescribed withdrawal pursuant to subsection (6) and is determined to have been an unnecessary withdrawal;

(*f*) the taxpayer files with the Minister, on or before the day on or before which the taxpayer is required (or would be required if tax under Part I of the Act were payable by the taxpayer for the taxation year in which the taxpayer pays the premium) by section 150 of the Act to file a return of income for the taxation year in which the taxpayer pays the premium, a written notice in which the taxpayer designates the premium as a recontribution of all or a portion of the withdrawn amount; and

(*g*) the taxpayer has not designated, pursuant to paragraph (*f*), any other premium as a recontribution of all or a portion of the withdrawn amount.

Interpretation Bulletins: *Secondary* — IT-124R6 Contributions to registered retirement savings plans.

8308. Special Rules

(1) Benefits Provided Before Registration. For the purposes of this Part and subsection 147.1(10) of the Act, benefits that became provided under a defined benefit provision of a pension plan before the day as of which the plan becomes a registered pension plan shall be deemed to have become provided as a consequence of an event occurring on that day and not to have been provided before that day.

(2) Prescribed Amount for Connected Persons. Where

(*a*) at any particular time in a calendar year after 1990,

(i) an individual becomes a member of a registered pension plan, or

(ii) lifetime retirement benefits commence to accrue to the individual under a defined benefit provision of a registered pension plan following a period in which lifetime retirement benefits did not accrue to the individual,

(*b*) the individual is connected at the particular time, or was connected at any time after 1989, with an employer who participates in the plan for the benefit of the individual,

(*c*) the individual did not have a pension adjustment for 1990 that was greater than nil, and

(*d*) this subsection did not apply before the particular time to prescribe an amount with respect to the individual,

an amount equal to the lesser of $11,500 and 18% of the individual's earned income (as defined in subsection 146(1) of the Act) for 1990 is prescribed with respect to the individual for the calendar year that includes the particular time for the purposes of the descriptions of B in the definitions "RRSP deduction limit" and "unused RRSP deduction room" in subsection 146(1) of the Act and the description of B in paragraph 204.2(1.1)(*b*) of the Act.

Interpretation Bulletins: *Secondary* — IT-124R6 Contributions to registered retirement savings plans.

(3) Remuneration for Prior Years. Where an individual who is entitled to benefits under a defined benefit provision of a registered pension plan receives remuneration at a particular time in a particular calendar year no part of which is pensionable service of the individual under the provision and the remuneration is treated for the purpose of determining benefits under the provision as if it were remuneration received in one or more calendar years preceding the particular calendar year for services rendered in those preceding years, the following rules apply:

(*a*) such portion of the remuneration as is treated under the provision as if it were remuneration received in a preceding calendar year for services rendered in that preceding year shall be deemed, for the purpose of determining, as of the particular time and any subsequent time, a redetermined benefit entitlement of the individual under the provision, to have been received in that preceding year for services rendered in that preceding year; and

(*b*) the pension credit of the individual for the particular year under the provision with respect to an employer is the aggregate of

(i) the amount that would otherwise be the individual's pension credit for the particular year, and

(ii) the amount that would, if the payment of the remuneration were a past service event, be the provisional PSPA (or a reasonable estimate thereof determined in a manner acceptable to the Minister) of the individual with respect to the employer that is associated with the payment of the remuneration.

(4) Period of Reduced Services — Retroactive Benefits. Where,

(*a*) as a consequence of a past service event, retirement benefits (in this subsection referred to as "retroactive benefits") become provided under a defined benefit provision of a registered pension plan (other than a plan that is a specified multi-employer plan) to an individual in respect of a period of reduced services of the individual,

(*b*) the period of reduced services was not, before the past service event, pensionable service of the individual under the provision, and

(*c*) the past service event occurs on or before April 30 of the year immediately following the calendar year in which ends the complete period of reduced services of the individual that includes the period of reduced services,

the following rules apply:

(*d*) each pension adjustment of the individual with respect to an employer for a year before the calendar year in which the past service event occurs shall be deemed to be, and to always have been, the aggregate of

(i) the amount that would otherwise be the individual's pension adjustment with respect to the employer for the year, and

(ii) such portion of the provisional PSPA of the individual with respect to the employer that is associated with the past service event as may reasonably be considered to be attributable to the provision of retroactive benefits in respect of the year, and

(*e*) each provisional PSPA of the individual with respect to an employer that is associated with the past service event shall be deemed (except for the purposes of this subsection) to be such portion of the amount that would otherwise be the individual's provisional PSPA as may reasonably be considered not to be attributable to the provision of retroactive benefits.

Information Circulars: IC 98-2 Prescribed compensation for registered pension plans.

(5) Period of Reduced Services — Retroactive Contributions. Where

(*a*) a contribution (in this subsection referred to as a "retroactive contribution") is made by an individual, or by an employer with respect to the individual, under a money purchase provision of a registered pension plan in respect of a period in a particular calendar year that is a period of reduced services of the individual, and

(*b*) the retroactive contribution is made after the particular year and on or before April 30 of the year immediately following the calendar year in which ends the complete period of reduced services of the individual that includes the period of reduced services,

the following rules apply:

(*c*) each pension adjustment of the individual for the particular year with respect to an employer shall be deemed to be, and to always have been, the amount that it would have been had the retroactive contribution been made at the end of the particular year, and

(*d*) the retroactive contribution shall be deemed, for the purpose of determining pension adjustments of the individual for any year after the particular year, to have been made at the end of the particular year and not to have been made at any subsequent time.

Information Circulars: IC 98-2 Prescribed compensation for registered pension plans.

(6) Commitment to Make Retroactive Contributions. Where

(*a*) an individual enters into a written commitment to make a contribution under a money purchase provision of a registered pension plan,

(*b*) the commitment is made to the administrator of the plan or to an employer who participates in the plan, and

(*c*) the rules in subsection (5) would apply in respect of the contribution if the contribution were made at the time at which the individual enters into the commitment,

the following rules apply for the purposes of this Part:

(*d*) the individual shall be deemed to have made the contribution to the plan at the time the individual enters into the commitment,

(*e*) if the individual subsequently pays all or a part of the contribution to the plan pursuant to the commitment, the amount paid to the plan is, for the purposes of paragraphs 8301(4)(*a*) and (8)(*e*), a contribution described in this paragraph,

(*f*) any contribution that an employer is required to make under the money purchase provision conditional on the individual making the contribution that the individual has committed to pay and in respect of which subsection (5) would apply if the contribution were made by the employer at the time the individual enters into the commitment shall be deemed to have been made by the employer at that time, and

Regulations

(*g*) if an employer subsequently pays to the plan all or a part of a contribution in respect of which paragraph (*f*) applies, the amount paid to the plan is, for the purposes of paragraph 8301(4)(*a*), a contribution described in this paragraph.

Information Circulars: IC 98-2 Prescribed compensation for registered pension plans.

(7) Loaned Employees. Where, pursuant to an arrangement between an employer (in this subsection referred to as the "lending employer") who is a participating employer in relation to a pension plan and an employer (in this subsection referred to as the "borrowing employer") who, but for this subsection, would not be a participating employer in relation to the plan,

(*a*) an employee of the lending employer renders services to the borrowing employer for which the employee receives remuneration from the borrowing employer, and

(*b*) while the employee renders services to the borrowing employer, benefits continue to accrue under a defined benefit provision of the plan to the employee, or the lending employer continues to make contributions under a money purchase provision of the plan with respect to the employee,

the following rules apply:

(*c*) for the purpose of the definition "participating employer" in subsection 147.1(1) of the Act as it applies in respect of the plan, the borrowing employer is a prescribed employer,

(*d*) the determination, for the purposes of this Part, of the portion of the employee's benefit accrual under a defined benefit provision of the plan in respect of a year that can reasonably be considered to be attributable to the employee's employment with each of the lending and borrowing employers shall be made with regard to the remuneration received by the employee for the year from each employer, and

(*e*) such portion of the contributions made under a money purchase provision of the plan by the lending employer as may reasonably be considered to be in respect of the employee's remuneration from the borrowing employer shall be deemed, for the purposes of this Part, to be contributions made by the borrowing employer.

(8) Successor Plans. Notwithstanding any other provisions of this Part, other than section 8310, where

(*a*) all benefits with respect to an individual under a defined benefit provision (in this subsection referred to as the "former provision") of a registered pension plan are replaced in a calendar year by identical benefits under a defined benefit provision of another registered pension plan,

(*b*) the replacement of benefits is consequent on a transfer of the individual's employment from one employer (in this subsection referred to as the "former employer") to another employer (in this subsection referred to as the "successor employer"), and

(*c*) the Minister consents in writing to the application of this subsection in respect of that replacement of benefits,

the individual's pension adjustments for the year with respect to the former employer and the successor employer shall be the amounts that they would be if all benefits with respect to the individual under the former provision had been attributable to employment with the successor employer and not to employment with the former employer.

(9) Special Downsizing Benefits. Where

(*a*) lifetime retirement benefits that do not comply with the condition in paragraph 8503(3)(*a*) are provided to an individual under a defined benefit provision of a registered pension plan, and

(*b*) the benefits are permissible only by reason of subsection 8505(3),

each pension credit of the individual under the provision and each provisional PSPA of the individual shall be determined without regard to the lifetime retirement benefits.

8308.1. Foreign Plans

(1) Definition. In this section, "foreign plan" means a plan or arrangement (determined without regard to subsection 207.6(5) of the Act) that would, but for paragraph (l) of the definition "retirement compensation arrangement" in subsection 248(1) of the Act, be a retirement compensation arrangement.

(2) Pension Credit. Subject to subsections (3) to (4.1), the pension credit of an individual for a calendar year with respect to an employer under a foreign plan is

(*a*) where paragraph (*b*) does not apply, nil; and

(*b*) where

(i) the year is 1992 or a subsequent year,

(ii) the individual became entitled in the year, either absolutely or contingently, to benefits under the foreign plan in respect of services rendered to the employer in a period throughout which the individual was resident in Canada and rendered services to the employer that were primarily services rendered in Canada or services rendered in connection with a business carried on by the employer in Canada, or a combination of those services,

(iii) the individual continued to be entitled at the end of the year, either absolutely or contingently, to all or part of the benefits, and

(iv) either

(A) no contribution was made under the foreign plan in the year in respect of the individual, except where

(I) no contribution was made because the foreign plan had an actuarial surplus, and

(II) had a contribution been made in respect of the benefits referred to in subparagraph (ii), it would have been a resident's contribution (as defined in subsection 207.6(5.1) of the Act), or

(B) a contribution that is not a resident's contribution was made under the foreign plan in the year in respect of the individual,

the lesser of

(v) the amount, if any, by which 18% of the individual's resident compensation from the employer for the year exceeds the PA offset for the year, and

(vi) the amount by which the money purchase limit for the year exceeds the PA offset for the year.

(2.1) Pension Credit — Tax Treaty. For the purposes of applying subsection (2) in determining an individual's pension credit for a calendar year with respect to an employer under a foreign plan, if any contributions made to, or benefits accruing under, the plan in respect of the individual and the calendar year benefit from the application of paragraph 8 of Article XVIII of the *Canada–United States Tax Convention* signed at Washington on September 26, 1980, or from the application of a similar provision in another tax treaty,

(*a*) subparagraph (2)(*b*)(ii) shall be read without reference to the words "was resident in Canada and"; and

(*b*) the portion of subsection (2) after subparagraph (*b*)(iv) shall be read as "the lesser of the money purchase limit for the year and 18% of the individual's resident compensation from the employer for the year".

History: S. 8308.1(2.1) was added by S.C. 2009, c. 2, s. 115(1), applicable in determining pension credits for the 2009 and subsequent calendar years.

(3) Pension Credit — Alternative Determination. Subject to subsection (4), where the Minister has, on the written application of an employer, approved in writing a method for determining pension credits for a year with respect to the employer under a foreign plan, the pension credits shall be determined in accordance with that method.

(4) Pension Credits for 1992, 1993 and 1994. The pension credit of an individual for 1992, 1993 or 1994 with respect to an employer under a foreign plan is the lesser of

(*a*) the amount that would, but for this subsection, be determined as the pension credit for the year, and

(*b*) the amount, if any, by which the lesser of

(i) 18% of the amount that would be the individual's compensation from the employer for the year if the definition "compensation" in subsection 147.1(1) of the Act were read without reference to paragraphs (*b*) and (*c*) of that definition, and

(ii) the money purchase limit for the year

exceeds the total of

(iii) $1,000, and

(iv) the amount that would be the pension adjustment of the individual for the year with respect to the employer if subsection 8301(1) were read without reference to paragraph (*b*) of that subsection.

(4.1) Pension Credits — 1996 to 2002. For the purpose of determining the pension credit of an individual for a calendar year after 1995 and before 2003 with respect to an employer under a foreign plan, subparagraph (2)(*b*)(vi) shall be read as

"(vi) the money purchase limit for the year."

(5) Foreign Plan PSPA. Subject to subsection (6), where the benefits to which an individual is entitled, either absolutely or contingently, under a foreign plan are modified, the foreign plan PSPA of the individual with respect to an employer associated with the modification of benefits is the amount, if any, by which

(*a*) the total of all amounts each of which is the amount that, if this section were read without reference to subsection (3), would be the pension credit of the individual with respect to the employer under the foreign plan for a calendar year before the year in which the individual's benefits are modified

exceeds the total of all amounts each of which is

(*b*) the pension credit of the individual with respect to the employer under the foreign plan for a calendar year before the year in which the individual's benefits are modified, or

(*c*) the foreign plan PSPA of the individual with respect to the employer associated with a previous modification of the individual's benefits under the foreign plan.

(6) Foreign Plan PSPA — Alternative Determination. Where the Minister has, on the written application of an employer, approved in writing a method for determining the foreign plan PSPA of an individual with respect to the employer associated with a modification of the individual's benefits under a foreign plan, the individual's foreign plan PSPA shall be determined in accordance with that method.

8308.2. Prescribed Amount for Member of Foreign Plan

(1) Prescribed Amount. For the purposes of the descriptions of B in the definitions "RRSP deduction limit" and "unused RRSP deduction room" in subsection 146(1) of the Act and the description of B in paragraph 204.2(1.1)(*b*) of the Act, there is prescribed in respect of an individual for a calendar year the lesser of the money purchase limit for the preceding calendar year (in this section referred to as the "service year") and the amount determined by subsection (2), if the individual

(*a*) rendered services to an employer (excluding services that were primarily services rendered in Canada or services rendered in connection with a business carried on by the employer in Canada, or a combination of those services) throughout a period in the service year in which the individual was resident in Canada;

(*b*) became entitled, either absolutely or contingently, in the service year to benefits under a foreign plan (as defined in subsection 8308.1(1)) in respect of the services; and

(*c*) continued to be entitled at the end of the service year, either absolutely or contingently, to all or part of the benefits.

History: S. 8308.2(1) was replaced by S.C. 2009, c. 2, s. 116(1), applicable in determining prescribed amounts for the 2009 and subsequent calendar years except that in determining prescribed amounts for 2009, the amount of the money purchase limit for 2008 is deemed to be reduced by $600. S. 8308.2(1) formerly read:

(1) Where

(*a*) throughout a period in a particular calendar year after 1992 an individual resident in Canada rendered services to an employer, other than services that were primarily services rendered in Canada or services rendered in connection with a business carried on by the employer in Canada, or a combination of those services,

Regulations

(*b*) the individual became entitled in the particular year, either absolutely or contingently, to benefits under a pension plan that is a foreign plan (as defined in subsection 8308.1(1)) in respect of the services, and

(*c*) the individual continued to be entitled at the end of the particular year, either absolutely or contingently, to all or part of the benefits,

subject to subsection (2), there is prescribed in respect of the individual for the year following the particular year, for the purposes of the descriptions of B in the definitions "RRSP deduction limit" and "unused RRSP deduction room" in subsection 146(1) of the Act and the description of B in paragraph 204.2(1.1)(*b*) of the Act, the lesser of

(*d*) the amount by which the money purchase limit for the particular year exceeds the PA offset for the particular year, and

(*e*) 10% of the portion of the individual's resident compensation from the employer for the particular year that is attributable to services rendered by the individual to the employer in periods throughout which the individual rendered services described in paragraph (*a*).

(2) Prescribed Amount. The amount determined for the purpose of subsection (1) is,

(*a*) if the only benefits to which the individual became entitled in the service year under the foreign plan were provided under one or more money purchase provisions of the foreign plan, the total of all amounts each of which is the individual's pension credit for the service year with respect to the employer under a money purchase provision of the foreign plan, determined

(i) as though the foreign plan were a registered pension plan,

(ii) without regard to any contributions made by the individual, and

(iii) if, under the laws of the country in which the foreign plan is established, any contributions made after the end of the service year are treated as having been made in the service year, as though those contributions were made in the service year and not when the contributions were actually made; and

(*b*) in any other case, the greater of

(i) the total that would be determined under paragraph (*a*) if the individual had not become entitled in the service year to any benefits under a defined benefit provision of the foreign plan, and

(ii) 10% of the portion of the individual's resident compensation from the employer for the service year that is attributable to services rendered to the employer and included under paragraph (1)(*a*).

History: S. 8308.2(2) was replaced by S.C. 2009, c. 2, s. 116(1), applicable in determining prescribed amounts for the 2009 and subsequent calendar years except that in determining prescribed amounts for 2009, the amount of the money purchase limit for 2008 is deemed to be reduced by $600. S. 8308.2(2) formerly read:

Prescribed Amounts — 1997 to 2003

(2) *Prescribed Amounts — 1997 to 2003.* For the purpose of determining the amount prescribed under subsection (1) in respect of an individual for a calendar year after 1996 and before 2004, paragraph (*d*) of that subsection shall be read as:

(*d*) the money purchase limit for the particular year, and.

8308.3. Specified Retirement Arrangements

(1) Definition. In this section, "specified retirement arrangement" means, in respect of an individual and an employer, a plan or arrangement under which payments that are attributable to the individual's employment with the employer are to be, or may be, made to or for the benefit of the individual after the termination of the individual's employment with the employer, but does not include

(*a*) a plan or arrangement referred to in any of paragraphs (*a*) to (*k*), (*m*) and (*n*) of the definition "retirement compensation arrangement" in subsection 248(1) of the Act;

(*b*) (Repealed.)

(*c*) a plan or arrangement that does not provide in any circumstances for payments to be made to or for the benefit of the individual after the later of the last day of the calendar year in which the individual attains 71 years of age and the day that is 5 years after the day of termination of the individual's employment with the employer;

(*d*) a plan or arrangement (in this paragraph referred to as the "arrangement") that is, or would be, but for paragraph (l) of the definition "retirement compensation arrangement" in subsection 248(1) of the Act, a retirement compensation arrangement where

(i) the funding of the arrangement is subject to the *Pension Benefits Standards Act, 1985* or a similar law of a province, or

(ii) the arrangement is funded substantially in accordance with the funding requirements that would apply if the arrangement were subject to the *Pension Benefits Standards Act, 1985*;

(*e*) a plan or arrangement that is deemed by subsection 207.6(6) of the Act to be a retirement compensation arrangement; or

(*f*) an arrangement established by the *Judges Act* or the *Lieutenant Governors Superannuation Act*.

(2) Pension Credit. Subject to subsections (3) and (3.1), the pension credit of an individual for a calendar year with respect to an employer under a specified retirement arrangement is

(*a*) where paragraph (*b*) does not apply, nil; and

(*b*) where

(i) the year is 1993 or a subsequent year,

(ii) the employer is, at any time in the year,

(A) a person who is exempt, because of section 149 of the Act, from tax under Part I of the Act on all or part of the person's taxable income, or

(B) the Government of Canada or the government of a province,

(iii) the individual became entitled in the year, either absolutely or contingently, to benefits under the arrangement in respect of employment with the employer,

(iv) at the end of the year, the individual is entitled, either absolutely or contingently, to benefits under the arrangement, and

(v) the amount determined by the formula

$$0.85A - B$$

is greater than nil where

A is the lesser of

(A) the amount, if any, by which 18% of the individual's resident compensation from the employer for the year exceeds the PA offset for the year, and

(B) the amount by which the money purchase limit for the year exceeds the PA offset for the year, and

B is the amount that would be the pension adjustment of the individual for the year with respect to the employer if subsection 8301(1) were read without reference to paragraph (*c*) of that subsection,

the amount that would be determined by the formula in subparagraph (v) if the reference to "0.85" in that formula were replaced by a reference to "1".

(3) Pension Credit — Alternative Determination. Where the Minister has, on the written application of an employer, approved in writing a method for determining pension credits for a year with respect to the employer under a specified retirement arrangement, the pension credits shall be determined in accordance with that method.

(3.1) Pension Credits — 1996 to 2002. For the purpose of determining the pension credit of an individual for a calendar year after 1995 and before 2003 with respect to an employer under a specified retirement arrangement, the portion of paragraph (2)(*b*) after subparagraph (iv) shall be read as

"(v) the amount determined by the formula

0.85A - B

is greater than nil where

A is the lesser of

(A) the amount, if any, by which 18% of the individual's resident compensation from the employer for the year exceeds the PA offset for the year, and

(B) the amount by which $15,500 exceeds the PA offset for the year, and

B is the amount that would be the pension adjustment of the individual for the year with respect to the employer if subsection 8301(1) were read without reference to paragraph (*c*),

the amount that would be determined by the formula in subparagraph (v) if

(vi) the reference to "0.85A" in that formula were read as a reference to "A", and

(vii) clause (B) of the description of A in that subparagraph were read as

'(B) the money purchase limit for the year, and'.".

(4) Specified Retirement Arrangement PSPA. Subject to subsection (5), where the benefits to which an individual is entitled, either absolutely or contingently, under a specified retirement arrangement are modified, the specified retirement arrangement PSPA of the individual with respect to an employer associated with the modification of benefits is the amount, if any, by which

(*a*) the total of all amounts each of which is the amount that, if this section were read without reference to subsection (3), would be the pension credit of the individual with respect to the employer under the arrangement for a calendar year before the year in which the individual's benefits are modified

exceeds the total of all amounts each of which is

(*b*) the pension credit of the individual with respect to the employer under the arrangement for a calendar year before the year in which the individual's benefits are modified, or

(*c*) the specified retirement arrangement PSPA of the individual with respect to the employer associated with a previous modification of the individual's benefits under the arrangement.

(5) Specified Retirement Arrangement PSPA — Alternative Determination. Where the Minister has, on the written application of an employer, approved in writing a method for determining the specified retirement arrangement PSPA of an individual with respect to the employer associated with a modification of the individual's benefits under a specified retirement arrangement, the individual's specified retirement arrangement PSPA shall be determined in accordance with that method.

8308.4. Government-Sponsored Retirement Arrangements

(1) Definitions. The definitions in this subsection apply in this section.

"administrator" means, in respect of a government-sponsored retirement arrangement, the government or other entity that has ultimate responsibility for the administration of the arrangement.

"government-sponsored retirement arrangement" means a plan or arrangement established to provide pensions directly or indirectly from the public money of Canada or a province to one or more individuals each of whom renders services in respect of which amounts that are included in computing the income from a business of any person or partnership are paid directly or indirectly from the public money of Canada or a province.

(2) Prescribed Amount. Where

(*a*) in a particular calendar year after 1992 an individual renders services in respect of which an amount that is included in computing the income from a business of any person was payable directly or indirectly by the Government of Canada or of a province, and

(*b*) at the end of the particular year, the individual is entitled, either absolutely or contingently, to benefits under a government-sponsored retirement arrangement that provides benefits in connection with such services,

there is prescribed in respect of the individual for the year following the particular year, for the purposes of the descriptions of B in the definitions "RRSP deduction limit" and "unused RRSP deduction room" in subsection 146(1) of the Act and the description of B in paragraph 204.2(1.1)(*b*) of the Act,

(*c*) where the particular year is before 1996, the amount by which the RRSP dollar limit for that following year exceeds $1,000, and

(*d*) in any other case, the RRSP dollar limit for that following year.

8309. Prescribed Amount for Lieutenant Governors and Judges

(1) Subject to subsection (3), where an individual is, at any time in a particular calendar year after 1989, a lieutenant governor of a province (other than a lieutenant governor who is not a contributor as defined in section 2 of the *Lieutenant Governors Superannuation Act*), there is prescribed in respect of the individual for the year following the particular year, for the purposes of the descriptions of B in the definitions "RRSP deduction limit" and "unused RRSP deduction room" in subsection 146(1) of the Act and the description of B in paragraph 204.2(1.1)(*b*) of the Act, the lesser of

(*a*) the amount, if any, by which 18% of the salary received by the individual for the particular year as a lieutenant governor exceeds the PA offset for the particular year, and

(*b*) the amount by which the money purchase limit for the particular year exceeds the PA offset for the particular year.

(2) Subject to subsection (3), where an individual is, at any time in a particular calendar year after 1990, a judge in receipt of a salary under the *Judges Act*, there is prescribed in respect of the individual for the year following the particular year, for the purposes of the descriptions of B in the definitions "RRSP deduction limit" and "unused RRSP deduction room" in subsection 146(1) of the Act and the description of B in paragraph 204.2(1.1)(*b*) of the Act, the lesser of

(*a*) the amount, if any, by which 18% of the portion of the salary received by the individual for the particular year under the *Judges Act* in respect of which contributions are required under subsection 50(1) or (2) of that Act exceeds the PA offset for the particular year; and

(*b*) the amount determined by the formula

$$A \times B/12$$

where

A is the amount by which the money purchase limit for the particular year exceeds the PA offset for the particular year, and

B is the number of months, in the particular year, for which the individual received salary in respect of which contributions were required under subsection 50(1) or (2) of the *Judges Act*.

(3) For the purpose of determining the amount prescribed under subsection (1) or (2) in respect of an individual for a calendar year after 2000 and before 2004,

(*a*) paragraph (1)(*b*) shall be read as follows:

"(*b*) the money purchase limit for the particular year.", and

(*b*) the description of A in paragraph (2)(*b*) shall be read as follows:

"A is the money purchase limit for the particular year, and".

8310. Minister's Powers

(1) Where more than one method for determining an amount under this Part complies with the rules in this Part, only such of those methods as are acceptable to the Minister shall be used.

(2) Where, in a particular case, the rules in this Part require the determination of an amount in a manner that is not appropriate having regard to the provisions of this Part read as a whole and the purposes for which the amount is determined, the Minister may permit or require the amount to be determined in a manner that, in the Minister's opinion, is appropriate.

Registered Plans Directorate Newsletters: No. 01-3, Tailored Individual Pension Plan (TIPPs).

(3) Where, pursuant to subsection (2), the Minister gives permission or imposes a requirement, the permission or requirement is not effective unless it is given or imposed in writing.

8311. Rounding of Amounts

Where a pension credit, provisional PSPA or PAR of an individual is not a multiple of one dollar, it shall be rounded to the nearest multiple of one dollar or, if it is equidistant from two such consecutive multiples, to the higher of the two multiples.

Regulations

Part LXXXIV
Retirement and Profit-Sharing Plans — Reporting and Provision of Information

8400. Definitions

(1) All words and expressions used in this Part that are defined in subsection 8300(1), 8308.4(1) or 8500(1) or in subsection 147.1(1) of the Act have the meanings assigned in those provisions.

(2) A reference in this Part to a pension credit of an individual means a pension credit of the individual as determined under Part LXXXIII.

(3) For the purposes of this Part, where the administrator of a pension plan is not otherwise a person, the administrator shall be deemed to be a person.

8401. Pension Adjustment

(1) Where the pension adjustment of an individual for a calendar year with respect to an employer is greater than nil, the employer shall, on or before the last day of February in the immediately following calendar year, file with the Minister an information return in prescribed form reporting the pension adjustment, other than the portion, if any, required by subsection (2) or (3) to be reported by the administrator of a registered pension plan.

(2) Where an individual makes a contribution in a particular calendar year to a registered pension plan that is a specified multi-employer plan in the year and the contribution is not remitted to the plan by any participating employer on behalf of the individual, the plan administrator shall, on or before the last day of February in the immediately following calendar year, file with the Minister an information return in prescribed form reporting the aggregate of all amounts each of which is the portion, if any, of the individual's pension adjustment for the particular year with respect to an employer that may reasonably be considered to result from the contribution.

(3) Where the portion of a pension credit of an individual for a calendar year that, pursuant to subsection (4), is reportable by the administrator of a registered pension plan is greater than nil, the administrator shall, on or before the last day of February in the immediately following calendar year, file with the Minister an information return in prescribed form reporting that portion of the pension credit.

(4) For the purpose of subsection (3), where, on application by the administrator of a registered pension plan that is, in a calendar year, a multi-employer plan (other than a specified multi-employer plan), the Minister consents in writing to the application of this subsection in respect of the plan in the year, such portion of each pension credit for the year under a defined benefit provision of the plan as may reasonably be considered to be attributable to benefits provided in respect of a period of reduced services of an individual is, to the extent permitted by the Minister, reportable by the administrator.

(5) Subsections (1) to (3) do not apply to require the reporting of amounts with respect to an individual for the calendar year in which the individual dies.

(6) Where the pension adjustment of an individual for a calendar year with respect to an employer is altered by reason of the application of paragraph 8308(4)(*d*) or (5)(*c*) and the amount (in this subsection referred to as the "redetermined amount") that a person would have been required to report based on the pension adjustment as altered exceeds

(*a*) if the person has not previously reported an amount in respect of the individual's pension adjustment, nil, and

(*b*) otherwise, the amount reported by the person in respect of the individual's pension adjustment,

the person shall, within 60 days after the day on which paragraph 8308(4)(*d*) or (5)(*c*), as the case may be, applies to alter the pension adjustment, file with the Minister an information return in prescribed form reporting the redetermined amount.

8402. Past Service Pension Adjustment

(1) Where a provisional PSPA (computed under section 8303, 8304 or 8308) of an individual with respect to an employer that is associated with a past service event (other than a certifiable past service event) is greater than nil, the administrator of each registered pension plan to which the past service event relates shall, within 120 days after the day on which the past service event occurs, file with the Minister an information return in prescribed form reporting such portion of the aggregate of all amounts each of which is the individual's PSPA with respect to an employer that is associated with the past service event as may reasonably be considered to be attributable to benefits provided under the plan, except that a return is not required to be filed by an administrator if the amount that would otherwise be reported by the administrator is nil.

(2) Where a foreign plan PSPA (computed under subsection 8308.1(5) or (6)) of an individual with respect to an employer associated with a modification of benefits under a foreign plan (as defined by subsection 8308.1(1)) is greater than nil, the employer shall, on or before the last day of February in the year following the calendar year in which the individual's benefits were modified, file with the Minister an information return in prescribed form reporting the foreign plan PSPA.

(3) Where a specified retirement arrangement PSPA (computed under subsection 8308.3(4) or (5)) of an individual with respect to an employer associated with a modification of benefits under a specified retirement arrangement (as defined by subsection 8308.3(1)) is greater than nil, the employer shall, on or before the last day of February in the calendar year following the calendar year in which the individual's benefits were modified, file with the Minister an information return in prescribed form reporting the specified retirement arrangement PSPA.

8402.01. Pension Adjustment Reversal

(1) Deferred Profit Sharing Plan. Where the PAR determined in connection with an individual's termination from a deferred profit sharing plan is greater than nil, each trustee under the plan shall file with the Minister an information return in prescribed form reporting the PAR

(*a*) where the termination occurs in the first, second or third quarter of a calendar year, on or before the day that is 60 days after the last day of the quarter in which the termination occurs, and

(*b*) where the termination occurs in the fourth quarter of a calendar year, before February of the following calendar year,

and, for this purpose, an information return filed by a trustee under a deferred profit sharing plan is deemed to have been filed by each trustee under the plan.

(2) Deferred Profit Sharing Plan — Employer Reporting. Where an amount included in an individual's pension credit in respect of an employer under a deferred profit sharing plan is included in determining a PAR in connection with the individual's termination from the plan, the employer is deemed to be a trustee under the plan for the purpose of reporting the PAR.

(3) Benefit Provision of a Registered Pension Plan. Subject to subsection (4), where the PAR determined in connection with an individual's termination from a benefit provision of a registered pension plan is greater than nil, the administrator of the plan shall file with the Minister an information return in prescribed form reporting the PAR

(*a*) where the termination occurs in the first, second or third quarter of a calendar year, on or before the day that is 60 days after the last day of the quarter in which the termination occurs; and

(*b*) where the termination occurs in the fourth quarter of a calendar year, before February of the following calendar year.

(4) Extended Deadline — PA Transfer Amount. Where, in determining an individual's PAR in connection with the individual's termination from a defined benefit provision of a registered pension plan, it is reasonable for the administrator of the plan to conclude, on the basis of information provided to the administrator by the administrator of another pension plan or by the individual, that the value of D in paragraph 8304.1(5)(*a*) in respect of the termination may be greater than nil, the administrator shall file with the Minister an information return in prescribed form reporting the PAR, if it is greater than nil, on or before the later of

(*a*) the day on or before which it would otherwise be required to be filed; and

(*b*) the day that is 60 days after the earliest day on which the administrator has all the information required to determine that value.

(5) Calendar Year Quarter. For the purposes of this section,

(*a*) the first quarter of a calendar year is the period beginning on January 1 and ending on March 31 of the calendar year;

(*b*) the second quarter of a calendar year is the period beginning on April 1 and ending on June 30 of the calendar year;

(*c*) the third quarter of a calendar year is the period beginning on July 1 and ending on September 30 of the calendar year; and

(*d*) the fourth quarter of a calendar year is the period beginning on October 1 and ending on December 31 of the calendar year.

8402.1. Government-Sponsored Retirement Arrangements

Where an amount is prescribed by subsection 8308.4(2) in respect of an individual for a calendar year because of the individual's entitlement (either absolute or contingent) to benefits under a government-sponsored retirement arrangement (as defined in subsection 8308.4(1)), the administrator of the arrangement shall, on or before the last day of February in the year, file with the Minister an information return in prescribed form reporting the prescribed amount.

8403. Connected Persons

Where, at any particular time after 1990,

(*a*) an individual becomes a member of a registered pension plan, or

(*b*) lifetime retirement benefits commence to accrue to the individual under a defined benefit provision of a registered pension plan following a period in which lifetime retirement benefits did not accrue to the individual,

each employer who participates in the plan for the benefit of the individual and with whom the individual is connected (within the meaning assigned by subsection 8500(3)) at the particular time, or was connected at any time after 1989, shall, within 60 days after the particular time, file with the Minister an information return in prescribed form containing prescribed information with respect to the individual unless the employer has previously filed an information return under this section with respect to the individual.

Registered Plans Directorate Newsletters: No. 91-5, Transitional rules and other administrative issues for pension plans.

8404. Reporting to Individuals

(1) Every person who is required by section 8401 or 8402.1 to file an information return with the Minister shall, on or before the day on or before which the return is required to be filed with the Minister, send to each individual to whom the return relates, two copies of the portion of the return that relates to the individual.

(2) Every person who is required by section 8402, 8402.01 or 8403 to file an information return with the Minister shall, on or before the day on or before which the return is required to be filed with the Minister, send to each individual to whom the return relates, one copy of the portion of the return that relates to the individual.

(3) Every person who obtains a certification from the Minister for the purposes of subsection 147.1(10) of the Act in respect of a past service event and an individual shall, within 60 days after receiving from the Minister the form submitted to the Minister pursuant to subsection 8307(1) in respect of the past service event and the individual, forward to the individual one copy of the form as returned by the Minister.

(4) Every person who is required by subsection (1), (2) or (3) to forward a copy of an information return or a form to an individual shall send the copy to the individual at the individual's latest known address or deliver the copy to the individual in person.

8405. Discontinuance of Business

Subsection 205(2) and section 206 are applicable, with such modifications as the circumstances require, in respect of returns required to be filed under this Part.

8406. Provision of Information

(1) Where a person who is required to file an information return under section 8401 requires information from another person in order to determine an amount that is to be reported or to otherwise complete the return and makes a written request to the other person for the information, the other person shall provide the person with the information that is available to that other person,

(*a*) where the information return is required to be filed in the calendar year in which the request is received, within 30 days after receipt of the request; or

(*b*) in any other case, by January 31 of the year immediately following the calendar year in which the request is received.

(2) Where the administrator of a registered pension plan requires information from a person in order to determine a provisional PSPA of an individual under section 8303, 8304 or 8308 and makes a written request to the person for the information, the person shall, within 30 days after receipt of the request, provide the administrator with the information that is available to the person.

(3) Where the administrator of a registered pension plan requires information from a person in order to complete an information return required to be filed under section 8409 and makes a written request to the person for the information, the person shall, within 30 days after receipt of the request, provide the administrator with the information that is available to that person.

(4) Where a person requires information from another person in order to determine a PAR under section 8304.1 in connection with an individual's termination in a calendar year from a deferred profit sharing plan or from a benefit provision of a registered pension plan (other than information that the other person is required to provide to the person under subsection (5)) and makes a written request to the other person for the information, the other person shall provide the person with the information that is available to the other person on or before

(*a*) if the request is received before December 17 of the year, the day that is 30 days after the day on which the request is received; and

(*b*) in any other case, the later of the day that is 15 days after the day on which the request is received and January 15 of the year following the year.

(5) Where benefits provided to an individual under a registered pension plan (in this subsection referred to as the "importing plan") as a consequence of a past service event result in a PA transfer amount in relation to the individual's termination from a defined benefit provision of another registered pension plan (in this subsection referred to as the "exporting plan"),

(*a*) the administrator of the importing plan shall, in writing on or before the day that is 30 days after the day on which the past service event occurred, notify the administrator of the exporting plan of the occurrence of the past service event and of its relevance in determining the individual's PAR in connection with the individual's termination from the defined benefit provision; and

(*b*) the administrator of the importing plan shall notify the administrator of the exporting plan of the PA transfer amount in writing on or before the day that is 60 days after

(i) in the case of a certifiable past service event, the day on which the Minister issues a certification for the purposes of subsection 147.1(10) of the Act in respect of the past service event and the individual, and

(ii) in any other case, the day on which the past service event occurred.

8407. Qualifying Withdrawals

Where

(*a*) an individual who has withdrawn an amount from a registered retirement savings plan under which the individual was, at the time of the withdrawal, the annuitant (as defined in subsection 146(1) of the Act) provides to the issuer (as defined in subsection 146(1) of the Act) of the plan, in the calendar year in which the amount was withdrawn or one of the two immediately following calendar years, the prescribed form referred to in subparagraph 8307(3)(*a*)(ii) accompanied by a request that the issuer complete the form in respect of the withdrawal, and

(*b*) the issuer has not, at the time of the receipt of the request, forwarded to the individual 2 copies of the information return required by subsection 214(1) to be made by the issuer in respect of the withdrawal, and does not, within 30 days after receipt of the request, forward to the individual 2 copies of that return,

the issuer shall, within 30 days after receipt of the request, complete those portions of the form that the form indicates are required to be completed by the issuer in respect of the withdrawal and return the form to the individual.

8408. Requirement to Provide Minister with Information

(1) The Minister may, by notice served personally or by registered or certified mail, require that a person provide the Minister, within such reasonable time as is stipulated in the notice, with

Regulations

(*a*) information relating to the determination of amounts under Part LXXXIII;

(*b*) where the person claims that paragraph 147.1(10)(*a*) of the Act is not applicable with respect to an individual and a past service event by reason of an exemption provided by regulation, information relevant to the claim; or

(*c*) information for the purpose of determining whether the registration of a pension plan may be revoked.

(2) Where a person fails to provide the Minister with information pursuant to a requirement under subsection (1), each registered pension plan and deferred profit sharing plan to which the information relates becomes a revocable plan as of the day on or before which the information was required to be provided.

8409. Annual Information Returns

(1) The administrator of a registered pension plan that is administered under the supervision of a government regulator shall file an information return for a fiscal period of the plan in prescribed form and containing prescribed information

(*a*) where an agreement concerning annual information returns has been entered into by the Minister and the regulator, as identified in subsection (2),

(i) in the case of the agreement with the Pension Commission of Ontario, with the Taxation Data Centre of the Ministry of Finance of Ontario, and

(ii) in any other case, with that regulator,

on or before the day that an information return required by that regulator is to be filed for the fiscal period; and

(*b*) in any other case, with the Minister on or before the day that is 180 days after the end of the fiscal period.

Forms: T244 — Registered Pension Plan Annual Information Return.

Registered Plans Directorate Newsletters: No. 96-2, Waiving the requirement to file a registered pension plan annual information return for an inactive plan; No. 95-4, New filing requirements for the registered pension plan annual information return; No. 94-4, Wind-up valuation report.

(2) For the purposes of paragraph (1)(*a*), the following government regulators have entered into an agreement concerning annual information returns with the Minister:

(*a*) the Pension Commission of Ontario, Province of Ontario;

(*b*) the Superintendent of Pensions, Province of Nova Scotia;

(*c*) the Superintendent of Pensions, Province of New Brunswick;

(*d*) the Superintendent of Pensions, Province of Manitoba; and

(*e*) the Superintendent of Pensions, Province of British Columbia.

Editorial Note: Registered Plans Directorate Newsletter No. 03-1 states that Regulation 8409(2) will be amended to add the Province of Quebec to the list of government regulators that have entered into an agreement concerning annual information returns with the Minister.

Registered Plans Directorate Newsletters: No. 03-1, Joint annual information return — New participating pension supervisory authority; No. 01-2, Joint annual information return — New participating pension supervisory authorities.

(3) The administrator of a registered pension plan shall, within 60 days after the final distribution of property held in connection with the plan, notify the Minister in writing of the date of the distribution and the method of settlement.

8410. Actuarial Reports

The administrator of a registered pension plan that contains a defined benefit provision shall, on demand from the Minister served personally or by registered or certified mail and within such reasonable time as is stipulated in the demand, file with the Minister a report prepared by an actuary on the basis of reasonable assumptions and in accordance with generally accepted actuarial principles and containing such information as is required by the Minister in respect of the defined benefit provisions of the plan.

Registered Plans Directorate Newsletters: No. 95-5, Conversion of a defined benefit provision to a money purchase provision; No. 94-4, Wind-up valuation report.

Part LXXXV
Registered Pension Plans

8500. Interpretation

(1) In this Part,

History: S. 8500(1), the definition "predecessor employer" was replaced by S.C. 2013, c. 34, s. 407(1), deemed to have come into force on November 6, 2010, except that it does not apply in respect of a sale, assignment or disposition of a business or undertaking that occurred before that date. S. 8500(1), the definition "predecessor employer" formerly read:

"predecessor employer" means, in relation to a particular employer, an employer (in this definition referred to as the "vendor") who has sold, assigned or otherwise disposed of all or part of the vendor's business or undertaking or all or part of the assets of the vendor's business or undertaking to the particular employer or to another employer who, at any time after the sale, assignment or other disposition, becomes a predecessor employer in relation to the particular employer, where one or more employees of the vendor have, in conjunction with the sale, assignment or disposition, become employees of the employer acquiring the business, undertaking or assets;

S. 8500(1), the definition "IPP minimum amount" was added by S.C. 2011, c. 24, s. 93(1), applicable to the 2012 and subsequent taxation years.

Information Circulars: IC 98-2 Prescribed compensation for registered pension plans.

Interpretation Bulletins: *Secondary* — IT-124R6 Contributions to registered retirement savings plans.

Registered Plans Directorate Newsletters: No. 96-1, Changes to retirement savings limits.

"active member" —"active member" of a pension plan in a calendar year means a member of the plan to whom benefits accrue under a defined benefit provision of the plan in respect of all or any portion of the year or who makes contributions, or on whose behalf contributions are made, in relation to the year under a money purchase provision of the plan;

Related Regulations: 8301(2); 8301(2.1). 8500(7).

"average Consumer Price Index" —"average Consumer Price Index" for a calendar year means the amount that is obtained by dividing by 12 the aggregate of all amounts each of which is the Consumer Price Index for a month in the 12-month period ending on September 30 of the immediately preceding calendar year;

"beneficiary" —"beneficiary" of an individual means a person who has a right, by virtue of the participation of the individual in a pension plan, to receive benefits under the plan after the death of the individual;

"benefit provision" —"benefit provision" of a pension plan means a money purchase or defined benefit provision of the plan;

"bridging benefits" —"bridging benefits" provided to a member under a benefit provision of a pension plan means retirement benefits payable to the member under the provision for a period ending no later than on a date determinable at the time the benefits commence to be paid;

"Consumer Price Index" —"Consumer Price Index" for a month means the Consumer Price Index for the month as published by Statistics Canada under the authority of the *Statistics Act*;

"defined benefit limit" —"defined benefit limit" for a calendar year means the greater of

(*a*) $1,722.22, and

(*b*) 1/9 of the money purchase limit for the year;

Related Sections: 60.03(1) eligible pension income.

"dependant" —"dependant" of an individual at the time of the individual's death means a parent, grandparent, brother, sister, child or grandchild of the individual who, at that time, is both dependent on the individual for support and

(*a*) under 19 years of age and will not attain 19 years of age in the calendar year that includes that time,

(*b*) in full-time attendance at an educational institution, or

(*c*) dependent on the individual by reason of mental or physical infirmity;

"designated plan" —"designated plan" has the meaning assigned by section 8515;

"disabled" —"disabled" means, in relation to an individual, suffering from a physical or mental impairment that prevents the individual from performing the duties of the employment in which the individual was engaged before the commencement of the impairment;

"eligible period of reduced pay" —"eligible period of reduced pay" of an employee with respect to an employer means a period (other than a period in which the employee is, at any time after 1990, connected with the employer or a period any part of which is a period of disability of the employee)

(*a*) that begins after the employee has been employed by the employer or predecessor employers to the employer for not less than 36 months,

(*b*) throughout which the employee renders services to the employer, and

(*c*) throughout which the remuneration received by the employee from the employer is less than the remuneration that it is reasonable to expect the employee would have received from the employer had the employee rendered services throughout the period on a regular basis (having regard to the services rendered by the employee to the employer before the period) and had the employee's rate of remuneration been commensurate with the employee's rate of remuneration before the period;

"eligible period of temporary absence" —"eligible period of temporary absence" of an individual with respect to an employer means a period throughout which the individual does not render services to the employer by reason of leave of absence, layoff, strike, lock-out or any other circumstance acceptable to the Minister, other than a period

(*a*) a part of which is a period of disability of the individual, or

(*b*) in which the individual is, at any time after 1990, connected with the employer;

"eligible survivor benefit period" —"eligible survivor benefit period", in relation to a person who is a dependant of an individual at the time of the individual's death,

Regulations

means the period beginning on the day of death of the individual and ending on the latest of

(*a*) where the dependant is under 19 years of age throughout the calendar year that includes the day of death of the individual, the earlier of

(i) December 31 of the calendar year in which the dependant attains 18 years of age, and

(ii) the day of death of the dependant,

(*b*) where the dependant is in full-time attendance at an educational institution on the later of the day of death of the individual and December 31 of the calendar year in which the dependant attains 18 years of age, the day on which the dependant ceases to be in full-time attendance at an educational institution, and

(*c*) where the dependant is dependent on the individual at the time of the individual's death by reason of mental or physical infirmity, the day on which the dependant ceases to be infirm or, if there is no such day, the day of death of the dependant;

Regulations

"existing plan" —"existing plan" means a pension plan that was a registered pension plan on March 27, 1988 or in respect of which an application for registration was made to the Minister before March 28, 1988, and includes a pension plan that was established before March 28, 1988 pursuant to an Act of Parliament that deems member contributions to be contributions to a registered pension plan;

"forfeited amount" —"forfeited amount" under a money purchase provision of a pension plan means an amount to which a member of the plan has ceased to have any rights, other than the portion thereof, if any, that is payable

(*a*) to a beneficiary of the member as a consequence of the member's death, or

(*b*) to a spouse or common-law partner or former spouse or common-law partner of the member as a consequence of the breakdown of their marriage or common-law partnership;

"grandfathered plan" —"grandfathered plan" means

(*a*) an existing plan that, on March 27, 1988, contained a defined benefit provision, or

(*b*) a pension plan that was established to provide benefits under a defined benefit provision to one or more individuals in lieu of benefits to which the individuals were entitled under a defined benefit provision of another pension plan that is a grandfathered plan, whether or not benefits are also provided to other individuals;

"IPP minimum amount" —"IPP minimum amount", for a year, for a person who is a member of an individual pension plan (or a beneficiary, in respect of the plan, who was, at the time of the member's death, a spouse or common-law partner of the member) means

(*a*) if there is only one such person in respect of the plan, the minimum amount that would be determined under subsection 146.3(1) of the Act for the year in respect of the plan if the plan were a registered retirement income fund that held the same property as the property held by the plan and the person were the annuitant of the fund, and

(*b*) in any other case, the minimum amount that would be determined under subsection 146.3(1) of the Act if the person were the annuitant of a registered retirement income fund and the fair market value of the property held in connection with the fund at the beginning of the year were determined by the formula

$$A \times B/C$$

where

A is the fair market value of all property held in connection with the plan at the beginning of the year,

B is the amount of the actuarial liabilities in respect of the benefits payable to the person under the terms of the plan at the beginning of the year, and

C is the amount of the actuarial liabilities in respect of all benefits payable under the terms of the plan at the beginning of the year;

"lifetime retirement benefits" —"lifetime retirement benefits" provided to a member under a benefit provision of a pension plan means

(*a*) retirement benefits provided to the member under the provision that, after they commence to be paid, are payable to the member until the member's death, unless the benefits are commuted or payment of the benefits is suspended, and

(*b*) for greater certainty, retirement benefits provided to the member under the provision in accordance with paragraph 8506(1)(*e.1*);

"multi-employer plan" —"multi-employer plan" in a calendar year means

(*a*) a pension plan in respect of which it is reasonable to expect, at the beginning of the year (or at the time in the year when the plan is established, if later), that at no time in the year will more than 95 per cent of the active members of the plan be employed by a single participating employer or by a related group of participating employers, other than a plan where it is reasonable to consider that one of the main reasons there is more than one employer participating in the plan is to obtain the benefit of any of the provisions of the Act or these Regulations that are applicable only in respect of multi-employer plans, or

(*b*) a pension plan that is, in the year, a specified multi-employer plan,

and, for the purposes of this definition, 2 corporations that are related to each other solely by reason that they are both controlled by Her Majesty in right of Canada or a province shall be deemed not to be related persons;

"pensionable service" —"pensionable service" of a member of a pension plan under a defined benefit provision of the plan means the periods in respect of which lifetime retirement benefits are provided to the member under the provision;

"period of disability"—"period of disability" of an individual means a period throughout which the individual is disabled;

"predecessor employer"—"predecessor employer" means, in relation to a particular employer, an employer (in this definition referred to as the "vendor") who has sold, assigned or otherwise disposed of all or part of the vendor's business or undertaking or all or part of the assets of the vendor's business or undertaking to the particular employer or to another employer who, at any time after the sale, assignment or other disposition, becomes a predecessor employer in relation to the particular employer, if all or a significant number of employees of the vendor have, in conjunction with the sale, assignment or disposition, become employees of the employer acquiring the business, undertaking or assets;

"public pension benefits"—"public pension benefits" means amounts that are payable on a periodic basis under the *Canada Pension Plan*, a provincial pension plan as defined in section 3 of the *Canada Pension Plan*, or Part I of the *Old Age Security Act*, but does not include disability, death or survivor benefits provided under those Acts;

"public safety occupation"—"public safety occupation" means the occupation of

(*a*) firefighter,

(*b*) police officer,

(*c*) corrections officer,

(*d*) air traffic controller,

(*e*) commercial airline pilot, or

(*f*) paramedic;

"retirement benefits"—"retirement benefits" provided to an individual under a benefit provision of a pension plan means benefits provided to the individual under the provision that are payable on a periodic basis;

"surplus"—"surplus" under a money purchase provision of a pension plan at any time means such portion, if any, of the amount held at that time in respect of the provision as has not been allocated to members and is not reasonably attributable to

(*a*) forfeited amounts under the provision or earnings of the plan that are reasonably attributable to those amounts,

(*b*) contributions made under the provision by an employer that will be allocated to members as part of the regular allocation of such contributions, or

(*c*) earnings of the plan (other than earnings that are reasonably attributable to the surplus under the provision before that time) that will be allocated to members as part of the regular allocation of such earnings;

"totally and permanently disabled"—"totally and permanently disabled" means, in relation to an individual, suffering from a physical or mental impairment that prevents the individual from engaging in any employment for which the individual is reasonably suited by virtue of the individual's education, training or experience and that can reasonably be expected to last for the remainder of the individual's lifetime;

"Year's Maximum Pensionable Earnings"—"Year's Maximum Pensionable Earnings" for a calendar year has the meaning assigned by section 18 of the *Canada Pension Plan*.

(1.1) The definition "surplus" in subsection (1) applies for the purpose of subsection 147.3(7.1) of the Act.

(1.2) The definition "predecessor employer" in subsection (1) applies for the purpose of subsection 147.2(8) of the Act.

History: S. 8500(1.2) was added by S.C. 2013, c. 34, s. 407(2), applicable to contributions made after 1990.

(2) All words and expressions used in this Part that are defined in subsection 147.1(1) of the Act or in Part LXXXIII have the meanings assigned in those provisions.

(3) For the purposes of this Part, a person is connected with an employer at any time where, at that time, the person

(*a*) owns, directly or indirectly, not less than 10% of the issued shares of any class of the capital stock of the employer or of any other corporation that is related to the employer,

(*b*) does not deal at arm's length with the employer, or

(*c*) is a specified shareholder of the employer by reason of paragraph (*d*) of the definition "specified shareholder" in subsection 248(1) of the Act,

and, for the purposes of this subsection,

(*d*) a person shall be deemed to own, at any time, each share of the capital stock of a corporation owned, at that time, by a person with whom the person does not deal at arm's length,

(*e*) where shares of the capital stock of a corporation are owned at any time by a trust,

(i) if the share of any beneficiary in the income or capital of the trust depends on the exercise by any person of, or the failure by any person to exercise, any discretionary power, each beneficiary of the trust shall be deemed to own, at that time, all the shares owned by the trust, and

(ii) in any other case, each beneficiary of a trust shall be deemed to own, at that time, that proportion of the shares owned by the trust that the fair market value at that time of the beneficiary's beneficial interest in the trust is of the fair market value at that time of all beneficial interests in the trust,

(*f*) each member of a partnership shall be deemed to own, at any time, that proportion of all shares of the capital stock of a corporation that are property of the partnership at that time that the fair market value at that time of the member's interest in the partnership is of the fair market value at that time of the interests of all members in the partnership, and

(*g*) a person who, at any time, has a right under a contract, in equity or otherwise, either immediately or in the future and either absolutely or contingently, to, or to acquire, shares of the capital stock of

Regulations

a corporation shall be deemed to own, at that time, those shares if one of the main reasons for the existence of the right may reasonably be considered to be that the person not be connected with an employer.

Interpretation Bulletins: *Secondary* — IT-124R6 Contributions to registered retirement savings plans.

Registered Plans Directorate Newsletters: No. 91-1, Transitional registration rules for pension plans; No. 91-4R, Registration rules for money purchase provisions.

(4) For the purposes of this Part, an officer who receives remuneration for holding an office shall, for any period that the officer holds the office, be deemed to render services to, and to be in the service of, the person from whom the officer receives the remuneration.

(5) For the purpose of this Part, "spouse" and "former spouse" of a particular individual include another individual who is a party to a void or voidable marriage with the particular individual.

(6) Where this Part provides that an amount is to be determined by aggregating the durations of periods that satisfy specified conditions, a period shall be included in determining the aggregate only if it is not part of a longer period that satisfies the conditions.

(7) For the purposes of the definition "active member" in subsection (1), subparagraph 8503(3)(*a*)(v) and paragraphs 8504(7)(*d*), 8506(2)(*c*.1) and 8507(3)(*a*), the portion of an amount allocated to an individual at any time under a money purchase provision of a registered pension plan that is attributable to

(*a*) forfeited amounts under the provision or earnings of the plan that are reasonably attributable to those amounts,

(*b*) a surplus under the provision,

(*c*) property transferred to the provision in respect of the actuarial surplus under a defined benefit provision of the plan or another registered pension plan, or

(*d*) property transferred to the provision in respect of the surplus under another money purchase provision of the plan or under a money purchase provision of another registered pension plan

shall be deemed to be a contribution made under the provision on behalf of the individual at that time.

(8) Where an individual who is entitled to receive benefits (in this subsection referred to as "member benefits") under a pension plan because of the individual's membership in the plan is also entitled to receive other benefits (in this subsection referred to as "non-member benefits") under the plan or under any other pension plan solely because of the participation of another individual in the plan or in the other plan, the following rules apply:

(*a*) for the purpose of determining whether the member benefits are permissible under this Part, the non-member benefits shall be disregarded;

(*b*) for the purpose of determining whether the non-member benefits are permissible under this Part, the member benefits shall be disregarded; and

(*c*) for the purpose of determining a pension adjustment, pension adjustment reversal or provisional past service pension adjustment of the individual under Part LXXXIII, the non-member benefits shall be disregarded.

(9) For the purposes of paragraph 147.3(6)(*b*) of the Act and subparagraphs 8502(*d*)(iv) and 8503(2)(*h*)(iii), if an amount is transferred in accordance with subsection 147.3(3) of the Act to a defined benefit provision (referred to in this subsection as the "current provision") of a registered pension plan from a defined benefit provision (referred to in this subsection as the "former provision") of another registered pension plan on behalf of all or a significant number of members whose benefits under the former provision are replaced by benefits under the current provision, each current service contribution made at a particular time under the former provision by a member whose benefits are so replaced is deemed to be a current service contribution made at that particular time under the current provision by the member.

History: S. 8500(9) was added by S.C. 2013, c. 34, s. 407(3), deemed to have come into force on January 1, 2000.

8501. Prescribed Conditions for Registration and Other Conditions Applicable to Registered Pension Plans

(1) Conditions for Registration. For the purposes of section 147.1 of the Act, and subject to sections 8509 and 8510, the prescribed conditions for the registration of a pension plan are

(*a*) the conditions set out in paragraphs 8502(*a*), (*c*), (*e*), (*f*) and (*l*),

(*b*) if the plan contains a defined benefit provision, the conditions set out in paragraphs 8503(4)(*a*) and (*c*), and

(*c*) if the plan contains a money purchase provision, the conditions set out in paragraphs 8506(2)(*a*) and (*d*),

and the following conditions:

(*d*) there is no reason to expect, on the basis of the documents that constitute the plan and establish the funding arrangements, that

(i) the plan may become a revocable plan pursuant to subsection (2), or

(ii) the conditions in subsection 147.1(10) of the Act may not be complied with, and

(*e*) there is no reason to expect that the plan may become a revocable plan under subsection 147.1(8) or (9) of the Act or subsections 8503(15) or (26) or 8506(4).

History: S. 8501(1)(*e*) was replaced by S.C. 2011, c. 24, s. 94(1), applicable to the 2012 and subsequent taxation years. S. 8501(1)(*e*) formerly read:

(*e*) there is no reason to expect that the plan may become a revocable plan pursuant to subsection 147.1(8) or (9) of the Act or subsection 8503(15) or 8506(4).

Related Regulations: 8502; 8506(2).

Information Circulars: IC 98-2 Prescribed compensation for registered pension plans.

Registered Plans Directorate Newsletters: No. 91-4R, Registration rules for money purchase provisions.

(2) Conditions Applicable to Registered Pension Plans. For the purposes of paragraph 147.1(11)(*c*) of the Act, and subject to sections 8509 and 8510, a registered

Regulations

pension plan becomes a revocable plan at any time that it fails to comply with

(*a*) a condition set out in any of paragraphs 8502(*b*), (*d*), (*g*) to (*k*) and (*m*);

(*b*) where the plan contains a defined benefit provision, a condition set out in paragraph 8503(3)(*a*), (*b*), (*d*), (*j*), (*k*) or (*l*) or (4)(*b*), (*d*), (*e*) or (*f*); or

(*c*) where the plan contains a money purchase provision, a condition set out in any of paragraphs 8506(2)(*b*) to (*c*.1) and (*e*) to (*i*).

Related Regulations: 8503(3).

Registered Plans Directorate Newsletters: No. 91-4R, Registration rules for money purchase provisions.

(3) Permissive Rules. The conditions in this Part do not apply in respect of a pension plan to the extent that they are inconsistent with the provisions of subsections 8503(6) and (8) and 8505(3) and (4).

(4) Supplemental Plans. Where

(*a*) the benefits provided under a pension plan (in this subsection referred to as the "supplemental plan") that contains one defined benefit provision and no money purchase provisions may reasonably be considered to be supplemental to the benefits provided under a defined benefit provision (in this subsection referred to as the "base provision") of another pension plan,

(*b*) the supplemental plan does not otherwise comply with the condition set out in paragraph 8502(*a*) or the condition set out in paragraph 8502(*c*), and

(*c*) the Minister has approved the application of this subsection, which approval has not been withdrawn,

for the purpose of determining whether the supplemental plan complies with the conditions in paragraphs 8502(*a*) and (*c*), the benefits provided under the base provision shall be considered to be provided under the supplemental plan.

(5) Benefits Payable after the Breakdown of the Marriage or Common-law Partnership. Where

(*a*) an individual who is a spouse or common-law partner or former spouse or common-law partner of a member of a registered pension plan is entitled to receive all or a portion of the benefits that would otherwise be payable under the plan to the member, and

(*b*) the entitlement was created

(i) by assignment of benefits by the member, on or after the breakdown of their marriage or common-law partnership, in settlement of rights arising out of their marriage or common-law partnership, or

(ii) by a provision of the law of Canada or a province applicable in respect of the division of property between the member and the individual, on or after the breakdown of their marriage or common-law partnership, in settlement of rights arising out of their marriage or common-law partnership,

the following rules apply:

(*c*) except where paragraph (*d*) applies, the benefits to which the individual is entitled are, for the purposes of this Part, deemed to be benefits provided and payable to the member, and

(*d*) the benefits to which the individual is entitled are, for the purposes of this Part, deemed to be benefits provided and payable to the individual and not provided or payable to the member where

(i) the entitlement of the individual was created by a provision of the law of Canada or a province described in subparagraph (*b*)(ii), and

(ii) that provision

(A) requires that benefits commence to be paid to the individual at a time that may be different from the time benefits commence to be paid to the member, or

(B) gives the individual any rights in respect of the benefits to which the individual is entitled in addition to the rights that the individual would have as a consequence of an assignment by the member, in whole or in part, of the member's right to benefits under the plan.

(6) Indirect Contributions. Where an employer or individual makes payments to a trade union or association of employers (in this subsection referred to as the "contributing entity") to enable the contributing entity to make contributions to a pension plan, such portion of a contribution made by the contributing entity to the plan as is reasonably attributable to a payment made to the contributing entity by an employer or individual shall, for the purposes of the conditions in this Part, be considered to be a contribution made by the employer or individual, as the case may be, and not by the contributing entity.

(6.1) Member Contributions for Unfunded Liability. For the purposes of the conditions in this Part (other than subparagraph 8510(9)(*b*)(i)), a contribution made by a member of a pension plan in respect of a defined benefit provision of the plan is deemed to be a current service contribution made by the member in respect of the member's benefits under the provision if

(*a*) the contribution cannot, but for this subsection, reasonably be considered to be made in respect of the member's benefits under the provision;

(*b*) the contribution is determined by reference to the actuarial liabilities under the provision in respect of periods before the time of the contribution; and

(*c*) the contribution is made pursuant to an arrangement

(i) under which all, or a significant number, of the active members of the plan are required to make similar contributions,

(ii) the main purpose of which is to ensure that the plan has sufficient assets to pay benefits under the provision, and

(iii) that is approved by the Minister.

(6.2) Prescribed Eligible Contributions. For the purpose of paragraph 147.2(4)(*a*) of the Act, a contribution

Regulations

described in subsection (6.1) is a prescribed eligible contribution.

(7) Benefits Provided with Surplus on Plan Wind-up. Where

(*a*) a single amount is paid in full or partial satisfaction of an individual's entitlement to retirement benefits (in this subsection referred to as the "commuted benefits") under a defined benefit provision of a registered pension plan,

(*b*) other benefits are subsequently provided to the individual under the provision as a consequence of an allocation, on full or partial wind-up of the plan, of an actuarial surplus under the provision,

(*c*) the other benefits include benefits (in this subsection referred to as "ancillary benefits") that, but for this subsection, would not be permissible under this Part,

(*d*) if the individual had previously terminated from the provision and the conditions in subsection 8304.1(14) were satisfied with respect to the termination, it is reasonable to consider that all of the ancillary benefits are in respect of periods before 1990, and

(*e*) the Minister has approved the application of this subsection in respect of the ancillary benefits,

for the purpose of determining whether the ancillary benefits are permissible under this Part, the individual is considered to have an entitlement under the provision to the commuted benefits.

8502. Conditions Applicable to All Plans

For the purposes of section 8501, the following conditions are applicable in respect of a pension plan:

(a) Primary purpose — the primary purpose of the plan is to provide periodic payments to individuals after retirement and until death in respect of their service as employees;

Registered Plans Directorate Newsletters: No. 01-3, Tailored individual pension plan (TIPPs).

Tax Window Files: Information Return — Real Estate Developer, *Technical Interpretation, Business and Partnerships Division, November 15, 2006*, CRA Document No. 2006-0202971I7.

(b) Permissible contributions — each contribution that is made to the plan after 1990 is an amount that

(i) is paid by a member of the plan in accordance with the plan as registered, where the amount is credited to the member's account under a money purchase provision of the plan or is paid in respect of the member's benefits under a defined benefit provision of the plan,

(ii) is paid in accordance with a money purchase provision of the plan as registered, by an employer with respect to the employer's employees or former employees,

(iii) is an eligible contribution that is paid in respect of a defined benefit provision of the plan by an employer with respect to the employer's employees or former employees,

(iv) is transferred to the plan in accordance with any of subsections 146(16), 146.3(14.1), 147(19), 147.3(1) to (8) and 147.5(21) of the Act,

(v) is acceptable to the Minister and that is transferred to the plan from a pension plan that is maintained primarily for the benefit of non-residents in respect of services rendered outside Canada, or

(v.1) is paid by the trustee of a trust described in paragraph 6802(*h*), where the amount would have been an eligible contribution if the amount had been paid in respect of a defined benefit provision of the plan by an employer with respect to the employer's employees or former employees,

and, for the purposes of this paragraph,

(vi) an eligible contribution is a contribution that is paid by an employer in respect of a defined benefit provision of a pension plan where it is an eligible contribution under subsection 147.2(2) of the Act or, in the case of a plan in which Her Majesty in right of Canada or a province is a participating employer, would be an eligible contribution under subsection 147.2(2) of the Act if all amounts held to the credit of the plan in the accounts of Canada or the province were excluded from the assets of the plan, and

(vii) the portion of each contribution that is made by Her Majesty in right of Canada or of a province, or by a person described in paragraph 4802(1)(*d*), in respect of a defined benefit provision of the plan and that can reasonably be considered to be made with respect to one or more employees or former employees of another person is deemed to be a contribution made by that other person;

History: S. 8502(*b*)(v.1) was added by S.C. 2013, c. 34, s. 408(1), deemed to have come into force on January 1, 2009.

S. 8502(*b*)(iv) was replaced by S.C. 2012, c. 31, s. 69(1), in force December 14, 2012, and formerly read:

> (iv) is transferred to the plan in accordance with any of subsections 146(16), 146.3(14.1), 147(19) and 147.3(1) to (8) of the Act, or

S. 8502(*b*)(vii) was replaced by P.C. 2011-936, SOR/2011-188, dated September 22, 2011, published in the *Canada Gazette* October 12, 2011, applicable after 2004. S. 8502(*b*)(vii) formerly read:

> (vii) such portion of the contributions that are made by Her Majesty in right of Canada or a province in respect of a defined benefit provision of the plan as can reasonably be considered to be made with respect to the employees or former employees of another person shall be deemed to be contributions that are made by that other person;

(c) Permissible benefits — the plan does not provide for, and its terms are such that it will not under any circumstances provide for, any benefits other than benefits

(i) that are provided under one or more defined benefit provisions and are in accordance with subsection 8503(2), paragraphs 8503(3)(*c*) and (*e*) to (*i*) and section 8504,

(ii) that are provided under one or more money purchase provisions and are in accordance with subsection 8506(1),

(iii) that the plan is required to provide by reason of a designated provision of the law of Canada or a province, or that the plan would be required to provide if each such provision were applicable to the plan with respect to all its members, or

(iv) that the plan is required to provide to an individual who is a spouse or common-law partner or former spouse or common-law partner of a member of the plan by reason of a provision of the law of Canada or a province applicable in respect of the division of property between the member and the individual, on or after the breakdown of their marriage or common-law partnership, in settlement of rights arising out of their marriage or common-law partnership;

Related Regulations: 8503(3); 8506(1).

Registered Plans Directorate Newsletters: No. 04-1, Transfers from a Defined Benefit Provision to a Money Purchase Provision, an RRSP, or a RRIF and Transfers between Defined Benefit Provisions; No. 98-2, Treating excess member contributions under a registered pension plan; No. 91-4R, Registration rules for money purchase provisions.

(d) Permissible distributions — each distribution that is made from the plan is

(i) a payment of benefits in accordance with the plan as registered,

(ii) a transfer of property held in connection with the plan where the transfer is made in accordance with subsection 147.3(3), (4.1), (7.1) or (8) of the Act,

(iii) a return of all or a portion of the contributions made by a member of the plan or an employer who participates in the plan, where the payment is made to avoid the revocation of the registration of the plan,

(iv) a return of all or a portion of the contributions made by a member of the plan under a defined benefit provision of the plan, where the return of contributions is pursuant to an amendment to the plan that also reduces the future contributions that would otherwise be required to be made under the provision by members,

(v) a payment of interest (computed at a rate not exceeding a reasonable rate) in respect of contributions that are returned as described in subparagraph (iv),

(vi) a payment in full or partial satisfaction of the interests of a person in an actuarial surplus that relates to a defined benefit provision of the plan,

(vii) a payment to an employer of property held in connection with a money purchase provision of the plan;

(viii) where the Minister has, under subsection 8506(2.1), waived the application of the condition in paragraph 8506(2)(*b*.1) in respect of a money purchase provision of the plan, a payment under the provision of an amount acceptable to the Minister;

(ix) a payment, other than a payment described in subparagraph (i), with respect to a member of a single amount that the plan is required to make because of the *Pension Benefits Standards Act, 1985* or a similar law of a province, where the single amount is not transferred directly to another registered pension plan, a registered retirement savings plan or a registered retirement income fund; or

(x) the portion of the IPP minimum amount for an individual that is not described in subparagraph (i).

History: S. 8502(*d*)(x) was added by S.C. 2011, c. 24, s. 95(1), applicable to the 2012 and subsequent taxation years.

(e) Payment of pension — the plan

(i) requires that the retirement benefits of a member under each benefit provision of the plan begin to be paid not later than the end of the calendar year in which the member attains 71 years of age except that,

(A) in the case of benefits provided under a defined benefit provision, the benefits may begin to be paid at any later time that is acceptable to the Minister, if the amount of benefits (expressed on an annualized basis) payable does not exceed the amount of benefits that would be payable if payment of the benefits began at the end of the calendar year in which the member attains 71 years of age, and

(B) in the case of benefits provided under a money purchase provision in accordance with paragraph 8506(1)(*e*.1), the benefits may begin to be paid not later than the end of the calendar year in which the member attains 72 years of age, and

(ii) provides that retirement benefits under each benefit provision are payable not less frequently than annually;

(f) Assignment of rights — the plan includes a stipulation that no right of a person under the plan is capable of being assigned, charged, anticipated, given as security or surrendered, and, for the purposes of this condition,

(i) assignment does not include

(A) assignment pursuant to a decree, order or judgment of a competent tribunal or a written agreement in settlement of rights arising out of a marriage or common-law partnership between an individual and the individual's spouse or common-law partner or former spouse or common-law partner, on or after the breakdown of their marriage or common-law partnership, or

(B) assignment by the legal representative of a deceased individual on the distribution of the individual's estate, and

(ii) surrender does not include a reduction in benefits to avoid the revocation of the registration of the plan;

(g) Funding media — the arrangement under which property is held in connection with the plan is acceptable to the Minister;

Registered Plans Directorate Newsletters: No. 91-4R, Registration rules for money purchase provisions.

Regulations

(h) Investments — the property that is held in connection with the plan does not include

(i) a prohibited investment under subsection 8514(1),

(ii) at any time that the plan is subject to the *Pension Benefits Standards Act, 1985* or a similar law of a province, an investment that is not permitted at that time under such laws as apply to the plan, or

(iii) at any time other than a time referred to in subparagraph (ii), an investment that would not be permitted were the plan subject to the *Pension Benefits Standards Act, 1985*;

Proposed Amendment

2019 Federal Budget Resolutions

The Act is modified to give effect to the proposals relating to permitting additional types of annuities under registered plans described in the budget documents tabled by the Minister of Finance in the House of Commons on Budget Day.

Explanatory Note:
Dentons Canada LLP Commentary

Budget 2019 proposes to provide "qualified investment" status to the following additional types of annuities for certain registered plans, effective for 2020 and subsequent taxation years:

- advanced life deferred annuities will be permitted under a registered retirement savings plan (RRSP), registered retirement income fund (RRIF), deferred profit sharing plan (DPSP), pooled registered pension plan (PRPP) and defined contribution registered pension plan (RPP); and
- variable payment life annuities will be permitted under a PRPP and defined contribution RPP.

Advanced Life Deferred Annuities (ALDA)

The tax rules generally require an annuity purchased with a registered plan to commence by the end of the year in which the annuitant attains 71 years of age. An ALDA will be a life annuity the commencement of which may be deferred until the end of the year in which the annuitant turns 85 and meets certain other prescribed conditions. A lifetime limit of 25% of the value of the plan (including payments for the ALDA) and $150,000 will apply.

Annuity payments to a surviving spouse or common-law partner will be taxable in the year of receipt. Lump-sum payments to a surviving spouse, common-law partner or dependent child or grandchild (provided that the child or grandchild is dependent by reason of physical or mental infirmity) will qualify for a tax-deferred transfer to an RRSP, RRIF or other eligible vehicle of the annuitant.

Variable Payment Life Annuity (VPLA)

Existing rules generally require retirement benefits from a PRPP or defined contribution RPP be provided to a member by means of a transfer of funds from the account to an RRSP or RRIF. Budget 2019 proposes that commencing in 2020 and subsequent years, PRPP and RPPs be able to provide a VPLA directly to members from the plan. A VPLA will provide payments that vary based on the investment performance of the underlying annuities fund and on the mortality experience of VPLA annuitants.

PRPP and defined contribution RPP administrators will be permitted to establish a separate annuities fund under the plan to receive transfers of amounts from members' accounts to provide for VPLAs. A minimum of 10 retired members will be required to participate in a VPLA. VPLAs will be required to comply with certain existing tax rules applicable to PRPPs and defined contribution RPPs, as well as additional requirements. On death, VPLAs will be subject to the existing tax treatment of annuities purchased with PRPP and defined contribution RPP savings.

(i) Borrowing — a trustee or other person who holds property in connection with the plan does not borrow money for the purposes of the plan, except where

(i) the borrowing is for a term not exceeding 90 days,

(ii) the borrowing is not part of a series of loans or other transactions and repayments, and

(iii) none of the property that is held in connection with the plan is used as security for the borrowed money (except where the borrowing is necessary to provide funds for the current payment of benefits or the purchase of annuities under the plan without resort to a distressed sale of the property that is held in connection with the plan),

or where

(iv) the money is borrowed for the purpose of acquiring real property that may reasonably be considered to be acquired for the purpose of producing income from property,

(v) the aggregate of all amounts borrowed for the purpose of acquiring the property and any indebtedness incurred as a consequence of the acquisition of the property does not exceed the cost to the person of the property, and

(vi) none of the property that is held in connection with the plan, other than the real property, is used as security for the borrowed money;

(j) Determination of amounts — except as otherwise provided in this Part, each amount that is determined in connection with the plan is determined, where the amount is based on assumptions, using such reasonable assumptions as are acceptable to the Minister, and, where actuarial principles are applicable to the determination, in accordance with generally accepted actuarial principles;

Registered Plans Directorate Newsletters: No. 95-5, Conversion of a defined benefit provision to a money purchase provision; No. 94-3R, Using assumptions to compute the present value of benefits.

(k) Transfer of property between provisions — property that is held in connection with a benefit provision of the plan is not made available to pay benefits under another benefit provision of the plan (including another benefit provision that replaces the first benefit provision), except where the transaction by which the property is made so available is such that if the benefit provisions were in separate registered pension plans, the transaction would constitute a transfer of property from one plan to the other in accordance with any of subsections 147.3(1) to (4.1), (6), (7.1) and (8) of the Act;

Registered Plans Directorate Newsletters: No. 91-4R, Registration rules for money purchase provisions.

(l) Appropriate pension adjustments — the plan terms are not such that an amount that is determined under Part LXXXIII in respect of the plan would be inappropriate having regard to the provisions of that Part read as a whole and the purposes for which the amount is determined; and

(m) Participants in GSRAs — no individual who, at any time after 1993, is entitled, either absolutely or contingently, to benefits under the plan because of employment with an employer with whom the individual is connected is entitled at that time, either absolutely or contingently, to benefits under a government-sponsored retirement arrangement (as defined in subsection 8308.4(1)).

8503. Defined Benefit Provisions

(1) Net Contribution Accounts. In this section and subsection 8517(2), the net contribution account of a member of a pension plan in relation to a defined benefit provision of the plan is an account that is

Registered Plans Directorate Newsletters: No. 04-1, Transfers from a defined benefit provision to a money purchase provision, an RRSP, or a RRIF and transfers between defined benefit provisions.

(*a*) credited with

(i) the amount of each contribution that is made by the member to the plan in respect of the provision,

(ii) each amount that is transferred on behalf of the member to the plan in respect of the provision in accordance with any of subsections 146(16), 147(19) and 147.3(2) and (5) to (7) of the Act,

(iii) such portion of each amount that is transferred to the plan in respect of the provision in accordance with subsection 147.3(3) of the Act as may reasonably be considered to derive from contributions that are made by the member to a registered pension plan or interest (computed at a reasonable rate) in respect of those contributions,

(iv) the amount of any property that was held in connection with another benefit provision of the plan and that has been made available to provide benefits under the provision, to the extent that if the provisions were in separate registered pension plans, the amount would be included in the member's net contribution account by reason of subparagraph (ii) or (iii), and

(v) interest (computed at a reasonable rate determined by the plan administrator) in respect of each period throughout which the account has a positive balance; and

(*b*) charged with

(i) each amount that is paid under the provision with respect to the member, otherwise than in respect of an actuarial surplus under the provision,

(ii) the amount of any property that is held in connection with the provision (other than property that is in respect of an actuarial surplus under the provision) and that is made available to provide benefits with respect to the member under another benefit provision of the plan, and

(iii) interest (computed at a reasonable rate determined by the plan administrator) in respect of each period throughout which the account has a negative balance.

(2) Permissible Benefits. For the purposes of paragraph 8502(*c*), the following benefits may, subject to the conditions set out in respect of each benefit, be provided under a defined benefit provision of a pension plan:

Registered Plans Directorate Newsletters: No. 94-2, Technical questions and answers; No. 92-12, Commutation and opting out of a pension plan; No. 92-6, Pre-reform disability and bridging benefits; No. 92-5, Pre-reform death benefits.

(a) Lifetime retirement benefits — lifetime retirement benefits provided to a member where the benefits are payable in equal periodic amounts, or are not so payable only by reason that

(i) the benefits payable to a member after the death of the member's spouse or common-law partner are less than the benefits that would be payable to the member were the member's spouse or common-law partner alive,

(ii) the plan provides for periodic cost-of-living adjustments to be made to the benefits, where the adjustments

(A) are determined in such a manner that they do not exceed cost-of-living adjustments warranted by increases in the Consumer Price Index after the benefits commence to be paid,

(B) consist of periodic increases at a rate not exceeding 4 per cent per annum after the time the benefits commence to be paid,

(C) are based on the rates of return on a specified pool of assets after the benefits commence to be paid, or

(D) consist of any combination of adjustments described in clauses (A) to (C),

and, in the case of adjustments described in clauses (C) and (D), the present value (at the time the member's benefits commence to be paid) of additional benefits that can reasonably be expected to be paid as a consequence of the adjustments does not exceed the greater of

(E) the present value (at the time the member's benefits commence to be paid) of additional benefits that could reasonably be expected to be paid as a consequence of adjustments warranted by increases in the Consumer Price Index after the member's benefits commence to be paid, and

(F) the present value (at the time the member's benefits commence to be paid) of additional benefits that would be paid as a consequence of adjustments at a fixed rate of 4 per cent per annum after the time the member's benefits commence to be paid,

(iii) where the plan does not provide for periodic cost-of-living adjustments to be made to the benefits, or provides only for such adjustments as are

Regulations

described in clause (ii)(A) or (B), the plan provides for cost-of-living adjustments to be made to the benefits from time to time at the discretion of any person, where the adjustments, together with periodic cost-of-living adjustments, if any, are warranted by increases in the Consumer Price Index after the benefits commence to be paid,

(iv) the amount of the benefits is increased as a consequence of additional lifetime retirement benefits becoming provided to the member under the provision,

(v) the amount of the benefits is determined with a reduction computed by reference to the member's age, duration of service, or both (or with any other similar reduction), and the amount is subsequently adjusted to reduce or eliminate the portion, if any, of the reduction that is not required for the benefits to comply with the conditions in paragraph (3)(*c*),

(vi) the amount of the benefits is determined with a reduction computed by reference to the following benefits and the amount is subsequently adjusted to reduce or eliminate the reduction:

(A) disability benefits to which the member is entitled under the *Canada Pension Plan* or a provincial pension plan as defined in section 3 of that Act,

(B) benefits to which the member is entitled under an employees' or workers' compensation law of Canada or a province in respect of an injury or disability, or

(C) benefits to which the member is entitled pursuant to a sickness or accident insurance plan or a disability insurance plan,

(vii) the amount of the benefits is determined with a reduction computed by reference to other benefits provided under the provision in respect of the member that are permissible under paragraph (*c*), (*d*), (*k*) or (*n*), and the amount is subsequently adjusted to reduce or eliminate the reduction,

(viii) the amount of the benefits is reduced as a consequence of benefits that are permissible under paragraph (*c*), (*d*), (*k*) or (*n*) becoming provided under the provision in respect of the member,

(ix) the amount of the benefits payable to the member while the member is in receipt of remuneration from a participating employer is less than the amount of the benefits that would otherwise be payable to the member if the member were not in receipt of the remuneration, or

(x) the amount of the benefits is adjusted in accordance with plan terms that were submitted to the Minister before April 19, 2000, where the benefits have commenced to be paid before 2003 and the adjustment is approved by the Minister;

(b) Bridging benefits — bridging benefits provided to a member where

(i) the bridging benefits are payable for a period beginning no earlier than the time lifetime retirement benefits commence to be paid under the provision to the member and ending no later than the end of the month immediately following the month in which the member attains 65 years of age, and

(ii) the amount of the bridging benefits payable for a particular month does not exceed the amount that is determined for that month by the formula

$$A \times (1 - .0025 \times B) \times C \times (D / 10)$$

where

A is the amount (or a reasonable estimate thereof) of public pension benefits that would be payable to the member for the month in which the bridging benefits commence to be paid to the member if

(A) the member were 65 years of age throughout that month,

(B) that month were the first month for which public pension benefits were payable to the member,

(C) the member were entitled to the maximum amount of benefits payable under the *Old Age Security Act*, and

(D) the member were entitled to that proportion, not exceeding one, of the maximum benefits payable under the *Canada Pension Plan* (or a provincial plan as defined in section 3 of the *Canada Pension Plan*) that the total of the member's remuneration for the 3 calendar years in which the remuneration is the highest is of the total of the Year's Maximum Pensionable Earnings for those 3 years (or such other proportion of remuneration to Year's Maximum Pensionable Earnings as is acceptable to the Minister),

B is,

(A) except where clause (B) is applicable, the number of months, if any, from the date on which the bridging benefits commence to be paid to the member to the date on which the member attains 60 years of age, and

(B) where the member is totally and permanently disabled at the time the bridging benefits commence to be paid to the member and the member was not, at any time after 1990, connected with an employer who has participated in the plan, nil,

C is the greatest of all amounts each of which is the ratio of the Consumer Price Index for a month not before the month in which the bridging benefits commence to be paid to the member and not after the particular month, to the Consumer Price Index for the month in which the bridging benefits commence to be paid to the member, and

D is

(A) except where clause (B) is applicable, the lesser of 10 and

(I) where the member was not, at any time after 1990, connected with an employer who has participated in the plan, the aggregate of all amounts each of which is the duration (measured in years, including any fraction of a year) of a period that is pensionable service of the member under the provision, and

(II) in any other case, the aggregate that would be determined under subclause (I) if the duration of each period were multiplied by a fraction (not greater than 1) that measures the services rendered by the member throughout the period to employers who participate in the plan as a proportion of the services that would have been rendered by the member throughout the period to such employers had the member rendered services on a full-time basis, and

(B) where the member is totally and permanently disabled at the time the bridging benefits commence to be paid to the member and the member was not, at any time after 1990, connected with an employer who has participated in the plan, 10;

(c) Guarantee period — retirement benefits (in this paragraph referred to as "continued retirement benefits") provided to one or more beneficiaries of a member who dies after retirement benefits under the provision commence to be paid to the member where

(i) the continued retirement benefits are payable for a period beginning after the death of the member and ending

(A) if retirement benefits permissible under paragraph (*d*) are provided under the provision to a spouse or common-law partner or former spouse or common-law partner of the member, no later than five years, and

(B) in any other case, no later than 15 years

after the day on which retirement benefits commence to be paid under the provision to the member, and

(ii) the aggregate amount of continued retirement benefits payable under the provision for each month does not exceed the amount of retirement benefits that would have been payable under the provision for the month to the member if the member were alive;

(d) Post-retirement survivor benefits — retirement benefits (in this paragraph referred to as "survivor retirement benefits") provided to one or more beneficiaries of a member who dies after retirement benefits under the provision commence to be paid to the member where

(i) each beneficiary is, at the time of the member's death, a spouse, a common-law partner, a former spouse, a former common-law partner or a dependant, of the member,

(ii) the survivor retirement benefits provided to a spouse or common-law partner or former spouse or common-law partner are payable for a period beginning after the death of the member and ending with the death of the spouse or common-law partner or former spouse or common-law partner,

(iii) the survivor retirement benefits provided to a dependant are payable for a period beginning after the death of the member and ending no later than at the end of the dependant's eligible survivor benefit period,

(iv) the amount of survivor retirement benefits payable for each month to a beneficiary does not exceed 66⅔ per cent of the amount of retirement benefits that would have been payable under the provision for the month to the member if the member were alive, and

(v) the aggregate amount of survivor retirement benefits and other retirement benefits payable under the provision for each month to beneficiaries of the member does not exceed the amount of retirement benefits that would have been payable under the provision for the month to the member if the member were alive;

(e) Pre-retirement survivor benefits — retirement benefits (in this paragraph referred to as "survivor retirement benefits") provided to one or more beneficiaries of a member who dies before retirement benefits under the provision commence to be paid to the member where

(i) no other benefits (other than benefits permissible under paragraph (*g*), (*j*), (*l.1*) or (*n*)) are payable as a consequence of the member's death,

(ii) each beneficiary is, at the time of the member's death, a spouse, a common-law partner, a former spouse, a former common-law partner or a dependant, of the member,

(iii) the survivor retirement benefits provided to a spouse or common-law partner or former spouse or common-law partner are payable for a period beginning after the death of the member and ending with the death of the spouse or common-law partner or former spouse or common-law partner,

(iv) the survivor retirement benefits provided to a dependant are payable for a period beginning after the death of the member and ending no later than at the end of the dependant's eligible survivor benefit period,

(v) the amount of survivor retirement benefits payable for a month to a beneficiary does not exceed $66^{2}/_{3}$ per cent of the amount that is determined in respect of the month by the formula set out in subparagraph (vi), and

(vi) the aggregate amount of survivor retirement benefits payable under the provision for a particular month to beneficiaries of the member does not exceed the amount that is determined for the particular month by the formula

$$((A + B)/12) \times C$$

where

A is the amount (expressed on an annualized basis) of lifetime retirement benefits that accrued under the provision to the member as of the member's day of death, determined without any reduction computed by reference to the member's age, duration of service, or both, and without any other similar reduction,

B is, in the case of a member who attains 65 years of age before the member's death or who was, at any time after 1990, connected with an employer who has participated in the plan, nil, and, otherwise, the amount, if any, by which the lesser of

(A) the amount (expressed on an annualized basis) of lifetime retirement benefits that could reasonably be expected to have accrued to the member to the day on which the member would have attained 65 years of age if the member had survived to that day and continued in employment and if the member's rate of remuneration had not increased after the member's day of death, and

(B) the amount, if any, by which $^{3}/_{2}$ of the Year's Maximum Pensionable Earnings for the calendar year in which the member dies exceeds such amount as is required by the Minister to be determined in respect of benefits provided, as a consequence of the death of the member, under other benefit provisions of the plan and under benefit provisions of other registered pension plans

exceeds the amount determined for A, and

C is the greatest of all amounts each of which is the ratio of the Consumer Price Index for a month not before the month in which the member dies and not after the particular month, to the Consumer Price Index for the month in which the member dies;

(f) Pre-retirement survivor benefits — Alternative rule — retirement benefits (in this paragraph referred to as "survivor benefits") provided to a beneficiary of a member who dies before retirement benefits under the defined benefit provision commence to be paid to the member where

(i) no other benefits (other than benefits permissible under paragraph (*g*), (*j*), (*l*.1) or (*n*)) are payable as a consequence of the member's death,

(ii) the beneficiary is a spouse or common-law partner or former spouse or common-law partner of the member,

(iii) the survivor benefits are payable for a period beginning not later than the later of

(A) the day that is one year after the day of death of the member, and

(B) the end of the calendar year in which the beneficiary attains 71 years of age,

and ending with the death of the beneficiary,

(iv) the survivor benefits would be in accordance with paragraph (*a*) if the beneficiary were a member of the plan, and

(v) the present value (at the time of the member's death) of all benefits provided as a consequence of the member's death does not exceed the present value (immediately before the member's death) of all benefits that have accrued under the provision with respect to the member to the day of the member's death;

(g) Pre-retirement survivor benefits — Guarantee period — retirement benefits provided to one or more individuals as a consequence of the death of a person who

(i) is a beneficiary of a member who died before retirement benefits under the provision commenced to be paid to the member,

(ii) was, at the time of the member's death, a spouse or common-law partner or former spouse or common-law partner of the member, and

(iii) dies after the member's death,

where the benefits would be in accordance with paragraph (*c*) if the person were a member of the plan;

(h) Lump sum payments on termination — the payment, with respect to a member in connection with the member's termination from the plan (otherwise than by reason of death), of one or more single amounts where

(i) the payments are the last payments to be made under the provision with respect to the member,

(ii) if subparagraph (iii) is not applicable, each single amount does not exceed the balance in the member's net contribution account immediately before the time of payment of the single amount, and

(iii) if

(A) the Minister has, pursuant to subsection (5), waived the application of the conditions in paragraph (4)(*a*) in respect of the provision, or

(B) the member's contributions under the provision for each calendar year after 1990 would have been in accordance with paragraph (4)(*a*) if the reference in clause (i)(B) thereof to "70 per cent" were read as a reference to "50 per cent",

each single amount does not exceed the amount that would be the balance in the member's net contribution account immediately before the time of the payment of the single amount if, for each current service contribution made by the member under the provision, the account were credited at the time of the contribution with an additional amount equal to the amount of the contribution (other than the portion of the contribution, if any, paid in respect of one or more periods that were not periods of regular employment and that would not have been required to be paid by the member if the periods were periods of regular employment);

(i) Payment of commuted value of benefits on death before retirement — the payment of one or more single amounts to one or more beneficiaries of a member who dies before retirement benefits under the provision commence to be paid to the member where

(i) no retirement benefits are payable as a consequence of the member's death, and

(ii) the aggregate of all amounts, each of which is such a single amount (other than the portion thereof, if any, that can reasonably be considered to be interest, computed at a rate not exceeding a reasonable rate, in respect of the period from the day of death of the member to the day the single amount is paid), does not exceed the present value, immediately before the death of the member, of all benefits that have accrued under the provision with respect to the member to the day of the member's death;

(j) Lump sum payments on death — the payment of one or more single amounts after the death of a member where

(i) the payments are the last payments to be made under the provision with respect to the member,

(ii) if the member dies before retirement benefits under the provision commence to be paid to the member and no retirement benefits are payable as a consequence of the member's death, the aggregate amount to be paid at any time complies with whichever of the conditions in subparagraphs (*h*)(ii) and (iii) would be applicable if the single amounts were paid in connection with the member's termination from the plan otherwise than by reason of death, and

(iii) if subparagraph (ii) is not applicable, the aggregate amount to be paid at any time does not exceed the balance, immediately before that time, in the member's net contribution account in relation to the provision;

(k) Additional post-retirement death benefits — retirement benefits (in this paragraph referred to as "additional death benefits") payable after the death of a member who dies after retirement benefits under the provision commence to be paid to the member where the additional death benefits are

(i) retirement benefits provided to a spouse or common-law partner or former spouse or common-law partner of the member that are in excess of the benefits that are permissible under paragraph (*d*), but that would be permissible under that paragraph if the reference in subparagraph (*d*)(iv) to "66⅔ per cent" were read as a reference to "100 per cent",

(ii) retirement benefits provided to one or more beneficiaries of the member that are in excess of the benefits that are permissible under paragraph (*c*), but that would be permissible under that paragraph if it were read without reference to clause (i)(A) thereof, or

(iii) a combination of retirement benefits described in subparagraphs (i) and (ii),

and where

(iv) the additional death benefits are provided in lieu of a proportion of the lifetime retirement benefits that would otherwise be payable under the provision to the member, and

(v) the present value of all benefits provided under the provision with respect to the member does not exceed the present value of the benefits that would be provided if

(A) the amount of the member's lifetime retirement benefits were determined without any reduction dependent on the benefits payable after the death of the member or on circumstances that are relevant in determining such death benefits,

(B) the maximum amount of retirement benefits that are permissible under paragraph (*d*) were payable to the member's spouse or common-law partner or former spouse or common-law partner after the death of the member, and

(C) those present values were determined as of

(I) except where subclause (II) applies, the particular time at which retirement benefits under the provision commence to be paid to the member, and

(II) where the additional death benefits become provided after the particular time, the time at which the additional death benefits become provided;

(l) Additional bridging benefits — bridging benefits in excess of bridging benefits that are permissible under paragraph (*b*) (referred to in this paragraph as "additional bridging benefits") provided to a member where

(i) the additional bridging benefits would be permissible under paragraph (*b*) if

(A) the formula in subparagraph (*b*)(ii) were replaced by the formula "A/12 × C", and

Regulations

(B) the description of A in subparagraph (*b*)(ii) were read as follows:

"A is 40% of the Year's Maximum Pensionable Earnings for the year in which the bridging benefits commence to be paid to the member,"

(ii) the additional bridging benefits are provided in lieu of all or a proportion of the benefits that would otherwise be payable under the provision with respect to the member, and

(iii) the present value (at the time retirement benefits under the provision commence to be paid to the member) of all benefits provided under the provision with respect to the member does not exceed the present value (at that time) of the benefits that would be so provided if the additional bridging benefits were not provided;

(l.1) Survivor bridging benefits — retirement benefits (in this paragraph referred to as "survivor bridging benefits") provided to a beneficiary of a member after the death of the member where

(i) the beneficiary is a spouse or common-law partner or former spouse or common-law partner of the member,

(ii) the survivor bridging benefits are payable at the election of the beneficiary, and

(iii) the survivor bridging benefits would be in accordance with paragraph (*l*) if the beneficiary were a member of the plan;

(m) Commutation of benefits — the payment with respect to a member of a single amount in full or partial satisfaction of the member's entitlement to other benefits under the provision, where the single amount does not exceed the total of

(i) the present value (at the particular time determined in accordance with subsection (2.1)) of

(A) the other benefits that, as a consequence of the payment, cease to be provided, and

(B) benefits, other than benefits referred to in clause (A), that it is reasonable to consider would cease to be provided as a consequence of the payment if

(I) where retirement benefits have not commenced to be paid under the provision to the member at the particular time, the plan provided for the retirement benefits that accrued to the member under the provision to be adjusted to reflect the increase in a general measure of wages and salaries from the particular time to the day on which the benefits commence to be paid, and

(II) the plan provided for periodic cost-of-living adjustments to be made to the retirement benefits payable under the provision to the member to reflect increases in the Consumer Price Index after the retirement benefits commence to be paid (other than increases before the particular time), and

(ii) interest (computed at a reasonable rate) from the particular time to the time the single amount is paid; and

(n) [Idem] — the payment, with respect to an individual after the death of a member, of a single amount in full or partial satisfaction of the individual's entitlement to other benefits under the provision, where

(i) the individual is a beneficiary of the member,

(ii) the single amount does not exceed the total of

(A) the present value (at the particular time determined in accordance with subsection (2.1)) of the other benefits that, as a consequence of the payment, cease to be provided, and

(B) interest (computed at a reasonable rate) from the particular time to the time the single amount is paid, and

(iii) if the other benefits in respect of which the single amount is paid include benefits described in paragraph (*e*) and the beneficiary was a spouse or common-law partner or former spouse or common-law partner of the member at the time of the member's death, the single amount is not transferred from the plan directly to another registered pension plan, a registered retirement savings plan or a registered retirement income fund except with the approval of the Minister.

(2.1) Rule for Commutation of Benefits. For the purpose of determining the limit on a single amount that can be paid with respect to an individual under paragraph (2)(*m*) or (*n*), the particular time referred to in that paragraph is

(*a*) except where paragraph (*b*) applies, the time the single amount is paid; and

(*b*) an earlier time than the time the single amount is paid, where

(i) the amount is based on a determination of the actuarial value (at the earlier time) of the individual's benefits,

(ii) the use of the earlier time in determining the actuarial value

(A) is required by the *Pension Benefits Standards Act, 1985* or a similar law of a province, or

(B) is reasonable having regard to accepted actuarial practice and the circumstances in which the individual acquires the right to the payment, and

(iii) except where clause (ii)(A) applies, the earlier time is no more than two years before the time the single amount is paid.

(3) Conditions Applicable to Benefits. For the purposes of subsection 8501(2) and subparagraph 8502(*c*)(i), the following conditions are applicable in respect of the benefits provided under each defined benefit provision of a pension plan:

Related Regulations: 8500(7).

Registered Plans Directorate Newsletters: No. 93-2, Foreign service newsletter; No. 92-8R, Eligible service; No. 92-7, Pre-reform early retirement provisions and post-retirement indexing; No. 92-6, Pre-reform disability and bridging benefits.

(a) **Eligible service** — the only lifetime retirement benefits provided under the provision to a member (other than additional lifetime retirement benefits provided to a member because the member is totally and permanently disabled at the time the member's retirement benefits commence to be paid) are lifetime retirement benefits provided in respect of one or more of the following periods (other than the portion of a period that is after the calendar year in which the member attains 71 years of age), namely,

(i) a period throughout which the member is employed in Canada by, and receives remuneration from, an employer who participates in the plan,

(ii) a period throughout which the member was employed in Canada by, and received remuneration from, a predecessor employer to an employer who participates in the plan,

(iii) an eligible period of temporary absence of the member with respect to an employer who participates in the plan or a predecessor employer to such an employer,

(iv) a period of disability of the member subsequent to a period described in subparagraph (i) where, throughout such part of the period of disability as is after 1990, the member is not connected with an employer who participates in the plan,

(v) a period in respect of which

> **Proposed Amendment**
>
> **2019 Federal Budget Resolutions**
>
> **The portion of subparagraph 8503(3)(*a*)(v) of the Regulations before clause (A) is replaced by the following:**
>
> (v) unless the provision is a provision of an individual pension plan, a period in respect of which
>
> **Applicable:** Deemed to have come into force on March 19, 2019. However, subsections (1) to (3) do not apply to a period that was pensionable service (as defined in subsection 8500(1) of the Regulations) in respect of a member under a defined benefit provision of an individual pension plan before March 19, 2019.

(A) both

(I) subparagraph (v.1) does not apply, and

(II) benefits that are attributable to employment of the member with a former employer accrued to the member under a defined benefit provision of another registered pension plan, or

(B) contributions were made by or on behalf of the member under a money purchase provision of another registered pension plan,

where the member has ceased to be a member of that other plan,

(v.1) a portion — determined by reference to the proportion of property that has been transferred, as described in clause (B) — of a period in respect of which

> **Proposed Amendment**
>
> **2019 Federal Budget Resolutions**
>
> **The portion of subparagraph 8503(3)(*a*)(v.1) of the Regulations before clause (A) is replaced by the following:**
>
> (v.1) unless the provision is a provision of an individual pension plan, a portion — determined by reference to the proportion of property that has been transferred, as described in clause (B) — of a period in respect of which
>
> **Applicable:** Deemed to have come into force on March 19, 2019. However, subsections (1) to (3) do not apply to a period that was pensionable service (as defined in subsection 8500(1) of the Regulations) in respect of a member under a defined benefit provision of an individual pension plan before March 19, 2019.

(A) benefits that are attributable to employment of the member with a former employer accrued to the member under a defined benefit provision of another registered pension plan, and

(B) pursuant to the *Pension Benefits Standards Act, 1985* or a similar law of a province, a portion of property held in connection with the benefits described in clause (A) has been transferred to the provision and the balance of property is required to be transferred to the provision at a later date,

(vi) a period throughout which the member was employed in Canada by a former employer where the period was an eligibility period for the participation of the member in another registered pension plan, and

> **Proposed Amendment**
>
> **2019 Federal Budget Resolutions**
>
> **Subparagraph 8503(3)(*a*)(vi) of the Regulations is replaced by the following:**
>
> (vi) unless the provision is a provision of an individual pension plan, a period throughout which the member was employed in Canada by a former employer where the period was an eligibility period for the participation of the member in another registered pension plan, and
>
> **Applicable:** Deemed to have come into force on March 19, 2019. However, subsections (1) to (3) do not apply to a period that was pensionable service (as defined in subsection 8500(1) of the Regulations) in respect of a member under a defined benefit provision of an individual pension plan before March 19, 2019.

(vii) a period acceptable to the Minister throughout which the member is employed outside Canada;

History: S. 8503(3)(*a*)(v)(A) was replaced by S.C. 2017, c. 33, s. 102(1), applicable in respect of transfers of property that occur after 2012, and formerly read:

(A) benefits that are attributable to employment of the member with a former employer accrued to the member under a defined benefit provision of another registered pension plan, or

S. 8503(3)(*a*)(v.1) was added by S.C. 2017, c. 33, s. 102(2), applicable in respect of transfers of property that occur after 2012.

Information Circulars: IC 98-2 Prescribed Compensation for Registered Pension Plans.

(b) Benefit accruals after pension commencement — benefits are not provided under the provision (in this paragraph referred to as the "particular provision") to a member in respect of a period that is after the day on which retirement benefits commence to be paid to the member under a defined benefit provision of

(i) the plan, or

(ii) any other registered pension plan if

(A) an employer who participated under the particular provision for the benefit of the member, or

(B) an employer who does not deal at arm's length with an employer referred to in clause (A)

has participated under the defined benefit provision of the other plan for the benefit of the member;

(c) Early retirement — where lifetime retirement benefits commence to be paid under the provision to a member at any time before

(i) in the case of a member whose benefits are provided in respect of employment in a public safety occupation, the earliest of

(A) the day on which the member attains 55 years of age,

(B) the day on which the member has 25 years of early retirement eligibility service in relation to the provision,

(C) the day on which the aggregate of the member's age (measured in years, including any fraction of a year) and years of early retirement eligibility service in relation to the provision is equal to 75, and

(D) if the member was not, at any time after 1990, connected with any employer who has participated in the plan, the day on which the member becomes totally and permanently disabled, and

(ii) in any other case, the earliest of

(A) the day on which the member attains 60 years of age,

(B) the day on which the member has 30 years of early retirement eligibility service in relation to the provision,

(C) the day on which the aggregate of the member's age (measured in years, including any fraction of a year) and years of early retirement eligibility service in relation to the provision is equal to 80, and

(D) if the member was not, at any time after 1990, connected with any employer who has participated in the plan, the day on which the member becomes totally and permanently disabled,

the amount (expressed on an annualized basis) of lifetime retirement benefits payable to the member for each calendar year does not exceed the amount that is determined for the year by the formula

$$X \times (1 - .0025 \times Y)$$

where

X is the amount (expressed on an annualized basis) of lifetime retirement benefits that would be payable to the member for the year if the benefits were determined without a reduction computed by reference to the member's age, duration of service, or both, and without any other similar reduction, and

Y is the number of months in the period from the day on which lifetime retirement benefits commence to be paid to the member to the earliest of the days that would be determined under clauses (i)(A) to (C) or (ii)(A) to (C), as the case may be, if the member continued in employment with an employer who participates in the plan,

and, for the purposes of this paragraph,

(iii) "early retirement eligibility service" of a member in relation to a defined benefit provision of a pension plan means one or more periods each of which is

(A) a period that is pensionable service of the member under the provision, or

(B) a period throughout which the member was employed by an employer who has participated in the plan or by a predecessor employer to such an employer, and

(iv) "years of early retirement eligibility service" of a member in relation to a defined benefit provision of a pension plan means the aggregate of all amounts each of which is the duration (measured in years, including any fraction of a year) of a period that is early retirement eligibility service of the member in relation to the provision;

(d) Increased benefits for disabled member — where the amount of lifetime retirement benefits provided under the provision to a member depends on whether the member is physically or mentally impaired at the time (in this paragraph referred to as the "time of commencement") at which retirement benefits under the provision commence to be paid to the member,

(i) the amount of lifetime retirement benefits payable if the member

(A) is not totally and permanently disabled at the time of commencement, or

(B) is totally and permanently disabled at the time of commencement and was, at any time after 1990, connected with an employer who has participated in the plan satisfies the limit that would be determined by the formula set out in paragraph (*c*) if the member were not impaired at the time of commencement, and

(ii) the amount of lifetime retirement benefits payable for a particular month to the member if subparagraph (i) is not applicable does not exceed the amount that is determined for the particular month by the formula

$$((A + B)/12) \times C$$

where

A is the amount (expressed on an annualized basis) of lifetime retirement benefits that have accrued under the provision to the member to the time of commencement, determined as if the member were not impaired at the time of commencement and without any reduction computed by reference to the member's age, duration of service, or both, and without any other similar reduction,

B is, in the case of a member who attains 65 years of age before the time of commencement, nil, and, otherwise, the amount, if any, by which the lesser of

(A) the amount (expressed on an annualized basis) of lifetime retirement benefits that could reasonably be expected to have accrued to the member to the day on which the member would have attained 65 years of age if the member had survived to that day and continued in employment and if the member's rate of remuneration had not increased after the time of commencement, and

(B) the amount, if any, by which the Year's Maximum Pensionable Earnings for the calendar year that includes the time of commencement exceeds such amount as is required by the Minister to be determined in respect of benefits provided to the member under other benefit provisions of the plan and under benefit provisions of other registered pension plans

exceeds the amount determined for A, and

C is the greatest of all amounts each of which is the ratio of the Consumer Price Index for a month not before the month that includes the time of commencement and not after the particular month to the Consumer Price Index for the month that includes the time of commencement;

(e) **Pre-1991 benefits** — all benefits provided under the provision in respect of periods before 1991 are acceptable to the Minister and, for the purposes of this condition, any benefits in respect of periods before 1991 that become provided after 1988 with respect to a member who is connected with an employer who participates in the plan or was so connected at any time before the benefits become provided, shall, unless the Minister is notified in writing that the benefits are provided with respect to the member, be deemed to be unacceptable to the Minister;

(f) **Determination of retirement benefits** — the amount of retirement benefits provided under the provision to a member is determined in such a manner that the member's pension credit (as determined under Part LXXXIII) under the provision for a calendar year with respect to an employer is determinable at the end of the year;

(g) **Benefit accrual rate** — if the amount of lifetime retirement benefits provided under the provision to a member is determined, in part, by multiplying the member's remuneration (or a function of the member's remuneration) by an annual benefit accrual rate, or in a manner that is equivalent to that calculation, the annual benefit accrual rate or the equivalent annual benefit accrual rate does not exceed

(i) in the case of a member whose benefits are provided in respect of employment in a public safety occupation and for whom the formula for determining the amount of the lifetime retirement benefits can reasonably be considered to take into account public pension benefits, 2.33 per cent, and

(ii) in any other case, 2 per cent;

(h) **Increase in accrued benefits** — where the amount of lifetime retirement benefits provided to a member in respect of a calendar year depends on

(i) the member's remuneration in subsequent years, or

(ii) the average wage (or other general measure of wages and salaries) for subsequent years,

and this condition has not been waived by the Minister, the formula for determining the amount of lifetime retirement benefits is such that

(iii) the percentage increase from year to year in the amount of lifetime retirement benefits that accrued to the member in respect of the year can reasonably be expected to approximate or be less than the percentage increase from year to year in the member's remuneration or in the average wage (or other general measure of wages and salaries), as the case may be, or

(iv) the condition in subparagraph (iii) is not satisfied only by reason that the formula can reasonably be considered to have been designed taking into account the public pension benefits payable to members,

and, for the purposes of this condition, where in determining the amount of lifetime retirement benefits provided under the provision to a member there is deducted an amount described in subparagraph (*j*)(i), it shall be assumed that the amount so deducted is nil;

(i) **[Idem]** — where the amount of lifetime retirement benefits provided to a member in respect of a cal-

Regulations

endar year depends on the member's remuneration in other years, the formula for determining the amount of the lifetime retirement benefits is such that any increase in the amount of lifetime retirement benefits that accrued to the member in respect of the year that is attributable to increased remuneration is primarily attributable to an increase in the rate of the member's remuneration;

(j) Offset benefits — where

(i) in determining the amount of lifetime retirement benefits provided under the provision to a member there is deducted

(A) the amount of lifetime retirement benefits provided to the member under a benefit provision of a registered pension plan, or

(B) the amount of a lifetime annuity that is provided to the member under a deferred profit sharing plan, and

(ii) a single amount is paid in full or partial satisfaction of the member's entitlement to benefits under the benefit provision referred to in clause (i)(A) or the deferred profit sharing plan referred to in clause (i)(B),

the amount that is so deducted in determining the amount of the member's lifetime retirement benefits under the defined benefit provision includes the amount of lifetime retirement benefits or lifetime annuity that may reasonably be considered to have been foregone as a consequence of the payment of the single amount;

(k) Bridging benefits — Cross-plan restriction — bridging benefits are not paid under the provision to a member who receives bridging benefits under another defined benefit provision of the plan (in this paragraph referred to as the "particular plan") or under a defined benefit provision of another registered pension plan, except that this condition is not applicable where it is waived by the Minister or where

(i) bridging benefits are paid to the member under only one defined benefit provision of the particular plan,

(ii) the decision to provide bridging benefits under the particular plan to the member was not made by the member, by persons with whom the member does not deal at arm's length or by the member and such persons, and

(iii) each employer who has participated in any registered pension plan (other than the particular plan) under a defined benefit provision of which the member receives bridging benefits

(A) has not participated in the particular plan, and

(B) has always dealt at arm's length with each employer who has participated in the particular plan,

and, for the purposes of this paragraph, bridging benefits provided under a defined benefit provision of a registered pension plan to the member do not include benefits that are provided on a basis no more favourable than an actuarially equivalent basis in lieu of all or a proportion of the benefits that would otherwise be payable under the provision with respect to the member; and

(l) Division of benefits on breakdown of the marriage or common-law partnership — if, by reason of a provision of a law described in subparagraph 8501(5)(*b*)(ii), an individual who is a spouse or common-law partner or former spouse or common-law partner of a member becomes entitled to receive all or a portion of the benefits that would otherwise be payable under the defined benefit provision to the member, and paragraph 8501(5)(*d*) applies with respect to the benefits,

(i) the present value of benefits provided under the provision with respect to the member (including, for greater certainty, benefits provided with respect to the individual) is not increased as a consequence of the individual becoming so entitled to benefits, and

(ii) the benefits provided under the provision to the member are not, at any time, adjusted to replace, in whole or in part, the portion of the member's benefits to which the individual has become entitled.

(4) Additional Conditions. For the purposes of section 8501, the following conditions are applicable in respect of each defined benefit provision of a pension plan:

Registered Plans Directorate Newsletters: No. 94-2, Technical questions and answers.

(a) Member contributions — where members are required or permitted to make contributions under the provision,

(i) the aggregate amount of current service contributions to be made by a member in respect of a calendar year after 1990, no part of which is a period of disability or an eligible period of reduced pay or temporary absence of the member, does not exceed the lesser of

(A) 9 per cent of the aggregate of all amounts each of which is the member's compensation for the year from an employer who participates in the plan in the year for the benefit of the member, and

(B) the aggregate of $1,000 and 70 per cent of the aggregate of all amounts each of which is the amount that would be the member's pension credit (as determined under Part LXXXIII) for the year under the provision with respect to an employer if section 8302 were read without reference to paragraphs (2)(*b*) and (3)(*g*) thereof,

(ii) the method for determining current service contributions to be made by a member in respect of a calendar year that includes a period of disability or an eligible period of reduced pay or temporary absence of the member (referred to in this subparagraph as "a period of reduced services") is consistent with that used for determining contributions in respect of years described in subparagraph (i), except that the member may be permitted or required to make, in respect of a period of reduced services, current service contributions not exceeding the amount reasonably necessary to fund the member's benefits in respect of the period of reduced services, and

(iii) the aggregate amount of contributions to be made by a member in connection with benefits that, as a consequence of a transaction, event or circumstance occurring at a particular time, become provided under the provision in respect of periods before that time does not exceed the amount reasonably necessary to fund such benefits;

(b) Pre-payment of member contributions — the contributions that are made under the provision by a member in respect of a calendar year are not paid before the year;

(c) Reduction in benefits and return of contributions — where the plan is not established by an enactment of Canada or a province, it includes a stipulation that permits, for the purpose of avoiding revocation of the registration of the plan,

(i) the plan to be amended at any time to reduce the benefits provided under the provision with respect to a member, and

(ii) a contribution that is made under the provision by a member or an employer to be returned to the person who made the contribution,

which stipulation may provide that an amendment to the plan, or a return of contributions, is subject to the approval of the authority administering the *Pension Benefits Standards Act, 1985* or a similar law of a province;

(d) Undue deferral of payment — each single amount that is payable after the death of a member is paid as soon as is practicable after the member's death (or, in the case of a single amount permitted by reason of paragraph (2)(*j*), after all other benefits have been paid);

(e) Evidence of disability — where additional lifetime retirement benefits are provided under the provision to a member because the member is totally and permanently disabled, the additional benefits are not paid before the plan administrator has received from a medical doctor or a nurse practitioner who is licensed to practise under the laws of a province or of the place where the member resides a written report providing the information on the medical condition of the member taken into account by the administrator in determining that the member is totally and permanently disabled; and

(f) Idem — where lifetime retirement benefits are provided under the provision to a member in respect of a period of disability of the member, the benefits, to the extent that they would not be in accordance with paragraph (3)(*a*) if that paragraph were read without reference to subparagraph (iv) thereof, are not paid before the plan administrator has received from a medical doctor or a nurse practitioner who is licensed to practise under the laws of a province or of the place where the member resides a written report providing the information on the medical condition of the member taken into account by the administrator in determining that the period is a period of disability.

History: S. 8503(4)(*e*) and (*f*) were replaced by S.C. 2017, c. 33, s. 102(3), applicable in respect of reports made after September 7, 2017, and formerly read:

(*e*) *Evidence of disability* — where additional lifetime retirement benefits are provided under the provision to a member because the member is totally and permanently disabled, the additional benefits are not paid before the plan administrator has received from a medical doctor who is licensed to practise under the laws of a province or of the place where the member resides a written report providing the information on the medical condition of the member taken into account by the administrator in determining that the member is totally and permanently disabled; and

(*f*) *Idem* — where lifetime retirement benefits are provided under the provision to a member in respect of a period of disability of the member, the benefits, to the extent that they would not be in accordance with paragraph (3)(*a*) if that paragraph were read without reference to subparagraph (iv) thereof, are not paid before the plan administrator has received from a medical doctor who is licensed to practise under the laws of a province or of the place where the member resides a written report providing the information on the medical condition of the member taken into account by the administrator in determining that the period is a period of disability.

(5) Waiver of Member Contribution Condition. The Minister may waive the conditions in paragraph (4)(*a*) where member contributions under a defined benefit provision of a pension plan are determined in a manner acceptable to the Minister and it is reasonable to expect that, on a long-term basis, the aggregate of the regular current service contributions made under the provision by all members will not exceed $1/2$ of the amount that is required to fund the aggregate benefits in respect of which those contributions are made.

(6) Pre-Retirement Death Benefits. A pension plan may provide, in the case of a member who dies before retirement benefits under a defined benefit provision of the plan commence to be paid to the member but after becoming eligible to have retirement benefits commence to be paid, benefits under the provision to the beneficiaries of the member where the benefits would be in accordance with subsection (2) if retirement benefits under the provision had commenced to be paid to the member immediately before the member's death.

Registered Plans Directorate Newsletters: No. 92-5, Pre-reform death benefits.

(7) Commutation of Lifetime Retirement Benefits. Where a pension plan permits a member to receive a single amount in full or partial satisfaction of the member's entitlement to lifetime retirement benefits under a defined benefit provision of the plan, the following rules apply:

(*a*) the condition in subparagraph (2)(*b*)(i) that the payment of bridging benefits under the provision not commence before lifetime retirement benefits commence to be paid under the provision to the member is not applicable where, before the member's lifetime retirement benefits commence to be paid, a single amount is paid in full satisfaction of the member's entitlement to the lifetime retirement benefits; and

Regulations

(*b*) such part of the member's lifetime retirement benefits as remains payable after a single amount is paid in full satisfaction of the member's entitlement to lifetime retirement benefits that would otherwise be payable after the member attains a particular age shall be deemed, for the purposes of the conditions in this section, to be lifetime retirement benefits and not to be bridging benefits.

Registered Plans Directorate Newsletters: No. 04-1, Transfers from a Defined Benefit Provision to a Money Purchase Provision, an RRSP, or a RRIF and Transfers between Defined Benefit Provisions; No. 94-2, Technical questions and answers.

(7.1) Bridging Benefits and Election. Where a pension plan permits a member, or a spouse or common-law partner or former spouse or common-law partner of the member, to elect to receive benefits described in any of paragraphs (2)(*b*), (*l*) or (*l*.1) under a defined benefit provision of the plan on a basis no more favourable than an actuarially equivalent basis in lieu of all or a proportion of the benefits that would otherwise be payable under the provision with respect to the member, the following rules apply:

(*a*) the condition in subparagraph (2)(*b*)(i) that the payment of bridging benefits under the provision not commence before lifetime retirement benefits commence to be paid under the provision to the member does not apply if, as a consequence of the election, no lifetime retirement benefits remain payable under the provision to the member; and

(*b*) for the purpose of determining whether retirement benefits provided under the provision to beneficiaries of the member are in accordance with paragraphs (2)(*c*), (*d*) and (*k*), the election may be disregarded.

(8) Suspension or Cessation of Pension. A pension plan may provide for

(*a*) the suspension of payment of a member's retirement benefits under a defined benefit provision of the plan where

(i) the retirement benefits payable to the member after the suspension are not altered by reason of the suspension, or

(ii) subsection (9) is applicable in respect of the member's retirement benefits; and

(*b*) the cessation of payment of any additional benefits that are payable to a member under a defined benefit provision of the plan because of a physical or mental impairment of the member or the termination of the member's employment under a downsizing program (within the meaning assigned by subsection 8505(1)).

(9) Re-Employed Member. Subject to subsection (10), where a pension plan provides, in the case of a member who becomes an employee of a participating employer after the member's retirement benefits under a defined benefit provision of the plan have commenced to be paid, that

(*a*) payment of the member's retirement benefits under the provision is suspended while the member is employed by a participating employer, and

(*b*) the amount of retirement benefits payable to the member after the suspension is redetermined

(i) to include benefits in respect of all or a part of the period throughout which payment of the member's benefits was suspended,

(i.1) where the retirement benefits payable under the provision to the member after the suspension are not adjusted by any cost-of-living or similar adjustments in respect of the period throughout which payment of the member's benefits was suspended, to take into account the member's remuneration from the employer for the period throughout which payment of the benefits was suspended,

(ii) where the member was totally and permanently disabled at the time the member's retirement benefits commenced to be paid, to include benefits in respect of all or a part of the period of disability of the member,

(iii) where the amount of the member's retirement benefits was previously determined with a reduction computed by reference to the member's age, duration of service, or both, or with any other similar reduction, by redetermining the amount of the reduction, or

(iv) where payment of the member's retirement benefits resumes after the member attains 65 years of age, by applying an adjustment for the purpose of compensating, in whole or in part, for the payments foregone by the member after attaining 65 years of age,

the following rules apply:

(*c*) the condition in paragraph (3)(*b*) is not applicable in respect of benefits provided under the provision to the member in respect of a period throughout which payment of the member's benefits is suspended,

(*d*) where the member was totally and permanently disabled at the time the member's retirement benefits commenced to be paid, the condition in paragraph (3)(*b*) is not applicable in respect of benefits provided under the provision to the member in respect of a period of disability of the member,

(*e*) the conditions in paragraphs (2)(*b*) and (3)(*c*) and (*d*) and section 8504 are applicable in respect of benefits payable under the provision to the member after a suspension of the member's retirement benefits as if the member's retirement benefits had not previously commenced to be paid,

(*f*) for the purpose of paragraph 8502(*c*) as it applies in respect of benefits provided under the provision on the death of the member during or after a period throughout which payment of the member's benefits is suspended, subsections (2) and (6) are applicable as if the member's retirement benefits had not commenced to be paid before the period, and

(*g*) the provisions in paragraph (2)(*m*), Part LXXXIII and subsection 8517(4) that depend on whether the member's retirement benefits have commenced to be paid apply to past service events, commutations and transfers occurring in the period in which the member's benefits are suspended as if the member's benefits had not previously commenced to be paid.

Registered Plans Directorate Newsletters: No. 92-6, Pre-reform disability and bridging benefits.

(10) Re-Employed Member — Special Rules Not Applicable. Subsection (9) does not apply in respect of benefits provided under a defined benefit provision of a pension plan to a member unless the terms of the plan that provide for the redetermination of the amount of the member's retirement benefits do not apply where retirement benefits have, at any time, been paid under the provision to the member while the member was an employee of a participating employer.

(11) Re-Employed Member — Anti-Avoidance. Where a member of a registered pension plan has become an employee of a participating employer after the member's retirement benefits under a defined benefit provision of the plan have commenced to be paid and it is reasonable to consider that one of the main reasons for the employment of the member is to enable the member to benefit from terms of the plan that provide for a redetermination of the amount of the member's retirement benefits provided in respect of a period before the benefits commenced to be paid, the plan becomes a revocable plan at the time the payment of the member's benefits resumes.

(11.1) Special Rules for Member Aged 70 or 71 in 2007. Where

(*a*) a member of a registered pension plan attained 69 years of age in 2005 or 2006,

(*b*) the member's retirement benefits under a defined benefit provision of the plan commenced to be paid to the member in the year in which the member attained 69 years of age,

(*c*) the member's retirement benefits are suspended as of any particular time in 2007, and

(*d*) the member was employed with a participating employer from the time the member's retirement benefits commenced to be paid to the particular time,

the following rules apply:

(*e*) subsections (9) and (11) shall apply with respect to the member as though the member became an employee of the participating employer at the particular time, and

(*f*) for the purpose of subsection (10), retirement benefits paid under the provision to the member before the particular time shall be disregarded.

(12) Limits Dependent On Consumer Price Index. Benefits provided under a defined benefit provision of a pension plan that are benefits to which a condition in any of subparagraphs (2)(*b*)(ii) and (*e*)(v) and (vi) and (3)(*d*)(ii) is applicable shall be deemed to comply with the condition where they would so comply if the Consumer Price Index ratio computed as part of the formula that applies for the purpose of the condition were replaced by a substantially similar measure of the change in the Consumer Price Index.

(13) Statutory Plans — Special Rules. Notwithstanding subsection (3),

(*a*) for the purposes of the condition in paragraph (3)(*b*) as it applies in respect of benefits provided under the pension plan established by the *Public Service Superannuation Act*, the reference to "any other registered pension plan" in subparagraph (3)(*b*)(ii) does not include the pension plans established by the *Canadian Forces Superannuation Act* and the *Royal Canadian Mounted Police Superannuation Act*; and

(*b*) the condition in paragraph (3)(*c*) does not apply in respect of benefits provided under the pension plan established by the *Canadian Forces Superannuation Act*.

(14) Artificially Reduced Pension Adjustments. Where

(*a*) the amount of lifetime retirement benefits provided under a defined benefit provision of a registered pension plan to a member depends on the member's remuneration,

(*b*) remuneration (in this subsection referred to as "excluded remuneration") of certain types is disregarded for the purpose of determining the amount of the member's lifetime retirement benefits, and

(*c*) it can reasonably be considered that one of the main reasons that remuneration in the form of excluded remuneration was paid to the member by an employer at any time was to artificially reduce a pension credit of the member under the provision with respect to the employer,

the following rules apply for the purposes of the conditions in subsection 8504(1):

(*d*) the member shall be deemed to have been connected with the employer while the member was employed by the employer, and

(*e*) the member shall be deemed not to have received such remuneration as is excluded remuneration.

(15) Past Service Employer Contributions. Where

(*a*) a contribution that is made by an employer to a registered pension plan is made, in whole or in part, in respect of benefits (in this subsection referred to as "past service benefits") provided under the plan to a member in respect of a period before 1990 and before the calendar year in which the contribution is made,

(*b*) the contribution is made

(i) after December 10, 1989, or

(ii) before December 11, 1989 where the contribution has not, before that date, been approved by the Minister under paragraph 20(1)(*s*) of the Act, and

(*c*) it is reasonable to consider that all or substantially all of such portion of the contribution as is in respect of past service benefits was paid by the employer, with the consent of the member, in lieu of a payment or other benefit to which the member would otherwise be entitled,

Regulations

the plan becomes, for the purposes of paragraph 147.1(11)(*c*) of the Act, a revocable plan on the later of December 11, 1989 and the day immediately before the day on which the contribution is made.

(16) Definitions. The following definitions apply in this subsection and in subsections (17) to (23).

"qualifying period" of a member under a defined benefit provision of a pension plan means a period throughout which the member is employed by an employer who participates in the plan but does not include any period that is before the day that is the first day, on or after the later of the following days, in respect of which retirement benefits are provided under the provision to the member:

(*a*) the day on which retirement benefits first commenced to be paid to the member under the provision; and

(*b*) the member's specified eligibility day under the provision.

"specified eligibility day" of a member under a defined benefit provision of a pension plan means the earlier of

(*a*) the later of

(i) the day on which the member attains 55 years of age, and

(ii) the day on which the member attains the earliest age at which payment of the member's lifetime retirement benefits may commence under the terms of the provision without a reduction computed by reference to the member's age, duration of service, or both (and without any other similar reduction), otherwise than because of the member being totally and permanently disabled; and

(*b*) the day on which the member attains 60 years of age.

(17) Bridging Benefits Payable on a Stand-alone Basis. The condition in subparagraph (2)(*b*)(i) that bridging benefits be payable to a member under a defined benefit provision of a pension plan for a period beginning no earlier than the time lifetime retirement benefits commence to be paid under the provision to the member does not apply where the following conditions are satisfied:

(*a*) the bridging benefits do not commence to be paid before the member's specified eligibility day under the provision;

(*b*) the plan provides that bridging benefits are payable under the provision to the member only for calendar months

(i) at any time in which the member is employed by an employer who participates in the plan, or

(ii) that begin on or after the time the member's lifetime retirement benefits under the provision commence to be paid;

(*c*) the member was not, at any time before the time at which the bridging benefits commence to be paid, connected with an employer who participates in the plan; and

(*d*) the plan is not a designated plan.

(18) Rules of Application. Where bridging benefits under a defined benefit provision of a pension plan commence to be paid to a member in circumstances to which subsection (17) applies, the following rules apply:

(*a*) if the member dies before lifetime retirement benefits under the provision commence to be paid to the member, subsections (2) and (6) apply in respect of benefits provided under the provision on the death of the member as if the bridging benefits had not commenced to be paid before the member's death; and

(*b*) the provisions in paragraph (2)(*m*), Part LXXXIII and subsection 8517(4) that depend on whether the member's retirement benefits have commenced to be paid apply to past service events, commutations and transfers occurring before lifetime retirement benefits under the provision commence to be paid to the member as if the bridging benefits had not commenced to be paid.

(19) Benefit Accruals After Pension Commencement. Paragraph (3)(*b*) does not apply to retirement benefits (in this subsection and in subsections (20) and (21) referred to as "additional benefits") provided under a defined benefit provision of a pension plan to a member of the plan if the following conditions are satisfied:

(*a*) the additional benefits are provided in respect of all or part of a qualifying period of the member under the provision;

(*b*) the amount of retirement benefits payable to the member under the provision for each whole calendar month in the qualifying period does not exceed 5% of the amount (expressed on an annualized basis) of retirement benefits that have accrued under the provision to the member to the beginning of the month, determined without a reduction computed by reference to the member's age, duration of service, or both, and without any other similar reduction (except that, if the plan limits the amount of pensionable service of a member or prohibits the provision of benefits in respect of periods after a member attains a specific age or combination of age and pensionable service, this condition does not apply to any calendar month in respect of which no benefits can be provided to the member because of the limit or prohibition, as the case may be);

(*c*) no part of the additional benefits are provided as a consequence of a past service event, unless the benefits are provided in circumstances to which subsection 8306(1) would apply if no qualifying transfers were made in connection with the past service event;

(*d*) the member was not, at any time before the additional benefits become provided, connected with an employer who participates in the plan; and

(*e*) the plan is not a designated plan.

(20) Redetermination of Benefits. Where the amount of retirement benefits payable under a defined benefit provision of a pension plan to a member is redetermined to include additional benefits provided to the member in respect of a qualifying period of the member under the provision, the conditions in paragraph (2)(*b*) and section 8504 apply in respect of benefits payable under the provision to the member after the redetermination as if the member's retirement benefits had first commenced to be paid at the time of the redetermination.

(21) Rules of Application. Where additional benefits are provided under a defined benefit provision of a pension plan to a member in respect of a qualifying period of the member under the provision, the following rules apply:

(*a*) if the qualifying period ends as a consequence of the member's death, subsections (2) and (6) apply in respect of benefits provided under the provision on the death of the member as if the member's retirement benefits had not commenced to be paid before the member's death; and

(*b*) the provisions in paragraph (2)(*m*), Part LXXXIII and subsection 8517(4) that depend on whether the member's retirement benefits have commenced to be paid apply to past service events, commutations and transfers occurring in the qualifying period as if the member's retirement benefits had not commenced to be paid.

(22) Anti-avoidance. Subsections (20) and (21) do not apply where it is reasonable to consider that one of the main reasons for the provision of additional benefits to the member is to obtain the benefit of any of those subsections.

(23) Cross-plan Rules. Where a member is provided with benefits under two or more associated defined benefit provisions, the determination of whether the conditions in subsections (17) and (19) are satisfied in respect of benefits payable or provided to the member under a particular associated provision shall be made on the basis of the following assumptions:

(*a*) benefits payable to the member under each of the other associated provisions were payable under the particular associated provision;

(*b*) if, before the member's specified eligibility day (determined without reference to this paragraph) under the particular associated provision, the member had commenced to receive retirement benefits under another associated provision on or after the member's specified eligibility day under that provision, the member's specified eligibility day under the particular associated provision were the member's specified eligibility day under that other associated provision; and

(*c*) if one or more of the other associated provisions is in a designated plan, the plan that includes the particular provision were also a designated plan.

(24) Associated Defined Benefit Provisions. For the purpose of subsection (23), a defined benefit provision is associated with another defined benefit provision (other than a provision that is not in a registered pension plan) if

(*a*) the provisions are in the same pension plan; or

(*b*) the provisions are in separate pension plans and

(i) there is an employer who participates in both plans, or

(ii) an employer who participates in one of the plans does not deal at arm's length with an employer who participates in the other plan.

(25) Subsection (24) Not Applicable. A particular defined benefit provision of a pension plan is not associated with a defined benefit provision of another pension plan if it is unreasonable to expect the benefits under the particular provision to be coordinated with the benefits under the other provision and the Minister has agreed not to treat the particular provision as being associated with the other provision.

(26) IPP — Minimum Withdrawal. An individual pension plan becomes a revocable plan at the end of a year if

(*a*) a person who is a member or a beneficiary, in respect of the plan, who was, at the time of the member's death, a spouse or common-law partner of the member, is in receipt of retirement benefits under the terms of the plan;

(*b*) the person has attained 71 years of age before the year; and

(*c*) the plan has not paid in the year an amount to the person equal to the greater of the retirement benefits payable to the person for the year and the IPP minimum amount for the person for the year.

History: S. 8503(26) was added by S.C. 2011, c. 24, s. 96(1), applicable to the 2012 and subsequent taxation years.

8504. Maximum Benefits

(1) Lifetime Retirement Benefits. For the purposes of subparagraph 8502(*c*)(i), the following conditions are applicable in respect of the lifetime retirement benefits provided to a member under a defined benefit provision of a pension plan:

(*a*) the amount (expressed on an annualized basis) of lifetime retirement benefits payable to the member for the calendar year (in this paragraph referred to as the "year of commencement") in which the lifetime retirement benefits commence to be paid does not exceed the aggregate of

(i) the aggregate of all amounts each of which is, in respect of a calendar year after 1990 (in this paragraph referred to as a "specified year") in which the member was, at any time, connected with an employer who participated in the plan in the year for the benefit of the member, the lesser of

(A) the amount determined by the formula

$$.02 \times A \times (B / C)$$

where

A is the aggregate of all amounts each of which is the member's compensation for the specified year from an employer who participated under the provision in the year for the benefit of the member,

B is the greatest of all amounts each of which is the average wage for a calendar year not before the specified year and not after the year of commencement, and

C is the average wage for the specified year, and

(B) the amount determined by the formula

$$D \times E$$

where

D is the defined benefit limit for the year of commencement, and

E is the fraction of the specified year that is pensionable service of the member under the provision, and

(ii) the amount determined by the formula

$$F \times G$$

where

F is the lesser of

(A) 2 per cent of the member's highest average compensation (computed under subsection (2)) for the purpose of the provision, indexed to the year of commencement, and

(B) the defined benefit limit for the year of commencement, and

G is the aggregate of all amounts each of which is the duration (measured in years, including any fraction of a year) of a period that is pensionable service of the member under the provision and no part of which is in a specified year; and

(*b*) the amount of lifetime retirement benefits payable to the member for a particular calendar year after the year in which the lifetime retirement benefits commence to be paid does not exceed the product of

(i) the aggregate of the amounts determined under subparagraphs (*a*)(i) and (ii), and

(ii) the greatest of all amounts each of which is the ratio of

(A) the average Consumer Price Index for a calendar year not earlier than the calendar year in which the lifetime retirement benefits commence to be paid and not later than the particular year

to

(B) the average Consumer Price Index for the calendar year in which the lifetime retirement benefits commence to be paid.

Information Circulars: IC 98-2 Prescribed compensation for registered pension plans.

Registered Plans Directorate Newsletters: No. 96-1, Changes to retirement savings limits; No. 92-11, Maximum pension limits; No. 92-7, Pre-reform early retirement provisions and post-retirement indexing.

(2) Highest Average Compensation. For the purposes of subsection (1) and paragraph 8505(3)(*d*), the highest average compensation of a member of a pension plan for the purpose of a defined benefit provision of the plan, indexed to the calendar year (in this subsection referred to as the "year of commencement") in which the member's lifetime retirement benefits under the provision commence to be paid, is,

(*a*) in the case of a member who has been employed for 3 non-overlapping periods of 12 consecutive months each by employers who participated under the provision for the benefit of the member, $1/3$ of the greatest of all amounts each of which is the aggregate of the member's total indexed compensation for the purpose of the provision for each of the 36 months in 3 such periods throughout which the member was so employed, and

(*b*) in any other case, the amount determined by the formula

$$12 \times (H / I)$$

where

H is the aggregate of all amounts each of which is the member's total indexed compensation for the purpose of the provision for a month throughout which the member was employed by an employer who participated under the provision for the benefit of the member, and

I is the number of months for which total indexed compensation is included in the amount determined for H,

and, for the purposes of this subsection, the member's total indexed compensation for a month for the purpose of the provision is the amount determined by the formula

$$J \times (K / L)$$

where

J is the aggregate of all amounts each of which is such portion of the member's compensation for the calendar year (in this subsection referred to as the "compensation year") that includes the month from an employer who participated under the provision for the benefit of the member as may reasonably be considered to have been received in the month or to otherwise relate to the month,

K is the greatest of all amounts each of which is the average wage for a calendar year not before the later of the compensation year and 1986 and not after the year of commencement, and

L is the average wage for the later of the compensation year and 1986.

Registered Plans Directorate Newsletters: No. 92-11, Maximum pension limits.

(2.1) Predecessor Employer. For the purposes of subsection (2), if the pensionable service of the member under the provision includes a period throughout which the member was employed by a predecessor employer to an employer who participates in the plan, the predecessor employer is deemed to have participated under the provision for the benefit of the member.

History: S. 8504(2.1) was added by S.C. 2013, c. 34, s. 409(1), deemed to have come into force on January 1, 1991.

(3) Alternative Compensation Rules. Lifetime retirement benefits provided to a member under a defined benefit provision of a pension plan shall be deemed to comply with the conditions in subsection (1) where they would so comply if either or both of the following rules were applicable:

(*a*) determine, for the purpose of subsection (2), the member's compensation from an employer for a calendar year by adding to the compensation otherwise determined such portion of the amount of each bonus and retroactive increase in remuneration paid by the employer to the member after the year as may reasonably be considered to be in respect of the year and by deducting therefrom such portion of the amount of each bonus and retroactive increase in remuneration paid by the employer to the member in the year as may reasonably be considered to be in respect of a preceding year; and

(*b*) determine, for the purpose of computing the amount J in subsection (2), the portion of the member's compensation from an employer for a calendar year that may reasonably be considered to relate to a month in the year by apportioning the compensation uniformly over the period in the year in respect of which it was paid.

(4) Part-Time Employees. Where the pensionable service of a member under a defined benefit provision of a pension plan includes a period throughout which the member rendered services on a part-time basis to an employer who participates in the plan, the lifetime retirement benefits provided under the provision to the member shall be deemed to comply with the conditions in subsection (1) where they would so comply or be deemed by subsection (3) to so comply if

(*a*) for the purpose of determining the amount J in subsection (2), the member's compensation from an employer for a calendar year in which the member rendered services on a part-time basis to the employer were the amount that it is reasonable to expect would have been the member's compensation for the year from the employer if the member had rendered services to the employer on a full-time basis throughout the period or periods in the year throughout which the member rendered services to the employer, and

(*b*) in determining the amount G in subparagraph (1)(*a*)(ii), the duration of each period were multiplied by a fraction (not greater than one) that measures the services rendered by the member throughout the period to employers who participate in the plan as a proportion of the services that would have been rendered by the member throughout the period to such employers had the member rendered services on a full-time basis,

and, for the purposes of this subsection,

(*c*) where a member of a pension plan has rendered services throughout a period to 2 or more employers who participate in the plan, the employers shall be deemed to be, throughout the period, the same employer, and

(*d*) where a period is

(i) an eligible period of reduced pay or temporary absence of a member of a pension plan with respect to an employer, or

(ii) a period of disability of the member,

the member shall be deemed to have

(iii) rendered services throughout the period on a regular basis (having regard to the services rendered by the employee before the period) to the employer or employers by whom the member was employed before the period, and

(iv) received remuneration throughout the period at a rate commensurate with the member's rate of remuneration before the period.

(5) Retirement Benefits Before Age 65. For the purposes of subparagraph 8502(*c*)(i), the following conditions are applicable in respect of retirement benefits payable under a defined benefit provision of a pension plan to a member of the plan for the period (in this subsection referred to as the "bridging period") from the time the benefits commence to be paid to the time the member attains 65 years of age:

(*a*) the amount (expressed on an annualized basis) of retirement benefits payable to the member for that part of the bridging period that is in the calendar year in which the benefits commence to be paid does not exceed the amount determined by the formula

$$(A \times B) + (0.25 \times C \times (D / 35))$$

where

A is the defined benefit limit for the calendar year in which the benefits commence to be paid,

B is the aggregate of all amounts each of which is the duration (measured in years, including any fraction of a year) of a period that is pensionable service of the member under the provision,

C is the average of the Year's Maximum Pensionable Earnings for the year in which the benefits commence to be paid and for each of the 2 immediately preceding years, and

D is the lesser of 35 and the amount determined for B; and

(*b*) the amount of retirement benefits (expressed on an annualized basis) payable to the member for that part of the bridging period that is in a particular calendar year after the year in which the retirement benefits commence to be paid does not exceed the product of

(i) the amount determined by the formula set out in paragraph (*a*), and

(ii) the greatest of all amounts each of which is the ratio of

(A) the average Consumer Price Index for a calendar year not earlier than the calendar year in which the retirement benefits commence to be paid and not later than the particular year

to

(B) the average Consumer Price Index for the calendar year in which the retirement benefits commence to be paid.

Registered Plans Directorate Newsletters: No. 91-5, Transitional rules and other administrative issues for pension plans.

(6) Pre-1990 Benefits. For the purposes of subparagraph 8502(*c*)(i), and subject to subsection (7), the lifetime

Regulations

retirement benefits provided under a defined benefit provision of a pension plan to a member of the plan in respect of pensionable service in a particular calendar year before 1990 (in this subsection referred to as the "benefit year") are subject to the condition that

(*a*) the amount (expressed on an annualized basis) of such lifetime retirement benefits payable to the member for a particular calendar year (in this subsection referred to as the "payment year")

does not exceed

(*b*) the amount determined by the formula

$$(2 / 3) \times A \times B \times C$$

where

A is the greater of $1,725 and the defined benefit limit for the year in which the benefits commence to be paid,

B is the aggregate of all amounts each of which is the duration (measured as a fraction of a year) of a period in the benefit year that is pensionable service of the member under the provision, and

C is the greatest of all amounts each of which is the ratio of

(i) the average Consumer Price Index for a calendar year not earlier than the calendar year in which the lifetime retirement benefits commence to be paid and not later than the payment year

to

(ii) the average Consumer Price Index for the calendar year in which the lifetime retirement benefits commence to be paid.

Registered Plans Directorate Newsletters: No. 91-5, Transitional rules and other administrative issues for pension plans.

(7) Limit Not Applicable. The condition in subsection (6) is not applicable in respect of lifetime retirement benefits provided to an individual in respect of periods of pensionable service in a particular calendar year if

(*a*) at any time before June 8, 1990, a period in the particular year was pensionable service of the individual under a defined benefit provision of a registered pension plan;

(*b*) on June 7, 1990, the individual was entitled, pursuant to an arrangement in writing, to be provided with lifetime retirement benefits under a defined benefit provision of a registered pension plan in respect of a period in the particular year, whether or not the individual's entitlement was conditional on the individual making contributions under the provision;

(*c*) at the beginning of the particular year, a period in a preceding year was pensionable service of the individual under a defined benefit provision of a registered pension plan, and the individual did not, by reason of disability or leave of absence, render services in the particular year to an employer who participated in the plan with respect to the individual;

(*d*) contributions were made before June 8, 1990 by or on behalf of the individual under a money purchase provision of a registered pension plan in respect of the year; or

(*e*) contributions were made in the year by or on behalf of the individual to a deferred profit sharing plan.

Related Regulations: 8500(7).

(8) Cross-Plan Restrictions. Where an individual is provided with benefits under more than one defined benefit provision, the determination of whether the benefits provided to the individual under a particular defined benefit provision comply with the conditions in subsections (5) and (6) shall be made on the assumption that benefits provided to the individual under each other defined benefit provision (other than a provision that is not included in a registered pension plan) associated with the particular provision were provided under the particular provision.

(9) Associated Defined Benefit Provisions. For the purposes of subsection (8), a defined benefit provision is associated with a particular defined benefit provision if

(*a*) the provisions are in the same pension plan, or

(*b*) the provisions are in separate pension plans and

(i) there is an employer who participates in both plans,

(ii) an employer who participates in one of the plans does not deal at arm's length with an employer who participates in the other plan, or

(iii) there is an individual who is provided with benefits under both provisions and the individual, or a person with whom the individual does not deal at arm's length, has the power to determine the benefits that are provided under the particular provision,

unless it is unreasonable to expect the benefits under the particular provision to be coordinated with the benefits under the other provision and the Minister has agreed not to treat the other provision as being associated with the particular provision.

(10) Excluded Benefits. For the purpose of determining whether lifetime retirement benefits provided under a defined benefit provision of a pension plan comply with the conditions in subsection (1), the following benefits shall be disregarded:

(*a*) additional lifetime retirement benefits payable to a member because the member is totally and permanently disabled at the time the member's retirement benefits commence to be paid; and

(*b*) additional lifetime retirement benefits payable to a member whose retirement benefits commence to be paid after the member attains 65 years of age, where the additional benefits result from an adjustment that is made to offset, in whole or in part, the decrease in the value of lifetime retirement benefits that would otherwise result by reason of the deferral of such benefits after the member attains 65 years of age and the adjustment is not more favourable than such an adjustment made on an actuarially equivalent basis.

Regulations

(11) [Idem]. For the purpose of determining whether retirement benefits provided under a defined benefit provision of a pension plan comply with the conditions in subsection (5), the following benefits shall be disregarded:

(*a*) additional lifetime retirement benefits that are described in paragraph (10)(*a*); and

(*b*) bridging benefits payable at the election of a member, where the benefits are provided on a basis that is not more favourable than an actuarially equivalent basis in lieu of all or a proportion of the benefits that would otherwise be payable under the provision with respect to the member.

(12) [Idem]. For the purpose of determining whether lifetime retirement benefits provided under a defined benefit provision of a pension plan comply with the condition in subsection (6), additional lifetime retirement benefits that are described in paragraph (10)(*b*) shall be disregarded.

(13) Alternative CPI Indexing. The lifetime retirement benefits provided to a member under a defined benefit provision of a pension plan shall be deemed to comply with the condition in paragraph (1)(*b*) where they would so comply, or would be deemed by subsection (3) or (4) to so comply, if the ratio that is determined under subparagraph (1)(*b*)(ii) were replaced by a substantially similar measure of the change in the Consumer Price Index.

(14) [Idem]. The retirement benefits provided to a member under a defined benefit provision of a pension plan shall be deemed to comply with the condition in paragraph (5)(*b*) where they would so comply if the ratio that is determined under subparagraph (5)(*b*)(ii) were replaced by a substantially similar measure of the change in the Consumer Price Index.

(15) [Idem]. The lifetime retirement benefits provided to a member under a defined benefit provision of a pension plan shall be deemed to comply with the condition in subsection (6) where they would so comply if the amount C in the formula set out in paragraph (6)(*b*) were replaced by a substantially similar measure of the change in the Consumer Price Index.

8505. Additional Benefits on Downsizing

(1) Downsizing Program. For the purposes of this section, "downsizing program" means the actions that are taken by an employer to bring about a reduction in the employer's workforce, including

(*a*) the termination of the employment of employees; and

(*b*) the payment of amounts and the provision of special benefits to employees who elect to or are required to terminate their employment.

Registered Plans Directorate Newsletters: No. 92-9, Downsizing programs.

(2) Applicability of Downsizing Rules. For the purposes of this section,

(*a*) a downsizing program is an approved downsizing program if the Minister has approved in writing the application of this section in respect of the program;

(*b*) subject to subsection (2.1), an individual is a qualifying individual in relation to an approved downsizing program if

(i) the employment of the individual is terminated while the downsizing program is in effect,

(ii) the individual was not, at any time before the termination of employment, connected with the employer from whom the individual terminated employment, and

(iii) the Minister has approved in writing the application of this section to the individual; and

(*c*) the specified day is, in respect of an approved downsizing program,

(i) the day that is designated by the Minister in writing for the purpose of subparagraph (3)(*c*)(ii), and

(ii) if no such day has been designated, the day that is 2 years after the day on which the Minister approves the application of this section in respect of the downsizing program.

(2.1) Qualifying Individual — Exclusion. An individual whose employment is terminated under an approved downsizing program is not a qualifying individual in relation to the program if, at the time the individual's employment is terminated, it is reasonable to expect that

(*a*) the individual will become employed by, or provide services to,

(i) a person or body of persons from whom the individual terminated employment under the downsizing program, or

(ii) a person or body of persons that does not deal at arm's length with a person or body of persons referred to in subparagraph (i), or

(*b*) a corporation with which the individual is connected will provide services to a person or body of persons referred to in paragraph (*a*) and the individual will be directly involved in the provision of the services,

except that this subsection does not apply with respect to an individual where

(*c*) it is reasonable to expect that

(i) the individual will not be employed or provide services, or

(ii) if paragraph (*b*) is applicable, the corporation will not provide services,

for a period exceeding 12 months, and

(*d*) the Minister has waived the application of this subsection with respect to the individual.

(3) Additional Lifetime Retirement Benefits. Lifetime retirement benefits (in this section referred to as "special retirement benefits") that do not comply with the condition in paragraph 8503(3)(*a*) may be provided under a defined benefit provision of a pension plan to a member of the plan who terminates employment after attaining 55 years of age where the following conditions are satisfied:

Regulations

(*a*) the special retirement benefits are provided pursuant to an approved downsizing program;

(*b*) the member is a qualifying individual in relation to the downsizing program;

(*c*) under the terms of the provision,

(i) retirement benefits will not commence to be paid to the member until the member ceases to be employed by all employers who participate in the plan, and

(ii) retirement benefits will commence to be paid to the member no later than on the specified day;

(*d*) the amount (expressed on an annualized basis) of special retirement benefits payable to the member for a particular calendar year does not exceed the amount that is determined by the formula

$$A \times B \times C$$

where

A is the lesser of

(i) 2 per cent of the member's highest average compensation (computed under subsection 8504(2)) for the purpose of the provision, indexed to the calendar year (in this paragraph referred to as the "year of commencement") in which retirement benefits commence to be paid under the provision to the member, and

(ii) the defined benefit limit for the year of commencement,

B is the lesser of 7 and the amount, if any, by which 65 exceeds the member's age (expressed in years, including any fraction of a year) at termination of employment, and

C is the greatest of all amounts each of which is the ratio of

(i) the average Consumer Price Index for a calendar year not earlier than the year of commencement and not later than the particular year

to

(ii) the average Consumer Price Index for the year of commencement;

(*e*) (Revoked.)

(*f*) the plan

(i) does not permit the commutation of retirement benefits payable to the member, or

(ii) permits the commutation of retirement benefits payable to the member only if the life expectancy of the member is significantly shorter than normal; and

(*g*) lifetime retirement benefits that are permissible only by reason of this subsection are not provided to the member under any other defined benefit provision, unless this condition has been waived by the Minister.

Information Circulars: IC 98-2 Prescribed Compensation for Registered Pension Plans.

(3.1) Re-employed Members. Where

(*a*) a member of a pension plan becomes an employee of a participating employer after lifetime retirement benefits that are permissible only by reason of subsection (3) have commenced to be paid under a defined benefit provision of the plan to the member, and

(*b*) payment of the member's retirement benefits under the provision is suspended while the member is so employed,

the condition in paragraph (3)(*d*) is applicable in respect of benefits payable under the provision to the member after the suspension as if

(*c*) the member had not become so employed, and

(*d*) payment of the member's retirement benefits had not been suspended.

(4) Early Retirement Reduction. Where a member of a pension plan is a qualifying individual in relation to an approved downsizing program, the terms of a defined benefit provision of the plan that determine the amount by which the member's lifetime retirement benefits under the provision are reduced because of the early commencement of the benefits may, under the downsizing program, be modified in such a way that the benefits do not comply with the condition in paragraph 8503(3)(*c*) but would so comply if the member's benefits were provided in respect of employment in a public safety occupation.

(5) Exception for Future Benefits. Subsection (4) does not apply with respect to benefits that are provided to an individual in respect of a period that is after the day on which the individual's employment was terminated under an approved downsizing program.

(6) Alternative CPI Indexing. Special retirement benefits provided to a member under a defined benefit provision of a pension plan shall be deemed to comply with the condition in paragraph (3)(*d*) where they would so comply if the amount C in that paragraph were replaced by a substantially similar measure of the change in the Consumer Price Index.

(7) Exclusion from Maximum Pension Rules. For the purpose of determining whether retirement benefits provided under a defined benefit provision of a pension plan comply with the conditions in subsections 8504(1) and (5), lifetime retirement benefits that are permissible only by reason of subsection (3) shall be disregarded.

(8) Exemption from Past Service Contribution Rule. Subsection 8503(15) does not apply in respect of a contribution that is made in respect of benefits provided to a qualifying individual pursuant to an approved downsizing program.

8506. Money Purchase Provisions

(1) Permissible Benefits. For the purposes of paragraph 8502(*c*), the following benefits may, subject to the conditions specified in respect of each benefit, be provided under a money purchase provision of a pension plan:

Registered Plans Directorate Newsletters: No. 94-2, Technical questions and answers; No. 92-12, Commutation and opting out of a pension plan; No. 91-4R, Registration rules for money purchase provisions.

(a) Lifetime retirement benefits — lifetime retirement benefits provided to a member where the benefits are payable in equal periodic amounts or are not so payable only by reason that

(i) the benefits payable to a member after the death of the member's spouse or common-law partner are less than the benefits that would be payable to the member were the member's spouse or common-law partner alive, or

(ii) the benefits are adjusted, after they commence to be paid, where those adjustments would be in accordance with any of subparagraphs 146(3)(*b*)(iii) to (v) of the Act if the annuity by means of which the lifetime retirement benefits are provided were an annuity under a retirement savings plan;

(b) Bridging benefits — bridging benefits provided to a member where the bridging benefits are payable for a period ending no later than the end of the month following the month in which the member attains 65 years of age;

(c) Guarantee period — retirement benefits (in this paragraph referred to as "continued retirement benefits") provided to one or more beneficiaries of a member who dies after retirement benefits under the provision commence to be paid to the member where

(i) the continued retirement benefits are payable for a period beginning after the death of the member and ending no later than 15 years after the day on which retirement benefits commence to be paid under the provision to the member, and

(ii) the total amount of continued retirement benefits payable under the provision for each month does not exceed the amount of retirement benefits (other than benefits permissible under paragraph (*e*.1)) that would have been payable under the provision for the month to the member if the member were alive;

(d) Post-retirement survivor benefits — retirement benefits (in this paragraph referred to as "survivor retirement benefits") provided to a beneficiary of a member who dies after retirement benefits under the provision commence to be paid to the member where

(i) the beneficiary is a spouse or common-law partner or former spouse or common-law partner of the member at the time the member's retirement benefits commence to be paid,

(ii) the survivor retirement benefits are payable for a period beginning after the death of the member and ending with the death of the beneficiary, and

(iii) the total amount of survivor retirement benefits and other retirement benefits (other than benefits permissible under paragraph (*e*.1)) payable under the provision for each month to beneficiaries of the member does not exceed the amount of retirement benefits (other than benefits permissible under paragraph (*e*.1)) that would have been payable under the provision for the month to the member if the member were alive;

(e) Pre-retirement survivor benefits — retirement benefits provided to a beneficiary of a member who dies before retirement benefits under the provision commence to be paid to the member, and benefits provided to other individuals after the death of the beneficiary, where

(i) the beneficiary is a spouse or common-law partner or former spouse or common-law partner of the member at the time of the member's death,

(ii) the benefits would be permissible under paragraphs (*a*) to (*c*) if the beneficiary were a member of the plan, and

(iii) the retirement benefits are payable to the beneficiary beginning no later than on the later of one year after the day of death of the member and the end of the calendar year in which the beneficiary attains 71 years of age;

(e.1) Variable benefits — retirement benefits (in this paragraph referred to as "variable benefits"), other than benefits permissible under any of paragraphs (*a*) to (*e*), provided to a member and, after the death of the member, to one or more beneficiaries of the member if

(i) the variable benefits are paid from the member's account,

(ii) the variable benefits provided to the member or a beneficiary (other than a beneficiary who is the specified beneficiary of the member in relation to the provision) are payable for a period ending no later than the end of the calendar year following the calendar year in which the member dies,

(iii) the variable benefits provided to a beneficiary who is the specified beneficiary of the member in relation to the provision are payable for a period ending no later than the end of the calendar year in which the specified beneficiary dies, and

(iv) the amount of variable benefits payable to the member and beneficiaries of the member for each calendar year is not less than the minimum amount for the member's account under the provision for the calendar year;

Related Regulations: 8506(5).

(f) Payment from account — the payment with respect to a member of a single amount from the member's account under the provision;

(g) Payment from account after death — the payment, with respect to one or more beneficiaries of a member, of one or more single amounts from the member's account under the provision;

(h) Commutation of benefits — the payment with respect to a member of a single amount in full or partial satisfaction of the member's entitlement to other benefits under the provision, where the single amount does not exceed the present value (at the

Regulations

time the single amount is paid) of the other benefits that, as a consequence of the payment, cease to be provided; and

(i) [Idem] — the payment, with respect to an individual after the death of a member, of a single amount in full or partial satisfaction of the individual's entitlement to other benefits under the provision, where the individual is a beneficiary of the member and the single amount does not exceed the present value (at the time the single amount is paid) of the other benefits that, as a consequence of the payment, cease to be provided.

(2) Additional Conditions. For the purposes of section 8501, the following conditions are applicable in respect of each money purchase provision of a pension plan:

Related Regulations: 8500(7).

Registered Plans Directorate Newsletters: No. 94-2, Technical questions and answers; No. 91-4R, Registration rules for money purchase provisions.

(a) Employer contributions acceptable to Minister — the amount of contributions that are to be made under the provision by each employer who participates in the plan is determined in a manner acceptable to the Minister;

(b) Employer contributions with respect to particular members — each contribution that is made under the provision by an employer consists only of amounts each of which is an amount that is paid by the employer with respect to a particular member;

(b.1) Allocation of employer contributions — each contribution that is made under the provision by an employer is allocated to the member with respect to whom it is made;

(c) Employer contributions not permitted — contributions are not made under the provision by an employer, and property is not transferred to the provision in respect of the actuarial surplus under a defined benefit provision of the plan or another registered pension plan,

(i) at a time when there is a surplus under the provision, or

(ii) at a time after 1991 when an amount that became a forfeited amount under the provision before 1990, or any earnings of the plan that are reasonably attributable to that amount, is being held in respect of the provision and has not been reallocated to members of the plan;

(c.1) Contributions not permitted — no contribution is made under the provision with respect to a member, and no amount is transferred for the benefit of a member to the provision from another benefit provision of the plan, at any time after the calendar year in which the member attains 71 years of age, other than an amount that is transferred for the benefit of the member to the provision

(i) in accordance with subsection 146.3(14.1) or 147.3(1) or (4) of the Act, or

(ii) from another benefit provision of the plan, where the amount so transferred would, if the benefit provisions were in separate registered pension plans, be in accordance with subsection 147.3(1) or (4) of the Act;

(d) Return of contributions — where the plan is not established by an enactment of Canada or a province, it includes a stipulation that permits, for the purpose of avoiding revocation of the registration of the plan, a contribution made under the provision by a member or by an employer to be returned to the person who made the contribution, which stipulation may provide that a return of contributions is subject to the approval of the authority administering the *Pension Benefits Standards Act, 1985* or a similar law of a province;

(e) Allocation of earnings — the earnings of the plan, to the extent that they relate to the provision and are not reasonably attributable to forfeited amounts or a surplus under the provision, are allocated to plan members on a reasonable basis and no less frequently than annually;

(f) Payment or reallocation of forfeited amounts — each forfeited amount under the provision (other than an amount forfeited before 1990) and all earnings of the plan that are reasonably attributable to the forfeited amount are

(i) paid to participating employers,

(ii) reallocated to members of the plan, or

(iii) paid as or on account of administrative, investment or similar expenses incurred in connection with the plan

on or before December 31 of the year immediately following the calendar year in which the amount is forfeited, or such later time as is permitted by the Minister under subsection (3);

(g) Retirement benefits — retirement benefits (other than benefits permissible under paragraph (1)(*e*.1)) under the provision are provided by means of annuities that are purchased from a licensed annuities provider;

(h) Undue deferral of payment — Death of member — each single amount that is payable after the death of a member (other than a single amount that is payable after the death of the specified beneficiary of the member in relation to the provision) is paid as soon as is practicable after the member's death; and

(i) Undue deferral of payment — Death of specified beneficiary — each single amount that is payable after the death of the specified beneficiary of a member in relation to the provision is paid as soon as is practicable after the specified beneficiary's death.

(2.1) Alternative Method for Allocating Employer Contributions. The Minister may, on the written application of the administrator of a pension plan, waive the application of the condition in paragraph (2)(*b*.1) in respect of a money purchase provision of the plan where contributions made under the provision by an employer are allocated to members of the plan in a manner acceptable to the Minister.

(3) Reallocation of Forfeitures. The Minister may, on the written application of the administrator of a registered pension plan, extend the time for satisfying the requirements of paragraph (2)(*f*) where

(*a*) the aggregate of the forfeited amounts that arise in a calendar year is greater than normal because of unusual circumstances; and

(*b*) the forfeited amounts are to be reallocated on a reasonable basis to a majority of plan members or paid as or on account of administrative, investment or similar expenses incurred in connection with the plan.

Registered Plans Directorate Newsletters: No. 91-4R, Registration rules for money purchase provisions.

(4) Non-payment of Minimum Amount — Plan Revocable. A registered pension plan that contains a money purchase provision becomes, for the purposes of paragraph 147.1(11)(*c*) of the Act, a revocable plan at the beginning of a calendar year if the total amount of retirement benefits (other than retirement benefits permissible under any of paragraphs (1)(*a*) to (*e*)) paid from the plan in the calendar year in respect of a member's account under the provision is less than the minimum amount for the account for the calendar year.

(5) Minimum Amount. For the purposes of paragraph (1)(*e*.1) and subsection (4), but subject to subsection (7), the minimum amount for a member's account under a money purchase provision of a registered pension plan for a calendar year is the amount determined by the formula

$$A \times B$$

where

A is the balance in the account at the beginning of the year; and

B is

(*a*) if there is a specified beneficiary of the member for the year in relation to the provision, the factor designated under subsection 7308(4) for the year in respect of the specified beneficiary,

(*b*) if paragraph (*a*) does not apply for the year, the factor designated under subsection 7308(4) for the year in respect of an individual where

(i) the individual was, at the time the designation referred to in subparagraph (ii) was made, the member's spouse or common-law partner,

(ii) the member had, before the beginning of the year, provided the administrator of the plan with a written designation of the individual for the purpose of this paragraph in relation to the provision, and

(iii) the member had not, before the beginning of the year, revoked the designation, and

(*c*) in any other case, the factor designated under subsection 7308(4) for the year in respect of the member.

Related Regulations: 7308(4).

(6) Determination of Account Balance. For the purpose of the description of A in subsection (5), the balance in a member's account at the beginning of a calendar year (in this subsection referred to as the "current year") is to be determined in accordance with the following rules:

(*a*) the determination is to be made in a manner that reasonably reflects the fair market value of the property held in connection with the account at the beginning of the current year, including an estimate of the portion of any unallocated earnings of the plan that arose in the preceding calendar year and that can reasonably be expected to be allocated to the account in the current year; and

(*b*) if retirement benefits (other than benefits permissible under paragraph (1)(*e*.1)) provided under the provision with respect to the member had commenced to be paid before the current year and continue to be payable in the current year, the determination is to be made without regard to the value of any property held in connection with those benefits.

(7) Special Rules for Minimum Amount. The minimum amount for a member's account under a money purchase provision of a registered pension plan for a calendar year is

(*a*) nil, if an individual who is either the member or the specified beneficiary of the member for the year in relation to the provision

(i) is alive at the beginning of the year, and

(ii) had not attained 71 years of age at the end of the preceding calendar year; and

(*b*) if paragraph (*a*) does not apply and the year is 2008, 75 per cent of the amount that would, in the absence of this subsection, be the minimum amount for the account for the year.

History: S. 8506(7) and the heading before it were replaced by S.C. 2009, c. 2, s. 117(1), in force on Royal Assent, March 12, 2009. S. 8506(7) and the heading before it formerly read:

When Minimum Amount is Nil

(7) *When Minimum Amount is Nil.* The minimum amount for a member's account under a money purchase provision of a registered pension plan for a calendar year is nil if

(*a*) an individual, who is either the member or the specified beneficiary of the member for the year in relation to the provision, is alive at the beginning of the year; and

(*b*) that individual had not attained 71 years of age at the end of the preceding calendar year.

(8) Specified Beneficiary. In this section, an individual is the specified beneficiary of a member for a calendar year in relation to a money purchase provision of a registered pension plan if

(*a*) the member died before the beginning of the year;

(*b*) the individual is a beneficiary of the member and was, immediately before the member's death, the member's spouse or common-law partner; and

(*c*) the member or the member's legal representative had, before the beginning of the year, provided the administrator of the plan with a written designation of the individual (and of no other individual) as the specified beneficiary of the member for the calendar year in relation to the provision.

(9) Recontribution — Adjusted Minimum Amount for 2008. If a contribution made by a member of a registered pension plan and credited to the member's account under a money purchase provision of the plan complies with the conditions in subsection (10), the contribution

(*a*) is deemed to have been made in accordance with the plan as registered;

(*b*) is to be disregarded for the purposes of paragraph (2)(*c.1*); and

(*c*) is deemed to be an excluded contribution for the purposes of paragraph 8301(4)(*a*).

History: S. 8506(9) was added by S.C. 2009, c. 2, s. 117(2), in force on Royal Assent, March 12, 2009. Contributions described in subsections 8506(9) and (10), that are made during the period that begins after 2008 and ends on the day that is 30 days after the day on which this Act is assented to (or such longer period as is acceptable to the Minister of National Revenue) are deemed for the purpose of subsection 8506(10) to have been made on December 31, 2008 and not when they were actually made, except that the amounts so deemed shall not exceed the amount that would be determined in respect of the account under paragraph 8506(10)(*c*), if the value of C in the formula in that paragraph were nil. [S.C. 2009, c. 2 was assented to on March 12, 2009. Due to statutory holidays in this 30-day period after Royal Assent, the period ends on April 14, 2009.]

(10) Conditions Referred to in Subsection (9). The conditions referred to in subsection (9) are as follows:

(*a*) the contribution is made in 2008;

(*b*) the contribution is designated for the purposes of this subsection in a manner acceptable to the Minister; and

(*c*) the amount of the contribution does not exceed the amount determined by the formula

$$A - B - C$$

where

A is the lesser of

(i) the total of all amounts each of which is the amount of a retirement benefit (other than a retirement benefit permissible under any of paragraphs (1)(*a*) to (*e*)) paid from the plan in 2008 in respect of the account and included, because of paragraph 56(1)(*a*) of the Act, in computing the taxpayer's income for the taxation year, and

(ii) the amount that would, in the absence of paragraph (7)(*b*), be the minimum amount for the account for 2008,

B is the minimum amount for the account for 2008, and

C is the total of all other contributions made by the member under the money purchase provision at or before the time of the contribution and designated for the purposes of this subsection.

History: S. 8506(10) was added by S.C. 2009, c. 2, s. 117(2), in force on Royal Assent, March 12, 2009. Contributions described in subsections 8506(9) and (10), that are made during the period that begins after 2008 and ends on the day that is 30 days after the day on which this Act is assented to (or such longer period as is acceptable to the Minister of National Revenue) are deemed for the purpose of subsection 8506(10) to have been made on December 31, 2008 and not when they were actually made, except that the amounts so deemed shall not exceed the amount that would be determined in respect of the account under paragraph 8506(10)(*c*), if the value of C in the formula in that paragraph were nil. [S.C. 2009, c. 2 was assented to on March 12, 2009. Due to statutory holidays in this 30-day period after Royal Assent, the period ends on April 14, 2009.]

(11) Recontribution for 2015. If a contribution made by a member of a registered pension plan and credited to the member's account under a money purchase provision of the plan complies with the conditions in subsection (12), the contribution

(*a*) is deemed to have been made in accordance with the plan as registered;

(*b*) is to be disregarded for the purposes of paragraph (2)(*c.1*); and

(*c*) is deemed to be an excluded contribution for the purposes of paragraph 8301(4)(*a*).

History: S. 8506(11) was added by S.C. 2015, c. 36, s. 24, in force on Royal Assent, June 23, 2015.

(12) Conditions Referred to in Subsection (11). The conditions referred to in subsection (11) are as follows:

(*a*) the contribution is made after December 31, 2014 and before March 1, 2016;

(*b*) the contribution is designated for the purposes of this subsection in a manner acceptable to the Minister; and

(*c*) the amount of the contribution does not exceed the amount determined by the formula

$$A - B - C$$

where

A is the lesser of

(i) the total of all amounts each of which is the amount of a retirement benefit (other than a retirement benefit permissible under any of paragraphs (1)(*a*) to (*e*)) paid from the plan in 2015 in respect of the account and included, because of paragraph 56(1)(*a*) of the Act, in computing the taxpayer's income for the taxation year, and

(ii) the amount that would be the minimum amount for the account for 2015 if it were determined using the factor designated under subsection 7308(4) as it read on December 31, 2014,

B is the minimum amount for the account for 2015, and

C is the total of all other contributions made by the member under the money purchase provision at or before the time of the contribution and designated for the purposes of this subsection.

History: S. 8506(12) was added by S.C. 2015, c. 36, s. 24, in force on Royal Assent, June 23, 2015.

8507. Periods of Reduced Pay

(1) Prescribed Compensation. For the purposes of paragraph (*b*) of the definition "compensation" in subsection 147.1(1) of the Act, there is prescribed for inclusion in the compensation of an individual from an employer for a calendar year after 1990

(*a*) where the individual has a qualifying period in the year with respect to the employer, the amount that is determined under subsection (2) in respect of the period; and

(*b*) where the individual has a period of disability in the year, the amount that would be determined under paragraph (2)(*a*) in respect of the period if the period were a qualifying period of the individual with respect to the employer.

Information Circulars: IC 98-2 Prescribed compensation for registered pension plans.

(2) Additional Compensation in Respect of Qualifying Period. For the purposes of paragraph (1)(*a*) and subsection (5), the amount that is determined in respect of a period in a calendar year that is a qualifying period of an individual with respect to an employer is the lesser of

(*a*) the amount, if any, by which

(i) the amount that it is reasonable to consider would have been the remuneration of the individual for the period from the employer if the individual had rendered services to the employer throughout the period on a regular basis (having regard to the services rendered by the individual to the employer before the complete period of reduced pay of which the period is a part) and the individual's rate of remuneration had been commensurate with the individual's rate of remuneration before the beginning of the complete period of reduced pay

exceeds

(ii) the remuneration of the individual for the period from the employer, and

(*b*) the amount determined by the formula

$$(5 + A + B - C) \times D$$

where

A is the lesser of 3 and the amount that would be the cumulative additional compensation fraction of the individual with respect to the employer, determined to the time that is immediately before the end of the period, if the individual's only qualifying periods had been periods that are also periods of parenting,

B is

(i) if no part of the period is a period of parenting, nil, and

(ii) otherwise, the lesser of

(A) the amount, if any, by which 3 exceeds the amount determined for A, and

(B) the ratio of

(I) the amount that would be determined under paragraph (*a*) if the remuneration referred to in subparagraphs (*a*)(i) and (ii) were the remuneration for such part of the period as is a period of parenting

to

(II) the amount determined for D,

C is the cumulative additional compensation fraction of the individual with respect to the employer, determined to the time that is immediately before the end of the period, and

D is the amount that it is reasonable to consider would have been the individual's remuneration for the year from the employer if the individual had rendered services to the employer on a full-time basis throughout the year and the individual's rate of remuneration had been commensurate with the individual's rate of remuneration before the beginning of the complete period of reduced pay of which the period is a part.

Information Circulars: IC 98-2 Prescribed compensation for registered pension plans.

(3) Qualifying Periods and Periods of Parenting. For the purposes of this section,

(*a*) a period in a calendar year is a qualifying period of an individual in the year with respect to an employer if

(i) the period is an eligible period of reduced pay or temporary absence of the individual in the year with respect to the employer,

(ii) either

(A) lifetime retirement benefits are provided to the individual under a defined benefit provision of a registered pension plan (other than a plan that is, in the year, a specified multi-employer plan) in respect of the period, or

(B) contributions are made by or on behalf of the individual under a money purchase provision of a registered pension plan (other than a plan that is, in the year, a specified multi-employer plan) in respect of the period,

pursuant to terms of the plan that apply in respect of periods that are not regular periods of employment,

(iii) the lifetime retirement benefits or the contributions, as the case may be, exceed the benefits that would otherwise be provided or the contributions that would otherwise be made if the benefits or contributions were based on the services actually rendered by the individual and the remuneration actually received by the individual,

(iv) the individual's pension adjustment for the year with respect to the employer includes an amount in respect of the lifetime retirement benefits or the contributions, as the case may be,

(v) no benefits are provided in respect of the period to the individual under a defined benefit provision of any registered pension plan in which the employer does not participate,

(vi) no contributions are made by or on behalf of the individual in respect of the period under a money purchase provision of a registered pension plan or a deferred profit sharing plan in which the employer does not participate, and

(vii) no part of the period is after the earlier of

(A) the time at which bridging benefits commence to be paid to the individual in circumstances to which subsection 8503(17) applied, and

(B) the earliest day in respect of which benefits have been provided to the individual in circumstances to which subsection 8503(19) applied; and

(*b*) a period of parenting of an individual is all or a part of a period that begins

(i) at the time of the birth of a child of whom the individual is a natural parent, or

(ii) at the time the individual adopts a child,

and ends 12 months after that time.

Related Regulations: 8500(7).

Information Circulars: IC 98-2 Prescribed compensation for registered pension plans.

(4) Cumulative Additional Compensation Fraction. For the purposes of this section, the cumulative additional compensation fraction of an individual with respect to an employer, determined to any time, is the aggregate of all amounts each of which is the additional compensation fraction that is associated with a period that ends at or before that time and that is a qualifying period of the individual in a calendar year after 1990 with respect to

(*a*) the employer;

(*b*) any other employer who does not deal at arm's length with the employer; or

(*c*) any other employer who participates in a registered pension plan in which the employer participates for the benefit of the individual.

(5) Additional Compensation Fraction. For the purposes of subsection (4), the additional compensation fraction associated with a qualifying period of an individual in a calendar year with respect to a particular employer is the amount determined by the formula

$$E / D$$

where

D is the amount that is determined for D under paragraph (2)(*b*) in respect of the qualifying period, and

E is

(*a*) if

(i) all or a part of the qualifying period is a period throughout which the individual renders services to another employer pursuant to an arrangement in respect of which subsection 8308(7) is applicable,

(ii) the particular employer is a lending employer for the purposes of subsection 8308(7) as it applies in respect of the arrangement, and

(iii) the particular employer and the other employer deal with each other at arm's length,

the amount that would be determined under subsection (2) in respect of the qualifying period if, in the determination of the amount under paragraph (2)(*a*), no remuneration were included in respect of the portion of the qualifying period referred to in subparagraph (*a*)(i), and

(*b*) otherwise, the amount that is determined under subsection (2) in respect of the qualifying period.

Information Circulars: IC 98-2 Prescribed compensation for registered pension plans.

(6) Exclusion of Subperiods. A reference in this section to a qualifying period of an individual in a calendar year with respect to an employer or to a period of disability of an individual in a calendar year does not include a period that is part of a longer such period.

(7) Complete Period of Reduced Pay. In subsection (2), "complete period of reduced pay" of an individual with respect to an employer means a period that consists of one or more periods each of which is

(*a*) a period of disability of the individual, or

(*b*) an eligible period of reduced pay or temporary absence of the individual with respect to the employer,

and that is not part of a longer such period.

8508. Salary Deferral Leave Plan

Where an employee and an employer enter into an arrangement in writing described in paragraph 6801(*a*) or (*b*),

(*a*) the period throughout which the employee defers salary or wages pursuant to the arrangement shall be deemed to be an eligible period of reduced pay of the employee with respect to the employer; and

(*b*) for the purposes of section 8507, the amount that it is reasonable to consider would have been the remuneration of the employee for any period from the employer shall be determined on the basis that the employee's rate of remuneration was the amount that it is reasonable to consider would, but for the arrangement, have been the employee's rate of remuneration.

Information Circulars: IC 98-2 Prescribed compensation for registered pension plans.

8509. Transition Rules

(1) Prescribed Conditions Applicable Before 1992 to Grandfathered Plan. The prescribed conditions for the registration of a grandfathered plan are, before 1992,

(*a*) the condition set out in paragraph 8502(*a*),

(*b*) the condition set out in paragraph 8502(*c*), but only in respect of benefits provided under a money purchase provision of the plan, and

(*c*) if the plan contains a money purchase provision, the condition set out in paragraph 8506(2)(*a*),

and the following conditions:

(*d*) the benefits provided under each defined benefit provision of the plan are acceptable to the Minister and, for the purposes of this condition, any benefits in respect of periods before 1991 that become provided after 1988 with respect to a member who is connected with an employer who participates in the plan, or was so connected at any time before the benefits become provided, shall, unless the Minister is notified in writing that the benefits are provided with respect to the member, be deemed to be unacceptable to the Minister, and (*e*) the plan contains such terms as may be required by the Minister.

Related Regulations: 8501(1).

(2) Conditions Applicable After 1991 to Benefits Under Grandfathered Plan. For the purpose of the condition in paragraph 8502(*c*) as it applies after 1991 in respect of a grandfathered plan,

(*a*) the condition in subparagraph 8503(2)(*b*)(ii) is replaced by the condition that the amount of bridging benefits payable to a member for a particular month does not exceed the amount that is determined in respect of the month by the formula

$$(A \times C \times (E / F)) + (G \times (1 - (E / F)))$$

where

A is the amount determined for A under subparagraph 8503(2)(*b*)(ii) with respect to the member for the month,

C is the amount determined for C under subparagraph 8503(2)(*b*)(ii) with respect to the member for the month,

E is the aggregate of all amounts each of which is the duration (measured in years, including any fraction of a year) of a period ending before 1992 that is pensionable service of the member under the provision,

F is the aggregate of all amounts each of which is the duration (measured in years, including any fraction of a year) of a period that is pensionable service of the member under the provision, and

G is the amount determined with respect to the member for the month by the formula set out in subparagraph 8503(2)(*b*)(ii);

(*b*) the conditions in paragraphs 8503(3)(*c*), (*h*) and (*i*) and 8504(1)(*a*) and (*b*) apply only in respect of lifetime retirement benefits provided in respect of periods after 1991; and

(*c*) for the purposes of the conditions in paragraphs 8504(1)(*a*) and (*b*),

(i) the aggregate that is determined under subparagraph 8504(1)(*a*)(i) does not include an amount in respect of 1991, and

(ii) the amount that is determined for G under subparagraph 8504(1)(*a*)(ii) is based only on periods of pensionable service after 1991.

(3) Additional Prescribed Condition for Grandfathered Plan After 1991. The prescribed conditions for the registration of a grandfathered plan include, after 1991, the condition that all benefits provided under each defined benefit provision of the plan in respect of periods before 1992 are acceptable to the Minister.

Registered Plans Directorate Newsletters: No. 92-8R, Eligible service.

(4) Defined Benefits Under Grandfathered Plan Exempt From Conditions. The Minister may, after 1991, exempt from the condition in paragraph 8502(*c*) the following benefits provided under a defined benefit provision of a grandfathered plan:

(*a*) benefits that are payable after the death of a member, to the extent that the benefits can reasonably be considered to relate to lifetime retirement benefits provided to the member in respect of periods before 1992; and

(*b*) bridging benefits in excess of bridging benefits that are permissible under paragraph 8503(2)(*b*), to the extent that the excess bridging benefits are vested in a member on December 31, 1991.

Registered Plans Directorate Newsletters: No. 92-6, Pre-reform disability and bridging benefits; No. 92-5, Pre-reform death benefits.

(4.1) Benefits under Grandfathered Plan — Pre-1992 Disability. Where benefits are provided under a defined benefit provision of a grandfathered plan to a member of the plan as a consequence of the member having become, before 1992, physically or mentally impaired, the following rules apply:

(*a*) the conditions in this Part (other than the condition in paragraph (*b*)) do not apply in respect of the benefits;

(*b*) the prescribed conditions for the registration of the plan include the condition that the benefits are acceptable to the Minister; and

(*c*) subsections 147.1(8) and (9) of the Act do not apply to render the plan a revocable plan where those subsections would not so apply if the member's pension credits under the provision were determined without regard to the benefits.

(5) Conditions Not Applicable to Grandfathered Plan. Where a pension plan is a grandfathered plan,

(*a*) the conditions referred to in paragraph 8501(2)(*b*) do not apply before 1992 in respect of the plan;

(*b*) the condition in paragraph 8502(*d*) does not apply in respect of distributions that are made before 1992 under a defined benefit provision of the plan; and

(*c*) the conditions in paragraphs 8503(3)(*a*) and (*b*) do not apply in respect of benefits provided under a defined benefit provision of the plan in respect of periods before 1992.

(6) PA Limits for Grandfathered Plan for 1991. Subsections 147.1(8) and (9) of the Act do not apply in respect of a grandfathered plan for a calendar year before 1992 if

(*a*) the plan does not contain a money purchase provision in that year; or

(*b*) no contributions are made in respect of that year under the money purchase provisions of the plan.

(7) Limit on Pre-Age 65 Benefits. Where a pension plan is a grandfathered plan or would be a grandfathered plan if the references to "March 27, 1988" in the definitions "existing plan" and "grandfathered plan" in subsection 8500(1) were read as references to "June 7, 1990" and the references to "March 28, 1988" in the definition "existing plan" in that subsection were read as references to "June 8, 1990",

(*a*) the conditions in paragraphs 8504(5)(*a*) and (*b*) apply only in respect of retirement benefits provided in respect of periods after 1991; and

Regulations

(*b*) the amounts that are determined for B and D under paragraph 8504(5)(*a*) are based only on periods of pensionable service after 1991.

(8) Benefit Accrual Rate Greater Than 2 Per Cent. Where a pension plan is a grandfathered plan or would be a grandfathered plan if the references to "March 27, 1988" in the definitions "existing plan" and "grandfathered plan" in subsection 8500(1) were read as references to "July 31, 1991" and the references to "March 28, 1988" in the definition "existing plan" in that subsection were read as references to "August 1, 1991",

(*a*) the condition in paragraph 8503(3)(*g*) applies only in respect of lifetime retirement benefits provided under a defined benefit provision of the plan in respect of periods after 1994; and

(*b*) subparagraph 8503(3)(*h*)(iv) is not applicable in respect of lifetime retirement benefits provided under a defined benefit provision of the plan to a member unless the formula for determining the amount of the member's lifetime retirement benefits complies with the condition in paragraph 8503(3)(*g*) as that condition would, but for this subsection, apply.

(9) Benefits Under Plan Other Than Grandfathered Plan. The following rules apply in respect of the benefits provided under a defined benefit provision of a pension plan that is not a grandfathered plan:

(*a*) the condition in paragraph 8502(*c*) does not apply in respect of benefits provided with respect to an individual

(i) to whom retirement benefits have commenced to be paid under the provision before 1992, or

(ii) who has died before 1992; and

(*b*) the prescribed conditions for the registration of the plan include the condition that all benefits referred to in paragraph (*a*) are acceptable to the Minister.

(10) Money Purchase Benefits Exempt From Conditions. The Minister may exempt from the condition in paragraph 8502(*c*) all or a portion of the benefits provided under a money purchase provision of a pension plan with respect to a member that may reasonably be considered to derive from contributions made before 1992 under a money purchase provision of a registered pension plan.

(10.1) Stipulation Not Required for Pre-1992 Plans. The conditions in paragraphs 8503(4)(*c*) and 8506(2)(*d*) do not apply in respect of a pension plan

(*a*) that was a registered pension plan on December 31, 1991,

(*b*) in respect of which an application for registration was made to the Minister before 1992, or

(*c*) that was established to provide benefits to one or more individuals in lieu of benefits to which the individuals were entitled under another pension plan that is a plan described in paragraph (*a*) or (*b*) or this paragraph, whether or not benefits are also provided to other individuals.

(11) Benefits Acceptable to Minister. For greater certainty, where benefits under a defined benefit provision of a pension plan are, by reason of paragraph 8503(3)(*e*) or subsection (3), subject to the condition that they be acceptable to the Minister, the provisions of this section shall not be considered to limit in any way the requirements that may be imposed by the Minister in respect of the benefits.

(12) PA Limits — 1996 to 2002. Neither subsection 147.1(8) nor (9) of the Act applies to render a registered pension plan a revocable plan at the end of any calendar year after 1995 and before 2003 solely because a pension adjustment, a total of pension adjustments or a total of pension credits of an individual for the year (each of which is, in this subsection, referred to as a "test amount") is excessive where the subsection would not apply to render the plan a revocable plan at the end of the year if each test amount were decreased by the lesser of

(*a*) the amount, if any, by which the lesser of

(i) the total of all amounts each of which is

(A) a pension credit under a defined benefit provision of a registered pension plan that is included in determining the test amount, or

(B) a pension credit under a money purchase provision of a registered pension plan or under a deferred profit sharing plan that is included in determining the test amount and that is taken into account, under paragraph 8302(2)(*c*), in determining a pension credit referred to in clause (A), and

(ii) $15,500

exceeds the money purchase limit for the year, and

(*b*) the total of all amounts each of which is a pension credit referred to in clause (*a*)(i)(A).

(13) Maximum Benefits Indexed Before 2005. Where

(*a*) a pension plan is a grandfathered plan or would be a grandfathered plan if the references to "March 27, 1988" in the definitions "existing plan" and "grandfathered plan" in subsection 8500(1) were read as references to "March 5, 1996" and the references to "March 28, 1988" in the definition "existing plan" in that subsection were read as references to "March 6, 1996",

(*b*) under the terms of the plan as they read immediately before March 6, 1996, the plan provided for benefits that are benefits to which a condition in any of subsections 8504(1), (5) and (6) and paragraph 8505(3)(*d*) applies and, at that time, the benefits complied with the condition, and

(*c*) as a consequence of the change in the defined benefit limit effective March 6, 1996, the benefits would, if this Part were read without reference to this subsection, cease to comply with the condition,

the following rules apply:

(*d*) for the purpose of determining at any time after March 5, 1996 and before 1998 whether the benefits comply with the condition, the defined benefit limit for each year after 1995 is deemed to be the amount that it would be if the definition "money purchase limit" in subsection 147.1(1) of the Act were applied as it read on December 31, 1995, and

(*e*) for the purpose of determining at any time after 1997 whether the benefits comply with the condition, the defined benefit limit for 1996 and 1997 is deemed to be the amount that it would be if it were determined in accordance with paragraph (*d*).

8510. Multi-employer Plans and other Special Plans

(1) Definition of "Multi-Employer Plan". The definition "multi-employer plan" in subsection 8500(1) is applicable for the purposes of subsection 147.1(1) of the Act.

Related Regulations: 8501(1).

(2) Definition of "Specified Multi-Employer Plan". For the purposes of this Part and subsection 147.1(1) of the Act, "specified multi-employer plan" in a calendar year means a pension plan

(*a*) in respect of which the conditions in subsection (3) are satisfied at the beginning of the year (or at the time in the year when the plan is established, if later),

(*b*) that has, on application by the plan administrator, been designated in writing by the Minister to be a specified multi-employer plan in the year, or

(*c*) that was, by reason of paragraph (*a*), a specified multi-employer plan in the immediately preceding calendar year (where that year is after 1989),

but does not include a pension plan where the Minister has, before the beginning of the year, given notice by registered mail to the plan administrator that the plan is not a specified multi-employer plan.

(3) Qualification as a Specified Multi-Employer Plan. The conditions referred to in paragraph (2)(*a*) are the following:

(*a*) it is reasonable to expect that at no time in the year will more than 95 per cent of the active members of the plan be employed by a single participating employer or by a related group of participating employers;

(*b*) where the year is 1991 or a subsequent year, it is reasonable to expect that

(i) at least 15 employers will contribute to the plan in respect of the year, or

(ii) at least 10 per cent of the active members of the plan will be employed in the year by more than one participating employer,

and, for the purposes of this condition, all employers who are related to each other shall be deemed to be a single employer;

(*c*) employers participate in the plan pursuant to a collective bargaining agreement;

(*d*) all or substantially all of the employers who participate in the plan are persons who are not exempt from tax under Part I of the Act;

(*e*) contributions are made by employers in accordance with a negotiated contribution formula that does not provide for any variation in contributions determined by reference to the financial experience of the plan;

(*f*) the contributions that are to be made by each employer in the year are determined, in whole or in part, by reference to the number of hours worked by individual employees of the employer or some other measure that is specific to each employee in respect of whom contributions are made to the plan;

(*g*) the administrator is a board of trustees or similar body that is not controlled by representatives of employers; and

(*h*) the administrator has the power to determine the benefits to be provided under the plan, whether or not that power is subject to the terms of a collective bargaining agreement.

(4) Minister's Notice. For the purpose of subsection (2), the Minister may give notice that a plan is not a specified multi-employer plan only if the Minister is satisfied that participating employers will be able to comply with all reporting obligations imposed by Part LXXXIV in respect of the plan if it is not a specified multi-employer plan, and

(*a*) the notice is given at or after a time when the conditions in subsection (3) are not satisfied in respect of the plan; or

(*b*) the plan administrator has applied to the Minister for the notice.

(5) Special Rules — Multi-Employer Plan. Where a pension plan is a multi-employer plan in a calendar year,

(*a*) each member of the plan who is connected at any time in the year with an employer who participates in the plan shall be deemed, for the purposes of applying the conditions in sections 8503 and 8504 in respect of the plan in the year and in each subsequent year, not to be so connected in the year;

(*b*) paragraph 8503(3)(*b*) shall, in its application in respect of benefits provided under a defined benefit provision of the plan in respect of a period in the year, be read without reference to subparagraph (ii) thereof; and

(*c*) the condition in paragraph 8503(3)(*k*) and the rule in subsection 8504(8) shall apply in the year in respect of the plan without regard to benefits provided under any other pension plan.

(6) Special Rules — Specified Multi-Employer Plan. Where a pension plan is a specified multi-employer plan in a calendar year,

(*a*) a contribution that is made in the year in respect of a defined benefit provision of the plan by an employer with respect to the employer's employees or former employees in accordance with the plan as registered shall be deemed, for the purpose of paragraph 8502(*b*), to be an eligible contribution;

(*b*) subparagraph 8502(*c*)(i) shall, in its application in the year in respect of the plan, be read as follows:

"(i) benefits that are in accordance with subsection 8503(2), paragraphs

8503(3)(*c*), (*e*) and (*g*) and subsections 8504(5) and (6);"

(*c*) the conditions in paragraphs 8503(3)(*j*) and (4)(*a*) do not apply in the year in respect of the plan, and

(*d*) a payment made in the year under a defined benefit provision of the plan with respect to a member is deemed to comply with the conditions in paragraph 8503(2)(*h*) (in the case of a payment made in connection with the member's termination from the plan otherwise than by reason of death) or (*j*) (in the case of a payment made after the death of the member) where it would comply if paragraph 8503(2)(*h*) were read as follows:

"(*h*) the payment, with respect to a member in connection with the member's termination from the plan (otherwise than by reason of death), of one or more single amounts where

(i) the payments are the last payments to be made under the provision with respect to the member, and

(ii) each single amount does not exceed the amount that would be the balance in the member's net contribution account immediately before the time of payment of the single amount if, for each contribution that is a specified contribution, the account were credited at the time of the specified contribution with an additional amount equal to the amount of the specified contribution and, for this purpose, a specified contribution is

(A) a contribution included in determining a pension credit of the member under the provision because of paragraph 8301(5)(*b*), or

(B) a contribution made before 1990 in respect of the provision by a participating employer, to the extent that the contribution can reasonably be considered to have been determined by reference to the number of hours worked by the member or some other measure specific to the member;".

(7) Additional Prescribed Conditions. Where a pension plan is a specified multi-employer plan in a calendar year, the prescribed conditions for the registration of the plan include, in that year, the following conditions:

(*a*) when employer and member contribution rates under the plan were last established, it was reasonable to expect that, for each calendar year beginning with the year in which the contribution rates were last established,

(i) the aggregate of all amounts each of which is the pension credit of an individual for the year with respect to an employer under a benefit provision of the plan

would not exceed

(ii) 18 per cent of the aggregate of all amounts each of which is, for an individual and an employer where the pension credit of the individual for the year with respect to the employer under a benefit provision of the plan is greater than nil, the compensation of the individual from the employer for the year,

except that this condition does not apply for years before 1992 in the case of a pension plan that is a grandfathered plan; and

(*b*) where the plan contains a money purchase provision,

(i) the plan terms are such that, if subsection 147.1(9) of the Act were applicable in respect of the plan, the plan would not under any circumstances become a revocable plan at the end of the year pursuant to that subsection, or

(ii) if the plan terms do not comply with the condition in subparagraph (i), the only circumstances that would result in the plan becoming a revocable plan at the end of the year pursuant to subsection 147.1(9) of the Act, if that subsection were applicable in respect of the plan, are circumstances acceptable to the Minister.

Proposed Amendment

2019 Federal Budget Resolutions

Subsection 8510(7) of the *Income Tax Regulations* (the "Regulations") is amended by striking out "and" at the end of paragraph (*a*), by adding "and" at the end of paragraph (*b*) and by adding the following after that paragraph:

(*c*) no contributions are made

(i) to the plan with respect to a member at any time after the end of the calendar year in which the member attains 71 years of age, or

(ii) to a defined benefit provision of the plan with respect to a member during a period (other than a *qualifying period*, as defined in subsection 8503(16)) in which the member is in receipt of retirement benefits from a defined benefit provision of the plan.

Applicable: In respect of contributions made pursuant to any collective bargaining agreement entered into after 2019, except that it does not apply in respect of contributions made on or before the date the agreement is entered into.

Information Circulars: IC 98-2 Prescribed compensation for registered pension plans.

(8) Purchase of Additional Benefits. Where, in the case of a pension plan that is a specified multi-employer plan in a calendar year,

(*a*) the amount of lifetime retirement benefits provided under a defined benefit provision of the plan to each member is determined by reference to the hours of employment of the member with participating employers,

(*b*) the plan permits a member whose actual hours of employment in a period are fewer than a specified number of hours for the period to make contributions to the plan in order to increase, to an amount not exceeding the specified number of hours for the period, the number of hours that are treated under the provision as hours of employment of the member in the period, and (*c*) the specified number of hours for a period does not exceed a reasonable measure of the actual hours of employment of members who render services throughout the period on a full-time basis,

the condition in paragraph 8503(3)(*a*) does not apply in respect of such portion of the lifetime retirement benefits provided under the provision to a member as is determined by reference to hours acquired by the member as a consequence of contributions made to the plan in the year by the member, as described in paragraph (*b*).

(9) Special Rules — Member-funded Pension Plans. Where a pension plan (other than a specified multi-employer plan) is a member-funded pension plan for the purposes of Division IX of the Regulation respecting the exemption of certain categories of pension plans from the provisions of the Supplemental Pension Plans Act of Quebec (R.Q., c. R.-15.1, r. 2), as amended from time to time,

(*a*) paragraph 8502(*c*) shall in its application in respect of the plan be read without reference to subparagraph (iii);

(*b*) the prescribed conditions for the registration of the plan include the following conditions:

(i) the plan terms are such that each contribution to be made by a member under a defined benefit provision of the plan would be an eligible contribution under subsection 147.2(2) of the Act if

(A) the contribution were made by an employer who participates in the plan for the benefit of the member, and

(B) this subsection were read without reference to paragraph (*c*),

(ii) unless this condition is waived by the Minister, the plan is maintained pursuant to a collective bargaining agreement,

(iii) the plan is not, and it is reasonable to expect that the plan will not become, a designated plan, and

(iv) the amount of benefits provided to members, the amount of contributions required to be made by members and the entitlement of members' [*sic*] to benefit from actuarial surplus are determined in a manner that is

(A) clearly established in the plan terms, and

(B) not more advantageous for members who, at any time after the plan is established, are specified individuals (within the meaning assigned by subsection 8515(4)) under the plan than for members who are not specified individuals; and

(*c*) a contribution made by an employer to the plan is a prescribed contribution for the purposes of subsection 147.2(2) of the Act if

(i) the contribution is a current service contribution that would be an eligible contribution under subsection 147.2(2) of the Act if no contributions were prescribed for the purposes of that subsection and if that subsection were read without reference to its subparagraph (*d*)(ii), and

(ii) the recommendation pursuant to which the contribution is made is such that the current service contributions to be made by the employer do not exceed,

(A) where the amount of actuarial surplus in respect of the employer is greater than the amount determined under subparagraph 147.2(2)(*d*)(ii) of the Act, 50% of the current service contribution that would be required to be made by the employer if there were no actuarial surplus under the provisions, and

(B) in any other case, the current service contributions that would be required to be made by the employer if there were no actuarial surplus under the provisions.

History: S. 8510(9)(*c*)(i) was replaced by S.C. 2010, c. 12, s. 24(1), applicable to contributions made after 2009 to fund benefits provided in respect of periods of pensionable service after 2009. S. 8510(9)(*c*)(i) formerly read:

(i) the contribution is a current service contribution that would be an eligible contribution under subsection 147.2(2) of the Act if no contributions were prescribed for the purposes of that subsection and if that subsection were read without reference to its subparagraphs (*d*)(ii) and (iii), and

S. 8510(9)(*c*)(ii)(A) was replaced by S.C. 2010, c. 12, s. 24(2), applicable to contributions made after 2009 to fund benefits provided in respect of periods of pensionable service after 2009. S. 8510(9)(*c*)(ii)(A) formerly read:

(A) where the amount of actuarial surplus in respect of the employer is greater than the greater of the amounts determined under subparagraphs 147.2(2)(*d*)(ii) and (iii) of the Act, 50% of the current service contributions that would be required to be made by the employer if there were no actuarial surplus under the provisions, and

8511. Conditions Applicable to Amendments

(1) For the purposes of paragraph 147.1(4)(*c*) of the Act, the following conditions are prescribed in respect of an amendment to a registered pension plan:

(*a*) where the amendment increases the accrued lifetime retirement benefits provided to a member under a defined benefit provision of the plan, the increase is not, in the opinion of the Minister, inconsistent with the conditions in paragraphs 8503(3)(*h*) and (*i*); and

(*b*) where the plan is a grandfathered plan and the amendment increases the bridging benefits provided to a member under a defined benefit provision of the plan, the member's bridging benefits, as amended, comply with the condition in subparagraph 8503(2)(*b*)(ii) that would apply if the plan were not a grandfathered plan.

(2) Where an amendment to a registered pension plan provides for the return to a member of all or a part of the contributions made by the member under a defined benefit provision of the plan, the plan becomes a revocable plan at any time that an amount (other than an amount that may be transferred from the plan in accordance with subsection 147.3(6) of the Act) that is payable to the member as a consequence of the amendment is not paid to the member as soon after the amendment as is practicable.

8512. Registration and Amendment

(1) For the purpose of subsection 147.1(2) of the Act, an application for registration of a pension plan shall be made by sending the following documents by registered mail to the Commissioner of Revenue at Ottawa:

Regulations

(*a*) an application in prescribed form containing prescribed information;

(*b*) certified copies of the plan text and any other documents that contain terms of the plan;

(*c*) certified copies of all trust deeds, insurance contracts and other documents that relate to the funding of benefits under the plan;

(*d*) certified copies of all agreements that relate to the plan; and

(*e*) certified copies of all resolutions and by-laws that relate to the documents referred to in paragraphs (*b*) to (*d*).

Registered Plans Directorate Newsletters: No. 04-2, Registered pension plan applications — Processing an incomplete application; No. 91-4R, Registration rules for money purchase provisions.

(2) Where an amendment is made to a registered pension plan, to the arrangement for funding benefits under the plan or to a document that has been filed with the Minister in respect of the plan, within 60 days after the day on which the amendment is made, the plan administrator shall send to the Commissioner of Revenue at Ottawa

(*a*) a prescribed form containing prescribed information; and

(*b*) certified copies of all documents that relate to the amendment.

(3) For the purpose of subsection 147.1(4) of the Act, an application for the acceptance of an amendment to a registered pension plan is made in prescribed manner if the documents that are required by subsection (2) are sent by registered mail to the Commissioner of Revenue at Ottawa.

8513. Designated Laws

For the purposes of paragraph 8302(3)(*m*), subparagraph 8502(*c*)(iii) and paragraph 8517(5)(*f*), "designated provision of the law of Canada or a province" means subsection 21(2) of the *Pension Benefits Standards Act, 1985* and any provision of a law of a province that is similar to that subsection.

8514. Prohibited Investments

(1) For the purposes of subparagraph 8502(*h*)(i) and subject to subsections (2), (2.1) and (3), a prohibited investment in respect of a registered pension plan is a share of the capital stock of, an interest in, or a debt of

(*a*) an employer who participates in the plan,

(*b*) a person who is connected with an employer who participates in the plan,

(*c*) a member of the plan,

(*d*) a person or partnership that controls, directly or indirectly, in any manner whatever, a person or partnership referred to in paragraph (*a*) or (*b*), or

(*e*) a person or partnership that does not deal at arm's length with a person or partnership referred to in paragraph (*a*), (*b*), (*c*) or (*d*),

or an interest in, or a right to acquire, such a share, interest or debt.

(2) A prohibited investment does not include

(*a*) a debt obligation described in paragraph (*a*) of the definition "fully exempt interest" in subsection 212(3) of the Act;

(*b*) a share listed on a designated stock exchange;

(*c*) a bond, debenture, note or similar obligation of a corporation any shares of which are listed on a designated stock exchange;

(*d*) an interest in, or a right to acquire, property referred to in paragraph (*b*) or (*c*); or

(*e*) a mortgage in respect of real property situated in Canada that

(i) where this condition has not been waived by the Minister and the amount paid for the mortgage, together with the amount of any indebtedness outstanding at the time the mortgage was acquired under any mortgage or hypothec that ranks equally with or superior to the mortgage, exceeds 75 per cent of the fair market value, at that time, of the real property that is subject to the mortgage, is insured under the *National Housing Act* or by a corporation that offers its services to the public in Canada as an insurer of mortgages,

(ii) where the registered pension plan in connection with which the mortgage is held would be a designated plan for the purposes of subsection 8515(5) if subsection 8515(4) were read without reference to paragraph (*b*) thereof, is administered by an approved lender under the *National Housing Act*, and

(iii) bears a rate of interest that would be reasonable in the circumstances if the mortgagor dealt with the mortgagee at arm's length.

(2.1) Where a share of the capital stock of, an interest in or a debt of, a person who is connected with a particular employer who participates in a registered pension plan that is a multi-employer plan would, but for this subsection, be a prohibited investment in respect of the plan, the property is not a prohibited investment in respect of the plan if

(*a*) the plan contains no money purchase provision other than a money purchase provision under which each member account is credited, on a reasonable basis and no less frequently than annually, an amount based on the income earned, losses incurred and capital gains and capital losses realized, on all of the property held by the plan;

(*b*) at the time the property is acquired by the plan, there are at least 15 employers who participate in the plan and, for this purpose,

(i) all employers who are related to each other are deemed to be a single employer, and

(ii) all the structural units of a trade union, including each local, branch, national and international unit, are deemed to be a single employer;

(*c*) at the time the property is acquired by the plan, no more than 10% of the active members of the plan are employed by the particular employer or by any person related to the particular employer;

(*d*) the property would not be a prohibited investment in respect of the plan if subsection (1) were read without reference to paragraph (1)(*b*); and

(*e*) immediately after the time the property is acquired by the plan, the total of all amounts each of which is the cost amount to a person of a property held in connection with the plan that would, but for this subsection, be a prohibited investment in respect of the plan does not exceed 10% of the total of all amounts each of which is the cost amount to a person of a property held in connection with the plan.

History: S. 8514(2.1)(*a*) was replaced by S.C. 2013, c. 34, s. 410(1), deemed to have come into force on January 1, 2011, and formerly read:

(*a*) the plan does not contain a money purchase provision;

(2.2) For the purposes of the conditions set out in paragraphs (2.1)(*b*) and (*c*), two corporations that are related to each other solely because they are both controlled by Her Majesty in right of Canada or a province are deemed not to be related to each other.

(3) A prohibited investment in respect of a registered pension plan does not include an investment that was acquired by the plan before March 28, 1988.

(4) For the purposes of subsection (3), where at any time after March 27, 1988, the principal amount of a bond, debenture, note, mortgage or similar obligation increases as a consequence of the advancement or lending of additional amounts or the maturity date of such an obligation is extended, the obligation shall, after that time, be deemed to have been issued at that time.

Department of Finance Comfort Letters

(June 12, 2017) [A person or partnership in which a Registered Pension Plan invests would not be a prohibited investment]

2016-TL-21

XXXX

Dear XXXX and Mr. XXXX:

I am writing in response to your letter of November 23, 2016 and further discussions in which you outline proposed transactions and identify certain technical issues with the income tax rules that would apply to the transactions.

In your letter, you advise that XXXX

- XXXX a corporation without share capital, was established to provide investment management services and investment advisory services to its members.
- The initial members of XXXX
- For the purposes of subsection 8514(1) of the *Income Tax Regulations* (the "Regulations"), none of the members have an "interest" in XXXX
- The members may enter into investment management agreements with XXXX if they wish to invest plan assets (XXXX

I understand that XXXX employees accrue pensionable service under the XXXX and that some XXXX employees will transfer their employment to XXXX. It is contemplated that XXXX will become a participating employer under the XXXX so that, among other things, the transferred employees will benefit from uninterrupted pension coverage.

I also understand that XXXX will manage the investment of XXXX assets in certain pooled investment corporations, pooled investment partnerships and pooled investment trusts (collectivelly the "Pooled Vehicles"). XXXX interest in any Pooled Vehicle would be limited to that consistent with its role as investment manager and advisor.

You have indicated that by virtue of its role as investment manager and advisor expected to factually not deal at arm's length with the Pooled Vehicles. As a result, if XXXX were a participating employer under the XXXX an investment in a Pooled Vehicle would be a prohibited investment described in paragraph 8514(1)(*e*) of the Regulations for the XXXX.

In this context, you have requested that we recommend amendments to section 8514 of the Regulations to permit XXXX to be a participating under the XXXX without causing the Pooled Vehicles to be prohibited investments for XXXX. We agree that the proposed transactions do not raise income tax policy concerns. In particular, we understand that, but for XXXX being a participating employer, the Pooled Vehicles would not be prohibited investments under the Regulations and would adhere to investment restrictions under XXXX.

We are prepared to recommend that a recommendation be made to the Governor General in Council that amendments to section 8514 of the Regulations be made such that a person or partnership in which a registered pension plan invests would not be a prohibited investment to the plan solely because the person or partnership does not deal at arm's length with a participating employer whose main object is the management of, and/or the provision of investment advice in respect of, the fund of a registered pension plan, Her Majesty in right of Canada, Her Majesty in right of a province, or an entity described in any of paragraphs 149(1)(*c*) and (*d*) to (*d.4*) of the *Income Tax Act*.

We would also recommend that the proposed amendments apply in respect of investments made after May 2017

While I cannot offer any assurance that the Governor General in Council will agree with our recommendations, I hope that this statement of our intention is helpful to you.

Thank you for writing to us on this matter

Yours sincerely,

Brian Ernewein

General Director, Legislation

Tax Policy Branch

8515. Special Rules for Designated Plans

(1) Designated Plans. For the purposes of subsections (5) and (9), and subject to subsection (3), a registered pension plan that contains a defined benefit provision is a designated plan throughout a calendar year if the plan is not maintained pursuant to a collective bargaining agreement and

(*a*) the aggregate of all amounts each of which is a pension credit (as determined under Part LXXXIII) for the year of a specified individual under a defined benefit provision of the plan

exceeds

(*b*) 50 per cent of the aggregate of all amounts each of which is a pension credit (as determined under Part LXXXIII) for the year of an individual under a defined benefit provision of the plan.

Registered Plans Directorate Newsletters: No. 94-2, Technical questions and answers.

(2) Designated Plan in Previous Year. For the purposes of subsections (5) and (9), a registered pension plan is a designated plan throughout a particular calendar year after 1990 if the plan was a designated plan at any time in the immediately preceding year, except where the Minister has waived in writing the application of this subsection in respect of the plan.

(3) Exceptions. A registered pension plan is not a designated plan in a calendar year pursuant to subsection (1) if

(*a*) the plan would not be a designated plan in the year pursuant to that subsection if the reference in paragraph (1)(*b*) to "50 per cent" were read as a reference to "60 per cent",

(*b*) the plan was established before the year, and

(*c*) the amount determined under paragraph (1)(*a*) in respect of the plan for the immediately preceding year did not exceed the amount determined under paragraph (1)(*b*).

History: S. 8515(3), the portion following paragraph (*c*) was repealed by P.C. 2011-936, SOR/2011-188, dated September 22, 2011, published in the *Canada Gazette* October 12, 2011, applicable after February 19, 2011. S. 8515(3), the portion following paragraph (*c*) formerly read:

or if

(*d*) there are more than 9 active members of the plan in the year, and

(*e*) the Minister has given written notice to the administrator of the plan that the plan is not a designated plan in the year.

(3.1) Exceptions. If a designated plan has more than nine active members, the Minister may waive the application of any provision of this Part or Part LXXXIII that would otherwise apply to the designated plan because of its status as a designated plan.

History: S. 8515(3.1) was added by P.C. 2011-936, SOR/2011-188, dated September 22, 2011, published in the *Canada Gazette* October 12, 2011, applicable after February 19, 2011.

(4) Specified Individuals. An individual is a specified individual for the purposes of paragraph (1)(*a*) in respect of a pension plan and a particular calendar year if

(*a*) the individual was connected at any time in the year with an employer who participates in the plan; or

(*b*) the aggregate of all amounts each of which is the remuneration of the individual for the year from an employer who participates in the plan, or from an employer who does not deal at arm's length with a participating employer, exceeds $2^1/_2$ times the Year's Maximum Pensionable Earnings for the year.

(5) Eligible Contributions. For the purpose of determining whether a contribution that is made by an employer to a registered pension plan at a time when the plan is a designated plan is an eligible contribution under subsection 147.2(2) of the Act, a prescribed condition is that

(*a*) the contribution satisfies the condition in subsection (6), or

(*b*) the contribution would satisfy the condition in subsection (6) if

(i) paragraph (6)(*b*) and subparagraph (7)(*e*)(i) were applicable only in respect of retirement benefits that became provided under the plan after 1990,

(ii) paragraph (6)(*c*) were applicable only in respect of those benefits payable after the death of a member that relate to retirement benefits that became provided under the plan to the member after 1990, and

(iii) the assumption as to the time retirement benefits (other than retirement benefits that became provided after 1990) will commence to be paid is the same for the purposes of the maximum funding valuation as for the purposes of the actuarial valuation that forms the basis for the recommendation referred to in subsection 147.2(2) of the Act pursuant to which the contribution is made.

(6) Funding Restriction. The condition referred to in subsection (5) is that the contribution would be required to be made for the plan to have sufficient assets to pay benefits under the defined benefit provisions of the plan, as registered, with respect to the employees and former employees of the employer if

(*a*) required contributions were determined on the basis of a maximum funding valuation prepared as of the same effective date as the actuarial valuation that forms the basis for the recommendation referred to in subsection 147.2(2) of the Act pursuant to which the contribution is made;

(*a*.1) each defined benefit provision of the plan provided that, with respect to restricted-funding members, retirement benefits are payable monthly in advance;

(*b*) each defined benefit provision of the plan provided that, after retirement benefits commence to be paid with respect to a restricted-funding member, the benefits are adjusted annually by a percentage increase for each year that is one percentage point less than the percentage increase in the Consumer Price Index for the year, in lieu of any cost-of-living adjustments actually provided;

(*c*) each defined benefit provision of the plan provided the following benefits after the death of a restricted-funding member who dies after retirement benefits under the provision have commenced to be paid to the member, in lieu of the benefits actually provided:

(i) where the member dies within 5 years after retirement benefits commence to be paid under the provision, the continuation of the retirement benefits for the remainder of the 5 years as if the member were alive, and

(ii) where an individual who is a spouse or common-law partner of the member when retirement benefits commence to be paid under the provision to the member is alive on the later of the day of death of the member and the day that is 5 years after the day on which the member's retirement benefits commence to be paid, retirement benefits payable to the individual for the duration of the individual's life, with the amount of the benefits payable for each month equal to 66⅔ per cent of the amount of retirement benefits that would have been payable under the provision for the month to the member if the member were alive;

(*d*) where more than one employer participates in the plan, assets and actuarial liabilities were apportioned in a reasonable manner among participating employers with respect to their employees and former employees; and

(*e*) the rule in paragraph 147.2(2)(*d*) of the Act that provides for the disregard of a portion of the assets of the plan apportioned to the employer with respect to the employer's employees and former employees were applicable for the purpose of determining required contributions pursuant to this subsection.

(7) Maximum Funding Valuation. For the purposes of subsection (6), a maximum funding valuation is a valuation prepared by an actuary in accordance with the following rules:

(*a*) the projected accrued benefit method is used for the purpose of determining actuarial liabilities and current service costs;

(*b*) the valuation rate of interest is 7.5 per cent per annum;

(*c*) it is assumed that

(i) the rate of increase in general wages and salaries and in each member's rate of remuneration will be 5.5 per cent per annum, and

(ii) the rate of increase in the Consumer Price Index will be 4 per cent per annum;

(*d*) each assumption made in respect of economic factors other than those referred to in paragraph (*c*) is consistent with the assumptions in that paragraph;

(*e*) in the case of a restricted-funding member, it is assumed that

(i) retirement benefits will commence to be paid to the member no earlier than the day on which the member attains 65 years of age,

(ii) the member will survive to the time the member's retirement benefits commence to be paid,

(iii) where the member is employed by a participating employer as of the effective date of the valuation, the member will continue in employment until the time the member's retirement benefits commence to be paid, and

(iv) when the member's retirement benefits commence to be paid, the member will be married to a person who is the same age as the member;

(*f*) the rate of mortality at each age is equal to

(i) in the case of a restricted-funding member, 80 per cent of the average of the rates at that age for males and females in the *1983 Group Annuity Mortality Table*, as published in Volume XXXV of the *Transactions of the Society of Actuaries*, and

(ii) in the case of any other member, 80 per cent of the rate at that age in the mortality table referred to in subparagraph (i) for individuals of the same sex as the member;

(*g*) it is assumed that where a member has a choice between receiving retirement benefits or a lump sum payment, retirement benefits will be paid to the member; and

(*h*) the plan's assets are valued at an amount equal to their fair market value as of the effective date of the valuation.

(8) Restricted-Funding Members. For the purposes of subsections (6) and (7) as they apply in respect of a contribution made to a registered pension plan, a member of the plan is a restricted-funding member if, at the time the maximum funding valuation is prepared,

(*a*) the member has a right, whether absolute or contingent, to receive retirement benefits under a defined benefit provision of the plan and the benefits have not commenced to be paid; or

(*b*) the payment of retirement benefits under a defined benefit provision of the plan to the member has been suspended.

(9) Member Contributions. Where

(*a*) a member of a registered pension plan makes a contribution to the plan to fund benefits that have become provided at a particular time under a defined benefit provision of the plan in respect of periods before that time,

(*b*) the contribution is made at a time when the plan is a designated plan, and

(*c*) the contribution would not be an eligible contribution under subsection 147.2(2) of the Act if it were made by an employer who participates in the plan on behalf of the member,

the plan becomes, for the purposes of paragraph 147.1(11)(*c*) of the Act, a revocable plan immediately before the time the contribution is made.

8516. Eligible Contributions

(1) Prescribed Contribution. For the purposes of subsection 147.2(2) of the Act, a contribution described in subsection (2) or (3) is a prescribed contribution.

History: S. 8516(1) was replaced by S.C. 2010, c. 12, s. 25(1), applicable to contributions made after 2009 to fund benefits provided in respect of periods of pensionable service after 2009. S. 8516(1) formerly read:

(1) For the purposes of subsection 147.2(2) of the Act, a contribution described in any of subsections (2) to (4) is a prescribed contribution.

(2) Funding on Termination Basis. A contribution that is made by an employer to a registered pension plan is described in this subsection if

(*a*) the contribution is made pursuant to a recommendation by an actuary in whose opinion the contribution is required to be made so that, if the plan is terminated immediately after the contribution is made, it will have sufficient assets to pay benefits accrued under the defined benefit provisions of the plan, as registered, to the time the contribution is made;

(*b*) the recommendation is based on an actuarial valuation that complies with the following conditions:

(i) the effective date of the valuation is not more than four years before the day on which the contribution is made,

(ii) all assumptions made for the purposes of the valuation are reasonable at the time the valuation is prepared and at the time the contribution is made,

(iii) the valuation is prepared in accordance with generally accepted actuarial principles applicable with respect to a valuation prepared on the basis that a plan will be terminated, and

(iv) where more than one employer participates in the plan, assets and actuarial liabilities are apportioned in a reasonable manner among participating employers;

(*c*) the recommendation is approved by the Minister; and

(*d*) at the time the contribution is made, the plan is not a designated plan.

Registered Plans Directorate Newsletters: No. 91-5, Transitional rules and other administrative issues for pension plans.

(3) Contributions Required by Pension Benefits Legislation. A contribution that is made by an employer to a registered pension plan is described in this subsection if

(*a*) the contribution

(i) is required to be made to comply with the *Pension Benefits Standards Act, 1985* or a similar law of a province,

(ii) is made in respect of benefits under the defined benefit provisions of the plan as registered, and

(iii) is made pursuant to a recommendation by an actuary;

(*b*) the recommendation is based on an actuarial valuation that complies with the following conditions:

(i) the effective date of the valuation is not more than four years before the day on which the contribution is made,

(ii) all assumptions made for the purposes of the valuation are reasonable at the time the valuation is prepared and at the time the contribution is made, and

(iii) where more than one employer participates in the plan, assets and actuarial liabilities are apportioned in a reasonable manner among participating employers;

(*c*) the recommendation is approved by the Minister; and

(*d*) at the time the contribution is made, the plan is not a designated plan.

(4) (Repealed.)

History: S. 8516(4) and the heading before it were repealed by S.C. 2010, c. 12, s. 25(2), applicable to contributions made after 2009 to fund benefits provided in respect of periods of pensionable service after 2009. S. 8516(4) formerly read:

(4) *Shared Funding Arrangement.* A contribution that is made by an employer to a registered pension plan is described in this subsection if

(*a*) responsibility for the governance of the plan is shared between the participating employers and the members of the plan;

(*b*) the contribution is made pursuant to an arrangement approved by the Minister under which it is reasonable to expect that, on a long-term basis, the members' entitlement to benefit from actuarial surplus, the members' obligation to fund actuarial deficiencies and the members' obligation to make regular current service contributions, under the defined benefit provisions of the plan, will not be less than 66 2/3% or more than 100% of each such entitlement or obligation of the participating employers;

(*c*) the contribution is a current service contribution that would be an eligible contribution under subsection 147.2(2) of the Act if no contributions were prescribed for the purposes of that subsection and if that subsection were read without reference to subparagraphs (*d*)(ii) and (iii);

(*d*) the recommendation pursuant to which the contribution is made is such that the current service contributions to be made by the employer and the employer's employees in respect of the provisions do not exceed,

(i) where the amount of actuarial surplus in respect of the employer is not more than 10% of the amount of actuarial liabilities apportioned to the employer in respect of the employer's employees and former employees, the current service contributions that would be required if there were no actuarial surplus under the provisions,

(ii) where the amount of actuarial surplus in respect of the employer is greater than 10%, but not more than 15%, of the amount of actuarial liabilities apportioned to the employer in respect of the employer's employees and former employees, 75% of the current service contributions that would be required if there were no actuarial surplus under the provisions,

(iii) where the amount of actuarial surplus in respect of the employer is greater than 15%, but not more than 20%, of the amount of actuarial liabilities apportioned to the employer in respect of the employer's employees and former employees, 50% of the current service contributions that would be required if there were no actuarial surplus under the provisions,

(iv) where the amount of actuarial surplus in respect of the employer is greater than 20%, but not more than 25%, of the amount of actuarial liabilities apportioned to the employer in respect of the employer's employees and former employees, 25% of the current service contributions that would be required if there were no actuarial surplus under the provisions, and

(v) where the amount of actuarial surplus in respect of the employer is greater than 25% of the amount of actuarial liabilities apportioned to the employer in respect of the employer's employees and former employees, nil; and

(*e*) at the time the contribution is made, the plan is not a designated plan.

(5) (Repealed.)

(6) (Repealed.)

(7) (Repealed.)

(8) (Repealed.)

(9) (Repealed.)

Regulations

8517. Transfer — Defined Benefit to Money Purchase

(1) Prescribed Amount. Subject to subsections (2) to (3.1), for the purpose of applying paragraph 147.3(4)(*c*) of the Act to the transfer of an amount on behalf of an individual in full or partial satisfaction of the individual's entitlement to benefits under a defined benefit provision of a registered pension plan, the prescribed amount is the amount that is determined by the formula

$$A \times B$$

where

A is the amount of the individual's lifetime retirement benefits under the provision commuted in connection with the transfer, as determined under subsection (4), and

B is

(*a*) the present value factor that corresponds to the age attained by the individual at the time of the transfer, determined pursuant to the table to this subsection, or

(*b*) where the present value factor referred to in paragraph (*a*) is less than the present value factor that corresponds to the next higher age, the present value factor determined by interpolation between those two factors on the basis of the age (expressed in years, including any fraction of a year) of the individual.

Attained Age	Present Value Factor
Under 50	9.0
50	9.4
51	9.6
52	9.8
53	10.0
54	10.2
55	10.4
56	10.6
57	10.8
58	11.0
59	11.3
60	11.5
61	11.7
62	12.0
63	12.2
64	12.4
65	12.4
66	12.0
67	11.7
68	11.3
69	11.0
70	10.6
71	10.3
72	10.1
73	9.8
74	9.4
75	9.1
76	8.7
77	8.4
78	8.0
79	7.7
80	7.3
81	7.0
82	6.7
83	6.4
84	6.1
85	5.8
86	5.5
87	5.2
88	4.9
89	4.7
90	4.4
91	4.2
92	3.9
93	3.7
94	3.5
95	3.2
96 or over	3.0

Interpretation Bulletins: *Secondary* — IT-528 Transfers of funds between registered plans.

Registered Plans Directorate Newsletters: No. 04-1, Transfers from a defined benefit provision to a money purchase provision, an RRSP, or a RRIF and transfers between defined benefit provisions.

(2) Minimum Prescribed Amount. Where an amount is transferred in full satisfaction of an individual's entitlement to benefits under a defined benefit provision of a registered pension plan, the prescribed amount for the purposes of paragraph 147.3(4)(*c*) of the Act in respect of the transfer is the greater of the amount that would, but for this subsection, be the prescribed amount, and the balance, at the time of the transfer, in the individual's net contribution account (within the meaning assigned by subsection 8503(1)) in relation to the provision.

Interpretation Bulletins: *Secondary* — IT-528 Transfers of funds between registered plans.

Registered Plans Directorate Newsletters: No. 04-1, Transfers from a defined benefit provision to a money purchase provision, an RRSP, or a RRIF and transfers between defined benefit provisions.

(3) Underfunded Pension. Subsection (3.01) applies in respect of a transfer of an amount on behalf of an individual in full or partial satisfaction of the individual's entitlement to benefits under a defined benefit provision of a registered pension plan if

(*a*) the individual is an employee or a former employee of an employer (or a predecessor employer of the employer);

(*b*) the employer

(i) was a participating employer under the provision,

(ii) is the subject of proceedings commenced under the *Bankruptcy and Insolvency Act* or the *Companies' Creditors Arrangement Act*, and

(iii) has ceased making regular contributions under the provision;

(*c*) after the commencement of the proceedings, lifetime retirement benefits paid or payable to the individual under the provision have been reduced because the assets of the plan are insufficient to pay the benefits provided under the provision of the plan as registered;

(*d*) the plan is not a designated plan; and

(*e*) the Minister has approved the application of subsection (3.01) in respect of the transfer.

History: S. 8517(3) and the heading before it were replaced by S.C. 2011, c. 24, s. 97(1), applicable after 2010. S. 8517(3) and the heading before it formerly read:

Plan Wind-Up or Replacement

(3) *Plan Wind-Up or Replacement.* Where an amount is transferred before January 1, 1993, or such later date as is acceptable to the Minister, on behalf of an individual as a consequence of the winding-up of a registered pension plan or as a consequence of the replacement of a defined benefit provision of a registered pension plan by a money purchase provision of another registered pension plan and either

(*a*) the winding-up of the plan or the replacement of the provision commenced at a time (in this subsection referred to as the "time of termination") before 1989,

(*b*) at the time of termination, the plan had at least 50 members, and

(*c*) the plan was established at least 5 years before the time of termination,

or the condition in paragraph (*a*) is satisfied and the Minister waives the conditions in paragraphs (*b*) and (*c*), the prescribed amount for the purposes of paragraph 147.3(4)(*c*) of the Act in respect of the transfer is the amount so transferred.

Interpretation Bulletins: *Secondary* — IT-528 Transfers of funds between registered plans.

Registered Plans Directorate Newsletters: No. 94-4, Wind-up valuation report.

(3.001) Subsection (3.01) applies in respect of a transfer of an amount on behalf of an individual in full or partial satisfaction of the individual's entitlement to benefits under a defined benefit provision of a registered pension plan if

(*a*) the individual is an employee or a former employee of an employer (or a predecessor employer of the employer) that was a participating employer under the provision;

(*b*) lifetime retirement benefits paid or payable to the individual under the provision have been reduced because the assets of the plan are insufficient to pay the benefits provided under the provision of the plan as registered;

(*c*) the Minister has approved the application of subsection (3.01) in respect of the transfer; and

(*d*) either

(i) the plan is not an individual pension plan and the reduction in the lifetime retirement benefits paid or payable to the individual has been approved under the *Pension Benefits Standards Act, 1985* or a similar law of a province, or

(ii) the plan is an individual pension plan, the amount transferred from the plan on behalf of the individual is the last payment from the plan to the individual and all the property held in connection with the plan is distributed from the plan on behalf of plan members within 90 days of the transfer.

History: S. 8517(3.001) was added by S.C. 2014, c. 20, s. 36(1), applicable in respect of transfers from registered pension plans made after 2012.

(3.01) If this subsection applies, the description of A in subsection (1) is to be read as follows in respect of the transfer:

"A is the amount of the individual's lifetime retirement benefits under the provision commuted in connection with the transfer, as determined under subsection (4), but without reference to the benefit reduction referred to in paragraph (3)(*c*) or (3.001)(*b*), as the case may be; and"

History: S. 8517(3.01) was replaced by S.C. 2014, c. 20, s. 36(1), applicable in respect of transfers from registered pension plans made after 2012, and formerly read:

(3.01) *Underfunded Pension.* If this subsection applies, the description of A in subsection (1) shall be read as follows in respect of the transfer:

"A is the amount of the individual's lifetime retirement benefits under the provision commuted in connection with the transfer, as determined under subsection (4), but without reference to the benefit reduction referred to in paragraph (3)(*c*); and"

S. 8517(3.01) was added by S.C. 2011, c. 24, s. 97(1), applicable after 2010.

(3.02) Underfunded Pension. If a particular amount is transferred in full or partial satisfaction of an individual's entitlement to benefits under a defined benefit provision of a registered pension plan and subsection (3.01) had applied in respect of a transfer (in this subsection referred to as the "initial transfer") of an amount on behalf of the individual under the provision, for the purpose of paragraph 147.3(4)(*c*) of the Act the prescribed amount in respect of the transfer of the particular amount is the lesser of

(*a*) the particular amount, and

(*b*) the amount, if any, by which the prescribed amount in respect of the initial transfer exceeds the total of all amounts each of which is the amount of a previous transfer to which this subsection or subsection (3.01) applied in respect of the individual's entitlement to benefits under the provision.

History: S. 8517(3.02) was added by S.C. 2011, c. 24, s. 97(1), applicable after 2010.

(3.1) Benefits Provided With Surplus on Plan Wind-up. Where an amount is transferred in full or partial satisfaction of an individual's entitlement to benefits under a defined benefit provision of a registered pension plan and the benefits include benefits (in this subsection referred to as "ancillary benefits") that are permissible solely because of subsection 8501(7), the prescribed amount for the purpose of paragraph 147.3(4)(*c*) of the Act in respect of the transfer is the total of

(*a*) the amount that would, but for this subsection, be the prescribed amount, and

(*b*) an amount approved by the Minister not exceeding the lesser of

(i) the present value (at the time of the transfer) of the ancillary benefits that, as a consequence of the transfer, cease to be provided, and

(ii) the total of all amounts each of which is, in respect of a previous transfer from the provision to a money purchase provision of a registered pension plan, a registered retirement savings plan or a registered retirement income fund in full or partial satisfaction of the individual's entitlement to other benefits under the defined benefit provision, the amount, if any, by which

(A) the prescribed amount for the purpose of paragraph 147.3(4)(*c*) of the Act in respect of the previous transfer

exceeds

(B) the amount of the previous transfer.

(4) Amount of Lifetime Retirement Benefits Commuted. For the purposes of subsection (1), and subject to subsection (7), the amount of an individual's lifetime retirement benefits under a defined benefit provision of a registered pension plan commuted in connection with the transfer of an amount on behalf of the individual in full or partial satisfaction of the individual's entitlement to benefits under the provision is the aggregate of

(*a*) where retirement benefits have commenced to be paid under the provision to the individual, the amount (expressed on an annualized basis) by which the individual's lifetime retirement benefits under the provision are reduced as a result of the transfer,

(*b*) where retirement benefits have not commenced to be paid under the provision to the individual, the amount (expressed on an annualized basis) by which the individual's normalized pension (computed in accordance with subsection (5)) under the provision at the time of the transfer is reduced as a result of the transfer, and

(*c*) where, in conjunction with the transfer, any other payment (other than an amount that is transferred in accordance with subsection 147.3(5) of the Act or that is transferred after 1991 in accordance with subsection 147.3(3) of the Act) is made from the plan in partial satisfaction of the individual's entitlement to benefits under the provision, the amount (expressed on an annualized basis) by which

(i) if paragraph (*a*) is applicable, the individual's lifetime retirement benefits under the provision are reduced, and

(ii) if paragraph (*b*) is applicable, the individual's normalized pension (computed in accordance with subsection (5)) under the provision at the time of the payment is reduced,

as a result of the payment, except to the extent that such reduction is included in determining, for the purposes of subsection (1), the amount of the individual's lifetime retirement benefits under the provision commuted in connection with the transfer of another amount on behalf of the individual.

Interpretation Bulletins: *Secondary* — IT-528 Transfers of funds between registered plans.

Registered Plans Directorate Newsletters: No. 04-1, Transfers from a defined benefit provision to a money purchase provision, an RRSP, or a RRIF and transfers between defined benefit provisions.

(5) Normalized Pensions. For the purposes of subsection (4), the normalized pension of an individual under a defined benefit provision of a registered pension plan at a particular time is the amount (expressed on an annualized basis) of lifetime retirement benefits that would be payable under the provision at the particular time if

(*a*) lifetime retirement benefits commenced to be paid to the individual at the particular time;

(*b*) where the individual has not attained 65 years of age before the particular time, the individual attained that age at the particular time;

(*c*) all benefits to which the individual is entitled under the provision were fully vested;

(*d*) where the amount of the individual's lifetime retirement benefits would otherwise be determined with a reduction computed by reference to the individual's age, duration of service, or both, or with any other similar reduction, no such reduction were applied;

(*e*) where the amount of the individual's lifetime retirement benefits depends on the amount of benefits provided under another benefit provision of the plan or under another plan or arrangement, a reasonable estimate were made of those other benefits;

(*f*) where the individual's lifetime retirement benefits would otherwise include benefits that the plan is required to provide by reason of a designated provision of the law of Canada or a province, or that the plan would be required to provide if each such provision were applicable to the plan with respect to all its members, such benefits were not included; and

(*g*) except as otherwise provided by subsection (6), where the amount of the individual's lifetime retirement benefits depends on

(i) the form of benefits provided with respect to the individual under the provision (whether or not at the option of the individual), including

(A) the benefits to be provided after the death of the individual,

(B) the amount of retirement benefits, other than lifetime retirement benefits, provided to the individual, or

(C) the extent to which the lifetime retirement benefits will be adjusted to reflect changes in the cost of living, or

(ii) circumstances that are relevant in determining the form of benefits,

the form of benefits and the circumstances were such as to maximize the amount of the individual's lifetime retirement benefits on commencement of payment.

Interpretation Bulletins: *Secondary* — IT-528 Transfers of funds between registered plans.

Regulations

(6) Optional Forms. Where

(*a*) the terms of a defined benefit provision of a registered pension plan permit an individual to elect to receive additional lifetime retirement benefits in lieu of benefits that would, in the absence of the election, be payable after the death of the individual if the individual dies after retirement benefits under the provision commence to be paid to the individual, and

(*b*) the elections available to the individual include an election

(i) to receive additional lifetime retirement benefits, not exceeding additional benefits determined on an actuarially equivalent basis, in lieu of all or a portion of a guarantee that retirement benefits will be paid for a minimum period of 10 years or less, or

(ii) to receive additional lifetime retirement benefits in lieu of retirement benefits that would otherwise be payable to a person who is a spouse or common-law partner or former spouse or common-law partner of the individual for a period beginning after the death of the individual and ending with the death of the person, where

(A) the election may be made only if the life expectancy of the person is significantly shorter than normal and has been so certified in writing by a medical doctor or a nurse practitioner licensed to practise under the laws of a province or of the place where the person resides, and

(B) the additional benefits do not exceed additional benefits determined on an actuarially equivalent basis and on the assumption that the person has a normal life expectancy,

paragraph (5)(*g*) applies as if

(*c*) the election described in subparagraph (*b*)(i) were not available to the individual, and

(*d*) where the particular time the normalized pension of the individual is determined under subsection (5) is after 1991, the election described in subparagraph (*b*)(ii) were not available to the individual.

History: S. 8517(6)(*b*)(ii)(A) was replaced by S.C. 2017, c. 33, s. 103(1), applicable in respect of certifications made after September 7, 2017, and formerly read:

(A) the election may be made only if the life expectancy of the person is significantly shorter than normal and has been so certified in writing by a medical doctor licensed to practise under the laws of a province or of the place where the person resides, and

Interpretation Bulletins: *Secondary* — IT-528 Transfers of funds between registered plans.

(7) Replacement Benefits. Where

(*a*) an amount is transferred on behalf of an individual in full or partial satisfaction of the individual's entitlement to benefits under a defined benefit provision (in this subsection referred to as the "particular provision") of a registered pension plan,

(*b*) in conjunction with the transfer, benefits become provided to the individual under another defined benefit provision of the plan or under a defined benefit provision of another registered pension plan, and

(*c*) an employer who participated under the particular provision for the benefit of the individual also participates under the other provision for the individual's benefit,

the amount of the individual's lifetime retirement benefits under the particular provision commuted in connection with the transfer is the amount that would be determined under subsection (4) if the benefits provided under the other provision were provided under the particular provision.

Interpretation Bulletins: *Secondary* — IT-528 Transfers of Funds Between Registered Plans.

8518. Transfer — Defined Benefit to Money Purchase

(Repealed.)

8519. Association of Benefits with Time Periods

Where, for the purposes of Part LXXXIII or this Part or subsection 147.1(10) of the Act, it is necessary to associate benefits provided under a defined benefit provision of a pension plan with periods of time, the association shall be made in a manner acceptable to the Minister.

8520. Minister's Actions

For the purposes of this Part, a waiver, extension of time or other modification of the requirements of this Part granted by the Minister or an approval by the Minister in respect of any matter is not effective unless it is in writing and expressly refers to the requirement that is modified or the matter in respect of which the approval is given.

Regulations

Part LXXXVI
Taxable Capital Employed in Canada

8600. [Definitions]

For the purposes of this Part and Part I.3 of the Act,

"attributed surplus" of a non-resident insurer for a taxation year has the meaning assigned by subsection 2400(1);

"Canadian assets" of a corporation that is a financial institution (as defined in subsection 181(1) of the Act) at any time in a taxation year means, in respect of the year, the amount, if any, by which

(*a*) the total of all amounts each of which is the amount at which an asset of the corporation (which asset is required, or, if the corporation were a bank to which the *Bank Act* applied, would be required, to be reflected in a return under subsection 223(1) of the *Bank Act*, as that Act read on May 31, 1992, if that return were prepared on a non-consolidated basis) would be shown on the corporation's balance sheet at the end of the year if its balance sheet were prepared on a non-consolidated basis

exceeds

(*b*) the investment allowance of the corporation for the year determined under subsection 181.3(4) of the Act;

"Canadian premiums" for a taxation year, in respect of an insurance corporation that was resident in Canada at any time in the year and throughout the year did not carry on a life insurance business, means the total of the insurance corporation's net premiums for the year

(*a*) in respect of insurance on property situated in Canada, and

(*b*) in respect of insurance, other than on property, from contracts with persons resident in Canada,

and, for the purposes of this definition, "net premiums" has the same meaning as in subsection 403(2), and subsection 403(3) applies as if the references therein to "province" were read as references to "country";

"Canadian reserve liabilities" of an insurer as at the end of a taxation year has the meaning assigned by subsection 2400(1);

"permanent establishment" has the same meaning as in subsection 400(2);

"total assets" of a corporation that is a financial institution (as defined in subsection 181(1) of the Act) at any time in a taxation year means, in respect of that year, the amount, if any, by which

(*a*) the total of all amounts each of which is the amount at which an asset of the corporation would be shown on the corporation's balance sheet at the end of the year if its balance sheet were prepared on a non-consolidated basis

exceeds

(*b*) the investment allowance of the corporation for the year determined under subsection 181.3(4) of the Act;

"total premiums" for a taxation year, in respect of an insurance corporation that was resident in Canada at any time in the year and throughout the year did not carry on a life insurance business, means the total of the corporation's net premiums for the year (as defined in subsection 403(2)) that are included in computing its income under Part I of the Act;

"total reserve liabilities" of an insurer as at the end of a taxation year means the amount determined by the formula

$$A - B$$

where

A is the total amount as at the end of the year of the insurer's liabilities and reserves (other than liabilities and reserves in respect of a segregated fund within the meaning assigned by subsection 138(12) of the Act) in respect of all its insurance policies, as determined for the purposes of the Superintendent of Financial Institutions, if the insurer is required by law to report to the Superintendent of Financial Institutions, or, in any other case, the superintendent of insurance or other similar officer or authority of the province under the laws of which the insurer is incorporated, and

B is the total of the reinsurance recoverable (within the meaning assigned by subsection 2400(1)) reported as a reinsurance asset by the insurer as at the end of the year relating to its liabilities and reserves in A.

History: S. 8600, the portion of the definition "Canadian assets" after paragraph (*a*) was replaced by S.C. 2013, c. 33, s. 38(1), applicable to taxation years that begin after March 20, 2013, and formerly read:

exceeds the total of

(*b*) the investment allowance of the corporation for the year determined under subsection 181.3(4) of the Act, and

(*c*) the total of all amounts each of which is the amount outstanding at the end of the year on account of a deposit made by the corporation that is described in paragraph (*c*) of the definition "eligible loan" in subsection 33.1(1) of the Act;

S. 8600, the definition "total reserve liabilities" was replaced by S.C. 2010, c. 25, s. 86(1), applicable to taxation years that begin after 2010. S. 8600, the definition "total reserve liabilities" formerly read:

"total reserve liabilities" of an insurer as at the end of a taxation year means the total amount as at the end of the year of the insurer's liabilities and reserves (other than liabilities and reserves in respect of a segregated fund) in respect of all its insurance policies, as determined for the purposes of the Superintendent of Financial Institutions, if the insurer is required by law to report to the Superintendent of Financial Institutions, or, in any other case, the superintendent of insurance or other similar officer or authority of the province under the laws of which the insurer is incorporated.

8601. [Prescribed proportion of taxable capital]

For the purpose of determining the taxable capital employed in Canada of a corporation for a taxation year under subsection 181.2(1) of the Act, the prescribed proportion of the corporation's taxable capital (as determined under Part I.3 of the Act) for the year is the amount determined by the formula

$$A \times (B / C)$$

where

A is the taxable capital (as determined under Part I.3 of the Act) of the corporation for the year,

Regulations

B is the total of all amounts each of which is the amount, determined in accordance with Part IV (or, in the case of an airline corporation, that would be so determined if the corporation had a permanent establishment in every province and if paragraphs 407(1)(*a*) and (*b*) were read without reference to the words "in Canada"), of the corporation's taxable income earned in the year in a particular province or the amount of its taxable income that would, pursuant to that Part, be earned in the year in a province if all permanent establishments of the corporation in Canada were in a province, and

C is the corporation's taxable income for the year,

except that, where the corporation's taxable income for the year is nil, the corporation shall, for the purposes of this section, be deemed to have a taxable income for the year of $1,000.

8602. [Prescribed proportion re Canadian surtax]

For the purposes of paragraph (*b*) of the definition "Canadian surtax payable" in subsection 125.3(4) of the Act, the prescribed proportion of the amount determined under section 123.2 of the Act in respect of a corporation for a taxation year is the amount determined by the formula

$$A \times (B / C)$$

where

A is the amount determined under section 123.2 of the Act in respect of the corporation for the year;

B is

(*a*) where the corporation carried on a life insurance business at any time in the year, the corporation's taxable capital (as determined under Part I.3 of the Act) for the year, and

(*b*) in any other case, the corporation's taxable capital employed in Canada (as would be determined under Part I.3 of the Act if that Part were read without reference to paragraphs 181.3(1)(*a*) and (*b*) thereof) for the year; and

C is the corporation's taxable capital (as determined under Part I.3 of the Act) for the year.

8603. [Interpretation]

For the purposes of Part VI of the Act,

(*a*) "Canadian assets" of a corporation that is a financial institution (as defined in subsection 190(1) of the Act) at any time in a taxation year means, in respect of that year, the amount that would be determined under the definition "Canadian assets" in section 8600 in respect of the corporation for the year if the reference in that definition to "subsection 181(1)" were read as a reference to "subsection 190(1)" and paragraph (*b*) of that definition were read as follows:

"(*b*) the total determined under section 190.14 of the Act in respect of the corporation's investments for the year in financial institutions related to it;";

(*b*) "total assets" of a corporation that is a financial institution (as defined in subsection 190(1) of the Act) at any time in a taxation year means, in respect of that year, the amount that would be determined under the definition "total assets" in section 8600 in respect of the corporation for the year if the reference in that definition to "subsection 181(1)" were read as a reference to "subsection 190(1)" and paragraph (*b*) of that definition were read as follows:

"(*b*) the total determined under section 190.14 of the Act in respect of the corporation's investments for the year in financial institutions related to it;"

(*c*) "attributed surplus", "Canadian reserve liabilities" and "total reserve liabilities" have the same respective meanings as in section 8600.

History: S. 8603(*a*) was replaced by S.C. 2013, c. 33, s. 39(1), applicable to taxation years that begin after March 20, 2013, and formerly read:

(*a*) "Canadian assets" of a corporation that is a financial institution (as defined in subsection 190(1) of the Act) at any time in a taxation year means, in respect of that year, the amount that would be determined under the definition "Canadian assets" in section 8600 in respect of the corporation for the year if the reference in that definition to "subsection 181(1)" were read as a reference to "subsection 190(1)" and paragraph (*b*) of that definition were read as follows:

"(*b*) the total determined under section 190.14 of the Act in respect of the corporation's investments for the year in financial institutions related to it, and"

8604. (Repealed by S.C. 2013, c. 34, s. 411(1).)

History: S. 8604 was repealed by S.C. 2013, c. 34, s. 411(1), deemed to have come into force on December 20, 2002, and formerly read:

8604. For the purposes of paragraph (*g*) of the definition "financial institution" in subsection 181(1) of the Act, each of the following corporations is a prescribed corporation:

(*a*) a corporation of which all or substantially all of the assets are shares or indebtedness of financial institutions (as defined in that subsection) to which the corporation is related;

(*b*) AVCO Financial Services Canada Limited;

(*c*) AVCO Financial Services Realty Limited;

(*d*) AVCO Financial Services Quebec Limited;

(*e*) General Motors Acceptance Corporation of Canada, Limited;

(*f*) Household Financial Corporation Limited;

(*g*) Household Finance Corporation of Canada;

(*h*) Household Realty Corporation Limited;

(*i*) Merchant Retail Services Limited;

(*j*) Superior Acceptance Corporation Limited;

(*k*) Superior Credit Corporation Limited;

(*l*) Crédit Industriel Desjardins;

(*m*) Beneficial Canada Inc.;

(*n*) Beneficial Realty Ltd.;

(*o*) RT Mortgage-Backed Securities Limited;

(*p*) RT Mortgage-Backed Securities II Limited;

(*q*) T. Eaton Acceptance Co. Limited;

(*r*) National Retail Credit Services Limited;

(*s*) Ford Credit Canada Limited;

(*t*) Principal Fund Incorporated;

(*u*) Farm Credit Canada;

(*v*) Canadian Cooperative Agricultural Financial Services;

(*w*) CU Credit Inc.;

(*x*) Household Commercial Canada Inc.;

(*y*) Canadian Home Income Plan Corporation;

(*z*) Hudson's Bay Company Acceptance Limited;

(*z*1) Bombardier Capital Ltd.;

(*z*2) Trans Canada Credit Corporation;

(*z*3) Norwest Financial Canada, Inc.;

(*z*4) Norwest Financial Capital Canada, Inc.;

(*z*5) GE Capital Canada Limited; and

(*z*6) GE Capital Canada Retailer Financial Services Company.

8605. [Prescribed amount – financial institution]

(1) For the purposes of subclause 181.3(1)(*c*)(ii)(A)(II) and clause 190.11(*b*)(i)(B) of the Act, the amount prescribed in respect of a particular corporation for a taxation year ending at a particular time is the total of all amounts each of which is the amount determined in respect of a corporation that is, at the particular time, a foreign insurance subsidiary of the particular corporation, equal to the amount, if any, by which

(*a*) the amount by which the total, at the end of the subsidiary's last taxation year ending at or before the particular time, of

(i) the amount of the subsidiary's long-term debt, and

(ii) the amount of the subsidiary's capital stock (or, in the case of an insurance corporation incorporated without share capital, the amount of its member's contributions), retained earnings, contributed surplus and any other surpluses

exceeds the total of

(iii) the amount of the subsidiary's deferred tax debit balance at the end of the year, and

(iv) the amount of any deficit deducted in computing the subsidiary's shareholders' equity at the end of the year

exceeds the total of all amounts each of which is

(*b*) the carrying value to its owner at the particular time for the taxation year that includes the particular time of a share of the subsidiary's capital stock or its long term debt that is owned at the particular time by

(i) the particular corporation,

(ii) a subsidiary of the particular corporation,

(iii) a corporation

(A) that is resident in Canada,

(B) that carried on a life insurance business in Canada at any time in its taxation year ending at or before the particular time, and

(C) that is

(I) a corporation of which the particular corporation is a subsidiary, or

(II) a subsidiary of a corporation described in subclause (I), or

(iv) a subsidiary of a corporation described in subparagraph (iii), or

(*c*) an amount included under paragraph (*a*) in respect of any surplus of the subsidiary contributed by a corporation described in any of subparagraphs (*b*)(i) to (iv), other than an amount included under paragraph (*b*).

(*d*) (Repealed.)

(2) For the purposes of subclause 181.3(1)(*c*)(ii)(A)(III) and clause 190.11(*b*)(i)(C) of the Act, the amount prescribed in respect of a particular corporation for a taxation year ending at a particular time is the total of all amounts each of which is the amount determined in respect of a corporation that is, at the particular time, a foreign insurance subsidiary of the particular corporation, equal to the amount, if any, by which

(*a*) the total of the amounts determined under paragraphs (1)(*b*) and (*c*) in respect of the subsidiary for the year

exceeds

(*b*) the amount determined under paragraph (1)(*a*) in respect of the subsidiary for the year.

(3) For the purposes of subclause 181.3(1)(*c*)(ii)(A)(V) and clause 190.11(*b*)(i)(E) of the Act, the amount prescribed in respect of a particular corporation for a taxation year ending at a particular time means the total of all amounts each of which would be the total reserve liabilities of a foreign insurance subsidiary of the particular corporation as at the end of the subsidiary's last taxation year ending at or before the particular time if the subsidiary were required by law to report to the Superintendent of Financial Institutions for that year.

(4) The definitions in this subsection apply in this section.

"foreign insurance subsidiary" of a particular corporation at any time means a non-resident corporation that

(*a*) carried on a life insurance business throughout its last taxation year ending at or before that time,

(*b*) did not carry on a life insurance business in Canada at any time in its last taxation year ending at or before that time, and

(*c*) is at that time

(i) a subsidiary of the particular corporation, and

(ii) not a subsidiary of any corporation that

(A) is resident in Canada,

(B) carried on a life insurance business in Canada at any time in its last taxation year ending at or before that time, and

(C) is a subsidiary of the particular corporation.

"subsidiary" of a corporation (in this definition referred to as the "parent corporation") means a corporation controlled by the parent corporation where shares of each class of the capital stock of the corporation having a fair market value of not less than 75% of the fair market value of all of the issued and outstanding shares of that class belong to

(*a*) the parent corporation,

(*b*) a corporation that is a subsidiary of the parent corporation, or

(*c*) any combination of corporations each of which is a corporation referred to in paragraph (*a*) or described in paragraph (*b*).

Regulations

Part LXXXVII
National Arts Service Organizations

8700. [Prescribed conditions]

For the purposes of paragraph 149.1(6.4)(*d*) of the Act, the following conditions are prescribed for a national arts service organization:

(*a*) the organization is an organization

(i) that is, because of paragraph 149(1)(*l*) of the Act, exempt from tax under Part I of the Act,

(ii) that represents, in an official language of Canada, a community of artists from one or more of the following sectors of activity in the arts community, that is, theatre, opera, music, dance, painting, sculpture, drawing, crafts, design, photography, the literary arts, film, sound recording and other audio-visual arts,

(iii) no part of the income of which may be payable to, or otherwise available for the personal benefit of, any proprietor, member, shareholder, trustee, or settlor of the organization, except where the payment is for services rendered or is an amount to which paragraph 56(1)(*n*) of the Act applies in respect of the recipient,

(iv) all of the resources of which are devoted to the activities and objects described in its application for its last designation by the Minister of Canadian Heritage pursuant to paragraph 149.1(6.4)(*a*) of the Act,

(v) more than 50 per cent of the directors, trustees, officers or other officials of which deal with each other at arm's length, and

(vi) no more than 50% of the property of which at any time has been contributed or otherwise paid into the organization by one person or members of a group of persons who do not deal with each other at arm's length and, for the purpose of this subparagraph, a reference to any person or to members of a group does not include a reference to Her Majesty in Right of Canada or a province, a municipality, a registered charity that is not a private foundation or any club, society or association described in paragraph 149(1)(*l*) of the Act; and

(*b*) the activities of the organization (which may include collective bargaining on behalf of its sector of activity under the *Status of the Artist Act*, provided it is not the organization's primary activity) are confined to one or more of

(i) promoting one or more art forms,

(ii) conducting research into one or more art forms,

(iii) sponsoring arts exhibitions or performances,

(iv) representing interests of the arts community or a sector thereof (but not of individuals) before governmental, judicial, quasi-judicial or other public bodies,

(v) conducting workshops, seminars, training programs and similar development programs relating to the arts for members of the organization, in respect of which the value of benefits received or enjoyed by members of the organization is required by paragraph 56(1)(*aa*) of the Act to be included in computing the incomes of those members,

(vi) educating the public about the arts community or the sector represented by the organization,

(vii) organizing and sponsoring conventions, conferences, competitions and special events relating to the arts community or the sector represented by the organization,

(viii) conducting arts studies and surveys of interest to members of the organization relating to the arts community or the sector represented by the organization,

(ix) acting as an information centre by maintaining resource libraries and data bases relating to the arts community or the sector represented by the organization,

(x) disseminating information relating to the arts community or the sector represented by the organization, and

(xi) paying amounts to which paragraph 56(1)(*n*) of the Act applies in respect of the recipient and which relate to the arts community or the sector represented by the organization.

History: S. 8700(*a*)(ii) was replaced by P.C. 2011-936, SOR/2011-188, dated September 22, 2011, published in the *Canada Gazette* October 12, 2011, applicable after February 19, 2011. S. 8700(*a*)(ii) formerly read:

(ii) that represents, in an official language of Canada, the community of artists from one or more of the following sectors of activity in the arts community, that is, theatre, opera, music, dance, painting, sculpture, drawing, crafts, design, photography, the literary arts, film, sound recording and other audio-visual arts, and such other sectors of artistic activity related to the creation or performance of works of art as the Minister of Communications may recognize,

S. 8700(*a*)(iv) was replaced by P.C. 2011-936, SOR/2011-188, dated September 22, 2011, published in the *Canada Gazette* October 12, 2011, applicable after February 19, 2011. S. 8700(*a*)(iv) formerly read:

(iv) all of the resources of which are devoted to the activities and objects described in its application for its last designation by the Minister of Communications pursuant to paragraph 149.1(6.4)(*a*) of the Act,

S. 8700(*b*), the portion before subparagraph (i) was replaced by P.C. 2011-936, SOR/2011-188, dated September 22, 2011, published in the *Canada Gazette* October 12, 2011, applicable after February 19, 2011. S. 8700(*b*), the portion before subparagraph (i) formerly read:

(*b*) the activities of the organization are confined to one or more of

Regulations

Part LXXXVIII
Disability-Related Modifications and Apparatus

8800. [Prescribed renovations and alterations]

The renovations and alterations that are prescribed for the purposes of paragraph 20(1)(*qq*) of the Act are

(*a*) the installation of

(i) an interior or exterior ramp, or

(ii) a hand-activated electric door opener; and

(*b*) a modification to a bathroom, elevator or doorway to accommodate its use by a person in a wheelchair.

8801. [Prescribed devices and equipment]

The devices and equipment that are prescribed for the purposes of paragraph 20(1)(*rr*) of the Act are

(*a*) an elevator car position indicator, such as a braille panel or an audio signal, for individuals having a sight impairment;

(*b*) a visual fire alarm indicator, a listening device for group meetings or a telephone device, for individuals having a hearing impairment; and

(*c*) a disability-specific computer software or hardware attachment.

Part LXXXIX
Entities Prescribed with Respect to Certain Rules

8900. International Organizations

(1) For the purposes of subparagraph 110(1)(*f*)(iii) and paragraph 126(3)(*a*) of the Act, the following international organizations are prescribed:

(*a*) the United Nations; and

(*b*) each international organization that is a specialized agency brought into relationship with the United Nations in accordance with Article 63 of the Charter of the United Nations.

History: S. 8900(1), the portion before paragraph (*a*) was replaced by S.C. 2013, c. 40, s. 115(1), applicable to the 2013 and subsequent taxation years, and formerly read:

(1) For the purpose of subparagraph 110(1)(*f*)(iii) of the Act, the following international organizations are prescribed:

(2) International Non-governmental Organizations. For the purpose of subparagraph 110(1)(*f*)(iv) of the Act, the following international non-governmental organizations are prescribed:

(*a*) the International Air Transport Association;

(*b*) the Société internationale de télécommunications aéronautiques; and

(*c*) the World Anti-Doping Agency.

8901. Partnership

(Repealed by S.C. 2013, c. 34, s. 411(1).)

History: S. 8901 and the preceding heading were repealed by S.C. 2013, c. 34, s. 412(1), applicable to fiscal periods that begin after June 26, 2013, and formerly read:

8901. *Partnership.* For the purpose of paragraph 249.1(1)(*b*) of the Act, Gaz Métropolitan and Company, Limited Partnership is a prescribed partnership.

Part XC
Financial Institutions — Prescribed Entities and Properties

9000. Prescribed Person not a Financial Institution

For the purposes of paragraph (*e*) of the definition "financial institution" in subsection 142.2(1) of the Act, the following are prescribed persons:

(*a*) the Business Development Bank of Canada;

(*b*) BDC Capital Inc.; and

(*c*) a trust, at any particular time, if at that particular time

(i) the trust is a related segregated fund trust (within the meaning assigned by paragraph 138.1(1)(*a*) of the Act),

(ii) the trust is deemed, under paragraph 138.1(1)(*a*) of the Act, to have been created at a time that is not more than two years before that particular time, and

(iii) the cost of the trustee's interest (as determined by paragraph 138.1(1)(*c*) and (*d*) of the Act) in the trust does not exceed $5,000,000.

History: S. 9000 and the heading before it were replaced by S.C. 2014, c. 20, s. 37(1), applicable to taxation years that end after November 29, 2013, and formerly read:

9000. *Prescribed Trust Not a Financial Institution.* For the purpose of paragraph (*e*) of the definition "financial institution" in subsection 142.2(1) of the Act, a trust is, at any particular time, a prescribed person if the following conditions are satisfied at that particular time:

(*a*) the trust is a related segregated fund trust (within the meaning assigned by paragraph 138.1(1)(*a*) of the Act);

(*b*) the trust is deemed, under paragraph 138.1(1)(*a*) of the Act, to have been created at a time that is not more than two years before that particular time; and

(*c*) the cost of the trustee's interest (as determined by paragraph 138.1(1)(*c*) and (*d*) of the Act) in the trust does not exceed $5,000,000.

The heading for Part XC was replaced, and s. 9000 was added by S.C. 2009, c. 2, s. 118(1), applicable to taxation years that end after February 22, 1994. The heading for Part XC formerly read: "Financial Institutions — Prescribed Entities"

9001. Prescribed Property Not Mark-To-Market Property

(1) In this section, "qualified small business corporation", at any time, means a corporation in respect of which the following conditions are satisfied at that time:

(*a*) the corporation is a Canadian-controlled private corporation;

(*b*) the corporation either is an eligible corporation (as defined in subsection 5100(1)) or would be an eligible corporation if the definition "eligible corporation" in subsection 5100(1) were read without reference to its paragraph (*e*);

(*c*) the carrying value of the total assets of the corporation and all corporations related to it (determined in accordance with generally accepted accounting principles on a consolidated or combined basis, where applicable) does not exceed $50,000,000; and

(*d*) the number of employees of the corporation and all corporations related to it does not exceed 500.

History: S. 9001(1) was added by S.C. 2009, c. 2, s. 118(1), applicable to taxation years that end after February 22, 1994, except that in applying section 9001 to taxation years that begin before October 2006, the reference in that section to "excluded property" is to be read as a reference to "mark-to-market property".

(2) For the purpose of paragraph (*e*) of the definition "excluded property" in subsection 142.2(1) of the Act, a share of the capital stock of a corporation is a prescribed property of a taxpayer if

(*a*) immediately after the time at which the taxpayer acquired the share, the corporation was a qualified small business corporation, and

(i) the corporation continued to be a qualified small business corporation for one year after that time, or

(ii) the taxpayer could not reasonably expect at that time that the corporation would cease to be a qualified small business corporation within one year after that time; or

(*b*) the share was issued to the taxpayer in exchange for one or more shares of the capital stock of the corporation that were, at the time of the exchange, prescribed property of the taxpayer under this subsection.

History: S. 9001(2) was added by S.C. 2009, c. 2, s. 118(1), applicable to taxation years that end after February 22, 1994, except that in applying section 9001 to taxation years that begin before October 2006, the reference in that section to "excluded property" is to be read as a reference to "mark-to-market property".

9002. Prescribed Property Not Mark-To-Market Property

(1) For the purposes of paragraph (*e*) of the definition "excluded property" in subsection 142.2(1) of the Act, and of subparagraph 142.6(4)(*a*)(ii) of the Act, a debt obligation held by a bank is a prescribed property of the bank if the obligation is

(*a*) an exposure to a designated country (within the meaning assigned by section 8006);

(*b*) a United Mexican States Collateralized Par Bond due 2019; or

(*c*) a United Mexican States Collateralized Discount Bond due 2019.

History: S. 9002(1) was added by S.C. 2009, c. 2, s. 118(1), applicable to taxation years that end after February 22, 1994, except that in applying section 9002 to taxation years that begin before October 2006, the references in that section to "excluded property" are to be read as references to "mark-to-market property".

(2) For the purpose of paragraph (*e*) of the definition "excluded property" in subsection 142.2(1) of the Act, a share is a prescribed property of a taxpayer for a taxation year if

(*a*) the share is a lending asset of the taxpayer in the year; or

(*b*) the share was, immediately after its issuance, a share described in paragraph (*e*) of the definition "term preferred share" in subsection 248(1) of the Act, and the share would, at any time in the year, be a term preferred share if

(i) that definition were read without reference to the portion following paragraph (*b*), and

(ii) where the share was issued or acquired on or before June 28, 1982, it were issued or acquired after that day.

History: S. 9002(2) was added by S.C. 2009, c. 2, s. 118(1), applicable to taxation years that end after February 22, 1994, except that in applying section 9002 to taxation years that begin before October 2006, the references in that section to "excluded property" are to be read as references to "mark-to-market property".

(3) For the purpose of paragraph (*e*) of the definition "excluded property" in subsection 142.2(1) of the Act, a share of the capital stock of a corporation that is held by a credit union is a prescribed property of the credit union for a taxation year if, throughout the period (referred to in this subsection as the "holding period") in that taxation year during which the credit union holds the share

(*a*) the corporation is a credit union; or

(*b*) the following conditions are satisfied:

(i) credit unions hold shares of the corporation that

(A) give those credit unions at least 50% of the votes that could be cast under all circumstances at an annual meeting of shareholders of the corporation, and

(B) have a fair market value of at least 50% of the fair market value of all the issued shares of the corporation,

(ii) the corporation is not controlled, directly or indirectly in any manner whatever, by any person that is not a credit union, and

(iii) the corporation would not be controlled by a person that is not a credit union if each share of the corporation that is not owned at any time in the holding period by a credit union were owned, at that time, by the person.

History: S. 9002(3) was replaced by S.C. 2009, c. 2, s. 118(2), applicable to taxation years that begin after February 2, 2009, except that

(a) it also applies to taxation years, of a taxpayer, that end after 2002 and begin before February 3, 2009, if the taxpayer so elects in writing and files the election with the Minister of National Revenue on or before the taxpayer's filing-due date for the taxpayer's taxation year in which this Act is assented to [R.A. March 12, 2009]; and

(b) if a taxpayer makes an election under paragraph (*a*) [above], in applying subsection 9002(3) for taxation years of the taxpayer that begin before October 2006, the reference in that subsection to "excluded property" is to be read as a reference to "mark-to-market property".

S. 9002(3) formerly read:

(3) For the purpose of paragraph (*e*) of the definition "excluded property" in subsection 142.2(1) of the Act, a share of the capital stock of a corporation that is held by a credit union is a prescribed property of the credit union for a taxation year if, throughout that taxation year,

(*a*) the corporation is a credit union; or

(*b*) credit unions hold

(i) shares of the corporation that give the credit unions more than 50% of the votes that could be cast under all circumstances at an annual meeting of shareholders of the corporation, and

(ii) shares of the corporation having a fair market value of more than 50% of the fair market value of all the issued shares of the corporation.

S. 9002(3) was added by S.C. 2009, c. 2, s. 118(1), applicable to taxation years that end after February 22, 1994, except that in applying section 9002 to taxation years that begin before October 2006, the reference in that subsection to "excluded property" is to be read as a reference to "mark-to-market property".

9002.1. Prescribed Payment Card Corporation Share Not Mark-To-Market Property

For the purpose of paragraph (*b*) of the definition "excluded property" in subsection 142.2(1) of the Act, a prescribed payment card corporation share of a taxpayer at any time means a share of the capital stock of a particular corporation if, at that time,

(*a*) the particular corporation is any one of the following

(i) MasterCard International Incorporated,

(ii) MasterCard Incorporated, or

(iii) Visa Inc.; and

(*b*) the share

(i) is of a class of shares that is not listed on a stock exchange,

(ii) is not convertible into or exchangeable for a share of the class of the capital stock of a corporation that is listed on a stock exchange, and

(iii) was issued by the particular corporation to the taxpayer or to a person related to the taxpayer.

History: S. 9002.1 was added by S.C. 2009, c. 2, s. 118(1), applicable to taxation years that end after February 22, 1994, except that in applying section 9002.1 to taxation years that begin before October 2006, the reference in that section to "paragraph (*b*) of the definition "excluded property"" is to be read as a reference to "paragraph (*d.1*) of the definition "mark-to-market property"".

Department of Finance Comfort Letters (January 30, 2018) [Shares held by financial institutions prescribed to be "excluded property" for purposes of 142.2(1)]

2018FIN468286

Dear XXXX:

I am writing further to your request that section 9002.1 of the *Income Tax Regulations* (the "Regulations") be amended so that shares of Interac Corp. ("Newco") that will be held by financial institutions as the result of a corporate reorganization will be prescribed payment card corporation shares for the purposes of paragraph (*b*) of the definition "excluded property" in subsection 142.2(1) of the *Income Tax Act*.

Our understanding of the request for relief and the facts relevant to the request is based on correspondence, and discussions, between you and officials of the Department of Finance, including with respect to the Amended and Restated Consent Agreement of the Competition Tribunal dated October 20, 2017 (the "Consent Agreement") and XXXXX

You describe a scenario in which your clients, Interac Inc., Acxsys Corporation, and ACX Corporation (the "Entities"), intend to participate in a proposed reorganization permitted under the terms of the Consent Agreement. As part of the reorganization, current shareholders of the Entities will exchange their shares of the Entities for common shares of a new corporation, Newco. In addition, members of the Interac Association (the "Association") will exchange certain rights as members of the Association for common shares of Newco. Common shares will be the only class of share issued by Newco.

The current shareholders of the Entities, and a number of the other taxpayers that will become shareholders of Newco, are financial institutions as defined in subsection 142.2(1). You have advised that, in the absence of the requested relief, the shares of Newco will be mark-to-market property of certain shareholders following the proposed reorganization.

You indicate that the Entities, together with the Association, develop and provide network services that facilitate payments, and develop and license software related thereto. XXXXX None of the shares of any of the Entities have ever been listed on a stock exchange.

You also indicate that Newco will generally be restricted to carrying on the same business as that carried on by the Entities and the Association prior to the reorganization. The initial shareholders of Newco will consist of the members of the Association immediately prior to the reorganization. The shares of Newco will be subject to ongoing transfer restrictions and will neither be listed on a stock exchange nor exchangeable for shares listed on a stock exchange. XXXXX

In your view, based on the above, including the restrictions imposed on Newco and its shareholders by the Consent Agreement and XXXXX shares of the capital stock of Newco will form part of the organizational infrastructure of its shareholders and will not be acquired or held by those shareholders in the ordinary course of their business. Your view is that the shares of Newco should be excluded property as defined in subsection 142.2(1).

As a result of your submissions and our own analysis, we have concluded that the proposed amendment would be consistent with the tax policy behind the mark-to-market rules. Therefore, we are prepared to recommend to the Minister of Finance that paragraph 9002.1(*a*) of the Regulations be amended so that a share of Newco may qualify as a "prescribed payment card corporation share" for purposes of the definition "excluded property" in subsection 142.2(1). The current requirements in paragraph 9002.1(*b*) of the Regulations would apply to the shares of Newco.

While we cannot offer any assurance that either the Minister of Finance or Parliament will agree with our recommendation in respect of this matter, we hope that this statement of our intention is helpful.

Yours sincerely,

Brian Ernewein

General Director – Legislation

Tax Policy Branch

9002.2. Prescribed Payment Card Corporation Share Not Mark-To-Market Property

(Repealed.)

History: The heading before s. 9002.2 was repealed by P.C. 2010-548, SOR/2010-93, dated April 29, 2010, published in the *Canada Gazette* May 12, 2010, applicable to taxation years that begin after 2007. The heading before s. 9002.2 formerly read:

Prescribed Securities Exchange Investment Not Mark-To-Market Property

S. 9002.2 was repealed by S.C. 2009, c. 2, s. 118(3), applicable to taxation years that begin after 2007. S. 9002.2 formerly read:

9002.2 For the purpose of paragraph (*c*) of the definition "excluded property" in subsection 142.2(1) of the Act, a prescribed securities exchange investment of a taxpayer at any time means a share of the capital stock of a corporation if, at that time, the corporation is not a public corporation and is

(*a*) The Toronto Stock Exchange Inc.;

(*b*) TSX Inc.;

(*c*) TSX Group Inc.;

(*d*) Bourse de Montréal Inc.; or

(*e*) Canadian Venture Exchange Inc.

S. 9002.2 was added by S.C. 2009, c. 2, s. 118(1), applicable to taxation years that begin after 1998 and before 2008, except that in applying that section to taxation years that begin before October 2006, the reference to "paragraph (*c*) of the definition "excluded property"" is to be read as a reference to "paragraph (*d.2*) of the definition "mark-to-market property"".

9003. Significant Interest in a Corporation

For the purpose of paragraph 142.2(3)(*c*) of the Act, a share described in paragraph 9002(2)(*b*) is prescribed in respect of all taxpayers.

History: S. 9003 was added by S.C. 2009, c. 2, s. 118(1), applicable to taxation years that end after February 22, 1994.

9004. Financing Arrangement Not a Specified Debt Obligation

For the purpose of paragraph (*c*) of the definition "specified debt obligation" in subsection 142.2(1) of the Act, a property is a prescribed property throughout a taxation year if

(*a*) the property is a direct financing lease, or any other financing arrangement, of a taxpayer that is reported as a loan in the taxpayer's financial statements for the year prepared in accordance with generally accepted accounting principles; and

(*b*) in computing the taxpayer's income for the year, an amount is deductible under paragraph 20(1)(*a*) of the Act in respect of the property that is the subject of the arrangement.

History: S. 9004 was replaced by S.C. 2009, c. 2, s. 118(1), applicable to taxation years that begin after February 2, 2009. S. 9004 formerly read:

9004. For the purpose of the definition "specified debt obligation" in subsection 142.2(1) of the Act, a property is a prescribed property throughout a taxation year if the property is a direct financing lease, or any other financing arrangement, of a taxpayer that is reported as a loan in the taxpayer's financial statement for the year prepared in accordance with generally accepted accounting principles and an amount is deductible under paragraph 20(1)(*a*) of the Act in respect of the property that is the subject of the lease or arrangement in computing the taxpayer's income for the year.

9005. Prescribed Non-reporting Financial Institution

For the purposes of the definition "non-reporting financial institution" in subsection 270(1) of the Act, the following entities are prescribed:

(*a*) a labour-sponsored venture capital corporation as prescribed in section 6701;

(*b*) a registered retirement savings plan;

(*c*) a registered retirement income fund;

(*d*) a pooled registered pension plan;

(*e*) a deferred profit sharing plan;

(*f*) a registered disability savings plan;

(*g*) a registered education savings plan;

(*h*) a registered pension plan;

(*i*) a trust governed by a registered pension plan;

(*j*) a trust described in paragraph 149(1)(*o*.4) of the Act, if all of the interests in the trust as a beneficiary are held by one or more registered pension plans;

(*k*) a corporation described in clause 149(1)(*o*.1)(i)(A) or subparagraph 149(1)(*o*.1)(ii) or (*o*.2)(i) of the Act;

(*l*) a corporation described in any of subparagraphs 149(1)(*o*.2)(ii) to (iii) of the Act, if all of the shares of the corporation are held by

(i) one or more registered pension plans or trusts governed by registered pension plans,

(ii) one or more trusts described in paragraph (*j*), or

(iii) one or more corporations described in this paragraph or paragraph (*k*);

(*m*) a trust, if all of the interests in the trust as a beneficiary are held by one or more plans, trusts or corporations described in paragraph (*i*), (*k*) or (*l*);

(*n*) a "central cooperative credit society", as defined in section 2 of the *Cooperative Credit Associations Act* and whose accounts are maintained for member financial institutions; and

(*o*) a TFSA.

History: S. 9005 was added by S.C. 2016, c. 12, s. 83(1), in force July 1, 2017.

9006. Prescribed Excluded Accounts

For the purposes of the definition "excluded account" in subsection 270(1) of the Act, the following accounts are prescribed:

(*a*) a registered retirement savings plan;

(*b*) a registered retirement income fund;

(*c*) a pooled registered pension plans;

(*d*) a registered pension plan;

(*e*) a registered disability savings plan;

(*f*) a registered education savings plan;

(*g*) a deferred profit sharing plan;

(*h*) a net income stabilization account, including a NISA Fund No. 2;

(*i*) an eligible funeral arrangement;

(*j*) a dormant account if the balance or value of the account does not exceed 1,000 USD; and

(*k*) a TFSA.

History: S. 9006 was added by S.C. 2016, c. 12, s. 83(1), in force July 1, 2017.

Part XCI
Financial Institutions — Income from Specified Debt Obligations

9100. Interpretation

Definitions

The following definitions apply in this Part.

"fixed payment obligation", of a taxpayer, means a specified debt obligation under which

(*a*) the amount and timing of each payment (other than a fee or similar payment or an amount payable because of a default by the debtor) to be made by the debtor were fixed when the taxpayer acquired the obligation and have not been changed; and

(*b*) all payments are to be made in the same currency.

History: S. 9100, the definition "fixed payment obligation" was added by P.C. 2009-1212, SOR/2009-222, dated July 30, 2009, published in the *Canada Gazette* August 19, 2009, applicable to taxation years that end after February 22, 1994.

"primary currency", of a specified debt obligation, means

(*a*) the currency with which the obligation is primarily connected; and

(*b*) if there is no such currency, Canadian currency.

History: S. 9100, the definition "primary currency" was added by P.C. 2009-1212, SOR/2009-222, dated July 30, 2009, published in the *Canada Gazette* August 19, 2009, applicable to taxation years that end after February 22, 1994.

"tax basis", of a specified debt obligation at any time to a taxpayer, has the meaning assigned by subsection 142.4(1) of the Act.

History: S. 9100, the definition "tax basis" was added by P.C. 2009-1212, SOR/2009-222, dated July 30, 2009, published in the *Canada Gazette* August 19, 2009, applicable to taxation years that end after February 22, 1994.

"total return", of a taxpayer from a fixed payment obligation, means the amount, measured in the primary currency of the obligation, by which

(*a*) the total of all amounts each of which is the amount of a payment (other than a fee or similar payment) required to be made by the debtor under the obligation after its acquisition by the taxpayer

exceeds

(*b*) the cost to the taxpayer of the obligation.

History: S. 9100, the definition "total return" was added by P.C. 2009-1212, SOR/2009-222, dated July 30, 2009, published in the *Canada Gazette* August 19, 2009, applicable to taxation years that end after February 22, 1994.

9101. Prescribed Inclusions and Deductions

(1) Inclusion. For the purpose of paragraph 142.3(1)(*a*) of the Act, where a taxpayer holds a specified debt obligation at any time in a taxation year, the amount prescribed in respect of the obligation for the year is the total of

(*a*) the taxpayer's accrued return from the obligation for the year,

(*b*) if the taxpayer's accrual adjustment determined under section 9102 in respect of the obligation for the year is greater than nil, the amount of the adjustment, and

(*c*) if a foreign exchange adjustment is determined under section 9104 in respect of the obligation for the year and is greater than nil, the amount of the adjustment.

History: S. 9101(1) was added by P.C. 2009-1212, SOR/2009-222, dated July 30, 2009, published in the *Canada Gazette* August 19, 2009, applicable to taxation years that end after February 22, 1994.

(2) Deduction. For the purpose of paragraph 142.3(1)(*b*) of the Act, where a taxpayer holds a specified debt obligation at any time in a taxation year, the amount prescribed in respect of the obligation is the total of

(*a*) if the taxpayer's accrual adjustment determined under section 9102 in respect of the obligation for the year is less than nil, the absolute value of the amount of the adjustment, and

(*b*) if a foreign exchange adjustment is determined under section 9104 in respect of the obligation for the year and is less than nil, the absolute value of the amount of the adjustment.

History: S. 9101(2) was added by P.C. 2009-1212, SOR/2009-222, dated July 30, 2009, published in the *Canada Gazette* August 19, 2009, applicable to taxation years that end after February 22, 1994.

9102. General Accrual Rules

(1) Fixed Payment Obligation Not in Default. For the purpose of paragraph 9101(1)(*a*), a taxpayer's accrued return for a taxation year from a fixed payment obligation, under which each payment required to be made before the end of the year was made by the debtor when it was required to be made, shall be determined in accordance with the following rules:

(*a*) determine, in the primary currency of the obligation, the portion of the taxpayer's total return from the obligation that is allocated to each day in the year using

(i) the level-yield method described in subsection (2), or

(ii) any other reasonable method that is substantially similar to the level-yield method;

(*b*) if the primary currency of the obligation is not Canadian currency, translate to Canadian currency the amount allocated to each day in the year, using a reasonable method of translation; and

(*c*) determine the total of all amounts each of which is the Canadian currency amount allocated to a day, in the year, at the beginning of which the taxpayer holds the obligation.

History: S. 9102(1) was added by P.C. 2009-1212, SOR/2009-222, dated July 30, 2009, published in the *Canada Gazette* August 19, 2009, applicable to taxation years that end after February 22, 1994.

(2) Level-yield Method. For the purpose of subsection (1), the level-yield method for allocating a taxpayer's total return from a fixed payment obligation is the method that allocates, to each particular day in the period that begins on the day following the day on which the taxpayer acquired the obligation and that ends on the day on which the obligation matures, the amount determined by the formula

$$(A + B - C) \times D$$

where

Regulations

A is the cost of the obligation to the taxpayer (expressed in the primary currency of the obligation);

B is the total of all amounts each of which is the portion of the taxpayer's total return from the obligation that is allocated to a day before the particular day;

C is the total of all payments required to be made under the obligation after it was acquired by the taxpayer and before the particular day; and

D is the rate of interest per day that, if used in computing the present value (as of the end of the day on which the taxpayer acquired the obligation and based on daily compounding) of all payments to be made under the obligation after it was acquired by the taxpayer, produces a present value equal to the cost to the taxpayer of the obligation (expressed in the primary currency of the obligation).

History: S. 9102(2) was added by P.C. 2009-1212, SOR/2009-222, dated July 30, 2009, published in the *Canada Gazette* August 19, 2009, applicable to taxation years that end after February 22, 1994.

(3) Other Specified Debt Obligations. For the purpose of paragraph 9101(1)(*a*), a taxpayer's accrued return for a taxation year from a specified debt obligation, other than an obligation to which subsection (1) applies, shall be determined

(*a*) using a reasonable method that,

(i) taking into account the extent to which the obligation differs from fixed payment obligations, is consistent with the principles implicit in the methods that can be used under subsection (1) for fixed payment obligations, and

(ii) is in accordance with generally accepted accounting practice for the measurement of profit from debt obligations; and

(*b*) on the basis of reasonable assumptions with respect to the timing and amount of any payments to be made by the debtor under the obligation that are not fixed in their timing or amount (expressed in the primary currency of the obligation).

History: S. 9102(3) was added by P.C. 2009-1212, SOR/2009-222, dated July 30, 2009, published in the *Canada Gazette* August 19, 2009, applicable to taxation years that end after February 22, 1994.

(4) Accrual Adjustment Nil. For the purposes of paragraphs 9101(1)(*b*) and (2)(*a*), if subsection 142.3(1) of the Act applies to a taxpayer for a particular taxation year in respect of a specified debt obligation and either the subsection did not apply in respect of the obligation for the taxpayer's immediately preceding taxation year or the taxpayer did not own the obligation at the end of that immediately preceding taxation year, the taxpayer's accrual adjustment in respect of the obligation for the particular taxation year is nil.

History: S. 9102(4) was added by P.C. 2009-1212, SOR/2009-222, dated July 30, 2009, published in the *Canada Gazette* August 19, 2009, applicable to taxation years that end after February 22, 1994.

(5) Accrual Adjustment. For the purposes of paragraphs 9101(1)(*b*) and (2)(*a*), if subsection (4) does not apply to determine a taxpayer's accrual adjustment in respect of a specified debt obligation for a particular taxation year, the taxpayer's accrual adjustment is the positive or negative amount determined by the formula

$$A - B$$

where

A is the total of all amounts each of which is the amount that would be the taxpayer's accrued return from the obligation for a taxation year, before the particular taxation year, for which subsection 142.3(1) of the Act applied to the taxpayer in respect of the obligation if the accrued return were redetermined on the basis of

(*a*) the information available at the end of the particular taxation year, and

(*b*) the assumptions, if any, with respect to the timing and amount of payments to be made under the obligation after the particular taxation year that were used for the purpose of determining the taxpayer's accrued return from the obligation for the particular taxation year; and

B is the total of

(*a*) the amount included under paragraph 9101(1)(*a*) as the taxpayer's accrued return from the obligation for the taxation year immediately preceding the particular taxation year, and

(*b*) if the taxpayer's accrual adjustment in respect of the obligation for that immediately preceding taxation year was determined under this subsection, the value of A for the purpose of determining that accrual adjustment.

History: S. 9102(5) was added by P.C. 2009-1212, SOR/2009-222, dated July 30, 2009, published in the *Canada Gazette* August 19, 2009, applicable to taxation years that end after February 22, 1994.

(6) Special Cases and Transition. The rules in this section for determining accrued returns and accrual adjustments are subject to section 9103.

History: S. 9102(6) was added by P.C. 2009-1212, SOR/2009-222, dated July 30, 2009, published in the *Canada Gazette* August 19, 2009, applicable to taxation years that end after February 22, 1994.

9103. Accrual Rules — Special Cases and Transition

(1) Convertible Obligation. For the purposes of section 9102, if the terms of a specified debt obligation of a taxpayer give the taxpayer the right to exchange the obligation for shares of the debtor or of a corporation related to the debtor

(*a*) subject to paragraph (*b*), the right shall be disregarded (whether it has been exercised or not); and

(*b*) if 5% or more of the cost of the obligation to the taxpayer is attributable to the right, the cost is deemed to equal the amount by which the cost exceeds the portion of the cost attributable to the right.

History: S. 9103(1) was added by P.C. 2009-1212, SOR/2009-222, dated July 30, 2009, published in the *Canada Gazette* August 19, 2009, applicable to taxation years that end after February 22, 1994.

(2) Default by Debtor. (Repealed.)

History: S. 9103(2) was repealed by P.C. 2009-1212, SOR/2009-222, dated July 30, 2009, published in the *Canada Gazette* August 19, 2009, applicable

(a) to taxation years that end after September 1997; and

(b) to a taxpayer's taxation years that end after 1995 and before October 1997 where the taxpayer has made an election under paragraph 81(11)(*b*) of the *Income Tax Amendment Act, 1997*, S.C. 1998, c. 19 [an election under s. 20(1)(*l*) of the *Income Tax Act*, to have been filed before October 1998].

S. 9103(2) formerly read:

(2) *Default by debtor.* For the purposes of section 9102, in determining amounts in respect of a specified debt obligation, no reduction shall be made on account of the possible or actual failure of the debtor to make any payments under the obligation.

Regulations

S. 9103(2) was added by P.C. 2009-1212, SOR/2009-222, dated July 30, 2009, published in the *Canada Gazette* August 19, 2009, applicable to taxation years that end after February 22, 1994.

(3) Amendment of Obligation. If the terms of a specified debt obligation of a taxpayer are amended at any time in a taxation year of the taxpayer to change the timing or amount of any payment to be made, at or after that time, under the obligation, the taxpayers's accrued returns for the taxation year and for each subsequent taxation year are to be redetermined under section 9102 using a reasonable method that fully gives effect, in those accrued returns, to the alteration to the payments under the obligation.

History: S. 9103(3) was added by P.C. 2009-1212, SOR/2009-222, dated July 30, 2009, published in the *Canada Gazette* August 19, 2009, applicable to taxation years that end after February 22, 1994, except that in respect of taxation years beginning before April 11, 2009 [the day of the prepublication of these regulations in Part I of the *Canada Gazette*], subsection 9103(3) is to be read as follows:

(3) For the purposes of determining accrued returns and accrual adjustments under section 9102, if the terms of a specified debt obligation of a taxpayer have been amended to change the timing or amount of any payment to be made under the obligation, the amendment shall be taken into account as if the obligation had been acquired at the time the amendment was made.

(4) Obligations Acquired before Financial Institution Rules Apply. If a taxpayer held a specified debt obligation at the beginning of the taxpayer's first taxation year (in this subsection referred to as the "initial year") for which subsection 142.3(1) of the Act applied to the taxpayer in respect of the obligation, the following rules apply:

(*a*) the taxpayer's accrued return from the obligation for the initial year or a subsequent taxation year shall not include an amount to the extent that the amount was included in computing the taxpayer's income for a taxation year preceding the initial year; and

(*b*) if interest on the obligation in respect of a period before the initial year becomes receivable or is received by the taxpayer in a particular taxation year that is the initial year or a subsequent taxation year, and all or part of the interest would not, but for this paragraph, be included in computing the taxpayer's income for any taxation year, there shall be included in determining the taxpayer's accrued return from the obligation for the particular taxation year the amount, if any, by which

(i) the portion of the interest that would not otherwise be included in computing the taxpayer's income for any taxation year

exceeds

(ii) the portion of the cost of the obligation to the taxpayer that is reasonably attributable to that portion of the interest.

History: S. 9103(4) was added by P.C. 2009-1212, SOR/2009-222, dated July 30, 2009, published in the *Canada Gazette* August 19, 2009, applicable to taxation years that end after February 22, 1994.

(5) Prepaid Interest — Transition Rule. If, before November 1994 and in a taxation year that ended after February 22, 1994, a taxpayer received an amount under a specified debt obligation in satisfaction, in whole or in part, of the debtor's obligation to pay interest in respect of a period after the taxation year,

(*a*) the amount may, at the election of the taxpayer, be included in determining the taxpayer's accrued return for the taxation year from the obligation; and

(*b*) if the amount is so included, the taxpayer's accrued returns for subsequent taxation years from the obligation shall not include any amount in respect of interest that, because of the payment of the amount, the debtor is no longer required to pay.

History: S. 9103(5) was added by P.C. 2009-1212, SOR/2009-222, dated July 30, 2009, published in the *Canada Gazette* August 19, 2009, applicable to taxation years that end after February 22, 1994.

9104. Foreign Exchange Adjustment

(1) Obligations Held at End of Taxation Year. For the purposes of paragraphs 9101(1)(*c*) and (2)(*b*), if, at the end of a taxation year, a taxpayer holds a specified debt obligation the primary currency of which is not Canadian currency, the taxpayer's foreign exchange adjustment in respect of the obligation for the taxation year is the positive or negative amount determined by the formula

$$(A \times B) - C$$

where

A is the amount that would be the tax basis of the obligation to the taxpayer at the end of the year if

(*a*) the tax basis were determined using the primary currency of the obligation as the currency in which all amounts are expressed,

(*b*) the definition "tax basis" in subsection 142.4(1) of the Act were read without reference to paragraphs (*f*), (*h*), (*o*) and (*q*), and

(*c*) the taxpayer's foreign exchange adjustment in respect of the obligation for each year were nil;

B is the rate of exchange at the end of the year of the primary currency of the obligation into Canadian currency; and

C is the amount that would be the tax basis of the obligation to the taxpayer at the end of the year if

(*a*) the definition "tax basis" in subsection 142.4(1) of the Act were read without reference to paragraphs (*h*) and (*q*), and

(*b*) the taxpayer's foreign exchange adjustment in respect of the obligation for the year were nil.

History: S. 9104(1) was added by P.C. 2009-1212, SOR/2009-222, dated July 30, 2009, published in the *Canada Gazette* August 19, 2009, applicable to taxation years that end after February 22, 1994.

(2) Disposition of Obligation. If a taxpayer disposes of a specified debt obligation the primary currency of which is not Canadian currency, the taxpayer's foreign exchange adjustment in respect of the obligation for the taxation year in which the disposition occurs is the amount that would be the foreign exchange adjustment if the taxation year had ended immediately before the disposition.

History: S. 9104(2) was added by P.C. 2009-1212, SOR/2009-222, dated July 30, 2009, published in the *Canada Gazette* August 19, 2009, applicable to taxation years that end after February 22, 1994.

(3) Disposition of Obligation before 1996. At the election of a taxpayer, subsection (2) does not apply to specified debt obligations disposed of by the taxpayer before 1996.

History: S. 9104(3) was added by P.C. 2009-1212, SOR/2009-222, dated July 30, 2009, published in the *Canada Gazette* August 19, 2009, applicable to taxation years that end after February 22, 1994.

Regulations

Part XCII

Financial Institutions — Disposition of Specified Debt Obligations

9200. Interpretation

(1) Definitions. The following definitions apply in this Part.

"gain", of a taxpayer from the disposition of a specified debt obligation, means the gain from the disposition determined under paragraph 142.4(6)(*a*) of the Act.

History: S. 9200(1), the definition "gain" was added by P.C. 2009-1212, SOR/2009-222, dated July 30, 2009, published in the *Canada Gazette* August 19, 2009, applicable to taxation years that end after February 22, 1994.

"loss", of a taxpayer from the disposition of a specified debt obligation, means the loss from the disposition determined under paragraph 142.4(6)(*b*) of the Act.

History: S. 9200(1), the definition "loss" was added by P.C. 2009-1212, SOR/2009-222, dated July 30, 2009, published in the *Canada Gazette* August 19, 2009, applicable to taxation years that end after February 22, 1994.

"residual portion", of a taxpayer's gain or loss from the disposition of a specified debt obligation, means the amount determined under subsection 142.4(8) of the Act in respect of the disposition.

History: S. 9200(1), the definition "residual portion" was added by P.C. 2009-1212, SOR/2009-222, dated July 30, 2009, published in the *Canada Gazette* August 19, 2009, applicable to taxation years that end after February 22, 1994.

(2) Amortization Date. For the purposes of this Part, the amortization date for a specified debt obligation disposed of by a taxpayer is the day determined as follows:

(*a*) subject to paragraphs (*b*) to (*d*), the amortization date is the later of the day of disposition and the day on which the debtor is required to make the final payment under the obligation, determined without regard to any option respecting the timing of payments under the obligation (other than an option that was exercised before the disposition);

(*b*) subject to paragraphs (*c*) and (*d*), the amortization date is the day of disposition if the day on which the debtor is required to make the final payment under the obligation is not determinable for the purpose of paragraph (*a*);

(*c*) subject to paragraph (*d*), the amortization date is the first day, if any, after the disposition on which the interest rate could change, if the obligation is one in respect of which the following conditions are satisfied:

(i) the obligation provides for stipulated interest payments,

(ii) the rate of interest for one or more periods after the issuance of the obligation was not fixed on the day of issue, and

(iii) when the obligation was issued, it was reasonable to expect that the interest rate for each period would equal or approximate a reasonable market rate of interest for that period; and

(*d*) if, for purposes of its financial statements, the taxpayer had a gain or loss from the disposition that is being amortized to profit, the amortization date is the last day of the amortization period.

History: S. 9200(2) was added by P.C. 2009-1212, SOR/2009-222, dated July 30, 2009, published in the *Canada Gazette* August 19, 2009, applicable to taxation years that end after February 22, 1994.

9201. Transition Amount

For the purpose of subsection 142.4(1) of the Act, "transition amount", of a taxpayer in respect of the disposition of a specified debt obligation, means,

(*a*) if neither paragraph (*b*) nor (*c*) applies, nil;

(*b*) if

(i) the taxpayer acquired the obligation before its taxation year that includes February 23, 1994,

(ii) neither paragraph 7000(2)(*a*) nor (*b*) has applied to the obligation, and

(iii) the principal amount of the obligation exceeds the cost of the obligation to the taxpayer (which excess is referred to in this paragraph as the "discount"),

the amount determined by the formula

$$A - B$$

where

A is the total of all amounts each of which is the amount included in respect of the discount in computing the taxpayer's profit for a taxation year that ended before February 23, 1994, and

B is the total of all amounts each of which is the amount included in respect of the discount in computing the taxpayer's income for a taxation year that ended before February 23, 1994; and

(*c*) where

(i) the conditions in subparagraphs (*b*)(i) and (ii) are satisfied, and

(ii) the cost of the obligation to the taxpayer exceeds the principal amount of the obligation (which excess is referred to in this paragraph as the "premium"),

the negative of the amount determined by the formula

$$A - B$$

where

A is the total of all amounts each of which is the amount deducted in respect of the premium in computing the taxpayer's profit for a taxation year that ended before February 23, 1994, and

B is the total of all amounts each of which is the amount deducted in respect of the premium in computing the taxpayer's income for a taxation year that ended before February 23, 1994.

History: S. 9201 was added by P.C. 2009-1212, SOR/2009-222, dated July 30, 2009, published in the *Canada Gazette* August 19, 2009, applicable to taxation years that end after February 22, 1994.

9202. Prescribed Debt Obligations

(1) Application of Related Election. The following rules apply with respect to an election made under subsection (3) or (4) by a taxpayer:

(*a*) the election applies only if

(i) it is in writing,

(ii) it specifies the first taxation year (in this subsection referred to as the "initial year") of the taxpayer to which it is to apply, and

(iii) either it is received by the Minister within six months after the end of the initial year, or the Minister has expressly accepted the later filing of the election;

(*b*) subject to paragraph (*c*), the election applies to dispositions of specified debt obligations in the initial year and subsequent taxation years; and

(*c*) if the Minister has approved, on written application by the taxpayer, the revocation of the election, the election does not apply to dispositions of specified debt obligations in the taxation year specified in the application and in subsequent taxation years.

History: S. 9202(1) was added by P.C. 2009-1212, SOR/2009-222, dated July 30, 2009, published in the *Canada Gazette* August 19, 2009, applicable to taxation years that end after February 22, 1994.

(2) Prescribed Specified Debt Obligation. For the purpose of subparagraph 142.4(5)(*a*)(ii) of the Act, a specified debt obligation disposed of by a taxpayer in a taxation year is prescribed in respect of the taxpayer if the amortization date for the obligation is not more than two years after the end of the taxation year.

History: S. 9202(2) was added by P.C. 2009-1212, SOR/2009-222, dated July 30, 2009, published in the *Canada Gazette* August 19, 2009, applicable to taxation years that end after February 22, 1994.

(3) Prescribed Specified Debt Obligation — Exception. Subsection (2) does not apply in respect of a taxpayer for a taxation year if

(*a*) generally accepted accounting principles require that the taxpayer's gains and losses arising on the disposition of a class of debt obligations be amortized to profit for the purpose of the taxpayer's financial statements;

(*b*) the taxpayer has elected not to have subsection (2) apply; and

(*c*) the election applies to dispositions in the year.

History: S. 9202(3) was added by P.C. 2009-1212, SOR/2009-222, dated July 30, 2009, published in the *Canada Gazette* August 19, 2009, applicable to taxation years that end after February 22, 1994.

(4) Prescribed Specified Debt Obligation. For the purpose of subparagraph 142.4(5)(*a*)(ii) of the Act, a specified debt obligation disposed of by a taxpayer in a taxation year is prescribed in respect of the taxpayer if

(*a*) the taxpayer has elected to have this subsection apply;

(*b*) the election applies to dispositions in the year; and

(*c*) the absolute value of the positive or negative amount determined by the formula (A - B) does not exceed the lesser of $5,000 and the amount, if any, specified in the election, where

A is the total of all amounts each of which is the residual portion of the taxpayer's gain from the disposition of the obligation or any other specified debt obligation disposed of in the same transaction, and

B is the total of all amounts each of which is the residual portion of the taxpayer's loss from the disposition of the obligation or any other specified debt obligation disposed of in the same transaction.

History: S. 9202(4) was added by P.C. 2009-1212, SOR/2009-222, dated July 30, 2009, published in the *Canada Gazette* August 19, 2009, applicable to taxation years that end after February 22, 1994.

(5) Prescribed Specified Debt Obligation. For the purpose of subparagraph 142.4(5)(*a*)(ii) of the Act, a specified debt obligation disposed of by a taxpayer in a taxation year is prescribed in respect of the taxpayer if

(*a*) the disposition resulted in an extinguishment of the obligation, other than an extinguishment that occurred because of a purchase of the obligation by the debtor in the open market;

(*b*) the taxpayer had the right to require the obligation to be settled at any time; or

(*c*) the debtor had the right to settle the obligation at any time.

History: S. 9202(5) was added by P.C. 2009-1212, SOR/2009-222, dated July 30, 2009, published in the *Canada Gazette* August 19, 2009, applicable to taxation years that end after February 22, 1994.

9203. Residual Portion of Gain or Loss

(1) Allocation of Residual Portion. Subject to section 9204, if subsection 142.4(4) of the Act applies to the disposition of a specified debt obligation by a taxpayer, the amount allocated to each taxation year in respect of the residual portion of the gain or loss from the disposition shall be determined, for the purpose of that subsection,

(*a*) by a method that complies with, or is substantially similar to a method that complies with, subsection (2); or

(*b*) if gains and losses from the disposition of debt obligations are amortized to profit for the purpose of the taxpayer's financial statements, by the method used for the purpose of the taxpayer's financial statements.

History: S. 9203(1) was added by P.C. 2009-1212, SOR/2009-222, dated July 30, 2009, published in the *Canada Gazette* August 19, 2009, applicable to taxation years that end after February 22, 1994.

(2) Proration Method. For the purpose of subsection (1), a method for allocating to taxation years the residual portion of a taxpayer's gain or loss from the disposition of a specified debt obligation complies with this subsection if the amount allocated to each taxation year is determined by the formula

$$A \times B/C$$

where

Regulations

A is the residual portion of the taxpayer's gain or loss;

B is the number of days in the taxation year that are in the period referred to in the description of C; and

C is the number of days in the period that,

(*a*) where subsection (3) applies in respect of the obligation, is determined under that subsection, and

(*b*) in any other case,

(i) begins on the day on which the taxpayer disposed of the obligation, and

(ii) ends on the earlier of

(A) the amortization date for the obligation, and

(B) the day that is 20 years after the day on which the taxpayer disposed of the obligation.

History: S. 9203(2) was added by P.C. 2009-1212, SOR/2009-222, dated July 30, 2009, published in the *Canada Gazette* August 19, 2009, applicable to taxation years that end after February 22, 1994.

(3) Single Proration Period. This subsection applies in respect of specified debt obligations disposed of by a taxpayer in a transaction in a taxation year, and the period determined under this subsection in respect of the obligations is the period that begins on the day of disposition and ends on the weighted average amortization date for those obligations so disposed of to which subsection 142.4(4) of the Act applies, if

(*a*) the taxpayer has elected in its return of income for the taxation year to have this subsection apply in respect of the obligations so disposed of;

(*b*) all the obligations so disposed of were disposed of at the same time; and

(*c*) the number of the obligations so disposed of to which subsection 142.4(4) of the Act applies is at least 50.

History: S. 9203(3) was added by P.C. 2009-1212, SOR/2009-222, dated July 30, 2009, published in the *Canada Gazette* August 19, 2009, applicable to taxation years that end after February 22, 1994.

(4) Weighted Average Amortization Date. For the purpose of subsection (3), the weighted average amortization date for a group of specified debt obligations disposed of on the same day by a taxpayer is,

(*a*) if paragraph (*b*) does not apply, the day that is the number of days after the day of disposition equal to the total of the number of days determined in respect of each obligation by the formula

$$A \times B/C$$

where

A is the number of days from the day of disposition to the amortization date for the obligation,

B is the residual portion of the gain or loss from the disposition of the obligation, and

C is the total of all amounts each of which is the residual portion of the gain or loss from the disposition of an obligation in the group; and

(*b*) the day that the taxpayer determines using a reasonable method for estimating the day determined under paragraph (*a*).

History: S. 9203(4) was added by P.C. 2009-1212, SOR/2009-222, dated July 30, 2009, published in the *Canada Gazette* August 19, 2009, applicable to taxation years that end after February 22, 1994.

9204. Special Rules for Residual Portion of Gain or Loss

(1) Application. This section applies for the purposes of subparagraphs 142.4(4)(*c*)(ii) and (*d*)(ii) of the Act.

History: S. 9204(1) was added by P.C. 2009-1212, SOR/2009-222, dated July 30, 2009, published in the *Canada Gazette* August 19, 2009, applicable to taxation years that end after February 22, 1994.

(2) Winding-up. If subsection 88(1) of the Act has applied to the winding-up of a taxpayer (in this subsection referred to as the "subsidiary"), the following rules apply in respect of the residual portion of a gain or loss of the subsidiary from the disposition of a specified debt obligation to which subsection 142.4(4) of the Act applies:

(*a*) the amount of that residual portion allocated to the taxation year of the subsidiary in which its assets were distributed to its parent on the winding-up shall be determined on the assumption that the taxation year ended when the assets were distributed to its parent;

(*b*) no amount shall be allocated in respect of that residual portion to any taxation year of the subsidiary after its taxation year in which its assets were distributed to its parent; and

(*c*) the amount of that residual portion allocated to the taxation year of the parent in which the subsidiary's assets were distributed to it shall be determined on the assumption that the taxation year began when the assets were distributed to it.

History: S. 9204(2) was added by P.C. 2009-1212, SOR/2009-222, dated July 30, 2009, published in the *Canada Gazette* August 19, 2009, applicable to taxation years that end after February 22, 1994.

(2.1) Winding-up. (Repealed.)

History: S. 9204(2.1) was repealed by P.C. 2009-1869, SOR/2009-302, dated November 19, 2009, published in the *Canada Gazette* December 9, 2009, applicable to windings-up that occur after June 14, 2004. S. 9204(2.1) formerly read:

(2.1) If subsection 142.7(13) of the Act applies in respect of the winding-up of a Canadian affiliate of an entrant bank,

(*a*) subsection (2) applies with respect to the winding-up and, for this purpose, the references in subsection (2) to "subsection 88(1)", "taxpayer" and "parent" are to be read as references to "subsection 142.7(13)", "Canadian affiliate" and "entrant bank", respectively; and

(*b*) in respect of the winding-up, the reference in paragraph (5)(*a*) to "subsection 88(1) of the Act" is to be read as a reference to "subsection 142.7(13) of the Act".

S. 9204(2.1) was added by P.C. 2009-1869, SOR/2009-302, dated November 19, 2009, published in the *Canada Gazette* December 9, 2009, applicable after June 27, 1999, except that before August 9, 2000, subsection 9204(2.1) applies only in respect of authorized foreign banks.

(3) Transfer of an Insurance Business. No amount in respect of the residual portion of a gain or loss of an insurer from the disposition of a specified debt obligation to which subsection 142.4(4) of the Act applies shall be allocated to any taxation year of the insurer that ends after the insurer ceased to carry on all or substantially all of an insurance business, if

(*a*) subsection 138(11.5) or (11.94) of the Act has applied to the transfer of that business; and (*b*) the person to whom that business was transferred is considered, because of paragraph 138(11.5)(*k*) of the Act, to be the same person as the insurer in respect of that residual portion.

History: S. 9204(3) was added by P.C. 2009-1212, SOR/2009-222, dated July 30, 2009, published in the *Canada Gazette* August 19, 2009, applicable to taxation years that end after February 22, 1994.

(4) Transfer to New Partnership. If subsection 98(6) of the Act deems a partnership (in this subsection referred to as the "new partnership") to be a continuation of another partnership (in this subsection referred to as the "predecessor partnership"), the following rules apply in respect of the residual portion of a gain or loss of the predecessor partnership from the disposition of a specified debt obligation to which subsection 142.4(4) of the Act applies:

(*a*) the amount of that residual portion allocated to the taxation year of the predecessor partnership in which its property was transferred to the new partnership shall be determined on the assumption that the taxation year ended when the property was transferred;

(*b*) no amount shall be allocated in respect of that residual portion to any taxation year of the predecessor partnership after its taxation year in which its property was transferred to the new partnership; and

(*c*) the amount of that residual portion allocated to the taxation year of the new partnership in which the predecessor partnership's property was transferred to it shall be determined on the assumption that the taxation year began when the property was transferred to it.

History: S. 9204(4) was added by P.C. 2009-1212, SOR/2009-222, dated July 30, 2009, published in the *Canada Gazette* August 19, 2009, applicable to taxation years that end after February 22, 1994.

(5) Ceasing to Carry on Business. There shall be allocated to a particular taxation year of a taxpayer the part, if any, of the residual portion of the taxpayer's gain or loss that is from a disposition of a specified debt obligation to which subsection 142.4(4) of the Act applies and that was not allocated to a preceding taxation year, if

(*a*) at any time in the particular taxation year the taxpayer ceases to carry on all or substantially all of a business, otherwise than as a result of a merger to which subsection 87(2) of the Act applies, a winding-up to which subsection 88(1) of the Act applies or a transfer of the business to which subsection 98(6) or 138(11.5) or (11.94) of the Act applies;

(*b*) the disposition occurred before that time; and

(*c*) the specified debt obligation was property used in the business.

History: S. 9204(5) was added by P.C. 2009-1212, SOR/2009-222, dated July 30, 2009, published in the *Canada Gazette* August 19, 2009, applicable to taxation years that end after February 22, 1994.

(5.1) Non-resident Taxpayer. For the purpose of subsection (5), a non-resident taxpayer is considered to cease to carry on all or substantially all of a business if the taxpayer ceases to carry on, or ceases to carry on in Canada, all or substantially all of the part of the business that was carried on in Canada.

History: S. 9204(5.1) was added by P.C. 2009-1869, SOR/2009-302, dated November 19, 2009, published in the *Canada Gazette* December 9, 2009, applicable after June 27, 1999, except that before August 9, 2000, subsection 9204(5.1) applies only in respect of authorized foreign banks.

(6) Ceasing to be a Financial Institution. There shall be allocated to a particular taxation year of a taxpayer the part, if any, of the residual portion of the taxpayer's gain or loss that is from a disposition of a specified debt obligation to which subsection 142.4(4) of the Act applies and that was not allocated to a preceding taxation year, if

(*a*) the particular taxation year ends immediately before the time at which the taxpayer ceases to be a financial institution, otherwise than because it has ceased to carry on a business; and

(*b*) the disposition occurred before that time.

History: S. 9204(6) was added by P.C. 2009-1212, SOR/2009-222, dated July 30, 2009, published in the *Canada Gazette* August 19, 2009, applicable to taxation years that end after February 22, 1994.

Part XCIII
Film or Video Production Services Tax Credit

9300. Accredited Production

(1) Subject to subsection (2), for the purpose of section 125.5 of the Act, accredited production means

(*a*) a film or video production in respect of which the aggregate expenditures, included in the cost of the production, in the period that ends 24 months after the time that the principal filming or taping of the production began, exceeds $1,000,000; and

(*b*) a film or video production that is part of a series of television productions that has two or more episodes, or is a pilot programme for such a series of episodes, in respect of which the aggregate expenditures included in the cost of each episode in the period that ends 24 months after the time that the principal filming or taping of the production began exceeds

(i) in the case of an episode whose running time is less than 30 minutes, $100,000, and

(ii) in any other case, $200,000.

(2) An accredited production does not include a production that is any of the following:

(*a*) news, current events or public affairs programming, or a programme that includes weather or market reports;

(*b*) a talk show;

(*c*) a production in respect of a game, questionnaire or contest;

(*d*) a sports event or activity;

(*e*) a gala presentation or awards show;

(*f*) a production that solicits funds;

(*g*) reality television;

(*h*) pornography;

(*i*) advertising; and

(*j*) a production produced primarily for industrial, corporate or institutional purposes.

Part XCIV
Prescribed Children's Programs

History: The heading before s. 9400 was replaced by S.C. 2011, c. 24, s. 98(1), applicable to the 2011 and subsequent taxation years. The heading before s. 9400 formerly read: "Prescribed Programs of Physical Activity".

9400. [Child Fitness Tax Credit]

(1) Interpretation. (Repealed by S.C. 2016, c. 7, s. 59(1).)

History: S. 9400(1) was repealed by S.C. 2016, c. 7, s. 59(1), applicable January 1, 2017, and formerly read:

(1) *Interpretation.* The following definitions apply in this Part.

"physical activity" means a supervised activity suitable for children (other than an activity where a child rides on or in a motorized vehicle as an essential component of the activity) that

(*a*) in the case of a qualifying child in respect of whom an amount is deductible under section 118.3 of the Act in computing any person's income for the taxation year, results in movement and in an observable expenditure of energy in a recreational context; and

(*b*) in the case of any other child, contributes to cardio-respiratory endurance and to one or more of the following:

(i) muscular strength,

(ii) muscular endurance,

(iii) flexibility, and

(iv) balance.

"qualifying child"—"qualifying child" has the meaning assigned by subsection 122.8(1) of the Act.

S. 9400(1), the definition "qualifying child" was replaced by S.C. 2014, c. 39, s. 89(1), applicable to the 2015 and subsequent taxation years, and formerly read:

"qualifying child" has the meaning assigned by subsection 118.03(1) of the Act.

(2) Prescribed Program of Physical Activity. (Repealed by S.C. 2016, c. 7, s. 59(1).)

History: S. 9400(2) was repealed by S.C. 2016, c. 7, s. 59(1), applicable January 1, 2017, and formerly read:

(2) *Prescribed Program of Physical Activity.* For the purpose of the definition "eligible fitness expense" in subsection 122.8(1) of the Act, a prescribed program of physical activity is

(*a*) a weekly program, that is not part of a school's curriculum, of a duration of eight or more consecutive weeks in which all or substantially all of the activities include a significant amount of physical activity;

(*b*) a program, that is not part of a school's curriculum, of a duration of five or more consecutive days of which more than 50% of the daily activities include a significant amount of physical activity;

(*c*) a program, that is not part of a school's curriculum, of a duration of eight or more consecutive weeks, offered to children by a club, association or similar organization (in this section referred to as an "organization") in circumstances where a participant in the program may select amongst a variety of activities if

(i) more than 50% of those activities offered to children by the organization are activities that include a significant amount of physical activity, or

(ii) more than 50% of the time scheduled for activities offered to children in the program is scheduled for activities that include a significant amount of physical activity; or

(*d*) a membership in an organization, that is not part of a school's curriculum, of a duration of eight or more consecutive weeks if more than 50% of all the activities offered to children by the organization include a significant amount of physical activity.

S. 9400(2), the portion before paragraph (*a*) was replaced by S.C. 2014, c. 39, s. 89(2), applicable to the 2015 and subsequent taxation years, and formerly read:

(2) *Prescribed Program of Physical Activity.* For the purpose of the definition "eligible fitness expense" in subsection 118.03(1) of the Act, a prescribed program of physical activity is

(3) Mixed-use Facility. (Repealed by S.C. 2016, c. 7, s. 59(1).)

History: S. 9400(3) was repealed by S.C. 2016, c. 7, s. 59(1), applicable January 1, 2017, and formerly read:

(3) *Mixed-use Facility.* For the purpose of the definition "eligible fitness expense" in subsection 122.8(1) of the Act, a prescribed program of physical activity is that portion of a program, which program does not meet the requirements of paragraph (2)(*c*) and is not part of a school's curriculum, of a duration of eight or more consecutive weeks, offered to children by an organization in circumstances where a participant in the program may select amongst a variety of activities

(*a*) that is the percentage of those activities offered to children by the organization that are activities that include a significant amount of physical activity; or

(*b*) that is the percentage of the time scheduled for activities in the program that is scheduled for activities that include a significant amount of physical activity.

S. 9400(3), the portion before paragraph (*a*) was replaced by S.C. 2014, c. 39, s. 89(3), applicable to the 2015 and subsequent taxation years, and formerly read:

(3) *Mixed-use Facility.* For the purpose of the definition "eligible fitness expense" in subsection 118.03(1) of the Act, a prescribed program of physical activity is that portion of a program, which program does not meet the requirements of paragraph (2)(*c*) and is not part of a school's curriculum, of a duration of eight or more consecutive weeks, offered to children by an organization in circumstances where a participant in the program may select amongst a variety of activities

(4) Membership. (Repealed by S.C. 2016, c. 7, s. 59(1).)

History: S. 9400(4) was repealed by S.C. 2016, c. 7, s. 59(1), applicable January 1, 2017, and formerly read:

(4) *Membership.* For the purpose of the definition "eligible fitness expense" in subsection 122.8(1) of the Act, a prescribed program of physical activity is that portion of a membership in an organization, which membership does not meet the requirements of paragraph (2)(*d*) and is not part of a school's curriculum, of a duration of eight or more consecutive weeks that is the percentage of all the activities offered to children by the organization that are activities that include a significant amount of physical activity.

S. 9400(4) was replaced by S.C. 2014, c. 39, s. 89(4), applicable to the 2015 and subsequent taxation years, and formerly read:

(4) *Membership.* For the purpose of the definition "eligible fitness expense" in subsection 118.03(1) of the Act, a prescribed program of physical activity is that portion of a membership in an organization, which membership does not meet the requirements of paragraph (2)(*d*) and is not part of a school's curriculum, of a duration of eight or more consecutive weeks that is the percentage of all the activities offered to children by the organization that are activities that include a significant amount of physical activity.

(5) Horseback Riding. (Repealed by S.C. 2016, c. 7, s. 59(1).)

History: S. 9400(5) was repealed by S.C. 2016, c. 7, s. 59(1), applicable January 1, 2017, and formerly read:

(5) *Horseback Riding.* For the purpose of the definition "physical activity" in subsection (1), horseback riding is deemed to be an activity that contributes to cardio-respiratory endurance and to one or more of muscular strength, muscular endurance, flexibility and balance.

9401. Program of Artistic, Cultural, Recreational or Developmental Activity

(1) Definition of "artistic, cultural, recreational or developmental activity". (Repealed by S.C. 2016, c. 7, s. 59(1).)

History: S. 9401(1) was repealed by S.C. 2016, c. 7, s. 59(1), in force January 1, 2017, and formerly read:

(1) *Definition of "artistic, cultural, recreational or developmental activity".* In this section, "artistic, cultural, recreational or developmental activity" means a supervised activity, including an activity adapted for children in respect of whom an amount is deductible under section 118.3 of the Act, suitable for children (other than a physical activity), that

(*a*) is intended to contribute to a child's ability to develop creative skills or expertise, acquire and apply knowledge, or improve dexterity or coordination, in an artistic or cultural discipline including

(i) literary arts,

(ii) visual arts,

(iii) performing arts,

(iv) music,

(v) media,

(vi) languages,

(vii) customs, and

(viii) heritage;

(*b*) provides a substantial focus on wilderness and the natural environment;

(*c*) assists with the development and use of intellectual skills;

(*d*) includes structured interaction among children where supervisors teach or assist children to develop interpersonal skills; or

(*e*) provides enrichment or tutoring in academic subjects.

S. 9401(1) was added by S.C. 2011, c. 24, s. 99(1), applicable to the 2011 and subsequent taxation years.

(2) Prescribed program of artistic, cultural, recreational or developmental activity. (Repealed by S.C. 2016, c. 7, s. 59(1).)

History: S. 9401(2) was repealed by S.C. 2016, c. 7, s. 59(1), in force January 1, 2017, and formerly read:

(2) *Prescribed program of artistic, cultural, recreational or developmental activity.* For the purpose of the definition "eligible expense" in subsection 118.031(1) of the Act, a prescribed program of artistic, cultural, recreational or developmental activity is

(*a*) a weekly program, that is not part of a school's curriculum, of a duration of eight or more consecutive weeks in which all or substantially all the activities include a significant amount of artistic, cultural, recreational or developmental activity;

(*b*) a program, that is not part of a school's curriculum, of a duration of five or more consecutive days of which more than 50% of the daily activities include a significant amount of artistic, cultural, recreational or developmental activity;

(*c*) a program, that is not part of a school's curriculum, of a duration of eight or more consecutive weeks, offered to children by a club, association or similar organization (in this section referred to as an "organization") in circumstances where a participant in the program may select amongst a variety of activities if

(i) more than 50% of those activities offered to children by the organization are activities that include a significant amount of artistic, cultural, recreational or developmental activity, or

(ii) more than 50% of the time scheduled for activities offered to children in the program is scheduled for activities that include a significant amount of artistic, cultural, recreational or developmental activity; or

(*d*) a membership in an organization, that is not part of a school's curriculum, of a duration of eight or more consecutive weeks if more than 50% of all the activities offered to children by the organization include a significant amount of artistic, cultural, recreational or developmental activity.

S. 9401(2) was added by S.C. 2011, c. 24, s. 99(1), applicable to the 2011 and subsequent taxation years.

(3) Mixed-use facility. (Repealed by S.C. 2016, c. 7, s. 59(1).)

History: S. 9401(3) was repealed by S.C. 2016, c. 7, s. 59(1), in force January 1, 2017, and formerly read:

(3) *Mixed-use facility.* For the purpose of the definition "eligible expense" in subsection 118.031(1) of the Act, a prescribed program of artistic, cultural, recreational or developmental activity is that portion of a program, which program does not meet the requirements of paragraph (2)(*c*) and is not part of a school's curriculum, of a duration of eight or more consecutive weeks, offered to children by an organization in circumstances where a participant in the program may select amongst a variety of activities

(*a*) that is the percentage of those activities offered to children by the organization that are activities that include a significant amount of artistic, cultural, recreational or developmental activity; or

(*b*) that is the percentage of the time scheduled for activities in the program that is scheduled for activities that include a significant amount of artistic, cultural, recreational or developmental activity.

S. 9401(3) was added by S.C. 2011, c. 24, s. 99(1), applicable to the 2011 and subsequent taxation years.

(4) Membership. (Repealed by S.C. 2016, c. 7, s. 59(1).)

History: S. 9401(4) was repealed by S.C. 2016, c. 7, s. 59(1), in force January 1, 2017, and formerly read:

(4) *Membership.* For the purpose of the definition "eligible expense" in subsection 118.031(1) of the Act, a prescribed program of artistic, cultural, recreational or developmental activity is that portion of a membership in an organization, which membership does not meet the requirements of paragraph (2)(*d*) and is not part of a school's curriculum, of a duration of eight or more consecutive weeks that is the percentage of all the activities offered to children by the organization that are activities that include a significant amount of artistic, cultural, recreational or developmental activity.

S. 9401(4) was added by S.C. 2011, c. 24, s. 99(1), applicable to the 2011 and subsequent taxation years.

Part XCV
Employee Life and Health Trusts

9500. Prescribed rights

For the purpose of subparagraph 144.1(2)(*g*)(iii) of the Act, prescribed payments are payments to General Motors of Canada Limited or Chrysler Canada Inc. by the employee life and health trust established for the benefit of retired automobile industry workers by the Canadian Auto Workers' Union that

(*a*) are reasonable in the circumstances;

(*b*) are made as consideration for administrative services provided to or on behalf of the trust or its beneficiaries, or as reimbursement for employee benefit payments made on behalf of, or in contemplation of the establishment of, the trust; and

(*c*) the recipient acknowledges in writing shall be included in computing the recipient's income in the year that they are receivable, to the extent that the recipient deducts in the year, or deducted in a prior year, in computing its income amounts in respect of the services or benefit payments described in paragraph (*b*).

History: S. 9500 was added by S.C. 2010, c. 25, s. 87(1), applicable after 2009.

Part XCVI
School Supplies Tax Credit

9600. Prescribed durable goods

For the purpose of the definition *teaching supplies* in subsection 122.9(1) of the Act, the following are prescribed durable goods:

(*a*) books;

(*b*) games and puzzles;

(*c*) containers (such as plastic boxes or banker boxes); and

(*d*) educational support software.

History: S. 9600 was added by S.C. 2016, c. 7, s. 60(1), applicable to the 2016 and subsequent taxation years.

Related Sections: S. 122.9(1) "teaching supplies".

Regulations

Schedule I
Ranges of Remuneration and of Total Remuneration, (Sections 100, 102 and 106)

1. For the purposes of paragraph 102(1)(*c*), the ranges of remuneration for each pay period in a taxation year shall be determined as follows:

(*a*) in respect of a daily pay period, the ranges of remuneration shall commence at $44 and increase in increments of $2 for each range up to and including $151.99;

(*b*) in respect of a weekly pay period, the ranges of remuneration shall commence at $202 and increase in increments of

(i) $2 for each range up to and including $309.99,

(ii) $4 for each range from $310 to $529.99,

(iii) $8 for each range from $530 to $969.99,

(iv) $12 for each range from $970 to $1,629.99,

(v) $16 for each range from $1,630 to $2,509.99,

(vi) $20 for each range from $2,510 to $3,609.99;

(*c*) in respect of a bi-weekly pay period, the ranges of remuneration shall commence at $403 and increase in increments of

(i) $4 for each range up to and including $618.99,

(ii) $8 for each range from $619 to $1,058.99,

(iii) $16 for each range from $1,059 to $1,938.99,

(iv) $24 for each range from $1,939 to $3,258.99,

(v) $32 for each range from $3,259 to $5,018.99,

(vi) $40 for each range from $5,019 to $7,218.99;

(*d*) in respect of a semi-monthly pay period, the ranges of remuneration shall commence at $437 and increase in increments of

(i) $4 for each range up to and including $652.99,

(ii) $8 for each range from $653 to $1,092.99,

(iii) $18 for each range from $1,093 to $2,082.99,

(iv) $26 for each range from $2,083 to $3,512.99,

(v) $34 for each range from $3,513 to $5,382.99,

(vi) $44 for each range from $5,383 to $7,802.99;

(*e*) in respect of 12 monthly pay periods, the ranges of remuneration shall commence at $873 and increase in increments of

(i) $8 for each range up to and including $1,304.99,

(ii) $18 for each range from $1,305 to $2,294.99,

(iii) $34 for each range from $2,295 to $4,164.99,

(iv) $52 for each range from $4,165 to $7,024.99,

(v) $70 for each range from $7,025 to $10,874.99,

(vi) $86 for each range from $10,875 to $15,604.99;

(*f*) in respect of 10 monthly pay periods, the ranges of remuneration shall commence at $1,048 and increase in increments of

(i) $10 for each range up to and including $1,587.99,

(ii) $20 for each range from $1,588 to $2,687.99,

(iii) $42 for each range from $2,688 to $4,997.99,

(iv) $62 for each range from $4,998 to $8,407.99,

(v) $84 for each range from $8,408 to $13,027.99,

(vi) $104 for each range from $13,028 to $18,747.99;

(*g*) in respect of four-week pay periods, the ranges of remuneration shall commence at $806 and increase in increments of

(i) $8 for each range up to and including $1,237.99,

(ii) $16 for each range from $1,238 to $2,117.99,

(iii) $32 for each range from $2,118 to $3,877.99,

(iv) $48 for each range from $3,878 to $6,517.99,

(v) $64 for each range from $6,518 to $10,037.99,

(vi) $80 for each range from $10,038 to $14,437.99;

(*h*) in respect of 22 pay periods per annum, the ranges of remuneration shall commence at $477 and increase in increments of

(i) $6 for each range up to and including $800.99,

(ii) $10 for each range from $801 to $1,350.99,

(iii) $18 for each range from $1,351 to $2,340.99,

(iv) $28 for each range from $2,341 to $3,880.99,

(v) $38 for each range from $3,881 to $5,970.99,

(vi) $48 for each range from $5,971 to $8,610.99.

2. For the purposes of paragraph 102(1)(*d*), the mid-point of the range of amount of personal credits for a taxation year shall be as follows:

(*a*) from $0 to $8,929, $8,929;

(*b*) from $8,929.01 to $10,817, $9,873.00;

(*c*) from $10,817.01 to $12,705, $11,761.00;

(*d*) from $12,705.01 to $14,593, $13,649.00;

(*e*) from $14,593.01 to $16,481, $15,537.00;

(*f*) from $16,481.01 to $18,369, $17,425.00;

(*g*) from $18,369.01 to $20,257, $19,313.00;

(*h*) from $20,257.01 to $22,145, $21,201.00;

(*i*) from $22,145.01 to $24,033, $23,089.00;

(*j*) from $24,033.01 to $25,921, $24,977.00;

(*k*) for amounts in excess of $25,921, the amount of the personal credits.

3. (Repealed.)

Schedule II

Capital Cost Allowances, (Sections 215, 700, 701, 1100 to 1105, 1205, 1206, 1700, 1704, 3900, 4600, 4601, 5202 and 5204)

Class 1. (4 per cent)

Property not included in any other class that is

(*a*) a bridge;

(*b*) a canal;

(*c*) a culvert;

(*d*) a dam;

(*e*) a jetty acquired before May 26, 1976;

(*f*) a mole acquired before May 26, 1976;

(*g*) a road, sidewalk, airplane runway, parking area, storage area or similar surface construction, acquired before May 26, 1976;

(*h*) railway track and grading, including components such as rails, ballast, ties and other track material,

(i) that is not part of a railway system, or

(ii) that was acquired after May 25, 1976;

(*i*) railway traffic control or signalling equipment, acquired after May 25, 1976, including switching, block signalling, interlocking, crossing protection, detection, speed control or retarding equipment, but not including property that is principally electronic equipment or systems software therefor;

(*j*) a subway or tunnel, acquired after May 25, 1976;

(*k*) electrical generating equipment (except as specified elsewhere in this Schedule);

(*l*) a pipeline, other than

(i) a pipeline that is gas or oil well equipment, and

(ii) a pipeline that is for oil or natural gas if the Minister, in consultation with the Minister of Natural Resources, is or has been satisfied that the main source of supply for the pipeline is or was likely to be exhausted within 15 years after the date on which the operation of the pipeline commenced;

(*m*) the generating or distributing equipment and plant (including structures) of a producer or distributor of electrical energy;

(*n*) manufacturing and distributing equipment and plant (including structures) acquired primarily for the production or distribution of gas, except

(i) a property acquired for the purpose of producing or distributing gas that is normally distributed in portable containers,

(ii) a property acquired for the purpose of processing natural gas, before the delivery of such gas to a distribution system, or

(iii) a property acquired for the purpose of producing oxygen or nitrogen;

(*o*) the distributing equipment and plant (including structures) of a distributor of water;

(*p*) the production and distributing equipment and plant (including structures) of a distributor of heat; or

(*q*) a building or other structure, or a part of it, including any component parts such as electric wiring, plumbing, sprinkler systems, air-conditioning equipment, heating equipment, lighting fixtures, elevators and escalators (except property described in any of paragraphs (*k*) and (*m*) to (*p*) of this Class or in any of paragraphs (*a*) to (*e*) of Class 8).

Interpretation Bulletins: *Primary* — IT-79R3 Capital cost allowance — Buildings or other structures; IT-482R Pipelines. *Secondary* — IT-195R4 Rental property — Capital cost allowance restrictions; IT-304R2 Condominiums; IT-476R Capital cost allowance — Equipment used in petroleum and natural gas activities.

Class 2. (6 per cent)

Property that is

(*a*) electrical generating equipment (except as specified elsewhere in this Schedule);

(*b*) a pipeline, other than gas or oil well equipment, unless, in the case of a pipeline for oil or natural gas, the Minister in consultation with the Minister of Energy, Mines and Resources, is or has been satisfied that the main source of supply for the pipeline is or was likely to be exhausted within 15 years from the date on which operation of the pipeline commenced;

(*c*) the generating or distributing equipment and plant (including structures) of a producer or distributor of electrical energy, except a property included in Class 10, 13, 14, 26 or 28;

(*d*) manufacturing and distributing equipment and plant (including structures) acquired primarily for the production or distribution of gas, except

(i) a property included in Class 10, 13 or 14,

(ii) a property acquired for the purpose of producing or distributing gas that is normally distributed in portable containers,

(iii) a property acquired for the purpose of processing natural gas, before delivery of such a gas to a distribution system, or

(iv) a property acquired for the purpose of producing oxygen or nitrogen;

(*e*) the distributing equipment and plant (including structures) of a distributor of water, except a property included in Class 10, 13 or 14; or

(*f*) the production and distributing equipment and plant (including structures) of a distributor of heat, except a property included in Class 10, 13 or 14;

acquired by the taxpayer

(*g*) before 1988, or

(*h*) before 1990

(i) pursuant to an obligation in writing entered into by the taxpayer before June 18, 1987,

(ii) that was under construction by or on behalf of the taxpayer on June 18, 1987, or

(iii) that is machinery or equipment that is a fixed and integral part of a building, structure, plant facility or other property that was under construction by or on behalf of the taxpayer on June 18, 1987.

Class 3. (5 per cent)

Property not included in any other class that is

(*a*) a building or other structure, or part thereof, including component parts such as electric wiring, plumbing, sprinkler systems, air-conditioning equipment, heating equipment, lighting fixtures, elevators and escalators, acquired by the taxpayer

(i) before 1988, or

(ii) before 1990

(A) pursuant to an obligation in writing entered into by the taxpayer before June 18, 1987,

(B) that was under construction by or on behalf of the taxpayer on June 18, 1987, or

(C) that is a component part of a building that was under construction by or on behalf of the taxpayer on June 18, 1987;

(*b*) a breakwater;

(*c*) a dock;

(*d*) a trestle;

(*e*) a windmill;

(*f*) a wharf;

(*g*) an addition or alteration, made during the period that is after March 31, 1967 and before 1988, to a building that would have been included in this class during that period but for the fact that it was included in Class 20;

(*h*) a jetty acquired after May 25, 1976;

(*i*) a mole acquired after May 25, 1976;

(*j*) telephone, telegraph or data communication equipment, acquired after May 25, 1976, that is a wire or cable;

(*k*) an addition or alteration, other than an addition or alteration described in paragraph (*k*) of Class 6, made after 1987, to a building included, in whole or in part,

(i) in this class,

(ii) in Class 6 by virtue of subparagraph (*a*)(viii) thereof, or

(iii) in Class 20,

to the extent that the aggregate cost of all such additions or alterations to the building does not exceed that lesser of

(iv) $500,000, and

(v) 25 per cent of the aggregate of the amounts that would, but for this paragraph, be the capital cost of the building and any additions or alterations thereto included in this class or Class 6 or 20; or

(*l*) ancillary to a wire or cable referred to in paragraph (*j*) or Class 42 and that is supporting equipment such as a pole, mast, tower, conduit, brace, crossarm, guy or insulator.

Interpretation Bulletins: *Primary* — IT-79R3 Capital cost allowance — Buildings or other structures.

Class 4. (6 per cent)

Property that would otherwise be included in another class in this Schedule that is

(*a*) a railway system or a part thereof, except automotive equipment not designed to run on rails or tracks, that was acquired after the end of the taxpayer's 1958 taxation year and before May 26, 1976; or

(*b*) a tramway or trolley bus system or a part thereof, except property included in Class 10, 13 or 14.

Class 5. (10 per cent)

Property that is

(*a*) a chemical pulp mill or ground wood pulp mill, including buildings, machinery and equipment, but not including hydro-electric power plants and their equipment, or

(*b*) an integrated mill producing chemical pulp or ground wood pulp and manufacturing therefrom paper, paper board or pulp board, including buildings, machinery and equipment, but not including hydro-electric power plants and their equipment,

but not including any property that was acquired after the end of the taxpayer's 1962 taxation year.

Class 6. (10 per cent)

Property not included in any other class that is

(*a*) a building of

(i) frame,

(ii) log,

(iii) stucco on frame,

(iv) galvanized iron, or

(v) corrugated metal

construction, including component parts such as electric wiring, plumbing, sprinkler systems, air-conditioning equipment, heating equipment, lighting fixtures, elevators and escalators, if the building

(vi) is used by the taxpayer for the purpose of gaining or producing income from farming or fishing,

(vii) has no footings or any other base support below ground level,

(viii) was acquired by the taxpayer before 1979 and is not a building described in subparagraph (vi) or (vii),

(ix) was acquired by the taxpayer after 1978 under circumstances such that

(A) he was obligated to acquire the building under the terms of an agreement in writing entered into before 1979, and

(B) the installation of footings or any other base support of the building was commenced before 1979, or

(x) was acquired by the taxpayer after 1978 under circumstances such that

Regulations

(A) he commenced construction of the building before 1979, or

(B) the construction of the building was commenced under the terms of an agreement in writing entered into by him before 1979, and

the installation of footings or any other base support of the building was commenced before 1979;

(*b*) a wooden breakwater;

(*c*) a fence;

(*d*) a greenhouse;

(*e*) an oil or water storage tank;

(*f*) a railway tank car acquired before May 26, 1976;

(*g*) a wooden wharf;

(*h*) an aeroplane hangar acquired after the end of the taxpayer's 1958 taxation year;

(*i*) an addition or alteration, made

(A) during the period that is after March 31, 1967 and before 1979, or

(B) after 1978 if the taxpayer was obligated to have it made under the terms of an agreement in writing entered into before 1979,

to a building that would have been included in this class during that period but for the fact that it was included in Class 20;

(*j*) a railway locomotive that is acquired after May 25, 1976 and before February 26, 2008 and that is not an automotive railway car;

(*k*) an addition or alteration, made after 1978 to a building included in this class by virtue of subparagraph (*a*)(viii), to the extent that the aggregate cost of all such additions and alterations to the building does not exceed $100,000.

History: Paragraph (*j*) of Class 6 was replaced by P.C. 2009-660, SOR/2009-126, dated April 30, 2009, applicable in respect of property acquired after February 25, 2008. Paragraph (*j*) of Class 6 formerly read:

(*j*) a railway locomotive acquired after May 25, 1976, but not including an automotive railway car; or

Interpretation Bulletins: *Primary* — IT-79R3 Capital cost allowance — Buildings or other structures. *Secondary* — IT-195R4 Rental property — Capital cost allowance restrictions; IT-476R Capital cost allowance — Equipment used in petroleum and natural gas activities.

Class 7. (15 per cent)

Property that is

(*a*) a canoe or rowboat;

(*b*) a scow;

(*c*) a vessel, but not including a vessel

(i) of a separate class prescribed by subsection 1101(2a), or

(ii) included in Class 41;

(*d*) furniture, fittings or equipment attached to a property included in this class, but not including radiocommunication equipment;

(*e*) a spare engine for a property included in this class;

(*f*) a marine railway;

(*g*) a vessel under construction, other than a vessel included in Class 41;

(*h*) subject to an election made under subsection 1103(2i), property acquired after February 27, 2000 that is

(i) a rail suspension device designed to carry trailers that are designed to be hauled on both highways and railway tracks, or

(ii) a railway car;

(*i*) property that is acquired after February 27, 2000 (other than property included in paragraph (*y*) of Class 10), that is a railway locomotive and that is not an automotive railway car;

(*j*) pumping or compression equipment, including equipment ancillary to pumping and compression equipment, acquired after February 22, 2005 if the equipment pumps or compresses petroleum, natural gas or a related hydrocarbon for the purpose of moving it

(i) through a transmission pipeline,

(ii) from a transmission pipeline to a storage facility, or

(iii) to a transmission pipeline from a storage facility, or

(*k*) pumping or compression equipment that is acquired after February 25, 2008, including equipment ancillary to pumping and compression equipment, that is on a pipeline and that pumps or compresses carbon dioxide for the purpose of moving it through the pipeline.

History: Class 7, paragraph (*i*) was replaced by P.C. 2009-660, SOR/2009-126, dated April 30, 2009, applicable in respect of property acquired after February 25, 2008. Class 7, paragraph (*i*) formerly read:

(*i*) property acquired after February 27, 2000 that is a railway locomotive, but not including an automotive railway car; or

Class 7, paragraph (*k*) was added by P.C. 2009-660, SOR/2009-126, dated April 30, 2009, applicable in respect of property acquired after February 25, 2008.

Interpretation Bulletins: *Secondary* — IT-267R2 Capital cost allowance — Vessels; Capital cost allowance — Equipment used in petroleum and natural gas activities.

Class 8. (20 per cent)

Property not included in Class 1, 2, 7, 9, 11, 17 or 30 that is

(*a*) a structure that is manufacturing or processing machinery or equipment;

(*b*) tangible property attached to a building and acquired solely for the purpose of

(i) servicing, supporting or providing access to or egress from, machinery or equipment,

(ii) manufacturing or processing, or

(iii) any combination of the functions described in subparagraphs (i) and (ii);

(*c*) a building that is a kiln, tank or vat, acquired for the purpose of manufacturing or processing;

(*d*) a building or other structure, acquired after February 19, 1973, that is designed for the purpose of preserving ensilage on a farm;

(*e*) a building or other structure, acquired after February 19, 1973, that is

(i) designed to store fresh fruits or fresh vegetables at a controlled level of temperature and humidity, and

(ii) to be used principally for the purpose of storing fresh fruits or fresh vegetables by or for the person or persons by whom they were grown;

(*f*) electrical generating equipment acquired after May 25, 1976, if

(i) the taxpayer is not a person whose business is the production for the use of or distribution to others of electrical energy,

(ii) the equipment is auxiliary to the taxpayer's main power supply, and

(iii) the equipment is not used regularly as a source of supply;

(*g*) electrical generating equipment, acquired after May 25, 1976, that has a maximum load capacity of not more than 15 kilowatts;

(*h*) portable electrical generating equipment acquired after May 25, 1976;

(*i*) a tangible capital property that is not included in another class in this Schedule except

(i) land or any part thereof or any interest therein,

(ii) an animal,

(iii) a tree, shrub, herb or similar growing thing,

(iv) an oil or gas well,

(v) a mine,

(vi) a specified temporary access road of the taxpayer,

(vii) radium,

(viii) a right of way,

(ix) a timber limit,

(x) a tramway track, or

(xi) property of a separate class prescribed by subsection 1101(2a);

(*j*) property not included in any other class that is radio-communication equipment acquired after May 25, 1976;

(*k*) a rapid transit car that is used for the purpose of public transportation within a metropolitan area and is not part of a railway system;

(*l*) an outdoor advertising poster panel or bulletin board; or

(*m*) a greenhouse constructed of a rigid frame and a replaceable, flexible plastic cover.

Editorial Note: For data network infrastructure equipment acquired after March 22, 2004, see Class 46 (30%).

Interpretation Bulletins: *Primary* — IT-79R3 Capital cost allowance — Buildings or other structures; IT-482R Pipelines. *Secondary* — IT-472 Capital cost allowance — Class 8 property; IT-476R Capital cost allowance — Equipment used in petroleum and natural gas activities.

Class 9. (25 per cent)

Property acquired before May 26, 1976, other than property included in Class 30, that is

(*a*) electrical generating equipment, if

(i) the taxpayer is not a person whose business is the production for the use of or distribution to others of electrical energy,

(ii) the equipment is auxiliary to the taxpayer's main power supply, and

(iii) the equipment is not used regularly as a source of supply,

(*b*) radar equipment,

(*c*) radio transmission equipment,

(*d*) radio receiving equipment,

(*e*) electrical generating equipment that has a maximum load capacity of not more than 15 kilowatts, or

(*f*) portable electrical generating equipment,

and property acquired after May 25, 1976 that is

(*g*) an aircraft;

(*h*) furniture, fittings or equipment attached to an aircraft; or

(*i*) a spare part for an aircraft, or for furniture, fittings or equipment attached to an aircraft.

Tax Window Files: , CRA Document No. 2016-0633111E5.

Class 10. (30 per cent)

Property not included in any other class that is

(*a*) automotive equipment, including a trolley bus, but not including

(i) an automotive railway car acquired after May 25, 1976,

(ii) a railway locomotive, or

(iii) a tramcar,

(*b*) a portable tool acquired after May 25, 1976 for the purpose of earning rental income for short terms, such as hourly, daily, weekly or monthly, except a property described in Class 12,

(*c*) harness or stable equipment,

(*d*) a sleigh or wagon,

(*e*) a trailer, including a trailer designed to be hauled on both highways and railway tracks,

(*f*) general-purpose electronic data processing equipment and systems software for that equipment, including ancillary data processing equipment, acquired after May 25, 1976 and before March 23, 2004 (or after March 22, 2004 and before 2005 if an election in respect of the property is made under subsection 1101(5q)), but not including property that is principally or is used principally as

(i) electronic process control or monitor equipment,

(ii) electronic communications control equipment,

(iii) systems software for a property referred to in subparagraph (i) or (ii), or

(iv) data handling equipment unless it is ancillary to general-purpose electronic data processing equipment,

(*f*.1) a designated underground storage cost, or

(*f*.2) an unmanned telecommunication spacecraft designed to orbit above the earth,

Regulations

and property (other than property included in Class 41, 41.1 or 41.2 or property included in Class 43 that is described in paragraph (*b*) of that Class) that would otherwise be included in another Class in this Schedule, that is

(*g*) a building or other structure (other than property described in paragraph (*l*) or (*m*)) that would otherwise be included in Class 1, 3 or 6 and that was acquired for the purpose of gaining or producing income from a mine, except

(i) a property included in Class 28,

(ii) a property acquired principally for the purpose of gaining or producing income from the processing of ore from a mineral resource that is not owned by the taxpayer,

(iii) an office building not situated on the mine property, or

(iv) a refinery that was acquired by the taxpayer

(A) before November 8, 1969, or

(B) after November 7, 1969 and that had been used before November 8, 1969 by any person with whom the taxpayer was not dealing at arm's length;

(v) (Revoked.)

(*h*) contractor's movable equipment, including portable camp buildings, acquired for use in a construction business or for lease to another taxpayer for use in that other taxpayer's construction business, except a property included in

(i) this Class by virtue of paragraph (*t*),

(ii) a separate class prescribed by subsection 1101(2b), or

(iii) Class 22 or 38;

(*i*) a floor of a roller skating rink;

(*j*) gas or oil well equipment;

(*k*) property (other than property included in Class 28 or property described in paragraph (*l*) or (*m*)) that was acquired for the purpose of gaining or producing income from a mine and that is

(i) a structure that would otherwise be included in Class 8, or

(ii) machinery or equipment,

except a property acquired before May 9, 1972 for the purpose of gaining or producing income from the processing of ore after extraction from a mineral resource that is not owned by the taxpayer;

(*l*) property acquired after the 1971 taxation year for the purpose of gaining or producing income from a mine and providing services to the mine or to a community where a substantial proportion of the persons who ordinarily work at the mine reside, if such property is

(i) an airport, dam, dock, fire hall, hospital, house, natural gas pipeline, power line, recreational facility, school, sewage disposal plant, sewer, street lighting system, town hall, water pipeline, water pumping station, water system, wharf or similar property,

(ii) a road, sidewalk, airplane runway, parking area, storage area or similar surface construction, or

(iii) machinery or equipment ancillary to any of the property described in subparagraph (i) or (ii),

but is not

(iv) a property included in Class 28, or

(v) a railway not situated on the mine property;

(*m*) property acquired after March 31, 1977, principally for the purpose of gaining or producing income from a mine, if such property is

(i) railway track and grading including components such as rails, ballast, ties and other track material,

(ii) property ancillary to the track referred to in subparagraph (i) that is

(A) railway traffic control or signalling equipment, including switching, block signalling, interlocking, crossing protection, detection, speed control or retarding equipment, or

(B) a bridge, culvert, subway, trestle or tunnel,

(iii) machinery or equipment ancillary to any of the property referred to in subparagraph (i) or (ii), or

(iv) conveying, loading, unloading or storing machinery or equipment, including a structure, acquired for the purpose of shipping output from the mine by means of the track referred to in subparagraph (i),

but is not

(v) property included in Class 28, or

(vi) for greater certainty, rolling stock,

(*n*) property that was acquired for the purpose of cutting and removing merchantable timber from a timber limit and that will be of no further use to the taxpayer after all merchantable timber that the taxpayer is entitled to cut and remove from the limit has been cut and removed, unless the taxpayer has elected to include another property of this kind in another class in this Schedule;

(*o*) mechanical equipment acquired for logging operations, except a property included in Class 7;

(*p*) an access road or trails for the protection of standing timber against fire, insects or disease;

(*q*) property acquired for a motion picture drive-in theatre;

(*r*) property included in this class by virtue of subsection 1102(8) or (9), except a property included in Class 28;

(*s*) a motion picture film or video tape acquired after May 25, 1976, except a property included in paragraph (*w*) or (*x*) or in Class 12;

(*t*) a property acquired after May 22, 1979 that is designed principally for the purpose of

(i) determining the existence, location, extent or quality of accumulations of petroleum or natural gas,

(ii) drilling oil or gas wells, or

(iii) determining the existence, location, extent or quality of mineral resources,

except a property included in a separate class prescribed by subsection 1101(2b);

(*u*) property acquired after 1980 to be used primarily in the processing in Canada of heavy crude oil recovered from a natural reservoir in Canada to a stage that is not beyond the crude oil stage or its equivalent that is

(i) property that would otherwise be included in Class 8 except railway rolling stock or a property described in paragraph (*j*) of Class 8,

(ii) an oil or water storage tank,

(iii) a powered industrial lift truck that would otherwise be included in paragraph (*a*), or

(iv) property that would otherwise be included in paragraph (*f*);

(*v*) property acquired after August 31, 1984 (other than property that is included in Class 30) that is equipment used for the purpose of effecting an interface between a cable distribution system and electronic products used by consumers of that system and that is designed primarily

(i) to augment the channel capacity of a television receiver or radio,

(ii) to decode pay television or other signals provided on a discretionary basis, or

(iii) to achieve any combination of functions described in subparagraphs (i) and (ii);

(*w*) a certified production acquired after 1987 and before March 1996;

(*x*) a Canadian film or video production; or

(*y*) a railway locomotive that is not an automotive railway car and that was not used or acquired for use for any purpose by any taxpayer before February 26, 2008.

History: Class 10, the portion after paragraph (*f.2*) and before paragraph (*g*) was replaced by S.C. 2013, c. 40, s. 116(1), applicable to property acquired after March 20, 2013, and formerly read:

> and property (other than property included in Class 41 or 41.1 or property included in Class 43 that is described in paragraph (*b*) of that Class) that would otherwise be included in another Class in this Schedule, that is

Class 10, the portion after paragraph (*f.2*) and before paragraph (*g*) was replaced by P.C. 2011-44, SOR/2011-9, dated February 4, 2011, published in the *Canada Gazette* February 16, 2011, applicable to property acquired after March 18, 2007. Class 10, the portion after paragraph (*f.2*) and before paragraph (*g*) formerly read:

> and property (other than property included in Class 41 or property included in Class 43 that is described in paragraph (*b*) of that Class) that would otherwise be included in another Class in this Schedule, that is

The portion of paragraph (*v*) of Class 10 before subparagraph (i) was replaced by S.C. 2010, c. 25, s. 88(1), applicable in respect of taxation years that end after March 4, 2010. The portion of paragraph (*v*) of Class 10 before subparagraph (i) formerly read:

> (*v*) property acquired after August 31, 1984 that is equipment used for the purpose of effecting an interface between a cable distribution system and electronic products used by consumers of that system and that is designed primarily

Class 10, paragraph (*y*) was added by P.C. 2009-660, SOR/2009-126, dated April 30, 2009, applicable in respect of property acquired after February 25, 2008.

Interpretation Bulletins: *Secondary* — IT-306R2 Capital cost allowance — Contractor's movable equipment; IT-501 Capital cost allowance — Logging assets.

Class 10.1. (30 per cent)

Property that would otherwise be included in Class 10 that is a passenger vehicle, the cost of which to the taxpayer exceeds $20,000 or such other amount as may be prescribed for the purposes of subsection 13(2) of the Act.

Class 11. (35 per cent)

Property not included in any other class that is used to earn rental income and that is

(*a*) an electrical advertising sign owned by the manufacturer thereof, acquired before May 26, 1976; or

(*b*) an outdoor advertising poster panel or bulletin board acquired by the taxpayer

(i) before 1988, or

(ii) before 1990

(A) pursuant to an obligation in writing entered into by the taxpayer before June 18, 1987, or

(B) that was under construction by or on behalf of the taxpayer on June 18, 1987.

Class 12. (100 per cent)

Property not included in any other class that is

(*a*) a book that is part of a lending library;

(*b*) chinaware, cutlery or other tableware;

(*c*) a kitchen utensil costing less than

(i) $100, if acquired before May 26, 1976,

(ii) $200, if acquired after May 25, 1976, and before May 2, 2006, or

(iii) $500, if acquired after May 1, 2006;

(*d*) a die, jig, pattern, mould or last;

(*e*) a medical or dental instrument costing less than

(i) $100, if acquired before May 26, 1976,

(ii) $200, if acquired after May 25, 1976, and before May 2, 2006, or

(iii) $500, if acquired after May 1, 2006;

(*f*) a mine shaft, main haulage way or similar underground work designed for continuing use, or any extension thereof, sunk or constructed after the mine came into production, to the extent that the property was acquired before 1988;

(*g*) linen;

(*h*) a tool (other than an electronic communication device or electronic data processing equipment that is acquired after May 1, 2006 and that can be used for a purpose other than any of measuring, locating and calculating) costing less than

(i) $100, if acquired before May 26, 1976,

(ii) $200, if acquired after May 25, 1976, and before May 2, 2006, or

(iii) $500, if acquired after May 1, 2006;

(*i*) a uniform;

(*j*) the cutting or shaping part in a machine;

(*k*) apparel or costume, including accessories used therewith, used for the purpose of earning rental income;

(*l*) a video tape acquired before May 26, 1976;

(*m*) a motion picture film or video tape that is a television commercial message;

(*n*) a certified feature film or certified production;

(*o*) computer software acquired after May 25, 1976, but not including systems software and property that is described in paragraph (*s*);

(*p*) a metric scale or a scale designed for ready conversion to metric weighing, acquired after March 31, 1977 and before 1984 for use in a retail business and having a maximum weighing capacity of 100 kilograms;

(*q*) a designated overburden removal cost; or

(*r*) a video-cassette, a video-laser disk or a digital video disk, that is acquired for the purpose of renting and that is not expected to be rented to any one person for more than 7 days in any 30-day period;

and property that would otherwise be included in another class in this Schedule that is

(*s*) acquired by the taxpayer after August 8, 1989 and before 1993, for use in a business of selling goods or providing services to consumers that is carried on in Canada, or for lease to another taxpayer for use by that other taxpayer in such a business, and that is

(i) electronic bar code scanning equipment designed to read bar codes applied to goods held for sale in the ordinary course of the business,

(ii) a cash register or similar sales recording device designed with the capability of calculating and recording sales tax imposed by more than one jurisdiction in respect of the same sale,

(iii) equipment or computer software that is designed to convert a cash register or similar sales recording device to one having the capability of calculating and recording sales tax imposed by more than one jurisdiction in respect of the same sale, or

(iv) electronic equipment or computer software that is ancillary to property described in subparagraph (i), (ii) or (iii) and all or substantially all the use of which is in conjunction with that property.

History: Subparagraph (*c*)(ii) of Class 12 was replaced, and subparagraph (iii) was added by P.C. 2011-935, SOR/2011-187, dated September 22, 2011, published in the *Canada Gazette* October 12, 2011, deemed to have come into force on May 2, 2006. Subparagraph (*c*)(ii) of Class 12 formerly read:

(ii) $200, if acquired after May 25, 1976;

Subparagraph (*e*)(ii) of Class 12 was replaced, and subparagraph (iii) was added by P.C. 2011-935, SOR/2011-187, dated September 22, 2011, published in the *Canada Gazette* October 12, 2011, deemed to have come into force on May 2, 2006. Subparagraph (*e*)(ii) of Class 12 formerly read:

(ii) $200, if acquired after May 25, 1976;

Paragraph (*h*) of Class 12 was replaced by P.C. 2011-935, SOR/2011-187, dated September 22, 2011, published in the *Canada Gazette* October 12, 2011, deemed to have come into force on May 2, 2006. Paragraph (*h*) of Class 12 formerly read:

(*h*) a tool costing less than

(i) $100, if acquired before May 26, 1976, or

(ii) $200, if acquired after May 25, 1976;

Paragraph (*o*) of Class 12 of Schedule II was replaced by P.C. 2010-548, SOR/2010-93, dated April 29, 2010, in force May 12, 2010, date of publication in the *Canada Gazette*. Paragraph (*o*) of Class 12 of Schedule II formerly read:

(*o*) computer software acquired after May 25, 1976, but not including systems software or property acquired after August 8, 1989 and before 1993 that is described in paragraph (*s*);

Interpretation Bulletins: *Secondary* — IT-422 Definition of tools.

Class 13. Property that is a leasehold interest and property acquired by a taxpayer that would, if that property had been acquired by a person with whom the taxpayer was not dealing at arm's length at the time the property was acquired by the taxpayer, be a leasehold interest of that person, except

(*a*) an interest in minerals, petroleum, natural gas, other related hydrocarbons or timber and property relating thereto or in respect of a right to explore for, drill for, take or remove minerals, petroleum, natural gas, other related hydrocarbons or timber;

(*b*) that part of the leasehold interest that is included in another class in this Schedule by reason of subsection 1102(5) or (5.1); or

(*c*) a property included in Class 23.

Interpretation Bulletins: *Secondary* — IT-195R4 Rental property — Capital cost allowance restrictions.

Class 14. Property that is a patent, franchise, concession or licence for a limited period in respect of property, except

(*a*) a franchise, concession or licence in respect of minerals, petroleum, natural gas, other related hydrocarbons or timber and property relating thereto (except a franchise for distributing gas to consumers or a licence to export gas from Canada or from a province) or in respect of a right to explore for, drill for, take or remove minerals, petroleum, natural gas, other related hydrocarbons or timber;

(*b*) a leasehold interest;

(*c*) a property included in Class 23;

(*d*) a licence to use computer software; or

(*e*) a property that is included in Class 44.

Tax Profile: July 2012 — Intangibles.

Interpretation Bulletins: *Secondary* — IT-143R3 Meaning of eligible capital expenditure; IT-477 (Consolid.) Capital cost allowance — Patents, franchises, concessions and licences.

Class 14.1. (5 per cent)

Property of a taxpayer that, in respect of a business of the taxpayer,

(*a*) is goodwill;

(*b*) was eligible capital property of the taxpayer immediately before January 1, 2017 and is owned by the taxpayer at the beginning of that day; or

(*c*) is acquired after 2016, other than

(i) property that is tangible or, for civil law, corporeal property,

(ii) property that is not acquired for the purpose of gaining or producing income from business,

(iii) property in respect of which any amount is deductible (otherwise than as a result of being included in this class) in computing the taxpayer's income from the business,

(iv) property in respect of which any amount is not deductible in computing the taxpayer's income from the business because of any provision of the Act (other than paragraph 18(1)(*b*)) or these Regulations,

(v) an interest in a trust,

(vi) an interest in a partnership,

(vii) a share, bond, debenture, mortgage, hypothecary claim, note, bill or other similar property, or

(viii) property that is an interest in, or for civil law a right in, or a right to acquire, a property described in any of subparagraphs (i) to (vii).

History: Class 14.1 in Schedule II was added by S.C. 2016, c. 12, s. 84(1), in force January 1, 2017.

Class 15. Property that would otherwise be included in another class in this Schedule and that

(*a*) was acquired for the purpose of cutting and removing merchantable timber from a timber limit, and

(*b*) will be of no further use to the taxpayer after all merchantable timber that the taxpayer is entitled to cut and remove from the limit has been cut and removed,

except

(*c*) property that the taxpayer has, in the taxation year or a preceding taxation year, elected not to include in this class, or

(*d*) a timber resource property.

Interpretation Bulletins: *Secondary* — IT-501 Capital cost allowance — Logging assets.

Class 16. (40 per cent)

Property acquired before May 26, 1976 that is

(*a*) an aircraft,

(*b*) furniture, fittings or equipment attached to an aircraft, or

(*c*) a spare part for a property included in this class,

property acquired after May 25, 1976 that is

(*d*) a taxicab,

property acquired after November 12, 1981 that is

(*e*) a motor vehicle that

(i) would be an automobile as that term is defined in subsection 248(1) of the Act, if that definition were read without reference to paragraph (*d*) thereof,

(ii) was acquired for the purpose of renting or leasing, and

(iii) is not expected to be rented or leased to any person for more than 30 days in any 12 month period,

property acquired after February 15, 1984 that is

(*f*) a coin-operated video game or pinball machine,

and property acquired after December 6, 1991 that is

(*g*) a truck or tractor designed for hauling freight, and that is primarily so used by the taxpayer or a person with whom the taxpayer does not deal at arm's length in a business that includes hauling freight, and that has a "gross vehicle weight rating" (as that term is defined in subsection 2(1) of the Motor Vehicle Safety Regulations) in excess of 11,788 kg.

Class 17. (8 per cent)

Property that would otherwise be included in another class in this Schedule that is

(*a*) a telephone system, telegraph system, or a part thereof, acquired before May 26, 1976, except

(i) radiocommunication equipment, or

(ii) a property included in Class 10, 13, 14 or 28, or

(*a*.1) property (other than a building or other structure) acquired after February 27, 2000 that has not been used for any purpose before February 28, 2000 and is

(i) electrical generating equipment (other than electrical generating equipment described in Class 43.1, 43.2 or 48 or in Class 8 because of paragraph (*f*), (*g*) or (*h*) of that Class), or

(ii) production and distribution equipment of a distributor of water or steam (other than such property described in Class 43.1 or 43.2) used for heating or cooling (including, for this purpose, pipe used to collect or distribute an energy transfer medium but not including equipment or pipe used to distribute water that is for consumption, disposal or treatment),

and property not included in any other class, acquired after May 25, 1976, that is

(*b*) telephone, telegraph or data communication switching equipment, except

(i) equipment installed on customers' premises, or

(ii) property that is principally electronic equipment or systems software therefor; or

(*c*) a road (other than a specified temporary access road of the taxpayer), sidewalk, airplane runway, parking area, storage area or similar surface construction.

Interpretation Bulletins: *Primary* — IT-482R Pipelines. *Secondary* — IT-476R Capital cost allowance — Equipment used in petroleum and natural gas activities.

Class 18. (60 per cent)

Property that is a motion picture film acquired before May 26, 1976, except

(*a*) a television commercial message; or

(*b*) a certified feature film.

Class 19. Property acquired by the taxpayer after June 13, 1963 and before January 1, 1967 that would otherwise be included in Class 8 if,

(*a*) in the taxation year in which the property was acquired,

(i) the taxpayer was an individual who was resident in Canada for not less than 183 days, or

(ii) the taxpayer was a corporation that had a degree of Canadian ownership;

(*b*) the property was acquired for use in Canada in a business carried on by the taxpayer that,

(i) for the fiscal period in which the property was acquired, or

(ii) for the fiscal period in which the business first commenced selling goods in reasonable commercial quantities,

whichever was later, was a business in which the aggregate of

(iii) its net sales, as they would be determined under paragraphs 71A(2)(*d*) and (*f*) of the former Act (within the meaning assigned by paragraph 8(*b*) of the *Income Tax Application Rules, 1971*), from the sale of goods processed or manufactured in Canada by the business,

(iv) an amount equal to that part of its gross revenue that is rent from goods processed or manufactured in Canada in the course of the business, and

(v) its gross revenue from advertisements in a newspaper or magazine produced by the business,

was not less than 2/3 of the amount by which the gross revenue from the business for the period exceeded the aggregate of each amount paid or credited in the period to a customer of the business as a bonus, rebate or discount or for returned or damaged goods, and was not a business that was principally

(vi) operating a gas or oil well,

(vii) logging,

(viii) mining,

(ix) construction, or

(x) a combination of two or more of the activities referred to in subparagraphs (vi) to (ix); and

(*c*) the property had not been used for any purpose whatever before it was acquired by the taxpayer.

Class 20. Property that would otherwise be included in Class 3 or 6

(*a*) that was acquired after December 5, 1963 and before April 1, 1967 that is

(i) a building,

(ii) an extension to a building, outside the previously existing walls or roof of the building, if the aggregate cost of the extensions added in the aforementioned period exceeded the lesser of

(A) $100,000, and

(B) 25 per cent of the capital cost to the taxpayer of the building on December 5, 1963, or

(iii) an addition or alteration to a property described in subparagraph (i) or (ii),

and that has been certified by the Minister of Industry, upon application by the taxpayer in such form as may be prescribed by the Minister of Industry,

(iv) to be situated in an area that was a designated area, as determined for the purposes of section 71A of the former Act (within the meaning assigned by paragraph 8(*b*) of the *Income Tax Application Rules, 1971*),

(A) at the time the property was acquired,

(B) in a case where the property was built by the taxpayer, at the time construction was commenced, or

(C) in a case where the property was built for the taxpayer pursuant to a contract entered into by the taxpayer, at the time the contract was entered into, and

(v) to have not been used for any purpose whatever before it was acquired by the taxpayer; or

(*b*) the capital cost of which was included in the approved capital costs as defined in the *Area Development Incentives Act* upon which approved capital cost the Minister of Industry has based the amount of a development grant authorized under that Act.

Class 21. Property that would otherwise be included in Class 8 or Class 19

(*a*) that was acquired after December 5, 1963 and before April 1, 1967 and that

(i) was acquired for use in a business carried on by the taxpayer that has been certified by the Minister of Industry, for the purposes of section 71A of the former Act (within the meaning assigned by paragraph 8(*b*) of the *Income Tax Application Rules, 1971*), to be a new manufacturing or processing business in a designated area for the fiscal period in which the property was acquired or for a subsequent fiscal period, and

(ii) had not been used for any purpose whatever before it was acquired by the taxpayer; or

(*b*) the capital cost of which was included in the approved capital costs as defined in the *Area Development Incentives Act* upon which approved capital cost the Minister of Industry has based the amount of a development grant authorized under that Act.

Class 22. (50 per cent)

Property acquired by the taxpayer after March 16, 1964 and

(*a*) before 1988, or

(*b*) before 1990

(i) pursuant to an obligation in writing entered into by the taxpayer before June 18, 1987, or

(ii) that was under construction by or on behalf of the taxpayer on June 18, 1987

that is power-operated movable equipment designed for the purpose of excavating, moving, placing or compacting earth, rock, concrete or asphalt, except a property included in Class 7.

Interpretation Bulletins: *Secondary* — IT-411R Meaning of "construction"; IT-469R Capital cost allowance — Earth-moving equipment.

Class 23. (100 per cent)

Property that is

(*a*) a leasehold interest or a concession in respect of land granted under or pursuant to an agreement in writing with the Canadian Corporation for the 1967 World Exhibition where such leasehold interest or concession is to expire not later than June 15, 1968;

(*b*) a building or other structure, including component parts, erected on land that is the subject matter of a leasehold interest or concession described in paragraph (*a*) where such building or other structure, including component parts, is of a temporary nature and is required by the agreement to be removed not later than June 15, 1968;

(*c*) a leasehold interest or licence in respect of land granted under or pursuant to an agreement in writing with the Expo 86 Corporation where such leasehold interest or licence is to expire not later than January 31, 1987; or

(*d*) a building or other structure, including component parts, erected on land that is the subject matter of a leasehold interest or licence described in paragraph (*c*) where such building or other structure, including component parts, is of a temporary nature and is required by the agreement to be removed not later than January 31, 1987.

Class 24. Property acquired after April 26, 1965 and before 1971

(*a*) that would otherwise be included in Class 2, 3, 6 or 8 and that

(i) was acquired primarily for the purpose of preventing, reducing or eliminating pollution of

(A) any of the inland, coastal or boundary waters of Canada, or

(B) any lake, river, stream, watercourse, pond, swamp or well in Canada,

by industrial waste, refuse or sewage created by operations in the course of carrying on a business by the taxpayer or that would be created by such operations if the property had not been acquired and used, and

(ii) had not been used for any purpose whatever before it was acquired by the taxpayer,

but not including property acquired for use in the production of by-products or the recovery of materials unless the by-products are produced from, or the materials are recovered from, materials that after April 26, 1965,

(iii) were being discarded as waste by the taxpayer, or

(iv) were commonly being discarded as waste by other taxpayers who carried on operations of a type similar to the operations carried on by the taxpayer,

and property acquired before 1999

(*b*) that would otherwise be included in another class in this Schedule

(i) that has not been included by the taxpayer in any other class,

(ii) that had not been used for any purpose whatever before it was acquired by the taxpayer,

(iii) that was acquired by the taxpayer after 1970 primarily for the purpose of preventing, reducing or eliminating pollution of

(A) any of the inland, coastal or boundary waters of Canada, or

(B) any lake, river, stream, watercourse, pond, swamp or well in Canada,

that is caused, or that, if the property had not been acquired and used, would be caused by

(C) operations carried on by the taxpayer at a site in Canada at which operations have been carried on by him from a time that is before 1974,

(D) the operation in Canada of a building or plant by the taxpayer, the construction of which was either commenced before 1974 or commenced under an agreement in writing entered into by him before 1974, or

(E) the operation of transportation or other movable equipment that has been operated by the taxpayer in Canada (including any of the inland, coastal or boundary waters of Canada) from a time that is before 1974,

or that was acquired by him after May 8, 1972, that would otherwise have been property referred to in this subparagraph except that

(F) it was acquired

(I) for the purpose of gaining or producing income from a business by a taxpayer whose business includes the preventing, reducing or eliminating of pollution of a kind referred to in this subparagraph that is caused or that otherwise would be caused primarily by operations referred to in clause (C), (D) or (E) carried on by other taxpayers (not including persons referred to in section 149 of the Act), and

(II) to be used in a business referred to in subclause (I) in the preventing, reducing or eliminating of pollution of a kind referred to in this subparagraph, or

(G) it was acquired

(I) for the purpose of gaining or producing income from a property by a corporation whose principal business is the purchasing of conditional sales contracts, accounts receivable, bills of sale, chattel mortgages, bills of exchange or other obligations representing part or all of the sale price of merchandise or services, the lending of money, or the leasing of property, or any combination thereof, and

(II) to be leased to a taxpayer (other than a person referred to in section 149 of the Act) to be used by him, in an operation referred to in clause (C), (D), (E) or (F), in the preventing, reducing or eliminating of pollution of a kind referred to in this subparagraph, and

(iv) that has, upon application by the taxpayer to the Minister of the Environment, been accepted by that Minister as property the primary use of which is to be the preventing, reducing or eliminating of pollution of a kind referred to in subparagraph (iii)

and for the purposes of paragraphs (*a*) and (*b*)

(*c*) where a corporation (in this paragraph referred to as the "predecessor corporation") has, as a result of an amalgamation within the meaning assigned by subsection 87(1) of the Act, merged at any time after 1973 with one or more other corporations to form one corporate entity (in this paragraph referred to as the "new corporation"), the new corporation

Regulations

shall be deemed to be the same corporation as, and a continuation of, the predecessor corporation;

(*d*) where a corporation (in this paragraph referred to as the "subsidiary") has been wound up at any time after 1973 in circumstances to which subsection 88(1) of the Act applies, the parent (within the meaning assigned by that subsection) shall be deemed to be the same corporation as, and a continuation of, the subsidiary; and

(*e*) this class shall be read without reference to subparagraph (*b*)(i) where paragraph (*c*) or (*d*) applies to the taxpayer and the property was acquired before 1992.

Class 25. (100 per cent)

Property that would otherwise be included in another class in this Schedule that is property acquired by the taxpayer

(*a*) before October 23, 1968, or

(*b*) after October 22, 1968 and before 1974, where the acquisition of the property may reasonably be regarded as having been in fulfilment of an obligation undertaken in an agreement made in writing before October 23, 1968 and ratified, confirmed or adopted by the legislature of a province by a statute that came into force before that date,

if the taxpayer was, on October 22, 1968, a corporation, commission or association to which, on the assumption that October 22, 1968 was in its 1969 taxation year, paragraph 62(1)(*c*) of the former Act (within the meaning assigned by paragraph 8(*b*) of the *Income Tax Application Rules, 1971*),

(*c*) would not apply; and

(*d*) would have applied but for subparagraph (i) or (ii) of that paragraph.

Class 26. (5 per cent)

Property that is

(*a*) a catalyst; or

(*b*) deuterium enriched water (commonly known as "heavy water") acquired after May 22, 1979.

Class 27. Property acquired before 1999 that would otherwise be included in another Class in this Schedule

(*a*) that has not been included by the taxpayer in any other class;

(*b*) that had not been used for any purpose whatever before it was acquired by the taxpayer;

(*c*) that was acquired by the taxpayer after March 12, 1970 primarily for the purpose of preventing, reducing or eliminating air pollution by

(i) removing particulate, toxic or injurious materials from smoke or gas, or

(ii) preventing the discharge of part or all of the smoke, gas or other air pollutant,

that is discharged or that, if the property had not been acquired and used, would be discharged into the atmosphere as a result of

(iii) operations carried on by the taxpayer at a site in Canada at which operations have been carried on by him from a time that is before 1974,

(iv) the operation in Canada of a building or plant by the taxpayer, the construction of which was either commenced before 1974 or commenced under an agreement in writing entered into by him before 1974, or

(v) the operation of transportation or other movable equipment that has been operated by the taxpayer in Canada (including any of the inland, coastal or boundary waters of Canada) from a time that is before 1974,

or that was acquired by him after May 8, 1972, that would otherwise have been property referred to in this paragraph except that

(vi) it was acquired

(A) for the purpose of gaining or producing income from a business by a taxpayer whose business includes the preventing, reducing or eliminating of air pollution that is caused or that otherwise would be caused primarily by operations referred to in subparagraph (iii), (iv) or (v) carried on by other taxpayers (not including persons referred to in section 149 of the Act), and

(B) to be used in a business referred to in clause (A) in the preventing, reducing or eliminating of air pollution in a manner referred to in this paragraph, or

(vii) it was acquired

(A) for the purpose of gaining or producing income from a property by a corporation whose principal business is the purchasing of conditional sales contracts, accounts receivable, bills of sale, chattel mortgages, bills of exchange or other obligations representing part or all of the sale price of merchandise or services, the lending of money, or the leasing of property, or any combination thereof, and

(B) to be leased to a taxpayer (other than a person referred to in section 149 of the Act) to be used by him, in an operation referred to in subparagraph (iii), (iv), (v) or (vi), in the preventing, reducing or eliminating of air pollution in a manner referred to in this paragraph; and

(*d*) that has, upon application by the taxpayer to the Minister of the Environment, been accepted by that Minister as property the primary use of which is to be the preventing, reducing or eliminating of air pollution in a manner referred to in paragraph (*c*);

and for the purposes of paragraphs (*a*) to (*d*),

(*e*) where a corporation (in this paragraph referred to as the "predecessor corporation") has, as a result of an amalgamation within the meaning assigned by subsection 87(1) of the Act, merged at any time after 1973 with one or more other corporations to form one corporate entity (in this paragraph referred to as the "new corporation"), the new corporation shall be deemed to be the same corporation as, and a continuation of, the predecessor corporation;

(*f*) where a corporation (in this paragraph referred to as the "subsidiary") has been wound up at any time after 1973 in circumstances to which subsection 88(1) of the Act applies, the parent (within the meaning assigned by that subsection) shall be deemed to be the same corporation as, and a continuation of, the subsidiary; and

(*g*) this class shall be read without reference to paragraph (*a*) where paragraph (*e*) or (*f*) applies to the taxpayer and the property was acquired before 1992.

Class 28. (30 per cent)

Property situated in Canada that would otherwise be included in another class in this Schedule that

(*a*) was acquired by the taxpayer

(i) before 1988, or

(ii) before 1990

(A) pursuant to an obligation in writing entered into by the taxpayer before June 18, 1987,

(B) that was under construction by or on behalf of the taxpayer on June 18, 1987, or

(C) that is machinery or equipment that is a fixed and integral part of a building, structure, plant facility or other property that was under construction by or on behalf of the taxpayer on June 18, 1987,

and that

(*b*) was acquired by the taxpayer principally for the purpose of gaining or producing income from one or more mines operated by the taxpayer and situated in Canada and each of which

(i) came into production in reasonable commercial quantities after November 7, 1969, or

(ii) was the subject of a major expansion after November 7, 1969

(A) whereby the greatest designed capacity, measured in weight of input of ore, of the mill that processed the ore from the mine was not less than 25% greater in the year following the expansion than it was in the year preceding the expansion, or

(B) where in the one year period preceding the expansion

(I) the Minister, in consultation with the Minister of Natural Resources, determines that the greatest designed capacity of the mine, measured in weight of output of ore, immediately after the expansion was not less than 25% greater than the greatest designed capacity of the mine immediately before the expansion, and

(II) either

1. no mill processed the ore from the mine at any time, or

2. the mill that processed the ore from the mine processed other ore,

(*c*) was acquired by the taxpayer

(i) after November 7, 1969,

(ii) before the coming into production of the mine or the completion of the expansion of the mine referred to in subparagraph (*b*)(i) or (ii), as the case may be, and

(iii) in the case of a mine that was the subject of a major expansion described in subparagraph (*b*)(ii), in the course of and principally for the purposes of the expansion,

(*d*) had not, before it was acquired by the taxpayer, been used for any purpose whatever by any person with whom the taxpayer was not dealing at arm's length, and

(*e*) is any of the following, namely,

(i) property that was acquired before the mine came into production and that would, but for this class, be included in Class 10 by virtue of paragraph (*g*), (*k*), (*l*) or (*r*) of that class or would have been so included in that class if it had been acquired after the 1971 taxation year,

(ii) property that was acquired before the mine came into production and that would, but for this class, be included in Class 10 by virtue of paragraph (*m*) of that class, or

(iii) property that was acquired after the mine came into production and that would, but for this class, be included in Class 10 by virtue of paragraph (*g*), (*k*), (*l*) or (*r*) of that class,

or that would be described in paragraphs (*b*) to (*e*) if in those paragraphs each reference to a "mine" were read as a reference to a "mine that is a location in a bituminous sands deposit, oil sands deposit or oil shale deposit from which material is extracted", and each reference to "after November 7, 1969" were read as "before November 8, 1969".

Class 29. Property (other than property included in Class 41 solely because of paragraph (*c*) or (*d*) of that Class or property included in Class 47 because of paragraph (*b*) of that Class) that would otherwise be included in another class in this Schedule

(*a*) that is property manufactured by the taxpayer, the manufacture of which was completed by him after May 8, 1972, or other property acquired by the taxpayer after May 8, 1972,

(i) to be used directly or indirectly by him in Canada primarily in the manufacturing or processing of goods for sale or lease, or

(ii) to be leased, in the ordinary course of carrying on a business in Canada of the taxpayer, to a lessee who can reasonably be expected to use, directly or indirectly, the property in Canada primarily in Canadian field processing carried on by the lessee or in the manufacturing or processing by the lessee of goods for sale or lease, if the taxpayer is a corporation whose principal business is

(A) leasing property,

(B) manufacturing property that it sells or leases,

(C) the lending of money,

(D) the purchasing of conditional sales contracts, accounts receivable, bills of sale, chattel mortgages, bills of exchange or other obligations representing part or all of the sale price of merchandise or services, or

(E) selling or servicing a type of property that it also leases,

or any combination thereof, unless use of the property by the lessee commenced before May 9, 1972;

(*b*) that is

(i) property that, but for this class, would be included in Class 8, except railway rolling stock or a property described in paragraph (*j*) of Class 8,

(ii) an oil or water storage tank,

(iii) a powered industrial lift truck,

(iv) electrical generating equipment described in Class 9,

(v) property that is described in paragraph (*b*) or (*f*) of Class 10, or

(vi) property that would be described in paragraph (*f*) of Class 10 if the portion of that paragraph before subparagraph (i) read as follows:

"(*f*) general-purpose electronic data processing equipment and systems software for that equipment, including ancillary data processing equipment, acquired after March 18, 2007 and before January 28, 2009, but not including property that is principally or is used principally as"; and

(*c*) that is property acquired by the taxpayer

(i) before 1988,

(ii) before 1990

(A) pursuant to an obligation in writing entered into by the taxpayer before June 18, 1987,

(B) that was under construction by or on behalf of the taxpayer on June 18, 1987, or

(C) that is machinery or equipment that is a fixed and integral part of a building, structure, plant facility or other property that was under construction by or on behalf of the taxpayer on June 18, 1987, or

(iii) after March 18, 2007 and before 2016 if the property is machinery, or equipment,

(A) that would be described in paragraph (*a*) if subparagraph (*a*)(ii) were read without reference to "in Canadian field processing carried on by the lessee or", or

(B) that is described in any of subparagraphs (*b*)(i) to (iii) and (vi).

History: Class 29, the portion of subparagraph (*c*)(iii) before clause (A) was replaced by S.C. 2013, c. 33, s. 40(1), deemed to have come into force on March 21, 2013, and formerly read:

(iii) after March 18, 2007 and before 2014 if the property is machinery, or equipment,

Class 29, the portion of subparagraph (*c*)(iii) before clause (A) was replaced by S.C. 2011, c. 24, s. 100(1) applicable after 2011. Class 29, the portion of subparagraph (*c*)(iii) before clause (A) formerly read:

(iii) after March 18, 2007 and before 2012 if the property is machinery, or equipment,

Class 29, subparagraph (*b*)(v) was replaced, and subparagraph (vi) was added by P.C. 2009-660, SOR/2009-126, dated April 30, 2009, applicable in respect of property acquired after March 18, 2007. Class 29, subparagraph (v) formerly read:

(v) property described in paragraph (*b*) or (*f*) of Class 10; and

Class 29, the portion of subparagraph (*c*)(iii) before clause (A) was replaced by P.C. 2009-660, SOR/2009-126, dated April 30, 2009, applicable in respect of property acquired after February 25, 2008. Class 29, the portion of subparagraph (*c*)(iii) before clause (A) formerly read:

(iii) after March 18, 2007 and before 2009 if the property is machinery, or equipment,

Class 29, clause (*c*)(iii)(B) was replaced by P.C. 2009-660, SOR/2009-126, dated April 30, 2009, applicable in respect of property acquired after March 18, 2007. Class 29, clause (*c*)(iii)(B) formerly read:

(B) that is described in any of subparagraphs (*b*)(i) to (iii).

The portion of Class 29 before paragraph (*a*) was replaced by P.C. 2009-581, SOR/2009-115, dated April 23, 2009, applicable to property acquired on or after March 19, 2007. The portion of Class 29 before paragraph (*a*) formerly read:

Property not included in Class 41 because of paragraph (*c*) or (*d*) of that Class that would otherwise be included in another class in this Schedule

Subparagraph (*c*)(iii) of Class 29 was added by P.C. 2009-581, SOR/2009-115, dated April 23, 2009, deemed to have come into force on March 19, 2007.

Income Tax Folios: S4-F15-C1 Manufacturing and Processing.

Interpretation Bulletins: *Secondary* — IT-411R Meaning of "construction".

Class 30. (40 per cent)

Property of a taxpayer that is

(*a*) an unmanned telecommunication spacecraft that was designed to orbit above the earth and that was acquired by the taxpayer

(i) before 1988, or

(ii) before 1990

(A) pursuant to an obligation in writing entered into by the taxpayer before June 18, 1987, or

(B) that was under construction by or on behalf of the taxpayer on June 18, 1987; or

(*b*) equipment used for the purpose of effecting an interface between a cable or satellite distribution system (other than a satellite radio distribution system) and electronic products used by consumers of that system if the equipment

(i) is designed primarily

(A) to augment the channel capacity of a television receiver, or

(B) to decode pay television or other signals provided on a discretionary basis,

(ii) is acquired by the taxpayer after March 4, 2010, and

(iii) has not been used or acquired for use for any purpose by any taxpayer before March 5, 2010.

History: Class 30 was replaced by S.C. 2010, c. 25, s. 89(1), applicable in respect of taxation years that end after March 4, 2010. Class 30 formerly read:

Class 30 *(40 per cent).* Property that is an unmanned telecommunication spacecraft designed to orbit above the earth and acquired by the taxpayer

(*a*) before 1988, or

(b) before 1990

(i) pursuant to an obligation in writing entered into by the taxpayer before June 18, 1987, or

(ii) that was under construction by or on behalf of the taxpayer on June 18, 1987.

Class 31. (5 per cent)

Property that is a multiple-unit residential building in Canada that would otherwise be included in Class 3 or Class 6 and in respect of which

(a) a certificate has been issued by Canada Mortgage and Housing Corporation certifying

(i) in respect of a building that would otherwise be included in Class 3, that the installation of footings or any other base support of the building was commenced

(A) after November 18, 1974 and before 1980, or

(B) after October 28, 1980 and before 1982,

as the case may be, and

(ii) in respect of a building that would otherwise be included in Class 6, that the installation of footings or any other base support of the building was commenced after December 31, 1977 and before 1979,

and that, according to plans and specifications for the building, not less than 80 per cent of the floor space will be used in providing self-contained domestic establishments and related parking, recreation, service and storage areas;

(b) not more than 20 per cent of the floor space is used for any purpose other than the purposes referred to in paragraph (a);

(c) the certificate referred to in paragraph (a) was issued on or before the later of

(i) December 31, 1981, and

(ii) the day that is 18 months after the day on which the installation of footings or other base support of the building was commenced; and

(d) the construction of the building proceeds, after 1982, without undue delay, taking into consideration acts of God, labour disputes, fire, accidents or unusual delay by common carriers or suppliers of materials or equipment;

and that was acquired by the taxpayer

(e) before June 18, 1987, or

(f) after June 17, 1987 pursuant to

(i) an obligation in writing entered into by the taxpayer before June 18, 1987, or

(ii) the terms of a prospectus, preliminary prospectus, registration statement, offering memorandum or notice required to be filed with a public authority in Canada and filed before June 18, 1987 with that public authority.

Interpretation Bulletins: *Secondary* — IT-195R4 Rental property — Capital cost allowance restrictions.

Class 32. (10 per cent)

Property that is a multiple-unit residential building in Canada that would otherwise be included in Class 6 if the reference to "1979" in subparagraph (a)(viii) of that Class were read as a reference to "1980", and in respect of which

(a) a certificate has been issued by Central Mortgage and Housing Corporation certifying

(i) that the installation of footings or any other base support of the building was commenced after November 18, 1974 and before 1978, and

(ii) that, according to plans and specifications for the building, not less than 80 per cent of the floor space will be used in providing self-contained domestic establishments and related parking, recreation, service and storage areas; and

(b) not more than 20 per cent of the floor space is used for any purpose other than the purposes referred to in subparagraph (a)(ii).

Interpretation Bulletins: *Secondary* — IT-195R4 Rental property — Capital cost allowance restrictions.

Class 33. (15 per cent)

Property that is a timber resource property.

Interpretation Bulletins: *Secondary* — IT-481 (Consolid.) Timber resource property and timber limits.

Class 34. Property that would otherwise be included in Class 1, 2 or 8

(a) that is

(i) electrical generating equipment,

(ii) production equipment and pipelines of a distributor of heat,

(iii) steam generating equipment that was acquired by the taxpayer primarily for the purpose of producing steam to operate property described in subparagraph (i), or

(iv) an addition to a property described in subparagraph (i), (ii) or (iii),

but not including buildings or other structures,

(b) that was acquired by the taxpayer after May 25, 1976,

(c) that

(i) was acquired by the taxpayer for use by him in a business carried on in Canada, or

(ii) is to be leased by the taxpayer to a lessee for use by the lessee in Canada, and

(d) that is property in respect of which a certificate has been issued

(i) before December 11, 1979 by the Minister of Industry, Trade and Commerce certifying that the property is part of a plan designed to

(A) produce heat derived primarily from the consumption of wood wastes or municipal wastes,

(B) produce electrical energy by the utilization of fuel that is petroleum, natural gas or related hydrocarbons, coal, coal gas, coke, lignite or peat (in this clause referred to as "fossil fuel"), wood wastes or municipal wastes, or any combination thereof, if the consumption of fossil fuel (expressed as the high heat value of the fossil fuel), if any, chargeable to electrical energy on an annual basis in respect of the property is no greater than 7,000 British Thermal Units per kilowatt-hour of electrical energy produced, or

Regulations

(C) recover heat that is a by-product of an industrial process, or

(ii) after December 10, 1979, by the Minister of Energy, Mines and Resources certifying that the property is part of a plan designed to

(A) produce heat derived primarily from the consumption of natural gas, coal, coal gas, lignite, peat, wood wastes or municipal wastes, or any combination thereof,

(B) produce electrical energy by the utilization of fuel that is petroleum, natural gas or related hydrocarbons, coal, coal gas, coke, lignite or peat (in this clause referred to as "fossil fuel"), wood wastes or municipal wastes, or any combination thereof, if the consumption of fossil fuel (expressed as the high heat value of the fossil fuel), if any, chargeable to electrical energy on an annual basis in respect of the property is no greater than 7,000 British Thermal Units per kilowatt-hour of electrical energy produced, or

(C) recover heat that is a by-product of an industrial process,

and property that was acquired by the taxpayer after December 10, 1979 (other than property described in paragraph (*a*)) and would otherwise be included in another Class in this Schedule

(*e*) that is

(i) active solar heating equipment including solar collectors, solar energy conversion equipment, storage equipment, control equipment, equipment designed to interface solar heating equipment with other heating equipment, and solar water heaters, used to

(A) heat a liquid or air to be used directly in the course of manufacturing or processing,

(B) provide space heating when installed in a new building or other new structure at the time of its original construction where that construction commenced after December 10, 1979, or

(C) heat water for a use other than a use described in clause (A) or (B),

(ii) a hydro electric installation of a producer of hydro electric energy with a planned maximum generating capacity not exceeding 15 megawatts upon completion of site development that is the generating equipment and plant (including structures) of that producer including a canal, a dam, a dyke, an overflow spillway, a penstock, a powerhouse complete with generating equipment and other equipment ancillary thereto, control equipment, fishways or fish bypasses and transmission equipment, except distribution equipment and a property included in Class 10 or 17,

(iii) heat recovery equipment that is designed to conserve energy or reduce the requirement to acquire energy by extracting and reusing heat from thermal waste including condensers, heat exchange equipment, steam compressors used to upgrade low pressure steam, waste heat boilers and ancillary equipment such as control panels, fans, instruments or pumps,

(iv) an addition or alteration to a hydro electric installation described in subparagraph (ii) that results in a change in generating capacity if the new maximum generating capacity at the hydro electric installation does not exceed 15 megawatts, or

(v) a fixed location device acquired after February 25, 1986, that is a wind energy conversion system designed to produce electrical energy, consisting of a wind-driven turbine, generating equipment and related equipment, including control and conditioning equipment, support structures, a powerhouse complete with equipment ancillary thereto, and transmission equipment, but not including distribution equipment, equipment designed to store electrical energy or property included in Class 10 or 17,

(*f*) that

(i) was acquired by the taxpayer for use by him for the purpose of gaining or producing income from a business carried on in Canada or from property situated in Canada, or

(ii) is to be leased by the taxpayer to a lessee for use by the lessee in Canada, and

(*g*) that is property in respect of which a certificate has been issued by the Minister of Energy, Mines and Resources,

but not including

(*h*) property in respect of which a certificate issued under paragraph (*d*) or (*g*) has been revoked pursuant to subsection 1104(11),

(*i*) property that had been used before it was acquired by the taxpayer unless the property had previously been included in Class 34 for the purpose of computing the income of the person from whom it was acquired.

(*j*) property acquired by the taxpayer after February 21, 1994 other than

(i) property acquired by the taxpayer

(A) pursuant to an agreement of purchase and sale in writing entered into by the taxpayer before February 22, 1994,

(B) in order to satisfy a legally binding obligation entered into by the taxpayer in writing before February 22, 1994 to sell electricity to a public power utility in Canada,

(C) that was under construction by or on behalf of the taxpayer on February 22, 1994, or

(D) that is machinery or equipment that is a fixed and integral part of a building, structure or other property that was under construction by or on behalf of the taxpayer on February 22, 1994, and

(ii) property acquired by the taxpayer before 1996

(A) pursuant to an agreement of purchase and sale in writing entered into before 1995 to acquire the property from a person or partnership in circumstances where

(I) the property was part of a project that was under construction by the person or partnership on February 22, 1994, and

(II) it is reasonable to conclude, having regard to all of the circumstances, that the person or partnership constructed the project with the intention of transferring all or part of the project to another taxpayer after completion, or

(B) pursuant to an agreement in writing entered into before 1995 by the taxpayer with a person or partnership where the taxpayer agrees to assume a legally binding obligation entered into by the person or partnership before February 22, 1994 to sell electricity to a public power utility in Canada, or

(*k*) property in respect of which a certificate has not been issued under paragraph (*d*) or (*g*) before the time that is the later of

(i) the end of 1995, and

(ii) 2 years after the property is acquired by the taxpayer or, where the property is property acquired in circumstances to which paragraph (*j*) applies, 2 years after substantial completion of the property.

Class 35. (7 per cent)

Property not included in any other class that is

(*a*) a railway car acquired after May 25, 1976; or

(*b*) a rail suspension device designed to carry trailers that are designed to be hauled on both highways and railway tracks.

Class 36. Property acquired after December 11, 1979 that is deemed to be depreciable property by virtue of paragraph 13(5.2)(*c*) of the Act.

Class 37. (15 per cent)

Property that would otherwise be included in another class in this Schedule that is property used in connection with an amusement park, including

(*a*) land improvements (other than landscaping) for or in support of park activities, including

(i) roads, sidewalks, parking areas, storage areas, or similar surface constructions, and

(ii) canals,

(*b*) buildings (other than warehouses, administration buildings, hotels or motels), structures and equipment (other than automotive equipment), including

(i) rides, attractions and appurtenances associated with a ride or attraction, ticket booths and facades,

(ii) equipment, furniture and fixtures, in or attached to a building included in this class,

(iii) bridges, and

(iv) fences or similar perimeter structures, and

(*c*) automotive equipment (other than automotive equipment designed for use on highways or streets),

and property not included in another class in this Schedule that is a waterway or a land improvement (other than landscaping, clearing or levelling land) used in connection with an amusement park.

Class 38. Property not included in Class 22 but that would otherwise be included in that class if that class were read without reference to paragraphs (*a*) and (*b*) thereof.

Interpretation Bulletins: *Secondary* — IT-411R Meaning of "construction"; IT-469R Capital cost allowance — Earth-moving equipment.

Class 39. Property acquired after 1987 and before February 26, 1992 that is not included in Class 29, but that would otherwise be included in that Class if that Class were read without reference to subparagraphs (*b*)(iii) and (v) and paragraph (*c*) thereof.

Interpretation Bulletins: *Secondary* — IT-411R Meaning of "construction".

Class 40. Property acquired after 1987 and before 1990 that is a powered industrial lift truck or property described in paragraph (*b*) or (*f*) of Class 10 and that is property not included in Class 29 but that would otherwise be included in that class if that class were read without reference to paragraph (*c*) thereof.

Class 41. (25 per cent)

Property (other than property included in Class 41.1 or 41.2)

(*a*) not included in Class 28 that would otherwise be included in that Class if that Class were read without reference to paragraph (*a*) of that Class and if subparagraphs (e)(i) to (iii) of that Class were read as follows:

"(i) property that was acquired before the mine came into production and that would, but for this Class, be included in Class 10 because of paragraph (*g*), (*k*), (*l*) or (*r*) of that Class or would have been so included in that Class if it had been acquired after the 1971 taxation year, and property that would, but for this Class, be included in Class 41 because of subsection 1102(8) or (9),

(ii) property that was acquired before the mine came into production and that would, but for this Class, be included in Class 10 because of paragraph (*m*) of that Class, or

(iii) property that was acquired after the mine came into production and that would, but for this Class, be included in Class 10 because of paragraph (*g*), (*k*), (*l*) or (*r*) of that Class, and property that would, but for this Class, be included in Class 41 because of subsection 1102(8) or (9);"

(*a*.1) that is the portion, expressed as a percentage determined by reference to capital cost, of property that

(i) would, but for this Class, be included in Class 10 because of paragraph (*g*), (*k*) or (*l*) of that Class, or

Regulations

that is included in this Class because of subsection 1102(8) or (9),

(ii) is not described in paragraph (*a*) or (*a*.2),

(iii) was acquired by the taxpayer principally for the purpose of gaining or producing income from one or more mines that are operated by the taxpayer and situated in Canada, and that became available for use for the purpose of subsection 13(26) of the Act in a taxation year, and

(iv) had not, before it was acquired by the taxpayer, been used for any purpose by any person or partnership with whom the taxpayer was not dealing at arm's length,

where that percentage is determined by the formula

100 × (([A - (B × 365 / C)]) / A)

where

A is the total of all amounts each of which is the capital cost of a property of the taxpayer that became available for use for the purpose of subsection 13(26) of the Act in the year and that is described in subparagraphs (i) to (iv) in respect of the mine or mines, as the case may be,

B is 5% of the taxpayer's gross revenue from the mine or mines, as the case may be, for the year, and

C is the number of days in the year;

(*a*.2) that

(i) is property that would, but for this Class, be included in Class 10 because of paragraph (*g*), (*k*) or (*l*) of that Class or that is included in his Class because of subsection 1102(8) or (9),

(ii) was acquired by the taxpayer in a taxation year principally for the purpose of gaining or producing income from one or more mines each of which

(A) is one or more wells operated by the taxpayer for the extraction of material from a deposit of bituminous sands or oil shales, operated by the taxpayer and situated in Canada.

(B) was the subject of a major expansion after March 6, 1996, and

(C) is a mine in respect of which the Minister, in consultation with the Minister of Natural Resources, determines that the greatest designed capacity of the mine, measured in volume of oil that is not beyond the crude oil stage or its equivalent, immediately after the expansion was not less than 25% greater than the greatest designed capacity of the mine immediately before the expansion,

(iii) was acquired by the taxpayer

(A) after March 6, 1996,

(B) before the completion of the expansion, and

(C) in the course of and principally for the purposes of the expansion, and

(iv) had not, before it was acquired by the taxpayer, been used for any purpose by any person or partnership with whom the taxpayer was not dealing at arm's length;

(*a*.3) that is property included in this Class because of subsection 1102(8) or (9), other than property described in paragraph (*a*) or (*a*.2) or the portion of property described in paragraph (*a*.1);

(*b*) that is property, other than property described in subsection 1101(2c),

(i) described in paragraph (*f*.1), (*g*), (*j*), (*k*), (*l*), (*m*), (*r*), (*t*) or (*u*) of Class 10 that would be included in that Class if this Schedule were read without reference to this paragraph; or

(ii) that is a vessel, including the furniture, fittings, radio communication equipment and other equipment attached thereto, that is designed principally for the purpose of

(A) determining the existence, location, extent or quality of accumulations of petroleum, natural gas or mineral resources, or

(B) drilling oil or gas wells,

and that was acquired by the taxpayer after 1987 other than property that was acquired before 1990

(iii) pursuant to an obligation in writing entered into by the taxpayer before June 18, 1987,

(iv) that was under construction by or on behalf of the taxpayer on June 18, 1987, or

(v) that is machinery and equipment that is a fixed and integral part of property that was under construction by or on behalf of the taxpayer on June 18, 1987.

(*c*) acquired by the taxpayer after May 8, 1972, to be used directly or indirectly by the taxpayer in Canada primarily in Canadian field processing, where the property would be included in Class 29 if

(i) Class 29 were read without reference to

(A) the words "property included in Class 41 solely because of paragraph (*c*) or (*d*) of that Class or",

(B) its subparagraphs (*b*)(iii) and (v), and

(C) its paragraph (*c*),

(ii) subsection 1104(9) were read without reference to paragraph (*k*) of that subsection, and

(iii) this Schedule were read without reference to this Class, Class 39 and Class 43; or

(*d*) acquired by the taxpayer after December 5, 1996 (otherwise than pursuant to an agreement in writing made before December 6, 1996) to be leased, in the ordinary course of carrying on a business in Canada of the taxpayer, to a lessee who can reasonably be expected to use, directly or indirectly, the property in Canada primarily in Canadian field processing carried on by the lessee, where the property would be included in Class 29 if

(i) Class 29 were read without reference to

(A) the words "property included in Class 41 solely because of paragraph (*c*) or (*d*) of that Class or",

(B) its subparagraphs (*b*)(iii) and (v), and

(C) its paragraph (*c*), and

(ii) this Schedule were read without reference to this Class, Class 39 and Class 43.

History: Class 41, the portion before paragraph (*a*) was replaced by S.C. 2013, c. 40, s. 117(1), applicable to property acquired after March 20, 2013, and formerly read:

Class 41 *(25 per cent).* Property (other than property included in Class 41.1)

The portion of Class 41 before paragraph (*a*) was replaced by P.C. 2011-44, SOR/2011-9, dated February 4, 2011, published in the *Canada Gazette* February 16, 2011, applicable to property acquired after March 18, 2007. The portion of Class 41 before paragraph (*a*) formerly read:

Class 41 *(25 per cent).* Property

Subparagraph (*c*)(i) of Class 41 was replaced by P.C. 2009-581, SOR/2009-115, dated April 23, 2009, applicable to property acquired on or after March 19, 2007. Subparagraph (*c*)(i) of Class 41 formerly read:

(i) Class 29 were read without reference to subparagraphs (*b*)(iii) and (v) and paragraph (*c*) of that Class,

Subparagraph (*d*)(i) of Class 41 was replaced by P.C. 2009-581, SOR/2009-115, dated April 23, 2009, applicable to property acquired on or after March 19, 2007. Subparagraph (*d*)(i) of Class 41 formerly read:

(i) Class 29 were read without reference to subparagraphs (*b*)(iii) and (v) and paragraph (*c*) of that Class, and

Interpretation Bulletins: *Primary* — IT-482R Pipelines. *Secondary* — IT-267R2 Capital cost allowance — Vessels; IT-476R Capital cost allowance — Equipment used in petroleum and natural gas activities.

Class 41.1. (25 per cent)

Oil sands property (other than specified oil sands property) that

(*a*) is acquired by a taxpayer after March 18, 2007 and before 2016 and that if acquired before March 19, 2007, would be included in paragraphs (*a*), (*a.1*) or (*a.2*) of Class 41, or

(*b*) is acquired by a taxpayer after 2015 and that if acquired before March 19, 2007 would be included in Class 41.

History: Class 41.1 was added by P.C. 2011-44, SOR/2011-9, dated February 4, 2011, published in the *Canada Gazette* February 16, 2011, applicable to property acquired after March 18, 2007.

Class 41.2. (25 per cent)

Property, other than an oil sands property or eligible mine development property,

(*a*) that is acquired by a taxpayer after March 20, 2013 and before 2021 and that, if acquired on March 20, 2013, would be included in paragraph (*a*) or (*a.1*) of Class 41; or

(*b*) that is acquired by a taxpayer after 2020 and that, if acquired on March 20, 2013, would be would be included in paragraph (*a*) or (*a.1*) of Class 41.

History: Class 41.2 was added by S.C. 2013, c. 40, s. 118(1), deemed to have come into force on March 21, 2013.

Class 42. (12 per cent)

Property that is

(*a*) fibre-optic cable; or

(*b*) telephone, telegraph or data communication equipment that is a wire or cable (other than a cable included in this class because of paragraph (*a*)), acquired after February 22, 2005, and that has not been used, or acquired for use, for any purpose before February 23, 2005.

Class 43. (30 per cent)

Property acquired after February 25, 1992 that

(*a*) is not included in Class 29 or 53, but that would otherwise be included in Class 29 if that Class were read without reference to its subparagraphs (*b*)(iii) and (v) and paragraph (*c*); or

History: Paragraph (*a*) of Class 43 of Schedule II was replaced by S.C. 2015, c. 36, s. 25, in force on Royal Assent, June 23, 2015, and formerly read:

(*a*) is not included in Class 29, but that would otherwise be included in that Class if that Class were read without reference to subparagraphs (*b*)(iii) and (v) and paragraph (*c*) thereof; or

(*b*) is property

(i) that is described in paragraph (*k*) of Class 10 and that would be included in that Class if this Schedule were read without reference to this paragraph and paragraph (*b*) of Class 41, and

(ii) that, at the time of its acquisition, can reasonably be expected to be used entirely in Canada and primarily for the purpose of processing ore extracted from a mineral resource located in a country other than Canada.

Income Tax Folios: S4-F15-C1 Manufacturing and Processing.

Interpretation Bulletins: *Primary* — IT-482R Pipelines. *Secondary* — IT-476R Capital cost allowance — Equipment used in petroleum and natural gas activities.

Class 43.1. (30 per cent)

Property, other than reconditioned or remanufactured equipment, that would otherwise be included in Class 1, 2, 8 or 48 or in Class 17 because of paragraph (*a*.1) of that Class

(*a*) that is

(i) electrical generating equipment, including any heat generating equipment used primarily for the purpose of producing heat energy to operate the electrical generating equipment,

(ii) equipment that generates both electrical and heat energy other than, for greater certainty, fuel cell equipment,

(ii.1) fixed location fuel cell equipment that uses hydrogen generated only from internal, or ancillary, fuel reformation equipment,

(iii) heat recovery equipment used primarily for the purpose of conserving energy, or reducing the requirement to acquire energy, by extracting for reuse thermal waste that is generated by equipment referred to in subparagraph (i) or (ii),

(iii.1) district energy equipment that is part of a district energy system that uses thermal energy that is primarily supplied by electrical cogeneration equipment that would be property described in paragraphs (*a*) to (*c*) if read without reference to this subparagraph,

(iv) control, feedwater and condensate systems and other equipment, if that property is ancillary to equipment described in any of subparagraphs (i) to (iii), or

(v) an addition to a property described in any of subparagraphs (i) to (iv),

other than buildings or other structures, heat rejection equipment (such as condensers and cooling water systems), transmission equipment, distribution equipment, fuel handling equipment that is not used

Regulations

to upgrade the combustible portion of the fuel and fuel storage facilities,

(*b*) that

(i) is situated in Canada,

(ii) is

(A) acquired by the taxpayer for use by the taxpayer for the purpose of gaining or producing income from a business carried on in Canada or from property situated in Canada, or

(B) leased by the taxpayer to a lessee for the use by the lessee for the purpose of gaining or producing income from a business carried on in Canada or from property situated in Canada, and

(iii) has not been used for any purpose before it was acquired by the taxpayer unless

(A) the property was depreciable property that

(I) was included in Class 34, 43.1 or 43.2 of the person from whom it was acquired, or

(II) would have been included in Class 34, 43.1 or 43.2 of the person from whom it was acquired had the person made a valid election to include the property in Class 43.1 or 43.2, as the case may be, under paragraph 1102(8)(*d*) or 1102(9)(*d*), and

(B) the property was acquired by the taxpayer not more than five years after the time it is considered to have become available for use, for the purpose of subsection 13(26) of the Act, by the person from whom it was acquired and remains at the same site in Canada as that at which that person used the property, and

(*c*) that is

(i) part of a system (other than an enhanced combined cycle system) that

(A) is used by the taxpayer, or by a lessee of the taxpayer, to generate electrical energy, or both electrical and heat energy, using only fuel that is eligible waste fuel, fossil fuel, producer gas, spent pulping liquor or any combination of those fuels, and

(B) has a heat rate attributable to fossil fuel (other than solution gas) not exceeding 6,000 BTU per kilowatt-hour of electrical energy generated by the system, which heat rate is calculated as the fossil fuel (expressed as the high heat value of the fossil fuel) used by the system that is chargeable to gross electrical energy output on an annual basis,

(ii) part of an enhanced combined cycle system that

(A) is used by the taxpayer, or by a lessee of the taxpayer, to generate electrical energy using only a combination of natural gas and thermal waste from one or more natural gas compressor systems located on a natural gas pipeline,

(B) has an incremental heat rate not exceeding 6,700 BTU per kilowatt-hour of electricity generated by the system, which heat rate is calculated as the natural gas (expressed as its high heat value) used by the system that is chargeable to gross electrical energy output on an annual basis, and

(C) does not have economically viable access to a steam host, or

(iii) equipment that is used by the taxpayer, or by a lessee of the taxpayer, to generate electrical energy in a process all or substantially all of the energy input of which is thermal waste, other than

(A) equipment that uses heat produced by a gas turbine that is part of the first stage of a combined cycle system, and

(B) equipment that, on the date of its acquisition, uses chlorofluorocarbons (CFCs) or hydrochlorofluorocarbons (HCFCs), within the meaning assigned by the *Ozone-Depleting Substances Regulations, 1998*,

and property, other than reconditioned or remanufactured equipment, that would otherwise be included in another Class in this Schedule

(*d*) that is

(i) property that meets the following conditions:

(A) it is used by the taxpayer, or by a lessee of the taxpayer, primarily for the purpose of heating an actively circulated liquid or gas and is

(I) active solar heating equipment, including such equipment that consists of above ground solar collectors, solar energy conversion equipment, solar water heaters, thermal energy storage equipment, control equipment and equipment designed to interface solar heating equipment with other heating equipment, or

(II) equipment that is part of a ground source heat pump system that transfers heat to or from the ground or groundwater (but not to or from surface water such as a river, a lake or an ocean) and that, at the time of installation, meets the standards set by the Canadian Standards Association for the design and installation of earth energy systems, including such equipment that consists of piping (including above or below ground piping and the cost of drilling a well, or trenching, for the purpose of installing that piping), energy conversion equipment, thermal energy storage equipment, control equipment and equipment designed to enable the system to interface with other heating or cooling equipment, and

(B) it is not a building, part of a building (other than a solar collector that is not a window and that is integrated into a building), equipment used to heat water for use in a swimming pool, energy equipment that backs up equipment described in subclause (A)(I) or (II) nor equipment that distributes heated or cooled air or water in a building,

(ii) a hydro-electric installation of a producer of hydro-electric energy, where that installation

(A) has, if acquired after February 21, 1994 and before December 11, 2001, an annual average generating capacity not exceeding 15 megawatts upon completion of the site development, or, if acquired after December 10, 2001, a rated capacity at the hydro-electric installation site that does not exceed 50 megawatts, and

(B) is the electrical generating equipment and plant (including structures) of that producer including a canal, a dam, a dyke, an overflow spillway, a penstock, a powerhouse (complete with electrical generating equipment and other ancillary equipment), control equipment, fishways or fish bypasses, and transmission equipment,

other than distribution equipment, property otherwise included in Class 10 and property that would be included in Class 17 if that Class were read without reference to its subparagraph (*a*.1)(i),

(iii) an addition or alteration, which is acquired after February 21, 1994 and before December 11, 2001, to a hydro-electric installation that is described in subparagraph (ii) or that would be so described if that installation were acquired by the taxpayer after February 21, 1994, and which results in an increase in generating capacity, if the resulting annual average generating capacity of the hydro-electric installation does not exceed 15 megawatts,

(iii.1) an addition or alteration, which is acquired after December 10, 2001, to a hydro-electric installation that is described in subparagraph (ii) or that would be so described if that installation were acquired by the taxpayer after February 21, 1994, and which results in an increase in generating capacity, if the resulting rated capacity at the hydro-electric installation site does not exceed 50 megawatts,

(iv) heat recovery equipment used by the taxpayer, or by a lessee of the taxpayer, primarily for the purpose of conserving energy, reducing the requirement to acquire energy or extracting heat for sale, by extracting for reuse thermal waste that is generated directly in an industrial process (other than an industrial process that generates or processes electrical energy), including such equipment that consists of heat exchange equipment, compressors used to upgrade low pressure steam, vapour or gas, waste heat boilers and other ancillary equipment such as control panels, fans, instruments or pumps, but not including property that is employed in reusing the recovered heat (such as property that is part of the internal heating or cooling system of a building or electrical generating equipment), is a building or is equipment that recovers heat primarily for use for heating water in a swimming pool,

(v) a fixed location device that is a wind energy conversion system that

(A) is used by the taxpayer, or by a lessee of the taxpayer, primarily for the purpose of generating electrical energy, and

(B) consists of wind-driven turbine, electrical generating equipment and related equipment, including

(I) control and conditioning equipment,

(II) support structures,

(III) powerhouse complete with other ancillary equipment, and

(IV) transmission equipment,

other than distribution equipment, auxiliary electrical generating equipment, property otherwise included in Class 10 and property that would be included in Class 17 if that Class were read without reference to its subparagraph (*a*.1)(i),

(vi) fixed location photovoltaic equipment that is used by the taxpayer, or a lessee of the taxpayer, primarily for the purpose of generating electrical energy from solar energy if the equipment consists of solar cells or modules and related equipment including inverters, control and conditioning equipment, support structures and transmission equipment, but not including

(A) a building or a part of a building (other than a solar cell or module that is integrated into a building),

(B) auxiliary electrical generating equipment, property otherwise included in Class 10 and property that would be included in Class 17 if that Class were read without reference to its subparagraph (*a*.1)(i), and

(C) distribution equipment,

(vii) equipment used by the taxpayer, or by a lessee of the taxpayer, primarily for the purpose of generating electrical energy or heat energy, or both electrical and heat energy, solely from geothermal energy, including such equipment that consists of piping (including above or below ground piping and the cost of completing a well (including the wellhead and production string), or trenching, for the purpose of installing that piping), pumps, heat exchangers, steam separators, electrical generating equipment and ancillary equipment used to collect the geothermal heat, but not including buildings, distribution equipment, equipment used to heat water for use in a swimming pool, equipment described in subclause (i)(A)(II), property otherwise included in Class 10 and property that would be included in Class 17 if that Class were read without reference to its paragraph (*a*.1),

(viii) equipment used by the taxpayer, or by a lessee of the taxpayer, primarily for the purpose of collecting landfill gas or digester gas, including such equipment that consists of piping (including

Regulations

above or below ground piping and the cost of drilling a well, or trenching, for the purpose of installing that piping), fans, compressors, storage tanks, heat exchangers and related equipment used to collect gas, to remove non-combustibles and contaminants from the gas or to store the gas, but not including property otherwise included in Class 10 or 17,

(ix) equipment used by the taxpayer, or by a lessee of the taxpayer, for the sole purpose of generating heat energy, primarily from the consumption of eligible waste fuel, producer gas or a combination of those fuels and not using any fuel other than eligible waste fuel, fossil fuel or producer gas, including such equipment that consists of fuel handling equipment used to upgrade the combustible portion of the fuel and control, feedwater and condensate systems, and other ancillary equipment, but not including equipment used for the purpose of producing heat energy to operate electrical generating equipment, buildings or other structures, heat rejection equipment (such as condensers and cooling water systems), fuel storage facilities, other fuel handling equipment and property otherwise included in Class 10 or 17,

(x) an expansion engine with one or more turbines, or cylinders, that convert the compression energy in pressurized natural gas into shaft power that generates electricity, including the related electrical generating equipment and ancillary controls, where the expansion engine

(A) is part of a system that is installed

(I) on a distribution line of a distributor of natural gas, or

(II) on a branch distribution line of a taxpayer primarily engaged in the manufacturing or processing of goods for sale or lease if the branch line is used to deliver natural gas directly to the taxpayer's manufacturing or processing facility, and

(B) is used instead of a pressure reducing valve,

(xi) equipment used by the taxpayer, or by a lessee of the taxpayer, in a system that converts wood waste or plant residue into bio-oil, if that bio-oil is used primarily for the purpose of generating heat that is used directly in an industrial process or a greenhouse, generating electricity or generating electricity and heat, other than equipment used for the collection, storage or transportation of wood waste or plant residue, buildings or other structures and property otherwise included in Class 10 or 17,

(xii) fixed location fuel cell equipment used by the taxpayer, or by a lessee of the taxpayer, that uses hydrogen generated only from ancillary electrolysis equipment (or, if the fuel cell is reversible, the fuel cell itself) using electricity all or substantially all of which is generated by using kinetic energy of flowing water or wave or tidal energy (otherwise than by diverting or impeding the natural flow of the water or by using physical barriers or dam-like structures) or by geothermal, photovoltaic, wind energy conversion, or hydro-electric equipment, of the taxpayer or the lessee, and equipment ancillary to the fuel cell equipment other than buildings or other structures, transmission equipment, distribution equipment, auxiliary electrical generating equipment and property otherwise included in Class 10 or 17,

(xiii) property that is part of a system that is used by the taxpayer, or by a lessee of the taxpayer, primarily to produce and store biogas, including equipment that is an anaerobic digester reactor, a buffer tank, a pre-treatment tank, biogas piping, a fan, a compressor, a heat exchanger, a biogas storage tank and equipment used to remove non-combustibles and contaminants from the gas, but not including

(A) property (other than a buffer tank) that is used to collect, move or store organic waste,

(B) equipment used to process the residue after digestion or to treat recovered liquids,

(C) buildings or other structures, and

(D) property otherwise included in Class 10 or 17,

(xiv) property that is used by the taxpayer, or by a lessee of the taxpayer, primarily for the purpose of generating electricity using kinetic energy of flowing water or wave or tidal energy (otherwise than by diverting or impeding the natural flow of the water or by using physical barriers or dam-like structures), including support structures, control and conditioning equipment, submerged cables and transmission equipment, but not including buildings, distribution equipment, auxiliary electricity generating equipment, property otherwise included in Class 10 and property that would be included in Class 17 if that class were read without reference to its subparagraph (*a*.1)(i),

(xv) district energy equipment that

(A) is used by the taxpayer or by a lessee of the taxpayer,

(B) is part of a district energy system that uses thermal energy that is primarily supplied by equipment that is described in subparagraphs (i), (iv), (vii) or (ix) or would be described in those subparagraphs if owned by the taxpayer, and

(C) is not a building,

(xvi) equipment used by the taxpayer, or by a lessee of the taxpayer, primarily for the purpose of generating producer gas (other than producer gas that is to be converted into liquid biofuels or chemicals), including related piping (including fans and compressors), air separation equipment, storage equipment, equipment used for drying or shredding eligible waste fuel, ash-handling equipment, equipment used to upgrade the producer gas into biomethane and equipment used to remove non-combustibles and contaminants from the producer gas, but not including buildings or other structures, heat rejection equipment (such as condensers and cooling water systems), equipment used to convert producer gas into liquid biofuels or chemicals and property otherwise included in Class 10 or 17,

(xvii) equipment used by the taxpayer, or by a lessee of the taxpayer, for the purpose of charging electric vehicles, including charging stations, transformers, distribution and control panels, circuit breakers, conduits and related wiring, if

(A) the equipment is situated

(I) on the load side of an electricity meter used for billing purposes by a power utility, or

(II) on the generator side of an electricity meter used to measure electricity generated by the taxpayer or the lessee, as the case may be,

(B) more than 75 per cent of the electrical equipment capacity is dedicated to charging electric vehicles, and

(C) the equipment is

(I) an electric vehicle charging station (other than a building) that supplies more than 10 kilowatts of continuous power, or

(II) used primarily in connection with one or more electric vehicle charging stations (other than buildings) each of which supplies more than 10 kilowatts of continuous power, or

(xviii) fixed location energy storage property that

(A) is used by the taxpayer, or by a lessee of the taxpayer, primarily for the purpose of storing electrical energy

(I) including batteries, compressed air energy storage, flywheels, ancillary equipment (including control and conditioning equipment) and related structures, and

(II) not including buildings, pumped hydroelectric storage, hydro electric dams and reservoirs, property used solely for backup electrical energy, batteries used in motor vehicles, fuel cell systems where the hydrogen is produced via steam reformation of methane and property otherwise included in Class 10 or 17, and

(B) either

(I) if the electrical energy to be stored is used in connection with property of the taxpayer or a lessee of the taxpayer, as the case may be, is described in paragraph (*c*) or would be described in this paragraph if it were read without reference to this subparagraph, or

(II) meets the condition that the efficiency of the electrical energy storage system that includes the property - computed by reference to the quantity of electrical energy supplied to and discharged from the electrical energy storage system - is greater than 50%, and

(*e*) that

(i) is situated in Canada,

(ii) is

(A) acquired by the taxpayer for use by the taxpayer for the purpose of gaining or producing income from a business carried on in Canada or from property situated in Canada, or

(B) leased by the taxpayer to a lessee for the use by the lessee for the purpose of gaining or producing income from a business carried on in Canada or from property situated in Canada, and

(iii) has not been used for any purpose before it was acquired by the taxpayer unless

(A) the property was depreciable property that

(I) was included in Class 34, 43.1 or 43.2 of the person from whom it was acquired, or

(II) would have been included in Class 34, 43.1 or 43.2 of the person from whom it was acquired had the person made a valid election to include the property in Class 43.1 or 43.2, as the case may be, under paragraph 1102(8)(*d*) or 1102(9)(*d*), and

(B) the property was acquired by the taxpayer not more than five years after the time it is considered to have become available for use, for the purpose of subsection 13(26) of the Act, by the person from whom it was acquired and remains at the same site in Canada as that at which that person used the property.

History: Class 43.1, subclauses (*d*)(i)(A)(I) and (II) were replaced by S.C. 2019, c. 29, s. 61(1), applicable to property acquired after March 21, 2016 that has not been used or acquired for use before March 22, 2016, and formerly read:

(I) active solar heating equipment, including such equipment that consists of above ground solar collectors, solar energy conversion equipment, solar water heaters, energy storage equipment, control equipment and equipment designed to interface solar heating equipment with other heating equipment, or

(II) equipment that is part of a ground source heat pump system that transfers heat to or from the ground or groundwater (but not to or from surface water such as a river, a lake or an ocean) and that, at the time of installation, meets the standards set by the Canadian Standards Association for the design and installation of earth energy systems, including such equipment that consists of piping (including above or below ground piping and the cost of drilling a well, or trenching, for the purpose of installing that piping), energy conversion equipment, energy storage equipment, control equipment and equipment designed to enable the system to interface with other heating or cooling equipment, and

Class 43.1, subclause (*d*)(v)(B)(I) was replaced by S.C. 2019, c. 29, s. 61(2), applicable to property acquired after March 21, 2016 that has not been used or acquired for use before March 22, 2016, and formerly read:

(I) control, conditioning and battery storage equipment,

Class 43.1, the portion of subparagraph (*d*)(vi) before clause (A) was replaced by S.C. 2019, c. 29, s. 61(3), applicable to property acquired after March 21, 2016 that has not been used or acquired for use before March 22, 2016, and formerly read:

(vi) fixed location photovoltaic equipment that is used by the taxpayer, or a lessee of the taxpayer, primarily for the purpose of generating electrical energy from solar energy if the equipment consists of solar cells or modules and related equipment including inverters, control, conditioning and battery storage equipment, support structures and transmission equipment, but not including

Class 43.1, subparagraph (*d*)(vii) was replaced by S.C. 2019, c. 29, s. 61(4), applicable to property acquired after March 21, 2016 that has not been used or acquired for use before March 22, 2016, and formerly read:

Regulations

(vii) equipment used by the taxpayer, or by a lessee of the taxpayer, primarily for the purpose of generating electrical energy or heat energy, or both electrical and heat energy, solely from geothermal energy, including such equipment that consists of piping (including above or below ground piping and the cost of completing a well (including the wellhead and production string), or trenching, for the purpose of installing that piping), pumps, heat exchangers, steam separators, electrical generating equipment and ancillary equipment used to collect the geothermal heat, but not including buildings, distribution equipment, equipment used to heat water for use in a swimming pool, equipment described in subclause (i)(A)(II), property otherwise included in Class 10 and property that would be included in Class 17 if that Class were read without reference to its paragraph (*a*.1),

Class 43.1, subparagraph (*d*)(vii) was replaced by S.C. 2019, c. 29, s. 61(5), applicable in respect of property acquired for use after March 21, 2017 that has not been used or acquired for use before March 22, 2017, and formerly read:

(vii) equipment used by the taxpayer, or by a lessee of the taxpayer, primarily for the purpose of generating electrical energy solely from geothermal energy, including such equipment that consists of piping (including above or below ground piping and the cost of drilling a well, or trenching, for the purpose of installing that piping), pumps, heat exchangers, steam separators, electrical generating equipment and ancillary equipment used to collect the geothermal heat, but not including buildings, transmission equipment, distribution equipment, property otherwise included in Class 10 and property that would be included in Class 17 if that Class were read without reference to its subparagraph (*a*.1)(i),

Class 43.1, subparagraph (*d*)(xii) was replaced by S.C. 2019, c. 29, s. 61(6), applicable to property acquired after March 21, 2016 that has not been used or acquired for use before March 22, 2016, and formerly read:

(xii) fixed location fuel cell equipment used by the taxpayer, or by a lessee of the taxpayer, that uses hydrogen generated only from ancillary electrolysis equipment (or, if the fuel cell is reversible, the fuel cell itself) using electricity all or substantially all of which is generated by photovoltaic, wind energy conversion or hydro-electric equipment, of the taxpayer or the lessee, and equipment ancillary to the fuel cell equipment other than buildings or other structures, transmission equipment, distribution equipment, auxiliary electrical generating equipment and property otherwise included in Class 10 or 17,

Class 43.1, subparagraph (*d*)(xiv) was replaced by S.C. 2019, c. 29, s. 61(7), applicable to property acquired after March 21, 2016 that has not been used or acquired for use before March 22, 2016, and formerly read:

(xiv) property that is used by the taxpayer, or by a lessee of the taxpayer, primarily for the purpose of generating electricity using kinetic energy of flowing water or wave or tidal energy (otherwise than by diverting or impeding the natural flow of the water or by using physical barriers or dam-like structures), including support structures, control, conditioning and battery storage equipment, submerged cables and transmission equipment, but not including buildings, distribution equipment, auxiliary electricity generating equipment, property otherwise included in Class 10 and property that would be included in Class 17 if that class were read without reference to its subparagraph (*a.1*)(i),

Class 43.1, subparagraph (*d*)(xvii) and (xviii) were addd by S.C. 2019, c. 29, s. 61(8), applicable to property acquired after March 21, 2016 that has not been used or acquired for use before March 22, 2016.

Class 43.1, subparagraph (*d*)(iv) was replaced by S.C. 2017, c. 33, s. 104(1), applicable to property acquired after March 3, 2010, and formerly read:

(iv) heat recovery equipment used by the taxpayer, or by a lessee of the taxpayer, primarily for the purpose of conserving energy, or reducing the requirement to acquire energy, by extracting for reuse thermal waste that is generated directly in an industrial process (other than an industrial process that generates or processes electrical energy), including such equipment that consists of heat exchange equipment, compressors used to upgrade low pressure steam, vapour or gas, waste heat boilers and other ancillary equipment such as control panels, fans, instruments or pumps, but not including property that is employed in re-using the recovered heat (such as property that is part of the internal heating or cooling system of a building or electrical generating equipment), is a building or is equipment that recovers heat primarily for use for heating water in a swimming pool.

Class 43.1, subparagraph (*d*)(vii) was replaced by S.C. 2017, c. 33, s. 104(2), applicable in respect of property acquired for use after March 21, 2017 that has not been used or acquired for use before March 22, 2017, and formerly read:

(vii) equipment used by the taxpayer, or by a lessee of the taxpayer, primarily for the purpose of generating electrical energy solely from geothermal energy, including such equipment that consists of piping (including above or below ground piping and the cost of drilling a well, or trenching, for the purpose of installing that piping), pumps, heat exchangers, steam separators, electrical generating equipment and ancillary equipment used to collect the geothermal heat, but not including buildings, transmission equipment, distribution equipment, equipment designed to store electrical energy, property otherwise included in Class 10 and property that would be included in Class 17 if that Class were read without reference to its subparagraph (*a*.1)(i),

Class 43.1, clause (*d*)(xv)(B) was replaced by S.C. 2017, c. 33, s. 104(3), applicable in respect of property acquired for use after March 21, 2017 that has not been used or acquired for use before March 22, 2017, and formerly read:

(B) is part of a district energy system that uses thermal energy that is primarily supplied by equipment that is described in subparagraphs (i), (iv) or (ix) or would be described in those subparagraphs if owned by the taxpayer, and

Class 43.1, clause (*c*)(i)(A) was replaced by S.C. 2014, c. 39, s. 90(1), applicable to property acquired after February 10, 2014 that has not been used or acquired for use before February 11, 2014, and formerly read:

(A) is used by the taxpayer, or by a lessee of the taxpayer, to generate electrical energy, or both electrical and heat energy, using only fuel that is fossil fuel, eligible waste fuel, spent pulping liquor, or any combination of those fuels, and

Class 43.1, subparagraph (*d*)(ix) was replaced by S.C. 2014, c. 39, s. 90(2), applicable to property acquired after February 10, 2014 that has not been used or acquired for use before February 11, 2014, and formerly read:

(ix) equipment used by the taxpayer, or by a lessee of the taxpayer, for the sole purpose of generating heat energy, primarily from the consumption of eligible waste fuel and not using any fuel other than eligible waste fuel or fossil fuel, including such equipment that consists of fuel handling equipment used to upgrade the combustible portion of the fuel and control, feedwater and condensate systems, and other ancillary equipment, but not including equipment used for the purpose of producing heat energy to operate electrical generating equipment, buildings or other structures, heat rejection equipment (such as condensers and cooling water systems), fuel storage facilities, other fuel handling equipment and property otherwise included in Class 10 or 17,

Class 43.1, subparagraph (*d*)(xiv) was replaced by S.C. 2014, c. 39, s. 90(3), applicable to property acquired after February 10, 2014 that has not been used or acquired for use before February 11, 2014, and formerly read:

(xiv) property that is used by the taxpayer, or by a lessee of the taxpayer, primarily for the purpose of generating electricity using wave or tidal energy (otherwise than by using physical barriers or dam-like structures), including support structures, control, conditioning and battery storage equipment, submerged cables and transmission equipment, but not including buildings, distribution equipment, auxiliary electricity generating equipment, property otherwise included in Class 10 and property that would be included in Class 17 if that class were read without reference to its subparagraph (*a.1*)(i), or

Class 43.1, subparagraph (*d*)(xvi) was added by S.C. 2014, c. 39, s. 90(4), applicable to property acquired after February 10, 2014 that has not been used or acquired for use before February 11, 2014.

Class 43.1, subparagraph (*d*)(viii) was replaced by S.C. 2013, c. 40, s. 119(1), applicable in respect of property acquired after March 20, 2013 that has not been used or acquired for use before March 21, 2013, and formerly read:

(viii) equipment used by the taxpayer, or by a lessee of the taxpayer, primarily for the purpose of collecting landfill gas or digester gas, including such equipment that consists of piping (including above or below ground piping and the cost of drilling a well, or trenching, for the purpose of installing that piping), fans, compressors, storage tanks, heat exchangers and other ancillary equipment used to collect gas, to remove non-combustibles and contaminants from the gas or to store the gas, but not including property otherwise included in Class 10 or 17,

Class 43.1, the portion of subparagraph (*d*)(xiii) before clause (A) was replaced by S.C. 2013, c. 40, s. 119(2), applicable in respect of property acquired after March 20, 2013 that has not been used or acquired for use before March 21, 2013, and formerly read:

(xiii) property that is part of a system that is used by the taxpayer, or by a lessee of the taxpayer, primarily to produce and store biogas, which property includes equipment that is an anaerobic digester reactor, a buffer tank, a pre-treatment tank, biogas piping, a biogas storage tank and a biogas scrubbing equipment, but not including

Class 43.1, subparagraph (*d*)(ix) was replaced by S.C. 2012, c. 31, s. 70(1), deemed to have come into force on March 29, 2012, and formerly read:

(ix) equipment used by the taxpayer, or by a lessee of the taxpayer, primarily for the purpose of generating heat energy from the consumption of eligible waste fuel, and not using any fuel other than eligible waste fuel or fossil fuel, if the heat energy is used directly in an industrial process, or in a greenhouse, including such equipment that consists of fuel handling equipment used to upgrade the combustible portion of the fuel and control, feedwater and condensate systems, and other ancillary equipment, but not including buildings or other structures, heat rejection equipment (such as condensers and cooling water systems), fuel storage facilities, other fuel handling equipment and electrical generating equipment, and property otherwise included in Class 10 or 17,

Class 43.1, clause (*d*)(xv)(B) was replaced by S.C. 2012, c. 31, s. 70(2), deemed to have come into force on March 29, 2012, and formerly read:

(B) is part of a district energy system that uses thermal energy that is primarily supplied by equipment that is described in subparagraph (i) or (iv) or would be described in subparagraph (i) or (iv) if owned by the taxpayer, and

Class 43.1, clause (*c*)(ii)(A) was replaced by S.C. 2011, c. 24, s. 101(2), applicable to property acquired on or after March 22, 2011. Class 43.1, clause (*c*)(ii)(A) formerly read:

(A) is used by the taxpayer, or by a lessee of the taxpayer, to generate electrical energy using only a combination of natural gas and waste heat from one or more natural gas compressor systems located on a natural gas pipeline,

Class 43.1, clause (*c*)(iii) was added by S.C. 2011, c. 24, s. 101(3), applicable to property acquired on or after March 22, 2011.

Class 43.1, subparagraphs (*a*)(iii) and (iii.1) were replaced by S.C. 2010, c. 25, s. 90(1), applicable to property acquired after March 3, 2010. Class 43.1, subparagraphs (*a*)(iii) and (iii.1) formerly read:

(iii) heat recovery equipment used primarily for the purpose of conserving energy, or reducing the requirement to acquire energy, by

(A) extracting thermal waste that is generated by equipment referred to in subparagraph (i) or (ii), and

(B) reusing the thermal waste to generate electrical energy from equipment referred to in subparagraph (i) or (ii),

(iii.1) district energy equipment,

Class 43.1, subclause (*d*)(i)(A)(II) was replaced by S.C. 2010, c. 25, s. 90(2), applicable to property acquired after February 25, 2008, except that in its application to property acquired before May 3, 2010, subclause (*d*)(i)(A)(II) of Class 43.1 in Schedule II to the Regulations shall be read as follows:

(II) equipment that is part of a ground source heat pump system that transfers heat to or from the ground or groundwater (but not to or from surface water such as a river, a lake or an ocean) and that, at the time of installation, meets the standards set by the Canadian Standards Association for the design and installation of earth energy systems, including such equipment that consists of underground piping, energy conversion equipment, energy storage equipment, control equipment and equipment designed to enable the system to interface with other heating or cooling equipment, and

Class 43.1, subclause (*d*)(i)(A)(II) formerly read:

(II) equipment that is a part of a ground source heat pump system that is used primarily for the purpose of heating a liquid or gas used directly in an industrial process or in a greenhouse, including such equipment that consists of underground piping, energy conversion equipment, energy storage equipment, control equipment and equipment designed to interface the system with other heating equipment, and

Class 43.1, clause (*d*)(i)(B) was replaced by S.C. 2010, c. 25, s. 90(3), applicable to property acquired after February 25, 2008. Class 43.1, clause (*d*)(i)(B) formerly read:

(B) it is not a building, part of a building (other than a solar collector that is not a window and that is integrated into a building), equipment used to heat water for use in a swimming pool, nor equipment that distributes heated air or water in a building,

Class 43.1, subparagraph (*d*)(iv) was replaced by S.C. 2010, c. 25, s. 90(4), applicable to property acquired after March 3, 2010. Class 43.1, subparagraph (*d*)(iv) formerly read:

(iv) heat recovery equipment used by the taxpayer, or by a lessee of the taxpayer, primarily for the purpose of conserving energy, or reducing the requirement to acquire energy, by

(A) extracting thermal waste that is generated directly in an industrial process (other than in an industrial process that generates or processes electrical energy), and

(B) reusing the thermal waste directly in an industrial process (other than in an industrial process that generates or processes electrical energy),

including such equipment that consists of heat exchange equipment, compressors used to upgrade low pressure steam, vapour or gas, waste heat boilers and other ancillary equipment such as control panels, fans, instruments or pumps, but not including buildings,

Class 43.1, subparagraphs (*d*)(vii) to (ix) were replaced by S.C. 2010, c. 25, s. 90(5), applicable to property acquired after February 25, 2008, except that in its application to property acquired before May 3, 2010, subparagraphs (*d*)(vii) and (viii) of Class 43.1 shall be read as follows:

(vii) above-ground equipment used by the taxpayer, or by a lessee of the taxpayer, primarily for the purpose of generating electrical energy solely from geothermal energy, including such equipment that consists of pumps, heat exchangers, steam separators, electrical generating equipment and ancillary equipment used to collect the geothermal heat, but not including buildings, transmission equipment, distribution equipment, equipment designed to store electrical energy, property otherwise included in Class 10 and property that would be included in Class 17 if that Class were read without reference to its subparagraph (*a.1*)(i),

(viii) above-ground equipment used by the taxpayer, or by a lessee of the taxpayer, primarily for the purpose of collecting landfill gas or digester gas, including such equipment that consists of fans, compressors, storage tanks, heat exchangers and other ancillary equipment used to collect gas, to remove non-combustibles and contaminants from the gas or to store the gas, but not including property otherwise included in Class 10 or 17,

Class 43.1, subparagraphs (*d*)(vii) to (ix) formerly read:

(vii) above-ground equipment used by the taxpayer, or by a lessee of the taxpayer, primarily for the purpose ofgenerating electrical energy solely from geothermal energy, including such equipment that consists of pumps, heat exchangers, steam separators, electrical generating equipment and ancillary equipment used to collect the geothermal heat, but not including buildings, transmission equipment, distribution equipment, equipment designed to store electrical energy, property otherwise included in Class 10 and property that would be included in Class 17 if that Class were read without reference to its subparagraph (*a.1*)(i),

(viii) above-ground equipment used by the taxpayer, or by a lessee of the taxpayer, primarily for the purpose of collecting landfill gas or digester gas, including such equipment that consists of fans, compressors, storage tanks, heat exchangers and other ancillary equipment used to collect the gas, to remove non-combustibles and contaminants from the gas or to store the gas, but not including buildings or property otherwise included in Class 10 or 17,

(ix) equipment used by the taxpayer, or by a lessee of the taxpayer, primarily for the purpose of generating heat energy from the consumption of eligible waste fuel, and using only fuel that is eligible waste fuel, fossil fuel or a combination of both, if the heat energy is used directly in an industrial process, or in a greenhouse, of the taxpayer or lessee, including such equipment that consists of fuel handling equipment used to upgrade the combustible portion of the fuel and control, feedwater and condensate systems, and other ancillary equipment, but not including buildings or other structures, heat rejection equipment (such as condensers and cooling water systems), fuel storage facilities, other fuel handling equipment and electrical generating equipment, and property otherwise included in Class 10 or 17,

Class 43.1, subparagraph (*d*)(xi) was replaced by S.C. 2010, c. 25, s. 90(6), applicable to property acquired after February 25, 2008. Class 43.1, subparagraph (*d*)(xi) formerly read:

(xi) equipment used in a system of the taxpayer that converts wood waste or plant residue into bio-oil, if that bio-oil is used by the taxpayer, or by a lessee of the taxpayer, primarily for the purpose of generating electricity, or electricity and heat, other than equipment used for the collection, storage or transportation of wood waste or plant residue, buildings or other structures and property otherwise included in Class 10 or 17,

Class 43.1, subparagraph (*d*)(xiii) was replaced by S.C. 2010, c. 25, s. 90(7), applicable to property acquired after February 25, 2008. Class 43.1, subparagraph (*d*)(xiii) formerly read:

(xiii) property that is part of a system that is used by the taxpayer, or by a lessee of the taxpayer, primarily to produce, store and use biogas if that biogas is used by the taxpayer or the lessee primarily to produce electricity, heat that is used directly in an industrial process or in a greenhouse, or electricity and such heat, which property

(A) includes equipment that is an anaerobic digester reactor, a buffer tank, a pre-treatment tank, biogas piping, a biogas storage tank, biogas scrubbing equipment and electrical generating equipment, and

(B) does not include property (other than a buffer tank) that is used to collect, move or store organic waste, equipment used to process the residue after digestion or to treat recovered liquids, auxiliary electrical generating equipment, buildings or other structures, transmission equipment, distribution equipment, equipment designed to store electrical energy, property otherwise included in Class 10 and property that would be included in Class 17 if that class were read without reference to its subparagraph (*a.1*)(i), or

Class 43.1, subparagraph (*d*)(xv) was added by S.C. 2010, c. 25, s. 90(8), applicable to property acquired after March 3, 2010.

Subparagraph (*a*)(ii.1) of Class 43.1 was replaced by P.C. 2009-581, SOR/2009-115, dated April 23, 2009, applicable to property acquired on or after March 19, 2007. Subparagraph (*a*)(ii.1) of Class 43.1 formerly read:

(ii.1) fixed location fuel cell equipment that has a peak capacity of not less than 3 kilowatts of electrical output and uses hydrogen generated only from internal, or ancillary, fuel reformation equipment,

The portion of paragraph (*a*) of Class 43.1 after subparagraph (v) was replaced by P.C. 2009-581, SOR/2009-115, dated April 23, 2009, applicable to property acquired on or after March 19, 2007. The portion of paragraph (*a*) of Class 43.1 after subparagraph (v) formerly read:

other than buildings or other structures, heat rejection equipment (such as condensers and cooling water systems), transmission equipment, distribution equipment, fuel storage facilities and fuel handling equipment,

Clause (*c*)(i)(A) of Class 43.1 was replaced by P.C. 2009-581, SOR/2009-115, dated April 23, 2009, applicable to property acquired on or after March 19, 2007. Clause (*c*)(i)(A) of Class 43.1 formerly read:

(A) is used by the taxpayer, or by a lessee of the taxpayer, to generate electrical energy, or both electrical and heat energy, using only fuel that is fossil fuel, wood waste, spent pulping liquor, municipal waste, land-fill gas, digester gas or bio-oil, or any combination of those fuels, and

Subparagraph (*d*)(i) of Class 43.1 was replaced by P.C. 2009-581, SOR/2009-115, dated April 23, 2009, applicable to property acquired on or after March 19, 2007. Subparagraph (*d*)(i) of Class 43.1 formerly read:

(i) active solar heating equipment used by the taxpayer, or by a lessee of the taxpayer, primarily for the purpose of heating a liquid or gas used directly in an industrial process or in a greenhouse, including such equipment that consists of solar collectors, solar energy conversion equipment, solar water heaters, energy storage equipment, control equipment and equipment designed to interface solar heating equipment with other heating equipment, but not including buildings,

Subparagraph (*d*)(vi) of Class 43.1 was replaced by P.C. 2009-581, SOR/2009-115, dated April 23, 2009, applicable to property acquired on or after March 19, 2007. Subparagraph (*d*)(vi) of Class 43.1 formerly read:

(vi) fixed location photovoltaic equipment that

(A) is used by the taxpayer, or by a lessee of the taxpayer, primarily for the purpose of generating electrical energy from solar energy,

(B) has a peak capacity of not less than 3 kilowatts of electrical output, and

(C) consists of solar cells or modules and related equipment including

(I) control, conditioning and battery storage equipment,

(II) support structures, and

(III) transmission equipment,

other than buildings, distribution equipment, auxiliaryelectrical generating equipment, property otherwise included in Class 10 and property that would be included in Class 17if that Class were read without reference to its subparagraph (*a*.1)(i),

Subparagraph (*d*)(ix) of Class 43.1 was replaced by P.C. 2009-581, SOR/2009-115, dated April 23, 2009, applicable to property acquired on or after March 19, 2007. Subparagraph (*d*)(ix) of Class 43.1 formerly read:

(ix) equipment used by the taxpayer, or by a lessee of the taxpayer, primarily for the purpose of generating heat energy from the consumption of wood waste, municipal waste, landfill gas, digester gas or bio-oil, if the heat energy is used directly in an industrial process, or in a greenhouse, of the taxpayer or lessee, including such equipment that consists of fuel handling equipment used to upgrade the combustible portion of the fuel and control, feedwater and condensate systems, and other ancillary equipment, but not including buildings or other structures, heat rejection equipment (such as condensers and cooling water systems), fuel storage facilities, other fuel handling equipment and electrical generating equipment, and property otherwise included in Class 10 or 17,

Subparagraph (*d*)(xii) of Class 43.1 was replaced by P.C. 2009-581, SOR/2009-115, dated April 23, 2009, applicable to property acquired on or after March 19, 2007, except that subparagraph (*d*)(xii) of Class 43.1 in Schedule II to the Regulations is to be read as follows with respect to property acquired before February 26, 2008:

(xii) fixed location fuel cell equipment used by the taxpayer, or by a lessee of the taxpayer, that uses hydrogen generated only from ancillary electrolysis equipment (or, if the fuel cell is reversible, the fuel cell itself) using electricity generated by photovoltaic, wind energy conversion or hydro-electric equipment, of the taxpayer or the lessee, and equipment ancillary to the fuel cell equipment other than buildings or other structures, transmission equipment, distribution equipment, auxiliary electrical generating equipment and property otherwise included in Class 10 or 17,

Subparagraph (*d*)(xii) of Class 43.1 formerly read:

(xii) fixed location fuel cell equipment used by the taxpayer, or by a lessee of the taxpayer, that has a peak capacity of not less than 3 kilowatts of electrical output and uses hydrogen generated only from ancillary electrolysis equipment (or, if the fuel cell is reversible, the fuel cell itself) using electricity generated by photovoltaic, wind energy conversion or hydro-electric equipment, of the taxpayer or the lessee, and equipment ancillary to the fuel cell equipment other than buildings or other structures, transmission equipment, distribution equipment, auxiliary electrical generating equipment and property otherwise included in Class 10 or 17, or

The portion of subparagraph (*d*)(xiii) of Class 43.1 before clause (A) was replaced by P.C. 2009-581, SOR/2009-115, dated April 23, 2009, applicable to property acquired on or after March 19, 2007. The portion of subparagraph (*d*)(xiii) of Class 43.1 before clause (A) formerly read:

(xiii) property of a taxpayer that is part of a system that is used by the taxpayer or a lessee of the taxpayer primarily to produce, store and use biogas produced from manure by anaerobic digestion if that biogas is used primarily by the taxpayer or the lessee to produce electricity, or to produce heat that is used directly in an industrial process or in a greenhouse, which property

Clause (*d*)(xiii)(B) of Class 43.1 was replaced by P.C. 2009-581, SOR/2009-115, dated April 23, 2009, applicable to property acquired on or after March 19, 2007. Clause (*d*)(xiii)(B) of Class 43.1 formerly read:

(B) does not include property that is used to collect manure, store manure (other than a buffer tank) or move manure to the system, equipment used to process the residue after digestion or to treat recovered liquids, auxiliary electrical generating equipment, buildings or other structures, transmission equipment, distribution equipment, equipment designed to store electrical energy, property otherwise included in Class 10 and property that would be included in Class 17 if that class were read without reference to its subparagraph (*a*.1)(i), and

Subparagraph (*d*)(xiv) of Class 43.1 was added by P.C. 2009-581, SOR/2009-115, dated April 23, 2009, applicable to property acquired on or after March 19, 2007.

Related Regulations: 1104(13) producer gas; 1104(13) Classes 43.1 and 43.2 — Energy Conservation Property.

Canadian Petroleum Tax Journal: Renewable Energy — Tax Developments and Opportunities, Leanne Sereda, 2000, Vol. 13, No. 1.

Income Tax Folios: *Primary* — S3-F8-C2 Tax Incentives for Clean Energy Equipment

Interpretation Bulletins: *Primary* — IT-482R Pipelines.

Tax Window Files: Geothermal Energy Project, *July 17, 2018*, CRA Document No. 2018-0747311E5.

Class 43.2. (50 per cent)

Property that is acquired after February 22, 2005 and before 2025 (other than property that was included, before it was acquired, in another class in this Schedule by any taxpayer) and that is property that would otherwise be included in Class 43.1

(*a*) otherwise than because of paragraph (*d*) of that Class, if the expression "6,000 BTU" in clause (*c*)(i)(B) of that Class were read as "4,750 BTU"; or

(*b*) because of paragraph (*d*) of that Class, if

(i) the expression "6,000 BTU" in clause (*c*)(i)(B) of that Class were read as "4,750 BTU",

(ii) subclauses (*d*)(xvii)(C)(I) and (II) of that Class were read as follows:

(I) an electric vehicle charging station (other than a building) that supplies at least 90 kilowatts of continuous power, or

(II) used

1. primarily in connection with one or more electric vehicle charging stations (other than buildings) each of which supplies more than 10 kilowatts of continuous power, and

2. in connection with one or more electric vehicle charging stations (other than build-

ings) each of which supplies at least 90 kilowatts of continuous power, or

and

(iii) clause (*d*)(xviii)(B) of that Class were read without reference to its subclause (II).

History: Paragraphs (*a*) and (*b*) were replaced by S.C. 2019, c. 29, s. 62(1), applicable to property acquired after March 21, 2016 that has not been used or acquired for use before March 22, 2016, and formerly read:

(*a*) if the expression "6,000 BTU" in clause (*c*)(i)(B) of that Class were read as the expression "4,750 BTU"; or

(*b*) because of paragraph (*d*) of that Class.

The portion of Class 43.2 before paragraph (*a*) was replaced by S.C. 2018, c. 12, s. 45, in force June 21, 2018, and formerly read:

Property that is acquired after February 22, 2005 and before 2020 (other than property that was included, before it was acquired, in another class in this Schedule by any taxpayer) and that is property that would otherwise be included in Class 43.1

The portion of Class 43.2 before paragraph (*a*) was replaced by P.C. 2009-581, SOR/2009-115, dated April 23, 2009, deemed to have come into force on March 19, 2007. The portion of Class 43.2 before paragraph (*a*) formerly read:

Property that is acquired after February 22, 2005 and before 2012 (other than property that was included, before it was acquired, in another Class in this Schedule by any taxpayer) and that is property that would otherwise be included in Class 43.1

Related Regulations: 1104(13) producer gas; 1104(13) Classes 43.1 and 43.2 — Energy Conservation Property.

Income Tax Folios: *Primary* — S3-F8-C2 Tax Incentives for Clean Energy Equipment.

Tax Window Files: Geothermal Energy Project, *July 17, 2018*, CRA Document No. 2018-0747311E5.

Class 44. (25 per cent)

Property that is a patent, or a right to use patented information for a limited or unlimited period.

Tax Profile: July 2012 — Intangibles.

Class 45. (45 per cent)

Property acquired after March 22, 2004 and before March 19, 2007 (other than property acquired before 2005 in respect of which an election is made under subsection 1101(5q)) that is general-purpose electronic data processing equipment and systems software for that equipment, including ancillary data processing equipment, but not including property that is principally or is used principally as

(*a*) electronic process control or monitor equipment;

(*b*) electronic communications control equipment;

(*c*) systems software for equipment referred to in paragraph (*a*) or (*b*); or

(*d*) data handling equipment (other than data handling equipment that is ancillary to general-purpose electronic data processing equipment).

History: The portion of Class 45 before paragraph (*a*) was replaced by P.C. 2009-581, SOR/2009-115, dated April 23, 2009, deemed to have come into force on March 19, 2007. The portion of Class 45 before paragraph (*a*) formerly read:

Property acquired after March 22, 2004 (other than property acquired before 2005 in respect of which an election is made under subsection 1101(5q)) that is general-purpose electronic data processing equipment and systems software for that equipment, including ancillary data processing equipment, but not including property that is principally or is used principally as

Class 46. (30 per cent)

Property acquired after March 22, 2004 that is data network infrastructure equipment, and systems software for that equipment, that would, but for this Class, be included in Class 8 because of paragraph (*i*) of that Class.

Class 47. (8 per cent)

Property that is

(*a*) transmission or distribution equipment (which may include for this purpose a structure) acquired after February 22, 2005 and that is used for the transmission or distribution of electrical energy, other than

(i) property that is a building, and

(ii) property that has been used or acquired for use for any purpose by any taxpayer before February 23, 2005; or

(*b*) equipment acquired after March 18, 2007 that is part of a liquefied natural gas facility that liquefies or regasifies natural gas, including controls, cooling equipment, compressors, pumps, storage tanks, vaporizers and ancillary equipment, loading and unloading pipelines on the facility site used to transport liquefied natural gas between a ship and the facility, and related structures, other than property that is

(i) acquired for the purpose of producing oxygen or nitrogen,

(ii) a breakwater, a dock, a jetty, a wharf, or a similar structure, or

(iii) a building.

History: Class 47 was replaced by P.C. 2009-581, SOR/2009-115, dated April 23, 2009, deemed to have come into force on March 19, 2007. Class 47 formerly read:

Property acquired after February 22, 2005 that is transmission or distribution equipment (which may include for this purpose a structure) used for the transmission or distribution of electrical energy, other than

(*a*) property that is a building; and

(*b*) property that has been used or acquired for use for any purpose by any taxpayer before February 23, 2005.

Class 48. (15 per cent)

Property acquired after February 22, 2005 that is a combustion turbine (including associated burners and compressors) that generates electrical energy, other than

(*a*) electrical generating equipment described in any of paragraphs (*f*) to (*h*) of Class 8;

(*b*) property acquired before 2006 in respect of which an election is made under subsection 1101(5t); and

(*c*) property that has been used or acquired for use for any purpose by any taxpayer before February 23, 2005.

Class 49. (8 per cent)

Property that is a pipeline, including control and monitoring devices, valves and other equipment ancillary to the pipeline, that

(*a*) is acquired after February 22, 2005, is used for the transmission (but not the distribution) of petroleum, natural gas or related hydrocarbons, and is not

(i) a pipeline described in subparagraph (*l*)(ii) of Class 1,

(ii) property that has been used or acquired for use for any purpose by any taxpayer before February 23, 2005,

Regulations

(iii) equipment included in Class 7 because of paragraph (*j*) of that Class, or

(iv) a building or other structure; or

(*b*) is acquired after February 25, 2008, is used for the transmission of carbon dioxide, and is not

(i) equipment included in Class 7 because of paragraph (*k*) of that Class, or

(ii) a building or other structure.

History: Class 49 was replaced by P.C. 2009-660, SOR/2009-126, dated April 30, 2009, applicable in respect of property acquired after February 25, 2008. Class 49 formerly read:

Property acquired after February 22, 2005 that is a pipeline, including control and monitoring devices, valves and other equipment ancillary to the pipeline, used for the transmission (but not the distribution) of petroleum, natural gas or related hydrocarbons, other than

(*a*) a pipeline described in subparagraph (*l*)(ii) of Class 1;

(*b*) property that has been used or acquired for use for any purpose by any taxpayer before February 23, 2005;

(*c*) equipment included in Class 7 because of paragraph (*j*) of that Class; and

(*d*) a building or other structure.

Interpretation Bulletins: *Secondary* — IT-476R Capital cost allowance — Equipment used in petroleum and natural gas activities.

Class 50. (55 per cent)

Property acquired after March 18, 2007 that is general-purpose electronic data processing equipment and systems software for that equipment, including ancillary data processing equipment, but not including property that is included in Class 52 or that is principally or is used principally as

(*a*) electronic process control or monitor equipment;

(*b*) electronic communications control equipment;

(*c*) systems software for equipment referred to in paragraph (*a*) or (*b*); or

(*d*) data handling equipment (other than data handling equipment that is ancillary to general-purpose electronic data processing equipment).

History: Class 50, the portion before paragraph (*a*) was replaced by P.C. 2009-660, SOR/2009-126, dated April 30, 2009, applicable in respect of property acquired after January 27, 2009. Class 50, the portion before paragraph (*a*) formerly read:

Property acquired after March 18, 2007 that is general-purpose electronic data processing equipment and systems software for that equipment, including ancillary data processing equipment, but not including property that is principally or is used principally as

Class 50 was added by P.C. 2009-581, SOR/2009-115, dated April 23, 2009, deemed to have come into force on March 19, 2007.

Class 51. (6 per cent)

Property acquired after March 18, 2007 that is a pipeline, including control and monitoring devices, valves and other equipment ancillary to the pipeline, used for the distribution (but not the transmission) of natural gas, other than

(*a*) a pipeline described in subparagraph (*l*)(ii) of Class 1 or in Class 49;

(*b*) property that has been used or acquired for use for any purpose by a taxpayer before March 19, 2007; and

(*c*) a building or other structure.

History: Class 51 was added by P.C. 2009-581, SOR/2009-115, dated April 23, 2009, deemed to have come into force on March 19, 2007.

Class 52. (100 per cent)

Property acquired by a taxpayer after January 27, 2009 and before February 2011 that

(*a*) is general-purpose electronic data processing equipment and systems software for that equipment, including ancillary data processing equipment, but not including property that is principally or is used principally as

(i) electronic process control or monitor equipment,

(ii) electronic communications control equipment,

(iii) systems software for equipment referred to in paragraph (i) or (ii), or

(iv) data handling equipment (other than data handling equipment that is ancillary to general- purpose electronic data processing equipment);

(*b*) is situated in Canada;

(*c*) has not been used, or acquired for use, for any purpose whatever before it is acquired by the taxpayer; and

(*d*) is acquired by the taxpayer

(i) for use in a business carried on by the taxpayer in Canada or for the purpose of earning income from property situated in Canada, or

(ii) for lease by the taxpayer to a lessee for use by the lessee in a business carried on by the lessee in Canada or for the purpose of earning income from property situated in Canada.

History: Class 52, the portion before paragraph (*a*) was amended by P.C. 2009-847 SOR/2009-155, dated May 28, 2009 to correct an error in P.C. 2009-660, SOR/2009-125 to refer to property acquired before February 2011, instead of before February 2010.

Class 52 was added by P.C. 2009-660, SOR/2009-126, dated April 30, 2009, applicable in respect of property acquired after January 27, 2009.

Class 53. Property acquired after 2015 and before 2026 that is not included in Class 29, but that would otherwise be included in that Class if

(*a*) subparagraph (*a*)(ii) of that Class were read without reference to "in Canadian field processing carried on by the lessee or"; and

(*b*) that Class were read without reference to its subparagraphs (*b*)(iv) to (vi) and paragraph (*c*).

History: Class 53 was added by S.C. 2015, c. 36, s. 26, in force on Royal Assent, June 23, 2015.

Related Regulations: 4600(2)(k).

Income Tax Folios: S4-F15-C1 Manufacturing and Processing.

Class 54. Property that is a zero-emission vehicle that is not included in Class 16 or 55.

History: Class 54 was added by S.C. 2019, c. 29, s. 63(1), deemed in force on March 19, 2019.

Class 55. Property that is a zero-emission vehicle that would otherwise be included in Class 16.

History: Class 55 was added by S.C. 2019, c. 29, s. 63(1), deemed in force on March 19, 2019.

Schedule III

Capital Cost Allowances, Class 13, (Section 1100)

1. For the purposes of paragraph 1100(1)(*b*), the amount that may be deducted in computing the income of a taxpayer for a taxation year in respect of the capital cost of property of Class 13 in Schedule II is the lesser of

(*a*) the aggregate of each amount determined in accordance with section 2 of this Schedule that is a prorated portion of the part of the capital cost to him, incurred in a particular taxation year, of a particular leasehold interest; and

(*b*) the undepreciated capital cost to the taxpayer as of the end of the taxation year (before making any deduction under section 1100) of property of the class.

2. Subject to section 3 of this Schedule, the prorated portion for the year of the part of the capital cost, incurred in a particular taxation year, of a particular leasehold interest is the lesser of

(*a*) 1/5 of that part of the capital cost; and

(*b*) the amount determined by dividing that part of the capital cost by the number of 12-month periods (not exceeding 40 such periods) falling within the period commencing with the beginning of the particular taxation year in which the capital cost was incurred and ending with the day the lease is to terminate.

3. For the purpose of determining, under section 2 of this Schedule, the prorated portion for the year of the part of the capital cost, incurred in a particular taxation year, of a particular leasehold interest, the following rules apply:

(*a*) where an item of the capital cost of a leasehold interest was incurred before the taxation year in which the interest was acquired, it shall be deemed to have been incurred in the taxation year in which the interest was acquired;

(*b*) where, under a lease, a tenant has a right to renew the lease for an additional term, or for more than one additional term, after the term that includes the end of the particular taxation year in which the capital cost was incurred, the lease shall be deemed to terminate on the day on which the term next succeeding the term in which the capital cost was incurred is to terminate;

(*c*) the prorated portion for the year of the part of the capital cost, incurred in a particular taxation year, of a particular leasehold interest shall not exceed the amount, if any, remaining after deducting from that part of the capital cost the aggregate of the amounts claimed and deductible in previous years in respect thereof;

(*d*) where, at the end of a taxation year, the aggregate of

(i) the amounts claimed and deductible in previous taxation years in respect of a particular leasehold interest, and

(ii) the proceeds of disposition, if any, of part or all of that interest

equals or exceeds the capital cost as of that time of the interest, the prorated portion of any part of that capital cost shall, for all subsequent years, be deemed to be nil; and

(*e*) where, at the end of a taxation year, the undepreciated capital cost to the taxpayer of property of Class 13 in Schedule II is nil, the prorated portion of any part of the capital cost as of that time shall, for all subsequent years, be deemed to be nil.

4. Where a taxpayer has acquired a property that would, if the property had been acquired by a person with whom the taxpayer was not dealing at arm's length at the time the property was acquired, be a leasehold interest of that person, a reference in this Schedule to a leasehold interest shall, in respect of the taxpayer, include a reference to that property, and the terms and conditions of the leasehold interest of that property in respect of the taxpayer shall be deemed to be the same as those that would have applied in respect of that person had that person acquired the property.

Interpretation Bulletins: *Secondary* — IT-464R Capital cost allowance — Leasehold interests.

Regulations

Schedule IV

Capital Cost Allowances, Class 15, (Sections 1100 and 1101)

1. For the purposes of paragraph 1100(1)(*f*), the amount that may be deducted in computing the income of a taxpayer for a taxation year in respect of property described in Class 15 in Schedule II is the lesser of

(*a*) an amount equal to

(i) if the property is an accelerated investment incentive property acquired in the year,

(A) if the property is acquired before 2024, 1.5 times an amount computed on the basis of a rate per cord, board foot or cubic metre cut in the taxation year, and

(B) if the property is acquired after 2023, 1.25 times an amount computed on the basis of a rate per cord, board foot or cubic metre cut in the taxation year, and

(ii) in any other case, an amount computed on the basis of a rate per cord, board foot or cubic metre cut in the taxation year, and

(*b*) the undepreciated capital cost to the taxpayer as of the end of the taxation year (before making any deduction under section 1100 for the taxation year) of property of that class.

History: Schedule IV, paragraph 1(*a*) was replaced by S.C. 2019, c. 29, s. 64, effective June 21, 2019, and formerly read:

(*a*) an amount computed on the basis of a rate per cord, board foot or cubic metre cut in the taxation year; and

2. Where all the property of the class is used in connection with one timber limit or section thereof, the rate per cord, board foot or cubic metre is the amount determined by dividing

(*a*) the undepreciated capital cost to the taxpayer as of the end of the taxation year (before making any deduction under section 1100 for the taxation year and computed as if subparagraph 1(*a*)(i) did not apply) of the property

by

(*b*) the number of cords, board feet or cubic metres of timber in the limit or section thereof as of the commencement of the taxation year, obtained by deducting the quantity cut up to that time from the amount shown by the latest cruise.

History: Schedule IV, paragraph 2(*a*) was replaced by S.C. 2019, c. 29, s. 65, effective June 21, 2019, and formerly read:

(*a*) the undepreciated capital cost to the taxpayer as of the end of the taxation year (before making any deduction under section 1100 for the taxation year) of the property

Related Regulations: Schedule IV 1(a).

3. Where a part of the property of the class is used in connection with one timber limit or a section thereof and a part is used in connection with another limit or section thereof, a separate rate shall be computed for each part of the property, in the manner provided in section 2 of this Schedule, as though each part of the property were the taxpayer's only property of that class.

Interpretation Bulletins: *Secondary* — IT-501 Capital cost allowance — Logging assets.

Regulations

Schedule V
Capital Cost Allowances, Industrial Mineral Mines, (Sections 1100, 1101 and 1104)

1. For the purposes of paragraph 1100(1)(*g*), the amount that may be deducted in computing the income of a taxpayer for a taxation year in respect of a property described in that paragraph that is an industrial mineral mine or a right to remove industrial minerals from an industrial mineral mine is the lesser of

(*a*) an amount computed on the basis of a rate (computed under section 2 or 3 of this Schedule, as the case may be) per unit of mineral mined in the taxation year; and

(*b*) the undepreciated capital cost to the taxpayer as of the end of the taxation year (before making any deduction under section 1100) of the mine or right.

2. If the taxpayer has not been granted an allowance in respect of the mine or right for a previous taxation year, the rate for a taxation year is determined by the formula

$$A(B - C)/D$$

where

A is

(*a*) 1.5, if the property is an accelerated investment incentive property acquired before 2024,

(*b*) 1.25, if the property is an accelerated investment incentive property acquired after 2023, and

(*c*) 1, in any other case;

B is the capital cost of the mine or right to the taxpayer;

C is the residual value, if any, of the mine or right; and

D is

(*a*) if the taxpayer has acquired a right to remove only a specified number of units, the specified number of units of material that the taxpayer acquired a right to remove, and

(*b*) in any other case, the number of units of commercially mineable material estimated as being in the mine when the mine or right was acquired.

History: Schedule V, section 2 was replaced by S.C. 2019, c. 29, s. 66, effective June 21, 2019, and formerly read:

2. Where the taxpayer has not been granted an allowance in respect of the mine or right for a previous taxation year, the rate for a taxation year is an amount determined by dividing the capital cost of the mine or right to the taxpayer minus the residual value, if any, by

(*a*) in any case where the taxpayer has acquired a right to remove only a specified number of units, the specified number of units of material that he acquired a right to remove; and

(*b*) in any other case, the number of units of commercially mineable material estimated as being in the mine when the mine or right was acquired.

3. Where the taxpayer has been granted an allowance in respect of the mine or right in a previous taxation year, the rate for the taxation year is

(*a*) if paragraph (*b*) does not apply,

(i) if section 2 applied in the previous year to determine the rate employed to determine the allowance for the year, the rate that would have been determined under section 2 if paragraph (*c*) of the description of A in that section applied, and

(ii) in any other case, the rate employed to determine the allowance for the most recent year for which an allowance was granted; and

(*b*) where it has been established that the number of units of material remaining to be mined in the previous taxation year was in fact different from the quantity that was employed in determining the rate for the previous year referred to in paragraph (*a*), or where it has been established that the capital cost of the mine or right is substantially different from the amount that was employed in determining the rate for that previous year, a rate determined by dividing the amount that would be the undepreciated capital cost to the taxpayer of the mine or right as of the commencement of the year if paragraph (*c*) of the description of A in section 2 had applied in respect of each previous taxation year minus the residual value, if any, by

(i) in any case where the taxpayer has acquired a right to remove only a specified number of units, the number of units of commercially mineable material that, at the commencement of the year, he had a right to remove, and

(ii) in any other case, the number of units of commercially mineable material estimated as remaining in the mine at the commencement of the year.

History: Schedule V, section 3(*a*) was replaced by S.C. 2019, c. 29, s. 67(1), effective June 21, 2019, and formerly read:

(*a*) where paragraph (*b*) does not apply, the rate employed to determine the allowance for the most recent year for which an allowance was granted; and

Schedule V, the portion of s. 3(*b*) before subparagraph (i) was replaced by S.C. 2019, c. 29, s. 67(2), effective June 21, 2019, and formerly read:

(*b*) where it has been established that the number of units of material remaining to be mined in the previous taxation year was in fact different from the quantity that was employed in determining the rate for the previous year referred to in paragraph (*a*), or where it has been established that the capital cost of the mine or right is substantially different from the amount that was employed in determining the rate for that previous year, a rate determined by dividing the undepreciated capital cost to the taxpayer of the mine or right as of the commencement of the year minus the residual value, if any, by

Related Regulations: Schedule V 2.

4. In lieu of the aggregate of deductions otherwise allowable under this Schedule, a taxpayer may elect that the deduction for the taxation year be the lesser of

(*a*) $100; and

(*b*) the amount received by him in the taxation year from the sale of mineral.

5. In this Schedule, "residual value" means the estimated value of the property if all commercially mineable material were removed.

Interpretation Bulletins: *Secondary* — IT-492 Capital cost allowance — Industrial mineral mines.

Schedule VI
Capital Cost Allowances, Timber Limits and Cutting Rights, (Sections 1100 and 1101)

1. For the purposes of paragraph 1100(1)(*e*), the amount that may be deducted in computing the income of a taxpayer for a taxation year in respect of the capital cost to him of a property, other than a timber resource property, that is a timber limit or a right to cut timber from a limit is the lesser of

(*a*) the aggregate of

(i) an amount computed on the basis of a rate (determined under section 2 or 3 of this Schedule) per cord, board foot or cubic metre cut in the year, and

(ii) the lesser of

(A) 1/10 of the amount expended by the taxpayer after the commencement of his 1949 taxation year that is included in the capital cost to him of the timber limit or right, for surveys, cruises or preparation of prints, maps or plans for the purpose of obtaining a licence or right to cut timber, and

(B) the amount expended as described in clause (A) minus the aggregate of amounts deducted under this subparagraph in computing the income of the taxpayer in previous years; and

(*b*) the undepreciated capital cost to the taxpayer as of the end of the year (before making any deduction under section 1100 for the year) of the timber limit or right.

2. If the taxpayer has not been granted an allowance in respect of the limit or right for a previous taxation year, the rate for a taxation year is an amount determined by the formula

$$A(B - (C + D))/E$$

where

A is

(*a*) 1.5, if the property is an accelerated investment incentive property acquired before 2024,

(*b*) 1.25, if the property is an accelerated investment incentive property acquired after 2023, and

(*c*) 1, in any other case;

B is the capital cost of the mine or right to the taxpayer;

C is the residual value of the timber limit;

D is the total of all amounts expended by the taxpayer after the commencement of the taxpayer's 1949 taxation year that are included in the capital cost to the taxpayer of the timber limit or right, for surveys, cruises or preparation of prints, maps or plans for the purpose of obtaining a licence or right to cut timber; and

E is the quantity of timber in the limit or the quantity of timber the taxpayer has obtained a right to cut, as the case may be, (expressed in cords, board feet or cubic metres) as shown by a cruise.

History: Section 2 of schedule VI was replaced by S.C. 2019, c. 29, s. 68, effective June 21, 2019, and formerly read:

2. If the taxpayer has not been granted an allowance in respect of the limit or right for a previous taxation year, the rate for a taxation year is an amount determined by dividing

(*a*) the capital cost of the limit or right to the taxpayer, minus the aggregate of the residual value of the timber limit and any amount expended by the taxpayer after the commencement of his 1949 taxation year that is included in the capital cost to him of the timber limit or right, for surveys, cruises or preparation of prints, maps or plans for the purpose of obtaining a licence or right to cut timber,

by

(*b*) the quantity of timber in the limit or the quantity of timber the taxpayer has obtained a right to cut, as the case may be, (expressed in cords, board feet or cubic metres) as shown by a cruise.

3. If the taxpayer has been granted an allowance in respect of the limit or right in a previous taxation year, the rate for a taxation year is

(*a*) if paragraph (*b*) does not apply,

(i) if section 2 applied in the previous year to determine the rate employed to determine the allowance for the year, the rate that would have been determined under section 2 if paragraph (*c*) of the description of A in that section applied, and

(ii) in any other case, the rate employed to determine the allowance for the most recent year for which an allowance was granted; and

(*b*) where it has been established that the quantity of timber that was in the limit or that the taxpayer had a right to cut was in fact substantially different from the quantity that was employed in determining the rate for the previous year referred to in paragraph (*a*), or where it has been established that the capital cost of the limit or right is substantially different from the amount that was employed in determining the rate for that previous year, a rate determined by dividing

(i) the amount that would be the undepreciated capital cost to the taxpayer of the limit or right as of the commencement of the year if paragraph (*c*) of the description of A in section 2 had applied in respect of each previous taxation year, minus the residual value,

by

(ii) the estimated remaining quantity of timber that is in the limit or that the taxpayer has a right to cut, as the case may be, (expressed in cords, board feet or cubic metres) at the commencement of the year.

History: Schedule VI, section 3(*a*) was replaced by S.C. 2019, c. 29, s. 69(1), effective June 21, 2019, and formerly read:

(*a*) where paragraph (*b*) does not apply, the rate employed to determine the allowance for the most recent year for which an allowance was granted; and

Schedule VI, section 3(*b*)(i) was replaced by S.C. 2019, c. 29, s. 69(2), effective June 21, 2019, and formerly read:

(i) the undepreciated capital cost to the taxpayer of the limit or right as of the commencement of the year, minus the residual value,

Related Regulations: Schedule VI 2.

4. In lieu of the deduction otherwise determined under this Schedule, a taxpayer may elect that the deduction for a taxation year be the lesser of

(*a*) $100; and

(*b*) the amount received by him in the taxation year from the sale of timber.

5. In this Schedule, "residual value" means the estimated value of the property if the merchantable timber were removed.

Interpretation Bulletins: *Secondary* — IT-481 (Consolid.) Timber resource property and timber limits.

Regulations

Schedule VII
Publicly-Traded Shares or Securities, (Section 4400)[1]

Column 1	Column 2	
A-1 Steel & Iron Foundry (Vancouver) Ltd.	Cl A.	6.75
A-1 Steel & Iron Foundry (Vancouver) Ltd.	Cl B.	6.50
Aabro Mining & Oils Ltd.	Com.	
Abbey Life Insurance Company of Canada	Com.	
Abcourt Metals Inc.	Com.	.28
Aberdeen Minerals Ltd.	Com.	
Abeta Mining Corp. Ltd.	Com.	.05
Abex Mines Ltd.	Com.	.01
Abino Gold Mines Ltd.	Com.	.03
Abitibi Asbestos Mining Co. Ltd.	Com.	1.75
Abitibi Copper Mines Ltd.	Com.	.13
Abitibi Paper Co. Ltd.	Com.	7.25
Abitibi Paper Co. Ltd.	7 1/2 pc cu A pr.	49.50
Abstainers Insurance Co.	Com.	11.00
Acadia Uranium Mines Ltd.	Com.	.06
Accra Explorations Limited	Com.	.07
Accurate Calculations Ltd.	Com.	1.13
Acheron Mines Ltd.	Com.	.16
Acklands Limited	Com.	7.50
Acklands Limited	6 pc cu pr.	15.75
Acklands Limited	6 pc cu cv 2nd pr.	11.25
Acme Gas & Oil Co. Ltd.	Com.	.22
Aconic	Com.	.02
Acres Limited	Com.	11.63
Acres Limited	7.20 pc A pr.	40.00
Acres Limited	Wt.	2.40
Acroll Oil & Gas Ltd.	Com.	.63
Adanac Mining & Exploration Ltd.	Com.	.46
Adera Mining Limited	Com.	.33
Admiral Corporation	Com.	18.50
Admiral Mines Limited	Com.	.15
Advance Red Lake Gold Mines Ltd.	Com.	.04
Advocate Mines Ltd.	Com.	1.80
Aetna Investment Ltd.	Com.	.85
Afton Mines Limited	Com.	1.21
A.G.F. Management Ltd.	Cl B pr.	5.75
AGF Special Fund Ltd.	Com.	3.00
Agressive Mining Limited	Com.	.11
Agnico Mines Ltd.	Com.	1.98
Agra Industries Ltd.	Com.	9.63
AGT Data Systems Ltd.	Com.	1.00
AHED Music Corp. Ltd.	Com.	4.70
Aiken-Russet Red Lake Mines Ltd.	Com.	.07
Aimco Industries Ltd.	Com.	16.00
A.I.S. Resources Ltd.	Com.	5.90
Ajax Mercury Mines Ltd.	Com.	.11
Ajax Minerals Limited	Com.	.23
Akaitcho Yellowknife Gold Mines Ltd.	Com.	.45
Alakon Metals Limited	Com.	.06
Albany Oil and Gas Ltd.	Com.	.45
Albarmont Mines Corporation	Com.	.27
Albatros Gold Mines Ltd.	Com.	

Alberta Copper Resources Ltd.	Com.	.40
Alberta Eastern Gas Ltd.	Com.	5.45
Alberta Gas Trunk Line Co. Ltd.	Com.	49.75
Alberta Gas Trunk Line Co. Ltd.	4 3/4 pc cu C pr.	76.00
Alberta Gas Trunk Line Co. Ltd.	5 3/8 pc cu cvD pr.	138.00
Alberta Gypsum Ltd.	Com.	.15
Alberta Natural Gas Co. Ltd.	Com.	20.00
Alcan Aluminium Ltd.	Com.	18.88
Alcan Aluminium Ltd.	4 1/4 pc cu cv pr.	26.75
Alchib Development Ltd.	Com.	.45
Alcor Minerals Limited	Com.	.12
Alexander Red Lake Mines Ltd.	Com.	.03
Algoma Central Railway Co.	Com.	8.25
Algoma Steel Corp. Ltd. The	Com.	13.38
Algonquin Building Credits Ltd.	Com.	4.05
Algonquin Building Credits Ltd.	6 pc cu pr.	4.00
Alice Arm Mining Ltd.	Com.	.11
Alice Lake Mines Limited	Com.	.23
Alina Mines & Oils Ltd.	Com.	.80
Aljo Mines Ltd.	Com.	
Allarco Developments Inc.	Com.	4.80
All Canadian-American Investments Limited	Com.	.55
All-Can Holdings Ltd.	Cl A.	
All-Can Holdings Ltd.	Cl B.	
Allcop Mines Ltd.	Com.	.02
Alliance Building Corp. Ltd.	Com.	3.20
Alliance Building Corp. Ltd.	7 pc cu cv A pr.	7.00
Allied Mining Corp.	Com.	3.25
Allied Roxana Minerals Limited	Com.	.65
Allied Telemedia Ltd.	Com.	.03
Alminex Ltd.	Com.	5.35
Alscope Consolidated Ltd.	Com.	1.25
Altair Mining Corp. Limited	Com.	.10
Aluminum Co. of Canada Ltd.	4 pc cu 1st pr.	18.00
Aluminum Co. of Canada Ltd.	4 1/2 pc cu 2nd pr.	36.13
Alvija Mines Ltd.	Com.	.07
Alwin Mining Co. Ltd.	Com.	.64
Amalgamated Beau Belle Mines Ltd.	Com.	.04
Amalgamated Kirkland Mines Ltd.	Com.	
Amalgamated Larder Mines Ltd.	Com.	.49
Amalgamated Properties Ltd.	Com.	.70
Amalgamated Rare Earth Mines Ltd.	Com.	.07
Amalgamated Resources Ltd.	Com.	.03
Amalta Oils & Minerals Ltd.	Com.	.13
Ambassador Development Corp. of Canada Ltd.	Com.	.70
Ambassador Mines Ltd.	Com.	.09
Amber Resources Ltd.	Com.	.30
Ameranium Mines Ltd.	Com.	.06
Americ Mines Ltd.	Com.	.17
American Chibougamau Mines Ltd.	Com.	

[1] Prices at Valuation Day — December 22, 1971.

American Copper & Smelting Ltd.	Com.	
American Eagle Petroleums Ltd.	Com.	.75
American Leduc Petroleums Ltd.	Com.	.09
American Metropolitan Enterprises Ltd.	Com.	1.15
American Quasar Petroleum Co.	Com.	4.80
American Uranium Limited	Com.	
Amigo Mines Ltd.	Com.	.06
Anaconda Petroleum Limited	Com.	
Anchor Mines Limited	Com.	.23
Anchor Petroleums Ltd.	Com.	.04
Andacollo Mining Co. Ltd.	Com.	
Andex Mines Ltd.	Com.	.30
Angelus Petroleums 1965 Ltd.	Com.	.23
Anglo American Nickel Mining Corp. Ltd.	Com.	
Anglo-Bomarc Mines Limited	Com.	.60
Anglo-Canadian Pulp & Paper Mills Ltd.	Com.	4.70
Anglo-Canadian Pulp & Paper Mills Ltd.	$4^1/2$ pc cu cv pr.	14.00
Anglo-Canadian Telephone Co.	$4^1/2$ pc cu pr.	30.75
Anglo-Canadian Telephone Co.	$2.65 cu pr.	34.00
Anglo-Canadian Telephone Co.	$2.90 cu pr.	38.00
Anglo-Canadian Telephone Co.	$3.15 cu pr.	42.63
Anglo-Permanent Corporate Holdings Limited	Com.	13.50
Anglo-Rouyn Mines Ltd.	Com.	.32
Anglo United Development Corp. Ltd.	Com.	.71
Anglo Western Minerals Ltd.	Com.	.17
Angot Group Limited, The	Com.	1.00
Annmar Mining Limited	Com.	.05
Ansil Mines Ltd.	Com.	.01
Anthes Imperial Limited	$5^1/2$ pc cu A 1st pr.	
Anthes Imperial Limited	$5^1/2$ pc cu B 1st pr.	80.00
Anthes Imperial Limited	$5^1/4$ pc cu C 1st pr.	80.00
Anthonian Mining Corp. Ltd.	Com.	.03
Anthony Gas & Oil Explorations Ltd.	Com.	1.43
Antoine Silver Mines Ltd.	Com.	.04
Anuk River Mines Ltd.	Com.	.25
Anuwon Uranium Mines Ltd.	Com.	.02
Aquablast Incorporated	Com.	3.65
Aquacare International Ltd.	Com.	
Aquitaine Co. of Canada Ltd.	Com.	24.50
Arcadia Explorations Ltd.	Com.	.11
Arctic Gold & Silver Mines Ltd.	Com.	.09
Arctic Yellowknife Mines Ltd.	Com.	.03
Ardel Explorations Limited	Com.	.08
Ardo Mines Ltd.	Com.	.16
Ardo Mines Ltd.	B wt.	
Argosy Mining Corp. Ltd.	Com.	.45
Argus Corporation Limited	Com.	13.00
Argus Corporation Limited	$2.50 cu A pr.	32.00
Argus Corporation Limited	$2.60 cu A pr.	34.13
Argus Corporation Limited	$2.70 cu B pr.	35.75
Argus Corporation Limited	C pr.	9.75
Arjon Gold Mines Ltd.	Com.	.01
Arlington Silver Mines Ltd.	Com.	.17
Armore Mines Ltd.	Com.	.14
Arno Mines Ltd.	Com.	.04
Arrowhead Gold Mines Ltd.	Com.	.01
Asamera Oil Corporation Ltd.	Com.	18.50
Asbestos Corporation Ltd.	Com.	25.50

Ascopex Explorations Ltd.	Com.	
Aselo Industries Ltd.	Com.	.13
Ashland Oil Canada Ltd.	Com.	11.88
Ashland Oil Canada Ltd.	6 pc cu cv pr.	29.50
Ashland Oil Inc.	Com.	20.38
Aspen Grove Mines Ltd.	Com.	.10
Associated Porcupine Mines Ltd.	Com.	.32
Astonish Lake Uranium Mining Corp. Ltd.	Com.	
Astrabrun Mines Ltd.	Com.	.03
Astral Communications Ltd.	Com.	1.97
Atco Industries Ltd.	Com.	8.13
Athabasca Columbia Resources Ltd.	Com.	1.65
Athena Mines Limited	Com.	.08
Atlanta Mines Ltd.	Com.	
Atlantic Coast Copper Corp. Ltd.	Com.	.46
Atlantic Nickel Mines Ltd.	Com.	.22
Atlantic Richfield Co.	Com.	64.13
Atlantic Sugar Refineries Co. Limited	Com.	6.38
Atlantic Sugar Refineries Co. Limited	A cu pr.	15.00
Atlantic Sugar Refineries Co. Limited	5 pc cu pr.	62.38
Atlantic Sugar Refineries Co. Limited	Wt.	1.40
Atlantic Trust Company	Com.	
Atlantic Tungsten Corp. Ltd.	Com.	.17
Atlas Explorations Limited	Com.	.32
Atlas Yellowknife Mines Ltd.	Com.	.05
Attila Resources Ltd.	Com.	1.13
Augdome Corp. Ltd.	Com.	.19
Augmitto Explorations Ltd.	Com.	
August Porcupine Gold Mines Ltd.	Com.	.02
Aunor Gold Mines Ltd.	Com.	2.30
Auscan Mining and Oil Corporation Limited	Com.	.90
Austin Investment Corp. Ltd.	Com.	.41
Auto Electric Services Co. Ltd.	Com.	6.00
Auto Marine Electric Ltd.	Com.	
Auto Marine Electric Ltd.	Pr.	.40
Automotive Hardware Limited	Com.	7.25
Autotelic Industries Ltd.	Com.	.65
Ava Gold Mining Co. Ltd.	Com.	
Avco Corporation	Com.	
Avilla International Explorations Ltd.	Com.	.28
Avino Mines & Resources Limited	Com.	.33
Avoca Mines Canada Ltd.	Com.	.65
Babine International Resources Ltd.	Com.	.14
Bahamas-Caribbean Development Corporation Limited	Com.	.16
Baker Talc Ltd.	Com.	.42
Balco Forest Products Ltd.	Com.	8.25
Bald Mountain Oil Co.	Com.	.03
Baldwin Consolidated Mines Ltd.	Com.	.01
Ballinderry Explorations Limited	Com.	.90
Bamboo Creek Gold Mines Ltd.	Com.	.80
Banco Finance Limited	Cl B.	
Bancroft Uranium Mines Ltd.	Com.	
Band-Ore Gold Mines Ltd.	Com.	.05
Bankeno Mines Ltd.	Com.	6.40
Bankfield Consolidated Mines Ltd.	Com.	.02
Bank of British Columbia	Com.	22.25
Bank of Montreal	Com.	18.50
Bank of Nova Scotia	Com.	31.13
Banner Porcupine Mines Ltd.	Com.	
Banque Canadienne Nationale	Com.	14.00

La Banque Provinciale du Canada	Com.	13.75
Bantam Mining Ltd.	Com.	.40
Barber-Ellis of Canada Ltd.	Com.	13.50
Barber Oil Corporation	Com.	48.50
Barbi Lake Copper Mines Ltd.	Com.	.15
Barcelona Traction Light & Power Co.	Com.	.20
Barclay Resources Ltd.	Com.	
Barex-Trust, The	Com.	.20
Barima Minerals Ltd.	Com.	.01
Barons Oil Limited	Com.	.05
Barrington Exploration Corp. Ltd.	Com.	.07
Bartaco Industries Limited	Com.	4.50
Barvallee Mines Ltd.	Com.	
Barymin Explorations Ltd.	Com.	1.20
Base Metals Mining Corp. Ltd.	Com.	.01
Bashaw Leduc Oil & Gas Limited	Com.	.05
Basic Resources International Limited	Com.	3.30
Baslen Petroleums Ltd.	Com.	.07
Bateman Bay Mining Co.	Com.	.06
Bathurst Norsemines Ltd.	Com.	.85
Bathurst Norsemines Ltd.	A wt.	
Bathurst Paper Ltd.	$5^1/_4$ pc cu 1963 pr.	6.75
Baton Broadcasting Ltd.	Com.	14.88
Bay Mills Ltd.	Com.	1.34
Bay Mills Ltd.	6 pc cu A 1st pr.	3.05
B.C. Turf Limited	Com.	4.00
Beacon Mining Co. Ltd.	Com.	.05
Bear International Industries Ltd.	Com.	.19
Beattie-Duquesne Mines Ltd.	Com.	.04
Beauce Placer Mining Co. Ltd.	Com.	.01
Beaumont Resources Limited	Com.	.09
Beauport Holdings Ltd.	Com.	.36
Beaver Engineering Ltd.	Com.	6.50
Beaver Lumber Co. Ltd.	Com.	19.50
Beaver Lumber Co. Ltd.	Cl A.	19.38
Beaver Lumber Co. Ltd.	$1.40 cu pr.	21.00
Becker Milk Co. Ltd.	Cl B pr.	10.00
Bel-Air Mining Ltd.	Com.	.92
Belcarra Explorations Ltd.	Com.	
Belding-Corticelli Limited	Com.	10.25
Belding-Corticelli Limited	7 pc cu pr.	10.34
Belding-Corticelli Limited	Wt.	2.80
Belgium Standard Ltd.	Com.	15.50
Belgium Standard Ltd.	5 pc cu pr.	
Bell Canada	Com.	46.88
Bell Canada	$3.20 cu cv pr.	52.38
Bell Canada	$3.34 cu cv cl B pr.	53.88
Bellechasse Mining Corp. Ltd.	Com.	.04
Belleterre Quebec Mines Ltd.	Com.	.15
Bellex Mines Ltd.	Com.	.02
Bell Knit Industries Ltd.	Com.	.88
Bell Molybdenum Mines Ltd.	Com.	.14
Belore Mines Ltd.	Com.	.16
Belra Explorations Ltd.	Com.	
Benson Mines Limited	Com.	.14
Berkley Hotel	Com.	1.75
Berncam International Industries Ltd.	Com.	6.13
Bethlehem Copper Corporation Ltd.	Com.	18.00
Betrust Investment Corporation Ltd.	Com.	16.50
Betrust Investment Corporation Ltd.	$5^3/_4$ pc cu A pr.	
Big I Mines Ltd.,The	Com.	
Big Jackpot Mines Ltd.	Com.	.01
Big Long Lac Gold Mining Co. Ltd.	Com.	.01
Big Nama Creek Mines Ltd.	Com.	.09
Big Town Copper Mines Ltd.	Com.	
Bilmac Gold Mines Ltd.	Com.	
Biltmore Hats Limited	Com.	13.00
Biltmore Hats Limited	Cl A cu pr.	10.50
Bio-Millet Laboratories	Com.	
Bird Construction Co. Ltd.	Com.	57.50
Bird River Mines Co. Ltd.	Com.	.65
Biroco Kirkland Mines Ltd.	Com.	.01
Biron Bay Gold Mines Ltd.	Com.	.23
Bison Petroleum & Minerals Ltd.	Com.	9.10
Black Bay Uranium Ltd.	Com.	
Black Cricket Mines Ltd.	Com.	.60
Black Giant Mines Ltd.	Com.	.30
Black Hawk Mining Ltd.	Com.	.50
Black Photo Corporation Ltd.	Com.	4.85
Blackwater Mines Ltd.	Com.	.30
Block Bros. Industries Ltd.	Com.	3.00
Block Bros. Industries Ltd.	A wt.	5.00
Block Bros. Industries Ltd.	B wt.	
Blue Bonnets Raceway Inc.	Com.	2.05
Blue Grass Uranium Mines Ltd.	Com.	.01
Blue Gulch Explorations Limited	Com.	.48
Blue Star Mines Limited	Com.	.06
Bluewater Oil & Gas Ltd.	Com.	.90
Bochawna Copper Mines Ltd.	Com.	
Bock & Frère Ltée	$6^3/_4$ pc cu pr.	
Boise Yellowknife Mines Ltd.	Com.	
Bombardier Limited	Cl A.	9.50
Bonanza Explorations Ltd.	Com.	
Bonnet Plume River Mines Ltd.	Com.	.15
Bon-Val Mines Ltd.	Com.	.44
Boraway Mines Ltd.	Com.	.11
Border Chemical Company Limited	Com.	10.38
Bordun Mining (Quebec) Limited	Com.	.30
Borealis Exploration Ltd.	Com.	.30
Borealis Exploration Ltd.	Wt.	
Boswell River Mines Ltd.	Com.	.22
Boundary Exploration Ltd.	Com.	.14
Bounty Exploration Ltd.	Com.	.13
Bourbeau Lake Mines Ltd.	Com.	.02
Bourlamaque Central Mines 1945 Ltd.	Com.	.02
Bovis Corporation Ltd.	Com.	1.90
Bowater Paper Corporation Ltd.	Com.	4.65
Bowaters Mersey Paper Company Ltd.	$5^1/_2$ pc cu pr.	32.00
Bowes Co. Ltd.	Com.	12.50
Bow Valley Industries Ltd.	Com.	28.38
Bow Valley Industries Ltd.	$5^1/_2$ pc cu A pr.	14.25
BP Canada Ltd.	5 pc pr.	75.00
BP Oil & Gas Limited	Com.	6.20
Bracemac Mines Ltd.	Com.	.03
Bralorne Can-Fer Resources Ltd.	Com.	1.75
Bralorne Oil & Gas Ltd.	Com.	2.25
Bralsaman Petroleums Ltd.	Com.	3.25
Bramalea Consolidated Development Ltd.	Com.	3.45
Bramalea Consolidated Development Ltd.	Wt.	2.10

Brameda Resources Limited	Com.	.92
Braminco Mines Ltd.	Com.	.03
Brandy Brook Mines Ltd.	Com.	.10
Brascan Limited	Com.	18.50
Brenda Mines Limited	Com.	4.55
Brenmac Mines Limited	Com.	.38
Brettland Mining Ltd.	Com.	
Brett Oils Limited	Com.	.23
Brewster Lake Mines Limited	Com.	.60
Briarcourt Mines Ltd.	Com.	.11
Bridge Hill Mines Limited	Com.	.38
Bridge & Tank Co. of Canada Ltd.	Com.	4.50
Bridge & Tank Co. of Canada Ltd.	$2.90 cu pr.	32.25
Bright & Co. Ltd. T.G.	Com.	16.00
Bright Red Lake Mines Ltd.	Com.	.01
Bright Star Trio Mining Ltd.	Com.	1.10
Brilund Mines Ltd.	Com.	8.00
Brinco Ltd.	Com.	5.63
British American Bank Note Co. Ltd.	Com.	13.00
British Columbia Forest Products Ltd.	Com.	19.75
British Columbia Forest Products Ltd.	6 pc cu pr.	41.50
British Columbia Oil Lands Limited	Com.	7.50
British Columbia Packers Ltd.	Cl A.	20.00
British Columbia Packers Ltd.	Cl B.	19.50
British Columbia Sugar Refinery Ltd.	Com.	19.38
British Columbia Sugar Refinery Ltd.	5 pc cu pr.	17.00
British Columbia Telephone Co.	Com.	63.75
British Columbia Telephone Co.	$4^{3}/_{8}$ pc cu pr.	63.00
British Columbia Telephone Co.	$4^{1}/_{2}$ pc cu pr.	63.00
British Columbia Telephone Co.	$4^{3}/_{4}$ pc C pr.	66.50
British Columbia Telephone Co.	$4^{3}/_{4}$ pc 1956 cu D pr.	66.00
British Columbia Telephone Co.	4.84 pc cu pr.	17.50
British Columbia Telephone Co.	5.15 pc cu pr.	71.50
British Columbia Telephone Co.	$5^{3}/_{4}$ pc cu pr.	80.50
British Columbia Telephone Co.	6 pc cu pr.	84.50
British Columbia Telephone Co.	6 pc cu 2nd pr.	82.00
British Columbia Telephone Co.	6.80 pc cu pr.	26.50
British Controlled Oilfields Ltd.	Com.	.20
British International Finance Canada Ltd.	Cl A.	
British Matachewan Gold Mines Ltd.	Com.	
Broken Hill Explorations Ltd.	Com.	.08
Brooke Bond Foods Ltd.	4.16 pc cu pr.	19.50
Brosnan Canadian Mines Ltd.	Com.	
Broulan Reef Mines Ltd.	Com.	.23
Brown-McDade Mines Ltd.	Com.	.10
Bruck Mills Ltd.	Cl A.	15.00
Bruck Mills Ltd.	Cl B.	8.00
Bruneau Mining Corporation 1970	Com.	.11
Brunswick Mining & Smelting Corp. Ltd.	Com.	3.05
Brycon Industries Ltd.	Com.	.18
Buchanan Mines Limited	Com.	.15
Buckeye Explorations Ltd.	Com.	.35
Budd Automotive Co. of Canada Ltd.	Com.	6.63
Budd Automotive Co. of Canada Ltd.	Wt.	2.40
Buffalo Gas & Oil Corporation Limited	Com.	1.05
Buffalo Lake Mines Ltd.	Com.	
Bullion Mountain Mining Ltd.	Com.	.65
Bullion Mountain Mining Ltd.	A wt.	
Bunker Hill Extension Mines Ltd.	Com.	.05
Burlington Mines & Enterprises Ltd.	Com.	

Burns Foods Limited	Com	12.75
Burnt Hill Tungsten & Metallurgical Ltd.	Com.	.18
Burrard Dry Dock Co. Ltd.	Com.	7.00
Burrard Mortgage Investments Ltd.	Com.	1.90
Burrex Mines Limited	Com.	.04
Bushnell Communications Limited	Com.	6.00
Buval Executive Mining Industries Ltd.	Com.	.40
Cable Copper Mines Limited	Com.	
Cabot Corporation	Com.	
Cadillac Development Corp. Ltd.	Com.	8.38
Cadillac Development Corp. Ltd.	$6^{1}/_{2}$ pc cu B pr.	20.25
Cadillac Explorations Ltd.	Com.	1.30
CAE Industries Ltd.	Com.	4.65
Calcorp Resources Ltd.	Com.	.14
Caledon Mountain Estates Ltd.	Com.	4.50
Calgary Power Ltd.	Com.	27.25
Calgary Power Ltd.	4 pc cu pr.	
Calgary Power Ltd.	$5.00 cu pr.	69.00
Calgary Power Ltd.	$5.40 cu cv pr.	91.00
Calico Silver Mines Ltd.	Com.	.18
Caliper Developments Limited	Com.	.75
Calix Mines Ltd.	Com.	.05
Calmark Industries Ltd.	Com.	
Calmor Iron Bay Mines Ltd.	Com.	.50
Calta Mines Limited	Com.	1.02
Calvert-Dale Estates Ltd.	Com.	.82
Calvert Gas & Oils Ltd.	Com.	.14
Cambridge Leaseholds Limited	Com.	11.50
Cambridge Mines Limited	Com.	.38
Cambridge Mining Corp. Ltd.	Com.	.02
Camdeck Mines Ltd.	Com.	.15
Camflo Mines Limited	Com.	2.51
Camindex Mines Ltd.	Com.	.13
Camlaren Mines Ltd.	Com.	.08
Cam Mines Ltd.	Com.	.30
Campbell Chibougamau Mines Ltd.	Com.	4.70
Campbell Red Lake Mines Ltd.	Com.	21.50
Campeau Corporation Ltd.	Com.	3.50
Canada & Dominion Sugar Co. Ltd.	Com.	32.50
Canada Cement Lafarge Ltd.	Com.	46.63
Canada Cement Lafarge Ltd.	$6^{1}/_{2}$ pc cu pr.	19.75
Canada Forgings Ltd.	Com.	4.50
Canada Geothermal Oil Ltd.	Com.	.68
Canada Machinery Corporation Ltd.	Com.	19.00
Canada Malting Co. Limited	Com.	26.00
Canada Malting Co. Limited	B pr.	.89
Canada Northwest Land Limited	Com.	1.50
Canada Packers Ltd.	Com.	18.50
Canada Permanent Mortgage Corporation	Com.	18.00
Canada Safeway Limited	$4.40 cu pr.	82.50
Canada Southern Petroleum Ltd.	Com.	6.20
Canada Southern Petroleum Ltd.	Wt.	3.10
Canada Steamship Lines Ltd.	Com.	40.00
Canada Steamship Lines Ltd.	5 pc cu pr.	5.13
Canada Tungsten Mining Corp. Ltd.	Com.	1.55
Canada Western Cordage Company Ltd.	Cl A.	
Canada Western Cordage Company Ltd.	Cl B.	
Canadex Mining Corp. Ltd.	Com.	.13
Canadian Allied Property Investments Limited	Com.	7.00

Canadian All-Metal Explorations Ltd.	Com.	
Canadian Arena Co.	Com.	15.00
Canadian Arrow Mines Limited	Com.	.14
Canadian Barranca Corp. Ltd.	Com.	.22
Canadian Bonanza Petroleums Ltd.	Com.	1.30
Canadian Breweries Limited	Com.	7.50
Canadian Breweries Limited	$2.20 cu A pr.	32.00
Canadian Breweries Limited	$2.65 cu B pr.	36.50
Canadian Cablesystems Ltd.	Com.	14.13
Canadian Cablesystems Ltd.	Wt.	2.25
Canadian Canners Ltd.	Cl A.	6.50
Canadian Converters Co. Ltd.	Cl A.	2.00
Canadian Converters Co. Ltd.	Cl B.	
Canadian Corporate Management Company Limited	Com.	16.00
Canadian Corporate Management Company Limited	Cl B.	
Canadian Curtiss-Wright Ltd.	Com.	.70
Canadian Delhi Oil Limited	Com.	5.00
Canadian Equity & Development Company Limited	Com.	12.00
Canadian Export Gas & Oil Ltd.	Com.	3.60
Canadian Food Products Ltd.	Com.	5.20
Canadian Food Products Ltd.	6 pc cu 1st pr.	32.50
Canadian Food Products Ltd.	6 pc cv 2nd pr.	32.00
Canadian & Foreign Securities Co. Ltd.	Com.	
Canadian Fortune Oil Limited	Com.	
Canadian Foundation Co. Ltd.	Com.	6.00
Canadian Foundation Co. Ltd.	6 pc cu A pr.	7.75
Canadian Gas & Energy Fund Ltd.	B wt.	7.25
Canadian General Electric Company Ltd.	Com.	22.50
Canadian General Electric Company Ltd.	Cu cv pr.	26.00
Canadian General Investments Ltd.	Com.	66.00
Canadian General Securities Limited	Cl A.	12.75
Canadian General Securities Limited	Cl B.	30.00
Canadian Goldale Corp. Ltd.	Com.	3.50
Canadian Hidrogas Resources Ltd.	Com.	.72
Canadian Homestead Oils Limited	Com.	8.60
Canadian Homestead Oils Limited	6 pc cu cv pr.	17.00
Canadian Hydrocarbons Ltd.	Com.	13.88
Canadian Hydrocarbons Ltd.	$5\frac{1}{2}$ pc cu A pr.	14.00
Canadian Imperial Bank of Commerce	Com.	25.75
Canadian Industrial Gas & Oil Ltd.	Com.	9.13
Canadian Industrial Gas & Oil Ltd.	$5\frac{1}{2}$ pc cu cv pr.	21.50
Canadian Industries Ltd.	Com.	13.88
Canadian Industries Ltd.	$7\frac{1}{2}$ pc cu pr.	52.50
Canadian International Investment Trust Ltd.	Com.	32.00
Canadian International Investment Trust Ltd.	5 pc cu pr.	
Canadian International Power Company Ltd.	Com.	22.50
Canadian International Power Company Ltd.	5.20 pc 1965 cu. pr.	13.50
Canadian Interurban Properties Limited	Com.	2.00
Canadian Interurban Properties Limited	7 pc cu cv A pr.	7.75
Canadian Jamieson Mines Ltd.	Com.	1.25
Canadian Javelin Limited	Com.	9.60
Canadian Keeley Mines Ltd.	Com.	.05
Canadian Leisure Industries Ltd.	Com.	.06
Canadian Lencourt Mines Ltd.	Com.	.07
Canadian Long Island Petroleums Ltd.	Com.	.65
Canadian Magnesite Mines Ltd.	Com.	.31
Canadian Malartic Gold Mines Ltd.	Com.	.27
Canadian Manoir Industries Limited	Com.	3.35
Canadian Manoir Industries Limited	6 pc cu pr.	
Canadian Marconi Company	Com.	3.05
Canadian Merrill Ltd.	Com.	4.75
Canadian Nistro Mines Ltd.	Com.	.09
Canadian Occidental Petroleum Ltd.	Com.	9.13
Canadian Pacific Investments Limited	Com.	12.00
Canadian Pacific Investments Limited	$4\frac{3}{4}$ pc cv A pr.	24.50
Canadian Pacific Investments Limited	Wt.	3.05
Canadian Pacific Limited	Ordinary	13.88
Canadian Pacific Limited	4 pc pr Canadian unit	9.63
Canadian Pacific Limited	4 pc pr United Kingdom unit	7.75
Canadian Pacific Limited	$7\frac{1}{4}$ pc A pr.	10.75
Canadian Provident, The	Com.	
Canadian Refractories Ltd.	Com.	
Canadian Reserve Oil & Gas Ltd.	Com.	5.60
Canadian Reynolds Metals Co. Limited	Pr.	
Canadian Salt Co. Ltd.	Com.	15.00
Canadian Scenic Oils Ltd.	Com.	.80
Canadian Security Management Ltd.	Cl A.	1.25
Canadian Southern Cross Mines (No Liability)	Com.	
Canadian Superior Oil Ltd.	Com.	43.25
Canadian Tire Corp. Ltd.	Com.	40.25
Canadian Tire Corp. Ltd.	Cl A.	35.38
Canadian Tricentrol Oils Ltd.	Com.	14.63
Canadian Union Insurance Company	Com.	
Canadian Utilities Limited	Com.	37.25
Canadian Utilities Limited	$4\frac{1}{4}$ pc cu pr.	57.25
Canadian Utilities Limited	5 pc cu pr.	66.50
Canadian Utilities Limited	6 pc cu pr.	78.75
Canadian Utilities Limited	Wt.	8.50
Canadian Vickers Ltd.	Com.	9.25
Canadian Wallpaper Manufacturers Ltd.	Com.	85.50
Canadian Western Natural Gas Company Limited	Com.	21.00
Canadian Western Natural Gas Company Limited	4 pc cu pr.	11.50
Canadian Western Natural Gas Company Limited	$5\frac{1}{2}$ pc cu pr.	15.00
Canadore Mining & Development Corp.	Com.	.10
Can-American Natural Resources Ltd.	Com.	
Can-American Petroleums Ltd.	Com.	
Canarctic Resources Ltd.	Com.	.27
Can-Base Industries Ltd.	Com.	.18
Canbridge Oil Explorations Ltd.	Com.	1.50
Can-Con Enterprises & Explorations Ltd.	Com.	.10
Candida Holdings Naamloze Vennootschap	Com.	16.75
Candore Explorations Ltd.	Com.	.04
Candy Mines & Investments Ltd.	Com.	.12
Caneonti Mines Ltd.	Com.	.01
Cannon Mines Limited	Com.	.07
Canol Metal Mines Ltd.	Com.	.02
Canol Mines Limited	Com.	.25
Canron Ltd.	Com.	19.38

Canron Ltd.	4 1/4 pc cu cv pr.	70.00
Canterra Development Corp. Ltd.	Com.	1.00
Cantol Ltd.	Com.	3.40
Cantrend Industries Ltd.	Cl A.	
Cantrend Industries Ltd.	Cl B.	
Canuc Mines Limited	Com.	.30
Canyon City Explorations Ltd.	Com.	.05
C-A Petroleums Ltd.	Com.	
Capital Diversified Industries Ltd.	Com.	.59
Capital Diversified Industries Ltd.	A wt.	.15
Capital Dynamics Ltd.	Com.	1.80
Capital Dynamics Ltd.	Wt.	.03
Capital Estates Inc.	Com.	
Capri Mining Corporation Ltd.	Com.	.14
Caprive Industries & Resources Limited	Com.	.09
Captain International Industries Limited	Com.	6.00
Captain Mines Limited	Com.	.11
Cara Operations Ltd.	Com.	4.60
Caravelle Mines Ltd.	Com.	.11
Card Lake Copper Mines Ltd.	Com.	.10
Cardwell Resources Limited	Com.	.15
Cariboo-Bell Copper Mines Limited	Com.	.25
Cariboo Gold Quartz Mining Co. Ltd.	Com.	.95
Carling Copper Mines Ltd.	Com.	.20
Carlson Mines Ltd.	Com.	
Carlton Cleaning Carousels Ltd.	Com.	.25
Carndesson Mines Ltd.	Com.	
Carnegie New Mining Corp. Ltd.	Com.	
Carolin Mines Limited	Com.	.20
Carrier Shoe Co. Ltd. J.D.	Com.	6.63
Carrier Shoe Co. Ltd. J.D.	Wt.	3.25
Carroll & Reed Ltd.	Com.	
Carter J. B. Ltd.	Cl A.	10.12
Carter J. B. Ltd.	Cl B.	60.00
Cartier Quebec Explorations Ltd.	Com.	.10
Casavant Brothers Limited	Cl A.	1.00
Cascade Molybdenum Mines Ltd.	Com.	.23
Casino Silver Mines Ltd.	Com.	.55
Cassiar Asbestos Corporation Limited	Com.	18.63
Cassiar Consolidated Mines Ltd.	Com.	.10
Cassidy's Ltd.	Com.	4.35
Cassidy's Ltd.	6 1/4 pc cu cv A 1st pr.	8.75
Castlebar Silver & Cobalt Mines Ltd.	Com.	.06
Castle Oil and Gas Limited	Com.	1.40
C & C Yachts Ltd.	Com.	2.50
CDP Computer Data Processors Ltd.	Com.	1.30
CDRH Limited	Com.	5.88
Cedarvale Mines Ltd.	Com.	.35
Celtic Minerals Ltd.	Com.	.79
Centex Mines Ltd.	Com.	.12
Central Dynamics Limited	Com.	.90
Central Fund of Canada Ltd.	Cl A.	6.25
Central Ontario Savings & Loan Corp.	Com.	8.00
Central Patricia Gold Mines Ltd.	Com.	1.70
Central Trust Company of Canada, The	Com.	13.75
Centura Mining Ltd.	Com.	.36
Cessland Corp. Ltd.	Com.	.28
CFTO-TV Limited	Com.	
CGC Mines Ltd.	Com.	
Chance Mining & Exploration Co. Ltd.	Com.	

Chapparal Mines Limited	Com.	.16
Charter Industries Ltd.	Com.	1.30
Charter Oil Company Ltd.	Com.	6.00
Chataway Exploration Co. Ltd.	Com.	.17
Chateau-Gai Wines Ltd.	Com.	16.88
Chemalloy Mineral Ltd.	Com.	2.06
Chemcell Ltd.	Com.	4.35
Chemcell Ltd.	$1.00 cu pr.	12.50
Chemcell Ltd.	$1.75 cu pt pr.	19.75
Chesbar Iron Powder Limited	Com.	2.00
Chesbar Iron Powder Limited	Wt.	.40
Chesterville Mines Limited	Com.	.10
Chibex Mining Corp.	Com.	.38
Chib-Kayrand Copper Mines Ltd.	Com.	.05
Chibougamau Mining & Smelting Co. Inc.	Com.	.29
Chiboug Copper Corp. Ltd.	Com.	.18
Chieftain Development Company Ltd.	Com.	8.10
Chimo Gold Mines Ltd.	Com.	1.20
Chinook Shopping Centre Limited	Com.	3.00
Chipman Mining & Energy Corp. Ltd.	Com.	.40
Choiceland Iron Mines Ltd.	Com.	.25
Chromex Nickel Mines Ltd.	Com.	.18
Chromium Mining & Smelting Corporation Limited	Com.	1.75
Chrysler Corporation	Com.	29.75
Chukuni Gold Mines Ltd.	Com.	.04
CHUM Limited	Com.	5.50
CHUM Limited	Cl B.	8.50
Churchill Copper Corporation Ltd.	Com.	.75
Cicada Mines Ltd.	Com.	.03
Cimco Limited	Cl A.	12.06
Cincinnati-Porcupine Mines Ltd.	Com.	.02
Cinola Mines Ltd.	Com.	.08
Citadel Mines Ltd.	Com.	.04
Citex Mines Ltd.	Com.	.05
Cities Service Company	Com.	
City Associated Enterprises Ltd.	Cl B.	.70
Clairtone Sound Corporation Limited	Com.	
Clarepine Development Ltd.	Com.	.20
Clark Canadian Exploration Co.	Com.	3.75
Clavos Porcupine Mines Ltd.	Com.	.02
Claw Lake Molybdenum Mines Ltd.	Com.	.03
Clearwater Mines Ltd.	Com.	.15
Clero Mines Ltd.	Com.	.06
Cleveland Mining & Smelting Co.	Com.	.05
Clicker Red Lake Mines Ltd.	Com.	
Clinger Gold Mines Ltd.	Com.	.02
Coast Copper Company Limited	Com.	3.00
Coast Interior Ventures	Com.	.75
Coast Silver Mines Ltd.	Com.	.14
Cochenour Willans Gold Mines Ltd.	Com.	.21
Cochrane-Dunlop Hardware Ltd.	Com.	35.00
Cochrane-Dunlop Hardware Ltd.	Cl A.	30.50
Cockfield Brown & Company Limited	Com.	6.00
Codville Distributors Ltd.	Cl A.	3.75
Coin Canyon Mines Ltd.	Com.	
Coin Canyon Mines Ltd.	A wt.	
Coin Lake Gold Mines Ltd.	Com.	.09
Coleman Collieries Ltd.	Cl A.	7.00
Coleman Collieries Ltd.	Cl B.	6.95
Coleman Collieries Ltd.	6 pc 1st cv pr.	.73

Coleman Collieries Ltd.	B wt.	2.51
Colleen Copper Mines Ltd.	Com.	.12
College Plumbing Supplies Ltd.	Com.	4.00
Collingwood Terminals Ltd.	Com.	
Collingwood Terminals Ltd.	Pr.	
Colonial Oil and Gas Ltd.	Com.	.65
Columbia Cellulose Company Limited	Com.	2.90
Columbia Cellulose Company Limited	$1.20 cu cv pr.	8.63
Columbia Gas System Inc.	Com.	
Columbia Metals Corporation Ltd.	Com.	.36
Columbia Placers Ltd.	Com.	.08
Columbia River Mines Limited	Com.	.28
Columbiere Mines Ltd.	Com.	
Comaplex Resources International Ltd.	Com.	1.80
Comaplex Resources International Ltd.	A wt.	.64
Combined Engineered Products Limited	Com.	2.60
Combined Engineered Products Limited	$1.10 cu cv pr.	11.88
Combined Insurance Co. of America	Com.	40.00
Combined Larder Mines Ltd.	Com.	.01
Combined Metal Mines Ltd.	Com.	.12
Comet Industries Ltd.	Com.	.70
Cominco Ltd.	Com.	22.88
Cominga Compagnie Minière de l'Ungava	Com.	.03
Commerce Nickel Mines Ltd.	Com.	.08
Commercial Finance Corporation Limited	Com.	
Commercial Holdings & Metals Corp.	Com.	2.00
Commercial Life Assurance Co. of Canada	Com.	
Commercial Oil & Gas Limited	Com.	.09
Commodore Business Machines (Canada) Limited	Com.	8.13
Commodore Business Machines (Canada) Limited	A wt.	4.25
Commonwealth Holiday Inns of Canada Ltd.	Com.	12.25
Compton Exploration Ltd.	Com.	
Computel Systems Ltd.	Com.	3.00
Computrex Centres Ltd.	Com.	.38
Comstock Keno Mines Ltd.	Com.	.07
Comtech Group International Limited	Com.	1.90
Comtech Group International Limited	5 pc cu pr.	
Concorde Explorations Ltd.	Com.	
Concourse Building Ltd.	Com.	
Condor Mines Limited	Com.	.11
Conduits National Co. Ltd.	Com.	3.00
Congress Mining Corporation Limited	Com.	.48
Coniagas Mines Ltd.	Com.	.28
Conigo Mines Ltd.	Com.	.13
Conoco Silver Mines Ltd.	Com.	.25
Con Quest Exploration Ltd.	Com.	.40
Consolidated Ad Astra Minerals Ltd.	Com.	.11
Consolidated Bathurst Limited	Com.	7.88
Consolidated Bathurst Limited	6 pc cu pr.	11.75
Consolidated Bathurst Limited	1968 Wt.	3.00
Consolidated Bathurst Limited	Wt.	.55
Consolidated Bellekemo Mines Ltd.	Com.	.01
Consolidated Brewis Minerals Ltd.	Com.	.08
Consolidated Buffalo Red Lake Mines Ltd.	Com.	.07
Consolidated Building Corp. Ltd.	Com.	1.50
Consolidated Building Corp. Ltd.	6 pc cu A pr.	
Consolidated Callinan Flin-Flon Mines Limited	Com.	.07
Consolidated Canadian Faraday Ltd.	Com.	.80
Consolidated Canorama Exploration Ltd.	Com.	.15
Consolidated Daering Mining Inc.	Com.	.09
Consolidated Developments Ltd.	Com.	.70
Consolidated Diversified Standard Securities Ltd.	Cl A.	2.50
Consolidated Diversified Standard Securities Ltd.	$2.50 1st pr.	25.00
Consolidated Dolsam Mines Ltd.	Com.	.12
Consolidated Durham Mines & Resources Ltd.	Com.	.73
Consolidated East Crest Oil Company Limited	Com.	1.52
Consolidated Fenimore Iron Mines Ltd.	Com.	.02
Consolidated Gem Exploration Ltd.	Com.	.05
Consolidated Harpers Malartic Gold Mines Ltd.	Com.	.05
Consolidated Imperial Minerals Ltd.	Com.	.07
Consolidated Manitoba Mines Ltd.	Com.	
Consolidated Marbenor Mines Ltd.	Com.	1.55
Consolidated Marcus Gold Mines Ltd.	Com.	.05
Consolidated Mogador Mines Ltd.	Com.	.03
Consolidated Monpas Mines Ltd.	Com.	
Consolidated Montclerg Mines Ltd.	Com.	.03
Consolidated Morrison Explorations Ltd.	Com.	1.58
Consolidated Negus Mines Ltd.	Com.	.07
Consolidated Nicholson Mines Ltd.	Com.	.05
Consolidated Northern Exploration Ltd.	Com.	.29
Consolidated Novell Mines Ltd.	Com.	.02
Consolidated Oil & Gas Inc.	Com.	
Consolidated Panther Mines Ltd.	Com.	.30
Consolidated Pershcourt Mining Ltd.	Com.	
Consolidated Professor Mines Ltd.	Com.	
Consolidated Proprietary Mines Holdings Ltd.	Com.	.06
Consolidated Prudential Mines Ltd.	Com.	.10
Consolidated Rambler Mines Ltd.	Com.	1.55
Consolidated Rexspar Minerals & Chemicals Limited	Com.	.16
Consolidated Ribago Mines Ltd.	Com.	.02
Consolidated Shunsby Mines Ltd.	Com.	.10
Consolidated Standard Mines Ltd.	Com.	.05
Consolidated Textile Mills Ltd.	Com.	4.75
Consolidated Theatres Ltd.	Cl A.	
Consolidated Vigor Mines Ltd.	Com.	.03
Consolidated Virginia Mining Corp.	Com.	
Consolidated West Petroleum Limited	Com.	1.28
Consumers Distributing Company Limited	Com.	23.88
Consumers Gas Company	Com.	19.50
Consumers Gas Company	$5^1/_2$ pc cu A pr.	83.25
Consumers Gas Company	$5^1/_2$ pc cu B pr.	84.00
Consumers Glass Co. Ltd.	Com.	10.50
Contact Ventures Ltd.	Com.	.55
Continental Can Company Inc.	Com.	32.00
Continental Cinch Mines Ltd.	Com.	.09
Continental Copper Mines Ltd.	Com.	.08
Continental McKinney Mines Ltd.	Com.	.08
Continental Potash Corporation Ltd.	Com.	.04
Continental Research & Development Ltd.	Com.	7.00
Controlled Foods International Ltd.	Com.	1.90
Conuco Limited	Com.	.35

Conwest Exploration Co. Ltd.	Com.	7.75
Cooper of Canada Ltd.	Com.	14.50
Copconda Mines Ltd.	Com.	
Copeland Process Ltd.	Com.	4.00
Cop-Mac Mines Ltd.	Com.	.23
Copp-Clark Publishing Co. Ltd.	Pr.	
Coppercorp Limited	Com.	.15
Copper Corp. of America	Com.	.08
Copperfields Mining Corp. Ltd.	Com.	1.25
Copper Giant Mining Corporation Ltd.	Com.	.10
Copper Horn Mining Ltd.	Com.	.04
Copper Lake Explorations Ltd.	Com.	.31
Copperline Mines Limited	Com.	.19
Copper-Lode Mines Ltd.	Com.	.09
Copper-Man Mines Ltd.	Com.	.04
Copper Pass Mines Ltd.	Com.	
Copper Queen Explorations Limited	Com.	.09
Copper Ridge Mines Ltd.	Com.	.22
Copperstream-Frontenac Mines Ltd.	Com.	
Copperville Mining Corp. Ltd.	Com.	.09
Corby Distilleries Limited	Cl A.	23.00
Corby Distilleries Limited	Cl B.	23.50
Corgemines Limited	Com.	.20
Cornat Industries Limited	Com.	1.65
Coronation Allied Industries Ltd.	Com.	.57
Coronation Credit Corp. Ltd.	Com.	1.20
Coronation Credit Corp. Ltd.	6 pc cu cv A pr.	1.75
Coronation Credit Corp. Ltd.	Wt. series 2	
Coronet Mines Limited	Com.	.25
Corporate Foods Ltd.	Com.	8.00
Corporate Foods Ltd.	$2.75 A cu pr.	28.00
Corporate Properties Ltd.	Com.	3.31
Corporation d'expansion financière	Com.	1.25
Coseka Resources Limited	Com.	1.01
Cosmic Nickel Mines Limited	Com.	.09
Cosmos Imperial Mills Limited	Com.	.85
Costain Richard Canada Ltd.	Com.	7.50
Coulee Lead & Zinc Mines Ltd.	Com.	.13
Courier Explorations Ltd.	Com.	.28
Courvan Mining Co. Ltd.	Com.	.07
Cove Uranium Mines Ltd.	Com.	
Cowl Limited	Com.	3.50
Crackingstone Mines Ltd.	Com.	.04
Craibbe Fletcher Gold Mines Ltd.	Com.	.01
Craig Bit Co. Ltd., The	Com.	4.75
Craigmont Mines Ltd.	Com.	7.00
Crain Limited, R. L.	Com.	11.13
Crawford Allied Industries Ltd.	Com.	1.85
Cream Silver Mines Limited	Com.	.24
Creative Patents & Products Limited	Com.	2.25
Credit Foncier Franco-Canadien	Com.	57.00
Credo Mining Limited	Com.	.05
Cree Lake Mining	Com.	.40
Crestbrook Forest Industries Ltd.	Com.	3.90
Crestland Mines Ltd.	Com.	.07
Crest Ventures Ltd.	Com.	.18
Crestwood Kitchens Ltd.	Com.	1.75
Cresus Mining Limited	Com.	.07
Creswell Mines Ltd.	Com.	
Cross Co. Ltd., W. B.	Com.	3.00
Crowbank Mines Ltd.	Com.	.12

Crownbridge Copper Mines Ltd.	Com.	.03
Crown Cork & Seal Co. Ltd.	Com.	150.00
Crown Life Insurance Company	Com.	30.25
Crown Trust Company	Com.	15.50
Crown Zellerbach Canada Ltd.	Cl A.	16.63
Crows Nest Industries Ltd.	Com.	26.00
Croydon Mines Ltd.	Com.	.14
Croydon Rouyn Mines Ltd.	Com.	.03
Crusade Petroleum Corp. Ltd.	Com.	.65
Crush International Ltd.	Com.	19.00
Cultus Exploration Ltd.	Com.	.20
Cumex Mines Ltd.	Com.	.45
Cummings Properties Limited	Com.	
Cumont Mines Ltd.	Com.	.32
Cunningham Drug Stores Limited	Com.	
Cuvier Mines Ltd.	Com.	.10
Cygnus Corporation Ltd.	Cl A.	5.75
Cygnus Corporation Ltd.	Cl B.	6.25
Dairy Barn Stores of Canada Limited	Com.	2.07
Dairy Barn Stores of Canada Limited	Wt.	.38
Dale-Ross Holdings Ltd.	Com.	7.50
Dale-Ross Holdings Ltd.	6 pc cu A pr.	7.50
Dalex Co. Limited	7 pc cu pr.	80.00
Dalex Mines Limited	Com.	.06
Dalfen's Ltd.	Com.	12.50
Dalhousie Oil Co. Ltd.	Com.	.18
Daniel Diversified Ltd.	Com.	.30
Dankoe Mines	Com.	.60
D'Aragon Mines Ltd.	Com.	.17
Darkhawk Mines Limited	Com.	.40
Darsi Mines Limited	Com.	.09
Dasson Copper Corp. Ltd.	Com.	.19
Dataline Systems Ltd.	Com.	1.83
Datapro Ltd.	Com.	2.25
Datateck Systems Ltd.	Com.	1.00
Dauphin Iron Mines Ltd.	Com.	.07
David Minerals Limited	Com.	.27
Davis Distributing & Vending Ltd.	Com.	1.30
Davis-Keays Mining Co. Ltd.	Com.	.70
Dawson Developments Ltd.	Com.	6.00
Debenture & Securities Corp. of Canada	5 pc cu pr.	
Debhold (Canada) Limited	$6\frac{1}{4}$ pc cu B pr.	78.00
Decca Resources Limited	Com.	2.20
Deerhorn Mines Ltd.	Com.	.03
Dejour Mines Ltd.	Com.	.17
Delahey Consolidated Nickel Mines Limited	Com.	.05
D'Eldona Gold Mines Ltd.	Com.	.45
Delhi Pacific Mines Ltd.	Com.	.07
Delkirk Mining Ltd.	Com.	.07
Delmico Mines Ltd.	Com.	.03
Delta-Benco	Com.	1.65
Delta Hotels Ltd.	Com.	2.30
Delta Hotels Ltd.	6 pc cl A pr.	1.35
Delta Hotels Ltd.	Rt.	
Delta Minerals Corp.	Com.	
Delta Petroleum Corporation Ltd.	Com.	.73
Deltan Corp. Ltd.	Com.	6.38
Deltec Panamerica (Sociedad Anonima)	Com.	1.00
Demsey Mines Ltd.	Com.	.17
Denison Mines Ltd.	Com.	24.50

Derby Mines Ltd.	Com.	
Derlak Red Lake Gold Mines Ltd.	Com.	.01
Deseret Peak Mines Ltd.	Com.	.18
Desjardins Mines Ltd.	Com.	.55
Despina Gold Mines Ltd.	Com.	
Destorbelle Mines Ltd.	Com.	.01
Devil's Elbow Mines Ltd.	Com.	.06
Dickenson Mines Ltd.	Com.	.85
Dictator Mines Ltd.	Com.	.33
Discovery Mines Ltd.	Com.	.75
Dison International Ltd.	Com.	1.34
Distillers Corporation-Seagrams Ltd.	Com.	31.25
District Trust Co.	Com.	15.00
Diversified Credit Corp. Ltd.	Com.	
Dixie-Carolina Mining Corp. Ltd.	Com.	
D L P Diversified Ltd.	Com.	
Dog'n Suds Food Services Ltd.	Com.	.25
Dolly Varden Mines Ltd.	Com.	.35
Doman Industries Ltd.	Com.	9.75
Doman Industries Ltd.	$6\frac{1}{2}$ pc cu cv A pr.	39.00
Doman Industries Ltd.	Wt.	22.00
Domco Industries Limited	Com.	5.00
Dome Mines Ltd.	Com.	54.50
Dome Petroleum Ltd.	Com.	34.00
Dominion & Anglo Investment Corporation Ltd.	Com.	
Dominion & Anglo Investment Corporation Ltd.	5 pc cu pr.	74.25
Dominion Bridge Co. Ltd.	Com.	23.75
Dominion Citrus & Drugs Ltd.	Com.	8.50
Dominion Coal Co. Ltd.	Pr.	23.38
Dominion Corset Co. Ltd.	Com.	6.00
Dominion Dairies Ltd.	Com.	34.00
Dominion Dairies Ltd.	5 pc pr.	25.00
Dominion Explorers Ltd.	Com.	1.40
Dominion Fabrics Limited	Com.	
Dominion Fabrics Limited	Cl A cu pt pr.	4.38
Dominion Foundries & Steel Ltd.	Com.	25.00
Dominion Foundries & Steel Ltd.	$4\frac{3}{4}$ pc cu A pr.	74.00
Dominion Glass Company Limited	Com.	10.25
Dominion Glass Company Limited	7 pc cu cv pr.	12.75
Dominion Jubilee Corp. Ltd.	Com.	.70
Dominion Leaseholds Ltd.	Com.	.06
Dominion Life Assurance Co.	Com.	95.00
Dominion Lime Limited	Com.	7.88
Dominion Lime Limited	Wt.	.50
Dominion Magnesium Ltd.	Com.	6.00
Dominion of Canada General Insurance Co.	Com.	
Dominion-Scottish Investments Ltd.	Com.	15.68
Dominion-Scottish Investments Ltd.	5 pc cu pr.	30.75
Dominion Stores Ltd.	Com.	15.00
Dominion Textile Limited	Com.	21.00
Dominion Textile Limited	7 pc cu pr.	101.00
Domtar Limited	Com.	12.25
Domtar Limited	$1.00 cu pr.	13.38
Donalda Mines Ltd.	Com.	.08
Donlee Manufacturing Industries Limited	Com.	4.50
Donna Mines Limited	Com.	.07
Donohue Company Limited	Com.	4.00
Donohue Company Limited	$6\frac{1}{4}$ pc cu pr.	15.75
Donrand Mines Ltd.	Com.	
Don-X Mines Ltd.	Com.	
Doral Mining Exploration Ltd.	Com.	
Dorion Red Lake Mines Ltd.	Com.	.01
Dorita Silver Mines Ltd.	Com.	.11
Douglas Leaseholds Limited	Com.	2.25
Dove Lake Mines Inc.	Com.	.40
Dover Industries Ltd.	Com.	15.00
Dover Industries Ltd.	6 pc cu pr.	8.00
DRG Limited	Com.	14.00
Drummond Die & Stamping Co. Ltd.	Com.	.16
Drummond Welding & Steel Works Ltd.	Cl A.	3.00
Dubuisson Goldfields Ltd.	Com.	.03
Ducros Mines Ltd.	Com.	.16
Duke Mining Company Limited	Com.	.20
Dumagami Mines Limited	Com.	.19
Dumont Nickel Corporation	Com.	.29
Duncan Range Iron Mines Ltd.	Com.	.10
Dundee Mines Ltd.	Com.	.18
Dunraine Mines Ltd.	Com.	.14
Dunterra Mines Ltd.	Com.	
Dunvegan Mines Ltd.	Com.	
Dupont of Canada Ltd.	Com.	20.25
Dupont of Canada Ltd.	$7\frac{1}{2}$ pc cu pr.	52.00
Duport Mining Co. Ltd.	Com.	
Dupuis Frères Limited	Cl A cu pr.	6.00
Dustbane Enterprises Ltd.	Com.	6.50
Dusty Mac Mines Limited	Com.	.10
Duvan Copper Co. Ltd.	Com.	.03
Duvex Oils & Mines Ltd.	Com.	.02
Dylex Diversified Limited	Com.	8.75
Dylex Diversified Limited	Cl A pt pr.	8.63
Dynacore Enterprises Ltd.	Com.	
Dynaco Resources Ltd.	Com.	.25
Dynalta Oil & Gas Co. Ltd.	Com.	1.25
Dynamic Mining Exploration Ltd.	Com.	.16
Dynamic Petroleum Products Ltd.	Com.	1.02
Dynamo Mines Limited	Com.	.17
Dynasty Exploration Ltd.	Com.	5.90
Eagle Gold Mines Ltd.	Com.	3.00
Eagle Industries Limited	Com.	5.63
Eagle River Mines Limited	Com.	.38
Earlcrest Resources Ltd.	Com.	.11
Early Bird Mines Ltd.	Com.	.13
East Amphi Gold Mines Ltd.	Com.	.01
East Bay Gold Ltd.	Com.	.04
Eastern Bakeries Ltd.	Com.	4.00
Eastern Bakeries Ltd.	4 pc cu pr.	
Eastern Canada Savings & Loan Company	Com.	12.50
Eastern Utilities Limited	$5\frac{1}{2}$ pc cu. pr.	
Eastgate	Com.	.73
East Lun Gold Mines Ltd.	Com.	.01
East Malartic Mines Ltd.	Com.	.95
Eastmont Larder Lake Gold Mines Ltd.	Com.	
Eastmont Silver Mines Ltd.	Com.	
Eastrock Explorations Ltd.	Com.	.40
East Sullivan Mines Ltd.	Com.	2.70
East Ventures Ltd.	Com.	.04
Eastview Mines Ltd.	Com.	
Eaton Corporation	Com.	42.00

Echo Bay Mining Ltd.	Com.	.15
Economic Investment Trust Ltd.	Com.	13.75
Economic Investment Trust Ltd.	5 pc cu A pr.	32.50
Eddy Match Co. Ltd.	Com.	10.25
Edmonton Concrete Block Co. Ltd.	Com.	
Edmonton International Speedway Ltd.	Com.	.65
EDP Industries Limited	Com.	.30
EDP Industries Limited	5 pc cu cv A pr.	
EDP Industries Limited	Wt.	
Ego Mines Ltd.	Com.	.09
El Bonanza Mining Corp. Ltd.	Com.	.12
El Coco Explorations Ltd.	Com.	.07
Electrohome Limited	Com.	41.00
Electrohome Limited	$5^3/_4$ pc cu A pr.	77.75
Electro-Knit Fabrics (Canada) Ltd.	Com.	5.38
Electronic Associates of Canada Limited	Com.	2.25
E-L Financial Corporation Limited	Com.	6.88
E-L Financial Corporation Limited	A cv pr.	9.75
E-L Financial Corporation Limited	Wt.	2.45
Elk Creek Waterworks Co. Ltd.	Com.	
Elmac Malartic Mines Ltd.	Com.	.03
El Paso Natural Gas Company	Com.	
Embassy Petroleums Ltd.	Com.	.43
Embassy Petroleums Ltd.	A wt.	.20
Emco Limited	Com.	6.25
Emperor Mines Ltd.	Com.	.10
Empire Life Insurance Co., The	Com.	8.00
Empire Metals Corporation Ltd.	Com.	.10
Empire Minerals Inc.	Com.	.05
Enamel & Heating Products Limited	Cl A.	2.25
Enamel & Heating Products Limited	Cl B.	1.25
Enex Mines Ltd.	Com.	.21
Entarea Management Ltd.	Com.	5.00
Equatorial Resources Limited	Com.	.19
Ericksen-Ashby Mines Ltd.	Com.	
Erie Diversified Industries Ltd.	Com.	8.00
Erie Diversified Industries Ltd.	Cl A.	8.00
ERI Explorations Inc.	Com.	.77
Eskimo Copper Mines Ltd.	Com.	.12
Essex Packers Limited	Com.	
Essex Packers Limited	5 pc cu 1st pr.	
Ethel Copper Mines Ltd.	Com.	
Evangeline Savings & Mortgage Co.	Com.	
Evenlode Mines Ltd.	Com.	.01
Excellence Life Insurance Co. (The)	Com.	
Excelsior Life Insurance Co.	Com.	
Exeter Mines Ltd.	Com.	.40
Expo Iron Limited	Com.	.45
Expo Ungava Mines Limited	Com.	.20
Exquisite Form Brassiere (Canada) Limited	Com.	4.10
Exquisite Form Brassiere (Canada) Limited	6 pc cu cv pr.	6.75
Extendicare (Canada) Ltd.	Com.	8.50
Extendicare (Canada) Ltd.	Wt.	3.50
Fab Metal Mines Ltd.	Com.	.04
Fairborn Mines Ltd.	Com.	.12
Fairway Explorations Ltd.	Com.	
Falaise Lake Mines Ltd.	Com.	.16
Falconbridge Nickel Mines Ltd.	Com.	81.00
Falcon Explorations Ltd.	Com.	.55
Fallinger Mining Corporation	Com.	1.32
Family Life Assurance Co.	50 pc paid	
Fannex Resources Ltd.	Com.	.37
Fanny Farmer Candy Shops Inc.	Com.	
Far East Minerals Ltd.	Com.	
Farmers & Merchants Trust Co. Ltd.	Com.	2.50
Farwest Mining Ltd.	Com.	.06
Fathom Oceanology Ltd.	Com.	.73
Fawn Bay Development Ltd.	Com.	.05
Federal Diversiplex Ltd.	Com.	1.20
Federal Grain Limited	Com.	8.00
Federated Mining Corp. Ltd.	Com.	.45
Federated Mining Corp. Ltd.	Rt.	
Fidelity Mining Investments Ltd.	Com.	.06
Fidelity Mortgage & Savings Corporation	Com.	
Fidelity Trust Co., The	Com.	1.55
Fidelity Trust Co., The	Wt.	.65
Fields Stores Limited	Com.	13.50
Financial Collection Agencies Ltd.	Com.	16.00
Financial Life Assurance Co.	Com.	
Finlayson Enterprises Ltd.	Cl A.	14.00
Finlayson Enterprises Ltd.	Cl B.	
Finning Tractor & Equipment Company Limited	Com.	12.50
First City Financial Corp. Ltd.	Com.	7.75
First Maritime Mining Corp. Ltd.	Com.	.60
First National City Corp.	Com.	
First National Uranium Mines Limited	Com.	.15
First Orenda Mines Ltd.	Com.	.08
Fiscal Investments Ltd.	Com.	9.00
Fiscal Investments Ltd.	Pr.	.20
Fittings Ltd.	Com.	15.00
Five Star Petroleum and Mines Ltd.	Com.	.16
Flagstone Mines Limited	Com.	.17
Fleet Manufacturing Ltd.	Com.	.86
Fleetwood Corporation	Com.	8.00
Flemdon Ltd.	Com.	1.40
Fleming Mines Ltd.	Com.	.01
Flin Flon Mines Ltd.	Com.	.27
Flint Rock Mines Ltd.	Com.	1.95
Foley Silver Mines Ltd.	Com.	.04
Fontana Mines 1945 Ltd.	Com.	.03
Ford Motor Company	Com.	70.00
Ford Motor Co. of Canada Ltd.	Com.	82.75
Forest Kerr Mines Ltd.	Com.	.04
Fort Norman Explorations Inc.	Com.	.53
Fort Reliance Minerals Ltd.	Com.	.32
Fort St. John Petroleums Ltd.	Com.	.67
Fortune Channel Mines Ltd.	Com.	.14
Fortune Channel Mines Ltd.	A wt.	
Fosco Mining Ltd.	Com.	1.18
Founders Group	Com.	.45
Fourbar Mines Limited	Com.	.10
4-F Foods Limited	Com.	.19
Four Seasons Hotels Ltd.	Com.	14.25
Four Seasons Hotels Ltd.	Wt.	6.50
Four Seasons Mining & Resources Ltd.	Com.	
Fox Lake Mines Ltd.	Com.	.03
FPE Pioneer Electric Ltd.	Cl A.	17.50
FPE Pioneer Electric Ltd.	$5^1/_2$ pc cu cv A pr.	69.00

Francana Oil & Gas Ltd.	Com.	4.55
Fraser Companies Limited	Com.	12.13
Frebert Mines Ltd.	Com.	.01
Freehold Gas & Oil Limited	Com.	1.76
Freehold Gas & Oil Limited	A wt.	
Freehold Gas & Oil Limited	B wt.	
Freiman Ltd., A. J.	Com.	5.88
Frobex Limited	Com.	.34
Frontier Explorations Limited	Com.	.16
Fruehauf Trailer Company of Canada Limited	Com.	16.50
Fulcrum Investments Co. Ltd.	Com.	3.65
Fulcrum Investments Co. Ltd.	6 pc cu pr.	7.50
Fundy Chemical Corporation Ltd.	Com.	8.75
Fundy Exploration Ltd.	Com.	.02
Futurity Oils Limited	Com.	.27
Galex Mines Limited	Com.	.45
Galt Malleable Iron Limited	Com.	7.50
Galt Malleable Iron Limited	6 pc cu 1st pr.	
Gan Copper Mines Ltd.	Com.	.02
Ganda Silver Mines Ltd.	Com.	
Garrison Creek Consolidated Mines Ltd.	Com.	.06
Gary Mines Ltd.	Com.	.10
Gaspé Copper Mines Ltd.	Com.	49.00
Gaspé Park Mines Ltd.	Com.	
Gaspé Quebec Mines Ltd.	Com.	.64
Gaspesie Mining Co. Limited	Com.	
Gaspex Mines Ltd.	Com.	
Gateford Mines Ltd.	Com.	.02
Gateway Uranium Mines Ltd.	Com.	.02
Gaz Métropolitain Inc.	Com.	5.50
Gaz Métropolitain Inc.	5.40 pc cu pr.	66.00
Gaz Métropolitain Inc.	$5^1/_2$ pc cu pr.	66.00
Gaz Métropolitain Inc.	1963 wt.	1.45
Gaz Métropolitain Inc.	1966 wt.	2.20
G & B Automated Equipment Limited	Com.	1.75
General Bakeries Ltd.	Com.	3.35
General Developments Corporation	Com.	25.50
General Distributors of Canada Ltd.	Com.	15.88
General Dynamics Corporation	Com.	
General Investment Corporation of Quebec	Com.	3.00
General Motors Corporation	Com.	80.50
General Products Mfg. Corporation Limited	Cl A.	82.00
General Products Mfg. Corporation Limited	Cl B.	81.00
General Resources Ltd.	Com.	.08
General Trust of Canada	Com.	23.75
Genesco Inc.	Com.	
Genstar Limited	Com.	13.13
Genstar Limited	Wt.	4.50
Geoquest Resources Ltd.	Com.	1.95
Georgia Lake Mines Ltd.	Com.	
Gesco Distributing Limited	Com.	3.50
Getty Oil Company	Com.	80.00
Giant Explorations Ltd.	Com.	.40
Giant Mascot Mines Ltd.	Com.	5.00
Giant Metallics Mines Ltd.	Com.	.11
Giant Reef Petroleums Limited	Com.	.21
Giant Yellowknife Mines Ltd.	Com.	7.05
Gibbex Mines Ltd.	Com.	.35

Gibraltar Mines Ltd.	Com.	4.70
Gibson Mines Ltd.	Com.	
Glenburk Mines Ltd.	Com.	.03
Glen Copper Mines Ltd.	Com.	.16
Glendale Mobile Homes Ltd.	Com.	5.25
Glengair Group Limited	Com.	1.90
Glengair Group Limited	6 pc cv B pr.	3.10
Glengair Group Limited	Cl A wt.	.85
Glengair Group Limited	Cl B wt.	.90
Glengair Group Limited	Unit	6.25
Glenlyon Mines Limited	Com.	.12
Goderich Elevator & Transit Co. Ltd.	Com.	
Gogama Minerals Ltd.	Com	.23
Golconda Mining Exploration	Com.	5.50
Goldcrest Products Ltd.	Com.	3.50
Golden Age Mines Ltd.	Com.	.40
Golden Gate Explorations Ltd.	Com.	.25
Golden Harker Explorations Ltd.	Com.	.07
Golden Shaft Mines Ltd.	Com.	
Golden Spike Western Petroleums Limited	Com.	.06
Golden West Resources Limited	Com.	.11
Goldex Mines Ltd.	Com.	1.20
Gold Hawk Exploration Ltd.	Com.	
Gold Hawk Mines Ltd.	Com.	.11
Goldray Mines Ltd.	Com.	.67
Goldrim Mining Company Ltd.	Com.	.10
Gold River Mines Ltd.	Com.	.15
Goldstar Explorations & Investments Limited	Com.	
Golsil Mines Ltd.	Com.	.46
Goodyear Tire & Rubber Co. of Canada Ltd.	Com.	153.00
Goodyear Tire & Rubber Co. of Canada Ltd.	4 pc cu pr.	34.50
Gordon-Lebel Mines Ltd.	Com.	.01
Gordon Mackay & Stores Ltd.	Cl A.	6.00
Gordon Mackay & Stores Ltd.	Cl B.	21.75
Governor Gold Mines Ltd.	Com.	
Gowganda Silver Mines	Com.	.23
Gradore Mines Ltd.	Com.	
Grafton Fraser Limited	6 pc cu pr.	17.25
Grafton Group Ltd.	Com.	20.75
Gramara Mercantile Corp. Ltd.	Com.	.18
Grand Bahama Developments Co. Ltd.	Com.	
Grandex Exploration and Investment Co. Ltd.	Com.	
Grandroy Mines Ltd.	Com.	.09
Granduc Mines Ltd.	Com.	4.50
Grandview Mines Ltd.	Com.	.12
Granisle Copper Limited	Com.	7.95
Granite Club Ltd.	Com.	14.75
Granite Mountain Mines Ltd.	Com.	.17
Grasset Lake Mines Ltd.	Com.	.20
Gray Industries Inc.	Com.	.40
Great Bear Silver Mines Ltd.	Com.	
Great Britain & Canada Investments Ltd.	Com.	18.75
Great Britain & Canada Investments Ltd.	$5^1/_4$ pc cu pr.	30.00
Great Canadian Oil Sands Limited	Com.	5.40
Great Eagle Explorations & Holdings Ltd.	Com.	
Great Eastern Resources Canada Ltd.	Com.	.39
Great Lakes Nickel Ltd.	Com.	1.37
Great Lakes Paper Company Limited	Com.	17.75

Great Lakes Paper Company Limited	Wt.	2.30
Great Lakes Power Corporation Ltd.	Com.	19.38
Great Lakes Silver Mines Ltd.	Com.	.11
Great National Land & Investment Corp. Ltd.	Com.	1.05
Great Northern Capital Corp. Ltd.	Com.	8.75
Great Northern Gas Utilities Ltd.	6 pc cu A pr.	19.00
Great Northern Petroleums & Mines Ltd.	Com.	.69
Great Northern Petroleums & Mines Ltd.	A wt.	
Great Pacific Industries Ltd.	Com.	1.30
Great Plains Development Co. of Canada Ltd.	Com.	29.75
Great Slave Mines Ltd.	Com.	.05
Great West International Equities Ltd.	Com.	
Great West Life Assurance Co.	Com.	43.00
Great West Mining & Smelting Corp. Ltd.	Com.	.16
Great West Steel Industries Ltd.	Com.	5.13
Greb Industries Limited	Com.	4.90
Green Coast Resources Limited	Com.	4.90
Green Eagle Mines Ltd.	Com.	.42
Greenfields Development Corporation Ltd.	Com.	
Green Point Mines Ltd.	Com.	.18
Grenache Inc.	Cl A.	3.37
Greyhound Computer of Canada Ltd.	Com.	1.65
Greyhound Lines of Canada Ltd.	Com.	15.75
Grissol Foods Ltd.	Com.	8.25
Grouse Mountain Resorts Ltd.	Com.	2.40
Grouse Mountain Resorts Ltd.	6 pc cv pr.	1.70
Growers Wine Co. Ltd.	Cl A.	3.90
Growers Wine Co. Ltd.	Cl B.	3.75
GSW Limited	Cl A.	9.13
GSW Limited	Cl B.	9.00
GSW Limited	5 pc cu pr.	71.63
Guarantee Co. of North America, The	Com.	
Guaranty Trust Company of Canada	Com.	14.88
Guaranty Trust Company of Canada	Rt.	.53
Guardian Growth Fund Ltd.	Pr.	8.84
Guardian Management Corporation Ltd.	Com.	7.00
Gubby Mines Ltd.	Com.	
Guichon Mine Ltd.	Com.	.03
Gui-Por Uranium Mines & Metals Ltd.	Com.	.15
Gulch Mines Ltd.	Com.	.06
Gulf Lead Mines Ltd.	Com.	
Gulf Oil Canada Limited	Com.	25.63
Gulf Oil Corporation	Com.	25.50
Gulf Titanium Ltd.	Com.	.25
Gunn Mines Ltd.	Com.	.24
Hahn Brass Limited	5 pc 1st pr.	
Halifax Developments Limited	Com.	1.85
Hallnor Mines Ltd.	Com.	.80
Halren Mines Ltd.	Com.	.10
Hambro Corp. of Canada Ltd.	Com.	13.00
Hambro Corp. of Canada Ltd.	$5^1/2$ pc cu A pr.	
Hamilton Group Limited, The	Com.	21.38
Hamilton Group Limited, The	5 pc cu A pr.	85.00
Hamilton Harvey Ltd.	Com.	8.00
Hamilton Trust & Savings Corp.	Com.	10.25
Hamilton Trust & Savings Corp.	Voting trust com.	10.50
Hamilton Trust & Savings Corp.	7 pc cu A Pr.	18.88
Hammond Investment Corporation	Com.	1.00
Hand Chemical Industries Limited	Com.	5.00
Hand Chemical Industries Limited	Pt pr.	5.00
Handy Andy Company	Com.	3.63
Hanna Gold Mines Ltd.	Com.	.19
Hansa Explorations Ltd.	Com.	
Hanson Mines Ltd.	Com.	.14
Hardee Farms International Ltd.	Com.	1.10
Hardee Farms International Ltd.	$6^1/2$ pc A pr.	80.00
Harding Carpets Ltd.	Com.	14.88
Harding Carpets Ltd.	Cl A.	14.50
Hardwicke Investment Corporation Ltd.	Com.	50.00
Harlequin Enterprises Ltd.	Com	3.80
Harris & Sons Ltd., J.	Com.	3.00
Hart River Mines Ltd.	Com.	.16
Harvest Petroleums Ltd.	Com.	.04
Harvey's Foods Ltd.	Com.	.82
Harvey Woods Ltd.	Cl A.	1.65
Harvey Woods Ltd.	Cl B.	.50
Hawker Industries Ltd.	Com.	
Hawker Siddeley Canada Ltd.	Com.	2.40
Hawker Siddeley Canada Ltd.	$5^3/4$ pc cu cv pr.	58.50
Hayes-Dana Limited	Com.	12.00
Headvue Mines Ltd.	Com.	
Headway Corporation Limited	Com.	3.45
Headway Red Lake Gold Mines Ltd.	Com.	.07
Hearne Coppermine Explorations Ltd.	Com.	.15
Heath Gold Mines Ltd.	Com.	.01
Hedman Mines Ltd.	Com.	.50
Hertz Industries Ltd.	Com.	.12
Hewbet Mines Ltd.	Com.	
Hibernia Mining Co. Ltd.	Com.	.11
Highland-Bell Limited	Com.	
Highland Chief Mines Ltd.	Com.	.12
Highland Lodge Mines Ltd.	Com.	.08
Highland Mercury Mines Ltd.	Com.	.15
Highland Queen Mines Ltd.	Com.	.23
Highland Queen Sportswear Ltd.	Com.	1.63
Highland Valley Mines Limited	Com.	.09
Highmont Mining Corporation Ltd.	Com.	2.10
Highpoint Mines Limited	Com.	.05
Hi-Lite Uranium Explorations Ltd.	Com.	
Hinde & Dauch Ltd.	Com.	125.00
H & M Tax Savers Ltd.	Com.	
Hobrough Ltd.	Com.	3.00
Hobrough Ltd.	6 pc cu pr.	1.70
Hogan Mines Ltd.	Com.	.12
Holberg Mines Limited	Com.	
Hollinger Mines Ltd.	Com.	36.50
Hollingsworth Mines Ltd.	Com.	
Home Oil Co. Ltd.	Cl A.	33.38
Home Oil Co. Ltd.	Cl B.	33.00
Home Smith International Ltd.	Com.	.75
Home Supermarket Ltd.	Com.	.30
Honda Mining Co. Ltd.	Com.	.29
Horne Fault Mines Ltd.	Com.	.07
Horne & Pitfield Foods Ltd.	Com.	2.50
Hotstone Minerals Ltd.	Com.	.01
House of Braemore Furniture Ltd.	Com.	3.50
Houston Oils Limited	Com.	1.94
Houston Oils Limited	Wt.	.65

Regulations

Howard Smith Paper Mills Ltd.	$2.00 cu pr.	25.38
Howden & Company Limited, D. H.	Com.	3.10
Hubbard Dyers Limited	Com.	45.00
Hubbard Dyers Limited	Pr.	
Hubert Lake Ungava Nickel Mines Ltd.	Com.	.01
Hub Mining Exploration Ltd.	Com.	.16
Hucamp Mines Ltd.	Com.	.27
Huclif Porcupine Mines Ltd.	Com.	
Hudson Bay Mines Ltd.	Com.	.16
Hudson Bay Mining & Smelting Co. Ltd.	Com.	21.00
Hudson Bay Mountain Silver Mines Ltd.	Com.	.08
Hudson's Bay Company	Com.	18.88
Hudson's Bay Oil & Gas Co. Ltd.	Com.	46.00
Hudson's Bay Oil & Gas Co. Ltd.	5 pc cu cv A pr.	55.50
Hughes-Owens Co. Ltd.	Cl B.	9.00
Hughes-Owens Co. Ltd.	6.40 pc cu pr.	21.13
Hugh-Pam Porcupine Mines Ltd.	Com.	.16
Humlin Red Lake Mines Ltd.	Com.	.01
Hummingbird Mines Ltd.	Com.	.85
Hunch Mines Ltd.	Com.	.03
Hunter Basin Mines Ltd.	Com.	.07
Hunter Douglas Limited	Com.	
Huron Bruce Mines Limited	Com.	
Huron & Erie Mortgage Corporation, The	Com.	25.00
Husky Oil Ltd.	Com.	16.38
Husky Oil Ltd.	6 pc cu A pr.	43.00
Husky Oil Ltd.	6 pc cu B pr.	44.25
Husky Oil Ltd.	D wt.	6.90
Husky Oil Ltd.	E wt.	5.60
Hydra Explorations Ltd.	Com.	.17
Hy's of Canada Limited	Com.	3.00
Hytec Electronics Ltd.	Com.	
I.A.C. Limited	Com.	19.75
I.A.C. Limited	4 1/2 pc cu pr.	69.00
I.A.C. Limited	5 3/4 pc cu pr.	23.00
I.A.C. Limited	Wt.	8.00
Ibes International Ltd.	Com.	.25
Ibsen Cobalt Silver Mines Ltd.	Com.	
Ice Station Resources Ltd.	Com.	.21
Ideal Bay Explorations Ltd.	Com.	.11
Imasco Limited	Com.	20.00
Imasco Limited	6 pc cu pr.	4.60
Imperial General Properties Limited	Com.	4.50
Imperial General Properties Limited	Wt.	1.00
Imperial Life Assurance Co. of Canada	Com.	137.00
Imperial Marine Industries Ltd.	Com.	1.05
Imperial Marine Industries Ltd.	A wt.	.16
Imperial Metals and Power Ltd.	Com.	.23
Imperial Metals and Power Ltd.	Wt.	
Imperial Oil Limited	Com.	31.50
Income Disability & Reinsurance Co. of Canada	Com.	6.00
Income Disability & Reinsurance Co. of Canada	Wt.	.58
Indal Canada Limited	Com.	8.38
Independent Mining Corp. Ltd.	Com.	.01
Index Mines Limited	Com.	1.40
Indian Mountain Metal Mines Ltd.	Com.	.49
Indusmin Limited	Com.	9.75
Industrial Adhesives Limited	Com.	13.38
Industrial Growth Management Limited	Com.	3.75
Industrial Life Insurance Company, The	Com.	
Ingersoll Machine & Tool Company Limited	4 pc cu pr.	
Inglis Co. Ltd., John	Com.	9.50
Initiative New Exploration Ltd.	Com.	2.25
Inland Chemicals Canada Ltd.	Com.	3.05
Inland Copper Ltd.	Com.	.23
Inland Natural Gas Co. Ltd.	Com.	13.00
Inland Natural Gas Co. Ltd.	5 pc cu pr.	14.50
In-Place Electronics Limited	Com.	.35
In-Place Electronics Limited	7 pc cv pr.	
Inqua Resources Ltd.	Com.	.50
Integrated Wood Products Ltd.	Com.	3.50
Inter-City Gas Limited	Com.	6.75
Inter-City Gas Limited	6 1/2 pc cu A 2nd pr.	16.50
Inter-City Gas Limited	B 2nd pr.	19.50
Inter-City Gas Limited	Wt.	2.90
Inter-City Gas Limited	1971 wt.	3.05
Inter-City Manufacturing Ltd.	Cl A.	
Interior Breweries Limited	Com.	3.35
Intermetco Ltd.	Com.	2.30
International Altas Development & Exploration Ltd.	Com.	.19
International Bibis Tin Mines Ltd.	Com.	.08
International Bond and Equity Corporation Ltd.	Com.	1.40
International Bond and Equity Corporation Ltd.	Cl A.	1.22
International Bond and Equity Corporation Ltd.	Wt.	.16
International Bornite Mines Ltd.	Com.	.19
International Business Machines Corp.	Com.	339.00
International Copper Corp. Ltd.	Com.	.16
International Halliwell Mines Ltd.	Com.	.21
International Hydrodynamics Company Ltd.	Com.	1.20
International Hydrodynamics Company Ltd.	B Wt.	
International Hydrodynamics Company Ltd	Rt.	
International Kenville Gold Mines Ltd.	Com.	.10
International Land Corporation Ltd.	Com.	5.75
International Mariner Resources Ltd.	Com.	.66
International Mariner Resources Ltd.	C wt.	.19
International Minerals & Chemical Corp. (Canada) Ltd.	Com.	16.88
International Mogul Mines Ltd.	Com.	7.40
International Nickel Co. of Canada Ltd.	Com.	32.63
International Norvalie Mines Ltd.	Com.	.06
International Obaska Mines Ltd.	Com.	.28
International Paper Co.	Com.	
International Space Modules Ltd.	Cl B.	.90
International Systcoms Ltd.	Com.	.57
International Utilities Corporation	Com.	42.75
International Utilities Corporation	Cl A. cv.	49.75
International Utilities Corporation	$1.32 cu cv pr.	
International Visual Systems Ltd.	Com.	1.25
International Visual Systems Ltd.	Wt.	.40
Interplex S.P.A. Industries Ltd.	Com.	.60
Interpool International Ltd.	Com.	20.00
Interprovincial Allied Properties Ltd.	Com.	1.35

Inter-Provincial Diversified Holdings Limited	Com.	3.25
Interprovincial Pipeline Co.	Com.	30.63
Interprovincial Pipeline Co.	Wt.	14.50
Interprovincial Steel & Pipe Corp. Ltd.	Com.	7.63
Interprovincial Steel & Pipe Corp. Ltd.	$1.20 cu cv pr.	23.75
Inter-Rock Oil Co. of Canada Limited	Com.	.15
Inter-Tech Development & Resources Ltd.	Com.	.80
Investment Foundation Ltd.	Com.	41.50
Investors Group, The	Com.	7.75
Investors Group, The	Cl A.	7.75
Investors Group, The	5 pc cu cv pr.	21.00
Invicta Explorations, Ltd.	Com.	.08
Ionarc Smelters Limited	Com.	1.40
I.O.S. Limited	Com.	
Irish Copper Mines Ltd.	Com.	.07
Iron Bay Trust	Com.	3.10
Iron City Mines Ltd.	Com.	.15
Iron Cliff Mines Ltd.	Com.	.17
Ironco Mining & Smelting Ltd.	Com.	
Iroquois Petroleum Co. Ltd.	Com.	
Irwin Toy Ltd.	Com.	17.00
Isec Canada Ltd.	Com.	.10
Iskut Silver Mines Ltd.	Com.	.16
Island Telephone Co. Ltd.	Com.	10.25
ISO Mines Ltd.	Com.	1.35
Israel Continental Oil Co. Ltd.	Com.	.21
I.T.L. Industries Limited	Com.	4.25
I.T.L. Industries Limited	$6\frac{1}{2}$ pc cu cv pr.	10.50
Ivaco Industries Limited	Com.	14.25
IWC Industries Limited	Com.	1.90
Jackpot Copper Mines Limited	Com.	.07
Jack Waite Mining Co.	Com.	.03
Jacobus Mining Corp. Ltd.	Com.	.03
Jacola Mines Ltd.	Com.	.04
Jagor Resources Limited	Com.	.20
Jahalla Lake Mines Ltd.	Com.	.04
Jamaican Mining Ltd.	Com.	
Jamaica Public Service Co. Ltd.	Com.	.23
Jameland Mines Ltd.	Com.	.05
James Bay Mining Corp.	Com.	.22
Jamex Explorations Limited	Com.	.32
Janus Explorations Ltd.	Com.	.06
Jason Explorers Ltd.	Com.	.13
Jason Explorers Ltd.	A wt.	
Jaye Explorations Ltd.	Com.	.06
J B Automatik Ltd.	Com.	
Jean Lake Lithium Mines Ltd.	Com.	.02
Jelex Mines Ltd.	Com.	.10
Jenkins Bros. Ltd.	Com.	
Jericho Mines Ltd.	Com.	.10
Jersey Consolidated Mines Ltd.	Com.	.11
Jespersen-Kay Systems Ltd.	Com.	3.00
Joburke Gold Mines Ltd.	Com.	.02
Jockey Club Ltd., The	Com.	5.25
Jockey Club Ltd., The	$5\frac{1}{2}$ pc cu B pr.	10.38
Jockey Club Ltd., The	5.60 pc cu 2nd pr.	10.38
Jockey Club Ltd., The	6 pc cu A 1st pr.	10.38
Johnson & Johnson	Com.	97.75
Joliet-Quebec Mines Ltd.	Com.	.19
Jolly Jumper Products of America Ltd.	Com.	1.30
Jolly Jumper Products of America Ltd.	Wt.	
Jonsmith Mines Ltd.	Com.	.07
Jorex Limited	Com.	1.36
Joutel Copper Mines Ltd.	Com.	.52
Jowsey Denton Gold Mines Ltd.	Com.	
Joy Mining Ltd.	Com.	.95
Joy Mining Ltd.	A wt.	.05
Juma Mining & Exploration Ltd.	Com.	.02
Juniper Mines Ltd.	Com.	.16
Kaiser Resources Ltd.	Com.	3.95
Kalco Valley Mines Ltd.	Com.	.15
Kallio Iron Mines Ltd.	Com.	5.00
Kal Resources Ltd.	Com.	.64
Kamad Silver Company Ltd.	Com.	.35
Kamco Developments Ltd.	Com.	
Kam-Kotia Mines Ltd.	Com.	.45
Kamloops Copper Consolidated Ltd.	Com.	.07
Kappa Explorations Ltd.	Com.	.36
Kaps Transport Limited	Com.	8.13
Kardar Canadian Oils Ltd.	Com.	1.88
KB Mining Co. Ltd.	Com.	.11
Keeprite Products Ltd.	Cl A.	11.75
Kelglen Mines Ltd.	Com.	.05
Kellcam Explorations Ltd.	Com.	
Kelly-Desmond Mining Corp. Ltd.	Com.	.01
Kelly-Deyong Sound Corporation Ltd.	Com.	.85
Kelly Douglas & Co. Ltd.	Cl A cu pr.	5.50
Kelsey-Hayes Canada Ltd.	Com.	7.00
Keltic Mining Corp. Ltd.	Com.	
Kelver Mines Limited	Com.	.18
Kelvinator of Canada Limited	Com.	5.00
Kendon Copper Mines Ltd.	Com.	
Kenogamisis Gold Mines Ltd.	Com.	.09
Kenting Limited	Com.	10.25
Kenwest Mines Ltd.	Com.	.02
Kerr Addison Mines Ltd.	Com.	7.40
Kewagama Gold Mines Que. Ltd.	Com.	.05
Key-Anacon Mines Ltd.	Com.	.25
Key Industries Limited	Com.	.22
Keystone Business Forms Limited	Com.	3.00
Key-Way Mining Co. Ltd.	Com.	.07
Kidd Copper Mines Ltd.	Com.	
Kiena Gold Mines Ltd.	Com.	.75
Kilarney Gas & Oil Development Co. Ltd.	Com.	
Kilembe Copper Cobalt Ltd.	Com.	2.25
Kimberlite Mining Corp. Ltd.	Com.	
King Island Mines Ltd.	Com.	.03
King Kirkland Gold Mines Ltd.	Com.	
Kingswood Explorations Ltd.	Com.	.14
Kingswood Explorations Ltd.	Wt.	
Kirkland Gateway Gold Mines Ltd.	Com.	
Kirkland Minerals Corp. Ltd.	Com.	.07
Kismet Mining Corporation Ltd.	Com.	.37
Knobby Lake Mines Limited	Com.	.20
Knogo Corp. Ltd.	Com.	.75
Koffler Stores Ltd.	Com.	15.38
Koffler Stores Ltd.	7 pc A 1st pr.	8.88
Koffler Stores Ltd.	Wt.	6.85

Komo Explorations Ltd.	Com.	.07
Kontiki Lead & Zinc Mines Ltd.	Com.	.03
Kopan Developments Ltd.	Com.	.06
KSF Chemical Processes Ltd.	Com.	1.80
KSF Chemical Processes Ltd.	1968 wt.	.50
K. T. Mining Ltd.	Com.	.11
Kukatush Mining Corp. (1960) Ltd.	Com.	1.75
Kupfer Mines Ltd.	Com.	.42
Labatt Limited, John	Com.	22.00
Labatt Limited, John	Cv A pr.	23.88
Labrador Mining & Exploration Co. Ltd.	Com.	35.25
Lacanex Mining Company Limited	Com.	.90
Lacanex Mining Company Limited	Wt.	.45
Laddie Gold Mines Ltd.	Com.	.04
Laduboro Oil Ltd.	Com.	.90
Laidlaw Motorways Ltd.	Com.	14.88
Laidlaw Motorways Ltd.	7 pc cu cv A pr.	15.38
Laidlaw Motorways Ltd.	Wt.	10.62
Laiteries Leclerc Inc., Les	Cl A.	10.75
Lake Beaverhouse Mines Limited	Com.	.12
Lake Dufault Mines Ltd.	Com.	12.13
Lake Erie Gas Ltd.	Com.	
Lake Expanse Gold Mines Ltd.	Com.	.09
Lakehead Mines Ltd.	Com.	.09
Lake Kozak Mines Ltd.	Com.	.04
Lakeland Natural Gas Ltd.	Wt.	
Lakelyn Mines Ltd.	Com.	.10
Lake Ontario Cement Ltd.	Com.	2.70
Lake-Osu Mines Ltd.	Com.	.09
Lake Shore Mines Ltd.	Com.	2.30
Lakeside Oil & Gas Ltd.	Com.	
La Luz Mines Ltd.	Com.	1.55
Lambert Inc., Alfred	Cl A.	15.25
Lambton Loan & Investment Co.	Com.	
Lancer of Canada Limited	Com.	1.85
Langis Silver & Cobalt Mining Co. Ltd.	Com.	.06
Larandona Mines Ltd.	Com.	
Larchmont Mines Ltd.	Com.	.08
Largo Mines Ltd.	Com.	.22
Laroma Midlothian Mines Ltd.	Com.	.04
Laronge Mining Ltd.	Com.	.81
Larum Mines Ltd.	Com.	.02
Lassie Red Lake Gold Mines Ltd.	Com.	.07
Lassiter Petroleums Ltd.	Com.	
Laura Mines Limited	Com.	.20
Laura Secord Candy Shops Ltd.	Com.	8.88
Laurentide Financial Corp. Ltd.	Com.	10.38
Laurentide Financial Corp. Ltd.	$1.25 cu pr.	17.50
Laurentide Financial Corp. Ltd.	$1.40 cu pr.	19.00
Laurentide Financial Corp. Ltd.	$2.00 cu cv 2nd pr.	25.88
Laurentide Financial Corp. Ltd.	6 1/4 pc cu pr.	17.00
La Verendrye Management Corp.	Com.	8.00
Lawson & Jones Ltd.	Cl A.	18.00
Lawson & Jones Ltd.	Cl B.	92.50
Leamoor Minerals Ltd.	Com.	1.10
Lederic Mines Ltd.	Com.	.18
Leeds Metals Co. Ltd.	Com.	.04
Leemac Mines Ltd.	Com.	.21
Leigh Instruments Limited	Com.	4.45

Leigh Instruments Limited	$2.60 cu cv A pr.	25.00
Leisure World Nursing Homes Ltd.	Com.	1.00
Leitch Mines Ltd.	Com.	
Lemtex Developments Limited	Com.	.55
Lennie Red Lake Gold Mines Ltd.	Com.	.03
Leon's Furniture Ltd.	Com.	6.13
Lequer Mines & Investments Ltd.	Com.	
Levack Mines Ltd.	Com.	
Levy Industries Ltd.	Com.	13.50
Levy Industries Ltd.	6 pc cu A pr.	6.50
Lewes River Mines Ltd.	Com.	.11
Lewis Red Lake Mines Ltd.	Com.	.22
Lexington Mines Limited	Com.	.25
Liberian Iron Ore Limited	Com.	10.13
Life Investors Ltd.	Com.	7.50
Life Investors Ltd.	Wt.	1.25
Lincoln Trust & Saving Company	Com.	12.13
Lingside Copper Mining Co. Limited	Com.	.03
Linland Equipment Sales Ltd.	Com.	1.25
Lion Mines Ltd.	Com.	
Lion Nickel Mines of Canada Ltd.	Com.	.25
Lithium Corporation of Canada Ltd.	Com.	.05
Little Hatchet Minerals Ltd.	Com.	.30
Little Long Lac Mines Limited	Com.	1.80
Livingston Industries Ltd.	Com.	9.00
Livingston Industries Ltd.	6 pc cu A 1st pr.	39.25
Livingston Industries Ltd.	Wt.	5.00
Lobell Mines Ltd.	Com.	
Loblaw Companies Limited	Cl A.	5.75
Loblaw Companies Limited	Cl B.	5.75
Loblaw Companies Limited	$2.40 cu pr.	30.00
Loblaw Groceterias Co. Limited	Com.	99.50
Loblaw Groceterias Co. Limited	$1.50 cu A pr.	18.50
Loblaw Groceterias Co. Limited	$1.60 cu B pr.	19.88
Loblaw Groceterias Co. Limited	$6.60 2nd pt pr.	60.00
Loblaw Inc.	Com.	7.00
Locana Corporation Ltd.	Com.	
Lochaber Oil Corp. Ltd.	Com.	
Lochiel Explorations Ltd.	Com.	1.54
Lodestar Mines Ltd.	Com.	.05
Loeb Ltd., M.	Com.	3.55
Logistec Corp.	Com.	8.25
Loisan Red Lake Gold Mines Ltd.	Com.	.04
London Life Insurance Co.	Com.	68.50
London Pride Silver Mines Ltd.	Com.	.09
Lone Creek Mines Ltd.	Com.	.50
Lord Simcoe Hotel Ltd.	Cl A.	
Lori Explorations Ltd.	Com.	.21
Lornex Mining Corporation Ltd.	Com.	6.80
Lost River Mining Corp. Ltd.	Com.	3.85
Louanna Gold Mines Ltd.	Com.	.05
Louisbourg Mines Ltd.	Com.	
Louisiana Land & Exploration Co.	Com.	
Louvicourt Goldfield Corp.	Com.	.11
Lower Valley Mines Ltd.	Com.	.12
Lucky Strike Mines Limited	Com.	.13
Lundor Mines Ltd.	Com.	.55
Luxor Red Lake Mines Ltd.	Com.	

Lynbar Mining Corp. Ltd.	Com.	.10
Lyndhurst Mining Co. Ltd.	Com.	.02
Lynx-Canada Explorations Limited	Com.	1.35
Lynx Yellowknife Gold Mines Ltd.	Com.	.04
Lytton Mineral Limited	Com.	1.30
Macandrews Red Lake Gold Mines Ltd.	Com.	
Macdonald Mines Ltd.	Com.	.08
Maclan Exploration Limited	Com.	.63
Maclaren Power & Paper Co.	Cl A.	15.00
Maclaren Power & Paper Co.	Cl B.	16.00
Maclaren Power & Paper Co.	1 pc pr.	.50
Maclean-Hunter Cable TV Limited	Com.	8.00
Maclean-Hunter Cable TV Limited	7 pc cu A pr.	18.62
Maclean-Hunter Limited	Com.	8.75
Maclean-Hunter Limited	Cl B.	9.50
Macmillan Bloedel Limited	Com.	25.50
Macmillan Bloedel Limited	3 pc pr.	.47
Madeleine Mines Ltd.	Com.	2.54
Madill Ltd., S.	Com.	6.50
Madison Oils Ltd.	Com.	.12
Madsen Red Lake Gold Mines Ltd.	Com.	.60
Magadyne Industries Limited	Com.	1.25
Magna Electronics Corp. Ltd.	Com.	4.05
Magna Electronics Corp. Ltd.	$6^1/2$ pc cu pr.	
Magnasonic Canada Ltd.	Com.	8.00
Magnetics International Ltd.	Com.	.80
Magnum Fund Ltd.	Com.	23.38
Magoma Mines Ltd.	Com.	.04
Maher Shoes Limited	Com.	20.25
Maher Shoes Limited	Pr.	8.00
Main Oka Mining Corp.	Com.	
Majestic Explorations Ltd.	Com.	
Major Holdings & Development Ltd.	Com.	1.60
Malartic Goldfields Quebec Ltd.	Com.	.55
Malartic Hygrade Gold Mines Ltd.	Com.	2.25
Mandarin Mines Ltd.	Com.	.16
M and M Porcupine Gold Mines Ltd.	Com.	.08
Maneast Uranium Corp. Ltd.	Com.	.01
Manhattan Continental Development Corporation	Com.	.31
Manitou-Barvue Mines Ltd.	Com.	.33
Manix Mining Co. Ltd.	Com.	.20
Manoka Mining & Smelting Co. Ltd.	Com.	
Manor Mines Ltd.	Com.	
Manterre Gold Mines Ltd.	Com.	.01
Maple Leaf Gardens Ltd.	Com.	30.50
Maple Leaf Mills Limited	$5^1/2$ pc cl B pr.	70.00
Maple Leaf Mills Limited	Com.	15.50
Maple Leaf Mines Ltd.	Com.	.13
Maracambeau Mines Ltd.	Com.	.07
Mara Lake Mines Ltd.	Com.	.09
Marchant Mining Co. Ltd.	Com.	.60
Marche Union Inc.	Com.	3.60
Mareast Explorations Ltd.	Com.	
Margaret Red Lake Mines 1940 Ltd.	Com.	
Maria Mining Corp. Ltd.	Com.	
Marigot Investments Ltd.	Com.	.25
Mariner Mines Limited	B wt.	
Maritime Electric Co. Ltd.	Com.	27.00
Maritime Telegraph & Telephone Co. Ltd.	Com.	22.13
Maritime Telegraph & Telephone Co. Ltd.	7 pc cu pr.	

Markborough Properties Ltd.	Com.	5.38
Markborough Properties Ltd.	Wt.	.70
Marlex Enviro-Systems & Resources Ltd.	Com.	.24
Marshall Boston Iron Mines Ltd.	Com.	.26
Marshall Creek Copper Co. Ltd.	Com.	.07
Martin-Bird Gold Mines Ltd.	Com.	.01
Martin-McNeely Mines Ltd.	Com.	.07
Marval Mines Ltd.	Com.	.35
Marvens Ltd.	Cl A.	
Massey-Ferguson Limited	Com.	11.63
Massval Mines Limited	Com.	.07
Master Metal Corp. Mining Ltd.	Com.	.55
Mastermet Cobalt Mines Ltd.	Com.	.05
Matachewan Consolidated Mines Ltd.	Com.	.07
Mate Yellowknife Gold Mines Limited	Com.	.05
Matrix Exploration Limited	Com.	.23
Mattagami Lake Mines Ltd.	Com.	27.88
Matt Berry Mines Ltd.	Com.	.09
Maverick Mines & Oils Limited	Com.	.12
Maverick Mountain Resources Ltd.	Com.	.20
Maybrun Mines Ltd.	Com.	.10
Maycor Mines Ltd.	Com.	.05
Mayfair Molly Mines Ltd.	Com.	.06
Mayfield Explorations Ltd.	Com.	.14
Maylac Gold Mines Ltd.	Com.	
McAdam Mining Corp. Ltd.	Com.	.41
McCarthy Milling Co. Ltd.	Cl A.	
McCarthy Milling Co. Ltd.	Cl B.	
McCoy Lake Mines Limited	Com.	
McCuaig Red Lake Gold Mines Ltd.	Com.	.02
McFinley Red Lake Gold Mines Ltd.	Com.	.05
McIntyre-Porcupine Mines Ltd.	Com.	74.75
McLaughlin Associates Ltd., S.B.	Com.	13.00
McLaughlin Associates Ltd., S.B.	Wt.	5.30
McManus Red Lake Gold Mines Ltd.	Com.	.01
McMarmac Red Lake Gold Mines Ltd.	Com.	.01
McVittie Graham Mining Co. Ltd.	Com.	1.55
Medipack Corp. Ltd.	Com.	1.45
Melchers Distilleries Limited	Com.	11.00
Melton Real Estate Ltd.	Com.	1.60
Melton Real Estate Ltd.	A Wt.	.48
Menorah Mines Ltd.	Com.	.11
Mentor Exploration & Development Co. Ltd.	Com.	.60
MEPC Canadian Properties Ltd.	Com.	7.38
MEPC Canadian Properties Ltd.	6 pc cu A pr.	18.88
MEPC Canadian Properties Ltd.	Wt.	2.40
MEPC Canadian Properties Ltd.	Rt.	
Mercuria Industries Limited	Com.	.80
Mercury Explorations Limited	Com.	.10
Merged Mining Enterprises Ltd.	Com.	.15
Meridian Mining & Exploration Co. Ltd.	Com.	.58
Merland Explorations Limited	Com.	.75
Meta Uranium Mines Ltd.	Com.	.11
Meteor Mining Company Limited	Com.	.04
Metropolitan Stores of Canada Ltd.	Com.	15.38
Metropolitan Stores of Canada Ltd.	$6^1/2$ pc cu 1961 pr.	18.50
Metropolitan Stores of Canada Ltd.	$1.30 cu 1967 pr.	19.50
Metropolitan Trust Company, The	Com.	18.75
Metropolitan Trust Company, The	Rt.	.90

Regulations

Mexican Light & Power Co. Limited	Com.	6.82
Mexican Light & Power Co. Limited	$1.00 cu pr.	11.38
Mextor Minerals Ltd.	Com.	.30
MGF Management Ltd.	Cl A.	1.95
Mica Company of Canada Ltd.	Com.	
Microsystems International Ltd.	Com.	5.38
Microsystems International Ltd.	Wt.	1.70
Midcon Oil & Gas Limited	Com.	.51
Middle Bay Mines Ltd.	Com.	.01
Midepsa Industries Ltd.	Com.	.16
Mid Industries & Explorations Ltd.	Com.	.40
Midland Nickel Corp. Ltd.	Com.	.18
Midland Petroleums Limited	Com.	.06
Mid Patepedia Mines Ltd.	Com.	.14
Midrim Mining Co. Ltd.	Com.	.12
Mid-West Mines Ltd.	Com.	.05
Mija Mines Limited	Com.	.12
Miles Red Lake Mines Ltd.	Com.	.02
Milestone Exploration Ltd.	Com.	.08
Mill City Petroleums Ltd.	Com.	2.06
Millerfields Silver Corp. Ltd.	Com.	
Milton Brick Company Ltd.	Com.	3.85
Mindustrial Corporation Ltd.	Com.	7.25
Minedel Mines Ltd.	Com.	.04
Mineral Exploration Corp. Ltd.	Com.	.12
Mineral Mountain Mining Co. Ltd.	Com.	.18
Mineral Resources International Ltd.	Com.	.35
Mines Iberville Ltée	Com.	
Minex Development Ltd.	Com.	.10
Min-Ore Mines Ltd.	Com.	.03
Mirado Nickel Mines Ltd.	Com.	.02
Miro Mines Ltd.	Com.	.05
Miron Company Ltd.	Cl A.	4.10
Mistango River Mines Ltd.	Com.	.12
Mistassini Uranium Mines Ltd.	Com.	.10
Mitchell Co. Ltd., Robert	Cl A.	11.50
Mitchell Co. Ltd., Robert	Cl B.	
MLW Worthington Limited	Com.	12.75
Mobilex Development Corporation Limited	Com.	.85
Mobil Oil Corporation	Com.	51.25
Mogar Mines Ltd.	Com.	
Mohawk Industries Ltd.	Com.	.90
Mohawk Industries Ltd.	6 pc cu cv pr.	1.95
Mohawk Mines Ltd.	Com.	.02
Mollie Mac Mines Ltd.	Com.	.09
Molson Industries Ltd.	Cl A.	19.75
Molson Industries Ltd.	Cl B.	19.75
Molson Industries Ltd.	Cl C.	
Molybdenite Corp. of Canada Limited	Com.	
Molymine Exploration Ltd.	Com.	.10
Moly-Ore Mines Ltd.	Com.	.32
Monarch Gold Mines Ltd.	Com.	.02
Monarch Investments Ltd.	Com.	23.38
Monarch Life Assurance	Com.	28.00
Monarch Metal Mines Ltd.	Com.	.07
Monenco Ltd.	Com.	6.00
Moneta Porcupine Mines Ltd.	Com.	.60
Monpre Iron Mines Ltd.	Com.	
Monteagle Minerals Ltd.	Com.	.35
Monterey Petroleum Corporation	Com.	.21
Mont Laurier Uranium Mines Ltd.	Com.	.86

Montreal City & District Savings Bank	Com.	14.88
Montreal Refrigerating & Storage Ltd.	Com.	
Montreal Trust Co.	Com.	18.13
Moore Corp. Ltd.	Com.	38.00
Mooshla Gold Mines Co. Ltd.	Com.	.01
More Mines Limited	Com.	.17
Moresby Mines Ltd.	Com.	.15
Morocco Mines Ltd.	Com.	.08
Morono Copper Mines Ltd.	Com.	.21
Morse Corporation Ltd., Robt.	Cl A.	14.00
Morse Corporation Ltd., Robt.	Cl B.	30.00
Morse Corporation Ltd., Robt.	$5^{1}/_{2}$ pc cu cv A pr.	33.00
Morse Corporation Ltd., Robt.	$5^{1}/_{2}$ pc cu cv B pr.	31.50
Motorcade Stores Limited	Com.	.25
Mount Jamie Mines Quebec Limited	Com.	.15
Mount Keno Mines Ltd.	Com.	.01
Mount Pleasant Mines Ltd.	Com.	.25
Mount Royal Rice Mills Ltd.	Com.	7.50
Mount Royal Rice Mills Ltd.	5.80 pc cu pr.	20.00
Mount Washington Copper Co. Ltd.	Com.	.07
Mount Wright Iron Mines Ltd.	Com.	.20
MPG Investment Corporation Limited	Com.	4.20
MPG Investment Corporation Limited	$1.30 cu pr.	15.00
MSN Industries Ltd.	Com.	6.13
Mt Hyland Mines Ltd.	Com.	.17
MTS International Services Inc.	Com.	3.00
Multi-Minerals Ltd.	Com.	.27
Multiple Access General Computer Corporation Limited	Com.	1.25
Murgor Explorations Ltd.	Com.	.09
Murky Fault Metal Mines Ltd.	Com.	.50
Murmac Lake Athabasca Mines Ltd.	Com.	.02
Murphy Oil Co. Ltd.	Com.	12.00
Murphy Oil Co. Ltd.	$5^{3}/_{4}$ pc cu cv A pr.	31.00
Murrit Photofax Ltd.	Com.	3.30
Murrit Photofax Ltd.	Wt.	.40
Muscocho Exploration Ltd.	Com.	.18
Mustang Mines Ltd.	Com.	.29
Mymar Mining & Reduction Ltd.	Com.	.27
My-Pitt Red Lake Gold Mines Ltd.	Com.	
Myteque Mines Limited	Com.	
Mytolon Chemical Inc.	Com.	2.75
Mytolon Chemical Inc.	Wt.	1.000
Nabors Drilling Limited	Com.	10.00
Na-Churs International Limited	Com.	6.00
Nadina Explorations Ltd.	Com.	.91
Naganta Mining & Development Co. Ltd.	Com.	.21
Nahanni Mines Ltd.	Com.	.20
Nasco Cobalt Silver Mines Ltd.	Com.	.01
National Drug & Chemical Co. of Canada Ltd.	Com.	6.00
National Drug & Chemical Co. of Canada Ltd.	Cu cv pr.	8.50
National Grocers Company Limited	$1.50 cu pr.	24.44
National Hees Enterprises Ltd.	Com.	2.75
National Hees Industries Ltd.	Com.	2.70
National Hees Industries Ltd.	6 pc cv 1st pr.	
National Nickel Limited	Com.	.17
National Nursing Homes Ltd.	Com.	1.75
National Nursing Homes Ltd.	Wt.	.35

Regulations

National Petroleum Corporation	Com.	2.35
National Sea Products Ltd.	Com.	9.50
National Sea Products Ltd.	$5\frac{1}{2}$ pc cu pr.	3.25
National Trust Co. Ltd.	Com.	32.50
Nation Lake Mines Ltd.	Com.	
Native Minerals Ltd.	Com.	.03
Native Mines Ltd.	Com.	.05
Navco Food Services Limited	Com.	
Negor Mines Ltd.	Com.	
Nello Mining Ltd.	Com.	
Nelson's Laundries Co. Ltd.	6 pc cu pr.	7.25
Nemrod Mining Co. Ltd.	Com.	.18
Neonex International Limited	Com.	3.70
Nesbitt Mining & Exploration Ltd.	Com.	.25
New Arnifield Mines Ltd.	Com.	
New Associated Developments Ltd.	Com.	
New Athona Mines Ltd.	Com.	.10
Newbaska Gold & Copper Mines Ltd.	Com.	
New Bedford Explorations Ltd.	Com.	.09
New Bidlamaque Gold Mines Ltd.	Com.	
New Brunswick Telephone Co. Ltd.	Com.	14.63
New Brunswick Uranium Metals & Mining Ltd.	Com.	2.90
New Calumet Mines Ltd.	Com.	.20
New Campbell Island Mines Ltd.	Com.	
New Cinch Uranium Ltd.	Com.	.19
Newconex Holdings Ltd.	Com.	4.70
New Continental Oil Company of Canada Limited	Com.	.69
New Cronin Babine Mines Ltd.	Com.	.06
New Davies Petroleums Ltd.	Com.	.06
New Digby Dome Mines Ltd.	Com.	.04
New Dimension Resources Ltd.	Com.	.58
New Dominion Nickel Mines Ltd.	Com.	.02
New Far North Exploration Ltd.	Com.	.04
New Formaque Mines Ltd.	Com.	.04
New Forty Four Mines Ltd.	Com.	
Newfoundland Light & Power Co. Ltd.	Com.	12.25
Newfoundland Light & Power Co. Ltd.	$5\frac{1}{2}$ pc cu A pr.	
New Gateway Oils & Minerals Ltd.	Com.	.11
New Glacier Explorers Ltd.	Com.	.05
New Gold Star Mines Limited	Com.	
New Goldvue Mines Ltd.	Com.	.06
New Harricana Mines Ltd.	Com.	
New Hope Porcupine Gold Mines Ltd.	Com.	
New Hosco Mines Ltd.	Com.	.62
New Indian Mines Ltd.	Com.	.06
New Insco Mines Ltd.	Com.	.40
New Jason Mines Ltd.	Com.	.03
New Kelore Mines Ltd.	Com.	.05
New Lorie Mines Ltd.	Com.	.04
Newlund Mines Ltd.	Com.	.13
New Mallen Red Lake Mines Ltd.	Com.	.01
New Marvel Oils Ltd.	Com.	.15
New Metalore Mining Co. Ltd.	Com.	.45
New Miller Pipe Lines & Mining Exploration Ltd.	Com.	.07
New Mount Costigan Mines Ltd.	Com.	.16
Newnorth Gold Mines Ltd.	Com.	.05
New Pascalis Mines Ltd.	Com.	.20
New Picton Uranium Mines Ltd.	Com.	
New Potterdoal Mines Ltd.	Com.	.04
New Privateer Mines Limited	Com.	.19
New Providence Development Co.	Com.	.36
New Quebec Raglan Mines Limited	Com.	6.90
New Redwood Gold Mines Ltd.	Com.	
Newrich Explorations Ltd.	Com.	.06
New Senator Rouyn Ltd.	Com.	.08
New Taku Mines Limited	Com.	.26
New Territorial Uranium Mines Ltd.	Com.	.11
New Unisphere Resources Limited	Com.	.42
Newvan Resources Ltd.	Com.	.28
New Walcord Mines Ltd.	Com.	.02
New Wellington Mines Ltd.	Com.	.21
New York Oils Limited	Com.	.65
Niagara Structural Steel Co. Ltd.	Com.	
Niagara Structural Steel Co. Ltd.	$6\frac{1}{2}$ pc cu cv A pr.	18.00
Niagara Wire Weaving Company Limited, The	Com.	11.00
Niagara Wire Weaving Company Limited, The	Cl B.	10.00
Nickel Hill Mines Limited	Com.	.14
Nickel Lake Mines Ltd.	Com.	.02
Nickel Offsets Ltd.	Com.	.14
Nickel Rim Mines Limited	Com.	.10
Nicoba Mines Ltd.	Com.	.02
Nicohal Mines Ltd.	Com.	
Nisson Mining & Development Limited	Com.	1.80
Nith River Petroleums Ltd.	Com.	.31
Nitracell Canada Ltd.	Com.	.30
Noble Mines & Oils Ltd.	Com.	1.15
Nocana Mines Ltd.	Com.	.03
Noctin Investment Corporation Ltd.	Com.	
Noland Mines Ltd.	Com.	
Nor-Acme Gold Mines Ltd.	Com.	.18
Noradco Mines Ltd.	Com.	
Noranda Mines Ltd.	Com.	32.75
Norbaska Mines Ltd.	Com.	.19
Norcan Mines Limited	Com.	.10
Norco Oil Corp.	Com.	1.19
Nordev Mines Ltd.	Com.	.10
Nordex Explosives Ltd.	Com.	.50
Nordic Industries Ltd.	Com.	.18
Norex Resources Limited	Com.	.20
Norgold Mines Limited	Com.	.03
Norlex Mines Ltd.	Com.	.26
Normont Copper Ltd.	Com.	
Norque Copper Mines Ltd.	Com.	
Norseman Mines Limited	Com.	.80
Northair Mines Ltd.	Com.	.15
North American Asbestos Co. Ltd.	Com.	.04
North American Land & Leisure Ltd.	Com.	
North American Rare Metals Ltd.	Com.	.18
North American Rockwell Corp.	Com.	29.00
Northcal Mines Ltd.	Com.	.41
North Canadian Oils Ltd.	Com.	5.50
North Canadian Oils Ltd.	$5\frac{1}{2}$ pc cu pr.	38.00
North Coldstream Mines Ltd.	Com.	.48
North Continental Oil & Gas Corporation Ltd.	Com.	.02
North D'Arcy Explorations Ltd.	Com.	.20
Northern Canada Mines Ltd.	Com.	.49
Northern & Central Gas Corporation Ltd.	Com.	14.00

Northern & Central Gas Corporation Ltd.	$1.06 cu cv pr.	22.00
Northern & Central Gas Corporation Ltd.	$1.50 cu cv pr.	28.75
Northern & Central Gas Corporation Ltd.	$2.60 cu 1st pr.	37.25
Northern & Central Gas Corporation Ltd.	$2.70 cu pr.	37.00
Northern & Central Gas Corporation Ltd.	Wt.	5.50
Northern Coal Mines Ltd.	Com.	.12
Northern Gem Mining Corp. Ltd.	Com.	.02
Northern Homestake Mines Ltd.	Com.	.24
Northern Homestake Mines Ltd.	Rt.	.01
Northern Metals Limited	Com.	
Northern Nuclear Mines Ltd.	Com.	
Northern Quebec Explorers Ltd.	Com.	.12
Northern Tar, Chemical & Wood Ltd.	Com.	3.25
Northern Tar, Chemical & Wood Ltd.	Cu A pr.	17.00
Northern Telephone Ltd.	5 1/2 pc cu A 1st pr.	
Northern Telephone Ltd.	5 1/2 pc cu B 1st pr.	
Northern Telephone Ltd.	5 1/2 pc cu C 1st pr.	14.50
North Expo Mines Ltd.	Com.	
Northgate Exploration Ltd.	Com.	4.70
North Island Mines Limited	Com.	.12
Northland Oils Ltd.	Com.	.82
Northland Trust Co.	Com.	
Northlode Explorations Ltd.	Com.	.16
North Pacific Mines Ltd.	Com.	.37
North Rock Explorations Ltd.	Com.	2.25
Northville Explorations Ltd.	Com.	.06
Northwest Canalask Nickel Mines Ltd.	Com.	.06
North Western Utilities Ltd.	4 pc cu pr.	54.00
Northwest Sports Enterprises Ltd.	Com.	6.00
Northwest Trust Co.	Com.	
Northwest Trust Co.	Pr.	
Northwest Ventures Limited	Com.	.52
North Whitney Mines Ltd.	Com.	
Nor-West Kim Resources Ltd.	Com.	.18
Nor-West Kim Resources Ltd.	B wt.	
Nouvelle Mining Exploration Ltd.	Com.	.10
Nova Beaucage Mines Ltd.	Com.	.26
Nova Scotia Light & Power Co. Ltd.	Com.	13.13
Nova Scotia Light & Power Co. Ltd.	4 pc cu pr.	
Nova Scotia Light & Power Co. Ltd.	4 1/2 pc cu pr.	
Nova Scotia Light & Power Co. Ltd.	5 pc cu pr.	
Nova Scotia Savings and Loan Co.	Com.	15.50
NQN Mines Ltd.	Com.	.17
NSI Marketing Ltd.	Com.	3.65
Nudulama Mines Ltd.	Com.	
Numac Oil & Gas Ltd.	Com.	12.75
Nu-West Development Corp. Ltd.	Com.	8.25
NWL Financial Corporation Ltd.	Com.	2.10
N W P Developments Ltd.	Com.	
N W T Copper Mines Ltd.	Com.	.15
Oakville Wood Specialties Limited	6 pc cu pr.	
Oakwood Petroleums Limited	Com.	1.00
O'Brien Gold Mines Limited	Com.	.14
Occidental Petroleum Corporation	Com.	12.25
Ocean Cement & Supplies Ltd.	Com.	29.50
Oceanic Iron Ore of Canada Ltd.	Com.	.15
Ogilvie Flour Mills Co. Ltd.	7 pc cu pr.	25.25
Oil Patch Equipment Sales & Rentals Ltd.	Com.	1.90
Okanagan Helicopters Ltd.	Com.	6.25
Okanagan Helicopters Ltd.	6 pc cu A pr.	
Okanagan Helicopters Ltd.	6 pc cv 2nd pr.	11.50
Okanagan Helicopters Ltd.	Wt.	3.00
Okanagan Holdings Ltd.	Com.	5.13
Okanagan Telephone Company	$0.40 cu pr.	5.25
Old Canada Investment Corporation Ltd.	Com.	.70
Old Canada Investment Corporation Ltd.	6 pc A 1st pr.	1.45
Old Canada Investment Corporation Ltd.	Wt.	.50
Olivet Gold Mines Ltd.	Com.	
Omega Hydrocarbons Ltd.	Com.	.07
Omega Mines Ltd.	Com.	.14
Onaco Petroleums Ltd.	Com.	.08
Onapping Mines Ltd.	Com.	.08
Ontex Mining Ltd.	Com.	.38
Opemiska Copper Mines Quebec Ltd.	Com.	8.10
Open End Mines Limited	Com.	.31
Orangeroof Canada Ltd.	Com.	5.25
Orchan Mines Ltd.	Com.	3.55
Ordala Mines Ltd.	Com.	
Orlando Realty Corporation Ltd.	Com.	4.95
Orofino Mines Ltd.	Com.	.13
Oro Mines Ltd.	Com.	.20
Ortega Minerals Ltd.	Com.	.05
Orvalley Gold Mines Ltd.	Com.	
OSF Industries Limited	Com.	4.75
Oshawa Group Ltd.	Cl A.	11.38
Oshawa Group Ltd.	Wt.	1.50
Osisko Lake Mines Ltd.	Com.	.27
Ourgold Mining Co. Ltd.	Com.	
Overland Express Ltd., The	Com.	10.50
Overland Express Ltd., The	$0.60 cu cv pr.	22.00
Overland Express Ltd., The	2nd pt pr.	4.45
Pace Industries Ltd.	Com.	.85
Pace Industries Ltd.	Wt.	
Pacific Asbestos Ltd.	Com.	1.32
Pacific Atlantic Canadian Investment Co. Ltd.	Com.	4.05
Pacific Atlantic Canadian Investment Co. Ltd.	5 pc cu A pr.	
Pacific Copper Mines Ltd.	Com.	1.85
Pacific Enterprises Ltd.	Com.	1.65
Pacific Gas Transmission Co.	Com.	
Pacific Nickel Mines Ltd.	Com.	.31
Pacific Northern Gas Ltd.	Cl A.	3.50
Pacific Northern Gas Ltd.	6 3/4 pc cu pr.	22.50
Pacific Northern Oils Ltd.	Com.	.07
Pacific Petroleums Limited	Com.	31.63
Pacific Silver Mines & Oils Ltd.	Com.	.06
Pacific Sulphur Ltd.	Com.	
Pacific Western Airlines Ltd.	Com.	12.63
Pacific Western Airlines Ltd.	6 pc cu pr.	30.88
Packard Pershing Mines Ltd.	Com.	
Paco Corporation of Canada Ltd.	Com.	1.85
Page Petroleum Ltd.	Com.	1.50
Palco Explorations Ltd.	Com.	.15
Palliser Petroleums Ltd.	Com.	
Palmer McLellan (United) Ltd.	Com.	
Palomino Explorations Ltd.	Com.	.10

Regulations

Pamike Mines Ltd.	Com.	.20
Pamour Porcupine Mines Ltd.	Com.	1.75
Panacan Resources Ltd.	Com.	.38
Panacea Mining & Exploration Ltd.	Com.	
Pan American Mines Ltd.	Com.	
Pan Canadian Petroleums Limited	Com.	15.25
Pancana Industries Ltd.	Com.	2.35
Pan Eastern Corporation Ltd.	Com.	.29
Pango Gold Mines Ltd.	Com.	
Pan Ocean Oil Corporation	Com.	11.38
Panther Mines Ltd.	Com.	.20
Paragon Properties Limited	Com.	3.10
Paramaque Mines Ltd.	Com.	.03
Paramount Mining Ltd.	Com.	.20
Parkland Beef Industries Ltd.	Com.	.30
Park Lawn Cemetery Company	Com.	
Parr Mines Ltd.	Com.	.14
Partridge River Mines Ltd.	Com.	
Pathfinder Resources Ltd.	Com.	.92
Pathfinder Resources Ltd.	B wt.	.16
Patino Naamloze Vennootschap	Com.	13.75
Pato Consolidated Gold Dredging Ltd.	Com.	6.50
Patricia Silver Mines Ltd.	Com.	.06
Paulpic Gold Mines Ltd.	Com.	.13
Pax International Mines Ltd.	Com.	.01
Payco Mines Ltd.	Com.	.05
Payette River Mines Limited	Com.	.06
Payfair Industries Ltd.	Com.	
PCE Explorations Limited	Com.	.52
Peace River Mining & Smelting Ltd.	Com.	
Peace River Petroleums Ltd.	Com.	.17
Peel-Elder Limited	Com.	14.13
Peel Resources Ltd.	Com.	.14
Pelangio Larder Mines Ltd.	Com.	.02
Pembina Pipe Line Ltd.	Cl A.	7.13
Pembina Pipe Line Ltd.	Cl B.	7.00
Pembina Pipe Line Ltd.	5 pc cu 1st pr.	48.00
Pembina Pipe Line Ltd.	6 pc cu A 2nd pr.	25.50
Pembroke Electric Light Co. Ltd.	Com.	27.50
Pend Oreille Mines & Metals Co.	Com.	.75
Pennbec Mining Corp.	Com.	
Pennington's Stores Limited	Com.	11.88
Peoples Credit Jewellers Ltd.	Com.	9.38
Peoples Credit Jewellers Ltd.	Cl A.	9.00
Peoples Credit Jewellers Ltd.	6 pc cu pr.	94.75
Peoples Department Stores Limited	Com.	11.75
P.E.P. Professional & Engineered Patents Ltd.	Com.	.35
Pere Marquette Petroleums Ltd.	Com.	.03
Permo Gas & Oil Limited	Com.	.38
Pershing Manitou Gold Mines Ltd.	Com.	
Pershon Gold Mines Ltd.	Com.	.01
Peruvian Oils & Minerals Ltd.	Com.	.29
Peso Silver Mines Ltd.	Com.	.14
Peterson Red Lake Mines Ltd.	Com.	
Petrofina Canada Ltd.	Com.	21.50
Petrol Oil & Gas Company Ltd., The	Com.	1.32
Petromines Ltd.	Com.	.26
Petroquest Ltd.	Com.	
Peyto Oils Limited	Com.	1.87

Pharaoh Mines Ltd.	Com.	
Phillips Cables Limited	Com.	9.75
Phillips Petroleum Co.	Com.	
Phoenix Canada Oil Company Ltd.	Com.	7.45
Photo Engravers & Electrotypers Ltd.	Com.	19.00
Pickel Crow Explorations Limited	Com.	.23
Pickering Metal Mines Ltd.	Com.	.01
Pick Mines Ltd.	Com.	
Picton Mines	Com.	
Pine Bell Mines Ltd.	Com.	.13
Pine Lake Mining Co. Ltd.	Com.	.13
Pine Pacific Mines Ltd.	Com.	.18
Pine Point Mines Ltd.	Com.	24.00
Pine Ridge Exploration Co. Ltd.	Com.	.13
Pine Tree Explorations Ltd.	Com.	.15
Pinex Mines Ltd.	Com.	.69
Pinnacle Mines Ltd.	Com.	.12
Pinnacle Petroleums Ltd.	Com.	.44
Pitchvein Mines Ltd.	Com.	.01
Pitt Gold Mining Co. Ltd.	Com.	.04
Pitts Engineering Construction Limited, C.A.	Com.	14.13
Pizza Pan International Corp.	Com.	
Place Gas & Oil Company Limited	Com.	1.00
Placer Development Ltd.	Com.	25.50
Plains Petroleum Ltd.	Com.	.27
Plateau Metals Limited	Com.	.33
Pleno Mines Ltd.	Com.	
Polaris Mines Ltd.	Com.	.05
Polcon Corp.	Com.	3.00
Polypump Ltd.	Com.	2.53
Ponderay Exploration Co. Ltd.	Com.	1.15
Ponder Oils Ltd.	Com.	.68
Popular Industries Ltd.	Com.	1.50
Port Arthur Iron Ore Corp.	Com.	
Portcomm Communications Corp. Ltd.	Com.	.75
Portcomm Communications Corp. Ltd.	A. Wt.	
Port Dover Gas & Oil Ltd.	Com.	
Porield Petroleums Limited	Com.	.10
Portland Yellowknife Gold Mines Limited	Com.	
Potter Distilleries Ltd.	Com.	3.50
Power Corp. of Canada Ltd.	Com.	5.50
Power Corp. of Canada Ltd.	$4^3/4$ pc 1st pr.	28.38
Power Corp. of Canada Ltd.	5 pc cv A 2nd pr.	8.88
Power Corp. of Canada Ltd.	6 pc 2nd pr.	
Prado Explorations Ltd.	Com.	1.12
Prairie Oil Royalties Company Ltd.	Com.	11.75
Prairie Royalty	Com.	
Prefac Concrete Co. Ltd.	Com.	1.45
Premier Cablevision Limited	Com.	10.60
Premier Trust Co., The	Fully paid	340.00
Premium Iron Ores Limited	Com.	1.75
Preston Mines Limited	Com.	6.70
Price Company Limited, The	Com.	7.25
Price Company Limited, The	4 pc cu pr.	50.00
Prime Potash Corporation of Canada Ltd.	Com.	.03
Primer Group Minerals Ltd.	Com.	.09
Probe Mines Limited	Com.	.20
Proflex Limited	Com.	2.20
Pronghorn Petroleum Corp. Ltd.	Com.	

Proto Explorations Ltd.	Com.	.15
Provident Assurance Company (The)	Com.	
Provigo Inc.	Com.	6.75
Provinces & Explorations Ltd.	Com.	.22
Puma Petroleums Ltd.	Com.	.84
Puma Petroleums Ltd.	A Wt.	.48
Purdex Minerals Ltd.	Com.	.01
Pure Silver Mines Ltd.	Com.	2.30
Pyramid Mining Co. Ltd.	Com.	.31
Q Broadcasting Ltd.	Cl A.	5.00
Q.S.P. Ltd.	Com.	11.25
Quadrate Explorations Ltd.	Com.	.02
Quatsino Copper-Gold Mines Ltd.	Com.	.11
Quebec Antimony Mines Ltd.	Com.	.24
Quebec Cobalt & Exploration Ltd.	Com.	.55
Quebec Explorers Corp. Ltd.	Com.	.15
Quebec Gold Belt Mines Ltd.	Com.	.08
Quebec Industrial Minerals Corp.	Com.	
Quebec Manitou Mines Ltd.	Com.	.12
Quebec Mattagami Minerals Ltd.	Com.	.25
Quebec Sturgeon River Mines Ltd.	Com.	.10
Quebec Telephone	Com.	13.75
Quebec Telephone	$6\,^1/_5$ pc cu cv A pr.	14.00
Quebec Telephone	5 pc cu pr 1951 series	5.50
Quebec Telephone	5 pc cu pr 1955 series	13.25
Quebec Telephone	5 pc cu pr 1956 series	
Quebec Telephone	$4\,^3/_4$ pc cu pr 1965 series	12.50
Quebec Uranium Mining Corp.	Com.	.18
Queenston Gold Mines Ltd.	Com.	.20
Quejo Mines Ltd.	Com.	.04
Quest Yellowknife Mines Limited	Com.	.01
Quilchena Mining & Development Co. Ltd.	Com.	
Quinte-Canlin Limited	Com.	1.95
Quinte-Canlin Limited	Cl A.	2.00
Rackla River Mines Ltd.	Com.	.06
Rackla River Mines Ltd.	Rt.	
Radex Minerals Ltd.	Com.	.08
Radex Minerals Ltd.	Wt.	
Radiation Development Co. Ltd.	Com.	3.50
Radio Hill Mines Co. Ltd.	Com.	
Radiore Uranium Mines Ltd.	Com.	.25
Ragged Chute Silver Mines Ltd.	Com.	
Ramada Resources Ltd.	Com.	
Rambler Exploration Co. Ltd.	Com.	
Ramid International Ltd.	Com.	.24
Ram Petroleums Ltd.	Com.	.64
Rancheria Mining Co. Ltd.	Com.	.08
Ranchmen's Resources Ltd.	Com.	.60
Rand Malartic Mines Ltd.	Com.	.02
Rand Resources Limited	Com.	.53
Ranger Oil Canada Limited	Com.	13.75
Rank Organization Ltd.	Com.	22.13
Ranney Gold Mines Ltd.	Com.	
Rapid Data Systems & Equipment Ltd.	Com.	4.50
Rapid Data Systems & Equipment Ltd.	6 pc cu cv pr.	5.25
Rapid Grip & Batten Limited	Com.	5.00
Rapid Grip & Batten Limited	Cl A.	7.00
Rapid River Resources Ltd.	Com.	.06
Rawhide U Mines Ltd.	Com.	.10
Rayfield Mining Co.	Com.	
Raylloyd Mines & Explorations Ltd.	Com.	.20
Raymond Tiblemont Gold Mines Ltd.	Com.	.02
Rayore Mines Ltd.	Com.	.40
Rayrock Mines Limited	Com.	1.15
Reactor Uranium Mines Ltd.	Com.	.15
Reader's Digest Association (Canada) Ltd.	Com.	7.88
Readyfoods Ltd.	Com.	1.88
Realm Mining Corporation Limited	Com.	
Realty Capital Corporation Ltd.	Cl A.	3.40
Realty Capital Corporation Ltd.	Wt.	.85
Reco Silver Mines Ltd.	Com.	.10
Redaurum Red Lake Gold Mines Ltd.	Com.	
Redcoat Mines Ltd.	Com.	
Redcon Gold Mines Ltd.	Com.	.03
Redhill Investment Corp. Ltd.	Com.	4.75
Red Metal Mines Ltd.	Com.	.06
Redruth Gold Mines Ltd.	Com.	.02
Redstone Mines Ltd.	Com.	.32
Reed Shaw Osler Limited	Com.	8.75
Reeves Macdonald Mines Ltd.	Com.	1.00
Regentbranch Holdings Limited	Com.	2.25
Reichhold Chemicals (Canada) Ltd.	Com.	9.00
Reichhold Chemicals (Canada) Ltd.	Wt.	2.75
Reid Lithographing Co. Ltd.	Com.	10.13
Reid Lithographing Co. Ltd.	$6\,^1/_4$ pc cu A pr.	41.13
Reitman's Canada Ltd.	Com.	19.13
Reitman's Canada Ltd.	Cl A.	19.25
Renold Chains Canada Ltd.	Cl A. cu pr.	
Renzy Mines Ltd.	Com.	.43
Reprox Corp. Ltd.	Com.	1.70
Republic Resources Ltd.	Com.	.17
Revelstoke Building Materials Ltd.	Com.	14.75
Revelstoke Building Materials Ltd.	6 pc cu pr.	15.00
Revenue Properties Co. Ltd.	Com.	.71
Rexdale Mines Ltd.	Com.	
Reynolds Aluminum Co. of Canada Ltd.	$4\,^3/_4$ pc cu 1st pr.	64.75
R.H.P. Canada Ltd.	Cu pt cl A.	
Rhyolite-Rouyn Mines Ltd.	Com.	
Richan Explorations Limited	Com.	.80
Richelieu Vaudreuil Farms Ltd.	Com.	
Richfault Explorations Ltd.	Com.	
Rich Group Yellowknife Mines Ltd.	Com.	.21
Richore Gold Mines Ltd.	Com.	
Richwood Industries Ltd.	Com.	2.10
Ridgefield Explorations Ltd.	Com.	
Riley's Datashare International Ltd.	Com.	1.95
Rimrock Mining Corporation Ltd.	Com.	.50
Rio-Algom Mines Ltd.	Com.	15.25
Rio-Algom Mines Ltd.	$5.80 cu A 1st pr.	75.50
Rio Plata Silver Mines Ltd.	Com.	.07
Rio Rupununi Mines Ltd.	Com.	.01
Ripley International Ltd.	Com.	3.80
Riverside Yarns Ltd.	Com.	2.25
Riverside Yarns Ltd.	Cl A cu cv pr.	2.75
Riviera Industries & Resources Ltd.	Com.	.22
Robb Montbray Mines Ltd.	Com.	.01

Robert Mines Ltd.	Com.	.50
Robin Red Lake Mines Ltd.	Com.	.50
Robinson, Little & Co. Ltd.	Com.	37.25
Robinson, Little & Co. Ltd.	Cl A.	36.75
Rocket Mines Limited	Com.	.18
Rockland Mining Ltd.	Com.	.23
Rodstrom Yellowknife Mines Ltd.	Com.	.07
Rokon Mines Ltd.	Com.	.29
Rolland Paper Co. Limited	Cl A.	3.10
Rolland Paper Co. Limited	Cl B.	2.75
Rolland Paper Co. Limited	$4\frac{1}{4}$ pc cu pr.	
Rolling Hills Copper Mines Ltd.	Com.	.34
Roman Corporation Ltd.	Com.	6.10
Romfield Building Corp. Ltd.	Com.	
Ronalds-Federated Ltd.	Com.	13.50
Ronnoco Gold Mines Ltd.	Com.	
Ron Roy Uranium Mines Limited	Com.	.12
Rose Gold Mining Co. Ltd.	Com.	.11
Rose Pass Mines Ltd.	Com.	.25
Rothmans of Pall Mall Canada Ltd.	Com.	16.63
Rothmans of Pall Mall Canada Ltd.	6.85 pc cu 1st pr.	82.50
Rothmans of Pall Mall Canada Ltd.	$6\frac{5}{8}$ pc cv 2nd pr.	19.88
Rothmans of Pall Mall Canada Ltd.	Wt.	3.50
Rouyn Exploration Ltd.	Com.	.07
Rowan Consolidated Mines Ltd.	Com.	.02
Roxmark Mines Ltd.	Com.	.04
Royal Agassiz Mines Ltd.	Com.	.28
Royal Bank of Canada, The	Com.	29.50
Royal Canadian Ventures Ltd.	Com.	1.02
Royal Oak Dairy Ltd.	Cl A.	12.75
Royal Oak Dairy Ltd.	Cl B.	
Royal Trust Company, The	Com.	37.50
Royal Trust Co. Mortgage Corp., The	5 pc cu A pr.	14.25
R R D Limited	Com.	5.00
R R D Limited	Wt.	.50
R S L Limited	Com.	3.10
Rugged Red Lake Mines Ltd.	Com.	.01
Russel Holdings Ltd.	Com.	1.08
Russel Ltd., Hugh	Cl A.	9.00
Russel Ltd., Hugh	$6\frac{1}{2}$ pc cv A 1st pr.	20.13
Russell Foods	Com.	
Ruttan Lake Explorations Ltd.	Com.	.37
Ryanor Mining Co. Ltd.	Com.	.14
Sabina Industries Ltd.	Com.	2.35
Safari Explorations Limited	Com.	.23
St. Anthony Mines Ltd.	Com.	
Saint Fabien Copper Mines Ltd.	Com.	.07
St. James Resources Ltd.	Com.	1.70
Saint Lawrence Cement Co. Ltd.	Cl A.	36.50
Saint Lawrence Columbium & Metals Corp.	Com.	1.00
Saint Lawrence Corp. Ltd.	Com.	21.00
Saint Lawrence Corp. Ltd.	5 pc cu A pr.	63.00
Saint Lawrence Diversified Co.	Com.	.65
Saint Luci Exploration Co. Ltd.	Com.	.16
St. Mary's Explorations Ltd.	Com.	.04
Saint Maurice Capital Corp. Ltd.	Com.	.70
Samson Mines Ltd.	Com.	.02
Sandwell & Company Limited	Com.	5.75
Sanelli Pools Limited	Unit	.45

Sangamo Co. Ltd.	Com.	14.38
San Jacinto Explorations Ltd.	Com.	.09
San Judas Molybdenum Corp. Ltd.	Com.	.40
Santack Mines Ltd.	Com.	
Santa Helena Mining Ltd.	Com.	.20
Santa Maria Mines Ltd.	Com.	.31
Santa's Village Ltd.	Com.	10.00
Santiago Mining & Exploration Ltd.	Com.	
Sapawe Gold Mines Ltd.	Com.	.03
Saratoga Processing Co. Ltd.	Com.	4.40
Sarimco Mines Ltd.	Com.	.02
Sarnoil Ltd.	Com.	
Saskatchewan Trust & Loan Co.	Com.	
Saskoba Mines Inc.	Com.	.34
Sastex Petro-Minerals Ltd.	Com.	.07
Satellite Metal Mines Ltd.	Com.	.06
Savanna Creek Gas & Oil Ltd.	Com.	
Sayvette Limited	Com.	4.70
Scandia Mining & Exploration Ltd.	Com.	.11
Schneider Limited, J. M.	Com.	11.00
Schneider Limited, J. M.	B cu cv pr.	8.25
Schneider Limited, J. M.	C cu cv pr.	
Schott Industries Inc.	Com.	5.50
Sciminex Limited	Com.	.53
Scintrex Limited	Com.	2.90
Scope Resources Ltd.	Com.	.13
Scott Chibougamau Mines Ltd.	Com.	.01
Scottish & York Holdings Ltd.	Com.	9.50
Scott-Lasalle Limited	Com.	9.13
Scott Misener Steamships Ltd.	Com.	2.50
Scott Misener Steamships Ltd.	$5\frac{1}{2}$ pc cu pr.	7.50
Scott Paper Limited	Com.	18.50
Scott's Restaurant Ltd.	Com.	15.13
SCU Industries Ltd.	Com.	1.75
Scurry-Rainbow Oil Limited	Com.	16.25
Scythes and Company Limited	Com.	16.00
Seaboard Life Insurance Co.	Com.	2.00
Seaway Copper Mines Limited	Com.	.83
Seaway Multi-Corp. Ltd.	Com.	8.00
Seaway Multi-Corp. Ltd.	Cu cv A pr.	5.88
Seaway Multi-Corp. Ltd.	Wt.	.94
Seco-Cemp. Ltd.	$7\frac{1}{4}$ pc.	10.31
Secondo Mining Ltd.	Com.	.10
Security Capital Corp. Ltd.	Cl B.	3.90
Seemar Mines Ltd.	Com.	.25
Seldore Mining Company Limited	Com.	.40
Select Properties Ltd.	Com.	2.45
Selkirk Holdings Ltd.	Cl A.	17.00
Senior Gas & Oil Ltd.	Com.	
September Mt. Copper Mines Ltd.	Com.	.10
Seton Lake Mines Ltd.	Com.	
Share Mines & Oils Ltd.	Com.	.12
Shasta Mines & Oils Ltd.	Com.	.50
Shaw Limited, L. E.	Com.	5.88
Shawmin Explorations Ltd.	Com.	
Shawnee Petroleums Ltd.	Com.	.09
Shawnex Mines Limited	Com.	.15
Shaw Pipe Industries Ltd.	Com.	8.00
Sheba Copper Mines Ltd.	Com.	.22
Sheba Mines Ltd.	Com.	.04
Sheldon-Larder Mines Ltd.	Com.	.07

Regulations

Shell Canada Limited	Cl A.	37.25
Shell Investments Ltd.	5 1/2 pc cu cv pr.	37.25
Shell Investments Ltd.	Wt.	17.00
Shell Oil Company	Com.	
Shelter Bay Mining Corp.	Com.	.21
Shepherd Casters Canada Ltd.	Com.	4.00
Sheritt-Lee Mines Ltd.	Com.	.28
Sherritt Gordon Mines Ltd.	Com.	15.13
Sherwin-Williams Co. of Canada Ltd.	Com.	13.50
Sherwin-Williams Co. of Canada Ltd.	7 pc cu pr.	89.00
Shewan Copper Mining Corp. Ltd.	Com.	
Shield Development Co. Ltd., The	Com.	.80
Shore to Shore Corporation Limited	Com.	3.50
Shully's Industries Limited	Com.	4.75
Siebens Oil & Gas Ltd.	Com.	9.00
Sierra Empire Mines Ltd.	Com.	1.50
Sifton Properties Ltd.	Com.	3.60
Sigma Mines Quebec Ltd.	Com.	3.75
Silbak Premier Mines Ltd.	Com.	.09
Sileurian Chieftain Mining Co. Ltd.	Com.	.09
Silknit Limited	Com.	22.00
Silknit Limited	5 pc pr.	37.00
Silmonac Mines Ltd.	Com.	.27
Silver Butte Mines Ltd.	Com.	.07
Silver Chief Minerals Ltd.	Com.	.27
Silver Christal Natural Gas & Minerals Ltd.	Com.	.45
Silver City Mines Ltd.	Com.	.12
Silver-Cup Mines Ltd.	Com.	.20
Silver Eureka Corp.	Com.	.38
Silver Key Mines Ltd.	Com.	.05
Silverknife Mines Ltd.	Com.	.05
Silver Lake Mines Ltd.	Com.	
Silvermaque Mining Ltd.	Com.	.18
Silver-Men Mines Ltd.	Com.	.03
Silver-Miller Mines Ltd.	Com.	.05
Silver Monarch Mines Ltd.	Com.	
Silver Pack Mines Ltd.	Com.	
Silverquick Development Co. BC Ltd.	Com.	.12
Silver Ridge Mining Co. Ltd.	Com.	.05
Silver Shield Mines Inc.	Com.	3.10
Silver Shield Mines Inc.	A wt.	2.19
Silver Shield Mines Inc.	B wt.	2.02
Silversides Mines Ltd.	Com.	.07
Silver Spring Mines Ltd.	Com.	.58
Silverstack Mines Ltd.	Com.	.26
Silver Standard Mines Ltd.	Com.	1.10
Silver Star Mines Ltd.	Com.	.10
Silver Summit Mines Ltd.	Com.	.02
Silverwood Industries Ltd.	Cl A.	15.63
Silverwood Industries Ltd.	Cl B.	14.75
Simpsons Limited	Com.	22.00
Simpsons-Sears Limited	Com.	28.63
Sintra Limited	Com.	5.50
Sirmac Mines Ltd.	Com.	
Skelly Oil Company	Com.	45.25
Sklar Manufacturing Ltd.	Com.	2.35
Sklar Manufacturing Ltd.	Wt.	.75
Skyline Hotels Limited	Com.	9.25
Sladen Quebec Ltd.	Com.	
Slate Bay Gold Mines Ltd.	Com.	.02
Slater Steel Industries Limited	Com.	10.00
Slater Steel Industries Limited	5 1/2 pc cu 1st pr.	13.88
Slater Steel Industries Limited	5 1/2 pc 2nd pr.	13.75
Slater Steel Industries Limited	$1.20 cu pr.	15.00
Slater Walker of Canada Ltd.	Com.	13.25
Slater Walker of Canada Ltd.	Rt.	
Slater Walker Securities Ltd.	Com.	8.00
Slave Point Mines Ltd.	Com.	.04
S L Diversified Corp. Ltd.	Com.	9.38
Slocan Ottawa Mines Ltd.	Com.	.69
S.M.A. Inc.	Com.	.50
S M Industries Ltd.	Com.	
Snowdrift Base Metal Mines Ltd.	Com.	.13
Sobeys Stores Limited	Com.	6.75
Soca Ltée.	Com.	.50
Sogena Inc.	Com.	14.50
Sogepet Ltd.	Com.	1.22
Solar Explorations Ltd.	Com.	
Solidarité Compagnie d'Assurance sur la Vie	Com.	
Solomon Development Ltd.	Com.	.38
Solomons Pillars Mines Ltd.	Com.	
Somerville Industries Ltd.	$2.80 cu pr.	40.00
Somex Ltée	Com.	.83
Southam Press Limited	Com.	73.13
South Dufault Mines Ltd.	Com.	.05
Southern Pacific Petroleum Ltd.	Com.	.08
Southern Union Oils Ltd.	Com.	
South Pacific Mines Ltd.	Com.	
South Seas Mining Ltd.	Com.	.22
South Winnipeg Limited	Com.	
Spacemaster Minerals Ltd.	Com.	.03
Spa Mines Ltd.	Com.	.05
Spanish River Mines Ltd.	Com.	
Spar Aerospace Products Ltd.	Com.	1.65
Sparling Ltd., George	Com.	2.40
Spartan Air Services Ltd.	Com.	.50
Spartan Explorations Ltd.	Com.	.13
Spartex Oil & Gas Ltd.	Com.	.08
Spectroair Explorations Ltd.	Com.	.13
Speculators Fund Ltd.	Com.	.42
Spenho Mines Ltd.	Com.	.06
Spina Porcupine Mines Ltd.	Com.	
Spirit Lake Mines Ltd.	Com.	
Spooner Mines & Oils Limited	Com.	1.10
Stability Life Insurance Co.	Com.	
Stafford Foods Ltd.	Com.	2.60
Stairs Exploration & Mining Co. Ltd.	Com.	.02
Stall Lake Mines Ltd.	Com.	.89
Stampede International Resources Ltd.	Com.	.68
Standard Broadcasting Corp. Ltd.	Com.	13.00
Standard Fuel Co. Ltd.	4 1/2 pc cu pr.	
Standard Gold Mines Ltd.	Com.	.07
Standard Nickel Mines Limited	Com.	.22
Standard Paving & Materials Ltd.	Com.	11.50
Stanfield's Ltd.	Cl A.	
Stanfield's Ltd.	Cl B.	
Stanford Mines Ltd.	Com.	.60
Stannex Minerals Ltd.	Com.	.14
Stanrock Uranium Mines Ltd.	Com.	.60

Star Lake Gold Mines Ltd.	Com.	.05
Steel Co. of Canada Ltd., The	Com.	26.75
Steeltree Group Inc.	Com.	.95
Steeltree Group Inc.	6 pc cu pr.	3.55
Steep Rock Iron Mines Ltd.	Com.	2.23
Steetley Industries Ltd.	Com.	7.00
Steinberg's Limited	Cl A.	22.88
Steinberg's Limited	5 1/4 pc cu A pr.	77.00
Steintron International Electronics Ltd.	Com.	3.35
Stellako Mining Company Ltd.	Com.	.11
Sterisystems Ltd.	Com.	15.25
Sterisystems Ltd.	Cl A.	15.50
Sterling Trust Corporation	Com.	8.25
Stewart Lake Iron Mines of Ontario Ltd.	Com.	.15
Stormy Mines Ltd.	Com.	.28
Stuart House International Ltd.	Com.	3.55
Stuart House International Ltd.	6 pc cu cv A pr.	6.75
Stuart Oil Company Ltd., D. A.	Com.	7.75
Studer Mines Limited	Com.	.10
Stump Mines Ltd.	Com.	.08
Sturdy Mines Ltd.	Com.	.14
Sturgeon Petroleums Ltd.	Com.	
Sturgex Mines Ltd.	Com.	.21
Subeo Limited	Com.	.10
Sudbury Contact Mines Ltd.	Com.	.25
Sullivan Mining Group Ltd.	Com.	2.70
Summit Explorations & Holdings Ltd.	Com.	.73
Sun Bear Mines Ltd.	Com.	.01
Sunburst Explorations Ltd.	Com.	.11
Sunburst Explorations Ltd.	Rt.	.01
Sunlite Oil Company Ltd.	Com.	5.00
Sunningdale Oils Ltd.	Com.	2.65
Sun Publishing Co. Limited	Cl A.	34.75
Sun Publishing Co. Limited	Cl B.	33.00
Sunrise Silver Mines Ltd.	Com.	.10
Sunset Yellowknife Mines Ltd.	Com.	
Superior Acid & Iron Ltd.	Com.	.12
Superior Electronics Industries Ltd.	Com.	2.05
Supermarché à Domicile Ltée	Com.	.30
Superpack Corporation Ltd.	Com.	4.00
Supersol Ltd.	Com.	
Supertest Petroleum Corporation Limited	Com.	16.25
Supertest Petroleum Corporation Limited	Ordinary	68.00
Surluga Gold Mines Ltd.	Com.	.07
Surpass Chemicals Limited	Com.	1.60
Swim Lake Mines Ltd.	Com.	.15
Swiss Oils of Canada 1959 Ltd.	Com.	.18
Systems Air Corp. Ltd.	Com.	.15
Systems Dimensions Ltd.	Com.	6.88
Tache Lake Mines Ltd.	Com.	.03
Tagami Mines Limited	Com.	.12
Takla Silver Mines Ltd.	Com.	.09
Talisman Mines Limited	Com.	.15
Taman Uranium Mines Ltd.	Com.	.07
Tamblyn Limited, G.	Com.	18.50
Tamblyn Limited, G.	4 pc cu pr.	25.00
Tancord Industries Limited	Com.	2.40
Tancord Industries Limited	A pr.	2.50
Taneloy Mines Ltd.	Com.	.08
Tanzilla Explorations Ltd.	Com.	.11
Tara Exploration & Development Company Limited	Com.	12.75
Target Mines Ltd.	Com.	.08
Tartan Explorations Ltd.	Com.	.19
Taseko Mines Ltd.	Com.	.22
Tashota-Nipigon Mines Ltd.	Com.	.22
Tasmaque Gold Mines Ltd.	Com.	
Taylor Windfall Gold Mining Co. Ltd.	Com.	.02
Tay River Mines Ltd.	Com.	.15
Teck Corporation Ltd.	Cl A.	4.75
Teck Corporation Ltd.	Cl B.	4.15
Teckora Mines Limited	Com.	.51
Teknol Mining Co. Ltd.	Com.	.34
Teledyne Canada Ltd.	Com.	4.65
Tenneco Inc.	Com.	
Terra Developers Ltd.	Com.	
Terra Mining & Exploration Ltd.	Com.	2.40
Terrasol	Com.	2.88
Terrex Mining Co. Ltd.	Com.	.15
Texacal Resources Ltd.	Com.	.24
Texaco Canada Limited	Com.	34.50
Texaco Canada Limited	4 pc cu pr.	60.00
Texal Development Ltd.	Com.	.30
Texas East Transmission	Com.	
Texas Gulf Sulphur Co. Inc.	Com.	14.38
Texmont Mines Ltd.	Com.	.39
Texore Mines Ltd.	Com.	.10
Tex-Sol Explorations Ltd.	Com.	.57
Thermatron Corporation Ltd.	Com.	
Thermatron Corporation Ltd.	Wt.	
Third Canadian General Investment Trust Ltd.	Com.	11.75
Third Canadian General Investment Trust Ltd.	Pr.	32.00
Thomas Nationwide Transport Limited	Com.	1.95
Thompson Lundmark Gold Mines Ltd.	Com.	.20
Thompson Paper Box Co. Limited	Com.	4.75
Thompson Paper Box Co. Limited	6 pc cu pr.	
Thomson Drilling Company Ltd.	Com.	1.50
Thomson Newspapers Limited	Com.	29.13
Thomson Newspapers Limited	6 3/4 pc cu pr.	51.13
Thor Explorations Ltd.	Com.	.68
Thorncrest Explorations Ltd.	Com.	
Timken Co.	Com.	43.00
Timrod Mining Co. Ltd.	Com.	.21
Tinex Development Exploration Ltd.	Com.	
Tobe Mines Ltd.	Com.	.12
Tokar Limited	Com.	1.40
Tombill Mines Ltd.	Com.	.55
Tomrose Mines Ltd.	Com.	
Tonecraft Limited	Com.	12.50
Tontine Mining Limited	Com.	.60
Tooke Bros. Ltd.	Com.	.75
Tooke Bros. Ltd.	A pr.	
Topley Criss Mines Limited	Com.	.09
Torcan Explorations Ltd.	Com.	.12
Tormex Mining Developers Ltd.	Com.	1.68
Toromont Industrial Holdings Ltd.	Com.	1.30
Toromont Industrial Holdings Ltd.	6 1/2 pc cu cv A pr.	
Toronado Mines Ltd.	Com.	.17
Toronto-Dominion Bank	Com.	30.00

Regulations

Toronto Iron Works Ltd. (The)	Com.	8.75
Toronto & London Investment Co. Ltd.	Com.	3.90
Toronto Star Limited	Cl B.	38.00
Toronto Star Limited	Cl C.	38.50
Torwest Resources 1962 Ltd.	Com.	.23
Total Petroleum (North America) Ltd.	Com.	6.20
Total Petroleum (North America) Ltd.	$3^1/2$ pc cv A pr.	14.25
Tower Resources Ltd.	Com.	.24
Towmart Holdings Limited	Com.	.45
Traders Building Association Ltd.	Com.	
Traders Group Limited	Cl A.	15.75
Traders Group Limited	Cl B.	15.00
Traders Group Limited	5 pc cu pr.	25.00
Traders Group Limited	5 pc cu cv A pr.	20.50
Traders Group Limited	$4^1/2$ pc cu pr.	56.25
Traders Group Limited	$2.16 cu pr.	26.00
Traders Group Limited	1965 wt.	2.05
Traders Group Limited	1966 wt.	4.70
Traders Group Limited	1969 wt.	5.00
Transair Limited	Com.	3.15
Transair Limited	Pr.	
Transair Limited	Wt.	.89
Transair Limited	Rt.	
Trans-American Mining Corp. Ltd.	Com.	
Trans Canada Glass Ltd.	Com.	5.13
Trans-Canada Pipe Lines Limited	Com.	36.25
Trans-Canada Pipe Lines Limited	$2.75 cu cv pr.	66.75
Trans-Canada Pipe Lines Limited	$2.80 cu pr.	42.25
Trans-Canada Pipe Lines Limited	Wt.	10.75
Trans-Canada Resources Ltd.	Com.	.82
Trans Columbia Exploration Ltd.	Com.	.11
Transcontinental Resources Ltd.	Com.	.27
Trans Eastern Oil & Gas Ltd.	Com.	
Trans Global Financial Services Ltd.	Com.	1.80
Trans-Mountain Oil Pipeline Company	Com.	20.38
Transocean Oil Incorporated	Com.	
Trans-Prairie Pipelines Ltd.	Com.	12.75
Transterre Exploration Ltd.	Com.	.20
Trans Yukon Exploration Ltd.	Com.	.06
Tresdor Larder Mines Ltd.	Com.	
Tribag Mining Co. Ltd.	Com.	.60
Tri-Bridge Mines Limited	Com.	.35
Trimac Ltd.	Com.	6.50
Trinity Chibougamau Mines Ltd.	Com.	.10
Triphope Resources Ltd.	Com.	
Triton Explorations Limited	Com.	.70
Trizec Corporation Limited	Com.	17.00
Trizec Corporation Limited	Wt.	.50
Troilus Mines Ltd.	Com.	.15
Trojan Consolidated Mines Ltd.	Com.	.25
Tromac Mines Ltd.	Com.	.03
Troy Silver Mines Ltd.	Com.	.08
Tru-Wall Concrete Forming Ltd.	Com.	2.90
Tundra Gold Mines Ltd.	Com.	.18
Turbo Resources Limited	Com.	.93
Turismo Industries Ltd.	Com.	.37
Turner Valley Oil Company Limited	Com.	.18
Twentieth Century Explorations Limited	Com.	.75
Twin Peak Mines Ltd.	Com.	.28
Twin Richfield Oils Ltd.	Com.	.21
Tyee Lake Resources Limited	Com.	.14
U.A.P. Inc.	Cl A.	16.25
Ulster Petroleums Ltd.	Com.	1.46
Ultramar Company Limited	Com.	6.13
Unas Investments Ltd.	Com.	16.63
Ungava Copper Corp. Ltd.	Com.	.04
Unican Security Systems Ltd.	Com.	4.05
Unigesco Inc.	Com.	
Unigesco Inc.	Cl A.	2.85
Unigesco Inc.	Cl B.	2.72
Union Acceptance Corporation Ltd.	6 pc cu C 1st pr.	40.44
Union Acceptance Corporation Ltd.	$6^1/4$ pc cu A 1st pr.	40.00
Union Acceptance Corporation Ltd.	$6^1/4$ pc cu B 1st pr.	42.50
Union Carbide Canada Limited	Com.	13.50
Union Gas Company of Canada Limited	Com.	14.75
Union Gas Company of Canada Limited	$5^1/2$ pc cu A pr.	43.00
Union Gas Company of Canada Limited	6 pc cu B pr.	44.13
Union Mining Corporation	Com.	.21
Union Oil Company of Canada Ltd.	Com.	44.00
United Asbestos Corp. Ltd.	Com.	4.05
United Canadian Shares Ltd.	Com.	
United Canso Oil & Gas Ltd.	Com.	4.25
United Canso Oil & Gas Ltd.	Wt.	.64
United Cobalt Mines Ltd.	Com.	.02
United Comstock Lode Mines Ltd.	Com.	
United Copper Corporation Ltd.	Com.	.10
United Corporations Ltd.	Cl A.	19.50
United Corporations Ltd.	Cl B.	15.00
United Corporations Ltd.	$1.50 cu A pr.	20.00
United Corporations Ltd.	5 pc cu 1963 pr.	19.00
United Equities Limited	Com.	2.00
United Funds Management Ltd.	Com.	8.38
United Grain Growers Limited	5 pc pr.	14.00
United Investment Life Assurance Co.	Com.	5.69
United Keno Hill Mines Ltd.	Com.	3.85
United Macfie Mines Ltd.	Com.	.04
United Mindamar Metals Ltd.	Com.	.16
United New Fortune Mines Ltd.	Com.	
United Provincial Investment Ltd.	Com.	1.30
United Reef Petroleums Ltd.	Com.	.18
United Siscoe Mines Ltd.	Com.	2.10
United Westburne Industries Ltd.	Com.	4.00
United Westburne Industries Ltd.	$6^1/4$ pc cu A 1st pr.	39.00
United Westburne Industries Ltd.	Wt.	1.00
Universal Factors Corp.	Com.	
Universal Gas Co. Ltd.	Com.	
Universal Minerals Corporation	Com.	.24
Universal Patent & Development Ltd.	Com.	.12
Universal Sections Ltd.	Com.	6.50
Univex Mining Corporation Ltd.	Com.	.41
Upper Canada Mines Ltd.	Com.	1.66
Uranium Ridge Mines Ltd.	Com.	.03
Uranium Valley Mines Ltd.	Com.	.20
Urban Quebec Mines Ltd.	Com.	.04
US-CA-MEX Explorations Ltd.	Com.	.20

Regulations

Utilities & Funding Corp. Ltd.	Com.	1.60
Utilities & Funding Corp. Ltd.	Cl A.	1.60
Valdex Mines Inc.	Com.	.13
Valley Copper Mines Ltd.	Com.	7.70
Val Mar Swimming Pools Ltd.	Cl A.	1.60
Val Nor Exploration Ltd.	Com.	
Vananda Exploration Ltd.	Com.	.06
Van Der Holt Associates Limited	Com.	7.25
Vandoo Consolidated Explorations Ltd.	Com.	.04
Van Ness Industries Ltd.	Com.	.83
Vargas Mines Limited	Com.	.53
Vastlode Mining Company Ltd.	Com.	.05
Velcro Industries Limited	Com.	17.63
Vencap Investments Ltd.	Com.	1.80
Venpower Limited	Com.	1.30
Ventures Mining Limited	Com.	.07
Vermont Mines Ltd.	Com.	
Versafood Services Ltd.	Com.	7.50
Versatile Manufacturing Ltd.	Com.	3.50
Versatile Manufacturing Ltd.	Cl A.	2.75
Vespar Mines Ltd.	Com.	.14
Vestor Explorations Ltd.	Com.	.33
Viau Limited	Com.	
Victoria Algoma Mineral Co. Ltd.	Com.	.11
Victoria & Grey Trust Co.	Com.	35.50
Victoria & Grey Trust Co.	5.35 pc cu A pr.	40.63
Victoria Wood Development Corp. Ltd.	Com.	
Victoria Wood Development Corp. Ltd.	$7^1/2$ pc cu A pr.	8.13
Victor Mining Corp. Ltd.	Com.	.08
Viking Mines Ltd.	Com.	.08
Villacentres Ltd.	Com.	9.88
Vimy Explorations Ltd.	Com.	.02
Visa Bella Inc.	Com.	
Volcanic Mines Ltd.	Com.	.10
Voyager Explorations Ltd.	Com.	
Voyager Petroleums Ltd.	Com.	4.90
Vulcan Industrial Packaging Limited	Com.	9.00
Wabasso Limited	Com.	18.50
Waco Petroleums Ltd.	Com.	.02
Wadge Mines Ltd.	Com.	.01
Waferboard Corp. Ltd.	Com.	1.50
Wainoco Oil & Chemicals Ltd.	Com.	5.63
Waite Dufault Mines Ltd.	Com.	.09
Wajax Limited	Com.	13.63
Walker-Gooderham & Worts Limited (Hiram)	Com.	42.38
Wall & Redekop Corporation Ltd.	Com.	2.75
Wardair Canada Ltd.	Com.	1.45
Warner Investments Ltd., E.C.	Cl A.	
Warner Investments Ltd., E.C.	Cl B.	
Warner West	Com.	.43
Warnock Hersey International Limited	Com.	3.65
Warnock Hersey International Limited	$1.50 cu A pr.	10.00
Warrington Products Ltd.	Pr.	3.50
Watson Lake Mines Ltd.	Com.	.04
Wavecom Development Ltd.	Com.	.75
W. C. P. Explorations Ltd.	Com.	10.13
W. C. P. Explorations Ltd.	5 pc cu cv A pr.	30.00
Webb & Knapp Canada Limited	Com.	.40
Webbwood Exploration Co. Ltd.	Com.	1.25
Webbwood Mobile Home Estates Ltd.	Com.	1.00
Wee-Gee Uranium Mines Ltd.	Com.	
Weldwood of Canada Limited	Com.	13.50
Weldwood of Canada Limited	Rt.	
Welland Consolidated Mining Ltd.	Com.	
Wellington Bank	Cl A.	.38
Wentworth Investment Corporation Ltd.	Com.	10.00
Werner Lake Nickel Mines Ltd.	Com.	.01
Wescorp Industries Ltd.	Com.	5.40
Wesley Mines Ltd.	Com.	
Westairs Mines Ltd.	Com.	
Westates Petroleum Company	Com.	5.05
Westburne International Industries Ltd.	Com.	10.75
Westburne International Industries Ltd.	8 pc cu cv pr.	36.00
Westburne International Industries Ltd.	Wt.	6.70
West Canadian Mineral Holdings Ltd.	Com.	1.10
Westcoast Petroleum Ltd.	Com.	10.13
Westcoast Petroleum Ltd.	6 pc cu pr.	30.00
West Coast Resources Ltd.	Com.	.06
Westcoast Transmission Co. Ltd.	Com.	25.88
Westcoast Transmission Co. Ltd.	Wt.	6.69
Westcoast Transmission Co. Ltd.	Rt.	.16
Westeel-Rosco Limited	Com.	13.88
Western Allenbee Oil & Gas Company Ltd.	Com.	.23
Western Broadcasting Co. Ltd.	Com.	12.13
Western Broadcasting Co. Ltd.	$5^3/4$ pc cu cv pr.	36.00
Western-Buff Mines & Oils Ltd.	Com.	.07
Western Canadian Seed Processors Ltd.	Com.	4.50
Western Decalta Petroleum Ltd.	Com.	6.55
Western Exploration Company Ltd.	Com.	.12
Western Mines Ltd.	Com.	2.55
Western Quebec Mines Co. Ltd.	Com.	.10
Western Realty Projects Limited	Com.	7.13
Western Standard Silver Mines Ltd.	Com.	.10
Western Supplies Ltd.	Cl A cu cv.	9.00
Western & Texas Oil Co. Ltd.	Com.	
Western Tin Mines Ltd.	Com.	.02
Western Warner Oils Limited	Com.	.47
Westfair Foods Ltd.	Cl A.	26.50
Westfair Foods Ltd.	7 pc cu pr.	19.00
Westfield Minerals Ltd.	Com.	.96
Westfield Minerals Ltd.	Wt.	.48
West Hill Enterprises & Mining Ltd.	Com.	.10
West Indies Plantation Ltd.	Com.	1.75
West Indies Plantation Ltd.	Cl A.	3.25
Westinghouse Canada Limited	Com.	14.50
Westland Mines Ltd.	Com.	.08
Weston Limited, George	Com.	18.00
Weston Limited, George	$4^1/2$ pc cu pr.	66.50
Weston Limited, George	6 pc cu pr.	82.00
West Red Lake Gold Mines Ltd.	Com.	
Westview Investment Corporation Ltd.	Com.	2.08
Westville Mines Ltd.	Com.	
West Wasa Mines Ltd.	Com.	.08
Whim Creek Consolidated No Liability	Com.	
Whipsaw Mines Limited	Com.	.10
Whistler Petroleums Ltd.	Com.	.32
Whitehorse Copper Mines Ltd.	Com.	1.75
White Pass & Yukon Corp. Ltd.	Com.	10.00

Regulations

White Pass & Yukon Corp. Ltd.	$6^3/4$ pc cu A pr.	22.00
White Pass & Yukon Corp. Ltd.	Wt.	.76
White River Mines Ltd.	Com.	.28
Whiterock Estates Development Corporation Limited	Com.	14.38
Whitesail Mines Ltd.	Com.	
White Star Copper Mines Ltd.	Com.	.14
Whitey Wilson Oil & Gas Ltd.	Com.	.31
Whonnock Industries Limited	Cl A.	13.50
Whonnock Industries Limited	Cl B	14.00
Wilco Mining Co. Ltd.	Com.	.15
Wildor Mines	Com.	.01
Wiley Oilfield Hauling Ltd.	Com.	7.00
Williams Creek Gold Quartze Mining Co. Ltd.	Com.	.46
Willow Lake Mines Ltd.	Com.	
Willroy Mines Ltd.	Com.	.70
Wilshire Oil Company of Texas	Com.	
Wilson Red Lake Gold Mines Ltd.	Com.	
Winco Steak & Burger Restaurants Limited	Com.	4.60
Windermere Exploration Limited	Com.	.20
Windfall Oils & Mines Ltd.	Com.	.09
Win-Eldrich Mines Ltd.	Com.	.09
Winnipeg Supply and Fuel Co. Ltd.	Com.	8.50
Win West Oil & Mining Ltd.	Com.	.25
Wisconsin Mining Company Ltd.	Com.	.10
Wolf Creek Mines Ltd.	Com.	
Wood, Alexander Ltd.	Com.	2.53
Wood-Croesus Gold Mines Ltd.	Com.	.02
Woodford Investment Ltd.	Cl A.	
Woodford Investment Ltd.	Cl B.	2.00
Woodward Stores Limited	Com.	25.00
Worldwide Energy Company Ltd.	Com.	2.16
Wosk's Ltd.	Com.	7.75
Wrightbar Mines Limited	Com.	.30
Wright-Hargreaves Mines Ltd.	Com.	1.15
Xoma Ltd.	Com.	4.05
Yankee Canuck Oil and Mining Corp. Ltd.	Com.	.04
Yarandry Silver Mines Ltd.	Com.	.05
Yellorex Mines Ltd.	Com.	.13
Yellowknife Base Metals Ltd.	Com.	
Yellowknife Bear Mines Ltd.	Com.	4.40
Yorbeau Mines Inc.	Com.	.05
York Lambton Corporation Limited	Cl A.	.80
York Lambton Corporation Limited	Cl B.	
Young-Davidson Mines Ltd.	Com.	.16
Young, H. G. Mines Ltd.	Com.	.06
Young-Shannon Gold Mines Ltd.	Com.	.01
Yreka Mines Ltd.	Com.	.17
Y & R Properties Ltd.	Com.	6.75
Yukon Consolidated Gold Corp. Ltd.	Com.	1.10
Yukon Properties Limited	Com.	
Yukon Revenue Mines Limited	Com.	.12
Zahamy Mines Ltd.	Com.	2.38
Zeller's Ltd.	Com.	17.00
Zeller's Ltd.	$4^1/2$ pc cu pr.	34.00
Zenith Electric Supply Ltd.	Com.	2.35
Zenith Mining Corporation Ltd.	Com.	.27
Zenmac Metal Mines Limited	Com.	.06
Zinat Mines Limited	Com.	.15
Zodiac Ltd.	Cl A.	1.90
Zodiac Mines Ltd.	Com.	
Zulapa Mining Corporation Ltd.	Com.	.12

Regulations

Schedule VIII
Universities Outside Canada, (Section 3503) [Repealed.]

History: Schedule VIII was repealed by S.C. 2018, c. 12, s. 46(1), deemed in force February 27, 2018.

1. (Repealed.)

History: S. 1 of Schedule VIII was repealed by S.C. 2018, c. 12, s. 46(1), deemed in force February 27, 2018, and formerly read:

1. The universities situated in the United States that are prescribed by section 3503 are the following:

Abilene Christian University, Abilene, Texas
Academy of the New Church, The, Bryn Athyn, Pennsylvania
Adams State College, Alamosa, Colorado
Adler School of Professional Psychology, Chicago, Illinois
Albany College of Pharmacy and Health Sciences, Albany, New York
Alfred University, Alfred, New York
American Film Institute, Los Angeles, California
American Film Institute Center for Advanced Film and Television Studies, Los Angeles, California
American International College, Springfield, Massachusetts
American Jewish University, Bel Air, California
American University, The, Washington, District of Columbia
American University in Cairo, The, New York, New York
Amherst College, Amherst, Massachusetts
Anabaptist Mennonite Biblical Seminary, Elkhart, Indiana
Anderson College, Anderson, South Carolina
Andover Newton Theological School, Newton Centre, Massachusetts
Andrews University, Berrien Springs, Michigan
Antioch College, Yellow Springs, Ohio
Arizona State University, Tempe, Arizona
Asbury Theological Seminary, Wilmore, Kentucky
Atlantic Union College, South Lancaster, Massachusetts
Aurora University, Aurora, Illinois
Azusa Pacific College, Azusa, California
Babson College, Babson Park, Massachusetts
Bacone College, Muskogee, Oklahoma
Bard College, Annandale-On-Hudson, New York
Barnard College, New York, New York
Bastyr University, Seattle, Washington
Bates College, Lewiston, Maine
Baylor College of Medicine, Houston, Texas
Baylor University, Waco, Texas
Bemidji State University, Bemidji, Minnesota
Bentley College, Waltham, Massachusetts
Berklee College of Music, Boston, Massachusetts
Beth Medrash Gevoha, Lakewood, New Jersey
Biola University, La Mirada, California
Bob Jones University, Greenville, South Carolina
Boston University, Boston, Massachusetts
Bowdoin College, Brunswick, Maine
Bowling Green State University, Bowling Green, Ohio
Brandeis University, Waltham, Massachusetts
Brigham Young University — Hawaii Campus, Laie, Hawaii
Brigham Young University — Idaho, Rexburg, Idaho
Brigham Young University, Provo, Utah
Brown University, Providence, Rhode Island
Bryn Mawr College, Bryn Mawr, Pennsylvania
Bucknell University, Lewisburg, Pennsylvania
California College of the Arts, San Francisco, California
California Institute of Technology, Pasadena, California
California Institute of the Arts, Valencia, California
California Lotheran University, Thousand Oaks, California
Calvin College, Grand Rapids, Michigan
Calvin Theological Seminary, Grand Rapids, Michigan
Canisius College, Buffalo, New York
Carleton College, Northfield, Minnesota
Carnegie-Mellon University, Pittsburgh, Pennsylvania
Carroll College, Helena, Montana
Case Western Reserve University, Cleveland, Ohio
Catholic University of America, The, Washington, District of Columbia
Cedarville College, Cedarville, Ohio
Centenary College, Hackettstown, New Jersey
Central Michigan University, Mount Pleasant, Michigan
Central Yeshiva Tomchei Tmimim-Lubavitch, Brooklyn, New York
Cranbrook Academy of Art, Bloomfield Hills, Michigan
Christendom College, Front Royal, Virginia
City University of New York, The, John Jay College of Criminal Justice, New York, New York
City University of Seattle, Bellevue, Washington
Claremont McKenna College, Claremont, California
Clark University, Worcester, Massachusetts
Clarkson University, Potsdam, New York
Colby College, Waterville, Maine
Colby-Sawyer College, New London, New Hampshire
Colgate-Rochester Divinity School, The, Rochester, New York
Colgate University, Hamilton, New York
College of William and Mary, Williamsburg, Virginia
Colorado College, The, Colorado Springs, Colorado
Colorado School of Mines, Golden, Colorado
Colorado State University, Fort Collins, Colorado
Columbia Union College, Takoma Park, Maryland
Columbia International University, Columbia, South Carolina
Columbia University in the City of New York, New York, New York
Concordia College, Moorhead, Minnesota
Concordia University, Mequon, Wisconsin
Connecticut College, New London, Connecticut
Conway School of Landscape Design, Conway, Massachusetts
Cooper Union for the Advancement of Science and Art, The, New York, New York
Cornell University, Ithaca, New York
Cornerstone College and Grand Rapids Baptist Seminary, Grand Rapids, Michigan
Covenant College, Lookout Mountain, Tennessee
Cranbrook Academy of Art, Bloomfield Hills, Michigan
Creighton University, Omaha, Nebraska
Curtis Institute of Music, The, Philadelphia, Pennsylvania
D'Youville College, Buffalo, New York
Dallas Theological Seminary, Dallas, Texas
Dartmouth College, Hanover, New Hampshire
Denison University, Granville, Ohio
De Paul University, Chicago, Illinois
Dordt College, Sioux Center, Iowa
Drake University, Des Moines, Iowa
Drew University, Madison, New Jersey
Drury College, Springfield, Missouri
Duke University, Durham, North Carolina
Duquensne University, Pittsburgh, Pennsylvania
Eastern College, St. Davids, Pennsylvania
Eastern Mennonite University, Harrisonburg, Virginia
Eastern Washington University, Cheney, Washington
Eckerd College, St. Petersburg, Florida

Ecumenical Theological Center, Detroit, Michigan
Elmira College, Elmira, New York
Embry-Riddle Aeronautical University, Daytona Beach, Florida
Emerson College, Boston, Massachusetts
Emmanuel School of Religion, Johnson City, Tennessee
Emmaus Bible College, Dubuque, Iowa
Emory University, Atlanta, Georgia
Emporia State University, Emporia, Kansas
Fairleigh Dickinson University, Teaneck, New Jersey
Ferris State University, Big Rapids, Michigan
Finlandia University, Hancock, Michigan
Florida Atlantic University, Boca Raton, Florida
Florida Gulf Coast University, Fort Myers, Florida
Florida State University, Tallahassee, Florida
Fordham University, New York, New York
Franciscan University of Steubenville, Steubenville, Ohio
Freed-Hardeman University, Henderson, Tennessee
Fresno Pacific College, Fresno, California
Fuller Theological Seminary, Pasadena, California
Gallaudet College, Washington, District of Columbia
Geneva College, Beaver Falls, Pennsylvania
Georgetown University, Washington, District of Columbia
George Washington University, The, Washington, District of Columbia
Georgia Institute of Technology, Atlanta, Georgia
Goddard College, Plainfield, Vermont
God's Bible School and College, Cincinnati, Ohio
Gonzaga University, Spokane, Washington
Gordon College, Wenham, Massachusetts
Gordon-Conwell Theological Seminary, South Hamilton, Massachusetts
Goshen College, Goshen, Indiana
Grace University, Omaha, Nebraska
Graceland College, Lamoni, Iowa
Greenville College, Greenville, Illinois
Grinnell College, Grinnell, Iowa
Hamilton College, Clinton, New York
Hampshire College, Amherst, Massachusetts
Harvard University, Cambridge, Massachusetts
Haverford College, Haverford, Pennsylvania
Hawaii Pacific University, Honolulu, Hawaii
Hebrew Union College — Jewish Institute of Religion, Cincinnati, Ohio
Hillsdale College, Hillsdale, Michigan
Hobart and William Smith Colleges, Geneva, New York
Holy Trinity Orthodox Seminary, The Jordanville, New York
Hope College, Holland, Michigan
Houghton College, Houghton, New York
Howard University, Washington, District of Columbia
Huntington University, Huntington, Indiana
Idaho State University, Pocatello, Idaho
Illinois Institute of Technology, Chicago, Illinois
Illinois State University, Normal, Illinois
Indiana University, Bloomington, Indiana
Iowa State University of Science and Technology, Ames, Iowa
Ithaca College, Ithaca, New York
Jacksonville State University, Jacksonville, Alabama
Jamestown College, Jamestown, North Dakota
Jewish Theological Seminary of America, The, New York, New York
John Brown University, Siloam Springs, Arkansas
Johns Hopkins University, The, Baltimore, Maryland
Juilliard School, The, New York, New York
Kansas State University, Manhattan, Kansas
Kent State University, Kent, Ohio
Kenyon College, Gambier, Ohio
Kettering University, Flint, Michigan
Kuyper College, Grand Rapids, Michigan
Lafayette College, Easton, Pennsylvania
Lake Superior State University, Sault Ste. Marie, Michigan
Lawrence Technological University, Southfield, Michigan
Lehigh University, Bethlehem, Pennsylvania
Leland Stanford Junior University (Stanford University), Stanford, California
LeMoyne College, Syracuse, New York
LeTourneau College, Longview, Texas
Liberty University, Lynchburg, Virginia
Life Chiropractic College West, Hayward, California
Life University, Marietta, Georgia
Limestone College, Gaffney, South Carolina
Logan College of Chiropractic, St. Louis, Missouri
Loma Linda University, Loma Linda, California
Louisiana State Univesity and Agricultural and Mechanical College, Baton Rouge, Louisiana
Loyola Marymount University, Los Angeles, California
Loyola University, Chicago, Illinois
Macalester College, St. Paul, Minnesota
Magdalen College, Warner, New Hampshire
Maharishi University of Management, Fairfield, Iowa
Manchester College, North Manchester, Indiana
Manhattanville College, Purchase, New York
Mankato State University, Mankato, Minnesota
Maranatha Baptist Bible College, Watertown, Wisconsin
Marian University, Fond du Lac, Wisconsin
Marquette University, Milwaukee, Wisconsin
Massachusetts Institute of Technology, Cambridge, Massachusetts
Mayo Foundation, Rochester, Minnesota
Mayo Graduate School of Medicine, Rochester, Minnesota
Meadville-Lombard Theological School, Chicago, Illinois
Medaille College, Buffalo, New York
Medical College of Ohio, Toledo, Ohio
Medical University of South Carolina, Charleston, South Carolina
Mercyhurst College, Erie, Pennsylvania
Mesivta Torah Vodaath Rabbinical Seminary, Brooklyn, New York
Mesivta Yshiva Rabbi Chaim Berlin, Brooklyn, New York
Messiah College, Grantham, Pennsylvania
Miami University, Oxford, Ohio
Michigan State University, East Lansing, Michigan
Michigan State University College of Law, East Lansing, Michigan
Michigan Technological University, Houghton, Michigan
Middlebury College, Middlebury, Vermont
Minot State University, Minot, North Dakota
Mirrer Yeshiva Central Institute, Brooklyn, New York
Montana Tech of the University of Montana, Butte, Montana
Montana State University, Bozeman, Montana
Moody Bible Institute, Chicago, Illinois
Moravian College, Bethlehem, Pennsylvania
Mount Holyoke College, South Hadley, Massachusetts
Mount Ida College, Newton Centre, Massachusetts
Mount Sinai School of Medicine, New York, New York
Multnomah Bible College, Portland, Oregon
Naropa University, Boulder, Colorado
National College of Chiropractic, The, Lombard, Illinois
Nazarene Theological Seminary, Kansas City, Missouri
Ner Israel Rabbinical College, Baltimore, Maryland
New England College, Henniker, New Hampshire
New School University, New York, New York
New York University, New York, New York
Niagara University, Niagara University, New York

North American Baptist Seminary, Sioux Falls, South Dakota
North Carolina State University at Raleigh, Raleigh, North Carolina
North Dakota State University of Agriculture and Applied Science, Fargo,
North Dakota
Northeastern University, Boston, Massachusetts
Northern Michigan University, Marquette, Michigan
Northwestern College, Orange City, Iowa
Northwestern College, St. Paul, Minnesota
Northwestern University, Evanston, Illinois
Northwood University, Midland, Michigan
Nova Southeastern University, Fort Lauderdale, Florida
Nyack College, Nyack, New York
Oakland University, Rochester, Michigan
Oakwood College, Huntsville, Alabama
Oberlin College, Oberlin, Ohio
Ohio State University, The, Columbus, Ohio
Ohio University, Athens, Ohio
Ohr Somayach/Joseph Tanenbaum Educational Center, Monsey, New York
Old Dominion University, Norfolk, Virginia
Olivet Nazarene University, Bourbonnais, Illinois
Oral Roberts University, Tulsa, Oklahoma
Oregon State University, Corvallis, Oregon
Pace University, New York, New York
Pacific Graduate School of Psychology, Menlo Park, California
Pacific Lutheran University, Tacoma, Washington
Pacific Union College, Angwin, California
Pacific University, Forest Grove, Oregon
Palm Beach Atlantic University, West Palm Beach, Florida
Palmer College of Chiropractic, Davenport, Iowa
Palmer College of Chiropractic-West, San Jose, California
Park University, Parkville, Missouri
Pennsylvania State University, The, University Park, Pennsylvania
Pepperdine University, Malibu, California
Philadelphia Biblical University, Langhorne, Pennsylvania
Pomona College, Claremont, California
Princeton Theological Seminary, Princeton, New Jersey
Princeton University, Princeton, New Jersey
Principia College, The, Elsah, Illinois
Providence College, Providence, Rhode Island
Purdue University, Lafayette, Indiana
Rabbinical College Bobover Yeshiva Bnei Zion, Brooklyn, New York
Rabbinical College of America, Morristown, New Jersey
Rabbinical College of Long Island, Long Beach, New York
Rabbinical Seminary of America, Forest Hills, New York
Reed College, Portland, Oregon
Reformed Theological Seminary, Jackson, Mississippi
Rensselaer Polytechnic Institute, Troy, New York
Rice University, Houston, Texas
Rio Grande Bible Institute, Edinburg, Texas
Roberts Wesleyan College, North Chili, New York
Rockefeller University, New York, New York
Rollins College, Winter Park, Florida
Rush University, Chicago, Illinois
Rutgers — The State University, New Brunswick, New Jersey
St. Bonaventure University, St. Bonaventure, New York
St. John's College, Annapolis, Maryland
St. John's College, Santa Fe, New Mexico
St. John's University, Jamaica, New York
St. Lawrence University, Canton, New York
St. Mary's University of San Antonio, San Antonio, Texas
St. Vladimir's Orthodox Theological Seminary, Crestwood, New York
Saint John's University, Collegeville, Minnesota
Saint Louis University, St. Louis, Missouri
Saint Mary's University of Minnesota, Winona, Minnesota
Saint Olaf College, Northfield, Minnesota
San Francisco State College, San Francisco, California
San José State University, San José, California
Santa Clara University, Santa Clara, California
Sarah Lawrence College, Bronxville, New York
Scripps College, Claremont, California
Scripps Research Institute, The, La Jolla, California
Seattle Pacific University, Seattle, Washington
Seattle University, Seattle, Washington
Simpson College, Indianola, Iowa
Simpson College, Redding, California
Skidmore College, Saratoga Springs, New York
Smith College, The, Northampton, Massachusetts
Southeastern University, Lakeland, Florida
Southern Adventist University, Collegedale, Tennessee
Southern Methodist University, Dallas, Texas
Southwestern Adventist University, Keene, Texas
Spring Arbor College, Spring Arbor, Michigan
State University College at Potsdam, Potsdam, New York
State University College at Oswego, Oswego, New York
State University of New York at Binghamton, Binghamton, New York
State University of New York at Buffalo, Buffalo, New York
State University of New York at Geneseo, Geneseo, New York
State University of New York College of Arts and Science at Plattsburgh, Plattsburgh, New York
Stephens College, Columbia, Missouri
Swarthmore College, Swarthmore, Pennsylvania
Syracuse University, Syracuse, New York
Tabor College, Hillsboro, Kansas
Talmudical Yeshiva of Philadelphia, Philadelphia
Taylor University, Upland, Indiana
Teachers College, Columbia University, New York, New York
Telshe Yeshiva Rabbinical College of Telshe, Inc., Wickcliffe, Ohio
Telshe Yeshiva-Chicago, Rabbinical College of Telshe-Chicago, Inc., Chicago, Illinois
Temple University, Philadelphia, Pennsylvania
Temple University School of Podiatric Medicine, Philadelphia, Pennsylvania
Texas A&M University, College Station, Texas
Texas Chiropractic College, Pasadena, Texas
Texas Woman's University, Denton, Texas
The Herman A. Finch University of Health Sciences/The Chicago Medical School, North Chicago, Illinois
Thomas Aquinas College, Santa Paula, California
Thunderbird School of Global Management, Glendale, Arizona
Touro College, New York, New York
Trinity Bible College, Ellendale, North Dakota
Trinity Christian College, Palos Heights, Illinois
Trinity College, Hartford, Connecticut
Trinity Episcopal School for Ministry, Ambridge, Pennsylvania
Trinity Evangelical Divinity School, Deerfield, Illinois
Trinity Lutheran College, Issaquah, Washington
Trinity University, San Antonio, Texas
Tufts University, Medford, Massachusetts
Tulane University, New Orleans, Louisiana
Union College, Lincoln, Nebraska
Union College, Schenectady, New York
Union Institute & University, Cincinnati, Ohio

Regulations

Union University, Jackson, Tennessee
University at Albany, State University of New York, Albany, New York
University of Alabama at Birmingham, The, Birmingham, Alabama
University of Alabama in Huntsville, Huntsville, Alabama
University of Arizona, The, Tucson, Arizona
University of California, Davis, California
University of California, Irvine, California
University of California, Los Angeles, California
University of California, Riverside, California
University of California, San Diego, California
University of California, Santa Barbara, California
University of California, Santa Cruz, California
University of California, Berkeley, California
University of California, San Francisco, California
University of Central Florida, Orlando, Florida
University of Chicago, The, Chicago, Illinois
University of Cincinnati, Cincinnati, Ohio
University of Colorado, Boulder, Colorado
University of Delaware, Newark, Delaware
University of Denver, Denver, Colorado
University of Detroit Mercy, Detroit, Michigan
University of Findlay, The, Findlay, Ohio
University of Florida, Gainesville, Florida
University of Georgia, The, Athens, Georgia
University of Houston, Houston, Texas
University of Idaho, Moscow, Idaho
University of Illinois, Urbana, Illinois
University of Kansas, Lawrence, Kansas
University of Kentucky, Lexington, Kentucky
University of Louisville, Louisville, Kentucky
University of Maine, Orono, Maine
University of Maryland, College Park, Maryland
University of Massachusetts at Amherst, Amherst, Massachusetts
University of Miami, Coral Gables, Florida
University of Michigan, The, Ann Arbor, Michigan
University of Minnesota, Minneapolis, Minnesota
University of Mississippi, The, Oxford, Mississippi
University of Missouri, Columbia, Missouri
University of Montana-Missoula, The, Misoula, Montana
University of Nebraska, The, Lincoln, Nebraska
University of Nevada-Reno, Reno, Nevada
University of North Carolina at Chapel Hill, Chapel Hill, North Carolina
University of North Dakota, Grand Forks, North Dakota
University of North Texas, Denton, Texas
University of Notre Dame du Lac, Notre Dame, Indiana
University of Oklahoma, Norman, Oklahoma
University of Oregon, Eugene, Oregon
University of Pennsylvania, Philadelphia, Pennsylvania
University of Pittsburgh, Pittsburgh, Pennsylvania
University of Portland, Portland, Oregon
University of Rhode Island, Kingston, Rhode Island
University of Rochester, Rochester, New York
University of San Diego, San Diego, California
University of Southern California, Los Angeles, California
University of Southern Mississippi, The, Hattiesburg, Mississippi
University of St. Thomas, Houston, Texas
University of St. Thomas, St. Paul, Minnesota
University of Tennessee, The, Knoxville, Tennessee
University of Texas, Austin, Texas
University of Texas at Arlington, Arlington, Texas
University of Texas Health Science Center at Houston, Houston, Texas
University of Texas Southwestern Medical Center at Dallas, The, Dallas, Texas
University of the Pacific, Stockton, California
University of Tulsa, Tulsa, Oklahoma
University of Utah, Salt Lake City, Utah
University of Vermont, Burlington, Vermont
University of Virginia, Charlottesville, Virginia
University of Washington, Seattle, Washington
University of Western States, Portland, Oregon
University of Wisconsin, Madison, Wisconsin
University of Wisconsin-Milwaukee, Milwaukee, Wisconsin
University of Wyoming, The, Laramie, Wyoming
Utah State University of Agriculture and Applied Science, Logan, Utah
Utah Valley University, Orem, Utah
Valparaiso University, Valparaiso, Indiana
Vanderbilt University, Nashville, Tennessee
Vassar College, Poughkeepsie, New York
Villanova University, Villanova, Pennsylvania
Wake Forest University, Winston-Salem, North Carolina
Walla Walla University, College Place, Washington
Washington and Lee University, Lexington, Virginia
Washington State University, Pullman, Washington
Washington University, St. Louis, Missouri
Wayne State University, Detroit, Michigan
Welch College, Nashville, Tennessee
Wellesley College, Wellesley, Massachusetts
Wesleyan University, Middletown, Connecticut
Western Illinois University, Macomb, Illinois
Western Seminary, Portland, Oregon
Western University of Health Sciences, Pomona, California
Western Washington University, Bellingham, Washington
Westminster Theological Seminary, Philadelphia, Pennsylvania
West Virginia University, Morgantown, West Virginia
Wheaton College, Norton, Massachusetts
Wheaton College, Wheaton, Illinois
Whitman College, Walla Walla, Washington
Whitworth College, Spokane, Washington
Williams College, Williamstown, Massachusetts
Wittenberg University, Springfield, Ohio
Woods Hole Oceanographic Institution, Woods Hole, Massachusetts
Yale University, New Haven, Connecticut
Yeshiva Ohr Elchonon Chabad West Coast Talmudic Seminary, Los Angeles, California
Yeshiva University, New York, New York

S. 1 of Schedule VIII was amended by P.C. 2015-862, SOR/2015-170, s. 4(1), dated June 19, 2015, published in the *Canada Gazette* July 1, 2015, by deleting: Augsburg College, Minneapolis, Minnesota; Beloit College, Beloit, Wisconsin; Bennington College, Bennington, Vermont; Bethel College, Mishawaka, Indiana; Bethel College, North Newton, Kansas; Bethel College and Seminary, St. Paul, Minnesota; Boston College, Chestnut Hill, Massachusetts, in force July 1, 2015.

S. 1 of Schedule VIII was amended by P.C. 2015-862, SOR/2015-170, s. 4(2), dated June 19, 2015, published in the *Canada Gazette* July 1, 2015, by adding: American Film Institute, Los Angeles, California; Brigham Young University — Idaho, Rexburg, Idaho; California College of the Arts, San Francisco, California; Concordia University, Mequon, Wisconsin; Fairleigh Dickinson University, Teaneck, New Jersey; Haverford College, Haverford, Pennsylvania; Marian University, Fond du Lac, Wisconsin; Rensselaer Polytechnic Institute, Troy, New York; Rockefeller University, New York, New York; Saint Louis University, St. Louis, Missouri; Syracuse University, Syracuse, New York; Texas Woman's University, Denton, Texas; University of Louisville, Louisville, Kentucky; University of Maryland, College Park, Maryland; University of Oregon, Eugene, Oregon; University of Texas at Arlington, Arlington, Texas; Utah Valley University, Orem, Utah, deemed to have come into force on January 1, 2014.

S. 1 of Schedule VIII was amended by P.C. 2015-862, SOR/2015-170, s. 4(3), dated June 19, 2015, published in the *Canada Gazette* July 1, 2015, by adding: Rio Grande Bible Institute, Edinburg, Texas, deemed to have come into force on January 1, 2009.

S. 1 of Schedule VIII was amended by P.C. 2015-862, SOR/2015-170, s. 4(4), dated June 19, 2015, published in the *Canada Gazette* July 1, 2015, by adding: Howard University, Washington, District of Columbia, deemed to have come into force on January 1, 2011.

S. 1 of Schedule VIII was amended by P.C. 2015-862, SOR/2015-170, s. 4(5), dated June 19, 2015, published in the *Canada Gazette* July 1, 2015, by adding: Bemidji State University, Bemidji, Minnesota; Embry-Riddle Aeronautical University, Daytona Beach, Florida; Hobart and William Smith Colleges, Geneva, New York; Olivet Nazarene University, Bourbonnais, Illinois, deemed to have come into force on January 1, 2013.

S. 1 of Schedule VIII was amended by P.C. 2014-358, SOR/2014-81, dated April 4, 2014, published in the *Canada Gazette* April 23, 2014, by striking out: Associated Mennonite Biblical Seminary, Elkhart, Indiana; Michigan State University, Detroit College of Law, East Lansing, Michigan; North Central College, Naperville, Illinois; Northwest College of The Assemblies of God, Kirkland, Washington; Ohio College of Podiatric Medicine, Cleveland, Ohio; Pennsylvania College of Podiatric Medicine, Philadelphia, Pennsylvania; Philadelphia University, Philadelphia, Pennsylvania; Pine Manor College, Chestnut Hill, Massachusetts; Reconstructionist Rabbinical College, Wyncote, Pennsylvania; Rensselaer Polytechnic Institute, Troy, New York; Rochester Institute of Technology, Rochester, New York; Rockefeller University, New York, New York; Saint Louis University, St. Louis, Missouri; Simmons College, Boston, Massachusetts; South Dakota School of Mines and Technology, Rapid City, South Dakota; Southern Illinois University of Carbondale, Carbondale, Illinois; State University of New York at Stony Brook, Stony Brook, New York; Stevens Institute of Technology, Hoboken, New Jersey; Syracuse University, Syracuse, New York; Talmudic College of Florida, Miami Beach, Florida; Texas Woman's University, Denton, Texas; Union Theological Seminary, New York, New York; University of Akron, The, Akron, Ohio; University of Arkansas at Little Rock, Little Rock, Arkansas; University of Hawaii, Honolulu, Hawaii; University of Iowa, Iowa City, Iowa; University of Maryland, College Park, Maryland; University of Missouri, St. Louis, Missouri; University of Oregon, Eugene, Oregon; Washington Bible College, Lanham, Maryland; Western Conservative Baptist Seminary, Portland, Oregon; Western Michigan University, Kalamazoo, Michigan; Westfield State College, Westfield, Massachusetts; Westminster Theological Seminary in California, Escondido, California; Wheelock College, Boston, Massachusetts; and Wright State University, Dayton, Ohio, in force April 23, 2014.

S. 1 of Schedule VIII was amended by P.C. 2014-358, SOR/2014-81, dated April 4, 2014, published in the *Canada Gazette* April 23, 2014, by adding: Anabaptist Mennonite Biblical Seminary, Elkhart, Indiana, deemed in force October 24, 2012.

S. 1 of Schedule VIII was amended by P.C. 2014-358, SOR/2014-81, dated April 4, 2014, published in the *Canada Gazette* April 23, 2014, by adding: Michigan State University College of Law, and East Lansing, Michigan, deemed in force September 12, 2012.

S. 1 of Schedule VIII was amended by P.C. 2014-358, SOR/2014-81, dated April 4, 2014, published in the *Canada Gazette* April 23, 2014, by adding: Bacone College, Muskogee, Oklahoma; Freed-Hardeman University, Henderson, Tennessee; Temple University School of Podiatric Medicine, Philadelphia, Pennsylvania; and University of Alabama in Huntsville, Huntsville, Alabama, deemed in force January 1, 2013.

S. 1 of Schedule VIII was amended by P.C. 2014-358, SOR/2014-81, dated April 4, 2014, published in the *Canada Gazette* April 23, 2014, by adding: Western Seminary, Portland, Oregon, deemed in force March 11, 2011.

S. 1 of Schedule VIII was amended by P.C. 2014-358, SOR/2014-81, dated April 4, 2014, published in the *Canada Gazette* April 23, 2014, by adding: University of Texas Health Science Center at Houston, Houston, Texas; and Western Illinois University, Macomb, Illinois, deemed in force January 1, 2011.

S. 1 of Schedule VIII was amended by P.C. 2014-358, SOR/2014-81, dated April 4, 2014, published in the *Canada Gazette* April 23, 2014, by adding: Cooper Union for the Advancement of Science and Art, The, New York, New York; Limestone College, Gaffney, South Carolina; Loyola Marymount University, Los Angeles, California; University of Wisconsin-Milwaukee, Milwaukee, Wisconsin; and Welch College, Nashville, Tennessee, deemed in force January 1, 2012.

S. 1 of Schedule VIII was amended by P.C. 2012-1330, SOR/2012-218, dated October 5, 2012, published in the *Canada Gazette* October 24, 2012, by striking out: American Graduate School of International Management, Glendale, Arizona; City University, Bellevue, Washington; Palm Beach Atlantic College, West Palm Beach, Florida; Palmer College of Chiropractic-West, Sunnyvale, California; Park College, Kansas City, Missouri; Philadelphia College of Bible, Langhorne, Pennsylvania; Reformed Bible College, Grand Rapids, Michigan; Sherman College of Straight Chiropractic, Spartanburq, South Carolina; Southwestern Adventist College, Keene, Texas; Springfield College, Springfield, Massachusetts; Sunbridge College, Chestnut Ridge, New York; University of Judaism, Los Angeles, California; Western Baptist College, Salem, Oregon; Western States Chiropractic College, Portland, Oregon; William Tyndale College, Farmington Hills, Michigan, in force October 24, 2012.

S. 1 of Schedule VIII was amended by P.C. 2012-1330, SOR/2012-218, dated October 5, 2012, published in the *Canada Gazette* October 24, 2012, by adding: Adler School of Professional Psychology, Chicago, Illinois; Berklee College of Music, Boston, Massachusetts; Pepperdine University, Malibu, California; Rabbinical College Bobover Yeshiva Bnei Zion, Brooklyn, New York; Saint Mary's University of Minnesota, Winona, Minnesota; Southeastern University, Lakeland, Florida, deemed to have come into force on January 1, 2009.

S. 1 of Schedule VIII was amended by P.C. 2012-1330, SOR/2012-218, dated October 5, 2012, published in the *Canada Gazette* October 24, 2012, by adding: Centenary College, Hackettstown, New Jersey; Kent State University, Kent, Ohio; Rollins College, Winter Park, Florida; State University of New York at Geneseo, Geneseo, New York; Thunderbird School of Global Management, Glendale, Arizona; University of Findlay, The, Findlay, Ohio; Woods Hole Oceanographic Institution, Woods Hole, Massachusetts, deemed to have come into force on January 1, 2010.

S. 1 of Schedule VIII was amended by P.C. 2012-1330, SOR/2012-218, dated October 5, 2012, published in the *Canada Gazette* October 24, 2012, by adding: American Jewish University, Bel Air, California; City University of Seattle, Bellevue, Washington; Kuyper College, Grand Rapids, Michigan; Manchester College, North Manchester, Indiana; Ohr Somayach/Joseph Tanenbaum Educational Center, Monsey, New York; Palm Beach Atlantic University, West Palm Beach, Florida; Philadelphia Biblical University, Langhorne, Pennsylvania; University at Albany, State University of New York, Albany, New York, deemed to have come into force on January 1, 2011.

S. 1 of Schedule VIII was amended by P.C. 2012-1330, SOR/2012-218, dated October 5, 2012, published in the *Canada Gazette* October 24, 2012, by adding: Park University, Parkville, Missouri; Southwestern Adventist University, Keene, Texas, deemed to have come into force on January 1, 2012.

S. 1 of Schedule VIII was amended by P.C. 2012-1330, SOR/2012-218, dated October 5, 2012, published in the *Canada Gazette* October 24, 2012, by adding: Palmer College of Chiropractic-West, San Jose, California, deemed to have come into force on January 1, 1999.

S. 1 of Schedule VIII was amended by P.C. 2012-1330, SOR/2012-218, dated October 5, 2012, published in the *Canada Gazette* October 24, 2012, by adding: University of Western States, Portland, Oregon, deemed to have come into force on March 2, 2010.

S. 1 of Schedule VIII was amended by P.C. 2010-551, SOR/2010-96, dated April 29, 2010, published in the *Canada Gazette* May 12, 2010, by striking out: Huntington College, Huntington, Indiana, Naropa Institute, The, Boulder, Colorado, and Union Institute, The, Cincinnati, Ohio, and by adding: Hawaii Pacific University, Honolulu, Hawaii, Huntington University, Huntington, Indiana, Idaho State University, Pocatello, Idaho, John Brown University, Siloam Springs, Arkansas, Naropa University, Boulder, Colorado and Union Institute & University, Cincinnati, Ohio, deemed to have taken effect on January 1, 2006.

S. 1 of Schedule VIII was amended by P.C. 2010-551, SOR/2010-96, dated April 29, 2010, published in the *Canada Gazette* May 12, 2010, by adding: Albany College of Pharmacy of Union University, Albany, New York, Jacksonville State University, Jacksonville, Alabama, Mesivta Torah Vodaath Rabbinical Seminary, Brooklyn, New York, Mount Sinai School of Medicine, New York, New York, Union University, Jackson, Tennessee and University of Mississippi, The, Oxford, Mississippi, deemed to have taken effect on January 1, 2007.

S. 1 of Schedule VIII was amended by P.C. 2010-551, SOR/2010-96, dated April 29, 2010, published in the *Canada Gazette* May 12, 2010, by striking out: Albany College of Pharmacy of Union University, Albany, New York, and by adding: Albany College of Pharmacy and Health Sciences, Albany, New York, deemed to have taken effect on August 21, 2008.

S. 1 of Schedule VIII was amended by P.C. 2010-551, SOR/2010-96, dated April 29, 2010, published in the *Canada Gazette* May 12, 2010, by striking out: Walla Walla College, College Place, Washington, and by adding: Walla Walla University, College Place, Washington, deemed to have taken effect on January 1, 2008.

S. 1 of Schedule VIII was amended by P.C. 2010-551, SOR/2010-96, dated April 29, 2010, published in the *Canada Gazette* May 12, 2010, by adding: Cranbrook Academy of Art, Bloomfield Hills, Michigan, deemed to have taken effect on January 1, 2009.

2. (Repealed.)

History: S. 2 of Schedule VIII was repealed by S.C. 2018, c. 12, s. 46(1), deemed in force February 27, 2018, and formerly read:

2. The universities situated in the United Kingdom of Great Britain and Northern Ireland that are prescribed by section 3503 are the following:

Aston University, Birmingham, England

Brunel University, Uxbridge, England

City University London, London, England

Cranfield University, Bedfordshire, England

Gateshead Talmudical College, Gateshead, England

Heriot-Watt University, Edinburgh, Scotland

Imperial College of Science, Technology and Medicine, London, England

Regulations

King's College London, London, England

London Business School, London, England

London School of Economics and Political Science, The, London, England

London School of Hygiene & Tropical Medicine, London, England

Loughborough University, Leicestershire, England

Queen's University of Belfast, The, Belfast, Northern Ireland

Swansea University, Swansea, Wales

University College London, London, England

University of Aberdeen, Aberdeen, Scotland

University of Birmingham, Birmingham, England

University of Bath, The, Bath, England

University of Bradford, Bradford, England

University of Bristol, Bristol, England

University of Buckingham, The, Buckingham, England

University of Cambridge, Cambridge, England

University of Dundee, The, Dundee, Scotland

University of Durham, Durham, England

University of Edinburgh, Edinburgh, Scotland

University of Exeter, Exeter, England

University of Glasgow, Glasgow, Scotland

University of Keele, Keele, England

University of Kent, Canterbury, England

University of Leeds, Leeds, England

University of Liverpool, Liverpool, England

University of London, London, England

University of Manchester, The, Manchester, England

University of Newcastle, The, Newcastle upon Tyne, England

University of Nottingham, The Nottingham, England

University of Oxford, Oxford, England

University of Reading, Reading, England

University of St. Andrews, St. Andrews, Scotland

University of Surrey, Guildford, Surrey, England

University of Sheffield, Sheffield, England

University of Southampton, Southampton, England

University of Strathclyde, Glasgow, Scotland

University of Sussex, Brighton, England

University of Ulster, Newtonabbey, Northern Ireland

University of Wales, Cardiff, Wales

University of York, York, England

S. 2 of Schedule VIII was amended by P.C. 2015-862, SOR/2015-170, s. 5(1), dated June 19, 2015, published in the *Canada Gazette* July 1, 2015, by adding: City University London, London, England; London School of Hygiene & Tropical Medicine, London, England; University of Buckingham, The, Buckingham, England, deemed to have come into force on January 1, 2014.

S. 2 of Schedule VIII was amended by P.C. 2015-862, SOR/2015-170, s. 5(2), dated June 19, 2015, published in the *Canada Gazette* July 1, 2015, by adding: Swansea University, Swansea, Wales, deemed to have come into force on January 1, 2013.

S. 2 of Schedule VIII was amended by P.C. 2014-358, SOR/2014-81, dated April 4, 2014, published in the *Canada Gazette* April 23, 2014, by striking out: University of North London, London, England, in force April 23, 2014.

S. 2 of Schedule VIII was amended by P.C. 2014-358, SOR/2014-81, dated April 4, 2014, published in the *Canada Gazette* April 23, 2014, by adding: University of York, York, England, deemed in force January 1, 2012.

S. 2 of Schedule VIII was amended by P.C. 2012-1330, SOR/2012-218, dated October 5, 2012, published in the *Canada Gazette* October 24, 2012, by adding: University of Ulster, Newtonabbey, Northern Ireland, deemed to have come into force on January 1, 2009.

S. 2 of Schedule VIII was amended by P.C. 2010-551, SOR/2010-96, dated April 29, 2010, published in the *Canada Gazette* May 12, 2010, by adding: London School of Economics and Political Science, The, London, England and University of Kent, Canterbury, England, deemed to have taken effect on January 1, 2005.

S. 2 of Schedule VIII was amended by P.C. 2010-551, SOR/2010-96, dated April 29, 2010, published in the *Canada Gazette* May 12, 2010, by adding: University of Keele, Keele, England, deemed to have taken effect on January 1, 2007.

S. 2 of Schedule VIII was amended by P.C. 2010-551, SOR/2010-96, dated April 29, 2010, published in the *Canada Gazette* May 12, 2010, by adding: Brunel University, Uxbridge, England, deemed to have taken effect on January 1, 2009.

3. (Repealed.)

History: S. 3 of Schedule VIII was repealed by S.C. 2018, c. 12, s. 46(1), deemed in force February 27, 2018, and formerly read:

3. The universities situated in France that are prescribed by section 3503 are the following:

American University in Paris, Paris

Catholic Faculties of Lyon, Lyon

Catholic Institute of Paris, Paris

Catholic University of Lille, The, Lille

École Nationale des Ponts et Chaussées, Paris

European Institute of Business Administration (INSEAD), Fontainebleau

Hautes Études Commerciales, Paris

S. 3 of Schedule VIII was amended by P.C. 2014-358, SOR/2014-81, dated April 4, 2014, published in the *Canada Gazette* April 23, 2014, by striking out: Paris Graduate School of Management, Paris, in force April 23, 2014.

4. (Repealed.)

History: S. 4 of Schedule VIII was repealed by S.C. 2018, c. 12, s. 46(1), deemed in force February 27, 2018, and formerly read:

4. The universities situated in Austria that are prescribed by section 3503 are the following:

WU Vienna University of Economics and Business, Vienna

S. 4 of Schedule VIII was amended by P.C. 2012-1330, SOR/2012-218, dated October 5, 2012, published in the *Canada Gazette* October 24, 2012, by striking out: University of Vienna, Vienna, in force October 24, 2012.

S. 4 of Schedule VIII was amended by P.C. 2010-551, SOR/2010-96, dated April 29, 2010, published in the *Canada Gazette* May 12, 2010, by adding: WU Vienna University of Economics and Business, Vienna, deemed to have taken effect on January 1, 2007.

5. (Repealed.)

History: S. 5 of Schedule VIII was repealed by S.C. 2018, c. 12, s. 46(1), deemed in force February 27, 2018, and formerly read:

5. The universities situated in Belgium that are prescribed by section 3503 are the following:

Catholic University of Louvain, Louvain

6. (Repealed.)

History: S. 6 of Schedule VIII was repealed by S.C. 2018, c. 12, s. 46(1), deemed in force February 27, 2018, and formerly read:

6. The universities situated in Switzerland that are prescribed by section 3503 are the following:

Franklin College of Switzerland, Sorengo (Lugano)

University of Lausanne, Lausanne

S. 6 of Schedule VIII was amended by P.C. 2014-358, SOR/2014-81, dated April 4, 2014, published in the *Canada Gazette* April 23, 2014, by striking out: University of Geneva, Geneva, in force April 23, 2014.

7. (Revoked.)

History: S. 7 of Schedule VIII was revoked by P.C. 2014-358, SOR/2014-81, dated April 4, 2014, published in the *Canada Gazette* April 23, 2014, in force April 23, 2014, and formerly read:

7. The universities situated in Vatican City that are prescribed by section 3503 are the following:

Pontifical Gregorian University

8. (Repealed.)

History: S. 8 of Schedule VIII was repealed by S.C. 2018, c. 12, s. 46(1), deemed in force February 27, 2018, and formerly read:

8. The universities situated in Israel that are prescribed by section 3503 are the following:

Bar-Ilan University, Ramat-Gan
Ben Gurion University of the Negev, Beersheba
École biblique et archéologique française, Jerusalem
Hebrew University of Jerusalem, The, Jerusalem
Interdisciplinary Center, The, Herzliya, Israel
Jerusalem College for Women, Bayit-Vegan, Jerusalem
Jerusalem College of Technology, Jerusalem
Technion-Israel Institute of Technology, Haifa
Tel-Aviv University, Tel-Aviv
University of Haifa, Haifa
Weizmann Institute of Science, Rehovot, Israel
Yeshivat Aish Hatorah, Jerusalem

S. 8 of Schedule VIII was amended by P.C. 2014-358, SOR/2014-81, dated April 4, 2014, published in the *Canada Gazette* April 23, 2014, by adding: Interdisciplinary Center, The, Herzliya, Israel, deemed in force January 1, 2012.

S. 8 of Schedule VIII was amended by P.C. 2014-358, SOR/2014-81, dated April 4, 2014, published in the *Canada Gazette* April 23, 2014, by adding: Weizmann Institute of Science, Rehovot, Israel, January 1, 2013.

S. 8 of Schedule VIII was amended by P.C. 2012-1330, SOR/2012-218, dated October 5, 2012, published in the *Canada Gazette* October 24, 2012, by striking out: Weizmann Institute of Science, Rehovot, in force October 24, 2012.

9. (Repealed.)

History: S. 9 of Schedule VIII was repealed by S.C. 2018, c. 12, s. 46(1), deemed in force February 27, 2018, and formerly read:

9. The universities situated in Lebanon that are prescribed by section 3503 are the following:

American University of Beirut, Riad El Solh, Beirut
St. Joseph University, Beirut

10. (Repealed.)

History: S. 10 of Schedule VIII was repealed by S.C. 2018, c. 12, s. 46(1), deemed in force February 27, 2018, and formerly read:

10. The universities situated in Ireland that are prescribed by section 3503 are the following:

National University of Ireland, Dublin
Royal College of Surgeons in Ireland, Dublin
University of Dublin, The, Trinity College, Dublin

11. (Repealed.)

History: S. 11 of Schedule VIII was repealed by S.C. 2018, c. 12, s. 46(1), deemed in force February 27, 2018, and formerly read:

11. The universities situated in the Federal Republic of Germany that are prescribed by section 3503 are the following:

Ukrainian Free University, Munich
University of Heidelberg, Heidelberg

12. (Repealed.)

History: S. 12 of Schedule VIII was repealed by S.C. 2018, c. 12, s. 46(1), deemed in force February 27, 2018, and formerly read:

12. The universities situated in Poland that are prescribed by section 3503 are the following:

Catholic University of Lublin, Lublin
Jagiellonian University, Krakow

13. (Repealed.)

History: S. 13 of Schedule VIII was repealed by S.C. 2018, c. 12, s. 46(1), deemed in force February 27, 2018, and formerly read:

13. The universities situated in Spain that are prescribed by section 3503 are the following:

University of Navarra, Pamplona

14. (Repealed.)

History: S. 14 of Schedule VIII was repealed by S.C. 2018, c. 12, s. 46(1), deemed in force February 27, 2018, and formerly read:

14. The universities situated in the People's Republic of China that are prescribed by section 3503 are the following:

Nanjing University, Nanjing
Peking University, Beijing

S. 14 of Schedule VIII was amended by P.C. 2012-1330, SOR/2012-218, dated October 5, 2012, published in the *Canada Gazette* October 24, 2012, by adding: Peking University, Beijing, deemed to have come into force on January 1, 2010.

15. (Repealed.)

History: S. 15 of Schedule VIII was repealed by S.C. 2018, c. 12, s. 46(1), deemed in force February 27, 2018, and formerly read:

15. The universities situated in Jamaica that are prescribed for the purposes of section 3503 are the following:

University of the West Indies, Mona Campus, Kingston

16. (Repealed.)

History: S. 16 of Schedule VIII was repealed by S.C. 2018, c. 12, s. 46(1), deemed in force February 27, 2018, and formerly read:

16. For the purposes of section 3503, the universities situated in Italy are the following:

John Cabot University, Rome
Pontifical University of the Holy Cross, Rome

S. 16 of Schedule VIII was amended by P.C. 2012-1330, SOR/2012-218, dated October 5, 2012, published in the *Canada Gazette* October 24, 2012, by adding: Pontifical University of the Holy Cross, Rome, deemed to have come into force on January 1, 2010.

S. 16 of Schedule VIII was added by P.C. 2010-551, SOR/2010-96, dated April 29, 2010, published in the *Canada Gazette* May 12, 2010, deemed to have taken effect on January 1, 2008.

17. (Repealed.)

History: S. 17 of Schedule VIII was repealed by S.C. 2018, c. 12, s. 46(1), deemed in force February 27, 2018, and formerly read:

17. The universities situated in Australia that are prescribed by section 3503 are the following:

Adelaide University, Adelaide
Australian National University, Canberra
Avondale College, Cooranbong
Monash University, Victoria
University of Melbourne, The, Parkville
University of Tasmania, Hobart

S. 17 of Schedule VIII was amended by P.C. 2014-358, SOR/2014-81, dated April 4, 2014, published in the *Canada Gazette* April 23, 2014, by striking out: Queensland University of Technology, Brisbane; and University of Queensland, The, Brisbane, in force April 23, 2014.

S. 17 of Schedule VIII was amended by P.C. 2012-1330, SOR/2012-218, dated October 5, 2012, published in the *Canada Gazette* October 24, 2012, by striking out: University of Sydney, The, Sydney, in force October 24, 2012.

S. 17 of Schedule VIII was amended by P.C. 2012-1330, SOR/2012-218, dated October 5, 2012, published in the *Canada Gazette* October 24, 2012, by adding: Avondale College, Cooranbong; Monash University, Victoria, deemed to have come into force on January 1, 2009.

S. 17 of Schedule VIII was amended by P.C. 2012-1330, SOR/2012-218, dated October 5, 2012, published in the *Canada Gazette* October 24, 2012, by adding: Australian National University, Canberra, deemed to have come into force on January 1, 2011.

18. (Repealed.)

History: S. 18 was repealed by P.C. 2012-1330, SOR/2012-218, dated October 5, 2012, published in the *Canada Gazette* October 24, 2012, in force October 24, 2012. S. 18 formerly read:

18. The university situated in the Republic of Croatia that is prescribed by section 3503 is the following:

University of Zagreb, Zagreb

19. (Repealed.)

History: S. 19 of Schedule VIII was repealed by S.C. 2018, c. 12, s. 46(1), deemed in force February 27, 2018, and formerly read:

19. The universities situated in South Africa that are prescribed by section 3503 are the following:

University of Cape Town, Rondebosch

University of KwaZulu-Natal, Durban

S. 19 of Schedule VIII was amended by P.C. 2014-358, SOR/2014-81, dated April 4, 2014, published in the *Canada Gazette* April 23, 2014, by striking out: University of the Witwatersrand, The, Johannesburg, in force April 23, 2014.

S. 19 of Schedule VIII was amended by P.C. 2012-1330, SOR/2012-218, dated October 5, 2012, published in the *Canada Gazette* October 24, 2012, by striking out: University of Natal, Durban, in force October 24, 2012.

S. 19 of Schedule VIII was amended by P.C. 2012-1330, SOR/2012-218, dated October 5, 2012, published in the *Canada Gazette* October 24, 2012, by adding: University of KwaZulu-Natal, Durban, deemed to have come into force on January 1, 2009.

20. (Repealed.)

History: S. 20 of Schedule VIII was repealed by S.C. 2018, c. 12, s. 46(1), deemed in force February 27, 2018, and formerly read:

20. For the purposes of section 3503 the universities situated in the Netherlands are the following:

Leiden University, Leiden

Nyenrode University, Breukelen

University of Groningen, Groningen

21. (Repealed.)

History: S. 21 of Schedule VIII was repealed by S.C. 2018, c. 12, s. 46(1), deemed in force February 27, 2018, and formerly read:

21. For the purposes of section 3503 the universities situated in Hong Kong are the following:

Chinese University of Hong Kong, The, Shatin, New Territories

Hong Kong University of Science and Technology, The, Kowloon

University of Hong Kong, The, Hong Kong

S. 21 of Schedule VIII was amended by P.C. 2010-551, SOR/2010-96, dated April 29, 2010, published in the *Canada Gazette* May 12, 2010, by adding: Chinese University of Hong Kong, The, Shatin, New Territories, deemed to have taken effect on January 1, 2007.

22. (Repealed.)

History: S. 22 of Schedule VIII was repealed by S.C. 2018, c. 12, s. 46(1), deemed in force February 27, 2018, and formerly read:

22. The universities situated in New Zealand that are prescribed by section 3503 are the following:

University of Auckland, The, Auckland

University of Otago, Dunedin

S. 22 of Schedule VIII was amended by P.C. 2014-358, SOR/2014-81, dated April 4, 2014, published in the *Canada Gazette* April 23, 2014, by striking out: Victoria University of Wellington, Wellington, in force April 23, 2014.

23. (Repealed.)

History: S. 23 of Schedule VIII was repealed by S.C. 2018, c. 12, s. 46(1), deemed in force February 27, 2018, and formerly read:

23. The university situated in Hungary that is prescribed by section 3503 is the following:

Central European University, Budapest

24. (Revoked.)

History: S. 24 of Schedule VIII was revoked by P.C. 2014-358, SOR/2014-81, dated April 4, 2014, published in the *Canada Gazette* April 23, 2014, in force April 23, 2014, and formerly read:

24. The university situated in India that is prescribed by section 3503 is the following:

Panjab University, Chandigarh

25. (Repealed.)

History: S. 25 of Schedule VIII was repealed by S.C. 2018, c. 12, s. 46(1), deemed in force February 27, 2018, and formerly read:

25. The university situated in Estonia that is prescribed by section 3503 is the following:

University of Tartu, Tartu

Schedule IX
Prescribed Areas — 1987 to 1992 [Revoked.]

(Revoked.)

Schedule X
Prescribed Areas [Revoked.]

(Revoked.)

Remission Orders

Locally Engaged Employees of the Canadian Embassy and Consulates in the United States Remission Order

P.C. 2018-345 March 26, 2018 (Registration SI/2018-30 April 18, 2018)

Her Excellency the Governor General in Council, considering that it is in the public interest to do so, on the recommendation of the Minister of Finance, pursuant to subsection 23(2) of the *Financial Administration Act*, makes the annexed *Locally Engaged Employees of the Canadian Embassy and Consulates in the United States Remission Order*.

INTERPRETATION

Definitions

1.

(1) The following definitions apply in this Order.

"Act" means the *Income Tax Act*.

"Canada-US Tax Convention" means the convention, as defined in the *Canada-United States Tax Convention Act, 1984*.

"Embassy or Consulate" means the Embassy of Canada located in Washington, D.C., United States or any one or more of the offices of the Consulate General of Canada that are located in the United States.

"locally engaged employee" means an individual who during the taxation year

(a) is a non-resident of Canada;

(b) is a Canadian citizen; and

(c) is paid by the government of Canada for services rendered by the individual in the discharge of functions of a governmental nature at an Embassy or Consulate.

Application of meanings in Act

Unless the context otherwise requires, words and expressions used in this Order have the same meaning as in the Act.

REMISSION

Remission of Income Tax

2. Subject to sections 3 and 4, remission is granted to each locally engaged employee with respect to tax payable under the Act for taxation years that begin after 2016 of the lesser of, in respect of remuneration that is taxable in Canada, and not in the United States, because of Article XIX of the Canada-US Tax Convention,

(a) the amount added to the tax payable under Part I of the Act by the employee under subsection 120(1) of the Act for the taxation year, and

(b) the amount, if any, of United States state-level income tax paid by the employee for the taxation year.

CONDITIONS

Amount not otherwise claimed

3. Remission is granted only to the extent the amount remitted has not otherwise been rebated, remitted, credited or refunded to any person under the Act, the *Financial Administration Act* or any other Act of Parliament.

Timing and Documentation

4. Remission is granted to a locally engaged employee in respect of a taxation year on the condition that

(a) the locally engaged employee applies for the remission in writing to the Minister on or before the day that is two years after their filing-due date for the taxation year; and

(b) the application is accompanied by the documentation required to determine both the eligibility for and the amount of the remission.

COMING INTO FORCE

Coming into Force

5. This Order comes into force on the day on which it is made.

EXPLANATORY NOTE

(*This note is not part of the Order.*)

Proposal

Pursuant to subsection 23(2) of the *Financial Administration Act*, the *Locally Engaged Employees of the Canadian Embassy and Consulates in the United States Remission Order* would grant remission to a specified group of individuals ("locally engaged employees" as described below) to alleviate the double taxation, which they are currently subjected to at the sub-national level. Specifically, locally engaged employees would be granted remission of the lesser of the amount of tax that is payable in Canada as "additional tax," and the amount, if any, that is paid as U.S. state-level income tax.

Objective

The objective of this Order is to relieve double taxation, to the extent that it arises, with respect to the tax liability of Canadian citizens who are locally engaged at the Canadian embassy in Washington, D.C. or at a Canadian consular office in the United States (the "Embassy or Consulate") on account of U.S. state-level income tax paid in addition to the "additional tax" that is payable in Canada, with respect to taxation years commencing on or after January 1, 2017.

Background

Under Article XIX of the *Convention between Canada and the United States of America with Respect to Taxes on Income and on Capital signed at Washington on September 26, 1980, as amended by the Protocols signed on June 14, 1983, March 28, 1984, March 17, 1995, July 29, 1997, and September 21, 2007* (the "Canada-US Tax Convention"), Canadian citizens who are locally engaged by the Embassy or Consulate are, by virtue of their status as Canadian citizens, taxable exclusively in Canada. This is a departure from the general rule that residence (as opposed to citizenship) is the criterion establishing an individual's liability for tax in a jurisdiction.

A locally engaged employee is an individual who during a taxation year commencing on or after January 1, 2017 is (i) a non-resident of Canada; (ii) a Canadian citizen; and (iii) paid by the government of Canada for services rendered in the discharge by the individual of functions of a governmental nature to an Embassy or a Consulate.

As a result of the provisions of Article XIX, locally engaged employees of the Embassy or Consulate do not pay U.S. federal tax. They are instead fully liable for Canadian federal tax. Included in their Canadian federal tax liability is an "additional tax" that is levied under subsection 120(1) of the *Income Tax Act*. Usually, when an individual is not resident in a province or territory, they are not liable for provincial or territorial tax.

In this particular case, the federal additional tax becomes payable. It is calculated to approximate the provincial or territorial tax that would otherwise be payable. The federal additional tax ensures that all individual Canadian taxpayers face a broadly comparable total income tax burden even in the case that they are not a resident of, and hence taxable in, any province or territory. Since locally engaged employees are not residents of any Canadian province or territory, they are not liable for any provincial or territorial tax. However, they are liable for the additional tax.

Some U.S. states levy an income tax against such employees. As a result these locally engaged employees are subject to double taxation because they are liable for both the Canadian federal additional tax and U.S. state-level income tax.

This Order does not apply to any sub-national level of tax liabilities other than state-level income tax.

Implications

The Remission Order applies to the 2017 taxation year and any subsequent taxation year; for 2017, this Order is expected to remit approximately $200,000 in federal income tax. The source of funds for the amounts remitted through this Order is the fiscal framework.

To obtain relief from double taxation under this Remission Order, locally engaged employees must apply in writing to the Minister of National Revenue on or before the day that is two years after their filing-due date for any given taxation year. The application must be accompanied by the documentation needed to determine both the eligibility for and the amount of the remission.

The Canada Revenue Agency will administer this Remission Order.

Consultation

No external consultations have been conducted. Global Affairs Canada will inform locally engaged employees working in the Embassy or Consulate of the implementation of this Remission Order.

Departmental contact

Stephanie Smith
Senior Director
Tax Treaties
Tax Legislation Division
Tax Policy Branch
Department of Finance
Telephone: 613-369-4081
Email: stephanie.smith@canada.ca

M-I Drilling Fluids Canada, Inc. Remission Order

P.C. 2016-937 October 21, 2016 (Registration SI/2016-61 November 2, 2016)

His Excellency the Governor General in Council, considering that it is in the public interest to do so, on the recommendation of the Minister of National Revenue, pursuant to subsection 23(2) of the *Financial Administration Act*, remits to M-I Drilling Fluids Canada, Inc. the following amounts:

(a) the amount of $689,691.86 in provincial sales tax that it mistakenly paid as tax under Part IX of the *Excise Tax Act* during the period beginning on March 1, 2004 and ending on April 30, 2010; and

(b)the amount of $26,349.11 that it paid in interest under Part IX of the *Excise Tax Act*.

Explanatory Note

(This note is not part of the Order.)

This Order remits $689,691.86 representing the provincial sales tax liability of M-I Drilling Fluids Canada, Inc. that was mistakenly remitted to the federal government as the goods and services tax (GST) rather than to provincial authorities during the period beginning on March 1, 2004, and ending on April 30, 2010. The Order also remits $26,349.11 interest assessed by the Canada Revenue Agency in respect of that amount. A rebate or credit of the amount under Part IX of the *Excise Tax Act* is not possible because statutory time limits have expired.

Remission Order in Respect of a Transfer of a Sahtu Dene and Metis Settlement Corporation's Assets under a Self-Government Agreement

P.C. 2015-637 May 28, 2015 (Registration SI/2015-45 June 17, 2015)

His Excellency the Governor General in Council, considering that it is in the public interest to do so, on the recommendation of the Minister of Finance, pursuant to section 23 of the *Financial Administration Act*, makes the annexed *Remission Order in Respect of a Transfer of a Sahtu Dene and Metis Settlement Corporation's Assets under a Self-Government Agreement*.

INTERPRETATION

Definitions

1.

(1) The following definitions apply in this Order.

"Act" means the *Income Tax Act*.

"Sahtu Dene and Metis Comprehensive Land Claim Agreement" means the Comprehensive Land Claim Agreement entered into by Her Majesty the Queen in right of Canada and the Sahtu Dene and Metis, as represented by the Sahtu Tribal Council, signed on September 6, 1993, as amended from time to time.

"Sahtu Dene and Metis First Nation Government" has the meaning assigned by 2.1 of Appendix B of the Sahtu Dene and Metis Comprehensive Land Claim Agreement.

"self-government agreement" has the meaning assigned by 2.1 of Appendix B of the Sahtu Dene and Metis Comprehensive Land Claim Agreement.

"settlement corporation" has the meaning assigned by 11.3.1 of the Sahtu Dene and Metis Comprehensive Land Claim Agreement.

Application of meanings in Act

Any word or expression used in this Order and not defined in subsection (1) has the same meaning as in the Act.

REMISSION

2. Remission is granted of

(*a*) the tax payable under the Act by a settlement corporation in respect of the settlement corporation ceasing to exist and all of its assets being transferred to, by way of vesting in, a Sahtu Dene and Metis First Nation Government under the self-government agreement that creates the Sahtu Dene and Metis First Nation Government;

(*b*) any penalties payable under the Act in respect of the settlement corporation ceasing to exist and all of its assets being transferred to, by way of vesting in, a Sahtu Dene and Metis First Nation Government under the self-government agreement that creates the Sahtu Dene and Metis First Nation Government; and

(*c*) any interest payable in respect of that tax and those penalties.

CONDITIONS

3. Remission is granted of an amount under this Order to a person on condition that

(*a*) the amount has not otherwise been rebated, credited, refunded or remitted to the person or any other person under the Act, the *Financial Administration Act* or any other Act of the Parliament of Canada; and

(*b*) the person applies in writing to the Minister of National Revenue for remission under this Order in respect of the transfer before the later of

(i) the day that is eighteen months after the day on which this order is made, and

(ii) the filing-due date of the person's taxation year in which the transfer occurs.

Explanatory Note

(*This note is not part of the Order.*)

Proposal

To make the annexed *Remission Order in Respect of a Transfer of a Sahtu Dene and Metis Settlement Corporation's Assets under a Self-Government Agreement*.

Objective

The objective of the Order is to enable a settlement corporation within the meaning of the Sahtu Dene and Metis Comprehensive Land Claim Agreement to cease to exist and all of its assets to be transferred to a Sahtu Dene and Metis First Nation Government under the self-government agreement that creates the Sahtu Dene and Metis First Nation Government, without tax implications.

Background

Canada and the Sahtu Dene and Metis entered into the Sahtu Dene and Metis Comprehensive Land Claim Agreement in 1993. Under the Sahtu Dene and Metis Comprehensive Land Claim Agreement, the Sahtu Dene and Metis received title to lands, financial payments, confirmation of harvesting rights, and guaranteed participation in specified land and resource management regimes. The Sahtu Dene and Metis Comprehensive Land Claim Agreement provides for rights to be exercised by and responsibilities to be performed by organizations referred to as "designated Sahtu organizations."

Under the Sahtu Dene and Metis Comprehensive Land Claim Agreement, a "settlement corporation" is a corporation that, among other things, is a designated Sahtu organization, has received no contributions of capital other than financial payments under the Sahtu Dene and Metis Comprehensive Land Claim Agreement, devotes all or substantially all of its resources to making permitted investments and carrying out permitted activities, has filed an election with the Minister of National Revenue to be a "settlement corporation" and has not had its status as a "settlement corporation" terminated.

Under chapter 11 of the Sahtu Dene and Metis Comprehensive Land Claim Agreement, a settlement corporation is exempt from federal and territorial income tax except as provided in that chapter. Under chapter 11, a settlement corporation is liable to pay federal and territorial income tax in certain circumstances. For example, it is liable to pay federal and territorial tax on any income it derives from a property that is not a permitted investment or acquired in the course of carrying on a permitted activity. It is also liable to pay federal and territorial tax in respect of any payment it makes that is not a permitted investment or made in the course of carrying on a permitted activity. In addition, if the settlement corporation commences to be wound-up, it is liable to pay federal and territorial income tax on the amount distributed on the winding-up, less the aggregate of the amount disbursed or expended in the course of the winding-up on its permitted activities, all amounts that may reasonably be considered to be original contributed capital and that are transferred to a designated settlement corporation or to another settlement corporation, and all other amounts transferred to another settlement corporation.

The Sahtu Dene and Metis Comprehensive Land Claim Agreement also provides for the negotiation of self-government agreements between Canada and the Government of the Northwest Territories and each of the five Sahtu Dene and Metis communities (Colville Lake, Déline, Fort Good Hope, Norman Wells and Tulita).

On February 18, 2015, Canada, the Government of the Northwest Territories and the Sahtu Dene and Metis of Déline signed the Déline Final Self-Government Agreement. The Déline Final Self-Government Agreement provides that, on the effective date of that agreement, the Déline Financial Corporation (a settlement corporation) will cease to exist and all of its claims, rights, titles, interests, assets, obligations and liabilities will vest in the Déline Got'ine Government (the government to be created by the Déline Final Self-Government Agreement).

The Déline Final Self-Government Agreement provides that a transfer of assets to the Déline Got'ine Government under the Déline Final Self-Government Agreement is not taxable. However, due to the conflict rules in the Sahtu Dene and Metis Comprehensive Land Claim Agreement, in the case of a conflict, the provisions of the Sahtu Dene and Metis Comprehensive Land Claim Agreement in respect of the taxation of settlement corporations would prevail over the provision of the Déline Final Self- Government Agreement providing that no transfer of assets to the Déline Got'ine Government under the Déline Final Self- Government Agreement is taxable.

The purpose of the Order is to ensure that the proposed transfer of assets by the Déline Financial Corporation to the Déline Got'ine Government under the Déline Final Self-Government Agreement, and any similar transfer of assets by a settlement corporation to a Sahtu Dene and Metis First Nation Government under a Sahtu Dene and Metis self-government agreement with another Sahtu Dene and Metis community, will not result in an obligation to pay income tax. The rationale for relieving the tax in these circumstances is two-fold. First, the tax provisions of the Sahtu Dene and Metis Comprehensive Land Claim Agreement were not intended to apply to a transfer under a self-government agreement. Second, it is in the public interest to enable the parties to determine the government structure on efficiency and other grounds, rather than tax considerations.

Implications

The Order remits the income tax payable, and any related penalties and interest, in respect of a settlement corporation ceasing to exist and all of its assets vesting in a Sahtu Dene and Metis First Nation Government under a self-government agreement. As a result, the Order permits the parties to a self-government negotiation to determine the most appropriate government structure based on efficiency and other grounds, rather than based on tax considerations. The cost of the Order is estimated to be nil because it is not expected that the parties to a self-government agreement would agree on the merger of a settlement corporation and a new government body created by the self-government agreement in the absence of the Order.

Consultation

The Government of the Northwest Territories and the Sahtu Secretariat Incorporated, which represents the Sahtu Dene and Metis, were consulted in relation to the proposal.

Departmental contact

For more information, please contact

Sara Gill
Senior Tax Policy Officer
Tax Policy Branch
Department of Finance
Telephone: 613-369-3808

Certain Flights Charge and Tax Remission Order

P.C. 2015-206 February 19 , 2015 (Registration SI/2015-15 March 11, 2015)

His Excellency the Governor General in Council, considering that it is in the public interest to do so, on the recommendation of the Minister of Finance, pursuant to subsection 23(2) of the *Financial Administration Act*, makes the annexed *Certain Flights Charge and Tax Remission Order*.

INTERPRETATION

1.

(1) The following definitions apply in this Order.

"qualified flight" means a flight that was provided by Air Canada on June 10, 2014 for no consideration solely to travellers who were attending a Royal Canadian Mounted Police regimental funeral in Moncton on that day if the flight was taking place either

(*a*) from Ottawa (Macdonald-Cartier International) or Toronto (Lester B. Pearson International) to Moncton; or

(*b*) from Moncton to Ottawa (Macdonald-Cartier International) or Toronto (Lester B. Pearson International).

"traveller" means an individual who, on June 10, 2014,

(*a*) was a member of the Royal Canadian Mounted Police, as defined in subsection 2(1) of the *Royal Canadian Mounted Police Act*;

(*b*) was a civilian employee of the Royal Canadian Mounted Police referred to in section 10 of the *Royal Canadian Mounted Police Act*; or

(*c*) if neither paragraph (*a*) nor (*b*) applies, was otherwise working in the core public administration, as defined in subsection 11(1) of the *Financial Administration Act*.

(2) Unless the context otherwise requires, words and expressions used in this Order have the same meaning as in the *Air Travellers Security Charge Act*.

REMISSION

2. Remission is granted of the charge imposed under section 11 of the *Air Travellers Security Charge Act* in respect of an air transportation service that included a chargeable emplanement of a traveller in a qualified flight.

3. Remission is granted of any tax imposed under section 165 of the *Excise Tax Act* in respect of the charge referred to in section 2.

4. Remission is granted of interest and penalties paid or payable on any amount for which remission is granted under section 2 or 3.

CONDITIONS

5. Remission is granted only to the extent to which the amount remitted has not otherwise been rebated, remitted, credited or refunded to any person under the *Financial Administration Act* or any other Act of Parliament.

6. If the charge referred to in section 2, or the tax referred to in section 3, was paid by the person acquiring the air transportation service, or was remitted by Air Canada to the Receiver General, remission is granted on the condition that

(*a*) a claim for remission is made in writing to the Minister of National Revenue not later than one year after the day on which this Order is made; and

(*b*) the person making the claim for remission provides the Minister of National Revenue with evidence or information that demonstrates that the charge or the tax has been paid or remitted by that person.

Explanatory Note

(*This note is not part of the Order.*)

Proposal

To make the *Certain Flights Charge and Tax Remission Order.*

Objectives

To provide relief from the Air Travellers Security Charge (ATSC) and the related Goods and Services Tax/Harmonized Sales Tax (GST/HST) in respect of special flights provided by Air Canada, for no consideration, to officers and officials of the Royal Canadian Mounted Police (RCMP) who were attending a regimental funeral in Moncton, New Brunswick on June 10, 2014.

Background

The ATSC came into effect in April 2002 to fund the air travel security system, including the Canadian Air Transport Security Authority (CATSA) — the federal authority responsible for the security screening of air passengers and their baggage. For air travel within Canada, the ATSC applies to flights between the 89 airports where air travel security services are provided by CATSA, including Toronto (Lester B. Pearson International), Ottawa (Macdonald-Cartier International) and Moncton.

The ATSC is payable by air travellers, who principally and directly benefit from the enhanced air travel security system. The charge is intended to provide revenues that are roughly equivalent to expenses for air travel security over time. All proceeds from the ATSC, including any related GST or the federal portion of the HST, are intended to fund the air travel security system. Currently, the charge for a round-trip domestic flight is $14.25 plus the related GST/HST.

On June 10, 2014, Air Canada provided special flights, for no consideration, solely for certain RCMP officers and officials to attend the regimental funeral for the three RCMP officers who had been killed in the line of duty in Moncton, New Brunswick.

The special flights provided by Air Canada occurred between the airports of Toronto (Lester B. Pearson International), Ottawa (Macdonald-Cartier International) and Moncton. The Governor General in Council considers that it is in the public interest to provide a one-time relief on the ATSC (and the related GST/HST) on these flights. A remission order is required to provide this relief as the ATSC legislation provides no exception for these particular circumstances.

Implications

In the case where the ATSC and the related GST/HST has already been paid, or remitted to the Receiver General, relief is granted on the condition that a written claim is made to the Minister of National Revenue not later than one year after the day on which this Order is made. Given that this ATSC relief is exceptional in nature and is provided on a one-time basis, this Remission Order has a negligible impact on government duty and tax revenues.

Departmental contact

Gervais Coulombe
Sales Tax Division
Department of Finance
90 Elgin Street
Ottawa, Ontario
K1P 0G6
Telephone: 613-369-3773

Estates of Kathleen McGowan and William F. McGowan Remission Order

P.C. 2014-1477 December 12, 2014 (Registration SI/2014-111 December 31, 2014)

His Excellency the Governor General in Council, considering that the collection of the penalties and interest is unjust, on the recommendation of the Minister of National Revenue, pursuant to subsection 23(2) of the *Financial Administration Act*, makes the annexed *Estates of Kathleen McGowan and William F. McGowan Remission Order*.

1.

(1) Remission is granted of the amounts set out in column 1 of Schedule 1, which represent penalties paid or payable by the Estate of Kathleen McGowan under Part I of the *Income Tax Act* for the taxation years listed in column 2, and all relevant interest on those amounts.

(2) Remission, in the amount of $7,660.97, is granted of interest paid or payable by the Estate of Kathleen McGowan under Part I of the *Income Tax Act* for the 1996, 1997, 1998 and 1999 taxation years, having accrued during the period beginning on January 23, 1997 and ending on December 31, 2000, and all relevant interest on that amount.

2.

(1) Remission is granted of the amounts set out in column 1 of Schedule 2, which represent penalties paid or payable by the Estate of William F. McGowan under Part I of the *Income Tax Act* for the taxation years listed in column 2, and all relevant interest on those amounts.

(2) Remission, in the amount of $132.67, is granted of interest paid or payable by the Estate of William F. McGowan under Part I of the *Income Tax Act* for the 2000 taxation year, having accrued during the period beginning on June 4, 2000 and ending on December 31, 2000, and all relevant interest on that amount.

SCHEDULE 1

(Subsection 1(1))

Column 1 Amount ($)	Column 2 Taxation Year
761.34	1996
644.56	1997
595.08	1998
6,855.49	1999
243.73	2000
185.76	2001
38.00	2002
27.21	2003

SCHEDULE 2

(Subsection 2(1))

Column 1 Amount ($)	Column 2 Taxation Year
381.95	2000
425.97	2001
86.43	2002

Explanatory Note

(This note is not part of the Order.)

This Order remits a portion of the arrears interest in respect of the 1996, 1997, 1998, 1999 and 2000 taxation years, and late-filing penalties in respect of the 1996, 1997, 1998, 1999, 2000, 2001, 2002 and 2003 taxation years and all relevant interest paid or payable thereon by the estates of Kathleen and William F. McGowan.

The amounts remitted represent the additional liabilities incurred by the estates as a result of circumstances that were beyond the executor's control.

BlackBerry Limited Income Tax Remission Order

P.C. 2013-1404 December 12, 2013 (Registration SI/2014-1 January 1, 2014)

His Excellency the Governor General in Council, considering that it is in the public interest to do so, on the recommendation of the Minister of Finance, pursuant to subsections 23(2) of the *Financial Administration Act*, makes the annexed *BlackBerry Limited Income Tax Remission Order*.

Interpretation

Definitions

1.

(1) The following definitions apply in this Order.

"Act" means the *Income Tax Act*.

"Minister" means the Minister of National Revenue.

Application of meanings in Act

(2) Unless the context otherwise requires, words and expressions used in this Order have the same meaning as in the Act.

Remission

2. Subject to section 3, remission is granted to BlackBerry Limited, in respect of tax paid for its 2009 to 2012 taxation years, of an amount equal to the amount by which

(*a*) the total tax and interest payable under the Act by BlackBerry Limited for those years

exceeds

(*b*) the total tax and interest that would be payable under the Act by BlackBerry Limited for those years if

(i) the reference to "3 taxation years" in paragraph 111(1)(*a*) of the Act were a reference to "4 taxation years" and BlackBerry Limited had, in computing taxable income for each of its 2011 and 2012 taxation years, claimed the lesser of

(A) the deduction that would have been available under that paragraph as a consequence, and

(B) the amount, if any, specified by BlackBerry Limited,

(ii) BlackBerry Limited had, in computing tax payable for each of its 2009 and 2010 taxation years, claimed the lesser of

(A) the deduction that would have been available under subsection 127(5) of the Act as a consequence of the deduction referred to or amount specified, as the case may be, in subparagraph (i), and

(B) the amount, if any, specified by Black- Berry Limited, and

(iii) the reference to "3 taxation years" in paragraph (*c*) of the definition "investment tax credit" in subsection 127(9) of the Act were a reference to "4 taxation years" and BlackBerry Limited had, in computing tax payable for each of its 2011 and 2012 taxation years, claimed the lesser of

(A) the deduction that would have been available under subsection 127(5) of the Act as a consequence, and

(B) the amount, if any, specified by BlackBerry Limited.

Conditions

3. Remission is granted under section 2 on condition that BlackBerry Limited

(*a*) has at least two taxation years that end after October 2013 and before March 2, 2014;

(*b*) files a waiver with the Minister under subparagraph 152(4)(*a*)(ii) of the Act with respect to each of its taxation years that end after 2010 and before March 1, 2015 and does not revoke any of them before 2020;

(*c*) does not claim, in computing its taxable income under the Act for any taxation year, a deduction in respect of any portion of a non-capital loss to the extent that the portion has resulted in an amount of tax being remitted under this Order;

(*d*) does not deduct, in computing its tax payable under the Act for any taxation year, an amount in respect of an investment tax credit to the extent that the amount has resulted in an amount of tax being remitted under this Order;

(*e*) for any amount specified under clause 2(*b*)(i)(B) or (iii)(B) that relates to the computation of taxable income or tax payable for its 2011 taxation year, provides that amount in writing to the Minister on or before the filing-due date for its second taxation year ending after October 2013;

(*f*) for any amount specified under clause 2(*b*)(ii)(B) that relates to the computation of tax payable for its 2009 taxation year, provides that amount in writing to the Minister on or before the filing-due date for its second taxation year ending after October 2013;

(*g*) for any amount specified under clause 2(*b*)(i)(B) or (iii)(B) that relates to the computation of taxable income or tax payable for its 2012 taxation year, provides that amount in writing to the Minister on or before the filing-due date for its third taxation year ending after October 2013; and

(*h*) for any amount specified under clause 2(*b*)(ii)(B) that relates to the computation of tax payable for its 2010 taxation year, provides that amount in writing to the Minister on or before the filing-due date for its third taxation year ending after October 2013.

EXPLANATORY NOTE

(*This note is not part of the Order.*)

Proposal

To make the *BlackBerry Limited Income Tax Remission Order.*

Objective

The Order makes a remission to BlackBerry Limited of taxes paid for the 2009 to 2012 taxation years. In effect, it enables the company to have undertaken a transaction to obtain early a portion of a refund that otherwise would have been received after its March 1, 2014, year-end without reducing the total amount of that refund.

Background

A transaction entered into by BlackBerry Limited resulted in it having a taxation year ending on November 3, 2013. This taxation year end enabled the company to apply the non-capital losses realized up to that date against taxable income earned in a prior year and obtain a refund of income tax paid for that prior year. If not for the transaction, its taxation year would have ended on March 1, 2014.

As a result of the transaction, BlackBerry Limited lost the ability it would otherwise have had under the *Income Tax Act* to apply non-capital losses and investment tax credits, that might be realized during the period from November 4, 2013, to March 1, 2014, against its taxable income and income tax payable, respectively, for its 2011 taxation year. BlackBerry Limited similarly lost the ability to apply, against its taxable income and income tax payable for the 2012 taxation year, non-capital losses and investment tax credits that might be realized in its second taxation year ending after November 3, 2013.

As a result of the inability to carry back these non-capital losses to its 2011 and 2012 taxation years, Blackberry Limited lost the ability to apply all or a portion of investment tax credits that it realized for its 2011 and 2012 taxation years against tax payable for its 2009 and subsequent taxation years.

The Order effectively preserves the carry-back abilities that would have existed had the company not undertaken the transaction to cause an early taxation year-end on November 3, 2013.

Financial implications

The Order in effect allows BlackBerry Limited to have undertaken a transaction to obtain an early refund of tax associated with the non-capital losses accrued over the first eight months of its taxation year beginning March 3, 2013, without losing the ability to carry back (to the extent that otherwise would have been permitted) any losses incurred and investment tax credits earned over the following four months. The transaction has enabled the company to obtain a portion of its anticipated tax refund earlier than normal. However, the Order will not result in the company receiving a total amount of tax refunds in excess of the amount that would have been obtained had the company not undertaken the transaction but instead had waited and claimed a refund following its normal taxation year end on March 1, 2014.

The Order will not have any impact on the amount of government tax revenues.

Consultation

The Canada Revenue Agency was consulted in relation to the proposal.

Departmental contact

Tobias Witteveen
Tax Legislation Division
Department of Finance
L'Esplanade Laurier
140 O'Connor Street
Ottawa, Ontario
K1A 0G5
Telephone: 613-992-4859

British Columbia Forestry Revitalization Remission Order

P.C. 2013-2 January 11, 2013 (Registration SI/2013-1 January 16, 2013)

His Excellency the Governor General in Council, considering that it is in the public interest to do so, on the recommendation of the Minister of Finance, pursuant to section 23 of the *Financial Administration Act*, makes the annexed *British Columbia Forestry Revitalization Remission Order*.

Interpretation

Definitions

1.

(1) The following definitions apply in this Order.

"Act" means the *Income Tax Act*.

"declaration of Subtrust" means the declaration, dated January 3, 2012, that sets out the terms and conditions of the Subtrust.

"eligible amount", in respect of an eligible taxpayer, means an amount paid by the Subtrust in respect of the eligible taxpayer's Eligible Income Tax, within the meaning assigned by section 2.02 of the declaration of Subtrust, that is attributable to an FRT Contractor Mitigation Amount.

"eligible taxpayer" has the meaning assigned by section 2.04 of the declaration of Subtrust.

"FRT Contractor Mitigation Amount" has the meaning assigned by section 2.01 of the declaration of Subtrust.

"Subtrust" means the 2011 Contractor Mitigation Account Subtrust that was established on January 3, 2012, and is a subtrust of the BC Forestry Revitalization Trust II.

Application of meanings in Act

(2) Unless the context otherwise requires, words and expressions used in this Order have the same meaning as in the Act.

Remission

Eligible amount

2. Remission is granted to each eligible taxpayer of the income tax paid or payable under Part I of the Act for a taxation year, and of any related interest and penalties, that are attributable to an eligible amount paid in the year by the Subtrust to, or for the benefit of, the eligible taxpayer.

FRT Contractor Mitigation Amount

3. Remission is granted to each eligible taxpayer in respect of whom an eligible amount has been paid by the Subtrust of the amount of any interest and penalties paid or payable to the extent that they relate to income tax under Part I of the Act that is attributable to an FRT Contractor Mitigation Amount paid to, or for the benefit of, the eligible taxpayer.

Explanatory Note

(This note is not part of the Order.)

Proposal

To make the annexed *British Columbia Forestry Revitalization Remission Order*.

The Order provides, first, for the remission to each eligible taxpayer of taxes paid or payable by the taxpayer under the *Income Tax Act* as a result of payments from the 2011 Contractor Mitigation Account Subtrust (the Subtrust), second for the remission of interest and penalties related to income taxes in respect of the previous payments from the BC Forest Revitalization Trust and the BC Forestry Revitalization Trust II (the Trusts), as well as in respect of the payments from the Subtrust.

Objective

To serve the public interest.

Background

In 2003 and 2008, the Province of British Columbia (the Province) created the Trusts to compensate eligible contractors for the loss of their contractual rights because of timber reallocation resulting from the restructuring of the Province's forestry sector under its *Forestry Revitalization Act*. Because of this restructuring, contractors suffered financial hardship. A purpose of the Trusts was to mitigate the adverse financial impacts that they suffered. The amount of compensation received by contractors was generally related to the value of lost contracts and redundant equipment. This amount was included in computing the income of contractors under Part I of the *Income Tax Act* and the net benefits to them were consequently lower. On the initiative of the Province, the Subtrust was created to make new payments to the contractors, or to the Receiver General for Canada for the benefit of contractors, to compensate for income taxes paid or payable by the contractors in respect of the previous payments from the Trusts.

Implications

The cost of this Remission Order is estimated to be $2.5 million. This cost includes the remission of taxes payable in respect of payments from the Subtrust (i.e. to compensate the tax paid or payable in respect of payments from the Trusts). The cost also includes interest and penalties in respect of income taxes payable on payments from the Trusts and the Subtrust.

Departmental contact

Ève Pentassuglia
Tax Legislation Division
Department of Finance
140 O'Connor Street
Ottawa, Ontario
K1A 0G5
Telephone: 613-992-5636

Quebec Domestic Help Charities Remission Order

P.C. 2011-1323 November 17, 2011 (SI/2011-100 December 7, 2011)

His Excellency the Governor General in Council, considering that it is in the public interest to do so, on the recommendation of the Minister of National Revenue, pursuant to subsection 23(2) of the *Financial Administration Act*, hereby makes the annexed *Quebec Domestic Help Charities Remission Order*.

Interpretation

1. The following definitions apply in this Order.

"registered charity" has the same meaning as in subsection 248(1) of the *Income Tax Act*.

"revocation tax" has the meaning assigned by subsection 188(1.1) of the *Income Tax Act*.

Remission

2. Remission of the revocation tax paid or payable is granted to a person on the condition that the person

(*a*) was a registered charity before the coming into force of this Order;

(*b*) was a participant in the Financial Assistance Program for Domestic Help Services, established by the Quebec Department of Health and Social Services, before the coming into force of this Order;

(*c*) makes a written application for revocation of its registration as a registered charity to the Minister of National Revenue within nine months after the day on which this Order comes into force; and

(*d*) makes a written application for remission under this Order to the Minister of National Revenue within nine months after the day on which this Order comes into force.

Explanatory Note

(*This note is not part of the Order.*)

The Order remits the revocation tax paid or payable under sub-section 188(1.1) of the *Income Tax Act* to certain charities that were, in addition to being a registered charity for the purposes of the *Income Tax Act*, concurrently participating in the *Programme d'exonération financière pour les services d'aide domestique* to provide subsidized domestic help services to residents of Quebec. Due to the requirements of the Income Tax Act, the organizations in question cannot retain their status as a registered charity and continue to participate in the program.

Wendy Drever Remission Order

P.C. 2009-299, February 26, 2009 (SI/2009-17 March 18, 2009.)

Her Excellency the Governor General in Council, considering that the collection of the tax is unjust, on the recommendation of the Minister of National Revenue, pursuant to subsection 23(2) of the *Financial Administration Act*, hereby remits tax in the amount of $2,891.00, and all relevant interest on it, paid or payable by Wendy Drever, for the 2002 taxation year, under Part I of the *Income Tax Act*.

Explanatory Note

(This note is not part of the Order.)

The Order remits a portion of income tax and all relevant interest paid or payable on it by Wendy Drever in respect of the 2002 taxation year.

Ms. Drever has been receiving taxable wage loss replacement benefits since 1995. In 2002, she received a retroactive lump sum disability payment from the Canada Pension Plan (CPP). This amount reduced her wage loss replacement benefit entitlements and she was required to repay the CPP lump sum payment to the wage loss replacement provider. She was taxed on the lump sum payment in 2002 and received a deduction from 2003 income for the repayment amount. Due to delays that were not within her control, the transaction bridged two taxation years. The amount remitted represents the additional tax liability incurred by Ms. Drever because of this timing difference.

Vera Henderson Income Tax Remission Order

P.C. 2008-983 May 29, 2008 (SI/2008-62 June 11, 2008.)

Her Excellency the Governor General in Council, considering that the collection of tax is unjust, on the recommendation of the Minister of National Revenue, pursuant to subsection 23(2) of the *Financial Administration Act*, hereby makes the annexed *Vera Henderson Income Tax Remission Order*.

Vera Henderson Income Tax Remission Order

Remission

1. Remission is hereby granted of the tax paid by Vera Henderson under Part I of the *Income Tax Act* in the amount of $4,000.70 for the 2001 taxation year.

Condition

2. The remission is granted on the condition that Vera Henderson does not claim a deduction under subsection 120.2(1) of the *Income Tax Act* in respect of the amount remitted.

Explanatory Note

(This note is not part of the Order.)

The Order remits $4,000.70 paid by Vera Henderson as income tax for the 2001 taxation year.

The amount remitted represents the additional tax paid by Mrs. Henderson due to unintended results of the legislation.

Certain Former Employees of SDL Optics, Inc. Remission Order No. 2

P.C. 2008-975 May 29, 2008 (SI/2008-60 June 11, 2008.)

Her Excellency the Governor General in Council, considering that it is in the public interest to do so, on the recommendation of the Minister of National Revenue, pursuant to subsection 23(2) of the *Financial Administration Act*, hereby makes the annexed *Certain Former Employees of SDL Optics, Inc. Remission Order No. 2*.

Certain Former Employees of SDL Optics, Inc. Remission Order No. 2

Interpretation

1. In this Order, “employment benefit” means a benefit under subsection 7(1) of the *Income Tax Act* in respect of the acquisition of shares, in 1999 and 2000, through the stock purchase plan for employees of SDL Optics, Inc.

Remission

2. Remission is granted to the taxpayers set out in column 1 of the schedule for the amount set out in column 2, in respect of the 1999 or 2000 taxation years, as the case may be, which represents all or a portion of tax paid or payable under Part I of the *Income Tax Act* in respect of an employment benefit.

3. The remission set out in section 2 is granted on the condition that the taxpayer agrees to reduce the adjusted cost base of any shares held at the close of the stock markets on December 29, 2006 that were, or are identical to those, purchased in 1999 or 2000 through the stock purchase plan for employees of SDL Optics, Inc. by the amount set out in column 2 of the schedule, divided by the taxpayer’s effective federal tax rate on the employment benefit.

Schedule (Sections 2 and 3)

SCHEDULE

Item	*Column 1 Taxpayer*	*Column 2 Amount ($)*
1.	*Jingjing Liu*	*9,882.91*
2.	*Mandeep Saini*	*6,075.70*
3.	*Shanna Wang*	*17,219.71*

Explanatory Note

(This note is not part of the Order.)

The Order remits all or a portion of federal income tax paid or payable in respect of the 1999 or 2000 taxation years, as the case may be, by certain former employees of SDL Optics, Inc. Those individuals qualify for tax remission if the tax assessed on the employment benefit associated with shares acquired in 1999 or 2000 through the stock purchase plan for employees of SDL Optics, Inc. exceeds the total of the proceeds of disposition realized on the disposition of those shares and the market value of any of those shares held at the close of stock markets on December 29, 2006. The remission is conditional and the amount remitted is subject to certain adjustments.

Doina-Florica Calin Remission Order

P.C. 2007-563 April 19, 2007 (SI/2007-53, May 2, 2007).

Her Excellency the Governor General in Council, considering that the collection of the tax is unjust, on the recommendation of the Minister of National Revenue, pursuant to subsection 23(2) of the *Financial Administration Act*, hereby remits tax under Part I of the *Income Tax Act* in the amount of $17,100.57 for the 2000 taxation year, and all relevant interest thereon, paid or payable by Doina-Florica Calin.

Explanatory Note

(This note is not part of the Order.)

This Order remits a portion of income tax and all relevant interest paid or payable thereon by Doina-Florica Calin in respect of her final return.

The executor of the estate was unable to take advantage of alleviating legislative agency-docs because he forfeited options after the legislated timeframe (first taxation year of the estate). The executor missed this deadline due to serious health problems.

Clara Reid Remission Order

P.C. 2006-372 May 31, 2006, (Registration SI/2006-78, May 11, 2006)

Her Excellency the Governor General in Council, considering that the collection of the tax is unjust, on the recommendation of the Minister of National Revenue, pursuant to subsection 23(2) of the *Financial Administration Act*, hereby remits tax under Part I of the Income Tax Act in the amount of $1,335.60 for the 2003 taxation year, and all relevant interest thereon, paid or payable by Clara Reid.

Explanatory Note

(This note is not part of the Order.)

This Order remits a portion of income tax and all relevant interest paid or payable thereon by Clara Reid in respect of the 2003 taxation year.

In 2003 Ms. Reid received Employment Insurance (EI) benefits. She reported them as income on her 2003 return and paid the applicable tax. In 2004 her claim for long-term disability payments was approved retroactive to 2003. Since the benefit periods overlapped, she was required to repay the EI benefits. She repaid the full amount.

In 2004 she was entitled to a deduction from income for the amount of the repayment. However, she had no income in 2004 from which to deduct it. As a result, she has been taxed in 2003 on benefits that she repaid in 2004. The inclusion in income of the EI benefits in 2003 that were later repaid unfairly caused Clara Reid additional tax liability.

McIntyre Lands Income Tax Remission Order

P.C. 2005-2230, November 28, 2005 (Registration SI/2005-128, December 14, 2005)

Her Excellency the Governor General in Council, considering that it is in the public interest to do so, on the recommendation of the Minister of Indian Affairs and Northern Development and Federal Interlocutor for Métis and Non-Status Indians, pursuant to subsection 23(2) of the *Financial Administration Act*, hereby makes the annexed McIntyre Lands Income Tax Remission Order.

McIntyre Lands Income Tax Remission Order

1. The following definitions apply in this Order.

"Indian" has the same meaning as in subsection 2(1) of the *Indian Act.* (Indien)

"McIntyre Lands" means the lands described in the Schedule. (terres de McIntyre)

"reserve" has the same meaning as in subsection 2(1) of the *Indian Act.* (réserve)

"Yukon First Nation Final Agreement" means a land claims agreement that is in effect pursuant to the *Yukon First Nations Land Claims Settlement Act.* (accord définitif d'une première nation du Yukon)

2. Subject to section 3, remission is hereby granted to an Indian in respect of each taxation year from 1999 to 2005 of the amount, if any, by which

(a) the tax, interest and penalties paid or payable by the Indian under Parts I, I.1 and I.2 of the *Income Tax Act* for the year exceeds

(b) the tax, interest and penalties that would have been payable by the Indian if the McIntyre Lands had been a reserve throughout that year.

3. This Order does not apply to an Indian who is enrolled throughout a taxation year referred to in section 2 under a Yukon First Nation Final Agreement.

Schedule (Section 1)

McIntyre Lands

FIRSTLY:

The whole of Lots numbered 567 to 669 inclusive, in the Hillcrest McIntyre Subdivision, in the City of Whitehorse in the Yukon Territory, as said lots are shown on a plan of survey of record number 66606 in the Canada Lands Surveys Records at Ottawa, a copy of which is filed in the Land Titles Office for the Yukon Land Registration District at Whitehorse under number 58624.

SECONDLY:

The whole of Lots numbered 791 to 901 inclusive, in the Hillcrest McIntyre subdivision, in the City of Whitehorse in the Yukon Territory, as said lots are shown on a plan of survey of record number 66607 in the Canada Land Surveys Records at Ottawa, a copy of which is filed in the Land Titles Office for the Yukon Land Registration District at Whitehorse under number 58625.

THIRDLY:

The whole of Lots number 710 to 735 inclusive, 748 to 762 inclusive, 766 to 790 inclusive and 741, in the Hillcrest McIntyre Subdivision, in the City of Whitehorse in the Yukon Territory, as said lots are shown on a plan of survey of record number 66607 in the Canada Lands Surveys Records at Ottawa, a copy of which is filed in the Land Titles Office for the Yukon Land Registration District at Whitehorse under number 58625.

FOURTHLY:

The whole of Lots number 326 to 566 inclusive, and 671, in the Hillcrest McIntyre Subdivision, in the City of Whitehorse in the Yukon Territory, as said lots are shown on a plan of survey of record number 66606 in the Canada Lands Surveys Records at Ottawa, a copy of which is filed in the Land Titles Office for the Yukon Land Registration District at Whitehorse under number 58624.

FIFTHLY:

The whole of Lots number 672 to 709 inclusive, 736 to 740 inclusive, 742 to 747 inclusive, and 763 to 765 inclusive, in the Hillcrest McIntyre Subdivision, in the City of Whitehorse in the Yukon Territory, as said lots are shown on a plan of survey of record number 66607 in the Canada Lands Surveys Records at Ottawa, a copy of which is filed in the Land Titles Office for the Yukon Land Registration District at Whitehorse under number 58625.

Explanatory Note

(This note is not part of the Order.)

The purpose of this Order is to provide relief from the amount of federal income tax paid or payable by an Indian that exceeds the amount of those taxes that would have been payable during the taxation years 1999 to 2005 if the Mount McIntyre area of the city of Whitehorse had been a reserve under the *Indian Act*. The Government of Canada made a commitment to grant this remission as part of an agreement to resolve outstanding litigation between the Kwanlin Dun First Nation and Canada.

ATA Woodworking Inc. Remission Order

P.C. 2005-1502, August 31, 2005.

Her Excellency the Governor General in Council, considering that the collection of the tax is unjust, on the recommendation of the Minister of National Revenue, pursuant to subsection 23(2) of the *Financial Administration Act*, hereby remits tax under Part I of the *Income Tax Act* in the amounts of $15,123.00, $15,305.00, $18,326.00, $20,198.00, $17,162.00 and $3,655.00 for the 1996, 1997, 1998, 1999, 2000 and 2001 taxation years, respectively, and all relevant interest thereon, paid or payable by ATA Woodworking Inc.

Explanatory Note

(This note is not part of the Order.)

This Order remits a portion of income tax and all relevant interest paid or payable thereon by ATA Woodworking Inc. (ATA) in respect of the 1996 to 2001 taxation years.

The Canada Customs and Revenue Agency made a material error in the calculation of tax payable, which created an additional tax liability for ATA.

David Lynds Remission Order

P.C. 2005-707, May 3, 2005.

Her Excellency the Governor General in Council, considering that the collection of certain amounts of tax is unjust, on the recommendation of the Minister of National Revenue, pursuant to subsection 23(2) of the *Financial Administration Act*, hereby makes the annexed David Lynds Income Tax Remission Order.

Interpretation

1. In this Order, "non-capital loss" has the meaning assigned by subsection 111(8) of the *Income Tax Act*.

Remission

2. Remission is hereby granted of the tax paid or payable by David Lynds under Part I of the *Income Tax Act* in the amount of $303.45, $5,050.75, $1,464.72, $2,783.04, $2,825.00 and $2,712.44 for the 1992, 1993, 1994, 1995, 1996 and 1997 taxation years, respectively, and all interest paid or payable on it.

Condition

3. The remission is granted on the condition that David Lynds does not claim a deduction for any portion of his non-capital loss relating to the repayment in 2001 of wage loss replacement benefits to Manulife Financial.

Explanatory Note

(This note is not part of the Order.)

The Order remits to David Lynds $15,139.40, which represents a portion of the tax paid or payable by Mr. Lynds under Part I of the *Income Tax Act* for the taxation years 1992 through 1997 and all interest paid or payable on it.

The amount remitted represents the additional tax liability incurred by Mr. Lynds as a result of the lengthy adjudication period involved in obtaining a workers' compensation award.

Dane Pocrnic Remission Order

P.C. 2005-624, April 19, 2005 (Registration SI/2005-38, May 4, 2005)

Her Excellency the Governor General in Council, considering that the collection of the tax is unjust, on the recommendation of the Minister of National Revenue, pursuant to subsection 23(2) of the *Financial Administration Act*, hereby remits tax under Part I.2 of the *Income Tax Act* in the amount of $3,161 for the 1999 taxation year, and all relevant interest thereon, paid or payable by Dane Pocrnic.

Explanatory Note

(This note is not part of the Order.)

This Order remits a portion of income tax and all relevant interest paid or payable by Dane Pocrnic in respect of the 1999 taxation year.

In 1999, Mr. Pocrnic received a taxable lump sum payment from a government agency, a portion of which he was entitled to receive in the years from 1992 to 1998. As a result of the income inclusion in 1999, Mr. Pocrnic was required to repay a significant portion of his Old Age Security benefits for that year. The amount remitted represents the additional tax liability incurred by Mr. Pocrnic as a result of the lengthy delay by the government agency in paying him the amounts to which he was entitled in the relevant years.

Karen Smedley and George Smedley Remission Order

P.C. 2004-0265, March 23, 2004 (Registration SI/2004-033, April 7, 2004).

Her Excellency the Governor General in Council, considering that the collection of the tax is unjust, on the recommendation of the Minister of National Revenue, pursuant to subsection 23(2) of the *Financial Administration Act*, hereby remits tax under Part I of the *Income Tax Act* in the amounts of $8,725.16 and $11,190.65 for the 1994 taxation year, and all relevant interest thereon, paid or payable by Karen Smedley and George Smedley, respectively.

Explanatory Note

(This note is not part of the Order.)

This Order remits a portion of income tax and all relevant interest paid or payable thereon by Karen Smedley and George Smedley in respect of the 1994 taxation year.

During the course of an audit in 1996 by Revenue Canada a portion of the Smedleys' 1994 claim for the capital gains exemption was disallowed because the disposition occurred after February 22, 1994. The Smedleys disputed the disposition date in court and were unsuccessful.

Both had already filed an "Election to Report a Capital Gain on Property Owned at the end of February 24, 1994" in respect of a similar property. The Revenue Canada auditor failed to advise the Smedleys that they could have amended their elections to include the first property and thereby take advantage of the capital gains exemption on its disposition. Incorrect action on the part of the auditor caused the Smedleys substantial additional tax liability.

Donald Potter Income Tax Remission Order

P.C. 2004-0264, March 23, 2004 (Registration SI/2004-032, April 7, 2004).

Her Excellency the Governor General in Council, considering that the collection of certain amounts of tax is unjust, on the recommendation of the Minister of National Revenue, pursuant to subsection 23(2) of the *Financial Administration Act*, hereby makes the annexed *Donald Potter Income Tax Remission Order.*

Interpretation

1. In this Order, "registered retirement savings plan" has the meaning assigned by subsection 146(1) of the *Income Tax Act.*

Remission

2. The remission referred to in section 2 is granted on condition that Donald Potter does not institute or proceed with any action, objection, appeal, application or other proceeding of any kind in respect of the taxation of funds withdrawn from his registered retirement savings plans in 2001.

Condition

3. The remission referred to in section 2 is granted on condition that Donald Potter does not institute or proceed with any action, objection, appeal, application or other proceeding of any kind in respect of the taxation of funds withdrawn from his registered retirement savings plans in 2001.

Explanatory Note

(This note is not part of the Order.)

This Order remits $2,517.61, representing a portion of the tax paid or payable by Donald Potter under Part I of the *Income Tax Act* for the 2001 taxation year and all interest paid or payable in respect of that portion.

The amount remitted is in relation to funds withdrawn by Mr. Potter from registered retirement savings plans based on incorrect information regarding the amount of non-capital losses he had available to be carried forward to the 2001 taxation year. The incorrect information was provided in writing by a Canada Customs and Revenue Agency (CCRA) official who also sent letters of authority to the financial institutions who issued those plans permitting them to pay the funds to Mr. Potter without withholding the required tax.

The amount remitted corresponds to the additional tax liability incurred by Mr. Potter in respect of the 2001 taxation year as a result of his reliance on the incorrect information provided by the CCRA official.

Order Declaring that all Provisions of Part X of the Financial Administration Act Apply to Parc Downsview Park Inc.

Order in Council P.C. 2003-1304, September 3, 2003 (Registration SI/2003-156, September 24, 2003).

Her Excellency the Governor General in Council, on the recommendation of the Prime Minister, pursuant to subsection 86(2) of the Financial Administration Act, hereby declares that all provisions of Part X of that Act that apply only to parent Crown corporations apply to Parc Downsview Park Inc. and that those provisions apply to Parc Downsview Park Inc. with such modifications as the circumstances require, as if it were a parent Crown corporation.

Explanatory Note

(This note is not part of the Order.)

This Order declares that all of the provisions of Part X of the *Financial Administration Act* that apply only to parent Crown corporations apply to Parc Downsview Park Inc. — a wholly-owned subsidiary of a parent Crown corporation — with such modifications as the circumstances require, as if it were a parent Crown corporation.

Certain Taxpayers Remission Order, 2003-1 [Pension Contributions by Members of the Memorial University Pension Plan]

Order in Council P.C. 2003-912, June 12, 2003 (Registration SI/2003-123, July 2, 2003).

Her Excellency the Governor General in Council, considering that it is in the public interest to do so, on the recommendation of the Minister of National Revenue, pursuant to subsection 23(2) of the *Financial Administration Act*, hereby makes the annexed Certain Taxpayers Remission Order, 2003-1.

Remission

1. Subject to section 2, remission is hereby granted of amounts payable under the *Income Tax Act* by a person who is or was a member of the Memorial University Pension Plan where those amounts would not be payable if the contributions paid by the person in respect of non-existent service pursuant to regulations made under section 29 of *The Memorial University (Pensions) Act*, R.S.N. 1970, c. 232, were deductible under the *Income Tax Act.*

Conditions

2. Remission is granted if the following conditions are met:

(*a*) the contributions for non-existent service were made pursuant to an agreement entered into prior to 1990;

(*b*) the contributions were made in accordance with the pension plan as registered;

(*c*) the contributions have not been deducted from income in prior years; and

(*d*) the person applies for this relief, in writing, to the Minister of National Revenue before January 1, 2004.

Explanatory Note

(This note is not part of the Order.)

This Order remits amounts payable under the *Income Tax Act* resulting from the disallowance of the deduction from income of pension contributions made in respect of the purchase of non-existent service, as provided for under the Memorial University Pension Plan at the time of purchase.

Saskatchewan Indian Federated College Remission Order, 2003

P.C. 2003-910, June 12, 2003 (Registration SI/2003-122, July 2, 2003).

Her Excellency the Governor General in Council, considering that it is in the public interest to do so, on the recommendation of the Minister of National Revenue, pursuant to subsection 23(2) of the *Financial Administration Act*, hereby makes the annexed Saskatchewan Indian Federated College Remission Order, 2003.

Interpretation

1. The following definitions apply in this Order.

"band" has the same meaning as in subsection 2(1) of the Indian Act.

"Indian" has the same meaning as in subsection 2(1) of the Indian Act.

"Indian Settlement" means the settlement named, and constituting the lands described, in the schedule.

"reserve" has the same meaning as in subsection 2(1) of the *Indian Act.*

APPLICATION

2. This Order applies in respect of the Indian Settlement until lands constituting that Indian Settlement are set apart as a reserve by an order of the Governor in Council.

PART 1 — INCOME TAX

Interpretation

3 In this Part,

(*a*) "tax" means a tax imposed under Part I, I.1 or I.2 of the *Income Tax Act*; and

(*b*) all other words and expressions not otherwise defined in section 1 have the same meaning as in the *Income Tax Act*.

Remission of Income Tax

4 Remission is hereby granted to an Indian, or a band, with income situated on the Indian Settlement, in respect of each taxation year or fiscal period beginning during or after the calendar year 2000, of the amount, if any, by which

(*a*) the taxes, interest and penalties paid or payable by the Indian or band, as the case may be, for the taxation year or fiscal period

exceed

(*b*) the taxes, interest and penalties that would have been payable by that Indian or band for the taxation year or fiscal period if the Indian Settlement had been a reserve throughout that taxation year or fiscal period.

PART 2 — GOODS AND SERVICES TAX

Interpretation

5 In this Part,

(*a*) "tax" means the goods and services tax imposed under subsection 165(1) of the *Excise Tax Act*; and

(*b*) all other words and expressions not otherwise defined in section 1 have the same meaning as in Part IX of the *Excise Tax Act*.

Remission of the Goods and Services Tax

6 Subject to sections 7 and 8, remission is hereby granted to an Indian or a band that is the recipient of a taxable supply made on or delivered to the Indian Settlement on or after the day on which this Order comes into force in the case of an Indian, and January 1, 2000 in the case of a band, of the amount, if any, by which

(*a*) the tax paid or payable by the recipient

exceeds

(*b*) the tax that would have been payable by the recipient if the Indian Settlement had been a reserve at the time the supply was made or delivered.

Conditions

7 Remission granted to an Indian under section 6 is on condition that

(*a*) the tax paid or payable has not otherwise been rebated, credited, refunded or remitted under Part IX of the *Excise Tax Act* or under the *Financial Administration Act*; and

(*b*) in respect of tax paid, a written claim for the remission is made to the Minister of National Revenue within two years after the day on which the tax was paid.

8. Remission granted to a band under section 6 is on condition that

(*a*) the tax paid or payable has not otherwise been rebated, credited, refunded or remitted under Part IX of the *Excise Tax Act* or under the *Financial Administration Act*; and

(*b*) in respect of tax paid on or after January 1, 2000 but before the day on which this Order comes into force, a written claim for the remission is made to the Minister of National Revenue within two years after the day on which this Order comes into force; and

(*c*) in respect of tax paid on or after the day on which this Order comes into force, a written claim for the remission is made to the Minister of National Revenue within two years after the day on which the tax was paid.

SCHEDULE (Section 1)

Settlement

Legal Description of Settlement Lands

Saskatchewan Indian Federated College Campus

In the City of Regina, in the North East and South East Quarters of Section 8, in Township 17, Range 19 West of the Second Meridian, Saskatchewan, all that portion shown as Block B on a Plan of record in the Saskatchewan Land Surveys Directory as No. 99RA08587, as amended by Master of Titles Order No. 01RA01057, containing 13.153 hectares (32.503 acres) more or less.

Explanatory Note

(This note is not part of the Order.)

The purpose of this Order is to provide relief from federal income tax and the goods and services tax to Indians and Indian Bands on the campus of the Saskatchewan Indian Federated College that would be available if that campus were a reserve under the *Indian Act*. The Government of Canada has made a public commitment to grant reserve status under the *Indian Act* to that land.

La Caisse des Mutuellistes, Épargne et Crédit Remission Order [Error in the Calculation of Capital Tax]

P.C. 2003-218 February 20, 2003 (Registration SI/2003-33, March 12, 2003).

Her Excellency the Governor General in Council, considering that the collection of the tax is unjust, on the recommendation of the Minister of National Revenue, pursuant to subsection 23(2) of the *Financial Administration Act*, hereby remits tax under Part I.3 of the *Income Tax Act* in the amount of $20,108.00 for the 1996 and 1997 taxation years, and all relevant interest thereon, paid by La Caisse des Mutuellistes, Épargne et Crédit.

Explanatory Note

(This note is not part of the Order.)

This Order remits tax on capital under Part I.3 of the *Income Tax Act* and any relevant interest paid by La Caisse des Mutuellistes, Épargne et Crédit (the Corporation) in respect of the 1996 and 1997 taxation years.

For a number of years, the Corporation included in the computation of its tax on capital amounts that should have been excluded and, as a result, it paid tax on capital where none would have been payable. This error was one that should have been easily detected and corrected in 1999, in the course of an audit carried out by the Canada Customs and Revenue Agency. However, the error went unnoticed until 2001. By then, only the 1998 to 2000 taxation years could be reassessed, the previous years being statute-barred. This Order remits tax on capital paid in respect of the 1996 and 1997 taxation years, since it would have been possible to issue reassessments for those years had the error been detected in 1999.

Remission Order for Payments to Employees Pursuant to 1998 Ice Storm

Order in Council P.C. 1998-2047, (T.B. Rec. 826537), dated November 19, 1998.

His Excellency the Governor General in Council, considering that it is in the public interest to do so, on the recommendation of the Minister of National Revenue and the Treasury Board, pursuant to subsections 23(2) and (2.1) of the *Financial Administration Act*, hereby remits amounts payable under the *Income Tax Act*, the Canada Pension Plan and the *Employment Insurance Act* as a result of an amount paid or advanced in 1998 as relief for loss because of the ice storm in January 1998 which caused extended power outages and extensive damage in Ontario, Quebec, New Brunswick and Nova Scotia in respect of which an amount is required to be included in the income from employment of a taxpayer by virtue of paragraph 6(1)(*a*) or (*b*) or subsection 6(9) of the *Income Tax Act*, where the employee deals at arm's length with the employer, the payment or advance is voluntary, reasonable in the circumstances and *bona fide* and does not exceed the damages suffered by the employee net of any other compensation the employee receives or is entitled to receive, is not based on employment factors such as performance, position or years of service or the fact that the employee is a shareholder and is not made in exchange for past or future services or to compensate for loss of income, plus relevant interest and penalties, on condition that the employee waive any benefit or right accruing under the said Acts as a result of the payment or advance.

Order Amending the Income Earned in Quebec Income Tax Remission Order, 1988

P.C. 1998-396; March 19, 1998.

His Excellency the Governor General in Council, considering that it is in the public interest to do so, on the recommendation of the Minister of Finance, pursuant to subsection 23(2) of the Financial Administration Act, hereby makes the annexed Order Amending the Income Earned in Quebec Income Tax Remission Order, 1988.

Amendments

Paragraph 3(*b*) of the Income Earned in Quebec Income Tax Remission Order, 1988 is amended by striking out the word "and" at the end of paragraph (c) of subsection 2602(1) of the Income Tax Regulations, as it reads for the purposes of paragraph 3(*b*) of the Order, by adding the word "and" at the end of paragraph (*d*) of that subsection and by adding the following after paragraph (d) of that subsection:

(*e*) the income of the individual for that year from the disposition of a life insurance policy under which a person resident in the province is, at the time the policy was issued or effected, the person whose life was insured.

2.

(1) Subparagraph 4(*d*)(ii) of the French version of the Order is replaced by the following:

(ii) soit par une société, une commission ou une association dont au moins 90% des actions, du capital ou des biens appartenaient à la province de Quéebec ou par une filiale en propriété exclusive d'une telle socieétee, commission ou association, si nul autre que Sa Majestée du chef de la province de Quéebec n'avait des droits sur les actions, le capital ou les biens de cette socieétee, commission, association ou filiale, ou n'avait le droit d'acquéerir ces actions, ce capital ou ces biens,

(2) Paragraphs 4(*f*) and (*g*) of the Order are replaced by the following:

(*f*) amounts that would be required by paragraph 56(1)(*n*) or (*o*) of the Act to be included in computing the individual's income for the year if

(i) the individual were resident in Canada throughout the year,

(ii) the references in subparagraph 56(1)(*n*)(i) and paragraph 56(1)(*o*) of the Act to "received by the taxpayer in the year" were read as references to "received by the taxpayer in the year from the Province of Quebec or any corporation, commission, association or institution referred to in paragraph 4(d) of the Income Earned in Quebec Income Tax Remission Order, 1988, other than an institution of the Government of Canada, or from a wholly-owned corporation subsidiary to such a corporation, commission or association", and

(iii) the reference to "$500" in paragraph 56(1)(*n*) of the Act were read as a reference to "the proportion of $500 that the amount determined under subparagraph (i) is of the amount that would be so determined if the requirements of subparagraphs 4(*f*)(i) and (ii) of the Income Earned in Quebec Income Tax Remission Order, 1988 were not taken into account",

(*g*) amounts that would be required by subsection 56(8) of the Act to be included in computing the individual's income for the year if the individual were resident in Canada throughout the year, and

3.

(1) Clause 5(2)(*c*)(ii)(B) of the French version of the Order is replaced by the following:

(B) soit d'une socieétee, commission ou association dont au moins 90% des actions, du capital ou des biens appartenaient à la province de Quéebec, ou d'une filiale en propriété exclusive d'une telle socieétee, commission ou association, si nul autre que Sa Majestée du chef de la province de Quéebec n'avait des droits sur les actions, le capital ou les biens de cette sociéetée, commission, association ou filiale, ou n'avait le droit d'acquerir ces actions, ce capital ou ces biens,

(2) Paragraph 5(2)(*e*) of the Order is replaced by the following:

(*e*) was, at any time in the year, a child of a person described in paragraph (*b*) or (*c*) and was living with the person in a self-contained domestic establishment that the person, whether alone or jointly with one or more other persons, maintained and in which the person lived and actually supported the child who at that time, was

(i) wholly dependent for support on the person, or the person and the other person or persons, and

(ii) either under 18 years of age or so dependent by reason of mental or physical infirmity.

4. Subparagraphs 6(1)(*b*)(ii) and (iii) of the Order are replaced by the following:

(ii) the definition "business-income tax" in subsection 126(7) of the Act read as follows:

""business-income tax" paid by a taxpayer for a taxation year in respect of businesses carried on by the taxpayer in a country other than Canada (in this definition referred to as the "business country") means such portion of 55% of any income or profits tax paid by the taxpayer for the year to the government of any country other than Canada or to the government of a state, province or other political subdivision of any such country as can reasonably be regarded as tax in respect of the income of the taxpayer from any business carried on by the taxpayer in the business country, but does not include a tax, or the portion of a tax, that can reasonably be regarded as relating to an amount that

(*a*) any other person or partnership has received or is entitled to receive from that government, or

(*b*) was deductible under subparagraph 110(1)(*f*)(i) in computing the taxpayer's taxable income for at he year", and

(iii) the definition "tax for the year otherwise payable under this Part" in subsection 126(7) of the Act read as follows:

""tax for the year otherwise payable under this Part" means the amount determined by the formula

A - B

where

is the tax payable under this Part for the year after taking into account the requirements of subparagraph 6(1)(b)(i) of the Income Earned in Quebec Income Tax Remission Order, 1988, but before making any deduction under any of sections 121, 122.3, 126.1, 127 and 127.2 to 127.4 and this section, and

B is the amount, if any, deemed by subsection 120(2) to have been paid on account of tax payable under this Part for the year after taking into account the requirements of subparagraph 6(1)(b)(i) of the Income Earned in Quebec Income Tax Remission Order, 1988";.

5. Paragraph 7(*b*) of the French version of the order is replaced by the following:

(*b*) dans le cas d'un particulier visée à l'alinéea 5(2)*b*), *c*), *d*) ou *e*), en ce qui concerne la réemunéeration reçue de la province de Quéebec ou d'une sociéetée, commission, association ou institution ou d'un éetablissement visées à l'alinéea 5(2)*c*), sauf une institution du gouvemement du Canada, ou d'une filiale en propriété exclusive d'une telle sociéetée, commission ou association.

6. The Order is amended by adding the following after section 7:

7.1 Every individual to whom an amount was remitted under section 5 for a taxation year shall reimburse that amount, plus interest thereon to the day of payment, to Her Majesty in right of Canada to the extent of the amount of tax payable under the *Taxation Act*, R.S.Q., c. I-3, for that year that the individual, as a result of an objection served on the Minister of Revenue of the Province of Quebec, a claim filed in any court or a complaint made to any tribunal, was declared not to be liable to pay on the ground that the individual was not subject to the tax levied under that Act because of the individual's place of residence.

7. Subsection 8(1) of the Order is replaced by the following:

8. **(1)** Sections 3 to 6 apply to the 1983 to 1996 taxation years.

Application

8.

(1) Sections 1 and 7 apply to the 1994 and subsequent taxation years.

(2) Paragraph 4(*f*) of the Order, as enacted by subsection 2(2), applies to the 1983 and subsequent taxation years.

(3) Paragraph 4(*g*) of the Order, as enacted by subsection 2(2), applies to the 1993 and subsequent taxation years.

(4) Subsection 3(2) applies to the 1988 and subsequent taxation years.

(5) Section 4 applies to the 1990 and subsequent taxation years.

Explanatory Note

(This note is not part of the Order.)

The Income Earned in Quebec Income Tax Remission Order, 1988 defines the expression "income earned in the year in a province" for the purposes of the *Income Tax Act* and remits to certain individuals who are deemed to be resident in Canada, to non-residents who realized capital gains in Quebec and to Quebec residents who earned business income from a foreign source the additional tax, interest and penalty arising both from the imposition of the federal surtax and from the loss of the federal tax abatement in respect of income earned in Quebec.

This Order extends, with the necessary changes, the application of the Income Earned in Quebec Income Tax Remission Order, 1988 with respect to the 1994, 1995 and 1996 taxation years in the case of sections 3 to 6 of that Order. The federal surtax and the federal tax abatement in respect of income earned in Quebec are respectively 52% and 16.5%.

Order Respecting the Remission of Income Tax in Respect of Certain Income of Individuals Earned in the Province of Quebec (1988)

Order in Council P.C. 1989-1204, SI/89-157, dated July 5, 1989, pursuant to section 17 of the Financial Administration Act, as amended by P.C. 1991-1661, SI/91-116, dated September 25, 1991.

Short Title

1. This Order may be cited as the *Income Earned in Quebec Income Tax Remission Order, 1988*.

Interpretation

In this Order,

"Act" means the *Income Tax Act*;

"Regulations" means the *Income Tax Regulations*.

Remission to Individuals who Did Not Reside in Canada at any Time in a Taxation Year

Remission is hereby granted to any individual who did not reside in Canada at any time in a taxation year of the amount, if any, by which

(*a*) the tax, interest and penalties paid or payable under the Act by that individual in respect of that taxation year

exceeds

(*b*) the tax, interest and penalties that would have been payable by that individual under the Act in respect of that taxation year if, for the purpose of determining that person's income earned in that year in the Province of Quebec, section 2602 of the Regulations read as follows:

"**2602.** (1) Except as provided in subsection (2), where an individual did not reside in Canada at any time in a taxation year, his income earned in the taxation year in a particular province is the aggregate of

(*a*) that part of the amount of his income from an office or employment that is included in computing his taxable income earned in Canada for the year by virtue of subparagraph 115(1)(*a*)(i) of the Act that is reasonably attributable to the duties performed by him in the province,

(*b*) his income for that year earned in the province as determined in the manner set forth in section 4 of the *Income Earned in Quebec Income Tax Remission Order, 1988*,

(*c*) his income for that year from carrying on business earned in the province, determined as hereinafter set forth in this Part, and

(*d*) the taxable capital gains in the province included in computing his taxable income earned in Canada for the year by virtue of subparagraph 115(1)(*a*)(iii) of the Act from dispositions of property, each of which was a disposition of a property or an interest therein that was

(i) real property situated in the province or an option in respect thereof, or

(ii) any other capital property used by him in carrying on a business in the province,

determined as hereinafter set forth in this Part.

(2) Where the aggregate of the amount of an individual's income as determined under subsection (1) for all provinces for a taxation year exceeds his income described in subsection 115(1) of the Act, the amount of his income earned in the taxation year in a particular province shall be that proportion of his income so described that the amount of his income earned in the taxation year in the province as determined under subsection (1) is of the aggregate of all those amounts.

(3) Where, in a taxation year, a non-resident individual has disposed of real property situated in a particular province or an interest therein, or an option in respect thereof, any taxable capital gain from that disposition shall be a taxable capital gain in that particular province.

(4) Except as provided in subsection (5), where, in a taxation year, a non-resident individual has disposed of any capital property, other than property referred to in subsection (3), used by him in carrying on a business in Canada, the proportion of any taxable capital gain from that disposition that

(*a*) his income for the year from carrying on that business in a particular province

is of

(*b*) his income for the year from carrying on that business in Canada,

shall be a taxable capital gain in that particular province.

(5) Where in a taxation year a non-resident individual

(*a*) had no permanent establishment in Canada, and

(*b*) disposed of any capital property, other than property referred to in subsection (3), used by him in a previous year in carrying on a business in Canada,

the proportion of any taxable capital gain from that disposition that

(*c*) his income from carrying on that business in a particular province for the last preceding taxation year in which he had income from carrying on that business in a province

is of

(*d*) his income for the year, referred to in paragraph (*c*), from carrying on that business in Canada,

shall be a taxable capital gain in that particular province."

4. Where an individual who did not reside in Canada at any time in a taxation year was

(*a*) a student in full-time attendance at an educational institution in the Province of Quebec that is a university, college or other educational institution providing courses at a post-secondary school level,

(*b*) a student attending, or a teacher teaching at, an educational institution outside Canada that is a university, college or other educational institution providing courses at a post-secondary school level who had, in any previous year, ceased to be resident in the Province of Quebec in the course of or subsequent to moving to attend or to teach at, as the case may be, that institution,

(*c*) an individual who had, in any previous year, ceased to be resident in the Province of Quebec in the course of or subsequent to moving to carry on research or any similar work under a grant received by him to enable him to carry on that research or work, or

(*d*) an individual who had, in any previous year, ceased to be resident in the Province of Quebec and who was, in the taxation year, in receipt of remuneration in respect of an office or employment that was paid to him directly or indirectly by

(i) the Province of Quebec,

(ii) any corporation, commission or association the shares, capital or property of which were at least 90 per cent owned by the Province of Quebec, or a wholly-owned subsidiary corporation to such a corporation, commission or association, on condition that no person other than Her Majesty in right of the Province of Quebec had any right to the shares, capital or property of that corporation, commission, association or subsidiary or a right to acquire the shares, capital or property,

(iii) an educational institution, other than an educational institution of the Government of Canada, in the Province of Quebec that was

(A) a university, college or other educational institution providing courses at a post-secondary school level that received or was entitled to receive financial support from the Province of Quebec,

(B) a school operated by the Province of Quebec, or by a municipality thereof or by a public body thereof performing a function of government, or a school operated on behalf of that Province, municipality or public body, or

(C) a secondary school providing courses leading to a certificate or diploma that is a requirement for entrance to a college or university, or

(iv) an institution in the Province of Quebec, other than an institution of the Government of Canada, supplying health services or social services, or both, that received or was entitled to receive financial support from the Province of Quebec,

there shall be included, for the purposes of this Order, in computing his income earned in the taxation year in the Province of Quebec, the aggregate of

(*e*) the amount of any remuneration in respect of an office or employment that was paid to him directly or indirectly by the Province of Quebec or any corporation, commission, association or institution referred to in paragraph (d), other than an institution of the Government of Canada, or by a wholly-owned corporation subsidiary to such corporation, commission or association, and that was received by the individual who did not reside in Canada in the year, except to the extent that such remuneration was attributable to the duties of an office or employment performed by him outside Canada, and that is

(i) subject to an income or profits tax imposed by the government of a country other than Canada, or

(ii) paid in connection with the selling of property, the negotiating of contracts or the rendering of services for his employer, or a foreign affiliate of his employer, or any other person with whom his employer does not deal at arm's length, in the ordinary course of a business carried on by his employer, that foreign affiliate or that other person,

(*f*) amounts that would be required by paragraph 56(1)(*n*) or (*o*) of the Act to be included in computing his income for the year if he were resident in Canada throughout the year and the references in subparagraph 56(1)(*n*)(i) and paragraph 56(1)(*o*) of the Act to "received by the taxpayer in the year" were read as references to "received by the taxpayer in the year from the Province of Quebec or any corporation, commission, association or institution referred to in paragraph 4(*d*) of the *Income Earned in Quebec Income Tax Remission Order, 1988*, other than an institution of the Government of Canada, or from a wholly-owned corporation subsidiary to such corporation, commission or association", and if the reference to "$500" in subparagraph 56(1)(*n*)(ii) of the Act were read as a reference to "the proportion of $500 that the amount that would be determined under subparagraph 56(1)(*n*)(i) if the requirements of this paragraph were taken into account is of the amount determined under subparagraph 56(1)(*n*)(i) without taking the requirements of this paragraph into account",

(*g*) amounts that would be required by subsection 56(5) or (8) of the Act to be included in computing his income for the year if he were resident in Canada throughout the year, and

(*h*) amounts that would be required by paragraph 56(1)(*q*) of the Act to be included in computing his income for the year if he were resident in Canada throughout the year,

minus the amount that would be deductible in computing his income for the year by virtue of section 62 of the Act if

(*I*) that section were read without reference to paragraph (1)(*a*) thereof,

(*j*) that section were applicable in computing the taxable income of individuals who did not reside in Canada, and

(*k*) the amounts described in subparagraph (1)(*f*)(ii) thereof were the amounts described in paragraph (*f*).

Remission to Individuals Who Did Not Reside in a Province, the Northwest Territories or the Yukon Territory on the Last Day of the Taxation Year 5.

5.

(1) Subject to subsection (2), remission is hereby granted to any individual who did not reside in a province on the last day of a taxation year of the amount, if any, by which

(*a*) income tax, interest and penalties paid or payable under the Act by that individual in respect of that taxation year

exceeds

(*b*) the tax, interest and penalties that would have been payable by that individual under the Act in respect of that taxation year if the individual had resided in the Province of Quebec on the last day of the taxation year.

(2) Subsection (1) is applicable to an individual who

(*a*) sojourned in the Province of Quebec for a period of, or periods the aggregate of which is, 183 days or more and was ordinarily resident outside Canada;

(*b*) was at any time in the year an agent-general, officer or servant of the Province of Quebec and was resident in that Province immediately prior to his appointment or employment by that Province;

(*c*) performed services at any time in the year under an international development assistance program prescribed under Part XXXIV of the Regulations and was at any time

(i) in the three month period preceding the day on which those services commenced, resident in the Province of Quebec, and

(ii) in the six month period preceding the day on which those services commenced, an officer or servant of

(A) the Province of Quebec,

(B) any corporation, commission or association the shares, capital or property of which were at least 90 per cent owned by the Province of Quebec, or a wholly-owned corporation subsidiary to such a corporation, commission or association, on condition that no person other than Her Majesty in right of the Province of Quebec had any right to those shares or that capital or property of such corporation, commission, association or subsidiary or a right to acquire those shares or that capital or property,

(C) an educational institution, other than an educational institution of the Government of Canada, in the Province of Quebec that was

(I) a university, college or other educational institution providing courses at a post-secondary school level that received or was entitled to receive financial support from the Province of Quebec,

(II) a school operated by the Province of Quebec, or by a municipality thereof or by a public body thereof performing a function of government, or a school operated on behalf of that Province, municipality or public body, or

(III) a secondary school providing courses leading to a certificate or diploma that is a requirement for entrance to a college or university, or

(D) an institution in the Province of Quebec, other than an institution of the Government of Canada, supplying health services or social services, or both, that received or was entitled to receive financial support from the Province of Quebec;

(*d*) was resident in Canada in any previous year and was, at any time in the year, the spouse of a person described in paragraph (*b*) or (*c*) living with that person; or

(*e*) was, at any time in the year, a child described in paragraph 109(1)(*d*) of the Act, as it applied in respect of the 1985 taxation year, of a person described in paragraph (*b*) or (*c*).

Paragraph (2)(*d*) is not applicable where the spouse of an individual described in paragraph (2)(*c*) is also an individual described in paragraph (2)(*c*).

Remission to Individuals who Resided in the Province of Quebec on the Last Day of a Taxation Year

6.

(1) Remission is hereby granted to any individual who resided in the Province of Quebec on the last day of a taxation year of the amount, if any, by which

(*a*) the tax, interest and penalties payable under the Act by that individual in respect of that taxation year

exceeds

(*b*) the tax, interest and penalties that would have been payable by that individual in respect of that taxation year if

(i) if subsections 2601(1) and (2) of the Regulations read as follows:

"**2601.** (1) Notwithstanding subsection (4) and section 2603, where an individual resided in a particular province on the last day of a taxation year and had no income for the year from a business with a permanent establishment in another province, his income earned in the taxation year in the province is his income for the year.

(2) Notwithstanding subsection (4) and section 2603, where an individual resided in a particular province on the last day of a taxation year and had income for the year from a business with a permanent establishment in any other province, his income earned in the taxation year in the province is the amount, if any, by which

(*a*) his income for the year

exceeds

(*b*) the aggregate of his income for the year from carrying on business earned in each other province, determined as hereinafter set forth in this Part.",

if paragraph 126(7)(*a*) of the Act read as follows:

(*a*) business-income tax paid by a taxpayer for a taxation year in respect of business carried on by him in a country other than Canada (in this paragraph referred to as the "business country") means such portion of 55/100ths of any income or profits tax paid by him for the year to the government of any country other than Canada or to the government of a state, province or other political subdivision of any such country as may reasonably be regarded as tax in respect of the income of the taxpayer from any business carried on by him in the business country; and",

and

if paragraph 126(7)(*d*) of the Act read as follows:

(*d*) tax for the year otherwise payable under this Part means the tax for the taxation year otherwise payable under this Part after taking into account the requirements of subparagraph 6(1)(*b*)(i) of the *Income Earned in Quebec Income Tax Remission Order, 1988*, but before making any deduction under sections 121, 126, 127 and 127.2 to 127.4."

(2) In subsection (1), a reference to the last day of a taxation year shall, in the case of an individual who resided in the Province of Quebec at any time in the year and ceased to reside in Canada before the end of the year, be deemed to be a reference to the last day in the year on which the individual resided in Canada.

Deductions and Remittances

7. Notwithstanding paragraph 102(1)(*a*), subsection 102(2), paragraph 103(1)(*m*) and subparagraphs 103(4)(*a*)(xiii), (*b*)(xiii) and (*c*)(xiii) of the Regulations, the amount to be deducted or withheld by an employer and remitted to the Receiver General pursuant to Part I of the Regulations shall, in the case of

(*a*) an individual referred to in section 4 in respect of the remuneration referred to in paragraph 4(*e*), and

(*b*) an individual referred to in paragraph 5(2)(*b*), (*c*), (*d*) or (*e*) in respect of remuneration received from the Province of Quebec or from any corporation, commission, association or institution referred to in paragraph 5(2)(*c*), other than an institution of the Government of Canada, or from a wholly-owned corporation subsidiary to such corporation, commission or association,

be determined as if the employee reported for work at an establishment of the employer in Quebec.

8.

(1) Sections 3 to 6 are applicable in respect of the 1983 to 1993 taxation years.

(2) Section 7 is applicable in respect of the 1989 and subsequent taxation years.

(SI/91-116, S. 1; SI/92-230, S. 1; SI/94-43, S. 1.)

Indians and Bands on Certain Indian Settlements Remission Order (1997)

Order in Council P.C. 1997-1529, SI/97-127, dated 23 October 1997.

His Excellency the Governor General in Council, considering that it is in the public interest to do so, on the recommendation of the Minister of National Revenue, pursuant to subsection 23(2)(*a*) of the Financial Administration Act, hereby makes the annexed Indians and Bands on Certain Indian Settlements Remission Order (1997).

Interpretation

1. The definitions in this section apply in this Order.

"band" has the same meaning as in subsection 2(1) of the *Indian Act*.

"Indian" has the same meaning as in subsection 2(1) of the *Indian Act*.

"Indian Settlement" means an area that is named and described in column 2 of the schedule.

"reserve" has the same meaning as in subsection 2(1) of the *Indian Act*.

Application

2. This Order applies to any Indian Settlement until the time when the area of that Indian Settlement is set aside, in whole or in part, as a reserve by Order of the Governor in Council.

Part 1 — Income Tax

Interpretation

3.

(1) For the purposes of this Part, "tax" means tax imposed under Parts I, I.1 and I.2 of the *Income Tax Act*.

(2) Subject to section 1, all other words and expressions used in this Part have the same meaning as in the *Income Tax Act*.

Remission of Income Tax

4. Remission is hereby granted to a taxpayer who is an Indian whose income is situated on an Indian Settlement, in respect of the taxation year set out in column 3 of the schedule in relation to that Indian Settlement and each taxation year after that year, of the amount, if any, by which

(*a*) the taxes, interest and penalties paid or payable by the taxpayer for the taxation year under the *Income Tax Act*

exceeds

(*b*) the taxes, interest and penalties that would have been payable by the taxpayer for the taxation year under that Act if the Indian Settlement were a reserve throughout the year.

Explanatory Note

(This note is not part of the Order.)

The purpose of this Order is to extend the benefits of relief from income tax and the goods and services tax (GST) to Indians, as though the specified Indian settlements were reserves. This Order applies to settlements for which a public commitment has been made by the Government of Canada to grant reserve status under the *Indian Act*. The Department of Indian and Northern Affairs has advised the Department of National Revenue of the settlements that have identified boundaries that should be included in this Order.

Schedule (Sections 1, 4, 6, 7 and 9)

Item	Column 1 Band	Column 2 Indian Settlement and Legal Description of Settlement Lands	Column 3 Taxation Year	Column 4 Date for Remission of GST for Individual Indians	Column 5 Date for Remission of GST for Bands
1.	Nibinamik First Nation	Summer Beaver, Ontario: District of Nakina, Ontario (52 degrees 45 minutes north latitude, 88 degrees 35 minutes west longitude) having an area of approximately 3.5 square miles. (Excluded are locations SN 160 and CL 6298, the sites of the old and new schools.)	1995	October 23, 1997	January 1, 1995
2.	Long Point First Nation	Winneway, Quebec: North-half portion of Lots 50 and 51 Range 8, the whole of Lot 46-5 Range 9 and the southeast corner of Lot 47 Range 9, 51770 CLSR and 59890 CLSR, Township of Devlin, having an area of approximately 47 hectares.	1996	October 23, 1997	January 1, 1996
3.	God's River First Nation	God's River, Manitoba: Parcel 5, Plan 4955 NLTO (situated in projected Township 67 Range 23, East of the principal meridian) having an area of approximately 2.83 acres.	1993	October 23, 1997	January 1, 1993

Income Tax as well as Canada Pension Plan and Employment Insurance Premiums Remission Order

Order in Council P.C. 1997-201, dated February 11, 1997, pursuant to subsection 23(2) of the Financial Administration Act.

His Excellency the Governor General in Council, considering that it is in the public interest to do so, on the recommendation of the Minister of National Revenue and the Treasury Board, pursuant to subsections 23(2) and 23(2.1) of the *Financial Administration Act*, hereby remits amounts payable under the *Income Tax Act*, the *Canada Pension Plan* and the *Employment Insurance Act* as a result of an amount paid as relief for loss because of torrential rains and wind in or near the region along the Saguenay River on or about July 20, 1996, that is required to be included in the income from employment of a taxpayer by virtue of paragraph 6(1)(*a*) or (*b*) of the *Income Tax Act*, where the payment is voluntary, reasonable and bona fide, is not based on employment factors such as performance, position or years of service and is not made in exchange for past or future services or to compensate for loss of income, plus relevant interest and penalties, on condition that the taxpayer waive any benefit or right accruing under the said Acts as a result of the payment.

Income Tax Paid by Investors, Other Than Promoters Remission Order

Order in Council P.C. 1996-1274, SI/96-80, dated August 7, 1996, pursuant to subsection 23(2) of the Financial Administration Act.

His Excellency the Governor General in Council, considering that it is in the public interest to do so, on the recommendation of the Minister of National Revenue, pursuant to subsection 23(2) of the *Financial Administration Act*, hereby remits to each taxpayer, other than a promoter, who has delivered or delivers to the Minister a timely and duly executed agreement letter (referred to in the details of the settlement project regarding general partnerships used as SR&ED tax shelters issued by the Minister on June 30, 1995) accepted by the Minister, amounts payable under the *Income Tax Act* by the taxpayer equal to (1) the difference between (a) 50% of the product of each payment made before executing the agreement on account of the tax liability resulting from adjustments made by the Minister to the taxpayer's claim in respect of the tax shelter and the prescribed rate of interest for income tax refunds, for the period from the date of the payment to the date of the assessment of the tax liability made as a result of the agreement, compounded daily, and (b) refund interest in respect of any such payment, (2) 50% of the product of that difference and that rate, for the period from the said date of assessment to the date this Order is implemented, so compounded, and (3) amounts that would not be payable if there were no such refund interest or if this Order were not made.

Income Tax Remission Order (Canada Pension Plan)

Order in Council P.C. 1995-201, SI/95-21, dated February 22, 1995, pursuant to subsection 23(2) of the Financial Administration Act.

His Excellency the Governor General in Council, considering that the collection of the tax is unjust, on the recommendation of the Minister of National Revenue, pursuant to subsection 23(2) of the *Financial Administration Act*, is pleased hereby to remit the net total of the taxes payable under Parts I and I.1 of the *Income Tax Act* for the 1987 to 1995 taxation years that, without regard to sections 122.2 and 122.4 to 122.64 thereof as they read at any time, would not be payable by a taxpayer if the part of any amount received by the taxpayer after 1987 and before 1996 by reason of section 63.1 of the *Canada Pension Plan* that was payable for a month in a year preceding the year in which it was received had been received in that preceding year, and all relevant penalties and interest.

Indian Income Tax Remission Order

Order in Council P.C. 1993-1649, SI/93-166, dated August 25, 1993, pursuant to subsection 23(2) of the Financial Administration Act.

His Excellency the Governor General in Council, considering that it is in the public interest to do so, on the recommendation of the Minister of National Revenue, pursuant to subsection 23(2) of the *Financial Administration Act*, is pleased hereby to remit amounts that would be remitted if the reference to subsection 87(1) of the *Indian Act* in the Indian Income Tax Remission Order included a reference to a provision similar to that subsection in an Act cited in that Order.

Farmers' Income Taxes Remission Order

Order in Council P.C. 1993-1647, SI/93-164, dated August 25, 1993, pursuant to subsection 23(2) of the Financial Administration Act.

His Excellency the Governor General in Council, considering that the collection of the tax is unreasonable, on the recommendation of the Minister of National Revenue, pursuant to subsection 23(2) of the *Financial Administration Act*, is pleased hereby to remit tax payable by a taxpayer under Parts I to I.2 of the *Income Tax Act* for the 1992 taxation year that would not be payable if that portion of each payment received in 1992 in respect of a gross revenue insurance program established under the *Farm Income Protection Act* that is required to be and is repaid were not included in computing the income of the taxpayer for the 1992 taxation year under paragraph 12(1)(*p*) of the *Income Tax Act*, and all relevant interest and penalties, on condition that the taxpayer file with the Minister an undertaking in a form acceptable to the Minister in which the taxpayer agrees not to deduct the amount repaid or required to be repaid in computing the taxpayer's income for any taxation year and waives all relevant rights of objection or appeal.

Order Respecting the Remission of Income Tax Paid or Payable on Income from Employers Residing on Reserves and Indian Settlements and on Certain Unemployment Insurance Benefits Received by Indians

Order in Council P.C. 1993-523, SI/93-44, dated April 7, 1993, pursuant to subsection 23(2) of the Financial Administration Act.

Short Title

1. This Order may be cited as the *Indian Income Tax Remission Order*.

Interpretation

2. In this Order,

"Act" means the *Income Tax Act*;

"Indian" has the same meaning as in subsection 2(1) of the *Indian Act*;

"Indian settlement" has the same meaning as in section 2 of the *Indians and Bands on Certain Indian Settlements Remission Order*;

"reserve" means

(*a*) a reserve as defined in subsection 2(1) of the *Indian Act*,

(*b*) Category IA land or Category IA-N land as defined in subsection 2(1) of the *Cree-Naskapi (of Quebec) Act*, and

(*c*) Sechelt lands as defined in subsection 2(1) of the *Sechelt Indian Band Self-Government Act*.

Remission in respect of Certain Employment Income

3.

(1) Remission is hereby granted to a taxpayer who is an Indian of the amounts payable by the taxpayer under Parts I to I.2 of the Act for a taxation year that would not be payable by the taxpayer if, in the calculation of the taxpayer's income for the year, there were not included an amount equal to the product obtained by multiplying the income for the year from each office or employment of the taxpayer by the proportion that

(*a*) the amounts that are required to be included in the computation of the income from that office or employment for the year and that are payable to the taxpayer by an employer residing on a reserve or Indian settlement

are of

(*b*) the amounts that are required to be included in the computation of the income from that office or employment for the year.

(2) Remission is hereby granted to a person for whom the amounts payable under Parts I to I.2 of the Act for a taxation year would be reduced if, in the calculation of the income of the taxpayer referred to in subsection (1) for the year, there were not included the product obtained under that subsection in respect of each office or employment of the taxpayer, of an amount equal to the amount, if any, by which

(*a*) total amount payable by the person under Parts I to I.2 of the Act for the year

exceeds

(*b*) total amount that would be payable by the person for the year if, in the calculation of the taxpayer's income for the year, there were not included the product obtained under subsection (1) in respect of each office or employment of the taxpayer.

(3) Subsections (1) and (2) apply to the 1992 and 1993 taxation years.

Remission in respect of Certain Unemployment Insurance Benefits

4.

(1) Subject to section 5, remission is hereby granted to a taxpayer who is an Indian of the amounts payable by the taxpayer under Parts I to I.2 of the Act for a taxation year that would not be payable by the taxpayer if, in the calculation of the taxpayer's income for the year for the purpose of an assessment, there were not included an amount equal to the product obtained by multiplying the total of the benefits referred to in subparagraph 56(1)(a)(iv) of the Act and included in the calculation of the taxpayer's income for the year for the purpose of an assessment, by the proportion that

(*a*) the income from employment during a relevant qualifying period that was taken into account in determining the amount of those benefits and that is exempt from taxation under subsection 87(1) of the Indian Act or in respect of which there is a remission of tax payable under the Act by a taxpayer who is an Indian

is of

(*b*) the total income from employment during a relevant qualifying period that was taken into account in determining the amount of those benefits.

(2) Subject to section 5, remission is hereby granted to a person for whom the amounts payable under Parts I to I.2 of the Act for a taxation year would be reduced if, in respect of the taxpayer referred to in subsection (1), an amount equal to the amount of the product referred to in that subsection were not included in the calculation of the taxpayer's income for the year for the purpose of an assessment, of an amount equal to the amount, if any, by which

(*a*) the total amount payable by the person under Parts I to I.2 of the Act for the year

exceeds

(*b*) the total amount that would be payable by the person for the year if, in respect of the taxpayer, an amount equal to the amount of the product referred to subsection (1) were not included in the calculation of the taxpayer's income for the year for the purpose of an assessment.

(3) Subsections (1) and (2) apply to taxation years 1985 to 1991.

Condition

5. Remission under subsection 4(1) or (2) is granted on condition that an application in writing establishing the applicant's right to that remission be submitted to the Minister of National Revenue.

Order Respecting the Remission of Income Tax, Interest and Penalties on Royalties or Fees Received from Canada by Residents of India for Technical Services

Order in Council P.C. 1991-1953, SI/91-137, dated October 23, 1991, pursuant to section 17 of the Financial Administration Act.

Short Title

1. This Order may be cited as the *Residents of India Remission Order*.

Interpretation

2. In this Order,

"Act" means the *Income Tax Act*;

"Agreement" means the *Agreement between the Government of Canada and the Government of India for the Avoidance of Double Taxation and the Prevention of Fiscal Evasion with respect to Taxes on Income* set out in Schedule III to chapter 7 of the Statutes of Canada, 1986;

"person" has the meaning assigned by paragraph 1(*c*) of Article 3 of the Agreement.

Remission

3. Remission is hereby granted to any person who is a resident of India, within the meaning of the Agreement, for any amount paid or credited to that person in respect of royalties in relation to a right or property that is granted after December 12, 1988 or in respect of fees for technical services under a contract that is signed after that date, of an amount equal to the amount by which

(*a*) the aggregate of the taxes, interest and penalties payable by that person under the Act with respect to the amount so paid or credited

exceeds

(*b*) the aggregate of the taxes, interest and penalties that would have been payable by that person under the Act with respect to the amount so paid or credited, if the reference to a rate of 30 per cent in paragraph 2 of Article 13 of the Agreement were read as a reference to a rate of 20 per cent.

Order Respecting the Remission of Certain Income Taxes Paid or Payable by Certain Persons in Respect of Interest from Government and Long-Term Corporate Debt Obligations

Order in Council P.C. 1985-3480, SI/85-214, dated December 11, 1985, pursuant to section 17 of the Financial Administration Act.

Short Title

1. This Order may be cited as the *Government and Long-Term Corporate Debt Obligations Remission Order.*

Interpretation

2. In this Order, "Act" means the *Income Tax Act*.

Remission

3. Remission is hereby granted to each non-resident person who is liable for tax under Part XIII of the Act in respect of any amount paid or credited to him as, on account or in lieu of payment of, or in satisfaction of, interest of an amount equal to the amount, if any, by which

(*a*) the tax payable by the non-resident person under Part XIII of the Act in respect of the amount so paid or credited

exceeds

(*b*) the tax that would be payable by the non-resident person under Part XIII of the Act in respect of the amount so paid or credited if the references to "1986" in subparagraphs 212(1)(b)(ii) and (vii) of the Act were read as references to "1987".

4. Where a person required to deduct or withhold a tax payable by a non-resident person under Part XIII of the Act is liable to pay as tax under Part XIII on behalf of the non-resident person the whole of the amount that should have been deducted or withheld, remission is hereby granted to that person of an amount equal to the amount, if any, by which

(*a*) the tax payable by the person so required to deduct or withhold under Part XIII of the Act

exceeds

(*b*) the tax that would be payable by the person so required to deduct or withhold under Part XIII of the Act if the references to "1986" in subparagraphs 212(1)(*b*)(ii) and (vii) of the Act were read as references to "1987".

Multilateral Instrument in Respect of Tax Conventions Act
S.C. 2019 c. 12

Her Majesty, by and with the advice and consent of the Senate and House of Commons of Canada, enacts as follows:

1. Short title. This Act may be cited as the *Multilateral Instrument in Respect of Tax Conventions Act*.

2. Definition of multilateral instrument. In this Act, ***multilateral instrument*** means the Multilateral Convention to Implement Tax Treaty Related Measures to Prevent Base Erosion and Profit Shifting set out in the schedule.

3. Multilateral instrument approved. The multilateral instrument is approved and has the force of law in Canada during the period that the multilateral instrument, by its terms, is in force for Canada.

4. (1) Inconsistent laws – general rule. Subject to subsection (2), in the event of any inconsistency between the provisions of this Act or the multilateral instrument and the provisions of any other law, the provisions of this Act and the multilateral instrument prevail to the extent of the inconsistency.

(2) Inconsistent laws – exception. In the event of any inconsistency between the provisions of the multilateral instrument and the provisions of the *Income Tax Conventions Interpretation Act*, the provisions of that Act prevail to the extent of the inconsistency.

5. Regulations. The Minister of National Revenue may make any regulations that are necessary for carrying out the multilateral instrument or for giving effect to any of its provisions.

6. Notifications. The Minister of Finance must cause to be published in the *Canada Gazette*

(*a*) on or before the 60th day following the day on which the multilateral instrument enters into force for Canada, a notice of the day on which the multilateral instrument so entered into force; and

(*b*) on or before the 60th day following the day on which Canada withdraws from the multilateral instrument, a notice of withdrawal and the date on which it takes effect.

Schedule (Section 2)
Multilateral Convention to Implement Tax Treaty Related Measures to Prevent Base Erosion and Profit Shifting

The Parties to this Convention,

Recognising that governments lose substantial corporate tax revenue because of aggressive international tax planning that has the effect of artificially shifting profits to locations where they are subject to non-taxation or reduced taxation;

Mindful that base erosion and profit shifting (hereinafter referred to as "BEPS") is a pressing issue not only for industrialised countries but also for emerging economies and developing countries;

Recognising the importance of ensuring that profits are taxed where substantive economic activities generating the profits are carried out and where value is created;

Welcoming the package of measures developed under the OECD/G20 BEPS project (hereinafter referred to as the "OECD/G20 BEPS package");

Noting that the OECD/G20 BEPS package included tax treaty-related measures to address certain hybrid mismatch arrangements, prevent treaty abuse, address artificial avoidance of permanent establishment status, and improve dispute resolution;

Conscious of the need to ensure swift, co-ordinated and consistent implementation of the treaty-related BEPS measures in a multilateral context;

Noting the need to ensure that existing agreements for the avoidance of double taxation on income are interpreted to eliminate double taxation with respect to the taxes covered by those agreements without creating opportunities for non-taxation or reduced taxation through tax evasion or avoidance (including through treaty-shopping arrangements aimed at obtaining reliefs provided in those agreements for the indirect benefit of residents of third jurisdictions);

Recognising the need for an effective mechanism to implement agreed changes in a synchronised and efficient manner across the network of existing agreements for the avoidance of double taxation on income without the need to bilaterally renegotiate each such agreement;

Have agreed as follows:

Part I
Scope and Interpretation of Terms

Article 1
Scope of the Convention

This Convention modifies all Covered Tax Agreements as defined in subparagraph a) of paragraph 1 of Article 2 (Interpretation of Terms).

Article 2
Interpretation of Terms

1. For the purpose of this Convention, the following definitions apply:

a) The term "Covered Tax Agreement" means an agreement for the avoidance of double taxation with respect to taxes on income (whether or not other taxes are also covered):

i) that is in force between two or more:

A) Parties; and/or

B) jurisdictions or territories which are parties to an agreement described above and for whose international relations a Party is responsible; and

Treaties and Related Legislation

ii) with respect to which each such Party has made a notification to the Depositary listing the agreement as well as any amending or accompanying instruments thereto (identified by title, names of the parties, date of signature, and, if applicable at the time of the notification, date of entry into force) as an agreement which it wishes to be covered by this Convention.

b) The term "Party" means:

i) A State for which this Convention is in force pursuant to Article 34 (Entry into Force); or

ii) A jurisdiction which has signed this Convention pursuant to subparagraph b) or c) of paragraph 1 of Article 27 (Signature and Ratification, Acceptance or Approval) and for which this Convention is in force pursuant to Article 34 (Entry into Force).

c) The term "Contracting Jurisdiction" means a party to a Covered Tax Agreement.

d) The term "Signatory" means a State or jurisdiction which has signed this Convention but for which the Convention is not yet in force.

2. As regards the application of this Convention at any time by a Party, any term not defined herein shall, unless the context otherwise requires, have the meaning that it has at that time under the relevant Covered Tax Agreement.

Part II
Hybrid Mismatches.

Article 3
Transparent Entities

1. For the purposes of a Covered Tax Agreement, income derived by or through an entity or arrangement that is treated as wholly or partly fiscally transparent under the tax law of either Contracting Jurisdiction shall be considered to be income of a resident of a Contracting Jurisdiction but only to the extent that the income is treated, for purposes of taxation by that Contracting Jurisdiction, as the income of a resident of that Contracting Jurisdiction.

2. Provisions of a Covered Tax Agreement that require a Contracting Jurisdiction to exempt from income tax or provide a deduction or credit equal to the income tax paid with respect to income derived by a resident of that Contracting Jurisdiction which may be taxed in the other Contracting Jurisdiction according to the provisions of the Covered Tax Agreement shall not apply to the extent that such provisions allow taxation by that other Contracting Jurisdiction solely because the income is also income derived by a resident of that other Contracting Jurisdiction.

3. With respect to Covered Tax Agreements for which one or more Parties has made the reservation described in subparagraph a) of paragraph 3 of Article 11 (Application of Tax Agreements to Restrict a Party's Right to Tax its Own Residents), the following sentence will be added at the end of paragraph 1: "In no case shall the provisions of this paragraph be construed to affect a Contracting Jurisdiction's right to tax the residents of that Contracting Jurisdiction."

4. Paragraph 1 (as it may be modified by paragraph 3) shall apply in place of or in the absence of provisions of a Covered Tax Agreement to the extent that they address whether income derived by or through entities or arrangements that are treated as fiscally transparent under the tax law of either Contracting Jurisdiction (whether through a general rule or by identifying in detail the treatment of specific fact patterns and types of entities or arrangements) shall be treated as income of a resident of a Contracting Jurisdiction.

5. A Party may reserve the right:

a) for the entirety of this Article not to apply to its Covered Tax Agreements;

b) for paragraph 1 not to apply to its Covered Tax Agreements that already contain a provision described in paragraph 4;

c) for paragraph 1 not to apply to its Covered Tax Agreements that already contain a provision described in paragraph 4 which denies treaty benefits in the case of income derived by or through an entity or arrangement established in a third jurisdiction;

d) for paragraph 1 not to apply to its Covered Tax Agreements that already contain a provision described in paragraph 4 which identifies in detail the treatment of specific fact patterns and types of entities or arrangements;

e) for paragraph 1 not to apply to its Covered Tax Agreements that already contain a provision described in paragraph 4 which identifies in detail the treatment of specific fact patterns and types of entities or arrangements and denies treaty benefits in the case of income derived by or through an entity or arrangement established in a third jurisdiction;

f) for paragraph 2 not to apply to its Covered Tax Agreements;

g) for paragraph 1 to apply only to its Covered Tax Agreements that already contain a provision described in paragraph 4 which identifies in detail the treatment of specific fact patterns and types of entities or arrangements.

6. Each Party that has not made a reservation described in subparagraph a) or b) of paragraph 5 shall notify the Depositary of whether each of its Covered Tax Agreements contains a provision described in paragraph 4 that is not subject to a reservation under subparagraphs c) through e) of paragraph 5, and if so, the article and paragraph number of each such provision. In the case of a Party that has made the reservation described in subparagraph g) of paragraph 5, the notification pursuant to the preceding sentence shall be limited to Covered Tax Agreements that are subject to that reservation. Where all Contracting Jurisdictions have made such a notification with respect to a Provision of a Covered Tax Agreement, that Provision shall be replaced by the provisions of paragraph 1 (as it may be modified by paragraph 3) to the extent provided in paragraph 4. In other cases, paragraph 1 (as it may be modified by paragraph 3) shall supersede the provisions of the Covered Tax Agreement only to the extent that those provisions are incompatible with paragraph 1 (as it may be modified by paragraph 3).

Article 4
Dual Resident Entities.

1. Where by reason of the provisions of a Covered Tax Agreement a person other than an individual is a resident of more than one Contracting Jurisdiction, the competent authorities of the Contracting Jurisdictions shall endeavour to determine by mutual agreement the Contracting Jurisdiction of which such person shall be deemed to be a resident for the purposes of the Covered Tax Agreement, having regard to its place of effective management, the place where it is incorporated or otherwise constituted and any other relevant factors. In the absence of such agreement, such person shall not be entitled to any relief or exemption from tax provided by the Covered Tax Agreement except to the extent and in such manner as may be agreed upon by the competent authorities of the Contracting Jurisdictions.

2. Paragraph 1 shall apply in place of or in the absence of provisions of a Covered Tax Agreement that provide rules for determining whether a person other than an individual shall be treated as a resident of one of the Contracting Jurisdictions in cases in which that person would otherwise be treated as a resident of more than one Contracting Jurisdiction. Paragraph 1 shall not apply, however, to provisions of a Covered Tax Agreement specifically addressing the residence of companies participating in dual-listed company arrangements.

3. A Party may reserve the right:

a) for the entirety of this Article not to apply to its Covered Tax Agreements;

b) for the entirety of this Article not to apply to its Covered Tax Agreements that already address cases where a person other than an individual is a resident of more than one Contracting Jurisdiction by requiring the competent authorities of the Contracting Jurisdictions to endeavour to reach mutual agreement on a single Contracting Jurisdiction of residence;

c) for the entirety of this Article not to apply to its Covered Tax Agreements that already address cases where a person other than an individual is a resident of more than one Contracting Jurisdiction by denying treaty benefits without requiring the competent authorities of the Contracting Jurisdictions to endeavour to reach mutual agreement on a single Contracting Jurisdiction of residence;

d) for the entirety of this Article not to apply to its Covered Tax Agreements that already address cases where a person other than an individual is a resident of more than one Contracting Jurisdiction by requiring the competent authorities of the Contracting Jurisdictions to endeavour to reach mutual agreement on a single Contracting Jurisdiction of residence, and that set out the treatment of that person under the Covered Tax Agreement where such an agreement cannot be reached;

e) to replace the last sentence of paragraph 1 with the following text for the purposes of its Covered Tax Agreements: "In the absence of such agreement, such person shall not be entitled to any relief or exemption from tax provided by the Covered Tax Agreement.";

f) for the entirety of this Article not to apply to its Covered Tax Agreements with Parties that have made the reservation described in subparagraph e).

4. Each Party that has not made a reservation described in subparagraph a) of paragraph 3 shall notify the Depositary of whether each of its Covered Tax Agreements contains a provision described in paragraph 2 that is not subject to a reservation under subparagraphs b) through d) of paragraph 3, and if so, the article and paragraph number of each such provision. Where all Contracting Jurisdictions have made such a notification with respect to a provision of a Covered Tax Agreement, that provision shall be replaced by the provisions of paragraph 1. In other cases, paragraph 1 shall supersede the provisions of the Covered Tax Agreement only to the extent that those provisions are incompatible with paragraph 1.

Article 5
Application of Methods for Elimination of Double Taxation.

1. A Party may choose to apply either paragraphs 2 and 3 (Option A), paragraphs 4 and 5 (Option B), or paragraphs 6 and 7 (Option C), or may choose to apply none of the Options. Where each Contracting Jurisdiction to a Covered Tax Agreement chooses a different Option (or where one Contracting Jurisdiction chooses to apply an Option and the other chooses to apply none of the Options), the Option chosen by each Contracting Jurisdiction shall apply with respect to its own residents.

2. Option A. Provisions of a Covered Tax Agreement that would otherwise exempt income derived or capital owned by a resident of a Contracting Jurisdiction from tax in that Contracting Jurisdiction for the purpose of eliminating double taxation shall not apply where the other Contracting Jurisdiction applies the provisions of the Covered Tax Agreement to exempt such income or capital from tax or to limit the rate at which such income or capital may be taxed. In the latter case, the first-mentioned Contracting Jurisdiction shall allow as a deduction from the tax on the income or capital of that resident an amount equal to the tax paid in that other Contracting Jurisdiction. Such deduction shall not, however, exceed that part of the tax, as computed before the deduction is given, which is attributable to such items of income or capital which may be taxed in that other Contracting Jurisdiction.

3. Paragraph 2 shall apply to a Covered Tax Agreement that would otherwise require a Contracting Jurisdiction to exempt income or capital described in that paragraph.

4. Option B. Provisions of a Covered Tax Agreement that would otherwise exempt income derived by a resident of a Contracting Jurisdiction from tax in that Contracting Jurisdiction for the purpose of eliminating double taxation because such income is treated as a dividend by that Contracting Jurisdiction shall not apply where such income gives rise to a deduction for the purpose of determining the taxable profits of a resident of the other Contracting Jurisdiction under the laws of that other Contracting Jurisdiction. In such case, the first-mentioned Contracting Jurisdiction shall allow as a deduction from the tax on the income of that resident an amount equal to the income tax paid in that other Contracting Jurisdiction. Such deduction shall not, however, exceed that part of the income tax, as computed before the deduction is given, which is attributable to such income which may be taxed in that other Contracting Jurisdiction.

5. Paragraph 4 shall apply to a Covered Tax Agreement that would otherwise require a Contracting Jurisdiction to exempt income described in that paragraph.

6. Option C.

a) Where a resident of a Contracting Jurisdiction derives income or owns capital which may be taxed in the other Contracting Jurisdiction in accordance with the provisions of a Covered Tax Agreement (except to the extent that these provisions allow taxation by that other Contracting Jurisdiction solely because the income is also income derived by a resident of that other Contracting Jurisdiction), the first-mentioned Contracting Jurisdiction shall allow:

i) as a deduction from the tax on the income of that resident, an amount equal to the income tax paid in that other Contracting Jurisdiction;

ii) as a deduction from the tax on the capital of that resident, an amount equal to the capital tax paid in that other Contracting Jurisdiction.

Such deduction shall not, however, exceed that part of the income tax or capital tax, as computed before the deduction is given, which is attributable to the income or the capital which may be taxed in that other Contracting Jurisdiction.

b) Where in accordance with any provision of the Covered Tax Agreement income derived or capital owned by a resident of a Contracting Jurisdiction is exempt from tax in that Contracting Jurisdiction, such Contracting Jurisdiction may nevertheless, in calculating the amount of tax on the remaining income or capital of such resident, take into account the exempted income or capital.

7. Paragraph 6 shall apply in place of provisions of a Covered Tax Agreement that, for purposes of eliminating double taxation, require a Contracting Jurisdiction to exempt from tax in that Contracting Jurisdiction income derived or capital owned by a resident of that Contracting Jurisdiction which, in accordance with the provisions of the Covered Tax Agreement, may be taxed in the other Contracting Jurisdiction.

8. A Party that does not choose to apply an Option under paragraph 1 may reserve the right for the entirety of this Article not to apply with respect to one or more identified Covered Tax Agreements (or with respect to all of its Covered Tax Agreements).

9. A Party that does not choose to apply Option C may reserve the right, with respect to one or more identified Covered Tax Agreements (or with respect to all of its Covered Tax Agreements), not to permit the other Contracting Jurisdiction(s) to apply Option C.

10. Each Party that chooses to apply an Option under paragraph 1 shall notify the Depositary of its choice of Option. Such notification shall also include:

a) in the case of a Party that chooses to apply Option A, the list of its Covered Tax Agreements which contain a provision described in paragraph 3, as well as the article and paragraph number of each such provision;

b) in the case of a Party that chooses to apply Option B, the list of its Covered Tax Agreements which contain a provision described in paragraph 5, as well as the article and paragraph number of each such provision;

c) in the case of a Party that chooses to apply Option C, the list of its Covered Tax Agreements which contain a provision described in paragraph 7, as well as the article and paragraph number of each such provision.

An Option shall apply with respect to a provision of a Covered Tax Agreement only where the Party that has chosen to apply that Option has made such a notification with respect to that provision.

Part III
Treaty Abuse

Article 6

Purpose of a Covered Tax Agreement

1. A Covered Tax Agreement shall be modified to include the following preamble text:

> Intending to eliminate double taxation with respect to the taxes covered by this agreement without creating opportunities for non-taxation or reduced taxation through tax evasion or avoidance (including through treaty-shopping arrangements aimed at obtaining reliefs provided in this agreement for the indirect benefit of residents of third jurisdictions),.

2. The text described in paragraph 1 shall be included in a Covered Tax Agreement in place of or in the absence of preamble language of the Covered Tax Agreement referring to an intent to eliminate double taxation, whether or not that language also refers to the intent not to create opportunities for non-taxation or reduced taxation.

3. A Party may also choose to include the following preamble text with respect to its Covered Tax Agreements that do not contain preamble language referring to a desire to develop an economic relationship or to enhance co-operation in tax matters:

> Desiring to further develop their economic relationship and to enhance their co-operation in tax matters,.

4. A Party may reserve the right for paragraph 1 not to apply to its Covered Tax Agreements that already contain preamble language describing the intent of the Contracting Jurisdictions to eliminate double taxation without creating opportunities for non-taxation or reduced taxation, whether that language is limited to cases of tax evasion or avoidance (including through treaty-shopping arrangements aimed at obtaining reliefs provided in the Covered

Tax Agreement for the indirect benefit of residents of third jurisdictions) or applies more broadly.

5. Each Party shall notify the Depositary of whether each of its Covered Tax Agreements, other than those that are within the scope of a reservation under paragraph 4, contains preamble language described in paragraph 2, and if so, the text of the relevant preambular paragraph. Where all Contracting Jurisdictions have made such a notification with respect to that preamble language, such preamble language shall be replaced by the text described in paragraph 1. In other cases, the text described in paragraph 1 shall be included in addition to the existing preamble language.

6. Each Party that chooses to apply paragraph 3 shall notify the Depositary of its choice. Such notification shall also include the list of its Covered Tax Agreements that do not already contain preamble language referring to a desire to develop an economic relationship or to enhance co-operation in tax matters. The text described in paragraph 3 shall be included in a Covered Tax Agreement only where all Contracting Jurisdictions have chosen to apply that paragraph and have made such a notification with respect to the Covered Tax Agreement.

Article 7

Prevention of Treaty Abuse.

1. Notwithstanding any provisions of a Covered Tax Agreement, a benefit under the Covered Tax Agreement shall not be granted in respect of an item of income or capital if it is reasonable to conclude; having regard to all relevant facts and circumstances, that obtaining that benefit was one of the principal purposes of any arrangement or transaction that resulted directly or indirectly in that benefit, unless it is established that granting that benefit in these circumstances would be in accordance with the object and purpose of the relevant provisions of the Covered Tax Agreement.

2. Paragraph 1 shall apply in place of or in the absence of provisions of a Covered Tax Agreement that deny all or part of the benefits that would otherwise be provided under the Covered Tax Agreement where the principal purpose or one of the principal purposes of any arrangement or transaction, or of any person concerned with an arrangement or transaction, was to obtain those benefits.

3. A Party that has not made the reservation described in subparagraph a) of paragraph 15 may also choose to apply paragraph 4 with respect to its Covered Tax Agreements.

4. Where a benefit under a Covered Tax Agreement is denied to a person under provisions of the Covered Tax Agreement (as it may be modified by this Convention) that deny all or part of the benefits that would otherwise be provided under the Covered Tax Agreement where the principal purpose or one of the principal purposes of any arrangement or transaction, or of any person concerned with an arrangement or transaction, was to obtain those benefits, the competent authority of the Contracting Jurisdiction that would otherwise have granted this benefit shall nevertheless treat that person as being entitled to this benefit, or to different benefits with respect to a specific item of income or capital, if such competent authority, upon request from that person and after consideration of the relevant facts and circumstances, determines that such benefits would have been granted to that person in the absence of the transaction or arrangement. The competent authority of the Contracting Jurisdiction to which a request has been made under this paragraph by a resident of the other Contracting Jurisdiction shall consult with the competent authority of that other Contracting Jurisdiction before rejecting the request.

5. Paragraph 4 shall apply to provisions of a Covered Tax Agreement (as it may be modified by this Convention) that deny all or part of the benefits that would otherwise be provided under the Covered Tax Agreement where the principal purpose or one of the principal purposes of any arrangement or transaction, or of any person concerned with an arrangement or transaction, was to obtain those benefits.

6. A Party may also choose to apply the provisions contained in paragraphs 8 through 13 (hereinafter referred to as the "Simplified Limitation on Benefits Provision") to its Covered Tax Agreements by making the notification described in subparagraph c) of paragraph 17. The Simplified Limitation on Benefits Provision shall apply with respect to a Covered Tax Agreement only where all Contracting Jurisdictions have chosen to apply it.

7. In cases where some but not all of the Contracting Jurisdictions to a Covered Tax Agreement choose to apply the Simplified Limitation on Benefits Provision pursuant to paragraph 6, then, notwithstanding the provisions of that paragraph, the Simplified Limitation on Benefits Provision shall apply with respect to the granting of benefits under the Covered Tax Agreement:

a) by all Contracting Jurisdictions, if all of the Contracting Jurisdictions that do not choose pursuant to paragraph 6 to apply the Simplified Limitation on Benefits Provision agree to such application by choosing to apply this subparagraph and notifying the Depositary accordingly; or

b) only by the Contracting Jurisdictions that choose to apply the Simplified Limitation on Benefits Provision, if all of the Contracting Jurisdictions that do not choose pursuant to paragraph 6 to apply the Simplified Limitation on Benefits Provision agree to such application by choosing to apply this subparagraph and notifying the Depositary accordingly.

8. **Simplified Limitation on Benefits Provision.** Except as otherwise provided in the Simplified Limitation on Benefits Provision, a resident of a Contracting Jurisdiction to a Covered Tax Agreement shall not be entitled to a benefit that would otherwise be accorded by the Covered Tax Agreement, other than a benefit under provisions of the Covered Tax Agreement:

a) which determine the residence of a person other than an individual which is a resident of more than one Contracting Jurisdiction by reason of provisions of the Covered Tax Agreement that define a resident of a Contracting Jurisdiction;

b) which provide that a Contracting Jurisdiction will grant to an enterprise of that Contracting Jurisdiction a corresponding adjustment following an initial adjustment made by the other Contacting Jurisdiction, in accordance with the Covered Tax Agreement, to the amount of tax charged in the first-mentioned Contracting Jurisdiction on the profits of an associated enterprise; or

c) which allow residents of a Contracting Jurisdiction to request that the competent authority of that Contracting Jurisdiction consider cases of taxation not in accordance with the Covered Tax Agreement,

unless such resident is a "qualified person", as defined in paragraph 9 at the time that the benefit would be accorded.

9. A resident of a Contracting Jurisdiction to a Covered Tax Agreement shall be a qualified person at a time when a benefit would otherwise be accorded by the Covered Tax Agreement if, at that time, the resident is:

a) an individual;

b) that Contracting Jurisdiction, or a political subdivision or local authority thereof, or an agency or instrumentality of any such Contracting Jurisdiction, political subdivision or local authority;

c) a company or other entity, if the principal class of its shares is regularly traded on one or more recognised stock exchanges;

d) a person, other than an individual, that:

i) is a non-profit organisation of a type that is agreed to by the Contracting Jurisdictions through an exchange of diplomatic notes; or

ii) is an entity or arrangement established in that Contracting Jurisdiction that is treated as a separate person under the taxation laws of that Contracting Jurisdiction and:

A) that is established and operated exclusively or almost exclusively to administer or provide retirement benefits and ancillary or incidental benefits to individuals and that is regulated as such by that Contracting Jurisdiction or one of its political subdivisions or local authorities; or

B) that is established and operated exclusively or almost exclusively to invest funds for the benefit of entities or arrangements referred to in subdivision A);

e) a person other than an individual, if, on at least half the days of a twelve-month period that includes the time when the benefit would otherwise be accorded, persons who are residents of that Contracting Jurisdiction and that are entitled to benefits of the Covered Tax Agreement under subparagraphs a) to d) own, directly or indirectly, at least 50 per cent of the shares of the person.

10.

a) A resident of a Contracting Jurisdiction to a Covered Tax Agreement will be entitled to benefits of the Covered Tax Agreement with respect to an item of income derived from the other Contracting Jurisdiction, regardless of whether the resident is a qualified person, if the resident is engaged in the active conduct of a business in the first-mentioned Contracting Jurisdiction, and the income derived from the other Contracting Jurisdiction emanates from, or is incidental to, that business. For purposes of the Simplified Limitation on Benefits Provision, the term "active conduct of a business" shall not include the following activities or any combination thereof:

i) operating as a holding company;

ii) providing overall supervision or administration of a group of companies;

iii) providing group financing (including cash pooling); or

iv) making or managing investments, unless these activities are carried on by a bank, insurance company or registered securities dealer in the ordinary course of its business as such.

b) If a resident of a Contracting Jurisdiction to a Covered Tax Agreement derives an item of income from a business activity conducted by that resident in the other Contracting Jurisdiction, or derives an item of income arising in the other Contracting Jurisdiction from a connected person, the conditions described in subparagraph a) shall be considered to be satisfied with respect to such item only if the business activity carried on by the resident in the first-mentioned Contracting Jurisdiction to which the item is related is substantial in relation to the same activity or a complementary business activity carried on by the resident or such connected person in the other Contracting Jurisdiction. Whether a business activity is substantial for the purposes of this subparagraph shall be determined based on all the facts and circumstances.

c) For purposes of applying this paragraph, activities conducted by connected persons with respect to a resident of a Contracting Jurisdiction to a Covered Tax Agreement shall be deemed to be conducted by such resident.

11. A resident of a Contracting Jurisdiction to a Covered Tax Agreement that is not a qualified person shall also be entitled to a benefit that would otherwise be accorded by the Covered Tax Agreement with respect to an item of income if, on at least half of the days of any twelve-month period that includes the time when the benefit would otherwise be accorded, persons that are equivalent beneficiaries own, directly or indirectly, at least 75 per cent of the beneficial interests of the resident.

12. If a resident of a Contracting Jurisdiction to a Covered Tax Agreement is neither a qualified person pursuant to the provisions of paragraph 9, nor entitled to benefits under paragraph 10 or 11, the competent authority of the other Contracting Jurisdiction may, nevertheless, grant the benefits of the Covered Tax Agreement, or benefits with respect to a specific item of income, taking into account the object and purpose of the Covered Tax Agreement, but only if such resident demonstrates to the satisfaction of such competent authority that neither its establishment, acquisition or maintenance, nor the conduct of its operations, had as one of its principal purposes the obtaining of benefits under the Covered Tax Agreement. Before either granting or denying a request made under this paragraph by a resident of a Contracting Jurisdiction, the competent authority of the other Contracting Jurisdiction to which the request has been made shall consult with the competent authority of the first-mentioned Contracting Jurisdiction.

13. For the purposes of the Simplified Limitation on Benefits Provision:

a) the term "recognised stock exchange" means:

i) any stock exchange established and regulated as such under the laws of either Contracting Jurisdiction; and

ii) any other stock exchange agreed upon by the competent authorities of the Contracting Jurisdictions;

b) the term "principal class of shares" means the class or classes of shares of a company which represents the majority of the aggregate vote and value of the company or the class or classes of beneficial interests of an entity which represents in the aggregate a majority of the aggregate vote and value of the entity;

c) the term "equivalent beneficiary" means any person who would be entitled to benefits with respect to an item of income accorded by a Contracting Jurisdiction to a Covered Tax Agreement under the domestic law of that Contracting Jurisdiction, the Covered Tax Agreement or any other international instrument which are equivalent to, or more favourable than, benefits to be accorded to that item of income under the Covered Tax Agreement; for the purposes of determining whether a person is an equivalent beneficiary with respect to dividends, the person shall be deemed to hold the same capital of the company paying the dividends as such capital the company claiming the benefit with respect to the dividends holds;

d) with respect to entities that are not companies, the term "shares" means interests that are comparable to shares;

e) two persons shall be "connected persons" if one owns, directly or indirectly, at least 50 per cent of the beneficial interest in the other (or, in the case of a company, at least 50 per cent of the aggregate vote and value of the company's shares) or another person owns, directly or indirectly, at least 50 per cent of the beneficial interest (or, in the case of a company, at least 50 per cent of the aggregate vote and value of the company's shares) in each person; in any case, a person shall be connected to another if, based on all the relevant facts and circumstances, one has control of the other or both are under the control of the same person or persons.

14. The Simplified Limitation on Benefits Provision shall apply in place of or in the absence of provisions of a Covered Tax Agreement that would limit the benefits of the Covered Tax Agreement (or that would limit benefits other than a benefit under the provisions of the Covered Tax Agreement relating to residence, associated enterprises or non-discrimination or a benefit that is not restricted solely to residents of a Contracting Jurisdiction) only to a resident that qualifies for such benefits by meeting one or more categorical tests.

15. A Party may reserve the right:

a) for paragraph 1 not to apply to its Covered Tax Agreements on the basis that it intends to adopt a combination of a detailed limitation on benefits provision and either rules to address conduit financing structures or a principal purpose test, thereby meeting the minimum standard for preventing treaty abuse under the OECD/G20 BEPS package; in such cases, the Contracting Jurisdictions shall endeavour to reach a mutually satisfactory solution which meets the minimum standard;

b) for paragraph 1 (and paragraph 4, in the case of a Party that has chosen to apply that paragraph) not to apply to its Covered Tax Agreements that already contain provisions that deny all of the benefits that would otherwise be provided under the Covered Tax Agreement where the principal purpose or one of the principal purposes of any arrangement or transaction, or of any person concerned with an arrangement or transaction, was to obtain those benefits;

c) for the Simplified Limitation on Benefits Provision not to apply to its Covered Tax Agreements that already contain the provisions described in paragraph 14.

16. Except where the Simplified Limitation on Benefits Provision applies with respect to the granting of benefits under a Covered Tax Agreement by one or more Parties pursuant to paragraph 7, a Party that chooses pursuant to paragraph 6 to apply the Simplified Limitation on Benefits Provision may reserve the right for the entirety of this Article not to apply with respect to its Covered Tax Agreements for which one or more of the other Contracting Jurisdictions has not chosen to apply the Simplified Limitation on Benefits Provision. In such cases, the Contracting Jurisdictions shall endeavour to reach a mutually satisfactory solution which meets the minimum standard for preventing treaty abuse under the OECD/G20 BEPS package.

17.

a) Each Party that has not made the reservation described in subparagraph a) of paragraph 15 shall notify the Depositary of whether each of its Covered Tax Agreements that is not subject to a reservation described in subparagraph b) of paragraph 15 contains a provision described in paragraph 2, and if so, the article and paragraph number of each such provision. Where all Contracting Jurisdictions have made such a notification with respect to a provision of a Covered Tax Agreement, that provision shall be replaced by the provisions of paragraph 1 (and where applicable, paragraph 4). In other cases, paragraph 1 (and where applicable, paragraph 4) shall supersede the provisions of the Covered Tax Agreement only to the extent that those provisions are incompatible with paragraph 1 (and where applicable, paragraph 4). A Party making a notification under this subparagraph may also include a statement that while such Party accepts the application of paragraph 1 alone as an interim measure, it intends where possible to adopt a limitation on benefits provision, in addition to or in replacement of paragraph 1, through bilateral negotiation.

b) Each Party that chooses to apply paragraph 4 shall notify the Depositary of its choice. Paragraph 4 shall apply to a Covered Tax Agreement only where all Contracting Jurisdictions have made such a notification.

c) Each Party that chooses to apply the Simplified Limitation on Benefits Provision pursuant to paragraph 6 shall notify the Depositary of its choice. Unless such Party has made the reservation described in subparagraph c) of paragraph 15, such notification shall also include the list of its Covered Tax Agreements which contain a provision described in paragraph 14, as well as the article and paragraph number of each such provision.

d) Each Party that does not choose to apply the Simplified Limitation on Benefits Provision pursuant to paragraph 6, but chooses to apply either subparagraph a) or b) of paragraph 7 shall notify the Depositary of its choice of subparagraph. Unless such Party has made the reservation described in subparagraph c) of paragraph 15, such notification shall also include the list of its Covered Tax Agreements which contain a provision described in paragraph 14, as well as the article and paragraph number of each such provision.

e) Where all Contracting Jurisdictions have made a notification under subparagraph c) or d) with respect to a provision of a Covered Tax Agreement, that provision shall be replaced by the Simplified Limitation on Benefits Provision. In other cases, the Simplified Limitation on Benefits Provision shall supersede the provisions of the Covered Tax Agreement only to the extent that those provisions are incompatible with the Simplified Limitation on Benefits Provision.

Article 8

Dividend Transfer Transactions

1. Provisions of a Covered Tax Agreement that exempt dividends paid by a company which is a resident of a Contracting Jurisdiction from tax or that limit the rate at which such dividends may be taxed, provided that the beneficial owner or the recipient is a company which is a resident of the other Contracting Jurisdiction and which owns, holds or controls more than a certain amount of the capital, shares, stock, voting power, voting rights or similar ownership interests of the company paying the dividends, shall apply only if the ownership conditions described in those provisions are met throughout a 365 day period that includes the day of the payment of the dividends (for the purpose of computing that period, no account shall be taken of changes of ownership that would directly result from a corporate reorganisation, such as a merger or divisive reorganisation, of the company that holds the shares or that pays the dividends).

2. The minimum holding period provided in paragraph 1 shall apply in place of or in the absence of a minimum holding period in provisions of a Covered Tax Agreement described in paragraph 1.

3. A Party may reserve the right:

a) for the entirety of this Article not to apply to its Covered Tax Agreements;

b) for the entirety of this Article not to apply to its Covered Tax Agreements to the extent that the provisions described in paragraph 1 already include:

i) a minimum holding period;

ii) a minimum holding period shorter than a 365 day period; or

iii) a minimum holding period longer than a 365 day period.

4. Each Party that has not made a reservation described in subparagraph a) of paragraph 3 shall notify the Depositary of whether each of its Covered Tax Agreements contains a provision described in paragraph 1 that is not subject to a reservation described in subparagraph b) of paragraph 3, and if so, the article and paragraph number of each such provision. Paragraph 1 shall apply with respect to a provision of a Covered Tax Agreement only where all Contracting Jurisdictions have made such a notification with respect to that provision.

Article 9

Capital Gains from Alienation of Shares or Interests of Entities Deriving their Value Principally from Immovable Property

1. Provisions of a Covered Tax Agreement providing that gains derived by a resident of a Contracting Jurisdiction from the alienation of shares or other rights of participation in an entity may be taxed in the other Contracting Jurisdiction provided that these shares or rights derived more than a certain part of their value from immovable property (real property) situated in that other Contracting Jurisdiction (or provided that more than a certain part of the property of the entity consists of such immovable property (real property)):

a) shall apply if the relevant value threshold is met at any time during the 365 days preceding the alienation; and

b) shall apply to shares or comparable interests, such as interests in a partnership or trust (to the extent that such shares or interests are not already covered) in addition to any shares or rights already covered by the provisions.

2. The period provided in subparagraph a) of paragraph 1 shall apply in place of or in the absence of a time period for determining whether the relevant value threshold in provisions of a Covered Tax Agreement described in paragraph 1 was met.

3. A Party may also choose to apply paragraph 4 with respect to its Covered Tax Agreements.

4. For purposes of a Covered Tax Agreement, gains derived by a resident of a Contracting Jurisdiction from the alienation of shares or comparable interests, such as interests in a partnership or trust, may be taxed in the other Contracting Jurisdiction if, at any time during the 365 days preceding the alienation, these shares or comparable interests derived more than 50 per cent of their value directly or indirectly from immovable property (real property) situated in that other Contracting Jurisdiction.

5. Paragraph 4 shall apply in place of or in the absence of provisions of a Covered Tax Agreement providing that gains derived by a resident of a Contracting Jurisdiction from the alienation of shares or other rights of participation in an entity may be taxed in the other Contracting Jurisdiction provided that these shares or rights derived more than a certain part of their value from immovable property (real property) situated in that other Contracting Jurisdiction, or provided that more than a certain part of the property of the entity consists of such immovable property (real property).

6. A Party may reserve the right:

a) for paragraph 1 not to apply to its Covered Tax Agreements;

b) for subparagraph a) of paragraph 1 not to apply to its Covered Tax Agreements;

c) for subparagraph b) of paragraph 1 not to apply to its Covered Tax Agreements;

d) for subparagraph a) of paragraph 1 not to apply to its Covered Tax Agreements that already contain a provision of the type described in paragraph 1 that includes a period for determining whether the relevant value threshold was met;

e) for subparagraph b) of paragraph 1 not to apply to its Covered Tax Agreements that already contain a provision of the type described in paragraph 1 that applies to the alienation of interests other than shares;

f) for paragraph 4 not to apply to its Covered Tax Agreements that already contain the provisions described in paragraph 5.

7. Each Party that has not made the reservation described in subparagraph a) of paragraph 6 shall notify the Depositary of whether each of its Covered Tax Agreements contains a provision described in paragraph 1, and if so, the article and paragraph number of each such provision. Paragraph 1 shall apply with respect to a provision of a Covered Tax Agreement only where all Contracting Jurisdictions have made a notification with respect to that provision.

8. Each Party that chooses to apply paragraph 4 shall notify the Depositary of its choice. Paragraph 4 shall apply to a Covered Tax Agreement only where all Contracting Jurisdictions have made such a notification. In such case, paragraph 1 shall not apply with respect to that Covered Tax Agreement. In the case of a Party that has not made the reservation described in subparagraph f) of paragraph 6 and has made the reservation described in subparagraph a) of paragraph 6, such notification shall also include the list of its Covered Tax Agreements which contain a provision described in paragraph 5, as well as the article and paragraph number of each such provision. Where all Contracting Jurisdictions have made a notification with respect to a provision of a Covered Tax Agreement under this paragraph or paragraph 7, that provision shall be replaced by the provisions of paragraph 4. In other cases, paragraph 4 shall supersede the provisions of the Covered Tax Agreement only to the extent that those provisions are incompatible with paragraph 4.

Article 10
Anti-abuse Rule for Permanent Establishments Situated in Third Jurisdictions.

1. Where:

a) an enterprise of a Contracting Jurisdiction to a Covered Tax Agreement derives income from the other Contracting Jurisdiction and the first-mentioned Contracting Jurisdiction treats such income as attributable to a permanent establishment of the enterprise situated in a third jurisdiction; and

b) the profits attributable to that permanent establishment are exempt from tax in the first-mentioned Contracting Jurisdiction,

the benefits of the Covered Tax Agreement shall not apply to any item of income on which the tax in the third jurisdiction is less than 60 per cent of the tax that would be imposed in the first-mentioned Contracting Jurisdiction on that item of income if that permanent establishment were situated in the first-mentioned Contracting Jurisdiction. In such a case, any income to which the provisions of this paragraph apply shall remain taxable according to the domestic law of the other Contracting Jurisdiction, notwithstanding any other provisions of the Covered Tax Agreement.

2. Paragraph 1 shall not apply if the income derived from the other Contracting Jurisdiction described in paragraph 1 is derived in connection with or is incidental to the active conduct of a business carried on through the permanent establishment (other than the business of making, managing or simply holding investments for the enterprise's own account, unless these activities are banking, insurance or securities activities carried on by a bank, insurance enterprise or registered securities dealer, respectively).

3. If benefits under a Covered Tax Agreement are denied pursuant to paragraph 1 with respect to an item of income derived by a resident of a Contracting Jurisdiction, the competent authority of the other Contracting Jurisdiction may, nevertheless, grant these benefits with respect to that item of income if, in response to a request by such resident, such competent authority determines that granting such benefits is justified in light of the reasons such resident did not satisfy the requirements of paragraphs 1 and 2. The competent authority of the Contracting Jurisdiction to which a request has been made under the preceding sentence by a resident of the other Contracting Jurisdiction shall consult with the competent authority of that other Contracting Jurisdiction before either granting or denying the request.

4. Paragraphs 1 through 3 shall apply in place of or in the absence of provisions of a Covered Tax Agreement that deny or limit benefits that would otherwise be granted to an enterprise of a Contracting Jurisdiction which derives income from the other Contracting Jurisdiction that is attributable to a permanent establishment of the enterprise situated in a third jurisdiction.

5. A Party may reserve the right:

a) for the entirety of this Article not to apply to its Covered Tax Agreements;

b) for the entirety of this Article not to apply to its Covered Tax Agreements that already contain the provisions described in paragraph 4;

c) for this Article to apply only to its Covered Tax Agreements that already contain the provisions described in paragraph 4.

6. Each Party that has not made the reservation described in subparagraph a) or b) of paragraph 5 shall notify the Depositary of whether each of its Covered Tax Agreements contains a provision described in paragraph 4, and if so, the article and paragraph number of each such provision. Where all Contracting Jurisdictions have made such a notification with respect to a provision of a Covered Tax Agreement, that provision shall be replaced by the provisions of paragraphs 1 through 3. In other cases, paragraphs 1 through 3 shall supersede the provisions of the Covered Tax Agreement only to the extent that those provisions are incompatible with those paragraphs.

Article 11

Application of Tax Agreements to Restrict a Party's Right to Tax its Own Residents.

1. A Covered Tax Agreement shall not affect the taxation by a Contracting Jurisdiction of its residents, except with respect to the benefits granted under provisions of the Covered Tax Agreement:

a) which require that Contracting Jurisdiction to grant to an enterprise of that Contracting Jurisdiction a correlative or corresponding adjustment following an initial adjustment made by the other Contracting Jurisdiction, in accordance with the Covered Tax Agreement, to the amount of tax charged in the first-mentioned Contracting Jurisdiction on the profits of a permanent establishment of the enterprise or the profits of an associated enterprise;

b) which may affect how that Contracting Jurisdiction taxes an individual who is a resident of that Contracting Jurisdiction if that individual derives income in respect of services rendered to the other Contracting Jurisdiction or a political subdivision or local authority or other comparable body thereof;

c) which may affect how that Contracting Jurisdiction taxes an individual who is a resident of that Contracting Jurisdiction if that individual is also a student, business apprentice or trainee, or a teacher, professor, lecturer, instructor, researcher or research scholar who meets the conditions of the Covered Tax Agreement;

d) which require that Contracting Jurisdiction to provide a tax credit or tax exemption to residents of that Contracting Jurisdiction with respect to the income that the other Contracting Jurisdiction may tax in accordance with the Covered Tax Agreement (including profits that are attributable to a permanent establishment situated in that other Contracting Jurisdiction in accordance with the Covered Tax Agreement);

e) which protect residents of that Contracting Jurisdiction against certain discriminatory taxation practices by that Contracting Jurisdiction;

f) which allow residents of that Contracting Jurisdiction to request that the competent authority of that or either Contracting Jurisdiction consider cases of taxation not in accordance with the Covered Tax Agreement;

g) which may affect how that Contracting Jurisdiction taxes an individual who is a resident of that Contracting Jurisdiction when that individual is a member of a diplomatic mission, government mission or consular post of the other Contracting Jurisdiction;

h) which provide that pensions or other payments made under the social security legislation of the other Contracting Jurisdiction shall be taxable only in that other Contracting Jurisdiction;

i) which provide that pensions and similar payments, annuities, alimony payments or other maintenance payments arising in the other Contracting Jurisdiction shall be taxable only in that other Contracting Jurisdiction; or

j) which otherwise expressly limit a Contracting Jurisdiction's right to tax its own residents or provide expressly that the Contracting Jurisdiction in which an item of income arises has the exclusive right to tax that item of income.

2. Paragraph 1 shall apply in place of or in the absence of provisions of a Covered Tax Agreement stating that the Covered Tax Agreement would not affect the taxation by a Contracting Jurisdiction of its residents.

3. A Party may reserve the right:

a) for the entirety of this Article not to apply to its Covered Tax Agreements;

b) for the entirety of this Article not to apply to its Covered Tax Agreements that already contain the provisions described in paragraph 2.

4. Each Party that has not made the reservation described in subparagraph a) or b) of paragraph 3 shall notify the Depositary of whether each of its Covered Tax Agreements contains a provision described in paragraph 2, and if so, the article and paragraph number of each such provision. Where all Contracting Jurisdictions have made such a notification with respect to a provision of a Covered Tax Agreement, that provision shall be replaced by the provisions of paragraph 1. In other cases, paragraph 1 shall supersede the provisions of the Covered Tax Agreement only to the extent that those provisions are incompatible with paragraph 1.

Part IV
Avoidance of Permanent Establishment Status.

Article 12
Artificial Avoidance of Permanent Establishment Status through Commissionnaire Arrangements and Similar Strategies

1. Notwithstanding the provisions of a Covered Tax Agreement that define the term "permanent establishment", but subject to paragraph 2, where a person is acting in a Contracting Jurisdiction to a Covered Tax Agreement on behalf of an enterprise and, in doing so, habitually concludes contracts, or habitually plays the principal role leading to the conclusion of contracts that are routinely concluded without material modification by the enterprise, and these contracts are:

a) in the name of the enterprise; or

b) for the transfer of the ownership of, or for the granting of the right to use, property owned by that enterprise or that the enterprise has the right to use; or

c) for the provision of services by that enterprise,

that enterprise shall be deemed to have a permanent establishment in that Contracting Jurisdiction in respect of any activities which that person undertakes for the enterprise unless these activities, if they were exercised by the enterprise through a fixed place of business of that enterprise situated in that Contracting Jurisdiction, would not cause that fixed place of business to be deemed to constitute a permanent establishment under the definition of permanent establishment included in the Covered Tax Agreement (as it may be modified by this Convention).

2. Paragraph 1 shall not apply where the person acting in a Contracting Jurisdiction to a Covered Tax Agreement on behalf of an enterprise of the other Contracting Jurisdiction carries on business in the first-mentioned Contracting Jurisdiction as an independent agent and acts for the enterprise in the ordinary course of that business. Where, however, a person acts exclusively or almost exclusively on behalf of one or more enterprises to which it is closely related, that person shall not be considered to be an independent agent within the meaning of this paragraph with respect to any such enterprise.

3.

a) Paragraph 1 shall apply in place of provisions of a Covered Tax Agreement that describe the conditions under which an enterprise shall be deemed to have a permanent establishment in a Contracting Jurisdiction (or a person shall be deemed to be a permanent establishment in a Contracting Jurisdiction) in respect of an activity which a person other than an agent of an independent status undertakes for the enterprise, but only to the extent that such provisions address the situation in which such person has, and habitually exercises, in that Contracting Jurisdiction an authority to conclude contracts in the name of the enterprise.

b) Paragraph 2 shall apply in place of provisions of a Covered Tax Agreement that provide that an enterprise shall not be deemed to have a permanent establishment in a Contracting Jurisdiction in respect of an activity which an agent of an independent status undertakes for the enterprise.

4. A Party may reserve the right for the entirety of this Article not to apply to its Covered Tax Agreements.

5. Each Party that has not made a reservation described in paragraph 4 shall notify the Depositary of whether each of its Covered Tax Agreements contains a provision described in subparagraph a) of paragraph 3, as well as the article and paragraph number of each such provision. Paragraph 1 shall apply with respect to a provision of a Covered Tax Agreement only where all Contracting Jurisdictions have made a notification with respect to that provision.

6. Each Party that has not made a reservation described in paragraph 4 shall notify the Depositary of whether each of its Covered Tax Agreements contains a provision described in subparagraph b) of paragraph 3, as well as the article and paragraph number of each such provision. Paragraph 2 shall apply with respect to a provision of a Covered Tax Agreement only where all Contracting Jurisdictions have made such a notification with respect to that provision.

Article 13
Artificial Avoidance of Permanent Establishment Status through the Specific Activity Exemptions.

1. A Party may choose to apply paragraph 2 (Option A) or paragraph 3 (Option B) or to apply neither Option.

2. Option A. Notwithstanding the provisions of a Covered Tax Agreement that define the term "permanent establishment", the term "permanent establishment" shall be deemed not to include:

a) the activities specifically listed in the Covered Tax Agreement (prior to modification by this Convention) as activities deemed not to constitute a permanent establishment, whether or not that exception from permanent establishment status is contingent on the activity being of a preparatory or auxiliary character;

b) the maintenance of a fixed place of business solely for the purpose of carrying on, for the enterprise, any activity not described in subparagraph a);

c) the maintenance of a fixed place of business solely for any combination of activities mentioned in subparagraphs a) and b),

provided that such activity or, in the case of subparagraph c), the overall activity of the fixed place of business, is of a preparatory or auxiliary character.

3. Option B. Notwithstanding the provisions of a Covered Tax Agreement that define the term "permanent establishment", the term "permanent establishment" shall be deemed not to include:

a) the activities specifically listed in the Covered Tax Agreement (prior to modification by this Convention) as activities deemed not to constitute a permanent establishment, whether or not that exception from permanent establishment status is contingent on the activity being of a preparatory or auxiliary character, except to the extent that the relevant provision of the Covered Tax Agreement provides explicitly that a specific activity shall be deemed not to constitute a permanent establishment provided that the activity is of a preparatory or auxiliary character;

b) the maintenance of a fixed place of business solely for the purpose of carrying on, for the enterprise, any activity not described in subparagraph a), provided that this activity is of a preparatory or auxiliary character;

c) the maintenance of a fixed place of business solely for any combination of activities mentioned in subparagraphs a) and b), provided that the overall activity of the fixed place of business resulting from this combination is of a preparatory or auxiliary character.

4. A provision of a Covered Tax Agreement (as it may be modified by paragraph 2 or 3) that lists specific activities deemed not to constitute a permanent establishment shall not apply to a fixed place of business that is used or maintained by an enterprise if the same enterprise or a closely related enterprise carries on business activities at the same place or at another place in the same Contracting Jurisdiction and:

a) that place or other place constitutes a permanent establishment for the enterprise or the closely related enterprise under the provisions of a Covered Tax Agreement defining a permanent establishment; or

b) the overall activity resulting from the combination of the activities carried on by the two enterprises at the same place, or by the same enterprise or closely related enterprises at the two places, is not of a preparatory or auxiliary character,

provided that the business activities carried on by the two enterprises at the same place, or by the same enterprise or closely related enterprises at the two places, constitute complementary functions that are part of a cohesive business operation.

5.

a) Paragraph 2 or 3 shall apply in place of the relevant parts of provisions of a Covered Tax Agreement that list specific activities that are deemed not to constitute a permanent establishment even if the activity is carried on through a fixed place of business (or provisions of a Covered Tax Agreement that operate in a comparable manner).

b) Paragraph 4 shall apply to provisions of a Covered Tax Agreement (as they may be modified by paragraph 2 or 3) that list specific activities that are deemed not to constitute a permanent establishment even if the activity is carried on through a fixed place of business (or provisions of a Covered Tax Agreement that operate in a comparable manner).

6. A Party may reserve the right:

(*a*) for the entirety of this Article not to apply to its Covered Tax Agreements;

(*b*) for paragraph 2 not to apply to its Covered Tax Agreements that explicitly state that a list of specific activities shall be deemed not to constitute a permanent establishment only if each of the activities is of a preparatory or auxiliary character;

(*c*) for paragraph 4 not to apply to its Covered Tax Agreements.

7. Each Party that chooses to apply an Option under paragraph 1 shall notify the Depositary of its choice of Option. Such notification shall also include the list of its Covered Tax Agreements which contain a provision described in subparagraph a) of paragraph 5, as well as the article and paragraph number of each such provision. An Option shall apply with respect to a provision of a Covered Tax Agreement only where all Contracting Jurisdictions have chosen to apply the same Option and have made such a notification with respect to that provision.

8. Each Party that has not made a reservation described in subparagraph a) or c) of paragraph 6 and does not choose to apply an Option under paragraph 1 shall notify the Depositary of whether each of its Covered Tax Agreements contains a provision described in subparagraph b) of paragraph 5, as well as the article and paragraph number of each such provision. Paragraph 4 shall apply with respect to a provision of a Covered Tax Agreement only where all Contracting Jurisdictions have made a notification with respect to that provision under this paragraph or paragraph 7.

Article 14

Splitting-up of Contracts.

1. For the sole purpose of determining whether the period (or periods) referred to in a provision of a Covered Tax Agreement that stipulates a period (or periods) of time after which specific projects or activities shall constitute a permanent establishment has been exceeded:

(*a*) where an enterprise of a Contracting Jurisdiction carries on activities in the other Contracting Jurisdiction at a place that constitutes a building site, construction project, installation project or other specific project identified in the relevant provision of the Covered Tax Agreement, or carries on supervisory or consultancy activities in connection with such a place, in the case of a provision of a Covered Tax Agreement that refers to such activities, and these activities are carried on during one or more periods of time that, in the aggregate, exceed 30 days without exceeding the period or periods referred to in the relevant provision of the Covered Tax Agreement; and

(*b*) where connected activities are carried on in that other Contracting Jurisdiction at (or, where the relevant provision of the Covered Tax Agreement applies to supervisory or consultancy activities, in connection with) the same building site, construction or installation project, or other place identified in the relevant provision of the Covered Tax Agreement during different periods of time, each exceeding 30 days, by one or more enterprises closely related to the first-mentioned enterprise,

these different periods of time shall be added to the aggregate period of time during which the first-mentioned enterprise has carried on activities at that building site, construction or installation project, or other place identified in the relevant provision of the Covered Tax Agreement.

2. Paragraph 1 shall apply in place of or in the absence of provisions of a Covered Tax Agreement to the extent that such provisions address the division of contracts into multiple parts to avoid the application of a time period or periods in relation to the existence of a permanent establishment for specific projects or activities described in paragraph 1.

3. A Party may reserve the right:

a) for the entirety of this Article not to apply to its Covered Tax Agreements;

b) for the entirety of this Article not to apply with respect to provisions of its Covered Tax Agreements relating to the exploration for or exploitation of natural resources.

4. Each Party that has not made a reservation described in subparagraph a) of paragraph 3 shall notify the Depositary of whether each of its Covered Tax Agreements contains a provision described in paragraph 2 that is not subject to a reservation under subparagraph b) of paragraph 3, and if so, the article and paragraph number of each such provision. Where all Contracting Jurisdictions have made such a notification with respect to a provision of a Covered Tax Agreement, that provision shall be replaced by the provisions of paragraph 1 to the extent provided in paragraph 2. In other cases, paragraph 1 shall supersede the provisions of the Covered Tax Agreement only to the extent that those provisions are incompatible with paragraph 1.

Article 15

Definition of a Person Closely Related to an Enterprise.

1. For the purposes of the provisions of a Covered Tax Agreement that are modified by paragraph 2 of Article 12 (Artificial Avoidance of Permanent Establishment Status through Commissionnaire Arrangements and Similar Strategies), paragraph 4 of Article 13 (Artificial Avoidance of Permanent Establishment Status through the Specific Activity Exemptions), or paragraph 1 of Article 14 (Splitting-up of Contracts), a person is closely related to an enterprise if, based on all the relevant facts and circumstances, one has control of the other or both are under the control of the same persons or enterprises. In any case, a person shall be considered to be closely related to an enterprise if one possesses directly or indirectly more than 50 per cent of the beneficial interest in the other (or, in the case of a company, more than 50 per cent of the aggregate vote and value of the company's shares or of the beneficial equity interest in the company) or if another person possesses directly or indirectly more than 50 per cent of the beneficial interest (or, in the case of a company, more than 50 per cent of the aggregate vote and value of the company's shares or of the beneficial equity interest in the company) in the person and the enterprise.

2. A Party that has made the reservations described in paragraph 4 of Article 12 (Artificial Avoidance of Permanent Establishment Status through Commissionnaire Arrangements and Similar Strategies), subparagraph a) or c) of paragraph 6 of Article 13 (Artificial Avoidance of Permanent Establishment Status through the Specific Activity Exemptions), and subparagraph a) of paragraph 3 of Article 14 (Splitting-up of Contracts) may reserve the right for the entirety of this Article not to apply to the Covered Tax Agreements to which those reservations apply.

Part V

Improving Dispute Resolution.

Article 16

Mutual Agreement Procedure

1. Where a person considers that the actions of one or both of the Contracting Jurisdictions result or will result for that person in taxation not in accordance with the provisions of the Covered Tax Agreement, that person may, irrespective of the remedies provided by the domestic law of those Contracting Jurisdictions, present the case to the competent authority of either Contracting Jurisdiction. The case must be presented within three years from the first notification of the action resulting in taxation not in accordance with the provisions of the Covered Tax Agreement.

2. The competent authority shall endeavour, if the objection appears to it to be justified and if it is not itself able to arrive at a satisfactory solution, to resolve the case by mutual agreement with the competent authority of the other Contracting Jurisdiction, with a view to the avoidance of taxation which is not in accordance with the Covered Tax Agreement. Any agreement reached shall be implemented notwithstanding any time limits in the domestic law of the Contracting Jurisdictions.

3. The competent authorities of the Contracting Jurisdictions shall endeavour to resolve by mutual agreement any difficulties or doubts arising as to the interpretation or application of the Covered Tax Agreement. They may also consult together for the elimination of double taxation in cases not provided for in the Covered Tax Agreement.

4.

a) i) The first sentence of paragraph 1 shall apply in place of or in the absence of provisions of a Covered Tax Agreement (or parts thereof) that provide that where a person considers that the actions of one or both of the Contracting Jurisdictions result or will result for that person in taxation not in accordance with the provisions of the Covered Tax Agreement, that person may, irrespective of the remedies provided by the domestic law of those Contracting Jurisdictions, present the case to the competent authority of the Contracting Jurisdiction of which that person is a resident including provisions under which, if the case presented by that person comes under the provisions of a Covered Tax Agreement relating to non-discrimination based on nationality, the case may be presented to the competent authority of the Contracting Jurisdiction of which that person is a national.

(ii) The second sentence of paragraph 1 shall apply in place of provisions of a Covered Tax Agreement that provide that a case referred to in the first sentence of paragraph 1 must be presented within a specific time period that is shorter than three years from the first notification of the action resulting in taxation not in accordance with the provisions of the Covered Tax Agreement, or in the absence of a provision of a Covered Tax Agreement describing the time period within which such a case must be presented.

b) i) The first sentence of paragraph 2 shall apply in the absence of provisions of a Covered Tax Agreement that provide that the competent authority that is presented with the case by the person referred to in paragraph 1 shall endeavour, if the objection appears to it to be justified and if it is not itself able to arrive at a satisfactory solution, to resolve the case by mutual agreement with the competent authority of the other Contracting Jurisdiction, with a view to the avoidance of taxation which is not in accordance with the Covered Tax Agreement.

ii) The second sentence of paragraph 2 shall apply in the absence of provisions of a Covered Tax Agreement providing that any agreement reached shall be implemented notwithstanding any time limits in the domestic law of the Contracting Jurisdictions.

c) i) The first sentence of paragraph 3 shall apply in the absence of provisions of a Covered Tax Agreement that provide that the competent authorities of the Contracting Jurisdictions shall endeavour to resolve by mutual agreement any difficulties or doubts arising as to the interpretation or application of the Covered Tax Agreement.

ii) The second sentence of paragraph 3 shall apply in the absence of provisions of a Covered Tax Agreement that provide that the competent authorities of the Contracting Jurisdictions may also consult together for the elimination of double taxation in cases not provided for in the Covered Tax Agreement.

5. A Party may reserve the right:

a) for the first sentence of paragraph 1 not to apply to its Covered Tax Agreements on the basis that it intends to meet the minimum standard for improving dispute resolution under the OECD/G20 BEPS Package by ensuring that under each of its Covered Tax Agreements (other than a Covered Tax Agreement that permits a person to present a case to the competent authority of either Contracting Jurisdiction), where a person considers that the actions of one or both of the Contracting Jurisdictions result or will result for that person in taxation not in accordance with the provisions of the Covered Tax Agreement, irrespective of the remedies provided by the domestic law of those Contracting Jurisdictions, that person may present the case to the competent authority of the Contracting Jurisdiction of which the person is a resident or, if the case presented by that person comes under a provision of a Covered Tax Agreement relating to non-discrimination based on nationality, to that of the Contracting Jurisdiction of which that person is a national; and the competent authority of that Contracting Jurisdiction will implement a bilateral notification or consultation process with the competent authority of the other Contracting Jurisdiction for cases in which the competent authority to which the mutual agreement procedure case was presented does not consider the taxpayer's objection to be justified;

b) for the second sentence of paragraph 1 not to apply to its Covered Tax Agreements that do not provide that the case referred to in the first sentence of paragraph 1 must be presented within a specific time period on the basis that it intends to meet the minimum standard for improving dispute resolution under the OECD/G20 BEPS package by ensuring that for the purposes of all such Covered Tax Agreements the taxpayer referred to in paragraph 1 is allowed to present the case within a period of at least three years from the first notification of the action resulting in taxation not in accordance with the provisions of the Covered Tax Agreement;

c) for the second sentence of paragraph 2 not to apply to its Covered Tax Agreements on the basis that for the purposes of all of its Covered Tax Agreements:

i) any agreement reached via the mutual agreement procedure shall be implemented notwithstanding any time limits in the domestic laws of the Contracting Jurisdictions; or

ii) it intends to meet the minimum standard for improving dispute resolution under the OECD/G20 BEPS package by accepting, in its bilateral treaty negotiations, a treaty provision providing that:

A) the Contracting Jurisdictions shall make no adjustment to the profits that are attributable to a permanent establishment of an enterprise of one of the Contracting Jurisdictions after a period that is mutually agreed between both Contracting Jurisdictions from the end of the taxable year in which the profits would have been attributable to the permanent establishment (this provision shall not apply in the case of fraud, gross negligence or wilful default); and

B) the Contracting Jurisdictions shall not include in the profits of an enterprise, and tax accordingly, profits that would have accrued to the enterprise but that by reason of the conditions referred to in a provision in the Covered Tax Agreement relating to associated enterprises have not so accrued, after a period that is mutually agreed between both Contracting Jurisdictions from the end of the taxable year in which the profits would have accrued to the enterprise (this provision shall not apply in the case of fraud, gross negligence or wilful default).

6.

a) Each Party that has not made a reservation described in subparagraph a) of paragraph 5 shall notify the Depositary of whether each of its Covered Tax Agreements contains a provision described in clause i) of subparagraph a) of paragraph 4, and if so, the article and paragraph number of each such provision. Where all Contracting Jurisdictions have made a notification with respect to a provision of a Covered Tax Agreement, that provision shall be replaced by the first sentence of paragraph 1. In other cases, the first sentence of paragraph 1 shall supersede the provisions of the Covered Tax Agreement only to the extent that those provisions are incompatible with that sentence.

b) Each Party that has not made the reservation described in subparagraph b) of paragraph 5 shall notify the Depositary of:

i) the list of its Covered Tax Agreements which contain a provision that provides that a case referred to in the first sentence of paragraph 1 must be presented within a specific time period that is shorter than three years from the first notification of the action resulting in taxation not in accordance with the provisions of the Covered Tax Agreement, as well as the article and paragraph number of each such provision; a provision of a Covered Tax Agreement shall be replaced by the second sentence of paragraph 1 where all Contracting Jurisdictions have made such a notification with respect to that provision; in other cases, subject to clause ii), the second sentence of paragraph 1 shall supersede the provisions of the Covered Tax Agreement only to the extent that those provisions are incompatible with the second sentence of paragraph 1;

ii) the list of its Covered Tax Agreements which contain a provision that provides that a case referred to in the first sentence of paragraph 1 must be presented within a specific time period that is at least three years from the first notification of the action resulting in taxation not in accordance with the provisions of the Covered Tax Agreement, as well as the article and paragraph number of each such provision; the second sentence of paragraph 1 shall not apply to a Covered Tax Agreement where any Contracting Jurisdiction has made such a notification with respect to that Covered Tax Agreement.

c) Each Party shall notify the Depositary of:

i) the list of its Covered Tax Agreements which do not contain a provision described in clause i) of sub-paragraph b) of paragraph 4; the first sentence of paragraph 2 shall apply to a Covered Tax Agreement only where all Contracting Jurisdictions have made such a notification with respect to that Covered Tax Agreement;

ii) in the case of a Party that has not made the reservation described in subparagraph c) of paragraph 5, the list of its Covered Tax Agreements which do not contain a provision described in clause ii) of subparagraph b) of paragraph 4; the second sentence of paragraph 2 shall apply to a Covered Tax Agreement only where all Contracting Jurisdictions have made such a notification with respect to that Covered Tax Agreement.

d) Each Party shall notify the Depositary of:

i) the list of its Covered Tax Agreements which do not contain a provision described in clause i) of subparagraph c) of paragraph 4; the first sentence of paragraph 3 shall apply to a Covered Tax Agreement only where all Contracting Jurisdictions have made such a notification with respect to that Covered Tax Agreement;

ii) the list of its Covered Tax Agreements which do not contain a provision described in clause ii) of subparagraph c) of paragraph 4; the second sentence of paragraph 3 shall apply to a Covered Tax Agreement only where all Contracting Jurisdictions have made such a notification with respect to that Covered Tax Agreement.

Article 17

Corresponding Adjustments

1. Where a Contracting Jurisdiction includes in the profits of an enterprise of that Contracting Jurisdiction — and taxes accordingly — profits on which an enterprise of the other Contracting Jurisdiction has been charged to tax in that other Contracting Jurisdiction and the profits so included are profits which would have accrued to the enterprise of the first-mentioned Contracting Jurisdiction if the conditions made between the two enterprises had been those which would have been made between independent enterprises, then that other Contracting Jurisdiction shall make an appropriate adjustment to the amount of the tax charged therein on those profits. In determining such adjustment, due regard shall be had to the other provisions of the Covered Tax Agreement and the competent authorities of the Contracting Jurisdictions shall if necessary consult each other.

2. Paragraph 1 shall apply in place of or in the absence of a provision that requires a Contracting Jurisdiction to make an appropriate adjustment to the amount of the tax charged therein on the profits of an enterprise of that Contracting Jurisdiction where the other Contracting Jurisdiction includes those profits in the profits of an enterprise of that other Contracting Jurisdiction and taxes those profits accordingly, and the profits so included are profits which would have accrued to the enterprise of that other Contracting Jurisdiction if the conditions made between the two enterprises had been those which would have been made between independent enterprises.

3. A Party may reserve the right:

a) for the entirety of this Article not to apply to its Covered Tax Agreements that already contain a provision described in paragraph 2;

b) for the entirety of this Article not to apply to its Covered Tax Agreements on the basis that in the absence of a provision referred to in paragraph 2 in its Covered Tax Agreement:

i) it shall make the appropriate adjustment referred to in paragraph 1; or

ii) its competent authority shall endeavour to resolve the case under the provisions of a Covered Tax Agreement relating to mutual agreement procedure;

c) in the case of a Party that has made a reservation under clause ii) of subparagraph c) of paragraph 5 of Article 16 (Mutual Agreement Procedure), for the entirety of this Article not to apply to its Covered Tax Agreements on the basis that in its bilateral treaty negotiations it shall accept a treaty provision of the type contained in paragraph 1, provided that the Contracting Jurisdictions were able to reach agreement on that provision and on the provisions described in clause ii) of subparagraph c) of paragraph 5 of Article 16 (Mutual Agreement Procedure).

4. Each Party that has not made a reservation described in paragraph 3 shall notify the Depositary of whether each of its Covered Tax Agreements contains a provision described in paragraph 2, and if so, the article and paragraph number of each such provision. Where all Contracting Jurisdictions have made such a notification with respect to a provision of a Covered Tax Agreement, that provision shall be replaced by the provisions of paragraph 1. In other cases, paragraph 1 shall supersede the provisions of the Covered Tax Agreement only to the extent that those provisions are incompatible with paragraph 1.

Part VI
Arbitration.

Article 18
Choice to Apply Part VI

A Party may choose to apply this Part with respect to its Covered Tax Agreements and shall notify the Depositary accordingly. This Part shall apply in relation to two Contracting Jurisdictions with respect to a Covered Tax Agreement only where both Contracting Jurisdictions have made such a notification.

Article 19
Mandatory Binding Arbitration

1. Where:

a) under a provision of a Covered Tax Agreement (as it may be modified by paragraph 1 of Article 16 (Mutual Agreement Procedure)) that provides that a person may present a case to a competent authority of a Contracting Jurisdiction where that person considers that the actions of one or both of the Contracting Jurisdictions result or will result for that person in taxation not in accordance with the provisions of the Covered Tax Agreement (as it may be modified by the Convention), a person has presented a case to the competent authority of a Contracting Jurisdiction on the basis that the actions of one or both of the Contracting Jurisdictions have resulted for that person in taxation not in accordance with the provisions of the Covered Tax Agreement (as it may be modified by the Convention); and

b) the competent authorities are unable to reach an agreement to resolve that case pursuant to a provision of a Covered Tax Agreement (as it may be modified by paragraph 2 of Article 16 (Mutual Agreement Procedure)) that provides that the competent authority shall endeavour to resolve the case by mutual agreement with the competent authority of the other Contracting Jurisdiction, within a period of two years beginning on the start date referred to in paragraph 8 or 9, as the case may be (unless, prior to the expiration of that period the competent authorities of the Contracting Jurisdictions have agreed to a different time period with respect to that case and have notified the person who presented the case of such agreement),

any unresolved issues arising from the case shall, if the person so requests in writing, be submitted to arbitration in the manner described in this Part, according to any rules or procedures agreed upon by the competent authorities of the Contracting Jurisdictions pursuant to the provisions of paragraph 10.

2. Where a competent authority has suspended the mutual agreement procedure referred to in paragraph 1 because a case with respect to one or more of the same issues is pending before court or administrative tribunal, the period provided in subparagraph b) of paragraph 1 will stop running until either a final decision has been rendered by the court or administrative tribunal or the case has been suspended or withdrawn. In addition, where a person who presented a case and a competent authority have agreed to suspend the mutual agreement procedure, the period provided in subparagraph b) of paragraph 1 will stop running until the suspension has been lifted.

3. Where both competent authorities agree that a person directly affected by the case has failed to provide in a timely manner any additional material information requested by either competent authority after the start of the period provided in subparagraph b) of paragraph 1, the period provided in subparagraph b) of paragraph 1 shall be extended for an amount of time equal to the period beginning on the date by which the information was requested and ending on the date on which that information was provided.

4.

a) The arbitration decision with respect to the issues submitted to arbitration shall be implemented through the mutual agreement concerning the case referred to in paragraph 1. The arbitration decision shall be final.

b) The arbitration decision shall be binding on both Contracting Jurisdictions except in the following cases:

Treaties and Related Legislation

i) if a person directly affected by the case does not accept the mutual agreement that implements the arbitration decision. In such a case, the case shall not be eligible for any further consideration by the competent authorities. The mutual agreement that implements the arbitration decision on the case shall be considered not to be accepted by a person directly affected by the case if any person directly affected by the case does not, within 60 days after the date on which notification of the mutual agreement is sent to the person, withdraw all issues resolved in the mutual agreement implementing the arbitration decision from consideration by any court or administrative tribunal or otherwise terminate any pending court or administrative proceedings with respect to such issues in a manner consistent with that mutual agreement.

ii) if a final decision of the courts of one of the Contracting Jurisdictions holds that the arbitration decision is invalid. In such a case, the request for arbitration under paragraph 1 shall be considered not to have been made, and the arbitration process shall be considered not to have taken place (except for the purposes of Articles 21 (Confidentiality of Arbitration Proceedings) and 25 (Costs of Arbitration Proceedings)). In such a case, a new request for arbitration may be made unless the competent authorities agree that such a new request should not be permitted.

iii) if a person directly affected by the case pursues litigation on the issues which were resolved in the mutual agreement implementing the arbitration decision in any court or administrative tribunal.

5. The competent authority that received the initial request for a mutual agreement procedure as described in subparagraph a) of paragraph 1 shall, within two calendar months of receiving the request:

a) send a notification to the person who presented the case that it has received the request; and

b) send a notification of that request, along with a copy of the request, to the competent authority of the other Contracting Jurisdiction.

6. Within three calendar months after a competent authority receives the request for a mutual agreement procedure (or a copy thereof from the competent authority of the other Contracting Jurisdiction) it shall either:

a) notify the person who has presented the case and the other competent authority that it has received the information necessary to undertake substantive consideration of the case; or

b) request additional information from that person for that purpose.

7. Where pursuant to subparagraph b) of paragraph 6, one or both of the competent authorities have requested from the person who presented the case additional information necessary to undertake substantive consideration of the case, the competent authority that requested the additional information shall, within three calendar months of receiving the additional information from that person, notify that person and the other competent authority either:

a) that it has received the requested information; or

b) that some of the requested information is still missing.

8. Where neither competent authority has requested additional information pursuant to subparagraph b) of paragraph 6, the start date referred to in paragraph 1 shall be the earlier of:

a) the date on which both competent authorities have notified the person who presented the case pursuant to subparagraph a) of paragraph 6; and

b) the date that is three calendar months after the notification to the competent authority of the other Contracting Jurisdiction pursuant to subparagraph b) of paragraph 5.

9. Where additional information has been requested pursuant to subparagraph b) of paragraph 6, the start date referred to in paragraph 1 shall be the earlier of:

a) the latest date on which the competent authorities that requested additional information have notified the person who presented the case and the other competent authority pursuant to subparagraph a) of paragraph 7; and

b) the date that is three calendar months after both competent authorities have received all information requested by either competent authority from the person who presented the case.

If, however, one or both of the competent authorities send the notification referred to in subparagraph b) of paragraph 7, such notification shall be treated as a request for additional information under subparagraph b) of paragraph 6.

10. The competent authorities of the Contracting Jurisdictions shall by mutual agreement (pursuant to the article of the relevant Covered Tax Agreement regarding procedures for mutual agreement) settle the mode of application of the provisions contained in this Part, including the minimum information necessary for each competent authority to undertake substantive consideration of the case. Such an agreement shall be concluded before the date on which unresolved issues in a case are first eligible to be submitted to arbitration and may be modified from time to time thereafter.

11. For purposes of applying this Article to its Covered Tax Agreements, a Party may reserve the right to replace the two-year period set forth in subparagraph b) of paragraph 1 with a three-year period.

12. A Party may reserve the right for the following rules to apply with respect to its Covered Tax Agreements notwithstanding the other provisions of this Article:

a) any unresolved issue arising from a mutual agreement procedure case otherwise within the scope of the arbitration process provided for by this Convention shall not be submitted to arbitration, if a decision on this issue has already been rendered by a court or administrative tribunal of either Contracting Jurisdiction;

b) if, at any time after a request for arbitration has been made and before the arbitration panel has delivered its decision to the competent authorities of the Contracting Jurisdictions, a decision concerning the issue is rendered by a court or administrative tribunal of one of the Contracting Jurisdictions, the arbitration process shall terminate.

Article 20

Appointment of Arbitrators

1. Except to the extent that the competent authorities of the Contracting Jurisdictions mutually agree on different rules, paragraphs 2 through 4 shall apply for the purposes of this Part.

2. The following rules shall govern the appointment of the members of an arbitration panel:

a) The arbitration panel shall consist of three individual members with expertise or experience in international tax matters.

b) Each competent authority shall appoint one panel member within 60 days of the date of the request for arbitration under paragraph 1 of Article 19 (Mandatory Binding Arbitration). The two panel members so appointed shall, within 60 days of the latter of their appointments, appoint a third member who shall serve as Chair of the arbitration panel. The Chair shall not be a national or resident of either Contracting Jurisdiction.

c) Each member appointed to the arbitration panel must be impartial and independent of the competent authorities, tax administrations, and ministries of finance of the Contracting Jurisdictions and of all persons directly affected by the case (as well as their advisors) at the time of accepting an appointment, maintain his or her impartiality and independence throughout the proceedings, and avoid any conduct for a reasonable period of time thereafter which may damage the appearance of impartiality and independence of the arbitrators with respect to the proceedings.

3. In the event that the competent authority of a Contracting Jurisdiction fails to appoint a member of the arbitration panel in the manner and within the time periods specified in paragraph 2 or agreed to by the competent authorities of the Contracting Jurisdictions, a member shall be appointed on behalf of that competent authority by the highest ranking official of the Centre for Tax Policy and Administration of the Organisation for Economic Co-operation and Development that is not a national of either Contracting Jurisdiction.

4. If the two initial members of the arbitration panel fail to appoint the Chair in the manner and within the time periods specified in paragraph 2 or agreed to by the competent authorities of the Contracting Jurisdictions, the Chair shall be appointed by the highest ranking official of the Centre for Tax Policy and Administration of the Organisation for Economic Co-operation and Development that is not a national of either Contracting Jurisdiction.

Article 21

Confidentiality of Arbitration Proceedings.

1. Solely for the purposes of the application of the provisions of this Part and of the provisions of the relevant Covered Tax Agreement and of the domestic laws of the Contracting Jurisdictions related to the exchange of information, confidentiality, and administrative assistance, members of the arbitration panel and a maximum of three staff per member (and prospective arbitrators solely to the extent necessary to verify their ability to fulfil the requirements of arbitrators) shall be considered to be persons or authorities to whom information may be disclosed. Information received by the arbitration panel or prospective arbitrators and information that the competent authorities receive from the arbitration panel shall be considered information that is exchanged under the provisions of the Covered Tax Agreement related to the exchange of information and administrative assistance.

2. The competent authorities of the Contracting Jurisdictions shall ensure that members of the arbitration panel and their staff agree in writing, prior to their acting in an arbitration proceeding, to treat any information relating to the arbitration proceeding consistently with the confidentiality and nondisclosure obligations described in the provisions of the Covered Tax Agreement related to exchange of information and administrative assistance and under the applicable laws of the Contracting Jurisdictions.

Article 22

Resolution of a Case Prior to the Conclusion of the Arbitration

. For the purposes of this Part and the provisions of the relevant Covered Tax Agreement that provide for resolution of cases through mutual agreement, the mutual agreement procedure, as well as the arbitration proceeding, with respect to a case shall terminate if, at any time after a request for arbitration has been made and before the arbitration panel has delivered its decision to the competent authorities of the Contracting Jurisdictions:

a) the competent authorities of the Contracting Jurisdictions reach a mutual agreement to resolve the case; or

b) the person who presented the case withdraws the request for arbitration or the request for a mutual agreement procedure.

Article 23

Type of Arbitration Process

1. Except to the extent that the competent authorities of the Contracting Jurisdictions mutually agree on different rules, the following rules shall apply with respect to an arbitration proceeding pursuant to this Part:

a) After a case is submitted to arbitration, the competent authority of each Contracting Jurisdiction shall submit to the arbitration panel, by a date set by agreement, a proposed resolution which addresses all unresolved issue(s) in the case (taking into account all agreements previously reached in that case between the competent authorities of the Contracting Jurisdictions). The proposed resolution shall be limited to a disposition of specific monetary amounts (for example, of income or expense) or, where specified, the maximum rate of tax charged pursuant to the Covered Tax Agreement, for each adjustment or similar issue in the case. In a case in which the competent authorities of the Contracting Jurisdictions have been unable to reach agreement on an issue regarding the conditions for application of a provision of the relevant Covered Tax Agreement (hereinafter referred to as a "threshold question"), such as whether an individual is a resident or whether a permanent establishment exists, the competent authorities may submit alternative proposed resolutions with respect to issues the determination of which is contingent on resolution of such threshold questions.

b) The competent authority of each Contracting Jurisdiction may also submit a supporting position paper for consideration by the arbitration panel. Each competent authority that submits a proposed resolution or supporting position paper shall provide a copy to the other competent authority by the date on which the proposed resolution and supporting position paper were due. Each competent authority may also submit to the arbitration panel, by a date set by agreement, a reply submission with respect to the proposed resolution and supporting position paper submitted by the other competent authority. A copy of any reply submission shall be provided to the other competent authority by the date on which the reply submission was due.

c) The arbitration panel shall select as its decision one of the proposed resolutions for the case submitted by the competent authorities with respect to each issue and any threshold questions, and shall not include a rationale or any other explanation of the decision. The arbitration decision will be adopted by a simple majority of the panel members. The arbitration panel shall deliver its decision in writing to the competent authorities of the Contracting Jurisdictions. The arbitration decision shall have no precedential value.

2. For the purpose of applying this Article with respect to its Covered Tax Agreements, a Party may reserve the right for paragraph 1 not to apply to its Covered Tax Agreements. In such a case, except to the extent that the competent authorities of the Contracting Jurisdictions mutually agree on different rules, the following rules shall apply with respect to an arbitration proceeding:

a) After a case is submitted to arbitration, the competent authority of each Contracting Jurisdiction shall provide any information that may be necessary for the arbitration decision to all panel members without undue delay. Unless the competent authorities of the Contracting Jurisdictions agree otherwise, any information that was not available to both competent authorities before the request for arbitration was received by both of them shall not be taken into account for purposes of the decision.

b) The arbitration panel shall decide the issues submitted to arbitration in accordance with the applicable provisions of the Covered Tax Agreement and, subject to these provisions, of those of the domestic laws of the Contracting Jurisdictions. The panel members shall also consider any other sources which the competent authorities of the Contracting Jurisdictions may by mutual agreement expressly identify.

c) The arbitration decision shall be delivered to the competent authorities of the Contracting Jurisdictions in writing and shall indicate the sources of law relied upon and the reasoning which led to its result. The arbitration decision shall be adopted by a simple majority of the panel members. The arbitration decision shall have no precedential value.

3. A Party that has not made the reservation described in paragraph 2 may reserve the right for the preceding paragraphs of this Article not to apply with respect to its Covered Tax Agreements with Parties that have made such a reservation. In such a case, the competent authorities of the Contracting Jurisdictions of each such Covered Tax Agreement shall endeavour to reach agreement on the type of arbitration process that shall apply with respect to that Covered Tax Agreement. Until such an agreement is reached, Article 19 (Mandatory Binding Arbitration) shall not apply with respect to such a Covered Tax Agreement.

4. A Party may also choose to apply paragraph 5 with respect to its Covered Tax Agreements and shall notify the Depositary accordingly. Paragraph 5 shall apply in relation to two Contracting Jurisdictions with respect to a Covered Tax Agreement where either of the Contracting Jurisdictions has made such a notification.

5. Prior to the beginning of arbitration proceedings, the competent authorities of the Contracting Jurisdictions to a Covered Tax Agreement shall ensure that each person that presented the case and their advisors agree in writing not to disclose to any other person any information received during the course of the arbitration proceedings from either competent authority or the arbitration panel. The mutual agreement procedure under the Covered Tax Agreement, as well as the arbitration proceeding under this Part, with respect to the case shall terminate if, at any time after a request for arbitration has been made and before the arbitration panel has delivered its decision to the competent authorities of the Contracting Jurisdictions, a person that presented the case or one of that person's advisors materially breaches that agreement.

6. Notwithstanding paragraph 4, a Party that does not choose to apply paragraph 5 may reserve the right for paragraph 5 not to apply with respect to one or more identified Covered Tax Agreements or with respect to all of its Covered Tax Agreements.

7. A Party that chooses to apply paragraph 5 may reserve the right for this Part not to apply with respect to all

Covered Tax Agreements for which the other Contracting Jurisdiction makes a reservation pursuant to paragraph 6.

Article 24

Agreement on a Different Resolution.

1. For purposes of applying this Part with respect to its Covered Tax Agreements, a Party may choose to apply paragraph 2 and shall notify the Depositary accordingly. Paragraph 2 shall apply in relation to two Contracting Jurisdictions with respect to a Covered Tax Agreement only where both Contracting Jurisdictions have made such a notification.

2. Notwithstanding paragraph 4 of Article 19 (Mandatory Binding Arbitration), an arbitration decision pursuant to this Part shall not be binding on the Contracting Jurisdictions to a Covered Tax Agreement and shall not be implemented if the competent authorities of the Contracting Jurisdictions agree on a different resolution of all unresolved issues within three calendar months after the arbitration decision has been delivered to them.

3. A Party that chooses to apply paragraph 2 may reserve the right for paragraph 2 to apply only with respect to its Covered Tax Agreements for which paragraph 2 of Article 23 (Type of Arbitration Process) applies.

Article 25

Costs of Arbitration Proceedings

. In an arbitration proceeding under this Part, the fees and expenses of the members of the arbitration panel, as well as any costs incurred in connection with the arbitration proceedings by the Contracting Jurisdictions, shall be borne by the Contracting Jurisdictions in a manner to be settled by mutual agreement between the competent authorities of the Contracting Jurisdictions. In the absence of such agreement, each Contracting Jurisdiction shall bear its own expenses and those of its appointed panel member. The cost of the chair of the arbitration panel and other expenses associated with the conduct of the arbitration proceedings shall be borne by the Contracting Jurisdictions in equal shares.

Article 26

Compatibility

1. Subject to Article 18 (Choice to Apply Part VI), the provisions of this Part shall apply in place of or in the absence of provisions of a Covered Tax Agreement that provide for arbitration of unresolved issues arising from a mutual agreement procedure case. Each Party that chooses to apply this Part shall notify the Depositary of whether each of its Covered Tax Agreements, other than those that are within the scope of a reservation under paragraph 4, contains such a provision, and if so, the article and paragraph number of each such provision. Where two Contracting Jurisdictions have made a notification with respect to a provision of a Covered Tax Agreement, that provision shall be replaced by the provisions of this Part as between those Contracting Jurisdictions.

2. Any unresolved issue arising from a mutual agreement procedure case otherwise within the scope of the arbitration process provided for in this Part shall not be submitted to arbitration if the issue falls within the scope of a case with respect to which an arbitration panel or similar body has previously been set up in accordance with a bilateral or multilateral convention that provides for mandatory binding arbitration of unresolved issues arising from a mutual agreement procedure case.

3. Subject to paragraph 1, nothing in this Part shall affect the fulfilment of wider obligations with respect to the arbitration of unresolved issues arising in the context of a mutual agreement procedure resulting from other conventions to which the Contracting Jurisdictions are or will become parties.

4. A Party may reserve the right for this Part not to apply with respect to one or more identified Covered Tax Agreements (or to all of its Covered Tax Agreements) that already provide for mandatory binding arbitration of unresolved issues arising from a mutual agreement procedure case.

Part VII

Final Provisions.

Article 27

Signature and Ratification, Acceptance or Approval

1. As of 31 December 2016, this Convention shall be open for signature by:

a) all States;

b) Guernsey (the United Kingdom of Great Britain and Northern Ireland); Isle of Man (the United Kingdom of Great Britain and Northern Ireland); Jersey (the United Kingdom of Great Britain and Northern Ireland); and

c) any other jurisdiction authorised to become a Party by means of a decision by consensus of the Parties and Signatories.

2. This Convention is subject to ratification, acceptance or approval.

Article 28

Reservations.

1. Subject to paragraph 2, no reservations may be made to this Convention except those expressly permitted by:

a) Paragraph 5 of Article 3 (Transparent Entities);

b) Paragraph 3 of Article 4 (Dual Resident Entities);

c) Paragraphs 8 and 9 of Article 5 (Application of Methods for Elimination of Double Taxation);

d) Paragraph 4 of Article 6 (Purpose of a Covered Tax Agreement);

e) Paragraphs 15 and 16 of Article 7 (Prevention of Treaty Abuse);

f) Paragraph 3 of Article 8 (Dividend Transfer Transactions);

g) Paragraph 6 of Article 9 (Capital Gains from Alienation of Shares or Interests of Entities Deriving their Value Principally from Immovable Property);

h) Paragraph 5 of Article 10 (Anti-abuse Rule for Permanent Establishments Situated in Third Jurisdictions);

i) Paragraph 3 of Article 11 (Application of Tax Agreements to Restrict a Party's Right to Tax its Own Residents);

j) Paragraph 4 of Article 12 (Artificial Avoidance of Permanent Establishment Status through Commissionnaire Arrangements and Similar Strategies);

k) Paragraph 6 of Article 13 (Artificial Avoidance of Permanent Establishment Status through the Specific Activity Exemptions);

l) Paragraph 3 of Article 14 (Splitting-up of Contracts);

m) Paragraph 2 of Article 15 (Definition of a Person Closely Related to an Enterprise);

n) Paragraph 5 of Article 16 (Mutual Agreement Procedure);

o) Paragraph 3 of Article 17 (Corresponding Adjustments);

p) Paragraphs 11 and 12 of Article 19 (Mandatory Binding Arbitration);

q) Paragraphs 2, 3, 6, and 7 of Article 23 (Type of Arbitration Process);

r) Paragraph 3 of Article 24 (Agreement on a Different Resolution);

s) Paragraph 4 of Article 26 (Compatibility);

t) Paragraphs 6 and 7 of Article 35 (Entry into Effect); and

u) Paragraph 2 of Article 36 (Entry into Effect of Part VI).

2.

a) Notwithstanding paragraph 1, a Party that chooses under Article 18 (Choice to Apply Part VI) to apply Part VI (Arbitration) may formulate one or more reservations with respect to the scope of cases that shall be eligible for arbitration under the provisions of Part VI (Arbitration). For a Party which chooses under Article 18 (Choice to Apply Part VI) to apply Part VI (Arbitration) after it has become a Party to this Convention, reservations pursuant to this subparagraph shall be made at the same time as that Party's notification to the Depositary pursuant to Article 18 (Choice to Apply Part VI).

b) Reservations made under subparagraph a) are subject to acceptance. A reservation made under subparagraph a) shall be considered to have been accepted by a Party if it has not notified the Depositary that it objects to the reservation by the end of a period of twelve calendar months beginning on the date of notification of the reservation by the Depositary or by the date on which it deposits its instrument of ratification, acceptance, or approval, whichever is later. For a Party which chooses under Article 18 (Choice to Apply Part VI) to apply Part VI (Arbitration) after it has become a Party to this Convention, objections to prior reservations made by other Parties pursuant to subparagraph a) can be made at the time of the first-mentioned Party's notification to the Depositary pursuant to Article 18 (Choice to Apply Part VI). Where a Party raises an objection to a reservation made under subparagraph a), the entirety of Part VI (Arbitration) shall not apply as between the objecting Party and the reserving Party.

3. Unless explicitly provided otherwise in the relevant provisions of this Convention, a reservation made in accordance with paragraph 1 or 2 shall:

a) modify for the reserving Party in its relations with another Party the provisions of this Convention to which the reservation relates to the extent of the reservation; and

b) modify those provisions to the same extent for the other Party in its relations with the reserving Party.

4. Reservations applicable to Covered Tax Agreements entered into by or on behalf of a jurisdiction or territory for whose international relations a Party is responsible, where that jurisdiction or territory is not a Party to the Convention pursuant to subparagraph b) or c) of paragraph 1 of Article 27 (Signature and Ratification, Acceptance or Approval), shall be made by the responsible Party and can be different from the reservations made by that Party for its own Covered Tax Agreements.

5. Reservations shall be made at the time of signature or when depositing the instrument of ratification, acceptance or approval, subject to the provisions of paragraphs 2, 6 and 9 of this Article, and paragraph 5 of Article 29 (Notifications). However, for a Party which chooses under Article 18 (Choice to Apply Part VI) to apply Part VI (Arbitration) after it has become a Party to this Convention, reservations described in subparagraphs p), q), r) and s) of paragraph 1 of this Article shall be made at the same time as that Party's notification to the Depositary pursuant to Article 18 (Choice to Apply Part VI).

6. If reservations are made at the time of signature, they shall be confirmed upon deposit of the instrument of ratification, acceptance or approval, unless the document containing the reservations explicitly specifies that it is to be considered definitive, subject to the provisions of paragraphs 2, 5 and 9 of this Article, and paragraph 5 of Article 29 (Notifications).

7. If reservations are not made at the time of signature, a provisional list of expected reservations shall be provided to the Depositary at that time.

8. For reservations made pursuant to each of the following provisions, a list of agreements notified pursuant to clause ii) of subparagraph a) of paragraph 1 of Article 2 (Interpretation of Terms) that are within the scope of the reservation as defined in the relevant provision (and, in the case of a reservation under any of the following provisions other than those listed in subparagraphs c), d) and n), the article and paragraph number of each relevant provision) must be provided when such reservations are made:

a) Subparagraphs b), c), d), e) and g) of paragraph 5 of Article 3 (Transparent Entities);

b) Subparagraphs b), c) and d) of paragraph 3 of Article 4 (Dual Resident Entities);

c) Paragraphs 8 and 9 of Article 5 (Application of Methods for Elimination of Double Taxation);

d) Paragraph 4 of Article 6 (Purpose of a Covered Tax Agreement);

e) Subparagraphs b) and c) of paragraph 15 of Article 7 (Prevention of Treaty Abuse);

f) Clauses i), ii), and iii) of subparagraph b) of paragraph 3 of Article 8 (Dividend Transfer Transactions);

g) Subparagraphs d), e) and f) of paragraph 6 of Article 9 (Capital Gains from Alienation of Shares or Interests of Entities Deriving their Value Principally from Immovable Property);

h) Subparagraphs b) and c) of paragraph 5 of Article 10 (Anti-abuse Rule for Permanent Establishments Situated in Third Jurisdictions);

i) Subparagraph b) of paragraph 3 of Article 11 (Application of Tax Agreements to Restrict a Party's Right to Tax its Own Residents);

j) Subparagraph b) of paragraph 6 of Article 13 (Artificial Avoidance of Permanent Establishment Status through the Specific Activity Exemptions);

k) Subparagraph b) of paragraph 3 of Article 14 (Splittingup of Contracts);

l) Subparagraph b) of paragraph 5 of Article 16 (Mutual Agreement Procedure);

m) Subparagraph a) of paragraph 3 of Article 17 (Corresponding Adjustments);

n) Paragraph 6 of Article 23 (Type of Arbitration Process); and

o) Paragraph 4 of Article 26 (Compatibility).

The reservations described in subparagraphs a) through o) above shall not apply to any Covered Tax Agreement that is not included on the list described in this paragraph.

9. Any Party which has made a reservation in accordance with paragraph 1 or 2 may at any time withdraw it or replace it with a more limited reservation by means of a notification addressed to the Depositary. Such Party shall make any additional notifications pursuant to paragraph 6 of Article 29 (Notifications) which may be required as a result of the withdrawal or replacement of the reservation. Subject to paragraph 7 of Article 35 (Entry into Effect), the withdrawal or replacement shall take effect:

a) with respect to a Covered Tax Agreement solely with States or jurisdictions that are Parties to the Convention when the notification of withdrawal or replacement of the reservation is received by the Depositary:

i) for reservations in respect of provisions relating to taxes withheld at source, where the event giving rise to such taxes occurs on or after 1 January of the year next following the expiration of a period of six calendar months beginning on the date of the communication by the Depositary of the notification of withdrawal or replacement of the reservation; and

ii) for reservations in respect of all other provisions, for taxes levied with respect to taxable periods beginning on or after 1 January of the year next following the expiration of a period of six calendar months beginning on the date of the communication by the Depositary of the notification of withdrawal or replacement of the reservation; and

b) with respect to a Covered Tax Agreement for which one or more Contracting Jurisdictions becomes a Party to this Convention after the date of receipt by the Depositary of the notification of withdrawal or replacement: on the latest of the dates on which the Convention enters into force for those Contracting Jurisdictions.

Article 29
Notifications

1. Subject to paragraphs 5 and 6 of this Article, and paragraph 7 of Article 35 (Entry into Effect), notifications pursuant to the following provisions shall be made at the time of signature or when depositing the instrument of ratification, acceptance or approval:

a) Clause ii) of subparagraph a) of paragraph 1 of Article 2 (Interpretation of Terms);

b) Paragraph 6 of Article 3 (Transparent Entities);

c) Paragraph 4 of Article 4 (Dual Resident Entities);

d) Paragraph 10 of Article 5 (Application of Methods for Elimination of Double Taxation);

e) Paragraphs 5 and 6 of Article 6 (Purpose of a Covered Tax Agreement);

f) Paragraph 17 of Article 7 (Prevention of Treaty Abuse);

g) Paragraph 4 of Article 8 (Dividend Transfer Transactions);

h) Paragraphs 7 and 8 of Article 9 (Capital Gains from Alienation of Shares or Interests of Entities Deriving their Value Principally from Immovable Property);

i) Paragraph 6 of Article 10 (Anti-abuse Rule for Permanent Establishments Situated in Third Jurisdictions);

j) Paragraph 4 of Article 11 (Application of Tax Agreements to Restrict a Party's Right to Tax its Own Residents);

k) Paragraphs 5 and 6 of Article 12 (Artificial Avoidance of Permanent Establishment Status through Commissionnaire Arrangements and Similar Strategies);

l) Paragraphs 7 and 8 of Article 13 (Artificial Avoidance of Permanent Establishment Status through the Specific Activity Exemptions);

m) Paragraph 4 of Article 14 (Splitting-up of Contracts);

n) Paragraph 6 of Article 16 (Mutual Agreement Procedure);

o) Paragraph 4 of Article 17 (Corresponding Adjustments);

p) Article 18 (Choice to Apply Part VI);

q) Paragraph 4 of Article 23 (Type of Arbitration Process);

r) Paragraph 1 of Article 24 (Agreement on a Different Resolution);

s) Paragraph 1 of Article 26 (Compatibility); and

t) Paragraphs 1, 2, 3, 5 and 7 of Article 35 (Entry into Effect).

2. Notifications in respect of Covered Tax Agreements entered into by or on behalf of a jurisdiction or territory for whose international relations a Party is responsible, where that jurisdiction or territory is not a Party to the Convention pursuant to subparagraph b) or c) of paragraph 1 of Article 27 (Signature and Ratification, Acceptance or Approval), shall be made by the responsible Party and can be different from the notifications made by that Party for its own Covered Tax Agreements.

3. If notifications are made at the time of signature, they shall be confirmed upon deposit of the instrument of ratification, acceptance or approval, unless the document containing the notifications explicitly specifies that it is to be considered definitive, subject to the provisions of paragraphs 5 and 6 of this Article, and paragraph 7 of Article 35 (Entry into Effect).

4. If notifications are not made at the time of signature, a provisional list of expected notifications shall be provided at that time.

5. A Party may extend at any time the list of agreements notified under clause ii) of subparagraph a) of paragraph 1 of Article 2 (Interpretation of Terms) by means of a notification addressed to the Depositary. The Party shall specify in this notification whether the agreement falls within the scope of any of the reservations made by the Party which are listed in paragraph 8 of Article 28 (Reservations). The Party may also make a new reservation described in paragraph 8 of Article 28 (Reservations) if the additional agreement would be the first to fall within the scope of such a reservation. The Party shall also specify any additional notifications that may be required under subparagraphs b) through s) of paragraph 1 to reflect the inclusion of the additional agreements. In addition, if the extension results for the first time in the inclusion of a tax agreement entered into by or on behalf of a jurisdiction or territory for whose international relations a Party is responsible, the Party shall specify any reservations (pursuant to paragraph 4 of Article 28 (Reservations)) or notifications (pursuant to paragraph 2 of this Article) applicable to Covered Tax Agreements entered into by or on behalf of that jurisdiction or territory. On the date on which the added agreement(s) notified under clause ii) of subparagraph a) of paragraph 1 of Article 2 (Interpretation of Terms) become Covered Tax Agreements, the provisions of Article 35 (Entry into Effect) shall govern the date on which the modifications to the Covered Tax Agreement shall have effect.

6. A Party may make additional notifications pursuant to sub-paragraphs b) through s) of paragraph 1 by means of a notification addressed to the Depositary. These notifications shall take effect:

a) with respect to Covered Tax Agreements solely with States or jurisdictions that are Parties to the Convention when the additional notification is received by the Depositary:

i) for notifications in respect of provisions relating to taxes withheld at source, where the event giving rise to such taxes occurs on or after 1 January of the year next following the expiration of a period of six calendar months beginning on the date of the communication by the Depositary of the additional notification; and

ii) for notifications in respect of all other provisions, for taxes levied with respect to taxable periods beginning on or after 1 January of the year next following the expiration of a period of six calendar months beginning on the date of the communication by the Depositary of the additional notification; and

b) with respect to a Covered Tax Agreement for which one or more Contracting Jurisdictions becomes a Party to this Convention after the date of receipt by the Depositary of the additional notification: on the latest of the dates on which the Convention enters into force for those Contracting Jurisdictions.

Article 30
Subsequent Modifications of Covered Tax Agreements

The provisions in this Convention are without prejudice to subsequent modifications to a Covered Tax Agreement which may be agreed between the Contracting Jurisdictions of the Covered Tax Agreement.

Article 31
Conference of the Parties

1. The Parties may convene a Conference of the Parties for the purposes of taking any decisions or exercising any functions as may be required or appropriate under the provisions of this Convention.

2. The Conference of the Parties shall be served by the Depositary.

3. Any Party may request a Conference of the Parties by communicating a request to the Depositary. The Depositary shall inform all Parties of any request. Thereafter, the Depositary shall convene a Conference of the Parties, provided that the request is supported by one-third of the Parties within six calendar months of the communication by the Depositary of the request.

Article 32
Interpretation and Implementation.

1. Any question arising as to the interpretation or implementation of provisions of a Covered Tax Agreement as they are modified by this Convention shall be determined in accordance with the provision(s) of the Covered Tax Agreement relating to the resolution by mutual agreement of questions of interpretation or application of the Covered Tax Agreement (as those provisions may be modified by this Convention).

2. Any question arising as to the interpretation or implementation of this Convention may be addressed by a Conference of the Parties convened in accordance with paragraph 3 of Article 31 (Conference of the Parties).

Article 33
Amendment.

1. Any Party may propose an amendment to this Convention by submitting the proposed amendment to the Depositary.

2. A Conference of the Parties may be convened to consider the proposed amendment in accordance with paragraph 3 of Article 31 (Conference of the Parties).

Article 34
Entry into Force.

1. This Convention shall enter into force on the first day of the month following the expiration of a period of three calendar months beginning on the date of deposit of the fifth instrument of ratification, acceptance or approval.

2. For each Signatory ratifying, accepting, or approving this Convention after the deposit of the fifth instrument of ratification, acceptance or approval, the Convention shall enter into force on the first day of the month following the expiration of a period of three calendar months beginning on the date of the deposit by such Signatory of its instrument of ratification, acceptance or approval.

Article 35
Entry into Effect.

1. The provisions of this Convention shall have effect in each Contracting Jurisdiction with respect to a Covered Tax Agreement:

a) with respect to taxes withheld at source on amounts paid or credited to non-residents, where the event giving rise to such taxes occurs on or after the first day of the next calendar year that begins on or after the latest of the dates on which this Convention enters into force for each of the Contracting Jurisdictions to the Covered Tax Agreement; and

b) with respect to all other taxes levied by that Contracting Jurisdiction, for taxes levied with respect to taxable periods beginning on or after the expiration of a period of six calendar months (or a shorter period, if all Contracting Jurisdictions notify the Depositary that they intend to apply such shorter period) from the latest of the dates on which this Convention enters into force for each of the Contracting Jurisdictions to the Covered Tax Agreement.

2. Solely for the purpose of its own application of subparagraph a) of paragraph 1 and subparagraph a) of paragraph 5, a Party may choose to substitute "taxable period" for "calendar year", and shall notify the Depositary accordingly.

3. Solely for the purpose of its own application of subparagraph b) of paragraph 1 and subparagraph b) of paragraph 5, a Party may choose to replace the reference to "taxable periods beginning on or after the expiration of a period" with a reference to "taxable periods beginning on or after 1 January of the next year beginning on or after the expiration of a period", and shall notify the Depositary accordingly.

4. Notwithstanding the preceding provisions of this Article, Article 16 (Mutual Agreement Procedure) shall have effect with respect to a Covered Tax Agreement for a case presented to the competent authority of a Contracting Jurisdiction on or after the latest of the dates on which this Convention enters into force for each of the Contracting Jurisdictions to the Covered Tax Agreement, except for cases that were not eligible to be presented as of that date under the Covered Tax Agreement prior to its modification by the Convention, without regard to the taxable period to which the case relates.

5. For a new Covered Tax Agreement resulting from an extension pursuant to paragraph 5 of Article 29 (Notifications) of the list of agreements notified under clause ii) of subparagraph a) of paragraph 1 of Article 2 (Interpretation of Terms), the provisions of this Convention shall have effect in each Contracting Jurisdiction:

a) with respect to taxes withheld at source on amounts paid or credited to non-residents, where the event giving rise to such taxes occurs on or after the first day of the next calendar year that begins on or after 30 days after the date of the communication by the Depositary of the notification of the extension of the list of agreements; and

b) with respect to all other taxes levied by that Contracting Jurisdiction, for taxes levied with respect to taxable periods beginning on or after the expiration of a period of nine calendar months (or a shorter period, if all Contracting Jurisdictions notify the Depositary that they intend to apply such shorter period) from the date of the communication by the Depositary of the notification of the extension of the list of agreements.

6. A Party may reserve the right for paragraph 4 not to apply with respect to its Covered Tax Agreements.

7.

a) A Party may reserve the right to replace:

i) the references in paragraphs 1 and 4 to "the latest of the dates on which this Convention enters into force for each of the Contracting Jurisdictions to the Covered Tax Agreement"; and

(ii) the references in paragraph 5 to "the date of the communication by the Depositary of the notification of the extension of the list of agreements";

with references to "30 days after the date of receipt by the Depositary of the latest notification by each Contracting Jurisdiction making the reservation described in paragraph 7 of Article 35 (Entry into Effect) that it has completed its internal procedures for the entry into effect of the provisions of this Convention with respect to that specific Covered Tax Agreement";

iii) the references in subparagraph a) of paragraph 9 of Article 28 (Reservations) to "on the date of the communication by the Depositary of the notification of withdrawal or replacement of the reservation"; and

iv) the reference in subparagraph b) of paragraph 9 of Article 28 (Reservations) to "on the latest of the dates on which the Convention enters into force for those Contracting Jurisdictions";

with references to "30 days after the date of receipt by the Depositary of the latest notification by each Contracting Jurisdiction making the reservation described in paragraph 7 of Article 35 (Entry into Effect) that it has completed its internal procedures for the entry into effect of the withdrawal or replacement of the reservation with respect to that specific Covered Tax Agreement";

v) the references in subparagraph a) of paragraph 6 of Article 29 (Notifications) to "on the date of the communication by the Depositary of the additional notification"; and

vi) the reference in subparagraph b) of paragraph 6 of Article 29 (Notifications) to "on the latest of the dates on which the Convention enters into force for those Contracting Jurisdictions";

with references to "30 days after the date of receipt by the Depositary of the latest notification by each Contracting Jurisdiction making the reservation described in paragraph 7 of Article 35 (Entry into Effect) that it has completed its internal procedures for the entry into effect of the additional notification with respect to that specific Covered Tax Agreement";

vii) the references in paragraphs 1 and 2 of Article 36 (Entry into Effect of Part VI) to "the later of the dates on which this Convention enters into force for each of the Contracting Jurisdictions to the Covered Tax Agreement";

with references to "30 days after the date of receipt by the Depositary of the latest notification by each Contracting Jurisdiction making the reservation described in paragraph 7 of Article 35 (Entry into Effect) that it has completed its internal procedures for the entry into effect of the provisions of this Convention with respect to that specific Covered Tax Agreement"; and

viii) the reference in paragraph 3 of Article 36 (Entry into Effect of Part VI) to "the date of the communication by the Depositary of the notification of the extension of the list of agreements";

ix) the references in paragraph 4 of Article 36 (Entry into Effect of Part VI) to "the date of the communication by the Depositary of the notification of withdrawal of the reservation", "the date of the communication by the Depositary of the notification of replacement of the reservation" and "the date of the communication by the Depositary of the notification of withdrawal of the objection to the reservation"; and

x) the reference in paragraph 5 of Article 36 (Entry into Effect of Part VI) to "the date of the communication by the Depositary of the additional notification";

with references to "30 days after the date of receipt by the Depositary of the latest notification by each Contracting Jurisdiction making the reservation described in paragraph 7 of Article 35 (Entry into Effect) that it has completed its internal procedures for the entry into effect of the provisions of Part VI (Arbitration) with respect to that specific Covered Tax Agreement".

b) A Party making a reservation in accordance with subparagraph a) shall notify the confirmation of the completion of its internal procedures simultaneously to the Depositary and the other Contracting Jurisdiction(s).

c) If one or more Contracting Jurisdictions to a Covered Tax Agreement makes a reservation under this paragraph, the date of entry into effect of the provisions of the Convention, of the withdrawal or replacement of a reservation, of an additional notification with respect to that Covered Tax Agreement, or of Part VI (Arbitration) shall be governed by this paragraph for all Contracting Jurisdictions to the Covered Tax Agreement.

Article 36

Entry into Effect of Part VI

1. Notwithstanding paragraph 9 of Article 28 (Reservations), paragraph 6 of Article 29 (Notifications), and paragraphs 1 through 6 of Article 35 (Entry into Effect), with respect to two Contracting Jurisdictions to a Covered Tax Agreement, the provisions of Part VI (Arbitration) shall have effect:

a) with respect to cases presented to the competent authority of a Contracting Jurisdiction (as described in subparagraph a) of paragraph 1 of Article 19 (Mandatory Binding Arbitration)), on or after the later of the dates on which this Convention enters into force for each of the Contracting Jurisdictions to the Covered Tax Agreement; and

b) with respect to cases presented to the competent authority of a Contracting Jurisdiction prior to the later of the dates on which this Convention enters into force for each of the Contracting Jurisdictions to the Covered Tax Agreement, on the date when both Contracting Jurisdictions have notified the Depositary that they have reached mutual agreement pursuant to paragraph 10 of Article 19 (Mandatory Binding Arbitration), along with information regarding the date or dates on which such cases shall be considered to have been presented to the competent authority of a Contracting Jurisdiction (as described in subparagraph a) of paragraph 1 of Article 19 (Mandatory Binding Arbitration)) according to the terms of that mutual agreement.

2. A Party may reserve the right for Part VI (Arbitration) to apply to a case presented to the competent authority of a Contracting Jurisdiction prior to the later of the dates on which this Convention enters into force for each of the Contracting Jurisdictions to the Covered Tax Agreement only to the extent that the competent authorities of both Contracting Jurisdictions agree that it will apply to that specific case.

3. In the case of a new Covered Tax Agreement resulting from an extension pursuant to paragraph 5 of Article 29 (Notifications) of the list of agreements notified under clause ii) of subparagraph a) of paragraph 1 of Article 2 (Interpretation of Terms), the references in paragraphs 1 and 2 of this Article to "the later of the dates on which this Convention enters into force for each of the Contracting Jurisdictions to the Covered Tax Agreement" shall be replaced with references to "the date of the communication by the Depositary of the notification of the extension of the list of agreements".

4. A withdrawal or replacement of a reservation made under paragraph 4 of Article 26 (Compatibility) pursuant to paragraph 9 of Article 28 (Reservations), or the withdrawal of an objection to a reservation made under paragraph 2 of Article 28 (Reservations) which results in the application of Part VI (Arbitration) between two Contracting Jurisdictions to a Covered Tax Agreement, shall have effect according to sub-paragraphs a) and b) of paragraph 1 of this Article, except that the references to "the later of the dates on which this Convention enters into force for each of the Contracting Jurisdictions to the Covered Tax Agreement" shall be replaced with references to "the date of the communication by the Depositary of the notification of withdrawal of the reservation", "the date of the communication by the Depositary of the notification of replacement of the reservation" or "the date of the communication by the Depositary of the notification of withdrawal of the objection to the reservation", respectively.

5. An additional notification made pursuant to subparagraph p) of paragraph 1 of Article 29 (Notifications) shall have effect according to subparagraphs a) and b) of paragraph 1, except that the references in paragraphs 1 and 2 of this Article to "the later of the dates on which this Convention enters into force for each of the Contracting Jurisdictions to the Covered Tax Agreement" shall be replaced with references to "the date of the communication by the Depositary of the additional notification".

Article 37
Withdrawal.

1. Any Party may, at any time, withdraw from this Convention by means of a notification addressed to the Depositary.

2. Withdrawal pursuant to paragraph 1 shall become effective on the date of receipt of the notification by the Depositary. In cases where this Convention has entered into force with respect to all Contracting Jurisdictions to a Covered Tax Agreement before the date on which a Party's withdrawal becomes effective, that Covered Tax Agreement shall remain as modified by this Convention.

Article 38
Relation with Protocols.

1. This Convention may be supplemented by one or more protocols.

2. In order to become a party to a protocol, a State or jurisdiction must also be a Party to this Convention.

3. A Party to this Convention is not bound by a protocol unless it becomes a party to the protocol in accordance with its provisions.

Article 39
Depositary.

1. The Secretary-General of the Organisation for Economic Co-operation and Development shall be the Depositary of this Convention and any protocols pursuant to Article 38 (Relation with Protocols).

2. The Depositary shall notify the Parties and Signatories within one calendar month of:

a) any signature pursuant to Article 27 (Signature and Ratification, Acceptance or Approval);

b) the deposit of any instrument of ratification, acceptance or approval pursuant to Article 27 (Signature and Ratification, Acceptance or Approval);

c) any reservation or withdrawal or replacement of a reservation pursuant to Article 28 (Reservations);

d) any notification or additional notification pursuant to Article 29 (Notifications);

e) any proposed amendment to this Convention pursuant to Article 33 (Amendment);

f) any withdrawal from this Convention pursuant to Article 37 (Withdrawal); and

g) any other communication related to this Convention.

3. The Depositary shall maintain publicly available lists of:

a) Covered Tax Agreements;

b) reservations made by the Parties; and

c) notifications made by the Parties.

In witness whereof the undersigned, being duly authorised thereto, have signed this Convention.

Done at Paris, the 24th day of November 2016, in English and French, both texts being equally authentic, in a single copy which shall be deposited in the archives of the Organisation for Economic Co-operation and Development.

United States

Canada–United States Tax Convention (1980)

Date Signed:	Convention — September 26, 1980 First Protocol — June 14, 1983 Second Protocol — March 28, 1984 Third Protocol — August 31, 1994; Revised Third Protocol — March 17, 1995 Fourth Protocol — July 29, 1997 Fifth Protocol — September 21, 2007
Statutory citation:	Convention — S.C. 1984, c. 20, Part I First Protocol — S.C. 1984, c. 20, Part II Second Protocol — S.C. 1984, c. 20, Part III Revised Third Protocol — S.C. 1995, c. 34 Fourth Protocol — S.C. 1997, c. 38, Part 7 Fifth Protocol — S.C. 2007, c. 32
Date entered into force:	Convention — August 16, 1984 First Protocol — August 16, 1984 Second Protocol — August 16, 1984 Revised Third Protocol — November 9, 1995 Fourth Protocol — December 16, 1997 Fifth Protocol — December 15, 2008
Effective date of provisions:	Convention and First and Second Protocols • For withholding taxes — Amounts paid or credited to non-residents on or after October 1, 1984 • For other taxes — Taxation years beginning on or after January 1, 1985 Third Protocol • For withholding taxes — Amounts paid or credited to non-residents on or after January 1, 1996 (See Article 21 of Third Protocol for details.) • For other taxes — Taxation years beginning on or after January 1, 1995 (See Article 21 of Third Protocol for details.) Fourth Protocol • For gains — April 26, 1995 (See Articles 1 and 3 of Fourth Protocol.) • For pensions and annuities — January 1, 1996 (See Article 3 of Fourth Protocol.) Fifth Protocol • For withholding taxes — Generally, on amounts paid or credited on or after February 1, 2009 (See paragraph 3 of Article 27 of Fifth Protocol for exceptions to certain specific provisions.) • For other taxes — Generally, for taxation years beginning after 2008 (See paragraph 3 of Article 27 of Fifth Protocol for exceptions to certain specific provisions.)
History:	Replaced the 1942 Canada–U.S. Convention
References:	See the CRA release "Guidelines for Taxpayers Requesting Treaty Benefits Pursuant to Paragraph 6 of Article XXIX A of the Canada–U.S. Tax Convention", dated May 22, 2009. See Department of Finance Press Release No. 2007-070, dated September 21, 2007, regarding the signing of the Fifth Protocol, which entered into force on December 15, 2008. A lengthy Backgrounder describing the Fifth Protocol is attached to the release.

Convention between Canada and the United States of America with Respect to Taxes on Income and on Capital[1]

Canada and the United States of America, desiring to conclude a Convention for the avoidance of double taxation and the prevention of fiscal evasion with respect to taxes on income and on capital, have agreed as follows:[2]

Article I — Personal Scope

This Convention is generally applicable to persons who are residents of one or both of the Contracting States.

Dentons Canada LLP Commentary: Article I describes the persons who may claim the benefits of the Convention. The Convention applies generally to residents of Canada and to residents of the United States. Article III (General Definitions) defines the term "person", while Article IV (Residence) defines the term "resident of a Contracting State". Specific exceptions designated in other Articles limit the benefits that may be claimed in certain circumstances (see, for example, Article XX (Students) and Article XXIX A (Limitation on Benefits)). This application generally follows the OECD Model Convention. The Convention also applies, in limited cases designated in other Articles (see, for example, paragraph 9 of Article V (Permanent Establishment)), to persons who are residents of neither Canada nor the United States. Article IV (Residence) defines the term "resident of a Contracting State".

Article II — Taxes Covered

1. This Convention shall apply to taxes on income and on capital imposed on behalf of each Contracting State, irrespective of the manner in which they are levied.

2. Notwithstanding paragraph 1, the taxes existing on March 17, 1995 to which the Convention shall apply are:

(*a*) In the case of Canada, the taxes imposed by the Government of Canada under the *Income Tax Act*; and

[1] The text of the Convention as it appears here has been consolidated to reflect the changes made by all five Protocols. The editorial comments on the provisions of the Convention are largely based on the revised technical explanation of the Convention issued by the U.S. Treasury Department on April 26, 1984 and on technical explanations issued with regard to the Third, Fourth, and Fifth Protocols. The technical explanations have been endorsed by the Canadian Department of Finance. See *Estate of William F. Kubicek Jr.*, 97 DTC 5454 (F.C.A.), regarding the Technical Explanation of the Convention. More recently, see the press release dated July 10, 2008 (No. 2008-052) by then Finance Minister Jim Flaherty in which the Minister indicated that Canada agrees that the Technical Explanation accurately reflects understandings reached in the course of negotiations with respect to the interpretation and application of the various provisions in the Protocol.

[2] The Supreme Court of Canada has stated that an ancillary goal of the Convention is to mitigate the administrative complexities arising from having to simultaneously comply with two uncoordinated taxation systems: See *The Queen v. Crown Forest Industries Limited*, 95 DTC 5389 (S.C.C.).

(*b*) In the case of the United States, the Federal income taxes imposed by the *Internal Revenue Code* of 1986. However, the Convention shall apply to:

(i) The United States accumulated earnings tax and personal holding company tax, to the extent, and only to the extent, necessary to implement the provisions of paragraphs 5 and 8 of Article X (Dividends);

(ii) The United States excise taxes imposed with respect to private foundations, to the extent, and only to the extent, necessary to implement the provisions of paragraph 4 of Article XXI (Exempt Organizations);

(iii) The United States social security taxes, to the extent, and only to the extent, necessary to implement the provisions of paragraph 2 of Article XXIV (Elimination of Double Taxation) and paragraph 4 of Article XXIX (Miscellaneous Rules); and

(iv) The United States estate taxes imposed by the *Internal Revenue Code* of 1986, to the extent, and only to the extent, necessary to implement the provisions of paragraph 3(*g*) of Article XXVI (Mutual Agreement Procedure) and Article XXIX B (Taxes Imposed by Reason of Death).

3. The Convention shall apply also to:

(*a*) Any taxes identical or substantially similar to those taxes to which the Convention applies under paragraph 2; and

(*b*) Taxes on capital;

which are imposed after March 17, 1995 in addition to, or in place of, the taxes to which the Convention applies under paragraph 2.

Dentons Canada LLP Commentary: Paragraph 1 of Article II states that the Convention applies to taxes "on income and on capital" imposed on behalf of Canada and the United States, irrespective of the manner in which such taxes are levied. As explained by the U.S. Treasury Department in its 1984 technical explanation, this paragraph is not intended either to broaden or to limit paragraph 2, which outlines the taxes existing at the time the Third Protocol was signed on March 17, 1995 to which the Convention applies.

In the case of Canada, the Convention applies to all taxes imposed under the *Income Tax Act* (Canada), not just income taxes. This is a change from the original provision in paragraph 2 that specified that the Convention applied to the taxes imposed by the Government of Canada under Parts I, XIII and XIV of the *Income Tax Act* (Canada).

In the case of the United States, the Convention applies to federal income taxes imposed by the *Internal Revenue Code*. Clauses 2(*b*)(i), (ii) and (iii) contain rules which provide that the Convention also applies to certain other U.S. taxes for certain specified purposes. The U.S. accumulated earnings tax and the personal holding company tax are subject to the Convention only to the extent provided in Article X (Dividends), which generally prevents imposition of these taxes with respect to a Canadian corporation unless non-Canadians hold more than half of the corporation's voting power. The U.S. excise tax imposed on private foundations is subject to the Convention but only to the extent necessary to implement the special provisions of paragraph 4 of Article XXI (Exempt Organizations), which exempts from the tax only Canadian organizations that receive substantially all of their support from persons other than citizens or residents of the United States. The U.S. social security tax is subject to the Convention but only to the extent necessary to implement the rules in paragraph 4 of Article XXIX (Miscellaneous Rules), which state that income from personal services not subject to tax by the United States under the 1942 Convention will not be subject to U.S. social security tax either. As well, clause 2(*b*)(iii) provides that the U.S. social security tax is subject to the Convention to the extent necessary to implement the provisions of paragraph 2 of Article XXIV (Elimination of Double Taxation) under which Canada agrees to give a foreign tax credit for U.S. social security taxes paid by individuals.

Clause 2(*b*)(iv), which provides that the Convention will apply to U.S. estate taxes imposed by the *Internal Revenue Code* to the extent necessary to implement the provisions of subparagraph 3(*g*) of Article XXVI (Mutual Agreement Procedure) and Article B (Taxes Imposed by Reason of Death). Subparagraph 3(*g*) of Article XXVI authorizes the two countries to provide relief from double taxation in situations concerning the distribution or disposal of property from a U.S. qualified domestic trust or a Canadian spousal trust, where relief is not otherwise available.

Paragraph 3 provides that the Convention also applies to any taxes identical or substantially similar to the taxes to which the Convention applies under paragraph 2 that are imposed after March 17, 1995 (the date of signature of the Third Protocol), which are imposed in addition to or in place of the taxes existing on that date. Similarly, taxes on capital imposed after that date are to be covered.

Article II refers only to federal taxes. Taxes imposed by the provinces of Canada, and by the states of the United States, are not generally covered by the Convention. However, if such taxes are substantially similar to the federal taxes, a foreign tax credit is ensured by paragraph 7 of Article XXIV (Elimination of Double Taxation). In addition, certain provinces incorporate federal treaty relief into the provincial statute.

Article II does not specifically refer to interest, fines and penalties. Thus, each Contracting State may, in general, impose interest, fines and penalties or pay interest pursuant to its domestic laws. Any question as to whether such items are being imposed or paid in connection with covered taxes in a manner consistent with provisions of the Convention, such as Article XXV (Non-Discrimination), may be resolved by the competent authorities pursuant to Article XXVI (Mutual Agreement Procedure).

History: Paragraphs 2 to 4 of Article II were amended by Article 1 of the Third Protocol, and formerly read:

2. The existing taxes to which the Convention shall apply are:

(*a*) In the case of Canada, the taxes imposed by the Government of Canada under Parts I, XIII and XIV of the *Income Tax Act*; and

(*b*) In the case of the United States, the Federal income taxes imposed by the *Internal Revenue Code*.

3. The Convention shall apply also to:

(*a*) Any identical or substantially similar taxes on income; and

(*b*) Taxes on capital; which are imposed after the date of signature of the Convention in addition to, or in place of, the existing taxes.

4. Notwithstanding the provisions of paragraphs 2(*b*) and 3, the Convention shall apply to:

(*a*) The United States accumulated earnings tax and personal holding company tax, to the extent, and only to the extent, necessary to implement the provisions of paragraphs 5 and 8 of Article X (Dividends);

(*b*) The United States excise taxes imposed with respect to private foundations, to the extent, and only to the extent, necessary to implement the provisions of paragraph 4 of Article XXI (Exempt Organizations); and

(*c*) The United States social security taxes, to the extent, and only to the extent, necessary to implement the provisions of paragraph 4 of Article XXIX (Miscellaneous Rules).

Article III — General Definitions

1. For the purposes of this Convention, unless the context otherwise requires:

(*a*) When used in a geographical sense, the term "Canada" means the territory of Canada, including any area beyond the territorial seas of Canada which, in accordance with international law and the laws of Canada, is an area within which Canada may exercise rights with respect to the seabed and subsoil and their natural resources;

(*b*) The term "United States" means:

(i) The United States of America, but does not include Puerto Rico, the Virgin Islands, Guam or any other United States possession or territory; and

(ii) When used in a geographical sense, such term also includes any area beyond the territorial seas of the United States which, in accordance with international law and the laws of the United States, is an area within which the United States may exercise rights with respect to the seabed and subsoil and their natural resources;

(*c*) The term "Canadian tax" means the taxes referred to in Article II (Taxes Covered) that are imposed on income by Canada;

(*d*) The term "United States tax" means the taxes referred to in Article II (Taxes Covered), other than in subparagraph (*b*)(i) to (iv) of paragraph 2 thereof, that are imposed on income by the United States;

(*e*) The term "person" includes an individual, an estate, a trust, a company and any other body of persons;

(*f*) The term "company" means any body corporate or any entity which is treated as a body corporate for tax purposes;

(*g*) The term "competent authority" means:

(i) In the case of Canada, the Minister of National Revenue or his authorized representative; and

(ii) In the case of the United States, the Secretary of the Treasury or his delegate;

(*h*) The term "international traffic" with reference to a resident of a Contracting State means any voyage of a ship or aircraft to

Treaties and Related Legislation

transport passengers or property (whether or not operated or used by that resident) except where the principal purpose of the voyage is to transport passengers or property between places within the other Contracting State;

(*i*) The term "State" means any national State, whether or not a Contracting State;

(*j*) The term "the 1942 Convention" means the Convention and Protocol between Canada and the United States for the Avoidance of Double Taxation and the Prevention of Fiscal Evasion in the case of Income Taxes signed at Washington on March 4, 1942, as amended by the Convention signed at Ottawa on June 12, 1950, by the Convention signed at Ottawa on August 8, 1956 and by the Supplementary Convention signed at Washington on October 25, 1966; and

(*k*) The term "national" of a Contracting State means:

(i) Any individual possessing the citizenship or nationality of that State; and

(ii) Any legal person, partnership or association deriving its status as such from the laws in force in that State.

2. As regards the application of the Convention by a Contracting State any term not defined therein shall, unless the context otherwise requires and subject to the provisions of Article XXVI (Mutual Agreement Procedure), have the meaning which it has under the law of that State concerning the taxes to which the Convention applies.

Dentons Canada LLP Commentary: Article III contains a group of definitions for terms used generally throughout the Convention. Articles IV and V define, at length, the terms "resident of a Contracting State" and "permanent establishment", respectively. Other definitions that are of importance to a particular Article may be found in that Article itself.

Paragraph 2 of Article III provides that, in the case of a term not defined in the Convention, the domestic tax law of Canada or the United States shall apply unless the context in which the term is used requires a definition independent of the domestic law, or the competent authorities reach agreement on a meaning pursuant to Article XXVI (Mutual Agreement Procedure). In determining the meaning of an undefined term, the Diplomatic Notes accompanying the Fifth Protocol (Annex B) clarify that the meaning under the tax laws of the relevant State is to take precedence over any non-tax meanings. This corresponds to paragraph 2 of Article 3 of the Organisation for Economic Cooperation and Development's Model Convention and would effectively codify within the Convention the existing principles of treaty interpretation adopted by both Canada and the United States. For example, the U.S. preference for a domestic tax meaning of an undefined term is reflected in the Technical Explanation to Article 3 of the U.S. Model Income Tax Convention. Moreover, paragraph 3 of the *Income Tax Conventions Interpretation Act* (Canada) (the "ITCIA"), which overrides any treaty provisions dealing with the interpretation of undefined terms, generally provides that an undefined term is to derive its meaning from the meaning that such term has for purposes of the *Income Tax Act* (Canada) unless the context otherwise requires.

If the meaning of a term cannot be readily determined under the law of a Contracting State, or if there is a conflict in meaning under the laws of the two States that creates difficulties in the application of the Convention, the competent authorities may establish a common meaning in order to prevent double taxation or to further any other purpose of the Convention. This common meaning presumably need not conform to the meaning of the term under the laws of either Contracting State.

Both the Diplomatic Notes (Annex "B") and the Technical Explanation to the Fifth Protocol confirm that the reference in paragraph 2 to the internal law of a Contracting State means the law in effect at the relevant time as opposed to the law in effect at the time the treaty was signed. This interpretation corresponds to section 3 of the ITCIA, which requires that undefined terms take their meaning from the *Income Tax Act* (Canada) as amended from time to time and not the meaning it had on the date the Convention was entered into or given the force of law in Canada. Inherent in the use of such "ambulatory" definitions (i.e., definitions that can evolve over time) is that it could lead to results that are at variance with the intentions of the Contracting States when the Convention was negotiated. Accordingly, both paragraph 2 of the Convention and section 3 of the ITCIA qualify the use of a domestic meaning to circumstances where the context does not otherwise require a different definition. Thus, flexibility in defining terms is both recognized and considered necessary in certain circumstances.

In subparagraphs 1(*a*) and (*b*), each country is defined in a geographical sense. The term "Canada" means the territory of Canada, including any area beyond the territorial seas of Canada which, in accordance with international law and the laws of Canada, is an area within which Canada may exercise rights with respect to the sea bed and subsoil and their natural resources. Therefore, income earned on the Canadian continental shelf would be covered. Under "the 1942 Convention" (as defined in subparagraph 1(*j*)), there is no reference to the Canadian continental shelf.

The "United States" means the United States of America, but not including Puerto Rico, the Virgin Islands, Guam or any other United States possession or territory. In addition, the definition of the United States also includes any area beyond the territorial seas of the United States which, in accordance with international law and the laws of the United States, is an area within which the United States may exercise its rights with respect to the sea beds and subsoil and their natural resources.

Subparagraphs 1(*c*) and (*d*) define the terms "Canadian tax" and "United States tax". These terms have always been defined as taxes on income as referred to in Article II (Taxes Covered). Article II provides that the Convention applies to some taxes other than income taxes. For example, for Canada the Convention applies to all taxes imposed under the *Income Tax Act* (Canada). Similarly, clauses 2(*b*)(i) to (iv) of Article II set out various U.S. taxes other than income taxes to which the Convention applies for certain purposes. As a result, the definition of "Canadian tax" was amended to mean only those taxes referred to in Article II (Taxes Covered) that are imposed on income. As well, the term "United States tax" includes taxes imposed on income and excludes the taxes imposed under clauses 2(*b*)(i) to (iv) of Article II. These other taxes are specified elsewhere as being eligible for credits. For example, the U.S. social security taxes are creditable under clause 2(*a*)(ii) of Article XXIV (Elimination of Double Taxation) and a Canadian tax credit is provided for U.S. estate taxes in paragraph 6 of Article XXIX B (Taxes Imposed by Reason of Death).

Subparagraph 1(*e*) provides that the term "person" includes an individual, an estate, a trust, a company, and any other body of persons. Although both Canada and the United States do not regard partnerships as taxable entities, the definition is broad enough to include partnerships where necessary. The OECD Model Convention contains a definition of the term "person" identical to that contained in the Canada–U.S. Income Tax Convention, except that the latter specifically covers an estate or trust.

The definition of the term "company" in subparagraph 1(*f*) is designed to cover any body corporate as well as any other taxable unit which is treated as a body corporate or a corporation according to the tax laws of the Contracting State in which it is organized. Reference may be made to the first paragraph of the letter exchanged between the two signatories on September 26, 1980, wherein it is stated that "in French, the term 'société' also means a 'corporation' within the meaning of Canadian law". This apparently ensures that there is no possible confusion in that the French term "société" actually covers the entity which is referred to in the French version of the *Income Tax Act* (Canada) as a "corporation".

A "company" includes a U.S. partnership that elects to be a taxable company in the United States, and may be eligible to claim treaty benefits. However, because Article XXIX A (Limitation on Benefits) imposes certain restrictions on the eligibility of treaty benefits, the application of the definitions in subparagraphs 1(*e*) and 1(*f*) should be applied carefully.

The term "competent authority" is defined in subparagraph 1(*g*) to mean, in the case of Canada, the Minister of National Revenue or his or her authorized representative, and in the case of the United States, the Secretary of the Treasury or his or her delegate. This term was similarly defined in paragraph 4 of the Protocol to the 1942 Convention and is referred to in the OECD Model Convention. This definition is of particular significance with respect to the provisions of Article XXVI (Mutual Agreement Procedure). In Canada, competent authority services are provided by a division of the Canada Revenue Agency ("CRA"), and the contact information for the specific individuals working in the Competent Authority Services Division is provided on the CRA website. Guidance for competent authority assistance under Canada's tax conventions is provided by the CRA in Information Circular 71-17R5. Where a double taxation problem may exist and a Competent Authority is asked to get involved, attention should be paid to limitation periods under the domestic statute and the treaty, and consideration given to the granting of waivers extending the time to reassess. This is discussed in the commentary to Article XXVI (Mutual Agreement Procedure).

Subparagraph 1(*h*) defines the term "international traffic" to mean, with reference to a resident of Canada or the United States, any voyage of a ship or aircraft to transport passengers or property except where the principal purpose of the voyage is to transport passengers or property between places within the other country. In general, profits that a resident of one country derives from the operation of ships or aircraft in international traffic are exempt from tax from the other country. A voyage of a resident from one country that has as its principal purpose the transportation of passengers or property within that country is in international traffic. For example, a flight of a Canadian airline that has as its principal purpose the transporting of property from Winnipeg to Toronto is not subject to U.S. tax, even if the flight continues for the secondary purpose of transporting property to Buffalo, New York. A similar flight of a U.S. airline would not be in international traffic and would not be exempt from Canadian tax. In addition, a resident of one country need not operate or use a ship or aircraft to benefit from the exemption for international traffic. Thus, the Canadian lessor of an aircraft that a Canadian airline flew in international traffic would not be subject to U.S. tax. It is perhaps worth noting that the definition applies only to ships and aircraft and is therefore of no use to determine whether a railway, bus or automobile is operated in international traffic. Profits from cross-border transportation by motor vehicle or railway may be covered by Article VIII (Transportation). Also, the definition of international traffic is to be applied on a voyage-by-voyage basis.

The term "State" is defined in subparagraph 1(*l*) as "any international state, whether or not a Contracting State". There is no counterpart of this definition in the 1942 Convention or in the OECD Model Convention. This term appears to be of use only with respect to paragraph 9 of Article V (Permanent Establishment) to determine for the purposes of that Article whether any person has a permanent establishment in any state.

Subparagraph 1(*j*) establishes "the 1942 Convention" as the term used throughout the Convention for referring to the pre-existing income tax treaty relationship between Canada and the United States. The term encompasses not only the Convention and Protocol signed on March 4, 1942, but also the amending Conventions signed on June 12, 1950, August 8, 1956 and October 25, 1966.

The Fifth Protocol added the definition of "national" in subparagraph 1(*k*), being an individual possessing the citizenship or nationality of that State and any legal person, partnership, or association deriving its status as such from the laws in force in that State. This definition is consistent with other U.S. tax treaties and was inserted at the request of the United States (with both Contracting States recognizing that Canadian tax law generally does not draw distinctions based on nationality) to ensure that both citizens and nationals are afforded benefits under the Convention. There are only two circumstances in which this term is used in the Convention:

(a) Paragraph 1 of Article XXV (Non-Discrimination) provides that a national of one Contracting State cannot be subject to a more burdensome tax liability in the other Contracting State than a national of that other State. Previously, paragraph 1 of Article XXV used the term "citizen" as opposed to "national". By broadening the non-discrimination provision to refer to nationals, the non-discrimination principle applies to any individual or legal person, whether or not such person is considered a citizen of either Contracting State.

(b) Paragraph 1 of Article XXVI (Mutual Agreement Procedure), provides that a person not resident in either Canada or the U.S. may commence a mutual agreement procedure in the Contracting State of which the person is a "national".

History: Subparagraph 1(*k*) of Article III was added by Article 1 of the Fifth Protocol to this Convention.

Subparagraphs 1(*c*) and (*d*) of Article III were amended by Article 2 of the Third Protocol to this Convention, and formerly read:

(*c*) The term "Canadian tax" means the Canadian taxes referred to in paragraphs 2(*a*) and 3(*a*) of Article II (Taxes Covered);

(*d*) The term "United States tax" means the United States taxes referred to in paragraphs 2(*b*) and 3(*a*) of Article II (Taxes Covered);

Subparagraph 1(*h*) of Article III was amended by Article I of the First Protocol to this Convention, and formerly read:

(*h*) The term "international traffic" means any voyage of a ship or aircraft to transport passengers or property except where the principal purpose of the voyage is to transport passengers or property between places within a Contracting State;

Article IV — Residence

1. For the purposes of this Convention, the term "resident" of a Contracting State means any person that, under the laws of that State, is liable to tax therein by reason of that person's domicile, residence, citizenship, place of management, place of incorporation or any other criterion of a similar nature, but in the case of an estate or trust, only to the extent that income derived by the estate or trust is liable to tax in that State, either in its hands or in the hands of its beneficiaries. For the purposes of this paragraph, an individual who is not a resident of Canada under this paragraph and who is a U.S. citizen or an alien admitted to the United States for permanent residence (a "green card" holder) is a resident of the United States only if the individual has a substantial presence, permanent home or habitual abode in the United States, and that individual's personal and economic relations are closer to the United States than to any third State. The term "resident" of a Contracting State is understood to include:

(*a*) The Government of that State or a political subdivision or local authority thereof or any agency or instrumentality of any such government, subdivision or authority, and

(*b*) (i) A trust, organization or other arrangement that is operated exclusively to administer or provide pension, retirement or employee benefits; and

(ii) A not-for-profit organization

that was constituted in that State and that is, by reason of its nature as such, generally exempt from income taxation in that State.

2. Where by reason of the provisions of paragraph 1 an individual is a resident of both Contracting States, then his status shall be determined as follows:

(*a*) He shall be deemed to be a resident of the Contracting State in which he has a permanent home available to him; if he has a permanent home available to him in both States or in neither State, he shall be deemed to be a resident of the Contracting State with which his personal and economic relations are closer (centre of vital interests);

(*b*) If the Contracting State in which he has his centre of vital interests cannot be determined, he shall be deemed to be a resident of the Contracting State in which he has an habitual abode;

(*c*) If he has an habitual abode in both States or in neither State, he shall be deemed to be a resident of the Contracting State of which he is a citizen; and

(*d*) If he is a citizen of both States or of neither of them, the competent authorities of the Contracting States shall settle the question by mutual agreement.

3. Where by reason of the provisions of paragraph 1, a company is a resident of both Contracting States, then

(*a*) If it is created under the laws in force in a Contracting State, but not under the laws in force in the other Contracting State, it shall be deemed to be a resident only of the first-mentioned State; and

(*b*) In any other case, the competent authorities of the Contracting States shall endeavor to settle the question of residency by mutual agreement and determine the mode of application of this Convention to the company. In the absence of such agreement, the company shall not be considered a resident of either Contracting State for purposes of claiming any benefits under this Convention.

4. Where by reason of the provisions of paragraph 1 an estate, trust or other person (other than an individual or a company) is a resident of both Contracting States, the Competent authorities of the States shall by mutual agreement endeavour to settle the question and to determine the mode of application of the Convention to such person.

5. Notwithstanding the provisions of the preceding paragraphs, an individual shall be deemed to be a resident of a Contracting State if:

(*a*) The individual is an employee of that state or of a political subdivision, local authority or instrumentality thereof rendering services in the discharge of functions of a governmental nature in the other Contracting State or in a third State; and

(*b*) The individual is subjected in the first-mentioned State to similar obligations in respect of taxes on income as are residents of the first-mentioned State.

The spouse and dependent children residing with such an individual and meeting the requirements of subparagraph (*b*) above shall also be deemed to be residents of the first-mentioned State.

6. An amount of income, profit or gain shall be considered to be derived by a person who is a resident of a Contracting State where:

(*a*) The person is considered under the taxation law of that State to have derived the amount through an entity (other than an entity that is a resident of the other Contracting State); and

(*b*) By reason of the entity being treated as fiscally transparent under the laws of the first-mentioned State, the treatment of the amount under the taxation law of that State is the same as its treatment would be if that amount had been derived directly by that person.

7. An amount of income, profit or gain shall be considered not to be paid to or derived by a person who is a resident of a Contracting State where:

(*a*) The person is considered under the taxation law of the other Contracting State to have derived the amount through an entity that is not a resident of the first-mentioned State, but by reason of the entity not being treated as fiscally transparent under the laws of that State, the treatment of the amount under the taxation law of that State is not the same as its treatment would be if that amount had been derived directly by that person; or (*b*) The person is considered under the taxation law of the other Contracting State to have received the amount from an entity that is a resident of that other State, but by reason of the entity being treated as fiscally transparent under the laws of the first-mentioned State, the treatment of the amount under the taxation law of that State is not the same as its treatment would be if that entity were not treated as fiscally transparent under the laws of that State.

Dentons Canada LLP Commentary: The concept of a "resident" of a contracting state serves various functions and is important in three cases:

- determining the treaty's application and personal scope, as the benefits of the Convention are generally available only to a "resident" of one of the contracting states, as set out in Article I
- solving cases where double taxation arises through the "tie breaker" rules contained in Article IV
- solving cases where double taxation arises as a consequence of taxation in the state of residence and the state of *situs*.

Paragraph 1 indicates that a person, either an individual or an entity such as a corporation or partnership, is considered to be a resident of that country if, under the laws of that country, the person is subject to taxation by that country because it is the person's country of domicile, residence, place of management, place of incorporation, or by reason of other criteria of a similar nature. An estate or trust will be considered to be a resident of a country only to the extent that the income it derives is subject to that country's tax, either in its hands or in the hands of its beneficiaries. To the extent that an estate or trust is considered a resident of a Contracting State under this provision, it can be a beneficial owner of items of income specified in other articles of the Convention such as paragraph 2 of Article X (Dividends).

The first sentence of paragraph 1 provides that a person will be considered a resident of Canada or the United States if the person is liable for tax in that country by reason of citizenship. Although the provision applies to both Canada and the United States, only the United States taxes its non-resident citizens as if they were residents. A "green card" holder is a person who has been admitted to the United States as a permanent resident and so is taxed in the United States as a resident regardless of where the person actually resides. As a result of the United States taxing its citizens and green card holders as residents even if they are not actually present in the United States, paragraph 1 provides that a U.S. citizen or green card holder who is not a Canadian resident will be treated as a U.S. resident for purposes of the Convention only if the individual has a substantial presence, permanent home, or habitual abode in the United States and the individual's personal and economic relations are closer to the United States than to any third State. If the individual is a resident of Canada, so that he or she is a resident of both countries, then the individual's residence status for purposes of the Convention is determined under the tie-breaker rules in paragraph 2 of Article IV.

Paragraph 2 of Article XXIX (Miscellaneous Rules) may still apply to a U.S. citizen who is not treated as a U.S. resident under Article IV because of the absence of close ties to the United States. However, a green card holder is treated as a resident of the United States for purposes of the saving clause in paragraph 2 of Article XXIX only if the individual qualifies as a resident under Article IV.

Paragraph 1 confirms that the term "resident" of a Contracting State includes the Government of that State or a political subdivision or local authority or any agency or instrumentality of the government, subdivision, or authority.

Because the definition of resident generally requires that a person be taxed in its state of residence, a specific rule is needed to extend treaty benefits to tax-exempt entities. Subparagraph 1(*b*) clarifies that for purposes of the Convention, the term "resident" of a Contracting State includes

(a) a trust, organization or other arrangement that is operated to administer or provide pension, retirement or employee benefits; and

(b) a not-for-profit organization.

Such a trust or organization is a resident of a Contracting State if it was constituted in that country and due to its nature, is generally tax exempt in the country in which it was constituted. Such an entity therefore qualifies for the benefits under the Convention as long as it satisfies the requirements of Article XXIX A. The requirement that a person be taxed in his or her state of residence in order to be considered a resident of that state for purposes of the treaty is a key distinguishing feature between the meaning of "resident" under a treaty and under domestic tax legislation. This means that certain types of U.S. entities whose income is not taxed in the United States at the entity level, but is flowed through to investors, will not be regarded as entities that are "resident" for purposes of the treaty and may be denied treaty benefits. For example, it has historically been the position of the CRA that U.S. limited liability companies ("LLCs") that are treated as flow-through entities for U.S. tax purposes do not qualify as residents of the United States for purposes of the Convention because they are not taxed in the U.S. as a separate legal entity. The CRA maintained this position despite the Tax Court of Canada providing otherwise in *TD Securities (USA) LLC v. The Queen*, 2010 DTC 1137. However, since the Fifth Protocol, it is the CRA's position that paragraph 6 of Article IV establishes the parameters under which the benefits of the Convention may be claimed by a fiscally transparent LLC, as will be discussed below. This case was decided after the Fifth Protocol entered into force, on December 15, 2008, but dealt with taxation years prior to the Fifth Protocol and the wording of the Treaty at that time. For this reason the case was not appealed.

In contrast, a corporation taxed under subchapter S of the *Internal Revenue Code* (an "S-Corp") will be considered a U.S. resident for purposes of the Convention by the CRA, because it is taxed at the entity level by default unless it elects to flow all income to its shareholders for tax purposes. (However, regardless of whether an S-Corp makes such an election, the CRA has indicated that it will regard it as a U.S. resident for purposes of the Convention.)

The CRA has taken a different position with respect to partnerships, generally disregarding the partnership in favour of determining the entitlement to benefits under the Convention based on the residency of the partners. This view is largely consistent with the position of the Organisation for Economic Cooperation and Development (see, e.g., paragraph 5 to the Commentary on Article 1 of the OECD Model Convention).

As described below, the Fifth Protocol introduced significant changes to the availability of benefits under the Convention in respect of amounts derived through certain fiscally transparent entities (including LLCs and partnerships) (see, e.g., paragraphs 6 and 7 of Article IV).

For a person to be considered a "resident of a Contracting State", the person must be subject to tax in that state by reason of its domicile, residence, citizenship, place of management, place of incorporation, or other criterion of a similar nature. In *The Queen v. Crown Forest Industries*, 85 DTC 5389, the Supreme Court of Canada confirmed that the United States branch of a third country corporation is not regarded as U.S. resident for purposes of the Convention. That U.S. branch was liable only to U.S. taxation on its U.S.-sourced income and the Convention applies only to entities bearing full tax liability on worldwide income in their state of residence. Taxation on U.S.-sourced income was not regarded as a criterion of a similar nature for purposes of this definition.

Paragraphs 2, 3, and 4 provide a set of rules to determine residence in the case of a person who, under the basic Convention definition, would be considered a resident of both countries (for example, an individual who is taxable as a resident under domestic law in both Canada and the United States). In the case of a dual resident individual, a series of "tie-breaker" rules would apply. If the first test does not determine a single residence, the second test comes into consideration, and so on. The individual will be deemed, for all purposes of the Convention, to be a resident of the country in which the individual has

(a) first, a permanent home (where, for example, an individual dwells with his or her family);

(b) second, the individual's centre of vital interests (his or her closest economic and personal relations);

(c) third, the individual's habitual abode; or

(d) fourth, the individual's citizenship.

These rules were considered by the Tax Court of Canada and the Federal Court of Appeal in *Trieste v. The Queen*, 2013 DTC 5020, affirming 2012 DTC 1125 (TCC). If the residence of an individual cannot be determined by these tests, the competent authorities of the countries will settle the question by mutual agreement (see Article XXVI (Mutual Agreement Procedure)). The CRA has outlined its position on determining an individual's residency in Income Tax Folio S5-F1-C1, "Determining an Individual's Residence Status".

A corporation that is a dual resident of Canada and the United States under the general rule of Article IV, and which is created under the laws of either country (or a political subdivision thereof, such as a province or state), will be treated as a resident of the country in which it was first created (the "tie-breaker" rule). Dual residence can arise under Canadian law because Canada treats a corporation as a resident if it is managed and controlled in Canada. Thus, for example, a U.S. incorporated company with its management in Canada would initially be characterized as resident in Canada under Canadian law. However, under the Convention, it would be resident only in the United States. Subsection 250(5) of the *Income Tax Act* (Canada) precludes a person having dual residence in Canada and a treaty country for purposes of that Act, by deeming that person to be resident in the other country if the treaty deems it to be resident in that other country. Paragraph 3 addresses the situation of a corporation that has been continued in the other Contracting State. Under Canadian law (subsection 250(5.1) of the *Income Tax Act* (Canada)), if a corporation is continued in another jurisdiction, it is deemed to have been incorporated in that other jurisdiction. For purposes of the Convention, the corporation is deemed to be a resident of the State in which it has been continued. Therefore, if a U.S.-incorporated company that is a resident of both Canada and the United States is continued in Canada, the corporation will be deemed to be a resident of Canada. This provision operates reciprocally and not just in terms of the Canadian law for continuance.

The Fifth Protocol changed the "tie-breaker" rule for determining the residency of a corporation that qualifies as a resident of both Contracting States, addressing a perceived abuse relating to "dually-chartered" corporations. Generally, a dually-chartered corporation is an entity incorporated under the laws of one Contracting State that continues under the laws of the other Contracting State without terminating its corporate status in the first-mentioned Contracting State. If, for example, a U.S. corporation continues into Canada without surrendering its U.S. corporate charter, subsection 250(5.1) of the *Income Tax Act* (Canada) would deem the corporation to have been incorporated in Canada upon continuation; the laws of both Canada and the U.S. would therefore consider the corporation to have been incorporated in their respective jurisdictions.

As discussed above, a dually-chartered corporation can currently claim benefits under the Convention as a resident of the State in which it is continued. However, the corporation may continue to qualify for certain benefits as a result of retaining its non-tax legal status as a domestic corporation in the other Contracting State. This situation was identified as potentially abusive as early as September 2000, when both Canada and the United States announced that this situation would be addressed in a subsequent protocol. From a domestic U.S. tax perspective, the Treasury Department has issued final Regulations to the *Internal Revenue Code* denying certain U.S. tax benefits that might be derived through a dually-chartered corporation. However, the U.S. Regulations do not affect the residency of such entities for purposes of tax treaties, leaving the tie-breaker rule in Article IV of the Convention as the sole means of determining the availability of treaty benefits to such entities.

In this respect, the Fifth Protocol redefined the tie-breaker test, providing at paragraph 3, where a corporation is found to be resident in both Contracting States under paragraph 1 of Article IV, then:

(a) It is to be regarded for purposes of the Convention as a resident only of the Contracting State in which it is legally created (see subparagraph IV(3)(*a*)). This rule only applies in instances where such a company is considered to have been created in only one of the Contracting States. For instance, a corporation continued from the United States to Canada that surrenders its U.S. corporate charter upon continuance is considered a resident of Canada. This rule is consistent with the tie-breaker rule in effect under Article IV of the Convention prior to the introduction of the Fifth Protocol.

(b) In situations where a corporation has been continued from one Contracting State into the other Contracting State and has not surrendered its corporate charter from the first country, the corporation is considered under the laws of both Contracting States to have been created in that State (i.e., a dually-chartered entity). In such a situation, pursuant to subparagraph IV(3)(*b*), the competent authorities of the Contracting States will endeavor to determine the residency of the corporation for purposes of the Convention. Failing an agreement between the competent authorities, the corporation will not be considered a resident of either Contracting State and will, therefore, be unable to claim any benefits under the Convention.

Subparagraph IV(3)(*b*) also applies to so-called "serial continuances" in which a corporation legally formed in a Contracting State continues to a third country without surrendering its corporate charter and subsequently continues into the other Contracting State.

The tie-breaker rules introduced by the Fifth Protocol are effective for corporate continuances effected after September 17, 2000, being the date upon which it was first publicly announced by Canada and the United States that this issue was under consideration.

Paragraph 4 provides that the residence of a dual resident partnership, trust, or estate, and the method of application of the provisions of the Convention to such persons, are to be determined by the competent authorities. The Supreme Court of Canada dealt with the residency of trusts in *Fundy Settlement v. Canada*, 2012 DTC 5063 (commonly referred to as the Garron Family Trust case), applying the corporate test originally set out in *De Beers Consolidated Mines v. Howe (Surveyor of Taxes)*, [1906] AC 455 (KB Div, CA, HL), to trusts in determining the residency of a trust based on where the central management and control of the trust actually takes place.

Paragraph 5 states that an individual who is an employee performing services of a governmental nature for either Canada or the United States will be treated as a resident of that country if the individual is subject to tax by that country as a resident. The same rule applies to an employee of a provincial, state, or local government of one of the Contracting States. Such an individual's spouse and dependent children are also residents of the country that employs the individual, provided they too are subject to tax by that country as residents. Under this rule, a Canadian resident who is employed by a Canadian governmental department or agency in any foreign country would be considered a Canadian resident for purposes of the Convention.

The Fifth Protocol added paragraphs 6 and 7 to Article IV of the Convention, addressing amounts derived through fiscally transparent entities (i.e., entities that are disregarded as a separate legal entity for tax purposes in one Contracting State and regarded as a separate legal entity in the other Contracting State). These paragraphs do not directly impact the residency status of a fiscally transparent entity; rather, they determine whether an amount of income, profits, or gains derived by a person through the fiscally transparent entity will be considered to have been paid to, or derived by, a resident of a Contracting State for purposes of claiming benefits under the Convention.

Entities that are "fiscally transparent" for U.S. tax purposes include partnerships, common investment trusts under section 584 of the *Internal Revenue Code*, grantor trusts, S-Corps that have elected to be treated as fiscally transparent, and business entities such as LLCs that are treated as partnerships or are disregarded as entities separate from their owners for U.S. tax purposes. Entities that are fiscally transparent for Canadian tax purposes are (except to the extent the law provides otherwise) partnerships and certain trusts that are akin to an agency relationship (i.e., "bare" trusts).

Paragraph 6 is a relieving provision designed to permit a resident of a Contracting State investing in the other Contracting State through fiscally transparent entities to claim all of the benefits under the Convention that are not currently available to that resident (including the reduction of withholding taxes under Articles X (Dividends), XI (Interest) and XII (Royalties), taxes on business profits under Article VII (Business Profits), capital gains under Article XIII (Gains) and branch taxes under paragraph 6 of Article X (Dividends)). Paragraph 6 achieves this objective by "looking-through" the entity to its members/shareholders in circumstances where the following criteria are met:

(a) the member/shareholder is a resident of a Contracting State;

(b) the member/shareholder is considered for tax purposes in its State of residence to have derived an amount (either income, profit, or gain) through an entity;

(c) the entity is not a resident of the other Contracting State for purposes of the Convention;

(d) the entity is treated as fiscally transparent under the tax laws of the Contracting State in which the member/shareholder is a resident; and

(e) the amount is taxed by the Contracting State in which the member/shareholder is resident in the same manner as if the member/shareholder had derived the amount directly.

The Technical Explanation indicates that the determination of whether an amount is taxed by the Contracting State "in the same manner" is to be made in accordance with the principles described in Code section 894 and the Treasury Regulations promulgated thereunder. Generally, this condition will be satisfied if (i) the laws of that jurisdiction require the member/shareholder to separately take into account on a current basis its respective share of the amounts derived by the entity, whether or not distributed to the member/shareholder; and (ii) the character and source of the amount in the hands of the member/shareholder is the same as the character and source of the amount in the hands of the entity. While Canada does not have comparable provisions in the *Income Tax Act* (Canada), the CRA has applied similar principles for this purpose.

For example, prior to the Fifth Protocol, a U.S. resident investing in Canada through a limited liability company (LLC) that is regarded as fiscally transparent for U.S. tax purposes could not claim benefits under the Convention in respect of amounts derived from Canada through the LLC (i.e., Canadian-source investment income). This result was based on the CRA's historic administrative position that a fiscally transparent LLC is not a resident of the U.S. for purposes of the Convention and, therefore, is not entitled to claim any benefits under the Convention. However, under paragraph 6, Canada must now regard that income as being earned directly by the U.S. resident in proportion to its ownership interest in the LLC and must allow the U.S. resident to claim treaty benefits in respect thereof (provided the U.S. resident is taxable in the U.S. in the same way as it would have been if it had earned the income directly).

Additionally, by specifically identifying partnerships as "fiscally transparent entities", the Fifth Protocol ensures that a U.S. corporate partner of a partnership that is not a resident of Canada for purposes of the Convention and that derives dividends from a Canadian corporation may be entitled to claim the lowest rate of withholding tax under Article X (5 per cent) in respect of that corporate partner's proportionate share of the dividends, where that corporate partner's proportion of the Canadian corporation's voting shares is 10 per cent or more (see the Commentary under Article X). This effectively nullifies the CRA's prior administrative position concerning a partner's entitlement to benefits under the Convention (discussed above).

These same principles apply if the fiscally transparent entity is resident in a third country. So long as the foreign entity is considered fiscally transparent under the tax laws of the Contracting State in which the member/shareholder is resident (and the other conditions in paragraph 6 are met), the source State must recognize the member/shareholder as having derived its proportionate amount of the income directly for purposes of allowing benefits under the Convention. It may also be possible for the entity to itself claim any available benefits under the applicable income tax convention between the third country and the source State (which may be advantageous if, for example, not all members/shareholders of the entity are resident in the other Contracting State), or for the member/shareholder to claim benefits directly under the Convention.

To the extent that any Canadian income tax filings are required in order to claim benefits in respect of amounts derived by a U.S. member/shareholder of a fiscally transparent entity, the entity is required to make such filing and provide any supporting documentation. This is because Canada regards the entity as the legal recipient of the amount, even though it looks through the entity for purposes of determining the availability of benefits under the Convention.

To the extent a fiscally transparent entity derives business profits in a Contracting State, the issue becomes one of determining whether the members/shareholders of the entity are entitled to relief from source-country taxation under Article VII of the Convention (i.e., on the basis that the business activities are not carried on through a permanent establishment in the source country). In the context of determining whether Canada will grant benefits under the Convention, it is only the presence and activities of the entity itself that are relevant and not the presence or activities of the members/shareholders. If the entity does not have a permanent establishment situated in Canada, then the U.S. members/shareholders of the entity will not be subject to Canadian taxation on their proportionate share of the entity's business profits. If the entity does have a permanent establishment situated in Canada, the entity itself will have a Canadian tax obligation in respect of any profits attributable to that permanent establishment.

By contrast, the U.S. takes the position that it is both the presence and activities of the entity and its members that are relevant in determining whether to grant benefits under the Convention to a fiscally transparent entity that carries on business in the U.S. For example, consider an Ontario limited partnership that is not treated as a fiscally transparent entity for U.S. tax purposes and that carries on business in the U.S. If the partnership does not have a permanent establishment in the U.S., a Canadian-resident partner would generally be eligible to claim the benefits of Article VII in respect of its proportionate share of the partnership's U.S. business profits, so long as such profits are not attributable to a permanent establishment of the Canadian partner. If the partnership does have a U.S. permanent establishment, the permanent establishment will be attributed to the Canadian partner, and the Canadian partner will be subject to U.S. tax on its proportionate share of the business profits.

In either case where a fiscally transparent entity is carrying on business in Canada or the U.S., any members/shareholders that are residents of third countries are not entitled to claim benefits under Article VII of the Convention, regardless of whether the entity has a permanent establishment in the source country.

Benefits under paragraph 6 with respect to withholding taxes were made available as of February 1, 2009. However, with respect to withholding tax on the payment of interest, the benefits under paragraph 6 were made available retroactively to interest paid or credited as of January 1, 2008 (see the discussion under Article XI (Interest) for the applicable rates of withholding tax on interest paid to related and unrelated parties). In respect of taxes on income and gains, benefits under paragraph 6 are available for taxation years that begin after 2008.

Whereas paragraph 6 extends benefits under the Convention in respect of amounts derived by a resident of a Contracting State through certain types of fiscally transparent entities (i.e., certain U.S. LLCs and partnerships), paragraph 7 denies benefits under the Convention in respect of amounts derived through certain other fiscally transparent entities. There are two distinct scenarios in which such benefits are denied.

First, subparagraph 7(*a*) of Article IV denies benefits under the Convention if the following criteria are met:

(a) an amount is derived by a resident of a Contracting State;

(b) the amount is considered under the taxation laws of the other Contracting State to have been derived by the recipient through an entity that is not a resident of the first-mentioned State (i.e., if the recipient is a U.S. resident and the country of source is Canada, Canada must not consider the entity to be a resident of the U.S.);

(c) the entity is not treated as fiscally transparent under the taxation laws of the first-mentioned State (i.e., if the recipient is a resident of the U.S., the U.S. must consider the entity as being a separate, taxable entity); and

(d) as a result of the entity not being treated as fiscally transparent under the taxation laws of the first-mentioned State, the amount is taxed in that State differently than if the amount had been derived directly by the recipient (i.e., the recipient is not directly subject to tax in the State of residence in respect of the amount because the entity is itself considered taxable in respect of the amount).

An entity within the ambit of subparagraph 7(*a*) from an "inbound to Canada" perspective is a Canadian partnership with U.S. partners that elects to be treated as a corporation for U.S. tax purposes. These partnerships are commonly used by U.S. taxpayers as part of a structure known as a synthetic non-resident-owned investment company, or "NRO". Synthetic NRO structures were developed primarily to deal with the abolishment under Canadian law of the "true" NRO structure in 2001. An NRO was a Canadian corporation that was favoured by U.S. residents seeking to invest in Canada because it qualified for a preferential Canadian tax regime if it satisfied certain foreign ownership requirements.

As a result of subparagraph 7(*a*) of Article IV, the reduced rate of withholding under Article XI no longer applies to interest paid by the Canadian subsidiary to the limited partnership with U.S. corporate partners, and instead the domestic 25 per cent rate now applies.

An "outbound from Canada" structure that was impacted by subparagraph 7(*a*) is a fiscally transparent U.S. LLC that earns U.S.-source income, shares of which are held by a Canadian resident. Currently, the Canadian resident would be liable for U.S. tax on its proportionate share of the LLC's income (owing to the fact that the U.S. disregards the LLC for tax purposes). Moreover, and as discussed further in the Commentary to Article X (Dividends), the Canadian shareholder may be liable for U.S. branch taxes at the domestic U.S. rate of 30 per cent, which is generally reduced under the Convention to 5 per cent. As a result of the differing classifications of the LLC under the tax laws of Canada and the U.S., the reduction of the branch tax rate under the Convention may not be available.

Second, subparagraph 7(*b*) denies benefits under the Convention if the following criteria are met:

(a) a resident of a Contracting State has received an amount that is considered under the taxation laws of the other Contracting State to have been received from an entity that is a resident of the other Contracting State (i.e., a U.S. resident that receives a distribution from a Canadian-resident company);

(b) the entity is treated as fiscally transparent under the taxation laws of the first-mentioned State (i.e., the U.S. resident has "checked-the-box" in respect of the Canadian-resident company for U.S. tax purposes); and

(c) as a result of the entity being treated as fiscally transparent under the taxation laws of the first-mentioned State, that State taxes the amount differently than if the amount were instead derived through an entity that was not fiscally transparent.

An entity that would be within the ambit of subparagraph 7(*b*) is an unlimited liability company ("ULC") formed under the laws of a Canadian province (e.g., Nova Scotia, Alberta, or British Columbia), which is treated as a corporation for Canadian tax purposes but is treated as fiscally transparent for U.S. tax purposes. These entities have been commonly used by U.S. residents seeking to invest, or carry on business, in Canada, primarily as a result of certain favourable U.S. tax treatment for such entities, as well as the ability of U.S. residents to claim benefits under the Convention in respect of amounts derived through such entities. For example, a U.S. resident may incorporate a ULC for purposes of acquiring a Canadian target company and would check the box to treat the ULC as disregarded for U.S. tax purposes. The U.S. resident may leverage the ULC with debt to fund the acquisition and then amalgamate with the target, thereby allowing the ULC's interest deduction to offset the operating income of the Canadian target (subject to thin capitalization rules). Interest paid by ULC to its U.S. shareholder would be subject to a reduced withholding tax rate under paragraph 2 of Article XI (Interest) but would be disregarded for U.S. tax purposes, resulting in no net U.S. tax in connection with the borrowing. Moreover, operating losses of the target could flow directly through to the U.S. shareholder for purposes of offsetting U.S. taxable income of the shareholder.

If the ULC is treated as a disregarded branch of a U.S.-resident corporation ("USco") for U.S. tax purposes and pays a dividend to USco, the conditions for application of subparagraph 7(*b*) of Article IV will be met and reduced rates of withholding tax will not be available under Article X because:

(a) Canada considers USco to have received an amount from ULC, being a resident of Canada;

(b) ULC is fiscally transparent under the tax laws of the U.S.; and

(c) the U.S. taxation of the amount would have been different had USco received the dividend from a non-fiscally transparent entity (i.e., because ULC is treated as a disregarded branch, the payment of the dividend is completely disregarded for U.S. tax purposes — had ULC been regarded by the U.S. as a corporation, USco would have been treated as having received a dividend from a Canadian corporation).

A similar result would be obtained if the ULC had paid interest or royalties to USco; such payments would be disregarded for U.S. tax purposes and, therefore, Canada would deny reduced rates of withholding tax under the relevant provision of the Convention.

If, however, the ULC is regarded as a partnership for U.S. tax purposes, the analysis is slightly different. For U.S. tax purposes, dividend payments from ULC to USco would be regarded as partnership distributions; partnership distributions are taxed differently than dividends in the U.S., meaning that subparagraph 7(*b*) of Article IV would apply to deny reduced rates of withholding tax under Article X. However, payments of interest and royalties would be subject to the same U.S. tax treatment when received by USco, either from a ULC regarded as a partnership for U.S. tax purposes or a non-fiscally transparent entity. Therefore, benefits under the Convention may still be available in respect of such amounts.

In certain circumstances, profits from the ULC can be distributed to U.S. shareholders without applying subparagraph 7(*b*) of Article IV by utilizing what is known as the two-step process. These transactions have been approved by the CRA on several occasions. The first step is the increase in the paid-up capital of the ULC in an amount equal to the desired amount of the dividend. This is accomplished pursuant to the relevant corporate law governing the ULC, generally by converting retained earnings or another surplus account to stated capital. This first step results in an increase in the adjusted cost base of the shares of the ULC as well as a deemed dividend for Canadian tax law purposes. However, in the United States, the treatment of the deemed dividend arising in these circumstances would be the same whether the ULC is a fiscally transparent entity or not and thus the operative elements of subparagraph 7(*b*) are not met. Accordingly, the reduced rates of withholding tax under Article X would apply. The second step is a return of capital on the shares of the ULC in an amount equal to the amount of increase in stated capital undertaken in the first step. For Canadian tax purposes, this would reduce the paid-up capital and the adjusted cost base of the ULC's shares but would not result in a dividend being paid, and thus no withholding tax would apply. For U.S. tax purposes, the return of capital would either be disregarded (in the case of a single shareholder ULC) or would be treated as a tax-free return of capital (in the case of a ULC with multiple shareholders).

The two-step process may not work when a ULC's shares are owned by an LLC in the U.S. This is because the increase in the paid-up capital of the ULC is not a taxable event for U.S tax purposes and, therefore, may not satisfy the operative provisions of Article IV(6). The CRA, in Document No. 2009-0345351C6, stated that "the better view is that Article IV(6) does not apply to treat a particular amount of Canadian-source income, profit or gain as being derived by the US resident member(s) of a LLC if that amount is 'disregarded' under the taxation laws of the US".

Residents of Canada investing in the U.S. through certain U.S. limited partnerships may also be affected by subparagraph 7(*b*) of Article IV. If a U.S. partnership has elected to be regarded as a U.S.-resident corporation for U.S. tax purposes, but is considered a U.S. branch of the Canadian-resident partners for Canadian tax purposes, the payment of dividends, interest, or royalties by the partnership would attract consequences similar to that described above in connection with payments from a single-owner ULC.

The usual rules apply in determining whether a person who derives an amount through a fiscally transparent entity is the "beneficial owner" of the amount for purposes of claiming reduced withholding tax rates under Articles X, XI, and XII of the Convention in respect of dividends, interest, and royalties, respectively. These reduced rates are only available if the recipient is considered by the source State to be the "beneficial owner" of the amount received. The term "beneficial owner" is to be defined under the domestic law of the source State that would have the right to impose withholding tax on the amount paid. A recipient will be regarded as the beneficial owner of the amount, generally, so long as the recipient is not acting as an agent or nominee on behalf of a person that is not a resident of that Contracting State. The Technical Explanation to the Fifth Protocol suggests that this interpretation conforms to the meaning of "beneficial owner" under the domestic laws of both Canada and the United States, as well as the meaning described in the Commentary to Article 10 of the OECD Model. If the amount is derived by a person through a fiscally transparent entity, the source State will look through the entity and determine whether the person considered under Article IV of the Convention to have derived the amount qualifies as the beneficial owner of the amount.

Editorial Note: Technical Interpretation, Document No. 2013-0486931E5, deals with a U.S. ULC that makes a distribution to a Canadian resident trust which, in turn, pays the distribution to a US resident. The CRA noted that the Canadian tax treatment of the distribution by the trust, and whether withholding relief was available under the Convention, depended on whether the trust is deemed under U.S. law to be fiscally transparent.

Technical Interpretation, Document No. 2005-0144621E5, dated January 28, 2008, confirms the CRA's previous position that a qualified subchapter S subsidiary of an S corporation is a resident of the United States for the purposes of Article IV of the Canada–United States Income Tax Convention (1980).

2007 Tax Executives Institute — Canada Revenue Agency Liaison Meeting, Document No. 2007-0259011C6, on December 4, 2007, deals with the CRA's position on a specific situation where business income earned in Canada by a U.S. limited liability company would be exempt from tax in Canada, by virtue of Articles V and VII and proposed paragraph 6 of Article IV of the Convention.

Technical Interpretation, Document No. 2003-0049781E5, dated January 8, 2004, deals with a specific scenario in determining whether a U.S. trust would be resident in the U.S. and, therefore, eligible for the lower rate of withholding on dividends paid to a U.S. resident under the Treaty.

Technical Interpretation, Document No. 2006-0194431I7, dated November 20, 2006, deals with whether a U.S. corporation using Canadian contract employees provided by an unrelated Canadian services provider to support sales of the corporation's products to the Canadian market would constitute a permanent establishment under Article IV of the Treaty.

Technical Interpretation, Document No. 2003-0025221E5, dated April 29, 2004, deals with whether the benefit of the Treaty would apply with respect to a U.S. Grantor Trust that owned shares in a Canadian-controlled private corporation (relating to Articles IV, X, and XIII of the Treaty).

Advance Income Tax Rulings, Documents No. 2009-0341681R3, dated December 15, 2009, and 2010-0360501R3, dated November 12, 2010, deal with the two-step process for distributing profits out of a ULC.

Canadian Tax Foundation — 2009 Round Table Question 4(d), Document No. 2009-0345351C6, dated February 11, 2010, deals with the CRA's position on the two-step process for an LLC shareholder of a ULC. More recently, the CRA discussed the matter in Advance Income Tax Ruling, Document No. 2014-0534751R3.

History: Paragraph 3 of Article IV was deleted and replaced by paragraph 1 of Article 2 of the Fifth Protocol to this Convention, and formerly read:

3. Where by reason of the provisions of paragraph 1 a company is a resident of both Contracting States, then if it was created under the laws in force in a Contracting State, it shall be deemed to be a resident of that State. Notwithstanding the preceding sentence, a company that was created in a Contracting State, that is a resident of both Contracting States and that is continued at any time in the other Contracting State in accordance with the corporate law in that other State shall be deemed while it is so continued to be a resident of that other State.

Paragraphs 6 and 7 of Article IV were added by paragraph 2 of Article 2 of the Fifth Protocol to this Convention.

Paragraph 1 of Article IV was amended by paragraph 1 of Article 3 of the Third Protocol to this Convention, and formerly read:

1. For the purposes of this Convention, the term "resident of a Contracting State" means any person who, under the laws of that State, is liable to tax therein by reason of his domicile, residence, place of management, place of incorporation or any other criterion of a similar nature, but in the case of an estate or trust, only to the extent that income, derived by such estate or trust is liable to tax in that State, either in its hands or in the hands of its beneficiaries.

The last sentence of paragraph 3 of Article IV was added by paragraph 2 of Article 3 of the Third Protocol to this Convention.

Article V — Permanent Establishment

1. For the purposes of this Convention, the term "permanent establishment" means a fixed place of business through which the business of a resident of a Contracting State is wholly or partly carried on.

2. The term "permanent establishment" shall include especially

(*a*) A place of management;

(*b*) A branch;

(*c*) An office;

(*d*) A factory;

(*e*) A workshop; and

(*f*) A mine, an oil or gas well, a quarry or any other place of extraction of natural resources.

3. A building site or construction or installation project constitutes a permanent establishment if, but only if, it lasts more than 12 months.

4. The use of an installation or drilling rig or ship in a Contracting State to explore for or exploit natural resources constitutes a permanent establishment if, but only if, such use is for more than three months in any twelve-month period.

5. A person acting in a Contracting State on behalf of a resident of the other Contracting State — other than an agent of an independent status to whom paragraph 7 applies — shall be deemed to be a permanent establishment in the first-mentioned State if such person has, and habitually exercises in that State, an authority to conclude contracts in the name of the resident.

6. Notwithstanding the provisions of paragraphs 1, 2, 5, and 9, the term "permanent establishment" shall be deemed not to include a fixed place of business used solely for, or a person referred to in paragraph 5 engaged solely in, one or more of the following activities:

(*a*) The use of facilities for the purpose of storage, display or delivery of goods or merchandise belonging to the resident;

(*b*) The maintenance of a stock of goods or merchandise belonging to the resident for the purpose of storage, display or delivery;

(*c*) The maintenance of a stock of goods or merchandise belonging to the resident for the purpose of processing by another person;

(*d*) The purchase of goods or merchandise, or the collection of information, for the resident; and

(*e*) Advertising, the supply of information, scientific research or similar activities which have a preparatory or auxiliary character, for the resident.

7. A resident of a Contracting State shall not be deemed to have a permanent establishment in the other Contracting State merely

because such resident carries on business in that other State through a broker, general commission agent or any other agent of an independent status, provided that such persons are acting in the ordinary course of their business.

8. The fact that a company which is a resident of a Contracting State controls or is controlled by a company which is a resident of the other Contracting State, or which carries on business in that other State (whether through a permanent establishment or otherwise), shall not constitute either company a permanent establishment of the other.

9. Subject to paragraph 3, where an enterprise of a Contracting State provides services in the other Contracting State, if that enterprise is found not to have a permanent establishment in that other State by virtue of the preceding paragraphs of this Article, that enterprise shall be deemed to provide those services through a permanent establishment in that other State if and only if:

(*a*) Those services are performed in that other State by an individual who is present in that other State for a period or periods aggregating 183 days or more in any twelve-month period, and, during that period or periods, more than 50 percent of the gross active business revenues of the enterprise consists of income derived from the services performed in that other State by that individual; or

(*b*) The services are provided in that other State for an aggregate of 183 days or more in any twelve-month period with respect to the same or connected project for customers who are either residents of that other State or who maintain a permanent establishment in that other State and the services are provided in respect of that permanent establishment.

10. For the purposes of this Convention, the provisions of this Article shall be applied in determining whether any person has a permanent establishment in any State.

Dentons Canada LLP Commentary: Article V provides a definition of "permanent establishment" that is needed for purposes of Article VII (Business Profits) which uses the long- established concept of the permanent establishment to determine in what circumstances a Contracting State has the right to tax an enterprise of the other Contracting State that is carrying on business within the territory of the first Contracting State. Both the Convention and the OECD Model Convention provide that the business profits of a resident of a Contracting State are taxable in the other Contracting State only to the extent that they are attributable to a "permanent establishment" situated in that other state. The concept of a "permanent establishment" is also of relevance for the purposes of determining the source of interest and royalty payments under the provisions of Article XI (Interest) and Article XII (Royalties).

In general, paragraph 1 provides that for purposes of the Convention, a "permanent establishment" is a fixed place of business through which a resident of one country engages in business in the other country. Paragraph 2 defines the term "permanent establishment" to include a place of management, a branch, an office, a factory, a workshop, and a mine, oil or gas well, quarry, or any other place of extraction of natural resources. Pursuant to paragraph 3, it also includes any building site, construction, or installation project if the site or project is in existence for more than 12 months.

In the digital age, determining whether there is a permanent establishment in a State where a business is partly or wholly carried on through digital mediums can be more difficult. That being said, both the CRA and the OECD commentary provide guidance that a distinction needs to be made between computer equipment, such as a computer server, which may be set up at a location so as to constitute a permanent establishment under certain circumstances, and the data, such as a website, which does not constitute tangible property. Therefore, a website itself does not have a location that can constitute a "place of business". Often, if a website is hosted on a third-party server, the website owner will not have a permanent establishment in the State where the server is located on this basis alone, since the server will not be at its disposal. On the other hand, if a website is hosted on a dedicated server owned or controlled by the website owner, this equipment could constitute a permanent establishment through which the business on the website is being carried on.

Pursuant to paragraph 4, the use of an installation, drilling rig, or ship in Canada or the United States to explore for or exploit natural resources also gives rise to a permanent establishment if the use in one of the States is for more than 3 months in any 12-month period. A competent authority agreement signed January 26, 1984 prescribes rules for the Canadian tax treatment of drilling rigs that constitute Canadian permanent establishments of U.S. residents.

Under paragraph 5, if a resident of one country maintains an agent in the other country who has and regularly exercises the authority to enter into contracts in that other country in the name of the resident, the resident agent will be deemed to constitute a permanent establishment in the other country with respect to the activities the agent undertakes. This rule does not apply where the contracting authority is limited to those activities such as storage, display, or delivery of merchandise which are excluded from the definition of permanent establishment. Paragraph 7 contains the provision that the agency rule will not apply if the agent is a broker, general commission agent, or other agent of independent status acting in the ordinary course of its business.

In *Knights of Columbus v. The Queen*, 2008 DTC 3648, and *American Income Life Insurance Company v. The Queen*, 2008 DTC 3631, the Tax Court of Canada provided meaningful guidance on the circumstances in which (i) a place of business will be considered a permanent establishment for purposes of paragraph 1 of Article V; and (ii) the activities of an agent will give rise to a permanent establishment under paragraph 5 of Article V. In respect of paragraph 1, the Tax Court concluded that there must be a place of business, the place must have some degree of permanence, and the business of the non-resident must be carried on through the place (meaning that the non-resident must have the place "at its disposal"). The Court suggested that the phrase "at its disposal" is intended to be descriptive of circumstances in which the non-resident might be viewed as having a sufficient measure of control over the premises or the business activities carried on through the premises, including:

(i) the use or control (or legal right to exercise control) of the premises by the non-resident;

(ii) the degree to which the premises are identified with the business of the non-resident (i.e., whether the premises has signage of the non-resident);

(iii) the degree to which the non-resident bears expenses in respect of the premises or equipment used at the premises;

(iv) whether the non-resident makes management decisions respecting the premises;

(v) what contracts were concluded at the premises;

(vi) what products of the non-resident were kept at the premises;

(vii) whether the non-resident has any Canadian employees;

(viii) whether the non-resident bore any risk of the operation of the premises;

(ix) whether agents of the non-resident were subject to detailed instructions or comprehensive control;

(x) whether the non-resident requires its agents to have home offices and stipulates what the home office must contain;

(xi) whether the non-resident requires its agents to meet with clients at their premises and client meetings are, in fact, held there; and

(xii) whether officers, directors, or employees of the non-resident visit or have regular access to the premises.

The Tax Court's analysis of the criteria giving rise to a permanent establishment under paragraph 5 generally focused on the types of contracts that an agent was authorized to conclude and whether such contracts were part of the "business proper" of the non-resident.

Paragraph 6 modifies the general rule to provide that a fixed place of business used solely for any of a number of specified activities will not constitute a permanent establishment. These activities include the use of facilities for storing, displaying, or delivering merchandise belonging to the resident, the maintaining of a stock of goods belonging to the resident for storage, display or delivery, or the maintaining of a stock of goods for processing by another person. Also exempted from the status of permanent establishment are activities such as the maintenance of a fixed place of business for the purchase of goods or merchandise, the collection of information, advertising of scientific research, or for any other preparatory or auxiliary activities for the resident.

Paragraph 7 excludes from the permanent establishment deeming rules any resident of a Contracting State that carries on business in the other State through a broker, general commission agent, or any other agent of an independent status, provided that such persons are acting in the ordinary course of their business. The CRA is generally of the view that where, for instance, a U.S. corporation has a wholly-owned subsidiary in Canada, if that subsidiary has the authority to negotiate and conclude contracts in Canada for its U.S. parent, the U.S. parent may be found to have a permanent establishment in Canada. This is due to the fact that the Canadian subsidiary is not an agent of independent status.

Under paragraph 8, the determination of whether a company of one country has a permanent establishment in the other country is to be made without regard to the fact that the company may control or be controlled by a resident of the other country, or by a person who engages in business in that other country. Only the activities of the company in question are relevant. It is noteworthy that the Convention differs from the 1942 Convention such that it could generally limit the cases in which a permanent establishment exists. The Convention eliminates the rule of the 1942 Convention that included as a permanent establishment the use by a resident of one country of substantial equipment in the other country. The Convention also eliminates the provision of the 1942 Convention under which a person was considered to have a permanent establishment if the person carried on business in a country through an agent or employee who had a stock of goods or merchandise from which he or she filled orders that the person received.

Paragraph 9 was introduced by the Fifth Protocol and deems a permanent establishment to exist for cross-border services providers satisfying one of two different tests. First, the enterprise will be deemed to have a permanent establishment in the other Contracting State under subparagraph V(9)(*a*) if:

(a) the services are provided by a single individual (i.e., a natural person) who is present in the other Contracting State for at least 183 days in any twelve-month period; and

(b) more than fifty per cent (50 per cent) of the "gross active business revenues" of the enterprise are derived from the services performed in the other State by that individual.

The term "gross active business revenues" refers to the gross revenues attributable to *all* active business activities of the enterprise (not simply activities relating to the provision of services) that have or should have been charged, regardless of billing or the timing of any income inclusion for domestic tax purposes.

The test under subparagraph V(9)(*a*) applies to services provided by a single natural person, including services provided by a single natural person on behalf of any entity. This test, however, does not apply where an enterprise performs services in the other Contracting State through multiple individuals, so long as none of those individuals is in the other state for at least 183 days in any 12-month period. In this situation, the non-resident enterprise will be deemed to have a permanent establishment under the test in subparagraph V(9)(*b*) where:

(a) the services are provided in the other State for at least 183 days in any 12-month period;

(b) the services are provided with respect to the same or a *connected project*; and

(c) the services are provided for customers that are either resident in the other State or are provided in respect of a permanent establishment that a customer may have in the other State (which is intended to reinforce the concept that, unless there is a customer in the other State, the enterprise will not be deemed as participating sufficiently in the economic life of the other State to warrant being deemed to have a permanent establishment there).

The Diplomatic Notes accompanying the Fifth Protocol provide that Canada and the United States will interpret the term "connected project" on a facts and circumstances basis, examining whether seemingly separate projects constitute a coherent whole. The projects must be coherent both (i) commercially; and (ii) geographically, in order to be aggregated for purposes of determining whether the enterprise will have a deemed permanent establishment in the other State. The Technical Explanation indicates that these determinations should be made from the perspective of the enterprise (not the customer) and will depend on the facts and circumstances of each case. Both the Technical Explanation and the OECD commentary have been cited by the CRA as being useful to the analysis from their perspective.

Factors relevant to the "commercial coherence" analysis include whether (absent tax planning) the projects would have been concluded pursuant to a single contract, whether the nature of the work involved under different contracts is the same, and whether the same individuals are used to perform the services. For example, an attempt to split a single 10-month services contract into two separate 5-month contracts in order to avoid the application of paragraph 9 could result in the contracts being aggregated, based on their commercial coherence. If the contracts also share a geographic coherence, the two 5-month contracts could give rise to a deemed permanent establishment. In this respect, "geographic coherence" requires that contracts for the same or similar services must relate to the same geographic location (i.e., separate contracts between a bank and a non-resident accounting firm for the provision of auditing services may lack geographic coherence, if the contracts relate to separate branches of the bank located in different cities).

The deeming rules in paragraph 9 only apply in respect of services physically rendered in the other State (i.e., it does not take into account services provided remotely by telephone or computer). In respect of the test described in subparagraph 9(*a*) relating to the performance of services by a single individual, the 183-day threshold takes into consideration all days that the individual is present in the other State (work days, weekends, holidays, etc.). On the other hand, the 183-day threshold in subparagraph 9(*b*) only takes into consideration the days which services are actually provided in the other State by representatives of the enterprise. Moreover, the 183-day threshold is to be determined irrespective of the number of representatives of the enterprise that are present in the other State (i.e., 50 representatives of the enterprise that are present in the other State for 5 days will only count as 5 days against the 183-day threshold).

The deeming rule in paragraph 9 was added at the same time that Article XIV (Independent Personal Services) was eliminated from the Convention. Article XIV allowed a Contracting State to tax income derived by a resident of the other State from the provision of independent personal services performed through a fixed base situated in the first-mentioned State. As indicated in the Diplomatic Notes accompanying the Fifth Protocol (Annex "B"), there was little practical distinction between a "fixed base" for purposes of Article XIV and a "permanent establishment" for purposes of Articles V and VII ("Business Profits"). As such, the Fifth Protocol eliminated Article XIV from the Convention on the basis that "personal services" income would be subject to tax as business profits under Article VII to the extent it is derived through a permanent establishment. This follows the approach of the OECD, which deleted the Independent Personal Services Article from the OECD Model Convention in 2000 on the basis that such activities should be dealt with as business profits.

Paragraph 9 of Article V can also be viewed as providing a corollary rule to Article XV (renamed *"Income from Employment"* by the Fifth Protocol), both of which link the ability of a Contracting State to tax income attributable to services performed by an enterprise resident in the other Contracting State to the period of time that the enterprise is considered to be present in that State.

This deeming rule appears to be in response to the decision of the Federal Court of Appeal in *The Queen v. Dudney*, 2000 DTC 6169 (F.C.A.). In that case, Mr. Dudney was a resident of the United States who spent 300 days in Canada in 1994 and approximately 40 days in 1995 performing services as an independent contractor. The Court held that Mr. Dudney was not subject to tax in Canada on his compensation for performing such independent personal services under Article XIV because he did not have a "fixed base" in Canada (which the Court analogized to a "permanent establishment" under Article V). Under paragraph 9, taxpayers such as Mr. Dudney would be deemed to have a permanent establishment in Canada for purposes of Article V and would be taxable on the business profits derived from that permanent establishment.

Paragraph 9 does not apply to service providers contemplated in paragraph 3 of Article V. Those providing services in connection with a building site or construction or installation project have a permanent establishment in the other Contracting State only if the building site or construction or installation project lasts for more than twelve months in the other State.

The CRA has stated that where a U.S. resident is hired to perform services in Canada and subcontracts those services to a related U.S. resident, both residents are deemed to have a permanent establishment in Canada pursuant to the rules in paragraphs 9 and 5 of Article V. In contrast, if the U.S. resident subcontracted the work to an arm's length independent resident of Canada, the U.S. resident would not be considered to have a permanent establishment in Canada.

Paragraph 10 specifically states that the provisions of Article V are to be applied in determining whether any person has a permanent establishment in any country. Thus, the provisions are to be applied to determine whether a resident of a country other than Canada or the U.S. has a permanent establishment in Canada or the U.S., and whether a person resident in Canada or the U.S. has a permanent establishment in any third country.

The definition of "permanent establishment" in the Convention differs from the definition of permanent establishment in Regulation 400, which applies for purposes of the *Income Tax Act* (Canada). It is also different from the definitions used in provincial tax legislation. Reference should be made to those definitions and the cases considering them. The CRA has published Interpretation Bulletin IT-177R2 "Permanent Establishment of a Corporation in a Province and of a Foreign Enterprise in Canada".

The OECD is currently working on a Base Erosion Profit Shifting ("BEPS") action plan comprising several focus areas, including Action 7 the artificial avoidance of permanent establishment status. Through a discussion draft released October 2014, the OECD has indicated that changes are needed to the wording in Articles 5(5) and 5(6) of the OECD Model Treaty.

Editorial Note: Income Tax Technical News No. 33, dated September 16, 2005, states that the factors considered by the Court in the *Dudney* decision in determining if a fixed base is regularly available to the individual, were the actual use made of the premises, the taxpayer's control over the premises, and the degree to which the premises were objectively identified with the taxpayer's business.

Income Tax Ruling, Document No. 2013-0475161I7, dated Februrary 24, 2014, deals with whether a U.S. corporation has a permanent establishment in Canada when hiring an associated enterprise to carry out services for it in Canada.

History: The first sentence of paragraph 6 of Article V was amended by paragraph 1 of Article 3 of the Fifth Protocol to this Convention by deleting the word "and" preceding the first reference to paragraph 5, inserting a comma, and adding the words "and 9" following that reference to paragraph 5.

Paragraph 9 of Article V was deleted and replaced with paragraphs 9 and 10 by paragraph 2 of Article 3 of the Fifth Protocol to this Convention. Paragraph 9 formerly read:

9. For the purposes of the Convention, the provisions of this Article shall be applied in determining whether any person has a permanent establishment in any State.

Paragraph 4 of Article V was amended by Article I of the First Protocol to this Convention and the Canada–United States Agreement Regarding

Canadian Taxation of Offshore Drilling Rigs. Paragraph 4 of Article V formerly read as follows:

4. The use of a drilling rig or ship in a Contracting State to explore for or exploit natural resources constitutes a permanent establishment if, but only if, such use is for more than 3 months in any twelve-month period.

Tax Window Files: Permanent Establishment, *15XXXX*, CRA Document No. 2014-0550611R3.

Article VI — Income from Real Property

1. Income derived by a resident of a Contracting State from real property (including income from agriculture, forestry or other natural resources) situated in the other Contracting State may be taxed in that other State.

2. For the purposes of this Convention, the term "real property" shall have the meaning which it has under the taxation laws of the Contracting State in which the property in question is situated and shall include any option or similar right in respect thereof. The term shall in any case include usufruct of real property, rights to explore for or to exploit mineral deposits, sources and other natural resources, and rights to amounts computed by reference to the amount or value of production from such resources; ships and aircraft shall not be regarded as real property.

3. The provisions of paragraph 1 shall apply to income derived from the direct use, letting or use in any other form of real property and to income from the alienation of such property.

Dentons Canada LLP Commentary: Under Article VI, income from real property may be taxed in the country where the real property is located. For purposes of this Article, income from real property includes income from any natural resources as well as income from agriculture and forestry. Real property will generally have the meaning provided under the laws of the country where the property is located, but will in any case include the right to use real property and the rights to explore for or to exploit mineral deposits, sources and other natural resources.

Unlike dividend, interest, and royalty income dealt with in Articles X, XI, and XII, the rate of withholding tax on real property rents is not limited or reduced.

The term "real property" also includes rights to amounts computed by reference to the amount or value of production of mineral deposits, sources and other natural resources. Thus, income from real property includes royalties and other payments in respect of the exploitation of natural resources (for example, an overriding royalty or, a net profits interest in a natural resources such as an oil or gas well) and gains on the sale, exchange, or other dispositions of any royalty rights or the underlining real property itself. Apparently, however, it will not include income in the form of rights to explore for or exploit natural resources which are received as compensation for services (for example, exploration services). This income is subject to the provisions of Article VII (Business Profits), XIV (Independent Personal Services), or XV (Dependent Personal Services), as the case may be.

Additionally, "real property" includes options for similar rights with respect to real property, but does not include ships and aircraft.

While income from real property includes income for the direct use, use in any form, renting, or alienation of the property, it will not include interest on loans secured by the real property.

Under Article XIII (Gains), gains on the sale, exchange or other disposition of real property may also be taxed by the country where the property is located. Also, gains from the disposition of stock in a company whose assets consist, directly or indirectly, principally of real estate, may generally be taxed in the country in which the company's real estate is located.

The 1942 Convention permitted a resident of one country to elect to be taxed on income from real property in the other country on a net basis. The Convention does not guarantee the right to such an election, but such an election is provided by section 216 of the *Income Tax Act* (Canada) with respect to certain income from Canadian real property but not for natural resource royalties other than timber royalties. The U.S. *Internal Revenue Code* also permits a net basis election with respect to U.S. real property. In addition, the 1942 Convention limited the tax a country may impose on rental or royalty income from real property to 15 per cent. There is no such limit in the current Convention. Under domestic law, Canada would impose a 25 per cent tax, while the United States would impose a 30 per cent tax. In an exchange of notes on June 14, 1983, the date of signing of the First Protocol, Canada and the United States agreed that if either country increases the statutory rate that then applied to natural resource royalties paid to non-residents, the two countries will, upon request by either country, promptly resume negotiations with a view to considering an amendment to the Convention to provide an appropriate limit to the rate of taxation upon such royalties.

History: Paragraphs 1 and 2 of Article VI were amended by Article III of the First Protocol to this Convention, and formerly read:

1. Income derived by a resident of a Contracting State from real property (including income from agriculture or forestry) situated in the other Contracting State may be taxed in that other State.

2. For the purposes of this Convention, the "real property"shall have the meaning which it has under the taxation laws of the Contracting State in which the property in question is situated and shall include any option or similar right in respect thereof. The term shall in any case include usufruct of real property and rights to explore for or to exploit mineral deposits, sources and other natural resources; ships and aircraft shall not be regarded as real property.

Article VII — Business Profits

1. The business profits of a resident of a Contracting State shall be taxable only in that State unless the resident carries on business in the other Contracting State through a permanent establishment situated herein. If the resident carries on, or has carried on, business as aforesaid, the business profits of the resident may be taxed in the other State but only so much of them as is attributable to that permanent establishment.

2. Subject to the provisions of paragraph 3, where a resident of a Contracting State carries on, or has carried on, business in the other Contracting State through a permanent establishment situated therein, there shall in each Contracting State be attributed to that permanent establishment the business profits which it might be expected to make if it were a distinct and separate person engaged in the same or similar activities under the same or similar conditions and dealing wholly independently with the resident and with any other person related to the resident (within the meaning of paragraph 2 of Article IX (Related Persons)).

3. In determining the business profits of a permanent establishment, there shall be allowed as deductions expenses which are incurred for the purposes of the permanent establishment, including executive and general administrative expenses so incurred, whether in the State in which the permanent establishment is situated, or elsewhere. Nothing in this paragraph shall require a Contracting State to allow the deduction of any expenditure which, by reason of its nature, is not generally allowed as a deduction under the taxation laws of that State.

4. No business profits shall be attributed to a permanent establishment of a resident of a Contracting State by reason of the use thereof for either the mere purchase of goods or merchandise or the mere provision of executive, managerial or administrative facilities or services for such resident.

5. For the purposes of the preceding paragraphs, the business profits to be attributed to a permanent establishment shall be determined by the same method year by year unless there is good and sufficient reason to the contrary.

6. Where business profits include items of income which are dealt with separately in other Articles of this Convention, then the provisions of those Articles shall not be affected by the provisions of this Article.

7. For the purposes of the Convention, the business profits attributable to a permanent establishment shall include only those profits derived from the assets or activities of the permanent establishment.

Dentons Canada LLP Commentary: Article VII sets out the circumstances in which tax may be imposed by one of the States on the business profits earned in that State by a resident of the other State. Paragraph 1 states that "business profits" of an enterprise of one country are taxable in the other country only to the extent that the profits are attributable to a permanent establishment (see Article V) in the other country through which the enterprise carries on, or has carried on, business. This is one of the basic limitations on the source country's right to tax income of a non-resident under the Convention.

The OECD encourages States to identify each source of profit for an enterprise and determine for each source whether or not the enterprise has a permanent establishment. Then, the State may only tax the profits of the enterprise resident in another State that arise from a source carried on through a permanent establishment in the first mentioned State.

The Convention permits a country to tax business profits attributable to a permanent establishment that no longer exists. Thus, either Canada or the United States may tax business profits received in a year after the permanent establishment to which those business profits are attributable has ceased to exist.

Under paragraph 2, the business profits of a permanent establishment are determined as if the permanent establishment were a distinct and separate entity which dealt at arm's length with the non-resident. There is to be attributed to a permanent establishment the business profits which it would reasonably expect to have derived if it were an independent entity engaged in the same or similar activities, under the same or similar conditions, and dealing at arm's length with the enterprise of which it is a permanent establishment or with any other person related to that enterprise. "Relationship" has the meaning provided in paragraph 2 of Article IX (Related Persons). Thus, for example, this arm's length rule applies to transactions between the permanent establishment and a branch or subsidiary of the enterprise located in a third country. Amounts may be attributed, whether they are from sources within or without the country in which the permanent establishment is located.

Paragraph 2 of Article VII also applies in circumstances where income may be attributable to a permanent establishment in a Contracting State that no longer exists. For example, if a resident of Canada sells all of the assets of its U.S. permanent establishment in year one in exchange for an installment obligation payable at the end of year three, the U.S. may tax the proceeds in year three, despite the fact that the Canadian resident may no longer have a permanent establishment in the U.S.

The OECD has endorsed the "distinct and separate entity" approach and, through the OECD Model Convention, has recommended that States employ language in their tax treaties similar to that which appears in paragraph 2 of the Convention. However, despite its widespread use, there has proven to be considerable international uncertainty regarding the application of the distinct and separate entity approach in allocating profits to a permanent establishment. For example, it is not uncommon for Contracting States to have separate legal, accounting, and regulatory regimes that prescribe contradictory rules for allocating income to permanent establishments. This lack of common interpretation can, in certain circumstances, lead to double taxation or less than single taxation.

The OECD has recognized this inconsistency and, since 2001, has been studying methods for improving the allocation of profits to permanent establishments. In December 2006, the OECD officially endorsed the use of its 1995 Transfer Pricing Guidelines for Multinational Enterprises and Tax Administrations (the "OECD Guidelines") (originally designed for use in the context of Article 9 of the OECD Model Convention) in determining the appropriate allocation of profits to most permanent establishments and is in the process of revising the Commentary to Article 7 to reflect its revised position. In this respect, the OECD recommends that the following two-step analysis be carried out:

(a) First, a functional and factual analysis must be conducted in accordance with the OECD Guidelines to attribute the assets used, risks assumed, and activities performed by the permanent establishment. The purpose of this test is to determine the economically significant activities and responsibilities performed by the permanent establishment in relation to the activities undertaken by the enterprise as a whole.

(b) Second, the appropriate arm's-length pricing of the various activities is to be determined through reference to the OECD Guidelines.

In 2010, the OECD published a report entitled "Attribution of Profits to Permanent Establishments." A modified version of a 2008 report, it adopted wholesale revisions to Article 7 of the OECD Model Tax Convention. These revisions were not captured in the Canada-U.S. Convention or in the Fifth Protocol. However, on June 26, 2012, the competent authorities of Canada and the United States entered into an agreement regarding Article VII pursuant to paragraph 3 of Article XXVI (Mutual Agreement Procedure). The agreement provides that the States agree to apply the OECD interpretation to determine the business profits attributable to a permanent establishment.

Applying the OECD interpretation follows the same approach generally taken by the United States in its treaty negotiation practice. For instance, the Technical Explanation to the Fifth Protocol indicates that Canada and the United States generally adopted the pre-2008 approaches recommended by the OECD. Similarly, the United States adopted this approach with other treaties (see, for example, the Belgium–United States treaty, signed on November 27, 2006).

Specifically, Canada and the United States have agreed to the following principles of profit attribution:

(a) The business profits to be attributed to a permanent establishment are only to include the profits derived from the assets used, risks assumed, and activities performed by the permanent establishment. This incorporates into Article VII the general principles of Article IX concerning the relationship between related (non-arm's length) parties.

(b) The principles of the OECD Guidelines are to apply in determining the profits allocable to a permanent establishment, taking into account the different economic and legal circumstances of a single entity. Any transfer pricing methodology described in the OECD Guidelines for determining an appropriate arm's length result may be used in allocating income to a permanent establishment so long as the method is applied in accordance with the OECD Guidelines. However, the use of the OECD Guidelines applies only for purposes of attributing profits within the legal entity. It does not create legal obligations or other tax consequences that would result from transactions having independent legal significance. For example, an entity that operates through branches rather than separate subsidiaries will have lower capital requirements because all of the assets of the entity are available to support all of the entity's liabilities (with some exceptions attributable to local regulatory restrictions). This is the reason that most commercial banks and some insurance companies operate through branches rather than subsidiaries. The benefit that comes from such lower capital costs must be allocated among the branches in an appropriate manner. This issue does not arise in the case of an enterprise that operates through separate entities, since each entity will have to be separately capitalized or will have to compensate another entity for providing capital (usually through a guarantee).

(c) For purposes of allocating the appropriate amount of profit to a permanent establishment, the permanent establishment must be treated as having the same amount of capital that it would need to carry out its activities if it were a distinct and separate enterprise engaged in the same or similar activities.

(d) In respect of financial institutions (other than insurance companies), a Contracting State may determine the appropriate amount of capital to be attributed to the permanent establishment by allocating the institution's total equity between its various offices proportionately to the institution's risk-weighted assets attributable to such offices. This recognizes the fact that financial institutions are in many cases required to risk-weight their assets for regulatory purposes and, in other cases, will do so for business reasons even if not required to do so by regulators. However, for U.S. tax purposes, such financial institutions can generally elect to apply the capital allocation principles in U.S. Treasury Regulation 1.882-5(c), as opposed to the rules in Article VII, which could ease the administrative burden that is commonly associated with the risk-weighting of assets (such election will not be available for Canadian tax purposes, unless the result conforms with the arm's length principle).

(e) The profits attributable to a permanent establishment of an insurance company are to include:

(i) insurance premiums earned through such permanent establishment; and

(ii) the portion of the insurance company's overall investment income from reserves and surplus that supports the risks assumed by the permanent establishment.

In certain circumstances, it may be beneficial, from a U.S. tax perspective, for a Canadian resident to use domestic U.S. tax rules to allocate income to a U.S. permanent establishment, as opposed to claiming relief under Article VII of the Treaty. For example, under section 864(c) of the *Internal Revenue Code*, the U.S. generally taxes a non-resident in respect of income that is "effectively connected" with the United States. Depending on the circumstances, the amount of income of a Canadian resident that would be "effectively connected" with the United States under U.S. domestic law could be greater or less than the income that would be "attributable to" a U.S. permanent establishment for purposes of Article VII. This is particularly relevant to financial institutions, where certain inter-branch transactions may be taken into account for purposes of the allocation rules in Article VII, but may be ignored under U.S. domestic law. However, a taxpayer seeking to use U.S. domestic law as opposed to the Convention to reduce its U.S. tax liability in respect of business profits may be limited in the use of the Convention in other respects; the Convention must be applied consistently and a taxpayer cannot "cherry pick" only the most beneficial treatment.

Paragraph 3 provides that in computing taxable business profits of a permanent establishment, deductions are allowed for expenses, wherever incurred, that are incurred for purposes of that permanent establishment. These deductions include a reasonable allocation of executive and general administrative expenses; interest, research and development, and other expenses which are incurred for purposes of the enterprise as a whole (or for purposes of that part of the enterprise which includes the permanent establishment). Thus, for example, a U.S. corporation that has a branch office in Canada and that has its head office in the United States will, in computing the Canadian tax liability of the branch, be entitled to deduct a portion of the executive and general administrative expenses incurred in the United States by the head office for the purpose of administering the Canadian branch. However, Canada will not be required to permit a deduction for an expense that is not by reason of its nature generally deductible under Canadian law.

In allocating business profits to a permanent establishment, it is appropriate to allow the permanent establishment deductions for certain notional or fictitious expenses (i.e., expenses intended to compensate a head office or another branch for services performed for the benefit of the permanent establishment). This arises because of the requirement that the permanent establishment be allocated the income it would reasonably be expected to have derived if it were an independent entity. For example, legal expenses incurred by the head office could be allocated to the permanent establishment according to the amount of services provided that relate to the business of the permanent establishment. This principle has been confirmed by the Federal Court of Appeal in *Cudd Pressure Control v. The Queen*, 98 DTC 6630. In that case however, the Court concluded that with respect to property owned by the entity, capital cost allowance was more appropriate in the particular circumstances than a notional rent deduction. In the case of *Wuslich v. MNR*, 91 DTC 704 (T.C.C.), an allocation of profits on the basis of time spent was considered appropriate in the circumstances.

Paragraph 4 provides that no business profits are to be attributed to the permanent establishment of a resident of a Contracting State by reason of the use of the permanent establishment for purchasing goods or merchandise or merely providing executive, managerial, or administrative facilities or services for the resident. Thus, where a permanent establishment purchases goods for its head office, the business profits attributable to the permanent establishment with respect to its other activities will not be increased by a profit element on its purchasing activities. Likewise, the permanent establishment could be the headquarters office for the corporation without being taxed in the country on profits generated by that activity. In addition, if business profits include management fees (other than excessive amounts), such fees should be taxable under the Convention by the payer's country only in the unlikely event that the recipient has a permanent establishment there. Paragraph 4 is unique to the Convention; it does not appear in any other tax treaty signed by either Canada or the United States.

Paragraph 5 provides that business profits are to be attributed to the permanent establishment by the same method in every taxable period unless there is good and sufficient reason to change such method.

Where business profits include items of income that are dealt with separately in other Articles of the Convention, paragraph 6 provides that those other Articles and not Article VII will govern the treatment on those items of income. Thus, for example, film rentals are taxed under the provisions of Article XII (Royalties), and not as business profits. Under the 1942 Convention, the terms "rentals" and "royalties" had a more limited definition than under the current Convention, and taxpayers were sometimes successful in relying on the predecessor to the business profits exemption in respect of income that would now be characterized as rent or royalty income. (See, for example, *The Queen v. Saint John Shipbuilding & Dry Dock Co. Ltd.*, 80 DTC 6272 (F.C.A.), and *MNR v. Paris Canada Films Limited*, 62 DTC 1338 (Ex. Ct.).)

In the event dividend interest or royalty income of a resident of one state is effectively connected with its permanent establishment in the other state, specific rules in Articles X, XI, and XII will cause that income to be included in business profits under Article VII and not as property income under those other Articles.

Under paragraph 7, the only business profits that can be attributed to a permanent establishment are those derived from the assets or activities of the permanent establishment itself. However, this paragraph does not preclude Canada or the United States from using appropriate rules of domestic law in determining the attribution.

To the extent a fiscally transparent entity derives business profits in a Contracting State, the issue becomes one of determining whether the members/shareholders of the entity are entitled to relief from source-country taxation under Article VII of the Convention (i.e., on the basis that the business activities are not carried on through a permanent establishment in the source country). In the context of determining whether Canada will grant benefits under the Convention, it is only the presence and activities of the entity itself that are relevant and not the presence or activities of the members/shareholders. If the entity does not have a permanent establishment situated in Canada, then the U.S. members/shareholders of the entity will not be subject to Canadian taxation on their proportionate share of the entity's business profits. The entity is itself required to file the necessary Canadian tax returns and provide any supporting documentation to claim protection for its members/shareholders under Article VII. This is because Canada regards the entity as the legal recipient of the amount, even though it looks through the entity for purposes of determining the availability of benefits under the Convention. If the entity does have a permanent establishment situated in Canada, the entity will have a Canadian tax obligation in respect of any profits attributable to that permanent establishment.

By contrast, the U.S. takes the position that it is both the presence and activities of the entity and its members that are relevant in determining whether to grant benefits under the Convention to a fiscally transparent entity that carries on business in the U.S. For example, consider an Ontario limited partnership that is not treated as a fiscally transparent entity for U.S. tax purposes and that carries on business in the U.S. If the partnership does not have a permanent establishment in the U.S., a Canadian-resident partner would generally be eligible to claim the benefits of Article VII in respect of its proportionate share of the partnership's U.S. business profits, so long as such profits are not attributable to a permanent establishment of the Canadian partner. If the partnership does have a U.S. permanent establishment, the permanent establishment will be attributed to the Canadian partner, and the Canadian partner will be subject to U.S. tax on its proportionate share of the business profits.

In either case where a fiscally transparent entity is carrying on business in Canada or the U.S., any members/shareholders that are residents of third countries are not entitled to claim benefits under Article VII of the Convention, regardless of whether the entity has a permanent establishment in the source country.

The Fifth Protocol eliminated Article XIV (Independent Services) from the Convention. The Diplomatic Notes accompanying the Fifth Protocol (Annex "B") confirm the shared understanding of Canada and the U.S. that there is no practical distinction between a "fixed base" (as that term was used in Article XIV) and a "permanent establishment" (as defined in Article V). Income derived by an independent service provider is therefore subject to the requirements of Article VII, meaning that the source State retains the ability to tax such income, to the extent it is derived through a permanent establishment situated in the source State. This change is consistent with the deletion in 2001 of Article 14 of the OECD Model Convention, which the OECD considered generally redundant of Article 7 (Business Profits).

Editorial Note: Technical Interpretation, Document No. 2007-0253321E5, dated November 14, 2007, deals with the requirement to withhold tax on a "franchise" fee paid to a company located in the United States. Where the franchise fee is for services provided to the franchisee, Article VII of the treaty (Business Profits) would apply and withholding is not required.

Technical Interpretation, Document No. 2005-0140621E5, dated November 29, 2006, deals with the application of Article XVIII of the treaty, where payments are made to the U.S. resident widow of a retired partner. It is the CRA's view that the allocations of partnership income would be business profits for the purposes of Article VII of the Treaty.

Technical Interpretation, Document No. 2006-0204171I7, dated October 19, 2006, deals with whether renewal commissions received by an insurance broker after emigrating to the U.S. would be attributable to a permanent establishment in Canada. It is the CRA's view that the individual's previous place of business would be a permanent establishment for the purposes of the Treaty.

Technical Interpretation, Document No. 2005-0161381I7, dated December 1, 2005, deals with payments to non-residents that are subject to Part XIII tax, but are not royalties under paragraph 4 of Article XII. Provided there is no permanent establishment, Article VII of the Treaty would apply to exempt the payments from tax.

Technical Interpretation, Document No. 2003-0054281I7, dated March 8, 2005, deals with whether the designation of out-of-country assets by the Minister, pursuant to paragraph 2400(1)(*f*) of the Regulations, is contrary to Article VII.

History: Paragraph 2 of Article VII was deleted and replaced by Article 4 of the Fifth Protocol to this Convention, and formerly read:

2. Subject to the provisions of paragraph 3, where a resident of a Contracting State carries on business in the other Contracting State through a permanent establishment situated therein, there shall in each Contracting State be attributed to that permanent establishment the business profits which it might be expected to make if it were a distinct and separate person engaged in the same or similar activities under the same or similar conditions and dealing wholly independently with the resident and with any other person related to the resident (within the meaning of paragraph 2 of Article IX (Related Persons)).

Article VIII — Transportation

1. Notwithstanding the provisions of Articles VII (Business Profits), XII (Royalties) and XIII (Gains), profits derived by a resident of a Contracting State from the operation of ships or aircraft in international traffic, and gains, derived by a resident of a Contracting State from the alienation of ships, aircraft or containers (including trailers and related equipment for the transport of containers) used principally in international traffic, shall be exempt from tax in the other Contracting State.

2. For the purposes of this Convention, profits derived by a resident of a Contracting State from the operation of ships or aircraft in international traffic include profits from:

(*a*) The rental of ships or aircraft operated in international traffic;

(*b*) The use, maintenance or rental of containers (including trailers and related equipment for the transport of containers) used in international traffic; and

(*c*) The rental of ships, aircraft or containers (including trailers and related equipment for the transport of containers) provided that such profits are incidental to profits referred to in paragraph 1, 2(*a*), or 2(*b*).

3. Notwithstanding the provisions of Article VII (Business Profits), profits derived by a resident of a Contracting State from a voyage of a ship where the principal purpose of the voyage is to transport passengers or property between places in the other Contracting State may be taxed in that other State.

4. Notwithstanding the provisions of Articles VII (Business Profits) and XII (Royalties), profits of a resident of a Contracting State engaged in the operation of motor vehicles or a railway as a common carrier or a contract carrier derived from:

(*a*) The transportation of passengers or property between a point outside the other Contracting State and any other point; or

(*b*) The rental of motor vehicles (including trailers) or railway rolling stock, or the use, maintenance or rental of containers (including trailers and related equipment for the transport of containers) used to transport passengers or property between a point outside the other Contracting State and any other point

shall be exempt from tax in that other Contracting State.

5. The provisions of paragraphs 1, 3 and 4 shall also apply to profits or gains referred to in those paragraphs derived by a resident of a Contracting State from the participation in a pool, a joint business or an international operating agency.

6. Notwithstanding the provisions of Article XII (Royalties), profits derived by a resident of a Contracting State from the use, maintenance or rental of railway rolling stock, motor vehicles, trailers or containers (including trailers and related equipment for the transport of containers) used in the other Contracting State for a period or periods not expected to exceed in the aggregate 183 days in any twelve-month period shall be exempt from tax in the other Contracting State except to the extent that such profits are attributable to a permanent establishment in the other State and liable to take in the other State by reason of Article VII (Business Profits).

Dentons Canada LLP Commentary: Paragraph 1 of Article VIII provides that profits derived by a resident of a Contracting State from the operation of ships or aircraft in "international traffic" (see the definition in Article III) are exempt from tax in the other Contracting State, even if, under Article VII (Business Profits), such profits are attributable to a "permanent establishment". This paragraph also provides the gains derived by a resident of a Contracting State from the alienation of ships, aircraft or containers (including trailers and related equipment for the transport of containers) used principally in international traffic are exempt from tax in the other Contracting State even if under Article XIII (Gains), the gains would be taxable in that other State. These rules differ from Article V of the 1942 Convention, which conditioned the exemption in the State of source on registration of the ship or aircraft in the other State.

For the purposes of the Convention, paragraph 2 provides that profits from the operation of ships or aircraft in international traffic will include those derived from the rental of ships or aircraft operating in international traffic (whether the rental is on a time, voyage or bareboat basis) and profits derived from the use, maintenance or rental of containers, including trailers and related equipment for the transport of containers provided such containers are used in international traffic. Also included will be the rental of ships, aircraft or containers, even if not operated in international traffic, as long as such profits are incidental to the profits derived from such activities in international traffic or the gains derived from the disposition of ships or aircraft used principally in international traffic. This exemption applies notwithstanding the provisions of Article XII (Royalties) which would otherwise apply to such rentals.

Paragraph 3 overrides the provisions of Article VII (Business Profits). Profits derived by a resident of a Contracting State from a voyage of a ship where the principal purpose of the voyage is to transport passengers or property between points in the other Contracting State are taxable in that other State whether or not the resident maintains a permanent establishment there. Such a voyage would not qualify for exemption under Article VIII by virtue of its exclusion from the definition of "international traffic" in subparagraph 1(*h*) of Article III (General Definitions). However, because paragraph 3 does not specifically mention aircraft, profits from a similar voyage by aircraft are taxable in the Contracting State of source pursuant to Article VII only if the profits are attributable to a permanent establishment maintained in that State.

Paragraph 4 allows an exemption with respect to profits derived from the operation of motor vehicles (i.e., cars, buses and trucks) or a railway as a common or contract carrier for the transportation of passengers or property between particular locales notwithstanding the existence of a permanent establishment. Thus, a resident of one of the Contracting States engaged in such operations may claim exemption from tax in the other State for profits derived from the transportation of passengers or property between a point outside the other State and any other point. In addition, such a person may claim exemption from tax in the other State for profits derived from the rental of motor vehicles (including trailers or railway rolling stock) used in such cross-border transportation activities. For example, a Canadian resident can claim exemption from U.S. tax in respect of the transportation of property by truck between Mexico City and San Francisco, between San Francisco and Vancouver, or between Mexico City and Vancouver even though the person may have a permanent establishment with respect to his transportation business in San Francisco. However, profits derived from his or her transportation of property between San Francisco and Chicago will not benefit from the exclusion from U.S. tax.

A resident of a Contracting State that participates in a pool, a joint business, or an international operating agency is, pursuant to paragraph 5, subject to the provisions of paragraphs 1, 3 and 4 with respect to the profits or gains derived through the pool, joint business or operating agency.

In certain circumstances, paragraph 6 overrides the provisions of Article XII (Royalties). Specifically, profits derived by a resident of a Contracting State from the use, maintenance or rental of railway rolling stock, motor vehicles, trailers or containers (including related equipment for the transport of containers) used in the other Contracting State for a period not expected to exceed 183 days in the aggregate in any 12-month period are exempt from tax in that other State, except where the profits are attributable to a permanent establishment. In such a case, Article VII (Business Profits) will apply. Unlike the provisions of paragraph 4, those of paragraph 6 apply whether or not the resident is engaged in the operation of motor vehicles or a railway as a common carrier or a contract carrier.

It should be noted that paragraphs 4 and 6 do not affect the taxation of gains from the alienation of motor vehicles and railway rolling stock derived by a resident of a Contracting State. Such gains would be taxable in the other Contracting State only if the motor vehicles or rolling stock form part of a permanent establishment maintained there (see paragraphs 2 and 4 of Article XIII).

History: Paragraph 1 of Article VIII was amended by Article IV of the First Protocol to this Convention, and formerly read:

1. Notwithstanding the provisions of Articles VII (Business Profits) and XIII (Gains), profits derived by a resident of a Contracting State from the operation of ships or aircraft in international traffic, and gains derived by a resident of a Contracting State from the alienation of ships or aircraft used principally in international traffic, shall be exempt from tax in the other Contracting State.

Article IX — Related Persons

1. Where a person in a Contracting State and a person in the other Contracting State are related and where the arrangements between them differ from those which would be made between unrelated persons, each State may adjust the amount of the income, loss or tax payable to reflect the income, deductions, credits or allowances which would, but for those arrangements, have been taken into account in computing such income, loss or tax.

2. For the purposes of this Article, a person shall be deemed to be related to another person if either person participates directly or indirectly in the management or control of the other, or if any third person or persons participate directly or indirectly in the management or control of both.

3. Where an adjustment is made or to be made by a Contracting State in accordance with paragraph 1, the other Contracting State shall (notwithstanding any time or procedural limitations in the domestic law of that other State) make a corresponding adjustment to the income, loss or tax of the related person in that other State if:

(*a*) It agrees with the first-mentioned adjustment; and

(*b*) Within six years from the end of the taxable year to which the first-mentioned adjustment relates, the competent authority of the other State has been notified of the first-mentioned adjustment. The competent authorities, however, may agree to consider cases where the corresponding adjustment would not otherwise be barred by any time or procedural limitations in the other State, even if the notification is not made within the six-year period.

4. In the event that the notification referred to in paragraph 3 is not given within the time period referred to therein, and the competent authorities have not agreed to otherwise consider the case in accordance with paragraph 3(*b*), the competent authority of the Contracting State which has made or is to make the first-mentioned adjustment may provide relief from double taxation where appropriate.

5. The provisions of paragraphs 3 and 4 shall not apply in the case of fraud, willful default or neglect or gross negligence.

Dentons Canada LLP Commentary: Article IX is the primary transfer pricing provision of the Treaty and deals with the tax treatment that is to be given where related persons (for example, parent and subsidiary companies and companies under common control) have not conducted transactions between themselves as if they were operating at arm's length and, as a result, their accounts do not show the true taxable profits arising in one or both of the Contracting States. Article IX provides that, in this case, the taxation authorities of a Contracting State may adjust the income (or loss) and tax calculations of a person to reflect the profit it would have normally made in the absence of any non-arm's length arrangements.

For the purposes of this Article, a person is deemed to be related to another person if either participates directly or indirectly in the management or control of the other, or if a third party or parties participate directly or indirectly in the management or control of both persons. The use of the words "management or control" appear to imply that this Article would not necessarily apply to individuals; however, subparagraph 1(*e*) of Article III (General Definitions) defines "person" to include an individual. It should also be noted that the test as to relationship does not look to direct or indirect legal control, but rather looks to a factual test of participation.

Where an adjustment is made or to be made by a Contracting State, the other Contracting State is required to make a corresponding adjustment to income, loss, or tax of the related person in that other State, provided that the other State agrees with the adjustment, and the competent authority of the other State has been notified in writing of the adjustment within six years from the end of the taxable year to which the adjustment relates. If one State was not immediately willing to make the corresponding adjustment, competent authority proceedings under Article XXVI would have to be requested.

A competent authority of the country making the adjustment is not required to advise the competent authority in the other country of the adjustment, although it may do so. Under the 1942 Convention, if the competent authority of the second country was not notified of the adjustment to be made by the first country, and if the taxpayer did not receive notification of the adjustment six months or more before the six-year period expired, then the first country could not make the initial adjustment to the extent that making it would give rise to double taxation.

Since the Third Protocol, there is no requirement that the taxpayer be notified at least six months before the expiration of the six-year period set out in paragraph 3 in order for an adjustment to be made. Paragraph 3 allows the competent authorities to agree to the adjustment as long as the year is not statute barred. Paragraph 4 was also amended to provide that if notification is not given within the six-year time period and if the competent authorities have not agreed to an adjustment, the competent authority of the first Contracting State may (but is not required to) make the adjustment unilaterally in order to provide relief from double taxation.

The burden of notifying the other competent authority is on the taxpayer, and the burden of giving the taxpayer timely notice is on the competent authority of the country making the initial adjustment. However, one competent authority may notify the other. The amendment from the Third Protocol effectively prevents taxpayers from using the notification requirements in the original Convention to avoid adjustments.

The provisions allowing relief if the competent authority originating an adjustment does not make notification do not apply if the adjustment, or the time lag, is due to fraud, willful default, neglect or gross negligence.

The relief provisions do not require that an adjustment must actually have been made or formally proposed. However, the taxpayer must be notified of a possible adjustment in writing with sufficient details to permit the taxpayer to notify the competent authority of the other country. Likewise, the notification to the competent authority of the other country must be in sufficient detail to apprise the competent authority of the nature of the adjustment.

Apart from the above procedural limitations, the provisions of the Convention are not intended to limit any law in either country which permits the distribution, apportionment, or allocation of income, deductions, credits or allowances between related persons when such law is necessary to prevent evasion of taxes or to clearly reflect the income of those persons.

While certain treaties have built-in limitation periods that prevent one Contracting State from making an adjustment after a certain period of time, Article IX of the Canada-U.S. Tax Convention removed the treaty limitation period in favour of the current rule contained in paragraph 3 of Article IX. This could result in double taxation if, for instance, the CRA makes an upward transfer pricing adjustment beyond the six-year rule in Article IX but within the seven-year domestic limitation period contained in subsection 152(4) of the *Income Tax Act* (Canada). It is understood that the CRA has an unpublished administrative practice to limit adjustments beyond the six-year treaty limitation period.

Several notable Canadian court cases have addressed the interpretation of treaty limitation periods. In *McKesson Canada Corporation v. The Queen*, 2014 DTC 1040, the Tax Court found that secondary adjustments (such as deemed dividends) that result from a primary (transfer pricing) adjustment are not subject to the limitation period found in many treaties. While the case discussed Canada's Treaty with Luxembourg, not the United States, the principle can be applied globally. *McKesson* was appealed to the Federal Court of Appeal but was withdrawn when the parties reached an out-of-court settlement.

In *Alberta Printed Circuits Ltd. v. the Queen*, 2011 DTC 1177, the Tax Court found that the shorter limitation period in the Canada-Barbados Treaty did not prevent a transfer pricing adjustment from being made so long as the adjustment was within the time set out in the *Income Tax Act* (Canada). In *Sundog Distributing Inc. v. The Queen*, 2010 DTC 1267 (TCC), the Tax Court found that both taxpayers need to be eligible under the particular treaty for the limitation periods to apply. In that case, only one of the two related parties was eligible for treaty protection and therefore the limitation period set out in Article IX of that treaty did not apply.

History: Paragraphs 3 and 4 of Article IX were amended by Article 4 of the Third Protocol to this Convention, and formerly read:

3. Where an adjustment is made or to be made by a Contracting State in accordance with paragraph 1, the other Contracting State shall (notwithstanding any time or procedural limitations in the domestic law of that other State) make a corresponding adjustment to the income, loss or tax of the related person in that other State if:

(*a*) It agrees with the first-mentioned adjustment; and

(*b*) Within six years from the end of the taxable year to which the first-mentioned adjustment relates, the competent authority of the other State has been notified of the first-mentioned adjustment.

4. In the event that the notification referred to in paragraph 3 is not given within the time period referred to therein, and if the person to whom the first-mentioned adjustment relates has not received, at least six months prior to the expiration of such time period, notification of such adjustment from the Contracting State which has made or is to make such adjustment that State shall, notwithstanding the provisions of paragraph 1, not make the first-mentioned adjustment to the extent that such adjustment would give rise to double taxation.

Article X — Dividends

1. Dividends paid by a company which is a resident of a Contracting State to a resident of the other Contracting State may be taxed in that other State.

2. However, such dividends may also be taxed in the Contracting State of which the company paying the dividends is a resident and according to the laws of the State; but if a resident of the other Contracting State is the beneficial owner of such dividends, the tax so charged shall not exceed:

(*a*) 5 percent of the gross amount of the dividends if the beneficial owner is a company which owns at least 10 percent of the voting stock of the company paying the dividends (for this purpose, a company that is a resident of a Contracting State shall be considered to own the voting stock owned by an entity that is considered fiscally transparent under the laws of that State and that is not a resident of the Contracting State of which the company paying the dividends is a resident, in proportion to the company's ownership interest in that entity);

(*b*) 15 per cent of the gross amount of the dividends in all other cases.

This paragraph shall not affect the taxation of the company in respect of the profits out of which the dividends are paid.

3. For the purposes of this Article, the term "dividends" means income from shares or other rights, not being debt-claims, participating in profits, as well as income that is subjected to the same taxation treatment as income from shares under the laws of the State of which the payer is a resident.

4. The provisions of paragraph 2 shall not apply if the beneficial owner of the dividends, being a resident of a Contracting State, carries on, or has carried on, business in the other Contracting State of which the company paying the dividends is a resident, through a permanent establishment situated therein, and the holding in respect of which the dividends are paid is effectively connected to such permanent establishment. In such case, the provisions of Article VII (Business Profits) shall apply.

5. Where a company is a resident of a Contracting State, the other Contracting State may not impose any tax on the dividends paid by the company, except insofar as such dividends are paid to a resident of that other State or insofar as the holding in respect of which the dividends are paid is effectively connected with a permanent establishment situated in that other State, nor subject the company's undistributed profits to a tax, even if the dividends paid or the undistributed profits consist wholly or partly of profits or income arising in such other State.

6. Nothing in this Convention shall be construed as preventing a Contracting State from imposing a tax on the earnings of a company attributable to permanent establishments in that State, in addition to the tax which would be chargeable on the earnings of a company which is a resident of that State, provided that any additional tax so imposed shall not exceed 5 per cent of the amount of such earnings which have not been subjected to such additional tax in previous taxation years. For the purposes of this paragraph, the term "earnings" means the amount by which the business profits attributable to per-

manent establishments in a Contracting State (including gains from the alienation of property forming part of the business property of such permanent establishments) in a year and previous years exceeds the sum of:

(*a*) Business losses attributable to such permanent establishments (including losses from the alienation of property forming part of the business property of such permanent establishments) in such year and previous years;

(*b*) All taxes, other than the additional tax referred to in this paragraph, imposed on such profits in that State;

(*c*) The profits reinvested in that State, provided that where that State is Canada, such amount shall be determined in accordance with the existing provisions of the law of Canada regarding the computation of the allowance in respect of investment in property in Canada, and any subsequent modification of those provisions which shall not affect the general principle hereof; and

(*d*) Five hundred thousand Canadian dollars ($500,000) or its equivalent in United States currency, less any amounts deducted by the company, or by an associated company with respect to the same or a similar business, under this subparagraph (*d*); for the purposes of this subparagraph (*d*) a company is associated with another company if one company directly or indirectly controls the other, or both companies are directly or indirectly controlled by the same person or persons, or if two companies deal with each other not at arm's length.

7. Notwithstanding the provisions of paragraph 2,

(*a*) Dividends paid by a company that is a resident of Canada and a non-resident-owned investment corporation to a company that is a resident of the United States, that owns at least 10 per cent of the voting stock of the company paying the dividends and that is the beneficial owner of such dividends, may be taxed in Canada at a rate not exceeding 10 per cent of the gross amount of the dividends;

(*b*) Paragraph 2(*b*) and not paragraph 2(*a*) shall apply in the case of dividends paid by a resident of the United States that is a Regulated Investment Company; and

(*c*) Subparagraph 2(*a*) shall not apply to dividends paid by a resident of the United States that is a Real Estate Investment Trust (REIT), and subparagraph 2(*b*) shall apply only if:

(i) The beneficial owner of the dividends is an individual holding an interest of not more than 10 percent in the REIT;

(ii) The dividends are paid with respect to a class of stock that is publicly traded and the beneficial owner of the dividends is a person holding an interest of not more than 5 percent in any class of the REIT's stock; or

(iii) The beneficial owner of the dividends is a person holding an interest of not more than 10 percent in the REIT and the REIT is diversified.

Otherwise, the rate of tax applicable under the domestic law of the United States shall apply. Where an estate or testamentary trust acquired its interest in a REIT as a consequence of an individual's death, for purposes of this subparagraph the estate or trust shall for the five-year period following the death be deemed with respect to that interest to be an individual.

8. Notwithstanding the provisions of paragraph 5, a company which is a resident of Canada and which has income subject to tax in the United States (without regard to the provisions of the Convention) may be liable to the United States accumulated earnings tax and personal holding company tax but only if 50 per cent or more in value of the outstanding voting shares of the company is owned, directly or indirectly, throughout the last half of its taxable year by citizens or residents of the United States (other than citizens of Canada who do not have immigrant status in the United States or who have not been residents in the United States for more than three taxable years) or by residents of a third State.

Dentons Canada LLP Commentary: Under paragraph 1 of Article X, dividends paid by a company resident in one of the Contracting States to a resident of the other Contracting State may be taxed in that other State. In addition, paragraph 2 of Article X allows each State to tax outbound dividends, although at significantly reduced rates in certain circumstances.

In Canada, subsection 212(2) of the *Income Tax Act* (Canada) provides a 25 per cent withholding tax on taxable and capital dividends paid or credited by a corporation resident in Canada to a non-resident person. In the United States, the *Internal Revenue Code* generally provides a 30 per cent withholding tax on dividends paid by a U.S. corporation to a non-resident shareholder.

Subsection 10(6) of the *Income Tax Application Rules* provides that, notwithstanding Part XIII of the *Income Tax Act*, where Canada has entered into a bilateral tax convention with a country and that convention provides for a maximum rate of Canadian withholding tax that is less than the Part XIII rate, the rate specified in the convention will apply to amounts paid or credited to a resident of that other country. Under the 1942 Convention, which did not require beneficial ownership of such income by a U.S. resident, the Tax Review Board held in *MacMillan Bloedel Limited v. MNR*, 79 DTC 297, that a Canadian payer's obligation to withhold under Part XIII was reduced to the convention rate, based on the address of the payee being in the United States. The CRA's administrative practices regarding reliance upon treaty reductions by payers for withholding tax purposes are set out in its Information Circular 76-12R6. The *Income Tax Application Rules* and *MacMillan Bloedel Limited* apply equally to all forms of withholding tax under Part XIII of the *Income Tax Act*, including interest and royalties, which are discussed in the following Articles.

Subparagraph 2(*a*) of Article X reduces the withholding tax rate on dividends to 5 per cent, if the "beneficial owner" is a corporation that owns at least 10 per cent of the voting stock of the payer corporation. Pursuant to subparagraph 2(*b*) withholding tax is limited to 15 per cent of the gross amount of the dividend in all other cases involving dividends paid to residents of the other country that qualify as the "beneficial owners" of the dividends.

For example, Canada can only impose a 5 per cent tax on gross dividends paid to a U.S. parent corporation by its Canadian subsidiary (assuming the subsidiary is the beneficial owner of the dividend). Likewise, Canada can only impose a 15 per cent tax on gross dividends paid to a U.S.-resident investor by a Canadian corporation (assuming the investor is the beneficial owner of the dividend).

The term "beneficial owner" is to be defined under the domestic law of the source State, being the State seeking to impose withholding tax on the amount paid. A recipient will be regarded as the beneficial owner of the amount, generally, so long as the recipient is not acting as an agent or nominee on behalf of a person that is not a resident of that Contracting State. The Technical Explanation to the Fifth Protocol suggests that this interpretation conforms to the meaning of "beneficial owner" under the domestic laws of both Canada and the United States, as well as the meaning described in the Commentary to Article 10 of the OECD Model. If the dividend is derived by a person through a fiscally transparent entity, the source State will look through the entity and determine whether the person considered under Article IV of the Convention to have derived the amount qualifies as the beneficial owner of the amount.

Beneficial ownership was considered in *The Queen v. Prévost Car Inc.*, 2009 DTC 5053, where the Federal Court of Appeal set out the "beneficial ownership test," which focuses on the attributes of ownership. This test requires the determination of who received possession of the payments for his or her own use and enjoyment and who assumed the risk and control of the payment received.

The Fifth Protocol added a "look-through" rule in subparagraph 2(*a*) for purposes of determining whether a person owns sufficient voting stock of the corporation paying the dividend in order to qualify for the reduced 5 per cent rate. The look-through provides that a corporation resident in a Contracting State will be considered to own any voting stock of a payer corporation resident in the other Contracting State if such stock is held through an entity that is not resident in the other State and is treated as fiscally transparent under the laws of the first-mentioned State. The resident will be considered to own that proportion of stock corresponding to its ownership interest in the fiscally transparent entity.

For example, the administrative position of the CRA is that a fiscally transparent U.S. limited liability company ("LLC") does not qualify as a resident of the United States for purposes of the Convention and therefore cannot claim the reduced 5 per cent dividend withholding tax rate in respect of dividends received from a Canadian corporation, regardless of the LLC's ownership percentage in the Canadian dividend payer. However, under paragraph 6 of Article IV, a U.S.-resident member of the LLC may be entitled to claim benefits as the person that derived the amount through the LLC. Subparagraph 2(*a*) of Article X works in conjunction with Article IV to ensure that a corporate member of an LLC will be treated as directly owning its proportionate number of voting shares of the Canadian dividend-payer that are held by the LLC, so that the member may potentially claim the 5 per cent withholding tax rate.

The term "dividends" is defined in paragraph 3 to include income from a share or other right (except a debt claim) that participates in profits. This broad definition includes, generally, any arrangement that yields a return on an equity investment, as determined under the tax law of the source State. For example, the term "dividends" includes payments which are deemed to be dividends by virtue of the taxation laws of the country of which the company making the distribution is resident. Therefore, this Article will apply to most deemed dividends under the *Income Tax Act* (Canada) (see, e.g., *RMM Canadian Enterprises Inc. and Equilease Corporation v. The Queen*, 97 DTC

302, where the Tax Court concluded that the definition of "dividends" in the Convention included deemed dividends under sections 84 and 212).

Other examples of payments that will be considered dividends for purposes of Article X include (i) interest payments in respect of debt that has been recharacterized by the source State as equity; and (ii) distributions by a U.S. publicly traded limited partnership that is taxed as a corporation under U.S. law. However, a distribution from a U.S. LLC that is not taxed as a corporation under U.S. law is not a dividend for purposes of Article X, since the source State (i.e., the U.S.) does not consider the payment to be a dividend under domestic law.

The Diplomatic Notes accompanying the Fifth Protocol (Annex "B") provide that the term "dividends" also includes distributions from Canadian income trusts and royalty trusts that are treated as dividends under Canadian tax law. As a result, U.S. investors receiving distributions from trusts that are deemed to be dividends pursuant to Canada's "specified investment flow-through" rules (enacted in June, 2007) retain their character as dividends for purposes of the Convention. Such distributions are subject to a 15 per cent withholding tax for most U.S. residents under Article X. However, subject to certain exceptions, U.S. tax-exempt investors (i.e., pension funds and retirement plans) are fully exempt from Canadian withholding tax in respect of dividends received from Canada.

Pursuant to paragraph 4, the reduced rates of withholding tax will not apply if, for example, the beneficial owner of the dividend is a resident of the United States who either carries on business in Canada or performs independent personal services in Canada through a permanent establishment in Canada, and the stock holding in respect of which the dividends are paid is effectively connected with that permanent establishment. Thus, dividends paid in respect of holdings which form part of the assets of a permanent establishment in Canada, or which are otherwise attributable to that permanent establishment, will be taxed in Canada as either business income (Article VII) or income from independent personal services (Article XIV), as the case may be. The Fifth Protocol amended paragraph 4 to clarify that the reduced withholding tax rates do not apply if the holding is connected with a permanent establishment in which a business had formerly been carried on. The Diplomatic Notes accompanying the Fifth Protocol (Annex "B") provide that this change is only for purposes of clarification and that the mutual understanding of Canada and the U.S. is that such holdings have always been within the ambit of paragraph 4.

Paragraph 5 limits the right of one of the countries to tax dividends paid by a corporation resident in the other country. For example, the United States may not tax a Canadian resident company's undistributed profits nor any dividends paid by it, except to the extent that the dividends are paid either to a resident of the United States, or to a stockholding which is effectively connected with a permanent establishment in the United States. Paragraphs 6 and 8 of this Article will, in some cases, qualify this rule.

Both Canada and the United States impose a branch profits tax. Canada levies a form of branch tax on the undistributed income of Canadian branches, or Canadian permanent establishments, of non-resident companies. The rules governing branch tax may be found in Part XIV of the *Income Tax Act* (Canada). Paragraph 6 of Article X restricts the branch tax to 5 per cent of the amount of the earnings which have not been subjected to branch tax in previous taxation years. This is a reduction from 10 per cent contained in the original Convention. Historically, the rate on branch taxes was 10 per cent for years to the end of 1995, 6 per cent for taxable years beginning on or after January 1, 1996 and ending before 1997, and 5 per cent for taxable years thereafter.

The term "earnings" as used in this Article means the amount by which business profits that are attributable to permanent establishments in the Contracting State (either Canada or the United States), including gains from the alienation of property forming part of the business property of such permanent establishments, for the year and previous years exceeds the sum of:

(a) business losses attributable to permanent establishments in the Contracting State (including losses from the alienation of property forming part of the business property of such permanent establishments) in the year and previous years;

(b) all taxes on profits imposed in the Contracting State, other than the branch tax;

(c) the profits reinvested in the Contracting State; and

(d) CDN $500,000, or its equivalent in United States currency, less any amount deducted under subparagraph 6(*d*) with respect to the same or similar business by the company or an associated company.

The threshold amount of $500,000 is cumulative. Thus, in effect, Canada cannot impose a branch tax on the earnings of a permanent establishment under this provision until it has earned $500,000 after the Convention became effective (see Article XXX (Entry Into Force)). The exclusion is available to Canadian permanent establishments of U.S. corporations that have earnings before the Convention is effective. Thus, all such permanent establishments in Canada will qualify for the exemption on their first $500,000 in earnings after the entry into force of this provision.

The $500,000 threshold amount must be shared among associated companies if the associated companies conduct the same or similar businesses in Canada. The term "associated companies" for the purpose of this Article differs from the definition of "related persons" in paragraph 2 of Article IX (Related Persons). It includes a company which directly or indirectly controls another company or two companies directly or indirectly controlled by the same person or persons, as well as two companies that do not deal with each other at arm's length.

As a result of the application of paragraph 6 of Article IV (Residence), a look-through rule applies for purposes of determining a person's entitlement to a reduction in branch taxes under the Convention if the branch activities are carried on through certain fiscally transparent entities. For example, a U.S.-resident member of a U.S. LLC that is regarded as fiscally transparent for U.S. tax purposes will generally be entitled to claim benefits under paragraph 6 of Article X with respect to that member's proportionate share of the branch taxes levied on the LLC's Canadian branch. Please refer to the commentary on Article IV for a discussion of the administrative procedures relating to the claiming of benefits in such circumstances.

On the other hand, paragraph 7 of Article IV (Residence) denies benefits under the Convention to amounts derived through certain fiscally transparent entities, which may negate the ability of a resident of a Contracting State to claim the 5 per cent branch tax rate under Article X in certain circumstances. An example is where a Canadian resident carries on business in the United States through an LLC that is fiscally transparent for U.S. tax purposes.

At the time the Convention was initially signed in 1980, the United States did not impose a branch tax *per se*. Therefore, former paragraph 7 of this Article provided that the United States may tax dividends paid by a Canadian resident company, if at least 50 per cent of the Canadian company's gross income from all sources, for the three-year period preceding the taxation year of the company in which the dividend is declared, was included in business profits attributable to permanent establishments that the Canadian company had in the United States. In order to be subject to U.S. tax, the dividend had to be attributable to profits earned by the company in taxation years beginning after September 26, 1980. Dividends were deemed to be distributed first out of the profits of the taxation year in which the dividend was paid, and then out of profits of preceding years. If a Canadian resident was the beneficial owner of the dividends paid by a Canadian company that was subject to this U.S. withholding tax, the broad dividend provisions of the Convention applied. Therefore, the 10 per cent or 15 per cent limitation found in paragraph 2 prior to the amendment by the Third Protocol, and the rules of paragraph 4, which provide that dividends may be taxed as either business income or income from independent personal services, applied.

Paragraph 7 of Article X was replaced by the Third Protocol. The former paragraph 7 is no longer relevant because it applied only in the case where a Contracting State does not impose a branch profits tax; however, both Canada and the United States now do impose such a tax. The revised paragraph 7 makes the 5 per cent withholding rate in subparagraph 2(*a*) inapplicable in certain situations.

Subparagraph 7(*a*) provides a special rule for dividends paid by a Canadian non-resident-owned investment corporation ("NRO"). An NRO was a specific type of corporation that was defined in former subsection 133(8) of the *Income Tax Act* (Canada). However, this provision is no longer relevant since the NRO structure was eliminated in Canada, with the creation of NROs having been prohibited since February 27, 2000.

Subparagraph 7(*b*) provides that the withholding tax rate on dividends paid by U.S. regulated investment companies (RICs) is 15 per cent, as allowed under subparagraph 2(*b*). Therefore, regardless of whether the Canadian beneficial owner of the RIC is a portfolio investor or an owner of 10 per cent or more of the stock, the rate of withholding tax remains at 15 per cent. This provision prevents a Canadian investor who holds portfolio investments in various U.S. shares from being entitled to a reduced rate of withholding tax by using an RIC as a conduit for the dividends from the portfolio investments. Dividends on the portfolio shares would be subject to the 15 per cent rate of withholding if held directly. If the Canadian investor places the portfolio of U.S. shares into an RIC, in which the investor owns 10 per cent or more of the shares, but for this provision, the investor could pass the portfolio investment dividends through the RIC and only be liable for withholding tax of 5 per cent.

Dividends paid by a U.S. real estate investment trust (REIT) to a Canadian resident are also subject to special withholding tax rules, under subparagraph 7(*c*). Generally, dividends paid by a U.S. REIT are not eligible for the 5 per cent maximum rate of withholding tax under subparagraph 2(*a*), but are instead subject to normal U.S. withholding tax rates (currently 30 per cent). As with the other rules in paragraph 7, this provision is intended to prevent the investor, in this case a Canadian resident, from paying a reduced rate of withholding tax by transforming other income into dividend income. This could be done by placing the real estate holding into a REIT. In this situation, if the REIT shareholder was a Canadian corporation, income from U.S. real estate that would otherwise be taxed at 30 per cent would be eligible for a 5 per cent withholding if the corporation held a 10 per cent or greater interest in the REIT, or 15 per cent if the holding was less than 10 per cent.

However, the 15 per cent rate provided under subparagraph 2(*b*) is available in respect of distributions from certain U.S. REITs if any of the following three conditions are met:

(a) The dividend is paid to an individual who qualifies as the beneficial owner of the dividend and who owns less than 10 per cent of the REIT. For this purpose, if an estate or trust acquires a less than 10 per cent interest in a REIT as a result of the death of an individual, dividends paid to the estate or trust for five years after the death will be deemed to be paid to an individual. Therefore, the dividends paid by the REIT to the estate or trust for a five-year period after the death will be eligible for the 15 per cent rate of withholding tax.

(b) The dividends are paid to a person who is the beneficial owner of the dividends and who does not hold more than 5 per cent of any class of a publicly traded REIT; or

(c) The dividends are paid to a person who is the beneficial owner of the dividends and does not hold more than 10 per cent of a "diversified" REIT. A REIT is considered "diversified" if the gross value of no single interest in real property held by the REIT exceeds 10 per cent of the gross value of the REIT's total interest in real property. For this purpose, foreclosure property is not considered an interest in real property. If a REIT holds an interest in a partnership, the REIT is treated as owning its proportionate share of any of the partnership's real property.

Generally, the 15 per cent rate is permitted in these limited circumstances, where the person's REIT holdings are not considered the equivalent of a direct holding in the underlying property (i.e., small interest holders).

Pursuant to paragraph 8, a Canadian resident company, which without the application of the Convention has income subject to U.S. tax, may be liable for U.S. accumulated earnings tax and the personal holding company tax. In order for these to apply, more than 50 per cent of the value of the Canadian company's shares must be owned, directly or indirectly, throughout the last half of its taxation year, by residents of a third country or by citizens or residents of the United States other than citizens of Canada who are resident in the United States, but who either do not have immigrant status in the United States or who have not been resident in the United States for more than three taxable years.

Subsection 10(6) of the *Income Tax Application Rules* provides that notwithstanding Part XIII of the *Income Tax Act* (Canada), where Canada has entered into a bilateral tax convention with a country and that convention provides for a maximum rate of Canadian withholding tax that is less than the Part XIII rate, the rate specified in the convention will apply to amounts paid or credited to a resident of that other country. Under the 1942 Convention, which did not require beneficial ownership of such income by a U.S. resident, the Tax Review Board held in *MacMillan Bloedel Limited v. MNR*, 79 DTC 297, that a Canadian payor's obligation to withhold under Part XIII was reduced to the Convention rate based on the address of the payee being in the United States. The CRA's administrative practices with respect to reliance upon treaty reductions by payors for withholding tax purposes is set out in its Information Circular 76-12R6.

The Fifth Protocol removed all references to "fixed base", "independent personal services" and Article XIV (Independent Services) from Article X (i.e., paragraphs 4 and 5) as a result of the elimination of Article XIV from the Convention. In this respect, the Diplomatic Notes accompanying the Fifth Protocol (Annex "B") confirm the shared understanding of Canada and the United States that there is no practical distinction between a "fixed base" and a "permanent establishment". This change is consistent with the deletion in 2001 of Article 14 of the OECD Model Convention, which the OECD considered generally redundant of Article 7 (Business Profits).

Editorial Note: Technical Interpretation, Document No. 2013-0497381E5, dated July 11, 2014, states that distributions from a SIFT trust in Canada would be treated as dividends pursuant to Article X.

Technical Interpretation, Document No. 2012-0440101E5, dated October 23, 2012, states that the CRA will permit an LLC to claim benefits available under Article X(6) on behalf of its members where a member is a qualifying person under paragraph 2 of Article XXIX A of the Convention or a U.S. resident company entitled to the benefits pursuant to paragraph 3 of Article XXIX A. See also CRA Roundtable, 2010 Canadian Tax Foundation Annual Conference, Document No. 2010-0386391C6, dated November 30, 2010.

Technical Interpretation, Document No. 2007-0262371I7, states that branch tax under Part XIV may be imposed, on a limited basis, on a corporation resident in the United States that has a permanent establishment in Canada. It is also the CRA's view that Article X(6) overrides Article XVI of the Treaty, which provides for the taxation of artists and athletes.

Technical Interpretation, Document No. 2003-0025221E5, dated April 29, 2004, deals with whether the benefit of the Treaty would apply with respect to a U.S. Grantor Trust that owned shares in a Canadian-controlled private corporation (relating to Articles IV, X, and XIII of the Treaty).

For CRA documents discussing the "two-step" process involving an LLC, see the Editorial Notes to Article IV.

History: Subparagraph 2(*a*) of Article X was deleted and replaced by paragraph 1 of Article 5 of the Fifth Protocol to this Convention, and formerly read:

(*a*) 5 per cent of the gross amount of the dividends if the beneficial owner is a company which owns at least 10 per cent of the voting stock of the company paying the dividends;

Paragraph 3 of Article X was deleted and replaced by paragraph 2 of Article 5 of the Fifth Protocol to this Convention, and formerly read:

3. The term 'dividends' as used in this Article means income from shares or other rights, not being debt-claims, participating in profits, as well as income subjected to the same taxation treatment as income from shares by the taxation laws of the State of which the company making the distribution is a resident.

Paragraph 4 of Article X was deleted and replaced by paragraph 3 of Article 5 of the Fifth Protocol to this Convention, and formerly read:

4. The provisions of paragraph 2 shall not apply if the beneficial owner of the dividends, being a resident of a Contracting State, carries on business in the other Contracting State of which the company paying the dividends is a resident, through a permanent establishment situated therein, or performs in that other State independent personal services from a fixed base situated therein, and the holding in respect of which the dividends are paid is effectively connected with such permanent establishment or fixed base. In such case, the provisions of Article VII (Business Profits) or Article XIV (Independent Personal Services), as the case may be, shall apply.

Paragraph 5 of Article X was amended by paragraph 4 of Article 5 of the Fifth Protocol to this Convention by deleting "or a fixed base" following "effectively connected with a permanent establishment".

Subparagraph 7(*c*) of Article X was deleted and replaced by paragraph 5 of Article 5 of the Fifth Protocol to this Convention, and formerly read:

(*c*) Paragraph 2(*a*) shall not apply to dividends paid by a resident of the United States that is a Real Estate Investment Trust, and paragraph 2(*b*) shall apply only where such dividends are beneficially owned by an individual holding an interest of less than 10 per cent in the trust; otherwise the rate of tax applicable under the domestic law of the United States shall apply. Where an estate or a testamentary trust acquired its interest in a Real Estate Investment Trust as a consequence of an individual's death, for the purposes of the preceding sentence the estate or trust shall for the five-year period following the death be deemed with respect to that interest to be an individual.

Paragraphs 2(*a*) and 6 were amended by paragraph 1 of Article 5 of the Third Protocol to the Convention by deleting references to a rate of tax of "10 per cent" and replacing them with references to a rate of tax of "5 per cent".

Paragraph 7 of Article X was amended by paragraph 2 of Article 5 of the Third Protocol to this Convention, and formerly read:

7. Notwithstanding the provisions of paragraph 5, a Contracting State, other than a Contracting State that imposes the additional tax on earnings referred to in paragraph 6, may tax a dividend paid by a company to the extent that the dividend is attributable to profits earned in taxable years beginning after the date of signature of the Convention if, for the three-year period ending with the close of the company's taxable period preceding the declaration of the dividend (or for such part of that three-year period as the company has been in existence, or for the first taxable year if the dividend was declared in that taxable year), at least 50 per cent of such company's gross income from all sources was included in the computation of the business profits attributable to a permanent establishment which such company had in that State; provided that where a resident of the other Contracting State is the beneficial owner of such dividend any tax so imposed on the dividend shall be subject to the limitations of paragraph 2 or the rules of paragraph 4, as the case may be.

Article XI — Interest

1. Interest arising in a Contracting State and beneficially owned by a resident of the other Contracting State may be taxed only in that other State.

2. The term "interest" as used in this Article means income from debt-claims of every kind, whether or not secured by mortgage, and whether or not carrying a right to participate in the debtor's profits, and in particular, income from government securities and income from bonds or debentures, including premiums or prizes attaching to such securities, bonds or debentures, as well as income assimilated to income from money lent by the taxation laws of the Contracting State in which the income arises. However, the term "interest" does not include income dealt with in Article X (Dividends).

3. The provisions of paragraph 1 shall not apply if the beneficial owner of the interest, being a resident of a Contracting State, carries

on, or has carried on, business in the other Contracting State in which the interest arises, through a permanent establishment situated therein, and the debt-claim in respect of which the interest is paid is effectively connected with such permanent establishment. In such case the provisions of Article VII (Business Profits) shall apply.

4. For the purposes of this Article, interest shall be deemed to arise in a Contracting State when the payer is that State itself, or a political subdivision, local authority or a resident of that State. Where, however, the person paying the interest, whether he is a resident of a Contracting State or not, has in a State other than that of which he is a resident a permanent establishment in connection with which the indebtedness on which the interest is paid was incurred, and such interest is borne by such permanent establishment, then such interest shall be deemed to arise in the State in which the permanent establishment is situated and not in the State of which the payer is a resident.

5. Where, by reason of a special relationship between the payer and the beneficial owner or between both of them and some other person, the amount of the interest, having regard to the debt-claim for which it is paid, exceeds the amount which would have been agreed upon by the payer and the beneficial owner in the absence of such relationship, the provisions of this Article shall apply only to the last-mentioned amount. In such case the excess part of the payments shall remain taxable according to the laws of each Contracting State, due regard being had to the other provisions of this Convention.

6. Notwithstanding the provisions of paragraph 1:

(*a*) Interest arising in the United States that is contingent interest of a type that does not qualify as portfolio interest under United States law may be taxed by the United States but, if the beneficial owner of the interest is a resident of Canada, the gross amount of the interest may be taxed at a rate not exceeding the rate prescribed in subparagraph (*b*) of paragraph 2 of Article X (Dividends);

(*b*) Interest arising in Canada that is determined with reference to receipts, sales, income, profits or other cash flow of the debtor or a related person, to any change in the value of any property of the debtor or a related person or to any dividend, partnership distribution or similar payment made by the debtor to a related person may be taxed by Canada, and according to the laws of Canada, but if the beneficial owner is a resident of the United States, the gross amount of the interest may be taxed at a rate not exceeding the rate prescribed in subparagraph (*b*) of paragraph 2 of Article X (Dividends); and

(*c*) Interest that is an excess inclusion with respect to a residual interest in a real estate mortgage investment conduit may be taxed by each State in accordance with its domestic law.

7. Where a resident of a Contracting State pays interest to a person other than a resident of the other Contracting State, that other State may not impose any tax on such interest except insofar as it arises in that other State or insofar as the debt-claim in respect of which the interest is paid is effectively connected with a permanent establishment situated in that other State.

Dentons Canada LLP Commentary: Under paragraph 212(1)(*b*) of the *Income Tax Act* (Canada), a 25 per cent withholding tax is imposed only with respect to: (i) interest paid to non-arm's length parties that is not "fully exempt interest"; or (ii) participating debt interest (as defined in subsection 212(3) of the *Income Tax Act* (Canada).

Under the *Internal Revenue Code*, the U.S. generally applies a 30 per cent withholding tax on outbound interest payments. In addition, the Fifth Protocol overhauled Article XI, eliminating withholding tax on most forms of interest paid on or after January 1, 2008 by a resident of a Contracting State to a beneficial owner resident in the other Contracting State, including payments between parties not dealing at arm's length. The Fifth Protocol also eliminated withholding taxes in respect of guarantee fees pursuant to paragraph 4 of Article XXII (Other Income).

Paragraph 1 of Article XI provides the general rule that interest arising in a Contracting State and beneficially owned by a resident of the other Contracting State may be taxed only in that other State. This elimination of withholding tax on outbound interest paid from Canada to related parties has provided for much greater flexibility in managing intra-group financings between related companies straddling the Canada-U.S. border. From a tax perspective, the most significant remaining restrictions on non-arm's length cross-border financing are the thin capitalization rules in subsection 18(4) of the *Income Tax Act*, which generally restrict interest deductions for any debt that exceeds a 1.5:1 debt/equity ratio. In addition, any interest arising on debt that exceeds the 1.5:1 ratio will result in a dividend being deemed to have been paid by the Canadian borrower to its non-arm's length, non-resident creditor.

The term "beneficial owner" is to be defined under the domestic law of the source State, being the State seeking to impose withholding tax on the amount paid. A recipient will be regarded as the beneficial owner of the amount, generally, so long as the recipient is not acting as an agent or nominee on behalf of a person that is not a resident of that Contracting State. The Technical Explanation to the Fifth Protocol suggests that this interpretation conforms to the meaning of beneficial owner under the domestic laws of both Canada and the United States, as well as the meaning described in the Commentary to Article 10 of the OECD Model. See the commentary to Article IV (Residence) for a discussion of beneficial owner in the context of amounts derived through a fiscally transparent entity. See also the discussion in the commentary to Article X (Dividends) and Article XII (Royalties) for the courts' application of the "beneficial ownership test".

In certain circumstances — for instance, where an LLC issues a loan to its wholly owned ULC (which is treated as fiscally transparent for U.S. tax purposes) — the payment of interest (or royalties or dividends) made by the ULC will be subject to Canadian withholding taxes under Part XIII of the *Income Tax Act* (Canada) but will not be recognized for U.S. tax purposes and will not be eligible for benefits under the Convention. This is pursuant to paragraph 7 of Article IV of the Convention, which deems a payment not to have been derived or received as an amount of income, profit, or gain in this situation. In such situations, benefits under the Convention could be obtained by issuing the loan by the members of the LLC to the ULC rather than issuing the loans to the ULC from its parent LLC.

Paragraph 2 defines "interest" as income from debt claims of every kind as well as amounts deemed to be interest by the taxation laws of a Contracting State. In no event, however, is income dealt with in Article X (Dividends) to be considered interest. Interest also includes amounts that would be considered interest under the tax laws of the source State. In the U.S., this would include, for example, original issue discount, amounts imputed on deferred sales contracts, a partner's distributive share of a partnership's interest income, certain amounts under a residual interest in a real estate mortgage investment conduit ("REMIC"), and interest with respect to notional principal contracts that are recharacterized as loans. In Canada, this would include, for example, amounts deemed to be interest under subsection 214(7) of the *Income Tax Act* (Canada) in respect of the premium received by a non-resident on the sale of certain obligations issued by a resident of Canada.

Paragraph 3 deals with interest that is effectively connected with a permanent establishment; the source State retains the right to tax such interest. The Fifth Protocol removed all references in paragraph 3 to "fixed base", "independent personal services" and Article XIV as a result of the elimination of Article XIV from the Convention.

Paragraphs 4, 5, and 7 deal with (i) the source of interest; (ii) situations in which there is a special relationship between the payer and the beneficial owner of the interest; and (iii) situations in which a Contracting State may tax interest paid by a resident of the other Contracting State to a person who is not a resident of the first-mentioned State. As with paragraph 3, the Fifth Protocol removed all references in these paragraphs to "fixed base", "independent personal services" and Article XIV as a result of the elimination of Article XIV from the Convention.

Paragraph 4 provides that interest has its source within a country if the payer is the government of that country, including political subdivisions and local authorities, or a resident of that country. Where a resident of one State has a permanent establishment in another State and interest is borne by that permanent establishment, the source of the interest will be the State in which that permanent establishment exists. The term "borne by" means allowable as a deduction in computing taxable income.

Pursuant to paragraph 5, if interest was paid between parties that did not deal with each other at arm's length, and the amount of the interest was in excess of an arm's length amount, the provisions of Article XI would not apply to the excess; instead, the excess would be taxed in accordance with the laws of each country with due regard to other provisions in the Convention.

Paragraph 6 provides exceptions to the withholding tax exemption (in addition to the exception contained in paragraph 7, dealing with interest paid by a debtor having a special relationship with the lender). Specifically:

(a) Contingent interest arising in the United States that does not qualify as portfolio interest under the laws of the United States is subject to tax in the United States at the normal domestic U.S. rates (currently 30 per cent). However, if the beneficial owner of the interest is a resident of Canada, then the gross amount of the dividend is taxed at a rate not exceeding the rate applicable to dividends under subparagraph 2(*b*) of Article X of the Convention, being 15 per cent.

(b) Certain types of participating interest arising in Canada are subject to tax in Canada at the rates normally applicable under Canadian law. However, if the beneficial owner of the interest is a resident of the United States, the gross amount of the dividend is taxed at a rate not exceeding the rate applicable to dividends under subparagraph 2(*b*) of Article X of the Convention, being 15 per cent. This reflects the amount of withholding tax that would be applicable in respect of dividends received on stock held as a portfolio investment. The types of interest within the ambit of this provision include:

(i) amounts determined with reference to receipts, sales, income profits, or cash-flows of the debtor or a person related to the debtor;

(ii) any change in the value of any property of the debtor or a related person; and

(iii) dividends, partnership distributions, or similar payments made by the debtor to a related person (the Technical Explanation to the Fifth Protocol confirmed that this paragraph will be interpreted as reading "made by the debtor *or* a related person", not "made by the debtor *to* a related person").

This definition is similar, but slightly narrower, than the definition of "participating debt interest" in subsection 212(3) of the *Income Tax Act* (Canada). Depending on the terms of the debt instrument, the payment of participating interest could be viewed as being more akin to the payment of a dividend than interest and therefore should not qualify for the reduced rate of interest withholding (although the Convention does not permit the recipient of participating interest to qualify for the lowest 5 per cent dividend withholding tax rate, even if the requisite shareholding condition is met).

With respect to convertible debentures, it is possible that the deemed interest arising pursuant to subsection 214(7) of the *Income Tax Act* (Canada) could be considered participating debt interest, as it may be derived based on the value of the equity of the corporation or the dividends paid on those shares. Accordingly, the concern exists that such interest may not be eligible for treatment under Article XI (Interest). The CRA has indicated that where there is a conversion of a "traditional convertible debenture" by its original holder for common shares of the issuer, there would be no excess under subsection 214(7) of the *Income Tax Act* (Canada), so no withholding tax would apply. The CRA specifically limited its position to so called "traditional convertible debentures." In order for the debentures to qualify, certain conditions must be met:

(a) the debentures are unsecured subordinated debts;

(b) the issuer is a public corporation;

(c) the debentures are issued for a fixed amount of money in Canadian dollars (for example, $1,000) that represents the face value of the debentures;

(d) the debentures bear interest at a commercial fixed rate per year calculated on their face value, and the interest on the debentures is paid by the issuer at least annually;

(e) the debentures are convertible at any time at the holders' option into the common shares of the issuer prior to maturity (some debentures have an initial non-conversion period);

(f) the terms of the debentures specifically provide either a fixed conversion price (specifying the fixed price paid per common share to acquire the common shares through the conversion of each debenture) or a fixed conversion ratio (specifying the number of common shares that can be obtained for each debenture);

(g) the conversion price exceeds the price at which the common shares of the issuer could have been purchased on the market at the time the debentures were issued (for example, with a 25% conversion premium);

(h) the debentures have a specified maturity date;

(i) at maturity, the debentures are redeemable by the issuer at a redemption price of 100 per cent of the face value, plus accrued and unpaid interest.

The CRA has also stated that it is not prepared to take the position that standard convertible debentures would in general constitute "excluded debt obligations," pursuant to paragraph 214(8)(*c*) of the *Income Tax Act* (Canada) unless the debentures otherwise meet that criteria, including meeting the 5/25 exception in subparagraph 212(1)(b)(vi) of the *Income Tax Act* (Canada), as it applied prior to January 1, 2008. This leaves certain private corporation convertible debentures at risk of producing participating debt interest, since they will not satisfy the CRA's definition of "traditional convertible debentures."

Paragraph 7 restricts the rights of the Contracting States to impose tax on interest paid by a resident of the other Contracting State. The first state cannot impose any tax on the interest except to the extent that the interest is paid to a resident of that state, arose in that state, or is effectively connected to a permanent establishment situated in that other state.

Editorial Note: Advance Income Tax Ruling, Document No. 2014-0521831R3, deals with a U.S. resident company having a permanent establishment in Canada and the application of paragraph 4 of Article XI of the Convention.

Update from the Income Tax Ruling Directorate, Document No.2013-0509061C6, dated November 26, 2013, dealing with Part XIII Tax & Standard Convertible Debentures.

Advance Income Tax Ruling, Document No. 2013-0514551R3, deals with convertible debentures and the meaning of "participating debt interest." Here the CRA stated that where participating debt interest is paid, residents of the United States can rely on paragraph 1 of Article XI of the Convention to eliminate any withholding tax.

Advance Income Tax Ruling, Document No. 2012-0444041C6, dated May 17, 2012, stated that where income is received by a recipient in the capacity as agent or nominee, the recipient is not the beneficial owner. Where income is not received in the capacity as agent or nominee, the recipient is the beneficial owner if the payment is received for the recipient's own use and enjoyment, and the recipient assumes risk and control over the payment.

Technical Interpretation, Document No. 2012-0436221I7, dated April 19, 2012, dealing with LLCs and ULCs and Treaty benefits.

International Fiscal Association–May 2009, Question 12, Document No. 2009-0320231C6, dated May 1, 2009, dealing with tax treatment under Part XIII of the *Income Tax Act* of convertible debt obligations held by non-residents.

History: Article XI was deleted and replaced by Article 6 of the Fifth Protocol to this Convention. In applying this amendment to interest paid or credited during the period January 1, 2008 to December 31, 2009, paragraph 1 of Article XI shall read:

1. Interest arising in a Contracting State and beneficially owned by a resident of the other Contracting State may be taxed only in that other State. However, if the interest is not exempt under paragraph 3 of Article XI (Interest) as it read on January 1, 2007, and the payer of the interest and the beneficial owner of the interest are related, or would be deemed to be related if the provisions of paragraph 2 of Article IX (Related Persons) applied for this purpose, such interest may also be taxed in the Contracting State in which it arises, and according to the laws of that State, but the tax so charged shall not exceed the following percentage of the gross amount of the interest:

(*a*) If the interest is paid or credited during the first calendar year that ends after entry into force [December 15, 2008] of this paragraph, 7 percent; and

(*b*) If the interest is paid or credited during the second calendar year that ends after entry into force [December 15, 2008] of this paragraph, 4 percent;

Article XI formerly read:

1. Interest arising in a Contracting State and paid to a resident of the other Contracting State may be taxed in that other State.

2. However, such interest may also be taxed in the Contracting State in which it arises, and according to the laws of that State; but if a resident of the other Contracting State is the beneficial owner of such interest, the tax so charged shall not exceed 10 per cent of the gross amount of the interest.

3. Notwithstanding the provisions of paragraph 2, interest arising in a Contracting State shall be exempt from tax in that State if:

(*a*) The interest is beneficially owned by the other Contracting State, a political subdivision or local authority thereof or an instrumentality of such other State, subdivision or authority, and is not subject to tax by that other State;

(*b*) The interest is beneficially owned by a resident of the other Contracting State and is paid with respect to debt obligations issued at arm's length and guaranteed or insured by that other State or a political subdivision thereof or an instrumentality of such other State or subdivision which is not subject to tax by that other State;

(*c*) The interest is beneficially owned by a resident of the other Contracting State and is paid by the first-mentioned State, a political subdivision or local authority thereof or an instrumentality of such first-mentioned State, subdivision or authority which is not subject to tax by that first-mentioned State;

(*d*) The interest is beneficially owned by a resident of the other Contracting State and is paid with respect to indebtedness arising as a consequence of the sale on credit by a resident of that other State of any equipment, merchandise or services except where the sale or indebtedness was between related persons; or

(*e*) The interest is paid by a company created under the laws in force in the other Contracting State with respect to an obligation entered into before the date of signature of this Convention, provided that such interest would have been exempt from tax in the first-mentioned State under Article XII of the 1942 Convention.

4. The term 'interest' as used in this Article means income from debt-claims of every kind, whether or not secured by mortgage, and whether or not carrying a right to participate in the debtor's profits, and in particular, income from government securities and income from bonds or debentures, including premiums and prizes attaching to such securities, bonds or debentures, as well as income assimilated to income from money lent by the taxation laws of the Contracting State in which the income arises. However, the term 'interest' does not include income dealt with in Article X Dividends.

5. The provisions of paragraphs 2 and 3 shall not apply if the beneficial owner of the interest, being a resident of a Contracting State, carries on business in the other Contracting State in which the interest arises, through a permanent establishment situated therein, or performs in that other State independent personal services from a fixed base situated therein, and the debt-claim in respect of which the interest is paid is effectively connected with such permanent establishment or fixed base. In such case, the provisions of Article VII (Business Profits) or Article XIV (Independent Personal Services), as the case may be, shall apply.

6. For the purposes of this Article, interest shall be deemed to arise in a Contracting State when the payer is that State itself, or a political subdivision, local authority or resident of that State. Where, however, the person paying the interest, whether a resident of a Contracting State or not, has, in a State other than that of which he or she is a resident, a permanent establishment or a fixed base in connection with which the indebtedness on which the interest is paid was incurred, and such interest is borne by such permanent establishment or fixed base, then such interest shall be deemed to arise in the State in which the permanent establishment or fixed base is situated and not in the State of which the payer is a resident.

7. Where, by reason of a special relationship between the payer and the beneficial owner or between both of them and some other person, the amount of the interest, having regard to the debt-claim for which it is paid, exceeds the amount which would have been agreed upon by the payer and the beneficial owner in the absence of such relationship, the provisions of this Article shall apply only to the last-mentioned amount. In such case, the excess part of the payments shall remain taxable according to the laws of each Contracting State, due regard being had to the other provisions of the Convention.

8. Where a resident of a Contracting State pays interest to a person other than a resident of the other Contracting State, that other State may not impose any tax on such interest except insofar as it arises in that other State, or insofar as the debt-claim in respect of which the interest is paid is effectively connected with a permanent establishment or a fixed base situated in that other State.

9. The provisions of paragraphs 2 and 3 shall not apply to an excess inclusion with respect to a residual interest in a Real Estate Mortgage Investment Conduit to which Section 860G of the United States *Internal Revenue Code*, as it may be amended from time to time without changing the general principle thereof, applies.

Paragraph 2 of Article XI was amended by paragraph 1 of Article 6 of the Third Protocol to this Convention by deleting the reference to "15 per cent" and replacing it with "10 per cent".

Subparagraph 3(*d*) of Article XI was amended by paragraph 2 of Article 6 of the Third Protocol to this Convention, and formerly read:

(*d*) The interest is beneficially owned by a seller who is a resident of the other Contracting State and is paid by a purchaser in connection with the sale on credit of any equipment, merchandise or services, except where the sale is made between persons dealing with each other not at arm's length; or.

Paragraph 9 was added to Article XI by paragraph 3 of Article 6 of the Third Protocol to this Convention.

Article XII — Royalties

1. Royalties arising in a Contracting State and paid to a resident of the other Contract State may be taxed in that other State.

2. However, such royalties may also be taxed in the Contracting State in which they arise, and according to the laws of that State; but if a resident of the other Contracting State is the beneficial owner of such royalties, the tax so charged shall not exceed 10 per cent of the gross amount of the royalties.

3. Notwithstanding the provisions of paragraph 2,

(*a*) Copyright royalties and other like payments in respect of the production or reproduction of any literary, dramatic, musical or artistic work (other than payments in respect of motion pictures and works on film, videotape or other means of reproduction for use in connection with television);

(*b*) Payments for the use of, or the right to use, computer software;

(*c*) Payments for the use of, or the right to use, any patent or any information concerning industrial, commercial or scientific experience (but not including any such information provided in connection with a rental or franchise agreement); and

(*d*) Payments with respect to broadcasting as may be agreed for the purposes of this paragraph in an exchange of notes between the Contracting States;

arising in a Contracting State and beneficially owned by a resident of the other Contracting State shall be taxable only in that other State.

4. The term "royalties" as used in this Article means payments of any kind received as a consideration for the use of, or the right to use, any copyright of literary, artistic or scientific work (including motion pictures and works on film, videotape or other means of reproduction for use in connection with television), any patent, trade mark, design or model, plan, secret formula or process, or for the use of, or the right to use, tangible personal property or for information concerning industrial, commercial or scientific experience, and, notwithstanding the provisions of Article XIII (Gains), includes gains from the alienation of any intangible property or rights described in this paragraph to the extent that such gains are contingent on the productivity, use or subsequent disposition of such property or rights.

5. The provisions of paragraphs 2 and 3 shall not apply if the beneficial owner of the royalties, being a resident of a Contracting State, carries on, or has carried on, business in the other Contracting State in which the royalties arise, through a permanent establishment situated therein, and the right or property in respect of which the royalties are paid is effectively connected to such permanent establishment. In such case the provisions of Article VII (Business Profits) shall apply.

6. For the purposes of this Article,

(*a*) Royalties shall be deemed to arise in a Contracting State when the payer is a resident of that State. Where, however, the person paying the royalties, whether he is a resident of a Contracting State or not, has in a State a permanent establishment in connection with which the obligation to pay the royalties was incurred, and such royalties are borne by such permanent establishment, then such royalties shall be deemed to arise in the State in which the permanent establishment is situated and not in any other State of which the payer is a resident; and

(*b*) Where subparagraph (*a*) does not operate to treat royalties as arising in either Contracting State and the royalties are for the use of, or the right to use, intangible property or tangible personal property in a Contracting State, then such royalties shall be deemed to arise in that State.

7. Where, by reason of a special relationship between the payer and the beneficial owner, or between both of them and some other person, the amount of the royalties, having regard to the use, right or information for which they are paid, exceeds the amount which would have been agreed upon by the payer and the beneficial owner in the absence of such relationship, the provisions of this Article shall apply only to the last-mentioned amount. In such cases, the excess part of the payments shall remain taxable according to the laws of each Contracting State, due regard being had to the other provisions of this Convention.

8. Where a resident of a Contracting State pays royalties to a person other than a resident of the other Contracting State, that other State may not impose any tax on such royalties except insofar as they arise in that other State or insofar as the right or property in respect of which the royalties are paid is effectively connected with a permanent establishment situated in that other State.

Dentons Canada LLP Commentary: Under paragraph 212(1)(*d*) of the *Income Tax Act* (Canada), a 25 per cent withholding tax is imposed on rents, royalties, or similar payments paid or credited by a resident of Canada to a non-resident person.

Paragraph 1 generally provides that royalties, other than those exempted under paragraph 3 of this Article, that arise (under the royalty source rule discussed below) in one of the Contracting States and are paid to a resident of the other Contracting State may be taxed by both countries. However, paragraph 2 provides that the withholding tax imposed by the source State may not exceed 10 per cent of the gross royalty if a resident of the other State is the "beneficial owner" of the royalty. Under the 1942 Convention the maximum withholding rate was 15 per cent. Therefore, for example, Canada may impose a tax on royalties arising in Canada and paid to a resident of the United States. If the beneficial owner of the royalty is a resident of the United States, the tax shall not exceed 10 per cent of the gross amount of the royalty.

However, resource royalties such as oil or mining royalty payments will not satisfy the requirements of Article XII and, therefore, will be subject to 25 per cent withholding tax pursuant to the *Income Tax Act* (Canada).

The term "beneficial owner" is to be defined under the domestic law of the source State, being the State seeking to impose withholding tax on the

Treaties and Related Legislation

amount paid. A recipient will be regarded as the beneficial owner of the amount, generally so long as the recipient is not acting as an agent or nominee on behalf of a person that is not a resident of that Contracting State. The Technical Explanation to the Fifth Protocol suggests that this interpretation conforms to the meaning of beneficial owner under the domestic laws of both Canada and the United States, as well as the meaning described in the Commentary to Article 10 of the OECD Model. See the commentary to Article IV (Residence) for a discussion of beneficial owner in the context of amounts derived through a fiscally transparent entity.

The concept of beneficial ownership in the context of royalties was most recently considered by the Tax Court of Canada in *Velcro Canada Inc. v. The Queen*, 2012 DTC 1100, where the Court applied the "beneficial ownership test" set out in *Prévost Car Inc. v. R.*, 2009 DTC 5053. Here the Court found that, when asserting who is the beneficial owner of the items being considered (e.g., a payment of dividends or royalties), one must determine who has received possession of the payments for his or her own use and enjoyment, and assumed the risk and control of the payment received. The focus is on the attributes of ownership of the payment or item to be considered.

Paragraph 3 exempts four classes of royalties from withholding tax. First, subparagraph 3(*a*) provides that withholding tax may not be imposed on what are known as "cultural royalties", which generally include copyright royalties and other like payments for the production or reproduction of any literary, dramatic, musical, or artistic work. Royalties for motion pictures and works on film, videotape, or other means of reproduction for use in connection with television are not cultural royalties. Thus, motion picture royalties can be taxed at the 10 per cent withholding rate. It should be noted that royalties for works for use in connection with television are not exempt cultural royalties whether or not the works appear on film or videotape. This treatment and characterization of motion picture and similar royalties is more broad than that under the 1942 Convention, which was addressed in *MCA Television Limited v. The Queen*, 94 DTC 6375 (F.C.T.D.), and in *MNR v. Paris Canadian Films Limited*, 62 DTC 1338 (Ex. Ct.).

Second, subparagraph 3(*b*) provides that payments for the use of, or the right to use, computer software are exempt from withholding tax. The specific reference to software is not intended to imply that the United States views the term "copyright" as excluding software in other U.S. treaties or in the 1980 Convention with Canada. The Tax Court of Canada has concluded that software royalties are copyright royalties: see *Angoss International Limited v. The Queen*, 99 DTC 567. The result in *Angoss* is that software royalties were exempt under Article XII even prior to the introduction of this exemption in the Third Protocol.

Third, subparagraph 3(*c*) provides that payments for the use of, or the right to use, any patent or any information concerning industrial, commercial, or scientific experience are not subject to withholding tax. Payments for information concerning industrial, commercial or scientific experience include royalties for the use of, or the right to use, designs, models, plans, secret formulas, or processes. Also qualifying for this exemption are payments for the use of, or the right to use, "know how". The Exchequer Court decision in *Western Electric Company Incorporated v. MNR*, 69 DTC 5204, supports a broad interpretation of this exemption. A royalty paid in a mixed contract that includes a royalty plus other payments will be exempt from withholding tax to the extent that the royalty portion that qualifies under subparagraph 3(*c*) can be identified. The exemption in subparagraph 3(*c*) does not apply to payments for the use of, or right to use any such information provided in connection with a rental or franchise agreement. A license to use intangibles in an area does not necessarily constitute a franchise agreement for purposes of subparagraph 3(*c*), unless there are other rights or obligations in the license agreement that would indicate that it is, in fact, a franchise agreement. The example given in the technical notes to the Third Protocol is that of a resident of one Contracting State who acquires a right to use a secret formula to manufacture perfume, along with the right to use the trademark for the perfume and to market it at a non-retail level in the other Contracting State. The royalty payment for the use of the secret formula would be exempt from withholding tax under subparagraph 3(*c*) as long as there are no other factors that would indicate that it was a franchise agreement. The payment for the use of, or the right to use the trademark would be subject to withholding tax at 10 per cent. Canada and the United States have confirmed their intention to collaborate to resolve any administrative issues arising from the application of subparagraph 3(*c*).

In an attempt to clarify the availability of this exemption, the Diplomatic Notes accompanying the Fifth Protocol (Annex "B") indicate that information provided in connection with a franchise agreement only refers to information that governs or otherwise deals with the operation of the franchise, whether by the payer or by another person (i.e., information relating to the operation of the franchise by the franchisee). Any other information concerning industrial, commercial, or scientific experience that is held for resale or license shall qualify for the exemption from withholding tax under subparagraph 3(*c*).

Fourth, subparagraph 3(*d*) provides that Canada and the U.S. may agree in an exchange of notes to exempt certain royalties relating to broadcasting. This exemption was added by the Third Protocol as the beginning of an attempt by the United States to broaden the exemption for all types of royalties. Canada was not prepared at the time of the negotiations of the Third Protocol to exempt broadcasting royalties from withholding tax and has not agreed to this exemption as of yet. However, this paragraph allows the two countries to agree to exempt such royalties without having to wait for another protocol. Stated U.S. policy is to pursue a zero rate of withholding for all royalties in future negotiations with Canada.

Paragraph 4 sets out a very wide definition of the term "royalties" for purposes of Article XII. "Royalties" means payments of any kind received as consideration for the use of, or the right to use:

- any copyright of literary, artistic, or scientific work (including motion pictures, films, and videotapes for use in connection with television broadcasting),
- any patent,
- any trademark,
- any design, model or plan,
- any secret formula or process, and
- any tangible personal property (for example equipment rentals).

"Royalties" also include payments made to obtain information concerning industrial, commercial or scientific experience and gains from the alienation of any intangible property, or rights described above, if the gain is contingent on the productivity, use, or subsequent disposition of such intangible property or right. Royalties do not include management fees or payments under a *bona fide* cost-sharing arrangement. Technical service may be royalties if the fees are periodic and dependent upon productivity or a similar measure.

This definition of royalties is broader than under the 1942 Convention and, for example, includes lump sum payments for indefinite use. Thus, it overrides the earlier decision in *Saint John Shipbuilding & Dry Dock Co. Ltd.*, 80 DTC 6272 (F.C.A.). Royalties do not, however, include amounts paid as an "application fee" for the consideration of a franchise agreement, and are therefore not subject to withholding under Article XII even though amounts paid under the franchise agreement itself would be considered royalties (see *Zainul & Shazma Holdings Ltd. v. The Queen*, 2004 DTC 3015 (T.C.C.)).

Paragraph 5 provides that the 10 per cent limitation on tax in the source State under paragraph 2 and the exemptions described in paragraph 3 for certain royalties do not apply if the beneficial owner of the royalties carries on (or carried on) business in the State of source through a permanent establishment and the right or property in respect of which the royalties are paid is effectively connected with such permanent establishment. In that event, the royalty income will be taxable under the provisions of Article VII (Business Profits). Thus, royalties paid to a resident of the United States in respect of property that forms (or formed) part of the assets of his or her permanent establishment in Canada, or that are otherwise attributable to that permanent establishment, will be taxed in Canada as business income.

Paragraph 6 specifies the rules for determining the source of a royalty payment (i.e., where the royalty is deemed to arise). Essentially, there are three rules:

(a) Subject to the rule in (b), royalties are deemed to arise in a Contracting State when the payer is a resident of that State. (The Convention originally referred to the payer being the State itself or a political subdivision or local authority thereof. The definition of "resident of a Contracting State" in Article IV, specifies that the term "resident" includes the Contracting States and their subdivisions and local authorities. Therefore, this reference was dropped from paragraph 6 in Article XII as being unnecessary.)

(b) Regardless of the payer's country of residence, royalties arise, or are deemed to arise, in the country in which there is a permanent establishment in connection with which the obligation to pay the royalty was incurred, if the royalty was borne by that permanent establishment. The term "borne by" means allowable as a deduction in computing taxable income. Thus, for example, if a royalty is paid to a Canadian company by another company that has a permanent establishment in the United States and the royalty obligation is incurred in connection with, and the royalty is borne by, the U.S. permanent establishment, there would be U.S. withholding tax on the royalty under the Convention, regardless of where the paying company is resident.

(c) If the conditions in (a) or (b) do not operate to treat the royalties as arising in either Contracting State, and the royalties are for the use of, or the right to use, intangible property or tangible personal property in a Contracting State, then the royalties are deemed to arise in that State. Therefore, royalties for the use of, or the right to use, intangible property or tangible personal property situated in a country, arise in that country. This means that if a resident of Canada receives a royalty from a resident of another (third) country for the use of, or right to use intangible property or tangible personal property in the United States, that royalty is considered to arise in the United States, and is, therefore, subject to tax in the United States. In the original Convention this rule overrode the preceding two rules. However, since the Third Protocol, this "place of use" rule applies only if the Convention does not otherwise deem the royalties to occur in one of the Contracting States. Therefore, if royalties are not paid by a resident of one of the Contracting States, nor borne by a permanent establishment in either State, then the "place of use" rule in (3) applies. Using the example in the technical notes to the Third Protocol, if a Canadian company granted franchise rights to a resident of

Chile for use in the United States, the royalty paid by the Chilean resident to the Canadian resident would be U.S. source income under this rule, subject to withholding tax at 10 per cent.

If royalties are paid between parties that do not deal with each other at arm's length, and the amount of the royalty is in excess of an arm's length amount value, the provisions of this Article will apply only to such arm's length amount. The excess will be taxable in accordance with the laws of each country with due regard to other provisions of the Convention.

Paragraph 8 restricts the right of a Contracting State to impose tax on royalties paid by a resident of the other Contracting State. The first State may not impose any tax on such royalties except insofar as they arise in that State or are paid to a resident of that State or the right or property in respect of which the royalties are paid is effectively connected with a permanent establishment situated in that State. Therefore, for example, Canada may not impose any tax on royalties by a resident of the United States to a resident of a third country unless the royalty arises in Canada, or unless the property in respect of which the royalty is paid is effectively connected with a permanent establishment situated in Canada.

Subsection 10(6) of the *Income Tax Application Rules* provides that notwithstanding Part XIII of the *Income Tax Act* (Canada), where Canada has entered into a bilateral tax convention with a country and that convention provides for a maximum rate of Canadian withholding tax that is less than the Part XIII rate, the rate specified in the convention will apply to amounts paid or credited to a resident of that other country. Under the 1942 Convention, which did not require beneficial ownership of such income by a U.S. resident, the Tax Review Board held in *MacMillan Bloedel Limited v. MNR*, 79 DTC 297, that a Canadian payer's obligation to withhold under Part XIII was reduced to the Convention rate based on the address of the payee being in the United States. CRA's administrative practices with respect to reliance upon treaty reductions by payers for withholding tax purposes is set out in its Information Circular 76-12R6.

Editorial Note: Technical Interpretation, Document No. 2011-0416181E5, dated August 27, 2012, deals with whether payments based on use in the form of online advertising "clicks", fitting within subparagraph 212(1)(*d*)(iii), constitute a royalty or business profits for the purposes of treaty relief.

Technical Interpretation, Document No. 2011-0422781E5, dated August 2, 2012, indicates that payments to use computer software generally constitute business profits and not royalties.

Technical Interpretation, Document No. 2007-0253321E5, dated November 14, 2007, deals with the requirement to withhold tax on a "franchise" fee paid to a company located in the United States. Where the franchise fee is for services provided to the franchisee, Article VII of the treaty (Business Profits) would apply and withholding is not required.

Technical Interpretation, Document No. 2004-0086631E5, dated June 14, 2005, deals with whether a royalty payment based on the net sales of reproduced artwork is exempt from Part XIII withholding within the meaning of subparagraph 212(1)(*d*)(vi) of the Act and under paragraph 3(*a*) of Article XII.

History: Paragraph 5 of Article XII was deleted and replaced by paragraph 1 of Article 7 of the Fifth Protocol to this Convention, and formerly read:

5. The provisions of paragraphs 2 and 3 shall not apply if the beneficial owner of the royalties, being a resident of a Contracting State, carries on business in the other Contracting State in which the royalties arise, through a permanent establishment situated therein, or performs in that other State independent personal services from a fixed base situated therein, and the right or property in respect of which the royalties are paid is effectively connected with such permanent establishment or fixed base. In such case the provisions of Article VII (Business Profits) or Article XIV (Independent Personal Services), as the case may be, shall apply.

Subparagraph 6(*a*) of Article XII was deleted and replaced by paragraph 2 of Article 7 of the Fifth Protocol to this Convention, and formerly read:

(*a*) Royalties shall be deemed to arise in a Contracting State when the payer is a resident of that State. Where, however, the person paying the royalties, whether he is a resident of a Contracting State or not, has in a State a permanent establishment or a fixed base in connection with which the obligation to pay the royalties was incurred, and such royalties are borne by such permanent establishment or fixed base, then such royalties shall be deemed to arise in the State in which the permanent establishment or fixed base is situated and not in any other State of which the payer is a resident; and

Paragraph 8 of Article XII was amended by paragraph 3 of Article 7 of the Fifth Protocol to this Convention by deleting "or a fixed base" following "effectively connected with a permanent establishment".

Paragraph 3 of Article XII was amended by paragraph 1 of Article 7 of the Third Protocol to this Convention, and formerly read:

3. Notwithstanding the provisions of paragraph 2, copyright royalties and other like payments in respect of the production or reproduction of any literary, dramatic, musical or artistic work (but not including royalties in respect of motion pictures and works on film, videotape or other means of reproduction for use in connection with television) arising in a Contracting State and beneficially owned by a resident of the other Contracting State shall be taxable only in that other State.

Paragraph 6 of Article XII was amended by paragraph 2 of Article 7 of the Third Protocol to this Convention, and formerly read:

6. For the purposes of this Article, royalties shall be deemed to arise in a Contracting State when the payer is that State itself, or a political subdivision, local authority or resident of that State. However:

(*a*) Except as provided in subparagraph (*b*), where the person paying the royalties, whether he is a resident of a Contracting State or not, has in a State other than that of which he is a resident a permanent establishment or a fixed base in connection with which the obligation to pay the royalties was incurred, and such royalties are borne by such permanent establishment or fixed base, then such royalties shall be deemed to arise in the State in which the permanent establishment or fixed base is situated and not in the State of which the payer is a resident; and

(*b*) Where the royalties are for the use of, or the right to use, intangible property or tangible personal property in a Contracting State, then such royalties shall be deemed to arise in that State and not in the State of which the payer is a resident.

Paragraphs 3 and 4 of Article XII were amended by Article V of the First Protocol to this Convention, and formerly read:

3. Notwithstanding the provisions of paragraph 2, copyright royalties and other like payments in respect of the production or reproduction of any literary, dramatic, musical or artistic work (but not including royalties in respect of motion picture films and of works on film or videotape for use in connection with television) arising in a Contracting State and beneficially owned by a resident of the other Contracting State shall be taxable only in that other State.

4. The term "royalties" as used in this Article means payments of any kind received as a consideration for the use of, or the right to use, any copyright of literary, artistic or scientific work (including motion picture films and works on film or videotape for use in connection with television), any patent, trade mark, design or model plan, secret formula or process, or for the use of, or the right to use, tangible personal property or for information concerning industrial, commercial or scientific experience, and, notwithstanding the provisions of Article XIII (Gains), includes gains from the alienation of any intangible property or rights described in this paragraph to the extent that such gains are contingent on the productivity, use or subsequent disposition of such property or rights.

Subparagraph 6(*b*) of Article XII was amended by Article V of the First Protocol to this Convention, and formerly read:

(*b*) Where the royalties are for the use of intangible property or tangible personal property in a Contracting State, then such royalties shall be deemed to arise in that State and not in the State of which the payer is a resident.

Article XIII — Gains

1. Gains derived by a resident of a Contracting State from the alienation of real property situated in the other Contracting State may be taxed in that other State.

2. Gains from the alienation of personal property forming part of the business property of a permanent establishment which a resident of a Contracting State has or had (within the twelve-month period preceding the date of alienation) in the other Contracting State, including such gains from the alienation of such a permanent establishment, may be taxed in that other State.

3. For the purposes of this Article the term "real property situated in the other Contracting State"

(*a*) In the case of real property situated in the United States, means a United States real property interest and real property referred to in Article VI (Income from Real Property) situated in the United States, but does not include a share of the capital stock of a company that is not a resident of the United States; and

(*b*) In the case of real property situated in Canada means:

(i) Real property referred to in Article VI (Income from Real Property) situated in Canada;

(ii) A share of the capital stock of a company that is a resident of Canada, the value of whose shares is derived principally from real property situated in Canada; and

(iii) An interest in a partnership, trust or estate, the value of which is derived principally from real property situated in Canada.

4. Gains from the alienation of any property other than that referred to in paragraphs 1, 2 and 3 shall be taxable only in the Contracting State of which the alienator is a resident.

5. The provisions of paragraph 4 shall not affect the right of a Contracting State to levy, according to its domestic law, a tax on gains from the alienation of any property derived by an individual who is a resident of the other Contracting State if:

(*a*) The individual was a resident of the first-mentioned State:

(i) For at least 120 months during any period of 20 consecutive years preceding the alienation of the property; and

(ii) At any time during the 10 years immediately preceding the alienation of the property; and

(*b*) The property (or property for which such property was substituted in an alienation the gain on which was not recognized for the purposes of taxation in the first-mentioned State):

(i) Was owned by the individual at the time the individual ceased to be a resident of the first-mentioned State; and

(ii) Was not a property that the individual was treated as having alienated by reason of ceasing to be a resident of the first-mentioned State and becoming a resident of the other Contracting State.

6. Where an individual (other than a citizen of the United States) who was a resident of Canada became a resident of the United States, in determining his liability to United States taxation in respect of any gain from the alienation of a principal residence in Canada owned by him at the time he ceased to be a resident of Canada, the adjusted basis of such property shall be no less than its fair market value at that time.

7. Where at any time an individual is treated for the purposes of taxation by a Contracting State as having alienated a property and is taxed in that State by reason thereof, the individual may elect to be treated for the purposes of taxation in the other Contracting State, in the year that includes that time and all subsequent years, as if the individual had, immediately before that time, sold and repurchased the property for an amount equal to its fair market value at that time.

8. Where a resident of a Contracting State alienates property in the course of a corporate or other organization, reorganization, amalgamation, division or similar transaction and profit, gain or income with respect to such alienation is not recognized for the purpose of taxation in that State, if requested to do so by the person who acquires the property, the competent authority of the other Contracting State may agree, in order to avoid double taxation and subject to terms and conditions satisfactory to such competent authority, to defer the recognition of the profit, gain or income with respect to such property for the purpose of taxation in that other State until such time and in such manner as may be stipulated in the agreement.

9. Where a person who is a resident of a Contracting State alienates a capital asset which may in accordance with this Article be taxed in the other Contracting State and

(*a*) That person owned the asset on September 26, 1980 and was resident in the first-mentioned State on that date; or

(*b*) The asset was acquired by that person in an alienation of property which qualified as a non-recognition transaction for the purposes of taxation in that other State;

the amount of the gain which is liable to tax in that other State in accordance with this Article shall be reduced by the proportion of the gain attributable on a monthly basis to the period ending on December 31 of the year in which the Convention enters into force, or such greater portion of the gain as is shown to the satisfaction of the competent authority of the other State to be reasonably attributable to that period. For the purposes of this paragraph the term "non-recognition transaction" includes a transaction to which paragraph 8 applies and, in the case of taxation in the United States, a transaction that would have been a non-recognition transaction but for Sections 897(*d*) and 897(*e*) of the *Internal Revenue Code*. The provisions of this paragraph shall not apply to

(*c*) An asset that on September 26, 1980 formed part of the business property of a permanent establishment of a resident of a Contracting State situated in the other Contracting State;

(*d*) An alienation by a resident of a Contracting State of an asset that was owned at any time after September 26, 1980 and before such alienation by a person who was not at all times after that date while the asset was owned by such person a resident of that State; or

(*e*) An alienation of an asset that was acquired by a person at any time after September 26, 1980 and before such alienation in a transaction other than a non-recognition transaction.

Dentons Canada LLP Commentary: The general rule, as provided in paragraph 4 of Article XIII, is that gains derived in one country, from the alienation of property (other than property referred to in paragraphs 1, 2, and 3) owned by a resident of the other country, will be taxed only in the alienator's country of residence. It is understood that the term "alienation" as used in this Article is intended to include sales, exchanges, and other dispositions or deemed dispositions (e.g., change of use, gifts, distributions, expropriations, death) that are taxable events under the taxation laws of the country applying the provisions of this Article.

The CRA has issued Interpretation Bulletin IT-173R2 (now archived) dealing with "Capital Gains Derived in Canada by Residents of the United States". This Bulletin discusses CRA's position with respect to the application of Article XIII.

There are several instances, however, where this general rule is not applicable. Firstly, under paragraph 1, gains derived by a resident of one country from the alienation of real property situated in the other country may be subject to tax in the country where the real property is situated. Therefore, the physical location of the real property is the critical factor in determining that the source country will tax the gain. Paragraph 3 of this Article defines the term "real property situated in the other Contracting State". Real property situated in Canada means:

(a) real property (as defined in Article VI) situated in Canada;

(b) a share of the capital stock of a company, that is a resident of Canada, if the value of the share is attributable principally to Canadian real property; and

(c) an interest in a partnership, trust or estate, the value of which is attributable principally to Canadian real property.

It is understood that the term "principally" is intended to mean more than 50 per cent of the value is attributable to real property.

"Real property situated in the United States" means:

(a) real property (as defined in Article VI) situated in the United States; and

(b) a U.S. real property interest. Under the provisions of the *Internal Revenue Code* the term "United States real property interest" includes shares in a United States corporation that owns sufficient United States real property interests to satisfy an asset-ratio test on certain testing dates. Consistently, subparagraph 3(*a*) explicitly excludes from the definition "real property situated in the United States" shares of the capital stock of a company that is not a resident of the United States.

As a result of the amendments in the Fourth Protocol to the definitions of "real property situated in the other Contracting State", effective April 26, 1995;

(a) Canada agrees not to tax U.S. residents' gains on shares of corporations that are not resident in Canada; and

(b) the U.S. agrees a "United States real property interest" does not include shares of corporations that are not resident in the U.S.

However, the term "share" does not include an "option in respect of a share," because paragraph 2 of Article III (Interpretation) provides that for the purposes of the Convention, domestic law should be used to interpret the meaning of "share." Pursuant to the *Income Tax Act* (Canada), there is currently no provision deeming an "option in respect of a share" to be a "share". Note that historically paragraph 115(1)(b) and subsection 115(3) of the *Income Tax Act* (Canada) provided a deeming rule that deemed an "option in respect of a share" to be a "share", but these provisions were repealed.

Secondly, paragraph 2 states that if a resident of one country has (or had) a permanent establishment (Article V) in the other country, that other country (or source country) may tax gains from the alienation of personal property realized by the non-resident which constituted business property, if the gains are attributable to the permanent establishment. The source country may tax any such gains that arise within a 12-month period after the permanent establishment ceases to exist.

The third exception, outlined in paragraph 5, concerns gains from the alienation of certain property which are realized by individuals. As was previously stated, most capital gains realized by an individual resident in one country may not be taxed in the other country. However, the main purpose of paragraph 5 is to ensure that gains that accrue while an individual is resident in a Contracting State (and that are not subject to taxation in that State upon emigration) remain taxable by that State for a defined period of time after the individual has emigrated to the other Contracting State. Pursuant to paragraph 5, a Contracting State may impose tax on gains derived by an individual who is a resident of the other Contracting State if:

(a) the individual was a resident of the first-mentioned State for 120 months (whether or not consecutive) during any period of any consecutive 20 years preceding alienation of the property;

(b) the individual was a resident of that State at any time during the 10-year period immediately preceding the alienation of the property;

(c) the property (or property received in substitution in a tax-free transaction in the first-mentioned State) was owned by the individual at the time the individual ceased to be a resident of the first-mentioned State; and

(d) the property was not property that was deemed to have been disposed of under the tax laws of the Contracting State as a result of ceasing to be a resident of that State and becoming a resident of the other State.

Therefore, for example, Canada may tax gains realized by an individual who is a resident of the United States if the individual was a resident of Canada for 120 months during any consecutive 20-year period preceding the date of alienation of property, *and* the individual was a resident of Canada at any time during the 10 years immediately preceding the alienation. However, for Canada to have a right to tax the gain, the property must have been owned by the individual at the time the individual ceased to be a resident of Canada and must not have been deemed to have been disposed of at the time of emigration for Canadian tax purposes. This last criteria was added by the Fifth Protocol and recognizes that if there is a taxable deemed disposition of property upon emigration from a Contracting State, that State should no longer have any jurisdiction to assert taxing authority over the property. For example, most forms of property are deemed under paragraph 128.1(4)(*b*) of the *Income Tax Act* (Canada) to have been disposed of by a resident of Canada immediately before the person ceases to be a Canadian resident, which generally allows Canada the right to tax any appreciation in the property that occurred while the person was a Canadian resident. Paragraph 5 prohibits Canada from subsequently taxing any appreciation in the property that occurs after the person emigrates from Canada to the United States.

Paragraph 5 generally allows Canada to impose tax on dispositions of taxable Canadian property by U.S. residents who were previously Canadian residents. However, gains that are taxable by one country following the rules in paragraph 5 have their source, for purposes of the Convention, in the country of residence (Article XXIV (2)(*c*)). Thus, the country of residence will have the primary right to tax the gain, while the country of former residence will allow a foreign tax credit for the tax paid to the country of residence.

Paragraph 6 concerns the taxation of gains realized on the alienation of a principal residence situated in Canada by a resident of the United States who was formerly a resident of Canada. An individual, other than a U.S. citizen, who was a resident of Canada but who becomes a resident of the United States, must adjust the cost base of his or her Canadian principal residence for U.S. tax purposes so that it is at least equal to the fair market value of the residence at the time he or she became resident of the United States.

Paragraph 7 provides a rule to coordinate U.S. and Canadian taxation of gains in the case of a timing mismatch, effective for alienations of property that occur after September 17, 2000. This provision would apply, for example, to an individual resident of one country (who is subject to tax in both countries) that alienates a property and one country treats the alienation as a taxable event and the other country defers taxation until a later year (i.e., a U.S. citizen who, for Canadian tax purposes, is deemed to recognize income upon emigration from Canada). As discussed above, a resident of Canada that emigrates to the United States is deemed under paragraph 128.1(4)(*b*) of the *Income Tax Act* (Canada) to have disposed of most types of property at fair market value immediately before the person ceases to be a Canadian resident. The person is therefore liable for Canadian tax on any gains deemed to have been realized on the disposition, and the adjusted cost basis of the property is "stepped-up" to fair market value for Canadian tax purposes. In such a case, the individual is permitted under paragraph 7 to elect to recognize the gains in the latter country and is deemed to have sold and immediately repurchased the property for an amount equal to its fair market value at that time.

The Fifth Protocol broadened the scope of paragraph 7 to ensure that the election is available to certain persons not subject to tax in both countries (i.e., a non-U.S. citizen that emigrates from Canada). If the individual is not subject to U.S. tax at the time of emigration from Canada, the election under paragraph 7 will give the individual an adjusted cost basis for U.S. tax purposes equal to the fair market value of the property as of the date of the deemed disposition. Accordingly, only post-emigration gain will be subject to U.S. taxation. If the person is a U.S. resident at the time of emigration, the election under paragraph 7 will accelerate U.S. taxation of the deemed disposition and allow the individual to offset its U.S. tax liability with foreign tax credits in respect of the Canadian tax paid. (See Article XXIV (Elimination of Double Taxation).)

The rule does not apply in the case of death, even though Canada deems death to be a taxable event. Article XXIX B (Taxes Imposed by Reason of Death) provides rules that coordinate the income tax that Canada imposes by reason of death with the U.S. estate tax. Moreover, this provision only applies if the deemed alienation of the property results in a net gain.

Paragraph 8 of Article XIII also provides special rules for reorganizations, amalgamations, and other such transactions, and is applicable to entities such as trusts and partnerships as well as corporations. Paragraph 8 applies where a resident of one country disposes of property in the course of a reorganization, amalgamation, division, or similar transaction and the profit, gain or income with respect to such disposition is not recognized by the Contracting State of which he or she is a resident. The competent authority of the other country may, upon request, agree to defer recognition of the profit gain or income with respect to the property. Such deferral, if permitted, is allowed to avoid double taxation and is subject to terms and conditions satisfactory to the competent authority. The CRA has confirmed, in Document No. 2012-0444161C6, that an agreement under this paragraph 8 of Article XIII will only be entered into where the agreement results in a deferral (to avoid double taxation) and not an exemption or exclusion of tax resulting from a gain.

The 1942 Convention generally exempted capital gains from tax while the current Convention does not. Paragraph 9 of Article XIII contains a transitional rule that takes this difference into account. In general, the transitional rule applies to certain property that was owned by a resident of the non-source country on September 26, 1980 (the date of signature of the Convention) and which was not part of a permanent establishment or fixed base in the source country (references to a "fixed base" were eliminated by the Fifth Protocol as a result of the deletion of Article XVI (Independent Personal Services). The effect of this transitional rule is to give the owner of the property a step-up in basis for purposes of computing the gain subject to tax in the other State. Under the transitional rule, for purposes of computing the taxable gain in the source country, the gain realized on the disposition is to be reduced by the portion of any gain attributable to the period up to December 31, 1984. (See Article XXX (Entry into Force).) This method gives taxpayers the benefit of the assumption that capital assets that appreciate do so in the same amount during each month of the holding period. If, however, the taxpayer shows to the satisfaction of the competent authority of the source country that a greater than proportional part of the gain is reasonably attributable to that period, then the competent authority is to permit that greater portion to be excluded from tax. In general, the excluded portion may be calculated one of two ways:

(a) $\dfrac{\text{Number of months owned before December 31, 1994}}{\text{Total months owned}} \times \text{Gain on alienation}$

(b) Obtain a valuation of the asset as at December 31, 1984.

Application of this transitional rule only applies if the resident who alienates the capital asset both owned it on September 26, 1980 and resided in the same country on September 26, 1980, or if the resident who alienates the asset acquired the asset in an alienation of property that qualified as a non-recognition transaction for purpose of taxation in the source country. Thus, for example, in order for paragraph 9 to be used by a Canadian resident who did not own the alienated asset on September 26, 1980, the asset must have been owned by other Canadian residents continuously since September 26, 1980 and must have been transferred only in transactions which were non-recognition transactions for U.S. tax purposes.

This transitional rule specifically does not apply to the alienation of property by a resident of one country if that asset:

(a) on September 26, 1980 formed part of the business property of a permanent establishment which the resident had in the other country;

(b) was owned at any time prior to the transaction in question and after September 26, 1980 by a person who was not a resident of that country;

(c) was acquired between September 26, 1980 and the time of alienation in a transaction other than a non-recognition transaction.

The proper application of the paragraph 9 transitional rule had been a source of some confusion in Canada. The CRA and Finance authorities, together with the Courts, seemed unnecessarily troubled when applying this transitional relief to Canadian property owned prior to December 31, 1971, when capital gains became taxable in Canada. The issue was whether the gain which is deemed to accrue over the period of ownership is the post-'71 taxable gain or the gain throughout the period the property was held. The Technical Explanation (and its predecessors), which have been confirmed by Canadian authorities, appear clearly worded to apply this rule to the gain accruing throughout the holding period. The CRA's IT-173 was amended by a Special Release in 1996 to depart from this view. In *Kaplan Estate v. The Queen*, 94 DTC 1816, the Tax Court confirmed that the gain was the entire gain and not simply the post-'71 taxable gain. Subsequently, and after the Interpretation Bulletin was amended without any change to the Technical Explanation, the Federal Court of Appeal in *Kubicek Estate v. Attorney General of Canada*, 97 DTC 5454, reversed the Tax Court and held that paragraph 9 applied to the post-'71 taxable gain. In *Haas Estate v. The Queen*, 2001 DTC 6701, the Federal Court of Appeal reiterated the conclusion it had reached in *Kubicek Estate*, presumably putting an end to the debate as to the proper interpretation of paragraph 9.

It must be remembered that, even if a non-Canadian's gain on the disposition of taxable Canadian property is exempt under Article XIII of the Convention, the notification, withholding and potential purchaser liability requirements of section 116 of the *Income Tax Act* (Canada) must still be complied with.

Editorial Note: International Fiscal Association (IFA) Conference, Canada Revenue Agency Roundtable, Document No. 2012-0444161C6, May 17, 2012, states that the CRA will not enter into an agreement pursuant to paragraph 8 of Article XIII that results in the exemption or exclusion of the gain from tax.

Technical Interpretation, Document No. 2011-0416521E5, dated June 22, 2012, states that following the repeal of paragraph 115(1)(*b*) and subsection 115(3) of the *Income Tax Act* (Canada), an option in respect of a share is not a share.

Technical Interpretation, Document No. 2004-0109171E5, dated September 5, 2007, states that where a partnership realizes a gain on the shares of a Canadian corporation that is not attributable to real property situated in Canada, it is the CRA's view that "Article XIII of the Convention would apply in determining if the member's share of the taxable capital gain realized by the partnership is taxable in Canada".

Technical Interpretation, Document No. 2003-0025221E5, dated April 29, 2004, deals with whether the benefit of the Treaty would apply with respect to a U.S. Grantor Trust that owned shares in a Canadian-controlled private corporation (relating to Articles IV, X, and XIII of the Treaty).

History: Paragraph 2 of Article XIII was deleted and replaced by paragraph 1 of Article 8 of the Fifth Protocol to this Convention, and formerly read:

2. Gains from the alienation of personal property forming part of the business property of a permanent establishment which a resident of a Contracting State has or had (within the twelve-month period preceding the date of alienation) in the other Contracting State or of personal property pertaining to a fixed base which is or was available (within the twelve-month period preceding the date of alienation) to a resident of a Contracting State in the other Contracting State for the purpose of performing independent personal services, including such gains from the alienation of such a permanent establishment or of such a fixed base, may be taxed in that other State.

Paragraph 5 of Article XIII was deleted and replaced by paragraph 2 of Article 8 of the Fifth Protocol to this Convention, and formerly read:

5. The provisions of paragraph 4 shall not affect the right of a Contracting State to levy tax on gains from the alienation of property derived by an individual who is a resident of the other Contracting State if such individual:

(*a*) Was a resident of the first-mentioned State for 120 months during any period of 20 consecutive years preceding the alienation of the property; and

(*b*) Was a resident of the first-mentioned State at any time during the ten years immediately preceding the alienation of the property;

and if such property (or property for which such property was substituted in an alienation the gain on which was not recognized for the purposes of taxation in the first-mentioned State) was owned by the individual at the time he ceased to be a resident of the first-mentioned State.

Paragraph 7 of Article XIII was deleted and replaced by paragraph 3 of Article 8 of the Fifth Protocol to this Convention, and formerly read:

7. Where at any time an individual is treated for the purposes of taxation by a Contracting State as having alienated a property and is taxed in that State by reason thereof and the domestic law of the other Contracting State at such time defers (but does not forgive) taxation, that individual may elect in his annual return of income for the year of such alienation to be liable to tax in the other Contracting State in that year as if he had, immediately before that time, sold and repurchased such property for an amount equal to its fair market value at that time.

Subparagraph 9(*c*) of Article XIII was amended by paragraph 4 of Article 8 of the Fifth Protocol to this Convention by deleting "or pertained to a fixed base" following "permanent establishment".

Subparagraph 3(*a*) was amended by the Fourth Protocol to this Convention, and formerly read:

(*a*) In the case of real property situated in the United States, means a United States real property interest and real property referred to in Article VI (Income from Real Property) situated in the United States; and

Subparagraph 3(*b*)(ii) was amended by the Fourth Protocol to this Convention, and formerly read:

(ii) A share of the capital stock of a company, the value of whose shares is derived principally from real property situated in Canada; and

Paragraph 8 of Article XIII was amended by Article 8 of the Third Protocol to this Convention, and formerly read:

8. Where a resident of a Contracting State alienates property in the course of a corporate organization, reorganization, amalgamation, division or similar transaction and profit, gain or income with respect to such alienation is not recognized for the purpose of taxation in that State, if requested to do so by the person who acquires the property, the competent authority of the other Contracting State may agree, in order to avoid double taxation and subject to terms and conditions satisfactory to such competent authority, to defer the recognition of the profit, gain or income with respect to such property for the purpose of taxation in that other State until such time and in such manner as may be stipulated in the agreement.

Paragraphs 3 and 5 of Article XIII were amended by Article VI of the First Protocol to this Convention, and formerly read:

3. Gains derived by a resident of a Contracting State from the alienation of:

(*a*) Shares forming part of a substantial interest in the capital stock of a company which is not a resident of that State the value of which shares is derived principally from real property situated in the other Contracting State; or

(*b*) An interest in a partnership, trust or estate the value of which is derived principally from real property situated in the other Contracting State may be taxed in that other State, provided that the laws in force in the first-mentioned State at the time of such alienation would, in comparable circumstances, be subject to taxation gains derived by a resident of that other State. For the purposes of this paragraph,

(*c*) The term "real property" includes the shares of a company the value of which shares is derived principally from real property or an interest in a partnership, trust or estate referred to in subparagraph (*b*), but does not include property (other than mines, oil or gas wells, rental property or property used for agriculture or forestry) in which the business of the company, partnership, trust or estate is carried on; and

(*d*) A substantial interest exists when the resident and persons related thereto own 10 per cent or more of the shares of any class of the capital stock of a company.

5. The provisions of paragraph 4 shall not affect the right of a Contracting State to levy a tax on gains from the alienation of property derived by an individual who is a resident of the other Contracting State if such individual:

(*a*) Was a resident of the first-mentioned State for 120 months during any period of 20 consecutive years; and

(*b*) Was a resident of the first-mentioned State at any time during the ten years immediately preceding the alienation of the property.

Paragraph 9 of Article XIII was amended by Article VI of the First Protocol to this Convention, and formerly read:

9. Where a resident of a Contracting State alienates property which may in accordance with this Article be taxed in the other Contracting State and which was owned by a resident of the first-mentioned State on the date of signature of this Convention, the amount of the gain which is liable to tax in that other State in accordance with this Article shall be reduced by the proportion of the gain attributable (on a monthly basis), or such greater portion of the gain as is shown to the satisfaction of the competent authority of the other State to be reasonably attributable, to the period ending on December 31 of the year in which the Convention enters into force; the provisions of this paragraph shall not apply to property which on the date of signature of the Convention formed part of the business property of a permanent establishment or pertained to a fixed base in the other Contracting State.

Article XIV — Independent Personal Services [Repealed.]

Dentons Canada LLP Commentary: The Fifth Protocol deleted Article XIV from the Convention. Previously, self-employed individuals (other than entertainers, musicians and athletes — see Article XVI) who were resident of one country could have been taxed in the other country (the source country) on their income from the performance of personal services under Article XIV, if the income was attributable to a fixed base in the source country. The 1942 Convention provided a limited exemption from tax by the source country and had a $5,000 threshold for source country taxation even when the services were performed through a fixed base.

Article XIV applied to services performed in an independent capacity and therefore did not contemplate services performed by an officer or an employee which are covered in Article XV (formerly referred to as "Dependent Personal Services").

The Federal Court of Appeal has held that criteria indicative of "independent personal services" as opposed to "dependent services" include the level of control exerted over the activities of the individual, the ownership of equipment necessary to perform the work, whether the taxpayer hired his/her own assistants, and the degree of financial risk that was assumed by the individual. Moreover, the common intentions of the payor/payee must be considered in order to assess whether the contract is genuinely entered into as a contract for services (see *Wolf v. The Queen*, 2002 DTC 6853 (F.C.A.)).

The income derived by an individual in respect of the performance of independent personal services would have been taxed by, for example, Canada, if the individual has, or had, a fixed base regularly available to him or her in Canada and the income was attributable to the fixed base. The term "has or had" ensured that the source country in which the fixed base existed had the right to tax income attributable to that fixed base even if there was a delay between the termination of the fixed base and the receipt or accrual of such income to the individual. There was, however, a total exemption from taxation by the source country if a fixed base did not exist.

The term "fixed base" was not defined in the Convention, but was given a meaning similar to the concept of "permanent establishment", which is defined in Article V (see commentary following Article V). In *The Queen v. Dudney*, 2000 DTC 6169 (F.C.A.), (confirming *Dudney v. The Queen*, 99 DTC 147 (T.C.C.)) Canadian courts had the opportunity to consider the meaning of "fixed base" as used in Article XIV. Both Courts, in reliance upon the commentaries to the OECD Model Convention, considered the meaning of fixed base to be based on principles similar to the meaning of "permanent establishment". In *Dudney*, an individual independent contractor who was provided with a Canadian office by one of his Canadian clients for purposes of performing his contracted services for that client was not considered to have a fixed base since the office did not constitute an identifiable location or base used by the non-resident for the operation of his own business.

When determining whether income from independent personal services was "attributable" to a fixed base, the principles used to determine business profits attributable to a permanent establishment were generally applicable. As a result, expenses incurred for the purposes of the fixed base, including executive and administrative expenses which were reasonably allocable to the fixed base, were deductible from independent personal services income without regard to where they were incurred.

The Fifth Protocol deleted Article XIV because there was no practical distinction between a "fixed base" and a "permanent establishment". This reflects the reasoning in the *Dudney* case, in which the Federal Court of Appeal confirmed that these concepts should generally be equated. All business income (including income from "independent personal services") derived by a resident of one Contracting State through the other Contracting State is now taxed pursuant to the conditions of Article VII (Business Profits). This deletion is in accordance with the position adopted by the OECD, which eliminated the corresponding independent personal services Article from its Model Convention in 2001. In doing so, the OECD noted that service businesses were appropriately addressed by Article 7 of the OECD Model Convention, dealing with the taxation of business profits, and that there was generally no need for a separate Article dealing with income from these types of services. In this respect, the Fifth Protocol also expanded the circumstances in which a service provider would be subject to tax in the source State under Article V (Permanent Establishment) by including a new deeming rule in paragraph 9 of that Article. This rule, discussed in the Commentary following Article V, deems a service provider to have a permanent establishment in the source State, and thereby be taxable in the source State under Article VII, in circumstances that would not have otherwise given rise to a "fixed base" under Article XIV or a permanent establishment under Article V.

History: Article XIV was deleted by Article 9 of the Fifth Protocol to this Convention, and formerly read:

Income derived by an individual who is a resident of a Contracting State in respect of independent personal services may be taxed in that State. Such income may also be taxed in the other Contracting State if the individual has or had a fixed base regularly available to him in that other State but only to the extent that the income is attributable to the fixed base.

Article XV — Income from Employment

1. Subject to the provisions of Articles XVIII (Pensions and Annuities) and XIX (Government Service), salaries, wages and other remuneration derived by a resident of a Contracting State in respect of an employment shall be taxable only in that State unless the employment is exercised in the other Contracting State. If the employment is so exercised, such remuneration as is derived therefrom may be taxed in that other State.

2. Notwithstanding the provisions of paragraph 1, remuneration derived by a resident of a Contracting State in respect of an employment exercised in the other Contracting State shall be taxable only in the first-mentioned State if:

(*a*) Such remuneration does not exceed ten thousand dollars ($10,000) in the currency of that other State; or

(*b*) The recipient is present in that other State for a period or periods not exceeding in the aggregate 183 days in any twelve-month period commencing or ending in the fiscal year concerned, and the remuneration is not paid by, or on behalf of, a person who is a resident of that other State and is not borne by a permanent establishment in that other State.

3. Notwithstanding the provisions of paragraphs 1 and 2, remuneration derived by a resident of a Contracting State in respect of an employment regularly exercised in more than one State on a ship, aircraft, motor vehicle or train operated by a resident of that Contracting State shall be taxable only in that State.

Dentons Canada LLP Commentary: Generally, employment income derived by a resident of a Contracting State shall be taxable only in that State unless the individual exercises employment duties in the other State. Subject to the limitations set out in paragraph 2 of Article XV, if a resident of one State works in the other State, the ensuing remuneration may be taxed in that other State.

The meaning of the word "derived," as it appears in paragraph 1 of Article XV, was the subject of the decision in *Garcia v. The Queen*, 2007 DTC 1593, where the Tax Court of Canada found that "derived" should be understood to mean something akin to "having its source." In that case, an individual was resident in the United States in 2002 and earned a bonus for employment duties exercised there. The bonus was paid to the individual in 2003, when the individual was resident in Canada. The individual argued that the bonus should not be taxable in Canada, because it related to employment exercised before the individual became a resident of Canada. The Court held that the bonus should be taxable when it is received regardless of when or where the employment to which it relates was exercised and would be included in the individual's income for Canadian tax purposes on that basis. Furthermore, since the employment was exercised in the United States, it may also have jurisdiction to tax the amount should it choose to do so.

A resident of one of the Contracting States who receives employment income for services performed in the other Contracting State (the source country) will be exempt from tax in the source country if either of the following two conditions are met:

(1) The remuneration for the employment performed in the source country does not exceed $10,000 in the calendar year. In all cases this limitation refers to the currency of the source country.

(2) The non-resident employee has not been present in the source State for more than 183 days in any twelve-month period commencing or ending in the fiscal year and his or her remuneration is not borne by a person who is a resident of the source country or by a permanent establishment in the source country. Prior to the Fifth Protocol, the 183 day test applied only in respect of a calendar year and did not contemplate a twelve-month period that spanned two different calendar years.

Therefore, employment income is generally exempt from tax in the source country in cases where the remuneration is $10,000 or less. If the remuneration is greater than $10,000 and the employee is present in the source country for a period greater than 183 days in any twelve-month period commencing or ending in the fiscal year, the entire amount of the remuneration is taxable in the source country. Consider a U.S.-resident employee of a U.S. company that performs employment services in Canada that are not connected to a Canadian permanent establishment of the U.S. company. Between August 1 of calendar year 1 and July 31 of calendar year 2, the employee is present in Canada for 184 days (92 days in each calendar year). The employee would be fully taxable in Canada in respect of remuneration relating to the Canadian employment rendered in both years, because the employee had been present in Canada for at least 183 days in any twelve-month period commencing in year 1 and ending in year 2.

If the remuneration is greater than $10,000 and the employee is not present in the source country for more than 183 days in any twelve-month period commencing or ending in the fiscal year, one must determine who the remuneration is "borne by" in order to determine if the income is taxable in the source country. The term "borne by" means allowable as a deduction in computing taxable income. If the employee's remuneration is borne by a person who is a resident of the source country, or by a permanent establishment in the source country, the earnings will be taxable in the source country if they exceed $10,000 in the calendar year. Thus, for example, if a Canadian resident employed at the Canadian permanent establishment of a U.S. company performs services in the United States, the income earned by the employee from such services is not exempt from U.S. tax if such income exceeds $10,000 (U.S.), because the U.S. company is entitled to a deduction for such wages in computing its taxable income.

The Tax Court of Canada's decision in *Sutcliffe v. The Queen*, 2006 DTC 2076 (T.C.C.), additional reasons at 2007 DTC 6, provides guidance on the manner in which income is to be attributed between source and residence States in connection with employment services that are carried out in both States. The taxpayer, an Air Canada pilot who was a resident of the United States, flew passengers from Toronto to destinations in both Canada and the United States. The pilot also received sick and vacation pay as well as compensation for layovers and travel time between various destinations. The flights between Canadian destinations routinely crossed into U.S. airspace. The Tax Court held that the pilot was taxable in Canada pursuant to Article XV of the Convention in respect of remuneration received for each flight (both domestic and international), but only to the extent that the plane was in Canadian airspace. Other compensation was to be similarly pro-rated on the basis that it was income from employment and would not have been received in the absence of the provision by the taxpayer of his employment services.

The use of the words "an employment" in paragraph 2 means this exemption applies to, and its requirements are to be met by, each employment, if a non-resident has more than one employment position: see *Prescott v. The Queen*, 96 DTC 1372 (T.C.C.).

Employees of international transport companies who work "regularly"on ships, aircraft, motor vehicles, and trains will not be taxed in the source country, provided that the employer and employee are resident in the other country. The term "regularly" is intended to distinguish crew members from persons who are occasionally employed on a ship, aircraft, motor vehicle, or train. The exemption from taxation at source is available to transportation employees even if the employee is present in the source country for more than 183 days in a calendar year. Accordingly, the exemption in paragraph 3 was unavailable to the taxpayer in *Sutcliffe v. The Queen*, 2006 DTC 2076 (T.C.C.), additional reasons at 2007 DTC 6, since the taxpayer pilot was a resident of the United States and was employed by a Canadian airline.

The Diplomatic Notes accompanying the Fifth Protocol (Annex "B") contain an apportionment rule for the taxation of income arising from employee stock options. Prior to the Fifth Protocol, there was no specific rule addressing apportionment issues in respect of employees who are granted stock options while employed in one country and who then work for the same or related employer in the other country before exercising or disposing of the option (or disposing of the share). The Fifth Protocol included a sourcing rule for the stock option benefit, which deems the benefit to have been derived in a country, to the extent that the individual's principal place of employment was in that country during the time between the granting of the option and the exercise (or the disposition of the shares).

For example, if an employee of a Canadian company ("Canco") is granted an option on January 1, 2009, and is permanently transferred to the head office of Canco's U.S. subsidiary ("USco") on January 1, 2010, and disposes of the option on December 31, 2010, Canada would be apportioned taxing authority over 1/3 of any gain realized on disposition and the U.S. would be apportioned taxing authority over the remaining 2/3 of any gain. This apportionment is carried out under the combined operation of paragraph 1 of Article XV and is subject to the exceptions in paragraph 2. Accordingly, if the employee is a resident of the United States at the time the options are exercised, Canada would only be permitted to tax the 1/3 portion of the gain to the extent paragraph 2 permits Canada to tax the gain (for this purpose, the tests in paragraph 2 are applied to the year or years in which the relevant services were performed in the other Contracting State and not the year in which the option is exercised or disposed). To the extent the same income is subject to taxation in both Contracting States after the application of Article XV, double taxation will be alleviated under the rules of Article XXIV (Elimination of Double Taxation).

The Diplomatic Notes also provide that the competent authorities of Canada and the United States could agree on other methods of apportionment in circumstances that warrant departing from this apportionment rule (i.e., if the terms of the option were such that the grant of the option is appropriately treated as transfer of ownership of the securities, because the options were in-the-money or not subject to a substantial vesting period).

The provisions of Article XV are over-ridden by the more specific rules of Article XVIII (Pensions and Annuities) and Article XIX (Government Service).

It must be remembered that whenever employment duties are performed in Canada, the withholding requirements set out in the *Income Tax Act* (Canada) will apply, even if paragraph 2 of Article XV exempts the employment services from income tax in Canada. Where an individual is a resident of a country with which Canada has a treaty, the individual may apply for a waiver of withholding tax from the CRA, and if granted, the waiver should be provided to the person making payment to the employee to alleviate this requirement. If a waiver is not obtained, the person paying the employee for services performed in Canada has an obligation to withhold. This applies equally to resident and non-resident employers.

As part of the 2015 federal Budget, the Minister of Finance has announced a plan to amend the *Income Tax Act* (Canada) to remove, in certain circumstances, the requirement to withhold tax on salary, wages, and other remuneration that may be eligible for protection under one of Canada's treaties. To qualify, the employer must be a "qualifying non-resident employer" (i.e., resident in a county with which Canada has an income tax treaty and register with the CRA for this program), and the employee must be a "qualifying non-resident employee" (i.e., resident in a country with which Canada has an income tax treaty and be in Canada for fewer than 90 days in the 12-month period or work in Canada for fewer than 45 days in the 12-month period that includes that time). Where parties qualify under these proposed changes, no waiver applications will be required.

Editorial Note: Technical Interpretation, Document No. 2013-0484501E5, dated February 10, 2015, states that employment income for the full calendar year is considered when deciding whether the income of Canadian residents who move mid-year to the U.S. exceeds the "safe harbour" limit in Article XV(2)(*a*) of the Convention.

Technical Interpretation, Document No. 2012-0436311I7, dated March 22, 2012, discusses the application of the Canadian income tax withholding requirements on U.S. resident employers.

Technical Interpretation, Document No. 2012-0440741I7, dated July 6, 2012, discusses the application of the Canadian income tax withholding requirements on U.S. resident employees receiving stock options that in part are derived from duties performed in Canada.

Technical Interpretation, Document No. 2005-0118521I7, dated February 14, 2006, deals with whether employees of a U.S. LLC can be considered to have a PE in Canada for the purposes of Article XV(2) of the Canada–U.S. Tax Convention.

Technical Interpretation, Document No. 9528647, dated January 3, 1996, deals with employment income earned on a U.S. Indian reserve. Article XV gives Canada the right to tax employment income earned in the U.S., regardless of whether the income is exempt in the U.S.

History: The title of Article XV was deleted and replaced by paragraph 1 of Article 10 of the Fifth Protocol to this Convention, and formerly read: "Dependent Personal Services."

Paragraphs 1 and 2 of Article XV were deleted and replaced by paragraph 2 of Article 10 of the Fifth Protocol to this Convention, and formerly read:

1. Subject to the provisions of Article XVIII (Pensions and Annuities) and XIX (Government Service), salaries, wages and other similar remuneration derived by a resident of a Contracting State in respect of an employment shall be taxable only in that State unless the employment is exercised in the other Contracting State. If the employment is so exercised, such remuneration as is derived therefrom may be taxed in that other State.

2. Notwithstanding the provisions of paragraph 1, remuneration derived by a resident of a Contracting State in respect of an employment exercised in a calendar year in the other Contracting State shall be taxable only in the first-mentioned State if:

(*a*) Such remuneration does not exceed ten thousand dollars ($10,000) in the currency of that other State; or

(*b*) The recipient is present in the other Contracting State for a period or periods not exceeding in the aggregate 183 days in that year and the remuneration is not borne by an employer who is a resident of that other State or by a permanent establishment or a fixed base which the employer has in that other State.

Article XVI — Artistes and Athletes

1. Notwithstanding the provisions of Articles VII (Business Profits) and XV (Income from Employment), income derived by a resident of a Contracting State as an entertainer, such as a theatre, motion picture, radio or television artiste, or a musician, or as an athlete, from his personal activities as such exercised in the other Contracting State, may be taxed in that other State, except where the amount of the gross receipts derived by such entertainer or athlete, including expenses reimbursed to him or borne on his behalf, from such activities do not exceed fifteen thousand dollars ($15,000) in the currency of that other State for the calendar year concerned.

2. Where income in respect of personal activities exercised by an entertainer or an athlete in his capacity as such accrues not to the entertainer or athlete but to another person, that income may, notwithstanding the provisions of Articles VII (Business Profits), and XV (Income from Employment), be taxed in the Contracting State in which the activities of the entertainer or athlete are exercised. For the purposes of the preceding sentence, income of an entertainer or athlete shall be deemed not to accrue to another person if it is established that neither the entertainer or athlete, nor persons related thereto, participate directly or indirectly in the profits of such other person in any manner, including the receipt of deferred remuneration, bonuses, fees, dividends, partnership distributions or other distributions.

3. The provisions of paragraphs 1 and 2 shall not apply to the income of:

(*a*) An athlete in respect of his activities as an employee of a team which participates in a league with regularly scheduled games in both Contracting States; or

(*b*) A team described in subparagraph (*a*).

4. Notwithstanding the provisions of Articles VII (Business Profits) and XV (Income from Employment) an amount paid by a resident of a Contracting State to a resident of the other Contracting State as an inducement to sign an agreement relating to the performance of the services of an athlete (other than an amount referred to in paragraph 1 of Article XV (Income from Employment)) may be taxed

in the first-mentioned State, but the tax so charged shall not exceed 15 per cent of the gross amount of such payment.

Dentons Canada LLP Commentary: Article XVI overrides Article XV (Income from Employment) to allow the taxation of an entertainer or athlete in cases where that Article would not permit such taxation.

Paragraph 1 provides that certain income of an entertainer or athlete may be taxed in the source country in all cases where the amount of gross receipts derived by the entertainer or athlete, including expenses reimbursed to him or her or borne on his or her behalf, exceeds $15,000 in the currency of the source country, for the calendar year concerned. Thus, for example, income earned by an entertainer, musician, or athlete who is a resident of Canada for such activities performed in the United States, may be taxed in the United States in all cases where the gross receipts derived by the entertainer, musician, or athlete, including expenses reimbursed to him or her, or borne on his or her behalf, exceed $15,000 (U.S.) for the calendar year.

The term "entertainer" is not exhaustively defined, but includes a theatre, motion picture, radio, or television artist. In *Cheek v. The Queen*, 2002 DTC 1283 (T.C.C.), the Tax Court held that a "play-by-play" radio announcer for a professional sports team was not a "radio artiste" or entertainer for purposes of Article XVI of the Convention, but was rather a radio journalist outside the scope of this provision. In order to qualify as an artiste or entertainer, the taxpayer must generally provide the performance that the audience seeks to experience. In *Cheek*, the taxpayer skillfully reported on-field events, but it was the on-field events and not the taxpayer's description thereof that the listener desired to experience.

Paragraph 2 provides that where income in respect of the personal activities of an entertainer, musician, or athlete accrues to another person (for example, a corporation), that income may be taxed in the country where the activities are performed. The person to whom the income accrues (the corporation in this example), is denied the exemptions of Articles VII (Business Profits) and XV (Income from Employment) with respect to such income. Paragraph 2 only applies, however, if it can be established that the entertainer, musician, or athlete, or persons related to him or her, participates directly or indirectly in the profits of that other person. Deferred remuneration, dividends, bonuses, fees, partnership distributions, or other distributions will constitute participating in profits. Paragraph 2 is apparently intended to prevent highly paid performers and athletes from avoiding tax in the country in which they perform by routing the compensation for their services through a third person such as a personal holding company or trust located in a country that would not tax such income. Paragraph 2 was applied to income shared between an entertainer/musician and a non-resident corporation which paid him to perform in Canada in *Sumner and Roxanne Music Inc. v. The Queen*, 2000 DTC 1667 (T.C.C.). This case involved both the U.S. and U.K. treaties with Canada because the entertainer was a U.K. resident and the corporation was a U.S. corporation. In *Sumner*, the Court concluded that, in the circumstances, an allocation of income from a North American tour should be done based upon gross revenues in Canada and not based upon number of concert nights in Canada.

Paragraphs 1 and 2 of Article XVI do not apply to the income of an athlete who is employed by a team that participates in a league with regularly scheduled games in both countries (including most major-league sports teams in North America). The athlete would be subject to the provisions of Article XV (Income from Employment). Such a Canadian resident athlete's remuneration for activities in the United States would be exempt from U.S. taxation if the athlete earns not more than $10,000 U.S., or if the athlete is present in the United States for not more than 183 days in any twelve-month period commencing or ending in the fiscal year and his or her remuneration is not borne by a person who is a resident of the source country or by a permanent establishment in the source country.

Paragraphs 1 and 2 of this Article would also not apply to the income of a team that participates in a league with regularly-scheduled games in both Canada and the United States. The team may be taxable pursuant to other Articles of the Convention, such as Article VII (Business Profits).

Paragraph 4 contains a rule governing any payment (other than salaries, wages, or similar remuneration) made as an inducement to sign an agreement relating to the performance of the services of an athlete. In the case of such a payment (sometimes called a "signing bonus") by a resident of one country to a resident of the other country, the payer's country may tax that payment, but that tax may not exceed 15 per cent of the gross amount of the payments. Therefore, for example, any amount paid by a resident of the United States to a resident of Canada, whether it be the athlete himself, or another person, as an inducement to sign an agreement relating to the performance of an athlete's services may be taxed in the United States. The withholding tax may not exceed 15 per cent of the gross amount of the payment. These inducement payments are not considered gross receipts for purposes of paragraph 1 of this Article. Thus, if an athlete earned less than $15,000 in a taxable year in salary but earned $100,000 as a signing bonus, the source country would not be entitled to tax the salary portion of the athlete's earnings for that year. Note that in *Khabibulin v The Queen*, 2000 DTC 1426, the Tax Court concluded that an NHL signing bonus was not in the circumstances a signing bonus but was remuneration for services. (Note that the *Khabibulin* case involved a Russian player and the corresponding article of the Canada-U.S.S.R. Convention differs significantly from the U.S. Convention.)

Editorial Note: Technical Interpretation, Document No. 2009-0345771I7, dated August 27, 2010, states that artists that are members of an LLC and derive income through the LLC may rely on Article XVI.

Technical Interpretation, Document No. 2007-0262371I7, states that branch tax under Part XIV may be imposed, on a limited basis, on a corporation resident in the United States that has a permanent establishment in Canada. It is also the CRA's view that Article X(6) of the Treaty overrides Article XVI of the Treaty, which provides for the taxation of artists and athletes.

History: Paragraph 1 of Article XVI was amended by paragraph 1 of Article 11 of the Fifth Protocol to this Convention by deleting "XIV (Independent Personal Services)" following "Notwithstanding the provisions of Articles" and substituting "VII (Business Profits)", and by deleting "XV (Dependent Personal Services)" and substituting "XV (Income from Employment)".

Paragraph 2 of Article XVI was amended by paragraph 2 of Article 11 of the Fifth Protocol to this Convention by deleting "XIV (Independent Personal Services)" following "notwithstanding the provisions of Articles VII (Business Profits)," and by deleting "XV (Dependent Personal Services)" and substituting "XV (Income from Employment)".

Paragraph 4 of Article XVI was amended by paragraph 3 of Article 11 of the Fifth Protocol to this Convention by deleting "XIV (Independent Personal Services)" following "Notwithstanding the provisions of Articles" and substituting "VII (Business Profits)", and by deleting "(Dependent Personal Services)" in both places in the paragraph and substituting "(Income from Employment)".

Paragraph 3 of Article XVI was amended by Article VII of the First Protocol to this Convention, and formerly read:

3. The provisions of this Article shall not apply to the income of an athlete in respect of an employment with a team which participates in a league with regularly scheduled games in both Contracting States.

Paragraph 4 of Article XVI was added by Article VII of the First Protocol to this Convention.

Article XVII — Withholding of Taxes in Respect of Personal Services [Repealed.]

Dentons Canada LLP Commentary: The Fifth Protocol eliminated Article XVII in its entirety to reflect the elimination of Article XIV (Independent Personal Services). Previously, Article XVII allowed a country to impose a withholding tax at source on remuneration paid to a resident of the other country who performs personal services in the source country. However, in the case of the first $5,000 paid for personal services during the year by each payer, the withholding was limited to 10 per cent of the payment.

When it was applicable, this provision in no way limited the particular individual's ultimate tax liability with respect to the source country. As an example, Canada may withhold tax on account of the ultimate Canadian tax liability of an individual who is a resident of the United States (including an entertainer or athlete) in respect of remuneration paid for the performance of services in Canada. However, the withholding tax was limited to 10 per cent on the first $5,000 (Canadian) of annual payments by any particular payor, which overrides the requirements of paragraph 153(1)(*g*) of the *Income Tax Act* (Canada) and Regulation 105 thereunder which impose a 15 per cent withholding obligation in such circumstances.

Where the competent authority of Canada or the United States believed that the normal rates of withholding in respect of independent personal services were excessive in terms of the individual's estimated tax liability to that country, the competent authority could have determined that a lesser amount was to be deducted or withheld.

The elimination of Article XVII allows both countries to impose withholding tax under the relevant domestic tax law in respect of remuneration for services performed in that country without any treaty limitation. In the event the withholding tax exceeds the amount of tax that the country is entitled to levy pursuant to other provisions of the Convention (e.g., under Article VII (Business Profits) or Article XVI (Artistes and Athletes)), the service provider could generally seek a refund of the overpayment.

A resident of the United States can make an application under subsection 153(1.1) of the *Income Tax Act* (Canada) for reduced Canadian withholding on the grounds of undue hardship. A withholding significantly greater than the reasonably expected tax liability is generally regarded as undue hardship.

History: Article XVII was deleted by Article 12 of the Fifth Protocol to this Convention, and formerly read:

1. Deduction and withholding of tax on account of the tax liability for a taxable year on remuneration paid to an individual who is a resident of a Contracting State (including an entertainer or athlete) in respect of the

performance of independent personal services in the other Contracting State may be required by that other State, but with respect to the first five thousand dollars ($5,000) in the currency of that other State, paid as remuneration in that taxable year by each payor, such deduction and withholding shall not exceed 10 per cent of the payment.

2. Where the competent authority of a Contracting State considers that an amount that would otherwise be deducted or withheld from any amount paid or credited to an individual who is a resident of the other Contracting State in respect of the performance of personal services in the first-mentioned State is excessive in relation to the estimated tax liability for the taxable year of that individual in the first-mentioned State, it may determine that a lesser amount will be deducted or withheld.

3. The provisions of this Article shall not affect the liability of a resident of a Contracting State referred to in paragraph 1 or 2 for tax imposed by the other Contracting State.

The title of Article XVII and paragraph 2 of that Article were amended by Article VIII of the First Protocol to this Convention, and formerly read:

Withholding of Taxes in Respect of Independent Personal Services

. . .

2. Where the competent authority of a Contracting State considers that an amount that would otherwise be deducted or withheld from any amount paid or credited to an individual who is a resident of the other Contracting State in respect of the performance of independent personal services in the first-mentioned State is excessive in relation to the estimated tax liability for the taxable year of that individual in the first-mentioned State, it may determine that a lesser amount will be deducted or withheld.

Article XVIII — Pensions and Annuities

1. Pensions and annuities arising in a Contracting State and paid to a resident of the other Contracting State may be taxed in that other State, but the amount of any such pension that would be excluded from taxable income in the first-mentioned State if the recipient were a resident thereof shall be exempt from taxation in that other State.

2. However:

(*a*) Pensions may also be taxed in the Contracting State in which they arise and according to the laws of that State; but if a resident of the other Contracting State is the beneficial owner of a periodic pension payment, the tax so charged shall not exceed 15 per cent of the gross amount of such payment; and

(*b*) Annuities may also be taxed in the Contracting State in which they arise and according to the laws of that State; but if a resident of the other Contracting State is the beneficial owner of an annuity payment, the tax so charged shall not exceed 15 per cent of the portion of such payment that would not be excluded from taxable income in the first-mentioned State if the beneficial owner were a resident thereof.

3. For the purposes of this Convention:

(*a*) The term "pensions" includes any payment under a superannuation, pension or other retirement arrangement, Armed Forces retirement pay, war veterans pensions and allowances and amounts paid under a sickness, accident or disability plan, but does not include payments under an income-averaging annuity contract or, except for the purposes of Article XIX (Government Service), any benefit referred to in paragraph 5; and

(*b*) The term "pensions" also includes a Roth IRA, within the meaning of section 408A of the *Internal Revenue Code*, or a plan or arrangement created pursuant to legislation enacted by a Contracting State after September 21, 2007 that the competent authorities have agreed is similar thereto. Notwithstanding the provisions of the preceding sentence, from such time that contributions have been made to the Roth IRA or similar plan or arrangement, by or for the benefit of a resident of the other Contracting State (other than rollover contributions from a Roth IRA or similar plan or arrangement described in the previous sentence that is a pension within the meaning of this subparagraph), to the extent of accretions from such time, such Roth IRA or similar plan or arrangement shall cease to be considered a pension for purposes of the provisions of this Article.

4. For the purposes of this Convention:

(*a*) The term "annuity" means a stated sum paid periodically at stated times during life or during a specified number of years, under an obligation to make the payments in return for adequate and full consideration (other than services rendered), but does not include a payment that is not a periodic payment or any annuity the cost of which was deductible for the purposes of taxation in the Contracting State in which it was acquired; and

(*b*) An annuity or other amount paid in respect of a life insurance or annuity contract (including a withdrawal in respect of the cash value thereof) shall be deemed to arise in a Contracting State if the person paying the annuity or other amount (in this subparagraph referred to as the "payer") is a resident of that State. However, if the payer, whether a resident of a Contracting State or not, has in a State other than that of which the payer is a resident a permanent establishment in connection with which the obligation giving rise to the annuity or other amount was incurred, and the annuity or other amount is borne by the permanent establishment, then the annuity or other amount shall be deemed to arise in the State in which the permanent establishment is situated and not in the State of which the payer is a resident.

5. Benefits under the social security legislation in a Contracting State (including tier 1 railroad retirement benefits but not including unemployment benefits) paid to a resident of the other Contracting State shall be taxable only in that other State, subject to the following conditions:

(*a*) a benefit under the social security legislation in the United States paid to a resident of Canada shall be taxable in Canada as though it were a benefit under the Canada Pension Plan, except that 15 per cent of the amount of the benefit shall be exempt from Canadian tax; and

(*b*) a benefit under the social security legislation in Canada paid to a resident of the United States shall be taxable in the United States as though it were a benefit under the *Social Security Act*, except that a type of benefit that is not subject to Canadian tax when paid to residents of Canada shall be exempt from United States tax.

6. Alimony and other similar amounts (including child support payments) arising in a Contracting State and paid to a resident of the other Contracting State shall be taxable as follows:

(*a*) Such amounts shall be taxable only in that other State;

(*b*) Notwithstanding the provisions of subparagraph (*a*), the amount that would be excluded from taxable income in the first-mentioned State if the recipient were a resident thereof shall be exempt from taxation in that other State.

7. A natural person who is a citizen or resident of a Contracting State and a beneficiary of a trust, company, organization or other arrangement that is a resident of the other Contracting State, generally exempt from income taxation in that other State and operated exclusively to provide pension or employee benefits may elect to defer taxation in the first-mentioned State, subject to rules established by the competent authority of that State, with respect to any income accrued in the plan but not distributed by the plan, until such time as and to the extent that a distribution is made from the plan or any plan substituted therefor.

8. Contributions made to, or benefits accrued under, a qualifying retirement plan in a Contracting State by or on behalf of an individual shall be deductible or excludible in computing the individual's taxable income in the other Contracting State, and contributions made to the plan by the individual's employer shall be allowed as a deduction in computing the employer's profits in that other State, where:

(*a*) The individual performs services as an employee in that other State the remuneration from which is taxable in that other State;

(*b*) The individual was participating in the plan (or another similar plan for which this plan was substituted) immediately before the individual began performing the services in that other State;

(*c*) The individual was not a resident of that other State immediately before the individual began performing the services in that other State;

(*d*) The individual has performed services in that other State for the same employer (or a related employer) for no more than 60 of the 120 months preceding the individual's current taxation year;

(*e*) The contributions and benefits are attributable to the services performed by the individual in that other State, and are made or accrued during the period in which the individual performs those services; and

(*f*) With respect to contributions and benefits that are attributable to services performed during a period in the individual's current taxation year, no contributions in respect of the period are made by or on behalf of the individual to, and no services performed in that other State during the period are otherwise taken into account for purposes of determining the individual's entitlement to benefits under, any plan that would be a qualifying retirement plan in that other State if paragraph 15 of this Article were read without reference to subparagraphs (*b*) and (*c*) of that paragraph.

This paragraph shall apply only to the extent that the contributions or benefits would qualify for tax relief in the first-mentioned State if the individual was a resident of and performed the services in that State.

9. For the purposes of United States taxation, the benefits granted under paragraph 8 to a citizen of the United States shall not exceed the benefits that would be allowed by the United States to its residents for contributions to, or benefits otherwise accrued under, a generally corresponding pension or retirement plan established in and recognized for tax purposes by the United States.

10. Contributions made to, or benefits accrued under, a qualifying retirement plan in a Contracting State by or on behalf of an individual who is a resident of the other Contracting State shall be deductible or excludible in computing the individual's taxable income in that other State, where:

(*a*) The individual performs services as an employee in the first-mentioned state the remuneration from which is taxable in that State and is borne by an employer who is a resident of that State or by a permanent establishment which the employer has in that State; and

(*b*) The contributions and benefits are attributable to those services and are made or accrued during the period in which the individual performs those services.

This paragraph shall apply only to the extent that the contributions or benefits qualify for tax relief in the first-mentioned State.

11. For the purposes of Canadian taxation, the amount of contributions otherwise allowed as a deduction under paragraph 10 to an individual for a taxation year shall not exceed the individual's deduction limit under the law of Canada for the year for contributions to registered retirement savings plans remaining after taking into account the amount of contributions to registered retirement savings plans deducted by the individual under the law of Canada for the year. The amount deducted by an individual under paragraph 10 for a taxation year shall be taken into account in computing the individual's deduction limit under the law of Canada for subsequent taxation years for contributions to registered retirement savings plans.

12. For the purposes of United States taxation, the benefits granted under paragraph 10 shall not exceed the benefits that would be allowed by the United States to its residents for contributions to, or benefits otherwise accrued under, a generally corresponding pension or retirement plan established in and recognized for tax purposes by the United States. For purposes of determining an individual's eligibility to participate in and receive tax benefits with respect to a pension or retirement plan or other retirement arrangement established in and recognized for tax purposes by the United States, contributions made to, or benefits accrued under, a qualifying retirement plan in Canada by or on behalf of the individual shall be treated as contributions or benefits under a generally corresponding pension or retirement plan established in and recognized for tax purposes by the United States.

13. Contributions made to, or benefits accrued under, a qualifying retirement plan in Canada by or on behalf of a citizen of the United States who is a resident of Canada shall be deductible or excludible in computing the citizen's taxable income in the United States, where:

(*a*) The citizen performs services as an employee in Canada the remuneration from which is taxable in Canada and is borne by an employer who is a resident of Canada or by a permanent establishment which the employer has in Canada; and

(*b*) The contributions and benefits are attributable to those services and are made or accrued during the period in which the citizen performs those services.

This paragraph shall apply only to the extent that the contributions or benefits qualify for tax relief in Canada.

14. The benefits granted under paragraph 13 shall not exceed the benefits that would be allowed by the United States to its residents for contributions to, or benefits otherwise accrued under, a generally corresponding pension or retirement plan established in and recognized for tax purposes by the United States. For purposes of determining an individual's eligibility to participate in and receive tax benefits with respect to a pension or retirement plan or other retirement arrangement established in and recognized for tax purposes by the United States, contributions made to, or benefits accrued under, a qualifying retirement plan in Canada by or on behalf of the individual shall be treated as contributions or benefits under a generally corresponding pension or retirement plan established in and recognized for tax purposes by the United States.

15. For purposes of paragraphs 8 to 14, a qualifying retirement plan in a Contracting State means a trust, company, organization or other arrangement:

(*a*) That is a resident of that State, generally exempt from income taxation in that State and operated primarily to provide pension or retirement benefits;

(*b*) That is not an individual arrangement in respect of which the individual's employer has no involvement; and

(*c*) Which the competent authority of the other Contracting State agrees generally corresponds to a pension or retirement plan established in and recognized for tax purposes by that other State.

16. For purposes of this Article, a distribution from a pension or retirement plan that is reasonably attributable to a contribution or benefit for which a benefit was allowed pursuant to paragraph 8, 10 or 13 shall be deemed to arise in the Contracting State in which the plan is established.

17. Paragraphs 8 to 16 apply, with such modifications as the circumstances require, as though the relationship between a partnership that carries on a business, and an individual who is a member of the partnership, were that of employer and employee.

Dentons Canada LLP Commentary: Under Article XVIII, pensions and annuities that arise in one country and are paid to a resident of the other country are taxable in the country of residence. However, the country of residence shall exempt from taxation the amount of any such pension that would be excluded from taxable income in the source country if the recipient were a resident of the source country. Thus, pensions arising in the United States and paid to a Canadian resident may be taxed in Canada but only to the extent that the pension would have been included in U.S. income if the recipient were a U.S. resident. For example, if a Canadian resident receives a $12,000 pension payment from the United States, and $5,000 of this payment would be excluded from U.S. taxable income as a return of capital if the recipient were a resident of the United States, the Canadian resident will not be required to pay Canadian tax on $5,000 of U.S. source pension income received. In *Coblentz v. The Queen*, 96 DTC 6531 (F.C.A.), the Court clarified that a U.S. sourced pension will not be exempt from Canadian taxation under paragraph 1 if an elective *Internal Revenue Code* provision would have permitted a deduction and deferral of U.S. tax on the pension income.

In addition to being subject to tax in the recipient's country of residence, pensions and annuities are also subject to tax in the country of payment, or the source country. Under paragraph 2, tax imposed at source on pensions and annuities is limited as follows:

(a) the tax imposed by the source country on pension payments to residents of the other country is not to exceed 15 per cent of the gross amount of the payment; and

(b) tax imposed by the source country on annuity payments to residents of the other country is not to exceed 15 per cent of the amount of the payment that would be taxable in the source country if the recipient were a resident thereof.

In *Meyer v. The Queen*, 2004 DTC 2393 (T.C.C.), the Tax Court of Canada held that a Canadian resident taxpayer (who was also a U.S. citizen) was not entitled to a credit for Canadian tax purposes in respect of the full amount of U.S. tax paid by the taxpayer on U.S.-source pension income. In that case, the taxpayer did not claim any treaty relief from U.S. tax on the pension income, with the result that the taxpayer paid an amount to the IRS in excess of the

15 per cent limitation contained in Article XVIII. The Tax Court did not permit the taxpayer to claim a deduction in Canada for the excess amount since the excess was considered to have been gratuitously paid. The onus was on the taxpayer to assert its entitlement to relief under the Convention first in the U.S. (as the State of source) and then seek the appropriate credit for Canadian tax purposes.

The term "pensions" is defined in paragraph 3 for the purposes of the Convention. It includes any payment, whether or not periodic, under a superannuation, pension, or retirement plan, armed forces retirement pay, war veterans pension allowance, and amounts paid under a sickness, accident, or disability plan. "Pensions" also includes, for example, payments from Individual Retirement Accounts (IRAs) in the United States and to provide that it includes, for example, registered retirement savings plans (RRSPs) and registered retirement income funds (RRIFs) in Canada. The term "pensions" also would include amounts paid by other retirement plans or arrangements, whether or not they are qualified plans under U.S. domestic law; this would include, for example, plans and arrangements described in section 457 or 414(d) of the *Internal Revenue Code*.

The definition of "pensions" specifically excludes payments under income-averaging annuity contracts. Consequently, any payments received under an income-averaging annuity contract will be subject to tax of 25 per cent in Canada under Part XIII of the *Income Tax Act* (Canada) rather than the reduced rate of 15 per cent under the Convention. Benefits paid under social security legislation are also specifically excluded from the term "pensions" except for the purposes of Article XIX (Government Service).

The Fifth Protocol extended the meaning of the term "pensions" to include a Roth IRA (within the meaning of section 408A of the *Internal Revenue Code*), or any plan or arrangement created pursuant to legislation enacted after September 21, 2007 that the competent authorities of Canada and the U.S. have agreed is similar thereto. However, such a plan generally ceases to be considered a "pension" for purposes of Article XVII (and will effectively be bifurcated into two separate pensions for purposes of Article XVIII) to the extent of accretions to the plan that accrue after a contribution has been made to the plan by or for the benefit of a resident of the other Contracting State (other than certain permitted rollover contributions).

The term "annuities" is specifically defined in paragraph 4 for the purposes of the Convention to mean a stated sum paid periodically at stated times during life or during a specified number of years, under an obligation to make payments in return for adequate and full consideration other than services rendered. The term "annuities" does not include an annuity the cost of which was deductible in computing taxable income in the country where the annuity was acquired. Like pensions, annuity payments must be periodic to qualify for the reduced taxation allowed by the Convention.

The Fifth Protocol added subparagraph 4(*b*), which is intended to relieve withholding taxes that would otherwise arise on the payment of certain annuities by an insurance company resident in one Contracting State to a resident of the other Contracting State through a branch of the insurance company situated in that other Contracting State. In this respect, subparagraph 4(*b*) provides that an amount paid in respect of a life insurance or annuity contract is deemed to arise in the State where the payer is resident. However, where the payer has in the other State a permanent establishment connected with the obligation giving rise to the annuity or other amount and the obligation is borne by the permanent establishment, the amount would be deemed to arise in the State in which the permanent establishment is situated, irrespective of the residency of the payer.

Paragraph 5, dealing with the taxation of social security benefits, was amended by both the Third and Fourth Protocols. Prior to such amendments (i.e., before January 1, 1996) one-half of a receipt of social security benefits was included in taxable income and subject to tax in the state of residence. The other half of the receipt was not subject to tax.

Social security benefits are defined to include tier 1 railroad retirement benefits but not unemployment benefits (which fall under Article XXII (Other Income) of the Convention). Pensions in respect of government service are covered not by this rule but by the rules of paragraphs 1 and 2 of this Article.

Article XVIII was amended by the Third Protocol to provide that benefits paid under the U.S. or Canadian social security legislation to a resident of the Other Contracting State, or, in the case of Canadian benefits, to a U.S. citizen, were taxable only in the State that paid the benefit. Accordingly, the state of residence did not have any right to tax such payments. However, under the Fourth Protocol, the taxation of social security benefits was revised again, allocating exclusive jurisdiction to tax such benefits to the country of residence.

Moreover, pursuant to the amendments contained in the Fourth Protocol social security benefits paid from the U.S. to a Canadian resident will be taxable in Canada as if it were a benefit under the *Canada Pension Plan*, except that 15 per cent of the benefit will not be subject to Canadian tax. Similarly, a benefit paid under the Canadian social security legislation to a U.S. resident is treated as though it were a benefit not subject to Canadian tax. The 15 per cent deduction is not applicable to private pensions (see, e.g., *Donnelly v. The Queen*, 2007 DTC 1281 (T.C.C.)).

The amendments to Article XVIII introduced by the Fourth Protocol also contained provision for the refund of excess tax paid under the amendments introduced by the Third Protocol before amendments to the Fourth Protocol were ratified.

Paragraph 6 provides that alimony and other similar amounts (including child support payments) are subject to tax only in the country of residence of the recipient. Thus, alimony and child support payments originating in the United States and paid to a resident of Canada shall be taxable only in Canada and not be subject to U.S. tax. Under the Convention, alimony and other similar amounts that are to be included in the taxable income of the recipient are limited to the same amount of income that would have been reported in the payer country if the recipient had been a resident of that country. Child support payments, for example, are generally not taxable to the recipient in the United States. Thus a Canadian recipient of such payments made from the United States will be able to claim exemption from Canadian tax thereon under the Convention.

Pursuant to paragraph 2 of Article III (General Definitions), "alimony" is to have the meaning it has under the tax law of that country whose taxes are being considered.

Paragraph 7 replaced paragraph 5 of Article XXIX (Miscellaneous Rules) as it existed prior to the Third Protocol. Paragraph 5 of Article XXIX provided that a U.S. citizen who was a resident of Canada and a beneficiary of a Canadian RRSP could elect, under rules established by the competent authority of the United States, to defer U.S. taxation with respect to any income accrued in the plan but not distributed by the plan, until such time as a distribution was made from such plan.

Paragraph 7 makes reciprocal the rule that it replaced and expands its scope, so that it no longer applies only to residents and citizens of the United States who are beneficiaries of Canadian RRSPs. Paragraph 7 applies to an individual who is a citizen or resident of a Contracting State and a beneficiary of a trust, company, organization, or other arrangement that is a resident of the other Contracting State and that is both generally exempt from income taxation in its State of residence and operated exclusively to provide pension or employee benefits.

The Fifth Protocol significantly altered the tax consequences associated with a contribution by a resident of one Contracting State to a pension plan in the other State. As discussed above, paragraph 7 generally permits a resident of a Contracting State to defer the taxation of income accrued on amounts contributed to certain pension plans in the other State. However, prior to the Fifth Protocol, there was no relief granted to the resident in respect of the deduction of actual contributions made to such plans (see, e.g., *Rodrigue v. Canada (Attorney General)*, 2001 DTC 5296 (F.C.A.), where the Federal Court of Appeal held that a Canadian resident could not deduct contributions made to a U.S. 401(k) pension plan because the words "income accrued" in paragraph 7 of Article XVIII did not extend to contributions of capital). This had long been considered a defect in the Convention.

The Fifth Protocol remedied this situation by providing a deduction (or exclusion), in certain circumstances, for contributions to (or benefits accrued under) a "qualifying retirement plan" (QRP) for purposes of determining the individual's taxable income in both Contracting States. For this purpose, a QRP in a Contracting State is defined in paragraph 15 of Article XVIII as a trust, company, organization, or other arrangement that is:

(a) a resident of that State; generally exempt from income taxation in that State and operated primarily to provide pension or retirement benefits;

(b) not an individual arrangement in respect of which the individual's employer has no involvement; and

(c) recognized by the competent authorities of both States as corresponding to a pension or retirement plan established in and recognized for tax purposes in the other State.

The Diplomatic Notes accompanying the Fifth Protocol (Annex "B") indicate that Canadian QRP's includes registered and tax-sheltered plans, such as RSPs (RRSPs, DPSPs, or RRIFs funded from contributions from one of the above plans). For U.S. purposes, a QRP includes, for example, 401(k) plans, certain retirement accounts such as 408(p), qualified plans under 401(a), simplified employee pensions under 408(k), certain qualified annuity plans and trusts, and the Thrift Savings Fund.

Paragraph 8 governs the ability of an individual resident in a Contracting State to deduct (or exclude) pension contributions made to (or benefits accrued under) a QRP in that State for purposes of determining its taxable income in the other Contracting State. Contributions made to the QRP by the individual's employer may similarly be deducted in computing the employer's profits in that other State. This paragraph is designed to apply to individuals that are on temporary work assignment to the other Contracting State for a period that is less than 5 years. In order for the contributions to be deductible (and the accrued benefits to be excludible), the following criteria must be met:

(a) the individual must perform employment services in the other State and the remuneration for such services must be taxable in the other State;

(b) the individual must have been participating in the QRP (or a similar substitute plan) before the individual began performing employment services in the other State;

(c) the individual must not have been a resident of the other State immediately before they began to perform the services in the other State;

(d) the individual performed services in the other State for the same or related employer for no more than 60 of the 120 months preceding the individual's current taxation year;

(e) the contributions to, and the benefits from, the QRP are attributable to the services performed in the other State and are made or accrued during the time the individual performs the services; and

(f) the individual generally does not participate in any other QRP during the taxation year.

Paragraph 8 only grants relief to the extent that it would have been granted in the State where the contributions are received as if the individual were a resident of and performed services in that State. Moreover, in a case where a Canadian resident is on a short-term work assignment in the U.S., paragraph 9 provides that the deduction for contributions under paragraph 8 are capped by the amount otherwise allowable by the United States to its residents for contributions to a similar U.S.-based plan.

Paragraph 10 provides relief to cross-border commuters who reside in one Contracting State and contribute to a QRP in the other State where they are employed. Such contributions are deductible (and benefits accrued thereunder would be excludible in computing the individual's taxable income in the other State) so long as the remuneration received is taxable in the other State and is borne by a resident (or permanent establishment) in the other State and the contributions and benefits attributable to the services are made or accrued during the period in which the individual performs the services. As in respect of paragraph 8, the deductions are capped at the amount that would otherwise be deductible if the contributions were made to a QRP in the State of residence. Pursuant to paragraph 11, which specifically deals with deductions for the purposes of Canadian taxation, the deduction is limited to the lesser of the actual contribution and the individual's RRSP contribution limit for the year, after taking into account the RRSP contributions otherwise deducted. This rule prevents double benefits for contributions to both an RRSP and a qualifying retirement plan in the United States with respect to the same services. For the purposes of U.S. taxation, paragraph 12 provides a reciprocal rule that generally limits the deductions that can be claimed by a Canadian resident for U.S. tax purposes.

Paragraph 13 specifically deals with U.S. citizens who are resident in Canada and who work for a Canadian employer. This rule allows such individuals to claim a deduction for U.S. tax purposes for contributions to Canadian QRPs (and to exclude benefits accrued thereunder for U.S. tax purposes), but only to the extent that such deductions (or exclusions) could have been claimed for Canadian tax purposes. The Canadian contribution must be made in respect of services rendered as an employee in Canada during the period in which the individual is resident in Canada, the remuneration from such services must be taxable in Canada, and the remuneration must be paid by a Canadian-resident employer or be borne by a Canadian permanent establishment of a foreign employer. Paragraph 14 further limits the benefits otherwise available under paragraph 13, generally to the amount that would be allowed under a similar pension or retirement plan established and recognized for tax purposes under U.S. law. This rule ensures that a U.S. citizen living and working in Canada does not receive better U.S. treatment than a U.S. citizen living and working in the United States.

Paragraph 16 deems the source of a distribution from a QRP to arise in the Contracting State in which the plan is established, to the extent the distribution is reasonably attributable to a contribution to which a benefit was allowed under either of paragraphs 8, 10, or 13. This ensures that the Contracting State in which the plan is established will have the right to tax the gross amount of the distribution under subparagraph 2(*a*) of Article XVIII, even if a portion of the services to which the distribution relates were not performed in such Contracting State.

For purposes of applying paragraphs 8 through 16, paragraph 17 equates the relationship of an individual partner and a partnership to that of an employee and employer, thus extending the benefits in the above-mentioned paragraphs to partners who have participated in a QRP.

Paragraphs 8, 10, and 13 are not subject to the saving clause of paragraph 2 of Article XXIX (Miscellaneous Rules) by reason of the exception in subparagraph 3(*a*) of Article XXIX.

Editorial Note: Technical Interpretation, Document No. 2014-0531441E5, dated September 26, 2014, states that long-term disability insurance payments from an employer-funded plan are salary, wages, or other remuneration. Where such payments are made to a non-resident, Canada would retain the ability to tax the payments, as they qualify as a pension under paragraph 3 of Article XVIII of the Convention.

Technical Interpretation, Document No. 2008-0304421I7, dated May 20, 2010, states that Article XVIII will apply in a situation where a Canadian resident inherits an IRA or U.S. pension plan.

Technical Interpretation, Document No. 2007-0228481E5, dated November 8, 2007, deals with Article XVIII(5) of the Treaty, which exempts 15 per cent of the amount of a benefit under U.S. social security legislation paid to a resident of Canada. It is the CRA's view that the exemption applies to a survivor benefit under the *U.S. Social Security Act* that is paid to a decedent's child, if the child is resident in Canada.

Technical Interpretation, Document No. 2005-0140621E5, dated November 29, 2006, deals with the application of Article XVIII of the treaty where payments are made to the U.S. resident widow of a retired partner. It is the CRA's view that the allocations of partnership income would be business profits for the purposes of Article VII of the treaty.

Technical Interpretation, Document Nos. 2002-0152515 and 2006-0186661M4, dated December 11, 2002 and July 11, 2006 respectively, deal with the treatment of a Roth IRA and the paragraph 7 election to defer taxation of income earned by a Canadian resident beneficiary until the income is distributed to the beneficiary.

Technical Interpretation, Document No. 2004-0101881E5, dated December 2, 2004, deals with whether a lump sum payment received by a Canadian resident from the World Bank pension plan is exempt from taxation in Canada. It is the CRA's view that the pension payment would not be exempt as the individual was deemed to be a resident of Canada while they were an employee of the World Bank.

Technical Interpretation, Document No. 2003-0047151E5, dated March 3, 2004, deals with whether amounts that were subject to U.S. estate tax could be excluded from income under clause 56(1)(*a*)(i)(C.1) of the *Income Tax Act* (Canada) or paragraph 1 of Article XVIII of the Treaty. It is the CRA's view that an amount equivalent to the U.S. estate taxes paid could not be deducted from income.

History: Paragraphs 3 and 4 of Article XVIII were deleted and replaced by paragraph 1 of Article 13 of the Fifth Protocol to this Convention, and formerly read:

3. For the purposes of this Convention, the term 'pensions' includes any payment under a superannuation, pension or other retirement arrangement, Armed Forces retirement pay, war veterans' pensions and allowances and amounts paid under a sickness, accident or disability plan, but does not include payments under an income-averaging annuity contract or, except for the purposes of Article XIX (Government Service), any benefit referred to in paragraph 5.

4. For the purposes of the Convention, the term 'annuities' means a stated sum paid periodically at stated times during life or during a specified number of years, under an obligation to make the payments in return for adequate and full consideration (other than services rendered), but does not include a payment that is not a periodic payment or any annuity the cost of which was deductible for the purposes of taxation in the Contracting State in which it was acquired.

Paragraph 7 of Article XVIII was deleted and replaced by paragraph 2 of Article 13 of the Fifth Protocol to this Convention, and formerly read:

7. A natural person who is a citizen or resident of a Contracting State and a beneficiary of a trust, company, organization or other arrangement that is a resident of the other Contracting State, generally exempt from income taxation in that other State and operated exclusively to provide pension, retirement or employee benefits may elect to defer taxation in the first-mentioned State, under rules established by the competent authority of that State, with respect to any income accrued in the plan but not distributed by the plan, until such time as and to the extent that a distribution is made from the plan or any plan substituted therefor.

Paragraphs 8 to 17 of Article XVIII were added by paragraph 3 of Article 13 of the Fifth Protocol to this Convention.

Paragraph 3 of Article XVIII was amended by the Fourth Protocol to this Convention, and formerly read:

3. For the purposes of this Convention, the term "pensions" includes any payment under a superannuation, pension or other retirement arrangement, Armed Forces retirement pay, war veterans' pensions and allowances and amounts paid under a sickness, accident or disability plan, but does not include payments under an income-averaging annuity contract or any benefit referred to in paragraph 5.

Paragraph 3 of Article XVIII was amended by paragraph 1 of Article 9 of the Third Protocol to this Convention, and formerly read:

3. For the purposes of this Convention, the term "pensions" includes any payment under a superannuation, pension or retirement plan, Armed Forces retirement pay, war veterans pensions and allowances and amounts paid under a sickness, accident or disability plan, but does not include payments under an income-averaging annuity contract or any benefit referred to in paragraph 5.

Paragraph 5 of Article XVIII was amended by paragraph 2 of Article 9 of the Third Protocol to this Convention, and formerly read:

5. Benefits under the social security legislation in a Contracting State paid to a resident of the other Contracting State shall be taxable as follows:

(*a*) Such benefits shall be taxable only in that other State;

(*b*) Notwithstanding the provisions of subparagraph (*a*), one-half of the total amount of any such benefit paid in a taxable year shall be exempt from taxation in that other State.

Paragraph 7 of Article XVIII was added by paragraph 3 of Article 9 of the Third Protocol to this Convention.

Paragraph 1 and subparagraph 2(*b*) of Article XVIII were amended by Article IX of the First Protocol to this Convention, and formerly read:

1. Pensions and annuities arising in a Contracting State and paid to a resident of the other Contracting State may be taxed in that other State, but the amount of any pension included in income for the purposes of taxation in that other State shall not exceed the amount that would be included in the first-mentioned State if the recipient were a resident thereof.

...

2.

...

(*b*) Annuities may also be taxed in the Contracting State in which they arise and according to the laws of that State; but if a resident of the other Contracting State is the beneficial owner of an annuity payment, the tax so charged shall not exceed 15 per cent of the portion of such payment that is liable to tax in the first-mentioned State.

Paragraph 5 of Article XVIII was amended by Article I of the Second Protocol to this Convention, and formerly read:

5. Benefits under the social security legislation in a Contracting State paid to a resident of the other Contracting State or a citizen of the United States shall be taxable only in the first-mentioned State.

Paragraph 6 of Article XVIII was amended by Article IX of the First Protocol to this Convention, and formerly read:

6. Alimony and other similar amounts (including child support payments) arising in a Contracting State and paid to a resident of the other Contracting State shall be taxable only in that other State, but the amount included in income for the purposes of taxation in that other State shall not exceed the amount that would be included in income in the first-mentioned State if the recipient were a resident thereof.

Article XIX — Government Service

Remuneration, other than a pension, paid by a Contracting State or a political subdivision or local authority thereof to a citizen of that State in respect of services rendered in the discharge of functions of a governmental nature shall be taxable only in that State. However, the provisions of Article VII (Business Profits), XV (Income from Employment) or XVI (Artistes and Athletes), as the case may be, shall apply, and the preceding sentence shall not apply, to remuneration paid in respect of services rendered in connection with a trade or business carried on by a Contracting State or a political subdivision or local authority thereof.

Dentons Canada LLP Commentary: Where government services are rendered in another State by a government employee, there may be double taxation based on the principle of taxation by source of payment and by residence in that State. In addition, a claim to impose taxation on the income from that office may be based on nationality. This situation may be remedied by either State foregoing the right to tax. In Canadian law and treaties, the tendency has been for the State to forego the right to tax where the employee resides and renders the service. Paragraph 149(1)(*a*) of the *Income Tax Act* (Canada) exempts from tax, on a reciprocal basis, foreign government employees whose duties require them to reside in Canada, provided that they have no other business or employment in Canada and are not Canadian citizens. This exemption extends to members of families and servants of such employees under paragraph 149(1)(*b*) of the *Income Tax Act* (Canada).

Article XIX of the Convention exempts U.S. citizens from Canadian income tax on remuneration (other than pensions) paid by the United States or any political subdivision or local authority of the United States for services rendered in discharge of government functions. This exemption applies only if the individual is a citizen of the United States. Article XIX allows Canada to impose tax on a person other than a citizen of the United States who earns remuneration paid by the United States in respect of services rendered in the discharge of governmental functions in Canada. The U.S. citizen will not be subject to Canadian tax on remuneration (other than pensions) paid by the United States in respect of services rendered in the discharge of governmental functions, even when that U.S. citizen is ordinarily resident in Canada for purposes other than rendering governmental services. As a result of this Article, a U.S. citizen resident in Canada and performing services in Canada in the discharge of the functions of a governmental nature for the United States is taxable on remuneration for such services only in the United States.

This exemption does not apply to remuneration paid to U.S. citizens for services rendered in respect of any trade or business carried on by the government, political subdivision, or local authority of the United States. If services are rendered in connection with a trade or business, then the provisions of Articles VII (Business Profits), XV (Income from Employment), and XVI (Artistes and Athletes), as the case may be, apply. The distinction between governmental functions and a trade or business carried on may be difficult to apply in circumstances where government policy and commercial undertakings are closely interwoven. Determination of whether functions are of a governmental nature could initially be made by comparison with the concept of a government function in the State in which the income arises.

Article XIX applies similarly to prevent the United States from taxing Canadian citizens receiving remuneration from the Canadian government, political subdivision, or local authority for services rendered in the discharge of functions of a governmental nature in the United States.

Editorial Note: Technical Interpretation, Document No. 2005-0153901E5, dated November 15, 2007, deal with a situation where a U.S. citizen was employed in Canada by a U.S. not-for-profit organization that was funded by the U.S. government. The Article XIX exemption on remuneration would not apply, as it is the CRA's view that a non-profit organization funded by the U.S. government is not "a Contracting State or a political subdivision or local authority thereof".

History: Article XIX was amended by Article 14 of the Fifth Protocol to this Convention by deleting "XIV (Independent Personal Services)" and substituting "VII (Business Profits)", and by deleting "XV (Dependent Personal Services)" and substituting "XV (Income from Employment)".

Article XX — Students

Payments received by an individual who is a student, apprentice, or business trainee, and is, or was immediately before visiting a Contracting State, a resident of the other Contracting State, and who is present in the first-mentioned State for the purpose of the individual's full-time education or full-time training, shall not be taxed in that State, provided that such payments arise outside that State, and are for the purpose of the maintenance, education or training of the individual. The provisions of this Article shall apply to an apprentice or business trainee only for a period of time not exceeding one year from the date the individual first arrives in the first-mentioned State for the purpose of the individual's training.

Dentons Canada LLP Commentary: An individual who is a resident of one of the Contracting States and who becomes a full-time student, apprentice, or business trainee in the other Contracting State (the "host State") will generally be exempt from tax in the host State on payments from abroad used for his or her maintenance, education, or training. Therefore, payments received from outside Canada by students, apprentices, or business trainees who are present in Canada for the purpose of full-time education or training are not taxable in Canada, provided the student, apprentice, or business trainee was a resident of the United States immediately before visiting Canada. The Fifth Protocol amended Article XX such that the exemption from tax only applies for a period of one year in respect of an apprentice or business trainee. The one-year period commences on the date the apprentice or business trainee arrives in the Contracting State where the training is received.

Students must be resident in Canada for the purpose of pursuing "full-time" education or training to enjoy this tax exemption and the payments must be received by them from sources outside Canada for the purpose of their maintenance or studies, although there is no requirement that the payments must be from the other country (i.e., the United States). Aside from apprentices and business trainees, there is no limitation on the number of years or the amount of income to which this exemption applies. It does not require residence in either State during the period of study or training.

A payment will be considered to arise outside the host State if the payer is located outside the host State. Where appropriate, a "substance over form" approach may be used to identify the payer (i.e., payments made directly or indirectly by a U.S. person with whom the visitor is training, but which have been routed through a source outside the United States, are not treated as arising outside the United States for this purpose).

History: Article XX was deleted and replaced by Article 15 of the Fifth Protocol to this Convention, and formerly read:

Payments which a student, apprentice or business trainee, who is or was immediately before visiting a Contracting State a resident of the other Contracting State, and who is present in the first-mentioned State for the purpose of his full-time education or training, receives for the purpose of his maintenance, education or training shall not be taxed in that State provided that such payments are made to him from outside that State.

Article XXI — Exempt Organizations

1. Subject to the provisions of paragraph 4, income derived by a religious, scientific, literary, educational or charitable organization shall be exempt from tax in a Contracting State if it is resident in the other Contracting State, but only to the extent that such income is exempt from tax in that other State.

2. Subject to the provisions of paragraph 4, income referred to in Articles X (Dividends) and XI (Interest) derived by a trust, company, organization or other arrangement that is a resident of a Contracting State, generally exempt from income taxation in a taxable year in that State and operated exclusively to administer or provide pension, retirement or employee benefits shall be exempt from income taxation in that taxable year in the other Contracting State.

3. Subject to the provisions of paragraph 4, income referred to in Articles X (Dividends) and XI (Interest) derived by a trust, company, organization or other arrangement that is a resident of a Contracting State, generally exempt from income taxation in a taxable year in that State and operated exclusively to earn income for the benefit of one or more of the following:

(*a*) An organization referred to in paragraph 1; or

(*b*) A trust, company, organization or other arrangement referred to in paragraph 2;

shall be exempt from income taxation in that taxable year in the other Contracting State.

4. The provisions of paragraphs 1, 2 and 3 shall not apply with respect to the income of a trust, company, organization or other arrangement from carrying on a trade or business or from a related person other than a person referred to in paragraphs 1, 2 or 3.

5. A religious, scientific, literary, educational or charitable organization which is resident in Canada and which has received substantially all of its support from persons other than citizens or residents of the United States shall be exempt in the United States from the United States excise taxes imposed with respect to private foundations.

6. For the purposes of United States taxation, contributions by a citizen or resident of the United States to an organization which is resident in Canada, which is generally exempt from Canadian tax and which could qualify in the United States to receive deductible contributions if it were resident in the United States shall be treated as charitable contributions; however, such contributions (other than such contributions to a college or university at which the citizen or resident or a member of his family is or was enrolled) shall not be deductible in any taxable year to the extent that they exceed an amount determined by applying the percentage limitations of the laws of the United States in respect of the deductibility of charitable contributions to the income of such citizen or resident arising in Canada. The preceding sentence shall not be interpreted to allow in any taxable year deductions for charitable contributions in excess of the amount allowed under the percentage limitations of the laws of the United States in respect of the deductibility of charitable contributions. For the purposes of this paragraph, a company that is a resident of Canada and that is taxable in the United States as if it were a resident of the United States shall be deemed to be a resident of the United States.

7. For the purposes of Canadian taxation, gifts by a resident of Canada to an organization that is a resident of the United States, that is generally exempt from United States tax and that could qualify in Canada as a registered charity if it were a resident of Canada and created or established in Canada shall be treated as gifts to a registered charity; however, no relief from taxation shall be available in any taxation year with respect to such gifts (other than such gifts to a college or university at which the resident or a member of the resident's family is or was enrolled) to the extent that such relief would exceed the amount of relief that would be available under the *Income Tax Act* if the only income of the resident for that year were the resident's income arising in the United States. The preceding sentence shall not be interpreted to allow in any taxation year relief from taxation for gifts to registered charities in excess of the amount of relief allowed under the percentage limitations of the laws of Canada in respect of relief for gifts to registered charities.

Dentons Canada LLP Commentary: The income of charities and similar non-profit organizations residing or carrying on business in Canada is exempt from Canadian tax pursuant to section 149 of the *Income Tax Act* (Canada). However, U.S. charitable and non-profit organizations deriving income from Canadian sources are generally required to pay withholding tax imposed by Part XIII of the *Income Tax Act* (Canada). Paragraph 1 of Article XXI exempts from Canadian tax, the income of religious, scientific, literary, educational, or charitable organizations that are resident in the United States to the extent that this income is exempt from tax in the United States.

Accordingly, to be exempt from tax in the State of source under this Article, income must:

(a) be derived by an organization, within the description of "religious, scientific, literary, educational or charitable", as used in this Article; and

(b) be exempt from income tax in the Contracting State in which the organization is resident.

Article XXI does not exempt an entity from tax in the State of source but rather exempts income to the extent that such income is exempt from tax in the State of residence.

In the second paragraph of the letter exchanged between the two signatories on September 26, 1980, it is indicated that the competent authorities of Canada and the United States will review the procedures and requirements for organizations to establish their exempt status. If the competent authorities of Canada and the United States determine that such procedures and requirements are similar to each other's, Canada's competent authority will accept the certification of the United States competent authority that the organization is an exempt organization and *vice versa*. Thus, an organization will not have to qualify as an exempt organization in both countries.

Paragraph 2, as amended by the Fifth Protocol, provides that dividends and interest received by a tax-exempt trust, company, organization, or other arrangement resident in a Contracting State and operated exclusively to administer or provide benefits to a pension, retirement, or employee benefit plan is exempt from taxation in the other Contracting State. The word "arrangement" was added by the Third Protocol to clarify that IRAs, for example, are eligible for the benefits of paragraph 2, as are Canadian RRSPs and RRIFs (provided that they are operated exclusively to administer or provide pension, retirement, or employee benefits). This exemption also applies to Canadian employee profit sharing plans, deferred profit sharing plans, registered supplementary unemployment benefit plans, and the like. It is a condition of this exemption that the entity generally be exempt from *income* taxation in the State in which it is resident in the taxation year that the dividend or interest income arose; being subject to excise tax will not disqualify an otherwise exempt organization.

Paragraph 3, added by the Fifth Protocol, clarifies that the exemption in paragraph 2 also applies to dividends and interest received by a tax-exempt trust, company, organization, or other arrangement resident in a Contracting State and operated exclusively to earn income for the benefit of one or more of:

(a) a tax-exempt religious, scientific, literary, educational, or charitable organization described in paragraph 1; or

(b) a tax-exempt trust, company, organization, or other arrangement resident in a Contracting State and operated exclusively to provide benefits to a pension, retirement, or employee benefit plan.

Paragraph 3 was added because it was previously unclear whether investment vehicles for charitable organizations described in paragraph 1 of Article XXI were exempt from tax in the other Contracting State on dividends and interest earned in that other State. In this respect, there was uncertainty as to whether an investment vehicle benefiting a combination of pension funds and charitable organizations would qualify for the Article XXI exemption. Moreover, it was unclear whether an investment vehicle would qualify for the exemption if it benefited multiple pension plans. For example, it is not uncommon for a "master trust" resident in a Contracting State, the units of which are held by various registered pension plans, to invest in several different subsidiary investment vehicles resident in the other State. Each subsidiary investment vehicle indirectly benefits several different pension plans, meaning that the investment vehicles may not technically have qualified for the exemption. Canada and the United States indicated that these ambiguities were unintended and, consequently, paragraph 3 was included under the Fifth Protocol.

The treaty exemptions for Article XXI entities cannot override the payer's withholding obligations under the *Income Tax Act* (Canada). However, the CRA maintains a list, available on its Web site, of entities to whom it has issued letters acknowledging that they are Article XXI exempt entities. The CRA's Information Circular 77-16R4 authorizes Canadian payors to rely upon the CRA's published list of treaty exempt investors under Article XXI. The CRA has also approved an electronic certification method for extending exemption at source to U.S. pension fund Article XXI investors on Canadian securities owned by them that are public securities registered in the name of a stock exchange depository and held by the investor's custodian (see paragraph 81 of IC 77-16R4).

Pursuant to paragraph 4, the above exemptions from withholding tax do not apply to income received from the carrying on of a trade or business in the other State or to income received from a related person that is also not an exempt organization. Thus, for example, a Canadian charity that owned a U.S. subsidiary that carried on a business would be subject to U.S. withholding tax on dividends and interest received from the subsidiary.

Pursuant to paragraph 5, a religious, scientific, literary, educational or charitable organization which is resident in Canada is exempt from U.S. excise taxes normally imposed on private foundations, but only if it has received "substantially all" of its support from persons who are not citizens or residents of the United States. Thus, Canadian private foundations will be exempt from the excise tax imposed on their gross U.S.-source investment income, provided they are not substantially funded by U.S. citizens or residents.

Paragraph 7 provides that Canada will allow its residents relief from taxation with regard to gifts made to U.S. organizations exempt from U.S. tax, but only if the U.S. organization, if it had been established and resident in Canada, would qualify as a registered charity. Under section 118.1 of the *Income Tax Act* (Canada), individuals are provided with a non-refundable tax credit for various donations; under subsection 110.1(1), corporations are permitted a deduction. The tax relief for gifts made to U.S. organizations (other than gifts to a college or university at which the Canadian resident or member of his or her family is or was enrolled) may not exceed the amount determined by applying to the income of a Canadian resident which arises in the United States, the percentage (presently 75 per cent) that is applied by Canada to income in determining the limitation of the tax credit for charitable gifts. The relief allowed by Article XXI does not increase the maximum credit that a Canadian taxpayer may receive for charitable donations from that allowed by the *Income Tax Act* (Canada).

The special limitation to income arising in the United States does not apply to contributions to a college or a university of which a Canadian citizen or resident or member of his or her family is, or was, enrolled. Contributions made to such colleges or universities are not limited by the Canadian resident's income derived from U.S. sources but are subject to the percentage limitation (presently 75 per cent) established by the *Income Tax Act* (Canada). A Canadian resident can claim a deduction in respect of a U.S. college or university at which the resident, or a member of his or her family, is or was enrolled although he or she has no U.S.-source income. The term "family" is defined to mean an individual's brothers and sisters whether by whole or half- blood or by adoption, as well as an individual's spouse, ancestors, lineal descendants, and adopted descendants. (See the letter exchanged on September 26, 1980.)

The U.S.-source income limitation also does not apply under subsection 118.1(9) of the *Income Tax Act* (Canada), which permits Canadian residents employed in the United States who commute to work to make creditable gifts to U.S. charities and similar organizations in accordance with its provisions.

Paragraph 6 of this Article provides rules for purposes of U.S. taxation with respect to the deductibility of gifts to a Canadian resident organization by a resident of the United States. The rules of this paragraph parallel the rules of paragraph 7. Paragraph 6 was amended by the Third Protocol to clarify that the benefits of the paragraph are available to a company that is a resident of Canada but is treated by the United States as a domestic corporation under the consolidated return rules of section 1504(d) of the *Internal Revenue Code*. Thus, such a company will be able to deduct, for U.S. income tax purposes, contributions to Canadian charities that are deductible to a U.S. resident, under the provisions of the paragraph.

Editorial Note: Technical Interpretation, Document No. 2005-0140291E5, dated January 18, 2008, deals with Article XXI(2) of the *Canada–United States Income Tax Convention (1980)*, where the income of a U.S. pension fund is exempt from tax in Canada in a situation where the pension fund was a member of a partnership that earned investment income.

CRA Tax Ruling, Document No. 2005-0149681R3, states that "income", for the purposes of Article XXI(1) of the Treaty, includes capital gains.

Technical Interpretation, Document No. 2006-0187461E5, dated August 23, 2006, deals with mutual fund distributions received by an IRA. The withholding tax exemption under Article XXI(2) does not apply to mutual fund distributions to an IRA.

History: Paragraphs 4, 5, and 6 of Article XXI were renumbered as paragraphs 5, 6, and 7, respectively, by paragraph 1 of Article 16 of the Fifth Protocol to this Convention.

Paragraphs 1 through 3 of Article XXI were deleted and replaced with paragraphs 1 through 4 by paragraph 2 of Article 16 of the Fifth Protocol to this Convention, and formerly read:

1. Subject to the provisions of paragraph 3, income derived by a religious, scientific, literary, educational or charitable organization shall be exempt from tax in a Contracting State if it is resident in the other Contracting State but only to the extent that such income is exempt from tax in that other State.

2. Subject to the provisions of paragraph 3, income referred to in Articles X (Dividends) and XI (Interest) derived by:

(*a*) A trust, company, organization or other arrangement that is a resident of a Contracting State, generally exempt from income taxation in a taxable year in that State and operated exclusively to administer or provide pension, retirement or employee benefits; or

(*b*) A trust, company, organization or other arrangement that is a resident of a Contracting State, generally exempt from income taxation in a taxable year in that State and operated exclusively to earn income for the benefit of an organization referred to in subparagraph (*a*);

shall be exempt from income taxation in that taxable year in the other Contracting State.

3. The provisions of paragraphs 1 and 2 shall not apply with respect to the income of a trust, company, organization or other arrangement from carrying on a trade or business or from a related person other than a person referred to in paragraph 1 or 2.

Paragraphs 2 and 3 of Article XXI were amended by paragraph 1 of Article X of the Third Protocol to this Convention, and formerly read:

2. Subject to the Provisions of paragraph 3, income referred to in Articles X (Dividends) and XI (Interest) derived by:

(*a*) A trust, company or other organization which is resident in a Contracting State, generally exempt from tax in a taxable year in that State and constituted and operated exclusively to administer or provide benefits under one or more funds or plans established to provide pension, retirement or other employee benefits; or

(*b*) A trust, company or other organization which is resident in a Contracting State, not taxed in a taxable year in that State and constituted and operated exclusively to earn income for the benefit of an organization referred to in subparagraph (*a*); shall be exempt from tax in that taxable year in the other Contracting State.

3. The provisions of paragraphs 1 and 2 shall not apply with respect to the income of a trust, company or other organization from carrying on a trade or business or from a related person other than a person referred to in paragraph 1 or 2.

Paragraph 5 of Article XXI was amended by paragraph 2 of Article 10 of the Third Protocol to this Convention by adding a new sentence at the end.

Paragraph 6 of Article XXI was amended by paragraph 3 of Article 10 of the Third Protocol to this Convention, and formerly read:

6. For the purposes of Canadian taxation, gifts by a resident of Canada to an organization which is resident in the United States, which is generally exempt from United States tax and which could qualify in Canada to receive deductible gifts if it were created or established and resident in Canada shall be treated as gifts to a registered charity; however, such gifts (other than such gifts to a college or university at which the resident or a member of his family is or was enrolled) shall not be deductible in any taxable year to the extent that they exceed an amount determined by applying the percentage limitations of the laws of Canada in respect of the deductibility of gifts to registered charities to the income of such resident arising in the United States. The preceding sentence shall not be interpreted to allow in any taxable year deductions for gifts to registered charities in excess of the amount allowed under the percentage limitations of the laws of Canada in respect of the deductibility of gifts to registered charities.

Paragraph 2 of Article XXI was amended by Article X of the First Protocol to this Convention, and formerly read:

2. Subject to the provisions of paragraph 3, income referred to in Articles X (Dividends) and XI (Interest) derived by a trust, company or other organization constituted and operated exclusively to administer or provide benefits under one or more funds or plans established to provide pension, retirement or other employee benefits shall be exempt from tax in a Contracting State if it is resident in the other Contracting State and its income is generally exempt from tax in that other State.

Tax Window Files: 2015 TEI Meeting Q7 Donations to qualifying US charity, *November 17, 2015*, CRA Document No. 2015-0614251C6.

Article XXII — Other Income

1. Items of income of a resident of a Contracting State, wherever arising, not dealt with in the foregoing Articles of this Convention shall be taxable only in that State, except that if such income arises in the other Contracting State it may also be taxed in that other State.

2. To the extent that income distributed by an estate or trust is subject to the provisions of paragraph 1, then, notwithstanding such provisions, income distributed by an estate or trust which is a resident of a Contracting State to a resident of the other Contracting State who is a beneficiary of the estate or trust may be taxed in the first-mentioned State and according to the laws of that State, but the tax so charged shall not exceed 15 per cent of the gross amount of the income; provided, however, that such income shall be exempt from tax in the first-mentioned State to the extent of any amount distributed out of income arising outside that State.

3. Losses incurred by a resident of a Contracting State with respect to wagering transactions the gains on which may be taxed in the other Contracting State shall, for the purpose of taxation in that other State, be deductible to the same extent that such losses would be deductible if they were incurred by a resident of that other State.

4. Notwithstanding the provisions of paragraph 1, compensation derived by a resident of a Contracting State in respect of the provision of a guarantee of indebtedness shall be taxable only in that State,

unless such compensation is business profits attributable to a permanent establishment situated in the other Contracting State, in which case the provisions of Article VII (Business Profits) shall apply.

Dentons Canada LLP Commentary: As a general rule, items of income not otherwise dealt with in the Convention which are derived by residents of either country shall be taxable only by the country of residence. However, if the income is sourced to the other country, it may also be taxed by that country.

The source of an item of income is determined under the domestic laws of the two countries unless the Convention contains a specific rule specifying where the income arises (for example, paragraph 6 of Article XI, with respect to interest). Therefore, items of income that are not specifically dealt with in the Convention and that arise in one country and are derived by a resident of the other country may be taxed in both countries.

There is a limitation under the provisions of the Convention as to the rate of tax that may be levied on such income by the source country. However, for example, Canadian residents that derive U.S.-source income that is taxed in both Canada and the United States can seek relief from double taxation under the provisions of Article XXIV (Elimination of Double Taxation). Article XXII would, for example, also give Canada the sole right to tax income sourced to a third country and paid to a resident of Canada.

In Canada, a trust or estate is taxed separately as an individual, but is allowed to deduct from its income the amount of income that has been distributed to beneficiaries in the year it is earned. Thus, in the normal course, income tax is imposed on either the trust or the beneficiary. Under Article XXII, tax may be withheld on the income of an estate or trust that is resident of one country and paid to a resident of the other country, but such tax is not to exceed 15 per cent. Tax may not be withheld by the first country in respect of trust income arising outside that country. A Canadian trust, for example, receiving U.K.-source income which is distributed to a U.S. income beneficiary need not withhold tax on such income. Article XXII recognizes that a trust or estate may simply be a means of channelling income from its various sources to its beneficiaries and that if both the source of income and the beneficiary are outside of the trust or estate's country of residence, no tax liability should arise from the mere presence there of the trust or estate administration.

Paragraph 3 entitles residents of one Contracting State who are taxable by the other State on gains from wagering transactions to deduct losses from wagering transactions for the purposes of taxation in that other State. However, losses are to be deductible only to the extent that they are incurred with respect to wagering transactions, the gains on which could be taxable in the other State, and only to the extent that such losses would be deductible if incurred by a resident of that other State. Canada does not generally tax gambling winnings, whereas the United States does.

The Fifth Protocol added paragraph 4, which provides that a guarantee fee received by a resident of a Contracting State from a resident of the other Contracting State are only taxable in the first-mentioned State, unless the amount is attributable to a permanent establishment of the recipient in the other State. For example, it is not uncommon for a U.S. parent company to guarantee the indebtedness of its Canadian subsidiary. Prior to the Fifth Protocol, the guarantee fee would have been subject to withholding tax in Canada pursuant to subsection 214(15) of the *Income Tax Act* (Canada). Under paragraph 4, the guarantee fee is only taxable in the United States, unless the fee is attributable to a Canadian permanent establishment of the U.S. parent. If attributable to a Canadian permanent establishment, the amount is subject to Canadian tax as business profits pursuant to Article VII of the Convention, meaning that the U.S. parent may be entitled to net certain expenses against the fee in determining its Canadian tax liability.

This Article does not affect the collection of tax by a Contracting State. Thus, in the case of a resident of Canada, it does not affect, for example, the imposition of U.S. withholding taxes under section 1441 or section 1442 of the *Internal Revenue Code* on the gross amount of gains from wagering transactions. However, in computing its U.S. income tax liability on net income for the taxable year concerned, the Canadian resident may reduce his or her gains from wagering transactions subject to taxation in the United States by any wagering losses incurred on such transactions, to the extent that those losses are deductible under the provisions of paragraph 3. Under United States domestic law, the deduction of wagering losses is governed by section 165 of the *Internal Revenue Code*. It is intended that the resident of Canada file a non-resident income tax return in order to substantiate the deduction for losses and to claim a refund of any overpayment of U.S. taxes collected by withholding.

History: Paragraph 4 of Article XXII was added by Article 17 of the Fifth Protocol to this Convention.

Paragraph 3 of Article XXI was added by Article 11 of the Third Protocol to this Convention.

Article XXIII — Capital

1. Capital represented by real property, owned by a resident of a Contracting State and situated in the other Contracting State, may be taxed in that other State.

2. Capital represented by personal property forming part of the business property of a permanent establishment which a resident of a Contracting State has in the other Contracting State may be taxed in that other State.

3. Capital represented by ships and aircraft operated by a resident of a Contracting State in international traffic, and by personal property pertaining to the operation of such ships and aircraft, shall be taxable only in that State.

4. All other elements of capital of a resident of a Contracting State shall be taxable only in that State.

Dentons Canada LLP Commentary: The following types of capital owned by a resident of one of the Contracting States may be subject to tax in the other State:

(a) real property (as defined for purposes of Article VI) situated in the other State; and

(b) personal property forming part of the business property of a permanent establishment in the other State (prior to the Fifth Protocol, capital also included personal property pertaining to a fixed base in the other State).

As a general rule, capital taxes would be imposed when the income from the capital would be taxed by the other State imposing the capital tax.

Capital represented by ships and aircraft operated by a resident of a Contracting State in international traffic (see Article III (General Definitions)) and personal property pertaining to the operation of such ships and aircraft can be taxed only by the State of residence and are specifically excluded from any capital tax imposed in the other State.

Any other capital owned by residents of a Contracting State can be taxed only in that State.

History: Paragraph 2 of Article XXIII was amended by Article 18 of the Fifth Protocol to this Convention by deleting ", or by personal property pertaining to a fixed base available to a resident of a Contracting State in the other Contracting State for the purpose of performing independent personal services,".

Article XXIV — Elimination of Double Taxation

1. In the case of the United States, subject to the provisions of paragraphs 4, 5 and 6, double taxation shall be avoided as follows: In accordance with the provisions and subject to the limitations of the law of the United States (as it may be amended from time to time without changing the general principle hereof), the United States shall allow to a citizen or resident of the United States, or to a company electing to be treated as a domestic corporation, as a credit against the United States tax on income the appropriate amount of income tax paid or accrued to Canada; and, in the case of a company which is a resident of the United States owning at least 10 per cent of the voting stock of a company which is a resident of Canada from which it receives dividends in any taxable year, the United States shall allow as credit against the United States tax on income the appropriate amount of income tax paid or accrued to Canada by that company with respect to the profits out of which such dividends are paid.

2. In the case of Canada, subject to the provisions of paragraphs 4, 5 and 6, double taxation shall be avoided as follows:

(*a*) Subject to the provisions of the law of Canada regarding the deduction from tax payable in Canada of tax paid in a territory outside Canada and to any subsequent modification of those provisions (which shall not affect the general principle hereof)

(i) Income tax paid or accrued to the United States on profits, income or gains arising in the United States, and

(ii) In the case of an individual, any social security taxes paid to the United States (other than taxes relating to unemployment insurance benefits) by the individual on such profits, income or gains

shall be deducted from any Canadian tax payable in respect of such profits, income or gains;

(*b*) In the case of a company which is a resident of Canada owning at least 10 percent of the voting stock of a company which is a resident of the United States from which it receives dividends in any taxable year, Canada shall allow as a credit against the Canadian tax on income the appropriate amount of income tax paid or accrued to the United States by the second company with respect to the profits out of which the dividends are paid.

(*c*) Notwithstanding the provisions of subparagraph (*a*), where Canada imposes a tax on gains from the alienation of property that, but for the provisions of paragraph 5 of Article XIII (Gains), would not be taxable in Canada, income tax paid or accrued to the United States on such gains shall be deducted from any Canadian tax payable in respect of such gains.

3. For the purposes of this Article:

(*a*) Profits, income or gains (other than gains to which paragraph 5 of Article XIII (Gains) applies) of a resident of a Contracting State which may be taxed in the other Contracting State in accordance with the Convention (without regard to paragraph 2 of Article XXIX (Miscellaneous Rules)) shall be deemed to arise in that other State; and

(*b*) Profits, income or gains of a resident of a Contracting State which may not be taxed in the other Contracting State in accordance with the Convention (without regard to paragraph 2 of Article XXIX (Miscellaneous Rules)) or to which paragraph 5 of Article XIII (Gains) applies shall be deemed to arise in the first-mentioned State.

4. Where a United States citizen is a resident of Canada, the following rules shall apply:

(*a*) Canada shall allow a deduction from the Canadian tax in respect of income tax paid or accrued to the United States in respect of profits, income or gains which arise (within the meaning of paragraph 3) in the United States, except that such deduction need not exceed the amount of the tax that would be paid to the United States if the resident were not a United States citizen; and

(*b*) For the purposes of computing the United States tax, the United States shall allow as a credit against United States tax the income tax paid or accrued to Canada after the deduction referred to in subparagraph (*a*). The credit so allowed shall not reduce that portion of the United States tax that is deductible from Canadian tax in accordance with subparagraph (*a*).

5. Notwithstanding the provisions of paragraph 4, where a United States citizen is a resident of Canada, the following rules shall apply in respect of the items of income referred to in Article X (Dividends), XI or XII (Royalties) that arise (within the meaning of paragraph 3) in the United States and that would be subject to United States tax if the resident of Canada were not a citizen of the United States, as long as the law in force in Canada allows a deduction in computing income for the portion of any foreign tax paid in respect of such items which exceeds 15 per cent of the amount thereof:

(*a*) The deduction so allowed in Canada shall not be reduced by any credit or deduction for income tax paid or accrued to Canada allowed in computing the United States tax on such items;

(*b*) Canada shall allow a deduction from Canadian tax on such items in respect of income tax paid or accrued to the United States on such items, except that such deduction need not exceed the amount of the tax that would be paid on such items to the United States if the resident of Canada were not a United States citizen; and

(*c*) For the purposes of computing the United States tax on such items, the United States shall allow as a credit against United States tax the income tax paid or accrued to Canada after the deduction referred to in subparagraph (*b*). The credit so allowed shall reduce only that portion of the United States tax on such items which exceeds the amount of tax that would be paid to the United States on such items if the resident of Canada were not a United States citizen.

6. Where a United States citizen is a resident of Canada, items of income referred to in paragraph 4 or 5 shall, notwithstanding the provisions of paragraph 3, be deemed to arise in Canada to the extent necessary to avoid the double taxation of such income under paragraph 4(*b*) or paragraph 5(*c*).

7. For the purposes of this Article, any reference to "income tax paid or accrued" to a Contracting State shall include Canadian tax and United States tax, as the case may be, and taxes of general application which are paid or accrued to a political subdivision or local authority of that State, which are not imposed by that political subdivision or local authority in a manner inconsistent with the provisions of the Convention and which are substantially similar to the Canadian tax or United States tax, as the case may be.

8. Where a resident of a Contracting State owns capital which, in accordance with the provisions of the Convention, may be taxed in the other Contracting State, the first-mentioned State shall allow as a deduction from the tax on the capital of that resident an amount equal to the capital tax paid in that other State. The deduction shall not, however, exceed that part of the capital tax, as computed before the deduction is given, which is attributable to the capital which may be taxed in that other State.

9. The provisions of this Article relating to the source of profits, income or gains shall not apply for the purpose of determining a credit against United States tax for any foreign taxes other than income taxes paid or accrued to Canada.

10. Where in accordance with any provision of the Convention income derived or capital owned by a resident of a Contracting State is exempt from tax in that State, such State may nevertheless, in calculating the amount of tax on other income or capital, take into account the exempted income or capital.

Dentons Canada LLP Commentary: One of the principal reasons for entering into an Income Tax Convention is to limit double taxation of income earned by a resident or citizen of one of the countries that may be taxed by the other country. Article XXIV provides for reciprocal credits and exemptions to avoid the imposition of double taxation on income that is taxable by both Canada and the United States. This Article provides separate rules for relief of double taxation by the United States and by Canada. In addition, it provides special rules for U.S. citizens resident in Canada.

Paragraph 1 provides that double taxation "shall be avoided" in the United States by allowing a U.S. citizen or resident, or a Canadian company electing under the *Internal Revenue Code* section 1504(d) to be treated as a domestic corporation, a credit against U.S. tax for the appropriate amount of Canadian income tax paid or accrued. Section 1504(d) applies only to Canadian corporations that are 100 per cent owned by U.S. parents and that are formed in Canada solely for the purpose of complying with the Canadian law concerning title and operation of property. In addition, U.S. corporations owning at least 10 per cent of the voting stock of a Canadian resident company (which for this purpose does not include a company electing under section 1504(d) to be treated as a domestic corporation) are entitled to a credit for Canadian income tax paid (or deemed to be paid by the *Internal Revenue Code*) by the Canadian company with respect to profits out of which dividends are paid to the U.S. company and included in its taxable income for U.S. tax purposes.

The direct and "deemed paid credits" allowed by paragraph 1 are to be computed in accordance with the provisions of and subject to the limitations of the U.S. *Internal Revenue Code* as they may be amended from time to time, without changing the general principles of paragraph 1.

The rules for avoiding double taxation in Canada are provided in paragraph 2 of this Article. These rules establish the priority of taxation at the source of income over taxation at the residence of the recipient. Under the Convention, Canada allows a foreign tax credit for U.S. income tax paid or accrued on income from U.S. sources. Subparagraph (*a*) of paragraph 2 obligates Canada to give a foreign tax credit for U.S. social security taxes paid by individuals. Subparagraph (*b*) of paragraph 2 provides that where a Canadian resident corporation receives dividends from a U.S. corporation in which it owns at least 10 per cent of the voting stock, a credit shall be provided equal to an *appropriate amount* of income tax paid or accrued to the United States by the U.S. dividend payer with respect to the profits out of which the dividends are paid (e.g., underlying foreign tax paid). Prior to the Fifth Protocol, subparagraph (*b*) referred to a deduction from income and "exempt surplus." In its current form, subparagraph (*b*) appears to prospectively grant Canada the flexibility to repeal its existing surplus rules relating to the taxation of distributions received from a foreign affiliate without the need to subsequently renegotiate the terms of Article XXIV. The change, introduced by the Fifth Protocol, is in conformity with other tax treaties negotiated by Canada.

The foreign tax credit allowed by the Convention is subject to the provisions and limitations of the *Income Tax Act* (Canada), or to any subsequent amendments of these provisions which do not affect the general principles of paragraph 2. Subsection 126(1) of the *Income Tax Act* (Canada) provides the rules which allow a Canadian resident taxpayer to deduct from Canadian tax certain non-business income tax paid by the taxpayer to another country, and subsection 126(2) provides rules to allow a Canadian resident taxpayer to deduct such foreign tax as he or she pays on business income earned in a foreign country. Under the provisions of the *Income Tax Act* (Canada), a Canadian resident taxpayer must calculate the foreign tax credit which he or she is entitled to deduct from Canadian tax on a country-by-country basis. Thus, the excess of U.S. tax paid over the foreign tax credit allowed in respect of U.S. tax cannot be used to reduce Canadian tax on income from another source. If the Canadian resident cannot obtain a full credit for U.S. business taxes paid, he or she may, subject to certain limitations, deduct the excess in another year. That amount of non-business tax for which a Canadian resident cannot obtain a foreign tax credit may be deducted from net income under subsection 20(12) of the *Income Tax Act* (Canada). If the non-business tax relates to property income, the Canadian resident is limited to a 15 per cent tax credit but may deduct that amount which exceeds 15 per cent of property income from net income under subsection 20(11) of the *Income Tax Act* (Canada).

These deductions were the subject of *FLSmidth Ltd. v. Canada*, 2013 DTC 5118, where the Federal Court of Appeal affirmed the Tax Court of Canada decision, 2012 DTC 1052. The Canadian taxpayer in the case utilized a "tower structure" to fund the acquisition of U.S. businesses and in doing so utilized "hybrid entities." Dividends were paid up the chain of companies, and for U.S. tax purposes income tax was paid as the amounts were recognized U.S. source income. In Canada, the amounts were recognized as tax-free exempt surplus, but the taxpayer attempted to deduct the U.S. taxes paid under subsection 20(12) of the *Income Tax Act* (Canada). The courts held that the deduction was unavailable, because the tax could not be reasonably regarded as having been paid in respect of income from the share of the capital stock of a foreign affiliate.

The CRA provides its administrative position on foreign tax credits in Income Tax Folio S5-F2-C1, "Foreign Tax Credit," which replaced and cancelled Interpretation Bulletin IT-270R3, "Foreign Tax Credit"; Interpretation Bulletin IT-395R2, "Foreign Tax Credit – Foreign-Source Capital Gains and Losses"; and Interpretation Bulletin IT-520 (consolidated), "Unused Foreign Tax Credits – Carryforward and Carryback."

Section 113 of the *Income Tax Act* (Canada) allows Canadian resident corporations to deduct from taxable income all or a portion of the dividends received from foreign affiliates. Paragraph 2 of Article XXIV confirms that Canadian-resident corporate shareholders are exempt (or will be provided with sufficient credit) from Canadian tax on dividends received from a foreign affiliate that is a U.S. resident which are paid out of "exempt surplus". Generally, "exempt surplus" represents after-tax business income arising in a jurisdiction with which Canada has a tax treaty.

Under paragraph 2 of Article XXIV, Canada will allow a foreign tax credit for income taxes paid or accrued to the United States on gains that would not normally be taxable in Canada except for the provision of paragraph 5 of Article XIII (Gains). Under paragraph 5 of Article XIII, Canada can impose tax on gains derived by U.S. residents on the alienation of certain Canadian property, if the U.S. resident was formerly a resident of Canada for 120 months during the 20-year period preceding the alienation of property and was also a U.S. resident at any time during the 10 years preceding the alienation of property. The Convention ensures that the U.S. resident will obtain a tax credit in Canada for U.S. taxes paid on these gains. The *Income Tax Act* (Canada) provides for this credit in subsection 126(2.2).

The term "income tax paid and accrued" used in this Article is defined in paragraph 7 to include certain specified taxes which are paid or accrued. Taxes which are creditable include "Taxes Covered" (defined in Article II (Taxes Covered) to include taxes imposed by the *Income Tax Act* (Canada), the U.S. *Internal Revenue Code*, and national taxes on capital) and taxes of general application that are paid to a political subdivision (a Canadian province or U.S. state) or local authority. In order for tax imposed by a political subdivision or local authority to fall within the definition of "income tax paid or accrued", such tax must apply to individuals, companies, or other persons generally, not only to a particular class of individuals or companies or a particular type of business. These taxes must be substantially similar to the national taxes covered in Article II of this Convention and must not be imposed in a manner inconsistent with the provisions of this Convention. For example, taxes of a political subdivision or local authority of the United States are not creditable if imposed on a resident of Canada earning business profits within the U.S. political subdivision or local authority but not having a permanent establishment there.

As a result of the definition of "income tax paid or accrued", it is possible for some Canadian tax not to be considered creditable tax. Thus, many provincial mining taxes, to the extent that they are not based on net income and contain other deviations from a net realized income concept, would not be creditable.

Source of Income

Income is sourced according to the rules of paragraph 3 of Article XXIV, and the source rules for income provided in this paragraph are to be used only for purposes of this Article. These source rules are as follows:

(1) Income (other than gains to which paragraph 5 of Article XIII (Gains) apply) of a resident of one country that may be taxed in the other country in accordance with this Convention is deemed to be sourced in that other country for domestic foreign tax credit purposes. Thus, income of a Canadian resident that may be taxed in the United States under the provisions of this Convention is deemed to be U.S.-source income. Accordingly, income taxes paid to the United States on this income will be creditable in Canada.

(2) Income that this Convention does not permit to be taxed in the other country has its source in the country of residence for domestic foreign tax credit purposes. Thus, when a Canadian resident has income from U.S. copyright royalties exempt from U.S. tax under paragraph 3 of Article XII (Royalties), the source of that income under Article XXIV becomes a Canadian source.

(3) Gains to which paragraph 5 of Article XIII (Gains) applies have their source in the taxpayer's country of residence. Thus, a U.S. resident can claim a foreign tax credit in Canada for U.S. taxes paid on gains from alienation of Canadian property that would otherwise be treated as Canadian source income.

Paragraph 6 allows U.S. citizens who are resident in Canada to treat U.S.-source income as Canadian source income to avoid double taxation of such U.S.-source income and ensure that the U.S. citizen obtains a foreign tax credit for Canadian taxes paid or accrued on such income. The provisions that allow a U.S. citizen, residing in Canada, to avoid double taxation of his or her U.S. source income are contained in paragraphs 4 and 5 of this Article and are discussed below.

Paragraph 9 provides that the source rules of paragraphs 3 and 6 shall not be used to determine the credit available to reduce U.S. tax for foreign taxes other than income taxes paid or accrued to Canada. Thus, creditable third country taxes may not offset the U.S. tax on income treated as arising in Canada.

U.S. Citizens Resident in Canada

The United States taxes its citizens on worldwide income, whereas Canada imposes tax based on residency. Therefore, double taxation often would occur from tax imposed as a result of being a citizen of the United States and a resident of Canada. Article XXIV attempts to order the three different interests of the source country, the country of residence, and the citizenship country. Generally speaking, the order set out is as follows:

(a) the source country has a limited right to tax;

(b) the residence country (i.e., Canada) has the right to tax but an obligation to give relief for source country taxes; and

(c) countries exercising their jurisdiction on the basis of citizenship (i.e., the United States) stand third in line and give relief for any taxes imposed by source and residence countries.

This is generally the order given to the above-noted three interests in paragraphs 4, 5, and 6 of the Convention. Paragraph 5 of this Article sets out the rules to avoid double tax for U.S. citizens residing in Canada on dividends (Article X), interest (Article XI), and royalties (Article XII) that arise in the United States. The mechanism for avoiding double taxation of other income (i.e., income other than dividends, interest, and royalties) and gains of U.S. citizens resident in Canada is provided for in paragraph 4. The allocation of tax between the United States and Canada is essentially as follows:

- The United States is allowed to impose U.S. tax on U.S.-source income in accordance with the provisions of the Convention.
- Canada can tax the total income of the U.S. citizen on the basis of residency but must allow a foreign tax credit for U.S. taxes imposed on other income and gains which arise in the United States, according to the rules of paragraph 3. The foreign tax credit allowed by Canada need not exceed the amount of U.S. tax that would be paid if the Canadian resident were not a U.S. citizen. In effect, this Convention requires Canada to allow a deduction for U.S. tax paid or accrued on U.S.-source income and gains at least equal to the U.S. tax that would be paid or accrued if the Canadian resident was not a U.S. citizen. A credit for U.S. tax paid in excess of the amount that would be imposed if the Canadian resident were not a U.S. citizen can only be claimed if it is allowed under the provisions of the *Income Tax Act* (Canada) and it is in fact paid or accrued by the U.S. citizen.
- The United States can impose tax on the total income of U.S. citizens residing in Canada. However, the United States must allow a foreign tax credit for net Canadian taxes paid or accrued (that is, Canadian tax computed after the deduction of a foreign tax credit for U.S. tax). The foreign tax credit allowed in respect of Canadian taxes cannot reduce U.S. tax below the amount which is creditable and deductible in Canada in accordance with subparagraph 4(*a*) of this Article; that is, below that amount that would be paid to the United States if the resident were not a U.S. citizen. Thus, the U.S. citizen residing in Canada will pay no less tax on his other income and gains from U.S. sources than he would if it was income earned in the United States by a non-resident Canadian citizen.
- Paragraph 6 of Article XXIV provides for a change in source rules to ensure the U.S. citizen obtains the maximum credit for Canadian taxes paid or accrued when computing his or her U.S. tax on worldwide income. Thus, a portion of the U.S. income can be treated as Canadian income for determining his or her foreign tax credit.

As noted above, paragraphs 4 and 5 of Article XXIV of the Convention provide double taxation relief rules, for both the United States and Canada, with respect to U.S.-source income derived by a U.S. citizen who is resident in

Canada. These rules address the fact that a U.S. citizen resident in Canada remains subject to U.S. tax on his or her worldwide income at ordinary progressive rates, and may, therefore, be subject to U.S. tax at a higher rate than a resident of Canada who is not a U.S. citizen. In essence, these paragraphs limit the foreign tax credit that Canada is obliged to allow such a U.S. citizen to the amount of tax on his or her U.S.-source income that the United States would be allowed to collect from a Canadian resident who is not a U.S. citizen. They also oblige the United States to allow the U.S. citizen a credit for any income tax paid to Canada on the remainder of his or her income. Paragraph 4 deals with items of income other than dividends, interest, and royalties. Paragraph 5 deals with dividends, interest, and royalties.

Paragraph 5 applies only to dividend, interest, and royalty income that would be subject to a positive rate of U.S. tax if paid to a Canadian resident who is not a U.S. citizen. This means that the rules of paragraph 4, not paragraph 5, will apply to items of interest and royalties, such as portfolio interest, that would be exempt from U.S. tax if paid to a non-U.S. citizen resident in Canada. Under paragraph 4, Canada will not allow a credit for the U.S. tax on such income, and the United States will credit the Canadian tax to the extent necessary to avoid double taxation.

Paragraph 5 provides special rules for the elimination of double taxation in the case of dividends, interest, and royalties earned by a U.S. citizen resident in Canada. These rules apply notwithstanding the provisions of paragraph 4, but only as long as the law in Canada allows a deduction in computing income for the portion of any foreign tax paid in respect of dividends, interest, or royalties which exceeds 15 per cent of the amount of such items of income, and only with respect to those items of income. The rules of paragraph 4 apply with respect to other items of income; moreover, if the law in force in Canada regarding the deduction for foreign taxes is changed so as to no longer allow such a deduction, the provisions of paragraph 5 shall not apply and the U.S. foreign tax credit for Canadian taxes and the Canadian credit for U.S. taxes will be determined solely pursuant to the provisions of paragraph 4.

The calculations under paragraph 5 are as follows:

(1) First, the deduction allowed in Canada in computing income shall be made with respect to U.S. tax on the dividends, interest, and royalties before any foreign tax credit by the United States with respect to income tax paid or accrued to Canada.

(2) Second, Canada shall allow a deduction from (credit against) Canadian tax for U.S. tax paid or accrued with respect to the dividends, interest, and royalties, but such credit need not exceed the amount of income tax that would be paid or accrued to the United States on such items of income if the individual were not a U.S. citizen after taking into account any relief available under the Convention.

(3) Third, for purposes of computing the U.S. tax on such dividends, interest, and royalties, the United States shall allow as a credit against the U.S. tax, the income tax paid or accrued to Canada after the credit against Canadian tax for income tax paid or accrued to the United States. The United States is in no event obliged to give a credit for Canadian income tax which will reduce the U.S. tax below the amount of income tax that would be paid or accrued to the United States on the amount of the dividends, interest, and royalties if the individual were not a U.S. citizen after taking into account any relief available under the Convention.

The rules of paragraph 5 are illustrated by the following examples.

Example 1.

- A U.S. citizen who is a resident of Canada has $100 of dividend income arising in the United States. The tentative U.S. tax before the foreign tax credit is $40.
- Canada, under its law, allows a deduction for the U.S. tax in excess of 15 per cent or, in this case, a deduction of $25 ($40 – $15). The Canadian taxable income is $75 and the Canadian tax on that amount is $35.
- Canada gives a credit of $15 (the maximum credit allowed is 15 per cent of the gross dividend taken into Canadian income) and collects a net tax of $20.
- The United States allows a credit for the net Canadian tax against its tax in excess of 15 per cent. Thus, the maximum credit is $25 ($40 – $15). But since the net Canadian tax paid was $20, the usable credit is $20.
- To be able to use a credit of $20 requires Canadian-source taxable income of $50 (50 per cent of the U.S. tentative tax of $40). Under paragraph 6, $50 of the U.S. dividend is deemed to be of Canadian source. The credit of $20 may then be offset against the U.S. tax of $40, leaving a net U.S. tax of $20.
- The combined tax paid to both countries is $40, $20 to Canada and $20 to the United States.

Example 2.

A U.S. citizen who is a resident of Canada receives $200 of income with respect to personal services performed within Canada and $100 of dividend income arising within the United States. Taxable income for U.S. purposes, taking into account the rules of *Internal Revenue Code* section 911, is $220. U.S. tax (before foreign tax credits) is $92. The $100 of dividend income is deemed to bear U.S. tax (before foreign tax credits) of $41.82 ($100/$220 × $92). Under Canadian law, a deduction of $26.82 (the excess of $41.82 over 15 per cent of the $100 dividend income) is allowed in computing income. The Canadian tax on $273.18 of income ($300 less the $26.82 deduction) is $130. Canada then gives a credit against the $130 for $15 (the U.S. tax paid or accrued with respect to the dividend, $41.82 but limited to 15 per cent of the gross amount of such income, or $15), leaving a final Canadian tax of $115. Of the $115, $30.80 is attributable to the dividend:

$$\frac{\$73.18 \text{ (\$100 dividend less \$26.82 deduction)}}{\$273.18 \text{ (\$300 income less \$26.82 deduction)}} \times \$115.$$

Of this amount, $26.82 is creditable against U.S. tax pursuant to paragraph 5. (Although the United States allows a credit for the Canadian tax imposed on the dividend, $30.80, the credit may not reduce the U.S. tax below 15 per cent of the amount of the dividend. Thus, the maximum allowable credit is the excess of $41.82, the U.S. tax imposed on the dividend income, over $15, which is 15 per cent of the $100 dividend. The remaining $3.98 (the Canadian tax of $30.80 less the credit allowed of $26.82) is a foreign tax credit carryover for U.S. purposes, subject to the limitations of paragraph 5. An additional $50.18 of Canadian tax with respect to Canadian source services income is creditable against U.S. tax pursuant to paragraph 3 and subparagraph 4(*b*). The $50.18 is computed as follows: tentative U.S. tax (before foreign tax credits) is $92; the U.S. tax on Canadian source services income is $50.18 ($92 less the U.S. tax on the dividend income of $41.82); the limitation on the services income is:

$$\frac{\$120 \text{ (taxable income from services)}}{\$220 \text{ (total taxable income)}} \times \$92,$$

or $50.18. The credit for Canadian tax paid on the services income is therefore $50.18; the remainder of the Canadian tax on the services income, or $34.02, is a foreign tax credit carryover for U.S. purposes, subject to the limitations of paragraph 5.

Paragraph 6 is necessary to implement the objectives of subparagraphs 4(*b*) and 5(*c*). Paragraph 6 provides that where a U.S. citizen is a resident of Canada, items of income referred to in paragraph 4 or 5 are deemed for the purposes of Article XXIV to arise in Canada to the extent necessary to avoid double taxation of income by Canada and the United States, consistent with the objectives of subparagraphs 4(*b*) and 5(*c*). Paragraph 6 can override the source rules of paragraph 3 to permit a limited resourcing of income.

The application of paragraph 6 is illustrated by the following example.

Example 3.

The facts are the same as in Example 2 above. The United States has undertaken, pursuant to subparagraph 5(*c*) and paragraph 6, to credit $26.82 of Canadian taxes on dividend income that has a U.S. source under both paragraph 3 and the *Internal Revenue Code*. (As illustrated in Example 2, the credit, however, only reduces the U.S. tax on the dividend income which exceeds the amount of income tax that would be paid or accrued to the United States on such income if the individual were not a U.S. citizen after taking into account any relief available under the Convention.) Pursuant to paragraph 6, for purposes of determining the U.S. foreign tax credit limitation under the Convention with respect to Canadian taxes, $64.13 of taxable income with respect to the dividends is deemed to arise in Canada:

$$\left(\frac{A}{\$220} \times \$92 = \$26.82;\ A = \$64.13\right).$$

Article XXIX B (Taxes Imposed by Reason of Death), added by the Third Protocol, also provides relief from double taxation in certain circumstances in connection with Canadian income tax imposed by reason of death and U.S. estate taxes. However, subparagraph 7(*c*) of Article XXIX B generally denies relief from U.S. estate tax under that Article to the extent that a credit or deduction has been claimed for the same amount in determining any other tax imposed by the United States. This restriction would operate to deny relief, for example, to the extent that relief from U.S. income tax is claimed under Article XXIV in respect of the same amount of Canadian tax. There is, however, no requirement that relief from U.S. tax be claimed first (or exclusively) under Article XXIV. Paragraph 6 of Article XXIX B also prevents the claiming of double relief from Canadian income taxation under both that Article and Article XXIV, by providing that the credit provided by Article XXIX B applies only after the application of the credit provided by Article XXIV.

Capital

Under paragraph 8 of Article XXIV, a Canadian resident owning capital which may be taxed in the United States is allowed a deduction from his or her Canadian tax for U.S. capital tax paid. This deduction, however, shall not exceed the amount of Canadian tax that would be due on that capital.

Exemption With Progression

Paragraph 10 of Article XXIV provides for the application of the rule of "exemption with progression" by a Contracting State in cases where an item of income of a resident of that State is exempt from tax in that State by virtue of a provision of the Convention. For example, where under Canadian law a tax benefit, such as the goods and services tax (GST) credit, to a Canadian resident individual is reduced as the income of that individual, or the individual's spouse or other dependant, increases, and any of these persons receives U.S. social security benefits that are exempt from tax in Canada under the Convention, Canada may, nevertheless, take the U.S. social security benefits into account in determining whether, and to what extent, the benefit should be reduced.

Editorial Note: 2013 STEP CRA Roundtable, Document No. 2013-0480301C6, dated June 10, 2013, states that paragraph 5 of Article XXIV will continue to apply to taxpayers subject to rate increases in the United States on dividend income where the U.S. rate exceeds the limit in Article X of the Convention.

Advance Income Tax Ruling, Document No. 2012-0462151I7, dated November 5, 2012, deals with mark-to-market rules, foreign tax credits, and Article XXIV of the Convention. The CRA stated that the income may not be considered qualifying income eligible for foreign tax credits under section 126 of the *Income Tax Act* (Canada).

Technical Interpretation, Document No. 2005-0125471E5, dated October 20, 2006, deals with social security taxes under Article XXIV(2). It is the CRA's view that the reference in the treaty to social security taxes would include Tier 1 railroad retirement taxes, but not Tier 2 taxes.

Technical Interpretation, Document No. 2003-0019751E5, dated December 7, 2004, deals with whether an individual is able to receive a Canadian FTC for U.S. AMT.

History: Subparagraph 2(*b*) of Article XXIV was deleted and replaced by Article 19 of the Fifth Protocol to this Convention, and formerly read:

(*b*) Subject to the existing provisions of the law of Canada regarding the taxation of income from a foreign affiliate and to any subsequent modification of those provisions — which shall not affect the general principle hereof — for the purpose of computing Canadian tax, a company which is a resident of Canada shall be allowed to deduct in computing its taxable income any dividend received by it out of the exempt surplus of a foreign affiliate which is a resident of the United States; and

Subparagraphs 2(*a*) and (*b*) of Article XXIV were amended by paragraph 1 of Article 12 of the Third Protocol to this Convention, and formerly read:

(*a*) Subject to the provisions of the law of Canada regarding the deduction from tax payable in Canada of tax paid in a territory outside Canada and to any subsequent modification of those provisions (which shall not affect the general principle hereof), and unless a greater deduction or relief is provided under the law of Canada, income tax paid or accrued to the United States on profits, income or gains arising in the United States shall be deducted from any Canadian tax payable in respect of such profits, income or gains;

(*b*) Subject to the provisions of the law of Canada regarding the determination of the exempt surplus of a foreign affiliate and to any subsequent modification of those provisions (which shall not affect the general principle hereof), for the purposes of computing Canadian tax, a company which is a resident of Canada shall be allowed to deduct in computing its taxable income any dividend received by it out of the exempt surplus of a foreign affiliate which is a resident of the United States; and.

Paragraph 5 of Article XXIV was amended by paragraph 2 of Article 12 of the Third Protocol to this Convention, and formerly read:

5. Notwithstanding the provisions of paragraph 4, where a United States citizen is a resident of Canada, the following rules shall apply in respect of the items of income referred to in Article X (Dividends), XI (Interest) or XII (Royalties) which arise (within the meaning of paragraph 3) in the United States, as long as the law in force in Canada allows a deduction in computing income for the portion of any foreign tax paid in respect of such items which exceeds 15 per cent of the amount thereof:

(*a*) The deduction so allowed in Canada shall not be reduced by any credit or deduction for income tax paid or accrued to Canada allowed in computing the United States tax on such items;

(*b*) Canada shall allow a deduction from the Canadian tax in respect of the income tax paid or accrued to the United States on such items, except that such deduction need not exceed 15 per cent of the gross amount of such items that has been included in computing the income of the citizen for Canadian tax purposes; and

(*c*) For the purposes of computing the United States tax on such items, the United States shall allow as a credit against United States tax the income tax paid or accrued to Canada after the deduction referred to in subparagraph (*b*). The credit so allowed shall reduce only that portion of the United States tax on such items which exceeds 15 per cent of the amount thereof included in computing United States taxable income.

Paragraph 7 of Article XXIV was amended by paragraph 3 of Article 12 of the Third Protocol to this Convention, and formerly read:

7. For the purposes of this Article, any reference to "income tax paid or accrued" to a Contracting State shall include Canadian tax and United States tax, as the case may be, and taxes of general application which are paid or accrued to a political subdivision or local authority of that State, which are not imposed by that political subdivision or local authority in a manner inconsistent with the provisions of the Convention and which are substantially similar to the taxes of that State referred to in paragraphs 2 and 3(*a*) of Article II (Taxes Covered).

Paragraph 10 of Article XXIV was added by paragraph 4 of Article 12 of the Third Protocol to this Convention.

Paragraphs 1 and 2 of Article XXIV were amended and paragraph 9 was added by Article XI of the First Protocol to this Convention. Paragraphs 1 and 2 of Article XXIV formerly read as follows:

1. In the case of the United States, subject to the provisions of paragraphs 4, 5 and 6, double taxation shall be avoided as follows: In accordance with the provisions and subject to the limitations of the law of the United States (as it may be amended from time to time without changing the general principle hereof), the United States shall allow to a citizen or resident of the United States, or to a company electing to be treated as a domestic corporation, as a credit against the United States tax on income the appropriate amount of income tax paid or accrued to Canada; and, in the case of a company which is a resident of the United States owning at least 10 per cent of the voting stock of a company which is a resident of Canada from which it receives dividends in any taxable year, the United States shall allow as a credit against the United States tax on income the appropriate amount of income tax paid or accrued to Canada by that company with respect to the profits out of which such dividends are paid. Such appropriate amount shall be based upon the amount of income tax paid or accrued to Canada, but shall not exceed that proportion of the United States tax that taxable income arising in Canada bears to the entire taxable income.

2. In the case of Canada, subject to the provisions of paragraphs 4, 5 and 6, double taxation shall be avoided as follows:

(*a*) Subject to the provisions of the law of Canada regarding the deduction from tax payable in Canada of tax paid in a territory outside Canada and to any subsequent modification of those provisions (which shall not affect the general principle hereof), and unless a greater deduction or relief is provided under the law of Canada, income tax paid or accrued to the United States on profits, income or gains arising in the United States shall be deducted from any Canadian tax payable in respect of such profits, income or gains; and

(*b*) Subject to the provisions of the law of Canada regarding the determination of the exempt surplus of a foreign affiliate and to any subsequent modification of those provisions (which shall not affect the general principle hereof), for the purposes of computing Canadian tax, a company which is a resident of Canada shall be allowed to deduct in computing its taxable income any dividend received by it out of the exempt surplus of a foreign affiliate which is a resident of the United States.

Article XXV — Non-Discrimination

1. Nationals of a Contracting State shall not be subjected in the other Contracting State to any taxation or any requirement connected therewith that is more burdensome than the taxation and connected requirements to which nationals of that other State in the same circumstances, particularly with respect to taxation on worldwide income, are or may be subjected. This provision shall also apply to individuals who are not residents of one or both of the Contracting States.

2. In determining the taxable income or tax payable of an individual who is a resident of a Contracting State, there shall be allowed as a deduction in respect of any other person who is a resident of the other Contracting State and who is dependent on the individual for support the amount that would be so allowed if that other person were a resident of the first-mentioned State.

3. Where a married individual who is a resident of Canada and not a citizen of the United States has income that is taxable in the United States pursuant to Article XV (Income from Employment), the United States tax with respect to such income shall not exceed such proportion of the total United States tax that would be payable for the taxable year if both the individual and his spouse were United States

citizens as the individual's taxable income determined without regard to this paragraph bears to the amount that would be the total taxable income of the individual and his spouse. For the purposes of this paragraph,

(*a*) The "total United States tax" shall be determined as if all the income of the individual and his spouse arose in the United States; and

(*b*) A deficit of the spouse shall not be taken into account in determining taxable income.

4. Any company which is a resident of a Contracting State, the capital of which is wholly or partly owned or controlled, directly or indirectly, by one or more residents of the other Contracting State, shall not be subjected in the first-mentioned State to any taxation or any requirement connected therewith which is other or more burdensome than the taxation and connected requirements to which other similar companies of the first-mentioned State, the capital of which is wholly or partly owned or controlled, directly or indirectly, by one or more residents of a third State, are or may be subjected.

5. Notwithstanding the provisions of Article XXIV (Elimination of Double Taxation), the taxation on a permanent establishment which a resident of a Contracting State has in the other Contracting State shall not be less favourably levied in the other State than the taxation levied on residents of the other State carrying on the same activities. This paragraph shall not be construed as obliging a Contracting State:

(*a*) To grant to a resident of the other Contracting State any personal allowances, reliefs and reductions for taxation purposes on account of civil status or family responsibilities which it grants to its own residents; or

(*b*) To grant to a company which is a resident of the other Contracting State the same tax relief that it provides to a company which is a resident of the first-mentioned State with respect to dividends received by it from a company.

6. Except where the provisions of paragraph 1 of Article IX (Related Persons), paragraph 7 of Article XI (Interest) or paragraph 7 of Article XII (Royalties) apply, interest, royalties and other disbursements paid by a resident of a Contracting State to a resident of the other Contracting State shall, for the purposes of determining the taxable profits of the first-mentioned resident, be deductible under the same conditions as if they had been paid to a resident of the first-mentioned State. Similarly, any debts of a resident of a Contracting State to a resident of the other Contracting State shall, for the purposes of determining the taxable capital of the first-mentioned resident, be deductible under the same conditions as if they had been contracted to a resident of the first-mentioned State.

7. The provisions of paragraph 7 shall not affect the operation of any provision of the taxation laws of a Contracting State:

(*a*) Relating to the deductibility of interest and which is in force on the date of signature of this Convention (including any subsequent modification of such provisions that do not change the general nature thereof); or

(*b*) Adopted after such date by a Contracting State and which is designed to ensure that a person who is not a resident of that State does not enjoy, under the laws of that State, a tax treatment that is more favorable than that enjoyed by residents of that State.

8. Expenses incurred by a citizen or resident of a Contracting State with respect to any convention (including any seminar, meeting, congress or other function of a similar nature) held in the other Contracting State shall, for the purposes of taxation in the first-mentioned State, be deductible to the same extent that such expenses would be deductible if the convention were held in the first-mentioned State.

9. Notwithstanding the provisions of Article II (Taxes Covered), this Article shall apply to all taxes imposed by a Contracting State.

Dentons Canada LLP Commentary: Article XXV contains provisions to protect persons of one Contracting State from discrimination by the other Contracting State with respect to all taxes of every kind imposed at the national level (i.e., taxes imposed by Canada under the *Income Tax Act* (Canada) and taxes imposed by the United States under the *Internal Revenue Code*). This Article is not a comprehensive non-discrimination Article in that it does not contain all the non-discrimination provisions found in the OECD Model Convention. Article XXV does contain a number of specific non-discrimination rules, some of which are limited in scope. These rules are discussed below.

Paragraph 1 provides a rule to prevent nationals of one Contracting State who are residents in the other Contracting State, from being discriminated against on the basis of their nationality. Thus, the United States cannot impose more burdensome taxes (or other requirements connected with taxes) on Canadian nationals residing in the United States than it imposes on U.S. nationals who are in the same circumstances, i.e., U.S. citizens residing in the United States. Prior to the Fifth Protocol, paragraph 1 referred to "citizens" of a Contracting State, as opposed to "nationals" of that State. Pursuant to subparagraph 1(*k*) of Article III of the Convention, a national of a Contracting State includes citizens of that State, as well as any legal person, partnership, or association deriving its status as such from the laws in force in that State. This change broadened the protection afforded under Article XXV and ensures that certain persons not otherwise considered citizens of a Contracting State are not subject to discrimination under the Convention.

As amended by the Fifth Protocol, the principles of non-discrimination in paragraph 1 apply equally to individuals who are not residents of either Contracting State. This principle was previously reflected in old paragraph 2, which was deleted by the Fifth Protocol. The major purpose of this provision is to guarantee a Canadian national, for example, resident in a third country, any benefits available to a U.S. national by virtue of an income tax Convention between the United States and that third country. Accordingly, the United States could discriminate against a Canadian national not resident in the United States *vis-à-vis* a U.S. national. However, the United States could not discriminate against a Canadian national resident in France, for example, *vis-à-vis* a French national resident in France. U.S. taxation with respect to the Canadian national resident in France may not be more burdensome than the taxation of the French national resident in France.

Paragraph 2 provides that, in computing taxable income on tax payable, an individual resident of a Contracting State will be entitled to the same deduction for dependants resident in the other Contracting State that would be allowed if the dependants were residents of the individual's State of residence. Consequently, Canada must allow its residents the same deduction in respect of any dependant residing in the United States that it would allow for a dependent person who is a resident of Canada. Under section 118 of the *Income Tax Act* (Canada), a resident individual can claim a reduction from tax for dependants, other than children or grandchildren, only if those dependants are residents of Canada. This provision of the Convention overrides the *Income Tax Act* (Canada), as it permits a Canadian resident a deduction for dependants who reside in the United States. Thus, the Convention expands the application of section 118 of the *Income Tax Act* (Canada) and sections 118.2 and 118.3 which allow credits in respect of medical expenses incurred on behalf of dependent persons and disabled dependants.

Paragraph 3 permits a married individual who is resident in Canada, but who is not a citizen of the United States, to file a joint U.S. return where the individual has income that is taxable in the United States pursuant to Article XV (Income From Employment), such as salary, wages, or other similar employee remuneration. This provision does not apply if the individual's earnings are exempt from tax under Article XV or the Canadian resident earns only income taxable in the United States under provisions of the Convention other than Article XV. By filing a joint tax return an individual may be in a position to take advantage of lower tax rates and other deductions that the individual would not have the benefit of if the only tax that was applicable was tax at source. This provision applies to the married Canadian resident who is not a U.S. citizen regardless of the residence of the spouse. In determining total taxable income of the individual and his or her spouse, a deficit of the spouse cannot be taken into account.

The benefit provided by paragraph 3 is limited by a formula designed to ensure the benefit is available solely with respect to persons whose U.S.-source income is entirely, or almost entirely, wage income. The formula limits the U.S. tax with respect to wage income to that portion of the total U.S. tax that would be payable for the tax year if both the Canadian resident and his or her spouse were U.S. citizens that the Canadian resident's taxable income bears to the total taxable income of the Canadian and his or her spouse. The term "total United States tax" used in the formula is total U.S. tax without regard to any foreign tax credits.

EXAMPLE:

	Canadian Resident and Citizen	Spouse
	$	$
Wages taxable in U.S. (Article XV)	12,000	
Wages taxable only in Canada	2,000	2,000
U.S. source Dividend Income		1,000
Total income	14,000	3,000
(i) U.S. tax when joint return not filed:		
		$
Wage income		12,000
Personal exemptions		(2,000)
Unused zero bracket amount		1,700
U.S. taxable income		11,700
U.S. tax payable on $11,700		1,600
Spouse's U.S. tax on dividends		150
Total U.S. tax		1,750
(ii) U.S. tax when joint return filed:		
		$
Total income ($14,000 + $3,000)		17,000
Personal exemptions		(2,000)
U.S. dividend exclusion		(200)
U.S. taxable income		14,800
U.S. tax payable:		
U.S. tax on combined income of $14,800 is $1,549		
U.S. tax on Canadian resident's wages is limited to:		
$\frac{(\$11{,}700 \times \$1{,}549)}{\$14{,}800} = \$1{,}225$		1,225
Spouse's U.S. tax on dividends		150
Total U.S. tax		1,375

An individual may elect to use the provisions of paragraph 3 on a year-by-year basis. These provisions are purely computational and do not make either or both spouses residents of the United States for the purposes of other U.S. income tax conventions.

Paragraph 4 provides limited protection from discrimination for corporations resident in one country which are owned by residents of the other country. This provision applies to corporations resident in one country that are wholly or partly owned or controlled, directly or indirectly, by one or more residents of the other Contracting State. For example, under this Article, a Canadian resident corporation which is owned by residents of the United States cannot be subject in Canada to other or more burdensome taxation (or other requirements connected with taxes) than that which similar Canadian resident corporations, that are wholly or partially owned by residents of a third country, may be subjected. Thus, a Canadian resident company owned by a U.S. resident, for example, cannot be taxed in a more burdensome manner than a Canadian resident company owned by French residents. However, a Canadian resident company owned by U.S. residents can be taxed at a more burdensome rate than a Canadian resident company owned by Canadians. This paragraph allows Canada to continue to apply lower corporate tax rates to Canadian-controlled private corporations than it applies to non-Canadian-controlled corporations.

Under paragraph 5, residents of one Contracting State which have a permanent establishment in the other Contracting State are protected against discrimination in that other Contracting State. The taxation of such a permanent establishment by the other Contracting State shall not be less favourable than the taxation of that Contracting State's own residents which carry on the same activities. Thus, the United States cannot tax a permanent establishment of a Canadian resident, which is situated in the United States, less favourably than it taxes its own residents carrying on the same activities. This paragraph specifically overrides the provisions of Article XXIV (Elimination of Double Taxation), thus ensuring that the permanent establishment of a Canadian resident in the United States will be entitled to relief from double taxation on a basis comparable to the relief afforded to U.S. residents. This provision, which protects a Canadian resident's permanent establishment in the United States from discrimination by the United States, does not obligate the United States to grant the Canadian resident any personal allowances, relief, or reductions for tax purposes on account of civil status or family responsibility which it grants to its own residents. In addition, the United States is not required to grant to a Canadian resident company the same tax relief that it provides to a company that is resident of the United States with respect to dividends received.

Paragraph 6 specifically allows that interest, royalties, and other disbursements paid by residents of Canada, for example, to a resident of the United States, will be deductible in computing Canadian taxable income as if they had been paid to a Canadian resident. This provision does not apply where paragraph 1 of Article IX (Related Persons), paragraph 7 of Article XI (Interest), or paragraph 7 of Article XII (Royalties) is applicable. In addition, for purposes of capital taxes, debts owed to residents of the United States are to be deductible to the extent they would be deductible if owed to residents of Canada.

Paragraph 7 provides that paragraph 6 of this Article will not affect the operation of national tax laws with respect to the deductibility of interest that were in force as of September 26, 1980. Paragraph 6 would also not affect any taxation laws regarding the deductibility of interest adopted after September 26, 1980, provided that the newly adopted provisions do not change the general nature of the provisions in effect as of September 26, 1980. Consequently, Canada can continue to apply the "thin capitalization" rules in subsection 18(4) of the *Income Tax Act* (Canada), which limit the deductibility of interest paid by a Canadian resident company to a non-resident in certain circumstances. In *Ramada Ontario Limited v. The Queen*, 94 DTC 1071 (T.C.C.), it was held that the subsequent changes to the Canadian thin capitalization rules which applied the three-to-one, debt-to-equity restriction to the non-resident's equity, and no longer to the total equity, did not change the general nature of the provisions.

Paragraph 8 provides that expenses incurred by citizens or residents of Canada with respect to any convention held in the United States shall be deductible in computing Canadian taxable income to the same extent as if that convention had been held in Canada. Similarly, U.S. citizens and residents are entitled to deduct expenses incurred in respect of conventions held in Canada on the same basis as convention expenses incurred in the United States.

Paragraph 9 ensures that Article XXV applies to all taxes imposed by a Contracting State. Before the Third Protocol, non-discrimination protection was limited in the case of Canadian taxes to taxes imposed under the *Income Tax Act* (Canada). Non-discrimination protection now extends, for example, to the Canadian goods and services tax (GST) and other Canadian excise taxes.

History: Paragraph 1 of Article XXV was deleted and replaced by paragraph 1 of Article 20 of the Fifth Protocol to this Convention, and formerly read:

1. Citizens of a Contracting State, who are residents of the other Contracting State, shall not be subject in that other State to any taxation or any requirement connected therewith which is other or more burdensome than the taxation and connected requirements to which citizens of that other State in the same circumstances are or may be subjected.

Paragraph 2 of Article XXV was deleted and paragraphs 3 to 10 were renumbered accordingly by paragraph 2 of Article 20 of the Fifth Protocol to this Convention. Paragraph 2 formerly read:

2. Citizens of a Contracting State, who are not residents of the other Contracting State, shall not be subjected in that other State to any taxation or any requirement connected therewith which is other or more burdensome than the taxation and connected requirements to which citizens of any third State in the same circumstances (including State of residence) are or may be subjected.

Paragraph 3 of Article XXV was amended by paragraph 3 of Article 20 of the Fifth Protocol to this Convention by deleting "Article XV (Dependent Personal Services)" and substituting "Article XV (Income from Employment)".

Paragraph 3 of Article XXV was amended by paragraph 1 of Article 13 of the Third Protocol to this Convention,and formerly read:

3. In determining the taxable income of an individual who is a resident of a Contracting State there shall be allowed as a deduction in respect of any other person who is a resident of the other Contracting State and who is dependent on the individual for support the amount that would be so allowed if that other person were a resident of the first-mentioned state.

Paragraph 10 of Article XXV was amended by paragraph 2 of Article 13 of the Third Protocol to this Convention, and formerly read:

10. Notwithstanding the provisions of Article II (Taxes Covered), this Article shall apply:

(*a*) In the case of Canada, to all taxes imposed under the *Income Tax Act*; and

(*b*) In the case of the United States, to all taxes imposed under the *Internal Revenue Code*.

Paragraph 6 of Article XXV was amended by Article XII of the First Protocol to this Convention, and formerly read:

6. Notwithstanding the provisions of Article XXIV (Elimination of Double Taxation), the taxation on a permanent establishment which a resident of a Contracting State has in the other Contracting State shall not be less favorably levied in the other State than the taxation levied on residents of the other State carrying on the same activities. This provision shall not be construed as obliging a Contracting State to grant to residents of the other Contracting State any personal allowances, reliefs and reductions for taxation purposes on account of civil status or family responsibilities which it grants to its own residents.

Article XXVI — Mutual Agreement Procedure

1. Where a person considers that the actions of one or both of the Contracting States result or will result for him in taxation not in accordance with the provisions of this Convention, he may, irrespective of the remedies provided by the domestic law of those States, present his case in writing to the competent authority of the Contracting State of which he is a resident or, if he is a resident of neither Contracting State, of which he is a national.

2. The competent authority of the Contracting State to which the case has been presented shall endeavor, if the objection appears to it to be justified and if it is not itself able to arrive at a satisfactory solution, to resolve the case by mutual agreement with the competent authority of the other Contracting State, with a view to the avoidance of taxation which is not in accordance with the Convention. Except where the provisions of Article IX (Related Persons) apply, any agreement reached shall be implemented notwithstanding any time or other procedural limitations in the domestic law of the Contracting States, provided that the competent authority of the other Contracting State has received notification that such a case exists within six years from the end of the taxable year to which the case relates.

3. The competent authorities of the Contracting States shall endeavor to resolve by mutual agreement any difficulties or doubts arising as to the interpretation or application of the Convention. In particular, the competent authorities of the Contracting States may agree:

(*a*) To the same attribution of profits to a resident of a Contracting State and its permanent establishment situated in the other Contracting State;

(*b*) To the same allocation of income, deductions, credits or allowances between persons;

(*c*) To the same determination of the source, and the same characterization, of particular items of income;

(*d*) To a common meaning of any term used in the Convention;

(*e*) To the elimination of double taxation with respect to income distributed by an estate or trust;

(*f*) To the elimination of double taxation with respect to a partnership;

(*g*) To provide relief from double taxation resulting from the application of the estate tax imposed by the United States or the Canadian tax as a result of a distribution or disposition of property by a trust that is a qualified domestic trust within the meaning of section 2056A of the *Internal Revenue Code*, or is described in subsection 70(6) of the *Income Tax Act* or is treated as such under paragraph 5 of Article XXIX B (Taxes Imposed by Reason of Death), in cases where no relief is otherwise available; or

(*h*) To increases in any dollar amounts referred to in the Convention to reflect monetary or economic developments.

They may also consult together for the elimination of double taxation in cases not provided for in the Convention.

4. Each of the Contracting States will endeavor to collect on behalf of the other Contracting State such amounts as may be necessary to ensure that relief granted by the Convention from taxation imposed by that other State does not enure to the benefit of persons not entitled thereto. However, nothing in this paragraph shall be construed as imposing on either of the Contracting States the obligation to carry out administrative measures of a different nature from those used in the collection of its own tax or which would be contrary to its public policy (*ordre public*).

5. The competent authorities of the Contracting States may communicate with each other directly for the purpose of reaching an agreement in the sense of the preceding paragraphs.

6. Where, pursuant to a mutual agreement procedure under this Article, the competent authorities have endeavored but are unable to reach a complete agreement in a case, the case shall be resolved through arbitration conducted in the manner prescribed by, and subject to, the requirements of paragraph 7 and any rules or procedures agreed upon by the Contracting States by notes to be exchanged through diplomatic channels, if:

(*a*) Tax returns have been filed with at least one of the Contracting States with respect to the taxable years at issue in the case;

(*b*) The case:

(i) Is a case that:

(A) Involves the application of one or more Articles that the competent authorities have agreed in an exchange of notes shall be the subject of arbitration; and

(B) Is not a particular case that the competent authorities agree, before the date on which arbitration proceedings would otherwise have begun, is not suitable for determination by arbitration; or

(ii) Is a particular case that the competent authorities agree is suitable for determination by arbitration; and

(*c*) All concerned persons agree according to the provisions of subparagraph 7(*d*).

7. For the purposes of paragraph 6 and this paragraph, the following rules and definitions shall apply:

(*a*) The term "concerned person" means the presenter of a case to a competent authority for consideration under this Article and all other persons, if any, whose tax liability to either Contracting State may be directly affected by a mutual agreement arising from that consideration;

(*b*) The "commencement date" for a case is the earliest date on which the information necessary to undertake substantive consideration for a mutual agreement has been received by both competent authorities;

(*c*) Arbitration proceedings in a case shall begin on the later of:

(i) Two years after the commencement date of that case, unless both competent authorities have previously agreed to a different date, and

(ii) The earliest date upon which the agreement required by subparagraph (*d*) has been received by both competent authorities;

(*d*) The concerned person(s), and their authorized representatives or agents, must agree prior to the beginning of arbitration proceedings not to disclose to any other person any information received during the course of the arbitration proceeding from either Contracting State or the arbitration board, other than the determination of such board;

(*e*) Unless a concerned person does not accept the determination of an arbitration board, the determination shall constitute a resolution by mutual agreement under this Article and shall be binding on both Contracting States with respect to that case; and

(*f*) For purposes of an arbitration proceeding under paragraph 6 and this paragraph, the members of the arbitration board and their staffs shall be considered "persons or authorities" to whom information may be disclosed under Article XXVII (Exchange of Information) of this Convention.

Dentons Canada LLP Commentary: Article XXVI contains the standard mutual agreement procedure ("MAP") provisions which authorize the competent authorities of Canada and the United States to consult together to attempt to alleviate individual cases of double taxation or cases of taxation not in accordance with the Convention.

Paragraph 1 provides that where a resident or citizen of one country who considers the action of one or both of the countries will cause taxation not in accordance with the Convention, that person may present his or her case to the competent authority of the country of which he or she is a resident, or, if that person is a resident of neither country, of which he or she is a citizen. The claim must be presented in writing. The competent authority then determines whether the claim has merit. If it determines that the claim does have merit and if the competent authority cannot unilaterally solve the problem, that competent authority is to endeavour to come to an agreement with the competent authority of the other country to limit the taxation which is not in accordance with the provisions of the Convention. Thus, a resident of Canada must present to the Minister of National Revenue (or his or her authorized representative) any claim that such resident is being subjected to taxation contrary to the Convention. See Information Circular 71-17R5, which sets out the manner in which a claim for competent authority consideration should be presented. Any person who requests assistance from the competent authority may, in addition, avail himself or herself of any avenues available under the respective domestic laws.

Canada's competent authority consists of a division of the CRA that, as of March 2015, employed 56 individuals. According to the CRA's website, in 2014-2015 its MAP caseload consisted of a beginning inventory of 344 cases and 347 new ones, with 170 cases completed during the year. Generally, over the last several years, MAP cases took 25 to 30 months to complete.

Any agreement reached between the competent authorities of Canada and the United States is to be implemented notwithstanding any time or other procedural limitations in the domestic laws of the countries, except where the special mutual agreement provisions of Article IX (Related Persons) apply, provided that the competent authority of the country asked to waive its domestic time or procedural limitations has received written notification within six years from the end of the taxable year in the first-mentioned country to which the case relates that such a case exists. Such notification may be given by the competent authority of the first-mentioned country, the taxpayer who has requested the competent authority to take action, or a person related to the taxpayer. However, Article XXVI does not require the competent authority of a country to grant unilateral relief to avoid double taxation in a case where timely notification is not given to the competent authority of the other country. In a case where the provisions of Article IX apply, the provisions in paragraphs 3, 4, and 5 of that Article are controlling with respect to adjustments of income, loss, or tax, and the effect of the Convention upon time or procedural limitations of the domestic law. Thus, if relief is not available under Article IX because of fraud, the provisions of paragraph 2 of this Article do not independently authorize such relief.

Paragraph 3 directs the competent authorities to resolve any difficulties or doubts arising as to the application of the Convention. Specifically, they are authorized to agree as to the attribution of profits to a resident of one country and its permanent establishment in the other country, the allocation of income, deductions, or credits, and the readjustment of taxes, the determination as to source of income, the characterization of items of income, and to the common meaning of terms. This paragraph also contains a provision, not found in most treaties, that permits the competent authorities to agree to increase dollar amounts mentioned in the Convention to reflect monetary or economic developments. For example, the competent authorities may agree to adjust the $500,000 threshold used in applying Canada's branch tax under Article X (Dividends) or the $10,000 remuneration limit with respect to dependent personal services (Article XV).

Subparagraph 3(*g*) specifically authorizes the competent authorities to provide relief from double taxation in certain cases involving the distribution or disposition of property by a U.S. qualified domestic trust or a Canadian spousal trust, where relief is not otherwise available.

The list of subjects of potential mutual agreement in paragraph 3 is not conclusive, as the competent authorities may also consult for the elimination of double taxation in cases not specifically provided for in the Convention.

Paragraph 4 provides that each country will endeavour to collect on behalf of the other country such amounts as may be necessary to ensure that relief granted by the Convention from taxation imposed by the other country does not enure to the benefit of persons not entitled to such relief. This provision does not, however, oblige either country to carry out administrative measures of a different nature from those that would be used in the collection of its own tax or which would be contrary to its public policy.

The competent authorities are also authorized to communicate with each other directly for purposes of reaching an agreement contemplated in the mutual agreement provisions. It also authorizes them to meet together for an oral exchange of opinions. These provisions make it clear that it is not necessary to go through normal diplomatic channels in order to discuss problems arising in the application of the Convention and also removes any doubt as to the restrictions that might otherwise arise by reason of the confidentiality rules of Canada and the United States.

Paragraph 6 was originally added by the Third Protocol, effective from January 1, 1996. Pursuant to the Third Protocol, paragraph 6 provided for a voluntary arbitration procedure that would be implemented only upon the exchange of Diplomatic Notes between the United States and Canada. Where the competent authorities were unable, pursuant to the other provisions of this Article, to resolve a disagreement regarding the interpretation or application of the Convention, the disagreement, with the consent of the taxpayer and both competent authorities, could have been submitted for arbitration, provided the taxpayer agreed in writing to be bound by the decision of the arbitration board. There was no requirement that any case be submitted for arbitration; however, if a case was submitted to an arbitration board, the board's decision would have been binding on both Contracting States and on the taxpayer with respect to that case.

The United States was reluctant to implement the arbitration procedure in the Convention at the time the Third Protocol was ratified; it first wanted to evaluate the arbitration process under other U.S. treaties (most notably, the 1989 U.S. treaty with Germany). It was contemplated that Canada and the U.S. would revisit the voluntary arbitration procedure shortly after the ratification of the Third Protocol to determine whether it should be implemented. However, there has never been an exchange of notes between Canada and the U.S. to implement the voluntary arbitration procedure. Moreover, while Canada has included similar voluntary arbitration procedures in other tax treaties, none have ever been fully implemented (see, e.g., Canada's treaties with France, Germany, Mexico, the Netherlands, and Peru).

Even though they did not implement the voluntary arbitration procedure, Canada and the U.S. began pursuing alternatives to effectively resolve cases under Article XXVI. In 2005, Canada and the U.S. entered into several memoranda of understanding ("MOU") concerning the manner in which MAP cases were to be handled.[3] These MOU set out the basic understanding that, among other things, all MAP cases are capable of resolution, the positions adopted by the competent authorities are to be principled, reasonable, and consistent, the facts of any particular MAP case should not be disputed (aside from exceptional cases), and compromise should be sought where necessary.

The MOU also created a process for the quasi-arbitration of factual issues through the appointment of a panel of tax administration officials chosen by representatives of the CRA and the IRS (the "independent review process"). The competent authorities are required to refer the factual issues in a MAP case to the independent review process if they have been unable to agree on the underlying facts and circumstances within six months after their first face-to-face negotiation. The joint panel must render its decision generally within five months of the date of referral of the factual issue by the competent authorities, which the competent authorities are required to adopt in resolving the MAP case.

[3] See, e.g., Memorandum of Understanding Between the Competent Authorities of Canada and the United States Regarding the Mutual Agreement Procedure, June 3, 2005 and Memorandum of Understanding Between the Competent Authorities of Canada and the United States Regarding Factual Disagreements under the Mutual Agreement Procedure, December 23, 2005.

It is unclear whether the competent authorities ever availed themselves of this procedure or whether there is any practical room for such a procedure alongside the mandatory arbitration procedure introduced under the Fifth Protocol (discussed below). However, the mere existence of the MOUs and the willingness to institute the joint panel approach demonstrates a growing desire between the States to streamline the resolution of MAP cases.

The Fifth Protocol deleted paragraph 6, eliminating the possibility of voluntary arbitration, and added a mandatory arbitration procedure in new paragraphs 6 and 7. This procedure is similar to the mandatory arbitration provisions recently included by the United States in its treaties with Germany, signed June 1, 2006, and Belgium, signed November 27, 2006. Canada and the United States exchanged Diplomatic Notes that accompanied the Fifth Protocol (Annex "A"), which describe the mandatory arbitration procedure in detail.

In November 2010, Canada and the United States entered into an MOU regarding the application of the arbitration procedure under paragraphs 6 and 7 of Article XXVI.[4]

Overview of Mandatory Arbitration in the Convention

The effective and efficient resolution of tax treaty disputes is of paramount importance to taxpayers. The arbitration procedures are intended to ensure that MAP cases proceed according to a schedule and that all cases will be resolved within a time period not exceeding approximately 35 months. However, the mandatory and binding arbitration procedures are new to the treaty networks of both Canada and the United States, meaning that it will take time to ascertain if these procedures are effective in meeting these objectives.

The Fifth Protocol generally requires arbitration of qualifying cases that are unresolved two years after submission to both competent authorities, unless both competent authorities agree that the case is not suitable for arbitration. One objective of the new procedure is the more efficient resolution of these cases by the competent authorities prior to the date that referral for arbitration is required. Another objective is the resolution of cases by arbitration within a guaranteed time period (notwithstanding the difficulty of one or both of the Contracting States in reaching agreement through the general mutual agreement procedure) so as to provide a measure of certainty and closure to the concerned taxpayers.

One potential drawback of the arbitration procedure is that it may encourage the competent authorities to slow down the MAP process in a number of cases with the expectation that the arbitrators will resolve difficult issues. The U.S. Senate has demanded periodic updates on the status and effectiveness of the mandatory arbitration provisions in the U.S. treaties with Canada, Germany, and Belgium as a condition to the ratification of the Fifth Protocol.

Background of Mandatory Arbitration

There have been several recent international developments concerning the arbitration of tax disputes. For example, on January 30, 2007, the OECD adopted proposed changes to its Model treaty and commentary, incorporating a mandatory and binding arbitration procedure (the "OECD mandatory arbitration procedure"). Some elements of the OECD mandatory arbitration procedure are similar to those of the Fifth Protocol.[5] The OECD mandatory arbitration procedure allows a taxpayer to require an issue to be submitted to arbitration after resort to the general mutual agreement procedure has not yielded a resolution after two years. The details of the OECD mandatory arbitration procedure are not specified in the OECD Model; rather, the competent authorities are charged with establishing the general procedure. An Annex to the proposed Commentary contains a Sample Mutual Agreement on Arbitration ("Sample Agreement") that may be varied by the treaty countries. (The Annex discusses a number of possible variations in a separate commentary on the issues raised by the Sample Agreement.)

The European Union has adopted certain mandatory and binding arbitration procedures that are applicable to transfer pricing disputes (the "EU mandatory arbitration procedure").[6] Under these procedures, two years after the case is submitted to one of the relevant competent authorities, the relevant competent authorities must set up an advisory commission charged with delivering an opinion within six months on the elimination of double taxation in the case under the arm's-length principle. The competent authorities must either reach an agreement to eliminate double taxation within six months of the advisory commission's opinion, or must accept and implement that opinion. The European Commission recently expressed its concern with the procedure:[7]

"The Commission considers that the number of long outstanding transfer pricing double tax cases means that, for reasons that need to be further explored, the Arbitration Convention is not eliminating transfer pricing related double taxation in the EU as well as it is supposed to. The proper functioning of the single market is therefore impaired. The Commission intends to consider how this failing can be addressed. It might well be that an instrument that ensures a more timely and effective elimination of double taxation is necessary from the perspective of the single market."

Commencing Arbitration

Generally, any MAP case may be the subject of arbitration, but there is no assurance that any given case will in fact be arbitrated. In this respect, paragraph 6 of Article XXVI of the Treaty requires the competent authorities to submit a case to binding arbitration if:

(a) the competent authorities have endeavored, but have been unable, to reach complete agreement in the case;

(b) tax returns have been filed with respect to the issues in the case in at least one of the Contracting States;

(c) all "concerned persons" agree prior to the commencement of arbitration to keep confidential all information disclosed during the course of the arbitration, except for the determination of the arbitrator (for this purpose, the term "concerned person" refers to the presenter of the case to the competent authorities and all other persons, if any, whose tax liability to either Contracting State may be directly affected by the outcome of the case — it does not include the competent authorities); and, most importantly,

(d) the case satisfies either of the following two separate tests:

(i) the case;

A. involves the application of a specific Article of the Treaty that the competent authorities have previously agreed in an exchange of diplomatic notes shall be the subject of arbitration (the Diplomatic Notes provide that cases involving Article IV (Residence),[8] Article V (Permanent Establishment), Article VII (Business Profits), Article IX (Related Persons) and Article XII (Royalties)[9] are *prima facie* subject to arbitration); and

B. the competent authorities have not agreed that arbitration is inappropriate in respect of that particular case; or

(ii) the case involves any other Article of the Treaty and the competent authorities have agreed that the case should be arbitrated.

Canada and the United States were clearly uncomfortable with requiring, as a default position, the arbitration of all unresolved MAP cases. Instead, a more conservative and flexible two-step approach was adopted, in which cases involving certain enumerated provisions of the Treaty are treated differently than non-enumerated provisions. A case involving one of the provisions identified in the Diplomatic Notes (which generally give rise to the most frequently encountered cases by the competent authorities) must be arbitrated, unless the competent authorities mutually agree that arbitration is inappropriate. This would, for example, allow the competent authorities to avoid arbitration in cases where it is agreed that a resolution is possible with further negotiation. Cases involving non-enumerated Articles cannot, *prima facie*, be arbitrated, unless the competent authorities agree otherwise.

Subparagraph 7(*c*) provides that arbitration proceedings shall begin on the later of:

(a) two years after the "commencement date" of the case (defined in subparagraph 7(*b*) as the earliest date on which the information necessary to undertake substantial consideration for a mutual agreement has been received by both competent authorities), unless the competent authorities have agreed to a different date; and

[4]See https://www.irs.gov/pub/irs-utl/2010_arbitration_mou_nov_8-10_-_final.pdf.

[5]See, e.g., the OECD Centre for Tax Policy and Administration, Report adopted by the Committee on Fiscal Affairs, *Improving the Resolution of Tax Treaty Disputes* (Jan. 30, 2007).

[6]See, e.g., the Convention on the elimination of double taxation in connection with the adjustment of profits of associated enterprises (90/436/EEC), 1990 O.J. (L 225) 10 (extended by Protocol amending the Convention of 23 July 1990 on the elimination of double taxation in connection with the adjustment of profits of associated enterprises, 1999 O.J. (C 202) 1).

[7]See the Communication from the Commission to the Council, the European Parliament and the European Economic and Social Committee on the work of the EU Joint Transfer Pricing Forum in the field of dispute avoidance and resolution procedures and on Guidelines for Advance Pricing Agreements within the EU, COM(2007) 71 final, at para. 28 (Feb. 26, 2007).

[8]But only insofar as the case relates to the residency of a natural person.

[9]But only insofar as the case involves: (i) the application of Article XII to transactions involving related persons under Article IX of the Treaty (i.e., transfer pricing disputes relating to royalties); or (ii) the allocation of amounts between royalties that are taxable under Article XII(2) of the Treaty and tax-exempt under Article XII(3) of the Treaty.

(b) the earliest date that both competent authorities have received confirmation that all "concerned persons" have agreed to keep confidential all information disclosed during the course of the arbitration. Confidentiality issues are described in greater detail below.

"Information necessary to undertake substantial consideration" is described in the Diplomatic Notes to mean the following, and will not be considered "received" until both competent authorities have exchanged all such information pursuant to the mutual agreement procedure in Article XXVI:

(a) in the United States, the information required to be submitted to competent authority under Revenue Procedure 2006-54, section 4.05 (or any analogous provision) (and, in the case of issues relating to advance pricing agreements, information described in Revenue Procedure 2006-9, section 4 (or any analogous provision));

(b) in Canada, information required to be submitted to competent authority under Information Circular IC 71-17 (or any applicable successor publication).

The 2010 MOU and the Diplomatic Notes accompanying the Fifth Protocol confirm that, notwithstanding the commencement of an arbitration proceeding, any concerned person may withdraw the request for the MAP, thereby terminating the arbitration. However, once terminated, the concerned person cannot access the MAP for the same matter and same years.

Composition of Arbitration Board

The arbitration board is to consist of three individual members, one appointed by each Contracting State and a third mutually appointed by the first two appointees. First, each Contracting State must send a written communication to the other Contracting State appointing one member of the arbitration board within 60 days from the date on which the arbitration proceeding begins. Second, within 60 days of receipt of the later of the two letters described above, the two appointed members of the arbitration board shall appoint a third member, who will also serve as chair of the arbitration committee. It is understood that the third member ordinarily should not be a citizen of either Contracting State.

If either Contracting State fails to appoint a member, or the two members fail to agree on the third member to be appointed in the prescribed manner, the appointment of the remaining member(s) is to be undertaken by the highest ranking member of the Secretariat at the Centre for Tax Policy and Administration of the OECD who is not a citizen of either Canada or the United States (the "OECD Representative"). The OECD Representative is to appoint the remaining member(s) within 60 days of the failure of the Contracting States or the other two appointees to appoint the remaining member(s), as the case may be. Either Contracting State may contact the OECD Representative for this purpose. To assist the OECD Representative in its task, both Contracting States are to provide a non-exclusive list of individuals with familiarity in international tax matters who may potentially serve as the chair of the arbitration board.

The arbitration board shall meet (to the extent necessary) in facilities provided by the Contracting State whose competent authority initiated the mutual agreement procedure in the case.

Arbitration Procedure

Once arbitration has commenced, the taxpayer has no further role to play in the procedure apart from exercising its option to reject the board's determination (discussed further below). Rather, all correspondence and representations to the arbitration board are to be made by the competent authorities. This is not dissimilar to the current level of involvement that a taxpayer has under the MAP process, which is generally restricted to the presentation of the initial request for MAP assistance.

Paragraph 6 requires that the arbitration be conducted in the manner prescribed by, and subject to, the requirements of paragraph 7 and any rules or procedures agreed upon by the Contracting States by exchange of Diplomatic Notes. As far as procedure is concerned, paragraph 7 generally only prescribes the timing of the commencement of the arbitration proceeding. The remaining procedures are described in the Diplomatic Notes.

Pursuant to the Diplomatic Notes, the arbitration board may adopt any procedures necessary that are not inconsistent with Article XXVI or the other requirements described in the Diplomatic Notes.

Prior to the commencement of arbitration, each Contracting State is required to ensure that all members of the arbitration board and their staff sign and send to each of the Contracting States notarized statements in which they agree to abide by and be subject to the confidentiality and nondisclosure provisions of Articles XXVI (Mutual Agreement Procedure) and XXVII (Exchange of Information) of the Convention and the applicable domestic laws of the Contracting States. In the event any of these provisions may conflict, the Diplomatic Notes confirm that the most restrictive conditions shall apply. These notarized statements must be executed and sent to the Contracting States by each member of the arbitration board prior to the member acting in the arbitration.

Within 60 days of the appointment of the chair of the arbitration board, each Contracting State may submit to the arbitration board a proposed resolution of the case (including a specific dollar amount of income, expense and/or tax liability) as well as submissions supporting the proposed resolution. Because the arbitration board must limit its determination to the amount of income, expense, or tax reportable to a Contracting State (and because the arbitration board must adopt one of the Contracting State's proposed resolutions as its determination, as discussed further below), Contracting States should ensure that the proposed resolution submitted to the board contains sufficient detail in all of these respects. The arbitration board shall distribute to each Contracting State the proposed resolution and submission of the other Contracting State once the board has received a proposed resolution and submission from both Contracting States. Each Contracting State may respond to the other State's proposed resolution and submission by submitting a reply to the arbitration board within 120 days of the appointment of the chair of the arbitration board. No other information may be submitted to the arbitration board unless it is requested by the board and any such requests and responses shall be shared with the other Contracting State. All communications between the arbitration board and the Contracting States shall be in writing between the competent authorities and the chair of the arbitration board.

In making its determination, the arbitration board may consider the following materials:

(a) the provisions of the Convention (as amended);

(b) any agreed commentaries or explanations of the Contracting States (such as any Technical Explanations of an Article);

(c) the laws of the Contracting States (to the extent they are not inconsistent); and

(d) OECD Commentary, Guidelines, or Reports regarding relevant analogous portions of the OECD Model Tax Convention.

Determinations of the Arbitration Board

All determinations made by the board will constitute a resolution by mutual agreement under Article XXVI, will be binding on both Contracting States with respect to that case but will not have precedential value. Within 30 calendar days of receiving the determination, each concerned person must accept the determination in writing with the competent authority in the State in which the concerned person is a resident. If the concerned person fails to accept the determination within 30 calendar days, the determination is considered rejected.

The arbitration board will adopt one of the proposed resolutions of the Contracting States as its decision — the arbitration board has no ability to come to any different, independent determination. Accordingly, it is critical that both Contracting States submit a proposed resolution and submission to the arbitration board within the 60-day time period. If only one Contracting State submits a proposal, it will be accepted by the arbitration board as the final determination of the case and the arbitration shall be terminated. This is a "baseball-style", or "last best offer" arbitration process which is intended to encourage the Contracting States to submit proposed resolutions that are reasoned and "fair" to all concerned persons and the other Contracting State.

Determinations of the arbitration board will be communicated by the chair of the board to the competent authorities of the Contracting States. The concerned persons are to be advised of the determination through the competent authorities.

This process is to be compared to the OECD Sample Agreement Commentary, which describes the various options open to treaty partners in structuring the arbitration process. One method is the "independent opinion" approach, under which the arbitrators are presented with the facts and arguments of the parties based on applicable law, and then reach their own independent decision based upon a written, reasoned analysis of the facts involved and applicable legal sources. The Sample Agreement Commentary explains that there are a number of variations between the independent opinion and the last best offer approaches. For example, the arbitrators could reach an independent decision but would not be required to submit a written decision, but simply their conclusions. The Sample Agreement Commentary states that "to some extent, the appropriate method depends on the type of issue to be decided". Although the Sample Agreement takes as its starting point the independent opinion approach, the Sample Agreement Commentary suggests that the last best offer approach may be better suited to factual questions rather than questions of law, and, alternatively, that competent authorities may agree to use this more "streamlined" process on a case-by-case basis.

One of the principal effects of the "last best offer" approach in the context of the Convention is that there will perhaps be more pressure on the competent authorities to negotiate reasonable settlements on an expedited basis rather than risk losing out completely should the arbitration board select the proposed resolution of the other competent authority.

Effect of Arbitration Board's Determination

Subparagraph 7(*e*) permits any "concerned person" to refuse to accept the determination of the arbitration board, which would result in nullifying the determination for all parties, including the competent authorities. There is no corresponding ability of a Contracting State to refuse to accept the determination. If all concerned persons accept the determination, the determination will constitute a mutual agreement for purposes of Article XXVI and will be binding on all parties. If the determination is not accepted, the case may not subsequently be taken before an arbitration board pursuant to Article XXVI.

Contracting States may levy interest and penalties under the relevant domestic law in connection with the determination of the arbitration board.

Confidential Information

As stated above, and pursuant to subparagraphs 7(*c*) and 7(*d*) of Article XXVI, an arbitration proceeding cannot commence without all concerned persons first agreeing in writing not to disclose to any other person any information received during the course of the arbitration proceeding from either Contracting State or the arbitration board (other than the determination of the board).

The 2010 MOU and the Diplomatic Notes accompanying the Fifth Protocol provide rules with respect to the disclosure of information by the arbitration board and the Contracting States. Notably, neither is permitted to disclose any information (not even the determination of the board), except as permitted by the Convention and the domestic laws of the Contracting States. All material prepared in the course of, or pertaining to, the arbitration shall be considered to be information exchanged between the Contracting States.

Subparagraph 7(*f*) of Article XXVI confirms that members of the arbitration board and their staff will be considered "persons or authorities" for purposes of Article XXVII (Exchange of Information). Article XXVII generally provides that any information received by a Contracting State from another Contracting State for purposes of carrying out the provisions of the Convention must be treated as secret in the same manner as if obtained by that Contracting State under the domestic taxation laws of that State. The information may only be disclosed to persons or authorities (including courts and administrative bodies) involved generally in (i) the assessment or collection of taxes to which the Convention applies; (ii) the administration and enforcement in respect of taxes to which the Convention applies; or (iii) the determination of appeals in relation to taxes to which the Convention applies. Article XXVII currently provides that such information may be released to an arbitration board and that any such information received by the arbitration board will be held secret in the same manner as described in Article XXVII.

In Canada, the disclosure of taxpayer information is dealt with in subparagraph 241(4)(*e*)(xii) of the *Income Tax Act* (Canada), which allows the Canada Revenue Agency to provide taxpayer information for the purposes of a provision contained in a tax treaty. The circumstances in which the Convention permits disclosure of such information is specifically limited by virtue of Article XXVII and the mandatory arbitration provisions.

Costs of the Arbitration

The Contracting States shall equally share the fees and expenses of the arbitration board, which are to be determined in accordance with the International Centre for Settlement of Investment Disputes (ICSID) Schedule of Fees for arbitrators (as in effect on the date the arbitration commences). Any language translation fees are similarly to be shared equally by the Contracting States.

As discussed above, the competent authority of the Contracting State that initiated the MAP must provide meeting facilities (if required) to carry out the arbitration. The Diplomatic Notes indicate that this competent authority must also bear all costs associated with providing such meeting facilities, as well as any related resources, financial management, logistical support, and general administrative costs associated with coordinating the arbitration.

Each Contracting State shall bear all of its own costs not described above.

Further Changes to the Arbitration Procedure

The Diplomatic Notes provide that the competent authorities of the Contracting States may modify or supplement any of the rules and procedures described in the Diplomatic Notes as necessary in order to more effectively implement the intent of Article XXVI(6) to eliminate double taxation.

History: Paragraph 6 of Article XXVI was deleted and replaced with paragraphs 6 and 7 by paragraph 1 of Article 21 of the Fifth Protocol to this Convention, and formerly read:

6. If any difficulty or doubt arising as to the interpretation or application of the Convention cannot be resolved by the competent authorities pursuant to the preceding paragraphs of this Article, the case may, if both competent authorities and the taxpayer agree, be submitted for arbitration, provided that the taxpayer agreed in writing to be bound by the decision of the arbitration board. The decision of the arbitration board in a particular case shall be binding on both States with respect to that case. The procedures shall be established in an exchange of notes between the Contracting States. The provisions of this paragraph shall have effect after the Contracting States have so agreed through the exchange of notes.

Subparagraphs 3(*f*) and (*g*) of Article XXVI were amended and paragraph (*h*) was added by paragraph 1 of Article 14 of the Third Protocol to this Convention. Paragraphs 3(*f*) and (*g*) formerly read:

(*f*) To the elimination of double taxation with respect to a partnership; or

(*g*) To increases in any dollar amounts referred to in the Convention to reflect monetary or economic developments.

Paragraph 6 was added to Article XXVI by paragraph 2 of Article 14 of the Third Protocol to this Convention.

Article XXVI A — Assistance in Collection

1. The Contracting States undertake to lend assistance to each other in the collection of taxes referred to in paragraph 9, together with interest, costs, additions to such taxes and civil penalties, referred to in this Article as a "revenue claim".

2. An application for assistance in the collection of a revenue claim shall include a certification by the competent authority of the applicant State that, under the laws of that State, the revenue claim has been finally determined. For the purposes of this Article, a revenue claim is finally determined when the applicant State has the right under its internal law to collect the revenue claim and all administrative and judicial rights of the taxpayer to restrain collection in the applicant State have lapsed or been exhausted.

3. A revenue claim of the applicant State that has been finally determined may be accepted for collection by the competent authority of the requested State and, subject to the provisions of paragraph 7, if accepted shall be collected by the requested State as though such revenue claim were the requested State's own revenue claim finally determined in accordance with the laws applicable to the collection of the requested State's own taxes.

4. Where an application for collection of a revenue claim in respect of a taxpayer is accepted

(*a*) By the United States, the revenue claim shall be treated by the United States as an assessment under United States laws against the taxpayer as of the time the application is received; and

(*b*) By Canada, the revenue claim shall be treated by Canada as an amount payable under the *Income Tax Act*, the collection of which is not subject to any restriction.

5. Nothing in this Article shall be construed as creating or providing any rights of administrative or judicial review of the applicant State's finally determined revenue claim by the requested State, based on any such rights that may be available under the laws of either Contracting State. If, at any time pending execution of a request for assistance under this Article, the applicant State loses the right under its internal law to collect the revenue claim, the competent authority of the applicant State shall promptly withdraw the request for assistance in collection.

6. Subject to this paragraph, amounts collected by the requested State pursuant to this Article shall be forwarded to the competent authority of the applicant State. Unless the competent authorities of the Contracting States otherwise agree, the ordinary costs incurred in providing collection assistance shall be borne by the requested State and any extraordinary costs so incurred shall be borne by the applicant State.

7. A revenue claim of an applicant State accepted for collection shall not have in the requested State any priority accorded to the revenue claims of the requested State.

8. No assistance shall be provided under this Article for a revenue claim in respect of a taxpayer to the extent that the taxpayer can demonstrate that

(*a*) Where the taxpayer is an individual, the revenue claim relates either to a taxable period in which the taxpayer was a citizen of the requested State or, if the taxpayer became a citizen of the requested State at any time before November 9, 1995 and is such a citizen at the time the applicant State applies for collection of the claim, to a taxable period that ended before November 9, 1995; and

(*b*) Where the taxpayer is an entity that is a company, estate or trust, the revenue claim relates to a taxable period in which the taxpayer derived its status as such an entity from the laws in force in the requested State.

9. Notwithstanding the provisions of Article II (Taxes Covered), the provisions of this Article shall apply to all categories of taxes collected, and to contributions to social security and employment insurance premiums levied, by or on behalf of the Government of a Contracting State.

10. Nothing in this Article shall be construed as:

(*a*) Limiting the assistance provided for in paragraph 4 of Article XXVI (Mutual Agreement Procedure); or (*b*) Imposing on either Contracting State the obligation to carry out administrative measures of a different nature from those used in the collection of its own taxes or that would be contrary to its public policy (*ordre public*).

11. The competent authorities of the Contracting States shall agree upon the mode of application of this Article, including agreement to ensure comparable levels of assistance to each of the Contracting States.

Dentons Canada LLP Commentary: Article XXVI A (Assistance in Collection) was added to the Convention by the Third Protocol. Collection assistance provisions are included in several other U.S. income tax treaties, including the treaty with the Netherlands, and in many U.S. estate tax treaties. However, such provisions appear in only a limited number of tax treaties concluded by Canada (for example, Canada's treaties with the Netherlands, Austria, Germany, Norway, and the United Kingdom). Canadian courts have generally followed the common law rule that they cannot be used to enforce the revenue laws of foreign countries. (See, for instance, *United States of America v. Harden* (1963), 36 D.L.R. (2d) 602, affirmed by the Supreme Court of Canada, [1963] S.C.R. 366, 63 DTC 1276.) As a result, this common law principle will have to yield to the provisions of Article XXVI A.

Under paragraph 1 of Article XXVI A, each Contracting State agrees, subject to the exercise of its discretion and to the conditions explicitly provided later in the Article, to lend assistance and support to the other in the collection of revenue claims. The term "revenue claim" is defined in paragraph 1 to include all taxes referred to in paragraph 9 of the Article, as well as interest, costs, additions to such taxes, and civil penalties. Paragraph 9 provides that, notwithstanding the provisions of Article II (Taxes Covered) of the Convention, Article XXVI A shall apply to all categories of taxes collected by or on behalf of the government of a Contracting State. That said, the CRA has concluded that certain civil penalties imposed under the U.S. *Bank Secrecy Act* (generally for failure to file a foreign bank account report, or "FBAR") are not penalties in respect of "taxes imposed" by the United States and are therefore not covered under the Treaty. See: CRA Document No. 2011-0427221E5.

Paragraph 2 of the Article requires the Contracting State applying for collection assistance (the "applicant State") to certify that the revenue claim for which collection assistance is sought has been "finally determined". A revenue claim has been finally determined when the applicant State has the right under its internal law to collect the revenue claim and all administrative and judicial rights of the taxpayer to restrain collection in the applicant State have lapsed or been exhausted.

Paragraph 3 of the Article clarifies that the Contracting State from which assistance was requested (the "requested State") has discretion as to whether to accept a particular application for collection assistance. However, if the application for assistance is accepted, paragraph 3 requires that the requested State grant assistance under its existing procedures as though the claim were the requested State's own revenue claim finally determined under the laws of that State. This obligation under paragraph 3 is limited by paragraph 7 of the Article, which provides that, although generally treated as a revenue claim of the requested State, a claim for which collection assistance is granted shall not have any priority accorded to the revenue claims of the requested State.

Paragraph 4 of Article XXVI A provides that, when the United States accepts a request for assistance in collection, the claim will be treated by the United States as an assessment as of the time the application was received. Similarly, when Canada accepts a request, a revenue claim shall be treated as an amount payable under the *Income Tax Act* (Canada), the collection of which is not subject to any restriction.

Paragraph 5 provides that nothing in Article XXVI A shall be construed as creating in the requested State any rights of administrative or judicial review of the applicant State's finally determined revenue claim. Thus, when an application for collection assistance has been accepted, the substantive validity of the applicant State's revenue claim cannot be challenged in an action in the requested State. Paragraph 5 furthers provides, however, that if the applicant State's revenue claim ceases to be finally determined, the applicant State is obligated to withdraw promptly any request that had been based on that claim.

Paragraph 6 provides that, as a general rule, the requested State is to forward the entire amount collected to the competent authority of the applicant State. The ordinary costs incurred in providing collection assistance will normally be borne by the requested State and only extraordinary costs will be borne by the applicant State. The application of this paragraph, including rules specifying which collection costs are to be borne by each State and the time and manner of payment of the amounts collected, will be agreed upon by the competent authorities, as provided for in paragraph 11.

Paragraph 8, as amended by the Fifth Protocol, imposes an important limitation on the assistance procedure. Subparagraph 8(*a*) provides that no assistance is to be given under this Article for a claim in respect of an individual taxpayer if either:

(a) the taxpayer can demonstrate that the claim relates to a taxable period in which the individual was a citizen of the requested State; or

(b) if the claim relates to a period in which the taxpayer was not a citizen of the requested State,

(i) the taxable period in question ended before November 9, 1995;

(ii) the individual became a citizen of the requested State at any time before November 9, 1995; and

(iii) the individual is a citizen of the requested State at the time the applicant State makes the application.

In other words, Canada will not help the United States collect U.S. taxes owed by Canadian citizens and *vice versa*, except in very limited circumstances.

Similarly, in the case of a company, estate, or trust, subparagraph 8(*b*) provides that no assistance is to be given to the extent that the entity can demonstrate that it derived its status as such under the laws in force in the requested State during the taxable period to which the claim relates.

Paragraph 9 of Article XXVI A, as amended by the Fifth Protocol, provides that the provisions of this Article apply to all categories of taxes collected, and to contributions to social security and employment insurance premiums levied, by or on behalf of the Government of a Contracting State. This paragraph ensures that contributions to the *Canada Pension Plan* and employment insurance programs (which are not considered "taxes" under Canadian law) are within the scope of Article XXVI A.

Subparagraph (*a*) of paragraph 10 clarifies that Article XXVI A supplements the provisions of paragraph 4 of Article XXVI (Mutual Agreement Procedure). The Mutual Agreement Procedure paragraph, which is more common in U.S. tax treaties, provides for collection assistance in cases in which a Contracting State seeks assistance in reclaiming treaty benefits that have been granted to a person that is not entitled to those benefits. Subparagraph (*b*) of paragraph 10 makes it clear that nothing in Article XXVI A can require a Contracting State to carry out administrative measures of a different nature from those used in the collection of its own taxes, or that would be contrary to its public policy ("*ordre public*").

Paragraph 11 requires the competent authorities to agree upon the mode of application of Article XXVI A, including agreement to ensure comparable levels of assistance to each of the Contracting States.

Paragraph 3 of Article 21 of the Third Protocol allows collection assistance under Article XXVI A to be sought for revenue claims that have been finally determined at any time within the 10 years preceding the date on which the Protocol came into force. The Protocol entered into force on November 9, 1995.

History: Subparagraph 8(*a*) of Article XXVI A was deleted and replaced by paragraph 1 of Article 22 of the Fifth Protocol to this Convention, and formerly read:

(*a*) Where the taxpayer is an individual, the revenue claim relates to a taxable period in which the taxpayer was a citizen of the requested State, and

Paragraph 9 of Article XXVI A was deleted and replaced by paragraph 2 of Article 22 of the Fifth Protocol to this Convention, and formerly read:

9. Notwithstanding the provisions of Article II (Taxes Covered), the provisions of this Article shall apply to all categories of taxes collected by or on behalf of the Government of a Contracting State.

Article XXVI A was added by Article 15 of the Third Protocol to this Convention.

Article XXVII — Exchange of Information

1. The competent authorities of the Contracting States shall exchange such information as may be relevant for carrying out the provisions of this Convention or of the domestic laws of the Contracting States concerning taxes to which this Convention applies insofar as the taxation thereunder is not contrary to this Convention. The exchange of information is not restricted by Article I (Personal Scope). Any information received by a Contracting State shall be treated as secret in the same manner as information obtained under the taxation laws of that State and shall be disclosed only to persons or authorities (including courts and administrative bodies) involved in the assessment or collection of, the administration and enforcement in respect of, or the determination of appeals in relation to the taxes to which this Convention applies or, notwithstanding paragraph 4, in relation to taxes imposed by a political subdivision or local authority of a Contracting State that are substantially similar to the taxes covered by this Convention under Article II (Taxes Covered). Such persons or authorities shall use the information only for such purposes. They may disclose the information in public court proceedings or in judicial decisions. The competent authorities may release to an arbitration board established pursuant to paragraph 6 of Article XXVI (Mutual Agreement Procedure) such information as is necessary for

carrying out the arbitration procedure; the members of the arbitration board shall be subject to the limitations on disclosure described in this Article.

2. If information is requested by a Contracting State in accordance with this Article, the other Contracting State shall use its information gathering measures to obtain the requested information, even though that other State may not need such information for its own tax purposes. The obligation contained in the preceding sentence is subject to the limitations of paragraph 3 but in no case shall such limitations be construed to permit a Contracting State to decline to supply information because it has no domestic interest in such information.

3. In no case shall the provisions of paragraph 1 and 2 be construed so as to impose on a Contracting State the obligation:

(*a*) To carry out administrative measures at variance with the laws and administrative practice of that State or of the other Contracting State;

(*b*) To supply information which is not obtainable under the laws or in the normal course of the administration of that State or of the other Contracting State; or

(*c*) To supply information which would disclose any trade, business, industrial, commercial or professional secret or trade process, or information the disclosure of which would be contrary to public policy (*ordre public*).

4. For the purposes of this Article, this Convention shall apply, notwithstanding the provisions of Article II (Taxes Covered):

(*a*) To all taxes imposed by a Contracting State; and

(*b*) To other taxes to which any other provision of this Convention applies, but only to the extent that the information may be relevant for the purposes of the application of that provision.

5. In no case shall the provisions of paragraph 3 be construed to permit a Contracting State to decline to supply information because the information is held by a bank, other financial institution, nominee or person acting in an agency or a fiduciary capacity or because it relates to ownership interests in a person.

6. If specifically requested by the competent authority of a Contracting State, the competent authority of the other Contracting State shall provide information under this Article in the form of depositions of witnesses and authenticated copies of unedited original documents (including books, papers, statements, records, accounts, and writings).

7. The requested State shall allow representatives of the requesting State to enter the requested State to interview individuals and examine books and records with the consent of the persons subject to examination.

Dentons Canada LLP Commentary: Article XXVII forms the basis for cooperation between the two countries in their attempt to deal with avoidance or evasion of their respective taxes and to enable them to obtain information so that they can properly administer the Convention. This Article provides for the exchange of information which is necessary to carry out the provisions of the Convention for the prevention of fraud or for the administration of statutory provisions concerning taxes to which the Convention applies. The exchange of information rules apply to any taxes imposed by Canada on estates and gifts (none have been effective for deaths or gifts after 1971), to taxes Canada imposes under the *Income Tax Act* (Canada), and to all taxes that the United States imposes under the *Internal Revenue Code*. Therefore, the United States would, under the provisions of this Article, be able to obtain information from Canada in order to assist, for example, in assessing its social security and excise taxes imposed under the *Internal Revenue Code*.

Paragraph 1 authorizes the competent authorities to exchange the information that may be relevant to the carrying out of the provisions of the Convention or the domestic laws of Canada and the United States concerning taxes to which the Convention applies, insofar as the taxation under those domestic laws is not contrary to the Convention. The authority to exchange information granted by paragraph 1 is not restricted by Article I (Personal Scope), and thus information can be exchanged with respect to persons not covered by the Convention, such as persons not resident in either country. Under paragraph 1, information may be exchanged for use in all phases of the taxation process, including assessments, collections, and appeals.

Paragraph 1 allows a Contracting State to provide information received from the other Contracting State to its states, provinces, or local authorities, if it relates to a tax imposed by that state, province, or local authority that is substantially similar to a national-level tax covered under Article II (Taxes Covered). However, this provision does not authorize a Contracting State to request information on behalf of a state, province, or local authority. Pparagraph 1 also authorizes the competent authorities to release information to any arbitration panel that may be established under the provisions of paragraph 6 of Article XXVI (Mutual Agreement Procedure). Any information provided to a state, province, or local authority or to an arbitration panel is subject to the same use and disclosure provisions as is information received by the national governments and used for their purposes. Paragraph 1 was revised by the Fifth Protocol to clarify that the information requested must not necessarily be relevant, but that may be of *potential* relevance to an ongoing investigation. However, as indicated in the Technical Explanation to the Fifth Protocol, this flexibility does not mean that a Contracting State may simply ask for any information relating to all bank accounts maintained by residents of that State in the other Contracting State — accordingly, there must be some basis to conclude that the request may yield potentially relevant information.

It is intended that Article XXVII be utilized by the competent authorities to exchange information upon request, routinely and spontaneously. In addition, in the *Canada-U.S. Intergovernmental Agreement* (the "IGA"), Canada and the United States agreed to exchange certain information regarding financial accounts held in each country. This exchange is to occur automatically under the provisions of Article XXVII. In *Hillis v. Canada (AG)*, 2015 DTC 5098 (F.C.), two petitioners sought to have the IGA and corresponding domestic legislation (Part XVIII of the *Income Tax Act* (Canada)) struck down by the Federal Court on the basis that it was unconstitutional and infringed certain rights under the *Canadian Charter of Rights and Freedoms*. The constitutional arguments had not been determined by the Court at the time of publication. However, certain non-constitutional arguments had been considered, and the Court and, in a lengthy judgment, concluded that the relevant provisions of the IGA and the *Income Tax Act* had been lawfully implemented. In addition, the Court held that the IGA was not inconsistent with Article XXVII.

Information exchanged is to be treated as secret in the same manner as information obtained under the domestic laws of the receiving country, except that it may be disclosed to persons involved in the assessment or collection of, the administration and enforcement in respect of, or litigation concerning the taxes to which the Convention applies. (See *Sherman v. Minister of National Revenue*, 2004 DTC 6694 (F.C.A.), for a discussion of the circumstances in which a taxpayer can seek disclosure of information prepared by a particular Contracting State.)

Paragraph 2 provides that a requested country will use its information gathering methods to obtain the information requested as if its own taxpayers were involved, notwithstanding the fact that the requested country does not, at that time, need the information. A Contracting State is not limited to providing only the information that is already has in its own files. What this means is that a requested country will use its audit, subpoena, or summons powers, or any other powers that it has under its own laws to collect information requested by the other country, even though it does not have or need the information for its own purposes. For example, in *Pacific Network Services v. Minister of National Revenue*, 2002 DTC 7585 (F.C.T.D.), it was held that the Canada Revenue Agency was permitted to use section 231.2 of the *Income Tax Act* (Canada) to make a demand for taxpayer information that had been requested by the U.S. Internal Revenue Service.

Paragraph 3 describes the circumstances in which a Contracting State would not be required to provide information to the other Contracting State. Specifically, Article XXVII cannot be interpreted so as to impose any obligation on a Contracting State (i) to carry out administrative duties at variance with its obligations under the domestic law of either Contracting State; (ii) to supply information not otherwise available under the normal administration of the laws of either Contracting State; or (iii) to generally disclose information that would disclose trade secrets or otherwise be against public policy. However, paragraph 3 does not permit a Contracting State to decline to obtain information and supply information merely because it has no domestic tax interest in such information.

Article XXVII was considered and applied in *Andison v. M.N.R.*, 95 DTC 5058 (F.C.T.D), and in *Montreal Aluminium Processing Inc. v. M.N.R.*, 91 DTC 5424 (F.C.T.D.). In each case, the Court upheld the Canada Revenue Agency's rights and obligations under Article XXVII.

Paragraph 4 describes the applicable taxes for the purposes of this Article. Under the Convention, as it read prior to the implementation of the Third Protocol, the Article applied in Canada to taxes imposed by the Government of Canada under the *Income Tax Act* (Canada) and on estates and gifts, and in the United States to all taxes imposed under the *Internal Revenue Code*. The Protocol broadened the scope of the Article to apply to "all taxes imposed by a Contracting State". This change allows information to be exchanged, for example, with respect to Canadian excise taxes. Paragraph 4 also authorizes the exchange of information with respect to other taxes, to the extent such information may be relevant to any other provision of the Convention. The CRA has concluded that certain civil penalties imposed under the U.S. *Bank Secrecy Act* (generally for failure to file a foreign bank account report, or "FBAR") are not penalties in respect of "taxes owing" by the US and are therefore not covered under the Treaty. See: CRA Document No. 2011-0427221E5.

Paragraph 5, added by the Fifth Protocol, clarifies that, notwithstanding paragraph 3, information held by banks, financial institutions, nominees, agents, or other fiduciaries shall be subject to the disclosure requirements of Article XXVII. This prevents a Contracting State from relying on any domestic bank secrecy laws or similar legislation to override its obligation to provide information under paragraph 1. Pursuant to paragraph 5, information regarding a person's beneficial interests are also subject to disclosure. This provision now dovetails with Canada's obligations under the IGA to report certain financial institution account information to the IRS on an annual basis.

Paragraph 6 was also added by the Fifth Protocol and refers to specific types of documents that may be requested (and should be provided, if so requested) by a Contracting State. This information had previously been contained in paragraph 1. Where specifically requested, the competent authority will attempt to provide the information in a form required by the other country. Specifically, the competent authority will attempt to provide depositions of witnesses and copies of unedited original documents (including books, papers, statements, records, accounts, or writings) to the extent that they can be obtained under the laws and practices of the requested country in the enforcement of its own tax laws.

The Fifth Protocol further added paragraph 7, which permits representatives of a requesting State to enter the other Contracting State in order to interview individuals and examine books and records with the consent of the persons subject to examination.

The Diplomatic Notes accompanying the Fifth Protocol provide that the standards and practices described in Article XXVII are to be in no respect less effective than those described by the Organisation for Economic Cooperation and Development (the "OECD") in its *Model Agreement on Exchange of Information on Tax Matters* (Paris: OECD, 2002) (the "OECD Model Exchange of Information Agreement"), which was developed by the OECD Global Forum Working Group on Effective Exchange of Information. The Working Group consisted of representatives of OECD countries as well as certain "tax havens", including Aruba, Bahrain, Bermuda, the Cayman Islands, Cyprus, the Isle of Man, Malta, Mauritius, the Netherlands Antilles, San Marino, and the Seychelles. The general purpose of the OECD Model Exchange of Information Agreement is to allow two (or more) States that would not otherwise enter into a comprehensive tax treaty with each other the opportunity to enter into a separate agreement governing only the exchange of information between those States. The direct linkage between the interpretation of Article XXVII of the Convention and the OECD Model Exchange of Information Agreement is logical since Article XXVII is intended to obviate the need for a separate exchange of information agreement between Canada and the United States. In this respect, both States clearly desired to clarify that the procedures governing an exchange of information under Article XXVII is to be no less rigorous or onerous than the procedures that would have existed under a stand-alone exchange of information agreement. The influence of the OECD Model Exchange of Information Agreement is evident in paragraph 5 of Article XXVII, dealing with information that may be obtained from financial institutions or agents, which was originally proposed by the OECD Global Forum Working Group on Effective Exchange of Information.

♦

History: Article XXVII was deleted and replaced by Article 23 of the Fifth Protocol to this Convention, and formerly read:

1. The competent authorities of the Contracting States shall exchange such information as is relevant for carrying out the provisions of this Convention or of the domestic laws of the Contracting States concerning taxes to which the Convention applies insofar as the taxation thereunder is not contrary to the Convention. The exchange of information is not restricted by Article I (Personal Scope). Any information received by a Contracting State shall be treated as secret in the same manner as information obtained under the taxation laws of that State and shall be disclosed only to persons or authorities (including courts and administrative bodies) involved in the assessment or collection of, the administration and enforcement in respect of, or the determination of appeals in relation to the taxes to which the Convention applies or, notwithstanding paragraph 4, in relation to taxes imposed by a political subdivision or local authority of a Contracting State that are substantially similar to the taxes covered by the Convention under Article II (Taxes Covered). Such persons or authorities shall use the information only for such purposes. They may disclose the information in public court proceedings or in judicial decisions. The competent authorities may release to an arbitration board established pursuant to paragraph 6 of Article XXVI (Mutual Agreement Procedure) such information as is necessary for carrying out the arbitration procedure; the members of the arbitration board shall be subject to the limitations on disclosure described in this Article.

2. If information is requested by a Contracting State in accordance with this Article, the other Contracting State shall endeavor to obtain the information to which the request relates in the same way as if its own taxation was involved notwithstanding the fact that the other State does not, at that time, need such information. If specifically requested by the competent authority of a Contracting State, the competent authority of the other Contracting State shall endeavor to provide information under this Article in the form requested, such as depositions of witnesses and copies of unedited original documents (including books, papers, statements, records, accounts, or writings), to the same extent such depositions and documents can be obtained under the laws and administrative practices of that other State with respect to its own taxes.

3. In no case shall the provisions of paragraphs 1 and 2 be construed so as to impose on a Contracting State the obligation:

(*a*) To carry out administrative measures at variance with the laws and administrative practice of that or of the other Contracting State;

(*b*) To supply information which is not obtainable under the laws or in the normal course of the administration of that or of the other Contracting State; or

(*c*) To supply information which would disclose any trade, business, industrial, commercial or professional secret or trade process, or information the disclosure of which would be contrary to public policy (*ordre public*).

4. For the purposes of this Article, the Convention shall apply, notwithstanding the provisions of Article II (Taxes Covered):

(*a*) To all taxes imposed by a Contracting State; and

(*b*) To other taxes to which any other provision of the Convention applies, but only to the extent that the information is relevant for the purposes of the application of that provision.

Paragraph 1 of Article XXVII was amended by paragraph 1 of Article 16 of the Third Protocol to this Convention, and formerly read:

1. The competent authorities of the Contracting States shall exchange such information as is necessary for carrying out the provisions of this Convention or of the domestic laws of the Contracting States concerning taxes covered by the Convention insofar as the taxation thereunder is not contrary to the Convention. The exchange of information is not restricted by Article I (Personal Scope). Any information received by a Contracting State shall be treated as secret in the same manner as information obtained under the taxation laws of that State and shall be disclosed only to persons or authorities (including courts and administrative bodies) involved in the assessment or collection of, the administration and enforcement in respect of, or the determination of appeals in relation to, the taxes covered by the Convention. Such persons or authorities shall use the information only for such purposes. They may disclose the information in public court proceedings or in judicial decisions.

Paragraph 4 of Article XXVII was amended by paragraph 2 of Article 16 of the Third Protocol to this Convention, and formerly read:

4. Notwithstanding the provisions of Article II (Taxes Covered), for the purposes of this Article the Convention shall apply:

(*a*) In the case of Canada, to all taxes imposed by the Government of Canada on estates and gifts and under the *Income Tax Act*; and

(*b*) In the case of the United States, to all taxes imposed under the *Internal Revenue Code*.

♦

Article XXVIII — Diplomatic Agents and Consular Officers

Nothing in this Convention shall affect the fiscal privileges of diplomatic agents or consular officers under the general rules of international law or under the provisions of special agreements.

Dentons Canada LLP Commentary: Article XXVIII provides that the Convention shall not affect the fiscal privileges of diplomatic agents or consular officers that are conferred on them under international law or special agreements. It is identical to Article 27 of the OECD Model Convention. It is intended to ensure that diplomatic agents and consular officers who are factually resident in one of the Contracting States to which they have been posted by the other Contracting State shall not receive less favourable tax treatment by virtue of the Convention than that to which they are entitled under international law or under special international agreements, such as the Vienna Conventions on Diplomatic Relations and on Consular Relations. It should be noted, however, that various provisions of the Convention could apply to such persons, such as those concerning the exchange of information, mutual agreement, and non-discrimination.

Article XXIX — Miscellaneous Rules

1. The provisions of this Convention shall not restrict in any manner any exclusion, exemption, deduction, credit or other allowance now or hereafter accorded by the laws of a Contracting State in the determination of the tax imposed by that State.

2.

(*a*) Except to the extent provided in paragraph 3, this Convention shall not affect the taxation by a Contracting State of its residents (as determined under Article IV (Residence)) and, in the case of the United States, its citizens and companies electing to be treated as domestic corporations.

(*b*) Notwithstanding the other provisions of this Convention, a former citizen or former long-term resident of the United States, may, for the period of ten years following the loss of such status, be taxed in accordance with the laws of the United States with respect to income from sources within the United States (including income deemed under the domestic law of the United States to arise from such sources).

3. The provisions of paragraph 2 shall not affect the obligations undertaken by a Contracting State:

(*a*) Under paragraphs 3 and 4 of Article IX (Related Persons), paragraphs 6 and 7 of Article XIII (Gains), paragraphs 1, 3, 4, 5, 6(*b*), 7, 8, 10 and 13 of Article XVIII (Pensions and Annuities), paragraph 5 of Article XXIX (Miscellaneous Rules), paragraphs 1, 5, and 6 of Article XXIX B (Taxes Imposed by Reason of Death), paragraphs 2, 3, 4, and 7 of Article XXIX B (Taxes Imposed by Reason of Death) as applied to estates of persons other than former citizens referred to in paragraph 2 of this Article, paragraphs 3 and 5 of Article XXX (Entry into Force), and Articles XIX (Government Service), XXI (Exempt Organizations), XXIV (Elimination of Double Taxation), XXV (Non-Discrimination) and XXVI (Mutual Agreement Procedure);

(*b*) Under Article XX (Students), toward individuals who are neither citizens of, nor have immigrant status in, that State.

4. With respect to taxable years not barred by the statute of limitations ending on or before December 31 of the year before the year in which the Social Security Agreement between Canada and the United States (signed in Ottawa on March 11, 1981) enters into force, income from personal services not subject to tax by the United States under this Convention or the 1942 Convention shall not be considered wages or net earnings from self-employment for purposes of social security taxes imposed under the *Internal Revenue Code*.

5. Where a person who is a resident of Canada and a shareholder of a United States S corporation requests the competent authority of Canada to do so, the competent authority may agree, subject to terms and conditions satisfactory to such competent authority, to apply the following rules for the purposes of taxation in Canada with respect to the period during which the agreement is effective:

(*a*) The corporation shall be deemed to be a controlled foreign affiliate of the person;

(*b*) All the income of the corporation shall be deemed to be foreign accrual property income;

(*c*) For the purposes of subsection 20(11) of the *Income Tax Act*, the amount of the corporation's income that is included in the person's income shall be deemed not to be income from a property; and

(*d*) Each dividend paid to the person on a share of the capital stock of the corporation shall be excluded from the person's income and shall be deducted in computing the adjusted cost base to the person of the share.

6. For purposes of paragraph 3 of Article XXII (Consultation) of the General Agreement on Trade in Services, the Contracting States agree that:

(*a*) A measure falls within the scope of the Convention only if:

(i) The measure relates to a tax to which Article XXV (Non-Discrimination) of the Convention applies; or

(ii) The measure relates to a tax to which Article XXV (Non-Discrimination) of the Convention does not apply and to which any other provision of the Convention applies, but only to the extent that the measure relates to a matter dealt with in that other provision of the Convention; and

(*b*) Notwithstanding paragraph 3 of Article XXII (Consultation) of the General Agreement on Trade in Services, any doubt as to the interpretation of subparagraph (*a*) will be resolved under paragraph 3 of Article XXVI (Mutual Agreement Procedure) of the Convention or any other procedure agreed to by both Contracting States.

7. The appropriate authority of a Contracting State may request consultations with the appropriate authority of the other Contracting State to determine whether change to the Convention is appropriate to respond to changes in the law or policy of that other State. Where domestic legislation enacted by a Contracting State unilaterally removes or significantly limits any material benefit otherwise provided by the Convention, the appropriate authorities shall promptly consult for the purpose of considering an appropriate change to the Convention.

Dentons Canada LLP Commentary: Article XXIX contains a number of special rules that amplify or modify other provisions of the Convention.

Paragraph 1 contains a general rule that the provisions of the Convention will not restrict any exclusion, exemption, deduction, credit, or other allowance, whether currently allowed or later enacted by one of the countries. Thus, if a deduction would be allowed for an item in computing the taxable income of a U.S. company under the *Income Tax Act* (Canada), such deduction is available to the company in computing taxable income under the Convention. This paragraph does not, however, authorize a taxpayer to make inconsistent choices between the applicable domestic laws and the rules of the Convention.

Subparagraph 2(*a*) contains a "saving clause" that provides, with specific exceptions, that the Convention is not to affect the taxation by the United States of its citizens and residents, or the taxation by Canada of its residents. This provision also applies to Canadian companies electing under section 1504 of the U.S. *Internal Revenue Code* to be treated as domestic corporations and thereby included in a consolidated U.S. return. Consequently, unless otherwise specifically provided in the Convention, the United States will continue to tax its citizens who are residents of Canada.

Subparagraph 2(*b*) contains an additional saving clause which provides that the United States may tax former citizens and former long-term residents for a period of ten years following the loss of such status. "Former long-term resident" is described in the Diplomatic Notes to the Fifth Protocol generally as an individual who was a lawful permanent resident of the United States in any eight of the prior fifteen taxable years. Any year in which the individual is considered a resident of Canada for purposes of the Convention (or any other country for purposes of the relevant tax treaty between that country and the United States) and the individual claims the benefits under the Convention (or the other treaty) as a non-resident of the United States shall not be considered in determining whether the threshold described above has been met. The Diplomatic Notes limit U.S. taxation of such individuals to income from sources within the United States (including income deemed, under U.S. domestic tax rules, to be from a source within the United States), including:

(a) gains from the sale or exchange of stock of U.S. corporations;

(b) debt obligations of U.S. persons and certain political subdivisions;

(c) gains from property situated in the U.S. (other than stock or debt obligations);

(d) income from the sale of stock of certain non-U.S. corporations (e.g., companies that would be considered controlled foreign affiliates if the individual were considered a resident of the United States);

(e) an exchange of property that would otherwise give rise to U.S.-source income for purposes of this Article for property that would not give rise to U.S.-source income. (A deeming rule would apply to consider the individual to have derived U.S.-source income on the exchange and also upon the ultimate disposition of the property received on the exchange.)

Exceptions to these savings clauses are provided in subparagraph 3(*a*) and relate to benefits confirmed by the Articles dealing with:

- related persons (Article IX);
- gains (Article XIII);
- pensions, annuities, and social security benefits (Article XVIII);
- Canadian resident shareholders in a U.S. S corporation (see commentary below on paragraph 5 of Article XXIX);
- taxes imposed by reason of death (Article XXIX B);
- certain transitional rules contained in paragraphs 3 and 5 of Article XXX (Entry into Force);
- government service (Article XIX);
- exempt organizations (Article XXI);
- elimination of double taxation (Article XXIV);
- non-discrimination (Article XXV); and
- the mutual agreement provisions (Article XXVI).

In addition, under subparagraph 3(*b*), the saving clauses do not apply to individuals who are subject to the provisions of Article XX (Students) and who are neither citizens of nor have immigrant status in the country in which they are temporarily present.

Paragraph 4 contains a provision intended to grant relief from U.S. social security taxes imposed on employers, employees, and self-employed persons under the U.S. *Internal Revenue Code*. Under its domestic laws, the United States imposes such social security taxes on account of some Canadian individuals exempt from U.S. income tax. Canada and the United States have negotiated a social security agreement that would limit such U.S. social security taxation for future years, once it comes into effect. This paragraph provides that, with respect to taxable years not barred by the U.S. statute of limitations ending on or before December 31 of the year before the year in which the proposed social security agreement enters into force, income from personal services that is not subject to tax by the United States under the 1942 Convention or the current Convention will not be considered wages or earnings from self-employment for purposes of social security taxes imposed under the U.S. *Internal Revenue Code*. This provision will therefore permit persons who have paid social security taxes for years which are still open to obtain a refund of those taxes.

Paragraph 5 provides a rule for the taxation by Canada of a Canadian resident that is a shareholder in a U.S. S corporation. The application of this rule is relatively limited, because U.S. domestic law requires that S corporation shareholders be either U.S. citizens or U.S. residents. Therefore, the rule provided by paragraph 5 would apply only to an S corporation shareholder who is a resident of both the United States and Canada (i.e., a "dual resident" who meets certain requirements), determined before the application of the "tie-breaker" rules of Article IV (Residence), or a U.S. citizen resident in Canada. Since the shareholder would be subject to U.S. tax on its share of the income of the S corporation as it is earned by the S corporation and, under Canadian statutory law, would be subject to tax only when the income is distributed, there could be a timing mismatch resulting in unrelieved double taxation. Under paragraph 5, the shareholder can make a request to the Canadian competent authority for relief under the special rules of the paragraph. Under these rules, the Canadian shareholder will be subject to Canadian tax on essentially the same basis as he or she is subject to U.S. tax, thus eliminating the timing mismatch.

Paragraph 6 provides a coordination rule for the Convention and the General Agreement on Trade in Services ("GATS"). Subparagraph 6(*a*) provides that, for purposes of paragraph 3 of Article XXII (Consultation) of the GATS, a measure falls within the scope of the Convention only if the measure relates to a tax

(1) to which Article XXV (Non-Discrimination) of the Convention applies, or

(2) to which Article XXV does not apply and to which any other provision of the Convention applies, but only to the extent that the measure relates to a matter dealt with in that other provision.

Under subparagraph 6(*b*), notwithstanding paragraph 3 of Article XXII of the GATS, any doubt as to the interpretation of subparagraph (*a*) will be resolved under paragraph 3 of Article XXVI (Mutual Agreement Procedure) of the Convention or any other procedure agreed to by both Contracting States.

The GATS generally obliges its Members to provide national treatment and most-favoured-nation treatment to services and service suppliers of other Members. A very broad exception from the national treatment obligation applies to direct taxes. An exception from the most-favoured-nation obligation applies to a difference in treatment resulting from an international agreement on the avoidance of double taxation (a "tax agreement") or from provisions on the avoidance of double taxation in any other international agreement or arrangement by which the Member is bound.

Article XXII (3) of the GATS specifically provides that there will be no access to the GATS procedures to settle a national treatment dispute concerning a measure that falls within the scope of a tax agreement. This provision preserves the exclusive application of non-discrimination obligations in the tax agreement and clarifies that the competent authority mechanism provided by the tax agreement will apply, instead of the GATS procedures, to resolve non-discrimination disputes involving the taxation of services and service suppliers.

In the event of a disagreement between Members as to whether a measure falls within the scope of a tax agreement that existed at the time of the entry into force of the Agreement establishing the World Trade Organization, Article XXII(2), footnote 11, of the GATS reserves the resolution of the dispute to the Contracting States under the tax agreement. In such a case, the issue of the scope of a tax agreement may be resolved under the GATS procedures (rather than tax treaty procedures) only if both parties to the existing tax agreement consent. With respect to subsequent tax agreements, the GATS provides that either Member may bring the jurisdictional matter before the Council for Trade in Services, which will refer the matter to arbitration for a decision that will be final and binding on the Members.

Both Canada and the United States agree that a Protocol to a convention that is grandfathered under Article XXII(2), footnote 11, of GATS is also grandfathered. Nevertheless, since the Third Protocol extends the application of the Convention, and particularly the non-discrimination Article, to additional taxes (e.g., some non-income taxes imposed by Canada), the negotiators sought to remove any ambiguity and agreed to a provision that clarified the scope of the Convention and the relationship between the Convention and the GATS.

The purpose of subparagraph 6(*a*) of the Convention is to provide the agreement of the Contracting States as to the measures considered to fall within the scope of the Convention in applying Article XXII (3) of GATS between the Contracting States. The purpose of subparagraph 6(*b*) is to reserve the resolution of the issue of the scope of the Convention for purposes of Article XXII (3) of the GATS to the competent authorities under the Convention rather than to settlement under the GATS procedures.

Paragraph 7 provides, first, that in response to a change in the law or policy of either State, the appropriate authority of either State may request consultations with its counterpart in the other State to determine whether a change in the Convention is appropriate. If a change in domestic legislation has unilaterally removed or significantly limited a material benefit provided by the Convention, the appropriate authorities are instructed by the paragraph to consult promptly to consider an appropriate amendment to the Convention. The "appropriate authorities" may be the Contracting States themselves or the competent authorities under the Convention. The consultations may be initiated by the authority of the Contracting State making the change in law or policy, or by the authority of the other State. Any change in the Convention recommended as a result of this process can be implemented only through the negotiation, signature, ratification, and entry into force of a new protocol to the Convention.

Editorial Note: Technical Interpretation, Document No. 2013-0477121E5, dated October 21, 2013, deals with the interaction of section 126 of the *Income Tax Act* and Articles XVIII(2) and XXIX(2) of the Convention.

2005 APFF Conference, Document No. 2005-0132441C6, dated October 7, 2005, deals with credit for United States estate or inheritance taxes payable at the time of death with respect to a property situated within the U.S., but held through an RRSP. The Treaty benefit cannot be claimed, as the Canadian tax on the income relates to the RRSP, which is situated in Canada.

◆

History: Paragraph 2 of Article XXIX was deleted and replaced by paragraph 1 of Article 24 of the Fifth Protocol to this Convention, and formerly read:

2. Except as provided in paragraph 3, nothing in the Convention shall be construed as preventing a Contracting State from taxing its residents (as determined under Article IV (Residence)) and, in the case of the United States, its citizens (including a former citizen whose loss of citizenship had as one of its principal purposes the avoidance of tax, but only for a period ten years following such loss) and companies electing to be treated as domestic corporations, as if there were no convention between the United States and Canada with respect to taxes on income and on capital.

Subparagraph 3(*a*) of Article XXIX was deleted and replaced by paragraph 2 of Article 24 of the Fifth Protocol to this Convention, and formerly read:

(*a*) Under paragraphs 3 and 4 of Article IX (Related Persons), paragraphs 6 and 7 of Article XIII (Gains), paragraphs 1, 3, 4, 5, 6 and 7 of Article XVIII (Pensions and Annuities), paragraph 5 of Article XXIX (Miscellaneous Rules), paragraphs 1, 5 and 6 XXIX B (Taxes Imposed by Reason of Death), paragraphs 2, 3, 4 and 7 XXIX B (Taxes Imposed by Reason of Death) as applied to the estates of persons other than former citizens referred to in paragraph 2 of this Article, paragraphs 3 and 5 of Article XXX (Entry into Force), and Articles XIX (Government Service), XXI (Exempt Organizations), XXIV (Elimination of Double Taxation), XXV (Non-Discrimination) and XXVI (Mutual Agreement Procedure);

Subparagraph 3(*a*) of Article XXIX was amended by paragraph 1 of Article 17 of the Third Protocol to this Convention, and formerly read:

(*a*) Under paragraphs 3 and 4 of Article IX (Related Persons), paragraphs 6 and 7 of Article XIII (Gains), paragraphs 1, 3, 4, 5(*b*) and 6(*b*) of Article XVIII (Pensions and Annuities), paragraphs 5 and 7 of Article XXIX (Miscellaneous Rules), paragraphs 3 and 5 of Article XXX (Entry into Force), and Articles XIX (Government Service), XXI (Exempt Organizations), XXIV (Elimination of Double Taxation), XXV (Non-Discrimination) and XXVI (Mutual Agreement Procedure); and.

Paragraphs 5 to 7 of Article XXIX were amended by paragraph 2 of Article 17 of the Third Protocol to this Convention, and formerly read:

5. A beneficiary of a Canadian registered retirement savings plan may elect, under rules established by the competent authority of the United States, to defer United States taxation with respect to any income accrued in the plan but not distributed by the plan, until such time as a distribution is made from such plan, or any plan substituted therefor. The provisions of the preceding sentence shall not apply to income which is reasonably attributable to contributions made to the plan by the beneficiary while he was not a resident of Canada.

6. Notwithstanding any other provision of the Convention,

(*a*) Where profits, income or gains derived by a trust is to be treated for the purposes of the Convention as income of a resident of a Contracting State, and a principal purpose for the establishment, acquisition or maintenance of the trust was to obtain a benefit under the Convention or the 1942 Convention for persons who are not residents of that state, Articles VI (Income from Real Property) through XXIV (Elimination of Double Taxation) shall not apply in relation to the profits, income or gains of the trust; and

(*b*) Articles VI (Income from Real Property) through XXIV (Elimination of Double Taxation) shall not apply to non-resident-owned investment corporations as defined under section 133 of the *Income Tax Act* of Canada, or under any similar provision enacted by Canada after the date of signature of the Protocol.

7. One-half of the total amount of benefits under the social security legislation in Canada paid in a taxable year to a resident of Canada who is a citizen of the United States shall be exempt from taxation in the United States.

Paragraph 2 of Article XXIX was amended by Article XIII of the First Protocol to this Convention, and formerly read:

2. Except as provided in paragraph 3, nothing in the Convention shall be construed as preventing a Contracting State from taxing its residents (as determined under Article IV (Residence)) and, in the case of the United States, its citizens (including a former citizen whose loss of citizenship had as one of its principal purposes the avoidance of income tax, but only for a period of ten years following such loss) and companies electing to be treated as domestic corporations, as if there were no convention between (the United States and Canada with respect to taxes on income and on capital.

Subparagraph 3(*a*) of Article XXIX was amended by Article II of the Second Protocol to this Convention. Subparagraph 3(*a*), as amended by Article XIII of the First Protocol to this Convention, formerly read as follows:

(*a*) Under paragraphs 3 and 4 of Article IX (Related Persons), paragraphs 6 and 7 of Article XIII (Gains), paragraphs 1, 3, 4, 5 and 6(*b*) of Article XVIII (Pensions and Annuities), paragraph 5 of Article XXIX (Miscellaneous Rules), paragraphs 3 and 5 of Article XXX (Entry into Force), and Articles XIX (Government Service), XXI (Exempt Organizations), XXIV (Elimination of Double Taxation), XXV (Non-Discrimination) and XXVI (Mutual Agreement Procedure); and.

Subparagraph 3(*a*) of Article XXIX was previously amended by Article XIII of the First Protocol to this Convention, and formerly read:

(*a*) Under paragraphs 3 and 4 of Article IX (Related Persons), paragraphs 6 and 7 of Article XIII (Gains), paragraph 5 of Article XXIX (Miscellaneous Rules), paragraphs 3 and 5 of Article XXX (Entry into Force), and Articles XVIII (Pensions and Annuities), XIX (Government Service), XXI (Exempt Organizations), XXIV (Elimination of Double Taxation), XXV (Non-Discrimination) and XXVI (Mutual Agreement Procedure); and.

Paragraphs 4, 5, and 6 of Article XXIX were amended by Article XIII of the First Protocol to this Convention, and formerly read:

4. With respect to taxable years not barred by the statute of limitations ending on or before December 31 of the year in which the Convention enters into force, income from personal services not subject to tax by the United States under the 1942 Convention shall not be considered wages or net earnings from self-employment for purposes of social security taxes imposed under the *Internal Revenue Code*.

5. A United States citizen who is a resident of Canada and a beneficiary of a Canadian registered retirement savings plan may elect, under rules established by the competent authority of the United States, to defer United States taxation with respect to any income accrued in the plan but not distributed by the plan, until such time as a distribution is made from such plan, or any plan substituted therefore.

6. If 25 per cent or more of the capital of a company which is a resident of a Contracting State is owned directly or indirectly by individuals who are not residents of that State, and if by reason of special measures the tax imposed in that State on that company with respect to dividends (other than dividends referred to in paragraph 2(*a*) of Article X (Dividends)), interest or royalties arising in the other Contracting State is substantially less than the tax generally imposed by the first-mentioned State on corporate business profits then, notwithstanding the provisions of Article X (Dividends), XI (interest) or XII (Royalties), that other State may tax such dividends, interest or royalties as if there were no convention between the United States and Canada with respect to taxes on income and on capital.

Paragraph 7 of Article XXIX was added by Article II of the Second Protocol to this Convention.

Article XXIX A — Limitation on Benefits

1. For the purposes of the application of this Convention by a Contracting State,

(*a*) a qualifying person shall be entitled to all of the benefits of this Convention; and

(*b*) except as provided in paragraphs 3, 4 and 6, a person that is not a qualifying person shall not be entitled to any benefits of this Convention.

2. For the purposes of this Article, a qualifying person is a resident of a Contracting State that is:

(*a*) a natural person;

(*b*) a Contracting State or a political subdivision or local authority thereof, or any agency or instrumentality of any such State, subdivision or authority;

(*c*) a company or trust whose principal class of shares or units (and any disproportionate class of shares or units) is primarily and regularly traded on one or more recognized stock exchanges;

(*d*) a company, if five or fewer persons each of which is a company or trust referred to in subparagraph (*c*) own directly or indirectly more than 50 percent of the aggregate vote and value of the shares and more than 50 percent of the vote and value of each disproportionate class of shares (in neither case including debt substitute shares), provided that each company or trust in the chain of ownership is a qualifying person;

(*e*) (i) a company, 50 percent or more of the aggregate vote and value of the shares of which and 50 percent or more of the vote and value of each disproportionate class of shares (in neither case including debt substitute shares) of which is not owned, directly or indirectly, by persons other than qualifying persons; or

(ii) a trust, 50 percent or more of the beneficial interest in which and 50 percent or more of each disproportionate interest in which, is not owned, directly or indirectly, by persons other than qualifying persons;

where the amount of the expenses deductible from gross income (as determined in the State of residence of the company or trust) that are paid or payable by the company or trust, as the case may be, for its preceding fiscal period (or, in the case of its first fiscal period, that period) directly or indirectly, to persons that are not qualifying persons is less than 50 percent of its gross income for that period;

(*f*) an estate;

(*g*) a not-for-profit organization, provided that more than half of the beneficiaries, members or participants of the organization are qualifying persons;

(*h*) a trust, company, organization or other arrangement described in paragraph 2 of Article XXI (Exempt Organizations) and established for the purpose of providing benefits primarily to individuals who are qualifying persons, or persons who were qualifying persons within the five preceding years; or

(*i*) a trust, company, organization or other arrangement described in paragraph 3 of Article XXI (Exempt Organizations) provided that the beneficiaries of the trust, company, organization or other arrangement are described in subparagraph (*g*) or (*h*).

3. Where a person is a resident of a Contracting State and is not a qualifying person, and that person, or a person related thereto, is engaged in the active conduct of a trade or business in that State (other than the business of making or managing investments, unless those activities are carried on with customers in the ordinary course of business by a bank, an insurance company, a registered securities dealer or a deposit-taking financial institution), the benefits of this Convention shall apply to that resident person with respect to income derived from the other Contracting State in connection with or incidental to that trade or business (including any such income derived directly or indirectly by that resident person through one or more other persons that are residents of that other State), but only if that trade or business is substantial in relation to the activity carried on in that other State giving rise to the income in respect of which benefits provided under this Convention by that other State are claimed.

4. A company that is a resident of a Contracting State shall also be entitled to the benefits of Articles X (Dividends), XI (Interest) and XII (Royalties) if:

(*a*) Its shares that represent more than 90 percent of the aggregate vote and value of all of its shares and at least 50 percent of the vote and value of any disproportionate class of shares (in neither case including debt substitute shares) are owned, directly or indirectly, by persons each of whom is a qualifying person or a person who:

(i) Is a resident of a country with which the other Contracting State has a comprehensive income tax convention and is entitled to all of the benefits provided by that other State under that convention;

(ii) Would qualify for benefits under paragraphs 2 or 3 if that person were a resident of the first-mentioned State (and, for the purposes of paragraph 3, if the business it carried on in the country of which it is a resident were carried on by it in the first-mentioned State); and

(iii) Would be entitled to a rate of tax in the other Contracting State under the convention between that person's country of residence and that other State, in respect of the particular class of income for which benefits are being claimed under this Convention, that is at least as low as the rate applicable under this Convention; and

(*b*) The amount of the expenses deductible from gross income (as determined in the company's State of residence) that are paid or payable by the company for its preceding fiscal period (or, in the case of its first fiscal period, that period) directly or indirectly to persons that are not qualifying persons is less than 50 percent of the company's gross income for that period.

5. For the purposes of this Article,

(*a*) The term "debt substitute share" means:

(i) A share described in paragraph (*e*) of the definition "term preferred share" in the *Income Tax Act*, as it may be amended from time to time without changing the general principle thereof; and

(ii) Such other type of share as may be agreed upon by the competent authorities of the Contracting States.

(*b*) The term "disproportionate class of shares" means any class of shares of a company resident in one of the Contracting States that entitles the shareholder to disproportionately higher participation, through dividends, redemption payments or otherwise, in the earnings generated in the other State by particular assets or activities of the company;

(*c*) The term "disproportionate interest in a trust" means any interest in a trust resident in one of the Contracting States that entitles the interest holder to disproportionately higher participation in, or claim to, the earnings generated in the other State by particular assets or activities of the trust;

(*d*) The term "not-for-profit organization" of a Contracting State means an entity created or established in that State and that is, by reason of its not-for-profit status, generally exempt from income taxation in that State, and includes a private foundation, charity, trade union, trade association or similar organization;

(*e*) The term "principal class of shares" of a company means the ordinary or common shares of the company, provided that such class of shares represents the majority of the voting power and value of the company. If no single class of ordinary or common shares represents the majority of the aggregate voting power and value of the company, the "principal class of shares" are those classes that in the aggregate represent a majority of the aggregate voting power and value of the company; and

(*f*) The term "recognized stock exchange" means:

(i) The NASDAQ System owned by the National Association of Securities Dealers, Inc. and any stock exchange registered with the Securities and Exchange Commission as a national securities exchange for purposes of the *Securities Exchange Act* of 1934;

(ii) Canadian stock exchanges that are "prescribed stock exchanges" or "designated stock exchanges" under the *Income Tax Act*; and

(iii) Any other stock exchange agreed upon by the Contracting States in an exchange of notes or by the competent authorities of the Contracting States.

6. Where a person that is a resident of a Contracting State is not entitled under the preceding provisions of this Article to the benefits provided under this Convention by the other Contracting State, the competent authority of that other State shall, upon that person's request, determine on the basis of all factors including the history, structure, ownership and operations of that person whether:

(*a*) Its creation and existence did not have as a principal purpose the obtaining of benefits under this Convention that would not otherwise be available; or

(*b*) It would not be appropriate, having regard to the purpose of this Article, to deny the benefits of this Convention to that person.

The person shall be granted the benefits of this Convention by that other State where the competent authority determines that subparagraph (*a*) or (*b*) applies.

7. It is understood that this Article shall not be construed as restricting in any manner the right of a Contracting State to deny benefits under this Convention where it can reasonably be concluded that to do otherwise would result in an abuse of the provisions of this Convention.

Dentons Canada LLP Commentary: Article XXIX A (Limitation on Benefits) was added to the Convention by the Third Protocol and was significantly modified by the Fifth Protocol.

Generally, Article XXIX A is designed to address the problem of "treaty shopping" by residents of third States. In a typical case of treaty shopping, a resident of a third State might establish an entity resident in Canada for the purpose of deriving income from the United States and claiming U.S. treaty benefits with respect to that income. Article XXIX A limits the benefits granted by the United States under the Convention to those persons whose residence in Canada is not considered to have been motivated by the existence of the Convention. Article XXIX A accomplishes this objective by imposing a series of ownership and "use of funds" tests that must be satisfied in order for the entity to obtain benefits under the Convention. In the absence of Article XXIX A, the entity would be entitled to U.S. benefits under the Convention as a resident of Canada, unless it were denied benefits as a result of domestic U.S. limitations (e.g., business purpose, substance-over-form, step transaction, or conduit principles or other anti-avoidance rules) applicable to a particular transaction or arrangement.

Prior to the Fifth Protocol, Article XXIX A generally only applied in determining whether a resident of Canada was entitled to a reduction of U.S. tax under the Convention; the tests in Article XXIX A were not reciprocal in determining whether a U.S. resident could claim a reduction of Canadian tax under the Convention. Rather, Canada's only ability to deny benefits under the Convention was in the limited (and difficult to administer) circumstances where it could reasonably be concluded that allowing the benefits would result in an abuse of the Convention. In the several years since the provision became reciprocal, the CRA has provided a number of rulings and technical interpretations on the application of the rules. See CRA Document No. 2013-0507961C6 for a list of many of these interpretations.

Canada has never included a comprehensive limitation on benefits provision in any income tax treaty. Generally, Canada's treaty policy has consisted of including only very specific and targeted limitation on benefits provision, such as limitations relating to entities benefiting from a preferential tax regime in the other Contracting State (see, e.g., Article XXX (3) of the *Canada–Barbados Income Tax Convention* (1980) and Article 26 (3) of the *Canada–Mexico Income Tax Convention* (2006)). Canada has also included a form of limitation in virtually all of its tax treaties in respect of amounts derived by a resident of a contracting state who is not considered the "beneficial owner" of the amount. Beyond these narrow limitation provisions, Canada has expressed its desire to apply general anti-avoidance rules (whether based under domestic tax law or inherent within the treaty itself) to deny treaty benefits. In this respect, Canada amended its domestic general anti-avoidance rule (the "GAAR") in 2005, providing that the GAAR applies to treaties retroactively to 1988, when the GAAR was originally introduced. Moreover, when Article XXIX A was originally introduced, Canada opted not to be bound by the comprehensive limitation provisions put forward by the United States; rather, it requested that paragraph 7 be included, generally permitting each Contracting State to deny benefits under the Convention where the State considers the granting of benefits to be abusive.

However, Canada has, as of yet, been unsuccessful in asserting the GAAR to deny treaty benefits. For example, in *MIL (Investments) S.A. v. The Queen*, 2006 DTC 3307 (T.C.C.), aff'd, 2007 F.C.A. 236 (F.C.A.), the Crown asserted that the treaty between Canada and Luxembourg (which did not contain any comprehensive limitation on benefits provision) had been abused. Generally, in that case, a corporation resident in Luxembourg sold shares of a Canadian company that derived their value principally from real property situated in Canada. The Luxembourg company had previously been a resident of Canada, but continued to Luxembourg prior to the sale. As a result of the continuation, the Luxembourg resident claimed that the capital gain realized on the sale of the shares was exempt from Canadian tax under the *Canada–Luxembourg Income Tax Convention*. The Crown argued that the GAAR should apply to deny the treaty benefit and, in the alternative, an inherent (and unwritten) anti-abuse provision within the Canada–Luxembourg Treaty itself should apply to deny the treaty benefits. The decision of the Tax Court of Canada, which was upheld by the Federal Court of Appeal, was that the transaction was not abusive, such that the GAAR had no application. Moreover, the Tax Court confirmed that there was no inherent anti-abuse provision within the Treaty itself.

While current U.S. treaty policy mandates the inclusion of such provisions (at least as far as the availability of U.S. treaty benefits is concerned), this would be the first bilateral income tax convention in which Canada has agreed to be bound by a comprehensive limitation on benefits provision. The adoption of a comprehensive limitation on benefits provision by Canada establishes bright-line tests in which benefits under the Convention will be denied. However, the possibility remains that either Canada or the United States could deny benefits that would otherwise satisfy these comprehensive limitation provisions based on the application of domestic anti-abuse principles in paragraph 7 of Article XXIX A.

Prior to the addition of Article XXIX A, the Convention dealt with treaty-shopping in a very limited manner (in paragraph 6 of Article XXIX) by denying benefits to Canadian residents that benefit from specified provisions of Canadian law. The Third Protocol removed that provision from Article XXIX in favour of the more general provisions of Article XXIX A.

The structure of Article XXIX A is as follows:

- Paragraph 1 states that, in determining whether a resident of a Contracting State is entitled to benefits under the Convention, a "qualifying person" is entitled to all of the benefits of the Convention, and other persons are not entitled to benefits, except where paragraphs 3, 4, or 6 provide otherwise.
- Paragraph 2 lists a number of characteristics, any one of which will make a resident of a Contracting State a "qualifying person". These are essentially mechanical tests.
- Paragraph 3 provides an alternative rule (the "active trade or business" exception), under which a resident of a Contracting State that is not a qualifying person under paragraph 2 may claim benefits with respect to items of income earned in the other Contracting State that are connected with the active conduct of a trade or business carried out in the first-mentioned State.
- Paragraph 4 provides another rule (the "derivative benefits" exception) for entitlement to benefits with respect to dividends, interest, and royalties derived in one Contracting State and beneficially owned by a resident of the other Contracting State that is not a qualifying person.
- Paragraph 5 defines certain terms used in the Article.
- Paragraph 6 requires the competent authorities to grant benefits to a resident of a Contracting State that does not qualify for benefits under any other provision of the Article where the competent authorities determine, on the basis of all factors, that benefits should be granted.
- Paragraph 7 clarifies the continuing application of domestic Canadian and U.S. anti-abuse doctrines in addition to the specific limitations contained in Article XXIX A.

Qualifying Persons

Before a determination of the availability of treaty benefits can be made under Article XXIX A, the look-through rules in Article IV (Residence) must be applied to first determine the identity of the person that is *prima facie* entitled to claim the relevant benefits (see the commentary to Article IV for a further discussion of this look-through principle). Once this person(s) has been positively identified, the next step is to determine whether the person(s) satisfy the requirements to be considered a "qualifying person", as described in paragraph 2 of Article XXIX A.

For example, assume that a U.S.-resident corporation ("USco") wishes to obtain benefits under the Convention in respect of Canadian-source income. USco is wholly-owned by a U.S. limited liability company that is treated as fiscally transparent for U.S. tax purposes ("LLC"). LLC is in turn wholly-owned by a U.S.-resident individual. Since the U.S. (i.e., the State of residence of the U.S. individual) views the LLC as being fiscally transparent, the U.S.-resident individual shall be regarded as the person entitled to claim the benefits under the Convention for purposes of applying the limitation on benefits rules in Article XXIX A (see, e.g., CRA Document Nos. 2008-0272361C6 and 2008-0272871C6).

(i) Individuals and governmental entities

Under subparagraphs 2(*a*) and (*b*), the first two categories of qualifying persons are (a) a natural person resident in a Contracting State; and (b) a Contracting State, a political subdivision or local authority thereof, or an agency or instrumentality of that Government, political subdivision, or local authority. It is considered unlikely that persons falling into either of these two categories can be used, as the beneficial owner of income, to derive treaty benefits on behalf of a third-country person. If a person is receiving income as a nominee on behalf of a third-country resident, benefits will be denied with respect to those items of income under the relevant Article of the Convention that grants the benefit (i.e., Articles X, XI, and XII concerning dividends, interest, and royalties, respectively), because of the requirements in those Articles that the beneficial owner of the income be a resident of a Contracting State.

(ii) Publicly traded entities

Under subparagraph (*c*) of paragraph 2, a company or trust resident in a Contracting State is a qualifying person if its principal class of shares or units (and any disproportionate class of shares or units) is primarily and regularly traded on a recognized stock exchange.

The term "principal class of shares" is defined in subparagraph 5(*e*) to mean the ordinary or common shares of the company representing the majority of the aggregate voting power and value of the company. In the absence of such a single class of shares, the "principal class of shares" is to be determined by aggregating the number of classes necessary to satisfy this vote and value test. For this purpose, a corporation that otherwise satisfies the "publicly-traded entity" test based on a particular aggregation of share classes will not be denied "qualifying person" status solely because a different aggregation of share classes also representing the majority of the aggregate voting power and value of the company and that are not listed on a recognized stock exchange could be identified.

However, regardless of where the principal class of shares is traded, the company will fail the "publicly-traded entity" test in subparagraph 2(*c*) if it has a disproportionate class of shares that is not regularly traded on a recognized stock exchange. "Disproportionate class of shares" is defined in subparagraph 5(*b*) to generally refer to an interest that entitles the holder to a disproportionately higher participation (e.g., dividends, distributions) of the company's earnings that are generated in the other Contracting State. An example would be tracking stock that pays dividends based on a formula that approximates the company's return on particular assets. A similar rule applies in respect of disproportionate interests in a trust.

The term "primarily traded" is not defined in the Convention. Consistent with the principles in Article III concerning the interpretation of undefined terms, primarily traded is therefore to be defined under the domestic law of the Contracting State from which the benefits of the Convention are sought (i.e., the source State). For U.S. tax purposes, a majority test is employed. In this respect, shares of a corporation are primarily traded if the number of shares in the corporation's principal class of stock that are traded during the year on all recognized stock exchanges exceeds the number of shares in the corporation's principal class of shares that are traded during the year on stock exchanges that do not qualify as "recognized stock exchanges".

The term "regularly traded" is also not defined in the Convention and, therefore, its meaning is to be taken from the domestic law of the Contracting State from which the benefits of the Convention are sought (i.e., the source State). For U.S. tax purposes, this term generally means shares that meet the following two conditions: (i) trades of the particular class of share are made in more than *de minimus* quantities on at least 60 days during the year; and (ii) the aggregate number of shares in the class traded during the year is at least 10 per cent of the average number of shares outstanding during the year. The regularly-traded requirement can be satisfied by aggregating trades that occur on multiple recognized stock exchanges.

Subject to the adoption by Canada of different definitions, the U.S. interpretations of "primarily traded" and "regularly traded" applies with such modifications as may be necessary for purposes of Canadian taxation.

The term "recognized stock exchange" is defined in subparagraph 5(*f*) of the Article to mean, in the United States, the NASDAQ System and any stock exchange registered as a national securities exchange with the Securities and Exchange Commission, and, in Canada, any Canadian stock exchange that is a "prescribed stock exchange" or "designated stock exchange" under the *Income Tax Act* (Canada). Pursuant to subsection 262 of the *Income Tax Act* (Canada), such exchanges include the Montreal Exchange, the TSX Venture Exchange (Tiers 1 and 2), and the Toronto Stock Exchange. Additional exchanges may be added by exchange of notes between the Contracting States or by agreement between the competent authorities.

Certain companies owned by publicly traded corporations also may be qualifying persons. Under subparagraph (*d*) of paragraph 2, a company resident in a Contracting State will be a qualifying person, even if not publicly traded, if more than 50 per cent of the vote and value of its shares (including each disproportionate class of shares) is owned (directly or indirectly) by five or fewer companies or trusts that would be qualifying persons under subparagraph (*c*). In addition, each company or trust in the chain of ownership must be a qualifying person. Thus, for example, a Canadian company that is not publicly traded but that is owned, one-third each, by three companies, two of which are Canadian resident corporations whose principal classes of shares are primarily and regularly traded on a recognized stock exchange, will be a qualifying person under subparagraph (*d*).

The 50 per cent test under subparagraph (*d*) applies only to shares other than "debt substitute shares". The term "debt substitute shares" is defined in paragraph 5 to mean shares defined in subparagraph (*e*) of the definition in the *Income Tax Act* (Canada) of "term preferred shares" (see subsection 248(1) of the *Income Tax Act* (Canada)), which relates to certain shares received in debt-restructuring arrangements undertaken by reason of financial difficulty or insolvency. Paragraph 5 also provides that the competent authorities may agree to treat other types of shares as debt substitute shares.

(iii) Ownership/base erosion test

Subparagraph (*e*) of paragraph 2 provides a two-part test under which companies or trusts may be "qualifying persons", based on ownership and "base erosion". Generally, the ownership/base erosion test requires that qualifying persons substantially own the company or trust and that a substantial part of any deductible payments made by the company or trust be made to qualifying persons.

Under the first branch of this test, 50 per cent or more of the vote and value of the company's shares (including each disproportionate class of shares, but excluding debt substitute shares) or 50 per cent or more of the beneficial interests in the trust (including each disproportionate interest) must be owned, directly or indirectly, by qualifying persons. The wording of this test is intended to make clear that, for example, if a Canadian company is more than 50 per cent owned by a U.S. resident corporation that is, itself, wholly owned by a third-country resident other than a U.S. citizen, the Canadian company would not pass the ownership test. This is because more than 50 per cent of its shares is owned indirectly by a person (the third-country resident) that is not a qualifying person.

The ownership test will be satisfied if 50 per cent or more of the vote and value of the company's or trust's shares or units (including each disproportionate class of shares or units, but excluding debt substitute shares) are owned by a public company or trust described in subparagraph 2(*c*); in such a case, no further analysis of the indirect ownership of the shares or units is required.

The term "shares" includes, in the case of a mutual insurance company, any certificate or contract entitling the holder to voting power in the corporation. This is consistent with the interpretation of similar limitation on benefits provisions in other U.S. treaties. In Canada, the principles reflected in subsection 256(8.1) of the *Income Tax Act* (Canada) will be applied, in effect treating memberships, policies, or other interests in a corporation incorporated without share capital as representing an appropriate number of shares.

The second branch of the test of subparagraph (*e*) is the so-called "base erosion" test. This test requires that the amount of expenses that are paid or payable by the company or trust in question to persons that are not qualifying persons and that are deductible from gross income, be less than 50 per cent of the gross income of the company or trust (for this purpose, deductibility and gross income are to be determined under the tax laws of the State of residence of the company or trust). This test is applied for the fiscal period immediately preceding the period for which the qualifying person test is being applied. If it is the first fiscal period of the person, the test is applied for the current period.

The CRA will apply the base erosion test to entities that are fiscally transparent under U.S. law; however, the test will be applied as if the entity were not fiscally transparent but is instead required to compute its gross income and expenses in its own right. See CRA Document No. 2010-0361251E5. Presumably, the CRA applies the Treaty this way to prevent the use of fiscally transparent entities (such as U.S. LLCs, subchapter S corporations, and qualified subchapter S subsidiaries) to defeat the policy objectives of the base erosion test.

The ownership/base erosion test recognizes that the benefits of the Convention can be enjoyed indirectly not only by equity holders of an entity, but also by that entity's obligees, such as lenders, licensors, service providers, insurers and reinsurers, and others. For example, a third-country resident could license technology to a Canadian-owned Canadian corporation to be sublicensed to a U.S. resident. The U.S.-source royalty income of the Canadian corporation would be exempt from U.S. withholding tax under Article XII (Royalties) of the Convention. While the Canadian corporation would be subject to Canadian corporation income tax, its taxable income could be reduced to near zero as a result of the deductible royalties paid to the third-country resident. If, under a Convention between Canada and the third country, those royalties were either exempt from Canadian tax or subject to tax at a low rate, the U.S. treaty benefit with respect to the U.S. source royalty income would have flowed to the third-country resident at little or no tax cost, with no reciprocal benefit to the United States from the third country.

Both the ownership and base erosion tests are to be applied by taking into account the look-through rules under Article IV (Residence) (see the commentary to Article IV for a discussion of these look-through rules). For example, in determining whether a U.S. C-corporation is a qualifying person, any shareholders of the C-corporation that are fiscally transparent for U.S. tax purposes will be looked-through in determining whether the ownership test is satisfied. Moreover, deductible payments made by the C-corporation to fiscally transparent entities are considered to have been made to the owners of the fiscally transparent entity for purposes of determining whether the base erosion test is satisfied.

(iv) Other qualifying persons

Under subparagraph (*f*) of paragraph 2, an estate resident in either Contracting State is a qualifying person.

Subparagraphs (*g*) and (*h*) specify the circumstances under which certain types of not-for-profit organizations will be qualifying persons. Subparagraph (*g*) of paragraph 2 provides that a not-for-profit organization resident in either Contracting State is a qualifying person if more than half of the beneficiaries, members, or participants in the organization are qualifying persons. The term "not-for-profit organization" of a Contracting State is defined in subparagraph (*b*) of paragraph 5 of the Article to mean an entity created or established in that State that is generally exempt from income taxation in that State by reason of its not-for-profit status. The term includes charities, private foundations, trade unions, trade associations, and similar organizations.

Subparagraph (*h*) of paragraph 2 specifies that certain organizations described in paragraph 2 of Article XXI (Exempt Organizations) are qualifying persons. To be a qualifying person, such an organization must be established primarily for the purpose of providing pension, retirement, or employee benefits to qualifying persons (or persons who were qualifying persons within any of the five preceding years). An organization will be considered to be established "primarily" for this purpose if more than 50 per cent of its beneficiaries, members, or participants are such persons. Thus, for example, a Canadian registered retirement savings plan (RRSP) of a former resident of Canada who is working temporarily outside of Canada would continue to be a qualifying person during the period of the individual's absence from Canada or for five years, whichever is shorter. A Canadian pension fund established to provide benefits to persons employed by a company would be a qualifying person only if most of the beneficiaries of the fund are (or were within the five preceding years) individual residents of Canada or residents or citizens of the United States.

Subparagraph (i) of paragraph 2 provides that a trust, company, organization, or other arrangement described in paragraph 3 of Article XXI (Exempt Organizations) is a qualified person, provided the beneficiaries are described in subparagraphs (*g*) or (*h*).

The provisions of paragraph 2 are self-executing, unlike the provisions of paragraph 6, discussed below. The tax authorities may, of course, on review, determine that the taxpayer has improperly interpreted the paragraph and is not entitled to the benefits claimed.

Active Trade or Business Test

Paragraph 3 provides an alternative rule (the "active trade or business" exception), under which a resident of a Contracting State that is not a qualifying person under paragraph 2 may claim benefits with respect to items of income earned in the other Contracting State that are connected with the active conduct of a trade or business carried out in the first-mentioned State.

Unlike the tests of paragraph 2, the active trade or business test looks not solely at the characteristics of the person deriving the income, but also at the nature of the activity engaged in by that person and the connection between the income and that activity.

Under the active trade or business test, a resident of a Contracting State (the "Residence State") that derives income from the other Contracting State (the "Source State") is entitled to benefits with respect to that income if:

- that person (or a person related to that person under the principles of the *Internal Revenue Code* section 482 in the case of the United States and under section 251 of the *Income Tax Act* (Canada) in the case of Canada) is engaged in an active trade or business in the Residence State;
- the income in question is derived in connection with, or is incidental to, that trade or business; and
- the size of the active trade or business in the Residence State is substantial relative to the activity in the Source State.

Income that is derived in connection with, or is incidental to, the business of making or managing investments will not qualify for benefits under this provision, unless those investment activities are carried on with customers in the ordinary course of the business of a bank, insurance company, registered securities dealer, or deposit-taking financial institution.

Income is considered derived "in connection" with an active trade or business in the Source State if, for example, the income-generating activity in the Source State is "upstream", "downstream", or parallel to that conducted in Canada. Thus, if the U.S. activity consisted of selling the output of a Canadian manufacturer or providing inputs to the manufacturing process, or of manufacturing or selling in the United States the same sorts of products that were being sold by the Canadian trade or business in Canada, the income generated by that activity would be treated as earned in connection with the Canadian trade or business. Income is considered "incidental" to a trade or business in the Residence State if, for example, it arises from the short-term investment of working capital in securities issued by persons in the Source State.

An item of income may be considered to be earned in connection with or to be incidental to an active trade or business in the Residence State if the income is derived directly or indirectly through one or more other persons that are residents of the Source State. Thus, for example, a Canadian resident could claim benefits with respect to an item of income earned by a U.S. operating subsidiary but derived by the Canadian resident indirectly through a wholly-owned U.S. holding company interposed between it and the operating subsidiary. This language would also permit a Canadian resident to derive income from the United States through one or more U.S. residents that it does not wholly own. For example, a Canadian partnership in which three unrelated Canadian companies each hold a one-third interest could form a wholly-owned U.S. holding company with a U.S. operating subsidiary. The "directly or indirectly" language would allow otherwise available treaty benefits to be claimed with respect to income derived by the three Canadian partners through the U.S. holding company, even if the partners were not considered to be related to the U.S. holding company under the principles of *Internal Revenue Code*, section 482. The CRA will interpret the test consistently with its interpretation of similar language in subparagraph 95(2)(*a*)(ii) of the *Income Tax Act* (Canada). See CRA Document No. 2009-0317941E5.

Income that is derived in connection with, or is incidental to, an active trade or business in the Residence State must pass an additional test to qualify for U.S. treaty benefits: the trade or business must be substantial in relation to the activity in the Source State that gave rise to the income in respect of which treaty benefits are being claimed. To be considered substantial, it is not necessary that the trade or business being carried out in the Residence State be as large as the income-generating activity in the Source State. The trade or business cannot, however, in terms of income, assets, or other similar measures, represent only a very small percentage of the size of the activity carried on in the Source State. The CRA has yet to deny the availability of Treaty benefits on the basis that the U.S. operations were not substantial in comparison to the Canadian activities. The factors the CRA will consider include the relative amount of assets and revenues, number of employees, and income and compensation expenses. See, for example, CRA Document No. 2014-0549621C6.

The substantiality requirement is intended to prevent treaty-shopping. For example, a third-country resident may want to acquire a U.S. company that manufactures television sets for worldwide markets; however, since its country of residence has no tax treaty with the United States, any dividends generated by the investment would be subject to a U.S. withholding tax of 30 per cent. Absent a substantiality test, the investor could establish a Canadian corporation that would operate a small outlet in Canada to sell a few of the television sets manufactured by the U.S. company and earn a very small amount of income. That Canadian corporation could then acquire the U.S. manufacturer with capital provided by the third-country resident and produce a very large number of sets for sale in several countries, generating a much larger amount of income. It might attempt to argue that the U.S. source income is generated from business activities in the United States related to the television sales activity of the Canadian parent and that the dividend income should be subject to U.S. tax at the 5 per cent rate provided by Article X (Dividends) of the Convention. However, the substantiality test would not be met in this example, so the dividends would remain subject to withholding in the United States at a rate of 30 per cent.

In general, it is expected that if a person qualifies for benefits under one of the tests of paragraph 2, no inquiry will be made into qualification for benefits under paragraph 3. Upon satisfaction of any of the tests of paragraph 2, any income derived by the beneficial owner from the other Contracting State is entitled to treaty benefits. Under paragraph 3, however, the test is applied separately to each item of income.

Derivative Benefits Test

Paragraph 4 provides an alternate means for a company resident in a Contracting State (the "residence State") that is not a qualifying person and cannot satisfy the requirements of the active trade or business exception to claim benefits under the Convention with respect to dividends, interest, and royalties derived from the other Contracting State (the "Source State").

This so-called "derivative benefits" rule is not generally found in U.S. treaties. This rule was introduced in the Third Protocol because of the special economic relationship between the United States and Canada and the close coordination between the tax administrations of the two countries.

To qualify under the derivative benefits rule, a company must satisfy both (i) an ownership test; and (ii) a base erosion test similar to the test under subparagraph (*e*) of paragraph 2.

The derivative benefits ownership test is similar to the test described in subparagraphs 2(*d*) and (*e*), but is considerably more onerous. This test requires that shares representing more than 90 per cent of the vote and value of a company resident in a Contracting State and at least 50 per cent of the vote and value of any disproportionate shares of that company (but in both cases excluding debt substitute shares) be owned directly or indirectly by either:

- a qualifying person; or
- a person who:
  - is a resident of a third State with which the Source State has a comprehensive Income Tax Convention and is entitled to *all* of the benefits under that Convention (the person will fail this test if a limitation on benefits provision in the relevant Convention would limit treaty benefits or if the person only qualifies for benefits under that Convention with respect to specific types of income);
  - would qualify for benefits with respect to the item of income for which benefits are sought under one or more of the tests of paragraph 2 or 3 of Article XXIX A of the Canada–U.S. Convention if the person were a resident of the Residence State and, for purposes of paragraph 3, the business were carried on in the Residence State (for example, a person resident in a third country would be deemed to be a person that would qualify under the publicly traded test of paragraph 2 of this Convention if the principal class of its shares were primarily and regularly traded on a stock exchange recognized either under the Canada–U.S. Convention or under the treaty between the third State and the Source State. Similarly, a company resident in a third country would be deemed to satisfy the ownership/base erosion test of paragraph 2 under this hypothetical analysis if, for example, it were wholly owned by an individual resident in that third country and most of its deductible payments were made to individual residents of that country); and
  - would be entitled to a rate of withholding tax levied by the Source State on the item of income in respect of which benefits are sought that is at least as low under the Convention between the person's country of residence and the Source State as under this Convention.

The second aspect of the derivative benefits rule is a base erosion test. This test requires that the amount of expenses that are paid or payable by the company in question to persons that are not qualifying persons and that are deductible from gross income, be less than 50 per cent of the gross income of the company (for this purpose, deductibility and gross income are to be determined under the tax laws of the State of residence of the company). This test is applied for the fiscal period immediately preceding the period for which the qualifying person test is being applied. If it is the first fiscal period of the person, the test is applied for the current period.

Competent Authority Discretion

Paragraph 6 provides that, when a resident of a Contracting State derives income from the other Contracting State and is not entitled to the benefits of the Convention under other provisions of the Article, benefits may, nevertheless be granted at the discretion of the competent authority of the other Contracting State. In making a determination under this paragraph, the competent authority will take into account all relevant facts and circumstances relating to the person requesting the benefits. In particular, the competent authority will consider the history, structure, ownership (including ultimate beneficial ownership), and operations of the person. In addition, the competent authority is to consider:

- whether the creation and existence of the person did not have as a principal purpose obtaining treaty benefits that would not otherwise be available to the person, and
- whether it would not be appropriate, in view of the purpose of the Article, to deny benefits.

If the competent authority determines that either of these two standards is satisfied, benefits shall be granted.

For purposes of implementing paragraph 6, a taxpayer will be expected to present his case to the competent authority for an advance determination based on the facts. The taxpayer will not be required to wait until it has been determined that benefits are denied under one of the other provisions of the Article. It is also expected that, if and when the competent authority determines that benefits are to be allowed, they will be allowed retroactively to the time of entry into force of the relevant treaty provision or the establishment of the structure in question, whichever is later (assuming that the taxpayer also qualifies under the relevant facts for the earlier period).

General Anti-Abuse Provisions

Paragraph 7 was originally added at Canada's request to confirm that the specific provisions of Article XXIX A apply only for the purposes of the application of the Convention by the United States, but should not be construed so as to limit the right of each Contracting State to invoke any applicable anti-abuse rules.

Thus, for example, Canada remains free to apply rules such as the general anti-avoidance rule in section 245 of the *Income Tax Act* (Canada) to counter perceived abusive arrangements involving "treaty-shopping" through the United States, and the United States remains free to apply its substance-over-form and anti-conduit rules, for example, in relation to Canadian residents. This principle is recognized by the Organization for Economic Cooperation and Development in the Commentaries to its Model Tax Convention on Income and on Capital, and the United States and Canada agree that it is inherent in the Convention. The agreement to state this principle explicitly in the Convention is not intended to suggest that the principle is not also inherent in other tax conventions concluded by either Canada or the United States.

In *RMM Canadian Enterprises Inc. and Equilease Corporation v. The Queen*, 97 DTC 302, the Tax Court in *obiter* confirmed that in appropriate circumstances, GAAR can apply to deal with tax avoidance or evasion by residents of treaty countries. However, in *MIL (Investments) S.A. v. The Queen*, 2006 DTC 3307 (T.C.C.), aff'd, 2007 F.C.A. 236 (F.C.A.), the Tax Court held (and the Federal Court of Appeal affirmed) that the GAAR did not apply in a specific fact scenario involving a pre-disposition reorganization of shareholdings that resulted in the elimination of Canadian capital gains tax on a subsequent sale of the shareholdings. Moreover, in that case, the Tax Court held that there was no inherent anti-abuse provision in the relevant treaty that would apply to deny the resulting treaty benefit.

Editorial Note: See the CRA release "Guidelines for Taxpayers Requesting Treaty Benefits Pursuant to Paragraph 6 of Article XXIX A of the Canada–U.S. Tax Convention", dated May 22, 2009, reproduced after the treaty.

History: Article XXIX A was deleted and replaced by Article 25 of the Fifth Protocol to this Convention, and formerly read:

1. For the purposes of the application of this Convention by the United States,

(*a*) A qualifying person shall be entitled to all of the benefits of this Convention, and

(*b*) Except as provided in paragraphs 3, 4 and 6, a person that is not a qualifying person shall not be entitled to any benefits of the Convention.

2. For the purposes of this Article, a qualifying person is a resident of Canada that is:

(*a*) A natural person;

(*b*) The Government of Canada or a political subdivision or local authority thereof, or any agency or instrumentality of any such government, subdivision or authority;

(*c*) A company or trust in whose principal class of shares or units there is substantial and regular trading on a recognized stock exchange;

(*d*) A company more than 50 per cent of the vote and value of the shares (other than debt substitute shares) of which is owned, directly or indirectly, by five or fewer persons each of which is a company or trust referred to in subparagraph (*c*), provided that each company or trust in the chain of ownership is a qualifying person or a resident or citizen of the United States;

(*e*)

(i) A company 50 per cent or more of the vote and value of the shares (other than debt substitute shares) of which is not owned, directly or indirectly, by persons other than qualifying persons or residents or citizens of the United States, or

(ii) A trust 50 per cent or more of the beneficial interest in which is not owned, directly or indirectly, by persons other than qualifying persons or residents or citizens of the United States,

where the amount of the expenses deductible from gross income that are paid or payable by the company or trust, as the case may be, for its preceding fiscal period (or, in the case of its first fiscal period, that period) to persons that are not qualifying persons or residents or citizens of the United States is less than 50 per cent of its gross income for that period;

(*f*) An estate;

(*g*) A not-for-profit organization, provided that more than half of the beneficiaries, members or participants of the organization are qualifying persons or residents or citizens of the United States; or

(*h*) An organization described in paragraph 2 of Article XXI (Exempt Organizations) and established for the purpose of providing benefits primarily to individuals who are qualifying persons, persons who were qualifying persons within the five preceding years, or residents or citizens of the United States.

3. Where a person that is a resident of Canada and is not a qualifying person of Canada, or a person related thereto, is engaged in the active conduct of a trade or business in Canada (other than the business of making or managing investments, unless those activities are carried on with customers in the ordinary course of business by a bank, an insurance company, a registered securities dealer or a deposit-taking financial institution), the benefits of the Convention shall apply to that resident person with respect to income derived from the United States in connection with or incidental to that trade or business, including any such income derived directly or indirectly by that resident person through one or more other persons that are residents of the United States. Income shall be deemed to be derived from the United States in connection with the active conduct of a trade or business in Canada only if that trade or business is substantial in relation to the activity carried on in the United States giving rise to the income in respect of which benefits provided under the Convention by the United States are claimed.

4. A company that is a resident of Canada shall also be entitled to the benefits of Articles X (Dividends), XI (Interest) and XII (Royalties) if

(*a*) Its shares that represent more than 90 per cent of the aggregate vote and value represented by all of its shares (other than debt substitute shares) are owned, directly or indirectly, by persons each of whom is a qualifying person, a resident or citizen of the United States or a person who

(i) Is a resident of a country with which the United States has a comprehensive income tax convention and is entitled to all of the benefits provided by the United States under that convention;

(ii) Would qualify for benefits under paragraphs 2 or 3 if that person were a resident of Canada (and, for the purposes of paragraph 3, if the business it carried on in the country of which it is a resident were carried on by it in Canada); and

(iii) Would be entitled to a rate of United States tax under the convention between that person's country of residence and the United States, in respect of the particular class of income for which benefits are being claimed under this Convention, that is at least as low as the rate applicable under this Convention; and

(*b*) The amount of the expenses deductible from gross income that are paid or payable by the company for its preceding fiscal period (or, in the case of its first fiscal period, that period) to persons that are not qualifying persons or residents or citizens of the United States is less than 50 per cent of the gross income of the company for that period.

5. For the purposes of this Article,

(*a*) The term "recognized stock exchange" means:

(i) The NASDAQ System owned by the National Association of Securities Dealers, Inc. and any stock exchange registered with the Securities and Exchange Commission as a national securities exchange for purposes of the *Securities Exchange Act* of 1934;

(ii) Canadian stock exchanges that are "prescribed stock exchanges" under the *Income Tax Act*; and

(iii) Any other stock exchange agreed upon by the Contracting States in an exchange of notes or by the competent authorities of the Contracting States;

(*b*) The term "not-for-profit organization" of a Contracting State means an entity created or established in that State and that is, by reason of its not-for-profit status, generally exempt from income taxation in that State, and includes a private foundation, charity, trade union, trade association or similar organization; and

(*c*) The term "debt substitute share" means:

(i) A share described in paragraph (*e*) of the definition "term preferred share" in the *Income Tax Act*, as it may be amended from time to time without changing the general principle thereof; and

(ii) Such other type of share as may be agreed upon by the competent authorities of the Contracting States.

6. Where a person that is a resident of Canada is not entitled under the preceding provisions of this Article to the benefits provided under the Convention by the United States, the competent authority of the United States shall, upon that person's request, determine on the basis of all factors including the history, structure, ownership and operations of that person whether

(*a*) Its creation and existence did not have as a principal purpose the obtaining of benefits under the Convention that would not otherwise be available; or

(*b*) It would not be appropriate, having regard to the purpose of this Article, to deny the benefits of the Convention to that person.

The person shall be granted the benefits of the Convention by the United States where the competent authority determines that subparagraph (*a*) or (*b*) applies.

7. It is understood that the fact that the preceding provisions of this Article apply only for the purposes of the application of the Convention by the United States shall not be construed as restricting in any manner the right of a Contracting State to deny benefits under the Convention where it can reasonably be concluded that to do otherwise would result in an abuse of the provisions of the Convention.

Article XXIX A was added by Article 18 of the Third Protocol to this Convention.

Article XXIX B — Taxes Imposed by Reason of Death

1. Where the property of an individual who is a resident of a Contracting State passes by reason of the individual's death to an organization that is referred to in paragraph 1 of Article XXI (Exempt Organizations) and that is a resident of the other Contracting State,

(*a*) If the individual is a resident of the United States and the organization is a resident of Canada, the tax consequences in the United States arising out of the passing of the property shall apply as if the organization were a resident of the United States; and

(*b*) If the individual is a resident of Canada and the organization is a resident of the United States, the tax consequences in Canada arising out of the passing of the property shall apply as if the individual had disposed of the property for proceeds equal to an amount elected on behalf of the individual for this purpose (in a manner specified by the competent authority of Canada), which amount shall be no less than the individual's cost of the property as determined for purposes of Canadian tax and no greater than the fair market value of the property.

2. In determining the estate tax imposed by the United States, the estate of an individual (other than a citizen of the United States) who was a resident of Canada at the time of the individual's death shall be allowed a unified credit equal to the greater of

(*a*) The amount that bears the same ratio to the credit allowed under the law of the United States to the estate of a citizen of the United States as the value of the part of the individual's gross estate that at the time of the individual's death is situated in the United States bears to the value of the individual's entire gross estate wherever situated; and

(*b*) The unified credit allowed to the estate of a non-resident not a citizen of the United States, under the law of the United States.

The amount of any unified credit otherwise allowable under this paragraph shall be reduced by the amount of any credit previously allowed with respect to any gift made by the individual. A credit otherwise allowable under subparagraph (*a*) shall be allowed only if all information necessary for the verification and computation of the credit is provided.

3. In determining the estate tax imposed by the United States on an individual's estate with respect to property that passes to the surviving spouse of the individual (within the meaning of the law of the United States) and that would qualify for the estate tax marital deduction under the law of the United States if the surviving spouse were a citizen of the United States and all applicable elections were properly made (in this paragraph and in paragraph 4 referred to as "qualifying property"), a non-refundable credit computed in accordance with the provisions of paragraph 4 shall be allowed in addition to the unified credit allowed to the estate under paragraph 2 or under the law of the United States, provided that

(*a*) The individual was at the time of death a citizen of the United States or a resident of either Contracting State;

(*b*) The surviving spouse was at the time of the individual's death a resident of either Contracting State;

(*c*) If both the individual and the surviving spouse were residents of the United States at the time of the individual's death, one or both was a citizen of Canada; and

(*d*) The executor of the decedent's estate elects the benefits of this paragraph and waives irrevocably the benefits of any estate tax marital deduction that would be allowed under the law of the United States on a United States Federal estate tax return filed for the individual's estate by the date on which a qualified domestic trust election could be made under the law of the United States.

4. The amount of the credit allowed under paragraph 3 shall equal the lesser of

(*a*) The unified credit allowed under paragraph 2 or under the law of the United States (determined without regard to any credit allowed previously with respect to any gift made by the individual), and

(*b*) The amount of estate tax that would otherwise be imposed by the United States on the transfer of qualifying property.

The amount of estate tax that would otherwise be imposed by the United States on the transfer of qualifying property shall equal the amount by which the estate tax (before allowable credits) that would be imposed by the United States if the qualifying property were included in computing the taxable estate exceeds the estate tax (before allowable credits) that would be so imposed if the qualifying property were not so included. Solely for purposes of determining other credits allowed under the law of the United States, the credit provided under paragraph 3 shall be allowed after such other credits.

5. Where an individual was a resident of the United States immediately before the individual's death, for the purposes of subsections 70(5.2) and (6) of the *Income Tax Act*, both the individual and the individual's spouse shall be deemed to have been resident in Canada immediately before the individual's death. Where a trust that would be a trust described in subsection 70(6) of that Act, if its trustees that were residents or citizens of the United States or domestic corporations under the law of the United States were residents of Canada, requests the competent authority of Canada to do so, the competent authority may agree, subject to terms and conditions satisfactory to such competent authority, to treat the trust for the purposes of that Act as being resident in Canada for such time and with respect to such property as may be stipulated in the agreement.

6. In determining the amount of Canadian tax payable by an individual who immediately before death was a resident of Canada, or by a trust described in subsection 70(6) of the *Income Tax Act* (or a trust which is treated as being resident in Canada under the provisions of paragraph 5), the amount of any Federal or state estate or inheritance taxes payable in the United States (not exceeding, where the individual was a citizen of the United States or a former citizen referred to in paragraph 2 of Article XXIX (Miscellaneous Rules), the amount of estate and inheritance taxes that would have been payable if the individual were not a citizen or former citizen of the United States) in respect of property situated within the United States shall,

(*a*) To the extent that such estate or inheritance taxes are imposed upon the individual's death, be allowed as a deduction from the amount of any Canadian tax otherwise payable by the individual for the taxation year in which the individual died on the total of

(i) Any income, profits or gains of the individual arising (within the meaning of paragraph 3 of Article XXIV (Elimination of Double Taxation)) in the United States in that year, and

(ii) Where the value at the time of the individual's death of the individual's entire gross estate wherever situated (determined under the law of the United States) exceeded 1.2 million U.S. dollars or its equivalent in Canadian dollars, any income, profits or gains of the individual for that year from property situated in the United States at that time, and

(*b*) To the extent that such estate or inheritance taxes are imposed upon the death of the individual's surviving spouse, be allowed as a deduction from the amount of any Canadian tax otherwise payable by the trust for its taxation year in which that spouse dies on any income, profits or gains of the trust for that year arising (within the meaning of paragraph 3 of Article XXIV (Elimination of Double Taxation)) in the United States or from property situated in the United States at the time of death of the spouse.

For purposes of this paragraph, property shall be treated as situated within the United States if it is so treated for estate tax purposes under the law of the United States as in effect on March 17, 1995, subject to any subsequent changes thereof that the competent authorities of the Contracting States have agreed to apply for the purposes of this paragraph. The deduction allowed under this paragraph shall take into account the deduction for any income tax paid or accrued to the United States that is provided under paragraph 2(*a*), 4(*a*) or 5(*b*) of Article XXIV (Elimination of Double Taxation).

7. In determining the amount of estate tax imposed by the United States on the estate of an individual who was a resident or citizen of the United States at the time of death, or upon the death of a surviving spouse with respect to a qualified domestic trust created by such an individual or the individual's executor or surviving spouse, a credit shall be allowed against such tax imposed in respect of property situated outside the United States, for the federal and provincial income taxes payable in Canada in respect of such property by reason of the death of the individual or, in the case of a qualified domestic trust, the individual's surviving spouse. Such credit shall be computed in accordance with the following rules:

(*a*) A credit otherwise allowable under this paragraph shall be allowed regardless of whether the identity of the taxpayer under the law of Canada corresponds to that under the law of the United States.

(*b*) The amount of a credit allowed under this paragraph shall be computed in accordance with the provisions and subject to the limitations of the law of the United States regarding credit for foreign death taxes (as it may be amended from time to time without changing the general principle hereof), as though the income tax imposed by Canada were a creditable tax under that law.

(*c*) A credit may be claimed under this paragraph for an amount of federal or provincial income tax payable in Canada only to the extent that no credit or deduction is claimed for such amount in determining any other tax imposed by the United States, other than the estate tax imposed on property in a qualified domestic trust upon the death of the surviving spouse.

8. Provided that the value, at the time of death, of the entire gross estate wherever situated of an individual who was a resident of Canada (other than a citizen of the United States) at the time of death does not exceed 1.2 million U.S. dollars or its equivalent in Canadian dollars, the United States may impose its estate tax upon property forming part of the estate of the individual only if any gain derived by the individual from the alienation of such property would have been subject to income taxation by the United States in accordance with Article XIII (Gains).

Dentons Canada LLP Commentary: The purpose of Article XXIX B is to better coordinate taxation on death for the two Contracting States. Such coordination is necessary because the United States imposes an estate tax on deceased individuals,, while Canada now applies an income tax on capital gains deemed realized by the individual at death. Article XXIX B also contains other provisions designed to alleviate the applicable taxes in certain situations.

For purposes of Article XXIX B, the term "resident" has the meaning provided by Article IV (Residence) of the Convention. The meaning of the term "resident" for purposes of Article XXIX B, therefore, differs in some respects from its meaning under the estate, gift, and generation-skipping transfer tax provisions of the *Internal Revenue Code*.

Charitable Bequests

Paragraph 1 of Article XXIX B facilitates certain charitable bequests by individuals resident in one Contracting State to an organization resident in the other State.

Prior to the Fifth Protocol, paragraph 1 generally provided that a Contracting State shall accord the same death tax treatment to a bequest by an individual resident in one of the Contracting States to a qualifying exempt organization resident in the other Contracting State as it would have accorded if the organization had been a resident of the first Contracting State. However, there existed confusion concerning the extent of Canadian tax relief available for bequests made by residents of Canada to organizations that did not qualify as "registered charities" for Canadian tax purposes.

The Fifth Protocol amended paragraph 1 by splitting it into separate subparagraphs for gifts by residents of the United States and gifts by residents of Canada. Subparagraph 1(*a*) provides that the U.S. tax consequences of a gift by a U.S. resident to an organization resident in Canada that is described in paragraph 1 of Article XXI (Exempt Organizations) of the Convention shall be determined as if the organization was a resident of the U.S. A bequest by a U.S. citizen or U.S. resident (as defined for estate tax purposes under the *Internal Revenue Code*) to such an exempt organization generally is deductible for U.S. estate tax purposes under section 2055 of the *Internal Revenue Code*, without regard to whether the organization is a U.S. corporation.

Subparagraph 1(*b*) provides that a Canadian-resident individual who, upon death, makes a charitable bequest to a U.S.-resident organization will be treated for Canadian tax purposes as having disposed of the property for proceeds equal to an amount elected on behalf of the individual. The elected amount must be no less than the individual's cost basis in the property, as determined for purposes of Canadian income tax, and must be no greater than the fair market value of the property. This election would provide the individual's estate with the option of either transferring the property to the organization free of Canadian tax or realizing all or a portion of the inherent gain in the property. The election is to be made in a manner to be specified by the competent authority of Canada.

If a decedent is not a U.S. citizen or U.S. resident (as defined for estate tax purposes under the *Internal Revenue Code*), a bequest is deductible for U.S. estate tax purposes, under section 2106(a)(2) of the *Internal Revenue Code*, only if the recipient organization is a U.S. corporation. This would prohibit a Canadian resident from claiming a deduction in respect of its U.S. estate tax liability in connection with the donation of U.S.-*situs* property to a Canadian charitable organization. Under paragraph 1 of Article XXIX B, a U.S. estate tax deduction will be allowed for a bequest by a Canadian resident (as defined under Article IV (Residence)) to a qualifying exempt organization that is a Canadian corporation. However, paragraph 1 does not allow a deduction for U.S. estate tax purposes with respect to any transfer of property that is not subject to U.S. estate tax.

Unified Credit

Paragraph 2 of Article XXIX B grants a "*pro rata*" unified credit to the estate of a Canadian resident decedent for purposes of computing U.S. estate tax. Although the Congress anticipated the negotiation of such *pro rata* unified credits in *Internal Revenue Code* section 2102(b)(3)(A), this is the first convention in which the United States has agreed to give such a credit. However, certain exemption provisions of existing estate and gift tax conventions have been interpreted as providing a *pro rata* unified credit.

Under the *Internal Revenue Code*, the estate of a non-resident not a citizen of the United States, is subject to U.S. estate tax only on its U.S. *situs* assets and is entitled to a unified credit of $13,000, while the estate of a U.S. citizen or U.S. resident is subject to U.S. estate tax on its entire worldwide assets and is entitled to a unified credit, which is indexed for inflation and at the time of publication was $2,117,800. (For purposes of these *Internal Revenue Code* provisions, the term "resident" has the meaning provided for estate tax purposes under the *Internal Revenue Code*.) A lower unified credit is provided for the former category of estates because it is assumed that the estate of a non-resident, not a citizen, generally will hold fewer U.S. *situs* assets, as a percentage of the estate's total assets, and thus will have a lower U.S. estate tax liability. The *pro rata* unified credit provisions of paragraph 2 increase the credit allowed to the estate of a Canadian resident decedent to an amount between $13,000 and $2,117,800 in appropriate cases, to take into account the extent to which the assets of the estate are situated in the United States. Paragraph 2 provides that the amount of the unified credit allowed to the estate of a Canadian resident decedent will in no event be less than the $13,000 allowed under the *Internal Revenue Code* to the estate of a non-resident not a citizen of the United States (subject to the adjustment for prior gift tax unified credits, discussed below). Paragraph 2 does not apply to the estates of U.S. citizen decedents, whether resident in Canada or elsewhere, because such estates receive a unified credit of $2,117,800 under the *Internal Revenue Code*.

Subject to the adjustment for gift tax unified credits, the *pro rata* credit allowed under paragraph 2 is determined by multiplying $2,117,800 by a fraction, the numerator of which is the value of the part of the gross estate situated in the United States and the denominator of which is the value of the entire gross estate wherever situated. Thus, if half of the entire gross estate (by value) of a decedent who was a resident and citizen of Canada were situated in the United States, the estate would be entitled to a *pro rata* unified credit of $1,058,900 (provided that the U.S. estate tax due is not less than that amount). For purposes of the denominator, the entire gross estate wherever situated (i.e., the worldwide estate, determined under U.S. domestic law) is to be taken into account for purposes of the computation. For purposes of the numerator, an estate's assets will be treated as situated in the United States if they are so treated under U.S. domestic law. For these purposes, property shall not be treated as situated in the United States if such property is exempt from the tax imposed for this purpose as a result of any U.S. treaty obligation.

Paragraph 2 restricts the availability of the *pro rata* unified credit in two respects. First, the amount of the unified credit otherwise allowable under paragraph 2 is reduced by the amount of any unified credit previously allowed against U.S. gift tax imposed on any gift by the decedent. This rule reflects the fact that, under U.S. domestic law, a U.S. citizen or U.S. resident individual is allowed a unified credit against the U.S. gift tax on lifetime transfers. However, as a result of the estate tax computation, the individual is entitled only to a total unified credit of $2,117,800, and the amount of the unified credit available for use against U.S. estate tax on the individual's estate is effectively reduced by the amount of any unified credit that has been allowed in respect of gifts by the individual. This rule is reflected by reducing the amount of the *pro rata* unified credit otherwise allowed to the estate of a decedent individual under paragraph 2 by the amount of any unified credit previously allowed with respect to lifetime gifts by that individual. This reduction will be relevant only in rare cases, where the decedent made gifts subject to the U.S. gift tax while a U.S. citizen or U.S. resident (as defined under the *Internal Revenue Code* for U.S. gift tax purposes).

Paragraph 2 also conditions allowance of the *pro rata* unified credit upon the provision of all information necessary to verify and compute the credit. Thus, for example, the estate's representatives will be required to demonstrate satisfactorily both the value of the worldwide estate and the value of the U.S. portion of the estate. Substantiation requirements also apply, of course, with respect to other provisions of the Convention. However, the negotiators believed it advisable to emphasize the substantiation requirements in connection with this provision, because the computation of the *pro rata* unified credit involves certain information not otherwise relevant for U.S. estate tax purposes.

In addition, the amount of the *pro rata* unified credit is limited to the amount of U.S. estate tax imposed on the estate (see section 2102(b)(4) of the *Internal Revenue Code*).

Marital Credit

Paragraph 3 of Article XXIX B allows a special "marital credit" against U.S. estate tax in respect of certain transfers to a surviving spouse. The purpose of this marital credit is to alleviate, in appropriate cases, the impact of the estate tax marital deduction restrictions enacted by the Congress in the *Technical and Miscellaneous Revenue Act* of 1988 ("TAMRA").

It is the firm position of the U.S. Treasury Department that the TAMRA provisions do not violate the non-discrimination provisions of this Convention or any other Convention to which the United States is a party. This is because the estate — not the surviving spouse — is the taxpayer, and the TAMRA provisions treat the estates of non-residents, not citizens, of the United States in the same manner as the estates of U.S. citizen and U.S. resident decedents. However, the U.S. negotiators believed that it was not inappropriate, in the context of the Third Protocol, to ease the impact of those TAMRA provisions upon certain estates of limited value.

Paragraph 3 allows a non-refundable marital credit in addition to the *pro rata* unified credit allowed under paragraph 2 (or, in the case of a U.S. citizen or U.S. resident decedent, the unified credit allowed under U.S. domestic law). However, the marital credit is allowed only in connection with transfers satisfying each of the five conditions set forth in paragraph 3:

- First, the property must be "qualifying property", i.e., it must pass to the surviving spouse (within the meaning of U.S. domestic law) and be property that would have qualified for the estate tax marital deduction under U.S. domestic law if the surviving spouse had been a U.S. citizen and all applicable elections specified by U.S. domestic law had been properly made.
- Second, the decedent must have been, at the time of death, either a resident of Canada or the United States or a citizen of the United States.

Treaties and Related Legislation

- Third, the surviving spouse must have been, at the time of the decedent's death, a resident of either Canada or the United States.
- Fourth, if both the decedent and the surviving spouse were residents of the United States at the time of the decedent's death, at least one of them must have been a citizen of Canada.
- Finally, to limit the benefits of paragraph 3 to relatively small estates, the executor of the decedent's estate is required to elect the benefits of paragraph 3, and to waive irrevocably the benefits of any estate tax marital deduction that would be allowed under U.S. domestic law, on a U.S. federal estate tax return filed by the deadline for making a qualified domestic trust election under *Internal Revenue Code* section 2056A(d). In the case of the estate of a decedent for which the U.S. Federal estate tax return is filed on or before the date on which the Third Protocol entered into force (November 9, 1995), this election and waiver must be made on any return filed to claim a refund pursuant to the special effective date applicable to such estates (discussed below).

Paragraph 4 governs the computation of the marital credit allowed under paragraph 3. It provides that the amount of the marital credit shall equal the lesser of:

(a) the amount of the unified credit allowed to the estate under paragraph 2 or, where applicable, under U.S. domestic law (before reduction for any gift tax unified credit), or

(b) the amount of U.S. estate tax that would otherwise be imposed on the transfer of qualifying property to the surviving spouse.

For this purpose, the amount of U.S. estate tax that would otherwise be imposed on the transfer of qualifying property equals the amount by which:

(a) the estate tax (before allowable credits) that would be imposed if that property were included in computing the taxable estate exceeds

(b) the estate tax (before allowable credits) that would be imposed if the property were not so included.

Property that, by reason of the provisions of paragraph 8 of this Article, is not subject to U.S. estate tax is not taken into account for purposes of this hypothetical computation.

Finally, paragraph 4 provides taxpayers with an ordering rule. The rule states that, solely for purposes of determining any other credits (e.g., the credits for foreign and state death taxes) that may be allowed under U.S. domestic law to the estate, the marital credit shall be allowed after such other credits.

In certain cases, the provisions of paragraphs 3 and 4 may affect the U.S. estate taxation of a trust that would meet the requirements for a qualified terminable interest property ("QTIP") election, for example, a trust with a life income interest for the surviving spouse and a remainder interest for other family members. If, in lieu of making the QTIP election and the qualified domestic trust election, the decedent's executor makes the election described in subparagraph 3(*d*) of this Article, the provisions of *Internal Revenue Code* sections 2044 (regarding inclusion in the estate of the second spouse of certain property for which the marital deduction was previously allowed), 2056A (regarding qualified domestic trusts), and 2519 (regarding dispositions of certain life estates) will not apply. To obtain this treatment, however, the executor is required, under paragraph 3, to irrevocably waive the benefit of any marital deduction allowable under the *Internal Revenue Code* with respect to the trust.

Canadian Treatment of Certain Transfers

The provisions of paragraph 5 relate to the operation of Canadian law. They are intended to provide deferral ("rollover") of the Canadian tax at death for certain transfers to a surviving spouse and to permit the Canadian competent authority to allow such deferral for certain transfers to a trust. For example, they would enable the competent authority to treat a trust that is a qualified domestic trust for U.S. estate tax purposes as a Canadian spousal trust as well for purposes of certain provisions of Canadian tax law and of the Convention. These provisions do not affect U.S. domestic law regarding qualified domestic trusts, nor do they affect the status of U.S. resident individuals for any other purpose.

The Fifth Protocol amended paragraph 5 to clarify that the trust is treated as resident in Canada only with respect to its Canadian property. For example, consider a U.S. decedent with a Canadian spouse who establishes a qualified U.S. trust holding both U.S. and Canadian real property. The decedent's executor elects for U.S. estate tax purposes to treat the entire trust as qualifying for the U.S. estate tax marital deduction. Since the decedent is not a Canadian resident, Canada would only impose capital gains tax on the deemed disposition of the Canadian-*situs* property immediately before death. To defer this Canadian tax, the competent authorities shall, at the request of the trustee, treat the trust as a Canadian spousal trust with respect to the Canadian-*situs* property.

Credit for U.S. Taxes

Under paragraph 6, Canada agrees to give Canadian residents and Canadian resident spousal trusts (or trusts treated as such by virtue of paragraph 5) a deduction from tax (i.e., a credit) for U.S. Federal or state estate or inheritance taxes imposed on U.S. *situs* property of the decedent or the trust. This credit is allowed against the income tax imposed by Canada, in an amount computed in accordance with subparagraph 6(*a*) or (*b*).

Subparagraph 6(*a*) covers the first set of cases — where the U.S. tax is imposed upon a decedent's death. Subparagraph 6(*a*)(i) allows a credit for U.S. tax against the total amount of Canadian income tax payable by the decedent in the taxable year of death on any income, profits, or gains arising in the United States (within the meaning of paragraph 3 of Article XXIV (Elimination of Double Taxation)). For purposes of subparagraph 6(*a*)(i), income, profits, or gains arising in the United States within the meaning of paragraph 3 of Article XXIV include gains deemed realized at death on U.S. *situs* real property and on personal property forming part of the business property of a U.S. permanent establishment or fixed base. (As explained below, these are the only types of property on which the United States may impose its estate tax if the estate is worth the equivalent of US$1.2 million or less.) Income, profits, or gains arising in the United States also include income and profits earned by the decedent during the taxable year of death, to the extent that the United States may tax such amounts under the Convention (e.g., dividends received from a U.S. corporation and wages from the performance of personal services in the United States).

Where the value of the decedent's entire gross estate exceeds US$1.2 million (or the equivalent in Canadian dollars), computed in accordance with the laws of the United States, subparagraph 6(*a*)(ii) allows a credit against the Canadian income tax on any income, profits, or gains from any U.S. *situs* property, in addition to any credit allowed by subparagraph 6(*a*)(i). This provision is broader in scope than is the general rule under subparagraph 6(*a*)(i), because the United States has retained the right to impose its estate tax on all types of property in the case of larger estates.

Subparagraph 6(*b*) provides rules for a second category of cases — where the U.S. tax is imposed upon the death of the surviving spouse. In these cases, Canada agrees to allow a credit against the Canadian tax payable by a trust for its taxable year during which the surviving spouse dies on any income, profits, or gains

(a) arising in the United States on U.S. *situs* real property or business property, or

(b) from property situated in the United States.

These rules are intended to provide a credit for taxes imposed as a result of the death of the surviving spouse in situations involving trusts. To the extent that taxes are imposed on the estate of the surviving spouse, subparagraph 6(*a*) would apply as well. In addition, the competent authorities are authorized to provide relief from double taxation in certain additional circumstances involving trusts, as described above in connection with Article XXVI of the Convention.

The credit allowed under paragraph 6 is subject to certain conditions. First, where the decedent was a U.S. citizen or former citizen (described in paragraph 2 of Article XXIX (Miscellaneous Rules)), paragraph 6 does not obligate Canada to provide a credit for U.S. taxes in excess of the amount of U.S. taxes that would have been payable if the decedent had not been a U.S. citizen or former citizen. Second, the credit allowed under paragraph 6 will be computed after taking into account any deduction for U.S. income tax provided under subparagraph 2(*a*), 4(*a*), or 5(*b*) of Article XXIV (Elimination of Double Taxation). This clarifies that no double credit will be allowed for any amount and provides an ordering rule. Finally, because Canadian domestic law does not contain a definition of U.S. *situs* property for purposes of taxation on death, such a definition is provided for purposes of paragraph 6. To maximize coordination of the credit provisions, the Contracting States agreed to follow the U.S. estate tax law definition as in effect on the date of signature of the Protocol and, subject to competent authority agreement, as it may be amended in the future.

The Diplomatic Notes accompanying the Fifth Protocol clarify the application of paragraph 6 in respect of taxes imposed by a Contracting State on certain types of property. First, if a share (or option in respect of a share) is considered to be property situated in the United States for purposes of Article XXIX B, any employment income attributable to the share (or option) shall also be considered to be income from property situated in the United States for purposes of subparagraph 6(*a*)(ii). Second, if U.S.-*situs* property is held by a tax-exempt Canadian-resident trust, organization, or other arrangement that is operated exclusively to administer pension, retirement, or employee benefits, any income derived through that entity that is attributable to the U.S.-*situs* property will be considered income from property situated in the United States for purposes of subparagraph 6(*a*)(ii). This ensures that the estate tax paid on the underlying property in the United States (if any) will be allowable as a deduction from Canadian income tax.

Credit for Canadian Taxes

Under paragraph 7, the United States agrees to allow a credit against U.S. federal estate tax imposed on the estate of a U.S. resident or U.S. citizen decedent, or upon the death of a surviving spouse with respect to a qualified domestic trust created by such a decedent (or the decedent's executor or surviving spouse). The credit is allowed for Canadian federal and provincial income taxes imposed at death with respect to property of the estate or trust that is situated outside of the United States. As in the case under paragraph 6, the competent authorities also are authorized to provide relief from double taxation in certain cases involving trusts.

The amount of the credit generally will be determined as though the income tax imposed by Canada were a creditable tax under the U.S. estate tax provisions regarding credit for foreign death taxes, in accordance with the provisions and subject to the limitations of *Internal Revenue Code* section 2014. However, subparagraph 7(*a*) clarifies that a credit otherwise allowable under paragraph 7 will not be denied merely because of inconsistencies between U.S. and Canadian law regarding the identity of the taxpayer in the case of a particular taxable event. For example, the fact that the taxpayer is the decedent's estate for purposes of U.S. estate taxation, and the decedent for purposes of Canadian income taxation will not prevent the allowance of a credit under paragraph 7 for Canadian income taxes imposed by reason of the death of the decedent.

In addition, subparagraph 7(*c*) clarifies that the credit against the U.S. estate tax generally may be claimed only to the extent that no credit or deduction is claimed for the same amount of Canadian tax in determining any other U.S. tax. This makes clear, for example, that a credit may not be claimed for the same amount under both this provision and Article XXIV (Elimination of Double Taxation). To prevent double taxation, an exception to this restriction is provided for certain taxes imposed with respect to qualified domestic trusts. Subject to the limitations of subparagraph 7(*c*), the taxpayer may choose between relief under Article XXIV, relief under this paragraph 7, or some combination of the two.

The Diplomatic Notes accompanying the Fifth Protocol provide some guidance in quantifying the credits available under paragraph 7 in respect of the deemed disposition of certain types of property under the *Income Tax Act* (Canada). Specifically, where a tax is imposed in Canada by reason of death in respect of a tax-exempt Canadian-resident trust, organization, or other arrangement that is operated exclusively to administer pension, retirement, or employee benefits, that tax shall be considered to be imposed in respect of property situated in Canada for purposes of paragraph 7. This ensures that Canadian income tax will be allowable as a credit against any U.S. estate tax.

Relief for Small Estates

Under paragraph 8, the United States agrees to limit the application of its estate tax in the case of certain small estates of Canadian resident decedents. This provision is intended to eliminate the "trap for the unwary" that exists for such decedents, in the absence of an estate tax Convention between the United States and Canada. In the absence of sophisticated estate tax planning, such decedents may inadvertently subject their estates to U.S. estate tax liability by holding shares of U.S. corporate stock or other U.S. *situs* property. U.S. resident decedents are already protected in this regard by the provisions of Article XIII (Gains) of the present Convention, which prohibit Canada from imposing its income tax on gains deemed realized at death by U.S. residents on such property.

Paragraph 8 provides relief only in the case of Canadian resident decedents whose entire gross estates wherever situated (i.e., worldwide gross estates determined under U.S. law) have a value, at the time of death, not exceeding $1.2 million. Paragraph 8 provides that the United States may impose its estate tax upon property forming part of such estates only if any gain on alienation of the property would have been subject to U.S. income taxation under Article XIII (Gains). For estates with a total value not exceeding $1.2 million, this provision has the effect of permitting the United States to impose its estate tax only on real property situated in the United States, within the meaning of Article XIII, and personal property forming part of the business property of a U.S. permanent establishment or fixed base.

Saving Clause Exceptions

Certain provisions of Article XXIX B are included in the list of exceptions to the general "saving clause" of Article XXIX (Miscellaneous Rules). To the extent that an exception from the saving clause is provided for a provision, each Contracting State is required to allow the benefits of that provision to its residents (and, in the case of the United States, its citizens), notwithstanding the saving clause. General saving clause exceptions are provided for paragraphs 1, 5, and 6 of Article XXIX B. Saving clause exceptions are provided for paragraphs 2, 3, 4, and 7, except for the estates of former U.S. citizens referred to in paragraph 2 of Article XXIX.

Effective Dates

Paragraphs 2 through 8 of Article XXIX B and the specified related provisions generally took effect with respect to deaths occurring after the date on which the Third Protocol entered into force (i.e., the date on which the instruments of ratification were exchanged, November 9, 1995). However, the benefits of those provisions were made available through special retroactive effective dates for deaths occurring after November 10, 1988, provided that a claim for refund due as a result of these provisions was filed within the required time frame of the later of one year from the date on which the Third Protocol entered into force or the date on which the applicable period for filing such a claim expired under the domestic law of the Contracting State concerned. The general effective dates set forth in Article 21 of the Protocol otherwise apply.

It is unusual for the United States to agree to retrospective effective dates. In this case, however, the negotiators believed that retrospective application was not inappropriate, given the fact that the TAMRA provisions were the impetus for negotiation of the Third Protocol and that the negotiations commenced soon after the enactment of TAMRA. The United States has agreed to retrospective effective dates in certain other instances (e.g., in the case of the U.S.–Germany Estate Tax Treaty). The retrospective effective dates apply reciprocally, so that they will benefit the estates of U.S. decedents as well as Canadian decedents.

History: Paragraph 1 of Article XXIX B was deleted and replaced by paragraph 1 of Article 26 of the Fifth Protocol of this Convention, and formerly read:

1. Where the property of an individual who is a resident of a Contracting State passes by reason of the individual's death to an organization referred to in paragraph 1 of Article XXI (Exempt Organizations), the tax consequences in a Contracting State arising out of the passing of the property shall apply as if the organization were a resident of that State.

Paragraph 5 of Article XXIX B was deleted and replaced by paragraph 2 of Article 26 of the Fifth Protocol of this Convention, and formerly read:

5. Where an individual was a resident of the United States immediately before the individual's death, for the purposes of subsection 70(6) of the *Income Tax Act*, both the individual and the individual's spouse shall be deemed to have been resident in Canada immediately before the individual's death. Where a trust that would be a trust described in subsection 70(6) of that Act, if its trustees that were residents or citizens of the United States or domestic corporations under the law of the United States were residents of Canada, requests the competent authority of Canada to do so, the competent authority may agree, subject to terms and conditions satisfactory to such competent authority, to treat the trust for the purposes of that Act as being resident in Canada for such time as may be stipulated in the agreement.

Article XXIX B was added by Article 19 of the Third Protocol to this Convention.

Article XXX — Entry into Force

1. This Convention shall be subject to ratification in accordance with the applicable procedures of each Contracting State and instruments of ratification shall be exchanged at Ottawa as soon as possible.

2. The Convention shall enter into force upon the exchange of instruments of ratification and, subject to the provisions of paragraph 3, its provisions shall have effect:

(*a*) For tax withheld at the source on income referred to in Articles X (Dividends), XI (Interest), XII (Royalties) and XVIII (Pensions and Annuities), with respect to amounts paid or credited on or after the first day of the second month next following the date on which the Convention enters into force;

(*b*) For other taxes, with respect to taxable years beginning on or after the first day of January next following the date on which the Convention enters into force; and

(*c*) Notwithstanding the provisions of subparagraph (*b*), for the taxes covered by paragraph 4 of Article XXIX (Miscellaneous Rules) with respect to all taxable years referred to in that paragraph.

3. For the purposes of applying the United States foreign tax credit in relation to taxes paid or accrued to Canada:

(*a*) Notwithstanding the provisions of paragraph 2(*a*) of Article II (Taxes Covered), the tax on 1971 undistributed income on hand imposed by Part IX of the *Income Tax Act* of Canada shall be considered to be an income tax for distributions made on or after the first day of January 1972 and before the first day of January 1979 and shall be considered to be imposed upon the recipient of a distribution, in the proportion that the distribution out of undistributed income with respect to which the tax has been paid bears to 85 per cent of such undistributed income;

(*b*) The principles of paragraph 6 of Article XXIV (Elimination of Double Taxation) shall have effect for taxable years beginning on or after the first day of January 1976; and

(*c*) The provisions of paragraph 1 of Article XXIV shall have effect for taxable years beginning on or after the first day of January 1981.

Any claim for refund based on the provisions of this paragraph may be filed on or before June 30 of the calendar year following that in which the Convention enters into force, notwithstanding any rule of domestic law to the contrary.

4. Subject to the provisions of paragraph 5, the 1942 Convention shall cease to have effect for taxes for which this Convention has effect in accordance with the provisions of paragraph 2.

5. Where any greater relief from tax would have been afforded by any provision of the 1942 Convention than under this Convention, any such provision shall continue to have effect for the first taxable year with respect to which the provisions of this Convention have effect under paragraph 2(*b*).

6. The 1942 Convention shall terminate on the last date on which it has effect in accordance with the preceding provisions of this Article.

7. The Exchange of Notes between the United States and Canada dated August 2 and September 17, 1928, providing for relief from double income taxation on shipping profits, is terminated. Its provisions shall cease to have effect with respect to taxable years beginning on or after the first day of January next following the date on which this Convention enters into force.

8. The provisions of the Convention between the Government of Canada and the Government of the United States of America for the Avoidance of Double Taxation and the Prevention of Fiscal Evasion with Respect to Taxes on the Estates of Deceased Persons signed at Washington on February 17, 1961 shall continue to have effect with respect to estates of persons deceased prior to the first day of January next following the date on which this Convention enters into force but shall cease to have effect with respect to estates of persons deceased on or after that date. Such Convention shall terminate on the last date on which it has effect in accordance with the preceding sentence.

Dentons Canada LLP Commentary: Article XXX of the Convention contains detailed transitional rules. However, the Convention was first subject to ratification in accordance with the applicable procedures of each country, and the instruments of ratification had to be exchanged. On June 28, 1984, the United States ratified the Convention and its first two Protocols while, on that same date, Bill S-14, the Canadian legislation to implement the 1980 Canada–U.S. Income Tax Convention together with its first two Protocols, received Royal Assent. On August 16, 1984, all necessary instruments of ratification were exchanged. Thus, the Convention, as amended by its two Protocols entered into force on that day. Therefore, pursuant to paragraph 3, and subject to paragraph 3 of Article XXX, as discussed below, the Convention has effect with respect to source country taxation of dividends, interest, royalties, pensions, annuities, alimony, and child support for amounts paid or credited on or after October 1, 1984 being the first day of the second calendar month after the date on which the instruments of ratification were exchanged. For other taxes, the Convention takes effect for the first taxable year beginning on or after January 1, 1985. With respect to relief from U.S. social security taxes as provided by paragraph 4 of Article XXIX (Miscellaneous Rules), the Convention has effect for prior taxable years provided they are not barred by the statute of limitations.

Paragraph 3 provides special effective dates for U.S. foreign tax credit computations with respect to taxes paid or accrued to Canada. It provides that the tax on 1971 undistributed income on hand (UIOH) imposed by Part IX of the *Income Tax Act* (Canada) is to be considered an income tax for distributions made on or after January 1, 1972 and before January 1, 1979. It also provides that the principle of paragraph 6 of Article XXIV (Elimination of Double Taxation), which provides for the sourcing of certain dividend, interest and royalty income to eliminate double taxation of U.S. citizens residing in Canada, has effect for taxable years beginning on or after January 1, 1976. In addition, the provisions of paragraph 1 of Article XXIV (Elimination of Double Taxation) and the source rules of that Article will have effect for taxable years beginning on or after January 1, 1981. For earlier taxable years, the Convention does not ensure the ability to claim a credit for Canadian tax. A claim for a refund based on the provisions of paragraph 3 may be filed on or before June 30, 1985 notwithstanding the U.S. statutes of limitations or other rules of U.S. domestic law to the contrary.

Paragraph 4 provides that, except as provided in paragraph 5, the 1942 Convention ceased to have effect for taxes for which the Convention has effect under the provisions of paragraph 2 of Article XXX. For example, under paragraph 2 of Article XXX, the Convention had effect with respect to taxes withheld at source on dividends paid as of October 1, 1984. Therefore, subject to paragraph 5, the provisions of the 1942 Convention will not have effect with respect to such withholding taxes. Therefore, the general 15 per cent withholding rate limitation on dividends that applied under the 1942 Convention ceased to have application with effect from October 1, 1984.

Generally, paragraph 5 provides that the provisions of the 1942 Convention that are more favourable than the provisions of the Convention will remain in effect for the period through the first taxable year beginning on or after January 1, 1985. Paragraph 5 applies to all provisions of the 1942 Convention, not just those provisions of the Convention known as "other taxes" under subparagraph 2(*b*) of Article XXIX. Thus, for example, a U.S. resident with a taxable year beginning on April 1, 1985 and ending on March 31, 1986 that receives natural resource royalties from Canada would be subject to a 25 per cent tax under Article VI (income from Real Property) and Part XIII of the *Income Tax Act* (Canada), but would be subject to only a 15 per cent tax under Article XI of the 1942 Convention. Under the provisions of paragraph 5, the greater benefits of the 1942 Convention would continue to apply to such royalties paid or credited to the U.S. resident through to March 31, 1986.

The 1942 Convention terminated on the last of the dates on which it has effect in accordance with the provisions of paragraphs 4 and 5 of this Article.

The Exchange of Notes between Canada and the United States on August 2 and September 17, 1928 concerning shipping profits was terminated for taxable years beginning on or after January 1, 1985. For all practical purposes, Article V of the 1942 Convention had previously superseded the effectiveness of the Exchange of Notes.

Paragraph 8 provides that the Estate Tax Treaty between Canada and the United States will continue to have effect for estates or persons who die prior to January 1, 1985. However, this Estate Tax Treaty will be terminated with respect to estates of persons who die on or after that date. This reflects the fact that Canada has repealed its federal estate tax law and now taxes transfers arising on death under provisions of the *Income Tax Act* (Canada).

Entry into Force of the Third, Fourth, and Fifth Protocols

Article 20 of the Third Protocol did not amend the text of the Convention. It states two understandings between the Contracting States regarding future action relating to matters dealt with in the Protocol. Paragraph 1 requires the appropriate authorities of the Contracting States to consult on two matters within three years from the date on which the Third Protocol entered into force. First, they will consult with a view to agreeing to further reductions in withholding rates on dividends, interest and royalties under Articles X, XI, and XII, respectively. This provision reflects the fact that, although the Third Protocol did significantly reduce withholding rates, the United States remains interested in even greater reductions, to further open the capital markets and fulfill the objectives of the North American Free Trade Agreement. Second, the appropriate authorities of the Contracting States will consult about the rules in Article XXIX A (Limitation on Benefits). It was anticipated that, by that time, both Contracting States would have had an opportunity to observe the operation of the Article, and the United States would have had greater experience with the corresponding provisions in other U.S. tax treaties containing similar limitations on benefits provisions.

Paragraph 2 of Article 20 also requires consultations between the appropriate authorities, after the three-year period from the date on which the Protocol entered into force (November 9, 1995), to determine whether to implement the arbitration procedure provided for in paragraph 6 of Article XXVI (Mutual Agreement Procedure), added by Article 14 of the Protocol. The three-year period was intended to give the authorities an opportunity to consider how arbitration has functioned in other tax conventions, such as the U.S.–Germany Convention, before implementing it under this Convention. The Fifth Protocol, and the exchange of Diplomatic Notes thereunder, clearly signals an end to the three-year observation period (which lasted for more than a decade). In the Fifth Protocol, Canada and the U.S. have introduced a mandatory arbitration mechanism significantly different than what Canada has ever previously agreed to include in a tax treaty (and to which the United States has only recently included in its recent treaties with Belgium and Germany).

Article 21 of the Third Protocol provides the rules for the entry into force of the Protocol provisions. The Protocol was subject to ratification according to the normal procedures in both Contracting States, and instruments of ratification were exchanged on November 9, 1995, at which time the Protocol entered into force.

Subparagraph 2(*a*) of Article 21 generally governs the entry into force of the provisions of the Protocol for taxes withheld at source, while subparagraph 2(*b*) generally governs for other taxes. Paragraphs 3, 4, and 5 provide special rules for certain provisions.

Subparagraph 2(*a*) provides that the Protocol generally will have effect for taxes withheld at source on dividends, interest, royalties, and pensions and annuities (other than social security benefits), under Articles X, XI, XII, and XVIII, respectively, with respect to amounts paid or credited on or after the first day of the second month following the date on which the Protocol entered into force (i.e., November 9, 1995). The effective date is, accordingly, January 1, 1996. However, with respect to direct investment dividends, the 5 per cent rate specified in subparagraph 2(*a*) of Article X will be phased in as follows:

(1) for dividends paid or credited after the first day of the second month referred to above, and during 1995, the rate of withholding will be 7 per cent;

(2) for dividends paid or credited after the first day of the second month, and during 1996, the rate will be 6 per cent; and

(3) for dividends paid or credited after the first day of the second month and after 1996, the rate will be 5 per cent.

For taxes other than those withheld at source and for the provisions of the Third Protocol relating to taxes withheld on social security benefits, the Protocol has effect with respect to taxable years beginning on or after January 1, 1996. However, the rate of tax applicable to the branch tax under paragraph 6 of Article X (Dividends) will be phased in a manner similar to the direct investment dividend withholding tax rate; that is, a rate of 6 per cent will apply for taxable years beginning in 1996 and a rate of 5 per cent will apply for taxable years beginning in 1997 and subsequent years.

Paragraph 3 of Article 21 provides a special effective date for the provisions of Article XXVI A (Assistance in Collection) of the Convention, introduced by Article 15 of the Third Protocol. Collection assistance may be granted by a Contracting State with respect to a request by the other Contracting State for a claim finally determined by the requesting State after the date that is 10 years before the date of the entry into force of the Protocol. Therefore, because instruments of ratification were exchanged on November 9, 1995, assistance may be given by Canada under Article XXVI A for a claim that was finally determined in the United States at any time after November 9, 1985.

Paragraph 4 of Article 21 provides special effective date provisions for paragraphs 2 through 7 of Article XXIX B (Taxes Imposed by Reason of Death) of the Convention, introduced by Article 19 of the Third Protocol, and certain related provisions elsewhere in the Convention. These special effective date provisions are discussed above in connection with Article XXIX B.

Finally, paragraph 5 of Article 21 provides a special effective date for paragraph 2 of Article 3 of the Third Protocol, which provides a residence rule for certain "continued" corporations. Under paragraph 5, the residence rule for such corporations has effect for taxable years beginning on or after January 1, 1996.

Similarly, Article 3 of the Fourth Protocol does not amend the text of the Convention but provides for the Protocol's entry into force. The Fourth Protocol was signed in 1997 and amends the provisions of Article XIII (Gains) relating to real property and Article XVIII (Pensions and Annuities) dealing with social security benefits. In appropriate circumstances, reference needs to be made to the provisions of Article 3 of the Fourth Protocol.

Paragraph 2 of Article 27 of the Fifth Protocol provides that the Fifth Protocol will enter into force on the date of the later of the receipt of notification from each of Canada and the United States confirming the domestic ratification of the Fifth Protocol, or January 1, 2008, whichever is later. Canada gave Royal Assent to the Fifth Protocol on December 14, 2007, and the U.S. Senate ratified the Fifth Protocol on September 23, 2008. All notification precedures were complete on December 15, 2008, meaning that the Fifth Protocol entered into force on that date.

Subparagraph 2(*a*) provides that the Protocol generally will have effect for taxes withheld at source with respect to amounts paid or credited on or after February 1, 2009 (i.e., the first day of the second month that began after the date on which the Protocol entered into force). However, with respect to interest payments under Article XI, the reduction/elimination of withholding tax would be effective at different dates, depending on whether the interest is paid between related or unrelated parties. In this respect, subparagraph 3(*d*) of the Fifth Protocol provides specific rules governing to the effective dates for withholding in respect of interest paid or credited during *the first two calendar years that end after the entry into force of the Fifth Protocol*, meaning that the elimination or reduction of withholding tax is intended to have retroactive effect to the beginning of the calendar year in which the Fifth Protocol is ratified.

In respect of interest paid between unrelated parties, the interest withholding tax rate would be nil as of the first day of the calendar year in which the Fifth Protocol entered into force. The Fifth Protocol entered into force on December 15, 2008, meaning that this exception became effective in respect of interest paid on January 1, 2008. If the payer is a resident of Canada, the exemption from withholding tax under domestic Canadian law (discussed above), became effective as of January 1, 2008. Accordingly, the effective date for the treaty-based elimination of withholding tax in respect of arm's length debt is generally relevant only insofar as the United States may levy a domestic withholding tax on interest paid by a resident of the United States to an arm's length resident of Canada or if the interest does not qualify for Canada's domestic withholding tax exemption.

In respect of interest paid on debt obligations between related parties and that was not otherwise exempt from withholding tax pursuant to former paragraph 3 (discussed above), the exemption is gradually phased in as follows:

(a) the withholding tax rate is reduced to 7 per cent during the first calendar year that ends after the entry into force of this paragraph (i.e., interest paid between January 1, 2008 and December 31, 2008);

(b) the withholding tax rate is reduced to 4 per cent during the second calendar year that ends after the entry into force of this paragraph (i.e., interest paid between January 1, 2009 and December 31, 2009); and

(c) the withholding tax rate is completely eliminated in respect of interest paid after December 31, 2009.

In respect of all other taxes, subparagraph 2(*b*) provides that the Protocol will have effect for taxation years that begin after 2008. Accordingly, a taxpayer that has a fiscal year end other than December 31 will not benefit from these amendments until the first day of its taxation year beginning in 2009.

Notwithstanding these general coming into force dates, the Fifth Protocol provides specific effective dates for certain provisions.

Subparagraph 3(*a*) of Article 27 of the Fifth Protocol provides that the amendments to paragraph 3 of Article IV (Residence), which address the residency of dually-chartered companies, shall have effect with respect to corporate continuances effected after September 7, 2000 (i.e., the date upon which Canada and the United States announced that such a change would be forthcoming).

Subparagraph 3(*b*) of Article 27 of the Fifth Protocol provides that new paragraph 7 of Article IV (Residence) comes into effect on January 1, 2010 (i.e., the first day of the third calendar year that ends after the Fifth Protocol enters into force). Paragraph 7 addresses the entitlement of a resident of a Contracting State to benefits under the Convention with respect to amounts derived through certain hybrid entities resident in the other Contracting State that are regarded as fiscally transparent in the first-mentioned State but a separate legal entity in the other State (i.e., Nova Scotia unlimited liability companies that have elected to be disregarded for U.S. tax purposes).

Subparagraph 3(*c*) of Article 27 of the Fifth Protocol provides that paragraph 9 of Article V of the Convention, which deems certain service providers resident in one Contracting State to have a permanent establishment in the other Contracting State, will have effect as of the third taxable year that ends after the Fifth Protocol enters into force. Accordingly, the effective date of this provision is dependent on the fiscal year end of the particular taxpayer. Regardless of this coming into force date, any days of presence, services rendered, or gross active business revenues that occur or arise prior to January 1, 2010 would not be taken into consideration in determining whether a non-resident service provider has a permanent establishment in the other State under paragraph 7.

Subparagraph 3(*e*) of Article 27 of the Fifth Protocol provides that the changes to paragraphs 5 and 7 of Article XIII (Gains), which deal respectively with the ability of a Contracting State to tax gains of a former resident and the requirement that a Contracting State recognized deemed gains realized in the other Contracting State upon emigration, would have effect with respect to alienations of property taking place after September 17, 2000.

Subparagraph 3(*f*) of Article 27 of the Fifth Protocol provides that the changes to Article XXVI (Mutual Agreement Procedure), governing the new mandatory arbitration procedure, are effective for cases that are under consideration by the competent authorities as of December 15, 2008 (i.e., the date on which the Fifth Protocol entered into force) and for all cases that come under consideration after that time.

Subparagraph 3(*g*) of Article 27 of the Fifth Protocol provides that the changes to subparagraph 8(*a*) of Article XXVI A (Assistance in Collection), which deals with the circumstances in which a Contracting State is not required to provide assistance to the other State, shall have effect for revenue claims finally determined by an applicant State after November 9, 1985.

The changes to Article XXIX A (Limitation on Benefits) come into effect according to the general effective dates described in paragraph 2 of Article 27 of the Fifth Protocol. Specifically, in respect of taxes withheld at source, the limitation on benefits provision applies for amounts paid on or after February 1, 2009. Even though subparagraph 3(*d*) of Article 27 of the Fifth Protocol provides reductions of interest withholding tax retroactively to January 1, 2008, there is no similar retroactive application of the limitation on benefits provision to deny the availability of these reduced withholding tax rates. In respect of all other taxes, the limitation on benefits provision applies for taxation years that begin after 2008.

History: Paragraph 3 of Article XXX was amended by Article XIV of the First Protocol to this Convention, and formerly read:

3. For the purposes of applying the United States foreign tax credit in relation to taxes paid or accrued to Canada:

(*a*) Notwithstanding the provisions of paragraph 2(*a*) of Article II (Taxes Covered), the tax on 1971 undistributed income on hand imposed by Part IX of the *Income Tax Act* of Canada shall be considered to be an income tax for distributions made on or after the first day of January 1972 and before the first day of January 1979, and shall be considered imposed upon the recipient of a distribution, in the proportion that the distribution out of undistributed income with respect to which the tax has been paid bears to 85 per cent of such undistributed income; and

(*b*) The principles of paragraph 6 of Article XXIV (Elimination of Double Taxation) shall have effect for taxable years beginning on or after the first day of January 1976.

Article XXXI — Termination

1. This Convention shall remain in force until terminated by a Contracting State.

2. Either Contracting State may terminate the Convention at any time after 5 years from the date on which the Convention enters into force provided that at least 6 months' prior notice of termination has been given through diplomatic channels.

3. Where a Contracting State considers that a significant change introduced in the taxation laws of the other Contracting State should be accommodated by a modification of the Convention, the Con-

tracting States shall consult together with a view to resolving the matter; if the matter cannot be satisfactorily resolved, the first-mentioned State may terminate the Convention in accordance with the procedures set forth in paragraph 2, but without regard to the 5-year limitation provided therein.

4. In the event the Convention is terminated, the Convention shall cease to have effect:

(*a*) For tax withheld at the source on income referred to in Articles X (Dividends), XI (Interest), XII (Royalties), XVIII (Pensions and Annuities) and paragraph 2 of Article XXII (Other Income), with respect to amounts paid or credited on or after the first day of January next following the expiration of the 6 months' period referred to in paragraph 2; and

(*b*) For other taxes, with respect to taxable years beginning on or after the first day of January next following the expiration of the 6 months' period referred to in paragraph 2.

Dentons Canada LLP Commentary: The Convention is to continue in force indefinitely, but either country may terminate it at any time after August 16, 1989 (five years from its entry into force) by giving at least six months' prior notice through diplomatic channels. If one of the countries determines that a significant change introduced in the laws of the other country should be accommodated by a modification to the Convention, the countries are to consult together with a view to resolving the matter. If the matter cannot be satisfactorily resolved, paragraph 3 of this Article provides a special termination rule. The country that feels that the other country has modified its laws in a significant way may terminate the Convention by giving six months' notice through diplomatic channels, even if the five-year period has not elapsed.

If terminated, paragraph 4 provides that the termination will be effective for tax withheld at source under Articles X (Dividends), XI (Interest), XII (Royalties), and XVI (Pensions and Annuities), and under paragraph 2 of Article XXII (Other income), with respect to amounts paid or credited on after the first day of January following the expiration of the six-month period of notice. On termination, in the case of other taxes, the Convention shall cease to have effect with respect to taxable years beginning on or after January 1 following the expiration of the six-month period.

IN WITNESS WHEREOF, the undersigned, being duly authorized thereto by their respective governments, have signed this Convention.

DONE in two copies at Washington this twenty-sixth day of September, 1980, in the French and English languages, each text being equally authentic.

FOR THE GOVERNMENT OF CANADA

Allan J. MacEachen

FOR THE GOVERNMENT OF THE UNITED STATES OF AMERICA

G. William Miller

Third Protocol — Entry into Force

[Articles 20 and 21 of the Third Protocol do not amend the text of the Convention and are therefore reproduced seperately in this Appendix. The Third Protocol was signed at Washington on August 31, 1994, and a revised version of this Third Protocol was signed at Washington on March 17, 1995. The Third Protocol of March 17, 1995 was ratified on November 9, 1995, on which day it also came into force.]

Article 20

1. The appropriate authorities of the Contracting States shall consult within a three-year period from the date on which this Protocol enters into force with respect to further reductions in withholding taxes provided in the Convention, and with respect to the rules in Article XXIX A (Limitation on Benefits) of the Convention.

2. The appropriate authorities of the Contracting States shall consult after a three-year period from the date on which the Protocol enters into force in order to determine whether it is appropriate to make the exchange of notes referred to in of Article XXVI (Mutual Agreement Procedure) of the Convention.

Article 21

1. This Protocol shall be subject to ratification in accordance with the applicable procedures in Canada and the United States and instruments of ratification shall be exchanged as soon as possible.

2. The Protocol shall enter into force upon the exchange of instruments of ratification, and shall have effect:

(*a*) For tax withheld at the source on income referred to in Articles X (Dividends), XI (Interest), XII (Royalties) and XVIII (Pensions and Annuities) of the Convention, except on income referred to in paragraph 5 of Article XVIII of the Convention (as it read before the entry into force of this Protocol), with respect to amounts paid or credited on or after the first day of the second month next following the date on which the Protocol enters into force, except that the reference in paragraph 2(*a*) of Article X (Dividends) of the Convention, as amended by the Protocol, to "5 per cent" shall be read, in its application to amounts paid or credited on or after that first day:

(i) Before 1996, as "7 per cent"; and

(ii) After 1995 and before 1997, as "6 per cent"; and

(*b*) For other taxes, with respect to taxable years beginning on or after the first day of January next following the date on which the Protocol enters into force, except that the reference in paragraph 6 of Article X (Dividends) of the Convention, as amended by the Protocol, to "5 per cent" shall be read, in its application to taxable years beginning on or after that first day and ending before 1997, as "6 per cent".

3. Notwithstanding the provisions of paragraph 2, Article XXVI A (Assistance in Collection) of the Convention shall have effect for revenue claims finally determined by a requesting State after the date that is 10 years before the date on which the Protocol enters into force.

4. Notwithstanding the provisions of paragraph 2, paragraphs 2 through 7 of Article XXIX B (Taxes Imposed by Reason of Death) of the Convention (and paragraph 2 of Article II (Taxes Covered) and paragraph 3(*a*) of Article XXIX (Miscellaneous Rules) of the Convention, as amended by the Protocol, to the extent necessary to implement paragraphs 2 through 7 of Article XXIX B (Taxes Imposed by Reason of Death) of the Convention) shall, notwithstanding any limitation imposed under the law of a Contracting State on the assessment, reassessment or refund with respect to a person's return, have effect with respect to deaths occurring after the date on which the Protocol enters into force and, provided that any claim for refund by reason of this sentence is filed within one year of the date on which the Protocol enters into force or within the otherwise applicable period for filing such claims under domestic law, with respect to benefits provided under any of those paragraphs with respect to deaths occurring after November 10, 1988.

5. Notwithstanding the provisions of paragraph 2, paragraph 2 of Article 3 of the Protocol shall have effect with respect to taxable years beginning on or after the first day of January next following the date on which the Protocol enters into force.

IN WITNESS WHEREOF, the undersigned, duly authorized thereto by their respective Governments, have signed this Protocol.

DONE in two copies at ________ this _____ day of _____ 199__ in the English and French languages, each text being equally authentic.

FOR THE GOVERNMENT OF CANADA

Robert Wright

FOR THE GOVERNMENT OF THE UNITED STATES OF AMERICA

Richard Hecklinger

Fourth Protocol — Entry into Force

[Article 3 of the Fourth Protocol does not amend the text of the Convention and is therefore reproduced separately in this Appendix. The Fourth Protocol was signed at Ottawa on July 29, 1997 and entered into force on December 16, 1997.]

Article 3

1. This Protocol shall be subject to ratification in accordance with the applicable procedures in Canada and the United States and instruments of ratification shall be exchanged as soon as possible.

2. This Protocol shall enter into force upon the exchange of instruments of ratification, and shall have effect as follows:

(*a*) Article 1 of this Protocol shall have effect as of April 26, 1995; and

(*b*) Article 2 of this Protocol shall have effect with respect to amounts paid or credited to a resident of the other Contracting State after 1995, except that where a Contracting State has, in accordance with the Convention read without reference to this Protocol, imposed a tax on benefits paid or credited under the social security legislation in that State, and those benefits are paid or credited after 1995 and

(i) before the calendar year in which this Protocol enters into force, if this Protocol enters into force before September 1 of that year, or

(ii) before the end of the calendar year in which this Protocol enters into force, if this Protocol enters into force after August 31 of that year,

Article 2 shall only have effect with respect to such benefits (referred to in this Article as "source-taxed benefits") as described in paragraphs 3, 4 and 5.

3. With respect to source-taxed benefits paid by a Contracting State to a resident of the other Contracting State, Article 2 applies only if the resident has, within three years after the date on which this Protocol enters into force, applied to the competent authority of the first-mentioned Contracting State for a refund of the tax imposed on the benefits. However, with respect to source-taxed benefits paid by the United States to a resident of Canada, the competent authority of Canada shall:

(*a*) apply for and receive such refund on behalf of the resident;

(*b*) remit to the resident, in accordance with the law of Canada governing refunds of income tax overpayments, such refund less any tax imposed in Canada on the benefits in accordance with Article 2 of this Protocol; and

(*c*) make the application referred to in subparagraph (*a*) only if the additional tax that would be imposed in Canada on the benefits, on the assumption that Article 2 of this Protocol applied, would be less than the tax imposed in the United States on the benefits as a result of paragraph 5 of Article XVIII (Pensions and Annuities) of the Convention read without reference to this Protocol.

4. All taxes refunded as a result of this Protocol shall be refunded without interest and interest on any taxes of a resident of a Contracting State assessed as a result of this Protocol shall be computed as though those taxes became payable no earlier than December 31 of the year following the year in which this Protocol enters into force.

5. The competent authorities of the Contracting States shall establish procedures for making or revoking the application referred to in paragraph 3 and shall agree on such additional procedures as are necessary to ensure the appropriate implementation of this Protocol.

IN WITNESS WHEREOF, the undersigned, being duly authorized thereto by their respective Governments, have signed this Protocol.

Done at Ottawa in duplicate, in the English and French languages, both texts being equally authentic, this 29th day of July, 1997.

FOR THE GOVERNMENT OF CANADA

Michael Leir

FOR THE GOVERNMENT OF THE UNITED STATES OF AMERICA

Vladimir Sambaiew

Fifth Protocol — Entry into Force

[Article 27 of the Fifth Protocol specifies the effective dates for the amendments in the Fifth Protocol and is reproduced separately in this Appendix. The Fifth Protocol was signed on September 21, 2007 at Chelsea, and entered into force on December 15, 2008.]

Article 27

1. This Protocol shall be subject to ratification in accordance with the applicable procedures in the United States and Canada. The Contracting States shall notify each other in writing, through diplomatic channels, when their respective applicable procedures have been satisfied.

2. This Protocol shall enter into force on the date of the later of the notifications referred to in paragraph 1, or January 1, 2008, whichever is later. The provisions of this Protocol shall have effect:

(*a*) In respect of taxes withheld at source, for amounts paid or credited on or after the first day of the second month that begins after the date on which this Protocol enters into force;

(*b*) In respect of other taxes, for taxable years that begin after (or, if the later of the notifications referred to in paragraph 1 is dated in 2007, taxable years that begin in and after) the calendar year in which this Protocol enters into force.

3. Notwithstanding paragraph 2,

(*a*) Paragraph 1 of Article 2 of this Protocol shall have effect with respect to corporate continuations effected after September 17, 2000;

(*b*) New paragraph 7 of Article IV (Residence) of the Convention as added by Article 2 of this Protocol shall have effect as of the first day of the third calendar year that ends after this Protocol enters into force;

(*c*) Article 3 of this Protocol shall have effect as of the third taxable year that ends after this Protocol enters into force, but in no event shall it apply to include, in the determination of whether an enterprise is deemed to provide services through a permanent establishment under paragraph 9 of Article V (Permanent Establishment) of the Convention, any days of presence, services rendered, or gross active business revenues that occur or arise prior to January 1, 2010;

(*d*) In applying Article 6 of this Protocol to interest paid or credited during the first two calendar years that end after entry into force of this Protocol, paragraph 1 of Article XI (Interest) of the Convention shall be read as follows:

1. Interest arising in a Contracting State and beneficially owned by a resident of the other Contracting State may be taxed only in that other State. However, if the interest is not exempt under paragraph 3 of Article XI (Interest) as it read on January 1, 2007, and the payer of the interest and the beneficial owner of the interest are related, or would be deemed to be related if the provisions of paragraph 2 of Article IX (Related Persons) applied for this purpose, such interest may also be taxed in the Contracting State in which it arises, and according to the laws of that State, but the tax so charged shall not exceed the following percentage of the gross amount of the interest:

(*a*) If the interest is paid or credited during the first calendar year that ends after entry into force of this paragraph, 7 percent; and

(*b*) If the interest is paid or credited during the second calendar year that ends after entry into force of this paragraph, 4 percent;

Treaties and Related Legislation

(*e*) Paragraphs 2 and 3 of Article 8 of this Protocol shall have effect with respect to alienations of property that occur (including, for greater certainty, those that are deemed under the law of a Contracting State to occur) after September 17, 2000;

(*f*) Article 21 of this Protocol shall have effect with respect to

(i) Cases that are under consideration by the competent authorities as of the date on which this Protocol enters into force; and

(ii) Cases that come under such consideration after that time,

and the commencement date for a case described in subparagraph (*f*)(i) shall be the date on which the Protocol enters into force; and

(*g*) Article 22 of this Protocol shall have effect for revenue claims finally determined by an applicant State after November 9, 1985.

IN WITNESS WHEREOF the undersigned, being duly authorized thereto by their respective Governments, have signed this Protocol.

DONE in duplicate at Chelsea this twenty-first day of September 2007 in the English and French languages, each text being equally authentic.

FOR THE GOVERNMENT OF CANADA

Jim Flaherty

FOR THE GOVERNMENT OF THE UNITED STATES OF AMERICA

Henry M. Paulson, Jr.

Diplomatic Notes to Fifth Protocol (Annex A)

Protocol Amending the Convention Between Canada and the United States of America With Respect to Taxes on Income and on Capital
Diplomatic Notes: Annex A to the Convention
September 21, 2007

Note no. JLAB-0111

Excellency,

I have the honor to refer to the Protocol (the "Protocol") done today between Canada and the United States of America amending the Convention with Respect to Taxes on Income and on Capital done at Washington on 26 September 1980, as amended by the Protocols done on 14 June 1983, 28 March 1984, 17 March 1995, and 29 July 1997 (the "Convention"), and to propose on behalf of the Government of Canada the following:

In respect of any case where the competent authorities have endeavored but are unable to reach a complete agreement under Article XXVI (Mutual Agreement Procedure) of the Convention regarding the application of one or more of the following Articles of the Convention: IV (Residence) (but only insofar as it relates to the residence of a natural person), V (Permanent Establishment), VII (Business Profits), IX (Related Persons), and XII (Royalties) (but only (i) insofar as Article XII might apply in transactions involving related persons to whom Article IX might apply, or (ii) to an allocation of amounts between royalties that are taxable under paragraph 2 thereof and royalties that are exempt under paragraph 3 thereof), binding arbitration shall be used to determine such application, unless the competent authorities agree that the particular case is not suitable for determination by arbitration. In addition, the competent authorities may, on an *ad hoc* basis, agree that binding arbitration shall be used in respect of any other matter to which Article XXVI applies. If an arbitration proceeding (the "Proceeding") under paragraph 6 of Article XXVI commences, the following rules and procedures shall apply:

1. The Proceeding shall be conducted in the manner prescribed by, and subject to the requirements of, paragraphs 6 and 7 of Article XXVI and these rules and procedures, as modified or supplemented by any other rules and procedures agreed upon by the competent authorities pursuant to paragraph 17 below.
2. The determination reached by an arbitration board in the Proceeding shall be limited to a determination regarding the amount of income, expense or tax reportable to the Contracting States.
3. Notwithstanding the initiation of the Proceeding, the competent authorities may reach a mutual agreement to resolve a case and terminate the Proceeding. Correspondingly, a concerned person may withdraw a request for the competent authorities to engage in the Mutual Agreement Procedure (and thereby terminate the Proceeding) at any time.
4. The requirements of subparagraph 7(*d*) of Article XXVI shall be met when the competent authorities have each received from each concerned person a notarized statement agreeing that the concerned person and each person acting on the concerned person's behalf, shall not disclose to any other person any information received during the course of the Proceeding from either Contracting State or the arbitration board, other than the determination of the Proceeding. A concerned person that has the legal authority to bind any other concerned person(s) on this matter may do so in a comprehensive notarized statement.
5. Each Contracting State shall have 60 days from the date on which the Proceeding begins to send a written communication to the other Contracting State appointing one member of the arbitration board. Within 60 days of the date on which the second such communication is sent, the two members appointed by the Contracting States shall appoint a third member, who shall serve as chair of the board. If either Contracting State fails to appoint a member, or if the members appointed by the Contracting States fail to agree upon the third member in the manner prescribed by this paragraph, a Contracting State shall ask the highest ranking member of the Secretariat at the Centre for Tax Policy and Administration of the Organisation for Economic Co-operation and Development (OECD) who is not a citizen of either Contracting State, to appoint the remaining member(s) by written notice to both Contracting States within 60 days of the date of such failure. The competent authorities shall develop a non-exclusive list of individuals with familiarity in international tax matters who may potentially serve as the chair of the board.
6. The arbitration board may adopt any procedures necessary for the conduct of its business, provided that the procedures are not inconsistent with any provision of Article XXVI or this note.
7. Each of the Contracting States shall be permitted to submit, within 60 days of the appointment of the chair of the arbitration board, a proposed resolution describing the proposed disposition of the specific monetary amounts of income, expense or taxation at issue in the case, and a supporting position paper, for consideration by the arbitration board. Copies of the proposed resolution and supporting position paper shall be provided by the board to the other Contracting State on the date on which the later of the submissions is submitted to the board. In the event that only one Contracting State submits a proposed resolution within the allotted time, then that proposed resolution shall be deemed to be the determination of the board in that case and the Proceeding shall be terminated. Each of the Contracting States may, if it so desires, submit a reply submission to the board within 120 days of the appointment of its chair, to address any points raised by the proposed resolution or position paper submitted by the other Contracting State. Additional information may be submitted to the arbitration board only at its request, and copies of the board's request and the Contracting State's response shall be provided to the other Contracting State on the date on which the request or the response is submitted. Except for logistical matters such as those identified in paragraphs 12, 14 and 15 below, all communications from the Contracting States to the arbitration board, and vice versa, shall take place only through

written communications between the designated competent authorities and the chair of the board.

8. The arbitration board shall deliver a determination in writing to the Contracting States within six months of the appointment of its chair. The board shall adopt as its determination one of the proposed resolutions submitted by the Contracting States.

9. In making its determination, the arbitration board shall apply, as necessary: (1) the provisions of the Convention as amended; (2) any agreed commentaries or explanations of the Contracting States concerning the Convention as amended; (3) the laws of the Contracting States to the extent they are not inconsistent with each other; and (4) any OECD Commentary, Guidelines or Reports regarding relevant analogous portions of the OECD Model Tax Convention.

10. The determination of the arbitration board in a particular case shall be binding on the Contracting States. The determination of the board shall not state a rationale. It shall have no precedential value.

11. As provided in subparagraph 7(*e*) of Article XXVI, the determination of an arbitration board shall constitute a resolution by mutual agreement under this Article. Each concerned person must, within 30 days of receiving the determination of the board from the competent authority to which the case was first presented, advise that competent authority whether that concerned person accepts the determination of the board. If any concerned person fails to so advise the relevant competent authority within this time frame, the determination of the board shall be considered not to have been accepted in that case. Where the determination of the board is not accepted, the case may not subsequently be the subject of a Proceeding.

12. Any meeting(s) of the arbitration board shall be in facilities provided by the Contracting State whose competent authority initiated the mutual agreement proceedings in the case.

13. The treatment of any associated interest or penalties shall be determined by applicable domestic law of the Contracting State(s) concerned.

14. No information relating to the Proceeding (including the board's determination) may be disclosed by the members of the arbitration board or their staffs or by either competent authority, except as permitted by the Convention and the domestic laws of the Contracting States. In addition, all material prepared in the course of, or relating to, the Proceeding shall be considered to be information exchanged between the Contracting States. The Contracting States shall ensure that all members of the arbitration board and their staffs sign and send to each Contracting State notarized statements, prior to their acting in the arbitration proceeding, in which they agree to abide by and be subject to the confidentiality and nondisclosure provisions of Articles XXVI and XXVII of the Convention and the applicable domestic laws of the Contracting States. In the event those provisions conflict, the most restrictive condition shall apply.

15. The fees and expenses of members of the arbitration board shall be set in accordance with the International Centre for Settlement of Investment Disputes (ICSID) Schedule of Fees for arbitrators, as in effect on the date on which the arbitration proceedings begin, and shall be borne equally by the Contracting States. Any fees for language translation shall also be borne equally by the Contracting States. Meeting facilities, related resources, financial management, other logistical support, and general administrative coordination of the Proceeding shall be provided, at its own cost, by the Contracting State whose competent authority initiated the mutual agreement proceedings in the case. Any other costs shall be borne by the Contracting State that incurs them.

16. For purposes of paragraphs 6 and 7 of Article XXVI and this note, each competent authority shall confirm in writing to the other competent authority and to the concerned person(s) the date of its receipt of the information necessary to undertake substantive consideration for a mutual agreement. Such information shall be:

(a) in the United States, the information required to be submitted to the U.S. competent authority under Revenue Procedure 2006-54, section 4.05 (or any applicable analogous provisions) and, for cases initially submitted as a request for an Advance Pricing Agreement, the information required to be submitted to the Internal Revenue Service under Revenue Procedure 2006-9, section 4 (or any applicable analogous provisions), and

(b) in Canada, the information required to be submitted to Canadian competent authority under Information Circular 71-17 (or any applicable successor publication).

However, this information shall not be considered received until both competent authorities have received copies of all materials submitted to either Contracting State by the concerned person(s) in connection with the mutual agreement procedure.

17. The competent authorities of the Contracting States may modify or supplement the above rules and procedures as necessary to more effectively implement the intent of paragraph 6 of Article XXVI to eliminate double taxation.

If the above proposal is acceptable to your Government, I further propose that this Note, which is authentic in English and in French, and your reply Note reflecting such acceptance shall constitute an agreement between our two Governments which shall enter into force on the date of entry into force of the Protocol and shall be annexed to the Convention as Annex A thereto and shall therefore be an integral part of the Convention.

Please accept, Excellency, the assurance of my highest consideration.

Maxime Bernier

Minister of Foreign Affairs

Excellency,

I have the honour to acknowledge receipt of your Note No. JLAB-0111 dated September 21, 2007, which states in its entirety as follows:

Excellency,

I have the honor to refer to the Protocol (the "Protocol") done today between Canada and the United States of America amending the Convention with Respect to Taxes on Income and on Capital done at Washington on 26 September 1980, as amended by the Protocols done on 14 June 1983, 28 March 1984, 17 March 1995, and 29 July 1997 (the "Convention"), and to propose on behalf of the Government of Canada the following:

In respect of any case where the competent authorities have endeavored but are unable to reach a complete agreement under Article XXVI (Mutual Agreement Procedure) of the Convention regarding the application of one or more of the following Articles of the Convention: IV (Residence) (but only insofar as it relates to the residence of a natural person), V (Permanent Establishment), VII (Business Profits), IX (Related Persons), and XII (Royalties) (but only (i) insofar as Article XII might apply in transactions involving related persons to whom Article IX might apply, or (ii) to an allocation of amounts between royalties that are taxable under paragraph 2 thereof and royalties that are exempt under paragraph 3 thereof), binding arbitration shall be used to determine such application, unless the competent authorities agree that the particular case is not suitable for determination by arbitration. In addition, the competent authorities may, on an *ad hoc* basis, agree that binding arbitration shall be used in respect of any other matter to which Article XXVI applies. If an arbitration proceeding (the "Proceeding") under paragraph 6 of Article XXVI commences, the following rules and procedures shall apply:

1. The Proceeding shall be conducted in the manner prescribed by, and subject to the requirements of, paragraphs 6 and 7 of Article XXVI and these rules and procedures, as modified or supplemented by any other rules and procedures agreed upon by the competent authorities pursuant to paragraph 17 below.

2. The determination reached by an arbitration board in the Proceeding shall be limited to a determination regarding the amount of income, expense or tax reportable to the Contracting States.

3. Notwithstanding the initiation of the Proceeding, the competent authorities may reach a mutual agreement to resolve a case and terminate the Proceeding. Correspondingly, a concerned person may withdraw a request for the competent authorities to engage in the Mutual Agreement

Procedure (and thereby terminate the Proceeding) at any time.

4. The requirements of subparagraph 7(*d*) of Article XXVI shall be met when the competent authorities have each received from each concerned person a notarized statement agreeing that the concerned person and each person acting on the concerned person's behalf, shall not disclose to any other person any information received during the course of the Proceeding from either Contracting State or the arbitration board, other than the determination of the Proceeding. A concerned person that has the legal authority to bind any other concerned person(s) on this matter may do so in a comprehensive notarized statement.

5. Each Contracting State shall have 60 days from the date on which the Proceeding begins to send a written communication to the other Contracting State appointing one member of the arbitration board. Within 60 days of the date on which the second such communication is sent, the two members appointed by the Contracting States shall appoint a third member, who shall serve as chair of the board. If either Contracting State fails to appoint a member, or if the members appointed by the Contracting States fail to agree upon the third member in the manner prescribed by this paragraph, a Contracting State shall ask the highest ranking member of the Secretariat at the Centre for Tax Policy and Administration of the Organisation for Economic Co-operation and Development (OECD) who is not a citizen of either Contracting State, to appoint the remaining member(s) by written notice to both Contracting States within 60 days of the date of such failure. The competent authorities shall develop a non-exclusive list of individuals with familiarity in international tax matters who may potentially serve as the chair of the board.

6. The arbitration board may adopt any procedures necessary for the conduct of its business, provided that the procedures are not inconsistent with any provision of Article XXVI or this note.

7. Each of the Contracting States shall be permitted to submit, within 60 days of the appointment of the chair of the arbitration board, a proposed resolution describing the proposed disposition of the specific monetary amounts of income, expense or taxation at issue in the case, and a supporting position paper, for consideration by the arbitration board. Copies of the proposed resolution and supporting position paper shall be provided by the board to the other Contracting State on the date on which the later of the submissions is submitted to the board. In the event that only one Contracting State submits a proposed resolution within the allotted time, then that proposed resolution shall be deemed to be the determination of the board in that case and the Proceeding shall be terminated. Each of the Contracting States may, if it so desires, submit a reply submission to the board within 120 days of the appointment of its chair, to address any points raised by the proposed resolution or position paper submitted by the other Contracting State. Additional information may be submitted to the arbitration board only at its request, and copies of the board's request and the Contracting State's response shall be provided to the other Contracting State on the date on which the request or the response is submitted. Except for logistical matters such as those identified in paragraphs 12, 14 and 15 below, all communications from the Contracting States to the arbitration board, and vice versa, shall take place only through written communications between the designated competent authorities and the chair of the board.

8. The arbitration board shall deliver a determination in writing to the Contracting States within six months of the appointment of its chair. The board shall adopt as its determination one of the proposed resolutions submitted by the Contracting States.

9. In making its determination, the arbitration board shall apply, as necessary: (1) the provisions of the Convention as amended; (2) any agreed commentaries or explanations of the Contracting States concerning the Convention as amended; (3) the laws of the Contracting States to the extent they are not inconsistent with each other; and (4) any OECD Commentary, Guidelines or Reports regarding relevant analogous portions of the OECD Model Tax Convention.

10. The determination of the arbitration board in a particular case shall be binding on the Contracting States. The determination of the board shall not state a rationale. It shall have no precedential value.

11. As provided in subparagraph 7(*e*) of Article XXVI, the determination of an arbitration board shall constitute a resolution by mutual agreement under this Article. Each concerned person must, within 30 days of receiving the determination of the board from the competent authority to which the case was first presented, advise that competent authority whether that concerned person accepts the determination of the board. If any concerned person fails to so advise the relevant competent authority within this time frame, the determination of the board shall be considered not to have been accepted in that case. Where the determination of the board is not accepted, the case may not subsequently be the subject of a Proceeding.

12. Any meeting(s) of the arbitration board shall be in facilities provided by the Contracting State whose competent authority initiated the mutual agreement proceedings in the case.

13. The treatment of any associated interest or penalties shall be determined by applicable domestic law of the Contracting State(s) concerned.

14. No information relating to the Proceeding (including the board's determination) may be disclosed by the members of the arbitration board or their staffs or by either competent authority, except as permitted by the Convention and the domestic laws of the Contracting States. In addition, all material prepared in the course of, or relating to, the Proceeding shall be considered to be information exchanged between the Contracting States. The Contracting States shall ensure that all members of the arbitration board and their staffs sign and send to each Contracting State notarized statements, prior to their acting in the arbitration proceeding, in which they agree to abide by and be subject to the confidentiality and nondisclosure provisions of Articles XXVI and XXVII of the Convention and the applicable domestic laws of the Contracting States. In the event those provisions conflict, the most restrictive condition shall apply.

15. The fees and expenses of members of the arbitration board shall be set in accordance with the International Centre for Settlement of Investment Disputes (ICSID) Schedule of Fees for arbitrators, as in effect on the date on which the arbitration proceedings begin, and shall be borne equally by the Contracting States. Any fees for language translation shall also be borne equally by the Contracting States. Meeting facilities, related resources, financial management, other logistical support, and general administrative coordination of the Proceeding shall be provided, at its own cost, by the Contracting State whose competent authority initiated the mutual agreement proceedings in the case. Any other costs shall be borne by the Contracting State that incurs them.

16. For purposes of paragraphs 6 and 7 of Article XXVI and this note, each competent authority shall confirm in writing to the other competent authority and to the concerned person(s) the date of its receipt of the information necessary to undertake substantive consideration for a mutual agreement. Such information shall be:

(a) in the United States, the information required to be submitted to the U.S. competent authority under Revenue Procedure 2006-54, section 4.05 (or any applicable analogous provisions) and, for cases initially submitted as a request for an Advance Pricing Agreement, the information required to be submitted to the Internal Revenue Service under Revenue Procedure 2006-9, section 4 (or any applicable analogous provisions), and

(b) in Canada, the information required to be submitted to Canadian competent authority under Information Circular 71-17 (or any applicable successor publication).

However, this information shall not be considered received until both competent authorities have received copies of all materials submitted to either Contracting State by the concerned person(s) in connection with the mutual agreement procedure.

17. The competent authorities of the Contracting States may modify or supplement the above rules and procedures as necessary to more effectively implement the intent of paragraph 6 of Article XXVI to eliminate double taxation.

If the above proposal is acceptable to your Government, I further propose that this Note, which is authentic in English and in French, and your reply Note reflecting such acceptance shall constitute an agreement between our two Governments which shall enter into force on the date of entry into force of the Protocol and shall be annexed to the Convention as Annex A thereto and shall therefore be an integral part of the Convention.

Please accept, Excellency, the assurance of my highest consideration.

I am pleased to inform you that the Government of the United States of America accepts the proposal set forth in your Note. The Government of the United States of America further agrees that your Note, which is authentic in English and in French, together with this reply, shall constitute an Agreement between the United States of America and Canada, which shall enter into force on the date of entry into force of the Protocol amending the Convention between the United States of America and Canada with Respect to Taxes on Income and on Capital done at Washington on 26 September 1980, as amended by the Protocols done on 14 June 1983, 28 March 1984, 17 March 1995, and 29 July 1997 (the "Convention"), and shall be annexed to the Convention as Annex A thereto, and shall therefore be an integral part of the Convention.

Accept, Excellency, the renewed assurances of my highest consideration.

Diplomatic Notes to Fifth Protocol (Annex B)

Protocol Amending the Convention Between Canada and the United States of America With Respect to Taxes on Income and on Capital
Diplomatic Notes: Annex B to the Convention
September 21, 2007

Note no. JLAB-0112

Excellency,

I have the honor to refer to the Protocol (the "Protocol") done today between Canada and the United States of America amending the Convention with Respect to Taxes on Income and on Capital done at Washington on 26 September 1980, as amended by the Protocols done on 14 June 1983, 28 March 1984, 17 March 1995, and 29 July 1997 (the "Convention").

In the course of the negotiations leading to the conclusion of the Protocol done today, the negotiators developed and agreed upon a common understanding and interpretation of certain provisions of the Convention. These understandings and interpretations are intended to give guidance both to the taxpayers and to the tax authorities of our two countries in interpreting various provisions contained in the Convention.

I, therefore, have the further honor to propose on behalf of the Government of Canada the following understandings and interpretations:

1. Meaning of undefined terms

For purposes of paragraph 2 of Article III (General Definitions) of the Convention, it is understood that, as regards the application at any time of the Convention, and any protocols thereto by a Contracting State, any term not defined therein shall, unless the context otherwise requires or the competent authorities otherwise agree to a common meaning pursuant to Article XXVI (Mutual Agreement Procedure), have the meaning which it has at that time under the law of that State for the purposes of the taxes to which the Convention, and any protocols thereto apply, any meaning under the applicable tax laws of that State prevailing over a meaning given to the term under other laws of that State.

2. Meaning of connected projects

For the purposes of applying subparagraph (*b*) of paragraph 9 of Article V (Permanent Establishment) of the Convention, it is understood that projects shall be considered to be connected if they constitute a coherent whole, commercially and geographically.

3. Definition of the term "dividends"

It is understood that distributions from Canadian income trusts and royalty trusts that are treated as dividends under the taxation laws of Canada shall be considered dividends for the purposes of Article X (Dividends) of the Convention.

4. Deletion of Article XIV (Independent Personal Services)

It is understood that the deletion of Article XIV (Independent Personal Services) of the Convention confirms the negotiators' shared understanding that no practical distinction can be made between a "fixed base" and a "permanent establishment", and that independent personal services of a resident of a Contracting State, to the extent that such resident is found to have a permanent establishment in the other Contracting State with respect to those services, shall be subject to the provisions of Article VII (Business Profits).

5. Former permanent establishments and fixed bases

It is understood that the modifications of paragraph 2 of Article VII (Business Profits), paragraph 4 of Article X (Dividends), paragraph 3 of Article XI (Interest) and paragraph 5 of Article XII (Royalties) of the Convention to refer to business having formerly been carried on through a permanent establishment confirm the negotiators' shared understanding of the meaning of the existing provisions, and thus are clarifying only.

6. Stock options

For purposes of applying Article XV (Income from Employment) and Article XXIV (Elimination of Double Taxation) of the Convention to income of an individual in connection with the exercise or other disposal (including a deemed exercise or disposal) of an option that was granted to the individual as an employee of a corporation or mutual fund trust to acquire shares or units ("securities") of the employer (which is considered, for the purposes of this Note, to include any related entity) in respect of services rendered or to be rendered by such individual, or in connection with the disposal (including a deemed disposal) of a security acquired under such an option, the following principles shall apply:

(a) Subject to subparagraph 6(*b*) of this Note, the individual shall be deemed to have derived, in respect of employment exercised in a Contracting State, the same proportion of such income that the number of days in the period that begins on the day the option was granted, and that ends on the day the option was exercised or disposed of, on which the individual's principal place of employment for the employer was situated in that Contracting State is of the total number of days in the period on which the individual was employed by the employer; and

(b) Notwithstanding subparagraph 6(*a*) of this Note, if the competent authorities of both Contracting States agree that the terms of the option were such that the grant of the option will be appropriately treated as transfer of ownership of the securities (e.g., because the options were in-the-money or not subject to a substantial vesting period), then they may agree to attribute income accordingly.

7. Taxes imposed by reason of death

It is understood that,

(a) Where a share or option in respect of a share is property situated in the United States for the purposes of Article XXIX

B (Taxes Imposed by Reason of Death) of the Convention, any employment income in respect of the share or option shall be, for the purpose of clause 6(*a*)(ii) of that Article, income from property situated in the United States;

(b) Where property situated in the United States for the purposes of Article XXIX B (Taxes Imposed by Reason of Death) of the Convention is held by an entity that is a resident of Canada and that is described in subparagraph 1(*b*) of Article IV (Residence) of the Convention, any income out of or under the entity in respect of the property shall be, for the purpose of subparagraph 6(*a*)(ii) of Article XXIX B (Taxes Imposed by Reason of Death), income from property situated in the United States; and

(c) Where a tax is imposed in Canada by reason of death in respect of an entity that is a resident of Canada and that is described in subparagraph 1(*b*) of Article IV (Residence) of the Convention, that tax shall be, for the purpose of paragraph 7 of Article XXIX B (Taxes Imposed by Reason of Death) of the Convention, imposed in respect of property situated in Canada.

8. Royalties — information in connection with franchise agreement

It is understood that the reference in subparagraph 3(*c*) of Article XII (Royalties) of the Convention to information provided in connection with a franchise agreement shall generally refer only to information that governs or otherwise deals with the operation (whether by the payer or by another person) of the franchise, and not to other information concerning industrial, commercial or scientific experience that is held for resale or license.

9. With reference to Article VII (Business Profits)

It is understood that the business profits to be attributed to a permanent establishment shall include only the profits derived from he assets used, risks assumed and activities performed by the permanent establishment. The principles of the OECD Transfer Pricing Guidelines shall apply for purposes of determining the profits attributable to a permanent establishment, taking into account the different economic and legal circumstances of a single entity. Accordingly, any of the methods described therein as acceptable methods for determining an arm's length result may be used to determine the income of a permanent establishment so long as those methods are applied in accordance with the Guidelines. In particular, in determining the amount of attributable profits, the permanent establishment shall be treated as having the same amount of capital that it would need to support its activities if it were a distinct and separate enterprise engaged in the same or similar activities. With respect to financial institutions other than insurance companies, a Contracting State may determine the amount of capital to be attributed to a permanent establishment by allocating the institution's total equity between its various offices on the basis of the proportion of the financial institution's risk-weighted assets attributable to each of them. In the case of an insurance company, there shall be attributed to a permanent establishment not only premiums earned through the permanent establishment, but that portion of the insurance company's overall investment income from reserves and surplus that supports the risks assumed by the permanent establishment.

10. Qualifying retirement plans

For purposes of paragraph 15 of Article XVIII (Pensions and Annuities) of the Convention, it is understood that

(a) In the case of Canada, the term "qualifying retirement plan" shall include the following and any identical or substantially similar plan that is established pursuant to legislation introduced after the date of signature of the Protocol: registered pension plans under section 147.1 of the *Income Tax Act*, registered retirement savings plans under section 146 that are part of a group arrangement described in subsection 204.2(1.32), deferred profit sharing plans under section 147, and any registered retirement savings plan under section 146 or registered retirement income fund under section 146.3 that is funded exclusively by rollover contributions from one or more of the preceding plans; and

(b) In the case of the United States, the term "qualifying retirement plan" shall include the following and any identical or substantially similar plan that is established pursuant to legislation introduced after the date of signature of the Protocol: qualified plans under section 401(*a*) of the *Internal Revenue Code* (including section 401(*k*) arrangements), individual retirement plans that are part of a simplified employee pension plan that satisfies section 408(*k*), section 408(*p*) simple retirement accounts, section 403(a) qualified annuity plans, section 403(b) plans, section 457(*g*) trusts providing benefits under section 457(*b*) plans, the Thrift Savings Fund (section 7701(*j*)), and any individual retirement account under section 408(*a*) that is funded exclusively by rollover contributions from one or more of the preceding plans.

11. Former long-term residents

The term "long-term resident" shall mean any individual who is a lawful permanent resident of the United States in eight or more taxable years during the preceding 15 taxable years. In determining whether the threshold in the preceding sentence is met, there shall not count any year in which the individual is treated as a resident of Canada under the Convention, or as a resident of any country other than the United States under the provisions of any other U.S. tax treaty, and, in either case, the individual does not waive the benefits of such treaty applicable to residents of the other country.

12. Special source rules relating to former citizens and long-term residents

For purposes of subparagraph 2(*b*) of Article XXIX (Miscellaneous Rules) of the Convention, "income deemed under the domestic law of the United States to arise from such sources" shall consist of gains from the sale or exchange of stock of a U.S. company or debt obligations of a U.S. person, the United States, a State, or a political subdivision thereof, or the District of Columbia, gains from property (other than stock or debt obligations) located in the United States, and, in certain cases, income or gain derived from the sale of stock of a non-U.S. company or a disposition of property contributed to such non-U.S. company where such company would be a controlled foreign corporation with respect to the person if such person had continued to be a U.S. person. In addition, an individual who exchanges property that gives rise or would give rise to U.S.-source income for property that gives rise to foreign-source income shall be treated as if he or she had sold the property that would give rise to U.S. source income for its fair market value, and any consequent gain shall be deemed to be income from sources within the United States.

13. Exchange of Information

It is understood that the standards and practices described in Article XXVII (Exchange of Information) of the Convention are to be in no respect less effective than those described in the Model Agreement on Exchange of Information on Tax Matters developed by the OECD Global Forum Working Group on Effective Exchange of Information.

14. Limitation on Benefits

The United States and Canada are part of the same regional free trade area and, as a result, the Convention reflects the fact that publicly traded companies resident in one country may be traded on a stock exchange of the other country. Nevertheless, the Contracting States agree that in making future amendments to the Convention, they shall consult on possible modifications to subparagraph 2(*c*) of Article XXIX A (Limitation on Benefits) of the Convention (including, modifications necessary to discourage corporate inversion transactions).

If the above proposal is acceptable to your Government, I further propose that this Note, which is authentic in English and in French, and your reply Note reflecting such acceptance shall constitute an agreement between our two Governments which shall enter into force on the date of entry into force of the Protocol and shall be annexed to the Convention as Annex B thereto and shall therefore be an integral part of the Convention.

Please accept, Excellency, the assurance of my highest consideration.

Maxime Bernier
Minister of Foreign Affairs

Excellency,

I have the honour to acknowledge receipt of your Note No. JLAB-0112 dated September 21, 2007, which states in its entirety as follows:

Excellency,

I have the honor to refer to the Protocol (the "Protocol") done today between Canada and the United States of America amending the Convention with Respect to Taxes on Income and on Capital done at Washington on 26 September 1980, as amended by the Protocols done on 14 June 1983, 28 March 1984, 17 March 1995, and 29 July 1997 (the "Convention").

In the course of the negotiations leading to the conclusion of the Protocol done today, the negotiators developed and agreed upon a common understanding and interpretation of certain provisions of the Convention. These understandings and interpretations are intended to give guidance both to the taxpayers and to the tax authorities of our two countries in interpreting various provisions contained in the Convention.

I, therefore, have the further honor to propose on behalf of the Government of Canada the following understandings and interpretations:

1. Meaning of undefined terms

For purposes of paragraph 2 of Article III (General Definitions) of the Convention, it is understood that, as regards the application at any time of the Convention, and any protocols thereto by a Contracting State, any term not defined therein shall, unless the context otherwise requires or the competent authorities otherwise agree to a common meaning pursuant to Article XXVI (Mutual Agreement Procedure), have the meaning which it has at that time under the law of that State for the purposes of the taxes to which the Convention, and any protocols thereto apply, any meaning under the applicable tax laws of that State prevailing over a meaning given to the term under other laws of that State.

2. Meaning of connected projects

For the purposes of applying subparagraph (*b*) of paragraph 9 of Article V (Permanent Establishment) of the Convention, it is understood that projects shall be considered to be connected if they constitute a coherent whole, commercially and geographically.

3. Definition of the term "dividends"

It is understood that distributions from Canadian income trusts and royalty trusts that are treated as dividends under the taxation laws of Canada shall be considered dividends for the purposes of Article X (Dividends) of the Convention.

4. Deletion of Article XIV (Independent Personal Services)

It is understood that the deletion of Article XIV (Independent Personal Services) of the Convention confirms the negotiators' shared understanding that no practical distinction can be made between a "fixed base" and a "permanent establishment", and that independent personal services of a resident of a Contracting State, to the extent that such resident is found to have a permanent establishment in the other Contracting State with respect to those services, shall be subject to the provisions of Article VII (Business Profits).

5. Former permanent establishments and fixed bases

It is understood that the modifications of paragraph 2 of Article VII (Business Profits), paragraph 4 of Article X (Dividends), paragraph 3 of Article XI (Interest) and paragraph 5 of Article XII (Royalties) of the Convention to refer to business having formerly been carried on through a permanent establishment confirm the negotiators' shared understanding of the meaning of the existing provisions, and thus are clarifying only.

6. Stock options

For purposes of applying Article XV (Income from Employment) and Article XXIV (Elimination of Double Taxation) of the Convention to income of an individual in connection with the exercise or other disposal (including a deemed exercise or disposal) of an option that was granted to the individual as an employee of a corporation or mutual fund trust to acquire shares or units ("securities") of the employer (which is considered, for the purposes of this Note, to include any related entity) in respect of services rendered or to be rendered by such individual, or in connection with the disposal (including a deemed disposal) of a security acquired under such an option, the following principles shall apply:

(a) Subject to subparagraph 6(*b*) of this Note, the individual shall be deemed to have derived, in respect of employment exercised in a Contracting State, the same proportion of such income that the number of days in the period that begins on the day the option was granted, and that ends on the day the option was exercised or disposed of, on which the individual's principal place of employment for the employer was situated in that Contracting State is of the total number of days in the period on which the individual was employed by the employer; and

(b) Notwithstanding subparagraph 6(*a*) of this Note, if the competent authorities of both Contracting States agree that the terms of the option were such that the grant of the option will be appropriately treated as transfer of ownership of the securities (e.g., because the options were in-the-money or not subject to a substantial vesting period), then they may agree to attribute income accordingly.

7. Taxes imposed by reason of death

It is understood that,

(a) Where a share or option in respect of a share is property situated in the United States for the purposes of Article XXIX B (Taxes Imposed by Reason of Death) of the Convention, any employment income in respect of the share or option shall be, for the purpose of clause 6(*a*)(ii) of that Article, income from property situated in the United States;

(b) Where property situated in the United States for the purposes of Article XXIX B (Taxes Imposed by Reason of Death) of the Convention is held by an entity that is a resident of Canada and that is described in subparagraph 1(*b*) of Article IV (Residence) of the Convention, any income out of or under the entity in respect of the property shall be, for the purpose of subparagraph 6(*a*)(ii) of Article XXIX B (Taxes Imposed by Reason of Death), income from property situated in the United States; and

(c) Where a tax is imposed in Canada by reason of death in respect of an entity that is a resident of Canada and that is described in subparagraph 1(*b*) of Article IV (Residence) of the Convention, that tax shall be, for the purpose of paragraph 7 of Article XXIX B (Taxes Imposed by Reason of Death) of the Convention, imposed in respect of property situated in Canada.

8. Royalties — information in connection with franchise agreement

It is understood that the reference in subparagraph 3(*c*) of Article XII (Royalties) of the Convention to information provided in connection with a franchise agreement shall generally refer only to information that governs or otherwise deals with the operation (whether by the payer or by another person) of the franchise, and not to other information concerning industrial, commercial or scientific experience that is held for resale or license.

9. With reference to Article VII (Business Profits)

It is understood that the business profits to be attributed to a permanent establishment shall include only the profits derived from the assets used, risks assumed and activities performed by the permanent establishment. The principles of the OECD Transfer Pricing Guidelines shall apply for purposes of determining the profits attributable to a permanent establishment, taking into account the different economic and legal circumstances of a single entity. Accordingly, any of the methods described therein as acceptable methods for determining an arm's length result may be used to determine the income of a permanent establishment so long as those methods are applied in accordance with the Guidelines. In particular, in determining the amount of attributable profits, the permanent establishment shall be treated as having the same amount of capital that it would need to support its activities if it were a distinct and separate enterprise engaged in the same or similar activities. With respect to financial institutions other than insurance companies, a Contracting State may determine the amount of capital to be attributed to a permanent establishment by allocating the institution's total equity between its various offices on the basis of the proportion of the financial institution's risk-weighted assets attributable to each of them. In the case of an insurance company, there shall be attributed to a permanent establishment not only premiums earned through the permanent establishment, but that portion of the insurance company's overall investment income from reserves and surplus that supports the risks assumed by the permanent establishment.

10. Qualifying retirement plans

For purposes of paragraph 15 of Article XVIII (Pensions and Annuities) of the Convention, it is understood that

(a) In the case of Canada, the term "qualifying retirement plan" shall include the following and any identical or substantially similar plan that is established pursuant to legislation introduced after the date of signature of the Protocol: registered pension plans under section 147.1 of the *Income Tax Act*, registered retirement savings plans under section 146 that are part of a group arrangement described in subsection 204.2(1.32), deferred profit sharing plans under section 147, and any registered retirement savings plan under section 146 or registered retirement income fund under section 146.3 that is funded exclusively by rollover contributions from one or more of the preceding plans; and

(b) In the case of the United States, the term "qualifying retirement plan" shall include the following and any identical or substantially similar plan that is established pursuant to legislation introduced after the date of signature of the Protocol: qualified plans under section 401(*a*) of the *Internal Revenue Code* (including section 401(k) arrangements), individual retirement plans that are part of a simplified employee pension plan that satisfies section 408(*k*), section 408(*p*) simple retirement accounts, section 403(*a*) qualified annuity plans, section 403(*b*) plans, section 457(*g*) trusts providing benefits under section 457(*b*) plans, the Thrift Savings Fund (section 7701(*j*)), and any individual retirement account under section 408(*a*) that is funded exclusively by rollover contributions from one or more of the preceding plans.

11. Former long-term residents

The term "long-term resident" shall mean any individual who is a lawful permanent resident of the United States in eight or more taxable years during the preceding 15 taxable years. In determining whether the threshold in the preceding sentence is met, there shall not count any year in which the individual is treated as a resident of Canada under the Convention, or as a resident of any country other than the United States under the provisions of any other U.S. tax treaty, and, in either case, the individual does not waive the benefits of such treaty applicable to residents of the other country.

12. Special source rules relating to former citizens and long-term residents

For purposes of subparagraph 2(*b*) of Article XXIX (Miscellaneous Rules) of the Convention, "income deemed under the domestic law of the United States to arise from such sources" shall consist of gains from the sale or exchange of stock of a U.S. company or debt obligations of a U.S. person, the United States, a State, or a political subdivision thereof, or the District of Columbia, gains from property (other than stock or debt obligations) located in the United States, and, in certain cases, income or gain derived from the sale of stock of a non-U.S. company or a disposition of property contributed to such non-U.S. company where such company would be a controlled foreign corporation with respect to the person if such person had continued to be a U.S. person. In addition, an individual who exchanges property that gives rise or would give rise to U.S.-source income for property that gives rise to foreign-source income shall be treated as if he or she had sold the property that would give rise to U.S. source income for its fair market value, and any consequent gain shall be deemed to be income from sources within the United States.

13. Exchange of Information

It is understood that the standards and practices described in Article XXVII (Exchange of Information) of the Convention are to be in no respect less effective than those described in the Model Agreement on Exchange of Information on Tax Matters developed by the OECD Global Forum Working Group on Effective Exchange of Information.

14. Limitation on Benefits

The United States and Canada are part of the same regional free trade area and, as a result, the Convention reflects the fact that publicly traded companies resident in one country may be traded on a stock exchange of the other country. Nevertheless, the Contracting States agree that in making future amendments to the Convention, they shall consult on possible modifications to subparagraph 2(*c*) of Article XXIX A (Limitation on Benefits) of the Convention (including, modifications necessary to discourage corporate inversion transactions).

If the above proposal is acceptable to your Government, I further propose that this Note, which is authentic in English and in French, and your reply Note reflecting such acceptance shall constitute an agreement between our two Governments which shall enter into force on the date of entry into force of the Protocol and shall be annexed to the Convention as Annex B thereto, and shall therefore be an integral part of the Convention.

Please accept, Excellency, the assurance of my highest consideration.

I am pleased to inform you that the Government of the United States of America accepts the proposal set forth in your Note. The Government of the United States of America further agrees that your Note, which is authentic in English and in French, together with this reply, shall constitute an Agreement between the United States of America and Canada, which shall enter into force on the date of entry into force of the Protocol amending the Convention between the United States of America and Canada with Respect to Taxes on Income and on Capital done at Washington on 26 September 1980, as amended by the Protocols done on 14 June 1983, 28 March 1984, 17 March 1995, and 29 July 1997 (the "Convention"), and shall be annexed to the Convention as Annex B thereto, and shall therefore be an integral part of the Convention.

Accept, Excellency, the renewed assurances of my highest consideration.

Technical Explanation of the Canada–U.S. Convention

Treasury Department Technical Explanation of the Convention Between the United States of America and Canada with Respect to Taxes on Income and on Capital Signed at Washington, D.C. on September 26, 1980, as Amended by the Protocol Signed at Ottawa on June 14, 1983 and the Protocol Signed at Washington on March 28, 1984.

Introduction

This is a technical explanation of the Convention between the United States and Canada signed on September 26, 1980, as amended by the Protocols signed on June 14, 1983 and March 28, 1984 ("the Convention"). References are made to the Convention and Protocol between Canada and the United States with respect to Income Taxes signed on March 4, 1942, as amended by the Convention signed on June 12, 1950, the Convention signed on August 8, 1956 and the Supplementary Convention signed on October 25, 1966 ("the 1942 Convention"). These references are intended to put various provisions of the Convention into context. The technical explanation does not, however, provide a complete comparison between the Convention and the 1942 Convention. Moreover, neither the Convention nor the technical explanation is intended to have implications for the interpretation of the 1942 Convention.

The technical explanation is an official guide to the Convention. It reflects policies behind particular Convention provisions, as well as understandings reached with respect to the interpretation and application of the Convention.

Article I — Personal Scope

Article I provides that the Convention is generally applicable to persons who are residents of either Canada or the United States or both Canada and the United States. The word "generally" is used because certain provisions of the Convention apply to persons who are residents of neither Canada nor the United States.

Article II — Taxes Covered

Paragraph 1 states that the Convention applies to taxes "on income and on capital" imposed on behalf of Canada and the United States, irrespective of the manner in which such taxes are levied. Neither Canada nor the United States presently impose taxes on capital. Paragraph 1 is not intended either to broaden or to limit paragraph 2, which provides that the Convention shall apply, in the case of Canada, to the taxes imposed by the Government of Canada under Parts I, XIII, and XIV of the *Income Tax Act* and, in the case of the United States, to the Federal income taxes imposed by the *Internal Revenue Code* ("the Code").

National taxes not generally covered by the Convention include, in the case of the United States, the estate, gift, and generation-skipping transfer taxes, the Windfall Profits Tax, Federal unemployment taxes, social security taxes imposed under sections 1401, 3101, and 3111 of the Code, and the excise tax on insurance premiums imposed under Code section 4371. The Convention also does not generally cover the Canadian excise tax on net insurance premiums paid by residents of Canada for coverage of a risk situated in Canada, the Petroleum and Gas Revenue Tax (PGRT) and the Incremental Oil Revenue Tax (IORT). However, the Convention has the effect of covering the Canadian social security tax in certain respects because under Canadian domestic tax law no such tax is due if there is no income subject to tax under the *Income Tax Act* of Canada. Taxes imposed by the states of the United States, and by the provinces of Canada, are not generally covered by the Convention. However, if such taxes are imposed in accordance with the provisions of the Convention, a foreign tax credit is ensured by paragraph 7 of Article XXIV (Elimination of Double Taxation).

Paragraph 2 contrasts with paragraph 1 of the Protocol to the 1942 Convention, which refers to "Dominion income taxes." In addition, unlike the 1942 Convention, the Convention does not contain a reference to "surtaxes and excess-profits taxes."

Paragraph 3 provides that the Convention also applies to any taxes identical or substantially similar to the taxes on income in existence on September 26, 1980 which are imposed in addition to or in place of the taxes existing on that date. Similarly, taxes on capital imposed after that date are to be covered.

It was agreed that Part I of the *Income Tax Act* of Canada is a covered tax even though Canada has made certain modifications in the *Income Tax Act* after the signature of the Convention and before the signature of the 1983 Protocol. In particular, Canada has enacted a low flat rate tax on petroleum production (the PGRT) which, at the time of the signature of the 1983 Protocol, is imposed generally at a statutory rate of 14.67 per cent for the period June 1, 1982 to May 31, 1983, and at 16 per cent thereafter, generally reduced to an effective rate of 11 per cent or 12 per cent after deducting a 25 per cent resource allowance. The PGRT is not deductible in computing income for Canadian income tax purposes. This agreement is not intended to have implications for any other convention or for the interpretation of Code sections 901 and 903. Further, the PGRT and IORT are not taxes described in paragraphs 2 or 3.

Paragraph 4 provides that, notwithstanding paragraphs 2 and 3, the Convention applies to certain United States taxes for certain specified purposes: the accumulated earnings tax and personal holding company tax are covered only to the extent necessary to implement the provisions of paragraphs 5 and 8 of Article X (Dividends); the excise taxes imposed with respect to private foundations are covered only to the extent necessary to implement the provisions of paragraph 4 of Article XXI (Exempt Organizations); and the social security taxes imposed under sections 1401, 3101, and 3111 of the Code are covered only to the extent necessary to implement the provisions of paragraph 4 of Article XXIX (Miscellaneous Rules). The pertinent provisions of Articles X, XXI, and XXIX are described below. Canada has no national taxes similar to the United States accumulated earnings tax, personal holding company tax, or excise taxes imposed with respect to private foundations.

Article II does not specifically refer to interest, fines and penalties. Thus, each Contracting State may, in general, impose interest, fines, and penalties or pay interest pursuant to its domestic laws. Any question whether such items are being imposed or paid in connection with covered taxes in a manner consistent with provisions of the Convention, such as Article XXV (Non-Discrimination), may, however, be resolved by the competent authorities pursuant to Article XXVI (Mutual Agreement Procedure). See, however, the discussion below of the treatment of certain interest under Articles XXIX (Miscellaneous Rules) and XXX (Entry Into Force).

Article III — General Definitions

Article III provides definitions and general rules of interpretation for the Convention. Paragraph 1(a) states that the term "Canada," when used in a geographical sense, means the territory of Canada, including any area beyond the territorial seas of Canada which, under international law and the laws of Canada, is an area within which Canada may exercise rights with respect to the seabed and subsoil and their natural resources. This definition differs only in form from the definition of Canada in the 1942 Convention; paragraph 1(a) omits the reference in the 1942 Convention to "the Provinces, the Territories and Sable Island" as unnecessary. Paragraph 1(b)(i) defines the term "United States" to mean the United States of America. The term does not include Puerto Rico, the Virgin Islands, Guam, or any other United States possession or territory.

Paragraph 1(b)(ii) states that when the term "United States" is used in a geographical sense the term also includes any area beyond the territorial seas of the United States which, under international law and the laws of the United States, is an area within which the United States may exercise rights with respect to the seabed and subsoil and their natural resources.

Paragraph 1(c) defines the term "Canadian tax" to mean the taxes imposed by the Government of Canada under Parts I, XIII, and XIV of the *Income Tax Act* as in existence on September 26, 1980 and any identical or substantially similar taxes on income imposed by the Government of Canada after that date and which are in addition to or in place of the then existing taxes. The term does not extend to capital taxes, if and when such taxes are ever imposed by Canada.

Paragraph 1(d) defines the term "United States tax" to mean the Federal income taxes imposed by the *Internal Revenue Code* as in existence on September 26, 1980 and any identical or substantially similar taxes on income imposed by the United States after that date in addition to or in place of the then existing taxes. The term does not extend to capital taxes, nor to the United States taxes identified in paragraph 4 of Article II (Taxes Covered).

Paragraph 1(e) provides that the term "person" includes an individual, an estate, a trust, a company, and any other body of persons. Although both the United States and Canada do not regard partnerships as taxable entities, the definition in the paragraph is broad enough to include partnerships where necessary.

Paragraph 1(f) defines the term "company" to mean any body corporate or any entity which is treated as a body corporate for tax purposes.

The term "competent authority" is defined in paragraph 1(g) to mean, in the case of Canada, the Minister of National Revenue or his authorized representative and, in the case of the United States, the Secretary of the Treasury or his delegate. The Secretary of the Treasury has delegated the general authority to act as competent authority to the Commissioner of the Internal Revenue Service, who has redelegated such authority to the Associate Commissioner (Operations). The Assistant Commissioner (Examination) has been delegated the authority to administer programs for simultaneous, spontaneous and industry wide exchanges of information. The Director, Foreign Operations District, has been delegated the authority to administer programs for routine and specific exchanges of information and mutual assistance in collection. The Assistant Commissioner (Criminal Investigations) has been delegated the authority to administer the simultaneous criminal investigation program with Canada.

Paragraph 1(h) defines the term "international traffic" to mean, with reference to a resident of a Contracting State, any voyage of a ship or aircraft to transport passengers or property (whether or not operated or used by that resident), except where the principal purpose of the voyage is transport between points within the other Contracting State. For example, in determining for Canadian tax purposes whether a United States resident has derived profits from the operation of ships or aircraft in international traffic, a voyage of a ship or aircraft (whether or not operated or used by that resident) that includes stops in both Contracting States will not be international traffic if the principal purpose of the voyage is to transport passengers or property from one point in Canada to another point in Canada.

Paragraph 1(i) defines the term "State" to mean any national State, whether or not a Contracting State.

Paragraph 1(j) establishes "the 1942 Convention" as the term to be used throughout the Convention for referring to the pre-existing income tax treaty relationship between the United States and Canada.

Paragraph 2 provides that, in the case of a term not defined in the Convention, the domestic tax law of the Contracting State applying to the Convention shall control, unless the context in which the term is used requires a definition independent of domestic tax law or the competent authorities reach agreement on a meaning pursuant to Article XXVI (Mutual Agreement Procedure). The term "context" refers to the purpose and background of the provision in which the term appears.

Pursuant to the provisions of Article XXVI, the competent authorities of the Contracting States may resolve any difficulties or doubts as to the interpretation or application of the Convention. An agreement by the competent authorities with respect to the meaning of a term used in the Convention would supersede conflicting meanings in the domestic laws of the Contracting States.

Article IV — Residence

Article IV provides a detailed definition of the term "resident of a Contracting State." The definition begins with a person's liability to tax as a resident under the respective taxation laws of the Contracting States. A person who, under those laws, is a resident of one Contracting State and not the other need look no further. However, the Convention definition is also designed to assign residence to one State or the other for purposes of the Convention in circumstances where each of the Contracting States believes a person to be its resident. The Convention definition is, of course, exclusively for purposes of the Convention.

Paragraph 1 provides that the term "resident of a Contracting State" means any person who, under the laws of that State, is liable to tax therein by reason of his domicile, residence, place of management, place of incorporation, or any other criterion of a similar nature. The phrase "any other criterion of a similar nature" includes, for U.S. purposes, an election under the Code to be treated as a U.S. resident. An estate or trust is, however, considered to be a resident of a Contracting State only to the extent that income derived by such estate or trust is liable to tax in that State either in its hands or in the hands of its beneficiaries. To the extent that an estate or trust is considered a resident of a Contracting State under this provision, it can be a "beneficial owner" of items of income specified in other articles of the Convention — e.g., paragraph 2 of Article X (Dividends).

Paragraphs 2, 3, and 4 provide rules to determine a single residence for purposes of the Convention for persons resident in both Contracting States under the rules set forth in paragraph 1. Paragraph 2 deals with individuals. A "dual resident" individual is initially deemed to be a resident of the Contracting State in which he has a permanent home available to him. If the individual has a permanent home available to him in both States or in neither, he is deemed to be a resident of the Contracting State with which his personal and economic relations are closer. If the personal and economic relations of an individual are not closer to one Contracting State than to the other, the individual is deemed to be a resident of the Contracting State in which he has an habitual abode. If he has such an abode in both States or in neither State, he is deemed to be a resident of the Contracting State of which he is a citizen. If the individual is a citizen of both States or of neither, the competent authorities are to settle the status of the individual by mutual agreement.

Paragraph 3 provides that if, under the provisions of paragraph 1, a company is a resident of both Canada and the United States, then it shall be deemed to be a resident of the State under whose laws (including laws of political subdivisions) it was created. Paragraph 3 does not refer to the State in which a company is organized, thus making clear that the tie-breaker rule for a company is controlled by the State of the company's original creation. Various jurisdictions may allow local incorporation of an entity that is already organized and incorporated under the laws of another country. Paragraph 3 provides certainty in both the United States and Canada with respect to the treatment of such an entity for purposes of the Convention.

Paragraph 4 provides that where, by reason of the provisions of paragraph 1, an estate, trust, or other person, other than an individual or a company, is a resident of both Contracting States, the competent authorities of the States shall by mutual agreement endeavor to settle the question and determine the mode of application of the Convention to such person. This delegation of authority to the competent authorities complements the provisions of Article XXVI (Mutual Agreement Procedure), which implicitly grant such authority.

Paragraph 5 provides a special rule for certain government employees, their spouses, and dependent children. An individual is deemed to be a resident of a Contracting State if he is an employee of that State or of a political subdivision, local authority, or instrumentality of that State, is rendering services in the discharge of functions of a governmental nature in any State, and is subjected in the first-mentioned State to "similar obligations" in respect of taxes on income as are residents of the first-mentioned State. Paragraph 5 provides further that a spouse and dependent children residing with a government employee and also subject to "similar obligations" in respect of income taxes as residents of the first-mentioned State are also deemed to be residents of that State. Paragraph 5 overrides the normal tie-breaker rule of paragraph 2. A U.S. citizen or resident who is an employee of the U.S. government in a foreign country or who is a spouse or dependent of such employee is considered to be subject in the United States to "similar obligations" in respect of taxes on income as those imposed on residents of the United States, notwithstanding that such person may be entitled to the benefits allowed by sections 911 or 912 of the Code.

Article V — Permanent Establishment

Paragraph 1 provides that for the purposes of the Convention the term "permanent establishment" means a fixed place of business through which the business of a resident of a Contracting State is wholly or partly carried on. Article V does not use the term "enterprise of a Contracting State," which appears in the 1942 Convention. Thus, paragraph 1 avoids introducing an additional term into the Convention. The omission of the term is not intended to have any implications for the interpretation of the 1942 Convention.

Paragraph 2 provides that the term "permanent establishment" includes especially a place of management, a branch, an office, a factory, a workshop, and a mine, oil or gas well, quarry, or any other place of extraction of natural resources. Paragraph 3 adds that a building site or construction or installation project constitutes a permanent establishment if and only if it lasts for more than 12 months. Paragraph 4 provides that a permanent establishment exists in a Contracting State if the use of an installation or drilling rig or drilling ship in that State to explore for or exploit natural resources lasts for more than 3 months in any 12 month period, but not if such activity exists for a lesser period of time. The competent authorities have entered into an agreement under the 1942 Convention setting forth guidelines as to certain aspects of Canadian taxation of drilling rigs owned by U.S. persons that constitute Canadian permanent establishments. The agreement will be renewed when this Convention enters into force.

Paragraph 5 provides that a person acting in a Contracting State on behalf of a resident of the other Contracting State is deemed to be a permanent establishment of the resident if such person has and habitually exercises in the first-mentioned State the authority to conclude contracts in the name of the resident. This rule does not apply to an agent of independent status, covered by paragraph 7. Under the provisions of paragraph 5, a permanent establishment may exist even in the absence of a fixed place of business. If, however, the activities of a person described in paragraph 5 are limited to the ancillary activities described in paragraph 6, then a permanent establishment does not exist solely on account of the person's activities.

There are a number of minor differences between the provisions of paragraphs 1 through 5 and the analogous provisions of the 1942 Convention. One important deviation is elimination of the rule of the 1942 Convention which deems a permanent establishment to exist in any circumstance where a resident of one State uses substantial equipment in the other State for any period of time. The Convention thus generally raises the threshold for source basis taxation of activities that involve substantial equipment (and that do not otherwise constitute a permanent establishment). Another deviation of some significance is elimination of the rule of the 1942 Convention that considers a permanent establishment to exist where a resident of one State carries on business in the other State through an agent or employee who has a stock of merchandise from which he regularly fills orders that he receives. The Convention provides that a person other than an agent of independent status who is engaged solely in the maintenance of a stock of goods or merchandise belonging to a resident of the other

State for the purpose of storage, display or delivery does not constitute a permanent establishment.

Paragraph 6 provides that a fixed place of business used solely for, or an employee described in paragraph 5 engaged solely in, certain specified activities is not a permanent establishment, notwithstanding the provisions of paragraphs 1, 2, and 5. The specified activities are: a) the use of facilities for the purpose of storage, display, or delivery of goods or merchandise belonging to the resident whose business is being carried on; b) the maintenance of a stock of goods or merchandise belonging to the resident for the purpose of storage, display, or delivery; c) the maintenance of a stock of goods or merchandise belonging to the resident for the purpose of processing by another person; d) the purchase of goods or merchandise, or the collection of information, for the resident; and e) advertising, the supply of information, scientific research, or similar activities which have a preparatory or auxiliary character, for the resident. Combinations of the specified activities have the same status as any one of the activities. Thus, unlike the OECD Model Convention, a combination of the activities described in subparagraphs 6(a) through 6(e) need not be of a preparatory or auxiliary character (except as required by subparagraph 6(e)) in order to avoid the creation of a permanent establishment. The reference in paragraph 6(e) to specific activities does not imply that any other particular activities — for example, the servicing of a patent or a know-how contract or the inspection of the implementation of engineering plans — do not fall within the scope of paragraph 6(e) provided that, based on the facts and circumstances, such activities have a preparatory or auxiliary character.

Paragraph 7 provides that a resident of a Contracting State is not deemed to have a permanent establishment in the other Contracting State merely because such resident carries on business in the other State through a broker, general commission agent, or any other agent of independent status, provided that such persons are acting in the ordinary course of their business.

Paragraph 8 states that the fact that a company which is a resident of one Contracting State controls or is controlled by a company which is either a resident of the other Contracting State or which is carrying on a business in the other State, whether through a permanent establishment or otherwise, does not automatically render either company a permanent establishment of the other.

Paragraph 9 provides that, for purposes of the Convention, the provisions of Article V apply in determining whether any person has a permanent establishment in any State. Thus, these provisions would determine whether a person other than a resident of Canada or the United States has a permanent establishment in Canada or the United States, and whether a person resident in Canada or the United States has a permanent establishment in a third State.

Article VI — Income from Real Property

Paragraph 1 provides that income derived by a resident of a Contracting State from real property situated in the other Contracting State may be taxed by that other State. Income from real property includes, for purposes of Article VI, income from agriculture, forestry or other natural resources. Also, while "income derived ... from real property" includes income from rights such as an overriding royalty or a net profits interest in a natural resource, it does not include income in the form of rights to explore for or exploit natural resources which a party receives as compensation for services (e.g., exploration services); the latter income is subject to the provisions of Article VII (Business Profits), XIV (Independent Personal Services), or XV (Dependent Personal Services), as the case may be. As provided by paragraph 3, paragraph 1 applies to income derived from the direct use, letting or use in any other form of real property and to income from the alienation of such property.

Generally speaking, the term "real property" has the meaning which it has under the taxation laws of the Contracting State in which the property in question is situated, in accordance with paragraph 2. In any case, the term includes any option or similar right in respect of real property, the usufruct of real property, and rights to explore for or to exploit mineral deposits, sources, and other natural resources. The reference to "rights to explore for or to exploit mineral deposits, sources and other natural resources" includes rights generating either variable (e.g., computed by reference to the amount of value or production) or fixed payments. The term "real property" does not include ships and aircraft.

Unlike Article XIIIA of the 1942 Convention, Article VI does not contain an election to allow a resident of a Contracting State to compute tax on income from real property situated in the other State on a net basis. Both the *Internal Revenue Code* and the *Income Tax Act* of Canada generally allow for net basis taxation with respect to real estate rental income, although Canada does not permit such an election for natural resource royalties. Also, unlike the 1942 Convention which in Article XI imposes a 15 per cent limitation on the source basis taxation of rental or royalty income from real property, Article VI of the Convention allows a Contracting State to impose tax on such income under its internal law. In Canada the rate of tax on resource royalties is 25 per cent of the gross amount of the royalty, if the income is not attributable to a business carried on in Canada. In an exchange of notes to the Protocol, the United States and Canada agreed to resume negotiations, upon request by either country, to provide an appropriate limit on taxation in the State of source if either country subsequently increases its statutory tax rate now applicable to such royalties (25 per cent in the case of Canada and 30 per cent in the case of the United States).

Article VII — Business Profits

Paragraph 1 provides that business profits of a resident of a Contracting State are taxable only in that State unless the resident carries on business in the other Contracting State through a permanent establishment situated in that other State. If the resident carries on, or has carried on, business through such a permanent establishment, the other State may tax such business profits but only so much of them as are attributable to the permanent establishment. The reference to a prior permanent establishment ("or has carried on") makes clear that a Contracting State in which a permanent establishment existed has the right to tax the business profits attributable to that permanent establishment, even if there is a delay in the receipt or accrual of such profits until after the permanent establishment has been terminated.

Any business profits received or accrued in taxable years in which the Convention has effect, in accordance with Article XXX (Entry Into Force), which are attributable to a permanent establishment that was previously terminated are subject to tax in the Contracting State in which such permanent establishment existed under the provisions of Article VII.

Paragraph 2 provides that where a resident of either Canada or the United States carries on business in the other Contracting State through a permanent establishment in that other State, both Canada and the United States shall attribute to that permanent establishment business profits which the permanent establishment might be expected to make if it were a distinct and separate person engaged in the same or similar activities under the same or similar conditions and dealing wholly independently with the resident and with any other person related to the resident. The term "related to the resident" is to be interpreted in accordance with paragraph 2 of Article IX (Related Persons). The reference to other related persons is intended to make clear that the test of paragraph 2 is not restricted to independence between a permanent establishment and a home office.

Paragraph 3 provides that, in determining business profits of a permanent establishment, there are to be allowed as deductions those expenses which are incurred for the purposes of the permanent establishment, including executive and administrative expenses, whether incurred in the State in which the permanent establishment is situated or in any other State. However, nothing in the paragraph requires Canada or the United States to allow a deduction for any expenditure which would not generally be allowed as a deduction under its taxation laws. The language of this provision differs from that of paragraph 1 of Article III of the 1942 Convention, which states that in the determination of net industrial and commercial profits of a permanent establishment there shall be allowed as deductions "all expenses, wherever incurred" as long as such expenses are reasonably allocable to the permanent establishment. Paragraph 3 of Article VII of the Convention is not intended to have any implications for interpretation of the 1942 Convention, but is intended to assure that under the Convention deductions are allowed by a Contracting State which are generally allowable by that State.

Paragraph 4 provides that no business profits are to be attributed to a permanent establishment of a resident of a Contracting State by reason of the use of the permanent establishment for merely purchasing goods or merchandise or merely providing executive, managerial, or administrative facilities or services for the resident. Thus, if a company resident in a Contracting State has a permanent establishment in the other State, and uses the permanent establishment for the mere performance of stewardship or other managerial services carried on for the benefit of the resident, this activity will not result in profits being attributed to the permanent establishment.

Paragraph 5 provides that business profits are to be attributed to a permanent establishment by the same method in every taxable period unless there is good and sufficient reason to change such method. In the United States, such a change may be a change in accounting method requiring the approval of the Internal Revenue Service.

Paragraph 6 explains the relationship between the provisions of Article VII and other provisions of the Convention. Where business profits include items of income which are dealt with separately in other Articles of the Convention, those other Articles are controlling.

Paragraph 7 provides a definition for the term "attributable to." Profits "attributable to" a permanent establishment are those derived from the assets or activities of the permanent establishment. Paragraph 7 does not preclude Canada or the United States from using appropriate domestic tax law rules of attribution. The "attributable to" definition does not, for example, preclude a taxpayer from using the rules of section 1.864-4(c)(5) of the Treasury Regulations to assure for U.S. tax purposes that interest arising in the United States is attributable to a permanent establishment in the United States. (Interest arising outside the United States is attributable to a permanent establishment in the United States based on the principles of Regulations sections 1.864-5 and 1.864-6 and Revenue Ruling 75-253, 1975-2 C.B. 203.) Income that would be taxable under the Code and that is "attributable to" a permanent establishment under paragraph 7 is taxable pursuant to Article VII, however, even if such income might under the Code be treated as fixed or determinable annual or periodical gains or income not effectively connected with the conduct of a trade or business within the United States. The "attributable to" definition means that the limited "force-of-attraction" rule of Code section 864(c)(3) does not apply for U.S. tax purposes under the Convention.

Article VIII — Transportation

Paragraph 1 provides that profits derived by a resident of a Contracting State from the operation of ships or aircraft in international traffic are exempt from tax in the other Contracting State, even if, under Article VII (Business Profits), such profits are attributable to a permanent establishment. Paragraph 1 also provides that gains derived by a resident of a Contracting State from the alienation of ships, aircraft or containers (including trailers and related equipment for the transport of containers) used principally in international traffic are exempt from tax in the other Contracting State even if, under Article XIII (Gains), those gains would be taxable in that other State. These rules differ from Article V of the 1942 Convention, which conditions the exemption in the State of source on registration of the ship or aircraft in the other State. Paragraph 1 also applies notwithstanding the provisions of Article XII (Royalties). Thus, to the extent that profits described in paragraph 2 would also fall within Article XII (Royalties) (e.g., rent from the lease of a container), the provisions of Article VIII are controlling.

Paragraph 2(a) provides that profits covered by paragraph 1 include profits from the rental of ships or aircraft operated in international traffic. Such rental profits are included whether the rental is on a time, voyage, or bareboat basis, and irrespective of the State of residence of the operator.

Paragraph 2(b) provides that profits covered by paragraph 1 include profits derived from the use, maintenance or rental of containers, including trailers and related equipment for the transport of containers, if such containers are used in international traffic.

Paragraph 2(c) provides that profits covered by paragraph 1 include profits derived by a resident of a Contracting State from the rental of ships, aircraft, or containers (including trailers and related equipment for the transport of containers), even if not operated in international traffic, as long as such profits are incidental to profits of such person referred to in paragraphs 1, 2(a), or 2(b).

Paragraph 3 states that profits derived by a resident of a Contracting State from a voyage of a ship where the principal purpose of the voyage is to transport passengers or property between points in the other Contracting State is taxable in that other State, whether or not the resident maintains a permanent establishment there. Paragraph 3 overrides the provisions of Article VII. Profits from such a voyage do not qualify for exemption under Article VIII by virtue of the definition of "international traffic" in paragraph 1(h) of Article III (General Definitions). However, profits from a similar voyage by aircraft are taxable in the Contracting State of source only if the profits are attributable to a permanent establishment maintained in that State.

Paragraph 4 provides that profits derived by a resident of a Contracting State engaged in the operation of motor vehicles or a railway as a common carrier or contract carrier, and attributable to the transportation of passengers or property between a point outside the other Contracting State and any other point are exempt from tax in that other State. In addition, profits of such a person from the rental of motor vehicles (including trailers) or railway rolling stock, or from the use, maintenance, or rental of containers (including trailers and related equipment for the transport of containers) used to transport passengers or property between a point outside the other Contracting State and any other point are exempt from tax in that other State.

Paragraph 5 provides that a resident of a Contracting State that participates in a pool, a joint business, or an international operating agency is subject to the provisions of paragraphs 1, 3, and 4 with respect to the profits or gains referred to in paragraphs 1, 3, and 4.

Paragraph 6 states that profits derived by a resident of a Contracting State from the use, maintenance, or rental of railway rolling stock, motor vehicles, trailers, or containers (including trailers and related equipment for the transport of containers) used in the other Contracting State for a period not expected to exceed 183 days in the aggregate in any 12-month period are exempt from tax in that other State except to the extent that the profits are attributable to a permanent establishment, in which case the State of source has the right to tax under Article VII. The provisions of paragraph 6, unlike the provisions of paragraph 4, apply whether or not the resident is engaged in the operation of motor vehicles or a railway as a common carrier or contract carrier. Paragraph 6 overrides the provisions of Article XII (Royalties), which would otherwise permit taxation in the State of source in the circumstances described.

Gains from the alienation of motor vehicles and railway rolling stock derived by a resident of a Contracting State are not affected by paragraph 4 or 6. Such gains would be taxable in the other Contracting State, however, only if the motor vehicles or rolling stock formed part of a permanent establishment maintained there. See paragraphs 2 and 4 of Article XIII.

Article IX — Related Persons

Paragraph 1 authorizes Canada and the United States, as the case may be, to adjust the amount of income, loss, or tax payable by a person with respect to arrangements between that person and a related person in the other Contracting State. Such adjustment may be made when arrangements between related persons differ from those that would obtain between unrelated persons. The term "person" encompasses a company resident in a third State with, for example, a permanent establishment in a Contracting State.

Paragraph 2 provides that, for the purposes of Article IX, a person is deemed to be related to another person if either participates directly or indirectly in the management or control of the other or if any third person or persons participate directly or indirectly in the management or control of both. Thus, if a resident of any State controls directly or indirectly a company resident in Canada and a company resident in the United States, such companies are considered to be related persons for purposes of Article IX. Article IX and the definition of "related person" in paragraph 2 may encompass situations that would not be covered by provisions in the domestic laws of the Contracting States. Nor is the paragraph 2 definition controlling for the definition of "related person" or similar terms appearing in other Articles of the Convention. Those terms are defined as provided in paragraph 2 of Article III (General Definitions).

Paragraph 3 provides that where, pursuant to paragraph 1, an adjustment is made or to be made by a Contracting State, the other Contracting State shall make a corresponding adjustment to the income, loss, or tax of the related person in that other State, provided that the other State agrees with the adjustment and, within six years from the end of the taxable year of the person in the first State to which the adjustment relates, the competent authority of the other State has been notified in writing of the adjustment. The reference to an adjustment which "is made or to be made" does not require a Contracting State to formally propose an adjustment before paragraph 3 becomes pertinent. The notification required by paragraph 3 may be made by any of the related persons involved or by the competent authority of the State which makes or is to make the initial adjustment. The notification must give details regarding the adjustment sufficient to apprise the competent authority receiving the notification of the nature of the adjustment. If the requirements of paragraph 3 are complied with, the corresponding adjustment will be made by the other Contracting State notwithstanding any time or procedural limitations in the domestic law of that State.

Paragraph 4 provides that in a case where the other Contracting State has not been notified as provided in paragraph 3 and if the person whose income, loss, or tax is being adjusted has not received notification of the adjustment within five and one-half years from the end of its taxable year to which the adjustment relates, such adjustment shall not be made to the extent that the adjustment would give rise to double taxation between the United States and Canada. Again, the notification referred to in this paragraph need not be a formal adjustment, but it must be in writing and must contain sufficient details to permit the taxpayer to give the notification referred to in paragraph 3.

If, for example, the Internal Revenue Service proposes to make an adjustment to the income of a U.S. company pursuant to Code section 482, and the adjustment involves an allocation of income from a related Canadian company, the competent authority of Canada must receive written notification of the proposed IRS adjustment within six years from the end of the taxable year of the U.S. company to which the adjustment relates. If such notification is not received in a timely fashion and if the U.S. company does not receive written notification of the adjustment from the IRS within 5-1/2 years from the end of its relevant taxable year, the IRS will unilaterally recede on the proposed section 482 adjustment to the extent that this adjustment would otherwise give rise to double taxation between the United States and Canada. The Internal Revenue Service will determine whether and to what extent the adjustment would give rise to double taxation with respect to income arising in Canada by examining the relevant facts and circumstances such as the amount of foreign tax credits attributable to Canadian taxes paid by the U.S. company, including any carryovers and credits for deemed paid taxes.

Paragraph 5 provides that neither a corresponding adjustment described in paragraph 3 nor the cancelling of an adjustment described in paragraph 4 will be made in any case of fraud, willful default, neglect, or gross negligence on the part of the taxpayer or any related person.

Paragraphs 3 and 4 of Article IX are exceptions to the "saving clause" contained in paragraph 2 of Article XXIX (Miscellaneous Rules), as provided in paragraph 3(a) of Article XXIX. Paragraphs 3 and 4 of Article IX apply to adjustments made or to be made with respect to taxable years for which the Convention has effect as provided in paragraphs 2 and 5 of Article XXX (Entry Into Force).

Article X — Dividends

Paragraph 1 allows a Contracting State to impose tax on its residents with respect to dividends paid by a company which is a resident of the other Contracting State.

Paragraph 2 limits the amount of tax that may be imposed on such dividends by the Contracting State in which the company paying the dividends is resident if the beneficial owner of the dividends is a resident of the other Contracting State. The limitation is 10 per cent of the gross amount of the dividends if the beneficial owner is a company that owns 10 per cent or more of the voting stock of the company paying the dividends; and 15 per cent of the gross amount of the dividends in all other cases. Paragraph 2 does not impose any restrictions with respect to taxation of the profits out of which the dividends are paid.

Paragraph 3 defines the term "dividends," as the term is used in this Article. Each Contracting State is permitted to apply its domestic law rules for differentiating dividends from interest and other disbursements.

Paragraph 4 provides that the limitations of paragraph 2 do not apply if the beneficial owner of the dividends carries on business in the State in which the company paying the dividends is a resident through a permanent establishment or fixed base situated there, and the stockholding in respect of which the dividends are paid is effectively connected with such permanent establishment or fixed base. In such a case, the dividends are taxable pursuant to the provisions of Article VII (Business Profits) or Article XIV (Independent Personal Services), as the case may be. Thus, dividends paid in respect of holdings forming part of the assets of a permanent establishment or fixed base or which are otherwise effectively connected with such permanent establishment or fixed base (i.e., dividends attributable to the permanent establishment or fixed base) will be taxed on a net basis using the rates and rules of taxation generally applicable to residents of the State in which the permanent establishment or fixed base is situated.

Paragraph 5 imposes limitations on the right of Canada or the United States, as the case may be, to impose tax on dividends paid by a company which is a resident of the other Contracting State. The State in which the company is not resident may not tax such dividends except insofar as they are paid to a resident of that State or the holding in respect of which the dividends are paid is effectively connected with a permanent establishment or fixed base in that State. In the case of the United States, such dividends may also be taxed in the hands of a U.S. citizen and certain former citizens, pursuant to the "saving clause" of paragraph 2 of Article XXIX (Miscellaneous Rules). In addition, the Contracting State in which the company is not resident may not subject such company's undistributed profits to any tax. See, however, paragraphs 6, 7, and 8 which, in certain circumstances, qualify the rules of paragraph 5. Neither paragraph 5 nor any other provision of the Convention restricts the ability of the United States to apply the provisions of the Code concerning foreign personal holding companies and controlled foreign corporations.

Paragraph 6 provides that, notwithstanding paragraph 5, a Contracting State in which is maintained a permanent establishment or permanent establishments of a company resident in the other Contracting State may impose tax on such company's earnings, in addition to the tax that would be charged on the earnings of a company resident in that State. The additional tax may not, however, exceed 10 per cent of the amount of the earnings which have not been subjected to such additional tax in previous taxation years. Thus, Canada, which has a branch profits tax in force, may impose that tax up to the 10 per cent limitation in the case of a United States company with one or more permanent establishments in Canada. This branch profits tax may be imposed notwithstanding other rules of the Convention, including paragraph 6 of Article XXV (Non-Discrimination).

For purposes of paragraph 6, the term "earnings" means the excess of business profits attributable to all permanent establishments for a year and previous years over the sum of: a) business losses attributable to such permanent establishments for such years; b) all taxes on profits, whether or not covered by the Convention (e.g., provincial taxes on profits and provincial resource royalties (which Canada considers "taxes") in excess of the mineral resource allowance provided for under the law of Canada), other than the additional tax referred to in paragraph 6; c) profits reinvested in such State; and d) $500,000 (Canadian, or its equivalent in U.S. dollars) less any amounts deducted under paragraph 6(d) with respect to the same or a similar business by the company or an associated company. The deduction under paragraph 6(d) is available as of the first year for which the Convention has effect, regardless of the prior earnings and tax expenses, if any, of the permanent establishment. The $500,000 deduction is taken into account after other deductions, and is permanent. For the purpose of paragraph 6, references to business profits and business losses include gains and losses from the alienation of property forming part of the business property of a permanent establishment. The term "associated company" includes a company which directly or indirectly controls another company or two companies directly or indirectly controlled by the same person or persons, as well as any two companies that deal with each other not at arm's length. This definition differs from the definition of "related persons" in paragraph 2 of Article IX (Related Persons).

Paragraph 7 provides that, notwithstanding paragraph 5, a Contracting State that does not impose a branch profits tax as described in paragraph 6 (i.e., under current law, the United States) may tax a dividend paid by a company which is a resident of the other Contracting State if at least 50 per cent of the company's gross income from all sources was included in the computation of business profits attributable to one or more permanent establishments which such company had in the first-mentioned State. The dividend subject to such a tax must, however, be attributable to profits earned by the company in taxable years beginning after September 26, 1980 and the 50 per cent test must be met for the three-year period preceding the taxable year of the company in which the dividend is declared (including years ending on or before September 26, 1980) or such shorter period as the company had been in existence prior to that taxable year. Dividends will be deemed to be distributed, for purposes of paragraph 7, first out of profits of the taxation year of the company in which the distribution is made and then out of the profits of the preceding year or years of the company. Paragraph 7 provides further that if a resident of the other Contracting State is the beneficial owner of such dividends, any tax imposed under paragraph 7 is subject to the 10 or 15 per cent limitation of paragraph 2 or the rules of paragraph 4 (providing for dividends to be taxed as business profits or income from independent personal services), as the case may be.

Paragraph 8 provides that, notwithstanding paragraph 5, a company which is a resident of Canada and which, absent the provisions of the Convention, has income subject to tax by the United States may be liable for the United States accumulated earnings tax and personal holding company tax. These taxes can be applied, however, only if 50 per cent or more in value of the outstanding voting shares of the company is owned, directly or indirectly, throughout the last half of its taxable year by residents of a third State or by citizens or residents of the United States, other than citizens of Canada who are resident in the United States but who either do not have immigrant status in the United States or who have not been resident in the United States for more than three taxable years. The accumulated earnings tax is applied to accumulated taxable income calculated without the benefits of the Convention. Similarly, the personal holding company tax is applied to undistributed personal holding company income computed as if the Convention had not come into force.

Article X does not apply to dividends paid by a company which is not a resident of either Contracting State. Such dividends, if they are income of a resident of one of the Contracting States, are subject to tax as provided in Article XXII (Other Income).

Article XI — Interest

Paragraph 1 allows interest arising in Canada or the United States and paid to a resident of the other State to be taxed in the latter State. Paragraph 2 provides that such interest may also be taxed in the Contracting State where it arises, but if a resident of the other Contracting State is the beneficial owner, the tax imposed by the State of source is limited to 15 per cent of the gross amount of the interest.

Paragraph 3 provides a number of exceptions to the right of the source State to impose a 15 per cent tax under paragraph 2. The following types of interest beneficially owned by a resident of a Contracting State are exempt from tax in the State of source: a) interest beneficially owned by a Contracting State, a political subdivision, or a local authority thereof, or an instrumentality of such State, subdivision, or authority, which interest is not subject to tax by such State; b) interest beneficially owned by a resident of a Contracting State and paid with respect to debt obligations issued at arm's length which are guaranteed or insured by such State or a political subdivision thereof, or by an instrumentality of such State or subdivision (not by a local authority or an instrumentality thereof, but only if the guarantor or insurer is not subject to tax by that State; c) interest paid by a Contracting State, a political subdivision, or a local authority thereof, or by an instrumentality of such State, subdivision, or authority, but only if the payor is not subject to tax by such State; and d) interest beneficially owned by a seller of equipment, merchandise, or services, but only if the interest is paid in connection with a sale on credit of equipment, merchandise, or services and the sale was made at arm's length. Whether such a transaction is made at arm's length will be determined in the United States under the facts and circumstances. The relationship between the parties is a factor, but not the only factor, taken into account in making this determination. Furthermore, interest paid by a company resident in the other Contracting State with respect to an obligation entered into before September 26, 1980 is exempt from tax in the State of source (irrespective of the State of residence of the beneficial owner), provided that such interest would have been exempt from tax in the Contracting State of source under Article XII of the 1942 Convention. Thus, interest paid by a United States corporation whose business is not managed and controlled in Canada to a recipient not resident in Canada or to a corporation not managed and controlled in Canada would be exempt from Canadian tax as long as the debt obligation was entered into before September 26, 1980. The phrase "not subject to tax by that ... State" in paragraph 3(a), (b), and (c) refers to taxation at the Federal levels of Canada and the United States.

The phrase "obligation entered into before the date of signature of this Convention" means: (1) any obligation under which funds were dispersed prior to September 26, 1980; (2) any obligation under which funds are dispersed on or after September 26, 1980, pursuant to a written contract binding prior to and on such date, and at all times thereafter until the obligation is satisfied; or (3) any obligation with respect to which, prior to September 26, 1980, a lender had taken every action to signify approval under procedures ordinarily employed by such lender in similar transactions and had sent or deposited for delivery to the person to whom the loan is to be made written evidence of such approval in the form of a document setting forth, or referring to a document sent by the person to whom the loan is to be made that sets forth, the principal terms of such loan.

Paragraph 4 defines the term "interest", as used in Article XI, to include, among other things, debt claims of every kind as well as income assimilated to income from money lent by the taxation laws of the Contracting State in which the income arises. In no event, however, is income dealt with in Article X (Dividends) to be considered interest.

Paragraph 5 provides that neither the 15 per cent limitation on tax in the Contracting State of source provided in paragraph 2 nor the various exemptions from tax in such State provided in paragraph 3 apply if the beneficial owner of the interest is a resident of the other Contracting State carrying on business in the State of source through a permanent establishment or fixed base, and the debt claim in respect of which the interest is paid is effectively connected with such permanent establishment or fixed base (i.e., the interest is attributable to the permanent establishment or fixed base). In this case, interest income is to be taxed in the Contracting State of source as business profits — that is, on a net basis.

Paragraph 6 establishes the source of interest for purposes of Article XI. Interest is considered to arise in a Contracting State if the payer is that State, or a political subdivision, local authority, or resident of that State. However, in cases where the person paying the interest, whether a resident of a Contracting State or of a third State, has in a State other than that of which he is a resident a permanent establishment or fixed base in connection with which the indebtedness on which the interest was paid was incurred, and such interest is borne by the permanent establishment or fixed base, then such interest is deemed to arise in the State in which the permanent establishment or fixed base is situated and not in the State of the payer's residence. Thus, pursuant to paragraphs 6 and 2, and Article XXII (Other Income), Canadian tax will not be imposed on interest paid to a U.S. resident by a company resident in Canada if the indebtedness is incurred in connection with, and the interest is borne by, a permanent establishment of the company situated in a third State. "Borne by" means allowable as a deduction in computing taxable income. Paragraph 7 provides that in cases involving special relationships between persons Article XI does not apply to amounts in excess of the amount which would have been agreed upon between persons having no special relationship; any such excess amount remains taxable according to the laws of Canada and the United States, consistent with any relevant provisions of the Convention.

Paragraph 8 restricts the right of a Contracting State to impose tax on interest paid by a resident of the other Contracting State. The first State may not impose any tax on such interest except insofar as the interest is paid to a resident of that State or arises in that State or the debt claim in respect of which the interest is paid is effectively connected with a permanent establishment or fixed base situated in that State. Thus, pursuant to paragraph 8 the United States has agreed not to impose tax on certain interest paid by Canadian companies to persons not resident in the United States, to the extent that such companies would pay U.S.-source interest under Code section 861(a)(1)(C) but not under the source rule of paragraph 6. It is to be noted that paragraph 8 is subject to the "saving clause" of paragraph 2 of Article XXIX (Miscellaneous Rules), so the United States may in all events impose its tax on interest received by U.S. citizens.

Article XII — Royalties

Generally speaking, under the 1942 Convention royalties, including royalties with respect to motion picture films, which are derived by a resident of one Contracting State from sources within the other Contracting State are taxed at a maximum rate of 15 per cent in the latter State; copyright royalties are exempt from tax in the State of source, if the resident does not have a permanent establishment in that State. See Articles II, III, XIIIC, and paragraph 1 of Article XI of the 1942 Convention, and paragraph 6(a) of the Protocol to the 1942 Convention.

Paragraph 1 of Article XII of the Convention provides that a Contracting State may tax its residents with respect to royalties arising in the other Contracting State. Paragraph 2 provides that such royalties may also be taxed in the Contracting State in which they arise, but that if a resident of the other Contracting State is the beneficial owner of the royalties the tax in the Contracting State of source is limited to 10 per cent of the gross amount of the royalties.

Paragraph 3 provides that, notwithstanding paragraph 2, copyright royalties and other like payments in respect of the production or reproduction of any literary, dramatic, musical, or artistic work, including royalties from such works on videotape or other means of reproduction for private (home) use, if beneficially owned by a resident of the other Contracting State, may not be taxed by the Contracting State of source. This exemption at source does not apply to royalties in respect of motion pictures, and of works on film, video tape or other means of reproduction for use in connection with television broadcasting. Such royalties are subject to tax at a maximum rate of 10 per cent in the Contracting State in which they arise, as provided in paragraph 2 unless the provisions of paragraph 5, described below, apply).

Paragraph 4 defines the term "royalties" for purposes of Article XII. "Royalties" means payments of any kind received as consideration for the use of or the right to use any copy right of literary, artistic, or scientific work, including motion pictures, and works on film, videotape or other means of reproduction for use in connection with television broadcasting, any patent, trademark, design or model, plan, secret formula or process, or any payment for the use of or the right to use tangible personal property or for information concerning industrial, commercial, or scientific experience. The term "royalties" also includes gains from the alienation of any intangible property or rights described in paragraph 4 to the extent that such gains are contingent on the productivity, use, or subsequent disposition of such intangible property or rights. Thus, a guaranteed minimum payment derived from the alienation of (but not the use of) any right or property described in paragraph 4 is not a "royalty." Any amounts deemed contingent on use by reason of Code section 871(e) are, however, royalties under paragraph 2 of Article III (General Definitions), subject to Article XXVI (Mutual Agreement Procedure). The term "royalties" does not encompass management fees, which are covered by the provisions of Article VII (Business Profits) or XIV (Independent Personal Services), or payments under a *bona fide* cost-sharing arrangement. Technical service fees may be royalties in cases where the fees are periodic and dependent upon productivity or a similar measure.

Paragraph 5 provides that the 10 per cent limitation on tax in the Contracting State of source provided by paragraph 2, and the exemption in the Contracting State of source for certain copyright royalties provided by paragraph 3, do not apply if the beneficial owner of the royalties carries on business in the State of source through a permanent establishment or fixed base and the right or property in respect of which the royalties are paid is effectively connected with such permanent establishment or fixed base (i.e., the royalties are attributable to the permanent establishment or fixed base). In that event, the royalty income would be taxable under the provisions of Article VII (Business Profits) or XIV (Independent Personal Services), as the case may be.

Paragraph 6 establishes rules to determine the source of royalties for purposes of Article XII. The first rule is that royalties arise in a Contracting State when the payer is that State, or a political subdivision, local authority, or resident of that State. Notwithstanding that rule, royalties arise not in the State of the payer's residence but in any State, whether or not a Contracting State, in which is situated a permanent establishment or fixed base in connection with which the obligation to pay royalties was incurred, if such royalties are borne by such permanent establishment or fixed base. Thus, royalties paid to a resident of the United States by a company resident in Canada for the use of property in a third State will not be subject to tax in Canada if the obligation to pay the royalties is incurred in connection with, and the royalties are borne by, a permanent establishment of the company in a third State. "Borne by" means allowable as a deduction in computing taxable income.

A third rule, which overrides both the residence rule and the permanent establishment rule just described, provides that royalties for the use of, or the right to use, intangible property or tangible personal property in a Contracting State arise in that State. Thus, consistent with the provisions of Code section 861(a)(4), if a resident of a third State pays royalties to a resident of Canada for the use of or the right to use intangible property or tangible personal property in the United States, such royalties are considered to arise in the United States and are subject to taxation by the United States consistent with the Convention. Similarly, if a resident of Canada pays royalties to a resident of a third State, such royalties are considered to arise in the United States and are subject to U.S. taxation if they are for the use of or the right to use intangible property or tangible personal property in the United States. The term "intangible property" encompasses all the items described in paragraph 4, other than tangible personal property.

Paragraph 7 provides that in cases involving special relationships between persons the benefits of Article XII do not apply to amounts in excess of the amount which would have been agreed upon between persons with no special relationship; any such excess amount remains taxable according to the laws of Canada and the United States, consistent with any relevant provisions of the Convention.

Paragraph 8 restricts the right of a Contracting State to impose tax on royalties paid by a resident of the other Contracting State. The first State may not impose any tax on such royalties except insofar as they arise in that State or they are paid to a resident of that State or the right or property in respect of which the royalties are paid is effectively connected with a permanent establishment or fixed base situated in that State. This rule parallels the rule in paragraph 8 of Article XI (Interest) and paragraph 5 of Article X (Dividends). Again, U.S. citizens remain subject to U.S. taxation on royalties received despite this rule, by virtue of paragraph 2 of Article XXIX (Miscellaneous Rules).

Article XIII — Gains

Paragraph 1 provides that Canada and the United States may each tax gains from the alienation of real property situated within that State which are derived by a resident of the other Contracting State. The term "real property situated in the other Contracting State" is defined for this purpose in paragraph 3 of this Article. The term "alienation" used in paragraph 1 and other paragraphs of Article XIII means sales, exchanges and other dispositions or deemed dispositions (e.g., change of use, gifts, distributions, death) that are taxable events under the taxation laws of the Contracting State applying the provisions of the Article.

Paragraph 2 of Article XIII provides that the Contracting State in which a resident of the other Contracting State "has or had" a permanent establishment or fixed base may tax gains from the alienation of personal property constituting business property if such gains are attributable to such permanent establishment or fixed base. Unlike paragraph 1 of Article VII (Business Profits), paragraph 2 limits the right of the source State to tax such gains to a twelve-month period following the termination of the permanent establishment or fixed base.

Paragraph 3 provides a definition of the term "real property situated in the other Contracting State." Where the United States is the other Contracting State, the term includes real property (as defined in Article VI (Income from Real Property)) situated in the United States and a United States real property interest. Thus, the United States retains the ability to exercise its full taxing right under the *Foreign Investment in Real Property Tax Act* (Code section 897). (For a transition rule from the 1942 Convention, see paragraph 9 of this Article).

Where Canada is the other Contracting State, the term means real property (as defined in Article VI) situated in Canada; shares of stock of a company, the value of whose shares consists principally of Canadian real property; and an interest in a partnership, trust or estate, the value of which consists principally of Canadian real property. The term "principally" means more than 50 per cent. Taxation in Canada is preserved through several tiers of entities if the value of the company's shares or the partnership, trust or estate is ultimately dependent principally upon real property situated in Canada.

Paragraph 4 reserves to the Contracting State of residence the sole right to tax gains from the alienation of any property other than property referred to in paragraphs 1, 2, and 3.

Paragraph 5 states that, despite paragraph 4, a Contracting State may impose tax on gains derived by an individual who is a resident of the other Contracting State if such individual was a resident of the first-mentioned State for 120 months (whether or not consecutive) during any period of 20 consecutive years preceding the alienation of the property, and was a resident of that State at any time during the 10-year period immediately preceding the alienation of the property. The property (or property received in substitution in a tax-free transaction in the first-mentioned State) must have been owned by the individual at the time he ceased to be a resident of the first-mentioned State.

Paragraph 6 provides a rule to coordinate Canadian and United States taxation of gains from the alienation of a principal residence situated in Canada. An individual (not a citizen of the United States) who was a resident of Canada and becomes a resident of the United States may determine his liability for U.S. income tax purposes in respect of gain from the alienation of a principal residence in Canada owned by him at the time he ceased to be a resident of Canada by claiming an adjusted basis for such residence in an amount no less than the fair market value of the residence at that time. Under paragraph 2(b) of Article XXX, the rule of paragraph 6 applies to gains realized for U.S. income tax purposes in taxable years beginning on or after the first day of January next following the date when instruments of ratification are exchanged, even if a particular individual described in paragraph 6 ceased to be a resident of Canada prior to such date. Paragraph 6 supplements any benefits available to a taxpayer pursuant to the provisions of the Code, e.g., section 1034.

Paragraph 7 provides a rule to coordinate U.S. and Canadian taxation of gains in circumstances where an individual is subject to tax in both Contracting States and one Contracting State deems a taxable alienation of property by such person to have occurred, while the other Contracting State at that time does not find a realization or recognition of income and thus defers, but does not forgive, taxation. In such a case the individual may elect in his annual return of income for the year of such alienation to be liable to tax in the latter Contracting State as if he had sold and repurchased the property for an amount equal to its fair market value at a time immediately prior to the deemed alienation. The provision would, for example, apply in the case of a gift by a U.S. citizen or a U.S. resident individual which Canada deems to be an income producing event for its tax purposes but with respect to which the United States defers taxation while assigning the donor's basis to the donee. The provision would also apply in the case of a U.S. citizen who, for Canadian tax purposes, is deemed to recognize income upon his departure from Canada, but not to a Canadian resident (not a U.S. citizen) who is deemed to recognize such income. The rule does not apply in the case of death, although Canada also deems that to be a taxable event, because the United States in effect forgives income taxation of economic gains at death. If in one Contracting State there are losses and gains from deemed alienations of different properties, then paragraph 7 must be applied consistently in the other Contracting State within the taxable period with respect to all such properties. Paragraph 7 only applies, however, if the deemed alienations of the properties result in a net gain.

Paragraph 8 concerns the coordination of Canadian and U.S. rules with respect to the recognition of gain on corporate organizations, reorganizations, amalgamations, divisions, and similar transactions. Where a resident of a Contracting State alienates property in such a transaction, and profit, gain, or income with respect to such alienation is not recognized for income tax purposes in the Contracting State of residence, the competent authority of the other Contracting State may agree, pursuant to paragraph 8, if requested by the person who acquires the property, to defer recognition of the profit, gain, or income with respect to such property for income tax purposes. This deferral shall be for such time and under such other conditions as are stipulated between the person who acquires the property and the competent authority. The agreement of the competent authority of the State of source is entirely discretionary and will be granted only to the extent necessary to avoid double taxation of income. This provision means, for example, that the United States competent authority may agree to defer recognition of gain with respect to a transaction if the alienator would otherwise recognize gain for U.S. tax purposes and would not recognize gain under Canada's law. The provision only applies, however, if alienations described in paragraph 8 result in a net gain. In the absence of extraordinary circumstances the provisions of the paragraph must be applied consistently within a taxable period with respect to alienations described in the paragraph that take place within that period.

Paragraph 9 provides a transitional rule reflecting the fact that under Article VIII of the 1942 Convention gains from the sale or exchange of capital assets are exempt from taxation in the State of source provided the taxpayer had no permanent establishment in that State. Paragraph 9 applies to deemed, as well as actual, alienations or dispositions. In addition, paragraph 9 applies to a gain described in paragraph 1, even though such gain is also income within the meaning of paragraph 3 of Article VI. Paragraph 9 will apply to transactions notwithstanding section 1125(c) of the *Foreign Investment in Real Property Tax Act*, Public Law 96-499 ("FIRPTA").

Paragraph 9 applies to capital assets alienated by a resident of a Contracting State if (a) that person owned the asset on September 26, 1980 and was a resident of that Contracting State on September 26, 1980 (and at all times after that date until the alienation), or (b) the asset was acquired by that person in an alienation of property which qualified as a non-recognition transaction for tax purposes in the other Contracting State. For purposes of subparagraph 9(b), a non-recognition transaction is a transaction in which gain resulting therefrom is, in effect, deferred for tax purposes, but is not permanently forgiven. Thus, in the United States, certain tax-free organizations, reorganizations, liquidations and like-kind exchanges will qualify as non-recognition transactions. However, a transfer of property at death will not constitute a non-recognition transaction, since any gain due to appreciation in the property is permanently forgiven in the United States due to the fair market value basis taken by the recipient of the property. If a transaction is a non-recognition transaction for tax purposes, the transfer of non-qualified property, or "boot," which may cause some portion of the gain on the transaction to be recognized, will not cause the transaction to lose its character as a non-recognition transaction for purposes of subparagraph 9(b). In addition, a transaction that would have been a non-recognition transaction in the United States but for the application of sections 897(d) and 897(e) of the Code will also constitute a non-recognition transaction for purposes of subparagraph 9(b). Further, a transaction which is not a non-recognition transaction under U.S. law, but to which non-recognition treatment is granted pursuant to the agreement of the competent authority under paragraph 8 of this Article, is a non-recognition transaction for purposes of subparagraph 9(b). However, a transaction which is not a non-recognition transaction under U.S. law does not become a non-recognition transaction for purposes of subparagraph 9(b) merely because the basis of the property in the hands of the transferee is reduced under section 1125(d) of FIRPTA.

The benefits of paragraph 9 are not available to the alienation or disposition by a resident of a Contracting State of an asset that (a) on September 26, 1980 formed part of the business property of a permanent establishment or pertained to a fixed base which a resident of that Contracting State had in the other Contracting State, (b) was alienated after September 26, 1980 and before the alienation in question in any transaction that was not a non-recognition transaction, as described above, or (c) was owned at any time prior to the alienation in question and after September 26, 1980 by a person who was not a resident of that same Contracting State after September 26, 1980 while such person held the asset. Thus, for example, in order for paragraph 9 to be availed of by a Canadian resident who did not own the alienated asset on September 26, 1980, the asset must have been owned by other Canadian residents continuously after September 26, 1980 and must have been transferred only in transactions which were non-recognition transactions for U.S. tax purposes.

The availability of the benefits of paragraph 9 is illustrated by the following examples. It should be noted that the examples do not purport to fully describe the U.S. and Canadian tax consequences resulting from the transactions described therein. Any condition for the application of paragraph 9 which is not discussed in an example should be assumed to be satisfied.

Example 1. A, an individual resident of Canada, owned an appreciated U.S. real property interest on September 26, 1980. On January 1, 1982, A transferred the U.S. real property interest to X, a Canadian corporation, in exchange for 100 per cent of X's voting stock. A's gain on the transfer to X is exempt from U.S. tax under Article VIII of the 1942 Convention. Since the transaction qualifies as a non-recognition transaction for U.S. tax purposes, as described above, X is entitled to the benefits of paragraph 9, pursuant to subparagraph 9(b), upon a subsequent disposition of the U.S. real property interest occurring after the entry into force of this Convention. If A's transfer to X had instead occurred after the entry into force of this Convention, A would be entitled to the benefits of paragraph 9, pursuant to subparagraph 9(a), with respect to U.S. taxation of that portion of the gain resulting from the transfer to X that is attributable on a monthly basis to the period ending on December 31 of the year in which the Convention enters into force (or a greater portion of the gain as is shown to the satisfaction of the U.S. competent authority). X would be entitled to the benefits of paragraph 9 pursuant to subparagraph 9(b), upon a subsequent disposition of the U.S. real property interest.

Example 2. The facts are the same as in *Example 1*, except that A is a corporation which is resident in Canada. Assuming that the transfer of the U.S. real property interest to X is a section 351 transaction or a tax-free reorganization for U.S. tax purposes, the results are the same as in *Example 1*.

Example 3. The facts are the same as in Example 1, except that X is a U.S. corporation. If the transfer to X by A took place on January 1, 1982, A's gain on the transfer to X would be exempt from tax under Article VIII of the 1942 Convention and A would be entitled to the benefits of paragraph 9, pursuant to subparagraph 9(b), upon a subsequent disposition of the stock of X occurring after the entry into force of this Convention. If the transfer to X by A took place after the entry into force of this Convention, A would be entitled to the benefits of paragraph 9, pursuant to subparagraph 9(a), with respect to U.S. taxation (if any) of the gain resulting from the transfer to X, and would also be entitled to the benefits of paragraph 9, pursuant to subparagraph 9(b), upon a subsequent disposition of the stock of X. For several reasons, including the fact that X is a U.S. corporation, paragraph 9 has no impact on the U.S. tax consequences of a subsequent disposition by X of the U.S. real property interest in either case.

Example 4. B, a corporation resident in Canada, owns all of the stock of C, which is also a corporation resident in Canada. C owns a U.S. real property interest. After the Convention enters into force, B liquidates C in a section 332 liquidation. The transaction is treated as a non-recognition transaction for U.S. tax purposes under the definition of a non-recognition transaction described above. C is entitled to the benefits of paragraph 9, pursuant to subparagraph 9(a), with respect to gain taxed (if any) under section 897(d), and B is entitled to the benefits of paragraph 9, pursuant to subparagraph 9(b), upon a subsequent disposition of the U.S. real property interest. Generally, the United States would not subject B to tax upon the liquidation of C.

Example 5. The facts are the same as in *Example 4*, except that C is a U.S. corporation. B is entitled to the benefits of paragraph 9, pursuant to subparagraph 9(a), with respect to U.S. taxation (if any) of the gain resulting from the liquidation of C. B is not entitled to the benefits of paragraph 9 upon a subsequent disposition of the U.S. real property interest since that asset was held after September 26, 1980 by a person who was not a resident of Canada. The U.S. tax consequences to C are governed by the internal law of the United States.

Example 6. D, an individual resident of the United States, owns Canadian real estate. On January 1, 1982, D transfers the Canadian real estate to E, a corporation resident in Canada, in exchange for all of E's stock. This transfer is treated as a taxable transaction under the *Income Tax Act* of Canada. However, D's gain on the transfer is exempt from Canadian tax under Article VIII of the 1942 Convention. D is not entitled to the benefits of subparagraph 9(b) upon a subsequent disposition of the stock of E since the stock was not transferred in a transaction which was a non-recognition transaction for Canadian tax purposes. E is not entitled to Canadian benefits under this paragraph since, *inter alia*, it is a Canadian resident. (However, under Canadian law, both D and E would have a basis for tax purposes equal to the fair market value of the property at the time of D's transfer). If the transfer to E had taken place after entry into force of this Convention, D would be entitled to the benefits of paragraph 9, pursuant to subparagraph 9(a), with respect to Canadian tax resulting from the transfer to E, but would not be entitled to the benefits of subparagraph 9(b) upon a subsequent disposition of the E stock. (Note that E could seek to have the transaction treated as a non-recognition transaction under paragraph 8 of this Article, with the result that, if the competent authority agrees, D will take a carryover basis in the stock of E and be entitled to the benefits of subparagraph 9(b) upon a subsequent disposition thereof).

Example 7. The facts are the same as in Example 6, except that E is a U.S. corporation. This transaction is also a recognition event under Canadian law at the shareholder level. The results are generally the same as in *Example 6*. However, if the transfer to E had been granted non-recognition treatment in Canada pursuant to paragraph 8, both D and E would be entitled to the benefits of paragraph 9 for Canadian tax purposes, pursuant to subparagraph 9(b), upon subsequent dispositions of the stock of E or the Canadian real estate, respectively.

Example 8. F, an individual resident of the United States, owns all of the stock of G, a Canadian corporation, which in turn owns Canadian real estate. F causes G to be amalgamated in a merger with another Canadian corporation. This is a non-recognition transaction under Canadian law and F is entitled, for Canadian tax purposes, to the benefits of paragraph 9, pursuant to subparagraph 9(b), upon a subsequent disposition of the stock of the other Canadian corporation.

Example 9. H, a U.S. corporation, owns all of the stock of J, another U.S. corporation. J owns Canadian real estate. H liquidates J. For Canadian tax purposes, no tax is imposed on H as a result of the liquidation and H receives a fair market value basis in the Canadian real estate. Accordingly, since gain has been forgiven due to the fair market value basis (rather than postponed in a non-recognition transaction), H would not be entitled to the benefits of subparagraph 9(b) upon the subsequent disposition of the Canadian real estate. Canada would impose a tax on J, but J would be entitled to the benefits of paragraph 9, pursuant to subparagraph 9(a), with respect to Canadian tax imposed on the liquidation.

Example 10. The facts are the same as in *Example 9*, except that J is a Canadian corporation. Paragraph 9 does not affect the Canadian taxation of J. While H is subject to Canadian tax on the liquidation of J, H is entitled to the benefits of paragraph 9, pursuant to subparagraph 9(a), with respect to such Canadian taxation. H will take a fair market value basis (rather than have gain postponed in a non-recognition transaction) in the Canadian real estate for Canadian tax purposes and is thus not entitled to the benefits of paragraph 9 upon a subsequent disposition of the Canadian real estate (since, *inter alia*, the gain has been forgiven due to the fair market value basis).

Example 11. K, a U.S. corporation, owns the stock of L, another U.S. corporation, which in turn owns Canadian real estate. K causes L to be merged into another U.S. corporation. For Canadian tax purposes, such a transaction is treated as a recognition event, but Canada will not impose a tax on K under its internal law. Canada would impose tax on L, but L is entitled to the benefits of paragraph 9, pursuant to subparagraph 9(a), with respect to Canadian taxation of gain resulting from the merger. The acquiring U.S. corporation would take a fair market value basis in the Canadian real estate, and would thus not be entitled to the benefits of subparagraph 9(b) upon a subsequent disposition of the real estate. (Note that the acquiring U.S. corporation could seek to obtain non-recognition treatment under paragraph 8 of this Article, with the result that, if approved by the competent authority, it would obtain a carryover basis in the property and be entitled to the benefits of subparagraph 9(b) upon a subsequent disposition of the Canadian real estate).

Paragraph 9 provides that where a resident of Canada or the United States is subject to tax pursuant to Article XIII in the other Contracting State on gains from the alienation of a capital asset, and if the other conditions of paragraph 9 are satisfied, the amount of the gain shall be reduced for tax purposes in that other State by the amount of the gain attributable to the period during which the property was held up to and including December 31 of the year in which the documents of ratification are exchanged. The gain attributable to such person is normally determined by dividing the total gain by the number of full calendar months the property was held by such person, including, in the case of an alienation described in paragraph 9(b), the number of months in which a predecessor in interest held the property, and multiplying such monthly amount by the number of full calendar months ending on or before December 31 of the year in which the instruments of ratification are exchanged.

Upon a clear showing, however, a taxpayer may prove that a greater portion of the gain was attributable to the specified period. Thus, in the United States the fair market value of the alienated property at the treaty valuation date may be established under paragraph 9 in the manner and with the evidence that is generally required by U.S. Federal income, estate, and gift tax regulations. For this purpose a taxpayer may use valid appraisal techniques for valuing real estate such as the comparable sales approach (see Rev. Proc. 79-24, 1979-1 C.B. 565) and the reproduction cost approach. If more than one property is alienated in a single transaction each property will be considered individually.

A taxpayer who desires to make this alternate showing for U.S. tax purposes must so indicate on his U.S. income tax return for the year of the sale or exchange and must attach to the return a statement describing the relevant evidence. The U.S. competent authority or his authorized delegate will determine whether the taxpayer has satisfied the requirements of paragraph 9.

The amount of gain which is reduced by reason of the application of paragraph 9 is not to be treated for U.S. tax purposes as an amount of "nontaxed gain" under section 1125(d)(2)(B) of FIRPTA, where that section would otherwise apply. (Note that gain not taxed by virtue of the 1942 Convention is "nontaxed gain").

U.S. residents, citizens and former citizens remain subject to U.S. taxation on gains as provided by the Code notwithstanding the provisions of Article XIII, other than paragraphs 6 and 7. See paragraphs 2 and 3(a) of Article XXIX (Miscellaneous Rules).

Article XIV — Independent Personal Services

Article XIV concerns the taxation of income derived by an individual in respect of the performance of independent personal services. Such income may be taxed in the Contracting State of which such individual is a resident. It may also be taxed in the other Contracting State if the individual has or had a fixed base regularly available to him in the other State for the purpose of performing his activities, but only to the extent that the income is attributable to that fixed base. The use of the term "has or had" ensures that a Contracting State in which a fixed base existed has the right to tax income attributable to that fixed base even if there is a delay between the termination of the fixed base and the receipt or accrual of such income.

Unlike Article VII of the 1942 Convention, which provides a limited exemption from tax at source on income from independent personal services, Article XIV does not restrict the exemption to persons present in the State of source for fewer than 184 days. Furthermore, Article XIV does not allow the $5,000 exemption at source of the 1942 Convention, which was available even if services were performed through a fixed base. However, Article XIV provides complete exemption at source if a fixed base does not exist.

Article XV — Dependent Personal Services

Paragraph 1 provides that, in general, salaries, wages, and other similar remuneration derived by a resident of a Contracting State in respect of an employment are taxable only in that State unless the employment is exercised in the other Contracting State. If the employment is exercised in the other Contracting State, the entire remuneration derived therefrom may be taxed in that other State but only if, as provided by paragraph 2, the recipient is present in the other State for a period or periods exceeding 183 days in the calendar year, or the remuneration is borne by an employer who is a resident of that other State or by a permanent establishment or fixed base which the employer has in that other State. However, in all cases where the employee earns $10,000 or less in the currency of the State of source, such earnings are exempt from tax in that State. "Borne by" means allowable as a deduction in computing taxable income. Thus, if a Canadian resident individual employed at the Canadian permanent establishment of a U.S. company performs services in the United States, the income earned by the employee from such services is not exempt from U.S. tax under paragraph 1 if such income exceeds $10,000 (U.S.) because the U.S. company is entitled to a deduction for such wages in computing its taxable income.

Paragraph 3 provides that a resident of a Contracting State is exempt from tax in the other Contracting State with respect to remuneration derived in respect of an employment regularly exercised in more than one State on a ship, aircraft, motor vehicle, or train operated by a resident of the taxpayer's State of residence. The word "regularly" is intended to distinguish crew members from persons occasionally employed on a ship, aircraft, motor vehicle, or train. Only the Contracting State of which the employee and operator are resident has the right to tax such remuneration. However, this provision is subject to the "saving clause" of paragraph 2 of Article XXIX (Miscellaneous Rules), which permits the United States to tax its citizens despite paragraph 3.

Article XV states that its provisions are overridden by the more specific rules of Article XVIII (Pensions and Annuities) and Article XIX (Government Services).

Article XVI — Artistes and Athletes

Article XVI concerns income derived by a resident of a Contracting State as an entertainer, such as a theatre, motion picture, radio, or television artiste, or a musician, or as an athlete, from his personal activities as such exercised in the other Contracting State. Article XVI overrides Articles XIV (Independent Personal Services) and XV (Dependent Personal Services) to allow source basis taxation of an entertainer or athlete in cases where the latter Articles would not permit such taxation. Thus, paragraph 1 provides that certain income of an entertainer or athlete may be taxed in the State of source in all cases where the amount of gross receipts derived by the entertainer or athlete, including expenses reimbursed to him or borne on his behalf, exceeds $15,000 in the currency of that other State for the calendar year concerned. For example, where a resident of Canada who is an entertainer derives income from his personal activities as an entertainer in the United States, he is taxable in the United States on all such income in any case where his gross receipts are greater than $15,000 for the calendar year. Article XVI does not restrict the right of the State of source to apply the provisions of Articles XIV and XV. Thus, an entertainer or athlete resident in a Contracting State and earning $14,000 in wages borne by a permanent establishment in the other State may be taxed in the other State as provided in Article XV.

Paragraph 2 provides that where income in respect of personal activities exercised by an entertainer or an athlete accrues not to the entertainer or athlete himself but to another person, that income may, notwithstanding the provisions of Article VII (Business Profits), Article XIV, and Article XV, be taxed in the Contracting State in which the activities are exercised. The anti-avoidance rule of paragraph 2 does not apply if it is established by the entertainer or athlete that neither he nor persons related to him participate directly or indirectly in the profits of the other person in any manner, including the receipt of deferred remuneration, bonuses, fees, dividends, partnership distributions, or other distributions.

Thus, if an entertainer who is a resident of Canada is under contract with a company and the arrangement between the entertainer and the company provides for payments to the entertainer based on the profits of the company, all of the income of the company attributable to the performer's U.S. activities may be taxed in the United States irrespective of whether the company maintains a permanent establishment in the United States. Paragraph 2 does not affect the rule of paragraph 1 that applies to the entertainer or athlete himself.

Paragraph 3 provides that paragraphs 1 and 2 of Article XVI do not apply to the income of an athlete in respect of an employment with a team which participates in a league with regularly scheduled games in both Canada and the United States, nor do those paragraphs apply to the income of such a team. Such an athlete is subject to the rules of Article XV. Thus, the athlete's remuneration would be exempt from tax in the Contracting State of source if he is a resident of the other Contracting State and earns $10,000 or less in the currency of the State of source, or if he is present in that State for a period or periods not exceeding in the aggregate 183 days in the calendar year, and his remuneration is not borne by a resident of that State or a permanent establishment or fixed base in that State. In addition, a team described in paragraph 3 may not be taxed in a Contracting State under paragraph 2 of this Article solely by reason of the fact that a member of the team may participate in the profits of the team through the receipt of a bonus based, for example, on ticket sales. The employer may be taxable pursuant to other articles of the Convention, such as Article VII.

Paragraph 4 provides that, notwithstanding Articles XIV and XV, an amount paid by a resident of a Contracting State to a resident of the other State as an inducement to sign an agreement relating to the performance of the services of an athlete may be taxed in the first-mentioned State. However, the tax imposed may not exceed 15 per cent of the gross amount of the payment. The provision clarifies the taxation of signing bonuses in a manner consistent with their treatment under U.S. interpretations of the 1942 Convention. Amounts paid as salary or other remuneration for the performance of the athletic services themselves are not taxable under this provision, but are subject to the provisions of paragraphs 1 and 3 of this Article, or Articles XIV or XV, as the case may be. The paragraph covers all amounts paid (to the athlete or another person) as an inducement to sign an agreement for the services of an athlete, such as a bonus to sign a contract not to perform for other teams. An amount described in this paragraph is not to be included in determining the amount of gross receipts derived by an athlete in a calendar year for purposes of paragraph 1. Thus, if an athlete receives a $50,000 signing bonus and a $12,000 salary for a taxable year, the State of source would not be entitled to tax the salary portion of the receipt of the athlete for that year under paragraph 1 of this Article.

Article XVII — Withholding of taxes in respect of personal services

Article XVII confirms that a Contracting State may require withholding of tax on account of tax liability with respect to remuneration paid to an individual who is a resident of the other Contracting State, including an entertainer or athlete, in respect of the performance of independent personal services in the first-mentioned State. However, withholding with respect to the first $5,000 (in the currency of the State of source) of such remuneration paid in that taxable year by each payor shall not exceed 10 per cent of such payment. In the United States, the withholding described in paragraph 1 relates to withholding with respect to income tax liability and does not relate to withholding with respect to other taxes, such as social security taxes. Nor is the paragraph intended to suggest that withholding in circumstances not specifically mentioned, such as withholding with respect to dependent personal services, is precluded by the Convention.

Paragraph 2 provides that in any case where the competent authority of Canada or the United States believes that withholding with respect to remuneration for the performance of personal services is excessive in relation to the estimated tax liability of an individual to that State for a taxable year, it may determine that a lesser amount will be deducted or withheld. In the case of independent personal services, paragraph 2 may thus result in a lesser withholding than the maximum authorized by paragraph 1.

Paragraph 3 states that the provisions of Article XVII do not affect the liability of a resident of a Contracting State for taxes imposed by the other Contracting State. The Article deals only with the method of collecting taxes and not with substantive tax liability.

Article XVIIIA of the 1942 Convention authorizes the issuance of regulations to specify circumstances under which residents of the United States temporarily performing personal services in Canada may be exempted from deduction and withholding of United States tax. This provision is omitted from the Convention as unnecessary. The Code and regulations provide sufficient authority to avoid excessive withholding of U.S. income tax. Further, paragraph 2 provides for adjustments in the amount of withholding where appropriate.

Article XVIII — Pensions and Annuities

Paragraph 1 provides that a resident of a Contracting State is taxable in that State with respect to pensions and annuities arising in the other Contracting State. However, the State of residence shall exempt from taxation the amount of any such pension that would be excluded from taxable income in the State of source if the recipient were a resident thereof. Thus, if a $10,000 pension payment arising in a Contracting State is paid to a resident of the other Contracting State and $5,000 of such payment would be excluded from taxable income as a return of capital in the first-mentioned State if the recipient were a resident of the first-mentioned State, the State of residence shall exempt from tax $5,000 of the payment. Only $5,000 would be so exempt even if the first-mentioned State would also grant a personal allowance as a deduction from gross income if the recipient were a resident thereof. Paragraph 1 imposes no such restriction with respect to the amount that may be taxed in the State of residence in the case of annuities.

Paragraph 2 provides rules with respect to the taxation of pensions and annuities in the Contracting State in which they arise. If the beneficial owner of a periodic pension payment is a resident of the other Contracting State, the tax imposed in the State of source is limited to 15 per cent of the gross amount of such payment. Thus, the State of source is not required to allow a deduction or exclusion for a return of capital to the pensioner, but its tax is limited in amount in the case of a periodic payment. Other pension payments may be taxed in the State of source without limit.

In the case of annuities beneficially owned by a resident of a Contracting State, the Contracting State of source is limited to a 15 per cent tax on the portion of the payment that would not be excluded from taxable income (i.e., as a return of capital) in that State if the beneficial owner were a resident thereof.

Paragraph 3 defines the term "pensions" for purposes of the Convention to include any payment under a superannuation, pension, or retirement plan, Armed-Forces retirement pay, war veterans pensions and allowances, and amounts paid under a sickness, accident, or disability plan. Thus, the term "pension" includes pensions paid by private employers as well as any pension paid by a Contracting State in respect of services rendered to that State. A pension for government service is covered. The term "pensions" does not include payments under an income averaging annuity contract or benefits paid under social security legislation. The latter benefits are taxed, pursuant to paragraph 5, only in the Contracting State paying the benefit. Income derived from an income averaging annuity contract is taxable pursuant to the provisions of Article XXII (Other Income).

Paragraph 4 provides that, for purposes of the Convention, the term "annuities" means a stated sum paid periodically at stated times during life or during a specified number of years, under an obligation to make payments in return for adequate and full consideration other than services rendered. The term does not include a payment that is not periodic or any annuity the cost of which was deductible for tax purposes in the Contracting State where the annuity was acquired. Items excluded from the definition of "annuities" are subject to the rules of Article XXII.

Paragraph 5, as amended by the 1984 Protocol, provides that benefits under social security legislation in Canada or the United States paid to a resident of the other Contracting State are taxable only in the State in which the recipient is resident. However, the State of residence must exempt from taxation one-half of the total amount of such benefits paid in a taxable year. Thus, if U.S. social security benefits are paid to a resident of Canada, the United States will exempt such benefits from tax and Canada will exempt one-half of the benefits from taxation. The exemption of one-half of the benefits in the State of residence is an exception to the saving clause under subparagraph 3(a) of Article XXIX (Miscellaneous Rules). The United States will not exempt U.S. social security benefits from tax if the Canadian resident receiving such benefits is a U.S. citizen. If a U.S. citizen and resident receives Canadian social security benefits, Canada will not tax such benefits and the United States will exempt from tax one-half of the total amount of such benefits. The United States will also exempt one-half of Canadian social security benefits from tax if the recipient is a U.S. citizen who is a resident of Canada, under paragraph 7 of Article XXIX. Paragraph 5 encompasses benefits paid under social security legislation of a political subdivision, such as a province of Canada.

Paragraph 6(a) provides that only the State of which a person is resident has the right to tax alimony and other similar amounts (including child support payments) arising in the other Contracting State and paid to such person. However, under paragraph 6(b), the State of residence shall exempt from taxation the amount that would be excluded from taxable income in the State of source if the recipient were a resident thereof. Thus, if child support payments are made by a U.S. resident to a resident of Canada, Canada shall exempt from tax the amount of such payments which would be excluded from taxable income under section 71(b) of the *Internal Revenue Code*. Paragraph 6 does not define the term "alimony"; the term is defined pursuant to the provisions of paragraph 2 of Article III (General Definitions).

Article XVIII does not provide rules to determine the State in which pensions, annuities, alimony, and other similar amounts arise. The provisions of paragraph 2 of Article III are used to determine where such amounts arise for purposes of determining whether a Contracting State has the right to tax such amounts.

Paragraphs 1, 3, 4, 5(b) and 6(b) of Article XVIII are, by reason of paragraph 3(a) of Article XXIX (Miscellaneous Rules), exceptions to the "saving clause." Thus, the rules in those paragraphs change U.S. taxation of U.S. citizens and residents.

Article XIX — Government Service

Article XIX provides that remuneration, other than a pension, paid by a Contracting State or political subdivision or local authority thereof to a citizen of that State in respect of services rendered in the discharge of governmental functions shall be taxable only in that State. (Pursuant to paragraph 5 of Article IV (Residence), other income of such a citizen may also be exempt from tax, or subject to reduced rates of tax, in the State in which he is performing services, in accordance with other provisions of the Convention.) However, if the services are rendered in connection with a trade or business, then the provisions of Article XIV (Independent Personal Services), Article XV (Dependent Personal Services), or Article XVI (Artistes and Athletes), as the case may be, are controlling. Whether functions are of a governmental nature may be determined by a comparison with the concept of a governmental function in the State in which the income arises.

Pursuant to paragraph 3(a) of Article XXIX (Miscellaneous Rules), Article XIX is an exception to the "saving clause." As a result, a U.S. citizen resident in Canada and performing services in Canada in the discharge of functions of a governmental nature for the United States is taxable only in the United States on remuneration for such services.

This provision differs from the rules of Article VI of the 1942 Convention. For example, Article XIX allows the United States to impose tax on a person other than a citizen of Canada who earns remuneration paid by Canada in respect of services rendered in the discharge of governmental functions in the United States. (Such a person may, however, be entitled to an exemption from U.S. tax as provided in Code section 893.) Also, under the provisions of Article XIX Canada will not impose tax on amounts paid by the United States in respect of services rendered in the discharge of governmental functions to a U.S. citizen who is ordinarily resident in Canada for purposes other than rendering governmental services. Under paragraph 1 of Article VI of the 1942 Convention, such amounts would be taxable by Canada.

Article XX — Students

Article XX provides that a student, apprentice, or business trainee temporarily present in a Contracting State for the purpose of his full-time education or training is exempt from tax in that State with respect to amounts received from outside that State for the purpose of his maintenance, education, or training, if the individual is or was a resident of the other Contracting State immediately before visiting the first-mentioned State. There is no limitation on the number of years or the amount of income to which the exemption applies.

The Convention does not contain provisions relating specifically to professors and teachers. Teachers are treated under the Convention pursuant to the rules established in Articles XIV (Independent Personal Services) and XV (Dependent Personal Services), in the same manner as other persons performing services. In Article VIIIA of the 1942 Convention there is a 2-year exemption in the Contracting State of source in the case of a professor or teacher who is a resident of the other Contracting State.

Article XXI — Exempt Organizations

Paragraph 1 provides that a religious, scientific, literary, educational, or charitable organization resident in a Contracting State shall be exempt from tax on income arising in the other Contracting State but only to the extent that such income is exempt from taxation in the Contracting State in which the organization is resident. Since this paragraph, and the remainder of Article XXI, deal with entities that are not normally taxable, the test of "resident in" is intended to be similar — but cannot be identical — to the one outlined in paragraph 1 of Article IV (Residence). Paragraph 3 provides that paragraph 1 does not exempt from tax income of a trust, company, or other organization from carrying on a trade or business, or income from a "related person" other than a person referred to in paragraph 1 or 2.

Paragraph 2 provides that a trust, company, or other organization that is resident in a Contracting State and constituted and operated exclusively to administer or provide employee benefits or benefits for the self-employed under one or more funds or plans established to provide pension or retirement benefits or other employee benefits is exempt from taxation on dividend and interest income arising in the other Contracting State in a taxable year, if the income of such organization is generally exempt from taxation for that year in the Contracting State in which it is resident. In addition, a trust, company, or other organization resident in a Contracting State and not taxed in a taxable year in that State shall be exempt from taxation in the other State in that year on dividend and interest income arising in that other State if it is constituted and operated exclusively to earn income for the benefit of an organization described in the preceding sentence. Pursuant to paragraph 3 the exemption at source provided by paragraph 2 does not apply to dividends or interest from carrying on a trade or business or from a "related person," other than a person referred to in paragraph 1 or 2. The term "related person" is not necessarily defined by paragraph 2 of Article IX (Related Persons).

Paragraph 4 provides an exemption from U.S. excise taxes on private foundations in the case of a religious, scientific, literary, educational, or charitable organization which is resident in Canada but only if such organization has received substantially all of its support from persons other than citizens or residents of the United States.

Paragraph 5 provides that contributions by a citizen or resident of the United States to an organization which is resident in Canada and is generally exempt from Canadian tax are treated as charitable contributions, but only if the organization could qualify in the United States to receive deductible contributions if it were resident in (i.e., organized in) the United States. Paragraph 5 generally limits the amount of contributions made deductible by the Convention to the income of the U.S. citizen or resident arising in Canada, as determined under the Convention. In the case of contributions to a college or university at which the U.S. citizen or resident or a member of his family is or was enrolled, the special limitation to income arising in Canada is not required. The percentage limitations of Code section 170 in respect of the deductibility of charitable contributions apply after the limitations established by the Convention. Any amounts treated as charitable contributions by paragraph 5 which are in excess of amounts deductible in a taxable year pursuant to paragraph 5 may be carried over and deducted in subsequent taxable years, subject to the limitations of paragraph 5.

Paragraph 6 provides rules for purposes of Canadian taxation with respect to the deductibility of gifts to a U.S. resident organization by a resident of Canada. The rules of paragraph 6 parallel the rules of paragraph 5. The current limitations in Canadian law provide that deductions for gifts to charitable organizations may not exceed 20 per cent of income. Excess deductions may be carried forward for one year.

The term "family" used in paragraphs 5 and 6 is defined in paragraph 2 of the Exchange of Notes accompanying the Convention to mean an individual's brothers and sisters (whether by whole or half-blood, or by adoption), spouse, ancestors, lineal descendants, and adopted descendants. Paragraph 2 of the Exchange of Notes also provides that the competent authorities of Canada and the United States will review procedures and requirements for organizations to establish their exempt status under paragraph 1 of Article XXI or as an eligible recipient of charitable contributions or gifts under paragraphs 5 and 6 of Article XXI. It is contemplated that such review will lead to the avoidance of duplicative administrative efforts in determining such status and eligibility.

The provisions of paragraph 5 and 6 generally parallel the rules of Article XIIID of the 1942 Convention. However, paragraphs 5 and 6 permit greater deductions for certain contributions to colleges and universities than do the provisions of the 1942 Convention.

Article XXII — Other Income

Paragraph 1 provides that a Contracting State of which a person is a resident has the sole right to tax items of income, wherever arising, if such income is not dealt with in the prior Articles of the Convention. If such income arises in the other Contracting State, however, it may also be taxed in that State. The determination of where income arises for this purpose is made under the domestic laws of the respective Contracting States unless the Convention specifies where the income arises (e.g., paragraph 6 of Article XI (Interest)) for purposes of determining the right to tax, in which case the provisions of the Convention control.

Paragraph 2 provides that to the extent that income distributed by an estate or trust resident in one Contracting State is deemed under the domestic law of that State to be a separate type of income "arising" within that State, such income distributed to a beneficiary resident in the other Contracting State may be taxed in the State of source at a maximum rate of 15 per cent of the gross amount of such distribution. Such a distribution will, however, be exempt from tax in the State of source to the extent that the income distributed by the estate or trust was derived by the estate or trust from sources outside that State. Thus, in a case where the law of Canada treats a distribution made by a trust resident in Canada as a separate type of income arising in Canada, Canadian tax is limited by paragraph 2 to 15 per cent of the gross amount distributed to a U.S. resident beneficiary. Although the Code imposes tax on certain domestic trusts (e.g., accumulation trusts) and such trusts are residents of the United States for purposes of Article IV (Residence) and paragraph 2 of Article XXII, paragraph 2 does not apply to distributions by such trusts because, pursuant to Code sections 667(e) and 662(b), these distributions have the same character in the hands of a non-resident beneficiary as they do in the hands of the trust. Thus, a distribution by a domestic accumulation trust is not a separate type of income for U.S. purposes. The taxation of such a distribution in the United States is governed by the distribution's character, the provisions of the Code and the provisions of the Convention other than the provision in paragraph 2 limiting the tax at source to 15 per cent.

Article XXIII — Capital

Although neither Canada nor the United States currently has national taxes on capital, Article XXIII provides rules for the eventuality that such taxes might be enacted in the future. Paragraph 1 provides that capital represented by real property (as defined in paragraph 2 of Article VI (Income From Real Property)) owned by a resident of a Contracting State and situated in the other Contracting State may be taxed in that other State.

Paragraph 2 provides that capital represented by either personal property forming part of the business property of a permanent establishment or personal property pertaining to a fixed base in a Contracting State may be taxed in that State.

Paragraph 3 provides that capital represented by ships and aircraft operated by a resident of a Contracting State in international traffic and by personal property pertaining to the operation of such ships and aircraft are taxable only in the Contracting State of residence.

Paragraph 4 provides that all elements of capital other than those covered by paragraphs 1, 2, and 3 are taxable only in the Contracting State of residence. Thus, capital represented by motor vehicles or railway cars, not pertaining to a permanent establishment or fixed base in a Contracting State, would be taxable only in the Contracting State of which the taxpayer is a resident.

Article XXIV — Elimination of Double Taxation

Paragraph 1 provides the general rules that will apply under the Convention with respect to foreign tax credits for Canadian taxes paid or accrued. The United States undertakes to allow to a citizen or resident of the United States, or to a company electing under Code section 1504(d) to be treated as a domestic corporation, a credit against the Federal income taxes imposed by the Code for the appropriate amount of income tax paid or accrued to Canada. In the case of a company which is a resident of the United States owning 10 per cent or more of the voting stock of a company which is a resident of Canada (which for this purpose does not include a company electing under Code section 1504(d) to be treated as a domestic corporation), and from which it receives dividends in a taxable year, the United States shall allow as a credit against income taxes imposed by the Code the appropriate amount of income tax paid or accrued to Canada by the Canadian company with respect to the profits out of which such company paid the dividends.

The direct and deemed-paid credits allowed by paragraph 1 are subject to the limitations of the Code as they may be amended from time to time without changing the general principle of paragraph 1. Thus, as is generally the case under U.S. income tax conventions, provisions such as Code sections 901(c), 904, 905, 907, 908, and 911 apply for purposes of computing the allowable credit under paragraph 1. In addition, the United States is not required to maintain the overall limitation currently provided by U.S. law.

The term "income tax paid or accrued" is defined in paragraph 7 of Article XXIV to include certain specified taxes which are paid or accrued. The Convention only provides a credit for amounts paid or

Treaties and Related Legislation

accrued. The determination of whether an amount is paid or accrued is made under the Code. Paragraph 1 provides a credit for these specified taxes whether or not they qualify as creditable under Code section 901 or 903. A taxpayer who claims credit under the Convention for Canadian taxes made creditable solely by paragraph 1 is not, as a result of the Protocol, subject to a per-country limitation with respect to Canadian taxes. Thus, credit for such Canadian taxes would be computed under the overall limitation currently provided by U.S. law. (However, see the discussion below of the source rules of paragraphs 3 and 9 for a restriction on the use of third country taxes to offset the U.S. tax imposed on resourced income.)

A taxpayer claiming credits for Canadian taxes under the Convention must apply the source rules of the Convention, and must apply those source rules in their entirety. Similarly, a taxpayer claiming credit for Canadian taxes which are creditable under the Code and who wishes to use the source rules of the Convention in computing that credit must apply the source rules of the Convention in their entirety.

Paragraph 3 provides source rules for purposes of applying Article XXIV. Profits, income or gains of a resident of a Contracting State which may be taxed in the other Contracting State in accordance with the Convention, for reasons other than the saving clause of paragraph 2 of Article XXIX (Miscellaneous Rules) (e.g., pensions and annuities taxable where arising pursuant to Article XVIII (Pensions and Annuities)), are deemed to arise in the latter State. This rule does not, however, apply to gains taxable under paragraph 5 of Article XIII (Gains) (i.e., gains taxed by a Contracting State derived from the alienation of property by a former resident of that State). Gains from such an alienation arise, pursuant to paragraph 3(b), in the State of which the alienator is a resident. Thus, if in accordance with paragraph 5 of Article XIII, Canada imposes tax on certain gains of a U.S. resident such gains are deemed, pursuant to paragraphs 2 and 3(b) of Article XXIV, to arise in the United States for purposes of computing the deduction against Canadian tax for the U.S. tax on such gain. Under the Convention such gains arise in the United States for purposes of the United States foreign tax credit. Paragraph 3(b) also provides that profits, income, or gains arise in the Contracting State of which a person is a resident if they may not be taxed in the other Contracting State under the provisions of the Convention (e.g., alimony), other than the "saving clause" of paragraph 2 of Article XXIX.

Paragraph 9 provides clarification that the source rules of this Article shall not be used to determine the credit available against U.S. tax for foreign taxes other than income taxes paid or accrued to Canada (i.e., taxes of third countries). Thus, creditable third country taxes may not offset the U.S. tax on income treated as arising in Canada under the source rules of the Convention. A person claiming credit for income taxes of a third country may not rely upon the rules of paragraphs 3 and 6 for purposes of treating income that would otherwise have a U.S. source as having a foreign source. Thus, if the taxpayer elects to compute the foreign tax credit for any year using the special source rules set forth in paragraphs 3 and 6, paragraph 9 requires that a separate limitation be computed for taxes not covered by paragraph 1 without regard to the source rules of paragraphs 3 and 6, and the credit for such taxes may not exceed such limitation. The credit allowed under this separate limitation may not exceed the proportion of the Federal income taxes imposed by the Code that the taxpayer's taxable income from foreign sources (under the Code) not included in taxable income arising in Canada (and not in excess of total foreign source taxable income under the Code) bears to the taxpayer's worldwide taxable income. In any case the credit for taxes covered by paragraph 1 and the credit for other foreign taxes is limited to the amount allowed under an overall limitation computed by aggregating taxable income arising in Canada and other foreign source taxable income.

If creditable Canadian taxes exceed the proportion of U.S. tax that taxable income arising in Canada bears to the entire taxable income, such taxes may qualify to be absorbed by any excess in the separate limitation computed with respect to other taxes.

In a case where a taxpayer has different types of income subject to separate limitations under the Code (e.g., section 904(d)(1)(B) DISC dividends) the Convention rules just described apply in the context of each of the separate Code limitations.

A taxpayer may, for any year, claim a credit pursuant to the rules of the Code. In such case, the taxpayer would be subject to the limitations established in the Code, and would forgo the rules of the Convention that determine where taxable income arises. In addition, any Canadian taxes covered by paragraph 1 which are not creditable under the Code would not be credited.

Thus, where a taxpayer elects to use the special source rules of this Article to compute the foreign tax credit for any year, the following computations must be made:

Step 1(a): Compute a hypothetical foreign tax credit limitation for Canadian income and taxes using the source rules of the Convention.

Step 1(b): Compute a hypothetical foreign tax credit limitation for third country income and taxes using the source rules of the Code.

Step 1(c): Compute an overall foreign tax credit limitation using the source rules of the Convention to the extent they resource Canadian source income as U.S. source income or U.S. source income as Canadian source income, and using the source rules of the Code with respect to any other income.

Step 2: Allocate the amount of creditable Canadian taxes to the amount of the limitation computed under step 1(a), and allocate the amount of creditable third country taxes to the amount of the limitation computed under step 1(b). The amount of credit to be so allocated may not exceed the amount of the respective limitation.

Step 3: (1) If the total credits allocated under step 2 exceed the amount of the limitation computed under step 1(c), the amount of allowable credits must be reduced to that limitation (see Rev. Rul. 82-215, 1982-2 Cum. Bull. 153 for the method of such reduction).

Step 3: (2) If the total credits allocated under step 2 are less than the amount of the limitation computed under step 1(c), then (a) any amount of creditable Canadian taxes in excess of the amount of the step 1(a) limitation may be credited to the extent of the excess of the step 1(c) limitation over the total step 2 allocation, and (b) any amount of third country taxes in excess of the amount of the step 1(b) limitation may not be credited.

The following examples (in which the taxpayer's U.S. tax rate is presumed to be 46%) illustrate the application of the source rules of Article XXIV:

Example 1.

(a) A U.S. corporate taxpayer has for the taxable year $100 of taxable income having a U.S. source under both the Convention and the Code; $100 of taxable income having a Canadian source under both the Convention and the Code; $50 of taxable income having a Canadian source under the Convention but a U.S. source under the Code (see, for example, paragraph 1 of Article VII (Business Profits) and paragraph 3(a) of Article XXIV); and $80 of taxable income having a foreign (non-Canadian) source under the Code. The taxpayer pays $75 of Canadian income taxes and $45 of third country income taxes. All the foreign source income of the taxpayer constitutes "other" income described in Code section 904(d)(1)(C).

The source rules of the Convention are applied as follows to compute the taxpayer's foreign tax credit:

Step 1(a):

$$\frac{\$150 \text{ (Canadian source taxable income under Convention)}}{\$330 \text{ (total taxable income)}} \times \$151.80 = \$69 \text{ limit for Canadian taxes.}$$

Step 1(b):

$$\frac{\$\ 80 \text{ (third country source taxable income under Code)}}{\$330 \text{ (total taxable income)}} \times \$151.80 = \$36.80 \text{ limit for third country taxes.}$$

Step 1(c):

$$\frac{\$230 \text{ (overall foreign taxable income under source rules described above)}}{\$330 \text{ (total taxable income)}} \times \$151.80 = \$105.80 \text{ total limit.}$$

Step 2: The taxpayer may tentatively credit $69 of the $75 Canadian income taxes under the step 1(a) limitation, and $36.80 of the third country income taxes under the step 1(b) limitation.

Step 3: Since the total amount of taxes credited under step 2 equals the taxpayer's total limitation of $105.80 under step 1(c), no additional taxes may be credited. The taxpayer has a $6 Canadian income tax carryover and a $8.20 third country income tax carryover for U.S. foreign tax credit purposes.

(b) If the taxpayer had paid only $30 of third country taxes, he would credit that $30 in step 2. Since the total amount of credits allowed under step 2 ($99) is less than the taxpayer's total limit of $105.80, and since the taxpayer has $6 of excess Canadian taxes not credited under step 2, he may also claim a credit for that $6 of Canadian income taxes, for a total credit of $105.

(c) If the taxpayer had paid $45 of third country income taxes and $65 of Canadian income taxes, the computation would be as follows:

Step 2: The taxpayer would credit the $65 of Canadian income taxes, and would also credit $36.80 of the $45 of third country income taxes.

Step 3: Although the total amount of credits computed under step 2 ($101.80) is less than the taxpayer's total limitation of $105.80, no additional credits can be claimed since the taxpayer has only excess third country income taxes. The excess third country income taxes are thus not permitted to offset U.S. tax on income that is Canadian source income under the Convention. The taxpayer would have $8.20 of third country income taxes as a carryover for U.S. foreign tax credit purposes.

Example 2.

A United States corporate taxpayer has for the taxable year $100 of taxable income having a Canadian source under the Convention but a U.S. source under the Code; $100 of taxable income having a U.S. source under both the Convention and the Code; $80 of taxable income having a foreign (non-Canadian) source under the Code; and ($50) of loss allocated or apportioned to Canadian source income. The taxpayer pays $50 of foreign (non-Canadian) income taxes, and $20 of Canadian income taxes.

The source rules of the Convention are applied as follows to compute the taxpayer's foreign tax credit:

Step 1(a):

$ 50 (Canadian source taxable income under Convention)

$230 (total taxable income)

x $105.80 = $23 limit for Canadian taxes.

Step 1(b):

$ 80 (third country source taxable income under Code)

$230 (total taxable income)

x $105.80 = $36.80 limit for third country taxes.

Step 1(c):

$130 (overall foreign taxable income under source rules described above)

$230 (total taxable income)

x $105.80 = $59.80 total limit.

Step 2: Since the taxpayer paid $20 of Canadian income taxes, he may credit that amount in full since the step 1(a) limit is $23. Since the step 1(b) limit is $36.80, the taxpayer may credit $36.80 of the $50 foreign income taxes paid.

Step 3: Although the total taxes credited under step 2 ($56.80) is less than the taxpayer's total limit of $59.80, no additional credits may be claimed since the only excess taxes are third country income taxes, and those may not be used to offset any excess limitation in step 3. The $13.20 of foreign taxes not allowed as a credit is available as a foreign tax credit carryover.

Example 3.

The facts are the same as in *Example 2,* except that foreign (non-Canadian) operations result in a loss of ($30) rather than taxable income of $80, and no foreign (non-Canadian) income taxes are paid. The taxpayers' credit is computed as follows:

Step 1(a):

$ 50
----- x $55.20 = $23 limit for $120 Canadian taxes.
$120

Step 1(b): Since there is no third country source taxable income under the Code, the limit for third country income taxes is zero.

Step 1(c):

$ 20
----- x $55.20 = $9.20 total limit.
$120

Step 2: Since the taxpayer paid $20 of Canadian income tax, he may tentatively credit that amount in full since the step 1(a) limit is $23.

Step 3: Since the total taxes credited under step 2 ($20) exceeds the taxpayer's total limit of $9.20, the taxpayer must reduce the total amount claimed as a credit to $9.20. The remaining $10.80 of Canadian income taxes are available as a foreign tax credit carryover.

Example 4.

The facts are the same as in *Example 2,* except that the first $100 of taxable income mentioned in *Example 2* has a Canadian source under both the Convention and the Code.

Step 1(a):

$ 50
----- x $105.80 = $23 limit for Canadian taxes.
$230

Step 1(b):

$ 80
----- x $105.80 = $36.80 limit for third country income taxes.
$230

Step 1(c):

$130
----- x $105.80 = $59.80 total limit.
$230

Step 2: The taxpayer credits the $20 of Canadian income tax and $36.80 of third country income tax.

Step 3: As explained in *Example 2,* the taxpayer's total credit is limited to $56.80. In this case, however, if the Canadian taxes covered by the Convention are creditable under the Code, the taxpayer could elect the Code limitation of $59.80 ($130 X $105.80), $230 which is more advantageous than the Convention limitation because that limitation does not permit third country income taxes to be credited against the U.S. tax on income arising in Canada under the Convention.

Example 5.

The facts are the same as in *Example 2,* except that the corporation pays $25 of Canadian income taxes and $12 of foreign (non-Canadian) income taxes. Under step 2, the taxpayer would credit $23 of the $25 of Canadian income taxes and the full $12 of third country income taxes. Since the total amount of income taxes credited under step 2 is $35, which is less than the taxpayer's total limit of $59.80, the taxpayer may credit an amount of Canadian income taxes up to the $24.80 excess. Here, the taxpayer may claim a credit for the additional $2 of Canadian income taxes not credited under step 2, and has a total credit of $37.

Example 6.

(a) A U.S. corporate taxpayer has for the taxable year $100 of taxable income having a Canadian source under the Convention and the Code; $50 of taxable income having a Canadian source under the Convention but a U.S. source under the Code; $80 of taxable income having a foreign (non-Canadian) source under the Code; and ($50) of loss allocated or apportioned to U.S. source income. The taxpayer pays $65 of Canadian income taxes, and $45 of third country income taxes.

Step 1(a):

$$\frac{\$150}{\$180} \times \$82.80 = \$69 \text{ limit for Canadian taxes.}$$

Step 1(b):

$$\frac{\$\ 80}{\$180} \times \$82.80 = \$36.80 \text{ limit for third country income taxes.}$$

Step 1(c):

$$\frac{\$180}{\$180} \times \$82.80 = \$82.80 \text{ total limit.}$$

Step 2: The taxpayer tentatively credits the $65 of Canadian income taxes against the $69 limit of step 1(a), and $36.80 of the $45 of third country income taxes against the $36.80 limit of step 1(b).

Step 3: Since the total amount of credits tentatively allowed under step 2 ($101.80) exceeds the taxpayer's total limit of $82.80 under step 1(c), the taxpayer's allowable credit is reduced to $82.80 under the method provided by Rev. Rul. 82-215.

(b) If the taxpayer had paid only $40 of Canadian income taxes, the total credits tentatively allowed under step 2 is $76.80. Although that amount is less than the $82.80 total limit under step 1(c), no additional taxes may be credited since the taxpayer only has excess third country income taxes. The $8.20 of excess third country income taxes would be allowed as a foreign tax credit carryover.

The general rule for avoiding double taxation in Canada is provided in paragraph 2. Pursuant to paragraph 2(a) Canada undertakes to allow to a resident of Canada a credit against income taxes imposed under the Income Tax Act for the appropriate amount of income taxes paid or accrued to the United States. Paragraph 2(b) provides for the deduction by a Canadian company, in computing taxable income, of any dividend received out of the exempt surplus of a U.S. company which is an affiliate. The provisions of paragraphs 2(a) and (b) are subject to the provisions of the *Income Tax Act* as they may be amended from time to time without changing the general principle of paragraph 2. Paragraph 2(c) provides that where Canada imposes a tax on the alienation of property pursuant to the provisions of paragraph 5 of Article XIII (Gains), Canada will allow a credit for the income tax paid or accrued to the United States on such gain.

The rules of paragraph 1 are modified in certain respects by rules in paragraphs 4 and 5 for income derived by United States citizens who are residents of Canada. Paragraph 4 provides two steps for the elimination of double taxation in such a case. First, paragraph 4(a) provides that Canada shall allow a deduction from (credit against) Canadian tax in respect of income tax paid or accrued to the United States in respect of profits, income, or gains which arise in the United States (within the meaning of paragraph 3(a)); the deduction against Canadian tax need not, however, exceed the amount of income tax that would be paid or accrued to the United States if the individual were not a U.S. citizen, after taking into account any relief available under the Convention.

The second step, as provided in paragraph 4(b), is that the United States allows as a credit against United States tax, subject to the rules of paragraph 1, the income tax paid or accrued to Canada after the Canadian credit for U.S. tax provided by paragraph 4(a). The credit so allowed by the United States is not to reduce the portion of the United States tax that is creditable against Canadian tax in accordance with paragraph 4(a).

The following example illustrates the application of paragraph 4.

Example A

— A U.S. citizen who is a resident of Canada earns $175 of income from the performance of independent personal services, of which $100 is derived from services performed in Canada and $75 from services performed in the United States. That is his total world-wide income.

— If he were not a U.S. citizen, the United States could tax $75 of that amount under Article XIV (Independent Personal Services). By reason of paragraph 3(a), the $75 that may be taxed by the United States under Article XIV is deemed to arise in the United States. Assume that the U.S. tax on the $75 would he $25 if the taxpayer were not a U.S. citizen.

— However, since the individual is a U.S. citizen, he is subject to U.S. tax on his worldwide income of $175. After excluding $75 under section 911, his taxable income is $100 and his U.S. tax is $40.

— Because he is a resident of Canada, he is also subject to Canadian tax on his worldwide income. Assume that Canada taxes the $175 at $75.

— Canada will credit against its tax of $75 the U.S. tax at source of $25, leaving a net Canadian tax of $50.

— The United States will credit against its tax of $40 the Canadian tax net of credit, but without reducing its source basis tax of $25; thus, the allowable credit is $40 – $25 = $15.

— To use a credit of $15 requires Canadian source taxable income of $37.50 ($37.50/$100 × $40 = $15). Without any special treaty rule, Canadian source taxable income would be only $25 ($100 less the section 911 exclusion of $75). Paragraph 6 provides for resourcing an additional $12.50 of income to Canada, so that the credit of $15 can be fully used.

Paragraph 5 provides special rules for the elimination of double taxation in the case of dividends, interest, and royalties earned by a U.S. citizen resident in Canada. These rules apply notwithstanding the provisions of paragraph 4, but only as long as the law in Canada allows a deduction in computing income for the portion of any foreign tax paid in respect of dividends, interest, or royalties which exceeds 15 per cent of the amount of such items of income, and only with respect to those items of income. The rules of paragraph 4 apply with respect to other items of income; moreover, if the law in force in Canada regarding the deduction for foreign taxes changes, the provisions of paragraph 5 shall not apply and the U.S. foreign tax credit for Canadian taxes and the Canadian credit for U.S. taxes will be determined solely pursuant to the provisions of paragraph 4.

The calculations under paragraph 5 are as follows. First, the deduction allowed in Canada in computing income shall be made with respect to U.S. tax on the dividends, interest, and royalties before any foreign tax credit by the United States with respect to income tax paid or accrued to Canada. Second, Canada shall allow a deduction from (credit against) Canadian tax for U.S. tax paid or accrued with respect to the dividends, interest, and royalties, but such credit need not exceed 15 per cent of the gross amount of such items of income that have been included in computing income for Canadian tax purposes. (The credit may, however, exceed the amount of tax that the United States would be entitled to levy under the Convention upon a Canadian resident who is not a U.S. citizen.) Third, for purposes of computing the U.S. tax on such dividends, interest, and royalties, the United States shall allow as a credit against the U.S. tax the income tax paid or accrued to Canada after the 15 per cent credit against Canadian tax for income tax paid or accrued to the United States. The United States is in no event obliged to give a credit for Canadian income tax which will reduce the U.S. tax below 15 per cent of the amount of the dividends, interest, and royalties.

The rules of paragraph 5 are illustrated by the following examples.

Example B

— A U.S. citizen who is a resident of Canada has $100 of royalty income arising in the United States. The tentative U.S. tax before foreign tax credit is $40.

— Canada, under its law, allows a deduction for the U.S. tax in excess of 15 per cent or, in this case, a deduction of $25 ($400 – $15). The Canadian taxable income is $75 and the Canadian tax on that amount is $35.

— Canada gives a credit of $15 (the maximum credit allowed is 15 per cent of the gross royalty taken into Canadian income) and collects a net tax of $20.

— The United States allows a credit for the net Canadian tax against its tax in excess of 15 per cent. Thus, the maximum credit is $25 ($400 – $15). But since the net Canadian tax paid was $20, the usable credit is $20.

— To be able to use a credit of $20 requires Canadian source taxable income of $50 (50% of the U.S. tentative tax of $40). Under paragraph 6, $50 of the U.S. royalty is resourced to be of Canadian source. The credit of $20 may then be offset against the U.S. tax of $40, leaving a net U.S. tax of $20.

— The combined tax paid to both countries is $40, $20 to Canada and $20 to the United States.

Example C

A U.S. citizen who is a resident of Canada receives $200 of income with respect to personal services performed within Canada and $100 of royalty income arising within the United States. Taxable income for U.S. purposes, taking into account the rules of Code section 911, is $220. U.S. tax (before foreign tax credits) is $92. The $100 of royalty income is deemed to bear U.S. tax (before foreign tax credits) of $41.82

$$\frac{(\$100 \text{ x } \$92)}{\$220}$$

Under Canadian law, a deduction of $26.82 (the excess of $41.82 over 15 per cent of the $100 royalty income) is allowed in computing income. The Canadian tax on $273.18 of income ($300 less the $26.82 deduction) is $130. Canada then gives a credit against the $130 for $15 (the U.S. tax paid or accrued with respect to the royalty, $41.82, but limited to 15 per cent of the gross amount of such income, or $15), leaving a final Canadian tax of $115. Of the $115, $30.80 is attributable to the royalty

$$\frac{\$\ 73.18\ (\$100 \text{ royalty less } \$26.82 \text{ deduction})}{\$273.18\ (\$300 \text{ income less } \$26.82 \text{ deduction})} \text{ x } \$115.$$

Of this amount, $26.82 is creditable against U.S. tax pursuant to paragraph 5. (Although the U.S. allows a credit for the Canadian tax imposed on the royalty, $30.80, the credit may not reduce the U.S. tax below 15 per cent of the amount of the royalty. Thus, the maximum allowable credit is the excess of $41.82, the U.S. tax imposed on the royalty income, over $15, which is 15 per cent of the $100 royalty). The remaining $3.98 (the Canadian tax of $30.80 less the credit allowed of $26.82) is a foreign tax credit carryover for U.S. purposes, subject to the limitations of paragraph 5. (An additional $50.18 of Canadian tax with respect to Canadian source services income is creditable against U.S. tax pursuant to paragraphs 3 and 4(b). The $50.18 is computed as follows: tentative U.S. tax (before foreign tax credits) is $92; the U.S. tax on Canadian source services income is $50.18 ($92 less the U.S. tax on the royalty income of $41.82); the limitation on the services income is:

$$\frac{\$120 \text{ (taxable income from services)}}{\$220 \text{ (total taxable income)}} \text{ x } \$92,$$

or $50.18. The credit for Canadian tax paid on the services income is therefore $50.18; the remainder of the Canadian tax on the services income, or $34.02, is a foreign tax credit carryover for U.S. purposes, subject to the limitations of paragraph 5).

Paragraph 6 is necessary to implement the objectives of paragraphs 4(b) and 5(c). Paragraph 6 provides that where a U.S. citizen is a resident of Canada, items of income referred to in paragraph 4 or 5 are deemed for the purposes of Article XXIV to arise in Canada to the extent necessary to avoid double taxation of income by Canada and the United States consistent with the objectives of paragraphs 4(b) and 5(c). Paragraph 6 can override the source rules of paragraph 3 to permit a limited resourcing of income. The principles of paragraph 6 have effect, pursuant to paragraph 3(b) of Article XXX (Entry Into Force), for taxable years beginning on or after January 1, 1976. See the discussion of Article XXX below.

The application of paragraph 6 is illustrated by the following example.

Example D

The facts are the same as in *Example C.* The United States has undertaken, pursuant to paragraph 5(c) and paragraph 6, to credit $26.82 of Canadian taxes on royalty income that has a U.S. source under both paragraph 3 and the *Internal Revenue Code.* (As illustrated in *Example C,* the credit, however, only reduces the U.S. tax on the royalty income which exceeds 15 per cent of the amount of such income included in computing U.S. taxable income.) Pursuant to paragraph 6, for purposes of determining the U.S. foreign tax credit limitation under the Convention with respect to Canadian taxes,

$$\left(\frac{A}{\$220} \text{ x } \$92 = \$26.82;\ A = \$64.13\right).$$

$64.13 of taxable income with respect to the royalties is deemed to arise in Canada.

Paragraph 7 provides that any reference to "income tax paid or accrued" to Canada or the United States includes Canadian tax or United States tax, as the case may be. The terms "Canadian tax" and "United States tax" are defined in paragraphs 1(c) and 1(d) of Article III (General Definitions). References to income taxes paid or accrued also include taxes of general application paid or accrued to a political subdivision or local authority of Canada or the United States which are not imposed by such political subdivision or local authority in a manner inconsistent with the provisions of the Convention and which are substantially similar to taxes of Canada or the United States referred to in paragraphs 2 and 3(a) of Article II (Taxes Covered).

In order for a tax imposed by a political subdivision or local authority to fall within the scope of paragraph 7, such tax must apply to individuals, companies, or other persons generally, and not only to a particular class of individuals or companies or a particular type of business. The tax must also be substantially similar to the national taxes referred to in paragraphs 2 and 3(a) of Article II. Finally, the political subdivision or local authority must apply its tax in a manner not inconsistent with the provisions of the Convention. For example, the political subdivision or local authority must not impose its tax on a resident of the other Contracting State earning business profits within the political subdivision or local authority but not having a permanent establishment there. It is understood that a Canadian provincial income tax that satisfied the conditions of paragraph 7 on September 26, 1980 also satisfied the conditions of that paragraph on June 14, 1983 — i.e., no significant changes have occurred in the taxes imposed by Canadian provinces.

Paragraph 8 relates to the provisions of Article XXIII (Capital). It provides that where a resident of a Contracting State owns capital which, in accordance with the provisions of Article XXIII, may be taxed in the other Contracting State, the State of residence shall allow as a deduction from (credit against) its tax on capital an amount equal to the capital tax paid in the other Contracting State. The deduction is not, however, to exceed that part of the capital tax, computed before the deduction, which is attributable to capital which may be taxed in the other State.

Article XXIX — Miscellaneous Rules

Paragraph 1 states that the provisions of the Convention do not restrict in any manner any exclusion, exemption, deduction, credit, or other allowance accorded by the laws of a Contracting State in the determination of the tax imposed by that State. Thus, if a deduction would be allowed for an item in computing the taxable income of a Canadian resident under the Code, such deduction is available to such person in computing taxable income under the Convention. Paragraph 1 does not, however, authorize a taxpayer to make inconsistent choices between rules of the Code and rules of the Convention. For example, if a resident of Canada desires to claim the benefits of the "attributable to" rule of paragraphs 1 and 7 of Article VII (Business Profits) with respect to the taxation of business profits of a permanent establishment, such person must use the "attributable to" concept consistently for all items of income and deductions and may not rely upon the "effectively connected" rules of the Code to avoid U.S. tax on other items of attributable income. In no event are the rules of the Convention to increase overall U.S. tax liability from what liability would be if there were no convention.

Paragraph 2 provides a "saving clause" pursuant to which Canada and the United States may each tax its residents, as determined under Article IV (Residence), and the United States may tax its citizens (including any former citizen whose loss of citizenship had as one of its principal purposes the avoidance of tax, but only for a period of 10 years following such loss) and companies electing under Code section 1504(d) to be treated as domestic corporations, as if there were no convention between the United States and Canada with respect to taxes on income and capital.

Paragraph 3 provides that, notwithstanding paragraph 2, the United States and Canada must respect certain specified provisions of the Convention in regard to residents, citizens, and section 1504(d) companies. Paragraph 3(a) lists certain paragraphs and Articles of the Convention that represent exceptions to the "saving clause" in all situations; paragraph 3(b) provides a limited further exception for students who have not acquired immigrant status in the State where they are temporarily present.

Paragraph 4 provides relief with respect to social security taxes imposed on employers, employees, and self-employed persons under

Code sections 1401, 3101 and 3111. Income from personal services not subject to tax by the United States under the provisions of this Convention or the 1942 Convention is not to be considered wages or net earnings from self-employment for purposes of the U.S. social security taxes with respect to taxable years of the taxpayer not barred by the statute of limitations relating to refunds (under the Code) ending on or before December 31 of the year before the year in which the Social Security Agreement between Canada and the United States (signed in Ottawa on March 11, 1981) enters into force. Thus, if that agreement enters into force in 1986, a resident of Canada earning income from personal services and such person's employer may apply for refunds of the employee's and employer's shares of U.S. social security tax paid attributable to the employee's income from personal services that is exempt from U.S. tax by virtue of this Convention or the 1942 Convention. In this example, the refunds would be available for social security taxes paid with respect to taxable years not barred by the statute of limitations of the Code ending on or before December 31, 1985. For purposes of Code section 6611, the date of overpayment with respect to refunds of U.S. tax pursuant to paragraph 4 is the later of the date on which the Social Security Agreement between Canada and the United States enters into force and the date on which instruments of ratification of the Convention are exchanged.

Under certain limited circumstances, an employee may, pursuant to paragraph 5 of Article XXX (Entry Into Force), claim an exemption from U.S. tax on wages under the 1942 Convention for one year after the Convention comes into force. The provisions of paragraph 4 would not, however, provide an exemption from U.S. social security taxes for such year.

Paragraph 4 does not modify existing U.S. statutes concerning social security benefits or funding. The Social Security Act requires the general funds of the Treasury to reimburse the social security trust funds on the basis of the records of wages and self-employment income maintained by the Social Security Administration. The Convention does not alter those records. Thus, any refunds of tax made pursuant to paragraph 4 would not affect claims for U.S. quarters of coverage with respect to social security benefits. And such refunds would be charged to general revenue funds, not social security trust funds.

Paragraph 5 provides a method to resolve conflicts between the Canadian and U.S. treatment of individual retirement accounts. Certain Canadian retirement plans which are qualified plans for Canadian tax purposes do not meet Code requirements for qualification. As a result, the earnings of such a plan are currently included in income, for U.S. tax purposes, rather than being deferred until actual distributions are made by the plan. Canada defers current taxes on the earnings of such a plan but imposes tax on actual distributions from the plan. Paragraph 5 is designed to avoid a mismatch of U.S. taxable income and foreign tax credits attributable to the Canadian tax on such distributions. Under the paragraph a beneficiary of a Canadian registered retirement savings plan may elect to defer U.S. taxation with respect to any income accrued in the plan but not distributed by the plan, until such time as a distribution is made from the plan or any substitute plan. The election is to be made under rules established by the competent authority of the United States. The election is not available with respect to income accrued in the plan which is reasonably attributable to contributions made to the plan by the beneficiary while he was not a Canadian resident.

Paragraph 6 provides rules denying the benefits of the Convention in certain situations where both countries believed that granting benefits would be inappropriate.

Paragraph 6(a) provides that Articles VI (Income from Real Property) through XXIV (Elimination of Double Taxation) shall not apply to profits, income or gains derived by a trust which is treated as the income of a resident of a Contracting State (see paragraph 1 of Article IV (Residence)), if a principal purpose of the establishment, acquisition or maintenance of the trust was to obtain a benefit under the Convention or the 1942 Convention for persons who are not residents of that State. For example, the provision could be applied to a case where a non-resident of the United States created a United States trust to derive dividend income from Canada and a principal purpose of the establishment or maintenance of the trust was to obtain the reduced rate of Canadian tax under Article X (Dividends) for the non-resident. Paragraph 6(b) provides that Articles VI through XXIV shall not apply to Canadian non-resident owned investment companies, as defined in section 133 of the *Income Tax Act*, or under a similar provision that is subsequently enacted. This provision operates to deny the benefits of the Convention to a Canadian non-resident owned investment company, and does not effect the grant of benefits to other persons. Thus, for example, a dividend paid by such a company to a shareholder who is a U.S resident is subject to the reduced rates of tax provided by Article X. The denial of the benefits of Articles VI through XXIV in such cases applies notwithstanding any other provision of the Convention. A Canadian non-resident owned investment company may, however, be entitled to claim the benefits of the 1942 Convention for an additional one-year period, pursuant to paragraph 5 of Article XXX (Entry into Force). Where the provisions of this paragraph apply, the Contracting State in which the income arises may tax such income under its domestic law.

Paragraph 7 provides rules for the U.S. taxation of Canadian social security benefits paid to a resident of Canada who is a U.S. citizen. These rules are described in the discussion of paragraph 5 of Article XVIII (Pensions and Annuities).

Article XXV — Non-discrimination

Paragraphs 1 and 2 of Article XXV protect individual citizens of a Contracting State from discrimination by the other Contracting State in taxation matters. Paragraph 1 provides that a citizen of a Contracting State who is a resident of the other Contracting State may not be subjected in that other State to any taxation or requirement connected with taxation which is other or more burdensome than the taxation and connected requirements imposed on similarly situated citizens of the other State.

Paragraph 2 assures protection in a case where a citizen of a Contracting State is not a resident of the other Contracting State. Such a citizen may not be subjected in the other State to any taxation or requirement connected to taxation which is other or more burdensome than the taxation and connected requirements to which similarly situated citizens of any third State are subjected. The reference to citizens of a third State "in the same circumstances" includes consideration of the State of residence. Thus, pursuant to paragraph 2, the Canadian taxation with respect to a citizen of the United States resident in, for example, the United Kingdom may not be more burdensome than the taxation of a U.K. citizen resident in the United Kingdom. Any benefits available to the U.K. citizen by virtue of an income tax convention between the United Kingdom and Canada would be available to the U.S. citizen resident in the United Kingdom if he is otherwise in the same circumstances as the U.K. citizen.

Paragraph 3 assures that, in computing taxable income, an individual resident of a Contracting State will be entitled to the same deduction for dependents resident in the other Contracting State that would be allowed if the dependents were residents of the individual's State of residence. The term "dependent" is defined in accordance with the rules set forth in paragraph 2 of Article III (General Definitions). For U.S. tax purposes, paragraph 3 does not expand the benefits currently available to a resident of the United States with a dependent resident in Canada. See Code section 152(b)(3).

Paragraph 4 allows a resident of Canada (not a citizen of the United States) to file a joint return in cases where such person earns salary, wages, or other similar remuneration as an employee and such income is taxable in the United States under the Convention. Paragraph 4 does not apply where the resident of Canada earns wages which are exempt in the United States under Article XV (Dependent Personal Services) or earns only income taxable by the United States under provisions of the Convention other than Article XV.

The benefit provided by paragraph 3 is available regardless of the residence of the taxpayer's spouse. It is limited, however, by a formula designed to ensure that the benefit is available solely with respect to persons whose U.S. source income is entirely, or almost entirely, wage income. The formula limits the United States tax with respect to wage income to that portion of the total U.S. tax that would be payable for the taxable year if both the individual and his spouse were United States citizens as the individual's taxable income (determined without any of the benefits made available by paragraph 4, such as the standard deduction) bears to the total taxable income of the individual and his spouse. The term "total United States tax" used in the formula is total United States tax without regard to any foreign tax credits, as provided in subparagraph 4(a). (Foreign income taxes may, however, be claimed as deductions in computing taxable income, to the extent allowed by the Code.) In determining total taxable income of the individual and his spouse, the benefits made available by paragraph 4 are taken into account, but a deficit of the spouse is not.

The following example illustrates the application of paragraph 4.

A, a Canadian citizen and resident, is married to B who is also a Canadian citizen and resident. A earns $12,000 of wages taxable in the U.S. under Article XV (Dependent Personal Services) and $2,000 of wages taxable only in Canada. B earns $1,000 of U.S. source dividend

Treaties and Related Legislation

income, taxed by the United States at 15 per cent pursuant to Article X (Dividends). B also earns $2,000 of wages taxable only in Canada. A's taxable income for U.S. purposes, determined without regard to paragraph 4, is $11,700 ($12,000 – $2,000 (Code sections 151(b) and 873(b)(3)) + $1,700 (Code section 63)). The U.S. tax (Code section 1(d)) with respect to such income is $2,084.50. The total U.S. tax payable by A and B if both were U.S. citizens and all their income arose in the United States would be $2,013 under Code section 1(a) on taxable income of $14,800 ($17,000 – $200 (Code section 116) – $2,000 (Code section 151)). Pursuant to paragraph 4, the U.S. tax imposed on A's wages from U.S. sources is limited to $1,591.36

($11,700 x $2.013)

$14,800

B's U.S. tax liability with respect to the U.S. source dividends remains $150.

The provisions of paragraph 4 may be elected on a year-by-year basis. They are purely computational and do not make either or both spouses residents of the United States for the purpose of other U.S. income tax conventions. The rules relating to the election provided by U.S. law under Code section 6013(g)(see section 1.6013–6 of the Treasury Regulations) do not apply to the election described in this paragraph.

Paragraph 5 protects against discrimination in a case where the capital of a company which is a resident of one Contracting State is wholly or partly owned or controlled, directly or indirectly, by one or more residents of the other Contracting State. Such a company shall not be subjected in the State of which it is a resident to any taxation or requirement connected therewith which is other or more burdensome than the taxation and connected requirements to which are subjected other similar companies which are residents of that State but whose capital is wholly or partly owned or controlled, directly or indirectly, by one or more residents of a third State.

Paragraph 6 protects against discrimination in the case of a permanent establishment which a resident of one Contracting State has in the other Contracting State. The taxation of such a permanent establishment by the other Contracting State shall not be less favorable than the taxation of residents of that other State carrying on the same activities. The paragraph specifically overrides the provisions of Article XXIV (Elimination of Double Taxation), thus ensuring that permanent establishments will be entitled to relief from double taxation on a basis comparable to the relief afforded to similarly situated residents. Paragraph 6 does not oblige a Contracting State to grant to a resident of the other Contracting State any personal allowances, reliefs, and reductions for taxation purposes on account of civil status or family responsibilities which it grants to its own residents. In addition, paragraph 6 does not require a Contracting State to grant to a company which is a resident of the other Contracting State the same tax relief that it grants to companies which are resident in the first-mentioned State with respect to intercorporate dividends. This provision is merely clarifying in nature, since neither the United States nor Canada would interpret paragraph 6 to provide for granting the same relief in the absence of a specific denial thereof. The principles of paragraph 6 would apply with respect to a fixed base as well as a permanent establishment. Paragraph 6 does not, however, override the provisions of Code section 906.

Paragraph 7 concerns the right of a resident of a Contracting State to claim deductions for purposes of computing taxable profits in the case of disbursements made to a resident of the other Contracting State. Such disbursements shall be deductible under the same conditions as if they had been made to a resident of the first-mentioned State. Thus, this paragraph does not require Canada to permit a deduction to a Canadian trust for disbursements made to a non-resident beneficiary out of income derived from a business in Canada or Canadian real property; granting such a deduction would result in complete exemption by Canada of such income and would put Canadian trusts with non-resident beneficiaries in a better position than if they had resident beneficiaries. These provisions do not apply to amounts to which paragraph 1 of Article IX (Related Persons), paragraph 7 of Article XI (Interest), or paragraph 7 of Article XII (Royalties) apply. Paragraph 7 of Article XXV also provides that, for purposes of determining the taxable capital of a resident of a Contracting State, any debts of such person to a resident of the other Contracting State shall be deductible under the same conditions as if they had been contracted to a resident of the first-mentioned State. This portion of paragraph 7 relates to Article XXIII (Capital).

Paragraph 8 provides that, notwithstanding the provisions of paragraph 7, a Contracting State may enforce the provisions of its taxation laws relating to the deductibility of interest, in force on September 26, 1980, or as modified subsequent to that date in a manner that does not change the general nature of the provisions in force on September 26, 1980; or which are adopted after September 26, 1980, and are designed to ensure that non-residents do not enjoy a more favorable tax treatment under the taxation laws of that State than that enjoyed by residents. Thus Canada may continue to limit the deductions for interest paid to certain non-residents as provided in section 18(4) of Part I of the *Income Tax Act*.

Paragraph 9 provides that expenses incurred by citizens or residents of a Contracting State with respect to any convention, including any seminar, meeting, congress, or other function of similar nature, held in the other Contracting State, are deductible for purposes of taxation in the first-mentioned State to the same extent that such expenses would be deductible if the convention were held in that first-mentioned State. Thus, for U.S. income tax purposes an individual who is a citizen or resident of the United States and who attends a convention held in Canada may claim deductions for expenses incurred in connection with such convention without regard to the provisions of Code section 274(h). Section 274(h) imposes special restrictions on the deductibility of expenses incurred in connection with foreign conventions. A claim for a deduction for such an expense remains subject, in all events, to the provisions of U.S. law with respect to the deductibility of convention expenses generally (e.g., Code sections 162 and 212). Similarly, in the case of a citizen or resident of Canada attending a convention in the United States, paragraph 9 requires Canada to allow a deduction for expenses relating to such convention as if the convention had taken place in Canada.

Paragraph 10 provides that, notwithstanding the provisions of Article II (Taxes Covered), the provisions of Article XXV apply in the case of Canada to all taxes imposed under the *Income Tax Act*; and, in the case of the United States, to all taxes imposed under the Code. Article XXV does not apply to taxes imposed by political subdivisions or local authorities of Canada or the United States.

Article XXV substantially broadens the protection against discrimination provided by the 1942 Convention, which contains only one provision dealing specifically with this subject. That provision, paragraph 11 of the Protocol to the 1942 Convention, states that citizens of one of the Contracting States residing within the other Contracting State are not to be subjected to the payment of more burdensome taxes than the citizens of the other State.

The benefits of Article XXV may affect the tax liability of a U.S. citizen or resident with respect to the United States. See paragraphs 2 and 3 of Article XXIX (Miscellaneous Rules).

Article XXVI — Mutual Agreement Procedure

Paragraph 1 provides that where a person considers that the actions of one or both of the Contracting States will result in taxation not in accordance with the Convention, he may present his case in writing to the competent authority of the Contracting State of which he is a resident or, if he is a resident of neither Contracting State, of which he is a national. Thus, a resident of Canada must present to the Minister of National Revenue (or his authorized representative) any claim that such resident is being subjected to taxation contrary to the Convention. A person who requests assistance from the competent authority may also avail himself of any remedies available under domestic laws.

Paragraph 2 provides that the competent authority of the Contracting State to which the case is presented shall endeavor to resolve the case by mutual agreement with the competent authority of the other Contracting State, unless he believes that the objection is not justified or he is able to arrive at a satisfactory unilateral solution. Any agreement reached between the competent authorities of Canada and the United States shall he implemented notwithstanding any time or other procedural limitations in the domestic laws of the Contracting States, except where the special mutual agreement provisions of Article IX (Related Persons) apply, provided that the competent authority of the Contracting State asked to waive its domestic time or procedural limitations has received written notification that such a case exists within six years from the end of the taxation year in the first-mentioned State to which the case relates. The notification may be given by the competent authority of the first-mentioned State, the taxpayer who has requested the competent authority to take action, or a person related to the taxpayer. Unlike Article IX, Article XXVI does not require the competent authority of a Contracting State to grant unilateral relief to avoid double taxation in a case where timely notification is not given to the competent authority of the other Contracting State. Such unilateral relief may, however, be granted by the competent authority in its discretion pursuant to the provisions of Article XXVI and in order to achieve the purposes of the Convention. In a case where the provisions of Article IX apply, the provisions of paragraphs 3, 4, and 5 of that Article are controlling with respect to adjustments and corresponding adjustments of income, loss, or tax and the effect of the Convention upon time or procedural limitations of domestic law. Thus, if relief is not available under Article IX because of fraud, the provisions of paragraph 2 of Article XXVI do not independently authorize such relief.

Paragraph 3 provides that the competent authorities of the Contracting States shall endeavor to resolve by mutual agreement any difficulties or doubts arising as to the interpretation or application of the Convention. In particular, the competent authorities may agree to the same attribution of profits to a resident of a Contracting State and its permanent establishment in the other Contracting State; the same allocation of income, deductions, credits, or allowances between persons; the same determination of the source of income; the same characterization of particular items of income; a common meaning of any term used in the Convention; rules, guidelines, or procedures for the elimination of double taxation with respect to income distributed by an estate or trust, or with respect to a partnership; or to increase any dollar amounts referred to in the Convention to reflect monetary or economic developments. The competent authorities may also consult and reach agreements on rules, guidelines, or procedures for the elimination of double taxation in cases not provided for in the Convention.

The list of subjects of potential mutual agreement in paragraph 3 is not exhaustive; it merely illustrates the principles set forth in the paragraph. As in the case of other U.S. tax conventions, agreement can be arrived at in the context of determining the tax liability of a specific person or in establishing rules, guidelines, and procedures that will apply generally under the Convention to resolve issues for classes of taxpayers. It is contemplated that paragraph 3 could be utilized by the competent authorities, for example, to resolve conflicts between the domestic laws of Canada and the United States with respect to the allocation and apportionment of deductions.

Paragraph 4 provides that each Contracting State will endeavor to collect on behalf of the other State such amounts as may be necessary to ensure that relief granted by the Convention from taxation imposed by the other State does not enure to the benefit of persons not entitled to such relief. Paragraph 4 does not oblige either Contracting State to carry out administrative measures of a different nature from those that would be used by Canada or the United States in the collection of its own tax or which would be contrary to its public policy.

Paragraph 5 confirms that the competent authorities of Canada and the United States may communicate with each other directly for the purpose of reaching agreement in the sense of paragraphs 1 through 4.

Article XXVII — Exchange of Information

Paragraph 1 authorizes the competent authorities to exchange the information necessary for carrying out the provisions of the Convention or the domestic laws of Canada and the United States concerning taxes covered by the Convention, insofar as the taxation under those domestic laws is not contrary to the Convention. The authority to exchange information granted by paragraph 1 is not restricted by Article I (Personal Scope), and thus need not relate solely to persons otherwise covered by the Convention. It is contemplated that Article XXVII will be utilized by the competent authorities to exchange information upon request, routinely, and spontaneously.

Any information received by a Contracting State pursuant to the Convention is to be treated as secret in the same manner as information obtained under the taxation laws of that State. Such information shall be disclosed only to persons or authorities, including courts and administrative bodies, involved in the assessment or collection of, the administration and enforcement in respect of, or the determination of appeals in relation to, the taxes covered by the Convention and the information may be used by such persons only for such purposes. (In accordance with paragraph 4, for the purposes of this Article the Convention applies to a broader range of taxes than those covered specifically by Article II (Taxes Covered).

In specific cases a competent authority providing information may, pursuant to paragraph 3, impose such other conditions on the use of information as are necessary. Although the information received by persons described in paragraph 1 is to be treated as secret, it may be disclosed by such persons in public court proceedings or in judicial decisions.

The provisions of paragraph 1 authorize the U.S. competent authority to continue to allow the General Accounting Office to examine tax return information received from Canada when GAO is engaged in a study of the administration of U.S. tax laws pursuant to a directive of Congress. However, the secrecy requirements of paragraph 1 must be met.

If a Contracting State requests information in accordance with Article XXVII, the other Contracting State shall endeavor, pursuant to paragraph 2, to obtain the information to which the request relates in the same manner as if its own taxation were involved, notwithstanding the fact that such State does not need the information. In addition, the competent authority requested to obtain information shall endeavor to provide the information in the particular from requested such as depositions of witnesses and copies of unedited original documents, to the same extent such depositions and documents can be obtained under the laws or administrative practices of that State with respect to its own taxes.

Paragraph 3 provides that the provisions of paragraph 1 and 2 do not impose on Canada or the United States the obligation to carry out administrative measures at variance with the laws and administrative practice of either State; to supply information which is not obtainable under the laws or in the normal course of the administration of either State; or to supply information which would disclose any trade, business industrial commercial or professional secret or trade process, or information the disclosure of which would be contrary to public policy. Thus, Article XXVII allows, but does not obligate, the United States and Canada to obtain and provide information that would not be available to the requesting State under its laws or administrative practice or that in different circumstances would not be available to the State requested to provide the information. Further, Article XXVII allows a Contracting State to obtain information for the other Contracting State even if there is no tax liability in the State requested to obtain the information. Thus, the United States will continue to be able to give Canada tax information even if there is no U.S. tax liability at issue.

Paragraph 4 provides that, for the purposes of Article XXVII, the Convention applies, in the case of Canada, to all taxes imposed by the Government of Canada on estates and gifts under the *Income Tax Act* and, in the case of the United States, to all taxes imposed under the *Internal Revenue Code*. Article XXVII does not apply to taxes imposed by political subdivisions or local authorities of the Contracting States. Paragraph 4 is designed to ensure that information exchange will extend to most national level taxes on both sides, and specifically to information gathered for purposes of Canada's taxes on estate and gifts (not effective for deaths or gifts after 1971). This provision is intended to mesh with paragraph 18 of Article XXX (Entry Into Force), which terminates the existing estate tax convention between the United States and Canada.

Article XXVIII — Diplomatic Agents and Consular Officers

Article XXVIII states that nothing in the Convention affects the fiscal privileges of diplomatic agents or consular officers under the general rules of international law or under the provisions of special agreements. However, various provisions of the Convention could apply to such persons such as those concerning exchange of information, mutual agreement, and non-discrimination.

Article XXX — Entry into Force

Paragraph 1 provides that the Convention is subject to ratification in accordance with the procedures of Canada and the United States. The exchange of instruments of ratification is to take place at Ottawa as soon as possible.

Paragraph 2 provides, subject to paragraph 3, that the Convention shall enter into force upon the exchange of instruments of ratification. It has effect, with respect to source State taxation of dividends, interest, royalties, pensions, annuities, alimony, and child support, for amounts paid or credited on or after the first day of the second calendar month after the date on which the instruments of ratification are exchanged. For other taxes, the Convention takes effect for taxable years beginning on or after January 1 next following the date when instruments of ratification are exchanged. In the case of relief from United States social security taxes provided by paragraph 4 of Article XXIX (Miscellaneous Rules), the Convention also has effect for taxable years before the date on which instruments of ratification are exchanged.

Treaties and Related Legislation

Paragraph 3 provides special effective date rules for foreign tax credit computations with respect to taxes paid or accrued to Canada. Paragraph 3(a) provides that the tax on 1971 undistributed income on hand imposed by Part IX of the *Income Tax Act* of Canada is considered to be an "income tax" for distributions made on or after January 1, 1972 and before January 1, 1979. Any such tax which is paid or accrued under U.S. standards is considered to be imposed at the time of distribution and on the recipient of the distribution, in the proportion that the distribution out of undistributed income with respect to which the tax has been paid bears to 85 per cent of such undistributed income. A person claiming a credit for tax pursuant to paragraph 3(a) is obligated to compute the amount of the credit in accordance with that paragraph.

Paragraph 3(b) provides that the principles of paragraph 6 of Article XXIV (Elimination of Double Taxation), which provides for resourcing of certain dividend, interest, and royalty income to eliminate double taxation of U.S. citizens residing in Canada, have effect for taxable years beginning on or after January 1, 1976. The paragraph is intended to grant the competent authorities sufficient flexibility to address certain practical problems that have arisen under the 1942 Convention. It is anticipated that the competent authorities will be guided by paragraphs 4 and 5 of Article XXIV in applying paragraph 3(b) of Article XXX. Paragraph 3(c) provides that the provisions of paragraph 1 of Article XXIV (and the source rules of that Article) shall have effect for taxable years beginning on or after January 1, 1981.

Any claim for refund based on the provisions of paragraph 3 may be filed on or before June 30 of the calendar year following the year in which instruments of ratification are exchanged, notwithstanding statutes of limitations or other rules of domestic law to the contrary. For purposes of Code section 6611, the date of overpayment is the date on which instruments of ratification are exchanged, with respect to any refunds of U.S. tax pursuant to paragraph 3.

Paragraph 4 provides that, subject to paragraph 5, the 1942 Convention ceases to have effect for taxes for which the Convention has effect under the provisions of paragraph 2. For example, if under paragraph 2 the Convention were to have effect with respect to taxes withheld at source on dividends paid as of October 1, 1984, the 1942 Convention will not have effect with respect to such taxes.

Paragraph 5 modifies the rule of paragraph 4 to allow all of the provisions of the 1942 Convention to continue to have effect for the period through the first taxable year with respect to which the provisions of the Convention would otherwise have effect under paragraph 2(b), if greater relief from tax is available under the 1942 Convention than under the Convention. Paragraph 5 applies to all provisions of the 1942 Convention, not just those provisions of the convention for which the Convention takes effect under paragraph 2(b) of this Article. Thus, for example, assume that the Convention has effect, pursuant to paragraph 2(b), for taxable years of a taxpayer beginning on or after January 1, 1985. Further assume that a U.S. resident with a taxable year beginning on April 1 and ending on March 31 receives natural resource royalties from Canada which are subject to a 25% tax under Article VI (Income from Real Property) of the Convention, as amended by the Protocol, and Canada's internal law, but which would be subject to a 15% tax under Article XI of the 1942 Convention. Pursuant to paragraph 5, the greater benefits of the 1942 Convention would continue to apply to royalties paid or credited to the U.S. resident through March 31, 1986.

Paragraph 6 provides that the 1942 Convention terminates on the last of the dates on which it has effect in accordance with the provisions of paragraphs 4 and 5.

Paragraph 7 terminates the Exchange of Notes between the United States and Canada of August 2 and September 17, 1928 providing for relief from double taxation of shipping profits. The provisions of the Exchange of Notes no longer have effect for taxable years beginning on or after January 1 following the exchange of instruments of ratification of the Convention. The 1942 Convention, in Article V, had suspended the effectiveness of the Exchange of Notes.

Paragraph 8 terminates the Convention between Canada and the United States for the Avoidance of Double Taxation with Respect to Taxes on the Estates of Deceased Persons signed on February 17, 1961. The provisions of that Convention cease to have effect with respect to estates of persons deceased on or after January 1 of the year following the exchange of instruments of ratification of the Convention.

Article XXXI — Termination

Paragraph 1 provides that the Convention shall remain in force until terminated by Canada or the United States.

Paragraph 2 provides that either Canada or the United States may terminate the Convention at any time after 5 years from the date on which instruments of ratification are exchanged, provided that notice of termination is given through diplomatic channels at least 6 months prior to the date on which the Convention is to terminate.

Paragraph 3 provides a special termination rule in situations where Canada or the United States changes its taxation laws and the other Contracting State believes that such change is significant enough to warrant modification of the Convention. In such a circumstance, the Canadian Ministry of Finance and the United States Department of the Treasury would consult with a view to resolving the matter. If the matter cannot be satisfactorily resolved, the Contracting State requesting an accommodation because of the change in the other Contracting State's taxation laws may terminate the Convention by giving the 6 months' prior notice required by paragraph 2, without regard to whether the Convention has been in force for 5 years.

Paragraph 4 provides that, in the event of termination, the Convention ceases to have effect for tax withheld at source under Articles X (Dividends), XI (Interest), XII (Royalties), and XVIII (Pensions and Annuities), and under paragraph 2 of Article XXII (Other Income), with respect to amounts paid or credited on or after the first day of January following the expiration of the 6 month period referred to in paragraph 2. In the case of other taxes, the Convention shall cease to have effect in the event of termination with respect to taxable years beginning on or after January 1 following the expiration of the 6 month period referred to in paragraph 2.

April 26, 1984

Technical Explanation of the Third Protocol to the Canada–U.S. Convention

Treasury Department Technical Explanation of the Protocol amending the convention between the United States of America and Canada with respect to taxes on income and on capital signed at Washington on September 26, 1980, as amended by the protocols signed on June 14, 1983 and March 28, 1984

The Protocol, signed at Washington on March 17, 1995 (the "Protocol"), amends the Convention Between the United States of America and Canada with Respect to Taxes on Income and on Capital, signed at Washington on September 26, 1980, as amended by the Protocols signed on June 14, 1983 and March 28, 1984 (collectively referred to as the "Convention"). This technical explanation is an official guide to the Protocol. It explains policies behind particular provisions, as well as understandings reached during the negotiations with respect to the interpretation and application of the Protocol. The technical explanation is not intended to provide a complete comparison between the Protocol and the Articles of the Convention that it amends. To the extent that the Convention has not been amended by the Protocol, the Technical Explanation of the Convention remains the official explanation. References to "he" or "his" should be read to mean "he" or "she" or "his" or "her."

Article 1

Article 1 of the Protocol amends Article II (Taxes Covered) of the Convention. Article II identifies the taxes to which the Convention applies. Paragraph 1 of Article 1 replaces paragraphs 2 through 4 of Article II of the Convention with new paragraphs 2 and 3. For each Contracting State, new paragraph 2 of Article II specifies the taxes existing on the date of signature of the Protocol to which the Convention applies. New paragraph 3 provides that the Convention will also apply to taxes identical or substantially similar to those specified in paragraph 2, and to any new capital taxes, that are imposed after the date of signature of the Protocol.

New paragraph 2(a) of Article II describes the Canadian taxes covered by the Convention. As amended by the Protocol, the Convention will apply to all taxes imposed by the Government of Canada under the *Income Tax Act*.

New paragraph 2(b) of Article II amends the provisions identifying the U.S. taxes covered by the Convention in several respects. The Protocol incorporates into paragraph 2(b) the special rules found in paragraph 4 of Article II of the present Convention. New paragraph 2(b)(iii) conforms the rule previously found in paragraph 4(c) of Article II to the amended provisions of Article XXIV (Elimination of Double Taxation), under which Canada has agreed to grant a foreign tax credit for U.S. social security taxes. In addition, the Protocol adds a fourth special rule to reflect the addition to the Convention of new Article XXIX B (Taxes Imposed by Reason of Death) and related provisions in new paragraph 3(g) of Article XXVI (Mutual Agreement Procedure).

Article 1 of the Protocol also makes minor clarifying, nonsubstantive amendments to paragraphs 2 and 3 of the Article.

Article 2

This Article of the Protocol amends paragraphs 1(c) and 1(d) of Article III (General Definitions) of the Convention. These paragraphs define the terms "Canadian tax" and "United States tax, "respectively. The present Convention defines "Canadian tax "to mean the Canadian taxes specified in paragraph 2(a) or 3(a) of Article II (Taxes Covered), i.e., Canadian income taxes. It similarly defines the term "United States tax" to mean the U.S. taxes specified in paragraph 2(b) or 3(a) of Article II, i.e., U.S. income taxes.

As amended by the Protocol, paragraph 2(a) of Article II of the Convention covers all taxes imposed by Canada under its *Income Tax Act*, including certain taxes that are not *income* taxes. As explained below, paragraph 2(b)is similarly amended by the Protocol to include certain U.S. taxes that are not *income* taxes. It was, therefore, necessary to amend the terms "Canadian tax" and "United States tax" so that they would continue to refer exclusively to the *income* taxes imposed by each Contracting State. The amendment to the definition of the term "Canadian tax" ensures, for example, that the Protocol will not obligate the United States to give a foreign tax credit under Article XXIV (Elimination of Double Taxation) for covered taxes other than income taxes.

The definition of "United States tax," as amended, excludes certain United States taxes that are covered in Article II only for certain limited purposes under the Convention. These include the accumulated earnings tax, the personal holding company tax, foundation excise taxes, social security taxes, and estate taxes. To the extent that these are to be creditable taxes in Canada, that fact is specified elsewhere in the Convention. A Canadian income tax credit for U.S. social security taxes is provided in new paragraph 2(a)(ii) of Article XXIV (Elimination of Double Taxation). A Canadian income tax credit for the U.S. estate taxes is provided in paragraph 6 of new Article XXIV B (Taxes Imposed by Reason of Death).

Article 3

Article 3 of the Protocol amends Article IV (Residence) of the Convention. It clarifies the meaning of the term "resident" in certain cases and adds a special rule, found in a number of recent U.S. treaties, for determining the residence of U.S. citizens and "green-card" holders.

The first sentence of paragraph 1 of Article IV sets forth the general criteria for determining residence under the Convention. It is amended by the Protocol to state explicitly that a person will be considered a resident of a Contracting State for purposes of the Convention if he is liable to tax in that Contracting State by reason of citizenship. Although the sentence applies to both Contracting States, only the United States taxes its non-resident citizens in the same manner as its residents. Aliens admitted to the United States for permanent residence ("green card" holders) continue to qualify as U.S. residents under the first sentence of paragraph 1, because they are taxed by the United States as residents, regardless of where they physically reside.

U.S. citizens and green card holders who reside outside the United States, however, may have relatively little personal or economic nexus with the United States. The Protocol adds a second sentence to paragraph 1 that acknowledges this fact by limiting the circumstances under which such persons are to be treated, for purposes of the Convention, as U.S. residents. Under that sentence, a U.S. citizen or green card holder will be treated as a resident of the United States for purposes of the Convention, and, thereby, be entitled to treaty benefits, only if (1) the individual has a substantial presence, permanent home, or habitual abode in the United States, and (2) the individual's personal and economic relations with the United States are closer than those with any third country. If, however, such an individual is a resident of both the United States and Canada under the first sentence of the paragraph, his residence for purposes of the Convention is determined instead under the "tie-breaker" rules of paragraph 2 of the Article.

The fact that a U.S. citizen who does not have close ties to the United States may not be treated as a U.S. resident under Article IV of the Convention does not alter the application of the saving clause of paragraph 2 of Article XXIX (Miscellaneous Rules) to that citizen. However, like any other individual that is a resident alien under U.S. law, a green card holder is treated as a resident of the United States for purposes of the saving clause only if he qualifies as such under Article IV.

New paragraph 1(a) confirms that the term "resident" of a Contracting State includes the Government of that State or a political subdivision or local authority of that State, as well as any agency or instrumentality of one of these governmental entities. This is implicit in the current Convention and in other U.S. and Canadian treaties, even where not specified.

New paragraph 1 also clarifies, in subparagraph (b), that trusts, organizations, or other arrangements operated exclusively to provide retirement or employee benefits, and other not-for-profit organizations, such as organizations described in section 501(c) of the *Internal Revenue Code*, are residents of a Contracting State if they are constituted in that State and are generally exempt from income taxation in that State by reason of their nature as described above. This change clarifies that the specified entities are to be treated as residents of one of the Contracting States. This corresponds to the interpretation that had previously been adopted by the Contracting States. Such entities, therefore, will be entitled to the benefits of the Convention with respect to the other Contracting State, provided that they satisfy the requirements of new Article XXIV A (Limitation on Benefits) (discussed below).

Article 3 of the Protocol adds a sentence to paragraph 3 of Article IV of the current Convention to address the residence of certain dual resident corporations. Certain jurisdictions allow local incorporation of an entity that is already organized and incorporated under the laws of another country. Under Canadian law, such an entity is referred to as having been "continued" into the other country. Although the Protocol uses the Canadian term, the provision operates reciprocally. The new sentence states that such a corporation will be considered a resident of the State into which it is continued. Paragraph 5 of Article 21 of the Protocol governs the effective date of this provision.

Article 4

Article 4 of the Protocol amends paragraphs 3 and 4 of Article IX (Related Persons) of the Convention. Paragraph 1 of Article IX authorizes a Contracting State to adjust the amount of income, loss, or tax payable by a person with respect to arrangements between that person and a related person in the other Contracting State, when such arrangements differ from those that would obtain between unrelated persons. Under the present Convention, if an adjustment is made or to be made by a Contracting State under paragraph 1, paragraph 3 obligates the other Contracting State to make a corresponding adjustment if two conditions are satisfied: (1) the other Contracting State agrees with the adjustment made or to be made by the first Contracting State, and (2) the competent authority of the other Contracting State has received notice of the first adjustment within six years of the end of the taxable year to which that adjustment relates. If notice is not given within the six-year period, and if the person to whom the first adjustment relates is not notified of the adjustment at least six months prior to the end of the six-year period, paragraph 4 of Article IX of the present Convention requires that the first Contracting State withdraw its adjustment, to the extent necessary to avoid double taxation.

Article 4 of the Protocol amends paragraphs 3 and 4 of Article IX to prevent taxpayers from using the notification requirements of the present Convention to avoid adjustments. Paragraph 4, as amended, eliminates the requirement that a Contracting State withdraw an adjustment if the notification requirement of paragraph 3 has not been met. Paragraph 4 is also amended to delete the requirement that the taxpayer be notified at least six months before expiration of the six-year period specified in paragraph 3.

As amended by the Protocol, Article IX also explicitly authorizes the competent authorities to relieve double taxation in appropriate cases, even if the notification requirement is not satisfied. Paragraph 3 confirms that the competent authorities may agree to a corresponding adjustment if such an adjustment is not otherwise barred by time or procedural limitations such as the statute of limitations. Paragraph 4 provides that the competent authority of the State making the initial adjustment may grant unilateral relief from double taxation in other cases, although such relief is not obligatory.

Article 5

Article 5 of the Protocol amends Article X (Dividends) of the Convention. Paragraph 1 of Article 5 amends paragraph 2(a) of Article X to reduce from 10 per cent to 5 per cent the maximum rate of tax that may be imposed by a Contracting State on the gross amount of dividends beneficially owned by a company resident in the other Contracting State that owns at least 10 per cent of the voting stock of the company paying the dividends. The rate at which the branch profits tax may be imposed under paragraph 6 is also reduced by paragraph 1 of Article 5 from 10 per cent to 5 per cent. Under the entry-into-force provisions of Article 21 of the Protocol, these reductions will be phased in over a three-year period.

Paragraph 2 of Article 5 of the Protocol replaces paragraph 7 of Article X of the Convention with a new paragraph 7. Paragraph 7 of the existing Convention is no longer relevant because it applies only in the case where a Contracting State does not impose a branch profits tax. Both Contracting States now do impose such a tax.

New paragraph 7 makes the 5 per cent withholding rate of new paragraph 2(a) inapplicable in certain situations. Under new paragraph 7(b), dividends paid by U.S. regulated investment companies (RICs) are denied the 5 per cent withholding rate even if the Canadian shareholder is a corporation that would otherwise qualify as a direct investor by satisfying the 10-per cent ownership requirement. Consequently, all RIC dividends to Canadian beneficial owners are subjected to the 15 per cent rate that applies to dividends paid to portfolio investors.

Dividends paid by U.S. real estate investment trusts (REITs) to Canadian beneficial owners are also denied the 5 per cent rate under the rules of paragraph 7(c). REIT dividends paid to individuals who own less than a 10 per cent interest in the REIT are subject to withholding at a maximum rate of 15 per cent. Paragraph 7(c) also provides that dividend distributions by a REIT to an estate or a testamentary trust acquiring the interest in the REIT as a consequence of the death of an individual will be treated as distributions to an individual, for the five-year period following the death. Thus, dividends paid to an estate or testamentary trust in respect of a holding of less than a 10 per cent interest in the REIT also will be entitled to the 15 per cent rate of withholding, but only for up to five years after the death. REIT dividends paid to other Canadian beneficial owners are subject to the rate of withholding tax that applies under the domestic law of the United States (i.e., 30 per cent).

The denial of the 5 per cent withholding rate at source to all RIC and REIT shareholders, and the denial of the 15 per cent rate to most shareholders of REITs, is intended to prevent the use of these non-taxable conduit entities to gain unjustifiable benefits for certain shareholders. For example, a Canadian corporation that wishes to hold a portfolio of U.S. corporate shares may hold the portfolio directly and pay a U.S. withholding tax of 15 per cent on all of the dividends that it receives. Alternatively, it may place the portfolio of U.S. stocks in a RIC, in which the Canadian corporation owns more than 10 per cent of the shares, but in which there are enough small shareholders to satisfy the RIC diversified ownership requirements. Since the RIC is a pure conduit, there are no U.S. tax costs to the Canadian corporation of interposing the RIC as an intermediary in the chain of ownership. It is unlikely that a 10 per cent shareholding in a RIC will constitute a 10 per cent shareholding in any company from which the dividends originate. In the absence of the special rules in paragraph 7(b), however, interposition of a RIC would transform what should be portfolio dividends into direct investment dividends taxable at source by the United States only at 5 per cent. The special rules of paragraph 7 prevent this.

Similarly, a resident of Canada may hold U.S. real property directly and pay U.S. tax either at a 30 per cent rate on the gross income or at the income tax rates specified in the *Internal Revenue Code* on the net income. By placing the real estate holding in a REIT, the Canadian investor could transform real estate income into dividend income and thus transform high-taxed income into much lower-taxed income. In the absence of the special rule, if the REIT shareholder were a Canadian corporation that owned at least a 10 per cent interest in the REIT, the withholding rate would be 5 per cent; in all other cases, it would be 15 per cent. In either event, with one exception, a tax rate of 30 per cent or more would be significantly reduced. The exception is the relatively small individual Canadian investor who might be subject to U.S. tax at a rate of only 15 per cent on the net income even if he earned the real estate income directly. Under the rule in paragraph 7(c), such individuals, defined as those holding less than a 10 per cent interest in the REIT, remain taxable at source at a 15 per cent rate.

Subparagraph (a) of paragraph 7 provides a special rule for certain dividends paid by Canadian non-resident-owned investment corporations ("NROs"). The subparagraph provides for a maximum rate of 10 per cent (instead of the standard rate of 5 per cent) for dividends paid by NROs that are Canadian residents to a U.S. company that owns 10 per cent or more of the voting stock of the NRO and that is the beneficial owner of the dividend. This rule maintains the rate available under the current Convention for dividends from NROS. Canada wanted the withholding rate for direct investment NRO dividends to be no lower than the maximum withholding rates under the Convention on interest and royalties, to make sure that a foreign investor cannot transform interest or royalty income subject to a 10 per cent withholding tax into direct dividends qualifying for a 5 per cent withholding tax by passing it through to an NRO.

Article 6

Article 6 of the Protocol amends Article XI (Interest) of the Convention. Paragraph 1 of the Article reduces the general maximum withholding rate on interest under paragraph 2 of Article XI from 15 per cent to 10 per cent.

Paragraph 3 of Article XI of the Convention provides that, notwithstanding the general withholding rate applicable to interest payments under paragraph 2, certain specified categories of interest are exempt from withholding at source. Paragraph 2 of Article 6 of the Protocol amends paragraph 3(d) of the Convention, which deals with interest paid on indebtedness arising in connection with a sale on credit of equipment, merchandise, or services. The exemption provided by that paragraph in the Convention is broadened under the Protocol to apply to interest that is beneficially owned either by the seller in the underlying transaction, asunder the present Convention, or by any beneficial owner of interest paid with respect to an indebtedness arising as a result of the sale on credit of equipment, merchandise, or services. This exemption, however, does not apply in cases where the purchaser is related to the seller or the debtor is related to the beneficial owner of the interest. The negotiators agreed that this exemption is subject, as are the other provisions of the Convention, to any anti-avoidance rules applicable under the respective domestic law of the Contracting States.

The reference to "related persons" in paragraph 3(d) of Article XI of the Convention, as amended, is a change from the present Convention, which refers to "persons dealing at arm's length." The term "related person" as used in this Article is not defined for purposes of the Convention. Accordingly, the meaning of the term, and, therefore, the application of this Article, will be governed by the domestic law of each Contracting State (as is true with the use of the term "arm's-length" under the current Convention) under the interpretative rule of paragraph 2 of Article III (General Definitions). The United States will define the term "related person" as under section 482 of the *Internal Revenue Code*, to include organizations, trades, or businesses (whether or not incorporated, whether or not organized in the United States, and whether or not affiliated) owned or controlled directly or indirectly by the same interests. The Canadian definition of "related persons" is found in section 251 of the *Income Tax Act*.

Paragraph 3 of Article 6 of the Protocol adds a new paragraph 9 to Article XI of the Convention. Although the definition of "interest" in paragraph 4 includes an excess inclusion with respect to a residual interest in a real estate mortgage investment conduit (REMIC) described in section 860G of the *Internal Revenue Code*, new paragraph 9 provides that the reduced rates of tax at source for interest provided for in paragraphs 2 and 3 do not apply to such income. This class of interest, therefore, remains subject to the statutory 30 per cent U.S. rate of tax at source. The legislation that created REMICs in 1986 provided that such excess inclusions were to be taxed at the full 30 per cent statutory rate, regardless of any then-existing treaty provisions to the contrary. The 30 per cent rate of tax on excess inclusions received by residents of Canada is consistent with this expression of Congressional intent.

Article 7

Article 7 of the Protocol modifies Article XII (Royalties) of the Convention by expanding the classes of royalties exempt from withholding of tax at source. Paragraph 3, as amended by the Protocol, identifies four classes of royalty payments arising in one Contracting State and beneficially owned by a resident of the other that are exempt at source: (1) subparagraph (a) preserves the exemption in paragraph 3 of the present Convention for copyright royalties in respect of literary and other works, other than certain such payments in respect of motion pictures, videotapes, and similar payments; (2) subparagraph (b) specifies that computer software royalties are also exempt; (3) subparagraph (c) adds royalties paid for the use of, or the right to use, patents and information concerning industrial, commercial, and scientific experience, other than payments in connection with rental or franchise agreements; and (4) subparagraph (d) allows the Contracting States to reach an agreement, through an exchange of Diplomatic Notes, with respect to the application of paragraph 3 of Article XII to payments in respect of certain live broadcasting transmissions.

The specific reference to software in subparagraph (b) is not intended to suggest that the United States views the term "copyright" as excluding software in other U.S. treaties (including the current treaty with Canada).

The negotiators agreed that royalties paid for the use of, or the right to use, designs or models, plans, secret formulas, or processes are included under subparagraph 3(c) to the extent that they represent payments for the use of, or the right to use, information concerning industrial, commercial, or scientific experience. In addition, they agreed that royalties paid for the use of, or the right to use, "know-how," as defined in paragraph 11 of the Commentary on Article 12 of the OECD Model Income Tax Treaty, constitute payments for the use of, or the right to use, information concerning industrial, commercial, or scientific experience. The negotiators further agreed that a royalty paid under a "mixed contract," "package fee," or similar arrangement will be treated as exempt at source by virtue of paragraph 3 to the extent of any portion that is paid for the use of, or the right to use, property or information with respect to which paragraph 3 grants an exemption.

The exemption granted under subparagraph 3(c) does not, however, extend to payments made for information concerning industrial, commercial, or scientific experience that is provided in connection with a rental or franchise agreement. For this purpose, the negotiators agreed that a franchise is to be distinguished from other arrangements resulting in the transfer of intangible property. They agreed that a license to use intangibles (whether or not including a trademark) in a territory, in and of itself, would not constitute a franchise agreement for purposes of subparagraph 3(c) in the absence of other rights and obligations in the license agreement or in any other agreement that would indicate that the arrangement in its totality constituted a franchise agreement. For example, a resident of one Contracting State may acquire a right to use a secret formula to manufacture a particular product (e.g., a perfume), together with the right to use a trademark for that product and to market it at anon-retail level, in the other Contracting State. Such an arrangement would not constitute a franchise in the absence of any other rights or obligations under that arrangement or any other agreement that would indicate that the arrangement in its totality constituted a franchise agreement. Therefore, the royalty payment under that arrangement would be exempt from withholding tax in the other Contracting State to the extent made for the use of, or the right to use, the secret formula or other information concerning industrial, commercial, or scientific experience; however, it would be subject to withholding tax at a rate of 10 per cent, to the extent made for the use of, or the right to use, the trademark.

The provisions of paragraph 3 do not fully reflect the U.S. treaty policy of exempting all types of royalty payments from taxation at source, but Canada was not prepared to grant a complete exemption for all types of royalties in the Protocol. Although the Protocol makes several important changes to the royalty provisions of the present Convention in the direction of bringing Article XII into conformity with U.S. policy, the United States remains concerned about the imposition of withholding tax on some classes of royalties and about the associated administrative burdens. In this connection, the Contracting States have affirmed their intention to collaborate to resolve in good faith any administrative issues that may arise in applying the provisions of subparagraph 3(c). The United States intends to continue to pursue a zero rate of withholding for all royalties in future negotiations with Canada, including discussions under Article 20 of the Protocol, as well as in negotiations with other countries.

As noted above, new subparagraph 3(d) enables the Contracting States to provide an exemption for royalties paid with respect to broadcasting through an exchange of notes. This provision was included because Canada was not prepared at the time of the negotiations to commit to an exemption for broadcasting royalties. Subparagraph 3(d) was included to enable the Senate to give its advice and consent in advance to such an exemption, in the hope that such an exemption could be obtained without awaiting the negotiation of another full protocol. Any agreement reached under the exchange of notes authorized by subparagraph 3(d) would lower the withholding rate from 10 per cent to zero and, thus, bring the Convention into greater conformity with established U.S. treaty policy.

Paragraph 2 of Article 7 of the Protocol amends the rules in paragraph 6 of Article XII of the Convention for determining the source of royalty payments. Under the present Convention, royalties generally are deemed to arise in a Contracting State if paid by a resident of that State. However, if the obligation to pay the royalties was incurred in connection with a permanent establishment or a fixed base in one of the Contracting States that bears the expense, the royalties are deemed to arise in that State.

The Protocol continues to apply these basic rules but changes the scope of an exception provided under the present Convention. Under the present Convention, a royalty paid for the use of, or the right to use, property in a Contracting State is deemed to arise in that State. Under the Protocol, this "place of use" exception applies only if the Convention does not otherwise deem the royalties to arise in one of the Contracting States. Thus, the "place of use" exception will apply only if royalties are neither paid by a resident of one of the Contracting States nor borne by a permanent establishment or fixed base in either State. For example, if a Canadian resident were to grant franchise rights to a resident of Chile for use in the United States, the royalty paid by the Chilean resident to the Canadian resident for those rights would be U.S. source income under this Article, subject to U.S. withholding at the 10 per cent rate provided in paragraph 2.

The rules of this Article differ from those provided under U.S. domestic law. Under U.S. domestic law, a royalty is considered to be from U.S. sources if it is paid for the use of, or the privilege of using, an intangible within the United States; the residence of the payor is irrelevant. If paid to a nonresident alien individual or other foreign person, a U.S. source royalty is generally subject to withholding tax at a rate of 30 per cent under U.S. domestic law. By reason of paragraph 1 of Article XXIX (Miscellaneous Rules), a Canadian resident would be permitted to apply the rules of U.S. domestic law to its royalty income if those rules produced a more favorable result in its case than those of this Article. However, under a basic principle of tax treaty interpretation recognized by both Contracting States, the prohibition against so-called "cherry-picking," the Canadian resident would be precluded from claiming selected benefits under the Convention (e.g., the tax rates only) and other benefits under U.S. domestic law (e.g., the source rules only) with respect to its royalties. See, e.g., Rev. Rul. 84-17, 1984-1 C.B. 308. For example, if a Canadian company granted franchise rights to a resident of the United States for use 50 per cent in the United States and 50 per cent in Chile, the Convention would permit the Canadian company to treat all of its royalty income from that single transaction as U.S. source income entitled to the withholding tax reduction under paragraph 2. U.S. domestic law would permit the Canadian company to treat 50 per cent of its royalty income as U.S. source income subject to a 30 per cent withholding tax and the other 50 per cent as foreign source income exempt from U.S. tax. The Canadian company could choose to apply either the provisions of U.S. domestic law or the provisions of the Convention to the transaction, but would not be permitted to claim both the U.S. domestic law exemption for 50 per cent of the income and the Convention's reduced withholding rate for the remainder of the income.

Royalties generally are considered borne by a permanent establishment or fixed base if they are deductible in computing the taxable income of that permanent establishment or fixed base.

Since the definition of "resident" of a Contracting State in Article IV (Residence), as amended by Article 3 of the Protocol, specifies that this term includes the Contracting States and their political subdivisions and local authorities, the source rule does not include a specific reference to these governmental entities.

Article 8

Article 8 of the Protocol broadens the scope of paragraph 8 of Article XIII (Gains) of the Convention to cover organizations, reorganizations, amalgamations, and similar transactions involving either corporations or other entities. The present Convention covers only transactions involving corporations. The amendment is intended to make the paragraph applicable to transactions involving other types of entities, such as trusts and partnerships.

As in the case of transactions covered by the present Convention, the deferral allowed under this provision shall be for such time and under such other conditions as are stipulated between the person acquiring the property and the competent authority. The agreement of the competent authority of the State of source is entirely discretionary and, when granted, will be granted only to the extent necessary to avoid double taxation.

Article 9

Article 9 of the Protocol amends Article XVIII (Pensions and Annuities) of the Convention. Paragraph 3 of Article XVIII defines the term "pensions" for purposes of the Convention, including the rules for the taxation of cross-border pensions in paragraphs 1 and 2 of the Article, the rules in paragraphs 2 and 3 of Article XXI (Exempt Organizations) for certain income derived by pension funds, and the rules in paragraph 1(b)(i) of Article IV (Residence) regarding the residence of pension funds and certain other entities. The Protocol amends the present definition by substituting the phrase "other retirement arrangement" for the phrase "retirement plan." The purpose of this change is to clarify that the definition of "pensions" includes, for example, payments from Individual Retirement Accounts (IRAs) in the United States and to provide that "pensions" includes, for example, Registered Retirement Savings Plans (RRSPs) and Registered Retirement Income Funds (RRIFs) in Canada. The term "pensions" also would include amounts paid by other retirement plans or arrangements, whether or not they are qualified plans under U.S. domestic law; this would include, for example, plans and arrangements described in section 457 or 414(d) of the *Internal Revenue Code*.

Paragraph 2 of Article 9 of the Protocol amends paragraph 5 of Article XVIII to modify the treatment of social security benefits under the Convention. Under the amended paragraph, benefits paid under the U.S. or Canadian social security legislation to a resident of the other Contracting State, or, in the case of Canadian benefits, to a U.S. citizen, are taxable exclusively in the paying State. This amendment brings the Convention into line with current U.S. treaty policy. Social security benefits are defined, for this purpose, to include tier 1 rail-road retirement benefits but not unemployment benefits (which therefore fall under Article XXII (Other Income) of the Convention). Pensions in respect of government service are covered not by this rule but by the rules of paragraphs 1 and 2 of Article XVIII.

The special rule regarding U.S. citizens is intended to clarify that only Canada, and not the United States, may tax a social security payment by Canada to a U.S. citizen not resident in the United States. This is consistent with the intention of the general rule, which is to give each Contracting State exclusive taxing jurisdiction over its social security payments. Since paragraph 5 is an exception to the saving clause, Canada will retain exclusive taxing jurisdiction over Canadian social security benefits paid to U.S. residents and citizens, and vice versa. It was not necessary to provide a special rule to clarify the taxation of U.S. social security payments to Canadian citizens, because Canada does not tax on the basis of citizenship and, therefore, does not include citizens within the scope of its saving clause.

A new paragraph 7 is added to Article XVIII by Article 9 of the Protocol. This paragraph replaces paragraph 5 of Article XXIX (Miscellaneous Rules) of the present Convention. The new paragraph makes reciprocal the rule that it replaced and expands its scope, so that it no longer applies only to residents and citizens of the United States who are beneficiaries of Canadian RRSPs. As amended, paragraph 7 applies to an individual who is a citizen or resident of a Contracting State and a beneficiary of a trust, company, organization, or other arrangement that is a resident of the other Contracting State and that is both generally exempt from income taxation in its State of residence and operated exclusively to provide pension, retirement, or employee benefits. Under this rule, the beneficiary may elect to defer taxation in his State of residence on income accrued in the plan until it is distributed or rolled over into another plan. The new rule also broadens the types of arrangements covered by this paragraph in a manner consistent with other pension-related provisions of the Protocol.

Article 10

Article 10 of the Protocol amends Article XXI (Exempt Organizations) of the Convention. Paragraph 1 of Article 10 amends paragraphs 2 and 3 of Article XXI. The most significant changes are those that conform the language of the two paragraphs to the revised definition of the term "pension" in paragraph 3 of Article XVIII (Pensions and Annuities). The revision adds the term "arrangement" to "trust, company or organization" in describing the residents of a Contracting State that may receive dividend and interest income exempt from current income taxation by the other Contracting State. This clarifies that IRAs, for example, are eligible for the benefits of paragraph 2, subject to the exception in paragraph 3, and makes Canadian RRSPs and RRIFs, for example, similarly eligible (provided that they are operated exclusively to administer or provide pension, retirement, or employee benefits).

The other changes, all in paragraph 2, are intended to improve and clarify the language. For example, the reference to "tax" in the present Convention is changed to a reference to "income taxation." This is intended to clarify that if an otherwise exempt organization is subject to an excise tax, for example, it will not lose the benefits of this paragraph. In subparagraph 2(b), the phrase "not taxed in a taxable year" was changed to "generally exempt from income taxation in a taxable year" to ensure uniformity throughout the Convention; this change was not intended to disqualify a trust or other arrangement that qualifies for the exemption under the wording of the present Convention.

Paragraph 2 of Article 10 adds a sentence to paragraph 5 of Article XXI of the Convention. The paragraph in the present Convention provides that a U.S. citizen or resident may deduct, for U.S. income tax purposes, contributions made to Canadian charities under certain circumstances. The added sentence makes clear that the benefits of the paragraph are available to a company that is a resident of Canada but is treated by the United States as a domestic corporation under the consolidated return rules of section 1504(d) of the *Internal Revenue Code*. Thus, such a company will be able to deduct, for U.S. income tax purposes, contributions to Canadian charities that are deductible to a U.S. resident under the provisions of the paragraph.

Paragraph 3 of Article 10 amends paragraph 6 of Article XXI of the Convention to replace references to "deductions" for Canadian tax purposes with references to "relief" from tax. These changes clarify that the provisions of paragraph 6 apply to the credit for charitable contributions allowed under current Canadian law. The Protocol also makes other non-substantive drafting changes to paragraph 6.

Article 11

Article 11 of the Protocol adds a new paragraph 3 to Article XXII (Other Income) of the Convention. This Article entitles residents of one Contracting State who are taxable by the other State on gains from wagering transactions to deduct losses from wagering transactions for the purposes of taxation in that other State. However, losses are to be deductible only to the extent that they are incurred with respect to wagering transactions, the gains on which could be taxable in the other State, and only to the extent that such losses would be deductible if incurred by a resident of that other State.

This Article does not affect the collection of tax by a Contracting State. Thus, in the case of a resident of Canada, this Article does not affect, for example, the imposition of U.S. withholding taxes under section 1441 or section 1442 of the *Internal Revenue Code* on the gross amount of gains from wagering transactions. However, in computing its U.S. income tax liability on net income for the taxable year concerned, the Canadian resident may reduce its gains from wagering transactions subject to taxation in the United States by any wagering losses incurred on such transactions, to the extent that those losses are deductible under the provisions of new paragraph 3. Under U.S. domestic law, the deduction of wagering losses is governed by section 165 of the *Internal Revenue Code*. It is intended that the resident of Canada file a nonresident income tax return in order to substantiate the deduction for losses and to claim a refund of any overpayment of U.S. taxes collected by withholding.

Article 12

Article 12 of the Protocol amends Article XXIV (Elimination of Double Taxation) of the Convention. Paragraph 1 of Article 12 amends the rules for Canadian double taxation relief in subparagraphs (a) and (b) of paragraph 2 of Article XXIV. The amendment to subparagraph (a) obligates Canada to give a foreign tax credit for U.S. social security taxes paid by individuals. The amendment to subparagraph (b) of paragraph 2 does not alter the substantive effect of the rule, but conforms the language to current Canadian law. Under the provision as amended, Canada generally continues to allow an exemption to a Canadian corporation for direct dividends paid from the exempt surplus of a U.S. affiliate.

Paragraphs 4 and 5 of Article XXIV of the Convention provide double taxation relief rules, for both the United States and Canada, with respect to U.S. source income derived by a U.S. citizen who is resident in Canada. These rules address the fact that a U.S. citizen resident in Canada remains subject to U.S. tax on his worldwide income at ordinary progressive rates, and may, therefore, be subject to U.S. tax at a higher rate than a resident of Canada who is not a U.S. citizen. In essence, these paragraphs limit the foreign tax credit that Canada is obliged to allow such a U.S. citizen to the amount of tax on his U.S. source income that the United States would be allowed to collect from a Canadian resident who is not a U.S. citizen. They also oblige the United States to allow the U.S. citizen a credit for any income tax paid to Canada on the remainder of his income. Paragraph 4 deals with items of income other than dividends, interest, and royalties and is not changed by the Protocol. Paragraph 5, which deals with dividends, interest, and royalties, is amended by paragraph 2 of Article 12 of the Protocol.

The amendments to paragraph 5 of the Article make that paragraph applicable only to dividend, interest, and royalty income that would be subject to a positive rate of U.S. tax if paid to a Canadian resident who is not a U.S. citizen. This means that the rules of paragraph 4, not paragraph 5, will apply to items of interest and royalties, such as portfolio interest, that would be exempt from U.S. tax if paid to a non-U.S. citizen resident in Canada. Under paragraph 4, Canada will not allow a credit for the U.S. tax on such income, and the United States will credit the Canadian tax to the extent necessary to avoid double taxation.

Paragraph 2 of Article 12 of the Protocol makes further technical amendments to paragraph 5 of Article XXIV of the Convention. The existing Technical Explanation of paragraphs 5 and 6 of Article XXIV of the Convention should be read as follows to reflect the amendments made by the Protocol:

Paragraph 5 provides special rules for the elimination of double taxation in the case of dividends, interest, and royalties earned by a U.S. citizen resident in Canada. These rules apply notwithstanding the provisions of paragraph 4, but only as long as the law in Canada allows a deduction in computing income for the portion of any foreign tax paid in respect of dividends, interest, or royalties which exceeds 15 per cent of the amount of such items of income, and only with respect to those items of income. The rules of paragraph 4 apply with respect to other items of income; moreover, if the law in force in Canada regarding the deduction for foreign taxes is changed so as to no longer allow such a deduction, the provisions of paragraph 5 shall not apply and the U.S. foreign tax credit for Canadian taxes and the Canadian credit for U.S. taxes will be determined solely pursuant to the provisions of paragraph 4.

The calculations under paragraph 5 are as follows. First, the deduction allowed in Canada in computing income shall be made with respect to U.S. tax on the dividends, interest, and royalties before any foreign tax credit by the United States with respect to income tax paid or accrued to Canada. Second, Canada shall allow a deduction from (credit against) Canadian tax for U.S. tax paid or accrued with respect to the dividends, interest, and royalties, but such credit need not exceed the amount of income tax that would be paid or accrued to the United States on such items of income if the individual were not a U.S. citizen after taking into account any relief available under the Convention. Third, for purposes of computing the U.S. tax on such dividends, interest, and royalties, the United States shall allow as a credit against the U.S. tax the income tax paid or accrued to Canada after the credit against Canadian tax for income tax paid or accrued to the United States. The United States is in no event obliged to give a credit for Canadian income tax which will reduce the U.S. tax below the amount of income tax that would be paid or accrued to the United States on the amount of the dividends, interest, and royalties if the individual were not a U.S. citizen after taking into account any relief available under the Convention.

The rules of paragraph 5 are illustrated by the following examples.

Example B

— A U.S. citizen who is a resident of Canada has $100 of dividend income arising in the United States. The tentative U.S. tax before foreign tax credit is $40.

— Canada, under its law, allows a deduction for the U.S. tax in excess of 15 per cent or, in this case, a deduction of $25 ($40 - $15). The Canadian taxable income is $75 and the Canadian tax on that amount is $35.

— Canada gives a credit of $15 (the maximum credit allowed is 15 per cent of the gross dividend taken into Canadian income) and collects a net tax of $20.

— The United States allows a credit for the net Canadian tax against its tax in excess of 15 per cent. Thus, the maximum credit is $25 ($40 - $15). But since the net Canadian tax paid was $20, the usable credit is $20.

— To be able to use a credit of $20 requires Canadian source taxable income of $50 (50% of the U.S. tentative tax of $40). Under paragraph 6, $50 of the U.S. dividend is resourced to be of Canadian source. The credit of $20 may then be offset against the U.S. tax of $40, leaving a net U.S. tax of $20.

— The combined tax paid to both countries is $40, $20 to Canada and $20 to the United States.

Example C

A U.S. citizen who is a resident of Canada receives $200 of income with respect to personal services performed within Canada and $100 of dividend income arising within the United States. Taxable income for U.S. purposes, taking into account the rules of Code section 911, is $220. U.S. tax (before foreign tax credits) is $92. The $100 of dividend income is deemed to bear U.S. tax (before foreign tax credits) of $41.82 ($100/$200 × $92). Under Canadian law, a deduction of $26.82 (the excess of $41.82 over 15 per cent of the $100 dividend income) is allowed in computing income. The Canadian tax on $273.18 of income ($300 less the $26.82 deduction) is $130. Canada then gives a credit against the $130 for $15 (the U.S. tax paid or accrued with respect to the dividend, $41.82 but limited to 15 per cent of the gross amount of such income, or $15), leaving a final Canadian tax of $115. Of the $115, $30.80 is attributable to the dividend:

$$\frac{\$73.18 \text{ (\$100 dividend less \$26.82 deduction)}}{\$273.18 \text{ (\$300 income less \$26.82 deduction)}} \times \$115.$$

Of this amount, $26.82 is creditable against U.S. tax pursuant to paragraph 5. (Although the U.S. allows a credit for the Canadian tax imposed on the dividend, $30.80, the credit may not reduce the U.S. tax below 15 per cent of the amount of the dividend. Thus, the maximum allowable credit is the excess of $41.82, the U.S. tax imposed on the dividend income, over $15, which is 15 per cent of the $100 dividend). The remaining $3.98 (the Canadian tax of $30.80 less the credit allowed of $26.82) is a foreign tax credit carryover for U.S. purposes, subject to the limitations of paragraph 5. (An additional $50.18 of Canadian tax with respect to Canadian source services income is creditable against U.S. tax pursuant to paragraphs 3 and 4(b). The $50.18 is computed as follows: tentative U.S. tax (before foreign tax credits) is $92; the U.S. tax on Canadian source services income is $50.18 ($92 less the U.S. tax on the dividend income of $41.82); the limitation on the services income is:

$$\frac{\$120 \text{ (taxable income from services)}}{\$220 \text{ (total taxable income)}} \times \$92$$

Treaties and Related Legislation

or $50.18. The credit for Canadian tax paid on the services income is therefore $50.18; the remainder of the Canadian tax on the services income, or $34.02, is a foreign tax credit carryover for U.S. purposes, subject to the limitations of paragraph 5.)

Paragraph 6 is necessary to implement the objectives of paragraphs 4(b) and 5(c). Paragraph 6 provides that where a U.S. citizen is a resident of Canada, items of income referred to in paragraph 4 or 5 are deemed for the purposes of Article XXIV to arise in Canada to the extent necessary to avoid double taxation of income by Canada and the United States consistent with the objectives of paragraphs 4(b) and 5(c). Paragraph 6 can override the source rules of paragraph 3 to permit a limited resourcing of income. The principles of paragraph 3 have effect, pursuant to paragraph 3(b) of Article XXX (Entry Into Force) of the Convention, for taxable years beginning on or after January 1, 1976. See the discussion of Article XXX below.

The application of paragraph 6 is illustrated by the following example.

Example D

The facts are the same as in Example C. The United States has undertaken, pursuant to paragraph 5(c) and paragraph 6, to credit $26.82 of Canadian taxes on dividend income that has a U.S. source under both paragraph 3 and the *Internal Revenue Code*. (As illustrated in Example C, the credit, however, only reduces the U.S. tax on the dividend income which exceeds the amount of income tax that would be paid or accrued to the United States on such income if the individual were not a U.S. citizen after taking into account any relief available under the Convention. Pursuant to paragraph 6, for purposes of determining the U.S. foreign tax credit limitation under the Convention with respect to Canadian taxes, $64.13

$$\frac{A}{\$220} \times \$92 = \$26.82;\ A = \$64.13$$

of taxable income with respect to the dividends is deemed to arise in Canada.

Paragraph 3 of Article 12 of the Protocol makes a technical amendment to paragraph 7 of Article XXIV. It conforms the reference to U.S. and Canadian taxes to the amended definitions of "United States tax" and "Canadian tax" in subparagraphs (c) and (d) of paragraph 1 of Article III (General Definitions). No substantive change in the effect of the paragraph is intended.

Paragraph 4 of Article 12 of the Protocol adds a new paragraph 10 to Article XXIV of the Convention. This paragraph provides for the application of the rule of "exemption with progression" by a Contracting State in cases where an item of income of a resident of that State is exempt from tax in that State by virtue of a provision of the Convention. For example, where under Canadian law a tax benefit, such as the goods and services tax credit, to a Canadian resident individual is reduced as the income of that individual, or the individual's spouse or other dependent, increases, and any of these persons receives U.S. social security benefits that are exempt from tax in Canada under the Convention, Canada may, nevertheless, take the U.S. social security benefits into account in determining whether, and to what extent, the benefit should be reduced.

New Article XXIX B (Taxes Imposed by Reason of Death), added by Article 19 of the Protocol, also provides relief from double taxation in certain circumstances in connection with Canadian income tax imposed by reason of death and U.S. estate taxes. However, subparagraph 7(c) of Article XXIX B generally denies relief from U.S. estate tax under that Article to the extent that a credit or deduction has been claimed for the same amount in determining any other tax imposed by the United States. This restriction would operate to deny relief, for example, to the extent that relief from U.S. income tax is claimed under Article XXIV in respect of the same amount of Canadian tax. There is, however, no requirement that relief from U.S. tax be claimed first (or exclusively) under Article XXIV. Paragraph 6 of Article XXIX B also prevents the claiming of double relief from Canadian income taxation under both that Article and Article XXIV, by providing that the credit provided by Article XXIX B applies only after the application of the credit provided by Article XXIV.

Article 13

Article 13 of the Protocol amends Article XXV (Non-Discrimination) of the Convention. Paragraph 1 of Article 13 amends paragraph 3 of Article XXV to conform the treaty language to a change in Canadian law. The paragraph is intended to allow the treatment of dependents under the income tax law of a Contracting State to apply with respect to dependents who are residents of the other Contracting State. As drafted in the present Convention, the rule deals specifically only with deductions; the amendments made by the Protocol clarify that it also applies to the credits now provided by Canadian law.

Paragraph 2 of Article 13 of the Protocol amends paragraph 10 of Article XXV of the Convention to broaden the scope of the non-discrimination protection provided by the Convention. As amended, Article XXV will apply to all taxes imposed by a Contracting State. Under the present Convention, non-discrimination protection is limited in the case of Canadian taxes to taxes imposed under the *Income Tax Act*. As amended by the Protocol, non-discrimination protection will extend, for example, to the Canadian goods and services tax and other Canadian excise taxes.

Article 14

Article 14 of the Protocol makes two changes to Article XXVI (Mutual Agreement Procedure) of the Convention. First, it adds a new subparagraph 3(g) specifically authorizing the competent authorities to provide relief from double taxation in certain cases involving the distribution or disposition of property by a U.S. qualified domestic trust or a Canadian spousal trust, where relief is not otherwise available.

Article 14 also adds a new paragraph 6 to Article XXVI (Mutual Agreement Procedure). Paragraph 6 provides for a voluntary arbitration procedure, to be implemented only upon the exchange of Diplomatic Notes between the United States and Canada. Similar provisions are found in the recent U.S. treaties with the Federal Republic of Germany, the Netherlands, and Mexico. Paragraph 6 provides that where the competent authorities have been unable, pursuant to the other provisions of Article XXVI, to resolve a disagreement regarding the interpretation or application of the Convention, the disagreement may, with the consent of the taxpayer and both competent authorities, be submitted for arbitration, provided the taxpayer agrees in writing to be bound by the decision of the arbitration board. Nothing in the provision requires that any case be submitted for arbitration. However, if a case is submitted to an arbitration board, the board's decision in that case will be binding on both Contracting States and on the taxpayer with respect to that case.

The United States was reluctant to implement an arbitration procedure until there has been an opportunity to evaluate the process in practice under other agreements that allow for arbitration, particularly the U.S.–Germany Convention. It was agreed, therefore, as specified in paragraph 6, that the provisions of the Convention calling for an arbitration procedure will not take effect until the two Contracting States have agreed through an exchange of Diplomatic Notes to do so. This is similar to the approach taken with the Netherlands and Mexico. Paragraph 6 also provides that the procedures to be followed in applying arbitration will be agreed through an exchange of notes by the Contracting States. It is expected that such procedures will ensure that arbitration will not generally be available where matters of either State's tax policy or domestic law are involved.

Paragraph 2 of Article 20 of the Protocol provides that the appropriate authorities of the Contracting State will consult after three years following entry into force of the Protocol to determine whether the Diplomatic Notes implementing the arbitration procedure should be exchanged.

Article 15

Article 15 of the Protocol adds to the Convention a new Article XXVI A (Assistance in Collection). Collection assistance provisions are included in several other U.S. income tax treaties, including the recent treaty with the Netherlands, and in many U.S. estate tax treaties. U.S. negotiators initially raised with Canada the possibility of including collection assistance provisions in the Protocol, because the Internal Revenue Service has claims pending against persons in Canada that would be subject to collection under these provisions. However, the ultimate decision of the U.S. and Canadian negotiators to add the collection assistance article was attributable to the confluence of several unusual factors.

Of critical importance was the similarity between the laws of the United States and Canada. The Internal Revenue Service, the Justice Department, and other U.S. negotiators were reassured by the close similarity of the legal and procedural protections afforded by the Contracting States to their citizens and residents and by the fact that these protections apply to the tax collection procedures used by each State. In addition, the U.S. negotiators were confident, given their extensive experience in working with their Canadian counterparts, that the agreed procedures could be administered appropriately, effectively, and efficiently. Finally, given the close cooperation already developed between the United States and Canada in the exchange of tax information, the U.S. and Canadian negotiators concluded that the potential benefits to both countries of obtaining such assistance would be immediate and substantial and would far outweigh any cost involved.

Under paragraph 1 of Article XXVI A, each Contracting State agrees, subject to the exercise of its discretion and to the conditions explicitly provided later in the Article, to lend assistance and support to the other in the collection of revenue claims. The term "revenue claim" is defined in paragraph 1 to include all taxes referred to in paragraph 9 of the Article, as well as interest, costs, additions to such taxes, and civil penalties. Paragraph 9 provides that, notwithstanding the provisions of Article II (Taxes Covered) of the Convention, Article XXVI A shall apply to all categories of taxes collected by or on behalf of the Government of a Contracting State.

Paragraph 2 of the Article requires the Contracting State applying for collection assistance (the "applicant State") to certify that the revenue claim for which collection assistance is sought has been "finally determined." A revenue claim has been finally determined when the applicant State has the right under its internal law to collect the revenue claim and all administrative and judicial rights of the taxpayer to restrain collection in the applicant State have lapsed or been exhausted.

Paragraph 3 of the Article clarifies that the Contracting State from which assistance was requested (the "requested State") has discretion as to whether to accept a particular application for collection assistance. However, if the application for assistance is accepted, paragraph 3 requires that the requested State grant assistance under its existing procedures as though the claim were the requested State's own revenue claim finally determined under the laws of that State. This obligation under paragraph 3 is limited by paragraph 7 of the Article, which provides that, although generally treated as a revenue claim of the requested State, a claim for which collection assistance is granted shall not have any priority accorded to the revenue claims of the requested State.

Paragraph 4 of Article XXVI A provides that, when the United States accepts a request for assistance in collection, the claim will be treated by the United States as an assessment as of the time the application was received. Similarly, when Canada accepts a request, a revenue claim shall be treated as an amount payable under the *Income Tax Act*, the collection of which is not subject to any restriction.

Paragraph 5 of the Article provides that nothing in Article XXVI A shall be construed as creating in the requested State any rights of administrative or judicial review of the applicant State's finally determined revenue claim. Thus, when an application for collection assistance has been accepted, the substantive validity of the applicant State's revenue claim cannot be challenged in an action in the requested State. Paragraph 5 furthers provides, however, that if the applicant State's revenue claim ceases to be finally determined, the applicant State is obligated to withdraw promptly any request that had been based on that claim.

Paragraph 6 provides that, as a general rule, the requested State is to forward the entire amount collected to the competent authority of the applicant State. The ordinary costs incurred in providing collection assistance will normally be borne by the requested State and only extraordinary costs will be borne by the applicant State. The application of this paragraph, including rules specifying which collection costs are to be borne by each State and the time and manner of payment of the amounts collected, will be agreed upon by the competent authorities, as provided for in paragraph XXVI A 11.

Paragraph 8 provides that no assistance is to be given under this Article for a claim in respect of an individual taxpayer, to the extent that the taxpayer can demonstrate that he was a citizen of the requested State during the taxable period to which the revenue claim relates. Similarly, in the case of a company, estate, or trust, no assistance is to be given to the extent that the entity can demonstrate that it derived its status as such under the laws in force in the requested State during the taxable period to which the claim relates.

Subparagraph (a) of paragraph 10 clarifies that Article XXVI A supplements the provisions of paragraph 4 of Article XXVI (Mutual Agreement Procedure). The Mutual Agreement Procedure paragraph, which is more common in U.S. tax treaties, provides for collection assistance in cases in which a Contracting State seeks assistance in reclaiming treaty benefits that have been granted to a person that is not entitled to those benefits. Subparagraph (b) of paragraph 10 makes clear that nothing in Article XXVI A can require a Contracting State to carry out administrative measures of a different nature from those used in the collection of its own taxes, or that would be contrary to its public policy (order public).

Paragraph 11 requires the competent authorities to agree upon the mode of application of Article XXVI A, including agreement to ensure comparable levels of assistance to each of the Contracting States.

Paragraph 3 of Article 21 of the Protocol allows collection assistance under Article XXVI A to be sought for revenue claims that have been finally determined at any time within the 10 years preceding the date on which the Protocol enters into force.

Article 16

Article 16 of the Protocol amends Article XXVII (Exchange of Information) of the Convention. Paragraph 1 of Article 16 amends paragraph 1 of Article XXVII. The first change is a wording change to make it clear that information must be exchanged if it is "relevant" for carrying out the provisions of the Convention or of the domestic laws of the Contracting States, even if it is not "necessary." Neither the United States nor Canada views this as a substantive change. The second amendment merely conforms the language of the paragraph to the language of Article II (Taxes Covered), as amended, by referring to the taxes "to which the Convention applies" rather than to the taxes "covered by the Convention."

The Protocol further amends paragraph 1 to allow a Contracting State to provide information received from the other Contracting State to its states, provinces, or local authorities, if it relates to a tax imposed by that state, province, or local authority that is substantially similar to a national-level tax covered under Article II (Taxes Covered). However, this provision does not authorize a Contracting State to request information on behalf of a state, province, or local authority. The Protocol also amends paragraph 1 to authorize the competent authorities to release information to any arbitration panel that may be established under the provisions of new paragraph 6 of Article XXVI (Mutual Agreement Procedure). Any information provided to a state, province, or local authority or to an arbitration panel is subject to the same use and disclosure provisions as is information received by the national Governments and used for their purposes.

Paragraph 2 of Article 16 amends paragraph 4 of Article XXVII, which describes the applicable taxes for the purposes of this Article. Under the present Convention, the Article applies in Canada to taxes imposed by the Government of Canada under the *Income Tax Act* and on estates and gifts and in the United States to all taxes imposed under the *Internal Revenue Code*. The Protocol broadens the scope of the Article to apply to "all taxes imposed by a Contracting State." This change allows information to be exchanged, for example, with respect to Canadian excise taxes, as is the case with respect to U.S. excise taxes under the present Convention. Paragraph 4 is also amended to authorize the exchange of information with respect to other taxes, to the extent relevant to any other provision of the Convention.

Article 17

Article 17 of the Protocol amends Article XXIX (Miscellaneous Rules) of the Convention. Paragraph 1 of Article 17 modifies paragraph 3(a), the exceptions to the saving clause, to conform the cross-references in the paragraph to changes in other parts of the Convention. The paragraph also adds to the exceptions to the saving clause certain provisions of Article XXIX B (Taxes Imposed by Reason of Death). Thus, certain benefits under that Article will be granted by a Contracting State to its residents and, in the case of the United States, to its citizens, notwithstanding the saving clause of paragraph 2 of Article XXIX.

Paragraph 2 of Article 17 replaces paragraphs 5 through 7 of Article XXIX of the present Convention with three new paragraphs. (Paragraph 5 in the present Convention was moved to paragraph 7 of Article XVIII (Pensions and Annuities), and paragraphs 6 and 7 were deleted as unnecessary.) New paragraph 5 provides a rule for the taxation by Canada of a Canadian resident that is a shareholder in a U.S. S corporation. The application of this rule is relatively limited, because U.S. domestic law requires that S corporation shareholders be either U.S. citizens or U.S. residents. Therefore, the rule provided by paragraph 5 would apply only to an S corporation shareholder who is a resident of both the United States and Canada (i.e., a "dual resident" who meets certain requirements), determined before application of the "tie-breaker" rules of Article IV (Residence), or a U.S. citizen resident in Canada. Since the shareholder would be subject to U.S. tax on its share of the income of the S corporation as it is earned by the S corporation and, under Canadian statutory law, would be subject to tax only when the income is distributed, there could be a timing mismatch resulting in unrelieved double taxation. Under paragraph 5, the shareholder can make a request to the Canadian competent authority for relief under the special rules of the paragraph. Under these rules, the Canadian shareholder will be subject to Canadian tax on essentially the same basis as he is subject to U.S. tax, thus eliminating the timing mismatch.

The Protocol adds to Article XXIX a new paragraph 6, which provides a coordination rule for the Convention and the General Agreement on Trade in Services ("GATS"). Paragraph 6(a) provides that, for purposes of paragraph 3 of Article XXII (Consultation) of the GATS, a measure falls within the scope of the Convention only if the measure relates to a tax (1) to which Article XXV (Non-Discrimination) of the Convention applies, or (2) to which Article XXV does not apply and to which any other provision of the Convention applies, but only to the extent that the measure relates to a matter dealt with in that other provision. Under paragraph 6(b), notwithstanding paragraph 3 of Article XXII of the GATS, any doubt as to the interpretation of subparagraph (a) will be resolved under paragraph 3 of Article XXVI (Mutual Agreement Procedure) of the Convention or any other procedure agreed to by both Contracting States.

GATS generally obliges its Members to provide national treatment and most-favored-nation treatment to services and service suppliers of other Members. A very broad exception from the national treatment obligation applies to direct taxes. An exception from the most-favored-nation obligation applies to a difference in treatment resulting from an international agreement on the avoidance of double taxation (a "tax agreement") or from provisions on the avoidance of double taxation in any other international agreement or arrangement by which the Member is bound.

Article XXII(3) of GATS specifically provides that there will be no access to GATS procedures to settle a national treatment dispute concerning a measure that falls within the scope of a tax agreement. This provision preserves the exclusive application of nondiscrimination obligations in the tax agreement and clarifies that the competent authority mechanism provided by the tax agreement will apply, instead of GATS procedures, to resolve nondiscrimination disputes involving the taxation of services and service suppliers.

In the event of a disagreement between Members as to whether a measure falls within the scope of a tax agreement that existed at the time of the entry into force of the Agreement establishing the World Trade Organization, Article XXII(2), footnote 11, of GATS reserves the resolution of the dispute to the Contracting States under the tax agreement. In such a case, the issue of the scope of a tax agreement may be resolved under GATS procedures (rather than tax treaty procedures) only if both parties to the existing tax agreement consent. With respect to subsequent tax agreements, GATS provides that either Member may bring the jurisdictional matter before the Council for Trade In Services, which will refer the matter to arbitration for a decision that will be final and binding on the Members.

Both Canada and the United States agree that a protocol to a convention that is grandfathered under Article XXII(2), footnote 11, of GATS is also grandfathered. Nevertheless, since the Protocol extends the application of the Convention, and particularly the nondiscrimination article, to additional taxes (e.g., some non-income taxes imposed by Canada), the negotiators sought to remove any ambiguity and agreed to a provision that clarified the scope of the Convention and the relationship between the Convention and GATS.

The purpose of new paragraph 6(a) of the Convention is to provide the agreement of the Contracting States as to the measures considered to fall within the scope of the Convention in applying Article XXII(3) of GATS between the Contracting States. The purpose of new paragraph 6(b) is to reserve the resolution of the issue of the scope of the Convention for purposes of Article XXII(3) of GATS to the competent authorities under the Convention rather than to settlement under GATS procedures.

The Protocol also adds to Article XXIX a new paragraph 7, relating to certain changes in the law or treaty policy of either of the Contracting States. Paragraph 7 provides, first, that in response to a change in the law or policy of either State, the appropriate authority of either State may request consultations with its counterpart in the other State to determine whether a change in the Convention is appropriate. If a change in domestic legislation has unilaterally removed or significantly limited a material benefit provided by the Convention, the appropriate authorities are instructed by the paragraph to consult promptly to consider an appropriate amendment to the Convention. The "appropriate authorities" may be the Contracting States themselves or the competent authorities under the Convention. The consultations may be initiated by the authority of the Contracting State making the change in law or policy or by the authority of the other State. Any change in the Convention recommended as a result of this process can be implemented only through the negotiation, signature, ratification, and entry into force of a new protocol to the Convention.

Article 18

In general

Article 18 of the Protocol adds a new Article XXIX A (Limitation on Benefits) to the Convention. Article XXIX A addresses the problem of "treaty shopping" by requiring, in most cases, that the person seeking U.S. treaty benefits not only be a Canadian resident but also satisfy other tests. In atypical case of treaty shopping, a resident of a third State might establish an entity resident in Canada for the purpose of deriving income from the United States and claiming U.S. treaty benefits with respect to that income. Article XXIX A limits the benefits granted by the United States under the Convention to those persons whose residence in Canada is not considered to have been motivated by the existence of the Convention. Absent Article XXIXA, the entity would be entitled to U.S. benefits under the Convention as a resident of Canada, unless it were denied benefits as a result of limitations (e.g., business purpose, substance-over-form, step transaction, or conduit principles or other anti-avoidance rules) applicable to a particular transaction or arrangement. General anti-abuse provisions of this sort apply in conjunction with the Convention in both the United States and Canada. In the case of the United States, such anti-abuse provisions complement the explicit anti-treaty-shopping rules of Article XXIX A. While the anti-treaty-shopping rules determine whether a person has a sufficient nexus to Canada to be entitled to treaty benefits, general anti-abuse provisions determine whether a particular transaction should be recast in accordance with the substance of the transaction.

The present Convention deals with treaty-shopping in a very limited manner, in paragraph 6 of Article XXIX, by denying benefits to Canadian residents that benefit from specified provisions of Canadian law. The Protocol removes that paragraph 6 from Article XXIX, because it is superseded by the more general provisions of Article XXIX A.

The Article is not reciprocal, except for paragraph 7. Canada prefers to rely on general anti-avoidance rules to counter arrangements involving treaty-shopping through the United States.

The structure of the Article is as follows: paragraph 1 states that, in determining whether a resident of Canada is entitled to U.S. benefits under the Convention, a "qualifying person" is entitled to all of the benefits of the Convention, and other persons are not entitled to benefits, except where paragraphs 3, 4, or 6 provide otherwise. Paragraph 2 lists a number of characteristics, any one of which will make a Canadian resident a qualifying person. These are essentially mechanical tests. Paragraph 3 provides an alternative rule, under which a Canadian resident that is not a qualifying person under paragraph 2 may claim U.S. benefits with respect to those items of U.S. source income that are connected with the active conduct of a trade or business in Canada. Paragraph 4 provides a limited "derivative benefits" test for entitlement to benefits with respect to U.S. source dividends, interest, and royalties beneficially owned by a resident of Canada that is not a qualifying person. Paragraph 5 defines certain terms used in the Article. Paragraph 6 requires the U.S. competent authority to grant benefits to a resident of Canada that does not qualify for benefits under any other provision of the Article, where the competent authority determines, on the basis of all factors, that benefits should be granted. Paragraph 7 clarifies the application of general anti-abuse provisions.

Individuals and governmental entities

Under paragraph 2, the first two categories of qualifying persons are (1) individual residents of Canada, and (2) the Government of Canada, a political subdivision or local authority thereof, or an agency or instrumentality of that Government, political subdivision, or local authority. It is considered unlikely that persons falling into these two categories can be used, as the beneficial owner of income, to derive treaty benefits on behalf of a third-country person. If a person is receiving income as a nominee on behalf of a third-country resident, benefits will be denied with respect to those items of income under the articles of the Convention that grant the benefit, because of the requirements in those articles that the beneficial owner of the income be a resident of a Contracting State.

Publicly traded entities

Under subparagraph (c) of paragraph 2, a Canadian resident company or trust is a qualifying person if there is substantial and regular trading in the company's principal class of shares, or in the trust's units, on a recognized stock exchange. The term "recognized stock exchange" is defined in paragraph 5(a) of the Article to mean, in the United States, the NASDAQ System and any stock exchange registered as a national securities exchange with the Securities and Exchange Commission, and, in Canada, any Canadian stock exchanges that are "prescribed stock exchanges" under the *Income Tax Act*. These are, at the time of signature of the Protocol, the Alberta, Montreal, Toronto, Vancouver, and Winnipeg Stock Exchanges. Additional exchanges may be added to the list of recognized exchanges by exchange of notes between the Contracting States or by agreement between the competent authorities.

Certain companies owned by publicly traded corporations also may be qualifying persons. Under subparagraph (d) of paragraph 2, a Canadian resident company will be a qualifying person, even if not publicly traded, if more than 50 per cent of the vote and value of its shares is owned (directly or indirectly) by five or fewer persons that would be qualifying persons under subparagraph (c). In addition, each company in the chain of ownership must be a qualifying person or a U.S. citizen or resident. Thus, for example, a Canadian company that is not publicly traded but that is owned, one-third each, by three companies, two of which are Canadian resident corporations whose principal classes of shares are substantially and regularly traded on a recognized stock exchange, will qualify under subparagraph (d).

The 50-per cent test under subparagraph (d) applies only to shares other than "debt substitute shares." The term "debt substitute shares" is defined in paragraph 5 to mean shares defined in paragraph (e) of the definition in the Canadian *Income Tax Act* of "term preferred shares" (see section 248(1) of the *Income Tax Act*), which relates to certain shares received in debt-restructuring arrangements undertaken by reason of financial difficulty or insolvency. Paragraph 5 also provides that the competent authorities may agree to treat other types of shares as debt substitute shares.

Ownership/base erosion test

Subparagraph (e) of paragraph 2 provides a two-part test under which certain other entities may be qualifying persons, based on ownership and "base erosion." Under the first of these tests, benefits will be granted to a Canadian resident company if 50 per cent or more of the vote and value of its shares (other than debt substitute shares), or to a Canadian resident trust if 50 per cent or more of its beneficial interest, is *not* owned, directly or indirectly, by persons other than qualifying persons or U.S. residents or citizens. The wording of these tests is intended to make clear that, for example, if a Canadian company is more than 50 per cent owned by a U.S. resident corporation that is, itself, wholly owned by a third-country resident other than a U.S. citizen, the Canadian company would not pass the ownership test. This is because more than 50 per cent of its shares is owned indirectly by a person (the third-country resident) that is not a qualifying person or a citizen or resident of the United States.

For purposes of this subparagraph (e) and other provisions of this Article, the term "shares" includes, in the case of a mutual insurance company, any certificate or contract entitling the holder to voting power in the corporation. This is consistent with the interpretation of similar limitation on benefits provisions in other U.S. treaties.

The second test of subparagraph (e) is the so-called "base erosion" test. A Canadian company or trust that passes the ownership test must also pass this test to be a qualifying person. This test requires that the amount of expenses that are paid or payable by the Canadian entity in question to persons that are not qualifying persons or U.S. citizens or residents, and that are deductible from gross income, be less than 50 per cent of the gross income of the company or trust. This test is applied for the fiscal period immediately preceding the period for which the qualifying person test is being applied. If it is the first fiscal period of the person, the test is applied for the current period.

The ownership/base erosion test recognizes that the benefits of the Convention can be enjoyed indirectly not only by equity holders of an entity, but also by that entity's obligees, such as lenders, licensors, service providers, insurers and reinsurers, and others. For example, a third-country resident could license technology to Canadian-owned Canadian corporation to be sublicensed to a U.S. resident. The U.S. source royalty income of the Canadian corporation would be exempt from U.S. withholding tax under Article XII (Royalties) of the Convention (as amended by the Protocol). While the Canadian corporation would be subject to Canadian corporation income tax, its taxable income could be reduced to near zero as a result of the deductible royalties paid to the third-country resident. If, under a Convention between Canada and the third country, those royalties were either exempt from Canadian tax or subject to tax at a low rate, the U.S. treaty benefit with respect to the U.S. source royalty income would have flowed to the third-country resident at little or no tax cost, with no reciprocal benefit to the United States from the third country. The ownership/base erosion test therefore requires both that qualifying persons or U.S. residents or citizens substantially own the entity and that the entity's deductible payments be made in substantial part to such persons.

Other qualifying persons

Under subparagraph (f) of paragraph 2, a Canadian resident estate is a qualifying person, entitled to the benefits of the Convention with respect to its U.S. source income.

Subparagraphs (g) and (h) specify the circumstances under which certain types of not-for-profit organizations will be qualifying persons. Subparagraph (g) of paragraph 2 provides that a not-for-profit organization that is a resident of Canada is a qualifying person, and thus entitled to U.S. benefits, if more than half of the beneficiaries, members, or participants in the organization are qualifying persons or citizens or residents of the United States. The term "not-for-profit organization" of a Contracting State is defined in subparagraph (b) of paragraph 5 of the Article to mean an entity created or established in that State that is generally exempt from income taxation in that State by reason of its not-for-profit status. The term includes charities, private foundations, trade unions, trade associations, and similar organizations.

Subparagraph (h) of paragraph 2 specifies that certain organizations described in paragraph 2 of Article XXI (Exempt Organizations), as amended by Article 10 of the Protocol, are qualifying persons. To be a qualifying person, such an organization must be established primarily for the purpose of providing pension, retirement, or employee benefits to individual residents of Canada who are (or were, within any of the five preceding years) qualifying persons, or to citizens or residents of the United States. An organization will be considered to be established "primarily" for this purpose if more than 50 per cent of its beneficiaries, members, or participants are such persons. Thus, for example, a Canadian Registered Retirement Savings Plan ("RRSP") of a former resident of Canada who is working temporarily outside of Canada would continue to be a qualifying person during the period of the individual's absence from Canada or for five years, whichever is shorter. A Canadian pension fund established to provide benefits to persons employed by a company would be a qualifying person only if most of the beneficiaries of the fund are (or were within the five preceding years) individual residents of Canada or residents or citizens of the United States.

The provisions of paragraph 2 are self-executing, unlike the provisions of paragraph 6, discussed below. The tax authorities may, of course, on review, determine that the taxpayer has improperly interpreted the paragraph and is not entitled to the benefits claimed.

Active trade or business test

Paragraph 3 provides an eligibility test for benefits for residents of Canada that are not qualifying persons under paragraph 2. This is the so-called "active trade or business" test. Unlike the tests of paragraph 2, the active trade or business test looks not solely at the characteristics of the person deriving the income, but also at the nature of the activity engaged in by that person and the connection between the income and that activity. Under the active trade or business test, a resident of Canada deriving an item of income from the United States is entitled to benefits with respect to that income if that person (or a person related to that person under the principles of *Internal Revenue Code* section 482) is engaged in an active trade or business in Canada and the income in question is derived in connection with, or is incidental to, that trade or business.

Income that is derived in connection with, or is incidental to, the business of making or managing investments will not qualify for benefits under this provision, unless those investment activities are carried on with customers in the ordinary course of the business of a bank, insurance company, registered securities dealer, or deposit-taking financial institution.

Income is considered derived "in connection" with an active trade or business in the United States if, for example, the income-generating activity in the United States is "upstream," "downstream," or parallel to that conducted in Canada. Thus, if the U.S. activity consisted of selling the output of a Canadian manufacturer or providing inputs to the manufacturing process, or of manufacturing or selling in the United States the same sorts of products that were being sold by the Canadian trade or business in Canada, the income generated by that activity would be treated as earned in connection with the Canadian trade or business. Income is considered "incidental" to the Canadian trade or business if, for example, it arises from the short-term investment of working capital of the Canadian resident in U.S. securities.

An item of income will be considered to be earned in connection with or to be incidental to an active trade or business in Canada if the income is derived by the resident of Canada claiming the benefits directly or indirectly through one or more other persons that are residents of the United States. Thus, for example, a Canadian resident could claim benefits with respect to an item of income earned by a U.S. operating subsidiary but derived by the Canadian resident indirectly through a wholly-owned U.S. holding company interposed between it and the operating subsidiary. This language would also permit a Canadian resident to derive income from the United States through one or more U.S. residents that it does not wholly own. For example, a Canadian partnership in which three unrelated Canadian companies each hold a one-third interest could form a wholly-owned U.S. holding company with a U.S. operating subsidiary. The "directly or indirectly" language would allow otherwise available treaty benefits to be claimed with respect to income derived by the three Canadian partners through the U.S. holding company, even if the partners were not considered to be related to the U.S. holding company under the principles of *Internal Revenue Code* section 482.

Income that is derived in connection with, or is incidental to, an active trade or business in Canada, must pass an additional test to qualify for U.S. treaty benefits. The trade or business in Canada must be substantial in relation to the activity in the United States that gave rise to the income in respect of which treaty benefits are being claimed. To be considered substantial, it is not necessary that the Canadian trade or business be as large as the U.S. income-generating activity. The Canadian trade or business cannot, however, in terms of income, assets, or other similar measures, represent only a very small percentage of the size of the U.S. activity.

The substantiality requirement is intended to prevent treaty-shopping. For example, a third-country resident may want to acquire a U.S. company that manufactures television sets for worldwide markets; however, since its country of residence has no tax treaty with the United States, any dividends generated by the investment would be subject to a U.S. withholding tax of 30 per cent. Absent a substantiality test, the investor could establish a Canadian corporation that would operate a small outlet in Canada to sell a few of the television sets manufactured by the U.S. company and earn a very small amount of income. That Canadian corporation could then acquire the U.S. manufacturer with capital provided by the third-country resident and produce a very large number of sets for sale in several countries, generating a much larger amount of income. It might attempt to argue that the U.S. source income is generated from business activities in the United States related to the television sales activity of the Canadian parent and that the dividend income should be subject to U.S. tax at the 5 per cent rate provided by Article X of the Convention, as amended by the Protocol. However, the substantiality test would not be met in this example, so the dividends would remain subject to withholding in the United States at a rate of 30 per cent.

In general, it is expected that if a person qualifies for benefits under one of the tests of paragraph 2, no inquiry will be made into qualification for benefits under paragraph 3. Upon satisfaction of any of the tests of paragraph 2, any income derived by the beneficial owner from the other Contracting State is entitled to treaty benefits. Under paragraph 3, however, the test is applied separately to each item of income.

Derivative benefits test

Paragraph 4 of Article XXIX A contains a so-called "derivative benefits" rule not generally found in U.S. treaties. This rule was included in the Protocol because of the special economic relationship between the United States and Canada and the close coordination between the tax administrations of the two countries.

Under the derivative benefits rule, a Canadian resident company may receive the benefits of Articles X (Dividends), XI (Interest), and XII (Royalties), even if the company is not a qualifying person and does not satisfy the active trade or business test of paragraph 3. To qualify under this paragraph, the Canadian company must satisfy both (i) the base erosion test under subparagraph (e) of paragraph 2, and (ii) an ownership test.

The derivative benefits ownership test requires that shares (other than debt substitute shares) representing more than 90 per cent of the vote and value of the Canadian company be owned directly or indirectly by either (i) qualifying persons or U.S. citizens or residents, or (ii) other persons that satisfy each of three tests. The three tests that must be satisfied by these other persons are as follows:

First, the person must be a resident of a third State with which the United States has a comprehensive income tax convention and be entitled to all of the benefits under that convention. Thus, if the person fails to satisfy the limitation on benefits tests, if any, of that convention, no benefits would be granted under this paragraph. Qualification for benefits under an active trade or business test does not suffice for these purposes, because that test grants benefits only for certain items of income, not for all purposes of the convention.

Second, the person must be a person that would qualify for benefits with respect to the item of income for which benefits are sought under one or more of the tests of paragraph 2 or 3 of this Convention, if the person were a resident of Canada and, for purposes of paragraph 3, the business were carried on in Canada. For example, a person resident in a third country would be deemed to be a person that would qualify under the publicly traded test of paragraph 2 of this Convention if the principal class of its shares were substantially and regularly traded on a stock exchange recognized either under the treaty between the United States and Canada or under the treaty between the United States and the third country. Similarly, a company resident in a third country would be deemed to satisfy the ownership/base erosion test of paragraph 2 under this hypothetical analysis if, for example, it were wholly owned by an individual resident in that third country and most of its deductible payments were made to individual residents of that country (i.e., it satisfied base erosion).

The third requirement is that the rate of U.S. withholding tax on the item of income in respect of which benefits are sought must be at least as low under the convention between the person's country of residence and the United States as under this Convention.

Competent authority discretion

Paragraph 6 provides that when a resident of Canada derives income from the United States and is not entitled to the benefits of the Convention under other provisions of the Article, benefits may, nevertheless be granted at the discretion of the U.S. competent authority. In making a determination under this paragraph, the competent authority will take into account all relevant facts and circumstances relating to the person requesting the benefits. In particular, the competent authority will consider the history, structure, ownership (including ultimate beneficial ownership), and operations of the person. In addition, the competent authority is to consider (1) whether the creation and existence of the person did not have as a principal purpose obtaining treaty benefits that would not otherwise be available to the person, and (2) whether it would not be appropriate, in view of the purpose of the Article, to deny benefits. The paragraph specifies that if the U.S. competent authority determines that either of these two standards is satisfied, benefits shall be granted.

For purposes of implementing paragraph 6, a taxpayer will be expected to present his case to the competent authority for an advance determination based on the facts. The taxpayer will not be required to wait until it has been determined that benefits are denied under one of the other provisions of the Article. It also is expected that, if and when the competent authority determines that benefits are to be allowed, they will be allowed retroactively to the time of entry into force of the relevant treaty provision or the establishment of the structure in question, whichever is later (assuming that the taxpayer also qualifies under the relevant facts for the earlier period).

General anti-abuse provisions

Paragraph 7 was added at Canada's request to confirm that the specific provisions of Article XXIX A and the fact that these provisions apply only for the purposes of the application of the Convention by the United States should not be construed so as to limit the right of each Contracting State to invoke applicable anti-abuse rules. Thus, for example, Canada remains free to apply such rules to counter abusive arrangements involving "treaty-shopping "through the United States, and the United States remains free to apply its substance-over-form and anticonduit rules, for example, in relation to Canadian residents. This principle is recognized by the Organization for Economic Cooperation and Development in the Commentaries to its Model Tax Convention on Income and on Capital, and the United States and Canada agree that it is inherent in the Convention. The agreement to state this principle explicitly in the Protocol is not intended to suggest that the principle is not also inherent in other tax conventions, including the current Convention with Canada.

Article 19

In general

Article 19 of the Protocol adds to the Convention a new Article XXIX B (Taxes Imposed by Reason of Death). The purpose of Article XXIX B is to better coordinate the operation of the death tax regimes of the two Contracting States. Such coordination is necessary because the United States imposes an estate tax, while Canada now applies an income tax on gains deemed realized at death rather than an estate tax. Article XXIX B also contains other provisions designed to alleviate death taxes in certain situations.

For purposes of new Article XXIX B, the term "resident" has the meaning provided by Article IV (Residence) of the Convention, as amended by Article 3 of the Protocol. The meaning of the term "resident" for purposes of Article XXIX B, therefore, differs in some respects from its meaning under the estate, gift, and generation-skipping transfer tax provisions of the *Internal Revenue Code*.

Charitable bequests

Paragraph 1 of new Article XXIX B facilitates certain charitable bequests. It provides that a Contracting State shall accord the same death tax treatment to a bequest by an individual resident in one of the Contracting States to a qualifying exempt organization resident in the other Contracting State as it would have accorded if the organization had been a resident of the first Contracting State. The organizations covered by this provision are those referred to in paragraph 1 of Article XXI (Exempt Organizations) of the Convention. A bequest by a U.S. citizen or U.S. resident (as defined for estate tax purposes under the *Internal Revenue Code*) to such an exempt organization generally is deductible for U.S. estate tax purposes under section 2055 of the *Internal Revenue Code*, without regard to whether the organization is a U.S. corporation. However, if the decedent is not a U.S. citizen or U.S. resident (as defined for estate tax purposes under the *Internal Revenue Code*), such a bequest is deductible for U.S. estate tax purposes, under section 2106(a)(2) of the *Internal Revenue Code*, only if the recipient organization is a U.S. corporation. Under paragraph 1 of Article XXIX B, a U.S. estate tax deduction also will be allowed for a bequest by a Canadian resident (as defined under Article IV (Residence)) to a qualifying exempt organization that is a Canadian corporation. However, paragraph 1 does not allow a deduction for U.S. estate tax purposes with respect to any transfer of property that is not subject to U.S. estate tax.

Unified credit

Paragraph 2 of Article XXIX B grants a "*pro rata*" unified credit to the estate of a Canadian resident decedent, for purposes of computing U.S. estate tax. Although the Congress anticipated the negotiation of such *pro rata* unified credits in *Internal Revenue Code* section 2102(c)(3)(A), this is the first convention in which the United States has agreed to give such a credit. However, certain exemption provisions of existing estate and gift tax conventions have been interpreted as providing a *pro rata* unified credit.

Under the *Internal Revenue Code*, the estate of a nonresident not a citizen of the United States is subject to U.S. estate tax only on its U.S. *situs* assets and is entitled to a unified credit of $13,000, while the estate of a U.S. citizen or U.S. resident is subject to U.S. estate tax on its entire worldwide assets and is entitled to a unified credit of $192,800. (For purposes of these *Internal Revenue Code* provisions, the term "resident" has the meaning provided for estate tax purposes under the *Internal Revenue Code*.) A lower unified credit is provided for the former category of estates because it is assumed that the estate of a nonresident not a citizen generally will hold fewer U.S. *situs* assets, as a percentage of the estate's total assets, and thus will have a lower U.S. estate tax liability. The pro rata unified credit provisions of paragraph 2 increase the credit allowed to the estate of a Canadian resident decedent to an amount between $13,000 and $192,800 in appropriate cases, to take into account the extent to which the assets of the estate are situated in the United States. Paragraph 2 provides that the amount of the unified credit allowed to the estate of a Canadian resident decedent will in no event be less than the $13,000 allowed under the *Internal Revenue Code* to the estate of a nonresident not a citizen of the United States (subject to the adjustment for prior gift tax unified credits, discussed below). Paragraph 2 does not apply to the estates of U.S. citizen decedents, whether resident in Canada or elsewhere, because such estates receive a unified credit of $192,800 under the *Internal Revenue Code*.

Subject to the adjustment for gift tax unified credits, the *pro rata* credit allowed under paragraph 2 is determined by multiplying $192,800 by a fraction, the numerator of which is the value of the part of the gross estate situated in the United States and the denominator of which is the value of the entire gross estate wherever situated. Thus, if half of the entire gross estate (by value) of a decedent who was a resident and citizen of Canada were situated in the United States, the estate would be entitled to a *pro rata* unified credit of $96,400 (provided that the U.S. estate tax due is not less than that amount). For purposes of the denominator, the entire gross estate wherever situated (i.e., the worldwide estate, determined under U.S. domestic law) is to be taken into account for purposes of the computation. For purposes of the numerator, an estate's assets will be treated as situated in the United States if they are so treated under U.S. domestic law. However, if enacted, a technical correction now pending before the Congress will amend U.S. domestic law to clarify that assets will not be treated as U.S. *situs* assets for purposes of the *pro rata* unified credit computation if the United States is precluded from taxing them by reason of a treaty obligation. This technical correction will affect the interpretation of both this paragraph 2 and the analogous provisions in existing conventions. As currently proposed, it will take effect on the date of enactment.

Paragraph 2 restricts the availability of the *pro rata* unified credit in two respects. First, the amount of the unified credit otherwise allowable under paragraph 2 is reduced by the amount of any unified credit previously allowed against U.S. gift tax imposed on any gift by the decedent. This rule reflects the fact that, under U.S. domestic law, a U.S. citizen or U.S. resident individual is allowed a unified credit against the U.S. gift tax on lifetime transfers. However, as a result of the estate tax computation, the individual is entitled only to a total unified credit of $192,800, and the amount of the unified credit available for use against U.S. estate tax on the individual's estate is effectively reduced by the amount of any unified credit that has been allowed in respect of gifts by the individual. This rule is reflected by reducing the amount of the *pro rata* unified credit otherwise allowed to the estate of a decedent individual under paragraph 2 by the amount of any unified credit previously allowed with respect to lifetime gifts by that individual. This reduction will be relevant only in rare cases, where the decedent made gifts subject to the U.S. gift tax while a U.S. citizen or U.S. resident (as defined under the *Internal Revenue Code* for U.S. gift tax purposes).

Paragraph 2 also conditions allowance of the *pro rata* unified credit upon the provision of all information necessary to verify and compute the credit. Thus, for example, the estate's representatives will be required to demonstrate satisfactorily both the value of the worldwide estate and the value of the U.S. portion of the estate. Substantiation requirements also apply, of course, with respect to other provisions of the Protocol and the Convention. However, the negotiators believed it advisable to emphasize the substantiation requirements in connection with this provision, because the computation of the *pro rata* unified credit involves certain information not otherwise relevant for U.S. estate tax purposes.

In addition, the amount of the *pro rata* unified credit is limited to the amount of U.S. estate tax imposed on the estate. See section 2102(c)(4) of the *Internal Revenue Code*.

Marital credit

Paragraph 3 of Article XXIX B allows a special "marital credit" against U.S. estate tax in respect of certain transfers to a surviving spouse. The purpose of this marital credit is to alleviate, in appropriate cases, the impact of the estate tax marital deduction restrictions enacted by the Congress in the Technical and Miscellaneous Revenue Act of 1988 ("TAMRA"). It is the firm position of the U.S. Treasury Department that the TAMRA provisions do not violate the non-discrimination provisions of this Convention or any other convention to which the United States is a party. This is because the estate — not the surviving spouse — is the taxpayer, and the TAMRA provisions treat the estates of nonresidents not citizens of the United States in the same manner as the estates of U.S. citizen and U.S. resident decedents. However, the U.S. negotiators believed that it was not inappropriate, in the context of the Protocol, to ease the impact of those TAMRA provisions upon certain estates of limited value.

Paragraph 3 allows a non-refundable marital credit in addition to the pro rata unified credit allowed under paragraph 2 (or, in the case of a U.S. citizen or U.S. resident decedent, the unified credit allowed under U.S. domestic law). However, the marital credit is allowed only in connection with transfers satisfying each of the five conditions set forth in paragraph 3. First, the property must be "qualifying property," i.e., it must pass to the surviving spouse (within the meaning of U.S. domestic law) and be property that would have qualified for the estate tax marital deduction under U.S. domestic law if the surviving spouse had been a U.S. citizen and all applicable elections specified by U.S. domestic law had been properly made. Second, the decedent must have been, at the time of death, either a resident of Canada or the United States or a citizen of the United States. Third, the surviving spouse must have been, at the time of the decedent's death, a resident of either Canada or the United States. Fourth, if both the decedent and the surviving spouse were residents of the United States at the time of the decedent's death, at least one of them must have been a citizen of Canada. Finally, to limit the benefits of paragraph 3 to relatively small estates, the executor of the decedent's estate is required to elect the benefits of paragraph 3, and to waive irrevocably the benefits of any estate tax marital deduction that would be allowed under U.S. domestic law, on a U.S. Federal estate tax return filed by the deadline for making a qualified domestic trust election under *Internal Revenue Code* section 2056A(d). In the case of the estate of a decedent for which the U.S. Federal estate tax return is filed on or before the date on which this Protocol enters into force, this election and waiver must be made on any return filed to claim a refund pursuant to the special effective date applicable to such estates (discussed below).

Paragraph 4 governs the computation of the marital credit allowed under paragraph 3. It provides that the amount of the marital credit shall equal the lesser of (i) the amount of the unified credit allowed to the estate under paragraph 2 or, where applicable, under U.S. domestic law (before reduction for any gift tax unified credit), or (ii) the amount of U.S. estate tax that would otherwise be imposed on the transfer of qualifying property to the surviving spouse. For this purpose, the amount of U.S. estate tax that would otherwise be imposed on the transfer of qualifying property equals the amount by which (i) the estate tax (before allowable credits) that would be imposed if that property were included in computing the taxable estate exceeds (ii) the estate tax (before allowable credits) that would be imposed if the property were not so included. Property that, by reason of the provisions of paragraph 8 of this Article, is not subject to U.S. estate taxis not taken into account for purposes of this hypothetical computation.

Finally, paragraph 4 provides taxpayers with an ordering rule. The rule states that, solely for purposes of determining any other credits (e.g., the credits for foreign and state death taxes) that may be allowed under U.S. domestic law to the estate, the marital credit shall be allowed after such other credits.

In certain cases, the provisions of paragraphs 3 and 4 may affect the U.S. estate taxation of a trust that would meet the requirements for a qualified terminable interest property ("QTIP") election, for example, a trust with a life income interest for the surviving spouse and a remainder interest for other family members. If, in lieu of making the QTIP election and the qualified domestic trust election, the decedent's executor makes the election described in paragraph 3(d) of this Article, the provisions of *Internal Revenue Code* sections 2044 (regarding inclusion in the estate of the second spouse of certain property for which the marital deduction was previously allowed), 2056A (regarding qualified domestic trusts), and 2519 (regarding dispositions of certain life estates) will not apply. To obtain this treatment, however, the executor is required, under paragraph 3, to irrevocably waive the benefit of any marital deduction allowable under the *Internal Revenue Code* with respect to the trust.

The following examples illustrate the operation of the marital credit and its interaction with other credits. Unless otherwise stated, assume for purposes of illustration that H, the decedent, and W, his surviving spouse, are Canadian citizens resident in Canada at the time of the decedent's death. Assume further that all conditions set forth in paragraphs 2 and 3 of this Article XXIX Bare satisfied (including the condition that the executor waive the estate tax marital deduction), that no deductions are available under the *Internal Revenue Code* in computing the U.S. estate tax liability, and that there are no adjusted taxable gifts within the meaning of *Internal Revenue Code* section 2001(b) or 2101(c). Also assume that the applicable U.S. domestic estate and gift tax laws are those that were in effect on the date the Protocol was signed.

Example 1. H has a worldwide gross estate of $1,200,000. He bequeaths U.S. real property worth $600,000 to W. The remainder of H's estate consists of Canadian *situs* property.

H's estate would be entitled to a *pro rata* unified credit of $96,400 (= $192,800 × (600,000/1,200,000)) and to a marital credit in the same amount (the lesser of the unified credit allowed ($96,400) and the U.S. estate tax that would otherwise be imposed on the property transferred to W ($192,800 tax on U.S. taxable estate of $600,000)). The *pro rata* unified credit and the marital credit combined would eliminate all U.S. estate tax with respect to the property transferred to W.

Example 2. H has a worldwide gross estate of $1,200,000, all of which is situated in the United States. He bequeaths U.S. real property worth $600,000 to W and U.S. real property worth $600,000 to a child, C. H's estate would be entitled to a *pro rata* unified credit of $192,800 (= $192,800 × 1,200,000/1,200,000) and to a marital credit of $192,800 (the lesser of the unified credit ($192,800) and the U.S. estate tax that would otherwise be imposed on the property transferred to W ($235,000, i.e., $427,800 tax on U.S. taxable estate of $1,200,000 less $192,800 tax on U.S. taxable estate of $600,000)). This would reduce the estate's total U.S. estate tax liability of $427,800 by $385,600.

Example 3. H has a worldwide gross estate of $700,000, of which $500,000 is real property situated in the United States. H bequeaths U.S. real property valued at $100,000 to W. The remainder of H's gross estate, consisting of U.S. and Canadian *situs* real property, is bequeathed to H's child, C. H's estate would be entitled to a *pro rata* unified credit of $137,714 ($192,800 × $500,000/$700,000). In addition, H's estate would be entitled to a marital credit of $34,000, which equals the lesser of the unified credit ($137,714) and $34,000 (the U.S. estate tax that would otherwise be imposed on the property transferred to W before allowance of any credits, i.e., $155,800 tax on U.S. taxable estate of $500,000 less $121,800 tax on U.S. taxable estate of $400,000).

Example 4. H has a worldwide gross estate of $5,000,000, $2,000,000 of which consists of U.S. real property situated in State X. State X imposes a state death tax equal to the federal credit allowed under *Internal Revenue Code* section 2011. H bequeaths U.S. *situs* real property worth $1,000,000 to W and U.S. *situs* real property worth $1,000,000 to his child, C. The remainder of H's estate ($3,000,000) consists of Canadian *situs* property passing to C. H's estate would be entitled to a *pro rata* unified credit of $77,120 ($192,800 × $2,000,000/$5,000,000). H's estate would be entitled to a state death tax credit under *Internal Revenue Code* section 2102 of $99,600 (determined under *Internal Revenue Code* section 2011(b) with respect to an adjusted taxable estate of $1,940,000). H's estate also would be entitled to a marital credit of $77,120, which equals the lesser of the unified credit ($77,120) and $435,000 (the U.S. estate tax that would otherwise be imposed on the property transferred to W before allowance of any credits, i.e., $780,000 tax on U.S. taxable estate of $2,000,000 less $345,800 tax on U.S. taxable estate of $1,000,000).

Example 5. The facts are the same as in Example 4, except that H and W are Canadian citizens who are resident in the United States at the time of H's death. Canadian Federal and provincial income taxes totalling $500,000 are imposed by reason of H's death. H's estate would be entitled to a unified credit of $192,800 and to a state death tax credit of $300,880 under *Internal Revenue Code* sections 2010 and 2011(b), respectively. Under paragraph 6 of Article XXIX B, H's estate would be entitled to a credit for the Canadian income tax imposed by reason of death, equal to the lesser of $500,000 (the Canadian taxes paid) or $1,138,272 ($2,390,800 (tax on $5,000,000 taxable estate) less total of unified and state death tax credits ($493,680) × $3,000,000/$5,000,000). H's estate also would be entitled to a marital credit of $192,800, which equals the lesser of the unified credit ($192,800) and $550,000 (the U.S. estate tax that would otherwise be imposed on the property transferred to W before allowance of any credits, i.e., $2,390,800 tax on U.S. taxable estate of $5,000,000 less $1,840,800 tax on U.S. taxable estate of $4,000,000).

Canadian treatment of certain transfers

The provisions of paragraph 5 relate to the operation of Canadian law. They are intended to provide deferral ("rollover") of the Canadian tax at death for certain transfers to a surviving spouse and to permit the Canadian competent authority to allow such deferral for certain transfers to a trust. For example, they would enable the competent authority to treat a trust that is a qualified domestic trust for U.S. estate tax purposes as a Canadian spousal trust as well for purposes of certain provisions of Canadian tax law and of the Convention. These provisions do not affect U.S. domestic law regarding qualified domestic trusts. Nor do they affect the status of U.S. resident individuals for any other purpose.

Credit for U.S. taxes

Under paragraph 6, Canada agrees to give Canadian residents and Canadian resident spousal trusts (or trusts treated as such by virtue of paragraph 5) a deduction from tax (i.e., a credit) for U.S. Federal or state estate or inheritance taxes imposed on U.S. *situs* property of the decedent or the trust. This credit is allowed against the income tax imposed by Canada, in an amount computed in accordance with subparagraph 6(a) or 6(b).

Subparagraph 6(a) covers the first set of cases — where the U.S. tax is imposed upon a decedent's death. Subparagraph 6(a)(i) allows a credit for U.S. tax against the total amount of Canadian income tax payable by the decedent in the taxable year of death on any income, profits, or gains arising in the United States (within the meaning of paragraph 3 of Article XXIV (Elimination of Double Taxation)). For purposes of subparagraph 6(a)(i), income, profits, or gains arising in the United States within the meaning of paragraph 3 of Article XXIV include gains deemed realized at death on U.S. *situs* real property and on personal property forming part of the business property of a U.S. permanent establishment or fixed base. (As explained below, these are the only types of property on which the United States may impose its estate tax if the estate is worth $1.2 million or less.) Income, profits, or gains arising in the United States also include income and profits earned by the decedent during the taxable year of death, to the extent that the United States may tax such amounts under the Convention (e.g., dividends received from a U.S. corporation and wages from the performance of personal services in the United States).

Where the value of the decedent's entire gross estate exceeds $1.2 million, subparagraph 6(a)(ii) allows a credit against the Canadian income tax on any income, profits, or gains from any U.S. *situs* property, in addition to any credit allowed by subparagraph 6(a)(i). This provision is broader in scope than is the general rule under subparagraph 6(a)(i), because the United States has retained the right to impose its estate tax on all types of property in the case of larger estates.

Subparagraph 6(b) provides rules for a second category of cases — where the U.S. tax is imposed upon the death of the surviving spouse. In these cases, Canada agrees to allow a credit against the Canadian tax payable by a trust for its taxable year during which the surviving spouse dies on any income, profits, or gains (i) arising in the United States on U.S. *situs* real property or business property, or (ii) from property situated in the United States. These rules are intended to provide a credit for taxes imposed as a result of the death of the surviving spouse in situations involving trusts. To the extent that taxes are imposed on the estate of the surviving spouse, subparagraph 6(a) would apply as well. In addition, the competent authorities are authorized to provide relief from double taxation in certain additional circumstances involving trusts, as described above in connection with Article 14 of the Protocol.

The credit allowed under paragraph 6 is subject to certain conditions. First, where the decedent was a U.S. citizen or former citizen (described in paragraph 2 of Article XXIX (Miscellaneous Rules)), paragraph 6 does not obligate Canada to provide a credit for U.S. taxes in excess of the amount of U.S. taxes that would have been payable if the decedent had not been a U.S. citizen or former citizen. Second, the credit allowed under paragraph 6 will be computed after taking into account any deduction for U.S. income tax provided under paragraph 2(a), 4(a), or 5(b) of Article XXIV (Elimination of Double Taxation). This clarifies that no double credit will be allowed for any amount and provides an ordering rule. Finally, because Canadian domestic law does not contain a definition of U.S. *situs* property for death tax purposes, such a definition is provided for purposes of paragraph 6. To maximize coordination of the credit provisions, the Contracting States agreed to follow the U.S. estate tax law definition as in effect on the date of signature of the Protocol and, subject to competent authority agreement, as it may be amended in the future.

Credit for Canadian taxes

Under paragraph 7, the United States agrees to allow a credit against U.S. Federal estate tax imposed on the estate of a U.S. resident or U.S. citizen decedent, or upon the death of a surviving spouse with respect to a qualified domestic trust created by such a decedent (or the decedent's executor or surviving spouse). The credit is allowed for Canadian Federal and provincial income taxes imposed at death with respect to property of the estate or trust that is situated outside of the United States. As in the case under paragraph 6, the competent authorities also are authorized to provide relief from double taxation in certain cases involving trusts (see discussion of Article 14, above).

The amount of the credit generally will be determined as though the income tax imposed by Canada were a creditable tax under the U.S. estate tax provisions regarding credit for foreign death taxes, in accordance with the provisions and subject to the limitations of *Internal Revenue Code* section 2014. However, subparagraph 7(a) clarifies that a credit otherwise allowable under paragraph 7 will not be denied merely because of inconsistencies between U.S. and Canadian law regarding the identity of the taxpayer in the case of a particular taxable event. For example, the fact that the taxpayer is the decedent's estate for purposes of U.S. estate taxation and the decedent for purposes of Canadian income taxation will not prevent the allowance of a credit under paragraph 7 for Canadian income taxes imposed by reason of the death of the decedent.

In addition, subparagraph 7(c) clarifies that the credit against the U.S. estate tax generally may be claimed only to the extent that no credit or deduction is claimed for the same amount of Canadian tax in determining any other U.S. tax. This makes clear, for example, that a credit may not be claimed for the same amount under both this provision and Article XXIV (Elimination of Double Taxation). To prevent double taxation, an exception to this restriction is provided for certain taxes imposed with respect to qualified domestic trusts. Subject to the limitations of subparagraph 7(c), the taxpayer may choose between relief under Article XXIV, relief under this paragraph 7, or some combination of the two.

Relief for small estates

Under paragraph 8, the United States agrees to limit the application of its estate tax in the case of certain small estates of Canadian resident decedents. This provision is intended to eliminate the "trap for the unwary "that exists for such decedents, in the absence of an estate tax convention between the United States and Canada. In the absence of sophisticated estate tax planning, such decedents may inadvertently subject their estates to U.S. estate tax liability by holding shares of U.S. corporate stock or other U.S. *situs* property. U.S. resident decedents are already protected in this regard by the provisions of Article XIII (Gains) of the present Convention, which prohibit Canada from imposing its income tax on gains deemed realized at death by U.S. residents on such property.

Paragraph 8 provides relief only in the case of Canadian resident decedents whose entire gross estates wherever situated (i.e., worldwide gross estates determined under U.S. law) have a value, at the time of death, not exceeding $1.2 million. Paragraph 8 provides that the United States may impose its estate tax upon property forming part of such estates only if any gain on alienation of the property would have been subject to U.S. income taxation under Article XIII (Gains). For estates with a total value not exceeding $1.2 million, this provision has the effect of permitting the United States to impose its estate tax only on real property situated in the United States, within the meaning of Article XIII, and personal property forming part of the business property of a U.S. permanent establishment or fixed base.

Saving clause exceptions

Certain provisions of Article XXIX B are included in the list of exceptions to the general "saving clause" of Article XXIX (Miscellaneous Rules), as amended by Article 17 of the Protocol. To the extent that an exception from the saving clause is provided for a provision, each Contracting State is required to allow the benefits of that provision to its residents (and, in the case of the United States, its citizens), notwithstanding the saving clause. General saving clause exceptions are provided for paragraphs 1, 5, and 6 of Article XXIX B. Saving clause exceptions are provided for paragraphs 2, 3, 4, and 7, except for the estates of former U.S. citizens referred to in paragraph 2 of Article XXIX.

Effective dates

Article 21 of the Protocol contains special retrospective effective date provisions for paragraphs 2 through 8 of Article XXIX B and certain related provisions of the Protocol. Paragraphs 2 through 8 of Article XXIX B and the specified related provisions generally will take effect with respect to deaths occurring after the date on which the Protocol enters into force (i.e., the date on which the instruments of ratification are exchanged). However, the benefits of those provisions will also be available with respect to deaths occurring after November 10, 1988, provided that a claim for refund due as a result of these provisions is filed by the later of one year from the date on which the Protocol enters into force or the date on which the applicable period for filing such a claim expires under the domestic law of the Contracting State concerned. The general effective dates set forth in Article 21 of the Protocol otherwise apply.

It is unusual for the United States to agree to retrospective effective dates. In this case, however, the negotiators believed that retrospective application was not inappropriate, given the fact that the TAMRA provisions were the impetus for negotiation of the Protocol and that the negotiations commenced soon after the enactment of TAMRA. The United States has agreed to retrospective effective dates in certain other instances (e.g., in the case of the U.S.–Germany estate tax treaty). The retrospective effective dates apply reciprocally, so that they will benefit the estates of U.S. decedents as well as Canadian decedents.

Article 20

Article 20 of the Protocol does not amend the text of the Convention. It states two understandings between the Contracting States regarding future action relating to matters dealt with in the Protocol. Paragraph 1 requires the appropriate authorities of the Contracting States to consult on two matters within three years from the date on which the Protocol enters into force. First, they will consult with a view to agreeing to further reductions in withholding rates on dividends, interest and royalties under Articles X, XI, and XII, respectively. This provision reflects the fact that, although the Protocol does significantly reduce withholding rates, the United States remains interested in even greater reductions, to further open the capital markets and fulfill the objectives of the North American Free Trade Agreement. Second, the appropriate authorities of the Contracting States will consult about the rules in Article XXIX A (Limitation on Benefits). By that time, both Contracting States will have had an opportunity to observe the operation of the Article, and the United States will have had greater experience with the corresponding provisions in other recent U.S. tax conventions.

Paragraph 2 of Article 20 also requires consultations between the appropriate authorities, after the three-year period from the date on which the Protocol enters into force, to determine whether to implement the arbitration procedure provided for in paragraph 6 of Article XXVI (Mutual Agreement Procedure), added by Article 14 of the Protocol. The three-year period is intended to give the authorities an opportunity to consider how arbitration has functioned in other tax conventions, such as the U.S.–Germany Convention, before implementing it under this Convention.

Article 21

Article 21 of the Protocol provides the rules for the entry into force of the Protocol provisions. The Protocol will be subject to ratification according to the normal procedures in both Contracting States and instruments of ratification will be exchanged as soon as possible. Upon the exchange of instruments, the Protocol will enter into force.

Paragraph 2(a) of Article 21 generally governs the entry into force of the provisions of the Protocol for taxes withheld at source, while paragraph 2(b) generally governs for other taxes. Paragraphs 3, 4, and 5 provide special rules for certain provisions.

Paragraph 2(a) provides that the Protocol generally will have effect for taxes withheld at source on dividends, interest, royalties, and pensions and annuities (other than social security benefits), under Articles X, XI, XII, and XVIII, respectively, with respect to amounts paid or credited on or after the first day of the second month following the date on which the Protocol enters into force (i.e., the date on which instruments of ratification are exchanged). However, with respect to direct investment dividends, the 5 per cent rate specified in paragraph 2(a) of Article X will be phased in as follows: (1) for dividends paid or credited after the first day of the second month referred to above, and during 1995, the rate of withholding will be 7 per cent; (2) for dividends paid or credited after the first day of the second month, and during 1996, the rate will be 6 per cent; and (3) for dividends paid or credited after the first day of the second month and after 1996, the rate will be 5 per cent.

For taxes other than those withheld at source and for the provisions of the Protocol relating to taxes withheld on social security benefits, the Protocol will have effect with respect to taxable years beginning on or after the first day of January following the date on which the Protocol enters into force. However, the rate of tax applicable to the branch tax under paragraph 6 of Article X (Dividends) will be phased in a manner similar to the direct investment dividend withholding tax rate; that is, a rate of 6 per cent will apply for taxable years beginning in 1996 and a rate of 5 per cent will apply for taxable years beginning in 1997 and subsequent years.

Paragraph 3 of Article 21 provides a special effective date for the provisions of the new Article XXVI A (Assistance in Collection) of the Convention, introduced by Article 15 of the Protocol. Collection assistance may be granted by a Contracting State with respect to a request by the other Contracting State for a claim finally determined by the requesting State after the date that is ten years before the date of the entry into force of the Protocol. Thus, for example, if instruments of ratification are exchanged on July 1, 1995, assistance may be given by Canada under Article XXVI A for a claim that was finally determined in the United States at any time after July 1, 1985.

Paragraph 4 of Article 21 provides special effective date provisions for paragraphs 2 through 7 of the new Article XXIX B (Taxes Imposed by Reason of Death) of the Convention, introduced by Article 18 of the Protocol, and certain related provisions elsewhere in the Convention. These special effective date provisions are discussed above in connection with Article 18.

Finally, paragraph 5 of Article 21 provides a special effective date for paragraph 2 of Article 3 of the Protocol, which provides a new residence rule for certain "continued" corporations. Under paragraph 5, the new residence rule for such corporations will have effect for taxable years beginning on or after the first day of January following the date on which the Protocol enters into force.

Technical Explanation of the Fourth Protocol to the Canada–U.S. Convention

Department of the Treasury Technical Explanation of the Protocol between the United States of America and Canada signed at Ottawa on July 29, 1997 amending the Convention between the United States of America and Canada with respect to taxes on Income and on capital signed at Washington on September 26, 1980 as amended by the Protocols signed on June 14, 1983, March 28, 1984 and March 17, 1995

Introduction

This document is a technical explanation of the Protocol Between the United States of America and Canada signed on July 29, 1997 (the "Protocol") amending the Convention Between the United States of America and Canada With Respect to Taxes on Income and on Capital Signed at Washington on September 26, 1980 as Amended by the Protocols Signed on June 14, 1983, March 28, 1984 and March 17, 1995 (the "Convention").

This technical explanation is an official guide to the Protocol. It reflects the policies behind particular Protocol provisions, as well as understandings reached with respect to the application and interpretation of the Protocol. References in this technical explanation to "he" or "his" should be read to mean "he or she" or "his or her."

Article 1

Article 1 of the Protocol amends paragraph 3 of Article XIII (Gains) of the Convention. Paragraph 1 of Article XIII of the Convention provides that gains derived by a resident of a Contracting State from the alienation of real property situated within the other Contracting State may be taxed in that other State. The term "real property situated in the other Contracting State" is defined for this purpose in paragraph 3 of Article XIII of the Convention.

Under paragraph 3(a) of Article XIII of the Convention, real property situated in the United States includes real property (as defined in Article VI (Income from Real Property) of the Convention) situated in the United States and a United States real property interest. Under section 897(c) of the *Internal Revenue Code* (the "Code") the term "United States real property interest" includes shares in a U.S. corporation that owns sufficient U.S. real property interests to satisfy an asset-ratio test on certain testing dates.

Under Paragraph 3(b) of Article XIII of the Convention, real property situated in Canada means real property (as defined in Article VI of the Convention) situated in Canada; shares of stock of a company, the value of whose shares consists principally of Canadian real property; and an interest in a partnership, trust or estate, the value of which consists principally of Canadian real property. The term "principally" means more than 50 per cent.

Under the Code, stock of a foreign corporation is not considered a "United States real property interest." Therefore, the United States does not tax a resident of Canada on the sale of stock of a foreign corporation, regardless of the composition of the corporation's assets. Although the Convention permits Canada to tax a U.S. resident on the sale of stock of a company that is not a resident of Canada if the value of the company's shares consists principally of Canadian real property, Canada does not currently impose such a tax. However, on April 26, 1995, amendments were proposed to the Canadian *Income Tax Act* that would impose Canadian income tax on gains realized on stock of certain companies that are not residents of Canada if (i) more than 50 per cent of the fair market value of all of the company's properties consists of any combination of taxable Canadian property, Canadian resource property, timber resource property in Canada and income interests in Canadian trusts, and (ii) more than 50 per cent of the fair market value of the shares in question is derived directly or indirectly from any combination of real property located in Canada, Canadian resource property, and timber resource property in Canada. This amendment is proposed to be effective as of April 26, 1995 with proration for gains that accrued before that date. Although the Canadian Parliament was dissolved before these amendments were passed, they are expected to be re-introduced in the current session with the same effective date.

The Protocol amends paragraphs 3(a) and 3(b)(ii) of Article XIII of the Convention to limit each State's right to tax the gains of a resident of the other State from the sale of stock of a real property holding company to cases where the company is resident in that State. Although the United States does not impose and is not currently considering imposing a tax under the Code on gains from the sale of stock of non-resident real property holding companies, the Protocol nevertheless amends the Convention to prohibit the imposition of such a tax on Canadian residents. Although Canada is considering imposing such a tax on gains from the sale of shares of companies that are not residents of Canada, this Protocol provision will cause the proposed amendments to the Canadian *Income Tax Act* to be inapplicable to U.S. residents who derive gains from the sale of stock of real property holding companies that are not residents of Canada. This provision will be retroactively effective to April 26, 1995, the date the previous Canadian legislation was proposed to be effective.

Article 2

Paragraph 1

Paragraph 1 of Article 2 of the Protocol amends paragraph 3 of Article XVIII (Pensions and Annuities) of the Convention to clarify that social security benefits paid by one Contracting State in respect of services rendered to that State or a subdivision or authority of that State are subject to the rules set forth in paragraph 5 of Article XVIII, and are not subject to Article XIX (Government Service). Thus, all social security benefits paid by a Contracting State will be subject to the same rules, regardless of whether the services were rendered to a private sector employer, the government, or both.

Paragraph 2

Paragraph 2 of Article 2 of the Protocol amends paragraph 5 of Article XVIII of the Convention, which provides rules for the taxation of social security benefits (including tier 1 railroad retirement benefits but not including unemployment benefits), and reverses changes made by the third protocol to the Convention, which was signed on March 17, 1995 and generally took effect as of January 1, 1996 (the "1995 Protocol"). Under the Convention prior to amendment by the 1995 Protocol, the State of residence of the recipient of social security benefits had the exclusive right to tax social security benefits paid by the other State on a net basis but exempted 50 per cent of the benefit. This was changed by the 1995 Protocol. Under the 1995 Protocol, effective January 1, 1996 benefits paid under the U.S. or Canadian social security legislation to a resident of the other Contracting State (or, in the case of Canadian benefits, paid to a U.S. citizen) are taxable exclusively in the paying State.

Canada and the United States impose different source-basis taxing regimes on social security benefits. Under Code section 871(a)(3), 85 per cent of social security benefits paid to a nonresident alien are includible in gross income. The taxable portion of social security benefits is subject to the regular 30 per cent withholding tax, with the result that the gross social security benefit is subject to an effective tax rate of 25.5 per cent. This is a final payment of tax and Canadian recipients of U.S. social security benefits, regardless of their level of income, may not elect to be taxed in the United States on a net basis at graduated rates.

In Canada, social security benefits paid to nonresidents are subject to a general withholding tax of 25 per cent. However, Canada permits U.S. recipients of Canadian benefits to file a Canadian tax return and pay tax at regular graduated rates on their net income. As a result, low-income U.S. recipients of Canadian social security typically pay little or no tax on their benefits.

The Protocol returns to a system of residence-based taxation in which social security benefits are exclusively taxable in the State where the recipient lives. Social security benefits will generally be taxed as if they were benefits paid under the social security legislation in the residence State. Therefore, social security benefits will be taxed on a net basis at graduated rates and low-income recipients will not pay any tax on these benefits. However, the Protocol modifies the residence

Treaties and Related Legislation

State's taxation of cross-border benefits in order to take into account how the benefits would have been taxed in the source State if paid to a resident of that State.

In the case of Canadian recipients of U.S. social security benefits, the Protocol provides that only 85 per cent of these benefits will be subject to tax in Canada. This reflects the fact that, although in Canada social security benefits are fully includible, a maximum of 85 per cent of United States social security benefits are includible in income for U.S. tax purposes. See Code section 86. This is also consistent with the taxation of social security benefits under the Convention prior to the effective date of the 1995 Protocol, since at the time the pre-1996 rule was adopted the United States included a maximum of 50 per cent of the social security benefits in income.

In the case of U.S. recipients of Canadian social security benefits, the Protocol provides that the benefits will be taxed as if they were payments under the Social Security Act. Therefore, a maximum of 85 per cent of the Canadian benefits will be included in the gross income of a U.S. recipient, even though the entire benefit would have been taxed by Canada if received by a Canadian resident. However, if the Canadian benefit is of a type that is not subject to Canadian tax when paid to a resident of Canada, it will not be subject to U.S. tax when received by a resident of the United States. This provision is necessary to take into account certain proposed changes to Canada's Old Age Security benefits. At present, Old Age Security benefits paid to U.S. residents are subject to both ordinary Canadian income tax and an additional "recovery tax" that has the effect of means-testing the benefit. Canada has proposed to change the Old Age Security benefit system so that the benefit would be means-tested at source and not subject to the recovery tax. Because the amount of such future benefits will have already been reduced to take into account the recipient's income, it would not be appropriate to subject such benefits to additional U.S. tax.

Article 3

Article 3 of the Protocol contains the rules for bringing the Protocol into force and giving effect to its provisions.

Paragraph 1

Paragraph 1 provides for the ratification of the Protocol by both Contracting States according to their constitutional and statutory requirements and instruments of ratification will be exchanged as soon as possible.

In the United States, the process leading to ratification and entry into force is as follows: Once a protocol has been signed by authorized representatives of the two Contracting States, the Department of State sends the protocol to the President who formally transmits it to the Senate for its advice and consent to ratification, which requires approval by two-thirds of the Senators present and voting. Prior to this vote, however, it generally has been the practice for the Senate Committee on Foreign Relations to hold hearings on the protocol and make a recommendation regarding its approval to the full Senate. Both Government and private sector witnesses may testify at these hearings. After receiving the advice and consent of the Senate to ratification, the protocol is returned to the President for his signature on the ratification document. The President's signature on the document completes the process in the United States.

Paragraph 2

Paragraph 2 of Article 3 provides that the Protocol will enter into force on the date on which the instruments of ratification are exchanged. However, the date on which the Protocol enters into force will not be the date on which its provisions will take effect. Paragraph 2, therefore, also contains rules that determine when the provisions of the Protocol will have effect.

Under paragraph 2(a), Article 1 of the Protocol will have effect as of April 26, 1995. As discussed above, this is the date on which certain proposed amendments to Canadian law would be effective.

Under paragraph 2(b), Article 2 of the Protocol will have effect as of January 1, 1996, which is the date as of which the changes to the taxation of social security benefits that were implemented by the 1995 Protocol became effective. Consequently, the source-basis taxation of social security benefits that was implemented by the 1995 Protocol will be retroactively eliminated and recipients of cross-border social security benefits will be entitled to a refund of any source-State tax withheld on their benefits for 1996 and later years. This return to residence-basis taxation of social security benefits means that some high-income recipients of cross-border benefits may be required to pay additional taxes to their State of residence if their average tax rate on these benefits in their State of residence is higher than the current rate of source-State withholding tax. It is only for future years, however, that such high-income recipients of benefits will be subject to a higher rate of tax. No one will be subject to a higher rate of tax for the retroactive period. If, as a result of the change, the residence-State tax would exceed the amount of the refund otherwise due, there will be neither a refund of source-State tax nor the imposition of additional residence-State tax.

Subparagraphs (b)(i) and (ii) provide rules that determine how the retroactive effect of the Protocol will generally be implemented for the year in which the Protocol enters into effect. As discussed below, these rules are required as a result of administrative limitations on the ability of the relevant Government organizations to effect the payment of refunds. Withholding taxes imposed by the United States on cross-border social security benefits are collected and administered by the Social Security Administration (SSA), not the Internal Revenue Service (IRS). However, any refunds of withholding tax improperly collected on social security benefits are ordinarily paid by the IRS. If the Protocol enters into force prior to September 1 of a calendar year, it is possible for the SSA to pay refunds of the tax withheld for the entire year directly to the individual Canadian recipient. If the Protocol enters into force after August 31 of a calendar year, it will not be possible for SSA to pay refunds of tax withheld for that year and refunds must be paid through the IRS.

Paragraphs 3, 4 and 5 of Article 3 establish administrative procedures to govern the payment of refunds through the IRS, including rules to ensure that benefits will not be subject to a higher rate of tax in the residence State for the retroactive period. The taxes withheld on social security benefits paid for years after 1995 and prior to the calendar year in which the Protocol enters into force (referred to in the Protocol as "source-taxed benefits") will be subject to the refund procedures set forth in paragraphs 3, 4, and 5, regardless of when the Protocol enters into force. Social security benefits paid for calendar years beginning after the Protocol enters into force will not be subject to the refund procedures set forth in paragraphs 3, 4, and 5 because source State tax will not be withheld.

If the Protocol enters into force after August 31 of a calendar year, subparagraph (b)(i) provides that social security benefits paid during such calendar year will be treated as benefits paid for calendar years ending before the year in which the Protocol enters into force (and thus will be treated as "source-taxed benefits"). In this case, the taxes withheld on these benefits will be subject to the refund procedures set forth in paragraphs 3, 4, and 5 of Article 3 and these benefits will not be subject to a higher rate of residence-State tax. If the Protocol enters into force before September 1 of a calendar year, subparagraph (b)(ii) provides that social security benefits paid during such calendar year will be treated as benefits paid for calendar years beginning after the year in which the Protocol enters into force. In this case, the taxes withheld on these benefits will be directly and automatically refunded by the source State and the potentially higher rate of residence-State tax will apply.

Paragraph 3

Paragraph 3 of Article 3 of the Protocol provides rules governing the payment of refunds of source-State tax with respect to "source-taxed benefits." In general, all applications for refund must be made to the competent authority of the source State within three years of entry into force of the Protocol.

Except as set forth in subparagraph (b) of paragraph 2, the retroactive effect of the Protocol is elective and applies only if a recipient of benefits applies for a refund of the tax paid or withheld. Consequently, if a recipient of benefits does not apply for a refund of the tax paid or withheld, the Protocol will not be given retroactive effect, except as set forth in subparagraph (b) of paragraph 2. If the residence-State tax that would be imposed on such source-taxed benefits is greater than the source-State tax imposed on such benefits, it is assumed that the recipient will not apply for a refund of the source-State tax and such benefits will not be subject to the retroactive effect of the Protocol. Because the application for refund may be made on a year-by-year basis, the recipient may elect the most beneficial treatment for each year. Therefore, social security benefits will not be subject to a higher rate of tax for the retroactive period, except as set forth in subparagraph (b) of paragraph 2.

The refund procedure depends on the recipient's State of residence. In the case of U.S. residents who received Canadian social security benefits that were subject to Canadian tax, a U.S. resident who elects to have the Protocol apply retroactively will apply directly to the Canadian competent authority for the refund of any Canadian tax not previously refunded. On the receipt of such refund, the Canadian social security benefits will be includible in the U.S. resident's gross income for the years with respect to which the refund was paid. Consequently, the U.S. recipient may be required to file an amended U.S. income tax return for such years and pay U.S. tax on such benefits. Pursuant to Article XXVII (Exchange of Information) of the Convention, the Canadian competent authority will provide the U.S. competent authority with information regarding the payment of refunds.

In the case of Canadian residents who received U.S. social security benefits, the Canadian competent authority shall be the only person entitled to apply for a refund of the U.S. taxes withheld on such benefits. Individual residents of Canada will not apply directly to the IRS for refunds. However, the Canadian competent authority may base its applications on information received from individual Canadians, as well as on information to be provided by the United State competent authority. The Protocol provides that the Canadian competent authority shall apply for and receive all such refunds on behalf of individual residents of Canada and shall remit such refunds to individual residents of Canada after deducting any additional Canadian tax that may imposed as a result of such social security benefits being subject to tax in Canada. The Canadian competent authority shall make such application for refund on behalf of an individual resident of Canada only if the additional Canadian tax that would be imposed is less than the amount of the U.S. tax to be refunded. If, with respect to an individual resident of Canada, the additional Canadian tax that would be imposed on the individual's social security benefits is equal to or greater than the U.S. tax withheld, the Canadian competent authority shall not apply for a refund of the U.S. tax withheld on the individual's benefits. This provision ensures that refunds of U.S. tax will be paid only when the refund will benefit an individual resident of Canada. A refund of U.S. tax will not be paid if it would simply result in a payment from the U.S. Treasury to the Government of Canada without any portion of the refund being paid to an individual resident of Canada.

Paragraph 4

Paragraph 4 provides that all taxes refunded as a result of the Protocol will be refunded without interest. Correspondingly, any additional taxes assessed as a result of the Protocol will be assessed without interest provided that the additional taxes are paid in a timely manner. However, interest and penalties on underpayments may be assessed for periods beginning after December 31 of the year following the year in which the Protocol enters into force.

Paragraph 5

Paragraph 5 provides that the competent authorities shall establish procedures for making or revoking the application for refund provided for in paragraph 3 and such other procedures as are necessary to ensure the appropriate implementation of the Protocol. It will be necessary to establish procedures for a taxpayer to revoke his application for refund because a taxpayer may apply for a refund and then determine that the residence-State tax imposed on his social security benefits pursuant to Article 2 of the Protocol exceeds the amount of source-State tax refunded. Such a taxpayer (or, in the case of a Canadian resident, the Canadian competent authority acting on behalf of such taxpayer) will be permitted to revoke his application for refund provided that the taxpayer returns the source-State refund and the three-year period established in paragraph 3 has not expired as of the date on which the revocation is filed. The competent authorities will also establish procedures to ensure that duplicate refunds are not paid.

Technical Explanation of the Fifth Protocol to the Canada–U.S. Convention

Department of the Treasury Technical Explanation of the Protocol done at Chelsea on September 21, 2007 amending the Convention between the United States of America and Canada with respect to taxes on income and on capital done at Washington on September 26, 1980, as amended by the Protocols done on June 14, 1983, March 28, 1984, March 17, 1995, and July 29, 1997

Introduction

This is a Technical Explanation of the Protocol signed at Chelsea on September 21, 2007 (the "Protocol"), amending the Convention between the United States of America and Canada with Respect to Taxes on Income and on Capital done at Washington on September 26, 1980, as amended by the Protocols done on June 14, 1983, March 28, 1984, March 17, 1995, and July 29, 1997 (the "existing Convention"). The existing Convention as modified by the Protocol shall be referred to as the "Convention."

Negotiation of the Protocol took into account the U.S. Treasury Department's current tax treaty policy and the Treasury Department's Model Income Tax Convention, published on November 15, 2006 (the "U.S. Model"). Negotiations also took into account the Model Tax Convention on Income and on Capital, published by the Organisation for Economic Cooperation and Development (the "OECD Model"), and recent tax treaties concluded by both countries.

The Technical Explanation is an official United States guide to the Protocol. The Government of Canada has reviewed this document and subscribes to its contents. In the view of both governments, this document accurately reflects the policies behind particular Protocol provisions, as well as understandings reached with respect to the application and interpretation of the Protocol and the Convention.

References made to the "existing Convention" are intended to put various provisions of the Protocol into context. The Technical Explanation does not, however, provide a complete comparison between the provisions of the existing Convention and the amendments made by the Protocol. The Technical Explanation is not intended to provide a complete guide to the existing Convention as amended by the Protocol. To the extent that the existing Convention has not been amended by the Protocol, the prior technical explanations of the Convention remain the official explanations. References in this Technical Explanation to "he" or "his" should be read to mean "he or she" or "his or her." References to the "Code" are to the *Internal Revenue Code*.

On the date of signing of the Protocol, the United States and Canada exchanged two sets of diplomatic notes. Each of these notes sets forth provisions and understandings related to the Protocol and the Convention, and comprises an integral part of the overall agreement between the United States and Canada. The first note, the "Arbitration Note", relates to the implementation of new paragraphs 6 and 7 of Article XXVI (Mutual Agreement Procedure), which provide for binding arbitration of certain disputes between the competent authorities. The second note, the "General Note", relates more generally to issues of interpretation or application of various provisions of the Protocol.

Article 1

Article 1 of the Protocol adds subparagraph 1(*k*) to Article III (General Definitions) to address the definition of "national" of a Contracting State as used in the Convention. The Contracting States recognize that Canadian tax law does not draw distinctions based on nationality as such. Nevertheless, at the request of the United States, the definition was added and contains references to both citizenship and nationality. The definition includes any individual possessing the citizenship or nationality of a Contracting State and any legal person, partnership or association whose status is determined by reference to the laws in force in a Contracting State. The existing Convention contains one reference to the term "national" in paragraph 1 of Article XXVI (Mutual Agreement Procedure). The Protocol adds another reference in paragraph 1 of Article XXV (Non-Discrimination) to ensure that nationals of the United States are covered by the non-discrimination provisions of the Convention. The definition added by the Protocol is consistent with the definition provided in other U.S. tax treaties.

The General Note provides that for purposes of paragraph 2 of Article III, as regards the application at any time of the Convention, any term not defined in the Convention shall, unless the context otherwise requires or the competent authorities otherwise agree to a common meaning pursuant to Article XXVI (Mutual Agreement Procedure), have the meaning which it has at that time under the law of that State for the purposes of the taxes to which the Convention apply, any meaning under the applicable tax laws of that State prevailing over a meaning given to the term under other laws of that State.

Article 2

Article 2 of the Protocol replaces paragraph 3 of Article IV (Residence) of the existing Convention to address the treatment of so-called dual resident companies. Article 2 of the Protocol also adds new paragraphs 6 and 7 to Article IV to determine whether income is considered to be derived by a resident of a Contracting State when such income is derived through a fiscally transparent entity.

Paragraph 3 of Article IV — Dual resident companies

Paragraph 3, which addresses companies that are otherwise considered resident in each of the Contracting States, is replaced. The provisions of paragraph 3, and the date upon which these provisions are effective, are consistent with an understanding reached between the United States and Canada on September 18, 2000, to clarify the residence of a company under the Convention when the company has engaged in a so-called corporate "continuance" transaction. The paragraph applies only where, by reason of the rules set forth in paragraph 1 of Article IV (Residence), a company is a resident of both Contracting States.

Subparagraph 3(*a*) provides a rule to address the situation when a company is a resident of both Contracting States but is created under the laws in force in only one of the Contracting States. In such a case, the rule provides that the company is a resident only of the Contracting State under which it is created. For example, if a company is incorporated in the United States but the company is also otherwise considered a resident of Canada because the company is managed in Canada, subparagraph 3(*a*) provides that the company shall be considered a resident only of the United States for purposes of the Convention. Subparagraph 3(*a*) is intended to operate in a manner similar to the first sentence of former paragraph 3. However, subparagraph 3(*a*) clarifies that such a company must be considered created in only one of the Contracting States to fall within the scope of subparagraph 3(*a*). In some cases, a company may engage in a corporate continuance transaction and retain its charter in the Contracting State from which it continued, while also being considered as created in the State to which the company continued. In such cases, the provisions of subparagraph 3(*a*) shall not apply because the company would be considered created in both of the Contracting States.

Subparagraph 3(*b*) addresses all cases involving a dual resident company that are not addressed in subparagraph 3(*a*). Thus, subparagraph 3(*b*) applies to continuance transactions occurring between the Contracting States if, as a result, a company otherwise would be considered created under the laws of each Contracting State, e.g., because the corporation retained its charter in the first State. Subparagraph 3(*b*) would also address so-called serial continuance transactions where, for example, a company continues from one of the Contracting States to a third country and then continues into the other Contracting State without having ceased to be treated as resident in the first Contracting State.

Subparagraph 3(*b*) provides that if a company is considered to be a resident of both Contracting States, and the residence of such company is not resolved by subparagraph 3(*a*), then the competent authorities of the Contracting States shall endeavor to settle the question of residency by a mutual agreement procedure and determine the mode of application of the Convention to such company. Subparagraph 3(*b*) also provides that in the absence of such agreement, the company shall not be considered a resident of either Contracting State for purposes of claiming any benefits under the Convention.

Paragraphs 6 and 7 of Article IV — income, profit, or gain derived through fiscally transparent entities

New paragraphs 6 and 7 are added to Article IV to provide specific rules for the treatment of amounts of income, profit or gain derived through or paid by fiscally transparent entities such as partnerships and certain trusts. Fiscally transparent entities, as explained more fully below, are in general entities the income of which is taxed at the beneficiary, member, or participant level. Entities that are subject to tax, but with respect to which tax may be relieved under an integrated system, are not considered fiscally transparent entities. Entities that are fiscally transparent for U.S. tax purposes include partnerships, common investment trusts under section 584, grantor trusts, and business entities such as a limited liability company ("LLC") that is treated as a partnership or is disregarded as an entity separate from its owner for U.S. tax purposes. Entities falling within this description in Canada are (except to the extent the law provides otherwise) partnerships and what are known as "bare" trusts.

United States tax law also considers a corporation that has made a valid election to be taxed under Subchapter S of Chapter 1 of the *Internal Revenue Code* (an "S corporation") to be fiscally transparent within the meaning explained below. Thus, if a U.S. resident derives income from Canada through an S corporation, the U.S. resident will under new paragraph 6 be considered for purposes of the Convention as the person who derived the income. Exceptionally, because Canada will ordinarily accept that an S corporation is itself resident in the United States for purposes of the Convention, Canada will allow benefits under the Convention to the S corporation in its own right. In a reverse case, however — that is, where the S corporation is owned by a resident of Canada and has U.S.-source income, profits or gains — the Canadian resident will not be considered as deriving the income by virtue of subparagraph 7(*a*) as Canada does not see the S corporation as fiscally transparent.

Under both paragraph 6 and paragraph 7, it is relevant whether the treatment of an amount of income, profit or gain derived by a person through an entity under the tax law of the residence State is "the same as its treatment would be if that amount had been derived directly." For purposes of paragraphs 6 and 7, whether the treatment of an amount derived by a person through an entity under the tax law of the residence State is the same as its treatment would be if that amount had been derived directly by that person shall be determined in accordance with the principles set forth in Code section 894 and the regulations under that section concerning whether an entity will be treated as fiscally transparent with respect to an item of income received by the entity. Treas. Reg. section 1.894-1(d)(3)(iii) provides that an entity will be fiscally transparent under the laws of an interest holder's jurisdiction with respect to an item of income to the extent that the laws of that jurisdiction require the interest holder resident in that jurisdiction to separately take into account on a current basis the interest holder's respective share of the item of income paid to the entity, whether or not distributed to the interest holder, and the character and source of the item in the hands of the interest holder are determined as if such item were realized directly from the source from which realized by the entity. Although Canada does not have analogous provisions in its domestic law, it is anticipated that principles comparable to those described above will apply.

Paragraph 6

Under paragraph 6, an amount of income, profit or gain is considered to be derived by a resident of a Contracting State (residence State) if 1) the amount is derived by that person through an entity (other than an entity that is a resident of the other Contracting State (source State), and 2) by reason of that entity being considered fiscally transparent under the laws of the residence State, the treatment of the amount under the tax law of the residence State is the same as its treatment would be if that amount had been derived directly by that person. These two requirements are set forth in subparagraphs 6(*a*) and 6(*b*), respectively.

For example, if a U.S. resident owns a French entity that earns Canadian-source dividends and the entity is considered fiscally transparent under U.S. tax law, the U.S. resident is considered to derive the Canadian-source dividends for purposes of Article IV (and thus, the dividends are considered as being "paid to" the resident) because the U.S. resident is considered under the tax law of the United States to have derived the dividend through the French entity and, because the entity is treated as fiscally transparent under U.S. tax law, the treatment of the income under U.S. tax law is the same as its treatment would be if that amount had been derived directly by the U.S. resident. This result obtains even if the French entity is viewed differently under the tax laws of Canada or of France (i.e., the French entity is treated under Canadian law or under French tax law as not fiscally transparent).

Similarly, if a Canadian resident derives U.S.-source income, profit or gain through an entity created under Canadian law that is considered a partnership for Canadian tax purposes but a corporation for U.S. tax purposes, U.S.-source income, profit or gain derived through such entity by the Canadian resident will be considered to be derived by the Canadian resident in considering the application of the Convention.

Application of paragraph 6 and related treaty provisions by Canada

In determining the entitlement of a resident of the United States to the benefits of the Convention, Canada shall apply the Convention within its own legal framework.

For example, assume that from the perspective of Canadian law an amount of income is seen as being paid from a source in Canada to USLLC, an entity that is entirely owned by U.S. persons and is fiscally transparent for U.S. tax purposes, but that Canada considers a corporation and, thus, under Canadian law, a taxpayer in its own right. Since USLLC is not itself taxable in the United States, it is not considered to be a U.S. resident under the Convention; but for new paragraph 6 Canada would not apply the Convention in taxing the income.

If new paragraph 6 applies in respect of an amount of income, profit or gain, such amount is considered as having been derived by one or more U.S. resident shareholders of USLLC, and Canada shall grant benefits of the Convention to the payment to USLLC and eliminate or reduce Canadian tax as provided in the Convention. The effect of the rule is to suppress Canadian taxation of USLLC to give effect to the benefits available under the Convention to the U.S. residents in respect of the particular amount of income, profit or gain.

However, for Canadian tax purposes, USLLC remains the only "visible" taxpayer in relation to this amount. In other words, the Canadian tax treatment of this taxpayer (USLLC) is modified because of the entitlement of its U.S. resident shareholders to benefits under the Convention, but this does not alter USLLC's status under Canadian law. Canada does not, for example, treat USLLC as though it did not exist, substituting the shareholders for it in the role of taxpayer under Canada's system.

Some of the implications of this are as follows. First, Canada will not require the shareholders of USLLC to file Canadian tax returns in respect of income that benefits from new paragraph 6. Instead, USLLC itself will file a Canadian tax return in which it will claim the benefit of the paragraph and supply any documentation required to support the claim. (The Canada Revenue Agency will supply additional practical guidance in this regard, including instructions for seeking to establish entitlement to Convention benefits in advance of payment.) Second, as is explained in greater detail below, if the income in question is business profits, it will be necessary to determine whether the income was earned through a permanent establishment in Canada. This determination will be based on the presence and activities in Canada of USLLC itself, not of its shareholders acting in their own right.

Determination of the existence of a permanent establishment from the business activities of a fiscally transparent entity

New paragraph 6 applies not only in respect of amounts of dividends, interest and royalties, but also profit (business income), gains and other income. It may thus be relevant in cases where a resident of one Contracting State carries on business in the other State through an entity that has a different characterization in each of the two Contracting States.

Application of new paragraph 6 and the provisions of Article V (Permanent Establishment) by Canada

Assume, for instance, that a resident of the United States is part owner of a U.S. limited liability company (USLLC) that is treated in the United States as a fiscally transparent entity, but in Canada as a corporation. Assume one of the other two shareholders of USLLC is resident in a country that does not have a tax treaty with Canada and that the remaining shareholder is resident in a country with which Canada does have a tax treaty, but that the treaty does not include a provision analogous to paragraph 6.

Assume further that USLLC carries on business in Canada, but does not do so through a permanent establishment there. (Note that from the Canadian perspective, the presence or absence of a permanent establishment is evaluated with respect to USLLC only, which Canada sees as a potentially taxable entity in its own right.) Regarding Canada's application of the provisions of the Convention, the portion of USLLC's profits that belongs to the U.S. resident shareholder will not be taxable in Canada, provided that the U.S. resident meets the Convention's limitation on benefits provisions. Under paragraph 6, that portion is seen as having been derived by the U.S. resident shareholder, who is entitled to rely on Article VII (Business Profits). The balance of USLLC's profits will, however, remain taxable in Canada. Since USLLC is not itself resident in the United States for purposes of the Convention, in respect of that portion of its profits that is not considered to have been derived by a U.S. resident (or a resident of another country whose treaty with Canada includes a rule comparable to paragraph 6) it is not relevant whether or not it has a permanent establishment in Canada.

Another example would be the situation where a USLLC that is wholly owned by a resident of the U.S. carries on business in Canada through a permanent establishment. If the USLLC is fiscally transparent for U.S. tax purposes (and therefore, the conditions for the application of paragraph 6 are satisfied) then the USLLC's profits will be treated as having been derived by its U.S. resident owner inclusive of all attributes of that income (e.g., such as having been earned through a permanent establishment). However, since the USLLC remains the only "visible" taxpayer for Canadian tax purposes, it is the USLLC, and not the U.S. shareholder, that is subject to tax on the profits that are attributable to the permanent establishment.

Application of new paragraph 6 and the provisions of Article V (Permanent Establishment) by the United States

It should be noted that in the situation where a person is considered to derive income through an entity, the United States looks in addition to such person's activities in order to determine whether he has a permanent establishment. Assume that a Canadian resident and a resident in a country that does not have a tax treaty with the United States are owners of CanLP. Assume further that CanLP is an entity that is considered fiscally transparent for Canadian tax purposes but is not considered fiscally transparent for U.S. tax purposes, and that CanLP carries on business in the United States. If CanLP carries on the business through a permanent establishment, that permanent establishment may be attributed to the partners. Moreover, in determining whether there is a permanent establishment, the activities of both the entity and its partners will be considered. If CanLP does not carry on the business through a permanent establishment, the Canadian resident, who derives income through the partnership, may claim the benefits of Article VII (Business Profits) of the Convention with respect to such income, assuming that the income is not otherwise attributable to a permanent establishment of the partner. In any case, the third country partner cannot claim the benefits of Article VII of the Convention between the United States and Canada.

Paragraph 7

Paragraph 7 addresses situations where an item of income, profit or gain is considered not to be paid to or derived by a person who is a resident of a Contracting State. The paragraph is divided into two subparagraphs.

Under subparagraph 7(*a*), an amount of income, profit or gain is considered not to be paid to or derived by a person who is a resident of a Contracting State (the residence State) if (1) the other Contracting State (the source State) views the person as deriving the amount through an entity that is not a resident of the residence State, and (2) by reason of the entity not being treated as fiscally transparent under the laws of the residence State, the treatment of the amount under the tax law of the residence State is not the same as its treatment would be if that amount had been derived directly by the person.

For example, assume USCo, a company resident in the United States, is a part owner of CanLP, an entity that is considered fiscally transparent for Canadian tax purposes, but is not considered fiscally transparent for U.S. tax purposes. CanLP receives a dividend from a Canadian company in which it owns stock. Under Canadian tax law USCo is viewed as deriving a Canadian-source dividend through CanLP. For U.S. tax purposes, CanLP, and not USCo, is viewed as deriving the dividend. Because the treatment of the dividend under U.S. tax law in this case is not the same as the treatment under U.S. law if USCo derived the dividend directly, subparagraph 7(*a*) provides that USCo will not be considered as having derived the dividend. The result would be the same if CanLP were a third-country entity that was viewed by the United States as not fiscally transparent, but was viewed by Canada as fiscally transparent. Similarly, income from U.S. sources received by an entity organized under the laws of the United States that is treated for Canadian tax purposes as a corporation and is owned by shareholders who are residents of Canada is not considered derived by the shareholders of that U.S. entity even if, under U.S. tax law, the entity is treated as fiscally transparent.

Subparagraph 7(*b*) provides that an amount of income, profit or gain is not considered to be paid to or derived by a person who is a resident of a Contracting State (the residence State) where the person is considered under the tax law of the other Contracting State (the source State) to have received the amount from an entity that is a resident of that other State (the source State), but by reason of the entity being treated as fiscally transparent under the laws of the Contracting State of which the person is resident (the residence State), the treatment of such amount under the tax law of that State (the residence State) is not the same as the treatment would be if that entity were not treated as fiscally transparent under the laws of that State (the residence State).

That is, under subparagraph 7(*b*), an amount of income, profit or gain is not considered to be paid to or derived by a resident of a Contracting State (the residence State) if: (1) the other Contracting State (the source State) views such person as receiving the amount from an entity resident in the source State; (2) the entity is viewed as fiscally transparent under the laws of the residence State; and (3) by reason of the entity being treated as fiscally transparent under the laws of the residence State, the treatment of the amount received by that person under the tax law of the residence State is not the same as its treatment would be if the entity were not treated as fiscally transparent under the laws of the residence State.

For example, assume that USCo, a company resident in the United States is the sole owner of CanCo, an entity that is considered under Canadian tax law to be a corporation that is resident in Canada but is considered under U.S. tax law to be disregarded as an entity separate from its owner. Assume further that USCo is considered under Canadian tax law to have received a dividend from CanCo.

In such a case, Canada, the source State, views USCo as receiving income (*i.e.*, a dividend) from a corporation that is a resident of Canada (CanCo), CanCo is viewed as fiscally transparent under the laws of the United States, the residence State, and by reason of CanCo being disregarded under U.S. tax law, the treatment under U.S. tax law of the payment is not the same as its treatment would be if the entity were regarded as a corporation under U.S. tax law. That is, the payment is disregarded for U.S. tax purposes, whereas if U.S. tax law regarded CanCo as a corporation, the payment would be treated as a dividend. Therefore, subparagraph 7(*b*) would apply to provide that the income is not considered to be paid to or derived by USCo.

The same result obtains if, in the above example, USCo is considered under Canadian tax law to have received an interest or royalty payment (instead of a dividend) from CanCo. Under U.S. law, because CanCo is disregarded as an entity separate from its owner, the payment is disregarded, whereas if CanCo were treated as not fiscally transparent, the payment would be treated as interest or a royalty, as the case may be. Therefore, subparagraph 7(*b*) would apply to provide that such amount is not considered to be paid to or derived by USCo.

The application of subparagraph 7(*b*) differs if, in the above example, USCo (as well as other persons) are owners of CanCo, a Canadian entity that is considered under Canadian tax law to be a corporation that is resident in Canada but is considered under U.S. tax law to be a partnership (as opposed to being disregarded). Assume that USCo is considered under Canadian tax law to have received a dividend from CanCo. Such payment is viewed under Canadian tax law as a dividend, but under U.S. tax law is viewed as a partnership distribution. In such a case, Canada views USCo as receiving income (*i.e.*, a dividend) from an entity that is a resident of Canada (CanCo), CanCo is viewed as fiscally transparent under the laws of the United States, the residence State, and by reason of CanCo being treated as a partnership under U.S. tax law, the treatment under U.S. tax law of the payment (as a partnership distribution) is not the same as the treatment would be if CanCo were not fiscally transparent under U.S. tax law (as a dividend). As a result, subparagraph 7(*b*) would apply to provide that such amount is not considered paid to or derived by the U.S. resident.

As another example, assume that CanCo, a company resident in Canada, is the owner of USLP, an entity that is considered under U.S. tax law (by virtue of an election) to be a corporation resident in the United States, but that is considered under Canadian tax law to be a branch of CanCo. Assume further that CanCo is considered under U.S. tax law to have received a dividend from USLP. In this case, the United States views CanCo as receiving income (*i.e.*, a dividend) from an entity that is resident in the United States (USLP), but by reason of USLP being a branch under Canadian tax law, the treatment under Canadian tax law of the payment is not the same as its treatment would be if USLP were a company under Canadian tax law. That is, the payment is treated as a branch remittance for Canadian tax purposes, whereas if Canadian tax law regarded USLP as a corporation, the payment would be treated as a dividend. Therefore, subparagraph 7(b) would apply to provide that the income is not considered to be paid to or derived by CanCo. The same result would obtain in the case of interest or royalties paid by USLP to CanCo.

Paragraphs 6 and 7 apply to determine whether an amount is considered to be derived by (or paid to) a person who is a resident of Canada or the United States. If, as a result of paragraph 7, a person is not considered to have derived or received an amount of income, profit or gain, that person shall not be entitled to the benefits of the Convention with respect to such amount. Additionally, for purposes of application of the Convention by the United States, the treatment of such payments under Code section 894(c) and the regulations thereunder would not be relevant.

New paragraphs 6 and 7 are not an exception to the saving clause of paragraph 2 of Article XXIX (Miscellaneous Rules). Accordingly, subparagraph 7(*b*) does not prevent a Contracting State from taxing an entity that is treated as a resident of that State under its tax law. For example, if a U.S. partnership with members who are residents of Canada elects to be taxed as a corporation for U.S. tax purposes, the United States will tax that partnership on its worldwide income on a net basis, even if Canada views the partnership as fiscally transparent.

Interaction of paragraphs 6 and 7 with the determination of "beneficial ownership"

With respect to payments of income, profits or gain arising in a Contracting State and derived directly by a resident of the other Contracting State (and not through a fiscally transparent entity), the term "beneficial owner" is defined under the internal law of the country imposing tax (*i.e.*, the source State). Thus, if the payment arising in a Contracting State is derived by a resident of the other State who under the laws of the first-mentioned State is determined to be a nominee or agent acting on behalf of a person that is not a resident of that other State, the payment will not be entitled to the benefits of the Convention. However, payments arising in a Contracting State and derived by a nominee on behalf of a resident of that other State would be entitled to benefits. These limitations are confirmed by paragraph 12 of the Commentary to Article 10 of the OECD Model.

Special rules apply in the case of income, profits or gains derived through a fiscally transparent entity, as described in new paragraph 6 of Article IV. Residence State principles determine who derives the income, profits or gains, to assure that the income, profits or gains for which the source State grants benefits of the Convention will be taken into account for tax purposes by a resident of the residence State. Source country principles of beneficial ownership apply to determine whether the person who derives the income, profits or gains, or another resident of the other Contracting State, is the beneficial owner of the income, profits or gains. The source State may conclude that the person who derives the income, profits or gains in the residence State is a mere nominee, agent, conduit, etc., for a third country resident and deny benefits of the Convention. If the person who derives the income, profits or gains under paragraph 6 of Article IV would not be treated under the source State's principles for determining beneficial ownership as a nominee, agent, custodian, conduit, etc., that person will be treated as the beneficial owner of the income, profits or gains for purposes of the Convention.

Assume, for instance, that interest arising in the United States is paid to CanLP, an entity established in Canada which is treated as fiscally transparent for Canadian tax purposes but is treated as a company for U.S. tax purposes. CanCo, a company incorporated in Canada, is the sole interest holder in CanLP. Paragraph 6 of Article IV provides that CanCo derives the interest. However, if under the laws of the United States regarding payments to nominees, agents, custodians and conduits, CanCo is found be a nominee, agent, custodian or conduit for a person who is not a resident of Canada, CanCo will not be considered the beneficial owner of the interest and will not be entitled to the benefits of Article XI with respect to such interest. The payment may be entitled to benefits, however, if CanCo is found to be a nominee, agent, custodian or conduit for a person who is a resident of Canada.

With respect to Canadian-source income, profit or gains, beneficial ownership is to be determined under Canadian law. For example, assume that LLC, an entity that is treated as fiscally transparent for U.S. tax purposes, but as a corporation for Canadian tax purposes, is owned by USCo, a U.S. resident company. LLC receives Canadian-source income. The question of the beneficial ownership of the income received by LLC is determined under Canadian law. If LLC is considered the beneficial owner of the income under Canadian law, paragraph 6 shall apply to extend benefits of the Convention to the income received by LLC to the extent that the Canadian-source income is derived by U.S. resident members of LLC.

Article 3

Article 3 of the Protocol amends Article V (Permanent Establishment) of the Convention. Paragraph 1 of Article 3 of the Protocol adds a reference in Paragraph 6 of Article IV [*sic* — V] to new paragraph 9 of Article V. Paragraph 2 of Article 3 of the Protocol sets forth new paragraphs 9 and 10 of Article V.

Paragraph 9 of Article V

New paragraph 9 provides a special rule (subject to the provisions of paragraph 3) for an enterprise of a Contracting State that provides services in the other Contracting State, but that does not have a permanent establishment by virtue of the preceding paragraphs of the Article. If (and only if) such an enterprise meets either of two tests as provided in subparagraphs 9(*a*) and 9(*b*), the enterprise will be deemed to provide those services through a permanent establishment in the other State.

The first test as provided in subparagraph 9(*a*) has two parts. First, the services must be performed in the other State by an individual who is present in that other State for a period or periods aggregating 183 days or more in any twelve-month period. Second, during that period or periods, more than 50 percent of the gross active business revenues of the enterprise (including revenue from active business activities unrelated to the provision of services) must consist of income derived from the services performed in that State by that individual. If the enterprise meets both of these tests, the enterprise will be deemed to provide the services through a permanent establishment. This test is employed to determine whether an enterprise is deemed to have a permanent establishment by virtue of the presence of a single individual (*i.e.*, a natural person).

For the purposes of subparagraph 9(*a*), the term "gross active business revenues" shall mean the gross revenues attributable to active business activities that the enterprise has charged or should charge for its active business activities, regardless of when the actual billing will occur or of domestic law rules concerning when such revenues should be taken into account for tax purposes. Such active business activities are not restricted to the activities related to the provision of services. However, the term does not include income from passive investment activities.

As an example of the application of subparagraph 9(*a*), assume that Mr. X, an individual resident in the United States, is one of the two shareholders and employees of USCo, a company resident in the United States that provides engineering services. During the 12-month period beginning December 20 of Year 1 and ending December 19 of Year 2, Mr. X is present in Canada for periods totaling 190 days, and during those periods, 70 percent of all of the gross active business revenues of USCo attributable to business activities are derived from the services that Mr. X performs in Canada. Because both of the criteria of subparagraph 9(*a*) are satisfied, USCo will be deemed to have a permanent establishment in Canada by virtue of that subparagraph.

The second test as provided in subparagraph 9(*b*) provides that an enterprise will have a permanent establishment if the services are provided in the other State for an aggregate of 183 days or more in any twelve-month period with respect to the same or connected projects for customers who either are residents of the other State or maintain a permanent establishment in the other State with respect to which the services are provided. The various conditions that have to be satisfied in order for subparagraph 9(*b*) to have application are described in detail below.

In addition to meeting the 183-day threshold, the services must be provided for customers who either are residents of the other State or maintain a permanent establishment in that State. The intent of this requirement is to reinforce the concept that unless there is a customer in the other State, such enterprise will not be deemed as participating sufficiently in the economic life of that other State to warrant being deemed to have a permanent establishment.

Assume for example, that CanCo, a Canadian company, wishes to acquire USCo, a company in the United States. In preparation for the acquisition, CanCo hires Canlaw, a Canadian law firm, to conduct a due diligence evaluation of USCo's legal and financial standing in the United States. Canlaw sends a staff attorney to the United States to perform the due diligence analysis of USCo. That attorney is present and working in the United States for greater than 183 days. If the remuneration paid to Canlaw for the attorney's services does not constitute more than 50 percent of Canlaw's gross active business revenues for the period during which the attorney is present in the United States, Canlaw will not be deemed to provide the services through a permanent establishment in the United States by virtue of subparagraph 9(*a*). Additionally, because the services are being provided for a customer (CanCo) who neither is a resident of the United States nor maintains a permanent establishment in the United States to which the services are provided, Canlaw will also not have a permanent establishment in the United States by virtue of subparagraph 9(*b*).

Paragraph 9 applies only to the provision of services, and only to services provided by an enterprise to third parties. Thus, the provision does not have the effect of deeming an enterprise to have a permanent establishment merely because services are provided to that enterprise. Paragraph 9 only applies to services that are performed or provided by an enterprise of a Contracting State within the other Contracting State. It is therefore not sufficient that the relevant services be merely furnished to a resident of the other Contracting State. Where, for example, an enterprise provides customer support or other services by telephone or computer to customers located in the other State, those would not be covered by paragraph 9 because they are not performed or provided by that enterprise within the other State. Another example would be that of an architect who is hired to design blueprints for the construction of a building in the other State. As part of completing the project, the architect must make site visits to that other State, and his days of presence there would be counted for purposes of determining whether the 183-day threshold is satisfied. However, the days that the architect spends working on the blueprint in his home office shall not count for purposes of the 183-day threshold, because the architect is not performing or providing those services within the other State.

For purposes of determining whether the time threshold has been met, subparagraph 9(*b*) permits the aggregation of services that are provided with respect to connected projects. Paragraph 2 of the General Note provides that for purposes of subparagraph 9(*b*), projects shall be considered to be connected if they constitute a coherent whole, commercially and geographically. The determination of whether projects are connected should be determined from the point of view of the enterprise (not that of the customer), and will depend on the facts and circumstances of each case. In determining the existence of commercial coherence, factors that would be relevant include: 1) whether the projects would, in the absence of tax planning considerations, have been concluded pursuant to a single contract; 2) whether the nature of the work involved under different projects is the same; and 3) whether the same individuals are providing the services under the different projects. Whether the work provided is covered by one or multiple contracts may be relevant, but not determinative, in finding that projects are commercially coherent.

The aggregation rule addresses, for example, potentially abusive situations in which work has been artificially divided into separate components in order to avoid meeting the 183-day threshold. Assume for example, that a technology consultant has been hired to install a new computer system for a company in the other country. The work will take ten months to complete. However, the consultant purports to divide the work into two five-month projects with the intention of circumventing the rule in subparagraph 9(*b*). In such case, even if the two projects were considered separate, they will be considered to be commercially coherent. Accordingly, subject to the additional requirement of geographic coherence, the two projects could be considered to be connected, and could therefore be aggregated for purposes of subparagraph 9(*b*). In contrast, assume that the technology consultant is contracted to install a particular computer system for a company, and is also hired by that same company, pursuant to a separate contract, to train its employees on the use of another computer software that is unrelated to the first system. In this second case, even though the contracts are both concluded between the same two parties, there is no commercial coherence to the two projects, and the time spent fulfilling the two contracts may not be aggregated for purposes of subparagraph 9(*b*). Another example of projects that do not have commercial coherence would be the case of a law firm which, as one project provides tax advice to a customer from one portion of its staff, and as another project provides trade advice from another portion of its staff, both to the same customer.

Additionally, projects, in order to be considered connected, must also constitute a geographic whole. An example of projects that lack geographic coherence would be a case in which a consultant is hired to execute separate auditing projects at different branches of a bank located in different cities pursuant to a single contract. In such an example, while the consultant's projects are commercially coherent, they are not geographically coherent and accordingly the services provided in the various branches shall not be aggregated for purposes of applying subparagraph 9(*b*). The services provided in each branch should be considered separately for purposes of subparagraph 9(*b*).

The method of counting days for purposes of subparagraph 9(*a*) differs slightly from the method for subparagraph 9(*b*). Subparagraph 9(*a*) refers to days in which an individual is present in the other country. Accordingly, physical presence during a day is sufficient. In contrast, subparagraph 9(*b*) refers to days during which services are provided by the enterprise in the other country. Accordingly, non-working days such as weekends or holidays would not count for purposes of subparagraph 9(*b*), as long as no services are actually being provided while in the other country on those days. For the purposes of both subparagraphs, even if the enterprise sends many individuals simultaneously to the other country to provide services, their collective presence during one calendar day will count for only one day of the enterprise's presence in the other country. For instance, if an enterprise sends 20 employees to the other country to provide services to a client in the other country for 10 days, the enterprise will be considered present in the other country only for 10 days, not 200 days (20 employees × 10 days).

By deeming the enterprise to provide services through a permanent establishment in the other Contracting State, paragraph 9 allows the application of Article VII (Business Profits), and accordingly, the taxation of the services shall be on a net-basis. Such taxation is also limited to the profits attributable to the activities carried on in performing the relevant services. It will be important to ensure that only the profits properly attributable to the functions performed and risks assumed by provision of the services will be attributed to the deemed permanent establishment.

In addition to new paragraph 9, Article 3 of the Protocol amends paragraph 6 of Article V of the Convention to include a reference to paragraph 9. Therefore, in no case will paragraph 9 apply to deem services to be provided through a permanent establishment if the services are limited to those mentioned in paragraph 6 which, if performed through a fixed place of business, would not make the fixed place of business a permanent establishment under the provisions of that paragraph.

The competent authorities are encouraged to consider adopting rules to reduce the potential for excess withholding or estimated tax payments with respect to employee wages that may result from the application of this paragraph. Further, because paragraph 6 of Article V applies notwithstanding paragraph 9, days spent on preparatory or auxiliary activities shall not be taken into account for purposes of applying subparagraph 9(*b*).

Paragraph 10 of Article V

Paragraph 2 of Article 3 of the Protocol also sets forth new paragraph 10 of Article V. The provisions of new paragraph 10 are identical to paragraph 9 of Article V as it existed prior to the Protocol. New paragraph 10 provides that the provisions of Article V shall be applied in determining whether any person has a permanent establishment in any State.

Article 4

Article 4 of the Protocol replaces paragraph 2 of Article VII (Business Profits).

New paragraph 2 provides that where a resident of either Canada or the United States carries on (or has carried on) business in the other Contracting State through a permanent establishment in that other State, both Canada and the United States shall attribute to permanent establishments in their respective states those business profits which the permanent establishment might be expected to make if it were a distinct and separate person engaged in the same or similar activities under the same or similar conditions and dealing wholly independently with the resident and with any other person related to the resident. The term "related to the resident" is to be interpreted in accordance with paragraph 2 of Article IX (Related Persons). The reference to other related persons is intended to make clear that the test of paragraph 2 is not restricted to independence between a permanent establishment and a home office.

New paragraph 2 is substantially similar to paragraph 2 as it existed before the Protocol. However, in addition to the reference to a resident of a Contracting State who "carries on" business in the other Contracting State, the Protocol incorporates into the Convention the rule of Code section 864(c)(6) by adding "or has carried on" to address circumstances where, as a result of timing, income may be attributable to a permanent establishment that no longer exists in one of the Contracting States. In such cases, the income is properly within the scope of Article VII. Conforming changes are also made in the Protocol to Articles X (Dividends), XI (Interest), and XII (Royalties) of the Convention where Article VII would apply. As is explained in paragraph 5 of the General Note, these revisions to the Convention are only intended to clarify the application of the existing provisions of the Convention.

The following example illustrates the application of paragraph 2. Assume a company that is a resident of Canada and that maintains a permanent establishment in the United States winds up the permanent establishment's business and sells the permanent establishment's inventory and assets to a U.S. buyer at the end of year 1 in exchange for an installment obligation payable in full at the end of year 3. Despite the fact that the company has no permanent establishment in the United States in year 3, the United States may tax the deferred income payment recognized by the company in year 3.

The "attributable to" concept of paragraph 2 provides an alternative to the analogous but somewhat different "effectively connected" concept in Code section 864(c). Depending on the circumstances, the amount of income "attributable to" a permanent establishment under Article VII may be greater or less than the amount of income that would be treated as "effectively connected" to a U.S. trade or business under Code section 864. In particular, in the case of financial institutions, the use of internal dealings to allocate income within an enterprise may produce results under Article VII that are significantly different than the results under the effectively connected income rules. For example, income from interbranch notional principal contracts may be taken into account under Article VII, notwithstanding that such transactions may be ignored for purposes of U.S. domestic law. A taxpayer may use the treaty to reduce its taxable income, but may not use both treaty and Code rules where doing so would thwart the intent of either set of rules. See Rev. Rul. 84-17, 1984-1 C.B. 308.

The profits attributable to a permanent establishment may be from sources within or without a Contracting State. However, as stated in the General Note, the business profits attributable to a permanent establishment include only those profits derived from the assets used, risks assumed, and activities performed by the permanent establishment.

The language of paragraph 2, when combined with paragraph 3 dealing with the allowance of deductions for expenses incurred for the purposes of earning the profits, incorporates the arm's length standard for purposes of determining the profits attributable to a permanent establishment. The United States and Canada generally interpret the arm's length standard in a manner consistent with the OECD Transfer Pricing Guidelines.

Paragraph 9 of the General Note confirms that the arm's length method of paragraphs 2 and 3 consists of applying the OECD Transfer Pricing Guidelines, but taking into account the different economic and legal circumstances of a single legal entity (as opposed to separate but associated enterprises). Thus, any of the methods used in the Transfer Pricing Guidelines, including profits methods, may be used as appropriate and in accordance with the Transfer Pricing Guidelines. However, the use of the Transfer Pricing Guidelines applies only for purposes of attributing profits within the legal entity. It does not create legal obligations or other tax consequences that would result from transactions having independent legal significance. Thus, the Contracting States agree that the notional payments used to compute the profits that are attributable to a permanent establishment will not be taxed as if they were actual payments for purposes of other taxing provisions of the Convention, for example, for purposes of taxing a notional royalty under Article XII (Royalties).

One example of the different circumstances of a single legal entity is that an entity that operates through branches rather than separate subsidiaries generally will have lower capital requirements because all of the assets of the entity are available to support all of the entity's liabilities (with some exceptions attributable to local regulatory restrictions). This is the reason that most commercial banks and some insurance companies operate through branches rather than subsidiaries. The benefit that comes from such lower capital costs must be allocated among the branches in an appropriate manner. This issue does not arise in the case of an enterprise that operates through separate entities, since each entity will have to be separately capitalized or will have to compensate another entity for providing capital (usually through a guarantee).

Under U.S. domestic regulations, internal "transactions" generally are not recognized because they do not have legal significance. In contrast, the rule provided by the General Note is that such internal dealings may be used to attribute income to a permanent establishment in cases where the dealings accurately reflect the allocation of risk within the enterprise. One example is that of global trading in securities. In many cases, banks use internal swap transactions to transfer risk from one branch to a central location where traders have the expertise to manage that particular type of risk. Under paragraph 2 as set forth in the Protocol, such a bank may also use such swap transactions as a means of attributing income between the branches, if use of that method is the "best method" within the meaning of regulation section 1.482-1(c). The books of a branch will not be respected, however, when the results are inconsistent with a functional analysis. So, for example, income from a transaction that is booked in a particular branch (or home office) will not be treated as attributable to that location if the sales and risk management functions that generate the income are performed in another location.

The understanding in the General Note also affects the interpretation of paragraph 3 of Article VII. Paragraph 3 provides that in determining the business profits of a permanent establishment, deductions shall be allowed for the expenses incurred for the purposes of the permanent establishment, ensuring that business profits will be taxed on a net basis. This rule is not limited to expenses incurred exclusively for the purposes of the permanent establishment, but includes expenses incurred for the purposes of the enterprise as a whole, or that part of the enterprise that includes the permanent establishment. Deductions are to be allowed regardless of which accounting unit of the enterprise books the expenses, so long as they are incurred for the purposes of the permanent establishment. For example, a portion of the interest expense recorded on the books of the home office in one State may be deducted by a permanent establishment in the other. The amount of the expense that must be allowed as a deduction is determined by applying the arm's length principle.

As noted above, paragraph 9 of the General Note provides that the OECD Transfer Pricing Guidelines apply, by analogy, in determining the profits attributable to a permanent establishment. Accordingly, a permanent establishment may deduct payments made to its head office or another branch in compensation for services performed for the benefit of the branch. The method to be used in calculating that amount will depend on the terms of the arrangements between the branches and head office. For example, the enterprise could have a policy, expressed in writing, under which each business unit could use the services of lawyers employed by the head office. At the end of each year, the costs of employing the lawyers would be charged to each business unit according to the amount of services used by that business unit during the year. Since this has the characteristics of a cost-sharing arrangement and the allocation of costs is based on the benefits received by each business unit, such a cost allocation would be an acceptable means of determining a permanent establishment's deduction for legal expenses. Alternatively, the head office could agree to employ lawyers at its own risk, and to charge an arm's length price for legal services performed for a particular business unit. If the lawyers were under-utilized, and the "fees" received from the business units were less than the cost of employing the lawyers, then the head office would bear the excess cost. If the "fees" exceeded the cost of employing the lawyers, then the head office would keep the excess to compensate it for assuming the risk of employing the lawyers. If the enterprise acted in accordance with this agreement, this method would be an acceptable alternative method for calculating a permanent establishment's deduction for legal expenses.

The General Note also makes clear that a permanent establishment cannot be funded entirely with debt, but must have sufficient capital to carry on its activities as if it were a distinct and separate enterprise. To the extent that the permanent establishment has not been attributed capital for profit attribution purposes, a Contracting State may attribute such capital to the permanent establishment, in accordance with the arm's length principle, and deny an interest deduction to the extent necessary to reflect that capital attribution. The method prescribed by U.S. domestic law for making this attribution is found in Treas. Reg. section 1.882-5. Both section 1.882-5 and the method prescribed in the General Note start from the premise that all of the capital of the enterprise supports all of the assets and risks of the enterprise, and therefore the entire capital of the enterprise must be allocated to its various businesses and offices.

However, section 1.882-5 does not take into account the fact that some assets create more risk for the enterprise than do other assets. An independent enterprise would need less capital to support a perfectly-hedged U.S. Treasury security than it would need to support an equity security or other asset with significant market and/or credit risk. Accordingly, in some cases section 1.882-5 would require a taxpayer to allocate more capital to the United States, and therefore would reduce the taxpayer's interest deduction more, than is appropriate. To address these cases, the General Note allows a taxpayer to apply a more flexible approach that takes into account the relative risk of its assets in the various jurisdictions in which it does business. In particular, in the case of financial institutions other than insurance companies, the amount of capital attributable to a permanent establishment is determined by allocating the institution's total equity between its various offices on the basis of the proportion of the financial institution's risk- weighted assets attributable to each of them. This recognizes the fact that financial institutions are in many cases required to risk-weight their assets for regulatory purposes and, in other cases, will do so for business reasons even if not required to do so by regulators. However, risk-weighting is more complicated than the method prescribed by section 1.882-5. Accordingly, to ease this administrative burden, taxpayers may choose to apply the principles of Treas. Reg. section 1.882-5(c) to determine the amount of capital allocable to its U.S. permanent establishment, in lieu of determining its allocable capital under the risk-weighted capital allocation method provided by the General Note, even if it has otherwise chosen the principles of Article VII rather than the effectively connected income rules of U.S. domestic law. It is understood that this election is not binding for purposes of Canadian taxation unless the result is in accordance with the arm's length principle.

As noted in the Convention, nothing in paragraph 3 requires a Contracting State to allow the deduction of any expenditure which, by reason of its nature, is not generally allowed as a deduction under the tax laws in that State.

Article 5

Article 5 makes a number of amendments to Article X (Dividends) of the existing Convention. As with other benefits of the Convention, the benefits of Article X are available to a resident of a Contracting State only if that resident is entitled to those benefits under the provisions of Article XXIX A (Limitation on Benefits).

See the Technical Explanation for new paragraphs 6 and 7 of Article IV (Residence) for discussion regarding the interaction between domestic law concepts of beneficial ownership and the treaty rules to determine when a person is considered to derive an item of income for purposes of obtaining benefits of the Convention such as withholding rate reductions.

Paragraph 1

Paragraph 1 of Article 5 of the Protocol replaces subparagraph 2(*a*) of Article X of the Convention. In general, paragraph 2 limits the amount of tax that may be imposed on dividends by the Contracting State in which the company paying the dividends is resident if the beneficial owner of the dividends is a resident of the other Contracting State. Subparagraph 2(*a*) limits the rate to 5 percent of the gross amount of the dividends if the beneficial owner is a company that owns 10 percent or more of the voting stock of the company paying the dividends.

The Protocol adds a parenthetical to address the determination of the requisite ownership set forth in subparagraph 2(*a*) when the beneficial owner of dividends receives the dividends through an entity that is considered fiscally transparent in the beneficial owner's Contracting State. The added parenthetical stipulates that voting stock in a company paying the dividends that is indirectly held through an entity that is considered fiscally transparent in the beneficial owner's Contracting State is taken into account, provided the entity is not a resident of the other Contracting State. The United States views the new parenthetical as merely a clarification.

For example, assume USCo, a U.S. corporation, directly owns 2 percent of the voting stock of CanCo, a Canadian company that is considered a corporation in the United States and Canada. Further, assume that USCo owns 18 percent of the interests in LLC, an entity that in turn owns 50 percent of the voting stock of CanCo. CanCo pays a dividend to each of its shareholders. Provided that LLC is fiscally transparent in the United States and not considered a resident of Canada, USCo's 9 percent ownership in CanCo through LLC (50 percent x 18 percent) is taken into account in determining whether USCo meets the 10 percent ownership threshold set forth in subparagraph 2(a). In this example, USCo may aggregate its voting stock interests in CanCo that it owns directly and through LLC to determine if it satisfies the ownership requirement of subparagraph 2(*a*). Accordingly, USCo will be entitled to the 5 percent rate of withholding on dividends paid with respect to both its voting stock held through LLC and its voting stock held directly. Alternatively, if, for example, all of the shareholders of LLC were natural persons, the 5 percent rate would not apply.

Paragraph 2

Paragraph 2 of Article 5 of the Protocol replaces the definition of the term "dividends" provided in paragraph 3 of Article X of the Convention. The new definition conforms to the U.S. Model formulation. Paragraph 3 defines the term dividends broadly and flexibly. The definition is intended to cover all arrangements that yield a return on an equity investment in a corporation as determined under the tax law of the source State, as well as arrangements that might be developed in the future.

The term dividends includes income from shares, or other corporate rights that are not treated as debt under the law of the source State, that participate in the profits of the company. The term also includes income that is subjected to the same tax treatment as income from shares by the law of the source State. Thus, for example, a constructive dividend that results from a non-arm's length transaction between a corporation and a related party is a dividend. In the case of the United States the term "dividend" includes amounts treated as a dividend under U.S. law upon the sale or redemption of shares or upon a transfer of shares in a reorganization. *See, e.g.,* Rev. Rul. 92-85, 1992-2 C.B. 69 (sale of foreign subsidiary's stock to U.S. sister company is a deemed dividend to extent of the subsidiary's and sister company's earnings and profits). Further, a distribution from a U.S. publicly traded limited partnership that is taxed as a corporation under U.S. law is a dividend for purposes of Article X. However, a distribution by a limited liability company is not considered by the United States to be a dividend for purposes of Article X, provided the limited liability company is not characterized as an association taxable as a corporation under U.S. law.

Paragraph 3 of the General Note states that distributions from Canadian income trusts and royalty trusts that are treated as dividends as a result of changes to Canada's taxation of income and royalty trusts enacted in 2007 (S.C. 2007, c. 29) shall be treated as dividends for the purposes of Article X.

Additionally, a payment denominated as interest that is made by a thinly capitalized corporation may be treated as a dividend to the extent that the debt is recharacterized as equity under the laws of the source State. At the time the Protocol was signed, interest payments subject to Canada's thin-capitalization rules were not recharacterized as dividends.

Paragraph 3

Paragraph 3 of Article 5 of the Protocol replaces paragraph 4 of Article X. New paragraph 4 is substantially similar to paragraph 4 as it existed prior to the Protocol. New paragraph 4, however, adds clarifying language consistent with the changes made in Articles 4, 6, and 7 of the Protocol with respect to income attributable to a permanent establishment that has ceased to exist. Paragraph 4 provides that the limitations of paragraph 2 do not apply if the beneficial owner of the dividends carries on or has carried on business in the State in which the company paying the dividends is a resident through a permanent establishment situated there, and the stockholding in respect of which the dividends are paid is effectively connected to such permanent establishment. In such a case, the dividends are taxable pursuant to the provisions of Article VII (Business Profits). Thus, dividends paid in respect of holdings forming part of the assets of a permanent establishment or which are otherwise effectively connected to such permanent establishment will be taxed on a net basis using the rates and rules of taxation generally applicable to residents of the State in which the permanent establishment is situated.

Paragraph 4

To conform with Article 9 of the Protocol, which deletes Article XIV (Independent Personal Services) of the Convention, paragraph 4 of Article 5 of the Protocol amends paragraph 5 of Article X by omitting the reference to a "fixed base."

Paragraph 5

Paragraph 5 of Article 5 of the Protocol replaces subparagraph 7(*c*) of Article X of the existing Convention. Consistent with current U.S. tax treaty policy, new subparagraph 7(*c*) provides rules that expand the application of subparagraph 2(*b*) for the treatment of dividends paid by a Real Estate Investment Trust (REIT). New subparagraph 7(*c*) maintains the rule of the existing Convention that dividends paid by a REIT are not eligible for the 5 percent maximum rate of withholding tax of subparagraph 2(*a*), and provides that the 15 percent maximum rate of withholding tax of subparagraph 2(*b*) applies to dividends paid by REITs only if one of three conditions is met.

First, the dividend will qualify for the 15 percent maximum rate if the beneficial owner of the dividend is an individual holding an interest of not more than 10 percent in the REIT. For this purpose, subparagraph 7(*c*) also provides that where an estate or testamentary trust acquired its interest in a REIT as a consequence of the death of an individual, the estate or trust will be treated as an individual for the five-year period following the death. Thus, dividends paid to an estate or testamentary trust in respect of a holding of less than a 10 percent interest in the REIT also will be entitled to the 15 percent rate of withholding, but only for up to five years after the death.

Second, the dividend will qualify for the 15 percent maximum rate if it is paid with respect to a class of stock that is publicly traded and the beneficial owner of the dividend is a person holding an interest of not more than 5 percent of any class of the REIT's stock.

Third, the dividend will qualify for the 15 percent maximum rate if the beneficial owner of the dividend holds an interest in the REIT of 10 percent or less and the REIT is "diversified." A REIT is diversified if the gross value of no single interest in real property held by the REIT exceeds 10 percent of the gross value of the REIT's total interest in real property. For purposes of this diversification test, foreclosure property is not considered an interest in real property, and a REIT holding a partnership interest is treated as owning its proportionate share of any interest in real property held by the partnership.

A resident of Canada directly holding U.S. real property would pay U.S. tax either at a 30 percent rate of withholding tax on the gross income or at graduated rates on the net income. By placing the real property in a REIT, the investor absent a special rule could transform real estate income into dividend income, taxable at the rates provided in Article X, significantly reducing the U.S. tax that otherwise would be imposed. Subparagraph 7(*c*) prevents this result and thereby avoids a disparity between the taxation of direct real estate investments and real estate investments made through REIT conduits. In the cases in which subparagraph 7(*c*) allows a dividend from a REIT to be eligible for the 15 percent maximum rate of withholding tax, the holding in the REIT is not considered the equivalent of a direct holding in the underlying real property.

Article 6

Article 6 of the Protocol replaces Article XI (Interest) of the existing Convention. Article XI specifies the taxing jurisdictions over interest income of the States of source and residence and defines the terms necessary to apply Article XI. As with other benefits of the

Convention, the benefits of Article XI are available to a resident of a Contracting State only if that resident is entitled to those benefits under the provisions of Article XXIX A (Limitation on Benefits).

Paragraph 1 of Article XI

New paragraph 1 generally grants to the residence State the exclusive right to tax interest beneficially owned by its residents and arising in the other Contracting State. See the Technical Explanation for new paragraphs 6 and 7 of Article IV (Residence) for discussion regarding the interaction between domestic law concepts of beneficial ownership and the treaty rules to determine when a person is considered to derive an item of income for purposes of obtaining benefits under the Convention such as withholding rate reductions.

Subparagraph 3(*d*) of Article 27 of the Protocol provides an additional rule regarding the application of paragraph 1 during the first two years that end after the Protocol's entry into force. This rule is described in detail in the Technical Explanation to Article 27.

Paragraph 2 of Article XI

Paragraph 2 of new Article XI is substantially identical to paragraph 4 of Article XI of the existing Convention.

Paragraph 2 defines the term "interest" as used in Article XI to include, *inter alia*, income from debt claims of every kind, whether or not secured by a mortgage. Interest that is paid or accrued subject to a contingency is within the ambit of Article XI. This includes income from a debt obligation carrying the right to participate in profits. The term does not, however, include amounts that are treated as dividends under Article X (Dividends).

The term "interest" also includes amounts subject to the same tax treatment as income from money lent under the law of the State in which the income arises. Thus, for purposes of the Convention, amounts that the United States will treat as interest include (i) the difference between the issue price and the stated redemption price at maturity of a debt instrument (i.e., original issue discount (OID)), which may be wholly or partially realized on the disposition of a debt instrument (section 1273), (ii) amounts that are imputed interest on a deferred sales contract (section 483), (iii) amounts treated as interest or OID under the stripped bond rules (section 1286), (iv) amounts treated as original issue discount under the below-market interest rate rules (section 7872), (v) a partner's distributive share of a partnership's interest income (section 702), (vi) the interest portion of periodic payments made under a "finance lease" or similar contractual arrangement that in substance is a borrowing by the nominal lessee to finance the acquisition of property, (vii) amounts included in the income of a holder of a residual interest in a real estate mortgage investment conduit (REMIC) (section 860E), because these amounts generally are subject to the same taxation treatment as interest under U.S. tax law, and (viii) interest with respect to notional principal contracts that are re-characterized as loans because of a "substantial non-periodic payment."

Paragraph 3 of Article XI

Paragraph 3 is in all material respects the same as paragraph 5 of Article XI of the existing Convention. New paragraph 3 adds clarifying language consistent with the changes made in Articles 4, 5, and 7 of the Protocol with respect to income attributable to a permanent establishment that has ceased to exist. Also, consistent with the changes described in Article 9 of the Protocol, discussed below, paragraph 3 does not contain references to the performance of independent personal services through a fixed base.

Paragraph 3 provides an exception to the exclusive residence taxation rule of paragraph 1 in cases where the beneficial owner of the interest carries on business through a permanent establishment in the State of source and the interest is effectively connected to that permanent establishment. In such cases the provisions of Article VII (Business Profits) will apply and the source State will retain the right to impose tax on such interest income.

Paragraph 4 of Article XI

Paragraph 4 is in all material respects the same as paragraph 6 of Article XI of the existing Convention. The only difference is that, consistent with the changes described below with respect to Article 9 of the Protocol, paragraph 4 does not contain references to a fixed base.

Paragraph 4 establishes the source of interest for purposes of Article XI. Interest is considered to arise in a Contracting State if the payer is that State, or a political subdivision, local authority, or resident of that State. However, in cases where the person paying the interest, whether a resident of a Contracting State or of a third State, has in a State other than that of which he is a resident a permanent establishment in connection with which the indebtedness on which the interest was paid was incurred, and such interest is borne by the permanent establishment, then such interest is deemed to arise in the State in which the permanent establishment is situated and not in the State of the payer's residence. Furthermore, pursuant to paragraphs 1 and 4, and Article XXII (Other Income), Canadian tax will not be imposed on interest paid to a U.S. resident by a company resident in Canada if the indebtedness is incurred in connection with, and the interest is borne by, a permanent establishment of the company situated in a third State. For the purposes of this Article, "borne by" means allowable as a deduction in computing taxable income.

Paragraph 5 of Article XI

Paragraph 5 is identical to paragraph 7 of Article XI of the existing Convention.

Paragraph 5 provides that in cases involving special relationships between the payer and the beneficial owner of interest income or between both of them and some other person, Article XI applies only to that portion of the total interest payments that would have been made absent such special relationships (*i.e.*, an arm's-length interest payment). Any excess amount of interest paid remains taxable according to the laws of the United States and Canada, respectively, with due regard to the other provisions of the Convention.

Paragraph 6 of Article XI

New paragraph 6 provides anti-abuse exceptions to exclusive residence State taxation in paragraph 1 for two classes of interest payments.

The first class of interest, dealt with in subparagraphs 6(*a*) and 6(*b*), is so-called "contingent interest." With respect to interest arising in the United States, subparagraph 6(*a*) refers to contingent interest of a type that does not qualify as portfolio interest under U.S. domestic law. The cross-reference to the U.S. definition of contingent interest, which is found in Code section 871(h)(4), is intended to ensure that the exceptions of Code section 871(h)(4)(C) will apply. With respect to Canada, such interest is defined in subparagraph 6(b) as any interest arising in Canada that is determined by reference to the receipts, sales, income, profits or other cash flow of the debtor or a related person, to any change in the value of any property of the debtor or a related person or to any dividend, partnership distribution or similar payment made by the debtor or a related person.[1] Any such interest may be taxed in Canada according to the laws of Canada.

Under subparagraph 6(*a*) or 6(*b*), if the beneficial owner is a resident of the other Contracting State, the gross amount of the "contingent interest" may be taxed at a rate not exceeding 15 percent.

The second class of interest is dealt with in subparagraph 6(*c*). This exception is consistent with the policy of Code sections 860E(e) and 860G(b) that excess inclusions with respect to a real estate mortgage investment conduit (REMIC) should bear full U.S. tax in all cases. Without a full tax at source, foreign purchasers of residual interests would have a competitive advantage over U.S. purchasers at the time these interests are initially offered. Also, absent this rule, the U.S. fisc would suffer a revenue loss with respect to mortgages held in a REMIC because of opportunities for tax avoidance created by differences in the timing of taxable and economic income produced by these interests.

Therefore, subparagraph 6(*c*) provides a bilateral provision that interest that is an excess inclusion with respect to a residual interest in a REMIC may be taxed by each State in accordance with its domestic law. While the provision is written reciprocally, at the time the Protocol was signed, the provision had no application in respect of Canadian- source interest, as Canada did not have REMICs.

Paragraph 7 of Article XI

Paragraph 7 is in all material respects the same as paragraph 8 of Article XI of the existing Convention. The only difference is that,

[1]New subparagraph 6(b) of Article XI erroneously refers to a "similar payment made by the debtor to a related person." The correct formulation, which the Contracting States agree to apply, is "similar payment made by the debtor or a related person."

consistent with the changes made in Article 9 of the Protocol, paragraph 7 removes the references to a fixed base.

Paragraph 7 restricts the right of a Contracting State to impose tax on interest paid by a resident of the other Contracting State. The first State may not impose any tax on such interest except insofar as the interest is paid to a resident of that State or arises in that State or the debt claim in respect of which the interest is paid is effectively connected with a permanent establishment situated in that State.

Relationship to other Articles

Notwithstanding the foregoing limitations on source State taxation of interest, the saving clause of paragraph 2 of Article XXIX (Miscellaneous Rules) permits the United States to tax its residents and citizens, subject to the special foreign tax credit rules of paragraph 5 of Article XXIV (Elimination of Double Taxation), as if the Convention had not come into force.

Article 7

Article 7 of the Protocol amends Article XII (Royalties) of the existing Convention. As with other benefits of the Convention, the benefits of Article XII are available to a resident of a Contracting State only if that resident is entitled to those benefits under the provisions of Article XXIX A (Limitation on Benefits).

See the Technical Explanation for new paragraphs 6 and 7 of Article IV (Residence) for discussion regarding the interaction between domestic law concepts of beneficial ownership and the treaty rules to determine when a person is considered to derive an item of income for purposes of obtaining benefits of the Convention such as withholding rate reductions.

Paragraph 1

Paragraph 1 of Article 7 of the Protocol replaces paragraph 5 of Article XII of the Convention. In all material respects, new paragraph 5 is the same as paragraph 5 of Article XII of the existing Convention. However, new paragraph 5 adds clarifying language consistent with the changes made in Articles 4, 5, and 6 of the Protocol with respect to income attributable to a permanent establishment that has ceased to exist. To conform with Article 9 of the Protocol, which deletes Article XIV (Independent Personal Services) of the Convention, paragraph 1 of Article 7 of the Protocol also amends paragraph 5 of Article XII by omitting the reference to a "fixed base."

New paragraph 5 provides that the 10 percent limitation on tax in the source State provided by paragraph 2, and the exemption in the source State for certain royalties provided by paragraph 3, do not apply if the beneficial owner of the royalties carries on or has carried on business in the source State through a permanent establishment and the right or property in respect of which the royalties are paid is attributable to such permanent establishment. In such case, the royalty income would be taxable by the source State under the provisions of Article VII (Business Profits).

Paragraph 2

Paragraph 2 of Article 7 of the Protocol sets forth a new subparagraph 6(*a*) of Article XII that is in all material respects the same as subparagraph 6(*a*) of Article XII of the existing Convention. The only difference is that, consistent with the changes made in Article 9 of the Protocol, new subparagraph 6(*a*) omits references to a "fixed base."

Paragraph 3

Paragraph 3 of Article 7 of Protocol amends paragraph 8 of Article XII of the Convention to remove references to a "fixed base." In addition, paragraph 8 of the General Note confirms the intent of the Contracting States that the reference in subparagraph 3(*c*) of Article XII of the Convention to information provided in connection with a franchise agreement generally refers only to information that governs or otherwise deals with the operation (whether by the payer or by another person) of the franchise, and not to other information concerning industrial, commercial or scientific experience that is held for resale or license.

Article 8

Paragraph 1

Paragraph 1 of Article 8 of the Protocol replaces paragraph 2 of Article XIII (Gains) of the existing Convention. Consistent with Article 9 of the Protocol, new paragraph 2 does not contain any reference to property pertaining to a fixed base or to the performance of independent personal services.

New paragraph 2 of Article XIII provides that the Contracting State in which a resident of the other Contracting State has or had a permanent establishment may tax gains from the alienation of personal property constituting business property if such gains are attributable to such permanent establishment. Unlike paragraph 1 of Article VII (Business Profits), paragraph 2 limits the right of the source State to tax such gains to a twelve-month period following the termination of the permanent establishment.

Paragraph 2

Paragraph 2 of Article 8 of the Protocol replaces paragraph 5 of Article XIII of the existing Convention. In general, new paragraph 5 provides an exception to the general rule stated in paragraph 4 that gains from the alienation of any property, other than property referred to in paragraphs 1, 2, and 3, shall be taxable only in the Contracting State of which the alienator is a resident. Paragraph 5 provides that a Contracting State may, according to its domestic law, impose tax on gains derived by an individual who is a resident of the other Contracting State if such individual was a resident of the first-mentioned State for 120 months (whether or not consecutive) during any period of 20 consecutive years preceding the alienation of the property, and was a resident of that State at any time during the 10-year period immediately preceding the alienation of the property. Further, the property (or property received in substitution in a tax-free transaction in the first-mentioned State) must have been owned by the individual at the time he ceased to be a resident of the first-mentioned State and must not have been property that the individual was treated as having alienated by reason of ceasing to be a resident of the first-mentioned State and becoming a resident of the other Contracting State.

The provisions of new paragraph 5 are substantially similar to paragraph 5 of Article XIII of the existing Convention. However, the Protocol adds a new requirement to paragraph 5 that the property not be "a property that the individual was treated as having alienated by reason of ceasing to be a resident of the first-mentioned State and becoming a resident of the other Contracting State." This new requirement reflects the fact that the main purpose of paragraph 5 — ensuring that gains that accrue while an individual is resident in a Contracting State remain taxable for the stated time after the individual has moved to the other State — is met if that pre-departure gain is taxed in the first State immediately before the individual's emigration. This rule applies whether or not the individual makes the election provided by paragraph 7 of Article XIII, as amended, which is described below.

Paragraph 3

Paragraph 3 of Article 8 of the Protocol replaces paragraph 7 of Article XIII.

The purpose of paragraph 7, in both its former and revised form, is to provide a rule to coordinate U.S. and Canadian taxation of gains in the case of a timing mismatch. Such a mismatch may occur, for example, where a Canadian resident is deemed, for Canadian tax purposes, to recognize capital gain upon emigrating from Canada to the United States, or in the case of a gift that Canada deems to be an income producing event for its tax purposes but with respect to which the United States defers taxation while assigning the donor's basis to the donee. The former paragraph 7 resolved the timing mismatch of taxable events by allowing the individual to elect to be liable to tax in the deferring Contracting State as if he had sold and repurchased the property for an amount equal to its fair market value at a time immediately prior to the deemed alienation.

The election under former paragraph 7 was not available to certain non-U.S. citizens subject to tax in Canada by virtue of a deemed alienation because such individuals could not elect to be liable to tax in the United States. To address this problem, the Protocol replaces the election provided in former paragraph 7, with an election by the taxpayer to be treated by a Contracting State as having sold and repurchased the property for its fair market value immediately before the taxable event in the other Contracting State. The election in new paragraph 7 therefore will be available to any individual who emigrates from Canada to the United States, without regard to whether the person is a U.S. citizen immediately before ceasing to be a resident of Canada. If the individual is not subject to U.S. tax at that time, the effect of the election will be to give the individual an adjusted basis for U.S. tax purposes equal to the fair market value of the property as of the date of the deemed alienation in Canada, with the result that only

Treaties and Related Legislation

post-emigration gain will be subject to U.S. tax when there is an actual alienation. If the Canadian resident is also a U.S. citizen at the time of his emigration from Canada, then the provisions of new paragraph 7 would allow the U.S. citizen to accelerate the tax under U.S. tax law and allow tax credits to be used to avoid double taxation. This would also be the case if the person, while not a U.S. citizen, would otherwise be subject to taxation in the United States on a disposition of the property.

In the case of Canadian taxation of appreciated property given as a gift, absent paragraph 7, the donor could be subject to tax in Canada upon making the gift, and the donee may be subject to tax in the United States upon a later disposition of the property on all or a portion of the same gain in the property without the availability of any foreign tax credit for the tax paid to Canada. Under new paragraph 7, the election will be available to any individual who pays taxes in Canada on a gain arising from the individual's gifting of a property, without regard to whether the person is a U.S. taxpayer at the time of the gift. The effect of the election in such case will be to give the donee an adjusted basis for U.S. tax purposes equal to the fair market value as of the date of the gift. If the donor is a U.S. taxpayer, the effect of the election will be the realization of gain or loss for U.S. purposes immediately before the gift. The acceleration of the U.S. tax liability by reason of the election in such case enables the donor to utilize foreign tax credits and avoid double taxation with respect to the disposition of the property.

Generally, the rule does not apply in the case of death. Note, however, that Article XXIX B (Taxes Imposed by Reason of Death) of the Convention provides rules that coordinate the income tax that Canada imposes by reason of death with the U.S. estate tax.

If in one Contracting State there are losses and gains from deemed alienations of different properties, then paragraph 7 must be applied consistently in the other Contracting State within the taxable period with respect to all such properties. Paragraph 7 only applies, however, if the deemed alienations of the properties result in a net gain.

Taxpayers may make the election provided by new paragraph 7 only with respect to property that is subject to a Contracting State's deemed disposition rules and with respect to which gain on a deemed alienation is recognized for that Contracting State's tax purposes in the taxable year of the deemed alienation. At the time the Protocol was signed, the following were the main types of property that were excluded from the deemed disposition rules in the case of individuals (including trusts) who cease to be residents of Canada: real property situated in Canada; interests and rights in respect of pensions; life insurance policies (other than segregated fund (investment) policies); rights in respect of annuities; interests in testamentary trusts, unless acquired for consideration; employee stock options; property used in a business carried on through a permanent establishment in Canada (including intangibles and inventory); interests in most Canadian personal trusts; Canadian resource property; and timber resource property.

Paragraph 4

Consistent with the provisions of Article 9 of the Protocol, paragraph 4 of Article 8 of the Protocol amends subparagraph 9(*c*) of Article XIII of the existing Convention to remove the words "or pertained to a fixed base."

Relationship to other Articles

The changes to Article XIII set forth in paragraph 3 were announced in a press release issued by the Treasury Department on September 18, 2000. Consistent with that press release, subparagraph 3(*e*) of Article 27 of the Protocol provides that the changes, jointly effectuated by paragraphs 2 and 3, will be generally effective for alienations of property that occur after September 17, 2000.

Article 9

To conform with the current U.S. and OECD Model Conventions, Article 9 of the Protocol deletes Article XIV (Independent Personal Services) of the Convention. The subsequent articles of the Convention are not renumbered. Paragraph 4 of the General Note elaborates that current tax treaty practice omits separate articles for independent personal services because a determination of the existence of a fixed base is qualitatively the same as the determination of the existence of a permanent establishment. Accordingly, the taxation of income from independent personal services is adequately governed by the provisions of Articles V (Permanent Establishment) and VII (Business Profits).

Article 10

Article 10 of the Protocol renames Article XV of the Convention as "Income from Employment" to conform with the current U.S. and OECD Model Conventions, and replaces paragraphs 1 and 2 of that renamed article consistent with the OECD Model Convention.

Paragraph 1

New paragraph 1 of Article XV provides that, in general, salaries, wages, and other remuneration derived by a resident of a Contracting State in respect of an employment are taxable only in that State unless the employment is exercised in the other Contracting State. If the employment is exercised in the other Contracting State, the entire remuneration derived therefrom may be taxed in that other State, subject to the provisions of paragraph 2.

New paragraph 1 of Article XV does not contain a reference to "similar" remuneration. This change was intended to clarify that Article XV applies to any form of compensation for employment, including payments in kind. This interpretation is consistent with paragraph 2.1 of the Commentary to Article 15 (Income from Employment) of the OECD Model and the Technical Explanation of the 2006 U.S. Model.

Paragraph 2

New paragraph 2 of Article XV provides two limitations on the right of a source State to tax remuneration for services rendered in that State. New paragraph 2 is divided into two subparagraphs that each sets forth a rule which, notwithstanding any contrary result due to the application of paragraph 1 of Article XV, prevents the source State from taxing income from employment in that State.

First, subparagraph 2(*a*) provides a safe harbor rule that the remuneration may not be taxed in the source State if such remuneration is $10,000 or less in the currency of the source State. This rule is identical to the rule in subparagraph 2(*a*) of Article XV of the existing Convention. It is understood that, consistent with the prior rule, the safe harbor will apply on a calendar-year basis.

Second, if the remuneration is not exempt from tax in the source State by virtue of subparagraph 2(*a*), subparagraph 2(*b*) provides an additional rule that the source State may not tax remuneration for services rendered in that State if the recipient is present in the source State for a period (or periods) that does not exceed in the aggregate 183 days in any twelve-month period commencing or ending in the fiscal year concerned, and the remuneration is not paid by or on behalf of a person who is a resident of that other State or borne by a permanent establishment in that other State. For purposes of this article, "borne by" means allowable as a deduction in computing taxable income.

Assume, for example, that Mr. X, an individual resident in Canada, is an employee of the Canadian permanent establishment of USCo, a U.S. company. Mr. X is sent to the United States to perform services and is present in the United States for less than 183 days. Mr. X receives more than $10,000 (U.S.) in the calendar year(s) in question. The remuneration paid to Mr. X for such services is not exempt from U.S. tax under paragraph 1, because his employer, USCo, is a resident of the United States and pays his remuneration. If instead Mr. X received less than $10,000 (U.S.), such earnings would be exempt from tax in the United States, because in all cases where an employee earns less than $10,000 in the currency of the source State, such earnings are exempt from tax in the source State.

As another example, assume Ms. Y, an individual resident in the United States is employed by USCo, a U.S. company. Ms. Y is sent to Canada to provide services in the Canadian permanent establishment of USCo. Ms. Y is present in Canada for less than 183 days. Ms. Y receives more than $10,000 (Canadian) in the calendar year(s) in question. USCo charges the Canadian permanent establishment for Ms. Y's remuneration, which the permanent establishment takes as a deduction in computing its taxable income. The remuneration paid to Ms. Y for such services is not exempt from Canadian tax under paragraph 1, because her remuneration is borne by the Canadian permanent establishment.

New subparagraph 2(*b*) refers to remuneration that is paid by or on behalf of a "person" who is a resident of the other Contracting State, as opposed to an "employer." This change is intended only to clarify that both the United States and Canada understand that in certain abusive cases, substance over form principles may be applied to recharacterize an employment relationship, as prescribed in paragraph 8 of the Commentary to Article 15 (Income from Employment) of the OECD Model. Subparagraph 2(*b*) is intended to have the same meaning as the analogous provisions in the U.S. and OECD Models.

Paragraph 6 of the General Note

Paragraph 6 of the General Note contains special rules regarding employee stock options. There are no similar rules in the U.S. Model or the OECD Model, although the issue is discussed in detail in paragraph 12 of the Commentary to Article 15 (Income from Employment) of the OECD Model.

The General Note sets forth principles that apply for purposes of applying Article XV and Article XXIV (Elimination of Double Taxation) to income of an individual in connection with the exercise or other disposal (including a deemed exercise or disposal) of an option that was granted to the individual as an employee of a corporation or mutual fund trust to acquire shares or units ("securities") of the employer in respect of services rendered or to be rendered by such individual, or in connection with the disposal (including a deemed disposal) of a security acquired under such an option. For this purpose, the term "employer" is considered to include any entity related to the service recipient. The reference to a disposal (or deemed disposal) reflects the fact that under Canadian law and under certain provisions of U.S. law, income or gain attributable to the granting or exercising of the option may, in some cases, not be recognized until disposition of the securities.

Subparagraph 6(*a*) of the General Note provides a specific rule to address situations where, under the domestic law of the Contracting States, an employee would be taxable by both Contracting States in respect of the income in connection with the exercise or disposal of the option. The rule provides an allocation of taxing rights where (1) an employee has been granted a stock option in the course of employment in one of the Contracting States, and (2) his principal place of employment has been situated in one or both of the Contracting States during the period between grant and exercise (or disposal) of the option. In this situation, each Contracting State may tax as Contracting State of source only that proportion of the income that relates to the period or periods between the grant and the exercise (or disposal) of the option during which the individual's principal place of employment was situated in that Contracting State. The proportion attributable to a Contracting State is determined by multiplying the income by a fraction, the numerator of which is the number of days between the grant and exercise (or disposal) of the option during which the employee's principal place of employment was situated in that Contracting State and the denominator of which is the total number of days between grant and exercise (or disposal) of the option that the employee was employed by the employer.

If the individual is a resident of one of the Contracting States at the time he exercises the option, that Contracting State will have the right, as the State of residence, to tax all of the income under the first sentence of paragraph 1 of Article XV. However, to the extent that the employee renders his employment in the other Contracting State for some period of time between the date of the grant of the option and the date of the exercise (or disposal) of the option, the proportion of the income that is allocated to the other Contracting State under subparagraph 6(*a*) of the General Note will, subject to paragraph 2, be taxable by that other State under the second sentence of paragraph 1 of Article XV of the Convention. For this purpose, the tests of paragraph 2 of Article XV are applied to the year or years in which the relevant services were performed in the other Contracting State (and not to the year in which the option is exercised or disposed). To the extent the same income is subject to taxation in both Contracting States after application of Article XV, double taxation will be alleviated under the rules of Article XXIV (Elimination of Double Taxation).

Subparagraph 6(*b*) of the General Note provides that notwithstanding subparagraph 6(*a*), if the competent authorities of both Contracting States agree that the terms of the option were such that the grant of the option is appropriately treated as transfer of ownership of the securities (e.g., because the options were in-the-money or not subject to a substantial vesting period), then they may agree to attribute income accordingly.

Article 11

Consistent with Article 9 and paragraph 1 of Article 10 of the Protocol, paragraphs 1, 2, and 3 of Article 11 of the Protocol revise paragraphs 1, 2, and 4 of Article XVI (Artistes and Athletes) of the existing Convention by deleting references to former Article XIV (Independent Personal Services) of the Convention and deleting and replacing other language in acknowledgement of the renaming of Article XV (Income from Employment).

Article 12

Article 12 of the Protocol deletes Article XVII (Withholding of Taxes in Respect of Personal Services) from the Convention. However, the subsequent Articles are not renumbered.

Article 13

Article 13 of the Protocol replaces paragraphs 3, 4, and 7 and adds paragraphs 8 through 17 to Article XVIII (Pensions and Annuities) of the Convention.

Paragraph 1

Roth IRAs

Paragraph 1 of Article 13 of the Protocol separates the provisions of paragraph 3 of Article XVIII into two subparagraphs. Subparagraph 3(*a*) contains the existing definition of the term "pensions," while subparagraph 3(*b*) adds a new rule to address the treatment of Roth IRAs or similar plan (as described below).

Subparagraph 3(*a*) of Article XVIII provides that the term "pensions" for purposes of the Convention includes any payment under a superannuation, pension, or other retirement arrangement, Armed-Forces retirement pay, war veterans pensions and allowances, and amounts paid under a sickness, accident, or disability plan, but does not include payments under an income-averaging annuity contract (which are subject to Article XXII (Other Income)) or social security benefits, including social security benefits in respect of government services (which are subject to paragraph 5 of Article XVIII). Thus, the term "pensions" includes pensions paid by private employers (including pre-tax and Roth 401(k) arrangements) as well as any pension paid in respect of government services. Further, the definition of "pensions" includes, for example, payments from individual retirement accounts (IRAs) in the United States and from registered retirement savings plans (RRSPs) and registered retirement income funds (RRIFs) in Canada.

Subparagraph 3(*b*) of Article XVIII provides that the term "pensions" generally includes a Roth IRA, within the meaning of Code section 408A (or a similar plan described below). Consequently, under paragraph 1 of Article XVIII, distributions from a Roth IRA to a resident of Canada generally continue to be exempt from Canadian tax to the extent they would have been exempt from U.S. tax if paid to a resident of the United States. In addition, residents of Canada generally may make an election under paragraph 7 of Article XVIII to defer any taxation in Canada with respect to income accrued in a Roth IRA but not distributed by the Roth IRA, until such time as and to the extent that a distribution is made from the Roth IRA or any plan substituted therefore [*sic*]. Because distributions will be exempt from Canadian tax to the extent they would have been exempt from U.S. tax if paid to a resident of the United States, the effect of these rules is that, in most cases, no portion of the Roth IRA will be subject to taxation in Canada.

However, subparagraph 3(*b*) also provides that if an individual who is a resident of Canada makes contributions to his or her Roth IRA while a resident of Canada, other than rollover contributions from another Roth IRA (or a similar plan described below), the Roth IRA will cease to be considered a pension at that time with respect to contributions and accretions from such time and accretions from such time will be subject to tax in Canada in the year of accrual. Thus, the Roth IRA will in effect be bifurcated into a "frozen" pension that continues to be subject to the rules of Article XVIII and a savings account that is not subject to the rules of Article XVIII. It is understood by the Contracting States that, following a rollover contribution from a Roth 401(k) arrangement to a Roth IRA, the Roth IRA will continue to be treated as a pension subject to the rules of Article XVIII.

Assume, for example, that Mr. X moves to Canada on July 1, 2008. Mr. X has a Roth IRA with a balance of 1,100 on July 1, 2008. Mr. X elects under paragraph 7 of Article XVIII to defer any taxation in Canada with respect to income accrued in his Roth IRA while he is a resident of Canada. Mr. X makes no additional contributions to his Roth IRA until July 1, 2010, when he makes an after-tax contribution of 100. There are accretions of 20 during the period July 1, 2008 through June 30, 2010, which are not taxed in Canada by reason of the election under paragraph 7 of Article XVIII. There are additional accretions of 50 during the period July 1, 2010 through June 30, 2015, which are subject to tax in Canada in the year of accrual. On July 1, 2015, while Mr. X is still a resident of Canada, Mr. X receives a lump-sum distribution of 1,270 from his Roth IRA. The 1,120 that was in the Roth IRA on June 30, 2010 is treated as a distribution from a pension plan that, pursuant to paragraph 1 of Article XVIII, is exempt from tax in Canada provided it would be exempt from tax in the United States under the *Internal Revenue Code* if paid to a resident of the United States. The remaining 150 comprises the after-tax contribution of 100 in 2010 and accretions of 50 that were subject to Canadian tax in the year of accrual.

The rules of new subparagraph 3(*b*) of Article XVIII also will apply to any plan or arrangement created pursuant to legislation enacted by either Contracting State after September 21, 2007 (the date of signature of the Protocol) that the competent authorities agree is similar to a Roth IRA.

Source of payments under life insurance and annuity contracts

Paragraph 1 of Article 13 also replaces paragraph 4 of Article XVIII. Subparagraph 4(*a*) contains the existing definition of annuity, while subparagraph 4(*b*) adds a source rule to address the treatment of certain payments by branches of insurance companies.

Subparagraph 4(*a*) provides that, for purposes of the Convention, the term "annuity" means a stated sum paid periodically at stated times during life or during a specified number of years, under an obligation to make the payments in return for adequate and full consideration other than services rendered. The term does not include a payment that is not periodic or any annuity the cost of which was deductible for tax purposes in the Contracting State where the annuity was acquired. Items excluded from the definition of "annuity" and not dealt with under another Article of the Convention are subject to the rules of Article XXII (Other Income).

Under the existing Convention, payments under life insurance and annuity contracts to a resident of Canada by a Canadian branch of a U.S. insurance company are subject to either a 15-percent withholding tax under subparagraph 2(*b*) of Article XVIII or, unless dealt with under another Article of the Convention, an unreduced 30-percent withholding tax under paragraph 1 of Article XXII, depending on whether the payments constitute annuities within the meaning of paragraph 4 of Article XVIII.

On July 12, 2004, the Internal Revenue Service issued Revenue Ruling 2004-75, 2004-2 C.B. 109, which provides in relevant part that annuity payments under, and withdrawals of cash value from, life insurance or annuity contracts issued by a foreign branch of a U.S. life insurance company are U.S.-source income that, when paid to a nonresident alien individual, is generally subject to a 30-percent withholding tax under Code sections 871(a) and 1441. Revenue Ruling 2004-97, 2004-2 C.B. 516, provided that Revenue Ruling 2004-75 would not be applied to payments that were made before January 1, 2005, provided that such payments were made pursuant to binding life insurance or annuity contracts issued on or before July 12, 2004.

Under new subparagraph 4(b) of Article XVIII, an annuity or other amount paid in respect of a life insurance or annuity contract (including a withdrawal in respect of the cash value thereof), will generally be deemed to arise in the Contracting State where the person paying the annuity or other amount (the "payer") is resident. However, if the payer, whether a resident of a Contracting State or not, has a permanent establishment in a Contracting State other than a Contracting State in which the payer is a resident, the payment will be deemed to arise in the Contracting State in which the permanent establishment is situated if both of the following requirements are satisfied: (i) the obligation giving rise to the annuity or other amount must have been incurred in connection with the permanent establishment, and (ii) the annuity or other amount must be borne by the permanent establishment. When these requirements are satisfied, payments by a Canadian branch of a U.S. insurance company will be deemed to arise in Canada.

Paragraph 2

Paragraph 2 of Article 13 of the Protocol replaces paragraph 7 of Article XVIII of the existing Convention. Paragraph 7 continues to provide a rule with respect to the taxation of a natural person on income accrued in a pension or employee benefit plan in the other Contracting State. Thus, paragraph 7 applies where an individual is a citizen or resident of a Contracting State and is a beneficiary of a trust, company, organization, or other arrangement that is a resident of the other Contracting State, where such trust, company, organization, or other arrangement is generally exempt from income taxation in that other State, and is operated exclusively to provide pension, or employee benefits. In such cases, the beneficiary may elect to defer taxation in his State of residence on income accrued in the plan until it is distributed from the plan (or from another plan in that other Contracting State to which the income is transferred pursuant to the domestic law of that other Contracting State).

Paragraph 2 of Article 13 of the Protocol makes two changes to paragraph 7 of Article XVIII of the existing Convention. The first change is that the phrase "pension, retirement or employee benefits" is changed to "pension or employee benefits" solely to reflect the fact that in certain cases, discussed above, Roth IRAs will not be treated as pensions for purposes of Article XVIII. The second change is that "under" is changed to "subject to" to make it clear that an election to defer taxation with respect to undistributed income accrued in a plan may be made whether or not the competent authority of the first-mentioned State has prescribed rules for making an election. For the U.S. rules, see Revenue Procedure 2002-23, 2002-1 C.B. 744. As of the date the Protocol was signed, the competent authority of Canada had not prescribed rules.

Paragraph 3

Paragraph 3 of Article 13 of the Protocol adds paragraphs 8 through 17 to Article XVIII to deal with cross-border pension contributions. These paragraphs are intended to remove barriers to the flow of personal services between the Contracting States that could otherwise result from discontinuities in the laws of the Contracting States regarding the deductibility of pension contributions. Such discontinuities may arise where a country allows deductions or exclusions to its residents for contributions, made by them or on their behalf, to resident pension plans, but does not allow deductions or exclusions for payments made to plans resident in another country, even if the structure and legal requirements of such plans in the two countries are similar.

There is no comparable set of rules in the OECD Model, although the issue is discussed in detail in the Commentary to Article 18 (Pensions). The 2006 U.S. Model deals with this issue in paragraphs 2 through 4 of Article 18 (Pension Funds).

Workers on short-term assignments in the other Contracting State

Paragraphs 8 and 9 of Article XVIII address the case of a short-term assignment where an individual who is participating in a "qualifying retirement plan" (as defined in paragraph 15 of Article XVIII) in one Contracting State (the "home State") performs services as an employee for a limited period of time in the other Contracting State (the "host State"). If certain requirements are satisfied, contributions made to, or benefits accrued under, the plan by or on behalf of the individual will be deductible or excludible in computing the individual's income in the host State. In addition, contributions made to the plan by the individual's employer will be allowed as a deduction in computing the employer's profits in the host State.

In order for paragraph 8 to apply, the remuneration that the individual receives with respect to the services performed in the host State must be taxable in the host State. This means, for example, that where the United States is the host State, paragraph 8 would not apply if the remuneration that the individual receives with respect to the services performed in the United States is exempt from taxation in the United States under Code section 893.

The individual also must have been participating in the plan, or in another similar plan for which the plan was substituted, immediately before he began performing services in the host State. The rule regarding a successor plan would apply if, for example, the employer has been acquired by another corporation that replaces the existing plan with its own plan, transferring membership in the old plan over into the new plan.

Treaties and Related Legislation

In addition, the individual must not have been a resident (as determined under Article IV (Residence)) of the host State immediately before he began performing services in the host State. It is irrelevant for purposes of paragraph 8 whether the individual becomes a resident of the host State while he performs services there. A citizen of the United States who has been a resident of Canada may be entitled to benefits under paragraph 8 if (a) he performs services in the United States for a limited period of time and (b) he was a resident of Canada immediately before he began performing such services.

Benefits are available under paragraph 8 only for so long as the individual has not performed services in the host State for the same employer (or a related employer) for more than 60 of the 120 months preceding the individual's current taxable year. The purpose of this rule is to limit the period of time for which the host State will be required to provide benefits for contributions to a plan from which it is unlikely to be able to tax the distributions. If the individual continues to perform services in the host State beyond this time limit, he is expected to become a participant in a plan in the host State. Canada's domestic law provides preferential tax treatment for employer contributions to foreign pension plans in respect of services rendered in Canada by short-term residents, but such treatment ceases once the individual has been resident in Canada for at least 60 of the preceding 72 months.

The contributions and benefits must be attributable to services performed by the individual in the host State, and must be made or accrued during the period in which the individual performs those services. This rule prevents individuals who render services in the host State for a very short period of time from making disproportionately large contributions to home State plans in order to offset the tax liability associated with the income earned in the host State. In the case where the United States is the host State, contributions will be deemed to have been made on the last day of the preceding taxable year if the payment is on account of such taxable year and is treated under U.S. law as a contribution made on the last day of the preceding taxable year.

If an individual receives benefits in the host State with respect to contributions to a plan in the home State, the services to which the contributions relate may not be taken into account for purposes of determining the individual's entitlement to benefits under any trust, company, organization, or other arrangement that is a resident of the host State, generally exempt from income taxation in that State and operated to provide pension or retirement benefits. The purpose of this rule is to prevent double benefits for contributions to both a home State plan and a host State plan with respect to the same services. Thus, for example, an individual who is working temporarily in the United States and making contributions to a qualifying retirement plan in Canada with respect to services performed in the United States may not make contributions to an individual retirement account (within the meaning of Code section 408(a)) in the United States with respect to the same services.

Paragraph 8 states that it applies only to the extent that the contributions or benefits would qualify for tax relief in the home State if the individual were a resident of and performed services in that State. Thus, benefits would be limited in the same fashion as if the individual continued to be a resident of the home State. However, paragraph 9 provides that if the host State is the United States and the individual is a citizen of the United States, the benefits granted to the individual under paragraph 8 may not exceed the benefits that would be allowed by the United States to its residents for contributions to, or benefits otherwise accrued under, a generally corresponding pension or retirement plan established in and recognized for tax purposes by the United States. Thus, the lower of the two limits applies. This rule ensures that U.S. citizens working temporarily in the United States and participating in a Canadian plan will not get more favorable U.S. tax treatment than U.S. citizens participating in a U.S. plan.

Where the United States is the home State, the amount of contributions that may be excluded from the employee's income under paragraph 8 for Canadian purposes is limited to the U.S. dollar amount specified in Code section 415 or the U.S. dollar amount specified in Code section 402(g)(1) to the extent contributions are made from the employee's compensation. For this purpose, the dollar limit specified in Code section 402(g)(1) means the amount applicable under Code section 402(g)(1) (including the age 50 catch-up amount in Code section 402(g)(1)(C)) or, if applicable, the parallel dollar limit applicable under Code section 457(e)(15) plus the age 50 catch-up amount under Code section 414(v)(2)(B)(i) for a Code section 457(g) trust.

Where Canada is the home State, the amount of contributions that may be excluded from the employee's income under paragraph 8 for U.S. purposes is subject to the limitations specified in subsections 146(5), 147(8), 147.1(8) and (9) and 147.2(1) and (4) of the *Income Tax Act* and paragraph 8503(4)(*a*) of the Income Tax Regulations, as applicable. If the employee is a citizen of the United States, then the amount of contributions that may be excluded is the lesser of the amounts determined under the limitations specified in the previous sentence and the amounts specified in the previous paragraph.

The provisions described above provide benefits to employees. Paragraph 8 also provides that contributions made to the home State plan by an individual's employer will be allowed as a deduction in computing the employer's profits in the host State, even though such a deduction might not be allowable under the domestic law of the host State. This rule applies whether the employer is a resident of the host State or a permanent establishment that the employer has in the host State. The rule also applies to contributions by a person related to the individual's employer, such as contributions by a parent corporation for its subsidiary, that are treated under the law of the host State as contributions by the individual's employer. For example, if an individual who is participating in a qualifying retirement plan in Canada performs services for a limited period of time in the United States for a U.S. subsidiary of a Canadian company, a contribution to the Canadian plan by the parent company in Canada that is treated under U.S. law as a contribution by the U.S. subsidiary would be covered by the rule.

The amount of the allowable deduction is to be determined under the laws of the home State. Thus, where the United States is the home State, the amount of the deduction that is allowable in Canada will be subject to the limitations of Code section 404 (including the Code section 401(a)(17) and 415 limitations). Where Canada is the home State, the amount of the deduction that is allowable in the United States is subject to the limitations specified in subsections 147(8), 147.1(8) and (9) and 147.2(1) of the *Income Tax Act*, as applicable.

Cross-border commuters

Paragraphs 10, 11, and 12 of Article XVIII address the case of a commuter who is a resident of one Contracting State (the "residence State") and performs services as an employee in the other Contracting State (the "services State") and is a member of a "qualifying retirement plan" (as defined in paragraph 15 of Article XVIII) in the services State. If certain requirements are satisfied, contributions made to, or benefits accrued under, the qualifying retirement plan by or on behalf of the individual will be deductible or excludible in computing the individual's income in the residence State.

In order for paragraph 10 to apply, the individual must perform services as an employee in the services State the remuneration from which is taxable in the services State and is borne by either an employer who is a resident of the services State or by a permanent establishment that the employer has in the services State. The contributions and benefits must be attributable to those services and must be made or accrued during the period in which the individual performs those services. In the case where the United States is the residence State, contributions will be deemed to have been made on the last day of the preceding taxable year if the payment is on account of such taxable year and is treated under U.S. law as a contribution made on the last day of the preceding taxable year.

Paragraph 10 states that it applies only to the extent that the contributions or benefits qualify for tax relief in the services State. Thus, the benefits granted in the residence State are available only to the extent that the contributions or benefits accrued qualify for relief in the services State. Where the United States is the services State, the amount of contributions that may be excluded under paragraph 10 is the U.S. dollar amount specified in Code section 415 or the U.S. dollar amount specified in Code section 402(g)(1) (as defined above) to the extent contributions are made from the employee's compensation. Where Canada is the services State, the amount of contributions that may be excluded from the employee's income under paragraph 10 is subject to the limitations specified in subsections 146(5), 147(8), 147.1(8) and (9) and 147.2(1) and (4) of the *Income Tax Act* and paragraph 8503(4)(*a*) of the Income Tax Regulations, as applicable.

However, paragraphs 11 and 12 further provide that the benefits granted under paragraph 10 by the residence State may not exceed certain benefits that would be allowable under the domestic law of the residence State.

Paragraph 11 provides that where Canada is the residence State, the amount of contributions otherwise allowable as a deduction under paragraph 10 may not exceed the individual's deduction limit for contributions to registered retirement savings plans (RRSPs) remaining after taking into account the amount of contributions to RRSPs deducted by the individual under the law of Canada for the year. The amount deducted by the individual under paragraph 10 will be taken into account in computing the individual's deduction limit for subsequent taxation years for contributions to RRSPs. This rule prevents double benefits for contributions to both an RRSP and a qualifying retirement plan in the United States with respect to the same services.

Paragraph 12 provides that if the United States is the residence State, the benefits granted to an individual under paragraph 10 may not exceed the benefits that would be allowed by the United States to its residents for contributions to, or benefits otherwise accrued under, a generally corresponding pension or retirement plan established in and recognized for tax purposes by the United States. For purposes of determining an individual's eligibility to participate in and receive tax benefits with respect to a pension or retirement plan or other retirement arrangement in the United States, contributions made to, or benefits accrued under, a qualifying retirement plan in Canada by or on behalf of the individual are treated as contributions or benefits under a generally corresponding pension or retirement plan established in and recognized for tax purposes by the United States. Thus, for example, the qualifying retirement plan in Canada would be taken into account for purposes of determining whether the individual is an "active participant" within the meaning of Code section 219(g)(5), with the result that the individual's ability to make deductible contributions to an individual retirement account in the United States would be limited.

Paragraph 10 does not address employer deductions because the employer is located in the services State and is already eligible for deductions under the domestic law of the services State.

U.S. citizens resident in Canada

Paragraphs 13 and 14 of Article XVIII address the special case of a U.S. citizen who is a resident of Canada (as determined under Article IV (Residence)) and who performs services as an employee in Canada and participates in a qualifying retirement plan (as defined in paragraph 15 of Article XVIII) in Canada. If certain requirements are satisfied, contributions made to, or benefits accrued under, a qualifying retirement plan in Canada by or on behalf of the U.S. citizen will be deductible or excludible in computing his or her taxable income in the United States. These provisions are generally consistent with paragraph 4 of Article 18 of the U.S. Model treaty.

In order for paragraph 13 to apply, the U.S. citizen must perform services as an employee in Canada the remuneration from which is taxable in Canada and is borne by an employer who is a resident of Canada or by a permanent establishment that the employer has in Canada. The contributions and benefits must be attributable to those services and must be made or accrued during the period in which the U.S. citizen performs those services. Contributions will be deemed to have been made on the last day of the preceding taxable year if the payment is on account of such taxable year and is treated under U.S. law as a contribution made on the last day of the preceding taxable year.

Paragraph 13 states that it applies only to the extent the contributions or benefits qualify for tax relief in Canada. However, paragraph 14 provides that the benefits granted under paragraph 13 may not exceed the benefits that would be allowed by the United States to its residents for contributions to, or benefits otherwise accrued under, a generally corresponding pension or retirement plan established in and recognized for tax purposes by the United States. Thus, the lower of the two limits applies. This rule ensures that a U.S. citizen living and working in Canada does not receive better U.S. treatment than a U.S. citizen living and working in the United States. The amount of contributions that may be excluded from the employee's income under paragraph 13 is the U.S. dollar amount specified in Code section 415 or the U.S. dollar amount specified in Code section 402(g)(1) (as defined above) to the extent contributions are made from the employee's compensation. In addition, pursuant to Code section 911(d)(6), an individual may not claim benefits under paragraph 13 with respect to services the remuneration for which is excluded from the individual's gross income under Code section 911(a).

For purposes of determining the individual's eligibility to participate in and receive tax benefits with respect to a pension or retirement plan or other retirement arrangement established in and recognized for tax purposes by the United States, contributions made to, or benefits accrued under, a qualifying retirement plan in Canada by or on behalf of the individual are treated as contributions or benefits under a generally corresponding pension or retirement plan established in and recognized for tax purposes by the United States. Thus, for example, the qualifying retirement plan in Canada would be taken into account for purposes of determining whether the individual is an "active participant" within the meaning of Code section 219(g)(5), with the result that the individual's ability to make deductible contributions to an individual retirement account in the United States would be limited.

Paragraph 13 does not address employer deductions because the employer is located in Canada and is already eligible for deductions under the domestic law of Canada.

Definition of "qualifying retirement plan"

Paragraph 15 of Article XVIII provides that for purposes of paragraphs 8 through 14, a "qualifying retirement plan" in a Contracting State is a trust, company, organization, or other arrangement that (a) is a resident of that State, generally exempt from income taxation in that State and operated primarily to provide pension or retirement benefits; (b) is not an individual arrangement in respect of which the individual's employer has no involvement; and (c) the competent authority of the other Contracting State agrees generally corresponds to a pension or retirement plan established in and recognized for tax purposes in that State. Thus, U.S. individual retirement accounts (IRAs) and Canadian registered retirement savings plans (RRSPs) are not treated as qualifying retirement plans unless addressed in paragraph 10 of the General Note (as discussed below). In addition, a Canadian retirement compensation arrangement (RCA) is not a qualifying retirement plan because it is not considered to be generally exempt from income taxation in Canada.

Paragraph 10 of the General Note provides that the types of Canadian plans that constitute qualifying retirement plans for purposes of paragraph 15 include the following and any identical or substantially similar plan that is established pursuant to legislation introduced after the date of signature of the Protocol (September 21, 2007): registered pension plans under section 147.1 of the *Income Tax Act*, registered retirement savings plans under section 146 that are part of a group arrangement described in subsection 204.2(1.32), deferred profit sharing plans under section 147, and any registered retirement savings plan under section 146, or registered retirement income fund under section 146.3, that is funded exclusively by rollover contributions from one or more of the preceding plans.

Paragraph 10 of the General Note also provides that the types of U.S. plans that constitute qualifying retirement plans for purposes of paragraph 15 include the following and any identical or substantially similar plan that is established pursuant to legislation introduced after the date of signature of the Protocol (September 21, 2007): qualified plans under Code section 401(a) (including Code section 401(k) arrangements), individual retirement plans that are part of a simplified employee pension plan that satisfies Code section 408(k), Code section 408(p) simple retirement accounts, Code section 403(a) qualified annuity plans, Code section 403(b) plans, Code section 457(g) trusts providing benefits under Code section 457(b) plans, the Thrift Savings Fund (Code section 7701(j)), and any individual retirement account under Code section 408(a) that is funded exclusively by rollover contributions from one or more of the preceding plans.

If a particular plan in one Contracting State is of a type specified in paragraph 10 of the General Note with respect to paragraph 15 of Article XVIII, it will not be necessary for taxpayers to obtain a determination from the competent authority of the other Contracting State that the plan generally corresponds to a pension or retirement plan established in and recognized for tax purposes in that State. A taxpayer who believes a particular plan in one Contracting State that is not described in paragraph 10 of the General Note nevertheless satisfies the requirements of paragraph 15 may request a determination from the competent authority of the other Contracting State that the plan generally corresponds to a pension or retirement plan established in and recognized for tax purposes in that State. In the case of the United States, such a determination must be requested under Revenue Procedure 2006-54, 2006-49 I.R.B. 655 (or any applicable analogous provision). In the case of Canada, the current version of Information Circular 71-17 provides guidance on obtaining assistance from the Canadian competent authority.

Source rule

Paragraph 16 of Article XVIII provides that a distribution from a pension or retirement plan that is reasonably attributable to a contribution or benefit for which a benefit was allowed pursuant to paragraph 8, 10, or 13 of Article XVIII will be deemed to arise in the Contracting State in which the plan is established. This ensures that the Contracting State in which the plan is established will have the right to tax the gross amount of the distribution under subparagraph 2(*a*) of Article XVIII, even if a portion of the services to which the distribution relates were not performed in such Contracting State.

Partnerships

Paragraph 17 of Article XVIII provides that paragraphs 8 through 16 of Article XVIII apply, with such modifications as the circumstances require, as though the relationship between a partnership that carries on a business, and an individual who is a member of the partnership, were that of employer and employee. This rule is needed because paragraphs 8, 10, and 13, by their terms, apply only with respect to contributions made to, or benefits accrued under, qualifying retirement plans by or on behalf of individuals who perform services as an employee. Thus, benefits are not available with respect to retirement plans for self-employed individuals, who may be deemed under U.S. law to be employees for certain pension purposes. Paragraph 17 ensures that partners participating in a plan established by their partnership may be eligible for the benefits provided by paragraphs 8, 10, and 13.

Relationship to other Articles

Paragraphs 8, 10, and 13 of Article XVIII are not subject to the saving clause of paragraph 2 of Article XXIX (Miscellaneous Rules) by reason of the exception in subparagraph 3(*a*) of Article XXIX.

Article 14

Consistent with Articles 9 and 10 of the Protocol, Article 14 of the Protocol amends Article XIX (Government Service) of the Convention by deleting the reference to "Article XIV (Independent Personal Services)" and replacing such reference with the reference to "Article VII (Business Profits)" and by reflecting the new name of Article XV (Income from Employment).

Article 15

Article 15 of the Protocol replaces Article XX (Students) of the Convention. Article XX provides rules for host-country taxation of visiting students and business trainees. Persons who meet the tests of Article XX will be exempt from tax in the State that they are visiting with respect to designated classes of income. Several conditions must be satisfied in order for an individual to be entitled to the benefits of this Article.

First, the visitor must have been, either at the time of his arrival in the host State or immediately before, a resident of the other Contracting State.

Second, the purpose of the visit must be the full-time education or training of the visitor. Thus, if the visitor comes principally to work in the host State but also is a part-time student, he would not be entitled to the benefits of this Article, even with respect to any payments he may receive from abroad for his maintenance or education, and regardless of whether or not he is in a degree program. Whether a student is to be considered full-time will be determined by the rules of the educational institution at which he is studying.

The host State exemption in Article XX applies to payments received by the student or business trainee for the purpose of his maintenance, education or training that arise outside the host State. A payment will be considered to arise outside the host State if the payer is located outside the host State. Thus, if an employer from one of the Contracting States sends an employee to the other Contracting State for full-time training, the payments the trainee receives from abroad from his employer for his maintenance or training while he is present in the host State will be exempt from tax in the host State. Where appropriate, substance prevails over form in determining the identity of the payer. Thus, for example, payments made directly or indirectly by a U.S. person with whom the visitor is training, but which have been routed through a source outside the United States (*e.g.*, a foreign subsidiary), are not treated as arising outside the United States for this purpose.

In the case of an apprentice or business trainee, the benefits of Article XX will extend only for a period of one year from the time that the individual first arrives in the host country for the purpose of the individual's training. If, however, an apprentice or trainee remains in the host country for a second year, thus losing the benefits of the Article, he would not retroactively lose the benefits of the Article for the first year.

Relationship to other Articles

The saving clause of paragraph 2 of Article XXIX (Miscellaneous Rules) does not apply to Article XX with respect to an individual who neither is a citizen of the host State nor has been admitted for permanent residence there. The saving clause, however, does apply with respect to citizens and permanent residents of the host State. Thus, a U.S. citizen who is a resident of Canada and who visits the United States as a full-time student at an accredited university will not be exempt from U.S. tax on remittances from abroad that otherwise constitute U.S. taxable income. However, an individual who is not a U.S. citizen, and who visits the United States as a student and remains long enough to become a resident under U.S. law, but does not become a permanent resident (*i.e.*, does not acquire a green card), will be entitled to the full benefits of the Article.

Article 16

Article 16 of the Protocol revises Article XXI (Exempt Organizations) of the existing Convention.

Paragraph 1

Paragraph 1 amends Article XXI by renumbering paragraphs 4, 5, and 6 as 5, 6, and 7, respectively.

Paragraph 2

Paragraph 2 replaces paragraphs 1 through 3 of Article XXI with four new paragraphs. In general, the provisions of former paragraphs 1 through 3 have been retained.

New paragraph 1 provides that a religious, scientific, literary, educational, or charitable organization resident in a Contracting State shall be exempt from tax on income arising in the other Contracting State but only to the extent that such income is exempt from taxation in the Contracting State in which the organization is resident.

New paragraph 2 retains the provisions of former subparagraph 2(*a*), and provides that a trust, company, organization, or other arrangement that is resident in a Contracting State and operated exclusively to administer or provide pension, retirement or employee benefits or benefits for the self-employed under one or more funds or plans established to provide pension or retirement benefits or other employee benefits is exempt from taxation on dividend and interest income arising in the other Contracting State in a taxable year, if the income of such organization or other arrangement is generally exempt from taxation for that year in the Contracting State in which it is resident.

New paragraph 3 replaces and expands the scope of former subparagraph 2(*b*) Former subparagraph 2(*b*) provided that, subject to the provisions of paragraph 3 (new paragraph 4), a trust, company, organization or other arrangement that was a resident of a Contracting State, generally exempt from income taxation in that State and operated exclusively to earn income for the benefit of one or more organizations described in subparagraph 2(*a*) (new paragraph 2) was exempt from taxation on dividend and interest income arising in the other Contracting State in a taxable year. The Internal Revenue Service concluded in private letter rulings (PLR 200111027 and PLR 200111037) that a pooled investment fund that included as investors one or more organizations described in paragraph 1 could not qualify for benefits under former subparagraph 2(*b*). New paragraph 3 now allows organizations described in paragraph 1 to invest in pooled funds with trusts, companies, organizations, or other arrangements described in new paragraph 2.

Former subparagraph 2(*b*) did not exempt income earned by a trust, company or other arrangement for the benefit of religious, scientific, literary, educational or charitable organizations exempt from tax under paragraph 1. Therefore, the Protocol expands the scope of paragraph 3 to include such income.

As noted above with respect to Article X (Dividends), paragraph 3 of the General Note explains that distributions from Canadian income trusts and royalty trusts that are treated as dividends as a result of changes to Canada's law regarding taxation of income and royalty trusts shall be treated as dividends for the purposes of Article X. Accordingly, such distributions will also be entitled to the benefits of Article XXI.

New paragraph 4 replaces paragraph 3 and provides that the exemptions provided by paragraphs 1, 2, 3 do not apply with respect to the income of a trust, company, organization or other arrangement from carrying on a trade or business or from a related person, other than a person referred to in paragraph 1, 2 or 3. The term "related person" is not necessarily defined by paragraph 2 of Article IX (Related Person).

Article 17

Article 17 of the Protocol amends Article XXII (Other Income) of the Convention by adding a new paragraph 4. Article XXII generally assigns taxing jurisdiction over income not dealt with in the other articles (Articles VI through XXI) of the Convention.

New paragraph 4 provides a specific rule for residence State taxation of compensation derived in respect of a guarantee of indebtedness. New paragraph 4 provides that compensation derived by a resident of a Contracting State in respect of the provision of a guarantee of indebtedness shall be taxable only in that State, unless the compensation is business profits attributable to a permanent establishment situated in the other Contracting State, in which case the provisions of Article VII (Business Profits) shall apply. The clarification that Article VII shall apply when the compensation is considered business profits was included at the request of the United States. Compensation paid to a financial services entity to provide a guarantee in the ordinary course of its business of providing such guarantees to customers constitutes business profits dealt with under the provisions of Article VII. However, provision of guarantees with respect to debt of related parties is ordinarily not an independent economic undertaking that would generate business profits, and thus compensation in respect of such related-party guarantees is, in most cases, covered by Article XXII.

Article 18

Article 18 of the Protocol amends paragraph 2 of Article XXIII (Capital) of the Convention by deleting language contained in that paragraph consistent with the changes made by Article 9 of the Protocol.

Article 19

Article 19 of the Protocol deletes subparagraph 2(*b*) of Article XXIV (Elimination of Double Taxation) of the Convention and replaces it with a new subparagraph.

New subparagraph 2(*b*) allows a Canadian company receiving a dividend from a U.S. resident company of which it owns at least 10 percent of the voting stock, a credit against Canadian income tax of the appropriate amount of income tax paid or accrued to the United States by the dividend paying company with respect to the profits out of which the dividends are paid. The third Protocol to the Convention, signed March 17, 1995, had amended subparagraph (*b*) to allow a Canadian company to deduct in computing its Canadian taxable income any dividend received by it out of the exempt surplus of a foreign affiliate which is a resident of the United States. This change is consistent with current Canadian tax treaty practice: it does not indicate any present intention to change Canada's "exempt surplus" rules, and those rules remain in effect.

Article 20

Article 20 of the Protocol revises Article XXV (Non-Discrimination) of the existing Convention to bring that Article into closer conformity to U.S. tax treaty policy.

Paragraphs 1 and 2

Paragraph 1 replaces paragraph 1 of Article XXV of the existing Convention. New paragraph 1 provides that a national of one Contracting State may not be subject to taxation or connected requirements in the other Contracting State that are more burdensome than the taxes and connected requirements imposed upon a national of that other State in the same circumstances. The OECD Model would prohibit taxation that is "other than or more burdensome" than that imposed on U.S. persons. Paragraph 1 omits the words "other than or" because the only relevant question under this provision should be whether the requirement imposed on a national of the other Contracting State is more burdensome. A requirement may be different from the requirements imposed on U.S. nationals without being more burdensome.

The term "national" in relation to a Contracting State is defined in subparagraph 1(*k*) of Article III (General Definitions). The term includes both individuals and juridical persons. A national of a Contracting State is afforded protection under this paragraph even if the national is not a resident of either Contracting State. Thus, a U.S. citizen who is resident in a third country is entitled, under this paragraph, to the same treatment in Canada as a national of Canada in the same or similar circumstances (i.e., one who is resident in a third State).

Whether or not the two persons are both taxable on worldwide income is a significant circumstance for this purpose. For this reason, paragraph 1 specifically refers to taxation or any requirement connected therewith, particularly with respect to taxation on worldwide income, as relevant circumstances. This language means that the United States is not obliged to apply the same taxing regime to a national of Canada who is not resident in the United States as it applies to a U.S. national who is not resident in the United States. U.S. citizens who are not resident in the United States but who are, nevertheless, subject to U.S. tax on their worldwide income are not in the same circumstances with respect to U.S. taxation as citizens of Canada who are not U.S. residents. Thus, for example, Article XXV would not entitle a national of Canada residing in a third country to taxation at graduated rates on U.S.-source dividends or other investment income that applies to a U.S. citizen residing in the same third country.

Because of the increased coverage of paragraph 1 with respect to the treatment of nationals wherever they are resident, paragraph 2 of this Article no longer has application, and therefore has been omitted.

Paragraph 3

Paragraph 3 makes changes to renumbered paragraph 3 of Article XXV in order to conform with Article 10 of the Protocol by deleting the reference to "Article XV (Dependent Personal Services)" and replacing it with a reference to "Article XV (Income from Employment)."

Article 21

Paragraph 1 of Article 21 of the Protocol replaces paragraph 6 of Article XXVI (Mutual Agreement Procedure) of the Convention with new paragraphs 6 and 7. New paragraphs 6 and 7 provide a mandatory binding arbitration proceeding (Arbitration Proceeding). The Arbitration Note details additional rules and procedures that apply to a case considered under the arbitration provisions.

New paragraph 6 provides that a case shall be resolved through arbitration when the competent authorities have endeavored but are unable through negotiation to reach a complete agreement regarding a case and the following three conditions are satisfied. First, tax returns have been filed with at least one of the Contracting States with respect to the taxable years at issue in the case. Second, the case (i) involves the application of one or more Articles that the competent authorities have agreed in an exchange of notes shall be the subject of arbitration and is not a case that the competent authorities agree before the date on which an Arbitration Proceeding would otherwise have begun, is not suitable for determination by arbitration; or (ii) is a case that the competent authorities agree is suitable for determination by arbitration. Third, all concerned persons and their authorized representatives agree, according to the provisions of subparagraph 7(*d*), not to disclose to any other person any information received during the course of the Arbitration Proceeding from either Contracting State or the arbitration board, other than the determination of the board (confidentiality agreement). The confidentiality agreement may also be executed by any concerned person that has the legal authority to bind any other concerned person on the matter. For example, a parent corporation with the legal authority to bind its subsidiary with respect to confidentiality may execute a comprehensive confidentiality agreement on its own behalf and that of its subsidiary.

The United States and Canada have agreed in the Arbitration Note to submit cases regarding the application of one or more of the following Articles to mandatory binding arbitration under the provisions of paragraphs 6 and 7 of Article XXVI: IV (Residence), but only insofar as it relates to the residence of a natural person, V (Permanent Establishment), VII (Business Profits), IX (Related Persons), and XII (Royalties) (but only (i) insofar as Article XII might apply in transactions involving related persons to whom Article IX might apply, or (ii) to an allocation of amounts between royalties that are taxable under paragraph 2 thereof and royalties that are exempt under paragraph 3 thereof). The competent authorities may, however, agree, before the date on which an Arbitration Proceeding would otherwise have begun, that a particular case is not suitable for arbitration.

New paragraph 7 provides six subparagraphs that detail the general rules and definitions to be used in applying the arbitration provisions.

Subparagraph 7(*a*) provides that the term "concerned person" means the person that brought the case to competent authority for consideration under Article XXVI (Mutual Agreement Procedure) and includes all other persons, if any, whose tax liability to either Contracting State may be directly affected by a mutual agreement arising from that consideration. For example, a concerned person does not only include a U.S. corporation that brings a transfer pricing case with respect to a transaction entered into with its Canadian subsidiary for resolution to the U.S. competent authority, but also the Canadian subsidiary, which may have a correlative adjustment as a result of the resolution of the case.

Subparagraph 7(*c*) provides that an Arbitration Proceeding begins on the later of two dates: two years from the "commencement date" of the case (unless the competent authorities have previously agreed to a different date), or the earliest date upon which all concerned persons have entered into a confidentiality agreement and the agreements have been received by both competent authorities. The "commencement date" of the case is defined by subparagraph 7(*b*) as the earliest date the information necessary to undertake substantive consideration for a mutual agreement has been received by both competent authorities.

Paragraph 16 of the Arbitration Note provides that each competent authority will confirm in writing to the other competent authority and to the concerned persons the date of its receipt of the information necessary to undertake substantive consideration for a mutual agreement. In the case of the United States, this information is (i) the information that must be submitted to the U.S. competent authority under Section 4.05 of Rev. Proc. 2006-54, 2006-49 I.R.B. 1035 (or any applicable successor publication), and (ii) for cases initially submitted as a request for an Advance Pricing Agreement, the information that must be submitted to the Internal Revenue Service under Rev. Proc. 2006-9, 2006-2 I.R.B. 278 (or any applicable successor publication). In the case of Canada, this information is the information required to be submitted to the Canadian competent authority under Information Circular 71-17 (or any applicable successor publication). The information shall not be considered received until both competent authorities have received copies of all materials submitted to either Contracting State by the concerned person(s) in connection with the mutual agreement procedure. It is understood that confirmation of the "information necessary to undertake substantive consideration for a mutual agreement" is envisioned to ordinarily occur within 30 days after the necessary information is provided to the competent authority.

The Arbitration Note also provides for several procedural rules once an Arbitration Proceeding under paragraph 6 of Article XXVI ("Proceeding") has commenced, but the competent authorities may modify or supplement these rules as necessary. In addition, the arbitration board may adopt any procedures necessary for the conduct of its business, provided the procedures are not inconsistent with any provision of Article XXVI of the Convention.

Paragraph 5 of the Arbitration Note provides that each Contracting State has 60 days from the date on which the Arbitration Proceeding begins to send a written communication to the other Contracting State appointing one member of the arbitration board. Within 60 days of the date the second of such communications is sent, these two board members will appoint a third member to serve as the chair of the board. It is agreed that this third member ordinarily should not be a citizen of either of the Contracting States.

In the event that any members of the board are not appointed (including as a result of the failure of the two members appointed by the Contracting States to agree on a third member) by the requisite date, the remaining members are appointed by the highest ranking member of the Secretariat at the Centre for Tax Policy and Administration of the Organisation for Economic Co-operation and Development (OECD) who is not a citizen of either Contracting State, by written notice to both Contracting States within 60 days of the date of such failure.

Paragraph 7 of the Arbitration Note establishes deadlines for submission of materials by the Contracting States to the arbitration board. Each competent authority has 60 days from the date of appointment of the chair to submit a Proposed Resolution describing the proposed disposition of the specific monetary amounts of income, expense or taxation at issue in the case, and a supporting Position Paper. Copies of each State's submissions are to be provided by the board to the other Contracting State on the date the later of the submissions is submitted to the board. Each of the Contracting States may submit a Reply Submission to the board within 120 days of the appointment of the chair to address points raised in the other State's Proposed Resolution or Position Paper. If one Contracting State fails to submit a Proposed Resolution within the requisite time, the Proposed Resolution of the other Contracting State is deemed to be the determination of the arbitration board. Additional information may be supplied to the arbitration board by a Contracting State only at the request of the arbitration board. The board will provide copies of any such requested information, along with the board's request, to the other Contracting State on the date the request is made or the response is received.

All communication with the board is to be in writing between the chair of the board and the designated competent authorities with the exception of communication regarding logistical matters.

In making its determination, the arbitration board will apply the following authorities as necessary: (i) the provisions of the Convention, (ii) any agreed commentaries or explanation of the Contracting States concerning the Convention as amended, (iii) the laws of the Contracting States to the extent they are not inconsistent with each other, and (iv) any OECD Commentary, Guidelines or Reports regarding relevant analogous portions of the OECD Model Tax Convention.

The arbitration board must deliver a determination in writing to the Contracting States within six months of the appointment of the chair. The determination must be one of the two Proposed Resolutions submitted by the Contracting States. The determination shall provide a determination regarding only the amount of income, expense or tax reportable to the Contracting States. The determination has no precedential value and consequently the rationale behind a board's determination would not be beneficial and shall not be provided by the board.

Paragraph 11 of the Arbitration Note provides that, unless any concerned person does not accept the decision of the arbitration board, the determination of the board constitutes a resolution by mutual agreement under Article XXVI and, consequently, is binding on both Contracting States. Each concerned person must, within 30 days of receiving the determination from the competent authority to which the case was first presented, advise that competent authority whether the person accepts the determination. The failure to advise the competent authority within the requisite time is considered a rejection of the determination. If a determination is rejected, the case cannot be the subject of a subsequent MAP procedure on the same issue(s) determined by the panel, including a subsequent Arbitration Proceeding. After the commencement of an Arbitration Proceeding but before a decision of the board has been accepted by all concerned persons, the competent authorities may reach a mutual agreement to resolve the case and terminate the Proceeding.

For purposes of the Arbitration Proceeding, the members of the arbitration board and their staffs shall be considered "persons or authorities" to whom information may be disclosed under Article XXVII (Exchange of Information). The Arbitration Note provides that all materials prepared in the course of, or relating to, the Arbitration Proceeding are considered information exchanged between the Contracting States. No information relating to the Arbitration Proceeding or the board's determination may be disclosed by members of the arbitration board or their staffs or by either competent authority, except as permitted by the Convention and the domestic laws of the Contracting States. Members of the arbitration board and their staffs must agree in statements sent to each of the Contracting States in confirmation of their appointment to the arbitration board to abide by and be subject to the confidentiality and nondisclosure provisions of Article XXVII of the Convention and the applicable domestic laws of the Contracting States, with the most restrictive of the provisions applying.

The applicable domestic law of the Contracting States determines the treatment of any interest or penalties associated with a competent authority agreement achieved through arbitration.

In general, fees and expenses are borne equally by the Contracting States, including the cost of translation services. However, meeting facilities, related resources, financial management, other logistical support, and general and administrative coordination of the Arbitration Proceeding will be provided, at its own cost, by the Contracting State that initiated the Mutual Agreement Procedure. The fees and expenses of members of the board will be set in accordance with the International Centre for Settlement of Investment Disputes (ICSID) Schedule of Fees for arbitrators (in effect on the date on which the arbitration board proceedings begin). All other costs are to be borne by the Contracting State that incurs them. Since arbitration of MAP cases is intended to assist taxpayers in resolving a governmental difference of opinion regarding the taxation of their income, and is merely an extension of the competent authority process, no fees will be chargeable to a taxpayer in connection with arbitration.

Article 22

Article 22 of the Protocol amends Article XXVI A (Assistance in Collection) of the existing Convention. Article XXVI A sets forth provisions under which the United States and Canada have agreed to assist each other in the collection of taxes.

Paragraph 1

Paragraph 1 replaces subparagraph 8(*a*) of Article XXVI A. In general, new subparagraph 8(*a*) provides the circumstances under which no assistance is to be given under the Article for a claim in respect of an individual taxpayer. New subparagraph 8(*a*) contains language that is in substance the same as subparagraph 8(*a*) of Article XXVI A of the existing Convention. However, the revised subparagraph also provides that no assistance in collection is to be given for a revenue claim from a taxable period that ended before November 9, 1995 in respect of an individual taxpayer, if the taxpayer became a citizen of the requested State at any time before November 9, 1995 and is such a citizen at the time the applicant State applies for collection of the claim.

The additional language is intended to avoid the potentially discriminating application of former subparagraph 8(*a*) as applied to persons who were not citizens of the requested State in the taxable period to which a particular collection request related, but who became citizens of the requested State at a time prior to the entry into force of Article XXVI A as set forth in the third protocol signed March 17, 1995. New subparagraph 8(*a*) addresses this situation by treating the citizenship of a person in the requested State at anytime prior to November 9, 1995 as comparable to citizenship in the requested State during the period for which the claim for assistance relates if 1) the person is a citizen of the requested state at the time of the request for assistance in collection, and 2) the request relates to a taxable period ending prior to November 9, 1995. As is provided in subparagraph 3(g) of Article 27, this change will have effect for revenue claims finally determined after November 9, 1985, the effective date of the adoption of collection assistance in the third protocol signed March 17, 1995.

Paragraph 2

Paragraph 2 replaces paragraph 9 of Article XXVI A of the Convention. Under paragraph 1 of Article XXVI A, each Contracting State generally agrees to lend assistance and support to the other in the collection of revenue claims. The term "revenue claim" is defined in paragraph 1 to include all taxes referred to in paragraph 9 of the Article, as well as interest, costs, additions to such taxes, and civil penalties. New paragraph 9 provides that, notwithstanding the provisions of Article II (Taxes Covered) of the Convention, Article XXVI A shall apply to all categories of taxes collected, and to contributions to social security and employment insurance premiums levied, by or on behalf of the Government of a Contracting State. Prior to the Protocol, paragraph 9 did not contain a specific reference to contributions to social security and employment insurance premiums. Although the prior language covered U.S. federal social security and unemployment taxes, the language did not cover Canada's social security (*e.g., Canada Pension Plan*) and employment insurance programs, contributions to which are not considered taxes under Canadian law and therefore would not otherwise have come within the scope of the paragraph.

Article 23

Article 23 of the Protocol replaces Article XXVII (Exchange of Information) of the Convention.

Paragraph 1 of Article XXVII

New paragraph 1 of Article XXVII is substantially the same as paragraph 1 of Article XXVII of the existing Convention. Paragraph 1 authorizes the competent authorities to exchange information as may be relevant for carrying out the provisions of the Convention or the domestic laws of Canada and the United States concerning taxes covered by the Convention, insofar as the taxation under those domestic laws is not contrary to the Convention. New paragraph 1 changes the phrase "is relevant" to "may be relevant" to clarify that the language incorporates the standard in Code section 7602 which authorizes the Internal Revenue Service to examine "any books, papers, records, or other data which *may be relevant* or material." (Emphasis added.) In *United States v. Arthur Young & Co.*, 465 U.S. 805, 814 (1984), the Supreme Court stated that "the language 'may be' reflects Congress's express intention to allow the Internal Revenue Service to obtain 'items of even *potential* relevance to an ongoing investigation, without reference to its admissibility.'" (Emphasis in original.) However, the language "may be" would not support a request in which a Contracting State simply asked for information regarding all bank accounts maintained by residents of that Contracting State in the other Contracting State, or even all accounts maintained by its residents with respect to a particular bank.

The authority to exchange information granted by paragraph 1 is not restricted by Article I (Personal Scope), and thus need not relate solely to persons otherwise covered by the Convention. Under paragraph 1, information may be exchanged for use in all phases of the taxation process including assessment, collection, enforcement or the determination of appeals. Thus, the competent authorities may request and provide information for cases under examination or criminal investigation, in collection, on appeals, or under prosecution.

Any information received by a Contracting State pursuant to the Convention is to be treated as secret in the same manner as information obtained under the tax laws of that State. Such information shall be disclosed only to persons or authorities, including courts and administrative bodies, involved in the assessment or collection of, the administration and enforcement in respect of, or the determination of appeals in relation to, the taxes covered by the Convention and the information may be used by such persons only for such purposes. (In accordance with paragraph 4, for the purposes of this Article the Convention applies to a broader range of taxes than those covered specifically by Article II (Taxes Covered)). Although the information received by persons described in paragraph 1 is to be treated as secret, it may be disclosed by such persons in public court proceedings or in judicial decisions.

Paragraph 1 also permits, however, a Contracting State to provide information received from the other Contracting State to its states, provinces, or local authorities, if it relates to a tax imposed by that state, province, or local authority that is substantially similar to a national-level tax covered under Article II (Taxes Covered). This provision does not authorize a Contracting State to request information on behalf of a state, province, or local authority. Paragraph 1 also authorizes the competent authorities to release information to any arbitration panel that may be established under the provisions of new paragraph 6 of Article XXVI (Mutual Agreement Procedure). Any information provided to a state, province, or local authority or to an arbitration panel is subject to the same use and disclosure provisions as is information received by the national Governments and used for their purposes.

The provisions of paragraph 1 authorize the U.S. competent authority to continue to allow legislative bodies, such as the tax-writing committees of Congress and the Government Accountability Office to examine tax return information received from Canada when such bodies or offices are engaged in overseeing the administration of U.S. tax laws or a study of the administration of U.S. tax laws pursuant to a directive of Congress. However, the secrecy requirements of paragraph 1 must be met.

It is contemplated that Article XXVII will be utilized by the competent authorities to exchange information upon request, routinely, and spontaneously.

Paragraph 2 of Article XXVII

New paragraph 2 conforms with the corresponding U.S. and OECD Model provisions. The substance of the second sentence of former paragraph 2 is found in new paragraph 6 of the Article, discussed below.

Paragraph 2 provides that if a Contracting State requests information in accordance with Article XXVII, the other Contracting State shall use its information gathering measures to obtain the requested information. The instruction to the requested State to "use its information gathering measures" to obtain the requested information communicates the same instruction to the requested State as the language of former paragraph 2 that stated that the requested State shall obtain the information "in the same way as if its own taxation was involved." Paragraph 2 makes clear that the obligation to provide information is limited by the provisions of paragraph 3, but that such limitations shall not be construed to permit a Contracting State to decline to obtain and supply information because it has no domestic tax interest in such information.

In the absence of such a paragraph, some taxpayers have argued that subparagraph 3(*a*) prevents a Contracting State from requesting information from a bank or fiduciary that the Contracting State does not need for its own tax purposes. This paragraph clarifies that paragraph 3 does not impose such a restriction and that a Contracting State is not limited to providing only the information that it already has in its own files.

Paragraph 3 of Article XXVII

New paragraph 3 is substantively the same as paragraph 3 of Article XXVII of the existing Convention. Paragraph 3 provides that the provisions of paragraphs 1 and 2 do not impose on Canada or the United States the obligation to carry out administrative measures at variance with the laws and administrative practice of either State; to supply information which is not obtainable under the laws or in the normal course of the administration of either State; or to supply information which would disclose any trade, business, industrial, commercial, or professional secret or trade process, or information the disclosure of which would be contrary to public policy.

Thus, a requesting State may be denied information from the other State if the information would be obtained pursuant to procedures or measures that are broader than those available in the requesting State. However, the statute of limitations of the Contracting State making the request for information should govern a request for information. Thus, the Contracting State of which the request is made should attempt to obtain the information even if its own statute of limitations has passed. In many cases, relevant information will still exist in the business records of the taxpayer or a third party, even though it is no longer required to be kept for domestic tax purposes.

While paragraph 3 states conditions under which a Contracting State is not obligated to comply with a request from the other Contracting State for information, the requested State is not precluded from providing such information, and may, at its discretion, do so subject to the limitations of its internal law.

As discussed with respect to paragraph 2, in no case shall the limitations in paragraph 3 be construed to permit a Contracting State to decline to obtain information and supply information because it has no domestic tax interest in such information.

Paragraph 4 of Article XXVII

The language of new paragraph 4 is substantially similar to former paragraph 4. New paragraph 4, however, consistent with new paragraph 1, discussed above, replaces the words "is relevant" with "may be relevant" in subparagraph 4(b).

Paragraph 4 provides that, for the purposes of Article XXVII, the Convention applies to all taxes imposed by a Contracting State, and to other taxes to which any other provision of the Convention applies, but only to the extent that the information may be relevant for the purposes of the application of that provision.

Article XXVII does not apply to taxes imposed by political subdivisions or local authorities of the Contracting States. Paragraph 4 is designed to ensure that information exchange will extend to taxes of every kind (including, for example, estate, gift, excise, and value added taxes) at the national level in the United States and Canada.

Paragraph 5 of Article XXVII

New paragraph 5 conforms with the corresponding U.S. and OECD Model provisions. Paragraph 5 provides that a Contracting State may not decline to provide information because that information is held by a financial institution, nominee or person acting in an agency or fiduciary capacity. Thus, paragraph 5 would effectively prevent a Contracting State from relying on paragraph 3 to argue that its domestic bank secrecy laws (or similar legislation relating to disclosure of financial information by financial institutions or intermediaries) override its obligation to provide information under paragraph 1. This paragraph also requires the disclosure of information regarding the beneficial owner of an interest in a person.

Paragraph 6 of Article XXVII

The substance of new paragraph 6 is similar to the second sentence of paragraph 2 of Article XXVII of the existing Convention. New paragraph 6 adopts the language of paragraph 6 of Article 26 (Exchange of Information and Administrative Assistance) of the U.S. Model. New paragraph 6 provides that the requesting State may specify the form in which information is to be provided (*e.g.*, depositions of witnesses and authenticated copies of original documents). The intention is to ensure that the information may be introduced as evidence in the judicial proceedings of the requesting State. The requested State should, if possible, provide the information in the form requested to the same extent that it can obtain information in that form under its own laws and administrative practices with respect to its own taxes.

Paragraph 7 of Article XXVII

New paragraph 7 is consistent with paragraph 8 of Article 26 (Exchange of Information and Administrative Assistance) of the U.S. Model. Paragraph 7 provides that the requested State shall allow representatives of the requesting State to enter the requested State to interview individuals and examine books and records with the consent of the persons subject to examination. Paragraph 7 was intended to reinforce that the administrations can conduct consensual tax examinations abroad, and was not intended to limit travel or supersede any arrangements or procedures the competent authorities may have previously had in place regarding travel for tax administration purposes.

Paragraph 13 of General Note

As is explained in paragraph 13 of the General Note, the United States and Canada understand and agree that the standards and practices described in Article XXVII of the Convention are to be in no respect less effective than those described in the Model Agreement on Exchange of Information on Tax Matters developed by the OECD Global Forum Working Group on Effective Exchange of Information.

Article 24

Article 24 amends Article XXIX (Miscellaneous Rules) of the Convention.

Paragraph 1

Paragraph 1 replaces paragraph 2 of Article XXIX of the existing Convention. New paragraph 2 is divided into two subparagraphs. In general, subparagraph 2(*a*) provides a "saving clause" pursuant to which the United States and Canada may each tax its residents, as determined under Article IV (Residence), and the United States may tax its citizens and companies, including those electing to be treated as domestic corporations (*e.g.* under Code section 1504(d)), as if there were no convention between the United States and Canada with respect to taxes on income and capital. Subparagraph 2(*a*) contains language that generally corresponds to former paragraph 2, but omits certain language pertaining to former citizens, which are addressed in new subparagraph 2(*b*).

New subparagraph 2(*b*) generally corresponds to the provisions of former paragraph 2 addressing former citizens of the United States. However, new subparagraph 2(*b*) also includes a reference to former long-term residents of the United States. This addition, as well as other changes in subparagraph 2(*b*), brings the Convention in conformity with the U.S. taxation of former citizens and long-term residents under Code section 877.

Similar to subparagraph 2(*a*), new subparagraph 2(*b*) operates as a "saving clause" and provides that notwithstanding the other provisions of the Convention, a former citizen or former long-term resident of the United States, may, for a period of ten years following the loss of such status, be taxed in accordance with the laws of the United States with respect to income from sources within the United States (including income deemed under the domestic law of the United States to arise from such sources).

Paragraphs 11 and 12 of the General Note provide definitions based on Code section 877 that are relevant to the application of paragraph 2 of Article XXIX. Paragraph 11 of the General Note provides that the term "long-term resident" means any individual who is a lawful permanent resident of the United States in eight or more taxable years during the preceding 15 taxable years. In determining whether the eight- year threshold is met, one does not count any year in which the individual is treated as a resident of Canada under this Convention (or as a resident of any country other than the United States under the provisions of any other U.S. tax treaty), and the individual does not waive the benefits of such treaty applicable to residents of the other country. This understanding is consistent with how this provision is generally interpreted in U.S. tax treaties.

Paragraph 12 of the General Note provides that the phrase "income deemed under the domestic law of the United States to arise from such sources" as used in new subparagraph 2(*b*) includes gains from the sale or exchange of stock of a U.S. company or debt obligations of a U.S. person, the United States, a State, or a political subdivision thereof, or the District of Columbia, gains from property (other than stock or debt obligations) located in the United States, and, in certain cases, income or gain derived from the sale of stock of a non-U.S. company or a disposition of property contributed to such non-U.S. company where such company would be a controlled foreign corporation with respect to the individual if such person had continued to be a U.S. person. In addition, an individual who exchanges property that gives rise or would give rise to U.S.-source income for property that gives rise to foreign-source income will be treated as if he had sold the property that would give rise to U.S.-source income for its fair market value, and any consequent gain shall be deemed to be income from sources within the United States.

Paragraph 2

Paragraph 2 replaces subparagraph 3(*a*) of Article XXIX of the existing Convention. Paragraph 3 provides that, notwithstanding paragraph 2 of Article XXIX, the United States and Canada must respect specified provisions of the Convention in regard to certain persons, including residents and citizens. Therefore, subparagraph 3(*a*) lists certain paragraphs and Articles of the Convention that represent exceptions to the "saving clause" in all situations. New subparagraph 3(*a*) is substantially similar to former subparagraph 3(*a*), but now contains a reference to paragraphs 8, 10, and 13 of Article XVIII (Pensions and Annuities) to reflect the changes made to that article in paragraph 3 of Article 13 of the Protocol.

Article 25

Article 25 of the Protocol replaces Article XXIX A (Limitation on Benefits) of the existing Convention, which was added to the Convention by the Protocol done on March 17, 1995. Article XXIX A addresses the problem of "treaty shopping" by residents of third States by requiring, in most cases, that the person seeking benefits not only be a U.S. resident or Canadian resident but also satisfy other tests. For example, a resident of a third State might establish an entity resident in Canada for the purpose of deriving income from the United States and claiming U.S. treaty benefits with respect to that income. Article XXIX A limits the benefits granted by the United States or Canada under the Convention to those persons whose residence in the other Contracting State is not considered to have been motivated by the existence of the Convention. As replaced by the Protocol, new Article XXIX A is reciprocal, and many of the changes to the former paragraphs of Article XXIX A are made to effectuate this reciprocal application.

Absent Article XXIX A, an entity resident in one of the Contracting States would be entitled to benefits under the Convention, unless it were denied such benefits as a result of limitations under domestic law (*e.g.*, business purpose, substance-over-form, step transaction, or conduit principles or other anti-avoidance rules) applicable to a particular transaction or arrangement. As noted below in the explanation of paragraph 7, general anti-abuse provisions of this sort apply in conjunction with the Convention in both the United States and Canada. In the case of the United States, such anti-abuse provisions complement the explicit anti-treaty-shopping rules of Article XXIX A. While the anti-treaty-shopping rules determine whether a person has a sufficient nexus to Canada to be entitled to benefits under the Convention, the anti-abuse provisions under U.S. domestic law determine whether a particular transaction should be recast in accordance with the substance of the transaction.

Paragraph 1 of Article XXIX A

New paragraph 1 of Article XXIX A provides that, for the purposes of the application of the Convention, a "qualifying person" shall be entitled to all of the benefits of the Convention and, except as provided in paragraphs 3, 4, and 6, a person that is not a qualifying person shall not be entitled to any benefits of the Convention.

Paragraph 2 of Article XXIX A

New paragraph 2 lists a number of characteristics any one of which will make a United States or Canadian resident a qualifying person. The "look-through" principles introduced by the Protocol (e.g. paragraph 6 of Article IV (Residence)) are to be applied in conjunction with Article XXIX A. Accordingly, the provisions of Article IV shall determine the person who derives an item of income, and the objective tests of Article XXIX A shall be applied to that person to determine whether benefits shall be granted. The rules are essentially mechanical tests and are discussed below.

Individuals and governmental entities

Under new paragraph 2, the first two categories of qualifying persons are (1) natural persons resident in the United States or Canada (as listed in subparagraph 2(*a*)), and (2) the Contracting States, political subdivisions or local authorities thereof, and any agency or instrumentality of such Government, political subdivision or local authority (as listed in subparagraph 2(*b*)). Persons falling into these two categories are unlikely to be used, as the beneficial owner of income, to derive benefits under the Convention on behalf of a third-country person. If such a person receives income as a nominee on behalf of a third-country resident, benefits will be denied with respect to those items of income under the articles of the Convention that would otherwise grant the benefit, because of the requirements in those articles that the beneficial owner of the income be a resident of a Contracting State.

Publicly traded entities

Under new subparagraph 2(*c*), a company or trust resident in a Contracting State is a qualifying person if the company's principal class of shares, and any disproportionate class of shares, or the trust's units, or disproportionate interest in a trust, are primarily and regularly traded on one or more recognized stock exchanges. The term "recognized stock exchange" is defined in subparagraph 5(*f*) of the Article to mean, in the United States, the NASDAQ System and any stock exchange registered as a national securities exchange with the Securities and Exchange Commission, and, in Canada, any Canadian stock exchanges that are "prescribed stock exchanges" or "designated stock exchanges" under the *Income Tax Act*. These are, at the time of signature of the Protocol, the Montreal Stock Exchange, the Toronto Stock Exchange, and Tiers 1 and 2 of the TSX Venture Exchange. Additional exchanges may be added to the list of recognized exchanges by exchange of notes between the Contracting States or by agreement between the competent authorities.

If a company has only one class of shares, it is only necessary to consider whether the shares of that class meet the relevant trading requirements. If the company has more than one class of shares, it is necessary as an initial matter to determine which class or classes constitute the "principal class of shares." The term "principal class of shares" is defined in subparagraph 5(*e*) of the Article to mean the ordinary or common shares of the company representing the majority of the aggregate voting power and value of the company. If the company does not have a class of ordinary or common shares representing the majority of the aggregate voting power and value of the company, then the "principal class of shares" is that class or any combination of classes of shares that represents, in the aggregate, a majority of the voting power and value of the company. Although in a particular case involving a company with several classes of shares it is conceivable that more than one group of classes could be identified that account for more than 50% of the voting power and value of the shares of the company, it is only necessary for one such group to satisfy the requirements of this subparagraph in order for the company to be entitled to benefits. Benefits would not be denied to the company even if a second, non-qualifying, group of shares with more than half of the company's voting power and value could be identified.

A company whose principal class of shares is regularly traded on a recognized stock exchange will nevertheless not qualify for benefits under subparagraph 2(*c*) if it has a disproportionate class of shares that is not regularly traded on a recognized stock exchange. The term "disproportionate class of shares" is defined in subparagraph 5(*b*) of the Article. A company has a disproportionate class of shares if it has outstanding a class of shares which is subject to terms or other arrangements that entitle the holder to a larger portion of the company's income, profit, or gain in the other Contracting State than that to which the holder would be entitled in the absence of such terms or arrangements. Thus, for example, a company has a disproportionate class of shares if it has outstanding a class of "tracking stock" that pays dividends based upon a formula that approximates the company's return on its assets employed in the United States. Similar principles apply to determine whether or not there are disproportionate interests in a trust.

The following example illustrates the application of subparagraph 5(*b*).

Example. OCo is a corporation resident in Canada. OCo has two classes of shares: Common and Preferred. The Common shares are listed and regularly traded on a designated stock exchange in Canada. The Preferred shares have no voting rights and are entitled to receive dividends equal in amount to interest payments that OCo receives from unrelated borrowers in the United States. The Preferred shares are owned entirely by a single investor that is a resident of a country with which the United States does not have a tax treaty. The Common shares account for more than 50 percent of the value of OCo and for 100 percent of the voting power. Because the owner of the Preferred shares is entitled to receive payments corresponding to the U.S.-source interest income earned by OCo, the Preferred shares are a disproportionate class of shares. Because the Preferred shares are not primarily and regularly traded on a recognized stock exchange, OCo will not qualify for benefits under subparagraph 2(*c*).

The term "regularly traded" is not defined in the Convention. In accordance with paragraph 2 of Article III (General Definitions) and paragraph 1 of the General Note, this term will be defined by reference to the domestic tax laws of the State from which benefits of the Convention are sought, generally the source State. In the case of the United States, this term is understood to have the meaning it has under Treas. Reg. section 1.884-5(d)(4)(i)(B), relating to the branch tax provisions of the Code, as may be amended from time to time. Under these regulations, a class of shares is considered to be "regularly traded" if two requirements are met: trades in the class of shares are made in more than *de minimis* quantities on at least 60 days during the taxable year, and the aggregate number of shares in the class traded during the year is at least 10 percent of the average number of shares outstanding during the year. Sections 1.884-5(d)(4)(i)(A), (ii) and (iii) will not be taken into account for purposes of defining the term "regularly traded" under the Convention.

The regularly-traded requirement can be met by trading on one or more recognized stock exchanges. Therefore, trading may be aggregated for purposes of this requirement. Thus, a U.S. company could satisfy the regularly traded requirement through trading, in whole or in part, on a recognized stock exchange located in Canada. Authorized but unissued shares are not considered for purposes of this test.

The term "primarily traded" is not defined in the Convention. In accordance with paragraph 2 of Article III (General Definitions) and paragraph 1 of the General Note, this term will have the meaning it has under the laws of the State concerning the taxes to which the Convention applies, generally the source State. In the case of the United States, this term is understood to have the meaning it has under Treas. Reg. section 1.884-5(d)(3), as may be amended from time to time, relating to the branch tax provisions of the Code. Accordingly, stock of a corporation is "primarily traded" if the number of shares in the company's principal class of shares that are traded during the taxable year on all recognized stock exchanges exceeds the number of shares in the company's principal class of shares that are traded during that year on all other established securities markets.

Subject to the adoption by Canada of other definitions, the U.S. interpretation of "regularly traded" and "primarily traded" will be considered to apply, with such modifications as circumstances require, under the Convention for purposes of Canadian taxation.

Subsidiaries of publicly traded entities

Certain companies owned by publicly traded corporations also may be qualifying persons. Under subparagraph 2(*d*), a company resident in the United States or Canada will be a qualifying person, even if not publicly traded, if more than 50 percent of the vote and value of its shares, and more than 50 percent of the vote and value of each disproportionate class of shares, is owned (directly or indirectly) by five or fewer persons that are qualifying persons under subparagraph 2(*c*). In addition, each company in the chain of ownership must be a qualifying person. Thus, for example, a company that is a resident of Canada, all the shares of which are owned by another company that is a resident of Canada, would qualify for benefits of the Convention if the principal class of shares (and any disproportionate classes of shares) of the parent company are regularly and primarily traded on a recognized stock exchange. However, such a subsidiary would not qualify for benefits under subparagraph 2(*d*) if the publicly traded parent company were a resident of a third state, for example, and not a resident of the United States or Canada. Furthermore, if a parent company qualifying for benefits under subparagraph 2(*c*) indirectly owned the bottom-tier company through a chain of subsidiaries, each subsidiary in the chain, as an intermediate owner, must be a qualifying person in order for the bottom-tier subsidiary to meet the test in subparagraph 2(*d*).

Subparagraph 2(*d*) provides that a subsidiary can take into account ownership by as many as five companies, each of which qualifies for benefits under subparagraph 2(*c*) to determine if the subsidiary qualifies for benefits under subparagraph 2(*d*). For example, a Canadian company that is not publicly traded but that is owned, one-third each, by three companies, two of which are Canadian resident corporations whose principal classes of shares are primarily and regularly traded on a recognized stock exchange, will qualify under subparagraph 2(*d*).

By applying the principles introduced by the Protocol (e.g. paragraph 6 of Article IV) in the context of this rule, one "looks through" entities in the chain of ownership that are viewed as fiscally transparent under the domestic laws of the State of residence (other than entities that are resident in the State of source).

The 50-percent test under subparagraph 2(*d*) applies only to shares other than "debt substitute shares." The term "debt substitute shares" is defined in subparagraph 5(a) to mean shares defined in paragraph (*e*) of the definition in the Canadian *Income Tax Act* of "term preferred shares" (see subsection 248(1) of the *Income Tax Act*), which relates to certain shares received in debt-restructuring arrangements undertaken by reason of financial difficulty or insolvency. Subparagraph 5(*a*) also provides that the competent authorities may agree to treat other types of shares as debt substitute shares.

Ownership/base erosion test

Subparagraph 2(*e*) provides a two-part test under which certain other entities may be qualifying persons, based on ownership and lack of "base erosion." A company resident in the United States or Canada will satisfy the first of these tests if 50 percent or more of the vote and value of its shares and 50 percent or more of the vote and value of each disproportionate class of shares, in both cases not including debt substitute shares, is not owned, directly or indirectly, by persons other than qualifying persons. Similarly, a trust resident in the United States or Canada will satisfy this first test if 50 percent or more of its beneficial interests, and 50 percent or more of each disproportionate interest, is not owned, directly or indirectly, by persons other than qualifying persons. The wording of these tests is intended to make clear that, for example, if a Canadian company is more than 50 percent owned, either directly or indirectly (including cumulative indirect ownership through a chain of entities), by a U.S. resident corporation that is, itself, wholly owned by a third-country resident other than a qualifying person, the Canadian company would not pass the ownership test. This is because more than 50 percent of its shares is owned indirectly by a person (the third-country resident) that is not a qualifying person.

It is understood by the Contracting States that in determining whether a company satisfies the ownership test described in subparagraph 2(*e*)(i), a company, 50 percent of more of the aggregate vote and value of the shares of which and 50 percent or more of the vote and value of each disproportionate class of shares (in neither case including debt substitute shares) of which is owned, directly or indirectly, by a company described in subparagraph 2(*c*) will satisfy the ownership test of subparagraph 2(*e*)(i). In such case, no further analysis of the ownership of the company described in subparagraph 2(*c*) is required. Similarly, in determining whether a trust satisfies the ownership test described in subparagraph 2(*e*)(ii), a trust, 50 percent or more of the beneficial interest in which and 50 percent or more of each disproportionate interest in which, is owned, directly or indirectly, by a trust described in subparagraph (2)(*c*) will satisfy the ownership test of subparagraph (2)(*e*)(ii), and no further analysis of the ownership of the trust described in subparagraph 2(*c*) is required.

The second test of subparagraph 2(*e*) is the so-called "base erosion" test. A company or trust that passes the ownership test must also pass this test to be a qualifying person under this subparagraph. This test requires that the amount of expenses that are paid or payable by the entity in question, directly or indirectly, to persons that are not qualifying persons, and that are deductible from gross income (with both deductibility and gross income as determined under the tax laws of the State of residence of the company or trust), be less than 50 percent of the gross income of the company or trust. This test is applied for the fiscal period immediately preceding the period for which the qualifying person test is being applied. If it is the first fiscal period of the person, the test is applied for the current period.

The ownership/base erosion test recognizes that the benefits of the Convention can be enjoyed indirectly not only by equity holders of an entity, but also by that entity's obligees, such as lenders, licensors, service providers, insurers and reinsurers, and others. For example, a third-country resident could license technology to a Canadian-owned Canadian corporation to be sub-licensed to a U.S. resident. The U.S.-source royalty income of the Canadian corporation would be exempt from U.S. withholding tax under Article XII (Royalties) of the Convention. While the Canadian corporation would be subject to Canadian corporation income tax, its taxable income could be reduced to near zero as a result of the deductible royalties paid to the third-country resident. If, under a convention between Canada and the third country, those royalties were either exempt from Canadian tax or subject to tax at a low rate, the U.S. treaty benefit with respect to the U.S.-source royalty income would have flowed to the third-country resident at little or no tax cost, with no reciprocal benefit to the United States from the third country. The ownership/base erosion test therefore requires both that qualifying persons substantially own the entity and that the entity's tax base is not substantially eroded by payments (directly or indirectly) to nonqualifying persons.

For purposes of this subparagraph 2(*e*) and other provisions of this Article, the term "shares" includes, in the case of a mutual insurance company, any certificate or contract entitling the holder to voting power in the corporation. This is consistent with the interpretation of similar limitation on benefits provisions in other U.S. treaties. In Canada, the principles that are reflected in subsection 256(8.1) of the *Income Tax Act* will be applied, in effect treating memberships, policies or other interests in a corporation incorporated without share capital as representing an appropriate number of shares.

The look-through principles introduced by the Protocol (e.g. new paragraph 6 of Article IV) are to be taken into account when applying the ownership and base erosion provisions of Article XXIX A. Therefore, one "looks through" an entity that is viewed as fiscally transparent under the domestic laws of the residence State (other than entities that are resident in the source State) when applying the ownership/base erosion test. Assume, for example, that USCo, a company incorporated in the United States, wishes to obtain treaty benefits by virtue of the ownership and base erosion rule. USCo is owned by USLLC, an entity that is treated as fiscally transparent in the United States. USLLC in turn is wholly owned in equal shares by 10 individuals who are residents of the United States. Because the United States views USLLC as fiscally transparent, the 10 U.S. individuals shall be regarded as the owners of USCo for purposes of the ownership test. Accordingly, USCo would satisfy the ownership requirement of the ownership/base erosion test. However, if USLLC were instead owned in equal shares by four U.S. individuals and six individuals who are not residents of either the United States or Canada, USCo would not satisfy the ownership requirement. Similarly, for purposes of the base erosion test, deductible payments made to USLLC will be treated as made to USLLC's owners.

Other qualifying persons

Under new subparagraph 2(*f*), an estate resident in the United States or Canada is a qualifying person entitled to the benefits of the Convention.

New subparagraphs 2(*g*) and 2(*h*) specify the circumstances under which certain types of not-for-profit organizations will be qualifying persons. Subparagraph 2(*g*) provides that a not-for-profit organization that is resident in the United States or Canada is a qualifying person, and thus entitled to benefits, if more than half of the beneficiaries, members, or participants in the organization are qualifying persons. The term "not-for-profit organization" of a Contracting State is defined in subparagraph 5(*d*) of the Article to mean an entity created or established in that State that is generally exempt from income taxation in that State by reason of its not-for-profit status. The term includes charities, private foundations, trade unions, trade associations, and similar organizations.

New subparagraph 2(*h*) specifies that certain trusts, companies, organizations, or other arrangements described in paragraph 2 of Article XXI (Exempt Organizations) are qualifying persons. To be a qualifying person, the trust, company, organization or other arrangement must be established for the purpose of providing pension, retirement, or employee benefits primarily to individuals who are (or were, within any of the five preceding years) qualifying persons. A trust, company, organization, or other arrangement will be considered to be established for the purpose of providing benefits primarily to such persons if more than 50 percent of its beneficiaries, members, or participants are such persons. Thus, for example, a Canadian Registered Retirement Savings Plan ("RRSP") of a former resident of Canada who is working temporarily outside of Canada would continue to be a qualifying person during the period of the individual's absence from Canada or for five years, whichever is shorter. A Canadian pension fund established to provide benefits to persons employed by a company would be a qualifying person only if most of the beneficiaries of the fund are (or were within the five preceding years) individual residents of Canada or residents or citizens of the United States.

New subparagraph 2(*i*) specifies that certain trusts, companies, organizations, or other arrangements described in paragraph 3 of Article XXI (Exempt Organizations) are qualifying persons. To be a qualifying person, the beneficiaries of a trust, company, organization or other arrangement must be described in subparagraph 2(*g*) or 2(*h*).

The provisions of paragraph 2 are self-executing, unlike the provisions of paragraph 6, discussed below. The tax authorities may, of course, on review, determine that the taxpayer has improperly interpreted the paragraph and is not entitled to the benefits claimed.

Paragraph 3 of Article XXIX A

Paragraph 3 provides an alternative rule, under which a United States or Canadian resident that is not a qualifying person under paragraph 2 may claim benefits with respect to those items of income that are connected with the active conduct of a trade or business in its State of residence.

This is the so-called "active trade or business" test. Unlike the tests of paragraph 2, the active trade or business test looks not solely at the characteristics of the person deriving the income, but also at the nature of the person's activity and the connection between the income and that activity. Under the active trade or business test, a resident of a Contracting State deriving an item of income from the other Contracting State is entitled to benefits with respect to that income if that person (or a person related to that person under the principles of Code section 482, or in the case of Canada, section 251 of the *Income Tax Act*) is engaged in an active trade or business in the State where it is resident, the income in question is derived in connection with, or is incidental to, that trade or business, and the size of the active trade or business in the residence State is substantial relative to the activity in the other State that gives rise to the income for which benefits are sought. Further details on the application of the substantiality requirement are provided below.

Income that is derived in connection with, or is incidental to, the business of making or managing investments will not qualify for benefits under this provision, unless those investment activities are carried on with customers in the ordinary course of the business of a bank, insurance company, registered securities dealer, or deposit-taking financial institution.

Income is considered derived "in connection" with an active trade or business if, for example, the income-generating activity in the State is "upstream," "downstream," or parallel to that conducted in the other Contracting State. Thus, for example, if the U.S. activity of a Canadian resident company consisted of selling the output of a Canadian manufacturer or providing inputs to the manufacturing process, or of manufacturing or selling in the United States the same sorts of products that were being sold by the Canadian trade or business in Canada, the income generated by that activity would be treated as earned in connection with the Canadian trade or business. Income is considered "incidental" to a trade or business if, for example, it arises from the short-term investment of working capital of the resident in securities issued by persons in the State of source.

An item of income may be considered to be earned in connection with or to be incidental to an active trade or business in the United States or Canada even though the resident claiming the benefits derives the income directly or indirectly through one or more other persons that are residents of the other Contracting State. Thus, for example, a Canadian resident could claim benefits with respect to an item of income earned by a U.S. operating subsidiary but derived by the Canadian resident indirectly through a wholly-owned U.S. holding company interposed between it and the operating subsidiary. This language would also permit a resident to derive income from the other Contracting State through one or more residents of that other State that it does not wholly own. For example, a Canadian partnership in which three unrelated Canadian companies each hold a one-third interest could form a wholly-owned U.S. holding company with a U.S. operating subsidiary. The "directly or indirectly" language would allow otherwise unavailable treaty benefits to be claimed with respect to income derived by the three Canadian partners through the U.S. holding company, even if the partners were not considered to be related to the U.S. holding company under the principles of Code section 482.

As described above, income that is derived in connection with, or is incidental to, an active trade or business in a Contracting State, must pass the substantiality requirement to qualify for benefits under the Convention. The trade or business must be substantial in relation to the activity in the other Contracting State that gave rise to the income in respect of which benefits under the Convention are being claimed. To be considered substantial, it is not necessary that the trade or business be as large as the income-generating activity. The trade or business cannot, however, in terms of income, assets, or other similar measures, represent only a very small percentage of the size of the activity in the other State.

The substantiality requirement is intended to prevent treaty shopping. For example, a third-country resident may want to acquire a U.S. company that manufactures television sets for worldwide markets; however, since its country of residence has no tax treaty with the United States, any dividends generated by the investment would be subject to a U.S. withholding tax of 30 percent. Absent a substantiality test, the investor could establish a Canadian corporation that would operate a small outlet in Canada to sell a few of the television sets manufactured by the U.S. company and earn a very small amount of income. That Canadian corporation could then acquire the U.S. manufacturer with capital provided by the third-country resident and produce a very large number of sets for sale in several countries, generating a much larger amount of income. It might attempt to argue that the U.S.-source income is generated from business activities in the United States related to the television sales activity of the Canadian parent and that the dividend income should be subject to U.S. tax at the 5 per cent rate provided by Article X (Dividends) of the Convention. However, the substantiality test would not be met in this example, so the dividends would remain subject to withholding in the United States at a rate of 30 percent.

It is expected that if a person qualifies for benefits under one of the tests of paragraph 2, no inquiry will be made into qualification for benefits under paragraph 3. Upon satisfaction of any of the tests of paragraph 2, any income derived by the beneficial owner from the other Contracting State is entitled to treaty benefits. Under paragraph 3, however, the test is applied separately to each item of income.

Paragraph 4 of Article XXIX A

Paragraph 4 provides a limited "derivative benefits" test that entitles a company that is a resident of the United States or Canada to the benefits of Articles X (Dividends), XI (Interest), and XII (Royalties), even if the company is not a qualifying person and does not satisfy the active trade or business test of paragraph 3. In general, a derivative benefits test entitles the resident of a Contracting State to treaty benefits if the owner of the resident would have been entitled to the same benefit had the income in question been earned directly by that owner. To qualify under this paragraph, the company must satisfy both the ownership test in subparagraph 4(*a*) and the base erosion test of subparagraph 4(*b*).

Under subparagraph 4(*a*), the derivative benefits ownership test requires that the company's shares representing more than 90 percent of the aggregate vote and value of all of the shares of the company, and at least 50 percent of the vote and value of any disproportionate class of shares, in neither case including debt substitute shares, be owned directly or indirectly by persons each of whom is either (i) a qualifying person or (ii) another person that satisfies each of three tests. The three tests of subparagraph 4(*a*) that must be satisfied by these other persons are as follows:

First, the other person must be a resident of a third State with which the Contracting State that is granting benefits has a comprehensive income tax convention. The other person must be entitled to all of the benefits under that convention. Thus, if the person fails to satisfy the limitation on benefits tests, if any, of that convention, no benefits would be granted under this paragraph. Qualification for benefits under an active trade or business test does not suffice for these purposes, because that test grants benefits only for certain items of income, not for all purposes of the convention.

Second, the other person must be a person that would qualify for benefits with respect to the item of income for which benefits are sought under one or more of the tests of paragraph 2 or 3 of Article XXIX A, if the person were a resident of the Contracting State that is not providing benefits for the item of income and, for purposes of paragraph 3, the business were carried on in that State. For example, a person resident in a third country would be deemed to be a person that would qualify under the publicly-traded test of paragraph 2 of Article XXIX A if the principal class of its shares were primarily and regularly traded on a stock exchange recognized either under the Convention between the United States and Canada or under the treaty between the Contracting State granting benefits and the third country. Similarly, a company resident in a third country would be deemed to satisfy the ownership/base erosion test of paragraph 2 under this hypothetical analysis if, for example, it were wholly owned by an individual resident in that third country and the company's tax base were not substantially eroded by payments (directly or indirectly) to nonqualifying persons.

The third requirement is that the rate of tax on the item of income in respect of which benefits are sought must be at least as low under the convention between the person's country of residence and the Contracting State granting benefits as it is under the Convention.

Subparagraph 4(*b*) sets forth the base erosion test. This test requires that the amount of expenses that are paid or payable by the company in question, directly or indirectly, to persons that are not qualifying persons under the Convention, and that are deductible from gross income (with both deductibility and gross income as determined under the tax laws of the State of residence of the company), be less than 50 percent of the gross income of the company. This test is applied for the fiscal period immediately preceding the period for which the test is being applied. If it is the first fiscal period of the person, the test is applied for the current period. This test is qualitatively the same as the base erosion test of subparagraph 2(*e*).

Paragraph 5 of Article XXIX A

Paragraph 5 defines certain terms used in the Article. These terms were identified and discussed in connection with new paragraph 2, above.

Paragraph 6 of Article XXIX A

Paragraph 6 provides that when a resident of a Contracting State derives income from the other Contracting State and is not entitled to the benefits of the Convention under other provisions of the Article, benefits may, nevertheless be granted at the discretion of the competent authority of the other Contracting State. This determination can be made with respect to all benefits under the Convention or on an item by item basis. In making a determination under this paragraph, the competent authority will take into account all relevant facts and circumstances relating to the person requesting the benefits. In particular, the competent authority will consider the history, structure, ownership (including ultimate beneficial ownership), and operations of the person. In addition, the competent authority is to consider (1) whether the creation and existence of the person did not have as a principal purpose obtaining treaty benefits that would not otherwise be available to the person, and (2) whether it would not be appropriate, in view of the purpose of the Article, to deny benefits. If the competent authority of the other Contracting State determines that either of these two standards is satisfied, benefits shall be granted.

For purposes of implementing new paragraph 6, a taxpayer will be permitted to present his case to the competent authority for an advance determination based on a full disclosure of all pertinent information. The taxpayer will not be required to wait until it has been determined that benefits are denied under one of the other provisions of the Article. It also is expected that, if and when the competent authority determines that benefits are to be allowed, they will be allowed retroactively to the time of entry into force of the relevant provision of the Convention or the establishment of the structure in question, whichever is later (assuming that the taxpayer also qualifies under the relevant facts for the earlier period).

Paragraph 7 of Article XXIX A

New paragraph 7 is in substance similar to paragraph 7 of Article XXIX A of the existing Convention and clarifies the application of general anti-abuse provisions. New paragraph 7 provides that paragraphs 1 through 6 of Article XXIX A shall not be construed as limiting in any manner the right of a Contracting State to deny benefits under the Convention where it can reasonably be concluded that to do otherwise would result in an abuse of the provisions of the Convention. This provision permits a Contracting State to rely on general anti-avoidance rules to counter arrangements involving treaty shopping through the other Contracting State.

Thus, Canada may apply its domestic law rules to counter abusive arrangements involving "treaty shopping" through the United States, and the United States may apply its substance-over-form and anti-conduit rules, for example, in relation to Canadian residents. This principle is recognized by the OECD in the Commentaries to its Model Tax Convention on Income and on Capital, and the United States and Canada agree that it is inherent in the Convention. The statement of this principle explicitly in the Protocol is not intended to suggest that the principle is not also inherent in other tax conventions concluded by the United States or Canada.

Article 26

Article 26 of the Protocol replaces paragraphs 1 and 5 of Article XXIX B (Taxes Imposed by Reason of Death) of the Convention. In addition, paragraph 7 of the General Note provides certain clarifications for purposes of paragraphs 6 and 7 of Article XXIX B.

Paragraph 1

Paragraph 1 of Article XXIX B of the existing Convention generally addresses the situation where a resident of a Contracting State passes property by reason of the individual's death to an organization referred to in paragraph 1 of Article XXI (Exempt Organizations) of the Convention. The paragraph provided that the tax consequences in a Contracting State arising out of the passing of the property shall apply as if the organization were a resident of that State.

The Protocol replaces paragraph 1, and the changes set forth in new paragraph 1 are intended to specifically address questions that have arisen about the application of former paragraph 1 where property of an individual who is a resident of Canada passes by reason of the individual's death to a charitable organization in the United States that is not a "registered charity" under Canadian law. Under one view, paragraph 1 of Article XXIX B requires Canada to treat the passing of the property as a contribution to a "registered charity" and thus to allow all of the same deductions for Canadian tax purposes as if the U.S. charity had been a "registered charity" under Canadian law. Under another view, paragraph 6 of Article XXI (Exempt Organizations) of the Convention continues to limit the amount of the income tax charitable deduction in Canada to the individual's income arising in the United States. The changes set forth in new paragraph 1 are intended to provide relief from the Canadian tax on gain deemed recognized by reason of death that would otherwise give rise to Canadian tax when the individual passes the property to a charitable organization in the United States, but, for purposes of the separate Canadian income tax, do not eliminate the limitation under paragraph 6 of Article XXI on the amount of the deduction in Canada for the charitable donation to the individual's income arising in the United States.

As revised, paragraph 1 is divided into two subparagraphs. New subparagraph 1(*a*) applies where property of an individual who is a resident of the United States passes by reason of the individual's death to a qualifying exempt organization that is a resident of Canada. In such case, the tax consequences in the United States arising from the passing of such property apply as if the organization were a resident of the United States. A bequest by a U.S. citizen or U.S. resident (as defined for estate tax purposes under the Code) to an exempt organization generally is deductible for U.S. federal estate tax purposes under Code section 2055, without regard to whether the organization is a U.S. corporation. Thus, generally, the individual's estate will be entitled to a charitable deduction for Federal estate tax purposes equal to the value of the property transferred to the organization. Generally, the effect is that no Federal estate tax will be imposed on the value of the property.

New subparagraph 1(*b*) applies where property of an individual who is a resident of Canada passes by reason of the individual's death to a qualifying exempt organization that is a resident of the United States. In such case, for purposes of the Canadian capital gains tax imposed at death, the tax consequences arising out of the passing of the property shall apply as if the individual disposed of the property for proceeds equal to an amount elected on behalf of the individual. For this purpose, the amount elected shall be no less than the individual's cost of the property as determined for purposes of Canadian tax, and no greater than the fair market value of the property. The manner in which the individual's representative shall make this election shall be specified by the competent authority of Canada. Generally, in the event of a full exercise of the election under new subparagraph 1(*b*), no capital gains tax will be imposed in Canada by reason of the death with regard to that property.

New paragraph 1 does not address the situation in which a resident of one Contracting State bequeaths property with a situs in the other Contracting State to a qualifying exempt organization in the Contracting State of the decedent's residence. In such a situation, the other Contracting State may impose tax by reason of death, for example, if the property is real property situated in that State.

Paragraph 2

Paragraph 2 of Article 26 of the Protocol replaces paragraph 5 of Article XXIX B of the existing Convention. The provisions of new paragraph 5 relate to the operation of Canadian law. Because Canadian law requires both spouses to have been Canadian residents in order to be eligible for the rollover, these provisions are intended to provide deferral ("rollover") of the Canadian tax at death for certain transfers to a surviving spouse and to permit the Canadian competent authority to allow such deferral for certain transfers to a trust. For example, they would enable the competent authority to treat a trust that is a qualified domestic trust for U.S. estate tax purposes as a Canadian spousal trust as well for purposes of certain provisions of Canadian tax law and of the Convention. These provisions do not affect U.S. domestic law regarding qualified domestic trusts. Nor do they affect the status of U.S. resident individuals for any other purpose.

New paragraph 5 adds a reference to subsection 70(5.2) of the Canadian *Income Tax Act*. This change is needed because the rollover in respect of certain kinds of property is provided in that subsection. Further, new paragraph 5 adds a clause "and with respect to such property" near the end of the second sentence to make it clear that the trust is treated as a resident of Canada only with respect to its Canadian property.

For example, assume that a U.S. decedent with a Canadian spouse sets up a qualified domestic trust holding U.S. and Canadian real property, and that the decedent's executor elects, for Federal estate tax purposes, to treat the entire trust as qualifying for the Federal estate tax marital deduction. Under Canadian law, because the decedent is not a Canadian resident, Canada would impose capital gains tax on the deemed disposition of the Canadian real property immediately before death. In order to defer the Canadian tax that might otherwise be imposed by reason of the decedent's death, under new paragraph 5 of Article XXIX B, the competent authority of Canada shall, at the request of the trustee, treat the trust as a Canadian spousal trust with respect to the Canadian real property. The effect of such treatment is to defer the tax on the deemed distribution of the Canadian real property until an appropriate triggering event such as the death of the surviving spouse.

Paragraph 7 of the General Note

In addition to the foregoing, paragraph 7 of the General Note provides certain clarifications for purposes of paragraphs 6 and 7 of Article XXIX B. These clarifications ensure that tax credits will be available in cases where there are inconsistencies in the way the two Contracting States view the income and the property.

Subparagraph 7(*a*) of the General Note applies where an individual who immediately before death was a resident of Canada held at the time of death a share or option in respect of a share that constitutes property situated in the United States for the purposes of Article XXIX B and that Canada views as giving rise to employment income (for example, a share or option granted by an employer). The United States imposes estate tax on the share or option in respect of a share, while Canada imposes income tax on income from employment. Subparagraph 7(*a*) provides that for purposes of clause 6(*a*)(ii) of Article XXIX B, any employment income in respect of the share or option constitutes income from property situated in the United States. This provision ensures that the estate tax paid on the share or option in the United States will be allowable as a deduction from the Canadian income tax.

Subparagraph 7(*b*) of the General Note applies where an individual who immediately before death was a resident of Canada held at the time of death a registered retirement savings plan (RRSP) or other entity that is a resident of Canada and that is described in subparagraph 1(*b*) of Article IV (Residence) and such RRSP or other entity held property situated in the United States for the purposes of Article XXIX B. The United States would impose estate tax on the value of the property held by the RRSP or other entity (to the extent such property is subject to Federal estate tax), while Canada would impose income tax on a deemed distribution of the property in the RRSP or other entity. Subparagraph 7(*b*) provides that any income out of or under the entity in respect of the property is, for the purpose of subparagraph 6(*a*)(ii) of Article XXIX B, income from property situated in the United States. This provision ensures that the estate tax paid on the underlying property in the United States (if any) will be allowable as a deduction from the Canadian income tax.

Subparagraph 7(*c*) of the General Note applies where an individual who immediately before death was a resident or citizen of the United States held at the time of death an RRSP or other entity that is a resident of Canada and that is described in subparagraph 1(*b*) of Article IV (Residence). The United States would impose estate tax on the value of the property held by the RRSP or other entity, while Canada would impose income tax on a deemed distribution of the property in the RRSP or other entity. Subparagraph 7(*c*) provides that for the purpose of paragraph 7 of Article XXIX B, the tax imposed in Canada is imposed in respect of property situated in Canada. This provision ensures that the Canadian income tax will be allowable as a credit against the U.S. estate tax.

Article 27

Article 27 of the Protocol provides the entry into force and effective date of the provisions of the Protocol.

Paragraph 1

Paragraph 1 provides generally that the Protocol is subject to ratification in accordance with the applicable procedures in the United States and Canada. Further, the Contracting States shall notify each other by written notification, through diplomatic channels, when their respective applicable procedures have been satisfied.

Paragraph 2

The first sentence of paragraph 2 generally provides that the Protocol shall enter into force on the date of the later of the notifications referred to in paragraph 1, or January 1, 2008, whichever is later. The relevant date is the date on the second of these notification documents, and not the date on which the second notification is provided to the other Contracting State. The January 1, 2008 date is intended to ensure that the provisions of the Protocol will generally not be effective before that date.

Subparagraph 2(*a*) provides that the provisions of the Protocol shall have effect in respect of taxes withheld at source, for amounts paid or credited on or after the first day of the second month that begins after the date on which the Protocol enters into force. Further, subparagraph 2(*b*) provides that the Protocol shall have effect in respect of other taxes, for taxable years that begin after (or, if the later of the notifications referred to in paragraph 1 is dated in 2007, taxable years that begin in and after) the calendar year in which the Protocol enters into force. These provisions are generally consistent with the formulation in the U.S. Model treaty, with the exception that a parenthetical was added in subparagraph 2(*b*) to address the contingency that the written notifications provided pursuant to paragraph 1 may occur in the 2007 calendar year. Further, subparagraph 3(*d*) of Article 27 of the Protocol contains special provisions with respect to the taxation of cross-border interest payments that have effect for the first two calendar years that end after the date the Protocol enters into force. Therefore, during this period, cross-border interest payments are not subject to the effective date provisions of subparagraph 2(*a*).

Paragraph 3

Paragraph 3 sets forth exceptions to the general effective date rules set forth in paragraph 2 of Article 27 of the Protocol.

Dual corporate residence tie-breaker

Subparagraph 3(*a*) of Article 27 of the Protocol provides that paragraph 1 of Article 2 of the Protocol relating to Article IV (Residence) shall have effect with respect to corporate continuations effected after September 17, 2000. This date corresponds to a press release issued on September 18, 2000 in which the United States and Canada identified certain issues with respect to these transactions and stated their intention to negotiate a protocol that, if approved, would address the issues effective as of the date of the press release.

Certain payments through fiscally transparent entities

Subparagraph 3(*b*) of Article 27 of the Protocol provides that new paragraph 7 of Article IV (Residence) set forth in paragraph 2 of Article 2 of the Protocol shall have effect as of the first day of the third calendar year that ends after the Protocol enters into force.

Permanent establishment from the provision of services

Subparagraph 3(*c*) of Article 27 of the Protocol sets forth the effective date for the provisions of Article 3 of the Protocol, pertaining to Article V (Permanent Establishment) of the Convention. The provisions pertaining to Article V shall have effect as of the third taxable year that ends after the Protocol enters into force, but in no event shall it apply to include, in the determination of whether an enterprise is deemed to provide services through a permanent establishment under paragraph 9 of Article V of the Convention, any days of presence, services rendered, or gross active business revenues that occur or arise prior to January 1, 2010. Therefore, the provision will apply beginning no earlier than January 1, 2010 and shall not apply with regard to any presence, services or related revenues that occur or arise prior to that date.

Withholding rates on cross-border interest payments

Subparagraph 3(*d*) of Article 27 of the Protocol sets forth special effective date rules pertaining to Article 6 of the Protocol relating to Article XI (Interest) of the Convention. Article 6 of the Protocol sets forth a new Article XI of the Convention that provides for exclusive residence State taxation regardless of the relationship between the payer and the beneficial owner of the interest. Subparagraph 3(*d*), however, phases in the application of paragraph 1 of Article XI during the first two calendar years that end after the date the Protocol enters into force. During that period, paragraph 1 of Article XI of the Convention permits source State taxation of interest if the payer and the beneficial owner are related or deemed to be related by reason of paragraph 2 of Article IX (Related Persons) of the Convention ("related party interest"), and the interest would not otherwise be exempt under the provisions of paragraph 3 of Article XI as it read prior to the Protocol. However, subparagraph 3(*d*) also provides that the source State taxation on such related party interest is limited to 7 percent in the first calendar year that ends after entry into force of the Protocol and 4 percent in the second calendar year that ends after entry into force of the Protocol.

Subparagraph 3(*d*) makes clear that the provisions of the Protocol with respect to exclusive residence based taxation of interest when the payer and the beneficial owner are not related or deemed related ("unrelated party interest") applies for interest paid or credited during the first two calendar years that end after entry into force of the Protocol.

The withholding rate reductions for related party interest and exemptions for unrelated party interest will likely apply retroactively. For example, if the Protocol enters into force on June 30, 2008, paragraph 1 of Article XI, as it reads under subparagraph 3(*d*) of Article 27, will have the following effect during the first two calendar years. First, unrelated party interest that is paid or credited on or after January 1, 2008 will be exempt from taxation in the source State. Second, related party interest paid or credited on or after January 1, 2008 and before January 1, 2009, will be subject to source State taxation but at a rate not to exceed 7 percent of the gross amount of the interest. Third, related party interest paid or credited on or after January 1, 2009 and before January 1, 2010, will be subject to source State taxation but at a rate not to exceed 4 percent of the gross amount of the interest. Finally, all interest paid or credited after January 1, 2010, will be subject to the regular rules of Article XI without regard to subparagraph 3(*d*) of Article 27.

Further, the provisions of subparagraph 3(*d*) ensure that even with respect to circumstances where the payer and the beneficial owner are related or deemed related under the provisions of paragraph 2 of Article IX, the source State taxation of such cross-border interest shall be no greater than the taxation of such interest prior to the Protocol.

Gains

Subparagraph 3(*e*) of Article 27 of the Protocol provides the effective date for paragraphs 2 and 3 of Article 8 of this Protocol, which relate to the changes made to paragraphs 5 and 7 of Article XIII (Gains) of the Convention. The changes set forth in those paragraphs shall have effect with respect to alienations of property that occur (including, for greater certainty, those that are deemed under the law of a Contracting State to occur) after September 17, 2000. This date corresponds to the press release issued on September 18, 2000 which announced the intention of the United States and Canada to negotiate a protocol that, if approved, would incorporate the changes set forth in these paragraphs to coordinate the tax treatment of an emigrant's gains in the United States and Canada.

Arbitration

Subparagraph 3(*f*) of Article 27 of the Protocol pertains to Article 21 of the Protocol which implements the new arbitration provisions. An arbitration proceeding will generally begin two years after the date on which the competent authorities of the Contracting States began consideration of a case. Subparagraph 3(*f*), however, makes clear that the arbitration provisions shall apply to cases that are already under consideration by the competent authorities when the Protocol enters into force, and in such cases, for purposes of applying the arbitration provisions, the commencement date shall be the date the Protocol enters into force. Further, the provisions of Article 21 of the Protocol shall be effective for cases that come into consideration by the competent authorities after the date that the Protocol enters into force. In order to avoid the potential for a large number of MAP cases becoming subject to arbitration immediately upon the expiration of two years from entry into force, the competent authorities are encouraged to develop and implement procedures for arbitration by January 1, 2009, and begin scheduling arbitration of otherwise unresolvable MAP cases in inventory (and meeting the agreed criteria) prior to two years from entry into force.

Assistance in collection

Subparagraph 3(*g*) of Article 27 of the Protocol pertains to the date when the changes set forth in Article 22 of the Protocol, relating to assistance in collection of taxes, shall have effect. Consistent with the third protocol that entered into force on November 9, 1995, and which had effect for requests for assistance on claims finally determined after November 9, 1985, the provisions of Article 22 of the Protocol shall have effect for revenue claims finally determined by an applicant State after November 9, 1985.

United States
Canada–U.S. Enhanced Tax Information Exchange Agreement

Date Signed:	February 5, 2014
Reference citation:	S.C. 2014, c. 20, Part 5
Date entered into force:	June 27, 2014
Effective date of provisions:	• Generally, including the requirements for Canadian financial institutions to institute due diligence procedures to identify accounts held by U.S. persons — July 1, 2014 • For reciprocal information exchange between the Canada Revenue Agency and the U.S. Internal Revenue Service — by the end of September 2015

Agreement Between the Government of the United States of America and the Government of Canada to Improve International Tax Compliance through Enhanced Exchange of Information under the Convention Between the United States of America and Canada with Respect to Taxes on Income and on Capital

Whereas, the Government of the United States of America and the Government of Canada (each, a "Party," and together, the "Parties") have a longstanding and close relationship with respect to mutual assistance in tax matters and desire to conclude an agreement to improve international tax compliance by further building on that relationship;

Whereas, Article XXVII of the Convention Between the United States and Canada with Respect to Taxes on Income and on Capital done at Washington on September 26, 1980, as amended by the Protocols done on June 14, 1983, March 28, 1984, March 17, 1995, July 29, 1997, and September 21, 2007 (the "Convention") authorizes the exchange of information for tax purposes, including on an automatic basis;

Whereas, the United States of America enacted provisions commonly known as the Foreign Account Tax Compliance Act ("FATCA"), which introduce a reporting regime for financial institutions with respect to certain accounts;

Whereas, the Governments of Canada and the United States of America are supportive of applying the underlying policy goal of FATCA on a reciprocal basis to improve tax compliance;

Whereas, FATCA has raised a number of issues, including that Canadian financial institutions may not be able to comply with certain aspects of FATCA due to domestic legal impediments;

Whereas, the Government of the United States of America collects information regarding certain accounts maintained by U.S. financial institutions held by residents of Canada and is committed to exchanging such information with the Government of Canada and pursuing equivalent levels of exchange;

Whereas, the Parties are committed to working together over the longer term towards achieving common reporting and due diligence standards for financial institutions;

Whereas, the Government of the United States of America acknowledges the need to coordinate the reporting obligations under FATCA with other U.S. tax reporting obligations of Canadian financial institutions to avoid duplicative reporting;

Whereas, an intergovernmental approach to FATCA implementation would facilitate compliance by Canadian financial institutions while protecting the ability of Canadians to access financial services;

Whereas, the Parties desire to conclude an agreement to improve international tax compliance and provide for the implementation of FATCA based on domestic reporting and reciprocal automatic exchange pursuant to the Convention and subject to the confidentiality and other protections provided for therein, including the provisions limiting the use of the information exchanged under the Convention;

Now, therefore, the Parties have agreed as follows:

Article 1 — Definitions

1. For purposes of this agreement and any annexes thereto ("Agreement"), the following terms shall have the meanings set forth below:

a) The term "United States" has the same meaning as in the Convention. Any reference to a "State" of the United States includes the District of Columbia.

b) The term "U.S. Territory" means American Samoa, the Commonwealth of the Northern Mariana Islands, Guam, the Commonwealth of Puerto Rico, or the U.S. Virgin Islands.

c) The term "IRS" means the U.S. Internal Revenue Service.

d) The term "Canada" has the same meaning as in the Convention.

e) The term "Partner Jurisdiction" means a jurisdiction that has in effect an agreement with the United States to facilitate the implementation of FATCA. The IRS shall publish a list identifying all Partner Jurisdictions.

f) The term "Competent Authority" means:

(1) in the case of the United States, the Secretary of the Treasury or the Secretary's delegate; and

(2) in the case of Canada, the Minister of National Revenue or the Minister of National Revenue's authorized representative.

g) The term "Financial Institution" means a Custodial Institution, a Depository Institution, an Investment Entity, or a Specified Insurance Company.

h) The term "Custodial Institution" means any Entity that holds, as a substantial portion of its business, financial assets for the account of others. An entity holds financial assets for the account of others as a substantial portion of its business if the entity's gross income attributable to the holding of financial assets and related financial services equals or exceeds 20 percent of the entity's gross income during the shorter of:

(1) the three-year period that ends on December 31 (or the final day of a non-calendar year accounting period) prior to the year in which the determination is being made; or

(2) the period during which the entity has been in existence.

i) The term "Depository Institution" means any Entity that accepts deposits in the ordinary course of a banking or similar business.

j) The term "Investment Entity" means any Entity that conducts as a business (or is managed by an entity that conducts as a business) one or more of the following activities or operations for or on behalf of a customer:

(1) trading in money market instruments (cheques, bills, certificates of deposit, derivatives, etc.); foreign exchange; exchange, interest rate and index instruments; transferable securities; or commodity futures trading;

(2) individual and collective portfolio management; or

(3) otherwise investing, administering, or managing funds or money on behalf of other persons.

This subparagraph 1(*j*) shall be interpreted in a manner consistent with similar language set forth in the definition of "financial institution" in the Financial Action Task Force Recommendations.

k) The term "Specified Insurance Company" means any Entity that is an insurance company (or the holding company of an insurance company) that issues, or is obligated to make payments with respect to, a Cash Value Insurance Contract or an Annuity Contract.

l) The term "Canadian Financial Institution" means

(1) any Financial Institution that is resident in Canada, but excluding any branch of such Financial Institution that is located outside Canada, and

(2) any branch of a Financial Institution that is not resident in Canada, if such branch is located in Canada.

m) The term "Partner Jurisdiction Financial Institution" means

(1) any Financial Institution that is established in a Partner Jurisdiction, but excluding any branch of such Financial Institution that is located outside the Partner Jurisdiction, and

(2) any branch of a Financial Institution that is not established in the Partner Jurisdiction, if such branch is located in the Partner Jurisdiction.

n) The term "Reporting Financial Institution" means a Reporting Canadian Financial Institution or a Reporting U.S. Financial Institution, as the context requires.

o) The term "Reporting Canadian Financial Institution" means any Canadian Financial Institution that is not a Non-Reporting Canadian Financial Institution.

p) The term "Reporting U.S. Financial Institution" means

(1) any Financial Institution that is resident in the United States, but excluding any branch of such Financial Institution that is located outside the United States, and

(2) any branch of a Financial Institution that is not resident in the United States, if such branch is located in the United States,

provided that the Financial Institution or branch has control, receipt, or custody of income with respect to which information is required to be exchanged under subparagraph (2)(*b*) of Article 2 of this Agreement.

q) The term "Non-Reporting Canadian Financial Institution" means any Canadian Financial Institution, or other Entity resident in Canada, that is identified in Annex II as a Non-Reporting Canadian Financial Institution or that otherwise qualifies as a deemed compliant FFI or an exempt beneficial owner under relevant U.S. Treasury Regulations in effect on the date of signature of this Agreement.

r) The term "Nonparticipating Financial Institution" means a nonparticipating FFI, as that term is defined in relevant U.S. Treasury Regulations, but does not include a Canadian Financial Institution or other Partner Jurisdiction Financial Institution other than a Financial Institution treated as a Nonparticipating Financial Institution pursuant to subparagraph 2(*b*) of Article 5 of this Agreement or the corresponding provision in an agreement between the United States and a Partner Jurisdiction.

s) The term "Financial Account" means an account maintained by a Financial Institution, and includes:

(1) in the case of an Entity that is a Financial Institution solely because it is an Investment Entity, any equity or debt interest (other than interests that are regularly traded on an established securities market) in the Financial Institution;

(2) in the case of a Financial Institution not described in subparagraph 1(*s*)(1) of this Article, any equity or debt interest in the Financial Institution (other than interests that are regularly traded on an established securities market), if

(A) the value of the debt or equity interest is determined, directly or indirectly, primarily by reference to assets that give rise to U.S. Source Withholdable Payments, and

(B) the class of interests was established with a purpose of avoiding reporting in accordance with this Agreement; and

(3) any Cash Value Insurance Contract and any Annuity Contract issued or maintained by a Financial Institution, other than a noninvestment-linked, nontransferable immediate life annuity that is issued to an individual and monetizes a pension or disability benefit provided under an account, product, or arrangement identified as excluded from the definition of "Financial Account" in Annex II.

Notwithstanding the foregoing, the term "Financial Account" does not include any account, product, or arrangement identified as excluded from the definition of Financial Account in Annex II. For purposes of this Agreement, interests are "regularly traded" if there is a meaningful volume of trading with respect to the interests on an ongoing basis, and an "established securities market" means an exchange that is officially recognized and supervised by a governmental authority in which the market is located and that has a meaningful annual value of shares traded on the exchange. For purposes of this subparagraph 1(*s*), an interest in a Financial Institution is not "regularly traded" and shall be treated as a Financial Account if the holder of the interest (other than a Financial Institution acting as an intermediary) is registered on the books of such Financial Institution. The preceding sentence will not apply to interests first registered on the books of such Financial Institution prior to July 1, 2014, and with respect to interests first registered on the books of such Financial Institution on or after July 1, 2014, a Financial Institution is not required to apply the preceding sentence prior to January 1, 2016.

t) The term "Depository Account" includes any commercial, checking, savings, time, or thrift account, or an account that is evidenced by a certificate of deposit, thrift certificate, investment certificate, certificate of indebtedness, or other similar instrument maintained by a Financial Institution in the ordinary course of a banking or similar business. A Depository Account also includes an amount held by an insurance company pursuant to a guaranteed investment contract or similar agreement to pay or credit interest thereon.

u) The term "Custodial Account" means an account (other than an Insurance Contract or Annuity Contract) for the benefit of another person that holds any financial instrument or contract held for investment (including, but not limited to, a share or stock in a corporation, a note, bond, debenture, or other evidence of indebtedness, a currency or commodity transaction, a credit default swap, a swap based upon a nonfinancial index, a notional principal contract, an Insurance Contract or Annuity Contract, and any option or other derivative instrument).

v) The term "Equity Interest" means, in the case of a partnership that is a Financial Institution, either a capital or profits interest in the partnership. In the case of a trust that is a Financial Institution, an Equity Interest is considered to be held by any person treated as a settlor or beneficiary of all or a portion of the trust, or any other natural person exercising ultimate effective control over the trust. A Specified U.S. Person shall be treated as being a beneficiary of a foreign trust if such Specified U.S. Person has the right to receive directly or indirectly (for example, through a nominee) a mandatory distribution or may receive, directly or indirectly, a discretionary distribution from the trust.

w) The term "Insurance Contract" means a contract (other than an Annuity Contract) under which the issuer agrees to pay an amount upon the occurrence of a specified contingency involving mortality, morbidity, accident, liability, or property risk.

x) The term "Annuity Contract" means a contract under which the issuer agrees to make payments for a period of time determined in whole or in part by reference to the life expectancy of one or more individuals. The term also includes a contract that is considered to be an Annuity Contract in accordance with the law, regulation, or practice of the jurisdiction in which the contract was issued, and under which the issuer agrees to make payments for a term of years.

y) The term "Cash Value Insurance Contract" means an Insurance Contract (other than an indemnity reinsurance contract between two insurance companies) that has a Cash Value greater than $50,000.

z) The term "Cash Value" means the greater of (i) the amount that the policyholder is entitled to receive upon surrender or termination of the contract (determined without reduction for any surrender charge or policy loan), and (ii) the amount the policyholder can borrow under or with regard to the contract. Notwithstanding the foregoing, the term "Cash Value" does not include an amount payable under an Insurance Contract as:

(1) a personal injury or sickness benefit or other benefit providing indemnification of an economic loss incurred upon the occurrence of the event insured against;

(2) a refund to the policyholder of a previously paid premium under an Insurance Contract (other than under a life insurance contract) due to policy cancellation or termination, decrease in risk exposure during the effective period of the Insurance Contract, or arising from a redetermination of the premium due to correction of posting or other similar error; or

(3) a policyholder dividend based upon the underwriting experience of the contract or group involved.

aa) The term "Reportable Account" means a U.S. Reportable Account or a Canadian Reportable Account, as the context requires.

bb) The term "Canadian Reportable Account" means a Financial Account maintained by a Reporting U.S. Financial Institution if:

(1) in the case of a Depository Account, the account is held by an individual resident in Canada and more than $10 of interest is paid to such account in any given calendar year; or

(2) in the case of a Financial Account other than a Depository Account, the Account Holder is a resident of Canada, including an Entity that certifies that it is resident in Canada for tax purposes, with respect to which U.S. source income that is subject to reporting under chapter 3 of subtitle A or chapter 61 of subtitle F of the U.S. Internal Revenue Code is paid or credited.

cc) The term "U.S. Reportable Account" means a Financial Account maintained by a Reporting Canadian Financial Institution and held by one or more Specified U.S. Persons or by a Non-U.S. Entity with one or more Controlling Persons that is a Specified U.S. Person. Notwithstanding the foregoing, an account shall not be treated as a U.S. Reportable Account if such account is not identified as a U.S. Reportable Account after application of the due diligence procedures in Annex I.

dd) The term "Account Holder" means the person listed or identified as the holder of a Financial Account by the Financial Institution that maintains the account. A person, other than a Financial Institution, holding a Financial Account for the benefit or account of another person as agent, custodian, nominee, signatory, investment advisor, or intermediary, is not treated as the Account Holder for purposes of this Agreement, and such other person is treated as the Account Holder. For purposes of the immediately preceding sentence, the term "Financial Institution" does not include a Financial Institution organized or incorporated in a U.S. Territory. In the case of a Cash Value Insurance Contract or an Annuity Contract, the Account Holder is any person entitled to access the Cash Value or change the beneficiary of the contract. If no person can access the Cash Value or change the beneficiary, the Account Holder is any person named as the owner in the contract and any person with a vested entitlement to payment under the terms of the contract. Upon the maturity of a Cash Value Insurance Contract or an Annuity Contract, each person entitled to receive a payment under the contract is treated as an Account Holder.

ee) The term "U.S. Person" means

(1) a U.S. citizen or resident individual,

(2) a partnership or corporation organized in the United States or under the laws of the United States or any State thereof,

(3) a trust if

(A) a court within the United States would have authority under applicable law to render orders or judgments concerning substantially all issues regarding administration of the trust, and

(B) one or more U.S. persons have the authority to control all substantial decisions of the trust, or

(4) an estate of a decedent that is a citizen or resident of the United States.

This subparagraph 1(*ee*) shall be interpreted in accordance with the U.S. Internal Revenue Code.

ff) The term "Specified U.S. Person" means a U.S. Person, other than:

(1) a corporation the stock of which is regularly traded on one or more established securities markets;

(2) any corporation that is a member of the same expanded affiliated group, as defined in section 1471(*e*)(2) of the U.S. Internal Revenue Code, as a corporation described in clause (1);

(3) the United States or any wholly owned agency or instrumentality thereof;

(4) any State of the United States, any U.S. Territory, any political subdivision of any of the foregoing, or any wholly owned agency or instrumentality of any one or more of the foregoing;

(5) any organization exempt from taxation under section 501(*a*) of the U.S. Internal Revenue Code or an individual retirement plan as defined in section 7701(*a*)(37) of the U.S. Internal Revenue Code;

(6) any bank as defined in section 581 of the U.S. Internal Revenue Code;

(7) any real estate investment trust as defined in section 856 of the U.S. Internal Revenue Code;

(8) any regulated investment company as defined in section 851 of the U.S. Internal Revenue Code or any entity registered with the U.S. Securities and Exchange Commission under the U.S. Investment Company Act of 1940;

(9) any common trust fund as defined in section 584(*a*) of the U.S. Internal Revenue Code;

(10) any trust that is exempt from tax under section 664(*c*) of the U.S. Internal Revenue Code or that is described in section 4947(*a*)(1) of the U.S. Internal Revenue Code;

(11) a dealer in securities, commodities, or derivative financial instruments (including notional principal contracts, futures, forwards, and options) that is registered as such under the laws of the United States or any State thereof;

(12) a broker as defined in section 6045(*c*) of the U.S. Internal Revenue Code; or

(13) any tax exempt trust under a plan that is described in section 403(*b*) or section 457(*b*) of the U.S. Internal Revenue Code.

gg) The term "Entity" means a legal person or a legal arrangement such as a trust.

hh) The term "Non-U.S. Entity" means an Entity that is not a U.S. Person.

ii) The term "U.S. Source Withholdable Payment" means any payment of interest (including any original issue discount), dividends, rents, salaries, wages, premiums, annuities, compensations, remunerations, emoluments, and other fixed or determinable annual or periodical gains, profits, and income, if such payment is from sources within the United States. Notwithstanding the foregoing, a U.S. Source Withholdable Payment does not include any payment that is not treated as a withholdable payment in relevant U.S. Treasury Regulations.

jj) An Entity is a "Related Entity" of another Entity if either Entity controls the other Entity, or the two Entities are under common control. For this purpose control includes direct or indirect ownership of more than 50 percent of the vote or value in an Entity. Notwithstanding the foregoing, Canada may treat an Entity as not a Related Entity of another Entity if the two Entities are not members of the same expanded affiliated group as defined in section 1471(*e*)(2) of the U.S. Internal Revenue Code.

kk) The term "U.S. TIN" means a U.S. federal taxpayer identifying number.

Treaties and Related Legislation

ll) The term "Canadian TIN" means a Canadian taxpayer identifying number.

mm) The term "Controlling Persons" means the natural persons who exercise control over an Entity. In the case of a trust, such term means the settlor, the trustees, the protector (if any), the beneficiaries or class of beneficiaries, and any other natural person exercising ultimate effective control over the trust, and in the case of a legal arrangement other than a trust, such term means persons in equivalent or similar positions. The term "Controlling Persons" shall be interpreted in a manner consistent with the Financial Action Task Force Recommendations.

2. Any term not otherwise defined in this Agreement shall, unless the context otherwise requires or the Competent Authorities agree to a common meaning (as permitted by domestic law), have the meaning that it has at that time under the law of the Party applying this Agreement, any meaning under the applicable tax laws of that Party prevailing over a meaning given to the term under other laws of that Party.

Article 2 — Obligations to Obtain and Exchange Information with Respect to Reportable Accounts

1. Subject to the provisions of Article 3 of this Agreement, each Party shall obtain the information specified in paragraph 2 of this Article with respect to all Reportable Accounts and shall annually exchange this information with the other Party on an automatic basis pursuant to the provisions of Article XXVII of the Convention.

2. The information to be obtained and exchanged is:

a) In the case of Canada with respect to each U.S. Reportable Account of each Reporting Canadian Financial Institution:

(1) the name, address, and U.S. TIN of each Specified U.S. Person that is an Account Holder of such account and, in the case of a Non-U.S. Entity that, after application of the due diligence procedures set forth in Annex I, is identified as having one or more Controlling Persons that is a Specified U.S. Person, the name, address, and U.S. TIN (if any) of such Entity and each such Specified U.S. Person;

(2) the account number (or functional equivalent in the absence of an account number);

(3) the name and identifying number of the Reporting Canadian Financial Institution;

(4) the account balance or value (including, in the case of a Cash Value Insurance Contract or Annuity Contract, the Cash Value or surrender value) as of the end of the relevant calendar year or other appropriate reporting period or, if the account was closed during such year, immediately before closure;

(5) in the case of any Custodial Account:

(A) the total gross amount of interest, the total gross amount of dividends, and the total gross amount of other income generated with respect to the assets held in the account, in each case paid or credited to the account (or with respect to the account) during the calendar year or other appropriate reporting period; and

(B) the total gross proceeds from the sale or redemption of property paid or credited to the account during the calendar year or other appropriate reporting period with respect to which the Reporting Canadian Financial Institution acted as a custodian, broker, nominee, or otherwise as an agent for the Account Holder;

(6) in the case of any Depository Account, the total gross amount of interest paid or credited to the account during the calendar year or other appropriate reporting period; and

(7) in the case of any account not described in subparagraph 2(*a*)(5) or 2(*a*)(6) of this Article, the total gross amount paid or credited to the Account Holder with respect to the account during the calendar year or other appropriate reporting period with respect to which the Reporting Canadian Financial Institution is the obligor or debtor, including the aggregate amount of any redemption payments made to the Account Holder during the calendar year or other appropriate reporting period.

b) In the case of the United States, with respect to each Canadian Reportable Account of each Reporting U.S. Financial Institution:

(1) the name, address, and Canadian TIN of any person that is a resident of Canada and is an Account Holder of the account;

(2) the account number (or the functional equivalent in the absence of an account number);

(3) the name and identifying number of the Reporting U.S. Financial Institution;

(4) the gross amount of interest paid on a Depository Account;

(5) the gross amount of U.S. source dividends paid or credited to the account; and

(6) the gross amount of other U.S. source income paid or credited to the account, to the extent subject to reporting under chapter 3 of subtitle A or chapter 61 of subtitle F of the U.S. Internal Revenue Code.

Article 3 — Time and Manner of Exchange of Information

1. For purposes of the exchange obligation in Article 2 of this Agreement, the amount and characterization of payments made with respect to a U.S. Reportable Account may be determined in accordance with the principles of Canada's tax laws, and the amount and characterization of payments made with respect to a Canadian Reportable Account may be determined in accordance with principles of U.S. federal income tax law.

2. For purposes of the exchange obligation in Article 2 of this Agreement, the information exchanged shall identify the currency in which each relevant amount is denominated.

3. With respect to paragraph 2 of Article 2 of this Agreement, information is to be obtained and exchanged with respect to 2014 and all subsequent years, except that:

a) In the case of Canada:

(1) the information to be obtained and exchanged with respect to 2014 is only the information described in subparagraphs 2(*a*)(1) through 2(*a*)(4) of Article 2 of this Agreement;

(2) the information to be obtained and exchanged with respect to 2015 is the information described in subparagraphs 2(*a*)(1) through 2(*a*)(7) of Article 2 of this Agreement, except for gross proceeds described in subparagraph 2(*a*)(5)(B) of Article 2 of this Agreement; and

(3) the information to be obtained and exchanged with respect to 2016 and subsequent years is the information described in subparagraphs 2(*a*)(1) through 2(*a*)(7) of Article 2 of this Agreement;

b) In the case of the United States, the information to be obtained and exchanged with respect to 2014 and subsequent years is all of the information identified in subparagraph 2(*b*) of Article 2 of this Agreement.

4. Notwithstanding paragraph 3 of this Article, with respect to each Reportable Account that is maintained by a Reporting Financial Institution as of June 30, 2014, and subject to paragraph 4 of Article 6 of this Agreement, the Parties are not required to obtain and include in the exchanged information the Canadian TIN or the U.S. TIN, as applicable, of any relevant person if such taxpayer identifying number is not in the records of the Reporting Financial Institution. In such a case, the Parties shall obtain and include in the exchanged information the date of birth of the relevant person, if the Reporting Financial Institution has such date of birth in its records.

5. Subject to paragraphs 3 and 4 of this Article, the information described in Article 2 of this Agreement shall be exchanged within nine months after the end of the calendar year to which the information relates.

6. The Competent Authorities of Canada and the United States shall enter into an agreement or arrangement under the mutual agreement procedure provided for in Article XXVI of the Convention, which shall:

a) establish the procedures for the automatic exchange obligations described in Article 2 of this Agreement;

b) prescribe rules and procedures as may be necessary to implement Article 5 of this Agreement; and

c) establish as necessary procedures for the exchange of the information reported under subparagraph 1(*b*) of Article 4 of this Agreement.

7. All information exchanged shall be subject to the confidentiality and other protections provided for in the Convention, including the provisions limiting the use of the information exchanged.

Article 4 — Application of FATCA to Canadian Financial Institutions

1. **Treatment of Reporting Canadian Financial Institutions**. Each Reporting Canadian Financial Institution shall be treated as complying with, and not subject to withholding under, section 1471 of the U.S. Internal Revenue Code if Canada complies with its obligations under Articles 2 and 3 of this Agreement with respect to such Reporting Canadian Financial Institution, and the Reporting Canadian Financial Institution:

a) identifies U.S. Reportable Accounts and reports annually to the Canadian Competent Authority the information required to be reported in subparagraph 2(*a*) of Article 2 of this Agreement in the time and manner described in Article 3 of this Agreement;

b) for each of 2015 and 2016, reports annually to the Canadian Competent Authority the name of each Nonparticipating Financial Institution to which it has made payments and the aggregate amount of such payments;

c) complies with the applicable registration requirements on the IRS FATCA registration website;

d) to the extent that a Reporting Canadian Financial Institution is

(1) acting as a qualified intermediary (for purposes of section 1441 of the U.S. Internal Revenue Code) that has elected to assume primary withholding responsibility under chapter 3 of subtitle A of the U.S. Internal Revenue Code,

(2) a foreign partnership that has elected to act as a withholding foreign partnership (for purposes of both sections 1441 and 1471 of the U.S. Internal Revenue Code), or

(3) a foreign trust that has elected to act as a withholding foreign trust (for purposes of both sections 1441 and 1471 of the U.S. Internal Revenue Code),

withholds 30 percent of any U.S. Source Withholdable Payment to any Nonparticipating Financial Institution; and

e) in the case of a Reporting Canadian Financial Institution that is not described in subparagraph 1(*d*) of this Article and that makes a payment of, or acts as an intermediary with respect to, a U.S. Source Withholdable Payment to any Nonparticipating Financial Institution, the Reporting Canadian Financial Institution provides to any immediate payor of such U.S. Source Withholdable Payment the information required for withholding and reporting to occur with respect to such payment.

Notwithstanding the foregoing, a Reporting Canadian Financial Institution with respect to which the conditions of this paragraph 1 are not satisfied shall not be subject to withholding under section 1471 of the U.S. Internal Revenue Code unless such Reporting Canadian Financial Institution is treated by the IRS as a Nonparticipating Financial Institution pursuant to subparagraph 2(*b*) of Article 5 of this Agreement.

2. **Suspension of Rules Relating to Recalcitrant Accounts**. The United States shall not require a Reporting Canadian Financial Institution to withhold tax under section 1471 or 1472 of the U.S. Internal Revenue Code with respect to an account held by a recalcitrant account holder (as defined in section 1471(*d*)(6) of the U.S. Internal Revenue Code), or to close such account, if the U.S. Competent Authority receives the information set forth in subparagraph 2(*a*) of Article 2 of this Agreement, subject to the provisions of Article 3 of this Agreement, with respect to such account.

3. **Specific Treatment of Canadian Retirement Plans**. The United States shall treat as deemed-compliant FFIs or exempt beneficial owners, as appropriate, for purposes of sections 1471 and 1472 of the U.S. Internal Revenue Code, Canadian retirement plans identified in Annex II. For this purpose, a Canadian retirement plan includes an Entity established or located in, and regulated by, Canada, or a predetermined contractual or legal arrangement, operated to provide pension or retirement benefits or earn income for providing such benefits under the laws of Canada and regulated with respect to contributions, distributions, reporting, sponsorship, and taxation.

4. **Identification and Treatment of Other Deemed-Compliant FFIs and Exempt Beneficial Owners**. The United States shall treat each Non-Reporting Canadian Financial Institution as a deemed-compliant FFI or as an exempt beneficial owner, as appropriate, for purposes of section 1471 of the U.S. Internal Revenue Code.

5. **Special Rules Regarding Related Entities and Branches That Are Nonparticipating Financial Institutions**. If a Canadian Financial Institution, that otherwise meets the requirements described in paragraph 1 of this Article or is described in paragraph 3 or 4 of this Article, has a Related Entity or branch that operates in a jurisdiction that prevents such Related Entity or branch from fulfilling the requirements of a participating FFI or deemed-compliant FFI for purposes of section 1471 of the U.S. Internal Revenue Code or has a Related Entity or branch that is treated as a Nonparticipating Financial Institution solely due to the expiration of the transitional rule for limited FFIs and limited branches under relevant U.S. Treasury Regulations, such Canadian Financial Institution shall continue to be in compliance with the terms of this Agreement and shall continue to be treated as a deemed-compliant FFI or exempt beneficial owner, as appropriate, for purposes of section 1471 of the U.S. Internal Revenue Code, provided that:

a) the Canadian Financial Institution treats each such Related Entity or branch as a separate Nonparticipating Financial Institution for purposes of all the reporting and withholding requirements of this Agreement and each such Related Entity or branch identifies itself to withholding agents as a Nonparticipating Financial Institution;

b) each such Related Entity or branch identifies its U.S. accounts and reports the information with respect to those accounts as required under section 1471 of the U.S. Internal Revenue Code to the extent permitted under the relevant laws pertaining to the Related Entity or branch; and

c) such Related Entity or branch does not specifically solicit U.S. accounts held by persons that are not resident in the jurisdiction where such Related Entity or branch is located or accounts held by Nonparticipating Financial Institutions that are not established in the jurisdiction where such branch or Related Entity is located, and such branch or Related Entity is not used by the Canadian Financial Institution or any other Related Entity to circumvent the obligations under this Agreement or under section 1471 of the U.S. Internal Revenue Code, as appropriate.

6. **Coordination of Timing**. Notwithstanding paragraphs 3 and 5 of Article 3 of this Agreement:

a) Canada shall not be obligated to obtain and exchange information with respect to a calendar year that is prior to the calendar year with respect to which similar information is required to be reported to the IRS by participating FFIs pursuant to relevant U.S. Treasury Regulations;

b) Canada shall not be obligated to begin exchanging information prior to the date by which participating FFIs are required to report similar information to the IRS under relevant U.S. Treasury Regulations;

c) the United States shall not be obligated to obtain and exchange information with respect to a calendar year that is prior to the first calendar year with respect to which Canada is required to obtain and exchange information; and

d) the United States shall not be obligated to begin exchanging information prior to the date by which Canada is required to begin exchanging information.

7. **Coordination of Definitions with U.S. Treasury Regulations**. Notwithstanding Article 1 of this Agreement and the definitions provided in the Annexes to this Agreement, in implementing this Agreement, Canada may use, and may permit Canadian Financial Institutions to use, a definition in relevant U.S. Treasury Regulations in lieu of a corresponding definition in this Agreement, provided that such application would not frustrate the purposes of this Agreement.

Article 5 — Collaboration on Compliance and Enforcement

1. **Minor and Administrative Errors**. A Competent Authority shall notify the Competent Authority of the other Party when the first-

mentioned Competent Authority has reason to believe that administrative errors or other minor errors may have led to incorrect or incomplete information reporting or resulted in other infringements of this Agreement. The Competent Authority of such other Party shall endeavor, including where appropriate by applying its domestic law (including applicable penalties), to obtain corrected and/or complete information or to resolve other infringements of this Agreement.

2. **Significant Non-Compliance.**

a) A Competent Authority shall notify the Competent Authority of the other Party when the first-mentioned Competent Authority has determined that there is significant non-compliance with the obligations under this Agreement with respect to a Reporting Financial Institution in the other jurisdiction. The Competent Authority of such other Party shall apply its domestic law (including applicable penalties) to address the significant non-compliance described in the notice.

b) If, in the case of a Reporting Canadian Financial Institution, such enforcement actions do not resolve the non-compliance within a period of 18 months after notification of significant non-compliance is first provided, the United States shall treat the Reporting Canadian Financial Institution as a Nonparticipating Financial Institution pursuant to this subparagraph 2(b).

3. **Reliance on Third Party Service Providers**. Each Party may allow Reporting Financial Institutions to use third party service providers to fulfill the obligations imposed on such Reporting Financial Institutions by a Party, as contemplated in this Agreement, but these obligations shall remain the responsibility of the Reporting Financial Institutions.

4. **Prevention of Avoidance.** The Parties shall implement as necessary requirements to prevent Financial Institutions from adopting practices intended to circumvent the reporting required under this Agreement.

Article 6 — Mutual Commitment to Continue to Enhance the Effectiveness of Information Exchange and Transparency

1. **Reciprocity**. The Government of the United States acknowledges the need to achieve equivalent levels of reciprocal automatic information exchange with Canada. The Government of the United States is committed to further improve transparency and enhance the exchange relationship with Canada by pursuing the adoption of regulations and advocating and supporting relevant legislation to achieve such equivalent levels of reciprocal automatic information exchange.

2. **Treatment of Passthru Payments and Gross Proceeds.** The Parties are committed to work together, along with Partner Jurisdictions, to develop a practical and effective alternative approach to achieve the policy objectives of foreign passthru payment and gross proceeds withholding that minimizes burden.

3. **Development of Common Reporting and Exchange Model.** The Parties are committed to working with Partner Jurisdictions and the Organisation for Economic Co-operation and Development on adapting the terms of this Agreement and other agreements between the United States and Partner Jurisdictions to a common model for automatic exchange of information, including the development of reporting and due diligence standards for financial institutions.

4. **Documentation of Accounts Maintained as of June 30, 2014.** With respect to Reportable Accounts maintained by a Reporting Financial Institution as of June 30, 2014:

a) The United States commits to establish, by January 1, 2017, for reporting with respect to 2017 and subsequent years, rules requiring Reporting U.S. Financial Institutions to obtain and report the Canadian TIN of each Account Holder of a Canadian Reportable Account as required pursuant to subparagraph 2(*b*)(1) of Article 2 of this Agreement; and

b) Canada commits to establish, by January 1, 2017, for reporting with respect to 2017 and subsequent years, rules requiring Reporting Canadian Financial Institutions to obtain the U.S. TIN of each Specified U.S. Person as required pursuant to subparagraph 2(*a*)(1) of Article 2 of this Agreement.

Article 7 — Consistency in the Application of FATCA to Partner Jurisdictions

1. Canada shall be granted the benefit of any more favorable terms under Article 4 or Annex I of this Agreement relating to the application of FATCA to Canadian Financial Institutions afforded to another Partner Jurisdiction under a signed bilateral agreement pursuant to which the other Partner Jurisdiction commits to undertake the same obligations as Canada described in Articles 2 and 3 of this Agreement, and subject to the same terms and conditions as described therein and in Articles 5 through 9 of this Agreement.

2. The United States shall notify Canada of any such more favorable terms, and such more favorable terms shall apply automatically under this Agreement as if such terms were specified in this Agreement and effective as of the date of signing of the agreement incorporating the more favorable terms, unless Canada declines the application thereof.

Article 8 — Consultations and Amendments

1. In case any difficulties in the implementation of this Agreement arise, either Party may request consultations to develop appropriate measures to ensure the fulfillment of this Agreement.

2. This Agreement may be amended by written mutual agreement of the Parties. Unless otherwise agreed upon, such an amendment shall enter into force through the same procedures as set forth in paragraph 1 of Article 10 of this Agreement.

Article 9 — Annexes

The Annexes form an integral part of this Agreement.

Article 10 — Term of Agreement

1. This Agreement shall enter into force on the date of Canada's written notification to the United States that Canada has completed its necessary internal procedures for entry into force of this Agreement.

2. Either Party may terminate this Agreement by giving notice of termination in writing to the other Party. Such termination shall become effective on the first day of the month following the expiration of a period of 12 months after the date of the notice of termination.

3. The Parties shall, prior to December 31, 2016, consult in good faith to amend this Agreement as necessary to reflect progress on the commitments set forth in Article 6 of this Agreement.

IN WITNESS WHEREOF, the undersigned, being duly authorized thereto by their respective Governments, have signed this Agreement.

Done in duplicate, at Ottawa, this 5th day of February 2014, in the English and French languages, each version being equally authentic.

FOR THE GOVERNMENT OF CANADA:
Brian Ernewein

FOR THE GOVERNMENT OF THE UNITED STATES OF AMERICA:
Richard M. Sanders

Annex I: Due Diligence Obligations for Identifying and Reporting on U.S. Reportable Accounts and on Payments to Certain Nonparticipating Financial Institutions

I. General.

A. Canada shall require that Reporting Canadian Financial Institutions apply the due diligence procedures contained in this Annex I to identify U.S. Reportable Accounts and accounts held by Nonparticipating Financial Institutions.

B. For purposes of the Agreement,

1. All dollar amounts are in U.S. dollars and shall be read to include the equivalent in other currencies.
2. Except as otherwise provided herein, the balance or value of an account shall be determined as of the last day of the calendar year or other appropriate reporting period.
3. Where a balance or value threshold is to be determined as of June 30, 2014, under this Annex I, the relevant balance or value shall be determined as of that day or the last day of the reporting period ending immediately before June 30, 2014, and where a balance or value threshold is to be determined as of the last day of a calendar year under this Annex I, the relevant balance or value shall be determined as of the last day of the calendar year or other appropriate reporting period.
4. Subject to subparagraph E(1) of section II of this Annex I, an account shall be treated as a U.S. Reportable Account beginning as of the date it is identified as such pursuant to the due diligence procedures in this Annex I.
5. Unless otherwise provided, information with respect to a U.S. Reportable Account shall be reported annually in the calendar year following the year to which the information relates.

C. As an alternative to the procedures described in each section of this Annex I, Canada may permit Reporting Canadian Financial Institutions to rely on the procedures described in relevant U.S. Treasury Regulations to establish whether an account is a U.S. Reportable Account or an account held by a Nonparticipating Financial Institution. Canada may permit Reporting Canadian Financial Institutions to make such election separately for each section of this Annex I either with respect to all relevant Financial Accounts or, separately, with respect to any clearly identified group of such accounts (such as by line of business or the location of where the account is maintained).

II. Preexisting Individual Accounts.

The following rules and procedures apply for purposes of identifying U.S. Reportable Accounts among Preexisting Accounts held by individuals ("Preexisting Individual Accounts").

A. **Accounts Not Required to Be Reviewed, Identified, or Reported.** Unless the Reporting Canadian Financial Institution elects otherwise, either with respect to all Preexisting Individual Accounts or, separately, with respect to any clearly identified group of such accounts, where the implementing rules in Canada provide for such an election, the following Preexisting Individual Accounts are not required to be reviewed, identified, or reported as U.S. Reportable Accounts:

1. Subject to subparagraph E(2) of this section, a Preexisting Individual Account with a balance or value that does not exceed $50,000 as of June 30, 2014.
2. Subject to subparagraph E(2) of this section, a Preexisting Individual Account that is a Cash Value Insurance Contract or an Annuity Contract with a balance or value of $250,000 or less as of June 30, 2014.
3. A Preexisting Individual Account that is a Cash Value Insurance Contract or an Annuity Contract, provided the law or regulations of Canada or the United States effectively prevent the sale of such a Cash Value Insurance Contract or an Annuity Contract to U.S. residents (e.g., if the relevant Financial Institution does not have the required registration under U.S. law, and the law of Canada requires reporting or withholding with respect to insurance products held by residents of Canada).
4. A Depository Account with a balance of $50,000 or less.

B. Review Procedures for Preexisting Individual Accounts With a Balance or Value as of June 30, 2014, that Exceeds $50,000 ($250,000 for a Cash Value Insurance Contract or Annuity Contract), But Does Not Exceed $1,000,000 ("Lower Value Accounts").

1. **Electronic Record Search.** The Reporting Canadian Financial Institution must review electronically searchable data maintained by the Reporting Canadian Financial Institution for any of the following U.S. indicia:
   a) Identification of the Account Holder as a U.S. citizen or resident;
   b) Unambiguous indication of a U.S. place of birth;
   c) Current U.S. mailing or residence address (including a U.S. post office box);
   d) Current U.S. telephone number;
   e) Standing instructions to transfer funds to an account maintained in the United States;
   f) Currently effective power of attorney or signatory authority granted to a person with a U.S. address; or
   g) An "in-care-of" or "hold mail" address that is the sole address the Reporting Canadian Financial Institution has on file for the Account Holder. In the case of a Preexisting Individual Account that is a Lower Value Account, an "in-care-of" address outside the United States or "hold mail" address shall not be treated as U.S. indicia.
2. If none of the U.S. indicia listed in subparagraph B(1) of this section are discovered in the electronic search, then no further action is required until there is a change in circumstances that results in one or more U.S. indicia being associated with the account, or the account becomes a High Value Account described in paragraph D of this section.
3. If any of the U.S. indicia listed in subparagraph B(1) of this section are discovered in the electronic search, or if there is a change in circumstances that results in one or more U.S. indicia being associated with the account, then the Reporting Canadian Financial Institution must treat the account as a U.S. Reportable Account unless it elects to apply subparagraph B(4) of this section and one of the exceptions in such subparagraph applies with respect to that account.
4. Notwithstanding a finding of U.S. indicia under subparagraph B(1) of this section, a Reporting Canadian Financial Institution is not required to treat an account as a U.S. Reportable Account if:
   a) Where the Account Holder information unambiguously indicates a U.S. place of birth, the Reporting Canadian Financial Institution obtains, or has previously reviewed and maintains a record of:
      (1) A self-certification that the Account Holder is neither a U.S. citizen nor a U.S. resident for tax purposes (which may be on an IRS Form W-8 or other similar agreed form);
      (2) A non-U.S. passport or other government-issued identification evidencing the Account Holder's citizenship or nationality in a country other than the United States; and
      (3) A copy of the Account Holder's Certificate of Loss of Nationality of the United States or a reasonable explanation of:
         (a) The reason the Account Holder does not have such a certificate despite relinquishing U.S. citizenship; or
         (b) The reason the Account Holder did not obtain U.S. citizenship at birth.
   b) Where the Account Holder information contains a current U.S. mailing or residence address, or one or more U.S. telephone numbers that are the only telephone numbers associated with the account, the Reporting Canadian Finan-

cial Institution obtains, or has previously reviewed and maintains a record of:

(1) A self-certification that the Account Holder is neither a U.S. citizen nor a U.S. resident for tax purposes (which may be on an IRS Form W-8 or other similar agreed form); and

(2) Documentary evidence, as defined in paragraph D of section VI of this Annex I, establishing the Account Holder's non-U.S. status.

c) Where the Account Holder information contains standing instructions to transfer funds to an account maintained in the United States, the Reporting Canadian Financial Institution obtains, or has previously reviewed and maintains a record of:

(1) A self-certification that the Account Holder is neither a U.S. citizen nor a U.S. resident for tax purposes (which may be on an IRS Form W-8 or other similar agreed form); and

(2) Documentary evidence, as defined in paragraph D of section VI of this Annex I, establishing the Account Holder's non-U.S. status.

d) Where the Account Holder information contains a currently effective power of attorney or signatory authority granted to a person with a U.S. address, has an "in-care-of" address or "hold mail" address that is the sole address identified for the Account Holder, or has one or more U.S. telephone numbers (if a non-U.S. telephone number is also associated with the account), the Reporting Canadian Financial Institution obtains, or has previously reviewed and maintains a record of:

(1) A self-certification that the Account Holder is neither a U.S. citizen nor a U.S. resident for tax purposes (which may be on an IRS Form W-8 or other similar agreed form); or

(2) Documentary evidence, as defined in paragraph D of section VI of this Annex I, establishing the Account Holder's non-U.S. status.

C. **Additional Procedures Applicable to Preexisting Individual Accounts That Are Lower Value Accounts.**

1. Review of Preexisting Individual Accounts that are Lower Value Accounts for U.S. indicia must be completed by June 30, 2016.

2. If there is a change of circumstances with respect to a Preexisting Individual Account that is a Lower Value Account that results in one or more U.S. indicia described in subparagraph B(1) of this section being associated with the account, then the Reporting Canadian Financial Institution must treat the account as a U.S. Reportable Account unless subparagraph B(4) of this section applies.

3. Except for Depository Accounts described in subparagraph A(4) of this section, any Preexisting Individual Account that has been identified as a U.S. Reportable Account under this section shall be treated as a U.S. Reportable Account in all subsequent years, unless the Account Holder ceases to be a Specified U.S. Person.

D. **Enhanced Review Procedures for Preexisting Individual Accounts With a Balance or Value That Exceeds $1,000,000 as of June 30, 2014, or December 31 of 2015 or Any Subsequent Year ("High Value Accounts").**

1. **Electronic Record Search.** The Reporting Canadian Financial Institution must review electronically searchable data maintained by the Reporting Canadian Financial Institution for any of the U.S. indicia described in subparagraph B(1) of this section.

2. **Paper Record Search.** If the Reporting Canadian Financial Institution's electronically searchable databases include fields for, and capture all of the information described in, subparagraph D(3) of this section, then no further paper record search is required. If the electronic databases do not capture all of this information, then with respect to a High Value Account, the Reporting Canadian Financial Institution must also review the current customer master file and, to the extent not contained in the current customer master file, the following documents associated with the account and obtained by the Reporting Canadian Financial Institution within the last five years for any of the U.S. indicia described in subparagraph B(1) of this section:

a) The most recent documentary evidence collected with respect to the account;

b) The most recent account opening contract or documentation;

c) The most recent documentation obtained by the Reporting Canadian Financial Institution pursuant to AML/KYC Procedures or for other regulatory purposes;

d) Any power of attorney or signature authority forms currently in effect; and

e) Any standing instructions to transfer funds currently in effect.

3. **Exception Where Databases Contain Sufficient Information.** A Reporting Canadian Financial Institution is not required to perform the paper record search described in subparagraph D(2) of this section if the Reporting Canadian Financial Institution's electronically searchable information includes the following:

a) The Account Holder's nationality or residence status;

b) The Account Holder's residence address and mailing address currently on file with the Reporting Canadian Financial Institution;

c) The Account Holder's telephone number(s) currently on file, if any, with the Reporting Canadian Financial Institution;

d) Whether there are standing instructions to transfer funds in the account to another account (including an account at another branch of the Reporting Canadian Financial Institution or another Financial Institution);

e) Whether there is a current "in-care-of" address or "hold mail" address for the Account Holder; and

f) Whether there is any power of attorney or signatory authority for the account.

4. **Relationship Manager Inquiry for Actual Knowledge.** In addition to the electronic and paper record searches described above, the Reporting Canadian Financial Institution must treat as a U.S. Reportable Account any High Value Account assigned to a relationship manager (including any Financial Accounts aggregated with such High Value Account) if the relationship manager has actual knowledge that the Account Holder is a Specified U.S. Person.

5. **Effect of Finding U.S. Indicia.**

a) If none of the U.S. indicia listed in subparagraph B(1) of this section are discovered in the enhanced review of High Value Accounts described above, and the account is not identified as held by a Specified U.S. Person in subparagraph D(4) of this section, then no further action is required until there is a change in circumstances that results in one or more U.S. indicia being associated with the account.

b) If any of the U.S. indicia listed in subparagraph B(1) of this section are discovered in the enhanced review of High Value Accounts described above, or if there is a subsequent change in circumstances that results in one or more U.S. indicia being associated with the account, then the Reporting Canadian Financial Institution must treat the account as a U.S. Reportable Account unless it elects to apply subparagraph B(4) of this section and one of the exceptions in such subparagraph applies with respect to that account.

c) Except for Depository Accounts described in subparagraph A(4) of this section, any Preexisting Individual Account that has been identified as a U.S. Reportable Account under this section shall be treated as a U.S. Reportable Account in all subsequent years, unless the Account Holder ceases to be a Specified U.S. Person.

E. **Additional Procedures Applicable to High Value Accounts.**

1. If a Preexisting Individual Account is a High Value Account as of June 30, 2014, the Reporting Canadian Financial Institution must complete the enhanced review procedures described in paragraph D of this section with respect to such account by June 30, 2015. If based on this review such account is identified

as a U.S. Reportable Account on or before December 31, 2014, the Reporting Canadian Financial Institution must report the required information about such account with respect to 2014 in the first report on the account and on an annual basis thereafter. In the case of an account identified as a U.S. Reportable Account after December 31, 2014, and on or before June 30, 2015, the Reporting Canadian Financial Institution is not required to report information about such account with respect to 2014, but must report information about the account on an annual basis thereafter.

2. If a Preexisting Individual Account is not a High Value Account as of June 30, 2014, but becomes a High Value Account as of the last day of 2015 or any subsequent calendar year, the Reporting Canadian Financial Institution must complete the enhanced review procedures described in paragraph D of this section with respect to such account within six months after the last day of the calendar year in which the account becomes a High Value Account. If based on this review such account is identified as a U.S. Reportable Account, the Reporting Canadian Financial Institution must report the required information about such account with respect to the year in which it is identified as a U.S. Reportable Account and subsequent years on an annual basis, unless the Account Holder ceases to be a Specified U.S. Person.

3. Once a Reporting Canadian Financial Institution applies the enhanced review procedures described in paragraph D of this section to a High Value Account, the Reporting Canadian Financial Institution is not required to re-apply such procedures, other than the relationship manager inquiry described in subparagraph D(4) of this section, to the same High Value Account in any subsequent year.

4. If there is a change of circumstances with respect to a High Value Account that results in one or more U.S. indicia described in subparagraph B(1) of this section being associated with the account, then the Reporting Canadian Financial Institution must treat the account as a U.S. Reportable Account unless it elects to apply subparagraph B(4) of this section and one of the exceptions in such subparagraph applies with respect to that account.

5. A Reporting Canadian Financial Institution must implement procedures to ensure that a relationship manager identifies any change in circumstances of an account. For example, if a relationship manager is notified that the Account Holder has a new mailing address in the United States, the Reporting Canadian Financial Institution is required to treat the new address as a change in circumstances and, if it elects to apply subparagraph B(4) of this section, is required to obtain the appropriate documentation from the Account Holder.

F. **Preexisting Individual Accounts That Have Been Documented for Certain Other Purposes.** A Reporting Canadian Financial Institution that has previously obtained documentation from an Account Holder to establish the Account Holder's status as neither a U.S. citizen nor a U.S. resident in order to meet its obligations under a qualified intermediary, withholding foreign partnership, or withholding foreign trust agreement with the IRS, or to fulfill its obligations under chapter 61 of Title 26 of the United States Code, is not required to perform the procedures described in subparagraph B(1) of this section with respect to Lower Value Accounts or subparagraphs D(1) through D(3) of this section with respect to High Value Accounts.

III. New Individual Accounts.

The following rules and procedures apply for purposes of identifying U.S. Reportable Accounts among Financial Accounts held by individuals and opened on or after July 1, 2014 ("New Individual Accounts").

A. **Accounts Not Required to Be Reviewed, Identified, or Reported.** Unless the Reporting Canadian Financial Institution elects otherwise, either with respect to all New Individual Accounts or, separately, with respect to any clearly identified group of such accounts, where the implementing rules in Canada provide for such an election, the following New Individual Accounts are not required to be reviewed, identified, or reported as U.S. Reportable Accounts:

1. A Depository Account unless the account balance exceeds $50,000 at the end of any calendar year or other appropriate reporting period.

2. A Cash Value Insurance Contract unless the Cash Value exceeds $50,000 at the end of any calendar year or other appropriate reporting period.

B. **Other New Individual Accounts.**

1. With respect to New Individual Accounts not described in paragraph A of this section, upon account opening (or within 90 days after the end of the calendar year in which the account ceases to be described in paragraph A of this section), the Reporting Canadian Financial Institution must obtain a self-certification, which may be part of the account opening documentation, that allows the Reporting Canadian Financial Institution to determine whether the Account Holder is resident in the United States for tax purposes (for this purpose, a U.S. citizen is considered to be resident in the United States for tax purposes, even if the Account Holder is also a tax resident of another jurisdiction) and confirm the reasonableness of such self-certification based on the information obtained by the Reporting Canadian Financial Institution in connection with the opening of the account, including any documentation collected pursuant to AML/KYC Procedures.

2. If the self-certification establishes that the Account Holder is resident in the United States for tax purposes, the Reporting Canadian Financial Institution must treat the account as a U.S. Reportable Account and obtain a self-certification that includes the Account Holder's U.S. TIN (which may be an IRS Form W-9 or other similar agreed form).

3. If there is a change of circumstances with respect to a New Individual Account that causes the Reporting Canadian Financial Institution to know, or have reason to know, that the original self-certification is incorrect or unreliable, the Reporting Canadian Financial Institution cannot rely on the original self-certification and must obtain a valid self-certification that establishes whether the Account Holder is a U.S. citizen or resident for U.S. tax purposes. If the Reporting Canadian Financial Institution is unable to obtain a valid self-certification, the Reporting Canadian Financial Institution must treat the account as a U.S. Reportable Account.

IV. Preexisting Entity Accounts.

The following rules and procedures apply for purposes of identifying U.S. Reportable Accounts and accounts held by Nonparticipating Financial Institutions among Preexisting Accounts held by Entities ("Preexisting Entity Accounts").

A. **Entity Accounts Not Required to Be Reviewed, Identified or Reported.** Unless the Reporting Canadian Financial Institution elects otherwise, either with respect to all Preexisting Entity Accounts or, separately, with respect to any clearly identified group of such accounts, where the implementing rules in Canada provide for such an election, a Preexisting Entity Account with an account balance or value that does not exceed $250,000 as of June 30, 2014, is not required to be reviewed, identified, or reported as a U.S. Reportable Account until the account balance or value exceeds $1,000,000.

B. **Entity Accounts Subject to Review.** A Preexisting Entity Account that has an account balance or value that exceeds $250,000 as of June 30, 2014, and a Preexisting Entity Account that does not exceed $250,000 as of June 30, 2014, but the account balance or value of which exceeds $1,000,000 as of the last day of 2015 or any subsequent calendar year, must be reviewed in accordance with the procedures set forth in paragraph D of this section.

C. **Entity Accounts With Respect to Which Reporting Is Required.** With respect to Preexisting Entity Accounts described in paragraph B of this section, only accounts that are held by one or more Entities that are Specified U.S. Persons, or by Passive NFFEs with one or more Controlling Persons who are U.S. citizens or residents, shall be treated as U.S. Reportable Accounts. In addition, accounts held by Nonparticipating Financial Institutions shall be treated as accounts for which aggregate payments as described in subparagraph 1(*b*) of Article 4 of the Agreement are reported to the Canadian Competent Authority.

D. **Review Procedures for Identifying Entity Accounts With Respect to Which Reporting Is Required**. For Preexisting Entity Accounts described in paragraph B of this section, the Reporting Canadian Financial Institution must apply the following review procedures to determine whether the account is held by one or more Specified U.S. Persons, by Passive NFFEs with one or more Controlling Persons who are U.S. citizens or residents, or by Nonparticipating Financial Institutions:

1. **Determine Whether the Entity Is a Specified U.S. Person**.
   a) Review information maintained for regulatory or customer relationship purposes (including information collected pursuant to AML/KYC Procedures) to determine whether the information indicates that the Account Holder is a U.S. Person. For this purpose, information indicating that the Account Holder is a U.S. Person includes a U.S. place of incorporation or organization, or a U.S. address.
   b) If the information indicates that the Account Holder is a U.S. Person, the Reporting Canadian Financial Institution must treat the account as a U.S. Reportable Account unless it obtains a self-certification from the Account Holder (which may be on an IRS Form W-8 or W-9, or a similar agreed form), or reasonably determines based on information in its possession or that is publicly available, that the Account Holder is not a Specified U.S. Person.
2. **Determine Whether a Non-U.S. Entity Is a Financial Institution**.
   a) Review information maintained for regulatory or customer relationship purposes (including information collected pursuant to AML/KYC Procedures) to determine whether the information indicates that the Account Holder is a Financial Institution.
   b) If the information indicates that the Account Holder is a Financial Institution, or the Reporting Canadian Financial Institution verifies the Account Holder's Global Intermediary Identification Number on the published IRS FFI list, then the account is not a U.S. Reportable Account.
3. **Determine Whether a Financial Institution Is a Nonparticipating Financial Institution Payments to Which Are Subject to Aggregate Reporting Under Subparagraph 1(*b*) of Article 4 of the Agreement**.
   a) Subject to subparagraph D(3)(b) of this section, a Reporting Canadian Financial Institution may determine that the Account Holder is a Canadian Financial Institution or other Partner Jurisdiction Financial Institution if the Reporting Canadian Financial Institution reasonably determines that the Account Holder has such status on the basis of the Account Holder's Global Intermediary Identification Number on the published IRS FFI list or other information that is publicly available or in the possession of the Reporting Canadian Financial Institution, as applicable. In such case, no further review, identification, or reporting is required with respect to the account.
   b) If the Account Holder is a Canadian Financial Institution or other Partner Jurisdiction Financial Institution treated by the IRS as a Nonparticipating Financial Institution, then the account is not a U.S. Reportable Account, but payments to the Account Holder must be reported as contemplated in subparagraph 1(*b*) of Article 4 of the Agreement.
   c) If the Account Holder is not a Canadian Financial Institution or other Partner Jurisdiction Financial Institution, then the Reporting Canadian Financial Institution must treat the Account Holder as a Nonparticipating Financial Institution payments to which are reportable under subparagraph 1(b) of Article 4 of the Agreement, unless the Reporting Canadian Financial Institution:
      (1) Obtains a self-certification (which may be on an IRS Form W-8 or similar agreed form) from the Account Holder that it is a certified deemed-compliant FFI, or an exempt beneficial owner, as those terms are defined in relevant U.S. Treasury Regulations; or
      (2) In the case of a participating FFI or registered deemed-compliant FFI, verifies the Account Holder's Global Intermediary Identification Number on the published IRS FFI list.
4. **Determine Whether an Account Held by an NFFE Is a U.S. Reportable Account**. With respect to an Account Holder of a Preexisting Entity Account that is not identified as either a U.S. Person or a Financial Institution, the Reporting Canadian Financial Institution must identify (i) whether the Account Holder has Controlling Persons, (ii) whether the Account Holder is a Passive NFFE, and (iii) whether any of the Controlling Persons of the Account Holder is a U.S. citizen or resident. In making these determinations the Reporting Canadian Financial Institution must follow the guidance in subparagraphs D(4)(a) through D(4)(d) of this section in the order most appropriate under the circumstances.
   a) For purposes of determining the Controlling Persons of an Account Holder, a Reporting Canadian Financial Institution may rely on information collected and maintained pursuant to AML/KYC Procedures.
   b) For purposes of determining whether the Account Holder is a Passive NFFE, the Reporting Canadian Financial Institution must obtain a self-certification (which may be on an IRS Form W-8 or W-9, or on a similar agreed form) from the Account Holder to establish its status, unless it has information in its possession or that is publicly available, based on which it can reasonably determine that the Account Holder is an Active NFFE.
   c) For purposes of determining whether a Controlling Person of a Passive NFFE is a U.S. citizen or resident for tax purposes, a Reporting Canadian Financial Institution may rely on:
      (1) Information collected and maintained pursuant to AML/KYC Procedures in the case of a Preexisting Entity Account held by one or more NFFEs with an account balance or value that does not exceed $1,000,000; or
      (2) A self-certification (which may be on an IRS Form W-8 or W-9, or on a similar agreed form) from the Account Holder or such Controlling Person in the case of a Preexisting Entity Account held by one or more NFFEs with an account balance or value that exceeds $1,000,000.
   d) If any Controlling Person of a Passive NFFE is a U.S. citizen or resident, the account shall be treated as a U.S. Reportable Account.

E. **Timing of Review and Additional Procedures Applicable to Preexisting Entity Accounts**.

1. Review of Preexisting Entity Accounts with an account balance or value that exceeds $250,000 as of June 30, 2014 must be completed by June 30, 2016.
2. Review of Preexisting Entity Accounts with an account balance or value that does not exceed $250,000 as of June 30, 2014, but exceeds $1,000,000 as of December 31 of 2015 or any subsequent year, must be completed within six months after the last day of the calendar year in which the account balance or value exceeds $1,000,000.
3. If there is a change of circumstances with respect to a Preexisting Entity Account that causes the Reporting Canadian Financial Institution to know, or have reason to know, that the self-certification or other documentation associated with an account is incorrect or unreliable, the Reporting Canadian Financial Institution must redetermine the status of the account in accordance with the procedures set forth in paragraph D of this section.

V. New Entity Accounts.

The following rules and procedures apply for purposes of identifying U.S. Reportable Accounts and accounts held by Nonparticipating Financial Institutions among Financial Accounts held by Entities and opened on or after July 1, 2014 ("New Entity Accounts").

A. **Entity Accounts Not Required to Be Reviewed, Identified or Reported**. Unless the Reporting Canadian Financial Institution elects otherwise, either with respect to all New Entity Accounts or, separately, with respect to any clearly identified group of such accounts, where the implementing rules in Canada provide for such election, a credit card account or a revolving credit facility treated as a New Entity Account is not required to be reviewed, identified, or reported, provided that the Reporting Canadian Financial Institution maintaining such account implements policies and procedures to prevent an account balance owed to the Account Holder that exceeds $50,000.

B. **Other New Entity Accounts**. With respect to New Entity Accounts not described in paragraph A of this section, the Reporting Canadian Financial Institution must determine whether the Account Holder is:

1. a Specified U.S. Person;
2. a Canadian Financial Institution or other Partner Jurisdiction Financial Institution;
3. a participating FFI, a deemed-compliant FFI, or an exempt beneficial owner, as those terms are defined in relevant U.S. Treasury Regulations; or
4. an Active NFFE or Passive NFFE.

C. Subject to paragraph D of this section, a Reporting Canadian Financial Institution may determine that the Account Holder is an Active NFFE, a Canadian Financial Institution, or other Partner Jurisdiction Financial Institution if the Reporting Canadian Financial Institution reasonably determines that the Account Holder has such status on the basis of the Account Holder's Global Intermediary Identification Number or other information that is publicly available or in the possession of the Reporting Canadian Financial Institution, as applicable.

D. If the Account Holder is a Canadian Financial Institution or other Partner Jurisdiction Financial Institution treated by the IRS as a Nonparticipating Financial Institution, then the account is not a U.S. Reportable Account, but payments to the Account Holder must be reported as contemplated in subparagraph 1(b) of Article 4 of the Agreement.

E. In all other cases, a Reporting Canadian Financial Institution must obtain a self-certification from the Account Holder to establish the Account Holder's status. Based on the self-certification, the following rules apply:

1. If the Account Holder is a Specified U.S. Person, the Reporting Canadian Financial Institution must treat the account as a U.S. Reportable Account.
2. If the Account Holder is a Passive NFFE, the Reporting Canadian Financial Institution must identify the Controlling Persons as determined under AML/KYC Procedures, and must determine whether any such person is a U.S. citizen or resident on the basis of a self-certification from the Account Holder or such person. If any such person is a U.S. citizen or resident, the Reporting Canadian Financial Institution must treat the account as a U.S. Reportable Account.
3. If the Account Holder is:
   a) a U.S. Person that is not a Specified U.S. Person;
   b) subject to subparagraph E(4) of this section, a Canadian Financial Institution or other Partner Jurisdiction Financial Institution;
   c) a participating FFI, a deemed-compliant FFI, or an exempt beneficial owner, as those terms are defined in relevant U.S. Treasury Regulations;
   d) an Active NFFE; or
   e) a Passive NFFE none of the Controlling Persons of which is a U.S. citizen or resident,

   then the account is not a U.S. Reportable Account and no reporting is required with respect to the account.
4. If the Account Holder is a Nonparticipating Financial Institution (including a Canadian Financial Institution or other Partner Jurisdiction Financial Institution treated by the IRS as a Nonparticipating Financial Institution), then the account is not a U.S. Reportable Account, but payments to the Account Holder must be reported as contemplated in subparagraph 1(b) of Article 4 of the Agreement.

VI. Special Rules and Definitions.

The following additional rules and definitions apply in implementing the due diligence procedures described above:

A. **Reliance on Self-Certifications and Documentary Evidence**. A Reporting Canadian Financial Institution may not rely on a self-certification or documentary evidence if the Reporting Canadian Financial Institution knows or has reason to know that the self-certification or documentary evidence is incorrect or unreliable.

B. **Definitions**. The following definitions apply for purposes of this Annex I.

1. **AML/KYC Procedures.** "AML/KYC Procedures" means the customer due diligence procedures of a Reporting Canadian Financial Institution pursuant to the anti-money laundering or similar requirements of Canada to which such Reporting Canadian Financial Institution is subject.
2. **NFFE**. An "NFFE" means any Non-U.S. Entity that is not an FFI as defined in relevant U.S. Treasury Regulations or is an Entity described in subparagraph B(4)(j) of this section, and also includes any Non-U.S. Entity that is resident in Canada or another Partner Jurisdiction and that is not a Financial Institution.
3. **Passive NFFE**. A "Passive NFFE" means any NFFE that is not
   a) an Active NFFE or
   b) a withholding foreign partnership or withholding foreign trust pursuant to relevant U.S. Treasury Regulations.
4. **Active NFFE**. An "Active NFFE" means any NFFE that meets any of the following criteria:
   a) Less than 50 percent of the NFFE's gross income for the preceding calendar year or other appropriate reporting period is passive income and less than 50 percent of the assets held by the NFFE during the preceding calendar year or other appropriate reporting period are assets that produce or are held for the production of passive income;
   b) The stock of the NFFE is regularly traded on an established securities market or the NFFE is a Related Entity of an Entity the stock of which is regularly traded on an established securities market;
   c) The NFFE is organized in a U.S. Territory and all of the owners of the payee are bona fide residents of that U.S. Territory;
   d) The NFFE is a government (other than the U.S. government), a political subdivision of such government (which, for the avoidance of doubt, includes a state, province, county, or municipality), or a public body performing a function of such government or a political subdivision thereof, a government of a U.S. Territory, an international organization, a non-U.S. central bank of issue, or an Entity wholly owned by one or more of the foregoing;
   e) Substantially all of the activities of the NFFE consist of holding (in whole or in part) the outstanding stock of, or providing financing and services to, one or more subsidiaries that engage in trades or businesses other than the business of a Financial Institution, except that an NFFE shall not qualify for this status if the NFFE functions (or holds itself out) as an investment fund, such as a private equity fund, venture capital fund, leveraged buyout fund or any investment vehicle whose purpose is to acquire or fund companies and then hold interests in those companies as capital assets for investment purposes;
   f) The NFFE is not yet operating a business and has no prior operating history, but is investing capital into assets with the intent to operate a business other than that of a Financial Institution, provided that the NFFE shall not qualify for this exception after the date that is 24 months after the date of the initial organization of the NFFE;
   g) The NFFE was not a Financial Institution in the past five years, and is in the process of liquidating its assets or is reorganizing with the intent to continue or recommence operations in a business other than that of a Financial Institution;
   h) The NFFE primarily engages in financing and hedging transactions with, or for, Related Entities that are not Financial Institutions, and does not provide financing or hedging services to any Entity that is not a Related Entity, provided that the group of any such Related Entities is primarily engaged in a business other than that of a Financial Institution;

i) The NFFE is an "excepted NFFE" as described in relevant U.S. Treasury Regulations; or

j) The NFFE meets all of the following requirements:

(1) It is established and operated in its jurisdiction of residence exclusively for religious, charitable, scientific, artistic, cultural, athletic, or educational purposes; or it is established and operated in its jurisdiction of residence and it is a professional organization, business league, chamber of commerce, labor organization, agricultural or horticultural organization, civic league or an organization operated exclusively for the promotion of social welfare;

(2) It is exempt from income tax in its jurisdiction of residence;

(3) It has no shareholders or members who have a proprietary or beneficial interest in its income or assets;

(4) The applicable laws of the NFFE's jurisdiction of residence or the NFFE's formation documents do not permit any income or assets of the NFFE to be distributed to, or applied for the benefit of, a private person or non-charitable Entity other than pursuant to the conduct of the NFFE's charitable activities, or as payment of reasonable compensation for services rendered, or as payment representing the fair market value of property which the NFFE has purchased; and

(5) The applicable laws of the NFFE's jurisdiction of residence or the NFFE's formation documents require that, upon the NFFE's liquidation or dissolution, all of its assets be distributed to a governmental entity or other non-profit organization, or escheat to the government of the NFFE's jurisdiction of residence or any political subdivision thereof.

5. **Preexisting Account**. A "Preexisting Account" means a Financial Account maintained by a Reporting Financial Institution as of June 30, 2014.

C. **Account Balance Aggregation and Currency Translation Rules**.

1. **Aggregation of Individual Accounts**. For purposes of determining the aggregate balance or value of Financial Accounts held by an individual, a Reporting Canadian Financial Institution is required to aggregate all Financial Accounts maintained by the Reporting Canadian Financial Institution, or by a Related Entity, but only to the extent that the Reporting Canadian Financial Institution's computerized systems link the Financial Accounts by reference to a data element such as client number or taxpayer identification number, and allow account balances or values to be aggregated. Each holder of a jointly held Financial Account shall be attributed the entire balance or value of the jointly held Financial Account for purposes of applying the aggregation requirements described in this paragraph 1.

2. **Aggregation of Entity Accounts**. For purposes of determining the aggregate balance or value of Financial Accounts held by an Entity, a Reporting Canadian Financial Institution is required to take into account all Financial Accounts that are maintained by the Reporting Canadian Financial Institution, or by a Related Entity, but only to the extent that the Reporting Canadian Financial Institution's computerized systems link the Financial Accounts by reference to a data element such as client number or taxpayer identification number, and allow account balances or values to be aggregated.

3. **Special Aggregation Rule Applicable to Relationship Managers**. For purposes of determining the aggregate balance or value of Financial Accounts held by a person to determine whether a Financial Account is a High Value Account, a Reporting Canadian Financial Institution is also required, in the case of any Financial Accounts that a relationship manager knows, or has reason to know, are directly or indirectly owned, controlled, or established (other than in a fiduciary capacity) by the same person, to aggregate all such accounts.

4. **Currency Translation Rule**. For purposes of determining the balance or value of Financial Accounts denominated in a currency other than the U.S. dollar, a Reporting Canadian Financial Institution must convert the U.S. dollar threshold amounts described in this Annex I into such currency using a published spot rate determined as of the last day of the calendar year preceding the year in which the Reporting Canadian Financial Institution is determining the balance or value.

D. **Documentary Evidence**. For purposes of this Annex I, acceptable documentary evidence includes any of the following:

1. A certificate of residence issued by an authorized government body (for example, a government or agency thereof, or a municipality) of the jurisdiction in which the payee claims to be a resident.

2. With respect to an individual, any valid identification issued by an authorized government body (for example, a government or agency thereof, or a municipality), that includes the individual's name and is typically used for identification purposes.

3. With respect to an Entity, any official documentation issued by an authorized government body (for example, a government or agency thereof, or a municipality) that includes the name of the Entity and either the address of its principal office in the jurisdiction (or U.S. Territory) in which it claims to be a resident or the jurisdiction (or U.S. Territory) in which the Entity was incorporated or organized.

4. With respect to a Financial Account maintained in a jurisdiction with anti-money laundering rules that have been approved by the IRS in connection with a QI agreement (as described in relevant U.S. Treasury Regulations), any of the documents, other than a Form W-8 or W-9, referenced in the jurisdiction's attachment to the QI agreement for identifying individuals or Entities.

5. Any financial statement, third-party credit report, bankruptcy filing, or U.S. Securities and Exchange Commission report.

E. **Alternative Procedures for Financial Accounts Held by Individual Beneficiaries of a Cash Value Insurance Contract**. A Reporting Canadian Financial Institution may presume that an individual beneficiary (other than the owner) of a Cash Value Insurance Contract receiving a death benefit is not a Specified U.S. Person and may treat such Financial Account as other than a U.S. Reportable Account unless the Reporting Canadian Financial Institution knows, or has reason to know, that the beneficiary is a Specified U.S. Person. A Reporting Canadian Financial Institution has reason to know that a beneficiary of a Cash Value Insurance Contract is a Specified U.S. Person if the information collected by the Reporting Canadian Financial Institution and associated with the beneficiary contains U.S. indicia as described in subparagraph (B)(1) of section II of this Annex I. If a Reporting Canadian Financial Institution knows, or has reason to know, that the beneficiary is a Specified U.S. Person, the Reporting Canadian Financial Institution must follow the procedures in subparagraph B(3) of section II of this Annex I.

F. **Reliance on Third Parties**. Regardless of whether an election is made under paragraph C of section I of this Annex I, Canada may permit Reporting Canadian Financial Institutions to rely on due diligence procedures performed by third parties, to the extent provided in relevant U.S. Treasury Regulations.

Annex II: Non-Reporting Canadian Financial Institutions and Products

I. General

A. This Annex may be modified by a mutual written decision entered into between the Competent Authorities of Canada and the United States:

1. To include additional Entities, accounts, and products that present a low risk of being used by U.S. Persons to evade U.S. tax and that have similar characteristics to the Entities, accounts, and products identified in this Annex as of the date of signature of the Agreement; or
2. To remove Entities, accounts, and products that, due to changes in circumstances, no longer present a low risk of being used by U.S. Persons to evade U.S. tax.

Any such addition or removal shall be effective on the date of signature of the mutual decision unless otherwise provided therein.

B. Procedures for reaching a mutual decision described in paragraph A of this section may be included in the mutual agreement or arrangement described in paragraph 6 of Article 3 of the Agreement.

II. Exempt Beneficial Owners

The following Entities shall be treated as Non-Reporting Canadian Financial Institutions and as exempt beneficial owners for the purposes of sections 1471 and 1472 of the U.S. Internal Revenue Code:

A. **Central Bank**

1. The Bank of Canada.

B. **International Organizations**

1. A Canadian office of an international organization as defined under paragraph (1) of Section 2 of the *Foreign Missions and International Organizations Act*.

C. **Retirement Funds**

1. Any plan or arrangement established in Canada and described in paragraph 3 of Article XVIII (Pensions and Annuities) of the Convention, including any plan or arrangement that the Competent Authorities may agree under subparagraph 3(b) of Article XVIII is similar to a plan or arrangement under that subparagraph.

D. **Investment Entity Wholly Owned by Exempt Beneficial Owners**

1. An Entity that is a Canadian Financial Institution solely because it is an Investment Entity, provided that each direct holder of an Equity Interest in the Entity is an exempt beneficial owner, and each direct holder of a debt interest in such Entity is either a Depository Institution (with respect to a loan made to such Entity) or an exempt beneficial owner.

III. Deemed-Compliant Financial Institutions

The following Financial Institutions are Non-Reporting Canadian Financial Institutions that shall be treated as deemed-compliant FFIs for the purposes of section 1471 of the U.S. Internal Revenue Code.

A. **Financial Institution with a Local Client Base**. A Financial Institution that qualifies as a local FFI as described in relevant U.S. Treasury Regulations, applying subparagraphs A(1), A(2) and A(3) of this section in lieu of the relevant paragraphs in those regulations:

1. Beginning on or before July 1, 2014, the Financial Institution must have policies and procedures, consistent with those set forth in Annex I, to prevent the Financial Institution from providing a Financial Account to any Nonparticipating Financial Institution and to monitor whether the Financial Institution opens or maintains a Financial Account for any Specified U.S. Person who is not a resident of Canada (including a U.S. Person that was a resident of Canada when the Financial Account was opened but subsequently ceases to be a resident of Canada) or any Passive NFFE with Controlling Persons who are U.S. residents or U.S. citizens who are not residents of Canada;
2. Such policies and procedures must provide that if any Financial Account held by a Specified U.S. Person who is not a resident of Canada or by a Passive NFFE with Controlling Persons who are U.S. residents or U.S. citizens who are not residents of Canada is identified, the Financial Institution must report such Financial Account as would be required if the Financial Institution were a Reporting Canadian Financial Institution (including by following the applicable registration requirements on the IRS FATCA registration website) or close such Financial Account;
3. With respect to a Preexisting Account held by an individual who is not a resident of Canada or by an Entity, the Financial Institution must review those Preexisting Accounts in accordance with the procedures set forth in Annex I applicable to Preexisting Accounts to identify any Financial Account held by a Specified U.S. Person who is not a resident of Canada, by a Passive NFFE with Controlling Persons who are U.S. residents or U.S. citizens who are not residents of Canada, or by a Nonparticipating Financial Institution, and must report such Financial Account as would be required if the Financial Institution were a Reporting Canadian Financial Institution (including by following the applicable registration requirements on the IRS FATCA registration website) or close such Financial Account;

B. **Local Bank**. A Financial Institution that qualifies as a nonregistering local bank as described in relevant U.S. Treasury Regulations, using the following definitions where applicable:

1. The term "bank" shall include any Depository Institution to which the *Bank Act* or the *Trust and Loan Companies Act* applies, or which is a trust or loan company regulated by a provincial Act; and
2. The term "credit union or similar cooperative credit organization that is operated without profit" shall include any credit union or similar cooperative credit organization that is entitled to tax-favored treatment with respect to distributions to its members under Canadian law, including any credit union as defined in subsection 137(6) of the *Income Tax Act*.

C. **Financial Institution with Only Low-Value Accounts**. A Canadian Financial Institution satisfying the following requirements:

1. The Financial Institution is not an Investment Entity;
2. No Financial Account maintained by the Financial Institution or any Related Entity has a balance or value in excess of $50,000, applying the rules set forth in Annex I for account aggregation and currency translation; and
3. The Financial Institution does not have more than $50 million in assets on its balance sheet, and the Financial Institution and any Related Entities, taken together, do not have more than $50 million in total assets on their consolidated or combined balance sheets.

D. **Sponsored Investment Entity and Controlled Foreign Corporation**. A Financial Institution described in subparagraph D(1) or D(2) of this section having a sponsoring entity that complies with the requirements of subparagraph D(3) of this section.

1. A Financial Institution is a sponsored investment entity if:
   a. It is an Investment Entity established in Canada that is not a qualified intermediary, withholding foreign partnership, or withholding foreign trust pursuant to relevant U.S. Treasury Regulations; and
   b. An Entity has agreed with the Financial Institution to act as a sponsoring entity for the Financial Institution.
2. A Financial Institution is a sponsored controlled foreign corporation if:
   a. The Financial Institution is a controlled foreign corporation[1] organized under the laws of Canada that is not a qualified intermediary, withholding foreign partnership, or with-

[1] A "controlled foreign corporation" means any foreign (i.e., non-U.S.) corporation if more than 50 percent of the total combined voting power of all classes of stock of such corporation entitled to vote, or the total value of the stock of such corporation, is owned, or is considered as owned, by "United States shareholders" on any day during the taxable year of such foreign corporation. The term a "United States shareholder" means, with respect to any foreign corporation, a United States person who owns, or is considered as owning, 10 percent or more of the total combined voting power of all classes of stock entitled to vote of such foreign corporation.

holding foreign trust pursuant to relevant U.S. Treasury Regulations;

b. The Financial Institution is wholly owned, directly or indirectly, by a Reporting U.S. Financial Institution that agrees to act, or requires an affiliate of the Financial Institution to act, as a sponsoring entity for the Financial Institution; and

c. The Financial Institution shares a common electronic account system with the sponsoring entity that enables the sponsoring entity to identify all Account Holders and payees of the Financial Institution and to access all account and customer information maintained by the Financial Institution including, but not limited to, customer identification information, customer documentation, account balance, and all payments made to the Account Holder or payee.

3. The sponsoring entity complies with the following requirements:

a. The sponsoring entity is authorized to act on behalf of the Financial Institution (such as a fund manager, trustee, corporate director, or managing partner) to fulfill applicable registration requirements on the IRS FATCA registration website;

b. The sponsoring entity has registered as a sponsoring entity with the IRS on the IRS FATCA registration website;

c. If the sponsoring entity identifies any U.S. Reportable Accounts with respect to the Financial Institution, the sponsoring entity registers the Financial Institution pursuant to applicable registration requirements on the IRS FATCA registration website on or before the later of December 31, 2015 and the date that is 90 days after such a U.S. Reportable Account is first identified;

d. The sponsoring entity agrees to perform, on behalf of the Financial Institution, all due diligence, reporting, and other requirements (including providing to any immediate payor the information described in subparagraph 1(e) of Article 4 of the Agreement), that the Financial Institution would have been required to perform if it were a Reporting Canadian Financial Institution;

e. The sponsoring entity identifies the Financial Institution and includes the identifying number of the Financial Institution (obtained by following applicable registration requirements on the IRS FATCA registration website) in all reporting completed on the Financial Institution's behalf; and

f. The sponsoring entity has not had its status as a sponsor revoked.

E. **Sponsored, Closely Held Investment Vehicle**. A Canadian Financial Institution satisfying the following requirements:

1. The Financial Institution is a Financial Institution solely because it is an Investment Entity and is not a qualified intermediary, withholding foreign partnership, or withholding foreign trust pursuant to relevant U.S. Treasury Regulations;

2. The sponsoring entity is a Reporting U.S. Financial Institution, Reporting Model 1 FFI, or Participating FFI, and is authorized to act on behalf of the Financial Institution (such as a professional manager, trustee, or managing partner);

3. The Financial Institution does not hold itself out as an investment vehicle for unrelated parties;

4. Twenty or fewer individuals own all of the debt interests and Equity Interests in the Financial Institution (disregarding debt interests owned by Participating FFIs and deemed-compliant FFIs and Equity Interests owned by an Entity if that Entity owns 100 percent of the Equity Interests in the Financial Institution and is itself a sponsored Financial Institution described in this paragraph E); and

5. The sponsoring entity complies with the following requirements:

a. The sponsoring entity has registered as a sponsoring entity with the IRS on the IRS FATCA registration website;

b. The sponsoring entity agrees to perform, on behalf of the Financial Institution, all due diligence, reporting, and other requirements (including providing to any immediate payor the information described in subparagraph 1(e) of Article 4 of the Agreement), that the Financial Institution would have been required to perform if it were a Reporting Canadian Financial Institution and retains documentation collected with respect to the Financial Institution for a period of six years;

c. The sponsoring entity identifies the Financial Institution in all reporting completed on the Financial Institution's behalf; and

d. The sponsoring entity has not had its status as a sponsor revoked.

F. **Restricted Fund**. A Financial Institution that qualifies as a restricted fund as described in relevant U.S. Treasury Regulations, applying the procedures set forth in, or required under, Annex I in lieu of the procedures set forth in, or required under, Treasury Regulation section 1.1471-4, and applying references to "report" or "reports" in lieu of references in relevant paragraphs in those regulations to "withhold and report" or "withholds and reports", provided that the Financial Institution provides to any immediate payor the information described in subparagraph 1(e) of Article 4 of the Agreement, or fulfills the requirements described in subparagraph 1(d) of Article 4 of the Agreement, as applicable.

G. Labour-Sponsored Venture Capital Corporations prescribed under section 6701 of the *Income Tax Regulations*.

H. Any Central Cooperative Credit Society as defined in section 2 of the *Cooperative Credit Associations Act* and whose accounts are maintained for member financial institutions.

I. Any entity described in paragraph 3 of Article XXI (Exempt Organizations) of the Convention.

J. An Investment Entity established in Canada that is regulated as a collective investment vehicle, provided that all of the interests in the collective investment vehicle (including debt interests in excess of $50,000) are held by or through one or more exempt beneficial owners, Active NFFEs described in subparagraph B(4) of section VI of Annex I, U.S. Persons that are not Specified U.S. Persons, or Financial Institutions that are not Nonparticipating Financial Institutions.

K. **Special Rules**. The following rules apply to an Investment Entity:

1. With respect to interests in an Investment Entity that is a collective investment vehicle described in paragraph J of this section, the reporting obligations of any Investment Entity (other than a Financial Institution through which interests in the collective investment vehicle are held) shall be deemed fulfilled.

2. With respect to interests in:

a. An Investment Entity established in a Partner Jurisdiction that is regulated as a collective investment vehicle, all of the interests in which (including debt interests in excess of $50,000) are held by or through one or more exempt beneficial owners, Active NFFEs described in subparagraph B(4) of section VI of Annex I, U.S. Persons that are not Specified U.S. Persons, or Financial Institutions that are not Nonparticipating Financial Institutions; or

b. An Investment Entity that is a qualified collective investment vehicle under relevant U.S. Treasury Regulations;

the reporting obligations of any Investment Entity that is a Canadian Financial Institution (other than a Financial Institution through which interests in the collective investment vehicle are held) shall be deemed fulfilled.

3. With respect to interests in an Investment Entity established in Canada that is not described in paragraph J or subparagraph K(2) of this section, consistent with paragraph 3 of Article 5 of the Agreement, the reporting obligations of all other Investment Entities with respect to such interests shall be deemed fulfilled if the information required to be reported by the first-mentioned Investment Entity pursuant to the Agreement with respect to such interests is reported by such Investment Entity or another person.

IV. Accounts Excluded from Financial Accounts

The following accounts and products established in Canada and maintained by a Canadian Financial Institution shall be treated as excluded from the definition of Financial Accounts, and therefore shall not be treated as U.S. Reportable Accounts under the Agreement:

A. Registered Retirement Savings Plans (RRSPs) – as defined in subsection 146(1) of the *Income Tax Act*

B. Registered Retirement Income Funds (RRIFs) – as defined in subsection 146.3(1) of the *Income Tax Act*

C. Pooled Registered Pension Plans (PRPPs) – as defined in subsection 147.5(1) of the *Income Tax Act*

D. Registered Pension Plans (RPPs) – as defined in subsection 248(1) of the *Income Tax Act*

E. Tax-Free Savings Accounts (TFSAs) – as defined in subsection 146.2(1) of the *Income Tax Act*

F. Registered Disability Savings Plans (RDSPs) – as defined in subsection 146.4(1) of the *Income Tax Act*

G. Registered Education Savings Plans (RESPs) – as defined in subsection 146.1(1) of the *Income Tax Act*

H. Deferred Profit Sharing Plans (DPSPs) – as defined in subsection 147(1) of the *Income Tax Act*

I. AgriInvest accounts – as defined under "NISA Fund No. 2" and "net income stabilization account" in subsection 248(1) of the *Income Tax Act* including Quebec's Agri-Quebec program as prescribed in section 5503 of the *Income Tax Regulations*

J. Eligible Funeral Arrangements – as defined under subsection 148.1 of the *Income Tax Act*

K. Escrow Accounts. An account maintained in Canada established in connection with any of the following:

1. A court order or judgment.
2. A sale, exchange, or lease of real or immovable property or of personal or movable property, provided that the account satisfies the following requirements:
   a. The account is funded solely with a down payment, earnest money, deposit in an amount appropriate to secure an obligation directly related to the transaction, or a similar payment, or is funded with a financial asset that is deposited in the account in connection with the sale, exchange, or lease of the property;
   b. The account is established and used solely to secure the obligation of the purchaser to pay the purchase price for the property, the seller to pay any contingent liability, or the lessor or lessee to pay for any damages relating to the leased property as agreed under the lease;
   c. The assets of the account, including the income earned thereon, will be paid or otherwise distributed for the benefit of the purchaser, seller, lessor, or lessee (including to satisfy such person's obligation) when the property is sold, exchanged, or surrendered, or the lease terminates;
   d. The account is not a margin or similar account established in connection with a sale or exchange of a financial asset; and
   e. The account is not associated with a credit card account.
3. An obligation of a Financial Institution servicing a loan secured by real or immovable property to set aside a portion of a payment solely to facilitate the payment of taxes or insurance related to the property at a later time.
4. An obligation of a Financial Institution solely to facilitate the payment of taxes at a later time.

L. An account maintained in Canada and excluded from the definition of Financial Account under an agreement between the United States and another Partner Jurisdiction to facilitate the implementation of FATCA, provided that such account is subject to the same requirements and oversight under the laws of such other Partner Jurisdiction as if such account were established in that Partner Jurisdiction and maintained by a Partner Jurisdiction Financial Institution in that Partner Jurisdiction.

United Kingdom

Canada–U.K. Income Tax Convention (1978)

Date Signed:	Convention — September 8, 1978 First Protocol — April 15, 1980 Second Protocol — October 16, 1985 Third Protocol — May 7, 2003 Fourth Protocol and Interpretative Protocol — July 21, 2014 Agreement Concerning Applications of Arbitration Provisions signed on July 27, 2015 by Canada and August 11, 2015 by the UK
Statutory citation:	Convention — S.C. 1980-81-82-83, c.44, Part X First Protocol — S.C. 1980-81-82-83, c.44, Part X Second Protocol — Order in Council P.C. 1985-3278 Third Protocol — Order in Council P.C. 2003-1374 Fourth Protocol — Order in Council P.C. 2014-1146
Date entered into force:	Convention — December 17, 1980 First Protocol — December 18, 1980 Second Protocol — December 23, 1985 Third Protocol — May 4, 2004 Fourth Protocol and Interpretative Protocol — December 18, 2014 Agreement Concerning Applications of Arbitration Provisions — December 21, 2016
Effective date of provisions:	Convention — • For withholding taxes — Amounts paid or credited to non-residents on or after January 1, 1976 • For other taxes — Taxation years beginning on or after January 1, 1976 First protocol – The provisions of Article 27A of the Convention, as added by Article IV of the Protocol, will have effect in Canada: • For withholding taxes — Amounts paid or credited to non-residents on or after January 1, 1981 • For other taxes — Taxation years beginning on or after January 1, 1981 Second protocol – • For withholding taxes on dividends, interest and royalties — Amounts paid or credited on or after February 1, 1986 • For pension and annuity payments — Amounts paid or credited after April 6, 1986 • For other payments — Taxation years beginning on or after January 1, 1986 Third protocol – • For withholding taxes — Amounts paid or credited to non-residents on or after January 1, 2005 • For other taxes — Taxation years beginning on or after January 1, 2005 • In the case of the United Kingdom, the Protocol will have effect in respect of income tax and capital gains tax, for any year of assessment beginning on or after April 6, 2005, and • In respect of corporation tax, for any financial year beginning on or after April 1, 2005 Fourth protocol and Interpretative Protocol (for certain exceptions, see Article XVI, paragraph 2 of the Protocol) – In Canada: • For withholding taxes — Amounts paid or credited to non-residents on or after January 1, 2015 • For other taxes — Taxation years beginning on or after January 1, 2015 In the United Kingdom: • For withholding taxes — Amounts paid or credited to non-residents on or after January 1, 2015 • For income tax and capital gains tax — for any year of assessment beginning on or after the April 6, 2015 • For corporation tax — for any financial year beginning on or after April 1, 2015
History:	The 1978 Canada–U.K. Convention replaced the 1966 Agreement. The 1978 convention has been amended by four protocols — see above for dates.
References:	See Related CRA Documents and Related Case Law following certain Articles of the Convention.

Convention between the Government of Canada and the Government of the United Kingdom of Great Britain and Northern Ireland for the Avoidance of Double Taxation and the Prevention of Fiscal Evasion with respect to Taxes on Income and Capital Gains[1]

[1] The text of the Convention as it appears here has been consolidated to reflect the changes made by all four Protocols.

Treaties and Related Legislation

The Government of Canada and the Government of the United Kingdom of Great Britain and Northern Ireland desiring to conclude a Convention for the avoidance of double taxation and the prevention of fiscal evasion with respect to taxes on income and capital gains, have agreed as follows:

Article 1 — Personal Scope

This Convention shall apply to persons who are residents of one or both of the Contracting States.

Article 2 — Taxes Covered

1. The taxes which are the subject of this Convention are:

(*a*) in Canada:

the income taxes which are imposed by the Government of Canada, (hereinafter referred to as "Canadian tax");

(*b*) in the United Kingdom of Great Britain and Northern Ireland:

the income tax, the corporation tax, the capital gains tax, the petroleum revenue tax and the development land tax (hereinafter referred to as "United Kingdom tax").

2. The Convention shall apply also to any identical or substantially similar taxes which are imposed after the date of signature of this Convention in addition to, or in place of, the existing taxes by either Contracting State or by the Government of any territory to which the present Convention is extended under Article 26. The Contracting States shall notify each other of changes which have been made in their respective taxation laws.

Editorial Note: Related CRA Documents: CRA Document No. 2002-0161767, dated December 20, 2002, notes that the Convention does not apply to U.K. inheritance tax paid by a Canadian resident, pursuant to subparagraph 1(*b*) of Article 2.

Article 3 — General Definitions

1. In this Convention, unless the context otherwise requires:

(*a*) (i) the term "Canada" used in a geographical sense, means the territory of Canada, including any area beyond the territorial waters of Canada which is an area where Canada may, in accordance with its national legislation and international law, exercise sovereign rights with respect to the sea-bed and sub-soil and their natural resources;

(ii) the term "United Kingdom" means Great Britain and Northern Ireland, including any area outside the territorial sea of the United Kingdom which in accordance with international law has been or may be hereafter designated, under the laws of the United Kingdom concerning the Continental Shelf, as an area within which the rights of the United Kingdom with respect to the sea-bed and sub-soil and their natural resources may be exercised;

(*b*) the terms "a Contracting State" and "the other Contracting State" mean, as the context requires, Canada or the United Kingdom;

(*c*) the term "person" includes an individual, a trust, a company, a partnership and any other body of persons;

(*d*) the term "company" means any body corporate or any other entity which is treated as a body corporate for tax purposes; in French, the term "sociéetée" also means a "corporation" within the meaning of Canadian law;

(*e*) the terms "enterprise of a Contracting State" and "enterprise of the other Contracting State" mean respectively an enterprise carried on by a resident of a Contracting State and an enterprise carried on by a resident of the other Contracting State;

(*f*) the term "competent authority" means:

(i) in the case of Canada, the Minister of National Revenue or the Minister's authorised representative;

(ii) in the case of the United Kingdom, the Commissioners for Her Majesty's Revenue and Customs or their authorised representative;

(*g*) the term "tax" means Canadian tax or United Kingdom tax, as the context requires;

(*h*) the term "national" means:

(i) in relation to the United Kingdom, any British citizen, or any British subject not possessing the citizenship of any other Commonwealth country or territory, provided that citizen or subject has the right of abode in the United Kingdom; and any legal person, partnership, association or other entity deriving its status as such from the law in force in the United Kingdom;

(ii) in relation to Canada, all citizens of Canada and all legal persons, partnerships and associations deriving their status as such from the law in force in Canada.

(*i*) the term "international traffic" means any transport by a ship or aircraft operated by an enterprise of a Contracting State, except when the ship or aircraft is operated solely between places in the other Contracting State.

2. As regards the application of the Convention by a Contracting State any term not otherwise defined shall, unless the context otherwise requires, have the meaning which it has under the laws of that Contracting State relating to the taxes which are the subject of the Convention;

Editorial Note: Related CRA Documents: CRA Technical Interpretation, Document No. 2003-0003125, dated July 17, 2003, states that, where a professional diver resident in the United Kingdom works off the Canadian coast in an area which falls within the definition of "Canada" under subparagraph 1(*a*)(i) of Article 3, the employment income earned by the diver will be considered to be earned in Canada for the purposes of the Convention; such income would be taxable by Canada under Article 15(1) or 27A(4) of the Convention.

History: Subparagraph (*c*) of paragraph 1 of Article 3 was deleted and replaced by paragraph 1 of Article I of the Fourth Protocol to this Convention. Subparagraph (*c*) of paragraph 1 of Article 3 of the Convention formerly read:

(*c*) the term "person" includes an individual, a trust, a company, any entity treated as a unit for tax purposes and any other body of persons, but does not include a partnership;

Subparagraph (*f*) of paragraph 1 of Article 3 was deleted and replaced by paragraph 2 of Article I of the Fourth Protocol to this Convention. Subparagraph (*f*) of paragraph 1 of Article 3 of the Convention formerly read:

(*f*) the term "competent authority" means:

(i) in the case of Canada, the Minister of National Revenue or his authorized representative,

(ii) in the case of the United Kingdom, the Commissioners of Inland Revenue or their authorized representative;

Subparagraph (*i*) of paragraph 1 of Article 3 was added by paragraph 3 of Article I of the Fourth Protocol to this Convention.

Subparagraph (*c*) of paragraph 1 of Article 3 was amended by Article 1 of the Protocol to this Convention, dated May 7, 2003. Subparagraph (*c*) of paragraph 1 of Article 3 of the Convention formerly read:

(*c*) the term "person" comprises an individual, a company, any entity treated as a unit for tax purposes or any other body of persons.

Clause (i) of subparagraph (*h*) of paragraph 1 of Article 3 was amended by Article 1 of the Protocol to this Convention, dated May 7, 2003. Clause (i) of subparagraph (*h*) of paragraph 1 of Article 3 of the Convention formerly read:

(i) in relation to the United Kingdom all citizens of the United Kingdom and Colonies, British Subjects under sections 2, 13(1) or 16 of the *British Nationality Act* 1948, and British Subjects by virtue of section 1 of the *British Nationality Act 1965*, provided they are patrial within the meaning of the *Immigration Act* 1971, so far as these provisions are in force on the date of entry into force of this Convention or have been modified only in minor respects, so as not to affect their general character; and all legal persons, partnerships, and associations deriving their status as such from the law in force in the United Kingdom.

Article 4 — Fiscal Domicile

1. For the purposes of this Convention, the term "resident of a Contracting State" means any person who, under the laws of that State, is liable to taxation therein by reason of his domicile, residence, place of management, place of incorporation or any other criterion of a similar nature. This term also includes that State and any political subdivision or local authority thereof, or any agency or instrumentality of that State, subdivision or local authority. But this term does not include any person who is liable to tax in that Contracting State in respect only of income from sources therein.

2. Where by reason of the provisions of paragraph 1 an individual is a resident of both Contracting States, then his status shall be determined as follows:

(*a*) he shall be deemed to be a resident of the Contracting State in which he has a permanent home available to him. If he has a permanent home available to him in both Contracting States, he shall be deemed to be a resident of the Contracting State with which his personal and economic relations are closer (centre of vital interests);

(*b*) if the Contracting State in which he has his centre of vital interests cannot be determined, or if he has not a permanent home available to him in either Contracting State, he shall be deemed to be a resident of the Contracting State in which he has an habitual abode;

(*c*) if he has an habitual abode in both Contracting States or in neither of them, he shall be deemed to be a resident of the Contracting State of which he is a national;

(*d*) if he is a national of both Contracting States or of neither of them, the competent authorities of the Contracting States shall settle the question by mutual agreement;

3. Where by reason of the provisions of paragraph 1 of this Article a person other than an individual is a resident of both Contracting States, the competent authorities of the Contracting States shall endeavour to determine by mutual agreement the State of which the person shall be deemed to be a resident, having regard to its place of effective management, the place where it is incorporated or otherwise constituted and any other relevant factors. If the competent authorities are unable to determine the matter by mutual agreement, they shall endeavour to determine by mutual agreement the mode of application of the Convention to that person.

Editorial Note: Related CRA Documents: CRA Document No. 830902, dated September 2, 1983, states that, in general, a "permanent home" referred to in paragraph 2 of Article 4, means a dwelling which an individual has arranged to have available for use at all times, and not on an occasional basis for a short duration only, including, for example, a house, apartment, or furnished room, rented or owned by the individual.

History: Paragraph 1 of Article 4 was deleted and replaced by Article II of the Fourth Protocol to this Convention. Paragraph 1 of Article 4 of the Convention formerly read:

1. For the purposes of this Convention, the term "resident of a Contracting State" means any person who, under the law of that State, is liable to taxation therein by reason of his domicile, residence, place of management or any other criterion of a similar nature. But this term does not include any person who is liable to tax in that Contracting State in respect only of income from sources therein.

Paragraph 3 of Article 4 was amended by Article 2 of the Protocol to this Convention, dated May 7, 2003. Paragraph 3 of Article 4 of the Convention formerly read:

3. Where by reason of the provisions of paragraph 1 a person other than an individual is a resident of both Contracting States, the competent authorities of the Contracting States shall by mutual agreement endeavour to settle the question and to determine the mode of application of the Convention to such person.

Article 5 — Permanent Establishment

1. For the purposes of this Convention, the term "permanent establishment" means a fixed placed of business in which the business of the enterprise is wholly or partly carried on.

2. The term "permanent establishment" shall include especially:

(*a*) a place of management;

(*b*) a branch;

(*c*) an office;

(*d*) a factory;

(*e*) a workshop;

(*f*) a mine, quarry or other place of extraction of natural resources;

(*g*) a building site or construction or assembly project which exists for more than 12 months.

3. The term "permanent establishment" shall not be deemed to include:

(*a*) the use of facilities solely for the purpose of storage, display or delivery of goods or merchandise belonging to the enterprise;

(*b*) the maintenance of a stock of goods or merchandise belonging to the enterprise solely for the purpose of storage, display or delivery;

(*c*) the maintenance of a stock of goods or merchandise belonging to the enterprise solely for the purpose of processing by another enterprise;

(*d*) the maintenance of a fixed place of business solely for the purpose of purchasing goods or merchandise or for collecting information, for the enterprise;

(*e*) the maintenance of a fixed place of business solely for the purpose of advertising, for the supply of information, for scientific research, or for similar activities which have a preparatory or auxiliary character, for the enterprise.

4. A person — other than an agent of an independent status to whom paragraph 5 applies — acting in a Contracting State on behalf of an enterprise of the other Contracting State shall be deemed to be a permanent establishment in the first-mentioned State if he has, and habitually exercises in that first-mentioned State, an authority to conclude contracts in the name of the enterprise, unless his activities are limited to the purchase of goods or merchandise for the enterprise.

5. An enterprise of a Contracting State shall not be deemed to have a permanent establishment in the other Contracting State merely because it carries on business in that other State through a broker, general commission agent or any other agent of an independent status, where such persons are acting in the ordinary course of their business.

6. The fact that a company which is a resident of a Contracting State controls or is controlled by a company which is a resident of the other Contracting State, or which carries on business in that other State (whether through a permanent establishment or otherwise), shall not of itself constitute either company a permanent establishment of the other.

Article 6 — Income from Immovable Property

1. Income from immovable property, including income from agriculture or forestry, may be taxed in the Contracting State in which such property is situated.

2. For the purposes of this Convention, the term "immovable property" shall be defined in accordance with the law of the Contracting State in which the property in question is situated. The term shall in any case include property accessory to immovable property, livestock and equipment used in agriculture and forestry, rights to which the provisions of general law respecting landed property apply, usufruct of immovable property and rights to variable or fixed payments as consideration for the working of, or the right to work, mineral deposits, sources and other natural resources; ships, boats and aircraft shall not be regarded as immovable property.

3. The provisions of paragraph 1 shall apply to income derived from the direct use, letting, or use in any other form of immovable property and to profits from alienation of such property.

4. The provisions of paragraphs 1 and 3 shall also apply to the income from immovable property of an enterprise and to income from immovable property used for the performance of professional services.

Editorial Note: Related CRA Documents: CRA Technical Interpretation, Document No. 2003-0028155, dated November 24, 2003, states that Article 6 would apply to the disposition of an option to acquire land in Canada by a U.K. resident company, so that the profits from the disposition are taxable in Canada; the rights or interest in the land created by the option are considered to fall within the definition of "immovable property" for the purposes of the Convention.

CRA Technical Interpretation, Document No. 2003-0020015, dated September 5, 2003, states that Article 6 would apply to rental income from a house located in the United Kingdom and owned by a Canadian resident, making such income taxable in both Canada and the United Kingdom as income from immovable property; the taxpayer may be able to claim a foreign tax credit for U.K. tax paid, for Canadian tax purposes.

CRA Technical Interpretation, Document No. 9802205, dated February 18, 1998, notes that Article 6 does not deny Canada the right to tax rental income received from a U.K. property by a Canadian resident.

Article 7 — Business Profits

1. Profits of an enterprise of a Contracting State shall be taxable only in that State unless the enterprise carries on business in the other Contracting State through a permanent establishment situated therein. If the enterprise carries on business as aforesaid, the profits that are

attributable to the permanent establishment in accordance with the provisions of paragraph 2 may be taxed in that other State.

2. For the purposes of this Article and Article 21, the profits that are attributable in each Contracting State to the permanent establishment referred to in paragraph 1 are the profits it might be expected to make, in particular in its dealings with other parts of the enterprise, if it were a separate and independent enterprise engaged in the same or similar activities under the same or similar conditions, taking into account the functions performed, assets used and risks assumed by the enterprise through the permanent establishment and through the other parts of the enterprise.

3. Where, in accordance with paragraph 2, a Contracting State adjusts the profits that are attributable to a permanent establishment of an enterprise of one of the Contracting States and taxes accordingly profits of the enterprise that have been charged to tax in the other State, the other State shall, to the extent necessary to eliminate double taxation on these profits, make an appropriate adjustment to the amount of the tax charged on those profits. In determining such adjustment, the competent authorities of the Contracting States shall if necessary consult each other.

4. Where profits include items of income or gains which are dealt with separately in other Articles of this Convention, then the provisions of those Articles shall not be affected by the provisions of this Article.

Editorial Note: Related CRA Documents: CRA Technical Interpretation, Document No. 2003-0020015, dated September 5, 2003, states that Article 7 would apply to business income of a Canadian resident derived from a U.K. partnership, making the profits from the partnership taxable only in Canada unless the partnership has a permanent establishment in the United Kingdom, in which case the profits would also be taxable in the United Kingdom, and the taxpayer would be eligible to claim a foreign tax credit for U.K. taxes paid for Canadian tax purposes.

CRA Document No. 5-3724, dated September 17, 1987, states that reasonable management fees paid by a Canadian corporation to a U.K. resident would fall within Article 7 or Article 14 of the Convention, so that such fees would only be taxable in Canada if the U.K. resident carries on business in Canada through a permanent establishment or a fixed base situated in Canada, to the extent that such fees are attributable thereto.

History: Article 7 was deleted and replaced by Article III of the Fourth Protocol to this Convention. Article 7 of the Convention formerly read:

Article 7

Business Profits.

1. The profits of an enterprise of a Contracting State shall be taxable only in that State unless the enterprise carries on business in the other Contracting State through a permanent establishment situated therein. If the enterprise carries on or has carried on business as aforesaid, the profits of the enterprise may be taxed in the other State but only so much of them as is attributable to that permanent establishment.

2. Subject to the provisions of paragraph 3, where an enterprise of a Contracting State carries on business in the other Contracting State through a permanent establishment situated therein, there shall be attributed to that permanent establishment profits which it might be expected to make if it were a distinct and separate enterprise engaged in the same or similar activities under the same or similar conditions and dealing wholly independently with the enterprise of which it is a permanent establishment.

3. In the determination of the profits of a permanent establishment situated in a Contracting State, there shall be allowed as deductions expenses of the enterprise (other than expenses which would not be deductible under the law of that State if the permanent establishment were a separate enterprise) which are incurred for the purposes of the permanent establishment including executive and general administrative expenses, whether incurred in the State in which the permanent establishment is situated or elsewhere.

4. Insofar as it has been customary in a Contracting State to determine the profits to be attributed to a permanent establishment on the basis of an apportionment of the total profits of the enterprise to its various parts, nothing in paragraph 2 shall preclude that Contracting State from determining the profits to be taxed by such an apportionment as may be customary; the method of apportionment adopted shall, however, be such that the result shall be in accordance with the principles embodied in this Article.

5. No profits shall be attributed to a permanent establishment by reason of the mere purchase by that permanent establishment of goods or merchandise for the enterprise.

6. For the purposes of the preceding paragraphs, the profits to be attributed to the permanent establishment shall be determined by the same method year by year unless there is good and sufficient reason to the contrary.

7. Where profits include items of income which are dealt with separately in other Articles of this Convention, the provisions of this Article shall not prevent the application of the provisions of those other Articles with respect to the taxation of such items of income.

Article 8 — Shipping and Air Transport

1. Profits derived by an enterprise of a Contracting State from the operation of ships or aircraft in international traffic shall be taxable only in that State.

2. Notwithstanding the provisions of paragraph 1 and Article 7, profits derived by an enterprise of a Contracting State from the carriage by a ship or aircraft of passengers or goods taken on board at a place in the other Contracting State for discharge at another place in that other Contracting State may be taxed in that other Contracting State, unless all or substantially all of the passengers or goods carried to that other place were taken on board at a place outside that other Contracting State.

3. Notwithstanding the provisions of Article 7, profits of an enterprise of a Contracting State from the use, maintenance or rental of containers (including trailers and related equipment for the transport of containers) used for the transport of goods or merchandise in international traffic shall be taxable only in that State.

4. The provisions of this Article shall also apply to profits derived by an enterprise of a Contracting State from its participation in a pool, a joint business or an international operating agency.

History: Paragraph 2 of Article 8 was deleted and replaced by Article IV of the Fourth Protocol to this Convention. Paragraph 2 of Article 8 formerly read:

2. Notwithstanding the provisions of paragraph 1 and Article 7, profits derived from the operation of ships used principally to transport passengers or goods exclusively between places in a Contracting State may be taxed in that State.

Article 8 was amended by Article 1 of the 1985 Protocol to this Convention. Article 8 formerly read:

1. Profits derived by an enterprise of a Contracting State from the operation of ships or aircraft in international traffic shall be taxable only in that State.

2. Notwithstanding the provisions of paragraph 1 and Article 7, profits derived from the operation of ships used principally to transport passengers or goods exclusively between places in a Contracting state may be taxed in that State.

3. The provisions of paragraphs 1 and 2 shall also apply to profits referred to in those paragraphs derived by an enterprise of a Contracting State from its participation in a pool, a joint business or in an international operating agency.

Article 9 — Associated Enterprises

1. Where:

(*a*) an enterprise of a Contracting State participates directly or indirectly in the management, control or capital of an enterprise of the other Contracting State; or

(*b*) the same persons participate directly or indirectly in the management, control or capital of an enterprise of a Contracting State and an enterprise of the other Contracting State;

and in either case conditions are made or imposed between the two enterprises in their commercial or financial relations which differ from those which would be made between independent enterprises, then any profits which would, but for those conditions, have accrued to one of the enterprises, but, by reason of those conditions, have not so accrued, may be included by a Contracting State in the profits of that enterprise and taxed accordingly.

2. Where a Contracting State includes in the profits of an enterprise of that State — and taxes accordingly — profits on which an enterprise of the other Contracting State has been charged to tax in that other State and the profits so included are profits which would have accrued to the enterprise of the first-mentioned State if the conditions made between the two enterprises had been those which would have been made between independent enterprises, then, subject to the provisions of paragraph 3 of this Article, that other State shall (notwithstanding any time limits in the domestic law of that other State) make an appropriate adjustment to the amount of tax charged therein on the profits. In determining such adjustment, due regard shall be had to the other provisions of this Convention and the com-

petent authorities of the Contracting States shall if necessary consult each other.

3. A Contracting State shall not make a primary adjustment to the profits of an enterprise in the circumstances referred to in paragraph 1 after the expiry of the time limits provided in its domestic laws and, in any case, after eight years from the end of the taxable year in which the profits which would be subject to such an adjustment would, but for the conditions referred to in paragraph 1, have been attributed to that enterprise.

4. The provisions of paragraphs 2 and 3 shall not apply in the case of fraud, wilful default or where a person's obligations have not been fulfilled owing to careless or deliberate behaviour.

History: Paragraphs 3 and 4 of Article 9 were deleted and replaced by Article V of the Fourth Protocol to this Convention. Paragraphs 3 and 4 of Article 9 formerly read:

3. Where a Contracting State makes or proposes to make an adjustment in accordance with the provisions of paragraph 1 of this Article, the other Contracting State shall be required to make the appropriate adjustment provided for under paragraph 2 of this Article to the profits of the associated enterprise in that other State only if within six years from the end of the taxation year (in Canada) or the chargeable period (in the United Kingdom) to which the first-mentioned adjustment relates, the competent authority of the other State has been notified that the first-mentioned adjustment has been made or proposed.

4. The provisions of paragraphs 2 and 3 of this Article shall not impose any obligation on Canada in the case of fraud, wilful default or gross negligence or on the United Kingdom in the case of fraudulent conduct.

Article 9 was amended by Article 3 of the Protocol to this Convention, dated May 7, 2003. Article 9 of the Convention formerly read:

Where

(*a*) an enterprise of a Contracting State participates directly or indirectly in the management, control or capital of an enterprise of the other Contracting State, or

(*b*) the same persons participate directly or indirectly in the management, control or capital of an enterprise of a Contracting State and an enterprise of the other Contracting State,; and in either case conditions are made or imposed between the two enterprises in their commercial or financial relations which differ from those which would be made between independent enterprises, then any income, deductions, receipts or outgoings which would, but for those conditions, have been attributed to one of the enterprises, but, by reason of those conditions, have not been so attributed, may be taken into account in computing the profits or losses of that enterprise and taxed accordingly.

Article 10 — Dividends

1. Dividends paid by a company which is a resident of a Contracting State to a resident of the other Contracting State may be taxed in that other State.

2. However, such dividends may also be taxed in the Contracting State of which the company paying the dividends is a resident and according to the laws of that State, but if the beneficial owner of the dividends is a resident of the other Contracting State the tax so charged shall not exceed:

(*a*) 5 per cent of the gross amount of the dividends if the beneficial owner is a company which controls, directly or indirectly, at least 10 per cent of the voting power in the company paying the dividends;

(*b*) 15 per cent of the gross amount of the dividends in all other cases.

The provisions of this paragraph shall not affect the taxation of the company in respect of the profits out of which the dividends are paid.

3. Notwithstanding the provisions of paragraph 2, dividends arising in a Contracting State and beneficially owned by an organisation that was constituted and is operated in the other Contracting State exclusively to administer or provide benefits under one or more recognized pension plans shall be exempt from tax in the first-mentioned State if:

(*a*) the organisation is the beneficial owner of the shares on which the dividends are paid, holds those shares as an investment and is generally exempt from tax in the other State;

(*b*) the organisation does not own directly or indirectly more than 10 per cent of the capital or 10 per cent of the voting power of the company paying the dividends; and

(*c*) each recognized pension plan provides benefits primarily to individuals who are resident of the other Contracting State.

4. For the purposes of paragraph 3, the term "recognized pension plan" means:

(*a*) in the case of Canada, a retirement or employee benefits plan described in paragraph (*a*) of the definition of "pension" under Article 5 of the *Income Tax Conventions Interpretation Act*;

(*b*) in the case of the United Kingdom, a pension scheme (other than a social security scheme) registered under Part 4 of the *Finance Act 2004*, including pension funds or pension schemes arranged through insurance companies and unit trusts where the unit holders are exclusively pension schemes; and

(*c*) any other pension plan agreed by the competent authorities of both Contracting States.

5. The term "dividends" as used in this Article means income from shares, "jouissance" shares or "jouissance" rights, mining shares, founders' shares or other rights, not being debt-claims, participating in profits, as well as income assimilated to or treated in the same way as income from shares by the taxation law of the State of which the company making the payment is a resident.

6. The provisions of paragraphs 1 and 2 of this Article shall not apply if the beneficial owner of the dividends, being a resident of a Contracting State, carries on business in the other Contracting State of which the company paying the dividends is a resident, through a permanent establishment situated therein, or performs in that other State professional services from a fixed base situated therein, and the holding in respect of which the dividends are paid is effectively connected with such permanent establishment or fixed base. In such a case, the provisions of Article 7 or Article 14, as the case may be, shall apply.

7. Where a company is a resident of only one Contracting State, the other Contracting State may not impose any tax on the dividends paid by the company, except insofar as such dividends are paid to a resident of that other State or insofar as the holding in respect of which the dividends are paid is effectively connected with a permanent establishment or a fixed base situated in that other State, nor subject the company's undistributed profits to a tax on undistributed profits, even if the dividends paid or the undistributed profits consist wholly or partly of profits or income arising in such other State.

Editorial Note: Related CRA Documents: CRA Document No. 2004-0099401I7, dated November 2, 2005, states that, in circumstances where a Canadian corporation pays dividends to a Bermuda trust (Bermuda being a non-treaty country), which are then paid by the trust to a U.K. resident, the payment of the Canadian dividends is considered to be made to the Bermuda trust under the Canadian *Income Tax Act*, and the Canada–U.K. Tax Convention is not applicable to reduce the withholding tax rate; however, it was also noted that in other circumstances, where a trust may reasonably be considered to act as an agent for beneficiaries, the CRA may "look through" an arrangement in determining the applicability of a tax treaty.

In CRA Document No. 5-2479, dated December 17, 1986, with respect to dividends paid by a Canadian corporation to a U.K. resident, which are remitted by the corporation to a bank account outside both Canada and the United Kingdom, it is noted that the provision in section 2 of Article 27 is restrictive in that, where income is taxed in the United Kingdom by reference to the amount that is remitted to or received in the United Kingdom, the relief granted under any other Article of the Convention is applicable only if the relevant income is received in the United Kingdom or remitted to the United Kingdom; consequently, the reduced witholding tax rate under Article 10 will only apply to the dividends if the amount is remitted to a U.K. address or it is known that the dividend income is taxed in the United Kingdom on a basis other than referred to in Article 27(2), otherwise the full witholding tax rate under the Canadian *Income Tax Act* will apply.

See *Prévost Car Inc. v. The Queen*, 2008 DTC 3080 (T.C.C.), affirmed 2009 DTC 5053 (F.C.A.). Dutch parent corporation, Prévost Holding, was held to be the beneficial owner of dividends from Canadian-resident corporation Prévost Car Inc., because Prévost Holding was free to use the dividends for its own use and enjoyment and assumed the risk and control of the dividends received. Prévost Car Inc. was correct in withholding tax at the Canada–Netherlands Tax Treaty rate of 5%.

History: Paragraphs 3 and 4 of Article 10 were added by paragraph 1 of Article VI of the Fourth Protocol to this Convention.

Paragraphs 4 to 7 of Article 10 were renumbered as paragraphs 5 to 8 by paragraph 2 of Article VI of the Fourth Protocol to this Convention.

Paragraphs 1 and 2 of Article 10 were amended by Article 4 of the Protocol to this Convention, dated May 7, 2003. Paragraphs 1 and 2 of the Convention formerly read:

1. Dividends paid by a company which is a resident of Canada to a resident of the United Kingdom may be taxed in the United Kingdom. Such dividends may also be taxed in Canada, and according to the laws of Canada, but provided that the beneficial owner of the dividends is a resident of the United Kingdom the tax so charged shall not exceed:

(*a*) 10 per cent of the gross amount of the dividends if the recipient is a company which controls, directly or indirectly, at least 10 per cent of the voting power in the company paying the dividends;

(*b*) 15 per cent of the gross amount of the dividends in all other cases.

2. Dividends paid by a company which is a resident of the United Kingdom to a resident of Canada may be taxed in Canada. Such dividends may also be taxed in the United Kingdom, and according to the laws of the United Kingdom, but provided that the beneficial owner of the dividends is a resident of Canada the tax so charged shall not exceed 15 per cent of the gross amount of the dividends.

Paragraph 3 of Article 10 was deleted by Article 4 of the Protocol to this Convention, dated May 7, 2003. Paragraph 3 of Article 10 of the Convention formerly read:

3. However, as long as an individual resident in the United Kingdom is entitled to a tax credit in respect of dividends paid by a company resident in the United Kingdom, the following provisions of this paragraph shall apply instead of the provisions of paragraph 2 of this Article:

(*a*) (i) Dividends paid by a company which is a resident of the United Kingdom to a resident of Canada may be taxed in Canada.

(ii) where a resident of Canada is entitled to a tax credit in respect of such a dividend under subparagraph (*b*) of this paragraph, tax may also be charged in the United Kingdom and according to the laws of the United Kingdom, on the aggregate of the amount or value of that dividend and the amount of that tax credit at a rate not exceeding 15 per cent.

(iii) Where a resident of Canada is entitled to a tax credit in respect of such a dividend under subparagraph (*c*) of this paragraph, tax may also be charged in the United Kingdom and according to the laws of the United Kingdom, on the aggregate of the amount or value of that dividend and the amount of that tax credit at a rate not exceeding 10 per cent.

(iv) Except as provided in subparagraph (*a*)(ii) and (*a*)(iii) of this paragraph, dividends paid by a company which is a resident of the United Kingdom to a resident of Canada who is the beneficial owner of those dividends shall be exempt from any tax which is chargeable in the United Kingdom on dividends.

(*b*) A resident of Canada who receives a dividend from a company which is a resident of the United Kingdom shall, subject to the provisions of subparagraph (*c*) of this paragraph and provided he is the beneficial owner of the dividend, be entitled to the tax credit in respect thereof to which an individual resident in the United Kingdom would have been entitled had he received that dividend, and to the payment of any excess of such credit over his liability to the United Kingdom tax.

(*c*) The provisions of subparagraph (*b*) of this paragraph shall not apply where the beneficial owner of the dividend is, or is associated with, a company which, either alone or together with one or more associated companies, controls, directly or indirectly, at least 10 per cent of the voting power in the company paying the dividend. In these circumstances a company which is a resident of Canada and receives a dividend from a company which is a resident of the United Kingdom shall, provided it is the beneficial owner of the dividend, be entitled to a tax credit equal to one-half of the tax credit to which an individual resident in the United Kingdom would have been entitled had he received that dividend, and to the payment of any excess of such credit over its liability to United Kingdom tax. For the purpose of this subparagraph, two companies shall be deemed to be associated if one controls, directly or indirectly, more than 50 per cent of the voting power in the other company, or a third company controls more than 50 per cent of the voting power in both of them.

Paragraph 5 of Article 10 was amended by Article 4 of the Protocol to this Convention, dated May 7, 2003. Paragraph 5 of Article 10 of the Convention formerly read:

5. The provisions of paragraphs 1, 2 and 3 shall not apply if the recipient of the dividends, being a resident of a Contracting State, carries on business in the other Contracting State of which the company paying the dividends is a resident, through a permanent establishment situated therein, or performs in that other State professional services from a fixed base situated therein, and the holding in respect of which the dividends are paid is effectively connected with such permanent establishment or fixed base. In such a case, the provisions of Article 7 or Article 14, as the case may be, shall apply.

Paragraph 7 of Article 10 was amended by Article 4 of the Protocol to this Convention, dated May 7, 2003. Paragraph 7 of Article 10 of the Convention formerly read:

7. If a resident of Canada does not bear Canadian tax on dividends derived from a company which is a resident of the United Kingdom and owns 10 per cent or more of the class of shares in respect of which the dividends are paid, then neither paragraph 2 nor 3 shall apply to the dividends to the extent that they can have been paid only out of profits which the company paying the dividends earned or other income which it received in a period ending twelve months or more before the relevant date. For the purposes of this paragraph the term "relevant date" means the date on which the beneficial owner of the dividends became the owner of 10 per cent or more of the class of shares referred to above.; Provided that this paragraph shall not apply if the shares were acquired for *bona fide* commercial reasons and not primarily for the purpose of securing the benefit of this Article.

Article 10 was amended by Article 2 of the 1985 Protocol to this Convention. Article 10 formerly read:

1. Dividends paid by a company which is a resident of Canada to a resident of the United Kingdom may be taxed in the United Kingdom. Such dividends may also be taxed in Canada, and according to the laws of Canada, but provided that the beneficial owner of the dividends is a resident of the United Kingdom the tax so charged shall not exceed 15 per cent of the gross amount of the dividends.

2. Dividends paid by a company which is a resident of the United Kingdom to a resident of Canada may be taxed in Canada. Such dividends may also be taxed in the United Kingdom, and according to the laws of the United Kingdom, but provided that the beneficial owner of the dividends is a resident of Canada the tax so charged shall not exceed 15 per cent of the gross amount of the dividends.

3. However, as long as an individual resident in the United Kingdom is entitled to a tax credit in respect of dividends paid by a company resident in the United Kingdom, the following provisions of this paragraph shall apply instead of the provisions of paragraph 2 of this Article:

(*a*) (i) Dividends paid by a company which is a resident of the United Kingdom to a resident of Canada may be taxed in Canada

(ii) Where a resident of Canada is entitled to a tax credit in respect of such a dividend under subparagraph (*b*) of this paragraph, tax may also be charged in the United Kingdom and according to the laws of the United Kingdom, on the aggregate of the amount or value of that dividend and the amount of that tax credit at a rate not exceeding 15 per cent.

(iii) Except as provided in subparagraph (*a*)(ii) of this paragraph, dividends paid by a company which is a resident of the United Kingdom to a resident of Canada who is the beneficial owner of those dividends shall be exempt from any tax which is chargeable in the United Kingdom on dividends.

(*b*) A resident of Canada who receives a dividend from a company which is a resident of the United Kingdom shall, subject to the provisions of subparagraph (*c*) of this paragraph and provided he is the beneficial owner of the dividend, be entitled to the tax credit in respect thereof to which an individual resident in the United Kingdom would have been entitled had he received that dividend, and to payment of any excess of such credit over his liability to United Kingdom tax.

(*c*) The provisions of subparagraph (*b*) of this paragraph shall not apply where the beneficial owner of the dividend is a company which, either alone or together with one or more associated companies, controls directly or indirectly at least 10 per cent of the voting power in the company paying the dividend. For the purposes of this subparagraph two companies shall be deemed to be associated if one is controlled directly or indirectly by the other or both are controlled directly or indirectly by a third company.

4. The term "dividends" as used in this Article means income from shares, "jouissance" shares or "jouissance" rights, mining shares, founders' shares or other rights, not being debt-claims, participating in profits, as well as income assimilated to or treated in the same way as income from shares by the taxation law of the State of which the company making the payment is a resident.

5. The provisions of paragraphs 1, 2 and 3 shall not apply if the recipient of the dividends, being a resident of a Contracting State, carries on business in the other Contracting State of which the company paying the dividends is a resident, through a permanent establishment situated therein, or performs in that other State professional services from a fixed base situated therein, and the holding in respect of which the dividends are paid is effectively connected with such permanent establishment or fixed base. In such a case, the provisions of Article 7 or Article 14, as the case may be, shall apply.

6. Where a company is a resident of only one Contracting State, the other Contracting State may not impose any tax on the dividends paid by the company, except insofar as such dividends are paid to a resident of that other State or insofar as the holding in respect of which the dividends are paid is effectively connected with a permanent establishment or a fixed base situated in that other State, nor subject the company's undistributed profits to a tax on undistributed profits, even if the

dividends paid or the undistributed profits consist wholly or partly of profits or income arising in such other State.

7. If a resident of Canada does not bear Canadian tax on dividends derived from a company which is a resident of the United Kingdom and owns 10 per cent or more of the class of shares in respect of which the dividends are paid, then neither paragraph 2 nor 3 shall apply to the dividends to the extent that they can have been paid only out of profits which the company paying the dividends earned or other income which it received in a period ending twelve months or more before the relevant date. For the purposes of this paragraph the term "relevant date" means the date on which the beneficial owner of the dividends became the owner of 10 per cent or more of the class of shares referred to above.; Provided that this paragraph shall not apply if the shares were acquired for *bona fide* commercial reasons and not primarily for the purpose of securing the benefit of this Article.

8. The provisions of this Article shall not apply if it was the main purpose or one of the main purposes of any person concerned with the creation or assignment of the shares or other rights in respect of which the dividend is paid to take advantage of this Article by means of that creation or assignment.

Article 11 — Interest

1. Interest arising in a Contracting State and paid to a resident of the other Contracting State may be taxed in that other State.

2. However, such interest may also be taxed in the Contracting State in which it arises and according to the laws of that State, but if the beneficial owner of the interest is a resident of the other Contracting State, the tax so charged shall not exceed 10 per cent of the gross amount of the interest.

3. Notwithstanding the provisions of paragraph 2:

(*a*) interest arising in the United Kingdom and paid to a resident of Canada shall be taxable only in Canada if it is paid in respect of a loan made, guaranteed or insured, or a credit extended, guaranteed or insured by Export Development Canada;

(*b*) interest arising in Canada and paid to a resident of the United Kingdom shall be taxable only in the United Kingdom if it is paid in respect of a loan made, guaranteed or insured, or a credit extended, guaranteed or insured by the United Kingdom Export Credits Guarantee Department; and

(*c*) interest arising in a Contracting State and paid to a resident of the other Contracting State shall not be taxable in the first-mentioned State if the beneficial owner of the interest is a resident of the other Contracting State and is dealing at arm's length with the payer.

4. Paragraph 3(*c*) shall not apply to interest, all or any portion of which is contingent or dependent on the use of or production from property or is computed by reference to revenue, profit, cash flow, commodity price or any other similar criterion or by reference to dividends paid or payable to shareholders of any class of shares of the capital stock of a company.

5. The term "interest" as used in this Article means income from debt-claims of every kind, whether or not secured by mortgage, and in particular, income from government securities and income from bonds or debentures, including premiums and prizes attaching to such securities, bonds or debentures, as well as income which is subjected to the same taxation treatment as income from money lent by the laws of the State in which the income arises. However, the term "interest" does not include income dealt with in Article 8 or Article 10.

6. The provisions of paragraphs 1, 2 and 3 shall not apply if the beneficial owner of the interest, being a resident of a Contracting State, carries on business in the other Contracting State in which the interest arises through a permanent establishment situated therein, or performs in that other State professional services from a fixed base situated therein, and the debt-claim in respect of which the interest is paid is effectively connected with such permanent establishment or fixed base. In such case the provisions of Article 7 or Article 14, as the case may be, shall apply.

7. Interest shall be deemed to arise in a Contracting State when the payer is a resident of that State. Where, however, the person paying the interest, whether the payer is a resident of a Contracting State or not, has in a Contracting State a permanent establishment or a fixed base in connection with which the indebtedness on which the interest is paid was incurred, and such interest is borne by such permanent establishment or fixed base, then such interest shall be deemed to arise in the State in which the permanent establishment or fixed base is situated.

8. Where, by reason of a special relationship between the payer and the beneficial owner or between both of them and some other person, the amount of the interest exceeds for whatever reason the amount which would have been agreed upon by the payer and the beneficial owner in the absence of such relationship, the provisions of this Article shall apply only to the last-mentioned amount. In such case, the excess part of the payments shall remain taxable according to the laws of each Contracting State, due regard being had to the other provisions of this Convention.

9. The provisions of this Article shall not apply if it was the main purpose or one of the main purposes of any person concerned with the creation or assignment of the debt-claim in respect of which the interest is paid to take advantage of this Article by means of that creation or assignment.

History: Article 11 was deleted and replaced by Article VII of the Fourth Protocol to this Convention. Article 11 of the Convention formerly read:

Article 11

Interest

1. Interest arising in a Contracting State and paid to a resident of the other Contracting State may be taxed in that other State.

2. However, such interest may be taxed in the Contracting State in which it arises, and according to the law of that State; but if the recipient is the beneficial owner of the interest, the tax so charged shall not exceed 10 per cent of the gross amount of the interest.

3. Notwithstanding the provisions of paragraph 2 of this Article,

(*a*) interest arising in the United Kingdom and paid to a resident of Canada shall be taxable only in Canada if it is paid in respect of a loan made, guaranteed or insured, or a credit extended, guaranteed or insured by Export Development Canada;

(*b*) interest arising in Canada and paid to a resident of the United Kingdom shall be taxable only in the United Kingdom if it is paid in respect of a loan made, guaranteed or insured, or a credit extended, guaranteed or insured by the United Kingdom Export Credits Guarantee Department; and

(*c*) interest arising in a Contracting State and paid with respect to indebtedness in connection with the sale on credit by a resident of the other State of any equipment, merchandise or services, except where the sale or indebtedness was between related persons, shall be taxable only in the other State.

4.

(*a*) Notwithstanding the provisions of paragraph 2 of this Article, interest arising in Canada and paid in respect of a bond, debenture or other similar obligation of the Government of Canada or of a political subdivision or local authority thereof shall, provided that the interest is beneficially owned by a resident of the United Kingdom, be taxable only in the United Kingdom;

(*b*) Notwithstanding the provisions of Article 29 Canada may, on or before the thirtieth day of June in any calendar year, give to the United Kingdom notice of termination of this paragraph and in such event this paragraph shall cease to have effect in respect of interest paid on obligations issued after 31 December of the calendar year in which the notice is given.

5. The term "interest" as used in this Article means income from debt-claims of every kind, whether or not secured by mortgage, and whether or not carrying a right to participate in the debtor's profits, and in particular, income from government securities and income from bonds or debentures, including premiums and prizes attaching to bonds or debentures, as well as income assimilated to income from money lent by the taxation law of the State in which the income arises. However, the term "interest" does not include income dealt with in Article 10.

6. The provisions of paragraphs 1, 2, 3 and 4 of this Article shall not apply if the beneficial owner of the interest, being a resident of a Contracting State, carries on business in the other Contracting State in which the interest arises through a permanent establishment situated therein, or performs in that other State professional services from a fixed base situated therein, and the debt-claim in respect of which the interest is paid is effectively connected with such permanent establishment or fixed base. In such a case, the provisions of Article 7 or Article 14, as the case may be, shall apply.

7. Interest shall be deemed to arise in a Contracting State when the payer is that State itself, a political subdivision, a local authority or a resident of that State. Where, however, the person paying the interest, whether he is a resident of a Contracting State or not, has in a Contracting State a permanent establishment in connection with which the indebtedness on which the interest is paid was incurred, and that

interest is borne by that permanent establishment, then such interest shall be deemed to arise in the Contracting State in which the permanent establishment is situated.

8. Where, owing to a special relationship between the payer and the person deriving the interest or between both of them and some other person, the amount of the interest paid exceeds for whatever reason the amount which would have been paid in the absence of such relationship, the provisions of this Article shall apply only to the last-mentioned amount. In that case, the excess part of the payments shall remain taxable according to the law of each Contracting State, due regard being had to the other provisions of this Convention.

9. Any provision in the law of a Contracting State relating only to interest paid to a non-resident company shall not operate so as to require such interest paid to a company which is a resident of the other Contracting State to be treated as a distribution of the company paying such interest. The preceding sentence shall not apply to interest paid to a company which is a resident of a Contracting State in which more than 50 per cent of the voting power is controlled, directly or indirectly, by a person or persons resident in the other Contracting State.

10. The provisions of paragraph 2 of this Article shall not apply to interest where the beneficial owner of the interest:

(*a*) does not bear tax in respect thereof in Canada; and

(*b*) sells (or makes a contract to sell) the holding from which the interest is derived within three months of the date on which such beneficial owner acquired that holding.

11. The provisions of this Article shall not apply if it was the main purpose or one of the main purposes of any person concerned with the creation or assignment of the debt-claim in respect of which the interest is paid to take advantage of this Article by means of that creation or assignment.

Paragraph 3 of Article 11 was amended by Article 5 of the Protocol to this Convention, dated May 7, 2003. Paragraph 3 of Article 11 of the Convention formerly read:

3. Notwithstanding the provisions of paragraph 2 of this Article,

(*a*) interest arising in the United Kingdom and paid to a resident of Canada shall be taxable only in Canada if it is paid in respect of a loan made, guaranteed or insured, or a credit extended, guaranteed or insured by the Export Development Corporation; and

(*b*) interest arising in Canada and paid to a resident of the United Kingdom shall be taxable only in the United Kingdom if it is paid in respect of a loan made, guaranteed or insured, or a credit extended, guaranteed or insured by the United Kingdom Export Credits Guarantee Department.

Paragraph 6 of Article 11 was amended by Article 5 of the Protocol to this Convention, dated May 7, 2003. Paragraph 6 of Article 11 of the Convention formerly read:

6. The provisions of paragraphs 1, 2 and 4 of this Article shall not apply if the recipient of the interest, being a resident of a Contracting State, carries on business in the other Contracting State in which the interest arises through a permanent establishment situated therein, or performs in that other State professional services from a fixed base situated therein, and the debt-claim in respect of which the interest is paid is effectively connected with such permanent establishment or fixed base. In such a case, the provisions of Article 7 or Article 14, as the case may be, shall apply.

Paragraph 11 of Article 11 was added by Article 5 of the Protocol to this Convention, dated May 7, 2003.

Paragraph 2 of Article 11 was amended by Article 3 of the 1985 Protocol to this Convention, to change "15 per cent" to "10 per cent".

Article 12 — Royalties

1. Royalties arising in a Contracting State and paid to a resident of the other Contracting State may be taxed in that other State.

2. However, such royalties may be taxed in the Contracting State in which they arise, and according to the laws of that State, but if the beneficial owner of the royalties is a resident of the other Contracting State, the tax so charged shall not exceed 10 per cent of the gross amount of the royalties.

3. Notwithstanding the provisions of paragraph 2 of this Article,

(*a*) copyright royalties and other like payments in respect of the production or reproduction of any literary, dramatic, musical or artistic work (other than payments in respect of motion pictures, and payments in respect of works on film, videotape or other means of reproduction for use in connection with television broadcasting);

(*b*) payments for the use of, or the right to use, any patent or for information concerning industrial, commercial or scientific experience (but not including any such payment provided in connection with a rental or franchise agreement);

(*c*) payments for the use of, or the right to use, computer software;

arising in a Contracting State and beneficially owned by a resident of the other Contracting State shall be taxable only in that other State.

4. The term "royalties" as used in this Article means payments of any kind received as a consideration for the use of, or the right to use, any copyright, patent, trade mark, design or model, plan, secret formula or process, or for the use of, or the right to use, industrial, commercial or scientific equipment, or for information concerning industrial, commercial or scientific experience, and includes payments of any kind in respect of motion pictures and works on film, videotape or other means of reproduction for use in connection with television broadcasting.

5. The provisions of paragraphs 1, 2 and 3 of this Article shall not apply if the beneficial owner of the royalties, being a resident of a Contracting State, carries on business in the other Contracting State in which the royalties arise through a permanent establishment situated therein, or performs in that other State professional services from a fixed base situated therein, and the right or property in respect of which the royalties are paid is effectively connected with such permanent establishment or fixed base. In such a case, the provisions of Article 7 or Article 14, as the case may be, shall apply.

6. Royalties shall be deemed to arise in a Contracting State when the payer is a resident of that State. Where, however, the person paying the royalties, whether he is a resident of a Contracting State or not, has in a Contracting State a permanent establishment or a fixed base in connection with which the obligation to pay the royalties was incurred, and those royalties are borne by that permanent establishment or fixed base, then such royalties shall be deemed to arise in the Contracting State in which the permanent establishment or fixed base is situated.

7. Where, owing to a special relationship between the payer and the person deriving the royalties or between both of them and some other person, the amount of the royalties paid exceeds for whatever reason the amount which would have been paid in the absence of such relationship, the provisions of this Article shall apply only to the last-mentioned amount. In that case, the excess part of the payments shall remain taxable according to the law of each Contracting State, due regard being had to the other provisions of this Convention.

8. The provisions of this Article shall not apply if it was the main purpose or one of the main purposes of any person concerned with the creation or assignment of the rights in respect of which the royalties are paid to take advantage of this Article by means of that creation or assignment.

Editorial Note: Related CRA Documents: CRA Technical Interpretation, Document No. 9421435, dated December 20, 1994, states that, royalties paid by a Canadian company to a U.K. resident for the right to reproduce movies and television series in video format for sale to distributors who subsequently rent or sell the videos to the general public for private viewing, would be exempt under paragraph 3 of Article 12 as payments representing copyright royalties.

History: Paragraph 2 of Article 12 was deleted and replaced by paragraph 1 of Article VIII of the Fourth Protocol to this Convention. Paragraph 2 of Article 12 of the Convention formerly read:

2. However, such royalties may be taxed in the Contracting State in which they arise, and according to the law of that State; but if the recipient is the beneficial owner of the royalties the tax so charged shall not exceed 10 per cent of the gross amount of the royalties.

Subparagraph (*a*) of paragraph 3 of Article 12 was deleted and replaced by paragraph 2 of Article VIII of the Fourth Protocol to this Convention. Subparagraph (*a*) of paragraph 3 of Article 12 of the Convention formerly read:

(*a*) copyright royalties and other like payments in respect of the production or reproduction of any literary, dramatic, musical or artistic work (other than payments in respect of motion pictures and works on film, videotape or other means of reproduction for use in connection with television broadcasting);

Paragraph 6 of Article 12 was deleted and replaced by paragraph 3 of Article VIII of the Fourth Protocol to this Convention. Paragraph 6 of Article 12 of the Convention formerly read:

6. Royalties shall be deemed to arise in a Contracting State when the payer is that State itself, a political subdivision, a local authority or a resident of that State. Where, however, the person paying the royalties, whether he is a resident of a Contracting State or not, has in a Contracting State a permanent establishment in connection with which the obligation to pay the royalties was incurred, and those royalties are borne as such by that permanent establishment, then such royalties

shall be deemed to arise in the Contracting State in which the permanent establishment is situated.

Paragraph 3 of Article 12 was amended by Article 6 of the Protocol to this Convention, dated May 7, 2003. Paragraph 3 of Article 12 of the Convention formerly read:

3. Notwithstanding the provisions of paragraph 2 of this Article, copyright royalties and other like payments in respect of the production or reproduction of any literary, dramatic, musical or artistic work (but not including royalties in respect of motion pictures and works on film, videotape or other means of reproduction for use in connection with television broadcasting) arising in a Contracting State and beneficially owned by a resident of the other Contracting State shall be taxable only in that other State.

Paragraph 5 of Article 12 was amended by Article 6 of the Protocol to this Convention, dated May 7, 2003. Paragraph 5 of Article 12 of the Convention formerly read:

5. The provisions of paragraphs 1, 2 and 3 shall not apply if the recipient of the royalties, being a resident of a Contracting State, carries on business in the other Contracting State in which the royalties arise through a permanent establishment situated therein, or performs in that other State professional services from a fixed base siuated therein, and the right or property in respect of which the royalties are paid is effectively connected with such permanent establishment or fixed base. In such a case, the provisions of Article 7 or Article 14, as the case may be, shall apply.

Paragraph 8 of Article 12 was added by Article 6 of the Protocol to this Convention, dated May 7, 2003.

Paragraphs 3 and 4 of Article 12 were amended by Article 4 of the 1985 Protocol to this Convention. Paragraphs 3 and 4 formerly read:

3. Notwithstanding the provisions of paragraphs 2, copyrights royalties and other like payments in respect of the production or reproduction of any literary, dramatic, musical or artistic work (but not including royalties in respect of motion picture films and works on film or videotape for use in connection with television) arising in a Contracting State and beneficially owned by a resident of the other Contracting State shall be taxable only in that other State.

4. The term "royalties" as used in this Article means payments of any kind received as a consideration for the use of, or the right to use, any copyright, patent, trade mark, design or model, plan, secret formula or process, or for the use of, or the right to use, industrial, commercial or scientific equipment, or for information concerning industrial, commercial or scientific experience, and includes payments of any kind in respect of motion picture films and works on film or videotape for use in connection with television.

Article 13 — Capital Gains

1. Gains derived by a resident of a Contracting State from the alienation of immovable property situated in the other Contracting State may be taxed in that other State.

2. Gains from the alienation of movable property forming part of the business property of a permanent establishment which an enterprise of a Contracting State has in the other Contracting State or of movable property pertaining to a fixed base available to a resident of a Contracting State in the other Contracting State for the purpose of performing professional services, including such gains from the alienation of such a permanent establishment (alone or with the whole enterprise) or of such fixed base, may be taxed in that other State.

3. Gains derived by a resident of a Contracting State from the alienation of ships or aircraft operated in international traffic or movable property pertaining to the operation of such ships or aircraft, shall be taxable only in that Contracting State.

4. Gains from the alienation of:

(*a*) any right, licence or privilege to explore for, drill for, or take petroleum, natural gas or other related hydrocarbons situated in a Contracting State, or

(*b*) any right to assets to be produced in a Contracting State by the activities referred to in subparagraph (*a*) above or to interests in or to the benefit of such assets situated in a Contracting State,

may be taxed in that State.

5. Gains from the alienation of:

(*a*) shares, other than shares quoted on an approved stock exchange, deriving their value or the greater part of their value directly or indirectly from immovable property situated in a Contracting State or from any right referred to in paragraph 4 of this Article, or

(*b*) an interest in a partnership or trust the assets of which consists principally of immovable property situated in a Contracting State, of rights referred to in paragraph 4 of this Article, or of shares referred to in subparagraph (*a*) above,

may be taxed in that State.

6. The provisions of paragraph 5 of this Article shall not apply:

(*a*) in the case of shares, where immediately before the alienation of the shares, the alienator owned, or the alienator and any persons related to or connected with him owned, less than 10 per cent of each class of the share capital of the company; or

(*b*) in the case of an interest in a partnership or trust, where immediately before the alienation of the interest, the alienator was entitled to, or the alienator and any persons related to or connected with him were entitled to, an interest of less than 10 per cent of the income and capital of the partnership or trust.

7. For the purposes of paragraph 5 of this Article:

(*a*) the term "an approved stock exchange" means a stock exchange prescribed for the purposes of the Canadian *Income Tax Act* or a recognized stock exchange within the meaning of the United Kingdom *Corporation Tax Acts*; and

(*b*) the term "immovable property" does not include any property (other than rental property) in which the business of the company, partnership or trust was carried on.

8. Gains from the alienation of any property, other than that referred to in paragraphs 1, 2, 3, 4 and 5 of this Article shall be taxable only in the Contracting State of which the alienator is a resident.

9. The provisions of paragraph 8 of this Article shall not affect the right of a Contracting State to levy according to its law a tax on or in respect of gains from the alienation of any property on a person who is a resident of that State at any time during the fiscal year in which the property is alienated, or has been so resident at any time during the six years immediately preceding the alienation of the property.

10. Where an individual ceases to be a resident of a Contracting State and by reason thereof is treated under the laws of that State as having alienated property before ceasing to be a resident of that State and is taxed in that State accordingly and at any time thereafter becomes a resident of the other Contracting State, the other Contracting State may tax gains in respect of the property only to the extent that such gains had not accrued while the individual was a resident of the first-mentioned State. However, this provision shall not apply to property, any gain from which that other State could have taxed in accordance with the provisions of this Article, other than this paragraph, if the individual had realized the gain before becoming a resident of that other State. The competent authorities of the Contracting States may consult to determine the application of this paragraph.

Editorial Note: Related CRA Documents: CRA Technical Interpretation, Document No. 2004-0098981E5, dated November 2, 2004, states that, in a situation where property situated in Scotland is transferred from a U.K. resident to a Canadian resident in a non-arm's length transfer, and then is subsequently sold by the Canadian resident to a non-arm's length purchaser, Article 13 would not to impinge on Canada's right to tax the Canadian resident on the taxable capital gain arising from the sale of the property.

CRA Technical Interpretation, Document No. 2003-0001995, dated April 8, 2003, states that the phrase "value or the greater part of their value" in paragraph 5(*a*) of Article 13 is interpreted to mean "more than 50 per cent" of the value of the shares.

CRA Technical Interpretation, Document No. 2000-0042545, dated January 9, 2001, states that, where a capital gain is realized by a U.K. resident on the disposition of shares of a private Canadian corporation carrying on a farming business, if the value of the shares is derived primarily from real property in which the business of the corporation is carried on, such shares will not constitute immovable property for the purposes of the Convention, by virtue of paragraph 7(*b*) of Article 13.

CRA Technical Interpretation, Document No. 9505185, dated July 13, 1995, states that, capital gains realized by a U.K. resident shareholder on the disposal of shares of a Canadian corporation, which shares derive most of their value from real property in Canada, will be exempt from taxation in Canada, provided that the shares are listed on a prescribed stock exchange in Canada and that the proceeds of disposition are received in the United Kingdom, pursuant to paragraphs 5(*a*) and 8 of Article 13.

CRA Technical Interpretation, Document No. 9500915, dated June 12, 1995, states that, both paragraph 5 and subparagraph 7(*b*) of Article 13 should be applied on a "look through" basis in determining what the value of shares is attributable to.

CRA Technical Interpretation, Document No. 9335425, dated June 6, 1994, states that, for the purposes of paragraph 8 of Article 13, "alienation" includes a deemed disposition of property at death, and that since paragraph 2 of Article 27 would not apply to a deemed disposition at death, relief from Canadian tax under paragraph 8 of Article 13 may be available to a U.K. resident on certain gains at death, notwithstanding that no income tax may be payable in the United Kingdom on these gains at that time.

CRA Document Nos. FE91_047, FE91_036, and FE91_040, each dated February 25, 1991, states that, for the purposes of subparagraph 7(*b*) of Article 13, mines and mineral reserves, rights to explore for and/or exploit mineral deposits, and mills used to process ore from mines may constitute "property in which the business of a company is carried on" provided that the mines, mineral reserves, or rights are not in respect of petroleum, natural gas or other related hydrocarbons referred to in paragraph 4 of Article 13; it is also noted that coal would be included in "other related hydrocarbons".

CRA Document No. 840308, dated March 8, 1984, states that, for the purposes of determining whether shares derive the greater part of their value from immovable property under subparagraph 4(*a*) of Article 13, a valuation method based on net asset values after assigning the debt will generally be accepted where it relates; however, where this test appears to be manipulated in contemplation of a share sale this method will not be accepted, particularly where an increase in value of shares is mainly attributed to an increase in the value of Canadian real estate.

History: Paragraph 9 of Article 13 was amended by Article 7 of the Protocol to this Convention, dated May 7, 2003. Paragraph 9 of Article 13 formerly read:

9. The provisions of paragraph 8 of this Article shall not affect the right of a Contracting State to tax, according to its domestic law, gains derived by an individual who is a resident of the other Contracting State from the alienation of any property, if the alienator:

(*a*) is a national of the first-mentioned Contracting State or was a resident of that State for 15 years or more prior to the alienation of the property, and

(*b*) was a resident of the first-mentioned Contracting State at any time during the five years immediately preceding such alienation.

Paragraph 10 of Article 13 was added by Article 7 of the Protocol to this Convention, dated May 7, 2003.

Article 13 was amended by Article 5 of the 1985 Protocol to this Convention. Article 13 formerly read:

1. Gains from the alienation of immovable property may be taxed in the Contracting State in which such property is situated.

2. Gains from the alienation of movable property forming part of the business property of a permanent establishment which an enterprise of a Contracting State has in the other Contracting State or of movable property pertaining to a fixed base available to a resident of a Contracting State in the other Contracting State for the purpose of performing professional services, including such gains from the alienation of such a permanent establishment (alone or together with the whole enterprise) or of such a fixed base may be taxed in the other State. However, gains derived by a resident of a Contracting State from the alienation of ships and aircraft operated in international traffic and movable property pertaining to the operation of such ships and aircraft, shall be taxable only in that Contracting State.

3. Gains from the alienation of:

(*a*) any right, licence or privilege to explore for, drill for, or take petroleum, natural gas or other related hydrocarbons situated in a Contracting State, or

(*b*) any right to assets to be produced in a Contracting State by the activities referred to in subparagraph (*a*) above or to interests in or to the benefit of such assets situated in a Contracting State,

may be taxed in that State.

4. Gains from the alienation of

(*a*) shares, other than shares quoted on an approved stock exchange, deriving their value or the greater part of their value directly or indirectly from immovable property situated in a Contracting State or from any right referred to in paragraph 3 of this Article, or

(*b*) an interest in a partnership or trust the assets of which consist principally of immovable property situated in a Contracting State, of rights referred to in paragraph 3 of this Article, or of shares referred to in subparagraph (*a*) above,

may be taxed in that State.

5. For the purposes of paragraph 4 of this Article "an approved stock exchange" means a stock exchange prescribed for the purposes of the Canadian *Income Tax Act* or a recognized stock exchange within the meaning of the United Kingdom *Corporation Tax Acts*.

6. Gains from the alienation of any property, other than those mentioned in paragraphs 1, 2, 3 and 4 shall be taxable only in the Contracting State of which the alienator is a resident.

7. The provisions of paragraph 6 of this Article shall not affect the right of a Contracting State to tax, according to its domestic law, gains derived by an individual resident in the other Contracting State from the alienation of any property, if the alienator:

(*a*) is a national of the first-mentioned Contracting State or was a resident of that State for 15 years or more prior to the alienation of the property, and

(*b*) was a resident of the first-mentioned Contracting State at any time during the five years immediately preceding such alienation.

Article 14 — Professional Services

1. Income derived by a resident of a Contracting State in respect of professional services or other independent activities of a similar character shall be taxable only in that State unless he has a fixed base regularly available to him in the other Contracting State for the purpose of performing his activities. If he has such a fixed base, the income may be taxed in the other Contracting State but only so much of it as is attributable to that fixed base.

2. The term "professional services" includes independent scientific, literary, artistic, educational or teaching activities as well as the independent activities of physicians, lawyers, engineers, architects, dentists and accountants.

Editorial Note: Related CRA Documents: CRA Document No. 5-3724, dated September 17, 1987, states that reasonable management fees paid by a Canadian corporation to a U.K. resident would fall within Article 7 or Article 14 of the Convention, so that such fees would only be taxable in Canada if the U.K. resident carries on business in Canada through a permanent establishment or fixed base situated in Canada, to the extent that such fees are attributable thereto.

Article 15 — Dependent Personal Services

1. Subject to the provisions of Articles 17 and 18, salaries, wages and other similar remuneration derived by a resident of a Contracting State in respect of an employment shall be taxable only in that State unless the employment is exercised in the other Contracting State. If the employment is so exercised, such remuneration as is derived therefrom may be taxed in that other State.

2. Notwithstanding the provisions of paragraph 1, remuneration derived by a resident of a Contracting State in respect of an employment exercised in the other Contracting State shall be taxable only in the first-mentioned State if:

(*a*) the recipient is present in the other State for a period or periods not exceeding in the aggregate 183 days in any 12 month period commencing or ending in the fiscal year concerned, and

(*b*) the remuneration is paid by, or on behalf of, an employer who is not a resident of the other State, and

(*c*) the remuneration is not borne by a permanent establishment or a fixed base which the employer has in the other State.

3. Notwithstanding the preceding provisions of this Article, remuneration derived in respect of an employment exercised aboard a ship or aircraft operated in international traffic by an enterprise of a Contracting State may be taxed in that State.

4. In relation to remuneration of a director of a company derived from the company the preceding provisions of this Article shall apply as if the remuneration were remuneration of an employee in respect of employment, and as if references to employer were references to the company.

5. [Deleted.]

Editorial Note: Related CRA Documents: CRA Technical Interpretation, Document No. 1999-0009425, dated February 21, 2000, notes that stock option benefits fall within "salary, wages and other similar remuneration" for the purposes of Article 15, and that the "calendar year concerned" in paragraph 2 of Article 15 refers to the year in which employment was exercised, rather than the year an option was exercised.

CRA Technical Interpretation, Document No. 9411805, dated September 22, 1994, states that a "retiring allowance" paid to a U.K. resident, in respect of wrongful dismissal by a Canadian employer, is not considered to be "salaries, wages and similar remuneration" for the purposes of Article 15, nor is it considered to be a "pension" under Article 17; such a payment would be subject to witholding tax in Canada pursuant to paragraph 212(1)(*j*.1) of the *Income Tax Act*, as there is no other relieving provision for such an allowance under the Convention.

Related Case Law: A lump sum received by a non-resident taxpayer on the exercise of stock option rights, which were earned under an executive stock option plan while the taxpayer was formerly employed in Canada, were taxable in Canada; subsection 7(4) of the *Income Tax Act* was found to be complementary to, and not in conflict with, Article 15(1) of the Convention. *John Hale v. The Queen*, 92 DTC 6473 (F.C.A.).

Income earned by a non-resident taxpayer, who was hired through an employment agency to perform services for a Canadian corporation, was taxable in Canada under Article15 as employment income earned in Canada; even if the taxpayer had been determined to be an independent contractor, the income would still be taxable in Canada under Article 14. *Jeffrey Hinkley v. The Queen*, 91 DTC 1336 (T.C.C.); aff'g 90 DTC 6481 (F.C.T.D.).

History: Subparagraph (*a*) of paragraph 2 of Article 15 was amended by paragraph 1 of Article IX of the Fourth Protocol to this Convention, by deleting and replacing the "183 days in the calendar year concerned" by "183 days in any 12 month period commencing or ending in the fiscal year concerned".

Paragraph 3 of Article 15 was deleted and replaced by paragraph 2 of Article IX of the Fourth Protocol to this Convention. Paragraph 3 of Article 15 of this Convention formerly read:

3. Notwithstanding the preceding provisions of this Article, remuneration in respect of an employment exercised aboard a ship or aircraft operated in international traffic may be taxed in the Contracting State in which the place of effective management of the enterprise is situated.

Paragraph 5 of Article 15 was deleted by paragraph 3 of Article IX of the Fourth Protocol to this Convention. Paragraph 5 of Article 15 of this Convention formerly read:

5. Where under the law of a Contracting State tax is required to be deducted and is so deducted from salaries, wages and other similar remuneration derived in respect of an employment exercised in that Contracting State, tax shall not be deducted therefrom on behalf of the other Contracting State.

Paragraph 5 of Article 15 was added by Article 1 of the 1980 Protocol to this Convention, which became effective at the same time as the main body of the Convention.

Article 16 — Artistes and Athletes

1. Notwithstanding the provisions of Articles 7, 14 and 15, income derived by entertainers, such as theatre, motion picture, radio or television artistes, and musicians, and by athletes, from their personal activities as such may be taxed in the Contracting State in which these activities are exercised.

2. Where income in respect of personal activities as such of an entertainer or athlete accrues not to that entertainer or athlete himself but to another person, that income may, notwithstanding the provisions of Articles 7, 14 and 15, be taxed in the Contracting State in which the activities of the entertainer or athlete are exercised.

3. The provisions of paragraphs 1 and 2 shall not apply:

(*a*) to income derived from activities performed in a Contracting State by entertainers or athletes if the visit to that Contracting State is wholly or substantially supported by public funds;

(*b*) to a non-profit making organization no part of the income of which is payable, or is otherwise available for the personal benefit of, any proprietor, member or shareholder thereof; or

(*c*) to an entertainer or athlete in respect of services provided to an organization referred to in subparagraph (*b*).

Article 17 — Pensions and Annuities

1. Periodic pension payments arising in a Contracting State and paid to a resident of the other Contracting State who is the beneficial owner thereof shall be taxable only in that other State.

2. Annuities arising in a Contracting State and paid to a resident of the other Contracting State may be taxed in that other State. However, such annuities may also be taxed in the Contracting State in which they arise and according to the laws of that State, but if the recipient is the beneficial owner of the annuities the tax so charged shall not exceed 10 per cent of the portion thereof that is subject to tax in that State.

3. For the purposes of this Convention, the term "pension" includes any payment under a superannuation, pension or retirement plan, Armed Forces retirement pay, war veterans' pensions and allowances, and any payment under a sickness, accident or disability plan, as well as any payment made under the social security legislation in a Contracting State.

4. For the purposes of this Convention, the term "annuity" means a stated sum payable periodically at stated times during life or during a specified or ascertainable period of time under an obligation to make the payments in return for adequate and full consideration in money or money's worth, but does not include any payment under a superannuation, pension or retirement plan or any payment under an income-averaging annuity contract.

5. Notwithstanding any other provision of this Convention, alimony and similar payments arising in a Contracting State and paid to a resident of the other Contracting State who is the beneficial owner thereof shall be taxable only in that other State.

Editorial Note: Related CRA Documents: CRA Technical Interpretation, Document No. 2005-0157981E5, dated April 6, 2006, states that under paragraph 1 of Article 17, U.K. pension payments made to a Canadian resident are taxable only in Canada, and should not be subject to withholding tax in the United Kingdom; however, lump-sum payments made in settlement of future U.K. pension plan entitlements are specifically excluded from the definition of a "pension" amount under this paragraph, and thereby may be subject to U.K. withholding tax.

CRA Technical Interpretation, Document No. 2004-0105071E5, dated December 8, 2004, states that, where a Canadian resident receives a payment under an individual buy-out contract on the wind-up of a U.K. pension plan, paragraphs 1 and 2 of Article 17 do not provide any specific relief, and do not preclude taxation of non-periodic pension or annuity payments by either Canada or the United Kingdom.

CRA Technical Interpretation, Document No. 2004-0077311E5, dated June 23, 2004, states that paragraph 1 of Article 17 does not to apply to irregular RRSP payments made to a U.K. resident, including non-mandatory monthly withdrawals made in unset amounts; such payments are considered to be in settlement of all future entitlements, and not within the definition of "periodic pension payments" as defined under the *Income Tax Conventions Interpretation Act*.

CRA Technical Interpretation, Document No. 2004-0074801E5, dated June 3, 2004, notes that, where a Canadian resident makes additional lump-sum contributions to a U.K. pension plan, no relief is available for deduction of such contributions from income for Canadian income tax purposes either under the *Income Tax Act* or under the Convention.

CRA Technical Interpretations, Document Nos. 2002-0162845, dated February 25, 2003, and 2002-0168355, dated February 19, 2003, note that, where a U.K. pension amount is paid to a Canadian resident, it is immaterial for Canadian income tax purposes, under both the Canadian *Income Tax Act* and under Article 17, whether or not the amount would be taxable had the recipient been a resident of the United Kingdom at the time the payment was received.

CRA Technical Interpretation, Document No. 9922715, dated September 23, 1999, notes that there is no relieving provision in the Convention relating to disability pension payments received, including payments from the U.K. Fire Brigade Basic Pension or the Injury Pension.

CRA Technical Interpretation, Document Nos. 9335755 and 9331415, both dated March 24, 1994, state that payments out of an RRIF made to a resident of the United Kingdom are exempt from tax under paragraph 1 of Article 17, providing the payments meet the definition of "periodic pension payments" under the *Income Tax Conventions Interpretation Act*, and notwithstanding the definition of "annuity" under that Act.

History: Paragraph 1 of Article 17 was amended by Article 8 of the Protocol to this Convention, dated May 7, 2003. Paragraph 1 of Article 17 of the Convention formerly read:

1. Pensions arising in a Contracting State and paid to a resident of the other Contracting State who is the beneficial owner thereof shall be taxable only in that other State.

Paragraph 3 of Article 17 was amended by Article 8 of the Protocol to this Convention, dated May 7, 2003. Paragraph 3 of Article 17 of the Convention formerly read:

3. For the purposes of this Convention, the term "pension" includes any payment under a superannuation, pension or retirement plan, Armed Forces retirement pay, war veterans pensions and allowances, and any payment under a sickness, accident or disability plan, as well as any payment made under the social security legislation in a Contracting State, but does not include any payment under a superannuation, pension or retirement plan in settlement of all future entitlements under such a plan or any payment under an income-averaging annuity contract.

Paragraph 4 of Article 17 was amended by Article 8 of the Protocol to this Convention, dated May 7, 2003. Paragraph 4 of Article 17 of the Convention formerly read:

4. For the purposes of this Convention, the term "annuity" means a stated sum payable periodically at stated times during life or during a specified or ascertainable period of time under an obligation to make the payments in return for adequate and full consideration in money or money's worth, but does not include a pension or any payment under a superannuation, pension or retirement plan in settlement of all future entitlements under such a plan or any payment under an income-averaging annuity contract.

Article 17 was amended by Article 6 of the 1985 Protocol to this Convention. Article 17 formerly read:

1. Pensions and annuities arising in a Contracting State and paid to a resident of the other Contracting State may be taxed in that other State. However, such pension and annuities may also be taxed in the first-mentioned Contracting State, but of the total amount thereof paid in any year of assessment or taxation year to a resident of the other Contracting State that first-mentioned Contracting State shall exempt from tax ten thousand Canadian dollars ($10,000) or five thousand pounds sterling (£5000), whichever is the greater. For the purposes of this paragraph the term "pensions" does not include lump sum payments out of a pension plan.

2. Notwithstanding the provisions of paragraph 1 of this Article, pensions paid out of public funds of the United Kingdom or Northern Ireland or of the funds of any local authority in the United Kingdom to any individual in respect of services rendered to the Government of the United Kingdom or Northern Ireland or a local authority in the United Kingdom in the discharge of functions of a governmental nature may be taxed in the United Kingdom.

3. The term "annuity" means a stated sum payable periodically stated times during life or during a specific or ascertainable period of time under an obligation to make the payments in return for adequate and full consideration in money or money's worth, but does not include payments of any kind under an income-averaging annuity contract.

4. Notwithstanding any other provision of this Convention, alimony and similar payments arising in a Contracting State and paid to a resident of the other Contracting State who is the beneficial owner thereof shall be taxable only in that other State.

Paragraph 1 of Article 17 was amended by Article 2 of the 1980 Protocol to this Convention, which became effective at the same time as the main body of the Convention. Paragraph 1 formerly read as follows:

Pensions and annuities arising in a Contracting State and paid to a resident of the other Contracting State may be taxed in that other State. However, such pensions and annuities may also be taxed in the first-mentioned Contracting State but only to the extent that the total amount thereof paid in any year of assessment or taxation year to the resident of the other Contracting State exceeds ten thousand Canadian dollars ($10,000) or five thousand pounds sterling (£5,000), whichever is the greater. However, the tax so charged in the first-mentioned Contracting State shall not exceed the tax chargeable on such pensions and annuities in the other Contracting State.

Article 18 — Government Service

1\.

(*a*) Remuneration, other than a pension, paid by a Contracting State or a political subdivision or a local authority thereof to any individual in respect of services rendered to that State or subdivision or local authority thereof shall be taxable only in that State.

(*b*) However, such remuneration shall be taxable only in the other Contracting State if the services are rendered in that State and the recipient is a resident of that State who:

(i) is a national of that State; or

(ii) did not become a resident of that State solely for the purpose of performing the services.

2. This Article shall not apply to remuneration in respect of services rendered in connection with any trade or business carried on by one of the Contracting States or a political subdivision or a local authority thereof.

3. [Deleted.]

Editorial Note: Related CRA Documents: In CRA Technical Interpretation, Document No. 2004-0065821E5, dated October 27, 2004, Article 18(1) was stated not to apply to an individual employed by the Ontario Securities Commission (OSC), on secondment to the U.K. Financial Services Authority (FSA), since the taxpayer continued to be resident in Canada under subparagraph 2(*a*) of Article 4, the taxpayer rendered services only to the FSA (and not to the OSC) while on assignment in the United Kingdom, and the OSC is not a "political subdivision" or "local authority" for the purposes of the Treaty.

History: Paragraph 3 of Article 18 was deleted by Article X of the Fourth Protocol to this Convention. Paragraph 3 of Article 18 of this Convention formerly read:

3. In this Article, the term "political subdivision" shall, in relation to the United Kingdom, include Northern Ireland.

Article 19 — Students

Payments which a student, apprentice or business trainee who is or was immediately before visiting one of the Contracting States a resident of a Contracting State and who is present in the other Contracting State solely for the purpose of his education or training receives for the purpose of his maintenance, education or training shall not be taxed in that other State, provided that such payments are made to him from sources outside that other State.

Article 20 — Estates and Trusts

1. Income received from an estate or trust resident in Canada by a resident of the United Kingdom who is the beneficial owner thereof may be taxed in Canada according to its law, but the tax so charged shall not exceed 15 per cent of the gross amount of the income.

2. The provisions of paragraph 1 of this Article shall not apply if the recipient of the income, being a resident of the United Kingdom, carries on business in Canada through a permanent establishment situated therein, or performs in Canada professional services from a fixed base situated therein, and the right of interest in the estate or trust in respect of which the income is paid is effectively connected with such permanent establishment or fixed base. In such a case, the provisions of Article 7 or Article 14, as the case may be, shall apply.

3. For the purposes of this Article, a trust does not include an arrangement whereby the contributions made to the trust are deductible for the purposes of taxation in Canada.

History: Paragraph 3 of Article 20 was added by Article 7 of the 1985 Protocol to this Convention.

Article 20A — Other Income

1. Items of income beneficially owned by a resident of a Contracting State, wherever arising, not dealt with in the foregoing Articles of this Convention shall be taxable only in that State.

2. The provisions of paragraph 1 of this Article shall not apply to income, other than income from immovable property, if the beneficial owner of such income, being a resident of a Contracting State, carries on business in the other Contracting State through a permanent establishment situated therein, or performs in that other State independent personal services from a fixed base situated therein, and the right or property in respect of which the income is paid is effectively connected with such permanent establishment or fixed base. In such case the provisions of Article 7 or Article 14 of this Convention, as the case may be, shall apply.

3. Notwithstanding the provisions of paragraphs 1 and 2 of this Article, items of income of a resident of a Contracting State not dealt with in the foregoing Articles of this Convention and arising in the other Contracting State may also be taxed in that other State.

History: Article 20A was added by Article 9 of the Protocol to this Convention, dated May 7, 2003.

Article 21 — Elimination of Double Taxation

1. In the case of Canada, double taxation shall be avoided as follows:

(*a*) subject to the existing provisions of the law of Canada regarding the deduction from tax payable in Canada of tax paid in a territory outside Canada and to any subsequent modification of those provisions — which shall not affect the general principle hereof — and unless a greater deduction or relief is provided under the laws of Canada, tax payable in the United Kingdom on profits, income or gains arising in the United Kingdom shall be deducted from any Canadian tax payable in respect of such profits, income or gains;

(*b*) subject to the existing provisions of the law of Canada regarding the allowance as a credit against Canadian tax of tax payable in a territory outside Canada and to any subsequent modification of those provisions — which shall not affect the general principle hereof — where a company that is a resident of the United Kingdom pays a dividend to a company that is a resident of Canada that controls directly or indirectly at least 10 per cent of the voting power in the first-mentioned company, the credit shall take into account the tax payable in the United Kingdom by that first-mentioned company in respect of the profits out of which such dividend is paid;

(*c*) where in accordance with any provision of this Convention income derived by a resident of Canada is exempt from tax in Canada, Canada may nevertheless, in calculating the amount of tax on other income take into account the exempted income.

2. Subject to the provisions of the law of the United Kingdom regarding the allowance as a credit against United Kingdom tax of tax payable in a territory outside the United Kingdom or, as the case may be, regarding the exemption from United Kingdom tax of a dividend arising in a territory outside the United Kingdom or of the profits of a permanent establishment situated in a territory outside the United Kingdom (which shall not affect the general principle of this Article):

(*a*) Canadian tax payable under the laws of Canada and in accordance with this Convention, whether directly or by deduction, on profits, income or chargeable gains from sources within Canada (excluding in the case of a dividend tax payable in respect of the profits out of which the dividend is paid) shall be allowed as a credit against any United Kingdom tax computed by reference to the same profits, income or chargeable gains by reference to which the Canadian tax is computed;

(*b*) a dividend which is paid by a company which is a resident of Canada to a company which is a resident of the United Kingdom shall be exempted from United Kingdom tax, when the exemption is applicable and the conditions for exemption under the law of the United Kingdom are met;

(*c*) the profits of a permanent establishment in Canada of a company which is a resident of the United Kingdom shall be exempted from United Kingdom tax when the exemption is applicable and the conditions for exemption under the law of the United Kingdom are met;

(*d*) in the case of a dividend not exempted from tax under subparagraph (*b*) which is paid by a company which is a resident of Canada to a company which is a resident of the United Kingdom and which controls directly or indirectly at least 10 per cent of the voting power in the company paying the dividend, the credit mentioned in subparagraph (*a*) shall also take into account the Canadian tax payable by the company in respect of its profits out of which such dividend is paid.

3. For the purposes of paragraphs 1 and 2 of this Article, income profits and capital gains owned by a resident of a Contracting State which are taxed in the other Contracting State in accordance with this Convention shall be deemed to arise from sources in that other Contracting State.

Editorial Note: Related CRA Documents: CRA Document No. AC59470, dated August 31, 1990, states that, for the purposes of paragraph 21(1)(*b*), "dividends" does not include dividends on term preferred shares.

History: Paragraph 2 of Article 21 was deleted and replaced by Article XI of the Fourth Protocol to this Convention. Paragraph 2 of Article 21 of this Convention formerly read:

2. In the case of the United Kingdom, double taxation shall be avoided as follows: subject to the provisions of the law of the United Kingdom regarding the allowance as a credit against United Kingdom tax of tax payable in a territory outside the United Kingdom (which shall not affect the general principle hereof)

(*a*) tax payable under the laws of Canada and in accordance with this Convention, whether directly or by deduction, on profits, income or chargeable gains from sources within Canada, (excluding in the case of a dividend, tax payable in respect of the profits out of which the dividend is paid) shall be allowed as a credit against any United Kingdom tax computed by reference to the same profits, income or chargeable gains by reference to which the Canadian tax is computed; and

(*b*) in the case of a dividend paid by a company which is a resident of Canada to a company which is resident in the United Kingdom and which controls directly or indirectly at least 10 per cent of the voting power in the Canadian company, the credit shall take into account (in addition to any tax creditable under (*a*)) tax payable under the laws of Canada by the company in respect of the profits out of which such dividend is paid.

Paragraph 1 of Article 21 was amended by Article 10 of the Protocol to this Convention, dated May 7, 2003. Paragraph 1 of Article 21 of the Convention formerly read:

1. In the case of Canada, double taxation shall be avoided as follows:

(*a*) Subject to the existing provisions of the law of Canada regarding the deduction from tax payable in Canada of tax paid in a territory outside Canada and to any subsequent modification of those provisions — which shall not affect the general principle hereof — and unless a greater deduction or relief is provided under the laws of Canada, tax payable in the United Kingdom on profits, income or gains arising in the United Kingdom shall be deducted from any Canadian tax payable in respect of such profits, income or gains.

(*b*) Subject to the existing provisions of the law of Canada regarding the determination of the exempt surplus of a foreign affiliate and to any subsequent modification of those provisions — which shall not affect the general principle hereof — for the purpose of computing Canadian tax, a company resident in Canada shall be allowed to deduct in computing its taxable income any dividend received by it out of the exempt surplus of a foreign affiliate resident in the United Kingdom.; The terms "foreign affiliate" and "exempt surplus" shall have the meaning which they have under the *Income Tax Act* of Canada.

Paragraph 4 of Article 21 was deleted by Article 10 of the Protocol to this Convention, dated May 7, 2003. Paragraph 4 of Article 21 of the Convention formerly read:

4. Where profits on which an enterprise of a Contracting State has been charged to tax in that State are also included in the profits of an enterprise of the other State and the profits so included are profits which would have accrued to that enterprise of the other State if the conditions made between the enterprises had been those which would have been made between independent enterprises dealing at arm's length, the amount included in the profits of both enterprises shall be treated for the purposes of this Article as income from a source in the other State of the enterprise of the first-mentioned State and relief shall be given accordingly under the provisions of paragraph 1 or paragraph 2 of this Article.

Paragraph 4 of Article 21 was added by Article 8 of the 1985 Protocol to this Convention.

Article 22 — Non-Discrimination

1. The nationals of a Contracting State shall not be subjected in the other Contracting State to any taxation or any requirement connected therewith which is other or more burdensome than the taxation and connected requirements to which nationals of that other State in the same circumstances are or may be subjected.

2. The taxation on a permanent establishment which an enterprise of a Contracting State has in the other Contracting State shall not be less favourably levied in that other State than the taxation levied on enterprises of that other State carrying on the same activities. This provision shall not be construed as obliging either Contracting State to grant to individuals not resident in its territory those personal allowances and reliefs for tax purposes which are by law available only to individuals who are so resident.

3. Nothing in this Convention shall be construed as preventing a Contracting State from imposing on the earnings attributable to permanent establishments in that State of a company which is a resident of the other Contracting State, tax in addition to the tax which would be chargeable on the earnings of a company which is a resident of the first-mentioned State, provided that the rate of any additional tax so imposed shall not exceed 5 per cent of the amount of such earnings which have not been subjected to such additional tax in previous taxation years.

4. For the purpose of paragraph 3 of this Article, the term earnings means the profits attributable to permanent establishments in a Contracting State (including gains from the alienation of property forming part of the business property of such permanent establishments) in a year and previous years after deducting therefrom:

(*a*) business losses attributable to such permanent establishments (including losses from the alienation of property forming part of the business property of such permanent establishments) in such year and previous years; and

(*b*) all taxes, other than the additional tax referred to in paragraph 3 of this Article, imposed on such profits in that State; and

(*c*) the profits reinvested in that State, provided that where that State is Canada, the amount of such deduction shall be determined in accordance with the existing provisions of the law of Canada regarding the computation of the allowance in respect of investment in property in Canada, and any subsequent modification of those provisions which shall not affect the general principle thereof; and

(*d*) five hundred thousand Canadian dollars, or two hundred and fifty thousand pounds sterling, whichever is the greater, less any amount deducted in that State under this sub-paragraph (*d*) by the company or a company associated therewith; for the purposes of this subparagraph (*d*) a company is associated with another company if one of them directly or indirectly has control of the other or both are directly or indirectly under the control of the same person, or if the two companies deal with each other not at arm's length.

5. In this Article, the term "taxation" means taxes which are the subject of this Convention.

History: The reference in paragraph 3 of Article 22 to "10 per cent" was amended by Article 11 of the Protocol to this Convention, dated May 7, 2003, to read "5 per cent".

Paragraph 3 of Article 22 was amended by Article 9 of the 1985 Protocol to this Convention. Paragraph 3 formerly read:

3. Nothing in this Convention shall be construed as preventing a Contracting State from imposing on the earnings attributable to permanent establishments in that State of a company which is a resident of the other Contracting State, tax in addition to the tax which would be chargeable on the earnings of a company which is a resident of the first-mentioned State, provided that the rate of any additional tax so imposed shall not exceed 15 per cent of the amount of such earnings which have not been subjected to such additional tax in previous taxation years.

Paragraphs 3 and 4 of Article 22 were amended by Article 3 of the 1980 Protocol to this Convention, which became effective at the same time as the main body of the Convention. Paragraphs 3 and 4 formerly read as follows:

3. Subject to the provisions of paragraph 4 of this Article, nothing in this Convention shall be construed as preventing a Contracting State from imposing on the earnings attributable to a permanent establishment in that State of a company which is a resident of the other Contracting State, tax in addition to the tax which would be chargeable on the earnings of a company which is a resident of the first-mentioned State, provided that the rate of any additional tax so imposed shall not exceed the lessor of:

(*a*) 15 per cent of the amount of such earnings which have not been subjected to such additional tax in previous taxation years, and

(*b*) the rate specified in respect of such additional tax in any agreement or convention entered into by Canada with any third State. For the purpose of this provision, the term earnings' means an amount not in excess of the profits attributable to a permanent establishment in a Contracting State in a year and previous years after deducting therefrom all taxes, other than the additional tax referred to herein, imposed on such profits in that State.

4. The provisions of paragraph 3 of this Article shall not apply where the profits attributable to a permanent establishment in a year or previous years do not exceed in the aggregate 500,000 Canadian dollars or 250,000 pounds sterling, whichever is the greater.

Article 23 — Mutual Agreement Procedure

1. Where a person considers that the actions of one or both of the Contracting States result or will result for that person in taxation not in accordance with the provisions of this Convention, that person may, irrespective of the remedies provided by the domestic law of those States, address to the competent authority of the Contracting State of which that person is a resident an application in writing stating the grounds for claiming the revision of such taxation. To be admissible, the application must be submitted within three years from the first notification of the action resulting in taxation not in accordance with the provisions of this Convention.

2. The competent authority referred to in paragraph 1 shall endeavour, if the objection appears to it to be justified and if it is not itself able to arrive at a satisfactory solution, to resolve the case by mutual agreement with the competent authority of the other Contracting State, with a view to the avoidance of taxation not in accordance with this Convention. Any agreement reached shall be implemented notwithstanding any time limits in the domestic law of the Contracting States.

3. For the purposes of Articles 6, 7 and 14 of this Convention, a Contracting State shall not, after the expiry of the time limits provided in its domestic laws and, in any case, after eight years from the end of the taxable period to which the income concerned was attributed, make a primary adjustment to the income of a resident of one of the Contracting States where that income has been charged to tax in the other Contracting State in the hands of that resident. The foregoing shall not apply in the case of fraud or wilful default or where a person's obligations have not been fulfilled owing to careless or deliberate behaviour.

4. The competent authorities of the Contracting States shall endeavour to resolve by mutual agreement any difficulties or doubts arising as to the interpretation or application of this Convention. They may also consult together for the elimination of double taxation in cases not provided for in this Convention.

5. The competent authorities of the Contracting States may communicate with each other directly for the purpose of applying this Convention.

6. Where,

(*a*) under paragraph 1, a person has presented a case to the competent authority of a Contracting State on the basis that the actions of one or both of the Contracting States have resulted for that person in taxation not in accordance with the provisions of this Convention, and

(*b*) the competent authorities are unable to reach an agreement to resolve that case pursuant to paragraph 2 within a period of three years from the date on which the information necessary to undertake substantive consideration for a mutual agreement has been received by both competent authorities or such other period from that date as is agreed by both competent authorities,

any unresolved issues arising from the case shall be submitted to arbitration. The arbitration shall be conducted in the manner prescribed by the rules and procedures agreed upon by the Contracting States through an exchange of diplomatic notes. These unresolved issues shall not, however, be submitted to arbitration if a decision on these issues has already been rendered by a court or administrative tribunal of either State. Unless a person whose taxation is directly affected by the arbitration decision does not accept that decision, the decision shall be binding on both States and shall constitute a resolution by mutual agreement under this Article.

7. The provisions of paragraph 6 shall apply only with respect to issues arising under Article 4 (but only insofar as the issue relates to the residence of an individual), Article 5, Article 7, Article 9, Article 12 (but only insofar as Article 12 might apply in transactions involving related persons to which Article 9 might apply), Article 14, and any other Articles subsequently agreed by the Contracting States through an exchange of diplomatic notes.

Editorial Note: Related CRA Documents: CRA Document No. FE91_097.098, dated February 20, 1991, states that, generally, the Canadian tax authority will only consider granting relief from Canadian taxation under paragraph 3 of Article 23 where income is taxed in the other Contracting State in which the taxpayer is resident, such that a case of "double taxation" exists.

History: Article 23 was deleted and replaced by Article XII of the Fourth Protocol to this Convention. Article 23 of the Convention formerly read:

Article 23

Mutual Agreement Procedure.

1. Where a resident of a Contracting State considers that the actions of one or both of the Contracting States result or will result for him in taxation not in accordance with this Convention, he may, without prejudice to the remedies provided by the national laws of those States, address to the competent authority of the Contracting State of which he is a resident an application in writing stating the grounds for claiming the revision of such taxation.

2. The competent authority referred to in paragraph 1 shall endeavour, if the objection appears to it to be justified and if it is not itself able to arrive at an appropriate solution, to resolve the case by mutual agreement with the competent authority of the other Contracting State, with a view to the avoidance of taxation not in accordance with the Convention.

3. The competent authorities of the Contracting States shall endeavour to resolve by mutual agreement any difficulties or doubts arising as to the interpretation or application of the Convention. In particular, the competent authorities of the Contracting States may reach agreement on:

(*a*) the same attribution of profits to a resident of a Contracting State and its permanent establishment situated in the other Contracting State;

(*b*) the same allocation of income between a resident of a Contracting State and any associated person provided for in Article 9.

Article 24 — Exchange of Information

1. The competent authorities of the Contracting States shall exchange such information as is foreseeably relevant for carrying out the provisions of this Convention or to the administration or enforcement of the domestic laws concerning taxes of every kind and descrip-

tion imposed on behalf of the Contracting States, insofar as the taxation thereunder is not contrary to this Convention. The exchange of information is not restricted by Articles 1 and 2.

2. Any information received under paragraph 1 by a Contracting State shall be treated as secret in the same manner as information obtained under the domestic laws of that State and shall be disclosed only to persons or authorities (including courts and administrative bodies) concerned with the assessment or collection of, the enforcement or prosecution in respect of, the determination of appeals in relation to taxes of every kind and description imposed by or on behalf of the Contracting States or of their political subdivisions, or the oversight of the above. Such persons or authorities shall use the information only for such purposes. They may disclose the information in public court proceedings or in judicial decisions. Notwithstanding the foregoing, information received by a Contracting State may be used for other purposes when such information may be used for such other purposes under the laws of both States and the competent authority of the supplying State authorises such use.

3. In no case shall the provisions of paragraphs 1 and 2 be construed so as to impose on a Contracting State the obligation

(*a*) to carry out administrative measures at variance with the laws and the administrative practice of that or of the other Contracting State;

(*b*) to supply information which is not obtainable under the laws or in the normal course of the administration of that or of the other Contracting State;

(*c*) to supply information which would disclose any trade, business, industrial, commercial or professional secret or trade process, or information the disclosure of which would be contrary to public policy (*ordre public*).

4. If information is requested by a Contracting State in accordance with this Article, the other Contracting State shall use its information gathering measures to obtain the requested information, even though that other State may not need such information for its own tax purposes. The obligation contained in the preceding sentence is subject to the limitations of paragraph 3 but in no case shall such limitations be construed to permit a Contracting State to decline to supply information solely because it has no domestic interest in such information.

5. In no case shall the provisions of paragraph 3 be construed to permit a Contracting State to decline to supply information solely because the information is held by a bank, other financial institution, nominee or person acting in an agency or a fiduciary capacity or because the information relates to ownership interests in a person.

6. Authorized representatives of a Contracting State shall be permitted to enter the other Contracting State to interview individuals or examine a person's books and records with their consent, in accordance with procedures mutually agreed upon by the competent authorities.

History: Article 24 was deleted and replaced by Article XIII of the Fourth Protocol to this Convention. Article 24 of the Convention formerly read:

Article 24

Exchange of Information.

1. The competent authorities of the Contracting States shall exchange such information as is necessary for carrying out the provisions of this Convention or of the domestic laws of the Contracting States concerning taxes covered by this Convention insofar as the taxation thereunder is not contrary to this Convention, in particular, to prevent fraud and to facilitate the administration of statutory provisions against legal avoidance. This includes information relating to the assessment or collection of, the enforcement or prosecution in respect of, or the determination of appeals in relation to, the taxes covered by this Convention. The exchange of information is not restricted by Article 1 of this Convention. Any information received by a Contracting State shall be treated as secret and shall be disclosed only to persons or authorities (including courts and administrative bodies) concerned with the assessment or collection of, the enforcement or prosecution in respect of, or the determination of appeals in relation to, the taxes covered by this Convention. Such persons or authorities shall use the information only for such purposes. They may disclose the information in public court proceedings or in judicial decisions.

2. In no case shall the provisions of paragraph 1 of this Article be construed so as to impose on a Contracting State the obligation:

(*a*) to carry out administrative measures at variance with the laws and administrative practice of that or of the other Contracting State;

(*b*) to supply information which is not obtainable under the laws or in the normal course of the administration of that or of the other Contracting State;

(*c*) to supply information which would disclose any trade, business, industrial, commercial or professional secret or trade process, or information the disclosure of which would be contrary to public policy.

3. If information is requested by a Contracting State in accordance with this Article, the other Contracting State shall obtain that information in the same manner and to the same extent as if the tax of the first-mentioned State were the tax of that other State and were being imposed by that other State, notwithstanding that the other State may not, at that time, need such information for the purposes of its own tax.

Article 24 was amended by Article 12 of the Protocol to this Convention, dated May 7, 2003. Article 24 of the Convention formerly read:

1. The competent authorities of the Contracting States shall exchange such information (being information which is at their disposal under their respective taxation laws in the normal course of administration) as is necessary for the carrying out of the provisions of this Convention or for the prevention of fraud or for the administration of statutory provisions against legal avoidance in relation to the taxes which are the subject of this Convention. Any information so exchanged shall be treated as secret and shall not be disclosed to persons other than persons (including a court or administrative tribunal) concerned with the assessment, collection or enforcement in respect of the taxes which are the subject of this Convention. No information as aforesaid shall be exchanged which would disclose any trade, business, industrial or professional secret or trade process.

Article 24A — Assistance in the Collection of Taxes

1. The Contracting States shall lend assistance to each other in the collection of revenue claims. This assistance is not restricted by Articles 1 and 2. The competent authorities of the Contracting States shall by mutual agreement settle the mode of application of this Article, including agreement to ensure comparable levels of assistance.

2. The term "revenue claim" as used in this Article means an amount owed in respect of taxes of every kind and description collected by or on behalf of the Contracting States, or on behalf of the political subdivisions of the Contracting States, insofar as the taxation thereunder is not contrary to this Convention or any other instrument to which the Contracting States are parties, as well as interest, administrative penalties and costs of collection or conservancy related to such amount.

3. When a revenue claim of a Contracting State is enforceable under the laws of that State and is owed by a person who, at that time, cannot, under the laws of that State, prevent its collection, that revenue claim shall, at the request of the competent authority of that State made in accordance with the mode of application referred to in paragraph 1, be accepted for purposes of collection by the competent authority of the other Contracting State. That revenue claim shall be collected by that other State in accordance with the provisions of its laws applicable to the enforcement and collection of its own taxes as if the revenue claim were a revenue claim of that other State.

4. Notwithstanding the provisions of paragraph 3, a revenue claim accepted by a Contracting State for purposes of paragraph 3 shall not, in that State, be accorded any priority applicable to a revenue claim under the laws of that State by reason of its nature as such. In addition, a revenue claim accepted by a Contracting State for the purposes of paragraph 3 shall not, in that State, have any priority applicable to that revenue claim under the laws of the other Contracting State.

5. Proceedings with respect to the existence, validity or the amount of a revenue claim of a Contracting State shall not be brought before the courts or administrative bodies of the other Contracting State.

6. Where, at any time after a request has been made by a Contracting State under paragraph 3 and before the other Contracting State has collected and remitted the relevant revenue claim to the first-mentioned State, the relevant revenue claim ceases to be a revenue claim of the first-mentioned State that is enforceable under the laws of that State and is owed by a person who, at that time, cannot, under the laws of that State, prevent its collection, the competent authority of the first-mentioned State shall promptly notify the competent authority of the other State of that fact and, at the option of the other State, the first-mentioned State shall either suspend or withdraw its request.

7. In no case shall the provisions of this Article be construed so as to impose on a Contracting State the obligation:

(*a*) to carry out administrative measures at variance with the laws and administrative practice of that or of the other Contracting State;

(*b*) to carry out measures which would be contrary to public policy (*ordre public*);

(*c*) to provide assistance if the other Contracting State has not pursued all reasonable measures of collection available under its laws or administrative practice;

(*d*) to provide assistance in those cases where the administrative burden for that State is clearly disproportionate to the benefit to be derived by the other Contracting State;

(*e*) to provide administrative assistance if and insofar as it considers the taxation in the other State to be contrary to generally accepted taxation principles.

History: Article 24A was added by Article XIV of the Fourth Protocol to this Convention.

Article 25 — Diplomatic and Consular Officials

1. Nothing in this Convention shall affect the fiscal privileges of members of diplomatic or consular missions under the general rules of international law or under the provisions of special agreements.

2. This Convention shall not apply to International Organizations, to organs or officials thereof and to persons who are members of a diplomatic or permanent mission or consular post of a third State, being present in a Contracting State and not treated in either Contracting State as residents in respect of taxes on income or capital gains.

Article 26 — Extension

1. This Convention may be extended, either in its entirety or with modifications to any territory for whose international relations either of the Contracting States is responsible, and which imposes taxes substantially similar in character to those which are the subject of this Convention and any such extension shall take effect from such date and subject to such modifications and conditions (including conditions as to termination) as may be specified and agreed between the Contracting States in notes to be exchanged for this purpose.

2. The termination of this Convention under Article 29 shall, unless otherwise expressly agreed by both Contracting States, terminate the application of this Convention to any territory to which it has been extended under this Article.

Article 27 — Miscellaneous Rules

1. The provisions of this Convention shall not be construed to restrict in any manner any exclusion, exemption, deduction, credit or other allowance now or hereafter accorded by the laws of a Contracting State in the determination of the tax imposed by that Contracting State.

2. Where under any provision of this Convention any income is relieved from tax in a Contracting State and, under the law in force in the other Contracting State a person, in respect of that income, is subject to tax by reference to the amount thereof which is remitted to or received in that other Contracting State and not by reference to the full amount thereof, then the relief to be allowed under this Convention in the first-mentioned Contracting State shall apply only to so much of the income as is taxed in the other Contracting State.

3. Nothing in this Convention shall be construed as restricting the right of a Contracting State to tax a resident of that State on that resident's share of any income or capital gains of a partnership, trust or controlled foreign affiliate in which that resident has an interest.

4. The competent authorities of the Contracting States may communicate with each other directly for the purpose of applying this Convention.

5. Contributions paid in a year by, or on behalf of, an individual who exercises employment in a Contracting State in that year to a pension arrangement established in the other Contracting State (including an arrangement created under the social security legislation in that other State) and in which the individual participates in order to secure retirement benefits in respect of those services shall, during a period not exceeding in the aggregate 60 months, and if the contributions to the arrangement would qualify for tax relief if they had been made in that other State, be treated in the same way for tax purposes in the first-mentioned State as contributions paid to a pension arrangement that is recognised for tax purposes in the first-mentioned State, provided that:

(*a*) immediately before the individual began to exercise employment in the first-mentioned State, that individual was not a resident of that State and contributions had been paid by or on behalf of that individual to the pension arrangement; and

(*b*) the pension arrangement is accepted by the competent authority of the first-mentioned State as generally corresponding to a pension arrangement recognised as such for tax purposes by that State.

Editorial Note: See CRA publication "Guidance for Taxpayers Requesting Tax Treaty Relief for Cross-Border Pension Contributions" for general guidance on how the CRA will administer tax treaty provisions dealing with recognizing foreign pension contributions.

Related CRA Documents: CRA Technical Interpretation, Document No. 9335425, dated June 6, 1994, states that for the purposes of paragraph 2 of Article 27, "income" includes capital gains; however, paragraph 2 of Article 27 would not apply to capital gains resulting from deemed dispositions on death since such gains are not "remitted or received".

In CRA Document No. 5-2479, dated December 17, 1986, with respect to dividends paid by a Canadian corporation to a U.K. resident, which are remitted by the corporation to a bank account outside both Canada and the United Kingdom, it is noted that the provision in paragraph 2 of Article 27 is restrictive in that, where income is taxed in the United Kingdom by reference to the amount that is remitted to or received in the United Kingdom, the relief granted under any other Article of the Convention is applicable only if the relevant income is received in the U.K. or remitted to the United Kingdom; consequently, the reduced witholding tax rate under Article 10 will only apply to the dividends if the amount is remitted to a U.K. address or it is known that the dividend income is taxed in the United Kingdom on a basis other than referred to in Article 27(2), otherwise the full witholding tax rate under the Canadian *Income Tax Act* will apply.

History: Paragraph 3 of Article 27 was deleted and replaced by paragraph 1 of Article XV of the Fourth Protocol to this Convention. Paragraph 3 of Article 27 of the Convention formerly read:

3. Nothing in this Convention shall be construed as restricting the right of Canada to tax a resident of Canada on that resident's share of any income or capital gains of a partnership, trust or controlled foreign affiliate in which that resident has an interest.

Paragraph 5 of Article 27 was deleted, and paragraphs 6 and 7 were renumbered as paragraphs 4 and 5 respectively, by paragraph 2 of Article XV of the Fourth Protocol to this Convention. Paragraph 5 of Article 27 of the Convention formerly read:

5. Each of the Contracting States will endeavour to collect on behalf of the other Contracting State such amounts as may be necessary to ensure that relief granted by this Convention from taxation imposed by that other State does not enure to the benefit of persons not entitled thereto. However, nothing in this paragraph shall be construed as imposing on either of the Contracting States the obligation to carry out administrative measures of a different nature from those used in the collection of its own tax or which would be contrary to its public policy.

Paragraphs 2 and 3 of Article 27 were amended by Article 13 of the Protocol to this Convention, dated May 7, 2003. Paragraphs 2 and 3 of Article 27 of the Convention formerly read:

2. Where under any provision of this Convention any person is relieved from tax in a Contracting State on certain income and, under the law in force in the other Contracting State, that person is subject to tax in that other State in respect of that income by reference to the amount thereof which is remitted to or received in that other State, the relief from tax to be allowed under this Convention in the first-mentioned State shall apply only to the amounts so remitted or received.

3. Nothing in this Convention shall be construed as preventing Canada from imposing a tax on amounts included in the income of a resident of Canada by virtue of the provisions of section 91 of the Canadian *Income Tax Act*, so far as they are in force on the date of entry into force of this Convention, or have been modified only in minor respects, so as not to affect their general character.

Paragraph 4 of Article 27 was deleted by Article 8 of the Protocol to this Convention, dated May 7, 2003. Paragraph 4 of Article 27 of the Convention formerly read:

4. The aggregate of the amount or value of the dividend and the amount of the tax credit referred to in paragraph 3(b) or 3(c) of Article 10 of this Convention shall be treated as a dividend for Canadian income tax purposes.

Paragraph 7 of Article 27 was added by Article 13 of the Protocol to this Convention, dated May 7, 2003.

Paragraph 4 of Article 27 was amended by Article 10 of the 1985 Protocol to this Convention. Paragraph 4 formerly read:

4. The aggregate of the amount or value of the dividend and the amount of the tax credit referred to in subparagraph 3(*b*) of this Convention shall be treated as a dividend for Canadian income tax purposes.

Article 27A — Miscellaneous Rules Applicable to Certain Offshore Activities

1. The provisions of this Article shall apply notwithstanding any other provision of this Convention.

2. A person who is a resident of a Contracting State and carries on activities in the other Contracting State in connection with the exploration or exploitation of the sea bed and sub-soil and their natural resources situated in that other Contracting State shall, subject to paragraph 3 of this Article, be deemed to be carrying on a business in that other Contracting State through a permanent establishment situated therein.

3. The provisions of paragraph 2 of this Article shall not apply where the activities referred to therein are carried on for a period or periods not exceeding in the aggregate 30 days in any 12-month period. For the purposes of this paragraph:

(*a*) where a person carrying on activities referred to in paragraph 2 of this Article is associated with an enterprise carrying on substantially similar activities, that person shall be deemed to be carrying on those substantially similar activities of the enterprise with which he is associated, in addition to his own activities;

(*b*) two enterprises shall be deemed to be associated if one enterprise participates directly or indirectly in the management or control of the other enterprise or if the same persons participate directly or indirectly in the management or control of both enterprises.

4. Salaries, wages and similar remuneration derived by a resident of a Contracting State in respect of an employment connected with the exploration or exploitation of the sea bed and sub-soil and their natural resources situated in the other Contracting State may, to the extent that the duties are performed offshore in that other Contracting State, be taxed in that other Contracting State.

Editorial Note: Related CRA Documents: CRA Technical Interpretation, Document No. 2003-0003125, dated July 17, 2003, notes that Article 27A(4) may apply to give Canada the right to tax remuneration earned by a U.K. resident professional diver, working off the Canadian coast in an area that falls within the definition of "Canada" under subparagraph 1(*a*)(i) of Article 3.

Related Case Law: A non-resident corporate taxpayer that operated a fully crewed supply vessel in Canadian waters, in connection with exploration or exploitation of natural resources, was found to be "carrying on activities" in Canada for the purposes of paragraph 2 of Article 27A, and thereby was deemed to be carrying on business in Canada through a permanent establishment. *Gulf Offshore N.S. Limited v. The Queen*, 2006 DTC 2705 (T.C.C.), aff'd. 2007 DTC 5563 (F.C.A.).

History: Article 27A was amended by Article 11 of the 1985 Protocol to this Convention. Article 27A formerly read:

1. The provisions of this Article shall apply notwithstanding any other provision of this Convention.

2. A person who is a resident of a Contracting State and carries on activities in the other Contracting State in connection with the exploration or exploitation of the sea bed and sub-soil and their natural resources situated in that other Contracting State shall, subject to paragraphs 3 and 4 of this Article, be deemed to be carrying on a business in that other Contracting State through a permanent establishment situated therein.

3. The provisions of paragraph 2 of this Article shall not apply where the activities referred to therein are carried on for a period or periods not exceeding in the aggregate 30 days in any 12-month period. For the purposes of this paragraph:

(*a*) where a person carrying on activities referred to in paragraph 2 of this Article is associated with an enterprise carrying on substantially similar activities, that person shall be deemed to be carrying on those substantially similar activities of the enterprise with which he is associated, in addition to his own activities;

(*b*) two enterprises shall be deemed to be associated if one enterprise participates directly or indirectly in the management or control of the other enterprise or if the same persons participate directly or indirectly in the management or control of both enterprises.

4. Profits derived by a resident of a Contracting State from the transportation of passengers or goods to a location where activities in connection with the exploration or exploitation of the sea bed and sub-soil and their natural resources are being carried on in a Contracting State, or from the operation of tugboats and similar vessels in connection with such activities, shall be taxable only in the Contracting State of which he is a resident.

5.

(*a*) Subject to subparagraph (*b*) of this paragraph, salaries, wages and similar remuneration derived by a resident of a Contracting State in respect of an employment connected with the exploration or exploitation of the sea bed and sub-soil and their natural resources situated in the other Contracting State may, to the extent that the duties are performed offshore in that other Contracting State, be taxed in that other Contracting State.

(*b*) Salaries, wages and similar remuneration derived by a resident of a Contracting State in respect of an employment exercised aboard a ship or aircraft engaged in the transportation of passengers or goods to a location where activities connected with the exploration or exploitation of the sea bed and sub-soil and their natural resources are being carried on in the other Contracting State, or in respect of an employment exercised aboard a tugboat or similar vessel in connection with such activities, may be taxed in that other Contracting State unless the person deriving the profits from the operation of the ship or aircraft is a resident of the first-mentioned Contracting State.

Article 28 — Entry into Force

1. The Convention shall come into force on the date when the last of all such things shall have been done in Canada and the United Kingdom as are necessary to give the Convention the force of law in Canada and the United Kingdom respectively and shall thereupon have effect:

(*a*) in Canada:

(i) in respect of tax withheld at the source on amounts paid or credited to non-residents on or after 1 January 1976;

(ii) in respect of other Canadian taxes, for the 1976 taxation year and subsequent years;

(*b*) in the United Kingdom:

(i) in relation to any dividend to which paragraph 3 of Article 10 applies in respect of income tax and payment of tax credit, for any year of assessment beginning on or after 6 April 1973. A dividend paid on or after 1 April 1973 but before 6 April 1973 shall be treated for tax credit purposes as paid on 6 April 1973;

(ii) in relation to any other provision of this Convention, in respect of income tax and capital gains tax, for any year of assessment beginning on or after 6 April 1976;

(iii) in respect of corporation tax, for any financial year beginning on or after 1 April 1976;

(iv) in respect of petroleum revenue tax for any chargeable period beginning on or after 1 January 1976;

(v) in respect of development land tax, for any realized development value accruing on or after 1 August 1976.

2. The Governments of the Contracting States shall, as soon as possible, inform one another in writing of the date when the last of all such things have been done as are necessary to give the Convention the force of law in Canada and the United Kingdom respectively. The date specified by the last Government to fulfil this requirement, being the date on which the Convention shall come into force in accordance with paragraph 1, shall be confirmed in writing by the Government so notified.

3. Subject to the provisions of paragraph 4 of this Article the existing Agreement shall cease to have effect as respects taxes to which this Convention applies in accordance with the provisions of paragraph 1 of this Article.

4. Where, however, any greater relief from tax would have been afforded by any provision of the existing Agreement than is due under this Convention, any such provision as aforesaid shall continue to have effect:

(a) in the United Kingdom for any year of assessment, chargeable period or financial year;

(b) in Canada for any taxation year;

beginning before the entry into force of this Convention.

5. The existing Agreement shall terminate on the last date on which it has effect in accordance with the foregoing provisions of this Article.

6. The termination of the existing Agreement as provided in paragraph 5 of this Article shall not revive the Agreement between the Government of the United Kingdom of Great Britain and Northern Ireland and the Government of Canada for the Avoidance of Double Taxation with respect to certain classes of Income signed at Ottawa on 6 December 1965. Upon the entry into force of this Convention that Agreement shall terminate.

7. In this Article the term "the existing Agreement" means the Agreement between the Government of the United Kingdom of Great Britain and Northern Ireland and the Government of Canada for the Avoidance of Double Taxation and the Prevention of Fiscal Evasion with respect to Taxes on Income and Capital Gains signed at Ottawa on 12 December 1966.

8. Notwithstanding any provisions of the respective domestic laws of the Contracting States imposing time limits for applications for relief from tax, an application for relief under the provisions of this Convention shall have effect, and any consequential refunds of tax made, if the application is made to the competent authority concerned within one year of the end of the calendar year in which this Convention enters into force.

History: Paragraph 8 of Article 28 was added by Article 5 of the 1980 Protocol, which became effective at the same time as the main body of the Convention.

Article 29 — Termination

This Convention shall continue in effect indefinitely but the Government of either Contracting State may, on or before 30 June in any calendar year after the year 1980 give notice of termination to the Government of the other Contracting State and, in such event, this Convention shall cease to be effective:

(a) in Canada:

(i) in respect of tax withheld at the source on amounts paid or credited to non-residents on or after 1 January in the calendar year next following that in which the notice is given; and

(ii) in respect of other Canadian taxes for any taxation year ending in or after the calendar year next following that in which the notice is given;

(b) in the United Kingdom:

(i) in respect of income tax and capital gains tax for any years of assessment beginning on or after 6 April in the calendar year next following that in which such notice is given;

(ii) in respect of corporation tax, for any financial year beginning on or after 1 April in the calendar year next following that in which such notice is given;

(iii) in respect of petroleum revenue tax for any chargeable period beginning on or after 1 January in the calendar year next following that in which such notice is given;

(iv) in respect of development land tax, for any realized development value accruing on or after 1 April in the calendar year next following that in which such notice is given.

IN WITNESS WHEREOF the undersigned, duly authorized thereto, have signed this Convention.

DONE in duplicate at London, this 8th day of September 1978, in the English and French languages, both texts being equally authoritative.

FOR THE GOVERNMENT OF CANADA

Paul Martin

FOR THE GOVERNMENT OF THE UNITED KINGDOM OF GREAT BRITAIN AND NORTHERN IRELAND

Frank Judd

Income Tax Conventions Interpretation Act

R.S.C. 1985, Chapter I-4, as amended by R.S.C. 1985 (1st Supp.) c. 48; S.C. 1991, c. 49; S.C. 1993 c. 24; S.C. 1998, c. 19; S.C. 1999, c. 22; S.C. 2005, c. 19; S.C. 2007, c. 35, s. 70(1); S.C. 2013, c. 34

Short Title

Sec. 1 Short title — This Act may be cited as the *Income Tax Conventions Interpretation Act*.

Definition

Sec. 2 Definition of "convention" — In this Act, "convention" means any convention or agreement between Canada and another state relating to tax on income, and includes any protocol or supplementary convention or agreement relating thereto.

Interpretation

Sec. 3 Meaning of undefined terms — Notwithstanding the provisions of a convention or the Act giving the convention the force of law in Canada, it is hereby declared that the law of Canada is that, to the extent that a term in the convention is

(*a*) not defined in the convention,

(*b*) not fully defined in the convention, or

(*c*) to be defined by reference to the laws of Canada,

that term has, except to the extent that the context otherwise requires, the meaning it has for the purposes of the *Income Tax Act*, as amended from time to time, and not the meaning it had for the purposes of the *Income Tax Act* on the date the convention was entered into or given the force of law in Canada if, after that date, its meaning for the purposes of the *Income Tax Act* has changed.

Sec. 4 Permanent establishments in Canada — Notwithstanding the provisions of a convention or the Act giving the convention the force of law in Canada, it is hereby declared that the law of Canada is that where, for the purposes of the application of the convention, the profits from a business activity, including an industrial or commercial activity, attributable or allocable to a permanent establishment in Canada are to be determined for any period,

(*a*) there shall, except where the convention expressly otherwise provides, be included in the determination of those profits all amounts with respect to that activity that are attributable or allocable to the permanent establishment and that would be required to be included under the *Income Tax Act*, as amended from time to time, by a person resident in Canada carrying on the activity in Canada in the computation of his income from a business for that period; and

(*b*) there shall, except to the extent that an agreement between the competent authorities of the parties to the convention expressly otherwise provides, not be deducted in the determination of those profits any amount with respect to that activity that is attributable or allocable to the permanent establishment and that would not be deductible under the *Income Tax Act*, as amended from time to time, by a person resident in Canada carrying on the activity in Canada in the computation of his income from a business for that period.

Sec. 4.1 Application of section 245 of the *Income Tax Act* — Notwithstanding the provisions of a convention or the Act giving the convention the force of law in Canada, it is hereby declared that the law of Canada is that section 245 of the Income Tax Act applies to any benefit provided under the convention.

(S.C. 2005, c. 19, s. 60(1).)

Sec. 4.2 Stock exchanges — Notwithstanding the provisions of a convention or the Act giving the convention the force of law in Canada, each reference in a convention to a stock exchange that is prescribed under, or for the purposes of, the *Income Tax Act* shall be read as a reference to a designated stock exchange, as defined in the *Income Tax Act*.

(S.C. 2007, c. 35, s. 70(1), applicable on and after December 14, 2007.)

Sec. 4.3 Application of section 94 of the *Income Tax Act* — Notwithstanding the provisions of a convention or the Act giving the convention the force of law in Canada, if a trust is deemed by subsection 94(3) of the *Income Tax Act* to be resident in Canada for a taxation year for the purposes of computing its income, the trust is deemed to be a resident of Canada, and not a resident of the other contracting state, for the purposes of applying the convention

(a) in respect of the trust for that taxation year; and

(b) in respect of any other person for any period that includes all or part of that taxation year.

(S.C. 2013, c. 34, s. 26(1).)

Sec. 5 Definitions — Notwithstanding the provisions of a convention or the Act giving the convention the force of law in Canada, in this section and in the convention,

"annuity" — *"annuity"* does not include any pension payment or any payment under a plan, arrangement or contract described in subparagraphs (*a*)(i) to (ix) of the definition "pension"; (S.C. 1999, c. 22, s. 84(1); S.C. 1993, c. 24, s. 147.)

"Canada" — *"Canada"* means the territory of Canada, and includes

(*a*) every area beyond the territorial seas of Canada that, in accordance with international law and the laws of Canada, is an area in respect of which Canada may exercise rights with respect to the seabed and subsoil and their natural resources, and

(*b*) the seas and airspace above every area described in paragraph (*a*);

"immovable property" and "real property" — *"immovable property"* and "real property", with respect to property in Canada, are hereby declared to include

(*a*) any right to explore for or exploit mineral deposits and sources in Canada and other natural resources in Canada, and

(*b*) any right to an amount computed by reference to the production, including profit, from, or to the value of production from, mineral deposits and sources in Canada and other natural resources in Canada;

"pension" — *"pension"* means, in respect of payments that arise in Canada,

(*a*) if the convention does not include a definition "pension", a payment under any plan, arrangement or contract that is

(i) a registered pension plan,

(ii) a registered retirement savings plan,

(iii) a registered retirement income fund,

(iv) a retirement compensation arrangement,

(v) a deferred profit sharing plan,

(vi) a plan that is deemed by subsection 147(15) of the *Income Tax Act* not to be a deferred profit sharing plan,

(vii) an annuity contract purchased under a plan referred to in subparagraph (v) or (vi),

(viii) an annuity contract where the amount paid by or on behalf of an individual to acquire the contract was deductible under paragraph 60(*l*) of the *Income Tax Act* in computing the individual's income for any taxation year (or would have been so deductible if the individual had been resident in Canada), or

(ix) a superannuation, pension or retirement plan not otherwise referred to in this paragraph, and

(*b*) if the convention includes a definition "pension", a payment that is a pension for the purposes of the convention or a payment (other than a payment of social security benefits) that would be a periodic pension payment if the convention did not include a definition "pension";

(S.C. 1999, c. 22)

"periodic pension payment" — *"periodic pension payment"* means, in respect of payments that arise in Canada, a pension payment other than (S.C. 1999, c. 22)

(*a*) a lump sum payment, or a payment that can reasonably be considered to be an instalment of a lump sum amount, under a registered pension plan,

(*b*) a payment before maturity, or a payment in full or partial commutation of the retirement income, under a registered retirement savings plan,

(*c*) a payment at any time in a calendar year under a registered retirement income fund, where the total of all payments (other than the specified portion of each such payment) made under the fund at or before that time and in the year exceeds the total of

(i) the amount that would be the greater of

(A) twice the amount that, if the value of C in the definition "minimum amount" in subsection 146.3(1) of the *Income Tax Act* were nil, would be the minimum amount under the fund for the year, and

(B) 10% of the fair market value of the property (other than annuity contracts that, at the beginning of the year, are not described in paragraph (*b*.1) of the definition "qualified investment" in subsection 146.3(1) of the *Income Tax Act*) held in connection with the fund at the beginning of the year

if all property transferred in the year and before that time to the carrier of the fund as consideration for the carrier's undertaking to make payments under the fund had been so transferred immediately before the beginning of the year and if the definition "minimum amount" in subsection 146.3(1) of the *Income Tax Act* applied with respect to all registered retirement income funds, and

(ii) the total of all amounts each of which is an annual or more frequent periodic payment under an annuity contract that is a qualified investment, as defined in subsection 146.3(1) of the *Income Tax Act*, (other than an annuity contract the fair market value of which is taken into account under clause (i)(B)) held by a trust governed by the fund that was paid into the trust in the year and before that time, or

(*d*) a payment to a recipient at any time in a calendar year under an arrangement, other than a plan or fund referred to in paragraphs (*a*) to (*c*), where

(i) the payment is not

(A) one of a series of annual or more frequent payments to be made over the lifetime of the recipient or over a period of at least 10 years,

(B) one of a series of annual or more frequent payments each of which is contingent on the recipient continuing to suffer from a physical or mental impairment, or

(C) a payment to which the recipient is entitled as a consequence of the death of an individual who was in receipt of periodic pension payments under the arrangement, and that is made under a guarantee that a minimum number of payments will be made in respect of the individual, or

(ii) at the time the payment is made, it can reasonably be concluded that

(A) the total amount of payments (other than excluded payments) under the arrangement to the recipient in the year will exceed twice the total amount of payments (other than excluded payments) made under the arrangement to the recipient in the immediately preceding year, otherwise than because of the fact that payments commenced to be made to the recipient in the preceding year and were made for a period of less than twelve months in that year, or

(B) the total amount of payments (other than excluded payments) under the arrangement to the recipient in the year will exceed twice the total amount of payments (other than excluded payments) to be made under the arrangement to the recipient in any subsequent year, otherwise than because of the termination of the series of payments or the reduction in the amount of payments to be made after the death of any individual,

and, for the purposes of this subparagraph, "excluded payment" means a payment that is neither a periodic payment nor a payment described in any of clauses (i)(A) to (C).

(S.C. 1993, c. 24, s. 147; S.C. 1998, c. 19, s. 286; S.C. 1999, c. 22, s. 84.)

Sec. 5.1 Definition of "pension" — (1) [Repealed by S.C. 1999, c. 22, s. 85(1)]

(2) *Definition of "specified portion"* — For the purpose of the definition "periodic pension payment" in section 5, the "specified portion" of a payment means the total of

(*a*) the portion of the payment that is not required by section 146.3 of the *Income Tax Act* to be included in computing the income of any person and that is not included under paragraph 212(1)(*q*) of that Act in respect of any person; and

(*b*) the portion of the payment in respect of which a deduction is available under paragraph 60(*l*) of the *Income Tax Act* in computing the income of any person.

(1993, c. 24, s. 148; S.C. 1998, c. 19, s. 287; S.C. 1999, c. 22, s. 85.)

Sec. 6 Meaning of "interest" — Notwithstanding section 3, the meaning of the term "interest" in any convention given the force of law in Canada before November 19, 1974 does not include any amount paid or credited, pursuant to an agreement in writing entered into before June 23, 1983, as consideration for a guarantee referred to in paragraph 214(15)(*a*) of the *Income Tax Act*.

Sec. 6.1 Transitional — Where a taxation year of a taxpayer includes June 23, 1983, the additional tax payable under the *Income Tax Act* (except Part XIII thereof) by the taxpayer for the taxation year by virtue of this Act shall be calculated in accordance with the following formula:

$$A = T \times (B/C)$$

where

A is the amount of additional taxes payable under the *Income Tax Act*, (except Part XIII thereof) by the taxpayer for the taxation year by virtue of this Act,

T is the amount of additional taxes payable under the *Income Tax Act*, (except Part XIII thereof) by the taxpayer for the taxation year by virtue of this Act (except this section),

B is the number of days in the taxation year after June 23, 1983, and

C is the number of days in the taxation year.

(R.S.C. 1985, 1st Supp., c. 48, s. 2.)

Sec. 6.2 Partnerships — Notwithstanding the provisions of a convention between Canada and another state or the Act giving it the force of law in Canada, it is hereby declared that the law of Canada is that, for the purposes of the application of the convention and the *Income Tax Act* to a person who is a resident of Canada, a partnership of which that person is a member is neither a resident nor an enterprise of that other state.

(1991, c. 49, s. 220.)

Sec. 6.3 Gains arising in Canada — Except where a convention expressly otherwise provides, any amount of income, gain or loss in respect of the disposition of a property that is taxable Canadian property within the meaning assigned by the *Income Tax Act* is deemed to arise in Canada.

(S.C. 1999, c. 22, s. 86)

Application

Sec. 7 Application — This Act applies

(*a*) in the case of tax under Part XIII of the *Income Tax Act*, to amounts paid or credited after June 23, 1983; and

(*b*) in all other cases, to taxation years ending after June 23, 1983.

Treaties and Related Legislation

Interpretation Act

R.S.C. 1985, c. I-21, as amended by R.S.C. 1985 (1st Supp.), c. 11; R.S.C. 1985 (1st Supp.), c. 27; R.S.C. 1985 (2nd Supp.), c. 27; SOR/86-532; S.C. 1990, c. 17; S.C. 1992, c. 1; S.C. 1992, c. 47; S.C. 1992, c. 51; S.C. 1993, c. 28; S.C. 1993, c. 34; S.C. 1993, c. 38; SOR/93-140; S.C. 1995, c. 39; SOR/95-366; S.C. 1996, c. 31; S.C. 1997, c. 39; S.C. 1998, c. 15; S.C. 1998, c. 30; S.C. 1999, c. 3; S.C. 1999, c. 28; S.C. 1999, c. 31; S.C. 2001, c. 4; S.C. 2002, c. 7; S.C. 2002, c. 8; S.C. 2003, c. 22; S.C. 2014, c. 2; S.C. 2015, c. 3

Short Title

Sec. 1 Short title — This Act may be cited as the *Interpretation Act*.

Interpretation

Sec. 2 Definitions — (1) In this Act,

"Act" —*"Act"* means an Act of Parliament;

"enact" —*"enact"* includes to issue, make or establish;

"enactment" —*"enactment"* means an Act or regulation or any portion of an Act or regulation;

"public officer" —*"public officer"*[1] includes any person in the federal public administration who is authorized by or under an enactment to do or enforce the doing of an act or thing or to exercise a power, or on whom a duty is imposed by or under an enactment; (S.C. 2003, c. 22, s. 224, in force April 1, 2005.)

"regulation" —*"regulation"* includes an order, regulation, rule, rule of court, form, tariff of costs or fees, letters patent, commission, warrant, proclamation, by-law, resolution or other instrument issued, made or established

(*a*) in the execution of a power conferred by or under the authority of an Act, or

(*b*) by or under the authority of the Governor in Council;

"repeal" —*"repeal"* includes revoke or cancel.

(2) *Expired and replaced enactments* — For the purposes of this Act, an enactment that has been replaced is repealed and an enactment that has expired, lapsed or otherwise ceased to have effect is deemed to have been repealed. (S.C. 1993, c. 34, s. 88; S.C. 1999, c. 31, s. 146.)

(S.C. 1993, c. 34, s. 88; S.C. 1999, c. 31, s. 146; S.C. 2003, c. 22, s. 224.)

Application

Sec. 3 Application — (1) Every provision of this Act applies, unless a contrary intention appears, to every enactment, whether enacted before or after the commencement of this Act.

(2) *Application to this Act* — The provisions of this Act apply to the interpretation of this Act.

(3) *Rules of construction not excluded* — Nothing in this Act excludes the application to an enactment of a rule of construction applicable to that enactment and not inconsistent with this Act.

Enacting Clause of Acts

Sec. 4 Enacting clause — (1) The enacting clause of an Act may be in the following form:

"Her Majesty, by and with the advice and consent of the Senate and House of Commons of Canada, enacts as follows:".

(2) *Order of clauses* — The enacting clause of an Act shall follow the preamble, if any, and the various provisions within the purview or body of the Act shall follow in a concise and enunciative form.

Operation

Royal Assent

Sec. 5 Royal assent — (1) The Clerk of the Parliaments shall endorse on every Act, immediately after its title, the day, month and year when the Act was assented to in Her Majesty's name and the endorsement shall be a part of the Act.

(2) *Date of commencement* — If no date of commencement is provided for in an Act, the date of commencement of that Act is the date of assent to the Act.

(3) *Commencement provision* — Where an Act contains a provision that the Act or any portion thereof is to come into force on a day later than the date of assent to the Act, that provision is deemed to have come into force on the date of assent to the Act.

(4) *Commencement when no date fixed* — Where an Act provides that certain provisions thereof are to come or are deemed to have come into force on a day other than the date of assent to the Act, the remaining provisions of the Act are deemed to have come into force on the date of assent to the Act.

Day Fixed for Commencement or Repeal

Sec. 6 Operation when date fixed for commencement or repeal — (1) Where an enactment is expressed to come into force on a particular day, it shall be construed as coming into force on the expiration of the previous day, and where an enactment is expressed to expire, lapse or otherwise cease to have effect on a particular day, it shall be construed as ceasing to have effect on the commencement of the following day.

(2) *When no date fixed* — Every enactment that is not expressed to come into force on a particular day shall be construed as coming into force

(*a*) in the case of an Act, on the expiration of the day immediately before the day the Act was assented to in Her Majesty's name; and

(*b*) in the case of a regulation, on the expiration of the day immediately before the day the regulation was registered pursuant to section 6 of the *Statutory Instruments Act* or, if the regulation is of a class that is exempted from the application of subsection 5(1) of that Act, on the expiration of the day immediately before the day the regulation was made.

(3) *Judicial notice* — Judicial notice shall be taken of a day for the coming into force of an enactment that is fixed by a regulation that has been published in the *Canada Gazette*.

(S.C. 1992, c. 1, s. 87.)

Regulation Prior to Commencement

Sec. 7 Preliminary proceedings — Where an enactment is not in force and it contains provisions conferring power to make regulations or do any other thing, that power may, for the purpose of making the enactment effective on its commencement, be exercised at any time before its commencement, but a regulation so made or a thing so done has no effect until the commencement of the enactment, except in so far as may be necessary to make the enactment effective on its commencement.

Territorial Operation

Sec. 8 Territorial operation — (1) Every enactment applies to the whole of Canada, unless a contrary intention is expressed in the enactment.

(2) *Amending enactment* — Where an enactment that does not apply to the whole of Canada is amended, no provision in the amending enactment applies to any part of Canada to which the amended enactment does not apply, unless it is provided in the amending enactment that it applies to that part of Canada or to the whole of Canada.

(2.1) *Exclusive economic zone of Canada* — Every enactment that applies in respect of exploring or exploiting, conserving or managing natural resources, whether living or non-living, applies, in addition to its application to Canada, to the exclusive economic zone of Canada, unless a contrary intention is expressed in the enactment. (S.C. 1996, c. 31, s. 86.)

(2.2) *Continental shelf of Canada* — Every enactment that applies in respect of exploring or exploiting natural resources that are

Treaties and Related Legislation

1 The definition of "public officer" in subsection 2(1) was amended by S.C. 2003, c. 22, s. 224(z.43) to replace the expression "public service of Canada" with the expression "federal public administration", coming into force on a day to be fixed by order of the Governor in Council.

(a) mineral or other non-living resources of the seabed or subsoil, or

(b) living organisms belonging to sedentary species, that is to say, organisms that, at the harvestable stage, either are immobile on or under the seabed or are unable to move except in constant physical contact with the seabed or subsoil

applies, in addition to its application to Canada, to the continental shelf of Canada, unless a contrary intention is expressed in the enactment.

(S.C. 1996, c. 31, s. 86.)

(3) *Extra-territorial operation* — Every Act now in force enacted prior to December 11, 1931 that expressly or by necessary or reasonable implication was intended, as to the whole or any part thereof, to have extra-territorial operation shall be construed as if, at the date of its enactment, the Parliament of Canada had full power to make laws having extra-territorial operation as provided by the *Statute of Westminster, 1931.* (S.C. 1996, c. 31, s. 86.)

(S.C. 1996, c. 31, s. 86.)

Rules of Construction

Property and Civil Rights

Sec. 8.1 Duality of legal traditions and application of provincial law — Both the common law and the civil law are equally authoritative and recognized sources of the law of property and civil rights in Canada and, unless otherwise provided by law, if in interpreting an enactment it is necessary to refer to a province's rules, principles or concepts forming part of the law of property and civil rights, reference must be made to the rules, principles and concepts in force in the province at the time the enactment is being applied.

(S.C. 2001, c. 4, s. 8.)

Sec. 8.2 Terminology — Unless otherwise provided by law, when an enactment contains both civil law and common law terminology, or terminology that has a different meaning in the civil law and the common law, the civil law terminology or meaning is to be adopted in the Province of Quebec and the common law terminology or meaning is to be adopted in the other provinces.

(S.C. 2001, c. 4, s. 8.)

Private Acts

Sec. 9 Provisions in private Acts — No provision in a private Act affects the rights of any person, except as therein mentioned or referred to.

Law Always Speaking

Sec. 10 Law always speaking — The law shall be considered as always speaking, and where a matter or thing is expressed in the present tense, it shall be applied to the circumstances as they arise, so that effect may be given to the enactment according to its true spirit, intent and meaning.

Imperative and Permissive Construction

Sec. 11 "Shall" and "may" — The expression "shall" is to be construed as imperative and the expression "may" as permissive.

Enactments Remedial

Sec. 12 Enactments deemed remedial — Every enactment is deemed remedial, and shall be given such fair, large and liberal construction and interpretation as best ensures the attainment of its objects.

Preambles and Marginal Notes

Sec. 13 Preamble — The preamble of an enactment shall be read as a part of the enactment intended to assist in explaining its purport and object.

Sec. 14 Marginal notes and historical references — Marginal notes and references to former enactments that appear after the end of a section or other division in an enactment form no part of the enactment, but are inserted for convenience of reference only.

Application of Interpretation Provisions

Sec. 15 Application of definitions and interpretation rules — (1) Definitions or rules of interpretation in an enactment apply to all the provisions of the enactment, including the provisions that contain those definitions or rules of interpretation.

(2) *Interpretation sections subject to exceptions* — Where an enactment contains an interpretation section or provision, it shall be read and construed

(a) as being applicable only if a contrary intention does not appear; and

(b) as being applicable to all other enactments relating to the same subject-matter unless a contrary intention appears.

Sec. 16 Words in regulations — Where an enactment confers power to make regulations, expressions used in the regulations have the same respective meanings as in the enactment conferring the power.

Her Majesty

Sec. 17 Her Majesty not bound or affected unless stated — No enactment is binding on Her Majesty or affects Her Majesty or Her Majesty's rights or prerogatives in any manner, except as mentioned or referred to in the enactment.

Proclamations

Sec. 18 Proclamation — (1) Where an enactment authorizes the issue of a proclamation, the proclamation shall be understood to be a proclamation of the Governor in Council.

(2) *Proclamation to be issued on advice* — Where the Governor General is authorized to issue a proclamation, the proclamation shall be understood to be a proclamation issued under an order of the Governor in Council, but it is not necessary to mention in the proclamation that it is issued under such an order.

(3) *Effective day of proclamations* — A proclamation that is issued under an order of the Governor in Council may purport to have been issued on the day of the order or on any subsequent day and, if so, takes effect on that day. (S.C. 1992, c. 1, s. 88.)

(4) *Judicial notice of proclamation*

(Repealed.) —

(Repealed by S.C. 1992, c. 1, s. 88.)

(S.C. 1992, c. 1, s. 88.)

Oaths

Sec. 19 Administration of oaths — (1) Where, by an enactment or by a rule of the Senate or House of Commons, evidence under oath is authorized or required to be taken, or an oath is authorized or directed to be made, taken or administered, the oath may be administered, and a certificate of its having been made, taken or administered may be given by

(a) any person authorized by the enactment or rule to take the evidence; or

(b) a judge of any court, a notary public, a justice of the peace or a commissioner for taking affidavits, having authority or jurisdiction within the place where the oath is administered.

(2) *Where justice of peace empowered* — Where power is conferred on a justice of the peace to administer an oath or solemn affirmation or to take an affidavit or declaration, the power may be exercised by a notary public or a commissioner for taking oaths.

Reports to Parliament

Sec. 20 Reports to Parliament — Where an Act requires a report or other document to be laid before Parliament and, in compliance with the Act, a particular report or document has been laid before Parliament at a session thereof, nothing in the Act shall be construed as requiring the same report or document to be laid before Parliament at any subsequent session.

Corporations

Sec. 21 Powers vested in corporations — (1) Words establishing a corporation shall be construed

(a) as vesting in the corporation power to sue and be sued, to contract and be contracted with by its corporate name, to have a common seal and to alter or change it at pleasure, to have perpetual succession, to acquire and hold personal property for the purposes for which the corporation is established and to alienate that property at pleasure;

(b) in the case of a corporation having a name consisting of an English and a French form or a combined English and French form, as vesting in the corporation power to use either the English or the French form of its name or both forms and to show on its seal both the English and French forms of its name or have two seals, one showing the English and the other showing the French form of its name;

(c) as vesting in a majority of the members of the corporation the power to bind the others by their acts; and

(d) as exempting from personal liability for its debts, obligations or acts individual members of the corporation who do not contravene the provisions of the enactment establishing the corporation.

(2) *Corporate name* — Where an enactment establishes a corporation and in each of the English and French versions of the enactment the name of the corporation is in the form only of the language of that version, the name of the corporation shall consist of the form of its name in each of the versions of the enactment.

(3) *Banking business* — No corporation is deemed to be authorized to carry on the business of banking unless that power is expressly conferred on it by the enactment establishing the corporation.

Majority and Quorum

Sec. 22 Majorities — (1) Where an enactment requires or authorizes more than two persons to do an act or thing, a majority of them may do it.

(2) *Quorum of board, court, commission, etc.* — Where an enactment establishes a board, court, commission or other body consisting of three or more members, in this section called an "association",

(a) at a meeting of the association, a number of members of the association equal to,

(i) if the number of members provided for by the enactment is a fixed number, at least one-half of the number of members, and

(ii) if the number of members provided for by the enactment is not a fixed number but is within a range having a maximum or minimum, at least one-half of the number of members in office if that number is within the range,

constitutes a quorum;

(b) an act or thing done by a majority of the members of the association present at a meeting, if the members present constitute a quorum, is deemed to have been done by the association; and

(c) a vacancy in the membership of the association does not invalidate the constitution of the association or impair the right of the members in office to act, if the number of members in office is not less than a quorum.

Appointment, Retirement and Powers of Officers

Sec. 23 Public officers hold office during pleasure — (1) Every public officer appointed by or under the authority of an enactment or otherwise is deemed to have been appointed to hold office during pleasure only, unless it is otherwise expressed in the enactment, commission or instrument of appointment.

(2) *Effective day of appointments* — Where an appointment is made by instrument under the Great Seal, the instrument may purport to have been issued on or after the day its issue was authorized, and the day on which it so purports to have been issued is deemed to be the day on which the appointment takes effect.

(3) *Appointment or engagement otherwise than under Great Seal* — Where there is authority in an enactment to appoint a person to a position or to engage the services of a person, otherwise than by instrument under the Great Seal, the instrument of appointment or engagement may be expressed to be effective on or after the day on which that person commenced the performance of the duties of the position or commenced the performance of the services, and the day on which it is so expressed to be effective, unless that day is more than sixty days before the day on which the instrument is issued, is deemed to be the day on which the appointment or engagement takes effect.

(4) *Remuneration* — Where a person is appointed to an office, the appointing authority may fix, vary or terminate that person's remuneration.

(5) *Commencement of appointments or retirements* — Where a person is appointed to an office effective on a specified day, or where the appointment of a person is terminated effective on a specified day, the appointment or termination is deemed to have been effected immediately on the expiration of the previous day.

Sec. 24 Implied powers respecting public officers — (1) Words authorizing the appointment of a public officer to hold office during pleasure include, in the discretion of the authority in whom the power of appointment is vested, the power to

(a) terminate the appointment or remove or suspend the public officer;

(b) re-appoint or reinstate the public officer; and

(c) appoint another person in the stead of, or to act in the stead of, the public officer.

(2) *Power to act for ministers* — Words directing or empowering a minister of the Crown to do an act or thing, regardless of whether the act or thing is administrative, legislative or judicial, or otherwise applying to that minister as the holder of the office, include

(a) a minister acting for that minister or, if the office is vacant, a minister designated to act in the office by or under the authority of an order in council;

(b) the successors of that minister in the office;

(c) his or their deputy; and

(d) notwithstanding paragraph (c), a person appointed to serve, in the department or ministry of state over which the minister presides, in a capacity appropriate to the doing of the act or thing, or to the words so applying.

(S.C. 1992, c. 1, s. 89(3).)

(3) *Restriction as to public servants* — Nothing in paragraph (2)(c) or (d) shall be construed as authorizing the exercise of any authority conferred on a minister to make a regulation as defined in the *Statutory Instruments Act.* (S.C. 1992, c. 1, s. 89(4).)

(4) *Successors to and deputy of public officer* — Words directing or empowering any public officer, other than a minister of the Crown, to do any act or thing, or otherwise applying to the public officer by his name of office, include his successors in the office and his or their deputy.

(5) *Powers of holder of public office* — Where a power is conferred or a duty imposed on the holder of an office, the power may be exercised and the duty shall be performed by the person for the time being charged with the execution of the powers and duties of the office.

(S.C. 1992, c. 1, s. 89.)

Evidence

Sec. 25 Documentary evidence — (1) Where an enactment provides that a document is evidence of a fact without anything in the context to indicate that the document is conclusive evidence, then, in any judicial proceedings, the document is admissible in evidence and the fact is deemed to be established in the absence of any evidence to the contrary.

(2) *Queen's Printer* — Every copy of an enactment having printed thereon what purports to be the name or title of the Queen's Printer and Controller of Stationery or the Queen's Printer is deemed to be a copy purporting to be printed by the Queen's Printer for Canada.

Computation of Time

Sec. 26 Time limits and holidays — Where the time limited for the doing of a thing expires or falls on a holiday, the thing may be done on the day next following that is not a holiday.

(S.C. 1999, c. 31, s. 147(F)).

Sec. 27 Clear days — (1) Where there is a reference to a number of clear days or "at least" a number of days between two events, in calculating that number of days the days on which the events happen are excluded.

(2) *Not clear days* — Where there is a reference to a number of days, not expressed to be clear days, between two events, in calculating that number of days the day on which the first event happens is excluded and the day on which the second event happens is included.

(3) *Beginning and ending of prescribed periods* — Where a time is expressed to begin or end at, on or with a specified day, or to continue to or until a specified day, the time includes that day.

(4) *After specified day* — Where a time is expressed to begin after or to be from a specified day, the time does not include that day.

(5) *Within a time* — Where anything is to be done within a time after, from, of or before a specified day, the time does not include that day.

Sec. 28 Calculation of a period of months after or before a specified day — Where there is a reference to a period of time consisting of a number of months after or before a specified day, the period is calculated by

(*a*) counting forward or backward from the specified day the number of months, without including the month in which that day falls;

(*b*) excluding the specified day; and

(*c*) including in the last month counted under paragraph (*a*) the day that has the same calendar number as the specified day or, if that month has no day with that number, the last day of that month.

Sec. 29 Time of the day — Where there is a reference to time expressed as a specified time of the day, the time is taken to mean standard time.

Sec. 30 Time when specified age attained — A person is deemed not to have attained a specified number of years of age until the commencement of the anniversary, of the same number, of the day of that person's birth.

Miscellaneous Rules

Sec. 31 Reference to provincial court judge, etc — (1) Where anything is required or authorized to be done by or before a judge, provincial court judge, justice of the peace or any functionary or officer, it shall be done by or before one whose jurisdiction or powers extend to the place where the thing is to be done. (R.S.C. 1985 (1st Supp.), c. 27, s. 203.)

(2) *Ancillary powers* — Where power is given to a person, officer or functionary to do or enforce the doing of any act or thing, all such powers as are necessary to enable the person, officer or functionary to do or enforce the doing of the act or thing are deemed to be also given.

(3) *Powers to be exercised as required* — Where a power is conferred or a duty imposed, the power may be exercised and the duty shall be performed from time to time as occasion requires.

(4) *Power to repeal* — Where a power is conferred to make regulations, the power shall be construed as including a power, exercisable in the same manner and subject to the same consent and conditions, if any, to repeal, amend or vary the regulations and make others. (R.S.C. 1985 (1st Supp.), c. 27, s. 203.)

(R.S.C. 1985 (1st Supp.), c. 27, s. 203.)

Sec. 32 Forms — Where a form is prescribed, deviations from that form, not affecting the substance or calculated to mislead, do not invalidate the form used.

Sec. 33 Gender — (1) Words importing female persons include male persons and corporations and words importing male persons include female persons and corporations. (S.C. 1992, c. 1, s. 90.)

(2) *Number* — Words in the singular include the plural, and words in the plural include the singular.

(3) *Parts of speech and grammatical forms* — Where a word is defined, other parts of speech and grammatical forms of the same word have corresponding meanings.

(S.C. 1992, c. 1, s. 90.)

Offences

Sec. 34 Indictable and summary conviction offences — (1) Where an enactment creates an offence,

(*a*) the offence is deemed to be an indictable offence if the enactment provides that the offender may be prosecuted for the offence by indictment;

(*b*) the offence is deemed to be one for which the offender is punishable on summary conviction if there is nothing in the context to indicate that the offence is an indictable offence; and

(*c*) if the offence is one for which the offender may be prosecuted by indictment or for which the offender is punishable on summary conviction, no person shall be considered to have been convicted of an indictable offence by reason only of having been convicted of the offence on summary conviction.

(2) *Criminal Code to apply* — All the provisions of the *Criminal Code* relating to indictable offences apply to indictable offences created by an enactment, and all the provisions of that Code relating to summary conviction offences apply to all other offences created by an enactment, except to the extent that the enactment otherwise provides.

(3) *Documents similarly construed* — In a commission, proclamation, warrant or other document relating to criminal law or procedure in criminal matters,

(*a*) a reference to an offence for which the offender may be prosecuted by indictment shall be construed as a reference to an indictable offence; and

(*b*) a reference to any other offence shall be construed as a reference to an offence for which the offender is punishable on summary conviction.

Powers to Enter Dwelling-Houses to Carry Out Arrests

Sec. 34.1 Authorization to enter dwelling-house — Any person who may issue a warrant to arrest or apprehend a person under any Act of Parliament, other than the *Criminal Code*, has the same powers, subject to the same terms and conditions, as a judge or justice has under the *Criminal Code*

(*a*) to authorize the entry into a dwelling-house described in the warrant for the purpose of arresting or apprehending the person, if the person issuing the warrant is satisfied by information on oath that there are reasonable grounds to believe that the person is or will be present in the dwelling-house; and

(*b*) to authorize the entry into the dwelling-house without prior announcement if the requirement of subsection 529.4(1) of the *Criminal Code* is met.

(S.C. 1997, c. 39, s. 4.)

Definitions

Sec. 35 General definitions — (1) In every enactment,

"Act" — *"Act"*, in respect of an Act of a legislature, includes a law of the Legislature of Yukon, of the Northwest Territories or for Nunavut; (S.C. 1993, c. 28, s. 78 (Sch. III, item 82); S.C. 1998, c. 15, s. 28; S.C. 2002, c. 7, s. 188; 2014, c. 2, s. 14(2).)

"bank" — *"bank"* means a bank listed in Schedule I or II to the *Bank Act*; (S.C. 1999, c. 28 s. 168.)

"British Commonwealth" or "British Commonwealth of Nations" — *"British Commonwealth"* or "British Commonwealth of Nations" has the same meaning as "Commonwealth";

"broadcasting" — *"broadcasting"* means any radiocommunication in which the transmissions are intended for direct reception by the general public;

"Canada" — *"Canada"*, for greater certainty, includes the internal waters of Canada and the territorial sea of Canada; (S.C. 1996, c. 31, s. 87.)

"Canadian waters" — *"Canadian waters"* includes the territorial sea of Canada and the internal waters of Canada; (S.C. 1996, c. 31, s. 87.)

"Clerk of the Privy Council" or "Clerk of the Queen's Privy Council" — *"Clerk of the Privy Council"* or "Clerk of the Queen's Privy Council" means the Clerk of the Privy Council and Secretary to the Cabinet;

"commencement" — *"commencement"*, when used with reference to an enactment, means the time at which the enactment comes into force;

"Commonwealth" or "Commonwealth of Nations" — *"Commonwealth"* or "Commonwealth of Nations" means the association of countries named in the schedule;

"Commonwealth and Dependent Territories" — *"Commonwealth and Dependent Territories"* means the several Commonwealth countries and their colonies, possessions, dependencies, protectorates, protected states, condominiums and trust territories;

"contiguous zone" — *"contiguous zone"*,

(*a*) in relation to Canada, means the contiguous zone of Canada as determined under the *Oceans Act*, and (*b*) in relation to any other state, means the contiguous zone of the other state as determined in accordance with international law and the domestic laws of that other state;

(S.C. 1996, c. 31, s. 87.)

"continental shelf" —*"continental shelf"*,

(*a*) in relation to Canada, means the continental shelf of Canada as determined under the *Oceans Act*, and

(*b*) in relation to any other state, means the continental shelf of the other state as determined in accordance with international law and the domestic laws of that other state;

(S.C. 1996, c. 31, s. 87.)

"contravene" —*"contravene"* includes fail to comply with; (S.C. 1992, c. 47, s. 79.)

"corporation" —*"corporation"* does not include a partnership that is considered to be a separate legal entity under provincial law;

"county" —*"county"* includes two or more counties united for purposes to which the enactment relates;

"county court"

(Repealed.) —

(Repealed by S.C. 1990, c. 17, s. 26(1).)

"diplomatic or consular officer" —*"diplomatic or consular officer"* includes an ambassador, envoy, minister, chargé d'affaires, counsellor, secretary, attaché, consul-general, consul, vice-consul, proconsul, consular agent, acting consul-general, acting consul, acting vice-consul, acting consular agent, high commissioner, permanent delegate, adviser, acting high commissioner, and acting permanent delegate;

"exclusive economic zone" —*"exclusive economic zone"*,

(*a*) in relation to Canada, means the exclusive economic zone of Canada as determined under the *Oceans Act* and includes the seabed and subsoil below that zone, and

(*b*) in relation to any other state, means the exclusive economic zone of the other state as determined in accordance with international law and the domestic laws of that other state;

(S.C. 1996, c. 31, s. 87.)

"Federal Court"

(Repealed.) —

(Repealed by S.C. 2002, c. 8, s. 151.)

"Federal Court–Appeal Division" or "Federal Court of Appeal"

(Repealed.) —

(Repealed by S.C. 2002, c. 8, s. 151.)

"Federal Court–Trial Division"

(Repealed.) —

(Repealed by S.C. 2002, c. 8, s. 151.)

"Governor", "Governor General" or "Governor of Canada" —*"Governor"*, "Governor General" or "Governor of Canada" means the Governor General of Canada or other chief executive officer or administrator carrying on the Government of Canada on behalf and in the name of the Sovereign, by whatever title that officer is designated;

"Governor General in Council" or "Governor in Council" —*"Governor General in Council"* or "Governor in Council" means the Governor General of Canada acting by and with the advice of, or by and with the advice and consent of, or in conjunction with the Queen's Privy Council for Canada;

"Great Seal" —*"Great Seal"* means the Great Seal of Canada;

"Her Majesty", "His Majesty", "the Queen", "the King" or "the Crown" —*"Her Majesty"*, "His Majesty", "the Queen", "the King", or "the Crown" means the Sovereign of the United Kingdom, Canada and Her or His other Realms and Territories, and Head of the Commonwealth; (S.C. 2015, c. 3, s. 124(1).)

"Her Majesty's Realms and Territories" or "His Majesty's Realms and Territories" —*"Her Majesty's Realms and Territories"* or "His Majesty's Realms and Territories" means all realms and territories under the sovereignty of Her or His Majesty; (S.C. 2015, c. 3, s. 124(1).)

"herein" —*"herein"* used in any section shall be understood to relate to the whole enactment, and not to that section only;

"holiday" —*"holiday"* means any of the following days, namely, Sunday; New Year's Day; Good Friday; Easter Monday; Christmas Day; the birthday or the day fixed by proclamation for the celebration of the birthday of the reigning Sovereign; Victoria Day; Canada Day; the first Monday in September, designated Labour Day; Remembrance Day; any day appointed by proclamation to be observed as a day of general prayer or mourning or day of public rejoicing or thanksgiving; and any of the following additional days, namely,

(*a*) in any province, any day appointed by proclamation of the lieutenant governor of the province to be observed as a public holiday or as a day of general prayer or mourning or day of public rejoicing or thanksgiving within the province, and any day that is a non-juridical day by virtue of an Act of the legislature of the province, and

(*b*) in any city, town, municipality or other organized district, any day appointed to be observed as a civic holiday by resolution of the council or other authority charged with the administration of the civic or municipal affairs of the city, town, municipality or district;

"internal waters" —*"internal waters"*,

(*a*) in relation to Canada, means the internal waters of Canada as determined under the *Oceans Act* and includes the airspace above and the bed and subsoil below those waters, and

(*b*) in relation to any other state, means the waters on the landward side of the baselines of the territorial sea of the other state;

(S.C. 1996, c. 31, s. 87.)

"legislative assembly", "legislative council" or "legislature"

(Repealed.) — (S.C. 1993, c. 28, Sched. III, s. 82(1); S.C. 2002, c. 7, s. 188; 2014, c. 2, s. 14(1).)

"legislative assembly" or "legislature" —*"legislative assembly" or "legislature"* includes the Lieutenant Governor in Council and the Legislative Assembly of the Northwest Territories, as constituted before September 1, 1905, and the Legislature of Yukon, of the Northwest Territories or for Nunavut; (S.C. 2014, c. 2, s. 14(3).)

"lieutenant governor" —*"lieutenant governor"* means the lieutenant governor or other chief executive officer or administrator carrying on the government of the province indicated by the enactment, by whatever title that officer is designated, and in Yukon, the Northwest Territories and Nunavut means the Commissioner; (S.C. 1993, c. 28, Sched. III, s. 82(1); S.C. 2002, c. 7, s. 188.)

"lieutenant governor in council" —*"lieutenant governor in council"* means

(*a*) the lieutenant governor of the province indicated by the enactment acting by and with the advice of, by and with the advice and consent of, or in conjunction with, the executive council,

(*b*) in Yukon, the Commissioner of Yukon acting with the consent of the Executive Council of Yukon,

(*c*) in the Northwest Territories, the Commissioner of the Northwest Territories acting with the consent of the Executive Council of the Northwest Territories, and

(*d*) in Nunavut, the Commissioner;

(S.C. 1993, c. 28, Sched. III, s. 82(1); S.C. 2002, c. 7, s. 188; 2014, c. 2, s. 14(2).)

"local time" —*"local time"*, in relation to any place, means the time observed in that place for the regulation of business hours;

"military" —*"military"* shall be construed as relating to all or any part of the Canadian Forces;

"month" —*"month"* means a calendar month;

"oath" —*"oath"* includes a solemn affirmation or declaration when the context applies to any person by whom and to any case in which a solemn affirmation or declaration may be made instead of an oath, and in the same cases the expression "sworn" includes the expression "affirmed" or "declared";

"Parliament" —*"Parliament"* means the Parliament of Canada;

"person" —*"person"*, or any word or expression descriptive of a person, includes a corporation;

"proclamation"—*"proclamation"* means a proclamation under the Great Seal;

"province"—*"province"* means a province of Canada, and includes Yukon, the Northwest Territories and Nunavut; (S.C. 1993, c. 28, Sched. III, s. 82(1); S.C. 2002, c. 7, s. 188.)

"radio" or "radiocommunication"—*"radio"* or "radiocommunication" means any transmission, emission or reception of signs, signals, writing, images, sounds or intelligence of any nature by means of electromagnetic waves of frequencies lower than 3000 GHz propagated in space without artificial guide;

"regular force"—*"regular force"* means the component of the Canadian Forces that is referred to in the *National Defence Act* as the regular force;

"reserve force"—*"reserve force"* means the component of the Canadian Forces that is referred to in the *National Defence Act* as the reserve force;

"security"—*"security"* means sufficient security, and "sureties" means sufficient sureties, and when those words are used one person is sufficient therefor, unless otherwise expressly required;

"standard time"—*"standard time"*[2], except as otherwise provided by any proclamation of the Governor in Council that may be issued for the purposes of this definition in relation to any province or territory or any part thereof, means

(*a*) in relation to the Province of Newfoundland and Labrador, Newfoundland standard time, being three hours and thirty minutes behind Greenwich time, (S.C. 2015, c. 3, s. 124(2).)

(*b*) in relation to the Provinces of Nova Scotia, New Brunswick and Prince Edward Island, that part of the Province of Quebec lying east of the sixty-third meridian of west longitude, and that part of Nunavut lying east of the sixty-eighth meridian of west longitude, Atlantic standard time, being four hours behind Greenwich time,

(*c*) in relation to that part of the Province of Quebec lying west of the sixty-third meridian of west longitude, that part of the Province of Ontario lying between the sixty-eighth and the ninetieth meridians of west longitude, Southampton Island and the islands adjacent to Southampton Island, and that part of Nunavut lying between the sixty-eighth and the eighty-fifth meridians of west longitude, eastern standard time, being five hours behind Greenwich time,

(*d*) in relation to that part of the Province of Ontario lying west of the ninetieth meridian of west longitude, the Province of Manitoba, and that part of Nunavut, except Southampton Island and the islands adjacent to Southampton Island, lying between the eighty-fifth and the one hundred and second meridians of west longitude, central standard time, being six hours behind Greenwich time,

(*e*) in relation to the Provinces of Saskatchewan and Alberta, the Northwest Territories and that part of Nunavut lying west of the one hundred and second meridian of west longitude, mountain standard time, being seven hours behind Greenwich time,

(*f*) in relation to the Province of British Columbia, Pacific standard time, being eight hours behind Greenwich time, and

(*g*) in relation to Yukon, Yukon standard time, being nine hours behind Greenwich time;

(S.C. 1993, c. 28, Sched. III, s. 82(2); S.C. 2002, c. 7, s. 188.)

"statutory declaration"—*"statutory declaration"* means a solemn declaration made pursuant to section 41 of the *Canada Evidence Act*;

"superior court"—*"superior court"* means

(*a*) in the Province of Newfoundland and Labrador, the Supreme Court, S.C. 1990, c. 17, s. 26(2); S.C. 1992, c. 51, s. 56(2); 2015, c. 3, s. 124(3).)

(*a.1*) in the Province of Ontario, the Court of Appeal for Ontario and the Superior Court of Justice, (S.C. 1990, c. 17, s. 26(2); S.C. 1998, c. 30, s. 15(i).)

(*b*) in the Province of Quebec, the Court of Appeal and the Superior Court in and for the Province,

(*c*) in the Province of New Brunswick, Manitoba, Saskatchewan or Alberta, the Court of Appeal for the Province and the Court of Queen's Bench for the Province,

(*d*) in the Provinces of Nova Scotia, British Columbia and Prince Edward Island, the Court of Appeal and the Supreme Court of the Province, and (S.C. 1992, c. 51, s. 56(2); 2015, c. 3, s. 124(4).)

(*e*) the Supreme Court of Yukon, the Supreme Court of the Northwest Territories and the Nunavut Court of Justice, (S.C. 1993, c. 28, Sched. III, s. 82(3); S.C. 1999, c. 3, s. 71; S.C. 2002, c. 7, s. 188.)

and includes the Supreme Court of Canada, the Federal Court of Appeal, the Federal Court and the Tax Court of Canada;

(S.C. 2002, c. 8, s. 151(2).)

"telecommunications"—*"telecommunications"* means the emission, transmission or reception of signs, signals, writing, images, sounds or intelligence of any nature by any wire, cable, radio, optical or other electromagnetic system, or by any similar technical system; (S.C. 1993, c. 38, s. 87.)

"territorial sea"—*"territorial sea"*,

(*a*) in relation to Canada, means the territorial sea of Canada as determined under the *Oceans Act* and includes the airspace above and the seabed and subsoil below that sea, and

(*b*) in relation to any other state, means the territorial sea of the other state as determined in accordance with international law and the domestic laws of that other state;

(S.C. 1996, c. 31, s. 87.)

"territory"—*"territory"* means Yukon, the Northwest Territories and Nunavut; (S.C. 1995, c. 39, s. 174; S.C. 2002, c. 7, s. 188.)

"two justices"—*"two justices"* means two or more justices of the peace, assembled or acting together;

"United Kingdom"—*"United Kingdom"* means the United Kingdom of Great Britain and Northern Ireland;

"United States"—*"United States"* means the United States of America;

"writing"—*"writing"*, or any term of like import, includes words printed, typewritten, painted, engraved, lithographed, photographed or represented or reproduced by any mode of representing or reproducing words in visible form.

(2) *Governor in Council may amend schedule*—The Governor in Council may, by order, amend the schedule by adding thereto the name of any country recognized by the order to be a member of the Commonwealth or deleting therefrom the name of any country recognized by the order to be no longer a member of the Commonwealth. (S.C. 1992, c. 1, s. 91.)

(R.S.C. 1985 (1st Supp.), c. 11; 1985 (2nd Supp.), c. 27; 1990, c. 17, s. 26; 1992, c. 1, s. 91; 1992, c. 47, s. 79; 1992 c. 51, s. 56; 1993, c. 28. Sched. III, s. 82; 1993, c. 38, s. 87; 1995, c. 39, s. 174; 1996, c. 31, s. 87; 1998, c. 15, s. 28; 1998, c. 30, s. 15; 1999, c. 3, s. 71; 1999, c. 28, s. 168; 2002, c. 7, s. 188; 2002, c. 8, s 151; 2014, c. 2, s. 14; 2015, c. 3, s. 124.)

Sec. 36 Construction of "telegraph"—The expression "telegraph" and its derivatives, in an enactment or in an Act of the legislature of any province enacted before that province became part of Canada on any subject that is within the legislative powers of Parliament, are deemed not to include the word "telephone" or its derivatives.

Sec. 37 Construction of "year"—(1) The expression "year" means any period of twelve consecutive months, except that a reference

(*a*) to a "calendar year" means a period of twelve consecutive months commencing on January 1;

(*b*) to a "financial year" or "fiscal year" means, in relation to money provided by Parliament, or the Consolidated Revenue Fund, or the accounts, taxes or finances of Canada, the period beginning on April 1 in one calendar year and ending on March 31 in the next calendar year; and

(*c*) by number to a Dominical year means the period of twelve consecutive months commencing on January 1 of that Dominical year.

2 See Proclamation SOR/2001-182, dated May 23, 2001, concerning time zones for Nunavut, reproduced at the end of this Act.

(2) *Governor in Council may define year* — Where in an enactment relating to the affairs of Parliament or the Government of Canada there is a reference to a period of a year without anything in the context to indicate beyond doubt whether a financial or fiscal year, any period of twelve consecutive months or a period of twelve consecutive months commencing on January 1 is intended, the Governor in Council may prescribe which of those periods of twelve consecutive months shall constitute a year for the purposes of the enactment.

Sec. 38 Common names — The name commonly applied to any country, place, body, corporation, society, officer, functionary, person, party or thing means the country, place, body, corporation, society, officer, functionary, person, party or thing to which the name is commonly applied, although the name is not the formal or extended designation thereof.

Sec. 39 Affirmative and negative resolutions — (1) In every Act,

(*a*) the expression "subject to affirmative resolution of Parliament", when used in relation to any regulation, means that the regulation shall be laid before Parliament within fifteen days after it is made or, if Parliament is not then sitting, on any of the first fifteen days next thereafter that Parliament is sitting and shall not come into force unless and until it is affirmed by a resolution of both Houses of Parliament introduced and passed in accordance with the rules of those Houses;

(*b*) the expression "subject to affirmative resolution of the House of Commons", when used in relation to any regulation, means that the regulation shall be laid before the House of Commons within fifteen days after it is made or, if the House is not then sitting, on any of the first fifteen days next thereafter that the House is sitting and shall not come into force unless and until it is affirmed by a resolution of the House of Commons introduced and passed in accordance with the rules of that House;

(*c*) the expression "subject to negative resolution of Parliament", when used in relation to any regulation, means that the regulation shall be laid before Parliament within fifteen days after it is made or, if Parliament is not then sitting, on any of the first fifteen days next thereafter that Parliament is sitting and may be annulled by a resolution of both Houses of Parliament introduced and passed in accordance with the rules of those Houses; and

(*d*) the expression "subject to negative resolution of the House of Commons", when used in relation to any regulation, means that the regulation shall be laid before the House of Commons within fifteen days after it is made or, if the House is not then sitting, on any of the first fifteen days next thereafter that the House is sitting and may be annulled by a resolution of the House of Commons introduced and passed in accordance with the rules of that House.

(2) *Effect of negative resolution* — Where a regulation is annulled by a resolution of Parliament or of the House of Commons, it is deemed to have been revoked on the day the resolution is passed and any law that was revoked or amended by the making of that regulation is deemed to be revived on the day the resolution is passed, but the validity of any action taken or not taken in compliance with a regulation so deemed to have been revoked shall not be affected by the resolution.

References and Citations

Sec. 40 Citation of enactment — (1) In an enactment or document,

(*a*) an Act may be cited by reference to its chapter number in the Revised Statutes, by reference to its chapter number in the volume of Acts for the year or regnal year in which it was enacted or by reference to its long title or short title, with or without reference to its chapter number; and

(*b*) a regulation may be cited by reference to its long title or short title, by reference to the Act under which it was made or by reference to the number or designation under which it was registered by the Clerk of the Privy Council.

(2) *Citation includes amendment* — A citation of or reference to an enactment is deemed to be a citation of or reference to the enactment as amended.

Sec. 41 Reference to two or more parts, etc — (1) A reference in an enactment by number or letter to two or more parts, divisions, sections, subsections, paragraphs, subparagraphs, clauses, subclauses, schedules, appendices or forms shall be read as including the number or letter first mentioned and the number or letter last mentioned.

(2) *Reference in enactments to parts, etc.* — A reference in an enactment to a part, division, section, schedule, appendix or form shall be read as a reference to a part, division, section, schedule, appendix or form of the enactment in which the reference occurs.

(3) *Reference in enactment to subsections, etc.* — A reference in an enactment to a subsection, paragraph, subparagraph, clause or subclause shall be read as a reference to a subsection, paragraph, subparagraph, clause or subclause of the section, subsection, paragraph, subparagraph or clause, as the case may be, in which the reference occurs.

(4) *Reference to regulations* — A reference in an enactment to regulations shall be read as a reference to regulations made under the enactment in which the reference occurs.

(5) *Reference to another enactment* — A reference in an enactment by number or letter to any section, subsection, paragraph, subparagraph, clause, subclause or other division or line of another enactment shall be read as a reference to the section, subsection, paragraph, subparagraph, clause, subclause or other division or line of such other enactment as printed by authority of law.

Repeal and Amendment

Sec. 42 Power of repeal or amendment reserved — (1) Every Act shall be so construed as to reserve to Parliament the power of repealing or amending it, and of revoking, restricting or modifying any power, privilege or advantage thereby vested in or granted to any person.

(2) *Amendment or repeal at same session* — An Act may be amended or repealed by an Act passed in the same session of Parliament.

(3) *Amendment part of enactment* — An amending enactment, as far as consistent with the tenor thereof, shall be construed as part of the enactment that it amends.

Sec. 43 Effect of repeal —Where an enactment is repealed in whole or in part, the repeal does not

(*a*) revive any enactment or anything not in force or existing at the time when the repeal takes effect,

(*b*) affect the previous operation of the enactment so repealed or anything duly done or suffered thereunder,

(*c*) affect any right, privilege, obligation or liability acquired, accrued, accruing or incurred under the enactment so repealed,

(*d*) affect any offence committed against or contravention of the provisions of the enactment so repealed, or any punishment, penalty or forfeiture incurred under the enactment so repealed, or

(*e*) affect any investigation, legal proceeding or remedy in respect of any right, privilege, obligation or liability referred to in paragraph (*c*) or in respect of any punishment, penalty or forfeiture referred to in paragraph (*d*),

and an investigation, legal proceeding or remedy as described in paragraph (*e*) may be instituted, continued or enforced, and the punishment, penalty or forfeiture may be imposed as if the enactment had not been so repealed.

Sec. 44 Repeal and substitution —Where an enactment, in this section called the "former enactment", is repealed and another enactment, in this section called the "new enactment", is substituted therefor,

(*a*) every person acting under the former enactment shall continue to act, as if appointed under the new enactment, until another person is appointed in the stead of that person;

(*b*) every bond and security given by a person appointed under the former enactment remains in force, and all books, papers, forms and things made or used under the former enactment shall continue to be used as before the repeal in so far as they are consistent with the new enactment;

(c) every proceeding taken under the former enactment shall be taken up and continued under and in conformity with the new enactment in so far as it may be done consistently with the new enactment;

(d) the procedure established by the new enactment shall be followed as far as it can be adapted thereto

(i) in the recovery or enforcement of fines, penalties and forfeitures imposed under the former enactment,

(ii) in the enforcement of rights, existing or accruing under the former enactment, and

(iii) in a proceeding in relation to matters that have happened before the repeal;

(e) when any punishment, penalty or forfeiture is reduced or mitigated by the new enactment, the punishment, penalty or forfeiture if imposed or adjudged after the repeal shall be reduced or mitigated accordingly;

(f) except to the extent that the provisions of the new enactment are not in substance the same as those of the former enactment, the new enactment shall not be held to operate as new law, but shall be construed and have effect as a consolidation and as declaratory of the law as contained in the former enactment;

(g) all regulations made under the repealed enactment remain in force and are deemed to have been made under the new enactment, in so far as they are not inconsistent with the new enactment, until they are repealed or others made in their stead; and

(h) any reference in an unrepealed enactment to the former enactment shall, with respect to a subsequent transaction, matter or thing, be read and construed as a reference to the provisions of the new enactment relating to the same subject-matter as the former enactment, but where there are no provisions in the new enactment relating to the same subject-matter, the former enactment shall be read as unrepealed in so far as is necessary to maintain or give effect to the unrepealed enactment.

Sec. 45 Repeal does not imply enactment was in force — (1) The repeal of an enactment in whole or in part shall not be deemed to be or to involve a declaration that the enactment was previously in force or was considered by Parliament or other body or person by whom the enactment was enacted to have been previously in force.

(2) *Amendment does not imply change in law* — The amendment of an enactment shall not be deemed to be or to involve a declaration that the law under that enactment was or was considered by Parliament or other body or person by whom the enactment was enacted to have been different from the law as it is under the enactment as amended.

(3) *Repeal does not declare previous law* — The repeal or amendment of an enactment in whole or in part shall not be deemed to be or to involve any declaration as to the previous state of the law.

(4) *Judicial construction not adopted* — A re-enactment, revision, consolidation or amendment of an enactment shall not be deemed to be or to involve an adoption of the construction that has by judicial decision or otherwise been placed on the language used in the enactment or on similar language.

Demise of Crown

Sec. 46 Effect of demise — (1) Where there is a demise of the Crown,

(a) the demise does not affect the holding of any office under the Crown in right of Canada; and

(b) it is not necessary by reason of the demise that the holder of any such office again be appointed thereto or, having taken an oath of office or allegiance before the demise, again take that oath.

(2) *Continuation of proceedings* — No writ, action or other process or proceeding, civil or criminal, in or issuing out of any court established by an Act is, by reason of a demise of the Crown, determined, abated, discontinued or affected, but every such writ, action, process or proceeding remains in full force and may be enforced, carried on or otherwise proceeded with or completed as though there had been no such demise.

Treaties and Related Legislation

Schedule —

(Section 35)

Antigua and Barbuda	Mauritius
Australia	Nauru
The Bahamas	New Zealand
Bangladesh	Nigeria
Barbados	Pakistan
Belize	Papua New Guinea
Botswana	St. Christopher and Nevis
Brunei Darussalam	St. Lucia
Canada	St. Vincent and the Grenadines
Cyprus	Seychelles
Dominica	Sierra Leone
Fiji	Singapore
Gambia	Solomon Islands
Ghana	South Africa
Grenada	Sri Lanka
Guyana	Swaziland
India	Tonga
Jamaica	Trinidad and Tobago
Kenya	Tuvalu
Kiribati	Uganda
Lesotho	United Kingdom
Malawi	Vanuatu
Malaysia	Western Samoa
Maldives	Zambia
Malta	Zimbabwe

(SOR/86-532; SOR/93-140; SOR/95-366.)

Proclamation
Interpretation Act

SOR/2001-182, May 23 2001,

Proclamation establishing three different time zones in Nunavut, for the purposes of the definition of "standard time" in the Interpretation Act

A Proclamation

Whereas "standard time", in relation to any province or territory, has the meaning set out in subsection 35(1) of the Interpretation Act, except as otherwise provided by a proclamation of the Governor in Council;

And Whereas the Government of Nunavut has expressed the desire to change the definition of standard time in relation to Nunavut;

Now Know You that We, by and with the advice of Our Privy Council for Canada, and pursuant to Order in Council P.C. 2001-804 of May 2, 2001, do by this Our Proclamation provide that, for the purpose of the definition "standard time" in subsection 35(1) of the Interpretation Act, "standard time" means

(*a*) in relation to that part of Nunavut that is east of the 85th meridian of west longitude, and in Southampton Island and the islands adjacent to Southampton Island, Eastern Standard Time, being five hours behind Greenwich time;

(*b*) in relation to that part of Nunavut that is between the 85th meridian of west longitude and the 102nd meridian of west longitude, except Southampton Island and the islands adjacent to Southampton Island and all areas lying within the Kitikmeot Region, Central Standard Time, being six hours behind Greenwich time; and

(*c*) in relation to that part of Nunavut that is west of the 102nd meridian of west longitude, and all areas lying within the Kitikmeot Region, Mountain Standard Time, being seven hours behind Greenwich time.

Of All Which Our Loving Subjects and all others whom these Presents may concern are hereby required to take notice and to govern themselves accordingly.

In Testimony Whereof, We have caused this Our Proclamation to be published and the Great Seal of Canada to be hereunto affixed Witness: Our Right Trusty and Well-beloved Adrienne Clarkson, Chancellor and Principal Companion of Our Order of Canada, Chancellor and Commander of Our Order of Military Merit, Governor General and Commander-in-Chief of Canada

At Our Government House, in Our City of Ottawa, this twenty-third day of May in the year of Our Lord two thousand and one and in the fiftieth year of Our Reign

By Command,

V. Peter Harder

Deputy Registrar General of Canada

TOPICAL INDEX

References are to sections of the Income Tax Act, the Income Tax Application Rules (A.R.), and to the Income Tax Regulations

Topical Index

Topical Index

Topical Index

Topical Index

Topical Index

Topical Index

Section

Section

Section

Topical Index

Topical Index

Topical Index

Topical Index

Topical Index

Topical Index

Topical Index

Topical Index

Topical Index

Topical Index

Topical Index

Topical Index

Topical Index

Topical Index

Topical Index

Topical Index

Topical Index

Topical Index

Topical Index

Topical Index

Topical Index

Topical Index

Topical Index